TOTAL BASEBALL

THE OFFICIAL ENCYCLOPEDIA
OF MAJOR LEAGUE BASEBALL

TOTAL
BASEBALL

FOURTH EDITION

EDITED BY
JOHN THORN AND PETE PALMER
WITH MICHAEL GERSHMAN

David Pietrusza, Managing Editor

VIKING

VIKING
Published by the Penguin Group
Penguin Books USA Inc., 375 Hudson Street,
New York, New York 10014, U.S.A.
Penguin Books Ltd, 27 Wrights Lane,
London W8 5TZ, England
Penguin Books Australia Ltd, Ringwood,
Victoria, Australia
Penguin Books Canada Ltd, 10 Alcorn Avenue,
Toronto, Ontario, Canada M4V 3B2
Penguin Books (N.Z.) Ltd, 182–190 Wairau Road,
Auckland 10, New Zealand

Penguin Books Ltd, Registered Offices:
Harmondsworth, Middlesex, England

This edition published in 1995 by Viking Penguin,
a division of Penguin Books USA Inc.

10 9 8 7 6 5 4 3 2 1

Official Publication – Major League Baseball

ISBN 0–670–86099–9
CIP data available

Printed in the United States of America
Set in Times Roman
Designed by Marc Cheshire with Ray Shaw

Contents

PART TWO

The Registers, Leaders, and Rosters

Appendixes

Acknowledgments

This fourth edition of *Total Baseball* could not have been published without the assistance of a legion of writers, researchers, and editorial/production staff. The principal contributors in these areas are credited on the preceding staff page and table of contents; others may be acknowledged within the text or in the separate introductions to the various sections of Part 2. Still others provided vital inspiration, investigative tips, and production help, yet go unmentioned in the body of the book; this page is for them, especially those who took part in the launch of the book back in 1989 and our new colleagues at Major League Baseball and Viking.

This book would not exist in its current form without the clear vision and dedicated effort of Michael Bernstein, Director of Publishing at Major League Baseball Properties. Michael was an indispensable editorial adviser and his staff, Dana Nicole Williams, Cindy McManus, and Jennifer Langness, made the book better with their careful review of the manuscript.

Rich Levin, Director of Public Relations in the Commissioner's Office of Major League Baseball, played a key role in sharpening the statistical focus of this edition and providing editorial guidance for the essays on business and law. Jim Small provided helpful information too.

Seymour Siwoff and Steve Hirdt of the Elias Sports Bureau gave us generous advice and offered their aid in creating, in the coming years, a unified statistical database of Major League Baseball.

Al Silverman, our editor at Viking, was a key contributor in shaping the new features of this edition and in enlisting the support of the company's marketing group, led by Cathy Hemming and ably abetted by Mary Ellen Curley and Paul Slovak. Similarly, Roni Axelrod and Cynthia Achar were invaluable on the production end.

We were fortunate to extend our relationship with Starkey & Henricks, which has been the typographer for every edition of *Total Baseball.* To Peter and Doug Bird and their extraordinary, beleaguered staff go our admiration and gratitude.

We were also fortunate to begin a new relationship with our printer, Courier Corporation. Bill Topaz, a veteran of other campaigns with us, provided us with assistance every step along the way. Peter Clifford, Tony Caruso, and Dave Barton solved the unanticipated problems that tend to arise with a mammoth book such as this one.

David Pietrusza has been an essential part of the team since the second edition; in addition to writing a fine piece on the business of baseball, he supervised the updating and copy-flow processes that in the second edition had been the province of Richard Puff. Susan Ray, another seasoned member of the team, came through yet again, as did rookies Heather Cumming and Susan Newkirk. Providing skillful professional advice were our longtime counselors, Robert Gold and Robert Stein.

Marc Cheshire's splendid design for the first edition has stood the test of time. Gypsy da Silva earned the *croix de guerre* for her production work on the second edition, and Jacquie Roland was important to the third edition. This time around, Ray Shaw provided us with handsome new designs for the title and part-title pages.

Thanks as well to Eric Pozzo and Corey Smith and all the pioneers at CMC (Creative Multimedia Corporation) who brought *Total Baseball* to the public in electronic form, through CD-ROM technology. At Microsoft, which incorporated much of this work in its *Complete Baseball*, our appreciation goes to Robert Lindsey, Mark Nieker, David Cole, and Jasen Emmons for bringing *Total Baseball* to an even wider audience. (We still can't quite believe that a compact disc weighing an ounce or so contains everything in this book.)

We are indebted to David Reuther, our friend and associate in many other books. His contributions to the editorial, production, and business aspects of *Total Baseball*— both the original and second editions—were truly awesome.

For research help, particularly into the years before 1920, we extend heartfelt thanks (alphabetically) to SABR colleagues Bill Carle, Bob McConnell, David Neft, Bob Tiemann, and Frank Williams. Bill helped us with biographical data, especially debut dates. Bob McConnell lent his personal expertise and his knowledge of the John Tattersall research collection to clear up a variety of perplexing areas. David supplied us with heretofore unknown RBI data for the National League of 1880-1885 and inspired us by his example, as the man who headed the Information Concepts, Inc., team that produced *The Baseball Encyclopedia* of 1969. Bob Tiemann provided game scores and sites for a host of pre-1900 games that were most helpful in deriving, for the first time, home-road stats for the nineteenth century; he also headed the SABR research project that yielded new National Association data. And Frank continued his remarkable efforts in correcting pitcher won-lost records before 1920.

Since our debut in 1989, a veritable army of readers has taken us up on our invitation to write with their corrections and suggestions, from the mathematical to the typographical; we thank them in the aggregate here and list them by name in the Notes on Contributors section near the end of the book.

And last, we thank some giants of baseball research whose work informs these pages but who are no longer with us to receive the tribute: in no particular order, Ernie Lanigan, John Tattersall, S.C. Thompson, Alex Haas, Preston D. Orem, Len Gettelson, Lee Allen, and Harold Seymour.

J.T.
P.P.
M.G.

DEDICATION

To the men of the Knickerbocker Base Ball Club of New York, who 150 years ago organized for play on the Elysian Fields of Hoboken, New Jersey. From their creation of the playing rules on September 23, 1845 to the inception of the National Association of Base Ball Players in 1857, they made the game.

The Knickerbockers, 1845-56

Daniel Lucius Adams
D. Anthony
Henry T. Anthony
Jacob Anthony, Jr.
—— Arthur
Walter T. Avery
Louis J. Belloni
Edward A. Bibby
E. H. Birdsall
Charles H. Birney
John A. Boyle
—— Broadhead
Benjamin K. Brotherson
George A. Brown
M. Bunker
H. L. Butler
Andrew J. Carl
Alexander Joy Cartwright, Jr.
G. D. Cassio
John Clancy
Edwin F. Cone
Richard S. Conover
Duncan F. Curry
James Whyte Davis
Charles S. Debost
George W. Devoe
—— DeWitt
E. Dick
Thomas W. Dick, Jr.
John D. Dixon
Alexander H. Drummond
Ebenezer R. Dupignac, Jr.
William B. Eager, Jr.
Edward A. Ebbets
Henry C. Ellis
Henry C. Flender

Edwin C. Fronk
A. T. Gourlie
William H. Grenelle
David Hart
—— Hatfield
Peter S. Henderson
George Ireland, Jr.
F. U. Johnston
Samuel E. Kissam
William F. Ladd
James P. Landsdowne
—— Langworthy
Edgar F. Lasak
Benjamin C. Lee
James Lee
W. Lippincott
Gershom Lockwood
William F. McCutcheon
—— McDonald
Napoleon B. McLaughlin
James Moncrief
James L. Montgomery
—— Moore
Henry T. Morgan
James Morrier
Augustus C. Morrill
J. Paige Mumford
J. Murphy
John Murray, Jr.
—— Nichols
Fraley C. Niebuhr
John O'Brien
R. O'Brien
William O'Brien, Jr.
Walter Oakley
Henry M. Onderdonk

C. H. Parisen
Otto W. Parisen
—— Paulding
Charles H. Peirson
Eugene Plunkett
James W. Purdy
—— Rogers
—— Rutherford
John Simpkins
D. D. Smith
J. Connor Smith
Daniel S. Stansbury
Richard F. Stevens
John G. Storm
—— Talmadge
Edward W. Talman
William L. Talman
Asa P. Taylor
A. D. Thompson
W. L. Thorne
G. Colden Tracy
Frank W. Tryon
Abraham W. Tucker
William H. Tucker
—— Turney
William A. Tyson
Alfred Vredenburgh
Lewis F. Wadsworth
G. Waller
H. Watson
Norman M. Welling
William H. Westervelt
William R. Wheaton
Albert H. Winslow
William A. Woodhull
Samuel Yates

viii

Introduction

When it first appeared, in 1989, *Total Baseball* was the most complete, most authoritative, and most informative—not to mention the biggest—baseball book ever published. It came into being because its creators saw that there was nothing else like it and because its publishers had faith that fans would want such a book—a virtual baseball library in one volume. In fact, it could be said that *Total Baseball* is the first true baseball encyclopedia because it offers not only the game's numbers but also the stories and statistical principles that underlie them.

In this fourth edition, *Total Baseball* builds upon that foundation to provide new stories, new stats, and a thorough review of all the data that went into the first three editions. We welcome, in a dramatic new development, the endorsement of this volume by Major League Baseball as the official encyclopedia of the game, and we also welcome a new publishing partner in Viking.

This book is divided into two parts. The first consists of prose features on subjects of interest to all baseball fans, from the general reader who wishes to know more about the game's trivia and lore to the advanced fan who wants to know about its business and law. The origins of the farm system; black baseball before Jackie Robinson; complete balloting for the Hall of Fame and major awards; ballparks; women in baseball . . . but why tease you with the pleasures that await?

Simply be assured that *Total Baseball* will be totally absorbing. The writers gathered together here are experts in their fields, as befits an encyclopedic reference work, and even the most erudite reader will learn countless new things about our great game.

The same holds true for Part 2, which contains the playing and pitching registers, a variety of rosters, a year-by-year statistical summary of major league play since 1871, home-road statistics, and more. The stats newly developed for this book—like the Total Player Ranking or Fielding Runs—will please the devotee of sabermetrics, who may know about Runs Created, Production, and the whole Linear Weights System but who has never before been offered these stats applied to all of baseball's 14,166 players. The traditional computations will appeal to baseball scholars, who know what a tangle of briars the historical record has become over the last two decades, as individual player records have been altered without corresponding changes to other players on the same team. (For more on this, see the essay, "The History of Major League Baseball Statistics.") And the cornucopia of stats old and new—for everyone from all-time leaders to cup-of-coffee nonentities—will provide days, months, and years of archaeological delight for baseball fans of all stripes.

Total Baseball joins the game's most knowledgeable writers, most of them members of the Society for American Baseball Research (SABR), with the game's great historical database, the one built up over two decades by Pete Palmer. Benefiting from the painstaking research of hundreds of friends and colleagues in SABR, we have corrected many errors and omissions in other reference works, relying not upon the numbers enshrined by tradition or official edict but upon the evidence. How many hours have been spent scanning the handwritten official records of the early years of the century, or reviewing box scores and scoresheets and game summaries! It would have been easier not to bother, to accept, for example, a game mistakenly entered twice in the record for 1910 so that Ty Cobb could keep his career total of 4,191 hits. But there can be no statute of limitations on historical error; the researcher and historian must go where the evidence leads them.

This book is as good as we know how to make it, but we do want to hear from you about our blunders (we know there will be some, as there were in the previous editions) or about your research (which may be as important to subsequent editions of *Total Baseball* as that of, say, Joe Wayman or Barbara Gregorich was for this). We believe that history is process, not product, and our aim has been for *Total Baseball* to reflect the state of the art in baseball research and to convey its editors' love for the game.

THE HISTORY

CHAPTER 1

Our Game

John Thorn

Baseball has been, most often for better but occasionally for worse, the American game. It has given our people rest and recreation, myths and memories, heroes and history and hope. It has mirrored our society, sometimes propelling it with models for democracy, community, commerce, and common humanity, sometimes lagging behind with equally instructive models of futility and resistance to change. And as our national game, baseball in no small measure defines us as Americans, connecting us with our countrymen across all barriers of generation, class, race, and creed.

Baseball in the Americas is more than a game, an observation to which the scope of this book is testimony and tribute. But it is first and foremost about *play*, a fact obscured amid today's ferment of free agency, salary caps, and threatened cataclysm. Some 150 years ago, an overly solemn America was first indebted to baseball for the freedom it gave to play. As overture to this volume's chronicle of baseball's history, let's look at how child's play came to be our national pastime.

America Learns to Play

Even when baseball was in its infancy in the 1850s—having just evolved from the boyhood game of rounders and its more formalized derivative, town ball—the sport was already shaping the life of the country. Americans of the previous generation had been blind to the virtue of play, much perplexing our European cousins. We permitted ourselves few amusements that could not be justified in terms of social or business utility, or "seriousness." Nonconformists like the Olympic Town Ball Club of Philadelphia in the 1830s had to put up with a lot of guff, as this contemporary account details:

The first day that the Philadelphia men took the field .... only four men were found to play, so they started in by playing a game called cat ball. All the players were over twenty-five years of age, and to see them playing a game like this caused much merriment among the friends of the players. It required "sand" in those days to go out on the field and play, as the prejudice against the game was very great. It took nearly a whole season to get men enough together to make a team, owing to the ridicule heaped upon the players for taking part in such childish sports.

What brought scorn upon the heads of these staunch devotees of town ball (also known as "Boston Ball" or the "Massachusetts Game") was that although the game had regularly positioned fielders and demanded a modicum of strategic play, it still bore the childish essence of rounders: the retirement of a baserunner by throwing the ball *at* him, which necessitated a softer, less resilient ball than that used in the manly sport of cricket. Who was the genius who came up with the idea of retiring a runner by touching him with the ball or securing it "in the hands of an adversary on the base"? Perhaps it was Alexander Cartwright, who is known to many as "the man who invented baseball," though baseball was not invented; it evolved. But it may have been Daniel Lucius Adams or William Wheaton or Lewis F. Wadsworth.

No matter—this was the first step toward making an American game that could challenge boys and men alike, and that could take its place in the life of our nation as cricket had done in England. Henry Chadwick, the English-born cricket reporter who coined the term "national pastime" and became known as the "Father of Baseball," wrote that early on he

... was struck with the idea that base ball was just the game for a national sport for Americans and ... that from this game of ball a powerful lever might be made by which our people could be lifted into a position of more devotion to physical exercise and healthful out-door recreation than they had, hitherto, been noted for.... In fact, as is well-known, we were the regular target for the shafts of raillery and even abuse from our outdoor-sport-loving cousins of England, in consequence of our national neglect of sports and pastimes, and our too great devotion to business and the "Almighty Dollar." But thanks to Base Ball ... we have been transformed into quite another people....

The transformation was from a hard-working but grim citizenry to a nation devoted to fresh air and exercise, not unlike the current rage for jogging, aerobics, and body building. Amateur baseball clubs sprang up like dandelions in the years immediately before the Civil War, but these were formed more for camaraderie and calisthenics than the pursuit of victory or the honing of skills. The demands of the new game on athleticism were few, as the one-bound rule remained in effect (an out was recorded if a ball was caught on a bounce), and a couple of weeks' practice were enough to make a novice of forty a creditable player. Men viewed baseball as a mild pastime, or relief from the mental strains of work; as a tonic, restorative of the physical energies needed for work; or as a release of the surplus nervous energy that impedes young men in their pursuit of purposeful work. America in the mid-1850s was learning how to play, but still viewed sport in terms of its salutary effects on commerce; not until the close of the War Between the States would the focus shift to learning how to play well—for its own sake.

The Charm of the Game

Today we think of baseball as an anachronism, a last vestige of America's agrarian paradise—an idyllic game that takes us back to a more innocent time. But baseball originated in New York City, not rural Cooperstown, and in truth it was an exercise in nostalgia from the beginning. Alexander Cartwright and his Knickerbockers began play in Madison Square in 1842, and the city's northward progress soon compelled them to move uptown to Murray Hill. When the grounds there were also threatened by the march of industry, the Knicks ferried across the Hudson River to the Elysian Fields of Hoboken, a landscaped retreat of picnic grounds and scenic vistas that was designed by its proprietors to relieve New Yorkers of city air and city care. In other words, the purpose of baseball's primal park was the same as that of New York's Central Park or, much later, Boston's Fenway Park—to give an increasingly urban populace a park within the city, a place reminiscent of the idealized farms that had sent all these lads to the metropolis.

Thus the attraction of the game in its earliest days was first the novelty and exhilaration of play; second the opportunity for deskbound city clerks to expend surplus energy in a sylvan setting, freed from the tyranny of the clock; and third, to harmonize with an American golden age that was almost entirely legendary.

Simple charms, simple pleasures. In the late 1860s, advancing skills led to heightened appetites for victory, which led to hot pursuit of the game's gifted players, which inevitably led to *sub rosa* payments and, by 1870, rampant professionalism. (Doesn't that chain reaction put one in mind of college football or basketball?) The gentlemanly players of baseball's first generation retreated from the field, shaking their heads in dismay at how greed had perverted the "grand old game"—now barely twenty years old—and probably ruined it forever.

Sound familiar? It should—the same dire and premature announcements of the demise of the game have been issued ever since, spurred by free-agent signings, long-term contracts, no-trade provisions, strikes and lockouts, integration, night ball, rival leagues, ad infinitum. The only conclusions a calm head might draw from this recurring cycle of disdain for the present and glorification of the past are that (a) things aren't what they used to be and never were; (b) accurate assessment of a present predicament is impossible, for it requires perspective; and (c) no matter what the owners or players or rulesmakers or fans do, they can't kill baseball. All three conclusions are correct. In baseball, the distinction between amateur and professional is not clear-cut: an amateur may play for devotion to the game (*amat* being the Latin for love), but a professional does not play for pursuit of gain alone; he plays for love, too.

*Oh, don't you remember the game of base-ball we saw
  twenty years ago played,*
When contests were true, and the sight free to all, and
home-runs in plenty were made?
*When we lay on the grass, and with thrills of delight,
  watched the ball squarely pitched at the bat,*
*And easily hit, and then mount out of sight along with our
  cheers and our hat?*
*And then, while the fielders raced after the ball, the men
  on the bases flew round,*
*And came in together—four batters in all. Ah! That was
  the old game renowned.*
*Now salaried pitchers, who throw the ball curved at pad-
  ded and masked catchers lame*
*And gate-money music and seats all reserved is all that is
  left of the game.*
*Oh, give us the glorious matches of old, when love of true
  sport made them great,*
*And not this new-fashioned affair always sold for the
  boodle they take at the gate.*

                                                    H. C. Dodge

That doomsday ditty was published in 1886.

The National Pastime

America before the Civil War was still populated by a handful of veterans of the Revolutionary War and many who remembered vividly the War of 1812. The era of Anglo-American amity had not yet dawned; our country's spiritual separation from the Mother Country, though effected by treaty in 1783, was still in process. And having baseball to rival and replace cricket was an important step in that process. Moreover when England, seeking to maintain its supply of cotton from the American South, appeared over-cordial to the Confederate cause, anti-British feeling swept the North. An America long suffering from an inferiority complex toward England now turned against cricket and embraced baseball with increased fervor.

From 1856 on, Henry Chadwick had been eager for baseball to rise to the status in America that cricket held in his native England. He championed the game tirelessly, helping to refine its rules and practices to make it the equal of cricket as a "manly" and "scientific" game. And baseball soon became, in his words, like cricket "a game requiring the mental powers of judgment, calculation and quick perception to excel in it—while in its demands upon the vigor, endurance and courage of manhood, its requirements excel those requisite to become equally expert as a cricketer."

Chadwick invented a method of scorekeeping and statistical compilation patterned on those which were inaugurated in cricket. Baseball was an elemental game—pitch, hit, catch, throw—like other games of ball; but keeping records of the contests and later printing box scores and individual averages elevated it from rounders and placed it on an equal footing with its transatlantic counterpart. (As important, the records served to legitimize men's concern with what had been merely a boys' exercise by making it more systematic, like the numerically annotated world of business.) Today a baseball without records is inconceivable: They are what keep Babe Ruth and Ty Cobb and Walter Johnson alive in our minds in a way that President James K. Polk, Walter Reed, or

Admiral Dewey—arguably greater men—are not.

By the end of the Civil War cricket in this country remained a pastime for a shrinking band of Anglophiles, while the New York Game of Baseball (as it was then called to differentiate it from the nearly vanished Massachusetts Game) was spreading across the country, courtesy of returning veterans whose first exposure to baseball might have come in a prisoner-of-war camp. In the press, baseball was typically proclaimed The National Game—the same term Britons used for cricket.

Play for Pay

From its creation in 1871 to its crash five years later, the National Association had a rocky time as America's first professional league. Franchises came and went with dizzying speed, often folding in midseason. Schedules were not played out if a club slated to go on the road saw little prospect of gain. Drinking and gambling and game-fixing were rife. And the Boston Red Stockings of Al Spalding and the Wright brothers dominated play, going 71-8 in the last of their four straight championship seasons; their predictable and one-sided victories crushed the competition and at last, interest in the entire circuit.

But from the ashes of the National Association emerged the Red Stockings' model of success and the entrepreneurial genius of Chicago's William Hulbert. After raiding Boston to obtain four of the biggest stars in the game—Spalding, Ross Barnes, Deacon White, and Cal McVey—and lining up the services of the Philadelphia Athletics' Adrian Anson, the White Stockings were ready to roll in the National League of Professional Base Ball Clubs, founded on February 2, 1876 in New York's Grand Central Hotel.

The first five years of the NL were nearly as unsettled as the final years of the NA, with franchises appearing and then disappearing in such cities as Syracuse, Indianapolis, and Hartford while major cities like New York and Philadelphia were, after the league's inaugural year, unrepresented. In 1878 the fledgling circuit was forced to cut back to six teams: Milwaukee, Indianapolis, Chicago, Providence, Cincinnati, and Boston. *National* League? *National* Game? It seemed Americans had plenty of appetite for playing the game, but not much for watching it.

Yet as the National League suffered with growing pains, it was introducing some elements that were critical to the explosion of interest that came with the 1880s. It created a professional (paid) umpiring crew; insisted that the league schedule be honored; banned pool selling and hard-liquor consumption in the stands; and created a system of management-owned teams as opposed to the player-run cooperatives that had largely characterized the NA. As the public's renewed faith in the integrity of the game coincided with an upswing in the national economy, not only did the National League flourish; along came an interloper, the rival American Association, to offer patrons 25-cent baseball (NL admissions were 50 cents), Sunday games, and beer. With the public's new appetite for the game seeming insatiable, a group of investors led by St. Louis' Henry Lucas launched a *third* major league, the Union Association, for 1884.

As brash stars like Cap Anson, Tim Keefe, Dan Brouthers, and the larger-than-life King Kelly captured the newspaper headlines and the nation's imagination, the age of the baseball idol arrived. Before this decade, men like Jim Creighton, Joe Start, and George Wright had been admired in New York and New England, but now a baseball hero's image could be mass-produced for nationwide sale, or licensed for advertising, or inspire odes and songs. Kelly inspired "Slide, Kelly, Slide," its arcane references now largely forgotten but once the most popular song in the land:

> *Slide, Kelly, slide!*
> *Your running's a disgrace!*
> *Slide, Kelly, slide!*
> *Stay there, hold your base!*
> *If someone doesn't steal ya,*
> *And your batting doesn't fail ya,*
> *They'll take you to Australia!*
> *Slide, Kelly, slide!*

And although Ernest Lawrence Thayer always denied it, Kelly could well have been the model for "Casey at the Bat," the immortal lyric ballad Thayer penned in 1888. ("Casey" was sometimes reprinted in the newspapers of the 1880s as "Kelly at the Bat," changing the locale from Mudville to Beantown.)

Baseball was ascendant in the 1880s, and like the budding nation whose pastime it was, pretty cocksure of itself. In the same year that "Casey" made his debut, Albert Spalding led a contingent of baseball players on a round the world tour, spreading the gospel of bat and ball to such places as Egypt, Italy, England, Hawaii, and the above-mentioned Australia. Baseball, America thought, was too grand a game to be merely a national pastime; it ought to be the international pastime.

At a New York banquet for Spalding's returning "world tourists" in 1889, speaker Mark Twain declared, "Baseball is the very symbol, the outward and visible expression of the drive and push and rush and struggle of the raging, tearing, booming nineteenth century." Spalding himself later wrote:

I claim that Base Ball owes its prestige as our National Game to the fact that as no other form of sport it is the exponent of American Courage, Confidence, Combativeness; American Dash, Discipline, Determination; American Energy, Eagerness, Enthusiasm; American Pluck, Persistency, Performance; American Spirit, Sagacity, Success; American Vim, Vigor, Virility.

In fact baseball had become more than the mere reflection of our rising industrial and political power and its propensity for bluster and hokum: the national game was beginning to *supply* emblems for democracy, industry, and community that would change America and the world—not in the ways that Spalding's Tourists may have envisioned, but indisputably for the better.

A Model Institution

Father Chadwick had been typically prescient when he wrote in 1876, the inaugural year of the National League and the centenary of America's birth:

What Cricket is to an Englishman, Base-Ball has become to an American.... On the Cricket-field—and there only—the Peer and the Peasant meet on equal terms; the possession of courage, nerve, judgment, skill, endurance and activity alone giving the palm of superiority. In fact, a more democratic institution does not exist in Europe than this self-same Cricket; and as regards its popularity, the records of the thousands of Commoners, Divines and Lawyers, Legislators and Artisans, as well as Mechanics and Laborers, show how great a hold it has on the people. If this is the characteristic of Cricket in aristocratic and monarchical England, how much more will the same characteristics mark Base-Ball in democratic and republican America.

Chadwick's vision of baseball as a model democratic institution would have to wait for the turn of the century to be fully articulated, and for Jackie Robinson and Branch Rickey to be fully realized. But Chadwick's belief that baseball could be more than a game, could become a model of and for American life, presaged baseball's golden age of 1903-30.

The tumultuous 1890s witnessed a player revolt against high-handed and monopolistic management, epitomized by a cap on salaries, followed by a nearly ruinous contraction from three major leagues to one twelve-team circuit. The national economy suffered a panic in 1893 and a sluggish recovery thereafter; baseball attendance dwindled; and the lack of postseason interleague competition after 1890 (as there had been since 1884) was sorely felt. The game was in a period of consolidation, or hibernation, or stagnation; one's perspective depended upon whether he were an owner, fan, or player.

But then Ban Johnson came along, fired by the same vision of a rival league that had inflamed the Players League and the American and Union Associations before him, and that would beckon to the Federal and Continental Leagues later on. With the declaration by the American League that it would conduct business as a major league in 1901, and the signing of a peace treaty with the Nationals two years later, the World Series was resumed, prosperity returned, and the popularity and influence of the game exploded.

Baseball mania seized America as new heroes like Christy Mathewson, Honus Wagner, Ty Cobb, Walter Johnson, and Nap Lajoie found a public hungry for knowledge of their every action, their every thought. A fan's affiliation with his team could exceed in vigor his attachment to his church, his trade, his political party—all but family and country, and even these were wrapped up in baseball. The national pastime became the great repository of national ideals, the symbol of all that was good in American life: fair play (sportsmanship); the rule of law (objective arbitration of disputes); equal opportunity (each side has its innings); the brotherhood of man (bleacher harmony); and more.

The baseball boom of the early twentieth century built on the game's simple charms of exercise and communal celebration, adding the psychological and social complexities of vicarious play: civic pride, role models, and hero worship. It became routine for the President to throw out the first ball of the season. Supreme Court Justices had inning-by-inning scores from the World Series relayed to their chambers. Business leaders, perhaps disingenuously, praised baseball as a model of competition and fair play. "Baseball," opined a writer for *American Magazine* in 1913, "has given our public a fine lesson in commercial morals.... Some day all business will be reorganized and conducted by baseball standards."

Leaders of recent immigrant groups advised their peoples to learn the national game if they wanted to become Americans, and foreign-language newspapers devoted space to educating their readers about America's strange and wonderful game. (New York's *Staats-Zeitung*, for example, applauded *Kraftiges Schlagen*—hard hitting—and cautioned German fans not to kill the *Unparteiischer*.) As historian Harold Seymour wrote, "The argot of baseball supplied a common means of communication and strengthened the bond which the game helped to establish among those sorely in need of it—the mass of urban dwellers and immigrants living in the anonymity and impersonal vortex of large industrial cities.... With the loss of the traditional ties known in a rural society, baseball gave to many the feeling of belonging." And rooting for a baseball team permitted city folk, newcomers and native-born, the sense of pride in community that in former times—when they may have lived in small towns—was commonplace.

Thus baseball offered a model of how to be an American, to be part of the team: Baseball was "second only to death as a leveler," wrote essayist Allen Sangree. Even in those horrifically leveling years of 1941-45, when so many of our bravest and best gave their lives to defend American ideals, baseball's role as a vital enterprise was confirmed by President Franklin Delano Roosevelt's "green light" for continued play. Many of baseball's finest players—Ted Williams, Joe DiMaggio, Hank Greenberg, Bob Feller, to name a few—swapped their baseball gear for Uncle Sam's, and served with military distinction or helped to boost the nation's morale. Even oldtimers like Babe Ruth, Walter Johnson, and Ty Cobb donned uniforms in service of their country—baseball uniforms, as they staged exhibitions on behalf of war bonds. Servicemen overseas looked to letters from home and the box scores in *The Sporting News* to keep them in touch with what they had left behind, and what they were fighting for—an American way of life that was a beacon for a world in which the light of freedom had been nearly extinguished.

I was one of the countless immigrants who from the 1860s on saw baseball as the "open sesame" to the door of their adopted land. A Polish Jew born in occupied Germany to Holocaust survivors, I arrived on these shores at age two. After checking in at Ellis Island, I happened by chance to spend the first night in my new land in the no-longer-elegant hotel where in 1876 the National League had been founded. I learned to read by studying the backs of Topps baseball cards, and to be an American by attaching myself passionately to the Brooklyn Dodgers (who also taught me about the fickleness of love).

The Brooklyn Dodgers, in the persons particularly of Rickey and Robinson, also taught America a lesson: that baseball's integrative and democratic models, by the 1940s long held to be verities, were hollow at the core.

David Halberstam has written:

...it was part of our folklore, basic to our national democratic myth, that sports was the great American equalizer, that money and social status did not matter upon the playing fields. Elsewhere life was assumed to be unfair: those who had privilege passed it on to their children, who in turn had easier, softer lives. Those without privilege were doomed to accept the essential injustices of daily life. But according to the American myth, in sports the poor but honest kid from across the tracks could gain (often in competition with richer, snottier kids) recognition and acclaim for his talents.

Until October 23, 1945, when Robinson signed a contract to play for the Montreal Royals, Brooklyn's top farm club, the myth as far as African Americans were concerned was not a sustaining legend but a mere falsehood.

Rickey's rectitude and Robinson's courage have become central parables of baseball and America, exemplars of decency and strength that inspire all of us. Their "great experiment" came too late for such heroes of black ball as Josh Gibson and Oscar Charleston and Ray Dandridge, but its success has been complete. Once the integrative or leveling model of baseball—all America playing and working in harmony—was extended to African Americans, the effect on the nation was profound. Eighty years after the Civil War, America had proved itself unable to practice the values for which it was fought; baseball showed the way. This is what Commissioner Ford Frick said to the St. Louis Cardinals, rumored to be planning a strike in May 1947:

If you do this you will be suspended from the league. You will find that the friends you think you have in the press box will not support you, that you will be outcasts. I do not care if half the league strikes. Those who do it will encounter quick retribution. They will be suspended and I don't care if it wrecks the National League for five years. This is the United States of America, and one citizen has as much right to play as any other. The National League will go down the line with Robinson whatever the consequence.

As Monte Irvin said, "Baseball has done more to move America in the right direction than all the professional patriots with their billions of cheap words." The Supreme Court decision of *Brown v. Topeka Board of Education*; civil rights heroes like Martin Luther King, Jr., James Meredith, Thurgood Marshall, and others; the freedom marches and the voting rights act—all were vital to America's progress toward unity, but the title of one of Jackie Robinson's books may not overstate the case: *Baseball Has Done It.*

A final way in which baseball supplies models for America is one that has been present from the game's beginning: a model for children wishing to be grownups, wrestling with their insecurities and wondering, *What does it mean to be a man? What does a man do?* (Most of us old boys occasionally wonder this as well.) The answers in baseball, at least, are unequivocal; as Satchel Paige said in his later years, "I loved baseball. There wasn't no 'maybe so' about it."

Baseball gives children a sense of how wide the world is, in its possibilities but also in its geography. Reading the summations of minor-league ball in *The Sporting News* each week piqued the curiosity of baseball-mad boys like me: where were Kokomo and Mattoon and Thibodeaux and Nogales? How did people behave in Salinas or Rocky Mount? What did they eat in Artesia? How many exciting, exotic places this enormous country contained! But a note of comfort—they couldn't be all that strange if baseball was played there.

And to that other vast *terra incognita*—the world of adults—baseball also offered a road map. How many boys and girls learned to talk with adults, principally their fathers, by nodding wisely at an assessment of a shortstop's range or a pitcher's heart, and mock-confidently venturing an opinion about the hometown team's chances? Our dads are our first heroes (and, decades later, our last); but in between, baseball players are what we want to be. For heroes are larger than life, and when as adults we have taken the measure of ourselves and found we are no more than life-size, and on our bad days seemingly less than that, baseball can puff us up a bit.

Douglass Wallop put it nicely:

... only yesterday the fan was a kid of nine or ten bolting his breakfast on Saturday morning and hurtling from the house with a glove buttoned over his belt and a bat over his shoulder, rushing to the nearest vacant lot, perhaps the nearest alley, where the other guys were gathering, a place where it would always be spring. For him, baseball would always have the sound and look and smell of that morning and of other mornings just like it. Only by an accident of chance would he find himself, in the years to come, up in the grandstand, looking on. But for a quirk of fate, he himself would be down on that field; it would be his likeness on the television screen and his name in the newspaper high on the list of .300 hitters. He was a fan, but a fan only incidentally. He was, first and always, himself a baseball player.

The Fifties

If the America that was survives anywhere as more than a memory, it is in baseball, that strangely pastoral game in no matter what setting—domed stadium or Little League field. As hindsight improves upon foresight, memory improves upon reality, so that the endless monotony and grinding physical labor of small-town life before the Civil War are now thought quite romantic. For all our complaints today, it may likewise be argued that America is better than it ever was.

Given the calamitous labor-management war of 1994, there are few who would say the same about baseball. However, today's players *are* better than those in the game's golden age; the strategy of the game and even its execution are more adept (forget all that moaning about how nobody knows the "fundamentals" any more ... the average player of fifty years ago didn't know them either); and the opportunities to watch baseball, if not to play it, far exceed those of say, the 1950s, today broadly regarded as the game's halcyon era. (A golden age may be defined flexibly, it seems, so as to coincide with the period of one's youth.) For all its pull toward the good old days, for all its statistical illusions of an Olympian era when titans strode the basepaths, for all its seeming permanence in a world aswirl with change, baseball has in fact moved with America, and improved with it.

The period after World War II was a heady time for the nation and its pastime, both of them buoyed by returning veterans and removed restrictions. But in 1946 the major leagues still represented only the sixteen cities that had participated in the National Agreement of 1903, none west of St. Louis; a handful of African Americans were just entering the minor leagues after a half-century's exclusion; and because television was not yet a staple of the American home, most baseball fans had never seen *even a single big-league game.*

Women had been courted as patrons (even nonpaying patrons) ever since the game's dawn. Baseball management hoped that their presence would lend "tone" to the proceedings and keep a lid on the rowdies, in the stands and on the field. But women's participation in the game's labor force and management was even more limited than their role in the nation's business and industry—Rosie the Riveter and Eleanor Roosevelt as yet had no counterparts in Organized Baseball. The All-American Girls Baseball League made its debut in 1943, the brainchild of Chicago Cubs' owner Philip K. Wrigley. The women's "league of their own" won many admirers over the next decade, but the majors always regarded it as separate and unequal.

On the amateur level, while American Legion Junior Baseball had begun as early as 1928, and Little League in 1939, neither attained their heights until after the War ended. Naysayers will point out that baseball has lost ground as more kids today play football, basketball, soccer, and tennis than fifty years ago—but far more play baseball, too, and not only in America. The annual pursuit of the Little League championship in Williamsport, Pennsylvania (like the Pan-American Games), has become an international affair, an instrument of diplomacy that State Department officials envy. Indeed, baseball may yet hold the key to neighborly relations with all nations in the hemisphere.

Baseball in the colleges, now so vibrant and so fertile with major league talent, was on the path to extinction by the end of the War, only to be brought back from the brink by the G.I. Bill: the explosive growth in enrollment that the returning veterans produced also created a sudden need for expanded athletic programs, and baseball was the prime beneficiary. The NCAA's introduction of the College World Series in 1947 affirmed the game's recovery on campus, and since locating in Omaha three years later it has grown steadily.

In 1951 Major League Baseball, as dated from the inception of the National League in 1876, reached the august age of 75 and proclaimed its "diamond jubilee." Celebratory banquets were held, a plaque was erected at the old hotel where the league was founded, and all NL players wore a commemorative patch on their sleeves. (Coincidentally but less flashily the American League marked its fiftieth birthday as a major circuit.) Let's take a moment to look at where baseball stood at that point.

There was no question it was booming. On the professional level, a whopping 59 leagues contained 448 teams employing about 8,000 players—or 19 minor leaguers

competing for each of the then 400 spots in the big show. Little League would soon send its first alumnus to the majors, which had already accepted hundreds of graduates from Legion and other programs. Happy Chandler secured from television a then mind-boggling but now quaint $6 million for broadcast rights to the next six World Series. And with the game's most powerful teams bunched in New York City—the Yankees, the Dodgers, and the Giants—the publicity mills and the turnstiles were spinning as they had never spun before.

But the excitement of the first five postwar years was not confined to New York: even such perennial tailenders as the Boston Braves, the Philadelphia Phillies, and the Cleveland Indians fought their way into the World Series; and staid old Cleveland, under Bill Veeck's carnival-barker aegis, set staggering new attendance records. Many of the newly admitted African-American players had become stars and—satisfyingly, though few but Branch Rickey had predicted it—box-office attractions: Jackie Robinson, Roy Campanella, and Don Newcombe of the Dodgers; Monte Irvin and rookie Willie Mays of the Giants; Sam Jethroe of the Braves; Larry Doby and Satchel Paige of the Indians. Many prewar stars continued to shine, like Bob Feller, Stan Musial, and Ted Williams (though with the Korean War he answered Uncle Sam's call yet again), and new ones like Gotham's center field trio of Duke Snider, Mickey Mantle, and Mays replenished the stock as heroes like Joe DiMaggio hung up their spikes.

But most of these blessings had their downside. Opening the game to African Americans was indubitably right, but it killed the Negro Leagues, ruining owners and abruptly ending many playing careers. The increasing organization of youth baseball, particularly the rise of Little League, heightened the stress of the game at its formative levels and drained much of the fun, as driven parents began to see their Junior as tomorrow's big leaguer, not as just a boy having fun while learning a thing or two. The game on the field was dominated by the home run, making for a brand of ball that some might term dull. League champs registered such stolen-base totals as Dom DiMaggio's 15 or Jackie Jensen's 22; Early Wynn led the AL in ERA one year with a mark of 3.20; and the three-base hit, despite the big old parks still prevalent, went the way of the dodo. And the pennant domination by the three New York teams—principally the Yankees, of course—made the national pastime a rather parochial pleasure; it was hard for fans in Pittsburgh or Detroit to wax rhapsodic over a Subway Series. No, the blessings of the 1950s were not unmitigated, any more than on the national scene the tranquility of the Eisenhower years was without cost.

Take television, for instance: the revenues were great, and so was the publicity value of electronically extending major league play to people in southern and western areas. But the novelty of big-time heroes on the small screen kept those folks at home when formerly they had gone to the local ballpark. The minors began their long decline, one that didn't bottom out until 1964; by then the 59 leagues of 1951 had become 19, and the 8,000-odd professional players had dwindled to fewer than 2,500.

Moreover, television whetted the baseball appetites of Californians and Texans (and Georgians and Washingtonians and more). That demand plus the development of faster passenger planes gave ideas to owners of two of baseball's decaying franchises. Walter O'Malley, owner of the Brooklyn Dodgers, and Giants' owner Horace Stoneham had seen the solidarity of the original sixteen-city composition broken in 1953, when the venerable Boston Braves (a franchise established in the first year of the National Association, 1871) became the darlings of Milwaukee, and further weakened by the defections in 1954-55 of the St. Louis Browns to Baltimore and the Philadelphia Athletics to Kansas City. Amid weeping and gnashing of teeth that continue to this day, the Dodgers and Giants left for the Golden West in 1958.

In a strange twist, the architect of the move, Walter O'Malley, was (and in the East, still is) widely reviled as the man responsible for ending the grand old game's paradisical age. Yet the placement of franchises in California, as distressing as it was for Brooklyn and Manhattan and as roundly condemned as it was by traditionalists, may now be seen as the best thing to happen to baseball in the decade. And Walter O'Malley, if you will permit your mind a considerable stretch, may be viewed not as the snake offering baseball the mortal apple but as a latter-day Johnny Appleseed (in the footsteps of Alexander Cartwright, who in 1849 also headed for California in pursuit of gold, yet who is remembered not for his venality but for bringing the New York Game to the West).

It was imperative that baseball take the game to where the people were, precisely as it had in 1903. America's population had already begun the westward and southward shift that was to become so pronounced in the 1960s and '70s. The move to Los Angeles and San Francisco, rather than confirming those cities' stature as "big-league," as is so often written, brought baseball into step with America, which had long recognized them as such. Baseball could now call itself the national pastime without apology.

The Sixties

A chaotic decade for our country, the 1960s were worrisome, stormy years for baseball as well, with dramatic changes in league composition, playing styles, competitive balance and, most distressingly, the game's appeal to the American people. Baseball endured its ordeal by fire, and came through not unscathed but strengthened.

The departure of the Dodgers and Giants in 1958 created a vacuum in New York and an increased hunger for baseball in new boomtowns like Houston, Atlanta, and Minneapolis. Enter Branch Rickey, nearly eighty but still possessed of a keen nose for new opportunity. The great innovator who had already brought baseball the farm system and integration now created the Continental League, a paper league with paper franchises. Nonetheless, Rickey's mirage worried Organized Baseball into expansion.

Two of the Continental "franchises"—the future New York Mets and Houston Colt .45s—were admitted for 1962. The American League was authorized to commence its western foray one year earlier with the expansion-draft Los Angeles Angels and the relocated Minnesota Twins (the latter being the transplanted Washington Senators, who were replaced in the nation's capital by an ill-fated expansion team).

Other franchise shifts and startups in the decade saw baseball's original vagabonds, the Milwaukee Braves by way of Boston, move to Atlanta in 1966. Two years later the erstwhile Athletics of Philadelphia, having failed in Kansas City, directed their caravan toward Oakland.

The A's were quickly replaced in KC by the Royals, one of two new teams introduced in each league with the expansion of 1969. This in turn precipitated divisional play and the League Championship Series, both inventions much decried at the time but now generally applauded. And in one of baseball's more forgettable debacles, the expansion Pilots of 1969 lost their course in Seattle after only one year and ran aground in Milwaukee, where they were rechristened as the Brewers. The National League's expansion into San Diego and Montreal proceeded more smoothly, although Padres' attendance lagged expectations and the Expos' Olympic Stadium (replacing the stopgap Jarry Park) took longer to open its dome than Michelangelo took to paint St. Peter's.

On the field, the big-bang game of the 1950s was giving way to a pitching-and-defense formula, at least in the National League, which began to outstrip its long-time tormentor at the box office and in World Series and All Star confrontations. Speed returned to the equation, too, as personified by first Maury Wills and then Lou Brock (though both were preceded, in the AL, by Luis Aparicio). And a revolution in baseball strategy was brewing, as the 1959 success of such relievers as Larry Sherry, Lindy McDaniel, and Roy Face paved the way for the universal adoption of the bullpen stopper in the 1960s.

In the American League expansion year of 1961, the first played to a 162-game schedule, the Bronx Bombers hit a whopping 240 homers. Sluggers Harmon Killebrew, Norm Cash, and Rocky Colavito all hit more than 40 homers; Mickey Mantle hit more than 50. These totals were troubling to Commissioner Ford Frick, but nowhere near as consternating as the 61 homers struck by Roger Maris to top the game's most famous record, the 60 that Babe Ruth had walloped in 1927. After seeing the National League's scoring increase in 1962, its first year of expansion, Frick became concerned that pitchers were becoming an endangered species. He said:

I would even like the spitball to come back. Take a look at the batting, home run, and slugging record for recent seasons, and you become convinced that the pitchers need help urgently.

Disastrously, Frick convinced the owners to widen the strike zone for 1963 to its pre-1950 dimensions: top of the armpit to bottom of the knee. The result was to increase strikeouts, reduce walks, and shrink batting averages within five years to levels unseen since 1908, the nadir of the deadball era. The once-proud Yankees, who had continued their long domination of the American League to mid-decade, saw their team batting average sink to an incredible .214 in 1968. That year produced an overall AL mark of .230 and a batting champion, Carl Yastrzemski, with an average of .301.

As pitchers vanquished batters, seemingly for all eternity, the bottom line was that the fans stayed away in droves. Attendance in the National League, which in 1966 reached 15 million, fell by 1968 to only 11.7 million. In fact, despite the addition of four new clubs in 1961-62, attendance in 1968 was only 3 million more than it had been in 1960. Critics charged that baseball was a geriatric vestige of an America that had vanished, a game too slow for a nation that was rushing toward the moon; its decline would only steepen, they claimed, as that more with-it national pastime, pro football, extended its mastery of the airwaves.

But the sky was not falling, despite the alarms. The owners acted quickly to redress the game's balance between offense and defense, reducing the strike zone and lowering the pitcher's mound. But the most important change may have been one that was introduced in 1965 and was only beginning to take effect: the amateur free-agent draft. Typically successful teams like the Yankees, Dodgers, Braves, and Cardinals had stayed successful because of their attention to scouting. Consistently they were able to garner more top prospects for their farm systems than clubs with less deep pockets or more volatile management. Now, teams that had fallen on hard times need not look toward a generation of famine before returning to the feast. Now, dynasties—awe-inspiring but not healthy for the game—were suddenly rendered implausible. Now, baseball had a competitive balance that could produce a rotation of electrifying successes among the leagues' cities, like the ascension of the Boston Red Sox from ninth place in 1966 to the pennant the next, and the amazing rise of the New York Mets from the netherworld they had known to World Champions in 1969. The game would still have some hard rows to hoe in the 1970s, but there was no mistaking the reversal of its downturn: in the new age of "relevance," baseball was back.

The Seventies

The 1970s saw a continuation of the trend toward new stadium construction that had marked the 1960s and may well have triggered that decade's batting drought, as hitter's havens like Ebbets Field, the Polo Grounds, and Sportsman's Park fell to the wrecker's ball. The 1960s had brought new ballparks to nine cities—San Francisco, Los Angeles, New York (NL), Houston, Atlanta, Anaheim, St. Louis, Oakland, and San Diego. In 1970-71, baseball bade farewell to old friends Crosley Field, Forbes Field, and Shibe Park as new stadiums—artificial-turf clones of each other—sprang up in Cincinnati, Pittsburgh, and Philadelphia. Other new parks were built in Arlington, Kansas City, Montreal, Seattle, and Toronto (the latter two, expansion franchises added to the American League in 1977), and Yankee Stadium underwent a massive facelift.

All this construction activity seemed to bespeak the game's profitability. Indeed, attendance was climbing in almost all major league cities, as heroes like Henry Aaron, Johnny Bench, Reggie Jackson, and Pete Rose, to name but a few, gave the fans plenty to cheer about. And the controversial adoption of the designated hitter innovation by the American League in 1973 gave a further boost to hitting while giving fans much to argue about, which after all is one of the game's great pleasures.

But the game's financial health was imperiled by rising unrest over labor issues, centered on the reserve clause which bound a player to his team in perpetuity while denying him the opportunity to gauge his worth in the free market. The reformulation of the relationship between players and management became the hallmark of the decade and sorely tested fans' devotion to the game.

It began with the momentous case brought against Organized Baseball by veteran outfielder Curt Flood in 1970, challenging the legality of the reserve clause. The Supreme Court ruled against Flood the following year, but the tenor for the 1970s had been set. A thirteen-day player strike delayed the opening of the 1972 season, and arbitrator Peter Seitz ruled in 1975 (in what has come to be known as the Messersmith-McNally case) that a player could establish his right of free agency by playing out his option year without a signed contract. The writing on the wall was clear: free agency was the wave of the future.

Big-name players like Jim Hunter, Reggie Jackson, and Rich Gossage migrated to New York and lesser lights like Wayne Garland and Oscar Gamble signed elsewhere for figures that seemed incredible. In the race to sign available talent some owners spun out of control while others like Minnesota's Cal Griffith, without corporate coffers behind them, had no choice but to sit on the sidelines. Player movement among stars jeopardized fan allegiances, pundits alleged, as Gossage and Jackson played for three teams in three years and championship teams like the Oakland A's and Boston Red Sox were broken up through trades that were forced by the specter of impending—and uncompensated—free-agent departures.

(Comfortingly to the historian, all this hubbub had occurred in very much the same way in 1869-70, before the advent of the reserve clause, when Henry Chadwick was fulminating about the perniciousness of players "revolving" from one team to another simply to advance their fortunes. Also, baseball's first avowedly professional team, Harry Wright's Cincinnati Red Stockings of 1869-70, were roundly abused for constructing their powerhouse team with "mercenaries" from other states—thus scorning baseball's core appeal to civic pride.)

What actually compromised fan loyalties in the '70s was not player movement—it took Yankee fans, oh, maybe, ten minutes to regard Reggie as a born pinstriper—but player salaries. When the major-league minimum was under $5,000 or so and only a Mantle, Williams, Musial, and DiMaggio made $100,000 a year, fans saw with their heroes as, by and large, working colleagues who had the supreme good fortune to play ball for a living. If a star made a splendiferous salary, that was socially useful as a proof that any worker could make it big if only he had sufficient ability to emerge from the pack. But when stars began routinely to command seven-figure salaries, and more importantly the annual wage of the average major leaguer rose to six-figure levels, and eventually seven figures, many adult breadwinners struggled to remain fans.

That they succeeded is testament to their love of the game, for fans have had a difficult assignment in reshaping their views of baseball players along the lines of media stars. The princely compensations of actors and pop musicians have long been accepted by the public as the verdict of the marketplace. If the movie *The Termina-*

tor makes hundreds of millions of dollars for its studio and distributor, then Arnold Schwarzenegger's multimillion-dollar fee for the film seems not out of line. Analogously, if the Dodgers were fabulously lucrative for ownership, then a lofty salary for Steve Garvey ought not to have given rise in the 1970s to resentment among the fans. This sort of reeducation is by no means complete, but barroom banter about baseball by, say, 1994, was not as bitterly one-note about "greedy players" as it had been fifteen years ago.

And one didn't hear a peep about pro football replacing baseball as the national game.

The Eighties and Nineties

The game on the field in the 1970s had been marked by an unprecedented commingling of power and speed; the great teams of Cincinnati, Baltimore, and Oakland; the return to prominence of the Yankees; and the historic exploits of Henry Aaron and Pete Rose. The game in the '80s would begin with the Philadelphia Phillies, led by free-agent Rose and future Hall of Famers Mike Schmidt and Steve Carlton, ridding themselves of a historic stain. Until their victory over the Kansas City Royals, the Phils were the only one of the original sixteen major-league franchises never to have won a World Series (the St. Louis Browns had to accept the help of their modern incarnation, the Baltimore Orioles).

The next year brought baseball's darkest moment since the Brotherhood revolt and ensuing Players League of 1890, as major-league players walked off their jobs at the height of the season and didn't return for fifty days. By that time even diehard fans were thoroughly fed up with baseball's seeming inability to resolve its problems fairly and with dispatch. Talk of a fan boycott never amounted to much, but as players and management looked toward their Basic Agreement negotiation in 1989—the centenary of the Brotherhood's break with Organized Baseball—both reflected back on the damage wrought in 1981.

The 1980s brought unprecedented parity on the playing field and misery off it. The drug problem endemic in our society struck baseball, inevitably as well, and Pete Rose's itch for gambling disgraced him and the game. Baseball's victims are highly publicized and their fall from grace is judged more reprehensible for all the advantages that today's players enjoy—but the game is an American institution reflecting what is wrong with our people as well as what is right with them. Let's hope that in this most difficult area of addictive behavior baseball can again—as it did with integration—lead America rather than follow it.

The year of 1989 became a nightmare, with Commissioner Bart Giamatti's expulsion of Rose followed by his own sudden and shocking death days later, a second finding of collusion by owners to undermine the free-agent market, and a Bay Area World Series rudely interrupted by an earthquake. But baseball recovered even from these calamities, as well as a spring training lockout in 1990, to embark upon an era that gave promise of unprecedented prosperity. The attendance of the Toronto Blue Jays exceeded the 4 million mark while the team captured back-to-back World Series, the first such feat since the Cincinnati Reds of 1975-1976. And in 1993 the National League expanded to fourteen teams, welcoming franchises in Miami and Colorado that were instantly and wildly prosperous, with the Rockies setting an all-time attendance peak of nearly 4.5 million fans.

And then came 1994, a year of wonderment on the playing fields, as Ken Griffey, Jr., Matt Williams, Frank Thomas, Jeff Bagwell, Tony Gwynn, Greg Maddux and a host of others appeared to be initiating a new golden age of baseball ... until play stopped on August 12 and did not resume. The leagues, which had divided into three divisions for the first time, now had no opportunity to try out their new idea of an additional round of postseason play, with the introduction of a wild-card team that had not been a division winner.

As fans, do we side with the players, who went on strike hoping to extend their gains of the previous two decades? Or do we side with the owners, who stood fast in insisting upon a balance between costs and revenues? As fans, we would do well to side with the game of baseball, and wish that its most intense contests reconvene to the field of play.

Baseball is not a conventional industry. It belongs neither to the players nor management, but to all of us. It is our national pastime, our national symbol, and our national treasure.

Each of us has deplored the present state of things, and has thought back to his personal version of the good old days. But make no mistake about it—our game, the American game, will become stronger than before for having passed through its crucible of 1994.

The Weather of Our Lives

Ever changing in ways that are so small as to preserve the illusion that "nothing changes in baseball," the game has introduced, in the lifetime of many of us: night ball, plane travel, television, integration, bullpen stoppers, expansion, the amateur draft, competitive parity, indoor stadiums, artificial turf, free agency, the designated hitter, and international play. Not far off, perhaps, are further expansion to thirty-two teams, interleague contests, and intercontinental championships.

For fans accustomed to the game's languorous rhythms and conservative resistance to innovation, the changes of the past twenty years in particular seem positively frenetic. Yet for all its changes, baseball has not strayed far from its origins, and in fact has changed far less than other American institutions of equivalent antiquity. What sustains baseball in the hearts of Americans, finally, is not its responsiveness to changes in society nor its propensity for novelty, but its myths, its lore, its records, and its essential stability. As historian Bruce Catton noted in 1959:

A gaffer from the era of William McKinley, abruptly brought back to the second half of the twentieth century, would find very little in modern life that would not seem new, strange, and rather bewildering, but put in a good grandstand seat back of first base he would see nothing that was not completely familiar.

It's still a game of bat and ball, played without regard for the clock; a game of ninety-foot basepaths, nine innings, nine men in the field; three outs, all out; and three strikes still send you to the bench, no matter whom you know in city hall. It's the national anthem before every game; it's playing catch with your son or daughter; it's learning how to win and how to deal with loss, and how to connect with something larger than our selves.

"Baseball," wrote Thomas Wolfe, "has been not merely 'the great national game' but really a part of the whole weather of our lives, of the thing that is our own, of the whole fabric, the million memories of America." Spring comes in America not on the vernal equinox but on open-ing day; summer sets in with a Memorial Day doubleheader and does not truly end until the last out of the regular season. Winter begins the day after the World Series.

Where were you when Bobby Thomson hit the shot heard 'round the world? Or the night Carlton Fisk hit his homer in the twelfth? Or when the Mets, with batter after batter one strike away from their loss in the World Series, staged their famous rally? These are milestones in the lives of America and Americans.

We grow up with baseball; we mark—and, for a moment, stop—the passage of time with it; and we grow old with it. It is our game, for all our days.

## CHAPTER 2

Team Histories

Frederick Ivor-Campbell

When the National League awarded expansion franchises to Denver and Miami in June 1991, the number of major league clubs reached 14 in each league—the most since 1884. When the Colorado Rockies and Florida Marlins began play in 1993, they brought to 110 the number of clubs (plus those of the Negro major leagues) that have played major league ball at one time or another since baseball's first professional league—the National Association—was organized in 1871. Some of the early teams dropped out after only a few games, but several have played for more than a century, and one—the present Atlanta Braves—has played every season from 1871 to the present. The only existing franchise older than Atlanta's (which originated as the Boston Red Stockings, then became the Boston and Milwaukee Braves before moving to Atlanta) is the Chicago Cubs, which organized in 1870, a year before league play began. The White Stockings (as they were first known) missed two seasons (1872–1873) in the aftermath of the great Chicago fire, but have since then continuously represented the same city longer than any other club in baseball history.

Here are brief histories of the 28 current big-league clubs, arranged alphabetically by city or state. These are followed by summary histories of the 82 other clubs—now defunct—that at one time also represented their cities in the major leagues.

Atlanta Braves

The Atlanta Braves, who first played in 1871 as Boston's Red Stockings, are the only club to field a team every season of professional league baseball. When the game's first openly professional club, the Cincinnati Red Stockings, decided to revert to amateur status, manager/outfielder Harry Wright and three of his teammates took their talents (and club nickname) to Boston, where, with infielders Ross Barnes and Harry Schafer and pitcher Al Spalding, they formed the nucleus of a team that would dominate the five-year history of the first professional league, the National Association. After a close second-place finish in their first year, the Red Stockings won four pennants in convincing fashion, including a 71–8 record in 1875 with an .899 winning percentage that has never since been approached in major league ball.

When the National League replaced the NA in 1876, four of Boston's best players (including Spalding and Barnes) deserted the club for Chicago. But after a fourth-place finish in 1876, the Red Stockings lured pitcher Tommy Bond from Hartford and finished at the top in 1877 and '78. Bond dominated NL pitching, winning 80 games (40 each year), 22 more than his nearest rival. Although he won another 43 in 1879, Boston slipped to second.

In 1880 the Red Stockings suffered their first losing season as they fell to sixth. After another sixth-place finish the next year, Wright left to manage Providence, but Boston rebounded to third in 1882 and surprised everyone in 1883 by outplaying favored Chicago and Providence to capture their seventh pennant.

Providence knocked them out of the race late in 1884, and Boston remained out of contention the next four seasons. In 1889, though, with several players signed from the defunct Detroit Wolverines (including batting champ Dan Brouthers), and 49 wins from pitcher John Clarkson, the Beaneaters (as they were now more commonly known) waged a two-team race for the championship with the New York Giants. Boston won as many games as the Giants, but lost two more and finished a game back.

Frank Selee, who had managed two straight minor league pennant winners, was hired from Omaha along with his star pitcher, Charles "Kid" Nichols. Their arrival in 1890 ushered in Boston's second golden era. Before they left the club twelve years later, the Beaneaters had won five more NL pennants. Nichols won 27 games in his rookie season, but Boston—decimated by defections to the outlaw Players League—finished only fifth. With the return of some of the defectors in 1891, Clarkson won 33 games, Nichols recorded the first of seven consecutive 30-win seasons, and the Beaneaters returned to the top.

When the NL expanded in 1892 from eight teams to twelve, the schedule too was expanded, and the season divided into two halves. Boston won the first half, and the Cleveland Spiders the second. In a World Series to determine the league champion, the Beaneaters (who at 102–48 had the best over-all season record) defeated the Spiders.

The split season was abandoned and the schedule reduced in 1893—and Boston captured its third straight pennant. Center fielder Hugh Duffy hit .363. The next year, when hitters exploded for a league BA of .309, Duffy led the way with a .440 that is still the major-league record. His Beaneaters didn't win the pennant, but they became the first club in a decade (and the last until 1920) to hit over 100 home runs. Five Beaneaters drove in 100 runs or more, and the team set a big league record for runs scored (1,221) that still stands.

Boston dropped out of contention for a couple of years,

but bounced back in 1897 to edge Baltimore for the pennant by two games. In the Temple Cup series, though (played between the first- and second-place teams for the world title), the Orioles overwhelmed Boston four games to one. The next year the schedule was expanded again, and again (as in 1892) Boston won 102 games to lead the league, winning their twelfth pennant. But as the league had abandoned the four-year-old Temple Cup play, there was no World Series.

After coming in second in 1899, Boston dropped out of pennant contention for fourteen years, finishing as far back as 66½ games (in 1906) and losing as many as 108 (in 1909). Five times the club finished last, including the four years from 1909 to 1912. The Braves (as they were now known) rose to fifth in 1913 under new manager George Stallings, but seemed through the first half of 1914 to be securing for themselves another bed in the cellar.

In mid-July they stood a last-place eighth in a tight field. Six days and six wins later they were third. By mid-August they had climbed to second; on August 26 they replaced the New York Giants in first. For two weeks they alternated between first and second, then took off to win the pennant by 10½ games.

Boston's heroes were pitchers Dick Rudolph and Bill James, both in only their second full big league seasons. Rudolph won 27 games in 1914 and James won 26; then they added two more each in the Braves' World Series sweep of the heavily favored Philadelphia Athletics. But Rudolph crafted only one more 20-win season, and James won only 5 games in two final major-league campaigns.

Classy fielding kept the Braves competitive the next two years. In 1915 they spurted once again out of the cellar—but only to second place this time. They began their climb earlier the next year, but a seven-game losing streak in early September dropped them out of a tie for first. They rallied, but finished third. It was the Braves' last close race for thirty-two years.

In the twenty-nine years from 1917 through 1945 the Braves finished only three seasons as high as fourth, and only once as close as nine games from the top. With four years in the cellar and eleven in seventh place, the team finished near the bottom of the league more than half the time. In 1935 slugger Wally Berger led the league in home runs and RBIs, but the Braves lost a club-record 115 games in their worst season ever.

In 1946, with dynamic new ownership headed by contractor Lou Perini, a new manager—Billy Southworth, who had led the Cardinals to three pennants and two world championships—and the return of war veterans like pitchers Warren Spahn and John Sain, the Braves neared the end of their long depression with their first winning season in eight years. At the end of the season Boston acquired third baseman Bob Elliott from Pittsburgh. He enjoyed a career year in 1947, powering the Braves to third place. Spahn and Sain won 21 games each.

Spahn dropped to 15 wins in 1948, but Sain won 24. Four veterans—plus rookie shortstop Alvin Dark—hit over .300. With the league's best pitching and hitting, the Braves moved out in front in June, and shook off their last challengers with a September spurt that made them champions by 6½ games.

But from there on, the Braves' path in Boston was downhill. Cleveland beat them in the World Series, and the club dropped to fourth for the next three years. Southworth resigned part way into the 1951 season. In 1952 the team fell to seventh; home attendance was less than one-fifth what it had been four years earlier. The next spring Perini moved the franchise to Milwaukee in the league's first realignment since 1900.

The move was a spectacular success. Not only did the Braves rebound to second place, but attendance jumped 649 percent over their previous year in Boston to set an NL record of more than 1.8 million. The league's best pitching staff was led by the trio that would anchor Milwaukee's years of greatness: veteran Warren Spahn, sophomore Lew Burdette, and rookie Bob Buhl. Sophomore third baseman Eddie Mathews led the league in home runs; with outfielder Henry Aaron, who came up the next year, Mathews would give the Braves a consistent source of power through their Milwaukee years.

A July-August surge in 1954 pulled the Braves within a few games of the top before they slipped back, but they set another attendance record and became the first NL club to draw more than two million at home in a season. In 1955 the Braves finished a distant second to the Dodgers, but 1956 produced a great three-way race that found the Braves slightly ahead through much of the season until five straight losses in early September brought them even with the surging Dodgers. It was a dogfight the rest of the way, not settled until the final day, when a Dodger victory over Pittsburgh left Milwaukee a game back in second.

The acquisition of veteran second baseman Red Schoendienst from St. Louis in June 1957 steadied the infield and gave the team a frequent baserunner for Mathews and Aaron to drive in. In August the Braves drew away from the pack, and recovered from a September slump to win the pennant by a convincing 8 games over St. Louis. The Yankees took them to seven games in the World Series, but Burdette's shutout in the finale brought the Braves their first world championship in forty-three years.

Milwaukee repeated as league champions just as convincingly in 1958, but in the autumn classic, after taking the first two games from the Yankees, they lost the Series in seven. The race was much tighter in 1959 until the Giants moved away from the Dodgers and Braves in August. But in September the Giants faltered as the others surged past them, and the season ended with the Braves and Dodgers tied. In a best-of-three playoff, the Dodgers took the pennant in two games—but both by only one run and the second only after twelve innings.

A portent for the Braves' future could be seen in the crowd of under 20,000 that attended the first playoff game in Milwaukee. After setting a third NL record in 1957, Milwaukee attendance had gradually declined, dropping below two million in 1958, the club's second pennant year, and even farther in this year of the tight pennant race. As the Braves declined on the field to a more distant second in 1960, then successively to fourth, fifth, and sixth, so too did the decline continue in the stands to well under a million. Perini sold his majority interest in the club. A tighter race in 1964 stirred a little more fan interest, but when attendance dropped in 1965 to a new Milwaukee low of just over half a million, the club pulled up stakes again and moved to Atlanta.

The Braves' won-lost records in 1965 and '66 were nearly identical. But in Atlanta attendance improved by almost a million. Of the Braves who had brought glory to Milwaukee, most were gone from the club or in decline. But Aaron was still at the height of his powers, and younger players were beginning to make their mark. Reliever Phil Niekro, for example, was converted to a starter in 1967 and responded with the league's best ERA.

After finishing no higher than fifth in their first three seasons in Atlanta, the Braves celebrated 1969, the first year of divisional play, with a late-season drive that carried them out of a tight five-team race to the championship of the West. Veteran Orlando Cepeda, newly acquired from St. Louis, joined Aaron in supplying power, and Niekro won 23 games as the Braves won ten in a row to clinch the title in their next-to-last game. In the league's first Championship Series, though, the "Miracle" Mets of New York swept Atlanta in three games.

Aaron remained a presence in Atlanta for five more years, and Niekro, after a relatively dismal season in 1970, established himself over the years as one of the game's most durable and effective pitchers. But the team went nowhere. When they enjoyed an occasional good season (as in 1974, when they won 88 games), at least two other clubs did much better. Aaron returned to Milwaukee (to the AL Brewers) in 1975, and attendance sank to an Atlanta low. Yachtsman Ted Turner bought the club in 1976 and attendance rose, but the team sank to the bottom of the division for four years.

In 1982, though, with power from outfielder Dale Murphy and third baseman Bob Horner, and exceptional pitching from Niekro (17–4) and reliever Gene Garber (30 saves, a club record), Atlanta grabbed the division lead with a season-opening 13-game winning streak, and recovered from a midsummer collapse to edge Los Angeles by one game for their second divisional crown. But they were swept in the LCS, this time by St. Louis.

For the next two seasons Murphy's league-leading slugging carried the Braves to second place—a close 3 games behind Los Angeles in 1983 (in a race which pushed Atlanta attendance over two million for the first time), and a tie with Houston 12 games behind San Diego the next year. By 1986, though, they had sunk into the division cellar. Murphy boosted them up a notch in 1987 with the most productive season of his career, but as his power at the plate dropped the next year, the Braves sunk to their worst finish in fifty-three years. Fans fell away, and Atlanta became the first big-league club in three seasons to attract fewer than a million spectators to its home games.

Veteran outfielder Lonnie Smith broke out of a five-year slump in 1989, his second Atlanta season, to become one of baseball's most potent hitters, and in 1990 strong seasons by young sluggers Ron Gant and rookie Dave Justice gave Atlanta hope for the future. But Dale Murphy, in the third year of his decline, was traded to Philadelphia in August, and the Braves, mired in the cellar for their third straight season, remained the weakest draw in major league baseball.

With the first bottom-to-top comeback in NL history, the Braves captured the West in 1991. As Atlanta's home attendance zoomed back above 2 million, the Braves won a battle with Los Angeles that saw eleven ties or lead changes in the season's final weeks, then took the city's first pennant in a seven-game playoff against Pittsburgh. Free agent Terry Pendleton joined Justice and Gant to power Atlanta's offense, while a trio of young pitchers—Tom Glavine, Steve Avery, and John Smoltz—anchored one of the league's best mound staffs.

In the World Series the Braves overcame a two-game deficit to take a Series lead before falling short by one extra-inning run in each of the final two games. Nineteen ninety-two was a near-repeat of 1991. Once again the Braves captured the NL East—although this time they built a more comfortable eight-game lead at the finish, after moving into first place in July with an eleven-game win streak. Once again they edged Pittsburgh for the pennant, although this time it took a come-from-behind win in the final at bat of Game Seven to do it. And once again they faltered in the World Series, this time succumbing to Toronto in six games.

For the third season in a row the Braves topped the NL West in 1993, this time charging from ten games back in July to a four-game lead in mid-September, then holding off resurgent San Francisco to clinch the crown on the season's final day. After building a 2-1 lead in the LCS, though, they fell to the Phillies in six games.

When the players' strike ended the 1994 season in August, pitcher Greg Maddux, en route to a record third consecutive Cy Young Award, was fashioning one of the greatest mound seasons in years. Atlanta's 68–46 record ranked second in the NL only to Montreal's 74–40. But a new divisional alignment had moved the Braves from the NL West to the East—Montreal's division—so they only finished second, six games behind the Expos.

Baltimore Orioles

The history of major league baseball in Baltimore dates back to 1872, to the Lord Baltimores of the National Association, and includes the great National League Orioles of the 1890s. The city was also represented in the American League's first big league seasons, 1901–1902. But when those Orioles moved to New York in 1903 and became the Highlanders (later the Yankees), Baltimore was left without a big league club for more than half a century, until the transfer of the Browns from St. Louis in 1954.

The current Orioles didn't get their start in St. Louis, though. Their first home was Milwaukee, where they finished in the AL cellar in 1901. When they moved to St. Louis the next year, they lured several valuable players from the city's NL Cardinals—including 1901 batting champ Jesse Burkett, star shortstop Bobby Wallace, and the Cards' three best pitchers. They also took on the Cardinals' discarded nickname, becoming the new St. Louis Browns.

The Browns finished a strong second to the Philadelphia Athletics in their first St. Louis season, but fell to sixth the next year and, except for a fourth-place finish in 1908 (thanks to the pitching of newly acquired veteran Rube Waddell), remained mired in the second division until 1920. Late in the 1913 season a young Branch Rickey was hired to manage the Browns. In his two full seasons he was unable to lift the club out of the second division, but he did sign college star George Sisler (whom he had coached at the University of Michigan), who became, as the Browns' first baseman, one of the game's all-time greats.

In 1916, his first full season, Sisler led the Browns in hitting as they caught fire in August to record their first winning season in eight years. Pitcher Urban Shocker was obtained from the Yankees two years later and by 1920 had developed into a 20-game winner. Also in 1920, Sisler connected for what is still a major league record 257 hits and batted .407 to help move the Browns up to fourth, their first finish that high since 1908 (though their won-lost record of 76–77 remained on the losing side). The next year Shocker's 27 victories brought them a winning season and third place. And in 1922 the team recorded its finest record ever in St. Louis: 93 wins and a .604 winning percentage.

The 1922 Browns, led by Sisler's sizzling .420 BA, hit .313 as a team to lead the league. Left fielder Ken Williams ran away with the RBI title and beat out Babe Ruth and Tilly Walker for the home run crown. (Ruth, to be honest, did miss nearly a third of the season that year.) Sisler and Williams even finished one-two in AL stolen bases. And though Shocker slipped a bit to 24 wins, he led a pitching staff that recorded the league's lowest ERA. The team led the league in the standings throughout July and into August before the Yankees nudged ahead of them. The Browns hung close, but didn't regain the lead, remaining second, a heartbreaking single game back, at season's end.

Falling back to fifth the next year, as Sisler missed the whole season with a sinus infection, the Browns remained out of contention for the next twenty-one years, dropping to their lowest point in 1939, 64½ games out of first, with 111 losses. They recovered for three winning seasons in the war years 1942–1945, finishing a distant third in 1942, and capturing their only St. Louis pennant in 1944, edging the Detroit Tigers on the final day after trailing them through most of September. The World Series—an all-St. Louis affair—proved anticlimactic for the Browns as they lost to the Cardinals in six games.

The Browns finished third in 1945 before sinking back into the second division. Even the club's purchase by the dynamic Bill Veeck in July 1951 couldn't rouse them out of the depths. (A month after buying the Browns, Veeck made his best-remembered move, bringing in midget Eddie Gaedel for one plate appearance—he walked.)

Unable to earn either victories or money in St. Louis, Veeck in September 1953 sold the club to a Baltimore group, who moved the Browns and renamed them the Orioles. The new owners hired the brilliant Paul Richards to rebuild the team as manager, both in the front office and on the field. It took him (and Lee MacPhail, who became general manager and president in 1958) several years to move the Orioles above .500, but in 1960, young third baseman Brooks Robinson found he could hit as well as field, and rookie Jim Gentile drove in 98 runs; the team made its first run for the pennant since 1944. In first place in early September, they finished second when the Yanks won fifteen straight to pass them by.

The next year the O's did even better, winning six more games than they had in 1960 as Gentile hit 46 home runs and drove in 141. But it was an even better year for New York and Detroit, and Baltimore finished a distant third.

When Hank Bauer was brought in to manage the Orioles in 1964, the team entered its golden decades—twenty years which saw them win seven division titles, six pennants, and three world championships, with only two finishes below third. With Robinson driving in runs and left fielder Boog Powell slugging at a league-leading pace, the O's finished 1964 with wins in seven of their final eight games. But the White Sox won their last nine and the Yankees put together an eleven-game streak near the end to take the flag and leave Baltimore third, two games back.

After another third-place finish in 1965, the Orioles acquired slugging Frank Robinson from Cincinnati and moved second-year pitcher Jim Palmer into the starting rotation. Palmer won 15 to lead a balanced staff, and Frank Robinson captured the Triple Crown. With both Robinsons and Powell driving in 100 runs or more, the O's romped to their first Baltimore pennant. They continued the romp in the World Series, holding Los Angeles to a total of just two runs as they swept to their first world title.

A drop in offensive production and the loss of Palmer to injuries for most of the season plunged Baltimore into a tie for sixth in 1967. Palmer was out the next year, too, but pitchers Dave McNally and Jim Hardin burst to the forefront with fine seasons to lift the club back to second.

Baltimore coach Earl Weaver, a pennant-winning manager in the O's farm system, replaced Hank Bauer at the Orioles' helm in mid-1968 to begin what became one of the longest and most successful managerial tenures of recent times. In fourteen full seasons Weaver led his club to six Eastern Division titles and six second-place finishes, with one season each in third and fourth. His teams featured fine hitters and fielders, but it is the pitching that stands out above the rest. In seven of the fourteen years the Oriole staff compiled the league's lowest ERA, including five consecutive seasons (1969-1973). Oriole pitchers put together in those fourteen years twenty-one 20-win seasons (eight of them by Jim Palmer), and garnered six Cy Young Awards.

In the first three years of divisional play (1969-71) Baltimore ran away with the East championship and swept to the pennant each time in the League Championship Series. The 1969 team (despite an embarrassingly easy loss to the New York Mets in the World Series) is often ranked among the greatest of all time. With overwhelming pitching and fielding, the Orioles took the division crown by 19 games, winning a club-record 109. In fielding, seven percentage points separated the AL's second-best team from the worst; the Orioles fielded three points better than the second-best team. And Oriole pitchers gave up nearly a run less per game than the league average.

Baltimore's performance in 1970 was nearly as impressive. Mike Cuellar and Dave McNally won 24 games each, and Jim Palmer contributed 20 more wins to the O's total of 108. This year they won the World Series as well as the pennant, rolling over Cincinnati in five games.

In the 1971 World Series, though, Pittsburgh came back from losses in the first two games to defeat the Orioles by a run in game seven. The O's captured divisional titles in 1973 and '74, but it was 1979 before they again triumphed in the LCS. Once again, however, they faced the Pittsburgh Pirates in the World Series, and once again took the Series lead, only to fall again in the seventh game.

The 1979 pennant was Weaver's last, as late-season Oriole surges in 1980 and '82 fell just short. But in 1983 the O's—paced by the pitching of veteran Scott McGregor and rookie Mike Boddicker, and the hitting and fielding of Cal Ripken, Jr., at short, and Eddie Murray at first—made new manager Joe Altobelli look good. After a comfortable divisional win, they trounced Chicago's White Sox in the LCS and the Philadelphia Phillies in the World Series.

Declining after 1983 despite the return of Earl Weaver in 1985–1986, the Orioles finished last in the East in 1986. Though they rose to sixth in 1987, their .414 winning percentage was their lowest in thirty-two years. Then in 1988 they hit rock bottom, not only finishing last but also beginning the season with an AL record-setting twenty-one consecutive defeats.

Baltimore's rebound was even more startling than its plummet. Under manager Frank Robinson (who had been handed the hapless O's early in the 1988 season) the 1989 Orioles took over first place in late April, held the lead through August, and stayed within the reach of the division title until Toronto defeated them in the season's penultimate game to clinch the crown. The newly potent bat of catcher Mickey Tettleton and splendid relief from rookie Gregg Olson highlighted the Baltimore resurgence. Olson remained effective in 1990, but the offense faltered, and an August-September slide dropped the Orioles out of the race.

The O's began slowly in 1991, and manager Robinson was replaced by coach Johnny Oates in May, with the club in last place. Although Cal Ripken put together an MVP season, the O's never caught fire, and finished sixth, 24 games out. In 1992, however, playing in the packed new Orioles Park at Camden Yards, Baltimore snapped back to challenge Toronto through much of the season before slipping to third, 7 games out.

At a bankruptcy auction in August 1993, a group led by Peter Angelos agreed to purchase the club for a record $173 million. On the field, 1993 was much like 1992. Only half a game out of first as late as September 9, the Orioles finished ten games back, tied for third with Detroit.

They challenged again in 1994; however, they slipped from just half a game behind the division-leading Yankees at midseason to 6½ games out by the time the players' strike brought the season to an early close in August. The second-place finish was not good enough to save manager Oates's job.

Boston Red Sox

Since the end of World War Two, the Red Sox have won the American League pennant four times, only to lose the World Series each time in the seventh game. It was not always thus. In their first two decades they were the league's most successful club, winners of six pennants and five world championships. (No World Series was played the year of their second pennant.)

Organized in 1901 as one of four new eastern clubs in Ban Johnson's newly major league AL, Boston's Americans (or Pilgrims, Puritans, Plymouth Rocks, or Somersets, as they were variously called) quickly established themselves as one of the game's strongest teams. Star third baseman Jimmy Collins was lured from Boston's NL club to manage the new Americans, and he assembled a team that included such former NL standouts as slugger Buck Freeman and pitcher Cy Young. Finishing a strong second in the AL's inaugural major league season, the Pilgrims quickly supplanted their mediocre NL counterparts in the hearts and wallets of Boston fans.

After a third-place finish in 1902, the Pilgrims ran away from the rest of the league in 1903 to take their first pennant by 14½ games over Philadelphia. Young led the league in victories for the third straight season, Freeman took titles in home runs, total bases, and RBIs, and second-year outfielder Patsy Dougherty finished first in hits and runs scored. In the first modern World Series, Boston overcame Pittsburgh's favored Pirates, thereby confirming the AL's claim to major league status.

Boston repeated as pennant winners in 1904, but by a much narrower margin, after a struggle with New York's Highlanders that wasn't settled until the next-to-last game of the season. The NL Giants refused to play Boston in a World Series that year.

Over the next few years, as the Pilgrims dropped into the league cellar, new owner John I. Taylor (whose father, *Boston Globe* publisher Charles Taylor, was said to have bought the club for his son to give him something useful to do) rid the team of many of the players who had brought it glory. Eventually Taylor was himself maneuvered out of the club presidency, but it turned out he had not been a wanton destroyer. In driving out the old guard he had been making room for new young players: pitcher Joe Wood, for example, and a sprightly outfield of Tris Speaker, Harry Hooper, and Duffy Lewis. The club—now known as the Red Sox—rose out of its depths in the final years of Taylor's presidency, even challenging the league leaders through much of 1909 before dropping away in late August. In 1911, in one of the last acts of his presidency, Taylor had, with his father, purchased land in Boston's Fenway section and built a new ballpark.

Sparked by the spectacular pitching of Joe Wood and Speaker's play at the bat and in center field, the Red Sox of 1912 took the league lead in early June and were never headed, finishing with a club-record 105 victories. In the World Series they edged John McGraw's Giants and Christy Mathewson in one of the most exciting Series ever, four games to three, with one tie. Three years later, with a staff that boasted the AL's four top pitchers in winning percentage (including rookie Babe Ruth), the Sox captured their fourth pennant, staving off a late-season surge by Detroit to finish 2½ games in front. After a first-game loss to the Phillies in the World Series, Boston recovered to sweep the next four by one run apiece.

Joe Wood's ailing arm finally gave out, and Tris Speaker was traded to Cleveland at the start of the 1916 season following a salary dispute. But with Ruth winning 23 games to lead the team, the Sox slid past the White Sox and Tigers in mid-September to take their fifth flag, and waltzed over Brooklyn in the Series.

Incipient disaster struck the Red Sox that December

when New York theatrical entrepreneurs Hugh Ward and Harry Frazee bought the club. They put little cash into the deal, counting on future profits to pay the bulk of the purchase price. Ward sailed for Australia, leaving Frazee to run the club. For a while the future looked bright. After a second-place finish in 1917, Frazee hired minor league executive Ed Barrow as manager, and when many of the team's regulars left for military service in World War One, Frazee bought and traded for worthy replacements. In a season shortened a month because of the war, the Sox edged Cleveland for their sixth pennant and defeated the Chicago Cubs for their fifth and, as it turned out, last world championship.

Frazee's theater losses put him in a financial bind and gradually forced him to sell off the best of his players—mostly to the Yankees, who had plenty of money, and an office just a short hop from Frazee's New York theater. Though the Sox fell to sixth place in 1919, Babe Ruth kept attention fixed on the team as he went to the outfield and startled the baseball world with a record 29 home runs. But that winter Frazee sold Ruth to the Yankees for $100,000 and a $300,000 mortgage on Fenway Park.

The Red Sox were embarked on a fifteen-year sojourn in the second division that even a 1923 change in ownership was powerless to end. In the eleven years from 1922 through 1932 the Sox emerged from last place only twice. In 1932 they reached their nadir, losing 111 games and finishing 64 games out of first.

But in 1933, young, wealthy Tom Yawkey bought the club and promptly began what would be a lifetime effort to restore Boston to its former glory. His first efforts to buy success ready-made with such established stars as Lefty Grove, Jimmie Foxx, and Joe Cronin pulled the club out of the cellar but failed to lift it into pennant contention. But as general manager Eddie Collins began turning up young players to join the veterans, the Sox' fortunes rose. The emergence between 1938 and 1942 of players like Bobby Doerr, Ted Williams, and pitcher Tex Hughson brought Boston a level of success not seen since 1918. In four of the five years they finished second to the Yankees, achieving in 1942 their highest winning percentage since 1915.

The loss of most of these newcomers to military service in World War Two delayed further progress. But with the arrival of rookie pitching sensation Dave Ferriss in 1945, and the acquisition of slugging first baseman Rudy York that winter, the club was prepared for its returning war veterans to join in bringing Boston its greatest season since 1912. With 104 victories, the 1946 Sox won their long-delayed seventh pennant by 12 games over second-place Detroit. Only in the World Series was there disappointment as the heavily favored Sox bowed in Game Seven to the Cardinals by one run.

The Yankees ran away from the pack in 1947, but the three years that followed saw the Red Sox three times in the throes of pennant fever. In 1948, after falling back a bit in late September, the Sox won four at the very end to tie Cleveland for first—but lost the one-game playoff. The next year they were 12 games behind the Yankees on July 4, but pulled up gradually to take a one-game lead into the final two-game series in New York. One Sox win would give them the flag, but the Yankees took both games. In 1950 Boston played the league's best ball through July and August, to pull within a game of the Yankees on

September 18, but then lost four in a row and all hope of the pennant.

In 1951 the Sox collapsed at season's end to finish third, 11 games back. They came no closer for the next fifteen years, finishing with eight consecutive losing seasons from 1959 through 1966, when they suffered their second successive ninth-place finish in a league now expanded to ten teams.

In 1967 the Sox awakened from their long slumber. A ten-game win streak in mid-July shot them out of mediocrity into the midst of a four-team race for the pennant that was not settled until Boston beat Minnesota and Detroit split a doubleheader on the final day, leaving the Sox on top. Carl Yastrzemski, who had replaced Ted Williams in left field seven years earlier, replaced him now in the fans' awe as he clinched the Triple Crown with a game-winning home run and six other hits in the final two must-win games. But Boston lost the World Series to St. Louis in seven games.

It was eight years before the Red Sox won another pennant, but they came close in 1972, losing the AL East crown by half a game to Detroit in the season's final series. They led the division two years later from mid-July through early September, then fell apart and finished third. But the next year, 1975, they maintained to the end the lead they first took in May, and swept Oakland in the League Championship Series for their ninth pennant. Television viewers will long remember Carlton Fisk's home run that won Game Six of the World Series from Cincinnati. But Red Sox fans also remember that the Sox lost Game Seven the next day, 4–3. Owner Tom Yawkey died the following July without the world championship he had sought for more than forty years.

Boston contended seriously in 1977 in a tight three-way race, pulling ahead for a time in June and again in August, but ultimately falling 2½ games short. The next year, though, the Sox pulled off another amazing finish. After blowing a 7½-game late-August lead to fall 3⅓ games behind New York in mid-September, they won their final eight scheduled games to tie the Yankees. But in the playoff, Yankee Bucky Dent's three-run pop-fly homer over Fenway's cozy left field wall proved Boston's ruin. The Sox rallied in the eighth to draw within a run, but with two out and a man on third in the ninth, Yastrzemski popped up and the season was history.

Yaz retired in 1983, full of years and honor, but outfielders Jim Rice and Dwight Evans remained from the 1975 champions. Joined by a new generation that included, in Wade Boggs, baseball's most consistent hitter since Ted Williams, and, in Roger Clemens, Boston's most exciting pitcher since Joe Wood, the Sox in 1986 won their tenth pennant, with an amazing comeback over California from a 3–1 deficit in the League Championship Series. In Game Six of the World Series they were within one pitch of capturing their first world title in 68 years. But they lost the game, and in Game Seven—once again—the Series.

When a pitching decline dropped the Sox to fifth place in 1987, and the All-Star break the next year found them barely above .500, manager John McNamara was replaced by coach Joe Morgan. The Sox responded with nineteen wins in their next twenty games and, despite a slump at season's end, took the title in the AL East by one game. In the LCS, though, Oakland swept to the pennant in four games.

In 1989 Boston moved to within half a game of the division lead in August before slipping back to third, but in 1990, with pitcher Clemens back in peak form after a season and a half below par, the Sox arrived at midseason in first place. After trading the lead back and forth with Toronto, they captured the crown of the East on the season's final day. But in the LCS Oakland again swept past them to the pennant.

Roger Clemens won his third Cy Young award in 1991 and the Sox came from 11½ games back in August to within half a game of first-place Toronto in September. But they dropped eleven of their remaining fourteen games to finish in a second-place tie with Detroit. Manager Joe Morgan was replaced by Butch Hobson for 1992, but the downhill slide continued. Dreadful hitting and fielding added insult to a season haunted by injury, and plunged the Sox into the AL East cellar for the first time since the advent of divisional play.

In 1993 the team's best start in years, coupled with a midseason surge after a long slump, saw the Sox in first place for three days in late July. However, a late-season decline dropped them below .500, into fifth place.

Another strong start gave Boston the best record in the majors through the first month of the 1994 season. But, by the time the players' strike ended the season in August, they had sunk below .500 for the third year in a row. The Sox finished fourth, just one game ahead of last-place Detroit, and manager Hobson was fired.

California Angels

Of the ten teams added to the major leagues in the 1960s and '70s, the Angels were quickest to put together a winning season, finishing third in the American League in only their second year of play.

Former cowboy actor and singer Gene Autry brought the club into being as the Los Angeles Angels in December 1960. Playing their first season, 1961, in Los Angeles's Wrigley Field, a former minor league park with power alleys only five feet deeper than the foul poles, five Angels hit 20 or more home runs. Though the team finished seventh in the standings, they were second in homers only to the mighty Yankees.

What the Angels lost in home runs in 1962 (when they moved out of Wrigley Field into the L.A. Dodgers' new stadium), they more than made up in pitching. Paced by rookie Dean Chance, the Angels nearly doubled their wins on the road, and as late as mid-August stood in second place, within striking distance of New York. Though they tailed off in September, they finished a respectable third, 10 games back.

The team collapsed to ninth the next year, but in 1964 Chance's pitching and splendid relief by rookie Bob Lee overcame the Angels' continuing inertia at the bat to lift them back into the first division. Among Chance's league-leading 11 shutouts were six 1–0 victories.

Los Angeles became the California Angels in 1965 in anticipation of their move south to a new stadium in Anaheim the following year, but neither the name change nor the new location stirred them out of the second divi-

sion. In 1967, though, with below-average run production but the league's third-best pitching, the Angels in midseason shot up from ninth to third before leveling off to fifth. After dismal seasons in 1968–1969, career years in 1970 by pitcher Clyde Wright (22 wins, including a no-hitter) and newly acquired left fielder Alex Johnson (202 hits and a league-high .329 BA) helped the Angels snap back with an 86–76 record that matched their previous best (1962).

The seven losing seasons which followed 1970 were somewhat redeemed by the arrival in 1972 of pitcher Nolan Ryan, who burst into superstardom as an Angel, setting a modern record of 383 strikeouts in 1973 and hurling four no-hitters in three years (1973–1975). Ryan's effectiveness dipped in 1978, but the club as a whole came to life, contending closely for the Western Division title until Kansas City shot ahead in September.

In 1979 Don Baylor became the first (and, so far, only) DH to be named league MVP, as a renewed offense powered California to its first division title. Baltimore stopped the Angels in the LCS, though. The team's run production dropped off dramatically the next year and the club followed up its best season with its worst.

After another losing season in 1981 (during which Jim Fregosi was replaced as manager by twenty-year veteran Gene Mauch), California lured free-agent slugger Reggie Jackson from the Yankees. With Jackson leading a resurgent offense and Geoff Zahn headlining the league's second-best pitching staff, the Angels rebounded to a new team high of 93 wins in 1982, and their second division title. They defeated Milwaukee in the first two games of the LCS, but lost the next three. A disappointed Mauch retired.

Again, in 1983, the Angels followed a championship with a poor season—not quite as bad as 1980, but still their third worst to that point. In 1984 they rebounded to .500, good enough for second in a weak division. As a foretaste of continuing improvement, pitcher Mike Witt concluded his rise to staff ace with a perfect game on the season's last day.

Gene Mauch came out of retirement to manage the Angels again in 1985. With pitching that featured splendid relief from newly acquired Donnie Moore (31 saves; 1.92 ERA), the team led the division much of the season, but lost three games of four to Kansas City in the final week to fall a game behind the Royals into second.

With Witt's 18 wins and 2.84 ERA pacing the staff and rookie first baseman Wally Joyner leading a revitalized offense, California won the 1986 division crown with ease. In the LCS against Boston, the Angels took three of the first four games, and in Game Five were within one pitch of capturing their first pennant. But the Boston Red Sox rallied to win.

In 1987 California for the third time followed up their division championship with a losing season, this time dropping the season finale to tie for last place in the AL West. Manager Mauch retired again, this time for good. After another losing season brought them home a distant fourth in 1988, the Angels signed Doug Rader to manage the club. They also acquired a veteran pitcher—Bert Blyleven—who led a resurgence of Angel pitching that lifted the club to its third best won-lost record ever. But as the West was now the stronger AL division, the team's 91 wins carried them only into third place, eight games back. In 1990 they dropped just one place in the standings, but finished again below .500, 23 games out of first.

The Angels began strong in 1991, even moving into into the division lead on July 3. But seven straight losses plunged them to fifth, and although they finished at .500 for the season, just 14 games out of first, they wound up in the division cellar. Their standing in the AL West improved in 1992 and 1993 with back-to-back ties for fifth place. But their won-lost records of 72-90 and 71-91, respectively, were their worst since 1983.

The Angels played even worse in strike-shortened 1994. Although they finished only 5½ games out of first in the weak AL West, their .409 winning percentage was the league's lowest, and the second lowest in club history.

Chicago Cubs

The Chicago Cubs have represented the same city in the major leagues longer than any other club. Organized in 1870 to provide a professional challenge to Cincinnati's Red Stockings, the next year the White Stockings (as they were originally known) were one of the founding members of the game's first professional league—the National Association.

Despite the great Chicago fire, which destroyed their ballpark, uniforms, and club business records late in the 1871 season, the White Stockings completed their schedule, finishing third to the Athletics of Philadelphia. But they dropped out of the NA for the next two years because of the fire's devastation. In 1875, in the midst of a second losing season following their return, the club arranged for four of champion Boston's best players to jump to Chicago for the 1876 season. That winter, White Stocking president William A. Hulbert and pitcher/manager Al Spalding (one of the jumpers) led in forming a new league to replace the NA.

Sparked by its Boston players and infielder Adrian "Cap" Anson (lured from the Athletics), the 1876 White Stockings outscored their opponents by more than five runs per game and handily won the first championship of the new National League. The next year, though, when Spalding (whose pitching had brought Chicago 47 of its 52 victories in 1876) switched over to first base, the club fell to fifth.

Spalding retired from the field in 1878 to attend to his young sporting goods firm (though he returned as club president from 1882 through 1891). In 1879 Anson was named to manage the team. Leading the league in batting, he restored the White Stockings to winning ways, and in 1880 back to the top.

For twelve years the White Stockings ranked among baseball's best, garnering five pennants (1880–1882, 1885–1886) and four second-place finishes. Anson's stern morality and strict discipline did not make him popular with his often rowdy teammates, but his consistency as a player set an example, and his innovative management made the most of his players' drive and aggressiveness. Anson's forcefulness, however, contributed to baseball's most grievous setback: his adamant refusal in the mid-1880s to take the field against black players prevented the racial integration of the major leagues that had up to then seemed imminent.

After a close finish behind Boston in 1891, the White Stockings' first era as an NL power ended. In each of the next eleven seasons they fell at least 15 games short of the top. The team's youthful ineptitude was reflected in the nicknames that succeeded "White Stockings": the "Colts," the "Orphans" (in 1898, after Anson—by then known as "Pop"—was fired after nineteen years at the helm), and finally, the "Cubs."

When Frank Selee (who had led Boston to greatness in the 1890s) was hired to manage the Cubs in 1902, he inherited a team that had ended the 1901 season 37 games out, its worst finish up to then. By 1903 he had turned catcher/outfielder Frank Chance into a first baseman, moved Joe Tinker from third to short, and brought up Johnny Evers from Troy to play second. The new double-play combination flourished not only in the field but at the bat. The Cubs finished third in 1903 with their best record since 1898.

That winter Selee traded for pitcher Mordecai "Three Finger" Brown, and in 1905 signed rookie hurler Ed Reulbach. After leading the Cubs to second place in 1904, Selee, ill with tuberculosis, took a leave of absence in the middle of the 1905 season. Chance took his place and brought the team to third.

Selee never returned, but he had gone a long way toward building a championship team. Trades for outfielder Jimmy Sheckard and third baseman Harry Steinfeldt, the signing of rookie pitcher Jack Pfiester, and the acquisition during the 1906 season of pitchers Orval Overall and Jack Taylor completed one of the greatest teams of all time. The Cubs passed the Giants to take the lead early in May and kept on rising. New York and Pittsburgh made a race of it through July, but the Cubs won 55 of their final 65 games to finish with a record 116 victories, 20 games ahead of second-place New York. The hitting of Steinfeldt and Chance led the Cubs to the top of the league in batting and slugging, and the club topped all others in fielding. But it was Cub pitching that stood out most. Brown's 1.04 ERA was the league's best, with those of Pfiester and Reulbach second and third. The team ERA of 1.76 was the first below 2.00 since the pitching distance was increased to 60'6" in 1893. Over all, Chicago scored 80 more runs than its nearest rival, and yielded 89 fewer.

But in the World Series, the crosstown "hitless wonder" White Sox matched the Cubs' hitting and pitched twice as effectively to take the crown in six games. It was the third time the Cubs had failed to win the world title: in two of the earliest Series, they had tied the St. Louis Browns by 3–3–1 in 1885, and lost to them the next year, 2–4.

The Cubs' hitting and run production fell off in 1907, but their pitching did not (ERA: 1.73). With 107 wins, they captured their second straight pennant, by 17 games. This time their dominance carried over into the World Series as they swept Detroit after an opening-game tie.

The pennant race of 1908, in sharp contrast to those of the previous two years, was one of the tightest in baseball history. On September 22 the Cubs won two from the Giants to pull into a virtual tie for first (with Pittsburgh third, 1½ games back). The next day the Giants appeared to have beaten the Cubs with an RBI single in the last of the ninth. But young Fred Merkle, on first when the hit was made, seeing the runner on third cross the plate, failed to continue on to second himself and was forced out by alert Cub second baseman Johnny Evers for the third out, which negated the Giant run. Because of increasing darkness and the mood of excited fans on the field, the game was called and ruled a tie. After another week and a half in which all three teams took turns in front, Chicago defeated Pittsburgh to pull ahead by half a game, leaving the Pirates and Giants tied for second. But New York had one more game—and defeated the Boston Braves to pull into a tie with the Cubs. The "Merkle boner" game thus had to be replayed, and this time the Cubs won to take their third straight pennant. In the World Series they again beat Detroit in five games. Their second straight world title was also, to date, their last.

In 1909 the Cubs won 104 games as their pitching staff for the third time in four years recorded an ERA under 2.00, but the club trailed Pittsburgh throughout the season and finished second. In 1910, however, their 104 wins carried them to another pennant, by a comfortable 13 games. It was their last championship of the Chance era. After a World Series loss to the Philadelphia Athletics, and seasons in second and third place, Chance resigned, protesting the unwillingness of owner Charles Murphy to spend money for top players.

The Cubs got a new owner in 1916, and with him a new ballpark. Charles Weeghman, who had owned the Chicago Whales in the short-lived Federal League, purchased the Cubs when the FL went under, and moved them into the park he had built for the Whales. Although there was talk in the 1980s of moving the Cubs out of what is now known as Wrigley Field, the introduction of night baseball in 1988 assured continuing play in this crown jewel of ballparks.

The team that next carried Chicago to the pennant, in the war-shortened season of 1918, featured only one name familiar to Cubs fans from earlier championship seasons—Fred Merkle. The man whose rookie boner as a Giant had made possible their pennant in 1908 was now their leading run producer. As in earlier pennant-winning seasons, fine pitching predominated, with veteran James "Hippo" Vaughn the league's best pitcher on the league's top staff.

Several years of decline followed the Cubs' World Series loss to the Boston Red Sox. The club hit bottom in 1925 with its first cellar finish in fifty-three years of league play, but a new era of greatness was at hand. In 1921 wealthy chewing-gum manufacturer William Wrigley had purchased control of the Cubs, with a determination to spend whatever was needed to produce a pennant winner.

The seeds Wrigley planted eventually bore fruit. In 1926 he hired Joe McCarthy—a successful minor league manager—to lead the club, and drafted outfielder Lewis "Hack" Wilson from Toledo. Wilson immediately became one of the league's leading offensive threats, and the Cubs rebounded to the first division. In 1927 they even led the league through August before dropping back to fourth. A postseason trade brought them outfielder Hazen "Kiki" Cuyler, and a close third-place finish in 1928. Then the Cubs traded with the Braves for second baseman Rogers Hornsby, and in 1929 returned to the top. Led by

Wilson's 159 RBIs and Hornsby's 149, five Cubs drove in more than 90 runs each. After battling Pittsburgh for the lead through mid-July, the Cubs hurtled ahead to take the pennant by 10½ games, despite a late-season slump. The slump continued through the World Series, though, as Connie Mack's Philadelphia Athletics humbled the Cubs in five games.

Just four games from the end of the hot pennant race in 1930 (the year Wilson set the major league RBI record with 190), McCarthy—still smarting from criticism arising from the World Series loss—quit as manager. With Hornsby at the helm, the Cubs preserved a second-place finish. They dropped to third the next year, but returned to the top in 1932. Hornsby, near the end of his playing days, was dropped as manager in August, with the Cubs in second, and replaced by first baseman Charlie Grimm. Pitcher Lon Warneke, in his first full season as a starter, led the league in wins and ERA. The club enjoyed a hot streak in August to move out in front of slumping Pittsburgh and hung on to take the flag by four games. The Yankees provided the World Series humiliation this time, a four-game sweep that provided McCarthy (now the Yankee manager) with sweet revenge for the Chicago fans' criticism three years earlier.

It had become a pattern: three years, another pennant. In 1935 a balanced offense (led by catcher "Gabby" Hartnett and second baseman Billy Herman) and the league's best pitching brought the Cubs up from fourth in late June to first in September. They clinched the pennant with three games to go, with their twentieth win of a 21-game streak. In the World Series, Detroit stopped the Cubs in six games.

After two seasons in second, it was time for another pennant. Bill Lee, the Cubs' top pitcher in 1935, was now the league's finest, as was the Cubs' staff. With the club languishing 6½ games back in midseason, Grimm quit as manager and was replaced by catcher Hartnett. In September the Cubs came to life, rising to second early in the month. They overtook Pittsburgh on September 28 with their ninth consecutive win—on Hartnett's homer against the Pirates in the growing darkness with two away in the bottom of the ninth—and clinched the pennant four games later, on the next-to-last day of the season. It was their fourth pennant at three-year intervals—and their sixth straight World Series loss, another New York Yankee sweep.

In 1940, after fourteen straight winning seasons, the Cubs began a five-year stretch below .500. Jimmie Wilson replaced Hartnett as manager in 1941; then Grimm returned near the start of the 1944 season. The club finished a distant fourth that year, but in 1945, after a middling start, they won twenty-six of thirty midseason games to take a lead they never relinquished. Balanced pitching (sparked by Hank Borowy, who went 11–2 after coming over from the Yankees in July) and the hitting of veteran first baseman Phil Cavarretta (.355) and center fielder Andy Pafko (110 RBIs) held off the pressing St. Louis Cardinals to preserve a sixteenth Cub pennant. But although they battled Detroit through a full seven games in the World Series, they ended up losing again—their ninth defeat in twelve tries.

For the next twenty-three years the Cubs remained out of pennant contention. But in 1969, the first year of divisional play, under the lively management of Leo Durocher, they took an early lead in the NL East. With a potent offense led by veteran sluggers Ron Santo, Ernie Banks, and Billy Williams, the team continued rising through early August. But the New York Mets rose even faster and farther; they didn't pause when Chicago leveled off in late August, and while the Cubs were losing eight straight in September the Mets were winning ten in a row. The Cubs wound up eight games back.

The next year Chicago started well, slumped in late June, then fought back into the thick of the race in September before fading to another second-place finish. Three years later, in 1973, the Cubs entered July with a substantial lead. Although they fell to fifth by season's end, in the tightly packed division they were only five games back. It was to be their closest finish for eleven years.

In 1981 the Wrigley family, no longer able to bankroll a winner, sold the club to the Chicago Tribune Company. Three years later, with a new manager, Jim Frey, and an almost wholly different roster, the new management capped its rebuilding program with the acquisition from Cleveland, in mid-June 1984, of pitcher Rick Sutcliffe. As Sutcliffe fashioned a 16–1 record for his new club, the Cubs moved in front to stay on August 1, and kept on rising to capture their first division title by 6½ games.

Their fall was as rapid as their rise. After winning the first two games of the League Championship Series against San Diego, the pennant was swept out from under them as the Padres took the final three. Four losing seasons followed, in which the Cubs finished no closer than 18½ games behind the division winner.

But in 1989 the team, now managed by Don Zimmer, bounced back to duplicate its 1984 success. With a balanced offense and pitching vastly improved over the previous season, the Cubs took the NL East lead for good on August 7, and finished six games ahead of New York. Once again, though, they were unable to persevere to the pennant, losing the League Championship Series to San Francisco in five games.

As they had done in 1989, Andre Dawson, Mark Grace, and Ryne Sandberg continued to provide offensive clout over the next three years, and in 1992 Cy Young Award winner Greg Maddux and newly acquired Mike Morgan excelled on the mound. But the team could not carve out a winning season, finishing tied for fourth in 1990, and fourth by themselves in 1991 and '92. The Cub owners snarled when Commissioner Fay Vincent proposed transferring the club from the NL East to the West in 1993 (trading places with Atlanta), a logical move geographically. But the threat passed when Vincent, under pressure from owners dissatisfied with his leadership, resigned before the end of the 1992 season.

Free agents Dawson and Maddux left for greener pastures in 1993, but catcher Rick Wilkins and outfielder Sammy Sosa blossomed into power hitters, and newly acquired closer Randy Myers garnered a league record 53 saves. While the Cubs once again finished only fourth, they put together their first winning season in four years. The improvement wasn't enough to satisfy management, though, and second-year manager Jim Lefebvre was replaced by coach Tom Treblehorn at the end of the season.

Ryne Sandberg, claiming to have lost his competitive drive, retired during the 1994 season, and the Cubs followed suit, settling themselves firmly in the cellar of the newly formed Central division with eight losses in the ten games that preceded the season-ending strike.

Chicago White Sox

When minor league owner Charlie Comiskey transferred his club from St. Paul to Chicago as part of the move to upgrade the American League to major league status, he called it the White Stockings, after the Chicago team that dominated the National League in its early years. The new Chicago team revived memories of the old White Stockings, winning the AL championship in 1900, and repeating the triumph in 1901, the league's first major league season. Manager Clark Griffith (who had jumped to the White Stockings from Chicago's NL Cubs) was the team's star pitcher in 1901, winning 24 of 31 decisions as his team took the lead in May and held off the threatening Boston Somersets the rest of the way.

Griffith's effectiveness fell off in 1902, as did the team, (now called the White Sox) which took a sizable lead in July, only to slide back to fourth in August. Griffith left the next year and the White Sox sank to seventh. It would take eighteen years and baseball's greatest scandal for the Sox to finish that low again.

In 1904, after center fielder Fielder Jones replaced left fielder Nixey Callahan as manager, they rose into first place for a moment in August before settling back to third. The next year they made up a seven-game deficit in September to catch the Philadelphia Athletics, but the loss of two games to the A's stalled their drive and left them in second.

Nothing stalled the White Sox drive in 1906. Although they ranked at the very bottom of the league in hitting and entered June five games below .500, their pitching and hustle pulled them through. "Big Ed" Walsh, who had finally mastered the spitball after two years of trying, won 17 games, including a league-high 10 shutouts. Doc White contributed 18 wins with a league-best 1.52 ERA, and Frank Owen and Nick Altrock won 22 and 20, respectively. The Sox shot to the top in August with a 19-game win streak (including 8 shutouts). Early in September, New York's Highlanders passed them, but after the two teams had traded the lead back and forth for a couple of weeks the Sox spurted to take the pennant by 3 games. If the race was close, so were the individual games: the Sox achieved nearly one-third of their victories by the margin of a single run. The "hitless wonders" carried their momentum through the World Series, shocking the mighty crosstown Cubs (who had won a record 116 games that year) four games to two.

In 1907, after leading the league much of the first half, the Sox slipped to third. The next year Walsh pitched in the final seven games on his way to a career-high 40 wins. In a tight finish he pulled the Sox to within a half game of first-place Detroit before they dropped back to third with a loss to the Tigers on the final day.

It was 1915 before the Sox (piloted by rookie manager Clarence H. "Pants" Rowland) next finished that high, and 1916 before they again challenged seriously for the pennant. Comiskey, though accused of pinching pennies in his payment of players, was willing to spend what was needed to acquire them. After the 1914 season he purchased star second baseman Eddie Collins from the A's, and promising young Oscar "Happy" Felsch from minor league Milwaukee. The following August he acquired the great Joe Jackson from Cleveland. Together with the league's best pitching staff, they carried the Sox into the thick of a three-way race and a close second-place finish in 1916, and in 1917 to the pennant with the best winning percentage the club has ever compiled. Ten-year veteran pitcher Eddie Cicotte enjoyed his first 20-win season with a league-high 28 victories, and a league- and career-best 1.53 ERA. After dueling the Boston Red Sox most of the season, Chicago streaked out of reach in late August to finish with 100 wins and a 9-game lead. In the World Series against the New York Giants they captured their second (and, to date, their last) world title, in six games.

With several key players out much of 1918 for military or civilian war service, the White Sox finished out of the running, a dismal sixth. But in 1919, with the team back at full strength, the race once again went to Chicago. If their pitching didn't have quite the depth of the 1917 squad, its best hurlers were in peak form. Cicotte, after an off-year in 1918, attained a career high with 29 wins, as did Lefty Williams with 23 victories. Collins and Jackson enjoyed their best seasons in several years, and infielder Buck Weaver had never been better. Old-time pitcher/second baseman Kid Gleason was a rookie as a big league manager, but his Sox began strong and, after slipping briefly into second in midseason, pulled ahead in July to stay.

When the Sox lost the World Series to underdog Cincinnati, there were rumors of a fix, but nothing came to light for nearly a year. The White Sox looked better than ever in 1920. Though they fell back in May after a hot April, by mid-August they had risen to the thick of a tight three-team race. Felsch, Collins, and Weaver had never played better, Jackson was enjoying one of his very best seasons, and four pitchers were on their way to more than 20 wins. Chicago might not have caught Cleveland's rampaging Indians, but it didn't help that talk of a White Sox scandal revived late in the season, or that the grand jury convened only eight games from the end, or that eight Sox players were indicted and suspended with just three games to play. The team finished two games back, in second place.

The indicted players—among whom were Cicotte, Felsch, Jackson, Weaver, and Williams—were acquitted in court when three crucial confessions disappeared, but they were banned for life from organized baseball by Commissioner K. M. Landis. The White Sox did not soon recover from the loss. In 1921 they began fifteen years of wandering in the second division, including three seasons in the cellar and one seventh-place finish (in 1932) that, while not the league's most distant, remains the farthest out Chicago has ever finished, 56½ games behind champion New York.

Two of the club's greatest and most durable players arrived during these years: pitcher Ted Lyons (who won 260 games for the Sox over twenty-one years) in 1923, and in 1930 shortstop Luke Appling (who averaged .310 in his twenty years with the club). Owner Comiskey died in 1931, in the midst of his Sox's most dismal era, but Lyons and Appling were around long enough to enjoy a

few fourth- and third-place seasons. But neither saw the Sox contend seriously for the pennant. After his playing career was over, Lyons managed the team for a few years—until 1948, when the Sox lost 101 games and finished last.

That year Frank Lane was lured from the presidency of the American Association to take charge as Chicago's general manager. He began reshaping the team, and after two more losing seasons the White Sox' fortunes began to rise. When Lane hired Paul Richards to manage the club in 1951, the Sox began what became a seventeen-year string of winning seasons.

In 1951, Richards's first season, the Sox spent a month in first place before drifting down to fourth, and the next year began a five-year stopover in third place. In 1954 they won 94 games but were out of the race by August—that was the year Cleveland won 111 and the second-place Yankees 103. Richards moved on to Baltimore, but Marty Marion, who replaced him, kept the Sox in third place. Their 91 wins in 1955 earned them a much tighter race than '54, one that found them in first place at the start of September, until four losses dropped them to third.

Frank Lane left at the end of the 1955 season, and young Chuck Comiskey (one of the grandchildren of Charlie Comiskey who now owned the club) took over the front office. A year later Comiskey replaced Marion with Al Lopez, who had piloted the great Cleveland club of 1954 and whose teams, in his six seasons of managing, had never finished below second. Lopez continued his success in Chicago: the Sox moved up to second (though well behind the Yankees) in 1957 and '58. In March 1959, Bill Veeck (who had in previous years owned the Cleveland Indians and the St. Louis Browns) bought a controlling interest in the White Sox from the Comiskey family and stepped into instant success.

With the Yankees suffering an off-year in 1959, Chicago and Cleveland battled for the lead throughout the summer, until the White Sox pulled away in late August. The same 94–60 record that had given them only a distant third in 1954 now carried them to their first pennant in forty years. The close and successful pennant race, and the club's dynamic new ownership, pushed Sox home attendance up more than 78 percent to a new club record.

As they had in 1906, pitching and hustle won the Sox their 1959 pennant. The league's best staff was led by veteran Early Wynn (enjoying his last big season with a league high of 22 wins) and young Bob Shaw (with a career high of 18), and featured the league's top relievers in Gerry Staley and Turk Lown. Shortstop Luis Aparicio, in the midst of a nine-year reign as stolen-base leader, set a personal high in runs scored as the club went 35–15 in one-run games. But in the World Series, Los Angeles stopped Chicago in six games.

The next year the Sox remained competitive until September, but finished third. After dropping to fourth and fifth the next two years (in a league now expanded to ten teams), they returned to second in 1963. The next year the Sox finished a season-long three-way race with nine straight wins, enough to pull them past Baltimore, but a game short of catching the Yankees, whose eleven-game streak a week earlier had put them out in front. After a third straight second-place finish in 1965, manager Lopez resigned for health reasons.

Under Eddie Stanky—and with the AL's stingiest pitching staff in forty-nine years—the Sox competed into the final week of a hot 1967 race, when five straight losses at the end dropped them to fourth. Only twice in the next thirteen years would they rise above .500; in 1970 they lost a club-record 106 games to finish at the bottom of the AL West. Two years later they took the division lead briefly in late August before dropping back to second, and in 1977 they held the lead through much of the summer before tailing off to third.

Bill Veeck had sold the club and repurchased it in 1976. But in January 1981, after three losing seasons and troubled by poor health and skyrocketing player salaries, he sold the Sox once again, to a group headed by Jerry Reinsdorf and Eddie Einhorn. With Reinsdorf heading the club's baseball operations and lawyer Tony LaRussa piloting the team on the field, the Sox became by 1983 one of the best teams in baseball. With their best record since 1920, the 1983 Sox carried the AL West by 20 games. Rookie slugger Ron Kittle led the attack, backed up by fourth-year outfielder Harold Baines and resurgent old-timers Greg Luzinski and Carlton Fisk. Pitchers LaMarr Hoyt and Rich Dotson attained personal bests to lead the majors in wins (with 24 and 22), and White Sox home attendance for the first time topped two million. In the League Championship Series, though, after a close win over Baltimore in the opener, Chicago lost the next three games and the pennant. The Sox pitching and offense (except for Baines) collapsed the next year, and the team remained out of serious contention for six years.

Most forecasters predicted another dismal season for the Sox in 1990, but as fans watched a new Comiskey Park arise next door, they also saw their club celebrate its final year in the old yard with an astonishing resurgence. With their best start in decades, the Sox stayed close to mighty Oakland through the first half of the season, and even took over first place for brief periods in June and July before Oakland pulled away. Anchoring a strong bullpen, closer Bobby Thigpen shattered the major league record for saves, passing the old record of 46 with a month to go and finishing with 57.

First baseman Frank Thomas, confirming in his first full season the offensive powers he had demonstrated as a rookie in 1990, helped keep the Sox competitive through much of 1991, the inaugural season of their new park. Rookie Wilson Alvarez's August 11 no-hitter capped a seven-game win streak that pulled the team to just a game from the top, but fifteen losses in their next seventeen games stifled their pennant hopes. Thomas continued his awesome offense in 1992, and Jack McDowell showed himself one of the American League's best pitchers, but the team won one game fewer than the year before, and finished third.

McDowell, Alvarez, and Alex Fernandez led the league's stingiest pitching staff in 1993, and Thomas turned in an MVP season as the Sox carried a narrow lead into the All-Star break, held it into late September, then pulled away to an eight-game margin of victory at the finish. In the postseason, though, the Sox came up short, losing the AL pennant to Toronto in six games.

In 1994, Frank Thomas was rising to yet new heights and became the first American Leaguer since Roger Maris in 1960 and 1961 to be named MVP in back-to-back seasons. The Sox were hanging on to a slim first-place lead over Cleveland in the new Central division, when the players struck to end the season.

Cincinnati Reds

The Red Stockings was the nickname of two pioneering Cincinnati ballclubs—the first avowedly professional team, which was undefeated in 1869, and the charter member club in the National League of 1876–1880. After a year on the sidelines, the reformed Reds joined the new American Association and captured the 1882 pennant by 11½ games, with a .688 winning percentage that is still the club record. Seven Reds enjoyed career highs in batting, pitcher Will White led the association with 40 wins, and rookie second baseman John "Bid" McPhee proved himself already one of the game's classiest fielders. The Reds even won one of a pair of postseason exhibition games with Chicago's White Stockings, champions of the older and stronger National League.

McPhee remained eighteen years with the Reds and established himself as the finest second baseman of the nineteenth century. But the club would go thirty-seven years before it won another pennant. Twice in their seven remaining years in the AA the Reds finished second, and they enjoyed six winning seasons. Transferring from the AA to the NL in 1890, they finished fourth; at 10½ games out of first, it was their closest finish in the thirty-four years between 1884 and their next pennant-winning season, 1919.

The Reds wound up in the cellar for the first time in 1901. The next year club owner John T. Brush sold out to a group of Cincinnati's political bosses, who in mid-August named August "Garry" Herrmann (formerly head of the water works commission) to run it. Herrmann promptly acquired two outfielders from Baltimore—Cy Seymour and Joe Kelley, who was appointed team manager—who helped pull the Reds up to .500 and to fourth place by season's end. Three winning seasons followed, but then came eleven years in which the Reds finished above .500 only once (and then by only one game). Herrmann, meanwhile had found his calling in baseball administration. He not only remained president of the Reds for twenty-five years, but he also chaired the three-man National Commission that oversaw organized baseball, from its establishment in 1903 until 1920 (when his resignation brought about the commission's demise).

A midseason trade in 1916 brought the Reds Christy Mathewson (at the end of his pitching career) to manage the team, plus outfielder Edd Roush. The next year, with Roush leading the league in batting, the Reds edged above .500 and into fourth place. In 1918 an August spurt boosted the Reds into third place, in a season shortened by a month at the end because of the World War. Roush enjoyed another banner year, but Mathewson left for the Army just before the season ended.

First baseman Hal Chase—suspected of throwing games—was traded away after the season and replaced by veteran Jake Daubert. Southpaw Slim Sallee was purchased from the Giants and righthander Ray Fisher from the Yankees. Pat Moran (who had led the Phillies to a pennant in 1915) was hired to replace Mathewson at the

Cincinnati helm. Thus fortified, the Reds in 1919 won their second pennant. Three pitchers—Sallee (21–7), Hod Eller (20–9), and Dutch Ruether (19–7, 1.82 ERA)—reached career peaks, Fisher (14–5) enjoyed one of his best years, Roush won another batting title and finished second in NL RBIs, and three Reds finished in the league's top four in runs scored. The Reds broke quickly at the start, but faltered in May and didn't pass the Giants into first place for good until late July. But from then on, they increased their lead to the end, finishing 9 games in front. Rumors of a White Sox fix to throw the World Series clouded the Reds' Series triumph—and spoiled it entirely when, a year later, the scandal became public and the truth of the rumors was confirmed.

In 1920 Cincinnati led the league entering September, but Brooklyn spurted and the Reds slumped to a third-place finish, 10½ games out. They dropped to sixth in 1921, but recovered for five years in the first division, including three second-place finishes. But only in 1926 did the Reds contend closely for the flag. After leading the league much of the first half of the season, they found themselves in the second half tangled in a three-way battle with St. Louis and Pittsburgh. But after surging into a narrow lead with seven straight wins in mid-September, they lost their next five games and wound up 2 games back of the Cardinals in second place.

The Reds finished the eleven years after 1926 in the second division, hitting bottom with four straight cellar finishes in 1931–1934. President Herrmann retired after the 1927 season, and within two years a controlling interest in the Reds was sold to a wealthy Cincinnatian, Sidney Weil. But Weil lost his fortune in the stock market crash of 1929 and the Depression that followed. While he continued to run the Reds for four years, his stock in the club was held by the Central Trust Company. In his efforts to turn the club around, Weil acquired catcher Ernie Lombardi from Brooklyn in March 1932, and pitcher Paul Derringer from the St. Louis Cardinals the following May. Derringer lost 25 games in his first Red season and 21 the next, but both remained with the club long enough to star in its return to glory. Owner Weil, however, relinquished his control to the bank in 1933, at the depth of the Depression and of the team's fortunes.

The bank hired Larry MacPhail (who had rescued minor league Columbus by introducing night baseball there) to run the Reds. MacPhail in turn hired Frank Lane to develop a minor league farm system, and persuaded Cincinnati industrialist Powel Crosley, Jr., to invest in the club. On May 24, 1935, Crosley and MacPhail brought night ball to the major leagues (the Reds, with Derringer pitching, beat the Phillies 2–1), and with it a sharp upswing in attendance at Crosley Field. By June 1936, Crosley's increased investment in the Reds had made him the majority owner. The temperamental MacPhail quit suddenly in mid-September 1936, but the Reds replaced him with another successful minor league executive, Warren Giles, who ran the club until his selection in 1952 as president of the NL.

After rising to sixth place in 1935 and fifth the next year, the Reds dropped back into the cellar in 1937. But the following year, under new manager Bill McKechnie, they rose into the first division once again—even holding second place briefly in September before slipping to

fourth. Derringer enjoyed the first of three peak seasons, young Johnny Vander Meer contributed 15 wins (including two consecutive no-hitters) and Bucky Walters, after his acquisition from the Phillies in June, compiled his first winning season since converting from third baseman to pitcher in 1935. Catcher Lombardi led the NL in batting, and first baseman Frank McCormick, in his first full season, led the team in RBIs and the league in hits. The stage was set for the club's first back-to-back pennants.

Several Reds reached the apex of their careers in 1939, among them Walters (27–11) and Derringer (25–7), who between them topped most of the league's pitching stats, and Frank McCormick, who led the league in RBIs and hits and finished second in batting. The club pulled out of the pack to the front before the end of May and held the lead to the end, although St. Louis closed the gap with a late-season surge before slipping 4½ games back.

Cincinnati's sweep by the Yankees in the World Series was something of a shock, but the club had recovered its poise by the next spring. Starting strong and—except for a small dip in August—pushing steadily upward throughout the season, the Reds shook off the persistent Dodgers in midseason and finished 12 games in front with their first 100-win season. McCormick and Lombardi powered the offense, and Walters for the second year in a row took NL crowns in wins and ERA. This time the team's triumph carried through the World Series as Walters and Derringer won two games apiece to edge the Detroit Tigers in seven games.

The Reds' pitching remained strong in 1941, but their hitting and run production fell off and the team struggled to finish third. They remained in the upper division through 1944, but then dropped into an eleven-year trough of losing seasons in which, while they never sank into the cellar, they never rose above fifth.

Ted Kluszewski was in his ninth season as the Reds' slugging first baseman when Cincinnati next offered a serious run for the pennant in 1956 under manager Birdie Tebbetts. Kluszewski led the club in hitting and RBIs, but his 35 home runs were good enough only for third behind rookie Frank Robinson's 38 and Wally Post's 36 on a team that hammered 221 during the season to tie the major league record set nine years earlier by the Giants. The Reds' offense (they led the league in runs scored) kept them in the thick of a three-team race throughout the season, and they finished only 2 games out. That same year, for the first time ever they drew more than a million fans at home.

The Reds dropped out of a tight race in August 1957, and suffered losing seasons the next three years. After the 1960 season, Gabe Paul, who had succeeded Warren Giles as club president and general manager, left to help organize the new Houston club, and the following spring owner Crosley died. Bill DeWitt, who replaced Paul as president (and ultimately purchased control of the club), acquired pitcher Joey Jay from the Milwaukee Braves and third baseman Gene Freese from the White Sox. Jay in 1961 won twelve games more than his previous season high—tying for the league lead with 21—and Freese homered 26 times and drove in 87 runs—both career highs. Most of the team improved on their 1960 stats, and despite a poor start that saw them enter May in last place, the Reds had risen to the top by mid-June. The streaking

Dodgers caught them briefly in August, but then fell away as the Reds pushed their pennant-winning margin to 4 games. In the World Series, though, it was the Yankees in five games.

The Reds next threatened in 1964 when, in a wild three-way finish, they won nine straight in late September to take first place for a day before slipping into a tie for second, one game behind St. Louis. In 1965 a young Pete Rose recorded the first of his ten 200-hit seasons as the Reds battled among the leaders through much of the summer before dropping off to fourth.

That December, after a decade of standout offense in Cincinnati, Frank Robinson was traded to Baltimore. The next year, while Robinson won the Triple Crown in assisting his new team to the world championship, the Reds suffered their first losing season in six years and sank to seventh place. That winter, owner DeWitt completed the sale of the team to a group led by Cincinnati newspaper publisher Francis Dale, and including brothers James and William Williams who later acquired a controlling interest in the club.

In 1969, the first year of divisional play, the Reds rose, after a slow start, into the thick of a five-way race in the NL West before stumbling as Atlanta and San Francisco surged in the final three weeks. But the season provided a foretaste of the decade to come as the team captured league crowns in slugging and home runs.

At midseason in 1970 the Reds moved out of Crosley Field—their home for fifty-eight years—into the new Riverfront Stadium. Catcher Johnny Bench and third baseman Tony Perez, with the finest seasons of their long careers, paced an overwhelming Red offense as the team hammered out a new club-high 102 wins to reward rookie manager Sparky Anderson with victory in the NL West by 14½ games, and gain the appelation "Big Red Machine." In the League Championship Series the Reds continued their triumph with a three-game sweep of East winner Pittsburgh. But mighty Baltimore humbled the Reds in the World Series, 4–1.

Cincinnati's hitting and run production fell off sharply the next year, and the club dropped to fourth with their only losing season of the decade. But in 1972—spurred on after a slow start by Johnny Bench's recovery of power, Gary Nolan's finest season on the mound, and the all-around mastery of newly acquired second baseman Joe Morgan—the Reds rebounded after a slow start to take a lead in June and pull away from everyone in July for an easy division win. Victory in the LCS came harder, as powerful Pittsburgh carried the series to the full five games before handing the Reds the pennant with a wild pitch in the last of the ninth inning of the final game. Cincinnati's defeat in the World Series was also close: the Reds won three, and Oakland's four wins were each achieved by a margin of just one run.

The Reds repeated as division titlists in 1973 with a second-half surge from fourth place that carried them past front-runner Los Angeles in September. But the much weaker New York Mets ended Cincinnati's pennant hopes in the LCS, 3–2.

In 1974 the Reds trailed the Dodgers all season and finished 4 games back in second place. But over the next two years the Big Red Machine flattened all opposition. In 1975, after hovering around .500 through mid-May, the Reds began an ascent that carried them to what are still club records: 108 victories and a winning margin of 20 games. The team featured balanced pitching (six starters won ten or more games), a balanced offense in which every regular drove in more than 45 runs (averaging nearly 77 apiece), the best fielding in the majors, and a big NL lead in stolen bases. After a three-game sweep of Pittsburgh in the LCS, the Reds subdued the stubborn Boston Red Sox in seven games for their first world title in thirty-five years, and their third overall.

They won their fourth the next year. Joe Morgan, at the peak of his career, led the NL in slugging, finished second to teammate George Foster in RBIs, and stole 60 bases. Balanced pitching and offense again put the Reds in front to stay in June, carrying the team to 102 wins and a 10-game lead over Los Angeles at the finish. The LCS produced another sweep—of Philadelphia this time. The World Series was also a sweep as the Reds dispatched the Yankees, outscoring them nearly three to one.

Two years of second-place finishes followed, and the Reds replaced Sparky Anderson at the helm with John McNamara, who led the club back to the top of the NL West in 1979. Pete Rose, after sixteen years in Cincinnati, had signed with the Phillies as a free agent, but Ray Knight (who replaced Rose at third base) minimized the loss with a team-high .318 batting average. Houston led the division much of the summer, but a sustained Reds' surge in August brought them even, then pulled them ahead in early September, where they hung on to take the title by just 1½ games. But that was the end of the Reds' decade of splendor, for Pittsburgh swept past them to the pennant in the LCS.

Joe Morgan left the club after the season, returning as a free agent to Houston, whence he had come eight years earlier. In 1980 the Reds dipped in midseason, recovering to make a race of it in August, only to fade a bit and finish third. The next year, in a season shortened and split in two by a players' strike, the Reds compiled the best overall record in the majors. But they came away empty-handed by finishing half a game behind Los Angeles in the first half-season and 1½ games back of Houston in the second half, losing a chance at postseason play when the powers that be decided to pit the half-season winners against each other for the right to play in the LCS.

As a penurious front office continued to trade away its stars or lose them to free agency, the dispirited Reds dropped to the bottom of the NL West in 1982 with a club-worst 101 losses. Manager McNamara yielded in midseason to coach Russ Nixon, who was himself replaced by Vern Rapp after another last-place finish in 1983. Robert Howsam, Sr., whose shrewd trading as general manager had been instrumental in building the mighty Reds of the 1970s, was called out of semiretirement to restore the club to respectability. Howsam signed free-agent slugger Dave Parker from Pittsburgh, and late in the 1984 season brought Pete Rose back as player-manager. Early in 1985 the NL approved the sale of the Reds to Marge Schott, a Cincinnati automobile dealer. With Parker enjoying his most productive seasons in several years, and newcomers Eric Davis and John Franco developing respectively into one of the league's leading run producers and one of its best relief pitchers, owner Schott's public enthusiasm for her team was rewarded with four straight second-place finishes (and a return in 1987 to a home attendance over two million for the first time in seven years). In 1987 the team even spent two months at the top of the NL West, until an August slump dropped them into a hole from which a late-season rally could not extricate them.

Turmoil ruled the Reds in 1989. Disabling injuries to no fewer than twelve players, including such 1988 stand-outs as pitcher Danny Jackson (whose 23 wins tied for the league high) and infielders Barry Larkin and Chris Sabo, contributed most to the team's drop to fifth place. But baseball's investigation of manager Pete Rose on charges of gambling on baseball games and other offenses—an investigation which resulted in Rose's lifetime banish-ment from the game in August—did nothing to bolster Cincinnati's play on the field.

The distress of 1989 was all but forgotten in 1990 as the Reds, under new manager Lou Piniella, leaped to a 9–0 start and, surviving threats from San Francisco in August and Los Angeles in September, held on to first place through the entire season. Larkin and Sabo—whole again—anchored a balanced offense, while pitchers Randy Myers (acquired from the Mets in a trade for John Franco) and Rob Dibble provided All-Star relief to a solid core of starters. In the LCS, the Reds overcame an open-ing-game loss to capture the pennant from Pittsburgh in six games, then startled Oakland's heavily favored Athlet-ics with a four-game sweep.

The Reds remained in the thick of the 1991 race through midseason, despite a 10-game losing streak in July. But as Atlanta rose to battle early leader Los Ange-les, Cincinnati settled into a long decline that at the end left them 20 games back, in fifth place. Barry Larkin and Bip Roberts sparked the league's strongest offense in 1992, as the Reds rebounded to win 90 games. But they let a 6-game mid-season lead get away from them and finished 8 games behind repeat champion Atlanta.

Manager Piniella was replaced by Cincinnati hero—but managing novice—Tony Perez for 1993. Perez lasted only until May 24, when veteran manager Davey Johnson took his place. Meanwhile, Marge Schott's fellow NL owners banned her for the season from active participa-tion in club affairs for making racial slurs. With their season further marred by injuries and backbiting, the Reds finished fifth, 31 games out.

With Kevin Mitchell pacing a strong, balanced offense, the Reds turned their fortunes around in 1994 and reached the All-Star break atop the new Central division by 2½ games. They were still clinging to a half-game lead over Houston when the season ended on August 12.

Cleveland Indians

Cleveland is the only club in the American League East without at least one divisional title. Since the advent of divisional play in 1969, the Indians have enjoyed only four winning seasons, finishing last in the East eight times. Their record was not always this dismal. Though no other major league club with their longevity has won as few pennants, the Indians before 1969 ranked consistently among the league's better teams. They finished in the top half of the league nearly 70 percent of the time through

their first sixty-eight years, and only once (in 1914) wound up in the cellar.

The Indians (who were at first called the Blues because of the color of their uniforms) succeeded Cleveland's National League Spiders, who in 1899, their final season, lost a major league record 134 games. When the NL dropped the Spiders at the end of the season, Ban John-son, president of the emerging American League, grasped the opportunity to move into this major market. In 1901, when Johnson proclaimed the AL a major league, Cleve-land lured several players from NL clubs and played much better than the Spiders had, but still finished next-to-last in their first big league season. The next year the Bronchos (as they decided to call themselves) languished in last place through June. But during the season they acquired several players through trade and purchase—most notably star second baseman Napoleon "Nap" La-joie and pitcher Bill Bernhard—who turned the Bronchos around in midseason and lifted them above .500 (and into fifth place) by season's end.

With Lajoie sparkling in the field and dominating the league at the plate, the fans soon settled on another nick-name for the club—the Naps—that lasted as long as Lajoie remained in Cleveland. Late in the 1904 season, Lajoie was named manager. After enjoying moderate suc-cess in two of the next three seasons, the Naps in 1908 experienced their best year yet, and one of the team's most exciting finishes ever.

With a ten-game winning streak near the end of the season, they moved from fourth to first, only to be sur-passed by Detroit's ten-game streak. Both teams won their season finale, but the Tigers, because they had not made up an earlier rainout, took the pennant by half a game. Cleveland protested that if Detroit had played the missed game and lost, Cleveland would have gained a tie, forcing a playoff that might have brought them the cham-pionship. The dispute led to a rules change requiring ties or washouts to be replayed if their outcome could deter-mine the pennant winner.

Poor seasons alternated with good the next few years. Lajoie quit as manager but remained as player. Pitching ace Addie Joss pitched a second no-hitter (he had hurled a perfect game at the height of the 1908 race), but before the start of the 1911 season, Joss was dead of tubercular meningitis. Outfielder Joe Jackson—acquired from the Athletics—hit .408 in his first full big league season. The club reached bottom in 1914 with a last-place finish that found them 18½ games out of *seventh* place, 48½ out of first. After the season Lajoie was waivered to Philadelphia (the fans then voted to rename the club the Indians), and the next August Jackson was sold to the Chicago White Sox as attendance dropped to its lowest level since 1901.

By the time the 1916 season began, though, new own-ership had acquired the great Tris Speaker from Boston and brought up from the minors a pair of promising pitchers, Jim Bagby (Sr.) and Stan Coveleski. The club rose only one place that year, to sixth. But they stayed in the pennant fight through July and wound up winning 20 games more than they had the previous year. Attendance more than tripled over 1915.

Sparked by the three newcomers, the Indians rose to third in 1917, and to close second-place finishes the next two years. In 1920 everything came together. Speaker, who had taken over as manager the previous July, hit .388 and enjoyed one of his best years, as did Coveleski with 24 wins. Bagby, in the finest season of his career, led the league with 31 victories, and veteran pitcher Ray Caldwell (picked up from the Boston Red Sox the previous summer) added another 20. Six regulars hit over .300; the club as a whole hit .303.

Involved from mid-June in a close race with the Yankees, joined in August by the White Sox, Cleveland saw its home attendance climb above 900,000 for the first time, to set a club record that would last twenty-six years. The Yankees dropped back a bit in mid-September, but the White Sox hung close until the final week, when eight of their players were indicted and suspended as suspects in the Black Sox scandal of 1919. The Sox lost two of their final three games and all hope of tying Cleveland to force a playoff. The Indians defeated Brooklyn in a World Series that is best remembered for second baseman Bill Wambsganss's unassisted triple play in Game Five.

Cleveland led much of the way in 1921 before a late slump and a New York surge gave the Yankees their first pennant. Through the next quarter century the Indians came close to a pennant only twice. In 1926, with two veteran Georges—pitcher Uhle and first baseman Burns—enjoying their finest seasons, the Indians came to life in midseason and drew within three games of the Yankees by season's end. Fourteen years later, in 1940, behind the 27 wins of twenty-one-year-old Bob Feller and the inspired play (in the field and at the bat) of second-year shortstop Lou Boudreau, Cleveland made an even closer run for the flag. Throughout the summer the Indians were in or near first place, but six losses in nine games with a resurgent Detroit in late August and September left them a game back at the finish.

Two years later Boudreau, at age twenty-four, was named to manage the Tribe. His team stirred little interest through the war years. But in 1946, with Feller back from military service and pitching his best ever, Cleveland fans boosted home attendance above a million for the first time, even though the team's won-lost record was its worst in eighteen years. The next year, their first full season under new president Bill Veeck, the Indians climbed to fourth. More significantly, Veeck hired the league's first black player, Larry Doby, who became a mainstay of the Indians for the next eight years.

In 1948 the Indians began a nine-year era of excellence with a victory in one of the closest pennant races ever. Through June they ran a three-way race with the Yankees and the surprisingly lively Philadelphia Athletics; in July the Red Sox rose out of nowhere to make it a four-way struggle. In September the A's fell behind, but the three remaining clubs stayed close, and on September 24 found themselves in a three-way tie. Cleveland moved ahead with a four-game win streak, but Boston, after a pair of losses, won their final four (including two to eliminate New York). Cleveland's final-day loss to Detroit left them tied with Boston. In a one-game playoff in Boston the next day (the first playoff in AL history), manager-short-stop Boudreau capped his MVP season with two home runs to help give rookie Gene Bearden his twentieth win and the Tribe their second pennant. The exciting race drew more than 2.6 million Cleveland fans to Municipal Stadium, a new major league record and still Cleveland's

season high. By contrast, the World Series against the Boston Braves was anticlimactic—a Cleveland triumph in six games.

By 1951 both owner Veeck and manager Boudreau had moved on, but under new manager Al Lopez the Indians fashioned a six-year stretch in which they finished second to the Yankees five times, and in 1954 they won their third pennant with 111 victories—the most in AL history. The Lopez years, 1951–1956, were punctuated by the power of players like Doby, Luke Easter, Al Rosen, and Vic Wertz. But it was pitching that gave the team its consistency. Bob Lemon and Early Wynn won between 17 and 23 games in every one of the six years, as did Mike Garcia through 1954. As Garcia and Feller (who won 22 in 1951) faded, Art Houtteman was acquired from Detroit for a couple of good years, and Herb Score came along for his two explosive seasons.

The 1954 season—Cleveland's year to break the Yankee grip on the AL—was in fact New York's best season in the eighteen years from 1943 through 1960, a period in which they won twelve pennants. The Yankees kept the race close until early September, and finished with 103 wins. But the Indians won an AL-record 111 games to beat New York by 8. Wynn and Lemon tied for the league lead with 23 wins apiece, and Garcia copped the ERA crown. Doby led the league in homers and RBIs, and second baseman Bobby Avila took the batting title. Heavily favored to defeat the Giants in the World Series, the Tribe and their fans were shocked when the NL champs swept them in four games.

After Lopez left to manage the White Sox in 1957, the Indians slipped below .500 for the first time in a decade. Rocky Colavito's power and Cal McLish's pitching brought them back in 1959, when they finished second to Lopez's Sox. Their next highest post-Lopez finish came nine years later, in 1968, when Luis Tiant and Sam Mc-Dowell pitched them into third.

From 1969 through 1989 the Indians completed every season in the bottom half of the AL East, rising above .500 in only four seasons while finishing seven years in the division cellar. In 1990, though, with three straight wins at season's end, they passed Baltimore by half a game to wind up a middle-of-the-divison fourth.

The effort proved too much. In July 1991 the Indians dropped into the cellar to stay, spiraling on down to a club-record 105 losses. With nowhere to go but up, the 1992 team, spurred by the offense of Carlos Baerga and Albert Belle, and the impressive pitching of Charles Nagy, played the best ball in the AL after the All Star break, lifting themselves out of the cellar into a fourth-place tie with the Yankees.

The tragic preseason deaths of relievers Tim Crews and Steve Olin—and severe injury to starter Bob Ojeda—in a boating accident cast a pall over the team's final season in Cleveland Stadium. With Nagy also out much of the season, the Indians' pitching was among the league's worst. Offensively, though, they ranked among the better clubs, paced by Baerga, Belle, and sophomore Kenny Lofton, whose league-leading 70 stolen bases set a new club record. The team finished sixth.

The Indians—playing in brand-new Jacobs Field—were up for 1994. Belle, who ranked among AL leaders in almost every offensive category, and Lofton, who added the league lead in hits to another stolen base title, paced a powerful offense that kept the team in the thick of a tight race with Chicago in the league's new Central division. With their best chance in decades to bring Cleveland a winner, the Indians trailed the White Sox by just one game when the season ended prematurely.

Colorado Rockies

Denver was one of two cities awarded a National League franchise in June 1991 (Miami was the other), in the league's first expansion since Montreal and San Diego were added in 1969. The new teams took the field for the first time in 1993, their rosters stocked primarily with players selected from the other major league clubs in a special expansion draft. Denver, which chose to call itself the Colorado Rockies, drew nearly 4.5 million fans to cavernous Mile High Stadium (its home until new Coors Field is completed in 1995), the highest season attendance in the history of sport.

Though their 5.41 ERA was by far the worst in the majors, the Rockies, under rookie manager Don Baylor, not only avoided the NL West cellar, but set a new record for wins by a first-year expansion team, with 67. Andres Galarraga, Charlie Hayes, and Dante Bichette headed a solid offense, with Galarraga hitting more than one hundred points above his previous major league career average to lead the NL in batting at .370.

Galarraga was in the midst of another fine season in 1994 when a pitch broke his hand on July 28. Despite a 50–54 record, the Rockies stood in second place in the weak NL West, just half a game out of first. By the time the season ended two weeks later, though, they had slipped to third, 6½ games out.

Detroit Tigers

One of the more successful clubs in the American League, the Tigers have enjoyed winning seasons nearly 70 percent of the time. In eighteen of their sixty-one winning seasons, they have remained in contention into the final days, eleven times emerging triumphant as league or division champions. They have finished last in the league or AL East only five times, and have never had more than four losing seasons in a row.

Detroit was one of the clubs from Ban Johnson's Western League that (renamed the American League) raised itself to major league status in 1901 with a talent raid on the long-established National League. In their first six big league seasons, the Tigers displayed little bite, finishing four times in the second division and never threatening for the league lead.

In 1907 all that changed. Sparked by a young right fielder, Ty Cobb (who in his first full big league season led the league in batting, slugging, hits, RBIs, and stolen bases) and led by a dynamic new manager, Hugh "Eeyah" Jennings (who knew enough not to try to tell Cobb how to play the game), the Tigers clawed their way to the pennant in a four-way race. The outcome might have been different if two late-season games with second-place Philadelphia had not been rained out and tied. Today's rules would require that the games be made up.

The 1908 race was even closer, with four teams contending into late September. The race wasn't settled until the final day, when Detroit beat Chicago to edge Cleveland by half a game. Once again the pennant hinged on a rainout that had not been made up. And once again Cobb dominated the league's hitters (though he slipped to fourth in stolen bases).

The Tigers had a slightly easier time of it the next year. It was a three-way race into September, but Detroit then pulled away to finish 3½ games ahead of Philadelphia. Cobb, in his best season yet, took the Triple Crown and returned to the top in stolen bases. But the Tigers were unable to win a World Series. In 1907, after an opening-game tie, the Chicago Cubs swept the next four. The Cubs lost Game Three the next year, but won the other four. And in 1909 Pittsburgh and Detroit alternated victories, with the Pirates emerging world champions in seven games.

Jennings managed Detroit for eleven more seasons; then Cobb took the reins for six years before leaving for Philadelphia. But the Tigers won no more pennants in the Cobb era. Cobb himself continued to dominate the league offensively through 1919. In 1911 he achieved career highs in most offensive categories, including a batting average of .420, but the Tigers managed no better than a distant second to the Athletics. In 1915 they started strong and remained in the race throughout the season. Cobb stole what was for forty-seven years a modern-record 96 bases, and the team's 100 wins proved to be the highest total in their first thirty-three years. But after running neck and neck with the Red Sox through most of August, the Tigers slumped a bit in early September—just enough for the Sox to take the flag by 2½ games. A close third-place finish the next year marked the Tigers' last serious challenge for eighteen years.

In 1934, after six straight years in the second division, and only three years after their most distant finish ever (47 games out), the Tigers turned themselves around to win the pennant with a 101–53 record and a .656 winning percentage, the highest in Tiger history. Two newly acquired veterans—manager/catcher Mickey Cochrane and outfielder Goose Goslin—enjoyed fine seasons at the bat, as did first baseman Hank Greenberg (.339, 139 RBIs) in his first full season, and long-time Tiger second baseman Charlie Gehringer (.356, 127 RBIs). The two other infielders, third baseman Marv Owen and shortstop Billy Rogell enjoyed their finest seasons at the plate for a club whose batting average led the league at .300. It took the Tigers a month to get going, but by mid-July they had shot ahead of the Yankees, pulling farther away through August and September to win by 7 games. But once again, victory in the World Series eluded them as the St. Louis Cardinals blew them away 11–0 in Game Seven.

The Tigers' hitting fell off ten points in 1935, but their slugging jumped eleven points. Paced by Greenberg's 170 RBIs, Detroit—after another slow start—shot up so sharply in July and August that even a September slump gave the Yankees no opportunity to catch them. And finally, in their fifth try, the Tigers won a world championship, overcoming Chicago in six games despite the loss of Greenberg, who broke his wrist in Game Two. Part-owner Frank Navin, who had run the club for three decades, had finally seen his Tigers reach the very top. A month later, after falling from a horse, he suffered a heart attack and died.

Del Baker had replaced Cochrane as manager when Detroit next made a run for the pennant in 1940. In a tight race the Tigers caught up with Cleveland in early September and traded the lead with them for two weeks before pulling ahead to stay with two wins in a three-game series. In the pennant clincher, Detroit's Floyd Giebell outdueled Cleveland great Bob Feller 2–0 for his third—and last—big league victory. In the World Series the Tigers lost once again, as Cincinnati came from behind in Game Seven for a 2–1 win.

Two losing seasons followed, and Steve O'Neill replaced Baker at the helm. In 1944, the wartime Tigers, behind the splendid pitching of workhorses Dizzy Trout and Hal Newhouser (one-two in ERA and innings pitched, and winners of 27 and 29 games), joined the race in late August and found themselves tied with the St. Louis Browns for first going into the last game of the season. But the Browns beat the Yankees and Detroit lost to Washington as Trout failed in his try for a twenty-eighth win.

Hank Greenberg's release from military service in mid-1945 sparked another Tiger run for the pennant. They held the lead from mid-June through August, but in September a surging Washington Senators club caught up with them. The race once again went down to the final day, and the final inning, when Greenberg's grand slam home run overcame a St. Louis Browns' lead to give Detroit the flag over the idle Senators. Newhouser, with 25 wins and a 1.81 ERA, was named American League MVP for the second straight year. In the World Series his ERA shot up to 6.10, but he still managed to win two games (including the finale) as the Tigers took the Cubs in seven for their second world title.

In the twenty-three years that passed before their next pennant, the Tigers came close only twice. In 1950 they led the race through the middle of the season, but were caught by the Yankees late in August. After retaking the lead in early September, the two clubs ran neck-and-neck for a while before Detroit fell away to second.

Two years later the Tigers reached their nadir: their first cellar finish, their most losses ever (104), and their lowest winning percentage (.325). After a decade in which they finished no higher than fourth, they rebounded in 1961 as first baseman Norm Cash and left fielder Rocky Colavito both enjoyed the most explosive seasons of their careers. Compiling their best season record since 1934, Detroit led the league through parts of June and July. But this was the year of Maris and Mantle and 109 Yankee victories; when the season ended, the Tigers' 101 wins had earned them only second place.

They came much closer six years later in the great four-way race of 1967 that saw three clubs still contending on the final day, when the Tigers split a doubleheader to tie with Minnesota for second. If 1967 was a scramble, 1968 was all Detroit's. In what is now known as the year of the pitcher, Tiger Denny McLain won 31 games (the last major leaguer to win 30) to lead the team to a 103-win finish, 12 games ahead of Baltimore. Down 1–3 to the Cardinals in the World Series, the pitching of McLain in Game Six and Mickey Lolich in Games Five and Seven brought the Tigers back and gave them their third world championship.

A strike at the start of 1972 contributed to the Tigers' first divisional title, which culminated a four-way race in the AL East. Detroit defeated Boston two games out of three at season's end, to edge the Sox by half a game. But if the strike had not wiped out an unequal number of games, the end of the season could have seen the two clubs tied.

The Tigers lost the pennant to Oakland with a 1–2 loss in the finale of a close League Championship Series, and dropped out of contention for a decade. In 1974 they finished at the bottom of the division, and the next year lost 102 games to post the worst record in the majors.

Finally, after seven seasons in the second division, Detroit put together a strong second half in strike-divided 1981, fading only at the end to tie for second. Three years later the Tigers were back on top with one of their best years. Opening the season with 9 wins, they ended April at 18–2, stretched their mark to 35–5 by late May, and were never headed, finishing a team-record 15 games in front, with 104 wins, their most ever. Their balanced pitching staff led the league in ERA, even though none of their starters finished among the top ten. Tiger newcomer Willie Hernandez (who with Aurelio Lopez compiled a 19–4 record from the bullpen, with 46 saves) earned both Cy Young and MVP awards. After sweeping Kansas City in the LCS, the Tigers took the world championship—their fourth—from San Diego in five games.

In 1987 the Tigers caught Toronto's Blue Jays in the season's final series, tying them for the lead in the first game, moving to the front with a twelve-inning win in the second game, and clinching the division crown in the finale, 1–0. In the LCS, though, Minnesota stopped the favored Tigers, four games to one.

Injuries sidelined veteran keystoners Alan Trammell and Lou Whitaker more than a month each and derailed the season of starter Jeff Robinson in August just as he was emerging as ace of Detroit's pitchers. All the same, the Tigers led the AL East much of the 1988 season before falling back and rallied at season's end to finish second, one game behind Boston.

The next year, though, as new waves of injury broke over an aging lineup, the Tigers dropped into the division cellar in June and kept sinking, finishing with 103 losses and the worst record in the majors. But in 1990 Trammell rebounded from one of his worst seasons with one of his best and, with newly acquired first baseman Cecil Fielder, sparked a Tiger recovery to third place. Fielder, back in the AL after a season in Japan, topped the majors in home runs (with 51, the most in the AL since 1961), slugging percentage, and runs batted in.

The 1991 Tigers clawed their way back from an 8-game deficit in mid-July into a tie with first-place Toronto seven weeks later. But their grip wouldn't hold, and they finished tied for second with Boston. In 1992, for the third year in a row, Detroit led the AL in home runs, but this time their big bats couldn't lift the club above sixth place. Texas edged the Tigers for the home run crown in 1993, but Detroit challenged for their division lead through August and, after a dip in September, surged to tie Baltimore for third place. In strike-shortened 1994 they finished last in the AL East, 18 games out.

Florida Marlins

One of two new clubs to join the National League in 1993, the Florida Marlins were formed after the selection, in June 1991, of Miami and Denver as cities for the league's first expansion teams since 1969. Headed by entertainment magnate H. Wayne Huizenga, the Marlins played in Joe Robbie Stadium (which Huizenga partially owns). In their first season the Marlins featured one of the game's premier relievers in Bryan Harvey, whose 45 saves ranked third in the NL and contributed to seventy per cent of the club's 64 victories. Though the Marlins lost their final six games, they finished ahead of the New York Mets for sixth place in the NL East. In 1994 they finished in the division cellar, 23½ games back.

Houston Astros

The Colt .45s (as the Astros were originally known) had hoped to begin their history in the Harris County Domed Stadium, but when the start of the vast project was delayed, a temporary outdoor park was built for them next door in time for their 1962 inaugural. Heat, humidity, and giant mosquitoes held Colt home attendance below a million in each of their three outdoor seasons, but when, in 1965, they brought big league baseball indoors for the first time, the fans arrived—more than two million the first year. The original grass under the dome was real, but when the skylight panels were coated over so fielders wouldn't lose sight of high flies, the grass died. In 1966 the club (now known as the Astros) and the stadium (now called the Astrodome) brought to baseball yet another innovation—AstroTurf.

The Houston franchise, conceived as an entry in the abortive Continental League, first took the field instead (along with New York's Mets) in the National League, as part of the league's first expansion since shrinking from twelve teams to eight in 1900. Shrewd player selection by general manager Paul Richards kept the new team from being as bad as the Mets. Although they suffered just as long playing below .500 (seven years), they finished only once below New York in the standings.

When the NL added two more teams in 1969 and split into two divisions, the Astros for the first time made a serious title run. Though they wound up fifth in the West (ahead of only the expansion San Diego Padres), they rose to within two games of the top in August, and again in September, before a six-game losing streak dropped them out of contention. With an 81–81 record, they finished out of the ranks of losers for the first time.

After dropping below .500 again in 1970 and '71, the Astros made their second run for the division title in 1972. At the end of June they were neck and neck with Cincinnati for the lead, but the Reds pulled away over the rest of the season while Houston leveled off for an eventual second-place finish 10½ games back. With a record of 84–69, the Astros had fashioned their first winning season.

In 1975 they endured their worst year ever, losing 97 games to finish at the bottom of the West, 43½ games behind the Reds. But the next year pitcher J. R. Richard, with the first of several fine seasons, brought the club up

to third with his 20 wins. By 1979 Richard was the NL's most overwhelming pitcher, leading the league with 313 strikeouts and a 2.71 ERA. His 18 wins and teammate Joe Niekro's 21 sparked a team that spent much of the summer in first place before falling to 1½ games behind Cincinnati at the end.

Houston and Los Angeles battled back and forth for the division lead throughout 1980. Richard began strong and seemed headed for his finest year. With a 10–4 record, he was starting pitcher in the All-Star Game. But shortly after midseason he suffered a stroke that ended his big league career. Led by Joe Niekro and Vern Ruhle (who replaced Richard in the rotation and finished 12–4), the best pitching staff in baseball kept the Astros in the race to season's end, although three straight losses to the Dodgers had left the clubs tied for first. In a one-game playoff, Houston rebounded with a 7–1 win (Niekro's twentieth) to capture the division title. In the League Championship Series, the Astros took the Phillies to the tenth inning of the final game before bowing two games to three.

When a player strike cut the middle out of the 1981 season, intradivisional playoffs were scheduled between the winners of the two halves. Houston, the second-half champion, defeated first-half victor Los Angeles in the first two games, but lost the next three, and with them the division title.

After four years in the middle of the division, the Astros stormed back in 1986 with their best season ever, winning fifteen of their last nineteen games to conquer the West by ten games. Pitcher Mike Scott, who had developed a deceptive split-finger fastball, won 18 to pace a strong Astro staff, leading the league in strikeouts and ERA. On September 25 he clinched the division crown with a no-hitter. In the LCS the Astros lost to the Mets, two games to four—but they held the New Yorkers at bay for fifteen innings of the final game before falling by a run in the sixteenth.

In each of the next three seasons the Astros drew within ½ to 1½ games of first place in August, only to tumble out of the race in the season's final weeks. While the team never challenged for the division lead in 1990, they overcame—with a winning second half—the worst first half in the league to tie for fourth in the NL West.

Rookie first baseman Jeff Bagwell's strong performance at the plate gave Astros fans one of their few reasons to cheer in 1991 as their team plummeted to last place. In 1992 Bagwell's continuing offensive leadership, plus strong relief pitching (especially a career-best season from newly acquired Doug Jones) ignited a fiery final two months that lifted the Astros from sixteen games below .500 to an unexpected 81-81 fourth-place finish.

The offense set club records in batting average and home runs in 1993, and the pitching staff compiled the second lowest ERA in the majors, as ace Mark Portugal concluded his brilliant 18–4 season with 12 straight wins. But the Astros couldn't approach powerful Atlanta and San Francisco, and finished third in their division, 19 games out.

Free agent Portugal departed for San Francisco in 1994, but pitcher Doug Drabek rebounded after an off year and MVP Bagwell's slugging dominated the NL. Playing in the Central division under new manager Terry Collins, the Astros struggled to catch division leader Cincinnati, and had drawn within half a game of the Reds when the season ended.

Kansas City Royals

Two years after the Athletics abandoned Kansas City for the West Coast, patent-medicine millionaire Ewing Kauffman bankrolled an expansion club for the city. Where the A's had been unable in thirteen years to fashion even one winning season, the Royals did it in 1971, their third year (when, ironically, they finished second in the AL West to the newly invincible Oakland A's). One of the most successful of all expansion clubs, the Royals in their first twenty years finished either first or second in their division fourteen times.

In their fifth season, 1973, the year they moved into new Royals Stadium, the Royals also made their first serious run for the division title. A midsummer spurt carried them into first place in August before they leveled off to another second-place finish behind Oakland.

After a third second-place race with Oakland in 1975 (during which manager Jack McKeon was replaced by Whitey Herzog), the Royals won the division crown in 1976, taking the lead two months into the season and holding it to the end. Third baseman George Brett won his first AL batting championship and carried his hot bat into the League Championship Series, but the Yankees snatched the pennant on Chris Chambliss's home run in the bottom of the ninth inning of the final game.

For two more years the Royals dominated the AL West but failed to stop the Yankees in the LCS. In 1977, with a pitching staff that led the league in ERA and a balanced offense that included four players with more than 20 home runs and 80 RBIs, the Royals compiled a record of 102–60—their finest to date. Though they didn't move into the division lead until mid-August, they were nearly unstoppable the rest of the way. In the LCS they once again battled New York all the way, only to lose the Series and pennant for the second time in the final inning of game five.

The divisional race was a bit tighter in 1978, as California hung close to K.C. through much of August and into September, before the Royals finally pulled away. In the LCS, the Royals tied the Series with a big win in Game Two, but the Yankees came back to take the next two by one run each for their third straight flag.

The Royals slipped to second place in 1979, but the next year (led now by rookie manager Jim Frey) they overwhelmed the rest of a weak division. Despite a month-long decline in September, K.C. finished the season 14 games ahead of Oakland for their fourth divisional title. This was the year Brett chased .400 (ending at .390, the highest major league average since Ted Williams hit .406 in 1941), reliever Dan Quisenberry enjoyed his first big season (12 wins, 33 saves), and starter Dennis Leonard came back from an off-year to record his third 20-win season in four years. It was also the year the Royals finally beat the Yankees to capture their first pennant—with a three-game sweep in the LCS. In the World Series, though, it was Philadelphia in six games.

The player strike of 1981 divided the season into two halves. In the first half the Royals finished fifth, but part

way through the second half Dick Howser (who had managed the Yankees to the East title the previous year) replaced Frey as Royals manager and brought the club in first, a game ahead of Oakland. But in the special playoffs, the A's (who had won the first-half race) beat K.C. for the division title with a three-game sweep.

Two more second-place finishes in 1982 (a close race with California) and 1983 (20 games behind the Chicago White Sox) were followed in 1984 by a fifth division championship in a three-way race with California and Minnesota. But Detroit swept away the Royals' pennant hopes in the LCS, in the minimum three games.

For Kansas City, 1985 was a season of catching up. Few picked the Royals to win the West, but with starters Charlie Leibrandt (17–9) and Bret Saberhagen (20–6) finishing two-three in the league ERA race, reliever Quisenberry leading the league in saves for the fourth straight year, and veteran George Brett healthy and enjoying one of his best seasons ever, the Royals chased California throughout the summer and caught them in the final week to take their sixth division crown by a single game. In the LCS against Toronto, K.C. fell behind 1–3, which would have eliminated them in earlier years. But, saved by the expansion of the Series from five games to seven, they came back with three straight wins for their second pennant. Repeating the suspense in the World Series, the Royals again fell behind 1–3, to St. Louis, before rallying once again to win three straight for their first world championship.

During the 1986 season, manager Howser left the club after he was found to have a brain tumor. The Royals dropped below .500 and finished third, their lowest rank in a dozen years. Howser was unable to return to the helm in 1987 as he had hoped and died during the summer. The Royals rallied at season's end to pull themselves above .500 and finish (for the eighth time) runner-up in the West, 2 games behind Minnesota. Although they improved on their 1987 won-lost record in 1988, they finished in third place.

In 1989 Bret Saberhagen, with his most sparkling season yet (23–6, 2.16 ERA), hurled the Royals to their best record since 1980, but their 92 wins earned them only a ninth second-place finish. Confounding predictions of another strong season, following free agent acquisitions Mark Davis and Storm Davis, the Royals in 1990 floundered in the division cellar much of the summer. They wound up in sixth place, 27½ games out. Thirty-seven-year-old George Brett, though, rallied from the worst start of his career (.200 BA in early May) to hit .329 and capture his third AL batting title.

Slugging outfielder Danny Tartabull enjoyed a peak season in 1991 and helped lift K.C. back above .500. But in the strong AL West no club suffered a losing season, so the Royals again had to settle for sixth. When Tartabull left for the Yankees in 1992, the Royals faltered again. But as the West was now the weaker division, the club's 72–90 record was good enough for a fifth-place tie.

In the twenty-first—and final—season of his playing career at Kansas City, George Brett led his team in RBIs in 1993, and Kevin Appier led AL pitchers in ERA, as the Royals returned above .500 to finish third. Ewing Kauffman, the club's founder and owner, died in August, and Royals Stadium was renamed in his honor.

In 1994, after a sluggish first half, the Royals picked up the pace to challenge Chicago and Cleveland in the new AL Central division. At season's end, the Royals were still third but—thanks largely to Cy Young Award winner David Cone's 16–5 season—only four games behind first-place Chicago.

Los Angeles Dodgers

When the Dodgers left Brooklyn for Los Angeles, an era ended. From baseball's earliest days Brooklyn had been prominent; the city's Atlantics were the nation's best in the mid-1860s, and since 1884 Brooklyn had been home to major league ball. But before the start of the 1958 season, its link to the big time was severed by an owner who saw greener fields to the west. He was right: the Dodgers in Los Angeles are one of the game's most profitable franchises, regularly attracting more than three million fans per year to Dodger Stadium.

The club's origins were modest. After winning the championship of the minor Inter-State Association in 1883, Brooklyn moved up to the major league American Association in 1884 and endured three losing seasons in its first four years. But in 1888, after signing three regulars from New York's newly defunct Mets and buying pitching/hitting stars Bob Caruthers and Dave Foutz from the AA champion St. Louis Browns, Brooklyn finished second to St. Louis, and the next year dethroned the Browns for their first big league pennant. In a projected ten-game World Series against the National League champion New York Giants, the Bridegrooms (as the Brooklyns had been nicknamed) won three of the first four games, but lost the next five.

Before the start of the 1890 season, Brooklyn transferred from the AA to the more prestigious NL. Many NL clubs performed below par that year, weakened by the loss of players to the outlaw Players League. But Brooklyn held on to most of its players and swept to its second straight pennant. In postseason play, poor weather and lack of fan support caused the World Series against AA winner Louisville to be called off after each team had won three games and tied one. The next year, with other NL teams renewed by players from the failed PL, Brooklyn finished sixth.

When the AA folded after the 1891 season, Brooklyn picked up slugger Dan Brouthers and pitcher George Haddock from pennant-winning Boston, and rebounded in 1892 to finish second and third in the two halves of a divided season. But for the next five years they finished no higher than fifth, and in 1898 sank to tenth in what was now a twelve-team league.

Help was on the way, however—help that today would be prohibited. Longtime Brooklyn president Charles Byrne had died, and the owners of the Baltimore Orioles—Harry Von der Horst and Ned Hanlon—seeing an opportunity to move into the more lucrative Brooklyn market, purchased a half interest in the Bridegrooms. Hanlon retained his Baltimore presidency, but took over as manager in Brooklyn, bringing along with him the core of his Oriole club—shortstop Hughie Jennings and outfielders Joe Kelley and Willie Keeler—plus its two best pitchers, Jim Hughes and Doc McJames.

The infusion of new talent worked wonders, as Brooklyn in 1899 (with a new nickname, the Superbas) took the NL lead in late May, during a twenty-two game winning streak, and held it the rest of the way. That winter, when Baltimore was dropped as the NL cut back from twelve teams to eight, Hanlon moved more Orioles to Brooklyn (including pitcher Joe "Iron Man" McGinnity), and once again led the Superbas to the pennant. That year they also won their first world championship in a series played with second-place Pittsburgh for the elegant Chronicle-Telegraph Cup.

Slow starts in 1901 and '02 kept the Superbas out of pennant contention, although they finished third and second. During this period Charley Ebbets, who had risen from ticket seller to president, took over majority ownership with the purchase of Von der Horst's stock, thereby quashing Hanlon's proposed move back to Baltimore. But Ebbets's clashes with Hanlon hastened the club's decline. In 1903 the team began a twelve-year sojourn in the second division, including a last-place finish in 1905 with their worst record ever (48–104, 56½ games out). Perhaps the most memorable events of these years were the change in nickname to Dodgers, and their move to brand-new Ebbets Field in 1913.

Hanlon was fired as manager after the disastrous 1905 season, but it was not until Wilbert Robinson took over in 1914 that the team began to pull out of its doldrums. Pitcher Jack Pfeffer, in his first full big-league season, won 23 games for the fifth-place Dodgers that year, and two years later led them to the pennant with 25 wins on a sparkling 1.92 ERA.

But the Dodgers lost the World Series to the Boston Red Sox, and in 1917 fell all the way to seventh. After three years in the second division, they bounced back in 1920, turning a three-way race into a rout with sixteen wins in their final eighteen games. After another World Series loss, to Cleveland, the Dodgers returned to the second division for another three years. In 1924 they began slowly, but leaped from twelve games back to an early-September lead, only to slip 1½ games behind the Giants at the finish.

Charley Ebbets died the following April, and Robinson was named to replace him. In his five years as president the club suffered on the field, finishing sixth each year. Fired as president but retained as manager, "Uncle Robbie" saw his Robins (as the Dodgers were now known) lead the league in 1930 most of the time from mid-May to a mid-August decline, then retake the lead for a day in mid-September before tailing off once more to finish fourth. That was Uncle Robbie's last hurrah. When the Robins provided no serious challenge in their fourth-place run the next year, he resigned after eighteen years at the wheel.

A succession of managers followed, but it was not until the Dodgers brought in the free-spending Larry MacPhail as general manager in 1938 that the club began to pull itself back into contention. The highlight of MacPhail's first year with the Dodgers was not the team's finish (seventh) but the introduction of night baseball to Ebbets Field (on June 15, when Cincinnati's Johnny Vander Meer defeated Brooklyn with his second consecutive no-hitter). MacPhail was also looking for new talent, and over the next couple of years he acquired a combination of youngsters and veterans that turned the Dodgers into one of the best teams in the league.

But MacPhail's most brilliant move may have been his conversion of shortstop Leo Durocher into manager Leo Durocher. The loud, driven Durocher alienated many (including MacPhail himself), but provided inspired leadership and a will to win that overcame complaints against him. After a third-place finish in 1939 and second place in 1940, the Dodgers battled the St. Louis Cardinals through all of 1941 before pulling ahead to clinch the pennant with just two games remaining. Veteran first baseman Dolf Camilli led the league in home runs and RBIs, sophomore outfielder Pete Reiser led the league in batting, slugging, and runs scored, and pitchers Kirby Higbe and Whitlow Wyatt tied for the league lead with 22 wins apiece, as the Dodgers for the first time since 1899 won 100 games. Only their loss to the Yankees in the World Series marred their finest season in forty-two years.

In 1942 they played even better, winning 104 games. But a late-season five-game slump dropped them behind the surging Cardinals, and they finished 2 games short of the flag.

MacPhail and many of his players left for the war, and though the club finished third in 1943 and 1945, it was not until 1946 that the Dodgers again presented a serious challenge. Once again the Cards and Dodgers made a two-team race of it, but this time the race ended in a tie, forcing the first league playoff ever. St. Louis won the pennant with wins in the first two games.

When MacPhail left for the Army, Branch Rickey was hired to run the club. MacPhail had left the club financially sound and a big drawing card; Rickey set about to make it a consistent winner. Famed as the developer of the Cardinal farm system, he was determined at Brooklyn to tap the one source of talent that the major leagues had willfully neglected: black players. He signed Jackie Robinson to Montreal (Brooklyn's leading farm team), and after a year there promoted him to the Dodgers for the 1947 season. Thus began the club's golden Brooklyn decade: ten years in which they won six pennants and—in 1955—a World Series. Two other races went right to the wire; only once did they finish as low as third.

With manager Durocher suspended from baseball for a year for consorting with gamblers, the Dodgers in 1947 were led by grandfatherly Burt Shotton, brought out of his Florida retirement. Robinson's hustle put him at the top of the league in stolen bases and second in runs scored. The team pulled up from fourth in June to first in July, and held the lead to the end. In the World Series they lost to the Yankees in an exciting seven games.

Durocher returned to the helm in 1948, but was replaced by Shotton in midsummer, with the Dodgers in fifth place. Shotton saw the team rise to third that season, then battle back and forth with the Cardinals throughout 1949 before edging them by a game on the final day. Robinson, in his finest season, led the NL in hitting and stolen bases, and finished among the leaders in most other offensive categories. Rookie pitcher Don Newcombe led the team in victories with 17, and Preacher Roe led the league in winning percentage. Again the World Series was a loss to the Yankees, this time in only five games.

In 1950 the Dodgers nearly caught the staggering Phillies, losing out only in the tenth inning of the final game.

President Rickey left the club for Pittsburgh and was replaced by Walter O'Malley, who replaced manager Shotton with Charlie Dressen. The slugging of catcher Roy Campanella and first baseman Gil Hodges, and 20-win seasons by Roe (22–3) and Newcombe (20–9) kept the Dodgers in front through most of 1951, but New York's surging Giants closed from thirteen games back in August to tie for the lead at the finish. The teams split the first two playoff games. In Game Three the Dodgers were leading by three runs in the last of the ninth when Bobby Thomson's three-run homer gave New York the flag.

The next year, though, the Giants fell short and Brooklyn took the pennant with relative ease. But not the World Series. Although Brooklyn held a 3–2 lead after five games, the Yankees came back to take the final two.

The Dodgers repeated as NL champions in 1953 with their best season ever. Dodger bats overwhelmed the league, hitting 19 points and slugging 63 points above the league average, as the team outscored its nearest rival by more than a run per game. With a club-record 105 wins, the Dodgers cruised to the pennant by 13 games. But again the Yankees took the World Series, in six games.

Dressen wanted a three-year contract and was let go when he turned down another for only one year. Minor league manager Walter Alston wasn't so demanding, and signed for 1954 the first of a historic string of twenty-three one-year Dodger contracts that would see him into the Hall of Fame. After a second-place finish in Alston's rookie season, the Dodgers in 1955 took the lead from the start and—never challenged—walked away with their eleventh pennant. Outfielder Duke Snider, with one of his most productive seasons, led the league's most powerful squad; Newcombe (20–5) paced the league's best pitching staff.

Once more in the World Series, Brooklyn faced the Yankees, and once more the Series went seven games. But this time there was joy in Brooklyn—Johnny Podres shut out New York in the finale! In an exciting three-way fight in 1956, the Dodgers repeated as pennant-winners, taking their final three games to edge Milwaukee's Braves. Newcombe, in his greatest year, clinched the flag on the final day with his twenty-seventh win. In the World Series, though, it was *déjà vu* time—a sixth Yankee triumph, in seven games. The golden decade was over.

The Dodgers (despite the league's best pitching) vacated the 1957 race in August, finishing third. Before the start of the next season, they had vacated Brooklyn as well, for Los Angeles. Playing in Memorial Coliseum (a converted football stadium) the L.A. Dodgers sank to seventh place in 1958. But the next year the reawakened bats of aging Duke Snider and Gil Hodges, the fiery pitching of young Don Drysdale, and the late-season pitching heroics of Roger Craig (recalled from Spokane) kept the team in the thick of a tight race that found them tied with the Braves at season's end. The Dodgers won the first playoff game in Milwaukee, and captured big league baseball's first West Coast pennant at home the next day, in the twelfth inning. Then they defeated the Chicago White Sox to give the West its first World Series winner.

After finishes of fourth and second, the Dodgers produced record-breaking excitement in 1962 as they moved into brand-new Dodger Stadium in the hills above Los Angeles. Between the new ballpark and the excitement generated on the field, more than 2.75 million fans passed through the turnstiles—a new attendance record that would last until the Dodgers themselves broke it fifteen years later. As pitcher Don Drysdale and left fielder Tommy Davis ignited the league with career-high seasons, and shortstop Maury Wills became the first major leaguer of the century to steal 100 bases, the team locked into a season-long struggle for first place with archrival San Francisco. But after holding a narrow lead much of the season, the Dodgers dropped their last four games to finish in yet another tie—their fourth.

The playoff must have reminded fans of 1951. As they had then, the Giants and Dodgers split the first two games, and the Dodgers once again brought a 4–2 lead into the ninth inning of Game Three. This time, though, it was not a home run that undid them, but a bases-loaded walk.

Sandy Koufax—who had won 14 games in 1962 (and the first of five straight ERA crowns) despite losing half the year with circulation problems in his fingers—rose to dominate the world of pitching the next four years. For three of those years his Dodgers dominated the NL. In 1963 Koufax's 25–5 season carried Los Angeles into the World Series against the Yankees, where two more wins helped put the New Yorkers away in the minimum four games. The next year Koufax slipped to 19 wins, but the Dodgers fell all the way to a tie for sixth.

They rebounded to the top in 1965. Koufax won 26 and Drysdale 23 in a tight four-team race that saw them fall behind the Giants in early September, only to retake the lead for good later in the month with 13 straight wins. The World Series against Minnesota went to the seventh game before Koufax nailed down another world title with his second shutout in three days.

The race in 1966 was just as close as in '65, with three teams switching leads throughout the season. But the Dodgers, third at the end of August, put together streaks of five and seven wins in September to move to the top, where Koufax clinched the pennant on the final day with his twenty-seventh victory. And then it was all over. After a losing effort in Game Two of the World Series (a Baltimore sweep), Koufax, at age thirty, retired because of arthritis in his pitching elbow. The Dodgers sank to eighth the next year and rose only to seventh in 1968.

In 1969, the first season of divisional play, Los Angeles found itself in the thick of a five-team race in the West until eight straight losses in late September dropped them to fourth. No one challenged Cincinnati in 1970, but the next year the Dodgers closed to within a game of the front-running Giants in September before their drive stalled.

A late-season Dodger slump let Cincinnati get to the top in 1973, but the Dodgers held their lead to the end in 1974. Newly acquired veteran outfielder Jimmy Wynn and first baseman Steve Garvey, in his first full season, led the club offensively; pitcher Mike Marshall set a modern major league record with 106 appearances in relief of a staff that was the league's best (which earned him the Cy Young award). The Dodgers beat Pittsburgh handily in the League Championship Series for their fifth Los Angeles pennant, but lost the World Series to Oakland in five games.

Cincinnati proved untouchable in 1975 and '76, but in 1977 the Dodgers—under new manager Tom Lasorda, who moved up from the coaching staff when Alston retired—jumped to an early lead and held it all the way. Garvey's 33 home runs led a balanced offense in which four players hit 30 or more homers and drove in over 85 runs. Again the Dodgers won the LCS (in four games, against Philadelphia), and again they lost the World Series (to the Yankees, in six games).

Although the divisional race was closer— and the Dodgers broke baseball's three million attendance barrier for the first time—1978 was in most respects a replay of 1977. Garvey again led the club offensively, the Dodgers again beat out Cincinnati in the West and Philadelphia in a four-game LCS, and the Yankees again defeated the Dodgers in a six-game World Series.

A season-long back-and-forth battle with Houston in 1980 ended in a tie for first—the fifth tie for the Dodgers, three more than any other club. In the playoff (reduced from three games to one to bring the NL into line with AL practice), Houston won easily.

When the players went out on strike part way through 1981, the Dodgers, paced by the spectacular pitching of rookie Fernando Valenzuela, found themselves half a game in front of Cincinnati. In a special playoff with poststrike leader Houston, the Dodgers defeated the Astros in five games for the division title, and also went the distance in beating Montreal for the pennant—their twenty-first. Facing the Yankees for the eleventh time in World Series play, they lost the first two games, but swept the next four games to capture their sixth world title.

In 1982, after a poor start, the Dodgers fought back to take the lead in August and again in September before dropping back to second, a game out. More successful drives in 1983 and '85 led to their fifth and sixth division titles, but culminated in defeat in the LCS—to Philadelphia in 1983 and St. Louis two years later. In 1986 and '87 they posted identical 73–89 won-lost records—the team's worst performance in two decades.

But then in 1988, with an infusion of talent from the American League—most notably slugger Kirk Gibson and relief ace Jay Howell—and a spectacular season from starter Orel Hershiser (who concluded his 23–8 year with a major-league record 59 consecutive scoreless innings), the Dodgers bounced back to the top of the NL West. It took them the full seven games to down the favored Mets in the LCS for their twenty-second pennant, but in the World Series they humbled Oakland's powerful Athletics in just five games for their seventh world crown.

Hershiser (whose 15–15 record belied another strong season on the mound) led a 1989 Dodger pitching staff that yielded the fewest runs in the majors, but with an offense last among major league clubs in *scoring* runs, the Dodgers could finish no better than fourth in the West. Hershiser's 1990 season ended almost as soon as it began when he underwent shoulder surgery in late April, but young Ramon Martinez took up the slack, winning 20 games. With a revived offense that topped the NL West in runs scored, the Dodgers bounced back from a slow first half to draw within 3½ games of Cincinnati in late September and finish second, 5 games out.

From early May to late August 1991, the Dodgers occupied first place in their division, paced by the majors' stingiest pitching staff and the hot bats of free agent signees Brett Butler and Darryl Strawberry. But the team never enjoyed more than a 6-game lead, and with seven straight losses after the All-Star break, began their descent into a great struggle with ascendant Atlanta. From August 21 through season's end the two clubs stayed within two games of each other. With four games to go, Los Angeles held a one-game lead. But they lost their next three games and all hope of the division crown.

In 1992 everything fell apart. Unable to parry the twin blows of injury and inexperience, the Dodgers stumbled to the worst record in the majors, and finished last for only the second time in their 109 years of major league play. Rookie catcher Mike Piazza burst upon the scene in 1993 to rank among NL leaders in batting, slugging, home runs and RBIs, as the Dodgers recovered to finish in fourth place. A final-game victory over San Francisco brought their season record to .500, and deprived the Giants of a tie for the division title.

In 1994, the Dodgers struggled to keep their record above .500. But their 58–56 record, while only the league's fifth best, was good enough for a 3½ game lead over runner-up San Francisco in the weak NL West.

Milwaukee Brewers

When in 1969 the new Seattle Pilots played their home opener in the refurbished minor league Sick's Stadium, 7,000 seats and the left field fence were still unfinished. The Pilots may not have needed the seats. Fewer than 700,000 fans came to see them play—the third worst attendance in the league—as they drifted into the cellar of the American League West with 98 losses. That winter the Pilots—renamed the Brewers—moved to Milwaukee, where a genuine big league stadium (vacated by the Braves five years earlier) awaited them.

Attendance improved nearly 38 percent in Milwaukee, although the Brewers of 1970 won only one game more than the Pilots had in Seattle. It would be eight more years before they experienced their first winning season. Meanwhile, in 1972, they switched divisions from West to East, trading places with the Washington Senators, who moved West to become the Texas Rangers.

At last—and with power—the Brewers broke their losing pattern in 1978. One key front-office move leading to the turnaround, the signing of free agent Larry Hisle (who the previous year with Minnesota had led the league in RBIs), was also a giant step in the escalation of major league player compensation. With a signing bonus and deferred payments on top of salary, Hisle's six-year contract averaged out to eleven times what he was paid in Minnesota, an annual average figure that would have paid almost 40 percent of the Brewers' player payroll the previous year.

Hisle proved his worth in 1978, leading an offense that sprang to life under rookie manager George Bamberger to top the league in hitting, slugging, homers, and runs scored. On the mound Mike Caldwell won 22 games in the best season of his career. Although the Brewers never threatened the Boston Red Sox or the New York Yankees for the lead, they did rise from below .500 in early June to finish a solid third, 24 games above .500.

A shoulder injury the next April marked the beginning of the end of Hisle's career and perhaps cost Milwaukee the division title. Even without Hisle the team compiled what is still their best winning percentage (.590), as outfielder Gorman Thomas (45 home runs, 123 RBIs) and several other Brewer hitters attained new career peaks of productivity. While they never seriously threatened front-running Baltimore, they rose past Boston in late August to finish second.

Most of the Milwaukee bats remained hot in 1980, but injuries, ragged pitching, and Bamberger's heart attack (which caused him to miss the first part of the season and retire in early September) contributed to a distant third-place finish. In strike-divided 1981, league-leading performances by two newly acquired pitchers—starter Pete Vuckovich (14–4) and reliever Rollie Fingers (28 saves)—helped give the Brewers the best overall record in the AL East, and the second-half championship. But in the special intradivisional playoffs with first-half winner New York, the Yankees captured the division crown three games to two.

The Brewers started slowly in 1982; at the end of May they were two games below .500, near the bottom of the division. A day later Buck Rodgers, the Milwaukee coach who had replaced Bamberger as manager two years earlier, was himself replaced by coach Harvey Kuenn. By mid-July the team had risen to first place, and they led the West by more than six games as September neared. But Baltimore had cut the lead to three games by the time Milwaukee arrived for the season's final four games. One win would give the Brewers their first division championship, but they lost the first three games by five, six, and eight runs. Don Sutton, who had been acquired from Houston a month earlier, faced Oriole Jim Palmer in the season finale: the Brewers made Sutton's job easy, scoring ten runs to Baltimore's two.

Milwaukee's offense—"Harvey's Wallbangers"—had been awesome, scoring more than a run per game above the league average. Just about every offensive category featured one or two Brewers among the league's top three: in hits they took all three top spots. Shortstop Robin Yount, who finished first in slugging, hits, total bases, and doubles, was named major league player of the year.

In postseason play California took a 2–1 lead in the League Championship Series, but Milwaukee came back to take the final two games and the pennant. In the World Series against St. Louis, the Brewers twice took the lead in games, but a Cardinal come-from-behind win in Game Seven ended Brewer hopes.

Milwaukee dropped to fifth in 1983, then to a last-place seventh the next year, 36½ games back—their most distant finish ever. It was not until 1987 that they returned to the winning track, finishing third with 91 victories. Had they remained in the AL West where they started, they would have won the division championship by 6 games.

As veterans Robin Yount and Paul Molitor continued to spark the team's offense, and starter Ted Higuera and reliever Dan Plesac headlined the AL East's best pitching staff, the Brewers in 1988 rose above .500 to stay at the end of August, and finished in a tie for third, just two games behind champion Boston. With Yount and Molitor enjoying even more productive seasons in 1989, and reliever Plesac on a club-record pace for saves, the Brewers drew within half a game of first place in August. But injuries and league-worst fielding took their toll, and the club finished fourth, right at .500. In 1990, as poor fielding led to more than 100 unearned runs, the Brewers dropped to sixth.

Paul Molitor enjoyed a banner season in 1991, and from the first week in August to the finish the Brewers played at a torrid .750 clip. But they had begun their comeback 15 games behind, and too late to raise themselves past fourth, 8 games out. With another sterling season from Molitor in 1992, and another strong finish (after a better first half), Milwaukee drew within 2 games of ultimately victorious Toronto in the season's final week. Still, the Brewers' 92–70 record and second-place finish were their best since their pennant-winning season a decade earlier. In 1993, though, free agent Molitor departed for Toronto, sparking the Blue Jays' run for a second straight world championship as the Brewers fell into the AL East cellar, 26 games behind the Jays.

In 1994 the Brewers were one of five clubs inserted into the AL's new Central Division, thus becoming the only club to play in three different divisions. They finished last once again, dropping behind Minnesota just three days before the season concluded in August.

Minnesota Twins

The Twins' beginnings as the Washington Senators were inauspicious. When American League president Ban Johnson established the Senators as part of his move in 1901 to raise the league to major league status, he staffed it with the manager and many of the players from his disbanded Kansas City franchise. Within a decade, four of the eight teams in the new major league had won two or more pennants, and three others had enjoyed at least one season in second place. But the Senators, after sixth-place finishes in their first two seasons, spent the next nine years in seventh or eighth. In 1904, their fourth season, they lost 113 games—still the team worst.

Even the arrival of promising young fireballer Walter Johnson didn't seem to help. By 1909 he was the league's second-best strikeout artist, but he lost 25 games and the Senators finished farther back than ever—56 games from the top. Johnson turned his record around the next two years, winning 25 games in 1910 and in 1911, but the team rose only to seventh.

When Clark Griffith—a forty-two-year-old former pitching great and one of the founders of the American League—was hired to manage the Senators after the 1911 season, the club's fortunes took an immediate turn for the better. Griffith revamped the lineup—most strikingly in the acquisition of first baseman Chick Gandil from minor league Montreal. The Senators in 1912 won seventeen straight games after Gandil was put into the lineup, and found themselves in the midst of a pennant race. Boston's Red Sox eventually ran away from the field, but the Senators held off Philadelphia for second place. Johnson won 33 games, and his 1.39 ERA led the league.

The next season was Johnson's finest. His league-leading 36 wins, 11 shutouts, and 1.14 ERA were also career bests and enabled Washington to overtake Cleveland late in the season for another second-place finish. But while Johnson continued to top 20 wins per season for several years before beginning to fade, his team was unable to

stay competitive, only once in the next decade making a serious run at the pennant (in war-shortened 1918, when they finished 4 games back, in third).

Griffith wanted the Senators to spend more to attract good players; when his demands were rejected, he bought into a controlling interest in the club and named himself president. A year later, in 1921, he retired as field manager. Under a succession of veteran player-managers the team showed some improvement over the next three years, but Griffith's surprise appointment of twenty-seven-year-old second baseman Bucky Harris to manage the team in 1924 worked wonders. Left fielder Goose Goslin drove in more runs than Babe Ruth, and Walter Johnson put together his best season in years to head the league's best pitching staff. A hot streak in June shot the team from fifth to first, and a strong stretch drive in August and September brought them to the finish 2 games ahead of the Yankees. In the World Series a ground ball's lucky bounce over the head of the Giants' third baseman brought the Senators victory in the last of the twelfth inning of the seventh game.

Though the Senators, aided by the acquisition of veteran pitcher Stan Coveleski from Cleveland, fought off the A's to repeat as pennant winners in 1925, they were less successful in postseason play. Once again the Series went the full seven games, but this time Pittsburgh won the world title.

The Senators enjoyed winning seasons in five of the next seven years, as Johnson retired from the mound and replaced Harris as manager. But it was not until 1933, when Johnson was replaced by twenty-six-year-old shortstop Joe Cronin, that the team again pursued the pennant beyond midseason. Two veteran pitchers at the top of their form—Alvin "General" Crowder and Earl Whitehill—and a balanced offense led by Cronin and first baseman Joe Kuhel kept the Senators close to New York through July, and then, as the Yankees leveled off in August, shot the team up out of reach. Although they tailed off a bit at the end, the Senators won the pennant handily, compiling a .651 winning percentage that is still the club record. The New York Giants, though, took Washington's measure in the World Series and overcame them in five games.

The following October, after a drop from third place in June to a distant seventh at season's end had plunged home attendance nearly 25 percent below the previous year, Griffith—always close to the edge financially—traded Joe Cronin, his manager, star shortstop, and (since September) son-in-law, to the Boston Red Sox for a lesser shortstop and $225,000.

Only twice in their remaining quarter century in Washington did the Senators rise higher than fourth or finish closer than 17 games from the top. In 1943 they placed second, 13½ games behind the runaway Yankees. And two years later, after a poor start, they caught up with frontrunner Detroit in September, only to stall and finish 1½ games out. In their final six Washington seasons, they wound up in the cellar four times.

Calvin Griffith, Clark's adopted son, assumed the club presidency when his father died in 1955. Within three years he was making plans to move the club to Minneapolis. There were threats from Congress and a plea from President Eisenhower not to move the Senators—and at first the league itself opposed the move. But Washington was not a good baseball town even when the Senators were playing well, and in October 1960 a solution was reached. The league would let Griffith move his club to Minnesota, and Washington would be granted a new expansion team.

Players like outfielders Bob Allison and Harmon Killebrew, and pitcher Camilo Pascual, who had enjoyed productive seasons before the move, were even more productive in Minnesota. Other standouts became regulars or joined the club after the move—Zoilo Versalles at shortstop, Rich Rollins at third, Jim Kaat on the mound, and (arriving in 1964) outfielder Tony Oliva and pitcher Jim "Mudcat" Grant. Infielder Rod Carew began his twelve-year stint with the Twins in 1967.

Former outfielder Sam Mele made his major league managerial debut during 1961, and in 1962 saw his Twins come close to catching the Yankees in mid-September, finishing second. The next year they didn't catch fire until August and wound up third. In 1964 they dropped below .500 into a tie for sixth. But after the end of June 1965 no one challenged them as they breezed to their first Minnesota pennant. Oliva led the league in batting for the second straight year, and Versalles (in what was far and away his finest season) led the league in total bases and runs scored. Mudcat Grant led the league with 21 victories (his only 20-win season) and 6 shutouts, and Kaat's 18 wins were the league's third best. In the World Series it took a three-hitter by Los Angeles's Sandy Koufax to stop the Twins in the seventh game.

After a poor start in 1966 that saw them enter July deep in fifth place, the Twins played better than anyone else the rest of the season to sneak ahead of Detroit into second. Killebrew, who had been injured much of the previous year, returned with his old power in '66, and Kaat enjoyed a career-high season with 25 wins.

The Twins began 1967 with another poor start. With the team in disarray and in sixth place, the easygoing Mele was replaced in June by hard-driving Cal Ermer, a longtime minor league manager. By mid-July the team had risen to second, and a month later (after dropping back to fourth) moved to the top in one of the greatest pennant races ever. Four clubs battled for the title, with three still in the running on the final day. But Boston defeated Minnesota to win the pennant, and Detroit split a doubleheader to tie the Twins for second. The next year Minnesota finished seventh.

Fiery rookie manager Billy Martin replaced Ermer in 1969 and, in this first season of divisional play, piloted the Twins to the championship of the West by a convincing 9 games. Killebrew exploded for the best season of his career (49 home runs, 140 runs driven in), and Carew won the first of his seven batting titles. The first League Championship Series, though, was a disaster for the Twins as Baltimore swept to the pennant in three games. Veteran manager Bill Rigney replaced the difficult Martin at the helm, and piloted Minnesota to an almost identical division crown in 1970, 9 games ahead of Oakland. Pitcher Jim Perry, with 24 victories, enjoyed his second straight 20-win season, and the best of his career. The LCS, though, was another repeat performance—a Baltimore sweep.

For the next thirteen years the Twins remained out of contention, although only in 1981 and '82 did they drop to the bottom of the division. Twice (in 1974 and '76) they recovered from poor starts to make a decent showing, and once (1979) they pushed into first in July before nosediving out of the race. But it was not until the flowering of a new generation of young players in 1984 that a Minnesota title threat could be taken seriously.

The Twins' decline on the field was matched by a decline in attendance, which even their move indoors in 1982 did not significantly redress. The Griffith family, unwilling to risk the high cost of luring proven talent, decided to give up the club after more than sixty years of family ownership. Early in 1984 a buyer was found in Carl Pohlad, a wealthy Minneapolis banker. By the time Pohlad's purchase was completed at the end of July, the Twins' young team had blossomed into the West's front-runner, paced by pitcher Frank Viola's sudden development into a winner, and by the arrival in May of rookie centerfield sparkplug Kirby Puckett. Although the Twins leveled off in August and lost their final six games, to fall to .500 and a tie for second, they had brought the crowds back to the ballpark. The team in 1984 for the first time ever drew more than 1.5 million fans to their home games, and remained well above a million the next two years despite a pair of losing seasons.

In 1987 the Minnesota fans were rewarded for their faithfulness. Although the Twins lost their last five games to finish only eight above .500 (and two ahead of surging Kansas City), their winning record at home was the best in the league, and their title in the West was never in doubt. More surprising was their decisive triumph over favored Detroit in the LCS, four games to one. In the first World Series to feature indoor play, the Twins won the four games played in their Metrodome to capture Minnesota's first world baseball championship in seven games.

Although the Twins in 1988 improved on their 1987 won-lost record—and Frank Viola, Kirby Puckett, and relief ace Jeff Reardon enjoyed career peaks—they finished well back of Oakland in the race for the division crown. But their home attendance, which had jumped 66 percent in 1987 to top 2 million for the first time, bounded another 45 percent in 1988 to make the Twins the first AL club ever to attract more than 3 million fans in a season.

As the team suffered a general decline in pitching and hitting in 1989, Viola—in the middle of a disappointing season—was traded to the Mets; the Twins finished fifth. Reardon, a free agent, left for Boston after the season. The Twins continued their downhill slide in 1990, slipping from fifth place at midseason to their first cellar finish in eight years.

On May 27, 1991, the Twins stood sixth in the AL West. Three weeks later, after winning eighteen of nineteen games, they were first. There they finished, becoming (like Atlanta in the NL) the first AL team to rise from last place to first in successive seasons. Minnesota's attack featured a balanced offense in which seven players drove in 50 runs or more, and a pitching revival that starred veteran free agent Jack Morris and a pair of young hurlers in their first full seasons, Scott Erickson and Kevin Tapani. In the ALCS, the Twins overcame Toronto in five games, then came back from a 2–3 World Series deficit to defeat Atlanta with a pair of extra-inning victories.

After his single starring season in Minnesota, pitcher Morris moved on to Toronto to hurl the Blue Jays to the championship. The Twins, meanwhile, led the AL West into midseason, before drifting back into a second-place finish behind Oakland. Veteran superstar Dave Winfield left Toronto for Minnesota in 1993, where in September he passed the 3,000 hit mark. But the Twins slid out of contention early, and finished tied for fifth.

In early August 1994, now playing in the new Central Division, they finished fourth.

Montreal Expos

In the spring of 1969, in an unfinished "temporary" ballpark that would be the Expos' home for eight years, major league baseball came to Canada. One of two clubs added to the National League in this first year of divisional play—Montreal in the East and San Diego in the West—the Expos finished 48 games out of first. But although they matched San Diego's 52–110 record and last-place divisional finish, they outdrew the Padres by better than two to one, with a home attendance of more than 1.2 million fans.

After a second last-place (but much improved at 73–89) season in 1970, the Expos moved a notch out of the cellar to fifth in 1971 and '72, and into pennant contention in 1973. Outfielder Ken Singleton became the first Expo to drive in 100 or more runs, rookie pitcher Steve Rogers compiled a sparkling 1.54 ERA (and a 10–5 won-lost record), and reliever Mike Marshall set a new major-league record with 92 pitching appearances (winning 14 games and saving a league-high 31). In the tightest race of the century, all six clubs remained in contention into September, when Philadelphia dropped away. In mid-September Montreal won six straight to catch front-running Pittsburgh, only to lose nine of the next ten and drop back to fifth. Three wins in the final four games lifted them to fourth place, just 3½ games behind the champion New York Mets.

Center fielder Willie Davis (acquired from Los Angeles in a trade for Mike Marshall) led the Expos' offense in another fourth-place season in 1974, but the club sank back to a tie for last in 1975 and sole possession of the cellar a year later, with a 55–107 record nearly as bad as their first season (and a home attendance little more than half that of 1969).

But with the acquisition of heavy-hitting Tony Perez from Cincinnati, a new manager—the controversial Dick Williams—and strong seasons from catcher Gary Carter, sophomore outfielder Ellis Valentine, and rookie Andre Dawson, the club snapped back in 1977 to win 20 more games than the previous year and rise to fifth. And with their move into the new Olympic Stadium (built for the 1976 Olympics), Expo attendance rebounded from a club low to a new high.

After climbing another notch to fourth in 1978 (as the newly acquired Ross Grimsley became their first—and, to date, only—20-game winner), the Expos put on a run for the title that drove attendance in 1979 to over two million. Third baseman Larry Parrish, with a career-high season, led the club in batting and home runs in a balanced attack that saw five players drive in more than 70 runs. The pitching too was balanced, with six pitchers winning 10 games or more on a staff that compiled the league's lowest ERA. With a fast start in April, the Expos led the East through much of June and into July, when a surging Pittsburgh caught up with them. Both clubs climbed away from the pack to the end of the season. Montreal fell back a bit in August but caught up with the Pirates in September and carried the race to the final day before dropping off to second. The Expos' 95 victories remain the club record to date.

The 1980 race was just as exciting. A three-way struggle with Philadelphia and Pittsburgh through most of the summer narrowed to two teams in September as the Pirates fell away. In a crucial late-September series, the Expos beat the Phillies two games of three to take a half-game lead, but in the final series a week later Philadelphia won two games to clinch the crown.

In a 1981 season divided by a players' strike, Montreal finished the first part of the season in third place, but held off St. Louis to win the second part by half a game. The Expos then won the division championship in a special playoff with first-half winner Philadelphia—their first title—but lost the League Championship Series to Los Angeles.

As the Expos declined gradually over the next five years, most of the regulars left through trade, free agency, or retirement. But in 1987, two 1981 rookies who had remained in Montreal—outfielder Tim Raines and third baseman Tim Wallach—stood out in an Expo comeback that left them in third place, just four games back, with 91 wins and the second-best record up to that point.

Strong midsummer surges in 1988 and 1989 propelled the Expos into the thick of the race in the NL East, in 1989 lifting them into the lead for six straight weeks following the acquisition from Seattle of mound ace Mark Langston. But in both years, late-season slumps dropped the club to identical 81–81 finishes. In 1990 strong pitching (despite the loss of free-agents Langston, Bryan Smith, and Pascual Perez) kept the Expos competitive well into September before they fell out of the race.

The collapse of a huge cement beam at Olympic Stadium in September 1991—which forced the Expos to play all their remaining games on the road—was emblematic of the team's collapse into the cellar with their worst record in fifteen years. But the club revived in 1992 under new manager Felipe Alou (who was promoted from coach in late May), rising from fifth place to second behind the pitching of Ken Hill and veteran ace Dennis Martinez, and the offensive leadership of right fielder Larry Walker. The Expos finished an even closer second in 1993, just three games behind Philadelphia, with a record of 94–68, their second best ever.

On August 7, 1994, pitcher Hill moved into the NL lead with his sixteenth win of the season. Walker and Moises Alou—manager Felipe's son—dueled for the club's offensive leadership. Montreal stood atop the mountain with the best record in the majors. Five days later, the season was over.

New York Mets

Branch Rickey's projected Continental League never materialized, but its New York and Houston franchises were admitted to the National League, expanding the league to ten clubs in 1962. Few major league teams have been as inept as the New York Mets were in their first season. Despite the presence on the club of such New York favorites as manager Casey Stengel, pitcher Roger Craig, and first baseman Gil Hodges, and of players like outfielders Richie Ashburn and Frank Thomas who were still near peak form, the Mets finished at the bottom of the league in batting, fielding, and pitching. They won only one game in four and suffered a twentieth-century record 120 losses. But New York fans—deprived of National League baseball since the defection of the Dodgers and Giants to the West Coast four years earlier—found their ineptitude lovable. By their third season, having moved out of the old Polo Grounds into brand-new Shea Stadium, the last-place Mets were regularly outdrawing the pennant-bound Yankees.

Former New York Giants catcher Wes Westrum replaced the aging Stengel as manager part way through the 1965 season, and the next year saw the club rise out of the cellar for the first time. But they fell back to tenth in 1967 (despite rookie Tom Seaver's 16 wins—then a club record), and Westrum was replaced at the helm by Gil Hodges (who had retired from playing after a few games in 1963). With Jerry Koosman joining Seaver in the starting rotation and setting a new club record with 19 victories, Hodges led the Mets in 1968 back up to ninth place with their first season of more than 70 victories.

In 1969 the majors inaugurated divisional play, but the Mets got off to their usual indifferent start. At the end of May, however, they began to win consistently. By early June they were second in the NL East, though well back of the explosive Chicago Cubs. By September, though, the Cubs were faltering. The "Miracle Mets" caught and passed them with a ten-game winning streak and continued on to take the division title by eight games. Among the many Met heroes, Tom Seaver stands out. He won his last ten starts, sparking the team's final push to triumph and finishing with a league-high 25 wins that still stands as the club record. After a three-game sweep of West champion Atlanta in the league's first Championship Series, the Mets faced the mighty Baltimore Orioles—regarded by many as one of baseball's all-time greatest teams—for the world championship. The Met miracle continued as, after an opening game loss, the New Yorkers humbled the Orioles with four straight wins.

The Mets of 1970 remained competitive into mid-September as they sought to repeat their '69 triumph. But they fell back at the end while Pittsburgh spurted, and finished third. Two more third-place finishes followed in 1971 and '72. Just before the start of the 1972 season, Met coach Yogi Berra moved up to manage the club after Hodges suffered a fatal heart attack two days before his forty-eighth birthday.

In 1973 the NL East experienced the tightest major league race of the century. Chicago moved out in front of the pack early in the season, but folded in July and August. So did the Mets, who fell from third to a last-place sixth. But although they were last late in August, they were less than seven games out of first. A series of bursts in September, culminating in a seven-game winning streak, shot the Mets through the division into first place by September 21. Although they finished the season only three games above .500, they topped the division by 1½

games. In the LCS they held off the favored Cincinnati Reds to take the pennant in the maximum five games, but lost the World Series when Oakland overcame a 2–3 deficit to win the final two contests.

The Mets then entered a decade-long decline. Though they won as often in 1975 and '76 as they had in 1973, they didn't come close to winning the East, and dropped into a seven-year trough in 1977 which included five seasons in last place. Seaver was traded to Cincinnati in 1977, and Koosman (after two disastrous seasons) was sent to Minnesota in the fall of 1978 (where he won 20 the next year). The heirs of original owner Joan Whitney Payson (who had died in 1975) sold the club to Nelson Doubleday (of the publishing company) and Fred Wilpon in January 1980. In February the new owners hired Frank Cashen as general manager, hoping he could rebuild the Mets as he had the Baltimore Orioles in the late 1960s.

It took a few years to achieve the right blend, but when outfielder Darryl Strawberry was brought up from the minors early in 1983 and first baseman Keith Hernandez was acquired from St. Louis in June, the mix had nearly all the needed ingredients. In 1984, under new manager Davey Johnson, and with rookie pitchers Dwight Gooden and Ron Darling combining for 29 wins, the Mets rebounded to second place with their second-best season record up till then.

The rise continued in 1985. With catcher Gary Carter (newly acquired from Montreal) leading the club in homers and RBIs, and Gooden cementing his superstardom at age twenty with a phenomenal 24–4, 1.53 ERA season, the Mets won 98 games—eight more than the year before—and came within a game of tying St. Louis late in September before slipping 3 games back at the finish.

When the Mets acquired pitcher Bob Ojeda from the Boston Red Sox after the season, many predicted an easy division title for them in 1986. For once, the pundits were right. With Carter, Strawberry, and Hernandez powering the offense, and Ojeda, Darling, and Gooden all placing among the league's top five pitchers in ERA, the Mets won two of every three games (108 in all) to capture the division title by 21½ games.

The postseason battles were tougher. The Mets won the pennant from Houston with a 16-inning victory in Game Six of the LCS, but came within a strike of elimination by the Red Sox in Game Six of the World Series before rallying to take that game and the next for their second world crown.

Strawberry enjoyed his finest season yet in 1987, and pitchers Terry Leach and Rick Aguilera put together a combined won-lost record of 22–4. But Ojeda was lost to injury early in the season, and the Mets, though they hung close and posted 92 wins, lost out—as in 1985—to St. Louis by 3 games.

David Cone (20–3, 2.22 ERA) emerged in 1988 as the ace of the league's best pitching staff, which, with the power of Darryl Strawberry and Kevin McReynolds behind it, carried the Mets back to the top of the NL East, 15 games ahead of runner-up Pittsburgh. But after taking a 3-2 lead in the LCS, they lost the pennant to underdog Los Angeles in seven games.

With co-captains Carter and Hernandez injured and in decline, the Mets floundered through 1989, salvaging a narrow second-place finish over St. Louis with four wins in the season's final three days. The two captains were released after the season. Next May, with the Mets mired 9½ games out, manager Davey Johnson was replaced by coach Bud Harrelson. In June the team—ignited by Strawberry's suddenly hot bat—took off: with a flight that included a club-record eleven-game win streak, the Mets propelled themselves into first place before the end of the month. Through July and August the Mets and Pittsburgh lobbed the division lead back and forth, until the Pirates consigned the New Yorkers to second place for good with a three-game sweep in early September.

Free agent Strawberry signed with Los Angeles for 1991, but the Mets competed strongly into July before tumbling to fifth place with their first losing season in eight years. Manager Harrelson was replaced by Jeff Torborg for 1992, and ex-Pirate star Bobby Bonilla signed with the club as a free agent. But injuries plagued the team throughout the season, and the finish found them once again a distant fifth.

Things only got worse in 1993, and even a six-game win streak at the end of the season couldn't keep them from the worst record in the majors and, with 103 losses, the club's worst season in twenty-eight years.

In 1994, pitcher Bret Saberhagen's fifth comeback of his eleven-year career (14–4, 2.74 ERA) propelled the Mets to something of a comeback of their own. They finished just three games below .500, good enough for third place in the NL East.

New York Yankees

In its first twenty seasons, the club that became the New York Yankees won no league championships, and finished second only twice. But for the next forty-four years the Yankees dominated the American League, winning nearly two of every three pennants and twenty World Series. After another pennant drought of twelve years, the club in six years won five division titles, four pennants, and their twenty-first and twenty-second World Series. Their current pennant drought, which has lasted thirteen years so far, is tied for the second longest in their history.

The Yankees began as the Baltimore Orioles in 1901. But AL president Ban Johnson really wanted a club in New York and, after outmaneuvering the politically influential Giants (who didn't want a competing big league team in their city), Johnson moved the Orioles to the northern end of Manhattan in 1903.

In 1904 the Highlanders (as they were known during their first years in New York because of the high land on which their park was built) chased the Boston Pilgrims through midsummer, catching them in August and trading first place back and forth into October. But after Jack Chesbro defeated Boston 3–2 on October 7 to give New York a half-game lead (it was his forty-first win, a twentieth-century major league record), the Pilgrims came back to win the next two. In the fourth game of the series, with Chesbro again pitching and the score tied 2–2 in the top of the ninth, a wild pitch over the New York catcher's head let in Boston's pennant-clinching run.

The Highlanders again led the league in late September two years later, before tailing off to finish 3 games behind Chicago. But that was the last time they contended seriously for the title for fourteen years. Meanwhile they finished last twice, in 1908 losing a club-worst 103 games, and in 1912 suffering their most distant finish ever—55 games behind the pennant-winning Boston Red Sox.

In 1914 Colonel Jake Ruppert and Tillinghast Huston bought the Yankees, and the next year they purchased pitcher Bob Shawkey from the Philadelphia A's. Shawkey's 24 victories in 1916 led the Yankees to their first winning season in six years, and in 1919, on returning from military service, his 20 wins (plus the 9 of Carl Mays, who came to the club in a controversial mid-season deal with the Red Sox) brought the Yankees to third—at 7½ games out, their closest finish in thirteen years.

That winter, on the recommendation of manager Miller Huggins, the Yankees paid a then-record $125,000 (plus a $300,000 loan) to the Red Sox for Babe Ruth. Ruth, with 54 home runs in 1920, obliterated the record of 29 he had set the year before, and Mays and Shawkey together won 46 games in a three-way pennant race that ended with New York a close third.

At season's end Ruppert hired Ed Barrow as Yankee general manager. While managing the Red Sox, Barrow had converted Ruth from a pitcher to outfielder. His December trade with Boston that gave the Yankees pitcher Waite Hoyt and catcher Wally Schang was just the improvement needed to bring the Yankees their first pennant in 1921. Ruth's 59 homers and his career-high 171 RBIs didn't hurt, either.

The prickly Carl Mays, staff ace in 1921 with a 27–9 record, slipped to 13–14 the next year. But the Yankees continued to decimate the Red Sox roster with trades that brought them pitchers "Bullet Joe" Bush and "Sad Sam" Jones, and infielders Everett Scott and Joe Dugan. Bush's 26 wins in 1922 made up for Mays's decline, and the Yankees captured their second straight league championship.

Both races had been tight two-way struggles—with Cleveland in 1921 and the St. Louis Browns in 1922—and both pennants had been followed by a World Series loss to the Giants. But in 1923 the Yankees at last put everything together. After sharing the Giants' Polo Grounds since 1913, they were at home in brand-new Yankee Stadium just across the Harlem River in the Bronx. With the addition of yet another pitcher from the Red Sox—Herb Pennock—and a .393 year from Ruth, they took the lead from the start and built it over the summer to a 16-game margin by the end. For the third time the Yankees faced the Giants in the World Series; this time they beat them, in six games, for their first world championship.

The Yankees lost a close race to Washington in 1924 and collapsed into seventh place in 1925—a year in which Ruth was lost much of the season to surgery and suspension. There were bright spots, though: center fielder Earle Combs, in his first full season, hit .342 to lead Yankee regulars, left fielder Bob Meusel filled Ruth's shoes as AL home run and RBI leader, and first baseman Lou Gehrig arrived to stay. With Ruth's return to full strength in 1926 and the establishment of a new middle infield of Tony Lazzeri and Mark Koenig, the Yankees took their fourth pennant in a race that was not as close as their 3-game winning margin would suggest. They lost a close World Series to the Cardinals.

Many observers rank the 1927 Yankees as baseball's greatest team ever. Certainly it was the Yankees' greatest team. They won more games (110) than any Yankee team before or since. Ruth hit his 60 home runs, and Gehrig drove in 175. Waite Hoyt led the league in ERA and rookie Wilcy Moore proved the league's premier reliever. As a team the Yankees led the league in hitting (.307) and slugging (.489, still a major league record); their pitchers compiled a 3.20 ERA that was ¾ of a run per game lower than the ERA of the next best team. In the World Series they swept the Pittsburgh Pirates.

The resurgent Athletics made the 1928 race much closer, but New York won three in a row from the A's in mid-September to pull ahead, and held on for their sixth pennant. Another Series sweep (this time against the Cardinals) gave them their third world title.

For three years the A's left the Yankees in the shade. An ill Huggins yielded the club's reins in September 1929 and died before the season had ended. By the time the Yankees returned to the top in 1932, their manager was Joe McCarthy. He had led Chicago's Cubs to the NL pennant in 1929; in fifteen seasons at New York he would lead his club to eight more pennants and seven world championships. Only once would his Yankees finish as low as fourth.

A Yankee pennant and World Series triumph over the Cubs in 1932 was followed by three second-place finishes to Washington (in 1933) and Detroit (in 1934 and 1935). Ruth had retired by the time the Bronx Bombers returned to the top in 1936, but Gehrig was still in top form, catcher Bill Dickey and outfielder George Selkirk developed into formidable sluggers, and Joe DiMaggio arrived to take over center field. New York finished a club-record 19½ games in front and buried the Giants in the World Series.

Three more pennants and three more world titles followed in 1937–1939. Lefty Gomez emerged as the league's premier pitcher in 1937, and DiMaggio picked up the home run and slugging crowns. Again the Giants were vanquished in the World Series. Rookie second baseman Joe Gordon and sophomore outfielder Tommy Henrich joined Dickey, DiMaggio, and a declining Gehrig in leading the slugging Yankees to the 1938 crown and a Series sweep of the Cubs. A balanced attack in 1939 saw seven of the eight starters (including Babe Dahlgren, who replaced the dying Gehrig at first) drive in 80 runs or more as the Yankees won 106 to run away with their eleventh pennant—and eighth World Series, another sweep, with Cincinnati the victim. For the fourth year in a row the offense topped the league in slugging, and overshadowed the steady—if unspectacular—Yankee pitchers, who for the *sixth* consecutive season compiled the league's stingiest ERA.

After catching the leaders with a 19–4 spurt in late summer, the 1940 Yankees fell away to finish a close third. But then came another three convincing pennant wins and a pair of Series triumphs as the nation moved into World War Two. Outfielders DiMaggio and Charlie Keller dominated the Yankee offense in 1941, and rookie shortstop Phil Rizzuto hit .307. Though no Yankee pitcher won more than 15 games, seven won 9 or more (and

reliever Johnny Murphy won 8 while saving a league-high 15). With 101 victories the team was lost from view to the rest of a league in which six of the eight clubs failed to break .500. In the World Series Brooklyn was the loser in five games.

Keller, DiMaggio, and Gordon provided the power, and Tiny Bonham (with 21 wins), Spud Chandler, and rookie Hank Borowy headed the league-leading pitching staff that propelled the Yankees to 103 wins and another easy pennant in 1942. But after winning their previous eight World Series, the Yankees were finally stopped, in five games, by the St. Louis Cardinals.

By 1943 many Yankees were in military service. But pitchers Chandler, Bonham, Borowy, and Murphy were not, and they led the charge to the team's seventh pennant in eight years. In the Series the Yankees reversed the results of the previous year, turning back St. Louis in five.

When Jake Ruppert died in 1939, general manager Barrow succeeded him as president, a position he held until January 1945, when Dan Topping and Del Webb bought the club and installed Larry MacPhail as president, giving him a third of the club and a ten-year contract to run it. The volatile, innovative MacPhail had previously brought new life to Cincinnati and Brooklyn, and did bring night ball to Yankee Stadium. But manager McCarthy, who couldn't get along with MacPhail, quit early in the 1946 season, and the team finished a distant third.

DiMaggio and the others were back from the war by 1946, but it was not until 1947—under new manager Bucky Harris, and with sparkling pitching from Allie Reynolds (acquired from Cleveland), rookie Frank "Spec" Shea, and reliever Joe Page—that the Yankees returned to the top of the heap with an easy pennant win and a narrow World Series triumph over Brooklyn. On the day the Yankees won the Series, though, president MacPhail embarrassed the club and undid himself by brawling in public. Topping and Webb bought out his contract and share of the ownership. Topping took over the presidency, but promoted farm director George Weiss to run the club as general manager.

After the Yankees dropped a pair of season-ending games to the Red Sox to finish third in a tight 1948 race, Weiss replaced manager Harris with Casey Stengel, who in nine years of managing the Braves and Dodgers had only twice seen his club finish as high as fifth. But with Weiss providing a steady stream of talented players via the farm system and canny trades, the Yankees under Stengel proved all but invincible into the '60s.

Stengel's Yankees began by putting together a record string of five world championships. No major league club had ever won five pennants in a row, let alone five World Series, and the Yankees didn't accomplish the feat easily. In 1949, for example, they saw the Red Sox come from 12 games back in midseason to pass them with a three-game series sweep in late September, only to rescue the flag with two close must-win victories over the Sox in the season's final games. In the World Series, Brooklyn was again the victim, in five games.

After losing much of 1949 to injury, DiMaggio returned with power in 1950, shortstop Rizzuto and catcher Yogi Berra enjoyed the finest seasons of their careers, and pitcher Whitey Ford broke into the majors, winning all nine of his decisions as a starter (he lost one game in relief). But the Yankees struggled even harder for the pennant than the year before, battling three other contenders before finally pulling in front to stay with five straight wins near to the end of the season. Though three of the games in the World Series were decided by just one run, New York took the Phillie "Whiz Kids" without a loss.

No Yankee drove in as many as 90 runs in 1951, and Whitey Ford was drafted for two years of military service. But the remaining pitchers doubled their shutout production and lowered the team ERA by more than half a run per game, enough to propel the club ahead of Cleveland in mid-September. In the World Series the Yankees shook the faith of the "miracle" Giants, four games to two. Cleveland challenged once again in 1952, and again fell just short, as did Brooklyn in carrying the World Series to seven games.

Finally, in 1953, Stengel's Yankees won with relative ease. Ford, back from the Army, won 18 to lead the club to a finish 8½ games up. Once again it was Brooklyn in the World Series, and once again the Yankees beat them.

In 1954 New York won 103 games—the most in Stengel's twelve-year tenure. But Cleveland won an AL-record 111 to take the flag by 8 games. In 1955, though, it was back to second place for Cleveland as New York, with Mickey Mantle now established as one of the game's most productive hitters, settled in for another four pennants. As August passed into September, three teams were within a game of each other at the top. But the Chicago White Sox faltered and fell away, leaving the Yankees and Indians to fight it out. With two weeks left, New York won eight straight to pass Cleveland for good. Facing the Dodgers in the World Series for the sixth time, the Yankees finally lost, as Johnny Podres shut them out in Game Seven to give Brooklyn its first world title since 1900.

From 1956 through 1958 the Yankees seldom found themselves out of first place. Only in 1957, when they leveled off in May before surging to the front in June, were they involved in anything resembling a close race. In postseason play, they went the full seven games all three years, winning twice—from the Dodgers for the sixth time in 1956, and from the Milwaukee Braves in 1958, after losing to them the year before.

In 1959 the Yankees started poorly and never did rise much above .500, finishing a distant third with their worst won-lost record in thirty-four years. After the season, George Weiss sent an aging Hank Bauer to Kansas City in a trade that brought Roger Maris to New York. In 1960 Maris, with AL titles in slugging and RBIs, won the MVP award. He and Mantle dominated the power stats and led the charge back to the top as the Yankees won their final fifteen games to bury the faltering Orioles.

New York's 1960 pennant was the first in another five-flag streak, but it was the last for Stengel. After Pittsburgh toppled the Yankees in the World Series on Bill Mazeroski's famous home run, president Topping retired both the seventy-year-old Stengel and general manager Weiss, sixty-five, who had been with the club for twenty-eight years.

With the season lengthened by eight games in 1961, Maris broke Ruth's home-run record and rookie manager Ralph Houk led the club to 109 wins, just one off the club

record. Once again Maris and Mantle finished among the best in offensive power, and once again New York took the pennant by 8 games. Ford enjoyed a splendid 25–4 season and celebrated with two more wins in the World Series as the Yankees humbled Cincinnati in five games.

Pitcher Ralph Terry moved out of Ford's shadow in 1962 with 23 wins. Though the Yankees finished just five games ahead of Minnesota, there was little doubt about the outcome from midseason on. In a close World Series with San Francisco, Terry won two, including the clincher with a four-hit shutout.

Though New York won pennants the next two years, the 1962 world title was to be their last until the Steinbrenner era fifteen years later. Despite the loss to injuries of Mantle and Maris for much of 1963, New York dominated the AL, winning by 10½ games with 104 wins. But in postseason play the Yankees were themselves dominated by the Dodgers (now in Los Angeles), who held them to just four runs in a Series sweep.

Yogi Berra replaced Houk as manager for 1964. In a season-long three-way race with the White Sox and Orioles that found the clubs virtually tied in mid-September, only an eleven-game win streak gave the Yankees the space they needed for their final one-game margin of victory. Pitcher Jim Bouton won a pair in the World Series, but the Cardinals took the crown in seven. Berra was fired.

During the 1964 season Topping had sold the Yankees to CBS. The next year the club, which had gone forty years without a losing season, dropped to sixth place, and in 1966 fell to a last-place tenth, their first cellar finish in more than half a century. Even Houk's return as manager in 1967—though it led to some winning seasons—failed to restore the once-proud club to pennant contention, except once, in 1972, when it was mid-September before they fell out of a tight race to finish fourth.

In January 1973 a syndicate headed by Cleveland shipping magnate George Steinbrenner purchased the Yankees from CBS. Although he had vowed not to take a prominent role in running the club, Steinbrenner soon emerged as one of baseball's most active owners. Through a series of shrewd trades, offers of big contracts to free agents, and what became a round robin of managerial changes, Steinbrenner's Yankees became competitive again in 1974 (finishing a close second to Baltimore after streaking from last in July to first in September) and returned to the top with three successive pennants and a pair of world championships.

Billy Martin (a former Yankee second baseman) in 1976, his first full season as manager, led the renewed club to a runaway division title. First baseman Chris Chambliss's homer in the last of the ninth of the final game of the League Championship Series gave the Yankees the pennant by the narrowest of margins over the Kansas City Royals. Cincinnati swept New York in the World Series, but the Yankees came back the next year to edge Baltimore and Boston in a three-way race that saw the teams shift back and forth in the standings throughout the season. Slugger Reggie Jackson, signed as a free agent the previous autumn, turned the club's power trio of Chambliss, Graig Nettles, and Thurman Munson into a quartet as the Yankees recorded their first hundred-victory season in fourteen years. After another ninth-inning win over Kansas City in the LCS finale, New York won the World Series in six games over Los Angeles, and Jackson became "Mr. October" with five home runs—three of them in successive at-bats in the final game.

The 1978 season provided as exciting a race as baseball is likely to see. In mid-July it looked like a Red Sox romp, but the fourth-place Yankees put on a great surge, catching the faltering Sox with a four-game series sweep in early September. Boston dropped 3½ games back, but won their final eight games to catch New York on the final day. In the one-game tiebreaker, Yankee shortstop Bucky Dent lofted a wind-blown three-run homer over Boston's close left field wall in the seventh, and Jackson homered an inning later for New York's final run in the 5–4 win. Again the Royals were the victims in the LCS, as were the Dodgers in the World Series.

After dropping to fourth in 1979, the Yankees held off Baltimore in 1980 to win their fourth division title—but this time Kansas City swept to the pennant in three games. In 1981 the Yankees found themselves in first place when the players struck in June and were thus admitted to an intradivisional playoff with the season's second-half winner, Milwaukee. Narrowly defeating the Brewers for the division title, New York swept Oakland for the pennant in the LCS. But after taking the first two games from Los Angeles in the World Series, they were stopped cold as the Dodgers won the next four.

The Yankees fell below .500 the next year, and although they revived to win 91 games in 1983, they failed to frighten the division leaders until 1985. First baseman Don Mattingly drove in more runs than any American leaguer since 1953 and newcomer (from Oakland) Rickey Henderson scored more often than any major leaguer since 1949—the team remained in the running until Toronto eliminated them with just one game to go.

But constant roster manipulation and managerial rotation (Billy Martin alone was hired and fired five times) at last set in motion a steady drop in Yankee effectiveness. While the team remained in the thick of a tight 1988 divisional race until three season-ending losses set them back into fifth place, their won-lost record showed a third straight season of decline. In 1989 the Yankees sank to their worst finish in twenty-two years and in 1990 they dropped to the floor of the AL East with the club's worst record since 1913.

Attempting to gain information damaging to longtime Yankee outfielder Dave Winfield, Steinbrenner dealt with a gambler named Howard Spira. As his penalty, Steinbrenner was forced to relinquish his controlling interest in the club in August 1990. The team improved a little over the next two years to finish fifth in 1991 and tie for fourth in 1992. But their string of consecutive losing seasons stretched to four, something that hadn't happened to the Yankees in seventy-six years. In 1993 the Yankees bounced back and—bolstered by the league's best hitting and a strong season from newly acquired pitcher Jimmy Key—contended seriously into September, finishing second to Toronto, seven games back.

They were even better in 1994. With Key in the midst of one of his best seasons ever, and a solid offense paced by right fielder Paul O'Neill (whose .603 slugging average stood 99 points above his previous career high), the Yankees were enjoying the league's best won-lost record

and a 6½-game lead in the AL East when the players' strike cut the season short in August.

Oakland Athletics

The history of the Athletics is a tale of three cities—a story of the best of teams and of the worst of teams. With a thirteen-year sojourn in Kansas City between residence in Philadelphia and Oakland, the A's are the only club to include a stop in Middle America in their trek from the East Coast to West. They have won fifteen American League pennants (plus four Western Division championships that didn't lead to a pennant), second in the AL only to the incomparable Yankees. But they have also finished last in the league or division twenty-seven times, and in sixteen seasons have lost 100 games or more—both AL worsts, by far. A club of extremes, they have been either at the top or at the bottom in nearly one season out of two.

When Ban Johnson in 1901 established four eastern clubs for his American League, he chose Connie Mack to manage the new Philadelphia Athletics and gave him a quarter ownership of the club. Mack, who had been managing the league's Milwaukee franchise, settled in at Philadelphia and set a record for managerial longevity—fifty years—that is unlikely ever to be surpassed.

In his first fourteen years the A's dominated the league, with six pennants and two close second-place finishes. After finishing fourth in 1901, the club won its first pennant the next year, pulling away from the field with spurts in August and September. Rube Waddell led the team with 24 wins, and six regulars hit over .300. The next two years saw the A's fade in August, but in 1905, after forging ahead in early August and hanging on to the lead with two crucial wins over Chicago's surging White Sox in late September, the A's opened October with a five-game winning streak to clinch their second flag. Waddell, with 26 wins, once again led the club (followed closely by Eddie Plank's 25) and compiled a league-leading 1.48 ERA. In the Athletics' first World Series appearance, though, New York's Christy Mathewson provided most of the pitching heroics, shutting out the A's three times in the Giants' 4–1 Series triumph.

Another August decline in 1906 was followed in 1907 by a comeback struggle from fifth place in late May to a 2½-game lead in mid-September. But the loss of a crucial game to Detroit several days later, and the failure to make up a rainout and a tie, left the A's 1½ games behind the Tigers at the finish.

In 1908 the A's suffered their first losing season, but they rebounded in 1909 to chase the Tigers throughout the summer before tailing off to second. In 1910, with a pitching staff that compiled a stunning 1.79 ERA (paced by Jack Coombs, whose 31 wins included 13 shutouts) and with league-leading fielding and hitting, the A's pulled ahead for good in June, increasing their lead through the rest of the season to finish 14½ games in front. In the World Series they continued to dominate, outscoring the Chicago Cubs 35–15 as they took their first world title, in five games. The A's repeated just as convincingly in 1911. With their "$100,000 infield" of Stuffy McInnis, Eddie Collins, Jack Barry, and Frank "Home Run" Baker averaging .323 at the bat, and Jack Coombs winning 28 games to again lead the club (and the league), the A's overtook Detroit in August to win by 13½ games. In the World Series, Baker hit two important home runs against the Giants, and the A's defeated Mathewson twice, avenging their 1905 humiliation with a victory in six games.

A third-place finish in 1912 broke the pennant streak, but the Athletics came back for two more in 1913 and '14, in both seasons pulling away in early June for easy wins. In the 1913 World Series the A's again felled the Giants, this time in just five games, but the next year they were in turn humiliated by the upstart Boston Braves, who stunned Philadelphia with the first sweep since the renewal of World Series play in 1903.

That winter, Mack began to dismantle his championship club, selling second baseman Collins to the White Sox and releasing pitchers Coombs, Eddie Plank, and Chief Bender. (Third baseman Baker, homesick for the country life, sat out the 1915 season before moving on to the Yankees). Though Mack received $50,000 for Collins, his unconditional release of the three pitchers suggests that he had another reason than financial need for purging his club. (Suspicion of corrupt play in the 1914 World Series has been hinted.)

Whatever Mack's reasons, the changes did not help the club. The A's sank immediately to last place, where they remained for seven years. In 1915 they lost 109 games and finished 58½ games out. The next year they lost 117 games to set a league record for ineptitude that has never been equalled.

It was a decade before Mack was able to restore the club to respectability. In 1924 he brought up Al Simmons, and the next year Jimmie Foxx and pitcher Lefty Grove. Thus renewed, the A's in 1925 battled Washington to the end of August before backing off to second. In 1927 they won 91 games, though their second-place finish was 19 games back of the overwhelming Yankees. In 1928 the A's battled from well back of New York in midseason to overtake them for a day or two in September, only to lose three of four games in a critical Yankee series and slip back to second.

From 1929 through 1931, though, the A's interrupted New York's domination of the AL with three spectacular seasons. In 1929 sophomore pitcher George Earnshaw blossomed into the league's big winner with 24 victories and Grove led the league's stingiest staff with a league-low 2.81 ERA. Six players drove in 79 runs or more (led by Simmons' league-high 157) in powering the A's to 104 wins and an impressive finish 18 games ahead of the second-place Yankees.

After swamping the Cubs in the World Series, the A's repeated as pennant winners in 1930. Simmons led the league in batting (.381), and Grove led its pitchers in just about everything: wins (28), ERA, strikeouts—even saves (9). Again the World Series was no contest as the A's downed the Cardinals in six.

Earnshaw won more than 20 games for his third successive season in 1931, Simmons repeated as batting leader (.390), and Grove enjoyed what would be the finest season of his career (31–4, 2.06 ERA) in carrying the A's to 107 wins—their best record ever. But in Game Seven of the World Series their dominance of the baseball world ended in a Cardinal victory.

Following a second-place finish in 1932, Mack began selling off his stars again. This time the reason was primarily economic. Home attendance—never robust—fell off sharply after 1931, as the Great Depression and the A's decline made their impact felt. By 1935 the Athletics were back in the cellar, where they finished in ten of Mack's final sixteen years as manager.

In 1946 Mack, who since 1940 had been the A's majority stockholder, divided his shares among his three sons, provoking a family squabble over control of the club. In 1950 the two eldest, Roy and Earle, bought out Connie Jr. and pressured their eighty-seven-year-old father to retire. But with Connie Sr. gone, attendance (which had risen to new highs in the baseball boom that followed World War Two) dropped off again. When in 1954 the A's finished 60 games behind champion Cleveland and attendance dropped to an eighteen-year low, the Macks sold the club to Chicagoan Arnold Johnson, who moved it to Kansas City.

Attendance jumped more than a million the first season in Kansas City (putting the A's over one million for the first time ever), and the team rose a couple of places to sixth. But 1955 was the high point of their thirteen-year stay in the Midwest; the K.C. A's never again rose above seventh, and they finished last six times.

Owner Johnson died in March 1960, and that December his heirs sold the club to the enterprising but abrasive Charles O. Finley. Finley brought in a succession of new managers over the next few years, and in 1965 outfitted his players in new bright green-and-yellow uniforms. But with the league's expansion to ten teams in 1961, the A's had two places lower to sink—and did. After finishing tenth in 1967 for the third time in four years, Finley moved the club to Oakland, California.

Attendance was slow to improve in Oakland—unlike the team. In 1968, their first year on the coast, they put together their first winning season in sixteen years. The next year, with the start of divisional play, the A's took second in the AL West. Reggie Jackson, in only his second full big league season, enjoyed his finest year, with 47 home runs, 118 RBIs, and AL highs in slugging (.608) and runs scored (123).

After another second-place finish in 1970, the A's were ready for a return to glory. In the next five years they won five division titles, winning both the AL pennant and the World Series in the three middle years, 1972–1974. In 1971, with a new manager, Dick Williams, and three pitchers (Vida Blue, Catfish Hunter, and reliever Rollie Fingers) who reached their prime all at once, the A's enjoyed their best season in forty years and won the West by 16 games. Baltimore swept them away in the League Championship Series, but they came back to take the West again the next year. Detroit took them to the limit in the LCS, as did Cincinnati in the World Series, but in both series the A's prevailed in the deciding game by the margin of a single run.

The next year, 1973, Jackson led the league in slugging, homers, and RBIs, Ken Holtzman joined Blue and Hunter in the 20-win column, and home attendance crept over a million (by a few hundred souls) for the first time in Oakland as the A's ran their string of Western Division titles to three. Once again they were pushed to the limit in the postseason—by Baltimore in the LCS and the New

York Mets in the World Series—and once again they emerged as world champions.

Manager Williams quit in a dispute with Finley and was replaced by Al Dark, but the outcome in 1974 (except for a drop in attendance to under a million) was the same. Hunter bore more of the pitching load and wound up tied for the AL lead with 25 wins. His 2.49 ERA also led the league, as the staff ended Baltimore's five-year hold on the ERA title. The A's toppled the Orioles in the LCS and (in the first World Series held entirely on the West Coast) won their third consecutive world title in five closely fought games with Los Angeles.

Free-agent Catfish Hunter deserted to the Yankees, and Baltimore regained the ERA crown in 1975, but pitchers Paul Lindblad and newcomer Dick Bosman combined for a 20–5 record to supplement the efforts of Blue, Holtzman, and Fingers and carry Oakland to an unprecedented fifth straight division title. But there the magic stopped, as Boston swept to the pennant in the LCS.

In the off-season Finley, with moves reminiscent of Connie Mack, tried to sell off his star players: Blue, Jackson, Fingers, Holtzman, and outfielder/first baseman Joe Rudi, one of the team's steadiest hitters. The proposed sales made some sense: the players planned to leave the club at the end of their 1976 option year, and Finley by disposing of them before they played out their option could at least be compensated for his loss. The Jackson and Holtzman deals were approved, but baseball commissioner Bowie Kuhn blocked the sale of the others, citing the "best interests of baseball."

The weakened A's came back from a poor start to close within 2½ games of the Kansas City Royals in 1976, but they dropped to last place the next year. After another last-place finish in 1979, Finley hired fiery Billy Martin to manage the club. Martin brought the A's in second in 1980, and first in the first half of strike-divided 1981. They won the Western Division championship by sweeping Kansas City in the special intradivisional playoffs, but were in turn swept by the Yankees in the LCS.

Finley's sale of the club in 1981 to the folks who bring us Levi's jeans signaled a turn toward normalcy and popularity. Despite a losing season in 1982, the club set a home attendance record as over 1.7 million fans came to watch Rickey Henderson's successful assault on the stolen-base record. In 1987 the A's finished right at .500—for the first time in their history a perfectly average team.

The next season they inaugurated a new multiyear reign as the league's best. Starter Dave Stewart and closer Dennis Eckersley anchored the league's strongest pitching staff and "bash brothers" Jose Canseco and Mark McGwire headlined an awesome offense. In 1988–90 the A's took title to the AL West with the majors' best won-lost record, then sailed past the East champion to the pennant. In 1988 they built a 13-game margin of victory over runner-up Minnesota, winning 104 games and drawing more than 2 million fans to their home games for the first time. They swept Boston in the ALCS, but faltered in the World Series, losing to underdog L.A. in five games.

Injuries to several key players—especially Canseco, who missed the first half of the season with a broken wrist—kept the A's from dominating AL play through most of 1989. But the preseason signing of free agent starter Mike Moore had strengthened the pitching, and a June trade that brought Rickey Henderson back after more than four years with the Yankees gave the A's the push they needed to prevail. At full strength by season's end, the A's overwhelmed Toronto in five games for their fourteenth pennant, then swept San Francisco for their world title.

Only Chicago's surprising White Sox challenged Oakland in 1990, and they too fell away in the latter half of the season as the A's walked to the division title with 103 wins. The potent offense was made even more formidable by the late-season acquisition of Harold Baines from Texas and Willie McGee from St. Louis. But the key to Oakland's dominance was its pitchers, who for the third year in a row compiled the league's lowest earned run average. Bob Welch led the majors with 27 wins, Dave Stewart put together his fourth straight 20-win season, and Dennis Eckersley rebounded from an injury-hampered 1989 with his finest relief year yet. The A's swept over Boston to their third straight pennant, but—shades of 1988!—floundered in the World Series, succumbing in just four games to Cincinnati's aroused Reds.

In 1991 the A's stayed at or near the top into late June before slipping to fourth. Eckersley remained in top form, however, and in 1992 proved almost invincible, with 7 wins and 51 saves. Jose Canseco's trade to Texas late in the season severed the bash brothers' tandem offense, but Mark McGwire enjoyed a banner season at the bat. Despite a wave of injuries that would have sunk most teams, the A's stayed afloat near the front through the first half of the season and held steady in the second half to win their fourth division title in five years. In the LCS the A's fell to Toronto in six games.

With an injury to McGwire that sidelined him more than four months, plus a general decline on the mound and at the bat that saw the team finish with the league's worst batting and earned run averages, Oakland in 1993 did what only two major league clubs before them (the 1915 Athletics and 1885 St. Louis Maroons) had ever done: tumble into the cellar after a first-place finish the year before.

The A's weren't winning much more often in 1994 when the players' strike halted play in August, but in the weak AL West their 51–63 record was good enough to land them in second place, just a game out of first.

Philadelphia Phillies

It took the Phillies thirty-two years to win their first pennant, and ninety-seven to win their first world championship. They have finished last in their league or division twenty-eight times—one season in four. In the nine years from 1975 through 1983, though, they were one of the most formidable teams in baseball.

Alfred J. Reach, a sporting goods entrepreneur and former player, and Colonel John Rogers, a Philadelphia lawyer and politician, organized the Phillies in 1883 to bring Philadelphia back into the National League after a six-year absence. In their first season, the Phillies won only 17 of 98 decisions to finish an eighth-place last, as far out of seventh as the seventh-place team was from first. Bad as the Phillies have sometimes been since, their

1883 winning percentage of .173 remains their very worst.

Reach hired the respected Harry Wright to manage the Phillies in 1884, and while Wright failed to lead them to a pennant in his ten years at the helm, he did make them respectable. His fourth-place 1886 team, in fact, compiled a winning percentage of .623 that remained the club's best for ninety years. In 1887 the Phillies, with three pitchers winning more than 20 games, finished second, just 3½ games behind Detroit—their closest finish until their first pennant twenty-eight years later.

The Phillies remained in the upper division twelve of the next fourteen years. For five years—1891–1895—they fielded an outfield of Ed Delahanty, Billy Hamilton, and Sam Thompson—Hall of Famers who rank among the top hitters of all time. In the three heavy-hitting seasons that followed the lengthening of the pitching distance to its present 60′6″ in 1893, Delahanty, Hamilton, and Thompson—with help from players like catcher Jack Clements (.394 in 1895) and utility outfielder Tuck Turner (.416 in 1894)—sparked the Phillies to three team batting titles with BAs of over .300. In 1894 the big three joined Turner in batting over .400 and the team hit .349—still the major league club record.

In 1899, with Delahanty's .410 leading the way, the Phillies once again topped .300 to lead the league. Though the team finished third, they won 94 games, a club high they would not surpass for seventy-seven years. President Reach sold his interest in the club after a dispute with co-owner Rogers, and Rogers lost star second baseman Larry Lajoie in a salary dispute to the Athletics (Philadelphia's new entry in the rival American League). But the Phillies chased front-runner Pittsburgh through much of 1901. Though they slumped in August, they recovered to finish second.

It was the end of an era. Delahanty deserted to the AL the next season, and the Phillies dropped to seventh. Rogers sold the club to a syndicate. By 1904 the team was in last place, losing 100 games for the first time.

They rose into the first division the next season, but didn't mount a serious pennant run until 1911, when the pitching of rookie Grover Cleveland Alexander kept them in the thick of the race into midseason. Two years later they enjoyed first place through most of June before fading to a distant second.

In 1915 Alexander brought his ERA down more than a run per game to a league- and career-best of 1.22, hurling 12 shutouts among his 31 wins. Right fielder Gavvy Cravath and first baseman Fred Luderus finished one-two among NL sluggers, and Cravath won home run and RBI crowns. For half a season all eight clubs were in the thick of a tight race, with the Cubs and Phillies at the top of the heap. But in July the Cubs folded, and in August and September the Phillies took off to outdistance the late-surging Boston Braves by 7 games for their first pennant.

The World Series was a Phillies' heartbreak. Four of the five games were decided by a single run—but the runs belonged to the Boston Red Sox, who swept four after the Phillies had taken the opener.

Alexander shut out a record-tying 16 opponents the following year, winning a career-high 33, and teammate Eppa Rixey had his first big year with 22 wins. Through most of the season, the club trailed the leading Dodgers,

but caught them in September, only to fall away again in the final week.

After Alexander's 30 wins had brought the Phillies another second-place finish in 1917, the club dealt him to Chicago and embarked on thirty-one years of wandering in the desert. After fourteen losing seasons (eight of them in last place), they climbed to fourth, two games above .500, in 1932, but dropped back the next year into the second division (including nine last-place finishes) for sixteen more years.

Several outstanding players spent time in Philadelphia during these years: Dave Bancroft (a rookie in their pennant season), Cy Williams, Freddy Leach, Chuck Klein, Lefty O'Doul, and Dick Bartell. Of these, only Williams and Klein retired as Phillies. The financially strapped management traded away the others at the height of their careers in deals that included cash as well as players. Even Klein—perhaps the greatest of them all—was sold twice before returning a third time to Philly to end his career.

The Phillies in 1930 produced a season that ranks among the most extraordinary of all time. With Klein and O'Doul leading the way at .386 and .383, every regular hit at least .280, to give the Phillies a team BA of .315. But Phillie pitchers yielded a record 1199 runs while compiling the worst big league ERA ever—6.71. The club lost 102 games and finished last.

The Phillies' move in 1938 out of tiny, antiquated Baker Bowl into the Athletics' Shibe Park did nothing for attendance—or for performance, as the team strung together a club-record five consecutive last-place finishes from 1938 to 1942, in which they averaged 107 losses per season and finished between 43 and 62½ games out of first.

In February 1943 the league took control of the debt-ridden club and sold it to a group headed by New York sportsman William D. Cox. Cox didn't last long; before the year was out he was barred from baseball for betting on the Phillies. His controlling interest was sold to Robert M. Carpenter, who installed his son, Robert Jr., as president. The younger Carpenter hired former pitcher Herb Pennock as general manager with instructions to build a farm system, and a new era began in the club's history.

Outfielder Del Ennis had come up to hit .313 in 1946, but Pennock died (in January 1948) before he could see the full fruits of his labor. First baseman Dick Sisler would be purchased in March; rookie outfielder Richie Ashburn would lead Phillie batters in 1948 with a .333 BA. Willie Jones wouldn't nail down third base for another year, and rookie pitchers Robin Roberts and Curt Simmons wouldn't overawe the opposition for a couple of seasons yet. But the team that would be dubbed the "Whiz Kids" was gathering. Triple-A manager Eddie Sawyer was brought up in late July.

In 1949, the loss of first baseman Eddie Waitkus (shot in the chest by a crazed young woman) and midseason complacency threatened to strand the Phillies in the second division. But Sawyer fired up his players in a special team meeting, and the Phillies rallied to finish third with the club's best record in thirty-two years.

With new red-pinstripe uniforms and a recovered Eddie Waitkus, the 1950 Phillies pulled away from a tightly bunched first division in July and August, but late in September fell to within two games of onrushing Brooklyn. The Dodgers took the first game of a season-ending two-game series to narrow the gap to one. But in the finale the Phillies' Sisler homered to break a tenth-inning tie. When Brooklyn failed to score in the bottom of the tenth, the Whiz Kids had their pennant.

Curt Simmons, who was called up for military service in September after winning 17 games, missed the World Series. As in 1915, the result for Philadelphia was frustration and heartbreak, as the Phillies were swept by the Yankees—in the first three games by a single run.

Roberts's pitching kept the Phillies in the first division for four of the next five years, but the team made no serious run at another pennant. And when Roberts began to lose his effectiveness the team sank farther, to fifth for two years, then to four years in the cellar, culminating in 1961 with the longest big league losing streak of the century: 23 games.

The club stuck with new manager Gene Mauch, and the 1962 Phillies edged above .500 for the first time in nine years (though finishing seventh in a league newly expanded to ten teams). In 1963 they moved up to fourth with a strong second half. In 1964, with the acquisition of pitcher Jim Bunning from Detroit and infielder Richie (later Dick) Allen's productive rookie season, Mauch's Phillies moved way out in front in August. But they blew their lead with ten straight losses in late September while Cincinnati was winning nine and St. Louis eight in a row. Only victories in their final two games salvaged a second-place tie.

The Phillies produced winning seasons the next three years but never challenged the leaders. With Mauch replaced as manager during the 1968 campaign, the team embarked on seven straight losing seasons, including three years at the bottom of the NL East.

Pitcher Steve Carlton, acquired from St. Louis in an off-season trade, accounted for nearly half the Phillies' 59 wins in 1972. His 27 victories for the league's worst team gave the club a ray of hope for the future and earned Carlton the Cy Young Award. Carlton lost a league-high 20 games the next year, but as he regained his form over the next three seasons, so too the Phillies gradually rose to the top of the division.

In 1974 sophomore third baseman Mike Schmidt burst to the forefront of the league's power hitters. The Phillies dropped out of contention in August, but wound up third, their best finish since the league split into divisions in 1969. The next year outfielder Greg Luzinski joined Schmidt among the league's top sluggers, and the club rose to second, with their first winning season since 1967.

The Phillies had entered their golden age—nine straight winning seasons (a club record), including five division titles, two pennants, and their first world championship. In 1976 they enjoyed their finest regular season ever. With Schmidt and Luzinski providing the power, Carlton returning to the ranks of 20-game winners and Jim Lonborg climaxing a long comeback with 18 wins, the Phillies took the division lead in May and pulled away, recovering from a late-season dive to finish well ahead of Pittsburgh. Their 101 wins, .624 winning percentage, and nine-game margin of victory remain club records.

The Phillies were swept by Cincinnati in the League Championship Series, but came back the next season to duplicate their record 101 wins for another comfortable first-place finish. Carlton won 23 (and his second Cy Young Award), and Luzinski enjoyed the best season of his career, driving in 130 runs. After defeating Los Angeles in the LCS opener, though, the Phillies lost the pennant with three straight losses.

In 1978, even though Schmidt and Carlton had off-years, the Phillies led much of the season and captured the division title a third straight time. But it was a tight race, and they barely survived a late-season Pittsburgh surge to finish 1½ games in front. For the third time, their triumph in the East was followed by defeat in the LCS—for the second time at the hands of Los Angeles in four games.

Danny Ozark, in his seventh year as Phillies manager, was replaced by Dallas Green late in a disappointing 1979 season that saw the club stumble after a strong start before rallying in September to finish fourth. But Schmidt was back in top form, and Pete Rose had arrived via free agency to add his bat and hustle.

In a three-way race in 1980 that remained close through August, the Phillies hung tight without being able to move into the lead. But as Pittsburgh folded in late August and early September, the Phillies edged in front briefly, then battled back and forth with Montreal. Tied with the Expos as the clubs met in Montreal for the season's final three games, Philadelphia took the first 2–1, then—in eleven innings—the second, to clinch their fourth division title in five years. Schmidt, with perhaps his finest season, drove in 121 runs and was named NL MVP; Carlton, with 24 wins, won his third Cy Young Award; and veteran reliever Tug McGraw enjoyed his best season in years.

In an LCS in which four of the five games went into extra innings, the Phillies prevailed over Houston, capturing their first pennant since the Whiz Kids era thirty years earlier. And in the World Series, fortune finally smiled on the team as they overcame Kansas City in six games.

The Phillies won the first half of the strike-divided 1981 season. In the special intradivisional playoff against Montreal, Philadelphia fought back to tie the series after losing the first two games—only to lose the finale.

The Carpenter family—citing the prohibitive cost of running a major league club—sold the team. Manager Dallas Green also left and was replaced by Pat Corrales, who kept the club in the thick of the 1982 race until the final month, when the Phillies slipped 3½ games back, to second. And Steve Carlton did it again: his 23 wins earned him a record fourth Cy Young trophy.

Mike Schmidt again dominated the Phillies' offense in 1983, but Carlton yielded to John Denny as the team's pitching ace. Newly acquired reliever Al Holland emerged as one of the league's best. After general manager Paul Owens took over for Corrales as manager in midseason, the Phillies came alive and took the division title by 6 games. Carlton dominated the LCS with an 0.66 ERA and two wins as the Phillies won their fourth pennant. But their golden age ended in the World Series, when Baltimore triumphed in five games.

The Phillies dropped to .500 and fourth place in 1984, and suffered a losing fifth-place season in 1985. They rebounded to second in 1986 (but 21½ games behind New York), then dropped back below .500 in 1987. Mike Schmidt continued to power the offense—the only member of the 1980 world champions still a Phillie. Despite an impressive lineup of everyday players in 1988, the Phils collapsed, finishing in the division cellar for the first time in fifteen years.

Unable to recover from a shoulder injury, Mike Schmidt retired in May 1989, and despite several mid-season trades the Phillies again finished last in the NL East. In 1990, though, the flaming start of one of the players acquired in mid-1989—outfielder Len Dykstra, who was batting above .400 as late as June—lit the Phillies' competitive fires. But as Dykstra cooled off to mere excellence, the Phillies fell out of contention and finished 18 games back, tied for fourth.

A thirteen-game win streak in July–August 1991 came too late to propel the Phillies into the thick of the race, and although they rose to third place in the season's final week, they finished 20 games out. In 1992 they played at the bottom of the NL East much of the season, and finished there for the third time in five years.

Strengthened by the signing of several free agents, and sustained by solid performances throughout the roster, the Phillies reversed course in 1993. Led by Dykstra's peak season at the plate, the team grabbed the division lead at the start of the year and never let go, fending off Montreal's late-season surge to take the NL East title by three games. In the LCS they won their fifth NL pennant, defeating Atlanta in six games, but in the World Series they blew a pair of late-inning leads and fell in six games to repeat champion Toronto. Plagued by illness and injury, the Phillies never caught fire in 1994, finishing a distant fourth in the NL East.

Pittsburgh Pirates

Pittsburgh became a big league city in 1882, when its Allegheny baseball club joined with five other teams to form the American Association. Allegheny president H. D. McKnight was named president of the new league, but Allegheny made little stir until the club hired Horace Phillips to manage it and replaced its team in 1885 with players from the defunct Columbus club, which had finished second in the AA the year before. The new Alleghenys finished a distant third in 1885, but after purchasing Pud Galvin from Buffalo they improved in 1886 to finish second behind the St. Louis Browns.

Flushed with success, Allegheny in 1887 became the first club to desert the AA for the older and more highly regarded National League. There they found the competition stiffer and sank back into the second division. In 1890, when most of the team jumped to the rival Pittsburgh Players' League club, Allegheny (known that year as the Innocents) suffered the worst season in Pittsburgh major league history, finishing last, 66½ games out of first place (and 23 out of seventh), with a won-lost record of 23–113.

When the PL folded after just one season, Allegheny merged with its PL counterpart to form the Pittsburgh Athletic Company, thereby retrieving many of its old regulars. The club also hired a second baseman—Lou Bierbauer—whose signing (or theft, as his old club saw it) gave the Innocents a new and more enduring nickname: the Pirates. The renewed club still finished last in 1891, but thirty-six games closer to the top than the year before, and only fractionally out of seventh place.

In 1893 a rules change moved the pitcher 10½ feet farther back from home plate. Of all the NL clubs, the Pirates benefited most from the change: their batting average jumped 63 points—28 more than that of the league as a whole—while their pitchers suffered less than most. The club finished second, with a .628 winning percentage that was their best of the century. Lefty Frank Killen, a twenty-two-year-old pitcher acquired from Washington, led the club's resurgence with a league-leading 34 wins.

Although catcher Connie Mack was called upon to manage the club toward the end of the 1894 season and led them to winning seasons the next two years, the Pirates did not make another serious run for the pennant until 1900. With a team transformed yet again by players from a defunct club—this time the Louisville Colonels—the Pirates battled Brooklyn's Superbas almost to the end of the season before dropping 4½ games back, a solid second. Although they lost the postseason Chronicle-Telegraph Cup games (that year's World Series) to the Superbas, the Pirates were embarked on an era of greatness.

In the merger that brought the Louisville players to Pittsburgh, the Colonels' owner Barney Dreyfuss acquired half ownership of the Pirates. A year later he bought the other half. His perennial hope for the club was a first-division finish; in twenty-six of his thirty-two years of Pirate ownership his hope was rewarded.

Four of the former Louisville players—outfielder-turned-shortstop Honus Wagner, outfielder/manager Fred Clarke, third baseman/outfielder Tommy Leach, and pitcher Deacon Phillippe—and one carryover from the old Pirates, pitcher Sam Leever, remained with Pittsburgh long enough to help lead them to four pennants and, in 1909, their first world championship. In the sixteen years Clarke managed the Pirates (a club record), they also finished second five times, and slipped out of the first division only in Clarke's final two seasons at the helm.

In contrast to the club's devastation by the Players' League raid of 1890, the Pirates were unaffected in 1901 by raiders from the American League (which that year turned itself into a major league largely by drawing off talent from National League clubs). Only third baseman Jimmy Williams defected to the Americans, and he was ably replaced by Tommy Leach, as the Pirates, with the league's best pitching (Jesse Tannehill and Deacon Phillippe finished one-two in ERA, and Jack Chesbro at 21–10 led in winning percentage), captured their first pennant by a comfortable 7½ games over the Philadelphia Phillies.

The Pirates repeated as pennant winners in 1902 and 1903. The 1902 team was one of the most overwhelming of all time. One Pirate or another led the league in nearly every offensive category: Ginger Beaumont in hits and batting; Tommy Leach in home runs (with 6); and Honus Wagner in slugging, RBIs, runs scored, doubles, and stolen bases. Pitcher Jack Chesbro's 28 wins led the league, and the top five NL pitchers in winning percentage were all Pirates. The club held the lead the whole season, finishing 27½ games ahead of second-place Brooklyn, still a major league record.

Pitchers Chesbro and Tannehill deserted to the AL's New York Highlanders the next season, but their loss merely made Pittsburgh's pennant-winning margin (6½ games) smaller than it might have been. Wagner beat out teammate Fred Clarke for the NL batting crown and finished second to Clarke in slugging. Beaumont took the titles in hits, runs, and total bases. Pitcher Sam Leever, with his finest season, led the club with 25 wins and the league in ERA and winning percentage. Owner Dreyfuss arranged with the AL champion Boston Pilgrims for a best-of-nine World Series—the first between NL and AL champions—but the Pirates lost it in eight games as their tired pitchers at last succumbed to overwork.

Although the Pirates twice finished second over the next four years, they didn't come close to capturing another pennant until 1908, when, in one of the tightest NL races ever, they were edged out by the Chicago Cubs and finished one game back, tied with New York's Giants for second. The following year, though, they moved in June into the new concrete-and-steel Forbes Field and celebrated by returning to the top of the league with a club record 110 wins—holding off the dogged Cubs throughout the season to take the flag by 6½ games. And this time they won the World Series, too, although they needed the full seven games to subdue Detroit's Tigers. Honus Wagner remained the league's dominant offensive force, but aging pitchers Leever and Phillippe were overshadowed by a new crop of standouts: Vic Willis, Howie Camnitz, Nick Maddox, and Lefty Leifield—and the astonishing rookie Babe Adams, who after going 12–3 (with a 1.11 ERA) during the season, won three more games in the World Series.

The Series triumph ended an era. Wagner was past his prime and wound down his long career over the next several seasons as the Pirates dropped out of contention for a dozen years, including four (1914–1917) in the hated second division. Only Babe Adams remained of the world championship team when Pittsburgh next made a contest of the pennant race in 1921, taking an early lead and holding it most of the summer until an August-September decline dropped them to second place, 4 games back.

Former Pirate infielder Bill McKechnie replaced George Gibson as manager during the following season with the club in fifth place, and saw the Pirates spurt to second before fading to third at the finish. Two more third-place seasons—with the Pirates finishing just 3 games out of first in 1924—paved the way for another pennant in 1925.

The 1925 Pirates fielded several stars: shortstop Glenn Wright, who led the club with 121 RBIs; sophomore right fielder Kiki Cuyler, who led the team in hitting (.357) and the league in runs scored; third baseman Pie Traynor, who shone on the field and at the bat; and Max Carey, who beat out Cuyler for the league stolen base title and enjoyed his finest season (.343) at the plate. The team as a whole hit .307 to lead the league and ran away with the pennant, spurting to catch the front-running Giants in midseason and pushing ahead to an 8½-game lead by season's end. The World Series was tougher, but the Pirates prevailed over the Washington Senators, defeating veteran Walter Johnson in a seventh-game slugfest 9–7. Babe Adams, hero of the 1909 Series and now, at forty-three, nearing the end of his long career, pitched one shutout inning in Game Four.

Rookie outfielder Paul Waner arrived the next season

and hit .336, but the team, which had led the race going into August, fell into decline late in the month and finished third, 4½ games out. Max Carey sparked an unsuccessful player uprising against the management and was sold to Brooklyn just before the Pirate collapse in August, and manager McKechnie was replaced after the season by former Washington manager Donie Bush.

In 1927, his first season at the helm, Bush sailed the Pirate ship to its sixth pennant, even though Kiki Cuyler was benched for half the season for refusing to bat second in the order. But Paul Waner's younger brother Lloyd arrived to join Paul in the outfield, and the pair tore up the league, finishing one-two in hits (237 and 223) as Paul also took crowns in batting (.380; Lloyd was third at .355), RBIs and total bases, while Lloyd led in runs scored. In and out of first place throughout the season, the Pirates moved into the lead a final time at the start of September and held on to edge the St. Louis Cardinals by 1½ games. In the World Series, though (played with Cuyler on the bench), the Pirates were swept by a Yankee team widely acclaimed as the greatest of all time.

Barney Dreyfuss died in February 1932. Ownership of the Pirates passed to his widow, who named their son-in-law Bill Benswanger president. The team finished a competitive second in 1932 and 1933, but then fell back until 1938, when—with Pie Traynor now manager—they moved out in front in midseason and held their lead comfortably until late September, when ten straight Chicago victories (including three against Pittsburgh) dropped the Pirates to second place, where they finished, 2 games back.

The Pirates showcased some great players in their lean years, like shortstop Arky Vaughan in the 1930s and early '40s, and slugger Ralph Kiner, who won or shared the league home run title all seven of his seasons with Pittsburgh in the 1940s and '50s. But after 1938 the club finished no closer than eight games from the top for twenty-one years. They finished as high as second only twice (in 1944 and 1958), and in the eight years 1950–1957 wound up each season either last or next-to-last, reaching their nadir in 1952 with 112 losses and a last-place finish 54½ games out of first.

The Pirates had been purchased in 1946 by a four-man syndicate that included singer Bing Crosby and real estate tycoon John W. Galbreath. Galbreath later bought a majority interest in the club and, as president, hired Branch Rickey to rebuild the Pirates into contenders. Barney Dreyfuss had resisted the development of minor league farm systems (a Rickey innovation at St. Louis and Brooklyn), preferring to scour unaffiliated minor league teams himself for young talent. Rickey's ministrations helped build a foundation for the Pirate resurgence of 1958–1960.

No one threatened the 1958 Milwaukee Braves' preeminence in the NL after July, but Pittsburgh came closer than anyone, finishing second, eight games back. Six of the eight regulars who would lead the Pirates to their next championship in 1960 were already in the lineup, including Dick Groat, Bill Mazeroski, and Roberto Clemente; and the leading pitchers of 1958—Bob Friend, Vern Law, and reliever Roy Face—topped the 1960 staff, too.

In 1959 the Pirates fell back to fourth place, barely above .500, but the next year they began strong and, shaking off their last challenger in late July, built up a 7-game margin of victory by season's end. League batting champion Groat paced a balanced offense that led the league in hitting, and pitcher Law, with 20 wins, enjoyed the finest season of his career. Facing the Yankees in the World Series, the Pirates were overwhelmed in the three games they lost, but they won the world title with four close wins, capped by Mazeroski's famous home run in the bottom of the ninth inning of the final game.

Pittsburgh again led the league in batting in 1961, with Clemente (whose .351 batting average led the league) and first baseman Dick Stuart (35 home runs, 117 RBIs) enjoying especially fine seasons. But the Pirate pitching fell apart (Vern Law lost most of the season to arm trouble), and the club dropped to sixth place.

When the Pirates next made a serious run for the pennant, in 1966, Harry Walker managed the team and center fielder Matty Alou (newly acquired from San Francisco) won the batting crown. (His brother Felipe of Atlanta was runner-up—the only one-two brother finish ever.) In a season-long three-way race, the Pirates took a lead in August but lost it early in September and finished third, 3 games out. They dropped to sixth again the next season and remained out of the pennant race for three years.

In 1970 the majors experienced their second season of divisional play, John Galbreath's son Daniel was named Pirates' president, and Danny Murtaugh returned a third time to pilot the Pirates. (His second stint was for half a season in 1967.) The team began slowly and entered June with a record under .500. But they were already on their way up, and by mid-July, when they moved out of aging Forbes Field into the brand-new Three Rivers Stadium, they were at the top of the NL East. They slipped into a three-way tangle in mid-September, but shot ahead later in the month to take the division title by 5 games. Most of the team was new since 1960—the power was now supplied by first baseman Bob Robertson and outfielder Willie Stargell. But Roberto Clemente was still in top form, and Bill Mazeroski was still at second base, though nearing the end of his career.

In the 1970 League Championship Series, the Pirates were swept by Cincinnati. But they came back the next season to overwhelm the East in a race that was no race after June, then defeated San Francisco for their eighth pennant, three games to one. Their slugging—paced by Stargell's league-leading 48 home runs—led the league, and reliever Dave Giusti saved a league-leading 30 games in support of a balanced pitching staff. Clemente hit .414 in the World Series (with half his hits going for extra bases) as the Pirates overcame a 0–2 deficit to edge Baltimore in seven games for their fourth world title.

In 1972, after a slow start, Pittsburgh (now managed by their former center fielder Bill Virdon) rocketed to their third straight division championship—by 11 games over Chicago. The club lost, narrowly, to Cincinnati in the LCS, then suffered an even greater loss when Clemente was killed that winter in a plane crash. They played poorly the next season, yet even with a losing record finished third, only 2½ games behind the champion New York Mets in a five-way divisional race. Danny Murtaugh returned as manager a fourth (and final) time late in the season and piloted the club to two more NL East titles the next two years.

The 1974 championship drive featured a comeback from last place in early July to first by late August, followed by a nip-and-tuck race in September with St. Louis that was settled by a tenth-inning Pirate victory over Chicago in the season's final game. Stargell's bat was joined by those of Al Oliver and Richie Zisk as the Pirates outhit the rest of the league. In the LCS, though, the Los Angeles Dodgers overcame Pittsburgh handily, three games to one.

The Pirates won the 1975 race more easily, holding the lead from early June as right fielder Dave Parker, in his first full big league season, led the club in home runs and RBIs, and the league in slugging. But once again, for the fourth time in five tries, Pittsburgh lost the pennant in the LCS—swept this time by the awesome Cincinnati Reds, winners of 108 regular season games.

A distant second-place finish in 1976 was followed that December by manager Murtaugh's untimely death. His successor, Chuck Tanner, kept the Pirates competitive in his first two seasons, steering them to within 5 games of the champion Phillies in 1977, then—with an amazing August-September spurt from way below .500—to within 1½ games of the Phillies in 1978.

In 1979 the Pirates again started slowly but began to move up in May and pushed to the front, ahead of Montreal, in late July. By mid-September, though, the Expos had caught up, and it was not until the final day that an Expo loss and Pirate win gave Pittsburgh its sixth NL East title. Parker and the aging Stargell (now called "Pops") were still the club's big bats, but submariner Kent Tekulve had emerged as the bullpen ace, and one of six Pirate pitchers to win 10 games or more.

In the National League Championship Series the Pirates repaid Cincinnati for their 1975 humiliation, sweeping to the pennant in three games. In the World Series they seemed to have met their match in the Baltimore Orioles of Earl Weaver, falling behind three games to one. But Pops rallied his "family" to victory in the final three must-win contests, and Pittsburgh for a fifth time reigned at the top of the baseball world.

For seven years the Pirates drifted downhill. The club's family spirit disintegrated, fans deserted the team, and it seemed for a time that the Pirates would leave Pittsburgh. But in 1985 a group of local corporations and individuals purchased the club from the Galbreaths, determined (with the assistance of a loan from the city of Pittsburgh) to keep the Pirates in town. Syd Thrift, a trader of consummate skill, was named general manager, and Chicago White Sox coach Jim Leyland was hired to his first job as a big league pilot. Under the new regime the club improved gradually, until in 1988 it once again proved itself a serious contender for the NL championship of the East. Thrift had built a team second only to New York's mighty Mets. But Thrift's unwillingness to share with his superiors the top-level decision making bulked larger, in the eyes of the Pirate directors, than his achievement and he was fired at the season's end.

Plagued all season by injuries, Pittsburgh plunged to fifth in 1989. But in 1990, as Doug Drabek put together a career season on the mound and the bats of Barry Bonds and Bobby Bonilla burst into full bloom, the Pirates arrived at the All-Star break in first place by half a game over New York. With Drabek and Zane Smith (newly acquired from Montreal) all but unbeatable down the stretch, the Pirates, after exchanging the lead with New York several times, swept a Met series in early September to extend a narrow lead and clinched the NL East title at the end of the month with eight straight wins.

The Pirates repeated as division champions in 1991 and 1992. Bonds and Bonilla again led the offense in 1991 and pitcher John Smiley won 20 games. In 1992, even the departure of Bonilla (who signed with the Mets as a free agent) and Smiley (dealt to Minnesota) didn't hamper the Pirates. Center fielder Andy Van Slyke took up the offensive slack with one of his best seasons, and pitcher Tim Wakefield rose from the minors at the end of July to compile an 8–1 record as the Pirate ship breezed to the title by 9 games. But the three-time division champions could not win a pennant. In the 1990 LCS they fell to Cincinnati in six games. The next year they built a 3–1 lead over Atlanta, but lost the final two games. And in 1992, down three games to two, they fought back to within one out of victory in Game Seven before an Atlanta pinch hit cut them down once again.

The departure of free agent Barry Bonds to San Francisco was the most crucial of many roster changes for 1993, which saw more than half the 1992 NL East championship squad replaced. The revamped Pirates fielded near the top of the league and batted near the middle, but their pitching fell apart and the team finished fifth.

When the strike ended the 1994 season, the Pirates' .465 winning percentage was only two points better than the year before, but in the NL's new Central Division, that was good enough for a third-place tie with St. Louis.

St. Louis Cardinals

The club that is now the Cardinals first fielded a team in 1881, and the next season became a charter member of the American Association, a new major league formed in part to offer fans the beer and Sunday baseball forbidden by the older National League. Chris Von der Ahe, one of the club's founders and its first president, at first saw in baseball simply a source of customers for his St. Louis saloon and beer garden, but he developed a love for the game itself as his Brown Stockings—or Browns—developed into one of the era's greatest teams.

After a losing season in 1882, Von der Ahe hired Ted Sullivan, a noted judge of baseball talent, to manage the Browns. Sullivan brought in third baseman Arlie Latham and pitcher Tony Mullane to strengthen a team that already boasted a fine pitcher in Jumbo McGinnis (25–18 in 1882) and one of the game's premier first baseman in Charlie Comiskey. Although Sullivan quit before the end of his first season because of the continued interference of the volatile Von der Ahe, the Browns finished second in the AA, just a game behind champion Philadelphia.

When Mullane bolted the Browns in 1884, the club slipped to fourth. But help was on the way. In July Von der Ahe purchased the Bay City, Michigan, club to acquire its heavy-hitting pitcher Dave Foutz, and in September added another hitting pitcher, "Parisian Bob" Caruthers, to the roster. In 1885—with Comiskey now the manager, left fielder Tip O'Neill blossoming into one of baseball's best hitters, and Caruthers and Foutz winning 40 and 33

games—the Browns rose to the top, 16 games ahead of second-place Cincinnati. They finished on top four years in a row, tying Chicago's White Stockings (3–3–1) in the 1885 World Series and defeating them four games to two the next year for the AA's only Series triumph over their NL rivals.

Pitcher Silver King joined the club in 1887, and outfielder Tommy McCarthy arrived the following year. They helped keep the Browns at the top of the AA through 1888 (although the team lost the World Series both years). But Von der Ahe's sale of Foutz and Caruthers to Brooklyn following the 1887 season boosted Brooklyn to second place in 1888. The next year Brooklyn edged the Browns for the pennant, and the club's first era of greatness was over.

When the AA folded after the 1891 season, the Browns were taken into the NL, but fared poorly there, finishing ninth and eleventh of the twelve clubs in the divided season of 1892. They rose no higher than ninth in the remaining years of Von der Ahe's ownership, dropping into the cellar (63½ games out) in 1897 and returning to the bottom with a club-worst 111 losses the next season.

New owners Frank and Stanley Robison (who also controlled the Cleveland club) transferred the best Cleveland players and their manager to St. Louis in 1899. Dubbed the Perfectos, the revitalized St. Louis club fell short of perfection, but did rise to a first-division fifth place that year and (now known as the Cardinals) rose to fourth in 1901 before sinking back into the second division for a dozen years.

After Stanley Robison died in 1911 (his brother Frank had died in 1905), the club passed into the possession of Frank's daughter Helene Britton, who ran it behind the scenes until, in 1916, she sold it to a syndicate headed by her attorney James C. Jones. Jones hired Branch Rickey away from the AL Browns to run the club.

Rickey took over a team with two chief assets: manager Miller Huggins and a promising young infielder, Rogers Hornsby. Huggins had managed the Cards to third place in 1914, before Hornsby arrived, and after a pair of losing seasons brought them up to third again in 1917. Huggins was lost to the New York Yankees the next year, and Rickey left the club temporarily for military service in the Great War. When Rickey returned in 1919, he took over as manager himself, and in 1921 and 1922 saw the team finish third, closer to the leaders than the club had finished since joining the NL in 1891. Led by Hornsby's .397 and .401 batting, the team hit over .300 both seasons.

Sam Breadon, one of the Jones group of owners, increased his investment in the Cardinals until by 1920 he was majority stockholder and club president, with Rickey as vice president and general manager. Breadon moved the Cards out of the inadequate wooden Cardinal Park during the 1920 season into the more modern Sportsman's Park, owned by the Browns (and built on the site of Von der Ahe's original grounds).

Early in the 1925 season, with the Cards in last place, Breadon replaced Rickey as field manager with second baseman Hornsby. The switch worked. In 1925 the Cards rebounded to fourth, and in 1926 they captured their first pennant since the glory days of the old Browns four decades earlier—edging Cincinnati in the final week of the season after an August spurt had shot them into pennant contention. The season was made perfect by victory in the World Series over Miller Huggins's Yankees.

But Breadon and his irascible player-manager had a falling out, and Hornsby found himself traded that winter to the New York Giants for second baseman Frank Frisch and pitcher Jimmy Ring. The trade enraged Cardinal fans, but the team finished a close second in 1927, and returned to the top (under new manager Bill McKechnie) in a tight race the following season.

McKechnie, fired after the Yankees swept the Cards in the 1928 World Series and rehired in the midst of a Cardinal slump the next season, left to manage the Boston Braves in 1930. Former catcher Gabby Street, who replaced him, led the Cards back to the top again for successive pennants in 1930 and 1931, and in 1931 to a World Series victory over the Philadelphia Athletics. The 1930 race saw the club shoot from below .500 in mid-June to 30 games above .500 by season's end, overtaking three other teams to clinch the flag just three games from the finish. The 1931 team ran away with the pennant, leading all the way and finishing 13 games in front. Outfielder Chick Hafey and first baseman Jim Bottomley finished first and third in NL batting, and pitcher Bill Hallahan led the league in strikeouts (for the second year in a row) and tied for the lead in wins, with 19. Four of the league's top five base stealers—led by Frank Frisch and including outfielder Pepper Martin in his first full season—were Cardinals.

When the Cards dropped to sixth place in 1932 and showed little improvement the following year, Breadon replaced manager Street with Frisch. As when he had named Hornsby to manage, Breadon's move paid immediate dividends. Though the club finished fifth that season, their record improved after Frisch took over, and the next year, in a season-long uphill struggle, the Cards won thirteen of their final fifteen games to pass the front-running New York Giants in the final week.

Writers labeled the 1934 Cardinals the "Gashouse Gang" for their rowdy and daring play. In addition to team veterans Frisch and Martin (who had been shifted from the outfield to third base), the gang included short-stop Leo Durocher, left fielder Joe "Ducky" Medwick, and the team's leading hitter and slugger, first baseman Rip Collins, who in a career-best season led the league in slugging average and tied for first in home runs.

Cardinal pitching was headed by the league-leading Jerome "Dizzy" Dean (30–7) and his rookie brother Paul (19–11). Of the team's final nine wins, Diz and Paul accounted for seven. Each won another pair in the Cards' World Series triumph over Detroit.

The next two seasons the Cardinals moved into the lead late in the season only to wind up second. After the team slipped into the second division in 1938, Breadon replaced Frisch as manager with Ray Blades, who led a late-season run for the flag in 1939 but finished second. When the Cards failed to contend in 1940, Breadon brought up Rochester manager Billy Southworth for a second time. Southworth had failed as McKechnie's replacement in 1929, but this time he stuck, becoming one of the club's greatest helmsmen.

Through all these years Branch Rickey was revolutionizing baseball as he built the game's first and most extensive "farm system" of minor league clubs. The Cardinals' farm teams would—until the other major league clubs caught on and caught up—provide St. Louis with a competitive advantage in the recruitment and development of young players.

In the closing days of the 1941 season, perhaps the Cardinal system's greatest product arrived at the big club: Stan Musial. Southworth brought the club in a close second that year after a season-long back-and-forth struggle with Brooklyn. The next year—Musial's first full season—the Cardinals enjoyed their winningest season ever: 106 victories. They needed them all, too, for Brooklyn won 104 games, leading the race until mid-September, when the Cardinals passed them and held on to a narrow lead by winning twelve of their final thirteen games. St. Louis pitchers Mort Cooper and Johnny Beazley finished one-two in National League wins and ERA, while Enos Slaughter and Musial paced the Cardinal offense. The club maintained its momentum in the World Series, taking the Yankees in five games.

St. Louis retained its preeminence for two more years as baseball gradually lost players to military service in World War Two. Slaughter and Beazley were gone by 1943. But Cooper remained to compile two more 20-plus winning seasons, and Musial was not called until after the 1944 season. With 105 wins in both 1943 and 1944, the Cards ran away with two more pennants, losing to the Yankees in the 1943 World Series, but taking their sixth world title the next year from their St. Louis landlords, the AL champion Browns.

Owner Breadon had fired Branch Rickey in 1942 (objecting to the personal profit Rickey made from selling the club's unneeded farm players), and Southworth left to manage the Boston Braves after the 1945 season (in which the Cards failed to catch the leading Chicago Cubs, finishing second). Rickey went to head the Brooklyn Dodgers, building for them a farm system and tapping the large reservoir of black players. In 1946, the last year of all-white major league ball, the Cards (managed now by Eddie Dyer) and the Dodgers waged a two-team pennant race, ending the season in the first major league tie for first place. St. Louis won the first two games in a best-of-three playoff and went on to surprise the favored Boston Red Sox in the World Series. With the war over, the team was back at full strength. Slaughter led the league in RBIs, and Musial led it in most other offensive categories; pitcher Howie Pollett led the league in ERA (as he had in 1943 before leaving for the war) and in wins, with 21.

But St. Louis was slow to integrate its club and lost ground to teams like Brooklyn, whose black players brought an immediate upswing in the club's success. The Cards began poorly in 1947, but recovered to finish second to Brooklyn, though never offering a serious challenge for the flag. After the season Breadon sold the club to Fred Saigh and Robert Hannegan (the U.S. Postmaster General). Musial enjoyed his finest season in 1948, but the club finished second again in a lackluster race. The next year, though, the Cards and Dodgers tangled in a season-long struggle for first place that was not resolved until the season's last day—with Brooklyn on top.

The Cardinals threatened to move to Milwaukee, but beer magnate August Busch, Jr., purchased the club early in 1953 and the same year bought Sportsman's Park from the Browns (who were moving to Baltimore). With

Busch's infusion of money and enthusiasm, the club slowly revived. They made runs for the pennant in 1957, 1960, and 1963, but each time tailed off sharply in the final week of the season.

The Cards were playing below .500, in seventh place, in mid-June 1964 when the arrival (via a trade with the Cubs) of speedy young Lou Brock sparked a revival of both the team and player. Brock, who had been hitting .251 in Chicago, with 10 stolen bases, hit .348 the rest of the season and stole 33 more bases as the Cards hurtled into the midst of a four-way race for the pennant that was settled only when they took the flag with an 11–5 win on the final day. After surprising the Yankees in the World Series, the Cardinals were themselves surprised when manager Johnny Keane left to take the Yankee helm. The club slipped into the second division for a couple of years under the management of their great former second baseman Red Schoendienst.

But owner Busch built them a striking new stadium in 1966, and the next season the team rebounded to the top again, running away from the field in the last half of the season behind the heavy hitting of Orlando Cepeda, the bat and speed of Lou Brock, and a pitching staff of remarkable breadth and balance. Bob Gibson's three World Series wins over Boston edged the Cards to a ninth world title and set the stage for Gibson's astonishing season the following year.

With his 22 wins leading the Cards to another pennant in 1968, Gibson hurled 13 shutouts and compiled an ERA of just 1.12—both feats the best in more than half a century, both ranking among the top five big league performances ever. After winning two World Series games, Gibson lost Game Seven as Detroit took the crown.

Red Schoendienst continued as Cardinal manager through 1976—a club record twelve years—but led the team to no more championships. When divisional play was inaugurated in 1969, geography was ignored as the Cards were installed in the East to add strength to what seemed the weaker division. But it was fourteen years before they won their first divisional championship. Four times they finished second, losing twice by only 1½ games, in the back-to-back tight races of 1973 and 1974.

Dorrel "Whitey" Herzog was in his first full season as Cardinal manager before the club again finished that near the top. In the strike-shortened divided season of 1981, the Cards compiled the best overall record in the NL East, but because they had finished the two halves of the season second to Philadelphia and Montreal they were ineligible for postseason play.

With the defensive wizard shortstop Ozzie Smith (acquired from San Diego) and rookie speedster Willie McGee bolstering an already strong team, the Cardinals of 1982, after prevailing against the Phillies in the race for the East, swept West champion Atlanta for the pennant and captured their tenth World Series crown in a seven-game struggle with Milwaukee.

After two seasons out of the running, the Cards in 1985 gained the power of veteran Jack Clark (acquired from San Francisco) and the speed of rookie Vince Coleman. With career-best seasons from Willie McGee and newly acquired pitcher John Tudor, the team edged New York for the division title and defeated Los Angeles for the pennant—but lost the World Series to Kansas City.

Jack Clark missed two-thirds of the 1986 season to injury, and the Cards finished below .500, but they rebounded to edge the Mets again for the championship of the East in 1987 as Clark and Vince Coleman enjoyed their finest seasons at the bat. But the reinjured Clark made only a token appearance as the Cards edged San Francisco for the league championship, and he missed the World Series entirely as St. Louis bowed to Minnesota in seven games. That winter Clark signed as a free agent with the Yankees and in 1988 the Cardinals dropped to fifth place, 25 games out.

With solid pitching and hitting, and the league's best fielding, the 1989 Cardinals drew within half a game of the division lead on September 8, then fell out of the race with six straight losses, finishing third. As the season drew to its close, long-time owner August Busch, Jr., died at age ninety. The next July, with the club uncharacteristically mired at the bottom of the National League East, manager Whitey Herzog resigned. Under new manager Joe Torre the Cards revived briefly, but then dropped their final seven games to insure their first basement finish in seventy-two years.

Reliever Lee Smith provided the key to St. Louis's 1991 rebound to second place: his 47 saves—a new NL record—preserved more than half the wins of a team that won 37 of its games by a single run. Smith saved another 43 games in 1992, but this time the Cards finished third. The defense developed a leak in 1993, and the pitching faltered, but four regulars—Bernard Gilkey, Todd Zeile, and newcomers Gregg Jefferies and Mark Whiten—scaled new heights offensively to keep the Cardinals competitive through much of the season and give them another third place finish. In 1994 the team—now playing in the NL's new Central Division—performed below .500 for the first time since 1990.

San Diego Padres

In their first fifteen years the Padres put together only one winning season. In their sixteenth, they won the National League pennant. Founded in the 1969 expansion that saw the two major leagues divide into East and West divisions, the Padres finished last in the six-team NL West their first six seasons, ending each year from 28½ to 42 games behind the division champion.

Their first season was their worst. With 110 losses, the Padres finished not only 41 games out of first but 29 games out of *fifth*. First baseman Nate Colbert, with 24 home runs, provided San Diego's brightest ray of hope. He proved to be one of the Padres' standout performers through their last-place years, and in 1972 became the first Padre to drive in more than 100 runs.

Big league baseball was not an instant hit in San Diego. Home attendance barely topped half a million in the Padres' first year, and though it rose a little over the next few seasons, the increase was not enough to make the club viable. Owner C. Arnholt Smith decided early in 1974 to sell the franchise to a buyer who planned to move the team to Washington, D.C. New uniforms had been manufactured and the club's files were packed for the move, when the builder of the McDonald's fast-food empire, longtime baseball fan Ray Kroc, stepped in with an offer to buy the Padres for cash and keep them in San Diego. His bid was accepted.

Though Kroc's 1974 Padres finished last with the same 60–102 record they had posted the year before, his sense of showmanship drew spectators. Home attendance shot up 76 percent, rising above a million for the first time. The Padres then began to draw fans on their own merits as they finally pulled themselves out of the cellar. Pitcher Randy Jones, who in 1974 had led the league with 22 losses, turned his record around and for two years shone as one of the game's finest pitchers. He halved his 1974 ERA to a league-leading 2.24, winning 20 games as the Padres rose to fourth place in 1975 and posted a winning percentage over .400 for the first time. The next year Jones won a league-high 22 games and earned the Cy Young Award—the first major award to come to a San Diego player.

Although 1976 proved to be Jones's last winning season, the Padres were by then attracting other top-quality players. Outfielder Dave Winfield came up as a rookie in 1973, and the following year became the team RBI leader, a position he held in six of his seven full seasons with the Padres. Reliever Rollie Fingers signed as a free agent. In each of his four seasons in San Diego (1977–1980) he led the team in saves, twice also leading the league. In 1978 the Padres acquired veteran pitcher Gaylord Perry from Texas and installed rookie Ozzie Smith at shortstop. Perry's sparkling 21–6 season gave San Diego its second Cy Young winner, and together with Smith's play in the field, Winfield's bat (.308, 97 RBIs) and Fingers's 37 saves, brought the Padres their first winning season.

All these stars had gone—and owner Kroc had recently died—by the time the Padres recorded a second winning season six years later, and won the division title and NL pennant with a new blend of experience and youth. Sparked by recently acquired veterans Steve Garvey at first, Graig Nettles at third, and Goose Gossage in the bullpen, and by a bevy of younger stars like batting champ Tony Gwynn and hard-hitting outfielder Kevin McReynolds, the Padres moved into first place to stay in early June. From August 3 to the end of the season, they played only .500 ball but still won the championship of the weak Western Division by 12 games. Underdogs in the League Championship Series, the Padres lost the first two games in Chicago, but pulled themselves together to take the pennant with three come-from-behind wins at home.

Their decline began with their World Series loss to Detroit. The end of 1985 saw them tied for third, and in 1986 they slipped below .500 and into fourth place. In 1987 Gwynn won his second batting title, and rookie catcher Benito Santiago capped the season with a 34-game hitting streak to cop Rookie of the Year honors. But with most of the 1984 standouts faded or traded, the Padres' decline was complete: the club for the ninth time in its nineteen years finished last.

In late May 1988, with the team at 16–30, Padre general manager Jack McKeon took over as field manager from Larry Bowa. Under McKeon the Padres went 67–48, with nine wins in their final ten games, shot from sixth place to third in the NL West.

In 1989 a trio of veteran pitchers—starters Bruce Hurst (lured from Boston as a free agent) and Ed Whitson, and closer Mark Davis—attained new peaks of performance. Slugger Jack Clark (newly acquired from the Yankees) turned on the power after a slow start to complement Tony Gwynn's fourth season as NL batting leader. The Padres stumbled through the first half, arriving at the All-Star break four games below .500, but climbed steadily through the final two months to a second-place finish with their second-best winning percentage ever.

With the loss of free agent Davis in 1990, plus injuries to Clark and catcher Santiago, even the new power of Joe Carter (traded from Cleveland) could not lift the club above a tie for fourth. New owners, headed by TV producer Tom Werner, took control of the Padres from Ray Kroc's widow Joan in mid-June. Jack McKeon resigned his managerial position, which went to coach Greg Riddoch a month later, and was fired as general manager in September.

Slugger Fred McGriff arrived for 1991 (in a trade that sent Carter to Toronto) and helped power the Padres into third place. In 1992 he was joined by Gary Sheffield, who revived after an injury-ridden season at Milwaukee to lead the NL in batting and rank with McGriff among the league leaders in home runs and RBIs. The Padres again finished third. But Sheffield and McGriff were traded away during the 1993 season in cost-cutting moves that, combined with poor team pitching and fielding, dumped the Padres into the NL West cellar, a club record 43 games out of first. Attendance also fell, to below 1.4 million, the club's lowest level in thirteen years.

Although the Padres had improved their winning percentage somewhat over 1993 by the time the 1994 season was cut short in August by the strike, their 47–70 record was the worst in the majors. One of San Diego's few reasons to cheer in 1994 was the hitting of Tony Gwynn, whose .394 batting average was the best in the NL since Bill Terry's .401 sixty-four years earlier.

San Francisco Giants

The expulsion of Troy and Worcester from the National League after the 1882 season cleared the way for the league to reestablish clubs in the major markets of Philadelphia and New York. Manufacturer John B. Day was awarded the New York franchise. Purchasing the defunct Troy club, he divided their players between the new NL Gothams and his other club, the Metropolitans of the American Association, and set them up on adjoining grounds north of Central Park, on a field once used for polo.

The Mets fared better than the Gothams, finishing fourth in 1883 to the Gothams' sixth, and winning the AA pennant the next year while the Gothams rose only to fifth in the NL. Since the NL, with greater prestige and higher ticket prices, offered potentially greater profit, Day switched some of his Mets to the Gothams in 1885, including ace hurler Tim Keefe and manager Jim Mutrie. The results were immediate: the Mets sank to seventh place while the Gothams (dubbed "my Giants" by an enthusiastic Mutrie) rose to the thick of a pennant race with Chicago. At the finish Chicago was on top by two games, but the Giants had won more than three games out of four for a .759 winning percentage that is not only the club's best ever, but one of the highest in major-league history. Pitchers Keefe and Mickey Welch together won

76 of the team's 85 victories, and first-baseman Roger Connor led the league in batting.

The Giants won their first pennant in 1888 by nine games over Chicago, and their second the next year in a one-game squeaker over Boston. Keefe and Welch, still going strong, combined for 61 wins in '88 and 55 in '89. Continuing their winning ways in the World Series, the Giants triumphed easily over St. Louis in 1888, and overcame a 1-3 deficit to vanquish Brooklyn the next year.

In 1890, ravaged by the loss of players to the rival Players League, the Giants finished sixth, but they recovered several players when the PL folded at the end of the season. (They also moved into the PL ballpark, named it after their original Polo Grounds, and played there 67 years). They rose to third in 1891, but Day could no longer afford to maintain the team and sold out to financier Edward Talcott. Talcott brought back former Giant star J. M. Ward to manage the club, and in 1894 saw the team rise to a close second-place finish behind Baltimore. Pitchers Amos Rusie and Jouett Meekin tied for the league lead with 36 wins apiece. In postseason Temple Cup play, the Giants swept Baltimore in four games for their third world championship.

That winter Talcott sold control of the club to Tammany Hall politician Andrew Freedman. Giant fortunes sank under Freedman's abrasive and heavy-handed rule. As he ran through a succession of managers, the Giants fell to ninth (of twelve clubs) in 1895 and—apart from a third-place finish in 1897—rose no higher than seventh while he controlled the franchise. In 1902, his final year of ownership, the Giants suffered their lowest winning percentage—.353—and most distant finish ever—53½ games behind champion Pittsburgh.

In the midst of the 1902 season, though, a skirmish in the war between the NL and the upstart American League led to a Giant turnaround. John T. Brush, owner of the NL Cincinnati Reds, bought the AL Baltimore Orioles, then released Oriole manager John McGraw and several key players to sign with NL clubs. Five joined the Giants, including McGraw, catcher Roger Bresnahan, and pitcher Joe "Iron Man" McGinnity. That winter, Brush sold the Reds and Orioles and bought the Giants.

In 1903, with Bresnahan hitting .350 and McGinnity winning a league-high 31 games (closely followed by third-year Giant Christy Mathewson's 30 wins), manager McGraw saw his Giants win thirty-six more games than they had in 1902 and finish a solid second in the standings. In McGraw's twenty-nine full seasons at the helm, the team would win ten pennants and finish second eleven times.

Just two years after their worst season ever, McGraw in 1904 led the Giants to one of their best. Their 106 wins and 13-game winning margin remain Giant highs to this day. The club led the NL in pitching, hitting, fielding, and base stealing. McGinnity led league pitchers in several categories with a career-best 35–8, 1.61 ERA season. Mathewson, right behind with 33 wins, led the league in strikeouts.

The only Giant disappointment of 1904 was McGraw's refusal to face Boston in a World Series. His rejection of the AL champions as worthy opponents was the last shot fired in the war between the two leagues. By the time the Giants had repeated as NL pennant winners a year later,

the World Series was an official and permanent feature of the baseball landscape. Mathewson led NL pitchers in 1905 with 31 wins and an ERA of 1.27, and outfielder "Turkey Mike" Donlin, acquired from Cincinnati the previous July, erupted with the best season of his career, batting a team-high .356 and scoring a league-high 124 runs. The Giants won only one game less than the year before and held a comfortable lead throughout the season. Matty's three shutouts against the Philadelphia Athletics in the World Series secured the club's fourth world crown.

It was 1911 before the Giants won their next pennant. Despite 96 wins in 1906 they finished a distant second to Chicago's mighty Cubs, who won a record 116 games. In 1908 the Giants came within a disputed play of the pennant. On September 23, playing Chicago (with whom they were tied at the top of a three-way race), Giant baserunner Fred Merkle failed to run to second on a single by Al Bridwell that would have driven in the winning run from third. Merkle was forced at second after the ball (or a second ball—the argument still rages) was recovered amid the horde of fans who overran the field. The force out at second negated the run, and the game was ruled a tie. At season's end, when the two clubs found themselves again tied at the top, the "Merkle boner" game was replayed. The Cubs won the game and flag, leaving the Giants in a second-place tie with Pittsburgh.

In 1911 the Giants pulled away from the Cubs in September for the first of three straight pennants. (Early in the season most of the Polo Grounds was rebuilt in concrete after fire destroyed the wooden stands.) The following year the Giants took the lead in May and held it comfortably the rest of the way. In 1913 they didn't move into first until late June, but then quickly put the flag out of reach and finished 12½ games ahead of the faltering Phillies. Mathewson led the team in victories over the three years, with 74, followed closely by Rube Marquard (who with 73 wins enjoyed the three best seasons of his career). Matty led the NL in ERA in 1911 and 1913; Giant rookie Jeff Tesreau took the honors in 1912 (winning 17 games that season and 22 the next). Giant pitching led the league all three seasons, as did their hitting, which featured a balanced offense paced by infielders Larry Doyle and Art Fletcher and catcher John "Chief" Meyers.

In the World Series, though, the Giants three times fell short of the title. Philadelphia's Athletics defeated them handily in 1911 and 1913, but the Giants carried the 1912 Series against the Boston Red Sox to the tenth inning of the final game before a pair of Giant fielding lapses enabled Boston to rally for the win.

Boston's "miracle" Braves, in their 1914 surge from last place to the pennant, passed the front-running Giants for good in early September. The next year, five of the eight NL clubs found themselves bunched within 3½ games of one another at the lower end of the standings as the season ended—with the Giants at the very bottom. And in a 1916 Giant season characterized by dips and surges, even a 26-game winning streak in September couldn't raise the team higher than fourth. But in 1917 a balanced pitching staff—paced by Ferdie Schupp's one big season (21–7, 1.95 ERA)—hurled the Giants to the front early in June and kept them there to the finish. Once more, though, the World Series proved a disappointment, with a loss to the Chicago White Sox in six games.

Three years of second-place finishes followed, in the midst of which the Giants changed owners. Brush had died in 1912 and was succeeded as president by his son-in-law Harry Hempstead. But in January 1919 Brush's heirs sold the club to financier and racehorse fancier Charles A. Stoneham, with manager McGraw a minority stockholder.

In 1921 McGraw brought home the first of four straight winners for Stoneham. Seven regulars hit over .300 (led by third baseman Frank Frisch's .341); first baseman George Kelly's 23 home runs topped the NL. The club hung close to Pittsburgh through August, then broke into a lead which the fading Pirates could not challenge. In postseason play the Giants lost the first two games to the Yankees, but charged back to win their fifth world title. The next year outfielder Emil "Irish" Meusel celebrated his first full season in New York with a team-high 132 RBIs, as the Giants fended off a midseason challenge from St. Louis to pull away to a comfortable margin at the end. The World Series was especially sweet: a four-game sweep of the Yankees.

Cincinnati and Pittsburgh hung just behind the Giants through much of 1923, but never quite caught up. The Giants' league-leading offense was led by individual NL highs in RBIs (Meusel), runs scored (outfielder Ross Youngs), and hits and total bases (Frisch). But the Yankees finally caught the Giants in the World Series, 4–2.

George Kelly took the NL RBI title in 1924. The club's hitting remained the league's best, and by early August the Giants had taken a ten-game lead. But they then leveled off while Brooklyn and Pittsburgh surged. Brooklyn, in fact, took over the lead for a day in early September, but the Giants emerged triumphant at the end by 1½ games. The World Series, though, was as heartbreaking as the pennant race had been heartstopping: the Giants lost to Washington in the last of the twelfth inning of the seventh game when a Senator grounder bounced over the head of rookie third baseman Fred Lindstrom to drive in the Series-ending run.

Close finishes—2 games out—in 1927 and 1928 were the nearest McGraw's Giants came to another pennant. Player relations with the demanding manager had seldom been harmonious, and they had reached a low point when, ill and tired, he quit early in the 1932 season with the team in last place, naming first baseman Bill Terry to replace him. Under Terry the Giants rose only to sixth that season, but McGraw had built a squad fit for a new era of greatness. He had persuaded Terry to leave a career with Standard Oil for one with the Giants; he had saved Mel Ott's unique but effective batting stance from revision by well-meaning minor league managers by keeping Ott out of the minors; and he had rescued pitcher Carl Hubbell from mediocrity by encouraging the screwball pitch other managers had tried to suppress.

Hubbell and Ott formed the heart of the club that would win a trio of pennants under Terry's management. In 1933 the Giants moved to the front in June and, despite a late-September slump, finished well ahead of runner-up Pittsburgh. Ott, with what was for him an off-year, powered the Giant offense with 23 homers and 103 RBIs, while Hubbell led the league in wins, shutouts, and ERA.

Hubbell also hurled two wins against Washington in the World Series, and Ott won it all for New York with a tenth-inning home run in Game Five. McGraw, still the club's vice president, threw a party for "his" Giants after the Series. The following February he died, at age sixty.

As they had the previous season, the Giants of 1934 emerged from the crowd to take and hold first place into late September. They rose higher than they had in 1933 and didn't slump as far at the end. But their five end-of-season losses were enough to drop them 2 games behind the surging Cardinals at the finish. Again in 1935 they led the league much of the season. But they had begun to level off in mid-July and finished the season well back in third. Charles Stoneham died in January 1936, and his son Horace—who at age thirty-three had already run the club for a year—assumed the club presidency.

In 1936, and again in 1937, the Giants came from behind to take the flag. Hubbell sparked their second-half resurgence in 1936, winning his final 16 decisions of the season as the Giants rose from fourth to first. In the World Series, though, Hubbell, after one win, was stopped by the Yankees in his try for a second. The Yankees took the Series in six games.

Again the next year the Giants hid behind the leaders most of the season until a surge in late August coincided with a Chicago decline and shot the Giants to the front. The Cubs recovered, but New York continued its winning ways and finished ahead by 3 games. But again the Yankees dominated the World Series, winning 4–1.

Hubbell's years of greatness were now over, and while the Giants led the NL through the first half of 1938, they finished third, 5 games out. It would be twelve years before they again finished that close to the top. Mel Ott replaced Terry as manager in 1942, but the Giants sank to the cellar in 1943 with their second-worst season ever, and finished last again three years later. One bright spot: in 1947 they rose to fourth with a barrage of 221 home runs (led by Johnny Mize's 51) that remained the major league record (though tied by Cincinnati in 1956) until the 1961 Yankees topped it with 240.

Halfway through the 1948 season the baseball world was startled to learn that Leo Durocher, the fiery manager of the Brooklyn Dodgers, had switched his allegiance to their arch foes, the Giants. Durocher discarded the three top Giant home run hitters of 1947 (but presciently retained the fourth, Bobby Thomson), and added agile infielders Alvin Dark and Eddie Stanky to the roster. By 1950, with the blossoming of Sal Maglie into a first-rank pitcher and the timely midseason purchase of hurler Jim Hearn, the Giants were once more a challenger, spurting in the second half from below .500 to within 5 games of the top.

After losing their first eleven games the next year, the Giants began a long climb. A sixteen-game August winning streak and a seven-game streak at season's end tied them with Brooklyn and forced a three-game playoff. After a win and a loss, the Giants entered the last of the ninth inning of Game Three trailing 1–4. Two singles and a double cut the deficit by a run and brought on Dodger Ralph Branca to face Bobby Thomson, whose two-run homer had provided the Giants' margin of victory in Game One. Thomson homered again, and the Giants won the pennant. Their defeat by the Yankees in the World

Series dimmed the miracle a bit, but couldn't detract from the career bests of pitchers Maglie and Larry Jansen, who tied for the NL lead with 23 wins apiece, and of former Negro League great Monte Irvin, who hit .312 and led the league in RBIs.

The next year Irvin was lost until August with a broken ankle, Jansen (with a back problem) fell off to 11–11, and Willie Mays—a promising rookie in 1951—left early in the season for a hitch in the Army. Still, the Giants hung close to Brooklyn for much of the summer and finished second. In 1953, though, they fell apart in midseason and wound up in fifth, 35 games out.

Mays returned in 1954 to enjoy one of his strongest seasons at the bat, and pitchers Johnny Antonelli (newly acquired from Milwaukee), sophomore Ruben Gomez, and reliever Marv Grissom all burst forth with the best seasons of their careers. The Giants pulled away from Brooklyn in July and held on with a late-season rush to finish 5 games up. Underdogs to powerful Cleveland in the World Series, they stunned the Indians (and the rest of the baseball world) with a four-game sweep. It was their eighth world title—and, so far, their last.

Manager Durocher retired after a distant third-place finish in 1955, and Bill Rigney, who replaced him (the first of seven straight rookie managers to be hired by the Giants over the next twenty years), presided over a pair of sixth-place seasons in the club's final years in New York. Persuaded by the Dodgers' Walter O'Malley that California was the land of baseball opportunity, Giant owner Horace Stoneham announced in August 1957 his decision to move the club to San Francisco before the next season.

The move succeeded. Home attendance doubled, even though the team had to play in a former minor league park that seated fewer than 23,000 fans. When new Candlestick Park opened in 1960 attendance climbed to nearly 1.8 million, a new club high. Better still, rookie sensations like Orlando Cepeda in 1958 and Willie McCovey in 1959, plus the continuing mastery of Willie Mays, made the Giants competitive once again. In their first fourteen San Francisco seasons, they compiled winning records—a longer string than they had known in all their years in New York.

Candlestick Park, though, proved a cold and windy place to watch baseball, and after its inaugural season fans began to drift away. Attendance picked up some in 1962, however, as the Giants battled for first all summer with the Los Angeles Dodgers. Mays, Cepeda, and Felipe Alou headlined the league's best offense, and a pair of veteran pitchers—Jack Sanford and Billy O'Dell—garnered the most wins of their careers (24 and 19) as part of a balanced staff that also got 16 wins from veteran Billy Pierce and 18 from the emerging great Juan Marichal. Still, the Giants trailed the Dodgers most of the season until a Dodger loss and Giant win on the final day threw the teams into a tie and another playoff. As in 1951, the Giants won the first game and lost the second, and overcame a ninth-inning deficit in the finale to win the pennant. Also as in 1951, they lost the World Series to the Yankees, although this time they held on until the final out of Game Seven—a screaming liner off the bat of Willie McCovey into the glove of Bobby Richardson—before losing their grip on the crown.

The 1963 Giants offered little challenge to the leaders after June, but the next three years found them locked to the end in tight struggles for the flag. Although they finished fourth in 1964, they were still in contention with just two games to play, in one of the closest four-way races ever. The next year they took the lead from the Dodgers early in September, only to lose it in the final week. And in 1966, in a season-long three-way race with the Dodgers and Pirates, the Giants weren't eliminated until the final day.

The turbulence of these races was reflected in the team itself. Cepeda (until traded to St. Louis in 1966) continually railed against his managers and his low pay. Alvin Dark, after four winning seasons as manager, was fired in 1964 when some of his racist comments ended up in print. And Marichal was fined and suspended for nine days in 1965 for hitting Dodger catcher John Roseboro over the head with his bat.

After a pair of distant second-place finishes, the Giants in 1969 (with the fine work of Marichal and McCovey augmented by the speed and power of young outfielder Bobby Bonds) found themselves in the thick of a five-way race for the championship of the newly created NL West. The race wasn't settled until the final week, when Atlanta's ten-game winning streak knocked the Giants out of first. Two years later, with Bonds the chief source of offensive power and fine pitching from starters Marichal and Gaylord Perry and reliever Jerry Johnson, the Giants moved out in front at the start of the season and held their lead all the way. A September slump coinciding with a Dodger surge narrowed the lead to one game in midmonth, but the Giants held on for the division crown. In their first experiences with a League Championship Series, though, they succumbed to Pittsburgh with three losses after an opening-game win.

The LCS loss signaled the end of an era. McCovey was past his prime and Marichal had enjoyed his last big year. Mays, after twenty Giant seasons, was sold to the Mets in 1972 so he could close out his career in New York, where it began. That year the Giants suffered their first losing season in San Francisco, and attendance for the first time dropped below what it had been in their final New York season.

Attendance had reached such a low point by the mid-1970s that Stoneham negotiated the club's sale to a Canadian brewery which planned to move it to Toronto. But San Francisco's mayor George Moscone delayed the sale until a buyer could be found who would keep the Giants in the city. San Francisco realtor Robert Lurie stepped forth with half the purchase price, and Arizona cattleman Arthur "Bud" Herseth provided the rest. (Toronto settled for an expansion club, the Blue Jays.)

After six years out of the running, the Giants in 1978 played at the top of the NL East through much of the summer before dropping to third (and home attendance jumped more than a million above the previous year). But they fell below .500 the next two years—making seven losing seasons in the nine that followed their division title of 1971.

In 1982 the Giants—paced by the slugging of Jack Clark and Greg Minton's sparkling relief pitching—made one of the most impressive comebacks since divisional play was instituted in 1969, driving from ten games below

.500 in late June to just 2 games from champion Atlanta at season's end. But they dropped to fifth the following year, and to a last-place sixth in 1984 and 1985.

When Roger Craig was called on to manage the final weeks of the 1985 season, there was no stopping the Giants' slide to a club-record 100 losses. But the next year, inspiring a "can do" spirit among the players, Craig turned the club around. Veteran hurler Mike Krukow won a career-high 20 games, eight players contributed more than 40 RBIs each, and the team captured 26 of their 83 wins in their final at-bat. In first place at midseason, the Giants slipped (in part because of injuries) to third by season's end, but the fans were back—over 700,000 more than a year earlier.

The club set a new home attendance record of more than 1.9 million in 1987 as it returned to the top of the NL West for the first time in sixteen years. Sophomore first baseman Will Clark led a balanced offense, and several shrewd in-season acquisitions by the front office spurred a second-half drive from five games back to a 6-game lead at the finish. But after taking a 3–2 advantage over St. Louis in the LCS, the Giants failed to score in the final two games and the Cardinals captured the flag.

Injuries contributed to the Giants' decline to fourth place the next year, but in 1989 Will Clark enjoyed his strongest season yet, and left fielder Kevin Mitchell erupted with league-high power (47 HRs, 125 RBIs, .635 slugging) to lead another successful Giant assault on the division title. For the first time, the Giants passed the 2 million mark in home attendance. After holding first place from mid-June to the finish, they pushed past the stubborn Cubs in the LCS to their first pennant in twenty-seven years, their nineteenth over all. But the earthquake that delayed Game 3 of the World Series only postponed a sweep by mighty Oakland.

The Giants' downward slide over the next three years—to third place in 1990, fourth in 1991, and fifth in 1992—coincided with futile efforts to persuade Bay area voters to approve public funding for a new stadium to replace unpopular Candlestick Park. In August 1992, Giant owner Bob Lurie arranged to sell the club to a group of investors who planned to move it to St. Petersburg, Florida. In November, though, the sale and move were blocked by the other major league owners.

The signing of free agent Barry Bonds ignited a Giant turnaround in 1993. As Bonds put together another Ruthian season, and Matt Williams rebounded from his worst season to his best, starting pitchers John Burkett and Bill Swift developed into twenty-game winners and closer Rod Beck saved the second most games (48) in NL history. The Giants lost their once-big lead to surging Atlanta in September, but revived to tie the Braves with three games to go. Although a final-game loss to Los Angeles cost them the division title, their 103 wins tied for third best in club history.

On August 11, 1994, the Giants stood five games below .500, but only 3½ games out of first place in the weak NL West. Barry Bonds was enjoying another fine season at the bat, but Matt Williams stole the headlines: with 43 home runs he was challenging Roger Maris's major league single season record of 61. When the players went out on strike the next day, one of the most exciting offensive seasons ever went down the drain.

Seattle Mariners

The Mariners began play in 1977, returning major league baseball to the Pacific Northwest eight years after the Seattle Pilots had moved to Milwaukee after only one season. With a 64–98 inaugural season, the Mariners avoided last place in the American League West only because the Oakland A's had plummeted faster and farther. The hitting of first baseman Dan Meyer, outfielder Leroy Stanton, and rookie center fielder Ruppert Jones—who combined for 73 home runs—and the relief pitching of rookie Enrique (Romo) Romero, who contributed 16 saves and 8 wins, provided most of the high points of that first season.

There was less to cheer about the next year as the production of the first-season heroes fell off and the Mariners took possession of the cellar from mid-May on, losing a club-record 104 games. They finished 12 games out of sixth place, 35 out of first. Much of the offense that was generated came from outfielder Leon Roberts. Acquired from Houston over the winter, Roberts put together his best season and became the Mariners' first .300 hitter.

The club moved up a notch in 1979, to sixth place. Meyer and Jones regained much of their 1977 power, first baseman Bruce Bochte hit .316 and drove in 100 runs, and DH Willie Horton, near the end of a long career, enjoyed one of his finest seasons, driving in 106 runs and leading the club with 29 homers.

As the Mariners, with the league's weakest hitting, dropped back into the cellar the next season, attendance fell to a new low, and some of the original owners decided to sell out. In January 1981 California real-estate magnate George Argyros purchased control of the club, and later bought out the remaining partners to take sole ownership.

In strike-divided 1981 the Mariners finished sixth and fifth in the two halves of the season. Second baseman Julio Cruz continued among the league's top base stealers, and right fielder Tom Paciorek's second-place .326 BA put a Seattle hitter high among the league's best for the first time. Paciorek was traded away that winter, but his replacement, veteran Al Cowens, came through with one of his best seasons in 1982. And Mariner pitching improved dramatically—from the bottom of the league in ERA in 1981 to fourth best in '82. Newcomers Bill Caudill and rookie Ed Vande Berg, working in relief, combined for 21 wins and 31 saves. Starter Floyd Bannister led the league in strikeouts while winning 12 games (tying Caudill for the team lead), and veteran Gaylord Perry added 10 victories, including his 300th career win in May. The team finished above .450 for the first time, fourth in the AL West, a new high.

Caudill's 26 saves in 1983 couldn't prevent a slide back into last place. But the club's farm system was beginning to produce quality talent, and 1984 saw the arrival of two standouts: first baseman Alvin Davis, whose 27 homers and 116 RBIs earned him AL Rookie of the Year honors, and pitcher Mark Langston, a 17-game winner in 1984 and AL strikeout leader in three of his first four seasons. Rookie third baseman Jim Presley hit 10 home runs in 70 games and proceeded to blossom into one of the Seattle club's leading power hitters the next year.

After sixth-place finishes in 1984 and '85, the Mariners

fell off to last again in 1986. Langston's 19 wins led the team's 1987 rebound to fourth, with Lee Guetterman's 11–4 pitching and the power of Davis and Presley providing valuable assists. Infielder Harold Reynolds stole his sixtieth base in the final game to preserve his lead in that department and to give the Mariners their first league leader in an offensive category.

After dropping back into the cellar in 1988 and rising a notch to sixth in 1989, the Mariners revived under new ownership in 1990 to challenge the .500 barrier. Center fielder Ken Griffey, Jr., began to fulfill the promise he had shown as a nineteen-year-old rookie the previous summer. Sophomore hurler Erik Hanson—with 18 wins and an ERA among the league's best—replaced the traded Mark Langston as ace of a young pitching staff that compiled the league's third lowest ERA. The Mariners entered August third in the strong AL West, with a winning record which they maintained through mid-month before stumbling to fifth place with their fourteenth straight losing season.

At last, in 1991, Seattle produced its first winning season, rising from an even .500 with six wins in the final eight games. Griffey Jr. overcame a lackluster first half to reach new Mariner heights in batting (.327) and slugging (.527), but the club still finished fifth, and manager Jim Lefebvre was fired. It also continued to lose money, so in June 1992, as the Mariners sailed for the sixth time toward the bottom of the AL West, the club was sold. The new ownership group included (for the first time) substantial local representation, but as major financing came from Hiroshi Yamauchi, the Japanese president of computer game giant Nintendo, and his son-in-law, a Washington State resident but Japanese national, the sale was delayed until jingoistic opposition to it subsided. The deal was restructured to insure American control of the club. On the field Griffey enjoyed another strong season, and third baseman Edgar Martinez hit .343 to give Seattle its first league batting champion.

A torn hamstring sidelined Martinez much of 1993, but Griffey shone brighter than ever at the bat, and pitcher Randy Johnson finished with nine straight wins (for a 19–8 season record) and 308 strikeouts (a fifteen-year AL high). Their exploits lifted the Mariners into third place for a day in late September before they settled into fourth, with their second winning season ever.

In 1994 the Mariners again enjoyed stellar performances from Griffey and Johnson, but despite six straight wins before the season ended in August, they wound up fourteen games below .500. In the weak AL West, though, their ministreak brought them within two games of division leader Texas—and a third place finish, their highest ever.

Texas Rangers

As part of the first American League expansion, a new Washington club was added to the league in November 1960, to replace the old Senators, who were moving to Minnesota to become the Twins. The old Senators had languished in the second division their final 14 years in Washington, and the new Senators scarcely improved on that record. In each of their first four seasons they lost 100 games or more, tying for last place in 1961 and holding down the bottom all by themselves for two years before rising to ninth in 1964.

Although as an expansion team the new Senators had to make do at first with expendable players from the established clubs, they were not devoid of talent. In their first season, pitcher Dick Donovan led the league with a 2.40 earned run average, though injuries and the lack of offensive support held his won-lost record to 10–10. Perhaps their most promising player, he was traded with two teammates to Cleveland for outfielder Jimmy Piersall. Piersall proved a major disappointment in Washington, batting only .244 while Donovan was winning 20 games for his new club.

Not all the Senators' trades proved disastrous. In late 1964 they sent another promising pitcher—Claude Osteen—to the Dodgers in a deal that brought them five players, including third baseman Ken McMullen and outfielder Frank Howard. Osteen blossomed into a consistent winner in Los Angeles, but at the same time, McMullen brought strength to the Washington infield and Howard became one of the league's offensive stars.

The Senators' blend of youth and experience jelled in 1969 under rookie manager Ted Williams, as several key players—including McMullen and Howard—enjoyed career-best seasons. The club finished above .500 for the first time, driving with a late-season spurt to within a game of third-place Boston in the league's Eastern Division.

But 1969 was a one-year phenomenon. After losing seasons in 1970 and '71 (and the loss of much of their fan support), owner Bob Short pulled up stakes and moved the club to Arlington, Texas (midway between Fort Worth and Dallas), where, as the Texas Rangers, they have been ever since. Their first summer in Texas resembled their first in Washington: they lost 100 games (despite a strike-shortened season) and finished last. Williams was replaced by a new rookie manager—Whitey Herzog—but the club did no better in 1973.

Before the season's end Herzog gave way to Billy Martin. Martin came too late to save the Rangers from another lost season, but the next year he spurred the team to the kind of turnaround Williams had managed five years earlier. Behind the 25–12 pitching of Ferguson Jenkins (acquired in the offseason from the Cubs) and the hitting of league MVP Jeff Burroughs and rookie first baseman Mike Hargrove, the Rangers spurted in the second half of 1974 from a sub-.500 record to second place in the American League West, only 5 games behind Oakland.

Since 1974 the Rangers' fortunes have been up and down. After two losing seasons they rebounded in 1977 to their finest season yet (94–68, .580) and second place, behind strong pitching and the blooming of Jim Sundberg as a hitter to go along with his league-leading catching. Fergie Jenkins's return to the club (after two years in Boston), the sparkling 11–5 season of rookie Steve Comer, and a September surge kept the club competitive in 1978. Jim Kern's brilliant relief work the next season helped the club recover from a nosedive in July and August to edge the Minnesota Twins for a strong third-place finish.

After a losing season in 1980, the Rangers bounced

back in 1981 to record their second-best winning percentage ever (.543)—and finishes of second and third in the two halves of the strike-divided season. Then they slipped below .500 again for four more years. Pitcher Charlie Hough's knuckleball, and strong seasons at the bat from Pete O'Brien, Larry Parrish, Scott Fletcher and rookie Pete Incaviglia helped new manager Bobby Valentine turn the Rangers around once again in 1986, lifting them to the club's fifth second-place finish after last-place seasons in 1984 and '85.

Once more, though, the turnaround was brief: in 1987 losses in their final games of the season dropped the Rangers into a tie at the bottom of the division, and in 1988 they finished only two games out of the cellar, in sixth place.

A group of investors headed by George W. Bush—the President's son—purchased control of the Rangers in March 1989, and strikeout king Nolan Ryan returned to the American League as a Ranger after nine years in Houston. The strong arms of starter Ryan (who recorded his 5,000th career strikeout during the season) and reliever Jeff Russell, the potent bats of outfielder Ruben Sierra and second baseman Julio Franco (newly acquired from the Cleveland Indians), and a 10–1 start that put the club in first place for a month highlighted a Ranger return to the winning side of the ledger. In 1990 Ryan hurled his 300th win and sixth no-hitter, first baseman Rafael Palmeiro peaked at the plate, and pitcher Bobby Witt enjoyed his finest season, with 17 wins. After a slow first half, the Rangers rose from sixth place to third, compiling an 83–79 record identical to that of the year before.

A fourteen-game win streak in May 1991 boosted the Rangers into first place for several days, although they again finished third. Jose Guzman joined Ryan (who threw a sixth no-hitter) among the league's top pitchers, and young slugger Juan Gonzalez formed with Franco, Palmeiro, and Sierra a powerful quartet that made the Rangers the top scoring team in the majors. In 1992 pitcher Kevin Brown won 21 games, and Gonzalez topped the majors in home runs. But an overall decline in offense, coupled with disastrous fielding and relief pitching, dropped the team below .500 after a competitive first half. In the year's biggest in-season trade, the club acquired Jose Canseco from Oakland for Sierra, Witt, and Russell.

The Rangers surged to within a game of first place in mid-July 1993, and remained competitive into September, finishing second, eight games out. Canseco injured his elbow in a relief pitching stint in June and was lost for the season, but Gonzalez again led the league in home runs (with 46), while also leading his team in batting and RBIs. Nolan Ryan retired after an injury-shortened season, and as the Rangers ended their tenure at Texas Stadium, their new home—"The Ballpark At Arlington"—arose on the other side of the parking lot.

In the weak American League West of 1994, it didn't matter that the Rangers played losing ball in their new park. Despite their worst record in six years—a .456 winning percentage that would have consigned them to the cellar of the East or Central divisions—season's end found the Rangers a game ahead of the Oakland Athletics, improbably in first place.

Toronto Blue Jays

For a while, in February 1976, it looked as if the National League's San Francisco Giants would move to Toronto, where there were buyers eager for the club. But when the Giants were sold in March to new owners determined to keep them in San Francisco, the American League jumped in to establish Toronto as an American League city, setting up an expansion club, the Blue Jays, who began play the next year.

It took seven years for the Jays to lift themselves out of last place in the seven-team American League East. For five years they had the cellar all to themselves, never finishing closer than 11 games behind the *sixth*-place club.

In their first season, the Jays' 107 losses left them 45½ games out of first, as the team performed at the bottom of the division in hitting, fielding, and pitching. In 1978 their fielding improved dramatically, but the Jays still lost over 100 games, and there was little doubt after April who would finish last.

The next year was the team's worst ever. While every other Eastern Division club was compiling a winning record, Toronto plunged relentlessly downward and, despite a brief rally in September, finished 28½ games out of sixth place (50½ out of first), with 109 losses.

The club's turnaround began in 1980. It was late June before the Jays began their drop away from the rest of the division, and for the first time they finished with fewer than 100 losses. Pitchers Jim Clancy and Dave Stieb lowered their ERAs below 4.00 for the first time, and newly acquired second baseman Damaso Garcia combined with shortstop Alfredo Griffin to form the league's best double-play combination. There were still two more seasons in the cellar, but in strike-divided 1981 the Jays played a creditable second half for the first time, and in 1982 they spurted in September to tie the Indians for sixth at season's end. Garcia in 1982 became a .300 hitter and a leading base stealer, Clancy put together his first winning season and Stieb his second, and Stieb's five shutouts led the league.

In 1983, with seven of the Blue Jays' eight principal pitchers enjoying winning seasons, and the Jays' hitters leading the league in team batting and slugging, Toronto recorded its first winning season—in fourth place, only 9 games out of first. Their balanced pitching and offense carried them to a repeat 89–73 record in 1984—this time for second place (though they finished a distant 15 games behind Detroit).

In 1985 the Blue Jays topped their division with 99 victories, edging the Yankees by 2 games. Their pitching was better than ever. Doyle Alexander won 17 games, Jimmy Key and Dave Stieb contributed 14 each, and reliever Dennis Lamp compiled an impressive 11–0 record. Stieb led the league in ERA, with Key fourth. Tony Fernandez, in his first full big league season, sparkled as expected at short, but also proved unexpectedly solid at the bat. Eight Jays drove in more than 50 runs, with outfielders George Bell (95), Jesse Barfield (84), and Lloyd Moseby (71) pacing the club's balanced attack.

In the LCS the Jays won three of their first four games against Kansas City, but lost the next three—and the pennant. Equally discouraging was their drop to fourth place in 1986. Barfield, Bell, and Fernandez all improved at the plate, but the league-leading pitchers of 1985 dropped back to the middle of the pack in '86 (though rookie Mark Eichorn sparkled in long relief).

Toronto sprang back stronger than ever in 1987. Jim Clancy (15–11, 3.54 ERA) enjoyed his best season yet, as did Jimmy Key (17–8), whose 2.76 ERA led the league. Once again, as in 1985, the team ERA was the league's lowest. And the offense remained strong. (George Bell, league RBI leader with 134, was named the American League MVP at season's end.) The Jays led their division going into the season's final series against second-place Detroit, though four straight losses had reduced the lead to just one game. Needing to win two of the three games to take the AL East title, or one to tie the Tigers and force a playoff, the Jays' slumping bats remained quiet, and Toronto lost the first two games. In the season finale, Jimmy Key hurled a three-hitter, striking out eight. But one of the hits was a home run—the only run of the game, as it turned out. Toronto's seven-game losing streak had cost them what would have been their second title in three years.

In 1988, a rocky season made worse by George Bell's feud with manager Jimy Williams (who wanted the unwilling outfielder to serve as designated hitter), the Jays surged at the end—with six straight wins—into a tie for third place, only two games out of first. The season was highlighted by the emergence of Fred McGriff as one of the game's most powerful batsmen, and by ace Dave Stieb's two successive one-hitters in late September—both of which were no-hitters through 8⅔ innings.

When Toronto's front office replaced manager Williams with batting coach Cito Gaston in mid-May 1989, the Jays were drowning near the bottom of the AL East with a record of 12–24. By mid-August they had bobbed above .500 to stay, and on September 1 replaced Baltimore in first place. With a pair of one-run victories over the Orioles at the end of September, the Jays preserved their narrow lead and clinched the division title. But Oakland outplayed them in the LCS, taking the pennant in five games.

From mid-June 1990 to the final day of the season, the Blue Jays battled Boston for the division lead before settling for second. Dave Stieb (after two more one-hitters in 1989) at last hurled a no-hitter, and third baseman Kelly Gruber confirmed a place with Bell and McGriff among Toronto's power elite. But the brightest Toronto star of 1989–90 was the new SkyDome, with its 11,000-ton retractable roof and its restaurants and hotel rooms above the outfield wall. After the Jays moved into the Dome on June 5, 1989, attendance zoomed, and by season's end the club set a new American League home attendance record of nearly 3.4 million. In 1990, with a full season in the Dome, the Jays attracted over a half million more fans than the year before, for a new major league record of 3,885,284.

SkyDome attendance continued to set new records in 1991 and 1992 as it rose above 4 million. McGriff and Bell had departed by 1991, but an improved Devon White, plus newly acquired slugger Joe Carter and second baseman Roberto Alomar, led an offense that—together with the league's stingiest pitching staff—brought the Jays to their third divisional title. For the third time,

though, they crashed in the LCS, this time trampled by Minnesota in five games. With the addition of a pair of free-agent veterans—pitcher Jack Morris (who went 21–6) and DH–outfielder Dave Winfield (108 RBIs)—Toronto in 1992 finally completed the puzzle. The Jays sported a balanced offense (six players drove in 60 runs or more) and outstanding pitching from starter Juan Guzman (16–5; 2.64 ERA) and relievers Tom Henke and Duane Ward. Thus armed, they fended off Baltimore's challenge for the lead through much of the summer and resisted Milwaukee's late-season surge to repeat as AL East titlists. They then felled Oakland in six games to bring Canada its first major league baseball pennant, and stopped stubborn Atlanta in six games to carry home the championship of the world.

Nearly half the team was new in 1993, but after a tight battle with several clubs through most of the season, the Blue Jays pulled away to capture their fourth divisional title in five years, by a comfortable seven-game margin. John Olerud, with his first full .300 season at the bat, hit over .400 through the first half of the season and finished with a league-high .363. Paul Molitor, signed from Milwaukee as a free agent, hit better than anyone else in the league from midseason on, and finished second over all. Together with Roberto Alomar, Olerud and Molitor became the first teammates since 1893 to take the top three spots in a major league batting race. In postseason play the Jays repeated their success of the previous year, with six-game victories over the Chicago White Sox for the AL pennant and over Philadelphia for the world title.

The glory faded fast in 1994. At the July All-Star break the Blue Jays lay at the bottom of the AL East. While they pulled themselves up to third before the players' strike ended the season in August, they remained sixteen games out of first, their most distant finish and first losing season in a dozen years.

Defunct Clubs

In addition to the many Negro League teams, some 110 ballclubs have played in the major leagues since the first professional association was formed in 1871. The twenty-eight that still do are described above; here are the other eighty-two, listed according to the league and year in which they first played major league baseball. The official club names precede the name of the city; nicknames follow.

National Association, 1871–1875

Two of the twenty-three clubs that played at one time or another in baseball's first professional league still play in the majors: the Atlanta Braves (then the Boston Red Stockings) and the Chicago Cubs (then the White Stockings). The other twenty-one:

Athletic of Philadelphia: NA 1871–1875, NL 1876. Organized in 1860 as an amateur club, the Athletics became one of the dominant teams of the decade. As professionals they won the first NA pennant in 1871. After one year in the NL, they were expelled for failing to make the final western trip of the season.

Forest City of Cleveland, NA 1871–1872. In the midst

of a second losing season, the club disbanded in August 1872.

Forest City of Rockford, Ill., NA 1871. As an amateur club, Forest City (with its sixteen-year-old pitcher Al Spalding) was the only team to defeat the famous Washington Nationals on their pioneering midwestern tour of 1867. As professionals, Forest City finished seventh of the nine NA teams in 1871.

Kekionga of Fort Wayne, NA 1871. The Kekiongas won the first NA game ever played, but dropped out of the association before the end of the season.

Mutual of New York, NA 1871–1875, NL 1876. Organized as an amateur club in 1857, the Mutuals were said to be backed financially by New York's notorious William M. "Boss" Tweed. Frequently accused of corrupt practices, the club was one of the leading eastern teams of the late 1860s. They were declared national champions of 1868, and proclaimed themselves national champions of 1870. On the demise of the NA the Mutuals entered the NL, but were expelled after one season (along with the Athletics) for failing to play their final games in the West.

Olympic of Washington, D.C., NA 1871–1872. Unsuccessful in 1872 after playing well the year before, the Olympics disbanded about midseason.

Union of Troy, N.Y., NA 1871–1872. The Haymakers, as they were popularly known, dropped out of the NA halfway through the 1872 season.

Atlantic of Brooklyn, NA 1872–1875. One of the greatest of the amateur clubs, the Atlantics (organized in 1855) went undefeated in 1864 and 1865, and won three successive national championships, 1864–1866. But in four NA seasons their combined won-lost record was only 49–139, including a dismal 2–42 in 1875.

Eckford of Brooklyn, NA 1872. Another great early amateur club—like the Atlantics, organized in 1855— they won the national championship in 1862, and again (with an undefeated season of ten games) the next year. The Eckfords actually joined the NA in August 1871, replacing Kekionga, but their 1871 games were later erased from the record because they had failed to enter the association at the start of the season.

Lord Baltimore of Baltimore, NA 1872–1874. After twice finishing third, the Lord Baltimores (or "Canaries," for their yellow silk jerseys) disbanded two games before the end of the 1874 season, while in last place.

Mansfield of Middletown, Ct., NA 1872. Disbanded in late August.

National of Washington, D.C., NA 1872–1873, 1875. Organized as amateurs in 1859, the Nationals were the first eastern club to tour as far west as Chicago and St. Louis. After skipping the 1874 race, the Nationals re-entered the NA in 1875, but dropped out in July.

Maryland of Baltimore, NA 1873. Dropped out after only six games.

Philadelphia, NA 1873–1875. Known successively as the "White Stockings," "Pearls," and "Phillies," the team finished a strong second to Boston in their first season, but slipped to fourth and fifth the next two years.

Resolute of Elizabeth, N.J., NA 1873. Disbanded in August with a 2–21 record.

Hartford Dark Blues, NA 1874–1875, NL 1876–1877. After a weak first year, Hartford finished third in its next three seasons, as standings are reckoned today. But by the 1876 guidelines (which used the number of games won rather than winning percentage), Hartford that year placed second. In 1877 the club played its home games in Brooklyn, N.Y.

Centennial of Philadelphia, NA 1875. Dropped out in late May.

New Haven Elm Citys, NA 1875. Failed to play out their schedule.

St. Louis Brown Stockings, NA 1875, NL 1876–1877. George Bradley pitched all but 5 of the Browns' 39 wins in 1875, when they finished fourth, and all 45 victories in 1876, when they finished a strong third (in number of victories; they were second in winning percentage). With Bradley lost to Chicago the next year, St. Louis dropped below .500—and out of the league.

St. Louis Red Stockings, NA 1875. A successful amateur club that decided to take a fling at pro ball, the Red Stockings played only a few games in the NA.

Western of Keokuk, Iowa, NA 1875. Disbanded in mid-June.

National League, 1876–

When the NL was founded to replace the ill-organized NA, it included six of the stronger NA clubs plus independent clubs in Cincinnati and Louisville. The league's composition was in continual flux to the end of the century as clubs were dropped and added, shrinking the league to as few as six teams and expanding it to as many as twelve. Two clubs that first played major league ball in the NL still do: the Philadelphia Phillies and the San Francisco (originally New York) Giants, both organized in 1883. (The Boston and Chicago franchises—that continue to this day as the Atlanta Braves and Chicago Cubs—had their starts in the National Association.) Those that have not survived:

Cincinnati Red Stockings, NL 1876–1880. From last place in 1876 (and 1877, when their games were not counted because of the club's reorganization and failure to pay its dues), the Reds—with seven new regulars—rose to second in 1878, only to fall back to fifth in 1879, and last again in 1880. That fall, when they refused to accept a new rule abolishing liquor sales and Sunday baseball, they were dropped from league membership.

Louisville Grays, NL 1876–1877. The strong Louisville team led the league in mid-August, 1877, but seven suspicious losses to chief rivals Boston and Hartford dropped the Grays out of first place. After Boston clinched the pennant, Louisville revived to secure second place, but four players—including pitching ace Jim Devlin—were expelled from baseball for throwing games. Their expulsion showed the NL's determination to wipe out corruption, but it also caused the St. Louis Browns, who had planned to sign three of the four Louisville players for 1878, to resign from the league. Louisville, too, dropped out of the league before the next season, unable to find adequate replacements for the four.

Indianapolis Browns, NL 1878. Finished fifth of six teams.

Milwaukee Grays (or Cream Citys), NL 1878. Finished a last-place sixth.

Providence Grays, NL 1878–1885. One of the great teams in the NL's early years, Providence won pennants in 1879 and 1884, finishing no lower than third in seven of their eight seasons. In 1884, pitcher Charlie "Old Hoss" Radbourn won a record 59 games, then pitched the Grays to victory in baseball's first World Series with a three-game sweep of the American Association champion New York Mets. But as they dropped to fourth place the next year, finishing for the first time below .500, their fans deserted them. Late that autumn the club was dissolved.

Buffalo Bisons, NL 1879–1885. Buffalo moved up to the majors after winning the International Association pennant in 1878. Jim "Pud" Galvin pitched nearly 70 percent of Buffalo's victories as he led them to four first-division finishes in seven big league seasons. First baseman Dan Brouthers, in his five years with Buffalo, twice won the batting title and led NL sluggers five times.

Cleveland Blues, NL 1879–1884. Cleveland's fortunes rested in large measure with pitcher Jim McCormick (who also managed the club their first two seasons). In 1880, their best season, McCormick won a career-high 45 games to bring the Blues in third. In 1883 Cleveland was in first place when McCormick's injured arm put him out for the season after he had won twenty-three games. The Blues dropped to fourth. The club folded after a seventh-place finish in 1884, a season that saw McCormick and two other Blues jump to the UA.

Star of Syracuse, NL 1879. After finishing a close second to Buffalo in the International League in 1878, the Stars moved up with the Bisons to the NL, but disbanded after a single unsuccessful season.

Troy, N.Y., Trojans, NL 1879–1882. After four losing seasons the franchise was expelled to make room for a club in New York City.

Worcester, Mass., Brown Stockings, NL 1880–1882. After a pair of losing minor league seasons, Worcester was admitted to the NL to replace the defunct Stars of Syracuse. After finishing a respectable fifth in 1880, Worcester dropped into the cellar for two seasons before being ousted in 1883 for a new Philadelphia club.

Detroit Wolverines, NL 1881–1888. Buffalo's sale of its "big four" (Dan Brouthers, Hardy Richardson, Jack Rowe, and Deacon White) to Detroit late in 1885 transformed a perennial also-ran into a contender. The club finished second in 1886 and won the pennant in 1887. In a World Series played in ten different cities, the Wolverines trounced St. Louis ten games to five. In 1888, after finishing fifth, they expired.

Kansas City Cowboys, NL 1886. They finished seventh, 58½ games out.

Washington Senators, NL 1886–1889. In their four seasons, the Senators finished out of the cellar only once: next to last in 1887.

Indianapolis Hoosiers, NL 1887–1889. After dropping below Washington into the cellar in 1887, the Hoosiers and Senators traded places for their final two years.

American Association, 1882–1891

Three of the six clubs that formed the AA in 1882 still represent their cities in the majors today: Allegheny (Pittsburgh), Cincinnati, and St. Louis. Brooklyn, which entered the AA two years later, today represents Los Angeles. The others:

Athletic of Philadelphia, AA 1882–1890. After finish-ing a distant second in the AA's first season, the Athletics in 1883 took the pennant from St. Louis by a single game. First baseman Harry Stovey, who led AA batters in most offensive categories that year, was even more productive in 1884. But the A's dropped to seventh and never again challenged for the crown. Expelled from the AA after the 1890 season for financial reasons, they were replaced by the Philadelphia club from the defunct Players League.

Baltimore Orioles, AA 1882–1889, 1890–1891, NL 1892–1899. After eight seasons out of pennant contention (including four in last place), the Orioles dropped out of the AA to play minor league ball in 1890. But toward the end of the season, when Brooklyn's new franchise went under, the Orioles returned to complete Brooklyn's season (finishing a combined last). After rising to third in 1891, the AA's final year, the Orioles were invited into the expanding NL, where they dropped to a twelfth-place last (54½ games out) in 1892.

Ned Hanlon, hired to manage Baltimore early in the 1892 season, set about building a championship club. By 1894, with a lineup that included six future Hall of Famers, Hanlon led his club to a narrow pennant victory over New York, though the Giants swept the Orioles in the first Temple Cup World Series, 4–0.

For five years Hanlon's brand of scrappy, hustling play made the Orioles the terror of the NL. Led by shortstop Hughie Jennings and outfielders Willie Keeler and Joe Kelley, the club repeated as NL champions in 1895 and 1896, and finished second to Boston the next two years. They lost the Temple Cup to Cleveland (1–4) in 1895, but swept the Spiders the next year 4–0, and took the cup again in 1897, defeating Boston 4–1 in what turned out to be the Series swan song.

Baltimore owners Hanlon and Harry Von der Horst purchased a half-interest in the Brooklyn club in 1899 (retaining a half-interest in Baltimore), and switched Jennings, Kelley, and Keeler to Brooklyn. Hanlon also went over as manager, leaving third baseman John McGraw in charge of the Orioles. McGraw hit .391 and rookie pitcher Joe McGinnity won 28 games to bring the team in fourth. But Hanlon's Superbas won the pennant, and when the NL cut back to eight teams after the season, Baltimore got the ax.

Eclipse of Louisville/Louisville Colonels (or Cyclones), AA 1882–1891, NL 1892–1899. The club, which changed its official name from Eclipse to Louisville after the 1883 season, was one of only two teams to play all ten seasons of the major league AA. (St. Louis—the present Cardinals—was the other.) Louisville finished above .500 in five of its first six years, but only once in that time closed within ten games of the top—in 1884, when Guy Hecker's 52 wins brought the team in third. Slugger Pete Browning paced the Colonel offense in their early years, winning batting titles in 1882 (his rookie season), 1885 and 1886, and hammering a second-best .402 in 1887. (A bat made for him by woodworker John Hillerich inspired the creation of the Louisville Slugger.)

By 1889, though, the club had sunk to last place, finishing 66½ games out of first, with 111 losses. The next year, although Hecker and Browning defected to the outlaw PL, the club was less affected by deserters than other AA teams. The Colonels (paced by the league's best hitter, William "Chicken" Wolf, and its best pitcher, Scott Stratton) made one of the greatest turnarounds in big league history, winning the pennant by 10 games over second-place Columbus. In the World Series against Brooklyn, poor weather and small crowds ended play after the teams had tied once and won three apiece.

Even though the Colonels finished next to last in 1891, they were one of four clubs taken into the NL after the AA folded. They never finished higher than ninth in the NL, and for three straight years (1894–1896) they occupied the cellar. When the league cut back from twelve teams to eight after the 1899 season, Louisville merged with the Pittsburgh Pirates.

Columbus Colts (or Senators), AA 1883–1884. From sixth place in 1883, Columbus climbed to second in 1884 behind the 34–13 pitching of rookie Ed Morris. But when the AA dropped back from twelve clubs to eight in 1885, Columbus was out.

Metropolitan of New York, AA 1883–1887. After success in minor league and independent play since 1880, the Mets entered the AA in 1883 as the association expanded from six clubs to eight. With 41 victories from pitcher Tim Keefe (who was picked up from disbanded Troy), the Mets finished fourth. The next season, with first baseman Dave Orr hitting .354 in his first full major league season and pitcher Jack Lynch matching Keefe with 37 wins apiece, the Mets won the AA pennant handily. But they lost baseball's first World Series to the Providence Grays. When manager Jim Mutrie, third baseman Dude Esterbrook, and pitcher Keefe were transferred in 1885 to the New York Giants (the two clubs had the same owner), the Mets sank to seventh place, where they finished in their final three seasons.

Indianapolis Blues, AA 1884. Finished eleventh of twelve clubs, 46 games behind.

Toledo Blue Stockings, AA 1884. Catcher Fleet Walker (who played in 42 games) and his brother Welday (5 games) were the major leagues' first black players—and the only blacks until Jackie Robinson broke the color bar for good in 1947.

Washington, D.C., AA 1884. The popularity of the city's UA Nationals proved too much for this inept AA club, which went under in early August.

Virginia of Richmond, AA 1884. When Washington disbanded in August, the Wilmington club of the Eastern League was invited to join the AA as its replacement. Wilmington declined (and later jumped to the UA), but Virginia—also a member of the EL—accepted the invitation and took over Washington's remaining games. Washington-Virginia finished a combined 24–81, in last place.

Cleveland Spiders, AA 1887–1888, NL 1889–1899. After two losing seasons in the AA, the Spiders moved to the NL, where they continued below .500 for three more years. But in 1892 Cy Young's league-leading pitching brought them the second-half championship of the league's experimental split season. Cleveland lost the World Series to first-half winner Boston, losing five after tying the first game.

Second-place finishes in 1895 and 1896 qualified the Spiders for the Temple Cup series against champion Baltimore. In 1895 they beat the Orioles for the world title four games to one, but were swept the next year 0–4.

In 1899, when owner Frank Robison transferred all the team's best players to St. Louis (which he also owned),

Cleveland suffered the worst season in major league history, winning only 20 games while losing a record 134. They finished 35 games behind eleventh-place Washington and 84 games out of first. After the season the Spiders died, as the National League cut back from twelve teams to eight.

Kansas City Blues, AA 1888–1889. Finished last in 1888, next to last in 1889.

Columbus Colts (or Solons), AA 1889–1891. In 1890, with the AA weakened by the replacement of half its franchises with new clubs and by defections to the outlaw PL, Columbus (which retained several of its regulars) rose from its 1889 sixth-place finish to second behind Louisville. When the PL folded and the defectors returned in 1891, Columbus dropped back to sixth.

Brooklyn Gladiators, AA 1890. Formed as a replacement for the Brooklyn club that forsook the AA for the NL in 1890, the Gladiators floundered and were replaced by Baltimore late in the season.

Rochesters, AA 1890. Played .500 ball, finishing fifth.

Syracuse Stars, AA 1890. Finished sixth.

Toledo Maumees, AA 1890. Finished fourth.

Cincinnati Porkers, AA 1891. Also known as "Kelly's Killers" for their manager Mike "King" Kelly, the club went bankrupt in August and was replaced by Milwaukee.

Milwaukee Brewers, AA 1891. This Western League club moved up to the AA in August. Taking five players and the 43–57 record from the defunct Cincinnati club, Milwaukee went 21–15 the rest of the way to lift the Cincinnati-Milwaukee combination from seventh to fifth by season's end.

Washington Senators, AA 1891, NL 1892–1899. Despite a cellar finish in the AA's final year, the Senators were taken into the expanding NL. Of its nine losing seasons, the best was a tie for sixth in the twelve-team NL of 1897.

Union Association, 1884

Formed in opposition to the reserve rule that governed players in the NL and AA, the UA struggled through one season. The first eight clubs listed here began the season. The other five are listed according to the month they entered the UA as replacement teams. All thirteen—like the UA itself—are long extinct:

Altoona, Pa., Unions, UA 1884. The first of several UA clubs to drop out of competition during the season, Altoona disbanded on May 31, but reorganized as an independent club two days later with many of the same players.

Baltimore Unions, UA 1884. Bill Sweeney's league-leading 40 wins accounted for 70 percent of third-place Baltimore's victories.

Boston Unions, UA 1884. Outfielder Tom McCarthy, the UA's only Hall of Famer, hit .215 in this, his rookie big league season. Boston finished fourth.

Chicago Browns/Pittsburgh Stogies, UA 1884. Financial woes caused the Chicago Browns to relocate in Pittsburgh in late August, but the club quit altogether less than a month later.

Cincinnati Outlaw Reds, UA 1884. With three 20-game winners—including Jim McCormick, who won 21 after defecting from the NL in midseason—Cincinnati compiled a strong 69–36 record, but still finished 21 games behind champion St. Louis.

Keystone of Philadelphia, UA 1884. In early August Keystone dropped out of the league and reorganized as an independent semipro club.

National of Washington, D.C., UA 1884. Finished sixth, 46½ games back.

St. Louis Maroons, UA 1884, NL 1885–1886. Batting 47 points above the league average, the Maroons scored 184 runs more than the next-best club to run away with the pennant. They were the only UA club to survive 1884 as a major league team, but in the NL, where they were dubbed "the black diamonds" because of their previously expelled players, they were unable to fashion a winning season or finish higher than sixth.

Kansas City Unions, UA 1884. Formed to replace Altoona, Kansas City went 16–63 in its partial season.

Wilmington, Del., UA 1884. After Wilmington had gone 51–12 to sew up the Eastern League championship, they jumped to the UA in August to replace Philadelphia's Keystones. But as several players failed to make the jump with them, the move was a disaster on the field (2–16) and financially. They failed in mid-September.

Milwaukee Grays, UA 1884. One of only two teams left in the deteriorating Northwestern League, Milwaukee moved up to the UA in September to complete the schedule of dropout Pittsburgh.

St. Paul White Caps, UA 1884. With the disbanding of the Northwestern League in September, St. Paul joined the UA to take over Wilmington's remaining games.

Players League, 1890

Formed in rebellion against the Brush classification plan, a scheme to limit players' pay, the PL drew many of the finest players from the NL and AA, and proved the most popular league with the fans. But when only one club turned a profit, the clubs' financial backers deserted and the league died. Two clubs were admitted to the AA, and many of the rest merged with their NL counterparts:

Boston Red Stockings, PL 1890, AA 1891. Boston won the PL pennant with such stars as Dan Brouthers, Old Hoss Radbourne, Hardy Richardson, and manager King Kelly. The only PL club to make money, Boston joined the AA the next year and won another pennant. But when the popular Kelly defected to Boston's NL Beaneaters (who also won a pennant for the city in 1891), the fans defected too, and the Red Stockings died along with the AA at the end of the season.

Brooklyn Wonders, PL 1890. At the end of a season in which they edged New York for second place, the Wonders merged with Brooklyn's NL pennant-winners.

Buffalo Bisons, PL 1890. After a last-place finish 20 games back of their nearest competitor, the Bisons simply went out of business.

Chicago Pirates, PL 1890. Mark Baldwin, with a league-high 34 wins, and Charles "Silver" King, with 30, pitched Chicago into fourth place. Both went to Pittsburgh the next year, although the franchise was absorbed by Chicago's NL Colts.

Cleveland Infants, PL 1890. Like Cleveland's NL Spiders of 1890, the Infants finished next to last. But one of their three managers, infielder Oliver Wendell "Patsy"

Tebeau, would go on to lead the Spiders to their finest seasons.

Philadelphia Quakers, PL 1890, *Athletic* AA 1891. Although they finished sixth in their PL season, the Quakers compiled a winning record. When the Athletics of the AA were expelled following the 1890 season, the Quakers were admitted in their place and awarded the name "Athletic." The team finished fourth in 1891, but was not among the four clubs taken into the NL when the AA folded, because Philadelphia already had an NL team (the Phillies).

New York Giants, PL 1890. Paced by the hitting of first baseman Roger Connor and outfielder Jim O'Rourke, New York's PL Giants finished third. In November the club merged with the city's NL Giants.

Pittsburgh Burghers, PL 1890. After a sixth-place finish, the Pittsburgh PL club and the NL Allegheny Club combined to form the new Pittsburgh Athletic Club, which still represents Pittsburgh in the NL.

American League, 1901–

When Western League president Ban Johnson renamed the circuit in 1900 and proclaimed it a major league the next year, he little knew how stable it would be. For over half a century (1903–1953) the same eight clubs represented the same eight cities. Even today, although the league has expanded and several clubs have moved to new cities, not one franchise has perished.

Federal League, 1914–1915

After an inaugural season as a six-team minor league in 1913, the FL expanded to eight teams and declared war on the NL and AL for their players. After two big league seasons, and despite two of the game's most exciting pennant races ever, the league died for lack of patronage, and with it went its eight franchises:

Baltimore Terrapins, FL 1914–1915. Jack Quinn and George Suggs, with 26 and 25 wins, pitched Baltimore to third place in 1914. But when Quinn and Suggs lost their stuff the next year, the club sank out of sight, 24 games behind seventh-place Brooklyn.

Brooklyn Tip-Tops (or Brookfeds), FL 1914–1915. The Brookfeds finished fifth in 1915 and not even the acquisition of batting and base-stealing champ Benny Kauff could stop Brooklyn from slipping to seventh the next year.

Buffalo Buffeds, FL 1914–1915. Finished fourth in 1914, sixth the next year.

Chicago Chifeds (or Whales), FL 1914–1915. After leading the league through July and much of August in 1914, only to lose out after a late-season struggle with Indianapolis, the Whales came back in 1915 to triumph in an even tighter race that saw the three top teams separated at the finish by only half a game. Owner Charles Weeghman was permitted to buy the NL Cubs in 1916, and many Whales joined the Cubs in play at what was then Weeghman Park and now is known as Wrigley Field.

Indianapolis Federals (or Hoosiers), FL 1914; *Newark Peps,* FL 1915. Five regulars hit over .300 (paced by Benny Kauff's league-leading .370) in 1914, and the team as a whole hit twenty-two points above the league average. From fourth place in August the Hoosiers fought back to capture the flag from Chicago by 1½ games, with seven consecutive wins at the end. The only major league pennant-winner to move to a new city the next year, the Hoosiers became the Peps in 1915. Though they remained competitive into September, an eight-game losing streak dropped them out of the race and they finished fifth.

Kansas City Packers, FL 1914–1915. After a sixth-place finish in 1914, the Packers competed in a five-way race through much of 1915. But from first place on August 21 they dropped to fifth a week later and finished fourth.

Pittsburgh Rebels, FL 1914–1915. After avoiding last place in 1914 only by St. Louis's late-season nosedive, Pittsburgh turned itself around the next year, luring first baseman Ed Konetchy from their NL rival Pirates, and pitcher Frank Allen from the NL Brooklyn Robins. Both enjoyed the best season of their careers to lead the Rebels into first place in late August, where they remained until they were dropped to third by losing three out of four at the end to the champion Whales.

St. Louis Terriers, FL 1914–1915. After finishing last in 1914, St. Louis added veteran pitcher Eddie Plank to its roster. From a club with two 20-game losers, the Terriers became in 1915 a team with three 20-game winners (including Plank), pulling up from fifth late in August to catch the leaders with a nine-game winning streak. At the finish, though, they ranked second—by less than one percentage point, the narrowest big league pennant margin ever. For 1916, Terriers' owner Phil Ball took over the AL St. Louis Browns.

## CHAPTER 3

Ballparks
Philip J. Lowry

What follows are the vital statistics of each of the current twenty-eight major league baseball stadiums and a selection of the storied parks of the past. My book, *Green Cathedrals,* from which much of this section is taken, encompasses the whole of major league history, from 1871 to the present, including the extraordinary variety of early playing sites, from cricket grounds and polo fields to agricultural fairgrounds and cow pastures. That book also covers Negro League ballparks in a depth beyond the scope possible here, including the vast array of barnstorming sites, even for official league games, that was characteristic of impoverished ballclubs looking to maximize their gate receipts in any way possible. All the same, despite the space constraints imposed upon this entry, the primary Negro League parks will be covered, as well as classic shrines such as Ebbets Field, Griffith Stadium, Forbes Field, and others.

The focus here is on ballpark geometry and the oddities in play that resulted from the unique configuration of the park. Dimensional changes are catalogued and dated, particularly in outfield fence distances and heights. This subject is crucial to an understanding of the statistical history of baseball, whether or not one is a devotee of the park-adjusted figures on display in this volume.

The following leagues are covered by this study. The accompanying abbreviations may be employed for the twentieth century's principal leagues:

NL   National League, 1876–
AL   American League, 1901–
FL   Federal League, 1914–1915
NNL   Negro National League, 1920–1931, 1933–1948
ECL   Eastern Colored League, 1923–1928
NAL   Negro American League, 1929, 1937–1950
NSL   Negro Southern League, 1932
NEWL   Negro East-West League, 1932

Before 1900, most parks were small wooden grandstands hastily constructed around recreation fields that often were not even enclosed by outfield fences. Beginning with the erection of Shibe park and Forbes Field in 1909, however, concrete-and-steel ballparks became the rule. These palaces signaled the growing prominence of baseball and constituted to my mind the best in ballpark design; the term I have applied to this type of park is "Major League Classic." Beginning in the 1950s, multipurpose stadiums were developed. "Multipurpose" means, for this essay, that a stadium was used for both football and baseball, a marriage not made in heaven.

"New Major League Classic" reflects the return to asymmetrical, baseball-only parks—in Baltimore, Cleveland, Texas, and Denver.

Diagrams are by Kevin Spleid.

Using the Outlines

"Style" defines the structural design of the park.

"A.K.A." (Also Known As) lists alternate names and nicknames used for the ballpark.

"Occupant" lists teams using the park in chronological order. Inclusive dates of play within the league follow.

"Event" contains neutral site and All-Star Games.

"Location" lists the surrounding streets. When possible, fields and bases are associated with the streets. Geographical directions, (N) for North, (S) for South, (E) for East, and (W) for West, are provided when available.

Because all older stadiums had grass "surfaces," information concerning carpet or grass is included only for modern ballparks.

Under "Dimensions" the distance is given in feet from home plate to the fences, and to the backstop. Dates, in parentheses, denote the *first* month and/or year when boundaries stood at the stated distance.

"Fences" lists the heights of the outfield fences in feet. Dates denote the *first* time the fences stood at the stated height.

"Former Use" describes how the site was utilized before stadium construction. Similarly, "Current Use" chronicles the development of the site after a ballpark was demolished or abandoned.

"Phenomena" is a more general category for historical data. Included here will be special features of the park's physical plant, important changes over the years, and events of note throughout the years of operation.

ANAHEIM, CALIFORNIA

ANAHEIM STADIUM
STYLE Multipurpose
A.K.A. Big A 1966, Bigger A 1980
OCCUPANT AL Angels April 19, 1966 to date
EVENT All-Star Game 1967, 1989
LOCATION *Left Field (N)* Katella Avenue; *3rd Base (W)* 2000 State College Boulevard, then Interstate 5; *1st Base (S)* Orangewood Avenue, then Santa Ana River; *Center Field (NE)* Amtrak Railroad Station
SURFACE Bluegrass

DIMENSIONS *Foul Lines:* 333; *Bullpens:* 362; *Power Alleys:* 375 (1966), 369 (1973), 374 (1974), 370 (1989); *Deep Alleys:* 386; *Center Field:* 406 (1966), 402 (1973), 404 (1974); *Backstop:* 55 (1966), 60.5 (1973)
FENCES *Majority of the Fence:* 10 (wire 1966), 7.86 (wire 1973), 7.86 (padded 1981); *Corners Between Foul Poles and Bullpens:* 4.75 (steel 1966); *Left-center Between 386 and 404 Marks:* 7.5 (padded 1981); *Padded Posts at the Left Sides of Both Left and Right Field; Bullpen Gates:* 9 (padded 1981); *Bullpen Gates:* 9.95 (wire 1966)
FORMER USE Four farms—Camille Allec's 39 acres of orange and eucalyptus trees, Roland Reynolds' 70 acres of alfalfa, John Knutgen's 20 acres of corn, Bill Ross and George Lenney's 19 acres of corn
CAPACITY 64,593

Anaheim Stadium

PHENOMENA
• Power hitter's park, the ball carries well.
• Huge 230-foot-high letter "A" stood behind the fence in left as a scoreboard support until 1980, then it was moved to the parking lot. The letter has a gold halo at its top.
• Sections 69 and 70 in center covered by green-canvas batters' background.
• Two thin black TV cables run in fair territory on the warning track from the left field corner bullpen gate to the foul pole, and then along the wall in foul territory about 50 feet toward third base, then into the stands.
• Outfield enclosed and tripledecked in 1980.
• 6 doors on ivy-covered wall in deep left-center behind outfield fence labeled: "warning track," "skin material," "screen clay mounds," "raw clay," "sand," "equipment."

ATLANTA, GEORGIA

ATLANTA-FULTON COUNTY STADIUM
STYLE Multipurpose
A.K.A. Atlanta Stadium 1965-74, Launching Pad
OCCUPANT NL Braves April 12, 1966 to date
EVENT All-Star Game 1972
LOCATION *Left Field (NE)* Pullman Street and Interstate 20; *3rd Base (NW)* Washington Street and Interstate 75/85 and Georgia Avenue; *1st Base (SW)* 521 Capitol Avenue; *Right Field (SE)* Fulton Street
SURFACE Grass
DIMENSIONS *Foul Lines:* 325 (1966), 330 (1967); *Power Alleys:* 385 (1966), 375 (1969), 385 (1974); *Center Field:* 402 (1966), 400 (1969), 402 (1973); Back Stop:

59.92 (1973); *Foul Territory:* Large (1966), Medium (1977)
FENCES 6 (wire 1966), 10 (4 plexiglass above 6 wire 1983), 10 (plexiglass 1985)
CAPACITY 52,007

Atlanta-Fulton County Stadium

PHENOMENA
• Three statues outside the stadium honor Ty Cobb, Hank Aaron, and Phil Niekro.
• Used by 1965 Triple A IL Crackers.
• Big Victor, a large totem-pole-styled figure, stood in the stadium in 1966. The huge head tilted and the eyes rolled whenever a Brave hit a home run.
• With an altitude of more than 1,000 feet above sea level, it was—until Colorado entered the major leagues—the highest park in the majors, which results in many homers and the nickname "the Launching Pad."
• Chief Noc-A-Homa's Wigwam replaced Big Victor in 1967. From 1967 to 1971 the teepee stood on a 20-foot-square platform behind the left field fence. In 1972 the teepee was moved to right field. From 1973 to 1977 it returned to left field. From 1978 to August 1982 the teepee was moved to left-center, occupying 235 seats between aisles 128 and 130, rows 18-30. From August to early September, 1982, it was removed in anticipation of additional revenue in the playoffs, "causing" a disastrous tailspin for the first-place Braves. Its replacement coincided with the Braves' comeback to win the division crown in 1982. The teepee's removal on August 11, 1983, saw another losing streak which could not be overcome by its return on September 16. It stands today, a permanent outfield installation.
• 22-foot outfield wall never in play.
• 80-year-old calliope organ installed 1971.

BALTIMORE, MARYLAND

ORIOLE PARK AT CAMDEN YARDS
STYLE New Major League Classic
A.K.A. Camden Yards
OCCUPANT AL Orioles April 6, 1992 to date
EVENT All-Star Game 1993
LOCATION *(N)* Camden Street; *(W)* Russell Street; *(E)* Howard Street; *(S)* Martin Luther King Boulevard
SURFACE Maryland Bluegrass ("Prescription Athletic Turf")
DIMENSIONS *Left Field:* 333; *Left Center:* 364; *Deepest Left Center:* 410; *Center Field:* 400; *Right Center:* 373; *Right Field:* 318; *Backstop:* 57

FENCES 25 in right, 7 elsewhere
FORMER USE Le Comte de Rochambeau, French general, camped his troops here on the way to Yorktown in 1781; former station of Baltimore & Ohio Railroad
CAPACITY 48,000

Oriole Park at Camden Yards

PHENOMENA

• Camden Yards complex includes the Baltimore & Ohio Warehouse, longest building on the East Coast (1,016 feet long but only 51 feet wide). Houses Orioles offices as well as a cafeteria, sports bar, and the exclusive Camden Club. Banks of lights are mounted on roof.
• Each aisle seat in the park features an 1890s Orioles logo.
• Unique doubledecked bullpens in left-center field.
• Hearing-impaired persons may hook into "hearing assistance channels" at their seats.
• Playing field is 16 feet below street level.
• Located only two blocks from Babe Ruth's birthplace; Babe's father operated Ruth's Cafe at 406 Conway Street, the site of which is now located in center field.
• Designed by HOK Sports Facility Group.
• Site of unique three league triple header on June 6, 1992. Fans could take in a morning game at Hagerstown, Md., an afternoon contest at Frederick, Md., and end up under the lights at Camden Yards.
• Built by Maryland Stadium Authority at an approximate cost of $105 million.
• Faced with brick to present a traditional appearance.
• Football stadium will be built adjacent to Camden Yards if an NFL team can be secured.
• Warehouse is 432 feet from home plate.
• Sportswriter John Steadman's unofficial measurements reveal that LCF is 352 rather than 364, deepest LCF is 397 rather than 410, and RCF is 363 rather than 373.

BOSTON, MASSACHUSETTS

FENWAY PARK

STYLE Major League Classic
OCCUPANT AL Red Sox April 20, 1912 to date
EVENT NL Braves vs. New York April 19, May 30, 1913; August 1 and 8, September 7 to 29, 1914; 1914 World Series; April 14 to July 26, 1915; All-Star Game 1946, 1961
LOCATION *Left Field (N)* Lansdowne Street, Boston & Albany Railroad tracks, and Mass. Turnpike/Interstate 90; *3rd Base (W)* Brookline Avenue and 24 Jersey Street, renamed 24 Yawkey Way in 1976, also bowling alley

building attached to park; *1st Base (S)* Van Ness Street (built after park was done); *Right Field (E)* Ipswich Street and Fenway Garage building
SURFACE Bluegrass
DIMENSIONS *Left Field:* 324 (1921), 320.5 (1926), 320 (1930), 318 (1931), 320 (1933), 312 (1934), 315 (1936); *Left-Center:* 379 (1934); *Deep Left-Center at Flagpole:* 388 (1934); *Flagpole Removed from Field of Play in 1970; Centerfield:* 488 (1922), 468 (1930), 388.67 (1934), 389.67 (1954); *Deepest Corner, Just Right of Center:* 550 (1922), 593 (1931), 420 (1934) [Note: 593 is cited in 1931-33 Bluebooks; this could be a misprint.]*Right-Center, Just Right of Deepest Corner Where the Bullpen Begins:* 380 (1938), 383 (1955); *Right of Right Center:* 405 (1939), 382 (1940), 381 (1942), 380 (1943); *Right Field:* 313.5 (1921), 358.5 (1926), 358 (1930), 325 (1931) 358 (1933), 334 (1934), 332 (1936), 322 (1938), 332 (1939), 304 (1940), 302 (1942); *Backstop:* 68 (1912), 60 (1934); *Foul Territory:* Very small, smallest in the majors
FENCES *Left Field:* 25 (wood 1912), 37.17 (tin over wood over concrete lower section 1934), 37.17 (hard plastic 1976); *Left Field Wall to Center Bleacher Wall Behind Flagpole:* 18 sloping to 17 (concrete 1934), (padding 1976) crash pad added from 18 inches to 6 feet on left and center field walls (1976); *Center Field to Bullpen Fence:* 8.75 (wood 1940); *Right-Center Bullpen Fence:* 5.25 (wood 1940); *Right Field Wall and Railing:* Bullpen 3.42 sloping to 5.37 at foul pole (steel 1940); *Right Field Belly:* the low railing and wall curve out sharply from the 302 marker at the right field foul pole into deep right field—many a right fielder has run toward the foul line and watched helplessly as a 310-foot pop fly falls over the railing for a home run.
CAPACITY 34,182

Fenway Park

PHENOMENA

• Seats made of oak.
• 1976 electronic scoreboard significantly altered the wind currents.
• 43 private 28-seat rooftop boxes added 1984.
• Duffy's Cliff was a 10-foot-high mound which formed an incline in front of the left field wall from 1912 to 1933, extending from the left field foul pole to the flag pole in center—named after Red Sox left fielder Duffy Lewis, who was the acknowledged master of defensive play on the cliff. It was greatly reduced but not completely eliminated in 1934.
• The Green Monster Wall in left completely dominates

the field of play—now all green, it used to be covered with advertisements.

• Ladder starts near upper-left corner of scoreboard, 13 feet above ground, and rises to top of the Green Monster to allow groundskeeper to remove batting practice home run balls from the netting above the Wall.

• Scoreboard numbers—runs and hits: 16 inches by 16 inches, 3 pounds; errors, innings, pitcher's numbers: 12 inches by 16 inches, 2 pounds.

• No ball has ever been hit over the right field roof.

• Balls that hit uprights above the Wall, and should have been homers, have been declared in play by the umpires.

• Wooden bleachers stood down the left field line in foul territory in the 1910s and 1920s, but burned down on May 8, 1926. The charred remains were removed, increasing the size of foul territory there. Wooden bleachers were completed in center and right-center by the 1912 World Series.

• Infield grass was transplanted from Huntington Avenue Baseball Grounds to Fenway in 1912.

• During the winter of 1933-34, all the wooden grandstands were replaced with concrete and steel. A big fire on January 5, 1934, destroyed much of what had already been built, but all was finished for the 1934 season opener on April 17.

• In 1936, a 23-foot seven-inch net was placed atop the wall in left to protect windows on Landsdowne Street.

• Wind usually helps the batters. New pressbox built in late 1980s above home plate causes wind swirl which pushes foul balls back into fair territory. This is the park with the tiniest foul territory in the majors.

• When tin covered the two-by-fours on the Wall, balls hitting the tin over two-by-fours had a live bounce, but balls hitting between the two-by-fours were dead and just dropped straight down.

• In 1940, in an effort to help Ted Williams hit home runs, the Red Sox added the right field bullpens, called Williamsburg, which reduced the distance to the fence by 23 feet.

• In 1947 all advertisements were removed from the left field wall, which was painted green.

• Tom A. Yawkey's and his wife Jean R. Yawkey's initials, TAY and JRY, appear in Morse code in two vertical stripes on the scoreboard in left. The 1946 roof boxes were replaced in 1982.

• The screen behind home plate, designed to protect fans and allow foul balls to roll back down onto the field of play, was the first of its kind in the majors.

• Left field scoreboard installed on the Wall in 1934, moved 20 feet to the right in 1976.

• The low concrete base of the left and center field walls was padded after the 1975 World Series, during which Fred Lynn crashed into the concrete wall in center.

• The left field foul line was measured by Art Keefe and George Sullivan, authors of *The Picture History of the Boston Red Sox,* in October 1975 as 309 feet 5 inches. On October 19, 1975, the Boston *Globe* used aerial photography and measured it at 304.779 feet. Osborn Engineering Co. blueprints document the distance at 308 feet.

• Fenway—"where you can sit for hours and feel a security that does not exist anywhere else in the world."

CHICAGO, ILLINOIS

NEW COMISKEY PARK

STYLE Superstructure with natural surface
A.K.A. Comiskey II
OCCUPANT AL White Sox April 18, 1991 to date
LOCATION West 36th Street (South); 333 West 35th Street (North); Dan Ryan Expressway (East); Wentworth Ave. (West)
SURFACE Natural Grass (Bluegrass)
DIMENSIONS *Left field:* 347; *Left Center:* 383; *Center Field:* 400; *Right Center:* 383; *Right Field:* 347; *Backstop:* 60
FENCES 8

FORMER USE Approximately 80 privately owned residential buildings
CAPACITY 44,321
PHENOMENA

• Contains eighty-four luxury skyboxes on two levels, renting for $55,000 to $90,000 annually.

• Unlike the Picnic Area at old Comiskey Park, entry to the new Picnic Area's buffet costs $30 over the ticket price.

• Echoing the nickname of Charles Comiskey, food court contains a shop called Old Roman Pizza.

• Management boasts "Ratio of washroom fixtures to fan capacity, one of the best in baseball" but fans complain of long washroom lines.

• During construction was visible from former Comiskey Park, to which it was adjacent.

• Large scoreboard in center field replicates one designed by Bill Veeck at former Comiskey Park.

• Infield dirt transported here from old park.

• Built at a cost of $134.9 million; paid for in large part by a new hotel tax.

• Park's exterior is of precast colored concrete and features arched windows reminiscent of former park.

• Seats in front row of the upper deck are farther from home plate than those in last row at old Comiskey.

WRIGLEY FIELD

STYLE Major League Classic
A.K.A. North Side Ball Park, 1914; Weeghman Park, 1914-15; Cubs' Park, 1916-26; Whales Park, 1915; Eddie Dorr's House
OCCUPANT FL Whales April 23, 1914 to October 3, 1915; NL Cubs April 20, 1916 to date
EVENT All-Star Game 1947, 1962, 1990
LOCATION *Left Field (N)* West Waveland Avenue; *3rd Base (W)* Seminary Avenue; *Home Plate (SW)* North

Clark Street; *1st Base (S)* 1060 West Addison Street; *Right Field (E)* North Sheffield Avenue

SURFACE   Grass, mixture of Merion Bluegrass and clover

DIMENSIONS   *Left Field:* 345 (April 1914), 310 (May 1914), 327 (June 1914), 343 (1921), 325 (1923), 348 (1926), 364 (1928), 355 (1938); *Left-Center Deepest:* 357 (1938); *Power Alleys:* 364 (1914), 368 (1938); *Center Field:* 440 (1914), 447 (1923), 436 (1928), 400 (1938); *Right-Center Deepest:* 363 (1938); *Right Field:* 356 (April 1914), 345 (June 1914), 321 (1915), 298 (1921), 399 (1922), 318 (1923), 321 (1928), 353 (1938); *Backstop:* 62.42 (1930), 60.5 (1957), 62.42 (1982); *Foul Territory:* Very small

FENCES   *Left Field Corner:* 15.92 (11.33 brick with Boston and Bittersweet Ivy, below 4.59 plywood), 3 wire basket in front 1985 (does not change height of fence); *Transition Between Left Field Corner and Bleachers:* 12.5 (screen and yellow railing on top of brick wall); *Left-Center to Right-Center:* 8 (screen 1914), 11.33 (brick with ivy 1938); in front is wire basket (May 1970); *Left Field Scoreboard:* 40 (wood July 9 to September 3, 1937); *Center Field Screen:* 1933 (8 wire above 11.33 brick June 18, 1963 to October 1964); *Right Center Triangle:* 17.5 in front of catwalk steps sloping down to 15.5 (screen 1928, plywood 1979, removed 1985); *Right Field Corner:* 15.5 (11.33 brick with ivy, below 4.17 plywood), wire basket in front (1985)

CAPACITY   38,765

Wrigley Field

PHENOMENA

• IBM Home Run Distance calculation appears on center field scoreboard after a home run.

• The only remaining Federal League ballpark.

• Beautiful ivy vines on the outfield wall.

• After the game, a blue flag with a white W flying from the center field flag pole signifies a Cub win, a white flag with a blue L a Cub loss.

• Sea breeze off the lake favors pitchers.

• 452 seats added July 1985 to catwalks near foul pole, in fair territory.

• The center field 400 sign is slightly right of straight-away center.

• The only park where it's more difficult to hit a homer down the foul line than to hit one 50 or so feet out in fair territory because the bleachers protrude into the outfield.

• In 1923, the foul lines were shifted slightly amidst park renovations.

• During the 1930s Bobby Dorr, the groundskeeper, lived in a 6 room apartment at the ballpark, adjacent to the left field corner gate; the apartment is still there.

• Eight-foot-high batter's background wire fence, 64 feet wide, stood on top of the center field wall from June 18, 1963 through the end of the 1964 season. Called the Whitlow fence because Cub Athletic Director Robert Whitlow put it up. The screen prevented 10 homers, 4 by Cubs and 6 by visitors, 1 each by 500+ homer hitters Ernie Banks and Willie McCovey.

• Current green Astroturf cover on center field seats used for batters' background and debuted on May 18, 1967.

• In the winter of 1926-27, the left field bleachers were removed, the grandstand was doubledecked, and the playing area was lowered several feet.

• For World Series in 1929, 1932, and 1935, extra bleachers were built on the street on Waveland and Sheffield.

• The park was located so it would be easy for fans to get there on the Milwaukee Road train.

• The 27-foot-high, 75-foot-wide scoreboard was built in 1937 by Bill Veeck. Its top is 85 feet above the field. The 10 foot diameter clock was added in 1941.

• In 1937, the bleacher stairstep was created to allow potted plants and eight huge Chinese elm trees to grow, complementing the ivy. The trees eventually died.

• Ivy planted on the outfield walls in 1937 by Bill Veeck. Originally 350 Japanese bittersweet plants and 200 Boston ivy plants.

• During the 1937 season, new outfield bleachers were built, and the six gates in the brick wall were emplaced. They were red, repainted blue in 1981.

• The bleachers were expanded to their present state in the 1940s; famous Bleacher Bums formed here in 1966 by 10 bleacher fans.

• Lights were inside the park in the early 1940s ready to be installed, but Mr. Wrigley donated them to the war effort instead on December 8, 1941, thus allowing Wrigley Field to remain dark at night until 1988.

• The right field wall was remodeled in 1950-51.

• On April 14, 1976, Met Dave "King Kong" Kingman hit a homer 550 feet over Waveland and against a frame house 3 doors down on the east side of Kenmore Avenue. If the ball had carried 3 feet higher, it would have crashed through a window and smashed a TV screen on which Ms. Naomi Martinez was watching Mr. Kingman round the bases.

• Park is affected by wind conditions more than any other major league park, with the possible exception of Candlestick.

• More home runs than normal are caused by high altitude of over 600 feet above sea level, and by the heat involved in playing so many daylight games.

• Water fountain moved to the Cub Hall of Fame under the first base stands, near the Friendly Confines cafe.

• Arched dormers on the roof.

• Outfield wall distances before 1981 were marked on plywood markers screwed into the brick. Since then they have been painted directly on the brick.

• Foul pole screens have distances marked on plywood vertically "355" and "353."

• The most distant current outfield measurement sign is at Wrigley Field. On the roof of a house across Sheffield Avenue in right-center, the sign says "495."

• Winds blowing toward the lake take homers with them.

CINCINNATI, OHIO

RIVERFRONT STADIUM

STYLE Multipurpose
OCCUPANT NL Reds June 30, 1970 to date
EVENT All-Star Game 1970
LOCATION *Left Field (E)* Riverfront Coliseum, Central Bridge and Broadway; *3rd Base (N)* 201 East Second Street, renamed Pete Rose Way on September 10, 1985; *1st Base (W)* Interstate 71 Suspension Bridge Approach Ramp; *Right Field (S)* Mehring Way, railroad tracks, and Ohio River
SURFACE Astroturf—hard, balls bounce high off it
DIMENSIONS *Foul Lines:* 330; *Power Alleys:* 375; *Center Field:* 404; *Backstop:* 51; *Foul Territory:* Small
FENCES 12 (wood, 1970); 8 (wood, 1984)
CAPACITY 52,952

Riverfront Stadium

PHENOMENA

• First to paint metric distances on outfield walls: 100.58 down the lines, 114.30 to the alleys, 123.13 to center.
• Uses Crosley Field's home plate.
• Parking garage beneath stadium.
• 4,192 circle in left center commemorates Pete Rose's 4,192nd hit here on 9/10/85 vs. the Padres.
• Reds and Pirates played slowest game ever here 8/30/78—80.6 minutes per inning, called off after 3½ innings and 3½ hours of rain delays at 12:47 A.M.
• Winds help righthanded hitters.

CLEVELAND, OHIO

JACOBS FIELD

STYLE New Major League Classic
OCCUPANT Cleveland Indians, April 1994 to present
AKA Gateway
LOCATION *Left Field (SW):* Ontario Avenue; *First Base (SE)* Carnegie Avenue; *Right Field (NE)* East 9th Street
SURFACE Natural Grass
DIMENSIONS *Left Field:* 325; *Left Center:* 368; *Center Field:* 410; *Right Center:* 375; *Right Field:* 325; *Foul Territory:* Small.
FENCES *Left Field:* 19; *Center and Right Field:* 8
CAPACITY 42,400
PHENOMENA
• Original plan was for a $100 million downtown domed stadium but local voters rejected an increase in property taxes to fund the proposal.

Jacobs Field

• Base of exterior facade consists of Atlantic green granite; remainder is Kasota stone, limestone, and buff-colored brick.
• Picnic Plaza will be located beyond Center Field fence.
• Executive Offices located in separate building in back of left field stands.
• Adjacent to new home of NBA's Cleveland Cavaliers, The Arena at Gateway.
• Club-level-seating tickets go for $28 each.
• Scoreboard located in left field.
• Indians bullpen in deep right center field; visitors in right field corner; each with 3 pitching mounds.
• Bullpens elevated 4'6" above playing field.
• Funded by a 15-year "luxury tax" on alcohol and cigarette sales passed in a May 1990 referendum.
• Part of $362 million dollar Gateway project to revitalize downtown Cleveland.
• Features "Kidsland" near the family seating area.
• First property for site acquired in December 1985; entire site acquired by Spring 1988.
• Home plate from Cleveland Stadium transplanted at end of 1993 season.
• Projected cost of $161 million.

DALLAS, TEXAS

THE BALLPARK AT ARLINGTON

STYLE New Major League Classic
OCCUPANT Texas Rangers, April 1994 to present
LOCATION Northwest corner of Stadium Drive and Randol Road
SURFACE Natural Grass
DIMENSIONS *Left Field:* 332; *Left Center:* 388; *Center Field:* 400; *Deepest Right Center:* 403; *Right Center:* 381; *Right Field:* 325; *Backstop:* 60; *Foul Territory:* Small.
FENCES *Left Field:* 14; *Center and Right Field:* 8
CAPACITY 49,292
PHENOMENA
• Granite and brick facade.
• Projected cost of $165 million.
• Funding authorized by a January 19, 1991 referendum which approved a one-half cent increase in the City of Arlington sales tax.
• Covered pavilion porch in right field features pillars reminiscent of Tiger Stadium.
• Playing field is 22 feet below street level.

The Ballpark at Arlington

• Bullpens raised five feet above playing surface so fans can see who is warming up.
• A total of 122 suites: 44 lower level; 78 upper level.
• Construction began April 2, 1992.
• Part of a complex that will include two manmade lakes and a Riverwalk area featuring shops and restaurants.
• Five levels: lower deck, lower suites, club deck, upper suites, and upper deck.
• Picnic area in front of four-story office building in center field.
• Site for 1995 All-Star Game.
• Outfield has many nooks and crannies reminiscent of Ebbets Field in Brooklyn.

DENVER, COLORADO

MILE HIGH STADIUM
STYLE   Expanded Minor League
A.K.A.   Bears Stadium 1948-1967
OCCUPANT   Colorado Rockies, April 9, 1993 to present

Mile High Stadium

LOCATION   Interstate 25, Routes 88 and 287, and Routes 70, 287 and 40; *Left Field* Clay Street; *3rd Base* West 20th Street; *1st Base* Elliot Street
SURFACE   Natural Grass ("Prescription Athletic Turf")
FENCES   10 (padded)
DIMENSIONS   *Left field:* 335; *Left Center:* 375; *Center Field:* 423; *Right Center:* 400; *Right Field:* 370
CAPACITY   19,000 (1960), 43,103 (1985), 75,123 (1985), 76,037 (1993)
PHENOMENA
• Temporary home of Colorado Rockies until 1995 com-

pletion of 43,800-seat Coors Field (*LF:* 347; *LC:* 390; *Deepest CF:* 420; *CF:* 415; *RF Corner:* 358; *RC:* 375; *RF:* 350; *Backstop:* 56.33).
• Home of American Association and Pacific Coast League's Denver Bears/Zephyrs, 1948–1992.
• Also home of NFL's Denver Broncos; former home of United States Football League's Denver Gold.
• Ownership assumed by City and County of Denver in 1968.
• Near McNichols Sports Arena, home of NBA Nuggets.
• Capacity: 19,000 (1960), 43,103 (1985), 75,123 (1985).
• Features 130 luxury suites.
• Entire east stands (built in 1977; capacity 21,000) are movable to accommodate both football and baseball; conversion time to football is ten hours; back to baseball, twelve hours.
• Playing field is heated electrically to prevent surface freezing and to allow year-round growth.
• First "fully distributed sound system" in any major US stadium—delivers "near stereo quality sound."
• Largest NL regular season paid crowd ever—80,227—against Expos on April 9, 1993. The only bigger AL regular season paid crowds have been:

84,587 - September 12, 1954 - Cleveland Stadium
82,781 - June 20, 1948 - Cleveland Stadium
81,841 - May 30, 1938 - Yankee Stadium
81,622 - September 9, 1928 - Yankee Stadium

• Rockies drew largest ever season attendance of 4,483,350 in 1993.

DETROIT, MICHIGAN

TIGER STADIUM
STYLE   Major League Classic
A.K.A.   Navin Field 1912 to 1937, Briggs Stadium 1938 to 1960
OCCUPANT   AL Tigers April 20, 1912 to date
EVENT   All-Star Game 1941, 1951, 1971
LOCATION   *Left Field (NW)* Cherry Street, later Kaline Drive, and Interstate 75; *3rd Base (SW)* National Avenue, later Cochrane Avenue; *1st Base (SE)* Michigan Avenue; *Right Field (NE)* 2121 Trumbull Avenue, same site as Bennett park but turned around 90 degrees, in the Corktown neighborhood
SURFACE   Bluegrass
DIMENSIONS   *Left Field:* 345 (1921), 340.58 (1926), 339 (1930), 367 (1931), 339 (1934), 340 (1938), 342 (1939), 340 (1942); *Left Center:* 365 (1942); *Center Field:* 467 (1927), 455 (1930), 464 (1931), 459 (1936), 450 (1937), 440 (1938), 450 (1939), 420 (1942), 440 (1944); *Right Center:* 370 (1942), 375 (1982); *Right Field:* 370 (1921), 370.91 (1926), 372 (1930), 367 (1931), 325 (1936), 315 (1939), 325 (1942), 302 (1954), 325 (1955); *Backstop:* 54.35 (1954), 66 (1955); *Foul Territory:* Small
FENCES   *All Fences:* 5 concrete topped by screen; *Left Field:* 20 (1935), 30 (1937), 10 (1938), 12 (1940), 15 (1946), 12 (1953), 14 (1954), 12 (1955), 11 (1958), 9 (1962); *Center Field:* 9 (1940), 15 (1946), 11 (1950), 9 (1953), 14 (1954), 9 (1955); *Right of Flag Pole:* 7 (1946);

Right Field: 8 (1940), 30 (1944), 10 (1945), 20 (1950), 8 (1953), 9 (1958), 30 (1961), 9 (1962); *Flag Pole:* 125 in play (5 feet in front of fence in center field, just left of dead center)

CAPACITY 52,416

Tiger Stadium

PHENOMENA

• First named for Frank Navin, a Tiger president.

• Right field second deck overhangs the lower deck by 10 feet. Screen in right in 1944 and in 1961 required balls to be hit into the second deck to be home runs.

• Only doubledecked bleachers in the majors—upper deck from left-center to center, lower deck from center to right-center.

• 125-foot-high flag pole in play in deep center, just to the left of the 440 mark—highest outfield obstacle ever in play in baseball history. The scoreboard now on the left field fence was originally placed at the 440 mark in dead center in 1961 but was moved when Norm Cash, Al Kaline, and Charlie Maxwell complained that it hindered the batters' view of the pitch.

• There is a string of spotlights mounted under the over-hang to illuminate the right field warning track which is shadowed from the normal light standards.

• Cobb's Lake—area in front of plate which was always soaked with water by the groundskeepers to slow down Ty Cobb's bunts.

• When slugging teams came to visit, manager Ty Cobb had the groundskeepers put in temporary bleachers in the outfield, so that long drives would be just ground-rule doubles.

• Sign above entrance to visitors' clubhouse: "Visitors' Clubhouse—No Visitors Allowed."

• Doubledecked in winter of 1923-24 from first to third base.

• Capacity increased in winter of 1935-36 by doubledecking the right field stands, and in the winter of 1937-38 by doubledecking both the left field stands and the center field bleachers.

• In the 1930s and 1940s, there was a 315 marker on the second deck in right field.

• In 1942 and 1943, the center field distance was only 420. The notches just left and right of dead center were closer than 420, at 405.

• Next-to-last classic old ballyard to put in lights, in 1948.

• Saved in 1974 when owner John Fetzer told the Pontiac Silverdome committee, "This franchise belongs to the inner city of Detroit; I'm just the caretaker." Now that mantle of caretaker has been forfeited to the Tiger Stadium Fan Club and the Cochrane Plan, an architectural

plan to preserve the ballpark.

• First homer at Navin Field, on May 5, 1912, came on a fluke bounce which hopped through the side door of the left-center scoreboard.

• Home plate and batters' boxes oriented towards right-center rather than straight out to the mound. This tends to give righthanded pitchers more outside corner strike calls and can disorient visiting batters.

HOUSTON, TEXAS

ASTRODOME

STYLE Dome

A.K.A. Harris County Domed Stadium 1965, Eighth Wonder of the World 1960s

OCCUPANT NL Astros April 12, 1965 to date

EVENT All-Star Game 1968, 1986

LOCATION *Center Field (E)* Fannin Street; *3rd Base (N)* Old Spanish Trail; *Home Plate (W)* Kirby Drive; *1st Base (S)* South Loop Freeway/Interstate 610; *Above:* Domed roof of 4796 Lucite panels and steel girders

SURFACE *Infield:* Grass (1965) Tifway 419 Bermuda grass specially selected for indoor play—died; Astroturf, fast (April 1966 to date); *Outfield:* Grass (April 12, 1965 to July 19, 1966)—died too; Astroturf, fast (July 19, 1966 to date)

DIMENSIONS *Foul Lines:* 340 (1965), 330 (1972), 340 (1977), 330 (1985), 325 (1992), 330 (1993), 325 (1994); *Power Alleys:* 375 (1965), 390 (1966), 378 (1972), 390 (1977), 378 (1985), 375 (1992), 380 (1993); *Center Field:* 406 (1965), 400 (1972), 406 (1977), 400 (1985); *Apex of Dome:* 208; *Backstop:* 60.5 (1965), 67 (1990), 52 (1993)

Astrodome

FENCES *Left and Right Field:* 16 (9 concrete below 3 wire, 2 concrete, and 2 wire plus railing, 1965), 12 (concrete, 1969), 10 (concrete, 1977); 10 (canvas, 1990); 19.5 (concrete, 1991); 10 canvas (1992); Between foul poles and scoreboards: 8 (canvas, 1994), Scoreboards 16 (canvas, 1994); *Center Field* 12 (concrete, 1965), 10 (concrete, 1977), 10 (padded 1990)

PHENOMENA

• The second major league covered stadium, the first being the field under the Queensboro 59th Street Bridge in New York City used by the New York Cubans of the Negro National League in the 1930s.

• Maximum height of the dome is 208 feet, just beyond second base.

• The roof had 4,796 clear panes of glass originally, but they caused a glare which prevented fielders from seeing the ball, thus two of the eight roof sections were painted white. This killed the grass and unfortunately introduced the world to Astroturf.

• Excepting Yankee Stadium's Death Valley, the most distant power alleys in the majors at 390 feet, until changed in 1985.

• Too much yellow, orange, and red.

• Hard to see through the screen from behind the plate.

• Site of 1992 Republican convention.

• In its inaugural season of 1965, the Astrodome was the scene of a unique groundskeeping argument. The New York Mets claimed that the groundskeepers were roof-keeping as well by manipulating the air conditioning system so that the air currents helped Astro long balls and hindered visitors' long balls.

• The first game on a carpet was versus the Dodgers on April 8, 1966.

• Shoeshine stands behind home plate in lower deck.

• On April 28, 1965, Met announcer Lindsey Nelson broadcast a game from a gondola suspended from the apex of the dome.

• On June 10, 1974, Phillie Mike Schmidt hit the public address speaker 117 feet up and 329 feet from home—what would have been a 500-plus-foot homer ended up as a single as the ball dropped in center field.

• On June 15, 1976, a game was rained out because of flooding in the streets.

• The old location of Colt Stadium (now rebuilt in Torreon, Mexico) is just northwest of the Astrodome; Astrohall and Astroarena are just south of the Astrodome.

KANSAS CITY, MISSOURI

KAUFFMAN STADIUM
STYLE   Traditional Baseball Only
A.K.A.   Harry S. Truman Sports Complex, Royals Stadium 1973 to 1993
OCCUPANT   AL Royals April 10, 1973 to date
EVENT   All-Star Game 1973

LOCATION   Center Field (N) Spectacular Drive, then Interstate 70; 3rd Base (W) Lancer Lane, then Dutton Brookfield Drive; Home Plate (S) Royal Way, then Chiefs Way, Arrowhead Stadium, Raytown Road, and CRI&P Railroad tracks; 1st Base (E) Red Coat Drive, then Blue Ridge Cut-Off; Stadium Drive encircles the park
SURFACE   Astroturf—very fast (1973-1994); Grass 1995

DIMENSIONS   Foul Lines: 330 (1973); 320 (1995); Power Alleys: 375 (1973); 385 (1990); 375 (1995);

Center Field: 410; Backstop: 60; Foul Territory: Small
FENCES   12 (canvas, 1973), 8 (canvas, 1995)
CAPACITY   40,625
PHENOMENA

• Waterfalls and fountains run for 322 feet on the embankment overlooking right-center.

• Best visibility for hitters in the majors.

• Homers few here because alleys are deep and the fence cuts away sharply from the 330 foul poles.

• Kenny Pippin, in his frogman suit, cleans the pond periodically in right-center.

• Royals 1985 World Series cup and other trophies are on display through the sixth inning of each game at Section 107.

• Upper deck fans near foul poles are in relative darkness.

• Best groundskeeper in baseball had the ironic job of maintaining an ugly plastic carpet. He kept busy maintaining the Runway and the Baja, the grassy running area and the 125-tree forest beyond the left-center fence.

LOS ANGELES, CALIFORNIA

DODGER STADIUM
STYLE   Traditional Baseball Only
A.K.A.   Chavez Ravine during AL use 1962 to 1965 by Angels, Taj O'Malley, O'Malley's Golden Gulch

OCCUPANT   NL Dodgers April 10, 1962 to date; AL Angels April 17, 1962 to September 22, 1965
EVENT   All-Star Game 1980
LOCATION   Left Field (NW) Glendale Boulevard; 3rd Base (SW) Sunset Boulevard; Home Plate (S) 1000 Elysian Park Avenue; 1st Base (SE) Pasadena Freeway; Right Field (NE) Los Angeles Police Academy, Elysian Park, and Golden State Freeway/Interstate; Stadium Way encircles the park; in Chavez Ravine, on a hill overlooking downtown Los Angeles
SURFACE   Santa Ana Bermuda grass
DIMENSIONS   Foul Lines: 330; Power Alleys: 380 (1962), 370 (1969), 385 (1983); Center Field: 410 (1962), 400 (1969); Back Stop: 65 (1962), 68.19 (1963), 75 (1969); Foul Territory: Large
FENCES   Left-Center to Right-Center: 10 (wood 1962), 8 (1973); Foul Poles to Bullpens in Left and Right Field Corners: 3.75 (steel 1962), 3.83 (1969); The Dip: (where low corner steel wall and screen bullpen fence meet) 3.42 (1962), 3.5 (1969)
FORMER USE   Used by squatters and goats.
CAPACITY   56,000

PHENOMENA

- A classic pitcher's park.
- Cleanest ballpark, bar none.
- Designed by architect Emil Praeger to be expandable to 85,000 seats.
- Painted every offseason.
- Infield dirt and outfield warning track made of 70 percent crushed red building brick and 30 percent mountain clay and calcium chlorate. Palm trees beyond the fence down the foul lines.
- See-through windows in bullpen fence installed in 1974.
- Although the center field 400 sign came down in 1980, the distance is still 400 to center; the two 395 signs are left and right of dead center.
- No drinking-water fountains when first built. Original design had a huge fountain in center field, like that in right-center at Royals Stadium.
- When foul poles were installed in 1962, discovered that they were positioned completely foul. Special dispensation was received from National League so they were recognized as fair, but the next year plate was moved so that poles are now actually fair.

MIAMI, FLORIDA

JOE ROBBIE STADIUM

STYLE   Multipurpose
A.K.A.   JRS
OCCUPANT   Florida Marlins April 5, 1993 to present
LOCATION   2269 N.W. 199th Street
SURFACE   Natural Grass ("Bermuda 419")
DIMENSIONS   *Left Field:* 335; *Power Alleys:* 380; *Center Field:* 410; *Right Field:* 345; *Backstop:* 58
FENCES   *Left Center scoreboard:* 33; *everywhere else:* 8
CAPACITY   56,000

Joe Robbie Stadium

PHENOMENA

- Opening Day for football: August 16, 1987 (Bears vs. Dolphins).
- First baseball game: Los Angeles Dodgers vs. Baltimore Orioles on March 11, 1988.
- Parking for 14,970 cars and 254 buses plus a helipad.
- Retrofitted for baseball at a cost of $10 million.
- All the second-deck outfield seats are covered by canvas and are not used.

MILWAUKEE, WISCONSIN

COUNTY STADIUM

STYLE   Multipurpose
OCCUPANT   NL Braves April 14, 1953 to September 22, 1965; AL White Sox for nine 1968 games and and eleven in 1969; games from May 15, 1968 to September 26, 1969; AL Brewers April 7, 1970 to date
EVENT   All-Star Game 1955, 1975
LOCATION   *Left Field (E)* Menominee River and South 44th Street, later US-41 Stadium Freeway; *3rd Base (N)* Story Parkway and Interstate 94; *1st Base (W)* General Mitchell Boulevard; *Right Field (S)* West National Avenue and the National Soldiers Home
SURFACE   Bluegrass
DIMENSIONS   *Left Field:* 320 (1953), 315 (1975); *Power Alleys:* 355 (1953), 362 (1962); *Deep Alleys:* 397 (1953), 392 (1955); *Center Field:* 404 (1953), 410 (1954), 402 (1955); *Right Field:* 320 (1953), 315.37 (1954); *Backstop:* 60

County Stadium

FENCES   *Left Field:* 4 (1953), 8 (1955), 8.33 (1959), 10 (1985); *Center Field:* 4 (1953), 8 (1955), 8.33 (1959), 10 (1985); *Right Field:* 4 (1953), 10 (1955)
FORMER USE   Stone Quarry
CAPACITY   53,192

PHENOMENA

- Surveyor's mark on right field foul pole: "315.37."
- Before the park was expanded from 1953 to 1973, hospital patients at the National Soldiers Home V.A. Hospital sat outside their rooms on Mockingbird Hill overlooking right field and watched the game for free.
- Perini's Woods, spruce and fir trees behind center field fence, planted in 1954, replaced by bleachers in 1961.
- Braves Reservation, a picnic area down the left field line, was inaugurated in 1961.
- Bernie Brewer slides into a huge beer stein in right-center whenever a Brewer hits a homer.
- Only homer ever hit over left field roof was hit by Cecil Fielder.
- Scene of Midwest League minor league game on August 27, 1966 between Fox Cities and Wisconsin Rapids.
- Braves hosted both the Reds and the Cards on September 24, 1954. The first game was the finish of a game two days earlier whose conclusion on a disputed double play was successfully protested by the Reds. The Reds tied the game after the protested game's resumption, but the Braves won 4-3 in the bottom of the ninth, and then beat the Cards 4-2.

MINNEAPOLIS, MINNESOTA

HUBERT H. HUMPHREY METRODOME
STYLE Dome
A.K.A. Minnedome, Bounce Dome, Hump Dome, Homer Dome, Hubie Dome, Sweat Box (before June 28, 1983, when air conditioning arrived), Domed Stadium, Thunderdome
OCCUPANT AL Twins April 6, 1982 to date
EVENT All-Star Game 1985
LOCATION *Left Field (SW)* Fourth Street South; *3rd Base (NW)* 501 Chicago Avenue South; *1st Base (NE)* Sixth Street South; *Right Field (SE)* Tenth Avenue South; *Above:* Domed roof
SURFACE SporTurf (1982 to 1986—liveliest bounce ever), Astroturf (1987 to date)
DIMENSIONS *Apex of Dome:* 186; *Left Field:* 344 (1982), 343 (1983); *Left-Center:* 385; *Center Field:* 407 (1982), 408 (1983); *Right Center:* 367; *Right Field:* 327; *Backstop:* 60; *Foul Territory:* Small
FENCES *Left Field:* 7 (canvas 1982), 13 (6 plexiglass above 7 canvas 1983); *Center Field:* 7 (canvas 1982); *Right Field:* 7 (canvas 1982), 13 (canvas early in 1983), 23 (canvas later in 1983)
CAPACITY 55,883
PHENOMENA
- A power hitter's park.
- Right field wall called Hefty Bag.
- Almost an exact duplicate of the domed stadiums in Seattle, Pontiac, and Vancouver. All four were built by the same engineering firm.
- Game on April 26, 1986 delayed as violent rainstorm knocked out the lights and had the scoreboard and roof swaying.
- The white air-supported fabric Teflon roof makes it difficult to see the ball when hit high in the air.

Metrodome

- Playoffs and World Series of 1987 set new decibel records for sound in the Thunderdome.
- Sections 107 to 113 are football seats which in baseball season are tilted up and back to create a 40-foot wall behind the right field fence.
- The roof collapsed on April 14, 1983 from the weight of heavy snow.
- Twin batter Randy Bush hit a ball off the roof in 1983. The ball was caught foul for an out by Blue Jays catcher Buck Martinez. Rob Deer hit two such fly-ball outs to shortstop on consecutive at bats on May 30, 1992.
- On May 4, 1984, in the top of the fourth inning, A's batter Dave Kingman hit a ball through the roof. It should have been a homer, but Kingman got only a double.
- Balls bounced very high off the carpet used from 1982 to 1986.
- More home runs tend to be hit when the air conditioning is turned off.
- Curvature of wall behind plate causes wild pitches and passed balls to bounce directly toward first base.

MONTREAL, QUEBEC

STADE OLYMPIQUE
STYLE Summer Olympics Stadium/Dome
A.K.A. Olympic Stadium, Big O, Big Owe
OCCUPANT NL Expos April 15, 1977 to date
EVENT All-Star Game 1982
LOCATION *Left Field (NW)* rue Sherbrooke; *3rd Base (SW)* boulevard Pie-IX; *1st Base (SE)* 4549, avenue Pierre-de-Coubertin; *Right Field (NE)* boulevard Viau
SURFACE Astroturf

Olympic Stadium

DIMENSIONS *Foul Lines:* 325 (1977), 330 (1981), 325 (1983); *Power Alleys:* 375; *Center Field:* 404 (1977), 405 (1979), 404 (1980), 400 (1981), 404 (1983); *Apex of Dome:* 180; *Backstop:* 62 (1977), 65 (1983), 53 (1989); *Foul Territory:* Large
FENCES 12 (wood 1977), 12 (foam 1989)
CAPACITY 43,739
PHENOMENA
- Labatt's Noise-Meter high above right field is baseball's answer to the NBA Sacramento Kings' Arco Arena Noise-Meter.
- Roof improves offense by keeping out extreme cold.
- Built for 1976 Olympics.
- Plaque inside and statue of Jackie Robinson at main entrance. Robinson starred at the Delorimer Downs for the IL Montreal Royals in 1946. Huge 623-foot-high umbrella tower in center field from section 766 in left-center to section 767 in right-center stood half finished from 1976 to 1987. Became a fixed-dome stadium in 1989. The once retractable dome is silver on top, and orange on the bottom, with 26 white cones which link the roof to the tower. It consists of 60,696 square feet of Kevlar, weighing 50 tons. Retractable roof not actually retractable until 1988 due to generator problems, then became balky and decision was made to keep it closed.
- Parts of the concrete upper section of the stadium fell down in 1991, forcing the Expos to reschedule their September home games for the road.

NEW YORK, NEW YORK

YANKEE STADIUM

STYLE Major League Classic
A.K.A. House That Ruth Built
OCCUPANT AL Yankees April 18, 1923 to September 30, 1973; NEWL Black Yankees 1932; NNL Black Yankees 1946 to 1948; Negro League World Series 3rd game, 1942; 1st game 1947; AL Yankees April 15, 1976 to date
EVENT All-Star Game 1939, 1960, 1977
LOCATION *Left Field (NE)* East 161st Street; *3rd Base (NW)* Doughty Street, later Ruppert Place; *Home Plate (W)* Major Degan Expressway/Interstate 87 and Harlem River; *1st Base (SW)* East 157th Street; *Right Field (SE)* River Avenue and IRT elevated tracks; In the southwest Bronx
SURFACE Grass—Merion Bluegrass
DIMENSIONS *Left Field:* 280.58 (1923), 301 (1928), 312 (1976), 318 (1988); *Left Side of Bullpen Gate in Short Left-Center:* 395 (1923), 402 (1928), 387 (1976), 379 (1985); *Right Side of Bullpen Gate:* 415 (1937); *Deepest Left-Center:* 500 (1923), 490 (1924), 457 (1937), 430 (1976), 411 (1985), 399 (1988); *Left Side of Center Field Screen:* 466 (1937); *Center Field:* 487 (1923), 461 (1937), 463 (1967), 417 (1976), 410 (1985), 408 (1988); *Deepest Right Center:* 429 (1923), 407 (1937), 385 (1976); *Left Side of Bullpen Gate in Short Right Center:* 350 (1923), 367 (1937), 353 (1976); *Right Side of Bullpen Gate:* 344 (1937); *Right Field:* 294.75 (1923), 295 (1930), 296 (1939), 310 (1976), 314 (1988); *Backstop:* 82 (1942), 80 (1953), 84 (1976); *Foul Territory:* Large for the catcher behind home plate, but small for fielders down the foul lines

Yankee Stadium

FENCES *Left Field–Foul Line:* 3.92 (3 wire above .92 concrete 1923), 8 (canvas 1976); *Left Center–Left of Visitors' Bullpen:* 3.58 (3 wire above .58 concrete); *Right of Visitors' Bullpen:* 7.83 (3 wire above 4.83 concrete), 7 (canvas 1976); *Center Field-Left Screen When Up for Hitters' Background:* 20 (1953), 22.25 (1959), 22.42 (1954); *Screen When Down:* 13.83,7 (canvas 1976); *Right Center-Right of Screen:* 14.5 (3 wire above 11.5 concrete 1923); *Left of Home Bullpen:* 7.83 (3 wire above 4.83 concrete 1923); *Right of Home Bullpen:* 3.58 (3 wire above .58 concrete 1923), 8 (canvas 1976), 9 (canvas 1979); *Right Field-Foul Line:* 3.75 (3 wire above .75 concrete 1923), 10 (canvas 1976)
CAPACITY 57,545

PHENOMENA

- Left-center field monuments and plaques: Yankee Stadium (I) Monuments in fair territory, Lou Gehrig on the left, Miller Huggins in the middle, Babe Ruth on the right; Yankee Stadium (II) Monuments beyond the fence; same as Yankee Stadium I. Plaques beyond the fence, Ed Barrow, Jacob Ruppert, Joe DiMaggio, Mickey Mantle, Casey Stengel, Joe McCarthy, Pope Paul VI, Thurman Munson, Pope John Paul II, Billy Martin, Whitey Ford, Lefty Gomez, Roger Maris, Allie Reynolds, Elston Howard, Phil Rizzuto, Bill Dickey, Thurman Munson, and Yogi Berra.
- A ball hitting the foul pole in the 1930s was in play, not a homer.
- "Death Valley" in left-center.
- Green curtain in center sometimes raised and lowered like a window shade to force visiting batters to face a background of white-shirted bleacher fans but allow Yankee hitters to face a dark green background. Removed in World Series to sell more seats.
- Bleachers in right-center often called Ruthville and Gehrigville.
- Warning track red cinders; later on, red brick dust.
- Extra grass kept near monuments in center, in play.
- Underneath second base in Yankee Stadium (I), there was a 15-foot-deep brick-lined vault with electrical, telephone, and telegraphic connections for boxing events.
- As originally constructed, from May 5, 1922, to April 18, 1923, three concrete decks extended from behind home plate to each corner, with a single deck in left-center, and wooden bleachers around the rest of the outfield.
- In the winter of 1927-28, second and third decks were added to left-center, and several rows of box seats were removed in left, extending the foul pole from 281 to 301.
- During the 1936 season, the winter of 1936-37, and continuing through the 1937 season, the wooden bleachers were replaced with concrete ones. During the 1937 season, second and third decks were added in right-center. The bleacher changes shortened straightaway center from 490 to 461 and reduced seating capacity from the 80,000s to the 70,000s.
- As the outfield bench seats were gradually replaced with chair seats, in the 1930s and 1940s, the seating capacity gradually dropped from over 70,000 to about 67,000.
- Bloody Angle—between bleachers and RF foul line in 1923 season was very asymmetric and caused crazy bounces. Eliminating this in 1924 caused the plate to be moved 13 feet, and the deepest left center corner to change from 500 to 490.
- Auxiliary scoreboards were built in the late 1940s, which covered up the 367 right-center sign and the 415 left-center sign.
- Minor modifications were made in the winter of 1966-67. During this work, a new 463 sign and a 433 sign appeared in the power alleys, and the exterior was painted blue and white.
- During 1974-75 renovation, iron third deck distinctive facade was removed, and a portion was placed in the bleachers.

SHEA STADIUM

STYLE Multipurpose
A.K.A. William A. Shea Municipal Stadium
OCCUPANT NL Mets April 17, 1964 to date; AL Yankees, April 6, 1974 to September 28, 1975
EVENT All-Star Game 1964
LOCATION *Centerfield (E)* 126th Street; *3rd Base (N)* Whitestone Expressway/Interstate 678, and Flushing Bay; *Home Plate (W)* Grand Central Parkway; *1st Base (S)* Roosevelt Avenue; In Queens, near Flushing Meadow Park, site of 1939 and 1964 World's Fairs, just southeast of La Guardia Airport
SURFACE Bluegrass

Shea Stadium

DIMENSIONS *Foul Line:* 330 (marked 1964), 341 (actual 1964), 341 (1965), 338 (1979); *Power Alleys:* 371; *Center Field:* 410; *Backstop:* 80 (1964); *Foul Territory:* Very large
FENCES *Foul Lines:* 16.33 (4 wire and railing above 12.33 brick 1964), 12.33 (brick 1965), 8 (wood 1979); *Power Alleys:* 8 (wood); *Center Field:* Small section 8.75 (wood), most 8 (wood)
CAPACITY 55,601
PHENOMENA
• Designed to be expandable to 90,000 seats.
• Noisiest outdoor ballpark; frequent La Guardia Airport air traffic noise overhead.
• Named for attorney William Shea, who obtained the Mets franchise for New York by organizing the Continental League.
• Right-center scoreboard is largest in majors, 86 feet high with Bulova clock on top, about 25 feet behind the outfield fence, and 175 feet long.
• Practice facilities under the right field stands.
• Behind fence in center, just to the right of the 410 mark, is a Mets Magic Top Hat. When a Met hits a homer, a red Big Apple rises out of the black top hat, which actually looks more like a big kettle.
• Foul lines from 1965 to 1978 had an orange home run line painted at the top of the 12-foot, 4-inch brick wall. Above this was a 4-foot wire screen and railing. A ball was a homer if it hit above the line. Like a similar ground rule at Crosley Field in center field, this caused many controversies, so in 1979 an inner 8-foot wooden fence was installed.
• Worst visibility for hitters in the majors.
• Churchlike spire beyond center field fence formerly graced "Serval Zippers" sign.
• Outfield fences also marked as 358 and 396. From 1973 to 1979, there were also distance markers, outside the field of play, on the rear bullpen walls at 428, base of left-center light tower at 442, bottom edge of right-center scoreboard at 405 on right field end and 420 on center field end.
• 1964 Mets Banner Day—"Mongolia Loves The Mets" (in Mongolian) banner carried by the author; other banners included "E=mc2" (or Errors = Mets times customers squared),"Eamus Metropoli" (Let's go Mets in Latin).
• Christened April 16, 1964 with Dodger Holy Water from the Gowanus Canal in Brooklyn and Giant Holy Water from the Harlem River at the exact location where it passed the old Polo Grounds.

OAKLAND, CALIFORNIA

OAKLAND-ALAMEDA COUNTY COLISEUM

STYLE Multipurpose
A.K.A. Oakland Coliseum Complex, Oakland Mausoleum
OCCUPANT AL Athletics April 17, 1968 to date
EVENT All-Star Game 1987
LOCATION *Center Field (NE)* San Leandro Street and Southern Pacific Railroad tracks; *3rd Base (NW)* 66th Avenue; *Home Plate (SW)* Oakland-Alameda County Coliseum Arena, Nimitz Freeway, and San Leandro Bay; *1st Base (SE)* Hegenberger Drive
SURFACE Bluegrass
DIMENSIONS *Foul Lines:* 330; *Power Alleys:* 378 (1968), 375 (1969), 372 (1981); *Center Field:* 410 (1968), 400 (1969), 396 (1981), 397 (1982), 400 (1990); *Backstop:* 90 (1968), 60 (1969); *Foul Territory:* Huge, largest in the majors
FENCES 8 (plywood 1968), 10 (canvas over plywood and plexiglass 1981), 8 (1986)
CAPACITY 48,219

Oakland-Alameda County Stadium

PHENOMENA
• Surrounded by beautiful green ivy slope.
• Backstop is a notch cut in stands.
• Possible to watch game for free from concourse behind the field seats by peering between wooden slats on cyclone fence.
• Steel shell of pitcher's mound was exposed on Opening Day April 17, 1968 and had to keep being covered between innings.
• Right field scoreboard installed June 1968.
• Finley Fun Board put in for 1969 season—24 feet high and 126 feet long.
• Named the Mausoleum in the 1970s when the

scoreboard didn't work, the entire stadium was gray concrete in color, and the A's were terrible.

• Huge foul territory area reduces batting average by roughly 5 to 7 points, making this the best pitcher's park in the AL.

• Fun picnic atmosphere is the very best in the majors of all new concrete circular ugly ashtray stadia.

• Best food in baseball.

• Winds favor lefthanded batters.

• Next door to Jewel Box, home of the NBA Golden State Warriors.

• Scoreboard shows upcoming home stands, with A's annihilating the opposition.

• Fans sitting at the foul poles can catch home run fair balls by reaching in front of the foul pole screens.

• Hand-operated scoreboard showing major league line scores installed in 1986.

PHILADELPHIA, PENNSYLVANIA

VETERANS STADIUM

STYLE Multipurpose
A.K.A. Vet
OCCUPANT April 10, 1971 to date
EVENT All-Star Game 1976
LOCATION *Left Field (NE)* Packer Street and Interstate 76; *3rd Base (NW)* Broad Street and Philadelphia Naval Hospital; *1st Base (SW)* Pattison Avenue, Spectrum, and JFK Stadium; *Right Field (SE)* Tenth Street
SURFACE Astroturf—fast, but slower since 1977
DIMENSIONS *Foul Lines:* 330; *Power Alleys:* 371; *Center Field:* 408; *Backstop:* 60; *Foul Territory:* Large
FENCES 6 (wood April 1972); 8 (wood June 1971); 12 (6 plexiglass above 6 wood 1972)
CAPACITY 62,382

Veterans Stadium

PHENOMENA

• The park's rounded rectangular shape is called an octorad by the architects.

• Connie Mack Stadium's home plate was transplanted here.

• Plastic tarp covered unfinished right field wall in April 1971.

• "Liberty Bell" used to hang from center field roof in fourth level—hit only by Greg Luzinski on May 16, 1972.

• First ball dropped from a helicopter on April 10, 1971.

• Smallest hot dogs and loudest boos in baseball.

• Statues of Connie Mack and a sliding runner outside the park.

PITTSBURGH, PENNSYLVANIA

THREE RIVERS STADIUM

STYLE Multipurpose
A.K.A. House That Clemente Built
OCCUPANT NL Pirates July 16, 1970 to date
EVENT All-Star Game 1974

Three Rivers Stadium

LOCATION *Left Field (E)* Interstate 279 Fort Duquesne Bridge approach ramp; *3rd Base (N)* Reedsdale Street; *1st Base (W)* Allegheny Avenue, Ohio River, and the original point where the Monongahela River joins the Allegheny River to form the Ohio River; *Right Field (S)* North Shore Avenue, Roberto Clemente Memorial Park, Allegheny River; Stadium Circle encircles the park
SURFACE Carpet—Tartanturf 1970 to 1982; Astroturf 1983 to date
DIMENSIONS *Foul Lines:* 340 (1970), 335 (1975); *Power Alleys:* 385 (1970), 375 (1975); *Center Field:* 410 (1970), 400 (1975); *Backstop:* 60; *Foul Territory:* Large
FENCES 10 (wood)
CAPACITY 47,971
PHENOMENA

• Roberto Clemente statue dedicated here in 1994.

• On a site that was an island during the French and Indian Wars. It had been an Indian burial ground, a fact discovered when the Big Flood of 1763 uncovered many graves. Named Kilbuck Island after a friendly Delaware Indian chief. Back channels filled with silt, and it was no longer an island in 1852.

• Numbers painted on seats in right field upper deck where Willie Stargell's homers landed.

• Without the inner fence, the outfield would be 342 down the lines and 434 to center.

• The Honus Wagner statue, which used to stand outside of Forbes Field, now stands outside of Three Rivers Stadium.

• An 8- by 12-foot area of the 406 marker section of the Forbes Field brick wall, 12 Romanesque window frames, and the Babe Ruth plaque showing where his 714th home run landed are in the Allegheny Club at Three Rivers.

• Original design by Erik Sirko was for a "Stadium Over the Monongahela," with stadium above two parking lot levels, all sitting above the Monongahela River with plenty of room for boats to pass beneath on the river.

ST. LOUIS, MISSOURI

BUSCH STADIUM (II)

STYLE   Multipurpose
A.K.A.   Civic Center Stadium 1966, Busch Memorial Stadium 1966 to 1983
OCCUPANT   NL Cardinals May 12, 1966 to date
EVENT   All-Star Game 1966

Busch Stadium

LOCATION   *Left Field (E)* Broadway, Interstate 70, Gateway Arch and Mississippi River; *3rd Base (N)* Walnut Street; *1st Base (W)* Seventh Street and 300 Stadium Plaza; *Right Field (S)* Spruce Street; Stadium Plaza surrounds the park
SURFACE   Grass 1966 to 1969. Carpet—very fast—1970 to date. From 1970 to 1976, the entire field was carpeted except for the part of the infield that is normally dirt on a grass field. In 1977, this was carpeted except for the sliding pits. This is one of only two instances where there was a full dirt infield, with an otherwise fully carpeted field, the other being Candlestick in 1971.
DIMENSIONS   *Foul Lines:* 330; *Power Alleys:* 386 (1966), 376 (1973), 386 (1977), 383 (July 1983), 375 (1992); *Center Field:* 414 (1966), 410 (1971), 414 (1972), 404 (1973), 414 (1977), 402 (1992); *Backstop:* 64 (Vin Scully's unofficial measurement during 1985 World Series showed this to be 50 rather than 64); *Foul Territory:* Large
FENCES   *Left and Right Fields:* 10.5 (padded concrete), 8 (padded canvas 1992); *Center Field:* 10.5 (padded concrete 1966), 8 (wood 1973), 10.5 (padded concrete 1977), 8 (padded canvas 1992)
CAPACITY   57,000
PHENOMENA

• A line drive park because of the deep alleys and deep center field and the quick turf.
• Open arches surround the field just below the roof.
• From 1966 to 1982 right field scoreboard lights showed a cardinal in flight when a Cardinal hit a home run; same show was put on each time Lou Brock set a new base-stealing record.
• Home plate transplanted from old Busch Stadium at opener on May 12, 1966.
• Next to the Gateway Arch and the Mississippi River; you can see the Arch from the top deck in right field.
• Statue of "Stan the Man" Musial outside the stadium was unveiled in 1968.
• Small sections of bleachers in the outfield.
• Chicken wire basket (à la Wrigley Field in Chicago), installed in front of left-center and right-center bleacher

sections in July 1983, is 2 feet high and reduces distance to fence by 3 feet (386 to 383 in power alleys). It does not raise the height of the 10½ foot wall. No basket in center field bleacher section since it was used only for professional football.
• At league direction, the site designated for any Cubs playoffs or World Series home games from 1986 until 1988, when Wrigley Field got lights.
• Most fans at the stadium seem to be wearing Cardinal red.
• Seventh inning brings the Clydesdale horses to the scoreboard.
• Only ballpark where the seventh-inning stretch does not bring on "Take Me Out to the Ballgame." Instead, here they play the "King of Beers" theme song on the organ.

SAN DIEGO, CALIFORNIA

SAN DIEGO JACK MURPHY STADIUM

STYLE   Multipurpose
A.K.A.   San Diego Stadium 1969 to 1980, Jack Murphy Stadium thereafter
OCCUPANT   NL Padres April 8, 1969 to date
EVENT   All-Star Games 1978, 1992
LOCATION   *Left Field (N)* 9449 Friars Road; *3rd Base (W)* Stadium Way and a quarry; *1st Base (S)* San Diego River, Camino del Rio North, and Interstate 8; *Right Field (E)* Interstate 15
SURFACE   Santa Ana Bermuda grass
DIMENSIONS   *Foul Lines:* 330 (1969), fence 327 (1982), foul poles 329 (1982); *Power Alleys:* 375 (1969), 370 (1982); *Center Field:* 420 (1969), 410 (1973), 420 (1978), 405 (1982); *Backstop:* 80 (1969), 75 (1982)

Jack Murphy Stadium

FENCES   *Left and Right Fields:* 17.5 (concrete 1969), 9 (line painted on concrete 1973), 18 (concrete 1974), 8.5 (canvas 1982); *Center Field:* 17.5 (concrete 1969), 10 (wood 1973), 18 (concrete 1978), 8.5 (canvas 1982), one section in right center 9 (canvas 1982)
FORMER USE   San Diego River ran through the area, which was then a marshy swampland.
CAPACITY   59,022
PHENOMENA

• Named for sports editor who campaigned to bring major league baseball to San Diego.
• Noticeable lack of Spanish-speaking fans and Spanish language advertisements in the only major league ballpark on the Mexican border.
• The stadium is circular but open in right.

- Foul poles sit two feet behind the fence, and one foot in front of the wall.
- The right-center scoreboard sits directly behind the right center seats, and is so hot that fans there feel the heat on their backs.
- Only park where bullpen dirt area touches the foul lines.
- Only park where a foul ball can be caught out of sight of all umpires and most players. Location is in either bullpen near the foul poles.
- After 1981 season, the plate was moved 5 feet back toward the backstop.
- Expanded during 1983 football season by adding seats in right and right-center.
- Ivy put on center field fence in 1980.
- 20-foot-wide black batter's eye section on both center field wall and fence July-October 1982.

SAN FRANCISCO, CALIFORNIA

CANDLESTICK PARK

STYLE Multipurpose
OCCUPANT NL Giants April 12, 1960 to date
EVENT All-Star Game 1961, 1984
LOCATION *Left Field (NW)* Giants Drive; *3rd Base (SW)* Jamestown Avenue and Bay View Hill; *1st Base (SE)* Jamestown Avenue, Candlestick Point and San Francisco; *Right Field (NE)* Hunters Point Expressway and San Francisco Bay; Candlestick Point, with its rock outcroppings, was leveled to fill in the water for the parking lots.
SURFACE Grass (1960), Carpet (1971), Bluegrass (1979)

Candlestick Park

DIMENSIONS *Left Field:* 330 (1960), 335 (1968); *Left-Center:* 397 (1960), 365 (1961); *Center Field:* 420 (1960), 410 (1961); *Right-Center:* 397 (1960), 365 (1961); *Right Field:* 330 (1965), 335 (1968), 330 (1991), 328 (1993); *Backstop:* 73 (1960), 70 (1961), 55 (1975), 65 (1982), 66 (1985); *Foul Territory:* Very large
FENCES 10 (wire 1960); 8 (wire 1972); 12 (6 canvas below 6 plexiglass 1975); 9 (6 canvas below 3 plexiglass 1982); 9 (wire 1984), 9.5 (fence posts 1984); 8 (canvas 1993)
CAPACITY 58,000
PHENOMENA
- Named for jagged rocks and trees which rise from the tidelands like giant candlesticks.
- Bay View Hill overlooks the park from behind 3rd base.

- Many fans arrived by boat in 1960s.
- Only hot-water-heated open-air stadium in the majors.
- Before the bleachers were enclosed, so many fans would stream out of the bleachers in right-center when Mays and McCovey batted and crowd up against the flimsy cyclone fence, that a white line was painted on the asphalt 20 feet behind the fence. Fans had to stand behind this line.
- Fifty-nine posts every 20 feet or so on the outfield fence can cause strange bounces—their tips extend 6 inches above the 9 foot wire fence.
- Wind, wind, and more wind! Before the stadium was enclosed, wind blew in from left-center and out toward right-center. Now that it is enclosed, the wind is a swirling monster, just as strong as before.
- Six Giants retired numbers on white baseballs on the right field fence.
- Maury's Lake—the basepath between first and second was drenched before the game to make it more difficult for Dodger Maury Wills to steal second.
- Umps protested location of foul poles completely in fair territory in third inning of opening game on April 12, 1960.
- Stu Miller was blown off the mound by the wind in the 1961 All-Star Game.
- The stadium was enlarged and fully enclosed in the winter of 1971-72 to house the 49ers.
- Architect John Bolles' boomerang-shaped concrete shell baffle behind the upper tier's last row of seats was intended to protect the park from wind; it didn't work.
- In the winter of 1978-79, the Giants ripped up their carpet and replaced it with grass.
- Coldest park in the majors, resulting in fewer home runs.
- Croix de Candlestick pin awarded to fans at conclusion of night extra-inning games.

SEATTLE, WASHINGTON

KINGDOME

STYLE Dome
A.K.A. King County Stadium, The Tomb (1980s), Puget Puke (1980s)
OCCUPANT AL Mariners April 6, 1977 to date
EVENT All-Star Game 1979
LOCATION *Left Field (N)* 201 South King Street; *3rd Base (W)* 589 Occidental Avenue South; *1st Base (S)* South Royal Brougham Way; *Right Field (E)* Fourth Avenue South and Burlington Northern Railroad tracks; *Above:* Domed roof
DIMENSIONS *Left Field:* 315 (1977), 316 (marked 1978), 314 (actual 1978), 324 (1990), 331 (1991); *Left Center:* 375 (1977), 365 (1978), 357 (1981), 362 (1990), 376 (1991); *Deep Left-Center:* 385 (1990), 389 (1991); *Center Field:* 405 (1977), 410 (1978), 405 (1981), 410 (1986), 405 (1991); *Deep Right Center:* 375 (1990), 380 (1991); *Right Center:* 375 (1977), 365 (1978), 357 (1981), 352 (1990); *Right Field:* 315 (1977), 316 (1978), 314 (1990), 312 (1991); *Speakers in Left (3), Left Center, and Center:* 110 (1977), 133.5 (1981); 11 other speakers 130; *Backstop:* 63; *Apex of Dome:* 250; *Foul Territory:* Large

FENCES *Left Field:* 11.5 (wood 1977), 17.5 (6 plexi-glass over wood 1988), 11.5 (wood 1990); *Center Field:* 11.5 (wood 1977); *Right Field:* 11.5 (wood 1977), 23.25 (wood 1982), 11.5 (wood 1988)
CAPACITY 58,150

Kingdome

PHENOMENA
• Large American flag flies above the concrete dome.
• 23-foot Mini-Green Monster in right and right-center is called the Walla Walla.
• Carpet is rolled out by the Rhinoceros machine, and smoothed by the Grasshopper machine after it has been zipped together.
• Baby-changing areas in aisles 111, 113, 201, 203.
• Domed roof looks from below like it's made of thousands of bricks.
• Sick's Stadium home plate on display in Royal Brougham trophy case.
• In the winter of 1980-81, the three speakers above left, left-center, and center were raised from 102 to 133.5 feet to reduce the chance of their being hit again.
• Two foul balls have gone up but never come down: August 4, 1979—Ruppert Jones of Mariners hit a foul ball that stuck in the speaker above the first base dugout, thus disproving the old adage of physics that what goes up must come down. On May 20, 1983, Brewer Ricky Nelson did the same. By some arcane logic, both fly balls were ruled strikes.
• Four foul balls have bounced off speakers and been caught for outs: August 3, 1979, caught by A's pitcher Matt Keough; September 3, 1979, caught by Mariners' first baseman; May 19, 1980, caught by Mariners' first baseman; April 25, 1985, caught by Mariners' pitcher Mark Langston.
• Other foul balls have bounced off the Seattle Supersonics basketball speakers above first base and the basketball scoreboard above and behind home plate, without being caught.
• One fair ball bounced off a roof support wire and remained in play on April 11, 1985—a ball hit by Dave Kingman of A's was caught for an out in deep left: it would have been a home run. One fair ball has struck the right field speaker—Ken Phelps of the Mariners hit a tape-measure homer on August 13, 1987—the ball landed foul.
• Seven fair balls have bounced off speakers and remained in play.
• Called the Tomb by visiting sportswriters because it's sickeningly gray concrete and quiet.
• Roof's hanging red, white, and blue streamers can tangle up an infield fly and deflect it from the pitcher's

mound to behind second base.
• U.S.S. *Mariner*—a huge yellow sailing ship behind the center-field fence which fires a cannon after every Mariner homer.
• 42 air-conditioning units, 16 in fair territory, 26 in foul territory, 8 ducts in each unit. These blow air in toward the field which means fewer home runs in what would normally be a "Homer Dome" because of the short 357 foot power alleys.
• Outfield distances marked on fences in both feet and fathoms 1977-80 (1 fathom = 6 feet).
• Third deck highest at third base and in right field. AL East and AL West standings posted on right field third deck facade.
• Plate moved 10 feet toward first base dugout in 1990 in a change that altered outfield distances.
• New classic "in-play" 123-feet by 11½-foot scoreboard placed on right field wall in 1990 in dramatic facelift.
• Scene of Funny Nose-Eye Glasses night.

TORONTO, ONTARIO

SKYDOME
STYLE Retractable Dome
OCCUPANT AL Blue Jays June 5, 1989 to date
EVENT All-Star Game 1991

SkyDome

LOCATION *Center Field (N)* Front Street West; *3rd Base (W)* Spadina Avenue; *Home Plate (S)* Gardiner Expressway; *1st Base (E)* John Street and CN Tower, the world's largest free-standing structure
SURFACE Astroturf
DIMENSIONS *Left Field:* 328; *Left Center:* 375; *Center Field:* 400; *Right Center:* 375; *Right Field:* 328
FENCES 10
FORMER USE Water Supply pumping station where second base is now
CAPACITY 50,516
PHENOMENA
• 400-foot sign in center is actually right of dead center.
• 31 stories high (Astrodome is just 18).
• SkyDome's $17 million Jumbotron scoreboard is the world's biggest video display board (115 by 33 feet).
• Hotel inside SkyDome has 348 rooms, 70 with a view of (and by) the stadium.
• SkyDome Fitness Club boasts the world's largest indoor running track (2.2 lap per mile circuit) at the top of the stadium.
• First park to draw over 4 million fans in a season.

- SkyDome's retractable four-panel, 11,000-ton roof takes twenty minutes to open or close; uses $500 in electricity in doing so.
- When roof is opened 91 percent of all seats are exposed to sky.
- Overruns ballooned costs from an estimated $202 million to $495 million.
- Facilities include a Hard Rock Cafe and the 650-seat Windows on SkyDome restaurant.
- Site of first World Series games played outside United States.
- Also home to the Toronto Argonauts of the Canadian Football League.
- Contains 161 private skyboxes on the 300 and 400 level, ranging in price from $150,000 to $225,000 yearly.

Storied Parks of the Past

BALTIMORE, MARYLAND

MEMORIAL STADIUM
STYLE   Multipurpose
OCCUPANT   AL Orioles April 15, 1954 to September 30, 1991
EVENT   All-Star Game 1958
LOCATION   *Center Field (N)* East 36th Street; *3rd Base (W)* Ellerslie Avenue; *Home Plate (S)* 1000 East 33rd Street, section of 33rd Street near ballpark is known as Babe Ruth Plaza; *1st Base (E)* Ednor Road
SURFACE   Bluegrass

Memorial Stadium
(Baltimore)

DIMENSIONS   *Foul Lines:* 309; where the 7-foot fence meets the 14-foot wall, 360; *Power Alleys:* 446 (1954), 447 (1955), 405 (1956), 380 (1958), 370 (1962), 385 (1970), 375 (1976), 378 (1977), 376 (1980), 378 (1990); *Center Field:* 445 (1954), 450 (1955), 425 (1956), 410 (1958), 400 (1976), 405 (1977), 410 (1978), 405 (1980); *Backstop:* 78 (1954), 58 (1961), 54 (1980), 75 (1987); *Foul Territory:* Large
FENCES   *Foul Line Corners:* 11.33 (concrete 1954), 14 (11 concrete below 3 plywood 1959); these walls bounce balls toward center, reducing triples; *Left-Center to Right-Center:* 10 (hedges April and May, 1954), 8 (wire June 1954), 7 (wire 1955), 6 (wire 1958), 14 (wire 1961), 6 (wire 1963), 7 (canvas 1977)
FORMER USE   Venable Stadium

PHENOMENA
- Beautiful trees on an embankment beyond the fence in center.
- Oriole Landing was a picnic area in the upper deck in the 1960s.
- At the beginning of the 1954 season, hedges served as the center field fence. In June 1954 a wire fence was erected which stood right in front of a row of high hedges. The top 6 feet of the fence were covered with canvas padding in 1958 after Harvey Kuenn cut his face trying to catch a home run ball by climbing the fence. The walls in the left and right field corners were also padded after Curt Blefary injured his hip chasing a Max Alvis fly.
- Fans yelled "O" (for Orioles) in unison when "The Star-Spangled Banner" reaches "O say does that star-spangled banner yet wave . . ."
- Wind usually helps lefthanded hitters.
- Venable Stadium, a football stadium also used for baseball after the July 4, 1944 fire destroyed Oriole Park (V), was torn down to make way for Memorial Stadium. Home plate was moved from where it had been in the north to its current location in the south.
- Home of the best crabcakes in baseball; crab races in the bottom of the sixth on the scoreboard between Wee Willie in orange, Paco in blue, and Mugsy in yellow.
- Inscribed into the concrete facade: "Dedicated as a memorial to all who so valiantly fought in the world wars with eternal gratitude to those who made the supreme sacrifice to preserve equality and freedom throughout the world—time will not dim the glory of their deeds."
- Used for Eastern League Bowie Baysox games in 1993.

BLOOMINGTON, MINNESOTA

METROPOLITAN STADIUM
STYLE   Expanded Minor League
A.K.A.   Met
OCCUPANT   AL Twins April 21, 1961 to September 30, 1981
LOCATION   *Left Field (E)* 24th Avenue South, and a cornfield during the 1960s; *3rd Base (N)* Interstate 494; *1st Base (W)* 8001 Cedar Avenue; *Right Field (S)* West 78th Street, later named Killebrew Drive in 1973
SURFACE   Grass

Metropolitan Stadium

DIMENSIONS   *Left Field:* 329 (1961), 330 (1962), 344 (1965), 346 (1967), 330 (1975), 343 (1977); *Short Left Center:* 365 (1961), 360 (1966), 373 (1972), 350 (1975), 346 (1976), 360 (1977); *Deep Left Center:* 402

(1961), 435 (1965), 430 (1968), 410 (1975), 406 (1976); *Deep Left Center Corner:* 430 (1965), 406 (1975); *Center Field:* 412 (1961), 430 (1965), 425 (1968), 410 (1975), 402 (1977); *Deep Right Center Corner:* 430 (1965); *Deep Right Center:* 402 (1961), 435 (1965), 430 (1968), 410 (1977); *Short Right Center:* 365 (1961), 373 (1968), 365 (1972), 370 (1977); *Right Field:* 329 (1961), 330 (1962); *Backstop:* 60

FENCES *Left Field:* 8 (wire 1961), 12 (1964), 7 (1974), 12 (1977); *Center Field:* 8 (wire 1961); *Right Field:* 8 (wire 1961), 12 (1964), 8 (1970)

FORMER USE Opened on April 24, 1956 by minor league Millers

CURRENT USE Razed 1984-1985. Future site of Convention Center and amusement park

PHENOMENA

• The 330 foot marker was curiously far away from the foul pole in right, raising the distinct possibility that the distance to right was actually less than 330.

• Most poorly maintained ballpark in the majors. In 1981, broken railings on the third deck overlooking the left field bleachers created a distinct safety hazard.

• First modern stadium to be abandoned.

BOSTON, MASSACHUSETTS

HUNTINGTON AVENUE BASEBALL GROUNDS
STYLE Wooden

OCCUPANT AL Red Sox May 8, 1901 to October 7, 1911

LOCATION *Left Field (N)* Huntington Avenue; *3rd Base (W)* Rogers Avenue, later Forsyth Street; *1st Base (S)* New York, New Haven and Hartford Railroad Tracks; *Right Field (E)* New Gravely Street and Gainsborough Street; just north of South End Grounds

DIMENSIONS *Left Field:* 440; *Center Field:* 635; *Right Field:* 280; *Backstop:* 60

Huntington Ave. Grounds

FORMER USE Circuses and carnivals

CURRENT USE Northeastern University's indoor athletic building, known officially as Godfrey Lowell Cabot Physical Education Center and informally as Cabot Cage. A room there, devoted to mementos of the 1901 to 1911 era, is called the World Series Exhibit Room. A plaque commemorating the former location of the right field foul pole was unveiled in May 1956.

PHENOMENA

• Scene of the first NL-AL World Series vs. Pittsburgh in 1903.

• The 635 distance to center is an approximation by Bob Bluthardt, working from a scale drawing.

BRAVES FIELD
STYLE Major League Classic

A.K.A. National League Field, 1936 to 1940; National League Ball Park, 1936 to 1940; Bee Hive, 1936 to 1940; Wigwam, Nickerson Field

OCCUPANT NL Braves August 18, 1915 to September 21, 1952 AL Red Sox 1915 and 1916 World Series, and Sunday games 1929 to June 1932

LOCATION *Left Field (NW)* Boston and Albany R.R. tracks, Storrow Drive, and Charles River; *3rd Base (SW)* Babcock Street; *1st Base (SE)* Commonwealth Avenue; *Right Field (NE)* 34 Gaffney Street

Braves Field

DIMENSIONS *Left Field:* 402.5 (early 1915), 396 (late 1915), 402.42 (1921), 404 (1922), 402.5 (1926), 320 (April 1928), 353.5 (July 1928), 340 (1930), 353.67 (1931), 359 (1933), 353.67 (1934), 368 (1936), 350 (1940), 337 (1941), 334 (1942), 340 (1943), 337 (1944); *Left Center:* 330 (April, 1928), 359 (July, 1928), 365 (1942); *Center Field:* 520 (1926), 387 (April 1928), 417 (July 1928), 387.17 (1929), 394.5 (1930), 387.25 (1931), 417 (1933), 426 (1936), 407 (1937), 408 (1939), 385 (1940), 401 (1941), 375 (1942), 370 (1943), 390 (1944), 380 (1945), 370 (1946); *Deepest Center Field corner,* just right of straightaway center: 550 (1915), 401 (1942), 390 (1943); *Right Center:* 362 (1942), 355 (1943); *Right Field:* 402 (early 1915), 375 (late 1915), 365 (1921), 364 (1928), 297.75 (1929), 297.92 (1931), 364 (1933), 297 (1936) 376 (1937), 378 (1938), 350 (1940), 340 (early 1943), 320 (late 1943), 340 (April 1944), 320 (May 1944), 340 (April 1946), 320 (May 1946), 318 (1947), 320 (1948), 319 (1948); *Backstop:* 75 (1915), 60 (1936)

FENCES *Left Field to Right Center:* 10 (concrete 1915), 8 (wood 1928), 20 (wood 1946), 25 (wood 1948), 19 (wood 1953); *Left Field scoreboard sides:* 64 (1949); *middle arch:* 68 (1949); *Left Center:* 1 (gravestones July, 1928); *Right Center:* exit gate 8 (wire); *Right Field:* 10 (6 screen above 4 wood)

FORMER USE Allston Golf Club

CURRENT USE Nickerson Field, a football stadium serving as home for the B.U. Terriers and the 1983 USFL Boston Breakers. Also Myles Standish Dorms, three Boston University dorm towers near 3rd base.

PHENOMENA

• In 1915, there was a ground level scoreboard in left.

• In 1928, plate was turned towards right and inner fences were added.

• The infield grass was transported from the old South End Grounds in 1915, and was kept very long by the groundskeepers.

• Left field bleachers installed April 1928, removed slowly in a process that took from mid-June to the end of the season. Scoreboard moved from top of the left center wall to the rear of right field in 1928; later moved to Kansas City Municipal Stadium in 1955.

• Jury Box—small bleachers section behind the fence in right with very vocal fans.

• In 1936, home plate was moved 15 feet closer to the backstop.

• In the 1940s, fir trees were planted beyond the fence in center in an unsuccessful attempt to hide from the fans the huge clouds of railroad locomotive smoke belching from the Boston and Albany tracks in left and center.

• In 1946, the field was turned again slightly toward right. In 1937, a notch was cut in the right field bleachers, which can still be seen today in the former home of the United States Football League Breakers, Nickerson Field.

• In 1946, 5,000 fans left the home opener with green paint on their clothing because that morning's paint job on the seats had not yet dried—the Braves paid $6,000 in claims to irate fans, and played the rest of their April home games at Fenway.

• In June, 1947, the field was lowered by 18 inches.

• Boston University purchased the field in the 1950s, and laid out a football carpet from the first base dugout to right center.

• The right field foul line bleachers, extending from first base to the right field foul pole, still stand.

• The Gaffney Street first base entrance still stands.

• The concrete outer wall in right and center still stands.

BROOKLYN, NEW YORK

EBBETS FIELD

STYLE Major League Classic

OCCUPANT NL Dodgers April 9, 1913 to September 24, 1957, NNL Eagles 1935

EVENT All-Star Game 1949

LOCATION *Left Field (NE)* Montgomery Street; *3rd Base (NW)* Franklin Avenue, later Cedar Place, later McKeever Place; *1st Base (SW)* 55 Sullivan Place; *Right Field (SE)* Bedford Avenue; in the Pigtown/Crown Heights district of Flatbush, near the Gowanus Canal.

DIMENSIONS *Left Field:* 419 (1913), 410 (1914), 418.75 (1921), 383.67 (1926), 382.83 (1930), 384 (1931), 353 (1932), 356.33 (1934), 365 (1938), 357 (1939), 365 (1940), 356 (1942), 357 (1947), 343 (1948), 348 (1953), 343 (1955), 348 (1957). There is some confusion about distances because the left field foul line and grandstand wall were the same near the corner between the 343 and 357 markers. *Left-Center:* 365 (1932), 351 (1948); *Deep Left-Center at Bend in Wall:* 407 (1932), 393 (1948), 395 (1954); *Center Field:* 450 (1914), 466 (1930), 460.79 (early 1931), 447 (late 1931), 399.42 (1932), 399 (1936), 402 (1938), 400 (1939), 399 (1947), 384 (1948), 393 (1955); *Right Side of Center Field Grandstand:* 390 (1932), 376 (1948); *Right-Center's Deepest Corner:* 500 (1913), 476.75 (1926), 415 (1932), 403 (1948), 405

(1950), 403 (1955); *Right Side of Right-Center Field Exit Gate:* 399 (1932); *Right-Center:* 352; *Scoreboard:* left side 344, right side 318; *Right Field:* 301 (1913), 300 (1914), 296.17 (1921), 292 (1922), 301 (1926), 296.08 (1930), 295.92 (1931), 296.5 (1934), 297 (1938); *Backstop:* 64 (1942), 70.5 (1954), 72 (1957)

FENCES *Left Field to Left-Center:* 20 (1913), 3 (wood 1920), 9.87 (concrete 1931); *Center Field:* 20 (1913), 393 marker: 9.87 (concrete 1931) sloping upward; 376 marker: 15 (concrete 1931); *Right-Center:* 9 (concrete 1913), from 376 point to screen: 15 sloping upward to 19, then down to 13; *Right-Center to Right Field:* 38 (top 19 screen, bottom 19 concave concrete wall, bent at 9.5 midpoint, vertical top half, concave angled bottom half); *Screen in Center Field:* 20 (screen above sloping concrete 1920s); *Right Field Before the Screen:* 9 (concrete 1913)

FORMER USE The Pigtown garbage dump

Ebbets Field

CURRENT USE Scoreboard clock now sits on top of right field scoreboard at McCormick Field, Asheville, North Carolina. Ebbets Field Apartments housing development built in 1963 and the I.S. 320 Intermediate School is across the road. Apartments renamed Jackie Robinson Apartments at Ebbets Field in 1972; renamed Ebbets Field Apartments in mid-1970s. Jackie Robinson School, previously known as Crown Heights, houses the Brooklyn Dodger Hall of Fame.

PHENOMENA

• Rotunda was 80-foot circle enclosed in Italian marble with floor tiled with stitches of a baseball, a chandelier with 12 baseball-bat arms holding 12 globes shaped like baseballs. There were 12 turnstiles and 12 gilded ticket windows. The domed ceiling was 27 feet high at its center.

• Little kids watched the game through a gap under the metal gate in right-center.

• Cobblestoned Bedford Avenue was a hill, climbing from a low point in right field to higher ground in center field.

• Right field wall and scoreboard had approximately 289 different angles—the scoreboard jutted out 5 feet from the wall at a 45-degree angle. Overhang of the center field second deck hung out over the field. Scoreboard built after 1930.

• Schaefer Beer sign on the top of the right-center scoreboard notified fans of official scorer's decision—the "H" in Schaefer lit up for a hit, an "E" for an error—the sign was erected after World War II.

• Abe Stark sign offered a free suit at 1514 Pitkin Avenue to any batter hitting the 3-foot-by-30-foot sign.

• Opened on April 5, 1913 for an exhibition game vs. the

Yankees; it was discovered that the flag, a press box, and the keys to the bleachers had been forgotten. A press box was finally added in 1929.

• In the winter of 1931-32, the double deck was extended from 3rd base to the left field corner and across to center field.

• According to Roger Kahn, the park was "a narrow cockpit of iron and concrete along a steep cobblestone slope."

• In the winter of 1937-38, box seats were added in center field.

• In the winter of 1947-48, more seats were added to left and center.

• Demolition began on February 23, 1960. Same wrecking ball used 4 years later to demolish Polo Grounds. Eight light towers were moved to Downing Stadium on Randall's Island.

• George Cutshaw of Dodgers hit groundball home run in 1916 which bounced crazily up the concave wall in right and over the fence, to the amazement of Phillies rightfielder Gavvy Cravath.

CHICAGO, ILLINOIS

COMISKEY PARK

STYLE   Major League Classic

A.K.A.   White Sox Park (II) 1910 to 1912, Charles A. Comiskey's Baseball Palace 1910, White Sox Park(III) May 1962 to 1975

OCCUPANT   AL White Sox July 1, 1910 through September 30, 1990; NL Cubs 1918 World Series; NAL American Giants 1941 to 1950

EVENT   First major league All-Star Game, 1933; all Negro League East-West All-Star games, 1933 to 1950; Negro League World Series, eighth through tenth games, 1926; third game, 1943; fifth game, 1946; fourth game, 1947

LOCATION   *Left Field (N)* West 34th; *3rd Base (W)* Portland Avenue, later called South Shield's Avenue; *1st Base (S)* 324 West 35th Street; *Right Field (E)* South Wentworth Avenue, later Dan Ryan Expressway/I-94

SURFACE   *Outfield:* Grass; *Infield:* Grass (1910), Carpet (1969), Grass (1976)

Old Comiskey Park

DIMENSIONS   *Foul Lines:* 363 (1910), 362 (1911), 365 (1927), 362 (1930), 342 (1934), 353 (1935), 340 (1936), 352 (1937), 332 (April 22, 1949), 352 (May 5, 1949), 335 (1969), 352 (marked 1971), 349 (actual 1971), 341 (1983), 347 (1986); *Power Alleys:* 382 (1910), 375

(1927), 370 (1934), 382 (1942), 362 (April 22, 1949), 375 (May 5, 1949), 382 (1954), 365 (1955), 375 (1956), 365 (1959), 375 (1968), 370 (1969), 375 (marked 1971), 382 (actual 1971), 374 (1983), 382 (1986); *Center Field:* 420 (1910), 450 (1926), 455 (1927), 450 (1930), 436 (1934), 422 (1936), 440 (1937), 420 (April 22, 1949), 415 (May 5, 1949), 410 (1951), 415 (1952), 400 (1969), 440 (1976), 445 (1977), 402 (marked 1981), 409 (actual 1981), 401 (1983), 409 (1986); *Backstop:* 98 (1910), 71 (1933), 85 (1934), 86 (1955); *Foul Territory:* Large

FENCES   *Foul Lines and Power Alleys:* 12 (concrete 1955), 9.83 (concrete 1959), 5 (wire 1969), 9.83 (concrete 1971); *Center Field:* 15 (1927), 30 (1948), 17 (1976), 18 (1980); *Left-Center to Right-Center Inner Fences:* 5 (canvas 1949), 6.5 (24-foot section in front of bullpens 1969), 9 (1974), 7 (canvas 1981), 7.5 (1982), 11 (1984), 7.5 (1986)

FORMER USE   A truck garden owned by Signor Scavado, and/or a city dump. South Side Park (II) was almost on the same site, across Wentworth Avenue.

PHENOMENA

• Foul lines were old water hoses, painted white and squished flat.

• In 1910, there were bleachers in left and right, but not in center.

• In the winter of 1926-27, wooden bleachers were replaced with concrete and steel, and the pavilions from left around home plate to right were doubledecked. The scoreboard was moved from right center to two locations on the left field and right field walls.

• Center field bleachers were eliminated in 1947 to improve batter's visibility.

• Section of grandstand collapsed May 17, 1913.

• Special elevator for Lou Comiskey, in use from 1931 to 1982, had an inlaid tile floor.

• In 1950 the bullpens were moved from foul territory down the lines to behind the center field fence.

• In 1960 Bill Veeck installed the first exploding scoreboard in the majors, high above the bleachers in center. In 1982, when the Diamond Vision Board replaced the original, the pinwheels were retained.

• Green cornerstone laid on St. Patrick's Day in 1910 stayed green until 1960 when the exterior was painted all white by Bill Veeck.

• Scene of many masterful groundskeeping tricks by Roger, Gene, and Emil Bossard: (a) Camp Swampy in 1967 referred to the area in front of the plate, dug up and soaked with water when White Sox sinkerball pitchers were on the mound, but mixed with clay and gasoline and burned to provide hard soil if a sinkerballer was pitching for the visiting team. (b) Opposing team bullpen mounds were lowered or raised from the standard 10-inch height to upset visiting pitchers' rhythm. (c) Under Eddie Stanky's managerial tenure, the grass in front of shortstop was cut long because the Sox shortstop had limited range, but at second the grass was cut short because the Sox second sacker had very good range. (d) When the Sox had a lousy defensive outfield, the grass was cut long to turn triples into doubles. (e) When the Sox had speedy line drive hitters, the outfield grass was cut long to turn singles into doubles. (f) When the Sox had good bunters, more paint was added to the foul line in order to tilt the ball back fair.

- Nine speaker horns on the center field bleacher wall.
- Clock on wall in center to left of flag pole.
- Picnic areas, including Bullring in left and Bullpens I and II in right and right-center, Bavarian and Mexican restaurants and beer halls under the stands behind the plate.
- Showers in the bleachers in center.
- Foul poles bend back slightly to join the top of the roof.
- 540 center field listing in 1931-33 *Baseball Guides* is a misprint.
- Organist Nancy Faust played "Na-na-na-na, hey-hey, Good bye."
- Open arches between first and second decks.

CINCINNATI, OHIO

CROSLEY FIELD
STYLE   Major League Classic
A.K.A.   Redland Field 1912 to 1933
OCCUPANT   NL Cincinnati Reds April 11, 1912 to June 24, 1970; NAL Tigers 1937; NAL Clowns 1942 to 1945
EVENT   All-Star Games 1938, 1953

Crosley Field

LOCATION   *Left Field* (N) York Street; *3rd Base* (W) McLean Avenue; *1st Base* (S) Findlay Street; *Center Field* (NE) Western Avenue
DIMENSIONS   *Left field:* 360 (1912), 320 (321), 352 (1926), 339 (1927), 328 (1938); *Scoreboard in Left Center* 380383 feet left to right; *Center Field:* 420 (1912), 417 (1926), 395 (1927), 393 (1930), 407 (1931), 393 (1933), 407 (1936), 387 (1938), 380 (1939), 387 (1940), 390 (1944), 387 (1955); *Right Center Field:* 383 (1955); *Deepest Corner:* 387 (1944); *Right Field:* 360 (1912), 384 (1921), 400 (1926), 383 (early 1927), 377 (late 1927), 366 (1938), 366 (1938), 342 (1942), 366 (June 30, 1950), 342 (1953), 366 (1958); *Backstop* 38 (1912), 58 (1927), 66 (1943), 78 (1953)
FENCES   *Center Field* Canvas shield above fence to protect against street light glare (1935 to June 7, 1940); *Left Field* 18 (1938), 12 (1957), 14 (1962), 18 (1963); *Clock on top of the Scoreboard* 58 (1957), 45 (1967); *Left Center to Right Center* 18 (1954), 14 (1962), 13.5 (1963), 23 (9.5 plywood over 13.5 concrete 1965); *Right Field 7.5 (4.5 wire above 3 concrete 1938), 7.5 (4.5 wire above 3 wood 1942), 10 (7 wire above 3 wood 1949), 12 (9 wire above 3 concrete (June 30, 1950), 10 (7 wire above 3 wood 1953), 10 (7 wire above 3 concrete 1958), 9 (6 wire above 3 concrete 1959); Flagpole in left center 82, in play*
FORMER USE   Brickyard, League Park (1884-1901), Palace of the Fans (1902-1911)

CURRENT USE   Reconstructed on farm near Union, Kentucky (a replica has also been constructed at Blue Ash, Ohio). Site used for an industrial park.
PHENOMENA
- Designed by Harry Hake; built at cost of $225,000.
- In the 1920s rented out for movies and dancing, leading to complaints of "immoral dancing" and "vulgar conduct between boys and girls in unlighted portions of the grandstand."
- Steep incline in front of the fence all around the outfield; a pratfall on it by Babe Ruth on May 28, 1935 helped speed his retirement.
- Renamed for Reds owner Powel Crosley, manufacturer of radios, refrigerators and autos.
- Scene of first major league night game (vs. Phillies) on May 24, 1935.
- In January 1937 the Mill Creek flooded, covering the playing field with twenty-one feet of water. Pitcher Lee Grissom and Reds traveling secretary John McDonald rowed a boat over the center field fence.
- Pressbox was not erected until 1938. Prior to that sportswriters sat in the front row of the second deck.
- Both home and visitor clubhouses were located behind left field stands.
- *"Hit this sign and win a Siebler suit"* prominently displayed on Superior Towel & Linen Service Building across street.
- Capacity rose from 20,000 in 1912 to 29,488 in 1970 (yet largest crowd was 36,691 for an April 27, 1947 doubleheader).
- A 65 ×50.2 foot scoreboard installed in left center field in 1957.

PALACE OF THE FANS
STYLE   Wooden
A.K.A.   League Park (III)
OCCUPANT   NL Reds April 17, 1902 to October 6, 1911
LOCATION   *Left Field* (N) York Street; *3rd Base* (W) McLean Avenue; *1st Base* (S) Findlay Street; *Right Field* (E) Western Avenue; *Center Field* (NE) Western Avenue

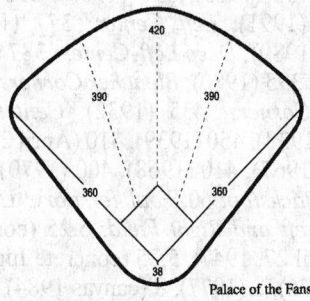

Palace of the Fans

PHENOMENA
- Pillars and columns patterned after those of the 1893 Columbian Exposition in Chicago.
- Rooters Row—beer drinkers' area next to the field down both foul lines.
- Burned down in the fall of 1911.

CLEVELAND, OHIO

CLEVELAND STADIUM
STYLE   Summer Olympics Stadium
A.K.A. Lakefront Stadium 1930s, Cleveland Public Municipal Stadium 1930s, Municipal Stadium 1940s and 1950s

Cleveland Stadium

OCCUPANT   AL Indians July 31, 1932 to September 24, 1933; August 2, 1936 vs. New York; AL Indians May 30 to September 6, 1937 Sundays and holidays only between Memorial Day and Labor Day; April 1938 to June 1939 Sundays, holidays and selected important games only; AL Indians June 27, 1939 to September 1947 nights, Sundays, holidays, and selected important games (this was a majority of home games in 1940, 1942-46); AL Indians April 15, 1947 to September 26, 1993.
EVENT   All-Star Game 1935, 1954, 1963, 1981
LOCATION   *Center Field (NE)* East Ninth Street; *3rd Base (NW)* Erieside Avenue and Donald Gray Lakefront Gardens Port Authority Dock 28 and Lake Erie; *Home Plate (SW)* West Third Street; *1st Base (SE)* Cleveland Memorial Shoreway, Amtrak/Conrail railroad tracks; Boudreau Boulevard encircles the park
SURFACE   Bluegrass
DIMENSIONS   *Foul Lines:* 322 (1932), 320 (1933), 321 (1948), 320 (1953); *Corners Where Inner Fence Meets Stadium Walls:* 362 (1947), 370 (1980); *Power Alleys:* 435 (1932), 365 (1947), 362 (1948), 385 (1949), 380 (1954), 400 (1965), 390 (1967), 395 (1968), 385 (1970), 395 (1991); *Left Center:* 377 (1980); *Right-Center:* 385 (1980); *Deep Left-Center:* 387 (1980); *Deep Right Center:* 395 (1980); *Bleacher Corners:* 463 (1932); *Grandstand Corners:* 435 (1932); *Center Field:* 470 (1932), 467 (1938), 450 (1939), 410 (April 27, 1947), 408 (1966), 407 (1967), 410 (1968), 400 (1970), 415 (1990), 404 (1992); *Backstop:* 60; *Foul Territory:* Large
FENCES   *Left and Right Field:* 5.25 (concrete 1932), 5.5 (wire April 27, 1947), 5.25 (concrete June 6, 1947), 6 (1955), 9 (1976), 8 (1977), 8 (canvas 1984)
PHENOMENA
• Architectural style has been called "stripped classicism," and has been compared to later Memorial and County Stadiums in Baltimore and Milwaukee.
• Groundskeepers' tools kept in foul territory in 1930s and 1940s.
• Before the inner fences were installed on April 27 after the first two weeks of the 1947 season, there was an incline in front of the center field bleacher wall; strange shape in power alleys caused by the end of the double-decked grandstand, where the fence jumped abruptly

deeper to the bleacher wall in center. The April 27 inner fence curved all the way to the foul poles. On June 6, 1947, it was changed so the inner fence just stretched across center field, hitting the permanent wall at 362 mark.
• Teepees erected in 1946 in center.
• Foul poles were 32 feet 8 inches high, 27 inches wide, and the screen on them is 22 inches wide.
• No one ever hit a ball into the center field bleachers.
• Music bandstand in center field between fence and bleachers set up in 1953.
• Wind usually blew out toward the lake.
• Center field standing-room area was a garden in 1957.
• Field was lowered 2 feet in 1976.
• Cleveland Stadium/League Park ratio of home games from 1936 to 1946—1/77, 15/63, 18/58, 30/47, 49/33, 32/45, 46/34, 48/29, 44/34, 46/31, 41/36.
• Featured in two movies—*The Kid from Cleveland* in 1949, *Fortune Cookie* in mid-1960s.
• Opened formally on July 1, 1931—13 months before the Indians' first home game on July 31, 1932.
• Largest regular season crowd ever—86,563 (84,587 paid)—for doubleheader against Yankees, September 12, 1954.

LEAGUE PARK
STYLE   Major League Classic
A.K.A.   Dunn Field 1916 to 1927
OCCUPANT   AL Indians April 21, 1910 to July 1932; AL Indians April 1934 to September 21, 1946; NAL Bears 1939 to 1940; NAL Buckeyes 1943 to 1948, 1950; Negro League World Series 1st game 1945; 2nd and 5th games 1947
LOCATION   *Left Field (E)* East 70th Street; *3rd Base (N)* Linwood Avenue; *1st Base (W)* Dunham Street, later East 66th Street; *Right Field (S)* Lexington Avenue Northeast
DIMENSIONS   *Left Field:* 385 (1910), 376 (1921), 374 (1930), 373 (1934) 374 (1938) 375 (1942); *Left Center:* 415 (1942); *Deepest corner, just left of Center Field:* 450 (1926), 467 (1930), 465 (1938), 460 (1939); *Center Field:* 420; *Right Center:* 400 (1942); *Right Field:* 290 (1921), 240 (when roped off for overflow crowds); *Backstop:* 76 (1910), 60 (1942)

League Park

FENCES   *Left Field:* 5 (concrete); *Left Center:* 10 (7 screen above 3 concrete); *Center Field Scoreboard:* 35; *Right Center Clock:* 20 (left and right sides), 22 (center of clock); *Right Field:* 45 (20 concrete topped by 25 screen 1920), 40 (20 concrete topped by 20 screen 1934)
CURRENT USE   Public park, stands were razed in 1950

PHENOMENA

• Named after owner James Dunn (1916 to 1927).
• Seats added in left and center in August 1920 which considerably reduced fence distances. Until that time, center field fence was as distant as center field at Polo Grounds.
• Steel beams protruded from the wall in right, causing balls to bounce at crazy angles. Only here did left fielders handle doubles to right field.
• Large green scoreboard in center field, and a clock just to the right of the scoreboard.
• Megaphone speakers on left center wall.
• Tepees erected in 1946.
• Ticket booths and part of left field stands remain as League Park Community Center.

DALLAS, TEXAS

ARLINGTON STADIUM

STYLE   Expanded Minor League
A.K.A.   Turnpike Stadium, 1965 to 1971
OCCUPANT   AL Rangers April 21, 1972 to October 3, 1993.
LOCATION   Arlington, Texas—between Dallas and Fort Worth; *Left Field (E)* Stadium Drive East and Six Flags Over Texas Amusement Park; *3rd Base (N)* 1500 South Copeland Road; *1st Base (W)* Stadium Drive West; *Right Field (S)* Randol Mill Road
SURFACE   419 Bermuda grass
DIMENSIONS   *Foul Lines:* 330; *Power Alleys:* 380 (1972), 370 (1974), 383 (1981), 380 (1982); *Center Field:* 400; *Backstop:* 60; *Foul Territory:* Small
FENCES   11 (1972), 12 (1981), 11 (1986)
FORMER USE   Minor league ballpark from 1965 to 1971 called Turnpike Stadium

Arlington Stadium

PHENOMENA

• Built in 1965 as Turnpike Stadium.
• Like Dodger Stadium, the field was below the surrounding parking lots. Before 1978, when the upper deck was added, fans would walk in at the top of the stadium.
• Wind blew in directly from the outfield.
• Hottest park in the majors, which increased the number of home runs hit here since the warm humid air is not as dense as cooler drier air elsewhere and therefore does not offer as much resistance to the ball in flight.
• More advertising signs than any other major league park.
• The Lone Ranger on Diamond Vision scoreboard rooted for the Rangers.

HOUSTON, TEXAS

COLT STADIUM

STYLE   For Temporary Use
A.K.A.   Mosquito Heaven
OCCUPANT   NL Colt .45s April 10, 1962 to September 27, 1964

Colt Stadium

LOCATION   *(N)* East/West Utility Road; *(E)* North Stadium Drive; *1st Base (S)* Astrodome—future site; *3rd Base* Loop 610 South, also called South Main Street; Home Plate Kirby Drive
DIMENSIONS   *Foul Lines:* 360; *Power Alleys:* 395; *Center Field:* 420; *Deepest corners in center just left and right of straightaway center:* 427; *Backstop:* 60
FENCES   Left and Right 8; Center Field Screen 30
CURRENT USE   Blacktop in northern Astrodome parking lot
PHENOMENA

• Scoreboard in center on both sides of 30-foot-high batters' background.
• Stiff wind blew in from right toward home.
• Power alley measurements not marked on the wall
• Home of largest and peskiest mosquitoes in major league history. Park was regularly sprayed by the ground crew between innings.
• Lay in decay until early 1970s when it was bought and moved to Mexico by a Mexican League team.

KANSAS CITY, MISSOURI

MUNICIPAL STADIUM

STYLE   Expanded Minor League
A.K.A.   Muehlebach Field 1923 to 1937, Ruppert Stadium 1938 to 1942, Blues Stadium 1943 to 1954
OCCUPANT   NAL Monarchs 1923 to 1950; AL Athletics April 12, 1955 to September 27, 1967; AL Royals April 8, 1969 to October 4, 1972; Negro World Series, Games 5-7, 1924; 1-4, 1925; 4, 1942, 3-4, 1946
LOCATION   *Left Field (N)* 21st Street; *3rd Base (W)* Euclid Avenue; *1st Base (S)* 22nd Street; *Right Field (E)* 2128 Brooklyn Avenue
DIMENSIONS   *Left Field:* 350 (1923), 312 (1955), 330 (1956), 370 (1961), 353 (1962), 331 (1963), 370 (1965), 369 (1967); *Left Center:* 408 (1923), 382 (1955), 375 (1957), 390 (1961), 364 (1963), 392 (1964), 409 (1965), 408 (1969); *Center Field:* 450 (1923), 432 (1950), 430 (1955), 421 (1956), 410 (1964), 421 (1965); *Right Center:* 382 (1955), 387 (1957), 364 (1962), 360 (1963), 392 (1964), 360 (1965), 382 (1969); *Right Field:*

350 (1923), 347 (1955), 352 (1956), 353 (1957), 338 (1963), 325 (1965), 338 (1966); *Backstop:* 60 (1955), 70 (1963)

FENCES *Left Field:* 24 (screen 1956), 18.5 (concrete 1958), 38.5 (20 screen over 18.5 concrete 1959), 10 (1961), 13.5 (1962), 10 (1963), 22 (1967), 13 (1969); *Center Field:* 12 (1958), 14 (1959), 12 (1961), 13.5 (1962), 10 (1963), 22 (screen 1966), 40 (screen 1969), 22 (screen 1970); *Right Field:* 12 (1956), 14 (1959), 12 (1961), 13.5 (1962), 10 (1963), 4.5 (plywood 1965), 40 (screen 1966), 13 (1969), 12 (screen 1970)

FORMER USE Swimming hole, frog pond, and ash heap

Municipal Stadium

PHENOMENA
- Opened on July 23, 1923.
- Originally named for owner George Muehlebach
- When rebuilt for 1955, home plate was moved 25 feet toward the outfield.
- In the spring of 1955, the right center field scoreboard was put into position. It had previously stood in Boston's Braves Field.
- The bottom of the left center light tower was in play—the warning track detoured around it.
- Right field embankment zoo—the mule Charlie O., sheep, China golden pheasants, Capuchin monkeys, German checker rabbits, peafowl, and a German shorthaired pointer dog all lived out there.
- Little Blowhard was a subterranean device that blew compressed air through the middle of the plate so that the umpire didn't have to brush it off.
- Harvey the Mechanical Rabbit rose out of the ground to the right of the plate to offer the umpire new baseballs from a basket between his ears.
- Pennant Porch: Charles O. Finley believed that one reason the Yankees won so many pennants was their 296-foot right field porch. In April 1965, he created his own 296-foot pennant porch in Municipal Stadium's right field.

LOS ANGELES, CALIFORNIA

LOS ANGELES MEMORIAL COLISEUM
STYLE Summer Olympics Stadium
A.K.A. O'Malley's Chinese Theatre, O'Malley's Alley
OCCUPANT NL Dodgers April 18, 1958 to September 20, 1961
EVENT All-Star Game 1959
LOCATION *Left Field (N)* Exposition Boulevard and museums; *3rd Base (W)* Merlo Avenue and Los Angeles Olympic Swimming Stadium; *1st Base (S)* Santa Barbara

Avenue, now Martin Luther King, Jr. Drive; *Right Field (E)* 3911 South Figueroa Street and Los Angeles Memorial Sports Arena

DIMENSIONS *Left Field:* 250 (1958), 251.6 (1959); *Left-Center:* 320 at end of screen rectangle; *Left-Center Where Fence Met Wall:* 425 (1958), 417 (1959); *Center Field:* 425 (1958), 420 (1959); *Right-Center:* 440 (1958), 375 (1959), 394 (1960), 380 (1961); *Right Field Where Fence Met Wall:* 390 (1958), 333 (1959), 340 (1960); *Right Field:* 301 (1958), 300 (1959); *Back-stop:* 60 (1958), 66 (1959); *Foul Territory:* Large; tremendous area on 3rd base line, but almost none on 1st base line

FENCES *Left Field:* 40 (screen 1958), 42 (screen 1959); 60 (2 support towers for screen 1958); *Left Center:* 40 (fence (1958); from foul pole 140 feet into left center, 42 sloping to ground at 30 degree angle from 320 mark to 348 mark for a distance of 24 feet (1959 to 1960); 4 steps down from 42 to 8: 1st step left corner 42 sloping to 41, 2nd step 31, 3rd step 20, 4th step 12 (1961); *Right of Screen in Left-Center:* 8 (wire); *Center Field to Right Field Corner:* 6 (wire); *Right Field Corner:* 4 (concrete)

FORMER USE Agriculture Park in 1890s—fairs, livestock shows, amusement park booths, horse-racing track and barns, saloons. Exposition Park—armory, museum, gardens from 1908 to 1921 along with gravel pit

Los Angeles Memorial Coliseum

PHENOMENA
- Wall in left-center jutted out twice, going from chest to thigh level, jutting out to ankle level, jutting out to thigh level, then back again to chest level.
- Concrete wall in the right field corner was the wall surrounding the football field. It sloped sharply away, creating a Fenway-like belly, and allowing a situation where a long drive near the right field foul line would be an out but a short fly down the line would be a home run.
- Huge tunnel behind home plate.
- First used for baseball by USC Trojans, who worked out here before the Dodgers opened the 1958 season.
- O'Malley considered using the Rose Bowl in Pasadena for the first years after the move from Brooklyn and before the Dodgers' Stadium opened. It would have been laid out differently from the Coliseum. Ten rows would have been removed in right and left to deepen the foul lines to 300 feet, and center field would have been 460. The field would have been symmetrical, because home plate would have been in one endzone and center field in the other endzone. Box seats were to have been added behind the plate and between 1st and 3rd.
- The 42-foot screen in left placed to prevent 251 foot popups from becoming homers.
- Commissioner Ford Frick attempted to order the Dodg-

ers to construct a second screen in left, in the seats at 333 feet. A ball clearing both screens would be a home run, but a ball clearing just the shorter screen would be a double. The California Earthquake Law made construction of such a screen illegal.

• 79 rows of seats.

• 700 feet to furthest seats under peristylum.

• Two stones are on exhibit under the peristylum atop the bleachers in right-center at one end of the oval—the one on the left from Altis, Olympia, Greece, and the one on the right from the Colosseum, Rome, Italy.

• Rim of stadium 110 feet above ground level, field 33 feet below ground level.

• Cable and towers and wires above screen in play.

• Small green light pole in field of play in right field.

• 74,000 seats built from 1921 to 1923, expanded to 105,000 seats for the 1932 Olympic games.

• The right-center fence was shortened in 1959 after 182 homers were hit to left but only 3 to center and 8 to right. In 1959, there were 132 homers to left, 1 to center, 39 to right. In 1960, 155 to left, 3 to center, 28 to right. In 1961, 147 to left, 7 to center, 38 to right.

• Largest World Series crowd ever—92,706 against White Sox on October 6, 1959.

WRIGLEY FIELD
STYLE Minor League
OCCUPANT AL Angels April 27 to October 1, 1961
LOCATION *Left Field (E)* Avalon Boulevard; *3rd Base (S)* East 42nd Place; *1st Base (W)* San Pedro Street; *Right Field (N)* East 41st Place
DIMENSIONS *Left Field:* 340; *Power Alleys:* 345; *Center Field:* 412; *Right Field:* 338.5; *Backstop:* 56
FENCES *Left Field to Center Field:* 14.5 (concrete); *Center Field to Right Field:* 9 (6 wire above 3 concrete)
CURRENT USE Gilbert Lindsay Park, a public playground, and City Center Community Mental Health Facility
PHENOMENA

• Dedicated on September 27, 1925.

• Named for Cubs owner William Wrigley when Los Angeles was a Cub farm team.

• In its minor league days, there were two walls and a picnic area in right. A large office tower stood just to the first base side of home plate above the grandstand. The bottom of the light tower in left center was in play.

• Rear wall at foul pole was 346.58 in 1961.

• In 1961, Wrigley Field set the current record for most homers in one park in one season—248. The reason was that the power alleys were only 5 feet more distant than the foul pole in left.

• Demolished in 1966.

MONTREAL, QUEBEC

PARC JARRY
STYLE For Temporary Use
A.K.A. Jarry Park
OCCUPANT NL Expos April 14, 1969 to September 26, 1976
LOCATION *Left Field (NW)* rue Jarry; *3rd Base (SW)* Canadian Pacific Railroad tracks; *1st Base (SE)* 285,

ouest rue Faillon; *Right Field (NE)* rue St. Laurent and a public swimming pool
DIMENSIONS *Left Field:* 340; *Left Center:* 368; *Center Field:* 415 (1969), 417 (1971), 420 (1974); *Right Center:* 368; *Right Field:* 340; *Backstop:* 62
FENCES 8 (wire 1969), 5 (wire 1970), 8 (wire 1976)

Jarry Park

CURRENT USE Municipal facility for athletic events
PHENOMENA

• Still under construction during the first two months of Expos home games in April and May 1969.

• Jet stream wind helped drives to left center. Homers to right landed in a swimming pool.

• On April 13, 1971, opening day, fans stood on snow plowed high in mounds behind the 8½-foot wall that stood behind the 5-foot wire screen fence in right field and viewed the game free.

NEW YORK, NEW YORK

HILLTOP PARK
STYLE Wooden
A.K.A. Highlanders Park, New York American League Ballpark, Rockpile, The Hilltop
OCCUPANT AL Highlanders-Yankees April 30, 1903 to October 5, 1912; NL Giants April 15 to May 30, 1911

Hilltop Park

LOCATION *(N)* West 168th Street; *(W)* Fort Washington Avenue; *(SW)* Deaf and Dumb Asylum; *(S)* West 165th Street; *(E)* Broadway
DIMENSIONS *Left Field:* 365; *Center Field:* 542; *Right Field:* 400
CURRENT USE Columbia Presbyterian Hospital
PHENOMENA

• Excellent view of the Hudson River and the New Jersey Palisades from the upper seats behind the plate.

• Scoreboard in left.

• Large exit gate in right from which fans left after the game.

• Bull Durham sign shaped like a bull in right center in 1909, twice the height of the rest of the fence.

• Memorial dedicated at site of home plate in 1993 through cooperation of the Society for American Baseball Research (SABR), the New York Yankees, and Columbia Presbyterian Hospital.

POLO GROUNDS (IV)

STYLE   Major League Classic

A.K.A.   Brush Stadium 1911 to 1919, Coogan's Bluff, Coogan's Hollow, Matty Schwab's House, Harlem Meadow

OCCUPANT   NL Giants June 28, 1911 to September 29, 1957; AL Yankees May 30, 1912 (morning game); April 17, 1913 to October 8, 1922; NL Mets April 13, 1962 to September 18, 1962

EVENT   Negro League World Series first game, 1946; All-Star Game 1934, 1942

LOCATION   *Center Field (SE)* Eighth Avenue, then IRT elevated tracks, Harlem River and Harlem River Drive; *3rd Base (NE)* West 159th Street and IRT Rail Yards; *Home Plate (NW)* Bridge Park, then Harlem River Speedway, Coogan's Bluff, and Croton Aqueduct; *1st Base (SW)* West 157th Street trace; Same site as Polo Grounds (III); In Coogan's Hollow, 115 feet below Coogan's Bluff, the last remaining portion of a farm granted to Mr. John Lion Gardiner by the King of England in the seventeenth century

DIMENSIONS   *Left Field:* 277 (1911), 286.67 (1921), 279.67 (1923), 279 (1930), 280 (1943), 279 (1955); *Left Field, Second Deck:* 250; *Left Center, Left of Bullpen:* 447; *Left-Center, Right of Bullpen:* 455; *Front Clubhouse Steps:* 460; *Center Field:* 433 (1911), 483 (1923), 484.75 (1927), 505 (1930), 430 (1931), 480 (1934), 430 (1938), 505 (1940), 490 (1943), 505 (1944), 480 (1945), 490 (1946), 484 (1947), 505 (1949), 483 (1952), 480 (1953), 483 (1954), 480 (1955), 475 (1962), 483 (1963); *Bleacher Corners:* 475; *Right-Center, Left of Bullpen:* 449; *Right-Center, Right of Bullpen:* 440; *Right Field:* 256.25 (1921), 257.67 (1923), 257.5 (1931), 257.67 (1942), 259 (1943), 257.67 (1944); *Right Field Photographers Perch:* 249; *Backstop:* 65 (1942), 70 (1943), 65 (1944), 70 (1946), 74 (1949), 65 (1954), 74 (1955), 65 (1962); *Foul Territory:* Very large. There's a lot of confusion here. During the Giants' stay it was 483 to the front of the clubhouse, and probably 505 to the rear clubhouse wall above the overhang. Why the 483 marker sometimes was changed to 480 or 475, is not known but it could have

been due to remeasurements or a slight shift of home plate's location. Or it could have been a measurement to the base of the Eddie Grant Memorial. In the Giants' time, reading from left to right, the markers read 315, 360, 414, 447, 455, 483, 455, 449, 395, 338, 294. In the Mets' time, they read 306, 405, 475, 405, 281. The foul lines were never marked. One possibility is that it was 433 feet to the front of the bleachers, 475 to the beginning of the clubhouse overhang, 483 to the rear wall under the overhang, and 505 to the front of the high wall. The 21-foot overhang of the second deck in left reduced the distance to the second deck from 279 to 250, not 258, because of the angle involved.

FENCES—1911-22   *Left to Center:* 10 (concrete); *Center:* 20 (tarp); *Right-Center:* 10 (concrete); *Right Field:* 12 sloping to 11 at pole (concrete)

FENCES—1923-63   *Left Field:* 16.81 (concrete); *Left-Center:* 18 (concrete); *Where Left-Center Wall Ended at Bleachers:* 12 (concrete); *Center Field Bleachers Wall:* 8.5 (4.25 wire on top of 4.25 concrete) on both sides of clubhouse runway; *Center Field Hitters' Background:* 16.5 on both sides of clubhouse runway; *Center Field Clubhouse:* 60 high and 60 wide—50 high in 1963; *Center Field Top of Longines Clock:* 80; *Center Field Top of Right Side of Scoreboard:* 71; *Center Field Top of Left Side of Scoreboard:* 68; *Center Field Top of Middle of Scoreboard:* 64; *Center Field Top of 5 Right Scoreboard Windows:* 57; *Center Field Top of 4 Left Scoreboard Windows:* 55; *Center Field Bottom of 5 Right Scoreboard Windows:* 53; *Center Field Bottom of 4 Left Scoreboard Windows:* 48; *Center Field Bottom of Clubhouse Scoreboard:* 31; *Center Field Top of Rear Clubhouse Wall:* 28; *Center Field Top of Front Clubhouse Wall:* 19; *Center Field Top of 14 Lower Clubhouse Windows:* 16; *Center Field Bottom of 14 Lower Clubhouse Windows:* 11; *Center Field Clubhouse floor Overhang:* 8; *Center Field Top of Eddie Grant Memorial:* 5; *Center Field Width of Little Office on Top of Lower Clubhouse:* 10; *Right Center:* 12 (concrete); *Right Field:* 10.64 (concrete)

FORMER USE   Underneath the Harlem River until filled in with dirt in the late 1870s.

CURRENT USE   Polo Grounds Towers—four 30-story apartment buildings. Willie Mays Field—an asphalt playground with 6 basketball backboards where center field used to be, a brass historical marker in place.

PHENOMENA

• Originally named for owner John T. Brush.

• Second deck in right had 9-foot photographer's perch overhang 60 feet from foul pole out into right-center.

• Bullpens in fair territory in left-center and right-center.

• There was no line on the 60-foot-high center field clubhouse above which a ball would be a home run.

• The outfield was slightly sunken. A manager, standing in his dugout, could see only the top half of his outfielders. At the wall, the field was 8 feet below the infield.

• The left field second deck overhang meant that a homer to left was easier than a homer to right, even though the wall in left was 279 and the wall in right was 258. The overhang was 21 feet, but it effectively shortened the distance required for a pop-fly homer to the second deck in left to 250 feet because of the angle involved.

• The overhangs here and at Tiger Stadium and Shibe Park have more significance than one might suspect, according to research published by the professional society for physicists, the American Physical Society. The batted ball's trajectory consists of two component vectors, horizontal and vertical. The vertical deceleration is constant over time due to gravity, but the horizontal deceleration increases over time due to wind resistance and atmospheric drag. Near the end of its flight, the ball is coming down sharply, rather than arcing down as it arched up, as would occur in a vacuum. So many outfielders have watched helplessly as a ball they could catch dropped into the 2nd deck.

• Hitter's background extended beyond the end of the bleacher wall, several feet into the clubhouse gap.

• The field sloped in a "turtle back" just beyond the infield dirt. It sloped down 1.5 feet to drains about 20 feet into the outfield, then back up again.

• Right-center wall sloped gradually from 11 feet at pole to 12 feet at the bleachers.

• Left-center wall sloped from 16 feet 9.75 inches at the pole to 18 feet in left center, then abruptly fell to 16 feet and then to 14 feet and sloped gradually to 12 feet at the bleachers. When ad signs were removed in the 1940s, the abrupt changes in height in left-center disappeared.

• After the all-wooden Polo Grounds (III) burned down April 14, 1911, Polo Grounds (IV) was built with temporary stands for 1911. The infield stands were rebuilt with concrete for 1912, and the outfield concrete double deck was finished in 1922. The bleachers in left-center and center were wood remaining from before the fire.

• In 1914, there were 2 bends in the wall in right-center.

• In 1917, the fans exited from the field through gates under the center field bleachers.

• Morris James Mansion sat up on Coogan's Bluff, overlooking the ballpark.

• Brush Stairway led down from Coogan's Bluff to the Speedway and the ticket booths behind home plate.

• Coats of arms of all the teams in the National League on the top of the grandstand. Removed in the 1920s.

• Dedicated on May 30, 1921, to a former Giant killed in World War I, the Eddie Grant Memorial stood in center at the base of the clubhouse wall. It was 5 feet high. The Memorial reads:

In Memory of
Capt. Edward Leslie Grant
307th Infantry - 77th Division
A.E.F.
Soldier - Scholar - Athlete
Killed in action
Argonne Forest
October 5, 1918
Philadelphia Nationals
1907-1908-1909-1910
Cincinnati Reds
1911-1912-1913
New York Giants
1913-1914-1915
Erected by friends in Baseball,
Journalism, and the Service.

• In the winter of 1922-23, the concrete double decks were extended all the way to either side of the new concrete bleachers in center, housing the clubhouse. Unfortunately, the Roman Colosseum facade frescoes were removed during that winter also.

• Bleachers in center remodeled in 1923.

• In 1929, the first attempt was made to wire the umpires for sound and reconnect them into the PA system. It didn't work too well.

• Speaker placed above Grant Memorial in 1931.

• Field raised 4½ feet in 1949 to help with drainage. In 1609 and 1874 maps, the location is shown to be underneath the Harlem River. The water table was only 2-6 feet below the playing surface, and drainage was complicated by rainwater cascading off the 115-foot-high Coogan's Bluff down onto the site.

• During the 1950s, groundskeeper Matty Schwab and his family lived in an apartment under Section 3 of the left field stands built for him by Horace Stoneham. The apartment was the main bait in Mr. Stoneham's successful offer to grab Mr. Schwab away from the hated Dodgers in 1950.

• A two-foot-square section of sod from center field was removed and taken to San Francisco in the fall of 1957.

• Home plate was moved out toward center several feet by the Mets in the winter of 1961-62.

• During the Mets' stay in 1962 and 1963, Johnny McCarthy and his crew of groundskeepers painted Schwab's four rooms pink, installed a shower and plywood on the floor and lockers, and called it their Pink Room.

• In 1962 and 1963, the Howard Clothes sign on the outfield wall promised a boat to any player hitting it.

• Demolition started on April 10, 1964, with same wrecking ball that demolished Ebbets Field.

PHILADELPHIA, PENNSYLVANIA

BAKER BOWL

STYLE   Major League Classic
A.K.A.   Huntingdon Street Baseball Grounds 1895 to July 1913, National League Park (III) 1895 to 1938, Hump, Cigar Box, Band Box, Philadelphia Park

Baker Bowl

OCCUPANT   NL Phillies April 14, 1904 to May 14, 1927; NL Phillies June 24, 1927 to June 20, 1938; also neutral use by NL Cleveland versus Baltimore July 29, July 30, and August 11, 1898; and versus Washington August 5, 6, and 8, 1898
EVENT   Negro League World Series first and second games 1924, fifth and sixth games 1925, fourth and fifth games 1926
LOCATION   *Left Field (N)* West Lehigh Avenue; *3rd Base (W)* North 15th Street; *1st Base (S)* West Huntingdon Street; *Right Field (E)* North Broad Street; *Beneath* Philadelphia and Reading Railroad tracks in a tunnel
DIMENSIONS   *Left Field:* 335 (1921), 341.5 (1926),

341 (1930), 341.5 (1931); *Center Field:* 408; *Right-Center:* 300; *Right Field:* 272 (1921), 279.5 (1924), 280.5 (1925); *Backstop:* 60
FENCES *Left Field:* 4 (1895), 12 July (1929); *Left-Center Field Clubhouse to Right-Center:* 35 (1895), 47 (with 12 screen on top 1915); *Right Field:* 40 (tin over brick 1895), 60 (40 tin over brick, topped by 20 screen 1915)
CURRENT USE Parking lot and car wash in right-center, gas station in center, bus garage from home down right field foul line
PHENOMENA
• Named after Phillie owner William F. Baker.
• Named the Hump because it was on an elevated piece of ground that had a railroad tunnel underneath the outfield.
• Swimming pool in the basement of the center field clubhouse prior to World War I.
• Coke and "Health Soap Stops B.O." Lifebuoy signs on the high right field wall.
• Extra seats added in front of the fence in center for the 1915 World Series led directly to the Phillies losing the Series' last game.
• During Prohibition, the outfield wall liquor ads were boarded over with dirty grimy blank boards.
• Home plate moved back a foot in 1925, making the right field foul pole 280.5 rather than 279.5.
• Torn down in 1950.

SHIBE PARK
STYLE Major League Classic
A.K.A. Connie Mack Stadium 1953 to 1970
OCCUPANT AL Athletics April 12, 1909 to September 19, 1954; NL Phillies May 16 to May 28, 1927; NL Phillies July 4, 1938 to October 1, 1970
EVENT Negro League World Series fifth game 1942; fourth game 1945; third game 1947; All-Star Game 1943, 1952
LOCATION *Left Field (N)* West Somerset Street; *3rd Base (W)* North 21st Street; *1st Base (S)* West Lehigh Avenue; *Right Field (E)* North 20th Street
DIMENSIONS *Left Field:* 360 (1909), 378 (late 1909), 380 (1921), 334 (1922), 312 (1926), 334 (1930); *Center:* 515 (1909), 502 (late 1909), 468 (1922), 448 (1950), 440 (1951), 460 (1953), 468 (1954), 447 (1956), 410 (1969); *Right Center:* 393 (1909), 390 (1969); *Right Center, Left of Scoreboard:* 400 (1942); *Right Field:* 360 (1909), 340 (late 1909), 380 (1921), 307 (1926), 331 (1931), 331 (to lower 1934), 329 (to upper iron fence 1934); *Backstop:* 90 (1942), 86 (1943), 78 (1956), 64 (1960)
FENCES *Left Field to Left Center:* 12 (4 screen above 8 concrete 1949); *Center Field, Small Section:* 20 (1955), 8 (wood 1956), 3 (canvas 1969); *Right-Center Scoreboard:* 50 (top of black scoreboard 1956), 60 (top of Ballantine Beer sign 1956); *Right Field:* 12 (concrete 1909), 34 (22 corrugated iron above 12 concrete 1935), 30 (1943), 50 (1949), 40 (1953), 30 (1954), 40 (1955), 32 (1956)
FORMER USE City dog pound, also a brickyard in the Swampoodle neighborhood nearby
CURRENT USE Vacant site. Several hundred of the seats are being used now in Duncan Park, home of the

Sally League Phillies in Spartanburg, South Carolina, and in War Memorial Stadium, Greensboro, North Carolina

Shibe Park

PHENOMENA
• The first concrete and steel stadium in the majors.
• Named for Ben Shibe, an A's stockholder and baseball manufacturer.
• French Renaissance churchlike dome on exterior roof behind the plate which housed Connie Mack's office.
• Sod transplanted here from Columbia Park.
• Highest pitcher's mound—20 inches high.
• Batting cage sat behind short fence in center when the measurement was only 447.
• Corrugated iron fence in right—balls bounced at crazy angles off it—top 22 feet of 34-foot fence—2-foot-deep frame—was 329 to front of frame, 231 to rear of frame where iron sheets were.
• Conduit on right field wall was in play.
• Slopes in front of the outfield fences in early years.
• Ladder in front of left field scoreboard, 1909—went all the way to the top.
• Doubledecked in 1925; also in that year left field stands added.
• Mezzanine added in 1929.
• Right field wall reinforcement in 1934 reduced distance to front of the frame from 331 to 329, but sign wasn't changed until 1956.
• Before 1935, 20th Street residents could sit in their front bedroom or on their roof and see the game free over the 12-foot right-field fence. Fans could see the lines of laundry on the roof of 20th Street houses. Connie Mack lost a suit to prevent this, so he built the high right-field fence.
• 1948 plans to add 18,000 seats in right field and reduce foul line to 315 feet never materialized.
• In 1956, the old Yankee Stadium scoreboard was installed in front of the right-center wall; later a clock was added—balls hitting the clock were homers—top of clock was 75 feet high; top of Ballantine Beer sign, 60 feet high.
• In 1956 the normal screen was replaced by see-through plexiglass—protected the fans behind the plate from foul balls.
• Home plate moved to Veterans Stadium in 1971.
• Fire damaged it on August 20, 1971.
• Last game on October 1, 1970.
• Torn down in June 1976.

PITTSBURGH, PENNSYLVANIA

FORBES FIELD

STYLE Major League Classic

A.K.A. Oakland Orchard, Dreyfuss' Folly

OCCUPANT NL Pirates June 30, 1909 to June 28, 1970; NNL Grays 1939 to 1948

EVENT Negro League World Series second game 1942; fourth and fifth games 1944; second game in 1945; All-Star Game 1944, 1959

LOCATION *Left Field (NE)* Schenley Park, then Bigelow Boulevard; *3rd Base (NW)* Sennott (also spelled "Sonnett" at times) Street, then Cathedral of Learning; *1st Base (SW)* Boquet (also spelled "Bouquet" at times) Street; *Right Field (SE)* Joncaire Street, Pierre Ravine, Junction Hollow, Junction Railroad tracks

DIMENSIONS *Left Field:* 360 (1909), 356.5 (1921), 356 (1922), 360 (1926), 365 (1930), 335 (1947), 365 (1954); *Deepest Corner, Left of Straightaway Center, at the Flag Pole:* 462 (1909), 457 (1930); *Center Field:* 442 (1926), 435 (1930); *Right-Center, Right Side of Exit Gate:* 416 (1955); *Right-Center:* 375 (1942); *Bend at Left End of Screen:* 375; *Right Field:* 376 (1909), 376.5 (1921), 376 (1922), 300 (1925); *Backstop:* 110 (1909), 84 (1938), 80 (1947), 84 (1953), 75 (1959)

FENCES *Left Field Front Fence:* 8 (5 screen above 3 wood 1947), 12 (9 screen on top of 3 wood 1949), 14 (screen 1950); *Left Field Wall:* 12 (1909), 12 (brick and ivy 1946); *Left Field Scoreboard:* 25.42 (steel left and right sides), 27 (middle); *Wooden Marine Sergeant at Parade Rest to Right of Scoreboard:* 32 (June 26, 1943 to end of season); *Side Wall Angling Back to Meet Brick Wall in Left-Center:* 12 (wood, when front fence was up); *Cages Around Light Tower Just Right of Scoreboard and in Power Alleys:* 16.5; *Center Field:* 12 (wood 1909), 12 (brick and ivy 1946); *Right-Center:* 9.5 (concrete 1925); *Screen—Left Side at 375 Mark:* 24 (14.5 wire above 9.5 concrete 1932); *Screen—Right Side at Flag Pole:* 27.67 (18.17 wire above 9.5 concrete 1932)

Forbes Field

FORMER USE Part of Schenley Farms, a hothouse and livery stable. Land for grazing cows. Ravine where right field would be. Football site for University of Pennsylvania vs. Carnegie Tech October 31, 1908, game. Penn won on the rocky field.

CURRENT USE Mervis Hall, out in right field, and the University of Pittsburgh's Forbes Quadrangle in the infield. The center field and right-center brick walls still stand, along with the base of the flag pole. Mazeroski Field, a Little League diamond beyond the left field brick wall, still remains. Roberto Clemente Drive now bisects the site, and runs about 10 feet under what used to be the playing surface of the infield.

PHENOMENA

• 1st base by a misspelled street: Boquet Street was named for General Henry Bouquet, a Swiss soldier who fought for the British in the French and Indian War's decisive battle at Fort Duquesne.

• Named for General John Forbes, a British general in the French and Indian War who captured Fort Duquesne and renamed it Fort Pitt in 1758.

• Ivy-covered brick wall in left and left-center.

• The 14-foot Longines clock with speaker horns on top of the left field scoreboard were out of play—a drive hitting it was a home run.

• Fans in the upper left corner of the left field bleachers could not see the plate because of the third base grandstand, which stood between them and the plate. Right field roof was 86 feet high.

• During World War II, the right field screen could not be replaced due to the priority given to the war effort. It deteriorated badly.

• No no-hitter was ever pitched here.

• Home plate remains in almost its exact original location, only now it is encased in glass on the first-floor walkway of the University of Pittsburgh's Forbes Quadrangle.

• The bottoms of the light-tower cages in left-center, center, and right-center were in play, as was the bottom of the center field flag pole.

• Just to the left of the flag pole stood the batting cage, also in play. Before being placed in left-center, it stood behind home plate.

• Very hard infield surface—ask Tony Kubek!

• Back in the 1910s, there was a small scoreboard on the center field wall.

• In 1920s, cars and trucks were repaired and sold beneath the left field bleachers.

• Right field stands built in 1925, reducing distance to right field foul pole by 76.5 feet. Right field screen added in 1932. It was taken down for a short period once, then put back up.

• Barney Dreyfuss Monument was just to the left of the exit gate in right-center where fans exited the ballpark into Schenley Park after a game. It was installed on June 30, 1934, on the park's 25th anniversary, and was made of granite with a bronze tablet.

• Greenberg Gardens, also called Kiner's Korner: the area between the scoreboard and a chicken coop wire short fence in left put there to increase home run production from 1947 to 1953—called Greenberg Gardens 1947, Kiner's Korner 1948 to 1953.

• When Greenberg Gardens were in place, a Western Union clock stood on top of the scoreboard, to the right of the familiar Gruen Clock. Torn down in 1972 and 1973.

• In 1938, with the Buccos apparently on their way to the World Series, they built a third deck of seats behind the plate called the Crow's Nest, which had the major leagues' first elevator. Bucs finally made the Series 22 years later.

• During World War II, from June 26 through the end of the 1943 season, a huge U.S. Marine made of wood stood against the left field wall, just to the right of the scoreboard. Standing at parade rest, the Marine sergeant

was 32 feet high, 15 feet wide across his feet, and in play.
• Honus Wagner statue in Schenley Park erected 1955—18 feet high, 1,800 pounds—moved to Three Rivers with Bucs in 1970.
• A plaque today marks the spot where Bill Mazeroski's World Series-winning homer left the park in 1960 and flew into the trees above Yogi Berra's head.
• Green foam rubber crash pads placed on concrete wall in right and right-center, first in majors. Wooden walls installed in left and center in 1909, replaced with brick and ivy in 1946.
• Street deadending into Sennott Street by 3rd base was called at various times Pennant Place and Forbes Field Avenue.
• Fires damaged park December 24, 1970, and July 17, 1971. Destruction began July 28, 1971.
• Site also occupied today by Deliverance Evangelistic Church.

ST. LOUIS, MISSOURI

SPORTSMAN'S PARK (IV)

STYLE Major League Classic
A.K.A. Busch Stadium (I) 1953 to 1966, Bill Veeck's House
OCCUPANT AL Browns April 14, 1909 to September 27, 1953; NL Cardinals July 1, 1920 to May 8, 1966; NAL New Orleans–St. Louis Stars one game 1941
EVENT All-Star Game 1940, 1948, 1957
LOCATION *Left Field (NE)* Sullivan Avenue; *3rd Base (NW)* North Spring Avenue; *1st Base (SW)* 3623 Dodier Street; *Right Field (SE)* 2911 North Grand Avenue, later North Grand Boulevard. Same as earlier Sportsman's Parks, but turned around so that home plate was in the west-southwest corner

Sportsman's Park

DIMENSIONS *Left Field:* 368 (1909), 340 (1921), 356 (1923), 355 (1926), 360 (1930), 351.1 (1931); *Left Center:* 379; *Center Field:* 430 (1926), 450 (1930), 445 (1931), 420 (1938), 422 (1939); *Deepest Corner Just Left of Dead Center:* 426 (1938); *Deepest Corner Just Right of Dead Center:* 422 (1938); *Right Center:* 354 (1942); *Right Field:* 335 (1909), 315 (1921), 320 (1926), 310 (1931), 332 (1938), 309.5 (1939); *Backstop:* 75 (1942), 67 (1953)
FENCES *Left to Center:* 11.5 (concrete); *354 Mark in Right-Center to Right:* 11.5 (1909), 33 (11.5 concrete below 21.5 wire July 5, 1929), 11.5 (1955), 36.67 (11.5

concrete below 25.17 wire 1956)
CURRENT USE Herbert Hoover Boys' Club, with a baseball diamond where the major league one used to be
PHENOMENA
• The local newspaper, the *Globe-Democrat*, had an ad on the right-center wall which showed the star of the previous game. Just to the right of this ad, the league standings for both leagues were listed.
• The Busch eagle would flap its wings after a Cardinal home run. It sat on top of the left-center scoreboard. During World War II, there was a War Chest sign there.
• Cards office was at 3623 Dodier, Browns office was at 2911 North Grand.
• Pavilion seats in the power alley in right center.
• Second deck from first to third added in 1909.
• Second deck expanded to foul poles in 1925.
• Bleachers were added to parts of outfield in 1926.
• Beginning in the 1940s, the outfield signs were 351, 358, 379, 400, 426, 425, 422, 422, 405, 354, 322, and 310. In the mid 1950s, the 426 and the right 422 signs that marked the corners just left and right of straightaway center were removed.
• Flag pole in fair territory until removed in the 1950s.
• Bill Veeck's family lived in an apartment under the stands in the 1950s.
• When he bought the stadium from the Browns in 1953, Card owner Gussie Busch almost named it Budweiser Stadium, but was prevented by league pressure.
• The wire screen in front of the right field pavilion was removed for the entire 1955 season. It had been installed on July 5, 1929.
• A helicopter carried home plate to Busch Memorial Stadium after the last game on May 8, 1966.
• The old 1902–8 grandstand behind home plate became the left field pavilion in this park from 1909 to 1925 when it was replaced.

SAN FRANCISCO, CALIFORNIA

SEALS STADIUM

STYLE Minor League
A.K.A. Home Plate Mine
OCCUPANT NL Giants April 15, 1958 to September 20, 1959
LOCATION *Left Field (E)* Potrero Avenue; *3rd Base (N)* Alameda Street; *1st Base (W)* Bryant Street; *Right Field (S)* 16th Street and Franklin Square Park

Seals Stadium

DIMENSIONS *Left Field:* 365 (1958), 361 (1959);

Left Center: 375 (1958), 364 (1959); *Just Left of Straight-away Center in the Corner:* 404; *Center Field:* 410 (1958), 400 (1959); *Just Right of Straightaway Center in the Corner:* 415; *Just Right of the 415 Mark Where the Seats Jutted Out:* 397; *Right Field:* 355 (1958), 350 (1959); *Back Stop:* 55.42

FENCES *Left Field:* 15 (5 concrete below 10 wire); *Center Field Scoreboard:* 30.5; *Right Field:* 16 (5 concrete below 11 wire)

CURRENT USE San Francisco Auto Center

PHENOMENA
- Opened April 7, 1931.
- The original deed for the land under the park was listed as "Home Plate Mine."
- No warning track.
- Wind blew from right to left.
- Nearby Hamms Brewery still standing.

SEATTLE, WASHINGTON

SICK'S STADIUM
STYLE Expanded Minor League
A.K.A. Sick's Select Stadium 1940s, Seattle Stadium 1940s
OCCUPANT AL Pilots April 11 to October 2, 1969
LOCATION *Left Field (E)* Empire Way South; *3rd Base (N)* South Bayview Street; *1st Base (W)* 2700 Ranier Avenue South; *Right Field (S)* South McClellan Street
DIMENSIONS *Left Field:* 305; *Power Alleys:* 345; *Corners just right and left of center:* 405; *Center Field:* 402; *Right Field:* 320; *Backstop:* 54
FENCES *Left Field:* 8 (3 concrete below 5 wire); *Center Field:* 12.55 (3 concrete below 9.55 wire); *Right Field:* 8 (3 concrete below 5 wire)

Sick's Stadium

PHENOMENA
- Opened June 15, 1938 for PCL franchise.
- Bleachers down the left field line just as at Forbes Field. Fans could see Mt. Rainier in the distance.
- On April 11, 1969, fans could get a free view of the Pilots' opening day game by looking through numerous openings in the unfinished left field fence. Seven thousand seats were unfinished and 700 fans had to wait an hour before they could take their seats while the carpenters finished their work.
- Insufficient water pressure if crowd was large.
- Used by Class A teams in early 1970s.

WASHINGTON, D.C.

GRIFFITH STADIUM
STYLE Major League Classic
A.K.A. National Park (III) 1911 to 1921, Clark Griffith Park 1922
OCCUPANT AL Senators (I) April 12, 1911 to October 2, 1960; ECL Potomacs 1924; NEWL Pilots 1932; NNL Elite Giants 1936 to 1937; NNL Washington-Homestead Grays half of their home games 1937 to 1948; NNL Black Senators 1938; AL Senators (II) April 10 to September 21, 1961; Negro League World Series first game 1942, first and second games 1943; third game 1945
EVENT All-Star Game 1937, 1956
LOCATION *Left Field (E)* Larch Street, later Fifth Street NW; *3rd Base (N)* Howard University, then W Street NW; *1st Base (W)* J. Frank Kelley Lumber and Mill Works, then Georgia Avenue NW, also called Seventh Street NW; *Right Field (S)* Spruce Street, later U Street NW

Griffith Stadium

DIMENSIONS *Left Field:* 407 (1911), 424 (1921), 358 (1926), 407 (1931), 402 (1936), 405 (1942), 375 (Opening Day 1947), 405 (remainder 1947), 402 (1948), 386 (1950), 408 (1951), 405 (1952), 388 (1954), 386 (1956), 350 (1957), 388 (1961); *Left of Left-Center at Corner:* 383 (1931), 366 (1954), 360 (1956); *Right of Left-Center at Bend in Bleachers: 409 (1942), 398 (1954), 383 (1955), 380 (1956); Left- Center:* 391 (1911), 380 (1950); *Center Field:* 421; *Center Field Corner to Left of Building Protection Wall:* 423 (1926), 441 (1930), 422 (1931), 426 (1936), 420 (1942), 426 (1948), 420 (1950), 394 (1951), 420 (1952) 421 (1953), 426 (1954), 421 (1955), 426 (1961); *Inner Tip of Building Protection Wall:* 409 (1943), 408 (1953); *Deepest Corner—Right End of Building Protection Wall*; *Right Center:* 378 (1954), 372 (1955), 373 (1956); *Right Field:* 328 (1909), 326 (1921), 328 (marked 1926), 320 (actual 1926), 320 (1956); *Backstop:* 61
FENCES *Left Field:* 11.25 (foul pole to 408 mark concrete 1953), 12 (from 410 corner near left field foul pole to 408 mark just right of dead center 1954), 8 to 10 (wood in the corner in front of the bullpen at the foul pole 1955), 6.5 (wire and plywood in front of bullpen 1956); *Center Field:* 30 (concrete 408 mark to 457 mark 1953), 31 (concrete 408 mark to 457 mark 1954), 6 (wire and plywood 1956); *Right-Center:* to the left of the scoreboard in front of the bullpen: 4 (wood from 457 mark to 435 mark 1953), 10 (wood 1955), 4 (wood 1959); *Right Center Scoreboard:* 41 (1946); *National Bohemian Beer Bottle:*

56 (1946); *Right Field:* 30 (concrete 1953), 31 (concrete 1954)

CURRENT USE   Howard University Medical Center and Howard University College of Dentistry, 909 seats now in use at Tinker Field in Orlando, Florida

PHENOMENA

• Loudspeaker horn high on the wall in center.

• The center field wall detoured around 5 houses and a huge tree in center, jutting into the field of play.

• Right field foul line was the grandstand wall for the last 15 or so feet in front of the foul pole, so there was no way to catch a foul ball there.

• It was downhill from the plate to first base, supposedly to help save a step for slow Washington batters.

• Right field clock out of play.

• Ball rolling between top of scoreboard and bottom of the clock was in play: if it didn't come out, it was a homer; if it did, the outfielder could throw it back into play.

• U.S. presidents traditionally opened each season here by throwing out the first ball.

• Memorials honoring Walter Johnson and Clark Griffith stood outside the main entrance to the first base grandstand. The former now stands at Walter Johnson High School in Bethesda, Maryland; the latter at RFK Stadium.

• Height of National Bohemian Beer Bottle, above right-center scoreboard, approximately 50 feet.

• Park rebuilt after March 17, 1911 fire; completed on July 24, 1911.

• Doubledecked in 1920 from the bases down to the foul poles with a roof higher than the original second deck roof behind the plate.

• Temporary seats placed in front of left field bleachers for the 1924 World Series.

• In 1954, the visitor's bullpen was enclosed behind a screen fence in the left field corner in fair territory.

• Clark Calvin Griffith Memorial, dedicated by Vice President Nixon on August 8, 1956, was later moved to R.F.K. Stadium.

• In 1956, all the distances to the outfield fences were remeasured, and it was discovered that right field had lost 8 feet over the years!

• Also in 1956, 10 rows of temporary seats were added in front of the left field bleacher section.

• Park demolished from January 26 to August 14, 1965.

Negro League and Auxilliary Major League Baseball Sites

ATLANTA, GEORGIA

PONCE DE LEON PARK

STYLE   Minor League

A.K.A.   Spiller Park 1924 to 1932, Poncey

OCCUPANT   NSL Black Crackers 1932; NAL Black Crackers 1938

LOCATION   *Left Field (N)* Parking lot; *3rd Base (W)* North Boulevard; *1st Base (S)* 650 Ponce de Leon Boulevard; *Right Field (E) Southern Railroad tracks*

DIMENSIONS   *Left Field:* 365 (1932), 330 (1949); *Left-Center, Left Side of Scoreboard:* 525; *Center Field:*

462 (1932), 448 (1938), 410 (1949); *Right Field:* 321 (1932), 324 (1938)

FENCES   *Left Field:* 2 (hedge, April 1949), 4 (cyclone fence, May 1949); *Left-Center:* 25 (scoreboard); *Center Field:* 6; *Right-Center:* Magnolia Tree halfway up very steep embankment, no fence; *Right Field:* 15

CURRENT USE   Parking lot opposite Sears department store since being torn down in 1967

PHENOMENA

• First Ponce de Leon Park, built in 1907, burned down September 9, 1923.

• A 2-foot-high hedge formed the outfield fence from the left field line to the right side of the left-center scoreboard in 1949. It reduced the foul line from 365 to 330 and caused numerous arguments because a left fielder had to stay within the hedge. If he fell over it, the hit was a homer.

BROOKLYN, NEW YORK

DEXTER PARK

STYLE   Negro League

A.K.A.   Sterling Oval

OCCUPANT   ECL Royal Giants 1923 to 1927

LOCATION   Woodhaven, Long Island *Left (N)* Simpson Street, now called Park Lane South; *3rd Base (NW)* Cypress Hills Cemetery; *1st Base (W)* Elderta Lane and 75th Street; *Center Field (E)* Lott Avenue, now called 76th Street

PHENOMENA

• Had probably the most creative outfield wall billboard ever. An optician's ad read: "Don't Kill the Umpire— Maybe It's Your Eyes."

• Owners Max and Milt Rosner operated the semipro Brooklyn Bushwicks.

• Huge incline in right field caused by horse buried under the grass.

• First lights installed on east coast, 1930.

CHICAGO, ILLINOIS

SOUTH SIDE PARK (III)

STYLE   Cricket Ground

A.K.A.   39th Street Grounds (II), White Stocking Park (III) 1901 to 1903, Chicago Cricket Club, White Sox Park (I) 1904 to 1910, American Giants Field 1911 to 1940, Schorling's Park 1920 to 1940

OCCUPANT   AL White Sox April 24, 1901 to June 27, 1910; NNL Giants 1920; NNL American Giants 1920 to 1931, 1933 to 1935; NSL American Giants 1932; NAL American Giants 1937 to 1940; Neutral site use by NNL Cleveland Tigers 1928, by NNL Kansas City Monarchs in 1920s, by NNL Cuban Stars West in 1920s

LOCATION   *Left Field (N)* West 38th Street; *3rd Base (W)* South Princeton Avenue; *1st Base (S)* West 39th Street, now West Pershing Road; *Right Field (E)* Wentworth Avenue

DIMENSIONS   *Left Field:* 355; *Left Center:* 400; *Center Field:* 450

FORMER USE   Home of Wanderers cricket team

CURRENT USE Housing project three blocks from Comiskey Park
PHENOMENA
• Opened in 1900.
• Overhanging roof added in 1902.
• Fence cut back sharply around J. F. Kidwell Greenhouse buildings in right center, making right-center relatively short compared to center and right.
• Used as a dog racing track during the summer of 1933, forcing the NNL American Giants to move all their home games from May 28 through the end of the 1933 season to Indianapolis.
• Burned down Christmas Day 1940.

EAST ORANGE, NEW JERSEY

GROVE STREET OVAL

STYLE Negro League
A.K.A. Grove Street Senior Ball Diamond, Monte Irvin Field, East Orange Oval
OCCUPANT NNL Cubans 1940 to 1948; NAL Cubans 1949 to 1950; also neutral site used by NNL Newark Eagles 1936 to 1948
LOCATION East Orange, New Jersey *Left Field (E)* Greenwood Avenue; *3rd Base (N)* Grove Place; *1st Base (W)* Grove Street North; *Right Field (S)* Eaton Place;
DIMENSIONS *Left Field:* 240; *Center Field:* 360 to the water fountain; *Right Field:* 280
FENCES *Left Field:* 25 (garage walls); *Center Field:* 4 (water fountain); *Right Field:* None
CURRENT USE Still used as a community ball diamond
PHENOMENA
• No fence in center field where there were some hedges.
• Water fountain in play in deepest center field.
• Trees in right, as well as tennis courts beyond.
• Scoreboard in left, as well as poplar trees.
• Clubhouse down right field line in foul territory.
• "Bujum" Jud Wilson hit longest ball ever hit over water fountain in center.
• Property purchased by city in October 1907 and park dedicated Labor Day 1908 in a game between the New Jersey State Senate and the New Jersey State General Assembly.
• Fire destroyed the first grandstand at 4 AM, May 3, 1925; new grandstand dedicated May 1, 1926.
• Renamed Monte Irvin Field at June 6, 1986 ceremony in culmination of 4 years effort initiated by this author and the SABR Negro Leagues Committee, who designed the plaque marking the site.

JERSEY CITY, NEW JERSEY

ROOSEVELT STADIUM

STYLE Minor League
OCCUPANT NL Dodgers for seven 1956 games and eight 1957 games from April 19, 1956 to September 3, 1957; some NNL New York Black Yankees games in 1940s
LOCATION *Left Field (NE)* Hackensack River; *3rd Base (NW)* Newark Bay; *1st Base (SW)* Danforth Avenue; *Right Field (SE)* State Highway 440; at Droyers Point
DIMENSIONS *Foul lines:* 330; *Power Alleys:* 397; *Center Field:* 411; *Backstop:* 60
FENCES *Foul Line Corners:* 11; *Left Field to Center Field:* 4; *Right-Center to Right Field:* 7
FORMER USE A landfill for dirt excavated from Holland Tunnel
PHENOMENA
• Built as a WPA project in 1937 and named for FDR.
• Newark Bay brought mosquitoes and mist into the outfield.
• Thanksgiving morning football games between St. Peter's and Dickinson were always sold out in the 1940s.
• Torn down in 1984.

NASHVILLE, TENNESSEE

SULPHUR DELL (II)

STYLE Minor League
A.K.A. Sulphur Springs Bottom, Sulphur Dell Park, Athletic Park, Dump, Suffer Hell
OCCUPANT NNL Elite Giants 1933 to 1934
LOCATION *Left Field (N)* Jackson Street; *3rd Base (W)* Summer Street, later 900 Fifth Avenue North; *1st Base (S)* Tennessee Central Railroad tracks; *Right Field (E)* Cherry Street, later Fourth Avenue North
DIMENSIONS *Left Field:* 334; *Center Field:* 421; *Right Field:* 262 (235 when fans sat behind ropes on the bank)
FENCES *All Around:* 16 (wood 1927); *Left and Center:* 16 (wood 1931); *Right Field:* 38.5 to 46 (16 wood below 22.5 to 30 screen to a point 186 feet from the right field foul line)
PHENOMENA
• Only one-quarter mile from the Cumberland River, the park was often flooded.
• Nicknamed "the Dump" in honor of the exceptional fragrance that drifted over from the nearby smoldering city dump and lent a unique character to Sulphur Dell hot dogs!
• Sulphur Dell had the craziest right field in history. Right fielders were called mountain goats because they had to go up and down the irregular hills in right-center and right. The incline in right rose 25 feet, beginning gradually behind first, then rising sharply at a 45-degree angle, then leveling off at a 10-foot-wide shelf one-third of the way up the incline, and then continuing at a 45-degree angle to the fence.
• Fielders used to play on the shelf, 235 feet from the plate. When overflow crowds were attracted to a game, a rope was extended in front of the shelf, and fans sat on the upper two thirds of the incline, reducing right field to 235 rather than 262.
• The stands were very close to the pancake-shaped diamond. First base was 42 feet from the seats; third base was 26 feet from the seats.
• Embankments began in left at 301 and in right at 224.
• Casey Stengel once joked that he hit a bunt home run down the 1st base line.

NEW YORK, NEW YORK

DYCKMAN OVAL

STYLE Negro League
OCCUPANT NNL Cuban Stars 1922; ECL Cuban Stars East 1923 to 1928; ECL Bachrach Giants many games 1923 to 1928; NAL Cuban Stars East 1929; NNL Cuban House of David 1931; NEWL Cuban Stars 1932
LOCATION *Left Field (NE)* West 204th Street; *3rd Base (NW)* Nagle Avenue; *1st Base (SW)* Academy Street; *Right Field (SE)* Tenth Avenue. In Upper Manhattan, 8 blocks east of the Henry Hudson Parkway, 5 blocks east of Inwood Hill Park, south of the Harlem Ship Canal, 4 blocks north of Dyckman Street, in Dyckman section
PHENOMENA
• The first major league park in New York to have lights for evening games. They were installed in 1930 by Cuban Stars owner Alex Pompez.

CAPITAL TEXTURE

STYLE Negro League
OCCUPANT ECL Lincoln Giants 1928; NAL Lincoln Giants 1929
LOCATION *(N)* East 138th Street; *(W)* Fifth Avenue; *(S)* East 135th Street; *(E)* Madison Avenue
CURRENT USE Riverton Apartments

CATHOLIC PROTECTORY OVAL

STYLE Amateur
OCCUPANT ECL Lincoln Giants 1923 to 1926; NNL Cubans 1935 to 1936
LOCATION *Left Field (E)* Hoguet Avenue; *3rd Base (N)* East Tremont Avenue; *1st Base (W)* White Plains Road; *Right Field (S)* McGraw Avenue. Bronx, 5 miles northeast of Yankee Stadium
CURRENT USE Parkchester Apartments, built by the Metropolitan Life Insurance Company—Unionport Road now crosses the site from home plate to center field; Metropolitan Avenue now runs from right field in to second base and then curves out to left field.
PHENOMENA
• The Protectory was a Catholic home and school for impoverished boys whose 50-piece marching band was much in demand. One of the students, Hank Greenberg, is now in the Hall of Fame.
• No grass in the infield.
• Leveled in 1939 so that Parkchester Apartments could be built.

TRIBOROUGH STADIUM

STYLE Football Stadium
A.K.A. Randall's Island Stadium, J. J. Downing Memorial Stadium
OCCUPANT NNL Black Yankees 1938
LOCATION *(N)* Bronx Kills and Harlem River, Eastern Parkway and Triborough Bridge; *(W)* House of Refuge, Vesta Avenue; *(S)* Little Hell Gate, East River, and Ward's Island, Sutter Avenue; *(E)* Sunken Meadow, Powell Street, Triborough Bridge
CURRENT USE Still standing, was used for WFL Stars football games in 1974 and NASL Cosmos soccer games in 1975

PHENOMENA
• A U-shaped stadium, open at the southwest end.
• Eight Ebbets Field light towers were moved here when Ebbets had new lights installed.

PATERSON, NEW JERSEY

HINCHCLIFFE STADIUM

STYLE Football Stadium
OCCUPANT NNL Black Yankees 1936 to 1937, 1939 to 1945
LOCATION Paterson, New Jersey *Center Field (SE)* Passaic River; *3rd Base (NE)* Redwood Avenue; *Home Plate (NW)* Liberty Street; *1st Base (SW)* Maple Street
CURRENT USE Community baseball, still standing, opened 1932

PHILADELPHIA, PENNSYLVANIA

HILLDALE PARK

STYLE High School
A.K.A. Darby Catholic School Stadium
OCCUPANT ECL Hilldales 1923 to 1927; NAL Hilldales 1929; NEWL Hilldales 1932
LOCATION Yeadon, Pennsylvania *Left Field (N)* Bunting Lane, later MacDade Boulevard; *3rd Base (W)* Greenhouses and Cedar Avenue; *1st Base (S)* Chester Avenue; *Right Field (E)* Yeadon School In the suburbs of Philadelphia at a Catholic school on the Darby-Yeadon borderline
DIMENSIONS *Left Field:* 315; *Right Center:* 400; *Right Field:* 370
CURRENT USE Acme Super Saver supermarket and drive-in bank
PHENOMENA
• A huge tree sat beyond the fence in right-center; branches hung over the fence and were in play.

PITTSBURGH, PENNSYLVANIA

GUS GREENLEE FIELD

STYLE Negro League
OCCUPANT NEWL Grays 1932; NEWL Crawfords 1932; NNL Grays 1933, 1935 to 1938; NNL Crawfords 1933 to 1938
LOCATION In the Hill District *Left Field (N)* Ridgeway Street; *3rd Base (W)* Junilla Street; *1st Base (S)* 2500 Bedford Avenue; *Right Field (E)* Municipal Hospital and Francis Street
FORMER USE Entress Brick Company factory
CURRENT USE Pittsburgh Housing Authority projects
PHENOMENA
• Opened on April 29, 1932.
• Tin fence in outfield.
• Left field foul line was longer than at Forbes Field, where it was 365.
• The structure was torn down on December 10, 1938.

## CHAPTER 4

Major League Attendance

Robert L. Tiemann and Pete Palmer

If you have the patience to sift through them, the figures on the following pages, dating from 1890 through 1994, tell a remarkable story. Season attendance has approached 4.5 million in Colorado in 1993, and it has been as little as 6,088 in Cleveland in 1899, when the awful Spiders went 20–134. The first club to pass the million mark was the New York Yankees of 1920, featuring a newcomer named Ruth and a ballpark borrowed from the Giants (who did not reach the mark themselves until 1945). In the depths of the Depression, the St. Louis Browns posted annual attendance figures (80,922 in 1935; 88,113 in 1933) below what a weekend set produces in many major-league venues.

Why did attendance stagnate in the 1890s? How much did the entry of the American League into National League strongholds New York, Chicago, Philadelphia, and St. Louis hurt the senior franchises? Were the Dodgers justified in leaving Brooklyn? How did baseball survive in Washington as long as it did, surpassing the million mark only once from 1892 to 1971? Did anyone notice that Atlanta's attendance of 1990 doubled, and then tripled, over the next two years? Or that while major league attendance increased by 25.8 percent from 1992 to 1993, almost all of that gain came from the senior circuit? (The American League rose a modest 5 percent while the National League posted a whopping gain of 53 percent; even if we subtract expansion clubs Florida and Colorado, the NL increase was an impressive 21.8 percent.)

You get the picture. There's stuff here that permits you to chart trends in baseball that you already know about, and if you are eagle-eyed you may pick up an anomalous figure that prompts you to rethink what you thought you knew.

A researcher's goldmine, the tables that follow tell an interesting story for the average fan as well. Does winning a pennant correlate with higher attendance? Are first-division teams more profitable than those in the second division? What is the impact on attendance of a new stadium?

By the time the next edition rolls around we may be able to gather figures going back to the dawn of professional baseball. Here are some scattered tidbits:

- In their first year of existence, 1871, the Boston Red Stockings counted 32,600 fans in 18 home games.
- In 1882, the last year of its existence as an NL franchise, the Troy Haymakers drew a whopping 26,000 attendees for its 42 home games, with one late season date posting a recorded crowd of 12 (that's not a typo).
- The 1891 American Association, in its final year of operation, counted 1,296,000 fans, or an average of 162,000 per team, a figure very comparable to the 169,060 of the National League. In 1892, with the AA gone and the NL a twelve-team circuit, the average team attendance was less than 152,000. Is there a lesson to be drawn from this?

Yes, and the lesson is plain for magnates no less than for fans and students of the game.

	1890	1891	1892	1893	1894	1895	1896	1897	1898	1899
NATIONAL LEAGUE										
BAL			93,589	143,000	328,000	293,000	249,448	273,046	123,416	121,935
BOS	147,539	184,472	146,421	193,300	152,800	242,000	240,000	334,800	229,275	200,384
BRO	121,412	181,477	183,727	235,000	214,000	230,000	201,000	220,831	122,514	269,641
CHI	102,536	201,188	109,067	223,500	239,000	382,300	317,500	327,160	424,352	352,130
CIN	131,980	97,500	196,473	194,250	158,000	281,000	373,000	336,800	336,378	259,536
CLE	47,478	132,000	139,928	130,000	82,000	143,000	152,000	115,250	70,496	6,088
LOU			131,159	53,683	75,000	92,000	133,000	145,210	128,980	109,319
NY	60,667	210,568	130,566	290,000	387,000	240,000	274,000	390,340	206,700	121,384
PHI	148,366	217,282	193,731	293,019	352,773	474,971	357,025	290,027	265,414	388,933
PIT	16,064	128,000	177,205	184,000	159,000	188,000	197,000	165,950	150,900	251,834
STL			192,442	195,000	155,000	170,000	184,000	136,400	151,700	373,909
WAS			128,279	90,000	125,000	153,000	223,000	151,028	103,250	86,392
TOT	776,042	1,352,487	1,822,587	2,224,752	2,427,573	2,889,271	2,900,973	2,886,842	2,313,375	2,541,485
ML	776,042	1,352,487	1,822,587	2,224,752	2,427,573	2,889,271	2,900,973	2,886,842	2,313,375	2,541,485

	1900	1901	1902	1903	1904	1905	1906	1907	1908	1909
AMERICAN LEAGUE										
BAL		141,952	174,606							
BOS		289,448	348,567	379,338	623,295	468,828	410,209	436,777	473,048	668,965
CHI		354,350	337,898	286,183	557,123	687,419	585,202	666,307	636,096	478,400
CLE		131,380	275,395	311,280	264,749	316,306	325,733	382,046	422,262	354,627
DET		259,430	189,469	224,523	177,796	193,384	174,043	297,079	436,199	490,490
MIL		139,034								
NY				211,808	438,919	309,100	434,700	350,020	305,500	501,700
PHI		206,329	420,078	422,473	512,294	554,576	489,129	625,581	455,062	674,915
STL			272,283	380,405	318,108	339,112	389,157	419,025	618,947	366,274
WAS		161,661	188,158	128,878	131,744	252,027	129,903	221,929	264,252	205,199
TOT		1,683,584	2,206,454	2,344,888	3,024,028	3,120,752	2,938,076	3,398,764	3,611,366	3,740,570
NATIONAL LEAGUE										
BOS	202,000	146,502	116,960	143,155	140,694	150,003	143,280	203,221	253,750	195,188
BRO	183,000	198,200	199,868	224,670	214,600	227,924	277,400	312,500	275,600	321,300
CHI	248,577	205,071	263,700	386,205	439,100	509,900	654,300	422,550	665,325	633,480
CIN	170,000	205,728	217,300	351,680	391,915	313,927	330,056	317,500	399,200	424,643
NY	190,000	297,650	302,875	579,530	609,826	552,700	402,850	538,350	910,000	783,700
PHI	301,913	234,937	112,066	151,729	140,771	317,932	294,680	341,216	420,660	303,177
PIT	264,000	251,955	243,826	326,855	340,615	369,124	394,877	319,506	382,444	534,950
STL	270,000	379,988	226,417	226,538	386,750	292,800	283,770	185,377	205,129	299,982
TOT	1,829,490	1,920,031	1,683,012	2,390,362	2,664,271	2,734,310	2,781,213	2,640,220	3,512,108	3,496,420
ML	1,829,490	3,603,615	3,889,466	4,735,250	5,688,299	5,855,062	5,719,289	6,038,984	7,123,474	7,236,990

	1910	1911	1912	1913	1914	1915	1916	1917	1918	1919
AMERICAN LEAGUE										
BOS	584,619	503,961	597,096	437,194	481,359	539,885	496,397	387,856	249,513	417,291
CHI	552,084	583,208	602,241	644,501	469,290	539,461	679,923	684,521	195,081	627,186
CLE	293,456	406,296	336,844	541,000	185,997	159,285	492,106	477,298	295,515	538,135
DET	391,288	484,988	402,870	398,502	416,225	476,105	616,772	457,289	203,719	643,805
NY	355,857	302,444	242,194	357,551	359,477	256,035	469,211	330,294	282,047	619,164
PHI	588,905	605,749	517,653	571,896	346,641	146,223	184,471	221,432	177,926	225,209
STL	249,889	207,984	214,070	250,330	244,714	150,358	335,740	210,486	122,076	349,350
WAS	254,591	244,884	350,663	325,831	243,888	167,332	177,265	89,682	182,122	234,096
TOT	3,270,689	3,339,514	3,263,631	3,526,805	2,747,591	2,434,684	3,451,885	2,858,858	1,707,999	3,654,236
NATIONAL LEAGUE										
BOS	149,027	116,000	121,000	208,000	382,913	376,283	313,495	174,253	84,938	167,401
BRO	279,321	269,000	243,000	347,000	122,671	297,766	447,747	221,619	83,831	360,721
CHI	526,152	576,000	514,000	419,000	202,516	217,058	453,685	360,218	337,256	424,430
CIN	380,622	300,000	344,000	258,000	100,791	218,878	255,846	269,056	163,009	532,501
NY	511,785	675,000	638,000	630,000	364,313	391,850	552,056	500,264	256,618	708,857
PHI	296,597	416,000	250,000	470,000	138,474	449,898	515,365	354,428	122,266	240,424
PIT	436,586	432,000	384,000	296,000	139,620	225,743	289,132	192,807	213,610	276,810
STL	355,668	447,768	241,759	203,531	256,099	252,666	224,308	288,491	110,599	167,059
TOT	2,935,758	3,231,768	2,735,759	2,831,531	1,707,397	2,430,142	3,051,634	2,361,136	1,372,127	2,878,203
ML	6,206,447	6,571,282	5,999,390	6,358,336	4,454,988	4,864,826	6,503,519	5,219,994	3,080,126	6,532,439

	1920	1921	1922	1923	1924	1925	1926	1927	1928	1929
AMERICAN LEAGUE										
BOS	402,445	279,273	259,184	229,688	448,556	267,782	285,155	305,275	396,920	394,620
CHI	833,492	543,650	602,860	573,778	606,658	832,231	710,339	614,423	494,152	426,795
CLE	912,832	748,705	528,145	558,856	481,905	419,005	627,426	373,138	375,907	536,210
DET	579,650	661,527	861,206	911,377	1,015,136	820,766	711,914	773,716	474,323	869,318
NY	1,289,422	1,230,696	1,026,134	1,007,066	1,053,533	697,267	1,027,675	1,164,015	1,072,132	960,148
PHI	287,888	344,430	425,356	534,122	531,992	869,703	714,508	605,529	689,756	839,176
STL	419,311	355,978	712,918	430,296	533,349	462,898	283,986	247,879	339,497	280,697
WAS	359,260	456,069	458,552	357,406	584,310	817,199	551,580	528,976	378,501	355,506
TOT	5,084,300	4,620,328	4,874,355	4,602,589	5,255,439	5,186,851	4,912,583	4,612,951	4,221,188	4,662,470

	1920	1921	1922	1923	1924	1925	1926	1927	1928	1929
NATIONAL LEAGUE										
BOS	162,483	318,627	167,965	227,802	177,478	313,528	303,598	288,685	227,001	372,351
BRO	808,722	613,245	498,865	564,666	818,883	659,435	650,819	637,230	664,863	731,886
CHI	480,783	410,107	542,283	703,705	716,922	622,610	885,063	1,159,168	1,143,740	1,485,166
CIN	568,107	311,227	493,754	575,063	473,707	464,920	672,987	442,164	490,490	295,040
NY	929,609	973,477	945,809	820,780	844,068	778,993	700,362	858,190	916,191	868,806
PHI	330,998	273,961	232,471	228,168	299,818	304,905	240,600	305,420	182,168	281,200
PIT	429,037	701,567	523,675	611,082	736,883	804,354	798,542	869,720	495,070	491,377
STL	326,836	384,773	536,998	338,551	272,885	404,959	668,428	749,340	761,574	399,887
TOT	4,036,575	3,986,984	3,941,820	4,069,817	4,340,644	4,353,704	4,920,399	5,309,917	4,881,097	4,925,713
ML	9,120,875	8,607,312	8,816,175	8,672,406	9,596,083	9,540,555	9,832,982	9,922,868	9,102,285	9,588,183

	1930	1931	1932	1933	1934	1935	1936	1937	1938	1939
AMERICAN LEAGUE										
BOS	444,045	350,975	182,150	268,715	610,640	558,568	626,895	559,659	646,459	573,070
CHI	406,123	403,550	233,198	397,789	236,559	470,281	440,810	589,245	338,278	594,104
CLE	528,657	483,027	468,953	387,936	391,338	397,615	500,391	564,849	652,006	563,926
DET	649,450	434,056	397,157	320,972	919,161	1,034,929	875,948	1,072,276	799,557	836,279
NY	1,169,230	912,437	962,320	728,014	854,682	657,508	976,913	998,148	970,916	859,785
PHI	721,663	627,464	405,500	297,138	305,847	233,173	285,173	430,738	385,357	395,022
STL	152,088	179,126	112,558	88,113	115,305	80,922	93,267	123,121	130,417	109,159
WAS	614,474	492,657	371,396	437,533	330,074	255,011	379,525	397,799	522,694	339,257
TOT	4,685,730	3,883,292	3,133,232	2,926,210	3,763,606	3,688,007	4,178,922	4,735,835	4,445,684	4,270,602
NATIONAL LEAGUE										
BOS	464,835	515,005	507,606	517,803	303,205	232,754	340,585	385,339	341,149	285,994
BRO	1,097,329	753,133	681,827	526,815	434,188	470,517	489,618	482,481	663,087	955,668
CHI	1,463,624	1,086,422	974,688	594,112	707,525	692,604	699,370	895,020	951,640	726,663
CIN	386,727	263,316	356,950	218,281	206,773	448,247	466,345	411,221	706,756	981,443
NY	868,714	812,163	484,868	604,471	730,851	748,748	837,952	926,887	799,633	702,457
PHI	299,007	284,849	268,914	156,421	169,885	205,470	249,219	212,790	166,111	277,973
PIT	357,795	260,392	287,262	288,747	322,622	352,885	372,524	459,679	641,033	376,734
STL	508,501	608,535	279,219	256,171	325,056	506,084	448,078	430,811	291,418	400,245
TOT	5,446,532	4,583,815	3,841,334	3,162,821	3,200,105	3,657,309	3,903,691	4,204,228	4,560,827	4,707,177
ML	10,132,262	8,467,107	6,974,566	6,089,031	6,963,711	7,345,316	8,082,613	8,940,063	9,006,511	8,977,779

	1940	1941	1942	1943	1944	1945	1946	1947	1948	1949
AMERICAN LEAGUE										
BOS	716,234	718,497	730,340	358,275	506,975	603,794	1,416,944	1,427,315	1,558,798	1,596,650
CHI	660,336	677,077	425,734	508,962	563,539	657,981	983,403	876,948	777,844	937,151
CLE	902,576	745,948	459,447	438,894	475,272	558,182	1,057,289	1,521,978	2,620,627	2,233,771
DET	1,112,693	684,915	580,087	606,287	923,176	1,280,341	1,722,590	1,398,093	1,743,035	1,821,204
NY	988,975	964,722	922,011	618,330	789,995	881,845	2,265,512	2,178,937	2,373,901	2,283,676
PHI	432,145	528,894	423,487	376,735	505,322	462,631	621,793	911,566	945,076	816,514
STL	239,591	176,240	255,617	214,392	508,644	482,986	526,435	320,474	335,564	270,936
WAS	381,241	415,663	403,493	574,694	525,235	652,660	1,027,216	850,758	795,254	770,745
TOT	5,433,791	4,911,956	4,200,216	3,696,569	4,798,158	5,580,420	9,621,182	9,486,069	11,150,099	10,730,647
NATIONAL LEAGUE										
BOS	241,616	263,680	285,332	271,289	208,691	374,178	969,673	1,277,361	1,455,439	1,081,795
BRO	975,978	1,214,910	1,037,765	661,739	605,905	1,059,220	1,796,824	1,807,526	1,398,967	1,633,747
CHI	534,878	545,159	590,972	508,247	640,110	1,036,386	1,342,970	1,364,039	1,237,792	1,143,139
CIN	850,180	643,513	427,031	379,122	409,567	290,070	715,751	899,975	823,386	707,782
NY	747,852	763,098	779,621	466,095	674,483	1,016,468	1,219,873	1,600,793	1,459,269	1,218,446
PHI	207,177	231,401	230,183	466,975	369,586	285,057	1,045,247	907,332	767,429	819,698
PIT	507,934	482,241	448,897	498,740	604,278	604,694	749,962	1,283,531	1,517,021	1,449,435
STL	324,078	633,645	553,552	517,135	461,968	594,630	1,061,807	1,247,913	1,111,440	1,430,676
TOT	4,389,693	4,777,647	4,353,353	3,769,342	3,974,588	5,260,703	8,902,107	10,388,470	9,770,743	9,484,718
ML	9,823,484	9,689,603	8,553,569	7,465,911	8,772,746	10,841,123	18,523,289	19,874,539	20,920,842	20,215,365

	1950	1951	1952	1953	1954	1955	1956	1957	1958	1959
AMERICAN LEAGUE										
BAL					1,060,910	852,039	901,201	1,029,581	829,991	891,926
BOS	1,344,080	1,312,282	1,115,750	1,026,133	931,127	1,203,200	1,137,158	1,181,087	1,077,047	984,102
CHI	781,330	1,328,234	1,231,675	1,191,353	1,231,629	1,175,684	1,000,090	1,135,668	797,451	1,423,144
CLE	1,727,464	1,704,984	1,444,607	1,069,176	1,335,472	1,221,780	865,467	722,256	663,805	1,497,976
DET	1,951,474	1,132,641	1,026,846	884,658	1,079,847	1,181,838	1,051,182	1,272,346	1,098,924	1,221,221
KC						1,393,054	1,015,154	901,067	925,090	963,683
NY	2,081,380	1,950,107	1,629,665	1,537,811	1,475,171	1,490,138	1,491,784	1,497,134	1,428,438	1,552,030
PHI	309,805	465,469	627,100	362,113	304,666					
STL	247,131	293,790	518,796	297,238						
WAS	699,697	695,167	699,457	595,594	503,542	425,238	431,647	457,079	475,288	615,372
TOT	9,142,361	8,882,674	8,293,896	6,964,076	7,922,364	8,942,971	7,893,683	8,196,218	7,296,034	9,149,454
NATIONAL LEAGUE										
BOS	944,391	487,475	281,278							
BRO	1,185,896	1,282,628	1,088,704	1,163,419	1,020,531	1,033,589	1,213,562	1,028,258		
CHI	1,165,944	894,415	1,024,826	763,658	748,183	875,800	720,118	670,629	979,904	858,255

	1950	1951	1952	1953	1954	1955	1956	1957	1958	1959
CIN	538,794	588,268	604,197	548,086	704,167	693,662	1,125,928	1,070,850	788,582	801,298
LA									1,845,556	2,071,045
MIL				1,826,397	2,131,388	2,005,836	2,046,331	2,215,404	1,971,101	1,749,112
NY	1,008,878	1,059,539	984,940	811,518	1,155,067	824,112	629,179	653,923		
PHI	1,217,035	937,658	755,417	853,644	738,991	922,886	934,798	1,146,230	931,110	802,815
PIT	1,166,267	980,590	686,673	572,757	475,494	469,397	949,878	850,732	1,311,988	1,359,917
STL	1,093,411	1,013,429	913,113	880,242	1,039,698	849,130	1,029,773	1,183,575	1,063,730	929,953
SF									1,272,625	1,422,130
TOT	8,320,616	7,244,002	6,339,148	7,419,721	8,013,519	7,674,412	8,649,567	8,819,601	10,164,596	9,994,525
ML	17,462,977	16,126,676	14,633,044	14,383,797	15,935,883	16,617,383	16,543,250	17,015,819	17,460,630	19,143,979

	1960	1961	1962	1963	1964	1965	1966	1967	1968	1969
AMERICAN LEAGUE										
BAL	1,187,849	951,089	790,254	774,343	1,116,215	781,649	1,203,366	955,053	943,977	1,062,069
BOS	1,129,866	850,589	733,080	942,642	883,276	652,201	811,172	1,727,832	1,940,788	1,833,246
CAL						566,727	1,400,321	1,317,713	1,025,956	758,388
CHI	1,644,460	1,146,019	1,131,562	1,158,848	1,250,053	1,130,519	990,016	985,634	803,775	589,546
CLE	950,985	725,547	716,076	562,507	653,293	934,786	903,359	662,980	857,994	619,970
DET	1,167,669	1,600,710	1,207,881	821,952	816,139	1,029,645	1,124,293	1,447,143	2,031,847	1,577,481
KC	774,944	683,817	635,675	762,364	642,478	528,344	773,929	726,639		902,414
LA		603,510	1,144,063	821,015	760,439					
MIN		1,256,723	1,433,116	1,406,652	1,207,514	1,463,258	1,259,374	1,483,547	1,143,257	1,349,328
NY	1,627,349	1,747,725	1,493,574	1,308,920	1,305,638	1,213,552	1,124,648	1,259,514	1,185,666	1,067,996
OAK									837,466	778,232
SEA										677,944
WAS	743,404	597,287	729,775	535,604	600,106	560,083	576,260	770,868	546,661	918,106
TOT	9,226,526	10,163,016	10,015,056	9,094,847	9,235,151	8,860,764	10,166,738	11,336,923	11,317,387	12,134,720
NATIONAL LEAGUE										
ATL							1,539,801	1,389,222	1,126,540	1,458,320
CHI	809,770	673,057	609,802	979,551	751,647	641,361	635,891	977,226	1,043,409	1,674,993
CIN	663,486	1,117,603	982,095	858,805	862,466	1,047,824	742,958	958,300	733,354	987,991
HOU			924,456	719,502	725,773	2,151,470	1,872,108	1,348,303	1,312,887	1,442,995
LA	2,253,887	1,804,250	2,755,184	2,538,602	2,228,751	2,553,577	2,617,029	1,664,362	1,581,093	1,784,527
MIL	1,497,799	1,101,441	766,921	773,018	910,911	555,584				
MON										1,212,608
NY			922,530	1,080,108	1,732,597	1,768,389	1,932,693	1,565,492	1,781,657	2,175,373
PHI	862,205	590,039	762,034	907,141	1,425,891	1,166,376	1,108,201	828,888	664,546	519,414
PIT	1,705,828	1,199,128	1,090,648	783,648	759,496	909,279	1,196,618	907,012	693,485	769,369
STL	1,096,632	855,305	953,895	1,170,546	1,143,294	1,241,201	1,712,980	2,090,145	2,011,167	1,682,783
SD										512,970
SF	1,795,356	1,390,679	1,592,594	1,571,306	1,504,364	1,546,075	1,657,192	1,242,480	837,220	873,603
TOT	10,684,963	8,731,502	11,360,159	11,382,227	12,045,190	13,581,136	15,015,471	12,971,430	11,785,358	15,094,946
ML	19,911,489	18,894,518	21,375,215	20,477,074	21,280,341	22,441,900	25,182,209	24,308,353	23,102,745	27,229,666

	1970	1971	1972	1973	1974	1975	1976	1977	1978	1979
AMERICAN LEAGUE										
BAL	1,057,069	1,023,037	899,950	958,667	962,572	1,002,157	1,058,609	1,195,769	1,051,724	1,681,009
BOS	1,595,278	1,678,732	1,441,718	1,481,002	1,556,411	1,748,587	1,895,846	2,074,549	2,320,643	2,353,114
CAL	1,077,741	926,373	744,190	1,058,206	917,269	1,058,163	1,006,774	1,432,633	1,755,386	2,523,575
CHI	495,355	833,891	1,177,318	1,302,527	1,149,596	750,802	914,945	1,657,135	1,491,100	1,280,702
CLE	729,752	591,361	626,354	615,107	1,114,262	977,039	948,776	900,365	800,584	1,011,644
DET	1,501,293	1,591,073	1,892,386	1,724,146	1,243,080	1,058,836	1,467,020	1,359,856	1,714,893	1,630,929
KC	693,047	910,784	707,656	1,345,341	1,173,292	1,151,836	1,680,265	1,852,603	2,255,493	2,261,845
MIL	933,690	731,531	600,440	1,092,158	955,741	1,213,357	1,012,164	1,114,938	1,601,406	1,918,343
MIN	1,261,887	940,858	797,901	907,499	662,401	737,156	715,394	1,162,727	787,878	1,070,521
NY	1,136,879	1,070,771	966,328	1,262,103	1,273,075	1,288,048	2,012,434	2,103,092	2,335,871	2,537,765
OAK	778,355	914,993	921,323	1,000,763	845,693	1,075,518	780,593	495,599	526,999	306,763
SEA								1,338,511	877,440	844,447
TEX			662,974	686,085	1,193,902	1,127,924	1,164,982	1,250,722	1,447,963	1,519,671
TOR								1,701,052	1,562,585	1,431,651
WAS	824,789	655,156								
TOT	12,085,135	11,868,560	11,438,538	13,433,604	13,047,294	13,189,423	14,657,802	19,639,551	20,529,965	22,371,979
NATIONAL LEAGUE										
ATL	1,078,848	1,006,320	752,973	800,655	981,085	534,672	818,179	872,464	904,494	769,465
CHI	1,642,705	1,653,007	1,299,163	1,351,705	1,015,378	1,034,819	1,026,217	1,439,834	1,525,311	1,648,587
CIN	1,803,568	1,501,122	1,611,459	2,017,601	2,164,307	2,315,603	2,629,708	2,519,670	2,532,497	2,356,933
HOU	1,253,444	1,261,589	1,469,247	1,394,004	1,090,728	858,002	886,146	1,109,560	1,126,145	1,900,312
LA	1,697,142	2,064,594	1,860,858	2,136,192	2,632,474	2,539,349	2,386,301	2,955,087	3,347,845	2,860,954
MON	1,424,683	1,290,963	1,142,145	1,246,863	1,019,134	908,292	646,704	1,433,757	1,427,007	2,102,173
NY	2,697,479	2,266,680	2,134,185	1,912,390	1,722,209	1,730,566	1,468,754	1,066,825	1,007,328	788,905
PHI	708,247	1,511,223	1,343,329	1,475,934	1,808,648	1,909,233	2,480,150	2,700,070	2,583,389	2,775,011
PIT	1,341,947	1,501,132	1,427,460	1,319,913	1,110,552	1,270,018	1,025,945	1,237,349	964,106	1,435,454
STL	1,629,736	1,604,671	1,196,894	1,574,046	1,838,413	1,695,270	1,207,079	1,659,287	1,278,215	1,627,256
SD	643,679	557,513	644,273	611,826	1,075,399	1,281,747	1,458,478	1,376,269	1,670,107	1,456,967
SF	740,720	1,106,043	647,744	834,193	519,987	522,919	626,868	700,056	1,740,477	1,456,402
TOT	16,662,198	17,324,857	15,529,730	16,675,322	16,978,314	16,600,490	16,660,529	19,070,228	20,106,921	21,178,419
ML	28,747,333	29,193,417	26,968,268	30,108,926	30,025,608	29,789,913	31,318,331	38,709,779	40,636,886	43,550,398

	1980	1981	1982	1983	1984	1985	1986	1987	1988	1989
AMERICAN LEAGUE										
BAL	1,797,438	1,024,247	1,613,031	2,042,071	2,045,784	2,132,387	1,973,176	1,835,692	1,660,738	2,535,208
BOS	1,956,092	1,060,379	1,950,124	1,782,285	1,661,618	1,786,633	2,147,641	2,231,551	2,464,851	2,510,012
CAL	2,297,327	1,441,545	2,807,360	2,555,016	2,402,997	2,567,427	2,655,872	2,696,299	2,340,925	2,647,291
CHI	1,200,365	946,651	1,567,787	2,132,821	2,136,988	1,669,888	1,424,313	1,208,060	1,115,749	1,045,651
CLE	1,033,827	661,395	1,044,021	768,941	734,079	655,181	1,471,805	1,077,898	1,411,610	1,285,542
DET	1,785,293	1,149,144	1,636,058	1,829,636	2,704,794	2,286,609	1,899,437	2,061,830	2,081,162	1,543,656
KC	2,288,714	1,279,403	2,284,464	1,963,875	1,810,018	2,162,717	2,320,794	2,392,471	2,350,181	2,477,700
MIL	1,857,408	874,292	1,978,896	2,397,131	1,608,509	1,360,265	1,265,041	1,909,244	1,923,238	1,970,735
MIN	769,206	469,090	921,186	858,939	1,598,692	1,651,814	1,255,453	2,081,976	3,030,672	2,277,438
NY	2,627,417	1,614,353	2,041,219	2,257,976	1,821,815	2,214,587	2,268,030	2,427,672	2,633,701	2,170,485
OAK	842,259	1,304,052	1,735,489	1,294,941	1,353,281	1,334,599	1,314,646	1,678,921	2,287,335	2,667,225
SEA	836,204	636,276	1,070,404	813,537	870,372	1,128,696	1,029,045	1,134,255	1,022,398	1,298,443
TEX	1,198,175	850,076	1,154,432	1,363,469	1,102,471	1,112,497	1,692,002	1,763,053	1,581,901	2,043,993
TOR	1,400,327	755,083	1,275,978	1,930,415	2,110,009	2,468,925	2,455,477	2,778,429	2,595,175	3,375,883
TOT	21,890,052	14,065,986	23,080,449	23,991,053	23,961,427	24,532,225	25,172,732	27,277,351	28,499,636	29,849,262
NATIONAL LEAGUE										
ATL	1,048,411	535,418	1,801,985	2,119,935	1,724,892	1,350,137	1,387,181	1,217,402	848,089	984,930
CHI	1,206,776	565,637	1,249,278	1,479,717	2,107,655	2,161,534	1,859,102	2,035,130	2,089,034	2,491,942
CIN	2,022,450	1,093,730	1,326,528	1,190,419	1,275,887	1,834,619	1,692,432	2,185,205	2,072,528	1,979,320
HOU	2,278,217	1,321,282	1,558,555	1,351,962	1,229,862	1,184,314	1,734,276	1,909,902	1,933,505	1,834,908
LA	3,249,287	2,381,292	3,608,881	3,510,313	3,134,824	3,264,593	3,023,208	2,797,409	2,980,262	2,944,653
MON	2,208,175	1,534,564	2,318,292	2,320,651	1,606,531	1,502,494	1,128,981	1,850,324	1,478,659	1,783,533
NY	1,192,073	704,244	1,323,036	1,112,774	1,842,695	2,761,601	2,767,601	3,034,129	3,055,445	2,918,710
PHI	2,651,650	1,638,752	2,376,394	2,128,339	2,062,693	1,830,350	1,933,335	2,100,110	1,990,041	1,861,985
PIT	1,646,757	541,789	1,024,106	1,225,916	773,500	735,900	1,000,917	1,161,193	1,866,713	1,374,141
STL	1,385,147	1,010,247	2,111,906	2,317,914	2,037,448	2,637,563	2,471,974	3,072,122	2,892,799	3,080,980
SD	1,139,026	519,161	1,607,516	1,539,815	1,983,904	2,210,352	1,805,716	1,454,061	1,506,896	2,009,031
SF	1,096,115	632,274	1,200,948	1,251,530	1,001,545	818,697	1,528,748	1,917,168	1,785,297	2,059,701
TOT	21,124,084	12,478,390	21,507,425	21,549,285	20,781,436	22,292,154	22,333,471	24,734,155	24,499,268	25,323,834
ML	43,014,136	26,544,376	44,587,874	45,540,338	44,742,863	46,824,379	47,506,203	52,011,506	52,998,904	55,173,096

	1990	1991	1992	1993	1994
AMERICAN LEAGUE					
BAL	2,415,189	2,552,753	3,567,819	3,644,965	2,535,359
BOS	2,528,986	2,562,435	2,468,574	2,422,021	1,775,826
CAL	2,555,688	2,416,236	2,065,444	2,057,460	1,512,622
CHI	2,002,357	2,934,154	2,681,156	2,581,091	1,697,398
CLE	1,225,240	1,051,863	1,224,094	2,177,908	1,995,174
DET	1,495,785	1,641,661	1,423,963	1,971,421	1,184,783
KC	2,244,956	2,161,537	1,867,689	1,934,578	1,400,494
MIL	1,752,900	1,478,729	1,857,351	1,688,080	1,268,397
MIN	1,751,584	2,293,842	2,482,428	2,048,673	1,398,565
NY	2,006,436	1,863,733	1,748,737	2,416,942	1,675,557
OAK	2,900,217	2,713,493	2,494,160	2,035,025	1,242,692
SEA	1,509,727	2,147,905	1,651,367	2,052,638	1,103,798
TEX	2,057,911	2,297,720	2,198,231	2,244,616	2,502,538
TOR	3,885,284	4,001,527	4,028,318	4,057,947	2,907,933
TOT	30,332,260	32,117,588	31,759,331	33,333,365	24,201,136
NATIONAL LEAGUE					
ATL	980,129	2,140,217	3,077,400	3,884,720	2,539,240
CHI	2,243,791	2,314,250	2,126,720	2,653,763	1,845,208
CIN	2,400,892	2,372,377	2,315,946	2,453,232	1,897,681
COL				4,483,350	3,281,511
FLA				3,064,847	1,937,467
HOU	1,310,927	1,196,152	1,211,412	2,084,618	1,561,136
LA	3,002,396	3,348,170	2,473,266	3,170,393	2,279,355
MON	1,373,087	934,742	1,669,127	1,641,437	1,276,250
NY	2,732,745	2,284,484	1,779,534	1,873,183	1,151,471
PHI	1,992,484	2,050,012	1,927,448	3,137,674	2,290,971
PIT	2,049,908	2,065,302	1,829,395	1,650,593	1,222,520
STL	2,573,225	2,448,699	2,418,483	2,844,977	1,866,544
SD	1,856,396	1,804,289	1,721,406	1,375,432	953,857
SF	1,975,528	1,737,478	1,560,998	2,606,354	1,704,608
TOT	24,491,508	24,696,172	24,111,135	36,924,573	25,807,819
ML	54,823,768	56,813,760	55,870,466	70,257,938	50,008,955

CHAPTER 5

The True Father of Baseball

John Thorn

The history of baseball is a lie from beginning to end, from its creation myth to its rosy models of commerce, community, and fair play. The game's epic feats and revered figures, its pieties about racial harmony and bleacher democracy, its artful blurring of sport and business—all of it is bunk, tossed up with a wink and a nudge. Yet Abner Doubleday, for example, will not be consigned to the dustbin of baseball history no matter how convincingly one argues that he did not invent baseball.

But if the history of baseball is a lie, it is a glorious, vibrant and, in the grand scheme of life, harmless lie, gripping us in a way that good, gray fact seldom can. The bearer of fact cannot hope to annihilate the legends in baseball's Elysian Fields, but simply to play alongside them, occasionally getting a turn at bat.

I believe that the conventional tale of the game's birth is substantially incorrect. By this I refer not to the Doubleday fable, pointless to attack, but to the scarcely less legendary development of the Knickerbocker game, ostensibly sired by Alexander Cartwright.

Let's look at the delicate condition of baseball's paternity. There would have been no need to establish Alexander Cartwright as a baseball deity had the Mills Commission report of 1907—created by Albert Spalding not to explore the origins of the game but to confirm its American roots—not named Abner Doubleday the father of the game; however, the absurdity of the Doubleday claim agitated Cartwright's son Bruce so much that he protested to Spalding, and to *Collier's* writer Will Irwin, that baseball did not exist before the advent of Cartwright and the Knickerbocker Base Ball Club of New York City. This claim came at a time when men were still alive who had seen some rural variant of baseball in the 1820s or 1830s or who had even played baseball in an urban setting with one of the several ball clubs that had preceded the formation of the Knicks in 1845, such as the New York Base Ball Club, the Brooklyn Ball Club, the Eagles of New York, or the Olympics of Philadelphia.

Earlier histories of baseball—from those published annually by Henry Chadwick in the Beadle, DeWitt, and Spalding Guides to book-length histories such as Charles Peverelly's *Book of American Pastimes* (1866) and Jacob Morse's *Sphere and Ash* (1888)—gave credit to the Knickerbockers for the eventual ascendance of the New York Game of baseball over the competing Massachusetts Game, but did not single out Cartwright as the sole creator. In 1860, in the premier edition of the Beadle *Dime Base Ball Player,* Chadwick acknowledged the existence of the New York Base Ball Club prior to the organization of the Knicks, but stated "we shall not be far wrong if we award to the Knickerbocker the honor of being the pioneers of the present game of base ball." Still, he never swerved from his assertion in that same essay that it was rounders, the English childhood game, "from which base ball is derived." Only in the next century did Cartwright become—no less than Doubleday—a tool of those who wished to establish baseball as the product of an identifiable spark of American ingenuity, without foreign or Darwinian taint.

What *did* Cartwright do? He suggested that the Knickerbockers, who had been playing informally since at least 1842, be organized as a club, with a constitution and playing rules that he did much to formulate (although not alone—three other Knickerbockers were equally involved in drafting the original fourteen playing rules). Notable among these rules—which simply codified the game that the Knicks were already playing—were the laying out of baseball on a "diamond" rather than a square, the concept of foul territory, and the elimination of the rounders and town-ball practice of retiring a runner by throwing the ball *at* him. These are critical differences from earlier games, sufficient in and of themselves to term the Knickerbocker game a landmark in the evolution of baseball. But what Cartwright assuredly did *not* do was any of the three central things credited to him on his plaque in the Baseball Hall of Fame: "Set bases 90 feet apart. Established 9 innings as a game and 9 players as a team." (More on this in a moment.) He also did not create the forty-five-foot pitching distance, nor the requirement that a ball be caught on the fly to register an out, nor a system for calling balls and strikes.

The truth of the paternity question? Eighty-year-old Henry Chadwick had it right when he said in 1904, only one year before the formation of the Mills Commission, "Like Topsy, baseball never had no 'fadder'; it jest growed." In fact, until Papa Doubleday was pulled out of the hat, it was Chadwick himself who had most frequently been honored with the sobriquet "Father of Baseball," not for any powers of invention but for his role in popularizing and shaping the game. Others to have been accorded patriarchal honors were Harry Wright, who organized the first openly professional team; Albert Spalding, the tireless player, magnate, and tour promoter; William Hulbert, founder of the National League in 1876; and Daniel L. Adams, whose name today is scarcely known. Allow me to introduce him.

Daniel Lucius Adams was born on November 1, 1814, in Mt. Vernon, New Hampshire, the younger of two sons of Dr. Daniel Adams and Nancy Mulliken Adams. He spent his first two years of college at Amherst, then graduated from Yale in 1835. Afterwards came a medical degree from Harvard in 1838, then a general practice in New York City, coupled with an active involvement with treating the poor at the New York Dispensaries. He resided and practiced at 14 Bond Street.

"Doc" Adams, as he was known to all, began to play baseball in 1839. "I was always interested in athletics while in college and afterward," he told an interviewer at the age of eighty-one, "and soon after going to New York I began to play base ball just for exercise, with a number of other young medical men. Before that there had been a club called the New York Base Ball Club, but it had no very definite organization and did not last long. Some of the younger members of that club got together and formed the Knickerbocker Base Ball Club, September 24, 1845 [actually September 23]. The players included merchants, lawyers, Union Bank clerks [like Cartwright], insurance clerks and others who were at liberty after 3 o'clock in the afternoon. They went into it just for exercise and enjoyment, and I think they used to get a good deal more solid fun out of it than the players in the big games do nowadays.

"About a month after the organization of this club, several of us medical fellows joined it, myself among the number. The following year I was made President and served as long as I was willing to retain the office."

What's new here? Plenty. According to Adams, the New York Base Ball Club not only preceded the Knickerbocker, but formed it; for example, such early New York Base Ball Club members as James Lee, Abraham Tucker, and William Wheaton all became Knickerbockers in 1845–1846. As early as 1840, Adams played a game in New York that he understood to be baseball. It was the same game as that played by the men who would become the Knickerbockers, played on a square, at first with eleven men on a side, as in cricket and perhaps the Massachusetts Game. This game—called base ball and not rounders or town ball—was played in New York City as early as 1832 by two clubs, one composed of residents of the first ward (the lower part of the city), the other in the upper part of the city (ninth and fifteenth wards). By 1843, when the Knicks were still playing at their original site in Madison Square, the teams had been reduced to eight—which included a "pitch," a "behind," three basemen and three in the field—and the playing field had been changed from a square to a diamond, as in rounders. According to Alphonse Martin, a prominent pitcher in the 1860s who left an unpublished manuscript "History of Base Ball," it was Cartwright who prompted this move. In later years, when asked how the game of baseball originated, Doc Adams declined to identify a distinct starting point; he believed it grew from rounders.

Actually, baseball as played by the Knicks in the years 1845–1849 (Cartwright left for California in the gold-rush spring of 1849) was almost never a nine-man game—eight, ten, and eleven were all more frequently employed numbers to the side. Play was conducted in accord with Cartwright's model of only three basemen, and on the rare occasions when nine or more fielding positions were created by a surfeit of players, the "extras" were put into the outfield. In a game in late May 1847, for example, when eleven men were available to each side, the Knickerbockers' response was to play with nine, including four outfielders, and hold two men out as substitutes.

The advent of the short fielder, or shortstop, was a crucial break with rounders, and this position was created in 1849 or 1850 by Adams. "I used to play shortstop," he reminisced, "and I believe I was the first one to occupy that place, as it had formerly been left uncovered." But when Adams first went out to short, it was not to bolster the infield but to assist in relays from the outfield. The early Knickerbocker ball was so light that it could not be thrown even 200 feet; thus the need for a short fielder to send the ball in to the pitcher's point.

"We had a great deal of trouble in getting balls made," Adams recalled, "and for six or seven years I made all the balls myself, not only for our club but also for other clubs when they were organized. [He also supervised the turning of the bats during this period.] I went all over New York to find someone who would undertake this work, but no one could be induced to try it for love or money. Finally I found a Scotch saddler who was able to show me a good way to cover the balls with horsehide, such as was used for whip lashes. I used to make the stuffing out of three or four ounces of rubber cuttings, wound with yarn and then covered with the leather. Those balls were, of course, a great deal softer than the balls now in use."

When the ball was wound tighter, gaining more hardness and resilience, it could be hit farther and, crucially, thrown farther. This permitted the shortstop to come into the infield, which Adams did. Even more important, the introduction of the hard ball permitted a change in the dimensions of the playing field. The Knickerbocker rules of 1845 had specified no pitching distance, and no baseline length; all that was indicated was: "from 'home' to second base, forty-two paces; from first to third base, forty-two paces, equidistant." It has been presumed by scholars that when a three-foot pace is plugged in, the resulting baselines of eighty-nine feet are close enough to the present ninety so that we can proclaim Cartwright's genius. In fact, the pace in 1845 was either an imprecise and variable measure—to gauge distances by "stepping off"—or precisely two and a half feet, in which case the distance from home to second would have been 105 feet and the Cartwright basepaths would have been 74.25 feet. The pace of 1845 could not have been interpreted as the equivalent of three feet. The alternate definition of a pace as a three-foot measure did not come into practice until much later in the century. (Here is the definition of a pace from An American Dictionary of the English Language, by Noah Webster, 1828: Pace: "1. A step. 2. The space between the two feet in walking, estimated at two feet and a half. But the geometrical pace is five feet, or the whole space passed over by the same foot from one step to another." This definition was not changed for Webster's 1853 revised edition.)

My research indicates that 75-foot basepaths were the norm well into the mid-1850s—when the basepaths were first prescribed as "42 paces or yards"—and were the standard for youth play well into the next decade.

In 1848 Adams, as Knickerbocker president, headed the Committee to Revise the Constitution and By-Laws; Alexander Cartwright served under him. Adams' interest in refining the rules of the game, already evident, was further piqued by the formation of additional clubs, beginning with the Washington Base Ball Club in 1850, which was constructed around several former New York

Base Ball Club members. In 1852 the Washingtons were renamed the Gothams and took in additional players, and the Eagle Club, which had been organized to play town ball in 1840, reconstituted itself to become the Eagle Base Ball Club. "The playing rules remained very crude up to this time," Adams said, "but in 1853 the three clubs united in a revision of the rules and regulations. At the close of 1856 there were twelve clubs in existence, and it was decided to hold a convention of delegates from all of these for the purpose of establishing a permanent code of rules by which all should be governed. A call was therefore issued, signed by the officers of the Knickerbocker Club as the senior organization, and the result was the assembling of the first convention of base ball players in May, 1857. I was elected presiding officer." It was at this meeting, eight years after Cartwright's western expedition, that the winner of a game was defined as the team that was ahead at the conclusion of nine innings, rather than the first team to score twenty-one runs. "In March of the next year the second convention was held, and at this meeting the annual convention was declared a permanent organization, and with the requisite constitution and by-laws became the 'National Association of Ball Players.'

"I was chairman of the Committee on Rules and Regulations from the start and so long as I retained membership. I presented the first draft of rules, prepared after much careful study of the matter, and it was in the main adopted. The distance between bases I fixed at 30 yards—the only previous determination of distance being 'the bases shall be from home to second base 42 paces, from first to third base 42 paces equidistant'—which was rather vague. In every meeting of the National Association while a member, I advocated the fly-game—that is, not to allow first-bound catches—but I was always defeated on the vote. The change was made, however, soon after I left, as I predicted in my last speech on the subject before the convention.

"The distance from home to pitcher's base I made 45 feet. Many of the old rules, such as those defining a foul, remain substantially the same today," he concluded in 1896, "while others are changed and, of course, many new ones added. I resigned in 1862, but not before thousands were present to witness matches, and any number of outside players standing ready to take a hand on regular playing days." In the 1840s players could not be relied upon to show up for practice. Adams recalled that the Knickerbockers frequently went to Hoboken to find only two or three members present, and were often obliged to take their exercise "in the form of 'old cat,' 'one' or 'two' as the case might be." But, he summed up in 1896, "we pioneers never expected to see the game so universal as it has now become."

On May 7, 1861, Adams married Cornelia A. Cook. Less than a year later he resigned from the Knickerbocker Base Ball Club, and in 1865 he retired from his practice in New York and moved to Ridgefield, Connecticut. He played his last formal game of baseball on September 27, 1875, in an oldtimers' contest arranged by longtime Knickerbocker comrade James Whyte Davis. Adams played backyard ball with his sons even into his eighth decade, when he moved his family to New Haven, where the boys attended Sheffield Scientific School. On January 3, 1899, Daniel Lucius Adams died in his home at 146 Edwards Street.

Success has many fathers, failure none. For his role in making baseball the success it is, Doc Adams may be counted as first among the Fathers of Baseball.

## CHAPTER 6

The Evolution of the Baseball Diamond

Tom Shieber

The modern baseball diamond has such familiar features as the coach's boxes, the catcher's box, the three-foot first base line, and so on; but its key components have always been the batter's box, the pitcher's mound, and the bases. By studying these three fundamental elements, one can trace the evolution of the baseball diamond.

What *is* the baseball diamond? More easily addressed is what the baseball diamond is not, for its shape does not conform to that of a geometrical diamond. A geometrical diamond is a four-sided figure, each side of equal length, with two acute angles and two obtuse angles. The baseball "diamond" is really a square, with each of its corners forming a ninety-degree angle. In fact, the shape of the infield has been the same ever since the rules of baseball were first published, one hundred fifty years ago. The term "diamond" was used early in the history of the game to differentiate the infield configuration of the "New York" version of the game of baseball from that used in the "Massachusetts" Game. In the New York Game, the batter stood at home base, which was located at the bottom corner of the infield. Looking toward fair territory, he would view a diamond-shaped infield. In contrast, the batter in the Massachusetts game was positioned at a point between the first and fourth bases, from which he would view a rectangular infield.

In 1845 the New York Knickerbocker Base Ball Club created the first codified set of baseball rules. The rules were twenty in number, fourteen pertaining to the playing of the game and six concerning club matters. Of the fourteen game rules, only the first related to the layout of the playing field: "The bases shall be from 'home' to second base, forty-two paces; from first to third base, forty-two paces, equidistant." By the mid-1850s, the batter's and pitcher's positions were noted in the rules, though only in rudimentary form: "The striker's stand is at the Home Base" and the distance "from 'Home' to pitcher [shall be] not less than fifteen paces." Thus, within the first decade of formal baseball rules, the three main components of the baseball diamond had been addressed.

The New Rules of 1857

At the first convention of baseball players, in 1857, the Knickerbocker rules were completely rewritten and reorganized. The rule that set the distance between opposite bases on the infield at forty-two paces was replaced by a new rule that called for the bases to be located "upon the four corners of a square, whose sides are respectively thirty yards." At the same time, the rule setting the pitching distance at fifteen paces from home was only slightly modified, essentially substituting the word "yard" for "pace." In making these particular changes, the members of the Rules Committee consciously avoided the word "pace." It is not clear that by changing the measure from "pace" to "yard" the new rules changed the size of the infield or the length of the pitching distance; scholars continue to debate the point of whether the pace was understood to be two-and-a-half feet or three feet. According to Daniel Lucius Adams, 1845 Knickerbocker club member and 1857 president of what would later be known as the National Association of Base Ball Players, the rules were rewritten to clarify the distances on the ball field, the word "pace" being "rather vague." (See "The True Father of Baseball," in this volume.)

The new rules of 1857 also defined more clearly the batter's and pitcher's positions and the size and shape of the bases. The bases were to "be so constructed as to be distinctly seen by the umpires and referee, and must cover a space equal to one square foot of surface; the first, second, and third bases shall be canvas bags, painted white, and filled with sand or saw-dust. . . ." In the 1860 *Beadle's Dime Base Ball Player*, editor Henry Chadwick elaborated on some of the rules of the game. He advised against filling bases with sand, as this made them unwieldy and quite heavy. By 1866, the rule was reworded to require only that the bases be "filled with some soft material."

Chadwick also stated that "the proper size of a base is about fourteen inches by seventeen; but as long as it covers one square foot of ground . . . the requirements of the rules will be fulfilled." Note that the rule required the base to "cover," not necessarily *be*, one square foot of surface. Thus, by Chadwick's interpretation of the rule, any base that covered an area greater than or equal to one square foot was acceptable. There is no evidence that Chadwick's rectangular bases were ever used.

The rules of 1857 also required that "the home base and pitcher's point . . . be each marked by a flat circular iron plate, painted or enameled white . . ." Though the size of these plates was not noted in the official rules, Chadwick stated that they were to be "not less than nine inches in diameter." Unfortunately, there are no surviving examples of a circular home plate or pitcher's point, though drawings and photographs show that they were commonly used.

The 1857 rules also stipulated that the pitcher deliver the ball from behind "a line four yards in length, drawn at right angles to a line from home to the second base."

Chadwick suggested marking this line with a six-foot long, two-inch wide piece of wood inserted into the ground, but it is unknown whether or not such a device was ever actually employed. The only required marker for the pitcher's position was the circular pitcher's point, placed at the center of the pitcher's line.

The pitcher's line should not be construed as an early form of the pitcher's rubber, as it was from *behind* this line that the pitcher was required to deliver the ball. Stepping beyond the line while in the act of pitching constituted a balk. However, the pitcher was not required to deliver the ball from directly behind the *center* of the line. For example, it was perfectly legal to pitch the ball from behind either extreme end of the line. This flexibility in the pitcher's delivery point gave the defense an advantage not found in today's game. The pitcher might pitch from the first base side of the line when an opposing left-hander was at bat. This tactic made it more likely that the batter would hit the ball to the first or second baseman, or into foul territory. The foul ball in baseball of this era was much more significant than it is today. During these early years, the batter could be retired on a foul ball caught on the fly *or* after the first bound. The fair territory bound-out was eliminated in 1865, but the foul-territory bound-out remained in vogue until the early 1880s.

In the modern game, a baserunner is allowed a leisurely return to his base after an uncaught foul ball; a baserunner of this early era had to return to his base quickly, because the ball was in play as soon as it was back in the hands of the pitcher (wherever the pitcher might be). The importance of this rule was well illustrated in an article in the 1869 *DeWitt's Guide*:

> When a foul ball has been hit, [the pitcher] should place himself in readiness to receive the ball as near any portion of the field as could render it serviceable in putting out any player who might be running the bases. For instance: Suppose a player is running from first base to second base at the time a foul ball is struck; if the ball be hit toward first base, the pitcher's play should be to take possession of the base—and there receive the ball, in which case the ball would be "alive" as soon as the pitcher had secured it, and by holding it on the base before the player could return, the latter would be put out. If the ball were knocked "foul" in any other direction, the pitcher should place himself in such a position that he could receive the ball and pass it quickly to any point at which it could be made effective.

With regard to the batter's position, the new rules of 1857 required the batter to stand on a line that extended three feet on either side of home base, the line being parallel to the pitcher's line. This defining feature of the batter's position was known as the line of the home base.

Though not stipulated in the rules, "Father" Chadwick suggested that the playing surface be level. However, a higher area or "mound" for the pitcher to pitch from would not necessarily have been an advantage at the time, since underhand pitching was still a requirement. Nevertheless, by this time swift pitching had been introduced to the game of baseball.

The pitcher most often credited with popularizing what was known as "speed" pitching is Jim Creighton. Creighton used a technically illegal snap of his wrist in his delivery, which caused the ball to speed to the plate much quicker than the commonly pitched ball. A number of pitchers were able to mimic this technique, but most sacrificed control. Creighton's talent was that he managed to maintain velocity *and* accuracy. At the time, the rules of the game did not allow a pitcher to "jerk" or "throw" the ball, but the wrist snap was difficult to discern and the pitch was allowed. If there is one thing that has been true of baseball since its very inception, it is that players will push the limit of, find loopholes in, and subtly break the rules. Pitching rules were no exception.

The 1860s

In 1863, the pitcher's position was redefined. The pitcher was required to deliver the ball from within an area defined by "two lines, four yards in length, drawn at right angles to a line from home to second base, having their centers on that line at two fixed iron plates placed at points fifteen and sixteen yards distant from the home base. The pitcher must stand within the lines, and must deliver the ball as near as possible over the center of the home base, and for the striker." It was also required that the pitcher have both feet in contact with the ground when delivering the ball. While the rule required only a front and back line for the pitcher's position, it marked the beginning of the pitcher's box. A box of some size would define the pitcher's position for the next thirty years.

During the early 1860s, a number of pitchers, in order to compensate for their inability to master Creighton's technique of accurate speed pitching, resorted to a pitching style characterized by intimidation. These pitchers threw *at* rather than *for* the batter. It was hoped that the more restrictive pitching rules of 1863 would check this technique, as well as decrease pitching speed. However, a new rule introduced that same season was more effective: it allowed the umpire to identify wide pitches as balls, and, when the pitcher repeatedly failed to pitch fairly, the batter was entitled to first base. (Interestingly, the rule awarding first base to a batter hit by a pitched ball was not introduced into the rules until the mid-1880s.)

In 1866, the pitcher's position was enlarged. The rear pitcher's line was moved back a foot so that the box was twelve feet wide by four feet deep. This spacious pitcher's box lasted only a single season. In 1867 the box was narrowed to six feet wide by four feet deep, half its previous size.

Before 1867, diagrams of the baseball diamond in newspapers and books did not accurately represent the ball field. Curlicues, asterisks, and other symbols were used to represent the bases, and often the infield was not shown to be square. The 1867 *Beadle's Guide* included a new, truly representational diagram of the baseball diamond. Home base was a circle, and the other bases were squares. Each base was shown centered on its corner of the infield square. Curiously, instead of having their sides parallel to the base lines, the first, second, and third bases were oriented such that two corners of each base touched the base lines. In other words, each base was rotated forty-five degrees from its more familiar, present-day orientation. While this orientation and positioning of the bases was implied in the diagram, it was not explicitly stated in the rules.

In 1867, the rule regarding the batter's position was amended. The batter was barred from taking a step forward or backward while in the act of striking. Thus, his feet had to remain in contact with the ground with one or both feet fixed on the line of the home base. The introduction of this rule was principally aimed at eliminating the backward step, which seems implausible today but was strategically related to the definition of foul balls at the time: if a ball initially hit the ground in foul territory, it was a foul ball, no matter whether the ball remained in foul territory or eventually ended up in fair territory (likewise, a ball hitting once in fair territory was a fair ball, even if it bounded off into foul ground). If the batter were allowed a backward step while in the act of hitting, balls chopped straight downward would more likely hit in foul territory than fair territory and thus be declared foul balls. If such a hit was unintentional, then the batter would not be subject to an easy putout at first base. If done intentionally, the technique might delay the game and wear out the pitcher until the batter received a pitch that he liked (foul balls were not counted as strikes until the start of the twentieth century). The rule disallowing a backward step in batting reduced the likelihood of both of these scenarios.

The following year, the rule requiring the pitcher to keep both feet on the ground was eliminated. Along with this change, the rule defining the batter's position was also altered. The batter, "when about to strike the ball, must stand astride of a line drawn through the center of the home base, not exceeding three feet from either side thereof . . . and he must not take any backward step when striking at the ball." This completely changed the purpose of the line of the home base. The batter was now required to stand *astride*, not *on*, the line. The penalty for a violation of this rule was the calling of a strike, though this type of strike was counted separately from the more familiar swing-and-miss strike. The violation would later be termed a "foul strike" but not did not signify the same thing as that term does today; it was akin to a pitcher's balk. If three such "foul strikes" were called, the batter was out.

In 1868, the words "circular iron" were dropped from the rule defining the home base and pitcher's points. With this subtle alteration of the rules, the shape of home base changed from a circle to a square. Like the first, second, and third bases, home was also required to "cover a space equal to one square foot of surface." The shape of the pitcher's points were now square, as well. The following year, Henry Chadwick suggested that these points be "about half the size of the home base plate. But it was not until 1874 that the exact size and shape of the pitcher's points would be explicitly stated in the rules, the plates being defined as six inches square.

The diagram in the 1868 *Beadle's Guide* failed to reflect the changes in the shapes of home base and the pitcher's points. While the *Beadle's* diagram of the following year corrected the mistake with regard to home base, the pitcher's points continued to be erroneously represented as being circular. And later, when the positions of the pitcher's points were altered and the number

of points increased, the *Beadle's* diagram still showed two circular pitcher's points centered on the front and rear lines of the box.

Though the official rules still failed to stipulate the exact positioning of the bases on the infield square, the 1869 *Beadle's* diagram implied that, unlike the first, second, and third bases, home base was to be oriented with its sides parallel to the baselines. Also, though no longer technically required to be made of iron, it is most likely that iron remained the material of choice for the home base and pitcher's points.

In 1869, the pitcher's position was resized for the fourth time in just seven seasons. This time the box was enlarged to six feet square, "so as to give [the pitcher] ample room for his preliminary movements in delivering the ball." This change apparently met with some approval, as the size of the box was not altered again for another ten years.

The 1870s

In 1870, a section was added to the rules calling for the lines of both "the striker's and pitcher's positions [to be] marked by the use of chalk, or other suitable material, so as to be distinctly seen by the umpire." Previous to this rule, the only lines specified to be marked with chalk were the foul lines, a requirement under the rules since 1861.

The year 1871 was the inaugural season of the National Association, the first professional baseball league. An addition to the rules for that season required that the batter remain at least one foot from the home base when at bat. The restriction barring the batter from taking a backward step was removed, though the batter still had to keep one foot on either side of the line of the home base.

The mid-1870s saw the introduction of a number of new rules addressing the exact placement of the bases and the pitcher's box on the baseball diamond. In 1874, the orientation of the home base was stated in the rules for the first time: Home base was required to have "one corner of it facing the pitcher's position." This placement gave the pitcher the greatest width of the plate over which to deliver the ball: seventeen inches from corner to corner. If the plate were oriented with a flat side facing the pitcher, the width of the strike zone would be just twelve inches. For the same season, the exact positioning of the home, first, and third (but not second) bases was implied in a new foul line rule: "The foul ball lines shall be unlimited in length, and shall run from the center of the home base through the center of the first and the third base to the foul ball posts. . . ." Thus, as had long been implied in diagrams of the ball field, each base was required to be centered on its corner of the infield square.

In 1874, the rule defining the placement of the pitcher's position was reworded to define more clearly its location on the baseball diamond. The front line of the pitcher's box was required to be forty-five feet from the center of the home base. Previously, the word "center" was not included in this rule, thus allowing as much as a seventeen-inch leeway in the positioning of the pitcher's box.

In 1872, two additional pitcher's points were required to mark the front corners of the pitcher's box, the plates that marked the centers of the front and rear pitcher's lines remaining unchanged. However, two years later, the four pitcher's points were rearranged such that each corner of the box was marked by a six-inch square plate.

The most important change made to the baseball diamond in 1874 was the introduction of the batter's box. Under the new rule, the batter was no longer required to keep one foot on either side of the line of home base, but was instead allowed to move and step however he pleased while confined "within a space of ground—located on either side of the home base—six feet long by three feet wide, extending three feet in front and behind of the line of the home base, and with its nearest line distant one foot from the home base." With this rule change, the line of the home base lost its original purpose and now served only to define the location of the batter's box.

In 1875, the foul ball rules prompted yet another change in the layout of the baseball diamond. The home base was moved from its location centered on the lower corner of the infield square to one wholly in foul territory, such that the front point of the home base "touch the foul ball lines where they meet at the home base corner." This amounted to a move of about eight and one-half inches. The repositioning of home base meant that the batter's box would be relocated, as well. However, since the batter's position was redefined in 1874 as "extending *two* feet in front of and *four* feet behind of the line of the home base," the batter's box was moved not eight and one-half inches, but over twenty inches away from fair territory. To further discourage the batter from stepping outside the lines of his position, he was now called out after only two foul strikes were called. The idea behind these changes was to make it more difficult for the batter to successfully perform what was known as a "fair-foul hit."

To execute a fair-foul hit, the batter hit the ball such that it first touched the ground in fair territory and then bounded into foul territory. Under the rules of the day, this was a fair ball. Dickey Pearce and Ross Barnes were known to be quite skilled at this hitting technique. The ramifications of the fair-foul hit were far reaching. Often the fielders would have to run a great distance into foul territory to retrieve these fair-foul hits. To shorten this distance, the first and third basemen would play quite close to the foul lines, which subsequently opened up large gaps in the infield and allowed what would otherwise be easy groundouts to penetrate the infield as hits. Chadwick, among others, was eager to lessen the impact of the fair-foul hit. He proposed adding a tenth man (or "right shortstop") to each team so that the large gaps in the infield would be filled. Chadwick popularized this idea by writing special sections in both the *Beadle's* and *DeWitt's* guides of 1874 suggesting the implementation of the ten-man rule. However, though Chadwick continued to lobby for the extra man well into the 1880s, and the experiment was tried in nonleague contests, the ten-man game was never adopted into the official rules of baseball. As it turned out, the move of home base to foul territory did not successfully check the "problem" of fair-foul hitting. Neither did the 1876 rule of reducing the number of foul strikes allowed to just one before the batter was called out. It was not until 1877, when the rules defining fair and foul balls were changed to essentially those of the modern era, that the fair-foul hit was eliminated from the game altogether.

The move of home base to foul territory in 1875 not only affected the position of the batter's box, but that of the pitcher's box as well. Since the front line of the pitcher's position was required to be forty-five feet from the center of the home base, the entire pitcher's box was required to move toward the lower end of the infield by eight and one-half inches.

A number of significant changes occurred to the layout of the baseball diamond in 1877. With the demise of the fair-foul hit, home base was once again repositioned. This time it was moved forward seventeen inches such that it lay wholly in fair territory, two sides of the base laying flush with the foul lines at home. As it did two years earlier, the relocation of the home base once again affected the positions of both the pitcher's and batter's boxes. As noted in the 1877 *DeWitt's Guide*: "The line of the home base . . . has been moved further forward with the base, but as the pitcher's position is measured from the centre of the base it follows that the pitcher's place has been moved back too."

The batter's position was moved with the relocation of home base as well; but, as was the case in 1875, the move was complicated by a change in the layout of the batter's box. This time the box reverted back to its original dimensions of three feet in front and three feet in back of the home base line. Thus, the batter's box moved toward second base an extra foot beyond the seventeen-inch move of home base. In summary, home base and the pitcher's box each moved toward second base by seventeen inches, while the batter's box moved toward second base a total of twenty-nine inches.

In 1877, the size of the first, second, and third bases was increased to fifteen square inches. The larger base helped guard against possible injury due to, for example, a runner stepping on a baseman's foot during a force play. Home base, however, remained a twelve-inch square, as a change in its size would have greatly altered the strike zone.

The year 1877 was also the first in which a major baseball annual showed the bases oriented such that their sides were parallel to the base lines. The diagrams in both the *Spalding* and *DeWitt's* guides showed this orientation, though the *Beadle's* diagram continued to show the bases with their corners touching the base lines. Nevertheless, the rules still did not specify the precise orientation of the first, second, and third bases.

In 1879 the size of the pitcher's box was altered for the first time in over a decade. The box was reduced in size such that it covered an area four feet wide by six feet long. This was the same size as it was in 1867 and 1868, but rotated by ninety degrees. The change was made to lessen the advantage the pitcher gained by pitching from an extreme side of the box. When the change was first proposed in the meeting of the Rules Committee, Boston manager Harry Wright spoke out against it. He claimed that the narrower box would adversely affect his star pitcher Tommy Bond. Bond was the dominant pitcher of the era, having led the National League in wins, winning percentage, and strikeouts in each of the previous two seasons. But Wright's complaint against the smaller pitcher's box backfired, as delegates of the Rules Committee from other teams, quite willing to hinder Bond in any way possible, heartily endorsed the change.

The following season Bond, apparently unaffected by the narrower pitcher's box, compiled a record of 43-19 while allowing fewer than two earned runs per game. The strain of pitching over 2000 innings from 1876 to 1879 (almost 500 more than the next most active pitcher) eventually ruined Bond's arm. Over the final four years of his career, he struggled to a record of 39-47.

The 1880s

In 1880, the official rules of the game were extensively rewritten and rearranged. Though much of the wording regarding the diamond was altered, the state of the infield itself remained unchanged. However, the positioning of the first, second, and third bases was now made explicit: ". . . the center of each [base] shall be upon a separate corner of the infield. . . ."

In the 1881 *Spalding Guide*, Chadwick wrote that "while the art of pitching in baseball has rapidly approached the point of perfection of late years, skill in handling the bat, or what may be termed 'scientific batting,' has progressed but little in comparison." In the decade of professional league ball played since 1871, the average number of runs per game had been cut in half, the average number of strikeouts per game had more than quadrupled, and batting averages had dropped over forty points. To bolster the league's sagging offense, the distance between batter and pitcher was increased by five feet, the front line of the pitcher's box now being located "fifty feet from the center of the Home Base."

The increased distance between batter and pitcher did aid the offense, but the effect was short-lived. By 1884 in the National League and 1885 in the American Association, all restrictions regarding the pitcher's delivery were dropped. As long as the pitcher remained within the lines of the pitcher's box, he could throw overhand, underhand, or however he pleased.

With the legalization of overhand pitching, offense was once again imperiled. In 1885, to balance the greater freedom given the pitcher, the National League resized and relocated the batter's box for the batter's advantage. The new box was increased in size to six feet long by four feet wide, and was moved half a foot closer to home base. The American Association adopted this larger batter's box the following year, and this configuration retains its size, shape, and location today.

In 1886, both the National League and the American Association enlarged the pitcher's position by moving the rear line of the box back by one foot. For the same season, the American Association also added a unique feature to the pitcher's position: a smooth, flat stone slab, four foot by one foot in size, laid even with the playing surface and in front of the pitcher's box. This slab thus marked the front line of the pitcher's position, though it was located completely *outside* of the box. The slab was used to aid the umpire in determining whether or not the pitcher had illegally stepped beyond the front line of his position. When the National League and American Association adopted a uniform set of rules the following year, the rule requiring the stone slab was eliminated.

In 1887, a number of major rule changes affected the layout of the baseball diamond. The rear line of the pitcher's position was moved toward home base by one and one-half feet, resulting in a pitcher's box four feet wide by five and one-half feet deep, the smallest size in its history. The reduction in the size of the box was less restrictive to the pitcher than a new rule which required the pitcher to begin his delivery with one foot on the back line of the pitcher's position. After the meeting of the Rules Committee, *The Sporting News* commented: "The pitchers will not dance the Highland fling every time they deliver a ball next season." With the introduction of this rule, the back line of the pitcher's box, though marked only by chalk and pitcher's points, truly became the precursor of the present-day pitcher's rubber.

A number of pitchers suffered under this new restriction. Guy Hecker, who won 140 games and lost only 95 in his career before the rule change, had employed the use of a running start in his delivery. With the new rule, he quickly lost his effectiveness and was never again a dominant pitcher. Ed Morris, who compiled a three-year record of 114 wins to just 57 losses before 1887, used a skipping motion in his delivery. He dropped to 14-22 in his first season under the new rule (eventually, Morris adjusted to the rule change and regained some success before a sore arm ended his career). And Lady Baldwin, whose 42 wins in 1886 remains the single-season record for a lefthanded pitcher, could not adapt to the new pitching restriction and won only 19 more games in his career.

Another rule change for the 1887 season called for the first, second, and third bases to be "so placed that the center of the second base shall be upon its corner of the infield, and the center of the first and third bases shall be on the lines running to and from second base and seven and one-half inches from the foul lines, providing that each base be entirely within the foul lines." That is, the first and third bases were moved to positions completely in fair territory. But why change the positions of these bases? Once again, the reason is linked to the foul ball rules. Before 1887, a batted ball hitting the half of the base that was in fair territory was a fair ball, while a ball hitting the other half of the base was a foul ball. Under such circumstances, the umpire was faced with an exceedingly difficult decision. Moving first and third base completely into fair territory made the decision academic: if the ball hit the base, it must be a fair ball.

According to the exact wording of the rule, the first and third bases were to be positioned such that they straddle the baselines to and from second base. However, the diagram that accompanied the rules in the 1887 *Spalding* guide shows the bases positioned as they are today, neatly nestled in their respective corners of the ninety-foot infield square. The original intent of the rulemakers was for the bases to be laid out as shown in the diagram, but, as was often the case, the wording of the rule was rather poor. In 1894, the inconsistency was resolved by a new rule essentially stating that the diamond should be laid out in such a way that it looked like the supplied diagram.

It was not necessary to change the position of second base, as it had no bearing on fair and foul ball rules. So, to this day, second base remains "upon its corner of the infield," while the first and third bases lie wholly within the diamond. This rather strange positioning of second base is often overlooked in many modern-day representations of the baseball diamond. Even the cover of Macmillan's *The Baseball Encyclopedia* shows an infield diamond with second base erroneously placed entirely within the ninety-foot infield square.

The 1870s and 1880s saw a number of changes in the composition of the home base and pitcher's plates. Beginning with the rules of 1857, both the home base and pitcher's points were required to be made of iron. But a rule change for the season of 1872 called for home base to be made of white marble or stone, while three years later the pitcher's points were allowed to be made of *iron* or stone. In 1885, to curtail injuries due to a slippery home base, the American Association required home plate to be made of white rubber. The National League allowed for a choice of rubber or stone. When the two rival leagues adopted the same rule book in 1887, the rubber-only home base rule prevailed. Finally, in 1890, the pitcher's points also were required to be composed solely of rubber, and were further changed from squares to circles, six inches in diameter.

The 1890s

The Players League of 1890 adopted its own rule book, though it differed only slightly from that of the National League and American Association. However, for reasons that are unclear, the new league decided to alter the pitcher's position significantly. The length of the pitcher's box was increased by half a foot, thus reverting to the six by four foot pitcher's box last used in 1885. Furthermore, the front line of the box was moved back a foot such that it was located fifty-one feet from the center of home base. Finally, each corner of the box was marked with a "wooden peg fixed in the ground even with the surface." Why the league decided to revert to the larger pitcher's box, increase the pitching distance by a single foot, and substitute wooden pegs for rubber pitcher's points is a mystery. Even Chadwick was confused by the modifications to the pitcher's mound: "What advantage this change is to yield I cannot conceive."

After the 1892 season, there was general concern regarding the lack of offense in the game. The National League's batting average had dropped for four consecutive years, and the perception was that the delicate balance between offense and pitching/defense had tilted away from the batter. In the offseason, there was a great deal of discussion in the newspapers regarding two main ideas to balance the scales: increase the size of the diamond to ninety-three square feet, and move the pitcher back a distance from home base. While the former idea was almost universally discounted, it *was* endorsed by Chadwick and thus carried some weight. But, when the annual league meeting was held in March 1893, the decision went in favor of the latter idea.

Another concern voiced over the winter was that of the danger of high-speed overhand pitching. Up-and-coming "cyclone" pitchers such as Pink Hawley, Bill Hutchinson, and Jack Stivetts were throwing with exceptional speed, and were all too often wild. Moving the pitcher farther from the batter addressed this problem as well.

It was originally suggested by the Rules Committee that the pitcher be moved to a location at the exact center of the diamond, which would amount to a backward move of approximately seven-and-one-half feet. However, the move that was finally endorsed by the National League was somewhat less than this distance. As the story goes, it was decided to set the pitching distance to sixty feet from home base. A surveyor supposedly misread the blueprint notation of "60 feet 0 inches" as "60 feet 6 inches" and thus misplaced the pitcher's rubber. Like many of baseball's more colorful tales, this one proves to be false. Actually, it was just the reverse that occurred. The pitching distance was set to sixty feet six inches from home base and this value was incorrectly typeset as sixty feet *and no inches* on both the 1893 and 1894 *Spalding Guide* diagrams. The erroneous diagram was corrected for the 1895 guide.

But why change the pitching distance to such a strange number as sixty feet six inches? Sources frequently state that the 1893 pitching distance was simply increased by some ten feet, from fifty feet to sixty feet six inches. This presumption fails to take into account the pitching rules of the era.

Before 1887 the pitcher was required to pitch within the lines of his position. With regard to the pitching distance, the important feature of this rule was the requirement that the pitcher not step beyond the front line of the box, located fifty feet from home base. Thus, it is fair to state that the pitching distance at the time was fifty feet. However, beginning in 1887, the rules called for the pitcher to pitch with one foot on the rear line of the pitcher's box. With this change, the pitching distance was no longer defined by the front line of the pitcher's box, but by the pitcher's starting point at the rear line of the box. As the rear line of the pitcher's box was set five-and-one-half feet behind the front line, the pitching distance was now fifty-five feet six inches.

The pitching distance of sixty feet six inches resulted from the lines of the pitcher's position moving back five feet from home base. Or so it would seem. However, a subtle change in the wording of the rules complicated this move. Since 1874, the pitcher's box had been defined in terms of distances from the *center* of the home base. But the new rules for 1893 placed the pitcher's position sixty feet six inches from the *outer corner* of the home base. This amounts to a difference of eight and one-half inches. Thus, the pitcher's distance was moved back not five feet, but actually only four feet three and one-half inches.

Previously, the only time that league batting averages had dropped in four consecutive seasons was from 1877 to 1880, after which similar measures to those of 1893 were taken, the front line of the pitcher's box being moved back from forty-five to fifty feet. With both the move of 1881 and that of 1893, batting averages jumped. The increase from 1880 to 1881 was from an average of .245 to .260. But, the increase from 1892 to 1893 was even more dramatic: from an average of .245 to .280. And batting averages remained consistently above .270 for the rest of the century.

Along with the new pitching distance, the 1893 season also introduced the pitcher's plate or rubber. Essentially, the back line of the pitcher's box was replaced with a twelve-inch-wide by four-inch-deep rubber plate. The front and side lines of the box were eliminated altogether. The pitcher's box, though gone from baseball for over a century, remains a part of the language of the modern game. "A hit through the box" and "knocked out of the box" are terms still used to this day.

During the summer of 1893, a number of individuals expressed their belief that the heavy batting experienced that season was not due to pitchers having trouble adjusting to the lengthier pitching distance. Rather, they felt that pitchers were being hampered by the requirement that they pitch with one foot fixed at essentially a single point: the pitcher's rubber. Washington manager Jim O'Rourke agreed:

[The pitcher] hasn't got the whole county to work in now, as heretofore, when he could step in either side of the box and pitch a ball at an angle. Now he has got to stand right in front of you, and when he draws back his arm you know what is going to happen. . . . Now the pitcher is king no more. He is only an ordinary every-day individual, and as a result honors are divided among nine men, instead of one. . . .

Before the introduction of the pitcher's rubber, Silver King used to stride from the back left to front right corner of the box as part of his pitching delivery. But under the new rule, this pitching technique was abolished. King posted a 180-127 career record before 1893, but never again won more than 10 games in a season with the pitcher's rubber.

Early during the 1893 season, pitcher Bill Hutchinson stated that the increased pitching distance did not have much of an effect on him: "I use no more speed than usual with straight balls . . . but I have to put an extra twist on my curves. The pitcher who uses a slow curve is at a decided disadvantage. This class of pitchers will be affected. I like the new distance." For the three-year period from 1890 to 1892, Hutchinson had more National League wins than anyone (30 more than runner-up Amos Rusie). Hutchinson averaged 4.35 strikeouts per nine innings pitched and a 2.75 ERA. But in 1893 his record was 16-24, his ERA soared to 4.75, and his strikeouts per nine innings pitched dropped to just over 2. He never again regained the success he had enjoyed when pitching from the box.

Before the 1893 season, Tony Mullane said: "As far as I am concerned, personally, I can stand [the increased pitching distance] as well as the other pitchers." Nicknamed "The Apollo of the Box," Mullane enjoyed a record before 1893 of 289 wins against 187 losses with a 2.79 ERA. However, his status on the rubber was less than godlike: 25-33 with a 5.08 ERA. Other pitchers had similar problems. Yet, a number of pitchers, including Sadie McMahon, Kid Nichols, Amos Rusie, and Cy Young, adapted to or were unaffected by the change.

In 1894, a new diagram of the baseball diamond was included with the rules. The diagram was precisely labeled with multiple points and angles, and was accompanied with mathematical and geometrical descriptions of how the infield was to be laid out. Chadwick found the new, complicated diagram a bit ridiculous:

The diagram of the diamond needs a surveyor to lay it out so that it might be made comprehensible to amateurs and novices in the game. What with its "arcs" and its "radiuses" and its algebraic style of descrip-

tion, it is likely to be a greek puzzle to foreign votaries of the game.

With the 1894 diagram and rules, the exact orientation of the bases was made explicit for the first time: the sides of each base were oriented such that they lay parallel to the baselines.

In 1895, the pitcher's rubber was enlarged to its current dimensions of twenty-four inches wide by six inches deep. Ned Hanlon, chairman of the Rules Committee at the time, was the author of the proposal to increase the size of the pitcher's rubber. He detailed his idea in an article published in a *New York Clipper* of March 1895:

I have found . . . that the "stride" of pitchers varies, and that when a tall man is officiating against a short one, the "bank" which the tall pitcher forms in making his delivery is out of the reach of the short man. With the rubber plate only a foot in length the short pitcher had no chance to make a new "bank" for himself, and many times the slipping of a pitcher placed in this awkward position, has been the chief cause of his ineffectiveness. If you lengthen the rubber it allows each pitcher to make a "bank" to suit himself. A rubber two feet long, and only four inches wide would, I think, soon warp and bend out of shape, and in order to give it stability it seems to me that it would be well to increase its breadth to six inches. That would make it more easily seen by the umpire, too, and he could better tell when the pitcher was standing on the plate, and when he was not.

As alluded to by Hanlon, the problem of the pitcher failing to make contact with the rubber was a common one in 1894. In fact, frequent abuse of the rule continued throughout the decade and was a major reason behind numerous calls for a return to the pitcher's box. Jouett Meekin, Dad Clarke, and Frank Killen, among others, were accused of violating the rule by inching away from the rubber and closer to the batter. Chadwick was not convinced that the larger pitcher's rubber would curb the infractions:

As to the change made in the Pitcher's Plate, nothing was gained by it. The pitcher will still violate the rule requiring him to have his foot in contact with the rubber plate, as he did last year. He cannot get a firm foothold by placing his foot on the rubber. What was wanted was a hollow, oblong square, 12x36 inches in which the pitcher could have obtained a good, firm foothold within the box. . . .

Chadwick's wording is a bit confusing. More simply stated, he was calling for the use of a small box, set as a slight concavity in the ground at the pitcher's position. The pitcher was to place his pivot foot in this box when delivering the ball. The suggestion was never seriously considered.

The final change made to the bases on the infield was the introduction of the five-sided home plate in 1900. Two triangular areas were added to the front of the square home base such that the pitcher was faced with a flat side, seventeen inches wide. The reason for the change was clearly explained in the 1900 *Spalding Guide*:

With the plate placed in accordance with the form of the diamond field, that is, with its corner facing the pitcher instead of one of its sides, a width of 17 inches was presented for the pitcher to throw the ball over instead of 12 inches, the width of each side of the base. But this left the pitcher handicapped by having to "cut the corners" as it is called, besides which the umpire, in judging called balls and strikes, found it difficult to judge the "cut the corner" balls. To obviate this difficulty, the Committee , while keeping the square plate in its old place—touching the lines of the diamond on two of its sides—gave it a new form in its fronting the pitcher, by making the front square with its width of 17 inches, the same as from corner to corner, from foul line to foul line. The change made is undoubtedly an advantage alike to the pitcher and umpire, as it enables the pitcher to see the width *of base he has to throw the ball over better than before, and the umpire can judge called balls and strikes with less difficulty.*

Fred "Crazy" Schmit, major league pitcher for a number of teams from 1890 to 1901, claimed that he invented the pentagonal home base. In a letter published in *The Sporting News* before the 1900 season, Schmit stated: "The idea was suggested by me to James A. Hart, chairman of the Rules Committee, two years ago. . . . The new invention belongs to me." Schmit also noted that dirt covering the side corners of the old home base effectively shortened the width of the strike zone. This problem was alleviated with the shape of the new five-sided plate. Though no other individual came forward to dispute the claim, it remains unclear whether or not Schmit was the true inventor of the present-day home plate. Today, Schmit is better remembered for having one of the worst winning percentages (7-36, .136) in major league history.

The Twentieth Century

The introduction of the five-sided home base was the last change made to the rules regarding the bases. Changes made to the baseball diamond in the twentieth century affected only the pitcher's position.

The pitcher's mound emerged during the late nineteenth century, though its exact beginnings are not known. A common theory is that soon after the allowance of overhand pitching, it became apparent that a downward slope over the range of the pitcher's stride increased the speed of a pitched ball. Groundskeepers, in an effort to aid the pitcher's footing after a rain storm, would often add dirt to the pitcher's box area, but soon dirt was requested with or without rain. Astute pitchers and managers eventually made the mound an integral part of the pitcher's position.

In his book *Pitching in a Pinch*, Christy Mathewson discussed the practice of altering or "doping" the pitcher's position:

The first time in my baseball career that I ever encountered [doping] was in Brooklyn when [Ned] Hanlon was the manager. Every time he thought I was going to

pitch there, he would have the diamond doctored for me in the morning. The groundkeeper sank the pitcher's box down so that it was below the level of all the bases instead of slightly elevated as it should be.

Hanlon knew that I used a lot of speed when I first broke into the league, getting some of it from my elevation on the diamond. He had a team of fast men who depended largely on a bunting game and their speed in getting to first base to win. With me fielding bunts out of the hollow, they had a better chance of making their goal. Then pitching from the lower level would naturally result in the batters getting low balls, because I would be more apt to misjudge the elevation of the plate. Low ones were made to bunt. Finally, Hanlon always put into the box to work against me a little pitcher who was not affected as much as I by the topographical changes.

Later in the book, Matty recounted the story of Philadelphia Athletics' manager Connie Mack doping the mound for his star pitcher, Rube Waddell. Mack had the normally low mound at Columbia Park built up two feet high for the tall lefthander, but when game time approached, Rube was nowhere to be found. By the time it became apparent that Rube was not going to pitch that day, it was too late to lower the mound. Mack started a much shorter pitcher, while the opposition pitched "a skyscraper." The Athletics were hammered and Rube was fined handsomely.

Matty felt that doping was "not so much in vogue" in the early 1910s as it had once been. At the turn of the century, tinkering with the pitcher's mound was not only commonplace, but extreme. In 1902 Ned Hanlon, no longer promoting the speed and bunting game described above, had a very high mound in use at Washington Park. And Cleveland manager Bill Armour admitted to using a mound of as high as twenty-four inches during the 1902 season.

Washington manager and Rules Committee member Tom Loftus was concerned that "the groundkeepers [were] playing the game by putting the pitcher on a hill, or tilting the base paths to help or hinder bunters." In 1903 he introduced a rule requiring that "the pitcher's box . . . be [no] more than fifteen inches higher than the base lines and home plate. The base lines and home plate shall be perfectly level and the slope from the pitcher's box toward the base lines and home plate be gradual." Note that the rule mistakenly refers to the pitcher's "box," an error that would be corrected the following year by substituting the word "plate" for "box."

Since the new rule for 1903 dictated only the maximum height of the pitcher's mound, mounds were allowed to vary in height from park to park, and even day to day. This was the case for the first five decades of the twentieth century.

After the 1946 season, *The Sporting News* featured an article detailing the different heights of mounds around the major leagues. Heights ranged from the maximum of fifteen inches at Briggs Stadium, Braves Field, and Shibe Park to a low of ten inches at Sportsman's Park. (So much for St. Louis' nickname of the "Mound City.") The author of the article, Fred Lieb, interviewed a number of pitchers regarding their opinions of pitcher's mounds around the major leagues. Bob Feller, Hal Newhouser, Spud Chandler, and Tex Hughson, among others, favored the high mounds. Mickey Haefner was the only pitcher to speak favorably of the low mounds, but being a sidearmed hurler he gained no advantage from a high mound. Several pitchers complained of the mound at Griffith Park—it was like "pitching out of a hollow." Yankee Stadium's mound, described as a "pitching peak," had an abrupt drop rather than a gentle slope. Perhaps most significantly, the majority of the interviewed pitchers favored a rule change requiring a mound of uniform height throughout the majors.

In the late 1940s, a number of other articles appeared in *The Sporting News* calling for the uniformity of pitcher's mounds. Finally, in 1950, a new rule was introduced: "The pitcher's plate shall be on a mound 15 inches higher than home plate." With this rule, the pitcher's mound was set to a standard height—no higher and no lower.

With the 1950 rule change came a detailed description of how the pitcher's mound was to be laid out. It was required that the mound be a circle eighteen feet in diameter with the pitcher's plate set on a leveled surface five feet wide by two feet deep. The front of the rubber was to be placed six inches back from the front of this leveled area, and ten feet five inches from the front of the mound. Thus, the front edge of the pitcher's mound was fifty feet one inch from the rear of the home plate.

The final change to the baseball diamond occurred twenty years later. In 1968 the ERA in both the National and American Leagues dropped below 3.00 for the first time in fifty years. The American League's batting average had dropped every year since 1961, and the National League's batting average was at its lowest since 1908. As in 1893, it was decided that rule changes would be required to regain a balance between offense and pitching/defense. The anemic batting was remedied by two major changes for the 1969 season: the strike zone was reduced in size, and the pitcher's mound was lowered by five inches to its current height of ten inches above the level of home plate. The combined effects of these rule changes were similar to the effects of the increased pitching distances of both 1881 and 1893: the offense improved.

The pitcher's mound rules introduced in 1969 (and still in effect today) also clarified and subtly changed the exact shape, slope, and position of the mound. The front of the mound must be graded in an exact fashion, whereas in the past it was simply noted that the slope be "gradual." The grade is linear for six feet in front of the edge of the flat area atop the mound, with a one inch drop in height for every foot closer to home base. Thus, the entire area onto which the pitcher strides is not curved, but simply angled. Also, an additional ten inches was added to the flat ground behind the pitcher's rubber, such that this leveled area covers five feet by thirty-four inches. Finally, the front of the rubber is placed ten feet six inches from the front edge of the mound, which sets the front edge of the pitcher's mound exactly fifty feet from the rear of the home plate. Technically, this means that the 1969 pitcher's mound (but not the rubber or the leveled area atop the mound) was one inch closer to home base than in previous seasons. It is unlikely that this rather obscure repositioning of the mound was actually made.

There is some evidence that the 1950 standardizations did not really force clubs to have uniform mounds. In a *Sports Illustrated* article published before the 1969 season, author William Leggett noted that in the past, Dodger Stadium always had a high mound, but, the Phillies' mound was low to aid sidearmed and three-quarter-style hurlers, specifically Jim Bunning. Old Comiskey Park (at that time, the only Comiskey Park) also was known to have a low mound.

No further changes have been made to the baseball diamond since 1969. However, in 1972, with the American League's attendance lagging significantly behind that of the National League, the junior circuit looked to attract more fans by boosting its offense. Alterations to the baseball diamond were considered, including an idea that was first proposed in 1885, which called for an increase in the angle of the infield at home base such that the foul lines would enclose a greater amount of fair territory. But, rather than make this or a more traditional change in the baseball diamond rules, the American League opted for the use of the designated hitter rule. While the designated hitter did aid the American League's offense, the rule change failed to affect the National League's lead in attendance. In fact, though they voted not to use the designated hitter, the National League's offense increased along with that of the American League.

Home base is a five-sided figure. Second base is half in and half out of the infield square. The pitcher's rubber is sixty feet six inches from the rear of home plate. With such haphazard shapes, sizes, placements, and distances, one might easily conclude that our present-day baseball diamond was conceived by a lunatic. In fact, the state of the diamond resulted from 150 years of evolution, and evolution works not toward simplicity, but toward perfection. Each change made to the diamond was in an effort to better the game. Whether it was to correct for the effects of baseball's quirky foul ball rules, or to balance offense with pitching and defense, the progress of the game of baseball toward perfection has been visible within the confines of its diamond.

Visual Timelines

The diagrams on the following pages are drawn to scale and represent, first, the baseball diamond and then the pitcher's position for the year(s) noted. Listed below the year(s) are the changes made to the baseball diamond that differentiate the diamond pictured from the previous year's diagram. Beginning with the diagram of the pitcher's position for 1903-1949, the scale has been reduced from previous diagrams by a factor of two, allowing for the entire pitcher's mound to be shown. Home base is always toward the bottom of the page.

The Diamond

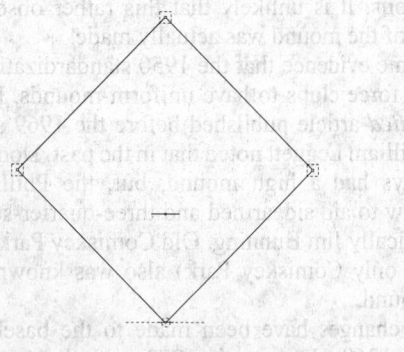

1857–1862
Rules adopted at convention of 1857.

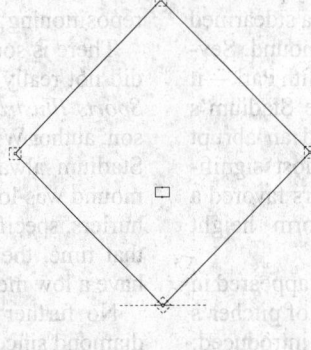

1868
Square home base and pitcher's points.

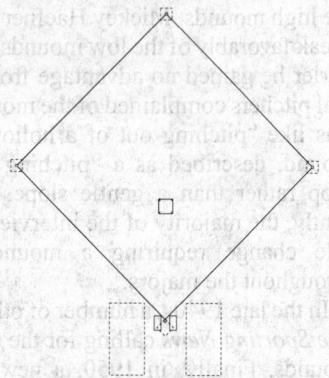

1875–1876
Home base moved to foul territory; batter's box redefined.

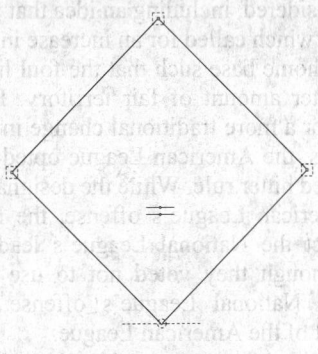

1863–1865
Rear pitcher's line introduced.

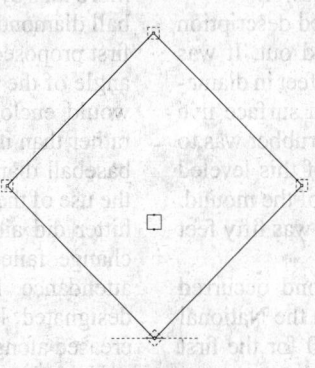

1869–1871
Six by six foot pitcher's box.

1877–1878
Home base moved to fair territory; batter's box redefined;
first, second, and third bases fifteen inches square.

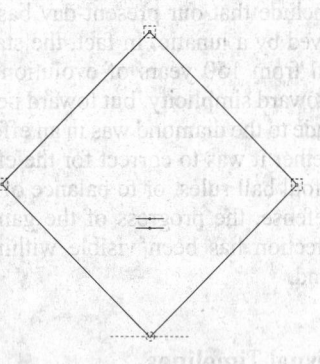

1866
Rear pitcher's line moved back one foot.

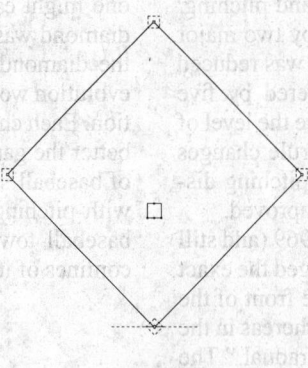

1872–1873
Two additional pitcher's points required.

1879–1880
Four by six foot pitcher's box.

1867
Six by four foot pitcher's box.

1874
Batter's box introduced; pitcher's points rearranged.

**1881–1884 National League
1881–1885 American Association**
Pitcher's box moved back five feet.

The Diamond *(continued)*

1885 National League
Four by six foot batter's box.

1890–1892
Six inch circular pitcher's points.

1900–1902
Five-sided home base.

1886 National League
Four by seven foot pitcher's box.

1890 Players League
Four by six foot pitcher's box; front line of
pitcher's box fifty-one feet from center of home base;
each corner of pitcher's box marked by wooden pegs.

1903–1949
Maximum height of pitcher's rubber is fifteen inches;
other dimensions of mound not defined.

1886 American Association
Four by seven foot pitcher's box;
four by one foot slab in front of pitcher's box;
four by six foot batter's box.

1893–1894
Twelve inch by four inch pitcher's rubber introduced;
pitching distance now sixty feet six inches.

1950–1968
Height of pitcher's rubber exactly fifteen inches;
dimensions of pitcher's mound defined.

1887–1889
Four by five and one-half foot pitcher's box;
first and third bases moved into fair territory.

1895–1899
Twenty-four inch by six inch pitcher's rubber.

1969–date
Height of pitcher's rubber exactly ten inches;
dimensions of pitcher's mound redefined.

The Pitcher's Position

1857–1862, Pitcher's point, 45' distance

1863–1865, Rear point introduced

1866, Rear line moved back one foot

1867, 6' × 4'

1868, square points

1869–1871, 6' × 6'

1872–1873,
Two extra points

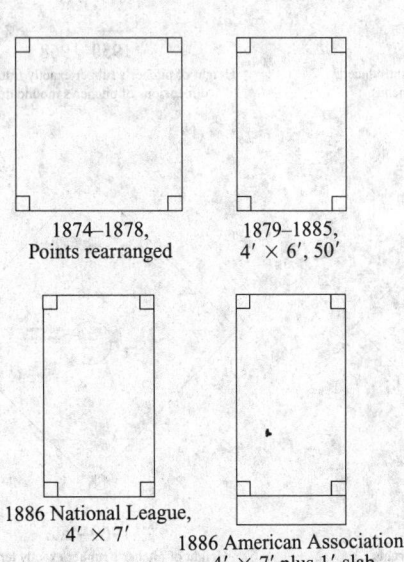

1874–1878,
Points rearranged

1879–1885,
4' × 6', 50'

1886 National League,
4' × 7'

1886 American Association,
4' × 7' plus 1' slab

1887–1889,
4' × 5.5'

1890 Players League,
4' × 6'; 51'

1893–1894, 12" × 4"; 60' 6"

1895–1902, 24" × 6"

1890–1892, 6" circular points

1903–1949, Max. ht. 15"

1950–1968, Ht. 15"

1969–date, Ht. 10"

THE PLAYERS

CHAPTER 7

The 100 Greatest Players

Michael Gershman

Picking baseball's hundred greatest players looks easy, which is why it's been tried more often than a Cub fan's patience. But in fact it requires the hand of a sculptor, the eye of an eagle, the nose of a sommelier, and the sensitivity of a redistricted Congressman up for reelection. Lacking these attributes, brass will suffice.

Part of the problem revolves around packing a hundred great players into just nine positions. It is easy to be blinded by power and pick just fireballing pitchers or slugging left fielders. Balance requires a different approach, with proper attention paid to fielding, baserunning, longevity, and other factors unrelated solely to batting or pitching statistics.

Accordingly, after poring over the contents of this volume, I have selected the players I considered the best:

- eight at each corner position (first and third base, left and right field);
- ten at each interior position (catcher, second base, shortstop, and center field);
- four who logged quality time in both infield and outfield (like Pete Rose);
- twenty-four pitchers (with representation for relievers).

One of the problems with this approach is that the eleventh best shortstop may very well be a better all-around ballplayer than the eighth best left fielder. Nevertheless, drawing the line—and thus obtaining focus—is what this exercise is all about. The great ones are easy to identify; the problem comes in separating the near great from the very good. Some of the players who didn't make the list were very good indeed—Johnny Mize, Pee Wee Reese, Early Wynn, and more.

It was tempting to pick a hundred Hall of Famers and let it go at that. But such a procedure would necessarily exclude players of today who are sure bets to make the Hall—such as Carlton Fisk, Nolan Ryan, and Ryne Sandberg. A second problem with an all-Hall top hundred is that I have the advantage of the records in this book, which are seemingly unfamiliar to those on the Hall of Fame Veterans Committee who place a Pop Haines in Cooperstown while keeping a Bid McPhee out, or those writers who persist in their snubs of Bill Mazeroski and Ron Santo.

Some members of the Baseball Hall of Fame are merely famous for being famous—like Candy Cummings, who may have invented the curveball—or famous for being pulled into the Hall by their more illustrious teammates, like the infield of the New York Giants of the 1920s. Such Hall of Famers are easy enough to exclude from any list of the top 100 baseball figures. But if fame alone is not enough to make the cut, how about great stats? While statistics are the lifeblood of *Total Baseball*, numbers can never adequately reflect the accomplishments of the game's pioneers, white or black. Dan Brouthers was the greatest offensive force in the game before 1900. His numbers would probably be very different if he were beamed down to play today, but then again he would not be playing the game of yesterday, and it could be said that he would not even be Dan Brouthers anymore. It is safe to assume, I believe, that while an average player of a century ago probably could not play in the 1990s, a star of an earlier period would be a star today. And as for Negro League baseball, statistics—even the scattered and fragmentary numbers unearthed by the Society for American Baseball Research—can only hint at the greatness of an Oscar Charleston or a Pop Lloyd. Such men were excluded during their active careers; they cannot be excluded here.

Having delivered the requisite caveats, it is now time to deliver the goods. I have tried to go beyond the stats and convey in each of these profiles a sense of the man, the era in which he performed, and why he deserves to be included in a list more elite than the roll call of the Baseball Hall of Fame.

Humorist Robert Benchley once said of baseball that "one of the chief duties of the fan is to engage in arguments with the man behind him. This department of the game has been allowed to run down fearfully." I hope this top hundred list stimulates a whole new bunch of arguments.

First Base (8)	*Second Base* (10)
Anson, Cap	Collins, Eddie
Brouthers, Dan	Evers, Johnny
Foxx, Jimmie	Frisch, Frankie
Gehrig, Lou	Gehringer, Charlie
Greenberg, Hank	Hornsby, Rogers
Killebrew, Harmon	Lajoie, Nap
McCovey, Willie	Mazeroski, Bill
Sisler, George	McPhee, Bid

Morgan, Joe
Sandberg, Ryne

Shortstop (10)
Aparicio, Luis
Appling, Luke
Banks, Ernie
Cronin, Joe
Lloyd, John Henry

Maranville, Rabbit
Ripken, Cal
Smith, Ozzie
Vaughan, Arky
Wagner, Honus

Third Base (8)
Baker, Home Run
Boggs, Wade

Brett, George
Mathews, Eddie
Robinson, Brooks
Santo, Ron
Schmidt, Mike
Traynor, Pie

DiMaggio, Joe
Hamilton, Billy
Mantle, Mickey
Mays, Willie
Murphy, Dale
Snider, Duke
Speaker, Tris

Rose, Pete
Yount, Robin

Fingers, Rollie
Ford, Whitey
Gibson, Bob
Grove, Lefty
Hubbell, Carl
Keefe, Tim
Johnson, Walter
Koufax, Sandy
Mathewson, Christy
Nichols, Kid
Paige, Satchel
Palmer, Jim
Rusie, Amos
Ryan, Nolan
Seaver, Tom
Spahn, Warren
Walsh, Ed
Wilhelm, Hoyt
Young, Cy

Catchers (10)
Bench, Johnny
Berra, Yogi
Campanella, Roy
Carter, Gary
Cochrane, Mickey
Dickey, Bill
Ewing, Buck
Fisk, Carlton
Gibson, Josh
Hartnett, Gabby

Left Field (8)
Brock, Lou
Henderson, Rickey
Jackson, Joe
Kiner, Ralph
Musial, Stan
Simmons, Al
Stargell, Willie
Williams, Ted

Right Field (8)
Aaron, Hank
Clemente, Roberto
Jackson, Reggie
Kaline, Al
Robinson, Frank
Ruth, Babe
Thompson, Sam
Winfield, Dave

Center Field (10)
Ashburn, Richie
Charleston, Oscar
Cobb, Ty

Utility (4)
Bell, Cool Papa
Robinson, Jackie

Pitchers (24)
Alexander, Grover
Brown, Mordecai
Carlton, Steve
Clemens, Roger
Feller, Bob

HANK AARON

Right Field. Born Feb. 5, 1934 Mobile, Ala. Holds major league record for most lifetime home runs (755). NL MVP 1957.

Even though he led the NL in hits and batting average in 1956, Henry Louis Aaron, Jr., was pictured backward—batting lefthanded—on his 1957 baseball card.

That was fitting symbolism for the man who did everything quietly, except break Babe Ruth's record for career home runs. Hank Aaron integrated the Sally League, set records for career RBIs (2,297) and total bases (6,856), won two batting titles and four RBI crowns, and hit .300 or better in fourteen seasons—all very quietly.

No one exclaimed over his fielding, either, although Aaron played errorless defense in fourteen World Series games, won three Gold Gloves, led the league's outfielders three times in double plays, and twice in fielding runs. According to the Total Baseball Ranking, he was baseball's leading player from 1961 to 1990 and fifth overall, behind only Babe Ruth, Napoleon Lajoie, Ty Cobb, and Ted Williams.

Aaron hit crosshanded in Mobile, Alabama, and with the Indianapolis Clowns of the Negro AL. After the Braves bought his contract, he hit .326 in the Northern League and .362 to lead the Sally League. When Bobby Thomson broke his ankle in spring training in 1954, Aaron became a major league regular at age twenty.

Three years later, with characteristically little fanfare, he was named the NL's MVP as the Braves won the pennant, and he hit .393 in the World Series, including 3 home runs to lead all batters. Always rising to the occasion, Aaron hit home runs in two of the twenty-four All-Star Games in which he played, homered in all three playoff games in 1969, and amassed a lifetime World Series average of .364.

Number 44 attracted attention only with his home runs, hitting 44 in four different seasons; he won three National League home run crowns and tied for a fourth. In 1973 he hit 40 home runs in just 392 at bats. He broke Ruth's record the following year with a rocket off Al

Downing in Atlanta, and finished his career with a record 755.

Although many fans discovered Aaron after most of his career was over, his colleagues knew how special he was. Stan Musial jumped onto the field to congratulate him when he joined the 3,000 hit club, and Mickey Mantle said of him, "Aaron was to my time what Joe DiMaggio was to the era when he played."

He was elected to the Hall of Fame in 1982.

GROVER CLEVELAND ALEXANDER

Pitcher. Born Feb. 26, 1887 St. Paul, Neb. Died Nov. 4, 1950 St. Paul,. Neb. Holds NL records for lifetime shutouts (90) and lifetime complete games (436).

Grover Cleveland Alexander got his big break when he was traded for a vote.

Charles Carr, owner of the American Association's Indianapolis team, had invested in a company that manufactured baseballs. Anxious to have his ball used in the New York State League, he told the owner of the Syracuse team, "If you'll vote for my ball, I'll give you a good pitcher for nothing."

The pitcher, Alexander, suffered from double vision at the time but recovered enough to win 29 games for Syracuse—13 of them shutouts. Drafted by the Phillies, he no-hit the Athletics in a five-inning exhibition game and won 28 games in 1911 to set the rookie record. He won 19, 22, and 27 his next three years to set the stage for the most successful three-year run enjoyed by any pitcher.

In 1915 he won 31 games (12 shutouts and a record 4 one-hitters) and outdid himself a year later by winning 33 games, 16 of them shutouts. In 1917 he won 30, two of them complete games in a Labor Day doubleheader against the Dodgers. If there were a "Triple Crown" for pitchers, as many have suggested, Alexander would have won it twice, leading the league in most wins, strikeouts, and lowest ERA for 1916 and 1920. The second time occurred after he returned from military duty deaf in one ear and suffering from epilepsy.

Occasional neurological fits and an eventually crippling fondness for liquor didn't ruin his pitching. He led the league in ERA twice after his trade to the Chicago Cubs, for whom he won 27 games in 1920. Waived to the Cardinals six years later, he pitched the 15–1 underdogs to complete game victories in the second and sixth games and recorded the most dramatic "save" in Series history, striking out Tony Lazzeri with the bases loaded in the seventh inning of the seventh game.

Alex averaged 19.6 wins for nineteen years, pitched 90 lifetime shutouts (second only to Walter Johnson's 110), and won 373 games to tie Christy Mathewson as the NL lifetime leader. Even more impressive, he recorded the bulk of them at hitter-friendly parks—Philadelphia's Baker Bowl with its 290-foot right field fence and Wrigley Field. He joined the other immortals in Cooperstown in 1938.

ADRIAN "CAP" ANSON

First Baseman. Born Apr. 11, 1852 Marshalltown, Ia. Died Apr. 14, 1922 Chicago. Holds NL record for most seasons batting .300 or more (18). Most seasons of big-league play, 27 (5 NA, 22, NL).

Adrian Constantine "Cap" Anson was the first man to reach 3,000 hits, the first manager to rotate pitchers, and the first player to draw the color line against blacks in baseball.

A hard-driving disciplinarian, Anson was perhaps the most influential player in the nineteenth century. He played in the first professional league, the National Association, from its inception in 1871 and hit .331 in the NL twenty-five years later. Using a split grip, he hit .300 or better in twenty-five seasons, won two batting titles and eight RBI crowns, averaging an RBI every five at-bats over the course of his career.

Anson spent a year at Notre Dame, turned pro with the NA Rockford Forest Citys, played third base for the Philadelphia Athletics for four years, and joined Chicago when White Stockings owner William Hulbert formed the NL. Anson became the White Sox captain in 1878 and switched to first base exclusively when he took over as manager in 1879.

He managed Chicago to pennants from 1880 to 1882, 1884, and 1885, rotating his pitchers and using signals to his hitters and fielders. He has a claim to originating platooning and initiated preseason training. He also was fined regularly by umpires and league officials, earning the nickname "Baby" (for crybaby) before cleaning up his act to earn the nickname "Cap" (for captain). He used bed checks to keep tabs on his charges but also got them first-class hotel rooms and personally marched them onto the field single file before every game.

In 1883, Anson refused to play in an exhibition game at Toledo because the home team had a black catcher, Moses Fleetwood Walker. Although Anson backed down when threatened with forfeiture of the gate, he used his position and popularity to ban black pitcher George Stovey in 1887 when John Montgomery Ward tried to sign him to the Giants; no one tried to upset this "gentleman's agreement" until 1947.

Despite this black mark on his character, Anson later mellowed and eventually became known as "Pop" Anson. When he was fired in 1897, Chicago briefly became known as the Orphans, because they'd lost their Pop.

Anson managed the Giants for just twenty-five days, turned down $50,000 donated by Chicago fans, opened a billiard saloon, tried to organize a rival major league—the abortive American Association of 1899, entered vaudeville (doing skits written by Ring Lardner), and served a term as city clerk in Chicago. He was voted into the Hall of Fame in 1939.

LUIS APARICIO

Shortstop. Born Apr. 29, 1934 Maracaibo, Venezuela. Holds major league records for most games at shortstop (2,581), assists (8,016), and double plays (1,553).

Hank Greenberg had a choice of Venezuelan shortstops in the 1950s and guessed wrong. The Indians' general manager didn't think Luis Aparicio was worth a $10,000 bonus and traded instead for his countryman, Alfonso "Chico" Carrasquel. Carrasquel's career ended in 1959, the same year Aparicio led the "Go-Go Sox" to a pennant, the first for Chicago since the scandal year of 1919.

While Maury Wills is generally given credit with reinventing the stolen base in 1962, Aparicio had made pilferage pay six years earlier. In his rookie year, Aparicio led the league in stolen bases with 21, handled more chances than any AL shortstop, and was named Rookie of the Year. Aparicio led the league in stolen bases his first nine years in the AL (1956–1964), once stole 26 consecutive bases, and was successful on 79 percent of his base stealing attempts.

In truth, Aparicio was not a prototypical leadoff man, sporting an on base average of only .313. Part of his success was due to the bat-handling ability of second baseman and second-place hitter Nelson Fox. Looie hollered like Fox, spat tobacco juice like Fox, and named his son for Fox. When Fox won the MVP award in 1959, the year the Sox won the pennant, Aparicio was right behind him in second place.

Fox and Aparicio won more fielding titles together than any other double play combination, and no shortstop ever led his league in the major defensive categories as often as Looie. He won nine Gold Gloves, was selected to the *Sporting News* All-Star team five times, and the All-Star fielding team ten times. Aparicio attributed his success to using a heavier glove in infield practice to make his own feel lighter during the game.

In January 1963, the White Sox broke up the double play combination, trading Looie to the Orioles. Aparicio provided some of the leadership that enabled the Orioles to win the 1966 pennant and sweep the World Series. He began a second hitch with the White Sox in 1968, hit better than .300 for the only time in his career in 1970 (.313), and finished up playing three years for the Red Sox, giving him eighteen consecutive seasons in which he played 100 or more games. Aparicio was voted into the Hall of Fame in 1984.

LUKE APPLING

Shortstop. Born Apr. 2, 1907 High Point, N.C. Died Jan. 3, 1991 Cumming, Ga. Won two batting titles, including a record for shortstops of .388 in 1936.

They called him Old Aches and Pains, Fumblefoot, and Old Tanglehoof. But by the time he had retired, Luke Appling had hit .300 or better nine straight years and sixteen times in all; had set a major league record by leading the AL in assists seven seasons in a row, and had played more games at shortstop than any ALer.

The hypochondriacal Appling would complain to White Sox manager Jimmy Dykes, saying "Honest, Jimmy, I'm dying." In actuality, over his long career Appling only broke a finger in 1930 and a leg in 1938. "Old Aches and Pains" was hung on him when he roomed with Chicago's trainer. The roomies would get to Comiskey Park early, and Appling would catch forty winks on the rubbing table; inquiring mates were told he was getting "special treatment for a muscle pull."

Lucius Benjamin Appling was healthy enough to consider pro football after playing fullback at Oglethorpe College, but joined the Atlanta Crackers instead. After hitting .326 in 104 games, he was told that the Cubs had bought his contract; however, Bill Veeck, Sr., had second thoughts, and Appling wound up with the Chicago White Sox instead.

Veeck must have felt relieved when the rookie started 1931 0-for-28 and averaged an error every other day; manager Lew Fonseca tried to trade him to no avail. He told Appling, "You're going to play 154 games if you hit .154 and field .154." By 1933, Luke was leading the AL in errors for the first of a record five times, but he also tied Billy Rogell for the lead in total chances and hit .322.

In 1936 he went 4-for-4 the final day of the season to become the first AL shortstop to win a batting title. He won his second in 1943 (.328) before going into the service. By 1949 he had become, at 42, the oldest regular shortstop in baseball history. He eclipsed Rabbit Maranville's record of 2,154 games at short, and retired with a career batting average of .310.

Appling won pennants managing Memphis (Southern Association) and Indianapolis (American Association) and managed the Kansas City A's in 1967. Elected to the Hall of Fame in 1964, he made an appearance in the Cracker Jack All-Star Game in 1984, homering at age 75 against Warren Spahn.

RICHIE ASHBURN
Center Field. Born Mar. 19, 1927 Tilden, Neb. Holds major league records for most years with 400 or more putouts (9) and 500 or more putouts (4).
When Richie Ashburn reported to spring training in 1948, all he had to do to win the center field job for the Phillies was beat out the man who had won the previous year's batting championship by 46 points—Harry "The Hat" Walker.

But Walker fouled a pitch off his foot one morning and was out of the lineup through May. By then, Ashburn was hitting .346 and had unseated him as the Phils' center fielder. The only rookie voted to the 1948 All-Star team, Ashburn had a pair of singles and a stolen base. Even though he broke a finger in August, no injury could spoil a year in which he had a 23-game hitting streak, led the league with 32 stolen bases, hit .333, and was named Rookie of the Year.

Some skeptics pointed out that, "He's not hitting .333; he's hitting .133 and running .200." But in a fifteen-year career, Ashburn hit .300 or better nine times, won two batting titles, got on base about 40 percent of the time, and posted a .308 career average, topping Pete Rose, Willie Mays, and Hank Aaron, among others. As an out-

fielder he set records by recording 500 or more putouts in four different seasons and 400 or more putouts in nine different seasons. He tied Max Carey's major league records by leading the league in that department nine times; he accepted the most chances nine times; he ranks fifth behind Carey, Willie Mays, Tris Speaker, and Ty Cobb in both career putouts and total chances.

"Whitey" Ashburn won batting titles in 1955 (.338) and 1958 (.350), but his greatest moment as a Phillie came in the field. On the last day of the 1950 season, the Dodgers, trailing Philadelphia by a game, played them at Ebbets Field. With the score tied, 1–1, in the bottom of the ninth inning, Brooklyn's Cal Abrams tried to score from second on Duke Snider's single; Ashburn cut him down by twenty feet, setting the stage for Dick Sisler's tenth-inning homer and clinching the Phils' first flag in thirty-five years.

Traded to the Cubs in 1961, Ashburn became one of the original Mets in 1962 and the expansion team's first All-Star, the fifth time he'd been named to an All-Star squad. Since retiring as a player, allegedly because the Mets were so bad at the time, Ashburn has become the Phillies' longest-running broadcaster.

FRANK "HOME RUN" BAKER
Third Baseman. Born Mar. 13, 1886 Trappe, Md., Died Jun. 28, 1963 Trappe, Md.
By the end of the 1910 season, Frank Baker had hit just six home runs in 1,133 at bats. Up to that point, he was more noted as a base stealer than a power hitter, having stolen 20 or more bases every year and having led the league in triples in 1909 with 19.

Then Baker hit 11 homers in 1911 to lead the league for the first of four straight years and helped Connie Mack's Athletics to their second straight pennant. In the World Series, the Giants' Christy Mathewson won the opener, 2–1. Game Two was tied 1–1 in the sixth; New York's Rube Marquard had retired thirteen batters in a row; but, after Eddie Collins doubled, Baker pulled an inside pitch over the short right field wall at the Polo Grounds to give the A's a 3–1 win. The next day, Mathewson's ghost writer, John Wheeler, second-guessed Marquard and advised that "Baker should be pitched *outside*." Later that day, in Game Three, Mathewson retired Baker on two harmless grounders and a fly ball. When Baker came to bat for the fourth time, with the Giants ahead 1–0 with one out in the ninth, Mathewson got two strikes, but then Baker pulled an outside pitch into the right field seats; the A's won, 3–1 in 11 innings, and Frank Baker suddenly became "Home Run" Baker.

Baker batted cleanup, behind Eddie Collins, and sportswriters suggested that Collins's antics on the basepaths made Baker a better hitter. Collins laughed. "When it came to hitting," he said, "Baker needed help like Carnegie needed money." A .300 hitter in six different seasons, he led the league in RBIs twice and might have done even more damage if he hadn't missed two whole seasons.

When the A's were swept in the 1914 Series, Mack decided to punish his players with stiff pay cuts; Baker sat out the season instead and was sold to the Yankees. He also didn't play in 1920, the year his wife died, but helped New York win pennants in 1921 and 1922 as a spot player.

In 1961 sportswriter Joe Williams asked Baker how many homers he would hit today. He replied, "I'd say 50 anyway. The year I hit 12, I also hit the right field fence at Shibe Park 38 times; all of those would have been home runs with the lively ball."

ERNIE "MR. CUB" BANKS

Shortstop/First Baseman. Born Jan. 31, 1931 Dallas, Tex. NL MVP 1958, 1959. Holds major league shortstop record for home runs in a season (47).

To the victors go the spoils—and most of the MVP Awards. Yet, once in baseball history, the shortstop of a club tied for fifth was named MVP two straight years. In 1958 Ernie Banks led the league in home runs (47), RBIs (129), and slugging percentage (.614), and played in every game. A year later, Banks led the league again with 143 ribbies. He hit 20 or more homers in thirteen seasons, hit .300 or better three times, and drove in 100 or more runs eight times. He led the league's shortstops in fielding three times and, after moving to first base in 1962, led all first basemen in putouts five times.

Banks never played minor league ball, jumping directly from the Kansas City Monarchs of the Negro AL to the Chicago Cubs. He hit .314 in ten games in 1953, took over as the Cubs' starting shortstop the following year, and had his first great season in 1955, knocking in 117 runs and hitting 44 homers, a record for shortstops; five of them came with the bases loaded, then a record (since broken by Don Mattingly).

By 1957 he was one of the most feared power hitters in the league. The late umpire Tom Gorman once recalled that, "in 1957 Banks was knocked down four times by four different pitchers—Don Drysdale, Bob Purkey, Bob Friend, and Jack Sanford. And each time he was knocked down, Banks hit their next pitch out of the park."

He led the league in RBIs in 1959 and homers again in 1960 (41). Only Eddie Mathews's 46th homer in a 1959 playoff game kept Banks, who had 45, from a share of three consecutive home run titles. He hit more home runs than any shortstop in the history of the game (293) and wound up with 512 for his career. Prior to his retirement in 1971, he was voted the Greatest Cub Player of All Time.

After becoming a minor league instructor for the Cubs, Banks belied his goody-two-shoes image by saying things like, "I like my players to be married and in debt. That's the way you motivate them." But Cub fans will always remember him as the ballplayer who said, "What a great day for baseball. Let's play two!"

JAMES "COOL PAPA" BELL

Infielder/Outfielder. Negro Leagues 1922–46; St. Louis Stars, Pittsburgh Crawfords, Detroit Wolves, Kansas City Monarchs, Chicago American Giants, Memphis Red Sox, Homestead Grays. Born May 17, 1903 Starkville, Miss. Died March 7, 1991 St. Louis, Mo.

Cool Papa Bell may have been the headiest and fastest baserunner of his time, and, maybe, all time.

He is credited with stealing 175 bases in 1933 and is said to have once rounded the bases in 12 seconds. (The official record is 13.3 seconds, set by Evar Swanson of the Reds in 1931.) Bell scored from first on a sacrifice in a 1940s exhibition against major leaguers. Satchel Paige bunted him over to second, then seeing third uncovered, Bell took off; catcher Roy Partee gave chase, but Bell slid home safely; he was forty-five at the time.

Originally a righthanded batter, Bell taught himself to switch hit and is credited with hitting .437 for Torreon of the Mexican League in 1940. Over an 89-game season, he led the league in runs (119), hits (167), triples (15), home runs (12) and RBIs (79). According to incomplete records, he hit .407 in 1944 and .402 in 1946.

Bill Veeck said, "Defensively, he was the equal of Tris Speaker, Joe DiMaggio or Willie Mays." Pro basketball pioneer and baseball scout Eddie Gottlieb said, "If he had played in the major leagues, he would have reminded the fans of Willie Keeler as a hitter and Ty Cobb as a baserunner—and he might have exceeded both."

Born in Starkville, Mississippi, James Bell played semipro ball with four of his brothers on the Compton Hill Cubs in St. Louis, breaking in as a lefthanded pitcher. After a particularly strong game in 1922, the St. Louis Stars signed him for $90 a month and switched him to the outfield to take advantage of his speed every day.

Named Cool Papa for his unflappability, he performed up to par in his few appearances against major league opposition. In 1929 he and other black stars barnstormed against a team headed by Hall of Famers Charlie Gehringer, Al Simmons, and Heinie Manush and won six games out of eight.

When his playing days were over, Bell had a hand in the development of Ernie Banks and others. Banks credits Bell with taking him from the Texas sandlots to Kansas City, and both Lou Brock and Maury Wills give Bell credit for helping them steal bases. He was elected to the Hall of Fame in 1974.

JOHNNY BENCH

Catcher. Born Dec. 7, 1947 Oklahoma City, Okla. NL MVP 1970, 1972.

Ted Williams has signed many autographs but none as prescient as one penned in spring training in 1965: "To Johnny Bench, a sure Hall of Famer."

Bench was named to the NL All-Star team fourteen times, played in every game from 1968 to 1975, and hit .409 with 3 home runs. He set a major league record for home runs by a catcher (327 plus 62 playing elsewhere), later broken by Carlton Fisk; won two home run crowns; led the league in RBIs three times; and was chosen MVP twice.

While Bench is remembered most for his offense, he may have had his greatest impact behind the bat. He was the first receiver to use a protective helmet in the field, popularized catching onehanded, kept his throwing hand behind his back to protect it from foul tips, and said his father "taught me to throw 254 feet—twice the distance to second base—from a crouch."

Not known for keeping his counsel, Bench once said flatly, "I can throw out any runner alive," and brashly predicted that he would be the first catcher to be named Rookie of the Year. He did just that in 1968, caught 154 games, a rookie record, and won the first of ten straight Gold Gloves. Bench hit 45 homers and was chosen MVP for the first time in 1970, the year Bob Hunter, a Los Angeles sportswriter, first called Cincinnati "the Big Red Machine."

That year, the Reds ran into Brooks Robinson and, the second time Bench was named MVP, in 1972, the Big Red Machine was derailed by the Oakland A's Mustache Gang. When the Reds squared off against the New York Yankees in 1976, the press played up the confrontation between Bench and the Yankees' catcher and captain, Thurman Munson.

Bench caught Mickey Rivers stealing in Game One, New York's only attempted theft in the Series, got two hits in each of the first three games, and hit two home runs in Game Four to lead the Reds to their first World Series sweep. Munson hit .529 with 2 RBIs; Bench hit .533 and knocked in 6 runs. Munson gave Bench his due, "The man deserves all the credit in the world."

Bench made Williams's prediction come true in 1989, the first year he was eligible. He is currently a broadcaster with CBS radio nationally and local station WLWT in Cincinnati.

LAWRENCE "YOGI" BERRA
Catcher. Born May 12, 1925 St. Louis, Mo. AL MVP, 1951, 1954, 1955.
Branch Rickey didn't make many mistakes, but declining to sign Yogi Berra for all of $250 was a real beaut.

In 1942 Rickey was the Cardinals' general manager and offered Berra $250 to sign, refusing to pay him the same $500 offered to his friend, Joe Garagiola. Berra turned down the $250 and, a year later, the Yankees signed him for the very same $500; not very long thereafter, they turned down a $50,000 offer from Giant manager Mel Ott, who had seen Berra play for the International League Newark Bears.

Berra eventually became a fifteen-time All-Star, a three-time MVP, and a Hall of Famer. He also holds numerous World Series records including games by a catcher (63), hits (71), and times on the winning team (10). Though lightly regarded as a manager, he was the first big league skipper to win pennants in both leagues in nearly forty years.

Born in "the Hill" section of St. Louis, Berra got his nickname when childhood friends watching a movie noted Berra's resemblance to a Hindu practicing yoga. Following stints in the navy and the minors, Yogi became a Yankee and shared catching duties with Aaron Robinson and Sherman Lollar until the Dodgers ran him ragged in the 1947 World Series. After being tutored by Bill Dickey, however, he became a standout catcher and accepted 950 errorless chances from July 28, 1957 to May 10, 1959.

Berra led AL catchers in putouts eight times, assists and fielding three times each, and handled the Yankee pitching staff masterfully. Although he never led the league in home runs or RBIs, Berra, a notorious bad-ball hitter, was a constant threat offensively, particularly with men on base; he was named Most Valuable Player in 1951, repeated in 1954 and 1955, and retired with a .285 lifetime average.

Named to manage the Yankees in 1964, he won the pennant but lost both a seven-game Series and his job to Johnny Keane. He joined the Mets as a coach and became the manager in 1973, taking them from fifth place to the pennant, ultimately losing the Series again in seven games, to the A's. He returned to the Yankees as coach and manager, was elected to the Hall of Fame in 1972 and ended his career as a coach with the Astros.

WADE BOGGS
Third Baseman. Born June 15, 1958 Omaha, Neb. Won four straight AL batting titles, 1985–1988, five straight on base percentage titles, 1985–1989.
Despite hitting a paltry .259 in 1992, Wade Boggs's lifetime average is still a robust .335, which places him 19th on the all-time list.

Boggs scored 100 or more runs seven straight times, led the AL in batting five times, and notched 200 or more hits in seven straight seasons, a modern record. Named to the All-Star team in 1985, he has been a starter every year from 1986 to 1994.

The son of a retired Marine, Boggs grew up an all-state kicker in Tampa, Florida, signed with the Red Sox in 1976, and was playing for Elmira of the NY-Penn League shortly after graduating from high school. In 1980 he lost the International League batting title on the last day of the season but won it the next year on the last day of the season. Boggs became a regular in 1982 when Carney Lansford was injured. He booted the first two ground balls hit to him in the majors but hit .349, splitting his time between first base and third.

In 1983 he made 27 errors but led the majors in hitting (.361) and on-base percentage (.449). A year later, he topped all AL third basemen in errors but also had the most chances, double plays, assists, putouts, and fielding runs. In 1985 he hit .368 to win the first of four straight batting titles, reached base safely 340 times, and had 240 hits, the most since Babe Herman's 241 in 1930. He batted .357 to help the Red Sox win the pennant in 1986 and has hit .311 in three playoffs and World Series.

The "Chicken Man," so named by Jim Rice for his love of fowl, lives a disciplined life, getting up at the same time, going to the ballpark at the same time, eating chicken daily, and doing the same things the same way as often as possible. He fields exactly 150 grounders in practice, steps into the batting cage at 5:17 and, after private time in the clubhouse bouncing a baseball off a wall, hits the field at precisely 7:17 for wind sprints.

Boggs says his eyesight is his greatest asset. He told *Newsweek*, "I can observe the spin on a breaking ball. If it happens to be a fastball, I can still hit it to left. And if the pitch happens to be off-speed enough, believe it or not, I'll pull it."

GEORGE BRETT
Third Baseman. May 15, 1953 Glen Dale, W. Va. In 1980 had highest batting average since Ted Williams' .406 of 1941.
George Brett joined the exclusive 3,000-hit club on September 30, 1992. He was already the only player to win batting titles in three different decades, a thirteen-time All-Star, and the last modern player to make a serious run at hitting .400.

The younger brother of pitcher Ken Brett, he led the league in hits and triples in 1975, repeated in both categories in 1976, and added his first batting title that year, hitting .333 to edge Rod Carew and teammate Hal McRae, later his manager. From 1976 to 1978 the Royals lost three straight playoffs to the Yankees despite Brett's three-run homer in 1976 and his three consecutive homers off Catfish Hunter in 1978.

Just before the All-Star break in 1980 Brett was hitting .337 when he strained ankle ligaments trying to steal a base; however, he got hot in July and even hotter in August, going 4-for-4 on the 17th to reach the magic figure of .400. With two weeks left, he slumped but finished strong (10-for-19), ending the season at .390; he also led the league in slugging (.664) and, to absolutely no one's surprise, was named MVP.

That year, the Royals broke the playoff jinx against the Yankees as Brett homered in Game One and hit an upper deck home run off Goose Gossage to win Game Three. Although the Phils beat KC in a six-game Series, Brett homered and went 9-for-24 in the Series. The Royals finally won a championship in 1985 as Brett starred offensively and defensively; he went 4-for-5 in Game Seven, robbed the Cardinals of five potential hits and went 10-for-27, scoring five runs.

On July 24, 1983, Brett made history in a different way. With New York leading Kansas City 4-3 in the ninth inning at Yankee Stadium, he homered with two out and a man on to put the Royals in front, 5-4. Yankee manager Billy Martin contended that Brett should be declared out and the runs shouldn't count, because his bat had pine tar more than 18 inches from the knob to the barrel; the umpires agreed, awarding the win to the Yankees. The Royals protested, however, and AL president Lee Mac-Phail ended the Great Pine Tar Incident by overruling his own umpires and declaring a resumption of play at a later date.

Brett won his third batting title in 1990.

He retired after the 1993 season and became a member of the Royals' front office.

LOU BROCK
Left Field. Born Jun. 18, 1939 ElDorado, Ark. Holds major league record for most consecutive years 50 or more stolen bases (12).
In 1978 the NL announced that its annual stolen base leader would receive the Lou Brock Award, making Brock the first active player to have an award named after him. The greatest base stealer baseball had produced to that time, Lou went on to break Ty Cobb's "modern" career record of 891 with 938 (Billy Hamilton had 912 in 1888–1901) although the record was eventually eclipsed, in turn, by Rickey Henderson.

Brock ensured that he'd get numerous chances to run by joining the exclusive 3,000-hit club (3,023) and finishing a nineteen-year career with seven .300 seasons and a lifetime batting average of .293. In 1968 he led the league in doubles, triples, and steals, the first NL player to accomplish that feat since Honus Wagner did it in 1908.

Lou could run, hit, and even hit with power occasionally; in 1967 he led the Cardinals in extra-base hits and knocked in 76 runs as a leadoff man. As a youngster with the Chicago Cubs, Brock even blasted a home run into the center field stands at the Polo Grounds, a startling feat that had been accomplished only once before, by certified slugger Joe Adcock.

After being traded from the Cubs to the Cardinals for Ernie Broglio in June 1964, he hit .348 and scored 81 runs in 103 games; during the stretch run, when the Phillies folded, he hit .461 to help the Cardinals win their first pennant in eighteen years. Although he hit .300, 1964 would prove to be his poorest offensive Series. In 1967 he batted .414 with 12 hits, stole a record 7 bases, and went 4-for-4 in Game One. A year later, he stole 7 bases again and improved to .464 with 13 hits, tying Bobby Richardson's record; his 14 steals is a World Series career record, tying Eddie Collins.

In 1966 he broke Maury Wills's stranglehold on the stolen base championship with 74 thefts. That was the first of four straight base-stealing crowns, and, after Bobby Tolan interrupted his string in 1970, Lou won four more in a row. In 1974 he smashed Maury Wills's season mark of 104 stolen bases, ending with 118, and was named Man of the Year by *The Sporting News*. He was elected to the Hall of Fame in 1985.

DENNIS "BIG DAN" BROUTHERS
First Baseman. Born May 8, 1858 Sylvan Lake, N.Y. Died Aug. 3, 1932 East Orange, N.J. Highest slugging average of any player to perform before 1900; led NL in slugging six years in a row (1881–1886).
Big Dan Brouthers holds the highest lifetime average of any first baseman (.342), batting .300 or better for fourteen straight years. He played on champions in three leagues, won five batting titles, and topped the NL in slugging six straight times.

Although he hit just 106 homers, the lefthanded Brouthers (rhymes with "soothers") was "the Babe Ruth of his era." John McGraw, his Oriole teammate, said, "When I first went with Baltimore there were little flags stuck on the fences of the different parks to show where Brouthers had driven balls out."

Brouthers got his baseball baptism with the semipro Wappingers Falls Actives. The Troy Haymakers brought him to the big leagues but, after he made 34 errors in 39 games in 1879, returned him to the minors. In 1881 Big Dan shuffled off to Buffalo, where he led the NL in homers (8) and topped all batsmen in 1882 (.368) and 1883 (.374).

Brouthers, James "Deacon" White, Hardy "Old True Blue" Richardson, and Jack Rowe constituted Buffalo's "Big Four." Although they failed to bring Buffalo a pennant, the quartet—sold as a unit to the Wolverines after the 1885 season—brought Detroit its first flag in 1887. Brouthers led the league in runs, doubles, and on-base percentage.

When the Wolverines disbanded a year later, Brouthers was awarded to the Boston Beaneaters, with whom he won his third batting title (.373) in 1889. The next year, he jumped to the Boston Reds, a Players League team; when it, too, disbanded, he joined a team of the same name that captured the American Association pennant and won the batting title again in 1891 (.350). Big Dan "revolved" (changed teams) and became a Brooklyn Superba, copped his fifth batting crown in 1892 (.335), and was traded to the Orioles with Willie Keeler. Brouthers had his last great year in 1894, hitting .347 and providing 128 RBIs to lead Baltimore to its first pennant.

After brief stops in Louisville and Philadelphia he continued his slugging exploits in the minors, winning the batting title of the Class D Hudson River League in 1904 at the age of 46, capping that incredible year with a two-game return to the big leagues for McGraw's Giants. He served as a press box attendant at the Polo Grounds until he died in 1932. He was elected to the Hall of Fame in 1945.

MORDECAI "THREE FINGER" BROWN

Pitcher. Born Oct. 19, 1876 Nyesville, Ind. Died Feb. 14, 1948 Terre Haute, Ind. ERA of 1.06 in 1906 stands as NL best since 1880.

Mordecai Brown's colorful nickname often obscures what a great pitcher he was.

He ranks third behind Ed Walsh and Addie Joss in lifetime ERA (2.06) and trails only Walsh, Joss, and Christy Mathewson in allowing the fewest runners per nine innings (9.80). Ty Cobb said of Brown's breaking ball, "It was the most devastating pitch I ever faced. Christy Mathewson's fadeaway was good, but it was nothing like that curve Three-Fingered Brown threw at you."

Brown was seven when he put the index finger of his right hand into his uncle's corn shredder; it was amputated just above the knuckle. A few weeks later he broke his third and fourth fingers while chasing a hog; they healed into a gnarled, unnatural shape. Despite his handicap, Brown became a semipro infielder. One day, the team's star pitcher broke his arm and Brown took over; in five innings, he struck out fourteen, using a curve ball that broke unusually because of the shape of his hand.

"Miner" Brown (so named because he was a coal miner before he became a ballplayer) joined the Cardinals, going 9–13 in his rookie season. Cubs' manager Frank Chance saw great potential and traded for the man he called "the greatest fielding pitcher the game ever had." Brown won 15 games in 1904, 18 in 1905, and 26 in 1906, posting a 1.04 ERA.

In 1908 Brown won 29 games against 9 losses, threw four consecutive shutouts, and helped Chicago catch the slumping Giants by winning both ends of a September doubleheader. The next day, Fred Merkle's baserunning boner turned a Giant victory in a tie, ultimately necessitating a playoff game. When the first three Giants hit safely and the next two walked, Brown took over from Jack Pfiester without warming up. He shut the Giants out the rest of the way and the Cubs won the game, 4–2, and the pennant.

In 1909 he led the league in wins (27), complete games (32), and saves (7) but wrenched a ligament in his right leg. He remained effective in 1910, but the glory years were behind him. Traded to the Reds in 1913, he won only 5 games. Following a stretch managing the St. Louis Federals, he rejoined the Cubs, and he and Mathewson pitched their finales against each other, Mathewson winning the atypically inept contest 10–7.

The great pitchers thus concluded their personal rivalry with Mathewson winning thirteen times against Brown's eleven. Matty was an original inductee into the Hall of Fame in 1936; Brown had to wait thirteen more years.

ROY CAMPANELLA

Catcher. Born Nov. 19, 1921 Philadelphia, Pa. Died Jun. 23, 1993 Woodland Hills, Cal. NL MVP 1951, 1953, 1955.

Baseball's all-time record crowd wasn't attracted by a red-hot playoff or a World Series game. Instead, 93,103 fans filled the Los Angeles Coliseum on May 7, 1959, to honor Roy Campanella, whose baseball career had ended the previous year when the car he was driving skidded into a telephone pole, leaving him paralyzed.

A decade after that unique tribute, Campanella received baseball's ultimate honor and was inducted into the Hall of Fame despite a major league career that had lasted a mere ten years. Then again, Campy was named MVP in three of the nine full seasons in which he played; 1951, 1953, and 1955 to rank with Stan Musial and Mike Schmidt as the only three-time MVPs in the National League.

An outstanding handler of pitchers, Campanella caught three no-hitters, led the league in putouts six times, caught 100 or more games a year his last nine years in the majors, and nailed two of every three runners that tried to steal on him. Although his batting average oscillated wildly (.312 to .207 to .318 to .219 between 1953 and 1956), he was more consistent at the power game, averaging 27 homers between 1949 and 1956.

He joined the Negro NL's Baltimore Elite Giants right out of high school and eventually made $3,000 a month as a full-fledged star, being named to All-Star teams in 1941, 1944, and 1945. After that season he became Brooklyn's second black signee, taking $185 a month to play with Nashua in the New England League; by 1949 he was the Dodgers' regular catcher.

In 1951 he hit .325 with 33 homers and 108 RBIs but pulled a leg muscle in the final regular season game, missing the last two games of the playoff. Monte Irvin says, "If Campanella hadn't injured himself in Philadelphia, he might have settled Ralph Branca down after one high strike to Bobby Thomson."

After a modest 1952 season, Campy hit 41 homers in 1953 (40 as a catcher to set the major league record), batted .312, and led the league with 142 RBIs. In 1955 he hit .318 with 32 homers and 107 RBIs and was named to *The Sporting News* All-Star Team for the fourth time. He hit two home runs as Brooklyn won its only World Series.

STEVE CARLTON

Pitcher. Born Dec. 22, 1944 Miami, Fla. NL Cy Young Award 1972, 1977, 1980, 1982.

Steve Carlton never won the hearts and minds of baseball writers, but he led the NL in innings pitched and strikeouts five times each, won 329 games, and captured four Cy Young Awards.

He trained by using isometrics, kung fu, and twisting his hands in three-foot deep buckets of rice. The powerful lefty made 30 or more starts in 16 seasons. "I've never paced myself," he said, "I've always thrown everything as hard as I can for as long as I can."

Offered $4,000 by the Pirates as a junior college freshman, Carlton was signed by Cards' scout Howie Pollet for $5,000. On a Cards trip to Japan in 1968, he began developing the slider that became his "out" pitch. He fanned 19 Mets in a September 1969 game to set an National League record, finished the season 17–11, and won 20 games in 1971.

Instead of the big raise he expected, Carlton got traded to the Phillies and responded with a historic season. Lefty won 27 games for the last place Phils, notching an all-time record 45 percent of the team's wins. A Triple Crown pitcher, he also led in ERA (1.97) and strikeouts (310), won his first Cy Young Award, and negotiated a salary of $167,000, then a record for pitchers.

The bounces didn't go his way the next year and he became a 20-game loser. He bounced back to win 59 games as the Phils won division titles in 1976, 1977, and 1978. In 1980, Carlton was 24–9 in the regular season, captured his third Cy Young Award, and beat the Royals twice in the World Series to give the Phillies their only world championship.

Three years after his last Cy Young Award (1982), Carlton went on the DL for the first time and was released by the Phils a year later. He pitched briefly for the Giants, White Sox, Indians, and Twins before retiring in 1988 as the NL leader in career strikeouts (4,000) and the leading lefty in the majors (4,136).

GARY CARTER

Catcher. Born Apr. 8, 1954 Culver City, Cal. All-Star Game MVP 1981, 1984.

In an earlier edition of Total Baseball, Bob Carroll wrote of Gary Carter, "The guy is friendly, open, cooperative, thoughtful, enthusiastic and has never been involved in a scandal. What's he hiding?"

Carter's gee-whiz personality has led observers to discount his achievements; clearly, however, he was the National League's leading catcher since Johnny Bench. A three-time Gold Glover, Carter led the league five times in assists and six straight years in games and putouts. Offensively, he drove in more than a hundred runs four times and hit 20 or more homers nine times.

Carter passed on more than a hundred football scholarship offers to sign with the Montreal Expos and was shocked to discover that they saw him not as a shortstop but as a catcher. In the beginning, Carter says, "I was the worst catcher you ever saw—a real joke." (One of his minor league managers charged him a quarter for every ball he dropped and often collected three or four dollars a game.)

He caught and played first and the outfield until the Expos traded Barry Foote in 1977. In 1978 he set a major league record by allowing just a single passed ball in 157 games. By 1981, "Kid" was the All-Star starter and homered off Ken Forsch and Ron Davis to be named MVP, joining Al Rosen, Arky Vaughan, Willie McCovey, and Ted Williams as the only men to homer twice in an All-Star Game. That fall, Carter hit .421 against the Phils in the divisional playoff and .438 against the Dodgers in the NLCS.

In the 1984 All-Star Game Carter homered off Dave Stieb to break a 1–1 tie and win his second All-Star MVP award. That season, despite knee problems which required postseason surgery, he tied Mike Schmidt for the RBI crown (106) and hit 27 homers. Traded to the Mets, he hit 24 homers to help the Mets win the pennant in 1986, drove in 3 runs in both Games Three and Four of the World Series, and singled to ignite the come-from-behind rally that won Game Six. After being released by the Mets in 1989, he played a year each with the Giants, Dodgers, and Expos.

In 1993 he became part of the original broadcasting crew for the expansion Florida Marlins, an alliance he continues to this day.

OSCAR CHARLESTON

Center Fielder. Born Oct. 14, 1896 Indianapolis, Ind. Died Oct. 5, 1954 Philadelphia, Pa. Batted .434 in the Negro National League of 1921.

Oscar Charleston is generally regarded as the greatest of all Negro League players.

It diminishes Negro Leaguers to equate them with white players as the "black" this or that; however, Charleston's preeminence is such that he is known equally as "the black Tris Speaker" for his fielding, "the black Ty Cobb" for his baserunning, and "the black Babe Ruth" for his hitting. John McGraw said that he was simply the best, adding, "If only I could calcimine him."

He started out as batboy for the Indianapolis ABCs in his home town, joined the army at age fifteen, and was stationed in the Philippines with the all-black 24th Infantry. Even at that age, he was skilled enough to play in the otherwise all-white Manila League. He also ran track and was timed at the 220-yard dash in 23 seconds flat, giving rise to his nickname, "the Hoosier Comet."

He started professional play with the Indianapolis ABC's in 1915 and later moved on to the Chicago American Giants and St. Louis Giants. In a five-game series between Charleston's St. Louis Giants and the white St. Louis Cardinals, he is reported to have hit four home runs in one game, two of them off Hall of Famer Jesse "Pop" Haines.

Charleston became player-manager of the Eastern Colored League Harrisburg Giants from 1922 to 1925 and moved to Philadelphia, where he became friends with catcher Biz Mackey and third baseman Judy Johnson. After stints with the Hilldales and the Homestead Grays, Johnson and Charleston moved to Pittsburgh when Gus Greenlee persuaded Charleston to manage and play for the Crawfords. Charleston hit .363, second only to Josh Gibson, and led the team to a 99–36 record, with the help of Gibson, Johnson, and Satchel Paige.

When the Crawfords moved to Toledo and Indianapolis, Charleston stayed with them through 1940, moving on to the Philadelphia Stars in 1941. After the war, Charleston was signed to Branch Rickey's Brooklyn Brown Dodgers, where he had a hand in corralling both Jackie Robinson and Roy Campanella. He joined them in the Hall of Fame in 1976.

ROGER CLEMENS

Pitcher. Born Aug. 4, 1962 Dayton, Oh. AL Cy Young Award 1986, 1987, 1991.

In 1987 Roger Clemens became the third pitcher, along with Sandy Koufax and Jim Palmer, to win back-to-back Cy Young Awards outright (Denny McLain won the award in 1968 and tied for it in 1969). He picked up his third Cy Young in 1991. Nicknamed "Rocket," or "Rocket Man," after an Elton John song, Clemens burst on the scene the night of April 29, 1986, when he struck out 20 Mariners. That broke the nine-inning record previously held by Tom Seaver, Steve Carlton, and Clemens's idol, Nolan Ryan.

Clemens was destined for stardom. Offered $1,500 by the Twins, Clemens instead entered San Jacinto Junior

College, then turned down a $20,000 bonus offered by the Mets and transferred to the University of Texas. (There he joined Bruce Ruffin, Calvin Schiraldi, and Greg Swindell.) After beating Alabama, 4–3, in the finals in 1983, Rocket became the Red Sox first pick in the June draft, signing for $121,000.

Called up the following May, Clemens was 9–4 in August when he strained a tendon in his right forearm and missed the rest of the season. He suffered a second arm injury in 1985 and required arthroscopic surgery in the rotator cuff of his right shoulder; yet eight months later he was striking out 20 Mariners on his way to winning his first 14 decisions. Starting for the American League in the All-Star Game, he retired nine straight batters to be named MVP. Clemens finished the 1986 season 24–4 to lead Boston to a division title and was the unanimous winner of the Cy Young Award. Pitching with the flu on three days' rest, Clemens beat the Angels, 8–1, to clinch the pennant. He left two World Series games ahead, 6–3 (after 4⅓ innings in Game Two) and 3–2 after 7 innings of the ill-fated Game Six.

In 1990 Clemens put together a 21–6 season but missed most of September because of a shoulder injury. The Sox won their division and Clemens left Game One of the playoffs after six shutout innings and got no decision. He gave up three runs in Game Four and was ejected after arguing with plate umpire Terry Cooney. In 1991 and 1992 Clemens won 18 games and remained the game's best active pitcher. Clemens returned to form with a mark of 9-7 and a splendid 2.85 ERA in run-crazy 1994.

ROBERTO CLEMENTE

Right Field. Born Aug. 18, 1934 Carolina, P.R. Died Dec. 31, 1972 San Juan, P.R. NL MVP, 1966.

When Roberto Clemente graduated from high school in Puerto Rico, he received not only the best wishes of his friends and family but also blessings in person from scouts for ten different big league teams.

He had played for Santurce in the Puerto Rican Winter League while still a student and had quickly attracted bird dogs with his hitting, fielding, and throwing ability. Although the Milwaukee Braves offered him a $30,000 signing bonus, he kept an earlier commitment to the Dodgers and signed for $10,000.

However, he never played for Brooklyn or Los Angeles. A rule then in effect required that any player signing for more than $4,000 be put on the big league roster after a year in the minors; otherwise, he could be signed by any other club for $4,000. Although the Dodgers tried to hide Clemente on their Montreal roster by not playing him, he was claimed by the Pirates on November 22, 1954, for $4,000.

It was the Bucs' best investment since Honus Wagner. Clemente batted over .300 in thirteen seasons, won four NL batting crowns, finished with an even 3,000 hits, and ended an eighteen-year career with a lifetime average of .317. The NL MVP in 1966, he was also selected for the All-Star game twelve times.

A textbook right fielder, Clemente won twelve straight Gold Gloves. In 1958 he threw out 22 runners to win the first of a NL record five assists titles. A World Series star, he led the Bucs to championships in 1960 and 1971 and hit safely in every World Series game in which he played.

In 1971 he homered in the sixth and seventh games, hit .414 with 12 hits, fielded flawlessly, and was chosen the Series MVP.

Throughout his career Clemente was plagued by back injuries, the result of an arthritic spine caused by an automobile accident. He died in an airplane crash on New Year's Eve, 1972, carrying food and medical supplies to earthquake-stricken Nicaragua.

The customary five-year waiting period was waived, and in 1973 he became the first Hispanic member of the Hall of Fame. Later he became the second baseball player, after Jackie Robinson, to be pictured on a U.S. postage stamp.

TY COBB

Center Field. Born Dec. 18, 1886 Narrows, Ga. Died July 17, 1961 Atlanta. Holds major league record for lifetime batting average (.366), most years leading league in batting (12) and hits (8).

When Ty Cobb was eighteen, his mother shot his father fatally at her bedroom window; some say she mistook him for a burglar, others that she suspected her of infidelity.

Either way, the tragedy probably spurred Cobb to become the fiercest competitor in baseball as well as the game's greatest hitter. Since 1947, only Stan Musial, Ted Williams, Rod Carew, George Brett, Tony Gwynn, Wade Boggs, Andres Galarraga, and Jeff Bagwell have, in single seasons, outhit Cobb's career average of .366. Virtually overlooked is his feat of leading the league in RBIs four out of five years and bettering 100 seven times, mostly in the dead-ball era.

One of the original five players elected to the Hall of Fame (he got seven more votes than Babe Ruth), Cobb is the only ALer to hit .400 or better in three different seasons. The Georgia Peach hit .300 or better every year from 1906 to 1928 and won the AL batting championship every year from 1907 to 1915 and from 1917 to 1919. (He slumped to .371 in 1916, when Tris Speaker hit .386.) Revisionist historians have deprived him of the batting titles in 1910 and 1914, but Cobb went to his grave with twelve batting championships.

While serving as player-manager of the Tigers in the mid-1920s Cobb benched himself when he was hitting .392. At the time, the Tigers had an all-.400 hitting outfield—Heinie Manush (.402), Fats Fothergill (.406), and Harry Heilmann (.410)—and Cobb didn't want to tamper with such statistics.

Although Pete Rose eclipsed Cobb's record for career hits, and Maury Wills, Lou Brock, and Rickey Henderson have broken most of his baserunning records, Cobb remains the career leader in steals of home (35); he also stole second, third, and home in the same inning three different times. While it cannot be documented statistically, his aggressive style produced balks, throwing errors, and lapses of concentration that counted as runs.

Cobb was shrewd as well as belligerent. He started the practice of swinging several bats in the on-deck circle so that one would feel light when it came time to hit. Similarly, he hunted in lead-weighted boots in the winter, practiced in them all spring, and switched to paper-thin shoes once the season started. (That same shrewdness led him to buy Coca-Cola at $1.18 a share and build a considerable fortune.)

Although Detroit won three straight pennants from 1907 to 1909, Cobb was never part of a world championship team and, as a manager, he never brought the Bengals home higher than second.

GORDON "MICKEY" COCHRANE

Catcher. Born Apr. 6, 1903 Bridgewater, Mass. Died Jun. 28, 1962 Lake Forest, Ill. AL MVP 1928, 1934.

Mickey Cochrane was a franchise player—literally. In 1924, Cochrane had hit .333 for Portland in the Pacific Coast League and carried a stiff $50,000 price tag. When Connie Mack found the whole club could be had for $200,000, he bought the franchise, sold the other players at a profit, and got Cochrane at a bargain price.

"Black Mike" hit .331, .357 and .349 from 1929 to 1931 to lead the A's to three pennants. A lifetime .320 hitter, he hit .300 or better nine times in his career. After he was sold to the Tigers in 1934 as a player-manager, he led them to a pennant in 1934 and a world championship in 1935.

Cochrane hit .400 in the 1929 Series, but Commissioner Landis threatened to suspend him for his brutal bench jockeying. Chastened, Cochrane greeted the Cubs with , "Hello, sweethearts! We're gonna serve tea this afternoon." After the A's won Game Five to secure the championship, Landis congratulated every Athletic except Cochrane. Just before he left, the Judge said to Mickey, "Hello, sweetheart. I came in after my tea. Will you pour?"

Mack sold Cochrane to the Tigers after the 1933 season. Just as he had sparked the A's, Black Mike led a fifth place team to the pennant his first year. As the season wore on, the exhausted Cochrane played but spent the night in a nearby hospital. The Gashouse Gang won the 1934 classic in seven games. Next year it was Cochrane's turn. He scored the run that clinched the World Series and later said, "It was my greatest day in baseball."

There would not be too many others. In a game against the Yankees in May 1937, Cochrane homered off Bump Hadley. On his next trip to the plate he took a fastball to his right temple and collapsed in a heap. He was unconscious for ten days but finally pulled through; he never played again. Elected to the Hall of Fame in 1947, he went on to serve as general manager of the A's under Mack and became a Tiger VP in 1961.

EDDIE "COCKY" COLLINS

Second Baseman. Born May 2, 1887 Millerton, N.Y. Died Mar. 25, 1951 Boston, Mass. Holds major league record for most years leading league in fielding (9). AL MVP 1914.

Eddie Collins may have been "Cocky," but as a member of four world championship teams he'd earned the right to be confident about his abilities. He hit an even .333 lifetime and batted .300 or better every year from 1909 to 1916 and the period 1919–1928.

Had Ty Cobb not been so dominant while Collins was playing, he might have enjoyed even greater recognition. As it was, Cocky hit .369, .365, and .360 without ever winning a batting title. He did lead the league in stolen bases four times, winding up with 744 career steals, behind only Cobb and Billy Hamilton during his lifetime.

Defensively he played more games (2,650) and had more putouts (6,526), assists (7,630) and total chances (14,591) than any other second baseman. Collins won nine fielding titles and, with the exception of 1918 when he missed 57 games because of injuries, he led the league in one or another fielding category every year from 1909 to 1922.

In 1906, he made his debut under the name Sullivan until it was revealed that Sullivan was, in reality, Columbia University's junior quarterback and star infielder Eddie Collins. He was allowed to continue at Columbia as nonplaying captain and joined the A's after graduation.

Collins quickly became the keystone of the A's infield. When shortstop Jack Barry, third baseman Frank "Home Run" Baker and first baseman John "Stuffy" McInnis joined the A's, the quartet became known as the "$100,000 infield" because Mack "wouldn't take that sum for all of them." The A's proceeded to roll to pennants in 1910, 1911, 1913, and 1914.

Sold to the White Sox in 1915 after winning the Chalmers Award as MVP in 1914, he hit .409 in the 1917 Series and scored the deciding run by slipping out of a rundown between third and home to beat the Giants' third baseman to the unprotected plate. Dispirited by some of his teammates' play in the Black Sox World Series of 1919, Collins batted only .226 but still stole a base to give him 14 career World Series thefts.

Inevitably, he became a manager, piloting the White Sox in 1925 and 1926 before returning to the Athletics as a pinch hitter—and leading the league in that department with a .353 average. He served as a highly placed Red Sox executive from 1932 until his death in 1951. Collins was elected to the Hall of Fame in 1939.

JOE CRONIN

Shortstop. Born Oct. 12, 1906 San Francisco, Cal. Died Sept. 7, 1984. AL MVP 1930.

Joe Cronin had 11 .300-plus seasons, hit .301 lifetime, won the Washington Senators' last pennant as a player-manager and, as a nonplaying manager, led the Red Sox to their only pennant in the 1940s.

Cronin grew up in San Francisco and signed with the Pirates but cooled his heels in the minors because the Bucs already had the league's leading shortstop in Glenn Wright. After Cronin signed with the Kansas City Blues, Joe Engel bought his contract for the Senators.

He finished 1928 in the big leagues, bettered .300 and 100 RBIs from 1930 to 1933, and also led the league in triples in 1932 (18) and in doubles in 1933 (45). Moreover, Cronin was the league's best shortstop in that time span, three times leading in putouts, assists, and double plays. Senators' owner Clark Griffith made him the manager at age twenty-six to replace Walter Johnson. Hailed as the Boy Manager, Cronin won the pennant in his first season, though the Senators lost the Series in five games to the Giants.

The Nats nosedived to seventh in 1934, and the high point of Cronin's season was marrying Griffith's adopted daughter, Mildred Robinson. While the two honeymooned, Red Sox boss Tom Yawkey angled to buy Cronin. When he offered a record $225,000 and shortstop Lyn Lary, the Boy Manager gave the go-ahead; in one move, Griffith had gotten rid of his shortstop, his manager and his son-in-law.

In 1938 Cronin hit a career high .325 and also led the league in doubles; however, the Sox finished second in four out of the five years between 1938 and 1942. Cronin stepped aside as shortstop in favor of Johnny Pesky, and prospered as a part-time player and pinch hitter, leading the league in 1943 with 18 hits in 42 at-bats, a .426 average. On one occasion he pinch hit home runs in both halves of a doubleheader. Ironically, the year he removed himself from the roster, 1946, the Red Sox won their first pennant since 1918, only to lose a seven-game Series to the Cardinals.

Cronin moved to the front office in 1948 and served as Boston's general manager until 1959 when he became AL president. He was named to the Hall of Fame in 1956.

BILL DICKEY

Catcher. Born Jun. 6, 1907 Bastrop, Ga. Died Nov. 12, 1993 Little Rock, Ark. Hit .362 in 1936, highest average for a catcher in this century.

Bill Dickey was the only Yankee quiet enough to play in the shadow of his roommate, the painfully shy Lou Gehrig, who had himself played in Babe Ruth's shadow.

Yet, with the passage of the years, it becomes clear that while Ruth started the Yankee mystique with his power and personality, the pinstriped legacy was passed along by quiet men—Gehrig, Dickey, Joe DiMaggio. An admiring Dan Daniel once wrote, "Dickey isn't just a catcher. He's a ball club. He isn't just a player. He's an influence."

With the Yanks and Reds scoreless in the ninth inning of the 1939 World Series opener, Charlie Keller tripled and Reds pitcher Paul Derringer walked Joe DiMaggio intentionally. Tommy Henrich says, "When I saw that— and this is the absolute gospel truth—I turned around and picked up my glove, because I knew the game was going to be over right now. And it was." (Dickey singled.)

One of the few nonpitchers in the Hall of Fame who never led the league in a single offensive category, he hit .300 or better eleven times—in 1936 a lofty .362, the highest mark for a backstop in this century—and compiled a lifetime average of .313. In the course of 6,300 at bats, he struck out only 289 times. As a bonus, Dickey caught 100 games in thirteen straight seasons, a record later tied by Johnny Bench.

At his best in October, Dickey hit .438 in the 1932 Classic, went 4-for-4 to open the 1938 edition, knocked in at least one run in every game in 1939, and finished off the Cardinals in Game Five of the 1943 Series with a two-run homer in the ninth.

Signed by Yankee scout Lena Blackburne on the back of an Elks Club card, Dickey tried to impress manager Miller Huggins with his home run swing. Huggins told him, "Stop unbuttoning your shirt on every pitch." With Ruth, Gehrig, and Lazzeri, the Yankees didn't need power from Dickey. What they wanted was steadiness. Dickey provided it, leading AL catchers three times each in assists and fielding and five times in putouts.

Given the job of turning Yogi Berra into a catcher, he looked up one day to find Joe Garagiola and Roy Campanella listening. In Yogi's phrase, Dickey "learned them all his experiences," too.

JOE DiMAGGIO

Center Field. Born Nov. 25, 1914 Martinez, Cal. Holds major league record for hitting in 56 consecutive games.

Babe Ruth played on seven pennant winners and four championship teams in his fifteen years as a Yankee; Joe DiMaggio played on ten pennant winners and nine championship teams in thirteen years.

At nineteen, he hit in 61 straight games for the San Francisco Seals, a Pacific Coast League record that still stands. Bought by the Yankees in 1936, he hit .323 as a rookie, led the league in home runs and runs scored the following year, and in 1939 led the league in batting and was named MVP for the first time.

He won the batting crown again in 1940 and the RBI title in 1941, the year he hit in 56 straight games, winning the MVP award despite Ted Williams' mark of .406. A disc jockey wrote a hit song called "Joltin' Joe DiMaggio." A Cincinnati high school class was asked to name the greatest American of all time; George Washington finished second to DiMaggio.

After his return from military service, DiMaggio had a sub-par 1946, hitting only .290. The next spring, he was almost traded for Williams. DiMaggio responded by winning his third MVP award in 1947 and blasting two home runs in the World Series.

On February 7, 1949, DiMaggio became the first $100,000 ballplayer and, despite serious injuries, helped the Yanks win the pennant. In 1951 he retired with a .325 career batting average, having played on All-Star teams in every year of major league service. He was named to the Hall of Fame in 1955.

Despite serving on the boards of the A's and Orioles, a turbulent marriage to Marilyn Monroe, commercials for banks and coffeemakers, and an involvement in signing memorabilia for profit, DiMaggio retains his aura of heroism. In 1989 former All-Star outfielder Andy Pafko said, "Even today I look up to him. And he's never disappointed me."

JOHNNY EVERS

Second Baseman. Born July 21, 1881 Troy, N.Y. Died Mar. 28, 1947 Albany, N.Y. NL MVP 1914.

When Johnny Evers joined the Cubs in 1902 he played both ends of a Labor Day doubleheader; yet his mates thought so little of him that they refused to let him on the team bus; he had to ride on top instead.

As things turned out, Evers was a Hall of Fame second baseman and a winner in every sinew of his 125-pound body. An early incarnation of Eddie Stanky or Billy Martin, Evers single-mindedly drove himself and his mates to victory and his opponents to distraction. He was on five pennant winners, and three of the four times he played his team won the Series. (A broken leg kept him out of the 1910 Series, which the Cubs lost.)

Born in Troy, he was "the Trojan," but that nickname soon gave way to "the Crab." Like many other bantam-sized battlers, Evers had a chip on his shoulder and never ran from a fight. He and shortstop Joe Tinker had a falling out on September 14, 1905, when Evers took a cab to the park without waiting for Tinker; although they didn't speak for thirty-three years, they won three championships together.

The third championship came in 1908 when Evers batted 1.000 in the rules department. On September 4, with one out in the bottom of the tenth of a scoreless tie, the Pirates loaded the bases; Owen "Chief" Wilson singled, Fred Clarke scored the winning run, and Warren Gill, the runner on first, started for the clubhouse. Evers called for the ball, touched second, and told umpire Hank O'Day the side had been retired because Gill had been "forced." O'Day disallowed that protest but, when the same situation arose on September 23, Evers's alertness caused the controversial "Merkle boner" game to end in a tie and, after a one-game playoff to break a final-day tie, give Chicago its third straight pennant.

In February 1914, Evers was sold to the Braves. He and Rabbit Maranville led the Miracle Braves from last place to the pennant, and Evers was named MVP and shone in the World Series, hitting .438 to lead the Braves to a sweep. He ended his career in Philadelphia, although he played one game each for the Braves and White Sox while coaching with them. He, Tinker, and Frank Chance were reunited in the Hall of Fame in 1946.

WILLIAM "BUCK" EWING

Catcher. Born Oct. 17, 1859 Hoaglands, Oh. Died Oct. 20, 1906, Cincinnati, Oh.

In the 1919 *Reach Guide*, sportswriter Francis Richter picked the three greatest players of all time—Ty Cobb, Honus Wagner, and Buck Ewing—and said that, in his prime (1884–1890), Ewing was "the greatest player of the game." In the 1930 *Spalding Guide*, editor John Foster said Ewing "was the greatest all-around player ever connected with the game."

For one thing, Ewing did play all around literally, all nine positions. In addition to catching 636 games and leading all catchers in assists three times and double plays twice, he played 253 at first, 212 at the other infield slots, and 112 in the outfield. Finally, with the Giants involved in the pennant race in 1889 and short of pitchers, Ewing even pitched and won two games.

A lifetime .303 hitter, Ewing was fast enough to lead the league in triples in 1884 (20), and strong enough to outhomer it in 1883 (10). One of the few catchers to bat leadoff and be considered a real threat to run, Ewing stole 40 or more bases four times in his career. In one famous instance, he stole second, stole third, announced, "Now I'm stealing home," and made it. The moment was later immortalized in a famous lithograph.

But Ewing's greatest fame came as a defensive catcher and strategist. Mickey Welch, a Hall of Fame pitcher, said Ewing was "the thinking man's player" and credited him with inventing the pregame clubhouse meeting. It is said that Ewing also originated the practice of throwing from a crouch, saving precious fractions of a second to catch larcenous runners.

In 1888 John Montgomery Ward resigned as team captain, a position closer to today's manager, and Ewing took over and led the Giants to their first pennant. For the 1889 season, Ewing was paid $5,000, a princely sum, and hit .327 as the Giants repeated. When the Players League was founded, Ewing jumped to be player-manager of the New York team, rejoined the Giants when the league folded, and later played at Cleveland and Cincinnati, where he succeeded Charles Comiskey as the Reds' manager.

Ewing died a wealthy man from real estate investments. In 1936 he tied Cap Anson for the most "old-timer" votes in the intial selection of men for the Hall of

Fame, and three years later, when the new museum opened, he and his old rival were immortalized with plaques.

BOB FELLER

Pitcher. Born Nov. 3, 1918 Van Meter, Ia. Threw three no-hitters and twelve one-hitters.

Bob Feller struck out 17 Athletics in a major league game in 1936, tying Dizzy Dean's record; then he went back to Van Meter, Iowa, to finish high school.

Feller generated statewide publicity at sixteen, and the Indians signed him to a contract before he completed high school, a violation of baseball rules. When he attracted attention pitching in Des Moines, the Tigers also offered him a bonus, and the truth was revealed. Commissioner Landis fined the Indians $7,500 and ruled that Feller was free to sign with any team. The bidding might have reached $100,000, an astronomical sum in those days, but Feller respected his contract and signed with the Indians.

Without any minor league experience, he faced the Cardinals in an exhibition game on July 6, 1936, and fanned eight members of the Gashouse Gang in three innings. "Rapid Robert" won his first big league start, 4–1, striking out 15 St. Louis Browns.

On the last day of the 1938 season, 30,000 people came to see Hank Greenberg try to break Babe Ruth's record of 60 home runs in a season. Instead, they saw Feller strike out 18 Tigers to set the major league record (since broken) and win the AL strikeout title, beating out Bobo Newsom. (He also led in bases on balls.)

By the time he was twenty-three Feller had won 107 games. He enlisted in the Navy the day after Pearl Harbor and was sworn in by former heavyweight champ Gene Tunney. Pitching anti-aircraft shells from the deck of the battleship *Alabama*, Feller missed nearly four full seasons but earned six battle citations as a gun crew chief.

Returning to baseball at the end of 1945, he had his best season ever in 1946, winning 26 games, striking out a record 348 batters in 371 innings, and recording 10 shutouts with an ERA of 2.18. In 1948, he two-hit the Braves in his only World Series game but lost. In 1951, he still had enough stuff to throw his third no-hitter and lead the league with a record of 22–8.

By the time he retired, Feller had pitched twelve one-hitters, won 20 or more games six times and rolled up 2,581 career strikeouts. Satchel Paige summed up his career this way: "If anybody threw that ball any harder than Rapid Robert, then the human eye couldn't follow it." He was elected to the Hall of Fame in 1962.

ROLLIE FINGERS

Pitcher. Born Aug. 25, 1946 Steubenville, Oh. AL Cy Young Award and MVP, 1981. Established major league record for saves, 341 (since surpassed).

If he hadn't been such a worrywart, Rollie Fingers might have been an average starter; instead, he fretted himself right into the bullpen and became a Hall of Fame fireman.

"I would plan my pitches days in advance of my start and get so wound up I couldn't sleep the night before my turn," he recalled. After finishing only four of thirty-five starts, he took immediately to the relief role in 1971 and finished with 17 saves. In 1972, he led the league with 11 relief wins and 21 saves to help Oakland win the division.

Fingers pitched in six of the seven games in the 1972 World Series, earning saves in Games Two and Seven and a win in Game Four. One year later, he pitched 3⅓ hitless innings in the Series opener against the Mets, saved Game Three for Paul Lindblad and Game Six for Catfish Hunter, and yielded only one unearned run in 3⅓ innings of relief in the finale.

In 1974, he led the A's to a third straight world championship. He got the win in Game One; for a change, Catfish Hunter got the save. The roles were reversed in Game Three when Fingers saved Hunter. Rollie got a second save the next day, and was named Series MVP.

When Fingers and the A's reached a contract impasse, owner Charlie Finley sold him to Boston, but Commissioner Bowie Kuhn voided the sale. With San Diego in 1977, Fingers appeared in 78 games and saved 35 (league-leading figures), and earned National League Fireman of the Year honors.

Four days after being traded to St. Louis in 1980, he moved again, to Milwaukee. During the strike-shortened 1981 season, he notched a league-leading 28 saves and posted a brilliant 1.04 ERA. Fingers won his fourth Fireman of the Year award, won the Cy Young Award, and was also named MVP.

After posting 29 saves in 1982, Fingers missed the World Series and the entire 1983 season because of tendinitis. He came back to notch 23 saves by July, 1984, when a herniated disk ended his season and career. He ranks first in wins plus saves (430) and was inducted into the Hall of Fame in 1992.

CARLTON FISK
Catcher. Born Dec. 26, 1947 Bellows Falls, Vt. Holds major league record for lifetime home runs by a catcher (351). Holds major league record for games caught (2,226).

During a Yankees–White Sox game in May 1990, Carlton Fisk blasted Deion Sanders for not running out a pop fly, starting a brawl but enhancing Fisk's role as Defender of the Game. Moreover, it came at a time when Fisk, a ten-time All-Star, was trying to push an unknown pitching staff to a division title.

That year Fisk, already the oldest regular catcher in baseball history, hit 18 homers to pass Johnny Bench as baseball's leading home run-hitting catcher, extended his AL record of games caught, and added to his total as modern baseball's best base-stealing catcher. Fisk, Bench, and Yogi Berra are the only three receivers to hit 300 homers and both score and drive in 1,000 runs.

Carlton Ernest Fisk grew up in Charlestown, New Hampshire on the heavy side (5'4", 155) and was dubbed "Pudge" by a female relative. A three-sport MVP in high school, he earned a basketball scholarship to the University of New Hampshire but signed instead with the Red Sox in 1967.

Brought up late in 1971 for a look-see, he was the All-Star catcher by the summer of '72. That fall he became the first AL Rookie of the Year to be chosen unanimously. In 1975 injuries limited him to only 79 games during the regular season, but he created one of baseball's enduring moments in the World Series with a twelfth-inning, body English home run off the Reds' Pat Darcy to end the now fabled Game Six.

After the 1980 season, free agent Fisk signed with the White Sox. He had worn number 27 in Boston but sported number 72 in Chicago, because "it represents a turn-around in my career." Following a workmanlike 1982 season, Fisk slumped in early 1983 and was hitting only .136. Replaced in both halves of a June 12 doubleheader in Oakland, Fisk jawed with manager Tony LaRussa. LaRussa said, "He came out fighting, the way a winner reacts to a challenge." In the next 71 games, Fisk hit 16 homers, drove in 49 runs, raised his average more than 100 points, and helped Chicago clinch the division.

An Opening Day abdominal muscle pull hampered him in 1984. The next year, however, at age thirty-seven, Fisk had his greatest campaign, knocking in 107 runs and hitting 37 homers.

ED "WHITEY" FORD
Pitcher. Born Oct. 21, 1928 New York, N.Y. Holds record for World Series wins (10); AL Cy Young Award, 1961.

Whitey Ford won 236 games and lost only 106 to register a lifetime .690 won-lost percentage, the highest recorded by any pitcher since 1900. He also broke Babe Ruth's forty-five-year-old record of 29⅔ scoreless innings in World Series competition, ending up with 32. Ford also holds the records for most Series wins (10), strikeouts (94), and innings pitched (146).

Ford's Series stats are so impressive that his regular season numbers tend to get buried. He won 20 games only twice in sixteen seasons; however, from 1953 to 1960, he averaged nearly 16 wins against 7 losses. Casey Stengel, who manipulated the rotation so Ford faced the toughies (though he kept him out of Boston's Fenway Park), said, "If you had one game to win and your life depended on it, you'd want him to pitch it."

Even though he led the league in wins, innings pitched, and won-lost percentage and won the Cy Young Award in 1961, Ford's 25–4 record was almost overshadowed by Roger Maris's quest for home run number 61. He got more recognition by going 24–7 in 1963 and repeating in all three categories.

Ford was inducted into the Hall of Fame on August 12, 1974, along with Mickey Mantle, his partner in the long-running "Mick and Slick" Show. When writers recalled the spitter Ford used to strike out Willie Mays in the 1964 All-Star Game, Ford said, "Look, they didn't call me Slick for nothing."

JIMMIE FOXX
First Baseman. Born Oct. 22, 1907 Sudlersville, Md. Died July 21, 1967 Miami, Fla. Holds major league record for most consecutive years with 30 or more home runs (12). AL MVP 1932, 1933, 1938.

Jimmie Foxx hit some of baseball's most awesome home runs. He homered over the two-tiered left field stands in Shibe Park, drove a ball out of Comiskey Park some 600 feet from home plate, broke a seat in the upper deck of left field at Yankee Stadium, and hit what he considered his longest shot over the left-center field fence in Sportsman's Park to win Game Five of the 1930 Series. Ted Williams, not known for admiring other hitters, said of Foxx, "I never saw anyone hit a baseball harder."

Nicknamed "The Beast" and "Double X," Foxx won three MVP awards (1932, 1933, 1938), knocked in 100 or more runs in thirteen straight seasons, won five slugging titles, hit .300 or better thirteen times, and ended his career with a lifetime batting average of .325, 534 homers, and 1,922 RBIs. He also set a record by hitting 30 or more home runs in 12 consecutive seasons.

Appropriately enough this great home run hitter was discovered at age sixteen by none other than Home Run Baker. He entered Organized Baseball as a catcher. After several .300-plus seasons as a utility player, Foxx was installed at first base in 1929 and hit .354 with 33 homers. In 1932 he mounted the first serious challenge to Babe Ruth's season record of 60 home runs with 58. (According to writer Fred Lieb, Foxx hit five doubles against the right field screen in Sportsman's Park, which hadn't been there in 1927 when Ruth hit 60 homers.) Foxx failed to win the Triple Crown when Dale Alexander was named batting champ, even though he didn't have 400 at bats. Nevertheless, the Beast led the league in homers (58), runs scored (151), RBIs (169), total bases (438) and slugging (.749) and finished second in batting average (.364) and hits (213) to win his first MVP award.

In 1933 he repeated as MVP, topped the league with a slugging percentage of .703, and captured the Triple Crown, hitting 48 homers, driving in 163 runs, and hitting .356. After tying Hank Greenberg for the home run crown in 1935, he was sold to the Red Sox. Foxx responded with another MVP year in 1938, leading the league with 175 RBIs and hitting 50 homers, second only to Greenberg's 58.

Foxx entered the pantheon at Cooperstown in 1951.

FRANKIE FRISCH

Second Baseman. Born Sept. 9, 1898 New York, N.Y. Died Mar. 12, 1973 Wilmington, Del. Holds major league records for most assists (641) and chances accepted (1,037) in a season, 1927; NL MVP 1931.

Frank Frisch, "The Fordham Flash," had something to prove in 1927.

Giants manager John McGraw, the man who had taken Frisch from Fordham to stardom, had traded him to the Cardinals after the 1926 season for Rogers Hornsby. McGraw had taught Frisch how to switch hit and play the hitters, and had been a father figure for Frisch, giving the trade a personal twist.

Frisch spent the winter toughening up and came out charging. He hit .337, led the league in steals, handled a record 1,037 chances (including a record 641 assists), made the most double plays, and just missed being named MVP, finishing second to Paul Waner. Cardinal catcher Bob O'Farrell, the MVP a year before, said, "The greatest player I ever saw in any one season was Frankie Frisch in 1927."

He'd served as captain of the baseball, football and basketball teams at Fordham and been a second-team All-America halfback when he joined the Giants in 1919. Frisch led the league in stolen bases in 1921 and hits in 1923, and the Giants won pennants every year from 1921–1924. He went 4-for-4 in the 1921 Series opener and averaged .363 in his first four Series.

The Flash also brought the Cardinals to three World Series as a player and one as a player-manager. The Yanks swept St. Louis in 1928 and the A's took them in six games in 1930, so 1931 was doubly sweet. Frisch sparked

the Cardinals to a seventh-game win over the A's and was also named MVP. In the first All-Star Game, in 1933, Frisch singled and hit the first NL homer.

Shortly thereafter, he took over as player-manager of the Gashouse Gang, riding herd over Pepper Martin, Dizzy Dean, and company. In 1934 he hit .305 (one of thirteen times he hit .300 or better) and led the Redbirds to a pennant. In Game Seven of the Series, the Tigers intentionally walked Jack Rothrock to load the bases; Frisch unloaded them with a double and the Cardinals went on to a rout, 11–0.

After retiring as a player to devote himself to managing full time, Frisch never won another pennant with the Cardinals, Pirates, or Cubs; however, in 1947 he began a third successful career as a Giants broadcaster. In that same year he was reunited with McGraw in the Hall of Fame.

LOU GEHRIG

First Base. Born Jun. 19, 1903 New York, N.Y. Died June 2, 1941 Riverdale, N.Y. Holds major league records for consecutive games played (2,130) and grand slams (23); AL MVP 1927, 1936.

Playing in Babe Ruth's shadow may have robbed Lou Gehrig of the spotlight, but, as he himself said, "It's a pretty big shadow. It gives me lots of room to spread myself." The year Ruth retired (1935), Gehrig began a three-year streak of leading the league in walks, a good measure of the respect pitchers still had for him when he was in his mid-thirties.

Gehrig had 200 or more hits in eight seasons, never hit below .300 from 1926 to 1937, and had a career average of .340. He tied Ruth for the RBI lead in 1928 and led the league outright four times; his 184 ribbies in 1931 is still the league record. The "Iron Horse" led in homers in 1934 and 1936 and tied Ruth for the lead in 1931 with 46, when Lyn Lary's baserunning mistake—passing a runner on the bases—robbed him of his 47th. He also holds the record for career grand slams (23). On June 3, 1932, he was the first modern slugger to hit four home runs in a game, an achievement that was somewhat eclipsed because it happened on the same day as John McGraw's retirement.

Although Gehrig originally went to Columbia on a football scholarship, Giant manager John McGraw persuaded him to play pro baseball under an assumed name (Lewis) in 1921, making him ineligible for college ball; however, Gehrig's coach, Andy Coakley, persuaded the faculty to give Lou another chance. The contract was dissolved, and Gehrig resumed collegiate play.

In 1934, Ruth's last year as a Yankee, Gehrig won the Triple Crown, leading the AL in homers (49), RBIs (165), and batting average (.363). He batted .361 in World Series play, averaging an RBI a game for 34 games with 43 hits, 10 of them homers.

Suffering from the effects of amyotrophic lateral sclerosis, Gehrig took himself out of the lineup on May 2, 1939, after playing in 2,130 consecutive games. He entered the Hall of Fame later that year when the Baseball Writers Association waived the existing rule which required a player to be retired one year before he could be elected.

On Lou Gehrig Day at Yankee Stadium, the stoical

slugger told a packed house, "I may have been given a bad break, but with all this I have a lot to live for. I consider myself the luckiest man on the face of the earth."

CHARLIE GEHRINGER
Second Baseman. Born May 11, 1903 Fowlerville, Mich. Died Jan. 21, 1993 Bloomfield Hills, Mich. American League MVP 1937.

Describing Charlie Gehringer, Mickey Cochrane said of his teammate, "He says hello on opening day and goodbye on closing day, and in between he hits .350."

Gehringer was so quiet that when he was given a "Day," the lefthander was given a set of righthanded golf clubs and learned to play the game righthanded. He celebrated the Day by homering on the first pitch thrown to him, getting three other hits, and stealing home to win the game.

"The Mechanical Man" had 200 or more hits seven times, bettered .300 fourteen times, and knocked in 100 or more runs seven times. In the field, he led the AL in fielding six times, putouts three times, and assists a record seven times. A measure of Gehringer's all-around excellence is the 1929 season, when he led the league in stolen bases, doubles, triples, hits, runs, games, putouts, and fielding while hitting .339. As for consistency, he hit .320 lifetime and .320 in twenty World Series games.

Like Bob Feller, Gehringer played his first baseball on a field carved out of a family farm. A third baseman at the University of Michigan, Gehringer was discovered by Tiger great Bobby Veach and, despite his quiet nature, became a favorite of manager Ty Cobb. Cobb resisted all efforts to change Gehringer's swing and said that, aside from Eddie Collins, Gehringer was "the best second baseman I ever saw."

After brief callups in 1924 and 1925, Gehringer became the Tigers' regular second baseman in 1926. In 1933 he started a string of six straight starts for the AL in the All-Star Game. He is the midsummer classic's lifetime batting leader with an even .500 average (10 for 20).

This splendid ballplaying machine was equally sparkling in World Series play, hitting .379, leading all Tiger hitters in a losing effort in 1934. In 1935, however, Detroit's "G-Men"—Hank Greenberg, Gehringer, and Goose Goslin—became champions, beating the Cubs as Gehringer hit .375 and handled 39 chances flawlessly.

In 1937 Gehringer reached the high-water mark of his career, hitting .371 and being named MVP. After three more .300-plus seasons, he played out the string during World War II. Elected to the Hall of Fame in 1949, he served as the Tigers' general manager from 1951 to 1953 and a vice president until 1959.

BOB GIBSON
Pitcher. Born Nov. 9, 1935 Omaha, Neb. Holds major league season record for lowest ERA in 300 or more innings (1.12), 1968. NL MVP 1968, Cy Young Award 1968, 1970.

Bob Gibson was a winner whether he was using his arm, his bat, or his glove.

In a fifteen-year career, he won 251 games, posted 56 shutouts, became the first major leaguer to strike out 200 or more in nine seasons, and posted a lifetime ERA of 2.91. He also hit 24 regular season home runs and earned

a Gold Glove every year from 1965 to 1973.

Gibson suffered from rickets and asthma while growing up in Omaha and because of a heart murmur needed a doctor's permission to play ball. Nevertheless, he starred as the switch-hitting catcher-shortstop of a YMCA team, won a basketball scholarship to Creighton University, played with the Harlem Globetrotters for a year, joined the Cards for good in 1961, and had his first big year in 1963, going 18–9.

In 1964 his 19–12 record helped the Cards win the pennant, and he began an unprecedented streak of seven straight World Series wins by taking Game Five and, on two days' rest, Game Seven. On his way to another big year in 1967 (13 wins), Gibson was out when Roberto Clemente's smash fractured his left leg. Incredibly, after being sidelined for eight weeks, he came back to win three World Series games against the Red Sox, allowing just three earned runs and pitching three complete games.

In 1968 he was even better, posting a record of 22–9 with an ERA of 1.12, breaking Walter Johnson's 1913 record for the lowest ERA with 300 or more innings pitched. That year Gibson pitched 13 shutouts, and surrendered just 2 runs during one 95-inning stretch during the regular season to win both the MVP and Cy Young Awards. Awesome in the 1968 Series, he struck out 17 Tigers, a World Series record, while winning the opener.

In 1970 he was 23–7 and took his second Cy Young Award. On July 17, 1974, he became only the second pitcher (Walter Johnson was the first) to notch 3,000 strikeouts. Shortly before Gibson retired, 55,000 people at Busch Stadium gave him a ten-minute standing ovation. He was named to the Hall of Fame in 1981.

JOSH GIBSON
Catcher. Born Dec. 21, 1911 Buena Vista, Ga. Died Jan. 20, 1947 Pittsburgh, Pa.

Josh Gibson may have been the greatest catcher of all time. Walter Johnson said of him, "He hits the ball a mile. Throws like a rifle. Bill Dickey isn't as good a catcher." Roy Campanella, who saw Gibson at his peak, said, "When I broke in with the Baltimore Elite Giants in 1937 there were already a thousand legends about him; once you saw him play you knew they were all true."

According to a 1967 article in *The Sporting News*, Gibson hit a ball two feet from the top of the stadium wall circling the bleachers at Yankee Stadium, some 580 feet from home plate. His Hall of Fame plaque credits him with "almost 800 home runs," and various authorities say he hit 69, 75, 84, and 89 home runs in a season, albeit sometimes against semipro pitching. Gibson could also hit for average, compiling a .412 mark in 34 at bats against big league pitching. And, while he wasn't a great handler of pitchers or catcher of popups, few baserunners tried to steal on him because of his great arm.

He was born in Buena Vista, Georgia, and moved to Pittsburgh when he was twelve. As a youngster he won numerous swimming medals. At maturity, he stood 6' 2" and weighed 210.

Unable to break into the lineup of Pittsburgh's Homestead Grays, Gibson organized the semipro Crawford Colored Giants; He was in the stands when the Grays' regular catcher, Buck Ewing, split a finger in June 1930; he changed into a uniform and never left the lineup again.

In 1931 Gus Greenlee founded the Pittsburgh Crawfords, signed Gibson and Satchel Paige, and wrote ads that promised, "Josh Gibson will hit a home run and Satchel Paige will strike out the side on nine pitches." They nearly always delivered. Gibson also played winter ball extensively and said his greatest thrill was being chosen MVP of the Puerto Rican League in 1941.

Pirate owner Bill Benswanger reportedly signed him to a contract in 1943, but Commissioner Landis vetoed the signing. On January 20, 1947, three months before Jackie Robinson's major league debut, Gibson died of a stroke. He was elected to the Hall of Fame in 1972.

HANK GREENBERG

First Baseman. Born Jan. 1, 1911 New York, N.Y. Died Sept. 4, 1986 Beverly Hills, Cal. AL MVP 1935, 1940.
In 1934, the big question in Detroit was, "Should Hank Greenberg play on Rosh Hashanah and Yom Kippur?"

With the Tigers involved in a hot pennant race with the Yankees, the Jewish slugger sought spiritual guidance. After due deliberation, Rabbi Leo Franklin ruled that Greenberg should play on Rosh Hashanah, the Jewish New Year, a happy occasion; he did and hit a tenth-inning homer to win the game. However, Rabbi Franklin said the slugger should pray, not play, on Yom Kippur, the Day of Atonement. Greenberg acquiesced. Poet Edgar Guest commented:

We shall miss him in the infield and shall miss him at the bat
But he's true to his religion—and I honor him for that.

The Tigers won the pennant, and Greenberg homered in the World Series, as he would in all four Series in which he played. A year later, his 36 homers and 170 RBIs earned him the MVP award, but he missed the last four games of the Series with a broken wrist. Greenberg had a null year in 1936—67 at bats; however, in 1937, he drove in a mind-boggling 183 runs and, in 1938 fell just short of Babe Ruth's season home run record, with 58.

After hitting 33 homers and knocking in 112 runs in 1939, he was forced to take a $10,000 pay cut—if he stayed at first base. Instead he moved to the outfield, making way for good-hit, no-field Rudy York, and got a $10,000 raise. He was named MVP again in 1940, when the Tigers lost the Series in seven games to Cincinnati.

In May 1941 Greenberg was drafted into the Army and returned in July 1945, winning the pennant for the Tigers on the last day of the season with a grand slam in the bottom of the ninth inning. In 1947 he had a last fling with the Pirates, hitting 25 homers and knocking in 74 runs in his only NL season. When he retired that fall, he had led the league in RBIs four times, won home run honors outright four times and tied for the lead once, and hit 331 career home runs, even though he had lost four and a half seasons to the war and injury. He was elected to the Hall of Fame in 1956.

ROBERT "LEFTY" GROVE

Pitcher. Born Mar. 6, 1900 Lonaconing, Md. Died May 22, 1975 Norwalk, Oh. AL MVP 1931.
In 1931 Lefty Grove was en route to his seventeenth straight victory, which would have broken the AL record

then shared by Walter Johnson and Smoky Joe Wood. Al Simmons had taken the day off, and the rookie outfielder subbing for him misjudged a fly ball, leading to an unearned run; Grove lost, 1–0. He said, "After that game I went in and tore the clubhouse up. Wrecked the place. Tore those stall lockers off the wall, giving Al Simmons hell all the while."

Grove recovered his composure, won another eight straight, was named MVP, and ended the season 31–4, possibly the single greatest season enjoyed by any hurler. The dominant pitcher of his era, he was the AL's strikeout leader his first seven years, led in ERA a record nine times, and went on to compile a won-lost record of 300–141, a winning percentage of .680. Normalized for league average and adjusted for home park, his 3.06 ERA is, quite simply, the best in baseball history.

He started in Organized Ball with Martinsburg, West Virginia, of the Blue Ridge League and joined the International League Orioles when Baltimore bartered for him, paying cash for Martinsburg's new center field fence. Owner Jack Dunn knew what he had in Grove and delayed his entry to the big leagues until the southpaw was twenty-five; he sold Grove to Connie Mack's A's for $100,600—$600 more than the Red Sox had paid for Babe Ruth in 1914.

Like Sandy Koufax after him, Grove had his troubles initially, winning 10 and losing 12 in 1925, his rookie year; however, the following year his ERA improved from 4.75 to 2.51, good enough to lead the league for the first time. By 1927, he was ready for his first 20-win season and tied George Pipgras for the league lead in wins (24) while losing only 8.

From 1929 to 1931 Grove was an awesome 79–15, and the A's won pennants every year as well as the Series the first two. By the time he was sold to the Red Sox for $125,000 in 1933, he had won 20, 24, 20, 28, 31, 25, and 24 games in seven consecutive seasons. Yet success didn't mellow him; in batting practice a teammate once hit a ball back through the box; on the next pitch the batter hit the dust. Grove was elected to the Hall of Fame in 1947.

"SLIDING BILLY" HAMILTON

Center Fielder. Born Feb. 16, 1866 Newark, N.J. Died Dec. 16, 1940 Worcester, Mass. Holds major league record for runs scored in a season (196), 1894; stole 912 bases, a mark that stood for nine decades.
Although he was nicknamed for his daring, head-first slides, looking at the records, it's clear that Billy Hamilton should properly have been nicknamed "Scoring Billy."

Hamilton notched a record 1,690 runs in 1,591 games, making him the most effective leadoff man of all time. (For comparison, Rickey Henderson had, at the end of the 1994 season, 1,652 in 2,080 games.) What's more, Billy could hit as well as run. He missed hitting .300 only in his first and last seasons, led the league in hitting twice, and retired with a lifetime average of .344.

He was also a part of history's only all-.400 outfield, the Phillies' 1894 edition; Hamilton's puny .404 was dwarfed by the lusty .407 achieved by both his oversized garden mates, "Big Sam" Thompson and "Big Ed" Delahanty. (Incredibly, spare outfielder Tuck Turner, in over 300 at bats, hit for .416.)

Equally oversized is Hamilton's stolen base total. The record credits him with 912 steals—100-plus each in the years from 1889 to 1891. At the time, however, if a runner tagged up on a fly ball, went from first to third on a single, or moved up on a ground ball to the right side, he was credited with a stolen base. Beginning in 1892, steals were awarded to a runner only if there were "a possible chance and a palpable attempt made to retire him." Sliding Billy slid to only 57 and 43 steals the next two years but rebounded with 98 and 97 in 1894 and 1895 to lead the league. He also topped all NLers in bases on balls, runs scored (a record 192 in 1894), and on-base percentage. In fact, his on-base percentage of .455 over nearly 1600 games is probably a greater achievement than all the stolen bases; he trails only Ted Williams, Babe Ruth, and John McGraw in this department.

Hamilton moved over to the Boston Beaneaters in 1896. He missed 59 games in 1899 because of injuries and played his last major league season in 1901. Far from ready to retire, he played ten more years in the Tri-State and New England Leagues. After becoming a Red Sox scout, he bought part of the Worcester team. Sliding Billy was named to the Hall of Fame in 1961.

CHARLES "GABBY" HARTNETT

Catcher. Born Dec. 20, 1900 Woonsocket, R.I. Died Dec. 20, 1972 Park Ridge, Ill. NL MVP 1935.

Gabby Hartnett had an active role in three of baseball's greatest moments. He caught Charlie Root when Babe Ruth "called his shot" in the 1932 World Series; flashed the signs when Carl Hubbell fanned Ruth and four other Hall of Fame sluggers in order in the 1934 All-Star Game; and, hit the "Homer in the Gloamin'" that put the Cubs ahead to stay in the 1938 pennant race.

The NL Bill Dickey, Hartnett was resilient, reliable, clever at picking pitches, and blessed with a shotgun for an arm. He caught 100 or more games twelve times, had a career average of .297, and set the standard for NL catchers defensively, leading four times in putouts, six times in assists, and six times in fielding percentage.

Hartnett was born in Woonsocket, Rhode Island to an unusual family; his mother had seven boys in a row and then seven girls in a row. Signed by the Cubs in high school, he was silent on his first train trip west to Catalina in 1922, and a reporter promptly dubbed him Gabby. His father had played semipro ball with Grover Cleveland Alexander, the Cubs' reigning star. Alexander insisted that Hartnett catch him on Opening Day, and Hartnett called the pitches for most of his starts thereafter.

By 1924 Gabby was doing the bulk of the catching, and Bob O'Farrell was traded to the Cardinals. Joe McCarthy became the Cubs' manager in 1926 and brought them a pennant winner in 1929 without Hartnett, who due to a dead arm caught in only one game. Hartnett's mother thought the pain in his arm was related to his wife's pregnancy; when the baby was born in December, the pain went away.

Hartnett came out charging in 1930. He led all the fielding categories, hit .339, and knocked in a career-high 122 runs; in 1935, he hit .344 and was named MVP. With the Cubs 5½ games behind Pittsburgh in July 1938, he became player-manager. On September 28, with darkness falling at Wrigley Field, Hartnett's homer to left in the bottom of the ninth off Pittsburgh's Mace Brown gave them a half-game lead they never relinquished. The famous blow was the highlight of a stretch drive that saw the Cubs leapfrog over three teams to win the pennant.

The Cubs faltered the next two years, and Hartnett was released, eventually catching on as a player-coach with Bill Terry's Giants. He later managed in the minors and was elected to the Hall of Fame in 1955.

RICKEY HENDERSON

Left Field. Born Dec. 25, 1958 Chicago, Ill. Holds major league records for stolen bases season (130), 1982, and lifetime (1,117). AL MVP, 1990.

The most powerful leadoff man in history, Rickey Henderson broke Bobby Bonds's career record for leadoff homers in 1989 and had 66 at the end of the 1994 season. He was named the American League MVP in 1990, broke Lou Brock's record for career steals on May 1, 1991, and, a year later to the day, became the first man to steal 1,000 bases.

None of this surprised long-time Henderson watchers, who became convinced of his gifts when he played for Modesto of the California League. In 1977 Henderson stole a a record 95 bases, led league outfielders in total chances (313), hit .345 to be named MVP, and became only the fourth man in professional baseball to steal seven bases in a single game.

Brought up to Oakland in 1979, the "Man of Steal" absconded with 33 bases in 89 games and, a year later, became the first ALer to steal 100 bases in a season, was second in the AL in walks, third in on-base percentage, and fourth in runs scored. A year later, during the strike-shortened 1981 season, he led the league in hits (135), runs (89), and steals (56); he also led the league's outfielders in putouts and total chances and won a Gold Glove, the first of many.

In 1982 Henderson broke Lou Brock's record of 118 steals in a season, set in 1974, winding up with 130. After the 1984 season he became a Yankee in exchange for Tim Birtsas, Eric Plunk, Stan Javier, Jay Howell, and Jose Rijo. Although he missed the first 10 games of the 1985 season with a sprained left ankle, he hit 24 homers, knocked in 72 runs, batted .314, and led the league in runs scored (146) for the second time, the highest total since Ted Williams scored 150 in 1949.

Henderson led the league in steals every year from 1980 to 1990 except in 1987, when he missed 57 games due to injuries. Traded back to Oakland in June 1989, Henderson helped the A's win the division and starred in the playoffs, tying Jim Rice's record of 8 runs scored in a single series, stealing a record 8 bases, and being named MVP. He was chosen World Series MVP as well and was named regular season MVP in 1990 when he hit .325 and hit 28 homers. In 1993 he was traded to the Blue Jays and helped them to their second straight championship. He has the highest Total Player Rating among active players and, with many years of optimum performance ahead, is already the twelfth greatest player of all time.

ROGERS HORNSBY

Second Baseman. Born Apr. 27, 1896 Winters, Tex. Died Jan. 5, 1963 Chicago, Ill. Holds modern major league record for highest batting average in a season (.424), 1924, and NL record for batting average, lifetime (.358). Rogers Hornsby was suspicious, short-tempered, and the greatest righthanded hitter that ever lived.

The Rajah hit .300 or better in fourteen full seasons, won the NL batting title six straight years (1920–1925), is the only righthanded hitter to bat .400 or better three times and ended his career with a lifetime average of .358, second only to Ty Cobb. Like Cobb, he was thorny and idiosyncratic, reserving the right to bet on horses and refusing to read books or see movies for fear it would hurt his eyesight.

His career didn't begin auspiciously; Hornsby made 58 errors at shortstop in the Texas League and was unimpressive in 18 games with the Cardinals in 1915. Manager Miller Huggins told him to put on weight and, 25 pounds heavier, the Rajah hit .313 to lead the Cardinals in 1916.

By the mid-1920s he was the dominant player in the NL, winning the Triple Crown in both 1922 and 1925, when he became the Cardinals player-manager and was also named MVP for the first time. For the five-year period 1921–1925 his batting average exceeded .400! In 1926 he slumped to .317 but he gave the Cardinals their first pennant and helped upset the Yanks in a seven-game Series.

Two months after his great triumph, on December 20, 1926, he was traded to the Giants for Frankie Frisch and Jimmy Ring. Before the trade could go through, Hornsby had to sell 1,000 shares of St. Louis stock lest a Giants player own stock in the Cardinals; he nearly tripled his money, finally settling for $120,000.

He was traded again to the Braves and then the Cubs. With Chicago in 1929, he hit .380 with 39 homers and 149 RBIs, to win his second MVP award in his last full year as a player. Hornsby managed the Cubs from the end of 1930 until August 2, 1932, when he was replaced by Charlie Grimm; the Cubs went on to win the pennant and demonstrated their affection for Hornsby by cutting him out of the World Series pool.

The Rajah finished up with the Browns and managed in the minor leagues for fifteen years before coming back to lead the Browns in 1952 and the Reds in 1953. He ended his career as a Mets scout and coach. Hornsby was elected to the Hall of Fame in 1942.

CARL HUBBELL
Pitcher. Born Jun. 22, 1903 Carthage, Mo. Died Nov. 21, 1988 Scottsdale, Ariz. NL MVP 1933, 1936.
Ty Cobb was convinced that Carl Hubbell's screwball, which Cobb called the "butterfly pitch," would ruin his arm and forbade Hubbell to throw it—even though the Tigers had paid Oklahoma City $20,000 for his services. The man who would later be known as the Giants' "Meal Ticket" languished without his favorite pitch and was eventually given his outright release.

Hubbell picked up the scroogie again with Beaumont of the Texas League and was signed by Dick Kinsella, a part-time Giant scout and bored Illinois delegate to the 1928 Democratic Convention in Houston. Hubbell won 10 of his 16 decisions that first season, no-hit the Pirates, 11–0, in his sophomore year, and really hit his stride in 1933. That year King Carl six-hit the Cardinals, 1–0, over eighteen innings, led the league in innings pitched (309),

wins (23), shutouts (10), and ERA (1.66), and was named MVP.

In the World Series he beat Joe Cronin's Senators twice, 4–2 and 2–1, and pitched twenty innings without allowing an earned run as the Giants won in five games. On July 10, 1934, Hubbell started the second All-Star Game by giving up a single to Charlie Gehringer and walking Heinie Manush. He then struck out Babe Ruth, Lou Gehrig, and Jimmie Foxx consecutively to end the first inning and got Al Simmons and Joe Cronin to start the second, one of baseball's greatest feats.

Equally commanding during the regular season that year, Hubbell led the league with a 2.30 ERA and a 21–12 record, the second of five straight 20-game seasons. In 1936, he went 26–6 and was named MVP again. That July 17, he started a string of 24 straight victories over two seasons, eventually snapped by the Dodgers on May 27, 1937; he also won games in both the 1936 and 1937 World Series to post a 1.97 ERA in October.

In 1938, Hubbell experienced arm trouble and won only 13 games; in four more years he would never win more than 11, and he finally ended his pitching career at age 40 with 253 wins and 36 shutouts. Named to the Hall of Fame in 1947, he ran the Giants' farm system, directing player development from 1943 to 1977 and scouting from 1978 to 1985, eventually seeing fellow Hall of Famers like Willie Mays, Willie McCovey, and Juan Marichal take his place as the Giants' meal tickets.

"SHOELESS JOE" JACKSON
Outfielder. Born July 16, 1888 Brandon Mills, S.C. Died Dec. 5, 1951 Greenville, S.C. In ten years as a regular, 1911–1920, never hit below .300.
Babe Ruth once said, "I decided to pick out the greatest hitter to watch and study and Jackson was good enough for me."

Joseph Jefferson Jackson never learned to read or write, but he could hit, field, and run. He hit .356 lifetime (third highest behind Cobb and Rogers Hornsby), and his glove was named "the place triples go to die." Yet he remains under a cloud for his part in the Black Sox series of 1919.

Signed by the A's but assailed by homesickness, Shoeless Joe blossomed in Cleveland, making the biggest rookie splash in history by hitting .408 in 1911 and finishing second only to Ty Cobb in batting, slugging, hits, doubles, and total bases. Although his stats were nearly as good in 1912 (.395) and 1913 (.373), Cleveland was a last place club; sold to Chicago in the middle of 1915, Jackson helped the Sox win the pennant in 1917 and the World Series.

When Sox first baseman Chick Gandil approached Jackson about throwing the 1919 Series, Jackson called owner Charles Comiskey and asked to be benched, but Comiskey refused to hear him out. While Jackson was the leading hitter (.375), set a Series record for hits (12), and knocked in 6 runs, pitcher Lefty Williams gave Jackson $5,000 for his part in the fix, and, to his eternal discredit, Jackson took it.

In 1920 Jackson hit .382 but, that September, a Chicago grand jury investigated the fix; Jackson confessed, denied doing anything to throw the Series, but admitted taking the money. Although acquitted after their confessions "disappeared," Jackson and the other Black Sox were barred from baseball for life by Commissioner Landis. Shoeless Joe sued Comiskey for back pay and won a judgment for $16,711.04, but it was overturned; the sitting judge ordered him to jail for perjury and, after a brief stay, he accepted a small settlement from Comiskey,

Jackson ran several successful businesses in his home town of Brandon Mills, South Carolina but never learned to write his name. When the Cleveland Hall of Fame was started, in 1951, Jackson became the fourth highest vote-getter even though his name wasn't on the ballot. TV host Ed Sullivan heard the story and asked Jackson to be on the show; the day before he was scheduled to appear, Jackson died of a heart attack.

REGGIE JACKSON

Right Field. Born May 18, 1946 Wyncote, Pa. AL MVP 1973.

The only player to be named MVP in two World Series, Reggie Jackson earned the nickname "Mr. October" by setting a Series record for slugging percentage (.755).

He's also baseball's all-time strikeout king, fanning 2,597 times, once every four at-bats. In addition to being all-or-nothing on offense, Jackson was next-to-nothing on defense. He is tied with Burt Shotton for leading the AL in errors the most times (five). Yet, from 1971 to 1982, Jackson helped three different clubs win ten division titles, six pennants, and five championships.

In 1968 he hit 29 homers, led the league in assists (14) and errors (12), and struck out 171 times in 553 at bats. In July 1969 he was two weeks ahead of Roger Maris's pace with 40, then hit only 7 more for the rest of the season and finished second to Harmon Killebrew. In 1973 he won the first of four home run crowns.

Jackson made his 1973 World Series debut memorable with four hits in Game Two, doubled twice to knock in both runs of Game Six, and hit a home run and made two spectacular catches to help Oakland win Game Seven; Jackson was voted MVP of the Series to go along with the MVP award he had won in the regular season.

He also homered in the opener of the 1974 Series, doubled in Game Two, and threw out a key base runner in Game Five. In the fall of 1977, Jackson fulfilled his destiny and truly became Mr. October. He homered in Games Four and Five and homered on three consecutive pitches in Game Six. Since he'd hit a homer on his last swing of Game Five and walked his first time up in Game Six, Jackson had hit four straight homers in four official at bats off four different pitchers. He set other Series records for homers in a Series (5), runs scored (10), and total bases (25).

After getting his name on a candy bar, Jackson won a third home run crown in 1980 with the Yankees, a fourth in 1982 with the Angels, and ended his career with the A's in 1987, retiring with 563 career homers to place sixth on the all-time list. Jackson was elected to the Hall of Fame in 1993.

WALTER JOHNSON

Pitcher. Born Nov. 6, 1887 Humboldt, Kan. Died Dec. 10, 1946 Washington, D.C. Holds major league record for lifetime shutouts (110). AL MVP 1913, 1924.

Walter Johnson and the Senators were baseball's odd couple. From 1907 to 1927, Johnson compiled a record of 417–279 while the Senators won just two pennants. He lost 27 games by the score of 1–0; in all, he lost 65 games in which his team failed to score.

Not that he needed much support. On thirty-eight occasions when the Senators managed only a single run, Johnson held the opposition scoreless. He pitched seven Opening Day shutouts and wound up with more career whitewashes (110) than most big league pitchers have career wins.

Twelve of those shutouts came in 1913, when he was at his peak, finishing 36–7 to win his first MVP award. His 1.14 ERA was a record for fifty-five years, and he struck out 243 batters in 346 innings. "Barney" (after race driver Barney Oldfield) led the league in wins, ERA, and strikeouts again in 1918 and 1924, won 20 games or more in ten straight seasons, and had the lowest lifetime ERA (2.17) among AL pitchers with more than 2,000 innings. Considering all pitchers in all eras, Johnson ranks first in Total Pitcher Index.

A high school sensation, Johnson was ready to sign with the Pirates but was refused a $9 signing bonus; instead, he agreed to sign with the Senators on the condition that they pay his way home to Fullerton, California, if he didn't make it in the big leagues. He made his debut on August 2, 1907, losing a five-hitter to Ty Cobb and the Tigers, 3–2. The following year, the "Big Train" arrived, shutting out the New York Highlanders (Yankees) three times in a four-day weekend series on four, three, and two hits.

Seventeen years later, when he should have been washed up, Johnson went 23–7 to win his second MVP award, and the hapless Senators finally reached the World Series. After losing twice to the Giants, Johnson won his first Series game by pitching four scoreless innings of relief in Game 7 as Washington beat the Giants, 4–3, in twelve innings. In the 1925 Series, Johnson won two games against the Pirates but lost the finale, 9–7, as his mates allowed four unearned runs.

When the first election was held for the Hall of Fame, Johnson joined Cobb, Babe Ruth, Honus Wagner, and Christy Mathewson as charter members, the "Five Immortals."

AL KALINE

Right Field. Born Dec. 19, 1934 Baltimore, Md. Won batting championship at age twenty.

He was never named MVP, never led the league in home runs or RBIs, and managed to win only one batting title in twenty-two major league seasons. Yet, in 1980, Al Kaline became only the tenth player named to the Hall of Fame in his first year of eligibility.

Kaline had 100 or more hits eighteen times, hit 20 or more home runs nine times, hit .300 or better eight times. The first player to win Gold Gloves at two positions, he won ten in all. In 1971 at age thirty-six, Kaline played the entire season errorless as part of a 242-game streak without a miscue.

One week after signing with the Tigers on his high school graduation day, Kaline got into the lineup when Steve Souchock broke his wrist. Soon after, in a game against the White Sox, Kaline threw runners out at second, third, and home in successive innings. the next year he became the youngest player to win the batting title (.340) and was named AL Player of the Year by *The Sporting News*.

He started in the All-Star Game for the first of ten times in 1955 and played in sixteen summer classics without committing an error, hit .324, and homered in the 1959 Game and the second Game in 1960. He also won the slugging championship in 1959 (.530) and was named *The Sporting News* Player of the Year a second time in 1963.

A's pitcher Lew Krausse hit him with a pitch in 1968, breaking his arm; six weeks later, Kaline returned as a first baseman and played the outfield during the Series. Down three games to one, the Tigers came back in Game Five when Kaline singled in the tying and go-ahead runs. In Game Six he singled twice in the ten-run third inning as the Tigers romped, 13–1. He wound up leading the eventual Champs with a .379 average and 8 RBIs.

In 1974 Kaline needed 139 hits to reach 3,000 and became a full-time DH. He got his 3,000th, doubling off Dave McNally, and retired with 3,007. While no Tiger uniform had been retired in deference to Ty Cobb, who didn't wear numerals, Kaline's number 6 was taken out of circulation in August 1980, after his election to the Hall of Fame.

TIM KEEFE

Pitcher. Born Jan. 1, 1857 Cambridge, Mass. Died Apr. 23, 1933 Cambridge, Mass. Posted all-time-low ERA of 0.80 in 1880.

The Mets' first great pitcher wasn't Tom Seaver. It was Tim Keefe, who won 41 games his first year and 37 in his second for the New York Metropolitans of the American Association.

Keefe notched 342 victories in just fourteen years, with a career ERA of 2.62, and established a major league record (since tied) by winning 19 straight games. In the 600 games Keefe pitched, he held the opposition to six or fewer hits on 235 occasions, more than a third of the time. In his streak season (1888), he managed this feat twenty-eight times in fifty-one starts, more than half the time.

His success depended partly on the changeup, of which he was the acknowledged pioneer, and partly on keeping meticulous records of opposing hitters in his own system of notation. (When fellow Giant John Montgomery Ward organized the Players League in 1890, Keefe was named secretary because he could take shorthand.)

Born in Cambridge, Massachusetts, he played with a string of semipro and minor-league New England teams before joining the Troy Haymakers in 1880. He first attracted national attention by going 41–27 with the Mets in 1883—including both ends of a doubleheader, a one-hitter and a two-hitter. He enjoyed even greater success with Jim Mutrie's New York Giants (42–20 in 1886) and became known as "Sir Timothy" for his pitching and manner.

Sir Tim's streak started on June 23, 1888, when he beat the Quakers (Phillies), 7–6, at the Baker Bowl. He went forty-five days before losing again, to the White Stockings (Cubs), 4–2, at the Polo Grounds. To cap off a dream season, Keefe was 4–0 in the World Series, yielding the American Association St. Louis Browns just 18 hits and 2 earned runs in 35 innings.

After jumping to the Players League, Keefe ended his playing days with the Phillies. He umpired in the NL before becoming a real estate mogul. He was elected to the Hall of Fame in 1964 and was proclaimed Cambridge's All-Time Greatest Athlete in a 1976 poll conducted by the Cambridge *Chronicle*.

HARMON KILLEBREW

First Baseman. Born Jun. 29, 1936 Payette, Ida. Holds AL record for most lifetime home runs, righthanded batter (573). AL MVP 1969.

Harmon Killebrew averaged a homer every 14.22 at-bats, more frequently than anyone but Babe Ruth and Ralph Kiner.

The fact is that Killebrew was better at hitting home runs than Ruth and Kiner—half the time—and worse than Rabbit Maranville and Nellie Fox the other half. Baseball has had many streak hitters for average, but Killebrew was a bonafide streak hitter for power.

In 1962 the Killer beat Norm Cash for the home run title, 48 to 39; after a horrendous summer slump, he hit 11 homers in the last eleven games to beat Cash. In 1963 he pulled the same stunt, missing twenty games with a twisted knee, then hit seven homers in the last six games to outhomer Dick Stuart, 45 to 42. In all, he hit 573 homers to place fifth on the all-time list. He led the league in homers five times.

Killebrew is also the only Washington Senator to be discovered by an Idaho senator. The Honorable Herman Welker tipped Clark Griffith about Killebrew in 1954, comparing him to Mickey Mantle. The last time Welker had boasted about an Idaho boy, it had been Vernon Law, and Griffith hadn't listened. This time he sent Ossie Bluege to investigate, and Bluege signed Killebrew the day he first saw him.

In 1959 the Senators gave Killebrew the third base job; he responded with five two-homer games from May 1 through May 17 and ended the year with 42 to tie Rocky Colavito for the league lead. The Senators moved him to first base for two years, then to the outfield the year after moving to Minnesota. From 1962 through 1964, he led the league with 48, 45, and 49 homers.

When the Twins won their first pennant in 1965, he missed 48 games with a dislocated elbow but still hit 25 homers and won a fifth home run crown in 1967 (44). After missing nearly half the 1968 season with injuries, he had a banner year in 1969, leading the league in homers (49) and RBIs (140) and helped bring the Twins a Western Division title.

He hit 41 homers in 1970, his eighth 40-plus year, homered in his third All-Star Game in 1971 and ended his career in a Kansas City uniform; he was elected to the Hall of Fame in 1984.

RALPH KINER

Left Field. Born Oct. 27, 1922 Santa Rita, N.M. Hit home runs at a clip (home run percentage) faster than anyone except Babe Ruth.

Ralph Kiner set a home run record that even Babe Ruth and Hank Aaron couldn't top by leading or tying for the league lead in home runs the first seven years of his career. He is also the only player who hit home runs in three consecutive All-Star Games (1949–1951), averaged

35 homers a year in his ten-year major league career, and tied Rogers Hornsby for the then National League record in career grand slams with 12.

Never noted for his finesse with either arm or glove, Kiner ushered in the era of the pure slugger. Kiner had led the NL in 1946 with 23 home runs, the first rookie to do so since Harry Lumley in 1906; however, he really blossomed after slugger Hank Greenberg joined the Pirates in 1947. "Hank put me in a better position in the batter's box, which enabled me to pull outside pitches, and changed my stance and my whole approach to hitting, getting me not to swing at bad pitches," Kiner recalls. He hit 51 homers in 1947, 48 of them after June 1.

The good-looking Kiner also attracted a new kind of woman fan to baseball and became linked with movie stars like Elizabeth Taylor. He began doing personal appearances and became one of the first ballplayers to host his own local TV show.

Kiner reached his peak as a long ball hitter in 1949, hitting 54 homers, four of them grand slams. His mighty blasts attracted fans despite the Pirates' second-division finishes, and, by 1951, Kiner topped Stan Musial as the league's highest salaried player, at $90,000. Two years later the romance was over, and Kiner was traded to the Cubs. He ended his playing career with Cleveland, retiring at thirty-three when a back sprain held him to just 18 homers in 113 games.

Adept at putting people in the seats, he learned the business side of baseball as general manager of the San Diego Padres of the Pacific Coast League from 1955 to 1960. After a year as the radio voice of the White Sox, Kiner became part of the expansion Mets' announcing troika, with Lindsey Nelson and Bob Murphy. Named to the Hall of Fame in 1975, Kiner recently celebrated his thirtieth anniversary as a Mets announcer.

SANFORD "SANDY" KOUFAX
Pitcher. Born Dec. 30, 1935 Brooklyn, N.Y. Holds major league record for most consecutive years leading league in ERA (five). NL MVP 1963 and Cy Young Award 1963, 1965, 1966.

Sandy Koufax was the best pitcher in baseball for five seasons. From 1962 to 1966, he was 111–34 with 100 complete games, 33 of them shutouts. He led the NL in ERA all five years, in wins and strikeouts in 1963, 1965, and 1966, and won the Cy Young Award all three years.

Born Sanford Braun, he took the name of his stepfather, attorney Irving Koufax. He went to the University of Cincinnati on a basketball scholarship, but chose baseball after striking out 51 batters in 32 innings. In 1955 the nineteen-year old lefty joined the Dodgers and mopped up for three seasons. The first sign that he might be special came on August 31, 1959, when Koufax struck out 18 Cubs to tie Bob Feller's record; yet, frustrated with his progress, he nearly quit in 1960 after going 8–13.

One day, scout Kenny Meyers and catcher Norm Sherry asked him to throw at a spot and noticed that Koufax's motion obstructed his vision. Meyers said, "How can you hit that spot when you can't even see it?" Sherry persuaded Koufax to throw more deliberately, and controlling the speed of his delivery made all the difference between getting behind the hitters and throwing strikes.

In 1961, Koufax was 18–13, leading the league with 269 strikeouts. He blossomed fully in 1963, winning 25 of 30 regular season decisions and taking the first and last games of the World Series sweep of the Yankees. He also won the Cy Young Award and was named MVP.

Adhesions in his pitching arm broke loose in 1964, leading to the traumatic arthritis which would end his career. After throwing his third no-hitter in late August, Koufax was forced to stop pitching with a record of 19–5 and an ERA of 1.74. On medical orders, he didn't throw between starts in 1965 and went 26–8, crowning the regular season by pitching a perfect game against the Cubs on September 9; he shut out Minnesota twice in the World Series as the Dodgers won in seven games.

Koufax's final season was 1966, when he won 27 and lost 9 and led the league in ERA for the fifth year in a row (1.73). In 1972 he became the youngest player ever elected to the Hall of Fame and was also named Player of the Decade in the 1960s.

NAPOLEON "LARRY" LAJOIE
Second Baseman. Born Sept. 5, 1875 Woonsocket, R.I. Died Feb. 7, 1959 Daytona Beach, Fla. Holds AL record for highest season batting average, (.426), 1901.

Napoleon Lajoie was the complete package. No other second baseman has ever shone so brilliantly in so many ways for so long (twenty-one years).

In addition to leading ALers in every fielding category in two different seasons, Lajoie won a Triple Crown and four batting titles, compiled 3,242 career hits and a lifetime batting average of .338. At one time or another, he led both leagues in RBIs, slugging average, and fielding percentage, and was so well-loved that his team adopted his nickname as its own.

Originally signed by the Phillies, Lajoie hit .361 in 1897 and won the slugging championship (.569). By 1900 he had gathered five straight .300 plus seasons but was earning only $2,400, the NL maximum. When Connie Mack offered him $4,000, he jumped to the new AL and won the Triple Crown in 1901, hitting .426 (still an AL record) with 14 home runs and 125 RBIs; it is a measure of his versatility that he also led in runs scored (145), hits (232), doubles (48) and slugging percentage (.643), putouts (395) and fielding percentage (.960).

The Phils sued Mack, and eventually the Pennsylvania Supreme Court enjoined Lajoie from playing with the Athletics. AL president Ban Johnson ordered that Lajoie be transferred to Cleveland where he could avoid Pennsylvania's jurisdiction but could still play in the AL; for the first few years, Lajoie always remained behind or went on to the next road stop when the Bronchos (Indians) traveled to Philadelphia.

He won batting titles in 1903 (.344) and 1904 (.376) and was named Cleveland's player-manager in 1905; the team was renamed the Naps in his honor. Although the Naps improved, they never won a pennant under Lajoie, who resigned during the 1909 season to concentrate on playing.

Nap might have won a fourth, albeit tainted batting championship when he got six bunt singles on the last day of the 1910 season, all because of the opposing manager's hatred for Cobb, who was four points ahead. In retaliation, sportswriter Hugh Fullerton changed his ruling on a

Cobb smash that he had ruled an error earlier in the season, helping to give Cobb a single extra hit and the championship. Seven decades later the controversy erupted anew as it was discovered that Cobb had been the beneficiary of a double entry of a game in which he had gone 2-for-3; Larry had the higher batting average in 1910, after all.

Lajoie was elected to the Hall of Fame in 1937.

JOHN HENRY "POP" LLOYD
Shortstop. Born Apr. 25, 1884 Palatka, Fla. Died Mar. 19, 1965 Atlantic City, N.J. At age forty-four, hit .564 and led the Negro NL in home runs.

Pop Lloyd was frequently called "the Black Honus Wagner." There is no record that Wagner was ever called "the white Pop Lloyd," but to have done so would have been high compliment indeed.

Wagner once commented about Lloyd, "After I saw him play, I felt honored that they should name such a great ballplayer after me." Connie Mack added, "You could put Wagner and Lloyd in a bag together and whichever one you pulled out, you couldn't go wrong."

Lloyd may have been the single greatest black player of all time. A lefthanded line drive hitter, he was a gifted base runner and base stealer in both the United States and Cuba, where he played for twelve years and was an idol to fans and youngsters. They called him "El Cuchara"—"the Shovel," and writers talk of him scooping ground balls with dirt, twigs, and anything else that populated the primitive infields.

Born in Florida, he played semipro ball in Georgia with the Macon Acmes and moved on to the Cuban-X Giants. In Cuba he played against Ty Cobb in an exhibition game, tagging him out three times on attempted steals with catcher Bruce Petway delivering the ball. Lloyd also outhit Cobb, .500 to .369, and Cobb was so embarrassed that he vowed never to play against blacks again.

Perhaps the highlight of Lloyd's playing career came from 1914 to 1917 when he played for Rube Foster's Chicago American Giants and batted cleanup on a team that included Oscar Charleston, Bingo DeMoss, Smokey Joe Williams, and Cannonball Dick Redding.

As Lloyd's legs began to go, he switched to first base and signed on with the Brooklyn Royal Giants as player-manager for three seasons. From 1921 to 1928, he played with the Columbus Buckeyes, Hilldale, the Bacharach Giants, and the New York Lincoln Giants. At age forty-four he hit .564 and led the league in home runs.

When announced Graham McNamee asked Babe Ruth to name the greatest player of all time, Ruth said, "You mean major leaguers?" "No," replied McNamee, "the greatest player anywhere." "In that case," said Ruth, "I'd pick John Henry Lloyd." Lloyd was elected to the Hall of Fame in 1977.

MICKEY MANTLE
Center Field. Born Oct. 20, 1931 Spavinaw, Okla. AL MVP 1956, 1957, 1962.

Despite a chronic bone infection in his legs and operations on both knees, Mickey Mantle became baseball's most powerful switch hitter, hitting 536 home runs in the regular season and setting a World Series record with 18 more.

Named for Mickey Cochrane, his father's favorite player, Mantle learned to switch hit at age five and starred in high school baseball and football, developing osteomyelitis after bruising a leg in a football game. After a short (and error-filled) career as a minor league shortstop, he became the Yankees' regular right fielder before his twentieth birthday. He suffered his first serious injury during the 1951 Series when he tripped on a drain at Yankee Stadium and required surgery for torn knee cartilage.

Joe DiMaggio retired that fall, and Mantle moved to center field, hitting .311 in 142 games. He led the league in home runs (37) in 1955 and, a year later, won the Triple Crown, hitting 52 homers, knocking in 130 runs, and batting .353. The only player besides Jimmie Foxx to hit 50 homers and win a batting title, Mantle won the MVP award and shone in the World Series, hitting three homers as the Yanks beat Brooklyn in seven games.

In 1957 he was chosen MVP again as he hit .365. He won home run crowns again in 1958 (42) and 1960 (40), finishing second to Roger Maris's 61 homers in 1961 with 54. Mantle was named MVP a third time in 1962 when he hit .321. On June 5, 1963, he broke his left foot in Baltimore, ending a season in which he had 15 home runs in 172 at-bats, although he returned in time to hit a home run in the World Series.

His personal choice for most memorable homer was his ninth-inning shot off Cardinal Barney Schultz in 1964, which broke Babe Ruth's record for lifetime Series home runs and won Game Three. Mickey went on to hit two more in that Series, his last, and wound up his tenth Series with 18 homers, 42 runs scored, 123 total bases, and 40 RBIs—all records.

Despite his injuries, Mantle holds the Yankee record for games played—2,401. He retired during spring training in 1969, and, on June 8, received a ten-minute standing ovation at Yankee Stadium. He was named to the Hall of Fame in 1974.

WALTER "RABBIT" MARANVILLE
Shortstop. Born Nov. 11, 1891 Springfield, Mass. Died Jan. 5, 1954 New York, N.Y. Holds major league shortstop record for most years leading league in putouts (6) and lifetime putouts (5,133).

If you thought Jimmy Blake was, in the words of *Casey at the Bat,* "much-despised," consider Walter James Vincent "Rabbit" Maranville.

Every time suggestions are made to "prune" the Hall of Fame of its many undeserving members, Maranville's name is invariably suggested, mostly due to his limitations with the bat. The possessor of just 28 career home runs in more than 10,000 at bats, "Rabbit" bettered .300 just once in seventeen seasons as a regular, and never led the league in an offensive category.

Yet, in 1914 and again in 1919, Maranville led the league in both Fielding Runs and Total Player Rating. He saved 50 runs more than an average shortstop in 1914 and personally accounted for more wins than any player in the league. Casey Stengel, who later managed Maranville, said of him, "Shortstops who stay around more than twenty years are not clowns."

Maranville finished a close second to fellow Miracle Brave Johnny Evers in the voting for the Chalmers (MVP) Award. There was no MVP voting for the NL in 1919, but

Maranville was third in 1913 and finished in the top twenty in MVP voting no less than seven times.

The colorful Maranville invented the "basket catch," but many of his antics were inspired by alcohol. He jumped into a water fountain fully clothed; dangled a teammate out of a twelfth-story hotel window; and, named manager of the Cubs in 1925, celebrated by pouring ice water on all his sleeping teammates. Waived to the Brooklyn Robins, Maranville was demoted to Rochester of the International League.

That's when he resolved to quit drinking. Asked to comment on the effects of Prohibition, he said, "There is much less drinking now than there was before 1927, because I quit drinking on May 24, 1927."

He joined the Cardinals later that year, started for the pennant-winning 1928 team, and hit .308 in the World Series. Back with the Braves in 1929, he started playing more second base; in 1932, at the age of forty-one, he led the league at that position in putouts and fielding. He still holds the major league record for career putouts by a shortstop and was elected to the Hall of Fame shortly after his death in 1954.

EDDIE MATHEWS

Third Baseman. Born Oct. 13, 1931 Texarkana, Tex. Holds NL record, most consecutive years with 30 or more home runs (nine).

Eddie Mathews played a game-within-the-game. He said, "I'd take on the other third baseman ... I wanted to beat him in every department—fielding, hitting, running the bases. I played that game all my life, and it kept me on my toes."

It did indeed. Mathews was a seven-time All-Star. He hit 30 or more homers for nine straight seasons and 512 lifetime, led the NL's third basemen three times in assists, and teamed with Henry Aaron to form the greatest one-two home run punch in baseball history; as Braves teammates, they accounted for 863 homers.

The only Brave to play in Boston, Milwaukee and Atlanta, Mathews could have had his choice of teams. He was scouted by nine, but because Boston had the oldest third baseman (Bob Elliott), Mathews became a Brave at 12:01 a.m. the day following his high school graduation in 1949 and was sent to Atlanta, where Dixie Walker was the manager. Walker helped Mathews deal with left-handed pitchers and Billy Jurges polished his fielding. By the fall of 1951, Ty Cobb said, "I've seen three or four perfect swings in my time. This lad has one of them."

In April 1952 Elliott was traded to the Giants, and Steady Eddie got his job. He became the first rookie to homer three times in a game, hit 25 homers, and proved there was no sophomore jinx by winning the home run title the following year with 47 round-trippers, finishing second only to Roy Campanella in the MVP voting.

Mathews starred in the 1957 World Series although the Yankees walked him eight times. He won Game Four with a tenth-inning homer, scored the only run in Game Five, and doubled in the first two runs of Game Seven; with the bases loaded and two out in the bottom of the ninth, he made a lunging stop on Bill Skowron's shot down the line and stepped on third to give the Milwaukee Braves their only championship.

In 1959 Mathews won his second home run crown. He was traded to the Astros on New Year's Eve, 1967, moved on to the Tigers, and played in his final World Series in 1968. He managed the Braves from 1972 to 1974 and entered the Hall of Fame in 1978.

CHRISTY MATHEWSON

Pitcher. Born Aug. 12, 1880 Factoryville, Pa. Died Oct. 7, 1925 Saranac Lake, N.Y. Holds NL record for most years winning 20 or more games (12).

If Mattel had made Barbie dolls in 1903, Christy Mathewson might have been the model for Ken.

Handsome, clean-cut, intelligent, clean-living, and heroic, Mathewson was one of the first players to attract women and children to the ballpark. An All-America college football player for Bucknell, he was nationally known as a checkers expert, too. Oh yes. He won 373 games in his major league career even though he didn't normally pitch on Sundays. (His mother had wanted him to become a minister.)

One of the "Five Immortals" elected when the Hall of Fame was established in 1936, Mathewson was called "Big Six" because his fastball reminded reporters of a famous New York fire engine. Nevertheless, it was his fadeaway (screwball) that drove National Leaguers crazy. He won 30 or more games four times, finished 434 of the 551 games he started, and completed 10 of 11 World Series games while posting an ERA of 1.15. A control whiz, he pitched 68 consecutive innings in 1913 without walking a batter.

Born to well-to-do parents in Factoryville, Pennsylvania, Mathewson studied forestry at Bucknell, headed two literary societies, was elected class president, and was the kicker on Walter Camp's 1900 All-America team. He became a Giant that fall, won 20 games in 1901, and became baseball's dominant pitcher starting in 1903, the first of three straight years in which he won 30 or more games.

In the 1905 World Series, Mathewson became a household name; in a Series decided entirely by shutouts, Matty contributed three—in five days. He four-hit Connie Mack's A's in the opener and, two days after Chief Bender blanked the Giants, four-hit the Mackmen again. Two days later Matty wound up the Series, giving up six hits this time, but nevertheless pitching his third shutout in six days. In 27 innings, Mathewson walked one man and struck out 18.

Over the next ten years, Mathewson won at least 20 games a season. When the fadeaway began to fade, Mathewson's manager and best friend, John McGraw, arranged a trade to Cincinnati so he could take the helm of the Reds. Joining a chemical warfare unit in France during World War I, he was accidentally exposed to poison gas that weakened his lungs; he later contracted tuberculosis, which ultimately proved fatal. He had served as general manager of the Braves despite his poor health but died on the opening day of the 1925 World Series.

WILLIE MAYS

Center Field. Born May 6, 1931 Westfield, Ala. NL Rookie of the Year 1951, MVP 1954, 1965.

In 1951 Willie Mays chased a 457-foot shot to dead center in Forbes Field, hit the warning track, saw the ball hook right, and, with no time to reach across his body, made the catch bare-handed. Pirates general manager Branch Rickey, in his forty-eighth year of baseball, sent Mays a note: "That was the finest catch I have ever seen and the finest catch I ever hope to see."

Mays started with the Birmingham Black Barons of the Negro AL and, after hitting .477 in the opening months of the 1951 season with the Minneapolis Millers, was promoted to the Giants. When Mays had trouble hitting big league pitching, manager Leo Durocher assured him that center field was his—whether he hit or not. Mays responded by leading the Giants to the pennant and was named Rookie of the Year.

He spent most of 1952 and all of 1953 in the service, returning in 1954 to win his only batting title (.345) and to belt 41 homers. The Giants won another pennant and Mays collected his first MVP award. In Game One of the World Series, Mays made one of baseball's most famous catches, snaring Vic Wertz's drive to deep center over his shoulder to keep the game tied, 3–3; the Giants swept the Indians, and Mays won the Hickok Belt as Pro Athlete of the Year.

The "Say Hey Kid" only got better, winning the first of four home run titles in 1955 and becoming the complete player in 1957—winning a Gold Glove, stealing a league-leading 38 bases, and hitting 26 doubles, 20 triples, and 35 homers. He hit four home runs in a game on April 30, 1961, and hit 49 homers in 1962 to lead the league and drive the Giants to another pennant.

Voted the All-Star MVP in 1963 and 1968, he holds the All-Star Game record for career hits (23) and stolen bases (6) and says the best catch he ever made was one that robbed Ted Williams of a home run in the 1955 game at Milwaukee's County Stadium.

Willie earned eleven Gold Gloves, set records for career putouts and total chances, was the first man to hit 300 home runs and steal 300 bases, had 660 lifetime homers, and sported a lifetime batting average of .302. He has considerable support as the best ever to play the game. He was elected to the Hall of Fame in 1979, his first year of eligibility.

BILL MAZEROSKI

Second Baseman. Born Sept. 5, 1936 Wheeling, West Va. Holds major league record for lifetime double plays by a second baseman (1,706).

Bill Mazeroski, remembered best for his Series-winning home run in 1960, may have been baseball's best fielder. In *Baseball Ratings*, Charles Faber awards points for percentage, assists, chances, and range factor to all players with ten years' experience; Mazeroski leads every player from every era, regardless of position.

He set records for second basemen by leading his league the most years in assists (9) and double plays (8) and holds the record for career double plays by a second baseman (1706). Only three *first basemen* took part in more double plays; Lou Gehrig, for instance, played in one game more and figured in 136 fewer double plays.

Mazeroski won the first of eight Gold Gloves in 1956 and became an All-Star for the first of seven times in 1958. After hitting 19 home runs that year, he tried to pull everything and wound up with just seven homers and thirty-four-point drop in his batting average. When the slump continued into 1960, George Sisler made him stand deeper in the box to hit curveballs after they broke. Hitting .237 on August 3, Mazeroski ended the regular season at .273 as the Pirates won their first pennant in thirty-three years.

He started a double play in the first inning of Game One, hit a two-run homer in the fourth inning (the margin of victory in a 6–4 Pirate win), and turned his third double play in the ninth inning to end the game. With the Yanks and Pirates even in the Series, in the seventh game the Pirates went ahead, 9–7, in the eighth inning. The Yankees tied it in the top of the ninth, but, leading off in the bottom, Mazeroski hit Ralph Terry's second pitch over the left field wall to win the Series.

Maz set an NL record for double plays by a second baseman (144) in 1961 and smashed Gerry Priddy's ML record of 150 double plays in 1966; that year, he (161) and Gene Alley (128) recorded the most double plays for a shortstop and a second baseman in a season. A utility man in 1971, he retired in 1972. He later became an unofficial infield instructor for the Expos, and the Pirates retired his number 9 in 1987.

WILLIE "STRETCH" McCOVEY

First Baseman. Born Jan. 10, 1938 Mobile, Ala. Holds National League record for most lifetime home runs by a lefthanded batter (521). NL Rookie of the Year 1959, MVP 1969.

The man who left his heart in San Francisco wasn't Tony Bennett but Willie McCovey. After three seasons in San Diego and 11 games in Oakland, McCovey returned on Opening Day in 1977 and received a standing ovation that moved him to tears. He responded to the fans by hitting 28 homers at age thirty-nine and was named Comeback Player of the Year.

The love affair began on July 30, 1959, when McCovey made a spectacular debut. Called up from Phoenix, where he'd been tutored by Ted Williams, McCovey went 4-for-4 against Robin Roberts with two singles and two triples. But there was a problem. The Giants already had a first baseman, Orlando Cepeda, who had been named Rookie of the Year the year before. McCovey won the same honor in 1959, hitting .354, and the two see-sawed back and forth between first and the outfield; Cepeda got the first base job until he was injured in 1965, then was traded to the Cardinals.

By then McCovey was a star, having led the league with 44 homers in 1963. When he returned to first base full time, Willie led the league in 1968 with 36 homers, 105 RBIs, and a .545 slugging average. For an encore, he headed the same categories in 1969 with even better numbers—45 homers, 126 RBIs and a .656 slugging average.

NL pitchers, rather than pitch to McCovey in 1970, decided to walk him instead—a league-leading 137 times, including a record 45 intentional walks. "Stretch" (for his ability to keep one foot on the bag and reach off-the-mark throws) still hit 39 homers and led the league in slugging for the third straight year.

A series of injuries plagued him in the 1970s, and when he did play, pitchers continued to pitch around him. The Giants traded him and he played for three teams without leaving California. When he hung up his spikes in 1980, McCovey had played in four decades and hit 521 homers to tie Ted Williams, his idol and former mentor, for ninth on the all-time list. He also set the NL career record for grand slams (18), second only to Lou Gehrig's 23. He was elected to the Hall of Fame in 1985.

JOHN "BID" McPHEE
Second Baseman. Born Nov. 1, 1859 Messina, N.Y. Died Jan. 3, 1943 San Diego, Cal. Holds major league record for putouts by a second baseman (6,545).
John Alexander "Bid" McPhee made more putouts than any other major league second baseman, ranks fifth in Fielding Wins, ahead of star glove men like Tris Speaker and Ozzie Smith, stole more bases than Davey Lopes or Luis Aparicio. and, in Total Player Rating, beats out Hall of Fame second basemen Frankie Frisch, Bobby Doerr, and Billy Herman.

So how come you never heard of this guy?

Sometimes greatness can be boring, and that's certainly the case with "King Bid," as he was known. As historian Bob Carroll has noted, "In all of his eighteen years he was never fined. He was never even thrown out of a game!... McPhee showed up every day in shape, stayed sober, did his job, and went home to a good night's sleep." About the only thing that made him colorful was the fact that he was the best defensive second baseman in the nineteenth century and for fourteen (of his eighteen) seasons he did it barehanded.

McPhee, who stood 5'8" and weighed 152 on a good day, was "biddy"—small. He joined the brand-new Cincinnati Reds of the brand-new American Association in 1882, leading the league in putouts, double plays, and fielding average, a habit he never quite broke. He was the double play champ eleven times and led in fielding nine times.

As you might expect, McPhee was a pesky hitter (.271 lifetime), speedy enough to steal 95 bases in 1887 and 568 lifetime. What might surprise is that Bid once "cranked out" 8 homers to lead the league in 1886. (Yes, they were all inside the park.) The other surprise is that McPhee's on-base percentage is .354, relatively low for a guy who walked 981 times.

When his contemporaries began using mitts, McPhee refused to go along. Although he toughened his hands every spring, he was no longer leading the league; however, he began 1896 with a sore finger and finally gave in. The results were instructive; at age 37, McPhee's fielding average was .978, a full 10 points above the recognized mark. The record stood until 1925 when Sparky Adams broke it.

He retired after the 1899 season, briefly managed the Reds, and scouted for them in Los Angeles, where he settled.

JOE MORGAN
Second Baseman. Born Sept. 19, 1943 Bonham, Tex. Holds major league record for seasons by a second baseman (22). NL MVP 1975, 1976.
When the Big Red Machine was operating in the 1970s, Joe Morgan was its generator. He got on base 41 percent of the time and, on a team with Johnny Bench and Pete Rose, was named MVP in both 1975 and 1976.

From 1972 through 1977, he averaged 60 stolen bases, scored more than 100 runs each year, and averaged 21

homers and 84 RBIs with a .301 batting average. Moreover, Little Joe won Gold Gloves in 1973–1977. Over twenty-two years, he helped his teammates win six divisional titles, four pennants and two world championships.

Born in Bonham, Texas, Morgan signed with the Astros and was named NL Rookie of the Year in 1965 by *The Sporting News.* Traded to Cincinnati before the 1972 season, he topped NL second basemen in putouts and fielding and led in walks (115) and runs scored (122).

In 1975 he hit .327, led all second basemen in fielding percentage, and stole 67 bases to be named MVP (he added six steals in the postseason). Morgan won Game Three of the World Series with a single in the bottom of the tenth and Game Seven with a single in the top of the ninth to give the Reds their first championship in thirty-five years.

The Reds repeated in 1976 and Morgan became the first back-to-back MVP since Ernie Banks. Little Joe won the slugging title (.576) and was runner-up in RBIs (111), runs scored (113), and steals (60). Morgan set a record for second basemen in 1977, making just five errors, but tailed off offensively in 1978 and 1979. He helped the Astros win their division in 1980 and went on to two solid years with the San Francisco Giants. Reunited with Pete Rose and Tony Perez in Philadelphia for 1983, he hit 16 homers to help the Phillies win the pennant and homered twice in the World Series.

He made his 1984 farewell with Oakland memorable by replacing Rogers Hornsby as the most prolific home-run hitting second baseman of all time (268). A first-year selection to the Hall of Fame in 1990, Morgan has also been successful as a broadcaster for ESPN.

DALE MURPHY
Center Field. Born Mar. 12, 1956 Portland, Ore. NL MVP 1982, 1983.
Dale Murphy hit 20 or more homers in twelve seasons, played in at least 154 games from 1982 to 1990, and became in 1983 the youngest player to be chosen MVP in two consecutive seasons.

He was the Braves' first-round draft choice two months after Hank Aaron set the record for career home runs. A catcher at the time, Murphy had impressed Atlanta management with his home run swing and rifle arm and was touted as "the next Johnny Bench." For a while, he wasn't even the next Biff Pocoroba. Shortly after being brought up to Atlanta, he developed a mysterious mental block about throwing to second base, and even tossing back to the pitcher.

Rather than let him languish behind Pocoroba and Bruce Benedict, manager Bobby Cox moved Murphy to first base, and he hit 23 homers in 1978. Moved again, to center field in 1980, Murphy became a superstar, hitting 33 homers and, two years later, leading the Braves to the Western Division championship. Murph finished second that year in homers (36 to Dave Kingman's 37), tied Al Oliver for the RBI lead with 109, won his first of five Gold Gloves, and was named MVP. Nolan Ryan said, "I can't imagine Joe DiMaggio was a better all-around player than Dale Murphy."

Five weeks later, he was working on his hitting; new manager Joe Torre was convinced that Murphy could become an even better hitter with two strikes. In 1983 he hit 36 home runs again, added 21 points to his batting average, and struck out 24 fewer times. He also stole 30 bases to become only the sixth 30–30 man in major league history. He was named MVP again at age twenty-seven—joining Ernie Banks, Joe Morgan, and Mike Schmidt as the only NLers to be named MVP in back-to-back seasons.

In 1984 Murphy hit 36 home runs yet again to tie Mike Schmidt for the league lead; a year later, he led the league in walks (90), runs scored (118), and home runs (37). After perhaps his best all-around season in 1987, when he hit 44 homers and achieved personal bests in slugging (.580) and on base percentage (.420), Murphy had calamitous declines in 1988–1990. In August 1990 he was traded to Philadelphia.

Dealt to the expansion Rockies in 1993, Murphy concluded his career with 398 lifetime homers to rank him twenty-fourth on the all-time list.

STAN "THE MAN" MUSIAL
Left Field. Born Nov. 21, 1920 Donora, Pa. Holds modern NL record for most years (seventeen) and consecutive years (sixteen) hitting .300 or better. NL MVP 1943, 1946, 1948.
In the bottom of the twelfth inning of the 1955 All-Star Game, Yogi Berra complained, "My feet are killing me." Stan Musial said, "Relax, I'll have you home in a minute." He hit a home run on the next pitch to win the game.

Musial's magic lit up twenty-four All-Star Games, and he holds the record for most All-Star homers (6), extra-base hits (8), and total bases (40). During the regular season he hit .300 or better in 17 of his 21 full years, won seven batting titles, and had a lifetime average of .331, with 475 homers and 1,951 RBIs.

His bat and glove helped the Cardinals reign over the NL in the 1940s as St. Louis won the pennant in 1943 and the World Series in 1942, 1944, and 1946. Musial was named MVP in 1942, 1946, and 1948 and won three straight batting titles from 1950 to 1952, around the time a Dodger fan nicknamed him by saying, "Uh, oh. Here comes that man again."

Musial's splendid hitting redeemed a promising pitching career that was ended by a shoulder injury. In 1940, Musial was 18–5 in the Florida State League when he fell on his arm and it went numb. Branch Rickey converted him to the outfield, and Musial's hitting got him to the big leagues in time to hit .426 in 12 games in 1941.

In twenty-two seasons as a Cardinal, he led the National League in runs scored five times, sharing the record with Rogers Hornsby and George Burns, and led the major leagues in total bases six times. At his retirement, he held major league records for most extra-base hits and total bases and the NL records for runs, hits, doubles, and RBIs.

Musial said his hitting secret was memory. "I consciously memorized the speed at which every pitcher in the league threw his fastball, curve, and slider; then, I'd pick up the speed of the ball in the first thirty feet of its flight and knew how it would move once it had crossed the plate."

When he retired, he became a Cardinal VP. The club honored him with a statue outside Busch Memorial Stadium in 1968, and he entered the Hall of Fame in 1969.

Fully ten years later, when consumers were asked whose endorsement they would trust, Stan the Man still ranked first among athletes.

CHARLES "KID" NICHOLS
Pitcher. Born Sep. 14, 1869 Madison, Wis. Died Apr. 11, 1953 Kansas City, Mo. Won 30 games or more in seven of eight straight years (1891–1898).
Little recalled today, Kid Nichols won 361 games, completed 531 (as many as Walter Johnson), and finished behind only Johnson and Cy Young in Adjusted Pitching Runs, a measurement of how many runs a pitcher saved his team, beyond what an average pitcher would have done in his stead.

No pitcher has had more 30-win seasons than Nichols (seven), who pitched with no wind-up and, scorning the curveball, changed speeds with surpassing skill. The righthander led the Boston Beaneaters to five pre-1900 pennants and became the youngest pitcher to win 300 games, marking the anniversary before his thirty-first birthday.

He made his debut with Kansas City in 1887, when that city was in the Western League, and made his mark two years later with Omaha of the Western Association, winning 36 games. When his manager, Frank Selee, went to Boston to manage the Beaneaters, Nichols went along and was an immediate sensation, winning 27 games his rookie year.

Called "Kid" for his slight build and baby face, Nichols soon became the workhorse of his era. He pitched more than 400 innings in each of his first five years, 300 or more in his first ten, and holds the record for most seasons with 300 innings pitched (twelve). He was relieved in only 24 of the 501 starts he made for Boston. Late in 1892, a year in which he finished at 35–16 in 453 innings, he pitched complete game wins three days in a row.

Named "Nervy Nick" for beating the Orioles twice in three days to win the 1897 pennant, Nichols held out for more than $2,400, the maximum allowable at the time, and was given a $285 bonus for winning the 1898 pennant. Nevertheless, he left the majors to buy a piece of the Kansas City team and returned after a two-year hiatus as player-manager of the Cardinals. Fading from the big leagues after the 1906 campaign, he returned to Kansas City and coached amateur clubs, one of which had a player named Charles Dillon "Casey" Stengel.

A vigorous man, he won the Kansas City bowling championship at age sixty-four and bowled competitively into his seventies. Elected to the Hall of Fame in 1949, he died in Kansas City four years later at the age of eighty-three.

LEROY "SATCHEL" PAIGE
Pitcher. Born July 7, 1905 Mobile, Ala. Died June 8, 1982 Kansas City, Mo. Pitched professionally from 1924 to 1959.
When the Cleveland Indians signed Satchel Paige to a contract in 1948, J.G. Taylor Spink, publisher of *The Sporting News,* wrote, "To bring in a pitching rookie of Paige's age is to demean the standards of baseball." Two days later, Paige demeaned the White Sox, holding them scoreless in two innings of relief. He pitched a shutout in his second start and finished his first big league season

6–1; since the Indians wound up in a tie with the Red Sox, they literally could not have won the pennant without him.

Satchel Paige had made it to the majors, but not when he was the best pitcher in baseball. In 1930 he struck out 22 big leaguers, including Hack Wilson and Babe Herman, in an exhibition game. A year later he joined the Pittsburgh Crawfords, who advertised—truthfully—that "Josh Gibson will hit two home runs and Satchel Paige will strike out the first nine batters."

As a member of the Crawfords in 1933 he was 31–4, winning 21 games in a row and once racking up 62 straight scoreless innings. In 1938 a sore arm threatened to put him out of baseball, but he learned to throw curves, and gradually his arm came back. He pitched the Kansas City Monarchs to five pennants, and, when one of his teammates, Jackie Robinson, made it to the majors, Paige figured rightly that his time had come.

After his sensational start with the Indians, Paige had a subpar season in 1949 and, following owner Bill Veeck's departure, was released. He rejoined Veeck as a member of the lowly Browns and, incredibly, became the AL's leading reliever in 1952 at age 46, winning 12 games and saving 10.

When the team moved to Baltimore, Satch pitched in the minors for seven more years. He came back at 59 to pitch three scoreless innings for the Kansas City A's in 1965. He was signed as a pitching coach in 1968 by the Braves to qualify for his pension. Fittingly, he was the first man elected to the Hall of Fame by the Committee on Negro Leagues formed in 1971.

JIM PALMER
Pitcher. Born Oct. 15, 1945 New York, N.Y. AL Cy Young Award 1973, 1975, 1976.
The best pitchers win the big ones. Jim Palmer clinched the first four pennants in Baltimore's post-1900 history and had a record of 8–3 and an ERA of 2.61 in postseason play. In 1983 he became the only pitcher to win a World Series game in three different decades.

Over eighteen years, Palmer won the Cy Young Award three times (1973, 1975, and 1976) and set Oriole records for career wins (268), shutouts (53), and complete games (211). He is, along with Walter Johnson and Lefty Grove, the only AL pitcher to win 20 games in eight or more seasons, and his ERA (2.86) ranks fifth among pitchers with 3,000 innings or more.

Palmer averaged 288 innings for nine straight years and led the league in that department four times. Despite this durability, he was frequently injured and acquired a reputation as a hypochondriac. When Oriole pitcher Steve Stone saw Palmer reading *Doctor Zhivago,* he quipped, "It must be about an elbow specialist."

Palmer led the Orioles in wins with 15 in 1966 and, before his twenty-first birthday, beat the Dodgers and Sandy Koufax in the southpaw's last game, 6–0, to become the youngest pitcher to throw a World Series shutout. The game was an apt symbol to divide the old and new orders of pitchers, but Palmer suffered a sore arm and was out of the majors for nearly two years.

He won 20 games eight out of nine years, from 1970 to 1973 and from 1975 to 1978. Numerous arm injuries slowed him down, and, when he sported an ERA of 7.44 in May 1982, it looked as though that might be his last

year; however, Palmer recovered and won 11 in a row, nearly leading the Orioles to another pennant. When the O's won in 1983, Palmer pitched only once, winning Game Three as a relief pitcher.

After starting the 1984 season 0–3, Palmer pitched his last game on May 12. Although his plan to make a comeback in 1991—one year after he was inducted into the Hall of Fame!—never materialized, he remains in the public eye as a TV talk show host and corporate spokesman.

CAL RIPKEN, JR.
Shortstop. Born Aug. 24, 1960 Havre De Grace, Md. AL Rookie of the Year 1982, American League MVP 1983.
Cal Ripken, Jr., has played more consecutive games at one position than any major leaguer (1,986) and hasn't been out of the Orioles' starting lineup since May 29, 1982, when he started at short in the second game of a doubleheader. His consecutive game streak (he started at third base) was at 2,009 at the end of the 1994 season; if he keeps playing, he will, barring injury, break Lou Gehrig's record of 2,130 consecutive games played late in 1995.

Ripken has taken criticism for keeping the streak alive, when he might not have been healthy enough to play effectively. Nevertheless, the streak has pushed Ripken beyond ordinary physical limits, sometimes with gratifying results. In 1983, he hurt his hand sliding on artificial turf in Seattle and was unable to grip the bat at first; he somehow gritted his teeth and got five hits that night, two of them home runs, and thirteen total bases to tie an Oriole club record.

At 6'4", he is the tallest regular shortstop in major league history and one of the most powerful. In 1986, Ripken became the only shortstop besides Ernie Banks to hit 20 or more homers in six straight seasons. (His streak of ten straight seasons was finally broken in 1992.) The first AL shortstop to start more than three straight All-Star Games (seven in all), he has also led the league four times in putouts and double plays, six times in assists, and set a new AL assist record (534) in 1983.

Although Ripken played 44 errorless games at third base and homered in his first at-bat in 1982, he suffered a deep batting slump (7-for-60). Reggie Jackson told him, "You look like you're fighting yourself ... stick with what got you here." Moved to shortstop on July 1 to fill Mark Belanger's shoes for good, he wound up with 28 homers and 93 RBIs to be named Rookie of the Year.

In 1983, Ripken led the majors in hits and doubles and the league in runs, extra base hits, assists, total chances, and double plays. He was named MVP and led Baltimore to a division title. He played errorless ball as the O's beat the White Sox in the playoffs and Philadelphia in the World Series.

BROOKS "HOOVER" ROBINSON
Third Baseman. Born May 18, 1937 Little Rock, Ark. Holds major league third baseman records for highest fielding average (.971), putouts (2,697), assists (6,205), and double plays (618). AL MVP 1964.
Brooks Calbert Robinson, Jr. wasn't nicknamed "Hoover" for his resemblance to Herbert or J. Edgar but rather for his ability to suck up everything hit towards third base.

He won Gold Gloves every year from 1960 to 1975, led AL third basemen eleven times in fielding and eight times each in putouts and assists, and made more putouts, assists, chances, and double plays than any third baseman in history. He also spent a record twenty-three years with one team, the Orioles. Sportswriter Gordon Beard said, "He never asked anyone to name a candy bar after him. In Baltimore people name their children after him."

Robinson made his debut as an Oriole in 1955 and collected 2,848 hits in the regular season; however, no amount of work could make up for his basic lack of speed; he grounded into more double plays than any other ALer (297) and stole only 28 bases in his entire career.

He won the MVP award in 1964, hitting .317 with 28 homers and shone in postseason play. In 39 playoff and World Series games, he hit 5 homers and went 44-for-145, a .303 average. He hit an even .500 in the 1969 playoffs and .583 in 1970 as the O's crushed the Twins.

The 1970 World Series was the Brooks Robinson Show. In the opener he backhanded Lee May's bullet to keep the go-ahead run off base in the sixth inning and, with the score tied 3–3 in the seventh, homered over the left field fence to give the Birds a 4–3 win; in Game Two he knocked in the game-winner in a 6–5 squeaker.

All that was prologue to Game Three when Robinson did for fielding what Esther Williams did for swimsuits. He made sparkling plays on Tony Perez's shot down the line in the first, Tommy Helms's slow roller in the second, Johnny Bench's line drive in the sixth. He went 4-for-4 in Game Four and was named MVP when the Orioles won Game Five and the Series. The ultimate accolade came from Johnny Bench: "I will become a lefthanded hitter to keep the ball away from that guy."

When he retired in 1977, the Orioles gave credit where it was due by holding Thanks Brooks Day on September 18. The occasion drew the largest regular season crowd in Memorial Stadium's history. He entered the Hall of Fame in 1983.

FRANK ROBINSON

Right Field. Born Aug. 31, 1935 Beaumont, Tex. NL Rookie of the Year 1956, MVP 1961. Won AL MVP and Triple Crown 1966.

Frank Robinson was in a class by himself as a two-league player. He's the only man to be chosen MVP in both leagues, to hit All-Star Game homers for both, to hit 200 or more home runs in both, and to become the first black manager in both, piloting Cleveland from 1975 to 1977 and San Francisco from 1981 to 1984. In 1989, while managing Baltimore, he matched the Manager of the Year award he'd won in 1982 with the Giants.

Robinson also holds the record for hitting home runs in the most ballparks and, while his 586 homers place him fourth on the all-time list, Robinson also ranks in the top ten in career runs, RBIs, and total bases. The complete player, he stole 20 bases or more three times, and even led the majors in intentional walks in four straight years (1961–1964).

Like all professionals, he produced under pressure. Robby made a dramatic debut as a player-manager, homering in his first at bat for the Indians. Similarly, he won the hearts of Baltimore fans shortly after joining the Orioles by hitting the first home run—a 540-foot shot—out of Memorial Stadium.

Robinson broke in with Cincinnati in 1956, tied Wally Berger's rookie record by hitting 38 homers, and was named Rookie of the Year. The first MVP award came in 1961, when he hit .323 with 37 homers, and stole 22 bases. In 1966 he hit 49 homers, knocked in 122 runs, and hit .316 to win the Triple Crown; that year he led Baltimore to a pennant and earned his second MVP award. Robby's home run off Don Drysdale in the World Series provided the only run in Game Four of an Oriole sweep, and he was named MVP of the Series as well.

He played in six All-Star Games for the National League and five for the American League. Yet, he will probably always be remembered as an Oriole. When he was traded to the Dodgers, number 20 became the first Baltimore uniform to be retired, and it's the one he wears in his 1982 Hall of Fame portrait.

JACKIE ROBINSON

Infielder/Outfielder. Born Jan. 31, 1919 Cairo, Ga. Died Oct. 24, 1972 Stamford, Conn. First black player in twentieth-century major leagues. NL Rookie of the Year 1947, MVP 1949.

If all Jackie Robinson did was to integrate baseball, that alone would have ensured his place in the game's history. For the story of his valiant effort and his role not only in baseball's history but that of our nation as well, see the essay by Jules Tygiel in this volume.

But Jackie Robinson did so much more than make baseball truly the national pastime. It is easy to overlook what a fabulous baseball player he was. He led the Brooklyn Dodgers to six pennants in ten years (plus their only world championship) and was named Rookie of the Year in 1947 and MVP in 1949.

While the Dodgers also had Hall of Famers Duke Snider, Pee Wee Reese, and Roy Campanella, Robinson forced them, by his example, to elevate their game, as he did all his other teammates. Cardinal second baseman Red Schoendienst once said, "If it wasn't for him, the Dodgers would be in the second division."

Driven by history and temperament, Robinson rattled pitchers by dancing off first base and had enough speed to steal home 19 times, 5 times in one season. He bettered .300 for six straight seasons, and retired with a .311 average. He was a regular at first, second, and third base and left field and led the league's second basemen in double plays four straight years (1949–1952).

UCLA's first four-letter man (baseball, basketball, football, and track), he went on to join the Army's Officer Candidate School. There he was court martialed, then acquitted, for refusing to sit in the back of a bus. After stints with the Kansas City Monarchs and the Dodgers' Montreal Royals farm club, he made his major league debut with the Dodgers in 1947 at the advanced age of twenty-eight; Robby hit .297, scored 125 runs, and led them to a pennant. That fall he finished second in a poll only to crooner Bing Crosby as the most popular man in America.

Robinson, in just his second year, became the Dodgers' team leader. He started on the All-Star team for the first of five times (four as a second baseman) in 1949, led the league in hitting, was named MVP, and led the Dodgers to another pennant.

On the last day of the 1951 season, with Brooklyn needing to win to force a playoff with the Giants, Robinson made a spectacular, game-saving grab of Eddie Waitkus's liner to send the game into extra innings, then won it with a homer in the fourteenth. The Dodgers fell short of the pennant that year thanks to Bobby Thomson, but recaptured the flag in four of Robinson's final five seasons.

Fifteen years after he'd integrated baseball, Robinson integrated the Baseball Hall of Fame.

PETE ROSE

Infielder/Outfielder. Born Apr. 14, 1941 Cincinnati, Oh. NL Rookie of the Year 1963, MVP 1973. Holds major league records for games played (3,562); most seasons, 200 or more hits (10); most lifetime hits (4,256).

In 1989 Commissioner A. Bartlett Giamatti suspended Pete Rose from baseball for life for gambling. In 1990 Rose served five months in prison for tax evasion. It all seemed a long way since spring training in 1963, when Rose ran out a walk and Whitey Ford dubbed him "Charlie Hustle."

Sadly, Rose is ineligible to be voted into the Hall of Fame, an honor he deserves for his accomplishments on the field. Rose was named Player of the Decade (1970–1979) by *The Sporting News*, played in sixteen All-Star Games, and holds the record for starting at most different positions (five)—first, second, and third bases, and left and right fields. He also played on three championship teams in six years—the 1975 and 1976 Reds and the 1980 Phillies. Rose holds playoff records for most hits (45) and batted .381 in 118 playoff at bats.

He grew up in Cincinnati and credited his father Harry, a former semipro football player, with influencing him to become an athlete. "He wanted me to share his love of sports and I did. One time Mom sent him to the store to buy a pair of shoes for my sister. Instead, he came back with a pair of boxing gloves for me."

In 1963 Rose hustled his way onto the Reds and turned out to be the sparkplug of the developing Big Red Machine. In 1970 Rose led the league in hits (205) for the third time. He repeated in 1972 and, in 1975 and 1976, he led the league in doubles and runs scored both times. In each of those years the Reds won the pennant.

In December 1978, the man who once said, "I'd go through hell in a gasoline suit to keep playing baseball," signed a four-year 3.2 million contract with the Phils to become the highest-paid player in team sports. Six years later, after playing briefly with the Expos, he returned to Cincinnati where he became a player-manager, breaking Ty Cobb's record for career hits. He retired as a player after the 1986 season and in six years as manager brought the Reds home second three times without winning a division title.

AMOS RUSIE

Pitcher. Born May 31, 1871 Indianapolis, Ind. Died Dec. 6, 1942 Seattle, Wash.

When Walter Johnson came along in 1907, writers seeking to compliment the young fireballer called him "another Rusie."

Baseball paid Rusie the ultimate compliment in 1893 when it changed the rules because of him. The mound was moved back from 50 feet to 60 feet, 6 inches, and several authorities claim the change was intended to make Rusie's heat less intimidating. (Rusie's first catcher, Dick Buckley, padded his glove with a thin sheet of lead to help absorb the impact of Rusie's hummer.) The Indianan led the league in strikeouts five years out of six and won 30 games or more four years in a row.

The stocky righthander (6'1", 200) beat Boston and Washington in exhibition games before joining Indianapolis of the NL in 1889; when the franchise folded, Rusie and seven other players became Giants for $60,000. He arrived as a star in 1890, striking out 341 batters to lead the league. The media hero of his day, "the Hoosier Thunderbolt" was mentioned in a Mr. Dooley story as well as a Weber and Fields vaudeville skit; Lillian Russell, the sex symbol of that era, begged for an introduction to Rusie and got it.

At the end of the 1892 season the Giants, hoping to save half a month's pay, released him under a "gentlemen's agreement" that no club would sign him ... but the White Stockings did, for $6,250 plus a $2,000 bonus. The Giants eventually bought the contract back, then tried to count the bonus as part of Rusie's salary.

Rusie prevailed but in crossing swords with Giant boss Andrew Freedman he had bought a heap of trouble. Rusie later was fined for missing curfew and for thumbing his nose at Freedman in public, who withheld $200 from his last paycheck of 1895. Rusie pioneered the holdout, missing the entire 1896 season. He sued for damages and, just before the 1897 season, the NL owners pooled $5,000 to settle the suit.

Rusie picked up where he'd left off and went 28–10. He won 20 in 1898; however, he hurt his arm making a pickoff throw, and 1898 was his last full season. He stayed home in Washington State to tend to his ailing wife and was disciplined by the Giants yet again. After sitting out a two-year suspension, he was traded to the Reds for Christy Mathewson. Matty at this point had no major league wins behind him but 373 ahead; Rusie had 245 in his pocket but, alas, none ahead. He started just two games, was blasted as he had never been in his prime, and retired. He was elected to the Hall of Fame in 1977.

GEORGE HERMAN "BABE" RUTH

Right Field. Born Feb. 6, 1895 Baltimore, Md. Died Aug. 16, 1948 New York, N.Y. Holds major league records for highest slugging percentage, season (.847, 1920) and lifetime (.690), most home runs by lefthanded batter (714), most years leading league in home runs (twelve).

Babe Ruth was one of baseball's best pitchers, its greatest player, greatest public figure, and the greatest hero in American sports.

When he was seven, George Herman Ruth was committed to Baltimore's St. Mary's Industrial School for repeated theft. Father Gilbert of St. Mary's later released him to pitch for the International League Baltimore Orioles and persuaded Orioles' owner-manager, Jack Dunn, to become Ruth's guardian, making Ruth his "Babe."

In 1914 Ruth was bought by the Red Sox, farmed out to Providence, and brought back to Boston after winning 22 games. He won 18 games for the big club in 1915, followed up with 23 wins in 1916, and pitched the longest complete game victory in World Series history that fall, a fourteen-inning 2–1 win over the Dodgers. The Babe became primarily an outfielder in 1918 (though he still pitched enough to go 13–7 in 1918 and 9–5 the following year). He left the mound in 1919 (not counting five cameo appearances over the next fourteen years, each of which he won) as the only man to have pitched more than 1,000 innings and have a lifetime batting average over .300 (.304).

In 1918 Ruth led the league in home runs (with 11) for the first of a record twelve times. Harry Frazee, Red Sox owner and a theatrical producer deep in debt, was forced to sell him to the Yankees that December. Now playing his home games in the friendly Polo Grounds, which the Yanks shared with the Giants, Ruth changed the game by hitting 54 homers; the rest of the American League had only 315. His slugging average of .847 has never been approached, except by the Babe himself the following year, when he produced a mark of .846.

Fans rushed to see him in his first year in New York, producing the first million-plus attendance in baseball history and spurring the Yankees to erect a superstadium in 1923, "The House That Ruth Built." That year he hit .393 to lead the Yankees to their third straight pennant and first World Series their first of twenty-two World Series titles. He dominated the 1923 Series, hitting three home runs and batting .368.

From 1926 to 1930, he led the league in home runs every year and tied Lou Gehrig for the lead in 1931. Three years later, Ruth asked to manage the Yankees and was chagrined when owner Jacob Ruppert offered him New York's top farm club instead. He signed with the Braves and had a final moment of glory on May 25, 1935, hitting 3 home runs in a game, one of them a prodigious shot over the right-field roof at Pittsburgh's Forbes Field. The Babe retired a few weeks later with 714 home runs, a lifetime average of .342, and the highest slugging percentage in history (.690). In the inaugural ballot for the Hall of Fame the following year, he became one of the Founding Five members.

NOLAN RYAN
Pitcher. Born Jan. 31, 1947 Refugio, Tex. Holds major league record for no-hitters (7) and lifetime strikeouts (5,714). Add up the lifetime strikeouts of Vida Blue (2,175), Hal Newhouser (1,796), and Carl Hubbell (1,677), and you still have 66 fewer than Nolan Ryan had all by himself.
The career of baseball's strikeout king parallels that of Sandy Koufax—the great fastball and overpowering curve, the control problems, early failure, final success— with Ryan's longevity being the obvious difference. Koufax retired at thirty-two, an age at which Ryan was leading the league in strikeouts for the sixth of twelve times.

Lynn Nolan Ryan was selected by the Mets on the eighth round of the free-agent draft in June 1965, when Tom Seaver was graduating from USC. In 1969 Seaver was the toast of the baseball world after winning 25 games in the regular season; Ryan was, by contrast, 6–3 as a relief pitcher although he saved Game Three of the World Series.

Traded to the Angels for Jim Fregosi, Ryan blossomed all at once, just as Koufax had a decade earlier. From 1972 to 1974, Ryan had a record of 62–48, with 1,079 strikeouts in 943 innings. In an eight-day period in 1972 he fanned 15 Rangers, 16 Red Sox, and 16 A's, on his way to winning 19 games, 9 of them shutouts. In 1973 he was even better, no-hitting the Royals and the Tigers. Despite a torn calf muscle, he fanned Rich Reese for his 383rd and final K of the season, breaking Koufax's record for strike-outs in a season.

On August 12, 1974, he struck out 19 Red Sox to tie the record held by former teammate Tom Seaver and Steve Carlton. One month later he notched his third no-hitter, against the Twins. He tied Koufax with number four on June 1, 1975, beating the Orioles, 1-0. In 1979 Ryan signed with the Astros as a free agent.

Back in the NL, he eclipsed Koufax's record for no-hitters by beating the Dodgers, 5–0, at the Astrodome on September 26, 1981 and he led NL pitchers in that strike-shortened year with a 1.69 ERA. In 1983 he broke Walter Johnson's record for career strikeouts. Signing with the Texas Rangers after the 1988 season for what was antici-pated to be his fading farewell tour, Ryan instead turned up the heat. He added a sixth no-hitter in 1990 on the road against the A's and a seventh at home against the Blue Jays.

RYNE SANDBERG
Second Baseman. Born Sept. 18, 1959 Spokane, Wash. NL MVP 1984.
The Cubs weren't looked upon as a contender in 1984, but Ryne Sandberg changed that in a nationally televised game against the Cardinals. In both the ninth and tenth innings, Sandberg homered against Bruce Sutter to tie the game and went 5-for-6 with seven RBIs in a game the Cubs won, 12–11. Cards manager Whitey Herzog said, "One day I thought he was one of the best players in the NL. The next day I think he's one of the best players I've ever seen."

Sandberg attracted a lot of attention for his defense in 1990, by which time he'd gone nearly a year without making an error. The streak started on June 21, 1989, and ended on May 17, 1990; by that time, Sandberg had played in 123 consecutive games and accepted 582 chances without making an error, both records for all infielders except first basemen. Even more incredible, Sandberg put together streaks of 30 or more errorless games fifteen times.

He grew up in Spokane, where he was the quarterback on *Parade* magazine's high school All-America team. Drafted by the Phillies, he played at Wichita, Spartan-burg, and Reading and spent winter ball learning all the infield positions, because the Phillies saw him as a utility man. Dealt to Chicago as a throw-in in a swap of short-stops Larry Bowa and Ivan DeJesus, Sandberg made the team as a third baseman, moving to second in 1983 when the Cubs signed Ron Cey.

Second baseman Sandberg became the first player to change positions and win a Gold Glove; he has since won eight more. In 1984 Jim Frey signed on as the manager and convinced Sandberg that he could become a power hitter by turning on 2–0 or 3–1 pitches. "Coaches and managers had always told me to hit the ball on the ground. He told me to swing for power and gave me confidence." Not coincidentally, the Cubs caught fire as a team, took the Eastern Division, and narrowly missed winning the pennant; Sandberg was named MVP.

After the 1991 season, Sandberg signed a contract which paid him $7.1 million a year. In 1992, he hit .304, his fourth .300-plus season, and hit 26 homers for the second straight year.

He retired early in the 1994 season.

RON SANTO
Third Baseman. Born Feb. 25, 1940 Seattle, Wash. Holds major league record for most times leading the league in total chances (nine), third baseman .

Ron Santo was the NL's best third baseman in the 1960s, the senior circuit's version of Brooks Robinson.

Although he won fewer Gold Gloves than Robinson, he set a major league record by leading third basemen in total chances the most times (nine) and shares NL records for leading the most times in putouts and assists (7) and double plays (6).

With 342 career homers, he was also a disciplined batter who led the league in walks four times and twice in on-base percentage.

The durable Santo missed just 23 games in a ten-year period and played from 1961 to 1971 without injury. Bill James has plumped for Santo as a Hall of Famer, as have the editors of *Total Baseball*; James ranks him as the seventy-first best player of all time, ahead of contemporaries Roberto Clemente and Billy Williams.

When Santo started out at San Antonio, he had such a wild arm, according to pitcher Jim Brosnan, that the GM "was going to sell first base box seats at a premium since fans who sat there were pretty sure to get a ball." Santo benefited from the coaching of Grady Hatton and was a polished third sacker by the time he reached Chicago. in his Cub debut he also knocked in five runs in a doubleheader.

If Billy Williams played in the shadow of Ernie Banks, Santo was even more invisible. Using the Total Player Rating, Santo was the best player in the NL in both 1966 and 1967 by a wide margin, yet finished thirteenth and fourth respectively in MVP voting. When the Cubbies came close to winning the division, in 1969, Santo led the league in runs produced (191) and drove in a career-high 123 runs.

Santo was also a success in business. He owned a printing company, started a baseball school, and got the rights to sell Pro's Pizza at Wrigley Field. (Every cover had a round baseball card of a Cub hero.) When the Cubs had a Day for him, he revealed that he had been diabetic since age eighteen; Santo buttons were sold, and all proceeds went to the Diabetes Association.

On December 11, 1973, he became the first ten-year veteran to veto a trade to another team, the Angels. (Given the timing, wits called this contract provision the "Santo clause.") Santo instead moved to the South Side and played second base with the White Sox, retiring after an unsatisfying 1974 season. He joined the Cub broadcast team in 1990.

MIKE SCHMIDT
Third Baseman. Born Sept. 27, 1949 Dayton, Oh. Holds major league record for most home runs by a third baseman (509 of his total 548).

Philadelphia's famous boobirds even booed baseball's greatest third baseman in 1978. They held Mike Schmidt's light hitting accountable for playoff losses to the Reds in 1976 and the Dodgers in 1977 and 1978.

When the Phillies beat Houston to face Kansas City in the 1980 World Series, Schmidt turned the boos to cheers. He:

• scored two runs in Game One;
• doubled in the winning run in Game Two;
• homered in a losing cause in Game Three;
• hit a two-run homer and singled to start a rally in the ninth inning of Game Five;
• singled in the first two runs in Game Six to win the championship.

Schmidt hit .381 and was named MVP of the Series to match the MVP award he'd won in the regular season, the first of three he earned. Over eighteen seasons, Schmidt homered more often than any other third baseman (509), hit 30 or more homers thirteen times, started seven All-Star Games, and won ten Gold Gloves, nine of them consecutively.

The shortstop on *The Sporting News* College All-America team for 1971 and the Pacific Coast League's All-Star second baseman the next year, he became the Phils' regular third baseman in 1973. He had a disastrous year, striking out 136 times in 367 at bats and hitting .196, the lowest average compiled that season by any major league regular.

One year later he led the NL in homers (36) for the first of three consecutive seasons and batted in 116 runs. He told *Sport* that winter ball in Puerto Rico had made the difference. "I found a swing that made things happen ... I was standing at the plate nice and relaxed and that sucker went off my bat a mile."

On April 17, 1976, he became the tenth major leaguer to hit four home runs in a game, as the Phillies beat the Cubs, 18–16. That same year he set a record for assists in a 162-game season (404) and topped the NL six more times to tie Ron Santo's record, as well as tying him in leading the league in double plays with six.

In the strike-shortened 1981 season, he led the majors in homers (31), RBIs (91), slugging (.644), and total bases (228) to earn his second consecutive MVP award. Fans named him the greatest Phillies player ever in 1983. Three years later, he led the league in homers (37) and RBIs (119) and became the only three-time NL MVP besides Stan Musial and Roy Campanella. He retired in 1989 and was named to the Hall of Fame in 1995.

TOM SEAVER
Pitcher. Born Nov. 17, 1944 Fresno, Cal. Holds major league record for most consecutive years with 200 or more strikeouts (9). NL Cy Young Award 1969, 1973, 1975.

Tom Seaver almost single-handedly turned the Mets from laughingstock to champion.

In their first four years, the Mets had a winning percentage of .294; four years later, thanks to Seaver, they won 100 games, swept the Braves in the playoffs, and stunned the Orioles in five games to become world champions. Over a decade after he last pitched for them, Seaver remains the Mets' team leader in wins (198), shutouts

(44), and strikeouts (2,541). He won 311 games in all and three Cy Young Awards, and struck out a record 200 batters in nine straight seasons (1968-76).

He almost began his career as a Brave, signing a contract with Atlanta that violated baseball's college rule, according to Commissioner William Eckert. Three clubs wanted to sign him—the Indians, Phillies, and Mets. On April 3, 1966, Eckert picked the Mets' name out of a hat, and the Mets signed Seaver to a $50,000 bonus and assigned him to Jacksonville.

Sixteen months later he made his first of eight All-Star Game appearances and capped the season by by being named National League Rookie of the Year. Seaver won 16 games each of his first two years and, in 1969, he was 25-7 to lead the Mets to the World Series. In the Mets' five-game defeat of the Baltimore Orioles, he won Game 4, 2-1 in ten innings.

On April 22, 1970, Seaver was presented with his first Cy Young Award at Shea Stadium and celebrated by setting the record for consecutive strikeouts in one game, fanning the last 10 Padres to reach a game total of 19. Seaver won 20 games or more in 1971, 1972, 1975, and 1977, when he was unexpectedly traded to the Reds.

He no-hit the Cardinals in 1978, and went 14-2 in 1981, his best won-lost percentage; however, injuries made 1982 his worst—a 5-13 record and a 5.50 ERA—and he improved only slightly upon his return to the Mets in 1983. After joining the White Sox, Tom turned Terrific again, and, at 39, wound up leading the Sox in wins (15) and shutouts (4), never missing a turn in the rotation. In 1985 he was even better, winning 16 games, among them his 300th.

He retired after the 1986 season with 61 career shutouts (seventh on the all-time list); was fourth in career strikeouts; and compiled a sterling 2.85 ERA. He entered the Hall of Fame in 1992.

AL SIMMONS

Left Field. Born May 22, 1902 Milwaukee, Wis. Died May 26, 1956 Milwaukee, Wis. AL MVP 1929.
Striding toward third base, leaving the impression that he hit with his "foot in the bucket" (a venerable baseball term for a frightened batter, going back to the days when a water bucket sat at the end of the players' bench) didn't bother Al Simmons. He bettered .300 for eleven straight years, won back-to-back batting titles, hit .329 in nineteen World Series games, and .334 lifetime. Though unheralded for his defense, Simmons led the league in fielding twice. Joe Cronin said, "There never was a better left fielder in hustling to the foul line to turn a double into a single."

Born Aloysius Szymanski in Milwaukee in 1902, he turned pro with the Milwaukee Brewers in 1922, taking the name Simmons from a newspaper ad. Sold to the A's, Simmons worried that Connie Mack would change his stance, but Mack told him, "You can hold the bat in your teeth, provided you hit safely and often." Simmons hit .387 as a sophomore and led the league in hits (253), still a record for righthanded batsmen.

In 1929, he helped the A's to a pennant with 34 homers and a league-leading 157 RBIs and was named MVP. He drove in four runs in Game Two of the Series with a single and a homer, homered to start the famous ten-run rally in

Game Four, and singled and doubled in Game Seven, scoring the Series-winning run on Bing Miller's double. If anything, Simmons improved in 1930, leading the league in runs (152) and hitting (.381), and homering in Games One and Six as the A's won their second straight championship.

Simmons held out in 1931, and, on Opening Day, Mack announced he would not play for the A's. Taking a cab to Shibe Park, Mack reached into his pocket to pay; the driver declined, saying, "If you can't afford Simmons, you can't afford me either." Hours later, Simmons signed a three-year contract and homered on the first pitch thrown to him.

In 1931, the Duke of Milwaukee hit .390 to lead the league for the second straight year and homered twice in the World Series, but he never again reached such heights. He said later, "When I finally decided I had it made, I was never again the ballplayer I was when I was hungry." Simmons went on to play with six other teams before finishing his career in a third tour of duty with the A's. He was named to the Hall of Fame in 1953.

GEORGE SISLER

First Baseman. Born Mar. 24, 1893 Manchester, Oh. Died Mar. 26, 1973 St. Louis, Mo. Holds major league record for hits in a season (257); AL MVP 1922.
George Sisler had the defensive ability, foot speed, and batting prowess to equal any first baseman. Originally a pitcher, Sisler was clearly more valuable as an everyday player. He led the league's first basemen in assists a record seven times, stole home nineteen times, and compiled a .340 career average.

In 1920 he played every inning of every game, had 140 assists, started 13 first-to-short-to-first double plays, stole 42 bases, batted .407, banged out 19 homers, and established what may be an unbeatable major league record with 257 hits. Two years later he led the league in hits, runs, doubles, and average, batting .420. Although Sisler earned the first League Award (MVP), the Yanks won the pennant by a single game, a sad end to a great season; Sisler never came close to another chance to play in a World Series.

Born in Manchester, Ohio, Sisler was an all-around athlete and signed with Akron of the Ohio-Penn League, although he received no money and never played for Akron. (He reported but was told the team didn't have a uniform small enough.) Instead, he starred for Branch Rickey at the University of Michigan. Rickey became a Browns scout in 1912, moved up to manager a year later, and signed Sisler when he graduated in 1915 with a degree in mechanical engineering.

The Pirates, who had purchased the Akron contract from Columbus, also claimed Sisler, and the case was brought before the three-man National Commission, a predecessor of the commissioner's office. The NL and AL presidents voted along party lines, but Reds president Garry Herrmann broke ranks, and Sisler became a Brown.

As great as he was, Sisler might have been even better had he not contracted poisonous sinusitis and missed the entire 1923 season. Although he had three more 200-plus-hit seasons thereafter, he said, "I didn't consider that real good hitting." He once told *Baseball* magazine that his ambition was to "hang up a higher average than Ty Cobb's," and, indeed, Sisler's .41979 average in 1922 did edge the .41962 Cobb had in 1911. In fact, Cobb called him "the nearest thing to a perfect ballplayer."

Sisler was elected to the Hall of Fame in 1939, and in the 1940s and 1950s tutored two other Hall of Famers—Duke Snider and Roberto Clemente.

OZZIE SMITH

Shortstop. Born Dec. 26, 1954 Mobile, Ala. Holds NL record for most Gold Gloves (13).

Thomas Boswell of the *Washington Post* once wrote of Ozzie Smith, "Instead of '1' his number should be '8,' but turned sideways because the possibilities he brings to his position are almost infinite."

Already the NL's career leader in Gold Gloves and arguably baseball's best-fielding shortstop of all time, Smith has also made himself into an above-average hitter and high-average base-stealer. But what makes him a lock for the Hall of Fame when he hangs up his glove is ... his glove. Through the 1994 season, he had saved his teams 236 runs beyond what an average shortstop would have done, a mark unequaled at the position in this century.

"The Wizard of Oz" attended Locke High School in Los Angeles with Eddie Murray, and the Padres picked him in the fourth round of the 1977 free agent draft. After winning two Gold Gloves for San Diego and setting a record for assists in 1980 (621), Smith was traded to the Cardinals. Two years later, the Cardinals won their first championship in fifteen years as Smith led the league's shortstops in fielding for the first of a record seven times. (He also whacked two home runs, doubling his four-year output in San Diego.)

Learning to fit his talents to Busch Stadium, the switch-hitting Smith improved his batting average to .276 by 1985, when the Cardinals won their division again. Smith blossomed in the playoffs against the Dodgers, batting .435. With the score tied, 2–2, in Game Five, he homered in the bottom of the ninth to give the Cardinals a 3–2 edge in games. (To date, it is his only lefthanded major league home run.)

In 1987, for the fifth time in Smith's six years in St. Louis, the Cardinals led the league in team fielding. They won another pennant but lost a seven-game Series to the Royals. That year, the Wizard of Ahs finally reached the .300 mark (.303), won the accustomed Gold Glove, and finished second to Andre Dawson in voting for the Most Valuable Player.

In 1991 he set a record for NL shortstops, committing just 8 errors in 150 games, and won his thirteenth consecutive Gold Glove in 1992 to break a tie with Willie Mays and Roberto Clemente. By the end of the 1994 season he had also amassed 569 stolen bases.

EDWIN "DUKE" SNIDER

Center Field. Born Sept. 19, 1926 Los Angeles, Cal. Hit 40 or more home runs in five consecutive seasons (1952-56).

When New York had Willie (Mays), Mickey (Mantle), and the Duke (Snider), Snider always got third billing. Yet he hit more home runs in the 1950s than Mays, Mantle, or any other major leaguer (326) and tied Ralph Kiner's NL record of hitting 40 or more homers in five straight sea-

sons. Kiner said of his fielding, "I'd say Duke covers more ground, wastes less motion, and is more consistent than anyone since DiMaggio."

Snider chose the Dodgers because of his admiration for Pete Reiser and Pee Wee Reese. General manager Branch Rickey put him in the batting cage three hours every day with Hall of Famer George Sisler—but not to hit. Snider recalls, "I was just supposed to call every pitch, ball or strike. It was amazing how wrong I was at the beginning. But I learned."

The Duke became a regular in 1949, hitting .292 with 23 homers, and clinched the pennant on the last day of the season by driving in the winning run. His World Series debut was a disaster (a .143 average and 8 strikeouts), but he redeemed himself in the 1952 World Series with ten hits, four of them home runs to tie the mark then shared by Babe Ruth and Lou Gehrig.

In 1955 Snider led the league in RBIs (136), led for a third time in runs scored (126), hit .309, and had 42 homers. He hit four more homers in the 1955 Series as Brooklyn won its only World Series and became the only man to hit four dingers in a Series twice. After the season, he was named Player of the Year by *The Sporting News*.

He led the league in home runs (43) in 1956, the only time he did so. The Dodgers moved to Los Angeles for the 1958 season, depriving the Duke of the cozy dimensions of Ebbets Field. In 1959 he still had enough muscle to send out 23 homers and propel Los Angeles to the world championship, in which he homered again. That was Snider's last Series; he still holds the NL record for career World Series homers (11) and RBIs (26).

After two seasons as a Met and, even more incongruously, as a Giant, he retired with a lifetime batting average of .295 and 407 homers. He managed several Dodger farm teams, scouted for the Dodgers and Padres, and broadcast games for those two teams as well as the Expos. He was elected to the Hall of Fame in 1980.

WARREN SPAHN

Pitcher. Born Apr. 23, 1921 Buffalo, N.Y. Holds major league record for most games won by lefthanded pitcher (363).

Stan Musial once said, "I don't think Spahn will ever get into the Hall of Fame. He'll never stop pitching."

Musial's point was well taken. Warren Spahn pitched long enough to be a Brave under Casey Stengel in 1942 and a Met under Stengel again in 1965. In between, he became the winningest lefthander in major league history, emerging victorious in 363 games. He put 15,741 batters out of their misery, won 20 games or more in thirteen seasons, and had a lifetime ERA of 3.09.

Not regarded as a strikeout artist, he nonetheless recorded 2,583 whiffs in his career and led the NL four straight years, from 1949 to 1952. He led the league in wins five times outright, had the most shutouts four times, and compiled the lowest ERA three times. He also started more double plays than any other major league pitcher (82) and also leads all NL pitchers in hitting home runs (35).

Brought up to the Boston Braves in 1942, he was sent back down when Stengel ordered him to throw at Pee Wee Reese and he refused. He enlisted in the Army, suffered shrapnel wounds in a battle along the Rhine, and was awarded the Purple Heart. He made his mark in 1947 by posting a 21–10 record, leading the league in ERA (2.33) and innings pitched (289⅔).

In 1948 the Braves won the pennant, fueled by the hopes for "Spahn and Sain and two days of rain." The franchise moved to Milwaukee in 1953. That year Spahn pitched in his third of seven All-Star Games and got the win. When the Braves won pennants in 1957 and 1958, he led the league in wins both years. He was given the Cy Young Award in 1957 (when there was only one award for both leagues) and won two games in the 1958 Series, shutting out the Yanks in Game 4.

When the 1960 season started, Spahn had won 267 major league games without pitching a no-hitter. He remedied this oversight on September 15, striking out 15 Phillies to win his 20th game of the season. Five days after his fortieth birthday, in 1961, Spahn pitched his second no-hitter.

After a losing season in 1964 (his first) and brief stays with the Mets and Giants in 1965, he coached in Mexico City and Japan. In line with Musial's prediction, Spahn interrupted his retirement to pitch in the Mexican League, thus delaying the onset of the mandatory five-year inactive period before induction into the Hall of Fame. Finally, however, Spahn left the mound for good and was elected to the Hall of Fame in 1973.

TRIS SPEAKER
Center Fielder. Born Apr. 4, 1888 Hubbard City, Tex. Died Dec. 8, 1958 Lake Whitney, Tex. Holds major league records for assists (450) and double plays (135) by an outfielder.

Like a wide receiver anticipating the throw of the quarterback, Tris Speaker revolutionized center fielding by moving before the pitch.

He acquired the knack as a Red Sox rookie, fielding fungos hit by Cy Young and trying to figure out which way the ball would go. He says, "In a few days I knew just by the way he swung whether the ball would go to my right or left. Then I began to study the batter during a game; when he started his swing, I knew if he would hit to my left or right and I was on my way."

Getting a head start allowed him to play shallow. The "Gray Eagle" participated in a record four unassisted double plays and set a record for outfielders with 448 career assists. He led AL outfielders seven times in putouts, five times in double plays (some of them 4–8–3 or 6–8–3), three times in assists, and twice in fielding. Just as much a threat offensively, Speaker hit .345 during a twenty-two-year career, had eighteen .300-plus seasons, and compiled 3,514 hits.

Two of baseball's shrewdest operators didn't sign him: Pirate boss Barney Dreyfuss because "he smoked cigarettes"; and Giant manager John McGraw because "I had all the outfielders I needed." Speaker paid his way to the Red Sox training camp in Little Rock, Arkansas. Boston optioned Speaker and bartered him to Little Rock in lieu of their $400 rental fee. Several months later, he was burning up the league and became the Red Sox starting center fielder in 1909.

A star by 1912, Speaker tied Home Run Baker for most home runs (10) that year, led the league in doubles (53), hit .383, and won the Chalmers Award (a forerunner of the MVP award), and hit .340 as the Red Sox beat the Giants in the World Series. In 1916 Speaker, newly arrived in Cleveland, won the batting title (.386) from Ty Cobb, interrupting what would have been an uninterrupted string of 13 titles, and also led the league in doubles (41), hits (211), and slugging percentage (.503).

He took over as manager of the Indians during the 1919 season; a year later he steered them to a pennant and a World Series win over the Dodgers. Speaker was elected to the Hall of Fame in 1937 and returned to the Tribe as a coach during the Bill Veeck era.

WILVER "WILLIE" STARGELL
Left Field. Born Mar. 6, 1941. Earlsboro, Okla. NL co-MVP 1979.

Wilver Stargell was the Pittsburgh Pirates' Gold Star Father in 1979.

When a teammate distinguished himself with a clutch hit, heads-up move on the basepaths, or fielding gem, "Pops" Stargell marked the occasion with a gold star ceremony. Soon ballplayers earning $300,000 a year were putting out a little bit extra to get a gold "Stargell Star" and by the end of the season, the Pirates had the whole country singing "We Are Family," earning enough gold stars to become World Champions.

At thirty-nine, two years after his career had apparently ended, Stargell set a record for most MVP awards in a season. He was named MVP of both the playoffs and the World Series, divided regular season MVP honors with Keith Hernandez, and shared *Sports Illustrated*'s Sportsman of the Year award with Steeler Terry Bradshaw.

Many of his 475 career home runs were titanic. Only eighteen balls were hit out of Forbes Field in sixty-one years (beginning with Babe Ruth's epic blast on May 25, 1935); Stargell hit seven of them. Only one player hit a ball completely out of Dodger Stadium—Stargell, who did it twice.

Stargell's 1977 season was plagued with injuries, but Pops hit 28 homers and drove in 97 runs in 1978 to earn Comeback Player of the Year. After the gold stars came out during spring training in 1979, Stargell hit 32 homers and the Pirates won the division, finishing two games ahead of Montreal.

In the playoffs against Cincinnati, he broke an 11-inning 2–2 tie with a three-run homer and homered again in Game Three as Pittsburgh swept the Big Red Machine. In the World Series against Baltimore, Stargell homered as the Orioles won the opener and went 3-for-5 with a homer in Game Four; however, Baltimore came up with six runs in the eighth inning to win, 9–6, and open up a 3–1 lead in games.

With the Pirates trailing, 1–0, in the bottom of the sixth inning of Game 5, Stargell hit a sacrifice fly to even the score and later singled to start a three-run inning. The Pirates won, 7–1. After John Candelaria and Kent Tekulve shut Baltimore out in Game Six to bring the Buccos even, Stargell put on a batting show in the finale, going 4-for-5 with a two-run homer. Overall, he set a Series record with seven extra-base hits. He became a Hall of Famer in 1988.

SAM THOMPSON
Right Field. Born Mar. 5, 1860 Danville, Ind. Died Nov. 7, 1922 Detroit, Mich.

Sam Thompson was the power hitter par excellence of the nineteenth century and set a record for lifetime home runs that wasn't broken until Babe Ruth came along. Also possessed of a legendary throwing arm, "Big Sam" Thompson was still so highly regarded that he played eight games alongside rookie Ty Cobb in the Tiger outfield in 1906—at age 46.

The fifth of eleven children, Thompson started his big league career late. He played on the Danville team and worked in his father's carpentry business. When a scout offered to pay him the magnificent sum of $2.50 per game, Thompson joined Evansville of the Northwest League and hit .391 before the league folded. He signed with Indianapolis and, at age twenty-five, joined the NL Detroit Wolverines. When Gene Moriarty crashed into an outfield wall, Thompson took over and got 11 hits in his first 26 at bats. Moriarty never played another game for Detroit.

Thompson was an innovator in the outfield, too. Possessed of a rifle arm, he is said to have originated the one-hop throw to the plate, trying to catch a runner from third. He was so successful at this technique that in 1886 he led the league's outfielders in double plays (11) for the first of two times. In 1887, "Big Sam" (6'2", 207) had an awesome season at the bat, leading the league in hits (203), triples (23), batting (.372), and slugging (.571). He drove in an astounding 1.31 runs per game. This was a record that only he would ever surpass, with 1.42 in 1894 and 1.39 in 1895; for comparison, Hack Wilson, when he drove in 190 in 1930, had a mark of 1.23.

A sore arm sidelined him for most of 1888, and he was unceremoniously sold to the Philadelphia Quakers (Phillies). In 1889 Thompson rebounded with 20 home runs to lead the league, picked up another hit crown in 1890 (172), and in 1891 managed to accumulate 32 assists. In 1894 he led the league in fielding (.977) and hit .407 as part of an all-.400-hitting outfield, along with Ed Delahanty, Billy Hamilton, and Tuck Turner. His last great offensive year was 1895, when Big Sam led the league in homers (18), RBIs (165), and slugging (.654).

He still holds the major league record for ratio of RBIs to games played (.923, nipping Lou Gehrig) and was named to the Hall of Fame in 1974.

HAROLD "PIE" TRAYNOR

Third Baseman. Born Nov. 11, 1899 Framingham, Mass. Died Mar. 16, 1972 Pittsburgh, Pa. Holds NL record for lifetime putouts by third baseman (2,288).

Pie Traynor was the first third baseman whom the baseball writers voted into the Hall of Fame. (The Veterans' Committee previously selected Jimmy Collins.)

Traynor was also named the major leagues' outstanding third baseman by *The Sporting News* seven times and finished in the top ten in MVP voting six times between 1925 and 1933. While some analysts downplay his offensive accomplishments today, Hall of Famers of his era— Mickey Cochrane, Bill Dickey, Charlie Gehringer, Rogers Hornsby, and Carl Hubbell—named him to their All-Time All-Star teams.

Traynor hit .320 lifetime with ten seasons above .300, knocked in 100 or more runs seven times, and never struck out more than 28 times in seventeen seasons. In the field, he led in assists three times, double plays four

straight years, led in putouts seven times (a record tied by Puddin' Head Jones and Ron Santo), and set the NL record for career putouts (2,289).

As a child Traynor yearned to play for the Somerville, Massachusetts, parish team coached by Father Nangle; instead, he chased balls. Taken to the grocery store as a reward, he would invariably say, "I'll take pie, Father," the source of his nickname. He was originally a shortstop, but after Traynor made 12 errors in his 17-game trial in 1920, the Pirates acquired Rabbit Maranville. Traynor's fielding improved when he moved to third base, and he began to hit with more power when Rogers Hornsby switched him to a forty-two-ounce bat.

The Pirates won the pennant in 1925. Traynor singled and homered against Walter Johnson in his first two World Series at bats and hit .346 as the Pirates won in seven. The Pie Man's bases-loaded single on the last day of the 1927 season gave the Pirates another pennant, but the Bucs were swept by the Yankees of Ruth and Gehrig.

Traynor hit .356 in 1929 and had his best batting average, .366, in 1930, but his career was essentially ended in 1934 when catcher Jimmy Wilson fell across his right arm and broke it. Pie took over as player-manager and just missed leading Pittsburgh to a pennant in 1938, when the Cubs' Gabby Hartnett hit his "Homer in the Gloamin'."

In retirement, Traynor ran a sporting goods store with Honus Wagner, coached at Duquesne, and was active as a sportscaster in Pittsburgh for thirty-three years. He was elected to the Hall of Fame in 1948.

ARKY VAUGHAN

Shortstop. Born Mar. 9, 1912 Clifty, Ark. Died Aug. 30, 1952 Eagleville, Cal. His .385 average of 1935 is not only the NL record for shortstops in this century but also a mark unequaled in the league since.

Arky Vaughan was, according to his Total Player Rating, the NL's leading player four times from 1934–1940.

Using a unique flat-footed stance, Vaughan hit well over .300 ten straight years, twelve times in all, and set an all-time record for the league's shortstops by hitting .385 in 1935. Although it has become chic to deride Vaughan's fielding, he led the league three times each in putouts and assists (and, yes, errors) when such slick-fielding shortstops as Billy Jurges, Dick Bartell, and Eddie Miller were in their prime.

Born in Clifty, Arkansas (hence his nickname), Joseph Floyd Vaughan grew up in California and was a football star at Fullerton High School. (Fellow student Richard M. Nixon picked Vaughan for his All-Time All-Stars.) Signed by the Pirates, he led the league in errors his first two years but improved with help from his roommate, coach Honus Wagner, and from Pie Traynor.

Vaughan was named to the All-Star team for the first of seven times in 1934 and became the first man to homer twice in the midsummer classic, in 1941. His lifetime All-Star Game average was .364.

Traded to the Dodgers after the 1941 season, Vaughan became embroiled in a dispute between pitcher Bobo Newsom and catcher Bobby Bragan in 1943. Manager Leo Durocher suspended Newsom, and Vaughan led a successful "strike," after which Durocher backed down. Despite leading the league in runs scored for the third time, Vaughan was fed up and retired.

When Durocher was suspended in 1947, Vaughan came back and hit .325 to help the Dodgers win a pennant. Jackie Robinson said, "He went out of his way to be nice to me when I was a rookie. I needed it." After a sub-par 1948, he played briefly for the San Francisco Seals and retired.

On August 30, 1952, while fishing in Lost Lake, his companion tipped the boat over; Vaughan tried to rescue him but both went under and drowned. He was elected to the Hall of Fame in 1985. Among Hall of Fame short-stops, only Honus Wagner (.329) has a higher lifetime batting average than Vaughan (.318).

JOHN PETER "HONUS" WAGNER

Shortstop. Born Feb. 24, 1874 Carnegie, Pa. Died Dec. 6, 1955 Carnegie, Pa. Holds NL records for most years leading league in batting (eight) and most consecutive years hitting .300 or better (seventeen).

Honus Wagner and Babe Ruth finished in a tie behind Ty Cobb when the first players were voted into the Hall of Fame in 1936. The fan of today may look at the stats of these men and wonder why Wagner stands alongside the other two. Yet Bill Deane, in his "Awards and Honors" piece in this volume, credits Wagner with six "hypothetical" MVP awards during his career—for the years 1901–1903, 1907, and 1909, years in which no award was given. Only Babe Ruth dominated a league for so long a time.

John Peter Wagner became "Johannes" and, later, "Honus" or "Hans," just as Wagner's nationality, German (a "Deutschman") became "Dutchman," hence Wagner's nickname, "the Flying Dutchman." Bowlegged, he "looked like a hoop rolling down the baselines" but reached the majors with Louisville. When the city was dropped from the league, owner Barney Dreyfuss bought Pittsburgh and took Wagner with him.

In 1900 Wagner won his first of eight batting titles, an NL record. He was stationed all over the diamond until Frederick "Bones" Ely, the regular shortstop, begged off. Wagner made three errors in an inning, then got lucky. With men on first and second, he gave the signal for a pickoff play and dashed toward second; the pitcher deliv-ered to the plate instead, resulting in a one-hopper that Wagner turned into a double play. Wagner called it "the best play I ever made."

The Dutchman led the Pirates to pennants in 1901, 1902, 1903, and 1909, when he outplayed Cobb, and his batting average didn't fall below .300 until 1914. Wagner led the league five times in RBIs and stolen bases, six times in slugging, and seven times in doubles. When he retired as a player in 1917, he led the NL in hits, runs, singles, doubles, and triples.

After coaching at Carnegie Tech and owning a sporting goods store with Pie Traynor, Wagner fell on hard times. Early in 1933, Fred Lieb wrote a column about Wagner's plight, and new Pirate owner Bill Benswanger made him a coach. Honus boosted attendance and was given "Days," even in opposing cities.

In Larry Ritter's *The Glory of Their Times*, Paul Waner remembered, "He must have been sixty.... [He'd] get out there every once in a while [and take infield practice] ... a hush would come over the whole ballpark, and every player on both teams would stand there, like a bunch of little kids ... I'll never forget it."

ED WALSH

Pitcher. Born May 14, 1881 Plains, Pa. Died May 26, 1959 Pompano Beach, Fla. Holds major league record for lowest lifetime ERA (1.82).

Ty Cobb said of Ed Walsh, "When this big moose had his stuff, he was just unbeatable, that's all."

The big spitballer (6'1", 193) won 40 games one year, led the league in saves five times, and is baseball's all-time leader in career ERA (1.82). He also set several fielding records for pitchers and was the first AL pitcher to steal home twice. Walsh, who also helped design Co-miskey Park, pleased the crowds by fungoing balls into the stands and was not entirely unaware of his talents. Sportswriter Charlie Dryden said of him, "He's the only man I ever saw who could strut standing still." He is thought by many students of the game and literature to have been Ring Lardner's model for Jack Keefe, the cocksure narrator of *You Know Me, Al.*

Walsh joined the White Sox soon after Elmer Stricklett taught him how to throw the spitball in 1904. Exhibiting the endurance which marked his career, he pitched two complete game wins against the Red Sox on September 6, 1905, and led the league in 1906 with 10 shutouts in the regular season. He also won two World Series games, striking out 12 Cubs in Game Three, a record which stood until 1929, and taking Game Five even though the "Hitless Wonders" made five errors behind him.

In 1907 lack of offense hurt Walsh, who was shut out eight times but still posted a 24–18 record and set major league season records for assists and total chances by a pitcher.

He had a nearly perfect year in 1908, leading the league in wins (40), shutouts (11), starts, complete games, strike-outs, and saves and set a post-1900 record for innings pitched (464) which still stands.

Chicago, Detroit, St. Louis, and Cleveland were neck-and-neck all season long, and Walsh pitched seven times in the last nine games. He won a doubleheader against Boston September 29 but lost his best-pitched game of the season on October 2; Walsh struck out 15 in eight innings only to lose 1–0 to Addie Joss's perfect game.

Bedeviled by a lack of offense again in 1910, Walsh became the only pitcher to lead the league in ERA (1.27) and lose 20 games. His team hit 7 homers all season long, batted .211, and made 314 errors.

After winning 27 games in both 1911 and 1912, he suffered arm trouble and retired in 1917. Walsh was named to the Hall of Fame in 1946.

HOYT WILHELM

Pitcher. Born July 26, 1923 Huntersville, N.C. Holds major league record for games pitched (1,070) and most games won as a relief pitcher (124).

Hoyt Wilhelm, the first relief pitcher elected to the Hall of Fame, threw 36,000 knuckleballs to get there.

Pitching in twenty-one seasons, Wilhelm delivered those dipsy-doodles as an NL reliever, AL starter, and AL reliever. All told, he pitched in more games than any player in history (1,070), won the most in relief, (123) and finished the most (651).

After languishing in the minors, Wilhelm stuck with the Giants as a twenty-nine-year-old rookie and made a sensational debut in 1952, going 15–3 with 11 saves. He led the league in won-lost percentage (.833) and ERA

(2.43) to become the first rookie ever to top his league in those two categories and the only rookie ever to win an ERA crown.

In 1955, Wilhelm was 4–1 but hadn't posted a single save in 59 appearances. He was traded to St. Louis, sold to Cleveland, and was picked up on waivers by Baltimore, mostly because Oriole manager Paul Richards had caught knuckleballer Dutch Leonard; after he lost three starts, Knuckles knew his days as an Oriole were numbered.

With his career hanging by a thread, Wilhelm got one last chance on September 20, 1958, against the Yankees. He pitched a no-hitter, winning 1–0 on Gus Triandos's homer. In 1959 he won his first nine starts and went on to lead the league in ERA (2.19), thus becoming the only pitcher to turn the trick in both circuits.

Traded to the White Sox, Wilhelm began his third career, posting a 2.64 ERA and a career-high 21 saves in 1963 and outdoing himself in 1964 with 27 saves, 12 wins and an ultra-stingy 1.99 ERA; his ERA didn't rise above 2.00 for four more seasons as he compiled 98 saves and 41 wins with the White Sox.

In the expansion draft of 1969 he was picked by the new Kansas City Royals, traded to the Angels, and passed along to the Braves, helping them take their division by winning 2 games and saving 4 in 8 appearances. After stints with the Cubs and Dodgers, he was released five days short of his 49th birthday. He was elected to the Hall of Fame in 1985.

TED WILLIAMS
Left Field. Born Aug. 30, 1918 San Diego, Cal. AL MVP 1946, 1949. Highest on base percentage of all time (.483), second only to Babe Ruth in slugging percentage and production.
He'll never be remembered for his fielding, throwing, running, or leadership, but by any measure Ted Williams is the greatest hitter of his era and perhaps of all time.

Despite missing five seasons to military service, the "Splendid Splinter" holds the records for most consecutive years leading the league in runs scored (five) and walks (six) and for career on-base percentage (.483) He also won four home run crowns, six batting titles, led the AL in slugging nine times, and finished with a career batting average of .344 and 521 home runs. At the close of the 1950s *The Sporting News* named him Player of the Decade.

Williams broke in with the San Diego Padres of the Pacific Coast League in 1936. In 1938 he won the Triple Crown at Minneapolis and became the Red Sox regular right fielder in 1939, moving to left later on. He set the rookie record for RBIs (145) to lead the AL. In 1941 his two-out, three-run homer off Claude Passeau won the All-Star Game and he concluded the year with a .406 batting average. He could have safeguarded his .400 average on the final day by sitting out, but instead he chose to play both ends of a doubleheader, going 6-for-8. He became the last player to top the magic number of .400, and the only one since 1930.

After winning the Triple Crown in 1942, the "Thumper" played for Uncle Sam from 1943 to 1945. He returned to star in the 1946 All-Star Game, hitting 2 homers and 2 singles, led the league in runs scored and slugging percentage, helped the Red Sox win the pennant,

and was named Most Valuable Player. He won his second Triple Crown in 1947. In 1949 he led the league in homers (43) and RBIs (159), hit .343, and was named Most Valuable Player for a second time.

At thirty-four, he flew thirty-nine combat missions for the Marines in Korea and returned late in 1953 to hit .407 with 13 homers in 37 games. He had one of his greatest seasons at age thirty-nine in 1957, hitting .388 to become the oldest player ever to lead the league in hitting. To prove it was no fluke, he led the league again in hitting in 1958 at age 40, hitting .328, and ended his career at 42, hitting .316 with 29 home runs, including one in his last at-bat. He entered the Hall of Fame in 1966.

DAVE WINFIELD
Right Field. Born Oct. 3, 1951 St. Paul, Minn. Oldest player to drive in 100 or more runs, 1992.
Dave Winfield was given a second chance and made the most of it.

Bedeviled by the memory a 1-for-22 batting slump in the 1981 World Series with the Yankees (and George Steinbrenner's subsequent characterization of him as "Mr. May," for his inability to produce in October), Winfield came to bat in the eleventh inning of Game Six in the 1992 Fall Classic as a member of the Toronto Blue Jays. With the score tied, 2–2, and two out, Winfield doubled down the left field line to give the Jays a 4–2 lead, and they hung on to win their first world championship.

It was sweet vindication for a man who had won seven Gold Gloves (two with the Padres, five with the Yankees), was an All-Star every year from 1977 to 1988, started All-Star Games in 1979, 1981, and every year from 1983 to 1988, and batted .361 in the twelve games.

Known as "Daddy Longlegs," the six-foot six-inch Winfield was a pitcher at the University of Minnesota, finished his senior year 13–1 and hit .400, and was the MVP of the College World Series. Drafted by the NBA's Atlanta Hawks, the ABA's Utah Stars, and the NFL's Minnesota Vikings—even though he had not played college football—Winfield was also selected by the Padres on June 5, 1973. Like Sandy Koufax and Al Kaline, Winfield had no minor league experience, and made his major league debut two weeks later.

In 1980, after leading the NL in RBIs (118), he signed a ten-year free agent contract with the Yankees; however, misinterpreting a cost-of-living clause led Steinbrenner to owe Winfield an extra $7 million and started a simmering feud which resulted in the Yankee owner paying a convicted felon, Howard Spira, for allegedly damaging information about Winfield. The damage instead was done to Steinbrenner, who was banished from baseball by Commissioner Fay Vincent.

Despite his problems with Steinbrenner, Winfield knocked in 100 runs or more from 1982 to 1986, the first Yankee to turn the trick in five consecutive seasons since Joe DiMaggio. In 1984, Winfield consciously shortened his stroke in an attempt to win a batting title and came close, hitting .340 to finish three points behind Don Mattingly. He underwent back surgery and missed the 1989 season; he joined the Angels for 1990. With the Angels, he drove in 72 runs in 112 games and won the Comeback Player of the Year Award. At the end of the 1994 season, Winfield had 463 career home runs to lead all active players and rank eighteenth behind Stan Musial and Willie Stargell on the all-time list.

DENTON TRUE "CY" YOUNG

Pitcher. Born Mar. 29, 1867 Gilmore, Oh. Died Nov. 4, 1955 Newcomerstown, Oh. Holds major league records for wins (511), starts (815), and complete games (749).

Had the honor been presented during his career, baseball's winningest pitcher might have had a shot at winning half a dozen Cy Young Awards.

He won at least 30 games in five seasons and, although he won a mere 26 in 1904, Young put together a string of 44 consecutive scoreless innings—23 of them hitless as well. He started with two hitless innings on April 25 against the A's, six on April 30 against Washington, and nine in the first post-1900 perfect game ever pitched, on May 5 against the A's. The streak ended on May 11 after he'd pitched six more hitless innings against the Tigers. (He did shut them out for fifteen innings.)

Pitching at a time when complete games were the rule, Young finished what he'd started 749 times. He'd take twelve warmup tosses and be ready to go. He pitched more than 400 innings in a season five times, more than 300 eleven other times, and said, "I never had a sore arm, and I pitched every third day. Once I pitched every other day for eighteen days."

Denton True Young was an instant sensation at Canton of the Tri-State League and got the name Cyclone (later shortened to Cy) after his pregame pitches splintered the fence that served as an outfield barrier.

Young threw a three-hitter in his big-league debut in 1890 and pitched both ends of a doubleheader that October, winning 5–1 and 7–3. In 1891, his first full season, he won 27 for the Cleveland Spiders, the first of nine straight seasons in which he won 20 games or more.

In 1903 Cy pitched the first of his three no-hitters and also won two games for the Boston Pilgrims (Red Sox) in the first World Series between the American and National leagues. He rebounded from losing seasons in 1905 and 1906 to win 21 games in 1907 and, at age forty-one, pitched his third no-hitter in 1908.

He retired with the most career victories (511), losses (316), innings pitched (7,354), and complete games (749) in history. In 1937 he was voted into the Hall of Fame.

ROBIN YOUNT

Infielder/Outfielder. Born Sept. 16, 1955 Danville, Ill. AL MVP 1982, 1989; joined 3,000-hit club in 1992.

Unlike the slowing veteran who moves from the outfield to first base, Robin Yount made a different move with different results. Seven years after being chosen MVP at one demanding defensive position, shortstop, Yount was selected as MVP again at another demanding position—center field.

After 1974 Yount was consistency itself, hitting in the high .280s (and over .300 six times) and playing 150 or more games eight times. He won fielding titles at both positions, led the league in doubles, triples, and runs created twice each, and reached the 3,000 hit mark in 1992.

A high school All-America in Woodland Hills, California, Yount was the Brewers' number one pick in 1973 and the third player picked overall, behind David Clyde and John Stearns (and just ahead of Dave Winfield). He hit .285 at Newark, New York, in the New York–Penn League and went to spring training with the Brewers in 1974. When Brewers manager Del Crandall saw Yount play, he won the starting job; by the age of twenty-two, Yount had already qualified for his big league pension by playing for four years. During spring training in 1978, he left the Brewers briefly to become a pro golfer, returned a few months later, and has been with the Brewers ever since. In 1981, he led the league in fielding (.985) and fielding runs (28) and batted .316 in the divisional playoff series.

In 1982 Yount was the starting shortstop in the All-Star Game and had a career year; he became the first shortstop to lead the league in slugging and total bases and also topped his colleagues in hits, doubles, production, and Total Player Rating. He batted .414 with 6 RBIs in the World Series, although the Brewers lost to the Cardinals, and was named MVP in the off-season.

An All-Star starter again in 1983, Yount suffered back problems so severe that he was briefly shifted to DH. He moved to the outfield in 1985 and led the league's outfielders in fielding (.997), making just one error. On September 9, 1992, he joined baseball's exclusive 3,000-hit club by singling against Cleveland's Jose Mesa in Milwaukee. He finished the 1993 season with 3,142 hits and retired.

CHAPTER 8

Baseball Families

Larry Amman

Just as the Wright brothers were first in flight, so were Wright brothers first in baseball. In the National Association's inaugural season of 1871, the Boston team featured Harry Wright as manager and reserve outfielder, and George at shortstop. Brother Sam joined them on the bench for the 1876 season, after an apprenticeship in New Haven the year before.

Since then there have been 343 brother combinations in the majors. The only season in which there was not at least one such pair was 1899. There were four new ones in 1991, two more in 1992, six more in 1993, and another two in 1994.

The first thing that strikes the eye as one reads the list is the large number who were teammates, however briefly—more than 25 percent.

Another observation one must make is how one-sided the big league performance was between so many of the combinations. For example, there are twenty-five members of the Hall of Fame who had brothers in the majors. Yet how many baseball fans have ever heard of the brothers of Bill Dickey, Christy Mathewson, or Honus Wagner? As another example, how many people remember the brothers of Steve Sax, Robin Yount, or Eddie Murray? These big names have brothers who played in the majors briefly.

Of course, being the brother of a major leaguer never guarantees success, nor even a shot at the big leagues. The five Delahantys, the three Boyers, and the two Ferrells all had other brothers who played minor league ball only.

Because the combinations in which more than one brother excelled are so rare, we can focus on the more outstanding ones.

In terms of balanced, outstanding achievement no group of three or more brothers can match the DiMaggios. The enduring folk hero status of Joe DiMaggio unfortunately has not done anything to keep alive the memory of his brothers, Vince and Dom. All three were gifted outfielders, good hitters, and fine all-around athletes. Vince, the oldest of these sons of a San Francisco fisherman, played for five different National League teams. In 1941 he had 21 homers and 100 RBIs for Pittsburgh. Four years later he hit four grand slams for the Phillies.

Dom DiMaggio was the youngest and smallest of the three brothers. Although lacking any of the power of the other two, he was the fastest on the bases and yielded nothing to his two brothers in the grace and skill he exhibited in the outfield. His lifetime batting average was just under .300.

In the 1941 All-Star Game, Dom went to right field as a late-inning substitute to play alongside Joe in center. This was a first in the midsummer classic. In the eighth inning, Joe doubled and Dom singled him home. In the 1949 All-Star Game, Joe drove in Dom with what proved to be the margin of victory for the junior circuit.

Dominic, or the "Little Professor" as he was called, started four different All-Star games, including the 1946 contest. That year he was voted to start in center field ahead of his brother. On the season, Dom outhit Joe by 26 points (.316 to .290).

In the 1943 All-Star Game, Vince went 3 for 3, including a ninth-inning home run. While Joe and Dom were away in the military, Vince was ". . . maintaining the family tradition of excellence in All-Star Games."

The first time two brothers played against each other in an All-Star Game was in 1969. Carlos May of the White Sox came to bat as a pinch-hitter with brother Lee of the Reds playing first base. In the 1990 midsummer classic, television cameras showed Sandy Alomar, Jr., at bat while Roberto Alomar set himself at second base, ready to field anything his brother might have hit his way. Both men were teammates for the junior circuit in the 1991 and 1992 games.

For the title of the best brother pitching combination, the competition is very close between the Niekros of Ohio and the Perrys of Williamston, North Carolina. In 1987 the ancient knuckleballing duo of Phil and Joe Niekro passed Jim and Gaylord Perry in wins. The two families remain very close in most statistical categories.

The Perry brothers had one full season as teammates—1974 with Cleveland, when the two combined for 39 victories, almost half of the team total. A year earlier, when Jim was with Detroit, the two made their only start against each other. Gaylord took the loss for Cleveland. Jim got a no-decision. In the 1970 All-Star Game, the National League pitcher in the sixth and seventh innings was Gaylord Perry of the Giants. On the mound for the American League in the seventh and eighth innings was Jim Perry of the Twins. This is the only time two brothers were rival pitchers in the midsummer classic. Both have also won the Cy Young Award.

For Joe and Phil Niekro, pitching against each other was not that uncommon. It happened nine different times. The most noteworthy occasion came on September 26, 1978, in Atlanta. Before this, his last start of the season, Phil was 19–17 for the Braves; Joe was 12–14 for the Astros. Houston won 2–0, much to the dismay of victor Joe. He loathed the idea of pitching against his brother in these circumstances.

Harry and Stan Coveleski of the coal-mining country in Pennsylvania were brother hurlers who refused to start games against each other. Stan, the younger, was in his first full season in the majors in 1916 at Cleveland while Harry was winning 20 for the third consecutive year at Detroit. Harry developed arm trouble and did not pitch another full season, but Stan went on to five 20-win seasons and a niche in the Hall of Fame.

Virtually every baseball fan has heard of the game on September 15, 1963, in which Felipe, Matty, and Jesus Alou formed the San Francisco outfield for one inning. A better story about this Dominican family, however, is the race for the 1966 National League batting title.

Going into the season, Felipe, with the Atlanta Braves, had established himself as a hitter of high average and respectable power. Younger brother Matty's career so far had been disappointing. With no power, his lifetime batting average was .260. In the off-season the Giants had traded him to Pittsburgh.

With the Bucs, Matty came under the special tutelage of manager Harry Walker. "Harry the Hat" taught his pupil to chop down on the ball and to hit to left field instead of trying to pull. This, plus over 20 bunt and 30 infield singles, propelled Matty to the top of the league batting race. Second or third to him almost all year was Atlanta leadoff man and first baseman Felipe Alou. Matty won the crown with a .342 average, while Felipe finished second at .327. The elder brother, however, led the circuit in runs, hits, and total bases.

It was only fitting that Harry Walker was the cause of the enormous jump in Matty's batting average. In 1947 Harry Walker the outfielder was traded from the Cardinals to the Phillies early in the season. There he won the batting title with an average 100 points higher than the year before. This was the second batting title in the family. In 1944 older brother Dixie had led the senior circuit with a .357 mark at Brooklyn.

Brother rivalries and brother teammates come into very sharp focus under the media glare of the World Series. The fall classics from 1921 to 1932 featured Bob Meusel of the Yankees versus older brother Emil or "Irish" of the Giants. These two outfielders were very similar in physical appearance and in capabilities.

Before the 1921 Series one writer summed up the pair:

Bob hits harder than Emil though he is not as consistent in garnering his hits. Bob also excels Emil as a thrower, but Emil is the more finished fielder. Bob is a left field hitter, and Emil often hits to right, so the play of "Meusel flied to Meusel" may be repeated frequently during the Series.

Indeed, it was so in all three series. In Game Three of the 1923 fall classic, each brother robbed the other of an extra-base hit. Over all, Irish emerged superior to Bob in every category—even in extra-base hits. Bob, however, had the last laugh, driving in the go-ahead run in Game Six of 1923 to give the Yankees their first world title.

For their entire careers, the Meusels startle the observer with the closeness of all their statistics. Irish averaged .310 to Bob's .309, both for 11 seasons. Bob leads in all other categories, but not by much. If Irish's totals were increased by prorating them based on his 100 fewer

games, the two would look like clones. Each man led his league in RBIs one time.

Two brothers whose lifetime batting averages are identical are Bob and Roy Johnson. Both of these Oklahoma Indians hit .296 as American League outfielders in the 1930s. Bob amassed 2,000 hits and almost 300 home runs, playing mostly for Connie Mack. Elder brother Roy was a speedy singles and doubles hitter. He exceeded his brother only in stolen bases in his shorter career.

The 1927 World Series featured Lloyd Waner leading off and playing center field for Pittsburgh while older brother Paul hit third and patrolled right field. In just his second season, Paul had won the batting title. Rookie Lloyd finished second in hits and third in batting average. The two combined for 460 hits during the season and were 11 for 30 in the World Series as the Yankees swept the Pirates in four games.

The Waners played parts of 16 seasons together, much longer than any other pair. Paul hit 17 points higher in batting and almost 70 points higher in slugging. However, "Big Poison" was actually shorter than Lloyd. Paul's moniker came from all the doubles and triples he delivered.

In 1934 Dizzy and Paul Dean had the greatest year any pitching brothers have ever enjoyed. "Me 'n' Paul" together won 49 games during the regular season and all four of the games the Cardinals won from the Tigers in the World Series. In 1935 their combined victory total was only two less. These two 19-win seasons were Paul's only full years in the majors.

An even more memorable year in St. Louis Cardinal history was 1942. In the last week of August, the Red Birds were five games behind the defending champion Brooklyn Dodgers. Five weeks later the Cardinals clinched first place with a record September rush. Winning five games in the last month for a total of 22 on the season was Mort Cooper. Catching him was younger brother Walker, in his first season as a regular. Mort won his September games with great flair. He was called the "fashion plate" for wearing the number on his back which equaled the victory he was seeking that day. The Cardinals beat the Yankees in a five-game World Series to shock all of baseball. Walker Cooper contributed several timely hits to the Series upset.

Mort also won 20 for the 1943 and 1944 pennant winners and had a victory in each of the World Series. Both brothers were named to *The Sporting News* All-Star team in 1944. Walker hit an even .300 for three Fall Classics.

The Coopers may have been the best of the 15 brother battery combinations, but Wes and Rick Ferrell have to be a close second. Rick caught his younger brother for five straight seasons. Wes won 20 the first two years together.

The next great brother act in the World Series was in 1964, when Ken and Clete Boyer were the opposing third basemen. Elder brother Ken was the National League's Most Valuable Player with a league-leading 119 RBIs for St. Louis. Clete had hit an anemic .219 for the Yankees. Still, this was his chance to show the baseball world he was Ken's equal in the field.

Although neither hit for a high average in the seven games, both did well with the glove. Ken gave his team all its runs in Game Four with a grand-slam homer. St. Louis won that contest 4–3. In the seventh game, Ken scored the first run and later homered. Brother Clete helped make the finish exciting as he hit one of the two solo home runs off Bob Gibson in the ninth inning. Like the Coopers, the Boyers were born and raised in the "Show Me" state. Both parents were in the stands maintaining their strict neutrality and feeling great pride.

The integrity of play when brothers square off against each other has been taken for granted for many years. This wasn't always the case. In 1933 Joe Sewell, playing third base for the Yankees, and Luke Sewell, catching for Washington, found themselves on opposite sides of a hot pennant race. They had been teammates at Cleveland for a number of years.

Reporting on a crucial game in the 1933 AL race, Shirley Povich of the *Washington Post* wrote:

> *It was brother versus brother in the seventh when Joe Sewell made a whale of a stop and throw to cut down Luke. It's things like that help prove the honesty of baseball.*

The shadow of the Black Sox Scandal still hung over the game.

Now for a trivia windup: There have been five brother shortstop–second base combinations in big league history: Granny and Garvin Hamner of the 1945 Phillies, Lou and Dino Chiozza of the 1935 Phillies, Milt and Frank Bolling of the 1958 Tigers, Eddie and Johnny O'Brien of the Pirates in the mid-1950s, and Cal and Bill Ripken of the Orioles from 1987 to 1992. The O'Briens were one of seven sets of twins in the majors.

Josh Clarke with Louisville in the National League in 1898 and George "White Wings" Tebeau of Cleveland in 1894–1895 must have felt some sense of constraint in criticizing their managers. In both cases it was a brother: Fred Clarke and Patsy Tebeau. Both pilots were regular players those seasons as well. Ed Hengle, who never played in the majors, managed his brother Moxie in the Union Association for the entry that began the season in Chicago. By the end of the campaign, both Mengels were gone, and the club had moved to Pittsburgh.

Wes and Rick Ferrell have something in common with Jesse and Lee Tannehill. In each case the pitching brother—Wes and Jesse—had a higher career batting average and more home runs than the brother who played every day.

No, Henry and Tommie Aaron were not the first "soul-brother" brother combination in major-league baseball. The game's first black siblings were Fleet and Welday Walker, who both played for Toledo of the American Association in 1884. That circuit was then considered a major league.

Brothers' Combined Totals (*Still active)

Seasons		Games		Hits		Doubles		Triples	
Alou	47	Alou	5,129	Waner	5,611	DiMaggio	906	Waner	308
Niekro	46	Waner	4,541	Alou	5,094	Waner	884	Delahanty	280
Delahanty	41	DiMaggio	4,245	DiMaggio	4,853	Delahanty	769	Wagner	256
Perry	39	Boyer	3,872	Delahanty	4,211	Alou	765	Clarke	233
Waner	38	Aaron	3,735	Aaron	3,987	Sewell	709	Connor	225
Boyer	36	Delahanty	3,595	Sewell	3,619	Johnson	671	DiMaggio	212
Sewell	35	Sewell	3,532	Boyer	3,559	Wagner	658	Johnson	178
Brett	35	May	3,236	Wagner	3,489	Brett	643	Ewing	178
DiMaggio	34	Cruz	3,077	Johnson	3,343	Meusel	618	Wheat	177
Ferrell	33	Johnson	3,016	Brett	3,245				
Forsch	32			Meusel	3,214				

Home Runs		Runs		RBIs		Batting Average (10 seasons)		Steals	
Aaron	768	DiMaggio	2,927	DiMaggio	2,739	Manush	.329	Wagner	726
DiMaggio	573	Waner	2,827	Aaron	2,391	Wagner	.326	Delahanty	685
*Murray	462	Delahanty	2,309	Delahanty	2,153	*Gwynn	.326	Clarke	557
Boyer	444	Aaron	2,276	Waner	1,907	Waner	.325	Milan	501
May	444	Alou	2,213	Meusel	1,887	Connor	.314	Sax	444
Nettles	406	Johnson	1,956	Johnson	1,839	Delahanty	.311	Cruz	322
Allen	358	Sewell	1,794	Boyer	1,803	Meusel	.309	Alou	294
Johnson	346	Wagner	1,762	May	1,780	Wheat	.309	*Gwynn	272
Brett	327	Boyer	1,761	Wagner	1,750	Clarke	.308	Yount	271
*Ripken	323	Clarke	1,744	Sewell	1,747	O'Rourke	.308	Meusel	253
						Brett	.303	Moriarty	250
								Aaron	249

Brother Pitching Totals

Games		Innings		Wins		Losses		Strikeouts		Shutouts		Complete Games	
Niekro	1,566	Niekro	8,690	Niekro	538	Niekro	478	Perry	5,110	Perry	85	Clarkson	571
Perry	1,407	Perry	8,637	Perry	529	Perry	439	Niekro	5,089	Niekro	74	Weyhing	455
Forsch	1,019	Clarkson	5,616	Clarkson	383	Forsch	249	Mathewson	2,504	Coveleski	51	Mathewson	436
McDaniel	1,006	Forsch	4,921	Coveleski	296	Weyhing	239	Clarkson	2,326	Clarkson	43	Perry	412
Reuschel	755	Mathewson	4,793	Forsch	282	Clarkson	232	Forsch	2,180	Forsch	37	Niekro	352
		Reuschel	3,865									Coveleski	308

Fathers and Sons

Shortly after breaking into the majors, Dale Berra was asked about similarities between himself and his famous father, Yogi. The younger Berra replied, "Our similarities are different."

Like the many malapropisms of Yogi Berra, this one by his son may appear foolish on the surface, but it contains quite a bit of underlying wisdom. In fact, it can serve as a metaphor for father-son combinations in major league baseball.

Of the 134 combinations, only forty-four feature both generations at the same position. There are twenty father-son pitcher combinations, five cases where both father and son caught, one where both played first, three where both played shortstop, and fourteen where both father and son were outfielders. Very few fathers and sons at any position have career totals that are at all close.

Another important generalization is the great increase in father-son combinations since World War Two, especially in the last twenty years. The first son of a former big leaguer to break into the majors was Jack Doscher in 1903 as a pitcher for the Chicago Cubs—one of the three teams with whom his father, Herm, had toiled as a utility player twenty years earlier. By 1945 the number of father-son combinations was 36. In 1965 the total was 66. That means almost 40 percent of today's number has been added in the last two decades.

Is the son of a big league ballplayer more apt to develop into a major leaguer than the average boy? Some people think not. In the 1950s, Hall of Famer George Sisler was asked this very question. The two-time .400 hitter shook his head over how two of his offspring had made the majors. He pointed out that baseball players are absentee fathers. They don't have much opportunity to teach their boys the fundamentals of the game or to practice with them.

If not their fathers, perhaps other well-qualified professionals have instructed the second generation. A worthwhile study could be conducted to determine how many second-generation players who have broken in during the last two decades attended baseball camps as boys. If the number is significant, this could explain the big increase during this period.

Certainly, the Sisler family deserves special attention. Father George broke into the majors just before World War One as a pitcher for the St. Louis Browns. After being switched to first base, he spent fifteen years as one of the greatest performers ever at that position. Accordingly, it is only fitting that he should have one son, Dick, who was a good hitter and another son, Dave, who pitched in the majors briefly. Dick's home run on the last day of the 1950 season, which gave the Philadelphia Whiz Kids the pennant, has given him an identity independent of his father. Also, these two men both managed in the majors for a short time. The Sislers and the Macks are the only families in which both father and son managed in the majors.

Baseball families fall into one of three categories: famous fathers only, famous sons only, and equals.

Let us consider the famous son category first. Another way of describing these men would be to call them "fathers of . . ." Two families stand out in this category. They are the Muellers and the Walkers.

Walter Mueller was a reserve outfielder for the Pirates for four seasons in the 1920s. His son, Don, hit .296 in twelve seasons as a National League outfielder. In 1954 Mueller and teammate Willie Mays battled all season for the batting title on the pennant-winning Giants. Mays finished first in hitting by three points, but Mueller led the league in hits with 212.

Dixie Walker was a pitcher for the Washington team from 1909 through 1912. His lifetime record was 24–30. Both his sons, Fred (or "Dixie") and Harry, won batting titles.

These two are the only clear cases of a son of All-Star quality who had a father whose career in the majors was forgettable. Other families with "fathers of . . . " are Coleman, Grimsley, and Smalley.

In contrast, the list of "sons of . . . " is a long one. There are eight baseball fathers in the Hall of Fame. Averill, Berra, Collins, Lindstrom, Mack, O'Rourke and Walsh had offspring who fit this category. Four more families—Bagby, Camilli, Trosky, and Wood—had fathers of All-Star quality and sons who are footnotes to their careers. Hegan, Wills, and Trout are families where the sons had respectable careers and characteristics similar to those of the fathers, but the older generation was clearly superior.

We must consider first whether some of the "sons of..." got to the majors, or second, stayed longer than they merited, because of the family name. I would cite Collins, Walsh, and Wood to prove the former proposition, and Dale Berra and Marc Sullivan as support for the latter.

The younger Berra and Sullivan not only had the temerity to go into their father's business, but, like Bill and Cal Ripken, Jr., of Baltimore, they had dad for their boss. The Ripkens (in 1988) and Dale Berra (in 1985) saw their fathers dismissed as managers early in the season. Cal Ripken, Sr., was not only the first father to manage two sons at once, but the first without major league playing experience to manage his sons.

Sullivan, whose father owned part of the Red Sox, traded his son to the Houston Astros organization before the 1988 season, where he could commiserate with the Berras on the difficulties of combining a baseball career with family obligations.

By far the most interesting category is that of the fathers and sons whose careers parallel or equal each other.

The two Billy Sullivans caught for both the White Sox and the Tigers. Both played other positions as well as caught in one World Series. Sullivan Senior caught the older Ed Walsh; Junior caught the younger Ed Walsh—both at Chicago. Junior hit for what appears a much higher average, but we must remember that Senior played in the Dead-Ball Era, and Junior in the high-hitting 1930s.

Jim and Mike Hegan were a father-son combination well known for defensive ability. Father Jim was a great handler of pitchers for Cleveland. Mike played first base and the outfield for several American League teams. Both appeared in two World Series. Mike broke into the majors just four seasons after his father's finale.

The father-son pitching combinations have few parallels. Both Thornton and Don Lee gave up home runs to Ted Williams. Only two families have had both father and son pitch in a World Series. Jim Bagby, Sr. pitched for Cleveland in the 1920 Series and his son for the Red Sox in 1946. Mel Stottlemyre went 1–1 for the Yankees in the 1964 Series. Todd Stottlemyre pitched for Toronto in the 1992 and 1993 fall classics.

Joe Schultz, Junior, received some unwanted publicity in Jim Bouton's book *Ball Four,* for being Bouton's manager. Schultz and his father, Joe Senior, each spent almost a decade in the majors as reserve players. Senior was 46 for 170 as a pinch-hitter. Junior went 43 for 160 in that same role.

It is only fitting that Buddy Bell spent a portion of his fine career with the Cincinnati Reds, the team on which his father Gus spent his best years. The two ended their careers with nearly identical batting averages and home run totals.

Six father-son combinations have played in All-Star Games. Prior to 1990 only the Bell and Boone families could have made that boast. Then Barry Bonds, Ken Griffey, Jr., and both Alomar sons made their debuts in the midsummer classic. The Bells and Boones have similar statistics. Gus was 2 for 6, hitting a home run his first time up; Buddy was 1 for 7, hitting a triple in his first plate appearance. Ray Boone went 1 for 5 in All-Star games with a homer; Bob is 2 for 5 in three games. Both Griffeys have been the Most Valuable Player in an All Star Game: Senior in 1980 and Junior in 1992. Currently the Seattle center fielder is 8 for 14 in the midsummer classic. His father was 5 for 7 in three games. Each has a home run to his credit. Barry Bonds is now 3 for 10 in All-Star competition. His father, Bobby, went 2 for 6 in three contests and was MVP in 1972.

Felipe Alou may have had some feelings of regret mixed with the great pride he felt when his son Moises drove in the winning run in the 1994 All-Star Game. Felipe's one appearance was in 1968. He played one inning in left field and did not have an official time at bat.

In Game One of the 1984 World Series, a two-run double by San Diego catcher Terry Kennedy was noted by the television announcers as something significant. This was the first time in the history of the fall classic that both a father and son had a World Series RBI. Terry's father, Bob, knocked in a run for Cleveland as an outfielder in the 1948 Series. There have been seven families in which the father and son both played in a World Series. Five have been mentioned already; there is also Ernie and Don Johnson. The father was a substitute infielder for the Yankees in the 1923 Series. Don was the regular second baseman for the Cubs in the 1945 fall classic. Stan Javier in 1988 and 1989 with Oakland makes seven; his father, Julian, played in four World Series.

An interesting father-son parallel to watch for in the future is that between Bobby and Barry Bonds. The son, an outfielder for San Francisco, has his father's penchant for home runs, stolen bases, and strikeouts.

The Bondses are not the first black father-son combination. That honor goes to the Hairstons. Father Sam caught two games for the White Sox in 1951. Son Jerry was a respected pinch-hitter for that team for over a decade.

Since the first edition of this book two significant events have taken place. In September 1990 Ken Griffey, Senior took a place in the Seattle Mariner outfield next to his son. Late in the 1992 season, Bret Boone made his major league debut as the Seattle second baseman. Baseball now has a three-generation family. Bret's father was Bob Boone and his grandfather was Ray Boone. It is hard to imagine what could top these two events in fan interest, but we are sure to see many more family combinations in the years to come.

Father-Son Hitters

	Years	Games	Runs	Hits	Homers	RBIs	BA	Steals
ALOMAR								
Sandy, Sr.	15	1,481	588	1,168	13	282	.245	227
Robby	7	1,020	526	1,174	64	433	.297	266
Sandy, Jr.	7	422	161	390	32	180	.268	18
AVERILL								
Earl, Sr.	13	1,669	1,224	2,020	238	1,165	.318	69
Earl, Jr.	9	449	137	249	44	159	.242	3
BELL								
Gus	15	1,741	865	1,823	206	942	.281	30
Buddy	18	2,405	1,150	2,514	201	1,106	.279	55
BERRA								
Yogi	19	2,120	1,175	2,150	358	1,430	.285	30
Dale	11	853	236	603	49	278	.236	32
BONDS								
Bobby	14	1,849	1,258	1,886	332	1,024	.268	461
Barry	9	1,281	890	1,287	259	760	.285	309
BOONE								
Ray	13	1,373	645	1,260	151	737	.275	21
Bob	19	2,264	679	1,838	105	826	.254	38
CAMILLI								
Dolf	12	1,490	936	1,482	239	950	.277	60
Doug	9	313	56	153	18	80	.199	0
GRIFFEY								
Ken, Sr.	19	2,090	1,129	2,143	152	859	.296	200
Ken, Jr.	6	842	518	972	172	543	.305	88
HEGAN								
Jim	17	1,666	550	1,087	92	525	.228	15
Mike	12	965	281	504	53	229	.242	28
KENNEDY								
Bob	16	1,483	514	1,176	63	514	.254	45
Terry	14	1,491	474	1,313	113	628	.264	6
McRAE								
Hal	19	2,084	940	2,091	191	1,097	.290	109
Brian	5	614	218	627	30	248	.259	93
SCHOFIELD								
Ducky	19	1,321	394	699	21	211	.227	12
Dick	12	1,333	501	978	56	351	.230	119
SISLER								
George	15	2,055	1,283	2,812	99	1,175	.340	375
Dick	8	799	302	720	55	360	.276	6
SMALLEY								
Roy, Jr.	11	872	277	601	61	305	.227	4
Roy, III	13	1,653	745	1,454	163	694	.257	27
SULLIVAN								
Billy, Sr.	16	1,146	363	777	20	378	.212	98
Billy, Jr.	12	962	347	820	29	388	.289	30
TRESH								
Mike	12	1,027	326	788	2	297	.249	19
Tom	9	1,192	595	1,041	153	530	.245	45
WILLS								
Maury	14	1,942	1,067	2,134	20	458	.281	586
Bump	6	831	472	807	36	302	.266	196

Father-Son Pitchers

	Years	Games	W-L	SO	CG	ERA
BAGBY						
Jim, Sr.	9	316	127–89	450	132	3.10
Jim, Jr.	10	303	97–96	431	84	3.96
COLEMAN						
Joe, Sr.	10	223	52–76	444	60	4.38
Joe, Jr.	15	484	142–135	1728	94	3.69
KRAUSSE						
Lew, Sr.	2	23	5–1	17	3	4.48
Lew, Jr.	12	321	68–91	721	21	4.00
LEE						
Thornton	16	374	117–124	937	155	3.56
Don	9	244	40–44	467	13	3.61
PILLETTE						
Herman	4	107	34–32	148	33	3.45
Duane	8	188	38–66	305	34	4.40

	Years	Games	W-L	SO	CG	ERA
QUEEN						
Mel, Sr.	8	146	27–40	328	15	5.09
Mel, Jr.	9	140	20–17	302	6	3.14
SISLER						
George	7	24	5–6	63	9	2.35
Dave	7	247	38–44	355	12	4.33
STOTTLEMYRE						
Mel, Sr.	11	360	164-139	1,257	152	2.97
Todd	7	206	69-70	662	25	4.22
TROUT						
Paul	15	521	170–161	1,256	158	3.23
Steve	12	301	88–92	656	32	4.18
WALSH						
Ed, Sr.	14	430	195–126	2,346	250	1.82
Ed, Jr.	4	79	11–24	107	15	5.57

Baseball Families

KEY

tm teammates
F-S father-son

BROTHERS
AARON Henry & Tommie *tm*
ACOSTA Jose & Merito
ADAMS Bobby & Dick *F-S also*
ALLEN Dick, Hank & Ron *tm*
ALLISON Art & Doug *tm*
ALOMAR Roberto & Sandy Jr.
ALOU Felipe, Matty & Jesus *tm*
ANDERSON Kent & Mike
ANDREWS Rob & Mike
ARMAS Tony & Marcos
ASPROMONTE Bob & Ken

BAILEY Ed & Jim *tm*
BAKER Dave & Doug
BANDO Chris & Sal
BANNON Jimmy & Tom
BARNES Jesse & Virgil
BARRETT Marty & Tom
BAXES Jim & Mike
BELL Charlie & Frank
BELL George & Juan
BENNETT Dave & Dennis *tm*
BERGEN Bill & Marty
BIGBEE Carson & Lyle *tm*
BLANKENSHIP Homer & Ted *tm*
BLUEGE Ossie & Otto
BOLLING Frank & Milt *tm*
BOONE Danny & Ike
BOYER Clete, Ken & Cloyd *tm*
BOYLE Buzz & Jim
BOYLE Eddie & Jack
BRASHEAR Kitty & Roy
BREEDEN Danny & Hal *tm*
BRETT George & Ken
BREWER Mike & Tony
BRINKMAN Chuck & Ed
BROWN Dick & Larry
BROWN Jackie & Paul
BROWN Oscar & Ollie
BROWN Curtis & Leon

CAMNITZ Harry & Howie *tm*
CAMP Kid & Llewellan *tm*
CAMPBELL Hugh & Mat *tm*
CANSECO Jose & Ozzie (twins)
CANTWELL Mike & John
CARLYLE Cleo & Roy
CASEY Dan & Dennis *tm*
CEDENO Andujar & Domingo
CHIOZZA Dino & Lou *tm*
CHRISTOPHER Lloyd & Russ
CLAPP Aaron & John
CLARK Jerald & Phil
CLARKE Fred & Josh *tm*
CLARKE Sumpter & Rufe
CLARKSON Dad, John & Walter *tm*
CLIBURN Stan & Stew (twins)
COFFMAN Dick & Slick

COHEN Andy & Syd
CONIGLIARO Billy & Tony
CONNELL Gene & Joe
CONNOR Joe & Roger
CONWAY Jim & Pete
CONWAY Bill & Dick *tm*
COONEY Jimmy & Johnny *tm F-S also*
COOPER Mort & Walker *tm*
CORCORAN Larry & Mike *tm*
COSCARART Joe & Pete
COVELESKI Harry & Stan
COVINGTON Sam & Tex
CROSS Amos, Frank & Lave *tm*
CRUZ Hector, Jose & Tommy *tm*
CUCCINELLO Al & Tony

DAILY Con & Ed
DALY Joe & Tom
DANNING Harry & Ike
DARINGER Cliff & Rolla
DARWIN Jeff & Danny
DAVALILLO Vic & Yo-Yo
DAVENPORT Claude & Dave
DAVIS Mark & Mike
DEAN Dizzy & Paul *tm*
DEASLEY John & Pat
DELAHANTY Ed, Frank, Jim, Joe & Tom *tm*
DEMONTREVILLE Gene & Lee
DICKEY Bill & George
DILLON Packy & John *tm*
DIMAGGIO Vince, Joe & Dom
DONAHUE Jiggs & Pat
DONNELLY Pete & John
DONOVAN Jerry & Tom
DORGAN Jerry & Mike
DOWNS Kelly & Dave
DOYLE Brian & Denny
DRAKE Sammy & Solly
DUGAN Bill & Ed *tm*

EDWARDS Dave, Marshall & Mike (twins)
ENS Jewel & Mutz
ERAUTT Eddie & Joe
EVERS Joe & Johnny
EWING Buck & John *tm*

FALK Bibb & Chet
FERRELL Rick & Wes *tm*
FERRY Cy & Jack
FINNEY Hal & Lou
FISHER Bob & Newt
FISHER Chauncey & Tom
FOGARTY Jim & Joe
FORD Gene & Russ
FOREMAN Brownie & Frank *tm*
FORSCH Bob & Ken
FOUTZ Dave & Frank
FOWLER Art & Jesse
FREESE Gene & George
FRIEL Bill & Pat
FULLER Harry & Shorty

FULMER Chick & Washington

GAGLIANO Phil & Ralph
GANZEL Charlie & John *F-S also*
GARBARK Bob & Mike
GARDELLA Al & Danny *tm*
GARRETT Adrian & Wayne
GASTON Alex & Milt *tm*
GEISS Bill & Emil
GENTRY Harvey & Rufe
GILBERT Harry & John *tm*
GILBERT Charlie & Tookie *F-S also*
GLEASON Bill & Jack *tm*
GLEASON Harry & Kid
GRABOWSKI Al & Reggie
GRAVES Joe & Sid
GREGG Dave & Vean
GRIMES Ray & Roy (twins) *F-S also*
GRISSOM Lee & Marv
GROH Heine & Lew
GUMBERT Ad & Billy
GWYNN Chris & Tony

HACKETT Mert & Walter *tm*
HAFEY Bud & Tom
HAIRSTON Jerry & John *F-S also*
HAMNER Garvin & Granny *tm*
HAMMOND Chris & Steve
HANDLEY Gene & Lee
HARGRAVE Bubbles & Pinky
HATFIELD Gil & John
HAYWORTH Ray & Red
HEMPHILL Charlie & Frank
HEVING Joe & Johnnie
HIGH Andy, Charlie & Hugh
HILL Hugh & Still Bill
HINCHMAN Bill & Harry *tm*
HITCHCOCK Billy & Jim
HOFFMAN Glenn & Trevor
HOGAN George & Happy
HOLMAN Brian & Brad
HOVLIK Hick & Joe
HOWARD Del & Ivon
HUGHES Jim & Mickey
HUGHES Ed & Tom
HUNTER Bill & George (twins)

IGNASIAK Gary & Mike
IORG Dane & Garth
IRWIN Arthur & John

JEFFCOAT George & Hal
JIMENEZ Elvio & Manny
JOHNSON Bob & Roy
JOHNSON Chet & Earl
JOHNSTON Doc & Jimmy
JONES Darryl & Lynn
JONES Gary & Steve
JONNARD Bubber & Claude (twins)
JORGENS Arndt & Orville

KAPPEL Heinie & Joe
KELL George & Skeeter
KELLER Charlie & Hal
KELLNER Alex & Walt *tm*
KELLY George & Ren
KENNEDY Jim & Junior
KEOUGH Marty & Joe *F-S also*
KIEFER Steve & Mark
KILLEFER Bill & Red
KILROY Matt & Mike *tm*
KLAUS Billy & Bobby
KLING Bill & Johnny
KNODE Mike & Ray
KNOTHE Fritz & George
KOPF Larry & Wally
KRSNICH Mike & Rocky

LACHEMANN Marcel & Rene
LANNING Johnny & Tom
LANSFORD Carney & Joe
LARY Al & Frank
LEITER Al & Mark
LELIVELT Bill & Jack
LILLARD Bill & Gene *tm*
LOBERT Frank & Hans
LOOK Bruce & Dean
LOWDERMILK Grover & Lou *tm*
LUSH Billy & Ernie

MACHA Ken & Mike
MACK Quinn & Shane
MADDUX Greg & Mike
MAHLER Mickey & Rick *tm*
MAISEL Fritz & George
MANCUSO Frank & Gus
MANGUAL Angel & Pepe
MANSELL John, Mike & Tom *tm*
MANUSH Frank & Heine
MANZANILLO Josias & Ravelo
MARION Marty & Red
MARTINEZ Pedro & Ramon *tm*
MASKREY Harry & Leech *tm*
MATHEWSON Christy & Henry *tm*
MATTOX Cloy & Jim
MAY Carlos & Lee
MAYER Erskine & Sam
MCDANIEL Lindy & Von *tm*
MCFARLAN Alex & Dan
MCFARLAND Lamont & Charles
MCGEEHAN Connie & Dan
MCLAUGHLIN Barney & Frank *tm*
MEUSEL Bob & Irish
MILAN Clyde & Horace *tm*
MILLER Jake & Russ
MILLER Bing & Ralph *tm*
MITCHELL John & Charlie
MOFFETT Joe & Sam
MORIARTY Bill & George
MORRISON Johnny & Phil *tm*
MORRISSEY John & Tom
MOTA Andy & Jose *F-S also*
MURRAY Eddie & Rich
MYERS Billy & Lynn

NETTLES Graig & Jim
NEWKIRK Floyd & Joel
NIEKRO Joe & Phil *tm*
NIXON Otis & Donnell
NYMAN Chris & Nyls

O'BRIEN Eddie & Johnny (twins) *tm*
OGDEN Curley & Jack
OLIVO Chi Chi & Diomedes
O'NEILL Jack, Jim, Mike & Steve *tm*
ONSLOW Eddie & Jack
O'ROURKE Jim & John *F-S also*
ORTIZ Baby & Roberto *tm*
O'TOOLE Denny & Jim
OWEN Dave & Spike

PACIOREK John, Tom & Jim
PARKER Jay & Doc
PARROTT Jiggs & Tom *tm*
PASCUAL Camilo & Carlos
PATTERSON Ham & Pat
PEITZ Heine & Joe *tm*
PENA Ramon & Tony
PEPLOSKI Henry & Pepper
PEREZ Pascual & Melido
PERRY Gaylord & Jim *tm*
PFEFFER Big Jeff & Jeff
PIERSON Dave & Dick
PIKE Jay & Lip
PIPGRAS Ed & George
POTTER Dykes & Squire

RAJSICH Dave & Gary
REACH Al & Bob
RECCIUS John & Phil *tm*
REUSCHEL Paul & Rick *tm*
REYNOLDS Harold & Don
RICKETTS Dick & Dave
RIDDLE Elmer & Johnny *tm*
RIPKEN Cal & Billy *tm*
ROBINSON Bruce & Dave
ROBINSON Fred & Wilbert
ROENICKE Gary & Ron
ROETTGER Oscar & Wally
ROMO Vicente & Romero Enrique
ROOF Gene & Phil
ROSENBERG Harry & Lou
ROTH Braggo & Frank
ROWE Dave & Jack
ROY Charlie & Luther
RUSSELL Allan & Lefty

SADOWSKI Bob, Eddie & Ted
SAUER Ed & Hank
SAX Dave & Steve *tm*
SAY Jimmie & Lou *tm*
SCANLAN Doc & Frank
SCHANG Bobby & Wally
SCHAREIN Art & George
SCHMIDT Boss & Walter
SCHULTE Herman & Leonard
SEWELL Luke, Joe & Tommie *tm*
SHAFFER Orator & Taylor *tm*
SHANNON Joe & Red (twins) *tm*
SHANTZ Billy & Bobby *tm*
SHERLOCK Monk & Vince
SHERRY Larry & Norm *tm*
SISLER Dave & Dick *F-S also*
SMITH Charlie & Fred
SOWDERS Bill, John & Len
STAFFORD John & Jim
STANICEK Steve & Pete
STANLEY Buck & Joe
STOTTLEMYRE Mel, Jr. & Todd

STOVALL George & Jessie
SURHOFF B.J. & Rick
SUTHERLAND Darrell & Gary

TANNEHILL Jesse & Lee
TEBEAU Patsy & White Wings *tm*
THIELMAN Henry & Jake
THOMAS Bill & Roy *tm*
THOMPSON Homer & Tommy *tm*
THRONEBERRY Faye & Marv
TOBIN Jim & Johnny
TORRE Frank & Joe *tm*
TRAFFLEY Bill & John
TREACEY Fred & Pete *tm*
TREVINO Alex & Bobby
TWOMBLY Babe & George
TYLER Fred & Lefty *tm*
TYRONE Jim & Wayne

UNDERWOOD Pat & Tom
UPTON Bill & Tom

VAN CUYK Chris & Johnny

WADE Ben & Jake
WAGNER Butts & Honus
WALKER Dixie Sr. & Ernie *F-S also*
WALKER Dixie Jr. & Harry
WALKER Gee & Hub *tm*
WALKER Fleet & Welday *tm*
WANER Lloyd & Paul *tm*
WATT Al & Frank
WEILAND Bob & Ed
WESTLAKE Jim & Wally
WEYHING Gus & John
WHEAT Mack & Zack
WHITE Deacon & Will *tm*
WHITNEY Art & Frank
WILLIAMS Gus & Harry
WILTSE Hooks & Snake
WINGO Al & Ivy
WOOD Fred & Pete *tm*
WORRELL Todd & Tim
WRIGHT George, Harry & Sam *tm*
YOCHIM Len & Ray
YOUNT Larry & Robin

FATHERS-SONS

ADAMS Bobby-Mike
ALOMAR Sandy-Roberto & Sandy Jr.
ALOU Felipe-Moises
AMARO Ruben Sr. & Jr.
ARAGON Angel-Jack
AVERILL Earl-Earl

BAGBY Jim Sr. & Jr.
BARNHART Clyde-Vic
BEAMON Charlie-Charlie
BELL Gus-Buddy
BERRA Yogi-Dale
BERRY Charlie-Charlie
BERRY Joe-Joe
BONDS Bobby-Barry
BOONE Ray-Bob
BOONE Bob-Bret
BORBON Pedro-Pedro
BRICKELL Fred-Fritzie
BRUCKER Earle Sr. & Jr.
BRUMLEY Mike-Mike
BUFORD Don-Damon

CAMILLI Dolf-Doug
CAMPANIS Alex-Jim
CARREON Camilo-Mark

COLEMAN Joe-Joe
COLLINS Ed Sr. & Jr.
CONNOLLY Ed Sr. & Jr.
COONEY Jimmy-Jimmy & John
CORRIDEN Red-John
CROUCH Bill-Wilmer

DOSCHER Herm-Jack

ELLSWORTH Dick-Steve
ESCHEN Jim-Larry

FLETCHER Tom-Darrin
FRANCONA Tito-Terry

GABRIELSON Len-Len
GANZEL Charlie-Babe
GILBERT Larry-Charlie & Tookie
GRAHAM Peaches-Jack
GREEN Fred-Gary
GRIFFEY Ken Sr. & Jr. *tm*
GRIMES Ray-Oscar
GRIMSLEY Ross-Ross

HAIRSTON Sam-Jerry & John
HANEY Larry-Chris
HEGAN Jim-Mike
HEINTZELMAN Ken-Tom
HOOD Wally Sr. & Jr.
HOWARD Bruce-David
HUNDLEY Randy-Todd

JAVIER Julian-Stan
JETER Johnny-Shawn
JOHNSON Adam-Adam
JOHNSON Ernie-Don

KENNEDY Bob-Terry
KEOUGH Marty-Matt
KESSINGER Don-Keith
KRAUSE Lew Sr. & Jr.
KUNKEL Bill-Jeff

LANDRUM Joe-Bill
LANIER Max-Hal
LAW Vern-Vance
LEE Thornton-Don
LERCHEN Dutch-George
LIEBHARDT Glenn-Glenn
LINDSTROM Fred-Charlie
LIVELY Jack-Bud

MACK Connie-Earle
MAGGERT Harl-Harl
MALAY Charlie-Joe
MARTIN Barney-Jerry
MATTICK Wally-Bobby
MAY Dave-Derrick
MAY Pinky-Milt
McKNIGHT Jim-Jeff
McRAE Hal-Brian
MEINKE Frank-Bob
MILLS Willie-Art
MONTEAGUDO Rene-Aurelio
MOORE Eugene Sr. & Jr.
MORTON Guy Sr. & Jr.
MOTA Manny-Andy & Jose
MUELLER Walter-Don

NARLESKI Bill-Ray
NAVARRO Julio-Jaime
NEN Dick-Robert
NICHOLS Chet Sr. & Jr.
NORTHEY Ron-Scott

O'DONOGHUE John Sr. & Jr.
OKRIE Frank-Len
OLIVARES Ed-Omar
OLIVER Bob-Darren
OLIVO Diomedes-Gilbert Rondon
O'ROURKE Patsy-Joe
O'ROURKE Jim-Queenie
OSBORNE Tiny-Bobo

PARTENHEIMER Steve-Stan
PEREZ Tony-Eduardo
PILLETTE Herman-Duane

QUEEN Mel-Mel

RIPLEY Walt-Allen

SAVIDGE Ralph-Don
SCHOFIELD Ducky-Dick
SCHULTZ Joe Sr. & Jr.
SEGUI Diego-David
SHEELY Earl-Bud
SHEELY Earl-Bub
SIEBERT Dick-Paul
SISLER George-Dick & Dave
SKINNER Bob-Joel
SMALLEY Roy Jr.-Roy III
SPRAGUE Ed Sr. & Jr.
ST. CLAIRE Ebba-Randy
STENHOUSE Dave-Mike
STEPHENSON Joe-Jerry
STILLWELL Ron-Kurt
STOTTLEMYRE Mel-Todd & Mel Jr.
SULLIVAN Billy Sr.-Jr.
SULLIVAN Haywood-Marc
SUSCE George-George

TANNER Chuck-Bruce
TARTABULL Jose-Danny
TORRES Ricardo-Gil
TRESH Mike-Tom
TROSKY Hal Sr. & Jr.
TROUT Paul-Steve

UNSER Al-Del

VIRGIL Ozzie Sr. & Jr.

WAKEFIELD Howard-Dick
WALKER Dixie-Dixie & Harry
WALSH Ed-Ed
WHITE JoJo-Mike
WILLS Maury-Bump
WINE Bobby-Robbie
WOOD Joe-Joe

YOUNG Del-Del

GREAT GRANDFATHER-GREAT GRANDSON

Jim Bluejacket & Bill Wilkinson

GRANDFATHER-GRANDSON

George Rooks-Lou Posselh
Shano Collins-Bob Gallagher
Bill Brubaker-Dennis Rasmussen
Marty & Ed Herrmann
Ben & Jim Spencer
Lloyd & Jim Spencer
Lennie & Matt Merullo
Ray & Bret Boone
Bill & Roger Salkeld

## CHAPTER 9

Tragedies and Shortened Careers

Joseph M. Overfield

If, of all words of tongue and pen,
The saddest are, "It might have been,"
More sad are these we daily see:
"It is, but hadn't ought to be."
— Bret Harte

In the eleventh century in the reign of William the Conqueror, detailed information about the landowners of England and their assets was gathered and then recorded in what were called *Domesday Books*. Much of what is known of the demographics of early England is derived from these books.

Baseball also has its *Domesday Books*, but they are called *Encyclopedias*. They list the name, vital statistics, and records of every player who ever appeared in a major league game, beginning with the formation of the National Association in 1871. So assiduously have baseball's *Domesday Books* been corrected, refined, and updated, it is safe to say that detailed information is more readily available about ballplayers, even the most obscure, than it is for statesmen, authors, artists, poets, or captains of industry.

Informative as they are, the *Encyclopedias* still leave much unsaid. For example, why did Bert Shepard play but a single game, while Jim McGuire played for twenty-six seasons? Short careers, like Shepard's, usually mean a lack of ability or, perhaps, the failure to receive a fair opportunity; but often they are short for other reasons—death, illness, injury, accident, suicide, or even murder. It is with such tragically shortened careers that this chapter will deal. Although the subject was carefully researched, no assertion of 100 percent completeness is proffered.

Since baseball's *Domesday Books* are limited to major league players and managers, no listing will be found there for minor leaguers like Bill Thomas of the 1906 Buffalo Bisons or Ralph Worrell of the 1918 Baltimore Orioles or Jeff Hoffman of the 1992 Albany-Colonie Yankees.

James Creighton was the star pitcher of the Excelsior Club, a famous Brooklyn amateur nine of the 1850s and 1860s. Before Creighton's day, it was customary for pitchers to toss the ball gently to the plate. Creighton changed all this by developing a snap throw that gave speed and spin to the ball. In addition, he was one of the most powerful hitters of his day. It is said that he completed one entire season without being put out. On October 14, 1862, the Excelsiors were playing the Union Club of Morrisania in their final match of the season. Creighton, at bat for the Excelsiors, swung mightily and sent the ball beyond the reach of the outfielders. As he crossed first base, he collapsed, obviously in great pain. Legend has it that he staggered around the bases for a home run. He was immediately taken home by his teammates. Four days later, the twenty-one-year-old pitcher was dead. According to an account in the *Brooklyn Eagle*, headlined "Obsequies of a Celebrated Ballplayer," Creighton had ruptured his bladder with the force of his final swing and died from internal bleeding.

A. G. Spalding, in his book *Baseball, America's National Game*, devoted two pages to Creighton, with his picture and a view of the towering granite monument his teammates erected in his memory on Tulip Hill in Brooklyn's Greenwood Cemetery. The monument is embossed with crossed bats, a cap, a base, and a scorebook.

The circumstances of the death of Bill Thomas, a twenty-five-year-old Buffalo pitcher, in April 1906, are still a mystery. Thomas had been a big winner in the Pacific Coast League, and manager George Stallings of Buffalo had brought him east to test his mettle in the stronger Eastern League. He was successful in his first start at Baltimore. The Bisons then finished a series at Providence and took a train to New Bedford, Massachusetts, from which point they boarded the night boat *Richard Peck*, en route to New York City. Thomas had left word with the porter and with his roommate, pitcher Joe Galaski, that he wanted an early call so he could see the New York skyline at sunrise. In the morning, when the porter came into the stateroom, the Thomas bunk, which had been slept in, was empty. Thomas was never seen again.

In 1918 Ralph Worrell, only nineteen, won 25 games for Jack Dunn's Baltimore Orioles, but he never pitched again. Instead of becoming another Lefty Grove (also a Jack Dunn discovery), Worrell failed to survive the winter, dying in the terrible World War One flu epidemic.

Just as tragic was the death of twenty-nine-year-old Yankee farmhand Jeff Hoffman of the Albany-Colonie Yankees, August 29, 1992. The young righthanded pitcher collapsed in his Binghamton (N.Y.) hotel room and died later that day in a local hospital. There was no evidence of foul play or drug or alcohol use. After several days it was determined he had died from a heart deficiency, previously undetected. He left his wife Teresa, who was expecting their first child.

The deaths of young, vigorous, and supposedly healthy athletes like Creighton, Thomas, Worrell, and Hoffman are sad and decidedly against the odds, but in the muster rolls of major league players in baseball's *Domesday Books*, such cases are far from rare.

Fatal Illnesses of Players and Managers

Elmer White was long thought to be a brother of James "Deacon" White and Will White. The early encyclopedias listed him as playing 15 games for the Forest Cities of Cleveland in 1872, but nothing more. A trip by the writer to the village of Caton in New York's southern tier and to the cemetery behind the Methodist Church there resulted in the finding of Elmer White's grave. The inscription on the tombstone, which showed he was Jim's and Will's cousin, not a brother, told with great economy of words the story of a short life and a short baseball career: "Born December 7, 1850. Died March 17, 1873."

Of all the deaths of active major leaguers to be recounted here, significantly, only one—that of Ray Chapman, who was killed by a Carl Mays pitch—resulted directly from activity on the diamond. Many of the deaths, especially those in the first fifty years, were from illnesses routinely controlled today. Typhoid fever, for example, killed first baseman Alex McKinnon of Pittsburgh (NL) on July 24, 1887. He played in the July 4 game, complained of not feeling well, and was taken home. He died twenty days later at the age of thirty. Less than a year later, on April 29, 1888, Charlie Ferguson, an outstanding young pitcher who had won 21, 26, 30, and 22 games for Philadelphia (NL) from 1884 through 1887 and was a strong hitter as well (.288 in four seasons), died from the same disease, twelve days after his twenty-fifth birthday.

On May 14, 1892 in a game at Boston, twenty-eight-old Brooklyn outfielder Hub Collins, who had played in the major leagues since 1886 and had led the American Association in doubles in 1888 and the National League in 1890, was pinch hit for because he was not feeling well. Five days later he died in Brooklyn, a victim of typhoid fever.

Edward "Sy" Sutcliffe, a catcher for most of his career, had shifted to first base for Baltimore (NL) in 1892 and had done quite well, batting .279 in 66 games. In the off-season, the twenty-nine-year-old native of Wheaton, Illinois, developed Bright's disease. He died February 13, 1893.

Joe Cassidy, an infielder for the Washington Senators in 1904 and 1905, was a fourth victim of the deadly typhoid. He was only twenty-three when he died at his home in Chester, Pennsylvania, March 25, 1906. Just a year and four days later, March 29, 1907, Patrick Henry "Cozy" Dolan, a nine-year outfielder in the majors, most recently with Boston (NL), also died of typhoid. He took ill during Boston's spring training trip, and died in a Louisville hospital, at age thirty-four. News of his death was overshadowed in the Boston papers by the extensive coverage given to the sensational suicide of manager Chick Stahl of the other Boston club, the day before in West Baden, Indiana.

Mike Powers, who caught in the majors from 1898 to 1909, mainly with the Philadelphia Athletics, was an anomaly in those hard-bitten days of the game's history, in that he held a degree from Holy Cross College and had also attended Notre Dame Medical School. Powers, incidentally, recruited the legendary Louis "Chief" Sockalexis for both of his alma maters, as shall be seen later. Powers was not a strong hitter (.216 lifetime), but he was considered a fine defensive catcher. He was behind the plate in an early season game in 1909, when he complained of nausea and asked to be taken to a hospital. He underwent three stomach operations, and then gangrene set in. "Doc" Powers died April 26, 1909, at the age of thirty-eight.

Alan Storke was an infielder for Pittsburgh and St. Louis (NL) from 1906 through 1909. He never made it to spring training in 1910. He was a mere twenty-five when he died in Newton, Massachusetts, March 18, 1910, following a lung operation. Less than two years later, February 1, 1912, another National League infielder, thirty-year-old Jimmy Doyle, who had batted .282 for the Cubs in 1911, died in Syracuse, New York, after an appendicitis operation.

Addie Joss pitched in the majors only eight seasons and part of a ninth, but his record was so extraordinary that he was elected to the Hall of Fame (in 1978), despite his short tenure. With Cleveland from 1902 to 1910, he won 160 games, lost 97, and compiled an ERA of 1.88 (second on the all-time list). He pitched a perfect game on October 2, 1908, defeating Big Ed Walsh, 1–0, with first place on the line. Joss had another no-hitter on April 20, 1910, also against the White Sox, just before his health began to fail.

Joss made only 13 appearances in 1910, and still felt weak when he went south in 1911. He collapsed on the bench during an exhibition game at Chattanooga, Tennessee, then became ill again when the team reached Cincinnati. Doctors said it was pleurisy and sent him home to Toledo. On April 14, 1911, two days after his team had opened the season in St. Louis, he died at the age of thirty-one. The cause of his death was given as tubercular meningitis. Famed ballplayer-preacher Billy Sunday presided at his funeral, said to have been the biggest ever seen in Toledo.

Leonard "King" Cole, a righthanded pitcher who had won 20 games for the Cubs in 1910 and 18 the following season, was, like Charlie Ferguson, to have a brilliant career nipped in the bud by a fatal illness. During the 1915 season, when Cole was with the Yankees, it was discovered that he had been suffering from tuberculosis. He returned to his home in Bay City, Michigan, where he died on January 6, 1916, at twenty-nine. He left a splendid 56–27 (.675) won–lost record.

Joe Leonard, a twenty-five-year-old infielder who began with Pittsburgh in 1914 and played for Washington in 1916, 1917, and 1919, appeared in only one game for the Senators in 1920, became ill, and was taken to George Washington Hospital. He died there on May 1, following an appendicitis operation.

In 1922, the St. Louis Cardinals lost two young ballplayers within nine months. First to go was William "Pickles" Dillhoefer, who had caught in the majors since 1917, usually in a backup role. He was twenty-seven when he died in a St. Louis hospital, February 22, 1922, of that old bugaboo, typhoid fever. Outfielder Austin McHenry had started with the Cardinals in 1918, but had not really blossomed until 1921, when he batted .350 and hit 37 doubles, 8 triples, and 17 home runs. The following year he began to have difficulties in judging fly balls. Manager Branch Rickey sent him to a doctor, who diagnosed his problem as a brain tumor. An operation proved unsuccessful, and he died at Jefferson Township, Ohio,

November 27, 1922. He was twenty-seven, the same age as Dillhoefer.

The 1924 season saw the deaths of two veterans of the Cincinnati Reds within eight months. Pat Moran was a catcher in the majors from 1901 to 1914 and then a highly successful manager, first with the Phillies and then with the Reds. In nine managerial seasons, he compiled a record of 748–586 and won a pennant with each team. His 1915 Phillies lost the World Series to the Boston Red Sox, in five games, while his 1919 Reds won the tainted 1919 Series from the White Sox, 5–3. Moran was forty-eight when he died of Bright's disease at Orlando, Florida, March 7, 1924, while at spring training with the Reds. The second Red to die that year was Jake Daubert, a fancy-fielding first baseman who could hit (.303 in fifteen years with the Dodgers and the Reds). Although forty years old, he played 102 games for the Reds in 1924, batted .281 and fielded .990. He became ill in October and was taken to Good Samaritan Hospital in Cincinnati, where he died on October 9 following an appendicitis operation, just as Jimmy Doyle and Joe Leonard had before him.

Legendary New York Giants outfielder and future Hall of Famer Ross Youngs was at the height of his career when he was struck down by Bright's disease, diagnosed during spring training in 1926. Despite his illness, he played 95 games and batted .306. All through the season, he was accompanied by a male nurse hired by manager John McGraw. Youngs was bedridden for the entire 1927 season and died on October 22 at the age of thirty. Despite his relatively short career, nine seasons and part of another, his record was impressive enough to earn him election to the Hall of Fame in 1972. McGraw said he was the greatest outfielder he had ever seen.

Urban Shocker was an outstanding pitcher for the great Yankee teams of the 1925–1927 period. His record was 18–6 for the 1927 Yankees, but illness kept him out of the World Series. His thirteen-year record with the St. Louis Browns and the Yankees is in Hall of Fame country—187–117 (.615)—and he never had a losing season. His health continued to fail in 1928, and he appeared in only one game before being released. On September 9, 1928, in Denver, he died of heart disease and pneumonia. He was thirty-eight.

Shocker's manager, Miller Huggins, was to survive him little more than a year. On September 20, 1929, Huggins, who had managed the Yankees since 1918 and had won six pennants and three world's championships, asked coach Art Fletcher to take over for him, so that he could check into a hospital. Five days later, he was dead of erysipelas, a streptococcal skin infection. Huggins, who was of Munchkin size at 5'6" and 140 pounds, had been in the majors since 1904, batting a career .265, and winning 1,413 games and losing 1,134 as a manager. His showdowns with his rambunctious slugger, Babe Ruth, are part of baseball lore. Huggins was elected to the Hall of Fame in 1964.

On May 28, 1930, Hal Carlson, thirty-eight-year-old righthanded pitcher of the Chicago Cubs, and a fourteen-year veteran of the National League, called several of his teammates to his apartment in a Chicago hotel, saying that he was in severe pain. Shortly after the team physician arrived, Carlson was dead from what was described as "an internal hemorrhage." He left a three-year-old son and his wife, who was expecting another child.

Twenty-nine-year-old infielder Mickey Finn, who had played for the Dodgers from 1930 to 1932 and then for the Phillies, became ill midway through the 1933 season. Owner Gerry Nugent of the Phillies summoned his brother-in-law, Dr. H. P. Boyle, who diagnosed Finn's trouble as a duodenal ulcer. Surgery was performed in an Allentown, Pennsylvania, hospital. He seemed on the road to recovery, but unforeseen medical problems arose, leading to his death on July 7, 1933.

On August 28, 1949, Ernie Bonham, who had pitched seven seasons for the Yankees and appeared in three World Series, but who was now with the Pirates, pitched his team to an 8–2 win over the Phillies. He had complained of some discomfort during the game, and as a precaution was taken to a Pittsburgh hospital, where appendicitis was diagnosed. The normally routine operation extended for three hours when complications developed. He was very weak when manager Billy Meyer visited him a few days later. "Billy, they are hitting me all over the field, and I can't get anybody out," he mumbled. On September 15, minutes before Meyer and coach Goldie Holt arrived for another visit, he passed away. Bonham, who was thirty-six, left an impressive 103–72 record.

Perhaps the closest parallel to the death of James Creighton in the preprofessional era was the shocking and tragic passing of first baseman Harry Agganis of the Boston Red Sox, on June 27, 1955 at the age of twenty-five. Like Creighton, Agganis was young and talented, with a glorious career seemingly assured.

At 6'2", 200 pounds, and lefthanded, Agganis was a drawing-board first baseman. "The Golden Greek," as he was called, was the most publicized athlete to come out of Boston University since Mickey Cochrane in 1923. Such were Agganis's skills as a quarterback that he was a first-round draft pick of the Cleveland Browns, who offered him $25,000 to sign. When the Boston Red Sox upped this figure by $10,000, he chose baseball. After the 1953 season at Louisville (American Association), where he batted .281, had 23 home runs, 108 RBIs, and played in 155 games, he took over at first base for the parent club in 1954. He batted only .251 his first season. In the early going in 1955, he was over .300 when he developed pneumonia and was hospitalized for ten days. He returned to the lineup, but became ill again in Kansas City. He flew back to Boston and checked into Santa Maria Hospital in nearby Cambridge. He was thought to be recovering nicely, when suddenly on June 27, he died. The cause of his death was given as a massive pulmonary embolism.

Agganis's body lay in state at St. George's Greek Orthodox Church in his home town of Lynn, Massachusetts. On the day before the funeral, ten thousand mourners passed the bier.

Righthanded pitcher Jim Umbricht of Houston underwent a cancer operation on March 8, 1963. By May 9 he was back in uniform, and he finished the year with a 4–3 record and an ERA of 2.61 in 35 appearances. He did not make it into the next season. The malignancy spread, and he died on April 8, 1964, at age thirty-three.

On April 13, 1965, twenty-five-year-old righthander Dick Wantz made his major league debut with the California Angels, giving up three hits and two runs in one inning of relief. Exactly one month later, he was dead, following an operation for a brain tumor.

According to present information, two active major leaguers succumbed to leukemia. Both were twenty-nine when they died and both at one time played with Minnesota. The first was giant 6'7" Walter Bond, who started with Cleveland in 1960, moved to Houston in 1964 and then to Minnesota in 1967, when illness forced him to quit. He died in Houston, September 14, 1967.

The second, infielder Danny Thompson, who broke in with Minnesota in 1970, had played for three years in the majors when he learned he had leukemia. He continued to play, however, and on June 1, 1976, he was involved in one of the big trades of the year, when he was bundled with pitcher Bert Blyleven and shipped to Texas for Roy Smalley, Bill Singer, Mike Cubbage, Jim Gideon, and $250,000. Thompson finished the season with Texas, but it was to be his last. Baseball's Most Courageous Performer (he was so voted in 1974) was only twenty-nine when he died December 10, 1976, at Rochester, Minnesota.

In a single year, 1966, the Detroit Tigers lost two managers to illness and subsequent death, a tragic sequence not duplicated in major league history. On May 16 Charley Dressen, who had managed in the majors for sixteen seasons, suffered a heart attack and was succeeded by coach Bob Swift. Dressen died three months later at the age of sixty-seven. Swift himself became ill in July and was hospitalized, with another coach, Frank Skaff, taking over. It was found that Swift had an advanced case of lung cancer. He died October 16 at the age of fifty-one.

Quiet, efficient, and soft-spoken Dick Howser was an American League infielder from 1961 to 1968 with Kansas City, Cleveland, and New York. He became manager of the Yankees in 1980 and led them to 103 wins and a division title. After the Yankees lost the league championship series to Kansas City, 0–3, owner George Steinbrenner made things so uncomfortable for Howser that he resigned. He moved to Kansas City in 1981, winning a division title in 1984, then a pennant and a world's championship in 1985.

Early in the 1986 season, Howser began to suffer from headaches and to experience visual and memory problems. On July 18, he learned he had a malignant brain tumor. Operations followed, and he recovered sufficiently to return to uniform in 1987. But his health continued to deteriorate and he was forced to give up his managerial duties. He was fifty years old when he died, June 17, 1987.

Suicides and Other Violent Deaths

According to present information, five active major leaguers and one league president ended their lives by their own hands. Four others killed themselves in the year after they had been sent to the minors. Another Johnny Mostil, attempted suicide but recovered. There is also some intimation that the violent deaths of Len Koenecke and Ed Delahanty might have been "death wish" situations.

On February 28, 1894, Edgar McNabb, a pitcher who had won eight games for the Baltimore Orioles in 1893,

checked in at the Eiffel Hotel on Smithfield Street in Pittsburgh. He told the clerk that his wife had gone to Braddock to visit her ailing parents and that he should give her the room key when she returned. Earlier that day, the McNabbs had run into a friend, one Louis Gillen, and the three had agreed to attend the theater that evening.

When the agreed time for the meeting passed, Gillen became concerned and went to the McNabbs' room. As he stood outside the door, he heard a woman's screams. He called for help, and when the room clerk opened the door, the two were shocked and sickened by the bloody and grisly scene before them. Mrs. McNabb lay on the floor, bleeding horribly from bullet holes in her neck and head, but still breathing. Lying beside her, dead, with bullet holes in the head, was Edgar McNabb. A pistol was still in his hand.

As the story unfolded, it became more than a tragic domestic confrontation. The dying woman was not Mrs. McNabb at all. She was Mrs. R. E. Rockwell, whose husband was a well-known West Coast baseball figure and had once been president of the Pacific Northwest Baseball League. She was an actress by profession and used the stage name of Louise Kellogg.

It appeared that Miss Kellogg, who had just finished a theatrical engagement in New York, had asked McNabb to meet her in Pittsburgh. According to a newspaper account, she was planning to break off her relationship with the ballplayer. Letters found in the room indicated that she had been sending him money to tide him over the winter, and further that there had been recent disagreements between them. In the judgment of the police who investigated, an argument had developed, culminating in McNabb's shooting of Miss Kellogg and then turning the gun on himself.

Among McNabb's possessions on the scene was a copy of a message which read: IN GREAT TROUBLE, TELEGRAPH $100 IMMEDIATELY. SEE YOU IN TWO WEEKS. It was probably this message that led Edgar McNabb and Louise Kellogg to their fateful rendezvous at the Eiffel Hotel. Miss Kellogg miraculously survived her wounds but was paralyzed.

Even more shocking than the McNabb affair was the sad denouement of Marty Bergen, first-string catcher for Frank Selee's Boston (NL) club from 1896 to 1899.

On the morning of January 19, 1900, Marty's father, Michael Bergen, who was staying at the house of a neighbor, walked to his son's property, which was called "Snowball Farm," to get some milk. Seeing no activity around the house, he left. He returned at noon and still saw no signs of life. He walked through the unlocked kitchen door, only to be confronted by a scene of unspeakable horror. On the kitchen floor, lay the body of his six-year-old granddaughter Florence. In the adjoining room, he found the body of his daughter-in-law Harriet Bergen and next to her that of her three-year-old son Joseph. Mrs. Bergen's hands were raised as though in supplication or as though trying to ward off a blow. A bloody ax, the apparent murder weapon, was found on the scene. Bergen himself had committed suicide with a straight razor, almost severing his head from his body.

Dr. W. E. Norwood, the medical examiner, made an almost on-the-spot judgment, ruling that the crime had been committed "in a fit of insanity," and that no autopsies would be necessary. According to the account in *The Sporting Life,* the funeral service at St. Joseph's Church in North Brookfield was somber and brief, and "only a few words suitable to the occasion were spoken." The only prominent baseball people present were Connie Mack of the Milwaukee club and Billy Hamilton, a Bergen teammate.

What triggered the carnage at Snowball Farm will never be known. Bergen's manager, Frank Selee, said that he seemed, at times, to act irrationally and to be pursued by hallucinations. It was also revealed that he had sought help from his pastor and his doctor, and that on one occasion he had accused the latter of trying to kill him. Bergen was not a drinker and apparently had no pressing money problems. He was buying the farm on the installment plan and had $2,000 in cash.

On January 12, 1903, not quite three years after the Bergen murder-suicide, the baseball world was stunned by the self-inflicted death of another prominent player. George Barclay "Win" Mercer was a versatile performer who had played every position but catcher in nine years in the majors, winning 131 games as a pitcher and batting .285. He was manager-designate for Detroit, where he had played in 1902.

Mercer was on the West Coast for a series of exhibition games between teams from the American and National leagues. A small man with striking good looks, he had a weakness for fast women and slow horses, a deadly combination that apparently was to do him in. On the fatal day, he did not appear when expected in the dining room of the San Francisco hotel where the players were staying. When the door of his room was opened, Mercer's body was found. A rubber hose was connected to a gas jet. He had died of self-inflicted asphyxiation.

Mercer left a suicide note in which he warned of the evils of women and gambling. He also left a note for his mother and one for his fiancée in East Liverpool, Ohio. Another letter was addressed to Tip O'Neill, manager of the ballplayer troupe, for which Mercer was in charge of finances. Even though Mercer had recently incurred heavy gambling losses, it was reported that his baseball accounts were in order.

Charles "Chick" Stahl had batted .307 in ten major league seasons and was considered one of the game's premier defensive outfielders. Stahl, a Marty Bergen teammate at Boston (NL) from 1897 to 1899, had been named manager of the Boston Puritans (AL) late in the 1906 season, succeeding his friend and roommate Jimmy Collins. Stahl was handsome, popular, well paid for his era, and recently married. Despite his oft-expressed distaste for managing and a recent attempt to resign, it seemed he had almost every reason to be on top of the world; but on March 28, 1907, in his room at the West Baden Hotel in West Baden, Indiana, he ingested a lethal dose of carbolic acid. As he staggered toward his bed, roommate Collins went to his assistance, just in time to hear him gasp: "Boys, I couldn't help it; it drove me to it."

For years, baseball historians pondered Stahl's cryptic words, then usually concluded it was the pressure of managing that forced him to swallow the poison. Dissenting was Harold Seymour, who, in his *Baseball, The Early Years,* strongly hints at the real reason: *cherchez la femme.* In the May 1986 issue of *Boston Magazine,* author Glenn

Stout dug out the rest of the Stahl story and wrote it.

Stahl, according to Stout, although in love with a young lady named Julia Harmon of Roxbury, Massachusetts, was also attracted to other young ladies, the groupies of his day. Furthermore, according to Stout, one of his admirers, a Lulu Ortman, demanded that Stahl marry her. When he spurned her, she twice tried to shoot him but missed. Meanwhile, on November 14, 1906, Stahl had married Miss Harmon at St. Francis de Sales Church in Roxbury. It seems that he had also been involved, late in the 1906 season, with another woman, who now claimed to be pregnant by him. She pressured Stahl to marry her on pain of exposure. He told her that marriage was impossible, since he was already married. She persisted that spring, and it was this pressure, concludes Stout, not the pressure of managing, that led to his suicide.

A sad postscript to the Stahl suicide was the fate of his wife, Julia. Shortly after his death, she attempted suicide herself, but survived. On November 15, 1908, she was found dead in the doorway of a house in South Boston, after a night on the town. An autopsy showed that she had died of edema of the brain.

Little more than two years after the Stahl tragedy, another suicide rocked the game, but it had none of the nasty characteristics of the McNabb, Bergen, or Stahl cases.

Richard Cory, in Edwin Arlington Robinson's poem of the same name, was young, elegant, and well thought of, but one summer night he "went home and put a bullet through his head." Harry Clay Pulliam, president of the National League, was baseball's Richard Cory. On June 28, 1909, Pulliam went to his room in the New York Athletic Club and fired a shot through his head. He died the next morning. The forty-year-old bachelor left no suicide note. Presumably it was a combination of poor health (he had been on leave of absence for health reasons) and the burdens of his job that caused him to do it.

On December 13, 1910, Dennis "Dan" McGann, former captain of the New York Giants and a premier first baseman for thirteen seasons, but most recently a member of the Milwaukee club of the American Association, was found dead in a Louisville hotel room, a bullet hole in his heart and a revolver in his hand. He had been seen around the hotel during the day and had appeared to be in good spirits. One explanation was that he was depressed over the suicide of a brother the past summer.

On March 28, 1927, at the Youree Hotel in Shreveport, Louisiana, spring training headquarters of the Chicago White Sox, Johnny Mostil, the team's star center fielder, slashed both wrists and wounded himself in the chest, throat, and legs with a razor blade and a knife. Early reports, giving him little chance to survive, were wrong. He did recover, played later that same season, and two more seasons thereafter, followed by a long career in the game as a scout. The only explanation for his act seems to have been his hypochondriacal nature. He constantly worried and brooded over his health, although a physical examination that spring had revealed no serious problems.

In eight major league seasons, Cincinnati righthander Benny Frey had struggled to a 57–82 record. At the end of the 1936 season, the best of his career (he was 10–8), he was sent to Nashville to work an ailing arm back into shape. Apparently despondent over the failure of his arm to recover, Frey, on November 1, 1937, at Jackson, Michigan, sat in his car with the motor running and a rubber hose attached to the exhaust pipe. When police found the thirty-one-year-old pitcher, he was dead from carbon monoxide poisoning.

It was August 3, 1940, and the Cincinnati Reds were in Boston. Pleading illness, catcher Willard Hershberger told his roommate, Bill Baker (some accounts say it was Lew Riggs), that he would not be able to come to the ballpark until later. When he did not appear and his telephone was not answered, manager Bill McKechnie sent Dan Cohen, Hershberger's close friend, to the hotel to get him. When the room was entered, Hershberger's body was found in the bathroom, his jugular vein severed by a razor.

Hershberger was young (just thirty), successful, and single, and there seemed no apparent reason for his act. As in the McGann case, there had been a previous suicide in the family. Hershberger's father had shot himself to death in 1928. It has been theorized that the catcher was depressed over his recent failures on the diamond. He had gone hitless in a crucial game, and on another occasion had supposedly called a wrong pitch to Harry Danning of the Giants, who then had hit a home run to beat the Reds in the ninth inning. On the other hand, it was no secret that he had been contemplating suicide. He had told manager McKechnie as much in recent weeks. Also, he had recently purchased a $500 bond, placed it in the hotel safe, and asked that it be given to his mother "if anything happens to me."

With all the obvious planning, it is curious that no suicide note was found. Suicidal tendencies notwithstanding, a hitless game and the call of a wrong pitch hardly seem sufficient to have provoked the deed. It took almost eighty years for the truth to be revealed about the Stahl suicide. Someday, perhaps, more light will be shed on the Hershberger story.

In seven seasons with the Chicago White Sox, Mexican-born righthander Francisco Barrios compiled a 38–38 record. After the 1981 season, during which he had entered a Chicago hospital for drug and alcohol treatment, he was released. On April 4, 1982, he died at his parents' home in Hermosillo, Mexico, of heart failure brought on by an overdose of heroin.

Donnie Ray Moore had a combined 52 saves in 1985 and 1986 for the California Angels, only to become the goat of the 1986 championship series loss to Boston when he gave up a two-out, two-run home run to Dave Henderson that helped cost the Angels the title. He spent most of the next season on the disabled list, was released by the Angels in 1988 and then signed with Omaha of the American Association. He was released by the Royals on June 12 after seven appearances and a 1–2 record. On July 18 he shot his estranged wife (she recovered) and then killed himself with a bullet to the brain as his ten-year-old son watched in horror. Moore's agent attributed all of Moore's troubles to his brooding over the Henderson home run.

Over the years, ballplayers have died violently, other than by suicide. The bizarre death of Hall of Famer Ed Delahanty is a case in point. In 1903 he was with Washington of the American League, but wanted to be with the Giants in New York, where he felt he could earn more money. He dealt with his unhappiness by consuming generous doses of alcohol, starting with a drinking spree in Cleveland. Later, in Detroit, where he took out an accident policy in favor of his daughter, he was heard to threaten to take his own life.

On July 2, 1903, Delahanty boarded a Michigan Central train at Detroit with a ticket to Buffalo, from where, it is believed, he planned to catch another train to Washington to meet his wife. The conductor said Delahanty was "under the weather" when he got on at Detroit and that he had downed at least five shots of whiskey along the way. Not only was he boisterous, but he also threatened some passengers with a razor. At Bridgeburg, Ontario, just across the Niagara River from Buffalo, the conductor ejected him from the train. Delahanty, in the darkness, began to walk across the International Bridge, a railroad bridge connecting Bridgeburg and Buffalo. Bridge watchman Sam Kingston had just escorted a freight across the bridge and, lantern in hand, was walking back to the Canadian side when he confronted Delahanty. Words were exchanged and a scuffle ensued. It is not clear (Kingston told conflicting stories) if Delahanty fell, jumped, or was pushed into the river. Eight days later, his body was found at Niagara Falls, below the Horseshoe Falls.

Subsequently, Delahanty's widow filed suit in the Ontario courts against the Michigan Central Railroad, seeking $20,000 damages for the wrongful death of her husband. She was awarded $3,000, and her daughter received $2,000.

When Walter "Big Ed" Morris won 19 games for the last-place Boston Red Sox in 1928 and then came back with 14 wins for another cellar Boston club in 1929, he became one of the most sought-after pitchers in the league. One story had the Red Sox turning down a $100,000 offer. A sore arm slowed Morris in 1930 and 1931, and his record retrogressed to 4–9 and 5–7. Confident that his arm had regained its strength, he prepared to go to spring training in 1932. As a going-away present, some of his buddies arranged a party for him at a tavern in Century, Florida, just across the state line from Morris's hometown of Flomaton, Alabama. Unfortunately, the party began to get out of hand, and soon the guest of honor was involved in a fight with Joe White, a gas station attendant from Brewton, Alabama. When Morris slipped to the floor, White pulled a knife and stabbed him twice, fatally. Morris was thirty-one and left a widow and two children.

Len Koenecke was an impressive-looking athlete—broad of shoulder, slim of waist, and ruggedly handsome. He was said to have been the last player personally scouted by John McGraw, who arranged for his purchase from Indianapolis (American Association) in 1931 for players valued at $75,000. The young outfielder failed to live up to his minor league billings and was farmed to Jersey City in 1932 and to Buffalo in 1933. An outstanding season for the Bisons in 1933 led to his sale to Brooklyn, where in 1934 he batted .320 and fielded a league-leading .994. But he slumped in 1935, and late that year manager Casey Stengel sent Koenecke and two other players home from St. Louis so that he could try out some young prospects.

On the flight from St. Louis to Detroit, Koenecke, who had been drinking, created a disturbance, and when the airport was reached he was ordered off the plane. Although it was late in the evening, he decided to charter a private plane and fly to Buffalo, where he had friends. The plane he chartered had an interesting past. It had once been owned by Smith Reynolds of the tobacco family and his wife, torch singer Libby Holman, who were principals in one of the most sensational murder cases of the 1930s. When Reynolds was shot to death at the family estate in Winston-Salem, N.C., his wife was charged with the crime but was later cleared.

While the plane was still over Canada, Koenecke tried to take over the controls from pilot William Mulqueeny. Irwin Davis, the copilot, attempted to restrain the husky ballplayer but was pushed to the floor. Mulqueeny, while trying to guide the plane with one hand, picked up a fire extinguisher with the other and bludgeoned Koenecke until he was dead. Mulqueeny had no idea where he was until he spotted the lights of Toronto. Seeing a racetrack on the outskirts of the city, he decided to use the backstretch as an airport and brought the plane safely down. Then, to cap their night of terror, the two men were attacked by watch dogs as they left the plane. The dogs eventually backed off, and they were able to summon help.

After two hearings in Canadian courts, Mulqueeny and Davis were absolved of all blame in Koenecke's death. Blood tests had shown that the dead ballplayer was drunk. At one of the hearings, Edward J. Murphy, attorney for the pilots, alleged that Koenecke was trying to commit suicide and to do it "in a grand and glorious manner."

In the early hours of January 5, 1975, Don Wilson, star righthanded pitcher of the Houston Astros, who had won 104 games in nine major league seasons and pitched two no-hitters, drove his luxury car into the garage of his suburban Houston home and left the motor running. At one P.M. his lifeless body was found slumped in the passenger seat. The ignition was on, the battery was dead, the gas tank was empty, and there were exhaust-fume stains on the garage floor. In the room above the garage, his five-year-old son Alexander was dead from the fumes. His wife, Bernice, and his daughter, Denise, were taken to the hospital in serious condition. Bernice Wilson also had a badly bruised jaw, which was never explained, but which could have been caused by a fall.

Mrs. Wilson and her daughter both recovered. Tests on the twenty-nine-year-old Don Wilson revealed a blood-alcohol content of .167. On February 5, 1975, the medical examiner ruled the deaths of father and son were accidental.

Mickey Fuentes, a righthanded pitcher who was 1–3 for Seattle in 1969, never made it to spring training in 1970. He was shot to death in a tavern brawl in his native Loiza Aldea, Puerto Rico, January 29, 1970, He was only twenty years old.

With Lyman Bostock, who had starred for Minnesota (in 1975–1977) and then had signed a lucrative free-agent contract with California, it was a case of being in the wrong place at the wrong time. On September 23, 1978, in Gary, Indiana, he was in a car being driven by his uncle when he was shot by a man named Leonard Smith, whose apparent target was Smith's estranged wife, seated next to

Bostock in the back seat. Three hours after the assault, the twenty-seven-year-old Bostock was dead. There was whispering that something was going on between Bostock and Mrs. Smith. Actually they had met only twenty minutes before and were heading for different destinations.

Leonard Smith was twice tried for murder. The first trial, in which insanity was pleaded, ended in a hung jury. In the second trial, he was found not guilty by reason of insanity, spent six months in a mental hospital, and then was a free man. Outrage over the outcome of the two trials resulted in a change in the Indiana law, whereby an accused can now be judged both insane and guilty of a crime.

Planes, Cars, Trucks, and a Dune Buggy

When superstars Roberto Clemente and Thurman Munson lost their lives in air crashes, it was front-page news all over the country. In Clemente's case, the coverage was international in scope because of the mercy mission in which he was involved.

Clemente and Munson were not the first active major leaguers to perish in airplane accidents. There were at least six prior air fatalities—seven if Koenecke is included. Marvin Goodwin, a righthanded spitball pitcher who saw action with the Senators, Cardinals, and Reds from 1916 through 1925, was the first. In 1925, nearing the end of his career, he was pitcher-manager of Houston of the Texas League, on assignment from the Cardinals. He did so well at Houston (21–9) that Cincinnati purchased him conditionally late in the season, with the understanding that final payment on the deal would be made only if he lasted thirty days into the 1926 season. He made four September appearances for the Reds with no wins and no losses.

Goodwin had been a flying instructor in World War One and was still a lieutenant in the reserve. On October 18, 1925, he took off on a practice flight from Ellington Field, near Houston, with a mechanic on board. The engine failed at 200 feet, and the plane crashed. The mechanic miraculously survived, but Goodwin, who suffered two broken legs and internal injuries, died four days later. The fatality had a ghoulish aftermath. The following year, the Cardinals demanded full payment for Goodwin's contract. The Reds refused on the grounds that he was not on their roster thirty days into the 1926 season. The case was referred to the commissioner's office. Judge Landis, citing the terms of the contract, ruled in favor of the Reds.

Elmer Joseph Gedeon played in the outfield for the Washington Senators in 1939. He had been a track star at the University of Michigan and had given up a chance to run in the Olympic Games to go into baseball. But then World War Two came along, and Gedeon gave up baseball to become an early volunteer in the Air Corps. He died April 15, 1944, when his plane was shot down over France. (Two others who played in the majors in 1939 also died in battle. Bob Neighbors, a shortstop for seven games with the St. Louis Browns, died in North Korea in 1952, and Harry O'Neill, who caught one game for the Philadelphia Athletics, perished in the assault on Iwo Jima in 1945.)

After his graduation from Boston University in 1955, catcher Tom Gastall pocketed a $40,000 bonus from the Baltimore Orioles. He was used sparingly, playing 20 games in 1955 and 32 in 1956. On September 20, 1956, he took off in a light plane from Harbor Field, near Baltimore. He landed at Easton, from where he later took off for the return flight over the Chesapeake Bay. Five days later, his body and the wreckage of the plane were found in the water off Riviera Beach. Gastall was just twenty-four.

A little over two months later, on November 27, 1956, outfielder Charlie Peete, who had played 23 games for the St. Louis Cardinals that summer, died in a plane crash in the mountains of Venezuela, near Caracas, while en route to play winter ball. His wife and three children also perished in the crash.

Another victim of a Venezuelan air disaster was twenty-one-year-old Nestor Chavez, a San Francisco Giant farmhand who played in two games for the Giants in 1967. On March 16, 1969, the young pitcher was on his way to join the Giants' Phoenix farm club when his plane crashed, killing 155 passengers. It was one of the worst accidents in aviation history.

Ken Hubbs, playing 160 games for the Chicago Cubs in 1962, handled 148 consecutive chances without an error and was Rookie of the Year. He tailed off in 1963 but was still rated one of the game's rising young stars. At the end of the 1963 season, he began to take flying lessons. In early February 1964, shortly after he had received his license, Hubbs, who lived in Colton, California, flew to Provo, Utah, with a friend, Dennis Doyle, to visit Doyle's in-laws. On February 15, Hubbs and Doyle took off in a snowstorm for their return trip to California. Only five miles from Provo, the plane crashed into Utah Lake, killing Hubbs and Doyle.

After investigation, the Civil Aeronautics Board reported the probable cause as "Hubbs's attempt to continue visual flight into an area of adverse weather." The twenty-two-year-old Hubbs, who was not licensed for instrument flying, left a log book which showed he had flown just 71 hours, 16 minutes.

On September 30, 1972, Roberto Clemente, who had batted .317 in eighteen seasons with Pittsburgh, touched Jon Matlack of the Mets for a base hit. It was Clemente's 3,000th and last hit. On December 31, 1972, Clemente and four others were killed when a plane carrying food, clothing, and medical supplies to earthquake-stricken Nicaragua crashed moments after takeoff from San Juan, Puerto Rico.

Clemente's career had all the elements of a Horatio Alger tale. Born August 18, 1934, in Carolina, Puerto Rico, the son of a sugar plantation foreman, he was signed by Al Campanis of the Dodgers as a teenager. The Dodgers tried to cover him up on the Montreal (International League) roster, but Pittsburgh general manager Branch Rickey, who knew all about him from his days with the Dodgers, drafted him for a piddling $4,000. It was one of the greatest bargains in baseball history. Clemente immediately became a regular and won all manner of plaudits for his hitting, fielding, and magnificent throwing arm. He was Most Valuable Player in 1966, batted .310 and .414 in two World Series (1960, 1971), and was *The Sporting News*'s Gold Glove outfielder twelve times. Twice he hit three home runs in one game, and five times he led National League outfielders in assists.

Clemente was voted into the Baseball Hall of Fame in 1973 in a special election, with the usual five-year waiting period waived by a change of the voting rules.

Thurman Munson was the only New York Yankee to win both Rookie of the Year (1970) and Most Valuable Player (1976) awards. He was the regular Yankee catcher from 1970, averaging more than 140 games a year, despite aching knees, a beaning, and a foul ball in the throat. He was one of the league's top clutch hitters, with 701 RBIs and a .292 average over eleven seasons. His clashes with Reggie Jackson over which of them was the straw that stirred the Yankee drink drew national attention.

On August 2, 1979, an off-day, Munson flew his new Cessna Citation jet from New York to Canton, Ohio, to visit his family. Late in the afternoon, he was practicing takeoffs and landings at the Akron-Canton Airport when the plane crashed a thousand feet short of the runway. Munson's flying companions, David Hall and Jerry Anderson, survived and at great danger to themselves, attempted to pull Munson from the flaming wreckage. But there was no chance. Munson, who was thirty-two, left his wife, Diane, and three children, not to mention millions of mourning baseball fans. On August 6 of that year, 51,000 fans at Yankee Stadium participated in an impressive nine-minute salute to the Yankee captain, who, with a few more years under his belt, could well have been a good bet for the Hall of Fame.

As far as is known, the first active major leaguer to die in a vehicular accident was Norman Boeckel, a .298 hitter for the 1923 Boston Braves. The thirty-one-year-old third baseman died February 16, 1924, in a San Diego hospital, from pelvic injuries sustained the day before, when he was standing alongside his car after it had been involved in a collision with a truck and he was struck by a passing motorist. Earlier, Boeckel had played a fringe role in another piece of baseball history. He had submitted an affidavit to National League President John Heydler, attesting that he had heard pitcher Rube Benton boast of winning $3,200 on the 1919 World Series on a tip from Hal Chase. Benton was thrown out of baseball, but was later reinstated by Judge Landis.

The year 1929 saw the deaths of two major leaguers in vehicular accidents. Denny Williams, a twenty-nine-year-old outfielder, who had played with the Reds in 1921 and the Red Sox in 1924, 1925 and 1928, was killed in Los Angeles, March 21. Seven months later, on October 22, Walter "Peck" Lerian, regular catcher for the Phillies in 1928 and 1929, died in a Baltimore hospital, after being hit by a truck that vaulted over a curb and pinned him against the wall of a building.

Catcher Al Montgomery was only twenty years old when he appeared in 42 games for the Boston Braves in 1941. While returning from spring training on April 26, 1942, having been assigned to Hartford of the Eastern League, he was involved in a car accident near Waverly, Virginia, and killed.

While Paul Edmondson, a twenty-seven-year-old pitcher who had been 1–6 with the 1969 White Sox, was en route to spring training, he was involved in a fatal auto accident February 13, 1970, near Santa Barbara, California. Another victim of a California crash was Chico Ruiz, who had been in the majors for eight years, first with Cincinnati and most recently with California. He was killed in San Diego February 9, 1972.

The pitching career of Bob Moose was a series of highs and lows. In ten years with the Pirates, he won 76 games and lost 71. One of his wins was a no-hitter against the New York Mets on September 20, 1969. On the other side of the coin is the wild pitch he uncorked in the final game of the 1972 league championship series that permitted Cincinnati to defeat Pittsburgh. He also made three appearances in the 1971 World Series, but had no decisions. On October 9, 1976, at Martin's Ferry, Ohio, he suffered fatal injuries in an automobile accident. It was his twenty-ninth birthday.

Righthanded pitcher Danny Frisella, who in ten years in the majors saw action with the Mets, Braves, Padres, Cardinals, and Brewers (34–40), took a dune buggy out in the desert near Phoenix on New Year's Day, 1977. When the buggy overturned, he was killed instantly.

Just six days later, on January 6, Mike Miley, a twenty-three-year-old shortstop with California in 1975 and 1976, was killed in a car crash at Baton Rouge.

On Friday night, December 19, 1986, Honolulu native Joe DeSa hit four doubles to help his Ponce Lions defeat the Mayaguez Indians, 11–8, in a Puerto Rico winter league game. At four A.M. on December 20, DeSa was killed in a head-on crash on the Las Americas Expressway. DeSa, who had played for Buffalo (American Association) in 1985 and 1986 and was the team's most valuable player in the latter year, had signed with Kansas City and was due to report in the spring for his third hitch in the majors.

The two known deaths of active players by drowning are separated by almost one hundred years. The first was England-born Al Thake, second baseman for the Brooklyn Atlantics. He drowned off Fort Hamilton, New York, while fishing, September 1, 1872. Almost a century later, on December 14, 1970, Herman Hill, twenty-five-year-old outfielder with Minnesota in 1969 and 1970, was in Venezuela to play winter ball when he drowned off Valencia.

On March 22, 1993, after a day of fishing on Little Lake Nellie, 27 miles north of Winter Haven, Florida, Cleveland Indians pitchers Tim Crews, Steve Olin, and Bob Ojeda were returning to shore in an open, eighteen-foot-base boat. In the darkness, Crews, who was returning the boat, did not see a dock that extended some 250 feet into the lake. He rammed it while traveling at an estimated 39 miles per hour. Olin was killed instantly and Crews died a few hours later. Ojeda came within an inch of having the top of his head sheared off, but though grievously injured did recover and returned to the mound late in the 1993 season, but is now out of baseball. Evidence in the boat and through blood tests indicated that alcohol was involved. Crews and Olin each left a wife and three small children. It was the only instance in major league history in which two players were killed in one accident.

Cleveland's cup of sorrow overflowed in the 1993 off-season as another member of its pitching staff lost his life in an accident. Reliever Cliff Young, a twenty-nine year-old veteran of three major league campaigns, was fatally injured in a November car crash.

Bean Balls

Every time a batter steps to the plate, it is an act of courage. With pitches hurtling toward him at 90 miles per hour, he has but a fraction of a second to decide if he should swing, take, or bail out. Modern helmets with ear flaps have removed much of the peril, but not all. Prior to the 1950s, batters had no head protection at all; and before 1893 the risk was even greater, since the pitching distance was only 50 feet.

Considering the danger involved, it is somewhat of a miracle that only one batter has been killed by a pitched ball in the long history of major league baseball. No definitive statistics are available, but it is known that many have been killed at the amateur level and at least seven in minor league play.

Major league baseball's only bean ball fatality, and its only diamond fatality for any reason, occurred on August 16, 1920, at the Polo Grounds, New York, in a game between the New York Yankees and the Cleveland Indians. It was the first half of the fifth inning, and shortstop Ray Chapman of the Indians was at bat, faced by Yankee submarine-baller Carl Mays. Chapman liked to crowd the plate and crouch over it. Mays, who had a mean streak, was not averse to throwing at any batter who encroached on his territory. Mays's first pitch was a strike, his second a ball, as Chapman seemed to edge even closer to the plate. Predictably the third pitch was high and inside. There was an ominous crack that was heard all over the Polo Grounds. Mays, thinking his pitch had hit Chapman's bat, fielded the ball and started to throw to Wally Pipp at first base, but then he saw Chapman slumped in the arms of catcher Muddy Ruel and he knew the batter had been hit. A doctor was summoned from the stands and Chapman was temporarily revived. Assisted by two of his teammates, he began the long walk to the clubhouse in center field, but he soon collapsed and was carried the rest of the way.

When a preliminary examination in the clubhouse showed the injury was extremely serious, he was taken to nearby St. Lawrence Hospital, where an operation was performed. He was still under ether when he died at five A.M. the following day, August 17.

The repercussions were immediate and furious. Mays, a surly sort and never popular among his peers, was strongly criticized. Detroit and Boston players demanded that he be barred for life, while those on the Washington and St. Louis clubs threatened to strike if Mays was allowed to pitch again. But Mays did have his defenders. Cleveland pitcher Ray Caldwell, a former Yankee, said it seemed to him that Chapman had turned his head right into the ball. Connie Mack, venerable skipper of the Philadelphia Athletics, while deploring the fatal accident, pleaded for sympathy for Mays. Catcher Muddy Ruel, who caught Chapman when he fell, said in later years that the pitch could have been a strike.

Mays appeared before the district attorney and, after a deposition, was cleared of any criminal charges. He said he was not trying to hit Chapman, only to pitch him tight. That spring, Mays pointed out, he had seen Yankee infielder Chick Fewster nearly killed by a pitch delivered by Jeff Pfeffer of the Dodgers, and from that time on he had been reluctant even to throw inside pitches, let alone throw at batters. He then suggested the fatality might have been averted had plate umpire Tom Connolly not refused to remove from play the scuffed ball that hit Chapman. This drew a sharp rejoinder from American League umpires Billy Evans and Bill Dinneen, who charged that Mays was one of the league's most notorious scuffers. They said further that club owners had complained to Ban Johnson, league president, that too many balls were being thrown out, and that Johnson had responded by sending out a directive, instructing umpires to keep balls in play, "except those which are dangerous."

In the *New York Times* of August 19, there was an impassioned plea for the development and use of batting helmets, but it was to be more than thirty years before this advice would be heeded.

At least seven minor leaguers have been killed by pitched balls. On August 9, 1906, Joe Yaeger of Fall River of the New England League hit Tom Burke of Lynn in the head with a pitch. Two days later, Burke was dead. Two days after attending Burke's funeral, Yaeger took his turn on the mound, only to be arrested by Lynn police on a manslaughter charge. Shortly thereafter, the charges were dropped. Jaeger, who had pitched for six years in the majors with Brooklyn and Detroit, completed the season with a 15–19 record.

In the second game of a Central League doubleheader, played in gathering darkness at Dayton, September 14, 1909, Charles "Cupid" Pinkney, twenty-year-old Dayton second baseman, was beaned by Casey Hageman of Grand Rapids. At first, it was thought he would recover, but his condition deteriorated, and he died following an operation. Pinkney's father, who had traveled from Cleveland to watch his son play, was at his side when he died.

On June 18, 1916, Johnny Dodge, infielder for Mobile of the Southern Association, was hit on the head by Tom "Shotgun" Rogers of Nashville and died the next day of a fractured skull. It is believed that Dodge was thrown at in retaliation for the beaning of a Nashville player the previous day. By the strangest of coincidences, Rogers and Carl Mays were to be teammates briefly on the 1921 Yankees.

On July 4, 1933, at Omaha, Jesse Batterton, nineteen-year-old third baseman for Springfield of the Western League, suffered a fractured skull when hit by a pitch thrown by Omaha's Floyd "Swede" Carlson. He was able to get to his feet and walk to the clubhouse, but then collapsed and was taken to a hospital. He died there following an operation, with pitcher Carlson at his bedside.

On July 21, 1938, Linus "Skeeter" Ebnet, twenty-three-year-old shortstop for Winnipeg of the Northern League, died in a Winnipeg hospital, five days after being hit by a pitched ball in a game against Grand Forks.

Twenty-year-old James (Stormy) Davis was off to a great start for Ballinger (Texas) of the Longhorn League. In 48 games he had hit 19 home runs and had 59 RBIs. On July 3, 1947 he was beaned by Stan (Midnight) Wilson of Sweetwater. The young outfielder died a week later.

A seventh fatality occurred in the Alabama-Florida League on June 2, 1951. Lefty Jack Clifton of Headland hit Ottis Johnson of the Dothan Browns on the head and killed him. In his next start, Clifton, who had already hit twelve batters that season, pitched a no-hit, no-run game against Panama City. According to Ken Brooks in his book *The Last Rebel Yell,* every Panama City batter had one foot in the dugout.

In major league history there have been countless beanings. In most cases, the batters came back, but often were not the same hitters as before. Lowell Reidenbaugh, in his *Cooperstown,* writes that Hughie Jennings survived three skull fractures. His most serious injury was from a pitch delivered by Amos Rusie of New York, said to have been the swiftest pitcher of his day. The blow left Jennings near death and unconscious for four days. Some historians say it was Rusie's speed and the fear that he might kill someone that brought about the lengthening of the pitching distance in 1893 to the present 60 feet, 6 inches.

At Ebbets Field on September 3, 1932, Giants shortstop Ed Marshall was beaned by a Van Lingle Mungo fastball. He survived despite lapsing into "unsafe condition." The incident ended his major league career although Marshall did play thereafter in the minors.

On May 25, 1937, future Hall of Famer Mickey Cochrane, player-manager of the Detroit Tigers, lost sight of a pitch by Bump Hadley of the Yankees. It hit him in the right temple and fractured his skull. He lay unconscious for ten days but eventually recovered, although he never played again. He did, however, resume his managerial duties and also served with distinction in the Navy in World War Two.

Tony Conigliaro of the Boston Red Sox, who hit 166 home runs in six full seasons and parts of two others (all with the Red Sox, except for 74 games and 4 home runs for California in 1971), surely would have racked up more impressive numbers had he not been hit in the face and nearly killed by a Jack Hamilton (of California) pitch on August 18, 1967. He was out of the game for a year and a half, but then came back to hit 20 home runs in 1969 and 36 in 1970. On October 11, 1970, in a most controversial deal, he was traded to California, where he was to see only limited duty. He returned to Boston for 21 games in 1975 and then was out of baseball. He died February 24, 1990.

Dickie Thon was the All-Star National League shortstop for Houston in 1983 and also led the league in game-winning hits. In the fifth game of the 1984 season, he was hit in the eye by a Mike Torrez (Mets) fastball. Despite permament damage to his eye, he was able to return to action and played more or less regularly for the Texas Rangers in 1992 and then briefly for Milwaukee in 1993.

Don Zimmer, 1988 manager of the Chicago Cubs, suffered two serious beanings and still carries a metal plate in his head from the injuries. Paul Blair, center field magician of the Baltimore Orioles, Minnie Minoso of the White Sox, and Wayne Terwilliger, utility player for several clubs, were others whose careers were interrupted or affected by bean balls.

Sore Arms, Illnesses, Injuries, and Accidents

Up to this point, the subject has been (with a few exceptions) deaths off or on the diamond. But fatalities are only part of the story. Many a baseball career has aborted for reasons not resulting in death, at least, not at once.

In the old days, sore arms were usually rested. If there was any treatment at all, it was by the likes of John D. "Bonesetter" Reese, a self-trained muscle manipulator of

Youngstown, Ohio. Nobody ever heard of the rotator cuff or even dreamed of such sophisticated operations as those which prolonged the careers of Tommy John, Ken Dayley, and others.

Charles "Lady" Baldwin was one old-timer who could have used a Tommy John bionic arm. In 1886 he won 42 games for Detroit (NL) and pitched 487 innings. He then developed arm trouble and dropped to 13 wins in 1887 and to 3 each in 1888 and 1890, after which he retired for good to his Michigan farm. Hall of Famer Christy Mathewson's arm went dead in 1916, but by then he was thirty-eight, had won 373 games, and had achieved immortality. Smoky Joe Wood was another sore arm victim, but he did beat the rap in a way. After winning 23 games for the Red Sox in 1911 and then 34 in 1912, including 16 in a row, he developed a sore arm the following spring. His days as an intimidating fireballer were over, although he did win 35 games for the Sox over the next three seasons. Realizing he could no longer pitch, he decided to become a sore-armed outfielder, and played that position with fair success for Cleveland through the 1922 season. Altogether he played in fourteen major league seasons and left a 116–57 pitching record and a career batting mark of .283.

Undocumented are the names of countless other pitchers of the game's early years who dropped out prematurely because of so-called dead arms. More is known of modern pitchers, like Dave Ferris and Karl Spooner. Ferris joined the Boston Red Sox in 1945, having been mustered out of the Army because of asthma. He raised plenty of eyebrows with a 21–10 record in the last year of wartime baseball, but then made believers out of everyone by winning 25 and losing just 6 in 1946. But in a night game in Cleveland in June of 1947, he suffered a shoulder injury, from which he never fully recovered although he did hang on until 1950. His career log shows 65–30 for a phenomenal .684 percentage.

No pitcher ever made a more dazzling entrance or faded as fast as Karl Spooner. The twenty-three-year-old lefthander was called up by Brooklyn from Fort Worth (Texas), late in the 1954 season. He pitched shutouts against New York and Pittsburgh in his first two starts, allowing just 7 hits and striking out 27. Hampered by a sore arm, he struggled to an 8–6 record in 1955, made two appearances in the World Series (0–1), then never pitched again.

In 1966 another Dodger lefthander, Hall of Famer Sandy Koufax was 27–9, with 5 shutouts and an ERA of 1.73 in 323 innings of work. Talk about going out on top! No pitcher in major league history ever matched that in a final season. He pitched against Baltimore in the 1966 World Series (0–1), but at the age of thirty his career was over. Traumatic arthritis in the left elbow, triggered by a fall on his left arm when attempting a pickoff during the 1964 season, made it impossible for him to continue. Had Koufax been able to pitch as long as, say Warren Spahn, there is no telling what his record might have been. As it was, he left an imposing mark of 165–87 (.655) and an ERA of 2.76.

Mark Fidrych, the colorful Detroit pitcher known as "the Bird," was 19–9 in 1976 and was the starting pitcher in the All-Star game. But plagued by arm trouble, he faded to a combined 10–11 record over the next four seasons. He was only twenty-six when he pitched his final big league game in 1980. Twice he tried comebacks in the minors, but failed.

Lefty Don Gullett, the only man to pitch the opening game in successive World Series for two different teams (Cincinnati Reds, 1976; and New York Yankees, 1977), was just twenty-seven when his career ended with a bad arm after the 1978 season. He had been one of the first free agents signed by the Yankees, and was certainly one of their most expensive, costing them $2 million for his 18 wins in two seasons.

Righthander Wayne Garland of the Indians was operated on for a rotator cuff tear on May 5, 1978. He had won 33 games the two previous seasons. After the operation, he came back, hanging on until 1981, but he was never the same pitcher. And like Gullett, he was working on a lucrative long-term contract.

The previous pages have told of the surprising number of active major leaguers who succumbed to illness. Many others became ill and were forced to give up the game or see their baseball livelihoods interrupted. An early example was Jimmy Wood, who played for Chicago, Brooklyn, and Philadelphia in the National Association from 1871 to 1873. In 1873 he developed a leg abscess which he attempted to lance with a penknife. A severe infection developed, resulting in the loss of his leg. His playing days, of course, were over, but he did return as a manager in 1874 and 1875.

In 1890 first baseman Dave Orr of Brooklyn (in the Players' League) batted .373, hit 32 doubles, 13 triples, and 6 home runs, while striking out only 11 times. For a nonpitcher, this was the ultimate in final seasons. In the off-season, the thirty-one-year-old Orr suffered a stroke and never played again. He died in Brooklyn on June 3, 1915.

Hall of Famer Amos Rusie won 243 games in nine seasons and part of a tenth, but saw his career shrouded by misfortune, some of his own making. The so-called "Hoosier Thunderbolt," who almost killed Hughie Jennings with a bean ball, himself took a line drive to the head which permanently damaged his hearing. He threw out his arm in 1898 and was out of the game for two years. He compounded his other problems with heavy drinking. Although he tried to come back in 1901, he failed. At the age of thirty he was through.

The aforementioned Jennings, another Hall of Famer, had a baseball life replete with illness and adversity. In addition to the almost fatal beaning by Rusie, he suffered a nervous breakdown in 1925, after taking over as manager of the New York Giants when John McGraw became ill. Jennings died of spinal meningitis in 1928 at the age of fifty-eight.

Often documented is the tragic accident that terminated the career of catcher Charley Bennett, who played in the majors from 1878 to 1893 (except for 1879). In January of 1894, while on a hunting trip, he tried to catch and board a moving train at Wellsville, Kansas, but lost his grip and fell under the wheels, losing both legs.

Shortstop Charlie Hollocher, who played for the Cubs from 1918 to 1924, was constantly bedeviled by illness, real and imaginary, blunting what some observers feel could have been a Hall of Fame–level career. His tormented life came to an end on August 14, 1940, when he parked his car on a quiet Clayton, Missouri, street, then tore his throat apart with a blast from a sixteen-gauge shotgun.

One of the strangest cases in which illness terminated a career involved pitcher-turned-outfielder Erwin (Zeke) Harvey. After batting .333 for Chicago and Cleveland of the new American League in 1901 and starting the 1902 season at a .348 clip in 12 games, he quit baseball, claiming he had such serious stomach pains that he could no longer play ball. He never returned to the diamond. Instead he became an entomologist on the west coast. He died in Santa Monica, in 1954 at the age of seventy-five.

On September 25, 1905, Dave Fultz was playing center field for the New York Highlanders when he collided with shortstop Norman "Kid" Elberfeld. His nose and jaw were broken, injuries which would end his baseball career. He had been studying law and he opened his own office in 1906. In 1912 he formed the Players Fraternity and later secured many benefits for players. In 1919 and 1920 he served as president of the International League.

Jackie Hayes, outstanding second baseman and shortstop for the Senators and the White Sox (1927–1940), was 3 for 3 in a 1940 Sox spring game; then in the shower room he noticed a cloudiness in one eye. He played 18 games that year, but by August he had lost his sight in the clouded eye. In a matter of three years, he had lost his sight in the other. Similarly, George "Specs" Toporcer, a former major league infielder, had lost his sight while managing Buffalo (International League) in 1951. Both men learned to live with their blindness and went on to lead productive lives, Hayes as the tax collector of Chilton County, Alabama, and Toporcer as a writer and lecturer.

Righthanded pitcher Monty Stratton (15–5 and 15–9 for the Chicago White Sox in 1937 and 1938) was hunting rabbits near his mother's home in Greenville, Texas, after the 1938 season, when he accidentally discharged a .22-caliber pistol. The slug lodged in his right knee, severing the main artery and necessitating amputation of the leg. Stratton did not pitch again in the majors, but he was a White Sox coach for three seasons. In 1946 he pitched for Sherman in the Class C East Texas League, where, remarkably, he won 18 games. Hollywood thought it saw a story in the courageous way he had faced his tragedy and made a much-acclaimed movie of his life, *The Stratton Story*, starring Jimmy Stewart.

A third victim of a leg injury was Joe Cronin, Hall of Fame shortstop who played twenty years for Washington and Boston, and probably would have played a few more had he not fractured his leg three games into the 1945 season. He never played again, but continued in the game for many years as a manager, front office executive, and as American League president.

He looked so indestructible that they called him "The Iron Horse." Henry Louis Gehrig, in seventeen years at first base for the New York Yankees, averaged .340, hit 535 doubles, 162 triples, and 493 home runs. He scored 1,888 runs, had 1,990 RBIs, and posted a slugging percentage of .632. His incredible record of playing in 2,130 consecutive games at one time seemed unassailable, but is now being challenged by Cal Ripken of the Baltimore Orioles, who played in 2,009 consecutive games through the end of the 1994 season. On May 2, 1939, Gehrig approached manager Joe McCarthy, told him he was not feeling well. Gehrig thought he was hurting the team, and

he asked to be taken from the lineup. McCarthy, of course, complied, and so for the first time since pinch-hitting for Pee-Wee Wanninger on May 31, 1925, Gehrig missed a Yankee game.

A few months later the bad news came from the Mayo Clinic. The indestructible one, "The Iron Horse," had been stricken with amyotrophic lateral sclerosis, a disease of the central nervous system for which no cure was known. On July 4, 1939, 61,000 gathered at Yankee Stadium for a gigantic Gehrig tribute. There he spoke his memorable words: "I consider myself the luckiest man on the face of the earth."

In the short time left to him, Gehrig devoted himself to public service. On June 2, 1941, exactly sixteen years from the day he replaced Wally Pipp at first base, he died. He was thirty-seven years old. The malady that killed him is now generally referred to as Lou Gehrig's disease. Unfortunately it is almost as much a medical mystery today as it was fifty years ago when it struck him.

Catcher Bill DeLancey was a product of the St. Louis Cardinal farm system. After playing eight games for the parent club in 1932 and then spending a year at Columbus (American Association), he became a regular member of the "Gas House Gang" in 1934. In 1935 he found that he had tuberculosis and faced a long recovery period. It was not until 1940 that he made it back, and then it was just for 15 games. By then, he knew it was no use. His career was over. He died November 28, 1946, on his thirty-fifth birthday.

When Don Black went to the mound for the Cleveland Indians against the St. Louis Browns on September 13, 1948, he could have looked back on an undistinguished six-year record with the Athletics and Indians (34–55). But there were two victories—one off the diamond—that he could recall with pride. The first was against the bottle; the second was a no-hit, no-run game against the Philadelphia Athletics on July 10, 1947.

In the late-season game against the Browns, upon retiring the Browns in the first two innings, Black came to bat against Bill Kennedy. After swinging mightily at the first pitch and fouling it back, he began to stagger and finally sank to his knees. Umpire Bill Summers bent over to assist Black and heard him whisper, "That last pitch to [Ed] Pellagrini did it." (He had struck out the Browns' shortstop with a curve ball to end the top of the second.) Apparently, that pitch plus the force of his swing had caused an aneurysm to rupture, sending blood to his brain and spinal cord. (Shades of James Creighton, who had injured himself fatally while batting on August 14, 1862.) An eminent neurosurgeon was summoned. He ruled out surgery as too risky, but said Black had just a 50-50 chance of surviving. But Black did survive and on September 22 he was recipient of a large purse from a benefit game against the Red Sox that attracted a crowd of 76,772.

The Indians went on to win the pennant and then defeated the Boston Braves in the World Series, but without Black, who never pitched again. He died April 21, 1959 at the age of 42.

Baseball's *Domesday Books* credit lefthanded pitcher Bert Shepard with one major league appearance. What the books do not say is that this game was pitched by a one-legged man. When Shepard's call to World War Two service came, he was a promising young pitcher. The fortunes of war took him to the European front, where he was downed over Germany on his thirty-fifth mission and taken prisoner. Doctors removed his shattered right leg, after which a fellow prisoner of war fashioned him a wooden leg. After his recapture and return to the States, he was signed by the Washington Senators as a batting practice pitcher. In his one appearance in a regular game, he allowed one run in 5⅓ innings for an ERA of 1.69.

Lou Brissie, like Bert Shepard, was a victim of World War Two combat. Brissie, who joined the Army in 1942 as a teenager, was badly wounded on the Italian front and forced to undergo twenty-three operations. Despite the handicap of a steel leg brace and a leather guard, he never gave up his dream of becoming a major league pitcher. In 1947, for Savannah of the Sally League, he won 23 games and earned a late-season call-up from the Philadelphia Athletics. From 1947 to 1953, he won 44 games for the A's and the Indians, to whom he was traded in 1951. His best year was 1949, when he won 16 games and pitched in the All-Star Game. He was only twenty-nine when his career came to a close. He then became national director of the American Legion baseball program.

Herb Score was a third American League lefty to see his career abbreviated by injury. In 1955, Score won 16 games for Cleveland and struck out 245; then in 1956 he improved to 20 wins and 263 strikeouts. Along the banks of Lake Erie, he was hailed as a lefthanded Bob Feller. But it was not to be. On May 7, 1957, at Municipal Stadium in Cleveland, he was hit in the eye by a torrid line drive off the bat of Gil McDougald of the New York Yankees and seriously injured.

His recovery was slow, and he did not return to the Indians until 1958 and then only for 12 games. On April 18, 1960, he was traded to the White Sox for Barry Latman. After three seasons of limited duty for the Sox, he called it a day. He remains in baseball as the play-by-play announcer for the Indians.

Brooklyn catcher Roy Campanella was thirty-six and in the twilight of a remarkable career that had seen him win three Most Valuable Player awards, when disaster struck on a January night in 1958. He was driving to his Long Island home in the early hours of the morning when his borrowed car skidded on a slippery spot in the road and slammed into a utility pole. The two broken vertebrae he suffered doomed him to a long and excruciatingly painful period of recovery and rehabilitation, not to mention lifelong confinement to a wheelchair.

On May 7, 1959, before a crowd of 93,103 fans at the Los Angeles Coliseum, the Dodgers and the Yankees met in a mammoth benefit for the paralyzed Campanella. It was an emotional affair, rivaling similar tributes to Yankee greats Gehrig and Ruth at Yankee Stadium.

The courage Campanella displayed in his rehabilitation was an inspiration to many others who suffered severe spinal injuries. He received baseball's highest honor in 1969—election to the Hall of Fame.

Mike Pazik, a lefthander from Lynn, Mass., who appeared briefly for Minnesota in 1975, 1976, and 1977, saw his pitching career terminated when he suffered multiple fractures of both legs in a 1977 automobile accident. He returned to the game in 1980 as a coach for the White Sox. Later, he served four years as a roving pitching instructor for the Milwaukee Brewers, and then in late 1987 he was named pitching coach for Charlotte of the Double-A Southern League.

Houston righthander J. R. Richard, at 6'8" and 222 pounds, was an intimidating figure on the mound. From 1976 through 1979, his strikeout log showed 214, 214, 303, and 313, respectively, while his victories totaled 74. In 1980, even though slowed by arm and shoulder injuries, he was chosen to start for the National League in the All-Star Game at Los Angeles. But, as fate would have it, he was to pitch just two more innings for the Astros before being laid low by a stroke. The rehabilitation was painfully slow, but there always seemed to be hope that his career could be salvaged, but such hopes proved to be futile. Twice (in 1982 and 1983) he tried to pitch in the lower minors, but the illness had taken too great a toll.

In 1988, while with the San Francisco Giants, lefty Dave Dravecky developed a cancerous growth on his pitching arm. An operation and a long recuperation followed. He tried to come back in 1989, but in a late-season game against Montreal his pitching arm broke as he was delivering a pitch. Subsequently his arm was amputated, bringing to an end a once promising career. His major league record was 64–57 with an ERA of 3.13.

First baseman Nick Esasky enjoyed a career year with the Boston Red Sox in 1989, with 30 home runs and 108 RBIs. He then signed a lucrative free agent contract with the Atlanta Braves. During spring training he began to suffer from vertigo. He played only nine regular season games in 1990 before being disabled. His failure to recover baffled a horde of medical experts. He did not play at all in 1991, tried to come back in '92, but was eventually released by the Braves.

Bo Jackson of the Kansas City Royals was one of the most exciting players to hit the majors in years. He could run, throw, field, and hit with power. He was also a superstar in football and that proved to be his downfall. An innocent-looking sideline tackle while he was playing for the Los Angeles Raiders in 1990 resulted in a serious hip injury. Released by the Royals, he was given another chance by the White Sox in 1991. He played in only 23 late-season games, batting .225 with three home runs. His hip continued to deteriorate and eventually had to be surgically replaced. He did not play at all in 1992, but, miraculously, returned to action in 1993, playing the entire season for the White Sox, mainly as a designated hitter, then in 1994 signed and played with the California Angels.

Careers cut short for psychological reasons are not common, but there have been a few. Steve Blass, hero of the 1971 Pittsburgh World Series victory over Baltimore and winner of 19 games in 1972, suddenly could not throw strikes. So severe was the mental block that his baseball life ended in 1974 when he was only thirty-two. Kevin Saucier, a lefthanded relief pitcher for Detroit, had 13 saves and 4 wins in 1981; then, inexplicably, he developed the Steve Blass syndrome and could not throw strikes. In his case it was a fear of hitting and injuring a batter. He could not overcome the problem, and at twenty-six he was out of baseball. Joe Cowley, who pitched for the Braves, Yankees, White Sox, and Phillies, and who has a no-hit game to his credit, simply could not throw strikes and was sent to the minors by the Phillies in 1987.

He could not throw strikes there either and finally was sent home.

At least one career came to a premature end because of a fear of flying. Jackie Jensen, who hit 199 home runs in eleven seasons with the Yankees, Senators, and Red Sox, retired first in 1959, tried again in 1961, but then quit for good at the age of thirty-four.

It was on July 30, 1991, eleven years to the day on which J. R. Richard of the Houston Astros was hit by a massive stroke, that twenty-eight-year-old Jeff Gray, Boston Red Sox pitcher, met the same fate. Stricken while sitting in front of his locker at Fenway Park, suddenly he was unable to walk, talk, or grip a baseball. After two years of excruciating rehabilitation, in which he had to relearn almost every normal activity, he even reached the point of being able to pitch with some authority, although not at his former level. In 1994 he was named a minor league pitching coach by the Red Sox.

Alcohol and Drugs

It is impossible to put a number on the baseball careers shortened or adversely affected by the excessive use of alcohol. In at least four cases (Delahanty, Koenecke, Morris, and Wilson), dealt with elsewhere in this chapter, fatalities resulted. Countless players of the game's early years were lushes. Liquor was readily available to them, often on the house, and there was plenty of time for carousing, especially when on the road. Some of the worst offenders were quietly blacklisted and faded from the game. Others who were heavy drinkers continued in uniform, because they were star players and the owners winked at their alcoholic escapades. Future Hall of Famer Michael "King" Kelly, for example, drank as hard as he played; yet in 1887 Boston paid an unheard of $10,000 to Chicago for his contract. Toward the end of his career, he opened a saloon in New York, which was like putting the fox in charge of the chicken coop. His performance level deteriorated rapidly, and by 1894 he was in the minors. That fall he developed pneumonia, and on November 8 he died at the age of thirty-six.

Terry Larkin, who won 29 games for Hartford in 1877, and 29 and 31, respectively, for Chicago in 1878 and 1879, was another nineteenth-century player whose career self-destructed from the ravages of strong drink. In 1883, while drunk, he shot his wife (she recovered) and then tried to commit suicide in jail. In 1886, while employed as a bartender in Brooklyn, he showed up for work with two pistols and challenged his employer to a duel. Police were called and he was thrown into jail until he sobered up. He died in Brooklyn in 1894.

Equally melancholy is the story of James (The Troy Terrier) Egan, who pitched, caught and played the outfield for Troy (NL) in 1882 and then was blacklisted for drunkenness. Supposedly rehabilitated, he was given a chance with Brooklyn (AA) in 1884, but before he played a game he was arrested for theft and jailed. He died of what was described as "brain fever" in a New Haven, Connecticut, jail, September 26, 1884.

Few players have come to the majors with more raw talent than Louis Sockalexis, a Penobscot Indian from Old Towne, Maine. He played college baseball at both Holy Cross and Notre Dame. While at the latter school in

1897, he and a companion broke up an establishment run by a certain "Popcorn Jennie" and threw the furniture out the windows. When the good fathers who ran Notre Dame read about this caper in the *South Bend Tribune,* they promptly threw him out. Future major league catcher Mike Powers, who had been instrumental in getting Sockalexis into both Holy Cross and Notre Dame, wired the Cleveland Club, with whom the Indian had signed a contract to take effect at the end of the school year, and suggested it send someone to South Bend to bail him out. Manager Patsy Tebeau caught the next train west, and in a few days Sockalexis was in a Cleveland uniform. He impressed with his strength, speed, and magnificent arm. In later years, both John McGraw and Hughie Jennings said he was the greatest natural talent they had ever seen. Even allowing for the hyperbole that often accompanies such reminiscence, it is apparent that he was a player of exceptional ability. But just as exceptional was his appetite for strong drink. Frequently interrupted by binges and injuries (once he jumped from a second-floor window and severely injured an ankle), his major league career was limited to 94 games in three seasons.

Sockalexis died in Burlington, Maine, on December 24, 1913, at the age of forty-two. His baseball monument is not his .313 batting average but the Cleveland Indians baseball club, which was nicknamed after him.

Hall of Famer Rube Waddell gained almost as much notoriety for his drinking as he did recognition for his pitching. Lowell Reidenbaugh, in his *Cooperstown,* tells how Waddell would come into a bar, penniless, and whisper to the bartender, "Give me a drink, and I will give you the ball I used to defeat Cy Young in twenty innings." According to Reidenbaugh, hundreds of bartenders "displayed what they considered to be the historic souvenir."

Despite the abuse he gave his body, the Rube lasted for thirteen major league seasons and won 191 games. But his indiscretions led to tuberculosis and he died in San Antonio, Texas, on April Fool's Day, 1914, at the age of thirty-seven.

Waddell contemporary Arthur (Bugs) Raymond was not the pitcher the Rube was, but he was his equal in the drinking department. The efforts of Giant manager John McGraw to rein him in are a part of the lore and legend of baseball. Raymond finally became so uncontrollable that the Giants let him go in the spring of 1912. Later that year Raymond, while drunk, was watching a sandlot game in Chicago when a spectator picked up a broken piece of pottery and threw it, hitting Raymond in the face. A fight ensued in which Raymond was badly beaten up. He went back to his hotel room, where six days later he died of a cerebral hemorrhage, caused by a skull fracture. He was only thirty years old. One former teammate said of him, "Bugs paid too much too soon for too many drinks."

The problem of alcoholism continues in the modern game, but added to it is an affliction even more virulent— the use of illegal drugs. Careers are being shortened or interrupted by excessive drinking or the ingestion of drugs, or by a combination of both. In the old days, when a player drank too much, he was either shunted aside or his problem was swept under the rug. Now, the usual pattern is a confession of the problem, or exposure, followed by treatment, rehabilitation, sometimes suspension, but then a return to the game.

In 1983 the baseball world was rocked by the news that four players on the Kansas City Royals—Willie Wilson, Willie Aikens, Jerry Martin, and Vida Blue (no longer with the team)—had been involved with illegal drugs. All were suspended for one year by Commissioner Bowie Kuhn, although later an arbitrator reduced the suspensions, except for Blue's. Meanwhile, indictments were handed down and all were convicted and sentenced to one year in jail, with the last nine months suspended. Eventually Wilson returned to the Royals. Aikens was traded to Toronto but then went to the minors. Martin and Blue are out of baseball.

Pitcher Steve Howe of the Los Angeles Dodgers was suspended for the 1984 season for alleged drug use and did not challenge it. After at least two relapses, he was signed by the Texas Rangers and appeared for them late in the 1987 season. He was out of baseball in '88 and '89, but made a comeback in 1991 and eventually worked himself up to a prominent place in the New York Yankee bullpen. After his conviction in 1992 in Kalispell, Montana, for drug possession, he was barred from baseball "for life" by Commissioner Fay Vincent, but was given yet another chance to play in 1993, by virtue of a ruling by an arbitrator. He pitched the entire season for the Yankees, with spotty results, and presumably passed all his required blood tests. In 1994 he became the ace of the Yankee bullpen.

Atlanta pitcher Pascual Perez spent three months in a Dominican Republic jail on drug charges during the 1983–1984 off-season and was also suspended by Commissioner Kuhn. Arbitrator Richard I. Bloch, who had also ruled in the Willie Wilson et al. cases, subsequently threw out the Perez suspension because of lack of evidence.

Also in 1983, pitcher Dickie Noles of the Cubs spent time in jail after a drunken brawl in Cincinnati. Outfielder Ron LeFlore was arrested on drug and weapons charges in 1982 while with the Chicago White Sox. Although found not guilty, he was released by the Sox in April 1983.

Bob Welch, talented righthanded pitcher of the Dodgers, best remembered for his classic confrontation with Reggie Jackson of the Yankees in the 1978 World Series, revealed that he had been an alcoholic for many years. After rehabilitation and relegation to the minors, he returned to the Dodgers in 1986 and Oakland two years later. He has written a book about his experiences, *Five O'Clock Comes Early*.

A much-publicized drug trial that began in Pittsburgh on September 5, 1985, exposed the drug involvement of numerous players, including Keith Hernandez of the Mets (formerly with the Cardinals) and Dave Parker of the Reds (formerly with the Pirates). After the trial, Commissioner Peter Ueberroth meted out penalties to twenty-one players, ranging from heavy fines to be paid to drug prevention programs, orders to participate in random drug testing, and the performance of drug-related community service.

The shocking disclosures of widespread drug use that came out of the 1985 trial and the severe penalties that followed seemed to have a favorable impact on the drug problem, but did not eliminate it entirely. In 1986 San Diego pitcher LaMarr Hoyt, a Cy Young Award winner in 1983 when he was with the White Sox, was arrested three times on drug-related charges, and after the third was sentenced to forty-five days in federal prison. Hoyt's suspension from baseball was later overturned, and he was ordered reinstated with back pay, much to the dismay of the baseball hierarchy.

Hoyt then signed with his old club, the Chicago White Sox, but his troubles were far from over. He tested positive for cocaine three times in October 1987, and then on December 4 he was arrested in his Columbia, S.C., apartment and charged with intent to distribute cocaine and marijuana. He was convicted the following year and sentenced to one year in prison. How widespread has been the use of illegal drugs by major league players? In a recent book, *Baseball Babylon*, author Dan Gutman lists eighty-three players who have been so involved, including such superstars as Dwight Gooden and Darryl Strawberry, whose problems surfaced again in 1994.

The list of tragedies and shortened careers has been a long one and sad. It has included paragons and playboys, teetotalers and tosspots, the great, the near-great, and the never-were; some who self-destructed and many more who were simply the victims of the cruelest of bad luck. However classified, for each player the hypothetical question remains: Had his tragedy not occurred, what might have been?

Careers Shortened by Blacklisting or Expulsion

Listed below, but not discussed in this chapter, are players blacklisted or expelled from baseball for gambling, dishonest play (or knowledge of same), criminal activity, or, in one case—that of Ray Fisher—violation of a contract. The players involved in the 1877 Louisville and 1919 Chicago White Sox scandals, all of whom were barred for life, are grouped; the others are listed alphabetically:

1877 Louisville players   Bill Craver, Jim Devlin, George Hall, Al Nichols.
1919 Chicago White Sox players   Eddie Cicotte, Oscar Felsch, Chick Gandil, Joe Jackson, Fred McMullin, Swede Risberg, Buck Weaver, Claude Williams.
Others   George Bechtel, Rube Benton (who was later reinstated and returned to the majors), Hal Chase, Cozy Dolan, Phil Douglas, Jean Dubuc (who returned as a coach with Detroit in 1931), Ray Fisher, Joe Gedeon, Claude Hendrix, Richard Higham (umpire), Benny Kauff, Hubert Leonard, Lee Magee, Jimmy O'Connell, Eugene Paulette, Pete Rose, Heinie Zimmerman. [Former major leaguers banned from baseball for their activities in the minor leagues include Babe Borton, Gene Dale, Jess Levan, Harl Maggert, Tom Seaton and Joe Tipton.]

## CHAPTER 10

Relief Pitching Strategy, 1952-92

Bill Felber

Three decades, three ballgames, three managers, three late-inning leads; three different decisions. Which manager made the right choices? September 7, 1952: Steve Gromek, pitching for the Cleveland Indians against the St. Louis Browns, completes seven innings in possession of a two-run, 3-1 lead. His manager, Al Lopez, sends Gromek out to start the final two innings in search of the complete-game victory.

September 7, 1972: Twenty years later to the day, Atlanta Braves rookie Jimmy Freeman also takes a two-run, 3-1 lead into the eighth inning against the Los Angeles Dodgers. Freeman's manager, Eddie Mathews, sends him back out to the mound, but he also warms up Ron Schueler in the event of trouble.

September 7, 1992: Another twenty years later, the Milwaukee Brewers hold a two-run lead over Cleveland after seven innings on the strength of four-hit pitching by rookie phenom Cal Eldred. His manager, Phil Garner, lifts Eldred before the start of the eighth, turning the game over to his setup man, Jeff Austin, and then at the start of the ninth to his closer, Doug Henry.

Which manager made the right decision? If the criteria for judging success is winning the game, then all three did. In 1952, Gromek completed his 3-1 victory without incident and without aid; in 1972, Freeman pitched a scoreless eighth, allowed a leadoff baserunner in the ninth and gave way to Schueler, who preserved the two-run win; and in 1992 both Austin and Henry pitched incident-free innings as the Brewers proceeded to shut out the Indians 2-0.

Three generations, three methods of bullpen use or nonuse, all equally successful. Although the styles managers employ to wrap up victories have changed over the decades—and although the salaries paid to relief pitchers have changed even more—the results have not. Major league teams today blow late-inning leads at almost precisely the same frequency they did twenty and even forty years ago, when there was no such thing as a closer or setup man, bullpens were commonly refuges for failed starters, and managers signaled for relief help only at the moment of absolute peril.

That assertion will probably surprise a generation of fans brought up on the theories of Tony LaRussa. His widely praised and ultrastructured Oakland pen—a lefty specialist, a righty specialist, and a setup man, all leading up to the closer (who starts the ninth inning any time his team leads by three runs or less) has become the model for virtually every major league team. Today, a major league manager is second-guessed if he doesn't do what Phil Garner did on that September day in 1992, pull a starting pitcher after seven innings no matter that he may be pitching a shutout.

Defying those widely held perceptions is a study of every game played in the major leagues during three complete seasons in which managers employed distinctly different bullpen usage patterns. In terms of victories (and winning or losing is all that concerns us in baseball), the eighth-inning and ninth-inning strategies of the 1990s represent no advance whatsoever upon those of the 1970s . . . or the 1950s.

The following table shows the percentage frequency with which teams won when they held the lead in each situation in 1952, 1972, and 1992.

	1952	1972	1992
Led by one run after seven innings	80.5	77.1	79.3
Led by two runs after seven innings	86.6	90.1	89.7
Led by three runs after seven innings	93.0	95.9	94.4
Led by one run after eight innings	89.1	89.4	85.3
Led by two runs after eight innings	95.1	95.5	95.5
Led by three runs after eight innings	95.0	97.8	97.5

In every instance, the differences are a matter of a couple of percentage points at most, and not statistically meaningful. The differences do not offer evidence that one usage pattern provides better results than another.

Take note that this is a study of the effectiveness of various strategies relating to bullpen use as they impact on teams that lead in the late innings of major league games. Accordingly, its focus is entirely on pitching changes that occurred in major league games after the final out was recorded in the seventh inning. It should not necessarily be inferred, in cases where no pitching change was made in the eighth or ninth innings, that the pitcher who continued on the mound was the starter. In some cases, pitching changes may have been made prior to the eighth inning. Since the study's focus is on use of the bullpen in the eighth and ninth innings, any earlier changes were not considered as part of the data.

Summary of Conclusions

Here is a summary of the conclusions drawn from the study.

1. There is no statistically significant evidence supporting the idea that the modern concept of a specialized bullpen—a save specialist, a setup man, and lefty-righty specialists—contributes to winning baseball games more frequently than other bullpen usage patterns that have been tried in previous years.

2. The clearest finding is that, contrary to what would appear to be the accepted notion, a highly structured bullpen—one in which roles are defined and adhered to in a reasonably rigid fashion—provides a team with no advantage. As a general proposition, teams with a highly structured bullpen lose late-inning leads in roughly the same proportion as teams of previous eras that had no structured system.

3. As a corollary to this, modern teams that invest heavily in "ensemble" bullpens or in "closers" (or in both) tend to lose leads at roughly the same percentage as modern teams that spend less money on bullpens, or closers, or both—particularly in the National League.

4. As an additional corollary, the evidence is substantial that a significant increase in the number of saves recorded in 1992 compared with previously studied seasons is wholly reflexive and gratuitous, and provides the saving team no actual advantage in the standings. The pitchers who accumulate these gratuitous saves, however, cost the average major league team in excess of $2 million in 1992.

5. This would seem to suggest that the value of a highly paid, structured bullpen, complete with a multimillion dollar "saver," is merely imitative and cosmetic.

Methodology

The study was conducted by examining box scores from games played in 1992, 1972, and 1952. These seasons provide contrast both across time and in the generally accepted patterns of bullpen use.

At the time the study was conducted, 1992 was the most recent season for which box score data was readily available. In 1992 managers generally employed a rigid system for bullpen work: one reliever was identified as the closer, another as the setup man, another as the lefty specialist, another as the "middle reliever," etc.; a manager assumed that his starting pitcher would not finish the game.

In 1972 bullpen roles were evolving, but not yet rigid; the concept of a closer (as opposed to the earlier "fireman," who was summoned in times of trouble) was in its early stages. There were a few—Sparky Lyle and Mike Marshall come to mind—but they tended to pitch under less rigid rules than the modern closer. They might commonly pitch three or four innings, and might enter a game while trailing. Beyond that, several teams did not yet utilize either a "closer" or a structured bullpen. In 1972, a manager hoped that his starting pitcher would finish the game, but was willing to use his bullpen if necessary.

In 1952, bullpen strategies had only begun to develop. Most teams still viewed relievers as failed starters or journeymen who should be used only as a last resort. Complete games were reasonably common, and only a few teams—the Yankees and Phillies being examples—had developed first-rate relief specialists. In 1952, a manager assumed his starting pitcher would finish the game, and turned to his bullpen only when forced to do so.

For each season, all games were studied in which a "save situation" occurred. A "save situation" was defined, for purposes of this study, as any game in which one team led by three or fewer runs at the end of either seven or eight innings. The studied games were divided into game situations in which a team:

A. led by one run after seven innings
B. led by two runs after seven innings
C. led by three runs after seven innings
D. led by one run after eight innings
E. led by two runs after eight innings
F. led by three runs after eight innings

A calculation was then made of the percentage of times the team that led in each of those situations actually won the game.

Notation was also made as to whether the team that led the game in each situation subsequently changed pitchers. An additional notation was made to determine the statistical correlation between changing pitchers and victories. For each category itemized above, the result was four bits of information concerning the percentage of games in which:

A. a leading team actually won.
B. a leading team changed pitchers.
C. a leading team that changed pitchers won.
D. a leading team that did not change pitchers won.

As described above, a total of 5,534 "save situations" were included in the study. This does not necessarily mean that the study consisted of 5,534 games, since a single game could theoretically have offered save situations—and in practice, numerous games did—after both the seventh and eighth innings.

Unknowns and Rule Changes

There was one major rules change over the course of the study that theoretically could have affected the results. This was imposition of the designated hitter rule in the American League in 1973. To determine whether there was any real impact, the games of 1992 were divided according to whether they were played in the American League, where the DH was in place, or the National League, where it was not. Theoretically, if the DH impacted the study, it seems logical that there would have been a greater percentage of lost leads in the American League than in the National League. In fact, the opposite was true: in 1992, National League teams lost 136 leads in "save situations," while American League teams lost 104. The DH rule seems not to have been a factor.

Several other factors of potential import are difficult if not impossible to quantify. Here is a summary of them.

A. *Improvement in the relative performance of players over the course of the study.* In the mid-1980s, Dick Cramer conducted a study in which he demonstrated that the performance of the average major league player had gradually improved over the course of years. His study, which included the years 1952 and 1972, showed that in order to equate batting averages for the years 1952 and 1972, it was necessary to adjust them upwards by approximately .039 in the American League, and .017 in the National League. There is no data measuring whether that trend has continued into 1992. Beyond that, it is not demonstrated that improvement in relative batting average necessarily equates to an overall improvement in the relative quality of the batters, since average is only one component of batting ability. It is also not possible to assert with certainty whether—and if so, to what degree—pitchers and fielders may have improved over time, although the commonly held view is that they have.

B. *Quality of starting pitching.* We know that starters pitched more innings in 1952 than in 1972, and more in 1972 than in 1992, but we do not know whether this is because the starting pitchers as a group were better in the earlier years. The study presents evidence supporting the theory that at least a substantial proportion of the falloff in starters' innings is a result of simple managerial reflex. League ERAs are roughly equivalent for the study years, but those do not necessarily measure starter quality either. Between 1952 and 1992, the four-man rotation has generally given way to the five-man rotation. If anything, however, that should argue that the starters of today should be better rested and more fit to complete their assignments than in previous years. Several new pitches have come into vogue—the slider and the split-fingered fastball especially—and it is possible that those pitches could create additional strain on pitchers' arms that did not exist in 1952 or 1972. However, the evidence arguing for or against any of these possibilities is anecdotal.

C. *Race.* This final nonquantifiable factor must be acknowledged. By 1952, baseball had been integrated. Yet not all major league teams had been integrated, and the inclusion of minority talent was not nearly as complete as it would become. Plainly, the broadening of the player talent pool over the course of intervening years has improved the general quality of on-field talent. It is theoretically possible that this broadening of talent could be a factor impacting on the ability of modern teams to hold leads over late innings at a rate no greater than earlier teams. While this is a fair topic for speculation, however, I believe the evidence suggests this theory cannot be used to deduce that 1952 teams, for example, would have held late leads at a rate greater than occurs today. By 1972, the major leagues already could be viewed as fully integrated. If the higher proportion of African Americans in the major leagues' racial makeup were properly isolated as a factor, those improvements should have shown up in the performance of teams in 1972 relative to 1952. Yet the data for 1972 is approximately the same as for both 1952 and 1992.

The Hemline Effect

For practical purposes, this two-generations-in-the-making shift in patterns of bullpen use can be compared to periodic and whimsical changes in dress hemlines: A lot of money is spent, but the gain is in the eye of the beholder. Note the lack of difference in how well an "average" team held leads in each of the years that were examined:

Up one after seven	W	L	Pct.
1952	12.94	3.13	.805
1992	14.42	3.77	.793
1972	14.46	4.29	.771

Up two after seven	W	L	Pct.
1952	12.46	1.38	.901
1992	12.38	1.42	.897
1972	12.19	1.88	.866

Up three after seven	W	L	Pct.
1952	9.67	0.42	.959
1992	10.31	0.62	.944
1972	9.12	0.69	.930

Up one after eight	W	L	Pct.
1952	14.75	1.75	.894
1992	13.31	1.63	.891
1972	14.54	2.50	.853

Up two after eight	W	L	Pct.
1952	14.29	0.67	.955
1992	13.08	0.61	.955
1972	12.38	0.63	.951

Up three after eight	W	L	Pct.
1972	11.29	0.25	.978
1992	11.92	0.31	.975
1952	9.44	0.50	.950

Although managers did not derive greater benefit from their bullpen in 1992 than in previous seasons, they clearly relied on it to a far greater extent. In 1952, managers who led by one run after eight innings went to their bullpen only 17.1 percent of the time. By 1972, this figure had risen to 29.0 percent. In 1992, however, managers who led by one run after eight innings went to their bullpen a whopping 66.1 percent of the time . . . while winning 4 percent less often.

An even more clear example of this trend to reflexive bullpen use is seen in the category of games in which a team led by three runs after eight innings. In 1952, managers in that situation called for a reliever only 21.4 percent of the time; by 1972, that percentage had actually fallen fractionally, to 21.3 percent. In 1992, however, managers of teams that led by three runs after eight innings went to their bullpen 54.7 percent of the time. They could hardly have achieved a significantly greater winning percentage, since teams in that advantageous position won 95.1 percent of the time in 1952, and 95.5 percent of the time in 1972. In fact, in 1992 teams that led by three runs after eight innings also won 95.5 percent of the time.

Money for Nothing

If the question were only the inability of modern-day closers to outperform old-time starters in holding late-inning leads, the findings would be amusing, but nothing more. Today, however, most teams invest millions of dollars on the assumption that having a first-rate bullpen and an expert "saver" is important. If that assumption is not valid, then those millions are essentially wasted. With specific respect to 1992, a comparison of the results of the study with the major league standings and with the salaries paid to major league players yields data relative to this point. For example:

In 1992 the average major league team devoted 17.17 percent of its total payroll to its bullpen. (*Note*: For all payroll issues, "bullpen" is defined as any pitcher who made more than one-half of his appearances during 1992 in relief.) This figure is based on payroll reports published in *USA Today*. Because comparable payrolls for previous years (1972 and 1952) are not available, it is impossible to know whether this represents a greater investment in bullpen than has historically been the case. Informally, however, it seems certain that 1952 teams did not invest an equal percentage of their payroll in relievers, and it also seems unlikely that 1972 teams did. It would contribute to the study if comparable data could be located.

The average salary of the highest-paid reliever on each major league team in 1992 was $2,203,846. Although it would seem logical that the highest paid reliever was the staff ace, this was frequently not the case. This may be can be attributed to a predisposition toward long-term contracts, injuries, poor front-office judgment, or changes from previously demonstrated levels of effectiveness.

Moreover, there was no consistent correlation between either the amount paid to a team's best-paid reliever, or to a team's bullpen as a group, and that same team's performance in the late innings of games in which it held a lead. This lack of correlation was especially noteworthy in the National League, where the three teams that invested the least in their bullpen aces ranked as the three best teams in holding late-inning leads. The Montreal Expos ranked third overall in bullpen effectiveness when leading after seven innings despite paying no reliever more than $160,000, and despite committing a mere 7 percent of its total payroll to the bullpen.

Below are the rankings for all NL teams based on percentages of leads that were held at the end of both seven innings and eight innings. The tables show the team and its ranking, the percentage of leads held after the seventh or eighth inning, the salary of the highest paid reliever (and who that reliever was), and the percentage of the total team payroll paid to the bullpen in 1992.

Team	Percent won when led after seven	Best paid reliever, 1992	Percent of payroll to bullpen
Houston	.946	$750,000 (Jones)	15.97
Pittsburgh	.887	$650,000 (Patterson)	6.34
Montreal	.872	$156,000 (Wetteland)	6.96
San Francisco	.868	$3,500,000 (Righetti)	21.69
Atlanta	.860	$2,650,000 (Pena)	11.82
St. Louis	.837	$2,666,667 (L. Smith)	27.83
Cincinnati	.827	$1,400,000 (Dibble)	11.16
New York	.825	$3,333,333 (Franco)	15.29
Chicago	.800	$2,500,000 (D. Smith)	18.38
Los Angeles	.769	$2,575,000 (Howell)	24.34
Philadelphia	.765	$3,200,000 (Williams)	15.73
San Diego	.743	$2,000,000 (Andersen)	14.37

Team	Percent won when led after eight	Best paid reliever, 1992	Percent of payroll to bullpen
Pittsburgh	.959	$650,000 (Patterson)	6.34
Philadelphia	.946	$3,200,000 (Williams)	15.73
Montreal	.935	$156,000 (Wetteland)	6.96
San Francisco	.919	$3,500,000 (Righetti)	21.69
Houston	.917	$750,000 (D Jones)	15.97
Cincinnati	.904	$1,400,000 (Dibble)	11.16
Atlanta	.887	$2,650,000 (Pena)	11.82
Chicago	.886	$2,500,000 (D Smith)	18.38
New York	.872	$3,333,334 (Franco)	15.29
(tie) L.A.	.868	$2,575,000 (Howell)	24.34
(tie) S.D.	.868	$2,000,000 (Andersen)	14.37
St. Louis	.865	$2,666,667 (L Smith)	27.83

The noteworthy aspect of this list is its suggestion of less than astute general managing in the National League. St. Louis, for instance, invested more as a proportion of its payroll in bullpen—27.83 percent—than any other major league team, and was the worst at

holding leads after eight innings. The situation in Los Angeles was much the same. In the cases of half the teams—San Diego, Cincinnati, Pittsburgh, San Francisco, Chicago, and Los Angeles—the highest paid reliever was not even the top saver. Los Angeles got four saves out of Howell, Chicago got none out of Dave Smith, and San Diego got two out of Larry Andersen. Montreal and Pittsburgh, on the other hand, spent virtually nothing on bullpens and wound up with two of the three most effective pens in the league after both the seventh and eighth innings. Atlanta won the National League pennant with a bullpen that ranked in the middle of the National League in holding late leads.

Here is the data for the American League in 1992:

Team	Percent won when led after seven	Best paid reliever, 1992	Percent of payroll to bullpen
Kansas City	.976	2,410,000 (Montgomery)	26.13
Toronto	.939	3,366,667 (Henke)	26.45
Oakland	.936	3,000,000 (Eckersley)	12.61
Cleveland	.923	300,000 (Olin)	14.01
Milwaukee	.914	2,766,000 (Plesac)	18.19
California	.897	3,125,000 (Harvey)	20.66
Baltimore	.894	1,450,000 (Olson)	25.90
Seattle	.888	800,000 (Schooler)	8.61
Detroit	.882	2,437,500 (Henneman)	24.20
New York	.872	2,400,000 (Farr)	20.40
Minnesota	.854	2,133,333 (Aguilera)	11.99
Boston	.850	2,633,000 (Reardon)	23.40
Chicago	.824	2,500,000 (Thigpen)	18.38
Texas	.810	2,600,000 (Russell)	10.38

Team	Percent won when led after eight	Best paid reliever, 1992	Percent of payroll to bullpen
Kansas City	1.000	2,410,000 (Montgomery)	26.13
Oakland	.978	3,000,000 (Eckersley)	12.61
Toronto	.977	3,366,667 (Henke)	26.45
Detroit	.969	2,437,000 (Henneman)	24.20
Milwaukee	.953	2,766,000 (Plesac)	18.19
(tie) N.Y.	.947	2,400,000 (Farr)	20.40
(tie) Cal.	.947	3,125,000 (Harvey)	20.66
Seattle	.941	800,000 (Schooler)	8.61
Boston	.933	2,633,000 (Reardon)	23.40
(tie) Texas	.915	2,600,000 (Russell)	10.38
(tie) Balt.	.915	1,450,000 (Olson)	25.90
Cleveland	.898	300,000 (Olin)	14.01
Chicago	.877	2,500,000 (Thigpen)	13.57
Minnesota	.860	2,133,333 (Aguilera)	11.99

As a general proposition, American League bullpens performed more in line with both pay and with their place in the standings than did National League teams. The two pennant winners, for example, ranked in the top three in bullpen efficiency after both seven and eight innings. Toronto spent a high proportion of its payroll on bullpen . . . but Toronto won the world championship. On the other hand, Kansas City spent about as much proportionally as Toronto, got an even better performance from its bullpen—the best in the majors, in fact—but still finished fifth in the AL West. The Kansas City anomaly is likely explained by the fact that management simply overinvested in relief pitching, to the neglect of other parts of its team.

What is the actual impact on the standings of these percentage discrepancies between teams? Here is a brief division-by-division look at the standings, with columns noting the number of leads lost after both the seventh inning and eighth inning *greater than the number of leads lost by the best club in the division in this category* (GBL stands for Games Behind Leader).

American League West

Kansas City achieved the best record in terms of holding leads after the seventh inning, on the basis of 41 victories in 42 opportunities. Texas achieved the worst percentage on the basis of a record of 34-8. That translates to a gain for Kansas City of 7 full games over Texas in the standings. More pertinently, Oakland, which won the AL West, achieved its .936 percentage of leads held after seven innings on the basis of a record of 44-3, which was 3.5 games better in that category than the actual second-place team, Minnesota (41-7, .854.). Oakland won the pennant by 6 games. When leading after eight innings, Oakland was 44-1 in 1992, while Minnesota was 37-6, six games worse. (The figures cannot be read cumulatively, since many games qualify for inclusion in the tables regarding both seventh-inning and eighth-inning performance.)

Team	W-L	GBL-7	GBL-8
Oakland	96-66	2	1
Minnesota	90-72	6	6
Chicago	86-76	8	7
Texas	77-85	7	4
Kansas City	72-90	—	—
California	72-90	3	2
Seattle	64-98	3	2

American League East

In the AL East, Toronto won the pennant by 4 games over Milwaukee, and also had a superior percentage in holding leads after seven innings. In this case, however, the figures must be analyzed more closely. Toronto's record in such games was 46-3, Milwaukee's was 32-3, nominally 7 games worse, but actually the equal of Toronto's in blown wins. The Brewers were done in by their failure to get in position to hold a late lead as often as the Blue Jays did. The statistics evened out after eight innings: Toronto's record of 43-1 was only slightly better than Milwaukee's 41-2 . . . a difference of 1.5 games in the standings. The difference between the best (Kansas City, 42-0) and worst (Minnesota, 37-6) teams was 5½ games. Again, however, it should be noted that the Royals—who devoted double the percentage of their payroll to bullpen that the Twins did—finished 18 games behind them in the actual standings.

Team	W-L	GBL-7	GBL-8
Toronto	96-66	—	—
Milwaukee	92-70	—	1
Baltimore	89-73	2	3
Cleveland	76-86	—	4
New York	76-86	3	1
Detroit	75-87	1	—
Boston	73-89	3	2

National League East

In the National League East, Pittsburgh's bullpen consistently performed at the best level. That is appropriate to the Pirates' pennant winning status, if not indicative of their spending priorities, since Pittsburgh devoted only 6.34 percent of its payroll to bullpen, the lowest figure in the majors. The impact in the standings, however, was much less significant. When leading after seven innings, Pittsburgh won 47 of 53 games for an .887 percentage; Philadelphia, which had the worst performance in that category in the National League East, lost only two more games (26-8) in which the Phils led after seven. But the Philly bullpen—cursed by a weaker offense—got 19 fewer chances than the Pirate staff. The picture was almost identical after eight innings: Pittsburgh's record of 47-2 compares favorably with Philadelphia's record of 35-2 except in opportunities.

Team	W-L	GBL-7	GBL-8
Pittsburgh	96-66	—	—
Montreal	87-75	—	1
St. Louis	83-79	1	3
Chicago	78-84	3	3
New York	72-90	1	3
Philadelphia	70-92	2	—

National League West

Houston's bullpen outperformed all others in the NL West in holding leads. The Astros' superiority was especially evident in leads held after seven innings; at .946, they ranked best by far in the National League and second best (behind Kansas City) in the majors. San Francisco, with the single highest-paid reliever (Dave Righetti) and the third highest proportion of bullpen pay to overall pay in the majors, got the second best performance. Both of these teams, however, finished in the second division of the standings. Atlanta, which won the pennant, ranked in the middle of the division in bullpen performance. Los Angeles, with the second-highest proportion of bullpen pay to overall pay, had the second-worst bullpen in the division (and league), ahead of only San Diego.

Team	W-L	GBL-7	GBL-8
Atlanta	98-64	6	3
Cincinnati	90-72	7	2
San Diego	82-80	7	2
Houston	81-81	—	—
San Francisco	72-90	3	—
Los Angeles	63-99	7	2

Six teams paid at least one reliever $3 million or more during 1992, thus forming an "elite" group. How did these six teams' bullpens perform? They ranged from very good to very poor, but on average were only slightly above the norms. Here are the six teams, along with their major league ranking for holding leads after the seventh and eighth innings:

Team	Rank, holding leads after seven	Rank, holding leads after eight
Toronto	3rd	3rd
Oakland	4th	2nd
California	7th	T-7th
San Francisco	14th	13th
Philadelphia	25th	9th
New York Mets	20th	22nd

The Gratuitous Save

In 1992, relief pitchers were credited with 1,109 major league saves. In 1972, the total was 733. In 1952, the total was 306. How do we account for this increase, which amounts to about 200 percent over four decades and roughly 50 percent since 1972?

First, more major league games were played in 1992 than there were in either of the previous years: 2,106 in 1992 compared with 1,859 in 1972 (a strike-shortened year) and 1,239 in 1952. But even a 70 percent increase in games played since 1952 accounts for less than half the 200 percent increase in saves. A 13 percent increase in games played since 1972 accounts for only a small proportion of the 50 percent increase in saves since that year.

Theoretically, teams might simply be playing more "close" games than in previous years, resulting in more save opportunities. But that is demonstrably not so; here is the data for average number of "save opportunity" games played per team in each of the studied years:

Year	Games led by three or fewer after seven	Games led by three or fewer after eight
1992	43	43
1972	42.5	43
1952	40	38

If close games are not being played with greater frequency, and if the schedule does not provide an answer, how, then, do we account for the increase in saves? It seems likely that the preponderance of these additional saves were credited in situations where the reliever was not actually needed. To determine the number of gratuitous saves awarded today, we first must determine a baseline number of saves that might be expected to be earned by a pitcher in any year.

In attempting to determine a baseline for saves, we can use the following facts and assumptions:

1. We can assume that in 1952 managers seldom used "savers" in cases other than actual necessity, and often enough not even then. "Actual necessity" is defined here as that point at which the game is in imminent danger of being lost.

2. We can assume that by approximately 1972, managers more readily used "savers", and did so in most if not all cases of relative necessity. "Relative necessity" is that point at which it is foreseeable that a game could be lost, although the game may not actually be imperiled.

3. Based on complete-game statistics, we can assume that in 1972 managers had not yet begun to employ the strategy of using relievers in preventative roles; that is, bringing a designated 'saver" into the game at the start of the ninth inning.

4. We know that in 1952, Al Brazle led the major leagues in saves with 16. We also know that the average major league team accumulated approximately 19 saves that season. We know that in 1972, Clay Carroll led the major leagues with 37 saves, and the average major league team accumulated 30.5 saves.

5. We know that the number of "save opportunities" per team has increased by about five since 1952—a factor that encompasses the lengthened schedule—but has not increased since 1972, despite changes in the scoring rule for crediting a save that came into the game in 1973 and 1975.

6. We know that teams blow leads in save opportunities with about the same frequency today that they did in 1952 and 1972.

In the context of the above facts and assumptions, we may thus deduce that the baseline figure for legitimate saves lies somewhere close to the actual save figures for 1972—that is, approximately 37 saves for the top saver, and approximately 30 saves for the average team.

That being the case, any significant number of saves earned by the best reliever in excess of 37, and any significant number of saves earned by the average staff in excess of about 30, may fairly be considered as probably gratuitous in the context of winning ballgames.

What's So Great About Being MVP?

The record of Dennis Eckersley in 1992 provides perhaps the best illustration of the concept of a "gratuitous save." In that year, Eckersley won the Cy Young and Most Valuable Player awards for appearing in 69 games and earning 51 saves for the Oakland A's. Let's take a look at those 51 saves.

A. To earn 7 of those saves, Eckersley protected a one-run lead for one inning. In an additional 3 games, he protected a one-run lead for 1.1 to 2 innings. In each of these games, he faced at least the tying run, and may theoretically—from the box scores we cannot always be certain—have had the tying run on base when he entered the game. By any definition, these 10 saves are "quality" saves.

B. To earn 15 of his 51 saves, however, Eckersley was only required to enter the game at the start of the ninth inning and protect a two-run lead. In each of these 15 games, he was not required to face the potential tying run unless he himself put that run on base. In eight of these games, Eckersley replaced a pitcher who had pitched at least one previous scoreless inning. In an additional four games, Eckersley pitched between 1.1 and 2 innings while protecting a two-run lead. Based on an examination of the box scores, it is possible that he faced the potential tying run in a maximum of one of those four games. In all four of those games, he replaced a pitcher who had not been scored upon. Taken together, these 19 games represent at least 18 times Eckersley received a save without ever facing the potential tying run, unless he himself brought it to the plate. In 12 of these 19 games, Eckersley replaced a pitcher who had pitched at least one inning without being scored upon. Many of these 18 to 19 saves, especially the ones in which Eckersley replaced a pitcher who had not been scored upon, might reasonably be characterized as gratuitous.

C. To earn an additional 10 saves, Eckersley pitched one inning or less and protected a three-run lead. In 9 of these games, he entered at the start of the ninth inning, needing only to record three outs before three runs scored in order to get credit for the save. In all of these games, Eckersley replaced a pitcher who had not given up a run in the previous inning. These saves can fairly be characterized as highly gratuitous.

D. To earn his final 12 saves, Eckersley protected a lead of four or five runs for between one-third of an inning and two innings. Recognizing that the lack of information regarding specific on-base situations at the time he entered the games in question makes an absolute judgment impossible, it still seems reasonable to assume that in most of these save situations Eckersley did not have to face the potential tying run unless he himself brought it to bat.

In summary, approximately only a dozen times in his 51 saves did Dennis Eckersley actually face the potential game-tying run. In the high proportion of his saves, perhaps 35 or more, the tying run never left the on-deck circle, and perhaps never left the dugout. In many of them, the pitcher relieved by Eckersley was in neither imminent nor proximate peril. In these situations, the practical impact of bringing Eckersley into the game was more on his save total than on the game. These are "gratuitous saves."

The often gratuitous nature of the save as utilized in 1992 can be illustrated in another way. In 13 of Eckersley's 69 appearances, he allowed one run or more. We might assume that his record in these 13 games was not impressive. In some respects that's an accurate assessment: His earned run average for those 13 games, for instance, was 10.69. Yet his record for those same 13 games was 2 wins, just 1 loss and 8 saves. Based solely on the save data, you would say Eckersley had pitched well over those 13 games. It's plausible that those eight saves, the difference between a 43-save and 51-save season, were also the margin by which he won the MVP and Cy Young Awards.

For forty-plus years, managers have wondered what to do with their bullpens, and have set their sails to the prevailing wind. What they have accomplished leaves fans to wonder.

THE HIGHLIGHTS
OF THE GAME

CHAPTER 11

Streaks and Feats

Jack Kavanagh

The past of baseball is accented by feats of accomplishment. The heroics of individual players or collective efforts of teams are listed in record books as bare statistics. It is the purpose of this section to clothe these with accounts of how such records were made.

These are the achievements of mortals whom we have made into heroes by giving great value to things they have done. Deeds of baseball players are valued more highly than scholarship, skills in creative crafts, or sustaining a precarious balance of world peace. We can name more Cy Young Award winners than we can list those given the Nobel Peace Prize; we can rattle off batting champions but not name holders of the Pulitzer Prize.

It is axiomatic that all records are made to be broken, yet it is wasteful to throw away old records which have been cherished by generations of fans and only replace them with a newly minted line of agate type. Those who have been on the top of the list, or came close to the peak, have been recognized by relying on lists which sustain enough depth to single out the most noteworthy performances in the many categories which are represented.

As the former mayor of New York City, the dapper, perceptive Jimmy Walker, once admonished Babe Ruth when he had fallen from grace in the eyes of fans, "The cheers of yesterday have a short echo."

The Streaks

Most records are, eventually, displaced by new ones. Some survive because the conditions under which they were made have been altered by changing circumstances in baseball. Some, such as the accumulation of sheer totals, are pushed higher. This is not so much a matter of accomplishment as it is of perseverance and lengthened seasons.

Longest Hitting Streaks

Joe DiMaggio's feat of hitting safely in 56 consecutive games is the type of record which is in jeopardy of being broken when each new baseball season begins. It is in jeopardy because every player has the same chance as DiMaggio to hit safely in every game he plays. Stringing enough of these games together to reach the level DiMaggio did in 1941 tests both a player's skill and his nerve.

The way baseball is played has not altered significantly since 1941. That year DiMaggio batted .357. In 1987 Wade Boggs was a threat to topple DiMaggio's record, batting .363. He even temporarily moved into DiMag-

gio's class as a home run hitter, with 24. In 1941 DiMaggio had hit 30. Boggs was also dropped from batting first or second to hitting third. Players with power have a different approach to collecting base hits than did Willie Keeler, whose nineteenth-century record of 44 consecutive games in which he hit safely was broken by Joe DiMaggio. Those with extra-base power are expected to sacrifice the string-extending single for a game-winning home run when the occasion rises. In setting his record, DiMaggio never once bunted for a base hit.

DiMaggio's streak is mind-boggling in its length, yet temptingly attainable by batters capable of hitting for high averages. And any player might get on a hot streak and sustain it long enough to challenge DiMaggio's total. However, those who have set extended streaks did it while accomplishing a high season's average. The trick is to string those games with base hits together. The more games in which a batter has hit safely, the greater the possibility these will come in succession for long stretches.

Until the New York press, wire services, and broadcast industry made Joe DiMaggio's consecutive-game hitting streak a matter of national awareness and interest, this kind of feat was not noted with a daily fanaticism. Streaks drew comment, but this was mostly reserved to be relished during the winter's Hot Stove League sessions among sport-starved fans.

Although Willie Keeler's consecutive-game string became the target for future attempts to exceed it, it might have been only one of the records made under special circumstances. Keeler's 44 consecutive games might only be unusual in retrospect because the string began on Opening Day, 1897. Had Bad Bill Dahlen not had a most peculiar bad day on August 7, 1894, even Joe DiMaggio's 56-game streak would only be a "modern record" set after 1900. As it is, Bill Dahlen appears high on the list with the 42 games in which he hit safely.

DiMaggio was stopped by stellar infield play. Bill Dahlen was stopped by his own inability to fatten his record in a game in which almost everyone else did. Dahlen's team, the Chicago Colts, had 17 hits, winning a ten-inning game from Cincinnati 13–11. Dahlen's blanking was more evident because it was sandwiched between the feats that day of his teammates, Jimmy Ryan and Walter Wilmot. Ryan, the leadoff batter, had five hits, three of them doubles, and Walter Wilmot, who followed Dahlen in the batting order, also had five hits, two of them triples.

Dahlen was at bat a half dozen times, but the Reds' pitchers, Chauncey Fisher and Tom Parrott, found him, uniquely that day, an easy out. Dahlen's feat was obscured when Willie Keeler, a star of greater national awareness, hit safely in 44 games three years later. The eclipsed record was simply noted but not recounted in the detail which was later paid to the strings which exceeded it. Although appearing in 121 games and batting .362, Dahlen was not a regular shortstop at that time, dividing his games between short and third.

It was Keeler's feat which caught the public fancy, particularly as it began on Opening Day, April 22, 1897, and continued for 44 games into the season. He was eventually stopped on June 18. Until then, it seemed he had found an unending series of opportunities to "hit 'em where they ain't"—his simplistic explanation for his base-hit totals. Keeler's record not only stood the test of time until Joe DiMaggio broke it in 1941, it still stands as the National League record, tied only by Pete Rose in 1978.

It wasn't until 1922 that the feat of hitting successfully in successive games became a real target for seekers of new records. Keeler's streak had been regarded more as evidence of his great ability to rap out base hits than as a model of daily consistency. He was a widely admired player, the leadoff batter for the Baltimore Orioles, three times pennant winners prior to the 1897 season.

When Ty Cobb came along, the fact that he nearly equaled Keeler's mark in 1911, when he set an American League record with 40 successive games in which he got at least one hit, was also taken as a sign of his superiority, not necessarily observed as a model event.

But in 1922 the public and press were ready for new records, and they had popular heroes to set them. In 1922 both George Sisler and Rogers Hornsby created new marks in hitting safely in consecutive games. Sisler broke Cobb's American League record and Hornsby notched 33 games in a row in which he had a base hit. This was hailed as a new record for righthanded batters, at least since 1900. Dahlen's 42 had been made before the turn of the century. While such a demarcation might be a dubious distinction, it serves to create new records. (Eventually those who are insatiable for "new records" will draw a line across some point in the twentieth century and begin proclaiming new records by ignoring those which, like DiMaggio's 56-game streak, seem unbreakable.)

Consider, too, that Ty Cobb, the American League record holder, whose 1911 mark was Sisler's target, was still quite capable of breaking his own record in 1922. Although the hit which raised his final average that year to .401 was argued about, he was still a high-average batter and needed only to string enough games together to set a new mark. Hitting safely in consecutive games was a trademark for Cobb. He hit in 20 or more games in a row seven times during his career.

George Sisler was a very popular player. A college product when the campus was not a direct line to the major leagues, with superlative skills and a gentlemanly manner, he was widely admired. In addition, his team, the St. Louis Browns, was engaged in a hot pennant battle with the New York Yankees.

Sisler began his string on July 27 and continued through August and past Labor Day, getting his base hit in game after game. Then, with his targets in sight—Cobb's American League record and Keeler's major league record, set in the National League—Sisler injured his right

shoulder. It was thought at first that not only might he not be able to keep his consecutive string going, but he might not be able to finish the season.

Ironically Sisler found himself at the threshold of Cobb's record while playing against the Detroit Tigers, managed by Cobb, who patrolled center field. Sisler notched games 37 and 38 when the Tigers came to Sportsman's Park in St. Louis. On September 11, struggling to keep his streak alive, Sisler tried for game 39, one short of Cobb's record.

Sisler had been granted a streak-extending single by a generous scorer on a fly ball which Bobby Veach had reached but couldn't hold, but in 1922 there were no message boards or public address systems to inform fans of scorer's decisions. So Cobb, playing center field, was too far away from the press box to see the scorer hold up one finger, the traditional sign of a safe hit. He didn't know Veach's muff had been ruled a hit. As far as he knew, Sisler, coming to bat in the bottom of the ninth, with two out, a runner on first, and the score 4–3 in favor of Detroit, was hitless.

Manager Cobb had a choice. He could order Sisler, the Browns' most dangerous hitter, walked. This would move the tying run into scoring position and put the winning run on base. It would have been bad baseball and worse sportsmanship to order an intentional walk. Cobb might have been tempted to deny his rival what he thought was a last chance, but he didn't. He did take the precaution of removing Bob "Fatty" Fothergill, a slow-footed fielder, and replacing him in right with a better defensive player, Ira Flagstead. Then he signaled Howard Ehmke to pitch. He did, and Sisler lined a triple between Cobb and Flagstead. He scored the game-winning run a moment later on a Marty McManus single. Cobb had lost a game he might have won by passing Sisler, and George had moved to within one game of tying Ty's record.

At this point Sisler's shoulder ached so much he couldn't play the next four games, a series against the last-place Boston Red Sox. It was one of those "might have been" situations. He might have set a new American League record then against the Red Sox. However, it was much more dramatically attained when the Yankees, a half game ahead of the Browns in a torrid pennant race's final stages, came to St. Louis for a crucial three-game series.

Sisler played. His shoulder and right arm were bandaged, and he could only swing his bat with one hand. But, he played and, in a 2–1 loss, he managed a lone hit off Bob Shawkey to tie Cobb's record. The next day, September 17, the Browns evened the series as Babe Ruth's nemesis, Hub Pruett, stopped the Yankees. Ruth did get a home run, but more importantly Sisler managed another one-handed base hit to break Cobb's record.

The final game of the series was won by the Yankees as Joe Bush gained his twenty-fifth victory and Sisler went hitless in four plate appearances, never making solid contact. The Yankees left town with an increased lead they nursed to a pennant by a one-game margin. With his team still in contention, Sisler was unable to play. He pinch-hit unsuccessfully the next day, as Walter Johnson defeated the Browns, then sat out games until he returned to action with a hit against the Athletics on September 23. He hit safely the next day, and then, in a peculiarity of the 1922 season, the whole league was idle for four days.

When the league resumed for the final Friday, Saturday, and Sunday, the Browns were unable to catch the Yankees, although George Sisler hit safely in the three final games. Leave out the pinch-hit effort against Walter Johnson, a desperate attempt by a player who, if he had been swinging with two hands, would have played the full game. Without an injured shoulder, Sisler arguably might have kept his string alive against Joe Bush. He might not have missed those four games against the pitching-poor Red Sox or the two final games against the Senators. He might have hit safely in all of those games as well as the three he added at the season's end. If he had, he would have finished the season, with no more games to play to extend his streak, with 52 games in which he hit consecutively. Think what a target that would have been for Joe DiMaggio in 1941.

The DiMaggio Streak

Joe DiMaggio was playing poorly when his epochal feat began. He wasn't thinking about hitting in 56 straight games; he was worrying about getting a hit in the game of May 15. In spring training DiMaggio hit safely in every exhibition game, a forecast of the record-setting year ahead. His momentum carried through the first eight games of the 1941 season. Then he was thrown into a slump by a junk-ball pitcher, Lester McCrabbe of the Philadelphia Athletics.

By mid-May DiMaggio was still floundering, hitting below .300 and without his usual authority. On May 15 he managed a scratch single. It was an unimpressive handle hit off Cotton Ed Smith of the Chicago White Sox. However, it began a streak that wouldn't end until another pitcher named Smith, Al Smith, paired with Jim Bagby, Jr., held Joe hitless in a game against the Cleveland Indians.

The well-known DiMaggio batting eye that had produced batting championships the two preceding seasons, grew sharper, although in most games he made only a single hit. There were to be 34 games in which the string was kept alive with a lone hit. Not only was this a precarious way to sustain a batting streak, it did not, in its opening stages, draw attention to the feat that was under way. Fans followed Joe's rising batting average but not his successive daily contributions to it. He was thought to be in a contest with Ted Williams, not with the ghosts of record holders whose feats had been both unchallenged and unnoticed since the 1920s. He never caught Williams, who was enjoying the last season a champion would bat over .400.

As DiMaggio's string lengthened, the days of another Yankee immortal, Lou Gehrig, grew fewer. The Iron Horse, who had set another sort of consecutive streak by appearing in 2,130 games, died on June 2, as DiMaggio's skein reached 19.

As the string stretched into the twenties, reporters began digging into record books. The last time this arcane event excited interest had been in 1922, when George Sisler broke Ty Cobb's American League record but was stopped short of Willie Keeler's total. In 1938 another St. Louis Browns first baseman, George McQuinn, had run off a string of 34 games in which he had hit safely. Since

McQuinn was playing in the anonymity of the second division, little attention was paid to his challenge.

Because there are two major leagues, record setters have two targets. DiMaggio was required first to set a league mark at 42 and then proceed to reach 45 and set an all-time mark by breaking Keeler's total set in the past century.

By regarding DiMaggio first as a righthanded batter, he could challenge the closer record of Rogers Hornsby, who had hit in 33 straight games in 1922. No mention was made of Bill Dahlen's record of 1894. Perhaps the reporters assumed it had been made under different playing conditions and shouldn't count. They were wrong; the pitching distance had been established at sixty feet, six inches in 1893, and bunts fouled off counted as strikes from 1894. In any case, Dahlen's 42 games was less than Keeler's total, which became the ultimate target.

When DiMaggio passed Rogers Hornsby's total, the public's attention was heightened. Sisler's American League record was only a week's play away. The hype went into full swing. Les Brown's orchestra hurried a phonograph record onto the market, "Jolting Joe DiMaggio." As banal a tune as ever came from Tin Pan Alley, the song became a pep rally number as the band chanted, "Joe, Joe, DiMaggio, we want you on our side."

Bill "Bojangles" Robinson, who had tap-danced in movies with little Shirley Temple, did routines atop the Yankees dugout while he sprinkled what he called "goofer dust" to enhance DiMaggio's luck.

Despite the distractions of people pressing their attention on the reserved, unemotional DiMaggio, he continued his consistent, game-after-game pursuit of the next milestone, Sisler's league record. At the same time, he was carrying the Yankees toward a pennant. They had lost the title in 1940 after four successive world championships under manager Joe McCarthy. They were out to recapture their league's title.

Interest in Joe DiMaggio's quest went beyond the readers of the sports pages. The wire services carried stories assuring newspaper readers that Joe had extended his string before they gave the account of the game in which he did it. Radio newscasts began with bulletins about Joe's progress.

Cynics and debunkers, who concentrated their suspicions on anything coming out of New York, particularly if it gave credit to the Yankees, watched closely for scoring decisions which would give DiMaggio a favored ruling.

Rival managers juggled pitching rotations to bring their best to the mound when DiMaggio and the Yankees came to town.

Dan Daniel, a prolific and conscientious sportswriter and editor, was the official scorer for games at Yankee Stadium in 1941, and he covered the team on the road for his paper. He has written extensively about DiMaggio's 56-game hitting streak. He saw every game.

The scorer's circumstances at Yankee Stadium, as described by Daniel, placed him in view of rabid Yankee supporters who gathered behind him to demand a base hit no matter how glaring the error which allowed DiMaggio to reach base.

Daniel wrote afterward that he had to have his home phone number changed. He also insisted both he and the other scorers around the league became hyperattentive every time DiMaggio came to bat once his string had become established as a potential record breaker.

Daniel also explained that players on the opposing teams were keyed up when DiMaggio batted, none wanting to contribute to extending the string by loafing on a ball and turning it into a hit. DiMaggio's streak lifted the quality of play, umpiring, and press coverage. Everyone, including DiMaggio, wanted him to earn a new record.

Years afterward, DiMaggio looked back on the 56 games and could only find one where he wished the play had not been as judgmental as it was. It came in the thirtieth game, when he was still short of Hornsby's record. The White Sox came to the Stadium, and Johnny Rigney was the pitcher. He had twice been DiMaggio's victim in earlier games in the streak but on this day had stopped the Yankee Clipper until the seventh inning.

Then DiMaggio hit a routine grounder to Luke Appling. The future Hall of Fame shortstop moved for the ball, but it took a bad bounce, hitting him in the shoulder. In his rush to recover, Appling grabbed at the ball, dropped it, then threw too late. A bad-hop single? Butter-fingered retrieval? The official scorer, Dan Daniel, ruled it a hit. Lucky for Joe and fortunate for legend, too, because on his last time up, in the ninth, Taft Wright made a leaping catch to snatch a home run out of the right field stands. Joe would have been blanked.

The next day DiMaggio got another streak-extending break, almost the same way. This time the ball was hard hit and Appling could only knock it down. He couldn't make a throw. Too hard to handle? Scorer Daniel ruled so and the fans relaxed. A few days later Hornsby's record for righthanded batters would be broken and DiMaggio would be headed for Sisler's mark. However, it took another break for DiMaggio to get there.

Eldon Auker, a St. Louis submarine-ball pitcher, held Joe hitless until the eighth inning at Yankee Stadium. Unless one of the first three batters kept the inning alive, Joe, due up fourth, would not bat again. The Yankees were ahead by two runs, and it did not appear as though there would be a bottom of the ninth.

Johnny Sturm popped up, but Red Rolfe drew a walk. Tommy Henrich, the next batter, had a dilemma. He could still deprive Joe of a chance to bat if he hit into a double play. With manager McCarthy's consent, Henrich bunted and moved Rolfe to second base. Now, with first base open, it was Auker who had a dilemma. He could walk DiMaggio, hit him with a pitch (a strategy as underhanded as his delivery), or pitch to him.

DiMaggio stood at the plate, unruffled. Coolly he smashed the first pitch into left field for a double. It was a close call, but now Sisler's record was in reach.

In a Sunday doubleheader with Washington at Griffith Stadium, on June 29, DiMaggio tied Sisler's record in the first game and broke it in the nightcap. The record-tying hit came off knuckleballer Dutch Leonard and was broken with a last-chance single off the unknown Arnold Anderson. DiMaggio was two games short of tying Willie Keeler's 1897 record.

The only mark left for DiMaggio to eclipse was tied in the second game of a July 1 doubleheader with the Boston Red Sox and broken the next day.

The day DiMaggio claimed the American League record was marked by two extremes of luck. It was fortunate

his record-tying hit came early in the game because a downpour deluged Yankee Stadium and the game was called after five innings. It was unfortunate that during the rain delay no one kept an eye on the bat rack. A souvenir hunter reached over the dugout and pulled out a bat. He grabbed DiMaggio's favorite club.

Although he was upset, the man who rarely showed emotion quietly borrowed a bat from teammate Tommy Henrich the next day. It was an identical thirty-six-inch, thirty-six-ounce bat, and Joe used it to break Keeler's record. His record-smashing hit was a prodigeous home run off Dick Newsome, a 19-game winner for the Red Sox. It carried high over the head of his rival, Ted Williams, into the left field stands.

Joe DiMaggio did not rest on his laurels. Actually, with the pressure to produce at least one base hit each game lifted, he began pounding out hits in clusters. He passed the 50-game mark and his luck still held. In the fifty-fourth game, he again came up against Johnny Rigney of the White Sox. This time he would have been stopped except for a topped roller. A typical lusty swing sent a dribbler slowly toward third base where Bob Kennedy was playing fearfully deep, a precaution normally taken by rival third baseman against DiMaggio. It worked to Joe's advantage that day as he beat out the slowly hit ball for his only hit. However, it would work to his disadvantage a few days later in Cleveland.

Although Joe DiMaggio said after his streak had ended, "I wish it could have gone on forever," like all good things it had to come to an end. Joe had reached 56 games when the kind of luck which occasionally had sustained him, such as the topped roller against Chicago, turned around. The Yankees came into Cleveland and crowds came, divided between fans' wishes to witness the streak extended and hometeam rooters' hopes that their team could bring the mighty DiMaggio to a halt.

What could only be a matter of time happened. As a minor league star in his native San Francisco, a nineteen-year-old Joe DiMaggio had been stopped after hitting in 61 consecutive games. After the 1941 streak ended, the *San Francisco Chronicle,* which had made daily reports of DiMaggio's record-breaking games, observed that the Pacific Coast League string had been ended by the son of a former major league pitching star, Bob Walsh, whose father, Big Ed Walsh, would be elected to the Hall of Fame. It was pointed out that DiMaggio's major league string was ended, in part, by Jim Bagby, Jr., another son of a successful major leaguer, a 31-game winner for the 1920 world champion Cleveland Indians.

It wasn't so much the pitching of starter Al Smith or reliever Bagby that halted DiMaggio as the glove work on the left side of the Indians' infield. Twice Ken Keltner, playing a very deep third base, took drives down the baseline and turned them into outs. And Joe's last chance found him deserted by luck on a bad bounce. A ball headed up the middle took an erratic hop, and shortstop Lou Boudreau grabbed it and flipped to second to start a double play that closed off DiMaggio's chance to keep safely intact the stretch of games in which he had hit.

Although the DiMaggio streak had been stopped, he was still a hot hitter, and even his favorite bat was back. An embarrassed fan from Newark admitted the theft and returned the bat, and Joe used it to continue his torrid

Joe DiMaggio's 1941 Hitting Streak

Game No.	Date	Club and Pitcher	AB	R	H
1	5-15	White Sox, Smith	4	0	1
2	5-16	White Sox, Lee	4	2	2
3	5-17	White Sox, Rigney	3	1	1
4	5-18	Browns, Harris, Niggeling	3	3	3
5	5-19	Browns, Galehouse	3	0	1
6	5-20	Browns, Auker	5	1	1
7	5-21	Tigers, Rowe, Benton	5	0	2
8	5-22	Tigers, McKain	4	0	1
9	5-23	Red Sox, Newsome	5	0	1
10	5-24	Red Sox, Johnson	4	2	1
11	5-25	Red Sox, Grove	4	0	1
12	5-27	Senators, Chase, Anderson, Carrasquel	5	3	4
13	5-28	Senators, Hudson	4	1	1
14	5-29	Senators, Sundra	3	1	1
15	5-30	Red Sox, Johnson	2	1	1
16	5-30	Red Sox, Harris	3	0	1
17	6-1	Indians, Milnar	4	1	1
18	6-1	Indians, Harder	4	0	1
19	6-2	Indians, Feller	4	2	2
20	6-3	Tigers, Trout	4	1	1
21	6-5	Tigers, Newhouser	5	1	1
22	6-7	Browns, Muncrief, Allen, Caster	5	2	3
23	6-8	Browns, Auker	4	3	2
24	6-8	Browns, Caster, Kramer	4	1	2
25	6-10	White Sox, Rigney	5	1	1
26	6-12	White Sox, Lee	4	1	2
27	6-14	Indians, Feller	2	0	1
28	6-15	Indians, Bagby	3	1	1
29	6-16	Indians, Milnar	5	0	1
30	6-17	White Sox, Rigney	4	1	1
31	6-18	White Sox, Lee	3	0	1
32	6-19	White Sox, Smith, Ross	3	2	3
33	6-20	Tigers, Newsom, McKain	5	3	4
34	6-21	Tigers, Trout	4	0	1
35	6-22	Tigers, Newhouser, Newsom	5	1	2
36	6-24	Browns, Muncrief	4	1	1
37	6-25	Browns, Galehouse	4	1	1
38	6-26	Browns, Auker	4	0	1
39	6-27	Athletics, Dean	3	1	2
40	6-28	Athletics, Babich, Harris	5	1	2
41	6-29	Senators, Leonard	4	1	1
42	6-29	Senators, Anderson	5	1	1
43	7-1	Red Sox, Harris, Ryba	4	0	2
44	7-1	Red Sox, Wilson	3	1	1
45	7-2	Red Sox, Newsome	5	1	1
46	7-5	Athletics, Marchildon	4	2	1
47	7-6	Athletics, Babich, Hadley	5	2	4
48	7-6	Athletics, Knott	4	0	2
49	7-10	Browns, Niggling	2	0	1
50	7-11	Browns, Harris, Kramer	5	1	4
51	7-12	Browns, Auker, Muncrief	5	1	2
52	7-13	White Sox, Lyons, Hallett	4	2	3
53	7-13	White Sox, Lee	4	0	1
54	7-14	White Sox, Rigney	3	0	1
55	7-15	White Sox, Smith	4	1	2
56	7-16	Indians, Milnar, Krakauskas	4	3	3
Totals			223	56	91

hitting. He kept pounding out hits on a daily basis until he had hit safely in 16 more consecutive games. This meant he would have reached an incredible 73 games had not Keltner and Boudreau pulled off outstanding defensive plays after game 56.

As it is, hitting safely in 72 of 73 games is almost unimaginable. Historians had to go back to the over-looked Bad Bill Dahlen to find a comparable feat for DiMaggio to eclipse almost half a century later. Back in 1894, after he had run up a string of 42 games, Dahlen ran off another stretch of 28 games in which he hit safely. He had left a neglected legacy of hitting in 70 of 71 games for DiMaggio to top with 72 in 73.

During his 56-game streak, Joe DiMaggio batted .408. Although he finished the 1941 season with a .357 average, he was second to Ted Williams's league-leading .406. However, DiMaggio had led his team to a championship

and this, with the incredible feat of hitting in 56 straight games, earned him the Most Valuable Player Award by a close margin.

Those whose interest in statistics match, if not exceed, a curiosity about the drama of making them, will want to know that, in hitting .408 during the 56 games, DiMaggio scored 56 runs and batted in 55. He hit 15 home runs, half his season's total, and had 35 extra-base hits among the 91 hits he collected in 223 at-bats. He walked 21 times, was hit by a pitch twice, and struck out only 7 times.

The Yankees went on to defeat the Brooklyn Dodgers in the World Series and, as the Japanese went on to bomb Pearl Harbor and involve the United States in World War Two, Joe was asked to take a $2,500 cut in salary for 1942. He managed to get a $5,000 raise and play the 1942 season before entering military service in possession of a unique feat which still attracts its new challengers.

The Pete Rose Challenge

The year 1978 was a tremendous one for Pete Rose, whose career with the Cincinnati Reds qualified him as a potential challenger for Joe DiMaggio's record of hitting safely in 56 consecutive games. Although he did not hit for the high averages of the other streakers who had held records—Keeler, Sisler, Hornsby, and DiMaggio—Rose batted leadoff and had amassed 10 seasons with 200 or more hits. Even more, he was the kind of player who would rise to any occasion. He loved a challenge.

Longest Hitting Streaks, NL

Player	Team	Year	G
Willie Keeler	BAL	1897	44
Pete Rose	CIN	1978	44
Bill Dahlen	CHI	1894	42
Tommy Holmes	BOS	1945	37
Billy Hamilton	PHI	1894	36
Fred Clarke	LOU	1895	35
Benito Santiago	SD	1987	34
George Davis	NY	1893	33
Rogers Hornsby	STL	1922	32
Ed Delahanty	PHI	1899	31
Willie Davis	LA	1969	31
Rico Carty	ATL	1970	31
Elmer Smith	CIN	1898	30
Stan Musial	STL	1950	30
Jerome Walton	CHI	1989	30

Longest Hitting Streaks, AL

Player	Team	Year	G
Joe DiMaggio	NY	1941	56
George Sisler	STL	1922	41
Ty Cobb	DET	1911	40
Paul Molitor	MIL	1987	39
Ty Cobb	DET	1917	35
George Sisler	STL	1925	34
George McQuinn	STL	1938	34
Dom DiMaggio	BOS	1949	34
Hal Chase	NY	1907	33
Heinie Manush	WAS	1933	33
Nap Lajoie	CLE	1906	31
Sam Rice	WAS	1924	31
Ken Landreaux	MIN	1980	31
Tris Speaker	BOS	1912	30
Bing Miller	PHI	1929	30
Goose Goslin	DET	1934	30
Ron LeFlore	DET	1976	30
George Brett	KC	1980	30

Pete Rose's 1978 Hitting Streak

Game No.	Date	Club and Pitcher	AB	R	H
1	6-14	Cubs, Roberts	4	1	2
2	6-16	Cardinals, Denny	4	1	2
3	6-17	Cardinals, Vuckovich, Schultz	4	2	2
4	6-18	Cardinals, Martinez	4	1	1
5	6-20	Giants, Montefusco	5	2	2
6	6-21	Giants, Halicki	4	0	1
7	6-22	Giants, Knepper	4	0	1
8	6-23	Dodgers, Hooton	4	0	1
9	6-24	Dodgers, Welch	5	1	4
10	6-25	Dodgers, John	3	1	2
11	6-26	Astros, Lemongello	5	1	1
12	6-27	Astros, Niekro	4	1	1
13	6-28	Astros, Dixon	4	0	1
14	6-29	Astros, Bannister	3	0	1
15	6-30	Dodgers, Rautzhan	4	1	1
16	6-30	Dodgers, Welch, Forster, Hough	5	1	3
17	7-1	Dodgers, Rhoden	5	0	1
18	7-2	Dodgers, Rau	4	1	1
19	7-3	Astros, Bannister, McLaughlin	5	1	3
20	7-4	Astros, Richard	4	1	1
21	7-5	Astros, Niekro	4	0	1
22	7-6	Giants, Blue, Curtis	5	1	3
23	7-7	Giants, Barr	4	0	1
24	7-8	Giants, Montefusco	4	1	1
25	7-9	Giants, Halicki, Knepper	4	1	3
26	7-13	Mets, Koosman, Lockwood	5	0	2
27	7-14	Mets, Zachry	5	0	2
28	7-15	Mets, Swan	2	2	1
29	7-16	Mets, Siebert	5	1	1
30	7-17	Expos, Bahnsen	4	0	1
31	7-18	Expos, Dues	4	0	2
32	7-19	Phillies, Reed	4	1	1
33	7-20	Phillies, Kaat	5	1	1
34	7-21	Expos, Grimsley	3	1	1
35	7-22	Expos, Schatzeder	3	0	1
36	7-23	Expos, Rogers, Knowles	6	0	2
37	7-24	Mets, Zachry, Lockwood	5	2	2
38	7-25	Mets, Swan	4	1	3
39	7-26	Mets, Espinosa	3	0	1
40	7-28	Phillies, Lerch	2	1	1
41	7-28	Phillies, Carlton	4	0	1
42	7-29	Phillies, Lonborg, Kaat	4	1	3
43	7-30	Phillies, Christenson	5	0	2
44	7-31	Braves, Niekro	4	0	1
Totals			182	30	70

Willie Keeler's 1897 Hitting Streak

Game No.	Date	AB	R	H
1	April 22	5	2	2
2	April 23	4	1	2
3	April 24	4	1	2
4	April 26	4	0	1
5	April 27	5	2	2
6	April 28	5	1	3
7	April 29	4	1	2
8	April 20	4	3	3
9	May 3	4	0	1
10	May 4	4	0	2
11	May 5	4	0	1
12	May 6	5	0	3
13	May 7	6	2	1
14	May 8	3	1	1
15	May 10	4	0	1
16	May 11	5	1	2
17	May 12	5	0	3
18	May 14	6	2	2
19	May 15	6	2	2
20	May 16	6	3	3
21	May 17	4	1	2
22	May 18	6	1	1
23	May 19	4	1	1
24	May 20	4	1	3
25	May 21	3	1	2
26	May 22	4	2	2
27	May 25	5	0	1
28	May 26	5	1	3
29	May 27	5	1	1
30	May 29	6	2	2
31	May 30	4	0	1
32	May 31	4	1	1
33	May 31	5	2	1
34	June 2	5	1	4
35	June 5	5	1	1
36	June 7	4	1	1
37	June 9	5	2	2
38	June 10	4	0	2
39	June 11	4	0	2
40	June 12	5	2	2
41	June 14	5	1	2
42	June 15	3	0	1
43	June 16	5	2	1
44	June 18	4	3	3
Totals		201	49	82

Before he got around to taking a swing at DiMaggio's record, Rose had, as his first order of business, the matter of making his 3,000th career base hit. He opened the 1978 season needing 34 hits to reach a plateau only twelve others had gained. On May 5 Rose reached 3,000 with a single off Montreal pitcher Steve Rogers, before a hometown crowd at Riverfront Stadium.

"Charlie Hustle" was having an epoch-making season and, with one landmark reached, he soon found himself en route to another. Consecutive-game hitting streaks begin without signaling their advent. It is only as they grow that they attract attention.

Pete Rose was only batting .267 when he got a pair of hits against the Cubs on June 14. He kept adding hits in the games he played and, eventually, it was decided he had enough in a row to start looking for a record to be broken.

DiMaggio's 56-game streak in 1941 loomed far beyond expectation. However, the record keepers had gerrymandered Willie Keeler, holder of the National League record at 44, out of the books. There was a modern mark of 37, set during the wartime year of 1945, by Tommy Holmes of the Boston Braves.

Pete Rose hustled onward and, as luck would have it, came into Shea Stadium for a series with the Mets on the verge of knocking Holmes out of the record book. The patron saint of hype was on the ball, and a now sixty-one-year-old Tommy Holmes was on hand to root for Rose. He was there in a dual capacity. Tommy Holmes was also the Mets' community relations director.

There was another reward in having Pete Rose break Holmes's record in front of the Mets' fans. In 1973 Pete had been *persona non grata* when he had wrestled on the ground with skinny shortstop Bud Harrelson in a League Championship Game after a takeout slide by Rose at second base. The Mets fans remembered Rose calling them "animals" as they threatened to avenge the honor of the team by challenging the wives and children of the Reds' players in field boxes behind the Cincinnati dugout. However, hype places a statute of limitations on vengeance in New York. Whipped to a frenzy of impartiality by the Mets' announcers and a record-hungry press, people filled Shea Stadium ready to cheer Rose on while trusting he'd not be so unappreciative as to make his record-extending safety a game-winning hit.

On July 24 Pete Rose equaled the record of Tommy Holmes and to chants of "Go, Pete, Go!" broke it the next night against Craig Swan. An appreciative Holmes, pleased to have been a short-term celebrity, came onto the field to shake the hand of the man who had erased him from the record books. Pete now held the "modern" National League record for hitting safely in consecutive games. In fairness, he would now try to reach Willie Keeler's mark of 44, a feat turned before the century began.

Pete continued his quest. He had the skill, the competitive instincts, and the attitude to do it. He was unruffled by press attention, accustomed to it as the consequence of being the game's most colorful player of his time. Would he break DiMaggio's seemingly unreachable mark? If anyone could, Pete Rose could do it. But first he had to lay the ghost of Willie Keeler and his 81-year-old record.

It was a struggle, as the whole streak had been, but Rose reached Keeler's mark on July 31 in Atlanta. His record-equaling hit came off the knuckleball pitching of Phil Niekro, a man whose own feats as a middle-aged ballplayer also merited recognition.

Keeler had been caught. Would he be passed? No. The next night a rookie lefthander, Larry McWilliams, held Pete Rose hitless through most of the game, and reliever Gene Garber provided the final denial. He struck Rose out.

Pete Rose is joined with Willie Keeler, linked now, regardless of the era when the feat was accomplished, as coholders of the National League record for hitting safely in consecutive games.

Consecutive Games Played

On May 31, 1925, no one thought the young substitute pinch-hitting for the New York Yankees was launching the most extraordinary streak of durability the game has yet seen. The next day Lou Gehrig took the place of the team's star first baseman, Wally Pipp, and continued his uncertain start toward a goal so distant it was unimaginable.

Gehrig had played for Hartford in the Eastern League after the Yankees signed him off the campus of Columbia University. It was thought he would make the major league grade, but he had not been handed a starting job. Only when Pipp complained of a headache and was given the day off by manager Miller Huggins did Gehrig get a chance to start a game. So uncertain of the rookie's skills was management that two days later Aaron Ward pinch-hit for Gehrig and Pipp finished the game in the field.

Before June ended, Gehrig had been taken out of games three times for pinch hitters, although he continued to start games. On July 5 he wasn't even the starting first baseman. Fred Merkle, who in 1908, as a rookie himself, had failed to run to second on what appeared to be a game-winning single, started the game. Merkle, whose gaffe eventually cost the New York Giants a pennant to the Chicago Cubs, had been forever more labeled Bonehead by unforgiving fans. Gehrig was destined for adulation. This day he made a ninth-inning appearance, an unsuspected extension of a fledgling feat.

Of course at the time there was no suspicion that young Lou Gehrig had launched a string of consecutive-game appearances which wouldn't end until fourteen years later. He began it as a young giant in the prime of his life and ended it a dying man, forced out of the lineup with a rare disease. From start to finish it became a matter of drama as the survival of the string became a compelling goal which Gehrig sustained despite injury, sickness, accident, and managed to avoid ending inadvertently.

Gehrig is remembered, or known to people who never saw him play, as the gentle giant who was portrayed by actor Gary Cooper in the movie *The Pride of the Yankees*. In reality, particularly in his early years, Gehrig was a hard-nosed, competitive player who would readily leap into argument with umpires and enemy players. He was ejected from a major league game a half dozen times without drawing a suspension which would have ended his string of games.

Durable, yes. Gehrig was well dubbed "the Iron Horse" for his rawboned toughness. However, he never spared himself. A statistic which astonishes fans is that he stole home 15 times, risking crashing into a plate-blocking catcher. He ran the bases with surprising speed and fearless abandon. Babe Ruth and Lou Gehrig are remembered for the home runs they hit; yet they were also daring baserunners.

Once Gehrig's penchant for never missing a game was established, just being in the boxscore was the goal. He could have simultaneously set records for consecutive games played at first base, while extending his string of boxscore appearances. However, while in the sixth year of his developing string, in a late-season game, the Yankees promoted a game in which Babe Ruth would pitch while Lou Gehrig took his place in the outfield. Harry Rice, an outfielder who sometimes spelled Gehrig late in one-sided games, played first base.

Gehrig's 2,130-game skein, stretched over fourteen seasons, was not simply a matter of having him go out to first base day after day. For one thing, there were times when he could hardly play. When the Iron Horse was no longer a frisky colt, he developed lumbago, and it hobbled him from time to time. In midseason of 1934, Lou was seized by an attack and, immobilized, had to be helped off the field.

There was an acute awareness on the part of the Yankees of the consecutive games Gehrig played, and this was kept alive by the sportswriters who covered the team. Everett Scott had astonished baseball with his consecutive-game appearances at shortstop, ending a string of 1,307 in 1925, the season Gehrig, his rookie roommate, began his string. Scott had started his run of games with the Boston Red Sox, and when he was bought by the Yankees in 1923, he carried on the string without interruption. He slowed down drastically early in 1925 and was first benched, then sold to the Senators. Unlike Scott, Lou Gehrig, the Iron Horse, would never be put out to pasture. However, Scott had left a legend behind, and it served to lead Gehrig toward new standards of durability.

The day after Gehrig had been helped off the field, with his string at 1,426, and Scott's record broken, he made a contrived appearance in the lineup. Hardly able to stand, he was in the lineup of the visiting Yankees in Detroit as the leadoff batter, penciled in to play shortstop. Despite his pain, he lined out a single and, with his appearance established in the boxscore, gave way to pinch runner Red Rolfe, who finished the game at short while Gehrig took his aching back to the hotel. Jack Saltzgaver, a utility infielder who, over the years, replaced Gehrig at first base more often than any other player, filled in at first that day.

Gehrig was back in the regular lineup the next day, collecting four hits, three of them doubles. He was on his way to the only batting title he ever won and the Triple Crown for 1934. But it wasn't a pain-free future ahead for Lou. Lumbago continued to be a problem. He left games early because he was feeling ill, and he had a thumb injury in 1938 which he ignored to keep his consecutive-game string going.

It was during 1938 that the perpetual machine began to show signs of wearing out. For the first time he batted below .300; his stats—a .295 average, 29 home runs, and 107 runs batted in—would have pleased most players. But they were substandard for Lou, and so was his general play. Just age catching up, it was thought, just the way it had slowed Everett Scott in 1925 when Gehrig was starting out.

In spring training the next season, it was evident that something was amiss, but manager Joe McCarthy left it to Gehrig to decide when to call it quits. It was on May 2, 1939, after eight feebly played games had brought his string to 2,130, that Gehrig advised McCarthy to replace him.

The longest streak of its kind, seemingly impossible to ever exceed despite the longer seasons, ended. For fourteen years Gehrig had played despite a broken thumb, a broken toe, back spasms, frequent colds, and recurring attacks of lumbago. He had been forced from the lineup by something no one could foresee and almost no one had ever heard about. When the tests at Mayo Clinic proved that he had amyotrophic lateral sclerosis, it was so singular an affliction that it was renamed Lou Gehrig's Disease. It was incurable then and still is. Gehrig was a doomed man. He knew it, as did his wife, Eleanor. They bravely pretended to each other that Lou would regain his strength.

He continued to carry the lineup card to home plate during the 1939 pennant-winning season, as the team captain, but soon he had to surrender even that role. On July 4, 1939, a Lou Gehrig Day was arranged at Yankee Stadium. The scene was repeated in the Gary Cooper movie and is seen often in filmed highlights of baseball history.

Babe Ruth, who had broken relations with Gehrig during a 1934 postseason tour to the Pacific and Japan, embraced his former teammate, and the occasion came to a climax as Gehrig, a man who knew his life was nearly over, stood at a microphone, surrounded by the Yankees who had been his fellow players. He told a choked-up audience, "Today, I consider myself the luckiest man on the face of the earth." He died on June 2, 1941.

Far in the Distance—But Closing In

Lou Gehrig's legacy of stamina and determination reached such a length that, at one time, historians could hardly imagine his record being broken. At best, they expected a change in the runner-up position. Then along came Cal Ripken, Jr. He had worked himself within 121 games of Gehrig's once seemingly insurmountable record when the strike-shortened 1994 season ended. Assuming the major leagues start playing in April, he will have an opportunity to break Gehrig's record sometime in late 1995.

Scott, whose record Gehrig had eclipsed, now is third on the list, just ahead of Steve Garvey's 1,207 games. For many years, Joe Sewell ranked third behind Scott. Sewell is best remembered for his avoidance of strikeouts. Twice he fanned only 4 times in a whole season. Once he went 115 games without striking out in 437 times at bat. He set his consecutive-game string with Cleveland, later moving to the Yankees where he played for three years as Lou Gehrig's teammate. He was elected to the Hall of Fame in 1977.

During the 1930s, Gus Suhr, a fine-fielding first baseman for the Pittsburgh Pirates, reached 822 consecutive games played. It was dwarfed, even as he made it, by Gehrig's string in progress, but he far exceeded earlier National League marks.

Gus Suhr's National League record was broken by Stan Musial, who played in 895 straight games, ending in 1957 at age thirty-six. This provided a target for Billy Williams when his career with the Cubs got under way in 1963 and daily appearances were part of his routine. He sailed past Musial to claim the National League record at 1,117. He stopped in 1970, and the occasional rest did him good. He led the National League in batting in 1972 and his career ended with Oakland in 1975. He has been elected to the Hall of Fame.

Williams's new National League record provided an attainable goal for Steve Garvey, who had the stamina and will power required to catch Gehrig. He just didn't get started soon enough. Gehrig was twenty-two when his streak began; Garvey was twenty-six.

Also, Garvey did not become an everyday regular with the Los Angeles Dodgers until 1975, his sixth season with the team. He had been regarded as erratic at third base but, once moved across the diamond in 1974, he delivered with consistency in the field, at the bat, with power, and refused to budge from the lineup.

He left the Dodgers with his string intact after the 1982 season and took his Iron Man act to San Diego, where he continued as a star with the Padres. A hand injury took him out of the lineup on July 29, 1983. He had broken Billy Williams's record the previous year, and all told he played in 1,207 consecutive games.

A special recognition is due to Pete Rose. Had he not paused to catch his breath during the 1978 season, when he was thirty-seven years old, he would hold the National League record. In 1978 Rose had more realistic aims than Gehrig's too distant goal. During that season he reached the 3,000-hit mark and set aim on Ty Cobb's all-time total. He also captured the headlines with his assault on Joe DiMaggio's 56-game hitting streak, ultimately falling 12 games short.

The year 1978 was also Rose's last season with the Cincinnati Reds and, in a celebrated case of free agency, he moved to Philadelphia. There he not only resumed his climb toward Cobb's hit totals, but played again on a daily basis. When he sat down for two games in 1978 with the Reds, he snapped a somewhat modest run of 678 games. When he finally left the daily lineup in Philadelphia, in 1983, he had run off an even longer string of 745 games. Add them together and Rose's total is 1,423 games, longer than anyone's stretch except Gehrig's and now Ripken's.

Most Consecutive Games Played

2,130	Lou Gehrig
2,009	Cal Ripken (through 1994)
1,307	Everett Scott
1,207	Steve Garvey
1,117	Billy Williams
1,103	Joe Sewell
895	Stan Musial
829	Eddie Yost
822	Gus Suhr
798	Nellie Fox

Successive Pitching Victories

The 1912 baseball season produced a bumper crop of pitchers winning successive victories. Rube Marquard of the New York Giants topped everyone by running up a total of 19. This tied the record set by Tim Keefe, also of New York. Keefe had won his games in 1888, when the pitching distance was only fifty feet between pitcher and batter, but he had won them in a row and that is the measurement of this feat. The present distance of sixty feet, six inches (actually, this is only about 55 feet from the pitcher's point of release) was set in 1893, Keefe's last season.

Marquard's mark remains unmatched within the confines of a single season. The record for consecutive wins beginning in the midst of one season and extending into the next season is held by Carl Hubbell, whose 24 consecutive victories, starting in 1936 and continuing into 1937, tops the list.

However, 1912 produced more than just Marquard's record. It also produced a new American League record and an immediate challenger to it. Even while Rube Marquard was engaged in his run in the National League, Walter Johnson, almost concurrently, was setting the American League record at 16. And by the time he was stopped, another streak was under way, this one by Smokey Joe Wood of the Boston Red Sox.

No one could ask for a better matchup in 1912 than the one which brought Walter Johnson, the record holder, to the mound at Fenway Park to face Joe Wood the challenger. Johnson was the premier pitcher in the American League and its strikeout king. Wood had dazzled the baseball world while en route to a 34–5 season, with 10 shutouts. He won three more games in the 1912 World Series. Then he injured his arm and never returned to his single-season pinnacle.

Walter Johnson, himself a 33-game winner in 1912, had broken the former American League record of 14 straight, set by Jack Chesbro in 1904. By winning his sixteenth straight game on August 23, he had set a new league mark and had his sights on the brand-new record of Rube Marquard. The New York lefthander had won his 19 by July 3. Johnson never caught Marquard.

Johnson was a victim of both bad luck and a scoring rule which today would not have cost him a loss. He lost a game in relief, taking over in the seventh inning of a tie game. There were two runners on base, and before Johnson could get the side out, one of them scored the winning run. Today the loss would be charged to the starting pitcher, Tom Hughes, who had allowed the runner to get on base. At that time the loss went against whoever was pitching when the winning run scored.

Even so, in 1912 the scorer's decision was denounced by the press and sympathetic fans. However, Ban Johnson, not only president of the American League but its iron-fisted founder, decreed the loss be placed against Walter Johnson's record, and there it remains forever. He had been stopped at 16.

When the 1912 penchant for pitchers winning consecutive victories identified the next challenger as Smokey Joe Wood of the pennant-bound Boston Red Sox, Johnson was called upon to stop him personally. The schedule brought the Washington Senators to Fenway Park to play the Red Sox, and the management was well aware they had a great gate attraction. Johnson was asked to pitch a day sooner so he would face Wood. He was glad to do it.

Whatever the capacity of Fenway Park in 1912, it was far exceeded when, on a weekday, over 30,000 baseball fans crowded the park. The crowd overflowed the stands. In fact, the players could not sit in their dugouts. Instead, they sat on chairs arranged in front of the throngs that stood just outside the baselines. Thousands more people stood in the outfield, behind ropes, reducing the area for the great Red Sox outfield to cover. Tris Speaker, Duffy Lewis, and Harry Hooper would not be able to roam back to catch deep fly balls. These would be automatic doubles if they reached the crowd herded behind the ropes.

Walter Johnson held the American League record, a string of 16 straight victories. Joe Wood had drawn nearer to Johnson's mark in his last start, beating New York on September 2 for his thirteenth win without a loss during the streak. Today he was after his fourteenth straight, Chesbro's old mark, and Walter Johnson didn't want him to get it. Unless Johnson himself stopped Wood, his own record, and possibly Marquard's, were in danger.

The game lived up to expectations. It was a pitcher's battle. Great defensive plays snuffed out rallies, and both pitchers stopped scoring threats with clutch strikeouts. A scoreless tie was broken in the sixth inning, when Tris Speaker hit a fly ball that reached the roped-back crowd for a ground-rule double and Duffy Lewis hit an opposite-field double down the right field foul line. It just eluded the grab of Danny Moeller and Speaker scored. And that was it. The game ended 1–0 as Walter Johnson lost another game in which his team failed to get him any runs. He lost 65 games during his career when his team was shut out.

When Wood pitched next, in Chicago, he was not in top form but held a 5–3 lead going into the bottom of the ninth. When the first two White Sox batters reached base with hits, manager Jake Stahl replaced Wood with reliever Charles "Sea Lion" Hall. A sacrifice fly made the final score 5–4, but Hall retired the White Sox without further damage and Joe Wood was within one game of tying Walter Johnson.

The Red Sox rode on to St. Louis in Pullman cars for a game on September 15, and Joe Wood pitched another strong game, a 2–1 victory in eight innings to tie Johnson's record. Darkness caused the game to be called after Wood himself had scored the go-ahead run in the top of the eighth inning.

It all came to an end on September 20 in Detroit. Wood

failed to break Walter Johnson's mark. He went the distance but mostly on the sufferance of manager Jake Stahl. Although two of the Tigers' runs were unearned, the 6–4 final score indicated Joe Wood's fastball lacked its usual smoke that day.

The Marquard Inheritance

When Rube Marquard wrote his way into the record books in 1912, with 19 consecutive victories, he established a benchmark which has been approached but never equaled, or excelled, since that time. Although Walter Johnson's American League mark, itself never beaten, took on extra importance because of the affection and awe he inspired in baseball fans, Marquard set the standard for all others to challenge.

The Johnson-Wood confrontation excited the imagination, and other challenges have created their own temporary focus, but always there stands the record of Marquard. It is the pinnacle toward which others climb and never reach, on a single-season, starting pitcher basis. It has only been exceeded by joining the end of one season to the start of the next.

Perhaps even more than the way Walter Johnson was revered in the American League, Rube Marquard's teammate, Christy Mathewson, overshadowed everyone. Marquard's record was the sort of achievement Matty should have had. Until 1912 all the heroics on the Giants' staff had been his. Rube's emergence took everyone by surprise; he was still living down the onerous nickname "the $11,000 Lemon."

Just a kid pitcher, only eighteen, when the Giants bought him from Indianapolis where he had won 28 games in 1908, Marquard had been a disappointment until the 1912 season. Then he began his streak with his first start of the season and, as he added to it, he began to attract favorable attention for the first time. When he won his sixth game, he exceeded any previous high; when he won the tenth game, he had won more than he had in his first two seasons combined.

Marquard had shed the label, "The $11,000 Lemon," the year before his record-breaking string, by winning 24 games and leading the league with a .774 winning percentage. Until then he had disappointed Giant fans, who had expected another Mathewson when John McGraw paid the largest amount shelled out for a player to date. The Giant manager had purposely topped the $10,000 price tag paid for Mike "King" Kelly, the leading nineteenth century gate attraction. In 1912, Marquard displaced Matty as the leading winner on the staff. While Mathewson won 23 games, Marquard led the league with 26, the first 19 of them in a row. He won his first start on April 11 and did not lose a game until July 8.

Actually, under the present scoring rules, Marquard's record would total 20 consecutive victories. McGraw inserted Rube in the eighth inning of a game at the Polo Grounds, against the Brooklyn Dodgers, which was tied at 3–3. Marquard inherited a bases-loaded situation but stopped Zack Wheat and Jake Daubert, both to become batting champions, and retired George Cutshaw, without a run being scored. The Giants won the game in the bottom of the ninth, but the rules then gave the victory to the starting pitcher.

The Giants, in 1912, were winning the middle of three successive pennants, and Marquard joined with Christy Mathewson to lead the Giants' staff. He was called "Rube," a nickname often given to lefthanders with a superior fastball. This was a tribute to Rube Waddell and had no bucolic significance: Marquard was no innocent country boy turned loose on Broadway.

Marquard married a vaudeville headliner, Blossom Seeley, who was even more popular than he was. Her life story was later made into a motion picture which ignored Marquard in favor of Blossom's subsequent husband, song-and-dance man Benny Fields.

However, Rube had held up his end of the vaudeville act, serving as a straight man for the comedienne and added female impersonations, in which he sang and danced as well. This too is a performance unlikely to be duplicated by a modern player.

Streakers Blurred by Time

Although it is convenient to separate the "modern era" of baseball from its ancient past at 1900, the better dividing line would be 1893. That year the pitcher was moved back from fifty feet to the still-prevailing sixty feet, six inches. He had been allowed to throw overhand since 1884.

Until the 1890s, teams rarely used more than two principal pitchers. More open dates existed in the schedules, and two strong-armed men could carry the bulk of the work. A third pitcher, or a general substitute, could help out in doubleheaders. However, the regular duo met most occasions and had many more opportunities to reel off long strings of victories.

When Tim Keefe set the mark at 19 straight, he required only seven weeks to do it. Between June 23 and August 10, 1888, he won all his starts, 17 of them complete games. He alternated on the mound with Mickey Welch, himself the owner of an impressive winning streak. In 1885 Smiling Mickey had run off 17 in a row. That had been one less than the record Hoss Radbourn set in 1884. Pitchers in those years were capable of putting together long winning streaks.

Another contemporary, Jim McCormick of Chicago, won 14 in a row in 1885 and 16 straight the next year. When Keefe set his mark in 1888, the public was impressed but not stunned by its magnitude. After all, it only topped the recent mark of Radbourn's by one.

The New York Giants of 1888 were the toast of the town. They were led by Jim Mutrie, who had dubbed them "my Giants," marveling at the magnitude of the star players. Such stalwarts as Roger Connor, Montgomery Ward, and Buck Ewing—all future Hall of Fame members— were in the lineup. Keefe and Welch, pitching in tandem, were also destined for Cooperstown and immortality. The Giants were easy pennant winners over Cap Anson's Chicago team.

Tim Keefe began his 19-game winning streak on June 23. He had lost his previous start to yet another star pitcher, John Clarkson. Also elected to the Hall of Fame, even before Keefe and Welch, Clarkson had won 13 straight in 1885.

Keefe's first win was a squeaker, 7–6, over Philadelphia. Then he marched along, and when he won his twelfth in a row, his opponent was Clarkson. During the streak Tim Keefe pitched 17 complete games. The two he failed to finish included one in which he was hit on the arm by a line drive while leading 8–3 in the sixth inning. A replacement with a name more domineering than the record he left behind, Cannonball Eddie Crane, held on for a 9–6 victory credited to Keefe.

The other incomplete game would not have been added to his string by today's scoring rules. On July 16, while leading Chicago 9–0, Keefe was excused for the day after two innings. The practices of the time gave him the win.

Tim Keefe's string came to an end on August 14, when his defense betrayed him and two unearned runs were the difference in a 4–2 loss. Gus Krock, of the Chicago White Stockings, was a lefthanded rookie who soon disappeared from the major leagues, but he had the satisfaction of stopping Keefe at 19.

Considering the winning streaks his contemporaries had run off, it was probably thought that Keefe's record was temporary. Had it not been for the victory gained in that two-inning start, it would have been. He would have been tied with Hoss Radbourn at 18 and eclipsed when Rube Marquard reached 19 in 1912. As it is, more than a century after his feat, Tim Keefe stands beside Marquard with a total no one has surpassed.

American League Record Tied

It wasn't until 1931 that the lesser American League record of 16 consecutive pitching victories was challenged. Lefty Grove came very close to setting a new record in the American League and narrowly missed being the pitcher to break Marquard's mark of 19. Grove had a 31–4 season, figures which could have accommodated both record-breaking streaks.

However, the luck even the best must have to sustain a long streak deserted Grove at the critical point. He was luckless in the game which would have moved him past Walter Johnson and Smokey Joe Wood, coholders of the American League mark.

The 1931 Philadelphia Athletics were awesome. Connie Mack's last championship team won its third pennant in a row. Responding to Depression-related financial pressures, Mack would break up the team, selling off its stars, including Grove, who went to the Red Sox. Future Hall of Famers Jimmie Foxx, Mickey Cochrane, Al Simmons, and Grove himself were at the peak of their careers. The members of the supporting cast—Max Bishop, Jimmie Dykes, Mule Haas, Bing Miller, and others—were all excellent role players. This was a team which did not beat itself.

As the season advanced into August, the Athletics were virtually coasting to a pennant. They would win 107 games and distance the runner-up New York Yankees by 13 games. Grove, pitching every fourth game and appearing in relief when needed, was on his personal roll. For the first time in many years, it appeared the American League record for consecutive victories could be broken by a pitcher. It was possible to project that Grove might go on and also catch Marquard's record. There was enough time left.

Lefty Grove tied the American League record on August 19 and was expected to break it four days later with his seventeenth straight win. The day the record coheld by Walter Johnson and Joe Wood since 1912 was to fall was Sunday, August 23.

The St. Louis Browns, a second-division team and perennial victim, would provide only token opposition, and the unheralded Dick Coffman would be the sacrificial pitching opponent. Grove pitched with close to his usual brilliance, limiting the Browns to six hits, allowing only one run, and striking out six.

However, Dick Coffman, on that particular day, outpitched Grove and shut out the Athletics with only three hits. Grove's streak came to an end at 16 straight victories. He had only joined Johnson and Wood at the top of the American League's list.

Lefty Grove had never been a gracious, philosophical loser. He refused to accept defeat gracefully. He blamed the loss on the absence of Al Simmons from the lineup. True, Simmons was at home, in Milwaukee, seeing a doctor, and his replacement, Jim Moore, was far from being a sure-handed defensive player. When Moore misjudged a fly ball, which became the game-winning hit, Grove fumed that Simmons would have caught the ball. Further, he complained, Simmons, the league-leading batter, would surely have knocked in a few runs as well as preventing the Browns from scoring a tainted one.

Grove complained every time he was asked about the end of his streak, and the image of Simmons idling away the afternoon, thumbing through *National Geographics* in a doctor's waiting room, persisted. Actually, Simmons had an infected ankle and had already been out of the lineup for a week.

What made the defeat more bitter in retrospect was that Grove went on to win his next five starts. These victories would have put the record at 21, eclipsing not only the American League record but topping Marquard's all-time total of 19. (Grove won his next two starts, incidentally, with Simmons still missing from the lineup.) He did not lose until the final game of the season, on September 27.

Schoolboy Rowe's Row

It was only a few years later, in 1934, when the next assault was made on the American League record, now held by Lefty Grove as well as by Walter Johnson and Joe Wood. This time it was the colorful Schoolboy Rowe, blessed with a rural candor that the press found refreshing and the public fascinating, who made the run.

Mickey Cochrane, Grove's former battery mate, was a first-term manager, having been sold by the Athletics to Detroit. Still a great player and catcher, Cochrane had his team headed for the pennant and Schoolboy Rowe led the way. Rowe had been a pitcher of promise and Cochrane had brought about its fulfillment. Rowe had made a slow start, splitting his first eight decisions. His inauspicious beginning offered no portent that when, on June 15, he won his fifth victory, it was the start of a record-equaling skein. During the summer months Rowe shared the spotlight with Dizzy Dean of the National League. However, while Dean was garnering the victories which would eventually reach 30 for the season, he did not string them together the way Rowe did.

Rowe won his sixteenth straight game on August 26 but then ran into the barrier which had blocked other American League pitchers at that point. He joined Grove, Johnson, and Wood at the top of the list but also joined them among the frustrated who could not go past that point.

Rowe stumbled from the path toward a new record on August 29, when the Tigers met the now lowly Philadelphia Athletics in a doubleheader. Gone from Connie Mack's A's were Lefty Grove, Mickey Cochrane, Al Simmons, George Earnshaw, and Rube Walberg. Only Jimmie Foxx remained from the recent championship teams.

It was the second game of an August 29 doubleheader, and Rowe was far off form. He was knocked out in the sixth inning. Unlike the contentious Lefty Grove, Rowe blamed no one but himself, saying without rancor that he'd just had an off-day. He refused the alibi offered by his manager, Mickey Cochrane, who contended that the demands of the press and public on the young pitcher had produced more turmoil than Schoolboy could handle. Rowe scoffed at the idea and went on to finish the season with 24 wins. He didn't face Dizzy Dean in the 1934 World Series, but he split two decisions, as the Cardinals won a seven-game series from Detroit. Another pennant year followed for Detroit, with Rowe winning 19 games. After that a chronic arm problem hindered his career, although he lasted a long while in the major leagues, winning 158 games, with a .610 winning average, over fifteen years.

Carl Hubbell's Fabulous Streak

When one adds the start of one season to the end of the preceding one, one finds a 17-game streak for Cleveland's Johnny Allen in 1936–1937 and another for Baltimore's Dave McNally in 1969–1970. But in this area Carl Hubbell claims all the records.

In the quirky way that records for consecutive victories by pitchers seem to come almost simultaneously, the same two seasons which provided Johnny Allen's 17 straight wins, also produced one of the most fabulous feats of all time. As had been the case with 1912, there was a magic about 1936–1937.

Carl Hubbell, between July 17, 1936, and May 27, 1937, won 24 games in a row. He won his last 16 decisions in 1936 and added 8 more victories before losing a game in 1937.

Carl Hubbell, and the team which would support him in his quest for a record, the New York Giants, were at their best in 1936 and 1937. They were the best in the National League at a time when their crosstown rivals, the Yankees, were dominant in the American League and also in the World Series. They beat the Giants both years despite Hubbell's presence. The Giants won only three World Series games in the two years and Hubbell won two of them.

Carl Hubbell was the ace of the Giants staff and the National League's most valuable player in 1936. He led the league in 1936 with 26 victories, an .813 winning percentage, and a 2.31 ERA. In 1937 he again topped the league in wins with 22 and percentage with .733 and added the strikeout crown with 159, his career high.

It was this kind of consistency that earned Carl Hubbell the nickname "the Meal Ticket." His manager, Bill Terry, knew Hubbell would pitch in rotation and stop any losing streak before it gained momentum.

The Giants were off to a bad start in 1936, although Hubbell was winning two of every three decisions. The day Hubbell's winning streak began, July 17, the Giants were in fifth place, barely over .500 at 42–41 and 10 games behind the defending champion Chicago Cubs. Hubbell had lost his last start, a tough two-hit 1–0 game, to the Cubs' Big Bill Lee. Chicago's run was unearned.

Appropriately Hubbell got the Giants back on a winning track by shutting out Pittsburgh, 6–0. The game contained a streak of another kind. In the first inning Joe Moore, Mel Ott, and Hank Leiber hit successive triples. Before the inning ended, Eddie Mayo, a utility infielder, added another triple. Not only was Hubbell off on a personal winning streak that wouldn't end until the next year, the Giants had found their own victory pace.

Oddly, considering the magnitude of Hubbell's record, the streak-starting shutout was the last one he pitched in 1936. He had a season-opening shutout the next year. However, low-run games predominated, and he produced an ERA of 1.95 for the run of 24 games.

Carl Hubbell's great rival was Dizzy Dean, and duels between the two were matchups between two titans. Hubbell's lefthanded screwball was matched against the fastball of the colorful screwball of the Cardinals. These confrontations were arranged as often as possible for their gate appeal, and Dean tried to head off Hubbell's march toward glory three times during the string.

Twice he failed gloriously and once ingloriously. During the 1936 portion of the skein, Dean lost 2–1 in an extra-inning game and lost another 2–1 game in the regulation nine innings. These were typical Hubbell-Dean matchups, with both pitchers rising to the occasion. Hubbell, over the years, rose higher more often.

Probably in frustration, when the streak reached 22 on May 19, 1937, Dean lost both the game and his temper when umpire George Barr called a balk against Dizzy for the third time. It gave a reprieve to the batter, Giant shortstop Dick Bartell, who had flied out. He then hit a line drive which Pepper Martin dropped, and a flurry of runs followed.

Dean's retaliation was to throw beanballs at every Giant batter who dared step to the plate. In this pre-helmet time such tactics were not viewed kindly, and outfielder Jimmy Ripple offered to take Dean on in a one-to-one fistfight. Dean, who spent a career vainly trying to find someone he could lick, accepted the challenge. He was engulfed by Giant bodies, topped by players in Cardinal uniforms, in what turned into one of the best displays of belligerence ever seen on a ballfield. Individual fights ranged all around the diamond. There were no peacemakers among the players. Among the few who chose to be spectators was Carl Hubbell. He had better use for his arm than swinging it at someone. When order was restored, Hubbell finished pitching a one-run, seven-hit game.

Dean protested his subsequent fine and threatened to boycott the upcoming All Star Game. As usual his threat was unfulfilled. It would have been far better for him if he had stayed away. It was in the 1937 All Star Game that Dean was hit on the foot by an Earl Averill line drive. He tried to pitch while favoring a broken toe and ruined a great right arm.

The end of Hubbell's streak came on May 31 at the hands of the team which considered any victory over the

Pitchers with 12 or More Straight Victories in Season

National League			American League		
Year	**Pitcher**	**Won**	**Year**	**Pitcher**	**Won**
1888	Timothy Keefe, N.Y.	19	1912	Walter Johnson, Wash.	16
1912	Richard Marquard, N.Y.	19	1912	Joseph Wood, Bos.	16
1884	Charles Radbourn, Provi.	18	1931	Robert Grove, Phila.	16
1885	Michael Welch, N.Y.	17	1934	Lynwood Rowe, Det.	16
1890	John Luby, Chi.	17	1932	Alvin Crowder, Wash.	15
1959	El Roy Face, Pitts.	17	1937	John Allen, Cleve.	15
1886	James McCormick, Chi.	16	1969	David McNally, Balt.	15
1936	Carl Hubbell, N.Y.	16	1974	Gaylord Perry, Cleve.	15
1947	Ewell Blackwell, Cinn.	16	1904	John Chesbro, N.Y.	14
1962	John Sanford, S.F.	16	1913	Walter Johnson, Wash.	14
1924	Arthur Vance, Brook.	15	1914	Charles Bender, Phila.	14
1968	Robert Gibson, St. L.	15	1928	Robert Grove, Phila.	14
1972	Steven Carlton, Phila.	15	1961	Edward Ford, N.Y.	14
1885	James McCormick, Chi.	14	1980	Steven Stone, Balt.	14
1886	John Flynn, Chi.	14	1986	W. Roger Clemens, Bos.	14
1904	Joseph McGinnity, N.Y.	14	1924	Walter Johnson, Wash.	13
1909	Edward Reulbach, Chi.	14	1925	Stanley Coveleski, Wash.	13
1984	Richard Sutcliffe, Chi.	14	1930	Wesley Ferrell, Cleve.	13
1985	Dwight Gooden, N.Y.	14	1940	Louis Newsom, Det.	13
1880	Lawrence Corcoran, Chi.	13	1949	Ellis Kinder, Bos.	13
1884	Charles Buffinton, Bos.	13	1971	David McNally, Balt.	13
1885	John Clarkson, Chi.	13	1973	James Hunter, Oak.	13
1892	Denton Young, Cleve.	13	1978	Ronald Guidry, N.Y.	13
1893	Frank Killen, Pitts.	13	1983	D. LaMarr Hoyt, Chi.	13
1896	Frank Dwyer, Cin.	13	1990	Bobby Witt, Tex.	13
1897	Fred Klobedanz, Bos.	13	1991	Scott Erickson, Minn.	13
1898	Ted Lewis, Bos.	13	1901	Denton Young, Bos.	12
1909	Chris. Mathewson, N.Y.	13	1910	Russell Ford, N.Y.	12
1910	Charles Phillippe, Pitts.	13	1914	Hubert Leonard, Bos.	12
1927	Burleigh Grimes, N.Y.	13	1929	Jonathan Zachary, N.Y.	12
1956	Brooks Lawrence, Cin.	13	1931	George Earnshaw, Phila.	12
1966	Philip Regan, L.A.	13	1938	John Allen, Cleve.	12
1971	Dock Ellis, Pitts.	13	1939	Atley Donald, N.Y.	12
1886	Charles Ferguson, Phila.	12	1946	David Ferriss, Bos.	12
1902	John Chesbro, Pitts.	12	1961	Luis Arroyo, N.Y.	12
1904	George Wiltse, N.Y.	12	1963	Edward Ford, N.Y.	12
1906	Edward Reulbach, Chi.	12	1968	David McNally, Balt.	12
1975	Burt Hooton, L.A.	12	1971	Patrick Dobson, Balt.	12
1992	Tom Glavine, Atl.	12	1985	Ronald Guidry, N.Y.	12

Giants as compensation for an otherwise dismal season. The Brooklyn Dodgers invaded the Polo Grounds for a doubleheader which drew the second-largest crowd that had ever crammed into the Giants home field.

The Dodgers had always been a tough team for Hubbell. He had beaten them five times during his 24-game streak, twice in relief, but in the opening game of the doubleheader Brooklyn closed the door on Hubbell's feat.

Carl Hubbell took the long walk from the mound to the clubhouse in center field during the third inning. Five runs had scored. There had been seven hits and three walks. In came Dick Coffman, who had been Lefty Grove's nemesis. It would have been fitting if he had stopped the Dodgers in their tracks and the Giants had rallied to save Hubbell's streak so he could extend it the next time. Neither happened; Brooklyn scored five more runs, the Giants only tallied three runs for the whole game.

Lost in the Crowd

By winning 24 games in a row over two seasons, Carl Hubbell obscured the feat of Roy Face in 1958 and 1959 when the forkballer won 22 consecutive games, all in relief. That stands as the best achievement for a reliever. Also in 1959, Face equaled Johnny Allen's mark of 17 consecutive wins, doing it all in one season.

Roy Face, only five-eight and weighing just 160 pounds, didn't lose his first decision in 1959 until September 11. He had entered the game in relief and gave up the winning run in the ninth inning of a game at Los Angeles when Charlie Neal hit a single. Until then, it appeared that Roy Face was destined to never lose a game. Even when his

forkball wasn't working its usual magic, he won.

A modest man, Face would point to six or seven games when the Pirates' hitters bailed him out. The most extreme of these times came in a June 11 game, when the San Francisco Giants played Pittsburgh. Face came in to protect a 7–5 lead in the eighth inning. The Giants had two men on base and Willie Mays came up as a pinch hitter. He homered and the Giants led, 8–7. In the bottom of the inning, the Pirates erupted with five runs and Face had a win instead of a loss.

During his string, Face won eleven of his games in extra innings.

Consecutive Base Hits

The feat of making a dozen consecutive base hits has been accomplished only twice in all the years major league baseball has been played. The record has rested there for over forty years and might never see the time when a batter delivers a baker's dozen to provide a new record. The hitter who reaches 13 will cap a slow, gradual climb toward a peak shared by Pinky Higgins and Walt Dropo, both American Leaguers. The National League's record is 10.

The history of consecutive base hits goes back to 1897, when Ed Delahanty, whom you would expect to set such standards, and Jake Gettman, whom you wouldn't, each got ten hits in a row during the season. Delahanty, one of five major-league-playing brothers, batted .377 for Philadelphia in 129 games. Gettman, who only played one season as a regular, got his ten straight while appearing in only 36 games for Washington. He hit .315 overall. The

National League record is still 10 consecutive hits, and seven others have joined the original pair.

Tris Speaker was the first to top 10, getting 11 straight hits in 1920. Speaker had eclipsed Doc Johnson's American League total of 9, hit in 1919, the same season Brooklyn's Ed Konetchy had joined Delahanty and Gettman with 10.

The next year, when Speaker moved the major league record up a notch, his feat came amid such epoch record-setting as Babe Ruth's 54 home runs. This had broken Ruth's own mark of 29 set the season before. It dwarfed Speaker's rattling off 11 straight hits. In fact, Speaker's own accomplishment, leading the Cleveland Indians to a World Series victory despite the loss of shortstop Ray

Most Consecutive Hits

American League

Player	Team	Year	H
Pinky Higgins	Bos.	1938	12
Walt Dropo	Det.	1952	12
Tris Speaker	Cleve.	1920	11
Johnny Pesky	Bos.	1946	11
George Sisler	St.L.	1921	10
Harry Heilmann	Det.	1922	10
Harry McCurdy	Chi.	1926	10
Rip Radcliff	Chi.	1938	10
Ken Singleton	Balt.	1981	10
Doc Johnston	Cleve.	1919	9
Ty Cobb	Det.	1925	9
Sam Rice	Wash.	1925	9
Hal Trosky	Cleve.	1936	9
Ted Williams	Bos.	1939	9
Tony Oliva	Minn.	1967	9
Jorge Orta	Cleve.	1980	9
Mickey Hatcher	Minn.	1985	9
Sammy Sosa	Chi.	1993	9

National League

Player	Team	Year	H
Ed Delahanty	Phila.	1897	10
Jake Gettman	Wash.	1897	10
Ed Konetchy	Brook.	1919	10
Kiki Cuyler	Pitts.	1925	10
Chick Hafey	St.L.	1929	10
Joe Medwick	St.L.	1936	10
Buddy Hassett	Bos.	1940	10
Woody Williams	Cin.	1943	10
Bip Roberts	Cin.	1992	10
Joe Kelley	Balt.	1894	9
Rogers Hornsby	St.L.	1924	9
Taylor Douthit	St.L.	1926	9
Babe Herman	Brook.	1926	9
Bill Jurges	N.Y.	1941	9
Terry Moore	St.L.	1947	9
Dick Sisler	Phila.	1950	9
Eddie Waitkus	Phila.	1950	9
Dave Philley	Phila.	1958-59	9
Felipe Alou	S.F.	1962	9
Willie Stargell	Pitts.	1966	9
Rennie Stennett	Pitts.	1975	9
Ron Cey	L.A.	1977	9
Andres Galarraga	Col.	1993	9

Chapman to a fatal beaning during the pennant chase, overshadowed his own batting feats. This included a runner-up .388 to George Sisler's league-leading batting average of .407.

However, Speaker's 11 straight stood the test of time. During the 1920s others made a run at the record but couldn't get beyond 10 straight hits. They included Sisler in 1921 and Harry Heilmann in 1922. Kiki Cuyler in 1925 and Chick Hafey in 1929, all future Hall of Famers, got up to 10 straight in the National League. In 1936 another Hall of Famer to be, Joe Medwick, hit in 10 straight times at bat.

One outsider who edged onto the list with those headed for baseball's Hall of Fame was a reserve catcher, Harry McCurdy. A rookie with the White Sox in 1926, he only played in 33 games, but cracked out 10 straight hits while batting .326. He might have played in more games, but he had a month's vacation in August. He was claimed by the Yankees on waivers, but when New York discovered this included an obligation for the rookie's bonus of $30,000, they refused to complete the deal. The White Sox insisted they were honor-bound. As is usual in baseball, honor lost and McCurdy remained a substitute catcher with Chicago.

Speaker's record finally tumbled in 1938, when Mike "Pinky" Higgins, the Boston Red Sox third baseman, began by going 4 for 4 against the White Sox in Chicago. The next day the team was in Detroit to play a doubleheader with the Tigers. When Higgins went 4 for 4, with a walk, against Roxie Lawson in the first game, and singled his first time up in the second game, Cal Hubbard, umpiring on the bases, observed, "That makes you 5 for 5 for the day."

Higgins told Hubbard he was 9 for 9, counting the previous day in Chicago. It wasn't enough that Higgins put pressure on himself, but after he got his tenth straight hit, the field announcer at Briggs Field, Ty Tyson, made a public-address announcement that Higgins could tie Speaker's record if he got another hit the next time up.

Higgins shook off the hex and got the hit and, with everyone knowing a new record was on the line, ripped a single off Tommy Bridges, the best curveballer in the league, the next time up. It was an unlucky 13, however, as Higgins fanned his last time at bat. The catcher in both games of the doubleheader was Rudy York. It was the year the Tigers tried to find a place for him to play.

Even though he was to be described by Tom Meany as "part Indian, part first baseman," when Hank Greenberg moved to the outfield so York could play where he'd do the least damage, the one season as a catcher had been a disaster. Higgins later confided he had little trouble guessing a fastball was coming as York had become known to avoid complications by refusing to call for curveballs.

In 1952 the slugging first baseman of the Red Sox, Walt Dropo, tied Higgins's record. He had debuted in 1950 with a sensational season, hitting .322, but he never hit above .300 again. Dropo had begun the season with Boston, but in a multiplayer deal in June, he had been traded to Detroit. Going along with Dropo was Johnny Pesky, longtime shortstop for the Red Sox and, in the way of coincidences in record setting, had reached 11 straight hits, one behind Higgins's record, in 1946. Pesky was at shortstop in the games when Dropo tied him first for runner-up, a spot he now shared with Speaker. He watched as Dropo got his twelfth straight.

Like Higgins, Walt Dropo made his run in a doubleheader. He had gone 5 for 5 against the Yankees in a single game on July 14, and the next day, in Griffith Stadium, he had four straight in the first game. All the hits had been singles, but starting off in the first inning of the nightcap, the powerful Dropo hit a triple with the bases loaded.

In the third inning he had his eleventh straight hit, another single, and Mickey Vernon, the Washington first baseman, told him he could tie the record with a hit the next time at bat. He did with a double. And he had another time at bat coming, in the seventh inning. Despite Dropo's hitting, the Tigers trailed, 7–6. He swung from the heels but only lifted a foul fly which catcher Mickey Grasso caught at the edge of the field boxes. The streak was over. Dropo added a single in the ninth inning but had to settle for a shared record which has stood against more recent assaults.

Ken Singleton of Baltimore got 10 in 1981, and Bip Roberts of Cincinnati managed the feat in 1992.

Team Winning Streaks

The two longest winning streaks by teams had different outcomes. Twice National League clubs won 21 in a row and the pennant. When the Chicago White Stockings did it, under Cap Anson, in 1880, they were simply running away from the pack. They won the pennant by 15 games.

However, when their descendants, the Chicago Cubs, won 21 in a row in 1935, the drive capped a sensational stretch battle that caught and passed their rivals, the St. Louis Cardinals, within a few days of the season's end.

These two 21-game streaks are not the longest on record. The record of 26 games won in a row by the 1916 New York Giants stands as the most perverse record of achievement in baseball. No other team has won so many games so convincingly to such little purpose. The Giants came in fourth, despite having had another win streak the same season of 17 straight. Even more peculiarly, the 26 games in a row were all played at home. Maybe the Giants could only win at the Polo Grounds? No. The 17 straight were all won on the road.

John McGraw did a remarkable thing in 1916. He rebuilt the team well into the season, after they had won 17 in a row. The season had started dismally, and before they hit their stride, they had lost thirteen of the first fifteen games played. When they ran off a streak of wins, it only made up for previously lost ground. Then they flattened out again. McGraw acted.

He had a flawed infield. Shortstop Art Fletcher was a gem, but the other positions were played by former stars, Fred Merkle at first and Larry Doyle at second. Bill McKechnie, the third baseman, would someday be a Hall of Famer, but as a manager.

John McGraw had a love-hate relationship with Buck Herzog. He loved him as a player, but hated him as an individual. Herzog had been a rookie with the Giants and was traded away to the Braves, then swapped back again to star on three successive pennant winners, in 1911 through 1913. Then he was exiled again.

McGraw coveted Herzog, an unrepentant infielder who could hit and play any place with superb skill. They met privately, agreed that the money and opportunity involved was more important than any blood feud, and McGraw swapped the immortal Christy Mathewson, whose fade-away pitch had failed, to Cincinnati, where he would become manager. He sent McKechnie along and a young outfielder of promise but little playing time, Edd Roush. The next year and two years later Roush won the batting championships. McGraw never regretted his move. He had laid the groundwork for the 1917 pennant.

Even though the season was well along, McGraw shipped his former captain, Larry Doyle, to Chicago for Heinie Zimmerman. Doyle, who had shouted in boyish enthusiasm, "It's great to be young and a Giant," was no longer young and no longer a Giant.

Fred Merkle, forgiven the blunder of 1908, when he failed to touch second as an apparent winning run scored and cost the Giants a pennant, had also grown old in McGraw's service and was shipped out so a rookie, Walter Holke, could finish the season at first base. When Zimmerman arrived, Herzog was shifted to second, and double plays began to be turned, base hits became infield outs, and the pitchers relished their new-found support. The Giants' drive began as late as September 7, when they were in fourth place, ten games out of third. Ferdie Schupp emerged as a star pitcher and won six games in the string. Pol Perritt won the first game of a doubleheader on September 9 and enjoyed it so much he came back and pitched a shutout in the second game. Regulars won, and rookies debuted and won. The Giants won, but they didn't move up.

The Giants ripped off 12 in a row and then paused for a rain-stopped tie game, 1–1, as Burleigh Grimes, who lost 13 in a row that season, managed a tie game for Pittsburgh. The streak resumed the next day and went on and on, although the Giants had been eliminated from catching Brooklyn in first place. It was the Phillies who were breathing on the necks of the Dodgers, with a chance to tie on the last day.

The Giants' streak was stopped in their last home game of the season, when they lost to the Boston Braves. They crossed the bridge to Brooklyn to close out the season on October 2, and McGraw set off wide speculation in the press by leaving the bench during the game and intimating afterward that the Giants had deliberately lost the game to ensure a Dodger pennant. Brooklyn was managed by Wilbert Robinson, once McGraw's closest crony, his coach and developer of pitchers. Some argument, some twist to the volatile McGraw temper had made them enemies. McGraw, who hated to lose, loathed losing to Brooklyn and Uncle Robbie. Maybe that's all there was to it, just another symptom of McGraw being a sore loser. Yet just ahead was the Black Sox scandal, and playing for the Giants were two non-Chicago players who were to be swept out of baseball when Judge Landis purged its suspect characters—Heinie Zimmerman and Bennie Kauff. McGraw's 1916 Giants finished in fourth place—right where they were when they began their 26-game streak!—and 7 games out of first place.

The 1935 Chicago Cubs, whose 21 straight wins carried them to a pennant, were a streaky team that year and the next year, too. In 1935 they faced a task made tougher by the schedule. The St. Louis Cardinals, the Gas House Gang world champions from 1934, not only led by 2 games, but the indomitable Deans, Dizzy and Paul, headed the staff. Even more comforting for the Cards, the schedule called for the Cubs to play the last five games of the season at Sportsman's Park in St. Louis.

In 1935 the Cubs picked up momentum, and it took them past the Cards in the middle of the streak. They took the lead on September 14 as they won their eleventh game and were three games ahead of the crumbling Cards when they reached St. Louis for the final five games. Lon

Warneke beat Paul Dean 1–0 in the opener, and Bill Lee won his twentieth game of the season, beating Dizzy Dean 6–3 to clinch the pennant. It was the first game of a doubleheader, and the Cubs reached 21 straight by taking the nightcap.

They lost the next game, a meaningless one in the pennant race, in extra innings on Joe Medwick's second home run of the game. The Cards won the season's finale, 2–1, but it was the Cubs who went on to the World Series.

The next year was also a season of streaks. Again the Cubs got in gear with an impressive run of victories, taking 15 straight before midseason was reached. It did not lead to a pennant. Another 15-game winning streak, by the New York Giants, brought the championship to the Polo Grounds.

It was a streak that started late in the season and ran, in part, concurrently with Carl Hubbell's own string of 16 wins. While the Giants were racking up 15 straight, Hubbell appeared in ten consecutive games. He never ran out of steam, only games to win. The season ended with Hubbell experiencing a 16-game streak. He extended it by winning his first 8 decisions the next year to reach 24 straight wins over two seasons.

Other very long winning streaks in the National League that added late-season zest to pennant races were those of the 1924 Dodgers and, of course, the 1951 Giants. It was Dazzy Vance against the world in 1924 when he dominated the league and was the MVP. The Dodgers came up short, unable to catch the leading Giants, who added a fourth straight pennant in 1924, when Brooklyn's 15 straight were not enough.

In 1951 the same traditional rivals reversed roles, but not results. It was the Dodgers who were far in front when the Giants, managed by former Dodger skipper Leo Durocher, began a late-season drive. The Giants had started with the wrong kind of a streak. They lost their first 11 games and spent the season trying to catch the fast-flying Dodgers. They were 13 games behind when they won the first of 16 straight decisions on August 12 and began to close the gap the Dodgers had opened.

The Giants slowly edged closer and into a tie with a game to play. When both teams won their final games, the Dodgers on Jackie Robinson's extra-inning heroics in Philadelphia, the stage was set for a playoff series. It was won by Bobby Thomson's dramatic home run in the last of the ninth of the third, and decisive, game.

The American League's consecutive winning streaks have been turned in mostly by powerhouse teams headed for easy pennant triumphs. However, the 1906 American League season produced long strings of wins by two teams locked in a hotly contested pennant race. The Chicago White Sox set a record, since tied by the 1947 Yankees and the 1988 Boston Red Sox, of 19 straight wins.

Dubbed "the Hitless Wonders" because of a .230 team batting average, the White Sox engaged in a dramatic scenario with the New York team, then called the Highlanders.

In early August the White Sox were in fourth place. Ahead of them were Philadelphia, New York, and Cleveland. Day after day the White Sox chipped away at the lead held by the teams ahead of them. They eventually passed Philadelphia and Cleveland.

The Highlanders proved the hardest to catch. They had benefited from a winning streak of their own, 15 in a row. However, in the final surge of the pennant race, it was the White Sox who came home in first place. New York became the only team to win 15 in a row and not win a pennant in the American League. In the National League since 1900, three teams have won at least 15 in a row and not won the pennant. The most glaring example, of course, was the 1916 Giants, winners of 26 and 17 straight. The 1936 Cubs won 15 in a row and finished second to the Giants, also winners of 15 straight. The 1907 Giants had the poorest finish. Despite 17 straight wins, they finished fourth, 25 games out of first place.

In the main, however, if a team wants to ensure winning a pennant, a good way to do it is rack up 15 or more consecutive victories along the way, preferably in the stretch run.

The Feats

What follows is a celebration of three of baseball's most rare and heroic feats: the triple crowns of batting and pitching, and the triple putout by one player, better known as the unassisted triple play. These feats do not rank with the central records of the game: Henry Aaron's 755 homers, Cy Young's 511 wins, Pete Rose's 4,256 hits, Ty Cobb's lifetime batting average of .366. They are not as distant in memory as a .400 hitter or a 40-game winner. But they are remarkable achievements and—unlike those mentioned above—are not evident from a perusal of the leaders tables found later in this book.

Triple Crown Winners—Batting

Baseball's first Triple Crown winner, Paul Hines, waited ninety years to be enthroned. The crown consists of three jewels: the batting, home run, and runs-batted-in titles must be won in a single season. The RBI count was a late starter among baseball stats and had to be reconstructed for earlier seasons. However, it was not for lack of the RBI distinction that Hines, of the Providence Grays, waited for belated recognition. His feat went unacknowledged until researchers turned up information which made him the true 1878 batting champion.

A special Baseball Records Committee met in 1968 and put a stamp of approval on statistics which had been in dispute or unverified from baseball's past. The new information appeared the next year when Macmillan published the first edition of *The Baseball Encyclopedia*.

Abner Dalrymple had gone to his grave in 1939, the year the Baseball Hall of Fame Museum opened in Cooperstown, New York, with one baseball honor to his name. He had won the National League batting championship in 1878. Paul Hines, who died in 1935, was remembered only as the winner of the 1879 title. But new data—coming from the two tie games he played and the one for Dalrymple—have revealed that Hines ought to have been a repeat batting champion, too, for under modern scoring rules, his batting average of .358 was higher than Dalrymple's .356.

Paul Hines enjoyed that distinction from 1969 through

1994, then lost it as Major League Baseball and *Total Baseball* adopted a new stance, acknowledging that the individual marks amassed in tie games were not counted in the NL of 1878, *by the practices of the day*—and thus the championship should return to Dalrymple, despite his lower average under modern reconstruction. Thus with hindsight, we can award Hines 1879 batting-average supremacy (though not the championship), the RBI leadership which resulted from reconstructed states, and the small but clearly superior total of 4 home runs. Thus Paul Hines can be said to have attained the first Triple Crown. In addition, when he won the batting title again in 1879, again through later research efforts, he became the first to repeat as hitting leader.

Another nineteenth-century player, Hugh Duffy, had—since 1969, when his RBI data first were published—been considered the first to wear the Triple Crown. In 1894 he had won the three necessary titles but had almost obscured his own feat by batting .438, later corrected upward to .440. This remains the highest batting average of all time and in Duffy's later years had always interested interviewers more than the Triple Crown. Duffy's 18 home runs and 145 runs batted in led the league in these departments in 1894, but the idea of linking them as a diadem had not yet been formed. No one knew Paul Hines had done it and few cared that Hugh Duffy had. Although the RBI was known as a baseball stat as early as 1879, it was not commonly used until the 1910s, and not an official measure until 1920.

Hugh Duffy, a twinkle-eyed New Englander, told about his batting record for the fifty subsequent years that he spent in major league baseball, the last several decades as a coach for the Boston Red Sox. When a rookie named Ted Williams arrived in the big leagues in 1939, Hugh Duffy became his first mentor. Duffy proclaimed Williams as the greatest hitter he ever saw and watched while Williams won two Triple Crowns and missed a third by the closest margin possible.

The player who placed the stamp of the superstar most firmly on the concept of the Triple Crown was Nap Lajoie, who was the dominant player in the game when the American League was formed and ushered in twentieth-century baseball. The great Napoleon Lajoie had become the star of the Philadelphia Phillies as the nineteenth century closed. He was the prize recruit for the new league, remaining in Philadelphia where Connie Mack was establishing a new franchise. Lajoie put the team and the American League on the baseball map in 1901, when he provided the league-leading totals in the three prize categories. He batted .426, hit 14 home runs in the dead-ball era of the time, as later research showed, and, batted in 145 runs. It was the greatest season the immortal would ever have. He would win two more batting titles and again lead the league in RBIs. However, home runs were not his specialty.

Still, his Triple Crown brought instant respect to the new league and, together with other stars who had switched leagues, forced acceptance that the American League was a full-fledged major league and would be part of the basis of baseball's structure from then on.

Lajoie was succeeded as the American League's superstar by Ty Cobb, who also laid claim to the Triple Crown in 1909. As with Lajoie, hitting home runs was not

Cobb's dominant ability, and despite ten batting championships and four RBI titles, he wore the Triple Crown but once. He came close two other times, in 1907 and 1911, finishing second in home runs each of those years.

Cobb's great rival was the National League's Honus Wagner, who never wore the Triple Crown, although he too missed it by a close margin. In 1908 he was second in home runs, the most difficult final jewel for the superstars of the dead-ball era to achieve. Wagner's eight batting titles and four RBI championships were never accompanied by a home run leadership.

While the list of those who have won the Triple Crown is short, it is a quality list. All but one Triple Crown holder in this century—the suspect Heinie Zimmerman—are in the Hall of Fame.

In 1912 Heinie Zimmerman, one of the best major league third basemen, put together the greatest season he would ever have. Honus Wagner failed to repeat as batting champion, and his 102 RBI total was one less than Zimmerman's, according to the tabulations of Ernie Lanigan. The 14 home runs Zimmerman hit edged teammate Wildfire Schulte, who had led the league in four-baggers the two previous seasons, by one. Only in batting average, where Zimmerman's .372 far distanced the field, did he have a clear superiority, but a Triple Crown by any measure is a rare treasure and it was Heinie's without dispute, that is until the researchers of Information Concepts, Inc., the group that compiled *The Baseball Encyclopedia,* downgraded his RBI total to 99. Later, an editor of *The Baseball Encyclopedia* fudged Zim's RBI count back up to 103 to restore his Triple Crown, but we cannot subscribe to such an arbitrary change.

It was 1922 before the Triple Crown would again rest on a player's head, but when it did, it landed on the brow of the royally nicknamed "Rajah" Hornsby and just eluded Babe Ruth, "the Sultan of Swat."

Hornsby strung together six successive batting titles, from 1920 through 1925, and added another in 1928. Although he had home run power to go with his high averages, the title escaped him in 1921, when George Kelly outhomered him by two. It would have been the first Triple Crown for the Rajah and would have given him an eventual three, a total no one has ever achieved.

Babe Ruth, who got two legs up on the Triple Crown seven times without ever winning one, had many home run titles and frequently topped the league in RBIs. However, the competition for batting championships in the 1920s, when Cobb, Sisler, and Heilmann topped .400 and Heilmann alone accounted for four batting titles, was tough. Ruth managed one hitting title but lost the RBI leg that year, 1924, to Goose Goslin. The Babe won many honors, but the Triple Crown was not among them.

In the 1930s a quartet of superstars and future Hall of Fame members competed for the Triple Crown during most of the decade, and each took a single turn wearing it.

The American League had two great first baseman, Jimmie Foxx and Lou Gehrig. Each was a threat to claim the Crown every year, but when Foxx narrowly failed on two occasions, it was not Gehrig who stymied him. In 1932 Jimmie came frustratingly close. He was edged out of the batting title by the clumsy-fielding Dale Alexander in 1932. Called "Moose," Alexander split the season between Detroit and Boston, the first player to win a batting title while appearing with two teams. Alexander barely qualified for the championship, but his .367 topped the .364 by Foxx. The following year, 1933, Foxx won his lone Triple Crown.

Alexander was long gone back to the minor leagues before Jimmie Foxx had his second near-miss of the Triple Crown in 1938. This time it was the home run lead that eluded him. Although Foxx hit 50 home runs in 1938, while winning the batting and RBI honors, Hank Greenberg hit 58 homers to almost equal Babe Ruth's record of 60.

While Gehrig and Foxx were trying on the Triple Crown for size in the American League, two sluggers in the National League were sharing domination of their league. Chuck Klein was the league's outstanding batter during the early 1930s and Joe Medwick took over for the final half of the decade. Both wore the Triple Crown, Klein getting his in 1933 when Jimmie Foxx was doing likewise. It was the only year that each league produced a Triple Crown winner. Medwick won his in 1937.

The next to claim the Triple Crown was Ted Williams. A brash rookie when he reported to the Boston Red Sox in 1939, he had little to learn from the old guy hitting fungos in practice. Hugh Duffy took one look at Williams's swing and knew the only part he could serve was as a role model. Williams had his eye on hitting .400. When he did it, in 1941, his .406 was far short of Duffy's .440, the all-time record.

Williams was also one leg short of the Triple Crown in 1941. He added the home run title to his batting championship, but his main rival, Joe DiMaggio, had topped the RBI column. DiMaggio had piled up his runs-batted-in totals largely during his 56-game hitting streak that season.

Ted Williams won all three titles for the Triple Crown the next season, 1942, and then went off to serve in World War Two. Several wartime players won two legs of the Triple Crown: Rudy York, with the Detroit Tigers in 1943, and Bill Nicholson, a Chicago Cubs outfielder in 1943 and 1944. Both hit home runs and batted in runs at league-leading levels, but they were far outdistanced for the batting-average honors.

Ted Williams returned from the war in 1946 and finished second in each of the Triple Crown categories. Mickey Vernon beat him out for the batting title, and Hank Greenberg, who had blocked Jimmie Foxx in 1938, had his last hurrah with the Tigers, topping Williams in both home runs and runs batted in.

The next year, with Greenberg gone to the National League, Ted Williams claimed his second Triple Crown. No one was close to him in any of the three prize categories, and despite three prime seasons lost to wartime service, the Red Sox star seemed most likely to be the first to wear the Triple Crown three times. He had won in 1942 and 1947.

In 1948 his old nemesis, Joe DiMaggio, who was never to win a Triple Crown, picked off two of the crown jewels, leading the American League in home runs with 39 and in runs batted in with 155. Ted Williams was far ahead of the pack as batting champion with a .369 average.

It was 1949 that proved the greatest disappointment to Williams. DiMaggio was injured much of the season and did not compete for individual honors. However, the pennant race was tightly contested between the Yankees and Red Sox, and more interest was focused on that than on the seemingly assured third Triple Crown to be worn by Ted Williams.

As the season reached the final weekend, Boston came to New York for two games between the Red Sox and Yankees. Boston was a game ahead and needed to win only one to gain the pennant. They lost on Saturday, and the teams were tied when Sunday's game began.

The biggest threat to Ted Williams' third Triple Crown came from teammate Vern Stephens, a slugging shortstop who was tied with Ted for RBIs. Williams held a small but probably secure batting lead over George Kell of the Detroit Tigers.

However, Williams and the Red Sox were in a slump, and it cost both the team and the individual their honors. The final game of the season between the Yankees and Red Sox was one of the most exciting of all time, if you were a Yankee fan. If you were among the generations of faithful Red Sox followers who have seen their team fail in the final situation, one frustrating season after another, it was a bitter end. The Yankees staved off a three-run Red Sox rally to win 5–3.

Williams had gone hitless and ended up not only missing a World Series appearance but his third Triple Crown. While Williams had sputtered in the final games, George Kell, who had missed two stretches of games with injuries, got back in the lineup for Detroit's final three games. With only a batting title at stake, Kell had two hits in his final game. When the final statistics were known, George Kell had batted .3429 and Ted Williams .3427. It was the closest any player ever came to a Triple Crown without actually winning it and the closest anyone has come to earning the honor three times.

The year before, in the National League, Stan Musial had narrowly missed his bid for a Triple Crown, when he was one behind Johnny Mize and Ralph Kiner, who tied for the home run title with 40.

In 1953 Al Rosen had a near-miss almost as tight as Ted Williams had had in 1949. Rosen won the home run and RBI titles but was edged out, .337 to .336, for the batting championship by Mickey Vernon, of the Washington Senators, who had blocked Williams's bid in that category in 1946.

Mickey Mantle hit his peak in 1956 when he put the necessary ingredients together to win a Triple Crown. He hit .353 for the only batting title he would win, had top totals in home runs with 52, and piled up 130 runs batted in.

Ten years later, in 1966, Frank Robinson reacted to being traded out of the National League by winning the Triple Crown in the American League. His .316 batting average was one of only two above .300 that year in the American League. He had switched leagues just in time. A .316 average wouldn't have made the top five in the National League in 1966. He won the home run and RBI titles comfortably.

In 1967, the year of the Red Sox "Impossible Dream," the team was driven to a surprise championship by the captain, Carl Yastrzemski, who had an astounding year. Yaz won the only home run title of his career and also the lone RBI championship he would record. He joined these with one of his three batting crowns and ended the season with what was to become an elusive honor, the Triple Crown.

He is the last player to wear the title, although a number of players have gained two legs, including Yaz's teammate, Jim Rice, who did this twice. In the American League the inability of power hitters to achieve a high batting average has resulted in a parade of sluggers leading in home runs and runs batted in but falling short in base-hit percentage.

Harmon Killebrew, who tied with Yaz for home runs in Yastrzemski's crown-winning season, Frank Howard, Dick Allen, Reggie Jackson, George Scott, Eddie Murray, Tony Armas, and Jose Canseco have won two legs but failed the batting title.

Since Yaz won the last Triple Crown, two National Leaguers have won batting titles and the RBI championship, but failed in home runs. Joe Torre in 1971 and Al Oliver in 1982 earned two legs one way, and Johnny Bench, Willie Stargell, George Foster, Andre Dawson, and Mike Schmidt have done it with the home run and RBI crowns. Foster did it twice and Schmidt four times.

Combining a high batting average with power is a rare characteristic in contemporary baseball. Players such as Rod Carew and Wade Boggs, who won frequent batting championships without expectation of adding the other elements of the Triple Crown, served to reduce the likelihood that a pure power hitter would also annex a batting title, especially in the course of the same season.

Carl Yastrzemski might not have been just part of a vanishing breed. He might have been the last example of a breed that has already vanished.

Triple Crown Winners—Pitching

Tommy Bond, the only nineteenth-century pitcher on the list of Triple Crown Winners who is not in the Hall of Fame, has, at least, the honor of turning the feat first. When the National League was formed in 1876, Bond was an established star in the National Association. The others who eventually won the pitchers' Triple Crown, for the most wins and strikeouts and the lowest ERA in a single season, began their careers in the National League.

Although he was only twenty-one when he won the Triple Crown in 1877, Bond had been pitching for prominent teams since he had been sixteen and joined the Athletics of Brooklyn. He entered the National League with Hartford but moved to Boston for his best seasons. He was Boston's only pitcher during 1877 and 1878 and pitched the great majority of games in 1879. He won 123 of the 204 games Boston played in those early years of short schedules.

Bond, who later coached baseball at Harvard, was celebrated for his victories and strikeouts. The measurement of earned runs was done retroactively.

As Bond's career lapsed, the next to claim the Triple Crown of pitching emerged. Old Hoss Radbourn reached the peak year that gave him his nickname for durability in 1884. He pitched the Providence Grays to the National League pennant, almost singlehandedly, after Charlie Sweeney's departure had left only Radbourn as the team's pitcher.

His 59 victories is the most ever won by a pitcher in a season. It shines brightest among all such jewels in the

Triple Crown Hitters

American League

Player	Team	Year	HR	RBI	BA
Nap Lajoie	Phila.	1901	14	125	.422
Ty Cobb	Det.	1909	9	115	.377
Jimmie Foxx	Phila.	1933	48	163	.356
Lou Gehrig	N.Y.	1934	49	165	.363
Ted Williams	Bos.	1942	36	137	.356
	Bos.	1947	32	114	.343
Mickey Mantle	N.Y.	1956	52	130	.353
Frank Robinson	Bal.	1966	49	122	.316
Carl Yastrzemski	Bos.	1967	44	121	.326

National League

Player	Team	Year	HR	RBI	BA
Paul Hines*	Prov.	1878	4	50	.358
Hugh Duffy	Bos.	1894	18	145	.438
Heinie Zimmerman**	Chi.	1912	14	103	.372
Rogers Hornsby	St.L.	1922	42	152	.401
	St. L.	1925	39	143	.403
Chuck Klein	Phila.	1933	28	120	.368
Joe Medwick	St.L.	1937	31	154	.374

*Hines's batting average was the highest in the NL, but Abner Dalrymple retains his title.

**Zimmerman ranked first in RBIs as calculated by Ernie Lanigan, but only third as calculated by ICI research in 1969.

Triple Crowns worn by those who came after him. Radbourn won 309 games in his big league career, but the 59 he totaled in his 1884 season—including a streak of 26 wins in 27 decisions—gave him a celebrity which was recognized when he was named to the Hall of Fame in its opening year, 1939.

A Triple Crown is an exacting measurement of a pitcher's superiority at any time. However, because of the circumstance that he started so many games for the league's best team, Radbourn's win totals and strikeout numbers can largely be attributed to sheer volume. However, it is his 1.38 ERA at a time when the league mark was 2.98 that stamps Old Hoss as truly remarkable for his time.

Tim Keefe, the next pitcher to annex a Triple Crown, wore his for a season that has kept his name in the active files of modern baseball writers. Whenever a pitcher runs off a string of victories, this prompts a review of the record book, and Keefe's 19 in a row is remembered as the highest total, shared with Rube Marquard's 1912 season total of 19 straight. In all, Tim Keefe won 35 games for the New York Giants in 1888, just edging out the man who would take the Triple Crown the next year.

John Clarkson pitched Boston to a pennant in 1889, winning the Triple Crown as the workhorse of a staff which included the worn Old Hoss Radbourn. Clarkson won 49 games and Radbourn 20.

Clarkson's career was overlapped by that of Amos Rusie, the most awesome pitcher of the 1890s. A burly farm boy, "the Hoosier Thunderbolt" was the principal reason the distance of the pitcher's box was pushed back in 1893. Rusie responded the following year by continuing to dominate the league in strikeouts, while topping all pitchers with 36 wins and an ERA of 2.78.

Probably because of the increased pitching distance, the league ERA ballooned to 5.32 and batters averaged .309 in 1894. This was the year Hugh Duffy won the batter's Triple Crown and set a still-unexcelled .440 batting record.

Rusie's career peaked in 1894. The next season one of the most oppressive men to own a big league team, Andrew Freedman, bought the Giants and began a blood feud with Rusie. Rusie sat out the 1896 season, but returned as a reluctant star for two more 20-game-winning seasons. Then he tore his arm muscles and retired. A token appearance in 1901 was the tenth season which qualified him for election to the Hall of Fame.

Just as Nap Lajoie marked the American League's inaugural in 1901 by winning a Triple Crown for batters, another established star, Cy Young, did the same for the pitchers' version. Young, in midcareer as a big league pitcher, won 33 games, a total almost dwarfed among the 511 he won in his career. This latter is a mark certain to stand permanently.

With two major leagues now offering the potential of a Triple Crown winner each year, it took only until 1905 to have both the American and National Leagues produce such winners. Christy Mathewson won the first of the two Triple Crowns he would win for the New York Giants, and the eccentric Rube Waddell had his last great year with the Philadelphia Athletics.

Matty won 31 games, struck out 206, and had an ERA of 1.43. The Rube produced 26 wins, 287 strikeouts, and an ERA of 1.48. The World Series, inaugurated in 1903 but boycotted by the Giants in 1904, was resumed in 1905. It would have provided marvelous theater for the two Triple Crown winners. The confrontation would have been the only one of its kind. Never since have two pennant winners also had pitching's Triple Crown winners. Alas, the colorful Rube Waddell injured his arm while wrestling a teammate just before the Series began.

Without Waddell to oppose him, Christy Mathewson won three games, all shutouts, and the Giants took the Series in five. Matty won the Triple Crown again in 1908 but lost his last start when the Chicago Cubs won the playoff game of a season which had ended in a tie. It was the failure of Fred Merkle to reach second as the winning run scored, resulting in his becoming an inning-ending force out, that deprived Matty of a second opportunity to wear his Triple Crown into a World Series.

Walter Johnson, the next to sport a Triple Crown, won three at widely spaced intervals in his long career. The first came in 1913, the next in 1918, and the last in 1924 when, in his eighteenth season, Johnson once more topped the American League in the three prize categories. This time it also brought a pennant to the Senators, the first in their history. The World Series came close to being a disappointing anticlimax for Johnson. He lost the opener to the Giants in extra innings, then lost again, but salvaged glory by winning the seventh game in relief.

Earlier, during Walter Johnson's widely spaced crown jewels, Grover Alexander produced the most impressive reign ever enjoyed by a Triple Crown winner. Pitching for the Philadelphia Phillies, he had three successive seasons with 30 or more victories, starting with the pennant-winning 1915 season; each time he led the NL in ERA and K's as well. What stopped Alexander's run of mastery was World War One. Old Pete swapped his baseball uniform for the khaki of the Army and his Triple Crown honors for a sergeant's stripes.

While Pete was in the Army, another pitcher claimed the Triple Crown. Hippo Vaughn in 1917 had achieved immortality by engaging in a double no-hit game, losing in the tenth inning. In 1918, with Alexander away, Vaughn won the Triple Crown pitching for the Cubs.

Ironically Grover Alexander had served his Army hitch as a new member of the Cubs. With his battery mate, Reindeer Bill Killefer, he had been sold to Chicago after winning his third Triple Crown, in 1917. He pitched only three games in 1918 while Vaughn was in the star's role, and in 1919 the two teammates competed for the Triple Crown. Alexander led the league in ERA and Vaughn in strikeouts. Between them they won 37 games, but neither came close to topping the league.

However, in 1920 Grover Alexander again emerged as the Triple Crown winner. It was his fourth, the most ever won by a pitcher. He continued to star, despite personal and physical problems, during the 1920s without again leading in any of the categories which make up the diadem of the Triple Crown.

Next to wear the Triple Crown of pitchers was Dazzy Vance. Like Rusie, Waddell, and Johnson, Vance began with expectation of finishing each season with a league-leading total in strikeouts. In 1924 he won the Most Valuable Player Award, even though the Brooklyn Dodgers as a team could not win the pennant. To his strikeout superiority, the Dazzler added leadership in wins with 24 and an ERA of 2.16. His domination of the league can best be measured by comparing his ERA to a league total of 3.87 as the lively ball bounded off hitters' bats.

Lefty Grove of the Philadelphia Athletics won back to back Triple Crowns in 1930 and 1931, having missed one of the three legs in 1929. The A's won pennants all three of those years, and Grove was their leading pitcher. In 1929 teammate George Earnshaw topped him in wins, 24 to 20, as Grove missed getting decisions in an unusual number of games.

Another southpaw ace, Lefty Gomez, succeeded Lefty Grove as a Triple Crown winner. Like Grove, he wore the title twice, but not consecutively. He won his first Triple Crown, oddly, in a season when his team, the New York Yankees, didn't win a pennant, 1934. His next came in 1937 as the Yankees were in the midst of a run of four straight pennants.

Gomez was only a spot starter in 1939, when the Yankees met the Reds in the World Series, but Cincinnati had a converted third baseman, Bucky Walters heading their staff, the first National Leaguer to win the Triple Crown in fifteen years.

During World War Two, Hal Newhouser emerged as a superlative pitcher who might have been equally impressive against peacetime competition. He missed the Triple Crown in 1944, winning two legs but coming in second to Detroit Tiger teammate Dizzy Trout for ERA honors. In 1945, the final wartime year, Newhouser topped the American League in the three prize categories, and winning the Triple Crown went into a long hiatus when the 1946 season resumed with the star pitchers back from service.

Despite leading the league in victories six times and in strikeouts seven, Bob Feller never won an official ERA title to match up with the other components of the Triple Crown. Although Feller's ERA in 1940 is today regarded as the lowest for that year, at that time Ernie Bonham won the title despite pitching only 99 innings.

Warren Spahn topped the National League in victories eight times, led in strikeouts four times, and even took ERA honors three times, but he could never link them up in a single season.

Robin Roberts, like Feller, never won an ERA title, so despite leading in victories four times and strikeouts twice, the singular honor of the Triple Crown eluded him, as it did all other pitchers once baseball had returned to the normalcy of peacetime play.

Triple Crown Pitchers

American League

Player	Team	Year	W	L	SO	ERA
Cy Young	Bos.	1901	33	10	158	1.62
Rube Waddell	Phila.	1905	26	11	287	1.48
Walter Johnson	Wash.	1913	36	7	303	1.09
	Wash.	1918	23	13	162	1.27
	Wash.	1924	23	7	158	2.72
Lefty Grove	Phila.	1930	28	5	209	2.54
	Phila.	1931	31	4	175	2.06
Lefty Gomez	N.Y.	1934	26	5	158	2.33
	N.Y.	1937	21	11	194	2.33
Hal Newhouser	Det.	1945	25	9	212	1.81

National League

Player	Team	Year	W	L	SO	ERA
Tommy Bond	Bos.	1877	40	17	170	2.11
Old Hoss Radbourn	Prov.	1884	59	12	441	1.38
Tim Keefe	N.Y.	1888	35	12	333	1.74
John Clarkson	Bos.	1889	49	19	284	2.73
Amos Rusie	N.Y.	1894	36	13	195	2.78
Christy Mathewson	N.Y.	1905	31	8	206	1.27
	N.Y.	1908	37	11	259	1.43
Grover Alexander	Phila.	1915	31	10	241	1.22
	Phila.	1916	33	12	167	1.55
	Phila.	1917	30	13	201	1.86
Hippo Vaughn	Chi.	1918	22	10	148	1.74
Grover Alexander	Chi.	1920	27	14	173	1.91
Dazzy Vance	Brook	1924	28	6	262	2.16
Bucky Walters	Cin.	1939	27	11	137	2.29
Sandy Koufax	L.A.	1963	25	5	306	1.88
	L.A.	1965	26	8	382	2.04
	L.A.	1966	27	9	317	1.73
Steve Carlton	Phila.	1972	27	10	310	1.97
Dwight Gooden	N.Y.	1985	24	4	268	1.53

It wasn't until Sandy Koufax reached stardom when the Dodgers were transplanted to Los Angeles and notched three Triple Crown titles that the distinction was again achieved. Koufax topped the three needed categories in 1963, 1965, and 1966. Unlike any other winner of the Triple Crown, Koufax retired with the honor. An aching arthritic arm caused his early retirement, leaving a final season of 27 victories, 317 strikeouts, and an ERA of 1.73.

A Triple Crown-winning pitcher has not always meant a pennant for his team, although the two have gone together more often than not. However, in 1972 Steve Carlton took the honor despite pitching for a last-place team. There has never been such a contrast in the success of a team's best pitcher and the rest of its staff. The Phillies won 59 games, and Carlton was responsible for 27 of them. He also led, for the only time, in ERA, with 1.97, and struck out 310.

Again a drought followed, despite the presence of such star pitchers as Tom Seaver, Fergie Jenkins, Juan Marichal, Jim Palmer, Gaylord Perry, and others who led in some of the prize-earning stats. Then in 1985 the New York Mets' Dwight Gooden took up the challenge and claimed the Triple Crown with a remarkable record: 24-4, 1.53, and 268 strikeouts. Gooden faltered the next year, but Roger Clemens came forward to just miss the honor by finishing second in strikeouts while winning the other two legs.

The Unassisted Triple Play

The unassisted triple play has been turned in regular season major league play only ten times in this century and just one questionable time in the nineteenth. (It also happened once in World Series play.)

On May 30, 1987, family and friends of ninety-three-year-old Jimmy Cooney gathered at his home to celebrate the sixtieth anniversary of his unassisted triple play. Rare? It was the last one made in the NL at that time.

Fate waited until Jimmy Cooney died two years later before ending the drought of TP-6UA scorebook entries. However, as wellwishers celebrated his sixty-year-old feat it seemed as though it might stand forever. Letters of congratulation had come for the the occasion from NL president A. Bartlett Giamatti and Dallas Green, the general manager of the Chicago Cubs. Cooney had worn a Chicago Cubs uniform the day destiny had decreed he be in the right place at the right time. A much-traveled infielder, he had worn six major league uniforms in seven seasons. It was a happy coincidence that he was Chicago's shortstop when he made his unassisted triple play. His father, the first Jimmy Cooney, had been Chicago's shortstop in 1890, '91, and part of '92.

Jimmy's younger brother John had logged twenty years in the big leagues as a pitcher, and after his arm went lame, he had become an outfielder and first baseman.

Jimmy Cooney was no stranger to unassisted triple plays. Two seasons earlier, when he was shortstop for the St. Louis Cardinals, he was doubled off second by the Pirate shortstop Glenn Wright, who next tagged out Rogers Hornsby coming from first base. Wright had snared a line drive off the bat of Jim Bottomley to start his triple play. He watched from the Pirates' bench the day Cooney emulated his feat in much the same manner.

Paul Waner provided the line drive to make the first out, with Cooney snaring it as he ran toward second base. Clyde Barnhart had broken for second on the pitch, and Lloyd Waner, the runner on second, had dashed for third as his brother, Paul, swung. Lloyd was doubled off second, and Cooney simply tagged the startled Barnhart, who thought the ball had gone into center field for a base hit.

There are certain similarities among ten of the eleven unassisted triple plays which have been recorded. These have occurred with runners on first and second, have been made by infielders, and have required the complicity of baserunners either attempting a double steal or running away on a hit-and-run play. The eleventh—which is soon to be revealed—was by an outfielder, with runners on second and third.

Even the most celebrated unassisted-triple-play feat had an explanation that almost absolved the victims, the Brooklyn Dodgers, of bonehead base running. This was the only such event to happen in a World Series, and it was turned in by Bill Wambsganss, the Cleveland Indian second baseman in 1920. Those who have examined the boxscore have questioned the tactics of Uncle Wilbert Robinson, the Brooklyn manager whose strategies often were charitably called "unusual." It was the fifth inning, and Brooklyn, behind 7–0, had the first two runners on base. Play it safe? Not Uncle Robbie.

Despite being scoreless, the Dodgers had been hitting the Cleveland pitcher, Jim Bagby, hard. It was a game in which they made thirteen hits and scored a lone run. Bill Wambsganss, who told the story hundreds of times, explained that he chose to play very deep when Clarence Mitchell, a very good-hitting pitcher came to bat in the fifth inning. He didn't think a seven-run lead was too secure the way the Dodgers had been hitting.

When Mitchell cracked the ball on a line, the batters took off, not thinking that Wamby was where the ball was going. He was and ran over and doubled Kilduff off second and turned and found a dumbfounded Otto Miller standing in the baseline. He tagged him out and, as has been the case after every unassisted triple play, trotted off the field in silence. It always takes the crowd a minute or more to realize what has happened.

In the early years of baseball, outfielder Paul Hines of the Providence Grays, had been credited with making an unassisted triple play. Later-day research indicated Hines had made an unassisted double play but had thrown to a base for the third out. But according to the rules of 1878, Hines did indeed register an unassisted triple play.

In 1928, Providence sportswriter W. D. "Bill" Perrin—who at that time had covered the Providence Grays for nearly half a century—described Hines' actions in the game played on May 8, 1878, in Providence. "The circumstances of this play have afforded more arguments than any other known play. That the play was made is not disputed, but whether Hines made the play unassisted or whether [second baseman Charles] Sweasy completed it by retiring the third man. . . . Here is what happened: [Jim] O'Rourke drew a base on balls and scored when Sweasy threw [Jack] Manning's drive over [Providence first baseman Tim] Murnane's head, Manning going to third on the error. Murnane muffed [Ezra] Sutton's fly, Manning holding third [as Sutton took second]. [Jack] Burdock was next up and dropped the ball just over [shortstop Tom] Carey's head for what looked like a safe hit. . . .

"The story in the *Providence Journal* of the next day thus describes the play: 'Manning and Sutton proceeded to the home plate,' meaning that both rounded third. 'Hines ran in and caught the ball, and kept going to tag third.' The rule then as now requires that when a base runner is forced to retrace his steps he must retouch the bases passed in reverse order. As Hines touched third with the ball in his hand, after making the catch, before either Manning or Sutton could get back, both were out automatically. It is true that Hines then on a signal from Sweasy threw the ball to second, but this was unnecessary as both runners were out at third."

To confirm Perrin's view, let's look at the playing rules for 1878, the year in which Hines made his celebrated play. Rule V, Section 1 reads: "Players running the bases must touch each base in regular order, viz., first, second, third, and home bases; and when obliged to return to bases they have occupied they must retouch them in reverse order. . . ." And Rule V, Section 15 reads: "Any base-runner failing to touch the base he runs for shall be declared out if the ball be held by a fielder, while touching said base, before the base-runner returns and touches it." Chadwick's gloss on the rule stated: ". . . it is only necessary for a fielder to hold the ball on the base, which should have been touched, in order to put the runner out."

Eureka! The controversy of over a century is thus resolved, and in favor of Paul Hines and his unassisted triple play. Rewrite the record books!

Johnny Neun had read in the morning paper of May 31, 1927, about Jimmy Cooney's unassisted triple play in the National League. As first baseman for the Detroit Tigers, known for his fielding and base stealing, Neun was alert to all possibilities when Homer Summa's line drive landed in his glove. Charlie Jamieson was a dead duck, caught off first and easily tagged for the second out. Shortstop Jackie Tavener was jumping up and down at second base calling for the ball. Slow-footed Glen Myatt was lumbering back from third base.

Neun waved his shortstop out of the way and raced toward second base, implausibly shouting, "I'm running into the Hall of Fame."

In a nice touch of journalistic enterprise, *Sports Illustrated,* in 1987, noted that both Jimmy Cooney and Johnny Neun were still alive and arranged for them to talk on the telephone about their unique plays made sixty years earlier. They had been contemporaries but had played in different leagues and had never met.

When each had gone back to the minor leagues, they played against each other in the International League but simply passed each other without fraternal comment, despite having shared such an extremely rare experience. They had a very nice talk, and months later, when Jimmy reached his anniversary a day ahead of Johnny, it was Neun who called to extend congratulations.

On July 30, 1968, Ron Hansen, playing shortstop for the Washington Senators, made an unassisted triple play, following the process all other shortstops have used. He grabbed a line drive off the bat of Joe Azcue, stepped on second to retire Dave Nelson, and tagged Russ Snyder coming from first. It was the first time the feat had been pulled since 1927, forty-one years earlier.

It was the most memorable event of Hansen's week, which was an unusual one in other ways as well. Following his play, he struck out six consecutive times, perhaps still stunned by the event. Then he regained his batting eye to hit a grand-slam home run. His unassisted triple play had been made on a road trip. He could expect applause when he came to bat the first time before hometown Washington fans when the team returned home. But he didn't get this. Instead, he was traded to the White Sox.

The first unassisted triple play of the twentieth century was made on July 19, 1909, by a Cleveland shortstop, Neal Ball. Overall Cleveland has been involved in five of the eleven unassisted triple plays in the major leagues. Three times the event has taken place there, twice executed by Cleveland players, and in all a Cleveland player has been involved somewhere five times. It all began with Neal Ball, who snagged a liner hit by Boston's Amby McConnell and retired Charley Wagner and Jake Stahl on the basepaths.

George Burns, playing for the Boston Red Sox between stints as a member of the Indians, turned the tables for Boston and made Cleveland the victim in 1923. He caught Frank Brower's liner, tagged Rube Lutzke off first, and ran to second to get Riggs Stephenson before he could return.

Burns made his play on September 14, and on October 6 another unassisted triple play occurred, making the feat which had been so rare appear almost commonplace, for a while. This time Ernie Padgett, a redheaded shortstop for the Boston Braves, turned the trick. Again the play was made in typical fashion—a line drive, a runner doubled off second base, and a surprised baserunner from first being tagged out.

Jimmy Cooney's claim on the last NL unassisted triple play ended late in the 1992 season. Rookie second baseman Mickey Morandini of the Philadelphia Phillies made a diving catch of a line drive off the bat of Pittsburgh's Jeff King. Morandini scrambled to second base to double off Andy Van Slyke. Then Barry Bonds, running from first base, bumbled into the surprised second baseman, who pushed him away with a climaxing third-out tag. Unaware of the rarity of his sudden feat, the rookie infielder rolled the ball toward the mound. The ball that was used to make the first play of its kind in the big leagues in twenty-four seasons was put into play the next inning.

In 1994 Boston's John Valentin replaced Ron Hansen as the last American Leaguer to perform the three-ply putout singlehandedly. On July 15 the Red Sox shortstop had an extraordinary day in an exceptionally well-played game. In the top of the sixth inning, after the Minnesota Twins had put the first two runners on base, Valentin speared Marc Newfield's line drive with the runners moving. He stepped on second to erase Mike Blowers, then noticed Keith Mitchell was about to run past him. It appeared as if the shortstop felt he had done enough to make an unassisted double play and only tagged the runner just in case the inning wasn't really over. As Morandini had done, Valentin nonchalantly dropped the ball on the mound and trotted off the field. Unlike Morandini, whose ball had negligently been put back into play, Valentin retrieved the ball and took it home as a souvenir.

In 1968 Ron Hansen had struck out six straight times after his one-man triple play, but Valentin homered to lead off the bottom of the sixth. The game ended with three game-saving defensive plays. Scott Cooper made a diving stop at third, and Tim Naehring sprawled to dig his throw out of the dirt. Lee Tinsley then made a Game of the Week super catch, grabbing a low line drive in right center, and, finally Wes Chamberlain went to the bullpen fence, leaped high in the air, and came down with a home run ball in the webbing of his glove. Sox fans left Fenway wondering if they would ever see the home team make so many defensive gems in one game again. Not likely.

Unassisted Triple Plays

Player/Team	Date	Pos.	Opp.	Opp. Batter
Paul Hines, Prov.	May 8, 1878	OF	Bos.	Jack Burdock
Neal Ball, Cleve.	July 19, 1909	SS	Bos.	Amby McConnell
Bill Wambsganss, Cleve.	October 10, 1920	2B	Brook.	Clarence Mitchell
George Burns, Bos.	September 14, 1923	1B	Cleve.	Frank Brower
Ernie Padgett, Bos.	October 6, 1923	SS	Phila.	Walter Holke
Glenn Wright, Pitts.	May 7, 1925	SS	St.L.	Jim Bottomley
Jimmy Cooney, Chi.	May 30, 1927	SS	Pitts.	Paul Waner
Johnny Neun, Det.	May 31, 1927	1B	Cleve.	Homer Summa
Ron Hansen, Wash.	July 29, 1968	SS	Cleve.	Joe Azcue
Mickey Morandini, Phi.	September 23, 1992	2B	Pitt.	Jeff King
John Valentin, Bos.	July 15, 1994	SS	Minn.	Marc Newfield

The No-Hitters

What follows is the traditional honor roll of the 200-plus pitchers who have attained the no-hit heights. Also provided is a list of those handful of ugly-duckling no-hitters that didn't go nine innings, and those 36 games in which a pitcher retired 27 or more batters in succession. Concerning the last-named group, only 14 are officially recognized as perfect games—the rest were deprived of perfection by their fielding support, their stars, or like Dick Bosman, simply themselves.

No-hit games, nine or more innings

(Number to left is career total if greater than one)
(Home team is that of pitcher, unless team is in italics)

Joe Borden, Phi vs. Chi NA, 4-0; July 28, 1875.
George Bradley, StL vs. Har NL, 2-0; July 15, 1876.
Lee Richmond, Wor vs. Cle NL, 1-0; June 12, 1880 (perfect game).
John Ward, Pro vs. Buf NL, 5-0; June 17, 1880.
Larry Corcoran, Chi vs. Bos NL, 6-0; August 19, 1880.
Jim Galvin, Buf vs. Wor NL, 1-0; August 20, 1880.
Tony Mullane, Lou vs. Cin AA, 2-0; September 11, 1882.
Guy Hecker, Lou vs. Pit AA, 3-1; September 19, 1882.
2 Larry Corcoran, Chi vs. Wor NL, 5-0; September 20, 1882
Hoss Radbourn, Pro vs. Cle NL, 8-0; July 25, 1883
Hugh (One Arm). Daily, Cle vs. Phi NL, 1-0; September 13, 1883.
Al Atkisson, Phi vs. Pit AA, 10-1; May 24, 1884.
Ed Morris, Col vs. Pit AA, 5-0; May 29, 1884.
Frank Mountain, Col vs. Was AA, 12-0; June 5, 1884.
3 Larry Corcoran, Chi vs. Pro NL, 6-0; June 27, 1884.
2 Jim Galvin, Buf vs. Det NL, 18-0; August 4, 1884.
Dick Burns, Cin vs. KC UA, 3-1; August 26, 1884.
Ed Cushman, Mil vs. Was UA, 5-0; September 28, 1884.
Sam Kimber, Bro vs. Tol AA, 0-0; October 4, 1884 (10 innings, tie).
John Clarkson, Chi vs. Pro NL, 4-0; July 27, 1885.
Charlie Ferguson, Phi vs. Pro NL, 1-0; August 29, 1885.
2 Al Atkisson, Phi vs. NY AA, 3-2; May 1, 1886.
Adonis Terry, Bro vs. StL AA, 1-0; July 24, 1886.
Matt Kilroy, Bal vs. Pit AA, 6-0; October 6, 1886.
2 Adonis Terry, Bro vs. Lou AA, 4-0; May 27, 1888.
Henry Porter, KC vs. Bal AA, 4-0; June 6, 1888.
Ed Seward, Phi vs. Cin AA, 12-2; July 26, 1888.
Gus Weyhing, Phi vs. KC AA, 4-0; July 31, 1888.
Silver King, eight innings, Chi vs. Bro PL, 0-1; June 21, 1890.
Cannonball Titcomb, Roch vs. Syr AA, 7-0; September 15, 1890.
Tom Lovett, Bro vs. NY NL, 4-0; June 22, 1891.
Amos Rusie, NY vs. Bro NL, 6-0; July 31, 1891.
Ted Breitenstein, StL vs. Lou AA, 8-0; October 4, 1891 (1st game). (first start in the major leagues).
Jack Stivetts, Bos vs. Bro NL, 11-0; August 6, 1892.
Ben Sanders, Lou vs. Bal NL, 6-2; August 22, 1892.
Bumpus Jones, Cin vs. Pit NL, 7-1; October 15, 1892. (first game in the major leagues).
Bill Hawke, Bal vs. Was NL, 5-0; August 16, 1893.
Cy Young, Cle vs. Cin NL, 6-0; September 18, 1897 (1st game).
2 Ted Breitenstein, Cin vs. Pit NL, 11-0; April 22, 1898.
Jim Hughes, Bal vs. Bos NL, 8-0; April 22, 1898.
Red Donahue, Phi vs. Bos NL, 5-0; July 8, 1898.
Walter Thornton, Chi vs. Bro NL, 2-0; August 21, 1898 (2nd game).
Deacon Phillippe, Lou vs. NY NL, 7-0; May 25, 1899.
Noodles Hahn, Cin vs. Phi NL, 4-0; July 12, 1900.
Earl Moore, Cle vs. Chi AL, 2-4; May 9, 1901 (lost on two hits in 10th).
Christy Mathewson, NY vs. StL NL, 5-0; July 15, 1901.
Jim Callahan, Chi vs. Det AL, 3-0; September 20, 1902 (1st game).
Chick Fraser, Phi vs. Chi NL, 10-0; September 18, 1903 (2nd game).
2 Cy Young, Bos vs. Phi AL, 3-0; May 5, 1904 (perfect game).
Bob Wicker, Chi vs. NY NL, 1-0; June 11, 1904. (won in 12 innings after allowing one hit in the 10th).
Jesse Tannehill, Bos vs. Chi AL, 6-0; August 17, 1904.
2 Christy Mathewson, NY vs. Chi NL, 1-0; June 13, 1905.
Weldon Henley, Phi vs. StL AL, 6-0; July 22, 1905 (1st game).
Frank Smith, Chi vs. Det AL, 15-0; September 6, 1905 (2nd game).
Bill Dinneen, Bos vs. Chi AL, 2-0; September 27, 1905 (1st game).
Johnny Lush, Phi vs. Bro NL, 6-0; May 1, 1906.

Mal Eason, Bro vs. *StL* NL, 2-0; July 20, 1906.
Harry McIntyre, Bro vs. Pit NL, 0-1; August 1, 1906. (lost on four hits in 13 innings after allowing first hit in 11th).
Frank (Jeff.) Pfeffer, Bos vs. Cin NL, 6-0; May 8, 1907.
Nick Maddox, Pit vs. Bro NL, 2-1; September 20, 1907.
3 Cy Young, Bos vs. *NY* AL, 8-0; June 30, 1908.
Hooks Wiltse, NY vs. Phi NL, 1-0; July 4, 1908 (first game, ten innings).
Nap Rucker, Bro vs. Bos NL, 6-0; September 5, 1908 (2nd game).
Dusty Rhoades, Cle vs. Bos AL, 2-1; September 18, 1908.
2 Frank Smith, Chi vs. Phi AL, 1-0; September 20, 1908.
Addie Joss, Cle vs. Chi AL, 1-0; October 2, 1908 (perfect game).
Red Ames, NY vs. Bro NL, 0-3; April 15, 1909. (lost on seven hits in 13 innings after allowing first hit in 10th).
2 Addie Joss, Cle vs. Chi AL, 1-0; April 20, 1910.
Chief Bender, Phi vs. Cle AL, 4-0; May 12, 1910.
Tom L. Hughes, NY vs. Cle AL, 0-5; August 30, 1910 (2nd game). (lost on seven hits in 11 innings after allowing first hit in 10th).
Joe Wood, Bos vs StL AL, 5-0; July 29, 1911 (1st game).
Ed Walsh, Chi vs. Bos AL, 5-0; August 27, 1911.
George Mullin, Det vs. StL AL, 7-0; July 4, 1912 (2nd game).
Earl Hamilton, StL vs. *Det* AL, 5-1; August 30, 1912.
Jeff Tesreau, NY vs. *Phi* NL, 3-0; September 6, 1912 (1st game).
Jim Scott, Chi vs. *Was* AL, 0-1; May 14, 1914 (lost on 2 two hits in 10th).
Joe Benz, Chi vs. Cle Al, 6-1; May 31, 1914.
George Davis, Bos vs. Phi NL, 7-0; September 9, 1914 (2nd game).
Ed Lafitte, Bro vs. KC FL, 6-2; September 19, 1914.
Rube Marquard, NY vs. Bro NL, 2-0; April 15, 1915.
Frank Allen, Pit vs. StL FL, 2-0; April 24, 1915
Claude Hendrix, Chi vs. Pit FL, 10-0; May 15, 1915.
Alex Main, KC vs Buf FL, 5-0; August 16, 1915.
Jimmy Lavender, Chi vs. *NY* NL, 2-0; August 31, 1915 (1st game).
Dave Davenport, StL vs. Chi FL, 3-0; September 7, 1915.
2 Tom L. Hughes, Bos vs. Pit NL, 2-0; June 16, 1916.
Rube Foster, Bos vs. NY AL, 2-0; June 16, 1916.
Joe Bush, Phi vs. Cle AL, 5-0; August 26, 1916.
Hubert (Dutch) Leonard, Bos vs. StL AL, 4-0; August 30, 1916
Eddie Cicotte, Chi vs. *StL* AL, 11-0; April 14, 1917.
George Mogridge, NY vs. *Bos* AL, 2-1; April 24, 1917.
Fred Toney, Cin vs. *Chi* NL, 1-0; May 2, 1917 (10 innings).
Hippo Vaughn, Chi vs. Cin NL, 0-1; May 2, 1917. (lost on two hits in 10th; Toney pitched a no-hitter in this game).
Ernie Koob, StL vs. Chi AL, 1-0; May 5, 1917.
Bob Groom, StL vs. Chi AL, May 6, 1917 (2nd game).
Ernie Shore, Bos vs. Was AL, 3-0; June 23, 1917 (1st game). (perfect game). (Shore relieved Babe Ruth in the first inning after Ruth had been thrown out of the game for protesting a walk to the first batter. The runner was caught stealing and Shore retired the remaining 26 batters in order).
2 Hubert (Dutch). Leonard, Bos vs. *Det* AL, 5-0; June 3, 1918.
Hod Eller, Cin vs. StL NL, 6-0; May 11, 1919.
Ray Caldwell, Cle vs. *NY* AL, 3-0; September 10, 1919 (1st game).
Walter Johnson, Was vs. *Bos* AL, 1-0; July 1, 1920.
Charlie Robertson, Chi vs. *Det* AL, 2-0; April 30, 1922 (perfect game).
Jesse Barnes, NY vs. Phi NL, 6-0; May 7, 1922.
Sam Jones, NY vs. *Phi* AL, 2-0; September 4, 1923.
Howard Ehmke, Bos vs. *Phi* AL, 4-0; September 7, 1923.
Jesse Haines, StL vs Bos NL, 5-0; July 17, 1924.
Dazzy Vance, Bro vs. Phi NL, 10-1; September 13, 1925 (1st game).
Ted Lyons, Chi vs. *Bos* AL, 6-0; August 21, 1926.
Carl Hubbell, NY vs. Pit NL, 11-0; May 8, 1929.
Wes Ferrell, Cle vs. StL AL, 9-0; April 29, 1931.
Bobby Burke, Was vs. Bos AL, 5-0; August 8, 1931.
Bobo Newsom, StL vs Bos AL, 1-2; September 18, 1934 (lost on one hit in 10th).
Paul Dean, StL vs. *Bro* NL, 3-0; September 21, 1934 (2nd game).
Vern Kennedy, Chi vs. Cle AL, 5-0; August 31, 1935.
Bill Dietrich, Chi vs. StL AL, 8-0; June 1, 1937.
Johnny Vander Meer, Cin vs. Bos NL, 3-0; June 11, 1938.
2 Johnny Vander Meer, Cin vs. *Bro* NL, 6-0; June 15, 1938 (next start after June 11).
Monte Pearson, NY vs. Cle AL, 13-0; August 27, 1938 (2nd game).
Bob Feller, Cle vs. *Chi* AL, 1-0; April 16, 1940 (opening day).
Tex Carleton, Bro vs. Cin NL, 3-0; April 30, 1940.
Lon Warneke, StL vs. Cin NL, 2-0; August 30, 1941.
Jim Tobin, Bos vs. Bro NL, 2-0; April 27, 1944.
Clyde Shoun, Cin vs. Bos NL, 1-0; May 15, 1944.
Dick Fowler, Phi vs. StL AL, 1-0; September 9, 1945 (2nd game).
Ed Head, Bro vs. Bos NL, 5-0; April 23, 1946.
2 Bob Feller, Cle vs. *NY* AL, 1-0; April 30, 1946.
Ewell Blackwell, Cin vs. Bos NL, 6-0; June 18, 1947.
Don Black, Cle vs. Phi AL, 3-0; July 10, 1947 (1st game).
Bill McCahan, Phi vs. Was AL, 3-0; September 3, 1947.
Bob Lemon, Cle vs. *Det* AL, 2-0; June 30, 1948.
Rex Barney, Bro vs. *NY* NL, 2-0; September 9, 1948.
Vern Bickford, Bos vs. Bro NL, 7-0; August 11, 1950.
Cliff Chambers, Pit vs. *Bos* NL, 3-0; May 6, 1951 (2nd game).
3 Bob Feller, Cle vs. Det AL, 2-1; July 1, 1951 (1st game).
Allie Reynolds, NY vs. *Cle* AL, 1-0; July 12, 1951.
2 Allie Reynolds, NY vs. Bos AL, 8-0; September 28, 1951 (1st game).
Virgil Trucks, Det vs. Was AL, 1-0; May 15, 1952.
Carl Erskine, Bro vs. Chi NL, 5-0; June 19, 1952.
2 Virgil Trucks, Det vs. *NY* AL, 1-0; August 25, 1952.
Bobo Holloman, StL vs. Phi AL, 6-0; May 6, 1953 (first start in the major leagues).

Jim Wilson, Mil vs. Phi NL, 2-0; June 12, 1954.
Sam Jones, Chi vs Pit NL, 4-0; May 12, 1955.
2 Carl Erskine, Bro vs. NY NL, 3-0; May 12, 1956.
Johnny Klippstein (7 innings), Hershell Freeman (1 inning) and Joe Black (3 innings)., Cin vs. *Mil* NL, 1-2; May 26, 1956. (lost on three hits in 11 innings after allowing first hit in 10th).
Mel Parnell, Bos vs. Chi AL, 4-0; July 14, 1956.
Sal Maglie, Bro vs. Phi NL, 5-0; September 25, 1956.
Don Larsen, NY AL vs. Bro NL, 2-0; October 8, 1956. (World Series). (perfect game).
Bob Keegan, Chi vs. Was AL, 6-0; August 20, 1957 (2nd game).
Jim Bunning, Det vs. *Bos* AL, 3-0; July 20, 1958 (1st game).
Hoyt Wilhelm, Bal vs. NY AL, 1-0; September 20, 1958.
Harvey Haddix, Pit vs. *Mil* NL, 0-1; May 26, 1959 (lost on one hit in 13 innings after pitching 12 perfect innings).
Don Cardwell, Chi vs. StL NL, 4-0; May 15, 1960 (2nd game).
Lew Burdette, Mil vs. Phi NL, 1-0; August 18, 1960.
Warren Spahn, Mil vs. Phi NL, 4-0; September 16, 1960.
2 Warren Spahn, Mil vs. SF NL, 1-0; April 28, 1961.
Bo Belinsky, LA vs. Bal AL, 2-0; May 5, 1962.
Earl Wilson, Bos vs. LA AL, 2-0; June 26, 1962.
Sandy Koufax, LA vs. NY NL, 5-0; June 30, 1962.
Bill Monbouquette, Bos vs. *Chi* AL, 1-0; August 1, 1962.
Jack Kralick, Min vs. KC AL, 1-0; August 26, 1962.
2 Sandy Koufax, LA vs. SF NL, 8-0; May 11, 1963.
Don Nottebart, Hou vs. Phi NL, 4-1; May 17, 1963.
Juan Marichal, SF vs. Hou NL, 1-0; June 15, 1963.
Ken T. Johnson, Hou vs. Cin NL, 0-1; April 23, 1964 (lost game).
3 Sandy Koufax, LA vs. *Phi* NL, 3-0; June 4, 1964.
2 Jim Bunning, Phi vs. *NY* NL, 6-0; June 21, 1964 (1st game; perfect game).
Jim Maloney, Cin vs. NY NL, 0-1; June 14, 1965 (lost on two hits in 11 innings after pitching 10 hitless innings).
Jim Maloney, Cin vs. *Chi* AL, 1-0; August 19, 1965 (1st game; 10 innings).
4 Sandy Koufax, LA vs. Chi NL, 1-0; September 9, 1965 (perfect game).
Dave Morehead, Bos vs. Cle AL, 2-0; September 16, 1965.
Sonny Siebert, Cle vs. Was AL, 2-0; June 10, 1966.
Steve D. Barber (8⅔ innings). and Stu Miller (⅓ inning) Bal vs. Det AL, 1-2; April 30, 1967 (1st game; lost game).
Don Wilson, Hou vs. Atl NL, 2-0; June 18, 1967.
Dean Chance, Min vs. *Cle* AL, 2-1; August 25, 1967 (2nd game).
Joe Horlen, Chi vs. Det AL, 6-0; September 10, 1967 (1st game).
Tom Phoebus, Bal vs. Bos AL, 6-0; April 27, 1968.
Catfish Hunter, Oak vs. Min AL, 4-0; May 8, 1968 (perfect game).
George Culver, Cin vs. *Phi* NL, 6-1; July 29, 1968 (2nd game).
Gaylord Perry, SF vs. StL NL, 1-0; Sept. 17, 1968.
Ray Washburn, StL vs. *SF* NL, 2-0; September 18, 1968.
Bill Stoneman, Mon vs. *Phi* NL, 7-0; April 17, 1969.
3 Jim Maloney, Cin vs. Hou NL, 10-0; April 30, 1969.
2 Don Wilson, Hou vs. Cin NL, 4-0; May 1, 1969.
Jim Palmer, Bal vs. Oak AL, 8-0; August 13, 1969.
Ken Holtzman, Chi vs. Atl NL, 3-0; August 19, 1969.
Bob Moose, Pit vs. *NY* NL, 4-0; September 20, 1969.
Dock Ellis, Pit vs. SD NL, 2-0; June 12, 1970 (1st game).
Clyde Wright, Cal vs. Oak AL, 4-0; July 3, 1970.
Bill Singer, LA vs. Phi NL, 5-0; July 20, 1970.
Vida Blue, Oak vs. Min AL, 6-0; September 21, 1970.
2 Ken Holtzman, Chi vs. Cin NL, 1-0; June 3, 1971.
Rick Wise, Phi vs. *Cin* NL, 4-0; June 23, 1971.
Bob Gibson, StL vs. *Pit* NL, 11-0; August 14, 1971.
Burt Hooton, Chi vs. Phi NL, 4-0; April 16, 1972.
Milt Pappas, Chi vs. SD NL, 8-0; September 2, 1972.
2 Bill Stoneman, Mon vs. NY NL, 7-0; October 2, 1972 (1st game).
Steve Busby, KC vs. *Det* AL, 3-0; April 27, 1973.
Nolan Ryan, Cal vs. *KC* AL, 3-0; May 15, 1973.
2 Nolan Ryan, Cal vs. *Det* AL, 6-0; July 15, 1973.
Jim Bibby, Tex vs. *Oak* AL, 6-0; July 20, 1973.
Phil Niekro, Atl vs. SD NL, 9-0; August 5, 1973.
2 Steve Busby, KC vs. *Mil* AL, 2-0; June 19, 1974.
Dick Bosman, Cle vs. Oak AL, 4-0; July 19, 1974.
3 Nolan Ryan, Cal vs. Min AL, 4-0; September 28, 1974
4 Nolan Ryan, Cal vs. Bal AL, 1-0; June 1, 1975.
Ed Halicki, SF vs. NY NL, 6-0; August 24, 1975 (2nd game).
Vida Blue (5 innings), Glenn Abbott (1 inning), Paul Lindblad (1 inning), and Rollie Fingers (2 innings), Oak vs. Cal AL, 5-0; September 28, 1975.
Larry Dierker, Hou vs. Mon NL, 5-0; July 9, 1976.
Blue Moon Odom (5 innings) and Francisco Barrios (4 innings), Chi vs. *Oak* AL, 6-0; July 28, 1976.
John Candelaria, Pit vs. LA NL, 2-0; August 9, 1976.
John Montefusco, SF vs. *Atl* NL, 9-0; September 29, 1976.
Jim Colborn, KC vs. Tex AL, 6-0; May 14, 1977.
Dennis Eckersley, Cle vs. Cal AL, 1-0; May 30, 1977.
Bert Blyleven, Tex vs. Cal AL, 6-0; September 22, 1977.
Bob Forsch, StL vs. Phi NL, 5-0; April 16, 1978.
Tom Seaver, Cin vs. StL NL, 4-0; June 16, 1978.
Ken Forsch, Hou vs. Atl NL, 6-0; April 7, 1979.
Jerry Reuss, LA vs. *SF* NL, 8-0; June 27, 1980.
Charlie Lea, Mon vs. SF NL, 4-0; May 10, 1981 (2nd game).
Len Barker, Cle vs. Tor AL, 3-0; May 15, 1981 (perfect game).
5 Nolan Ryan, Hou vs. LA NL, 5-0; September 26, 1981.
Dave Righetti, NY vs. Bos AL, 4-0; July 4, 1983.
2 Bob Forsch, StL vs. Mon NL, 3-0; September 26, 1983.
Mike Warren, Oak vs. Chi AL, 3-0; September 29, 1983.
Jack Morris, Det vs. *Chi* AL, 4-0; April 7, 1984.

Mike Witt, Cal vs. *Tex* AL, 1-0; September 30, 1984 (perfect game).
Joe Cowley, Chi vs. *Cal* AL, 7-1; September 19, 1986.
Mike Scott, Hou vs. SF NL, 2-0; September 25, 1986.
Juan Nieves, Mil vs. Bal AL, 7-0; April 15, 1987.
Tom Browning, Cin vs. LA NL, 1-0; September 16, 1988 (perfect game).
Mark Langston (7 innings) and Mike Witt (2 innings), Cal vs Sea AL, 1-0; April 11, 1990.
Randy Johnson, Sea vs. Det AL, 2-0; June 2, 1990.
6 Nolan Ryan, Tex vs. *Oak* AL, 5-0; June 11, 1990.
Dave Stewart, Oak vs. *Tor* AL, 5-0; June 29, 1990.
Fernando Valenzuela, LA vs. StL NL, 6-0; June 29, 1990.
Andy Hawkins, NY vs. *Chi* AL, 0-4; July 1, 1990 (8 innings, lost the game).
Terry Mulholland, Phi vs. SF NL, 6-0; August 15, 1990.
Dave Stieb, Tor vs. *Det* AL, 3-0; September 2, 1990.
7 Nolan Ryan, Tex vs. *Tor* AL, 3-0; May 1, 1991.
Tommy Greene, Phi vs. *Mon* NL, 2-0; May 23, 1991.
Bob Milacki, Bal (6 innings), Mike Flanagan (1 inning), Mark Williamson (1 inning), Gregg Olson (1 inning) vs. *Oak* AL, 2-0; July 13, 1991.
Mark Gardner, Mon vs. *LA* NL, 0-1; July 26, 1991 (9 innings, lost game in 10th).
Dennis Martinez, Mon vs. *LA* NL, 2-0; July 28, 1991 (perfect game).
Wilson Alvarez, Chi vs. *Bal* AL, 7-0; August 11, 1991.
Bret Saberhagen, KC vs. *Chi* AL, 7-0; August 26, 1991.
Kent Mercker (6 innings), Mark Wohlers (2 innings), Alejandro Pena (1 inning), Atl vs. *SD* NL, 1-0; September 11, 1991.
Matt Young, Bos vs. *Cle* AL, 1-2; April 12, 1992 (8 innings, lost game).
Kevin Gross, LA vs. *SF* NL, 2-0; August 17, 1992.
Chris Bosio, Sea vs. Bos AL, 7-0; April 22, 1993.
Jim Abbott, NY vs. Cle AL, 4-0; September 4, 1993.
Darryl Kile, Hou vs. NY NL, 7-1; September 8, 1993.
Kent Mercker, Atl vs. *LA*, NL, 6-0; April 8, 1994.
Scott Erickson, Minn vs. Mil AL, 6-0; April 27, 1994.
Kenny Rogers, Tex vs. Cal AL, 4-0; July 29, 1994 (perfect game).

No-hit games, fewer than nine innings

(Home team is that of pitcher, unless team is in italics)

Larry McKeon, six innings, Ind vs. *Cin* AA, 0-0; May 6, 1884.
Charlie Gagus, eight innings, Was vs. Wil UA, 12-1; August 21, 1884.
Charlie Getzien, six innings, Det vs. Phi NL, 1-0; October 1, 1884.

Charlie Sweeney (3 innings) and Henry Boyle (2 innings), five innings, StL vs. StP U.A., 0-1; October 5, 1884.
Dupee Shaw, five innings, Pro vs. *Buf* NL, 4-0; October 7, 1885 (1st game).
George Van Haltren, six innings, Chi vs. Pit NL, 1-0; June 21, 1888.
Cannonball Crane, seven innings, NY vs. Was NL, 3-0; September 27, 1888.
Matt Kilroy, seven innings, Bal vs. StL AA, 0-0; July 29, 1889 (2nd game).
George Nicol, seven innings, StL vs. Phi AA, 21-2; September 23, 1890.
Hank Gastright, eight innings, Col vs. Tol AA, 6-0; October 12, 1890.
Jack Stivetts, five innings, Bos vs. *Was* NL, 6-0; October 15, 1892 (2nd game).
Icebox Chamberlain, seven innings, Cin vs. Bos NL, 6-0; September 23, 1893 (2nd game).
Ed Stein, six innings, Bro vs. Chi NL, 6-0; June 2, 1894.
Red Ames, five innings, NY vs. *StL* NL, 5-0; September 14, 1903 (2nd game).
Rube Waddell, five innings, Phi vs. StL AL, 2-0; August 15, 1905.
Jake Weimer, seven innings, Cin vs. Bro NL, 1-0; August 24, 1906 (2nd game).
Jimmy Dygert (3 innings) and Rube Waddell (2 innings), five innings, Phi vs. Chi, AL, 4-3; August 29, 1906.
Stoney McGlynn, seven innings, StL vs. *Bro* NL, 1-1; September 24, 1906 (2nd game).
Lefty Leifield, six innings, Pit vs. *Phi* NL, 8-0; September 26, 1906, (2nd game).
Ed Walsh, five innings, Chi vs. NY AL, 8-1; May 26, 1907.
Ed Karger, seven perfect innings, StL vs. Bos NL, 4-0; August 11, 1907 (2nd game).
Howie Camnitz, five innings, Pit vs. *NY* NL, 1-0; August 23, 1907 (2nd game).
Rube Vickers, five perfect innings, Phi vs. *Was* AL, 4-0; October 5, 1907 (2nd game).
Johnny Lush, six innings, StL vs. *Bro* NL, 2-0; August 6, 1908.
King Cole, seven innings, Chi vs. *StL* NL, 4-0; July 31, 1910 (2nd game).
Jay Cashion, six innings, Was vs. Cle AL, 2-0; August 20, 1910 (2nd game).
Walter Johnson, seven innings, Was vs. StL Al, 2-0; August 25, 1910.
Fred Frankhouse, seven and two-thirds innings, Bro vs. Cin NL, 5-0; August 27, 1937.
John Whitehead, six innings, StL vs. Det AL, 4-0; August 5, 1940 (2nd game).
Jim Tobin, five innings, Bos vs. Phi NL, 7-0; June 22, 1944 (2nd game).
Mike McCormick, five innings, SF vs. *Phi* NL, 3-0; June 12, 1959.
Sam Jones, seven innings, SF vs. StL NL, 4-0; September 26, 1959.
Dean Chance, five perfect innings, Min vs. Bos AL, 2-0; August 6, 1967.
Dave Palmer, five perfect innings, Mon vs. *StL* NL, 4-0; April 21, 1984 (2nd game).
Pascual Perez, five innings, Mon vs. *Phi* NL, 1-0; September 24, 1988.
Melido Perez, five innings, rain, Chi vs. NY AL, 8-0; July 12, 1990.

Perfection Plus

Year	Pitcher	Batters	Opponent	Notes
1959	Harvey Haddix	36	Milwaukee	(12 innings)
1919	Waite Hoyt	34	Yanks	(2nd-13th inning)
1880	Pud Galvin	33	Worcester	(6 errors)
1884	Charlie Buffinton	32	Providence	(5 errors)
1971	Rick Wise	32	Chicago	(2nd-12th inning)
1908	Nap Rucker	30	Braves	(3 errors)
1885	John Clarkson	29	Providence	(3 errors, 1 DP)
1970	Bill Singer	29	Philadelphia	(2 errors, both his own)
1883	Hoss Radbourn	28	Cleveland	(1 error)
1884	Pud Galvin	28	Detroit	(1 error)
1905	Christy Mathewson	28	Cubs	(2 errors, one DP)
1910	Tom Hughes	28	Cleveland	(1 error)
1920	Walter Johnson	28	Red Sox	(1 error)
1947	Bill McCahan	28	Washington	(1 error)
1967	Joel Horlen	28	Detroit	(1 error)
1974	Dick Bosman	28	Oakland	(1 error, his own)
1980	Jerry Reuss	28	San Francisco	(1 error)
1880	J. L. Richmond	27	Cleveland	
1880	J. M. Ward	27	Buffalo	
1904	Cy Young	27	Philadelphia	
1906	Lefty Leifield	27	Cubs	(8 innings, 3 errors)
1908	Addie Joss	27	White Sox	

Year	Pitcher	Batters	Opponent	Notes
1919	Walter Johnson	28**	New York	
1922	Charlie Robertson	27	Detroit	
1953	Curt Simmons	27*	Milwaukee	
1956	Don Larsen	27	Brooklyn	
1964	Jim Bunning	27	Mets	
1965	Sandy Koufax	27	Cubs	
1968	Catfish Hunter	27	Minnesota	
1981	Len Barker	27	Toronto	
1984	Mike Witt	27	Texas	
1988	Tom Browning	27	Los Angeles	
1991	Dennis Martinez	27	Los Angeles	
1994	Kenny Rogers	27	California	
1954	Robin Roberts	27*	Cincinnati	
1981	Jim Bibby	27*	Atlanta	
1917	Ernie Shore	26†	Washington	

*Retired last twenty-seven batters in a row after giving up a hit to leadoff man.
**Retired twenty-eight batters in a row after allowing a one-out single in the first inning, then allowed a two-out single in the tenth.
†Starter Babe Ruth walked the first man and promptly slugged the umpire in the jaw and was banished. Ernie Shore rushed in from the bull pen, got the runner on a steal attempt, and retired the next twenty-six.
Note: Hooks Wiltse in 1908 and Lew Burdette in 1960 missed perfection because each hit a batter, with Wiltse hitting the *last* batter—the opposing pitcher—with an 0-2 count.

## CHAPTER 12

Awards and Honors

Bill Deane

This chapter presents the history and voting results of baseball's most prestigious awards and honors, including the complete balloting and current constituency of the Baseball Hall of Fame. This material will be of interest to the fan who wonders how a player of the past was viewed by his contemporaries. I have ventured an additional section of "what if" awards: what if the Cy Young Award had been instituted long before its actual inception in 1956, or the Rookie of the Year before its real debut in 1947, and so on. What follows is divided into seven sections:

MVP Award: history and balloting.
Rookie of the Year Award: history and balloting.
Cy Young Award: history and balloting.
Hypothetical Awards: explanation and selections.
Gold Glove Award: history, discussion, and list of winners.
Special MVP Awards: All-Star Game, League Championship Series, World Series.
Hall of Fame: history of elections and balloting.

Balloting tables and lists of winners include each player's first initial, last name, and club city abbreviation (and point total, if applicable).

Most Valuable Player Award: History

The concept of most valuable player awards dates back more than a century. The first documented MVP-type honor in pro ball was bestowed upon James "Deacon" White of the 1875 Boston Red Stockings in the National Association. Catcher White sparked Boston to a remarkable 71–8 record that year, scoring 77 runs in 80 games and batting .355. An ardent Red Stockings' admirer presented Deacon with a silver tray, water pitcher, and loving cup inscribed with the words: WON BY JIM WHITE AS MOST VALUABLE PLAYER TO BOSTON TEAM, 1875.

The first official MVP honor was initiated some thirty-five years later. Prior to the 1910 season, baseball fan Hugh Chalmers, president and general manager of the Chalmers Motor Company, announced that he would present one of his company's automobiles—a Chalmers "30"—to the major league player who compiled the highest batting average. What appeared to be a harmless promotional gimmick was to soon turn into a public relations disaster.

The rules specified that players must accumulate a specific minimum number of times at bat, depending on position, to qualify for the award. For infielders and outfielders, it was a minimum of 350 at-bats; for catchers,

250 at-bats; and for pitchers, 100 at-bats. Interest in the award was tremendous from the outset. Ty Cobb, who already owned a Chalmers "30" roadster, wrote: "I am glad that something besides medals and trophies is offered for the championship in batting. I think the offer of a Chalmers "30" is simply great and I hope to be lucky enough to own a new Chalmers next fall."

It developed into a two-man race, with Detroit's Cobb and Cleveland's Napoleon Lajoie, both American Leaguers, the only serious challengers for the coveted prize. Throughout the season there were charges and counter-charges of favoritism by scorers in various cities. Furthermore, the general consensus of the press was that Cobb's selfish pursuit of this individual honor had cost his team the pennant. The controversy was capped by scandalous circumstances on the final day of the season.

Through games of September 16, Cobb held a solid lead over Lajoie, .368 to .357 (although, because of the era's sloppy record keeping, few actually knew the official figures at the time). From then through October 8, Cobb batted a torrid .532 (25 for 47) to seemingly lock up the crown with a .383 average. But Lajoie refused to surrender, going 30 for 54 (.556) in that same span to enter the final day, October 9, with a .376 mark. Cobb chose to sit out his final game, while Lajoie played the infamous doubleheader with the St. Louis Browns in which he went 8 for 8, including *seven bunt hits*—remarkable for a slow-footed slugger—to apparently edge out Cobb in the batting race. Browns' manager Jack O'Connor had instructed his rookie third baseman, Red Corriden, to play deep on Lajoie, advice with which Corriden complied. Lajoie took advantage of the strange defensive arrangement with the repeated safe bunts. Although neither Lajoie nor Corriden were implicated, there were charges of a Browns' frame-up to give the coveted batting title (and car) to the respected Lajoie over the disliked Cobb.

O'Connor lost his job due to his role in the alleged fix. Subsequently, AL President Ban Johnson announced that a "discrepancy" had been found in the official records, and that Cobb had actually won the batting crown after all (although this point is challenged by many current researchers, who have evidence that Cobb was credited wrongly for a 2 for 3 game). Meanwhile, Hugh Chalmers, attempting to divorce himself from the controversy, presented autos to both Cobb and Lajoie. It was generally acknowledged that this fiasco doomed the future of individual awards of any kind.

Hoping to salvage some goodwill out of the whole idea, Chalmers came up with a new proposal for the 1911 season. This time he would award an auto to one player in each league who "should prove himself as the most important and useful player to his club and to the league at large in point of deportment and value of services rendered." The decision for this honor was to be made by a committee of baseball writers, one writer from each club city in each league. Each writer was to make eight selections, with a first-place ballot scoring eight points, on down to an eighth-place vote counting one point. Thus was born the short-lived Chalmers Award, with Ty Cobb and Frank Schulte earning recognition in 1911. Both Cobb and Schulte voluntarily withdrew from the competition in 1912, although the former received seventeen points anyway.

Interest in the award diminished within a few years. By 1914 the public was distracted by baseball's battles with the new Federal League and the escalation of the World War in Europe. The timing was right for the Chalmers Award to quietly disappear; it was noted that Mr. Chalmers had agreed to present vehicles for five years and that the 1914 awards marked the fifth presentations.

On July 15, 1922, the newly formed American League Trophy Committee adopted a set of rules governing the selection of an annual award-winner. The rules specified that "the purpose of the American League Trophy is to honor the baseball player who is of greatest all-round service to his club and credit to the sport during each season; to recognize and reward uncommon skill and ability when exercised by a player for the best interests of his team, and to perpetuate his memory." The rules further instructed voters to seek out the "winning ball player," reminding them that "combined offensive and defensive ability is not always indicated by any system of records."

Eight baseball writers, one from each AL city, were enfranchised, with each required to select exactly one player from each team, for a total of eight selections. Player-managers and previous winners were to be excluded from consideration. Points were distributed the same as in the Chalmers Award: eight for first place, down to one for eighth.

The intention of AL President Ban Johnson was to have a monument to baseball erected in East Potomac Park, Washington, D.C., engraved with the names of winners of the AL Award. This proposal was introduced as a congressional resolution in 1924, and passed in the House of Representatives before dying on the Senate Floor.

The AL voting rules led to growing criticism for several reasons, one of which was the limitation on the number of vote-getters from each team. For example, when the Browns' George Sisler won the first AL Award in 1922, he was named on all eight ballots—thus disqualifying his teammates from receiving any votes. As a result, fellow Brownie Ken Williams, who led the league in home runs (39), RBIs (155), and total bases (367) and became the first player ever to have 30 homers and 30 stolen bases in the same season, was shut out in the League Award voting.

Secondly, the rule prohibiting player-managers from eligibility drew fire. In 1925, when this rule eliminated five solid candidates from consideration, *The New York Times* wrote, "to say that it is impossible or impractical to divorce a man's managerial skill from his talents purely as a player is to reflect on the intelligence of the committee that awards the prize."

The *Times* further editorialized on the fallacy of assuming that no player can be the "most valuable" more than one year: "the purpose, of course, is to pass the honor around, but the effect is to pass an empty honor around." This rule became increasingly ridiculous when it eliminated Babe Ruth (and his 60 home runs) from consideration in 1927; by the following year, both Ruth and teammate Lou Gehrig, who were in the process of finishing one-two in the AL home run derby in five consecutive seasons, were ineligible for the League Award.

In 1924 the National League instituted its own award, with radical differences in the selection method: each writer voted for ten players rather than eight (ten points for first place, and so on); he was not bound to vote for a certain number of players from each team; he was free to select a player-manager; and, later, he was allowed to consider previous winners of the award. Additionally, the NL offered a cash "present" of $1,000 to the award-winner.

At various times between 1925–51, writers were permitted to name "honorable mention" candidates, whose vote totals were listed but not counted in the balloting. Another feature of early voting reports was the listing of "cumulative vote leaders"—a forerunner to Bill James's "award shares"—over a period of years.

A number of factors led to the demise of the AL Award, including the award's loss of credibility due to the previously mentioned shortsighted voting rules. Secondly, Ban Johnson, having failed to secure the erection of his proposed monument, felt the award had fallen short of its aim. Finally, management was concerned with the efforts of award-winners to parlay their honors into substantial pay raises. The AL Award was officially voted out at a special league meeting on May 6, 1929.

The National League followed suit with the AL's decision, but agreed to continue its award through the 1929 season.

In October 1929, the Baseball Writers' Association of America (BBWAA) announced the results of an "unofficial" AL most valuable player poll, whose winner was Lew Fonseca of Cleveland. Two months later, *The Sporting News* (TSN) conducted a poll of the eight writers who had previously voted on the League Award, thereby reporting Al Simmons as the "unofficial" AL Award-winner. Combining the results of these two unofficial polls gives Fonseca 77 points, followed by Heinie Manush (57), Simmons (56), Tony Lazzeri (55) and Charlie Gehringer (44).

The Sporting News announced that, thereafter, they would take it upon themselves to conduct an annual poll to substitute for the defunct league awards. However, they retained the stipulation that each voter must select just one player on each team. In 1930, TSN chose Joe Cronin in the AL and Bill Terry in the NL. Earlier, the Associated Press also had a special committee of writers make an unofficial AL selection for 1930, while the BBWAA did the same for the NL (adding a check for $1,000 for the winner). The respective selections here were Cronin in the AL and Hack Wilson in the NL. Again combining the two sets of polls, the AL leaders were Cronin (100), Al Simmons (85), Lou Gehrig (68), Charlie Gehringer (67), and Ted Lyons (56). The NL pace-setters were Hack Wilson (111), Frankie Frisch (107), Bill Terry (105), Chuck Klein (57), and Floyd "Babe" Herman (52).

In an effort to standardize MVP voting, the BBWAA, in its annual winter meeting in New York on December 11, 1930, decided to appoint two committees (one in each league) to elect most valuable players, with the association to "award suitable emblems to the players selected." Thus was born what is considered the modern MVP Award, with most of the flaws of its forerunners eliminated.

TSN, however, continued to make its own selections in bitter competition with the BBWAA. Finally, beginning in 1938, TSN agreed to unify the award by abiding with BBWAA balloting, and presenting The Sporting News Trophy to the winner. Among the various prizes awarded to the winners were wristwatches and shotguns.

At a meeting during the 1944 World Series, the BBWAA decided to begin issuing its own trophy, the Kenesaw Mountain Landis Award, in honor of the ailing commissioner. Landis died a month later and the official MVP Award has born his name ever since. A plaque engraved with the names of the winners hangs in the National Baseball Library in Cooperstown, New York.

The Sporting News went back to naming its own MVPs in 1944 and '45. Then, at the request of the new commissioner, Happy Chandler, TSN "withdrew from the field to cooperate in making the Landis Awards, provided by the major leagues, the official designations of the year." In 1948, however, TSN went back to its own awards, selecting a Player of the Year and Pitcher of the Year in each league, as they have done ever since. For some reason, TSN awards have never received the public recognition that the BBWAA honors have.

Two major changes in the MVP voting began in 1938. The BBWAA began polling three writers in each major league city, rather than just one, which remained in effect until it was reduced to two writers per city, starting in 1961. Also in 1938, the process was initiated to award fourteen points for each first-place vote, rather than ten.

"Split votes," which have since infiltrated all the major awards, first appeared in MVP Awards in 1959. The American League MVP race that year, by consensus, was between second baseman Nellie Fox and shortstop Luis Aparicio of the champion Chicago White Sox. Late in the season, the suggestion often arose that the two ought to share the award. When the votes were in, Fox had received fourteen first-place votes, Aparicio had gotten six, and four writers had split their votes between the two. Tickled with the idea of a split vote, one NL writer also resorted to this option, dividing his first-place nomination between Ernie Banks and Ed Mathews. The cop-out vote, having been allowed in '59, has since surfaced in sixteen more MVP Awards, ten Rookie of the Year, and six Cy Young Award elections. The ultimate folly of this practice was best exemplified in 1979. One NL writer split his fourth-place vote between pitching brothers Phil and Joe Niekro, evidently convinced that the two were identical twins. But

the writer was still permitted to make six more selections. That meant that his fifth-, sixth-, and seventh-place selections received more points (six, five and four, respectively) than his fourth-place co-selections, who were credited with just three and a half points apiece!

There has long been debate about the consideration of pitchers for the MVP Award, the theory (by some) that a man who plays every fourth game cannot be as valuable as a man who plays every day. The debate escalated after the inception of the Cy Young Award in 1956, giving pitchers their own exclusive honor, and the increasing practice of five-man rotations in the 1970s, giving starting pitchers even less of a chance to contribute. As far as Jack Lang, executive secretary of the BBWAA, is concerned, there is no room for controversy. "The rules that are sent out to the voters on the [MVP] committee state: 'Keep in mind that all players are eligible. That includes pitchers, starters and relievers,'" says Lang. "Anybody on the committee that feels they cannot vote for a pitcher, we replace them. In my twenty-four years running the elections, only two writers have said that to me." Since 1931, pitchers have won the award ten times in the AL and nine times in the NL.

There have been fourteen occasions in which one player received all of the available first-place MVP votes in his league. The AL players so honored are Ty Cobb (1911), Babe Ruth (1923), Hank Greenberg (1935), Al Rosen (1953), Mickey Mantle (1956), Frank Robinson (1966), Denny McLain (1968), Reggie Jackson (1973), Jose Canseco (1988), and Frank Thomas (1993). The four unanimous NL selections are Carl Hubbell (1936), Orlando Cepeda (1967), Mike Schmidt (1980), and Jeff Bagwell (1994). Hubbell's distinction is disputable, as two of the eight writers did not submit ballots that year and were not replaced on the selection committee.

Following are the maximum possible point totals that could have been earned by an individual receiving the first-place nomination of every writer polled:

National League		American League	
1911–14	64	1911–14	64
1924–29	80	1922–28	64
1931–37	80	1931–37	80
1938–60	336	1938–60	336
1961	224	1961–68	280
1962–68	280	1969–76	336
1969–1992	336	1977–present	392
1993–present	392		

There have been numerous cases in which the MVP vote point totals did not add up to the correct figure. Reasons for this include inaccuracies in tabulation, inaccuracies in reporting, and writers who failed to vote or to complete their ballots. However, the total impact of all these errors is a small fraction of 1 percent of the total voting over the years.

Following is a complete tabulation of all the recognized MVP elections since 1911:

MVP Award
Chalmers Award, 1911–14

1911 NATIONAL							
F. Schulte, CHI	29	F. Merkle, NY	19	M. Doolan, PHI	6	B. Sweeney, BOS	3	J. Kling, BOS	1	E. Collins, PHI	32
C. Mathewson, NY	25	R. Marquard, NY	19	B. Harmon, SL	6	O. Knabe, PHI	2	B. Adams, PIT	1	J. Jackson, CLE	28
L. Doyle, NY	23	J. Daubert, BRO	16	J. Archer, CHI	5	E. Konetchy, SL	2	N. Rucker, BRO	1	W. Johnson, WAS	19
H. Wagner, PIT	23	J. Tinker, CHI	11	H. Lobert, PHI	4	D. Hoblitzell, CIN	2			B. Cree, NY	16
G. Alexander, PHI	23	C. Meyers, NY	11	G. Gibson, PIT	4	J. Walsh, PHI	2	**1911 AMERICAN**		T. Speaker, BOS	16
M. Huggins, SL	21	J. Sheckard, CHI	9	M. Brown, CHI	4	J. Devore, NY	2	T. Cobb, DET	64	I. Thomas, PHI	12
		M. Mitchell, CIN	9	B. Bescher, CIN	4	F. Luderus, PHI	1	E. Walsh, CHI	35	C. Milan, WAS	10

V. Gregg, CLE 9
F. Baker, PHI 8
J. Coombs, PHI..... 6
N. Lajoie, CLE 5
J. Knight, NY 4
S. Crawford, DET 4
B. Lord, PHI 4
D. Bush, DET 4
R. Ford, NY 3
J. Barry, PHI........ 3
J. Austin, SL 2
F. LaPorte, SL 2
S. McInnis, PHI 1
G. McBride, WAS ... 1

1912 NATIONAL
L. Doyle, NY 48
H. Wagner, PIT 43
C. Meyers, NY 25
J. Tinker, CHI 22
B. Bescher, CIN 17
B. Sweeney, BOS ... 16
H. Zimmerman, CHI 16
R. Marquard, NY 13
O. Wilson, PIT 13
J. Daubert, BRO 13
O. Knabe, PHI 10
E. Konetchy, SL 8
C. Mathewson, NY .. 8
D. Paskert, PHI 6

J. Tesreau, NY 6
R. Murray, NY 5
M. Huggins, SL 5
A. Marsans, CIN 4
F. Merkle, NY 4
J. Evers, CHI 2
C. Hendrix, PIT 2
J. Archer, CHI 1
G. Alexander, PHI ... 1

1912 AMERICAN
T. Speaker, BOS .. 59
E. Walsh, CHI 30
W. Johnson, WAS .. 28
C. Milan, WAS 23
J. Wood, BOS 22
E. Collins, PHI 18
F. Baker, PHI 17
T. Cobb, DET 17
J. Jackson, CLE 16
H. Wagner, BOS 12
C. Gandil, WAS 7
B. Shotton, SL 6
D. Pratt, SL 5
E. Foster, WAS 4
L. Gardner, BOS 4
S. Crawford, DET ... 4
J. Barry, PHI 4
B. Carrigan, BOS 3

G. Moriarty, DET 3
J. Birmingham, CLE .. 2
D. Moeller, WAS 1
G. McBride, WAS ... 1
S. McInnis, PHI 1
B. Daniels, NY 1

1913 NATIONAL
J. Daubert, BRO 50
G. Cravath, PHI 40
R. Maranville, BOS .. 23
C. Mathewson, NY .. 21
C. Meyers, NY 20
V. Saier, CHI 15
L. Cheney, CHI 12
D. Miller, PIT 11
H. Wagner, PIT 11
J. Evers, CHI 10
T. Seaton, PHI 9
A. Fletcher, NY 7
J. Archer, CHI 6
M. Doolan, PHI 6
B. Sweeney, BOS ... 6
J. Viox, PIT 6
L. Doyle, NY 5
T. Shafer, NY 5
R. Murray, NY 4
H. Zimmerman, CHI .. 4
O. Knabe, PHI 4

B. Adams, PIT 3
G. Cutshaw, BRO.... 3
G. Burns, NY 2
A. Marsans, CIN 2
B. Humphries, CHI.... 2
M. Brown, CIN 1

1913 AMERICAN
W. Johnson, WAS .. 54
J. Jackson, CLE 43
E. Collins, PHI 30
T. Speaker, BOS ... 26
F. Baker, PHI 21
C. Gandil, WAS 14
S. McInnis, PHI 12
W. Schang, PHI..... 11
C. Milan, WAS 8
J. Barry, PHI 8
N. Lajoie, CLE 7
D. Bush, DET 6
H. Wagner, BOS 6
R. Russell, CHI 5
B. Shotton, SL 5
G. McBride, WAS ... 5
J. Scott, CHI 5
G. Stovall, SL 5
S. Crawford, DET ... 5
T. Cobb, DET 3
R. Schalk, CHI 3

C. Bender, PHI 2
T. Turner, CLE 2
S. O'Neill, CLE....... 1
H. Hooper, BOS 1

1914 NATIONAL
J. Evers, BOS 50
R. Maranville, BOS.. 44
B. James, BOS 33
G. Burns, NY 31
J. Miller, SL 18
J. Tesreau, NY 15
D. Rudolph, BOS ... 14
S. Magee, PHI 14
Z. Wheat, BRO 10
G. Alexander, PHI .. 9
R. Bresnahan, CHI .. 7
L. Magee, SL 6
B. Doak, SL 5
J. Viox, PIT 5
A. Fletcher, NY 5
C. Mathewson, NY .. 4
V. Saier, CHI 4
B. Schmidt, BOS 4
J. Daubert, BRO 4
L. McCarty, BRO ... 3
H. Groh, CIN....... 2
T. Clarke, CIN 1
G. Cravath, PHI 1

1914 AMERICAN
E. Collins, PHI 63
S. Crawford, DET ... 35
D. Bush, DET 17
F. Baker, PHI 17
J. Jackson, CLE 15
R. Schalk, CHI 13
E. Foster, WAS 11
B. Weaver, CHI 11
S. McInnis, PHI 11
D. Pratt, SL 10
W. Schang, PHI.... 10
T. Speaker, BOS ... 9
T. Walker, SL 9
T. Cobb, DET 7
E. Scott, BOS 7
J. Barry, PHI 6
D. Leonard, BOS ... 6
E. Plank, PHI 5
G. McBride, WAS ... 5
D. Lewis, BOS 4
H. Hooper, BOS 4
F. Maisel, NY 3
R. Peckinpaugh, NY .. 2
C. Milan, WAS 2
S. Agnew, SL 2
R. Hartzell, NY 2
E. Cicotte, CHI 1
G. Moriarty, DET 1

(No official awards, 1915–21)

MVP Award
League Awards, 1922–29

1922 AMERICAN
G. Sisler, SL 59
E. Rommel, PHI..... 31
R. Schalk, CHI....... 26
L. Bush, NY 19
E. Collins, CHI 18
J. Bassler, DET 13
S. O'Neill, CLE..... 13
J. Judge, WAS....... 12

W. Pipp, NY 12
L. Blue, DET 11
C. Galloway, PHI 10
H. Heilmann, DET.... 8
D. Pratt, BOS 7
W. Schang, NY 7
B. Meusel, NY 6
E. Scott, NY 6
W. Johnson, WAS ... 5

U. Shocker, SL 5
C. Jamieson, CLE ... 4
J. Sewell, CLE 4
G. Burns, BOS 2
J. Dykes, PHI 2
J. Harris, WAS 2
R. Peckinpaugh, WAS 2
B. Wambsganss, CLE 2
G. Cutshaw, DET 1

C. Perkins, PHI 1

1923 AMERICAN
B. Ruth, NY.......... 64
E. Collins, CHI 37
H. Heilmann, DET.... 31
W. Gerber, SL 20
J. Sewell, CLE 20
C. Jamieson, CLE ... 19

J. Bassler, DET 17
C. Galloway, PHI 13
G. Uhle, CLE 13
G. Burns, BOS 8
H. Ehmke, BOS 7
M. Ruel, WAS....... 7
R. Peckinpaugh,
　WAS 6
U. Shocker, SL 5

J. Judge, WAS....... 4
M. McManus, SL 4
K. Williams, SL 4
J. Harris, BOS 3
B. Harris, WAS 3
J. Hauser, PHI 1
W. Johnson, WAS ... 1
C. Perkins, PHI 1

(No National League awards, 1922–23)

1924 NATIONAL
D. Vance, BRO 74
R. Hornsby, SL 62
F. Frisch, NY 40
Z. Wheat, BRO 40
R. Youngs, NY 35
G. Kelly, NY 34
R. Maranville, PIT 33
K. Cuyler, PIT 25
J. Fournier, BRO 21
E. Roush, CIN 12
G. Wright, PIT 10
A. High, BRO 9
B. Pinelli, CIN...... 7
R. Bressler, CIN 6
G. Hartnett, CHI 5
B. Grimes, BRO 5
J. Bottomley, SL 4
J. Johnston, BRO ... 3
M. Carey, PIT 3
T. Jackson, NY 3
E. Yde, PIT 2
C. Williams, PHI 1
E. Rixey, CIN 1
G. Alexander, CHI 1
H. DeBerry, BRO ... 1

1924 AMERICAN
W. Johnson, WAS ... 55
E. Collins, CHI 49
C. Jamieson, CLE ... 25
H. Pennock, NY 24
J. Bassler, DET 22
H. Severeid, SL 17
J. Hauser, PHI 13
W. Jacobson, SL ... 11
H. Heilmann, DET ... 9
J. Sewell, CLE 9
M. Ruel, WAS 7
W. Schang, NY 7
A. Simmons, PHI ... 7
W. Pipp, NY 6
H. Ehmke, BOS 5
I. Flagstead, BOS ... 5
W. Gerber, SL 4

E. Whitehill, DET 4
L. Blue, DET 3
I. Boone, BOS 2
J. Harris, BOS 2
C. Galloway, PHI 1
K. Williams, SL 1

1925 NATIONAL
R. Hornsby, SL 73
K. Cuyler, PIT 61
G. Kelly, NY 52
G. Wright, PIT 43
D. Vance, BRO 42
D. Bancroft, BOS ... 41
J. Bottomley, SL ... 28
T. Traynor, PIT 27
F. Frisch, NY 13
E. Roush, CIN 12
M. Carey, PIT 11
I. Meusel, NY 6
D. Luque, CIN 5
C. Grimm, CHI 5
Z. Wheat, BRO 4
P. Donohue, CIN 4
B. Hargrave, CIN ... 4
G. Harper, PHI...... 3
J. Sand, PHI 3
W. Gautreau, BOS ... 2
V. Aldridge, PIT 1

1925 AMERICAN
R. Peckinpaugh,
　WAS 45
A. Simmons, PHI ... 41
J. Sewell, CLE 21
H. Heilmann, DET ... 20
H. Rice, SL 18
E. Sheely, CHI 17
I. Flagstead, BOS ... 10
W. Jacobson, SL ... 10
J. Mostil, CHI 10
O. Bluege, WAS 8
M. Cochrane, PHI ... 8
L. Blue, DET 7
S. Coveleski, WAS ... 7

W. Kamm, CHI 7
E. Rommel, PHI..... 7
R. Schalk, CHI 7
A. Wingo, DET 7
E. Combs, NY 6
B. Meusel, NY 6
T. Lyons, CHI 5
G. Burns, CLE 4
M. McManus, SL 4
H. Pennock, NY 4
H. Bengough, NY ... 2
H. Ehmke, BOS 2
L. Gehrig, NY 2
I. Boone, BOS 1
J. Dugan, NY 1
P. Todt, BOS 1

1926 NATIONAL
B. O'Farrell, SL 79
H. Critz, CIN 60
R. Kremer, PIT 32
T. Thevenow, SL.... 30
H. Wilson, CHI 25
L. Bell, SL 24
B. Hargrave, CIN ... 24
F. Rhem, SL 20
T. Lindstrom, NY ... 17
D. Bancroft, BOS ... 17
H. Carlson, PHI 16
P. Waner, PIT 15
P. Traynor, PIT 14
W. Pipp, CIN 12
E. Brown, BOS 10
H. Ferman, BRO 8
C. Root, CHI 8
R. Hornsby, SL 7
J. Butler, BRO 5
B. Southworth,
　NY-SL 5
G. Alexander, CHI-SL. 5
C. Mays, CIN 4
G. Kelly, NY 2
C. Walker, CIN 1

1926 AMERICAN
G. Burns, CLE 63
J. Mostil, CHI 33
H. Pennock, NY 32
S. Rice, WAS 18
H. Heilmann, DET ... 16
H. Manush, DET 16
A. Simmons, PHI ... 16
L. Grove, PHI 12
G. Goslin, WAS 9
L. Gehrig, NY 7
T. Lazzeri, NY...... 7
B. Falk, CHI 6
F. Fothergill, DET ... 6
O. Melillo, SL 6
H. Rice, SL 6
O. Bluege, WAS 5
P. Todt, BOS 5
M. Cochrane, PHI ... 4
J. Judge, WAS..... 4
M. McManus, SL 4
B. Meusel, NY 3
E. Rigney, BOS 3
I. Flagstead, BOS ... 2
W. Gerber, SL 2
T. Zachary, SL 2
W. Jacobson,
　SL-BOS 1

1927 NATIONAL
P. Waner, PIT 72
F. Frisch, SL 66
R. Hornsby, NY 54
C. Root, CHI 46
T. Jackson, NY 42
L. Waner, PIT 25
P. Traynor, PIT 18
J. Haines, SL 16
R. Kremer, PIT 14
G. Hartnett, CHI 12
R. Lucas, CIN 10
H. Wilson, CHI 9
B. Terry, NY 6
J. Bottomley, SL 6
B. Hargrave, CIN ... 6

F. May, CIN 6
C. Williams, PHI 6
E. Farrell, NY-BOS ... 4
B. Grimes, NY 4
M. Carey, BRO 3
R. Stephenson, CHI .. 3
G. Alexander, SL ... 3
C. Hill, PIT 2
J. Petty, BRO 2
F. Ulrich, PHI 2
C. Hafey, SL 1

1927 AMERICAN
L. Gehrig, NY 56
H. Heilmann, DET ... 35
T. Lyons, CHI 34
M. Cochrane, PHI ... 18
A. Simmons, PHI ... 18
G. Goslin, WAS 15
M. Ruel, WAS...... 15
J. Dykes, PHI 14
L. Sewell, CLE 13
J. Sewell, CLE 13
T. Lazzeri, NY...... 8
R. Reeves, WAS 7
F. O'Rourke, SL 6
D. Tavener, DET 5
H. Lisenbee, WAS ... 5
E. Miller, SL 5
A. Metzler, CHI 3
I. Flagstead, BOS ... 3
C. Jamieson, CLE ... 3
W. Schang, SL 3
F. Schulte, SL 3
W. Hudlin, CLE 2
W. Regan, BOS 2
J. Rothrock, BOS ... 2
B. Harriss, BOS 1
P. Todt, BOS 1

1928 NATIONAL
J. Bottomley, SL.... 76
F. Lindstrom, NY ... 70
B. Grimes, PIT 53
L. Benton, NY 37

H. Critz, CIN 37
P. Traynor, PIT 28
H. Wilson, CHI 21
S. Hogan, NY 17
T. Jackson, NY 16
R. Maranville, SL ... 14
D. Vance, BRO 13
C. Hafey, SL 11
R. Hornsby, BOS ... 10
G. Hartnett, CHI 5
P. Waner, PIT 5
L. Richbourg, BOS.... 5
T. Douthit, SL 5
D. Bissonette, BRO .. 3
D. Flowers, BRO.... 3
J. Wilson, PHI-SL ... 3
A. Whitney, PHI 3
H. Ford, CIN 2
L. Thompson, PHI ... 1

1928 AMERICAN
M. Cochrane, PHI ... 53
H. Manush, SL..... 51
J. Judge, WAS..... 27
T. Lazzeri, NY....... 27
W. Kamm, CHI 15
G. Goslin, WAS 13
E. Combs, NY 13
C. Gehringer, DET .. 12
C. Myer, BOS...... 11
W. Hoyt, NY 8
J. Foxx, PHI 7
J. Sewell, CLE 6
L. Sewell, CLE 6
I. Flagstead, BOS ... 5
E. Morris, BOS 4
H. Heilmann, DET ... 4
C. Lind, CLE 4
W. Cissell, CHI 4
A. Thomas, CHI 4
O. Carroll, DET 3
H. Rice, DET 3
L. Fonseca, CLE 2
T. Lyons, CHI 2
J. Hodapp, CLE 2

A. Metzler, CHI 1
W. Regan, BOS 1

1929 NATIONAL
R. Hornsby, CHI 60

L. O'Doul, PHI ... 54
B. Terry, NY 48
B. Grimes, PIT 35
L. Waner, PIT 30
R. Lucas, CIN 29

P. Traynor, PIT 27
H. Wilson, CHI 24
F. Herman, BRO 24
G. Bush, CHI 16
C. Klein, PHI 15

M. Ott, NY 15
T. Douthit, SL 14
C. Grimm, CHI 13
T. Jackson, NY 8
R. Maranville, BOS ... 8

H. Critz, CIN 5
B. Friberg, PHI 4
P. Malone, CHI 3
F. Frisch, SL 2

P. Whitney, PHI 2
J. Frederick, BRO 2
R. Stephenson, CHI ... 1
Z. Taylor, BOS-CHI ... 1

(There were no official selections for the American League in 1929 or for either league in 1930.)

MVP Award
Baseball Writers' Association of America Awards, 1931–Present

1931 NATIONAL
F. Frisch, SL 65
C. Klein, PHI 55
B. Terry, NY 53
W. English, CHI 30
C. Hafey, SL 29
J. Wilson, SL 28
T. Jackson, NY 24
C. Grimm, CHI 21
E. Adams, SL 18
E. Brandt, BOS 15
R. Maranville, BOS .. 15
K. Cuyler, CHI 14
P. Traynor, PIT 12
R. Lucas, CIN 10
L. Waner, PIT 8
J. Bottomley, SL 8
J. Elliott, PHI........ 6
J. Quinn, BRO 6
N. Finn, BRO 5
W. Clark, BRO 3
P. Derringer, SL 3
C. Root, CHI 3
D. Bartell, PHI 2
J. Vergez, NY 2
F. Fitzsimmons, NY ... 1
L. O'Doul, BRO 1
G. Wright, BRO 1
T. Cuccinello, CIN ... 1
C. Gelbert, SL 1

1931 AMERICAN
L. Grove, PHI 78
L. Gehrig, NY 59
A. Simmons, PHI 51
E. Averill, CLE 43
B. Ruth, NY 40
E. Webb, BOS 22
J. Cronin, WAS 18
O. Melillo, SL 17
S. West, WAS 16
M. Cochrane, PHI ... 16
G. Earnshaw, PHI ... 12
W. Ferrell, CLE 12
F. Marberry, WAS.... 11
H. Rhyne, BOS 10
B. Chapman, NY 7
J. Stone, DET 6
C. Gehringer, DET ... 4
L. Blue, CHI 4
R. Kress, SL 3
C. Reynolds, CHI ... 2
W. Stewart, SL 2
G. Goslin, SL 2
D. MacFayden, BOS . 2
T. Oliver, BOS 2
J. Foxx, PHI 1

1932 NATIONAL
C. Klein, PHI 78
L. Warneke, CHI 68
L. O'Doul, BRO 58
P. Waner, PIT 37
R. Stephenson, CHI .. 32
B. Terry, NY 25
D. Hurst, PHI 24
P. Traynor, PIT 17
B. Herman, CHI 16
M. Ott, NY 15
R. Brown, BOS 10
F. Herman, CIN 10
L. Waner, PIT 6
W. Berger, BOS 6
H. Wilson, BRO 6
E. Orsatti, SL 6
R. Maranville, BOS .. 5
J. Wilson, SL 5
T. Cuccinello, BRO ... 4
J. Dean, SL 4
F. Frisch, SL 3
R. Collins, SL 3
A. Vaughan, PIT 1

G. Bush, CHI 1

1932 AMERICAN
J. Foxx, PHI 75
L. Gehrig, NY 55
H. Manush, WAS 41
E. Averill, CLE 37
L. Gomez, NY 27
J. Cronin, WAS 26
B. Ruth, NY 26
T. Lazzeri, NY....... 21
A. Simmons, PHI 13
C. Gehringer, DET ... 13
D. Alexander,
  DET-BOS 10
W. Cissell, CHI-CLE . 10
R. Ferrell, SL........ 9
L. Grove, PHI 8
J. Allen, NY 8
B. Dickey, NY....... 8
G. Goslin, SL 7
M. Weaver, WAS 6
H. Davis, DET....... 5
D. Harris, WAS 5
W. Ferrell, CLE 5
J. Levey, SL 5
T. Lyons, CHI 5
B. Sullivan, CHI 3
E. McNair, PHI 3
S. Jolley, CHI-BOS ... 3
G. Crowder, WAS 2
M. McManus, BOS ... 2
G. Walker, DET 1
J. Sewell, NY 1

1933 NATIONAL
C. Hubbell, NY 77
C. Klein, PHI 48
W. Berger, BOS 44
B. Terry, NY 35
P. Martin, SL 31
G. Mancuso, NY 24
J. Dean, SL 23
P. Traynor, PIT 20
B. Ryan, NY 19
A. Lopez, BRO 18
B. Cantwell, BOS .. 18
H. Schumacher, NY .. 11
R. Maranville, BOS .. 11
G. Bush, CHI 11
L. French, PIT 10
F. Frisch, SL 7
J. Bottomley, CIN.... 6
J. Medwick, SL 5
G. Hartnett, CHI 5
L. Warneke, CHI 4
R. Lucas, CIN....... 3
D. Bartell, PHI 3
A. Vaughan, PIT 2
R. Moore, BOS 2
V. Davis, PHI 1
C. Hafey, CIN 1
D. Luque, NY 1

1933 AMERICAN
J. Foxx, PHI 74
J. Cronin, WAS 62
H. Manush, WAS ... 54
L. Gehrig, NY 39
L. Grove, PHI 35
C. Gehringer, DET ... 32
G. Crowder, WAS... 28
A. Simmons, CHI ... 19
E. Whitehill, WAS .. 18
O. Melillo, SL 12
S. West, SL 11
R. Ferrell, SL-BOS .. 9
B. Dickey, NY 9
T. Lazzeri, NY 6
J. Kuhel, WAS 5
E. Averill, CLE 5
C. Myer, WAS 5

M. Cochrane, PHI ... 5
B. Johnson, PHI 5
B. Chapman, NY 4
M. Bishop, PHI 1
L. Appling, CHI 1
W. Kamm, CLE 1

1934 NATIONAL
J. Dean, SL 78
P. Waner, PIT 50
J. Moore, NY 42
T. Jackson, NY 39
M. Ott, NY 37
R. Collins, SL 32
B. Terry, NY 30
C. Davis, PHI 18
P. Dean, SL........ 16
H. Schumacher, NY . 16
C. Hubbell, NY 16
W. Berger, BOS 13
L. Warneke, CHI ... 10
G. Hartnett, CHI 9
G. Slade, CIN 5
K. Cuyler, CHI 5
B. Frey, CIN 4
F. Frankhouse, BOS .. 4
R. Boyle, BRO 4
B. Herman, CHI 4
F. Frisch, SL 4
W. Hoyt, PIT 2
A. Lopez, BRO 1
V. Mungo, BRO ... 1
A. Vaughan, PIT ... 1

1934 AMERICAN
M. Cochrane, DET ... 67
C. Gehringer, DET .. 65
L. Gomez, NY 60
S. Rowe, DET...... 59
L. Gehrig, NY 54
H. Greenberg, DET .. 29
H. Trosky, CLE...... 18
W. Ferrell, BOS 16
M. Owen, DET 13
J. Foxx, PHI 11
A. Simmons, CHI ... 9
W. Werber, BOS ... 8
R. Johnson, BOS ... 8
G. Goslin, DET 6
S. West, SL 5
M. Harder, CLE 4
F. Higgins, PHI 3
E. Averill, CLE 3
B. Knickerbocker,
  CLE 2

1935 NATIONAL
G. Hartnett, CHI 75
J. Dean, SL......... 66
A. Vaughan, PIT 45
B. Herman, CHI 38
J. Medwick, SL 37
C. Hubbell, NY 20
W. Berger, BOS 20
B. Terry, NY 20
A. Galan, CHI 18
P. Martin, SL 16
H. Leiber, NY 11
L. Warneke, CHI ... 9
E. Lombardi, CIN ... 8
F. Frisch, SL....... 7
C. Blanton, PIT 5
J. Moore, PHI 5
J. Allen, PHI 5
G. Mancuso, NY.... 4
P. Derringer, CIN ... 4
M. Ott, NY......... 3
P. Dean, SL........ 2
R. Collins, SL 2
C. Davis, PHI 2
P. Waner, PIT 1
B. Lee, CHI 1

T. Jackson, NY 1
D. Camilli, PHI 1

1935 AMERICAN
H. Greenberg, DET .. 80
W. Ferrell, BOS 62
J. Vosmik, CLE 39
C. Myer, WAS 36
L. Gehrig, NY 29
C. Gehringer, DET .. 26
M. Cochrane, DET ... 24
R. Cramer, PHI 18
M. Solters, BOS-SL.. 16
R. Hemsley, SL 16
J. Foxx, PHI 11
T. Bridges, DET..... 11
T. Lyons, CHI 10
L. Grove, BOS 8
Z. Bonura, CHI 7
L. Appling, CHI 7
L. Sewell, CHI 7
J. Allen, NY 5
J. Whitehead, CHI .. 4
F. Higgins, PHI 3
J. Marcum, PHI 3
E. Auker, DET 2
M. Harder, CLE 2
L. Lary, WAS-SL ... 1

1936 NATIONAL
C. Hubbell, NY 60
J. Dean, SL 53
B. Herman, CHI..... 37
J. Medwick, SL 30
P. Waner, PIT 29
M. Ott, NY 28
F. Demaree, CHI ... 17
G. Mancuso, NY ... 13
D. MacFayden,
  BOS 12
L. Durocher, SL 8
P. Derringer, CIN ... 6
G. Hartnett, CHI 6
B. Whitehead, NY... 6
A. Lopez, BOS 5
V. Mungo, BRO ... 5
W. Berger, BOS ... 4
D. Camilli, PHI..... 4
G. Phelps, BRO 3
D. Bartell, NY 2
E. Lombardi, CIN ... 1
T. Moore, SL....... 1

1936 AMERICAN
L. Gehrig, NY 73
L. Appling, CHI 65
E. Averill, CLE 48
C. Gehringer, DET .. 39
B. Dickey, NY...... 29
V. Kennedy, CHI ... 27
J. Kuhel, WAS 27
J. DiMaggio, NY 26
T. Bridges, DET 25
H. Trosky, CLE...... 19
J. Foxx, BOS 16
G. Walker, DET 14
S. Bell, SL 10
W. Moses, PHI 7
L. Grove, BOS 5
J. Dykes, CHI 3
R. Radcliff, CHI 3
S. West, SL 2
Z. Bonura, CHI 1
E. McNair, BOS.... 1

1937 NATIONAL
J. Medwick, SL 70
G. Hartnett, CHI 68
C. Hubbell, NY 52
J. Turner, BOS...... 30
L. Fette, BOS 29
D. Bartell, NY 26

M. Ott, NY 24
P. Waner, PIT 21
B. Herman, CHI..... 19
J. Mize, SL 18
C. Melton, NY 17
C. Root, CHI 15
P. Whitney, PHI 10
H. Danning, NY 10
F. Demaree, CHI ... 9
L. Warneke, CHI ... 6
B. Jurges, CHI 4
J. Cooney, BRO ... 4
B. Myers, CIN 2
L. Grissom, CIN.... 2
H. Manush, BRO ... 1

1937 AMERICAN
C. Gehringer, DET .. 78
J. DiMaggio, NY 74
H. Greenberg, DET . 48
L. Gehrig, NY 42
L. Sewell, CHI 22
B. Dickey, NY...... 22
J. Cronin, BOS 19
R. Ruffing, NY 18
L. Gomez, NY 14
M. Kreevich, CHI ... 13
C. Travis, WAS 12
W. Moses, PHI 12
J. Allen, CLE 11
H. Clift, SL 11
R. Radcliff, CHI 10
B. Lewis, WAS..... 7
L. Appling, CHI 5
B. Bell, SL 5
E. Averill, CLE 4
L. Lary, CLE 4
R. Lawson, DET ... 4
G. Walker, DET 3
R. York, DET 1
P. Fox, DET....... 1

1938 NATIONAL
E. Lombardi, CIN ...229
B. Lee, CHI 166
A. Vaughan, PIT ...163
M. Ott, NY 132
F. McCormick, CIN 130
J. Rizzo, PIT 96
S. Hack, CHI 87
P. Derringer, CIN ... 70
M. Brown, PIT 62
G. Hartnett, CHI ... 61
J. Medwick, SL 55
J. Mize, SL 28
T. Cuccinello, BOS .. 23
P. Young, PIT 19
C. Bryant, CHI 16
H. Danning, NY 13
I. Goodman, CIN ... 11
J. VanderMeer, CIN . 7
L. Durocher, BRO... 6
D. Coffman, NY 6
A. Lopez, BOS 5
L. Waner, PIT 5
D. Garms, BOS 5
D. Camilli, BRO 5
C. Root, CHI 3
J. Moore, NY 3
J. Hudson, BRO ... 3
H. Mulcahy, PHI ... 3
L. Handley, PIT 2
L. Warneke, CHI ... 1
F. Fitzsimmons, BRO . 1
H. Martin, PHI 1

1938 AMERICAN
J. Foxx, BOS 305
B. Dickey, NY......196
H. Greenberg,
  DET 162
R. Ruffing, NY 146

B. Newsom, SL.....111
J. DiMaggio, NY 106
J. Cronin, BOS 92
E. Averill, CLE 34
C. Travis, WAS 33
C. Gehringer, DET .. 27
J. Heath, CLE..... 24
J. Gordon, NY 23
H. Trosky, CLE..... 22
K. Keltner, CLE 16
M. Stratton, CHI ... 15
M. Harder, CLE 14
B. Johnson, PHI ... 13
H. Clift, SL........ 11
L. Gehrig, NY 10
P. Fox, DET....... 9
J. Vosmik, BOS ... 7
G. McQuinn, SL ... 7
L. Grove, BOS 7
B. Lewis, WAS 5
R. Rolfe, NY 5
C. Myer, WAS 5
E. Brucker, PHI 5
J. Allen, CLE 2
F. Crosetti, NY 2
L. Gomez, NY 1
D. Cramer, BOS ... 1

1939 NATIONAL
B. Walters, CIN 303
J. Mize, SL 178
P. Derringer, CIN ...174
F. McCormick, CIN 159
C. Davis, SL 106
J. Brown, SL....... 99
J. Medwick, SL 81
L. Durocher, BRO... 52
H. Danning, NY 33
L. Hamlin, BRO ... 32
M. Ott, NY 21
B. Jurges, NY 20
D. Camilli, BRO 20
W. Myers, CIN 18
S. Hack, CHI 17
A. Galan, CHI 15
T. Moore, SL...... 15
M. Arnovich, PHI ... 10
L. Frey, CIN 8
B. Lee, CHI 8
E. Slaughter, SL ... 8
W. Werber, CIN ... 6
M. West, BOS 5
G. Hartnett, CHI ... 5
I. Goodman, CIN.... 4
B. Hassett, BOS 4
P. Coscarart, BRO .. 4
E. Fletcher, BOS-PIT . 4
C. Lavagetto, BRO ... 3
R. Bowman, SL..... 2
E. Miller, BOS 1
B. Herman, CHI.... 1

1939 AMERICAN
J. DiMaggio, NY 280
J. Foxx, BOS 170
B. Feller, CLE......155
T. Williams, BOS...126
R. Ruffing, NY 116
B. Dickey, NY......110
E. Leonard, WAS ... 71
B. Johnson, PHI ... 52
J. Gordon, NY 43
M. Kreevich, CHI ... 38
C. Brown, CHI 34
K. Keltner, CLE 26
G. McQuinn, SL ... 24
C. Gehringer, DET .. 21
L. Grove, BOS 17
J. Cronin, BOS 15
T. Lyons, CHI 13
H. Greenberg, DET . 12
B. Newsom, SL-DET . 11

J. Rigney, CHI 9
J. Kuhel, CHI 8
C. Keller, NY 7
J. Heath, CLE........ 7
G. Walker, CHI........ 7
F. Hayes, PHI........ 7
T. Bridges, DET 7
R. Rolfe, NY 6
B. McCosky, DET.... 6
E. McNair, CHI 5
H. Trosky, CLE........ 4
G. Case, WAS 3
M. Hoag, SL 3
R. York, DET 1
L. Appling, CHI 1

1940 NATIONAL

F. McCormick, CIN 274
J. Mize, SL 209
B. Walters, CIN 146
P. Derringer, CIN ... 121
F. Fitzsimmons, BRO 84
D. Walker, BRO 71
H. Danning, NY 64
S. Hack, CHI 61
E. Lombardi, CIN ... 38
W. Werber, CIN 36
J. Cooney, BOS 31
D. Camilli, BRO 30
E. Miller, BOS 28
D. Garms, PIT 28
A. Vaughan, PIT 27
C. Passeau, CHI 26
J. Beggs, CIN 19
T. Moore, SL........ 18
E. Fletcher, PIT 16
B. Nicholson, CHI 12
K. Higbe, PHI 10
C. Rowell, BOS 10
A. Lopez, BOS-PIT ... 9
M. Van Robays, PIT ... 8
R. Sewell, PIT........ 7
M. West, BOS 6
B. Young, NY 6
W. Wyatt, BRO 3
J. Rizzo, PHI 3
P. May, PHI 3
H. Mulcahy, PHI 3
J. Martin, SL........ 2
F. Gustine, PIT........ 1

1940 AMERICAN

H. Greenberg, DET .292
B. Feller, CLE........ 222
J. DiMaggio, NY 151
B. Newsom, DET ... 120
L. Boudreau, CLE...119
J. Foxx, BOS 110
S. Rowe, DET........ 62
R. York, DET 61
R. Radcliff, SL........ 55
L. Appling, CHI 54
R. Weatherly, CLE ... 34
D. Bartell, DET 26
J. Kuhel, CHI 18
S. Hudson, WAS........ 16
T. Williams, BOS........ 16
B. McCosky, DET.... 11
E. Bonham, NY 8
W. Judnich, SL 6
J. Babich, PHI 5
M. Tresh, CHI 4
F. Hayes, PHI 4
R. Mack, CLE........ 4
J. Gordon, NY 3
C. Travis, WAS........ 3
B. Kennedy, CHI 3
C. Gehringer, DET 3
R. Hemsley, CLE 2
T. Lyons, CHI 2
L. Finney, BOS 1
E. Auker, SL 1

1941 NATIONAL

D. Camilli, BRO ...300
P. Reiser, BRO 183
W. Wyatt, BRO 151
J. Brown, SL........ 107
E. Riddle, CIN 98
E. White, SL........ 77
K. Higbe, BRO 64
J. Hopp, SL........ 61
J. Mize, SL 48
D. Walker, BRO 34
B. Herman, CHI-BRO 27
T. Moore, SL 26
S. Hack, CHI 26
E. Fletcher, PIT 22
J. Cooney, BOS 20
B. Nicholson, CHI ... 16
G. Mancuso, SL 14
F. Crespi, SL 13
M. Ott, NY 12
E. Slaughter, SL 12
B. Young, NY 10
V. DiMaggio, PIT ... 10
J. Tobin, BOS 10
A. Lopez, PIT 8
M. Marion, SL 8
M. Cooper, SL 8
L. Warneke, SL 7
N. Etten, PHI 6
B. Walters, CIN 6
B. Dahlgren, BOS-CHI 6
W. Werber, CIN 6
E. Crabtree, SL 5
J. Rucker, NY 4
D. Litwhiler, PHI 3
H. Danning, NY 2
C. Hubbell, NY 2
C. Lavagetto, BRO ... 2
A. Vaughan, PIT 2

1941 AMERICAN

J. DiMaggio, NY 291
T. Williams, BOS....254
B. Feller, CLE........174
T. Lee, CHI 144
C. Keller, NY 126
C. Travis, WAS........ 101
J. Gordon, NY 60
J. Heath, CLE........ 37
H. Newsome, BOS ... 32
R. Cullenbine, SL 29
J. Cronin, BOS 26
S. Chapman, PHI 25
B. Dickey, NY........ 18
T. Henrich, NY 16
B. McCosky, DET.... 12
T. Lyons, CHI 12
D. Siebert, PHI........ 10
L. Boudreau, CLE... 10
A. Benton, DET 8
P. Rizzuto, NY 7
E. Leonard, WAS 7
B. Campbell, DET 4
R. York, DET 3
F. Hayes, PHI........ 3
T. Wright, CHI 2
R. Ruffing, NY 2
E. Auker, SL 1
F. Higgins, DET........ 1
D. DiMaggio, BOS ... 1

1942 NATIONAL

M. Cooper, SL....263
E. Slaughter, SL 200
M. Ott, NY 190
A. Owen, BRO 103
J. Mize, NY 97
P. Reiser, BRO 91
M. Marion, SL 81
D. Camilli, BRO 42
R. Elliott, PIT........ 39
C. Passeau, CHI 33
W. Cooper, SL........ 28
S. Musial, SL 26
E. Lombardi, BOS ... 24
J. Beazley, SL 24
J. Brown, SL........ 24
W. Wyatt, BRO 22
J. Medwick, BRO ... 20
T. Moore, SL........ 15
B. Nicholson, CHI ... 14
S. Hack, CHI 11
J. VanderMeer, CIN .. 11
T. Hughes, PHI 10
R. Starr, CIN 9
L. French, BRO 7
B. Reese, BRO 6
W. Kurowski, SL........ 6
R. Lamanno, CIN 4
M. West, BOS 4
L. Frey, CIN 4
F. McCormick, CIN 4
A. Javery, BOS 3

E. Miller, BOS 1

1942 AMERICAN

J. Gordon, NY 270
T. Williams, BOS....249
J. Pesky, BOS 143
V. Stephens, SL 140
E. Bonham, NY 102
T. Hughson, BOS........ 92
J. DiMaggio, NY 86
S. Spence, WAS 65
P. Marchildon, PHI... 39
L. Boudreau, CLE... 34
B. Doerr, BOS 24
T. Lyons, CHI 23
G. Case, WAS 17
K. Keltner, CLE 15
C. Keller, NY 15
W. Judnich, SL 14
B. Dickey, NY........ 12
D. Gutteridge, SL 12
P. Rizzuto, NY 9
C. Laabs, SL........ 9
R. Ferrell, SL........ 8
H. Borowy, NY 8
J. Bagby, CLE 6
T. Wright, CHI 6
T. Lupien BOS 4
L. Fleming, CLE 4
S. Chandler, NY 3
R. York, DET 3
B. McCosky, DET.... 1

1943 NATIONAL

S. Musial, SL 267
W. Cooper, SL........192
B. Nicholson, CHI ..181
B. Herman, BRO....140
M. Cooper, SL........ 130
R. Sewell, PIT........ 127
E. Riddle, CIN 68
R. Elliott, PIT........ 52
F. McCormick, CIN .. 26
C. Shoun, CIN 24
E. Miller, CIN 24
M. Witek, NY 21
M. Marion, SL........ 20
S. Rowe, PHI 18
W. Wyatt, BRO 15
A. Vaughan, BRO ... 15
R. Mueller, CIN 12
A. Javery, BOS 12
S. Hack, CHI 10
M. Ott, NY 9
E. Fletcher, PIT 7
A. Adams, NY 7
L. Klein, SL 6
A. Galan, BRO 5
D. Walker, BRO 5
J. Tobin, BOS........ 5
D. Bartell, NY 5
P. Cavaretta, CHI 4
T. Holmes, BOS 2
R. Northey, PHI 2
B. Dahlgren, PHI........ 2
H. Bithorn, CHI 1
B. Walters, CIN 1
L. Frey, CIN 1

1943 AMERICAN

S. Chandler, NY 246
L. Appling, CHI 215
R. York, DET........152
W. Johnson, NY 135
B. Johnson, WAS....116
D. Wakefield, DET ... 72
N. Etten, NY 61
B. Dickey, NY........ 58
V. Stephens, SL 49
L. Boudreau, CLE... 40
D. Trout, DET 38
G. Case, WAS 37
C. Keller, NY........ 31
B. Doerr, BOS 21
A. Smith, CLE 19
G. Priddy, WAS........ 14
O. Hockett, CLE 14
D. Gutteridge, SL 13
E. Wynn, WAS 13
J. Bagby, CLE 11
R. Cramer, DET 8
F. Higgins, DET 8
C. Laabs, SL........ 6
J. Early, WAS 6
J. Gordon, NY 4

R. Wolff, PHI........ 4
L. Newsome, BOS 3
J. Cronin, BOS 3
J. Flores, PHI 3
G. Maltzberger, CHI .. 3
F. Crosetti, PHI 2
K. Keltner, CLE 2
P. Fox, BOS 2
R. Hodgin, CHI 1
J. Murphy, NY 1
D. Siebert, PHI........ 1
J. Tabor, BOS 1
H. Wagner, PHI 1

1944 NATIONAL

M. Marion, SL 190
B. Nicholson, CHI ..189
D. Walker, BRO 145
S. Musial, SL 136
B. Walters, CIN 107
B. Voiselle, NY 107
R. Mueller, CIN 85
W. Cooper, SL........ 72
M. Cooper, SL........ 63
R. Elliott, PIT........ 57
R. Sewell, PIT........ 49
B. Dahlgren, PIT 33
F. McCormick, CIN ... 32
P. Cavaretta, CHI ... 27
R. Sanders, SL 25
M. Ott, NY 20
J. Tobin, BOS 13
J. Hopp, SL........ 10
R. Northey, PHI 10
J. Medwick, NY 9
J. Barrett, PIT 8
E. Miller, CIN 8
T. Holmes, BOS 6
T. Wilks, SL........ 4
T. Lupien, PHI 3
S. Hack, CHI 2
M. Lanier, SL 2
C. Ryan, BOS 2
A. Galan, BRO 1
W. Kurowski, SL 1
J. Russell, PIT 1

1944 AMERICAN

H. Newhouser, DET 236
D. Trout, DET 232
V. Stephens, SL 193
S. Stirnweiss, NY 129
D. Wakefield, DET .. 128
L. Boudreau, CLE... 84
R. Doerr, BOS 75
S. Spence, WAS 56
N. Potter, SL........ 52
B. Johnson, BOS 51
M. Christman, SL 27
T. Hughson, BOS 22
D. Cramer, DET 14
F. Hayes, PHI 13
P. Fox, BOS 12
J. Kramer, SL........ 9
J. Lindell, NY 8
P. Richards, DET 8
D. Gutteridge, SL 7
F. Higgins, DET 7
G. McQuinn, SL 7
G. Kell, PHI 6
R. Cullenbine, CLE ... 5
N. Etten, NY 5
R. York, DET 5
R. Hemsley, NY........ 4
M. Kreevich, SL 4
W. Moses, CHI 4
E. Mayo, DET 3
D. Siebert, PHI........ 3
H. Borowy, NY 2
F. Crosetti, NY 2
R. Hodgin, CHI 2
B. Muncrief, SL 1

1945 NATIONAL

P. Cavaretta, CHI ...279
T. Holmes, BOS ...175
C. Barrett, BOS-SL .151
A. Pafko, CHI 131
W. Kurowski, SL........ 90
H. Borowy, CHI 84
H. Wyse, CHI 72
M. Marion, SL 69
D. Walker, BRO 66
G. Rosen, BRO 56

S. Hack, CHI 42
H. Brecheen, SL 31
M. Ott, NY 22
A. Galan, BRO 18
J. Hopp, SL........ 17
R. Elliott, PIT........ 15
L. Olmo, BRO 13
B. Adams, PHI-SL ... 12
C. Passeau, CHI 9
P. Lowrey, CHI 5
A. Adams, NY 4
A. Karl, PHI 4
A. Lopez, PIT 2
P. Masi, BOS 2
E. Miller, CIN 2
V. DiMaggio, PIT 1
E. Stanky, BRO 1

1945 AMERICAN

H. Newhouser, DET 236
E. Mayo, DET 164
S. Stirnweiss, NY 161
B. Ferriss, BOS 148
G. Myatt, WAS 98
V. Stephens, SL 94
R. Wolff, WAS 78
L. Boudreau, CLE... 70
G. Case, WAS 60
P. Richards, DET 35
M. Tresh, CHI 33
J. Kuhel, WAS 29
R. Cullenbine, DET ... 26
H. Greenberg, DET ... 25
N. Etten, NY 21
T. Cuccinello, CHI ... 18
D. Trout, DET 17
E. Leonard, WAS 16
R. Schalk, CHI 13
J. Heath, CLE........ 10
G. Binks, WAS........ 9
B. Muncrief, SL 8
A. Benton, DET 6
R. Ferrell, WAS 6
B. Johnson, BOS 6
M. Christman, SL 5
B. Estalella, PHI 5
F. Hayes, PHI-CLE ... 5
D. Cramer, DET 4
W. Moses, CHI 4
E. Lake, BOS 2
R. Christopher, PHI ... 1
L. Newsome, BOS ... 1
R. York, DET 1

1946 NATIONAL

S. Musial, SL 319
D. Walker, BRO 159
E. Slaughter, SL 144
H. Pollet, SL........116
J. Sain, BOS........ 95
P. Reese, BRO 79
E. Stanky, BRO 67
D. Ennis, PHI 61
P. Reiser, BRO 58
P. Cavaretta, CHI 49
B. Kerr, NY 37
J. Hopp, BOS 34
E. Waitkus, CHI 21
B. Edwards, BRO 20
K. Higbe, BRO 18
H. Brecheen, SL 14
J. Mize, NY 14
G. Hatton, CIN 12
T. Holmes, BOS 11
J. Tabor, PHI........ 10
E. Verban, SL-PHI ... 10
H. Walker, SL 9
L. Rowe, PHI 9
P. Masi, BOS 7
J. VanderMeer, CIN ... 7
R. Schoendienst, SL .. 6
B. Cox, PIT 5
F. Gustine, PIT 4
M. Marion, SL 4
R. Kiner, PIT 3
W. Kurowski, SL 3
R. Mueller, CIN 3

J. Schmitz, CHI 3
P. Lowrey, CHI 2
F. McCormick, PHI ... 2
C. Furillo, BRO 1
O. Judd, PHI 1

1946 AMERICAN

T. Williams, BOS....224
H. Newhouser, DET 197
B. Doerr, BOS 158
J. Pesky, BOS 141
M. Vernon, WAS 134
B. Feller, CLE........ 105
B. Ferriss, BOS 94
H. Greenberg, DET .. 91
D. DiMaggio, BOS ... 56
L. Boudreau, CLE... 37
R. York, BOS 28
L. Appling, CHI 26
T. Hughson, BOS 19
E. Caldwell, CHI 18
C. Keller, NY 17
G. Kell, PHI-DET 12
S. Chandler, NY 12
A. Robinson, NY 12
J. DiMaggio, NY 6
B. Newsom, PHI-WAS 6
V. Stephens, SL 6
P. Marchildon, PHI... 5
B. Rosar, PHI 4
S. Spence, WAS 4
J. Berardino, SL 2
T. Henrich, NY 1
H. Wagner, BOS 1

1947 NATIONAL

R. Elliott, BOS 205
E. Blackwell, CIN ...175
J. Mize, NY 144
B. Edwards, BRO...140
J. Robinson, BRO ... 106
R. Kiner, PIT 101
L. Jansen, NY 91
P. Reese, BRO 80
W. Kurowski, SL 45
H. Walker, SL-PHI ... 45
R. Branca, BRO 40
H. Casey, BRO 37
E. Leonard, PHI........ 32
E. Stanky, BRO 32
W. Spahn, BOS 26
W. Marshall, NY 20
J. Sain, BOS........ 20
W. Cooper, NY 19
D. Walker, BRO 14
E. Slaughter, SL 12
S. Musial, SL 12
E. Verban, PHI 9
P. Cavaretta, CHI 4
P. Lowrey, CHI 2
E. Miller, CIN 2
A. Pafko, CHI 1

1947 AMERICAN

J. DiMaggio, NY 202
T. Williams, BOS....201
L. Boudreau, CLE...168
J. Page, NY 167
G. Kell, DET 132
G. McQuinn, NY 77
J. Gordon, CLE 59
B. Feller, CLE........ 58
P. Marchildon, PHI... 47
L. Appling, CHI 43
E. Joost, PHI 35
B. McCosky, PHI 35
T. Henrich, NY 33
F. Shea, NY 23
Y. Berra, NY 18
A. Reynolds, NY 18
B. Dillinger, SL........ 13
J. Pesky, BOS 11
F. Fain, PHI 9
W. Johnson, NY 9
S. Spence, WAS 9
F. Hutchison, DET 8
E. Wynn, WAS 7
B. Doerr, BOS 6
B. Rosar, PHI 6
M. Christman, WAS ... 4
B. McCahan, PHI 4
D. Mitchell, CLE 4
R. Cullenbine, DET ... 3

J. Dobson, BOS 3
J. Heath, SL 1
E. Lopat, SL 1
V. Stephens, SL 1
T. Wright, CHI 1

1948 NATIONAL
S. Musial, SL 303
J. Sain, BOS 223
A. Dark, BOS 174
S. Gordon, NY 72
H. Brecheen, SL 61
P. Reese, BRO 60
R. Kiner, PIT 55
E. Slaughter, SL 55
D. Murtaugh, PIT 52
D. Rojek, PIT 51
R. Ashburn, PHI 48
J. Schmitz, CHI 37
R. Elliott, BOS 33
W. Spahn, BOS 31
J. Robinson, BRO 30
A. Pafko, CHI 25
J. Mize, NY 22
R. Barney, BRO 15
J. VanderMeer, CIN ... 13
J. Wyrostek, CIN 9
R. Branca, BRO 8
R. Campanella, BRO... 8
B. Chesnes, PIT 8
P. Cavaretta, CHI 6
E. Miller, PHI 4
D. Ennis, PHI 3
G. Hatton, CIN 3
L. Jansen, NY 2
D. Walker, PIT 2
G. Hodges, BRO 1
W. Lockman, NY 1
H. Sauer, CIN......... 1

1948 AMERICAN
L. Boudreau, CLE..324
J. DiMaggio, NY 213
T. Williams, BOS ...171
V. Stephens, BOS ...121
B. Lemon, CLE 101
J. Gordon, CLE 63
T. Henrich, NY 63
G. Bearden, CLE.... 52
H. Newhouser, DET.. 48
E. Joost, PHI 39
H. Majeski, PHI 23
B. Tebbetts, BOS ... 23
V. Raschi, NY 23
K. Keltner, CLE 18
J. Priddy, SL....... 16
G. Kell, DET 14
W. Evers, DET 13
A. Zarilla, SL 11
B. Doerr, BOS 10
B. Dillinger, SL.... 10
J. Hegan, CLE 10
L. Appling, CHI 8
B. Feller, CLE 6
L. Brissie, PHI 5
F. Fain, PHI 5
J. Dobson, BOS 5
B. Goodman, BOS.... 4
R. McCosky, PHI 4
Y. Berra, NY 3
D. DiMaggio, BOS ... 3
L. Doby, CLE 3
C. Fannin, SL 2
P. Mullin, DET 1
P. Rizzuto, NY 1

1949 NATIONAL
J. Robinson, BRO ..264
S. Musial, SL 226
E. Slaughter, SL ...181
R. Kiner, PIT 133
P. Reese, BRO 118
C. Furillo, BRO ... 68
W. Spahn, BOS 60
D. Newcombe,
BRO 55
K. Heintzelman,
PHI 48
R. Schoendienst,
SL 30
G. Hodges, BRO.... 29
H. Pollet, SL 29
D. Ennis, PHI 28
B. Thomson, NY 25
R. Campanella, BRO.. 22

P. Roe, BRO 21
G. Hamner, PHI...... 9
W. Lockman, NY 9
R. Meyer, PHI....... 8
K. Raffensberger,
CIN 8
H. Sauer, CIN-CHI ... 8
T. Wilks, SL........ 8
R. Ashburn, PHI 6
J. Schmitz, CHI 6
A. Dark, BOS 3
M. Marion, SL 3
W. Jones, PHI 2
W. Marshall, NY 2
E. Torgeson, BOS.... 2
S. Gordon, NY 1
D. Sisler, PHI 1

1949 AMERICAN
T. Williams, BOS...272
P. Rizzuto, NY 175
J. Page, NY........166
M. Parnell, BOS ...151
E. Kinder, BOS 122
T. Henrich, NY 121
V. Stephens, BOS ..100
G. Kell, DET 80
B. Lemon, CLE 57
V. Wertz, DET...... 51
V. Raschi, NY...... 19
J. DiMaggio, NY ... 18
E. Joost, PHI 11
L. Boudreau, CLE... 10
Y. Berra, NY 9
D. DiMaggio, BOS ... 7
B. Doerr, BOS 7
A. Kellner, PHI ... 6
E. Robinson, WAS ... 6
R. Sievers, SL 6
B. Tebbetts, BOS .. 6
L. Appling, CHI ... 3
A. Houtteman, DET ... 3
J. Priddy, SL...... 3
V. Trucks, DET 3
D. Mitchell, CLE ... 2
A. Reynolds, NY 2

1950 NATIONAL
J. Konstanty, PHI ...286
S. Musial, SL 158
E. Stanky, NY 144
D. Ennis, PHI 104
R. Kiner, PIT 91
G. Hamner, PHI..... 79
R. Roberts, PHI ... 68
G. Hodges, BRO.... 55
D. Snider, BRO 53
S. Maglie, NY 51
E. Blackwell, CIN ... 41
A. Pafko, CHI...... 38
R. Campanella,
BRO 29
A. Seminick, PHI ... 25
J. Robinson, BRO .. 23
C. Simmons, PHI ... 22
P. Roe, BRO........ 15
T. Kluszewski, CIN.. 14
W. Spahn, BOS..... 14
D. Newcombe,
BRO 14
J. Sain, BOS 12
S. Gordon, BOS 11
J. Hearn, SL-NY ... 10
P. Reese, BRO 8
E. Waitkus, PHI ... 8
R. Elliott, BOS ... 8
E. Torgeson, BOS.... 6
S. Jethroe, BOS ... 6
H. Sauer, CHI 5
V. Bickford, BOS ... 4
C. Furillo, BRO ... 4
W. Westrum, NY 3
D. Sisler, PHI 2
H. Thompson, NY ... 2
L. Jansen, NY 2
W. Jones, PHI 1

1950 AMERICAN
P. Rizzuto, NY 284
B. Goodman,
BOS 180
Y. Berra, NY 146
G. Kell, DET 127
B. Lemon, CLE 102

W. Dropo, BOS 75
V. Raschi, NY 63
L. Doby, CLE 57
J. DiMaggio, NY ... 54
V. Wertz, DET...... 50
W. Evers, DET 38
C. Carrasquel, CHI ... 21
D. Trout, DET 21
D. DiMaggio, BOS ... 17
I. Noren, WAS 16
B. Doerr, BOS 15
J. Mize, NY 11
J. Priddy, DET 11
A. Rosen, CLE 11
E. Yost, WAS 8
M. Parnell, BOS ... 7
N. Ford, NY 7
T. Williams, BOS... 7
N. Garver, SL 6
V. Stephens, BOS .. 6
A. Houtteman, DET ... 6
S. Lollar, SL 4
E. Lopat, SL 3
K. Wood, SL 2
S. Dente, WAS 1
D. Philley, CHI ... 1

1951 NATIONAL
R. Campanella,
BRO 243
S. Musial, SL 191
M. Irvin, NY 166
S. Maglie, NY 153
P. Roe, BRO........138
J. Robinson, BRO .. 92
R. Ashburn, PHI ... 69
B. Thomson, NY 62
M. Dickson, PIT.... 59
R. Kiner, PIT 49
W. Spahn, BOS 45
A. Dark, NY 30
R. Roberts, PHI ... 27
L. Jansen, NY 26
P. Reese, BRO 15
G. Hodges, BRO.... 10
S. Gordon, BOS 10
K. Raffensberger,
CIN 8
J. Wyrostek, CIN .. 6
E. Blackwell, CIN . 6
C. Furillo, BRO ... 6
D. Newcombe, BRO .. 3
P. Cavaretta, CHI . 1
H. Sauer, CHI 1

1951 AMERICAN
Y. Berra, NY 184
N. Garver, SL 157
A. Reynolds, NY ...125
M. Minoso,
CLE-CHI 120
B. Feller, CLE 118
F. Fain, PHI 103
E. Kinder, BOS 66
V. Raschi, NY 64
G. McDougald, NY .. 63
B. Avila, CLE 49
P. Rizzuto, NY 47
E. Lopat, NY 44
T. Williams, BOS .. 35
E. Joost, PHI 32
G. Kell, DET 30
E. Wynn, CLE 29
N. Fox, CHI 25
B. Goodman, BOS ... 21
D. DiMaggio, BOS .. 16
G. Zernial, CHI-PHI ... 15
S. Shantz, PHI 14
M. Garcia, CLE 11
G. Coan, WAS 8
M. Parnell, BOS ... 7
E. Robinson, CHI .. 7
G. Woodling, NY ... 5
J. Pesky, BOS 5
I. Noren, WAS 4
D. Mitchell, CLE .. 4
V. Trucks, DET 2
E. Yost, WAS 2
J. Busby, CHI...... 2
J. Mize, NY 2

1952 NATIONAL
H. Sauer, CHI......226
R. Roberts, PHI ...211
J. Black, BRO 208

H. Wilhelm, NY 133
S. Musial, SL 127
E. Slaughter, SL .. 92
J. Robinson, BRO .. 31
P. Reese, BRO 29
D. Snider, BRO 29
R. Campanella,
BRO 25
R. Schoendienst,
SL 25
A. Dark, NY 24
M. Dickson, PIT.... 22
D. Ennis, PHI 18
W. Lockman, NY 18
B. Thomson, NY 17
F. Baumholtz, CIN .. 16
T. Kluszewski, CIN .. 16
G. Hodges, BRO.... 15
R. McMillan, CIN .. 15
E. Mathews, BOS ... 13
B. Adams, CIN 9
B. Cox, BRO........ 8
W. Hacker, CHI 8
R. Kiner, PIT 8
S. Maglie, NY 8
K. Raffensberger,
CIN 8
W. Spahn, BOS..... 8
P. Roe, BRO........ 7
S. Gordon, BOS 6
G. Hamner, PHI..... 5
S. Hemus, SL 5
M. Irvin, NY 5
G. Shuba, BRO 5
E. Yuhas, SL 5
A. Brazle, SL 3
J. Logan, BOS 3
T. Atwell, CHI 2
C. Metkovich, PIT... 2
W. Cooper, BOS 1

1952 AMERICAN
B. Shantz, PHI 280
A. Reynolds, NY ...183
M. Mantle, NY 143
Y. Berra, NY 104
E. Wynn, CLE 99
F. Fain, PHI 66
N. Fox, CHI 59
B. Lemon, CLE 58
M. Garcia, CLE 52
A. Rosen, CLE 51
E. Robinson, CHI .. 47
L. Doby, CLE 46
L. Easter, CLE 40
P. Rizzuto, NY 33
E. Joost, PHI 20
B. Goodman, BOS... 18
J. Jensen, NY-WAS.. 12
S. Paige, SL 12
V. Raschi, NY 12
D. Mitchell, CLE .. 11
H. Bauer, NY 10
G. Woodling, NY ... 10
P. Runnels, WAS ... 8
C. Courtney, SL ... 7
D. Gernert, BOS ... 6
W. Dropo, BOS-DET.. 5
S. Rogovin, CHI ... 4
S. White, BOS 4
B. Avila, CLE 3
B. Pierce, CHI 3
J. Sain, NY 3
B. Young, SL 3
J. Collins, NY 2
C. Marrero, WAS ... 1
B. Porterfield, WAS ... 1

1953 NATIONAL
R. Campanella,
BRO 297
E. Mathews, MIL ...216
D. Snider, BRO 157
R. Schoendienst,
SL 155
W. Spahn, MIL 120
R. Roberts, PHI ...106
T. Kluszewski, CIN.. 69
S. Musial, SL 62
C. Erskine, BRO ... 54
C. Furillo, BRO ... 54
P. Reese, BRO 27
J. Robinson, BRO .. 19
D. Ennis, PHI 14
G. Hodges, BRO.... 13

M. Irvin, NY 11
D. O'Connell, PIT .. 10
H. Haddix, SL 9
F. Thomas, PIT 6
R. Ashburn, PHI ... 5
G. Bell, CIN 4
J. Logan, MIL 3
R. Gomez, NY 2
G. Hamner, PHI 2
D. Crandall, MIL .. 1
H. Thompson, NY ... 1

1953 AMERICAN
A. Rosen, CLE 336
Y. Berra, NY 167
M. Vernon, WAS 162
M. Minoso, CHI 100
V. Trucks, SL-CHI .. 81
P. Rizzuto, NY 76
B. Porterfield, WAS . 64
R. Boone,
CLE-DET 59
J. Piersall, BOS .. 56
B. Pierce, CHI 55
E. Kinder, BOS 41
H. Bauer, NY 37
A. Reynolds, NY ... 37
M. Parnell, BOS ... 27
H. Kuenn, DET 23
B. Lemon, CLE 22
E. Lopat, NY 18
G. Zernial, PHI ... 16
D. Philley, PHI ... 11
W. Ford, NY 8
B. Goodman, BOS... 5
M. Mantle, NY 4
G. Woodling, NY ... 3
E. Yost, WAS 3
B. Martin, NY 2
C. Carrasquel, CHI . 1
G. Kell, BOS 1
T. Williams, BOS... 1

1954 NATIONAL
W. Mays, NY 283
T. Kluszewski,
CIN 217
J. Antonelli, NY ..154
D. Snider, BRO 135
A. Dark, NY 110
S. Musial, SL 97
R. Roberts, PHI ... 70
J. Adcock, MIL 60
P. Reese, BRO 53
G. Hodges, BRO.... 40
W. Spahn, MIL 38
D. Mueller, NY 30
R. Schoendienst,
SL 24
F. Thomas, PIT 24
H. Wilhelm, NY 17
E. Banks, CHI 14
D. Crandall, MIL .. 13
J. Logan, MIL 9
E. Mathews, MIL ... 9
G. Hamner, PHI 5
R. Ashburn, PHI ... 5
S. Maglie, NY 4
G. Conley, MIL 3
M. Grissom, NY 2
R. McMillan, CIN .. 2
D. Rhodes, NY 1
H. Sauer, CHI 1

1954 AMERICAN
Y. Berra, NY 230
L. Doby, CLE 210
B. Avila, CLE 203
M. Minoso, CHI 186
B. Lemon, CLE 179
E. Wynn, CLE 72
T. Williams, BOS .. 65
H. Kuenn, DET 37
M. Vernon, WAS 30
N. Fox, CHI 30
B. Grim, NY 25
J. Finigan, PHI ... 19
V. Trucks, CHI 19
J. Jensen, BOS 17
M. Mantle, NY 16
I. Noren, NY 16
A. Rosen, CLE 16
J. Busby, WAS 7
J. Coleman, NY-BAL . 6
B. Goodman, BOS.... 6

M. Garcia, CLE 6
J. Hegan, CLE 5
H. Bauer, NY 4
A. Kaline, DET 4
B. Turley, BAL 4
S. Gromek, DET 1
C. Abrams, BAL 1
R. Boone, DET 1
R. Sievers, WAS ... 1

1955 NATIONAL
R. Campanella,
BRO 226
D. Snider, BRO 221
E. Banks, CHI 195
W. Mays, NY 165
R. Roberts, PHI ...159
T. Kluszewski,
CIN 111
D. Newcombe,
BRO 89
S. Musial, SL 46
H. Aaron, MIL 36
P. Reese, BRO 36
J. Logan, MIL 24
W. Post, CIN 23
D. Ennis, PHI 21
R. Ashburn, PHI ... 17
C. Labine, BRO 11
B. Friend, PIT 10
D. Crandall, MIL .. 8
E. Mathews, MIL ... 6
D. Long, PIT 3
J. Meyer, PHI 3
G. Baker, CHI 2
C. Furillo, BRO ... 2
V. Law, PIT 1
F. Thomas, PIT 1

1955 AMERICAN
Y. Berra, NY 218
A. Kaline, DET 201
A. Smith, CLE 200
T. Williams, BOS...143
M. Mantle, NY 113
R. Narleski, CLE .. 90
N. Fox, CHI 84
H. Bauer, NY 64
V. Power, KC 53
J. Jensen, BOS 39
S. Lollar, CHI 37
G. McDougald, NY .. 34
B. Klaus, BOS 27
T. Byrne, NY 24
W. Ford, NY 21
R. Boone, DET 16
R. Sievers, WAS ... 9
H. Kuenn, DET 8
B. Pierce, CHI 8
D. Philley, CLE-BAL . 6
E. Wynn, CLE 6
E. Valo, KC 5
M. Vernon, WAS 4
B. Hoeft, DET 1
B. Mossi, CLE 1
F. Sullivan, BOS .. 1
G. Triandos, BAL .. 1
J. Valdivielso, WAS . 1
S. White, BOS 1

1956 NATIONAL
D. Newcombe,
BRO 223
S. Maglie, BRO 183
H. Aaron, MIL 146
W. Spahn, MIL 126
J. Gilliam, BRO ...103
R. McMillan, CIN .. 96
F. Robinson, CIN .. 79
P. Reese, BRO 71
S. Musial, SL 62
D. Snider, BRO 55
J. Adcock, MIL 54
B. Friend, PIT 38
H. Freeman, CIN ... 25
J. Antonelli, NY .. 18
T. Kluszewski, CIN . 18
J. Robinson, BRO .. 17
W. Mays, NY 14
E. Bailey, CIN 13
S. Virdon, SL-PIT . 13
S. Lopata, PHI 11
C. Furillo, BRO ... 9
L. Burdette, MIL .. 8
B. Buhl, MIL 7

R. Roberts, PHI 7
B. Lawrence, CIN 6
D. Long, PIT 4
W. Moon, SL 3
E. Banks, CHI 2
K. Boyer, SL 2
C. Labine, BRO 1
J. Logan, MIL 1
R. Ashburn, PHI 1

1956 AMERICAN
M. Mantle, NY 336
Y. Berra, NY 186
A. Kaline, DET 142
H. Kuenn, DET 80
B. Pierce, CHI 75
T. Williams, BOS..... 70
B. Nieman,
  CHI-BAL 55
G. McDougald, NY ... 55
V. Wertz, CLE 45
B. Lemon, CLE 40
H. Simpson, KC 37
W. Ford, NY 33
E. Wynn, CLE 32
J. Piersall, BOS 28
N. Fox, CHI 28
S. Lollar, CHI 27
F. Lary, DET 24
P. Runnels, WAS 24
H. Score, CLE 18
J. Jensen, BOS 15
M. Vernon, BOS 14
T. Brewer, BOS 11
H. Bauer, NY 8
C. Maxwell, DET 8
L. Aparicio, CHI 7
G. Triandos, BAL 6
F. Bolling, DET 3
M. Minoso, CHI 3
V. Power, KC 3
J. Kucks, NY 2
R. Sievers, WAS 1

1957 NATIONAL
H. Aaron, MIL 239
S. Musial, SL 230
R. Schoendienst,
  NY-MIL 221
W. Mays, NY 174
W. Spahn, MIL 131
E. Banks, CHI 60
G. Hodges, BRO..... 54
E. Mathews, MIL..... 45
F. Robinson, CIN 42
J. Sanford, PHI 39
D. Hoak, CIN 31
D. Blasingame, SL 26
E. Bouchee, PHI 26
B. Buhl, MIL 15
D. Ennis, SL 13
D. Groat, PIT 13
A. Dark, SL 12
D. Snider, BRO 10
F. Thomas, PIT 8
D. Drysdale, BRO..... 8
R. McMillan, CIN 6
D. Drott, CHI 6
G. Hamner, PHI 3
L. Burdette, MIL 2
J. Logan, MIL 1
H. Anderson, PHI 1

1957 AMERICAN
M. Mantle, NY 233
T. Williams, BOS..... 209
R. Sievers, WAS 205
N. Fox, CHI 193
G. McDougald,
  NY 165
V. Wertz, CLE 61
F. Malzone, BOS 58
M. Minoso, CHI 55
J. Bunning, DET 46
A. Kaline, DET 40
B. Pierce, CHI 35
B. Gardner, BAL 22
D. Donovan, CHI...... 19
Y. Berra, NY 18
G. Woodling, CLE..... 13
B. Grim, NY 9
B. Boyd, BAL 9
C. Maxwell, DET 5
W. Held, NY-KC 4
W. Ford, NY 4

V. Power, KC 3
J. Piersall, BOS 2
B. Skowron, NY 2
H. Kuenn, DET 2
S. Lollar, CHI 2
T. Kubek, NY 1
B. Shantz, NY 1

1958 NATIONAL
E. Banks, CHI 283
W. Mays, SF 185
H. Aaron, MIL...... 166
F. Thomas, PIT 143
W. Spahn, MIL...... 108
B. Friend, PIT 98
R. Ashburn, PHI 62
B. Mazeroski, PIT 61
O. Cepeda, SF 57
D. Crandall, MIL 48
L. Burdette, MIL 47
S. Musial, SL 39
K. Boyer, SL 31
J. Temple, CIN 26
B. Skinner, PIT 18
W. Covington, MIL..... 16
E. Face, PIT 8
H. Anderson, PHI 5
J. Gilliam, LA 4
B. Purkey, CIN 4
F. Robinson, CIN 4
J. Adcock, MIL 2
C. Furillo, LA........ 1

1958 AMERICAN
J. Jensen, BOS 233
B. Turley, NY 191
R. Colavito, CLE 181
B. Cerv, KC........ 164
M. Mantle, NY 127
R. Sievers, WAS 95
T. Williams, BOS..... 89
N. Fox, CHI 88
S. Lollar, CHI 57
P. Runnels, BOS..... 29
G. Triandos, BAL 27
D. Hyde, WAS 26
H. Kuenn, DET...... 24
C. McLish, CLE 18
V. Power, KC-CLE ... 15
F. Bolling, DET 10
E. Howard, NY 9
Y. Berra, NY 6
M. Minoso, CLE 6
A. Kaline, DET 5
G. McDougald, NY ... 5
R. Duren, NY 4
F. Lary, DET 3
J. Harshman, BAL 2
D. Donovan, CHI...... 1
F. Malzone, BOS 1

1959 NATIONAL
E. Banks, CHI 232½
E. Mathews,
  MIL.............. 189½
H. Aaron, MIL...... 174
W. Moon, LA 161
S. Jones, SF 130
W. Mays, SF 85
E. Face, PIT 67
C. Neal, LA 64
F. Robinson, CIN 52
K. Boyer, SL 37
D. Crandall, MIL 27
L. Burdette, MIL 14
R. Craig, LA 12
J. Cunningham, SL .. 12
V. Pinson, CIN 11
J. Temple, CIN 8
D. Hoak, PIT 6
G. Hodges, LA...... 4
O. Cepeda, SF 3
V. Law, PIT 3
W. Spahn, MIL...... 3
G. Conley, PHI 1
W. McCovey, SF 1
D. Snider, LA 1

1959 AMERICAN
N. Fox, CHI 295
L. Aparicio, CHI 255
E. Wynn, CHI 123
R. Colavito, CLE 117
T. Francona, CLE .. 102
A. Kaline, DET 84

J. Landis, CHI 66
H. Kuenn, DET 64
S. Lollar, CHI 44
J. Jensen, BOS 40
C. McLish, CLE..... 35
Y. Berra, NY 26
M. Minoso, CLE 26
F. Malzone, BOS 24
H. Killebrew, WAS ... 21
G. Woodling, BAL.... 18
M. Mantle, NY 13
B. Richardson, NY .. 11
C. Pascual, WAS 9
B. Shaw, CHI 8
G. Triandos, BAL 8
B. Daley, KC........ 7
V. Power, CLE 5
B. Tuttle, KC........ 5
J. Lemon, WAS 4
P. Runnels, BOS..... 2
T. Williams, BOS..... 2
B. Allison, WAS 1
G. Staley, CHI 1

1960 NATIONAL
D. Groat, PIT 276
D. Hoak, PIT 162
W. Mays, SF........ 155
E. Banks, CHI 100
L. McDaniel, SL...... 95
K. Boyer, SL 80
V. Law, PIT 80
R. Clemente, PIT 62
E. Broglio, SL........ 58
E. Mathews, MIL..... 52
H. Aaron, MIL....... 49
E. Face, PIT 47
D. Crandall, MIL 31
W. Spahn, MIL....... 27
N. Larker, LA 21
S. Musial, SL 18
M. Wills, LA 7
V. Pinson, CIN 6
J. Adcock, MIL 5
S. Burgess, PIT 2
F. Robinson, CIN 2
L. Sherry, LA 2
P. Herrera, PHI 1

1960 AMERICAN
R. Maris, NY 225
M. Mantle, NY 222
B. Robinson, BAL.. 211
M. Minoso, CHI.... 141
R. Hansen, BAL 110
A. Smith, CHI 73
R. Sievers, CHI 58
E. Battey, WAS 57
B. Skowron, NY 56
J. Lemon, WAS 36
T. Kubek, NY 29
C. Estrada, BAL 28
T. Williams, BOS..... 25
V. Wertz, BOS 22
Y. Berra, NY 21
J. Gentile, BAL 21
P. Runnels, BOS..... 18
N. Fox, CHI 11
V. Power, CLE 11
S. Barber, BAL 7
L. Aparicio, CHI...... 6
J. Perry, CLE 6
G. Staley, CHI 4
J. Bunning, DET 3
G. Woodling, BAL.... 3
H. Kuenn, CLE...... 3
B. Daley, KC.......... 3
M. Fornieles, BOS ... 2
C. Maxwell, DET 2
J. Piersall, CLE 2

1961 NATIONAL
F. Robinson, CIN 219
O. Cepeda, SF 117
V. Pinson, CIN 104
R. Clemente, PIT 81
J. Jay, CIN 74
W. Mays, SF........ 70
K. Boyer, SL 43
H. Aaron, MIL....... 39
M. Wills, LA 36
J. O'Toole, CIN 31
W. Spahn, MIL....... 31
S. Miller, SF 26
W. Moon, LA 22

G. Altman, CHI 9
J. Podres, LA 9
R. McMillan, MIL 8
E. Mathews, MIL..... 7
S. Koufax, LA 5
J. Roseboro, LA 4
J. Brosnan, CIN 3
J. Torre, MIL 3
L. Jackson, SL........ 1
J. Lynch, CIN 1
J. Malkmus, PHI 1
D. Stuart, PIT 1

1961 AMERICAN
R. Maris, NY 202
M. Mantle, NY 198
J. Gentile, BAL 157
N. Cash, DET 151
W. Ford, NY 102
L. Arroyo, NY 95
F. Lary, DET 53
R. Colavito, DET 51
A. Kaline, DET 35
E. Howard, NY 30
H. Killebrew, MIN ... 29
L. Aparicio, CHI...... 16
J. Piersall, CLE 10
S. Barber, BAL 7
D. Schwall, BOS 7
N. Siebern, KC 7
D. Donovan, WAS 5
B. Phillips, CLE 5
B. Robinson, BAL.... 4
C. Schilling, BOS 4
T. Morgan, LA 3
A. Smith, CHI 3
Y. Berra, NY 2
B. Richardson, NY .. 1
J. Romano, CLE 1
L. Thomas, NY-LA ... 1
H. Wilhelm, BAL 1

1962 NATIONAL
M. Wills, LA 209
W. Mays, SF........ 202
T. Davis, LA 175
F. Robinson, CIN 164
D. Drysdale, LA 85
H. Aaron, MIL....... 72
J. Sanford, SF 62
B. Purkey, CIN 33
F. Howard, LA 32
S. Musial, SL 19
J. Pagan, SF 13
D. Demeter, PHI 12
F. Alou, SF 10
B. White, SL 10
O. Cepeda, SF 9
D. Groat, PIT 7
R. Clemente, PIT 6
E. Banks, CHI 5
K. Boyer, SL 5
J. Callison, PHI 5
H. Kuenn, SF 5
J. Marichal, SF 4
B. Skinner, PIT 4
J. Davenport, SF..... 3
S. Koufax, LA........ 3
D. Crandall, MIL 2
A. Mahaffey, PHI..... 2
E. Roebuck, LA 2
E. Kasko, CIN 1
E. Mathews, MIL..... 1

1962 AMERICAN
M. Mantle, NY 234
B. Richardson,
  NY 152
H. Killebrew, MIN ... 99
L. Wagner, LA 85
D. Donovan, CLE 64
A. Kaline, DET 58
N. Siebern, KC 53
R. Rollins, MIN 47
B. Robinson, BAL.... 41
F. Robinson, CHI 33
L. Thomas, LA 32
T. Tresh, NY 30
B. Moran, LA 28
R. Terry, NY 19
C. Pascual, MIN 14
R. Colavito, DET 14
H. Aguirre, DET 10
J. Cunningham, CHI .. 9
P. Runnels, BOS 9

C. Yastrzemski,
  BOS 9
V. Power, MIN 8
D. Radatz, BOS 8
J. Bunning, DET 8
Z. Versalles, MIN..... 8
J. Lumpe, KC 7
E. Bressoud, BOS ... 6
B. Rodgers, LA 6
W. Ford, NY 6
R. Herbert, CHI 5
C. Hinton, WAS 5
F. Malzone, BOS 3
N. Cash, DET 3
A. Smith, CHI 1

1963 NATIONAL
S. Koufax, LA 237
D. Groat, SL 190
H. Aaron, MIL....... 135
R. Perranoski, LA 130
W. Mays, SF........ 102
J. Gilliam, LA 62
B. White, SL 56
T. Davis, LA 41
R. Santo, CHI 41
V. Pinson, CIN 32
J. Marichal, SF 31
W. Spahn, MIL....... 30
K. Boyer, SL 19
R. Clemente, PIT 12
J. Callison, PHI 11
T. Taylor, PHI 10
W. McCovey, SF..... 9
M. Wills, LA 9
D. Ellsworth, CHI 7
J. Maloney, CIN 7
D. Demeter, PHI 3
D. Drysdale, LA 3
T. Gonzalez, PHI..... 2
C. Flood, SL 1

1963 AMERICAN
E. Howard, NY 248
A. Kaline, DET 148
W. Ford, NY 125
H. Killebrew, MIN ... 85
D. Radatz, BOS 84
C. Yastrzemski,
  BOS 81
E. Battey, MIN 57
G. Peters, CHI 55
P. Ward, CHI 52
B. Richardson, NY .. 43
T. Tresh, NY 38
C. Pascual, MIN 29
D. Stuart, BOS 25
A. Pearson, LA 22
B. Allison, MIN 15
J. Bouton, NY 11
M. Alvis, CLE 10
J. Pepitone, NY 10
L. Wagner, LA 9
S. Miller, BAL 9
W. Causey, KC 5
R. Rollins, MIN...... 5
L. Aparicio, BAL 3
B. Dailey, MIN 3
J. Fregosi, LA 3
N. Fox, CHI 2
T. Kubek, NY 1
F. Robinson, CHI 1
N. Siebern, KC 1

1964 NATIONAL
K. Boyer, SL 243
J. Callison, PHI 187
B. White, SL 106½
F. Robinson, CIN ... 98
J. Torre, MIL 85
W. Mays, SF........ 66
R. Allen, PHI 63
R. Santo, CHI 59
R. Clemente, PIT 56
L. Brock, CHI-SL 40
C. Flood, SL 38
L. Jackson, CHI 26
J. Bunning, PHI..... 23
H. Aaron, MIL....... 22
J. Marichal, SF 14
S. Ellis, CIN 13
S. Koufax, LA........ 7½
V. Pinson, CIN 7
J. Hart, SF 6
B. Williams, CHI 6

R. Amaro, PHI 5
T. Davis, LA 4
B. Gibson, SL 2
C. Short, PHI 2
R. Hunt, NY 1
B. Schultz, SL 1

1964 AMERICAN
B. Robinson, BAL.. 269
M. Mantle, NY 171
E. Howard, NY 124
T. Oliva, MIN 99
D. Chance, CAL 97
P. Ward, CHI 67½
B. Freehan, DET 44
G. Peters, CHI 44
D. Radatz, BOS 37
H. Killebrew, MIN ... 31
B. Powell, BAL 28
W. Bunker, BAL 23
J. Fregosi, LA....... 21
A. Kaline, DET 17
F. Robinson, CHI 14
R. Hansen, CHI 10
B. Richardson, NY .. 9
L. Wagner, CLE 9
J. Pizarro, CHI 8
H. Wilhelm, CHI..... 7
J. Horlen, CHI 7
W. Ford, NY 7
B. Allison, MIN...... 5
R. Colavito, KC 5
M. Stottlemyre, NY .. 4
R. Maris, NY 4
W. Causey, KC 4
L. Aparicio, BAL 3½
D. Stuart, BOS...... 3
E. Bressoud, BOS ... 2
C. Osteen, WAS..... 2
D. Wickersham,
  DET 2
D. Lock, WAS......... 1

1965 NATIONAL
W. Mays, SF........ 224
S. Koufax, LA 177
M. Wills, LA........ 164
D. Johnson, CIN 108
D. Drysdale, LA 77
P. Rose, CIN 67
H. Aaron, MIL....... 58
R. Clemente, PIT 56
J. Marichal, SF 26
W. McCovey, SF..... 25
J. Torre, MIL 23
B. Williams, CHI 21
F. Linzy, SF 16
W. Stargell, PIT 15
C. Flood, SL 13
J. Hart, SF 13
V. Law, PIT 12
F. Robinson, CIN 11
R. Santo, CHI 11
E. Mathews, MIL..... 8
L. Cardenas, CIN 7
J. Maloney, CIN 7
J. Lefebvre, LA 7
J. Callison, PHI 6
L. Johnson, LA 6
C. Rojas, PHI 5
J. Roseboro, LA 5
R. Allen, PHI 4
T. Cloninger, MIL 4
J. Gilliam, LA 3
J. Morgan, HOU 1

1965 AMERICAN
Z. Versalles, MIN.... 275
T. Oliva, MIN 174
B. Robinson, BAL.. 150
E. Fisher, CHI....... 122
R. Colavito, CLE 89
J. Grant, MIN 74
S. Miller, BAL 45
W. Horton, DET 24
T. Tresh, NY 23
E. Battey, MIN 22
D. Wert, DET........ 22
C. Yastrzemski,
  BOS 22
J. Hall, MIN 19
M. Stottlemyre, NY .. 17
H. Killebrew, MIN ... 15
A. Kaline, DET 9
J. Adair, BAL 7

R. Hansen, CHI 7
S. McDowell, CLE ... 7
B. Richardson, NY 6
V. Davalillo, CLE 5
J. Fregosi, CAL 5
F. Whitfield, CLE 5
B. Knoop, CAL 4
D. Buford, CHI 3
M. Mantle, NY 3
P. Richert, WAS 3
F. Robinson, CHI 3
B. Campaneris, KC 2
F. Howard, WAS 2
R. Kline, WAS......... 2
F. Mantilla, BOS 2
N. Cash, DET 1
T. Conigliaro, BOS.... 1

1966 NATIONAL
R. Clemente, PIT ...218
S. Koufax, LA.......208
W. Mays, SF 111
R. Allen, PHI 107
F. Alou, ATL 83
J. Marichal, SF 74
P. Regan, LA 66
H. Aaron, ATL 57
M. Alou, PIT 36
P. Rose, CIN 31
G. Alley, PIT 24
R. Santo, CHI 23
J. Roseboro, LA 22
O. Cepeda, SF-SL .. 22
W. Stargell, PIT 19
J. Torre, ATL 18
W. McCovey, SF..... 12
J. Lefebvre, LA 8
G. Perry, SF 8
C. Flood, SL 7
M. Wills, LA.......... 5
R. Staub, HOU 4
B. Mazeroski, PIT 3
G. Beckert, CHI 3
J. Maloney, CIN 3
B. White, PHI 3
L. Brock, SL 2
B. Shaw, SF-NY 1
C. Short, PHI 1
W. Davis, LA.......... 1

1966 AMERICAN
F. Robinson, BAL ...280
B. Robinson, BAL...153
B. Powell, BAL 122
H. Killebrew, MIN 96
J. Kaat, MIN 84
T. Oliva, MIN 71
A. Kaline, DET 66
T. Agee, CHI 63
L. Aparicio, BAL 51
B. Campaneris, KC .. 36
S. Miller, BAL 27
N. Cash, DET 23
J. Aker, KC 22
E. Wilson,
  BOS-DET 13
D. McLain, DET...... 12
B. Freehan, DET 7
A. Etchebarren, BAL .. 7
B. Knoop, CAL 6
M. Mantle, NY 5
T. Tresh, NY 5
J. Sanford, CAL 4
R. Reichardt, CAL 4
F. Valentine, WAS 4
W. Horton, DET 4
L. Wagner, CLE....... 4
P. Richert, WAS 3
J. Pepitone, NY 2
T. Conigliaro, BOS.... 1
S. Siebert, CLE 1
C. Yastrzemski,
  BOS 1
J. Fregosi, CAL 1

1967 NATIONAL
O. Cepeda, SL....280
T. McCarver, SL... 136
R. Clemente, PIT ...129
R. Santo, CHI 103
H. Aaron, ATL 79
M. McCormick, SF... 73
L. Brock, SL 49
T. Perez, CIN 43
J. Javier, SL 41

P. Rose, CIN.... 40
J. Wynn, HOU 29
F. Jenkins, CHI 26
C. Flood, SL 24
E. Banks, CHI 22
N. Briles, SL 20
R. Staub, HOU 12
D. Hughes, SL 10
J. Hart, SF 10
R. Allen, PHI 9
T. Abernathy, CIN 8
C. Boyer, ATL........ 6
B. Gibson, SL 5
R. Hundley, CHI 5
J. Bunning, PHI 5
T. Seaver, NY 5
T. Davis, NY 3
G. Alley, PIT 3
T. Gonzalez, PHI 3
W. McCovey, SF..... 2

1967 AMERICAN
C. Yastrzemski,
  BOS 275
H. Killebrew, MIN ...161
B. Freehan, DET 137
J. Horlen, CHI 91
A. Kaline, DET 88
J. Lonborg, BOS..... 82
C. Tovar, MIN 70
J. Fregosi, CAL 70
G. Peters, CHI 37
G. Scott, BOS 33
F. Robinson, BAL 31
E. Wilson, DET....... 20
D. Chance, MIN 19
R. Hansen, CHI 13
J. Adair, CHI-BOS ... 11
P. Blair, BAL......... 9
R. Petrocelli, BOS ... 7
E. Howard, NY-BOS .. 7
T. Oliva, MIN 6
J. Kaat, MIN 4
P. Casanova, WAS ... 3
D. Mincher, CAL 3
M. Lolich, DET 2
M. Rojas, CAL 1

1968 NATIONAL
B. Gibson, SL 242
P. Rose, CIN........205
W. McCovey, SF....135
C. Flood, SL 116
J. Marichal, SF 93
L. Brock, SL 73
M. Shannon, SL 55
B. Williams, CHI 48
G. Beckert, CHI...... 40
F. Alou, ATL 33
M. Alou, PIT 32
H. Aaron, ATL 29
W. Mays, SF 14
E. Banks, CHI 14
J. Koosman, NY 14
J. Bench, CIN 11
P. Regan, LA-CHI 7
F. Jenkins, CHI 6
T. Perez, CIN 5
N. Briles, SL 4
D. Maxvill, SL........ 4
S. Blass, PIT 3
J. Haller, LA 3
R. Santo, CHI 2
C. Carroll, ATL-CIN .. 1
T. Helms, CIN 1

1968 AMERICAN
D. McLain, DET 280
B. Freehan, DET 161
K. Harrelson, BOS ..103
W. Horton, DET 102
D. McNally, BAL 78
L. Tiant, CLE........ 78
D. McAuliffe, DET ... 71
F. Howard, WAS 63
C. Yastrzemski,
  BOS 50
M. Stottlemyre, NY .. 43
B. Campaneris, OAK. 39
R. White, NY........ 17
J. Northrup, DET 15
L. Aparicio, CHI...... 13
J. Fregosi, CAL 11
D. Buford, BAL 11
B. Robinson, BAL.... 8

R. Jackson, OAK 8
T. Oliva, MIN 5
D. Cater, OAK 5
M. Andrews, BOS 4
B. Powell, BAL 4
N. Cash, DET 3
C. Tovar, MIN 3
M. Stanley, DET 2
W. Wood, CHI 2
T. Uhlaender, MIN ... 1

1969 NATIONAL
W. McCovey, SF....265
T. Seaver, NY.......243
H. Aaron, ATL 188
P. Rose, CIN 127
R. Santo, CHI 124
T. Agee, NY 89
C. Jones, NY 82
R. Clemente, PIT 51
P. Niekro, ATL 47
T. Perez, CIN 28
M. Wills, MON-LA ... 17
E. Banks, CHI 15
R. Carty, ATL 12
J. Bench, CIN 12
D. Kessinger, CHI.... 8
T. Gonzalez,
  SD-ATL 8
R. Hunt, SF 8
D. Menke, HOU 8
W. Granger, CIN 8
J. Wynn, HOU 8
W. Davis, LA......... 7
W. Stargell, PIT 7
J. Marichal, SF 6
B. Williams, CHI 6
J. Koosman, NY 6
J. Torre, SL 6
M. Alou, PIT 6
L. Dierker, HOU 6
J. Haller, LA 3
B. Gibson, SL 2
B. Bonds, SF 2
R. Hundley, CHI 2
L. May, CIN.......... 2
T. Sizemore, LA....... 2
W. Parker, LA........ 2
J. Edwards, HOU 1
R. Staub, MON 1
O. Cepeda, ATL...... 1

1969 AMERICAN
H. Killebrew, MIN ...294
B. Powell, BAL 227
F. Robinson, BAL ...162
F. Howard, WAS ...115
R. Jackson, OAK 110
D. McLain, DET 85
R. Petrocelli, BOS ... 71
M. Cuellar, BAL...... 55
J. Perry, MIN 40
R. Carew, MIN 30
P. Blair, BAL 28
L. Cardenas, MIN ... 27
R. Perranoski, MIN .. 25
D. McNally, BAL 25
T. Oliva, MIN 21
S. Bando, OAK 18
C. Tovar, MIN 9
M. Stottlemyre, NY .. 8
C. Yastrzemski, BOS.. 8
E. Brinkman, WAS ... 7
J. Fregosi, CAL 7
R. Smith, BOS 6
D. Unser, WAS 5
B. Robinson, BAL.... 5
M. Epstein, WAS..... 4
M. Andrews, BOS ... 3
D. Bosman, WAS 3
B. Freehan, DET 3
T. Harper, SEA 2
A. Messersmith, CAL. 2
R. Reese, MIN 2
K. Tatum, CAL 2
R. White, NY 2
M. Belanger, BAL.... 2
G. Green, OAK....... 1
J. Northrup, DET 1
L. Piniella, KC 1

1970 NATIONAL
J. Bench, CIN 326
B. Williams, CHI ...218
T. Perez, CIN 149

B. Gibson, SL 110
W. Parker, LA........ 91
D. Giusti, PIT 72
P. Rose, CIN 54
J. Hickman, CHI 52
W. McCovey, SF..... 47
R. Carty, ATL 43
M. Sanguillen, PIT ... 36
R. Clemente, PIT 33
D. Clendenon, NY ... 26
G. Perry, SF 24
W. Stargell, PIT 20
B. Tolan, CIN 17
H. Aaron, ATL 16
J. Torre, SL 15
T. Agee, NY 13
B. Harrelson, NY 10
F. Jenkins, CHI 8
J. Merritt, CIN 8
D. Kessinger, CHI.... 6
C. Gaston, SD 5
D. Johnson, PHI 4
L. Walker, PIT 4
C. Morton, MON 3
B. Robertson, PIT.... 3
T. Seaver, NY 2
W. Granger, CIN 1

1970 AMERICAN
B. Powell, BAL 234
T. Oliva, MIN 157
H. Killebrew, MIN ...152
C. Yastrzemski,
  BOS 136
F. Howard, WAS 91
T. Harper, MIL 78
B. Robinson, BAL.... 75
A. Johnson, CAL 70
J. Perry, MIN 63
F. Robinson, BAL 60
M. Cuellar, BAL...... 45
R. Perranoski, MIN .. 35
J. Fregosi, CAL 35
L. Aparicio, CHI...... 35
R. White, NY 25
D. McNally, BAL 22
S. McDowell, CLE ... 22
C. Tovar, MIN 16
T. Munson, NY 15
D. Buford, BAL 12
C. Wright, CAL 8
L. McDaniel, NY 8
R. Fosse, CLE 7
B. Campaneris, OAK.. 5
J. Palmer, BAL 4
R. Smith, BOS 3
S. Bando, OAK 1
H. Horton, CLE 1
R. Oliver, KC 1

1971 NATIONAL
J. Torre, SL 318
W. Stargell, PIT 222
H. Aaron, ATL 180
B. Bonds, SF 139
R. Clemente, PIT 87
M. Wills, LA.......... 74
F. Jenkins, CHI 71
M. Sanguillen, PIT ... 49
T. Seaver, NY 46
A. Downing, LA 36
G. Beckert, CHI...... 35
L. May, CIN.......... 28
L. Brock, SL 26
D. Giusti, PIT 16
W. McCovey, SF..... 15
T. Simmons, SL 13
W. Davis, LA......... 13
J. Johnson, SF 12
W. Mays, SF 11
R. Staub, MON 11
B. Williams, CHI 10
B. Harrelson, NY 4
B. Gibson, SL 3
B. Garr, ATL 3
D. Roberts, SD 1
P. Rose, CIN 1

1971 AMERICAN
V. Blue, OAK 268
S. Bando, OAK 182
F. Robinson, BAL ...170
B. Robinson, BAL...163
M. Lolich, DET 155
F. Patek, KC 77

B. Murcer, NY 72
A. Otis, KC 67
W. Wood, CHI 54
T. Oliva, MIN 36
D. McNally, BAL 26
N. Cash, DET 21
B. Melton, CHI 18
R. Jackson, OAK 15
C. Rojas, KC 15
K. Sanders, MIL 13
P. Dobson, BAL 9
R. Smith, BOS 9
D. Johnson, BAL 9
M. Rettenmund,
  BAL 8
H. Killebrew, MIN 5
J. Palmer, BAL 5
L. Cardenas, MIN ... 5
M. Cuellar, BAL...... 4
C. Tovar, MIN 4
G. Scott, BOS 3
D. Buford, BAL 2
J. Hunter, OAK 1
G. Nettles, CLE-MIN. 1

1972 NATIONAL
J. Bench, CIN 263
B. Williams, CHI 211
W. Stargell, PIT 201
J. Morgan, CIN 197
S. Carlton, PHI 124
C. Cedeno, HOU ...112
A. Oliver, PIT 52
N. Colbert, SD 45
L. May, HOU 30
T. Simmons, SL 22
M. Marshall, MON ... 22
P. Rose, CIN 19
R. Clemente, PIT 16
C. Carroll, CIN 16
L. Brock, SL 13
H. Aaron, ATL 12
M. Sanguillen, PIT ... 12
S. Blass, PIT 9
R. Garr, ATL 7
G. Clines, PIT 6
B. Tolan, CIN 6
D. Baker, ATL 5
M. Mota, LA 4
D. Kingman, SF 3
T. McGraw, NY 2
R. Staub, NY 2
T. Seaver, NY 2
J. Cardenal, CHI 1
F. Jenkins, Chi....... 1
C. Speier, SF 1

1972 AMERICAN
R. Allen, CHI 321
J. Rudi, OAK........164
S. Lyle, NY 158
C. Fisk, BOS........ 96
B. Murcer, NY 89
G. Perry, CLE....... 88
W. Wood, CHI 78
L. Tiant, BOS 70½
E. Brinkman, DET.... 62
M. Lolich, DET...... 60
J. Hunter, OAK 57
J. Mayberry, KC 27
J. Palmer, BAL 21
B. Grich, BAL 16
R. Carew, MIN 16
B. Campaneris, OAK. 11
M. Epstein, OAK 11
L. Aparicio, BOS ... 9½
R. Petrocelli, BOS ... 9
R. Jackson, OAK ... 9
C. May, CHI 6
G. Scott, MIL 6
D. Thompson, MIN .. 5
T. Harper, BOS 4
A. Kaline, DET 4
B. Freehan, DET 3
K. McMullen, CAL .. 3
B. Robinson, BAL.... 3
R. Smith, BOS 3
S. Bando, OAK 2
N. Ryan, CAL 2
A. Otis, KC 1
L. Piniella, KC 1

1973 NATIONAL
P. Rose, CIN.......274
W. Stargell, PIT 250

B. Bonds, SF 174
J. Morgan, CIN ... 102
M. Marshall, MON ... 93
L. Brock, SL 65
T. Perez, CIN 59
T. Seaver, NY 57
K. Singleton, MON .. 52
J. Bench, CIN 41
J. Cedeno, HOU ... 39
H. Aaron, ATL 35
D. Johnson, ATL ... 34
T. Simmons, SL ... 20
T. McGraw, NY ... 17
F. Millan, NY 12
W. Davis, LA 11
D. Evans, ATL 11
L. May, HOU 9
T. Fuentes, SF 8
B. Watson, HOU ... 7
J. Ferguson LA 7
J. Cardenal, CHI ... 6
J. Billingham, CIN .. 6
A. Oliver, PIT 5
R. Hunt, MON 5
R. Bryant, SF 3
G. Maddox, SF 3
B. Harrelson, NY ... 2
B. Williams, CHI ... 2
G. Luzinski, PHI ... 2
B. Russell, LA 1

1973 AMERICAN
R. Jackson, OAK ...336
J. Palmer, BAL 172
A. Otis, KC 112
R. Carew, MIN 83
J. Hiller, DET 83
S. Bando, OAK 83
J. Mayberry, KC ... 76
D. May, MIL 65
B. Murcer, NY 53
T. Davis, BAL 47
J. Hunter, OAK 47
T. Munson, NY 43
T. Harper, BOS 33
G. Scott, MIL 25
O. Cepeda, BOS.... 21
F. Robinson, CAL... 21
N. Ryan, CAL 20
C. Fisk, BOS....... 16
B. Grich, BAL 9
C. Yastrzemski,
  BOS 9
M. Belanger, BAL... 8
D. Johnson, OAK .. 8
J. Briggs, MIL 8
J. Coleman, DET ... 6
C. Rojas, KC....... 5
B. Blyleven, MIN ... 4
G. Perry, CLE...... 4
B. Campaneris, OAK. 4
V. Blue, OAK 3
C. May, CHI 3
W. Horton, DET 3
B. North, OAK 3
P. Blair, BAL 2
D. Nelson, TEX 2
R. Allen, CHI....... 1

1974 NATIONAL
S. Garvey, LA......270
L. Brock, SL 233
M. Marshall, LA 146
J. Bench, CIN 141
J. Wynn, LA 137
M. Schmidt, PHI ...136
A. Oliver, PIT 87
J. Morgan, CIN ... 72
R. Zisk, PIT 54
W. Stargell, PIT 43
R. Smith, SL 39
R. Garr, ATL 11
T. Simmons, SL ... 7
D. Cash, PHI....... 6
D. Concepcion, CIN. 5
J. Billingham, CIN .. 4
C. Cedeno, HOU .. 4
A. Hrabosky, SL ... 4
A. Messersmith, LA.. 4
B. Capra, ATL 3
L. McGlothen, SL... 2
B. McBride, SL 2
R. Hebner, PIT...... 2
R. Stennett, PIT.... 2
B. Buckner, LA 1

R. Cey, LA 1

1974 AMERICAN
J. Burroughs, TEX .. 248
J. Rudi, OAK....... 161½
S. Bando, OAK ...143½
R. Jackson, OAK ...119
F. Jenkins, TEX 118
J. Hunter, OAK 107
R. Carew, MIN 70
E. Maddox, NY 59
B. Grich, BAL 49
M. Cuellar, BAL 42
L. Tiant, BOS 41
B. Robinson, BAL....30
P. Blair, BAL 27
N. Ryan, CAL 24
B. Campaneris, OAK. 23
R. Fingers, OAK 21
G. Perry, CLE 18
C. Yastrzemski,
  BOS 14
K. Henderson, CHI...12
J. Hiller, DET 11
L. Randle, TEX 10
B. Murcer, NY 10
L. Piniella, NY...... 8
R. Allen, CHI......... 8
S. Lyle, NY 7
T. Munson, NY 6
T. Davis, BAL 6
M. Belanger, BAL.... 6
D. Money, MIL 5
T. Murphy, MIL 3
H. McRae, KC 3
S. Busby, KC 3
G. Scott, MIL 2
P. Dobson, NY....... 1

1975 NATIONAL
J. Morgan, CIN ...321½
G. Luzinski, PHI ...154
D. Parker, PIT.......120
J. Bench, CIN 117
P. Rose, CIN 114
T. Simmons, SL 103
W. Stargell, PIT 69
A. Hrabosky, SL 66
T. Seaver, NY....... 65
R. Jones, SD 54
S. Garvey, LA....... 50
B. Madlock, CHI 45
D. Cash, PHI 26
R. Staub, NY 20
T. Perez, CIN 18
M. Schmidt, PHI 16
M. Sanguillen, PIT ... 16
R. Cey, LA 11½
D. Kingman, NY 9
B. Watson, HOU 8
L. Brock, SL 6
L. Bowa, PHI 3
J. Reuss, PIT 2
A. Messersmith, LA .. 1
W. Montanez,
  PHI-SF 1

1975 AMERICAN
F. Lynn, BOS 326
J. Mayberry, KC ...157
J. Rice, BOS 154
R. Fingers, OAK 129
R. Jackson, OAK ...118
J. Palmer, BAL 82
T. Munson, NY 69
G. Scott, MIL 64½
R. Carew, MIN 54½
K. Singleton, BAL... 44
G. Brett, KC 37½
J. Hunter, NY 31
R. Burleson, BOS ... 28
C. Washington,
  OAK 22
T. Harrah, TEX 16
M. Torrez, BAL 12
R. Gossage, CHI 11
P. Lindblad, OAK ... 7
G. Tenace, OAK 7
B. Powell, CLE 6½
D. Baylor, BAL...... 6
B. Campaneris, OAK.. 6
B. Lee, BOS 5
J. Todd, OAK 5
D. Doyle, CAL-BOS .. 5
R. Wise, BOS 4

J. Rudi, OAK 3
J. Kaat, CHI 2
L. May, BAL 2
B. Bonds, NY 1
C. Yastrzemski,
  BOS 1

1976 NATIONAL
J. Morgan, CIN 311
G. Foster, CIN 221
M. Schmidt, PHI ...179
P. Rose, CIN 131
G. Maddox, PHI 98
B. Madlock, CHI 51
S. Garvey, LA....... 51
K. Griffey, CIN 49
R. Jones, SD 48
B. Watson, HOU 38
A. Oliver, PIT 30
R. Eastwick, CIN 26
J. Koosman, NY 20
S. Carlton, PHI 16
D. Cash, PHI....... 15
J. Richard, HOU 12
R. Monday, CHI 11
D. Kingman, NY 11
D. Parker, PIT...... 10
B. Robinson, PIT ... 9
D. Sutton, LA 7
R. Cey, LA 6
W. Montanez,
  SF-ATL............. 4
L. Brock, SL 3
C. Cedeno, HOU 3
C. Geronimo, CIN.... 3
R. Zisk, PIT 3
L. Bowa, PHI 3

1976 AMERICAN
T. Munson, NY 304
G. Brett, KC 217
M. Rivers, NY 179½
H. McRae, KC 99
C. Chambliss,
  NY 71½
R. Carew, MIN 71
A. Otis, KC 58
B. Campbell, MIN ... 56
L. May, BAL 51
J. Palmer, BAL 47
M. Fidrych, DET 41
J. Rudi, OAK........ 35
S. Bando, OAK 31
C. Yastrzemski,
  BOS 26
F. Tanana, CAL 19
R. Jackson, BAL.... 17
G. Nettles, NY 17
G. Tenace, OAK 13
R. Fingers, OAK 12
V. Blue, OAK 10
E. Figueroa, NY 9
S. Lyle, NY 8
R. LeFlore, DET 6
M. Littell, KC........ 5
R. Carty, CLE 5
R. White, NY 3
L. Tiant, BOS 3
J. Mayberry, KC 1
B. Wynegar, MIN ... 1

1977 NATIONAL
G. Foster, CIN 291
G. Luzinski, PHI ...255
D. Parker, PIT.......156
R. Smith, LA 112
S. Carlton, PHI 100
S. Garvey, LA...... 98
B. Sutter, CHI 68
R. Cey, LA 60
T. Simmons, SL 58
M. Schmidt, PHI ... 48
B. Robinson, PIT ... 34
T. John, LA 33
G. Templeton, SL ... 20
R. Fingers, SD 17
P. Rose, CIN 15
J. Burroughs, ATL ... 9
A. Oliver, PIT 9
J. Candelaria, PIT ... 8
R. Stennett, PIT 7
W. McCovey, SF 5
J. Bench, CIN 3
R. Reuschel, CHI ... 3

E. Valentine, MON ... 3
T. McGraw, PHI 2
L. Bowa, PHI 1
T. Seaver, NY-CIN ... 1

1977 AMERICAN
R. Carew, MIN 273
A. Cowens, KC 217
K. Singleton, BAL...200
J. Rice, BOS 163
G. Nettles, NY 112
S. Lyle, NY 79
T. Munson, NY 70
R. Jackson, NY 67
C. Fisk, BOS....... 67
B. Campbell, BOS ... 65
M. Rivers, NY....... 59
L. Hisle, MIN 54
G. Brett, KC 51
R. Zisk, CHI 34
J. Sundberg, TEX ... 30
B. Bonds, CAL..... 28
C. Yastrzemski,
  BOS 25
R. Guidry, NY...... 11
J. Palmer, BAL 9
R. LeFlore, DET 7
J. Thompson, DET ... 6
R. Burleson, BOS... 5
B. Hobson, BOS..... 4
N. Ryan, CAL 3
G. Scott, BOS 3
H. McRae, KC 3
L. Bostock, MIN 2
T. Johnson, MIN 2
C. Chambliss, NY.... 1
O. Gamble, CHI..... 1
D. Leonard, KC 1

1978 NATIONAL
D. Parker, PIT.......320
S. Garvey, LA.......194
L. Bowa, PHI 189
R. Smith, LA 164
J. Clark, SF 107
G. Foster, CIN 104
G. Luzinski, PHI 48
G. Perry, SD 45
W. Stargell, PIT 39
D. Winfield, SD 37
P. Rose, CIN....... 35
V. Blue, SF........ 33
K. Tekulve, PIT..... 23
R. Fingers, SD 16
B. Hooton, LA 15
D. Lopes, LA 12
P. Niekro, ATL 8
B. Buckner, CHI 8
J. Burroughs, ATL ... 7
B. Sutter, CHI 5
G. Maddox, PHI 4
E. Cabell, HOU 2
B. Boone, PHI - 1

1978 AMERICAN
J. Rice, BOS........352
R. Guidry, NY......291
L. Hisle, MIL 201
A. Otis, KC 90
R. Staub, DET 88
G. Nettles, NY 86
D. Baylor, CAL..... 51
E. Murray, BAL 50
C. Fisk, BOS....... 49
D. Porter, KC 48
R. Carew, MIN 46
M. Caldwell, MIL ... 41
R. Gossage, NY 39
A. Oliver, TEX 26½
J. Sundberg, DET ... 24
R. LeFlore, DET 21
R. Jackson, NY 18
C. Yastrzemski,
  BOS 17
G. Brett, KC 14
A. Thornton,
  CLE 12½
L. Piniella, NY..... 11
T. Munson, NY 9
L. Bostock, CAL.... 8
L. Gura, KC 8
F. Lynn, BOS 6
M. Rivers, NY 6
B. Stanley, BOS ... 6
D. LaRoche, CAL ... 6

D. Money, MIL 5
W. Randolph, NY 5
D. Eckersley, BOS ... 4
H. McRae, KC 4
L. Roberts, SEA ... 3
R. Gale, KC........ 2
K. Singleton, BAL... 2
R. Burleson, BOS ... 1
F. Tanana, CAL ... 1

1979 NATIONAL
W. Stargell, PIT 216
K. Hernandez, SL...216
D. Winfield, SD 155
L. Parrish, MON 128
R. Knight, CIN 82
J. Niekro, HOU 75½
B. Sutter, CHI 69
K. Tekulve, PIT..... 64
D. Concepcion,
  CIN 63
D. Parker, PIT...... 56
D. Kingman, CHI 53
G. Foster, CIN 34
M. Schmidt, PHI ... 32
S. Garvey, LA...... 30
O. Moreno, PIT 23
P. Rose, PHI....... 23
G. Carter, MON ... 15
B. Madlock,
  SF-PIT 14
J. Richard, HOU 12
P. Niekro, ATL 11½
J. Sambito, HOU ... 9
T. Seaver, CIN 9
J. Bench, CIN 7
A. Dawson, MON ... 6
G. Templeton, SL .. 5
G. Matthews, ATL... 4
D. Collins, CIN 3
B. Horner, ATL 1

1979 AMERICAN
D. Baylor, CAL......347
K. Singleton, BAL...241
G. Brett, KC 226
F. Lynn, BOS 160½
J. Rice, BOS.......124
M. Flanagan, BAL ..100
G. Thomas, MIL ..87
D. Porter, KC 52
B. Bell, TEX 48
E. Murray, BAL ...25½
J. Kern, TEX 25
M. Marshall, MIN .. 25
B. Downing, CAL ... 24
S. Lezcano, MIL ... 18
R. Smalley, MIN ... 16
W. Wilson, KC 15
S. Kemp, DET 15
M. Clear, CAL 12
P. Molitor, MIL..... 8
R. Burleson, BOS... 7
T. John, NY....... 5
C. Cooper, MIL 4
R. Jackson, NY ... 3
W. Horton, SEA ... 3
D. Ford, CAL 1
R. Guidry, NY...... 1
M. Hargrove, CLE ... 1

1980 NATIONAL
M. Schmidt, PHI ...336
G. Carter, MON ...193
J. Cruz, HOU 166
D. Baker, LA 138
S. Carlton, PHI 134
S. Garvey, LA......131
A. Dawson, MON ... 72
G. Hendrick, SL 50
B. Horner, ATL 42
B. McBride, PHI ... 32
K. Hernandez, SL... 29
D. Murphy, ATL 23
C. Cedeno, HOU ... 14
J. Bibby, PIT...... 11
J. Buckner, CHI ... 11
T. McGraw, PHI ... 10
J. Bench, CIN 7
J. Clark, SF 6
J. Niekro, HOU 3
M. Easler, PIT...... 2
J. Reuss, LA 2
K. Griffey, CIN ... 1

R. LeFlore, MON 1
G. Richards, SD 1
R. Scott, MON 1

1980 AMERICAN
G. Brett, KC 335
R. Jackson, NY 234
R. Gossage, NY 218
W. Wilson, KC 169
C. Cooper, MIL 160
E. Murray, BAL 106
R. Cerone, NY 77
D. Quisenberry,
  KC 76½
S. Stone, BAL 53
R. Henderson,
  OAK 51
A. Oliver, TEX 31½
T. Armas, OAK 29
A. Bumbry, BAL ... 27
B. Oglivie, MIL 27
W. Randolph, NY ... 10
M. Norris, OAK 10
R. Yount, MIL 8
M. Rivers, TEX 7
B. Bell, TEX....... 7
A. Trammell, DET .. 6
K. Singleton, BAL... 4
T. Perez, BOS 2
M. Dilone, CLE 2
F. Lynn, BOS 1
J. Wathan, KC 1

1981 NATIONAL
M. Schmidt, PHI ...321
A. Dawson, MON ...215
G. Foster, CIN ...146
D. Concepcion,
  CIN 108
F. Valenzuela, LA ... 90
G. Carter, MON 77
D. Baker, LA 65
B. Sutter, SL 59
S. Carlton, PHI ... 41
T. Seaver, CIN ... 35
P. Rose, PHI 35
B. Buckner, CHI ... 35
G. Matthews, PHI... 31
J. Cruz, HOU 25
G. Hendrick, SL ... 25
N. Ryan, HOU 23
B. Madlock, PIT ... 20
A. Howe, HOU 16
T. Raines, MON..... 15
R. Camp, ATL...... 9
K. Hernandez, SL... 9
T. Herr, SL 7
G. Minton, SF..... 4
W. Cromartie, MON.. 3
S. Garvey, LA 1
M. May, SF 1

1981 AMERICAN
R. Fingers, MIL 319
R. Henderson,
  OAK 308
D. Evans, BOS......140
T. Armas, OAK.....139
E. Murray, BAL 137
C. Lansford, BOS ...109
D. Winfield, NY 98
C. Cooper, MIL 96
R. Gossage, NY ... 62
T. Paciorek, SEA... 46
D. Murphy, OAK ... 45
K. Gibson, DET 40
S. McCatty, OAK ... 22
B. Grich, CAL 19
J. Morris, DET 17
A. Oliver, TEX 8
R. Yount, MIL 7
B. Bell, TEX...... 7
B. Almon, CHI 6
J. Mumphrey, NY ... 5
M. Hargrove, CLE... 4
A. Trammell, DET .. 4
K. Singleton, BAL... 3
S. Kemp, DET 3
D. Martinez, BAL .. 3
G. Luzinski, CHI ... 3
D. Stieb, TOR..... 1
G. Brett, KC 1

1982 NATIONAL
D. Murphy, ATL 283

L. Smith, SL 218
P. Guerrero, LA 175
A. Oliver, MON 175
B. Sutter, SL.......134
M. Schmidt, PHI 54
J. Clark, SF...... 53
G. Minton, SF..... 44
S. Carlton, PHI ... 41
B. Buckner, CHI ... 38
B. Madlock, PIT ... 37
G. Carter, MON ... 35
O. Smith, SL 25
G. Hendrick, SL ... 20
T. Kennedy, SD ... 20
J. Morgan, SF 17
K. Hernandez, SL... 12
J. Thompson, PIT... 12
G. Garber, ATL 6
J. Andujar, SL 6
F. Valenzuela, LA ... 3
A. Dawson, MON ... 3
C. Chambliss, ATL... 2
G. Matthews, PHI .. 2
R. Knight, HOU ... 1

1982 AMERICAN
R. Yount, MIL 385
E. Murray, BAL 228
D. DeCinces, CAL ..178
H. McRae, KC 175
C. Cooper, MIL 152
R. Jackson, CAL...107
D. Evans, BOS...... 57
G. Thomas, MIL ... 44½
D. Quisenberry, KC .. 39
R. Henderson,
  OAK 38
D. Winfield, NY 33
P. Molitor, MIL ...29½
L. Parrish, DET ... 26
B. Downing, CAL ... 22
W. Wilson, KC ... 16
R. Fingers, MIL ... 12
B. Boone, CAL ... 12
P. Vuckovich, MIL ... 11
J. Rice, BOS 10
T. Harrah, CLE 9
H. Baines, CHI 9
G. Brett, KC 9
D. Baylor, CAL..... 8
A. Thornton, CLE ... 8
B. Stanley, BOS ... 6
J. Palmer, BAL ... 5
D. Garcia, TOR ... 5
R. Carew, CAL 5
B. Caudill, SEA ... 4
B. Bell, TEX 3
C. Ripken, BAL ... 3
C. Lansford, BOS .. 1
R. Sutcliffe, CLE ... 1
G. Ward, MIN 1

1983 NATIONAL
D. Murphy, ATL 318
A. Dawson, MON ...213
M. Schmidt, PHI ...191
P. Guerrero, LA 182
T. Raines, MON ... 83
J. Cruz, HOU 76
D. Thon, HOU 67
B. Madlock, PIT ... 45
A. Holland, PHI 42
T. Kennedy, SD ... 37
G. Hendrick, SL ... 33
T. Pena, PIT 25
J. Denny, PHI 24
M. Soto, CIN 16
D. Evans, SF..... 16
R. Ramirez, ATL ... 15
J. Orosco, NY 14
L. Smith, CHI 8½
A. Oliver, MON ... 3
J. Leonard, SF ... 2
L. Smith, SL 1½
J. Davis, CHI 1
K. Hernandez, SL-NY. 1
B. Horner, ATL..... 1
O. Smith, SL...... 1

1983 AMERICAN
C. Ripken, BAL 322
E. Murray, BAL 290
C. Fisk, CHI 209
J. Rice, BOS........150
C. Cooper, MIL 123

D. Quisenberry, KC 107½
D. Winfield, NY 85
L. Whitaker, DET 84
L. Parrish, DET 66
H. Baines, CHI 49
W. Upshaw, TOR 41½
W. Boggs, BOS 25
L. Hoyt, CHI 24½
L. Moseby, TOR 21
B. Stanley, BOS ... 11½
A. Trammell, DET ... 11
G. Luzinski, CHI 9
R. Yount, MIL 6
T. Simmons, MIL 4
R. Dotson, CHI 3½
R. Law, CHI 2
R. Guidry, NY 2
J. Morris, DET 2
J. Cruz, SEA-CHI 1
R. Henderson, OAK ... 1
G. Wright, TEX 1
T. Martinez, BAL ..... ½

1984 NATIONAL
R. Sandberg, CHI ... 326
K. Hernandez, NY ... 195
T. Gwynn, SD 184
R. Sutcliffe, CHI ... 151
G. Matthews, CHI ... 70
B. Sutter, SL 67
M. Schmidt, PHI ... 55½
J. Cruz, HOU 53
J. Davis, CHI 49
T. Raines, MON 41
L. Durham, CHI 38
R. Gossage, SD 34
G. Carter, MON 32
D. Gooden, NY 28
A. Wiggins, SD 14
R. Cey, CHI 6
K. McReynolds, SD ... 6
B. Dernier, CHI 6
S. Garvey, SD 5
B. Brenly, SF 1
J. Samuel, PHI 1
J. Leonard, SF 1

1984 AMERICAN
W. Hernandez, DET 306
K. Hrbek, MIN 247
D. Quisenberry, KC 235
E. Murray, BAL 197
D. Mattingly, NY 113
K. Gibson, DET 96
T. Armas, BOS ... 87½
D. Winfield, NY 83
A. Trammell, DET ... 76½
W. Wilson, KC 61
D. Evans, BOS...... 39
A. Davis, SEA 26
J. Rice, BOS 10
H. Baines, CHI 10
D. Kingman, OAK 10
L. Parrish, DET 8
W. Upshaw, TOR 8
B. Downing, CAL 6
S. Balboni, KC 5
A. Thornton, CLE 5
J. Bell, TOR.......... 5
B. Bell, TEX 4
D. Stieb, TOR 4
L. Moseby, TOR 4
J. Beniquez, CAL 2
M. Boddicker, BAL ... 2
D. Alexander, TOR ... 1
C. Ripken, BAL 1

1985 NATIONAL
W. McGee, SL 280
D. Parker, CIN 220
P. Guerrero, LA 208
D. Gooden, NY 162
T. Herr, SL......... 119
G. Carter, NY 116
D. Murphy, ATL 63
K. Hernandez, NY ... 61
J. Tudor, SL........ 61
J. Clark, SL 20
V. Coleman, SL 16
T. Raines, MON 15
R. Sandberg, CHI 14

M. Marshall, LA 11
H. Brooks, MON 11
O. Hershiser, LA 9
K. Moreland, CHI 8
O. Smith, SL 5
M. Scioscia, LA 5
J. Reardon, MON 4
J. Cruz, HOU 2
B. Doran, HOU 2
M. Duncan, LA 1
T. Gwynn, SD......... 1
F. Valenzuela, LA 1
G. Wilson, PHI 1

1985 AMERICAN
D. Mattingly, NY 367
G. Brett, KC 274
R. Henderson, NY ... 174
W. Boggs, BOS 159
E. Murray, BAL 130
D. Moore, CAL...... 96
J. Barfield, TOR..... 88
J. Bell, TOR 84
H. Baines, CHI 49
B. Saberhagen, KC ... 45
D. Quisenberry, KC ... 39
D. Winfield, NY 35
C. Fisk, CHI 29
Da. Evans, DET 17
R. Guidry, NY 15
P. Bradley, SEA 12
C. Ripken, BAL 9
K. Gibson, DET 7
S. Balboni, KC 6
T. Henke, TOR....... 5
K. Puckett, MIN 3
D. Alexander, TOR ... 3
D. Garcia, TOR 2
R. Gedman, BOS 1

1986 NATIONAL
M. Schmidt, PHI 287
G. Davis, HOU 231
G. Carter, NY 181
K. Hernandez, NY ... 179
D. Parker, CIN 144
T. Raines, MON..... 99
K. Bass, HOU 73
V. Hayes, PHI 41
T. Gwynn, SD....... 34
M. Scott, HOU 33
B. Doran, HOU 32
E. Davis, CIN 21
S. Sax, LA 13
R. Knight, NY 9
M. Krukow, SF...... 8
T. Worrell, SL....... 7
R. McDowell, NY 5
D. Smith, HOU 5
F. Valenzuela, LA 4
L. Dykstra, NY 4
B. Ojeda, NY 2
D. Murphy, ATL 2
C. Maldonado, SF ... 2

1986 AMERICAN
R. Clemens, BOS ... 339
D. Mattingly, NY ... 258
J. Rice, BOS 241
J. Bell, TOR........ 125
J. Barfield, TOR.... 107
K. Puckett, MIN..... 105
W. Boggs, BOS..... 87
W. Joyner, CAL..... 74
J. Carter, CLE 72
D. Righetti, NY...... 71
D. DeCinces, CAL ... 56
M. Witt, CAL....... 34
D. Baylor, BOS 32
T. Fernandez, TOR ... 17
T. Higuera, MIL 7
G. Gaetti, MIN 6
P. O'Brien, TEX 5
S. Fletcher, TEX 5
M. Barrett, BOS 5
J. Canseco, OAK 3
J. Presley, SEA 2
D. Schofield, CAL.... 1

1987 NATIONAL
A. Dawson, CHI 269
O. Smith, SL 193
J. Clark, SL 186
T. Wallach, MON ... 165

W. Clark, SF 128
D. Strawberry, NY ... 95
T. Raines, MON...... 80
T. Gwynn, SD...... 75
E. Davis, CIN 73
H. Johnson, NY..... 42
D. Murphy, ATL 34
V. Coleman, SL... 20
J. Samuel, PHI..... 19
M. Schmidt, PHI.... 13
P. Guerrero, LA 12
S. Bedrosian, PHI.... 6
M. Thompson, PHI... 4
B. Doran, HOU 1
T. Pendleton, SL ... 1

1987 AMERICAN
J. Bell, TOR........ 332
A. Trammell, DET... 311
K. Puckett, MIN..... 201
Dw. Evans, BOS ... 127
P. Molitor, MIL..... 125
M. McGwire, OAK ... 109
D. Mattingly, NY 92
T. Fernandez, TOR ... 79
W. Boggs, BOS..... 64
G. Gaetti, MIN...... 47
J. Reardon, MIN..... 37
Da. Evans, DET..... 21
D. Alexander, DET ... 17
T. Henke, TOR 17
R. Clemens, BOS 7
J. Morris, DET 5
K. Seitzer, KC 5
R. Sierra, TEX 5
J. Canseco, OAK 4
M. Nokes, DET 1

1988 NATIONAL
K. Gibson, LA....... 272
D. Strawberry, NY .. 236
K. McReynolds, NY 162
A. Van Slyke, PIT ... 160
W. Clark, SF 135
O. Hershiser, LA 111
A. Galarraga, MON . 105
G. Davis, HOU 72
D. Jackson, CIN 41
D. Cone, NY 37
T. Gwynn, SD...... 29
J. Franco, CIN 23
E. Davis, CIN 14
B. Bonilla, PIT 7
A. Dawson, CHI 6
R. Myers, NY 3
B. Butler, SF 2
S. Sax, LA 1

1988 AMERICAN
J. Canseco, OAK ... 392
M. Greenwell, BOS . 242
K. Puckett, MIN..... 219
D. Winfield, NY..... 164
D. Eckersley, OAK .. 156
W. Boggs, BOS..... 107
A. Trammell, DET ... 62
P. Molitor, MIL..... 50
Dw. Evans, BOS 49
F. Viola, MIN....... 39
R. Yount, MIL 34
G. Brett, KC 29
D. Henderson, OAK.. 28
B. Hurst, BOS 15
D. Jones, CLE 11
J. Reardon, MIN 11
F. McGriff, TOR..... 9
R. Henderson, NY ... 8
M. McGwire, OAK ... 6
J. Carter, CLE 5
L. Smith, BOS 4
G. Gaetti, MIN 3
D. Plesac, MIL 3
D. Stewart, OAK 3
J. Franco, CLE 2
T. Fernandez, TOR ... 1

1989 NATIONAL
K. Mitchell, SF 314
W. Clark, SF 225
P. Guerrero, SL ... 190

R. Sandberg, CHI ... 157
H. Johnson, NY..... 153
M. Davis, SD 64
G. Davis, HOU 64
T. Gwynn, SD...... 57
E. Davis, CIN 45
M. Williams, CHI ... 41
L. Smith, ATL 34
J. Clark, SD........ 16
J. Walton, CHI 14
M. Grace, CHI 9
M. Scott, HOU...... 5
B. Bonilla, PIT 5
B. Butler, SF 3
T. Raines, MON..... 3
M. Thompson, SL ... 3
S. Garrelts, SF 2

1989 AMERICAN
R. Yount, MIL...... 256
R. Sierra, TEX...... 228
C. Ripken, BAL..... 216
J. Bell, TOR........ 205
D. Eckersley, OAK .. 116
F. McGriff, TOR..... 96
K. Puckett, MIN..... 84
B. Saberhagen, KC .. 82
R. Henderson,
  NY-OAK 67
B. Jackson, KC 46
D. Parker, OAK..... 44
G. Olson, BAL..... 35
B. Blyleven, CAL.... 32
D. Stewart, OAK 30
D. Mattingly, NY 25
J. Carter, CLE 23
C. Lansford, OAK ... 20
N. Esasky, BOS 19
T. Fernandez, TOR .. 9
M. Moore, OAK 6
W. Boggs, BOS 3
S. Sax, NY 3
A. Davis, SEA 3
N. Ryan, TEX 2
C. Davis, CAL 1
M. McGwire, OAK ... 1
M. Wilson, TOR...... 1

1990 NATIONAL
B. Bonds, PIT....... 331
B. Bonilla, PIT 212
D. Strawberry, NY .. 167
R. Sandberg, CHI .. 151
E. Murray, LA 123
M. Williams, SF 95
B. Larkin, CIN 82
D. Drabek, PIT 59
L. Dykstra, PHI 41
T. Wallach, MON ... 36
K. Mitchell, SF 20
E. Davis, CIN 12
C. Sabo, CIN 11
R. Gant, ATL 10
D. Gooden, NY 10
R. Martinez, LA 9
J. Carter, SD....... 7
R. Myers, CIN 7
P. O'Neill, CIN 6
J. Rijo, CIN 6
A. Dawson, CHI 6
D. Magadan, NY 4
B. Santiago, SD 3
B. Butler, SF........ 2
D. Justice, ATL 2
P. Guerrero, SL 2
K. Daniels, LA 1
A. Van Slyke, PIT ... 1

1990 AMERICAN
R. Henderson, OAK 317
C. Fielder, DET 286
R. Clemens, BOS ... 212
K. Gruber, TOR 175
B. Thigpen, CHI 170
D. Eckersley, OAK .. 112
G. Brett, KC 60
D. Stewart, OAK 56
B. Welch, OAK..... 54
F. McGriff, TOR..... 30
M. McGwire, OAK ... 29
J. Canseco, OAK ... 26
E. Burks, BOS 25
R. Palmeiro, TEX ... 22
C. Fisk, CHI 16
D. Parker, MIL 11

O. Guillen, CHI ... 10
J. Reed, BOS 9
K. Griffey, Jr., SEA . 7
A. Trammell, DET 7
T. Pena, BOS 6
W. Boggs, BOS..... 5
D. Jones, CLE 3
C. Ripken, BAL 2
N. Ryan, TEX 1
D. Stieb, TOR 1

1991 NATIONAL
T. Pendleton, ATL .. 274
B. Bonds, PIT.......259
B. Bonilla, PIT 191
W. Clark, SF 118
H. Johnson, NY..... 112
R. Gant, ATL 110
B. Butler, LA 103
L. Smith, SL 89
D. Strawberry, LA ... 76
F. McGriff, SD 23
T. Glavine, ATL 16
D. Justice, ATL 11
J. Bell, PIT 11
A. Dawson, CHI 5
J. Smiley, PIT 5
T. Gwynn, SD...... 5
J. Kruk, PHI 2
R. Sandberg, CHI ... 2
B. Larkin, CIN 2
R. Martinez, MON ... 1
C. Sabo, CIN 1
O. Smith, SL 1

1991 AMERICAN
C. Ripken, BAL 318
C. Fielder, DET 286
F. Thomas, CHI 181
J. Canseco, OAK ... 145
J. Carter, TOR 136
R. Alomar, TOR.... 128
K. Puckett, MIN 78
R. Sierra, TEX...... 63
K. Griffey, Jr., SEA .. 62
R. Clemens, BOS ... 57
P. Molitor, MIL..... 51
D. Tartabull, KC 32
J. Morris, MIN 29
C. Davis, MIN 21
J. Franco, TEX..... 17
D. White, TOR..... 15
S. Erickson, MIN ... 12
R. Aguilera, MIN ... 11
R. Palmeiro, TEX ... 6
R. Ventura, CHI 3
D. Henderson, OAK... 1

1992 NATIONAL
B. Bonds, PIT.......304
T. Pendleton, ATL...232
G. Sheffield, SD ...204
A. Van Slyke, PIT ... 145
L. Walker, MON..... 111
D. Daulton, PHI 100
F. McGriff, SD 100
B. Roberts, CIN 64
M. Grissom, MON ... 54
T. Glavine, ATL 18
G. Maddux, CHI 14
R. Sandberg, CHI ... 12
B. Larkin, CIN 12
D. Jones, HOU 8
J. Kruk, PHI 8
M. Grace, PHI 6
D. DeShields, MON ... 6
R. Lankford, SL 5
J. Bagwell, HOU 4
D. Hollins, PHI 3
B. Butler, LA 2
O. Smith, SL 2
O. Nixon, ATL 1
J. Wetteland, MON ... 1

1992 AMERICAN
D. Eckersley, OAK .. 306
K. Puckett, MIN 209
J. Carter, TOR 201
M. McGwire, OAK ... 155
D. Winfield, TOR ... 141
R. Alomar, TOR 118
M. Devereaux, BAL 109
F. Thomas, CHI 108
C. Fielder, DET 83
P. Molitor, MIL....... 63

C. Baerga, CLE 31
E. Martinez, SEA 29
J. Morris, TOR 18
R. Clemens, BOS ... 16
B. Anderson, BAL ... 16
J. Gonzalez, TEX ... 15
K. Griffey, Jr., SEA .. 13
P. Listach, MIL 8
J. McDowell, CHI ... 5
J. Bell, CHI 3
M. Bordick, OAK.... 2
M. Mussina, BAL ... 2
A. Belle, CLE 1

1993 NATIONAL
B. Bonds, SF 372
L. Dykstra, PHI 267
D. Justice, ATL 183
F. McGriff, SD-ATL . 177
R. Gant, ATL...... 176
M. Williams, SF 103
D. Daulton, PHI 79
M. Grissom, MON .. 66
M. Piazza, LA 49
A. Galarraga, COL ... 45
G. Jefferies, STL.... 28
R. Beck, SF........ 23
G. Maddux, ATL 17
B. Harvey, FLA..... 14
R. Thompson, SF ... 11
J. Blauser, ATL..... 9
J. Kruk, PHI 9
M. Grace, CHI 8
J. Bell, PIT 4
J. Bagwell, HOU 3
T. Gwynn, SD...... 2
R. Myers, CHI 2
J. Rijo, CIN 2
J. Burkett, SF 1
T. Glavine, ATL 1
J. Wetteland, MON ... 1

1993 AMERICAN
F. Thomas, CHI 392
P. Molitor, TOR 209
J. Olerud, TOR 198
J. Gonzalez, TEX ... 185
K. Griffey, Jr., SEA .. 182
R. Alomar, TOR.... 102
A. Belle, CLE 81
R. Palmeiro, TEX.... 52
J. McDowell, CHI ... 51
C. Baerga, CLE 50
J. Key, NY 29
J. Carter, TOR 25
M. Stanley, NY 15
J. Montgomery, KC . 15
C. Lofton, CLE...... 11
T. Phillips, DET 10
C. Hoiles, BAL...... 10
M. Vaughn, BOS ... 8
D. Mattingly, NY ... 7
C. Ripken, BAL 7
A. Fernandez, CHI ... 4
D. Ward, TOR..... 3
E. Gagne, KC 3
K. Appier, KC 1
C. Fielder, DET 1
R. Johnson, SEA ... 1

1994 NATIONAL
J. Bagwell, Hou 392
M. Williams, SF 201
M. Alou, Mtl 183
B. Bonds, SF 144
G. Maddux, Atl 133
M. Piazza, LA 121
T. Gwynn, SD...... 112
F. McGriff, Atl 96
K. Mitchell, Cin 86
A. Galarraga, Col ... 42
L. Walker, Mtl 23
K. Hill, Mtl 22
M. Grissom, Mtl 22
D. Bichette, Col ... 19
H. Morris, Cin 18
C. Biggio, Hou 17
G. Jefferies, StL ... 9
J. Conine, Fla 5
T. Wallach, LA 4
J. Franco, NY 3
J. Boone, Cin 2
A. Benes, SD 1
B. Butler, LA 1
B. Saberhagen, NY ... 1

1994 AMERICAN				
F. Thomas, Chi 372	P. O'Neill, NY 150	D. Cone, KC 40	W. Boggs, NY 19	M. Vaughn, Bos....10	M. Mussina, Bal 8
K. Griffey, Jr., Sea ..233	J. Key, NY 102	J. Carter, Tor 35	L. Smith, Bal 18	D. Mattingly, NY 9	C. Davis, Cal 3
A. Belle, Cle 225	K. Puckett, Min 100	J. Canseco, Tex 27	W. Clark, Tex 17	P. Molitor, Tor 9	J. Bere, Chi 1
K. Lofton, Cle 181	J. Franco, Chi 49	C. Ripken, Bal 24	R. Palmeiro, Bal 11	C. Knoblauch, Min 8	R. Sierra, Oak 1

Rookie of the Year Award: History

The Chicago chapter of the Baseball Writers' Association of America (BBWAA) established an award recognizing the major leagues' top rookie following the 1940 season, selecting Lou Boudreau for the honor. This procedure continued for six more years before going national. The subsequent winners of the Chicago chapter's award were Pete Reiser (1941), Johnny Beazley (1942), Bill Johnson (1943), Bill Voiselle (1944), Boo Ferriss (1945), and Eddie Waitkus (1946).

The Sporting News began naming its own Rookie of the Year in 1946, with the selection of Del Ennis of the Philadelphia Phillies. Their award has competed with that of the BBWAA ever since. In 1949 they began recognizing a winner from each league and in 1957 they started selecting both a rookie player and a rookie pitcher of the year for each league.

In 1947 thirty-three baseball writers were asked to name five rookies in order of preference, with votes distributed on a 5–4–3–2–1 basis. Thus, Jackie Robinson became the first nationally recognized winner of the BBWAA Rookie of the Year Award, or the J. Louis Comiskey Memorial Award, as it was called. During the 1987 Hall of Fame induction ceremony, Commissioner Peter Ueberroth announced that, hereafter, the Rookie of the Year Award would be officially known as the Jackie Robinson Award.

In 1948 forty-eight writers took part in the award, this time naming only a single candidate on each ballot. In 1949 the BBWAA began the process of choosing a top rookie in each league. Three writers from each league city, the same men who decided on the MVP Awards, participated in the voting. Voters were free to use their individual judgments as to the eligibility of rookie candidates, which created some problems, especially in 1950 when Al Rosen, and his league-leading 37 homers, was ignored by Rookie of the Year voters. Apparently they felt that Rosen's 58 previous major league at-bats were tanta-

mount to veteran status, while winner Walt Dropo's 41 previous at-bats were not.

In 1957 formal guidelines were finally established for determining rookie status. A player could not have accumulated more than 75 at-bats, 45 innings pitched, or have been on a major league roster between May 15 and September 1 of any previous season. Shortly after, the guidelines were changed to 90 at-bats, 45 innings pitched or 45 days on a major league roster before September 1. Finally, in 1971, the guidelines were set at 130 at-bats, 50 innings, or 45 days on a roster.

There were several instances, especially in the early days of the award, in which some Rookie of the Year voters didn't bother to exercise their franchise. In 1961, as with the MVP Award, the number of voters was reduced from three to two writers from each league city.

Following two tie votes in four years (1976 NL, 1979 AL), the writers adopted the system used in Cy Young Award balloting: naming three rookies on each ballot, in order of preference, with votes distributed on a 5–3–1 basis. This system began in 1980, although it had been scheduled to start ten years earlier.

The maximum possible point total available to Rookie of the Year candidates was 165 in 1947, 48 in 1948, and 24 in each league in 1949–60. In the National League, it was 16 in 1961, 20 in 1962–68, 24 in 1969–79, 120 in 1980-92, and 140 from 1993 to the present. In the American League, it was 20 in 1961–68, 24 in 1969–76, 28 in 1977–79, and 140 from 1980 to the present.

There have been eleven unanimous Rookie of the Year selections since 1947: Frank Robinson (NL, 1956), Orlando Cepeda (NL, 1958), Willie McCovey (NL, 1959), Carlton Fisk (AL, 1972), Vince Coleman (NL, 1985), Benito Santiago (NL, 1987), Mark McGwire (AL, 1987), Sandy Alomar (AL, 1990), Mike Piazza (NL, 1993), Tim Salmon (AL, 1993), and Raul Mondesi (NL, 1994). Technically, Tony Kubek's 1957 AL selection was also unanimous, as the lone dissenting vote went to an ineligible player.

Rookie of the Year Award

1947
J. Robinson, BRO
 (NL) 129
L. Jansen, NY
 (NL) 105
F. Shea, NY (AL) 67
F. Fain, PHI (AL) 43
F. Baumholtz, CIN
 (NL) 42
(Rest of voting
 unknown)

1948
A. Dark, BOS (NL) ...27
G. Bearden, CLE
 (AL) 8
R. Ashburn, PHI (NL)..7
L. Brissie, PHI (AL)...3
B. Goodman, BOS
 (AL) 3

1949 NATIONAL
D. Newcombe,
 BRO 21
D. Crandall, BOS 3

1949 AMERICAN
R. Sievers, SL 10
A. Kellner, PHI 5
G. Coleman, NY 4
B. Kuzava, CHI 1
J. Groth, DET 1
M. Garcia, CLE 1

1950 NATIONAL
S. Jethroe, BOS 11
B. Miller, PHI 5
D. O'Connell, PIT 4
E. Church, PHI 2
B. Serena, CHI 1

1950 AMERICAN
W. Dropo, BOS 15
W. Ford, NY 6
C. Carrasquel, CHI ...2

1951 NATIONAL
W. Mays, NY 18
C. Nichols, BOS 4
C. Labine, BRO 2

1951 AMERICAN
G. McDougald, NY ..13

M. Minoso, CLE-CHI. 11

1952 NATIONAL
J. Black, BRO 19
H. Wilhelm, NY 3
D. Groat, PIT 1
E. Mathews, BOS.....1

1952 AMERICAN
H. Byrd, PHI 9
C. Courtney, SL 8
S. White, BOS 7

1953 NATIONAL
J. Gilliam, BRO 11
H. Haddix, SL 4
R. Jablonski, SL 3
R. Repulski, SL 2
B. Bruton, MIL 2
F. Baczewski, CIN 1
J. Greengrass, CIN ...1

1953 AMERICAN
H. Kuenn, DET 23
T. Umphlett, BOS.....1

1954 NATIONAL
W. Moon, SL 17
E. Banks, CHI 4
G. Conley, MIL 2
H. Aaron, MIL.........1

1954 AMERICAN
B. Grim, NY 15
J. Finigan, PHI 8
A. Kaline, DET 1

1955 NATIONAL
B. Virdon, SL 15
J. Meyer, PHI 7
D. Bessent, BRO 2

1955 AMERICAN
H. Score, CLE 18
B. Klaus, BOS 5
N. Zauchin, BOS......1

1956 NATIONAL
F. Robinson, CIN 24

1956 AMERICAN
L. Aparicio, CHI......22
T. Francona, BAL 1

R. Colavito, CLE 1

1957 NATIONAL
J. Sanford, PHI 16
E. Bouchee, PHI 4
D. Drott, CHI..........3
B. Hazle, MIL 1

1957 AMERICAN
T. Kubek, NY 23
F. Malzone, BOS 1

1958 NATIONAL
O. Cepeda, SF.......21

1958 AMERICAN
A. Pearson, WAS 14
R. Duren, NY 7
G. Bell, CLE 3

1959 NATIONAL
W. McCovey, SF.....24

1959 AMERICAN
B. Allison, WAS 18
J. Perry, CLE 5
R. Snyder, KC 1

1960 NATIONAL
F. Howard, LA 12
P. Herrera, PHI 4
A. Mahaffey, PHI......3
R. Santo, CHI.........2
T. Davis, LA 1

1960 AMERICAN
R. Hansen, BAL 22
C. Estrada, BAL 1
J. Gentile, BAL 1

1961 NATIONAL
B. Williams, CHI 10
J. Torre, MIL 5
J. Curtis, CHI 1

1961 AMERICAN
D. Schwall, BOS 7
D. Howser, KC........6
Fl. Robinson, CHI 2
C. Schilling, BOS 2
L. Thomas, LA 2
J. Wood, DET.........1

1962 NATIONAL
K. Hubbs, CHI 19

D. Clendenon, PIT 1

1962 AMERICAN
T. Tresh, NY 13
B. Rodgers, LA 4
B. Allen, MIN 1
D. Chance, LA 1
D. Radatz, BOS....... 1

1963 NATIONAL
P. Rose, CIN......... 17
R. Hunt, NY 2
R. Culp, PHI 1

1963 AMERICAN
G. Peters, CHI 10
P. Ward, CHI 6
J. Hall, MIN 4

1964 NATIONAL
R. Allen, PHI 18
R. Carty, MIL 1
J. Hart, SF 1

1964 AMERICAN
T. Oliva, MIN 19
W. Bunker, BAL 1

1965 NATIONAL
J. Lefebvre, LA 13
J. Morgan, HOU 4
F. Linzy, SF 3

1965 AMERICAN
C. Blefary, BAL 12
M. Lopez, CAL 8

1966 NATIONAL
T. Helms, CIN 12
S. Jackson, HOU 3
T. Fuentes, SF 2
R. Hundley, CHI 1
C. Jones, NY 1
L. Jaster, SL 1

1966 AMERICAN
T. Agee, CHI 16
J. Nash, KC 2
D. Johnson, BAL 1
G. Scott, BOS 1

1967 NATIONAL
T. Seaver, NY 11
D. Hughes, SL 6
G. Nolan, CIN 3

1967 AMERICAN
R. Carew, MIN 19
R. Smith, BOS 1

1968 NATIONAL
J. Bench, CIN 10½
J. Koosman, NY ... 9½

1968 AMERICAN
S. Bahnsen, NY...... 17
D. Unser, WAS 3

1969 NATIONAL
T. Sizemore, LA..... 14
C. Laboy, MON 3
A. Oliver, PIT 3
B. Didier, ATL 2
L. Hisle, PHI 2

1969 AMERICAN
L. Piniella, KC 9
M. Nagy, BOS 6
C. May, CHI 5
K. Tatum, CAL 4

1970 NATIONAL
C. Morton, MON ... 11
B. Carbo, CIN 8
L. Bowa, PHI 3
W. Simpson, CIN ... 1

C. Cedeno, HOU 1

1970 AMERICAN
T. Munson, NY 23
R. Foster, CLE........ 1

1971 NATIONAL
E. Williams, ATL 18
W. Montanez, PHI 6

1971 AMERICAN
C. Chambliss, CLE ... 11
B. Parsons, MIL 5
A. Mangual, OAK 4
D. Griffin, BOS........ 3
P. Splittorff, KC 1

1972 NATIONAL
J. Matlack, NY 19
Dv. Rader, SF 4
J. Milner, NY 1

1972 AMERICAN
C. Fisk, BOS......... 24

1973 NATIONAL
G. Matthews, SF..... 11
S. Rogers, MON 3½
B. Boone, PHI 2
E. Sosa, SF 2
D. Driessen, CIN 2
R. Cey, LA 1
D. Lopes, LA 1
J. Grubb, SD 1
R. Zisk, PIT .... ½

1973 AMERICAN
A. Bumbry, BAL ... 13½
P. Garcia, MIL 3
D. Porter, MIL 3
S. Busby, KC 2
D. Medich, NY 2
R. Coggins, BAL 1½

1974 NATIONAL
B. McBride, SL 16
G. Gross, HOU 7
B. Madlock CHI...... 1

1974 AMERICAN
M. Hargrove,
TEX 16½
B. Dent, CHI 3
G. Brett, KC 2
R. Burleson, BOS ... 1½
J. Sundberg, TEX 1

1975 NATIONAL
J. Montefusco, SF ... 12
G. Carter, MON 9
Lr. Parrish, MON..... 1
R. Eastwick, CIN 1
M. Trillo, CHI 1

1975 AMERICAN
F. Lynn, BOS 23½
J. Rice, BOS.......... ½

1976 NATIONAL
B. Metzger, SD 11
P. Zachry, CIN 11
H. Cruz, SL 2

1976 AMERICAN
M. Fidrych, DET 22
B. Wynegar, MIN 2

1977 NATIONAL
A. Dawson, MON ... 10
S. Henderson, NY 9
G. Richards, SD 4
F. Bannister, HOU ... 1

1977 AMERICAN
E. Murray, BAL 12½
M. Page, OAK 9½

B. Wills, TEX.......... 4
D. Rozema, DET 2

1978 NATIONAL
B. Horner, ATL..... 12½
O. Smith, SD 8½
D. Robinson, PIT 3

1978 AMERICAN
L. Whitaker, DET..... 21
P. Molitor, MIL 3
C. Lansford, CAL 2
R. Gale, KC 1
A. Trammell, DET 1

1979 NATIONAL
R. Sutcliffe, LA...... 20
J. Leonard, HOU..... 3
S. Thompson, CHI 1

1979 AMERICAN
J. Castino, MIN 7
A. Griffin, TOR 7
M. Clear, CAL 5
R. Davis, NY 3
R. Baumgarten, CHI .. 3
P. Putnam, TEX 3

1980 NATIONAL
S. Howe, LA 80
B. Gullickson,
MON 53
L. Smith, PHI 49
R. Oester, CIN 16
D. Smith, HOU...... 13
J. Reardon, NY 3
A. Holland, SF 1
L. Durham, SL 1
B. Walk, PHI 1

1980 AMERICAN
J. Charboneau,
CLE 102
D. Stapleton, BOS ... 40
D. Corbett, MIN..... 38
D. Garcia, TOR 35
B. Burns, CHI....... 33
R. Peters, DET 3
R. Dotson, CHI 1

1981 NATIONAL
F. Valenzuela, LA ... 107
T. Raines, MON 85
H. Brooks, NY 8½
B. Berenyi, CIN 5
J. Bonilla, SD 5
T. Pena, PIT 4
M. Wilson, NY 1½

1981 AMERICAN
D. Righetti, NY......127
R. Gedman, BOS 64
B. Ojeda, BOS 36
M. Jones, KC 8
D. Engle, MIN...... 4½
M. Witt, CAL........ 4
S. Babitt, OAK 4
J. Bell, TOR.......... 2
G. Ward, MIN 1½
B. Havens, MIN 1

1982 NATIONAL
S. Sax, LA 63
J. Ray, PIT.......... 57
W. McGee, SL 39
C. Davis, SF 32
L. DeLeon, SD 10
R. Sandberg, CHI 9
S. Bedrosian, ATL ... 4
D. LaPoint, SL 1
E. Show, SD 1

1982 AMERICAN
C. Ripken, BAL 132
K. Hrbek, MIN 90
W. Boggs, BOS.... 10½

E. Vande Berg, SEA... 9
G. Gaetti, MIN 4
D. Hostetler, TEX 3
V. Hayes, CLE 2
J. Barfield, TOR.... 1½

1983 NATIONAL
D. Strawberry, NY ..106
C. McMurtry, ATL ... 49
M. Hall, CHI 32
G. Redus, CIN 8
B. Doran, HOU 7
F. DiPino, HOU 6
G. Brock, LA........ 3
J. DeLeon, PIT....... 3
M. Thurmond, SD.... 1
L. Tunnell, PIT 1

1983 AMERICAN
R. Kittle, CHI 104
J. Franco, CLE....... 78
M. Boddicker, BAL .. 70

1984 NATIONAL
D. Gooden, NY 118
J. Samuel, PHI....... 67
O. Hershiser, LA 15
D. Gladden, SF 9
R. Darling, NY 3
C. Martinez, SD..... 2
J. Stone, PHI 1
T. Pendleton, SL..... 1

1984 AMERICAN
A. Davis, SEA 134
M. Langston, SEA ... 82
K. Puckett, MIN 23
T. Teufel, MIN 5
M. Young, BAL 3
R. Clemens, BOS 2
M. Gubicza, KC...... 1
A. Nipper, BOS 1
R. Romanick, CAL ... 1

1985 NATIONAL
V. Coleman, SL 120
T. Browning, CIN 72
M. Duncan, LA...... 9
C. Brown, SF 3
G. Davis, HOU....... 3
R. McDowell, NY 2
J. Orsulak, PIT....... 2
J. Hesketh, MON 1

1985 AMERICAN
O. Guillen, CHI 101
T. Higuera, MIL 67
E. Riles, MIL 29
O. McDowell, TEX ... 25
S. Cliburn, CAL 16
B. Fisher, NY 7
T. Henke, TOR...... 5
M. Salas, MIN 2

1986 NATIONAL
T. Worrell, SL 118
R. Thompson, SF 46
K. Mitchell, NY...... 22
C. Kerfeld, HOU 17
W. Clark, SF 5
B. Bonds, PIT........ 4
J. Deshaies, HOU.... 1
B. Larkin, CIN 1
B. Ruffin, PHI 1
J. Kruk, SD 1

1986 AMERICAN
J. Canseco, OAK ...110
W. Joyner, CAL 98
M. Eichhorn, TOR ... 23
C. Snyder, CLE 16
D. Tartabull, SEA.... 4
R. Sierra, TEX....... 1

1987 NATIONAL
B. Santiago, SD 120

M. Dunne, PIT 66
J. Magrane, SL 10
C. Candaele, MON ... 9
G. Young, HOU 7
C. James, PHI 1
L. Lancaster, CHI 1
G. Mathews, SL 1
R. Myers, NY 1

1987 AMERICAN
M. McGwire, OAK ..140
K. Seitzer, KC 64
M. Nokes, DET 32
M. Greenwell, BOS .. 9
D. White, CAL 5
M. Henneman, DET... 1
N. Liriano, TOR 1

1988 NATIONAL
C. Sabo, CIN 79
M. Grace, CHI 61
T. Belcher, LA 35
R. Gant, ATL 22
R. Alomar, SD 11
D. Berryhill, CHI 3
G. Jefferies, NY..... 3
R. Jordan, PHI 2

1988 AMERICAN
W. Weiss, OAK 103
B. Harvey, CAL 49
J. Reed, BOS 48
D. August, MIL 22
D. Gallagher, CHI ... 18
M. Perez, CHI....... 9
M. Schooler, SEA ... 2
C. Espy, TEX 1

1989 NATIONAL
J. Walton, CHI 116
D. Smith, CHI...... 68
G. Jefferies, NY..... 18
D. Lilliquist, ATL 6
A. Benes, SD 3
C. Hayes, PHI 3
G. Harris, SD 2

1989 AMERICAN
G. Olson, BAL 136
T. Gordon, KC...... 67
K. Griffey, SEA...... 21
C. Worthington, BAL . 16
J. Abbott, CAL...... 10
K. Brown, TEX 2

1990 NATIONAL
D. Justice, ATL 118
D. DeShields, MON .. 60
H. Morris, CIN 13
J. Burkett, SF....... 12
M. Harkey, CHI 7
T. Zeile, SL 4
M. Grissom, MON ... 1
L. Walker, MON...... 1

1990 AMERICAN
S. Alomar, CLE 140
K. Maas, NY 47
K. Appier, KC 31
J. Olerud, TOR 13
K. Tapani, MIN 9
T. Fryman, DET 7
R. Ventura, CHI 3
B. McDonald, BAL... 2
A. Cole, CLE........ 1
S. Radinsky, CHI 1

1991 NATIONAL
J. Bagwell, HOU 118
O. Merced, PIT 53
R. Lankford, SL..... 28
B. Hunter, ATL 7
B. Barberie, MON.... 3
W. Chamberlain, PHI . 3
C. McElroy, CHI 3

M. Stanton, ATL 1

1991 AMERICAN
C. Knoblauch, MIN 136
J. Guzman, TOR 68
M. Cuyler, DET 22
I. Rodriguez, TEX ... 10
B. DeLucia, SEA 7
M. Timlin, TOR 2
M. Whiten, TOR-CLE . 2
L. Gomez, BAL 1
D. Henry, MIL 1
B. Mayne, KC....... 1
C. Nagy, CLE....... 1
P. Plantier, BOS 1

1992 NATIONAL
E. Karros, LA 116
M. Alou, MON 30
T. Wakefield, PIT.... 29
R. Sanders, CIN 23
D. Osborne, SL..... 12
M. Perez, SL....... 2
B. Rivera, PHI 1
F. Seminara, SD 1
B. Williams, HOU ... 1
M. Wohlers, ATL 1

1992 AMERICAN
P. Listach, MIL 122
K. Lofton, CLE 85
D. Fleming, SEA 23
C. Eldred, MIL 22

1993 NATIONAL
M. Piazza, LA 140
G. McMicheal, ATL .. 40
J. Conine, FLA 31
C. Carr, FLA 18
A. Martin, PIT 6
K. Stocker, PHI 4
W. Cordero, MON ... 3
K. Rueter, MON 3
C. Garcia, PIT 2
P. Martinez, LA 2
S. Cooke, PIT....... 1
R. Guttierrez, SD..... 1
A. Reynoso, COL 1

1993 AMERICAN
T. Salmon, CAL 140
J. Bere, CHI 59
A. Sele, BOS 19
W. Kirby, CLE 12
R. Amaral, SEA 8
B. Gates, OAK 7
T. Neel, OAK 5
J. DiPoto, CLE...... 1
D. Hulse, TEX....... 1

1994 NATIONAL
R. Mondesi, LA 140
J. Hudek, HOU 27
R. Klesko, ATL 25
S. Trachsel, CHI 22
C. Floyd, MON 10
J. Hamilton, SD..... 10
W. Van Landingham,
SF 9
H. Carrasco, CIN ... 3
B. Jones, NY 3
J. Lopez, ATL....... 2
S. Reynolds, HOU ... 1

1994 AMERICAN
B. Hamelin, KC 134
M. Ramirez, CLE..... 44
R. Greer, TEX 42
D. Hall, TOR 9
C. Gomez, DET 6
B. Risley, SEA 6
B. Anderson, CAL ... 4
J. Edmonds, CAL.... 2
J. Valentin, MIL 1

Cy Young Award: History

Commissioner Ford Frick, troubled by pitchers' lack of representation in MVP voting, spearheaded the 1956 effort to initiate a "most valuable pitcher" award. Cy Young, baseball's winningest pitcher, who had died the previous November, was the logical choice to name the honor after. At a special meeting on July 9, 1956, the Baseball Writers' Association of America approved, by the slim margin of 14-12, the establishment of the Cy Young Memorial

Award, designed to honor the major leagues' outstanding pitcher each year beginning in '56. Ironically, the first winner, Brooklyn's Don Newcombe, also won his league's MVP Award.

One writer from each major league city participated in the balloting. In case of a tie vote, a second balloting was to be taken between the deadlocked pitchers. Hurlers were not to be eligible to win the award more than once, a rule which was evidently scrapped within two years.

Frick was adamantly opposed to the commonly voiced idea to recognize a Cy Young winner in each league but, not long after his December 1965 retirement, the idea became a reality. On March 1, 1967, Frick's successor William Eckert approved the plan for dual awards, with two writers from each league city to select.

The system of having each writer make only one selection prevailed until 1969, when Detroit's Denny McLain and Baltimore's Mike Cuellar tied for the AL Cy Young Award. Thereafter, writers were instructed to name three pitchers in each league, with 5 points allotted for each first-place vote, 3 for second, and 1 for third.

The maximum number of points available for one pitcher was 16 from 1956–60, 18 in 1961, 20 in 1962–68,

24 in 1969, 120 in 1970–76 (AL) and 1970–1992 (NL), and 140 in 1977–present (AL) and 1993–present (NL). As with every other major award, there have been a few instances in Cy Young voting where at least one writer failed to return a ballot.

Unanimous winners of the Cy Young Award are Sandy Koufax (NL, 1963, '65, and '66), Bob Gibson (NL, 1968), Denny McLain (AL, 1968), Steve Carlton (NL, 1972), Ron Guidry (AL, 1978), Rick Sutcliffe (NL, 1984), Dwight Gooden (NL, 1985), Roger Clemens (AL, 1986), Orel Hershiser (NL, 1988), and Greg Maddux (NL, 1994).

Relief pitchers, once overlooked in Cy Young balloting, have become strong candidates in recent years. Until 1970 only one reliever — Lindy McDaniel in 1960 — had received even a single vote. The new voting system helped open opportunities for bullpen aces and in 1974 the Dodgers' Mike Marshall became the first reliever to win the Cy Young Award. He has been followed in that distinction by Sparky Lyle (AL, 1977), Bruce Sutter (NL, 1979), Rollie Fingers (AL, 1981), Willie Hernández (AL, 1984), Steve Bedrosian (NL, 1987), Mark Davis (NL, 1989), and Dennis Eckersley (AL, 1992).

Cy Young Award

1956
D. Newcombe, BRO (NL) 10
S. Maglie, BRO (NL) .. 4
W. Spahn, MIL (NL) .. 1
W. Ford, NY (AL) 1

1957
W. Spahn, MIL (NL) .. 15
D. Donovan, CHI (AL) 1

1958
B. Turley, NY (AL) 5
W. Spahn, MIL (NL) ... 4
B. Friend, PIT (NL) 3
L. Burdette, MIL (NL) 3

1959
E. Wynn, CHI (AL).... 13
S. Jones, SF (NL) 2
B. Shaw, CHI (AL) 1

1960
V. Law, PIT (NL) 8
W. Spahn, MIL (NL) .. 4
E. Broglio, SL (NL) 1
L. McDaniel, SL (NL) .. 1

1961
W. Ford, NY (AL) 9
W. Spahn, MIL (NL) .. 6
F. Lary, DET (AL) 2

1962
D. Drysdale, LA (NL) 14
J. Sanford, SF (NL) ... 4
B. Purkey, CIN (NL) ... 1
B. Pierce, SF (NL) 1

1963
S. Koufax, LA (NL) ... 20

1964
D. Chance, LA (AL) .. 17
L. Jackson, CHI (NL).. 2
S. Koufax, LA (NL) 1

1965
S. Koufax, LA (NL) ... 20

1966
S. Koufax, LA (NL) ... 20

1967 NATIONAL
M. Mc Cormick, SF .. 18
F. Jenkins, CHI 1
J. Bunning, PHI 1

1967 AMERICAN
J. Lonborg, BOS 18
J. Horlen, CHI 2

1968 NATIONAL
B. Gibson, SL 20

1968 AMERICAN
D. McLain, DET 20

1969 NATIONAL
T. Seaver, NY 23
P. Niekro, ATL 1

1969 AMERICAN
M. Cuellar, BAL 10
D. McLain, DET 10
J. Perry, MIN 3
D. McNally, BAL 1

1970 NATIONAL
B. Gibson, SL 118
G. Perry, SF 51
F. Jenkins CHI 16
D. Giusti, PIT 8
J. Merritt, CIN 8
G. Nolan, CIN 5
T. Seaver, NY 3
W. Granger, CIN 3
C. Morton, MON 2
L. Walker, PIT 1

1970 AMERICAN
J. Perry, MIN 55
D. McNally, BAL 47
S. McDowell, CLE ... 45
M. Cuellar, BAL 44
J. Palmer, BAL 11
C. Wright, CAL 9
R. Perranoski, MIN ... 5

1971 NATIONAL
F. Jenkins, CHI 97
T. Seaver, NY 61
A. Downing, LA 40
D. Ellis, PIT 9
B. Gibson, SL 3
J. Johnson, SF 2
D. Roberts, SD 2
J. Marichal, SF 1
B. Stoneman, MON .. 1

1971 AMERICAN
V. Blue, OAK 98
M. Lolich, DET 85
W. Wood, CHI 23
D. McNally, BAL 8
D. Drago, KC 1
A. Messersmith, CAL 1

1972 NATIONAL
S. Carlton, PHI 120
S. Blass, PIT 35
F. Jenkins, CHI 23
M. Marshall, MON ... 8
G. Nolan, CIN 6
T. Seaver, NY 6
C. Carroll, CIN 6
D. Sutton, LA 6
B. Gibson, SL 3
M. Pappas, CHI 3

1972 AMERICAN
G. Perry, CLE 64
W. Wood, CHI 58
M. Lolich, DET 27
J. Hunter, OAK 26
J. Palmer, BAL 20
L. Tiant, BOS 16
S. Lyle, NY 3
N. Ryan, CAL 2

1973 NATIONAL
T. Seaver, NY 71
M. Marshall, MON ... 54
R. Bryant, SF 50
J. Billingham, CIN ... 30
D. Sutton, LA 7
F. Norman, SD-CIN ... 3
D. Giusti, PIT 1

1973 AMERICAN
J. Palmer, BAL 88
N. Ryan, CAL 62
J. Hunter, OAK 52
J. Hiller, DET 6
W. Wood, CHI 3
J. Colborn, MIL 2
V. Blue, OAK 1
B. Blyleven, MIN 1
G. Perry, CLE 1

1974 NATIONAL
M. Marshall, LA 96
A. Messersmith, LA 66
P. Niekro, ATL 15

1974 AMERICAN
J. Hunter, OAK 90
F. Jenkins, TEX 75
N. Ryan, CAL 28
G. Perry, CLE 8
L. Tiant, BOS 8
M. Cuellar, BAL 6
J. Hiller, DET 1

1975 NATIONAL
T. Seaver, NY 98
R. Jones, SD 80
A. Hrabosky, SL 33
J. Montefusco, SF ... 2
D. Gullett, CIN 1
A. Messersmith, LA ... 1
D. Sutton, LA 1

1975 AMERICAN
J. Palmer, BAL 98
J. Hunter, NY 74
R. Fingers, OAK 25
F. Tanana, CAL 7
J. Kaat, CHI 7
V. Blue, OAK 2
R. Gossage, CHI 2
R. Wise, BOS 1

1976 NATIONAL
R. Jones, SD 96
J. Koosman, NY ... 69½
D. Sutton, LA 25½
S. Carlton, PHI 11
R. Eastwick, CIN 6
J. Matlack, NY 5
J. Richard, HOU 2
T. Seaver, NY 1

1976 AMERICAN
J. Palmer, BAL 108
M. Fidrych, DET 51
F. Tanana, CAL 18
E. Figueroa, NY 12
L. Tiant, BOS 10
V. Blue, OAK 8
B. Campbell, MIN 7
R. Fingers, OAK 1

D. Sutton, LA 12
A. Hrabosky, SL 9
J. Billingham, CIN 8
D. Gullett, CIN 5
C. Carroll, CIN 2
D. Giusti, PIT 1
B. Capra, ATL 1
L. McGlothen, SL 1

1977 NATIONAL
S. Carlton, PHI 104
T. John, LA 54
T. Seaver, NY-CIN .. 18
R. Reuschel, CHI 18
J. Candelaria, PIT.... 17
B. Sutter, CHI........ 5

1977 AMERICAN
S. Lyle, NY 56½
J. Palmer, BAL 48
N. Ryan, CAL 46
D. Leonard, KC 45
B. Campbell, BOS 25½
D. Goltz, MIN 19
R. Guidry, NY........ 5
D. Rozema, DET 4
F. Tanana, CAL 3

1978 NATIONAL
G. Perry, SD 116
B. Hooton, LA 38
V. Blue, SF 17
J. Richard, HOU 13
K. Tekulve, PIT....... 12
P. Niekro, ATL 10
R. Grimsley, MON ... 7
R. Fingers, SD 1
T. John, LA 1
D. Robinson, PIT 1

1978 AMERICAN
R. Guidry, NY........140
M. Caldwell, MIL..... 76
J. Palmer, BAL 14
D. Eckersley, BOS ... 10
R. Gossage, NY 4
F. Jenkins, TEX 2
E. Figueroa, NY 1
L. Gura, KC 1
D. Leonard, KC 1
M. Marshall, MIN 1
P. Splittorff, KC 1
B. Stanley, BOS 1

1979 NATIONAL
B. Sutter, CHI........ 72
J. Niekro, HOU 66
J. Richard, HOU 41
T. Seaver, CIN 20
K. Tekulve, PIT...... 14
P. Niekro, ATL 3

W. Garland, BAL...... 1

1979 AMERICAN
M. Flanagan, BAL ..136
T. John, NY.......... 51
R. Guidry, NY 26
J. Kern, TEX 25
M. Marshall, MIN 7
J. Koosman, MIN 5
D. Eckersley, BOS 1
A. Lopez, DET 1

1980 NATIONAL
S. Carlton, PHI 118
J. Reuss, LA 55
J. Bibby, PIT 28
J. Niekro, HOU 11
T. McGraw, PHI 1
S. Rogers, MON 1
J. Sambito, HOU 1
M. Soto, CIN 1

1980 AMERICAN
S. Stone, BAL 100
M. Norris, OAK 91
R. Gossage, NY .. 37½
T. John, NY......... 14
D. Quisenberry, KC 7½
L. Gura, KC.......... 1
S. McGregor, BAL ... 1

1981 NATIONAL
F. Valenzuela, LA 70
T. Seaver, CIN 67
S. Carlton, PHI 50
N. Ryan, HOU 28
B. Sutter, SL.......... 1

1981 AMERICAN
R. Fingers, MIL 126
S. McCatty, OAK .. 84½
J. Morris, DET 21
P. Vuckovich, MIL .. 8½
D. Martinez, BAL ... 3½
R. Gossage, NY 3
R. Guidry, NY........ 2½
B. Burns, CHI........ 2
L. Gura, KC.......... 1

1982 NATIONAL
S. Carlton, PHI 112
S. Rogers, MON 29
F. Valenzuela, LA .. 25½
B. Sutter, SL......... 25
P. Niekro, ATL 18
G. Minton, SF........ 4
J. Andujar, SL 1

G. Garber, ATL 1
M. Soto, CIN .... ½

1982 AMERICAN
P. Vuckovich, MIL ... 87
J. Palmer, BAL 59
D. Quisenberry, KC .. 40
D. Stieb, TOR 36
R. Sutcliffe, CLE 14
G. Zahn, CAL 7
B. Stanley, BOS 4
B. Caudill, SEA 4
D. Petry, DET 1

1983 NATIONAL
J. Denny, PHI 103
M. Soto, CIN 61
J. Orosco, NY 19
S. Rogers, MON 15
L. McWilliams, PIT ... 7
A. Holland, PHI 4
C. McMurtry, ATL 3
B. Welch, LA 1
N. Ryan, HOU 1
L. Smith, CHI 1

1983 AMERICAN
L. Hoyt, CHI 116
D. Quisenberry, KC .. 81
J. Morris, DET 38
R. Dotson, CHI 9
R. Guidry, NY 5
S. McGregor, BAL 3

1984 NATIONAL
R. Sutcliffe, CHI 120
D. Gooden, NY 45
B. Sutter, SL........ 33½
J. Andujar, SL 12½
R. Gossage, SD 3
M. Soto, CIN 2

1984 AMERICAN
W. Hernandez,
  DET 88
D. Quisenberry, KC .. 71
B. Blyleven, CLE..... 45
M. Boddicker, BAL .. 41
D. Petry, DET 3
F. Viola, MIN 2
J. Morris, DET 1
D. Stieb, TOR 1

1985 NATIONAL
D. Gooden, NY 120
J. Tudor, SL 65
O. Hershiser, LA 17
J. Andujar, SL 6
F. Valenzuela, LA 4
T. Browning, CIN 3
J. Reardon, MON 1

1985 AMERICAN
B. Saberhagen,
  KC 127
R. Guidry, NY 88
B. Blyleven, MIN 9
D. Quisenberry, KC ... 9
C. Leibrandt, KC...... 7
D. Alexander, TOR... 5
D. Burns, CHI 2
D. Moore, CAL........ 2
D. Stieb, TOR 2
M. Moore, SEA 1

1986 NATIONAL
M. Scott, HOU 98
F. Valenzuela, LA 88
M. Krukow, SF....... 15
B. Ojeda, NY 9
R. Darling, NY 2
R. Rhoden, PIT 2

D. Gooden, NY 1
S. Fernandez, NY 1

1986 AMERICAN
R. Clemens, BOS ...140
T. Higuera, MIL 42
M. Witt, CAL......... 35
D. Righetti, NY....... 20
J. Morris, DET 13
M. Eichhorn, TOR 2

1987 NATIONAL
S. Bedrosian, PHI.... 57
R. Sutcliffe, CHI 55
R. Reuschel, SF 54
O. Hershiser, LA 14
D. Gooden, NY 12
N. Ryan, HOU 12
M. Scott, HOU 9
B. Welch, LA.......... 3

1987 AMERICAN
R. Clemens, BOS ...124
J. Key, TOR 64
D. Stewart, OAK 32
D. Alexander, DET ... 8
M. Langston, SEA ... 7
T. Higuera, MIL 5
F. Viola, MIN 5
J. Reardon, MIN 4
J. Morris, DET 3

1988 NATIONAL
O. Hershisher, LA ...120
D. Jackson, CIN 54
D. Cone, NY 42

1988 AMERICAN
F. Viola, MIN 138
D. Eckersley, OAK .. 52

M. Gubicza, KC...... 26
D. Stewart, OAK..... 16
B. Hurst, BOS 12
R. Clemens, BOS 8

1989 NATIONAL
M. Davis, SD 107
M. Scott, HOU....... 65
G. Maddux, CHI 17
O. Hershiser, LA 7
J. Magrane, SL 7
T. Belcher, LA 4
S. Garrelts, SF 4
R. Reuschel, SF 3
M. Bielecki, CHI 1
M. Williams, CHI 1

1989 AMERICAN
B. Saberhagen,
  KC 138
D. Stewart, OAK 80
M. Moore, OAK 10
B. Blyleven, CAL..... 9
N. Ryan, TEX 5
J. Ballard, BAL....... 3
D. Eckersley, OAK ... 3
G. Olson, BAL 3
J. Russell, TEX 1

1990 NATIONAL
D. Drabek, PIT 118
R. Martinez, LA 70
F. Viola, NY 19
D. Gooden, NY 8
R. Myers, CIN 1

1990 AMERICAN
B. Welch, OAK.......107
R. Clemens, BOS 77
D. Stewart, OAK 43

B. Thigpen, CHI 20
D. Eckersley, OAK ... 2
B. Stieb, TOR 2
C. Finley, CAL 1

1991 NATIONAL
T. Glavine, ATL 110
L. Smith, SL 60
J. Smiley, PIT 26
J. Rijo, CIN 13
D. Martinez, MON ... 4
S. Avery, ATL 1
A. Benes, SD 1
M. Williams, PHI 1

1991 AMERICAN
R. Clemens, BOS ...119
S. Erickson, MIN..... 56
J. Abbott, CAL....... 26
J. Morris, MIN 17
B. Harvey, CAL 10
M. Langston, CAL ... 7
K. Tapani, MIN 6
B. Gullickson, DET ... 5
J. McDowell, CHI 3
D. Ward, TOR 3

1992 NATIONAL
G. Maddux, CHI 112
T. Glavine, ATL 78
B. Tewksbury, SL.... 22
L. Smith, SL 3
D. Drabek, PIT 1

1992 AMERICAN
D. Eckersley, OAK ..107
J. McDowell, CHI ... 51
R. Clemens, BOS 48
M. Mussina, BAL 26
J. Morris, TOR 10

K. Brown, TEX 9
C. Nagy, CLE 1

1993 NATIONAL
G. Maddux, ATL ...119
B. Swift, SF......... 61
T. Glavine, ATL 49
J. Burkett, SF........ 9
J. Rijo, CIN 3
T. Greene, PHI 2
M. Portugal, HOU..... 2
B. Harvey, FLA 1
R. Myers, CHI 1

1993 AMERICAN
J. McDowell, CHI ...124
R. Johnson SEA 75
K. Appier, KC 30
J. Key, NY 14
D. Ward, TOR......... 5
P. Hentgen, TOR 3
J. Guzman, TOR 1

1994 NATIONAL
G. Maddux, ATL ...140
K. Hill, MON 56
B. Saberhagen, NY .. 42
M. Freeman, COL..... 4
D. Drabek, HOU 4
D. Jackson, PHI 3
J. Franco, NY 2
R. Beck, SF.......... 1

1994 AMERICAN
D. Cone, KC 108
J. Key, NY 96
R. Johnson, SEA 24
M. Mussina, BAL ... 23
L. Smith, BAL........ 1

Hypothetical Awards

As the "expert" in baseball award-voting, I have been asked to make a set of hypothetical award selections for the years no official honors were given; i.e., pre-1956 Cy Young, pre-1947 Rookie of the Year, and pre-1911 MVP Awards, along with awards for any other "missing" years.

While this assignment gave me unusual freedom, I felt a certain responsibility to make my selections consistent with the perceptions and voting trends of a particular era. For example, although there were better NL players than Cincinnati's Edd Roush in 1919, he did two things which, combined, would have virtually guaranteed him the MVP Award: he won the batting crown, which was *the* individual title in the dead-ball era; and he played on a pennant-winner, which has always been a key factor in MVP voting. Thus, I felt obliged to make Roush my hypothetical selection.

Besides my own opinions and intuitions, several sources were instrumental in my selection process, including:

1. SABR retroactive award surveys, which have been done for pre-1949 Rookie of the Year and pre-1967 Cy Young Awards. SABR (the Society for American Baseball Research) is comprised of more than six thousand hard-core fans, hundreds of whom chose to participate in these surveys. The ballots were tremendously helpful in screening candidates and the voting results were carefully compared to my own choices.

2. Linear Weights, an overall player rating system devised by Pete Palmer, first used in *The Hidden Game of Baseball* (Doubleday, 1984, 1985), and continued in *Total Baseball*.

3. MVP voting results, for comparing Cy Young and Rookie candidates. If rookie "A" receives 75 points in the

MVP election, while comparable rookie "B" receives just 10, I am forced to conclude that the on-the-spot observers discerned some important difference that we can't see in the statistics and that "A" is probably the better choice. (Incidentally, the criteria used to determine rookies was a maximum of 90 at-bats or 45 innings pitched in any previous seasons.)

4. Unofficial awards, including 1940–46 Rookie and 1929–30 MVP selections.

5. Cy Young (1956–66) and Rookie of the Year (1947–48) balloting, for years in which one league had no official winner.

The resulting selections are not necessarily ones the average reader will agree with, nor even that the *writer* agrees with; rather, they are the ones which can be *best justified with the available evidence*. I am prepared to defend any of my choices.

In comparison with the Palmer system, my selections concurred 54 percent with top player selections and 59 percent with top pitcher nominations. In comparison with the SABR surveys, my selections agreed 84 percent in the Rookie of the Year Award and 79 percent in the Cy Young Award.

The big winner in the hypothetical awards is Christy Mathewson, who picks up a Rookie of the Year, two MVPs, and eight Cy Young Awards. Other pitchers capturing at least three Cy Youngs are Walter Johnson (7); Lefty Grove (6, consecutively); Warren Spahn (4, to add to the one he actually did win); Grover Cleveland Alexander (4); Burleigh Grimes, Carl Hubbell, Bob Feller, Bucky Walters, Bob Lemon, and appropriately, Cy Young himself (3 each).

Notable Rookies of the Year include Grover Cleveland Alexander, Babe Ruth, Rogers Hornsby, Dizzy Dean, Joe DiMaggio, and Ted Williams.

Honus Wagner cops six MVP Awards, including four in succession. Three-time MVPs are Nap Lajoie, Alexander, Ruth, and Hornsby. Ruth (once) and Hornsby (twice) also won official MVP Awards.

The following pages contain my hypothetical Cy Young (124), Rookie of the Year (97), and MVP (42) selections for this century.

Hypothetical Cy Young Award

American League Pitcher/Club	Year	American League Pitcher/Club	Year	American League Pitcher/Club	Year	National League Pitcher/Club	Year	National League Pitcher/Club	Year	National League Pitcher/Club	Year
C. Young, BOS	1901	G. Uhle, CLE	1923	D. Trout, DET	1944	J. McGinnity, BRO	1900	J. Vaughn, CHI	1918	B. Walters, CIN	1939
C. Young, BOS	1902	W. Johnson, WAS	1924	H. Newhouser, DET	1945	N. Hahn, CIN	1901	J. Vaughn, CHI	1919	B. Walters, CIN	1940
C. Young, BOS	1903	S. Coveleski, WAS	1925	H. Newhouser, DET	1946	J. Taylor, CHI	1902	G. Alexander, CHI	1920	W. Wyatt, BRO	1941
J. Chesbro, NY	1904	G. Uhle, CLE	1926	J. Page, NY	1947	C. Mathewson, NY	1903	B. Grimes, BRO	1921	M. Cooper, SL	1942
R. Waddell, PHI	1905	W. Moore, NY	1927	B. Lemon, CLE	1948	J. McGinnity, NY	1904	W. Cooper, PIT	1922	M. Cooper, SL	1943
A. Orth, NY	1906	L. Grove, PHI	1928	M. Parnell, BOS	1949	Mathewson, NY	1905	D. Luque, CIN	1923	B. Walters, CIN	1944
E. Walsh, CHI	1907	L. Grove, PHI	1929	B. Lemon, CLE	1950	M. Brown, CHI	1906	D. Vance, BRO	1924	C. Barrett, BOS-SL	1945
E. Walsh, CHI	1908	L. Grove, PHI	1930	N. Garver, SL	1951	Mathewson, NY	1907	D. Vance, BRO	1925	H. Pollet, SL	1946
F. Smith, CHI	1909	L. Grove, PHI	1931	B. Shantz, PHI	1952	Mathewson, NY	1908	R. Kremer, PIT	1926	E. Blackwell, CIN	1947
J. Coombs, PHI	1910	L. Grove, PHI	1932	B. Pierce, CHI	1953	Mathewson, NY	1909	C. Root, CHI	1927	J. Sain, BOS	1948
W. Johnson, WAS	1911	L. Grove, PHI	1933	B. Lemon, CLE	1954	Mathewson, NY	1910	B. Grimes, PIT	1928	W. Spahn, BOS	1949
J. Wood, BOS	1912	L. Gomez, NY	1934	R. Narleski, CLE	1955	Mathewson, NY	1911	B. Grimes, PIT	1929	J. Konstanty, PHI	1950
W. Johnson, WAS	1913	W. Ferrell, BOS	1935	B. Pierce, CHI	1956	R. Marquard, NY	1912	P. Malone, CHI	1930	S. Maglie, NY	1951
W. Johnson, WAS	1914	T. Bridges, DET	1936	J. Bunning, DET	1957	Mathewson, NY	1913	E. Brandt, BOS	1931	R. Roberts, PHI	1952
W. Johnson, WAS	1915	L. Gomez, NY	1937	C. Estrada, BAL	1960	B. James, BOS	1914	L. Warneke, CHI	1932	W. Spahn, MIL	1953
B. Ruth, BOS	1916	R. Ruffing, NY	1938	D. Donovan, CLE	1962	G. Alexander, PHI	1915	C. Hubbell, NY	1933	J. Antonelli, NY	1954
E. Cicotte, CHI	1917	B. Feller, CLE	1939	W. Ford, NY	1963	G. Alexander, PHI	1916	D. Dean, SL	1934	R. Roberts, PHI	1955
W. Johnson, WAS	1918	B. Feller, CLE	1940	E. Fisher, CHI	1965	G. Alexander, PHI	1917	D. Dean, SL	1935	W. Spahn, MIL	1958
W. Johnson, WAS	1919	B. Feller, CLE	1941	J. Kaat, MIN	1966			C. Hubbell, NY	1936	S. Jones, SF	1959
J. Bagby, CLE	1920	T. Hughson, BOS	1942					C. Hubbell, NY	1937	W. Spahn, MIL	1961
R. Faber, CHI	1921	S. Chandler, NY	1943					B. Lee, CHI	1938	L. Jackson, CHI	1964
E. Rommel, PHI	1922										

Hypothetical Federal League Awards

	1914	1915
Most Valuable Player	B. Kauff, IND	D. Zwilling, CHI
Cy Young	C. Hendrix, CHI	G. McConnell, CHI
Rookie of the Year	B. Kauff, IND	E. Johnson, SL

Hypothetical Rookie of the Year Award

American League Player/Club	Year	American League Player/Club	Year	American League Player/Club	Year	National League Player/Club	Year	National League Player/Club	Year	National League Player/Club	Year
S. Seybold, PHI	1901	J. Bagby, CLE	1916	J. Allen, NY	1932	E. Scott, CIN	1900	T. Long, SL	1915	W. Berger, BOS	1930
A. Joss, CLE	1902	A. Sothoron, SL	1917	B. Johnson, PHI	1933	C. Mathewson, NY	1901	R. Hornsby, SL	1916	P. Derringer, SL	1931
C. Bender, PHI	1903	S. Perry, PHI	1918	H. Trosky, CLE	1934	H. Smoot, SL	1902	L. Cadore, BRO	1917	D. Dean, SL	1932
F. Glade, SL	1904	D. Kerr, CHI	1919	J. Powell, WAS	1935	J. Weimer, CHI	1903	C. Hollocher, CHI	1918	F. Demaree, CHI	1933
G. Stone, SL	1905	B. Meusel, NY	1920	J. DiMaggio, NY	1936	H. Lumley, BRO	1904	O. Tuero, SL	1919	C. Davis, PHI	1934
C. Rossman, CLE	1906	J. Sewell, CLE	1921	Y. York, DET	1937	E. Reulbach, CHI	1905	J. Haines, SL	1920	C. Blanton, PIT	1935
S. Nicholls, PHI	1907	H. Pillette, DET	1922	K. Keltner, DET	1938	J. Pfiester, CHI	1906	R. Grimes, CHI	1921	J. Mize, SL	1936
E. Summers, DET	1908	H. Summa, CLE	1923	T. Williams, BOS	1939	N. Rucker, BRO	1907	H. Miller, CHI	1922	J. Turner, BOS	1937
F. Baker, PHI	1909	A. Simmons, PHI	1924	W. Judnich, SL	1940	G. McQuillan, PHI	1908	G. Grantham, CHI	1923	J. Rizzo, PIT	1938
R. Ford, NY	1910	E. Combs, NY	1925	P. Rizzuto, NY	1941	D. Miller, PIT	1909	K. Cuyler, PIT	1924	H. Casey, BRO	1939
V. Gregg, CLE	1911	T. Lazzeri, NY	1926	J. Pesky, BOS	1942	K. Cole, CHI	1910	J. Welsh, BOS	1925	B. Young, NY	1940
D. Pratt, SL	1912	W. Moore, NY	1927	B. Johnson, NY	1943	G. Alexander, PHI	1911	P. Waner, PIT	1926	E. Riddle, CIN	1941
R. Russell, CHI	1913	E. Morris, BOS	1928	J. Berry, PHI	1944	L. Cheney, CHI	1912	L. Waner, PIT	1927	J. Beazley, SL	1942
R. Bressler, PHI	1914	D. Alexander, DET	1929	B. Ferriss, BOS	1945	J. Viox, PIT	1913	D. Bissonette, BRO	1928	L. Klein, SL	1943
B. Ruth, BOS	1915	S. Jolley, CHI	1930	B. Lemon, CLE	1946	J. Pfeffer, BRO	1914	J. Frederick, BRO	1929	B. Voiselle, NY	1944
		J. Vosmik, CLE	1931	F. Shea, NY	1947					K. Burkhart, SL	1945
				G. Bearden, CLE	1948					D. Ennis, PHI	1946

Hypothetical Most Valuable Player Award

American League Player/Club	Year	American League Player/Club	Year	American League Player/Club	Year	National League Player/Club	Year	National League Player/Club	Year	National League Player/Club	Year
N. Lajoie, PHI	1901	T. Cobb, DET	1907	B. Ruth, BOS	1918	H. Wagner, PIT	1900	H. Wagner, PIT	1907	J. Vaughn, CHI	1918
C. Young, BOS	1902	E. Walsh, CHI	1908	J. Jackson, CHI	1919	H. Wagner, PIT	1901	C. Mathewson, NY	1908	E. Roush, CIN	1919
N. Lajoie, CLE	1903	T. Cobb, DET	1909	B. Ruth, NY	1920	H. Wagner, PIT	1902	H. Wagner, PIT	1909	R. Hornsby, SL	1920
J. Chesbro, NY	1904	J. Coombs, PHI	1910	B. Ruth, NY	1921	H. Wagner, PIT	1903	S. Magee, PHI	1910	R. Hornsby, SL	1921
R. Waddell, PHI	1905	E. Collins, PHI	1915	L. Fonseca, CLE	1929	J. McGinnity, NY	1904	G. Alexander, PHI	1915	R. Hornsby, SL	1922
N. Lajoie, CLE	1906	T. Speaker, CLE	1916	J. Cronin, WAS	1930	C. Mathewson, NY	1905	G. Alexander, PHI	1916	D. Luque, CIN	1923
		E. Cicotte, CHI	1917			F. Chance, CHI	1906	G. Alexander, PHI	1917	H. Wilson, CHI	1930

Gold Glove Award: History

In a 1956 spring training survey, Elmer A. Blasco—employed by Rawlings Sporting Goods as advertising, public relations and sales manager—found that 83 percent of the active regular major league players wore Rawlings gloves or mitts. Noting that Hillerich & Bradsby (the major leagues' leading baseball bat supplier) awarded Silver Bats to the leagues' top hitters, Blasco reasoned that Rawlings ought to sponsor some sort of fielding award. After his idea was accepted by Rawlings' management, Blasco contacted the Brown Shoe Company of St. Louis and obtained from them a hide of gold lamé-tanned leather used to make ladies' formal slippers. A glove was crafted from this hide, laced and stamped as a regular fielders glove, and attached to a metal fixture on a walnut base with an appropriate engraved plate.

Thus was born the Gold Glove Award.

The October 2, 1957, edition of *The Sporting News* featured a full-page advertisement/announcement: "Recognizing the importance of superior individual fielding performance to the advancement of baseball as America's national game, Rawlings (Sporting Goods Company) has established Annual Gold Glove Awards beginning with the 1957 season.

"Each of the nine Major League players chosen for *The Sporting News* All-Star Fielding Team will be honored with a Rawlings Gold Glove Award. Selections will be made by a Committee named by *The Sporting News*.

"Awards will be Rawlings custom-built gloves or mitts hand-crafted of special metallic gold-finished leather, each mounted on a suitable hardwood stand bearing an engraved plate."

TSN publisher J. G. Taylor Spink appointed nineteen noted sportswriters for the selection task. They included Shirley Povich, Edgar Munzel, Hy Hurwitz, Earl Lawson, Bob Broeg, Allen Lewis, and Hal Lebowitz. A contest to predict the winners, open to baseball-playing boys, was sponsored by Rawlings.

The first Gold Glove winners were announced with great pomp and circumstance in the December 18, 1957, issue of TSN. "Too long neglected, the magicians of the defense have had no real recognition," the article explained, adding that the selections were made "solely on the basis of their defensive ability."

Rawlings and TSN also joined forces that year in the establishment of the Silver Glove Award, given to the top minor league fielder at each position—based entirely on fielding averages.

In 1958 the Gold Glove selection privilege was turned over to the major league players and an All-Star Fielding Team was selected for each league (as it still is).

In 1961 the method for selecting outfielders was changed. Rather than choosing a left-, center-, and right fielder for each league, each voter was instructed to name three outfielders regardless of position (still the practice today).

In 1965 the managers and coaches of each team took over the voting responsibility, which they have retained ever since. Voters are not permitted to select players on their own teams. In 1987, 139 different managers and coaches took part in the balloting.

Perhaps because of its originality, the Gold Glove is the one *Sporting News* award that has gained universal acceptance and prestige in the baseball world. However, as with any award, the selections often draw criticism.

One complaint is that too much importance is given to fielding average. Most of us realize that FA is not always a reliable indicator of defensive ability, but how much does it influence the Gold Glove voters?

Of the 366 FA leaders at the various positions between 1957–87 (discounting pitchers and counting only one outfielder per league each year), 118 (32 percent) also won their respective Gold Glove Awards (see Table 1). We can say, then, that if a player leads his league in FA, he has about a one-in-three chance of winning the Gold Glove—not an overwhelming correlation, but about four times better than random chance.

This raises some interesting questions. Since official fielding statistics are not published until months *after* Gold Gloves are voted on, any voter relying on fielding

stats would probably have to consult (or remember) the *previous* year's data. Therefore, if FA itself really does impress voters, we should expect to see many players winning a Gold Glove the year *after* they lead in FA. Do they? Well, no (see Table 2). The percentage here is 25 percent or one-in-four—again, considerably better than chance, but less of a factor than leading in FA in the current year.

And what about the influence of Gold Gloves on fielding averages? Is an official scorer less likely to charge an error against a player simply because he won a Gold Glove the previous year? Apparently not (see Table 3). The percentage of Gold Glove recipients leading in FA the following year is 23 percent.

"It is my belief that a lot more is considered than fielding percentage," said *TSN* editor Tom Barnidge, citing "range, throwing arm, the headiness of the ballplayer." Pete Rose, a two-time Gold Glove winner and later a voter, concurred: "There are a lot of intangibles involved in voting for the Gold Glove. Take an outfielder. The coaches and managers watch these guys all the time. How they play the hitters, how strong their arms are, how often they hit the cutoff man, and all that is taken into consideration—things that do not show up in the statistics."

Another criticism of the Gold Glove is that batting performance plays a role in the selections, contrary to the award's philosophy. As *USA Today* baseball editor Hal Bodley put it, "A player who is outstanding on defense and respectable on offense has a much better chance of getting a Gold Glove than a counterpart whose forte is fielding alone."

Other factors can be distractions to the voters: flashiness, reputations, and the selection process itself. For insight on some of these and their effects, I consulted an expert on the Gold Glove: Wes Parker, a six-time winner of the award at first base.

Parker, it should be noted, would seem to have no reason to gripe about the award. He grasped the honor from a seven-time winner; he won it even when he batted as low as .239; and he became one of only two nonpitchers (Roberto Clemente is the other) to win the award in his final major league season.

"I would say many, if not most, coaches and managers fail to take their voting responsibility seriously," said Parker. "They don't treat it as a vital act. They are usually much more concerned with their team and the pennant race and, as a result, tend to zip through the ballots (distributed in September). So they wind up voting for the most recognizable names."

Parker brought out another rarely discussed procedural problem: "Since players [when they were voting] and coaches are forbidden to vote for anyone on their own team, they often won't vote for the guy who is contending with their team's leading candidate for the same award. That increases their teammate's chances."

On the subject of reputation, Parker asserted that it "has a lot to do with it, absolutely. In 1966, Bill White won the award (for the seventh consecutive time), although even White admitted that I probably deserved it. It takes a couple of years for your reputation to catch up with you, but that can work to your advantage at the end of your career.

"Flashiness is a factor too," continued Parker. "It puts the player's name in the forefront of the voter's minds." Wes also concurred with the theory that a player's bat can be the difference in winning this 'fielding' award.

"[Four-time Gold Glove winner Steve] Garvey is a good example of someone who won it with his bat and notoriety, a perfect example, in fact," opines Parker. "Garvey was vastly overrated defensively . . . he had no range, no arm, and no aggressiveness. He would hold the ball and allow opposing runners to take extra bases to avoid throwing errors. That's how he compiled his high [fielding] averages at first base. Remember, he was a terrible third baseman, worst I ever saw." (In 1972, Garvey's last season as a third-sacker, he led the NL with 28 errors in just 85 games, posting a woeful .902 percentage.)

"Amazingly, despite these prejudices," Parker concluded, "I think the Gold Glove choices have been excellent. At first base I think they have been perfect, with the exception of Garvey."

TABLE 1   Fielding Average Leaders Winning Gold Glove, 1957-87 (Maximum 61 Each Position).

POS.	NL	AL	TOT.	PCT.
C	7	7	14	23
1B	13	13	26	43
2B	14	5	19	31
3B	4	15	19	31
SS	14	12	26	43
OF	6	8	14	23
TOT.	58	60	118	32

TABLE 2   Fielding Average Leaders Winning Gold Glove in Following Season, 1956-86 (Maximum 61 Each Position).

POS.	NL	AL	TOT.	PCT.
C	7	7	14	23
1B	8	11	19	31
2B	9	6	15	25
3B	3	13	16	26
SS	11	9	20	33
OF	2	5	7	11
TOT.	40	51	91	25

TABLE 3   Fielding Average Leaders Who Won Gold Glove in Previous Season, 1958-87 (Maximum 59 Each Position).

POS.	NL	AL	TOT.	PCT.
C	3	7	10	17
1B	11	8	19	32
2B	8	2	10	17
3B	2	12	14	24
SS	10	9	19	32
OF	6	5	11	19
TOT.	40	43	83	23

While the Gold Glove Award has adequately filled the need for a subjective fielding award, there is still something to be said about fielding statistics. It is fashionable to say that fielding stats are meaningless, but, as analyst Bill James said, "If a baseball statistic is meaningless to you, that is simply because you don't know what it means."

With the understanding of which fielding statistics *are* meaningful for each position, it is possible to make a pretty reliable judgment of a player's defensive skills based on stats alone. In recent years, several analysts have attempted to measure individual fielding performance on the basis of numbers.

One newer method is Linear Weights, Pete Palmer's translation of individual batting, pitching, and fielding statistics into runs gained and thus games won. The fielding portion of the system, Fielding or Defensive Wins, incorporates data (variously weighted according to position) on putouts, assists, errors, and double plays, comparing a player's totals against the league averages.

The formula first determines how many runs a player saves (or costs) his team as compared to an "average" player at the same position. Runs are then translated into wins, based on the league average of runs per win. For example, second baseman Glenn Hubbard was computed to have won about three and a half games for the Braves with his glove in 1986, the top Defensive Wins total in the majors.

Of the sixty players identified by the Palmer system as the best fielders in their leagues between 1957-86, twenty-eight also won their respective Gold Glove Awards.

Palmer has drawn criticism for comparing players with average, rather than replacement-level, players; for overemphasizing the double play; and for the use of arbitrary weighting schemes. It is particularly—and admittedly—inadequate in evaluating catchers.

Bill James has also presented a fielding measurement system, Defensive Won/Lost Percentage (DW/L%), although he hasn't used it since 1984. The formula varies from position to position, using four arbitrarily weighted components at each. These components range from readily available statistics (fielding average, assists per game, and so on) to abstruse estimations and calculations, using some data unavailable to the average researcher. The formula is not designed for cross-era comparisons.

The results of these calculations produce the DW/L%, which in turn is translated into defensive wins and losses, based on still more arbitrary assignments of defensive games at each position (ranging from 3 at first base to 11 at shortstop).

Of the thirty-two players identified by DW/L% as the best at their positions and leagues for the 1983-84 seasons, twelve (38 percent) also won their respective Gold Gloves.

The use of a series of arbitrary values is the glaring flaw of DW/L%. Criticism is also due for the complexity and lack of adaptability of the system(s).

The Elias Sports Bureau has demonstrated a simple and generally effective system for evaluating fielders: comparing the number of runs scored per nine innings while a player is on the field to the number scored when he isn't. For example, Elias calculated that the 1982-86 Cardinals averaged allowing 3.85 runs per nine innings with Ozzie Smith at shortstop, as compared to 4.04 per game with other shortstops.

There is nothing new or brilliant about this concept; the difference is that Elias has the data available to make this type of measurement, right down to thirds of an inning, at least since 1975. Since they generally choose not to share this data with the public, however, it is of no value at present.

So, when all is said and done about modern statistical fielding measurements, a subjective measurement—the Gold Glove—is probably still the best tool we have available to rate fielders.

The following pages list the winners of the Gold Glove at each position since 1957. Complete balloting for Gold Glove elections is, unfortunately, neither available nor researchable.

Gold Glove Award

Pitchers

Year	National League	American League
1957	(No selection)	B. Shantz, NY
1958	H. Haddix, CIN	B. Shantz, NY
1959	H. Haddix, PIT	B. Shantz, NY
1960	H. Haddix, PIT	B. Shantz, NY
1961	B. Shantz, PIT	F. Lary, DET
1962	B. Shantz, SL	J. Kaat, MIN
1963	B. Shantz, SL	J. Kaat, MIN
1964	B. Shantz, PHI	J. Kaat, MIN
1965	B. Gibson, SL	J. Kaat, MIN
1966	B. Gibson, SL	J. Kaat, MIN
1967	B. Gibson, SL	J. Kaat, MIN
1968	B. Gibson, SL	J. Kaat, MIN
1969	B. Gibson, SL	J. Kaat, MIN
1970	B. Gibson, SL	J. Kaat, MIN
1971	B. Gibson, SL	J. Kaat, MIN
1972	B. Gibson, SL	J. Kaat, MIN
1973	B. Gibson, SL	J. Kaat, MIN
1974	A. Messersmith, LA	J. Kaat, CHI
1975	A. Messersmith, LA	J. Kaat, CHI
1976	J. Kaat, PHI	J. Palmer, BAL
1977	J. Kaat, PHI	J. Palmer, BAL
1978	P. Niekro, ATL	J. Palmer, BAL
1979	P. Niekro, ATL	J. Palmer, BAL
1980	P. Niekro, ATL	M. Norris, OAK
1981	S. Carlton, PHI	M. Norris, OAK
1982	P. Niekro, ATL	R. Guidry, NY
1983	P. Niekro, ATL	R. Guidry, NY
1984	J. Andujar, SL	R. Guidry, NY
1985	R. Reuschel, PIT	R. Guidry, NY
1986	F. Valenzuela, LA	R. Guidry, NY
1987	R. Reuschel, SF	M. Langston, SEA
1988	O. Hershiser, LA	M. Langston, SEA
1989	R. Darling, NY	B. Saberhagen, KC
1990	G. Maddux, CHI	M. Boddicker, BOS
1991	G. Maddux, CHI	M. Langston, CAL
1992	G. Maddux, CHI	M. Langston, CAL
1993	G. Maddux, CHI	M. Langston, CAL
1994	G. Maddux, ATL	M. Langston, CAL

Catchers

Year	National League	American League
1957	(No selection)	S. Lollar, CHI
1958	D. Crandall, MIL	S. Lollar, CHI
1959	D. Crandall, MIL	S. Lollar, CHI
1960	D. Crandall, MIL	E. Battey, WAS
1961	J. Roseboro, LA	E. Battey, MIN
1962	D. Crandall, MIL	E. Battey, MIN
1963	J. Edwards, CIN	E. Howard, NY
1964	J. Edwards, CIN	E. Howard, NY
1965	J. Torre, MIL	B. Freehan, DET
1966	J. Roseboro, LA	B. Freehan, DET
1967	R. Hundley, CHI	B. Freehan, DET
1968	J. Bench, CIN	B. Freehan, DET
1969	J. Bench, CIN	B. Freehan, DET
1970	J. Bench, CIN	R. Fosse, CLE
1971	J. Bench, CIN	R. Fosse, CLE
1972	J. Bench, CIN	C. Fisk, BOS
1973	J. Bench, CIN	T. Munson, NY
1974	J. Bench, CIN	T. Munson, NY
1975	J. Bench, CIN	T. Munson, NY
1976	J. Bench, CIN	J. Sundberg, TEX
1977	J. Bench, CIN	J. Sundberg, TEX
1978	B. Boone, PHI	J. Sundberg, TEX
1979	B. Boone, PHI	J. Sundberg, TEX
1980	G. Carter, MON	J. Sundberg, TEX
1981	G. Carter, MON	J. Sundberg, TEX
1982	G. Carter, MON	B. Boone, CAL
1983	T. Pena, PIT	Lc. Parrish, DET
1984	T. Pena, PIT	Lc. Parrish, DET
1985	T. Pena, PIT	Lc. Parrish, DET
1986	J. Davis, CHI	B. Boone, CAL
1987	M. LaValliere, PIT	B. Boone, CAL
1988	B. Santiago, SD	B. Boone, CAL
1989	B. Santiago, SD	B. Boone, KC
1990	B. Santiago, SD	S. Alomar, CLE
1991	T. Pagnozzi, SL	T. Pena, BOS
1992	T. Pagnozzi, SL	I. Rodriguez, TEX
1993	K. Manwaring, SF	I. Rodriguez, TEX
1994	T. Pagnozzi, SL	I. Rodriguez, TEX

First Basemen

Year	National League	American League
1957	G. Hodges, BRO	(No selection)
1958	G. Hodges, LA	V. Power, CLE
1959	G. Hodges, LA	V. Power, CLE
1960	B. White, SL	V. Power, CLE
1961	B. White, SL	V. Power, CLE
1962	B. White, SL	V. Power, MIN
1963	B. White, SL	V. Power, MIN
1964	B. White, SL	V. Power, LA
1965	B. White, SL	J. Pepitone, NY
1966	B. White, PHI	J. Pepitone, NY
1967	W. Parker, LA	G. Scott, BOS
1968	W. Parker, LA	G. Scott, BOS
1969	W. Parker, LA	J. Pepitone, NY
1970	W. Parker, LA	J. Spencer, CAL
1971	W. Parker, LA	G. Scott, BOS
1972	W. Parker, LA	G. Scott, MIL
1973	M. Jorgenson, MON	G. Scott, MIL
1974	S. Garvey, LA	G. Scott, MIL
1975	S. Garvey, LA	G. Scott, MIL
1976	S. Garvey, LA	G. Scott, MIL
1977	S. Garvey, LA	J. Spencer, CHI
1978	K. Hernandez, SL	C. Chambliss, NY
1979	K. Hernandez, SL	C. Cooper, MIL
1980	K. Hernandez, SL	C. Cooper, MIL
1981	K. Hernandez, SL	M. Squires, CHI
1982	K. Hernandez, SL	E. Murray, BAL
1983	K. Hernandez, SL-NY	E. Murray, BAL
1984	K. Hernandez, NY	E. Murray, BAL
1985	K. Hernandez, NY	D. Mattingly, NY
1986	K. Hernandez, NY	D. Mattingly, NY
1987	K. Hernandez, NY	D. Mattingly, NY
1988	K. Hernandez, NY	D. Mattingly, NY
1989	A. Galarraga, MON	D. Mattingly, NY
1990	A. Galarraga, MON	M. McGwire, OAK
1991	W. Clark, SF	D. Mattingly, NY
1992	M. Grace, CHI	D. Mattingly, NY
1993	M. Grace, CHI	D. Mattingly, NY
1994	J. Bagwell, HOU	D. Mattingly, NY

Second Basemen

Year	National League	American League
1957	(No selection)	N. Fox, CHI
1958	B. Mazeroski, PIT	F. Bolling, DET
1959	C. Neal, LA	N. Fox, CHI
1960	B. Mazeroski, PIT	N. Fox, CHI
1961	B. Mazeroski, PIT	B. Richardson, NY
1962	K. Hubbs, CHI	B. Richardson, NY
1963	B. Mazeroski, PIT	B. Richardson, NY
1964	B. Mazeroski, PIT	B. Richardson, NY
1965	B. Mazeroski, PIT	B. Richardson, NY
1966	B. Mazeroski, PIT	B. Knoop, CAL
1967	G. Beckert, CHI	B. Knoop, CAL
1968	F. Millan, ATL	B. Knoop, CAL
1969	T. Helms, CIN	D. Johnson, BAL
1970	T. Helms, CIN	D. Johnson, BAL
1971	F. Millan, ATL	D. Johnson, BAL
1972	J. Morgan, CIN	D. Griffin, BOS
1973	J. Morgan, CIN	B. Grich, BAL
1974	J. Morgan, CIN	B. Grich, BAL
1975	J. Morgan, CIN	B. Grich, BAL
1976	J. Morgan, CIN	B. Grich, BAL
1977	J. Morgan, CIN	F. White, KC
1978	D. Lopes, LA	F. White, KC
1979	M. Trillo, PHI	F. White, KC
1980	D. Flynn, NY	F. White, KC
1981	M. Trillo, PHI	F. White, KC
1982	M. Trillo, PHI	F. White, KC
1983	R. Sandberg, CHI	L. Whitaker, DET
1984	R. Sandberg, CHI	L. Whitaker, DET
1985	R. Sandberg, CHI	L. Whitaker, DET
1986	R. Sandberg, CHI	F. White, KC
1987	R. Sandberg, CHI	F. White, KC
1988	R. Sandberg, CHI	H. Reynolds, SEA
1989	R. Sandberg, CHI	H. Reynolds, SEA
1990	R. Sandberg, CHI	H. Reynolds, SEA
1991	R. Sandberg, CHI	R. Alomar, TOR
1992	J. Lind, PIT	R. Alomar, TOR
1993	R. Thompson, SF	R. Alomar, TOR
1994	C. Biggio, HOU	R. Alomar, TOR

Third Basemen

Year	National League	American League
1957	(No selection)	F. Malzone, BOS
1958	K. Boyer, SL	F. Malzone, BOS
1959	K. Boyer, SL	F. Malzone, BOS
1960	K. Boyer, SL	B. Robinson, BAL
1961	K. Boyer, SL	B. Robinson, BAL
1962	J. Davenport, SF	B. Robinson, BAL
1963	K. Boyer, SL	B. Robinson, BAL
1964	R. Santo, CHI	B. Robinson, BAL
1965	R. Santo, CHI	B. Robinson, BAL
1966	R. Santo, CHI	B. Robinson, BAL
1967	R. Santo, CHI	B. Robinson, BAL
1968	R. Santo, CHI	B. Robinson, BAL
1969	C. Boyer, ATL	B. Robinson, BAL
1970	D. Rader, HOU	B. Robinson, BAL
1971	D. Rader, HOU	B. Robinson, BAL
1972	D. Rader, HOU	B. Robinson, BAL
1973	D. Rader, HOU	B. Robinson, BAL
1974	D. Rader, HOU	B. Robinson, BAL
1975	K. Reitz, SL	B. Robinson, BAL
1976	M. Schmidt, PHI	A. Rodriguez, DET
1977	M. Schmidt, PHI	G. Nettles, NY
1978	M. Schmidt, PHI	G. Nettles, NY
1979	M. Schmidt, PHI	B. Bell, TEX
1980	M. Schmidt, PHI	B. Bell, TEX
1981	M. Schmidt, PHI	B. Bell, TEX
1982	M. Schmidt, PHI	B. Bell, TEX
1983	M. Schmidt, PHI	B. Bell, TEX
1984	M. Schmidt, PHI	B. Bell, TEX
1985	T. Wallach, MON	G. Brett, KC
1986	M. Schmidt, PHI	G. Gaetti, MIN
1987	T. Pendleton, SL	G. Gaetti, MIN
1988	T. Wallach, MON	G. Gaetti, MIN
1989	T. Pendleton, SL	G. Gaetti, MIN
1990	T. Wallach, MON	K. Gruber, TOR
1991	M. Williams, SF	R. Ventura, CHI
1992	T. Pendleton, ATL	R. Ventura, CHI
1993	M. Williams, SF	R. Ventura, CHI
1994	M. Williams, SF	W. Boggs, NY

Shortstops

Year	National League	American League
1957	R. McMillan, CIN	(No selection)
1958	R. McMillan, CIN	L. Aparicio, CHI
1959	R. McMillan, CIN	L. Aparicio, CHI
1960	E. Banks, CHI	L. Aparicio, CHI
1961	M. Wills, LA	L. Aparicio, CHI
1962	M. Wills, LA	L. Aparicio, CHI
1963	B. Wine, PHI	Z. Versalles, MIN
1964	R. Amaro, PHI	L. Aparicio, BAL
1965	L. Cardenas, CIN	Z. Versalles, MIN
1966	G. Alley, PIT	L. Aparicio, BAL
1967	G. Alley, PIT	J. Fregosi, CAL
1968	D. Maxvill, SL	L. Aparicio, CHI
1969	D. Kessinger, CHI	M. Belanger, BAL
1970	D. Kessinger, CHI	L. Aparicio, CHI
1971	B. Harrelson, NY	M. Belanger, BAL
1972	L. Bowa, PHI	E. Brinkman, DET
1973	R. Metzger, HOU	M. Belanger, BAL
1974	D. Concepcion, CIN	M. Belanger, BAL
1975	D. Concepcion, CIN	M. Belanger, BAL
1976	D. Concepcion, CIN	M. Belanger, BAL
1977	D. Concepcion, CIN	M. Belanger, BAL
1978	L. Bowa, PHI	M. Belanger, BAL
1979	D. Concepcion, CIN	R. Burleson, BOS
1980	O. Smith, SD	A. Trammell, DET
1981	O. Smith, SD	A. Trammell, DET
1982	O. Smith, SL	R. Yount, MIL
1983	O. Smith, SL	A. Trammell, DET
1984	O. Smith, SL	A. Trammell, DET
1985	O. Smith, SL	A. Griffin, OAK
1986	O. Smith, SL	T. Fernandez, TOR
1987	O. Smith, SL	T. Fernandez, TOR
1988	O. Smith, SL	T. Fernandez, TOR
1989	O. Smith, SL	T. Fernandez, TOR
1990	O. Smith, SL	O. Guillen, CHI
1991	O. Smith, SL	C. Ripken, BAL
1992	O. Smith, SL	C. Ripken, BAL
1993	J. Bell, PIT	O. Vizquel, SEA
1994	B. Larkin, CIN	O. Vizquel, SEA

National League Outfielders

YEAR	PLAYERS		
1957	W. Mays, NY (CF)	(No other selections)	
1958	F. Robinson, CIN (LF)	W. Mays, SF (CF)	H. Aaron, MIL (RF)
1959	J. Brandt, SF (LF)	W. Mays, SF (CF)	H. Aaron, MIL (RF)
1960	W. Moon, LA (LF)	W. Mays, SF (CF)	H. Aaron, MIL (RF)
1961	W. Mays, SF	R. Clemente, PIT	V. Pinson, CIN
1962	W. Mays, SF	R. Clemente, PIT	B. Virdon, PIT
1963	W. Mays, SF	R. Clemente, PIT	C. Flood, SL
1964	W. Mays, SF	R. Clemente, PIT	C. Flood, SL
1965	W. Mays, SF	R. Clemente, PIT	C. Flood, SL
1966	W. Mays, SF	C. Flood, SL	R. Clemente, PIT
1967	R. Clemente, PIT	C. Flood, SL	W. Mays, SF
1968	W. Mays, SF	R. Clemente, PIT	C. Flood, SL
1969	R. Clemente, PIT	C. Flood, SL	P. Rose, CIN
1970	R. Clemente, PIT	T. Agee, NY	P. Rose, CIN
1971	R. Clemente, PIT	B. Bonds, SF	W. Davis, LA
1972	R. Clemente, PIT	C. Cedeno, HOU	W. Davis, LA
1973	B. Bonds, SF	C. Cedeno, HOU	W. Davis, LA
1974	C. Cedeno, HOU	C. Geronimo, CIN	B. Bonds, SF
1975	C. Cedeno, HOU	C. Geronimo, CIN	G. Maddox, PHI
1976	C. Cedeno, HOU	C. Geronimo, CIN	G. Maddox, PHI
1977	C. Geronimo, CIN	G. Maddox, PHI	D. Parker, PIT
1978	G. Maddox, PHI	D. Parker, PIT	E. Valentine, MON
1979	G. Maddox, PHI	D. Parker, PIT	D. Winfield, SD
1980	A. Dawson, MON	G. Maddox, PHI	D. Winfield, SD
1981	A. Dawson, MON	G. Maddox, PHI	D. Baker, LA
1982	A. Dawson, MON	D. Murphy, ATL	G. Maddox, PHI
1983	A. Dawson, MON	D. Murphy, ATL	W. McGee, SL
1984	D. Murphy, ATL	B. Dernier, CHI	A. Dawson, MON
1985	W. McGee, SL	D. Murphy, ATL	A. Dawson, MON
1986	T. Gwynn, SD	D. Murphy, ATL	W. McGee, SL
1987	E. Davis, CIN	T. Gwynn, SD	A. Dawson, CHI
1988	A. Van Slyke, PIT	E. Davis, CIN	A. Dawson, CHI
1989	A. Van Slyke, PIT	E. Davis, CIN	T. Gwynn, SD
1990	A. Van Slyke, PIT	T. Gwynn, SD	B. Bonds, PIT
1991	A. Van Slyke, PIT	T. Gwynn, SD	B. Bonds, PIT
1992	A. Van Slyke, PIT	L. Walker, MON	B. Bonds, PIT
1993	B. Bonds, SF	L. Walker, MON	M. Grissom, MON
1994	B. Bonds, SF	D. Lewis, SF	M. Grissom, MON

American League Outfielders

YEAR	PLAYERS		
1957	M. Minoso, CHI (LF)	A. Kaline, DET (RF)	(No other selection)
1958	N. Siebern, NY (LF)	J. Piersall, BOS (CF)	A. Kaline, DET (RF)
1959	M. Minoso, CLE (LF)	A. Kaline, DET (CF)	J. Jensen, BOS (RF)
1960	M. Minoso, CHI (LF)	J. Landis, CHI (CF)	R. Maris, NY (RF)
1961	A. Kaline, DET	J. Piersall, CLE	J. Landis, CHI
1962	J. Landis, CHI	M. Mantle, NY	A. Kaline, DET
1963	A. Kaline, DET	C. Yastrzemski, BOS	J. Landis, CHI
1964	A. Kaline, DET	J. Landis, CHI	V. Davalillo, CLE
1965	A. Kaline, DET	T. Tresh, NY	C. Yastrzemski, BOS
1966	A. Kaline, DET	T. Agee, CHI	T. Oliva, MIN
1967	C. Yastrzemski, BOS	P. Blair, BAL	A. Kaline, DET
1968	M. Stanley, DET	C. Yastrzemski, BOS	R. Smith, BOS
1969	P. Blair, BAL	M. Stanley, DET	C. Yastrzemski, BOS
1970	M. Stanley, DET	P. Blair, BAL	K. Berry, CHI
1971	P. Blair, BAL	A. Otis, KC	C. Yastrzemski, BOS
1972	P. Blair, BAL	B. Murcer, NY	K. Berry, CAL
1973	P. Blair, BAL	A. Otis, KC	M. Stanley, DET
1974	P. Blair, BAL	A. Otis, KC	J. Rudi, OAK
1975	P. Blair, BAL	J. Rudi, OAK	F. Lynn, BOS
1976	J. Rudi, OAK	Dw. Evans, BOS	R. Manning, CLE
1977	J. Beniquez, TEX	C. Yastrzemski, BOS	A. Cowens, KC
1978	F. Lynn, BOS	Dw. Evans, BOS	R. Miller, CAL
1979	Dw. Evans, BOS	S. Lezcano, MIL	F. Lynn, BOS
1980	F. Lynn, BOS	D. Murphy, OAK	W. Wilson, KC
1981	D. Murphy, OAK	Dw. Evans, BOS	R. Henderson, OAK
1982	Dw. Evans, BOS	D. Winfield, NY	D. Murphy, OAK
1983	Dw. Evans, BOS	D. Winfield, NY	D. Murphy, OAK
1984	Dw. Evans, BOS	D. Winfield, NY	D. Murphy, OAK
1985	G. Pettis, CAL	D. Winfield, NY	Dw. Evans, BOS & D. Murphy, OAK
1986	G. Pettis, CAL	J. Barfield, TOR	K. Puckett, MIN
1987	J. Barfield, TOR	K. Puckett, MIN	D. Winfield, NY
1988	K. Puckett, MIN	D. White, CAL	G. Pettis, DET
1989	D. White, CAL	G. Pettis, DET	K. Puckett, MIN
1990	G. Pettis, TEX	K. Griffey, Jr., SEA	E. Burks, BOS
1991	K. Puckett, MIN	K. Griffey, Jr., SEA	D. White, TOR
1992	K. Puckett, MIN	K. Griffey, Jr., SEA	D. White, TOR
1993	K. Griffey, Jr., SEA	D. White, TOR	K. Lofton, CLE
1994	K. Griffey, Jr., SEA	D. White, TOR	K. Lofton, CLE

Special MVP Awards

The All-Star Game

The All-Star Game MVP Award began in 1962, the last year in which two All-Star Games were played. It was called the Arch Ward Memorial Award, in honor of the late Chicago newspaper writer credited with conceiving the Mid-Summer Classic. In Bowie Kuhn's tenure, 1970-84, the award was called the Commissioner's Trophy.

1962	Maury Wills, LA (NL) [Game 1]	1970	Carl Yastrzemski, BOS (AL)
	Leon Wagner, LA (AL) [Game 2]	1971	Frank Robinson, BAL (AL)
1963	Willie Mays, SF (NL)	1972	Joe Morgan, CIN (NL)
1964	Johnny Callison, PHI	1973	Bobby Bonds, SF (NL)
1965	Juan Marichal, SF	1974	Steve Garvey, LA (NL)
1966	Brooks Robinson, BAL (AL)	1975	Bill Madlock, CHI (NL)
1967	Tony Perez, CIN (NL)		Jon Matlack, NY (NL)
1968	Willie Mays, SF (NL)	1976	George Foster, CIN (NL)
1969	Willie McCovey, SF (NL)	1977	Don Sutton, LA (NL)

League Championship Series

MVP Awards for the League Championship Series were instituted by the National League in 1977, and in the American three years later. A committee of writers and executives in attendance does the voting.

Year	National League	American League
1977	Dusty Baker, LA	
1978	Steve Garvey, LA	
1979	Willie Stargell, PIT	
1980	Manny Trillo, PHI	Frank White, KC
1981	Burt Hooton, LA	Graig Nettles, NY
1982	Darrell Porter, SL	Fred Lynn, CAL
1983	Gary Matthews, PHI	Mike Boddicker, BAL
1984	Steve Garvey, SD	Kirk Gibson, DET
1985	Ozzie Smith, SL	George Brett, KC
1986	Mike Scott, HOU	Marty Barrett, BOS

World Series

There are two major World Series MVP Awards. The New York chapter of the Baseball Writers' Association of America established one in memory of Babe Ruth in 1949, the year after the Bambino's death. Six years later, *Sport* magazine introduced its version, presented in cooperation with the Chevrolet Motor Company (which typically presented a Corvette to the winner).

The winner of the *Sport* award was originally chosen by the magazine's editors, but the voting process eventually went to a committee of sports reporters and officials. The award is now sanctioned by Major League Baseball, and

Year	Babe Ruth Award	Sport Magazine Award
1949	Joe Page, NY (AL)	
1950	Jerry Coleman, NY (AL)	
1951	Phil Rizzuto, NY (AL)	
1952	Johnny Mize, NY (AL)	
1953	Billy Martin, NY (AL)	
1954	Dusty Rhodes, NY (NL)	
1955	Johnny Podres, BRO (NL)	Johnny Podres, BRO (NL)
1956	Don Larsen, NY (AL)	Don Larsen, NY (AL)
1957	Lew Burdette, MIL (NL)	Lew Burdette, MIL (NL)
1958	Elston Howard, NY (AL)	Bob Turley, NY (AL)
1959	Larry Sherry, LA (NL)	Larry Sherry, LA (NL)
1960	Bill Mazeroski, PIT (NL)	Bobby Richardson, NY (AL)
1961	Whitey Ford, NY (AL)	Whitey Ford, NY (AL)
1962	Ralph Terry, NY (AL)	Ralph Terry, NY (AL)
1963	Sandy Koufax, LA (NL)	Sandy Koufax, LA (NL)
1964	Bob Gibson, SL (NL)	Bob Gibson, SL (NL)
1965	Sandy Koufax, LA (NL)	Sandy Koufax, LA (NL)
1966	Frank Robinson, BAL (AL)	Frank Robinson, BAL (AL)
1967	Lou Brock, SL (NL)	Bob Gibson, SL (NL)
1968	Mickey Lolich, DET (AL)	Mickey Lolich, DET (AL)
1969	Al Weis, NY (NL)	Donn Clendenon, NY (NL)
1970	Brooks Robinson, BAL (AL)	Brooks Robinson, BAL (AL)
1971	Roberto Clemente, PIT (NL)	Roberto Clemente, PIT (NL)
1972	Gene Tenace, OAK (AL)	Gene Tenace, OAK (AL)

A committee of writers and executives in attendance votes on the recipient of the game's award. Only twice—Brooks Robinson in 1966 and Carl Yastrzemski in 1970—has a member of the losing team been honored. Two-time winners are Willie Mays, Steve Garvey, and Gary Carter.

Following are the winners of the All-Star Game MVP Awards. Complete voting breakdowns are not available.

1978	Steve Garvey, LA (NL)	1987	Tim Raines, MON (NL)
1979	Dave Parker, PIT (NL)	1988	Terry Steinbach, OAK (AL)
1980	Ken Griffey, CIN (NL)	1989	Bo Jackson, KC (AL)
1981	Gary Carter, MON (NL)	1990	Julio Franco, TEX (AL)
1982	Dave Concepcion, CIN (NL)	1991	Cal Ripken, BAL (AL)
1983	Fred Lynn, CAL (AL)	1992	Ken Griffey, Jr., SEA (AL)
1984	Gary Carter, MON (NL)	1993	Kirby Puckett, MIN (AL)
1985	LaMarr Hoyt, SD (NL)	1994	Fred McGriff, ATL (NL)
1986	Roger Clemens, BOS (AL)		

Steve Garvey and Dave Stewart are the only two-time winners thus far. Winners from losing teams are Fred Lynn (1982), Mike Scott (1986), and Jeffrey Leonard (1987).

Following are the winners of LCS MVP Awards. Complete voting breakdowns are not available.

Year	National League	American League
1987	Jeffrey Leonard, SF	Gary Gaetti, MIN
1988	Orel Hershiser, LA	Dennis Eckersley, OAK
1989	Will Clark, SF	Rickey Henderson, OAK
1990	Rob Dibble, CIN	Dave Stewart, OAK
	Randy Myers, CIN	
1991	Steve Avery, ATL	Kirby Puckett, MIN
1992	John Smoltz, ATL	Roberto Alomar, TOR
1993	Curt Schilling, PHI	Dave Stewart, TOR
1994	(No Series)	(No Series)

has eclipsed the Babe Ruth Award in prestige and public recognition. The *Sport* award is voted on during the final game of the Series and presented immediately following its conclusion, whereas the Ruth Award is voted on during a local chapter meeting some time after the Series.

Following are the winners of the two World Series MVP Awards. Two-time winners of the *Sport* award are Sandy Koufax, Bob Gibson, and Reggie Jackson; double-winners of the Ruth award are Koufax and Jack Morris. Winners from losing teams are Bobby Richardson (*Sport*, 1960), and Luis Tiant (Ruth, 1975). Complete voting breakdowns on either award are not available.

Year	Babe Ruth Award	Sport Magazine Award
1973	Bert Campaneris, OAK (AL)	Reggie Jackson, OAK (AL)
1974	Dick Green, OAK (AL)	Rollie Fingers, OAK (AL)
1975	Luis Tiant, BOS (AL)	Pete Rose, CIN (NL)
1976	Johnny Bench, CIN (NL)	Johnny Bench, CIN (NL)
1977	Reggie Jackson, NY (AL)	Reggie Jackson, NY (AL)
1978	Bucky Dent, NY (AL)	Bucky Dent, NY (AL)
1979	Willie Stargell, PIT (NL)	Willie Stargell, PIT (NL)
1980	Tug McGraw, PHI (NL)	Mike Schmidt, PHI (NL)
1981	Ron Cey, LA (NL)	Ron Cey, LA (NL)
		Pedro Guerrero, LA (NL)
		Steve Yeager, LA (NL)
1982	Bruce Sutter, SL (NL)	Darrell Porter, SL (NL)
1983	Rick Dempsey, BAL (AL)	Rick Dempsey, BAL (AL)
1984	Jack Morris, DET (AL)	Alan Trammell, DET (AL)
1985	Bret Saberhagen, KC (AL)	Bret Saberhagen, KC (AL)
1986	Ray Knight, NY (NL)	Ray Knight, NY (NL)
1987	Frank Viola, MIN (AL)	Frank Viola, MIN (AL)
1988	Orel Hershiser, LA (NL)	Orel Hershiser, LA (NL)
1989	Dave Stewart, OAK (AL)	Dave Stewart, OAK (AL)
1990	Billy Hatcher, CIN (NL)	Jose Rijo, CIN (NL)
1991	Jack Morris, MIN (AL)	Jack Morris, MIN (AL)
1992	Dave Winfield, TOR (AL)	Pat Borders, TOR (AL)
1993	Paul Molitor, TOR (AL)	Paul Molitor, TOR (AL)
1994	(No Series)	(No Series)

Hall of Fame Elections: History

In the 1930s plans were being made to celebrate baseball's 100th anniversary, based on the ill-advised findings of the Mills Commission three decades earlier: "The first scheme for playing baseball, according to the best evidence obtainable to date, was devised by Abner Doubleday at Cooperstown, New York, in 1839." A small-scale baseball museum was established in Cooperstown, and a Centennial Committee composed of six baseball bigwigs ordered the first Hall of Fame election. On January 29, 1936, the results of this election were announced, with five immortals qualifying for enshrinement (although actual induction was delayed until formal opening of the Hall on June 12, 1939).

Actually, there were two elections in 1936: one a poll of 226 members of the Baseball Writers' Association of America (BBWAA), and the other held by a special veterans' committee of 78 designed to choose from among "old-timers." No specific guidelines were set as to who was eligible for consideration (several active players received strong support), nor to which committee would consider whom (resulting in Cy Young's split vote: 49 percent in the writers' election, 41 percent in the veterans'). A 75 percent majority was necessary for election by either committee, a voting feature which survives.

Elections were held by both the BBWAA and an old-timers' committee for each of the next three years, resulting in a total of 26 inductees in 1939. After that, BBWAA elections were scheduled at three-year intervals, with only one player elected in 1942 and none in 1945. A decision was made to hold annual elections beginning in 1946. This continued through 1956, when it was decided to hold elections only every other year. Annual elections were resumed a decade later and continue to this day.

A nominating system was installed after the 1945 election, providing for the top twenty vote-getters in a preliminary balloting to be listed alphabetically on a second and final ballot. The preliminary election's vote totals were not to be divulged until after the final balloting (so as not to influence voters), nor would they assure anyone of automatic election. However, this system proved an utter failure in 1946 and was amended in December of that year. Thereafter, anyone receiving 75 percent of the votes on the nominating ballot would be automatically elected, eliminating the runoff election.

No runoff was required until 1949, when Charlie Gehringer was elected on the second ballot. The nominating system was discontinued after that year but revived from 1960-68 (providing for reconsideration of the top thirty vote-getters), being put into practice in 1964-67.

Currently, an eligible candidate must have played at least ten seasons in the majors and been active at some point during a period beginning twenty years and ending five years before a given election. The five-year wait rule was first implemented in 1954 (excepting candidates who had already received 100 or more votes in a previous election); a one-year wait had been in effect from 1946–53, and no wait was specified before then (due to World War II, it was sometimes unclear who was still "active"). At the other end of the span, the twenty-year rule has been in effect since 1962; the cutoff was thirty years in 1956-62, and twenty-five years in 1946-56.

Following Roberto Clemente's tragic death, a rule was passed in 1973 providing for the immediate consideration of an eligible candidate who dies while still active, or before the five-year waiting period has elapsed. Clemente was inducted overwhelmingly (393 of 424 votes) in a special election held that March. A few months later, the new rule was amended to allow consideration at least six months after a player's death (or five years after his retirement, whichever is less).

The "Pete Rose Rule" was added to the books in February 1991: "Any player on Baseball's ineligible list shall not be an eligible candidate."

Ten-year active and honorary members of the BBWAA are eligible to vote in the annual election (the ten-year restriction was installed in 1947). About 450 writers submit ballots each year, voting for up to ten eligible candidates apiece. At various times over the past three decades, it has been suggested that the enfranchisement be limited to a few dozen of the top baseball writers.

A candidate Screening Committee was first employed in 1968, limiting the ballot to forty candidates. Standards were relaxed somewhat after former pitcher Milt Pappas vociferously objected to his elimination by this committee (Pappas was allowed on the ballot in 1979, receiving 5 of 432 votes). Nomination by two of the six members of the Screening Committee now ensures a candidate at least one try on the BBWAA ballot; however, if he receives less than 5 percent of the vote, he is eliminated from future consideration. (Fortunately for many, this rule has not always been existent; more than seventy current Hall of Famers received less than 5 percent of the vote in their first tries!)

The Baseball Hall of Fame Committee on Baseball Veterans was established in July 1953. Previously, special old-timers' committees had elected new members in 1936–39, 1944–46, and 1949.

The new committee was composed of eleven members. This number was increased to twelve in 1960, eighteen in 1979, and twenty in 1987; then it was reduced to 18 in 1988. Elections were held every other year at first, but have been held annually since 1961.

In most years the committee has been limited to naming no more than two new inductees per election. Exceptions occurred in the elections of 1953 (six), 1963 (four), 1964 (six), 1970 (three), 1971 (seven), and 1972–77 (three each). In a move announced in 1995, two additional slots have been opened for 1995-99, one for pre-1920 players, the other for Negro Leaguers. Voting details are not released to the public.

Individuals considered by the Veterans Committee include managers, umpires, executives, and certain players no longer eligible through the BBWAA (except members of the committee). For eligibility under the former three groups, a person must have been retired five years, or six months if he has reached the age of sixty-five (a rule tailor-made for Casey Stengel's election in 1966). For players, the minimum wait is twenty-three years; previously, it was twenty-five years (1953–56, 1974–84), thirty years (1957–62), or twenty years (1963–73).

On June 10, 1971, a nine-member Baseball Hall of Fame Committee on Negro Baseball Leagues was established. Candidates were to have totaled at least ten years of service in the pre-1946 Negro Leagues and/or the major leagues, without being eligible for BBWAA election. A rule specified that the "Committee shall serve until it shall dissolve itself of its own motion or until further notice from the Board of Directors" of the Hall.

At least one new member was inducted by this committee in each year between 1971 and 1977, after which the committee dissolved and was absorbed into the Veterans Committee. Only two Negro League representatives have been enshrined since 1977.

As far back as 1944, it was suggested that a special "Roll of Honor," distinct from actual Hall of Fame induction, be established for distinguished baseball writers and similar contributors to the baseball world. In 1962 the J. G. Taylor Spink Award was initiated to honor individuals "for meritorious contributions to baseball writing." In 1978 the Ford C. Frick Award was established to dignify broadcasters "for major contributions to the game of Baseball." The awards are presented annually during the Hall of Fame induction ceremonies and the winners' names are engraved on a plaque hanging in the National Baseball Library (explaining references to a writers' or broadcasters' "wing" at the Hall of Fame). Through 1994 there had been forty-six winners of the Spink Award, and eighteen recipients of the Frick trophy. But, contrary to what you hear and read elsewhere, these men are not members of the Hall of Fame.

There have been a total of 220 men inducted into the National Baseball Hall of Fame and Museum through January 1995, including 170 major league players, twenty-one classified as pioneers or executives, eleven Negro Leaguers, eleven managers and seven umpires (many of the latter four groups also played in the majors or minors); eighty-six individuals have been elected by

the BBWAA, 125 by the various veterans committees, and nine by the Negro Leagues Committee.

What follows is, first, a roster of the 220 members of the Hall of Fame named between 1936 and early 1995; second, an index of every man who ever received so much as a single vote for the Hall of Fame, detailing each man's total for each year he received support; and third, the top ten finishers in the voting for each year of balloting since 1936. Men named to the Hall of Fame by special committee action, such as Alexander Cartwright or Josh Gibson, may not have received votes in an election, but they are included in this index as well. (There have been four such committee groupings: the Centennial Commission of 1937–1938, the Old Timers' Committee of 1939–1949, the Veterans Committee of 1953–present, and the Negro Leagues Committee of 1971–1977.)

Of special interest are some prominent players who were not elected or named to the Hall: Gil Hodges, who received the most votes for the Hall of Fame but remains outside it; Herman Long, who finished among the top ten vote-getters in the Veterans Ballot of 1936, which during later years produced twenty-nine future Hall of Famers; Hank Gowdy, who in the 1950s experienced a fate similar to Long's; and Marty Marion and Allie Reynolds, other long-term vote-getters who were not able to bunch their support in a given year. And don't get White Sox fans talking about Nellie Fox and the election of 1985, when, in his final year of eligibility for the Baseball Writers Election, Fox fell only two votes short of the 297 that would have granted him enshrinement—the closest any man has ever come without making it.

The Hall of Fame balloting results were researched and compiled by Pete Palmer.

Hall of Fame Roster

FIRST BASEMEN
Anson, Cap
Beckley, Jake
Bottomley, Jim
Brouthers, Dan
Chance, Frank
Connor, Roger
Foxx, Jimmie
Gehrig, Lou
Greenberg, Hank
Kelly, George
Killebrew, Harmon
McCovey, Willie
Mize, Johnny
Sisler, George
Terry, Bill

SECOND BASEMEN
Carew, Rod
Collins, Eddie
Doerr, Bobby
Evers, Johnny
Frisch, Frankie
Gehringer, Charlie
Herman, Billy
Hornsby, Rogers
Lajoie, Nap
Lazzeri, Tony
Morgan, Joe
Robinson, Jackie
Schoendienst, Red

SHORTSTOPS
Aparicio, Luis
Appling, Luke
Bancroft, Dave
Banks, Ernie
Boudreau, Lou
Cronin, Joe
Jackson, Travis
Jennings, Hugh
Maranville, Rabbit

Reese, Pee Wee
Rizzuto, Phil
Sewell, Joe
Tinker, Joe
Vaughan, Arky
Wagner, Honus
Wallace, Bobby
Ward, Monte

THIRD BASEMEN
Baker, Frank
Collins, Jimmy
Kell, George
Lindstrom, Fred
Mathews, Eddie
Robinson, Brooks
Schmidt, Mike
Traynor, Pie

LEFT FIELDERS
Brock, Lou
Burkett, Jesse
Clarke, Fred
Delahanty, Ed
Goslin, Goose
Hafey, Chick
Kelley, Joe
Kiner, Ralph
Manush, Heinie
Medwick, Joe
Musial, Stan
O'Rourke, Jim
Simmons, Al
Stargell, Willie
Wheat, Zack
Williams, Billy
Williams, Ted
Yastrzemski, Carl

CENTER FIELDERS
Averill, Earl

Carey, Max
Cobb, Ty
Combs, Earle
DiMaggio, Joe
Duffy, Hugh
Hamilton, Billy
Mantle, Mickey
Mays, Willie
Roush, Edd
Snider, Duke
Speaker, Tris
Waner, Lloyd
Wilson, Hack

RIGHT FIELDERS
Aaron, Hank
Clemente, Roberto
Crawford, Sam
Cuyler, Kiki
Flick, Elmer
Heilmann, Harry
Hooper, Harry
Kaline, Al
Keeler, Willie
Kelly, King
Klein, Chuck
McCarthy, Tommy
Ott, Mel
Rice, Sam
Robinson, Frank
Ruth, Babe
Slaughter, Enos
Thompson, Sam
Waner, Paul
Youngs, Ross

CATCHERS
Bench, Johnny
Berra, Yogi
Bresnahan, Roger
Campanella, Roy

Cochrane, Mickey
Dickey, Bill
Ewing, Buck
Ferrell, Rick
Hartnett, Gabby
Lombardi, Ernie
Schalk, Ray

PITCHERS
Alexander, Grover
Bender, Chief
Brown, Mordecai
Carlton, Steve
Chesbro, Jack
Clarkson, John
Coveleski, Stan
Dean, Dizzy
Drysdale, Don
Faber, Red
Feller, Bob
Fingers, Rollie
Ford, Whitey
Galvin, Pud
Gibson, Bob
Gomez, Lefty
Grimes, Burleigh
Grove, Lefty
Haines, Jess
Hoyt, Waite
Hubbell, Carl
Hunter, Catfish
Jenkins, Fergie
Johnson, Walter
Joss, Addie
Keefe, Tim
Koufax, Sandy
Lemon, Bob
Lyons, Ted
Marichal, Juan
Marquard, Rube
Mathewson, Christy

McGinnity, Joe
Newhouser, Hal
Nichols, Kid
Palmer, Jim
Pennock, Herb
Perry, Gaylord
Plank, Eddie
Radbourn, Charles
Rixey, Eppa
Roberts, Robin
Ruffing, Red
Rusie, Amos
Seaver, Tom
Spahn, Warren
Vance, Dazzy
Waddell, Rube
Walsh, Ed
Welch, Mickey
Wilhelm, Hoyt
Wynn, Early
Young, Cy

FROM NEGRO LEAGUES
Bell, Cool Papa
Charleston, Oscar
Dandridge, Ray
Dihigo, Martin
Foster, Rube
Gibson, Josh
Irvin, Monte
Johnson, Judy
Leonard, Buck
Lloyd, John
Paige, Satchel

MANAGERS
Alston, Walter
Durocher, Leo
Harris, Bucky
Huggins, Miller

Lopez, Al
Mack, Connie
McCarthy, Joe
McGraw, John
McKechnie, Bill
Robinson, Wilbert
Stengel, Casey

UMPIRES
Barlick, Al
Conlan, Jocko
Connolly, Tom
Evans, Billy
Hubbard, Cal
Klem, Bill
McGowan, Bill

PIONEERS AND EXECUTIVES
Barrow, Ed
Bulkeley, Morgan
Cartwright, Alexander
Chadwick, Henry
Chandler, Albert
Comiskey, Charles
Cummings, Candy
Frick, Ford
Giles, Warren
Griffith, Clark
Harridge, Will
Johnson, Ban
Landis, Kenesaw
MacPhail, Larry
Rickey, Branch
Spalding, Al
Veeck, Bill
Weiss, George
Wright, George
Wright, Harry
Yawkey, Tom

Hall of Fame Balloting: Vote Totals of All Candidates

Hank Aaron
Inducted in 1982
1982 406

Babe Adams
1937 8
1938 11
1939 11
1942 11
1945 7
1946 NOM 6
1947 22
1948 4
1949 5
1950 6
1951 12
1952 9
1953 17
1954 13
1955 24

Sparky Adams
1958 1
1960 1

Bobby Adams
1966 1

Pete Alexander
Inducted in 1938
1936 55
1937 125
1938 212

Dick Allen
1983 14
1985 28
1986 41
1987 55
1988 52
1989 35
1990 58
1991 59
1992 69
1993 70
1994 66
1995 72

Johnny Allen
1955 1

Doug Allison
1936 V 1

Felipe Alou
1980 3

Jesus Alou
1985 1

Matty Alou
1980 5

Walt Alston
Inducted in 1983
Manager
1983 .... Vet. Com.

Nick Altrock
1937 3
1938 7
1939 6
1953 1
1954 2
1958 20
1960 18

Cap Anson
Inducted in 1939
1936 V 40
1939 .... O/T Com.

Luis Aparicio
Inducted in 1984
1979 120

1980 124
1981 48
1982 174
1983 252
1984 341

Luke Appling
Inducted in 1964
1953 2
1955 3
1956 14
1958 77
1960 72
1962 48
1964 142
1964 RO 189

Jimmy Archer
1937 6
1938 7
1939 3

Richie Ashburn
1968 6
1969 10
1970 11
1971 10
1972 11
1973 25
1974 56
1975 76
1976 85
1977 139
1978 158
1979 130
1980 134
1981 142
1982 126

Jimmy Austin
1958 1

Earl Averill
Inducted in 1975
1949 1
1952 2
1955 2
1956 3
1958 14
1960 11
1962 3
1975 .... Vet. Com.

Bob Bailey
1984 1

Dusty Baker
1992 4

Frank Baker
Inducted in 1955
1936 1
1937 13
1938 32
1939 30
1942 39
1945 26
1946 NOM 39
1946 36
1947 49
1948 4
1950 4
1951 8
1955 .... Vet. Com.

Dave Bancroft
Inducted in 1971
1937 3
1938 2
1939 1
1946 NOM 1
1948 4
1949 5
1950 9
1951 9
1952 11
1953 10
1954 10

1955 19
1956 15
1958 43
1960 30
1971 .... Vet. Com.

Sal Bando
1987 3

Ernie Banks
Inducted in 1977
1977 321

Al Barlick
Inducted in 1989
Umpire
1989 .... Vet. Com.

Ross Barnes
1936 V 3

Ed Barrow
Inducted in 1953
Executive
1953 .... Vet. Com.

Jack Barry
1938 3
1939 1

Dick Bartell
1948 1
1951 1
1958 1
1960 1

Joe Battin
1936 V 1

Don Baylor
1994 12
1995 12

Hank Bauer
1967 23
1967 RO 9

Ginger Beaumont
1938 1
1942 1
1945 1
1946 NOM 1

Glenn Beckert
1981 1

Jake Beckley
Inducted in 1971
1936 V 1
1942 1
1971 .... Vet. Com.

Mark Belanger
1988 16

Buddy Bell
1995 8

Cool Papa Bell
Inducted in 1974
1974 .... Neg. Com.

Johnny Bench
Inducted in 1989
1989 431

Chief Bender
Inducted in 1953
1936 2
1937 17
1938 33
1939 40
1942 55
1945 40

1946 NOM 39
1946 35
1947 72
1948 5
1949 2
1950 6
1951 35
1952 70
1953 104
1953 .... Vet. Com.

Charlie Bennett
1936 V 3

Larry Benton
1958 1

Moe Berg
1958 3
1960 5

Marty Bergen
1937 2
1938 1
1939 1

Wally Berger
1956 1
1958 2

Yogi Berra
Inducted in 1972
1971 242
1972 339

Charlie Berry
1955 1
1958 3

Jim Bibby
1990 1

Carson Bigbee
1948 1

Jack Billingham
1986 1

Max Bishop
1955 1
1956 1
1958 4
1960 5

Ewell Blackwell
1968 5
1969 11
1970 14

Ray Blades
1958 1
1960 1

Paul Blair
1986 8

Steve Blass
1980 2

Lu Blue
1954 1

Vida Blue
1992 23
1993 37
1994 14
1995 26

Ossie Bluege
1948 2
1949 1
1954 1
1956 2
1958 1

1960 3

Ping Bodie
1937 2
1949 1

Joe Boley
1942 1

Tommy Bond
1936 V 1

Bobby Bonds
1987 24
1988 27
1989 29
1990 30
1991 39
1992 40
1993 45
1994 37
1995 35

Jim Bottomley
Inducted in 1974
1948 4
1949 8
1950 8
1951 6
1952 7
1953 10
1954 16
1955 26
1956 42
1958 57
1960 89
1962 20
1974 .... Vet. Com.

Lou Boudreau
Inducted in 1970
1956 2
1958 64
1960 35
1962 12
1964 68
1964 RO 43
1966 115
1967 143
1967 RO 68
1968 146
1969 218
1970 232

Jim Bouton
1984 3

Larry Bowa
1991 11

Clete Boyer
1978 1
1979 3

Ken Boyer
1975 9
1976 15
1977 14
1978 18
1979 20
1985 68
1986 95
1987 96
1988 109
1989 62
1990 78
1991 58
1992 71
1993 69
1994 56

Bill Bradley
1936 1
1937 5
1938 1
1939 1
1942 1

1946 NOM 1

Harry Brecheen
1960 7
1968 3
1969 2
1970 3
1971 7
1972 5
1973 3

Ted Breitenstein
1937 1

Roger Bresnahan
Inducted in 1945
1936 47
1937 43
1938 67
1939 67
1942 57
1945 133
1945 .... O/T Com.

Jim Brewer
1982 2

Tommy Bridges
1956 3
1958 11
1960 4
1962 1
1964 15
1964 RO 1
1966 16

Lou Brock
Inducted in 1985
1985 315

Dan Brouthers
Inducted in 1945
1936 V 2
1945 .... O/T Com.

Gates Brown
1981 1

Mordecai Brown
Inducted in 1949
1936 6
1937 31
1938 54
1939 54
1942 63
1945 46
1946 NOM 56
1946 48
1949 .... O/T Com.

Bill Bruton
1971 1

Morgan Bulkeley
Inducted in 1937
Executive
1937 .... Cen. Com.

Jim Bunning
1977 146
1978 181
1979 147
1980 177
1981 164
1982 138
1983 138
1984 201
1985 214
1986 279
1987 289
1988 317
1989 283
1990 257
1991 282

Lew Burdette
1973 12
1974 7
1975 11
1976 21
1977 85
1978 76
1979 53
1980 66
1981 48
1982 43
1983 43
1984 97
1985 82
1986 96
1987 96

Smoky Burgess
1973 1
1974 2

Jesse Burkett
Inducted in 1946
1936 V 1
1937 1
1938 2
1942 4
1945 2
1946 NOM 2
1946 .... O/T Com.

George J. Burns
1937 3
1938 3
1939 1
1949 1
1950 2

Jeff Burroughs
1991 1

Guy Bush
1956 2

Joe Bush
1958 5

Donie Bush
1937 1
1939 2
1942 2
1945 1
1946 NOM 2
1953 1

Leon Cadore
1948 1

Johnny Callison
1979 1

Dolf Camilli
1948 1
1956 1
1958 4
1960 3

Howie Camnitz
1945 1

Roy Campanella
Inducted in 1969
1964 115
1964 RO 138
1966 197
1967 204
1967 RO 170
1968 205
1969 270

Bert Campaneris
1989 14

Bill Campbell
1993 1

Jose Cardenal
1986 1

Leo Cardenas
1981 1
1982 1

Rod Carew
Inducted in 1991
1991 401

Max Carey
Inducted in 1961
1937 6
1938 6
1939 7
1945 1
1948 9
1949 12
1950 14
1951 27
1952 36
1953 55
1954 55
1955 119
1956 65
1958 136
1961 .... Vet. Com.

Steve Carlton
Inducted in 1994
1994 436

Chico Carrasquel
1966 1

Bill Carrigan
1937 5
1938 4
1939 2
1945 3

Clay Carroll
1984 1

Rico Carty
1985 1

Alex Cartwright
Inducted in 1938
Pioneer
1938 .... Cen. Com.

George Case
1958 1
1960 1
1962 1
1964 2

Dave Cash
1986 2

Norm Cash
1980 6

Phil Cavaretta
1962 2
1964 22
1964 RO 1
1966 9
1967 15
1967 RO 4
1968 23
1969 37
1970 51
1971 83
1972 61
1973 73
1974 61
1975 129

Cesar Cedeno
1992 2

Orlando Cepeda
1980 48
1981 77
1982 42
1983 59
1984 124
1985 114

1986 152
1987 179
1988 199
1989 176
1990 211
1991 192
1992 246
1993 252
1994 335

Ron Cey
1993 8

Henry Chadwick
Inducted in 1938
Pioneer
1938 .... Cen. Com.

Frank Chance
Inducted in 1946
1936 5
1937 49
1938 133
1939 158
1942 136
1945 179
1946 NOM 144
1946 150
1946 .... O/T Com.

Happy Chandler
Inducted in 1982
Executive
1982 .... Vet. Com.

Spud Chandler
1950 2
1951 1
1956 1
1962 2
1964 6

Ben Chapman
1949 1
1952 1

Ray Chapman
1938 1

Sam Chapman
1958 1

Oscar Charleston
Inducted in 1976
1976 .... Neg. Com.

Hal Chase
1936 11
1937 18

Jack Chesbro
Inducted in 1946
1937 1
1938 2
1939 6
1946 NOM 1
1946 .... O/T Com.

Bill Cissell
1937 1

Watty Clark
1958 1

Fred Clarke
Inducted in 1945
1936 V 9
1936 1
1937 22
1938 63
1939 59
1942 58
1945 53
1945 .... O/T Com.

John Clarkson
Inducted in 1963
1936 V 5

1946 NOM 1
1963 .... Vet. Com.

Roberto Clemente
Inducted in 1973
1973 .... Spec. El.

Andy Coakley
1938 1

Ty Cobb
Inducted in 1936
1936 222

Mickey Cochrane
Inducted in 1947
1936 80
1939 28
1942 88
1945 125
1946 NOM 80
1946 65
1947 128

Rocky Colavito
1974 2
1975 1

Eddie Collins
Inducted in 1939
1936 60
1937 115
1938 175
1939 213

Jimmy Collins
Inducted in 1945
1936 V 8
1936 58
1937 66
1938 79
1939 72
1942 68
1945 121
1945 .... O/T Com.

Shano Collins
1937 1

Earle Combs
Inducted in 1970
1937 4
1938 7
1939 3
1945 1
1948 6
1949 6
1950 3
1952 1
1953 3
1955 1
1956 14
1958 34
1960 43
1962 6
1970 .... Vet. Com.

Charlie Comiskey
Inducted in 1939
Executive
1936 V 6
1939 .... O/T Com.

Dave Concepcion
1994 31
1995 43

Jocko Conlan
Inducted in 1974
Umpire
1974 .... Vet. Com.

Tommy Connolly
Inducted in 1953
Umpire
1953 .... Vet. Com.

Roger Connor
Inducted in 1976
1976 .... Vet. Com.

Wid Conroy
1945 1

Jack Coombs
1937 2
1938 2
1946 NOM 2
1948 2
1951 1

Mort Cooper
1956 2
1958 3
1960 1
1969 3

Walker Cooper
1968 8
1969 5
1970 9
1971 7
1972 8
1973 8
1974 9
1975 13
1976 56
1977 45

Wilbur Cooper
1938 1
1939 1
1948 2
1949 4
1951 1
1952 2
1953 9
1954 7
1955 11

Clint Courtney
1967 1

Stan Coveleski
Inducted in 1969
1938 1
1948 2
1949 3
1950 1
1958 34
1969 .... Vet. Com.

Billy Cox
1962 1

Doc Cramer
1956 4
1958 2
1960 1
1962 1
1964 12

Del Crandall
1976 15
1977 8
1978 6
1979 9

Doc Crandall
1938 1

Gavvy Cravath
1937 2
1938 2
1939 2
1946 NOM 1
1947 2

Sam Crawford
Inducted in 1957
1936 1
1937 5
1938 11
1939 6
1942 2
1945 4

1946 NOM 9
1957 .... Vet. Com.

Lou Criger
1936 V 1
1936 7
1937 16
1938 11
1939 2
1946 NOM 6

Hughie Critz
1956 2

Joe Cronin
Inducted in 1956
1947 6
1948 25
1949 33
1949 RO 16
1950 33
1951 44
1952 48
1953 69
1954 85
1955 135
1956 152

Frank Crosetti
1950 1
1952 1
1956 1
1958 5
1960 8
1968 15

Lave Cross
1939 1
1942 1

Al Crowder
1958 1
1960 1

Walt Cruise
1938 1

Jose Cruz
1994 2

Tony Cuccinello
1956 1
1958 3

Candy Cummings
Inducted in 1939
Pioneer
1939 .... O/T Com.

Kiki Cuyler
Inducted in 1968
1948 3
1949 4
1950 11
1951 8
1952 10
1953 18
1954 20
1955 35
1956 55
1958 90
1960 72
1962 31
1968 .... Vet. Com.

Bill Dahlen
1936 V 1
1938 1

Ray Dandridge
Inducted in 1987
1987 .... Vet. Com.

Harry Danning
1958 1
1960 1

Alvin Dark

1966	17
1967	38
1967 RO	7
1968	36
1969	48
1970	55
1971	54
1972	55
1973	53
1974	54
1975	48
1976	62
1977	66
1978	60
1979	80
1980	43

Jake Daubert

1936 V	1
1937	2
1938	1
1939	1
1951	1
1955	1

Curt Davis

1958	1

Harry Davis

1945	1
1946 NOM	2

Tommy Davis

1982	5

Spud Davis

1948	1
1949	1

Dizzy Dean
Inducted in 1953

1945	17
1946 NOM	40
1946	45
1947	88
1948	40
1949	88
1949 RO	81
1950	85
1951	145
1952	152
1953	209

Doug DeCinces

1993	2

Ed Delahanty
Inducted in 1945

1936 V	22
1936	17
1937	70
1938	132
1939	145
1942	104
1945	111
1945	O/T Com.

Jerry Denny

1936 V	6

Bucky Dent

1990	3

Paul Derringer

1948	1
1950	1
1951	1
1955	1
1956	12
1958	15
1960	8

Bill Dickey
Inducted in 1954

1945	17
1946 NOM	40
1946	32
1948	39

1949	65
1949 RO	39
1950	78
1951	118
1952	139
1953	179
1954	202

Martin Dihigo
Inducted in 1977

1977	Neg. Com.

Dom DiMaggio

1960	4
1962	2
1964	12
1968	8
1969	13
1970	15
1971	15
1972	36
1973	43

Joe DiMaggio
Inducted in 1955

1945	1
1953	117
1954	175
1955	223

Bill Dinneen

1938	4
1939	7
1942	1
1945	1
1946 NOM	1

Bill Doak

1958	3

Larry Doby

1966	7
1967	10
1967 RO	1

Bobby Doerr
Inducted in 1986

1953	2
1956	5
1958	25
1960	15
1962	10
1964	24
1964 RO	5
1966	30
1967	35
1967 RO	15
1968	48
1969	62
1970	75
1971	78
1986	Vet. Com.

Mike Donlin

1937	6
1938	5
1939	5
1945	1

Bill Donovan

1937	3
1938	1
1939	2
1945	1
1946 NOM	4

Red Dooin

1937	1
1938	1

Jack Doyle

1936 V	1

Larry Doyle

1937	2
1938	4
1939	1

Walt Dropo

1967	1

Don Drysdale
Inducted in 1984

1975	76
1976	114
1977	197
1978	219
1979	233
1980	238
1981	243
1982	233
1983	242
1984	316

Hugh Duffy
Inducted in 1945

1936 V	4
1937	7
1938	24
1939	34
1942	77
1945	64
1945	O/T Com.

Joe Dugan

1937	1
1938	1
1948	3
1949	2
1956	1
1958	5
1960	8

Fred Dunlap

1936 V	2

Jack Dunn

1942	1
1945	1
1946 NOM	1

Leo Durocher
Inducted in 1994
Manager

1948	1
1949	1
1952	1
1956	1
1958	28
1960	10
1962	1
1964	15
1964 RO	2
1994	Vet. Com.

Eddie Dyer

1947	1

Jimmy Dykes

1948	5
1949	7
1950	2
1951	3
1952	5
1953	5
1955	1
1956	1
1958	26
1960	27
1962	6

George Earnshaw

1948	3
1949	2
1950	2
1955	2
1956	3

Hank Edwards

1960	2

Howard Ehmke

1938	1
1949	1
1951	1
1952	1
1953	3
1954	4

1955	8
1956	8
1958	7
1960	12

Kid Elberfeld

1936	1
1937	1
1938	2
1942	1
1945	2

Jumbo Elliott

1958	1

Bob Elliott

1960	2
1962	1
1964	4

Dock Ellis

1985	1

Del Ennis

1966	3
1967	2

Jewel Ens

1950	1

Carl Erskine

1966	6
1968	9
1969	4
1970	2
1971	3
1972	4
1973	4
1974	11

Billy Evans
Inducted in 1973
Umpire

1973	Vet. Com.

Darrell Evans

1995	8

Johnny Evers
Inducted in 1946

1936	6
1937	44
1938	91
1939	107
1942	91
1945	134
1946 NOM	130
1946	110
1946	O/T Com.

Buck Ewing
Inducted in 1939

1936 V	40
1939	2
1939	O/T Com.

Red Faber
Inducted in 1964

1937	3
1938	1
1939	1
1942	1
1948	3
1949	6
1950	9
1951	8
1952	9
1953	9
1954	12
1955	27
1956	34
1958	68
1960	83
1962	30
1964	Vet. Com.

Elroy Face

1976	23
1977	33

1978	27
1979	35
1980	21
1981	23
1982	22
1983	32
1984	65
1985	62
1986	74
1987	78
1988	79
1989	47
1990	50

Ron Fairly

1985	3

Cy Falkenberg

1937	1

Bob Feller
Inducted in 1962

1962	150

Rick Ferrell
Inducted in 1984

1956	1
1958	1
1960	1
1984	Vet. Com.

Wes Ferrell

1948	1
1949	1
1956	7
1960	8
1962	1

Rollie Fingers
Inducted in 1992

1991	291
1992	349

Fred Fitzsimmons

1948	2
1949	2
1950	1
1956	3
1958	16
1960	13
1962	1

Art Fletcher

1937	2
1938	3
1939	1
1947	3
1948	3
1949	1
1950	1
1951	4

Elmer Flick
Inducted in 1963

1938	1
1963	Vet. Com.

Curt Flood

1977	16
1978	8
1979	14
1985	28
1986	45
1987	50
1988	48
1989	27
1990	35
1991	23
1992	42
1993	36
1994	40
1995	59

Lew Fonseca

1948	1
1950	2
1956	2
1958	3
1960	3

Whitey Ford
Inducted in 1974

1973	255
1974	284

Bob Forsch

1995	2

Eddie Foster

1938	2

George Foster

1992	24
1993	29
1994	16
1995	19

Rube Foster
Inducted in 1981
Manager

1981	Vet. Com.

Nellie Fox

1971	39
1972	64
1973	73
1974	79
1975	76
1976	174
1977	152
1978	149
1979	174
1980	161
1981	168
1982	127
1983	173
1984	246
1985	295

Jimmie Foxx
Inducted in 1951

1936	21
1946 NOM	26
1947	10
1948	50
1949	85
1949 RO	89
1950	103
1951	179

Chick Fraser

1939	1

Bill Freehan

1982	2

Jim Fregosi

1984	4

Ford Frick
Inducted in 1970
Executive

1970	Vet. Com.

Frankie Frisch
Inducted in 1947

1936	14
1939	26
1942	84
1945	101
1946 NOM	104
1946	67
1947	136

Carl Furillo

1966	2
1967	2
1970	2
1971	5
1972	2

Augie Galan

1968	2
1970	3

Jim Galvin
Inducted in 1965

1965	Vet. Com.

Phil Garner
1994 ... 2

Ned Garver
1967 ... 1

Steve Garvey
1993 ... 176
1994 ... 166
1995 ... 196

Lou Gehrig
Inducted in 1939
1936 ... 51
1939 ... Spec. El.

Charlie Gehringer
Inducted in 1949
1945 ... 10
1946 NOM ... 43
1946 ... 23
1947 ... 105
1948 ... 52
1949 ... 102
1949 RO ... 159

Charlie Gelbert
1947 ... 1
1949 ... 2
1950 ... 1
1951 ... 1

Josh Gibson
Inducted in 1972
1972 ... Neg. Com.

Bob Gibson
Inducted in 1981
1981 ... 337

Warren Giles
Inducted in 1979
Executive
1979 ... Vet. Com.

Dave Giusti
1983 ... 1

Jack Glasscock
1936 V ... 2

Kid Gleason
1937 ... 1
1938 ... 1
1939 ... 1
1945 ... 1

Lefty Gomez
Inducted in 1972
1945 ... 7
1946 NOM ... 4
1947 ... 1
1948 ... 16
1949 ... 17
1950 ... 18
1951 ... 23
1952 ... 29
1953 ... 35
1954 ... 38
1955 ... 71
1956 ... 89
1958 ... 76
1960 ... 51
1962 ... 20
1972 ... Vet. Com.

Mike Gonzales
1950 ... 1
1952 ... 1
1953 ... 1
1958 ... 3
1960 ... 2

Joe Gordon
1945 ... 1
1955 ... 1
1956 ... 4
1958 ... 11
1960 ... 11
1962 ... 4
1964 ... 30
1964 RO ... 1
1966 ... 31
1967 ... 66
1967 RO ... 13
1968 ... 77
1969 ... 97
1970 ... 79

Goose Goslin
Inducted in 1968
1948 ... 1
1949 ... 4
1950 ... 2
1954 ... 1
1955 ... 7
1956 ... 26
1958 ... 26
1960 ... 30
1962 ... 14
1968 ... Vet. Com.

Hank Gowdy
1937 ... 2
1938 ... 8
1939 ... 4
1942 ... 8
1945 ... 3
1947 ... 1
1948 ... 3
1949 ... 10
1950 ... 6
1951 ... 26
1952 ... 34
1953 ... 58
1954 ... 51
1955 ... 90
1956 ... 49
1958 ... 45
1960 ... 38

Eddie Grant
1938 ... 1
1939 ... 2
1942 ... 3
1945 ... 2
1946 NOM ... 1

George Grantham
1958 ... 1

Hank Greenberg
Inducted in 1956
1945 ... 3
1949 ... 67
1949 RO ... 44
1950 ... 64
1951 ... 67
1952 ... 75
1953 ... 80
1954 ... 97
1955 ... 157
1956 ... 164

Bobby Grich
1992 ... 11

Clark Griffith
Inducted in 1946
Executive
1937 ... 4
1938 ... 10
1939 ... 20
1942 ... 71
1945 ... 108
1946 NOM ... 73
1946 ... 82
1946 ... O/T Com.

Burleigh Grimes
Inducted in 1964
1937 ... 1
1938 ... 1
1939 ... 1
1948 ... 7
1949 ... 8
1950 ... 6
1951 ... 5
1952 ... 9
1953 ... 9
1955 ... 3
1956 ... 25
1958 ... 71
1960 ... 92
1962 ... 43
1964 ... Vet. Com.

Charlie Grimm
1939 ... 1
1945 ... 1
1946 NOM ... 1
1948 ... 6
1949 ... 10
1950 ... 13
1951 ... 9
1952 ... 6
1953 ... 9
1958 ... 26
1960 ... 13
1962 ... 2

Marv Grissom
1966 ... 2

Dick Groat
1973 ... 7
1974 ... 4
1975 ... 4
1976 ... 7
1977 ... 4
1978 ... 3

Heinie Groh
1937 ... 1
1938 ... 3
1945 ... 1
1948 ... 1
1950 ... 2
1954 ... 1
1955 ... 5
1960 ... 1

Steve Gromek
1964 ... 1

Orval Grove
1958 ... 5
1960 ... 7

Lefty Grove
Inducted in 1947
1936 ... 12
1945 ... 28
1946 NOM ... 71
1946 ... 61
1947 ... 123

Ron Guidry
1994 ... 24
1995 ... 25

Frank Gustine
1958 ... 3

Mule Haas
1955 ... 1
1956 ... 1
1958 ... 1
1960 ... 1

Stan Hack
1948 ... 2
1949 ... 4
1950 ... 8
1951 ... 3
1956 ... 1
1958 ... 6
1960 ... 6

Harvey Haddix
1971 ... 10
1972 ... 9
1973 ... 1
1974 ... 8
1975 ... 8
1976 ... 8
1977 ... 7
1978 ... 7
1979 ... 7
1985 ... 15

Chick Hafey
Inducted in 1971
1948 ... 1
1949 ... 2
1950 ... 4
1951 ... 1
1952 ... 1
1953 ... 2
1954 ... 2
1955 ... 4
1956 ... 16
1958 ... 12
1960 ... 29
1962 ... 2
1971 ... Vet. Com.

Noodles Hahn
1939 ... 1

Jesse Haines
Inducted in 1970
1939 ... 1
1947 ... 1
1948 ... 2
1949 ... 2
1950 ... 11
1953 ... 4
1954 ... 6
1955 ... 10
1956 ... 14
1958 ... 22
1960 ... 20
1962 ... 3
1970 ... Vet. Com.

Bill Hallahan
1948 ... 1
1956 ... 1
1958 ... 1
1960 ... 2

Billy Hamilton
Inducted in 1961
1936 V ... 2
1942 ... 1
1961 ... Vet. Com.

Mel Harder
1949 ... 4
1950 ... 2
1951 ... 1
1952 ... 10
1953 ... 8
1958 ... 6
1960 ... 12
1962 ... 7
1964 ... 51
1964 RO ... 14
1966 ... 34
1967 ... 52
1967 RO ... 14

Bubbles Hargrave
1947 ... 1
1958 ... 1
1960 ... 1

Mike Hargrove
1991 ... 1

Toby Harrah
1992 ... 1

Bud Harrelson
1986 ... 1

Will Harridge
Inducted in 1972
Executive
1972 ... Vet. Com.

Bucky Harris
Inducted in 1975
Manager
1938 ... 1
1939 ... 1
1948 ... 3
1949 ... 11
1950 ... 4
1951 ... 9
1952 ... 12
1953 ... 21
1958 ... 45
1960 ... 31
1975 ... Vet. Com.

Gabby Hartnett
Inducted in 1955
1945 ... 2
1946 NOM ... 2
1947 ... 33
1948 ... 33
1949 ... 35
1949 RO ... 7
1950 ... 54
1951 ... 57
1952 ... 77
1953 ... 104
1954 ... 151
1955 ... 195

Grady Hatton
1966 ... 4
1967 ... 1

Jim Hearn
1966 ... 1
1967 ... 1

Richie Hebner
1991 ... 1

Jim Hegan
1966 ... 5
1967 ... 2

Harry Heilmann
Inducted in 1952
1937 ... 10
1938 ... 14
1939 ... 8
1942 ... 4
1945 ... 5
1946 NOM ... 23
1947 ... 65
1948 ... 40
1949 ... 59
1949 RO ... 52
1950 ... 87
1951 ... 153
1952 ... 203

Tommy Helms
1983 ... 1

Solly Hemus
1966 ... 1

Tommy Henrich
1952 ... 4
1953 ... 10
1956 ... 2
1958 ... 11
1960 ... 10
1962 ... 3
1964 ... 13
1968 ... 22
1969 ... 50
1970 ... 62

Babe Herman
1942 ... 1
1948 ... 2
1949 ... 5
1950 ... 2
1951 ... 1
1952 ... 3
1953 ... 2
1954 ... 1
1955 ... 5
1956 ... 11
1958 ... 13
1960 ... 7

Billy Herman
Inducted in 1975
1948 ... 1
1956 ... 2
1958 ... 7
1962 ... 4
1964 ... 26
1964 RO ... 9
1966 ... 28
1967 ... 59
1967 RO ... 14
1975 ... Vet. Com.

Willie Hernandez
1995 ... 2

Buck Herzog
1938 ... 1

Jim Hickman
1980 ... 1

Mike Higgins
1950 ... 2
1951 ... 1
1958 ... 6
1960 ... 3

John Hiller
1986 ... 11

Bill Hinchman
1937 ... 1

Gil Hodges
1969 ... 82
1970 ... 145
1971 ... 180
1972 ... 161
1973 ... 218
1974 ... 198
1975 ... 188
1976 ... 233
1977 ... 224
1978 ... 226
1979 ... 242
1980 ... 230
1981 ... 241
1982 ... 205
1983 ... 237

Tommy Holmes
1958 ... 2
1960 ... 2

Ken Holtzman
1985 ... 4
1986 ... 5

Harry Hooper
Inducted in 1971
1937 ... 6
1938 ... 4
1939 ... 5
1948 ... 2
1950 ... 2
1951 ... 3
1971 ... Vet. Com.

Burt Hooton
1991 ... 1

Rogers Hornsby
Inducted in 1942
1936 ... 105
1937 ... 53
1938 ... 46
1939 ... 176
1942 ... 182

Willie Horton
1986 ... 4

Art Houtteman
1964 ... 2

Elston Howard
1974 ... 19
1975 ... 23
1976 ... 55
1977 ... 43
1978 ... 41
1979 ... 30
1980 ... 29

1981 83
1982 40
1983 32
1984 45
1985 54
1986 51
1987 44
1988 53

Frank Howard

1979 6

Waite Hoyt
Inducted in 1969

1939 1
1942 1
1946 NOM 1
1948 7
1949 7
1950 11
1951 13
1952 12
1953 14
1954 14
1955 33
1956 37
1958 37
1960 29
1962 18
1969 .... Vet. Com.

Al Hrabosky

1988 1

Cal Hubbard
Inducted in 1976
Umpire

1976 .... Vet. Com.

Carl Hubbell
Inducted in 1947

1945 24
1946 NOM 101
1946 75
1947 140

Miller Huggins
Inducted in 1964
Manager

1937 5
1938 48
1939 97
1942 111
1945 133
1946 NOM 129
1946 106
1948 4
1950 2
1964 .... Vet. Com.

Catfish Hunter
Inducted in 1987

1985 212
1986 289
1987 315

Fred Hutchinson

1962 1
1964 10

Monte Irvin
Inducted in 1973

1973 .... Neg. Com.

Charlie Irwin

1938 1
1939 1

Joe Jackson

1936 2
1946 NOM 2

Reggie Jackson
Inducted in 1993

1993 396

Sonny Jackson

1980 1

Travis Jackson
Inducted in 1982

1948 5
1949 6
1950 6
1951 4
1952 1
1953 2
1954 1
1955 5
1956 14
1958 11
1960 11
1962 1
1982 .... Vet. Com.

Fergie Jenkins
Inducted in 1991

1989 234
1990 296
1991 334

Hughie Jennings
Inducted in 1945

1936 V 11
1937 4
1938 23
1939 33
1942 64
1945 92
1945 .... O/T Com.

Jackie Jensen

1967 3
1968 3
1969 1
1970 1
1971 2
1972 1

Tommy John

1995 98

Ban Johnson
Inducted in 1937
Executive

1937 .... Cen. Com.

Dave Johnson

1984 3

Judy Johnson
Inducted in 1975

1975 .... Neg. Com.

Bob Johnson

1948 1
1956 1

Walter Johnson
Inducted in 1936

1936 189

Fielder Jones

1946 NOM 1

Sam P. Jones

1939 1
1955 1
1956 1

Tim Jordan

1951 1

Mike Jorgensen

1991 1

Addie Joss
Inducted in 1978

1937 11
1938 18
1939 28
1942 33
1945 23
1946 NOM 14
1960 1
1978 .... Vet. Com.

Joe Judge

1937 1
1938 2
1949 1
1955 2
1956 2
1958 9
1960 15

Billy Jurges

1949 2
1958 1

Jim Kaat

1989 87
1990 79
1991 62
1992 114
1993 125
1994 98
1995 100

Al Kaline
Inducted in 1980

1980 340

Willie Kamm

1958 3
1960 1

Tim Keefe
Inducted in 1964

1936 V 1
1964 .... Vet. Com.

Willie Keeler
Inducted in 1939

1936 V 33
1936 40
1937 115
1938 177
1939 207

George Kell
Inducted in 1983

1964 33
1964 RO 8
1966 29
1967 40
1967 RO 11
1968 47
1969 60
1970 90
1971 105
1972 115
1973 114
1974 94
1975 114
1976 129
1977 141
1983 .... Vet. Com.

Charlie Keller

1953 1
1956 2
1958 9
1960 7
1962 1
1964 12
1968 11
1969 14
1970 7
1971 14
1972 24

Joe Kelley
Inducted in 1971

1939 1
1942 1
1971 .... Vet. Com.

George Kelly
Inducted in 1973

1947 1
1949 1
1956 2
1958 2
1960 5
1962 1

1973 .... Vet. Com.

Mike Kelly
Inducted in 1945

1936 V 15
1945 .... O/T Com.

Ken Keltner

1958 1
1960 1

Dickie Kerr

1937 1
1938 3
1939 5
1942 1
1945 1
1949 1
1951 3
1952 9
1953 13
1954 13
1955 25

Don Kessinger

1985 2

Harmon Killebrew
Inducted in 1984

1981 239
1982 246
1983 269
1984 335

Bill Killefer

1946 NOM 1

Matt Kilroy

1936 V 1

Ellis Kinder

1964 3

Ralph Kiner
Inducted in 1975

1962 5
1964 31
1964 RO 3
1966 74
1967 124
1967 RO 41
1968 118
1969 137
1970 167
1971 212
1972 235
1973 235
1974 215
1975 273

Dave Kingman

1992 3

Chuck Klein
Inducted in 1980

1948 3
1949 9
1950 14
1951 15
1952 19
1954 11
1955 25
1956 44
1958 36
1960 37
1962 18
1964 56
1964 RO 18
1980 .... Vet. Com.

Bill Klem
Inducted in 1953
Umpire

1953 .... Vet. Com.

Johnny Kling

1936 8
1937 20
1938 26

1939 14
1942 15
1945 12
1946 NOM 20
1948 2
1953 1

Ted Kluszewski

1967 9
1968 14
1969 11
1970 8
1971 9
1972 10
1973 14
1974 28
1975 33
1976 50
1977 55
1978 51
1979 58
1980 50
1981 56

Otto Knabe

1939 1
1946 NOM 1

Ray Knight

1994 1

Jerry Koosman

1991 4

Sandy Koufax
Inducted in 1972

1972 344

Ray Kremer

1948 1
1958 2

Red Kress

1958 1
1960 3

Mike Krukow

1995 1

Harvey Kuenn

1977 57
1978 58
1979 63
1980 83
1981 93
1982 62
1983 77
1984 106
1985 125
1986 144
1987 144
1988 168
1989 115
1990 107
1991 100

Joe Kuhel

1956 1

Bob Kuzava

1964 1

Nap Lajoie
Inducted in 1937

1936 V 2
1936 146
1937 168

Judge Landis
Inducted in 1944
Executive

1944 .... O/T Com.

Bill Lange

1936 V 6
1953 1

Hal Lanier

1979 1

Don Larsen

1974 29
1975 23
1976 47
1977 39
1978 32
1979 53
1980 31
1981 33
1982 32
1983 22
1984 25
1985 32
1986 33
1987 30
1988 31

Arlie Latham

1936 V 1
1938 1
1942 1

Cookie Lavagetto

1958 4
1960 2

Vern Law

1973 9
1974 5
1975 6
1976 9
1977 5
1978 6
1979 9

Tony Lazzeri
Inducted in 1991

1945 1
1947 1
1948 21
1949 20
1949 RO 6
1950 21
1951 27
1952 29
1953 28
1954 30
1955 66
1956 64
1958 80
1960 59
1962 8
1991 .... Vet. Com.

Fred Leach

1958 2
1960 1

Tommy Leach

1937 1
1939 1

Bill Lee

1988 3

Sam Leever

1937 1

Bob Lemon
Inducted in 1976

1964 24
1964 RO 3
1966 21
1967 35
1967 RO 7
1968 47
1969 56
1970 70
1971 90
1972 117
1973 177
1974 190
1975 233
1976 305

Buck Leonard
Inducted in 1972

1972 .... Neg. Com.

Dennis Leonard

1992 1

Emil Leonard

1960 2
1968 5
1969 4
1970 5
1971 3
1972 5
1973 6

Duffy Lewis

1937 3
1938 5
1939 6
1945 1
1951 2
1952 11
1953 20
1954 20
1955 34

Fred Lindstrom
Inducted in 1976

1949 1
1956 3
1958 5
1960 6
1962 7
1976 .... Vet. Com.

John Henry Lloyd
Inducted in 1977

1977 .... Neg. Com.

Hans Lobert

1937 2
1938 1
1939 2
1960 1

Whitey Lockman

1966 4

Mickey Lolich

1985 78
1986 86
1987 84
1988 109
1989 47
1990 27
1991 33
1992 45
1993 43
1994 23
1995 26

Ernie Lombardi
Inducted in 1986

1950 3
1951 3
1956 8
1958 4
1960 6
1962 5
1964 33
1964 RO 9
1966 34
1967 43
1967 RO 25
1986 .... Vet. Com.

Jim Lonborg

1985 3
1986 3

Herman Long

1936 V 16
1937 1
1938 1
1939 1
1945 1
1946 NOM............1

Ed Lopat

1968 2
1969 2
1970 1
1971 4
1972 2

Davey Lopes

1993 2

Al Lopez
Inducted in 1977
Manager

1949 1
1952 2
1953 2
1956 1
1958 34
1960 26
1962 11
1964 57
1964 RO 34
1966 109
1967 114
1967 RO 50
1977 .... Vet. Com.

Bobby Lowe

1936 V 2
1942 1
1945 2

John Lowenstein

1991 1

Red Lucas

1949 2
1950 1
1958 1

Dolph Luque

1937 1
1938 1
1939 1
1950 1
1952 1
1953 1
1956 1
1958 15
1960 4

Greg Luzinski

1990 1

Sparky Lyle

1988 56
1989 25
1990 25
1991 15

Ted Lyons
Inducted in 1955

1945 4
1946 NOM............3
1948 15
1949 29
1949 RO 14
1950 42
1951 71
1952 101
1953 139
1954 170
1955 217

Connie Mack
Inducted in 1937
Manager

1936 1
1937 .... Cen. Com.

Larry MacPhail
Inducted in 1978
Executive

1978 .... Vet. Com.

Bill Madlock

1993 19

Sherry Magee

1937 2
1938 2
1939 1
1942 1
1945 1
1946 NOM............1
1950 1
1951 2

Sal Maglie

1964 13
1968 11

Jim Maloney

1978 2
1979 2

Gus Mancuso

1958 1

Mickey Mantle
Inducted in 1974

1974 322

Heinie Manush
Inducted in 1964

1948 1
1949 1
1956 13
1958 22
1960 20
1962 15
1964 .... Vet. Com.

Rabbit Maranville
Inducted in 1954

1937 25
1938 73
1939 82
1942 66
1945 51
1946 NOM 50
1946 29
1947 91
1948 38
1949 58
1949 RO 39
1950 66
1951 110
1952 133
1953 164
1954 209

Firpo Marberry

1938 1
1950 1
1958 5
1960 2
1962 2

Juan Marichal
Inducted in 1983

1981 233
1982 305
1983 313

Marty Marion

1956 1
1960 37
1962 16
1964 50
1964 RO 17
1966 86
1967 90
1967 RO 22
1968 89
1969 112
1970 120
1971 123
1972 120
1973 127

Roger Maris

1974 78
1975 70
1976 87
1977 72
1978 83
1979 127

Sherry Magee (cont. column)

1980 111
1981 94
1982 69
1983 69
1984 107
1985 128
1986 177
1987 176
1988 184

Rube Marquard
Inducted in 1971

1936 1
1937 13
1938 10
1939 4
1946 NOM............6
1947 18
1948 6
1949 4
1951 3
1952 9
1953 19
1954 15
1955 35
1971 .... Vet. Com.

Mike Marshall

1987 6

Billy Martin

1967 1

Pepper Martin

1942 2
1945 1
1946 NOM............1
1948 7
1949 16
1950 7
1951 19
1952 31
1953 43
1956 7
1958 46
1960 29
1962 6
1964 19
1964 RO 5

Morrie Martin

1966 2

Eddie Mathews
Inducted in 1978

1974 118
1975 148
1976 189
1977 239
1978 301

Christy Mathewson
Inducted in 1936

1936 205

Lee May

1988 2

Carl Mays

1958 6

Willie Mays
Inducted in 1979

1979 409

Bill Mazeroski

1978 23
1979 36
1980 33
1981 38
1982 28
1983 48
1984 74
1985 87
1986 100
1987 125
1988 143
1989 134
1990 131
1991 142

Jim McAleer

1936 V 1

Joe McCarthy
Inducted in 1957
Manager

1939 3
1947 2
1951 1
1953 1
1958 2
1957 .... Vet. Com.

Tommy McCarthy
Inducted in 1946

1936 V 1
1946 .... O/T Com.

Tim McCarver

1986 16

Frank McCormick

1956 3
1962 1
1964 6
1968 3

Willie McCovey
Inducted in 1986

1986 346

Lindy McDaniel

1981 1
1982 3

Gil McDougald

1966 5
1967 4
1968 4
1969 3
1970 1
1971 4
1972 4
1973 2
1974 3

Joe McGinnity
Inducted in 1946

1937 12
1938 36
1939 32
1942 59
1945 44
1946 NOM 53
1946 47
1946 .... O/T Com.

Bill McGowan
Inducted in 1992
Umpire

1992 .... Vet. Com.

John McGraw
Inducted in 1937
Manager

1936 V 17
1936 4
1937 35
1937 .... Cen. Com.

Tug McGraw

1990 6

Stuffy McInnis

1937 1
1938 4
1939 4
1948 5
1949 8
1950 1
1951 3

Bill McKechnie
Inducted in 1962
Manager

1945 2
1946 NOM............2

1950 1
1951 8
1962 .... Vet. Com.

Denny McLain

1978 1
1979 3
1985 2

Larry McLean

1937 1

Don McMahon

1980 1

Marty McManus

1958 2
1960 2

Roy McMillan

1972 9
1973 5
1974 4

Dave McNally

1981 5
1982 5
1985 7
1986 12

Cal McVey

1936 V 1

Lee Meadows

1958 2

Ducky Medwick
Inducted in 1968

1948 1
1956 31
1958 50
1960 38
1962 34
1964 108
1964 RO 130
1966 187
1967 212
1967 RO 248
1968 240

Andy Messersmith

1985 3
1986 3

Bob Meusel

1937 1
1938 1
1945 1
1948 6
1949 3
1950 2
1952 1
1955 2
1956 1
1958 5
1960 10

Eddie Miksis

1964 1

Clyde Milan

1938 1
1950 1
1951 1
1952 1
1953 1
1954 3
1955 6

Felix Millan

1983 1

Bing Miller

1958 1
1960 6

Dots Miller

1948 1

(next to McAleer column)

1992 182

Hack Miller
1937 ... 1

Minnie Minoso
1969 ... 6
1986 ... 89
1987 ... 82
1988 ... 90
1989 ... 59
1990 ... 51
1991 ... 38
1992 ... 69
1993 ... 67
1994 ... 45
1995 ... 66

Johnny Mize
Inducted in 1981
1960 ... 45
1962 ... 14
1964 ... 54
1964 RO ... 12
1966 ... 81
1967 ... 89
1967 RO ... 14
1968 ... 103
1969 ... 116
1970 ... 126
1971 ... 157
1972 ... 157
1973 ... 157
1981 ... Vet. Com.

Rick Monday
1990 ... 2

Don Money
1989 ... 1

Wally Moon
1971 ... 2

Jo-Jo Moore
1950 ... 1

Terry Moore
1950 ... 1
1953 ... 1
1958 ... 12
1960 ... 7
1962 ... 1
1964 ... 14
1967 ... 3
1968 ... 33

Pat Moran
1937 ... 1
1938 ... 1
1939 ... 1
1945 ... 1

Joe Morgan
Inducted in 1990
1990 ... 363

Wally Moses
1958 ... 1
1960 ... 1
1968 ... 4
1969 ... 4
1970 ... 5
1971 ... 7

Johnny Mostil
1956 ... 1
1958 ... 1

Manny Mota
1988 ... 18
1989 ... 9

Hugh Mulcahy
1948 ... 1

Van Mungo
1945 ... 1
1948 ... 1
1958 ... 2

1960 ... 2

Thurman Munson
1981 ... 62
1982 ... 26
1983 ... 18
1984 ... 29
1985 ... 32
1986 ... 35
1987 ... 28
1988 ... 32
1989 ... 31
1990 ... 33
1991 ... 28
1992 ... 32
1993 ... 40
1994 ... 31
1995 ... 30

Bobby Murcer
1989 ... 3

Danny Murphy
1937 ... 1
1945 ... 1

Red Murray
1937 ... 1
1938 ... 1

Stan Musial
Inducted in 1969
1969 ... 317

Buddy Myer
1949 ... 1

Art Nehf
1937 ... 3
1938 ... 5
1939 ... 1
1949 ... 1
1950 ... 2
1951 ... 4
1952 ... 3
1953 ... 4
1954 ... 7
1955 ... 7
1958 ... 13

Graig Nettles
1994 ... 38
1995 ... 28

Don Newcombe
1966 ... 7
1967 ... 18
1967 RO ... 2
1968 ... 9
1969 ... 3
1970 ... 5
1971 ... 8
1972 ... 7
1973 ... 11
1974 ... 7
1975 ... 11
1976 ... 21
1977 ... 43
1978 ... 48
1979 ... 52
1980 ... 59

Hal Newhouser
Inducted in 1992
1962 ... 4
1964 ... 26
1964 RO ... 3
1966 ... 32
1967 ... 62
1967 RO ... 13
1968 ... 67
1969 ... 82
1970 ... 80
1971 ... 94
1972 ... 92
1973 ... 79
1974 ... 73
1975 ... 155
1992 ... Vet. Com.

Bobo Newsom
1960 ... 6
1962 ... 3
1964 ... 17
1964 RO ... 1
1966 ... 25
1967 ... 19
1967 RO ... 6
1968 ... 22
1969 ... 32
1970 ... 12
1971 ... 17
1972 ... 31
1973 ... 33

Kid Nichols
Inducted in 1949
1936 V ... 3
1938 ... 3
1939 ... 7
1942 ... 5
1945 ... 5
1946 NOM ... 1
1949 ... O/T Com.

Bill Nicholson
1960 ... 1

Joe Niekro
1994 ... 6

Phil Niekro
1993 ... 278
1994 ... 273
1995 ... 286

Ron Northey
1964 ... 1

Jim Northrup
1981 ... 1

Lefty O'Doul
1948 ... 4
1949 ... 4
1950 ... 9
1951 ... 13
1952 ... 19
1953 ... 11
1956 ... 5
1958 ... 27
1960 ... 45
1962 ... 13

Joe Oeschger
1948 ... 1

Bob O'Farrell
1950 ... 4
1958 ... 3
1960 ... 3

Charlie O'Leary
1953 ... 1
1958 ... 1
1960 ... 1

Tony Oliva
1982 ... 63
1983 ... 75
1984 ... 124
1985 ... 114
1986 ... 154
1987 ... 160
1988 ... 202
1989 ... 135
1990 ... 142
1991 ... 160
1992 ... 175
1993 ... 157
1994 ... 158
1995 ... 149

Al Oliver
1991 ... 19

Steve O'Neill
1948 ... 2
1949 ... 6

1950 ... 1
1951 ... 3
1952 ... 10
1953 ... 13
1958 ... 10

Jim O'Rourke
Inducted in 1945
1945 ... O/T Com.

Claude Osteen
1981 ... 2

Mel Ott
Inducted in 1951
1949 ... 94
1949 RO ... 128
1950 ... 115
1951 ... 197

Charlie Pabor
1936 V ... 1

Andy Pafko
1966 ... 2
1967 ... 1

Satchel Paige
Inducted in 1971
1951 ... 1
1971 ... Neg. Com.

Jim Palmer
Inducted in 1990
1990 ... 411

Milt Pappas
1979 ... 5

Larry Parrish
1994 ... 2

Camilo Pascual
1977 ... 3
1978 ... 1

Dode Paskert
1937 ... 1

Monte Pearson
1958 ... 1

Roger Peckinpaugh
1937 ... 3
1938 ... 2
1939 ... 1
1942 ... 2
1949 ... 1
1952 ... 2
1953 ... 2
1954 ... 1
1955 ... 1

Heinie Peitz
1939 ... 1

Herb Pennock
Inducted in 1948
1937 ... 15
1938 ... 37
1939 ... 40
1942 ... 72
1945 ... 45
1946 NOM ... 41
1946 ... 16
1947 ... 86
1948 ... 94

Hub Perdue
1938 ... 1
1939 ... 1

Tony Perez
1992 ... 215
1993 ... 233
1994 ... 263
1995 ... 259

Cy Perkins
1958 ... 2

Ron Perranoski
1979 ... 6

Gaylord Perry
Inducted in 1991
1989 ... 304
1990 ... 320
1991 ... 342

Jim Perry
1981 ... 6
1983 ... 7

Johnny Pesky
1960 ... 1

Rico Petrocelli
1982 ... 3

Deacon Phillippe
1939 ... 1
1942 ... 1
1945 ... 2
1946 NOM ... 1

Billy Pierce
1970 ... 5
1971 ... 7
1972 ... 4
1973 ... 4
1974 ... 4

Lip Pike
1936 V ... 1

Lou Piniella
1990 ... 2

Vada Pinson
1981 ... 18
1982 ... 6
1983 ... 12
1985 ... 19
1986 ... 43
1987 ... 48
1988 ... 67
1989 ... 33
1990 ... 36
1991 ... 30
1992 ... 36
1993 ... 38
1994 ... 46
1995 ... 32

Wally Pipp
1958 ... 1

Eddie Plank
Inducted in 1946
1937 ... 23
1938 ... 38
1939 ... 28
1942 ... 63
1945 ... 33
1946 NOM ... 34
1946 ... O/T Com.

Johnny Podres
1975 ... 3
1976 ... 2
1977 ... 3

Bob Porterfield
1966 ... 1

Boog Powell
1983 ... 5

Vic Power
1971 ... 2
1972 ... 3

Herb Pruett
1949 ... 1

1950 ... 1
1951 ... 1
1952 ... 1
1953 ... 1

Jack Quinn
1948 ... 2
1958 ... 9
1960 ... 2

Charlie Radbourn
Inducted in 1939
1936 V ... 16
1939 ... O/T Com.

Vic Raschi
1962 ... 1
1964 ... 8
1968 ... 1
1969 ... 3
1971 ... 2
1972 ... 4
1973 ... 7
1974 ... 3
1975 ... 37

Bugs Raymond
1937 ... 1

Pee Wee Reese
Inducted in 1984
1964 ... 73
1964 RO ... 47
1966 ... 95
1967 ... 89
1967 RO ... 16
1968 ... 81
1969 ... 89
1970 ... 97
1971 ... 127
1972 ... 129
1973 ... 126
1974 ... 141
1975 ... 154
1976 ... 186
1977 ... 163
1978 ... 169
1984 ... Vet. Com.

Pete Reiser
1958 ... 6
1960 ... 8

Jack Remsen
1936 V ... 1

Jerry Remy
1990 ... 1

Allie Reynolds
1956 ... 1
1960 ... 24
1962 ... 15
1964 ... 35
1964 RO ... 6
1966 ... 60
1967 ... 77
1967 RO ... 19
1968 ... 95
1969 ... 98
1970 ... 89
1971 ... 110
1972 ... 105
1973 ... 93
1974 ... 101

Del Rice
1966 ... 2

Jim Rice
1995 ... 137

Sam Rice
Inducted in 1963
1938 ... 1
1948 ... 1
1949 ... 3
1950 ... 1
1951 ... 1
1952 ... 1

1953 3
1954 9
1955 28
1956 45
1958 90
1960 143
1962 81
1963 ...... Vet. Com.

J. R. Richard

1986 7

Hardy Richardson

1936 V 1

Bobby Richardson

1972 8
1973 2
1974 5

Branch Rickey
Inducted in 1967
Executive

1942 3
1945 2
1967 .... Vet. Com.

Jimmy Ring

1949 1

Claude Ritchey

1945 1

Mickey Rivers

1990 2

Eppa Rixey
Inducted in 1963

1937 1
1938 2
1945 1
1947 2
1948 5
1949 4
1950 6
1951 5
1952 3
1953 3
1954 5
1955 8
1956 27
1958 32
1960 142
1962 49
1963 .... Vet. Com.

Phil Rizzuto
Inducted in 1994

1956 1
1962 44
1964 45
1964 RO........... 11
1966 54
1967 71
1967 RO........... 14
1968 74
1969 78
1970 79
1971 92
1972 103
1973 111
1974 111
1975 117
1976 149
1994 .... Vet. Com.

Robin Roberts
Inducted in 1976

1973 213
1974 224
1975 263
1976 337

Dave Robertson

1953 1

Brooks Robinson
Inducted in 1983

1983 344

Frank Robinson
Inducted in 1982

1982 370

Jackie Robinson
Inducted in 1962

1962 124

Wilbert Robinson
Inducted in 1945
Manager

1936 V 6
1937 5
1938 17
1939 46
1942 89
1945 81
1945 .... O/T Com.

Preacher Roe

1960 1
1962 1
1968 2
1970 1
1971 3
1972 2

Red Rolfe

1950 7
1951 6
1952 4
1953 5
1956 3
1958 13
1960 10
1962 1

Eddie Rommel

1948 3
1949 2
1950 1
1951 1
1952 1
1953 1
1958 7
1960 12

Charlie Root

1945 1
1948 3
1949 1
1950 1
1958 6
1960 2

Pete Rose

1992 41
1993 14
1994 19

Edd Roush
Inducted in 1962

1936 2
1937 10
1938 9
1939 8
1942 1
1945 5
1946 NOM....... 11
1947 25
1948 17
1949 14
1950 16
1951 21
1952 24
1953 32
1954 52
1955 97
1956 91
1958 112
1960 146
1962 .... Vet. Com.

Schoolboy Rowe

1958 12
1960 3
1968 6
1969 17

Nap Rucker

1936 1
1937 11
1938 12
1939 13
1942 15
1945 10
1946 NOM.......... 13

Dick Rudolph

1937 1
1951 1

Muddy Ruel

1946 NOM...........1
1950 4
1951 1
1952 1
1953 8
1954 5
1955 11
1956 16
1958 10
1960 9

Red Ruffing
Inducted in 1967

1948 4
1949 22
1949 RO........... 4
1950 12
1951 9
1952 10
1953 24
1954 29
1955 60
1956 97
1958 99
1960 86
1962 72
1964 141
1964 RO......... 184
1966 208
1967 212
1967 RO......... 266

Amos Rusie
Inducted in 1977

1936 V 12
1937 1
1938 8
1939 6
1942 1
1945 1
1977 .... Vet. Com.

Bill Russell

1992 3

Babe Ruth
Inducted in 1936

1936 215

Ray Sadecki

1983 2

Johnny Sain

1962 1
1964 3
1968 7
1969 8
1970 9
1971 11
1972 21
1973 47
1974 51
1975 123

Manny Sanguillen

1986 2

Ron Santo

1980 15
1985 53
1986 64
1987 78
1988 108
1989 75
1990 96
1991 116

1992 136
1993 155
1994 150
1995 139

Hank Sauer

1966 4

Al Schacht

1939 1
1948 2
1951 4
1956 1

Germany Schaefer

1942 1
1953 1

Ray Schalk
Inducted in 1955

1936 4
1937 24
1938 45
1939 35
1942 53
1945 33
1946 NOM....... 36
1947 50
1948 22
1949 24
1949 RO.......... 17
1950 16
1951 37
1952 44
1953 52
1954 54
1955 113
1955 .... Vet. Com.

Wally Schang

1948 1
1950 1
1956 1
1958 8
1960 11

Mike Schmidt
Inducted in 1995

1995 444

Red Schoendienst
Inducted in 1989

1969 65
1970 97
1971 123
1972 104
1973 96
1974 110
1975 94
1976 129
1977 105
1978 130
1979 159
1980 164
1981 166
1982 135
1983 146
1989 .... Vet. Com.

Ossie Schreckengost

1937 2
1938 2
1939 2

Frank Schulte

1937 1

Hal Schumacher

1948 1
1955 1
1956 2
1958 1
1960 11
1962 1
1964 10

Everett Scott

1937 2
1938 2
1939 1

1942 1
1947 1
1948 3
1949 3
1950 3
1951 2
1952 4
1953 5
1954 4
1955 8
1956 1

George Scott

1986 1

Jack Scott

1958 1

Tom Seaver
Inducted in 1992

1992 425

George Selkirk

1948 1
1949 1
1950 1
1951 2
1952 1
1953 1

Hank Severeid

1948 1

Joe Sewell
Inducted in 1977

1937 1
1948 1
1954 1
1955 1
1956 3
1958 1
1960 23
1977 .... Vet. Com.

Luke Sewell

1948 1
1958 3
1960 3
1962 1

Rip Sewell

1958 1
1962 1
1964 1

Cy Seymour

1945 1

Bobby Shantz

1970 7
1971 5
1972 9
1973 5
1974 3

Jim Sheckard

1938 1
1945 1
1946 NOM...........1

Bill Sherdel

1948 1
1949 1
1950 1
1951 1
1953 1
1955 1
1956 1
1958 2
1960 2

Urban Shocker

1938 1
1939 1
1948 1
1949 2
1958 4

Chris Short

1979 1

Sonny Siebert

1981 1

Roy Sievers

1971 4
1972 3

Al Simmons
Inducted in 1953

1936 4
1946 NOM...........1
1947 6
1948 60
1949 89
1949 RO.......... 76
1950 90
1951 116
1952 141
1953 199

Curt Simmons

1973 5
1974 3

Ted Simmons

1994 17

George Sisler
Inducted in 1939

1936 77
1937 106
1938 179
1939 235

Sibby Sisti

1960 1

Enos Slaughter
Inducted in 1985

1966 100
1967 123
1967 RO.......... 48
1968 129
1969 128
1970 133
1971 165
1972 149
1973 145
1974 145
1975 177
1976 197
1977 222
1978 261
1979 297
1985 .... Vet. Com.

Roy Smalley

1964 1

Earl Smith

1948 1
1956 1

Reggie Smith

1988 3

Sherry Smith

1948 1

Duke Snider
Inducted in 1980

1970 51
1971 89
1972 84
1973 101
1974 111
1975 129
1976 159
1977 212
1978 254
1979 308
1980 333

Billy Southworth

1945 1

1946 NOM.............1
1949................7
1950................1
1951................4
1952................1
1953................2
1958...............18

Warren Spahn
Inducted in 1973

1973.............316

Al Spalding
Inducted in 1939
Pioneer

1936 V..............4
1939.........O/T Com.

Tully Sparks

1946 NOM.............1

Tris Speaker
Inducted in 1937

1936.............133
1937.............165

Chris Speier

1995................1

Jake Stahl

1938................1
1939................1

Eddie Stanky

1960................3

Mickey Stanley

1984................2

Willie Stargell
Inducted in 1988

1988.............352

Rusty Staub

1991...............28
1992...............26
1993...............32
1994...............36
1995...............23

Harry Steinfeldt

1937................1
1939................1
1942................1

Casey Stengel
Inducted in 1966
Manager

1938................2
1939................6
1945................2
1948................1
1949................3
1950................3
1951................8
1952...............27
1953...............61
1966.........Vet. Com.

Riggs Stephenson

1956................2
1958................1
1960................4
1962................1

Mel Stottlemyre

1980................3

Harry Stovey

1936 V..............6

Gabby Street

1937................1
1938................1
1953................1

Gus Suhr

1956................1
1958................1
1960................1

Clyde Sukeforth

1958................1

Billy Sullivan

1937................1
1946 NOM.............1

Jim Sundberg

1995................1

Bruce Sutter

1994.............109
1995.............137

Don Sutton

1994.............259
1995.............264

Bill Sweeney

1945................1

Jess Tannehill

1946 NOM.............1

Birdie Tebbetts

1958................8
1960................1

Kent Tekulve

1995................6

Gene Tenace

1989................1

Fred Tenney

1936 V..............1
1937................5
1938................8
1939................3
1942................1
1946 NOM.............1

Bill Terry
Inducted in 1954

1936................9
1938................7
1939...............16
1942...............36
1945...............32
1946 NOM............31
1947...............46
1948...............52
1949...............81
1949 RO............48
1950.............105
1951.............148
1952.............155
1953.............191
1954.............195

Tommy Thevenow

1950................2

Ira Thomas

1938................1

Sam Thompson
Inducted in 1974

1974.........Vet. Com.

Bobby Thomson

1966...............12
1967...............10
1967 RO.............1
1968...............13
1969................6
1970................4
1971................4
1972...............10
1973................3
1974................6
1975...............10

1976................9
1977...............10
1978................5
1979...............11

Andre Thornton

1993................2

Luis Tiant

1988.............132
1989...............47
1990...............42
1991...............32
1992...............50
1993...............62
1994...............42
1995...............45

Joe Tinker
Inducted in 1946

1937...............15
1938...............16
1939...............12
1942...............36
1945...............49
1946 NOM............55
1946...............45
1946.........O/T Com.

Jim Tobin

1956................2

Fred Toney

1949................1

Earl Torgeson

1967................2

Joe Torre

1983...............20
1984...............45
1985...............44
1986...............60
1987...............47
1988...............60
1989...............40
1990...............55
1991...............41
1992...............62
1993...............63
1994...............53
1995...............50

Mike Torrez

1990................1

Pie Traynor
Inducted in 1948

1936...............16
1938................3
1939...............10
1942...............45
1945...............81
1946 NOM............65
1946...............53
1947.............119
1948...............93

Dizzy Trout

1964................1

Virgil Trucks

1964................4

Jim Turner

1956................1

Terry Turner

1947................2

George Uhle

1956................1
1958................4
1960................4

Ellis Valentine

1991................1

Elmer Valo

1967................2

Dazzy Vance
Inducted in 1955

1936................1
1937...............10
1938...............10
1939...............15
1942...............37
1945...............18
1946 NOM............31
1947...............50
1948...............23
1949...............33
1949 RO............15
1950...............52
1951...............70
1952.............105
1953.............150
1954.............158
1955.............205

Johnny Vander Meer

1945................1
1956................3
1958...............35
1960...............31
1962................5
1964...............51
1964 RO............20
1966...............72
1967...............87
1967 RO............35
1968...............79
1969...............95
1970...............88
1971...............98

George Van Haltren

1936 V..............1

Arky Vaughan
Inducted in 1985

1953................1
1954................2
1955................4
1956................9
1958................6
1960...............10
1962................6
1964...............17
1964 RO.............6
1966...............36
1967...............46
1967 RO............19
1968...............82
1985.........Vet. Com.

Bobby Veach

1937................1

Bill Veeck
Inducted in 1991
Executive

1991.........Vet. Com.

Mickey Vernon

1966...............20
1967...............14
1967 RO.............2
1968...............22
1969...............21
1970...............10
1971...............12
1972...............12
1973...............23
1974...............27
1975...............22
1976...............52
1977...............52
1978...............66
1979...............88
1980...............96

Bill Virdon

1974................3
1975................1

Rube Waddell
Inducted in 1946

1936...............33
1937...............67
1938.............148
1939.............179
1942.............126
1945.............154
1946 NOM..........122
1946...............87
1946.........O/T Com.

Honus Wagner
Inducted in 1936

1936 V..............5
1936.............215

Rube Walberg

1958................1
1960................1

Dixie Walker

1962................1
1964................6
1968................6
1969................9

Harry Walker

1958................1

Bobby Wallace
Inducted in 1953

1936 V..............1
1937................1
1938................7
1939................5
1942................2
1945................3
1953.........Vet. Com.

Ed Walsh
Inducted in 1946

1936...............20
1937...............56
1938.............110
1939.............132
1942.............113
1945.............137
1946 NOM..........115
1946.............106
1946.........O/T Com.

Bucky Walters

1950................4
1952................3
1953...............10
1956................5
1958...............33
1960...............19
1962................5
1964...............35
1964 RO.............8
1966...............56
1967...............65
1967 RO............24
1968...............67
1969...............20
1970...............29

Bill Wambsganss

1942................1
1950................1
1953................1
1954................4
1955................5
1956................1

Lloyd Waner
Inducted in 1967

1949................3
1950................1
1951................1
1952................2
1956...............18
1958...............39
1960...............22
1962................5
1964...............47
1964 RO............12
1967.........Vet. Com.

Paul Waner
Inducted in 1952

1946 NOM.............4
1948...............51
1949...............73
1949 RO............63
1950...............95
1951.............162
1952.............195

Monte Ward
Inducted in 1964

1936 V..............3
1964.........Vet. Com.

Lon Warneke

1949................2
1958................2
1960................4
1962................2
1964...............13

Bob Watson

1990................3

George Weiss
Inducted in 1971
Executive

1971.........Vet. Com.

Mickey Welch
Inducted in 1973

1973.........Vet. Com.

Billy Werber

1949................1
1950................1
1952................1
1958................3

Vic Wertz

1970................2
1971................2
1972................4
1973................2
1974................2
1975................5
1976................5
1977................4
1978................4

Sam West

1948................1

Wes Westrum

1964................2

Zach Wheat
Inducted in 1959

1937................5
1938................7
1939................4
1942................3
1945................2
1946 NOM.............6
1947...............37
1948...............15
1949...............15
1950...............17
1951...............19
1952...............30
1953...............32
1954...............33
1955...............51
1956...............26
1959.........Vet. Com.

Deacon White

1936 V..............1

Will White

1975................7
1976................7
1977................4

Burgess Whitehead

1956................1

Earl Whitehill

1956 ... 1
1958 ... 2
1960 ... 3

Hoyt Wilhelm
Inducted in 1985

1978 ... 158
1979 ... 168
1980 ... 209
1981 ... 238
1982 ... 236
1983 ... 243
1984 ... 290
1985 ... 331

Billy Williams
Inducted in 1987

1982 ... 97
1983 ... 153
1984 ... 202
1985 ... 252
1986 ... 315
1987 ... 354

Fred Williams

1938 ... 1
1945 ... 1
1948 ... 1
1949 ... 2
1950 ... 9
1951 ... 7
1952 ... 4
1953 ... 4
1954 ... 4
1955 ... 3
1956 ... 11
1958 ... 6
1960 ... 11

Ken Williams

1956 ... 1
1958 ... 1

Ted Williams
Inducted in 1966

1966 ... 282

Ned Williamson

1936 V ... 2

Maury Wills

1978 ... 115
1979 ... 166
1980 ... 146
1981 ... 163
1982 ... 91
1983 ... 77
1984 ... 104
1985 ... 93
1986 ... 124
1987 ... 113
1988 ... 127
1989 ... 95
1990 ... 95
1991 ... 61
1992 ... 110

Jimmie Wilson

1948 ... 8
1949 ... 6
1950 ... 4
1951 ... 2
1952 ... 7
1953 ... 10
1954 ... 8
1955 ... 13
1956 ... 17
1958 ... 3
1960 ... 6
1962 ... 4

Jim Wilson

1964 ... 2

Hack Wilson
Inducted in 1979

1937 ... 1
1939 ... 1
1942 ... 1

1948 ... 2
1949 ... 24
1949 RO ... 12
1950 ... 16
1951 ... 21
1952 ... 21
1953 ... 43
1954 ... 48
1955 ... 81
1956 ... 74
1958 ... 94
1960 ... 72
1962 ... 39
1979 ... Vet. Com.

Whitey Witt

1949 ... 1

Joe Wood

1937 ... 13
1938 ... 6
1939 ... 2
1942 ... 1
1946 NOM ... 5
1947 ... 29
1948 ... 5
1950 ... 1
1951 ... 5

Wilbur Wood

1984 ... 14
1985 ... 16
1986 ... 23
1987 ... 26
1988 ... 30
1989 ... 14

Glenn Wright

1948 ... 2
1949 ... 1
1950 ... 2
1951 ... 1
1952 ... 1
1953 ... 3
1954 ... 1
1955 ... 4
1956 ... 3
1958 ... 8
1960 ... 18
1962 ... 1

George Wright
Inducted in 1937
Pioneer

1936 V ... 6
1937 ... Cen. Com.

Harry Wright
Inducted in 1953
Pioneer

1953 ... Vet. Com.

Whit Wyatt

1958 ... 1

Early Wynn
Inducted in 1972

1969 ... 95
1970 ... 140
1971 ... 240
1972 ... 301

Tom Yawkey
Inducted in 1980
Executive

1980 ... Vet. Com.

Carl Yastrzemski
Inducted in 1989

1989 ... 423

Steve Yeager

1992 ... 2

Steve Yerkes

1945 ... 1

Rudy York

1962 ... 1

1964 ... 10

Cy Young
Inducted in 1937

1936 V ... 32
1936 ... 111
1937 ... 153

Pep Young

1958 ... 1

Ross Youngs
Inducted in 1972

1936 ... 10
1937 ... 16
1938 ... 40
1939 ... 34
1942 ... 44
1945 ... 22
1946 NOM ... 25
1947 ... 36
1948 ... 19
1949 ... 20
1949 RO ... 11
1950 ... 17
1951 ... 34
1952 ... 34
1953 ... 31
1954 ... 34
1955 ... 48
1956 ... 19
1972 ... Vet. Com.

Tom Zachary

1958 ... 1
1960 ... 1

Chief Zimmer

1938 ... 1

1936 Veterans
Needed to Elect: 59

Cap Anson ... 40
Buck Ewing ... 40
Willie Keeler ... 33
Cy Young ... 32
Ed Delahanty ... 22
John McGraw ... 17
Herman Long ... 16
Charlie Radbourn ... 16
Mike Kelly ... 15
Amos Rusie ... 12

1936
Needed to Elect: 170

Ty Cobb ... 222
Babe Ruth ... 215
Honus Wagner ... 215
Christy Mathewson ... 205
Walter Johnson ... 189
Nap Lajoie ... 146
Tris Speaker ... 133
Cy Young ... 111
Rogers Hornsby ... 105
Mickey Cochrane ... 80

1937
Needed to Elect: 151

Nap Lajoie ... 168
Tris Speaker ... 165
Cy Young ... 153
Pete Alexander ... 125
Eddie Collins ... 115
Willie Keeler ... 115
George Sisler ... 106
Ed Delahanty ... 70
Rube Waddell ... 67
Jimmy Collins ... 66

1938
Needed to Elect: 197

Pete Alexander ... 212
George Sisler ... 179
Willie Keeler ... 177
Eddie Collins ... 175
Rube Waddell ... 148
Frank Chance ... 133
Ed Delahanty ... 132
Ed Walsh ... 110
Johnny Evers ... 91
Jimmy Collins ... 79

1939
Needed to Elect: 206

George Sisler ... 235
Eddie Collins ... 213
Willie Keeler ... 207
Rube Waddell ... 179
Rogers Hornsby ... 176
Frank Chance ... 158
Ed Delahanty ... 145
Ed Walsh ... 132
Johnny Evers ... 107
Miller Huggins ... 97

1942
Needed to Elect: 175

Rogers Hornsby ... 182
Frank Chance ... 136
Rube Waddell ... 126
Ed Walsh ... 113
Miller Huggins ... 111
Ed Delahanty ... 104
Johnny Evers ... 91
Wilbert Robinson ... 89
Mickey Cochrane ... 88
Frankie Frisch ... 84

1945
Needed to Elect: 186

Frank Chance ... 179
Rube Waddell ... 154
Ed Walsh ... 137
Johnny Evers ... 134
Roger Bresnahan ... 133
Miller Huggins ... 133
Mickey Cochrane ... 125
Jimmy Collins ... 121
Ed Delahanty ... 111
Clark Griffith ... 108

1946 Nominating Total Voting: 202

Frank Chance ... 144
Johnny Evers ... 130
Miller Huggins ... 129
Rube Waddell ... 122
Ed Walsh ... 115
Frankie Frisch ... 104
Carl Hubbell ... 101
Mickey Cochrane ... 80
Clark Griffith ... 73
Lefty Grove ... 71

1946
Needed to Elect: 198

Frank Chance ... 150
Johnny Evers ... 110
Miller Huggins ... 106
Ed Walsh ... 106
Rube Waddell ... 87
Clark Griffith ... 82
Carl Hubbell ... 75
Frankie Frisch ... 67
Mickey Cochrane ... 65
Lefty Grove ... 61

1947
Needed to Elect: 121

Carl Hubbell ... 140
Frankie Frisch ... 136
Mickey Cochrane ... 128
Lefty Grove ... 123
Pie Traynor ... 119
Charlie Gehringer ... 105
Rabbit Maranville ... 91
Dizzy Dean ... 88
Herb Pennock ... 86
Chief Bender ... 72

1948
Needed to Elect: 91

Herb Pennock ... 94
Pie Traynor ... 93
Al Simmons ... 60
Charlie Gehringer ... 52
Bill Terry ... 52
Paul Waner ... 51
Jimmie Foxx ... 50
Dizzy Dean ... 40
Harry Heilmann ... 40
Bill Dickey ... 39

1949
Needed to Elect: 115

Charlie Gehringer ... 102
Mel Ott ... 94
Al Simmons ... 89
Dizzy Dean ... 88
Jimmie Foxx ... 85
Bill Terry ... 81
Paul Waner ... 73
Hank Greenberg ... 67
Bill Dickey ... 65
Harry Heilmann ... 59

1949 Run Off
Needed to Elect: 141
One Player Maximum

Charlie Gehringer ... 159
Mel Ott ... 128
Jimmie Foxx ... 89
Dizzy Dean ... 81
Al Simmons ... 76
Paul Waner ... 63
Harry Heilmann ... 52
Bill Terry ... 48
Hank Greenberg ... 44
Bill Dickey ... 39
Rabbit Maranville ... 39

1950
Needed to Elect: 126

Mel Ott ... 115
Bill Terry ... 105
Jimmie Foxx ... 103
Paul Waner ... 95
Al Simmons ... 90
Harry Heilmann ... 87
Dizzy Dean ... 85
Bill Dickey ... 78
Rabbit Maranville ... 66
Hank Greenberg ... 64

1951
Needed to Elect: 170

Mel Ott ... 197
Jimmie Foxx ... 179
Paul Waner ... 162
Harry Heilmann ... 153
Bill Terry ... 148
Dizzy Dean ... 145
Bill Dickey ... 118
Al Simmons ... 116
Rabbit Maranville ... 110
Ted Lyons ... 71

1952
Needed to Elect: 176

Harry Heilmann ... 203
Paul Waner ... 195
Bill Terry ... 155
Dizzy Dean ... 152
Al Simmons ... 141
Bill Dickey ... 139
Rabbit Maranville ... 133
Dazzy Vance ... 105
Ted Lyons ... 101
Gabby Hartnett ... 77

1953
Needed to Elect: 198

Dizzy Dean ... 209
Al Simmons ... 199
Bill Terry ... 191
Bill Dickey ... 179
Rabbit Maranville ... 164
Dazzy Vance ... 150
Ted Lyons ... 139
Joe DiMaggio ... 117
Chief Bender ... 104
Gabby Hartnett ... 104

1954
Needed to Elect: 189

Rabbit Maranville ... 209
Bill Dickey ... 202
Bill Terry ... 195
Joe DiMaggio ... 175
Ted Lyons ... 170
Dazzy Vance ... 158
Gabby Hartnett ... 151
Hank Greenberg ... 97
Joe Cronin ... 85
Max Carey ... 55

1955
Needed to Elect: 189

Joe DiMaggio ... 223
Ted Lyons ... 217
Dazzy Vance ... 205
Gabby Hartnett ... 195
Hank Greenberg ... 157
Joe Cronin ... 135
Max Carey ... 119
Ray Schalk ... 113
Edd Roush ... 97
Hank Gowdy ... 90

1956
Needed to Elect: 145

Hank Greenberg ... 164
Joe Cronin ... 152
Red Ruffing ... 97
Edd Roush ... 91
Lefty Gomez ... 89
Hack Wilson ... 74
Max Carey ... 65
Tony Lazzeri ... 64
Kiki Cuyler ... 55
Hank Gowdy ... 49

1958
Needed to Elect: 200

Max Carey ... 136
Edd Roush ... 112
Red Ruffing ... 99
Hack Wilson ... 94
Kiki Cuyler ... 90
Sam Rice ... 90
Tony Lazzeri ... 80
Luke Appling ... 77
Lefty Gomez ... 76
Burleigh Grimes ... 71

1960
Needed to Elect: 202

Edd Roush ... 146
Sam Rice ... 143
Eppa Rixey ... 142
Burleigh Grimes ... 92
Jim Bottomley ... 89
Red Ruffing ... 86
Red Faber ... 83
Luke Appling ... 72
Kiki Cuyler ... 72
Hack Wilson ... 72

1962
Needed to Elect: 120

Bob Feller ... 150
Jackie Robinson ... 124
Sam Rice ... 81
Red Ruffing ... 72
Eppa Rixey ... 49
Luke Appling ... 48
Phil Rizzuto ... 44
Burleigh Grimes ... 43
Hack Wilson ... 39
Ducky Medwick ... 34

1964
Needed to Elect: 151

Luke Appling ... 142
Red Ruffing ... 141
Roy Campanella ... 115
Ducky Medwick ... 108
Pee Wee Reese ... 73
Lou Boudreau ... 68
Al Lopez ... 57
Chuck Klein ... 56
Johnny Mize ... 54
Mel Harder ... 51
Johnny Vander Meer ... 51

1964 Run Off
Needed to Elect: 170
One Player Maximum

Luke Appling ... 189
Red Ruffing ... 184
Roy Campanella ... 138
Ducky Medwick ... 130
Pee Wee Reese ... 47
Lou Boudreau ... 43
Al Lopez ... 34
Johnny Vander Meer ... 20
Chuck Klein ... 18
Marty Marion ... 17

1966
Needed to Elect: 227

Ted Williams 282
Red Ruffing 208
Roy Campanella 197
Ducky Medwick 187
Lou Boudreau 115
Al Lopez 109
Enos Slaughter 100
Pee Wee Reese 95
Marty Marion 86
Johnny Mize 81

1967
Needed to Elect: 219

Ducky Medwick 212
Red Ruffing 212
Roy Campanella 204
Lou Boudreau 143
Ralph Kiner 124
Enos Slaughter 123
Al Lopez 114
Marty Marion 90
Johnny Mize 89
Pee Wee Reese 89

1967 Run Off
Needed to Elect: 230
One Player Maximum

Red Ruffing 266
Ducky Medwick 248
Roy Campanella 170
Lou Boudreau 68
Al Lopez 50
Enos Slaughter 48
Ralph Kiner 41
Johnny Vander Meer . 35
Ernie Lombardi 25
Bucky Walters 24

1968
Needed to Elect: 213

Ducky Medwick 240
Roy Campanella 205
Lou Boudreau 146
Enos Slaughter 129
Ralph Kiner 118
Johnny Mize 103
Allie Reynolds 95
Marty Marion 89
Arky Vaughan........ 82
Pee Wee Reese 81

1969
Needed to Elect: 255

Stan Musial 317
Roy Campanella 270
Lou Boudreau 218
Ralph Kiner 137
Enos Slaughter 128
Johnny Mize 116
Marty Marion 112
Allie Reynolds 98
Joe Gordon 97
Johnny Vander Meer . 95
Early Wynn 95

1970
Needed to Elect: 225

Lou Boudreau 232
Ralph Kiner 167
Gil Hodges 145
Early Wynn 140
Enos Slaughter 133
Johnny Mize 126
Marty Marion 120
Pee Wee Reese 97
Red Schoendienst .. 97
George Kell 90

1971
Needed to Elect: 270

Yogi Berra 242
Early Wynn 240
Ralph Kiner 212
Gil Hodges 180
Enos Slaughter 165
Johnny Mize 157
Pee Wee Reese 127
Marty Marion 123
Red Schoendienst .. 123
Allie Reynolds 110

1972
Needed to Elect: 297

Sandy Koufax 344
Yogi Berra 339
Early Wynn 301
Ralph Kiner 235
Gil Hodges 161
Johnny Mize 157
Enos Slaughter 149
Pee Wee Reese 129
Marty Marion 120
Bob Lemon 117

1973
Needed to Elect: 285

Warren Spahn 316
Whitey Ford 255
Ralph Kiner 235
Gil Hodges 218
Robin Roberts 213
Bob Lemon 177
Johnny Mize 157
Enos Slaughter 145
Marty Marion 127
Pee Wee Reese 126

1974
Needed to Elect: 274

Mickey Mantle 322
Whitey Ford 284
Robin Roberts 224
Ralph Kiner 215
Gil Hodges 198
Bob Lemon 190
Enos Slaughter 145
Pee Wee Reese 141
Eddie Mathews 118
Phil Rizzuto 111
Duke Snider 111

1975
Needed to Elect: 272

Ralph Kiner 273
Robin Roberts 263
Bob Lemon 233
Gil Hodges 188
Enos Slaughter 177
Hal Newhouser 155
Pee Wee Reese 154
Eddie Mathews 148
Phil Cavaretta 129
Duke Snider 129

1976
Needed to Elect: 291

Robin Roberts 337
Bob Lemon 305
Gil Hodges 233
Enos Slaughter 197
Eddie Mathews 189
Pee Wee Reese 186
Nellie Fox 174
Duke Snider 159
Phil Rizzuto 149
George Kell 129
Red Schoendienst .. 129

1977
Needed to Elect: 288

Ernie Banks 321
Eddie Mathews 239
Gil Hodges 224
Enos Slaughter 222
Duke Snider 212
Don Drysdale 197
Pee Wee Reese 163
Nellie Fox 152
Jim Bunning 146
George Kell 141

1978
Needed to Elect: 285

Eddie Mathews 301
Enos Slaughter 261
Duke Snider 254
Gil Hodges 226
Don Drysdale 219
Jim Bunning 181
Pee Wee Reese 169
Richie Ashburn 158
Hoyt Wilhelm 158
Nellie Fox 149

1979
Needed to Elect: 324

Willie Mays 409
Duke Snider 308
Enos Slaughter 297
Gil Hodges 242
Don Drysdale 233
Nellie Fox 174
Hoyt Wilhelm 168
Maury Wills 166
Red Schoendienst .. 159
Jim Bunning 147

1980
Needed to Elect: 289

Al Kaline 340
Duke Snider 333
Don Drysdale 238
Gil Hodges 230
Hoyt Wilhelm 209
Jim Bunning 177
Red Schoendienst .. 164
Nellie Fox 161
Maury Wills 146
Richie Ashburn 134

1981
Needed to Elect: 301

Bob Gibson 337
Don Drysdale 243
Gil Hodges 241
Harmon Killebrew .. 239
Hoyt Wilhelm 238
Juan Marichal 233
Nellie Fox 168
Red Schoendienst .. 166
Jim Bunning 164
Maury Wills 163

1982
Needed to Elect: 312

Hank Aaron 406
Frank Robinson 370
Juan Marichal 305
Harmon Killebrew .. 246
Hoyt Wilhelm 236
Don Drysdale 233
Gil Hodges 205
Luis Aparicio 174
Jim Bunning 138
Red Schoendienst .. 135

1983
Needed to Elect: 281

Brooks Robinson ... 344
Juan Marichal 313
Harmon Killebrew .. 269
Luis Aparicio 252
Hoyt Wilhelm 243
Don Drysdale 242
Gil Hodges 237
Nellie Fox 173
Billy Williams 153
Red Schoendienst .. 146

1984
Needed to Elect: 303

Luis Aparicio 341
Harmon Killebrew .. 335
Don Drysdale 316
Hoyt Wilhelm 290
Nellie Fox 246
Billy Williams 202
Jim Bunning 201
Orlando Cepeda 124
Tony Oliva 124
Roger Maris 107

1985
Needed to Elect: 297

Hoyt Wilhelm 331
Lou Brock 315
Nellie Fox 295
Billy Williams 252

1986
Needed to Elect: 319

Willie McCovey 346
Billy Williams 315
Catfish Hunter 289
Jim Bunning 279
Roger Maris 177
Tony Oliva 154
Orlando Cepeda ... 152
Harvey Kuenn 144
Maury Wills 124
Bill Mazeroski 100

1987
Needed to Elect: 310

Billy Williams 354
Catfish Hunter 315
Jim Bunning 289
Orlando Cepeda ... 179
Roger Maris 176
Tony Oliva 160
Harvey Kuenn 144
Bill Mazeroski 125
Maury Wills 113
Ken Boyer 96
Lew Burdette 96

1988
Needed to Elect: 321

Willie Stargell 352
Jim Bunning 317
Tony Oliva 202
Orlando Cepeda ... 199
Roger Maris 184
Harvey Kuenn 168
Bill Mazeroski 143
Luis Tiant 132
Maury Wills 127
Ken Boyer 109
Mickey Lolich 109

1989
Needed to Elect: 336

Johnny Bench 431
Carl Yastrzemski.... 423
Gaylord Perry 304
Jim Bunning 283
Fergie Jenkins 234
Orlando Cepeda ... 176
Tony Oliva 135
Bill Mazeroski 134
Harvey Kuenn 115
Maury Wills 95

1990
Needed to Elect: 333

Jim Palmer 411
Joe Morgan 363
Gaylord Perry....... 320
Fergie Jenkins 296

Jim Bunning 214
Catfish Hunter 212
Roger Maris 128
Harvey Kuenn 125
Orlando Cepeda ... 114
Tony Oliva 114

Jim Bunning 257
Orlando Cepeda ... 211
Tony Oliva 142
Bill Mazeroski 131
Harvey Kuenn 107
Ron Santo 96

1991
Needed to Elect: 333

Rod Carew 401
Gaylord Perry 342
Fergie Jenkins 334
Rollie Fingers 291
Jim Bunning 282
Orlando Cepeda ... 192
Tony Oliva 160
Bill Mazeroski 142
Ron Santo 116
Harvey Kuenn 100

1992
Needed to Elect: 323

Tom Seaver 425
Rollie Fingers 349
Orlando Cepeda ... 246
Tony Perez 215
Bill Mazeroski 182
Tony Oliva 175
Ron Santo 136
Jim Kaat 114
Maury Wills 110
Ken Boyer 71

1993
Needed to Elect: 318

Reggie Jackson 396
Phil Niekro 278
Orlando Cepeda ... 252
Tony Perez 233
Steve Garvey 176
Tony Oliva 157
Ron Santo 155
Jim Kaat 125
Dick Allen 70
Ken Boyer 69

1994
Needed to Elect: 342

Steve Carlton 436
Orlando Cepeda ... 335
Phil Niekro 273
Tony Perez 263
Don Sutton 259
Steve Garvey 166
Tony Oliva 158
Ron Santo 150
Bruce Sutter 109
Jim Kaat 98

1995
Needed to Elect: 345

Mike Schmidt...... 444
Phil Niekro.......... 286
Don Sutton 264
Tony Perez 259
Steve Garvey 196
Tony Oliva 149
Ron Santo 139
Jim Rice 137
Bruce Sutter........ 137
Jim Kaat............ 100

## CHAPTER 13

The All-Star Game

Frederick Ivor-Campbell

Although the tradition of All-Star Games in baseball dates back to an 1858 series between teams of stars from Brooklyn and New York (they were called "picked nines" in those days), the current All-Star series began when Arch Ward, sports editor of the *Chicago Tribune*, persuaded hesitant league owners to go along with his proposal for a game between stars from the American and National leagues, to be played in Chicago during that city's Century of Progress Exposition in 1933.

All-Star managers (who, except for the first game, have been the pilots of the previous year's pennant winners) shared with fans the selection of players for the first two games. From 1935 through 1946 the manager selected his whole squad. Since 1947, he has chosen his pitchers and all other players except the eight members of the starting lineup. The fans chose the starters in 1947–1957; after an incident of ballot-box stuffing by Cincinnati partisans in 1957, the major league players, coaches, and managers made the choice in 1958–1969; in 1970 the selection of starting lineups was returned to the fans.

The American League dominated the early years of the series, winning the first three games, and extending their winning margin to eight games (12–4) by 1949. The National League cut the lead in half with four straight wins, and by 1964 had drawn even in the series (17–17–1). From 1965 through 1985 the National Leaguers continued their drive, winning 19 All-Star Games while losing only two, to build a commanding 36–19 lead in the series. In recent years, though, the American Leaguers have begun to come back, winning in 1993 their seventh game in eight years, and their sixth in a row. The National League won in 1994, but it took extra innings to break the American League streak.

GAME 1
Comiskey Park, Chicago
July 6, 1933
AL, 4–2

```
NL   000 002 000   2 8 0
AL   012 001 00X   4 9 1
```

Pitchers: HALLAHAN, Warneke (3), Hubbell (7) vs GOMEZ, Crowder (4), Grove (7)
Home Runs: Ruth-A, Frisch-N
Attendance: 49,200

Baseball's two grand old managers—Connie Mack and John McGraw—were chosen to lead the American and National League squads in the first All-Star Game, and American starting pitcher Lefty Gomez of the Yankees took home honors both as the first All-Star winning pitcher and as the first player to drive in an All-Star run (singling in Jimmie Dykes in the second inning). But it was another "grand old man"—Babe Ruth—who made the game's headlines. At thirty-eight, in his next-to-last season as a Yankee, he lined a two-run homer in the third to make the score 3–0, and as right fielder in the eighth he robbed Chick Hafey of a hit with a remarkable running catch of Hafey's line drive.

Frank Frisch homered for the Nationals, following up Pepper Martin's RBI with a solo shot in the National League's two-run sixth. But the American stars countered with an insurance run in the bottom of the sixth, as Earl Averill singled in Joe Cronin to end the scoring. Carl Hubbell for the Nationals and Lefty Grove for the Americans blanked the opposition through the final innings.

GAME 2
Polo Grounds, New York
July 10, 1934
AL, 9–7

```
AL   000 261 000   9 14 1
NL   103 030 000   7  8 1
```

Pitchers: Gomez, Ruffing (4), HARDER (5) vs Hubbell, Warneke (4), MUNGO (5), J.Dean (6), Frankhouse (9)
Home Runs: Frisch-N, Medwick-N
Attendance: 48,363

This was the game in which Carl Hubbell struck out Babe Ruth, Lou Gehrig, Jimmie Foxx, Al Simmons, and Joe Cronin in order in the first two innings. Hubbell also walked two and gave up two hits in his three innings of work, but allowed no run to score as his Nationals took a 4–0 lead on homers by Frank Frisch in the first and Joe Medwick (for three runs) in the third off American starter (and first-game winner) Lefty Gomez.

But with Hubbell gone, the Americans pounced on Lon Warneke and Van Lingle Mungo for four runs each in the fourth and fifth innings. The Nationals battled back for three off Red Ruffing in their half of the fifth, to come within a run of tying the game. But Mel Harder relieved Ruffing with none out and put out the fire, one-hitting the National stars over the final five innings. The Americans picked up an insurance run in the sixth off Dizzy Dean before Dean and Fred Frankhouse shut them down, too, through the final three frames.

GAME 3
Municipal Stadium, Cleveland
July 8, 1935
AL, 4–1

```
NL   000 100 000   1 4 1
AL   210 010 00X   4 8 0
```

Pitchers: WALKER, Schumacher (3), Derringer (7), J.Dean (8) vs GOMEZ, Harder (7)
Home Runs: Foxx-A
Attendance: 69,812

Lefty Gomez started his third All-Star Game, and pitched a record six innings to pick up his second All-Star win. For three innings he shut out the Nationals as the Americans built a lead behind him on Jimmie Foxx's two-run homer in the first, and Rollie Hemsley's triple and Joe Cronin's run-scoring fly in the second.

The National Leaguers tried to catch up in the fourth, when they put together two of their three hits off Gomez—a double by Arky Vaughan and a single by Bill Terry—and scored a run. But an inning later Foxx nullified the National run, singling Joe Vosmik home for his third RBI.

Gomez blanked the National stars through two more innings before yielding to Mel Harder, who came in to close his second All-Star Game. Harder had created an All-Star record the previous year with his five consecutive scoreless innings pitched, and extended the record to eight, with three more shutout innings to end the game.

GAME 4
Braves Field, Boston
July 7, 1936
NL, 4–3

```
AL   000 000 300   3 7 1
NL   020 020 00X   4 9 0
```

Pitchers: GROVE, Rowe (4), Harder (7) vs J.DEAN, Hubbell (4), C.Davis (7), Warneke (7)
Home Runs: Galan-N, Gehrig-A
Attendance: 25,534

The National League, which had not yet won an All-Star Game, scored first in the second when Gabby Hartnett tripled in a run off Lefty Grove—rookie Joe DiMaggio missing his try for a shoe-top catch of Hartnett's drive to right field. Pinky Whitney then singled in Hartnett. Augie Galan homered off Schoolboy Rowe (and the right field foul pole) in the fifth, and DiMaggio's bobble of Billy Herman's single a batter later put Herman in position to score an unearned fourth run, on Joe Medwick's single, that proved to be the margin of victory.

The Americans, shut out through six by Dizzy Dean and Carl Hubbell, nearly tied the game in the seventh off Curt Davis as Lou Gehrig homered and Luke Appling singled in two more. But Lon Warneke took over and, after loading the bases with a walk, escaped disaster as shortstop Leo Durocher snared DiMaggio's vicious line drive to his right for the third out. Warneke shut the Americans out over the final two innings to preserve the one-run lead and the National League's first All-Star win.

GAME 5
Griffith Stadium, Washington
July 7, 1937
AL, 8–3

```
NL   000 111 000    3 13 0
AL   002 312 00X    8 13 2
```
Pitchers: J.DEAN, Hubbell (4), Blanton (4), Grissom (5), Mungo (6), Walters (8) vs GOMEZ, Bridges (4), Harder (7)
Home Runs: Gehrig-A
Attendance: 31,391

President Franklin Roosevelt attended the game. Lou Gehrig homered and doubled to drive in half the American League's eight runs in an easy American win. Lefty Gomez started his fourth All-Star Game in five years, winning his third. And AL reliever Mel Harder pitched the final innings for the fourth All-Star Game in a row, pushing his record for consecutive All-Star shutout innings to 13. But the game is remembered not for any of these things, but for Earl Averill's line drive in the third inning which fractured Dizzy Dean's toe and led to the premature end of his spectacular career. (Dean recovered from the broken toe, but tried to resume his pitching too soon. In favoring the toe, he changed his delivery and irreparably injured his pitching arm.)

The Americans began their scoring when Gehrig, who preceded Averill in the batting order, homered off Dean in the third, with one aboard. They added to their score in each of the next three innings, so that although the Nationals countered with single runs in the three middle innings, they only fell farther behind.

GAME 6
Crosley Field, Cincinnati
July 6, 1938
NL, 4–1

```
AL   000 000 001    1 7 4
NL   100 100 20X    4 8 0
```
Pitchers: GOMEZ, Allen (4), Grove (7) vs VANDER MEER, Lee (4), Brown (7)
Attendance: 27,607

For the fifth (and final) time, Lefty Gomez started for the American League, and although he gave up only two hits and no earned runs in his three innings, he was saddled with the loss when an error by shortstop Joe Cronin paved the way for a National League run in the first.

The Nationals scored their only earned run in the fourth when Mel Ott tripled and Ernie Lombardi singled him home. But in the seventh they recorded two more unearned runs when Leo Durocher bunted to move Frank McCormick to second. Both McCormick and Durocher scored as third baseman Jimmie Foxx threw wildly to first and right fielder Joe DiMaggio (who chased the ball down) missed home plate with his throw.

In the ninth DiMaggio singled and Cronin doubled him home in partial atonement for their errors. But as Johnny Vander Meer and Big Bill Lee had each blanked the American stars on one hit in their three-inning stints, and some fine outfield catches had kept them from scoring more than this one run off Mace Brown, the Americans' errors cost them the game.

GAME 7
Yankee Stadium, New York
July 11, 1939
AL, 3–1

```
NL   001 000 000    1 7 1
AL   000 210 00X    3 6 1
```
Pitchers: Derringer, LEE (4), Fette (7) vs Ruffing, BRIDGES (4), Feller (6)
Home Runs: J.DiMaggio-A
Attendance: 62,892

Six Yankees started for the American League, and one of them—Joe DiMaggio—hit the game's only home run. But it was a young Cleveland pitcher—twenty-year-old Bob Feller, playing in his first All-Star Game—who turned in the most memorable performance.

The Nationals scored first, with a run in the third on three hits off the American League starter, Red Ruffing. But the Americans came back with two runs in the fourth on a walk, two singles, and a bobbled grounder by shortstop Arky Vaughan. DiMaggio hit his insurance homer an inning later.

In the top of the sixth, after two singles and an error had loaded the bases with National stars, with only one out, Feller replaced Tommy Bridges to face Vaughan (who had earlier singled and scored his team's only run). One pitch got Feller out of the inning as Vaughan grounded into a 4–6–3 double play. Feller shut out the National stars over the final three innings, striking out Johnny Mize and Stan Hack in the ninth to end the game and give the Americans their fifth All-Star victory.

GAME 8
Sportsman's Park, St. Louis
July 9, 1940
NL, 4–0

```
AL   000 000 000    0 3 1
NL   300 000 01X    4 7 0
```
Pitchers: RUFFING, Newsom (4), Feller (7) vs DERRINGER, Walters (3), Wyatt (5), French (7), Hubbell (9)
Home Runs: West-N
Attendance: 32,373

The National Leaguers made short work of the Americans, scoring three times in the first inning and holding the opposing stars to three hits for the All-Star Game's first shutout. Before American League starter Red Ruffing retired a single National batter in the bottom of the first inning, three of the game's four runs had been scored, on singles by Arky Vaughan and Billy Herman and Max West's home run to right center.

Ruffing then settled down, and he and Buck Newsom held the Nationals to just three additional hits through the seventh. Bob Feller gave up the Nationals' fourth run in the eighth, on a walk, a sacrifice, and Harry Danning's single.

Five National League pitchers combined for the shutout, permitting only five batters to reach base while striking out seven. Starter Paul Derringer, who struck out three men in his two innings, was awarded the win.

GAME 9
Briggs Stadium, Detroit
July 8, 1941
AL, 7–5

```
NL   000 001 220   5 10 2
AL   000 101 014   7 11 3
```
Pitchers: Wyatt, Derringer (3), Walters (5), PASSEAU (7) vs Feller, Lee (4), Hudson (7), SMITH (8)
Home Runs: Vaughn-N (2), Williams-A
Attendance: 54,674

The National Leaguers entered the last of the ninth with a 5–3 lead and hopes of nailing down their first back-to-back All-Star victories. The American stars had scored their first run in the fourth. The Nationals tied the score in the top of the sixth, but the Americans countered with a run later in the inning. The Nationals' Arky Vaughan then made a bid to be the game's hero, homering in the seventh off Sid Hudson with a man aboard to restore the National lead, and homering again an inning later off Edgar Smith for two more runs.

A double and single by the DiMaggio brothers Joe and Dom brought the Americans a run closer in the eighth, but they still needed two to tie as they faced Claude Passeau in the bottom of the ninth. Two one-out singles and a walk loaded the bases, and a force play at second (that just missed being a game-ending double play) scored Ken Keltner from third. With two men now out and the Americans still down a run, Ted Williams homered on a letter-high fastball against the upper parapet in right for three more runs and another American League victory.

GAME 10
Polo Grounds, New York
July 6, 1942
AL, 3–1

```
AL   300 000 000   3 7 0
NL   000 000 010   1 6 1
```
Pitchers: CHANDLER, Benton (5) vs M.COOPER, Vander Meer (4), Passeau (7), Walters (9)
Home Runs: Boudreau-A, York-A, Owen-N
Attendance: 33,694

Home runs accounted for all the scoring as the American League, in something of a reverse of the 1940 game, scored three times in the top of the first to defeat the Nationals. Lou Boudreau, leading off, hit the game winner off Mort Cooper's second pitch, into the upper deck in left field. A double and two outs later, Rudy York put one over the fence near the short right field foul line for two more runs.

The Americans hit safely only four more times, and scored no more runs, but they already had more than enough, as Spud Chandler and Al Benton combined to shut out the National League stars for seven innings, until Mickey Owen, pinch-hitting for pitcher Claude Passeau in the eighth, hit his only home run of the summer.

This was the second All-Star Game played in the Polo Grounds. It had been Brooklyn's turn to host the game at Ebbets Field, but because the proceeds were destined for the war effort, the site was shifted to the larger stadium. The game might as well have been held in Brooklyn, though, as a pregame rain held attendance to well below the Polo Grounds' capacity.

GAME 11
Shibe Park, Philadelphia
July 13, 1943
AL, 5–3

```
NL   100 000 101   3 10 3
AL   031 010 00X   5 8 1
```
Pitchers: M.COOPER, Vander Meer (3), Sewell (6), Javery (7) vs LEONARD, Newhouser (4), Hughson (7)
Home Runs: Doerr-A, V.DiMaggio-N
Attendance: 31,938

For the first time, the All-Star Game was played at night. And for the only time in All-Star history, no Yankee played—although six had been named to the American League squad. But Yankee Joe Mc-Carthy (serving for the sixth time as American manager) was piqued by criticism that he favored his own players, and retaliated by keeping them all on the bench.

The only DiMaggio in this war-time game was Pittsburgh's Vince, and he provided most of the National League power—batting 3 for 3, with eight total bases and two of his team's three runs. But after the Nationals had jumped to a one-run lead in the first, Bobby Doerr of the Americans homered off Mort Cooper with two aboard in the second to put the American stars ahead. They added to their lead with a run in the third and another in the fifth. DiMaggio scored in the seventh after tripling off Tex Hughson and added a homer against Hughson in the ninth, but his heroics were not enough to overcome the American League's march to its third win in a row, and its eighth in eleven tries.

GAME 12
Forbes Field, Pittsburgh
July 11, 1944
NL, 7–1

```
AL   010 000 000   1 6 3
NL   000 040 21X   7 12 1
```
Pitchers: Borowy, HUGHSON (4), Muncrief (5), Newhouser (7), Newsom (8) vs Walters, RAFFENSBERGER (4), Sewell (6), Tobin (9)
Attendance: 29,589

For the second time the game was played at night, and for the seventh time Joe McCarthy managed the American League team. But this time—unlike Game 11—he let his Yankees play. He started Yankee pitcher Hank Borowy, who not only shut out the Nationals in his three innings but drove in a run in the second to give his team the lead.

But that was all the American stars got. For the first four innings it was enough, but in the fifth a double, four singles, a walk, an error, and a stolen base brought in four National League runs. In the seventh, Whitey Kurowski doubled in two more National runs, and in the eighth a missed third strike, two walks, and a fly ball produced a seventh and final tally.

No home runs were hit in the game, only the second time that had happened in All-Star play. But Phil Cavarretta of the Nationals tripled—and reached base four additional times on a single and three walks for a new All-Star on-base record.

GAME 13
Fenway Park, Boston
July 9, 1946
AL, 12–0

```
NL  000 000 000    0  3  0
AL  200 130 24X   12 14  1
```
Pitchers: PASSEAU, Higbe (4),
 Blackwell (5), Sewell (8) vs FELLER,
 Newhouser (4), Kramer (7)
Home Runs: Keller-A, Williams-A (2)
Attendance: 34,906

No All-Star Game was played in 1945 because of restrictions on wartime travel, but when the classic resumed in 1946 the American stars avenged their 1944 loss with the most decisive All-Star victory to date: 12–0. American pitchers Bob Feller, Hal Newhouser, and Jack Kramer combined to hold the National stars to three singles and a walk, as their teammates pounded National pitching for 14 hits, including two doubles and three home runs.

But the game belonged to Ted Williams. Back after three years at war, and playing before his hometown fans, he equaled Phil Cavarretta's 1944 on-base record in spectacular fashion, with one walk, two singles, and two home runs: one a drive into the center field bleachers and the other the first homer ever hit off Rip Sewell's looping "eephus" pitch. He scored the game's first run in the first inning as Charlie Keller followed his walk with a homer, and went on to break an All-Star record by scoring three more times, while driving in a record five runs.

GAME 14
Wrigley Field, Chicago
July 8, 1947
AL, 2–1

```
AL  000 001 100    2  8  0
NL  000 100 000    1  5  1
```
Pitchers: Newhouser, SHEA (4),
 Masterson (7), Page (8) vs Blackwell,
 Brecheen (4), SAIN (7), Spahn (8)
Home Runs: Mize-N
Attendance: 41,123

Johnny Mize homered for the National League off rookie Spec Shea in the fourth inning for the game's first run, after three one-hit innings by the two lanky starters, Ewell Blackwell of the Nationals and Hal Newhouser of the Americans. Mize's run remained the only score until the sixth inning, when the American Leaguers tied the game on two singles and a double-play grounder.

Sharp baserunning by Bobby Doerr—plus a little luck—led to the Americans' second run an inning later. Doerr singled, then stole second. He took third when pitcher Johnny Sain's pickoff throw bounced off Doerr's back into the outfield. Pinch hitter Stan Spence then singled Doerr home with what proved to be the game's final—and winning—run. The Nationals put men on first and third in the eighth, but shortstop Lou Boudreau's spectacular stop of a hot grounder and sharp throw to first retired the side and ended the threat.

GAME 15
Sportsman's Park, St. Louis
July 13, 1948
AL, 5–2

```
NL  200 000 000    2  8  0
AL  011 300 00X    5  6  0
```
Pitchers: Branca, SCHMITZ (4),
 Sain (4), Blackwell (6) vs Masterson,
 RASCHI (4), Coleman (7)
Home Runs: Musial-N, Evers-A
Attendance: 34,009

Vic Raschi pitched three shutout innings for the American stars and drove in two go-ahead runs with a fourth-inning single as the American League—for the third time since the All-Star Game originated in 1933—won its third classic in a row. The Nationals scored first on Stan Musial's two-run homer in the top of the first. But that was all they got, as starter Walt Masterson settled down and shut out the Nationals through the second and third innings. Raschi then came on for his shutout stint, and Joe Coleman stopped the Nationals without even a hit over the final three innings.

Meanwhile, the Americans scored a run in the second on Hoot Evers's homer, and tied the game with another run in the third on two walks, a double steal, and an outfield fly. Then in the fourth, when two walks and a single had loaded the bases, pitcher Raschi singled in the third and fourth American runs. Joe DiMaggio's pinch-hit fly scored a fifth run. Johnny Sain and Ewell Blackwell shut out the Americans the rest of the way, but the damage had been done.

GAME 16
Ebbets Field, Brooklyn
July 12, 1949
AL, 11–7

```
AL  400 202 300   11 13  1
NL  212 002 000    7 12  5
```
Pitchers: Parnell, TRUCKS (2),
 Brissie (4), Raschi (7) vs Spahn,
 NEWCOMBE (2), Munger (5),
 Bickford (6), Pollet (7), Blackwell (8),
 Roe (9)
Home Runs: Musial-N, Kiner-N
Attendance: 32,577

Each team scored seven earned runs in this game which saw a total of 25 hits, including seven doubles and two home runs. But two first-inning National League errors let in four unearned American runs to provide the margin for the American League's fourth consecutive All-Star win. Stan Musial and Ralph Kiner each drove in two National runs with homers, but Eddie Joost singled in two runs for the Americans and Joe DiMaggio singled and doubled in three more to lead the American attack. For the second year in a row, Vic Raschi shut out the National stars for three innings, this time holding the American lead over the final third of the game.

The game was notable as the first to include black players: three Dodgers (Jackie Robinson, Roy Campanella, and Don Newcombe) for the National League, and Larry Doby for the American. With the Americans now ahead 12–4, it also marked the farthest extent of American League domination of the midsummer classic.

GAME 17
Comiskey Park, Chicago
July 11, 1950
NL, 4–3

```
NL    020 000 001 000  01   4 10 0
AL    001 020 000 000  00   3  8 1
```

Pitchers: Roberts, Newcombe (4), Konstanty (6), Jansen (7), BLACKWELL (12) vs Raschi, Lemon (4), Houtteman (7), Reynolds (10), GRAY (13), Feller (14)
Home Runs: Kiner-N, Schoendienst-N
Attendance: 46,127

For the first time, the All-Star Game went into extra innings, and for the first time the National League won a game as the visiting team. Three pitchers each hurled three innings of shutout ball: Bob Lemon and Allie Reynolds for the American League and Ewell Blackwell (who finished the game and got the win) for the Nationals. But top pitching honors were earned by National Leaguer Larry Jansen, who struck out six and gave up only one hit over *five* shutout innings (7–11).

The National stars scored first with two runs in the second. The Americans came back with one in the third, and tied and took the lead in the fifth on George Kell's run-scoring fly and an RBI single by Ted Williams (who, it was later learned, had broken his left elbow making an off-the-wall catch in the first inning). But in the top of the ninth, Ralph Kiner of the Nationals hit a game-tying homer, and 4½ scoreless innings later Red Schoendienst—on the first pitch of the fourteenth inning—homered off American Ted Gray with what proved to be the game winner.

GAME 18
Briggs Stadium, Detroit
July 10, 1951
NL, 8–3

```
NL    100 302 110   8 12 1
AL    010 110 000   3 10 2
```

Pitchers: Roberts, MAGLIE (3), Newcombe (6), Blackwell (9) vs Garver, LOPAT (4), Hutchinson (5), Parnell (8), Lemon (9)
Home Runs: Musial-N, Elliott-N, Wertz-A, Kell-A, Hodges-N, Kiner-N
Attendance: 52,075

In a game moved from Philadelphia to help Detroit celebrate its 250th birthday, hometowners Vic Wertz and George Kell of the Tigers hit solo homers in the fourth and fifth innings to bring the American stars within a run of the Nationals. But they came no closer, as the National Leaguers pulled away for a convincing 8–3 victory.

The Nationals, aided by six innings of shutout pitching (including three by Don Newcombe), produced four home runs of their own to drive in six of their eight runs. With the score tied 1–1 going into the fourth inning, Stan Musial greeted Ed Lopat's first pitch with a shot to the right field upper deck, and Bob Elliott added two more runs later in the inning with a homer to left. Gil Hodges increased the National League lead to 6–3 with a two-run homer in the sixth, and Ralph Kiner concluded the Nationals' scoring with a solo upper-deck shot to left center in the eighth. For the first time in All-Star play, the National League had won two games in a row.

GAME 19
Shibe Park, Philadelphia
July 8, 1952
NL, 3–2

```
AL    000 20   2 5 0
NL    100 20   3 3 0
```

Pitchers: Raschi, LEMON (3), Shantz (5) vs Simmons, RUSH (4)
Home Runs: J.Robinson-N, Sauer-N
Attendance: 32,785

No sun shone for this rain-shortened game, but two hometown pitchers did. Curt Simmons of the Phillies held the American stars to one hit as he shut them out over the first three innings. And the Athletics' Bobby Shantz—in the midst of an MVP season—struck out the side in the fifth for the Americans.

But home runs and rain determined the final outcome. Jackie Robinson opened the scoring with a homer off Vic Raschi in the bottom of the first to give the Nationals a 1–0 lead. In the fourth the Americans came back to take the lead briefly with two runs on a double, a walk, and two singles off eventual winner Bob Rush. But in the bottom of the inning, Hank Sauer's home run off Bob Lemon with one aboard returned the lead to the National League. And there it stayed through a scoreless fifth, when the rain, which had fallen throughout the game, at last brought the soggy festivities to the All-Star series' first premature conclusion.

GAME 20
Crosley Field, Cincinnati
July 14, 1953
NL, 5–1

```
AL    000 000 001   1 5 0
NL    000 020 12X   5 10 0
```

Pitchers: Pierce, REYNOLDS (4), Garcia (6) Paige (8) vs Roberts, SPAHN (4), Simmons (6), Dickson (8)
Attendance: 30,846

For the first 4½ innings, pitchers for both sides held the opposition scoreless, with one hit each. Then the National Leaguers got to Allie Reynolds for two runs in the bottom of the fifth on a hit batsman, a walk, and two singles.

This proved margin enough for the National League's fourth consecutive victory, as four National pitchers held the Americans to just two hits through eight innings before three singles in the ninth gave the American Leaguers their only run. For good measure, though, the National stars added a run in the seventh, and two more in the eighth (with three singles and a walk off Satchel Paige in his only All-Star appearance).

Enos Slaughter of the Nationals provided much of the game's excitement. With two singles, a walk, and a stolen base, he drove in one run and scored two others, and defensively made a spectacular diving catch in right field. Pee Wee Reese's double in the seventh (scoring Slaughter) was the game's only extra-base hit.

GAME 21
Municipal Stadium, Cleveland
July 13, 1954
AL, 11–9

```
NL  000 520 020   9 14 0
AL  004 121 03X  11 17 1
```
Pitchers: Roberts, Antonelli (4), Spahn (6), Grissom (6), CONLEY (8), Erskine (8) vs Ford, Consuegra (4), Lemon (4), Porterfield (5), Keegan (8), STONE (8), Trucks (9)
Home Runs: Rosen-A (2), Boone-A, Kluszewski-N, Bell-N, Doby-A
Attendance: 68,751

American starter Whitey Ford gave up only one hit in three shutout innings, and National starter Robin Roberts shut out the American stars through two. But in the bottom of the third Al Rosen tagged Roberts for a three-run homer, and Ray Boone followed with a solo shot. By the end of the game new All-Star records had been set for hits (31), runs (20), and pitchers used (13), and the record of 6 home runs had been equaled.

The Nationals topped the American four-run third with five straight hits off Sandy Consuegra in the fourth, for five runs. The Americans tied the game with a run in their half of the fourth, but Ted Kluszewski homered in the fifth for two more National League runs. In the bottom of the fifth, Rosen homered again, for two, to bring the Americans even again.

A run in the sixth put the Americans ahead, but Gus Bell's two-run blast in the eighth returned the Nationals to the top by one. They were threatening to lengthen that lead when Dean Stone entered the contest in relief of Bob Keegan with two out and Red Schoendienst on third. Before Stone's first delivery, Schoendienst broke for home and was tagged out, setting the stage for Stone to become the winning pitcher without making a pitch. American Larry Doby tied it up again later in the eighth with a home run, and Nellie Fox drove in the game's final two runs a few batters later with a bases-loaded single.

In the ninth, the Nationals' Stan Musial blasted two over the fence—both foul—with a man aboard. But Virgil Trucks retired him and Gil Hodges, who followed, to preserve the American League's first victory in five games.

GAME 22
County Stadium, Milwaukee
July 12, 1955
NL, 6–5

```
AL  400 001 000 000  5 10 2
NL  000 000 230 001  6 13 1
```
Pitchers: Pierce, Wynn (4), Ford (7), SULLIVAN (8) vs Roberts, Haddix (4), Newcombe (7), Jones (8), Nuxhall (8), CONLEY (12)
Home Runs: Mantle-A, Musial-N
Attendance: 45,314

Down 5–0 in the seventh inning, the National Leaguers came back to tie the game and send it into extra innings. The Americans attacked early, scoring four runs off Robin Roberts (three of them on Mickey Mantle's home run to center) before the game's first out had been recorded. They added a fifth run in the sixth inning. Meanwhile, pitchers Billy Pierce and Early Wynn were shutting the Nationals down on four hits.

In the seventh, though, two singles, a walk, and an American error gave the Nationals two runs, and in the eighth, four two-out singles and another error tied the game. Joe Nuxhall for the Nationals and the Americans' Frank Sullivan prevented further scoring through the eleventh. In the top of the twelfth, Gene Conley replaced Nuxhall and struck out the side: Al Kaline, Mickey Vernon, and Al Rosen. Sullivan returned for the Americans to face Stan Musial in the bottom of the twelfth. Musial hit the first pitch—a fastball—over the screen in right and the game was over.

GAME 23
Griffith Stadium, Washington
July 10, 1956
NL, 7–3

```
NL  001 211 200  7 11 0
AL  000 003 000  3 11 0
```
Pitchers: FRIEND, Spahn (4), Antonelli (6) vs PIERCE, Ford (4), Wilson (5), Brewer (6), Score (8), Wynn (9)
Home Runs: Mays-N, Williams-A, Mantle-A, Musial-N
Attendance: 28,843

Four of the game's greatest sluggers—Willie Mays, Stan Musial, Ted Williams, and Mickey Mantle—hit home runs, three of them off two of the game's greatest pitchers—Whitey Ford and Warren Spahn. But the star of the game was National League third baseman Ken Boyer, who went 3 for 5, scoring one run and driving in another, while making three spectacular diving and leaping plays in the field.

The National stars scored five times—including twice in the fourth on Mays's homer off Ford—before the Americans put a run on the board. But in the bottom of the sixth, Williams homered for two runs off Spahn, and Mantle followed him with another homer to bring the Americans within two. But that was the end of their scoring, as Johnny Antonelli relieved Spahn to stop the American stars the rest of the way. The Nationals scored twice more in the seventh—one of the runs coming on Musial's homer—ensuring them a comfortable 7–3 victory.

GAME 24
Sportsman's Park, St. Louis
July 9, 1957
AL, 6–5

```
AL  020 001 003  6 10 0
NL  000 000 203  5  9 1
```
Pitchers: BUNNING, Loes (4), Wynn (7), Pierce (7), Mossi (9), Grim (9) vs SIMMONS, Burdette (2), Sanford (6), Jackson (7), Labine (9)
Attendance: 30,693

Cincinnati fans stuffed the ballot boxes and elected Reds to start everywhere but first base. Commissioner Ford Frick removed two elected starters, but left five Reds in the lineup. They could not bring the National League the victory, though.

The Americans scored twice in the second on singles and walks to take a lead they held to the finish. Although reliever Lew Burdette—after walking in the second run—stopped the American stars through the fifth, Jim Bunning and Billy Loes were combining to keep the Nationals from scoring through the first six innings. The Americans, meanwhile, added a third run in the top of the sixth on a double, a wild pitch, and a single.

The Nationals scored their first two in the seventh, on two singles and a double, to draw within a run of a tie. But in the top of the ninth the Americans combined two singles, an error, a sacrifice bunt, and Minnie Minoso's pinch double for three more runs. They needed them all, for the Nationals responded in their half of the ninth with three runs of their own on a blend of walks, hits (including Willie Mays's triple), and a wild pitch. With two out and a runner at second, Gil Hodges lined one deep to left center. But Minoso, now in left field, snared the drive on the run to end the game.

GAME 25
Memorial Stadium, Baltimore
July 8, 1958
AL, 4–3

```
NL   210 000 000    3 4 2
AL   110 011 00X    4 9 2
```

Pitchers: Spahn, FRIEND (4), Jackson (6), Farrell (7) vs Turley, Narleski (2), WYNN (6), O'Dell (7)
Attendance: 48,829

Although American League pitchers held the National Leaguers to only four hits (all singles), the Nationals took a quick lead, and held it for half the game before they were overtaken. Willie Mays and Stan Musial singled in the top of the first, both scoring as American starter Bob Turley proceeded to give up a sacrifice fly, hit a batter, walk a man, and unload a wild pitch.

The Americans came back with one run in their half of the first, but the Nationals drove Turley out with their third run as Mays (who had reached on a fielder's choice) worked his way around the bases on a steal, an error, and Bob Skinner's single. Once again the Americans answered with a run, but they didn't tie the game until Mickey Vernon scored on a bases-loaded ground out in the fifth. An inning later they took the lead when pinch hitter Gil McDougald singled home Frank Malzone.

Billy O'Dell set down the Nationals in order over the final three innings to preserve the lead and give the American Leaguers their second consecutive victory.

GAME 26
Forbes Field, Pittsburgh
July 7, 1959
NL, 5–4

```
AL   000 100 030    4 8 0
NL   100 000 22X    5 9 1
```

Pitchers: Wynn, Duren (4), Bunning (7), FORD (8), Daley (8) vs Drysdale, Burdette (4), Face (7), ANTONELLI (8), Elston (9)
Home Runs: Mathews-N, Kaline-A
Attendance: 35,277

For the third year in a row, the game was decided by one run, with the National League celebrating the city of Pittsburgh's bicentennial by breaking the American League's win streak at two.

Eddie Mathews homered for the Nationals in the bottom of the first for the only run in the first three innings, as Don Drysdale stopped the Americans without a hit or walk, fanning four. Al Kaline tied the game in the top of the fourth with an American home run for the only score of the middle three innings, as Ryne Duren one-hit the Nationals, like Drysdale striking out four.

In the last of the seventh, though, a double and two singles off Jim Bunning put the Nationals ahead by two runs. The NL lead lasted only briefly, however, as the Americans moved back into the lead with three runs in the eighth off Roy Face, with two singles, a walk, and a double after Face had retired the first two men. But in their half of the eighth the Nationals hit on Whitey Ford, tying the game with a single-sacrifice-single, and scoring the game winner on Willie Mays's triple to center.

GAME 27
Memorial Coliseum, Los Angeles
August 3, 1959
AL, 5–3

```
AL   012 000 110    5 6 0
NL   100 010 100    3 6 3
```

Pitchers: WALKER, Wynn (4), Wilhelm, (6), O'Dell (7), McLish (8) vs DRYSDALE, Conley (4), Jones (6), Face (8)
Home Runs: Malzone-A, Berra-A, F. Robinson-N, Gilliam-N, Colavito-A
Attendance: 55,105

To raise extra money for the players' pension fund and other causes, a second All-Star Game was scheduled for 1959, the first ever to be played in August, and the first on the West Coast. The American stars avenged their earlier defeat with a 5–3 win, out-homering the Nationals three to two.

The National Leaguers scored first on a first-inning double and sacrifice fly, but Frank Malzone tied the score with the game's first home run. Yogi Berra homered an inning later with one on for a 3–1 American lead, but Frank Robinson brought the Nationals back to within one with his homer in the fifth. The Americans replaced that run in the top of the seventh on a walk, two errors, and a single, but Junior Gilliam countered with a home run in the last of the inning. Rocky Colavito scored the game's final run for the Americans in the eighth with the game's final homer.

Don Drysdale, the pitching standout of the July game, struck out five this time, but also walked three and gave up three runs on homers to take the loss.

GAME 28
Municipal Stadium, Kansas City
July 11, 1960
NL, 5–3

```
NL   311 000 000    5 12 4
AL   000 001 020    3  6 1
```

Pitchers: FRIEND, McCormick (4), Face (6), Buhl (8), Law (9) vs MONBOUQUETTE, Estrada (3), Coates (4), Bell (6), Lary (8), Daley (9)
Home Runs: Banks-N, Crandall-N, Kaline-A
Attendance: 30,619

The day was hot—the temperature broke 100—and so were the National League bats. Willie Mays went 3 for 4, including a leadoff triple and a double; Ernie Banks homered and doubled; Del Crandall homered and singled; and Joe Adcock doubled and singled for three-fourths of the Nationals' 12 hits as the National League scored five unanswered runs in the first three innings to take an unbeatable lead. Starter Bob Friend, meanwhile, blanked the Americans on one hit through three innings and Mike McCormick held them scoreless for two more before yielding the first American run in the sixth on Nellie Fox's bases-loaded single. Roy Face then came on to douse the fire, getting Luis Aparicio to ground into a double play.

Four American League pitchers stopped the National stars after the third inning, and Al Kaline homered for two more American runs in the eighth. In the ninth the Americans put men on first and second with one away. But their comeback fell short, as Vern Law came on to retire Brooks Robinson and Harvey Kuenn and preserve the National victory.

GAME 29
Yankee Stadium, New York
July 13, 1960
NL, 6–0

NL	021	000	102	6	10	0
AL	000	000	000	0	8	0

Pitchers: LAW, Podres (3), S.Williams (5), Jackson (7), Henry (8), McDaniel (9) vs FORD, Wynn (4), Staley (6), Lary (8), Bell (9)
Home Runs: Mathews-N, Mays-N, Musial-N, Boyer-N
Attendance: 38,362

Only two days after the first All-Star Game, the squads met a second time before fewer than 39,000 fans in capacious Yankee Stadium. It was no contest. Vern Law, who had completed and saved the first game, started and won this one. His two shutout innings set the pace for the five National pitchers who followed him to fashion the first National League shutout in twenty years. The American stars got only two fewer hits than the Nationals (8 to 10), but only one was for extra bases, whereas four of the National League hits were home runs.

Eddie Mathews began the scoring with a two-run homer in the second, and Willie Mays (on his way to a second straight 3-for-4 game) homered for the third National run an inning later. No one scored through the three middle innings, but in the seventh Stan Musial broke his own record with his sixth All-Star homer—a mighty shot three tiers up in right—and in the ninth Ken Boyer completed the rout with a two-run shot to left.

GAME 30
Candlestick Park,
San Francisco
July 11, 1961
NL, 5–4

AL	000	001	002	1	4	4	2
NL	010	100	010	2	5	11	5

Pitchers: Ford, Lary (4), Donovan (4), Bunning (6), Fornieles (8), WILHELM (8) vs Spahn, Purkey (4), McCormick (6), Face (9), Koufax (9), MILLER (9)
Home Runs: Killebrew-A, Altman-N
Attendance: 44,115

National League pitchers began the game where they had left off the year before. For five innings Warren Spahn and Bob Purkey shut out the American stars without a hit or base on balls. In the sixth, Harmon Killebrew homered off Mike McCormick to end the American drought, but it was the only hit McCormick yielded through the eighth.

Meanwhile, the Nationals had taken a 3–1 lead with runs in the second and fourth innings and George Altman's homer in the eighth. But in the top of the ninth, Candlestick's notorious winds helped put the Americans back in the game. Their second and third hits of the game brought in one run, and their fourth (and last) hit put another man on base. The tying run came in when the wind first of all blew pitcher Stu Miller off the mound for a balk to advance the runners, and then twisted a grounder out of third baseman Ken Boyer's grasp for a run-scoring error. In the tenth, the wind may have contributed to the Americans' go-ahead run as Boyer's throw to first sailed into the outfield, allowing Nellie Fox (who had walked) to score from first.

But in the last of the tenth the wind finally came to the aid of the Nationals, rendering useless the famous knuckleball of American reliever Hoyt Wilhelm, who gave up the tying run on hits by Hank Aaron and Willie Mays and lost the game when Roberto Clemente singled in Mays from second.

GAME 31
Fenway Park, Boston
July 31, 1961
Tie, 1–1

NL	000	001	000	1	5	1
AL	100	000	000	1	4	0

Pitchers: Purkey, Mahaffey (3), Koufax (5), Miller (7) vs Bunning, Schwall (4), Pascual (7)
Home Runs: Colavito-A
Attendance: 31,851

In the second All-Star Game of 1961, the weather again played a crucial role, as heavy rain at the end of the ninth inning forced the first (and, so far, only) All-Star tie.

Rocky Colavito's home run for the Americans in the first inning turned out to be his squad's only run, as four National League pitchers combined to shut out the American stars on only three singles the rest of the way. The American League pitching was just as effective, with starter Jim Bunning and finisher Camilo Pascual each pitching three no-hit innings. Don Schwall, who pitched the middle three innings, gave up all five National hits and the Nationals' one run. But even that might have been prevented.

In the sixth, with two on and two out, American shortstop Luis Aparicio waited for a slow grounder, failing to get the ball in time to throw the batter out and end the inning. The Nationals scored on the next play, Bill White's hot ground single up the middle, which Aparicio stopped brilliantly to prevent more than one run from scoring, but which did drive in the game's tying—and final—run.

GAME 32
D.C. Stadium, Washington
July 10, 1962
NL, 3–1

NL	000	002	010	3	8	0
AL	000	001	000	1	4	0

Pitchers: Drysdale, MARICHAL (4), Purkey (6), Shaw (8) vs Bunning, PASCUAL (4), Donovan (7), Pappas (9)
Attendance: 45,480

The stadium was new, President Kennedy threw out the first ball, and starters Don Drysdale of the Nationals and Jim Bunning of the Americans both pitched three innings of one-hit shutout ball. But Maury Wills stole the show. Entering the game in the sixth inning to run for forty-one-year-old Stan Musial, who had singled, Wills stole second, then scored on Dick Groat's single up the middle for the game's first run. Another single, a long fly out, and a ground out scored Groat with the second (and, as it turned out, winning) run.

Two singles and a fly out by Roger Maris brought in an American run in the bottom of the sixth off Bob Purkey. But that was all they got, as Purkey and Bob Shaw one-hit the American stars through the final three innings.

In the eighth inning Wills manufactured an insurance run for the Nationals. On first with a leadoff single, he somehow reached third on Jim Davenport's single to short left, racing from second to third as left fielder Rocky Colavito threw in to second. He scored after tagging on a foul out to right.

GAME 33
Wrigley Field, Chicago
July 30, 1962
AL, 9–4

```
AL   001 201 302   9 10 0
NL   010 000 111   4 10 4
```

Pitchers: Stenhouse, HERBERT (3), Aguirre (6), Pappas (9) vs Podres, MAHAFFEY (3), Gibson (5), Farrell (7), Marichal (8)
Home Runs: Runnels-A, Wagner-A. Colavito-A, Roseboro-N
Attendance: 38,359

With this second game of 1962, the leagues ended their four-year experiment of playing two All-Star games a year. The Americans out-homered the Nationals to spoil the National League's attempt to even the series at 16 wins apiece. But no matter—the American stars would win only once again in the next twenty years.

The National stars scored first on a double and single in the second, but Pete Runnels evened the score in the third with a solo homer, and Leon Wagner put the Americans ahead with a two-run shot an inning later. After Tom Tresh doubled home a fourth American run in the sixth, Rocky Colavito put the game out of reach with a three-run blast in the seventh.

The Nationals tried to come back with runs in the seventh and eighth, but the Americans neutralized them with two more of their own in the ninth (on two errors, two Juan Marichal wild pitches, a double, and a long fly out). With the score now 9–3, John Roseboro's solo homer in the last of the ninth put the Nationals in the home-run column, but that was all.

GAME 34
Municipal Stadium, Cleveland
July 9, 1963
NL, 5–3

```
NL   012 010 010   5 6 0
AL   012 000 000   3 11 1
```

Pitchers: O'Toole, JACKSON (3), Culp (5), Woodeshick (6), Drysdale (8) vs McBride, BUNNING (4), Bouton (6), Pizarro (7), Radatz (8)
Attendance: 44,160

Willie Mays sparked the National League to victory with his baserunning and timely hitting. Although he had only one hit—a single—he scored two runs and drove in two others in the Nationals' 5–3 win.

The National stars scored first when Mays walked in the second inning, stole second, and came in on a single by Dick Groat. The Americans tied the game in the last of the second, but in the top of the third Mays singled in one run, stole second again, and scored his second run on Ed Bailey's single.

Once again the Americans came back in the bottom of the third to tie the game on Albie Pearson's double, followed by two singles sandwiched around an infield out. But these were their last runs, as four National pitchers shut them out on four singles the rest of the way. Meanwhile, Mays drove in what proved to be the winning run with a ground out in the fifth. In the eighth the Nationals scored a final run when Ron Santo singled home Bill White, who had singled and stolen second.

GAME 35
Shea Stadium, New York
July 7, 1964
NL, 7–4

```
AL   100 002 100   4 9 1
NL   000 210 004   7 8 0
```

Pitchers: Chance, Wyatt (4), Pascual (5), RADATZ (7) vs Drysdale, Bunning (4), Short (6), Farrell (7), MARICHAL (9)
Home Runs: B.Williams-N, Boyer-N, Callison-N
Attendance: 50,850

A new stadium in the midst of a World's Fair was the venue for this game in which the National League at last drew even with the American at 17 wins apiece.

The American stars jumped into the lead with an unearned run in the first, but the Nationals (after Dean Chance had shut them out through three innings) overtook the Americans in the fourth, on home runs by Billy Williams and Ken Boyer, and Dick Groat doubled in a third run in the fifth. In the top of the sixth the Americans tied the score when Brooks Robinson tripled in a pair, and took the lead again an inning later on a sacrifice fly that barely scored Elston Howard ahead of Willie Mays's throw from center.

The Americans held their slim lead into the bottom of the ninth. But Mays walked (after fouling off five third strikes), stole second, and scored the tying run on a single to short right and an errant throw home. One intentional walk and two outs later, Johnny Callison hit Dick Radatz's 1–2 fastball over the fence in right to win the game.

GAME 36
Metropolitan Stadium, Bloomington, Minnesota
July 13, 1965
NL, 6–5

```
NL   320 000 100   6 11 0
AL   000 140 000   5 8 0
```

Pitchers: Marichal, Maloney (4), Drysdale (5), KOUFAX (6), Farrell (7), Gibson (8) vs Pappas, Grant (2), Richert (4), McDOWELL (6), Fisher (8)
Home Runs: Mays-N, Torre-N, Stargell-N, McAuliffe-A, Killebrew-A
Attendance: 46,706

For a while it looked as though the Nationals would run away with the game. Willie Mays led off with a home run in the first, and Joe Torre added two runs with a homer later in the inning. In the second Willie Stargell homered for two more runs to make the score 5–0. National starter Juan Marichal stopped the Americans on one hit through three innings.

But the American stars battled back. A single, a walk, and another single off Marichal's replacement, Jim Maloney, brought in one run in the fourth. Maloney retired the first two men in the fifth, but then he gave up a walk followed by a home run to Dick McAuliffe, and a scratch single followed by a Harmon Killebrew homer—and the score was tied at 5–5.

Only one more run was scored. In the seventh, Willie Mays, who had walked and gone to third on Hank Aaron's single, scored on Ron Santo's infield hit to short. The Nationals held off American threats in the eighth and ninth to take the All-Star series lead for the first time.

GAME 37
Busch Memorial Stadium, St. Louis
July 12, 1966
NL, 2–1

```
AL    010 000 000 0    1 6 0
NL    000 100 000 1    2 6 0
```

Pitchers: McLain, Kaat (4), Stottlemyre (6), Siebert (8), RICHERT (10) vs Koufax, Bunning (4), Marichal (6), G.PERRY (9)
Attendance: 49,936

The celebration of another new stadium and the city's bicentennial—and a temperature of 106 Fahrenheit—greeted participants in the 1966 classic. Pitching dominated: seven pitchers hurled two innings or more each of shutout ball. American starter Denny McLain threw three perfect innings, but the National League's Sandy Koufax gave the Americans a run in the second when he let loose a wild pitch after Brooks Robinson had tripled.

The Nationals tied the score in the fourth with three singles off Jim Kaat, but that ended the scoring for both sides through the regulation nine innings. In the top of the tenth, Gaylord Perry stopped the American stars. But in the last half of the inning, National Leaguer Tim McCarver singled off Pete Richert, was sacrified to second, and came across with the winning run on Maury Wills's single to right.

GAME 38
Anaheim Stadium, Anaheim, California
July 11, 1967
NL, 2–1

```
NL    010 000 000 000 001    2 9 0
AL    000 001 000 000 000    1 8 0
```

Pitchers: Marichal, Jenkins (4), Gibson (7), Short (9), Cuellar (11), DRYSDALE (13), Seaver (15) vs Chance, McGlothlin (4), Peters (6), Downing (9), HUNTER (11)
Home Runs: Allen-N, B.Robinson-A, Perez-N
Attendance: 46,309

This was a game of strikeouts, home runs, and extra innings. Every one of the twelve pitchers used in the game struck out at least one batter. American Leaguers Gary Peters (who pitched three perfect middle innings) and Catfish Hunter struck out four apiece, while Ferguson Jenkins of the Nationals tied the All-Star record with six. The game total of 30 strikeouts shattered the previous record of 20 set in 1955.

Apart from the splendid pitching, three home runs provided the only excitement—and the only scoring—in this longest All-Star Game. Richie Allen of the Nationals scored first, homering to center off Dean Chance in the second inning. The Americans' Brooks Robinson tied the score in the sixth with a shot off Jenkins. And 8½ innings later, in the top of the fifteenth, National Leaguer Tony Perez homered off Hunter for the game's third and final run. Tom Seaver set down the Americans in the bottom of the fifteenth, and the game—after a record 3 hours and 41 minutes—was history.

GAME 39
Astrodome, Houston
July 9, 1968
NL, 1–0

```
AL    000 000 000    0 3 1
NL    100 000 00X    1 5 0
```

Pitchers: TIANT, Odom (3), McLain (5), McDowell (7), Stottlemyre (8), John (8) vs DRYSDALE, Marichal (4), Carlton (6), Seaver (7), Reed (9), Koosman (9)
Attendance: 48,321

This game could be described by what was missing: fresh air and real grass (it was the first All-Star Game held indoors), hitting (the eight hits were a new low for a nine-inning All-Star Game), and earned runs (the game's only run came with the help of an error). In fact, if it weren't for thirty-seven-year-old Willie Mays, the game might not have had any runs at all. Starting only because of an injury to Pete Rose, National Leaguer Mays led off the bottom of the first with a single, and took second when first baseman Harmon Killebrew mishandled pitcher Luis Tiant's pickoff throw for an error. Mays took third as the rattled Tiant threw a wild pitch to walk Curt Flood, and scored when Willie McCovey grounded into a double play.

The pitching on both sides was superb, but the National Leaguers shone especially bright. Tom Seaver gave up two of the Americans' three hits (all of which were doubles), but struck out five in his two innings. Juan Marichal hurled two perfect innings, fanning three. And none of the six National pitchers walked a man. One American, Killebrew, couldn't walk. Stretching for a throw at first, the slugger tore a hamstring and missed the next two months, the most serious All-Star Game casualty since Ted Williams's broken elbow 18 years earlier.

GAME 40
R.F.K. Memorial Stadium, Washington, D.C.
July 23, 1969
NL, 9–3

```
NL    125 100 000    9 11 0
AL    011 100 000    3  6 .2
```

Pitchers: CARLTON, Gibson (4), Singer (5), Koosman (7), Dierker (8), P.Niekro (9) vs STOTTLEMYRE, Odom (3), Knowles (3), McLain (4), McNally (5), McDowell (7), Culp (9)
Home Runs: Bench-N, Howard-A, McCovey-N (2), Freehan-A
Attendance: 45,259

After four one-run victories in a row, the National Leaguers finally broke loose, massing 10 of their 11 hits in the first four innings for nine runs and a crushing win. Scoring an unearned run in the first on a dropped outfield fly, and two in the second on Johnny Bench's home run, the Nationals erupted in the third for five runs off Blue Moon Odom before two outs had been recorded. Willie McCovey's two-run homer began the third-inning scoring, and an error, single, and two doubles added three more runs before Odom was mercifully relieved. McCovey homered again in the fourth for the Nationals' final tally.

The American bats were not wholly silent, but the solo homers by Frank Howard and Bill Freehan in the second and third, and a third run in the fourth, couldn't counter the Nationals' attack.

The final five innings of the game were as quiet as the opening four had been noisy. No runs scored, and the two teams together managed only three hits.

GAME 41
Riverfront Stadium, Cincinnati
July 14, 1970
NL, 5–4

```
AL  000 001 120 000   4 12 0
NL  000 000 103 001   5 10 0
```

Pitchers: Palmer, McDowell (4), J.Perry (7), Hunter (9), Peterson (9), Stottlemyre (9), WRIGHT (11) vs Seaver, Merritt (4), G.Perry (6), Gibson (8), OSTEEN (10)
Home Runs: Dietz-N
Attendance: 51,838

In a new stadium, opened only two weeks earlier, no one scored for the first five innings, as Jim Palmer and Sam McDowell of the Americans and Tom Seaver and Jim Merritt of the Nationals held the opposition to two hits per team. The Americans finally scored a run in the sixth, and another in the seventh. The Nationals got one back in the last of the seventh, but the Americans increased their lead to 4–1 in the eighth when Brooks Robinson tripled home two baserunners.

Fans had already begun to leave the park when the Nationals' Dick Dietz homered off Catfish Hunter to lead off the last of the ninth. Two pitchers, three singles, and a sacrifice fly later, the game was tied and headed for extra innings. Claude Osteen held the Americans scoreless from the tenth through the twelfth, and the Nationals also failed to score in the tenth and eleventh. But in the last of the twelfth, with two out, Pete Rose, Billy Grabarkewitz, and Jim Hickman singled. Hometowner Rose, racing home from second on Hickman's hit, crashed into catcher Ray Fosse with a force that injured both players and still provokes controversy—but which also gave the National League its eighth straight victory.

GAME 42
Tiger Stadium, Detroit
July 13, 1971
AL, 6–4

```
NL  021 000 010   4 5 0
AL  004 002 00X   6 7 0
```

Pitchers: ELLIS, Marichal (4), Jenkins (6), Wilson (7) vs BLUE, Palmer (4), Cuellar (6), Lolich (8)
Home Runs: Bench-N, Aaron-N, Jackson-A, F.Robinson-A, Killebrew-A, Clemente-N
Attendance: 53,559

With an assist from a favorable wind, six all-time greats homered to account for all the scoring as the American League broke its eight-game All-Star drought with a 6–4 victory. Johnny Bench put the Nationals in front with a two-run homer in the second inning off Vida Blue, and Hank Aaron—with his first All-Star home run—added a third run off Blue an inning later. But the Americans, shut out by Dock Ellis through the first two innings, rocked him in the bottom of the third as Reggie Jackson and Frank Robinson wrested the lead from the Nationals with a pair of two-run homers. (Robinson's made him the first player to hit an All-Star home run for both leagues.)

Ferguson Jenkins yielded the game's fifth homer, Harmon Killebrew's two-run shot for the Americans in the sixth. Roberto Clemente brought the Nationals a run closer with his solo homer off Mickey Lolich in the eighth, but that ended the team's scoring, and (for a year, anyway) the National League's All-Star stranglehold.

GAME 43
Atlanta-Fulton County Stadium, Atlanta
July 25, 1972
NL, 4–3

```
AL  001 000 020 0   3 6 0
NL  000 002 001 1   4 8 0
```

Pitchers: Palmer, Lolich (4), G.Perry (6), Wood (8), McNALLY (10) vs Gibson, Blass (3), Sutton (4), Carlton (6), Stoneman (7), McGRAW (9)
Home Runs: Aaron-N, Rojas-A
Attendance: 53,107

The American Leaguers tried to extend their All-Star win streak to two games, and for a time it looked as though they might do it. In the third, they scored the only run of the first half of the game as Jim Palmer and Mickey Lolich held the Nationals to two hits through the first five innings. In the sixth Hank Aaron thrilled the hometown crowd with a two-run homer deep to left to shift the lead to the National League. But Cookie Rojas restored the American lead with his own two-run shot in the eighth.

The Americans held their lead into the bottom of the ninth, but after two singles and a force out, the score was tied. Tug McGraw set down the American stars in order in the tenth, but American reliever Dave McNally was not so fortunate. He walked leadoff batter Nate Colbert, who was sacrificed to second. Joe Morgan then sent the American Leaguers back into the ranks of losers with a sharp RBI single to right center. His single also gave the Nationals their seventh win in seven extra-inning games.

GAME 44
Royals Stadium, Kansas City
July 24, 1973
NL, 7–1

```
NL  002 122 000   7 10 0
AL  010 000 000   1 5 0
```

Pitchers: WISE, Osteen (3), Sutton (5), Twitchell (6), Giusti (7), Seaver (8), Brewer (9) vs Hunter, Holtzman (2), BLYLEVEN (3), Singer (4), Ryan (6), Lyle (8), Fingers (9)
Home Runs: Bench-N, Bonds-N, W.Davis-N
Attendance: 40,849

Once again a new stadium was chosen to host the All-Star Game, and once again the National League emerged victorious. The Americans scored first, with a run in the second when Reggie Jackson scored from second on a single after doubling off the center field wall. But that was the beginning and end of their offense, as six National pitchers shut them out on three hits the rest of the way.

Meanwhile the National League hitters came to life, producing seven runs in four innings. Two walks and two singles in the third brought in two runs, and Johnny Bench's homer in the fourth made the score 3–1. In the fifth, Bobby Bonds—in the midst of his finest season—homered for two more National runs. And in the sixth, Willie Davis's home run completed the game's scoring, bringing in the Nationals' sixth and seventh runs.

The final third of the game was anticlimactic, as only two hits were made after the sixth inning. But Bonds brought the crowd to life briefly in the seventh, stretching one of those hits into a double with some audacious baserunning (ensuring his selection as the game's MVP).

GAME 45
Three Rivers Stadium, Pittsburgh
July 23, 1974
NL, 7–2

AL	002 000 000	2	4	1
NL	010 210 12X	7	10	1

Pitchers: G.Perry, TIANT (4), Hunter (6), Fingers (8) vs Messersmith, BRETT (4), Matlack (6), McGlothen (7), Marshall (8)
Home Runs: R.Smith-N
Attendance: 50,706

Steve Garvey, who was elected to the National League starting lineup on write-in votes (his name was omitted from the fans' All-Star ballot), sparked the Nationals to yet another convincing win over the hapless American stars. After singling in the second inning, he scored the game's first run on Ron Cey's double.

The Americans took the lead with two runs in the top of the third, capitalizing on two walks and an error sandwiched between Thurman Munson's leadoff double and Dick Allen's single. They might have scored more had not Garvey snared Bobby Murcer's hot grounder for an assist on the third out.

Garvey doubled in the tying run in the fourth, and Cey's RBI ground out restored the Nationals' lead. Lou Brock added a run in the fifth with a single and some inspired baserunning, and Reggie Smith homered for another in the seventh. Don Kessinger's triple and a wild pitch by Rollie Fingers in the eighth contributed to two final National League runs.

GAME 46
County Stadium, Milwaukee
July 15, 1975
NL, 6–3

NL	021 000 003	6	13	1
AL	000 003 000	3	10	1

Pitchers: Reuss, Sutton (4), Seaver (6), MATLACK (7), R.Jones (9) vs Blue, Busby (3), Kaat (5), HUNTER (7), Gossage (9)
Home Runs: Garvey-N, Wynn-N, Yastrzemski-A
Attendance: 51,480

When National stars Steve Garvey and Jim Wynn led off the second with back-to-back homers and their teammates added another run in the third, it looked as if the National League might be on its way to another easy win. But the American pitchers shut down the National League offense for the next five innings, and Carl Yastrzemski made a contest of it with a three-run homer in the sixth off Tom Seaver to tie the score.

In the top of the ninth, though, the Americans all but gave the game away. Left fielder Claudell Washington dropped a fly on the run (it was scored a hit) and misplayed a line drive that went for a double. Goose Gossage came in to relieve Catfish Hunter on the mound and hit the next batter to load the bases. Bill Madlock then drove in two of the baserunners with a single through the drawn-in infield, and Pete Rose knocked in the third run of the inning with a sacrifice fly.

Randy Jones set the Americans down in order in the bottom of the ninth, and—voilà!—the National League had won again.

GAME 47
Veterans Stadium, Philadelphia
July 13, 1976
NL, 7–1

AL	000 100 000	1	5	0
NL	202 000 03X	7	10	0

Pitchers: FIDRYCH, Hunter (3), Tiant (5), Tanana (7) vs R.JONES, Seaver (4), Montefusco (6), Rhoden (8), K.Forsch (9)
Home Runs: Foster-N, Lynn-A, Cedeno-N
Attendance: 63,974

Tom Seaver gave up a home run to Fred Lynn in the fourth inning, but that was the Americans' only score as the Nationals held the American stars to five hits while celebrating the nation's bicentennial with ten hits and seven runs.

Rookie standout Mark Fidrych was chosen to start for the Americans and was promptly rapped for two runs. Pete Rose led off with a single and was tripled home by Steve Garvey, who scored himself on a ground out. The Nationals doubled their score in the third inning as George Foster tagged Catfish Hunter for two runs with a mighty home run to left center, and capped their assault with three more in the eighth off Frank Tanana, including a two-run homer by Cesar Cedeno.

The fans had elected five members of Cincinnati's "big red machine" to the National League starting lineup, and Sparky Anderson, the Reds' and National squad's manager, added two more. They provided the bulk of the Nationals' offense, with seven hits, four RBIs, and four runs scored.

GAME 48
Yankee Stadium, New York
July 19, 1977
NL, 7–5

NL	401 000 020	7	9	1
AL	000 002 102	5	8	0

Pitchers: SUTTON, Lavelle (4), Seaver (6), R.Reuschel (8), Gossage (9) vs PALMER, Kern (3), Eckersley (4), LaRoche (6), Campbell (7), Lyle (8)
Home Runs: Morgan-N, Luzinski-N, Garvey-N, Scott-A
Attendance: 56,683

The Nationals' Joe Morgan homered off Jim Palmer to open the game, and before Palmer escaped the first inning three more National Leaguers had crossed the plate on a single, double, and Greg Luzinski's homer. Palmer got through the second inning without further damage, but before he was relieved in the third Steve Garvey had homered to give the Nationals a 5–0 lead.

The Americans fought back against Tom Seaver in the sixth and seventh. Seaver retired two in the sixth, but then gave up two singles, and two runs as Richie Zisk doubled the runners home. Two more singles in the seventh produced a third American run.

But the Nationals—assisted by pitcher Sparky Lyle's wild pitch and hit batsman—put a sixth and seventh run on the board in the eighth with a double and single. The Americans added two final runs of their own in the bottom of the ninth on George Scott's homer off Goose Gossage, but fell short of victory once again.

GAME 49
San Diego Stadium,
July 11, 1978
NL, 7–3

AL	201	000	000	3	8	1
NL	003	000	04X	7	10	0

Pitchers: Palmer, Keough (3), Sorensen (4), Kern (7), Guidry (7), GOSSAGE (8) vs Blue, Rogers (4), Fingers (6), SUTTER (8), P. Niekro (9)
Attendance: 51,549

Rod Carew led off both the first and third innings with triples—an All-Star record— scoring both times as the Americans took a 3–0 lead into the bottom of the third. But then Jim Palmer, who had shut the Nationals out on one hit through the first two innings, lost his touch. After yielding a leadoff single, he retired two batters, but then issued three walks to force in a run, and when Steve Garvey singled past the shortstop two more runs scored to tie the game.

No one scored through the next 4½ innings, with Larry Sorensen turning in the game's top pitching performance as he shut the Nationals out on one hit through the three middle innings. But in the last of the eighth, Goose Gossage (the National League closer the previous year) took the mound this year for the Americans. Garvey greeted him with a leadoff triple and scored what proved to be the winning run on a wild pitch. A walk and three singles added three insurance runs before the inning ended. Bruce Sutter and Phil Niekro blanked the Americans in the ninth, and the Nationals had extended their current win streak to seven.

GAME 50
Kingdome, Seattle
July 17, 1979
NL, 7–6

NL	211	001	011	7	10	0
AL	302	001	000	6	10	0

Pitchers: Carlton, Andujar (2), Rogers (4), G. Perry (6), Sambito (6), LaCoss (6), SUTTER (8) vs Ryan, Stanley (3), Clear (5), KERN (7), Guidry (9)
Home Runs: Lynn-A, Mazzilli-N
Attendance: 58,905

Mike Schmidt tripled and George Foster doubled to drive in the game's first runs as the Nationals began their scoring in the top of the first. The Americans fought back to take the lead later in the inning as Don Baylor doubled home one run and Fred Lynn homered for two more. The Nationals tied the score with a run in the second and went ahead again in the third when Schmidt scored after doubling. But the Americans recaptured the lead in the bottom of the third, scoring twice on a single, wild pitch, ground out, hit batsman, single, and error.

Three innings later the Nationals again tied the game, but the Americans went ahead for the third time with a run in their half of the sixth. Outstanding throws by right fielder Dave Parker, who notched two assists, helped to keep the Americans from pulling away. In the eighth the Nationals' Lee Mazzilli homered for yet another tie, and an inning later Ron Guidry walked Mazzilli with the bases loaded to force in the Nationals' go-ahead seventh run. When Bruce Sutter kept the Americans from scoring in the bottom of the ninth, the National Leaguers had for the second time defeated the Americans eight years in a row.

GAME 51
Dodger Stadium,
Los Angeles
July 8, 1980
NL, 4–2

AL	000	020	000	2	7	1
NL	000	012	10X	4	7	0

Pitchers: Stone, JOHN (4), Farmer (6), Stieb (7), Gossage (8) vs Richard, Welch (3), REUSS (6), Bibby (7), Sutter (8)
Home Runs: Lynn-A, Griffey-N
Attendance: 56,088

For 4⅔ innings J.R. Richard and Bob Welch held the American stars scoreless. But then Rod Carew singled and Fred Lynn drove in the game's first runs with his third All-Star homer.

The Americans' Steve Stone and Tommy John pitched even better, setting the Nationals down in order through four innings. John continued the perfect streak through the first two outs of the fifth, but then Ken Griffey homered, and the Americans' spell on the National Leaguers was broken.

While three National pitchers limited the Americans to a single and a walk over the final four innings, three singles and an error sent the Nationals into the lead in the sixth. A passed ball surrounded by two wild pitches moved Dave Concepcion around the bases in the seventh (he had reached on a fielder's choice) for the Nationals' fourth run. They didn't really need it, though, as Bruce Sutter—the winning pitcher in the two previous All-Star games—saved this one with two final innings of no-hit ball for the Nationals' ninth successive win.

GAME 52
Municipal Stadium,
Cleveland
August 9, 1981
NL, 5–4

NL	000	011	120	5	9	1
AL	010	003	000	4	11	1

Pitchers: Valenzuela, Seaver (2), Knepper (3), Hooton (5), Ruthven (6), BLUE (7), Ryan (8), Sutter (9) vs Morris, Barker (3), K.Forsch (5), Norris (6), Davis (7), FINGERS (8), Stieb (8)
Home Runs: Singleton-A, Carter-N (2), Parker-N, Schmidt-N
Attendance: 72,086

The game, delayed until August by the midseason players' strike, drew an All-Star record crowd of more than 72,000 fans, and the managers set a new record by using 56 players. But the game itself followed a familiar pattern.

The Americans scored first in the second inning on Ken Singleton's home run off Tom Seaver, and held their slim lead into the fifth on Len Barker's two innings of perfect pitching. But Ken Forsch replaced Barker in the fifth and Gary Carter homered off his first pitch to tie the score. Dave Parker's homer off Mike Norris an inning later put the Nationals ahead for the first time, but the Americans came right back in the bottom of the inning, putting together four singles and a sacrifice fly for three runs and a two-run advantage.

Gary Carter's second home run of the game—this time off Ron Davis's first pitch—brought the Nationals within one in the seventh, and Mike Schmidt's two-run blast off Rollie Fingers in the eighth restored their lead. Three National pitchers shut out the Americans without a hit over the final three innings as closer Bruce Sutter picked up his second consecutive All-Star save and the National Leaguers their tenth consecutive victory.

GAME 53
Olympic Stadium, Montreal
July 13, 1982
NL, 4–1

AL	100 000 000	1	8	2
NL	021 001 00X	4	8	1

Pitchers: ECKERSLEY, Clancy (4), Bannister (5), Quisenberry (6), Fingers (8) vs ROGERS, Carlton (4), Soto (6), Valenzuela (8), Minton (8), Howe (9), Hume (9)
Home Runs: Concepcion-N
Attendance: 59,057

In the first All-Star Game held outside the United States, the American League for the third year in a row put the first run on the board, but for the eleventh year in a row the final score showed the National League the winner. Two singles, a wild pitch, and a sacrifice fly gave the Americans a run in the top of the first. But starter Steve Rogers of the host Expos held the Americans scoreless for the remainder of his three innings while the Nationals struck back for two runs in the second on Dave Concepcion's home run, and added another in the third when Ruppert Jones—who had tripled to open the inning—scored on a sacrifice fly.

Six National League pitchers (and shortstop Ozzie Smith's spectacular stop and throw to first with two on in the eighth) joined Rogers in holding the American stars scoreless after the first inning. Two hometowners put together the Nationals' final run in the sixth. Al Oliver, leading off, doubled down the line in left and took third as the ball got by left fielder Rickey Henderson. Two outs later Gary Carter lined a pitch to center, scoring Oliver as Willie Wilson's dive for the ball came up short.

GAME 54
Comiskey Park, Chicago
July 6, 1983
AL, 13–3

NL	100 110 000	3	8	3
AL	117 000 22X	13	15	2

Pitchers: SOTO, Hammaker (3), Dawley (3), Dravecky (5), Perez (7), Orosco (7), L.Smith (8) vs STIEB, Honeycutt (4), Stanley (6), Young (8), Quisenberry (9)
Home Runs: Rice-A, Lynn-A
Attendance: 43,801

The game returned to the park where it had originated fifty years earlier, and the American League, after eleven years of All-Star losses, unleashed its pent-up fury to produce the greatest margin of victory in thirty-seven years. The game began, though, as an embarrassment of errors. American starter Dave Stieb struck out the side in the first, but along the way two errors (one of them Stieb's) let in a run. An unearned run in the bottom of the first tied the score and another in the second put the American League ahead for good (making a loser out of the unfortunate National starter Mario Soto).

The hitting began in earnest in the last of the third as the Americans scored seven times for a new one-inning record. Among their six hits (also a record for an All-Star inning) were a homer by Jim Rice, a triple by George Brett, and a bases-loaded blast by Fred Lynn—his fourth All-Star home run and the first grand slam in All-Star history. With the score now 9–1, the National League's single runs in the fourth and fifth were exercises in futility, and the Americans' two each in the seventh and eighth served chiefly to boost the winning total to 13—another All-Star high.

GAME 55
Candlestick Park, San Francisco
July 10, 1984
NL, 3–1

AL	010 000 000	1	7	2
NL	110 000 01X	3	8	0

Pitchers: STIEB, Morris (3), Dotson (5), Caudill (7), Hernandez (8) vs LEA, Valenzuela (3), Gooden (5), Soto (7), Gossage (9)
Home Runs: Brett-A, Carter-N, Murphy-N
Attendance: 57,756

Only four times in the previous fifty-four All-Star Games had a pitcher struck out the side in order. In this game, three more pitchers did it. And, on this fiftieth anniversary of Carl Hubbell's five consecutive strikeouts, two of those pitchers combined to break Hubbell's record with six back-to-back whiffs. Hubbell, who threw out the first ball, also saw an All-Star nine-inning record set with 21 total Ks (11 by National League pitchers, 10 by American).

In the fourth inning, National star Fernando Valenzuela mowed down three of the game's premier sluggers: Dave Winfield, Reggie Jackson, and George Brett. If the three men Dwight Gooden retired on strikes an inning later (Lance Parrish, Chet Lemon, and rookie Alvin Davis) were slightly less formidable, still, it was an impressive performance for a nineteen-year-old rookie (the youngest player in All-Star history). The three that American Leaguer Bill Caudill struck out in the seventh were no slouches either: Tim Raines, Ryne Sandberg (in the midst of an MVP season), and Keith Hernandez.

Three of the four runs scored in the game were homers. The National League's run in the first was unearned, but the Americans' George Brett homered to center to tie the game in the second, and the Nationals' go-ahead run later in the inning came on Gary Carter's blast to left. In the eighth, National Leaguer Dale Murphy also put one over the left field fence to end the scoring.

GAME 56
H. Humphrey Metrodome, Minneapolis
July 16, 1985
NL, 6–1

NL	011 020 002	6	9	1
AL	100 000 000	1	5	0

Pitchers: HOYT, Ryan (4), Valenzuela (7), Reardon (8), Gossage (9) vs MORRIS, Key (3), Blyleven (4), Stieb (6), Moore (7), Petry (9), Hernandez (9)
Attendance: 54,960

The American Leaguers scored first, as Rickey Henderson led off the bottom of the first with a single and circled the bases on a steal, error, and sacrifice fly. But the five National pitchers blanked the Americans the rest of the way on only four more singles.

Meanwhile, the National stars methodically dismantled the Americans for their thirty-sixth All-Star victory. In the top of the second, after Darryl Strawberry singled and stole second, Terry Kennedy, whose error had led to the American League run, redeemed himself by singling Strawberry home. An inning later, with two out, Tom Herr doubled and scored the go-ahead (and winning) run on Steve Garvey's single.

In the fifth the Nationals scored two more runs on a hit batsman, Tim Wallach's ground-rule double, and Ozzie Virgil's single, and finished their scoring in the ninth with another pair on three walks and Willie McGee's double—another ground-rule bounce out of play off the lively Metrodome surface. Goose Gossage struck out the final two American batters in the bottom of the ninth, and the Nationals had increased their winning margin in the series to a new high of seventeen games.

GAME 57
Astrodome, Houston
July 15, 1986
AL, 3–2

```
AL   020 000 100   3 5 0
NL   000 000 020   2 5 1
```

Pitchers: CLEMENS, Higuera (4), Hough (7), Righetti (8), Aase (9) vs GOODEN, Valenzuela (4), Scott (7), Fernandez (8), Krukow (9)
Home Runs: Whitaker-A, White-A
Attendance: 45,774

National League pitchers struck out 12 Americans, led by Fernando Valenzuela's five in a row, which matched the mark set by Carl Hubbell in 1934. (Two years earlier Valenzuela had helped set a multipitcher All-Star record of six consecutive strikeouts.) In the eighth inning Sid Fernandez, after walking two, struck out the next three.

Though the American Leaguers struck out fewer men, their pitching was more effective over all. Starter Roger Clemens hurled three perfect innings (3 balls and 21 strikes), and Teddy Higuera one-hit the Nationals over the next three. Charlie Hough struck out three in the eighth after yielding the Nationals' only extra-base hit (a double) to Chris Brown. But catcher Rich Gedman couldn't handle Hough's knuckleball, and Brown advanced to third on the first strikeout (ruled a wild pitch) and scored on the second, a passed ball which also enabled batter Hubie Brooks to reach first safely. Brooks moved up on a balk and scored the Nationals' second run on Steve Sax's single.

But home runs had already undone the Nationals. With two gone in the second, Dave Winfield doubled off starter Dwight Gooden, and Lou Whitaker clubbed an 0–2 pitch over the fence in right. And in the seventh, Frank White (hitting for Whitaker) knocked Mike Scott's 0–2 pitch over the fence in left center for what proved the margin of American League victory.

GAME 58
Oakland-Alameda County
Stadium, Oakland
July 14, 1987
NL, 2–0

```
NL   000 000 000 000 2   2 8 2
AL   000 000 000 000 0   0 6 1
```

Pitchers: Scott, Sutcliffe (3), Hershiser (5), R.Reuschel (7), Franco (8), Bedrosian (9), L.SMITH (10), S. Fernandez (13) vs Saberhagen, Morris (4), Langston (6), Plesac (8), Righetti (9), Henke (9), J.HOWELL (12)
Attendance: 49,671

None of the previous fifty-seven All-Star Games had gone more than five innings without at least one run crossing the plate. But this game went more than twice that before National Leaguer Tim Raines tripled in two runs in the top of the thirteenth for the game's only scoring. It was the National League's eighth win in eight extra-inning All-Star games.

Both teams missed scoring opportunities in the ninth inning. Raines singled for the Nationals with only one out, and became the game's first runner to reach third when a throw from first on his attempted steal went into center field. But a fly to short right and a foul out left him stranded. In the bottom of the ninth, the Americans came close to winning the game as Dave Winfield headed for home from second on a missed 4–6–1 double play. But National pitcher Steve Bedrosian, covering first, snared the off-center throw from short and fired it home to catch Winfield for the third out.

The Americans again reached third in the eleventh as Larry Parrish singled and moved around on a sacrifice and ground out. But pitcher Lee Smith (whose three shutout innings earned him the win) struck out Tony Fernandez to end the threat.

GAME 59
Riverfront Stadium,
Cincinnati
July 12, 1988
AL, 2–1

```
AL   001 100 000   2 6 2
NL   000 100 000   1 5 0
```

Pitchers: VIOLA, Clemens (3), Gubicza (4), Stieb (6), Russell (7), Jones (8), Plesac (8), Eckersley (9) vs GOODEN, Knepper (4), Cone (5), Gross (6), Davis (7), Walk (7), Hershiser (8), Worrell (9)
Home Run: Steinbach-A
Attendance: 55,837

Oakland's Terry Steinbach was not among the ten top American League catchers in batting; because of time lost to injuries, he was not even his club's leading catcher in games played. But the fans voted him to start in the All-Star Game, and he won it for the American Leaguers with a home run in his first trip to the plate and a sacrifice fly his next time up. Steinbach's homer—a drive off Dwight Gooden that led off the third inning—caromed off the glove of a leaping Darryl Strawberry over the wall in right for the game's first score. His sacrifice fly—high and deep to left in the fourth inning—scored Dave Winfield (aboard with his record seventh All-Star double) to put the Americans ahead 2–0.

Steinbach also contributed negatively to the National League run later in the fourth. His throwing error on Vince Coleman's steal of second enabled Coleman to advance to third, whence he scored on a wild pitch by Mark Gubicza.

American starter Frank Viola, the midseason league leader in wins, was awarded the victory for his two perfect innings pitched. Dennis Eckersley, the majors' top reliever, preserved the win for the Americans with a perfect ninth inning.

GAME 60
Anaheim Stadium,
Anaheim
July 11, 1989
AL, 5–3

```
NL   200 000 010   3 9 1
AL   212 000 00X   5 12 0
```

Pitchers: Reuschel, SMOLTZ (2), Sutcliffe (3), Burke (4), M. Davis (6), Howell (7), Williams (8) vs Stewart, RYAN (2), Gubicza (4), Moore (5), Swindell (6), Russell (7), Plesac (8), Jones (8)
Home Runs: Jackson-A, Boggs-A
Attendance: 64,036

The National stars struck early with a pair of two-out runs in the top of the first inning, and a double steal put two more runners in scoring position. But left fielder Bo Jackson stifled the assault with a fine running catch, then opened the American half of the first with a massive home run to center field off Rick Reuschel. Wade Boggs, the next man up, added insult to the forty-year-old Reuschel's first All-Star start, tying the game with another homer. In the second inning Jackson drove in the American League's go-ahead run with a slow grounder off young John Smoltz, and an inning later four American singles produced two more runs. A quartet of National League pitchers held the Americans scoreless on just three hits over the final six innings, and their teammates rallied for a third National run in the eighth. But Doug Jones (the majors' top reliever in 1989) came on to get the final out of the eighth, and in the ninth preserved the American lead to give the American Leaguers their first repeat All-Star victory in thirty-one years.

National League hurler Smoltz, at age twenty-two the youngest player in the lineup, took the loss. Nolan Ryan, back in the American League after nine National League seasons, earned the win with two shutout innings. Not only was he the oldest player on either side, at forty-two he was the oldest All-Star winning pitcher ever.

GAME 61
Wrigley Field, Chicago
July 10, 1990
AL, 2–0

```
AL   000 000 200    2 7 0
NL   000 000 000    0 2 1
```

Pitchers: Welch, Stieb (3), SABERHAGEN (5), Thigpen (7), Finley (8), Eckersley (9) vs Armstrong, R. Martinez (3), D. Martinez (4), Viola (5), D. Smith (6), BRANTLEY (6), Dibble (7), Myers (8), Franco (9)
Attendance: 39,071

Back-to-back American League singles off Jeff Brantley had put men on third and first and brought Julio Franco to the plate in the seventh inning, when heavy rain halted the game for more than an hour. During the delay Brantley's side stiffened, so when Franco finally got his turn at bat he faced a new National pitcher, Rob Dibble. Franco lined Dibble's third pitch into the gap in right center for a double—the only extra-base hit of the game—driving in what proved to be the game's only runs.

Damp air and a stiff breeze in from left field helped tame the offense. American League batters managed to accumulate seven hits, but the Nationals were held to two—an All-Star all-time low. No runner advanced as far as third base until the sixth inning, when American stars Kelly Gruber and Jose Canseco pulled off a double steal. No National Leaguer reached that far, and if it weren't for Barry Larkin's third-inning steal, no National runner would even have stood on second base.

American hurler Bret Saberhagen's two perfect middle innings earned him the win, and Dennis Eckersley, after yielding a leadoff hit in the ninth, retired the final three batters to record his second All-Star save in three years. The victory was the third in a row for the American Leaguers, the first time they had put together such a string of triumphs in forty-one years.

GAME 62
SkyDome, Toronto
July 9, 1991
AL, 4–2

```
NL   100 100 000    2 10 1
AL   003 000 10X    4 8 0
```

Pitchers: Glavine, MARTINEZ (3), Viola (5), Harnisch (6), Smiley (7), Dibble (7), Morgan (8) vs Morris, KEY (3), Clemens (4), McDowell (5), Reardon (7), Aguilera (7), Eckersley (9)
Home Runs: Ripken-A, Dawson-N
Attendance: 52,383

The National League took an early 1–0 lead on singles by Tony Gwynn, Will Clark, and Bobby Bonilla in the top of the first, and held it for two innings on Tom Glavine's strong pitching, which included three strikeouts. But Dennis Martinez yielded successive singles to Rickey Henderson and Wade Boggs in the third inning, and the next batter, Cal Ripken, Jr., homered to center to give the Americans all the runs they would need for victory.

National Leaguer Andre Dawson led off the fourth inning with a massive home run to center off Roger Clemens. This brought the Nationals within a run of tying the game, but they scored no more, as a succession of American pitchers shut them down on a walk and four singles the rest of the way. In the seventh inning the Americans added an insurance run when Joe Carter singled and moved around the bases on a call of catcher interference (the first in All-Star history), a sacrifice bunt, and Harold Baines's sacrifice liner to right.

Jimmy Key, the pitcher of record when Ripken's three-run homer put the American League ahead, was awarded the win. Dennis Eckersley, who pitched a perfect ninth, earned a record third All-Star save.

It was only the second time in All-Star history that the American League had won four games in a row.

GAME 63
Jack Murphy Stadium, San Diego
July 14, 1992
AL, 13–6

```
AL   411 004 030    13 19 1
NL   000 001 032     6 12 1
```

Pitchers: BROWN, McDowell (2), Guzman (3), Clemens (4), Mussina (5), Langston (5), Nagy (7), Montgomery (8), Aguilera (8), Eckersley (9) vs GLAVINE, Maddux (2), Cone (4), Tewksbury (5), Smoltz (6), Martinez (7), Jones (8), Charlton (9)
Home Runs: Sierra-A, Griffey-A, Clark-N
Attendance: 59,372

By the time the National Leaguers pushed across their first run in the sixth inning, the Americans had already scored ten times, and although National bats caught fire for five more runs in the eighth and ninth, they were powerless to prevent the American League from stretching its All-Star win streak to five games. National starting pitcher Tom Glavine could not repeat his strong 1991 start: before his relief after 1⅔ innings he was tagged for nine singles and five runs. In the third inning, Ken Griffey, Jr., who had driven in one of the first-inning runs, added the sixth American score with a homer off Greg Maddux. When he came up again to lead off the sixth inning, Griffey doubled to initiate a new American scoring spree, which included two-out doubles by Carlos Baerga and Robin Ventura, capped by Ruben Sierra's home run—all off Bob Tewksbury, who had set down the Americans 1–2–3 an inning earlier. Travis Fryman's RBI single and Roberto Kelly's two-run double in the eighth closed out the American League scoring.

Will Clark's two-out blast off Rick Aguilera in the last of the eighth was the National League's first three-run homer since 1964, but it was too little to make more than a dent in the American lead. With two men out in the ninth, a pair of singles off Dennis Eckersley loaded the bases, and Bip Roberts' single drove in two of the baserunners to bring the NL run total to six (enough to have defeated the AL in the seven previous All-Star Games).

Starter Kevin Brown was awarded the win; Glavine took the loss.

GAME 64
Oriole Park at Camden Yards, Baltimore
July 13, 1993
AL, 9–3

```
AL   011 033 10X    9 10 0
NL   200 001 000    3 7 2
```

Pitchers: Mulholland, Benes (3), BURKETT (5), Avery (5), Smoltz (6), Beck (7), Harvey (8) vs Langston, Johnson (3), McDOWELL (5), Key (6), Montgomery (7), Aguilera (8), Ward (9)
Home Runs: Sheffield-N, Alomar-A, Puckett-A
Attendance: 48,147

Barry Bonds doubled off Mark Langston with one out in the first inning and Gary Sheffield followed with a home run to left that gave the National League two runs before the American Leaguers came to bat. In the bottom of the second inning, though, Kirby Puckett's solo shot over the center field wall off Terry Mulholland narrowed the gap, and an inning later Roberto Alomar led off with a homer to right off Andy Benes that evened the score.

The Americans pushed ahead in the last of the fifth when, with John Burkett pitching, Ivan Rodriguez lined a ground rule double to left and Albert Belle singled him home. Belle took second on an error, and scored on Ken Griffey Jr.'s single; Griffey scored on Puckett's double into the gap at left center. A half inning later, Barry Larkin drove Bonds home with a sacrifice fly to narrow the score to 5–3, but the Americans blew the game open in the sixth with a trio of unearned runs. After shortstop Jeff Blauser failed to field a grounder by Carlos Baerga—depriving pitcher Steve Avery of a 1–2–3 inning—Avery walked Belle and Devon White doubled, sending Baerga home and Bell to third. John Smoltz, who relieved Avery, unloaded a pair of wild pitches that enabled Belle and White to score.

In the bottom of the seventh inning, Terry Steinbach tagged Rod Beck for a double high off the wall in right to drive in the ninth—and final—AL run. The Nationals got runners to second and third in the eighth with just one out, but failed to score, and when they fell to closer Duane Ward in order in the ninth, the American League had its sixth straight All-Star victory.

GAME 65
Three Rivers Stadium, Pittsburgh
July 12, 1994
NL, 8–7

AL	100 003 300 0	7	15	0
NL	103 001 002 1	8	12	1

Pitchers: Key, Cone (3), Mussina (5), Johnson (6) Hentgen (7), Alvarez (8), Smith (9), BERE (10) vs Maddux, Hill (4), Drabek (6), Hudek (6), Jackson (7), Beck (7), Myers (9), JONES (10)
Home Runs: Grissom-N, McGriff-N
Attendance: 59,568

A blend of youth and experience enabled the National League to snap the American Leaguers' six-game winning streak with one of the tightest finishes in All-Star history. In the bottom of the tenth inning, with the score tied, 7–7, Tony Gwynn, a veteran of ten All-Star games, led off by chopping a single to center off Jason Bere. He took off when novice All-Star Moises Alou drove Bere's second pitch to the base of the wall in left center. AL catcher Ivan Rodriguez received the ball—relayed sharply from the outfield—just as Gwynn slipped between the catcher's legs with the winning run.

It was a close game all the way. The teams traded single runs in the first inning. In the third, the National Leaguers grabbed the biggest lead of the evening when they sandwiched a hit batsman and Gwynn's double between a pair of singles to knock David Cone for three runs. In the top of the sixth the Americans evened the score again with a trio of runs off Doug Drabek. Then Marquis Grissom hit a home run off Randy Johnson a half inning later.

Once again the Americans knotted the game when Scott Cooper doubled home Ivan Rodriguez in the seventh and took their first (and, as it turned out, only) lead when Ken Lofton singled to score Chuck Knoblauch and Cooper. A fourth run would have scored in the seventh, however, if shortstop Ozzie Smith—thirty-nine years old and playing in his thirteenth All-Star contest—had not made a spectacular diving stop of Knoblauch's drive and recovered to force Mickey Tettleton at second. The run prevented by Smith's play would have given the American Leaguers their seventh straight victory.

The Americans maintained their 7–5 advantage into the last of the ninth. Pinch hitter Fred McGriff, after fouling off a third strike, brought National League fans to their feet with a game-tying home run. NL closer Doug Jones held the Americans scoreless in the top of the tenth, and the stage was set for the Gwynn–Alou finish.

## CHAPTER 14

The All-Star Roster

The first All-Star Game, played in Chicago on July 6, 1933, featured eighteen stars from each eight-team league, selected by the fans with help from the managers of the squads. The most recent All-Star Game, played in Pittsburgh on July 12, 1994, displayed twenty-eight stars from each fourteen-team circuit. Who was selected? Did they appear in the game? The answers are here, with each year's teams listed alphabetically. Players tagged with an asterisk were named to the team but were replaced due to injury; those whose names are followed by a dagger were on the squad but did not get into the game.

For details of the All-Star Game(s) of a particular year, refer to the accounts in the preceding section. For further details about a particular individual, refer to the Player and Pitcher Registers.

1933 AL
Earl Averill
Ben Chapman
Joe Cronin
General Crowder
Bill Dickey†
Jimmy Dykes
Rick Ferrell
Wes Ferrell†
Jimmie Foxx†
Lou Gehrig
Charlie Gehringer
Lefty Gomez
Lefty Grove
Oral Hildebrand†
Tony Lazzeri†
Babe Ruth
Al Simmons
Sam West

1933 NL
Dick Bartell
Wally Berger
Tony Cuccinello
Woody English
Frankie Frisch
Chick Hafey
Bill Hallahan
Gabby Hartnett
Carl Hubbell
Chuck Klein
Pepper Martin
Lefty O'Doul
Hal Schumacher†
Bill Terry
Pie Traynor
Paul Waner
Lon Warneke
Jimmie Wilson

1934 AL
Earl Averill
Tommy Bridges†
Ben Chapman
Mickey Cochrane
Joe Cronin
Bill Dickey
Jimmy Dykes†
Rick Ferrell†
Jimmie Foxx
Lou Gehrig
Charlie Gehringer
Lefty Gomez
Mel Harder
Pinky Higgins†
Heinie Manush
Red Ruffing
Jack Russell†
Babe Ruth
Al Simmons
Sam West

1934 NL
Wally Berger
Kiki Cuyler
Dizzy Dean
Fred Frankhouse
Frankie Frisch
Gabby Hartnett
Billy Herman
Carl Hubbell
Travis Jackson
Chuck Klein
Al Lopez
Pepper Martin
Joe Medwick
Jo-Jo Moore*
Van Mungo
Mel Ott
Bill Terry
Pie Traynor
Arky Vaughan
Paul Waner
Lon Warneke

1935 AL
Earl Averill*
Ossie Bluege
Tommy Bridges†
Ben Chapman
Mickey Cochrane†
Doc Cramer
Joe Cronin
Rick Ferrell†
Jimmie Foxx
Lou Gehrig
Charlie Gehringer
Lefty Gomez
Lefty Grove†
Mel Harder
Rollie Hemsley
Bob Johnson
Buddy Myer†
Schoolboy Rowe†
Al Simmons
Joe Vosmik
Sam West†

1935 NL
Wally Berger
Ripper Collins
Dizzy Dean
Paul Derringer
Frankie Frisch†
Gabby Hartnett
Billy Herman
Carl Hubbell†
Gus Mancuso
Pepper Martin
Joe Medwick
Jo-Jo Moore
Mel Ott
Hal Schumacher
Bill Terry

Arky Vaughan
Bill Walker
Paul Waner
Burgess Whitehead
Jimmie Wilson

1936 AL
Luke Appling
Earl Averill
Tommy Bridges*
Ben Chapman
Frankie Crosetti
Bill Dickey
Joe DiMaggio
Rick Ferrell
Jimmie Foxx
Lou Gehrig
Charlie Gehringer
Lefty Gomez†
Goose Goslin
Lefty Grove
Mel Harder
Rollie Hemsley†
Pinky Higgins
Vern Kennedy†
Monte Pearson†
Rip Radcliff
Schoolboy Rowe
George Selkirk

1936 NL
Wally Berger†
Ripper Collins
Curt Davis
Dizzy Dean
Frank Demaree
Leo Durocher
Augie Galan
Gabby Hartnett
Billy Herman
Carl Hubbell
Ernie Lombardi†
Stu Martin†
Joe Medwick
Jo-Jo Moore†
Van Mungo†
Mel Ott
Lew Riggs
Gus Suhr†
Arky Vaughan†
Lon Warneke
Pinky Whitney

1937 AL
Earl Averill
Beau Bell†
Tommy Bridges
Harlond Clift†
Doc Cramer†
Joe Cronin
Bill Dickey
Joe DiMaggio

Rick Ferrell†
Wes Ferrell†
Jimmie Foxx
Lou Gehrig
Charlie Gehringer
Lefty Gomez
Hank Greenberg†
Lefty Grove†
Mel Harder
Wally Moses†
Johnny Murphy†
Buddy Myer†
Red Rolfe
Luke Sewell†
Monty Stratton*
Gee Walker*
Sam West

1937 NL
Dick Bartell
Cy Blanton
Ripper Collins
Dizzy Dean
Frank Demaree
Lee Grissom
Gabby Hartnett
Billy Herman
Carl Hubbell
Billy Jurges†
Ernie Lombardi†
Gus Mancuso
Pepper Martin†
Joe Medwick
Johnny Mize
Gene Moore†
Jo-Jo Moore
Van Mungo
Mel Ott
Arky Vaughan
Bucky Walters
Paul Waner
Burgess Whitehead

1938 AL
Johnny Allen
Earl Averill
Doc Cramer
Joe Cronin
Bill Dickey
Joe DiMaggio
Bob Feller†
Rick Ferrell†
Jimmie Foxx
Lou Gehrig
Charlie Gehringer
Lefty Gomez
Hank Greenberg*
Lefty Grove
Bob Johnson
Vern Kennedy†
Mike Kreevich
Buddy Lewis

Rick Ferrell†
Wes Ferrell†
Jimmie Foxx
Lou Gehrig
Charlie Gehringer
Lefty Gomez
Hank Greenberg†
Lefty Grove†
Mel Harder
Wally Moses†
Johnny Murphy†
Bobo Newsom†
Red Rolfe†
Red Ruffing†
Cecil Travis†
Rudy York

1938 NL
Mace Brown
Tony Cuccinello†
Harry Danning†
Paul Derringer†
Leo Durocher
Ival Goodman
Stan Hack
Gabby Hartnett†
Billy Herman
Carl Hubbell†
Cookie Lavagetto†
Bill Lee
Hank Leiber
Ernie Lombardi
Hersh Martin†
Frank McCormick
Joe Medwick
Jo-Jo Moore†
Mel Ott
Babe Phelps*
Jim Turner†
Johnny Vander Meer
Arky Vaughan†
Lloyd Waner†

1939 AL
Luke Appling†
Tommy Bridges
George Case†
Doc Cramer
Joe Cronin
Frankie Crosetti†
Bill Dickey
Joe DiMaggio
Bob Feller
Jimmie Foxx†
Lou Gehrig†
Lefty Gomez†
Joe Gordon
Hank Greenberg
Lefty Grove†
Frankie Hayes†
Rollie Hemsley†
Myril Hoag
Bob Johnson†
Ted Lyons†
George McQuinn†
Johnny Murphy†
Bobo Newsom†
Red Rolfe
Red Ruffing
George Selkirk

1939 NL
Morrie Arnovich†
Dolph Camilli
Harry Danning†
Curt Davis†
Paul Derringer
Lou Fette
Lonny Frey
Ival Goodman
Stan Hack
Billy Herman
Billy Jurges†
Cookie Lavagetto†
Bill Lee
Ernie Lombardi
Frank McCormick
Joe Medwick
Johnny Mize
Terry Moore
Mel Ott
Babe Phelps
Johnny Vander Meer†
Arky Vaughan
Bucky Walters†
Lon Warneke†
Whit Wyatt†

1940 AL
Luke Appling
Lou Boudreau
Tommy Bridges†
Doc Cramer†
Bill Dickey
Joe DiMaggio
Bob Feller
Lou Finney
Jimmie Foxx
Joe Gordon
Hank Greenberg
Frankie Hayes
Rollie Hemsley
Bob Johnson†
Charlie Keller
Ken Keltner
Dutch Leonard†
Ray Mack
George McQuinn†
Al Milnar†
Bobo Newsom
Monte Pearson†
Red Rolfe*
Red Ruffing
Cecil Travis
Ted Williams

1940 NL
Pete Coscarart
Harry Danning
Paul Derringer
Leo Durocher†
Larry French
Billy Herman

Kirby Higbe†
Carl Hubbell
Billy Jurges*
Cookie Lavagetto
Hank Leiber*
Ernie Lombardi
Pinky May
Frank McCormick
Joe Medwick
Eddie Miller
Johnny Mize
Jo-Jo Moore
Terry Moore
Hugh Mulcahy†
Bill Nicholson
Mel Ott
Babe Phelps
Arky Vaughan
Bucky Walters
Max West
Whit Wyatt

1941 AL
Luke Appling†
Al Benton†
Lou Boudreau
Joe Cronin
Roy Cullenbine
Bill Dickey
Dom DiMaggio
Joe DiMaggio
Bobby Doerr
Bob Feller
Jimmie Foxx
Joe Gordon
Frankie Hayes
Jeff Heath
Sid Hudson
Charlie Keller
Ken Keltner
Thornton Lee
Red Ruffing†
Marius Russo†
Eddie Smith
Birdie Tebbetts†
Cecil Travis
Ted Williams
Rudy York

1941 NL
Cy Blanton†
Dolph Camilli*
Harry Danning
Paul Derringer
Bob Elliott
Lonny Frey
Stan Hack
Billy Herman
Carl Hubbell†
Cookie Lavagetto
Hank Leibe.*
Al Lopez
Frank McCormick
Joe Medwick
Eddie Miller
Johnny Mize
Terry Moore
Bill Nicholson
Mel Ott
Mickey Owen
Claude Passeau
Pete Reiser
Enos Slaughter
Arky Vaughan
Bucky Walters
Lon Warneke†
Whit Wyatt

1942 AL
Jim Bagby†
Al Benton
Tiny Bonham†
Lou Boudreau
Spud Chandler
Bill Dickey*
Dom DiMaggio†
Joe DiMaggio
Bobby Doerr†
Joe Gordon
Tommy Henrich
Sid Hudson†
Tex Hughson†
Bob Johnson

Ken Keltner
George McQuinn†
Hal Newhouser†
Phil Rizzuto†
Buddy Rosar†
Red Ruffing†
Eddie Smith†
Stan Spence†
Birdie Tebbetts
Hal Wagner†
Ted Williams
Rudy York

1942 NL
Jimmy Brown
Mort Cooper
Walker Cooper
Paul Derringer*
Bob Elliott
Billy Herman
Carl Hubbell†
Danny Litwhiler
Ernie Lombardi
Willard Marshall
Frank McCormick
Joe Medwick
Cliff Melton*
Eddie Miller
Johnny Mize
Terry Moore
Mel Ott
Mickey Owen
Claude Passeau
Pee Wee Reese
Pete Reiser
Enos Slaughter
Ray Starr†
Johnny Vander Meer
Arky Vaughan
Bucky Walters
Whit Wyatt†

1943 AL
Luke Appling†
Jim Bagby†
Tiny Bonham†
Lou Boudreau†
George Case
Spud Chandler†
Bill Dickey†
Bobby Doerr
Jake Early
Joe Gordon†
Jeff Heath
Tex Hughson
Bob Johnson
Oscar Judd†
Charlie Keller*
Ken Keltner
Chet Laabs
Dutch Leonard
Johnny Lindell†
Hal Newhouser
Buddy Rosar†
Dick Siebert
Al Smith†
Vern Stephens
Dick Wakefield
Rudy York

1943 NL
Ace Adams†
Mort Cooper
Walker Cooper
Babe Dahlgren
Vince DiMaggio
Elbie Fletcher
Lonny Frey
Augie Galan
Stan Hack
Billy Herman
Al Javery
Whitey Kurowski†
Max Lanier†
Ernie Lombardi
Marty Marion
Frank McCormick*
Eddie Miller
Stan Musial
Bill Nicholson
Mel Ott
Mickey Owen†
Claude Passeau†

Howie Pollet*
Rip Sewell
Johnny Vander Meer
Dixie Walker
Harry Walker

1944 AL
Hank Borowy
Lou Boudreau†
George Case*
Roy Cullenbine†
Bobby Doerr
Rick Ferrell†
Pete Fox†
Orval Grove†
Frankie Hayes
Rollie Hemsley
Pinky Higgins
Oris Hockett†
Tex Hughson
Bob Johnson
Ken Keltner
Dutch Leonard†
George McQuinn
Bob Muncrief
Hal Newhouser
Bobo Newsom
Joe Page†
Stan Spence
Vern Stephens
Dizzy Trout†
Thurman Tucker
Rudy York†

1944 NL
Nate Andrews†
Phil Cavarretta
Walker Cooper
Vince DiMaggio
Bob Elliott
Augie Galan
Al Javery†
Don Johnson†
Whitey Kurowski
Max Lanier*
Marty Marion
Frank McCormick†
Joe Medwick
Eddie Miller*
Ray Mueller
Red Munger*
Stan Musial
Bill Nicholson
Mel Ott
Mickey Owen†
Ken Raffensberger
Connie Ryan
Rip Sewell
Jim Tobin
Bill Voiselle†
Dixie Walker
Bucky Walters
Frankie Zak†

1945 AL
Hank Borowy†
Lou Boudreau†
George Case†
Russ Christopher†
Tony Cuccinello†
Nick Etten†
Rick Ferrell†
Dave Ferriss†
Hank Greenberg†
Oscar Grimes†
Steve Gromek†
Frankie Hayes†
Jeff Heath†
Bob Johnson†
Jack Kramer†
Thornton Lee†
Dutch Leonard†
Eddie Mayo†
George McQuinn†
Wally Moses†
Hal Newhouser†
Allie Reynolds†
Vern Stephens†
Snuffy Stirnweiss†
Mike Tresh†

1945 NL
Red Barrett†

Phil Cavarretta†
Mort Cooper†
Bob Elliott†
Hal Gregg†
Stan Hack†
Tommy Holmes†
Don Johnson†
Whitey Kurowski†
Ernie Lombardi†
Marty Marion†
Phil Masi†
Frank McCormick†
Van Mungo†
Bill Nicholson†
Ken O'Dea†
Mel Ott†
Andy Pafko†
Claude Passeau†
Preacher Roe†
Goody Rosen†
Rip Sewell†
Emil Verban†
Dixie Walker†
Hank Wyse†

1946 AL
Luke Appling
Spud Chandler†
Sam Chapman
Bill Dickey
Dom DiMaggio
Joe DiMaggio†
Bobby Doerr
Bob Feller
Dave Ferriss†
Joe Gordon
Mickey Harris†
Frankie Hayes
Charlie Keller
Ken Keltner
Jack Kramer
Hal Newhouser
Johnny Pesky
Buddy Rosar
Stan Spence
Vern Stephens
Snuffy Stirnweiss
Mickey Vernon
Hal Wagner
Ted Williams
Rudy York

1946 NL
Ewell Blackwell
Phil Cavarretta
Mort Cooper†
Walker Cooper
Del Ennis
Frankie Gustine
Kirby Higbe
Johnny Hopp
Whitey Kurowski
Ray Lamanno
Peanuts Lowrey
Marty Marion
Phil Masi
Frank McCormick
Eddie Miller*
Johnny Mize
Stan Musial
Claude Passeau
Howie Pollet†
Pee Wee Reese*
Pete Reiser†
Johnny Schmitz†
Red Schoendienst
Rip Sewell
Enos Slaughter
Emil Verban
Dixie Walker

1947 AL
Luke Appling
Lou Boudreau
Spud Chandler†
Joe DiMaggio
Bobby Doerr
Bob Feller*
Joe Gordon
Jim Hegan†
Tommy Henrich
Billy Johnson
George Kell

Charlie Keller*
Jack Kramer†
Buddy Lewis
Walt Masterson
George McQuinn
Pat Mullin†
Hal Newhouser
Joe Page
Aaron Robinson†
Buddy Rosar
Spec Shea
Stan Spence
Dizzy Trout†
Ted Williams
Early Wynn†
Rudy York†

1947 NL
Ewell Blackwell
Ralph Branca†
Harry Brecheen
Phil Cavarretta
Walker Cooper
Bruce Edwards
Bob Elliott*
Frankie Gustine
Bert Haas
Whitey Kurowski
Marty Marion
Willard Marshall
Phil Masi
Eddie Miller*
Johnny Mize
Red Munger†
Stan Musial
Andy Pafko
Pee Wee Reese
Schoolboy Rowe
Johnny Sain
Enos Slaughter
Warren Spahn
Eddie Stanky
Emil Verban
Dixie Walker
Harry Walker

1948 AL
Yogi Berra†
Lou Boudreau
Joe Coleman
Joe DiMaggio
Joe Dobson†
Bobby Doerr
Hoot Evers
Bob Feller*
Joe Gordon
Joe Haynes†
Tommy Henrich
George Kell†
Ken Keltner
Bob Lemon†
Walt Masterson
George McQuinn
Pat Mullin
Hal Newhouser
Joe Page†
Vic Raschi
Buddy Rosar
Vern Stephens
Birdie Tebbetts
Mickey Vernon
Ted Williams
Al Zarilla

1948 NL
Richie Ashburn
Ewell Blackwell
Ralph Branca
Harry Brecheen†
Walker Cooper
Bob Elliott
Sid Gordon†
Frankie Gustine
Tommy Holmes
Buddy Kerr
Ralph Kiner
Marty Marion*
Phil Masi
Clyde McCullough†
Johnny Mize
Stan Musial
Andy Pafko

Pee Wee Reese
Elmer Riddle†
Bill Rigney
Johnny Sain
Johnny Schmitz
Red Schoendienst
Enos Slaughter
Eddie Stanky*
Bobby Thomson
Eddie Waitkus

1949 AL
Yogi Berra
Lou Brissie
Bob Dillinger
Dom DiMaggio
Joe DiMaggio
Larry Doby
Billy Goodman
Joe Gordon
Jim Hegan†
Tommy Henrich†
Eddie Joost
George Kell
Alex Kellner†
Bob Lemon†
Cass Michaels
Dale Mitchell
Mel Parnell
Vic Raschi
Allie Reynolds†
Eddie Robinson
Vern Stephens
Birdie Tebbetts
Virgil Trucks
Vic Wertz
Ted Williams

1949 NL
Vern Bickford
Ewell Blackwell
Ralph Branca†
Roy Campanella
Walker Cooper†
Sid Gordon
Gil Hodges
Eddie Kazak
Ralph Kiner
Marty Marion†
Willard Marshall
Johnny Mize
Red Munger
Stan Musial
Don Newcombe
Andy Pafko
Howie Pollet
Pee Wee Reese
Jackie Robinson
Preacher Roe
Red Schoendienst
Andy Seminick
Enos Slaughter
Warren Spahn
Bobby Thomson
Eddie Waitkus†

1950 AL
Yogi Berra
Tommy Byrne†
Jerry Coleman
Dom DiMaggio
Joe DiMaggio
Larry Doby
Bobby Doerr
Walt Dropo
Hoot Evers
Ferris Fain
Bob Feller
Ted Gray
Jim Hegan
Tommy Henrich
Art Houtteman
George Kell
Bob Lemon
Sherm Lollar†
Cass Michaels
Vic Raschi
Allie Reynolds
Phil Rizzuto
Ray Scarborough†
Vern Stephens†
Ted Williams

1950 NL
Ewell Blackwell
Roy Campanella
Walker Coopert
Gil Hodges†
Larry Jansen
Willie Jones
Ralph Kiner
Jim Konstanty
Marty Marion
Stan Musial
Don Newcombe
Andy Pafko
Pee Wee Reese
Robin Roberts
Jackie Robinson
Preacher Roe†
Bob Rush†
Hank Sauer
Red Schoendienst
Dick Sisler
Enos Slaughter
Duke Snider
Warren Spahn†
Eddie Stanky†
Johnny Wyrostek

1951 AL
Yogi Berra
Jim Busby
Chico Carrasquel
Dom DiMaggio
Joe DiMaggio†
Larry Doby
Bobby Doerr
Ferris Fain
Nellie Fox
Ned Garver
Randy Gumpert†
Jim Hegan
Fred Hutchinson
George Kell
Bob Lemon
Ed Lopat
Connie Marrero†
Minnie Minoso
Mel Parnell
Phil Rizzuto
Eddie Robinson
Bobby Shantz†
Vern Stephens
Vic Wertz
Ted Williams

1951 NL
Richie Ashburn
Ewell Blackwell
Roy Campanella
Alvin Dark
Bruce Edwards†
Bob Elliott
Del Ennis
Gil Hodges
Larry Jansen†
Willie Jones
Ralph Kiner
Dutch Leonard†
Sal Maglie
Stan Musial
Don Newcombe
Pee Wee Reese
Robin Roberts
Jackie Robinson
Preacher Roe†
Red Schoendienst
Enos Slaughter
Duke Snider
Warren Spahn†
Wally Westlake
Johnny Wyrostek

1952 AL
Bobby Avila
Hank Bauer
Yogi Berra
Dom DiMaggio
Larry Doby
Ferris Fain†
Nellie Fox†
Mike Garcia†
Jim Hegan†
Jackie Jensen
Eddie Joost†

George Kell*
Bob Lemon
Mickey Mantle†
Gil McDougald
Minnie Minoso
Dale Mitchell
Satchel Paige†
Vic Raschi
Allie Reynolds†
Phil Rizzuto
Eddie Robinson
Al Rosen
Bobby Shantz
Vic Wertz†
Eddie Yost†

1952 NL
Toby Atwell†
Roy Campanella
Alvin Dark†
Carl Furillo†
Granny Hamner
Grady Hatton†
Jim Hearn†
Gil Hodges†
Monte Irvin†
Ralph Kiner†
Whitey Lockman
Sal Maglie†
Stan Musial
Pee Wee Reese
Robin Roberts†
Jackie Robinson
Preacher Roe†
Bob Rush
Hank Sauer
Red Schoendienst†
Curt Simmons
Enos Slaughter
Duke Snider†
Warren Spahn†
Gerry Staley†
Bobby Thomson
Wes Westrum†

1953 AL
Hank Bauer
Yogi Berra
Chico Carrasquel
Larry Doby
Ferris Fain
Nellie Fox
Mike Garcia
Billy Goodman
Billy Hunter
George Kell
Harvey Kuenn
Bob Lemon†
Mickey Mantle
Minnie Minoso
Johnny Mize
Satchel Paige
Billy Pierce
Allie Reynolds
Phil Rizzuto
Eddie Robinson
Al Rosen
Johnny Sain†
Mickey Vernon
Sammy White†
Ted Williams†
Gus Zernial

1953 NL
Richie Ashburn
Gus Bell
Roy Campanella
Del Crandall*
Murry Dickson
Carl Furillo†
Harvey Haddix†
Granny Hamner
Gil Hodges
Ralph Kiner
Ted Kluszewski
Eddie Mathews
Clyde McCullough†
Stan Musial
Pee Wee Reese
Del Rice*
Robin Roberts
Jackie Robinson
Red Schoendienst

Curt Simmons
Enos Slaughter
Duke Snider
Warren Spahn
Gerry Staley†
Wes Westrum†
Hoyt Wilhelm†
Davey Williams

1954 AL
Bobby Avila
Hank Bauer
Yogi Berra
Ray Boone
Chico Carrasquel
Sandy Consuegra
Larry Doby
Ferris Fain*
Jim Finigan†
Whitey Ford
Nellie Fox
Mike Garcia*
Bob Keegan
George Kell*
Harvey Kuenn†
Bob Lemon
Sherm Lollar†
Mickey Mantle
Minnie Minoso
Irv Noren
Jim Piersall
Bob Porterfield
Allie Reynolds*
Al Rosen
Dean Stone
Virgil Trucks
Bob Turley†
Mickey Vernon
Ted Williams

1954 NL
Johnny Antonelli
Gus Bell
Smoky Burgess
Roy Campanella
Gene Conley
Del Crandall†
Alvin Dark
Carl Erskine
Marv Grissom
Harvey Haddix*
Granny Hamner
Gil Hodges
Ray Jablonski
Randy Jackson
Ted Kluszewski
Willie Mays
Don Mueller
Stan Musial
Pee Wee Reese†
Robin Roberts
Jackie Robinson
Red Schoendienst
Duke Snider
Warren Spahn
Frank Thomas
Jim Wilson†

1955 AL
Bobby Avila
Yogi Berra
Chico Carrasquel
Larry Doby†
Dick Donovan†
Jim Finigan
Whitey Ford
Nellie Fox
Billy Hoeft†
Jackie Jensen
Al Kaline
Harvey Kuenn
Sherm Lollar†
Mickey Mantle
Billy Pierce
Vic Power
Al Rosen
Herb Score†
Al Smith
Frank Sullivan
Bob Turley†
Mickey Vernon
Ted Williams
Jim Wilson†

Early Wynn

1955 NL
Hank Aaron
Luis Arroyo†
Gene Baker
Ernie Banks
Smoky Burgess
Roy Campanella*
Gene Conley
Del Crandall
Del Ennis
Harvey Haddix
Gil Hodges
Randy Jackson
Sam Jones
Ted Kluszewski
Johnny Logan
Stan Lopata
Eddie Mathews
Willie Mays
Don Mueller
Stan Musial
Don Newcombe
Joe Nuxhall
Robin Roberts
Red Schoendienst
Duke Snider
Frank Thomas

1956 AL
Yogi Berra
Ray Boone
Tom Brewer
Whitey Ford
Nellie Fox
Al Kaline
George Kell
Johnny Kucks†
Harvey Kuenn
Sherm Lollar
Mickey Mantle
Billy Martin
Charlie Maxwell†
Gil McDougald†
Ray Narleski*
Billy Pierce
Jim Piersall
Vic Power
Herb Score
Roy Sievers
Harry Simpson
Frank Sullivan†
Mickey Vernon
Ted Williams
Jim Wilson
Early Wynn

1956 NL
Hank Aaron
Johnny Antonelli
Ed Bailey
Ernie Banks†
Gus Bell
Ken Boyer
Roy Campanella
Del Crandall*
Bob Friend
Jim Gilliam†
Ted Kluszewski
Clem Labine†
Brooks Lawrence†
Dale Long
Stan Lopata†
Eddie Mathews†
Willie Mays
Roy McMillan
Stan Musial
Joe Nuxhall†
Rip Repulski
Robin Roberts†
Frank Robinson
Duke Snider
Warren Spahn
Johnny Temple

1957 AL
Yogi Berra
Jim Bunning
Joe De Maestri†
Nellie Fox
Bob Grim
Elston Howard†

Al Kaline
George Kell
Harvey Kuenn
Billy Loes
Frank Malzone
Mickey Mantle
Charlie Maxwell
Gil McDougald
Minnie Minoso
Don Mossi
Billy Pierce
Bobby Richardson†
Bobby Shantz†
Roy Sievers†
Bill Skowron
Gus Triandos†
Vic Wertz
Ted Williams
Early Wynn

1957 NL
Hank Aaron
Johnny Antonelli†
Ed Bailey
Ernie Banks
Gus Bell
Lew Burdette
Gino Cimoli
Hank Foiles
Don Hoak
Gil Hodges
Larry Jackson
Clem Labine
Johnny Logan†
Eddie Mathews
Willie Mays
Roy McMillan
Wally Moon
Stan Musial
Frank Robinson
Jack Sanford
Red Schoendienst
Curt Simmons
Hal Smith†
Warren Spahn†
Johnny Temple

1958 AL
Luis Aparicio
Yogi Berra
Rocky Bridges†
Bob Cerv
Ryne Duren†
Whitey Ford†
Nellie Fox
Elston Howard†
Jackie Jensen
Al Kaline
Tony Kubek†
Harvey Kuenn†
Sherm Lollar†
Frank Malzone
Mickey Mantle
Gil McDougald
Ray Narleski
Billy O'Dell
Billy Pierce†
Bill Skowron
Gus Triandos
Bob Turley
Mickey Vernon
Ted Williams
Early Wynn

1958 NL
Hank Aaron
Johnny Antonelli†
Richie Ashburn†
Ernie Banks
Don Blasingame
Del Crandall
George Crowe†
Turk Farrell
Bob Friend
Larry Jackson
Johnny Logan
Eddie Mathews†
Willie Mays
Bill Mazeroski
Don McMahon†
Walt Moryn†
Stan Musial
Johnny Podres†

Bob Purkey†
Johnny Roseboro†
Bob Schmidt†
Bob Skinner
Warren Spahn
Frank Thomas
Lee Walls

1959 AL (GAME 1)
Luis Aparicio
Yogi Berra†
Jim Bunning
Rocky Colavito
Bud Daley
Ryne Duren
Whitey Ford
Nellie Fox
Al Kaline
Harmon Killebrew
Harvey Kuenn
Sherm Lollar
Frank Malzone
Mickey Mantle
Gil McDougald
Minnie Minoso
Billy Pierce†
Vic Power
Pete Runnels
Roy Sievers
Bill Skowron
Gus Triandos
Hoyt Wilhelm†
Ted Williams
Early Wynn

1959 NL (GAME 1)
Hank Aaron
Johnny Antonelli
Ernie Banks
Ken Boyer
Lew Burdette
Smoky Burgess†
Orlando Cepeda
Gene Conley†
Del Crandall
Joe Cunningham†
Don Drysdale
Don Elston
Roy Face
Dick Groat
Eddie Mathews
Willie Mays
Bill Mazeroski
Vinegar Bend Mizell*
Wally Moon
Stan Musial
Vada Pinson†
Frank Robinson†
Hal Smith†
Warren Spahn†
Johnny Temple
Bill White†

1959 AL (GAME 2)
Bob Allison†
Luis Aparicio
Yogi Berra
Rocky Colavito
Bud Daley†
Ryne Duren†
Nellie Fox
Elston Howard†
Al Kaline
Harmon Killebrew†
Tony Kubek
Harvey Kuenn*
Sherm Lollar
Frank Malzone
Mickey Mantle
Roger Maris
Gil McDougald*
Cal McLish
Minnie Minoso†
Billy O'Dell
Camilo Pascual*
Vic Power
Pedro Ramos†
Bobby Richardson†
Pete Runnels
Roy Sievers†
Bill Skowron*
Gus Triandos*
Jerry Walker

Hoyt Wilhelm
Ted Williams
Gene Woodling
Early Wynn

1959 NL (GAME 2)
Hank Aaron
Johnny Antonelli†
Ernie Banks
Ken Boyer
Lew Burdette†
Smoky Burgess
Orlando Cepeda*
Gene Conley
Del Crandall
Joe Cunningham
Don Drysdale
Don Elston†
Roy Face
Jim Gilliam
Dick Groat
Sam Jones
Johnny Logan†
Eddie Mathews
Willie Mays
Bill Mazeroski†
Wally Moon
Stan Musial
Charlie Neal
Vada Pinson
Frank Robinson
Hal Smith
Warren Spahn†
Johnny Temple
Bill White*

1960 AL (GAME 1)
Luis Aparicio
Gary Bell
Yogi Berra
Jim Coates
Bud Daley
Chuck Estrada
Whitey Ford†
Nellie Fox
Jim Gentile
Ron Hansen
Elston Howard
Al Kaline
Harvey Kuenn
Frank Lary
Jim Lemon
Sherm Lollar
Frank Malzone
Mickey Mantle
Roger Maris
Minnie Minoso
Bill Monbouquette
Camilo Pascual*
Vic Power†
Brooks Robinson
Pete Runnels
Bill Skowron
Al Smith
Gerry Staley†
Dick Stigman†
Ted Williams
Early Wynn†

1960 NL (GAME 1)
Hank Aaron
Joe Adcock
Ed Bailey†
Ernie Banks
Ken Boyer
Bob Buhl
Smoky Burgess
Orlando Cepeda
Roberto Clemente
Del Crandall
Roy Face
Bob Friend
Dick Groat
Bill Henry†
Larry Jackson†
Norm Larker
Vern Law
Eddie Mathews
Willie Mays
Bill Mazeroski
Mike McCormick
Lindy McDaniel†
Stan Musial

Charlie Neal
Vada Pinson
Johnny Podres†
Bob Skinner
Tony Taylor
Bill White
Stan Williams†

1960 AL (GAME 2)
Luis Aparicio†
Gary Bell
Yogi Berra
Jim Coates†
Bud Daley†
Chuck Estrada†
Whitey Ford
Nellie Fox
Jim Gentile†
Ron Hansen
Elston Howard†
Al Kaline
Harvey Kuenn
Frank Lary
Jim Lemon†
Sherm Lollar
Frank Malzone
Mickey Mantle
Roger Maris
Minnie Minoso
Bill Monbouquette†
Camilo Pascual*
Vic Power
Brooks Robinson
Pete Runnels
Bill Skowron
Al Smith
Gerry Staley
Dick Stigman†
Ted Williams
Early Wynn

1960 NL (GAME 2)
Hank Aaron
Joe Adcock
Ed Bailey
Ernie Banks
Ken Boyer
Bob Buhl†
Smoky Burgess
Orlando Cepeda
Roberto Clemente
Del Crandall
Roy Face†
Bob Friend†
Dick Groat
Bill Henry
Larry Jackson
Norm Larker
Vern Law
Eddie Mathews
Willie Mays
Bill Mazeroski
Mike McCormick†
Lindy McDaniel
Stan Musial
Charlie Neal
Vada Pinson
Johnny Podres
Bob Skinner
Tony Taylor
Bill White
Stan Williams

1961 AL (GAME 1)
Yogi Berra
Jackie Brandt
Jim Bunning
Norm Cash
Rocky Colavito
Dick Donovan
Ryne Duren†
Whitey Ford
Mike Fornieles
Nellie Fox
Jim Gentile
Elston Howard
Dick Howser
Al Kaline
Harmon Killebrew
Tony Kubek
Frank Lary
Mickey Mantle
Roger Maris

Jim Perry†
Billy Pierce†
Brooks Robinson
Johnny Romano
Johnny Temple
Hoyt Wilhelm

1961 NL (GAME 1)
Hank Aaron
George Altman
Frank Bolling
Ken Boyer
Smoky Burgess
Orlando Cepeda
Roberto Clemente
Roy Face
Joey Jay†
Eddie Kasko†
Sandy Koufax
Art Mahaffey†
Eddie Mathews
Willie Mays
Mike McCormick
Stu Miller
Stan Musial
Bob Purkey
Frank Robinson
Johnny Roseboro†
Warren Spahn
Dick Stuart
Bill White
Maury Wills
Don Zimmer

1961 AL (GAME 2)
Luis Aparicio
Luis Arroyo†
Yogi Berra†
Jackie Brandt†
Jim Bunning
Norm Cash
Rocky Colavito
Dick Donovan†
Whitey Ford†
Nellie Fox†
Tito Francona†
Jim Gentile†
Elston Howard
Dick Howser†
Al Kaline
Harmon Killebrew†
Tony Kubek*
Barry Latman†
Mickey Mantle
Roger Maris
Ken McBride†
Camilo Pascual
Brooks Robinson
Johnny Romano
Don Schwall
Roy Sievers
Bill Skowron†
Johnny Temple
Hoyt Wilhelm†

1961 NL (GAME 2)
Hank Aaron
George Altman
Ed Bailey†
Ernie Banks
Frank Bolling
Ken Boyer†
Smoky Burgess
Orlando Cepeda
Roberto Clemente
Don Drysdale†
Roy Face†
Joey Jay†
Eddie Kasko
Sandy Koufax
Art Mahaffey
Eddie Mathews
Willie Mays
Mike McCormick†
Stu Miller
Stan Musial
Bob Purkey
Frank Robinson†
Johnny Roseboro
Warren Spahn†
Dick Stuart
Bill White
Maury Wills

Don Zimmer†

1962 AL (GAME 1)
Hank Aguirre†
Luis Aparicio
Earl Battey
Jim Bunning
Rocky Colavito
Dick Donovan
Jim Gentile
Elston Howard†
Jim Landis
Mickey Mantle
Roger Maris
Bill Monbouquette†
Billy Moran
Milt Pappas
Camilo Pascual
Bobby Richardson
Brooks Robinson
Rich Rollins
Johnny Romano
Norm Siebern
Dave Stenhouse†
Ralph Terry†
Lee Thomas
Tom Tresh†
Leon Wagner
Hoyt Wilhelm*

1962 NL (GAME 1)
Hank Aaron*
Felipe Alou
Richie Ashburn†
Ernie Banks
Frank Bolling
Ken Boyer
Johnny Callison
Orlando Cepeda
Roberto Clemente
Del Crandall
Jim Davenport
Tommy Davis
Don Drysdale
Turk Farrell†
Bob Gibson†
Dick Groat
Sandy Koufax†
Juan Marichal
Willie Mays
Bill Mazeroski
Stan Musial
Bob Purkey
Johnny Roseboro†
Bob Shaw
Warren Spahn†
Maury Wills

1962 AL (GAME 2)
Hank Aguirre
Luis Aparicio
Earl Battey
Yogi Berra
Jim Bunning†
Rocky Colavito
Dick Donovan†
Jim Gentile
Ray Herbert
Elston Howard
Jim Kaat†
Al Kaline
Jim Landis*
Mickey Mantle†
Roger Maris
Ken McBride*
Billy Moran
Milt Pappas
Camilo Pascual†
Bobby Richardson
Brooks Robinson
Rich Rollins
Johnny Romano†
Pete Runnels
Norm Siebern†
Dave Stenhouse
Ralph Terry†
Lee Thomas
Tom Tresh
Leon Wagner
Hoyt Wilhelm*

1962 NL (GAME 2)
Hank Aaron

George Altman
Richie Ashburn
Ernie Banks
Frank Bolling
Ken Boyer
Johnny Callison
Orlando Cepeda
Roberto Clemente
Del Crandall
Jim Davenport†
Tommy Davis
Turk Farrell
Bob Gibson
Dick Groat
Art Mahaffey
Juan Marichal
Eddie Mathews
Willie Mays
Bill Mazeroski
Stan Musial
Johnny Podres
Bob Purkey†
Frank Robinson
Johnny Roseboro
Warren Spahn†
Billy Williams
Maury Wills

1963 AL
Bob Allison
Luis Aparicio
Steve Barber*
Earl Battey
Jim Bouton
Jim Bunning
Nellie Fox
Mudcat Grant†
Elston Howard
Al Kaline
Harmon Killebrew
Don Leppert†
Frank Malzone
Mickey Mantle*
Ken McBride
Bill Monbouquette†
Albie Pearson
Joe Pepitone
Juan Pizarro
Dick Radatz
Bobby Richardson
Brooks Robinson
Norm Siebern†
Tom Tresh
Zoilo Versalles
Leon Wagner
Carl Yastrzemski

1963 NL
Hank Aaron
Ed Bailey
Ken Boyer
Orlando Cepeda†
Roberto Clemente
Ray Culp
Tommy Davis
Don Drysdale
Johnny Edwards
Dick Groat
Larry Jackson
Julian Javier
Sandy Koufax†
Juan Marichal†
Willie Mays
Bill Mazeroski*
Willie McCovey
Stan Musial
Jim O'Toole
Ron Santo
Duke Snider
Warren Spahn†
Joe Torre†
Bill White
Maury Wills†
Hal Woodeshick

1964 AL
Bob Allison
Luis Aparicio*
Eddie Bressoud†
Dean Chance
Rocky Colavito
Whitey Ford†
Bill Freehan†

Jim Fregosi
Jimmie Hall
Chuck Hinton
Elston Howard
Al Kaline*
Harmon Killebrew
Jack Kralick†
Jerry Lumpe†
Frank Malzone†
Mickey Mantle
Tony Oliva
Camilo Pascual
Joe Pepitone
Gary Peters†
Juan Pizarro†
Dick Radatz
Bobby Richardson
Brooks Robinson
Norm Siebern
John Wyatt

1964 NL
Hank Aaron
Ken Boyer
Jim Bunning
Smoky Burgess†
Johnny Callison
Leo Cardenas
Orlando Cepeda
Roberto Clemente
Don Drysdale
Johnny Edwards
Dick Ellsworth†
Turk Farrell
Curt Flood
Dick Groat
Ron Hunt
Sandy Koufax†
Juan Marichal
Willie Mays
Bill Mazeroski†
Ron Santo†
Chris Short
Willie Stargell
Joe Torre
Bill White
Billy Williams

1965 AL
Max Alvis
Earl Battey
Rocky Colavito
Vic Davalillo
Eddie Fisher
Bill Freehan
Mudcat Grant
Jimmie Hall
Willie Horton
Elston Howard†
Al Kaline
Harmon Killebrew
Bob Lee†
Felix Mantilla
Mickey Mantle*
Dick McAuliffe
Sam McDowell
John O'Donoghue†
Tony Oliva
Milt Pappas
Joe Pepitone
Bobby Richardson
Pete Richert
Brooks Robinson
Bill Skowron†
Mel Stottlemyre†
Zoilo Versalles
Carl Yastrzemski*

1965 NL
Hank Aaron
Dick Allen
Ernie Banks
Johnny Callison†
Leo Cardenas
Roberto Clemente
Don Drysdale
Johnny Edwards†
Sammy Ellis†
Turk Farrell
Bob Gibson
Sandy Koufax
Ed Kranepool†
Jim Maloney

Juan Marichal
Willie Mays
Frank Robinson
Cookie Rojas
Pete Rose
Ron Santo
Willie Stargell
Joe Torre
Bob Veale†
Billy Williams
Maury Wills

1966 AL
Tommie Agee
Steve Barber†
Earl Battey
Gary Bell†
Norm Cash
Rocky Colavito
Andy Etchebarren†
Bill Freehan
Jim Fregosi
Catfish Hunter†
Jim Kaat
Al Kaline
Harmon Killebrew
Bobby Knoop
Dick McAuliffe
Sam McDowell*
Denny McLain
Tony Oliva
Bobby Richardson
Pete Richert
Brooks Robinson
Frank Robinson
George Scott
Sonny Siebert
Mel Stottlemyre
Carl Yastrzemski†

1966 NL
Hank Aaron
Dick Allen
Felipe Alou†
Jim Bunning
Leo Cardenas
Roberto Clemente
Curt Flood
Bob Gibson*
Tom Haller†
Jim Ray Hart
Ron Hunt
Sandy Koufax
Jim Lefebvre
Juan Marichal
Willie Mays
Tim McCarver
Billy McCool†
Willie McCovey
Joe Morgan*
Gaylord Perry
Claude Raymond†
Phil Regan†
Ron Santo
Willie Stargell
Joe Torre
Bob Veale†
Maury Wills

1967 AL
Tommie Agee
Max Alvis
Ken Berry
Rod Carew
Paul Casanova†
Dean Chance
Tony Conigliaro†
Al Downing
Andy Etchebarren†
Bill Freehan
Jim Fregosi
Steve Hargan†
Joe Horlen†
Catfish Hunter
Al Kaline*
Harmon Killebrew
Jim Lonborg†
Mickey Mantle
Dick McAuliffe
Jim McGlothlin
Don Mincher
Tony Oliva
Gary Peters

Rico Petrocelli
Brooks Robinson
Frank Robinson*
Carl Yastrzemski

1967 NL
Hank Aaron
Dick Allen
Gene Alley
Ernie Banks
Lou Brock
Orlando Cepeda
Roberto Clemente
Mike Cuellar
Don Drysdale
Bob Gibson
Tom Haller
Tommy Helms
Fergie Jenkins
Denny Lemaster*
Juan Marichal
Willie Mays
Bill Mazeroski
Tim McCarver
Claude Osteen†
Tony Perez
Pete Rose
Tom Seaver
Chris Short
Rusty Staub
Joe Torre
Jim Wynn

1968 AL
Joe Azcue
Gary Bell†
Bert Campaneris
Rod Carew
Bill Freehan
Jim Fregosi
Ken Harrelson
Willie Horton
Frank Howard
Tommy John
Davey Johnson
Duane Josephson
Harmon Killebrew
Mickey Mantle
Sam McDowell
Denny McLain
Rick Monday
Blue Moon Odom
Tony Oliva
Boog Powell
Brooks Robinson
Jose Santiago*
Mel Stottlemyre
Luis Tiant
Don Wert
Carl Yastrzemski

1968 NL
Hank Aaron
Gene Alley*
Felipe Alou
Matty Alou
Johnny Bench
Leo Cardenas
Steve Carlton
Don Drysdale
Curt Flood
Woodie Fryman†
Bob Gibson†
Jerry Grote
Tom Haller
Tommy Helms
Julian Javier
Don Kessinger
Jerry Koosman
Juan Marichal
Willie Mays
Willie McCovey
Tony Perez
Ron Reed
Pete Rose*
Ron Santo
Tom Seaver
Rusty Staub
Billy Williams

1969 AL
Mike Andrews
Sal Bando

Paul Blair
Rod Carew
Ray Culp
Bill Freehan
Jim Fregosi
Mike Hegan*
Frank Howard
Reggie Jackson
Davey Johnson*
Harmon Killebrew
Darold Knowles
Mickey Lolich†
Carlos May
Sam McDowell
Denny McLain
Dave McNally
Don Mincher
Blue Moon Odom
Tony Oliva*
Rico Petrocelli
Boog Powell
Brooks Robinson
Frank Robinson
Ellie Rodriguez†
Johnny Roseboro
Reggie Smith
Mel Stottlemyre
Roy White
Carl Yastrzemski

1969 NL
Hank Aaron
Matty Alou
Ernie Banks
Glenn Beckert
Johnny Bench
Chris Cannizzaro†
Steve Carlton
Roberto Clemente
Larry Dierker
Bob Gibson
Randy Hundley
Grant Jackson†
Cleon Jones
Don Kessinger
Jerry Koosman
Juan Marichal†
Lee May
Willie Mays
Willie McCovey
Denis Menke
Felix Millan
Phil Niekro
Tony Perez
Pete Rose
Ron Santo
Tom Seaver†
Bill Singer
Rusty Staub†

1970 AL
Sandy Alomar
Luis Aparicio
Rod Carew*
Mike Cuellar†
Ray Fosse
Bill Freehan
Jim Fregosi
Tommy Harper
Willie Horton
Frank Howard
Catfish Hunter
Alex Johnson
Davey Johnson
Harmon Killebrew
Sam McDowell
Dave McNally†
Jerry Moses†
Tony Oliva
Amos Otis
Jim Palmer
Jim Perry
Fritz Peterson
Boog Powell
Brooks Robinson
Frank Robinson
Mel Stottlemyre
Roy White†
Clyde Wright
Carl Yastrzemski

1970 NL
Hank Aaron

Dick Allen
Glenn Beckert
Johnny Bench
Rico Carty
Roberto Clemente
Dick Dietz
Cito Gaston
Bob Gibson
Billy Grabarkewitz
Bud Harrelson
Jim Hickman
Joe Hoerner†
Don Kessinger
Willie Mays
Willie McCovey
Denis Menke
Jim Merritt
Felix Millan*
Joe Morgan
Claude Osteen
Tony Perez
Gaylord Perry
Pete Rose
Tom Seaver
Wayne Simpson†
Rusty Staub
Joe Torre
Hoyt Wilhelm†

1971 AL
Luis Aparicio
Vida Blue
Don Buford
Leo Cardenas†
Rod Carew
Norm Cash
Mike Cuellar
Dave Duncan†
Ray Fosse*
Bill Freehan
Frank Howard
Reggie Jackson
Al Kaline
Harmon Killebrew
Mickey Lolich
Sam McDowell*
Bill Melton†
Andy Messersmith†
Thurman Munson
Bobby Murcer
Tony Oliva*
Amos Otis
Jim Palmer
Marty Pattin†
Jim Perry†
Boog Powell*
Brooks Robinson
Frank Robinson
Cookie Rojas
Sonny Siebert†
Wilbur Wood†
Carl Yastrzemski

1971 NL
Hank Aaron
Glenn Beckert
Johnny Bench
Bobby Bonds
Lou Brock
Steve Carlton†
Clay Carroll†
Roberto Clemente
Nate Colbert
Willie Davis
Larry Dierker*
Dock Ellis
Bud Harrelson
Fergie Jenkins
Don Kessinger
Juan Marichal
Lee May
Willie Mays
Willie McCovey
Felix Millan
Pete Rose
Manny Sanguillen†
Ron Santo
Tom Seaver†
Willie Stargell
Rusty Staub†
Joe Torre
Don Wilson
Rick Wise†

1972 AL
Dick Allen
Luis Aparicio*
Sal Bando
Bert Campaneris†
Rod Carew
Norm Cash
Joe Coleman†
Pat Dobson†
Carlton Fisk
Bill Freehan
Bobby Grich
Toby Harrah*
Ken Holtzman†
Catfish Hunter†
Reggie Jackson
Mickey Lolich
Carlos May†
Dave McNally
Bobby Murcer
Amos Otis*
Jim Palmer
Freddie Patek*
Gaylord Perry
Lou Piniella
Brooks Robinson
Ellie Rodriguez†
Cookie Rojas
Joe Rudi
Nolan Ryan†
Richie Scheinblum
Reggie Smith
Wilbur Wood
Carl Yastrzemski

1972 NL
Hank Aaron
Glenn Beckert
Johnny Bench
Steve Blass
Lou Brock†
Steve Carlton
Clay Carroll†
Cesar Cedeno
Roberto Clemente*
Nate Colbert
Bob Gibson
Fergie Jenkins†
Don Kessinger
Lee May
Willie Mays
Tug McGraw
Joe Morgan
Gary Nolan*
Al Oliver
Manny Sanguillen
Ron Santo
Tom Seaver†
Ted Simmons†
Chris Speier
Willie Stargell
Bill Stoneman
Don Sutton
Joe Torre
Billy Williams

1973 AL
Dick Allen*
Sal Bando
Buddy Bell
Paul Blair
Bert Blyleven
Ed Brinkman
Bert Campaneris
Rod Carew
Jim Colborn†
Rollie Fingers
Carlton Fisk
Bill Freehan†
Ken Holtzman
Willie Horton
Catfish Hunter
Reggie Jackson
Pat Kelly
Bill Lee†
Sparky Lyle
Dave May
John Mayberry
Thurman Munson
Bobby Murcer
Dave Nelson
Amos Otis
Brooks Robinson

Cookie Rojas
Nolan Ryan
Bill Singer
Jim Spencer
Carl Yastrzemski*

1973 NL
Hank Aaron
Johnny Bench
Jack Billingham†
Bobby Bonds
Jim Brewer
Cesar Cedeno
Nate Colbert
Dave Concepcion*
Willie Davis
Darrell Evans
Ron Fairly
Dave Giusti
Davey Johnson
Willie Mays
Joe Morgan
Manny Mota
Claude Osteen
Pete Rose
Bill Russell
Ron Santo
Tom Seaver
Ted Simmons
Chris Speier
Willie Stargell
Don Sutton
Joe Torre
Wayne Twitchell
Bob Watson
Billy Williams
Rick Wise

1974 AL
Dick Allen
Sal Bando*
Jeff Burroughs
Steve Busby†
Bert Campaneris
Rod Carew
Dave Chalk
Mike Cuellar†
Rollie Fingers
Carlton Fisk*
Bobby Grich
George Hendrick
Ed Herrmann†
John Hiller†
Catfish Hunter
Reggie Jackson
Al Kaline
John Mayberry
Don Money†
Thurman Munson
Bobby Murcer
Gaylord Perry
Darrell Porter†
Brooks Robinson
Frank Robinson
Cookie Rojas†
Joe Rudi
Jim Sundberg†
Luis Tiant
Wilbur Wood†
Carl Yastrzemski

1974 NL
Hank Aaron
Johnny Bench
Larry Bowa
Ken Brett
Lou Brock
Buzz Capra†
Steve Carlton†
Dave Cash
Cesar Cedeno
Ron Cey
Ralph Garr
Steve Garvey
Jerry Grote
Johnny Grubb
Don Kessinger
Mike Marshall
Jon Matlack
Lynn McGlothen
Andy Messersmith
Joe Morgan
Tony Perez

Steve Rogers†
Pete Rose
Mike Schmidt
Ted Simmons†
Reggie Smith
Chris Speier†
Jim Wynn

1975 AL
Hank Aaron
Vida Blue
Bobby Bonds
Steve Busby
Bert Campaneris
Rod Carew
Dave Chalk†
Bucky Dent
Rollie Fingers†
Bill Freehan†
Rich Gossage
Mike Hargrove
Toby Harrah†
George Hendrick
Catfish Hunter
Reggie Jackson
Jim Kaat
Fred Lynn
Hal McRae
Thurman Munson
Graig Nettles
Jorge Orta*
Jim Palmer†
Joe Rudi
Nolan Ryan†
George Scott
Gene Tenace
Claudell Washington
Carl Yastrzemski

1975 NL
Johnny Bench
Larry Bowa
Lou Brock
Gary Carter
Dave Cash
Ron Cey
Dave Concepcion
Steve Garvey
Randy Jones
Greg Luzinski
Bill Madlock
Mike Marshall†
Jon Matlack
Tug McGraw†
Andy Messersmith†
Joe Morgan
Bobby Murcer
Phil Niekro†
Al Oliver
Tony Perez
Jerry Reuss
Pete Rose
Manny Sanguillen†
Tom Seaver
Reggie Smith
Don Sutton
Bob Watson
Jim Wynn

1976 AL
Mark Belanger
George Brett
Rod Carew
Chris Chambliss
Mark Fidrych
Rollie Fingers†
Carlton Fisk
Phil Garner
Rich Gossage†
Bobby Grich
Toby Harrah
Catfish Hunter
Dave La Roche†
Ron Le Flore
Sparky Lyle†
Fred Lynn
Hal McRae
Don Money
Thurman Munson
Amos Otis
Freddie Patek
Willie Randolph*
Mickey Rivers

Rusty Staub
Frank Tanana
Luis Tiant
Bill Travers†
Butch Wynegar
Carl Yastrzemski

1976 NL
Johnny Bench
Bob Boone
Larry Bowa
Dave Cash
Cesar Cedeno
Ron Cey
Dave Concepcion
Ken Forsch
George Foster
Woodie Fryman†
Steve Garvey
Ken Griffey
Randy Jones
Dave Kingman
Greg Luzinski
Jon Matlack†
Bake McBride†
Andy Messersmith*
John Montefusco
Joe Morgan
Al Oliver
Tony Perez
Rick Rhoden
Pete Rose
Bill Russell
Dick Ruthven†
Mike Schmidt
Tom Seaver
Steve Swisher†

1977 AL
Vida Blue*
George Brett
Rick Burleson
Bert Campaneris
Bill Campbell
Rod Carew
Dennis Eckersley
Ron Fairly
Mark Fidrych*
Carlton Fisk
Wayne Gross†
Larry Hisle
Reggie Jackson
Ruppert Jones
Jim Kern
Dave La Roche
Sparky Lyle
Fred Lynn
Don Money*
Thurman Munson
Graig Nettles
Jim Palmer
Willie Randolph
Jim Rice
Nolan Ryan†
George Scott
Ken Singleton
Jim Slaton†
Frank Tanana*
Jason Thompson†
Butch Wynegar
Carl Yastrzemski
Richie Zisk

1977 NL
Joaquin Andujar†
Johnny Bench
John Candelaria†
Steve Carlton†
Ron Cey
Dave Concepcion
George Foster
Steve Garvey
Rich Gossage
Ken Griffey†
Gary Lavelle
Greg Luzinski
Willie Montanez
Jerry Morales
Joe Morgan
Dave Parker
Rick Reuschel
Pete Rose
Mike Schmidt

Tom Seaver
Ted Simmons
Reggie Smith
John Stearns
Bruce Sutter*
Don Sutton
Garry Templeton
Manny Trillo
Ellis Valentine
Dave Winfield

1978 AL
George Brett
Rick Burleson*
Rod Carew
Dwight Evans
Carlton Fisk
Mike Flanagan†
Rich Gossage
Ron Guidry
Larry Hisle
Roy Howell
Reggie Jackson*
Matt Keough
Jim Kern
Chet Lemon
Fred Lynn
Don Money
Thurman Munson*
Eddie Murray†
Graig Nettles
Jim Palmer
Freddie Patek
Darrell Porter
Jerry Remy†
Craig Reynolds†
Jim Rice
Lary Sorensen
Jim Sundberg
Frank Tanana†
Jason Thompson
Frank White
Carl Yastrzemski*
Richie Zisk

1978 NL
Johnny Bench*
Vida Blue
Bob Boone
Larry Bowa
Jeff Burroughs†
Ron Cey
Jack Clark
Dave Concepcion
Rollie Fingers
George Foster
Steve Garvey
Ross Grimsley†
Tommy John†
Davey Lopes
Greg Luzinski
Rick Monday
Joe Morgan
Phil Niekro
Biff Pocoroba
Terry Puhl†
Steve Rogers
Pete Rose
Tom Seaver†
Ted Simmons
Reggie Smith
Willie Stargell
Bruce Sutter
Dave Winfield
Pat Zachry†

1979 AL
Don Baylor
Bruce Bochte
George Brett
Rick Burleson
Rod Carew*
Mark Clear
Cecil Cooper
Brian Downing
Bobby Grich
Ron Guidry
Reggie Jackson
Tommy John†
Steve Kemp
Jim Kern
Dave Lemanczyk†
Chet Lemon

Fred Lynn
Sid Monge†
Graig Nettles
Jeff Newman†
Darrell Porter
Jim Rice
Nolan Ryan
Ken Singleton
Roy Smalley
Don Stanhouse†
Bob Stanley
Frank White
Carl Yastrzemski

1979 NL
Joaquin Andujar
Johnny Bench*
Bob Boone
Larry Bowa
Lou Brock
Steve Carlton
Gary Carter
Ron Cey
Jack Clark
Dave Concepcion*
George Foster
Steve Garvey
Keith Hernandez
Dave Kingman*
Mike La Coss
Davey Lopes
Gary Matthews
Lee Mazzilli
Joe Morgan
Joe Niekro†
Dave Parker
Larry Parrish
Gaylord Perry
Craig Reynolds
Steve Rogers
Pete Rose
Joe Sambito
Mike Schmidt
Ted Simmons*
John Stearns†
Bruce Sutter
Garry Templeton†
Dave Winfield

1980 AL
Buddy Bell
George Brett*
Al Bumbry
Tom Burgmeier†
Rod Carew
Cecil Cooper
Bucky Dent
Ed Farmer
Carlton Fisk
Rich Gossage
Bobby Grich
Larry Gura†
Rickey Henderson
Rick Honeycutt†
Reggie Jackson
Tommy John
Ken Landreaux
Fred Lynn
Paul Molitor*
Graig Nettles
Ben Oglivie
Al Oliver
Jorge Orta†
Lance Parrish
Darrell Porter
Willie Randolph
Jim Rice*
Dave Stieb
Steve Stone
Alan Trammell
Robin Yount

1980 NL
Johnny Bench
Jim Bibby
Vida Blue*
Steve Carlton†
Gary Carter
Dave Concepcion
Jose Cruz†
Phil Garner
Steve Garvey
Ken Griffey

George Hendrick
Keith Hernandez
Dave Kingman
Ray Knight
Davey Lopes
Dale Murphy
Dave Parker
Ken Reitz
Jerry Reuss
J.R. Richard
Pete Rose
Bill Russell
Mike Schmidt*
Reggie Smith
John Stearns
Bruce Sutter
Kent Tekulve†
Bob Welch
Ed Whitson†
Dave Winfield

1981 AL
Tony Armas
Len Barker
Buddy Bell
George Brett
Rick Burleson
Britt Burns†
Rod Carew
Doug Corbett†
Ron Davis
Bucky Dent
Bo Diaz
Dwight Evans
Rollie Fingers
Carlton Fisk
Ken Forsch
Rich Gossage*
Reggie Jackson
Fred Lynn
Scott McGregor†
Jack Morris
Eddie Murray
Mike Norris
Al Oliver
Tom Paciorek
Willie Randolph
Ted Simmons
Ken Singleton
Dave Stieb
Gorman Thomas
Frank White
Dave Winfield

1981 NL
Dusty Baker
Bruce Benedict
Vida Blue
Bill Buckner
Steve Carlton†
Gary Carter
Dave Concepcion
Andre Dawson
Mike Easler
George Foster
Phil Garner
Steve Garvey
Pedro Guerrero
Burt Hooton
Terry Kennedy
Bob Knepper
Davey Lopes
Bill Madlock
Dave Parker
Tim Raines
Pete Rose
Dick Ruthven
Nolan Ryan
Mike Schmidt
Tom Seaver
Ozzie Smith
Bruce Sutter
Manny Trillo
Fernando Valenzuela
Joel Youngblood

1982 AL
Floyd Bannister
Buddy Bell
George Brett
Rod Carew*
Jim Clancy
Mark Clear†

Cecil Cooper
Dennis Eckersley
Rollie Fingers
Carlton Fisk
Rich Gossage†
Bobby Grich
Ron Guidry†
Toby Harrah†
Rickey Henderson
Kent Hrbek
Reggie Jackson
Fred Lynn
Hal McRae
Eddie Murray
Ben Oglivie
Lance Parrish
Dan Quisenberry
Andy Thornton
Frank White
Willie Wilson
Dave Winfield
Carl Yastrzemski
Robin Yount

1982 NL
Dusty Baker
Steve Carlton
Gary Carter
Dave Concepcion
Andre Dawson
Leon Durham†
Bob Horner
Steve Howe
Tom Hume
Ruppert Jones
Ray Knight
Greg Minton
Dale Murphy
Phil Niekro†
Al Oliver
Tony Pena
Tim Raines
Steve Rogers
Pete Rose
Steve Sax
Mike Schmidt
Lonnie Smith
Ozzie Smith
Mario Soto
John Stearns
Jason Thompson
Manny Trillo
Fernando Valenzuela

1983 AL
Bob Boone
George Brett
Rod Carew
Cecil Cooper
Doug De Cinces
Ron Guidry*
Rickey Henderson
Rick Honeycutt
Reggie Jackson*
Ron Kittle
Aurelio Lopez†
Fred Lynn
Tippy Martinez†
Eddie Murray
Ben Oglivie
Lance Parrish
Dan Quisenberry
Jim Rice
Cal Ripken
Ted Simmons
Bob Stanley
Dave Stieb
Rick Sutcliffe†
Manny Trillo
Gary Ward
Lou Whitaker
Willie Wilson
Dave Winfield
Carl Yastrzemski
Matt Young
Robin Yount

1983 NL
Johnny Bench
Bruce Benedict
Gary Carter
Bill Dawley
Andre Dawson

Dave Dravecky
Leon Durham
Darrell Evans
Pedro Guerrero
Atlee Hammaker
George Hendrick†
Glenn Hubbard
Terry Kennedy†
Gary Lavelle†
Bill Madlock
Willie McGee
Dale Murphy
Al Oliver
Jesse Orosco
Pascual Perez
Tim Raines
Steve Rogers†
Steve Sax
Mike Schmidt
Lee Smith
Ozzie Smith
Mario Soto
Dickie Thon
Fernando Valenzuela†

1984 AL
Tony Armas†
Buddy Bell
Mike Boddicker†
George Brett
Rod Carew
Bill Caudill
Alvin Davis
Richard Dotson
Dave Engle†
Damaso Garcia
Alfredo Griffin
Rickey Henderson
Willie Hernandez
Reggie Jackson
Chet Lemon
Don Mattingly
Jack Morris
Eddie Murray
Phil Niekro†
Lance Parrish
Dan Quisenberry†
Jim Rice
Cal Ripken
Dave Stieb
Jim Sundberg
Andy Thornton
Alan Trammell*
Lou Whitaker
Dave Winfield

1984 NL
Joaquin Andujar*
Bob Brenly
Gary Carter
Chili Davis
Jody Davis
Steve Garvey
Dwight Gooden
Rich Gossage
Tony Gwynn
Keith Hernandez
Al Holland†
Charlie Lea
Mike Marshall†
Jerry Mumphrey
Dale Murphy
Jesse Orosco†
Tony Pena
Tim Raines
Rafael Ramirez†
Juan Samuel†
Ryne Sandberg
Mike Schmidt
Ozzie Smith
Mario Soto
Darryl Strawberry
Bruce Sutter†
Fernando Valenzuela
Tim Wallach
Claudell Washington

1985 AL
Harold Baines
Bert Blyleven
Wade Boggs
Phil Bradley
George Brett

Tom Brunansky
Cecil Cooper
Carlton Fisk
Damaso Garcia
Rich Gedman
Rickey Henderson
Willie Hernandez
Jay Howell†
Jimmy Key
Don Mattingly
Paul Molitor
Donnie Moore
Jack Morris
Eddie Murray
Lance Parrish*
Dan Petry
Jim Rice
Cal Ripken
Dave Stieb
Alan Trammell
Gary Ward
Lou Whitaker
Ernie Whitt
Dave Winfield

1985 NL
Joaquin Andujar†
Gary Carter*
Jack Clark
Jose Cruz
Ron Darling†
Scott Garrelts†
Steve Garvey
Dwight Gooden†
Rich Gossage
Pedro Guerrero*
Tony Gwynn
Tom Herr
La Marr Hoyt
Terry Kennedy
Willie McGee
Dale Murphy
Graig Nettles
Dave Parker
Tony Pena
Tim Raines
Jeff Reardon
Pete Rose
Nolan Ryan
Ryne Sandberg
Ozzie Smith
Darryl Strawberry
Garry Templeton
Fernando Valenzuela
Ozzie Virgil
Tim Wallach
Glenn Wilson

1986 AL
Don Aase
Harold Baines
Jesse Barfield
Wade Boggs
George Brett*
Jose Canseco†
Roger Clemens
Tony Fernandez
Rich Gedman
Rickey Henderson
Willie Hernandez†
Teddy Higuera
Charlie Hough
Brook Jacoby
Wally Joyner
Don Mattingly
Lloyd Moseby
Eddie Murray†
Lance Parrish
Jim Presley†
Kirby Puckett
Jim Rice
Dave Righetti
Cal Ripken
Ken Schrom†
Lou Whitaker
Frank White
Dave Winfield
Mike Witt†

1986 NL
Kevin Bass
Hubie Brooks
Chris Brown

Gary Carter
Chili Davis
Glenn Davis
Jody Davis
Sid Fernandez
John Franco†
Dwight Gooden
Tony Gwynn
Keith Hernandez
Mike Krukow
Dale Murphy
Dave Parker
Tony Pena
Tim Raines
Shane Rawley†
Jeff Reardon†
Rick Rhoden†
Ryne Sandberg
Steve Sax
Mike Schmidt
Mike Scott
Dave Smith†
Ozzie Smith
Darryl Strawberry
Fernando Valenzuela

1987 AL
Harold Baines
George Bell
Wade Boggs
Dwight Evans
Tony Fernandez
Rickey Henderson
Tom Henke
Jay Howell
Bruce Hurst†
Terry Kennedy
Mark Langston
Don Mattingly
Mark McGwire
Jack Morris
Matt Nokes
Larry Parrish
Dan Plesac
Kirby Puckett
Willie Randolph
Harold Reynolds
Dave Righetti
Cal Ripken
Bret Saberhagen
Kevin Seitzer
Pat Tabler
Alan Trammell
Lou Whitaker*
Dave Winfield
Mike Witt†

1987 NL
Steve Bedrosian
Hubie Brooks
Gary Carter
Jack Clark
Eric Davis
Andre Dawson
Bo Diaz
Sid Fernandez
John Franco
Pedro Guerrero
Tony Gwynn
Keith Hernandez
Orel Hershiser
Jeffrey Leonard
Willie McGee
Dale Murphy
Tim Raines
Rick Reuschel
Juan Samuel
Ryne Sandberg
Mike Schmidt
Mike Scott
Lee Smith
Ozzie Smith
Darryl Strawberry
Rick Sutcliffe
Ozzie Virgil
Tim Wallach

1988 AL
Doyle Alexander†
Wade Boggs
George Brett
Jose Canseco
Roger Clemens

Dennis Eckersley
Gary Gaetti
Mike Greenwell
Mark Gubicza
Ozzie Guillen*
Rickey Henderson
Doug Jones
Carney Lansford
Tim Laudner
Don Mattingly
Mark McGwire
Paul Molitor
Dan Plesac
Kirby Puckett
Johnny Ray
Jeff Reardon†
Harold Reynolds
Cal Ripken
Jeff Russell
Terry Steinbach
Dave Stieb
Kurt Stillwell
Alan Trammell*
Frank Viola
Dave Winfield

1988 NL
Bobby Bonilla
Gary Carter
Will Clark
Vince Coleman
David Cone
Mark Davis
Andre Dawson
Shawon Dunston†
Andres Galarraga
Dwight Gooden
Kevin Gross
Orel Hershiser
Danny Jackson†
Bob Knepper
Barry Larkin
Vance Law
Greg Maddux†
Willie McGee
Rafael Palmeiro
Lance Parrish
Gerald Perry
Chris Sabo
Ryne Sandberg
Ozzie Smith
Darryl Strawberry
Robby Thompson*
Andy Van Slyke
Bob Walk
Todd Worrell

1989 AL
Harold Baines
Wade Boggs
Jose Canseco*
Tony Fernandez
Chuck Finley†
Julio Franco
Gary Gaetti
Mike Greenwell
Kelly Gruber†
Mark Gubicza
Mike Henneman†
Bo Jackson
Doug Jones
Jeffrey Leonard
Don Mattingly
Mark McGwire
Mike Moore
Dan Plesac
Kirby Puckett
Cal Ripken
Jeff Russell
Nolan Ryan
Steve Sax
Ruben Sierra
Terry Steinbach
Dave Stewart
Greg Swindell
Mickey Tettleton
Devon White

1989 NL
Bobby Bonilla
Tim Burke
Will Clark
Vince Coleman

Eric Davis
Glenn Davis
Mark Davis
Andre Dawson
John Franco†
Pedro Guerrero
Tony Gwynn
Von Hayes
Orel Hershiser†
Jay Howell
Howard Johnson
Barry Larkin†
Kevin Mitchell
Tony Pena
Willie Randolph
Rick Reuschel
Ryne Sandberg
Benito Santiago
Mike Schmidt*
Mike Scioscia
Mike Scott*
Ozzie Smith
John Smoltz
Darryl Strawberry*
Rick Sutcliffe
Tim Wallach
Mitch Williams

1990 AL
Sandy Alomar
George Bell
Wade Boggs
Ellis Burks*
Jose Canseco
Roger Clemens†
Dennis Eckersley
Cecil Fielder
Chuck Finley
Julio Franco
Ken Griffey
Kelly Gruber
Ozzie Guillen
Rickey Henderson
Brook Jacoby
Randy Johnson†
Doug Jones†
Mark McGwire
Gregg Olson†
Dave Parker†
Lance Parrish
Kirby Puckett
Cal Ripken
Bret Saberhagen
Steve Sax
Dave Stieb
Bobby Thigpen
Alan Trammell
Bob Welch

1990 NL
Roberto Alomar
Jack Armstrong
Barry Bonds
Bobby Bonilla
Jeff Brantley
Will Clark
Andre Dawson
Rob Dibble
Shawon Dunston
Lenny Dykstra
John Franco
Tony Gwynn
Neal Heaton†
Barry Larkin
Dennis Martinez
Ramon Martinez
Kevin Mitchell
Randy Myers
Greg Olson
Chris Sabo
Ryne Sandberg
Benito Santiago*
Mike Scioscia
Dave Smith
Ozzie Smith
Darryl Strawberry
Frank Viola
Tim Wallach
Matt Williams

1991 AL
Rick Aguilera
Roberto Alomar

Sandy Alomar
Harold Baines
Wade Boggs
Joe Carter
Roger Clemens
Dennis Eckersley
Cecil Fielder
Carlton Fisk
Julio Franco†
Ken Griffey
Ozzie Guillen
Bryan Harvey†
Dave Henderson
Rickey Henderson
Jimmy Key
Mark Langston†
Jack McDowell
Mark McGwire*
Paul Molitor
Jack Morris
Rafael Palmeiro
Kirby Puckett
Jeff Reardon
Cal Ripken
Scott Sanderson†
Ruben Sierra
Danny Tartabull

1991 NL
George Bell
Craig Biggio
Bobby Bonilla
Tom Browning†
Brett Butler
Ivan Calderon
Will Clark
Andre Dawson
Rob Dibble
Tom Glavine
Tony Gwynn
Pete Harnisch
Howard Johnson
Felix Jose
John Kruk†
Barry Larkin
Dennis Martinez
Mike Morgan
Eddie Murray
Paul O'Neill
Chris Sabo
Juan Samuel
Ryne Sandberg
Benito Santiago
John Smiley
Lee Smith†
Ozzie Smith
Darryl Strawberry*
Frank Viola

1992 AL
Rick Aguilera
Roberto Alomar
Sandy Alomar
Brady Anderson
Carlos Baerga
Wade Boggs
Kevin Brown
Jose Canseco*
Joe Carter
Roger Clemens
Dennis Eckersley
Travis Fryman
Ken Griffey
Juan Guzman
Roberto Kelly
Chuck Knoblauch
Mark Langston
Edgar Martinez
Jack McDowell
Mark McGwire
Paul Molitor
Jeff Montgomery
Mike Mussina
Charles Nagy
Kirby Puckett
Cal Ripken
Ivan Rodriguez
Ruben Sierra
Robin Ventura

1992 NL
Craig Biggio
Barry Bonds

Norm Charlton
Will Clark
David Cone
Darren Daulton
Tony Fernandez
Ron Gant
Tom Glavine
Tony Gwynn
Doug Jones
John Kruk
Greg Maddux
Dennis Martinez
Fred McGriff
Tom Pagnozzi
Terry Pendleton
Bip Roberts
Ryne Sandberg
Benito Santiago
Mike Sharperson
Gary Sheffield
Lee Smith†
Ozzie Smith
John Smoltz
Bob Tewksbury
Andy Van Slyke
Larry Walker

1993 AL
Rick Aguilera
Roberto Alomar
Carlos Baerga
Albert Belle
Wade Boggs
Joe Carter
Scott Cooper
Cecil Fielder
Travis Fryman
Juan Gonzalez
Ken Griffey
Pat Hentgen†
Randy Johnson
Jimmy Key
Mark Langston
Jack McDowell
Paul Molitor
Jeff Montgomery
Mike Mussina†
John Olerud
Kirby Puckett
Cal Ripken
Ivan Rodriguez
Terry Steinbach

Frank Thomas
Greg Vaughn
Duane Ward
Devon White

1993 NL
Steve Avery
Rod Beck
Jay Bell
Andy Benes
Jeff Blauser
Barry Bonds
Bobby Bonilla
John Burkett
Darren Daulton
Andres Galarraga
Tom Glavine†
Mark Grace
Marquis Grissom
Tony Gwynn
Bryan Harvey
Dave Hollins
Gregg Jefferies
David Justice
Roberto Kelly

Darryl Kile†
John Kruk
Barry Larkin
Terry Mulholland
Mike Piazza
Ryne Sandberg
Gary Sheffield
Lee Smith†
John Smoltz
Robby Thompson*
Andy Van Slyke*

1994 AL
Roberto Alomar
Wilson Alvarez
Albert Belle
Jason Bere
Wade Boggs
Ricky Bones†
Joe Carter
Will Clark
David Cone
Scott Cooper
Chili Davis
Travis Fryman

Ken Griffey
Pat Hentgen
Randy Johnson
Jimmy Key
Chuck Knoblauch
Kenny Lofton
Paul Molitor
Mike Mussina
Paul O'Neill
Kirby Puckett
Cal Ripken
Ivan Rodriguez
Ruben Sierra
Lee Smith
Mickey Tettleton
Frank Thomas

1994 NL
Moises Alou
Jeff Bagwell
Rod Beck
Dante Bichette
Craig Biggio
Barry Bonds
Ken Caminiti

Jeff Conine†
Wil Cordero
Doug Drabek
Mariano Duncan
Lenny Dykstra*
Darrin Fletcher
Carlos Garcia
Marquis Grissom
Tony Gwynn
Ken Hill
John Hudek
Danny Jackson
Gregg Jefferies
Doug Jones
David Justice
Barry Larkin*
Greg Maddux
Fred McGriff
Randy Myers
Mike Piazza
Jose Rijo*
Bret Saberhagen†
Ozzie Smith
Matt Williams

## CHAPTER 15

Postseason Play

Frederick Ivor-Campbell

When Major League Baseball and the striking players were unable to work out a settlement of their dispute in 1994, they interrupted a tradition of major league postseason play that traced back to 1871, the first year there was a professional league. National Association teams in the 1870s typically followed the conclusion of their championship (regularly scheduled) season with exhibition games against amateur clubs. In the 1880s nearly every major league club played a couple of weeks of postseason games, generally against major- and minor-league teams they hadn't faced during the regular season. In the twentieth century there had been a World Series every year for ninety years, prefaced since 1969 by League Championship Series to determine the American and National League winners.

Before there was a World Series there were city and regional series. In 1882 Cleveland defeated Cincinnati for the championship of Ohio, and the next year teams in Philadelphia and New York played for the championships of those cities. These were informal series, arranged by the clubs themselves without official league sanction, and varied in the number of games scheduled according to the desires of the clubs involved.

The same held true for the early World Series, which had their beginnings in 1884. Two years earlier, the champions of the National League and the brand-new American Association played a pair of postseason contests (in which each team recorded a shutout against the other). Some would like to call these games the first World Series, but no one in 1882 saw them as more than exhibition games. In fact, because the NL didn't yet recognize the legitimacy of the AA and forbade its clubs to play those of the new league, the NL champion Chicago White Stockings had to release their players from their season contracts so they could face AA champion Cincinnati as technically independent players.

That winter the two major leagues made their peace, and although a proposed series between the 1883 NL and AA titlists was called off, the 1884 champion Providence Grays (NL) and the Metropolitan Club of New York (AA) played three games "for the championship of the United States." The winning Grays were acclaimed in the press as "champions of the world," and the World Series was born.

The brief 1884 Series set the stage for more elaborate World Series to follow. From 1885 through 1890 the NL and AA pennant-winners met in Series that ranged in length from six games to fifteen.

The demise of the AA after the 1891 season caused a one-year gap in World Series play. When the National League expanded from eight clubs to twelve the next year (by absorbing four teams from the defunct AA), it divided the regular season into two halves, with the first-half winner playing the winner of the second half for the world title. Boston defeated Cleveland in the first official World Series, but the unpopular divided season was not repeated (that is, until the strike year of 1981).

Two years later a new World Series scheme was devised when one William C. Temple offered a prize cup to the winner of a postseason series between the first- and second-place finishers in the NL. For four years these best-of-seven Temple Cup games served as the officially recognized world championship. But by the end of four lopsided Series (only one of which was won by the pennant-winning club), fan interest—never robust—had declined so much that the trophy was returned to its donor and the series abandoned.

In 1900, partisans of second-place Pittsburgh felt that their Pirates were the equal of pennant-winning Brooklyn, and a Pittsburgh newspaper, the *Chronicle-Telegraph*, offered a silver trophy cup to the winner of a best-of-five series between the clubs, to be played entirely in Pittsburgh. Described in the press as the "world's championship series," the games confirmed the superiority of Brooklyn's Superbas, who needed only four games to subdue the hometown Pirates.

The upgrading of the American League from minor- to major-league status in 1901 made a return to interleague World Series play theoretically possible, but it was not until after the NL and AL had made peace in 1903 that the first modern Series was contested. The owners of NL champion Pittsburgh and AL champion Boston arranged a best-of-nine postseason Series in 1903, which proved both popular and financially successful—a firm foundation for future Series. When the NL pennant-winning Giants refused to meet repeating AL titlist Boston in 1904, press and fan disappointment led baseball's National Commission to establish the World Series officially in 1905.

The end of the 1903 season saw not only the first modern World Series, but also a revival of city and regional series (which had lapsed when the AA folded) in Chicago, Philadelphia, St. Louis, and Ohio. In 1905 the National Commission offered to oversee these series, too, and give them the stability of official sanction. Until the manpower needs of the World War halted the 1918 season a month early (discouraging postseason play apart from the World Series), most of the city and regional series—and occasional series between other clubs, like Cleveland and Pittsburgh, and the Boston Red Sox and New York Giants—were played under National Commission auspices.

After the war's end, only Chicago's Cubs and White Sox resumed a city series; they played sixteen series between 1921 and 1942, when World War II intervened. For twenty-six years thereafter the World Series alone remained of the

once multifaceted major-league postseason—until the AL
and NL split into two divisions each in 1969 and ushered in a
new layer of playoffs: the League Championship Series. (In
1981, to recoup some of the money and fan interest lost
during a midseason players' strike that split the season in half,
a one-time third layer of postseason playoffs was added,
pitting the first-half and second-half winners in each division
against each other for the division titles—an aberration that
made the divisional races even more surreal than the strike
itself had done.) From 1969 through 1984 the LCS were
played as best-of-five series, but in 1985 they were expanded
to match the best-of-seven World Series.

In 1993, the club owners voted to realign each league into
three divisions—East, Central, and West—and to install a
preliminary layer of playoffs for each league. The three divisional champions and the second-place team with the best
record would determine, through a pair of best-of-five series,
which two teams would compete for the pennant in the
League Championship Series. When the 1994 postseason was
canceled, however, the introduction of the new playoffs was
among the casualties.

Key to the Statistics

The statistics in this section of *Total Baseball* are standard—
there is little point in applying newer analytical measures to
performances that run to seven games or fewer. We do offer,
however, stats that were not standard at the time, such as
earned run averages for years before 1912 and runs batted in
before 1920 (which were determined from box scores and
play-by-plays) and saves before 1969. Beyond our powers of
reconstruction were the following: runs batted in, stolen
bases, and batter strikeouts for the World Series of 1885.

Ignoring the odd 1887 custom of counting walks as base
hits, we present the cumulative box score for that year's

World Series in accordance with modern practice. Other curi-
osities of early postseason play include the use of neutral sites
for some games in 1885 and 1888 and for the majority of
games in 1887, and the use of players who did not appear in
so much as an inning for that team during the regular season
(Tom Forster, New York Mets, 1884; Bug Holliday, Chicago,
1885; Sy Sutcliffe, Detroit, 1887; Jumbo Davis, Brooklyn
1889).

The length of the World Series varied from three games in
1884 all the way up to fifteen in 1887 and ten the following
year. The best-of-seven format came in with the Temple Cup
Series of 1894 and has been the norm for World Series ever
since (excepting 1900, 1903, and 1919–1921). In recent years
this format has become the norm for League Championship
Series as well.

If a player appeared at more than one position during the
Series, the number of games he played at each is noted (for
example, a man who divided seven games at shortstop and
third base would carry the notation *ss-4, 3b-3*). Other abbreviations are as follows:

POS	Position	SB	Stolen Bases
AVG	Batting average	W	Wins
G	Games	L	Losses
AB	At bats	ERA	Earned run average
R	Runs	GS	Games started
H	Hits	CG	Complete games
2B	Doubles	SHO	Shutouts
3B	Triples	SV	Saves
HR	Home runs	IP	Innings pitched
RB	Runs batted in	ER	Earned runs
BB	Bases on Balls	SO	Strikeouts

Individual postseason records, annual and cumulative, may
be found in the Registers that follow.

After a flurry of boasts and challenges, Met manager Jim Mutrie and the Grays' Frank Bancroft arranged a three-game series in New York to determine which team was the nation's best. These were not the first games between NL and AA pennant winners. In 1882, the AA's first season, champion Cincinnati met NL titlist Chicago twice as part of its postseason schedule, in games viewed simply as exhibition contests. (Each team won one). The next year a postseason series was proposed between champions Boston (NL) and the Athletics of Philadelphia (AA), but the Athletics fared so poorly in exhibitions against lesser NL teams that they refused to face Boston.

The 1884 Series was touted as "for the championship of the United States," but the influential weekly *Sporting Life* established precedent for future Series hype by naming victorious Providence "Champions of the World." The weather turned cold and windy as the Series got under way. A hardy opening game crowd of 2,500 saw the Grays' great Charlie "Old Hoss" Radbourn blank the Mets on two singles. Met pitcher Tim Keefe, wild at the start, paved the way for two first-inning Providence runs by hitting the first two men to face him and assisted them around the bases with a pair of wild pitches. Paul Hines singled in the third for the Grays' first hit and scored as a passed ball and two more wild pitches brought him home. Keefe yielded only four other hits, but they came back to back in the seventh to produce the Grays' final three runs.

The 1,000 spectators at Game Two witnessed the Series' closest contest. Keefe and Radbourn overwhelmed their opposition for four innings, but in the top of the fifth the Grays bunched three of their five hits for three two-out runs as Jerry Denny homered over the center field fence. The Mets responded with a run in the last of the fifth, but scored no more before darkness ended the game after seven innings.

The Grays had clinched the championship with their second win, and when they saw only a few hundred diehards in the stands for Game Three, they wanted to go home. The Mets must have regretted their insistence on playing the game. Although darkness halted it after only six innings, rookie Met pitcher Buck Becannon (replacing Keefe, who umpired) and awful Mets fielding gave Providence eleven or twelve runs (scorers disagreed), while Radbourn held the New Yorkers to a pair of unearned tallies.

Providence Grays (NL), 3; New York Mets (AA), 0

PRO (N)

PLAYER/POS	AVG	G	AB	R	H	2B	3B	HR	RB	BB	SO	SB
Cliff Carroll, of	.100	3	10	2	1	0	0	0	1	1	1	0
Jerry Denny, 3b	.444	3	9	3	4	0	1	1	2	0	3	0
Jack Farrell, 2b	.444	3	9	3	4	2	0	0	0	0	0	1
Barney Gilligan, c	.444	3	9	3	4	2	0	0	2	0	1	0
Paul Hines, of	.250	3	8	5	2	0	0	0	1	3	0	2
Arthur Irwin, ss	.222	3	9	2	2	0	1	0	2	0	2	0
Charlie Radbourn, p	.100	3	10	1	1	0	0	0	2	1	3	0
Paul Radford, of	.000	3	7	1	0	0	0	0	1	0	1	0
Joe Start, 1b	.100	3	10	0	1	0	0	0	1	0	2	0
TOTAL	.235		81	20	19	4	2	1	12	5	13	3

PITCHER	W	L	ERA	G	GS	CG	SV	SHO	IP	H	ER	BB	SO
Charlie Radbourn	3	0	0.00	3	3	3	0	1	22.0	11	0	0	16
TOTAL	3	0	0.00	3	3	3	0	1	22.0	11	0	0	16

NY (A)

PLAYER/POS	AVG	G	AB	R	H	2B	3B	HR	RB	BB	SO	SB
Buck Becannon, p	.500	1	2	0	1	0	0	0	0	0	0	0
Steve Brady, of	.000	3	10	1	0	0	0	0	0	0	1	0
Dude Esterbrook, 3b	.300	3	10	0	3	1	0	0	0	0	3	1
Tom Forster, 2b	.000	1	3	0	0	0	0	0	0	0	1	0
Bill Holbert, c	.000	1	2	0	0	0	0	0	0	0	0	0
Tim Keefe, p	.200	2	5	0	1	0	0	0	0	0	4	0
Ed Kennedy, of	.000	3	7	0	0	0	0	0	0	0	2	0
Candy Nelson, ss	.100	3	10	0	1	0	0	0	0	0	1	0
Dave Orr, 1b	.111	3	9	0	1	0	0	0	0	0	0	0
Charlie Reipschlager, c	.000	2	5	1	0	0	0	0	0	0	1	0
Chief Roseman, of	.333	3	9	1	3	0	0	0	1	0	1	0
Dasher Troy, 2b	.200	2	5	0	1	0	0	0	1	0	1	0
TOTAL	.143		77	3	11	1	0	0	2	0	16	1

PITCHER	W	L	ERA	G	GS	CG	SV	SHO	IP	H	ER	BB	SO
Buck Becannon	0	1	10.50	1	1	1	0	0	6.0	9	7	2	1
Tim Keefe	0	2	3.60	2	2	2	0	0	15.0	10	6	3	12
TOTAL	0	3	5.57	3	3	3	0	0	21.0	19	13	5	13

GAME 1 AT NY OCT 23

NY	000 000 000	0	2	0
PRO	201 000 30X	6	5	2

Pitchers: KEEFE vs RADBOURN
Attendance: 2,500

GAME 2 AT NY OCT 24

PRO	000 030 0	3	5	4
NY	000 010 0	1	3	1

Pitchers: RADBOURN vs KEEFE
Home Runs: Denny-PRO
Attendance: 1,000
(Game called at end of seventh, darkness)

GAME 3 AT NY OCT 25

PRO	120 144	12	9	3
NY	000 011	2	6	9

Pitchers: RADBOURN vs BECANNON
Attendance: 300
(Game called at end of sixth, darkness)

Before the start of the final game, the two clubs agreed to throw out Game Two, which had been forfeited to Chicago, leaving the Series tied at two wins apiece, plus the one tie. But after the Browns won the seventh game for their third victory, Chicago manager Cap Anson decided his club should retain its forfeit win after all, and a select committee agreed, leaving the Series in a tie instead of a White Stocking defeat.

Game One, in Chicago, was called for darkness after eight innings, with the score tied 5–5. The Browns scored first with a run in the second and added four more in the top of the fourth. But Chicago came back with a run in the last of the fourth, and in the bottom of the eighth scored four more on a walk, two singles, and Fred Pfeffer's game-tying three-run homer.

The Series moved to St. Louis for the next three games. Chicago was leading 5–4 in the sixth inning of Game Three when Browns manager Charlie Comiskey pulled his team off the field, objecting to the umpiring of David Sullivan. Umpire Sullivan later forfeited the game to the White Stockings; he worked no more in the Series. The Browns won Game Three, scoring five unearned runs with two out in the top of the first, and holding on for a 7–4 win. Chicago lost again the next day in a much closer game. The Browns scored first with a run in the third inning, but Abner Dalrymple's two-run homer in the fifth gave the White Stockings a 2–1 lead. In the bottom of the eighth, however, St. Louis scored twice and held on for the 3–2 win.

The Series took to the road for its final three games. In Pittsburgh for Game Five, Chicago overwhelmed the Browns 9–2, scoring four runs in the first inning, and their final three just before darkness ended the game after seven innings.

Game Six and Seven were played in Cincinnati. The White Stockings won the sixth game by the same 9–2 score as Game Five. The Browns' two runs were unearned, as Chicago's Jim McCormick stopped St. Louis on just two hits, both singles. The Browns' victory in the finale was a runaway 13–4, called in the eighth for darkness. St. Louis' six-run fourth inning typified the game's sloppy play, the runs scoring on five hits, four errors, and two passed balls.

Chicago White Stockings (NL), 3;
St. Louis Browns (AA), 3; tie, 1

CHI (N)

PLAYER/POS	AVG	G	AB	R	H	2B	3B	HR	RB	BB	SO	SB
Cap Anson, 1b	.423	7	26	8	11	1	1	0		2		
Tom Burns, ss-4,3b-3	.080	7	25	3	2	0	1	0		0		
John Clarkson, p-2,of-2	.154	4	13	1	2	1	0	0		0		
Abner Dalrymple, of	.269	7	26	4	7	2	0	1		2		
Silver Flint, c	.143	4	14	0	2	0	0	0		0		
George Gore, of	.000	1	3	1	0	0	0	0		1		
Bug Holliday, of	.000	1	4	0	0	0	0	0		0		
King Kelly, of-4,c-3	.346	7	26	9	9	3	1	0		2		
Jim McCormick, p	.176	5	17	1	3	0	0	0		0		
Fred Pfeffer, 2b	.407	7	27	5	11	2	0	1		0		
Billy Sunday, of	.273	6	22	5	6	2	0	0		2		
N. Williamson, 3b-4,ss-3	.087	7	23	1	2	0	0	0		4		
TOTAL	.243		226	38	55	11	3	2		13		

PITCHER	W	L	ERA	G	GS	CG	SV	SHO	IP	H	ER	BB	SO
John Clarkson	0	1	1.13	2	2	2	0	0	16.0	15	2	1	15
Jim McCormick	3	2	2.00	5	5	5	0	0	36.0	27	8	6	19
TOTAL	3	3	1.73	7	7	7	0	0	52.0	42	10	7	34

STL (A)

PLAYER/POS	AVG	G	AB	R	H	2B	3B	HR	RB	BB	SO	SB
Sam Barkley, 2b	.087	7	23	3	2	0	0	0		2		
Doc Bushong, c	.154	4	13	1	2	0	0	0		0		
Bob Caruthers, p-3,of-2	.200	5	15	1	3	0	1	0		1		
Charlie Comiskey, 1b	.292	7	24	6	7	0	0	0		0		
Dave Foutz, p	.167	4	12	1	2	0	0	0		0		
Bill Gleason, ss	.231	7	26	5	6	2	0	0		1		
Arlie Latham, 3b	.318	7	22	5	7	3	0	0		2		
Hugh Nicol, of	.000	1	2	0	0	0	0	0		0		
Tip O'Neill, of	.208	7	24	4	5	0	0	0		0		
Yank Robinson, of-4,c-3	.174	7	23	5	4	0	1	0		1		
Curt Welch, of	.148	7	27	5	4	1	1	0		0		
TOTAL	.199		211	36	42	6	3	0		7		

PITCHER	W	L	ERA	G	GS	CG	SV	SHO	IP	H	ER	BB	SO
Bob Caruthers	1	1	2.42	3	3	3	0	0	26.0	25	7	4	16
Dave Foutz	2	2	0.61	4	4	4	0	0	29.1	30	2	9	14
TOTAL	3	3	1.46	7	7	7	0	0	55.1	55	9	13	30

GAME 1 AT CHI OCT 14

STL	010	400	00	5	7 2
CHI	000	100	04	5	10

Pitchers: CARUTHERS vs CLARKSON
Home Runs: Pfeffer-CHI
Attendance: 2,000
(Game called at end of eighth, darkness)

GAME 2 AT STL OCT 15

CHI	110	003		5	6 5
STL	300	10X		4	2 4

Pitchers: McCORMICK vs FOUTZ
Attendance: 2,000
(Game forfeited to Chicago in bottom of sixth)

GAME 3 AT STL OCT 16

CHI	111	000	001	4	8 7
STL	500	002	00X	7	8 4

Pitchers: CLARKSON vs CARUTHERS
Attendance: 3,000

GAME 4 AT STL OCT 17

CHI	000	020	000	2	8 3
STL	001	000	02X	3	6 7

Pitchers: McCORMICK vs FOUTZ
Home Runs: Dalrymple-CHI
Attendance: 3,000

GAME 5 AT PIT A OCT 22

CHI	400	110	3	9	7 1
STL	010	000	1	2	4 7

Pitchers: CLARKSON vs FOUTZ
Attendance: 500
(Game called at end of seventh, darkness)

GAME 6 AT CIN A OCT 23

CHI	200	111	040	9	11 7
STL	002	000	000	2	2 7

Pitchers: McCORMICK vs CARUTHERS
Attendance: 1,500

GAME 7 AT CIN A OCT 24

CHI	200	020	00	4	9 9
STL	004	621	0X	13	13 5

Pitchers: McCORMICK vs FOUTZ
Attendance: 1,200
(Game called in eighth, darkness)

It was a winner-take-all Series, with the club that won four games pocketing the entire proceeds. Attendance, very good for those days, averaged over 7,000 per game and brought the victorious Browns about $14,000.

The first three games were played in Chicago. The White Stockings won the opener on a sparkling five-hit shutout by their ace John Clarkson. But St. Louis's Bob Caruthers improved on Clarkson's performance the next day, blanking Chicago on just two singles as his Browns turned thirteen hits and thirteen Chicago errors into twelve runs (in a game shortened by darkness to eight innings). The White Stockings improved their fielding in the next game (which was also called after eight innings), and this time their bats came alive. With eleven hits (including home runs by Mike "King" Kelly and George Gore) combining with seven St. Louis errors, they regained the Series advantage with an easy 11–4 win.

When the venue shifted to St. Louis, though, the Browns battled back. In a back-and-forth battle in Game Four, Chicago tied the game at 5–5 with a pair of runs in the sixth, but St. Louis scored three final runs a half inning later, winning when darkness ended play in the middle of the seventh.

Game Five repeated Game Two's innovation: two umpires (instead of the usual one), plus a "referee" who stood between the pitcher and second base. The umpiring satisfied everyone, but Chicago, handicapped by their scheduled pitcher's sore arm, lost when they sent shortstop Ned Williamson and right fielder Jimmy Ryan into the box. In the 6½ innings before dark, St. Louis got to Williamson and Ryan for eleven hits and ten runs as their Nat Hudson held Chicago batters to three hits and three unearned runs.

The finale proved to be the Series' best-played and closest game. Chicago's Clarkson shut out the Browns through seven innings as his mates built a three-run lead—one of them scored on Fred's Pfeffer's homer in the fourth. Rain (and a rowdy crowd which poured onto the field) halted play for a while in the fifth. But the game resumed and the rain subsided. In the last of the eighth, Charlie Comiskey scored the Browns' first run on a single, errant throw and run-scoring fly out, and Arlie Latham tripled home two more runners later in the inning to tie the game. The score remained 3–3 into the last of the tenth, when the Browns' Curt Welch singled (for

only the fourth St. Louis hit), went to second on an infield hit, and took third on a sacrifice. Welch then attempted to steal home but catcher Kelly had smelled out the play and called for a pitch out. Clarkson's delivery was poor and bobbled by Kelly, allowing Welch to steal home with a "$15,000 slide" for the Browns' triumph.

St. Louis Browns (AA), 4; Chicago White Stockings (NL), 2

STL (A)

PLAYER/POS	AVG	G	AB	R	H	2B	3B	HR	RB	BB	SO	SB
Doc Bushong, c	.188	6	16	4	3	1	0	0	2	4	5	0
Bob Caruthers, p-3,of-3	.250	6	24	6	6	1	2	0	5	1	4	1
Charlie Comiskey, 1b	.292	6	24	2	7	1	0	0	2	0	4	0
Dave Foutz, p-2,of-2	.200	4	15	2	3	1	1	0	3	0	3	0
Bill Gleason, ss	.208	6	24	3	5	0	0	0	5	1	3	0
Nat Hudson, p-1,of-1	.167	2	6	1	1	0	1	0	0	1	3	0
Arlie Latham, 3b-6,c-1	.174	6	23	4	4	0	1	0	3	3	4	2
Tip O'Neill, of	.400	6	20	4	8	0	2	2	5	4	5	2
Yank Robinson, 2b	.316	6	19	5	6	1	1	0	3	2	3	2
Curt Welch, of	.350	6	20	7	7	2	0	0	1	3	4	2
TOTAL	.262		191	38	50	7	8	2	29	19	38	9

PITCHER	W	L	ERA	G	GS	CG	SV	SHO	IP	H	ER	BB	SO
Bob Caruthers	2	1	2.42	3	3	3	0	1	26.0	18	7	6	12
Dave Foutz	1	1	3.60	2	2	2	0	0	15.0	16	6	6	7
Nat Hudson	1	0	2.57	1	1	1	0	0	7.0	3	2	3	3
TOTAL	4	2	2.81	6	6	6	0	1	48.0	37	15	15	22

CHI (N)

PLAYER/POS	AVG	G	AB	R	H	2B	3B	HR	RB	BB	SO	SB
Cap Anson, 1b-6,c-2	.238	6	21	3	5	1	0	0	1	4	0	1
Tom Burns, 3b-6,of-1	.286	6	21	2	6	2	1	0	1	0	2	0
John Clarkson, p-4,of-1	.067	4	15	0	1	0	0	0	1	0	2	1
Abner Dalrymple, of	.190	6	21	2	4	1	1	0	2	0	5	1
Silver Flint, c	.000	1	3	0	0	0	0	0	1	0	1	0
George Gore, of	.174	6	23	4	4	0	0	1	2	3	3	0
King Kelly, c-5,ss-2,1b-1,3b-1	.208	6	24	4	5	0	0	1	1	2	2	1
Jim McCormick, p	.000	1	3	0	0	0	0	0	0	0	0	0
Fred Pfeffer, 2b	.286	6	21	7	6	0	0	1	4	2	1	2
Jimmy Ryan, of-6,p-1,ss-1	.250	6	20	4	5	1	0	0	2	0	1	1
Ned Williamson, ss-6,p-2,c-1,of-1	.056	6	18	2	1	0	1	0	3	4	5	1
TOTAL	.195		190	28	37	5	3	3	18	15	22	8

PITCHER	W	L	ERA	G	GS	CG	SV	SHO	IP	H	ER	BB	SO
John Clarkson	2	2	2.01	4	4	3	0	1	31.1	25	7	12	28
Jim McCormick	0	1	6.75	1	1	1	0	0	8.0	13	6	2	4
Jimmy Ryan	0	0	9.00	1	0	0	0	0	5.0	8	5	4	4
Ned Williamson	0	1	4.50	2	1	0	0	0	2.0	4	1	1	2
TOTAL	2	4	3.69	8	6	4	0	1	46.1	50	19	19	38

GAME 1 AT CHI OCT 18

STL	000 000 000	0	5	3
CHI	200 001 03X	6	10	4

Pitchers: FOUTZ vs CLARKSON
Attendance: 6,000

GAME 2 AT CHI OCT 19

STL	200 230 50	12	13	2
CHI	000 000 00	0	2	10

Pitchers: CARUTHERS vs McCORMICK
Home Runs: O'Neill-STL (2)
Attendance: 8,000
(Game called at end of eighth, darkness)

GAME 3 AT CHI OCT 20

CHI	200 112 32	11	11	2
STL	010 002 01	4	9	7

Pitchers: CLARKSON, Williamson (8) vs CARUTHERS
Home Runs: Kelly-CHI, Gore-CHI
Attendance: 6,000
(Game called at end of eighth, darkness)

GAME 4 AT STL OCT 21

CHI	300 002 0	5	6	4
STL	011 033 X	8	7	4

Pitchers: CLARKSON vs FOUTZ
Attendance: 8,000
(Game called in seventh, darkness)

GAME 5 AT STL OCT 22

CHI	011 100 00	3	3	3
STL	214 003 0X	10	11	3

Pitchers: WILLIAMSON, Ryan (2) vs HUDSON
Attendance: 10,000
(Game called in eighth, darkness)

GAME 6 AT STL OCT 23

CHI	010 101 000 0	3	6	2
STL	000 000 030 1	4	5	3

Pitchers: CLARKSON vs CARUTHERS
Home Runs: Pfeffer-CHI
Attendance: 8,000

Even though their star slugger Dan Brouthers was sidelined for all but one game by a sprained ankle, the Wolverines—in baseball's longest World Series, played in ten different cities—followed up their only pennant with an easy triumph over repeating AA champion St. Louis. The Browns won the opener at home, though, 6–1. They played errorless ball (rare in that era) as pitcher Bob Caruthers held Detroit scoreless until the ninth inning, and drove in the Browns' second run himself with a first-inning single.

The Wolverines came back to win the next three games. They took an early lead in Game Two and held on for a 5–3 win in St. Louis to even the Series. Then, in the Series' tightest game (played in Detroit) the Wolverines defeated Caruthers 2–1 in the last of the thirteenth when their pitcher Charlie Getzien led off with a single, advanced to second and third on ground outs, and scored on an infield error. In Game Four (in Pittsburgh) Detroit's Charles "Lady" Baldwin stopped the Browns on two hits for an easy 8–0 win.

Caruthers hurled a seven-hitter in Brooklyn for St. Louis's second win, but Detroit took the next four. Getzien contributed a two-hit shutout in New York, and Baldwin overcame Caruthers 3–1 in Philadelphia the next day. Getzien yielded eight hits the day after that in Boston, but Caruthers gave up thirteen, including two home runs to Sam Thompson, and Detroit took the game 9–2. Back in Philadelphia for Game Nine, St. Louis broke a 1–1 tie with a run in the top of the sixth. But the Wolverines scored two in the seventh and a final run in the eighth. The win gave Detroit a 7–2 Series advantage.

Game Ten, scheduled for the next day in Washington, was postponed because of rain until the following morning. Detroit's Hardy Richardson opened the game with a home run, but the Wolverines lost an opportunity to clinch the Series as the Browns overwhelmed Getzien with sixteen hits for an 11–4 victory featuring a triple play. But that afternoon, in Baltimore, Detroit took the deciding game as decisively as they had lost in the morning, knocking the Browns' Dave Foutz for fourteen hits (including four by Richardson and three—including a home run—by Larry Twitchell) as Baldwin held St. Louis to two hits in a 13–3 win.

The Browns and Wolverines split the final four meaningless games, played in Brooklyn,

Detroit Wolverines (NL), 10;
St. Louis Browns (AA), 5

DET (N)

PLAYER/POS	AVG	G	AB	R	H	2B	3B	HR	RB	BB	SO	SB
Lady Baldwin, p	.235	5	17	1	4	1	0	0	1	2	2	1
Charlie Bennett, c-10,1b-3	.262	11	42	6	11	2	1	0	9	3	5	5
Dan Brouthers, 1b	.667	1	3	0	2	0	0	0	0	0	0	0
Pete Conway, p	.000	4	12	0	0	0	0	0	0	0	2	0
Fred Dunlap, 2b	.150	11	40	5	6	0	1	0	1	0	4	4
Charlie Ganzel, 1b-10,c-7	.224	14	58	5	13	1	0	0	2	1	2	3
Charlie Getzien, p	.300	6	20	5	6	2	0	0	2	3	6	1
Ned Hanlon, of	.220	15	50	5	11	1	1	0	4	5	1	7
Hardy Richardson, of-10,2b-5,3b-1	.197	15	66	12	13	5	2	1	4	1	9	7
Jack Rowe, ss	.333	15	63	12	21	1	1	0	7	2	1	5
Cy Sutcliffe, 1b-3,c-1	.091	4	11	1	1	0	0	0	0	1	1	1
Sam Thompson, of	.362	15	58	8	21	2	0	2	7	3	3	5
Larry Twitchell, of	.250	6	20	5	5	1	0	1	3	0	1	1
Deacon White, 3b-14,1b-1	.207	15	58	8	12	1	1	0	3	2	0	2
TOTAL	.243		518	73	126	17	7	4	43	23	37	42

PITCHER	W	L	ERA	G	GS	CG	SV	SHO	IP	H	ER	BB	SO
Lady Baldwin	4	1	1.50	5	5	5	0	1	42.0	28	7	10	4
Pete Conway	2	2	3.00	4	4	4	0	0	33.0	31	11	6	10
Charlie Getzien	4	2	2.48	6	6	6	0	1	58.0	61	16	15	17
TOTAL	10	5	2.30	15	15	15	0	2	133.0	120	34	31	31

STL (A)

PLAYER/POS	AVG	G	AB	R	H	2B	3B	HR	RB	BB	SO	SB
Jack Boyle, c	.208	6	24	1	5	0	0	0	1	0	4	0
Doc Bushong, c	.241	9	29	3	7	0	0	0	1	4	1	0
Bob Caruthers, p-8,of-3	.239	10	46	2	11	0	0	0	3	1	1	3
Charlie Comiskey, 1b-14,of-1	.306	15	62	8	19	2	0	0	2	1	1	4
Dave Foutz, of-11,p-3,1b-1	.169	15	59	4	10	2	1	0	1	2	3	0
Bill Gleason, ss	.163	13	49	3	8	0	0	0	1	3	2	1
Silver King, p	.071	4	14	0	1	0	0	0	0	0	3	0
Arlie Latham, 3b	.293	15	58	12	17	1	0	1	9	1	2	15
Harry Lyons, ss	.286	2	7	3	2	0	0	0	0	1	0	0
Tip O'Neill, of	.200	15	65	7	13	2	1	1	5	0	2	0
Yank Robinson, 2b	.326	15	46	5	15	5	1	0	4	10	6	4
Curt Welch, of	.207	15	58	6	12	3	1	1	6	0	2	1
TOTAL	.232		517	54	120	15	4	2	25	31	27	28

PITCHER	W	L	ERA	G	GS	CG	SV	SHO	IP	H	ER	BB	SO
Bob Caruthers	4	4	2.13	8	8	8	0	0	71.2	64	17	12	19
Dave Foutz	0	3	3.46	3	3	3	0	0	26.0	36	10	9	6
Silver King	1	3	2.03	4	4	4	0	0	31.0	26	7	2	21
TOTAL	5	10	2.38	15	15	15	0	0	128.2	126	34	23	46

Detroit, Chicago, and St. Louis. For the first time in a World Series, two umpires officiated at all the games.

GAME 1 AT STL OCT 10

```
STL   200 040 000    6 12 0
DET   000 000 001    1  4 5
```
Pitchers: CARUTHERS vs GETZIEN
Attendance: 4,208

GAME 2 AT STL OCT 11

```
DET   022 000 100    5 10 2
STL   000 000 120    3  8 7
```
Pitchers: CONWAY vs FOUTZ
Attendance: 6,408

GAME 3 AT DET OCT 12

```
STL   010 000 000 000 0    1 13 7
DET   000 000 010 000 1    2  6 1
```
Pitchers: CARUTHERS vs GETZIEN
Attendance: 4,509

GAME 4 AT PIT OCT 13

```
DET   410 012 000    8 11 1
STL   000 000 000    0  2 6
```
Pitchers: BALDWIN vs KING
Attendance: 2,447

GAME 5 AT BRO OCT 14

```
STL   200 002 100    5  5 4
DET   000 020 000    2  7 5
```
Pitchers: CARUTHERS vs CONWAY
Attendance: 6,796

GAME 6 AT NY OCT 15

```
DET   330 000 003    9 12 1
STL   000 000 000    0  2 8
```
Pitchers: GETZIEN vs FOUTZ
Attendance: 5,797

GAME 7 AT PHI OCT 17

```
STL   000 000 001    1  8 1
DET   030 000 00X    3  6 1
```
Pitchers: CARUTHERS vs BALDWIN
Home Runs: O'Neill-STL
Attendance: 6,478

GAME 8 AT BOS OCT 18

```
DET   031 003 200    9 13 2
STL   100 001 000    2  8 5
```
Pitchers: GETZIEN vs CARUTHERS
Home Runs: Thompson-DET (2)
Attendance: 2,891

GAME 9 AT PHI OCT 19

```
STL   000 101 000    2  9 2
DET   000 100 21X    4  6 3
```
Pitchers: KING vs CONWAY
Attendance: 2,389

GAME 10 AT WAS OCT 21 (AM)

```
DET   200 010 001    4  8 3
STL   200 031 41X   11 16 5
```
Pitchers: GETZIEN vs CARUTHERS
Home Runs: Latham-STL, Welch-STL, Richardson-DET
Attendance: 1,261

GAME 11 AT BAL OCT 21 (PM)

```
STL   110 010 000    3  2 7
DET   100 344 10X   13 14 7
```
Pitchers: FOUTZ vs BALDWIN
Home Runs: Twitchell-DET
Attendance: 2,707
(Detroit wins best of 15 series 8 to 3)

GAME 12 AT BRO OCT 22

```
DET   000 100 0    1  5 3
STL   410 000 X    5 10 2
```
Pitchers: CONWAY vs KING
Attendance: 1,138
(Game called in seventh, darkness)

GAME 13 AT DET OCT 24

```
DET   020 100 120    6 12 3
STL   100 010 001    3  4 5
```
Pitchers: BALDWIN vs CARUTHERS
Attendance: 3,389

GAME 14 AT CHI OCT 25

```
STL   000 002 100    3 10 5
DET   300 100 00X    4  4 4
```
Pitchers: KING vs GETZIEN
Attendance: 378

GAME 15 AT STL OCT 26

```
STL   340 110    9 11 5
DET   011 000    2  8 7
```
Pitchers: CARUTHERS vs BALDWIN
Attendance: 659
(Game called after sixth, cold)

St. Louis, AA champions for the fourth straight year, battled the Giants closely through several games, but blowout losses in Games Six and Eight undid them. The first three games were played in New York. In a splendidly pitched opener, Brown ace Charles "Silver" King held New York to two hits and a walk while Giant ace Tim Keefe limited the Browns to three hits and a walk, striking out nine on his way to a narrow 2–1 win. St. Louis evened the Series in Game Two behind the shutout pitching of Elton "Icebox" Chamberlain. Tommy McCarthy scored the Browns' first run in the second inning when, after singling, he moved around to third on two passed balls by Giant catcher Buck Ewing and came home on Ewing's failed attempt to throw out a runner stealing second. Two more runs in the ninth gave St. Louis more than enough insurance for the win.

The Giants scored twice in the first inning of Game Three, and increased their lead to 4–0 before allowing St. Louis a pair of harmless runs in the final innings. They also scored first and led all the way in Game Four (played in Brooklyn) as another St. Louis rally fell short. The Browns took a 4–1 lead into the bottom of the eighth in Game Five (in New York), but a five-run Giant rally reversed the lead—and the outcome—as the game was called for darkness with St. Louis at bat in the ninth.

Giant Mickey Welch hurled a three-hitter (in Philadelphia) two days later, but St. Louis, capitalizing on walks and a questionable "safe" call at home, carried a 4–1 lead into the sixth inning. New York exploded in the late innings for 11 runs, however, and when darkness ended the game after eight the Giants were just one win away from the title.

The final four games were played in St. Louis. The Browns spoiled New York's hope of quick victory in Game Seven, coming from behind to tie the score with three runs in the fourth, and—after New York had scored twice in the sixth—recovering again with a four-run eighth for a 7–5 lead before darkness again halted play after eight innings. But the Browns' win only delayed the inevitable. The Giants hammered Icebox Chamberlain for twelve hits in Game Eight (including home runs by Buck Ewing and Mike Tiernan) to clinch their first world championship with an 11–3 win.

New York Giants (NL), 6;
St. Louis Browns (AA), 4

NY (N)

PLAYER/POS	AVG	G	AB	R	H	2B	3B	HR	RBI	BB	SO	SB
Willard Brown, c	.375	2	8	1	3	1	0	0	0	0	0	0
Roger Connor, 1b	.304	7	23	7	7	1	2	0	3	4	0	4
Ed Crane, p	.143	2	7	1	1	0	0	0	2	0	1	0
Buck Ewing, c-6,1b-1	.346	7	26	5	9	0	2	1	6	1	3	5
Bill George, p-1,1b-1	.333	2	9	2	3	1	0	1	4	0	2	0
George Gore, of-2,3b-1	.455	3	11	5	5	1	0	0	0	2	2	2
Gil Hatfield, p-1,2b-1,ss-1	.250	2	8	2	2	0	0	0	1	1	2	1
Tim Keefe, p	.091	4	11	2	1	0	0	0	0	0	2	1
Pat Murphy, c	.100	3	10	1	1	0	0	0	1	0	0	0
Jim O'Rourke, of-7,1b-2,ss-1	.222	10	36	4	8	0	0	0	1	4	2	3
Danny Richardson, 2b	.167	9	36	6	6	2	0	0	6	3	5	3
Mike Slattery, of-10,2b-1	.205	10	39	6	8	2	0	0	5	0	5	6
Mike Tiernan, of	.342	10	38	8	13	0	0	1	6	8	2	5
Ledell Titcomb, p-1,of-1	.500	1	4	1	2	1	0	0	1	0	0	0
Monte Ward, ss	.379	8	29	4	11	1	0	0	6	1	0	6
Mickey Welch, p	.286	2	7	2	2	0	0	0	1	0	0	0
Art Whitney, 3b-9,of-1	.324	10	37	7	12	0	1	0	12	1	4	2
TOTAL	.277		339	64	94	10	5	3	55	27	30	38

PITCHER	W	L	ERA	G	GS	CG	SV	SHO	IP	H	ER	BB	SO
Ed Crane	1	1	2.12	2	2	2	0	0	17.0	15	4	6	12
Bill George	0	1	7.20	1	1	1	0	0	10.0	15	8	3	4
Gil Hatfield	0	0	12.60	1	0	0	0	0	5.0	12	7	3	2
Tim Keefe	4	0	0.51	4	4	4	0	0	35.0	18	2	9	30
Ledell Titcomb	0	1	6.75	1	1	0	0	0	4.0	5	3	2	2
Mickey Welch	1	1	2.65	2	2	2	0	0	17.0	10	5	9	2
TOTAL	6	4	2.97	11	10	9	0	0	88.0	75	29	32	52

STL (A)

PLAYER/POS	AVG	G	AB	R	H	2B	3B	HR	RBI	BB	SO	SB
Jack Boyle, c-4,of-1	.438	4	16	4	7	0	1	0	4	2	2	3
Icebox Chamberlain, p	.000	5	13	3	0	0	0	0	0	4	3	1
Charlie Comiskey, 1b-10,of-1	.268	10	41	6	11	1	1	0	3	1	1	4
Jim Devlin, p	.000	1	3	0	0	0	0	0	0	0	0	0
Ed Herr, of	.091	3	11	2	1	0	0	0	0	0	5	1
Silver King, p	.067	5	15	1	1	0	0	0	0	1	6	0
Arlie Latham, 3b	.250	10	40	10	10	0	0	0	3	5	6	11
Harry Lyons, of	.118	5	17	0	2	0	0	0	1	1	5	0
Tommy McCarthy, of	.244	10	41	10	10	1	0	1	9	0	0	6
Jocko Milligan, c-8,1b-1	.400	8	25	5	10	2	1	0	4	3	3	0
Tip O'Neill, of	.243	10	37	8	9	1	0	2	11	6	3	0
Yank Robinson, 2b	.250	10	36	7	9	2	1	0	7	6	12	2
Bill White, ss	.143	10	35	4	5	1	0	0	4	3	6	1
TOTAL	.227		330	60	75	8	4	3	46	32	52	29

PITCHER	W	L	ERA	G	GS	CG	SV	SHO	IP	H	ER	BB	SO
Icebox Chamberlain	2	3	5.32	5	5	5	0	1	44.0	52	26	16	13
Jim Devlin	1	0	2.57	1	0	0	0	0	7.0	5	2	2	5
Silver King	1	3	2.31	5	5	4	0	0	35.0	37	9	9	12
TOTAL	4	6	3.87	11	10	9	0	1	86.0	94	37	27	30

The final two games meant nothing to the outcome, and both clubs used reserve pitchers in Game Nine. But St. Louis rewarded the small crowd with a two-run rally in the ninth to tie the game at 11-all and scored three more runs in the tenth to win it. The finale the next day again featured heavy hitting on both sides, including a trio of home runs (one of them Tip O'Neill's second in two days) and an 18–7 St. Louis romp.

Six wins was the magic number this year, and it was agreed that—unlike most previous Series—play would not continue beyond the deciding game. At first it seemed Brooklyn might prevail, with an assist from the dark of night. The Giants wanted the opening game called for darkness after the seventh inning, when they led 10–8. But the umpires held off until Brooklyn, in the deepening gloom, had scored four runs in the last of the eighth to go ahead 12–10.

The next day, in Brooklyn before more than 16,000 spectators (by far the largest World Series crowd to that time), Giant Ed "Cannonball" Crane held the Grooms to four hits as New York evened the Series. But Brooklyn won the next two for a 3–1 Series advantage. In Game Three, ahead 8–7 in the sixth inning, the Grooms began stalling, waiting for darkness to fall. The score was still 8–7 when the game was finally halted in the top of the ninth with one out and three Giants on base.

Darkness for a third time gave Brooklyn the victory in Game Four. New York overcame a 7–2 Bridegroom lead to tie the score with five runs in the top of the sixth, but in the bottom of the inning Brooklyn's Tom "Oyster" Burns homered in the dark for three runs. The umpires then halted the game.

The five remaining contests went the distance, and the Giants won them all. Cannonball Crane in Game Five gave up eight hits, but homered in his own behalf, driving in two runs in his Giants' 11–3 rout. Game Six was a pitching duel between New York's Hank O'Day and Brooklyn's William "Adonis" Terry. The Grooms scored a run in the second inning, but New York tied the game with two outs in the last of the ninth (when Monte Ward singled, stole second and third, and scored on Roger Connor's single), and won it two out away in the eleventh as Ward drove in a speedy Mike Slattery from second with an infield hit.

Back-to-back homers by Giants Dan Richardson and Jim O'Rourke highlighted an eight-run second inning in Game Seven. The Giants' eventual 11–7 win gave them their first Series advantage. In Game Eight, two of Brooklyn's five hits were home runs. But the Giants outscored the Grooms 12–2 over the first four innings and beat them 16–7.

With their backs to the wall, the Bridegrooms scored first in

New York Giants (NL), 6;
Brooklyn Bridegrooms (AA), 3

NY (N)

PLAYER/POS	AVG	G	AB	R	H	2B	3B	HR	RB	BB	SO	SB
Willard Brown, c	.600	1	5	3	3	0	0	1	2	0	0	0
Roger Connor, 1b	.343	9	35	9	12	2	2	0	12	3	2	8
Ed Crane, p	.278	5	18	3	5	1	1	1	5	1	2	0
Buck Ewing, c	.250	8	36	5	9	4	0	0	7	2	5	1
George Gore, of	.333	5	21	5	7	1	1	0	1	3	0	2
Tim Keefe, p	.500	2	4	1	2	1	0	0	0	1	1	0
Hank O'Day, p	.167	3	6	0	1	0	0	0	0	2	2	0
Jim O'Rourke, of	.389	9	36	7	14	2	2	2	7	2	2	3
Danny Richardson, 2b	.314	9	35	8	11	1	1	3	8	3	5	3
Mike Slattery, of	.188	4	16	6	3	0	0	0	1	3	1	1
Mike Tiernan, of	.289	9	38	12	11	1	1	1	5	5	3	3
Monte Ward, ss	.417	9	36	10	15	0	1	0	7	5	2	10
Mickey Welch, p	.333	1	3	0	1	0	0	0	0	0	1	0
Art Whitney, 3b	.229	9	35	4	8	2	1	0	3	1	0	0
TOTAL	.315		324	73	102	16	10	8	58	31	26	31

PITCHER	W	L	ERA	G	GS	CG	SV	SHO	IP	H	ER	BB	SO
Ed Crane	4	1	3.72	5	5	4	0	0	38.2	29	16	32	19
Tim Keefe	0	1	8.18	2	1	1	1	0	11.0	17	10	2	4
Hank O'Day	2	0	1.17	3	2	2	0	0	23.0	10	3	14	12
Mickey Welch	0	1	9.00	1	1	0	0	0	5.0	11	5	3	1
TOTAL	6	3	3.94	11	9	7	1	0	77.2	67	34	51	36

BRO (A)

PLAYER/POS	AVG	G	AB	R	H	2B	3B	HR	RB	BB	SO	SB
Oyster Burns, of	.229	9	35	8	8	3	0	2	11	5	6	0
Doc Bushong, c	.000	3	8	0	0	0	0	0	0	1	0	0
Bob Caruthers, p	.250	4	8	1	2	0	0	0	1	3	3	0
Bob Clark, c	.417	4	12	3	5	2	0	0	3	2	2	0
Hub Collins, 2b	.371	9	35	13	13	3	0	1	2	7	5	6
Pop Corkhill, of	.208	9	24	4	5	1	0	1	5	6	2	1
Jumbo Davis, ss	.000	1	4	0	0	0	0	0	0	0	0	0
Dave Foutz, 1b-9,p-1	.286	9	35	7	10	2	0	1	9	4	2	3
Mickey Hughes, p	.333	1	3	1	1	1	0	0	0	0	1	0
Tom Lovett, p	.000	1	1	0	0	0	0	0	0	0	0	0
Darby O'Brien, of	.161	9	31	8	5	0	1	0	4	12	6	6
George Pinckney, 3b	.258	9	31	8	8	2	0	0	3	4	2	2
Germany Smith, ss	.172	8	29	2	5	2	1	0	2	3	2	2
Adonis Terry, p-5,1b-1	.167	5	18	1	3	0	0	0	1	1	1	1
Joe Visner, c-3,of-2	.125	5	16	2	2	1	0	0	0	2	3	0
TOTAL	.231		290	52	67	17	2	5	41	51	36	21

PITCHER	W	L	ERA	G	GS	CG	SV	SHO	IP	H	ER	BB	SO
Bob Caruthers	0	2	3.75	4	2	2	1	0	24.0	28	10	6	6
Dave Foutz	0	0	7.20	1	0	0	0	0	5.0	5	4	2	2
Mickey Hughes	1	0	7.71	1	1	0	0	0	7.0	14	6	3	3
Tom Lovett	0	1	24.00	1	1	0	0	0	3.0	8	8	2	1
Adonis Terry	2	3	5.97	5	5	4	0	0	37.2	47	25	18	14
TOTAL	3	6	6.22	12	9	6	1	0	76.2	102	53	31	26

Game Nine and held a 2–1 lead after five innings. But New York tied the score in the sixth and went ahead 3–2 on a passed ball in the seventh. Meanwhile Giant pitcher Hank O'Day (although he walked five batters) blanked the Grooms on just two hits after the first inning to bring New York its second straight world championship.

GAME 1 AT NY OCT 18

NY	020 210 50	10 12 2
BRO	510 000 24	12 16 3

Pitchers: KEEFE vs TERRY
Home Runs: Collins-BRO, Richardson-NY
Attendance: 8,848
(Game called at end of eighth, darkness)

GAME 2 AT BRO OCT 19

NY	111 120 000	6 10 4
BRO	110 000 000	2 4 8

Pitchers: CRANE vs CARUTHERS
Attendance: 16,172

GAME 3 AT NY OCT 22

NY	200 032 00	7 15 2
BRO	023 120 00	8 12 3

Pitchers: WELCH, O'Day (6) vs HUGHES, Caruthers (8)
Home Runs: Corkhill-BRO, O'Rourke-NY
Attendance: 5,181
(Game called at end of eighth, darkness)

GAME 4 AT BRO OCT 23

NY	001 105	7 9 8
BRO	202 033	10 7 1

Pitchers: CRANE vs TERRY
Home Runs: Burns-BRO
Attendance: 3,045
(Game called at end of sixth, darkness)

GAME 5 AT BRO OCT 24

NY	004 040 021	11 12 2
BRO	000 111 000	3 8 2

Pitchers: CRANE vs CARUTHERS
Home Runs: Brown-NY, Richardson-NY, Crane-NY
Attendance: 2,901

GAME 6 AT NY OCT 25

BRO	010 000 000 00	1 6 4
NY	000 000 001 01	2 7 1

Pitchers: TERRY vs O'DAY
Attendance: 2,556

GAME 7 AT NY OCT 26

BRO	004 030 000	7 5 3
NY	180 001 10X	11 14 4

Pitchers: LOVETT, Caruthers (4) vs CRANE, Keefe (5)
Home Runs: Richardson-NY, O'Rourke-NY
Attendance: 3,312

GAME 8 AT BRO OCT 28

NY	541 203 001	16 15 4
BRO	200 000 023	7 5 4

Pitchers: CRANE vs TERRY, Foutz (5)
Home Runs: Foutz-BRO, Tiernan-NY, Burns-BRO
Attendance: 2,584

GAME 9 AT NY OCT 29

BRO	200 000 000	2 4 2
NY	100 001 10X	3 8 5

Pitchers: TERRY vs O'DAY
Attendance: 3,067

The Bridegrooms, AA pennant winners in 1889, switched to the NL and returned to World Series play as champions of their new league. Louisville, meanwhile, rose from a last-place finish in 1889 to replace Brooklyn at the top of the AA. The Series, though, seemed meaningless to many who believed that pennant-winning Boston of the outlaw Players League (which had drawn off many of the best NL and AA players) could beat both Louisville and Brooklyn if given the opportunity.

The first four games of the Series were played in Louisville before an ever decreasing number of spectators. The largest crowd—5,600—saw the Cyclones humiliated in the opener 9–0 as Brooklyn's Adonis Terry stopped them on two singles. The Grooms won the second game, too, breaking a 2–2 tie with a pair of runs in the fourth and holding on for a 5–3 win.

Louisville played catch-up throughout Game Three and entered the last of the eighth still behind 7–4. But a walk, three hits, a sacrifice fly, and a passed ball brought to score to 7-all—where it remained when darkness ended the game. Only 1,050 spectators attended the final contest in Louisville, but they saw the first Louisville win. The Cyclones scored three runs in the first inning, but Brooklyn countered with three an inning later, and both teams scored single runs in the third. Louisville's Red Ehret blanked the Grooms the rest of the way, but Brooklyn's Tom Lovett yielded the Cyclones a winning run in the seventh when Tim Shinnick tripled and was sacrificed home.

Rain postponed the first game in Brooklyn for two days, but when it was played—on a cold, muddy day before a small crowd of 1,000—the Grooms took the lead on Oyster Burns's two-run homer in the first inning and held it all the way for their third win. As the weather grew colder, the crowds declined for the final two games. Louisville captured its second win by a 9–8 margin when a three-run Brooklyn rally in the eighth inning of Game Six stalled one run short of a tie. Only abut 300 diehards saw the Cyclones even the Series in the finale, 6–2 behind Red Ehret's four-hitter. A tie-breaking eighth game seemed called for, but there was not enough interest in playing any further in the bitter cold.

Brooklyn Bridegrooms (NL), 3; Louisville Cyclones (AA), 3; tie, 1

BRO (N)

PLAYER/POS	AVG	G	AB	R	H	2B	3B	HR	RB	BB	SO	SB
Oyster Burns, of-4,3b-3	.222	7	27	6	6	2	0	1	5	3	4	0
Doc Bushong, c	.000	2	6	0	0	0	0	0	0	0	1	0
Bob Caruthers, of	.000	2	6	0	0	0	0	0	0	2	0	0
Bob Clark, c	.667	1	3	2	2	0	1	0	1	0	0	0
Hub Collins, 2b	.310	7	29	7	9	0	1	0	1	3	0	2
Tom Daly, c-6,1b-1	.182	6	22	1	4	2	0	0	3	0	4	2
Patsy Donovan, of	.471	5	17	5	8	1	0	0	3	2	1	3
Dave Foutz, 1b-7,of-1	.300	7	30	6	9	2	1	0	4	0	1	1
Tom Lovett, p-4,of-1	.067	5	15	0	1	0	0	0	0	0	4	0
Darby O'Brien, of	.125	6	24	3	3	0	1	0	3	1	5	3
George Pinckney, 3b	.357	4	14	4	5	0	2	0	3	2	1	1
Germany Smith, ss	.276	7	29	3	8	0	2	0	7	0	3	1
Adonis Terry, p-3,of-3	.050	6	20	5	1	1	0	0	0	6	3	1
TOTAL	.231		242	42	56	8	8	1	30	19	27	14

PITCHER	W	L	ERA	G	GS	CG	SV	SHO	IP	H	ER	BB	SO
Tom Lovett	2	2	2.83	4	4	4	0	0	35.0	29	11	6	14
Adonis Terry	1	1	3.60	3	3	3	0	1	25.0	25	10	10	8
TOTAL	3	3	3.15	7	7	7	0	1	60.0	54	21	16	22

LOU (A)

PLAYER/POS	AVG	G	AB	R	H	2B	3B	HR	RB	BB	SO	SB
Ned Bligh, c	.000	2	3	0	0	0	0	0	0	0	1	0
Ed Daily, of-4,p-2	.136	6	22	1	3	1	1	0	3	1	2	2
Red Ehret, p	.429	3	7	1	3	0	1	0	0	0	0	0
Charlie Hamburg, of	.269	7	26	3	7	1	0	0	2	0	3	0
George Meakim, p	.500	1	2	0	1	0	0	0	0	0	0	0
Harry Raymond, ss-5,ss-3	.148	7	27	5	4	1	1	0	1	2	5	1
John Ryan, c	.053	6	19	0	1	0	0	0	2	0	1	1
Tim Shinnick, 2b	.292	7	24	3	7	1	1	0	3	2	2	2
Scott Stratton, p-3,of-1	.222	4	9	4	2	1	0	0	0	2	1	3
Harry Taylor, 1b	.300	7	30	6	9	1	0	0	2	2	3	1
Phil Tomney, ss	.200	3	5	1	1	0	0	0	0	0	3	1
Farmer Weaver, of	.259	7	27	4	7	1	0	0	4	1	2	5
Pete Weckbecker, c	.000	1	4	0	0	0	0	0	0	0	1	0
Chicken Wolf, 3b-5,of-3	.360	7	25	4	9	3	1	0	8	3	0	2
TOTAL	.235		230	32	54	10	5	0	25	16	22	19

PITCHER	W	L	ERA	G	GS	CG	SV	SHO	IP	H	ER	BB	SO
Ed Daily	0	2	2.65	2	2	2	0	0	17.0	12	5	8	5
Red Ehret	2	0	1.35	3	2	2	1	0	20.0	12	3	6	13
George Meakim	0	0	0.00	1	0	0	0	0	4.0	6	0	1	1
Scott Stratton	1	1	2.37	3	3	1	0	0	19.0	26	5	4	8
TOTAL	3	3	1.95	9	7	5	1	0	60.0	56	13	19	27

GAME 1 AT LOU OCT 17

BRO	300 030 30	9	11	1
LOU	000 000 00	0	2	6

Pitchers: TERRY vs STRATTON
Attendance: 5,600

GAME 2 AT LOU OCT 18

BRO	020 201 000	5	5	3
LOU	101 000 001	3	6	5

Pitchers: LOVETT vs DAILY
Attendance: 2,860

GAME 3 AT LOU OCT 20

BRO	020 130 10	7	10	2
LOU	001 012 03	7	11	3

Pitchers: Terry vs Stratton, Meakim (4)
Attendance: 2,500
(Game called at end of eighth, darkness)

GAME 4 AT LOU OCT 21

BRO	031 000 000	4	7	2
LOU	301 000 10X	5	9	2

Pitchers: LOVETT vs EHRET
Attendance: 1,050

GAME 5 AT BRO OCT 25

LOU	010 010 000	2	5	6
BRO	210 200 20X	7	7	0

Pitchers: DAILY vs LOVETT
Home Runs: Burns-BRO
Attendance: 1,000

GAME 6 AT BRO OCT 27

LOU	012 101 220	9	13	3
BRO	100 004 030	8	12	3

Pitchers: STRATTON, Ehret (7) vs TERRY
Attendance: 600

GAME 7 AT BRO OCT 28

LOU	103 000 020	6	8	3
BRO	200 000 000	2	4	1

Pitchers: EHRET vs LOVETT
Attendance: 300

Interleague squabbling prevented a World Series in 1891, and the AA folded before the next season. Four AA clubs were taken into the NL, expanding the NL to twelve teams. To create a postseason championship series, the regular season was divided in half, with first-half winner Boston meeting second-half victor Cleveland for both the league and world titles.

The first game, in Cleveland, was a pitching and fielding classic. Boston's Jack Stivetts and Cleveland's Cy Young blanked the opposition for eleven innings before darkness halted the game. Young yielded just six hits and Stivetts four—all singles. Just as remarkable in an era when errors were commonplace, Cleveland committed only one and Boston none; several outstanding plays were made in the field.

Boston center fielder Hugh Duffy was the offensive and defensive star of Game Two. He drove in three of the Beaneaters' four runs (with a fly out, a triple, and a double), and scored the fourth himself after tripling a second time. And in the bottom of the ninth he snared a leadoff liner with a great running catch. As it was, Cleveland scored once in the inning to pull within a run of a tie; Duffy's catch prevented a certain tie and a possible Cleveland win. Game Three was just as close. Pitchers Stivetts and Young each gave up two early runs, but then blanked their foes until the seventh inning, when Boston's Tommy McCarthy singled in Stivetts (who had doubled) with what proved the winning run.

The Series moved to Boston for the next three games. In Game Four, Boston ace Kid Nichols shut out the Spiders, scattering seven hits and fanning eight. Cleveland's Nig Cuppy yielded only six hits, but one was a home run ball to Hugh Duffy for two runs in the third inning, and another was a two-run single to Joe Quinn in the sixth. Cleveland pitcher John Clarkson helped his own cause the next day with a three-run homer in the Spider's six-run second inning. But Boston pitcher Jack Stivetts—with the score now 7–5 Cleveland in the sixth—tripled in a run and scored the tying run. In the seventh, Stivetts scored Boston's twelfth (and final) run after singling, while holding Cleveland scoreless through the final four innings.

Two days later the Beaneaters brought the Series to an end with their fifth straight win. The Spiders scored first, with a three-run third, but pitcher Kid Nichols held them

scoreless after that and singled home Boston's tying and go-ahead runs himself as the Beaneaters tagged Cy Young for eight runs over the final six innings.

Boston Beaneaters, 5;
Cleveland Spiders, 0; tie, 1

BOS (N)

PLAYER/POS	AVG	G	AB	R	H	2B	3B	HR	RB	BB	SO	SB
Charlie Bennett, c	.286	2	7	2	2	0	0	1	1	0	2	1
Hugh Duffy, of	.462	6	26	3	12	3	2	1	9	1	0	3
Charlie Ganzel, c	.500	2	8	1	4	0	0	0	2	1	0	0
King Kelly, c	.000	2	8	0	0	0	0	0	0	0	2	1
Herman Long, ss	.222	6	27	4	6	0	0	0	1	0	0	2
Bobby Lowe, of	.130	6	23	8	3	0	0	0	0	1	2	1
Tommy McCarthy, of	.381	6	21	2	8	2	0	0	2	6	1	3
Billy Nash, 3b	.167	6	24	3	4	0	0	0	4	2	3	2
Kid Nichols, p	.286	2	7	1	2	0	0	0	2	0	1	1
Joe Quinn, 2b	.286	6	21	2	6	1	1	0	4	1	2	0
Harry Staley, p	.000	1	4	0	0	0	0	0	0	0	3	0
Jack Stivetts, p	.250	3	12	3	3	1	1	0	1	0	2	0
Tommy Tucker, 1b	.261	6	23	2	6	0	0	1	2	0	1	0
TOTAL	.265		211	31	56	7	4	3	28	12	19	14

PITCHER	W	L	ERA	G	GS	CG	SV	SHO	IP	H	ER	BB	SO
Kid Nichols	2	0	1.00	2	2	2	0	1	18.0	17	2	4	13
Harry Staley	1	0	3.00	1	1	1	0	0	9.0	10	3	1	0
Jack Stivetts	2	0	0.93	3	3	3	0	1	29.0	21	3	7	17
TOTAL	5	0	1.29	6	6	6	0	2	56.0	48	8	12	30

CLE (N)

PLAYER/POS	AVG	G	AB	R	H	2B	3B	HR	RB	BB	SO	SB
Jesse Burkett, of	.320	6	25	3	8	1	0	0	1	0	2	4
Cupid Childs, 2b	.409	6	22	3	9	0	2	0	0	5	1	0
John Clarkson, p	.250	2	8	1	2	0	0	1	3	0	1	0
Nig Cuppy, p	.000	1	3	0	0	0	0	0	0	0	2	0
George Davis, 3b-2	.167	3	6	0	1	0	0	0	0	0	1	0
Jimmy McAleer, of	.182	6	22	0	4	0	0	0	1	2	2	1
Ed McKean, ss	.440	6	25	2	11	0	0	0	6	1	3	0
Jack O'Connor, of	.136	6	22	1	3	0	0	0	0	2	3	0
Patsy Tebeau, 3b	.000	5	18	1	0	0	0	0	0	0	2	1
Jake Virtue, 1b	.125	6	24	1	3	0	0	0	0	2	5	1
Cy Young, p	.091	3	11	1	1	0	0	0	0	0	5	0
Chief Zimmer, c	.261	6	23	2	6	1	1	0	2	0	3	0
TOTAL	.230		209	15	48	2	3	1	13	12	30	7

PITCHER	W	L	ERA	G	GS	CG	SV	SHO	IP	H	ER	BB	SO
John Clarkson	0	2	5.29	2	2	2	0	0	17.0	24	10	5	9
Nig Cuppy	0	1	1.13	1	1	1	0	0	8.0	6	1	4	1
Cy Young	0	2	3.00	3	3	3	0	1	27.0	26	9	3	9
TOTAL	0	5	3.46	6	6	6	0	1	52.0	56	20	12	19

GAME 1 AT CLE OCT 17

CLE	000 000 000 00	0	4	1
BOS	000 000 000 00	0	6	0

Pitchers: YOUNG vs STIVETTS
Attendance: 6,000
(Game called at end of eleventh, darkness)

GAME 2 AT CLE OCT 18

BOS	101 010 010	4	10	2
CLE	001 100 001	3	10	2

Pitchers: STALEY vs CLARKSON
Attendance: 6,700

GAME 3 AT CLE OCT 19

CLE	200 000 000	2	8	0
BOS	110 000 10X	3	9	2

Pitchers: YOUNG vs STIVETTS
Attendance: 5,000

GAME 4 AT BOS OCT 21

CLE	000 000 000	0	7	3
BOS	002 002 00X	4	6	0

Pitchers: CUPPY vs NICHOLS
Home Runs: Duffy-BOS
Attendance: 6,547

GAME 5 AT BOS OCT 22

CLE	060 010 000	7	9	4
BOS	000 324 30X	12	14	3

Pitchers: CLARKSON vs STIVETTS
Home Runs: Clarkson-CLE, Tucker-BOS
Attendance: 3,466

GAME 6 AT BOS OCT 24

CLE	003 000 000	3	10	5
BOS	002 211 11X	8	11	5

Pitchers: YOUNG vs NICHOLS
Home Runs: Bennett-BOS
Attendance: 2,300

As the divided season of 1892 was not repeated, no "world series" was held in 1893. But in 1894 Pittsburgh sportsman William C. Temple offered an elegant trophy to the winner of a series between the NL's first- and second-place finishers. For four years the Temple Cup games determined the world championship. In this first matchup, second-place New York swept the feisty pennant-winning Orioles.

Game One, in Baltimore, was a shutout through four innings as New York's Amos Rusie and Baltimore's Duke Esper held their opponents at bay. But Giant George Van Haltren tripled in the fifth inning and scored the game's first run on a fly to left. The Giants also scored single runs in the sixth, seventh, and eighth innings, while Rusie continued his shutout pitching through the eighth. In the ninth Oriole John McGraw singled, and he came around on a sacrifice, stolen base, and single to spoil the shutout. But the Oriole effort was too little to deprive Rusie of his win.

Some two hundred policemen patrolled the second game the next day to protect the umpires and New York's players and fans from the abusive Orioles and the crowd in the stands whom the Oriole players egged on. Baltimore scored first with two runs in the second and, after losing and regaining the lead, completed the eighth inning tied 5–5. But in the top of the ninth, the Giants put together their second four-run inning of the game. Once again the Orioles came up with a run in the last of the ninth, but once again came up short.

More than 22,000 spectators showed up for Game Three as the Series shifted to New York—a huge crowd for that era, even for a Saturday. As in Game One, the Giants' Amos Rusie hurled a 4–1 victory. New York broke a 1–1 tie with a run in the fifth on a throwing error and a ground out, and scored the game's final runs an inning later. Threatening weather held down attendance at Game Four to about 12,000. Baltimore jumped to a quick lead with two runs in the top of the first, but New York pitcher Jouett Meekin held the Orioles to just one run after that as the Giants piled up runs for a 16–3 advantage by the time darkness forced an end to play after eight innings. Meekin, in winning his second game of the Series, connected for three hits himself—half as many as he permitted the whole Oriole team.

New York Giants, 4; Baltimore Orioles, 0

NY (N)

PLAYER/POS	AVG	G	AB	R	H	2B	3B	HR	RB	BB	SO	SB
Eddie Burke, of	.389	4	18	3	7	1	0	0	2	1	0	1
George Davis, 3b	.313	4	16	5	5	2	2	0	5	2	0	2
Jack Doyle, 1b	.588	4	17	4	10	1	1	0	6	1	1	6
Duke Farrell, c	.400	4	15	5	6	0	0	0	2	1	1	1
Shorty Fuller, ss	.286	4	14	4	4	0	0	0	2	2	0	1
Jouett Meekin, p	.556	2	9	2	5	0	0	0	3	0	1	0
Yale Murphy, of	.000	1	1	0	0	0	0	0	0	0	0	0
Amos Rusie, p	.429	2	7	1	3	1	0	0	1	0	1	0
Mike Tiernan, of	.294	4	17	5	5	0	1	0	3	2	2	0
George Van Haltren, of	.500	4	14	3	7	1	1	0	0	2	2	2
Monte Ward, 2b	.294	4	17	1	5	0	0	0	6	0	0	0
TOTAL	.393		145	33	57	6	5	0	30	11	8	13

PITCHER	W	L	ERA	G	GS	CG	SV	SHO	IP	H	ER	BB	SO
Jouett Meekin	2	0	1.59	2	2	2	0	0	17.0	13	3	8	6
Amos Rusie	2	0	0.50	2	2	2	0	0	18.0	14	1	3	9
TOTAL	4	0	1.03	4	4	4	0	0	35.0	27	4	11	15

BAL (N)

PLAYER/POS	AVG	G	AB	R	H	2B	3B	HR	RB	BB	SO	SB
Frank Bonner, ss-1,of-1	.000	2	5	0	0	0	0	0	0	0	2	0
Steve Brodie, of	.000	4	15	2	0	0	0	0	0	2	1	1
Dan Brouthers, 1b	.188	4	16	2	3	0	0	0	0	1	0	3
Duke Esper, p	.000	1	2	0	0	0	0	0	0	1	1	0
Kid Gleason, p	.200	2	5	0	1	0	1	0	1	0	1	0
Bill Hawke, p	.000	1	2	0	0	0	0	0	0	0	0	0
George Hemming, p	.000	1	3	0	0	0	0	0	0	1	1	0
Hughie Jennings, ss	.143	4	14	0	2	0	0	0	1	0	2	0
Willie Keeler, of	.250	3	12	1	3	0	0	0	1	1	0	0
Joe Kelley, of	.333	4	15	2	5	1	1	0	0	3	2	1
John McGraw, 3b	.250	4	16	2	4	0	0	0	2	0	0	1
Heinie Reitz, 2b	.333	4	15	1	5	0	0	0	4	1	3	1
Wilbert Robinson, c	.267	4	15	1	4	0	0	0	1	1	1	1
TOTAL	.200		135	11	27	1	2	0	10	11	15	8

PITCHER	W	L	ERA	G	GS	CG	SV	SHO	IP	H	ER	BB	SO
Duke Esper	0	1	4.00	1	1	1	0	0	9.0	13	4	1	3
Kid Gleason	0	1	9.69	2	1	1	0	0	13.0	25	14	6	3
Bill Hawke	0	1	9.00	1	1	0	0	0	4.0	9	4	1	0
George Hemming	0	1	1.13	1	1	1	0	0	8.0	10	1	3	2
TOTAL	0	4	6.09	5	4	3	0	0	34.0	57	23	11	8

GAME 1 AT BAL OCT 4

NY	000	011	110	4	13	2
BAL	000	000	001	1	7	1

Pitchers: RUSIE vs ESPER
Attendance: 9,000

GAME 2 AT BAL OCT 5

NY	004	000	014	9	14	3
BAL	022	000	101	6	7	2

Pitchers: MEEKIN vs GLEASON
Attendance: 11,000

GAME 3 AT NY OCT 6

BAL	000	100	000	1	7	4
NY	100	012	00X	4	10	4

Pitchers: HEMMING vs RUSIE
Attendance: 22,000

GAME 4 AT NY OCT 8

BAL	201	000	00	3	6	3
NY	101	351	50	16	20	4

Pitchers: HAWKE, Gleason (5) vs MEEKIN
Attendance: 12,000
(Game called at end of eighth, darkness)

Baltimore, repeating as NL pennant winner, returned to Temple Cup play against new runner-up Cleveland. The first 4½ innings of the opener—played in Cleveland—featured a scoreless duel between Baltimore veteran John "Sadie" McMahon and the Spiders' great Cy Young. After Cleveland scored the game's first run in the last of the fifth, the teams traded runs and the lead, completing the eighth inning tied 3–3. In the top of the ninth, doubles by Wilbert Robinson and John McGraw restored the edge to Baltimore. But in the bottom of the inning, four straight Spider hits pushed across the tying run and filled the bases. One runner was forced at home for the first out, but a grounder that just missed being a double-play ball drove in the winning Cleveland run.

The next three games were not so closely contested. A large and enthusiastic Cleveland crowd watched its Spiders jump on Baltimore for three runs in the bottom of the first inning of Game Two and coast to a 7–2 win behind the strong pitching of Nig Cuppy, who held the Orioles to five singles. Cleveland repeated itself in Game Three, again exploding for three runs in the bottom of the first on the way to a seven-run total. Cy Young was just as effective in the box as Cuppy had been, scattering four hits over seven shutout innings before Baltimore put together three singles in the eighth for their only run.

When the teams shifted to Baltimore for Game Four, the Orioles sprang to life. While their pitcher Duke Esper strangled the Spiders on just five singles—only two Cleveland runners advanced as far as second base—Oriole batters tagged Nig Cuppy for five runs and their first Temple Cup win in two years of trying.

It proved to be their only win of the Series. The next day, in the first close struggle since the opener, Cy Young and Baltimore's rookie ace Bill Hoffer dueled scorelessly through six innings. But in the top of the seventh, Young doubled to start what became a three-run rally, and an inning later the Spiders scored twice more. Baltimore scored a single run in the last of the seventh, and, with two out in the ninth, loaded the bases on two walks and a hit batsman. A Cleveland error brought in the Orioles' second run as the bases remained full for Steve Brodie. But despite the pleas of Baltimore partisans to hit a homer or triple, Brodie "failed miserably" and Cleveland copped the cup.

Cleveland Spiders, 4;
Baltimore Orioles, 1

CLE (N)

PLAYER/POS	AVG	G	AB	R	H	2B	3B	HR	RB	BB	SO	SB
Harry Blake, of	.250	5	20	1	5	3	0	0	2	0	2	0
Jesse Burkett, of	.450	5	20	3	9	2	0	0	2	0	0	1
Cupid Childs, 2b	.190	5	21	4	4	1	0	0	2	1	0	1
Nig Cuppy, p	.167	2	6	1	1	1	0	0	1	0	0	0
Jimmy McAleer, of	.286	5	21	2	6	0	0	0	2	0	0	1
Chippy McGarr, 3b	.368	5	19	3	7	2	0	0	1	1	0	2
Ed McKean, ss	.300	5	20	2	6	1	1	0	4	3	0	1
Patsy Tebeau, 1b	.286	5	21	3	6	1	0	0	3	1	1	0
Cy Young, p	.250	3	12	3	3	1	0	0	1	0	1	0
Chief Zimmer, c	.333	4	18	2	6	2	0	0	3	3	4	0
TOTAL	.298		178	24	53	14	1	0	21	9	9*	6

PITCHER	W	L	ERA	G	GS	CG	SV	SHO	IP	H	ER	BB	SO
Nig Cuppy	1	1	3.18	2	2	2	0	0	17.0	14	6	4	6
Cy Young	3	0	2.33	3	3	3	0	0	27.0	28	7	4	2
TOTAL	4	1	2.66	5	5	5	0	0	44.0	42	13	8	8

BAL (N)

PLAYER/POS	AVG	G	AB	R	H	2B	3B	HR	RB	BB	SO	SB
Steve Brodie, of	.200	5	20	1	4	0	0	0	2	0	0	0
Scoops Carey, 1b	.263	5	19	0	5	1	0	0	1	0	0	0
Boileryard Clarke, c	.286	2	7	1	2	0	0	0	0	0	0	2
Duke Esper, p	.000	1	3	0	0	0	0	0	0	1	2	0
Kid Gleason, 2b	.105	5	19	0	2	0	0	0	0	0	1	0
Bill Hoffer, p	.000	2	7	0	0	0	0	0	0	0	2	0
Hughie Jennings, ss	.368	5	19	3	7	2	0	0	2	1	0	1
Willie Keeler, of	.235	5	17	3	4	0	0	0	1	3	1	0
Joe Kelley, of	.368	5	19	1	7	0	0	0	5	1	1	1
John McGraw, 3b	.400	5	20	4	8	2	0	0	1	2	0	2
Sadie McMahon, p	.000	2	7	0	0	0	0	0	0	0	0	0
Wilbert Robinson, c	.250	3	12	1	3	1	0	0	0	0	1	0
TOTAL	.249		169	14	42	6	0	0	12	8	8	6

PITCHER	W	L	ERA	G	GS	CG	SV	SHO	IP	H	ER	BB	SO
Duke Esper	1	0	0.00	1	1	1	0	1	9.0	5	0	0	3
Bill Hoffer	0	2	4.24	2	2	2	0	0	17.0	21	8	6	4
Sadie McMahon	0	2	5.94	2	2	2	0	0	16.2	27	11	3	2
TOTAL	1	4	4.01	5	5	5	0	1	42.2	53	19	9	9

* While the total strikeouts for the team have been confirmed as 9, research has failed, to this point, to identify the missing batter strikeout.

GAME 1 AT CLE OCT 2

BAL	000 001 021	4	12	0
CLE	000 011 012	5	14	3

Pitchers: McMAHON vs YOUNG
Attendance: 8,000

GAME 2 AT CLE OCT 3

BAL	010 001 000	2	5	4
CLE	300 012 10X	7	10	5

Pitchers: HOFFER vs CUPPY
Attendance: 10,000

GAME 3 AT CLE OCT 5

BAL	000 000 010	1	7	1
CLE	300 000 31X	7	13	1

Pitchers: McMAHON vs YOUNG
Attendance: 12,000

GAME 4 AT BAL OCT 7

CLE	000 000 000	0	5	1
BAL	012 000 20X	5	9	1

Pitchers: CUPPY vs ESPER
Attendance: 9,100

GAME 5 AT BAL OCT 8

CLE	000 000 320	5	11	3
BAL	000 000 101	2	9	5

Pitchers: YOUNG vs HOFFER
Attendance: 5,000

Baltimore captured its third consecutive pennant and for the second year in a row faced runner-up Cleveland in the Temple Cup games. But this time the Orioles emerged triumphant—with a sweep in which their margin of victory was never less than four runs.

Aces Bill Hoffer of Baltimore and the Spiders' Cy Young faced each other in the opener, in Baltimore. Hoffer walked four men, but gave up only five hits while the Orioles bombarded Young for thirteen. When the game ended, Hoffer and Baltimore had a 7-1 win.

Bobby Wallace (who had not yet discovered his role at shortstop that would propel him into the Hall of Fame) pitched for Cleveland in Game Two. He lost the game in the first inning when two Spider errors, a hit batsman, three hits, and a steal of home put four Baltimore runs on the board. The Orioles added two runs in the third and another in the fifth, while their promising twenty-year-old pitcher Joe Corbett held the Spiders to two runs on seven hits.

The Orioles' Hoffer gave up ten hits to Cleveland in Game Three—two more than the Birds made off Spider Nig Cuppy. But all the hits off Hoffer were singles, and he walked only one. Half of Cleveland's hits went toward producing just two runs. Their second run tied the score in the fifth inning, but in the sixth Baltimore regained the lead as John McGraw singled, stole second, took third on an error, and came home on an outfield fly. In the eighth the Orioles bunched four of their eight hits for three insurance runs.

The Series moved to Cleveland for the fourth game. Young Joe Corbett was again sent into the box for Baltimore, this time to face Nig Cuppy. For six innings the game was a scoreless duel. Baltimore hit safely in every inning but the second, but failed to score until the seventh, when Joe Kelley's double and Jack Doyle's single scored the only run they would need. But the Orioles added a second run in that inning and three more in the eighth. Two of the four Cleveland hits against Corbett put men on base in the eighth inning, and Corbett walked two in the ninth to raise Cleveland's hopes. But no Spider scored, and with the 5-0 win the Orioles were world champions at last.

Baltimore Orioles, 4; Cleveland Spiders, 0

BAL (N)

PLAYER/POS	AVG	G	AB	R	H	2B	3B	HR	RB	BB	SO	SB
Steve Brodie, of	.067	4	15	1	1	0	0	0	3	0	0	1
Joe Corbett, p	.500	2	6	1	3	1	0	0	0	1	1	0
Jack Doyle, 1b	.294	4	17	3	5	1	0	0	4	0	0	2
Bill Hoffer, p	.286	2	7	1	2	0	2	0	0	0	1	0
Hughie Jennings, ss	.333	4	15	5	5	2	0	0	3	1	2	1
Willie Keeler, of	.471	4	17	4	8	1	2	0	4	0	0	1
Joe Kelley, of	.471	4	17	3	8	1	0	0	4	0	1	2
John McGraw, 3b	.267	4	15	4	4	0	0	0	1	0	0	4
Joe Quinn, 3b	.000	1	3	1	0	0	0	0	0	0	0	0
Heinie Reitz, 2b	.133	4	15	1	2	0	0	0	2	1	0	0
Wilbert Robinson, c	.267	4	15	1	4	1	0	0	2	0	3	0
TOTAL	.296		142	25	42	7	4	0	23	3	8	11

PITCHER	W	L	ERA	G	GS	CG	SV	SHO	IP	H	ER	BB	SO
Joe Corbett	2	0	0.50	2	2	2	0	1	18.0	11	1	7	10
Bill Hoffer	2	0	1.50	2	2	2	0	0	18.0	15	3	5	10
TOTAL	4	0	1.00	4	4	4	0	1	36.0	26	4	12	20

CLE (N)

PLAYER/POS	AVG	G	AB	R	H	2B	3B	HR	RB	BB	SO	SB
Harry Blake, of	.071	4	14	1	1	0	0	0	0	1	1	1
Jesse Burkett, of	.333	4	15	1	5	0	0	0	0	2	3	0
Cupid Childs, 2b	.231	4	13	2	3	0	0	0	0	4	0	1
Nig Cuppy, p	.143	2	7	0	1	0	0	0	0	0	1	0
Jimmy McAleer, of	.133	4	15	2	0	0	0	0	1	1	2	1
Chippy McGarr, 3b	.063	4	16	0	1	0	0	0	0	0	3	2
Ed McKean, ss	.313	4	16	0	5	1	1	0	1	1	1	1
Jack O'Connor, 1b	.286	4	14	1	4	0	0	0	1	1	2	0
Patsy Tebeau, 1b	.000	1	1	0	0	0	0	0	0	0	0	0
Bobby Wallace, p-1	.200	3	5	0	1	0	0	0	0	0	0	0
Cy Young, p	.000	1	3	0	0	0	0	0	0	0	0	0
Chief Zimmer, c	.214	4	14	0	3	1	0	0	1	2	6	0
TOTAL	.195		133	5	26	2	1	0	4	12	20	6

PITCHER	W	L	ERA	G	GS	CG	SV	SHO	IP	H	ER	BB	SO
Nig Cuppy	0	2	4.76	2	2	2	0	0	17.0	19	9	0	4
Bobby Wallace	0	1	4.50	1	1	1	0	0	8.0	10	4	2	4
Cy Young	0	1	6.00	1	1	1	0	0	9.0	13	6	1	0
TOTAL	0	4	5.03	4	4	4	0	0	34.0	42	19	3	8

GAME 1 AT BAL OCT 2

BAL	002 001 310	7 13 1
CLE	000 001 000	1 5 4

Pitchers: HOFFER vs YOUNG
Attendance: 4,000

GAME 2 AT BAL OCT 3

BAL	402 010 00	7 10 3
CLE	001 001 00	2 7 3

Pitchers: CORBETT vs WALLACE
Attendance: 3,100
(Game called at end of eighth, darkness)

GAME 3 AT BAL OCT 5

BAL	011 001 030	6 8 2
CLE	001 010 000	2 10 2

Pitchers: HOFFER vs CUPPY
Attendance: 2,000

GAME 4 AT CLE OCT 8

CLE	000 000 000	0 4 2
BAL	000 000 23X	5 11 1

Pitchers: CUPPY vs CORBETT
Attendance: 1,500

Boston had edged Baltimore in a close race for the NL pennant, but the Orioles turned the tables on the Beaneaters in Temple Cup play. The Series was a high-scoring affair, the winner of each game averaging eleven runs, the loser eight.

The opener, in Boston, set the tone for the games. Baltimore sent four runners across the plate in the top of the first inning, and Boston followed in its half with three. The Beaneaters recorded only twelve hits in the game to the Orioles' twenty, but they also received seven walks from Baltimore hurler Jerry Nops, and five of those runners scored. The lead switched back and forth in the middle innings, but Boston scored two final runs in the eighth and hung on for a 13–12 win.

Baltimore's Joe Corbett gave up sixteen hits (one a home run) and four walks in Game Two as Boston scored eleven times. But Boston's two pitchers, Fred Klobedanz and Jack Stivetts, were even more generous, handing out seventeen hits (including three homers—one of them to opposing pitcher Corbett, who also hit a double and two singles) and five walks as the Orioles evened the Series with their thirteen-run attack.

Game Three was the Series' lowest in run production, with Baltimore scoring four in the second inning and another four in the third for an 8–3 win. But rain ended the game before Boston could complete its time at bat in the last of the eighth, which erased from the record four more Oriole runs scored earlier in the inning. Rather than waste the two free days before the Series resumed in Baltimore, the two clubs played a pair of exhibition games in Worcester and Springfield, Massachusetts. Baltimore won them both, 11–10 and 8–6.

The Orioles continued their roll in Series Game Four, with another close but high-scoring victory, 12–11. It looked at first like a blowout as Baltimore scored six runs in the first inning and five more in the second. But Ted Lewis relieved Boston starter Jack Stivetts and held Baltimore to just one further run as the Beaneaters fought back to within one run of a tie before faltering in the ninth.

Boston batters hit Oriole Bill Hoffer safely fifteen times in Game Five, but only three Beaneaters scored. Baltimore, with two fewer hits, garnered six more runs than Boston and, with their fourth win, the right to hold the cup for another year. But attendance at the final game was so small the embarrassed Baltimore management refused to release the figures, and the league gave the cup back to Mr. Temple rather than sponsor another unprofitable Series. There was no postseason championship contest in 1898 or 1899.

Baltimore Orioles, 4;
Boston Beaneaters, 1

BAL (N)

PLAYER/POS	AVG	G	AB	R	H	2B	3B	HR	RBI	BB	SO	SB
Frank Bowerman, c-1,1b-1	.500	2	8	2	4	0	1	0	4	0	0	0
Boileryard Clarke, c	.563	4	16	5	9	1	1	1	4	1	0	0
Joe Corbett, p	.667	2	6	2	4	1	0	1	2	0	1	0
Jack Doyle, 1b	.526	5	19	7	10	2	0	0	9	0	1	2
Bill Hoffer, p	.250	2	8	2	2	1	0	0	0	0	0	0
Hughie Jennings, ss	.318	5	22	5	9	1	1	0	3	4	0	0
Willie Keeler, of	.391	5	23	5	9	2	0	0	2	4	0	0
Joe Kelley, of	.313	4	16	7	5	3	0	0	5	5	0	0
John McGraw, 3b	.300	5	20	6	6	1	1	0	6	7	0	0
Jerry Nops, p	.286	2	7	0	2	0	0	0	1	1	5	0
Tom O'Brien, of	.400	1	5	2	2	1	0	0	0	0	0	0
Heinie Reitz, 2b	.250	5	20	4	5	1	0	1	4	2	0	0
Jake Stenzel, of	.381	5	21	7	8	1	1	0	3	2	0	2
TOTAL	.382		191	54	73	16	4	3	43	26	7	4

PITCHER	W	L	ERA	G	GS	CG	SV	SHO	IP	H	ER	BB	SO
Joe Corbett	1	0	9.00	2	1	1	0	0	12.0	21	12	8	5
Bill Hoffer	2	0	3.38	2	2	2	0	0	16.0	25	6	4	2
Jerry Nops	1	1	12.86	2	2	1	0	0	14.0	23	20	9	3
TOTAL	4	1	8.14	6	5	4	0	0	42.0	69	38	21	10

BOS (N)

PLAYER/POS	AVG	G	AB	R	H	2B	3B	HR	RBI	BB	SO	SB
Marty Bergen, c	.500	1	4	0	2	0	0	0	1	0	1	1
Jimmy Collins, 3b	.182	5	22	2	4	0	0	0	4	1	0	0
Hugh Duffy, of	.524	5	21	6	11	2	0	0	7	1	0	0
Billy Hamilton, of	.500	4	16	6	8	1	0	0	2	5	3	2
Charlie Hickman, p-1,of-1	.250	1	4	0	1	1	0	0	1	0	0	0
Fred Klobedanz, p	1.000	2	5	3	5	0	0	0	0	0	0	0
Fred Lake, c	.000	1	3	0	0	0	0	0	0	1	0	0
Ted Lewis, p	.500	3	6	1	3	1	0	0	1	1	0	0
Herman Long, ss	.286	5	21	4	6	1	1	1	5	2	2	1
Bobby Lowe, 2b	.391	5	23	6	9	2	0	0	6	1	0	1
Kid Nichols, p	.000	1	3	0	0	0	0	0	0	1	0	0
Chick Stahl, of	.381	5	21	6	8	1	0	0	6	3	2	2
Jack Stivetts, p-2,of-1	.000	3	7	1	0	0	0	0	0	1	0	1
Jim Sullivan, p	.000	1	1	0	0	0	0	0	0	0	0	0
Fred Tenney, 1b	.300	5	21	4	6	0	0	0	2	4	1	2
George Yeager, c	.500	3	12	2	6	1	1	0	2	2	0	0
TOTAL	.365		189	41	69	10	2	1	38	21	10	10

PITCHER	W	L	ERA	G	GS	CG	SV	SHO	IP	H	ER	BB	SO
Charlie Hickman	0	1	3.60	1	1	0	0	0	5.0	7	2	2	0
Fred Klobedanz	0	1	9.35	2	1	0	0	0	8.2	12	9	8	0
Ted Lewis	1	1	6.00	3	1	0	0	0	12	18	8	9	4
Kid Nichols	0	0	12.00	1	1	0	0	0	6.0	14	8	0	3
Jack Stivetts	0	1	18.47	2	1	0	0	0	6.1	16	13	7	0
Jim Sullivan	0	0	3.00	1	0	0	0	0	3.0	6	1	0	0
TOTAL	1	4	9.00	10	5	0	0	0	41.0	73	41	26	7

GAME 1 AT BOS OCT 4

BAL   401 023 200   12 20 4
BOS   300 125 02X   13 12 4

Pitchers: NOPS vs Nichols, LEWIS (7)
Attendance: 9,600

GAME 2 AT BOS OCT 5

BAL   130 160 110   13 17 2
BOS   002 620 100   11 16 3

Pitchers: CORBETT vs KLOBEDANZ, Stivetts (5)
Home Runs: Reitz-BAL, Clarke-BAL, Corbett-BAL, Long-BOS
Attendance: 6,500

GAME 3 AT BOS OCT 6

BAL   044 000 0   8 9 2
BOS   003 000 0   3 10 2

Pitchers: HOFFER vs LEWIS, Klobedanz (4)
Attendance: 5,000
(Game called in eighth, rain)

GAME 4 AT BAL OCT 9

BOS   000 024 320   11 16 3
BAL   650 001 00X   12 14 3

Pitchers: STIVETTS, Lewis (3) vs NOPS, Corbett (7)
Attendance: 2,500

GAME 5 AT BAL OCT 11

BOS   020 000 001   3 15 3
BAL   023 000 22X   9 13 2

Pitchers: HICKMAN, Sullivan (7) vs HOFFER
Attendance: 700

Pennant-winning Brooklyn led the NL in hitting, but runner-up Pittsburgh claimed the best pitching. Honus Wagner was the only Pirate regular to hit over .300, but he enjoyed what turned out to be his finest season offensively, leading the league with a .381 batting average. Pittsburghers believed their club superior to Brooklyn and a best-of-five "world championship" series was arranged, with all the games to be played in Pittsburgh for a silver cup donated by the *Pittsburgh Chronicle-Telegraph*. Brooklyn, however, proved that its pennant was no fluke.

Two of the game's best pitchers faced off in the opener: Pittsburgh's Rube Waddell, who had led the league in ERA, and Joe "Iron Man" McGinnity, whose 28 regular-season wins totaled eight more than those of the league's runners-up. McGinnity prevailed, shutting out the Pirates until two unearned runs came across in the top of the ninth. Pirate errors also gave Brooklyn a pair of unearned runs, but Waddell lost the game on hits—thirteen in all, including six in the Superbas' three-run third inning.

In Game Two, Brooklyn's Frank Kitson held Pittsburgh to four hits, and although his Superbas scored only one earned run, six Pirate errors gave them their second win, 4–2.

The Pirates staved off a Series sweep with sharp pitching and heavy hitting in Game Three. Deacon Phillippe shut out Brooklyn on six hits as the Pirates jumped on Harry Howell for thirteen. All the Pirate hits were singles, but combined with Brooklyn errors they were good for ten runs, seven of them unearned.

Three Brooklyn singles and a fumble by Pirate pitcher Sam Leever in the fourth inning of Game Four gave the Superbas three runs and a 4–0 lead the Pirates could not overcome. Brooklyn hurler McGinnity scattered nine Pirate hits and, supported by flawless fielding, held Pittsburgh to a single run to bring Brooklyn its first World Series triumph in three tries—and its last until 1955. The Brooklyn players voted to award their trophy to McGinnity for his fine pitching. The cup may be seen today—along with the Temple Cup and the current World Series trophy—at the Baseball Hall of Fame in Cooperstown.

Brooklyn Superbas, 3; Pittsburgh Pirates, 1

BRO (N)

PLAYER/POS	AVG	G	AB	R	H	2B	3B	HR	RB	BB	SO	SB
Lave Cross, 3b	.278	4	18	2	5	0	1	0	1	0	0	1
Bill Dahlen, ss	.176	4	17	3	3	0	1	0	2	0	3	1
Tom Daly, 2b	.154	4	13	2	2	1	0	0	1	3	1	0
Duke Farrell, c	.375	2	8	0	3	0	0	0	1	0	0	1
Harry Howell, p	.000	1	3	0	0	0	0	0	0	0	2	0
Hughie Jennings, 1b	.167	4	18	1	3	1	0	0	2	1	1	0
Fielder Jones, of	.278	4	18	3	5	0	0	0	4	1	1	1
Willie Keeler, of	.353	4	17	0	6	0	0	0	0	1	0	0
Joe Kelley, of	.176	4	17	2	3	0	0	0	1	2	3	0
Frank Kitson, p	.000	1	3	0	0	0	0	0	0	1	2	0
Joe McGinnity, p	.143	2	7	1	1	0	0	0	1	0	2	0
Deacon McGuire, c	.375	2	8	1	3	1	0	0	0	0	1	0
TOTAL	.231		147	15	34	3	2	0	13	9	16	4

PITCHER	W	L	ERA	G	GS	CG	SV	SHO	IP	H	ER	BB	SO
Harry Howell	0	1	3.38	1	1	1	0	0	8.0	13	3	2	3
Frank Kitson	1	0	1.00	1	1	1	0	0	9.0	4	1	1	2
Joe McGinnity	2	0	0.00	2	2	2	0	0	18.0	14	0	3	5
TOTAL	3	1	1.03	4	4	4	0	0	35.0	31	4	6	10

PIT (N)

PLAYER/POS	AVG	G	AB	R	H	2B	3B	HR	RB	BB	SO	SB
Ginger Beaumont, of	.267	4	15	2	4	0	0	0	1	1	0	1
Fred Ely, ss	.286	4	14	1	4	1	0	0	0	1	1	2
Tommy Leach, of	.176	4	17	4	3	0	0	0	1	1	2	0
Sam Leever, p	.250	2	4	0	1	0	0	0	0	0	1	1
Tom O'Brien, 1b	.125	4	16	1	2	1	0	0	2	0	1	0
Jack O'Connor, c	.250	2	4	0	1	0	0	0	1	1	0	0
Deacon Phillippe, p	.000	1	4	1	0	0	0	0	0	0	1	0
Claude Ritchey, 2b	.333	4	15	3	5	1	0	0	1	1	0	0
Pop Schriver, ph	.000	1	1	0	0	0	0	0	0	0	0	0
Rube Waddell, p	.200	2	5	0	1	0	0	0	0	0	1	0
Honus Wagner, of	.400	4	15	2	6	1	0	0	3	0	1	2
Jimmy Williams, 3b	.214	4	14	0	3	0	0	0	1	0	1	0
Chief Zimmer, c	.111	3	9	1	1	0	0	0	1	0	2	1
TOTAL	.233		133	15	31	4	0	0	10	6	10	7

PITCHER	W	L	ERA	G	GS	CG	SV	SHO	IP	H	ER	BB	SO
Sam Leever	0	2	1.38	2	2	1	0	0	13.0	13	2	4	4
Deacon Phillippe	1	0	0.00	1	1	1	0	1	9.0	6	0	2	5
Rube Waddell	0	1	1.93	2	1	1	0	0	14.0	15	3	3	7
TOTAL	1	3	1.25	5	4	3	0	1	36.0	34	5	9	16

GAME 1 AT PIT OCT 15

BRO	003	101	000	5	13	1
PIT	000	000	002	2	5	4

Pitchers: McGINNITY vs WADDELL
Attendance: 4,000

GAME 2 AT PIT OCT 16

BRO	010	003	000	4	7	0
PIT	000	100	100	2	4	6

Pitchers: KITSON vs LEEVER
Attendance: 1,800

GAME 3 AT PIT OCT 17

BRO	000	000	000	0	6	3
PIT	310	020	13X	10	13	1

Pitchers: HOWELL vs PHILLIPPE
Attendance: 2,500

GAME 4 AT PIT OCT 18

BRO	100	311	000	6	8	0
PIT	000	001	000	1	9	3

Pitchers: McGINNITY vs LEEVER, Waddell (5)
Attendance: 2,335

When the Boston Pilgrims of the young American League accepted a challenge from owner Barney Dreyfuss of the National League Pirates, the modern World Series was born. (In 1901–02, the National and American Leagues were warring, and did not stage a post-season series.) Pittsburgh was favored to win but entered the Series weakened by injuries to pitching ace Sam Leever and shortstop Honus Wagner, and by the loss of pitcher Ed Doheny to mental illness.

Deacon Phillippe, the Pirates' one healthy starter, faced Cy Young in the opener, winning handily as Pirate batters, with two out in the top of the first, jumped on Young (and a porous defense) for four runs. Right fielder Jimmy Sebring starred offensively for the Pirates, with four RBIs and the Series's first home run. Boston came back in Game Two as Bill Dinneen shut out the Pirates on three hits. His teammates scored three runs off the sore-armed Leever and reliever Bucky Veil, two coming on homers by Patsy Dougherty. (They were the last World Series home runs for five years.)

Phillippe, with only a day's rest, started Game Three and again pitched Pittsburgh into the Series lead, holding Boston to four hits. After a Sunday travel day to Pittsburgh and a day of rain, Phillippe defeated Boston a third time, though he yielded three ninth-inning runs before emerging with a 5–4 win.

The tide began to turn against the Pirates the next day, as Boston knocked five ground-rule triples into the overflow crowd, scoring ten runs in the sixth and seventh innings to give Young an 11–2 victory. Dinneen bested Leever for a second time in Game Six, holding the Pirates scoreless in eight of their nine innings for a 6–3 win. And in Game Seven, Phillippe finally lost, Young winning his second game as Boston numbered 5 more triples among its 11 hits.

After another travel Sunday and another rainout, Phillippe for the fifth time faced the Pilgrims. He pitched well, giving up three runs (only two of them earned). But Bill Dinneen pitched better, holding the Pirates to four hits as he shut them out for the second time to give Boston the Series.

Boston Pilgrims (AL), 5;
Pittsburgh Pirates (NL), 3

BOS (A)

PLAYER/POS	AVG	G	AB	R	H	2B	3B	HR	RB	BB	SO	SB
Jimmy Collins, 3b	.250	8	36	5	9	1	2	0	1	1	1	3
Lou Criger, c	.231	8	26	1	6	0	0	0	4	2	3	0
Bill Dinneen, p	.250	4	12	1	3	0	0	0	0	2	2	0
Patsy Dougherty, of	.235	8	34	3	8	0	2	2	5	2	6	0
Duke Farrell, ph	.000	2	2	0	0	0	0	0	1	0	0	0
Hobe Ferris, 2b	.290	8	31	3	9	0	1	0	5	0	6	0
Buck Freeman, of	.281	8	32	6	9	0	3	0	4	2	2	0
Tom Hughes, p	.000	1	0	0	0	0	0	0	0	0	0	0
Candy La Chance, 1b	.222	8	27	5	6	2	1	0	4	3	2	0
Jack O'Ben, ph	.000	2	2	0	0	0	0	0	0	0	1	0
Freddy Parent, ss	.281	8	32	8	9	0	3	0	4	1	1	0
Chick Stahl, of	.303	8	33	6	10	1	3	0	3	1	2	2
Cy Young, p	.133	4	15	1	2	0	1	0	3	0	3	0
TOTAL	.252		282	39	71	4	16	2	34	14	29	5

PITCHER	W	L	ERA	G	GS	CG	SV	SHO	IP	H	ER	BB	SO
Bill Dinneen	3	1	2.06	4	4	4	0	2	35.0	29	8	8	28
Tom Hughes	0	1	9.00	1	1	0	0	0	2.0	4	2	2	0
Cy Young	2	1	1.85	4	3	3	0	0	34.0	31	7	4	17
TOTAL	5	3	2.15	9	8	7	0	2	71.0	64	17	14	45

PIT (N)

PLAYER/POS	AVG	G	AB	R	H	2B	3B	HR	RB	BB	SO	SB
Ginger Beaumont, of	.265	8	34	6	9	0	1	0	1	2	4	2
Kitty Bransfield, 1b	.207	8	29	3	6	0	2	0	1	1	6	1
Fred Clarke, of	.265	8	34	3	9	2	1	0	2	1	5	1
Brickyard Kennedy, p	.500	1	2	0	1	1	0	0	0	0	0	0
Tommy Leach, 3b	.273	8	33	3	9	0	4	0	7	1	4	1
Sam Leever, p	.000	2	4	0	0	0	0	0	0	0	0	0
Ed Phelps, c-7	.231	8	26	1	6	2	0	0	1	1	6	0
Deacon Phillippe, p	.222	5	18	1	4	0	0	0	1	0	3	0
Claude Ritchey, 2b	.111	8	27	2	3	1	0	0	2	4	7	1
Jimmy Sebring, of	.367	8	30	3	11	0	1	1	3	1	4	0
Harry Smith, c	.000	1	3	0	0	0	0	0	0	0	0	0
Gus Thompson, p	.000	1	1	0	0	0	0	0	0	0	0	0
Bucky Veil, p	.000	1	2	0	0	0	0	0	0	0	2	0
Honus Wagner, ss	.222	8	27	2	6	1	0	0	3	3	4	3
TOTAL	.237		270	24	64	7	9	1	21	14	45	9

PITCHER	W	L	ERA	G	GS	CG	SV	SHO	IP	H	ER	BB	SO
Brickyard Kennedy	0	1	5.14	1	1	0	0	0	7.0	11	4	3	3
Sam Leever	0	2	5.40	2	2	1	0	0	10.0	13	6	3	2
Deacon Phillippe	3	2	2.86	5	5	5	0	0	44.0	38	14	3	22
Gus Thompson	0	0	4.50	1	0	0	0	0	2.0	3	1	0	1
Bucky Veil	0	0	1.29	1	0	0	0	0	7.0	6	1	5	1
TOTAL	3	5	3.34	10	8	6	0	0	70.0	71	26	14	29

GAME 1 AT BOS OCT 1

PIT	401	100	100	7	12	2
BOS	000	000	201	3	6	4

Pitchers: PHILLIPPE vs YOUNG
Home Runs: Sebring-PIT
Attendance: 16,242

GAME 2 AT BOS OCT 2

PIT	000	000	000	0	3	2
BOS	200	001	00X	3	9	0

Pitchers: LEEVER, Vail (2) vs DINNEEN
Home Runs: Dougherty-BOS(2)
Attendance: 9,415

GAME 3 AT BOS OCT 3

PIT	012	000	010	4	7	0
BOS	000	100	010	2	4	2

Pitchers: PHILLIPPE vs HUGHES, Young (3)
Attendance: 18,801

GAME 4 AT PIT OCT 6

BOS	000	010	003	4	9	1
PIT	100	010	30X	5	12	1

Pitchers: DINNEEN vs PHILLIPPE
Attendance: 7,600

GAME 5 AT PIT OCT 7

BOS	000	006	410	11	14	2
PIT	000	000	020	2	6	4

Pitchers: YOUNG vs KENNEDY, Thompson (8)
Attendance: 12,322

GAME 6 AT PIT OCT 8

BOS	003	020	100	6	10	1
PIT	000	000	300	3	10	3

Pitchers: DINNEEN vs LEEVER
Attendance: 11,556

GAME 7 AT PIT OCT 10

BOS	200	202	010	7	11	4
PIT	000	101	001	3	10	3

Pitchers: YOUNG vs PHILLIPPE
Attendance: 17,038

GAME 8 AT BOS OCT 13

PIT	000	000	000	0	4	3
BOS	000	201	00X	3	8	0

Pitchers: PHILLIPPE vs DINNEEN
Attendance: 7,455

After a year's gap caused by the Giants' refusal to play the American League champion Boston Pilgrims, the World Series—now established on an official and permanent basis—resumed with a pitching classic. Even though the A's ERA league leader Rube Waddell had ostensibly injured his shoulder and could not pitch in the Series—rumor had it that gamblers had reached him—the Philadelphia staff recorded a Series ERA of only 1.47. But the Giants' staff—led by Christy Mathewson's three shutouts—registered a matchless ERA of 0.00, permitting only three unearned runs to score in their only Series loss. Every victory in the Series was a shutout.

Mathewson, a 31-game winner in the regular season, continued his winning ways in the Series opener. Though three of the four hits he yielded were doubles, he permitted no more than one hit in any inning, and stopped the only scoring threat, fielding a squeeze bunt to throw out the runner at the plate in the sixth inning.

The A's came back to tie the Series the next day. This time it was Chief Bender's turn to hurl a four-hit shutout. Joe McGinnity also pitched well for the Giants, but New York errors in the third and eighth innings let in three unearned runs—the only runs, as it turned out, to be scored against the Giants in the Series.

Mathewson, pitching with only two days' rest in Game Three, once again permitted only four hits (all singles this time), and Philadelphia's flawed fielding let in seven unearned runs to help give Matty an easy 9–0 win. In Game Four, McGinnity, the hard-luck loser of Game Two, tried again. This time the Giants supported him almost flawlessly, while he gave up only five singles on his way to victory in the Series' tightest game. An A's error led to a single Giant run, and a loss for Eddie Plank, who had pitched even better than McGinnity, giving up only four hits while fanning six.

Chief Bender, the A's winner in Game Two, pitched a five-hitter in Game Six, but he also yielded three walks, all of which contributed to the two Giant runs. Mathewson, though he gave up six hits, walked none, retiring the final ten batters to conclude his record third shutout—and the Series.

New York Giants (NL), 4; Philadelphia Athletics (AL), 1

NY (N)

PLAYER/POS	AVG	G	AB	R	H	2B	3B	HR	RB	BB	SO	SB
Red Ames, p	.000	1	0	0	0	0	0	0	0	0	0	0
Roger Bresnahan, c	.313	5	16	3	5	2	0	0	1	4	0	1
George Browne, of	.182	5	22	2	4	0	0	0	1	0	2	2
Bill Dahlen, ss	.000	5	15	1	0	0	0	0	1	3	2	3
Art Devlin, 3b	.250	5	16	0	4	1	0	0	1	1	3	3
Mike Donlin, of	.263	5	19	4	5	1	0	0	1	2	1	2
Billy Gilbert, 2b	.235	5	17	1	4	0	0	0	2	0	2	1
Christy Mathewson, p	.250	3	8	1	2	0	0	0	0	1	1	0
Dan McGann, 1b	.235	5	17	1	4	2	0	0	4	2	7	0
Joe McGinnity, p	.000	2	5	0	0	0	0	0	0	0	2	0
Sam Mertes, of	.176	5	17	2	3	1	0	0	2	2	5	0
Sammy Strang, ph	.000	1	1	0	0	0	0	0	0	0	1	0
TOTAL	.203		153	15	31	7	0	0	13	15	26	12

PITCHER	W	L	ERA	G	GS	CG	SV	SHO	IP	H	ER	BB	SO
Red Ames	0	0	0.00	1	0	0	0	0	1.0	1	0	1	1
Christy Mathewson	3	0	0.00	3	3	3	0	3	27.0	14	0	1	18
Joe McGinnity	1	1	0.00	2	2	1	0	1	17.0	10	0	3	6
TOTAL	4	1	0.00	6	5	4	0	4	45.0	25	0	5	25

PHI (A)

PLAYER/POS	AVG	G	AB	R	H	2B	3B	HR	RB	BB	SO	SB
Chief Bender, p	.000	2	5	0	0	0	0	0	0	0	1	0
Andy Coakley, p	.000	1	2	0	0	0	0	0	0	0	1	0
Lave Cross, 3b	.105	5	19	0	2	0	0	0	0	1	1	0
Monte Cross, ss	.176	5	17	0	3	0	0	0	0	0	7	0
Harry Davis, 1b	.200	5	20	0	4	1	0	0	0	0	1	0
Topsy Hartsel, of	.294	5	17	1	5	1	0	0	0	2	1	2
Danny Hoffman, ph	.000	1	1	0	0	0	0	0	0	0	1	0
Bris Lord, of	.100	5	20	0	2	0	0	0	2	0	5	0
Danny Murphy, 2b	.188	5	16	0	3	1	0	0	0	0	2	0
Eddie Plank, p	.167	2	6	0	1	0	0	0	0	0	2	0
Mike Powers, c	.143	3	7	0	1	1	0	0	0	0	0	0
Ossee Schreckengost, c	.222	3	9	2	2	1	0	0	0	0	0	0
Socks Seybold, of	.125	5	16	0	2	0	0	0	0	2	3	0
TOTAL	.161		155	3	25	5	0	0	2	5	25	2

PITCHER	W	L	ERA	G	GS	CG	SV	SHO	IP	H	ER	BB	SO
Chief Bender	1	1	1.06	2	2	2	0	1	17.0	9	2	6	13
Andy Coakley	0	1	2.00	1	1	1	0	0	9.0	8	2	5	2
Eddie Plank	0	2	1.59	2	2	2	0	0	17.0	14	3	4	11
TOTAL	1	4	1.47	5	5	5	0	1	43.0	31	7	15	26

GAME 1 AT PHI OCT 9

NY	000	020	001		3	10	1
PHI	000	000	000		0	4	0

Pitchers: MATHEWSON vs PLANK
Attendance: 17,955

GAME 2 AT NY OCT 10

PHI	001	000	020		3	6	2
NY	000	000	000		0	4	2

Pitchers: BENDER vs McGINNITY, Ames (9)
Attendance: 24,992

GAME 3 AT PHI OCT 12

NY	200	050	002		9	9	1
PHI	000	000	000		0	4	5

Pitchers: MATHEWSON vs COAKLEY
Attendance: 10,991

GAME 4 AT NY OCT 13

PHI	000	000	000		0	5	2
NY	000	100	00X		1	4	1

Pitchers: PLANK vs McGINNITY
Attendance: 13,598

GAME 5 AT NY OCT 14

PHI	000	000	000		0	6	0
NY	000	010	01X		2	5	1

Pitchers: BENDER vs MATHEWSON
Attendance: 24,187

The Cubs and White Sox have played more postseason City Series than any other clubs, but this was their only all-Chicago World Series. The Cubs were the clear favorites: league leaders in batting, fielding, and pitching (with a team ERA of only 1.76). They were one of baseball's greatest teams ever, with a still-record 116 wins, finishing 20 games ahead of the second-place Giants. The White Sox, by contrast, although their pitching and fielding were good enough to rank second in the American League, were the junior circuit's weakest hitters, batting as a team only .230, 32 points below the Cubs. But in the Series the "hitless wonders" prevailed. Though they hit only .198 and yielded eight unearned runs to the Cubs' two, the Sox bunched their hits for 20 earned runs—double the Cubs' total. Meanwhile, Sox pitchers held the Cubs to a .196 BA, and produced a team ERA less than half that of Cub pitchers.

Game One was a pitcher's duel as the Cubs' Mordecai (Three Finger) Brown and the Sox' Nick Altrock traded four-hitters and one earned run apiece. But Brown lost the game when his error in the seventh led to the Sox' second run. The Cubs snapped back to take Game Two on Ed Reulbach's one-hit 7–1 win. Although Reulbach issued six walks, he didn't really need the five unearned runs handed his club by Sox errors.

In Game Three the Sox regained the Series lead as Ed Walsh two-hit the Cubs, fanning 12 for the Series' first shutout. The Cubs' Jack Pfiester also pitched shutout ball in eight of his nine innings, but George Rohe's bases-loaded triple in the sixth gave the Sox more than enough to defeat him. Brown brought the Cubs back the next day, evening the Series with a two-hit shutout of his own, winning when Altrock yielded his only run on pairs of singles and sacrifice bunts in the seventh.

The rest of the Series belonged to the hitless wonders, who rocked three Cub pitchers for 12 hits and eight runs to take Game Five, and buried Brown and Orval Overall under 14 hits and another eight runs in Game Six to capture their first world championship.

Chicago White Sox (AL), 4;
Chicago Cubs (NL), 2

CHI (A)

PLAYER/POS	AVG	G	AB	R	H	2B	3B	HR	RB	BB	SO	SB
Nick Altrock, p	.250	2	4	0	1	0	0	0	0	1	1	0
George Davis, ss	.308	3	13	4	4	3	0	0	6	0	1	1
Jiggs Donahue, 1b	.333	6	18	0	6	2	1	0	4	3	3	0
Patsy Dougherty, of	.100	6	20	1	2	0	0	0	1	3	4	2
Eddie Hahn, of	.273	6	22	4	6	0	0	0	0	1	1	0
Frank Isbell, 2b	.308	6	26	4	8	4	0	0	4	0	6	1
Fielder Jones, of	.095	6	21	4	2	0	0	0	0	3	3	0
Ed McFarland, ph	.000	1	1	0	0	0	0	0	0	0	0	0
Bill O'Neill, of	.000	1	1	1	0	0	0	0	0	0	0	0
Frank Owen, p	.000	1	2	0	0	0	0	0	0	0	1	0
George Rohe, 3b	.333	6	21	2	7	1	2	0	4	3	1	2
Billy Sullivan, c	.000	6	21	0	0	0	0	0	0	0	9	0
Lee Tannehill, ss	.111	3	9	1	1	0	0	0	0	0	2	0
Babe Towne, ph	.000	1	1	0	0	0	0	0	0	0	0	0
Ed Walsh, p	.000	2	4	1	0	0	0	0	0	0	3	0
Doc White, p	.000	3	3	0	0	0	0	0	0	0	1	0
TOTAL	.198		187	22	37	10	3	0	19	18	35	6

PITCHER	W	L	ERA	G	GS	CG	SV	SHO	IP	H	ER	BB	SO
Nick Altrock	1	1	1.00	2	2	2	0	0	18.0	11	2	2	5
Frank Owen	0	0	3.00	1	0	0	0	0	6.0	6	2	3	2
Ed Walsh	2	0	1.20	2	2	1	0	1	15.0	7	2	6	17
Doc White	1	1	1.80	3	2	1	1	0	15.0	12	3	7	4
TOTAL	4	2	1.50	8	6	4	1	1	54.0	36	9	18	28

CHI (N)

PLAYER/POS	AVG	G	AB	R	H	2B	3B	HR	RB	BB	SO	SB
Mordecai Brown, p	.333	3	6	0	2	0	0	0	0	0	4	0
Frank Chance, 1b	.238	6	21	3	5	1	0	0	0	2	1	2
Johnny Evers, 2b	.150	6	20	2	3	1	0	0	1	1	3	2
Doc Gessler, ph	.000	2	1	0	0	0	0	0	0	1	0	0
Solly Hofman, of	.304	6	23	3	7	1	0	0	2	3	5	1
Johnny Kling, c	.176	6	17	2	3	1	0	0	0	4	3	0
Pat Moran, ph	.000	2	2	0	0	0	0	0	0	0	0	0
Orval Overall, p	.250	2	4	1	1	1	0	0	0	1	1	0
Jack Pfiester, p	.000	2	2	0	0	0	0	0	0	0	1	0
Ed Reulbach, p	.000	2	3	0	0	0	0	0	0	1	0	0
Frank Schulte, of	.269	6	26	1	7	3	0	0	3	1	3	0
Jimmy Sheckard, of	.000	6	21	0	0	0	0	0	1	2	4	1
Harry Steinfeldt, 3b	.250	6	20	2	5	1	0	0	2	1	0	0
Joe Tinker, ss	.167	6	18	4	3	0	0	0	1	2	2	3
TOTAL	.196		184	18	36	9	0	0	11	18	28	9

PITCHER	W	L	ERA	G	GS	CG	SV	SHO	IP	H	ER	BB	SO
Mordecai Brown	1	2	3.20	3	3	2	0	1	19.2	14	7	4	12
Orval Overall	0	0	2.25	2	0	0	0	0	12.0	10	3	3	8
Jack Pfiester	0	2	6.10	2	1	1	0	0	10.1	7	7	3	11
Ed Reulbach	1	0	2.45	2	2	1	0	0	11.0	6	3	8	4
TOTAL	2	4	3.40	9	6	4	0	1	53.0	37	20	18	35

GAME 1 AT CHI-N OCT 9

CHI-A	000	011	000	2	4	1
CHI-N	000	001	000	1	4	2

Pitchers: ALTROCK vs BROWN
Attendance: 12,693

GAME 2 AT CHI-A OCT 10

CHI-N	031	001	020	7	10	2
CHI-A	000	010	000	1	1	2

Pitchers: REULBACH vs WHITE, Owen (4)
Attendance: 12,595

GAME 3 AT CHI-N OCT 11

CHI-A	000	003	000	3	4	1
CHI-N	000	000	000	0	2	2

Pitchers: WALSH vs PFIESTER
Attendance: 13,667

GAME 4 AT CHI-A OCT 12

CHI-N	000	000	100	1	7	1
CHI-A	000	000	000	0	2	1

Pitchers: BROWN vs ALTROCK
Attendance: 18,385

GAME 5 AT CHI-N OCT 13

CHI-A	102	401	000	8	12	6
CHI-N	300	102	000	6	6	0

Pitchers: WALSH, White (7) vs Reulbach, PFIESTER (3), Overall (4)
Attendance: 23,257

GAME 6 AT CHI-A OCT 14

CHI-N	100	010	001	3	7	0
CHI-A	340	000	01X	8	14	3

Pitchers: BROWN, Overall (2) vs WHITE
Attendance: 19,249

The two-run lead that Detroit took into the bottom of the ninth inning of Game One proved to be its biggest of the Series. And it was short-lived, as Chicago—after Frank Chance's leadoff single—took advantage of a hit batsman, a fumble at third base, and a dropped third strike to even the score. Three scoreless extra innings later, darkness ended the game in a 3–3 tie.

The Tigers pitched well enough in the Series. Wild Bill Donovan and George Mullin, who provided more than 80 percent of Detroit's pitching, allowed only four earned runs each for a combined 1.89 ERA. But Cub pitchers gave up only four earned runs *as a team,* suffocating the Tigers with a team ERA of 0.75. And while Tiger fielders made one less error than the Cubs, their misplays proved more costly, permitting eight unearned runs to the Cubs' two.

Detroit's three-run eighth in the opener provided half of their Series scoring. Nine Tiger hits in Game Two produced only one run, while the Cubs bunched six of their nine hits into two innings for three runs and the Series' first win. In Games Three and Four, while the Tigers were twice again limited to a single run, the Cubs increased their run production to five and six, clustering 40 percent of their hits into two three-run innings, one in each game. Mordecai (Three Finger) Brown wrapped up the Series for Chicago with a shutout, as his Cubs blended a hit in each of the first two innings with three stolen bases and a Tiger error for the game's only two runs.

Detroit's twenty-year-old Ty Cobb, the American League batting, RBI, and stolen base leader in his first full big league season, hit an anemic .200 in the World Series, stealing no bases and driving in no Tiger runs. If there was an offensive hero, it was Cub centerfielder Jimmy Slagle. At age thirty-four, nearing the end of a ten-year major league career, he led both clubs with four RBIs (nearly quadruple his season's per-game output) and six stolen bases.

Chicago Cubs (NL), 4;
Detroit Tigers (AL), 0; tie, 1

CHI (N)

PLAYER/POS	AVG	G	AB	R	H	2B	3B	HR	RB	BB	SO	SB
Mordecai Brown, p	.000	1	3	0	0	0	0	0	0	1	0	0
Frank Chance, 1b	.214	4	14	3	3	1	0	0	0	3	2	3
Johnny Evers, 2b-5,ss-1	.350	5	20	2	7	2	0	0	1	0	1	3
Del Howard, 1b-1	.200	2	5	0	1	0	0	0	0	0	2	1
Johnny Kling, c	.211	5	19	2	4	0	0	0	1	1	4	0
Pat Moran, ph	.000	1	0	0	0	0	0	0	0	0	0	0
Orval Overall, p	.200	2	5	0	1	0	0	0	2	0	1	0
Jack Pfiester, p	.000	1	2	0	0	0	0	0	0	0	1	0
Ed Reulbach, p	.200	2	5	0	1	0	0	0	1	0	0	0
Frank Schulte, of	.250	5	20	3	5	0	0	0	2	1	2	0
Jimmy Sheckard, of	.238	5	21	5	5	2	0	0	2	0	4	1
Jimmy Slagle, of	.273	5	22	3	6	0	0	0	4	2	3	6
Harry Steinfeldt, 3b	.471	5	17	2	8	1	1	0	2	1	2	1
Joe Tinker, ss	.154	5	13	4	2	0	0	0	1	3	3	1
Heinie Zimmerman, 2b	.000	1	1	0	0	0	0	0	0	0	1	0
TOTAL	.257		167	19	43	6	1	0	16	12	26	16

PITCHER	W	L	ERA	G	GS	CG	SV	SHO	IP	H	ER	BB	SO
Mordecai Brown	1	0	0.00	1	1	1	0	1	9.0	7	0	1	4
Orval Overall	1	0	1.00	2	2	1	0	0	18.0	14	2	4	11
Jack Pfiester	1	0	1.00	1	1	1	0	0	9.0	9	1	1	3
Ed Reulbach	1	0	0.75	2	1	1	0	0	12.0	6	1	3	4
TOTAL	4	0	0.75	6	5	4	0	1	48.0	36	4	9	22

DET (A)

PLAYER/POS	AVG	G	AB	R	H	2B	3B	HR	RB	BB	SO	SB
Jimmy Archer, c	.000	1	3	0	0	0	0	0	0	0	1	0
Ty Cobb, of	.200	5	20	1	4	0	1	0	0	0	3	0
Bill Coughlin, 3b	.250	5	20	0	5	0	0	0	0	1	4	1
Sam Crawford, of	.238	5	21	1	5	1	0	0	3	0	3	0
Bill Donovan, p	.000	2	8	0	0	0	0	0	0	0	3	0
Davy Jones, of	.353	5	17	1	6	0	0	0	0	4	0	3
Ed Killian, p	.500	1	2	1	1	0	0	0	0	0	0	0
George Mullin, p	.000	2	6	0	0	0	0	0	0	0	1	0
Charley O'Leary, ss	.059	5	17	0	1	0	0	0	0	1	3	0
Fred Payne, c-1	.250	2	4	0	1	0	0	0	1	0	0	1
Claude Rossman, 1b	.400	5	20	1	8	0	1	0	2	1	0	1
Germany Schaefer, 2b	.143	5	21	1	3	0	0	0	0	0	3	0
Boss Schmidt, c-3	.167	4	12	0	2	0	0	0	0	2	1	0
Ed Siever, p	.000	1	1	0	0	0	0	0	0	0	0	0
TOTAL	.209		172	6	36	1	2	0	6	9	22	6

PITCHER	W	L	ERA	G	GS	CG	SV	SHO	IP	H	ER	BB	SO
Bill Donovan	0	1	1.71	2	2	2	0	0	21.0	17	4	5	16
Ed Killian	0	0	2.25	1	0	0	0	0	4.0	3	1	1	1
George Mullin	0	2	2.12	2	2	2	0	0	17.0	16	4	6	8
Ed Siever	0	1	4.50	1	1	0	0	0	4.0	7	2	0	1
TOTAL	0	4	2.15	6	5	4	0	0	46.0	43	11	12	26

The Tigers won their final game of the season to take their second straight pennant, and the Cubs won their third pennant in a row by defeating the Giants in a replay of an earlier tie. Ty Cobb and Detroit improved on their 1907 Series performance, as Cobb led his club in batting, hits, and RBIs, and the Tigers won a game. But the Cubs as a team hit 90 percentage points higher than Detroit, and outscored them 24–15, to take the Series with relative ease.

In Game One, the Tigers took advantage of the Cubs' ragged fielding to score two runs in the eighth for a 6–5 lead. But in the top of the ninth, the Cubs erupted for five runs on six consecutive singles and a double steal, to win the game. The next day Chicago's Orval Overall held Detroit to four hits and one ninth-inning run. The Tigers' Wild Bill Donovan pitched even better for seven innings, holding Pittsburgh to a single in the sixth. But in the eighth, Joe Tinker's two-run homer—the first in a World Series since 1903—began an assault that ended only after six Cubs had crossed the plate.

Detroit finally manufactured a Series win, pummeling Jack Pfiester in Game Three for ten hits (six of them in the sixth inning) and an 8–3 victory. But that was their last burst. As the Series moved to Detroit for Games Four and Five, the Tiger offense collapsed. Three Finger Brown, the winner as a reliever in Game One, won Game Four as a starter, shutting out the Tigers on four hits. The Cubs needed only three of their ten hits, combining them with a couple of walks and stolen bases, and a muffed fly ball, to score twice in the third inning and once in the ninth.

Only 6,210 spectators—the smallest World Series crowd of the century—saw Overall strike out four Tigers in the first inning of Game Five (one reached first on a wild pitch) in what became a three-hit shutout. Meanwhile, his Cubs unloaded for ten hits, defeating Donovan a second time, scoring runs in the first and fifth innings. Overall—after yielding a leadoff walk to Cobb in the fifth—retired Cobb on a force play and set down the final 11 men to face him.

Chicago Cubs (NL), 4;
Detroit Tigers (AL), 1

CHI (N)

PLAYER/POS	AVG	G	AB	R	H	2B	3B	HR	RB	BB	SO	SB
Mordecai Brown, p	.000	2	4	0	0	0	0	0	0	0	2	0
Frank Chance, 1b	.421	5	19	4	8	0	0	0	2	3	1	5
Johnny Evers, 2b	.350	5	20	5	7	1	0	0	2	1	2	2
Solly Hofman, of	.316	5	19	2	6	0	1	0	4	1	4	2
Del Howard, ph	.000	1	1	0	0	0	0	0	0	0	0	0
Johnny Kling, c	.250	5	16	2	4	1	0	0	2	2	2	0
Orval Overall, p	.333	3	6	0	2	0	0	0	0	0	1	0
Jack Pfiester, p	.000	1	2	0	0	0	0	0	0	0	2	0
Ed Reulbach, p	.000	2	3	0	0	0	0	0	0	0	1	0
Frank Schulte, of	.389	5	18	4	7	0	1	0	2	2	1	2
Jimmy Sheckard, of	.238	5	21	2	5	2	0	0	1	2	3	1
Harry Steinfeldt, 3b	.250	5	16	3	4	0	0	0	3	2	5	1
Joe Tinker, ss	.263	5	19	2	5	0	0	1	4	0	2	2
TOTAL	.293		164	24	48	4	2	1	20	13	26	15

PITCHER	W	L	ERA	G	GS	CG	SV	SHO	IP	H	ER	BB	SO
Mordecai Brown	2	0	0.00	2	1	1	0	1	11.0	6	0	1	5
Orval Overall	2	0	0.98	3	2	2	0	1	18.1	7	2	7	15
Jack Pfiester	0	1	7.87	1	1	0	0	0	8.0	10	7	3	1
Ed Reulbach	0	0	4.70	2	1	0	0	0	7.2	9	4	1	5
TOTAL	4	1	2.60	8	5	3	0	2	45.0	32	13	12	26

DET (A)

PLAYER/POS	AVG	G	AB	R	H	2B	3B	HR	RB	BB	SO	SB
Ty Cobb, of	.368	5	19	3	7	1	0	0	4	1	2	2
Bill Coughlin, 3b	.125	3	8	0	1	0	0	0	1	0	1	0
Sam Crawford, of	.238	5	21	2	5	1	0	0	1	1	2	0
Bill Donovan, p	.000	2	4	0	0	0	0	0	0	1	1	1
Red Downs, 2b	.167	2	6	1	1	1	0	0	1	1	2	0
Davy Jones, ph	.000	3	2	1	0	0	0	0	0	1	1	0
Ed Killian, p	.000	1	0	0	0	0	0	0	0	0	0	0
Matty McIntyre, of	.222	5	18	2	4	1	0	0	0	3	2	1
George Mullin, p	.333	1	3	1	1	0	0	0	1	1	0	0
Charley O'Leary, ss	.158	5	19	2	3	0	0	0	0	0	3	0
Claude Rossman, 1b	.211	5	19	3	4	0	0	0	3	1	4	1
Germany Schaefer, 2b-3,3b-2	.125	5	16	0	2	0	0	0	0	1	4	1
Boss Schmidt, c	.071	4	14	0	1	0	0	0	1	0	2	0
Ed Summers, p	.200	2	5	0	1	0	0	0	1	0	2	0
Ira Thomas, c-1	.500	2	4	0	2	1	0	0	1	1	0	0
George Winter, p-1	.000	2	0	0	0	0	0	0	0	0	0	0
TOTAL	.203		158	15	32	5	0	0	14	12	26	6

PITCHER	W	L	ERA	G	GS	CG	SV	SHO	IP	H	ER	BB	SO
Bill Donovan	0	2	4.24	2	2	2	0	0	17.0	17	8	4	10
Ed Killian	0	0	11.57	1	1	0	0	0	2.1	5	3	3	1
George Mullin	1	0	0.00	1	1	1	0	0	9.0	7	0	1	8
Ed Summers	0	2	4.30	2	1	0	0	0	14.2	18	7	4	7
George Winter	0	0	0.00	1	0	0	0	0	1.0	1	0	1	0
TOTAL	1	4	3.68	7	5	3	0	0	44.0	48	18	13	26

GAME 1 AT DET OCT 10

CHI	004	000	105	10	14	2
DET	100	000	320	6	10	4

Pitchers: Reulbach, Overall (7), BROWN (8) vs Killian, SUMMERS (3)
Attendance: 10,812

GAME 2 AT CHI OCT 11

DET	000	000	001	1	4	1
CHI	000	000	06X	6	7	1

Pitchers: DONOVAN vs OVERALL
Home Runs: Tinker-CHI
Attendance: 17,760

GAME 3 AT CHI OCT 12

DET	100	005	020	8	11	4
CHI	000	300	000	3	7	2

Pitchers: MULLIN vs PFIESTER, Reulbach (9)
Attendance: 14,543

GAME 4 AT DET OCT 13

CHI	002	000	001	3	10	0
DET	000	000	000	0	4	1

Pitchers: BROWN vs SUMMERS, Winter (9)
Attendance: 12,907

GAME 5 AT DET OCT 14

CHI	100	010	000	2	10	0
DET	000	000	000	0	3	0

Pitchers: OVERALL vs DONOVAN
Attendance: 6,210

Babe Adams, a twenty-seven-year-old rookie pitcher, was only the fifth biggest winner on the Pittsburgh staff. But his fine 12–3 record was supported by a team-best 1.11 ERA, and manager Fred Clarke started him in the Series opener against Detroit's ace George Mullin (who had led the American League with a career-high 29 wins). Mullin pitched well, giving up only one earned run—manager/outfielder Clarke's homer in the fourth inning. But four Tiger errors led to three Pirate runs in the fifth and sixth. Meanwhile, Adams, after yielding a run in the first, pitched shutout ball the rest of the way for the win.

Detroit came back in Game Two with seven runs (including Ty Cobb's theft of home) as Wild Bill Donovan held the Pirates to two runs on five hits. In Game Three the Pirates took an early lead, which Detroit, despite rallies in the seventh and ninth innings, was unable to overcome. Errors determined most of the scoring, as only one of Detroit's six runs and two of Pittsburgh's eight runs were earned.

Mullin shut out the Pirates on five hits in Game Four, striking out ten men as Detroit scored five runs (all earned, despite Pittsburgh's six errors) to drive out starter Lefty Leifield after four innings. The seesaw Series continued in Game Five, with Babe Adams winning his second game behind his Pirates' ten-hit, eight-run attack. Adams gave up leadoff homers to Davy Jones in the first and Sam Crawford in the eighth. But Pittsburgh's Clarke more than countered these with his three-run shot in the seventh. (All three homers were hit into temporary seats in center field.)

Back in Detroit for Game Six, the Tigers evened the Series for the third time, Mullin winning his second game in a close contest that saw Pittsburgh pull within a run of tying the game in the ninth before a runner thrown out at home and a game-ending double play cut their rally dead.

In the finale it was Babe Adams once again, scattering six Tiger hits for an easy 8–0 win, his third of the Series. Detroit had done better than ever, but still lost their third World Series in three consecutive attempts. A quarter century would pass before they would have a chance to try again.

Pittsburgh Pirates (NL), 4; Detroit Tigers (AL), 3

PIT (N)

PLAYER/POS	AVG	G	AB	R	H	2B	3B	HR	RB	BB	SO	SB
Ed Abbaticchio, ph	.000	1	1	0	0	0	0	0	0	0	0	0
Bill Abstein, 1b	.231	7	26	3	6	2	0	0	2	3	10	1
Babe Adams, p	.000	3	9	0	0	0	0	0	0	1	1	0
Bobby Byrne, 3b	.250	7	24	5	6	1	0	0	0	1	4	1
Howie Camnitz, p	.000	2	1	0	0	0	0	0	0	0	0	0
Fred Clarke, of	.211	7	19	7	4	0	0	2	7	5	3	3
George Gibson, c	.240	7	25	2	6	2	0	0	2	1	1	2
Ham Hyatt, of-1	.000	2	4	1	0	0	0	0	1	1	0	0
Tommy Leach, of-7,3b-1	.360	7	25	8	9	4	0	0	2	2	1	1
Lefty Leifield, p	.000	1	1	0	0	0	0	0	0	0	1	0
Nick Maddox, p	.000	1	4	0	0	0	0	0	0	0	1	0
Dots Miller, 2b	.250	7	28	2	7	1	0	0	4	2	5	3
Paddy O'Connor, ph	.000	1	1	0	0	0	0	0	0	0	1	0
Deacon Phillippe, p	.000	2	1	0	0	0	0	0	0	0	1	0
Honus Wagner, ss	.333	7	24	4	8	2	1	0	6	4	2	6
Vic Willis, p	.000	2	4	0	0	0	0	0	0	0	1	0
Chief Wilson, of	.154	7	26	2	4	1	0	0	1	0	2	1
TOTAL	.224		223	34	50	13	1	2	25	20	34	18

PITCHER	W	L	ERA	G	GS	CG	SV	SHO	IP	H	ER	BB	SO
Babe Adams	3	0	1.33	3	3	3	0	1	27.0	18	4	6	11
Howie Camnitz	0	1	9.82	2	1	0	0	0	3.2	8	4	2	2
Lefty Leifield	0	1	11.25	1	1	0	0	0	4.0	7	5	1	0
Nick Maddox	1	0	1.00	1	1	1	0	0	9.0	10	1	2	4
Deacon Phillippe	0	0	0.00	2	0	0	0	0	6.0	2	0	1	2
Vic Willis	0	1	3.97	2	1	0	0	0	11.1	10	5	8	3
TOTAL	4	3	2.80	11	7	4	0	1	61.0	55	19	20	22

DET (A)

PLAYER/POS	AVG	G	AB	R	H	2B	3B	HR	RB	BB	SO	SB
Donie Bush, ss	.261	7	23	5	6	1	0	0	3	5	3	1
Ty Cobb, of	.231	7	26	3	6	3	0	0	5	2	2	2
Sam Crawford, of-7,1b-1	.250	7	28	4	7	3	0	1	4	1	1	1
Jim Delahanty, 2b	.346	7	26	2	9	4	0	0	4	2	5	0
Bill Donovan, p	.000	2	4	0	0	0	0	0	0	0	1	0
Davy Jones, of	.233	7	30	6	7	0	0	1	1	2	1	1
Tom Jones, 1b	.250	7	24	3	6	1	0	0	2	2	0	1
Matty McIntyre, of-1	.000	4	3	0	0	0	0	0	0	0	1	0
George Moriarty, 3b	.273	7	22	4	6	1	0	0	1	3	1	0
George Mullin, p-4	.188	6	16	1	3	1	0	0	0	1	3	0
Charley O'Leary, 3b	.000	1	3	0	0	0	0	0	0	0	0	0
Boss Schmidt, c	.222	6	18	4	4	2	0	0	4	2	0	0
Oscar Stanage, c	.200	2	5	0	1	0	0	0	2	0	2	0
Ed Summers, p	.000	2	3	0	0	0	0	0	0	0	2	0
Ed Willett, p	.000	2	2	0	0	0	0	0	0	0	0	0
Ralph Works, p	.000	1	0	0	0	0	0	0	0	0	0	0
TOTAL	.236		233	28	55	16	0	2	26	20	22	6

PITCHER	W	L	ERA	G	GS	CG	SV	SHO	IP	H	ER	BB	SO
Bill Donovan	1	1	3.00	2	2	1	0	0	12.0	7	4	8	7
George Mullin	2	1	2.25	4	3	3	0	1	32.0	23	8	8	20
Ed Summers	0	2	8.59	2	2	0	0	0	7.1	13	7	4	4
Ed Willett	0	0	0.00	2	0	0	0	0	7.2	3	0	0	1
Ralph Works	0	0	9.00	1	0	0	0	0	2.0	4	2	0	2
TOTAL	3	4	3.10	11	7	4	0	1	61.0	50	21	20	34

GAME 1 AT PIT OCT 8

DET	100	000	000	1	6	4
PIT	000	121	00X	4	5	0

Pitchers: MULLIN vs ADAMS
Home Runs: Clarke-PIT
Attendance: 29,264

GAME 2 AT PIT OCT 9

DET	023	020	000	7	9	3
PIT	200	000	000	2	5	1

Pitchers: DONOVAN vs CAMNITZ, Willis (3)
Attendance: 30,915

GAME 3 AT DET OCT 11

PIT	510	000	002	8	10	3
DET	000	000	402	6	10	5

Pitchers: MADDOX vs SUMMERS, Willett (1), Works (8)
Attendance: 18,277

GAME 4 AT DET OCT 12

PIT	000	000	000	0	5	6
DET	020	300	00X	5	8	0

Pitchers: LEIFIELD, Phillippe (5) vs MULLIN
Attendance: 17,036

GAME 5 AT PIT OCT 13

DET	100	002	010	4	6	1
PIT	111	000	41X	8	10	2

Pitchers: SUMMERS, Willett (8) vs ADAMS
Home Runs: D.Jones-DET, Crawford-DET, Clarke-PIT
Attendance: 21,706

GAME 6 AT DET OCT 14

PIT	300	000	001	4	7	3
DET	100	211	00X	5	10	3

Pitchers: WILLIS, Camnitz (6), Phillippe (7) vs MULLIN
Attendance: 10,535

GAME 7 AT DET OCT 16

PIT	020	203	010	8	7	0
DET	000	000	000	0	6	3

Pitchers: ADAMS vs DONOVAN, Mullin (4)
Attendance: 17,562

Pitcher Jack Coombs burst into stardom in 1910, emerging as the ace of a Philadelphia pitching staff which dominated the American League with an ERA of only 1.79. Coombs himself led league pitchers with 31 wins and 13 shutouts, and finished second to Chicago's Ed Walsh with an ERA of 1.30—all career bests. He continued his domination into the World Series, pitching three complete-game victories in the Athletics' surprisingly easy triumph over the Cubs.

The Series' finest pitching performance, though, was turned in by the A's Chief Bender in the opener. Only two batters reached base over the first eight innings—on a single and walk—and both of them were cut down trying to steal second. In the ninth, two Cub singles and two Athletic errors produced an unearned run, but as the A's had scored four runs (Bender himself providing the margin of victory with the game's second RBI in the second inning), the Cubs' run did no damage.

Coombs started Game Two and gave up a Cub run in the top of the first inning. But Athletic bats were hot in the Series (their team .316 batting average stood as a Series record for fifty years), and their 14 hits in this game (including four doubles and six runs in the seventh) sank Three Finger Brown and gave Coombs an easy win. Connie Mack also started Coombs in Game Three, two days later, and again the result was a lopsided win. Coombs himself drove in three of his team's 12 runs, and right fielder Danny Murphy added three more with the Series' only home run.

Bender pitched Game Four and suffered the A's only loss, as the Cubs tied the game at 3–3 with a run in the bottom of the ninth, and won it for reliever Three Finger Brown with a two-out RBI single an inning later.

Coombs faced Brown a second time in Game Five. Both clubs made nine hits, but the A's put four of them together with a walk, a wild pitch, and two stolen bases for five runs in the eighth to sink Brown as they had in Game Two, breaking a tight game wide open for Coombs's third win and the Athletics' first world championship.

Philadelphia Athletics (AL), 4; Chicago Cubs (NL), 1

PHI (A)

PLAYER/POS	AVG	G	AB	R	H	2B	3B	HR	RB	BB	SO	SB
Frank Baker, 3b	.409	5	22	6	9	3	0	0	4	2	1	0
Jack Barry, ss	.235	5	17	3	4	2	0	0	3	1	3	0
Chief Bender, p	.333	2	6	1	2	0	0	0	1	1	1	0
Eddie Collins, 2b	.429	5	21	5	9	4	0	0	3	2	0	4
Jack Coombs, p	.385	3	13	0	5	1	0	0	3	0	3	0
Harry Davis, 1b	.353	5	17	5	6	3	0	0	2	3	4	0
Topsy Hartsel, of	.200	1	5	2	1	0	0	0	0	0	1	2
Jack Lapp, c	.250	1	4	0	1	0	0	0	1	0	2	0
Bris Lord, of	.182	5	22	3	4	2	0	0	1	1	3	0
Danny Murphy, of	.350	5	20	6	7	3	0	1	9	1	0	1
Amos Strunk, of	.278	4	18	2	5	1	1	0	2	2	5	0
Ira Thomas, c	.250	4	12	2	3	0	0	0	1	4	1	0
TOTAL	.316		177	35	56	19	1	1	30	17	24	7

PITCHER	W	L	ERA	G	GS	CG	SV	SHO	IP	H	ER	BB	SO
Chief Bender	1	1	1.93	2	2	2	0	0	18.2	12	4	4	14
Jack Coombs	3	0	3.33	3	3	3	0	0	27.0	23	10	14	17
TOTAL	4	1	2.76	5	5	5	0	0	45.2	35	14	18	31

CHI (N)

PLAYER/POS	AVG	G	AB	R	H	2B	3B	HR	RB	BB	SO	SB
Jimmy Archer, c-2,1b-1	.182	3	11	1	2	1	0	0	0	0	3	0
Ginger Beaumont, ph	.000	3	2	1	0	0	0	0	0	1	1	0
Mordecai Brown, p	.000	3	7	0	0	0	0	0	0	0	1	0
Frank Chance, 1b	.353	5	17	1	6	1	1	0	4	0	3	0
King Cole, p	.000	1	2	0	0	0	0	0	0	0	2	0
Solly Hofman, of	.267	5	15	2	4	0	0	0	2	4	3	0
Johnny Kane, pr	.000	1	0	0	0	0	0	0	0	0	0	0
Johnny Kling, c-3	.077	5	13	0	1	0	0	0	1	1	2	0
Harry McIntire, p	.000	2	1	0	0	0	0	0	0	0	1	0
Tom Needham, ph	.000	1	1	0	0	0	0	0	0	0	0	0
Orval Ovall, p	.000	1	1	0	0	0	0	0	0	0	0	0
Jack Pfiester, p	.000	1	2	0	0	0	0	0	0	0	1	0
Ed Reulbach, p	.000	1	0	0	0	0	0	0	0	0	0	0
Lew Richie, p	.000	1	0	0	0	0	0	0	0	0	0	0
Frank Schulte, of	.353	5	17	3	6	3	0	0	2	2	3	0
Jimmy Sheckard, of	.286	5	14	5	4	2	0	0	1	7	2	1
Harry Steinfeldt, 3b	.100	5	20	2	2	1	0	0	1	0	4	0
Joe Tinker, ss	.333	5	18	2	6	2	0	0	0	2	2	1
Heinie Zimmerman, 2b	.235	5	17	0	4	1	0	0	2	1	3	1
TOTAL	.222		158	15	35	11	1	0	13	18	31	3

PITCHER	W	L	ERA	G	GS	CG	SV	SHO	IP	H	ER	BB	SO
Mordecai Brown	1	2	5.50	3	2	1	0	0	18.0	23	11	7	14
King Cole	0	0	3.38	1	1	0	0	0	8.0	10	3	3	5
Harry Mc Intire	0	1	6.75	2	0	0	0	0	5.1	4	4	3	3
Orval Overall	0	1	9.00	1	1	0	0	0	3.0	6	3	1	1
Jack Pfiester	0	0	0.00	1	0	0	0	0	6.2	9	0	1	1
Ed Reulbach	0	0	9.00	1	1	0	0	0	2.0	3	2	2	0
Lew Richie	0	0	0.00	1	0	0	0	0	1.0	1	0	0	0
TOTAL	1	4	4.70	10	5	1	0	0	44.0	56	23	17	24

GAME 1 AT PHI OCT 17

CHI	000 000 001	1	3	1
PHI	021 000 01X	4	7	2

Pitchers: OVERALL, McIntire (4) vs BENDER
Attendance: 26,891

GAME 2 AT PHI OCT 18

CHI	100 000 101	3	8	3
PHI	002 010 60X	9	14	4

Pitchers: BROWN, Richie (8) vs COOMBS
Attendance: 24,597

GAME 3 AT CHI OCT 20

PHI	125 000 400	12	15	1
CHI	120 000 020	5	6	5

Pitchers: COOMBS vs Reulbach, McINTIRE (3), Pfiester (3)
Home Runs: Murphy-PHI
Attendance: 26,210

GAME 4 AT CHI OCT 22

PHI	001 200 000 0	3	11	3
CHI	100 100 001 1	4	9	1

Pitchers: BENDER vs Cole, BROWN (9)
Attendance: 19,150

GAME 5 AT CHI OCT 23

PHI	100 010 050	7	9	1
CHI	010 000 010	2	9	2

Pitchers: COOMBS vs BROWN
Attendance: 27,374

Connie Mack's pitching aces out-dueled Christy Mathewson, and Frank Baker hit two crucial home runs to become "Home Run" Baker forever more, as the A's avenged their 1905 Series loss to the Giants. Game One, though, belonged to Matty and New York. Philadelphia scored first, but the Giants tied the game with an unearned run in the fourth inning, and won it with two doubles in the seventh, setting at naught Chief Bender's otherwise splendid 11-strikeout performance.

The A's came back to take three in a row. In Game Two Eddie Plank held the Giants to one run and Baker hit the first of his homers, breaking a tie in the sixth with a two-run blast off Rube Marquard. The next day, the A's and Jack Coombs handed Mathewson his first World Series loss. Both pitchers went the distance in an 11-inning duel that saw Matty hold the A's scoreless through eight, only to give up a game-tying home run to Baker in the ninth, and two unearned runs in the eleventh. Coombs, meanwhile, pitched two-hit, one-run ball through ten innings. In the last of the eleventh, a third Giant hit and an A's error let in a second Giant run, but the rally died when Beals Becker was cut down for the final out trying to steal second.

After a week of rain, Mathewson and Bender squared off in Game Four. The Giants jumped on Bender for two runs in the first, and held the lead until the fourth. But in the last of the fourth, three successive A's doubles and a run-scoring fly put the A's in front to stay as Bender held New York scoreless over the final 8 innings.

In Game Five, a three-run homer by the A's Rube Oldring off Rube Marquard in the third provided the only scoring through 6½ innings. But the Giants crept back with one run in the seventh, and two more in the last of the ninth tied the score. Plank replaced Coombs for the A's in the tenth and took the loss as Larry Doyle led off with a double, took third on a missed force play, and scored on Fred Merkle's fly to deep right.

After five closely contested games, Game Six was a laugher. It, too, was close at first—tied 1–1 after 3½ innings. But the A's scored four runs in the fourth on singles and errors, once in the sixth, and seven times in the seventh on a barrage of hits, an error, and a two-run wild pitch. Chief Bender, who gave up only four hits and two unearned runs, was the beneficiary of this largesse, taking his second win of the Series and giving the A's their second consecutive world title.

Philadelphia Athletics (AL), 4; New York Giants (NL), 2

PHI (A)

PLAYER/POS	AVG	G	AB	R	H	2B	3B	HR	RB	BB	SO	SB
Frank Baker, 3b	.375	6	24	7	9	2	0	2	5	1	5	0
Jack Barry, ss	.368	6	19	2	7	4	0	0	2	0	2	2
Chief Bender, p	.091	3	11	0	1	0	0	0	0	0	1	0
Eddie Collins, 2b	.286	6	21	4	6	1	0	0	1	2	2	2
Jack Coombs, p	.250	2	8	1	2	0	0	0	0	0	0	0
Harry Davis, 1b	.208	6	24	3	5	1	0	0	5	0	3	0
Jack Lapp, c	.250	2	8	1	2	0	0	0	0	0	1	0
Bris Lord, of	.185	6	27	3	5	2	0	0	1	0	5	0
Stuffy McInnis, 1b	.000	1	0	0	0	0	0	0	0	0	0	0
Danny Murphy, of	.304	6	23	4	7	3	0	0	3	0	3	0
Rube Oldring, of	.200	6	25	2	5	2	0	1	3	0	5	0
Eddie Plank, p	.000	2	3	0	0	0	0	0	0	0	0	0
Amos Strunk, pr	.000	1	0	0	0	0	0	0	0	0	0	0
Ira Thomas, c	.083	4	12	1	1	0	0	0	1	1	2	0
TOTAL	.244		205	27	50	15	0	3	21	4	31	4

PITCHER	W	L	ERA	G	GS	CG	SV	SHO	IP	H	ER	BB	SO
Chief Bender	2	1	1.04	3	3	3	0	0	26.0	16	3	8	20
Jack Coombs	1	0	1.35	2	2	1	0	0	20.0	11	3	6	16
Eddie Plank	1	1	1.86	2	1	1	0	0	9.2	6	2	0	8
TOTAL	4	2	1.29	7	6	5	0	0	55.2	33	8	14	44

NY (N)

PLAYER/POS	AVG	G	AB	R	H	2B	3B	HR	RB	BB	SO	SB
Red Ames, p	.500	2	2	0	1	0	0	0	0	0	1	0
Beals Becker, ph	.000	3	3	0	0	0	0	0	0	0	0	0
Doc Crandall, p-2	.500	3	2	1	1	1	0	0	1	0	0	0
Josh Devore, of	.167	6	24	1	4	1	0	0	3	1	8	0
Larry Doyle, 2b	.304	6	23	3	7	3	1	0	1	2	1	2
Art Fletcher, ss	.130	6	23	1	3	1	0	0	1	0	4	0
Buck Herzog, 3b	.190	6	21	3	4	2	0	0	0	2	3	2
Rube Marquard, p	.000	3	2	0	0	0	0	0	0	0	0	0
Christy Mathewson, p	.286	3	7	0	2	0	0	0	0	1	3	0
Fred Merkle, 1b	.150	6	20	1	3	1	0	0	1	2	6	0
Chief Meyers, c	.300	6	20	2	6	2	0	0	2	0	3	0
Red Murray, of	.000	6	21	0	0	0	0	0	0	2	5	0
Fred Snodgrass, of	.105	6	19	1	2	0	0	0	1	2	7	0
Art Wilson, c	.000	1	1	0	0	0	0	0	0	0	0	0
Hooks Wiltse, p	.000	2	1	0	0	0	0	0	0	0	1	0
TOTAL	.175		189	13	33	11	1	0	10	14	44	4

PITCHER	W	L	ERA	G	GS	CG	SV	SHO	IP	H	ER	BB	SO
Red Ames	0	1	2.25	2	1	0	0	0	8.0	6	2	1	6
Doc Crandall	1	0	0.00	2	0	0	0	0	4.0	2	0	0	2
Rube Marquard	0	1	1.54	3	2	0	0	0	11.2	9	2	1	8
Christy Mathewson	1	2	2.00	3	3	2	0	0	27.0	25	6	2	13
Hooks Wiltse	0	0	18.90	2	0	0	0	0	3.1	8	7	0	2
TOTAL	2	4	2.83	12	6	2	0	0	54.0	50	17	4	31

GAME 1 AT NY OCT 14

PHI	010	000	000	1	6	2
NY	000	100	10X	2	5	0

Pitchers: BENDER vs MATHEWSON
Attendance: 38,281

GAME 2 AT PHI OCT 16

NY	010	000	000	1	5	3
PHI	100	002	00X	3	4	0

Pitchers: MARQUARD, Crandall (8) vs PLANK
Home Runs: Baker-PHI
Attendance: 26,286

GAME 3 AT NY OCT 17

PHI	000	000	001	02	3	9	2
NY	001	000	000	01	2	3	5

Pitchers: COOMBS vs MATHEWSON
Home Runs: Baker-PHI
Attendance: 37,216

GAME 4 AT PHI OCT 24

NY	200	000	000	2	7	3
PHI	000	310	00X	4	11	1

Pitchers: MATHEWSON, Wiltse (8) vs BENDER
Attendance: 24,355

GAME 5 AT NY OCT 25

PHI	003	000	000	0	3	7	1
NY	000	000	102	1	4	9	2

Pitchers: Coombs, PLANK (10) vs Marquard, Ames (4), CRANDALL (8)
Home Runs: Oldring-PHI
Attendance: 33,228

GAME 6 AT PHI OCT 26

NY	100	000	001	2	4	3
PHI	001	401	70X	13	13	5

Pitchers: AMES, Wiltse (5), Marquard (7) vs BENDER
Attendance: 20,485

The Giants outhit the Red Sox by 50 percentage points, and their pitchers let in one less earned run per game. But this was the Series in which Fred Snodgrass's famous muff of a routine fly to center in the tenth inning of the final game helped turn a slim Giant lead into a Red Sox world championship. In all fairness, it must be admitted that Snodgrass followed his muff with a brilliant catch off the next batter, and indecision by the catcher and first baseman permitted a pop foul to drop, keeping the Sox alive to score the tying and winning runs. For that matter, this final game might not have been needed at all if Snodgrass and Beals Becker hadn't both been cut down trying to steal second in the eleventh inning of Game Two, which ended in a tie because of darkness. If either had gone on to score, the Giants would have won the Series in seven games.

Boston's Smokey Joe Wood followed up his spectacular 34–5 regular season with Series wins in Games One and Four, before being rocked for six runs in the first inning of Game Seven for a loss. Relieving in the eighth inning of the finale, he stopped the Giants for two innings, but gave up what would have been the losing run in the tenth had not the Giants' fielding in the last of the inning turned the game around, giving Wood the win and the Sox the Series.

Although Wood won three games, the best pitching of the Series was turned in by the Giants' Rube Marquard and Boston's Hugh Bedient. Marquard (who in the regular season had tied a major league record with 19 consecutive wins) won two of his club's three victories (Games Three and Six), allowing three runs—only one of them earned. Bedient, in two starts and two relief appearances, matched Marquard's 0.50 earned run average, winning a duel with Christy Mathewson in Game Five, and hurling seven effective innings against Matty in the finale.

Mathewson was the Series' hard-luck pitcher: his one tie and two losses were all decided by unearned runs.

Boston Red Sox (AL), 4; New York Giants (NL), 3; tie, 1

BOS (A)

PLAYER/POS	AVG	G	AB	R	H	2B	3B	HR	RB	BB	SO	SB
Neal Ball, ph	.000	1	1	0	0	0	0	0	0	0	1	0
Hugh Bedient, p	.000	4	6	0	0	0	0	0	0	0	0	0
Hick Cady, c	.136	7	22	1	3	0	0	0	1	0	3	0
Bill Carrigan, c	.000	2	7	0	0	0	0	0	0	0	0	0
Ray Collins, p	.000	2	5	0	0	0	0	0	0	0	2	0
Clyde Engle, ph	.333	3	3	1	1	1	0	0	2	0	0	0
Larry Gardner, 3b	.179	8	28	4	5	2	1	1	4	2	5	0
Charley Hall, p	.750	2	4	0	3	1	0	0	0	1	0	0
Olaf Henricksen, ph	1.000	2	1	0	1	1	0	0	1	0	0	0
Harry Hooper, of	.290	8	31	3	9	2	1	0	2	4	4	2
Duffy Lewis, of	.156	8	32	4	5	3	0	0	2	2	2	0
Buck O'Brien, p	.000	2	2	0	0	0	0	0	0	0	2	0
Tris Speaker, of	.300	8	30	4	9	1	2	0	2	4	2	1
Jake Stahl, 1b	.281	8	32	3	9	2	0	0	2	0	6	2
Heinie Wagner, ss	.167	8	30	1	5	1	0	0	0	3	6	1
Joe Wood, p	.286	4	7	1	2	0	0	0	1	1	0	0
Steve Yerkes, 2b	.250	8	32	3	8	0	2	0	4	2	3	0
TOTAL	.220		273	25	60	14	6	1	21	19	36	6

PITCHER	W	L	ERA	G	GS	CG	SV	SHO	IP	H	ER	BB	SO
Hugh Bedient	1	0	0.50	4	2	1	0	0	18.0	10	2	7	7
Ray Collins	0	0	1.88	2	1	0	0	0	14.1	14	3	0	6
Charley Hall	0	0	3.38	2	0	0	0	0	10.2	11	4	9	1
Buck O'Brien	0	2	5.00	2	2	0	0	0	9.0	12	5	3	4
Joe Wood	3	1	3.68	4	3	2	0	0	22.0	27	9	3	21
TOTAL	4	3	2.80	14	8	3	0	0	74.0	74	23	22	39

NY (N)

PLAYER/POS	AVG	G	AB	R	H	2B	3B	HR	RB	BB	SO	SB
Red Ames, p	.000	1	0	0	0	0	0	0	0	0	0	0
Beals Becker, of-1	.000	2	4	1	0	0	0	0	0	2	0	0
Doc Crandall, p	.000	1	0	0	0	0	0	0	0	0	1	0
Josh Devore, of	.250	7	24	4	6	0	0	0	0	7	5	4
Larry Doyle, 2b	.242	8	33	5	8	1	0	1	2	3	2	2
Art Fletcher, ss	.179	8	28	1	5	1	0	0	3	1	4	1
Buck Herzog, 3b	.400	8	30	6	12	4	1	0	4	1	3	2
Rube Marquard, p	.000	2	4	0	0	0	0	0	0	1	0	0
Christy Mathewson, p	.167	3	12	0	2	0	0	0	0	0	4	0
Moose McCormick, ph	.250	5	4	0	1	0	0	0	1	0	0	0
Fred Merkle, 1b	.273	8	33	9	9	2	1	0	3	0	7	1
Chief Meyers, c	.357	8	28	2	10	1	0	0	3	2	3	1
Red Murray, of	.323	8	31	5	10	4	1	0	5	2	2	0
Tillie Shafer, ss	.000	3	0	0	0	0	0	0	0	0	0	0
Fred Snodgrass, of	.212	8	33	2	7	2	0	0	2	2	5	1
Jeff Tesreau, p	.375	3	8	0	3	0	0	0	2	1	3	0
Art Wilson, c	1.000	2	1	0	1	0	0	0	0	0	0	0
TOTAL	.270		274	31	74	14	4	1	25	22	39	12

PITCHER	W	L	ERA	G	GS	CG	SV	SHO	IP	H	ER	BB	SO
Red Ames	0	0	4.50	1	0	0	0	0	2.0	3	1	1	0
Doc Crandall	0	0	0.00	1	0	0	0	0	2.0	1	0	0	2
Rube Marquard	2	0	0.50	2	2	2	0	0	18.0	14	1	2	9
Christy Mathewson	0	2	1.26	3	3	3	0	0	28.2	23	4	5	10
Jeff Tesreau	1	2	3.13	3	3	1	0	0	23.0	19	8	11	15
TOTAL	3	4	1.71	10	8	6	0	0	73.2	60	14	19	36

GAME 1 AT NY OCT 8

BOS	000	001	300	4	6	1
NY	002	000	001	3	8	1

Pitchers: WOOD vs TESREAU, Crandall (8)
Attendance: 35,730

GAME 2 AT BOS OCT 9

NY	010	100	030	10	6	11	5
BOS	300	010	010	10	6	10	1

Pitchers: Mathewson vs Collins, Hall (8), Bedient (11)
Attendance: 30,148
(Game called at end of eleventh, darkness)

GAME 3 AT BOS OCT 10

NY	010	010	000	2	7	1
BOS	000	000	100	1	7	0

Pitchers: MARQUARD vs O'BRIEN, Bedient (9)
Attendance: 34,624

GAME 4 AT NY OCT 11

BOS	010	100	001	3	8	1
NY	000	000	100	1	9	1

Pitchers: WOOD vs TESREAU, Ames (8)
Attendance: 36,502

GAME 5 AT BOS OCT 12

NY	000	000	100	1	3	1
BOS	002	000	00X	2	5	1

Pitchers: MATHEWSON vs BEDIENT
Attendance: 34,683

GAME 6 AT NY OCT 14

BOS	020	000	000	2	7	2
NY	500	000	00X	5	11	2

Pitchers: O'BRIEN, Collins (2) vs MARQUARD
Attendance: 30,622

GAME 7 AT BOS OCT 15

NY	610	002	101	11	16	4
BOS	010	000	210	4	9	3

Pitchers: TESREAU vs WOOD, Hall (2)
Home Runs: Doyle-NY, Gardner-BOS
Attendance: 32,694

GAME 8 AT BOS OCT 16

NY	001	000	000	1	2	9	2
BOS	000	000	100	2	3	8	5

Pitchers: MATHEWSON vs Bedient, WOOD (8)
Attendance: 17,034

Third baseman Frank Baker and catcher Wally Schang drove in more than 60 percent of the Athletics' runs, as Philadelphia dispatched the Giants in five games. Chief Bender led A's pitchers with two wins, and rookie Bullet Joe Bush hurled a nifty five-hitter in Game Three, but the Series highlights were two duels between the A's Eddie Plank and the Giant's Christy Mathewson. The A's heavy hitting made Bender's wins possible and Bush's win easy, but pitching dominated the Plank-Matty games.

Bender yielded 11 hits in the opener, as did the Giants' pitchers. But five of the game's six extra-base hits belonged to the A's—including Baker's two-run homer and triples by Schang and Eddie Collins—and Bender emerged victorious. In Game Two, Plank and Mathewson pitched shutout ball through nine innings, but in the top of the tenth Matty himself singled in the game's first run and scored the second. Taking a 3–0 lead into the bottom of the inning, he set the A's down in order for New York's only Series win.

In Game Three, Schang's solo homer and Collins's three hits (including his second Series triple) and three RBIs led a 12-hit A's attack which, with Bush's fine pitching, put Philadelphia back into the Series lead. Bender won again in Game Four, shutting out the Giants through six innings as his A's scored six runs. But in the seventh, New York's Fred Merkle homered for three runs, and a single, double, and triple in the eighth brought in two more Giant runs. With his lead cut to a single run, Bender bore down in the ninth and retired the side in order.

Plank avenged his earlier loss with a brilliant two-hitter in Game Five, facing the minimum three batters in eight of the nine innings. (His own error in the fifth—a dropped pop-up—led to the Giants' only run.) Mathewson pitched well, too, yielding only six singles. But four of them came in the first and third innings, combining with two sacrifice flies and an error for three runs. Only one Athletic batter reached base in the final six innings, but with Plank pitching as he was, the game and the title were in Philadelphia's pocket.

Philadelphia Athletics (AL), 4;
New York Giants (NL), 1

PHI (A)

PLAYER/POS	AVG	G	AB	R	H	2B	3B	HR	RB	BB	SO	SB
Frank Baker, 3b	.450	5	20	2	9	0	0	1	7	0	2	1
Jack Barry, ss	.300	5	20	3	6	3	0	0	2	0	0	0
Chief Bender, p	.000	2	8	0	0	0	0	0	1	0	1	0
Joe Bush, p	.250	1	4	0	1	0	0	0	0	0	1	0
Eddie Collins, 2b	.421	5	19	5	8	0	2	0	3	1	2	3
Jack Lapp, c	.250	1	4	0	1	0	0	0	0	0	1	0
Stuffy McInnis, 1b	.118	5	17	1	2	1	0	0	2	0	2	0
Eddie Murphy, of	.227	5	22	2	5	0	0	0	0	2	0	0
Rube Oldring, of	.273	5	22	5	6	0	1	0	0	0	1	1
Eddie Plank, p	.143	2	7	0	1	0	0	0	0	0	0	0
Wally Schang, c	.357	4	14	2	5	0	1	1	6	2	4	0
Amos Strunk, of	.118	5	17	3	2	0	0	0	0	2	2	0
TOTAL	.264		174	23	46	4	4	2	21	7	16	5

PITCHER	W	L	ERA	G	GS	CG	SV	SHO	IP	H	ER	BB	SO
Chief Bender	2	0	4.00	2	2	2	0	0	18.0	19	8	1	9
Joe Bush	1	0	1.00	1	1	1	0	0	9.0	5	1	4	3
Eddie Plank	1	1	0.95	2	2	2	0	0	19.0	9	2	3	7
TOTAL	4	1	2.15	5	5	5	0	0	46.0	33	11	8	19

NY (N)

PLAYER/POS	AVG	G	AB	R	H	2B	3B	HR	RB	BB	SO	SB
George Burns, of	.158	5	19	2	3	2	0	0	1	1	5	1
Claude Cooper, pr	.000	2	0	0	0	0	0	0	0	0	0	1
Doc Crandall, p-2	.000	4	4	0	0	0	0	0	0	0	0	0
Al Demaree, p	.000	1	1	0	0	0	0	0	0	0	0	0
Larry Doyle, 2b	.150	5	20	1	3	0	0	0	2	0	1	0
Art Fletcher, ss	.278	5	18	1	5	0	0	0	4	1	1	1
Eddie Grant, ph	.000	2	1	1	0	0	0	0	0	0	0	0
Buck Herzog, 3b	.053	5	19	1	1	0	0	0	0	0	1	0
Rube Marquard, p	.000	2	1	0	0	0	0	0	0	0	0	0
Christy Mathewson, p	.600	2	5	1	3	0	0	0	1	1	0	0
Moose McCormick, ph	.500	2	2	1	1	0	0	0	0	0	0	0
Larry McLean, c-4	.500	5	12	0	6	0	0	0	2	0	0	0
Fred Merkle, 1b	.231	4	13	3	3	0	0	1	3	1	2	0
Chief Meyers, c	.000	1	4	0	0	0	0	0	0	0	0	0
Red Murray, of	.250	5	16	2	4	0	0	0	1	2	2	2
Tillie Shafer, of-5,3b-1	.158	5	19	2	3	1	1	0	1	2	3	0
Fred Snodgrass, 1b-1,of-1	.333	2	3	0	1	0	0	0	0	0	0	0
Jeff Tesreau, p	.000	2	2	0	0	0	0	0	0	0	1	0
Art Wilson, c	.000	3	3	0	0	0	0	0	0	0	2	0
Hooks Wiltse, 1b	.000	2	2	0	0	0	0	0	0	0	1	0
TOTAL	.201		164	15	33	3	1	1	15	8	19	5

PITCHER	W	L	ERA	G	GS	CG	SV	SHO	IP	H	ER	BB	SO
Doc Crandall	0	0	3.86	2	0	0	0	0	4.2	4	2	0	2
Al Demaree	0	1	4.50	1	1	0	0	0	4.0	7	2	1	0
Rube Marquard	0	1	7.00	2	1	0	0	0	9.0	10	7	3	3
Christy Mathewson	1	1	0.95	2	2	2	0	1	19.0	14	2	2	7
Jeff Tesreau	0	1	6.48	2	1	0	0	0	8.1	11	6	1	4
TOTAL	1	4	3.80	9	5	2	0	1	45.0	46	19	7	16

GAME 1 AT NY OCT 7

PHI	000	320	010	6	11 1
NY	001	030	000	4	11 0

Pitchers: BENDER vs MARQUARD, Crandall (6), Tesreau (8)
Home Runs: Baker-PHI
Attendance: 36,291

GAME 2 AT PHI OCT 8

NY	000	000	000 3	3	7 2
PHI	000	000	000	0	8 2

Pitchers: MATHEWSON vs PLANK
Attendance: 20,563

GAME 3 AT NY OCT 9

PHI	320	000	210	8	12 1
NY	000	010	100	2	5 1

Pitchers: BUSH vs TESREAU, Crandall (7)
Home Runs: Schang-PHI
Attendance: 36,896

GAME 4 AT PHI OCT 10

NY	000	000	320	5	8 2
PHI	010	320	00X	6	9 0

Pitchers: DEMAREE, Marquard (5) vs BENDER
Home Runs: Merkle-NY
Attendance: 20,568

GAME 5 AT NY OCT 11

PHI	102	000	000	3	6 1
NY	000	010	000	1	2 2

Pitchers: PLANK vs MATHEWSON
Attendance: 36,682

The Athletics, easy winners of their fourth pennant in five years, were clear favorites over Boston. But the "Miracle Braves"—who moved from last place to first between July 18 and August 25 and kept going to take the pennant by 10½ games—had the momentum and swept the Series.

Boston pitcher Dick Rudolph (who won 27 games during the season) limited the A's to five hits and an unearned run, to take the opener behind the Braves' heavy hitting, 7–1. But the rest of the games were not won so easily.

Philadelphia's Eddie Plank held the Braves scoreless through eight innings of Game Two, and gave up only one run in the ninth. But the Braves' Bill James (26–7 during the season) allowed only two hits and no runs at all.

Game Three was a seesaw affair not settled until the twelfth inning. Through ten innings, starters Lefty Tyler of Boston and Joe Bush of the A's traded runs. Philadelphia scored one in the top of the first, but Braves' catcher Hank Gowdy doubled in the tying run in the second. The teams traded runs again in the fourth, but no one else crossed the plate until the tenth, when Frank Baker's bases-loaded single drove in two. For the third time, the Braves came back to tie it up. Gowdy opened the last of the tenth with the Series' only home run, and after a walk and single, a sacrifice fly knotted the score. Bill James came on to pitch no-hit ball through the eleventh and twelfth. Bush remained in for the A's, retiring the side in the eleventh. But an inning later Gowdy opened with his third crucial hit of the game, a double. Les Mann replaced him as runner, and after a walk, bunt, and wild throw to third, Mann scampered home with the winning run.

Two of Connie Mack's most promising young pitchers, Bob Shawkey and Herb Pennock (who would later find stardom as New York Yankees), shared the A's pitching in Game Four, and gave up only six hits between them. But a walk and an error led to a Boston run in the fourth, and although Shawkey himself doubled in the tying run a half inning later, two more Braves scored in the last of the fifth on Johnny Evers's single. Pennock came on to pitch three innings of shutout relief, but Rudolph held the A's hitless over the final four innings to preserve his second win and the Braves' crown.

Boston Braves (NL), 4;
Philadelphia Athletics (AL), 0

BOS (N)

PLAYER/POS	AVG	G	AB	R	H	2B	3B	HR	RB	BB	SO	SB
Ted Cather, of	.000	1	5	0	0	0	0	0	0	0	1	0
Joe Connolly, of	.111	3	9	1	1	0	0	0	1	1	1	0
Charlie Deal, 3b	.125	4	16	1	2	2	0	0	0	0	0	2
Josh Devore, ph	.000	1	1	0	0	0	0	0	0	0	1	0
Johnny Evers, 2b	.438	4	16	2	7	0	0	0	2	2	2	1
Larry Gilbert, ph	.000	1	0	0	0	0	0	0	0	1	0	0
Hank Gowdy, c	.545	4	11	3	6	3	1	1	3	5	1	1
Bill James, p	.000	2	4	0	0	0	0	0	0	0	4	0
Les Mann, of-2	.286	3	7	1	2	0	0	0	1	0	1	0
Rabbit Maranville, ss	.308	4	13	1	4	0	0	0	3	1	1	2
Herbie Moran, of	.077	3	13	2	1	1	0	0	0	1	1	1
Dick Rudolph, p	.333	2	6	1	2	0	0	0	0	1	1	0
Butch Schmidt, 1b	.294	4	17	2	5	0	0	0	2	0	2	1
Lefty Tyler, p	.000	1	3	0	0	0	0	0	0	0	1	0
Possum Whitted, of	.214	4	14	2	3	0	1	0	2	3	1	1
TOTAL	.244		135	16	33	6	2	1	14	15	18	9

PITCHER	W	L	ERA	G	GS	CG	SV	SHO	IP	H	ER	BB	SO
Bill James	2	0	0.00	2	1	1	0	1	11.0	2	0	6	9
Dick Rudolph	2	0	0.50	2	2	2	0	0	18.0	12	1	4	15
Lefty Tyler	0	0	3.60	1	1	0	0	0	10.0	8	4	3	4
TOTAL	4	0	1.15	5	4	3	0	1	39.0	22	5	13	28

PHI (A)

PLAYER/POS	AVG	G	AB	R	H	2B	3B	HR	RB	BB	SO	SB
Frank Baker, 3b	.250	4	16	0	4	2	0	0	2	1	3	0
Jack Barry, ss	.071	4	14	1	1	0	0	0	0	1	3	1
Chief Bender, p	.000	1	2	0	0	0	0	0	0	0	0	0
Joe Bush, p	.000	1	5	0	0	0	0	0	0	0	2	0
Eddie Collins, 2b	.214	4	14	0	3	0	0	0	1	2	1	1
Jack Lapp, c	.000	1	1	0	0	0	0	0	0	0	0	0
Stuffy McInnis, 1b	.143	4	14	2	2	1	0	0	0	3	3	0
Eddie Murphy, of	.188	4	16	2	3	2	0	0	0	2	2	0
Rube Oldring, of	.067	4	15	0	1	0	0	0	0	0	5	0
Herb Pennock, p	.000	1	1	0	0	0	0	0	0	0	0	0
Eddie Plank, p	.000	1	2	0	0	0	0	0	0	0	1	0
Wally Schang, c	.167	4	12	1	2	1	0	0	0	1	4	0
Bob Shawkey, p	.500	1	2	0	1	1	0	0	1	0	1	0
Amos Strunk, of	.286	2	7	0	2	0	0	0	0	0	2	0
Jimmy Walsh, of-2	.333	3	6	0	2	1	0	0	1	3	1	0
Weldon Wyckoff, p	1.000	1	1	0	1	1	0	0	0	0	0	0
TOTAL	.172		128	6	22	9	0	0	5	13	28	2

PITCHER	W	L	ERA	G	GS	CG	SV	SHO	IP	H	ER	BB	SO
Chief Bender	0	1	10.13	1	1	0	0	0	5.1	8	6	2	3
Joe Bush	0	1	3.27	1	1	1	0	0	11.0	9	4	4	4
Herb Pennock	0	0	0.00	1	0	0	0	0	3.0	0	0	2	3
Eddie Plank	0	1	1.00	1	1	1	0	0	9.0	7	1	4	6
Bob Shawkey	0	1	3.60	1	1	0	0	0	5.0	4	2	2	0
Weldon Wyckoff	0	0	2.45	1	0	0	0	0	3.2	3	1	1	2
TOTAL	0	4	3.41	6	4	2	0	0	37.0	33	14	15	18

GAME 1 AT PHI OCT 9

BOS	020 013 010	7 11 2
PHI	010 000 000	1 5 0

Pitchers: RUDOLPH vs BENDER, Wyckoff (6)
Attendance: 20,562

GAME 2 AT PHI OCT 10

BOS	000 000 001	1 7 1
PHI	000 000 000	0 2 1

Pitchers: JAMES vs PLANK
Attendance: 20,562

GAME 3 AT BOS OCT 12

PHI	100 100 000 200	4 8 2
BOS	010 100 000 201	5 9 1

Pitchers: BUSH vs Tyler, JAMES (11)
Home Runs: Gowdy-BOS
Attendance: 35,520

GAME 4 AT BOS OCT 13

PHI	000 010 000	1 7 0
BOS	000 120 00X	3 6 0

Pitchers: SHAWKEY, Pennock (6) vs RUDOLPH
Attendance: 34,365

In a Series characterized by outstanding pitching, Boston's five runs in Game Five were the most scored by either team. It was also one of the most closely contested Series: the deciding run was not scored until the ninth inning in three of the games, and only in Game One was the margin of victory as much as two runs.

Grover Cleveland Alexander pitched the opener for the Phillies, and while the Red Sox tagged him for eight hits, they were all singles, and not until the eighth inning did one manage to drive a runner home. Boston's Ernie Shore pitched just as well, giving up only five singles and four walks. But two Phillie hits produced a run in the fourth, and an alternating pair of walks and infield hits in the eighth broke the tie with two runs for the Phillies' only win.

The next three games were 2–1 Boston victories. Rube Foster held the Phillies to three hits in Game Two, and led his team at the bat, going 3 for 4, including a double in the fifth. But it was his single in the ninth with a man on second that produced what proved to be the winning run as he retired the side in the bottom of the ninth to preserve his win. Dutch Leonard duplicated Foster's three-hit pitching two days later as the Series moved to Boston's spacious new Braves Field for Game Three. Before a new Series record crowd of 42,300, Leonard defeated the great Alexander, as the Sox' Duffy Lewis—with his third hit of the game—singled over second base to score Harry Hooper from third with two out in the bottom of the ninth.

Ernie Shore returned to the mound for Boston in Game Four, and although he gave up more hits (seven) than he had in Game One, his Sox had scored their two runs before the Phillies put across their one in the eighth.

Rube Foster was not as effective in Game Five as he had been in Game Two, twice giving the Phillies a two-run lead as Phillie first baseman Fred Luderus drove in three runs with a double and a home run. But from the fifth inning on, Foster held Philadelphia scoreless on two hits, while Duffy Lewis evened the score with a two-run homer in the eighth, and Harry Hooper (who had tied the score earlier with a home run in the third) won the game and the Series with a second homer in the top of the ninth.

Boston Red Sox (AL), 4; Philadelphia Phillies (NL), 1

BOS (A)

PLAYER/POS	AVG	G	AB	R	H	2B	3B	HR	RBI	BB	SO	SB
Jack Barry, 2b	.176	5	17	1	3	0	0	0	1	1	2	0
Hick Cady, c	.333	4	6	0	2	0	0	0	0	1	2	0
Bill Carrigan, c	.000	1	2	0	0	0	0	0	0	1	1	0
Rube Foster, p	.500	2	8	0	4	1	0	0	1	0	2	0
Del Gainer, 1b	.333	1	3	1	1	0	0	0	0	0	0	0
Larry Gardner, 3b	.235	5	17	2	4	0	1	0	4	0	1	0
Olaf Henricksen, ph	.000	2	2	0	0	0	0	0	0	0	0	0
Dick Hoblitzel, 1b	.313	5	16	1	5	0	0	0	1	0	1	1
Harry Hooper, of	.350	5	20	4	7	0	0	2	3	2	4	0
Hal Janvrin, ss	.000	1	1	0	0	0	0	0	0	0	0	0
Dutch Leonard, p	.000	1	3	0	0	0	0	0	0	0	2	0
Duffy Lewis, of	.444	5	18	1	8	1	0	1	5	1	4	0
Babe Ruth, ph	.000	1	1	0	0	0	0	0	0	0	0	0
Everett Scott, ss	.056	5	18	0	1	0	0	0	0	0	3	0
Ernie Shore, p	.200	2	5	0	1	0	0	0	0	0	3	0
Tris Speaker, of	.294	5	17	2	5	0	1	0	0	4	1	0
Pinch Thomas, c	.200	2	5	0	1	0	0	0	0	0	0	0
TOTAL	.264		159	12	42	2	2	3	11	11	25	1

PITCHER	W	L	ERA	G	GS	CG	SV	SHO	IP	H	ER	BB	SO
Rube Foster	2	0	2.00	2	2	2	0	0	18.0	12	4	2	13
Dutch Leonard	1	0	1.00	1	1	1	0	0	9.0	3	1	0	6
Ernie Shore	1	1	2.12	2	2	2	0	0	17.0	12	4	8	6
TOTAL	4	1	1.84	5	5	5	0	0	44.0	27	9	10	25

PHI (N)

PLAYER/POS	AVG	G	AB	R	H	2B	3B	HR	RBI	BB	SO	SB
Pete Alexander, p	.200	2	5	0	1	0	0	0	0	0	1	0
Dave Bancroft, ss	.294	5	17	2	5	0	0	0	1	2	2	0
Beals Becker, of	.000	2	0	0	0	0	0	0	0	0	0	0
Ed Burns, c	.188	5	16	1	3	0	0	0	0	1	2	0
Bobby Byrne, ph	.000	1	1	0	0	0	0	0	0	0	0	0
George Chalmers, p	.333	3	0	1	0	0	0	0	0	0	1	0
Gavvy Cravath, of	.125	5	16	2	2	1	1	0	1	2	6	0
Oscar Dugey, pr	.000	2	0	0	0	0	0	0	0	0	0	1
Bill Killefer, ph	.000	1	1	0	0	0	0	0	0	0	0	0
Fred Luderus, 1b	.438	5	16	1	7	2	0	1	6	1	4	0
Erskine Mayer, p	.000	2	4	0	0	0	0	0	0	0	2	0
Bert Niehoff, 2b	.063	5	16	1	1	0	0	0	0	1	5	0
Dode Paskert, of	.158	5	19	2	3	0	0	0	0	1	2	0
Eppa Rixey, p	.500	1	2	0	1	0	0	0	0	0	0	0
Milt Stock, 3b	.118	5	17	1	2	1	0	0	0	1	0	0
Possum Whitted, of-5,1b-1	.067	5	15	0	1	0	0	0	1	1	0	1
TOTAL	.182		148	10	27	4	1	1	9	10	25	2

PITCHER	W	L	ERA	G	GS	CG	SV	SHO	IP	H	ER	BB	SO
Pete Alexander	1	1	1.53	2	2	2	0	0	17.2	14	3	4	10
George Chalmers	0	1	2.25	1	1	1	0	0	8.0	8	2	3	6
Erskine Mayer	0	1	2.38	2	2	1	0	0	11.1	16	3	2	7
Eppa Rixey	0	1	4.05	1	0	0	0	0	6.2	4	3	2	2
TOTAL	1	4	2.27	6	5	4	0	0	43.2	42	11	11	25

GAME 1 AT PHI OCT 8

BOS	000	000	010	1	8	1
PHI	000	100	02X	3	5	1

Pitchers: SHORE vs ALEXANDER
Attendance: 19,343

GAME 2 AT PHI OCT 9

BOS	100	000	001	2	10	0
PHI	000	010	000	1	3	1

Pitchers: FOSTER vs MAYER
Attendance: 20,306

GAME 3 AT BOS OCT 11

PHI	001	000	000	1	3	0
BOS	000	100	001	2	6	1

Pitchers: ALEXANDER vs LEONARD
Attendance: 42,300

GAME 4 AT BOS OCT 12

PHI	000	000	010	1	7	0
BOS	001	001	00X	2	8	1

Pitchers: CHALMERS vs SHORE
Attendance: 41,096

GAME 5 AT PHI OCT 13

BOS	011	000	021	5	10	1
PHI	200	200	000	4	9	1

Pitchers: FOSTER vs Mayer, RIXEY (3)
Home Runs: Hooper-BOS (2),
Lewis-BOS, Luderus-PHI
Attendance: 20,306

In close pennant races, the Red Sox repeated as league champions and Brooklyn won its first pennant since 1900. The first three games of the Series were tightly contested, and the outcomes were determined by only one run apiece. For 6½ innings in the opener, Brooklyn's Rube Marquard dueled Boston's Ernie Shore about equally. But in the last of the seventh the Sox capitalized on a double, some sloppy Brooklyn fielding, and a couple of sacrifice hits for three runs, adding another off reliever Jeff Pfeffer in the eighth for a 6–1 lead. The Robins fought back in the ninth, driving out Shore and drawing within one run of a tie before reliever Carl Mays retired the final man with the bases loaded.

Game Two was even tighter. Boston starter Babe Ruth gave up a first-inning inside-the-park homer to Hy Myers, but in the third he drove in Everett Scott (who had tripled) to tie the game at 1–1. Then for the next ten innings he and Robin pitcher Sherry Smith shut off all scoring. Ruth continued to blank Brooklyn in the fourteenth, and in the last of the inning a walk, sacrifice, and single over the head of the third baseman gave Boston and Ruth the victory.

Brooklyn veteran Jack Coombs took a 4–0 lead into the sixth inning of Game Three before weakening. But after giving up a third Boston run on Larry Gardner's one-out homer in the seventh, he was relieved by Jeff Pfeffer, who set the Sox down in order the rest of the way. In saving what proved to be Coombs's last World Series appearance (as well as the Robins' only Series win), Pfeffer preserved Coombs's perfect Series won-lost record at 5–0.

Games Four and Five proved anticlimactic. In Game Four, Gardner's second homer of the Series— inside the park for three runs in the second inning—overcame the Robins' two runs in the first. The Sox added a run here and there to increase their lead, while Sox starter Dutch Leonard shut Brooklyn out through the final eight innings for a comfortable 6–2 win. And in what became the Series finale, Ernie Shore held the Robins to three singles and one unearned run as his Sox took advantage of a bad-hop triple in the second and two third-inning errors by Robin shortstop Ivy Olson to take the lead—and their fourth world championship.

Boston Red Sox (AL), 4;
Brooklyn Robins (NL), 1

BOS (A)

PLAYER/POS	AVG	G	AB	R	H	2B	3B	HR	RB	BB	SO	SB
Hick Cady, c	.250	2	4	1	1	0	0	0	0	3	0	0
Bill Carrigan, c	.667	1	3	0	2	0	0	0	1	0	1	0
Rube Foster, p	.000	1	1	0	0	0	0	0	0	0	1	0
Del Gainer, ph	1.000	1	1	0	1	0	0	0	1	0	0	0
Larry Gardner, 3b	.176	5	17	2	3	0	0	2	6	0	2	0
Olaf Henricksen, ph	.000	1	0	1	0	0	0	0	0	1	0	0
Dick Hoblitzel, 1b	.235	5	17	3	4	1	1	0	2	6	0	0
Harry Hooper, of	.333	5	21	6	7	1	1	0	1	3	1	1
Hal Janvrin, 2b	.217	5	23	2	5	3	0	0	1	0	6	0
Dutch Leonard, p	.000	1	3	0	0	0	0	0	0	1	3	0
Duffy Lewis, of	.353	5	17	3	6	2	1	0	1	2	1	0
Carl Mays, p	.000	2	1	0	0	0	0	0	0	0	1	0
Mike McNally, pr	.000	1	0	1	0	0	0	0	0	0	0	0
Babe Ruth, p	.000	1	5	0	0	0	0	0	1	0	2	0
Everett Scott, ss	.125	5	16	1	2	0	1	0	1	1	1	0
Ernie Shore, p	.000	2	7	0	0	0	0	0	0	0	2	0
Chick Shorten, of	.571	2	7	0	4	0	0	0	2	0	1	0
Pinch Thomas, c	.143	3	7	0	1	0	1	0	0	0	1	0
Tilly Walker, of	.273	3	11	1	3	0	1	0	1	1	2	0
Jimmy Walsh, of	.000	1	3	0	0	0	0	0	0	0	0	0
TOTAL	.238		164	21	39	7	6	2	18	18	25	1

PITCHER	W	L	ERA	G	GS	CG	SV	SHO	IP	H	ER	BB	SO
Rube Foster	0	0	0.00	1	0	0	0	0	3.0	3	0	0	1
Dutch Leonard	1	0	1.00	1	1	1	0	0	9.0	5	1	4	3
Carl Mays	0	1	5.06	2	1	0	1	0	5.1	8	3	3	2
Babe Ruth	1	0	0.64	1	1	1	0	0	14.0	6	1	3	4
Ernie Shore	2	0	1.53	2	2	1	0	0	17.2	12	3	4	9
TOTAL	4	1	1.47	7	5	3	1	0	49.0	34	8	14	19

BRO (N)

PLAYER/POS	AVG	G	AB	R	H	2B	3B	HR	RB	BB	SO	SB
Larry Cheney, p	.000	1	0	0	0	0	0	0	0	0	0	0
Jack Coombs, p	.333	1	3	0	1	0	0	0	1	0	0	0
George Cutshaw, 2b	.105	5	19	2	2	1	0	0	2	1	1	0
Jake Daubert, 1b	.176	4	17	1	3	0	1	0	0	2	3	0
Wheezer Dell, p	.000	1	0	0	0	0	0	0	0	0	0	0
Gus Getz, ph	.000	1	1	0	0	0	0	0	0	0	0	0
Jimmy Johnston, of-2	.300	3	10	1	3	0	0	0	0	1	0	0
Rube Marquard, p	.000	2	3	0	0	0	0	0	0	0	1	0
Fred Merkle, 1b-1	.250	3	4	0	1	0	0	0	1	2	0	0
Chief Meyers, c	.200	3	10	0	2	0	1	0	0	1	0	0
Otto Miller, c	.125	2	8	0	1	0	0	0	0	0	1	0
Harry Mowery, 3b	.176	5	17	2	3	0	0	0	1	3	2	0
Hy Myers, of	.182	5	22	2	4	0	1	1	3	0	3	0
Ivy Olson, ss	.250	5	16	1	4	0	1	0	2	2	2	0
Ollie O'Mara, ph	.000	1	1	0	0	0	0	0	0	0	1	0
Jeff Pfeffer, p-3	.250	4	4	0	1	0	0	0	0	0	2	0
Nap Rucker, p	.000	1	0	0	0	0	0	0	0	0	0	0
Sherry Smith, p	.200	1	5	0	1	0	0	0	0	0	0	0
Casey Stengel, of-3	.364	4	11	2	4	0	0	0	0	1	0	0
Zack Wheat, of	.211	5	19	2	4	0	1	0	1	2	2	1
TOTAL	.200		170	13	34	2	5	1	11	14	19	1

PITCHER	W	L	ERA	G	GS	CG	SV	SHO	IP	H	ER	BB	SO
Larry Cheney	0	0	3.00	1	0	0	0	0	3.0	4	1	1	5
Jack Coombs	1	0	4.26	1	1	0	0	0	6.1	7	3	1	1
Wheezer Dell	0	0	0.00	1	0	0	0	0	1.0	1	0	0	0
Rube Marquard	0	2	6.55	2	2	0	0	0	11.0	12	8	6	9
Jeff Pfeffer	0	1	1.69	3	1	0	1	0	10.2	7	2	4	5
Nap Rucker	0	0	0.00	1	0	0	0	0	2.0	1	0	0	3
Sherry Smith	0	1	1.35	1	1	1	0	0	13.1	7	2	6	2
TOTAL	1	4	3.04	10	5	1	1	0	47.1	39	16	18	25

GAME 1 AT BOS OCT 7

BRO	000 100 004	5	10	4
BOS	001 010 31X	6	8	1

Pitchers: MARQUARD, Pfeffer (8) vs SHORE, Mays (9)
Attendance: 36,117

GAME 2 AT BOS OCT 9

BRO	100 000 000 000 00	1	6	2
BOS	001 000 000 000 01	2	7	1

Pitchers: SMITH vs RUTH
Home Runs: H.Myers-BRO
Attendance: 41,373

GAME 3 AT BRO OCT 10

BOS	000 002 100	3	7	1
BRO	001 120 00X	4	10	0

Pitchers: MAYS, Foster (6) vs COOMBS, Pfeffer (7)
Home Runs: Gardner-BOS
Attendance: 21,087

GAME 4 AT BRO OCT 11

BOS	030 110 100	6	10	1
BRO	200 000 000	2	5	4

Pitchers: LEONARD vs MARQUARD, Cheney (5), Rucker (8)
Home Runs: Gardner-BOS
Attendance: 21,662

GAME 5 AT BOS OCT 12

BRO	010 000 000	1	3	3
BOS	012 010 00X	4	7	2

Pitchers: PFEFFER, Dell (8) vs SHORE
Attendance: 42,620

Easy winners in their pennant races, the White Sox and Giants traded pairs of victories in the Series before the Sox came up with a second pair to take the title in six games. In the opener, Happy Felsch's solo homer in the fourth inning gave Sox starter Eddie Cicotte the margin he needed to defeat Giant Slim Sallee 2–1, and in Game Two Red Faber went all the way, as his Sox broke a 2–2 tie in the fourth inning with five runs on six singles for Chicago's second win.

The clubs traveled to New York for Games Three and Four, and Giant pitchers rewarded their fans with a pair of shutouts to even the Series. In Game Three, a triple, double, and single against the Sox' Cicotte in the fourth inning produced the only scoring, as Giant Rube Benton blanked the Sox on five hits, walking none. Giant ace Ferdie Schupp (a 21-game winner during the season) did the honors in Game Four, scattering seven hits, as teammate Benny Kauff, with his first Series hit in the fourth inning, homered inside the park to deep center against Red Faber for the deciding run. Two later runs against Faber and two more in the eighth (on Kauff's second homer) against reliever Dave Danforth made Schupp's win easy.

But Faber, the loser in Game Four, came in to pitch two innings of perfect relief two days later in Chicago for his second win, as the Sox rebounded from a 2–5 deficit with three runs in the bottom of the seventh to tie the game and three more an inning later to win it.

After a day of rest and a return to New York, Faber was given his third start. He pitched well enough, but his third win and the Series clincher was really the gift of some infamous Giant fielding. In the fourth inning, the first two Sox batters—Eddie Collins and Joe Jackson—reached on a high throw to first and a dropped fly. Happy Felsch, the third man up, reached on a fielder's choice as Giant third baseman Heinie Zimmerman chased Collins across the plate in a botched rundown. Jackson and Felsch scored the second and third unearned runs as Chick Gandil singled off the hapless Rube Benton. The Giants recovered to score two runs an inning later, but Faber shut them out the rest of the way to give his Sox the Series.

Chicago White Sox (AL), 4; New York Giants (NL), 2

CHI (A)

PLAYER/POS	AVG	G	AB	R	H	2B	3B	HR	RB	BB	SO	SB
Eddie Cicotte, p	.143	3	7	0	1	0	0	0	0	1	2	0
Eddie Collins, 2b	.409	6	22	4	9	1	0	0	2	2	3	3
Shano Collins, of	.286	6	21	2	6	1	0	0	0	0	2	0
Dave Danforth, p	.000	1	0	0	0	0	0	0	0	0	0	0
Red Faber, p	.143	4	7	0	1	0	0	0	0	2	3	0
Happy Felsch, of	.273	6	22	4	6	1	0	1	3	1	5	0
Chick Gandil, 1b	.261	6	23	1	6	1	0	0	5	0	2	1
Joe Jackson, of	.304	6	23	4	7	0	0	0	2	1	0	1
Nemo Leibold, of	.400	2	5	1	2	0	0	0	2	1	1	0
Byrd Lynn, ph	.000	1	1	0	0	0	0	0	0	0	1	0
Fred McMullin, 3b	.125	6	24	1	3	1	0	0	2	1	6	0
Swede Risberg, ph	.500	2	2	0	1	0	0	0	1	0	0	0
Reb Russell, p	.000	1	0	0	0	0	0	0	0	0	0	0
Ray Schalk, c	.263	6	19	1	5	0	0	0	0	2	1	1
Buck Weaver, ss	.333	6	21	3	7	1	0	0	1	0	2	0
Lefty Williams, p	.000	1	0	0	0	0	0	0	0	0	0	0
TOTAL	.274		197	21	54	6	0	1	18	11	28	6

PITCHER	W	L	ERA	G	GS	CG	SV	SHO	IP	H	ER	BB	SO
Eddie Cicotte	1	1	1.96	3	2	2	0	0	23.0	23	5	2	13
Dave Danforth	0	0	18.00	1	0	0	0	0	1.0	3	2	0	2
Red Faber	3	1	2.33	4	3	2	0	0	27.0	21	7	3	9
Reb Russell	0	0	INF	1	1	0	0	0	0.0	2	1	1	0
Lefty Williams	0	0	9.00	1	0	0	0	0	1.0	2	1	0	3
TOTAL	4	2	2.77	10	6	4	0	0	52.0	51	16	6	27

NY (N)

PLAYER/POS	AVG	G	AB	R	H	2B	3B	HR	RB	BB	SO	SB
Fred Anderson, p	.000	1	0	0	0	0	0	0	0	0	0	0
Rube Benton, p	.000	2	4	0	0	0	0	0	0	0	3	0
George Burns, of	.227	6	22	3	5	0	0	0	2	2	6	1
Art Fletcher, ss	.200	6	25	2	5	1	0	0	0	0	2	0
Buck Herzog, 2b	.250	6	24	1	6	0	1	0	2	1	4	0
Walter Holke, 1b	.286	6	21	2	6	2	0	0	1	0	6	0
Benny Kauff, of	.160	6	25	2	4	1	0	2	5	0	2	1
Lew McCarty, c-2	.400	3	5	1	2	0	1	0	1	0	0	0
Pol Perritt, p	1.000	3	2	0	2	0	0	0	0	0	0	0
Bill Rariden, c	.385	5	13	2	5	0	0	0	2	2	1	0
Dave Robertson, of	.500	6	22	3	11	1	1	0	1	0	0	2
Slim Sallee, p	.167	2	6	0	1	0	0	0	0	1	2	0
Ferdie Schupp, p	.250	2	4	0	1	0	0	0	0	1	1	0
Jeff Tesreau, p	.000	1	0	0	0	0	0	0	0	0	0	0
Jim Thorpe, of	.000	1	0	0	0	0	0	0	0	0	0	0
Joe Wilhoit, ph	.000	2	1	0	0	0	0	0	0	1	0	0
Heinie Zimmerman, 3b	.120	6	25	1	3	0	1	0	0	0	0	0
TOTAL	.256		199	17	51	5	4	2	16	6	27	4

PITCHER	W	L	ERA	G	GS	CG	SV	SHO	IP	H	ER	BB	SO
Fred Anderson	0	1	18.00	1	0	0	0	0	2.0	5	4	0	3
Rube Benton	1	1	0.00	2	2	1	0	1	14.0	9	0	1	8
Pol Perritt	0	0	2.16	3	0	0	0	0	8.1	9	2	3	3
Slim Sallee	0	2	5.28	2	2	1	0	0	15.1	20	9	4	4
Ferdie Schupp	1	0	1.74	2	2	1	0	1	10.1	11	2	2	9
Jeff Tesreau	0	0	0.00	1	0	0	0	0	1.0	0	0	1	1
TOTAL	2	4	3.00	11	6	3	0	2	51.0	54	17	11	28

GAME 1 AT CHI OCT 6

NY	000 010 000	1	7	1
CHI	001 100 00X	2	7	1

Pitchers: SALLEE vs CICOTTE
Home Runs: Felsch-CHI
Attendance: 32,000

GAME 2 AT CHI OCT 7

NY	020 000 000	2	8	1
CHI	020 500 00X	7	14	1

Pitchers: Schupp, ANDERSON (2), Perritt (4), Tesreau (8) vs FABER
Attendance: 32,000

GAME 3 AT NY OCT 10

CHI	000 000 000	0	5	3
NY	000 200 00X	2	8	2

Pitchers: CICOTTE vs BENTON
Attendance: 33,616

GAME 4 AT NY OCT 11

CHI	000 000 000	0	7	0
NY	000 110 12X	5	10	1

Pitchers: FABER, Danforth (8) vs SCHUPP
Home Runs: Kauff-NY (2)
Attendance: 27,746

GAME 5 AT CHI OCT 13

NY	200 200 100	5	12	3
CHI	001 001 33X	8	14	6

Pitchers: SALLEE, Perritt (8) vs Russell, Cicotte (1), Williams (7), FABER (8)
Attendance: 27,323

GAME 6 AT NY OCT 15

CHI	000 300 001	4	7	1
NY	000 020 000	2	6	3

Pitchers: FABER vs BENTON, Perritt (6)
Attendance: 33,969

Although both clubs had lost key players to military service, so had other major league teams, and after a season shortened by a month because of the war, the Red Sox and Cubs found themselves opponents in an early-September World Series.

In the opener, Babe Ruth pushed his string of consecutive scoreless World Series innings to 22, holding the Cubs to six singles as he went the distance. The Cubs' Hippo Vaughn pitched just as well, but two of the five singles he yielded followed a leadoff walk in the fourth and produced the game's only run. Chicago evened the Series in Game Two, bunching four of their seven hits after a walk in the second inning to take a 3–0 lead. Successive triples in Boston's ninth spoiled Lefty Tyler's shutout but not his victory.

Hippo Vaughn lost another close one in Game Three when he gave up two runs in the fourth inning on a hit batsman and a succession of singles. The Cubs got him one run back in the fifth, but the Sox' Carl Mays held Chicago to that one run as he hurled Boston back into the Series lead. Ruth pushed the Sox farther ahead the next day in another squeaker. As he continued his mastery over Cub hitters, he drove Boston into the lead with a two-run triple in the fourth inning (his only Series hit). But in the eighth a run-scoring ground out ended his record setting string of scoreless innings at 29⅔, and a single drove in another run to tie the game. The Sox, though, scored a third run on a Chicago error in the last of the eighth, and reliever Bullet Joe Bush shut down a threat in the ninth to save Ruth's win.

Vaughn, in his third start, finally found what was needed for victory—a shutout, on five hits, as the Cubs added hits to walks from Boston's Sad Sam Jones in the third and eighth to push across their three runs. But in Game Six the Sox scored two unearned runs on a dropped line drive to right in the third inning. It was their only scoring off Lefty Tyler, but Boston's Carl Mays was on his way to a one-run three-hitter that brought the Red Sox their fifth world championship in five tries. To date, although they have tried four more times, they have not won a sixth.

Boston Red Sox (AL), 4;
Chicago Cubs (NL), 2

BOS (A)

PLAYER/POS	AVG	G	AB	R	H	2B	3B	HR	RB	BB	SO	SB
Sam Agnew, c	.000	4	9	0	0	0	0	0	0	0	0	0
Joe Bush, p	.000	2	2	0	0	0	0	0	0	1	0	0
Jean Dubuc, ph	.000	1	1	0	0	0	0	0	0	0	1	0
Harry Hooper, of	.200	6	20	0	4	0	0	0	0	2	2	0
Sam Jones, p	.000	1	1	0	0	0	0	0	0	1	0	0
Carl Mays, p	.200	2	5	1	1	0	0	0	0	1	0	0
Stuffy McInnis, 1b	.250	6	20	2	5	0	0	0	1	1	1	0
Hack Miller, ph	.000	1	1	0	0	0	0	0	0	0	0	0
Babe Ruth, p-2,of-2	.200	3	5	0	1	0	1	0	2	0	2	0
Wally Schang, c	.444	5	9	1	4	0	0	0	1	2	3	1
Everett Scott, ss	.095	6	21	0	2	0	0	0	1	1	1	0
Dave Shean, 2b	.211	6	19	2	4	1	0	0	0	4	3	1
Amos Strunk, of	.174	6	23	1	4	1	1	0	0	0	5	0
Fred Thomas, 3b	.125	6	16	0	2	0	0	0	0	1	2	0
George Whiteman, of	.250	6	20	2	5	0	1	0	1	2	1	1
TOTAL	.186		172	9	32	2	3	0	6	16	21	3

PITCHER	W	L	ERA	G	GS	CG	SV	SHO	IP	H	ER	BB	SO
Joe Bush	0	1	3.00	2	1	1	1	0	9.0	7	3	3	0
Sam Jones	0	1	3.00	1	1	1	0	0	9.0	7	3	5	5
Carl Mays	2	0	1.00	2	2	2	0	0	18.0	10	2	3	5
Babe Ruth	2	0	1.06	2	2	1	0	1	17.0	13	2	7	4
TOTAL	4	2	1.70	7	6	5	1	1	53.0	37	10	18	14

CHI (N)

PLAYER/POS	AVG	G	AB	R	H	2B	3B	HR	RB	BB	SO	SB
Turner Barber, ph	.000	3	2	0	0	0	0	0	0	0	0	0
Charlie Deal, 3b	.176	6	17	0	3	0	0	0	0	0	1	0
Phil Douglas, p	.000	1	0	0	0	0	0	0	0	0	0	0
Max Flack, of	.263	6	19	2	5	0	0	0	0	4	1	1
Claude Hendrix, p-1	1.000	2	1	0	1	0	0	0	0	0	0	0
Charlie Hollocher, ss	.190	6	21	2	4	0	1	0	1	1	1	1
Bill Killefer, c	.118	6	17	2	2	1	0	0	2	2	0	0
Les Mann, of	.227	6	22	0	5	2	0	0	2	0	0	0
Bill McCabe, ph	.000	3	1	1	0	0	0	0	0	0	0	0
Fred Merkle, 1b	.278	6	18	1	5	0	0	0	1	4	3	0
Bob O'Farrell, c-1	.000	3	3	0	0	0	0	0	0	0	0	0
Dode Paskert, of	.190	6	21	0	4	1	0	0	2	2	2	0
Charlie Pick, 2b	.389	6	18	2	7	1	0	0	0	1	1	1
Lefty Tyler, p	.200	3	5	0	1	0	0	0	2	2	0	0
Hippo Vaughn, p	.000	3	10	0	0	0	0	0	0	0	5	0
Chuck Wortman, 2b	.000	1	1	0	0	0	0	0	0	0	0	0
Rollie Zeider, 3b	.000	2	0	0	0	0	0	0	0	0	2	0
TOTAL	.210		176	10	37	5	1	0	10	18	14	3

PITCHER	W	L	ERA	G	GS	CG	SV	SHO	IP	H	ER	BB	SO
Phil Douglas	0	1	0.00	1	0	0	0	0	1.0	1	0	0	0
Claude Hendrix	0	0	0.00	1	0	0	0	0	1.0	0	0	0	0
Lefty Tyler	1	1	1.17	3	3	1	0	0	23.0	14	3	11	4
Hippo Vaughn	1	2	1.00	3	3	3	0	1	27.0	17	3	5	17
TOTAL	2	4	1.04	8	6	4	0	1	52.0	32	6	16	21

GAME 1 AT CHI SEPT 5

BOS	000	100	000	1	5	0
CHI	000	000	000	0	6	0

Pitchers: RUTH vs VAUGHN
Attendance: 19,274

GAME 2 AT CHI SEPT 6

BOS	000	000	001	1	6	1
CHI	030	000	000	3	7	1

Pitchers: BUSH vs TYLER
Attendance: 20,040

GAME 3 AT CHI SEPT 7

BOS	000	200	000	2	7	0
CHI	000	010	000	1	7	1

Pitchers: MAYS vs VAUGHN
Attendance: 27,054

GAME 4 AT BOS SEPT 9

CHI	000	000	020	2	7	1
BOS	000	200	01X	3	4	0

Pitchers: Tyler, DOUGLAS (8) vs RUTH, Bush (9)
Attendance: 22,183

GAME 5 AT BOS SEPT 10

CHI	001	000	002	3	7	0
BOS	000	000	000	0	5	0

Pitchers: VAUGHN vs JONES
Attendance: 24,694

GAME 6 AT BOS SEPT 11

CHI	000	100	000	1	3	2
BOS	002	000	00X	2	5	0

Pitchers: TYLER, Hendrix (8) vs MAYS
Attendance: 15,238

In the bottom of the first inning of Game One, White Sox pitcher Eddie Cicotte hit the first batter to face him, a prearranged signal to gamblers that "the fix was on"—that the Sox would throw the Series. The eight Chicago conspirators—pitching aces Cicotte and Lefty Williams, outfielders Joe Jackson and Happy Felsch, and infielders Chick Gandil, Buck Weaver, Fred McMullin and Swede Risberg—received no more than a fraction of the $100,000 promised them but "honored" their end of the deal. Cicotte (winner of 29 regular-season games, with a 1.82 ERA) gave up seven hits and six runs in the opening innings of Game One en route to a 1–9 loss, and Williams, though he held the Reds to four hits in Game Two, uncharacteristically walked six and fanned only one, a performance bad enough for a 2–4 loss.

Dickie Kerr, Chicago's third-best pitcher and not in on the fix, won Game Three with a three-hit shutout. But although Cicotte pitched well in Game Four, Chicago lost a third time as the Reds' Jimmy Ring hurled a three-hit shutout of his own (all three hits coming, ironically, off the bats of conspirators Jackson, Felsch, and Gandil).

Cincinnati's Hod Eller beat Chicago in Game Five with the Series' third successive three-hit shutout. Loser Lefty Williams once again yielded only four hits, but three came in a four-run sixth inning which also saw a walk and a throwing error by Felsch. (The win, the Reds' fourth, did not decide the Series, which had been expanded to the best five of nine in the exuberance which followed the end of the Great War.)

Chicago exerted itself to win the next two games. In Game Six, Kerr's second win depended on crucial hits by Jackson and Gandil in the tenth inning; and in Game Seven Cicotte held the Reds to one run as Jackson and Felsch drove in all the Sox' four.

But in Game Eight, Williams gave up two singles and two doubles before being pulled with only one away in the first. Jackson homered in the third. And he doubled and Gandil tripled to drive in three Chicago runs in the eighth. But by then the Reds had scored ten runs on their way to an easy win and their tainted world title.

Cincinnati Reds (NL), 5; Chicago White Sox (AL), 3

CIN (N)

PLAYER/POS	AVG	G	AB	R	H	2B	3B	HR	RBI	BB	SO	SB
Jake Daubert, 1b	.241	8	29	4	7	0	1	0	1	1	2	1
Pat Duncan, of	.269	8	26	3	7	2	0	0	8	2	2	0
Hod Eller, p	.286	2	7	2	2	1	0	0	0	0	2	0
Ray Fisher, p	.500	2	2	0	1	0	0	0	0	0	0	0
Heinie Groh, 3b	.172	8	29	6	5	2	0	0	2	6	4	0
Larry Kopf, ss	.222	8	27	3	6	0	2	0	3	3	2	0
Dolf Luque, p	.000	2	1	0	0	0	0	0	0	0	1	0
Sherry Magee, ph	.500	2	2	0	1	0	0	0	0	0	0	0
Greasy Neale, of	.357	8	28	3	10	1	1	0	4	2	5	1
Bill Rariden, c	.211	5	19	0	4	0	0	0	2	0	0	1
Morrie Rath, 2b	.226	8	31	5	7	1	0	0	2	4	1	2
Jimmy Ring, p	.000	2	5	0	0	0	0	0	0	0	2	0
Edd Roush, of	.214	8	28	6	6	2	1	0	7	3	0	2
Dutch Ruether, p-2	.667	3	6	2	4	1	2	0	4	1	0	0
Slim Sallee, p	.000	2	4	0	0	0	0	0	0	0	0	0
Jimmy Smith, pr	.000	1	0	0	0	0	0	0	0	0	0	0
Ivey Wingo, c	.571	3	7	1	4	0	0	0	1	3	1	0
TOTAL	.255		251	35	64	10	7	0	34	25	22	7

PITCHER	W	L	ERA	G	GS	CG	SV	SHO	IP	H	ER	BB	SO
Hod Eller	2	0	2.00	2	2	2	0	1	18.0	13	4	2	15
Ray Fisher	0	1	2.35	2	1	0	0	0	7.2	7	2	2	2
Dolf Luque	0	0	0.00	2	0	0	0	0	5.0	1	0	0	6
Jimmy Ring	1	1	0.64	2	1	1	0	1	14.0	7	1	6	4
Dutch Ruether	1	0	2.57	2	2	1	0	0	14.0	12	4	4	1
Slim Sallee	1	1	1.35	2	2	1	0	0	13.1	19	2	1	2
TOTAL	5	3	1.63	12	8	5	0	2	72.0	59	13	15	30

CHI (A)

PLAYER/POS	AVG	G	AB	R	H	2B	3B	HR	RBI	BB	SO	SB
Eddie Cicotte, p	.000	3	8	0	0	0	0	0	0	0	3	0
Eddie Collins, 2b	.226	8	31	2	7	1	0	0	1	1	2	1
Shano Collins, of	.250	4	16	2	4	1	0	0	0	0	0	0
Happy Felsch, of	.192	8	26	2	5	1	0	0	3	1	4	0
Chick Gandil, 1b	.233	8	30	1	7	0	1	0	5	1	3	1
Joe Jackson, of	.375	8	32	5	12	3	0	1	6	1	2	0
Bill James, p	.000	1	2	0	0	0	0	0	0	0	1	0
Dickie Kerr, p	.167	2	6	0	1	0	0	0	0	0	0	0
Nemo Leibold, of	.056	5	18	0	1	0	0	0	0	2	3	1
Grover Lowdermilk, p	.000	2	0	0	0	0	0	0	0	0	0	0
Byrd Lynn, c	.000	1	1	0	0	0	0	0	0	0	0	0
Erskine Mayer, p	.000	1	0	0	0	0	0	0	0	0	0	0
Fred McMullin, ph	.500	2	2	0	1	0	0	0	0	0	0	0
Eddie Murphy, ph	.000	3	2	0	0	0	0	0	0	0	1	0
Swede Risberg, ss	.080	8	25	3	2	0	1	0	0	5	3	1
Ray Schalk, c	.304	8	23	1	7	0	0	0	2	4	2	1
Buck Weaver, 3b	.324	8	34	4	11	4	1	0	0	0	2	0
Roy Wilkinson, p	.000	2	2	0	0	0	0	0	0	0	1	0
Lefty Williams, p	.200	3	5	0	1	0	0	0	0	0	3	0
TOTAL	.224		263	20	59	10	3	1	17	15	30	5

PITCHER	W	L	ERA	G	GS	CG	SV	SHO	IP	H	ER	BB	SO
Eddie Cicotte	1	2	2.91	3	3	2	0	0	21.2	19	7	5	7
Bill James	0	0	5.79	1	0	0	0	0	4.2	8	3	3	2
Dickie Kerr	2	0	1.42	2	2	2	0	1	19.0	14	3	3	6
Grover Lowdermilk	0	0	9.00	1	0	0	0	0	1.0	2	1	1	0
Erskine Mayer	0	0	0.00	1	0	0	0	0	1.0	0	0	1	0
Roy Wilkinson	0	0	1.23	2	0	0	0	0	7.1	9	1	4	3
Lefty Williams	0	3	6.61	3	3	1	0	0	16.1	12	12	8	4
TOTAL	3	5	3.42	13	8	5	0	1	71.0	64	27	25	22

The Indians outscored the Robins in the Series, 21 runs to 8. Yet after losing the opener in Brooklyn, the Robins fought back to take the next two, and held the Series lead as the teams traveled to Cleveland for the next four games.

Both clubs garnered five hits in Game One, but an error, walk, single, and double gave the Indians two runs in the second and a lead they never yielded, as Stan Coveleski outlasted Rube Marquard for the win. In Game Two, both clubs increased their hit totals to seven, but the Robins bunched six of theirs into three innings for three runs, while Burleigh Grimes, only once yielding two hits in an inning, shut the Indians out. The two runs Brooklyn scored in the first inning of Game Three were all Sherry Smith needed to give the Robins their second win behind his three-hit pitching. But Brooklyn scored only twice more in the Series as the Indians swept to the championship with four wins in Cleveland.

With the Indians scoring four runs in Game Four before Brooklyn put its one run on the board, Coveleski breezed to his second five-hit Series run. Jim Bagby had it even easier the next day. The Robins tagged him for 13 hits, but not until the ninth inning were they able to put them together for a run. Meanwhile Bagby and his teammates were registering a couple of Series firsts as they moved to an eight-run lead. Right fielder Elmer Smith opened the scoring in the first inning with the first World Series grand slam, and Bagby himself homered for three more in the fourth—the first pitcher to hit a Series home run.

But the 1920 Series is best remembered for second baseman Bill Wambsganss's unassisted triple play in the fifth inning. With runners on first and second going on pitcher Clarence Mitchell's liner, Wambsganss snared the ball for the first out, stepped on second to force one runner, and tagged the runner coming in from first to retire the side.

In Game Six Duster Mails, a late-season addition to the team, shut out Brooklyn on three hits in a 1–0 squeaker over Sherry Smith. Coveleski won the clincher the next day, also via the shutout, with his third five-hitter of the Series and his third Series win.

Cleveland Indians (AL), 5; Brooklyn Robins (NL), 2

CLE (A)

PLAYER/POS	AVG	G	AB	R	H	2B	3B	HR	RB	BB	SO	SB
Jim Bagby, p	.333	2	6	1	2	0	0	1	3	0	0	0
George Burns, 1b-4	.300	5	10	1	3	1	0	0	2	3	3	0
Ray Caldwell, p	.000	1	0	0	0	0	0	0	0	0	0	0
Stan Coveleski, p	.100	3	10	2	1	0	0	0	0	0	4	0
Joe Evans, of	.308	4	13	0	4	0	0	0	0	1	0	0
Larry Gardner, 3b	.208	7	24	1	5	1	0	0	2	1	1	0
Jack Graney, of-2	.000	3	3	0	0	0	0	0	0	0	2	0
Charlie Jamieson, of-5	.333	6	15	2	5	1	0	0	1	1	0	1
Doc Johnston, 1b	.273	5	11	1	3	0	0	0	0	2	1	1
Harry Lunte, 2b	.000	1	0	0	0	0	0	0	0	0	0	0
Duster Mails, p	.000	2	5	0	0	0	0	0	0	0	1	0
Les Nunamaker, c-1	.500	2	2	0	1	0	0	0	0	0	0	0
Steve O'Neill, c	.333	7	21	1	7	3	0	0	2	4	3	0
Joe Sewell, ss	.174	7	23	0	4	0	0	0	0	2	1	0
Elmer Smith, of	.308	5	13	1	4	0	1	1	5	1	1	0
Tris Speaker, of	.320	7	25	6	8	2	1	0	1	3	1	0
Pinch Thomas, c	.000	1	0	0	0	0	0	0	0	0	0	0
George Uhle, p	.000	2	0	0	0	0	0	0	0	0	0	0
Bill Wambsganss, 2b	.154	7	26	3	4	0	0	0	1	2	1	0
Joe Wood, of	.200	4	10	2	2	1	0	0	0	1	2	0
TOTAL	.244		217	21	53	9	2	2	17	21	21	2

PITCHER	W	L	ERA	G	GS	CG	SV	SHO	IP	H	ER	BB	SO
Jim Bagby	1	1	1.80	2	2	1	0	0	15.0	20	3	1	3
Ray Caldwell	0	1	27.00	1	1	0	0	0	0.1	2	1	1	0
Stan Coveleski	3	0	0.67	3	3	3	0	1	27.0	15	2	2	8
Duster Mails	1	0	0.00	2	2	1	0	1	15.2	6	0	6	6
George Uhle	0	0	0.00	2	0	0	0	0	3.0	1	0	0	3
TOTAL	5	2	0.89	10	7	5	0	2	61.0	44	6	10	20

BRO (N)

PLAYER/POS	AVG	G	AB	R	H	2B	3B	HR	RB	BB	SO	SB
Leon Cadore, p	.000	2	0	0	0	0	0	0	0	0	0	0
Tommy Griffith, of	.190	7	21	1	4	2	0	0	3	0	2	0
Burleigh Grimes, p	.333	3	6	1	2	0	0	0	0	0	0	0
Jimmy Johnston, 3b	.214	4	14	2	3	0	0	0	0	0	2	1
Pete Kilduff, 2b	.095	7	21	0	2	0	0	0	1	4	0	0
Ed Konetchy, 1b	.174	7	23	0	4	0	1	0	2	3	2	0
Ernie Krueger, c-3	.167	4	6	0	1	0	0	0	0	0	0	0
Bill Lamar, ph	.000	3	3	0	0	0	0	0	0	0	0	0
Al Mamaux, p	.000	3	1	0	0	0	0	0	0	0	1	0
Rube Marquard, p	.000	2	1	0	0	0	0	0	0	0	0	0
Bill McCabe, pr	.000	1	0	0	0	0	0	0	0	0	0	0
Otto Miller, c	.143	6	14	0	2	0	0	0	0	1	2	0
Clarence Mitchell, p-1	.333	2	3	0	1	0	0	0	0	0	0	0
Hy Myers, of	.231	7	26	0	6	0	0	0	1	0	1	0
Bernie Neis, of-2	.000	4	5	0	0	0	0	0	0	1	0	0
Ivy Olson, ss	.320	7	25	2	8	1	0	0	0	3	1	0
Jeff Pfeffer, p	.000	1	1	0	0	0	0	0	0	0	0	0
Ray Schmandt, ph	.000	1	1	0	0	0	0	0	0	0	0	0
Jack Sheehan, 3b	.182	3	11	0	2	0	0	0	0	0	1	0
Sherry Smith, p	.000	2	6	0	0	0	0	0	0	0	2	0
Zack Wheat, of	.333	7	27	2	9	2	0	0	2	1	2	0
TOTAL	.205		215	8	44	5	1	0	8	10	20	1

PITCHER	W	L	ERA	G	GS	CG	SV	SHO	IP	H	ER	BB	SO
Leon Cadore	0	1	9.00	2	1	0	0	0	2.0	4	2	1	1
Burleigh Grimes	1	2	4.19	3	3	1	0	1	19.1	23	9	9	4
Al Mamaux	0	0	4.50	3	0	0	0	0	4.0	2	2	0	5
Rube Marquard	0	1	1.00	2	1	0	0	0	9.0	7	1	3	6
Clarence Mitchell	0	0	0.00	1	0	0	0	0	4.2	3	0	3	1
Jeff Pfeffer	0	0	3.00	1	0	0	0	0	3.0	4	1	2	1
Sherry Smith	1	1	0.53	2	2	2	0	0	17.0	10	1	3	3
TOTAL	2	5	2.44	14	7	3	0	1	59.0	53	16	21	21

GAME 1 AT BRO OCT 5

CLE	020	100	000	3	5	0
BRO	000	000	100	1	5	1

Pitchers: COVELESKI vs MARQUARD, Mamaux (7), Cadore (9)
Attendance: 23,753

GAME 2 AT BRO OCT 6

CLE	000	000	000	0	7	1
BRO	101	010	00X	3	7	0

Pitchers: BAGBY, Uhle (7) vs GRIMES
Attendance: 22,559

GAME 3 AT BRO OCT 7

CLE	000	100	000	1	3	1
BRO	200	000	00X	2	6	1

Pitchers: CALDWELL, Mails (1), Uhle (8) vs SMITH
Attendance: 25,088

GAME 4 AT CLE OCT 9

BRO	000	100	000	1	5	1
CLE	202	000	00X	5	12	2

Pitchers: CADORE, Mamaux (2), Marquard (3), Pfeffer (6) vs COVELESKI
Attendance: 25,734

GAME 5 AT CLE OCT 10

BRO	000	000	001	1	13	1
CLE	400	310	00X	8	12	2

Pitchers: GRIMES, Mitchell (4) vs BAGBY
Home Runs: E.Smith-CLE, Bagby-CLE
Attendance: 26,884

GAME 6 AT CLE OCT 11

BRO	000	000	000	0	3	0
CLE	000	001	00X	1	7	3

Pitchers: SMITH vs MAILS
Attendance: 27,194

GAME 7 AT CLE OCT 12

BRO	000	000	000	0	5	2
CLE	000	110	10X	3	7	3

Pitchers: GRIMES, Mamaux (8) vs COVELESKI
Attendance: 27,525

Since both the Giants and Yankees called the Polo Grounds home, all eight games were played there, with the two clubs alternating from game to game as the hometeam. Pitching dominated the first two games—especially Yankee pitching. In Game One, Giant third baseman Frank Frisch went 4 for 4 against Carl Mays. But Mays gave up only one other hit and walked no one, to fashion a shutout. The next day Art Nehf of the Giants allowed the Yankees only three singles. But the Yankees capitalized on two of them, together with one of Nehf's seven walks, a couple of Giant errors, and Bob Meusel's steal of home to score three times, as pitcher Waite Hoyt shut out the Giants on two singles to put the Yanks two up in the Series.

In Game Three the hitters finally came alive. With the score tied 4-4 in the last of the seventh, the Giants unloaded for eight hits which, with two walks and a sacrifice fly, produced eight runs and the first Giant win. They evened the Series the next day, scoring three runs in the eighth to take a 3-1 lead, adding another in the ninth. Babe Ruth's first World Series home run, a solo shot in the bottom of the ninth, thrilled the fans but had no effect on the game's outcome.

The Yankees regained the Series lead in Game Five. Waite Hoyt was not as sharp as he had been in the opener, yielding ten hits. But the only run scored against him came as the result of a first-inning error, a deficit his Yankee teammates overcame for a 3-1 win. In Game Six the Yankees took a quick 3-0 lead in the first. The Giants tied it in the top of the second on home runs by Irish Meusel and Frank Snyder, but Chick Fewster hit a two-run shot a half inning later to restore the Yankee lead. In the fourth inning, though, the Giants parlayed four singles and an error into four runs and a lead that held up for a Series-tying win.

The Yankees scored only one run the rest of the way as the Giants took the final two games on unearned runs. In Game Seven, Mays and the Giants' Phil Douglas dueled into the seventh tied 1-1. But in the last of the seventh, Giant Frank Snyder's double drove in Johnny Rawlings, who had reached on an error, for the game's deciding run. In Game Eight, Hoyt held the Giants to four hits and completed his third game without giving up an earned run. But a Giant runner had scored in the first inning when a grounder shot through the legs of shortstop Roger Peckinpaugh. It turned out to be the game's only run, as Art Nehf and his Giants' flawless fielding blanked the Yankees to give manager John McGraw his first world championship since 1905.

New York Giants (NL), 5; New York Yankees (AL), 3

NY (N)

PLAYER/POS	AVG	G	AB	R	H	2B	3B	HR	RB	BB	SO	SB
Dave Bancroft, ss	.152	8	33	3	5	1	0	0	3	1	5	0
Jesse Barnes, p	.444	3	9	3	4	0	0	0	0	0	0	0
George Burns, of	.333	8	33	2	11	4	1	0	2	3	5	1
Phil Douglas, p	.000	3	7	0	0	0	0	0	0	0	2	0
Frankie Frisch, 3b	.300	8	30	5	9	0	1	0	1	4	3	3
George Kelly, 1b	.233	8	30	3	7	1	0	0	4	3	10	0
Irish Meusel, of	.345	8	29	4	10	2	1	1	7	2	3	1
Art Nehf, p	.000	3	9	0	0	0	0	0	0	1	3	0
Johnny Rawlings, 2b	.333	8	30	2	10	3	0	0	4	0	3	0
Earl Smith, c-2	.000	3	7	0	0	0	0	0	0	0	1	0
Frank Snyder, c-6	.364	7	22	4	8	1	0	1	3	0	2	0
Fred Toney, p	.000	2	0	0	0	0	0	0	0	0	0	0
Ross Youngs, of	.280	8	25	3	7	1	1	0	4	7	2	2
TOTAL	.269		264	29	71	13	4	2	28	22	38	7

PITCHER	W	L	ERA	G	GS	CG	SV	SHO	IP	H	ER	BB	SO
Jesse Barnes	2	0	1.65	3	0	0	0	0	16.1	10	3	6	18
Phil Douglas	2	1	2.08	3	3	2	0	0	26.0	20	6	5	17
Art Nehf	1	2	1.38	3	3	3	0	1	26.0	13	4	13	8
Fred Toney	0	0	23.63	2	2	0	0	0	2.2	7	7	3	1
TOTAL	5	3	2.54	11	8	5	0	1	71.0	50	20	27	44

NY (A)

PLAYER/POS	AVG	G	AB	R	H	2B	3B	HR	RB	BB	SO	SB
Frank Baker, 3b-2	.250	4	8	0	2	0	0	0	0	1	0	0
Rip Collins, p	.000	1	0	0	0	0	0	0	0	0	0	0
Al DeVormer, c-1	.000	2	1	0	0	0	0	0	0	0	0	0
Chick Fewster, of	.200	4	10	3	2	0	0	1	2	3	3	0
Harry Harper, p	.000	1	0	0	0	0	0	0	0	0	0	0
Waite Hoyt, p	.222	3	9	0	2	0	0	0	1	0	1	0
Carl Mays, p	.111	3	9	0	1	0	0	0	0	0	1	0
Mike McNally, 3b	.200	7	20	3	4	1	0	0	1	1	3	2
Bob Meusel, of	.200	8	30	3	6	2	0	0	3	2	5	1
Elmer Miller, of	.161	8	31	3	5	1	0	0	2	2	5	0
Roger Peckinpaugh, ss	.179	8	28	2	5	1	0	0	0	4	3	0
Bill Piercy, p	.000	1	0	0	0	0	0	0	0	0	0	0
Wally Pipp, 1b	.154	8	26	1	4	1	0	0	2	2	3	1
Jack Quinn, p	.000	1	2	0	0	0	0	0	0	0	1	0
Tom Rogers, p	.000	1	0	0	0	0	0	0	0	0	0	0
Babe Ruth, of	.313	6	16	3	5	0	0	1	4	5	8	2
Wally Schang, c	.286	8	21	1	6	1	1	0	1	5	4	0
Bob Shawkey, p	.500	2	4	2	2	0	0	0	0	0	1	0
Aaron Ward, 2b	.231	8	26	1	6	0	0	0	4	2	6	0
TOTAL	.207		241	22	50	7	1	2	20	27	44	6

PITCHER	W	L	ERA	G	GS	CG	SV	SHO	IP	H	ER	BB	SO
Rip Collins	0	0	54.00	1	0	0	0	0	0.2	4	4	1	0
Harry Harper	0	0	20.25	1	1	0	0	0	1.1	3	3	2	1
Waite Hoyt	2	1	0.00	3	3	3	0	1	27.0	18	0	11	18
Carl Mays	1	2	1.73	3	3	3	0	1	26.0	20	5	0	9
Bill Piercy	0	0	0.00	1	0	0	0	0	1.0	2	0	0	2
Jack Quinn	0	1	9.82	1	0	0	0	0	3.2	8	4	2	2
Tom Rogers	0	0	6.75	1	0	0	0	0	1.1	3	1	0	1
Bob Shawkey	0	1	7.00	2	1	0	0	0	9.0	13	7	6	5
TOTAL	3	5	3.09	13	8	6	0	2	70.0	71	24	22	38

GAME 1 AT NY -N OCT 5

NY-A	100 011 000	3	7	0
NY-N	000 000 000	0	5	0

Pitchers: MAYS vs DOUGLAS, Barnes (9)
Attendance: 30,202

GAME 2 AT NY -A OCT 6

NY-N	000 000 000	0	2	3
NY-A	000 100 02X	3	3	0

Pitchers: NEHF vs HOYT
Attendance: 34,939

GAME 3 AT NY -N OCT 7

NY-A	004 000 010	5	8	0
NY-N	004 000 81X	13	20	0

Pitchers: Shawkey, QUINN (3), Collins (7), Rogers (8) vs Toney, BARNES (3)
Attendance: 36,509

GAME 4 AT NY -A OCT 9

NY-N	000 000 031	4	9	1
NY-A	000 010 001	2	7	1

Pitchers: DOUGLAS vs MAYS
Home Runs: Ruth-NY(A)
Attendance: 36,372

GAME 5 AT NY -N OCT 10

NY-A	001 200 000	3	6	1
NY-N	100 000 000	1	10	1

Pitchers: HOYT vs NEHF
Attendance: 35,758

GAME 6 AT NY -A OCT 11

NY-N	030 401 000	8	13	0
NY-A	320 000 000	5	7	2

Pitchers: Toney, BARNES (1) vs Harper, SHAWKEY (2), Piercy (9)
Home Runs: E.Meusel-NY(N), Snyder-NY(N), Fewster-NY(A)
Attendance: 34,283

GAME 7 AT NY -N OCT 12

NY-A	010 000 000	1	8	1
NY-N	000 100 10X	2	6	0

Pitchers: MAYS vs DOUGLAS
Attendance: 36,503

GAME 8 AT NY -A OCT 13

NY-N	100 000 000	1	6	0
NY-A	000 000 000	0	4	1

Pitchers: NEHF vs HOYT
Attendance: 25,410

The Giants didn't quite sweep the Series—a tie in Game Two interrupted their string of victories—but they shut down the Yankee offense, holding Yankee scoring to three runs or less per game, and Babe Ruth to two hits and a .118 BA. This Series restored the best-of-seven-games format after three years of best-of-nine.

The Giants had to come from behind to take Game One. Yankee Bullet Joe Bush and Giant Art Nehf hurled shutout ball through five innings before the Yankees scored single runs in the sixth and seventh innings (Ruth driving in the Series' first run for the second year in a row with his single in the sixth). But in the eighth, Bush gave up four straight singles and two runs before Waite Hoyt relieved him with the score tied and men on first and third. Hoyt set down all three men he faced, but the first out—Ross Youngs's fly to center—drove in what proved to be the Giants' winning run.

The Giants led off Game Two with three first-inning runs on Irish Meusel's home run, but scored no more as Bob Shawkey stopped them for nine innings while his Yankees picked up runs in the first, fourth (on Aaron Ward's homer), and eighth to tie it all up. At the end of the tenth, with forty-five minutes left before sundown, the umpires called the game for darkness and provoked a storm of seat cushions and bottles from the stands.

The Giants resumed their winning ways in Game Three behind Jack Scott's shutout. Scott—picked up by the Giants in midseason—gave up only four Yankee hits, walking one, in the Series' top pitching performance. In Game Four the Yankees scored twice in the first inning, but in the fifth the Giants pounced on Carl Mays for four hits and two runs before the first out was recorded. Before the inning ended, a ground out and another hit had brought two more Giants across the plate, enough to survive Aaron Ward's second Series home run for a 4–3 win.

Game Five, the clincher, showed Nehf the winner by two runs at game's end, but the game went back and forth before the outcome was decided. Nehf gave up only five hits—all singles—but all of them contributed toward scoring Yankee runs in the first, fifth, and seventh innings. The Giants took the lead in the second with a pair of runs, but again fell behind until four hits and a walk in the eighth undid Yankee pitcher Joe Bush's fine effort, giving the Giants three additional runs and John McGraw his third world title.

New York Giants (NL), 4;
New York Yankees (AL), 0; tie, 1

NY (N)

PLAYER/POS	AVG	G	AB	R	H	2B	3B	HR	RB	BB	SO	SB
Dave Bancroft, ss	.211	5	19	4	4	0	0	0	2	2	1	0
Jesse Barnes, p	.000	1	4	0	0	0	0	0	0	0	1	0
Bill Cunningham, of	.200	4	10	0	2	0	0	0	2	2	1	0
Frankie Frisch, 2b	.471	5	17	3	8	1	0	0	2	1	0	1
Heinie Groh, 3b	.474	5	19	4	9	0	1	0	0	2	1	0
George Kelly, 1b	.278	5	18	0	5	0	0	0	2	0	3	0
Lee King, of	1.000	2	1	0	1	0	0	0	1	0	0	0
Hugh McQuillan, p	.250	1	4	1	1	1	0	0	0	0	1	0
Irish Meusel, of	.250	5	20	3	5	0	0	1	7	0	1	0
Art Nehf, p	.000	2	3	0	0	0	0	0	0	2	0	0
Rosy Ryan, p	.000	1	0	0	0	0	0	0	0	0	0	0
Jack Scott, p	.250	1	4	0	1	0	0	0	0	0	1	0
Earl Smith, c-1	.143	4	7	0	1	0	0	0	0	0	2	0
Frank Snyder, c	.333	4	15	1	5	0	0	0	0	0	1	0
Casey Stengel, of	.400	2	5	0	2	0	0	0	0	0	1	0
Ross Youngs, of	.375	5	16	2	6	0	0	0	2	3	1	0
TOTAL	.309		162	18	50	2	1	1	18	12	15	1

PITCHER	W	L	ERA	G	GS	CG	SV	SHO	IP	H	ER	BB	SO
Jesse Barnes	0	0	1.80	1	1	1	0	0	10.0	8	2	2	6
Hugh McQuillan	1	0	3.00	1	1	1	0	0	9.0	8	3	2	4
Art Nehf	1	0	2.25	2	2	1	0	0	16.0	11	4	3	6
Rosy Ryan	1	0	0.00	1	0	0	0	0	2.0	1	0	0	2
Jack Scott	1	0	0.00	1	1	1	0	1	9.0	4	0	1	2
TOTAL	4	0	1.76	6	5	4	0	1	46.0	32	9	8	20

NY (A)

PLAYER/POS	AVG	G	AB	R	H	2B	3B	HR	RB	BB	SO	SB
Frank Baker, ph	.000	1	1	0	0	0	0	0	0	0	0	0
Joe Bush, p	.167	2	6	0	1	0	0	0	1	0	0	0
Joe Dugan, 3b	.250	5	20	4	5	1	0	0	0	0	1	0
Waite Hoyt, p	.500	2	2	0	1	0	0	0	0	0	0	0
Sam Jones, p	.000	2	0	0	0	0	0	0	0	0	0	0
Carl Mays, p	.000	1	2	0	0	0	0	0	0	0	0	0
Norm McMillan, of	.000	1	2	0	0	0	0	0	0	0	0	0
Mike McNally, 2b	.000	1	0	0	0	0	0	0	0	0	0	0
Bob Meusel, of	.300	5	20	2	6	1	0	0	2	1	3	1
Wally Pipp, 1b	.286	5	21	0	6	1	0	0	3	0	2	1
Babe Ruth, of	.118	5	17	1	2	1	0	0	1	2	3	0
Wally Schang, c	.188	5	16	0	3	1	0	0	0	0	3	0
Everett Scott, ss	.143	5	14	0	2	0	0	0	1	1	0	0
Bob Shawkey, p	.000	1	4	0	0	0	0	0	0	0	1	0
Elmer Smith, ph	.000	2	2	0	0	0	0	0	0	0	2	0
Aaron Ward, 2b	.154	5	13	3	2	0	0	2	3	3	3	0
Whitey Witt, of	.222	5	18	1	4	1	1	0	0	1	2	0
TOTAL	.203		158	11	32	6	1	2	11	8	20	2

PITCHER	W	L	ERA	G	GS	CG	SV	SHO	IP	H	ER	BB	SO
Joe Bush	0	2	4.80	2	2	1	0	0	15.0	21	8	5	6
Waite Hoyt	0	1	1.13	2	1	0	0	0	8.0	11	1	2	4
Sam Jones	0	0	0.00	2	0	0	0	0	2.0	1	0	1	0
Carl Mays	0	1	4.50	1	1	0	0	0	8.0	9	4	2	1
Bob Shawkey	0	0	2.70	1	1	1	0	0	10.0	8	3	2	4
TOTAL	0	4	3.35	8	5	2	0	0	43.0	50	16	12	15

GAME 1 AT NY -N OCT 4

NY-A	000 001 100	2	7	0
NY-N	000 000 03X	3	11	3

Pitchers: BUSH, Hoyt (8) vs Nehf, RYAN (8)
Attendance: 36,514

GAME 2 AT NY -A OCT 5

NY-N	300 000 000 0	3	8	1
NY-A	100 100 010 0	3	8	0

Pitchers: Barnes vs Shawkey
Home Runs: E.Meusel-NY(N), Ward-NY(A)
Attendance: 37,020

GAME 3 AT NY -N OCT 6

NY-A	000 000 000	0	4	1
NY-N	002 000 10X	3	12	1

Pitchers: HOYT, Jones (8) vs J.SCOTT
Attendance: 37,620

GAME 4 AT NY -A OCT 7

NY-N	000 040 000	4	9	1
NY-A	200 000 100	3	8	0

Pitchers: McQUILLAN vs MAYS, Jones (9)
Home Runs: Ward-NY(A)
Attendance: 36,242

GAME 5 AT NY -N OCT 8

NY-A	100 010 100	3	5	0
NY-N	020 000 03X	5	10	0

Pitchers: BUSH vs NEHF
Attendance: 38,551

After two Series played entirely in the Polo Grounds, the Giants and Yankees in 1923 had Yankee Stadium across the river to play alternate games in. Celebrating the opener in the new "house that Ruth built," the Yankees took an early three-run lead. In the third inning, though, the Giants drove out starter Waite Hoyt, emerging with four runs. Yankee reliever Joe Bush prevented further Giant scoring for several innings as the Yankees picked up a tying run in the seventh. But with the game still knotted in the top of the ninth, Giant Casey Stengel legged out an inside-the-park homer to win it.

Babe Ruth gave Herb Pennock his first World Series win with a pair of homers in Game Two. The first, a solo blast over the roof in right, broke a 1–1 tie in the fourth, and the second, an inning later, concluded Yankee scoring in their 4–2 win that evened the Series. Stengel sent the Giants ahead in the seventh inning of Game Three, lifting a home run over the fence this time for the game's only score. The run gave Art Nehf the win in his duel with Sad Sam Jones, and again gave the Giants the Series lead.

Giant Ross Youngs's fourth hit of Game Four, an inside-the-park homer into the Polo Grounds' deep outfield, gave the Giants a fourth run to lead off the bottom of the ninth, but as a rally it fell short; the Yankees, who had already scored eight, took the game to even the Series. In Game Five Joe Bush gave up only three Giant hits—a single, double, and triple to Irish Meusel. Irish scored the only Giant run, but his Yankee brother Bob drove in three runs with his three hits—sharing RBI honors with Joe Dugan, whose four hits included the Series' third inside-the-park home run, a three-run shot in the second inning. Final score: 8–1.

In Game Six, Herb Pennock yielded four Giant runs in his seven innings on the mound and seemed on the edge of defeat. But in the top of the eighth, Art Nehf (who had pitched one-hit ball since Ruth homered for a Yankee run in the first) lost his stuff. With one out, two singles followed by two walks (on eight pitches) forced in a run. Rosy Ryan replaced Nehf and walked in another run. Ruth struck out, but Bob Meusel's single and a wild throw from center cleared the bases to put the Yankees ahead 6–4, where they remained to game's end for the first of their twenty-two world championships.

New York Yankees (AL), 4; New York Giants (NL), 2

NY (A)

PLAYER/POS	AVG	G	AB	R	H	2B	3B	HR	RB	BB	SO	SB
Joe Bush, p-3	.429	4	7	2	3	1	0	0	1	1	1	0
Joe Dugan, 3b	.280	6	25	5	7	2	1	1	5	3	0	0
Hinky Haines, of	.000	2	1	1	0	0	0	0	0	0	0	0
Harvey Hendrick, ph	.000	1	1	0	0	0	0	0	0	0	0	0
Fred Hofmann, ph	.000	2	1	0	0	0	0	0	0	1	0	0
Waite Hoyt, p	.000	1	1	0	0	0	0	0	0	0	1	0
Ernie Johnson, ss-1	.000	2	0	1	0	0	0	0	0	0	0	0
Sam Jones, p	.000	2	2	0	0	0	0	0	0	0	1	0
Bob Meusel, of	.269	6	26	1	7	1	2	0	8	0	3	0
Herb Pennock, p	.000	3	6	0	0	0	0	0	0	0	2	0
Wally Pipp, 1b	.250	6	20	2	5	0	0	0	2	4	1	0
Babe Ruth, of-6,1b-1	.368	6	19	8	7	1	1	3	3	8	6	0
Wally Schang, c	.318	6	22	3	7	1	0	0	1	0	2	0
Everett Scott, ss	.318	6	22	2	7	0	0	0	3	0	1	0
Bob Shawkey, p	.333	1	3	0	1	0	0	0	1	0	0	0
Aaron Ward, 2b	.417	6	24	4	10	0	0	1	2	1	3	1
Whitey Witt, of	.240	6	25	1	6	2	0	0	4	1	1	0
TOTAL	.293		205	30	60	8	4	5	29	20	22	1

PITCHER	W	L	ERA	G	GS	CG	SV	SHO	IP	H	ER	BB	SO
Joe Bush	1	1	1.08	3	1	1	0	0	16.2	7	2	4	5
Waite Hoyt	0	0	15.43	1	1	0	0	0	2.1	4	4	1	0
Sam Jones	0	1	0.90	2	1	0	0	0	10.0	5	1	2	3
Herb Pennock	2	0	3.63	3	2	1	1	0	17.1	19	7	1	8
Bob Shawkey	1	0	3.52	1	1	0	0	0	7.2	12	3	4	2
TOTAL	4	2	2.83	10	6	2	2	0	54.0	47	17	12	18

NY (N)

PLAYER/POS	AVG	G	AB	R	H	2B	3B	HR	RB	BB	SO	SB
Dave Bancroft, ss	.083	6	24	1	2	0	0	0	1	1	2	1
Virgil Barnes, p	.000	2	1	0	0	0	0	0	0	0	1	0
Jack Bentley, p-2	.600	5	5	0	3	1	0	0	0	0	0	0
Bill Cunningham, of-3	.143	4	7	0	1	0	0	0	1	0	1	0
Frankie Frisch, 2b	.400	6	25	2	10	0	1	0	1	0	0	0
Dinty Gearin, pr	.000	1	0	0	0	0	0	0	0	0	0	0
Hank Gowdy, c-2	.000	3	4	0	0	0	0	0	0	0	1	0
Heinie Groh, 3b	.182	6	22	3	4	0	1	0	2	3	1	0
Travis Jackson, ph	.000	1	1	0	0	0	0	0	0	0	0	0
Claude Jonnard, p	.000	2	0	0	0	0	0	0	0	0	0	0
George Kelly, 1b	.182	6	22	1	4	0	0	0	1	1	2	0
Freddie Maguire, pr	.000	2	0	1	0	0	0	0	0	0	0	0
Hugh McQuillan, p	.000	2	3	0	0	0	0	0	0	0	1	0
Irish Meusel, of	.280	6	25	3	7	1	1	1	2	0	2	0
Art Nehf, p	.167	2	6	0	1	0	0	0	0	0	4	0
Jimmy O'Connell, ph	.000	2	1	0	0	0	0	0	0	0	0	0
Rosy Ryan, p	.000	3	2	0	0	0	0	0	0	0	1	0
Jack Scott, p	.000	2	1	0	0	0	0	0	0	0	0	0
Frank Snyder, c	.118	5	17	1	2	0	0	1	2	0	2	0
Casey Stengel, of	.417	6	12	3	5	0	0	2	4	4	0	0
Mule Watson, p	.000	1	0	0	0	0	0	0	0	0	0	0
Ross Youngs, of	.348	6	23	2	8	0	0	1	3	2	0	0
TOTAL	.234		201	17	47	2	3	5	17	12	18	1

PITCHER	W	L	ERA	G	GS	CG	SV	SHO	IP	H	ER	BB	SO
Virgil Barnes	0	0	0.00	2	0	0	0	0	4.2	4	0	0	4
Jack Bentley	0	1	9.45	2	1	0	0	0	6.2	10	7	4	1
Claude Jonnard	0	0	0.00	2	0	0	0	0	2.0	1	0	1	1
Hugh McQuillan	0	1	5.00	2	1	0	0	0	9.0	11	5	4	3
Art Nehf	1	1	2.76	2	2	1	0	1	16.1	10	5	6	7
Rosy Ryan	1	0	0.96	3	0	0	0	0	9.1	11	1	3	3
Jack Scott	0	1	12.00	2	1	0	0	0	3.0	9	4	1	2
Mule Watson	0	0	13.50	1	1	0	0	0	2.0	4	3	1	1
TOTAL	2	4	4.25	16	6	1	0	1	53.0	60	25	20	22

GAME 1 AT NY -A OCT 10

NY-N	004 000 001	5	8	0
NY-A	120 000 100	4	12	1

Pitchers: Watson, RYAN (3) vs Hoyt, BUSH (3)
Home Runs: Stengel-NY(N)
Attendance: 55,307

GAME 2 AT NY -N OCT 11

NY-A	010 210 000	4	10	0
NY-N	010 001 000	2	9	2

Pitchers: PENNOCK vs McQUILLAN, Bentley (4)
Home Runs: Ward-NY(A), E.Meusel-NY(N), Ruth-NY(A) (2)
Attendance: 40,402

GAME 3 AT NY -A OCT 12

NY-N	000 000 100	1	4	0
NY-A	000 000 000	0	6	1

Pitchers: NEHF vs JONES, Bush (8)
Home Runs: Stengel-NY(N)
Attendance: 62,430

GAME 4 AT NY -N OCT 13

NY-A	061 100 000	8	13	1
NY-N	000 000 031	4	13	1

Pitchers: SHAWKEY, Pennock (8) vs J.SCOTT, Ryan (2), McQuillan (3), Jonnard (8), Barnes (9)
Home Runs: Youngs-NY(N)
Attendance: 46,302

GAME 5 AT NY -A OCT 14

NY-N	010 000 000	1	3	2
NY-A	340 100 00X	8	14	0

Pitchers: BENTLEY, J.Scott (2), Barnes (4), Jonnard (8) vs BUSH
Home Runs: Dugan-NY(A)
Attendance: 62,817

GAME 6 AT NY -N OCT 15

NY-A	100 000 050	6	5	0
NY-N	100 111 000	4	10	1

Pitchers: PENNOCK, Jones (8) vs NEHF, Ryan (8)
Home Runs: Ruth-NY(A), Snyder-NY(N)
Attendance: 34,172

Four of the seven games in this exciting Series were decided by one run—two of them after twelve innings. Pitcher Walter Johnson, in his first World Series after eighteen big-league seasons and 376 victories, opened for Washington against the Giants' Art Nehf. Although fourteen Giants reached base on hits or walks in the first nine innings, only two scored—George Kelly and Bill Terry, both of whom homered. In the bottom of the ninth, the Senators scored their second run to send the game into extra innings. Johnson shut out the Giants for two more frames, but in the top of the twelfth, two walks and three singles put New York ahead by two. Washington came back with a run and had a man on third. But Kelly at second base stopped Goose Goslin's grounder with his bare hand, and Nehf had the Giants' first win.

Goslin and manager/second baseman Bucky Harris homered in Game Two to give the Senators a 3–0 lead through six innings. The Giants scored once in the seventh and drove out starter Tom Zachary with two more in the ninth to tie the game, but in the last of the ninth Senator Roger Peckinpaugh doubled in the tie breaker to even the Series.

The Giants took an early lead in Game Three and held it to retake the Series lead, but Washington (led by Goslin's three-run homer in the third) unleashed a 13-hit, seven-run attack the next day to even the Series once more. In Game Five, though, New York pulled ahead again, defeating Johnson a second time as winning pitcher Jack Bentley put the Giants into the lead for good with a two-run homer in the fifth. In Game Six, Washington's two runs in the fifth inning overcame a first-inning Giant run and gave Tom Zachary all he needed for the Senators' third win, which set the stage for one of the most memorable games in Series history.

Washington scored first in Game Seven on manager Harris's homer in the fourth inning, but the Giants scored three runs in the sixth (two of them on Senator errors) to go ahead 3–1. In the last of the eighth, though, Harris's grounder to third bounced over the head of rookie Freddie Lindstrom for two more Senator runs and a 3–3 tie. Walter Johnson came in to face the Giants in the ninth, and shut them out through the twelfth, fanning five. Then in the bottom of the twelfth, with one out, Muddy Ruel (given a second chance after Giant catcher Hank Gowdy caught his foot in his mask and missed Ruel's pop foul) doubled to left. Pitcher Johnson then reached first when shortstop Travis Jackson bobbled what ought to have been a third-out grounder.

Washington Senators (AL), 4;
New York Giants (NL), 3

WAS (A)

PLAYER/POS	AVG	G	AB	R	H	2B	3B	HR	RB	BB	SO	SB
Ossie Bluege, ss-5,3b-4	.192	7	26	2	5	0	0	0	2	3	4	1
Goose Goslin, of	.344	7	32	4	11	1	0	3	7	0	7	0
Bucky Harris, 2b	.333	7	33	5	11	0	0	2	7	1	4	0
Walter Johnson, p	.111	3	9	0	1	0	0	0	0	0	0	0
Joe Judge, 1b	.385	7	26	4	10	1	0	0	0	5	2	0
Nemo Leibold, of-1	.167	3	6	1	1	1	0	0	0	1	0	0
Firpo Marberry, p	.000	4	2	0	0	0	0	0	0	0	0	0
Joe Martina, p	.000	1	0	0	0	0	0	0	0	0	0	0
Earl McNeely, of	.222	7	27	4	6	3	0	0	1	4	4	1
Ralph Miller, 3b	.182	4	11	0	2	0	0	0	2	1	0	0
George Mogridge, p	.000	2	5	0	0	0	0	0	0	0	5	0
Curly Ogden, p	.000	1	0	0	0	0	0	0	0	0	0	0
Roger Peckinpaugh, ss	.417	4	12	1	5	2	0	0	2	1	0	1
Sam Rice, of	.207	7	29	2	6	0	0	0	1	3	2	2
Muddy Ruel, c	.095	7	21	2	2	1	0	0	0	6	1	0
Allan Russell, p	.000	1	0	0	0	0	0	0	0	0	0	0
Mule Shirley, ph	.500	3	2	1	1	0	0	0	1	0	0	0
By Speece, p	.000	1	0	0	0	0	0	0	0	0	0	0
Bennie Tate, ph	.000	3	0	0	0	0	0	0	1	3	0	0
Tommy Taylor, 3b	.000	3	2	0	0	0	0	0	0	0	2	0
Tom Zachary, p	.000	2	5	0	0	0	0	0	0	1	3	0
TOTAL	.246		248	26	61	9	0	5	24	29	34	5

PITCHER	W	L	ERA	G	GS	CG	SV	SHO	IP	H	ER	BB	SO
Walter Johnson	1	2	2.25	3	2	2	0	0	24.0	30	6	11	20
Firpo Marberry	0	1	1.13	4	1	0	2	0	8.0	9	1	4	10
Joe Martina	0	0	0.00	1	0	0	0	0	1.0	0	0	0	1
George Mogridge	1	0	2.25	2	1	0	0	0	12.0	7	3	6	5
Curly Ogden	0	0	0.00	1	1	0	0	0	0.1	0	0	1	1
Allan Russell	0	0	3.00	1	0	0	0	0	3.0	4	1	0	0
By Speece	0	0	9.00	1	0	0	0	0	1.0	3	1	0	0
Tom Zachary	2	0	2.04	2	2	1	0	0	17.2	13	4	3	3
TOTAL	4	3	2.15	15	7	3	2	0	67.0	66	16	25	40

NY (N)

PLAYER/POS	AVG	G	AB	R	H	2B	3B	HR	RB	BB	SO	SB
Harry Baldwin, p	.000	1	0	0	0	0	0	0	0	0	0	0
Virgil Barnes, p	.000	2	4	0	0	0	0	0	0	1	2	0
Jack Bentley, p-3	.286	5	7	1	2	0	0	1	2	1	1	0
Wayland Dean, p	.000	1	0	0	0	0	0	0	0	0	0	0
Frankie Frisch, 2b-7,3b-1	.333	7	30	1	10	4	1	0	4	1	1	1
Hank Gowdy, c	.259	7	27	4	7	0	0	0	1	2	2	0
Heinie Groh, ph	1.000	1	1	0	1	0	0	0	0	0	0	0
Travis Jackson, ss	.074	7	27	3	2	0	0	0	1	1	4	1
Claude Jonnard, p	.000	1	0	0	0	0	0	0	0	0	0	0
George Kelly, 1b-4,of-4,2b-1	.290	7	31	7	9	1	0	1	4	1	8	0
Fred Lindstrom, 3b	.333	7	30	1	10	2	0	0	4	3	6	0
Hugh McQuillan, p	1.000	3	1	0	1	0	0	0	0	0	0	0
Irish Meusel, of	.154	4	13	0	2	0	0	0	1	2	0	0
Art Nehf, p	.429	3	7	1	3	0	0	0	0	0	0	0
Rosy Ryan, p	.500	2	2	1	1	0	0	1	2	0	0	0
Frank Snyder, ph	.000	1	1	0	0	0	0	0	0	0	0	0
Billy Southworth, of-2	.000	5	1	1	0	0	0	0	0	0	0	0
Bill Terry, 1b-4	.429	5	14	3	6	0	1	1	1	3	1	0
Mule Watson, p	.000	1	0	0	0	0	0	0	0	0	0	0
Hack Wilson, of	.233	7	30	1	7	1	0	0	3	1	9	0
Ross Youngs, of	.185	7	27	3	5	1	0	0	2	5	6	1
TOTAL	.261		253	27	66	9	2	4	22	25	40	3

PITCHER	W	L	ERA	G	GS	CG	SV	SHO	IP	H	ER	BB	SO
Harry Baldwin	0	0	0.00	1	0	0	0	0	2.0	1	0	0	1
Virgil Barnes	0	1	5.68	2	2	0	0	0	12.2	15	8	1	9
Jack Bentley	1	2	3.71	3	2	1	0	0	17.0	18	7	8	10
Wayland Dean	0	0	4.50	1	0	0	0	0	2.0	3	1	0	2
Claude Jonnard	0	0	INF	1	0	0	0	0	0.0	0	1	0	0
Hugh McQuillan	0	0	2.57	3	1	0	1	0	7.0	2	2	6	2
Art Nehf	1	1	1.83	3	2	1	0	0	19.2	15	4	9	7
Rosy Ryan	1	0	3.18	2	0	0	0	0	5.2	7	2	4	3
Mule Watson	0	0	0.00	1	0	0	1	0	0.2	0	0	1	0
TOTAL	3	4	3.24	17	7	2	2	0	66.2	61	24	29	34

With men on second and first, Earl McNeely bounced to Lindstrom at third. But again the ball bounded over Lindstrom's head, and Ruel raced home with Johnson's first Series win and Washington's first world championship.

GAME 1 AT WAS OCT 4

NY	010 100 000 002	4	14	1
WAS	000 001 001 001	3	10	1

Pitchers: NEHF vs JOHNSON
Home Runs: Kelly-NY, Terry-NY
Attendance: 35,760

GAME 2 AT WAS OCT 5

NY	000 000 102	3	6	0
WAS	200 010 001	4	6	1

Pitchers: BENTLEY vs ZACHARY, Marberry (9)
Home Runs: Goslin-WAS, Harris-WAS
Attendance: 35,922

GAME 3 AT NY OCT 6

WAS	000 200 011	4	9	2
NY	021 101 01X	6	12	0

Pitchers: MARBERRY, Russell (4), Martina (7), Speece (8) vs McQUILLAN, RYAN (4), Jonnard (9), Watson (9)
Home Runs: Ryan-NY
Attendance: 47,608

GAME 4 AT NY OCT 7

WAS	003 020 020	7	13	3
NY	100 001 011	4	6	1

Pitchers: MOGRIDGE, Marberry (8) vs BARNES, Baldwin (6), Dean (8)
Home Runs: Goslin-WAS
Attendance: 49,243

GAME 5 AT NY OCT 8

WAS	000 100 010	2	9	1
NY	001 020 03X	6	13	0

Pitchers: JOHNSON vs BENTLEY, McQuillan (8)
Home Runs: Bentley-NY, Goslin-WAS
Attendance: 49,211

GAME 6 AT WAS OCT 9

NY	100 000 000	1	7	1
WAS	000 020 00X	2	4	0

Pitchers: NEHF, Ryan (8) vs ZACHARY
Attendance: 34,254

GAME 7 AT WAS OCT 10

NY	000 003 000 000	3	8	3
WAS	000 100 020 001	4	10	4

Pitchers: Barnes, McQuillan (8), Nehf (10), BENTLEY (11) vs Ogden, Mogridge (1), Marberry (6), JOHNSON (9)
Home Runs: Harris-WAS
Attendance: 31,667

Repeating as pennant winners, the Senators found themselves again locked in a tight Series, this time with the Pirates, who hadn't won a pennant since 1909. Again Walter Johnson pitched the Series opener, winning this time with a strong five-hit, ten-strikeout performance, giving up only one run on Pie Traynor's homer in the fifth. Home runs by Pirates Kiki Cuyler and Glenn Wright and Senator Joe Judge accounted for four of the five runs scored in Game Two, in which Pirate Vic Aldridge dueled Senator Stan Coveleski to a narrow 3–2 win, evening the Series.

Washington took Games Three and Four, though, for a 3–1 Series advantage, Goose Goslin's solo homer in the sixth inning providing the margin of victory in Game Three, and homers by Goslin (for three runs) and Joe Harris the next day providing all the scoring as Johnson shut the Pirates out.

Harris hit his third Series homer in Game Five, but Pirate bats overwhelmed Coveleski as he lost to Aldridge for a second time. And although Goslin's third homer gave the Senators an early lead in Game Six, Pittsburgh's Ray Kremer shut Washington out from the third inning on as his teammates pulled even with two runs in the bottom of the third, and Eddie Moore's homer in the fifth gave him the run he needed for a win that sent the Series into a seventh game.

Both clubs went with their best in the finale as Johnson, winner of Games One and Four, faced Aldridge, victor in Games Two and Five. But Aldridge was wild, issuing three walks and two wild pitches in addition to two hits before being yanked with only one out in the top of the first. Johnson was hardly more effective: although he lasted the whole game, he gave up 15 hits and five earned runs. But if there was a Series goat, it would have to be Senator shortstop Roger Peckinpaugh, the American League MVP. Though he drove in a run in the first and homered for another in the eighth, his dropped pop fly in the seventh and wild throw in the eighth (his seventh and eighth errors of the Series) opened the way to four unearned runs and Pittsburgh's 9–7 triumph.

Pittsburgh Pirates (NL), 4; Washington Senators (AL), 3

PIT (N)

PLAYER/POS	AVG	G	AB	R	H	2B	3B	HR	RB	BB	SO	SB
Babe Adams, p	.000	1	0	0	0	0	0	0	0	0	0	0
Vic Aldridge, p	.000	3	7	0	0	0	0	0	0	0	0	0
Clyde Barnhart, of	.250	7	28	1	7	1	0	0	5	3	5	1
Carson Bigbee, of-1	.333	4	3	1	1	1	0	0	1	0	0	1
Max Carey, of	.458	7	24	6	11	4	0	0	2	2	3	3
Kiki Cuyler, of	.269	7	26	3	7	3	0	1	6	1	4	0
Johnny Gooch, c	.000	3	3	0	0	0	0	0	0	0	0	0
George Grantham, 1b-4	.133	5	15	0	2	0	0	0	0	0	3	1
Ray Kremer, p	.143	3	7	0	1	0	0	0	0	1	5	0
Stuffy McInnis, 1b-3	.286	4	14	0	4	0	0	0	1	0	2	0
Lee Meadows, p	.000	1	1	0	0	0	0	0	0	0	1	0
Eddie Moore, 2b	.231	7	26	7	6	1	0	1	2	5	2	0
Johnny Morrison, p	.500	3	2	1	1	0	0	0	0	0	0	0
Red Oldham, p	.000	1	0	0	0	0	0	0	0	0	0	0
Earl Smith, c	.350	6	20	0	7	1	0	0	0	1	2	0
Pie Traynor, 3b	.346	7	26	2	9	0	2	1	4	3	1	1
Glenn Wright, ss	.185	7	27	3	5	1	0	1	3	1	4	0
Emil Yde, p-1	.000	2	1	1	0	0	0	0	0	0	0	0
TOTAL	.265		230	25	61	12	2	4	25	17	32	7

PITCHER	W	L	ERA	G	GS	CG	SV	SHO	IP	H	ER	BB	SO
Babe Adams	0	0	0.00	1	0	0	0	0	1.0	2	0	0	0
Vic Aldridge	2	0	4.42	3	3	2	0	0	18.1	18	9	9	9
Ray Kremer	2	1	3.00	3	2	2	0	0	21.0	17	7	4	9
Lee Meadows	0	1	3.38	1	1	0	0	0	8.0	6	3	0	4
Johnny Morrison	0	0	2.89	3	0	0	0	0	9.1	11	3	1	7
Red Oldham	0	0	0.00	1	0	0	1	0	1.0	0	0	0	2
Emil Yde	0	1	11.57	1	1	0	0	0	2.1	5	3	3	1
TOTAL	4	1	3.69	13	7	4	1	0	61.0	59	25	17	32

WAS (A)

PLAYER/POS	AVG	G	AB	R	H	2B	3B	HR	RB	BB	SO	SB
Spencer Adams, 2b-1	.000	2	1	0	0	0	0	0	0	0	0	0
Win Ballou, p	.000	2	0	0	0	0	0	0	0	0	0	0
Ossie Bluege, 3b	.278	5	18	2	5	1	0	0	2	1	4	0
Stan Coveleski, p	.000	2	3	0	0	0	0	0	0	0	2	0
Alex Ferguson, p	.000	2	4	0	0	0	0	0	0	0	3	0
Goose Goslin, of	.308	7	26	6	8	1	0	3	6	3	3	0
Joe Harris, of	.440	7	25	5	11	2	0	3	6	3	4	0
Bucky Harris, 2b	.087	7	23	2	2	0	0	0	0	1	3	0
Walter Johnson, p	.091	3	11	0	1	0	0	0	0	0	3	0
Joe Judge, 1b	.174	7	23	2	4	1	0	1	3	3	2	0
Nemo Leibold, ph	.500	3	2	1	1	1	0	0	0	1	0	0
Firpo Marberry, p	.000	2	0	0	0	0	0	0	0	0	0	0
Earl McNeely, of-2	.000	4	2	0	0	0	0	0	0	0	0	1
Buddy Myer, 3b	.250	3	8	0	2	0	0	0	0	0	1	0
Roger Peckinpaugh, ss	.250	7	24	1	6	1	0	1	3	1	2	1
Sam Rice, of	.364	7	33	5	12	0	0	0	3	0	1	0
Muddy Ruel, c	.316	7	19	0	6	1	0	0	1	3	2	0
Dutch Ruether, ph	.000	1	1	0	0	0	0	0	0	0	1	0
Hank Severeid, c	.333	1	3	0	1	0	0	0	0	0	0	0
Bobby Veach, ph	.000	2	1	0	0	0	0	0	0	1	0	0
Tom Zachary, p	.000	1	0	0	0	0	0	0	0	0	0	0
TOTAL	.262		225	26	59	8	0	8	25	17	32	2

PITCHER	W	L	ERA	G	GS	CG	SV	SHO	IP	H	ER	BB	SO
Win Ballou	0	0	0.00	2	0	0	0	0	1.2	0	0	1	1
Stan Coveleski	0	2	3.77	2	2	1	0	0	14.1	16	6	5	3
Alex Ferguson	1	1	3.21	2	2	1	0	0	14.0	13	5	6	11
Walter Johnson	2	1	2.08	3	3	3	0	1	26.0	26	6	4	15
Firpo Marberry	0	0	0.00	2	0	0	1	0	2.1	3	0	0	2
Tom Zachary	0	0	10.80	1	0	0	0	0	1.2	3	2	1	0
TOTAL	3	4	2.85	12	7	5	1	1	60.0	61	19	17	32

GAME 1 AT PIT OCT 7

WAS	010	020	001	4	8	1
PIT	000	010	000	1	5	0

Pitchers: JOHNSON vs MEADOWS, Morrison (9)
Home Runs: J.Harris-WAS, Traynor-PIT
Attendance: 41,723

GAME 2 AT PIT OCT 8

WAS	010	000	001	2	8	2
PIT	000	100	02X	3	7	0

Pitchers: COVELESKI vs ALDRIDGE
Home Runs: Judge-WAS, Wright-PIT, Cuyler-PIT
Attendance: 43,364

GAME 3 AT WAS OCT 10

PIT	010	101	000	3	8	3
WAS	001	001	20X	4	10	1

Pitchers: KREMER vs FERGUSON, Marberry (8)
Home Runs: Goslin-WAS
Attendance: 36,495

GAME 4 AT WAS OCT 11

PIT	000	000	000	0	6	1
WAS	004	000	00X	4	12	0

Pitchers: YDE, Morrison (3), Adams (8) vs JOHNSON
Home Runs: Goslin-WAS, J.Harris-WAS
Attendance: 38,701

GAME 5 AT WAS OCT 12

PIT	002	000	211	6	13	0
WAS	100	100	100	3	8	1

Pitchers: ALDRIDGE vs COVELESKI, Ballou (7), Zachary (8), Marberry (9)
Home Runs: J.Harris-WAS
Attendance: 35,899

GAME 6 AT PIT OCT 13

WAS	110	000	000	2	6	2
PIT	002	010	00X	3	7	1

Pitchers: FERGUSON, Ballou (8) vs KREMER
Home Runs: Goslin-WAS, Moore-PIT
Attendance: 43,810

GAME 7 AT PIT OCT 15

WAS	400	200	010	7	7	2
PIT	003	010	23X	9	15	2

Pitchers: JOHNSON vs Aldridge, Morrison (1), KREMER (5), Oldham (9)
Home Runs: Peckinpaugh-WAS
Attendance: 42,856

The Yankees, returning to the World Series after a two-year absence, faced the Cardinals, who had won their first pennant since joining the National League in 1892. Both clubs led their league in slugging and runs scored; this power erupted occasionally in the Series, but over all, pitching dominated as each staff bettered its regular-season earned run average by nearly a run per game.

Herb Pennock of the Yankees pitched a splendid three-hitter in the opener. After yielding two hits and a run in the first inning, he shut out the Cards the rest of the way, holding them hitless until the ninth. Cardinal starter Bill Sherdel also pitched effectively, but three walks in the first and a hit-sacrifice-hit sandwich in the sixth brought in enough runs to beat him.

In Game Two, the veteran Grover Cleveland Alexander evened the Series, striking out ten and holding the Yankees to four singles (three of them in the two-run second) as Billy Southworth and Tommy Thevenow homered for four of St. Louis's six runs. Two days later Jesse Haines put the Cards into the lead, winning the game both ways with a five-hit shutout and a two-run homer.

New York's big bats finally awoke in Game Four. Five Yankees doubled, and Babe Ruth hit three home runs (a World Series record) in a 14-hit, 10-run assault on half the Cardinal pitching staff. Yankee pitcher Waite Hoyt also gave up 14 hits, but 12 were singles and only five runs scored. In contrast, Game Five was a pitchers' duel. Pennock and Sherdel again faced each other and held the opposition to two runs apiece through nine innings. But in the tenth, rookie Tony Lazzeri's sacrifice fly gave New York a 3–2 lead, which Pennock held in the last of the tenth for his second win.

With St. Louis down three games to two, the Series moved to hostile New York for the final games. This didn't seem to trouble the Cardinals, who erupted in Game Six for their own ten-run game, four of them driven in by Les Bell's first-inning single and seventh-inning home run. Alexander pitched a complete game for his second Series win, and came back the next day to relieve Haines in the seventh with a 3–2 lead and the bases full. He struck out Lazzeri to end the inning and kept the Yankees off the bases until he issued Babe Ruth his eleventh Series walk with two away in the ninth. But Ruth, trying to steal second, was caught, and the Cards were world champions.

St. Louis Cardinals (NL), 4; New York Yankees (AL), 3

STL (N)

PLAYER/POS	AVG	G	AB	R	H	2B	3B	HR	RB	BB	SO	SB
Pete Alexander, p	.000	3	7	1	0	0	0	0	0	0	2	0
Hi Bell, p	.000	1	0	0	0	0	0	0	0	0	0	0
Les Bell, 3b	.259	7	27	4	7	1	0	1	6	2	5	0
Jim Bottomley, 1b	.345	7	29	4	10	3	0	0	5	1	2	0
Taylor Douthit, of	.267	4	15	3	4	2	0	0	1	3	2	0
Jake Flowers, ph	.000	3	3	0	0	0	0	0	0	0	1	0
Chick Hafey, of	.185	7	27	2	5	2	0	0	0	0	7	0
Jesse Haines, p	.600	3	5	1	3	0	0	1	2	0	1	0
Bill Hallahan, p	.000	1	0	0	0	0	0	0	0	0	0	0
Wattie Holm, of-4	.125	5	16	1	2	0	0	0	1	1	2	0
Rogers Hornsby, 2b	.250	7	28	2	7	1	0	0	4	2	2	1
Vic Keen, p	.000	1	0	0	0	0	0	0	0	0	0	0
Bob O'Farrell, c	.304	7	23	2	7	1	0	0	2	2	2	0
Art Reinhart, p	.000	1	0	0	0	0	0	0	0	0	0	0
Flint Rhem, p	.000	1	1	0	0	0	0	0	0	0	1	0
Bill Sherdel, p	.000	2	5	0	0	0	0	0	0	0	2	0
Billy Southworth, of	.345	7	29	6	10	1	1	1	4	0	0	1
Tommy Thevenow, ss	.417	7	24	5	10	1	0	1	4	0	1	0
Specs Toporcer, ph	.000	1	0	0	0	0	0	0	0	1	0	0
TOTAL	.272		239	31	65	12	1	4	30	11	30	2

PITCHER	W	L	ERA	G	GS	CG	SV	SHO	IP	H	ER	BB	SO
Pete Alexander	2	0	1.33	3	2	2	1	0	20.1	12	3	4	17
Hi Bell	0	0	9.00	1	0	0	0	0	2.0	4	2	1	1
Jesse Haines	2	0	1.08	3	2	1	0	1	16.2	13	2	9	5
Bill Hallahan	0	0	4.50	1	0	0	0	0	2.0	2	1	3	1
Vic Keen	0	0	0.00	1	0	0	0	0	1.0	0	0	0	0
Art Reinhart	0	1	INF	1	0	0	0	0	0.0	1	4	4	0
Flint Rhem	0	0	6.75	1	1	0	0	0	4.0	7	3	2	4
Bill Sherdel	0	2	2.12	2	2	1	0	0	17.0	15	4	8	3
TOTAL	4	3	2.71	13	7	4	1	1	63.0	54	19	31	31

NY (A)

PLAYER/POS	AVG	G	AB	R	H	2B	3B	HR	RB	BB	SO	SB
Spencer Adams, ph	.000	2	0	0	0	0	0	0	0	0	0	0
Pat Collins, c	.000	3	2	0	0	0	0	0	0	0	1	0
Earle Combs, of	.357	7	28	3	10	2	0	0	2	5	2	0
Joe Dugan, 3b	.333	7	24	2	8	1	0	0	2	1	1	0
Mike Gazella, 3b	.000	1	0	0	0	0	0	0	0	0	0	0
Lou Gehrig, 1b	.348	7	23	1	8	2	0	0	4	5	4	0
Waite Hoyt, p	.000	2	6	0	0	0	0	0	0	0	1	0
Sam Jones, p	.000	1	0	0	0	0	0	0	0	0	0	0
Mark Koenig, ss	.125	7	32	2	4	1	0	0	2	0	6	0
Tony Lazzeri, 2b	.192	7	26	2	5	1	0	0	3	1	6	0
Bob Meusel, of	.238	7	21	3	5	1	0	0	1	0	6	1
Ben Paschal, ph	.250	5	4	0	1	0	0	0	0	1	2	0
Herb Pennock, p	.143	3	7	1	1	1	0	0	0	0	0	0
Dutch Ruether, p-1	.000	3	4	0	0	0	0	0	0	0	0	0
Babe Ruth, of	.300	7	20	6	6	0	0	4	5	11	2	1
Hank Severeid, c	.273	7	22	1	6	1	0	0	1	1	2	0
Bob Shawkey, p	.000	3	2	0	0	0	0	0	0	0	1	0
Urban Shocker, p	.000	2	2	0	0	0	0	0	0	0	2	0
Myles Thomas, p	.000	2	0	0	0	0	0	0	0	0	0	0
TOTAL	.242		223	21	54	10	1	4	20	31	31	1

PITCHER	W	L	ERA	G	GS	CG	SV	SHO	IP	H	ER	BB	SO
Waite Hoyt	1	1	1.20	2	2	1	0	0	15.0	19	2	1	10
Sam Jones	0	0	9.00	1	0	0	0	0	1.0	2	1	2	1
Herb Pennock	2	0	1.23	3	2	2	0	0	22.0	13	3	4	8
Dutch Ruether	0	1	4.15	1	1	0	0	0	4.1	7	2	2	1
Bob Shawkey	0	1	5.40	3	1	0	0	0	10.0	8	6	2	7
Urban Shocker	0	1	5.87	2	1	0	0	0	7.2	13	5	0	3
Myles Thomas	0	0	3.00	2	0	0	0	0	3.0	3	1	0	0
TOTAL	3	4	2.86	14	7	3	0	0	63.0	65	20	11	30

GAME 1 AT NY OCT 2

STL	100 000 000	1	3	1
NY	100 001 00X	2	6	0

Pitchers: SHERDEL, Haines (8) vs PENNOCK
Attendance: 61,658

GAME 2 AT NY OCT 3

STL	002 000 301	6	12	1
NY	020 000 000	2	4	0

Pitchers: ALEXANDER vs SHOCKER, Shawkey (8), Jones (9)
Home Runs: Southworth-STL, Thevenow-STL
Attendance: 63,600

GAME 3 AT STL OCT 5

NY	000 000 000	0	5	1
STL	000 310 00X	4	8	0

Pitchers: RUETHER, Shawkey (5), Thomas (8) vs HAINES
Home Runs: Haines-STL
Attendance: 37,708

GAME 4 AT STL OCT 6

NY	101 142 100	10	14	1
STL	100 300 001	5	14	0

Pitchers: HOYT vs Rhem, REINHART (5), H.Bell (5), Hallahan (7), Keen (9)
Home Runs: Ruth-NY (3)
Attendance: 38,825

GAME 5 AT STL OCT 7

NY	000 001 001 1	3	9	1
STL	000 100 100 0	2	7	1

Pitchers: PENNOCK vs SHERDEL
Attendance: 39,552

GAME 6 AT NY OCT 9

STL	300 010 501	10	13	2
NY	000 100 100	2	8	1

Pitchers: ALEXANDER vs SHAWKEY, Shocker (7), Thomas (8)
Home Runs: L.Bell-STL
Attendance: 48,615

GAME 7 AT NY OCT 10

STL	000 300 000	3	8	0
NY	001 001 000	2	8	3

Pitchers: HAINES, Alexander (7) vs HOYT, Pennock (7)
Home Runs: Ruth-NY
Attendance: 38,093

The Pirates, who struggled to a narrow pennant win in a four-team race, were no slouches at the bat. Their team BA of .305 led the National League, and in the Waner brothers—Paul and Lloyd—and Pie Traynor they had three of the league's five top hitters. But in the World Series they came up against a Yankee team that is still widely regarded as the game's greatest ever. With 110 season victories and a 19-game margin over second-place Philadelphia, the Yankees led the American League in nearly every offensive category. Three Yankees—Earle Combs, Lou Gehrig, and Babe Ruth—hit over .350, and divided among them league crowns in runs, hits, doubles, triples, home runs (Ruth's 60), RBIs, and slugging average. The Yankees not only hit: their pitching staff boasted the league's lowest earned run average.

In the Series, though, it was Pittsburgh's erratic play that brought about the first American League sweep. The Pirates scored four times off Yankee starter Waite Hoyt in Game One, and might have won the game. But Paul Waner misplayed a Gehrig fly for a run-scoring triple in the first, and in the third, two Pirate errors led to three more Yankee runs. A final run in the fifth was all New York needed to win, 5–4.

The Yankees won the next two games more convincingly, with strong pitching and timely hitting. George Pipgras held Pittsburgh to two runs in Game Two as his Yankees bunched seven of their 11 hits into the third and eighth innings (also taking advantage of two walks and a hit batsman in the eighth) for their six runs. And in Game Three—as Herb Pennock pitched perfectly into the eighth inning before yielding two hits and a run—Yankee batters again bunched most of their hits into two innings, scoring two runs on Gehrig's first-inning triple and six more in the seventh, climaxed by Ruth's three-run homer.

Pittsburgh took advantage of two Yankee errors in the seventh inning of Game Four to score two runs and tie the game at three-all. But in the last of the ninth, after the Pirates' Johnny Miljus had struck out Gehrig and Bob Meusel with the bases loaded, his second wild pitch of the inning undid him—Combs scored from third with the Series' winning run.

New York Yankees (AL), 4; Pittsburgh Pirates (NL), 0

NY (A)

PLAYER/POS	AVG	G	AB	R	H	2B	3B	HR	RB	BB	SO	SB
Benny Bengough, c	.000	2	4	1	0	0	0	0	0	1	0	0
Pat Collins, c	.600	2	5	0	3	1	0	0	0	3	0	0
Earle Combs, of	.313	4	16	6	5	0	0	0	2	1	2	0
Joe Dugan, 3b	.200	4	15	2	3	0	0	0	0	0	0	0
Cedric Durst, ph	.000	1	1	0	0	0	0	0	0	0	0	0
Lou Gehrig, 1b	.308	4	13	2	4	2	2	0	4	3	3	0
Johnny Grabowski, c	.000	1	2	0	0	0	0	0	0	0	0	0
Waite Hoyt, p	.000	1	3	0	0	0	0	0	0	0	0	0
Mark Koenig, ss	.500	4	18	5	9	2	0	0	2	0	2	0
Tony Lazzeri, 2b	.267	4	15	1	4	1	0	0	2	1	4	0
Bob Meusel, of	.118	4	17	1	2	0	0	0	1	1	7	1
Wilcy Moore, p	.200	2	5	0	1	0	0	0	0	0	3	0
Herb Pennock, p	.000	1	4	1	0	0	0	0	1	0	1	0
George Pipgras, p	.333	1	3	0	1	0	0	0	0	0	1	0
Babe Ruth, of	.400	4	15	4	6	0	0	2	7	2	2	1
TOTAL	.279		136	23	38	6	2	2	19	13	25	2

PITCHER	W	L	ERA	G	GS	CG	SV	SHO	IP	H	ER	BB	SO
Waite Hoyt	1	0	4.91	1	1	0	0	0	7.1	8	4	1	2
Wilcy Moore	1	0	0.84	2	1	1	1	0	10.2	11	1	2	2
Herb Pennock	1	0	1.00	1	1	1	0	0	9.0	3	1	0	1
George Pipgras	1	0	2.00	1	1	1	0	0	9.0	7	2	1	2
TOTAL	4	0	2.00	5	4	3	1	0	36.0	29	8	4	7

PIT (N)

PLAYER/POS	AVG	G	AB	R	H	2B	3B	HR	RB	BB	SO	SB
Vic Aldridge, p	.000	1	2	0	0	0	0	0	0	0	0	0
Clyde Barnhart, of	.313	4	16	0	5	1	0	0	4	0	0	0
Fred Brickell, ph	.000	2	2	1	0	0	0	0	0	0	0	0
Mike Cvengros, p	.000	2	0	0	0	0	0	0	0	0	0	0
Joe Dawson, p	.000	1	0	0	0	0	0	0	0	0	0	0
Johnny Gooch, c	.000	3	5	0	0	0	0	0	0	1	1	0
George Grantham, 2b	.364	3	11	0	4	1	0	0	0	1	1	0
Heinie Groh, ph	.000	1	1	0	0	0	0	0	0	0	0	0
Joe Harris, 1b	.200	4	15	0	3	0	0	0	1	0	0	0
Carmen Hill, p	.000	1	1	0	0	0	0	0	0	1	0	0
Ray Kremer, p	.500	1	2	1	1	1	0	0	0	0	1	0
Lee Meadows, p	.000	1	2	0	0	0	0	0	0	0	0	0
Johnny Miljus, p	.000	2	2	0	0	0	0	0	0	0	2	0
Hal Rhyne, 2b	.000	1	4	0	0	0	0	0	0	0	0	0
Earl Smith, c-2	.000	3	8	0	0	0	0	0	0	0	0	0
Roy Spencer, c	.000	1	1	0	0	0	0	0	0	0	0	0
Pie Traynor, 3b	.200	4	15	1	3	1	0	0	0	0	1	0
Lloyd Waner, of	.400	4	15	5	6	1	1	0	0	1	0	0
Paul Waner, of	.333	4	15	0	5	0	1	0	3	0	1	0
Glenn Wright, ss	.154	4	13	1	2	0	0	0	2	0	0	0
Emil Yde, pr	.000	1	0	1	0	0	0	0	0	0	0	0
TOTAL	.223		130	10	29	6	1	0	10	4	7	0

PITCHER	W	L	ERA	G	GS	CG	SV	SHO	IP	H	ER	BB	SO
Vic Aldridge	0	1	7.36	1	1	0	0	0	7.1	10	6	4	4
Mike Cvengros	0	0	3.86	2	0	0	0	0	2.1	3	1	0	2
Joe Dawson	0	0	0.00	1	0	0	0	0	1.0	0	0	0	0
Carmen Hill	0	0	4.50	1	1	0	0	0	6.0	9	3	1	6
Ray Kremer	0	1	3.60	1	1	0	0	0	5.0	5	2	3	1
Lee Meadows	0	1	9.95	1	1	0	0	0	6.1	7	7	1	6
Johnny Miljus	0	1	1.35	2	0	0	0	0	6.2	4	1	4	6
TOTAL	0	4	5.19	9	4	0	0	0	34.2	38	20	13	25

GAME 1 AT PIT OCT 5

NY	103	010	000	5	6	1
PIT	101	010	010	4	9	2

Pitchers: HOYT, Moore (8) vs KREMER, Miljus (6)
Attendance: 41,467

GAME 2 AT PIT OCT 6

NY	003	000	030	6	11	0
PIT	101	000	010	2	7	2

Pitchers: PIPGRAS vs ALDRIDGE, Cvengros (8), Dawson (9)
Attendance: 41,634

GAME 3 AT NY OCT 7

PIT	000	000	010	1	3	1
NY	200	000	60X	8	9	0

Pitchers: MEADOWS, Cvengros (7) vs PENNOCK
Home Runs: Ruth-NY
Attendance: 60,695

GAME 4 AT NY OCT 8

PIT	100	000	200	3	10	1
NY	100	020	001	4	12	2

Pitchers: Hill, MILJUS (7) vs MOORE
Home Runs: Ruth-NY
Attendance: 57,909

After squandering a 13½-game lead and falling briefly behind the Athletics in early September, the Yankees recovered to meet the Cardinals—winners of another tight National League race—in the Series. With Herb Pennock lost to arm trouble, the Yankees made do with just three pitchers in extending their Series win streak to eight games.

The four games offered little suspense, but for Yankee fans there were thrills aplenty. The Bronx Bombers' nine home runs (including four by Lou Gehrig and three by Babe Ruth) nearly equalled St. Louis's total scoring (ten runs), and Gehrig himself drove in as many runs (nine) as the entire Cardinal offense. Ruth and Gehrig started things off with successive doubles and a run in the first inning of the opener, and when Bob Meusel followed Ruth's second double with a home run in the fourth, the Yanks had more than they would need to support Waite Hoyt's three-hitter. The Cardinals' Jim Bottomley homered off Hoyt in the seventh, but successive singles by Mark Koenig, Ruth, and Gehrig produced a fourth Yankee run and concluded the scoring.

Gehrig homered in the first inning of Game Two to get New York off to a 3–0 lead against forty-one-year-old Grover Cleveland Alexander. The Cards snapped back to tie the game, but the Yankees retook the lead with a run in the last of the second and put together four hits, two walks, and a hit batsman for four more in the third. A final Yankee run in the seventh capped a 9–3 four-hit win for pitcher George Pipgras.

Jim Bottomley gave St. Louis its first lead of the Series with a two-run triple in the first inning of Game Three. But Yankee Tom Zachary gave up only one more run, taking the third Yankee win as Gehrig drove in three runs with homers in the second and fourth, and his teammates scored three more in the sixth (thanks in large part to two Cardinal errors and Meusel's steal of home) and a final (unearned) run an inning later.

New York completed its second straight Series sweep with another 7–3 win two days later. Waite Hoyt gained his second victory, mostly on the strength of five solo Yankee homers, including three by Babe Ruth.

New York Yankees (AL), 4;
St. Louis Cardinals (NL), 0

NY (A)

PLAYER/POS	AVG	G	AB	R	H	2B	3B	HR	RB	BB	SO	SB
Benny Bengough, c	.231	4	13	1	3	0	0	0	1	1	1	0
Pat Collins, c	1.000	1	1	0	1	1	0	0	0	0	0	0
Earle Combs, ph	.000	1	0	0	0	0	0	0	0	1	0	0
Joe Dugan, 3b	.167	3	6	0	1	0	0	0	1	0	0	0
Leo Durocher, 2b	.000	4	2	0	0	0	0	0	0	0	1	0
Cedric Durst, of	.375	4	8	3	3	0	0	1	2	0	1	0
Lou Gehrig, 1b	.545	4	11	5	6	1	0	4	9	6	0	0
Waite Hoyt, p	.143	2	7	0	1	0	0	0	0	0	0	0
Mark Koenig, ss	.158	4	19	1	3	0	0	0	0	0	1	0
Tony Lazzeri, 2b	.250	4	12	2	3	1	0	0	0	1	0	2
Bob Meusel, of	.200	4	15	5	3	1	0	1	3	2	5	2
Ben Paschal, of	.200	3	10	0	2	0	0	0	1	1	0	0
George Pipgras, p	.000	1	2	0	0	0	0	0	0	1	0	0
Gene Robertson, 3b	.125	3	8	1	1	0	0	0	2	1	0	0
Babe Ruth, of	.625	4	16	9	10	3	0	3	4	1	2	0
Tom Zachary, p	.000	1	4	0	0	0	0	0	0	0	1	0
TOTAL	.276		134	27	37	7	0	9	25	13	12	4

PITCHER	W	L	ERA	G	GS	CG	SV	SHO	IP	H	ER	BB	SO
Waite Hoyt	2	0	1.50	2	2	2	0	0	18.0	14	3	6	14
George Pipgras	1	0	2.00	1	1	1	0	0	9.0	4	2	4	8
Tom Zachary	1	0	3.00	1	1	1	0	0	9.0	9	3	1	7
TOTAL	4	0	2.00	4	4	4	0	0	36.0	27	8	11	29

STL (N)

PLAYER/POS	AVG	G	AB	R	H	2B	3B	HR	RB	BB	SO	SB
Pete Alexander, p	.000	2	1	0	0	0	0	0	1	0	0	0
Ray Blades, ph	.000	1	1	0	0	0	0	0	0	0	1	0
Jim Bottomley, 1b	.214	4	14	1	3	0	1	1	3	2	6	0
Taylor Douthit, of	.091	3	11	1	1	0	0	0	1	1	1	0
Frankie Frisch, 2b	.231	4	13	1	3	0	0	0	1	2	2	2
Chick Hafey, of	.200	4	15	0	3	0	0	0	0	1	4	0
Jesse Haines, p	.000	1	2	0	0	0	0	0	0	0	0	0
George Harper, of	.111	3	9	1	1	0	0	0	0	2	2	0
Andy High, 3b	.294	4	17	1	5	2	0	0	1	1	3	0
Wattie Holm, of-1	.167	3	6	0	1	0	0	0	1	0	1	0
Syl Johnson, p	.000	2	0	0	0	0	0	0	0	0	0	0
Rabbit Maranville, ss	.308	4	13	2	4	1	0	0	0	1	1	1
Pepper Martin, pr	.000	1	0	1	0	0	0	0	0	0	0	0
Clarence Mitchell, p	.000	1	2	0	0	0	0	0	0	0	0	0
Ernie Orsatti, of-1	.286	4	7	1	2	1	0	0	0	1	3	0
Flint Rhem, p	.000	1	0	0	0	0	0	0	0	0	0	0
Bill Sherdel, p	.000	2	5	0	0	0	0	0	0	0	2	0
Earl Smith, c	.750	1	4	0	3	0	0	0	0	0	0	0
Tommy Thevenow, ss	.000	1	0	0	0	0	0	0	0	0	0	0
Jimmie Wilson, c	.091	3	11	1	1	0	0	0	1	0	3	0
TOTAL	.206		131	10	27	5	1	1	9	11	29	3

PITCHER	W	L	ERA	G	GS	CG	SV	SHO	IP	H	ER	BB	SO
Pete Alexander	0	1	19.80	2	1	0	0	0	5.0	10	11	4	2
Jesse Haines	0	1	4.50	1	1	0	0	0	6.0	6	3	3	3
Syl Johnson	0	0	4.50	2	0	0	0	0	2.0	4	1	1	1
Clarence Mitchell	0	0	1.59	1	0	0	0	0	5.2	2	1	2	2
Flint Rhem	0	0	0.00	1	0	0	0	0	2.0	0	0	0	1
Bill Sherdel	0	2	4.72	2	2	0	0	0	13.1	15	7	3	3
TOTAL	0	4	6.09	9	4	0	0	0	34.0	37	23	13	12

GAME 1 AT NY OCT 4

STL	000	000	100	1	3	1
NY	100	200	01X	4	7	0

Pitchers: SHERDEL, Johnson (8) vs HOYT
Home Runs: Meusel-NY, Bottomley-STL
Attendance: 61,425

GAME 2 AT NY OCT 5

STL	030	000	000	3	4	1
NY	314	000	10X	9	8	2

Pitchers: ALEXANDER, Mitchell (3) vs PIPGRAS
Home Runs: Gehrig-NY
Attendance: 60,714

GAME 3 AT STL OCT 7

NY	010	203	100	7	7	2
STL	200	010	000	3	9	3

Pitchers: ZACHARY vs HAINES, Johnson (7), Rhem (8)
Home Runs: Gehrig-NY (2)
Attendance: 39,602

GAME 4 AT STL OCT 9

NY	000	100	420	7	15	2
STL	001	100	001	3	11	0

Pitchers: HOYT vs SHERDEL, Alexander (7)
Home Runs: Ruth-NY (3), Durst-NY, Gehrig-NY
Attendance: 37,331

The surprising success of a surprise starter and the ultimate in big innings highlighted the return of the Athletics to World Series play after a gap of fifteen years. In the opener, A's manager Connie Mack passed over the aces of his pitching staff in favor of Howard Ehmke, an aging journeyman who that season had started only eight times and pitched under 55 innings. But Ehmke, who (per Mack's instructions) had studied the Cubs' hitters in a series of late-season games, held the Cubs scoreless through the first eight innings of Game One (yielding an unearned run in the last of the ninth) while fanning 13 batters for a new Series record. Chicago's Charlie Root also pitched effectively until Jimmie Foxx's solo homer in the seventh gave the A's the game's first score. A pair of errors by Cub shortstop Woody English in the ninth set up two unearned runs against reliever Guy Bush and gave Ehmke and the A's all the lead they needed.

Home runs by Foxx and Al Simmons drove in five of the A's nine runs in Game Two as Philadelphia took a 2–0 Series lead. But Guy Bush held Mack's sluggers to nine singles and one run in Game Three as his Cubs scored three runs in the sixth to take their first win.

The Cubs seemed well on their way to tying the Series in Game Four as they entered the last of the seventh with an 8–0 lead. But Simmons led off with a homer to erase Charlie Root's shutout, and five of the next six batters singled. Art Nehf relieved Root, but the first batter to face him—Mule Haas—lofted a fly to center which Hack Wilson lost in the sun for a three-run inside-the-park homer, and the score was 8–7. After walking Mickey Cochrane, Nehf was replaced by Sheriff Blake, who gave up two singles and saw the tying run come home before Pat Malone took the mound with two men still on base and only one away. Malone struck out two in a row to end the inning—but not until he first hit a batter and gave up a double by Jimmy Dykes for the two runs that gave the A's a 10–8 win and a 3–1 Series advantage.

Game Five, although inevitably anticlimactic, was not decided until the final at-bat. Chicago scored twice off Ehmke in the fourth as Malone shut out the A's with only two hits through eight. But in the last of the ninth a single and Haas's home run tied the score, and—with two men out—Simmons doubled, Foxx was walked intentionally, Bing Miller doubled, and the Series was history.

Philadelphia Athletics (AL), 4; Chicago Cubs (NL), 1

PHI (A)

PLAYER/POS	AVG	G	AB	R	H	2B	3B	HR	RB	BB	SO	SB
Max Bishop, 2b	.190	5	21	2	4	0	0	0	1	2	3	0
Joe Boley, ss	.235	5	17	1	4	0	0	0	1	0	3	0
George Burns, ph	.000	1	2	0	0	0	0	0	0	0	1	0
Mickey Cochrane, c	.400	5	15	5	6	1	0	0	0	7	0	0
Jimmy Dykes, 3b	.421	5	19	2	8	1	0	0	4	1	1	0
George Earnshaw, p	.000	2	5	1	0	0	0	0	0	0	4	0
Howard Ehmke, p	.200	2	5	0	1	0	0	0	0	0	0	0
Jimmie Foxx, 1b	.350	5	20	5	7	1	0	2	5	1	1	0
Lefty Grove, p	.000	2	2	0	0	0	0	0	0	0	1	0
Mule Haas, of	.238	5	21	3	5	0	0	2	6	1	3	0
Bing Miller, of	.368	5	19	1	7	1	0	0	4	0	2	0
Jack Quinn, p	.000	1	2	0	0	0	0	0	0	0	2	0
Eddie Rommel, p	.000	1	0	0	0	0	0	0	0	0	0	0
Al Simmons, of	.300	5	20	6	6	1	0	2	5	1	4	0
Homer Summa, ph	.000	1	1	0	0	0	0	0	0	0	1	0
Rube Walberg, p	.000	2	1	0	0	0	0	0	0	0	0	0
TOTAL	.281		171	26	48	5	0	6	26	13	27	0

PITCHER	W	L	ERA	G	GS	CG	SV	SHO	IP	H	ER	BB	SO
George Earnshaw	1	1	2.63	2	2	1	0	0	13.2	14	4	6	17
Howard Ehmke	1	0	1.42	2	2	1	0	0	12.2	14	2	3	13
Lefty Grove	0	0	0.00	2	0	0	2	0	6.1	3	0	1	10
Jack Quinn	0	0	9.00	1	1	0	0	0	5.0	7	5	2	2
Eddie Rommel	1	0	9.00	1	0	0	0	0	1.0	2	1	1	0
Rube Walberg	1	0	0.00	2	0	0	0	0	6.1	3	0	0	8
TOTAL	4	1	2.40	10	5	2	2	0	45.0	43	12	13	50

CHI (N)

PLAYER/POS	AVG	G	AB	R	H	2B	3B	HR	RB	BB	SO	SB
Footsie Blair, ph	.000	1	1	0	0	0	0	0	0	0	0	0
Sheriff Blake, p	1.000	2	1	0	1	0	0	0	0	0	0	0
Guy Bush, p	.000	2	3	1	0	0	0	0	0	1	3	0
Hal Carlson, p	.000	2	0	0	0	0	0	0	0	0	0	0
Kiki Cuyler, of	.300	5	20	4	6	1	0	0	4	1	7	0
Woody English, ss	.190	5	21	1	4	2	0	0	0	1	6	0
Mike Gonzalez, c-1	.000	2	1	0	0	0	0	0	0	0	1	0
Charlie Grimm, 1b	.389	5	18	2	7	0	0	1	4	1	2	0
Gabby Hartnett, ph	.000	3	3	0	0	0	0	0	0	0	3	0
Cliff Heathcote, ph	.000	2	1	0	0	0	0	0	0	0	0	0
Rogers Hornsby, 2b	.238	5	21	4	5	1	1	0	1	1	8	0
Pat Malone, p	.250	3	4	0	1	1	0	0	0	0	2	0
Norm McMillan, 3b	.100	5	20	0	2	0	0	0	0	2	6	1
Art Nehf, p	.000	2	0	0	0	0	0	0	0	0	0	0
Charlie Root, p	.000	2	5	0	0	0	0	0	0	0	3	0
Riggs Stephenson, of	.316	5	19	3	6	1	0	0	3	2	2	0
Zack Taylor, c	.176	5	17	0	3	0	0	0	0	3	3	0
Chick Tolson, ph	.000	1	1	0	0	0	0	0	0	0	0	0
Hack Wilson, of	.471	5	17	2	8	0	1	0	0	4	3	0
TOTAL	.249		173	17	43	6	2	1	15	13	50	1

PITCHER	W	L	ERA	G	GS	CG	SV	SHO	IP	H	ER	BB	SO
Sheriff Blake	0	1	13.50	2	0	0	0	0	1.1	4	2	0	1
Guy Bush	1	0	0.82	2	1	1	0	0	11.0	12	1	2	4
Hal Carlson	0	0	6.75	2	0	0	0	0	4.0	7	3	1	3
Pat Malone	0	2	4.15	3	2	1	0	0	13.0	12	6	7	11
Art Nehf	0	0	18.00	2	0	0	0	0	1.0	1	2	1	0
Charlie Root	0	1	4.72	2	2	0	0	0	13.1	12	7	2	8
TOTAL	1	4	4.33	13	5	2	0	0	43.2	48	21	13	27

GAME 1 AT CHI OCT 8

PHI	000 000 102	3	6	1
CHI	000 000 001	1	8	2

Pitchers: EHMKE vs ROOT, Bush (8)
Home Runs: Foxx-PHI
Attendance: 50,740

GAME 2 AT CHI OCT 9

PHI	003 300 120	9	12	0
CHI	000 030 000	3	11	1

Pitchers: EARNSHAW, Grove (5) vs MALONE, Blake (4), Carlson (6), Nehf (9)
Home Runs: Simmons-PHI, Foxx-PHI
Attendance: 49,987

GAME 3 AT PHI OCT 11

CHI	000 003 000	3	6	1
PHI	000 010 000	1	9	1

Pitchers: BUSH vs EARNSHAW
Attendance: 29,921

GAME 4 AT PHI OCT 12

CHI	000 205 100	8	10	2
PHI	000 000 10X	10	15	2

Pitchers: Root, Nehf (7), BLAKE (7), Malone (7), Carlson (8) vs Quinn, Walberg (6), ROMMEL (7), Grove (8)
Home Runs: Grimm-CHI, Haas-PHI, Simmons-PHI
Attendance: 29,921

GAME 5 AT PHI OCT 14

CHI	002 000 000	2	8	1
PHI	000 000 003	3	6	0

Pitchers: MALONE vs Ehmke, WALBERG (4)
Home Runs: Haas-PHI
Attendance: 29,921

Pitching 85 percent of the Series with a combined ERA of 1.02, Philadelphia aces George Earnshaw and Lefty Grove chilled the hot Cardinals, who had hit .314 and averaged 6½ runs per game during the season. The A's hit only .197 themselves in the Series, but more than half their hits went for extra bases as they outscored St. Louis 21–12 and took their second consecutive world championship in six games.

Grove faced Cardinal spitballer Burleigh Grimes in the opener, giving up nine hits, including four singles in the Cards' two-run third. The Athletics, for their part, touched Grimes for only five hits, all in separate innings. But every hit—a double, two triples, and home runs by Al Simmons and Mike Cochrane—resulted in a run, and Grove and the A's emerged 5–2 victors. In the first inning of Game Two, Cochrane again homered, sending Earnshaw on his way to Philadelphia's second win, 6–1.

When the Series moved to St. Louis, though, the Cards came alive. Wild Bill Hallahan (their leading winner during the season, with 15) spaced seven hits for a shutout. Taylor Douthit's fourth-inning home run off Rube Walberg was the first Cardinal hit, but the Cards knocked out nine more for four more runs before they were finished. A pair of unearned runs evened the Series the next day when A's third baseman Jimmy Dykes's wild throw to first in the fourth inning let in a tie-breaking second Cardinal run and led to a third against the ultimate loser Lefty Grove. Meanwhile, Cardinal veteran Jesse Haines, after yielding three Philadelphia hits and a run in the first inning, shut out the A's on one hit the rest of the way.

Earnshaw and Grove combined to restore the Series lead to the Athletics in Game Five with a three-hit shutout. Grove, who took over when Earnshaw left for a pinch hitter in the eighth, garnered his second Series win as Jimmie Foxx homered off Grimes in the top of the ninth for the game's only runs. After a travel day to Philadelphia, Earnshaw pitched again for the A's in Game Six, and pushed the Cardinals' scoreless streak to 21 innings before allowing them a token run in the ninth. But by then seven A's had crossed the plate and the Series was theirs.

Philadelphia Athletics (AL), 4;
St. Louis Cardinals (NL), 2

PHI (A)

PLAYER/POS	AVG	G	AB	R	H	2B	3B	HR	RB	BB	SO	SB
Max Bishop, 2b	.222	6	18	5	4	0	0	0	0	7	3	0
Joe Boley, ss	.095	6	21	1	2	0	0	0	1	0	1	0
Mickey Cochrane, c	.222	6	18	5	4	1	0	2	4	5	2	0
Jimmy Dykes, 3b	.222	6	18	2	4	3	0	1	5	5	3	0
George Earnshaw, p	.000	3	9	0	0	0	0	0	0	0	5	0
Jimmie Foxx, 1b	.333	6	21	3	7	2	1	1	3	2	4	0
Lefty Grove, p	.000	3	6	0	0	0	0	0	0	0	3	0
Mule Haas, of	.111	6	18	1	2	0	1	0	1	1	3	0
Eric McNair, ph	.000	1	1	0	0	0	0	0	0	0	0	0
Bing Miller, of	.143	6	21	0	3	2	0	0	3	0	4	0
Jim Moore, of-1	.333	3	3	0	1	0	0	0	0	0	1	0
Jack Quinn, p	.000	1	0	0	0	0	0	0	0	0	0	0
Bill Shores, p	.000	1	0	0	0	0	0	0	0	0	1	0
Al Simmons, of	.364	6	22	4	8	2	0	2	4	2	2	0
Rube Walberg, p	.000	1	2	0	0	0	0	0	0	0	1	0
TOTAL	.197		178	21	35	10	2	6	21	24	32	0

PITCHER	W	L	ERA	G	GS	CG	SV	SHO	IP	H	ER	BB	SO
George Earnshaw	2	0	0.72	3	3	2	0	0	25.0	13	2	7	19
Lefty Grove	2	1	1.42	3	2	2	0	0	19.0	15	3	3	10
Jack Quinn	0	0	4.50	1	0	0	0	0	2.0	3	1	0	1
Bill Shores	0	0	13.50	1	0	0	0	0	1.1	3	2	0	0
Rube Walberg	0	1	3.86	1	1	0	0	0	4.2	4	2	1	3
TOTAL	4	2	1.73	9	6	4	0	0	52.0	38	10	11	33

STL (N)

PLAYER/POS	AVG	G	AB	R	H	2B	3B	HR	RB	BB	SO	SB
Sparky Adams, 3b	.143	6	21	0	3	0	0	0	0	1	4	0
Hi Bell, p	.000	1	0	0	0	0	0	0	0	0	0	0
Ray Blades, of-3	.111	5	9	2	1	0	0	0	0	2	2	0
Jim Bottomley, 1b	.045	6	22	1	1	1	0	0	0	2	9	0
Taylor Douthit, of	.083	6	24	1	2	0	0	1	2	0	2	0
George Fisher, ph	.500	2	2	0	1	1	0	0	0	0	1	0
Frankie Frisch, 2b	.208	6	24	0	5	2	0	0	0	0	0	1
Charlie Gelbert, ss	.353	6	17	2	6	0	1	0	2	3	3	0
Burleigh Grimes, p	.400	2	5	0	2	0	0	0	0	0	1	0
Chick Hafey, of	.273	6	22	2	6	5	0	0	2	1	3	0
Jesse Haines, p	.500	1	2	0	1	0	0	0	1	0	0	0
Bill Hallahan, p	.000	2	2	0	0	0	0	0	0	1	1	0
Andy High, 3b	.500	1	2	1	1	0	0	0	0	0	0	0
Syl Johnson, p	.000	2	0	0	0	0	0	0	0	0	0	0
Jim Lindsey, p	1.000	2	1	0	1	0	0	0	0	0	0	0
Gus Mancuso, c	.286	2	7	1	2	0	0	0	0	1	2	0
Ernie Orsatti, ph	.000	1	1	0	0	0	0	0	0	0	0	0
George Puccinelli, ph	.000	1	1	0	0	0	0	0	0	0	0	0
Flint Rhem, p	.000	1	1	0	0	0	0	0	0	0	1	0
George Watkins, of	.167	4	12	2	2	0	0	1	1	1	3	0
Jimmie Wilson, c	.267	4	15	0	4	1	0	0	2	0	1	0
TOTAL	.200		190	12	38	10	1	2	11	11	33	1

PITCHER	W	L	ERA	G	GS	CG	SV	SHO	IP	H	ER	BB	SO
Hi Bell	0	0	0.00	1	0	0	0	0	1.0	0	0	0	0
Burleigh Grimes	0	2	3.71	2	2	2	0	0	17.0	10	7	6	13
Jesse Haines	1	0	1.00	1	1	1	0	0	9.0	4	1	4	2
Bill Hallahan	1	1	1.64	2	2	1	0	1	11.0	9	2	8	8
Syl Johnson	0	0	7.20	2	0	0	0	0	5.0	4	4	3	4
Jim Lindsey	0	0	1.93	2	0	0	0	0	4.2	1	1	1	2
Flint Rhem	0	1	10.80	1	1	0	0	0	3.1	7	4	2	3
TOTAL	2	4	3.35	11	6	4	0	1	51.0	35	19	24	32

GAME 1 AT PHI OCT 1

STL	002	000	000	2	9	0
PHI	010	101	11X	5	5	0

Pitchers: GRIMES vs GROVE
Home Runs: Cochrane-PHI, Simmons-PHI
Attendance: 32,295

GAME 2 AT PHI OCT 2

STL	010	000	000	1	6	2
PHI	202	200	00X	6	7	2

Pitchers: RHEM, Lindsey (4), Johnson (7) vs EARNSHAW
Home Runs: Cochrane-PHI, Watkins-STL
Attendance: 32,295

GAME 3 AT STL OCT 4

PHI	000	000	000	0	7	0
STL	000	110	21X	5	10	0

Pitchers: WALBERG, Shores (5), Quinn (7) vs HALLAHAN
Home Runs: Douthit-STL
Attendance: 36,944

GAME 4 AT STL OCT 5

PHI	100	000	000	1	4	1
STL	001	200	00X	3	5	1

Pitchers: GROVE vs HAINES
Attendance: 39,946

GAME 5 AT STL OCT 6

PHI	000	000	002	2	5	0
STL	000	000	000	0	3	1

Pitchers: Earnshaw, GROVE (8) vs GRIMES
Home Runs: Foxx-PHI
Attendance: 38,844

GAME 6 AT PHI OCT 8

STL	000	000	001	1	5	1
PHI	201	211	00X	7	7	0

Pitchers: HALLAHAN, Johnson (3), Lindsey (6), Bell (8) vs EARNSHAW
Home Runs: Dykes-PHI, Simmons-PHI
Attendance: 32,295

For the second year in a row, the A's met the Cardinals in the Series, and once again pitchers Lefty Grove and George Earnshaw provided more than 80 percent of the Athletics' pitching, performing splendidly and winning three games between them. But this time Cardinal pitchers Wild Bill Hallahan and Burleigh Grimes outshone them, winning two games apiece to bring St. Louis the world championship.

Grove gave up four hits and two runs in the first inning of the opener, but shut out the Cards the rest of the way as the A's scored six off Paul Derringer to take the Series lead. Earnshaw also held St. Louis to two runs the next day—both manufactured by Pepper Martin's daring baserunning. But they were more than enough for Hallahan, who shut out the A's on three singles.

The Cardinals took their first Series lead in Game Three, scoring five times off Grove and reliever Roy Mahaffey while Grimes held the A's hitless through seven innings and scoreless through eight before giving up a harmless two-run homer to Al Simmons in the bottom of the ninth. But the A's came back to even the Series the next day on Earnshaw's two-hit shutout.

Pepper Martin, the Cardinal hero of Game Two, homered for two runs in Game Five, and drove in two more of St. Louis's five runs with a sacrifice fly and a single. Meanwhile pitcher Hallahan held Philadelphia to a lone run, returning the Series lead to the Cardinals with his second win.

Game Six pitted Grove and Derringer against each other again as in the opener, and again Grove emerged the victor, holding the Cardinals to one run and five hits. The Athletics scored four unearned runs in the fifth off the unfortunate Derringer who, after an error put a runner on base to open the inning, gave up two singles and walked four, including two with the bases full, before leaving the game. Four more Philadelphia runs in the seventh (two of them scoring on a dropped fly ball) gave the A's the Series' only lopsided win.

In the finale, Grimes once again held the A's scoreless through eight before giving up two runs in the ninth. And once again the runs proved harmless against an early Cardinal lead, as Hallahan came on to retire Max Bishop for the final out.

St. Louis Cardinals (NL), 4;
Philadelphia Athletics (AL), 3

STL (N)

PLAYER/POS	AVG	G	AB	R	H	2B	3B	HR	RB	BB	SO	SB
Sparky Adams, 3b	.250	2	4	0	1	0	0	0	0	0	1	0
Ray Blades, ph	.000	2	2	0	0	0	0	0	0	0	2	0
Jim Bottomley, 1b	.160	7	25	2	4	1	0	0	2	2	5	0
Ripper Collins, ph	.000	2	2	0	0	0	0	0	0	0	1	0
Paul Derringer, p	.000	3	2	0	0	0	0	0	0	0	1	0
Jake Flowers, 3b-4	.091	5	11	1	1	1	0	0	0	0	1	0
Frankie Frisch, 2b	.259	7	27	2	7	2	0	0	1	1	2	1
Charlie Gelbert, ss	.261	7	23	0	6	1	0	0	3	0	4	0
Burleigh Grimes, p	.286	2	7	0	2	0	0	0	2	0	2	0
Chick Hafey, of	.167	6	24	1	4	0	0	0	0	0	5	1
Bill Hallahan, p	.000	3	6	0	0	0	0	0	0	0	3	0
Andy High, 3b	.267	4	15	3	4	0	0	0	0	0	2	0
Syl Johnson, p	.000	3	2	0	0	0	0	0	0	0	2	0
Jim Lindsey, p	.000	2	0	0	0	0	0	0	0	0	0	0
Gus Mancuso, c-1	.000	2	1	0	0	0	0	0	0	0	0	0
Pepper Martin, of	.500	7	24	5	12	4	0	1	5	2	3	5
Ernie Orsatti, of	.000	1	3	0	0	0	0	0	0	0	3	0
Flint Rhem, p	.000	1	0	0	0	0	0	0	0	0	0	0
Wally Roettger, of	.286	3	14	1	4	1	0	0	1	0	3	0
George Watkins, of	.286	5	14	4	4	1	0	2	2	2	1	0
Jimmie Wilson, c	.217	7	23	0	5	0	0	0	2	1	1	0
TOTAL	.236		229	19	54	11	0	2	17	9	41	8

PITCHER	W	L	ERA	G	GS	CG	SV	SHO	IP	H	ER	BB	SO
Paul Derringer	0	2	4.26	3	2	0	0	0	12.2	14	6	7	14
Burleigh Grimes	2	0	2.04	2	2	1	0	0	17.2	9	4	9	11
Bill Hallahan	2	0	0.49	3	2	2	1	1	18.1	12	1	8	12
Syl Johnson	0	1	3.00	3	1	0	0	0	9.0	10	3	1	6
Jim Lindsey	0	0	5.40	2	0	0	0	0	3.1	4	2	3	2
Flint Rhem	0	0	0.00	1	0	0	0	0	1.0	1	0	0	1
TOTAL	4	3	2.32	14	7	3	1	1	62.0	50	16	28	46

PHI (A)

PLAYER/POS	AVG	G	AB	R	H	2B	3B	HR	RB	BB	SO	SB
Max Bishop, 2b	.148	7	27	4	4	0	0	0	0	3	5	0
Joe Boley, ph	.000	1	1	0	0	0	0	0	0	0	1	0
Mickey Cochrane, c	.160	7	25	2	4	0	0	0	1	5	2	0
Doc Cramer, ph	.500	2	2	0	1	0	0	0	2	0	0	0
Jimmy Dykes, 3b	.227	7	22	2	5	0	0	0	2	5	1	0
George Earnshaw, p	.000	3	8	0	0	0	0	0	0	0	2	0
Jimmie Foxx, 1b	.348	7	23	3	8	0	0	1	3	6	5	0
Lefty Grove, p	.000	3	10	0	0	0	0	0	0	0	7	0
Mule Haas, of	.130	7	23	1	3	1	0	0	2	3	5	0
Johnnie Heving, ph	.000	1	1	0	0	0	0	0	0	0	0	0
Waite Hoyt, p	.000	1	2	0	0	0	0	0	0	0	0	0
Roy Mahaffey, p	.000	1	0	0	0	0	0	0	0	0	0	0
Eric McNair, 2b-1	.000	2	2	1	0	0	0	0	0	0	1	0
Bing Miller, of	.269	7	26	3	7	1	0	0	1	0	4	0
Jim Moore, of-1	.333	2	3	0	1	0	0	0	0	0	0	0
Eddie Rommel, p	.000	1	0	0	0	0	0	0	0	0	0	0
Al Simmons, of	.333	7	27	4	9	2	0	2	8	3	3	0
Phil Todt, ph	.000	1	0	0	0	0	0	0	0	1	0	0
Rube Walberg, p	.000	2	0	0	0	0	0	0	0	0	0	0
Dib Williams, ss	.320	7	25	2	8	1	0	0	1	2	9	0
TOTAL	.220		227	22	50	5	0	3	20	28	46	0

PITCHER	W	L	ERA	G	GS	CG	SV	SHO	IP	H	ER	BB	SO
George Earnshaw	1	2	1.88	3	3	2	0	1	24.0	12	5	4	20
Lefty Grove	2	1	2.42	3	3	2	0	0	26.0	28	7	2	16
Waite Hoyt	0	1	4.50	1	1	0	0	0	6.0	7	3	0	1
Roy Mahaffey	0	0	9.00	1	0	0	0	0	1.0	1	1	1	0
Eddie Rommel	0	0	9.00	1	0	0	0	0	1.0	3	1	0	0
Rube Walberg	0	0	3.00	2	0	0	0	0	3.0	3	1	2	4
TOTAL	3	4	2.66	11	7	4	0	1	61.0	54	18	9	41

GAME 1 AT STL OCT 1

PHI	004	000	200	6 11	0
STL	200	000	000	2 12	0

Pitchers: GROVE vs DERRINGER, Johnson (8)
Home Runs: Simmons-PHI
Attendance: 38,529

GAME 2 AT STL OCT 2

PHI	000	000	000	0 3	0
STL	010	000	10X	2 6	1

Pitchers: EARNSHAW vs HALLAHAN
Attendance: 35,947

GAME 3 AT PHI OCT 5

STL	020	200	001	5 12	0
PHI	000	000	002	2 2	0

Pitchers: GRIMES vs GROVE, Mahaffey (9)
Home Runs: Simmons-PHI
Attendance: 32,295

GAME 4 AT PHI OCT 6

STL	000	000	000	0 2	1
PHI	100	002	00X	3 10	0

Pitchers: JOHNSON, Lindsey (6), Derringer (8) vs EARNSHAW
Home Runs: Foxx-PHI
Attendance: 32,295

GAME 5 AT PHI OCT 7

STL	100	002	011	5 12	0
PHI	000	000	100	1 9	0

Pitchers: HALLAHAN vs HOYT, Walberg (7), Rommel (9)
Home Runs: Martin-STL, Watkins-STL
Attendance: 32,295

GAME 6 AT STL OCT 9

PHI	000	040	400	8 8	1
STL	000	001	000	1 5	2

Pitchers: GROVE vs DERRINGER, Johnson (5), Lindsey (7), Rhem (9)
Attendance: 39,401

GAME 7 AT STL OCT 10

PHI	000	000	002	2 7	1
STL	202	000	00X	4 5	0

Pitchers: EARNSHAW, Walberg (8) vs GRIMES, Hallahan (9)
Attendance: 20,805

Lou Gehrig, who hit .529 and scored nearly a quarter of New York's runs, led both clubs in batting, slugging, hits, runs, and RBIs as the Yankees crushed the Cubs in four games. But the Series is best remembered for Babe Ruth's "called" shot in Game Three, when he pointed his bat at pitcher Charlie Root in the fifth inning and broke the game's 4–4 tie a moment later with a massive home run into the center field bleachers. Debate has raged ever since about whether Ruth intended his gesture as a home run prediction. Whether intended or not, it erased from public memory Gehrig's home run that followed Ruth's (and the homers both men had hit earlier in the game), and made memorable an otherwise undistinguished Series.

Chicago scored in the first inning of each game, taking early leads in three of the four, but held no lead beyond the sixth inning. In Game One, the Cubs connected for ten hits to the Yankees' eight, but managed to score only half as many runs as the New Yorkers, who put what had been a close game out of reach with five runs in the sixth (on four walks, two singles, and a ground out) and three more in the seventh (a walk, two singles, a hit batsman, a sacrifice fly, and a wild pitch).

Chicago's Lon Warneke walked four batters in Game Two, and three of them went on to score as the Yankees countered single Cub runs in the first and third with pairs of their own on two walks and two singles in each frame. (A fifth Yankee run—on two singles without bases on balls—concluded the scoring for the game.)

Game Three featured not only the two homers each by Ruth and Gehrig, but home runs by the Cubs' Kiki Cuyler and Gabby Hartnett. Hartnett's solo shot in the last of the ninth brought Chicago to within two runs of New York for the Series' closest finish.

Four first-inning singles, Frank Demaree's three-run homer, and a Yankee error gave the Cubs a 4–1 advantage early in Game Four—their biggest lead of the Series. But by game's end, 19 Yankee hits (including two home runs by Tony Lazzeri and one by Earle Combs) had created 13 Yankee runs, and the world title was theirs.

New York Yankees (AL), 4;
Chicago Cubs (NL), 0

NY (A)

PLAYER/POS	AVG	G	AB	R	H	2B	3B	HR	RB	BB	SO	SB
Johnny Allen, p	.000	1	0	0	0	0	0	0	0	0	0	0
Sammy Byrd, of	.000	1	0	0	0	0	0	0	0	0	0	0
Ben Chapman, of	.294	4	17	1	5	2	0	0	6	2	4	0
Earle Combs, of	.375	4	16	8	6	1	0	1	4	4	3	0
Frankie Crosetti, ss	.133	4	15	2	2	1	0	0	0	2	3	0
Bill Dickey, c	.438	4	16	2	7	0	0	0	4	2	1	0
Lou Gehrig, 1b	.529	4	17	9	9	1	0	3	8	2	1	0
Lefty Gomez, p	.000	1	3	0	0	0	0	0	0	0	2	0
Myril Hoag, pr	.000	1	0	1	0	0	0	0	0	0	0	0
Tony Lazzeri, 2b	.294	4	17	4	5	0	0	2	5	2	1	0
Wilcy Moore, p	.333	3	3	0	1	0	0	0	0	0	2	0
Herb Pennock, p	.000	2	1	0	0	0	0	0	0	0	0	0
George Pipgras, p	.000	1	5	0	0	0	0	0	0	0	5	0
Red Ruffing, p-1	.000	2	4	0	0	0	0	0	0	1	1	0
Babe Ruth, of	.333	4	15	6	5	0	0	2	6	4	3	0
Joe Sewell, 3b	.333	4	15	4	5	1	0	0	3	4	0	0
TOTAL	.313		144	37	45	6	0	8	36	23	26	0

PITCHER	W	L	ERA	G	GS	CG	SV	SHO	IP	H	ER	BB	SO
Johnny Allen	0	0	40.50	1	1	0	0	0	0.2	5	3	0	0
Lefty Gomez	1	0	1.00	1	1	1	0	0	9.0	9	1	1	8
Wilcy Moore	1	0	0.00	1	0	0	0	0	5.1	2	0	0	1
Herb Pennock	0	0	2.25	2	0	0	2	0	4.0	2	1	1	4
George Pipgras	1	0	4.50	1	1	0	0	0	8.0	9	4	3	1
Red Ruffing	1	0	4.00	1	1	1	0	0	9.0	10	4	6	10
TOTAL	4	0	3.25	7	4	2	2	0	36.0	37	13	11	24

CHI (N)

PLAYER/POS	AVG	G	AB	R	H	2B	3B	HR	RB	BB	SO	SB
Guy Bush, p	.000	2	1	0	0	0	0	0	0	1	0	0
Kiki Cuyler, of	.278	4	18	2	5	1	1	1	2	0	3	1
Frank Demaree, of	.286	2	7	1	2	0	0	1	4	1	0	0
Woody English, 3b	.176	4	17	2	3	0	0	0	1	2	2	0
Burleigh Grimes, p	.000	2	1	0	0	0	0	0	0	0	1	0
Charlie Grimm, 1b	.333	4	15	2	5	2	0	0	1	2	2	0
Marv Gudat, ph	.000	2	2	0	0	0	0	0	0	0	1	0
Stan Hack, ph	.000	1	0	0	0	0	0	0	0	0	0	0
Gabby Hartnett, c	.313	4	16	2	5	2	0	1	1	1	3	0
Rollie Hemsley, c-1	.000	3	3	0	0	0	0	0	0	0	3	0
Billy Herman, 2b	.222	4	18	5	4	1	0	0	1	1	3	0
Billy Jurges, ss	.364	3	11	1	4	1	0	0	1	0	1	2
Mark Koenig, ss-1	.250	2	4	1	1	0	1	0	1	1	0	0
Pat Malone, p	.000	1	0	0	0	0	0	0	0	0	0	0
Jakie May, p	.000	2	0	0	0	0	0	0	0	0	0	0
Johnny Moore, of	.000	2	7	1	0	0	0	0	0	2	1	0
Charlie Root, p	.000	1	2	0	0	0	0	0	0	0	1	0
Bob Smith, p	.000	1	0	0	0	0	0	0	0	0	0	0
Riggs Stephenson, of	.444	4	18	2	8	1	0	0	4	0	0	0
Bud Tinning, p	.000	2	0	0	0	0	0	0	0	0	0	0
Lon Warneke, p	.000	2	4	0	0	0	0	0	0	0	3	0
TOTAL	.253		146	19	37	8	2	3	16	11	24	3

PITCHER	W	L	ERA	G	GS	CG	SV	SHO	IP	H	ER	BB	SO
Guy Bush	0	1	14.29	2	2	0	0	0	5.2	5	9	6	2
Burleigh Grimes	0	0	23.63	2	0	0	0	0	2.2	7	7	2	0
Pat Malone	0	0	0.00	1	0	0	0	0	2.2	1	0	4	4
Jakie May	0	1	11.57	2	0	0	0	0	4.2	9	6	3	4
Charlie Root	0	1	10.38	1	1	0	0	0	4.1	6	5	3	4
Bob Smith	0	0	9.00	1	0	0	0	0	1.0	2	1	0	1
Bud Tinning	0	0	0.00	2	0	0	0	0	2.1	0	0	0	3
Lon Warneke	0	1	5.91	2	1	1	0	0	10.2	15	7	5	8
TOTAL	0	4	9.26	13	4	1	0	0	34.0	45	35	23	26

GAME 1 AT NY SEPT 28

CHI	200 000 220	6 10 1
NY	000 305 31X	12 8 2

Pitchers: BUSH, Grimes (6), Smith (8) vs RUFFING
Home Runs: Gehrig-NY
Attendance: 41,459

GAME 2 AT NY SEPT 29

CHI	101 000 000	2 9 0
NY	202 010 00X	5 10 1

Pitchers: WARNEKE vs GOMEZ
Attendance: 50,709

GAME 3 AT CHI OCT 1

NY	301 020 001	7 8 1
CHI	102 100 001	5 9 4

Pitchers: PIPGRAS, Pennock (9) vs ROOT, Malone (5), May (7), Tinning (9)
Home Runs: Ruth-NY (2), Gehrig-NY (2), Cuyler-CHI, Hartnett-CHI
Attendance: 49,986

GAME 4 AT CHI OCT 2

NY	102 002 404	13 19 4
CHI	400 001 001	6 9 1

Pitchers: Allen, MOORE (1), Pennock (7) vs Bush, Warneke (1), MAY (4), Tinning (7), Grimes (9)
Home Runs: Demaree-CHI, Lazzeri-NY (2), Combs-NY
Attendance: 49,844

Although John McGraw had retired from managing the Giants in 1932, he continued to regard them as "his" team. Led now by first baseman Bill Terry, the Giants faced a club also led by an active player, shortstop Joe Cronin in his rookie managerial season.

Giant ace Carl Hubbell dominated the first game, striking out ten while limiting the Senators to five singles and a pair of unearned runs. Mel Ott set the tone for New York with a two-out two-run homer in the first inning, and singled home a third Giant run in the third to build a lead Washington would not overcome. The next day the Senators scored first, on Goose Goslin's solo homer in the third. But that was the only run scored off Giant pitcher Hal Schumacher, and when the Giants drove out Senator starter Alvin Crowder with six runs in the sixth they had their second win well in hand.

The Senators revived when the Series moved to Washington for Game Three. Each of second baseman Buddy Myer's three hits scored or drove in a run, providing a growing cushion for pitcher Earl Whitehill, who recorded the Series' only shutout.

Games Four and Five went to New York, but not without a struggle. In the fourth game, manager Terry's home run broke the ice in the fourth inning, but Giant pitcher Hubbell muffed a bunt in the seventh which led to the tying run. Hubbell and Senator starter Monty Weaver dueled without further scoring until shortstop Blondy Ryan's single in the top of the eleventh put New York up by one. Hubbell let men reach second and third with one out in the last of the eleventh, but an intentional walk set up the hoped-for double play to end the game.

New York had built a three-run lead in Game Five when Senator Fred Schulte evened the score in the last of the sixth with a three-run homer. Relievers Jack Russell and Dolf Luque then dueled scorelessly into the tenth, when Giant Mel Ott (whose homer had begun the Series' scoring in the first inning of Game One) homered once again for what proved the Series' final run. Luque shut down the Senators in their half of the tenth, and "McGraw's Giants" were for the fourth time the world's finest. But before the advent of another spring, McGraw was dead.

New York Giants (NL), 4;
Washington Senators (AL), 1

NY (N)

PLAYER/POS	AVG	G	AB	R	H	2B	3B	HR	RB	BB	SO	SB
Hi Bell, p	.000	1	0	0	0	0	0	0	0	0	0	0
Hughie Critz, 2b	.136	5	22	2	3	0	0	0	0	1	0	0
Kiddo Davis, of	.368	5	19	1	7	1	0	0	0	0	3	0
Freddie Fitzsimmons, p	.500	1	2	0	1	0	0	0	0	0	0	0
Carl Hubbell, p	.286	2	7	0	2	0	0	0	0	0	0	0
Travis Jackson, 3b	.222	5	18	3	4	1	0	0	2	1	3	0
Dolf Luque, p	1.000	1	1	0	1	0	0	0	0	0	0	0
Gus Mancuso, c	.118	5	17	2	2	1	0	0	2	3	0	0
Jo-Jo Moore, of	.227	5	22	1	5	1	0	0	1	1	3	0
Lefty O'Doul, ph	1.000	1	1	1	1	0	0	0	2	0	0	0
Mel Ott, of	.389	5	18	3	7	0	0	2	4	4	4	0
Homer Peel, of-1	.500	2	2	0	1	0	0	0	0	0	0	0
Blondy Ryan, ss	.278	5	18	0	5	0	0	0	1	1	5	0
Hal Schumacher, p	.286	2	7	0	2	0	0	0	0	3	0	0
Bill Terry, 1b	.273	5	22	3	6	1	0	1	1	0	0	0
TOTAL	.267		176	16	47	5	0	3	16	11	21	0

PITCHER	W	L	ERA	G	GS	CG	SV	SHO	IP	H	ER	BB	SO
Hi Bell	0	0	0.00	1	0	0	0	0	1.0	0	0	0	0
Freddie Fitzsimmons	0	1	5.14	1	1	0	0	0	7.0	9	4	0	2
Carl Hubbell	2	0	0.00	2	2	2	0	0	20.0	13	0	6	15
Dolf Luque	1	0	0.00	1	0	0	0	0	4.1	2	0	2	5
Hal Schumacher	1	0	2.45	2	2	1	0	0	14.2	13	4	5	3
TOTAL	4	1	1.53	7	5	3	0	0	47.0	37	8	13	25

WAS (A)

PLAYER/POS	AVG	G	AB	R	H	2B	3B	HR	RB	BB	SO	SB
Ossie Bluege, 3b	.125	5	16	1	2	1	0	0	0	1	6	0
Cliff Bolton, ph	.000	2	2	0	0	0	0	0	0	0	0	0
Joe Cronin, ss	.318	5	22	1	7	0	0	0	2	0	2	0
General Crowder, p	.250	2	4	0	1	0	0	0	0	0	0	0
Goose Goslin, of	.250	5	20	2	5	1	0	1	1	1	3	0
Dave Harris, of-1	.000	3	2	0	0	0	0	0	0	2	0	0
John Kerr, pr	.000	1	0	0	0	0	0	0	0	0	0	0
Joe Kuhel, 1b	.150	5	20	1	3	0	0	0	1	1	4	0
Heinie Manush, of	.111	5	18	2	2	0	0	0	0	2	1	0
Alex McColl, p	.000	1	0	0	0	0	0	0	0	0	0	0
Buddy Myer, 2b	.300	5	20	2	6	1	0	0	2	2	3	0
Sam Rice, ph	1.000	1	1	0	1	0	0	0	0	0	0	0
Jack Russell, p	.000	3	2	0	0	0	0	0	0	1	2	0
Fred Schulte, of	.333	5	21	1	7	1	0	1	4	1	1	0
Luke Sewell, c	.176	5	17	1	3	0	0	0	1	2	0	1
Lefty Stewart, p	.000	1	1	0	0	0	0	0	0	0	1	0
Tommy Thomas, p	.000	2	0	0	0	0	0	0	0	0	0	0
Monte Weaver, p	.000	1	4	0	0	0	0	0	0	0	2	0
Earl Whitehill, p	.000	1	3	0	0	0	0	0	0	0	0	0
TOTAL	.214		173	11	37	4	0	2	11	13	25	1

PITCHER	W	L	ERA	G	GS	CG	SV	SHO	IP	H	ER	BB	SO
General Crowder	0	1	7.36	2	2	0	0	0	11.0	16	9	5	7
Alex McColl	0	0	0.00	1	0	0	0	0	2.0	0	0	0	0
Jack Russell	0	1	0.87	3	0	0	0	0	10.1	8	1	0	7
Lefty Stewart	0	1	9.00	1	1	0	0	0	2.0	6	2	0	0
Tommy Thomas	0	0	0.00	2	0	0	0	0	1.1	1	0	0	2
Monte Weaver	0	1	1.74	1	1	0	0	0	10.1	11	2	4	3
Earl Whitehill	1	0	0.00	1	1	1	0	1	9.0	5	0	2	3
TOTAL	1	4	2.74	11	5	1	0	1	46.0	47	14	11	21

GAME 1 AT NY OCT 3

WAS	000	100	001	2	5	3
NY	202	000	00X	4	10	2

Pitchers: STEWART, Russell (3), Thomas (8) vs HUBBELL
Home Runs: Ott-NY
Attendance: 46,672

GAME 2 AT NY OCT 4

WAS	001	000	000	1	5	0
NY	000	006	00X	6	10	0

Pitchers: CROWDER, Thomas (6), McColl (7) vs SCHUMACHER
Home Runs: Goslin-WAS
Attendance: 35,461

GAME 3 AT WAS OCT 5

NY	000	000	000	0	5	0
WAS	210	000	10X	4	9	1

Pitchers: FITZSIMMONS, Bell (8) vs WHITEHILL
Attendance: 25,727

GAME 4 AT WAS OCT 6

NY	000	100	000	01	2	11	1
WAS	000	000	100	00	1	8	0

Pitchers: HUBBELL vs WEAVER, Russell (11)
Home Runs: Terry-NY
Attendance: 26,762

GAME 5 AT WAS OCT 7

NY	020	001	000	1	4	11	1
WAS	000	003	000	0	3	10	0

Pitchers: Schumacher, LUQUE (6) vs Crowder, RUSSELL (6)
Home Runs: Schulte-WAS, Ott-NY
Attendance: 28,454

Pitching brothers Dizzy and Paul Dean won seven games in ten days to give the Cardinals the pennant on the final day of the season. In the Series they continued their winning ways, chalking up all four Cardinal victories. Dizzy pitched the opener in Detroit. Given a 3–0 lead, thanks to five Tiger errors in the first three innings, he breezed to an 8–3 win.

Detroit's Schoolboy Rowe brought the Tigers back with a pitching masterpiece in Game Two. After giving up single runs in the second and third innings, he allowed only one runner to reach base over the next nine as his Tigers tied the score in the ninth, and won it on two walks and a single in the twelfth.

Paul Dean nearly pitched a shutout in Game Three, yielding a harmless run with two out in the ninth after the Cards had built him a 4–0 lead. Brother Diz figured in a curious and painful play in Game Four. Pinch-running in the fourth inning, he was beaned by a would-be double-play throw as he ran to second. The tying run scored from third on the play, but Detroit's pitcher Eldon Auker shut out the Cards through the final five innings, and his teammates scored six more runs to bury St. Louis 10–4, evening the Series at two apiece. Diz was rushed to the hospital, but as no damage was found he started Game Five the next day. He pitched well enough, but Detroit's Tommy Bridges pitched better, giving the Cardinals only one run to the Tigers' three.

Paul Dean evened the Series again with a win against Rowe in a closely contested sixth game. A grounder through Dean's legs allowed the Tigers to tie the game in the sixth inning, but Paul redeemed his error in the seventh when he singled in the tie-breaking—and as it turned out, winning—run. Dizzy came back after only a day's rest to hurl a six-hit shutout in the finale. He also scored the game's first run and drove in the sixth with a double and single in his team's seven-run third. Three innings later, frustrated Tiger fans, angered by Cardinal Joe Medwick's rough slide into their third baseman, pelted Medwick with food and bottles, halting the game for twenty minutes until Commissioner Landis ordered Medwick from the game. The delay only forestalled Detroit's defeat, as the Cards took the title game 11–0.

St. Louis Cardinals (NL), 4; Detroit Tigers (AL), 3

STL (N)

PLAYER/POS	AVG	G	AB	R	H	2B	3B	HR	RB	BB	SO	SB
Tex Carleton, p	.000	2	1	0	0	0	0	0	0	0	0	0
Ripper Collins, 1b	.367	7	30	4	11	1	0	0	3	1	2	0
Pat Crawford, ph	.000	2	2	0	0	0	0	0	0	0	0	0
Spud Davis, ph	1.000	2	2	0	2	0	0	0	1	0	0	0
Dizzy Dean, p-3	.250	4	12	3	3	2	0	0	1	0	3	0
Paul Dean, p	.167	2	6	0	1	0	0	0	2	0	1	0
Bill DeLancey, c	.172	7	29	3	5	3	0	1	4	2	8	0
Leo Durocher, ss	.259	7	27	4	7	1	1	0	0	0	0	0
Frankie Frisch, 2b	.194	7	31	2	6	1	0	0	4	0	1	0
Chick Fullis, of	.400	3	5	0	2	0	0	0	0	0	0	0
Jesse Haines, p	.000	1	0	0	0	0	0	0	0	0	0	0
Bill Hallahan, p	.000	1	3	0	0	0	0	0	0	0	1	0
Pepper Martin, 3b	.355	7	31	8	11	3	1	0	4	3	3	2
Joe Medwick, of	.379	7	29	4	11	0	1	1	5	1	7	0
Jim Mooney, p	.000	1	0	0	0	0	0	0	0	0	0	0
Ernie Orsatti, of	.318	7	22	3	7	0	1	0	2	3	1	0
Jack Rothrock, of	.233	7	30	3	7	3	1	0	6	1	2	0
Dazzy Vance, p	.000	1	0	0	0	0	0	0	0	0	0	0
Bill Walker, p	.000	2	2	0	0	0	0	0	0	0	2	0
Burgess Whitehead, ss	.000	1	0	0	0	0	0	0	0	0	0	0
TOTAL	.279		262	34	73	14	5	2	32	11	31	2

PITCHER	W	L	ERA	G	GS	CG	SV	SHO	IP	H	ER	BB	SO
Tex Carleton	0	0	7.36	2	1	0	0	0	3.2	5	3	2	2
Dizzy Dean	2	1	1.73	3	3	2	0	1	26.0	20	5	5	17
Paul Dean	2	0	1.00	2	2	2	0	0	18.0	15	2	7	11
Jesse Haines	0	0	0.00	1	0	0	0	0	0.2	1	0	0	2
Bill Hallahan	0	0	2.16	1	1	0	0	0	8.1	6	2	4	6
Jim Mooney	0	0	0.00	1	0	0	0	0	1.0	1	0	0	0
Dazzy Vance	0	0	0.00	1	0	0	0	0	1.1	2	0	1	3
Bill Walker	0	2	7.11	2	0	0	0	0	6.1	6	5	6	2
TOTAL	4	3	2.34	13	7	4	0	1	65.1	56	17	25	43

DET (A)

PLAYER/POS	AVG	G	AB	R	H	2B	3B	HR	RB	BB	SO	SB
Eldon Auker, p	.000	2	4	0	0	0	0	0	0	0	2	0
Tommy Bridges, p	.143	3	7	0	1	0	0	0	0	1	4	0
Mickey Cochrane, c	.214	7	28	2	6	1	0	0	1	4	3	0
General Crowder, p	.000	2	1	0	0	0	0	0	0	0	0	0
Frank Doljack, of-1	.000	2	2	0	0	0	0	0	0	0	0	0
Pete Fox, of	.286	7	28	1	8	6	0	0	2	1	4	0
Charlie Gehringer, 2b	.379	7	29	5	11	1	0	1	2	3	0	1
Goose Goslin, of	.241	7	29	2	7	1	0	0	2	3	1	0
Hank Greenberg, 1b	.321	7	28	4	9	2	1	1	7	4	9	1
Ray Hayworth, c	.000	1	0	0	0	0	0	0	0	0	0	0
Chief Hogsett, p	.000	3	0	0	0	0	0	0	0	0	1	0
Firpo Marberry, p	.000	2	0	0	0	0	0	0	0	0	0	0
Marv Owen, 3b	.069	7	29	0	2	0	0	0	1	0	5	1
Billy Rogell, ss	.276	7	29	3	8	1	0	0	4	1	4	1
Schoolboy Rowe, p	.000	3	7	0	0	0	0	0	0	0	5	0
Gee Walker, ph	.333	3	3	0	1	0	0	0	1	0	1	0
Jo-Jo White, of	.130	7	23	6	3	0	0	0	0	8	4	1
TOTAL	.224		250	23	56	12	1	2	20	25	43	5

PITCHER	W	L	ERA	G	GS	CG	SV	SHO	IP	H	ER	BB	SO
Eldon Auker	1	1	5.56	2	2	1	0	0	11.1	16	7	5	2
Tommy Bridges	1	1	3.63	3	2	1	0	0	17.1	21	7	1	12
General Crowder	0	1	1.50	2	1	0	0	0	6.0	6	1	1	2
Chief Hogsett	0	0	1.23	3	0	0	0	0	7.1	6	1	3	3
Firpo Marberry	0	0	21.60	2	0	0	0	0	1.2	5	4	1	0
Schoolboy Rowe	1	1	2.95	3	2	2	0	0	21.1	19	7	0	12
TOTAL	3	4	3.74	15	7	4	0	0	65.0	73	27	11	31

GAME 1 AT DET OCT 3

STL	021	014	000	8	13	2
DET	001	001	010	3	8	5

Pitchers: J.DEAN vs CROWDER, Marberry (6), Hogsett (6)
Home Runs: Medwick-STL, Greenberg-DET
Attendance: 42,505

GAME 2 AT DET OCT 4

STL	011	000	000	000	2	7	3
DET	000	100	001	001	3	7	0

Pitchers: Hallahan, W.WALKER (9) vs ROWE
Attendance: 43,451

GAME 3 AT STL OCT 5

DET	000	000	001	1	8	2
STL	110	020	00X	4	9	1

Pitchers: BRIDGES, Hogsett (5) vs P.DEAN
Attendance: 34,073

GAME 4 AT STL OCT 6

DET	003	100	150	10	13	1
STL	011	200	000	4	10	5

Pitchers: AUKER vs Carleton, Vance (3), W.WALKER (5), Haines (8), Mooney (9)
Attendance: 37,492

GAME 5 AT STL OCT 7

DET	010	002	000	3	7	0
STL	000	000	100	1	7	1

Pitchers: BRIDGES vs J.DEAN, Carleton (9)
Home Runs: Gehringer-DET, Delancey-STL
Attendance: 38,536

GAME 6 AT DET OCT 8

STL	100	020	100	4	10	2
DET	001	002	000	3	7	1

Pitchers: P.DEAN vs ROWE
Attendance: 44,551

GAME 7 AT DET OCT 9

STL	007	002	200	11	17	1
DET	000	000	000	0	6	3

Pitchers: J.DEAN vs AUKER, Rowe (3), Hogsett (3), Bridges (4), Marberry (8), Crowder (9)
Attendance: 40,902

With a 21-game September winning streak, the Cubs vaulted over the Giants and Cardinals to face Detroit in the Series, and for a moment it seemed as if their momentum might carry them past the Tigers as well. Chicago scored two runs off Schoolboy Rowe in the top of the first in the opener, and right fielder Frank Demaree homered to open the ninth as Lon Warneke blanked the Tigers on four hits. But Detroit retaliated quickly in Game Two, driving out starter Charlie Root in the first inning with four runs (including Hank Greenberg's two-run homer) before Root had had a chance to record even one out. Tiger pitcher Rocky Bridges gained an easy 8–3 win, but Greenberg broke a wrist and was finished for the Series.

In Game Three the Cubs scored three times before Detroit countered with their first run in the sixth. But a walk and four Tiger hits in the eighth put the Bengals ahead 4–3, and Billy Rogell's baserunning as he turned a foiled steal into a rundown permitted a fifth Tiger to cross the plate. Two Cub runs in the last of the ninth tied the score, but Detroit pulled out the victory in the eleventh as a pair of singles sandwiched Fred Lindstrom's error at third to give them an unearned run.

Detroit's Alvin "General" Crowder followed up the Tigers' advantage the next day with a neat five-hit 2–1 win. Once again the Cubs bobbled away the game, this time with two sixth-inning errors that enabled Detroit to score the winning run without a hit. Chuck Klein's two-run homer saved Chicago from elimination in Game Five as Lon Warneke and Bill Lee shut out the Tigers through eight before letting in a harmless run in the ninth.

Chicago's Larry French and Tiger Rocky Bridges yielded 12 hits apiece in Game Six. Cub second baseman Billy Herman singled in a run in the third to tie the score, and homered for two more runs in the fifth to put the Cubs ahead. But the Tigers tied it up an inning later, and took their first world title ever when Goose Goslin singled in Mickey Cochrane with two out in the bottom of the ninth.

Detroit Tigers (AL), 4; Chicago Cubs (NL), 2

DET (A)

PLAYER/POS	AVG	G	AB	R	H	2B	3B	HR	RB	BB	SO	SB
Eldon Auker, p	.000	1	2	0	0	0	0	0	0	0	1	0
Tommy Bridges, p	.125	2	8	1	1	0	0	0	1	0	3	0
Flea Clifton, 3b	.000	4	16	1	0	0	0	0	0	2	4	0
Mickey Cochrane, c	.292	6	24	3	7	1	0	0	1	4	1	0
General Crowder, p	.333	1	3	1	1	0	0	0	0	1	0	0
Pete Fox, of	.385	6	26	1	10	3	1	0	4	0	1	0
Charlie Gehringer, 2b	.375	6	24	4	9	3	0	0	4	2	1	1
Goose Goslin, of	.273	6	22	2	6	1	0	0	3	5	0	0
Hank Greenberg, 1b	.167	2	6	1	1	0	0	1	2	1	0	0
Chief Hogsett, p	.000	1	0	0	0	0	0	0	0	0	0	0
Marv Owen, 1b-4,3b-2	.050	6	20	2	1	0	0	0	1	2	3	0
Billy Rogell, ss	.292	6	24	1	7	2	0	0	1	2	5	0
Schoolboy Rowe, p	.250	3	8	0	2	1	0	0	0	0	1	0
Gee Walker, of-1	.250	3	4	1	1	0	0	0	0	1	0	0
Jo-Jo White, of	.263	5	19	3	5	0	0	0	1	5	7	0
TOTAL	.248		206	21	51	11	1	1	18	25	27	1

PITCHER	W	L	ERA	G	GS	CG	SV	SHO	IP	H	ER	BB	SO
Eldon Auker	0	0	3.00	1	1	0	0	0	6.0	6	2	2	1
Tommy Bridges	2	0	2.50	2	2	2	0	0	18.0	18	5	4	9
General Crowder	1	0	1.00	1	1	1	0	0	9.0	5	1	3	5
Chief Hogsett	0	0	0.00	1	0	0	0	0	1.0	0	0	1	0
Schoolboy Rowe	1	2	2.57	3	2	2	0	0	21.0	19	6	1	14
TOTAL	4	2	2.29	8	6	5	0	0	55.0	48	14	11	29

CHI (N)

PLAYER/POS	AVG	G	AB	R	H	2B	3B	HR	RB	BB	SO	SB
Tex Carleton, p	.000	1	1	0	0	0	0	0	0	1	1	0
Phil Cavaretta, 1b	.125	6	24	1	3	0	0	0	0	0	5	0
Frank Demaree, of	.250	6	24	2	6	1	0	2	2	1	4	0
Larry French, p	.250	2	4	1	1	0	0	0	0	0	2	0
Augie Galan, of	.160	6	25	2	4	1	0	0	2	2	2	0
Stan Hack, 3b-6,ss-1	.227	6	22	2	5	1	1	0	0	2	2	1
Gabby Hartnett, c	.292	6	24	1	7	0	0	1	2	0	3	0
Roy Henshaw, p	.000	1	1	0	0	0	0	0	0	0	0	0
Billy Herman, 2b	.333	6	24	3	8	2	1	1	6	0	2	0
Billy Jurges, ss	.250	6	16	3	4	0	0	0	1	4	4	0
Chuck Klein, of-3	.333	5	12	2	4	0	0	1	2	0	2	0
Fabian Kowalik, p	.500	2	2	1	1	0	0	0	0	0	0	0
Bill Lee, p	.000	2	1	0	0	0	0	0	0	1	0	0
Fred Lindstrom, of-4,3b-1	.200	4	15	0	3	1	0	0	0	1	1	0
Ken O'Dea, ph	1.000	1	1	0	1	0	0	0	1	0	0	0
Charlie Root, p	.000	2	0	0	0	0	0	0	0	0	0	0
Walter Stephenson, ph	.000	1	1	0	0	0	0	0	0	0	1	0
Lon Warneke, p	.200	3	5	0	1	0	0	0	0	0	0	0
TOTAL	.238		202	18	48	6	2	5	17	11	29	1

PITCHER	W	L	ERA	G	GS	CG	SV	SHO	IP	H	ER	BB	SO
Tex Carleton	0	1	1.29	1	1	0	0	0	7.0	6	1	7	4
Larry French	0	2	3.38	2	1	1	0	0	10.2	15	4	2	8
Roy Henshaw	0	0	7.36	1	0	0	0	0	3.2	5	3	5	2
Fabian Kowalik	0	0	2.08	1	0	0	0	0	4.1	3	1	1	1
Bill Lee	0	0	3.48	2	1	0	1	0	10.1	11	4	5	5
Charlie Root	0	1	18.00	2	1	0	0	0	2.0	5	4	1	2
Lon Warneke	2	0	0.54	3	2	1	0	1	16.2	9	1	4	5
TOTAL	2	4	2.96	12	6	2	1	1	54.2	51	18	25	27

The Giants managed to win two games, but this first Series between the cross-river rivals in thirteen years was really no contest. Babe Ruth was gone, but Lou Gehrig was still there, and Joe DiMaggio had arrived. The Yankees outhit the Giants by 56 percentage points and outscored them by 20 runs.

Giant ace Carl Hubbell, who had won his final 16 decisions of the regular season, continued his streak in the Series opener. The Yankees scored first on George Selkirk's third-inning homer, but Giant shortstop Dick Bartell homered to even things in the fifth. Hubbell held the Yankees to that one run, but the Giants roughed up Red Ruffing for five more runs, to give the Polo Grounders a brief Series advantage.

Game Two was a Yankee blow-out, as the Yankees hammered five Giant pitchers for 18 runs—four of them on Tony Lazzeri's grand slam in the third—to give Lefty Gomez an easy win. By contrast, Game Three was a pitchers' duel. Although the Giants touched Bump Hadley and Pat Malone for 11 hits, only Jimmy Ripple's fifth-inning homer produced a run. Giant Freddie Fitzsimmons was much more stingy with hits, yielding only four. But one was Gehrig's home run in the second inning, and another was Frank Crosetti's game-winning RBI single in the eighth.

Gehrig homered again in the third inning of Game Four to give the Yankees an insurmountable lead—and Hubbell his first loss in months. Down three games to one, the Giants struggled back in Game Five. They took a first-inning 3–0 lead, but the Yankees clawed their way back, and by the end of six the score was 4–4. There it stayed until the tenth, when a double, sacrifice, and fly to center put the Giants ahead by a run. Hal Schumacher, who had pitched the whole game, held the Yankees scoreless one more time for the win.

Fitzsimmons, who had pitched so well in his third-game loss, didn't last four innings in Game Six. Though the Giants scored first, Yankee Jake Powell (who led all Series hitters at .455) tied the game with a two-run homer in the top of the second. Two more runs in the fourth drove out Fitzsimmons, but the game stayed close until the top of the ninth, when five Yankees singles and three walks produced seven runs and a Series-ending 13–5 rout.

New York Yankees (AL), 4;
New York Giants (NL), 2

NY (A)

PLAYER/POS	AVG	G	AB	R	H	2B	3B	HR	RB	BB	SO	SB
Frankie Crosetti, ss	.269	6	26	5	7	2	0	0	3	3	5	0
Bill Dickey, c	.120	6	25	5	3	0	0	1	5	3	4	0
Joe DiMaggio, of	.346	6	26	3	9	3	0	0	3	1	3	0
Lou Gehrig, 1b	.292	6	24	5	7	1	0	2	7	3	2	0
Lefty Gomez, p	.250	2	8	1	2	0	0	0	3	0	3	0
Bump Hadley, p	.000	1	2	0	0	0	0	0	0	0	1	0
Roy Johnson, ph	.000	2	1	0	0	0	0	0	0	0	1	0
Tony Lazzeri, 2b	.250	6	20	4	5	0	0	1	7	4	4	0
Pat Malone, p	1.000	2	1	0	1	0	0	0	0	0	0	0
Johnny Murphy, p	.500	1	2	1	1	0	0	0	1	0	1	0
Monte Pearson, p	.500	1	4	0	2	1	0	0	0	0	0	0
Jake Powell, of	.455	6	22	8	10	1	0	1	5	4	4	1
Red Rolfe, 3b	.400	6	25	5	10	0	0	0	4	3	1	0
Red Ruffing, p-2	.000	3	5	0	0	0	0	0	0	1	2	0
Bob Seeds, pr	.000	1	0	0	0	0	0	0	0	0	0	0
George Selkirk, of	.333	6	24	6	8	0	1	2	3	4	4	0
TOTAL	.302		215	43	65	8	1	7	41	26	35	1

PITCHER	W	L	ERA	G	GS	CG	SV	SHO	IP	H	ER	BB	SO
Lefty Gomez	2	0	4.70	2	2	1	0	0	15.1	14	8	11	9
Bump Hadley	1	0	1.13	1	1	0	0	0	8.0	10	1	1	2
Pat Malone	0	1	1.80	2	0	0	1	0	5.0	2	1	1	2
Johnny Murphy	0	0	3.38	1	0	0	1	0	2.2	1	1	1	1
Monte Pearson	1	0	2.00	1	1	1	0	0	9.0	7	2	2	7
Red Ruffing	0	1	4.50	2	2	0	0	0	14.0	16	7	5	12
TOTAL	4	2	3.33	9	6	2	2	0	54.0	50	20	21	33

NY (N)

PLAYER/POS	AVG	G	AB	R	H	2B	3B	HR	RB	BB	SO	SB
Dick Bartell, ss	.381	6	21	5	8	3	0	1	3	4	4	0
Slick Castleman, p	.500	1	2	0	1	0	0	0	0	0	0	0
Dick Coffman, p	.000	2	0	0	0	0	0	0	0	0	0	0
Harry Danning, c-1	.000	2	2	0	0	0	0	0	0	0	1	0
Kiddo Davis, ph	.500	4	2	2	1	0	0	0	0	0	0	0
Freddie Fitzsimmons, p	.500	2	4	0	2	0	0	0	0	0	1	0
Frank Gabler, p	.000	2	0	0	0	0	0	0	0	1	0	0
Harry Gumbert, p	.000	2	0	0	0	0	0	0	0	0	0	0
Carl Hubbell, p	.333	2	6	0	2	0	0	0	1	0	0	0
Travis Jackson, 3b	.190	6	21	1	4	0	0	0	1	1	3	0
Mark Koenig, 2b-1	.333	3	3	0	1	0	0	0	0	0	1	0
Hank Leiber, of	.000	2	6	0	0	0	0	0	0	2	2	0
Sam Leslie, ph	.667	3	3	0	2	0	0	0	0	0	0	0
Gus Mancuso, c	.263	6	19	3	5	2	0	0	1	3	3	0
Eddie Mayo, 3b	.000	1	1	0	0	0	0	0	0	0	0	0
Jo-Jo Moore, of	.214	6	28	4	6	3	0	1	1	1	4	0
Mel Ott, of	.304	6	23	4	7	2	0	1	3	3	1	0
Jimmy Ripple, of	.333	5	12	2	4	0	0	1	3	3	3	0
Hal Schumacher, p	.000	2	4	0	0	0	0	0	0	1	3	0
Al Smith, p	.000	1	0	0	0	0	0	0	0	0	0	0
Bill Terry, 1b	.240	6	25	1	6	0	0	0	5	1	4	0
Burgess Whitehead, 2b	.048	6	21	1	1	0	0	0	2	1	3	0
TOTAL	.246		203	23	50	9	0	4	20	21	33	0

PITCHER	W	L	ERA	G	GS	CG	SV	SHO	IP	H	ER	BB	SO
Slick Castleman	0	0	2.08	1	0	0	0	0	4.1	3	1	2	5
Dick Coffman	0	0	32.40	2	0	0	0	0	1.2	5	6	1	1
Freddie Fitzsimmons	0	2	5.40	2	2	1	0	0	11.2	13	7	2	6
Frank Gabler	0	0	7.20	2	0	0	0	0	5.0	7	4	4	0
Harry Gumbert	0	0	36.00	2	0	0	0	0	2.0	7	8	4	2
Carl Hubbell	1	1	2.25	2	2	1	0	0	16.0	15	4	2	10
Hal Schumacher	1	1	5.25	2	2	1	0	0	12.0	13	7	10	11
Al Smith	0	0	81.00	1	0	0	0	0	0.1	2	3	1	0
TOTAL	2	4	6.79	14	6	3	0	0	53.0	65	40	26	35

GAME 1 AT NY -N SEPT 30

NY-A	001 000 000	1	7	2
NY-N	000 011 04X	6	9	1

Pitchers: RUFFING vs HUBBELL
Home Runs: Bartell-NY(N), Selkirk-NY(A)
Attendance: 39,419

GAME 2 AT NY -N OCT 2

NY-A	207 001 206	18	17	0
NY-N	010 300 000	4	6	1

Pitchers: GOMEZ vs SCHUMACHER, Smith (3), Coffman (3), Gabler (5), Gumbert (9)
Home Runs: Dickey-NY(A), Lazzeri-NY(A)
Attendance: 43,543

GAME 3 AT NY -A OCT 3

NY-N	000 010 000	1	11	0
NY-A	010 000 01X	2	4	0

Pitchers: FITZSIMMONS vs HADLEY, Malone (9)
Home Runs: Gerhig-NY(A), Ripple-NY(N)
Attendance: 64,842

GAME 4 AT NY -A OCT 4

NY-N	000 100 010	2	7	1
NY-A	013 000 01X	5	10	1

Pitchers: HUBBELL, Gabler (8) vs PEARSON
Home Runs: Gehrig-NY(A)
Attendance: 66,669

GAME 5 AT NY -A OCT 5

NY-N	300 001 000 1	5	8	3
NY-A	011 002 000 0	4	10	1

Pitchers: SCHUMACHER vs Ruffing, MALONE (7)
Home Runs: Selkirk-NY(A)
Attendance: 50,024

GAME 6 AT NY -N OCT 6

NY-A	021 200 017	13	17	2
NY-N	200 010 110	5	9	1

Pitchers: GOMEZ, Murphy (7) vs FITZSIMMONS, Castleman (4), Coffman (9), Gumbert (9)
Home Runs: Moore-NY(N), Ott-NY(N), Powell-NY(A)
Attendance: 38,427

For the second year in a row, the Yankees overwhelmed the Giants, this time in just five games. Giant ace Carl Hubbell, who took the opener in 1936, was unable to repeat this year. For five innings he held the Yankees to one hit. But in the sixth everything fell apart. Before Hubbell was taken out, two walks, five singles, and a Giant error had let in five runs. And the two runners Hubbell left on base scored later on a second Giant error and two walks by reliever Dick Coffman. The Yankees' Lefty Gomez also yielded six hits, but wider spacing and better field support held the Giants to one run in the fifth. Tony Lazzeri's homer in the eighth made the final score 8–1.

The Yankees spread their runs a bit more evenly in Game Two. For the second time the Giants gained a 1–0 lead. Rookie phenom Cliff Melton held the Yankees scoreless through four, but four straight hits for two runs at the start of the fifth drove him out. Reliever Ad Gumbert stopped the Yankees in the rest of the inning but gave up four more hits—and four more runs—in the sixth before Coffman stepped in to stop the assault. But Coffman gave up two final Yankee runs in the seventh, to complete a second straight 8–1 Yankee win, as Red Ruffing held the Giants scoreless through the final eight innings.

The Yankees had scored five times off Hal Schumacher in Game Three before the Giants got their one run in the seventh. But Yankee starter Monte Pearson made the game tighter as he yielded a single and two walks to load the bases in the ninth before Johnny Murphy came on to record the final out.

Giant bats finally came alive in the second inning of Game Four. Seven singles, plus a walk and a missed play at the plate gave the club a 6–1 lead, which starter Hubbell protected for the only Giant win of the Series.

Solo homers by Myril Hoag in the second and Joe DiMaggio in the third gave the Yankees a 2–0 lead early in Game Five, but Giant Mel Ott tied it up with a two-run shot off Lefty Gomez in the last of the third. But Gomez shut the Giants down the rest of the way, and singled in Lazzeri in the fifth with what proved the game winner (scoring himself on Lou Gehrig's double for the final run of the Series).

New York Yankees (AL), 4;
New York Giants (NL), 1

NY (A)

PLAYER/POS	AVG	G	AB	R	H	2B	3B	HR	RBI	BB	SO	SB
Ivy Andrews, p	.000	1	2	0	0	0	0	0	0	0	1	0
Frankie Crosetti, ss	.048	5	21	2	1	0	0	0	0	3	2	0
Bill Dickey, c	.211	5	19	3	4	0	1	0	3	2	2	0
Joe DiMaggio, of	.273	5	22	2	6	0	0	1	4	0	3	0
Lou Gehrig, 1b	.294	5	17	4	5	1	1	1	3	5	4	0
Lefty Gomez, p	.167	2	6	2	1	0	0	0	1	2	1	0
Bump Hadley, p	.000	1	0	0	0	0	0	0	0	0	0	0
Myril Hoag, of	.300	5	20	4	6	1	0	1	2	0	1	0
Tony Lazzeri, 2b	.400	5	15	3	6	0	1	1	2	3	3	0
Johnny Murphy, p	.000	1	0	0	0	0	0	0	0	0	0	0
Monte Pearson, p	.000	1	3	0	0	0	0	0	0	1	1	0
Jake Powell, ph	.000	1	1	0	0	0	0	0	0	0	1	0
Red Rolfe, 3b	.300	5	20	3	6	2	1	0	1	3	2	0
Red Ruffing, p	.500	1	4	0	2	1	0	0	3	0	0	0
George Selkirk, of	.263	5	19	5	5	1	0	0	6	2	0	0
Kemp Wicker, p	.000	1	0	0	0	0	0	0	0	0	0	0
TOTAL	.249		169	28	42	6	4	4	25	21	21	0

PITCHER	W	L	ERA	G	GS	CG	SV	SHO	IP	H	ER	BB	SO
Ivy Andrews	0	0	3.18	1	0	0	0	0	5.2	6	2	4	1
Lefty Gomez	2	0	1.50	2	2	2	0	0	18.0	16	3	2	8
Bump Hadley	0	1	33.75	1	1	0	0	0	1.1	6	5	0	0
Johnny Murphy	0	0	0.00	1	0	0	1	0	0.1	0	0	0	0
Monte Pearson	1	0	1.04	1	1	0	0	0	8.2	5	1	2	4
Red Ruffing	1	0	1.00	1	1	1	0	0	9.0	7	1	3	8
Kemp Wicker	0	0	0.00	1	0	0	0	0	1.0	0	0	0	0
TOTAL	4	1	2.45	8	5	3	1	0	44.0	40	12	11	21

NY (N)

PLAYER/POS	AVG	G	AB	R	H	2B	3B	HR	RBI	BB	SO	SB
Dick Bartell, ss	.238	5	21	3	5	1	0	0	1	0	3	0
Wally Berger, ph	.000	3	3	0	0	0	0	0	0	0	1	0
Don Brennan, p	.000	2	0	0	0	0	0	0	0	0	0	0
Lou Chiozza, of	.286	2	7	0	2	0	0	0	0	1	1	0
Dick Coffman, p	.000	2	1	0	0	0	0	0	0	0	1	0
Harry Danning, c	.250	3	12	0	3	1	0	0	2	0	2	0
Harry Gumbert, p	.000	2	0	0	0	0	0	0	0	0	0	0
Carl Hubbell, p	.000	2	6	1	0	0	0	0	0	1	0	0
Hank Leiber, of	.364	3	11	2	4	0	0	0	2	1	1	0
Sam Leslie, ph	.000	2	1	0	0	0	0	0	0	1	0	0
Gus Mancuso, c-2	.000	3	8	0	0	0	0	0	1	0	1	0
Johnny McCarthy, 1b	.211	5	19	1	4	1	0	0	1	1	2	0
Cliff Melton, p	.000	3	2	0	0	0	0	0	0	1	1	0
Mel Ott, 3b	.200	5	20	1	4	0	0	1	3	1	4	0
Jo-Jo Moore, of	.391	5	23	1	9	1	0	0	1	0	1	0
Jimmy Ripple, of	.294	5	17	2	5	0	0	0	0	3	1	0
Blondy Ryan, ph	.000	1	1	0	0	0	0	0	0	0	1	0
Hal Schumacher, p	.000	1	1	0	0	0	0	0	0	0	1	0
Al Smith, p	.000	2	0	0	0	0	0	0	0	0	0	0
Burgess Whitehead, 2b	.250	5	16	1	4	2	0	0	0	2	0	1
TOTAL	.237		169	12	40	6	0	1	12	11	21	1

PITCHER	W	L	ERA	G	GS	CG	SV	SHO	IP	H	ER	BB	SO
Don Brennan	0	0	0.00	2	0	0	0	0	3.0	1	0	1	1
Dick Coffman	0	0	4.15	2	0	0	0	0	4.1	2	2	5	1
Harry Gumbert	0	0	27.00	2	0	0	0	0	1.1	4	4	1	1
Carl Hubbell	1	1	3.77	2	2	1	0	0	14.1	12	6	4	7
Cliff Melton	0	2	4.91	3	2	0	0	0	11.0	12	6	6	7
Hal Schumacher	0	1	6.00	1	1	0	0	0	6.0	9	4	4	3
Al Smith	0	0	3.00	2	0	0	0	0	3.0	2	1	0	1
TOTAL	1	4	4.81	14	5	1	0	0	43.0	42	23	21	21

GAME 1 AT NY -A OCT 6

```
NY-N   000 010 000   1 6 2
NY-A   000 007 01X   8 7 0
```

Pitchers: HUBBELL, Gumbert (6), Coffman (6), Smith (8) vs GOMEZ
Home Runs: Lazzeri-NY(A)
Attendance: 60,573

GAME 2 AT NY -A OCT 7

```
NY-N   100 000 000   1 7 0
NY-A   000 024 20X   8 12 0
```

Pitchers: MELTON, Gumbert (5), Coffman (6) vs RUFFING
Attendance: 57,675

GAME 3 AT NY -N OCT 8

```
NY-A   012 110 000   5 9 0
NY-N   000 000 100   1 5 4
```

Pitchers: PEARSON, Murphy (9) vs SCHUMACHER, Melton (7), Brennan (9)
Attendance: 37,385

GAME 4 AT NY -N OCT 9

```
NY-A   101 000 001   3 6 0
NY-N   060 000 10X   7 12 3
```

Pitchers: HADLEY, Andrews (2), Wicker (8) vs HUBBELL
Home Runs: Gehrig-NY(A)
Attendance: 44,293

GAME 5 AT NY -N OCT 10

```
NY-A   011 020 000   4 8 0
NY-N   002 000 000   2 10 0
```

Pitchers: GOMEZ vs MELTON, Smith (6), Brennan (8)
Home Runs: DiMaggio-NY(A), Hoag-NY(A), Ott-NY(N)
Attendance: 38,216

As they had six years earlier, the Cubs faced the Yankees in the World Series, and as they had six years earlier, New York swept the Series in four games. Although Cub batters made nearly as many hits as the Yankees, they did much less damage, driving in 13 fewer runs. In Game One, Yankee ace Red Ruffing scattered nine Cub hits, holding Chicago to a single run. The Cubs' Bill Lee was nearly as effective in scattering hits, but a base on balls in the second (the game's only walk) followed by a pair of singles sandwiched around an error accounted for two runs—all the Yankees would need for the win (though they scored once more in the sixth).

In Game Two the Cubs outhit the Yankees 11 to 7, but scored only half as many runs as the New Yorkers. Chicago's Dizzy Dean, pitching on craft and guile with his fastball gone, managed to keep the game close until the final innings. With a 3–2 lead going into the eighth, though, he gave up a two-run homer to Frank Crosetti, and the same to Joe DiMaggio in the ninth before being relieved. Yankee fireman Johnny Murphy, meanwhile, held Chicago scoreless over the final two innings to preserve Lefty Gomez's win.

Utility outfielder Joe Marty drove in both Chicago runs in Game Three with a grounder to third in the fifth and a homer in the eighth. (His .500 BA was tops for both teams, and he drove in five of the Cubs' nine Series runs.) But again the Cubs fell short, as Yankee rookie second baseman Joe Gordon homered to tie the score in the bottom of the fifth with the first of what would be five Yankee runs by the time Bill Dickey's homer in the eighth ended the scoring for the day.

Cub second baseman Billy Herman's wild throw with two out in the second inning of Game Four led to three unearned runs, and a Yankee lead they would not relinquish. Though their lead was cut to one run (4–3) when Chicago scored twice in the top of the eighth, the Yankees took advantage of two wild pitches and two walks to turn their four hits into four runs that crushed Cub hopes and gave the New Yorkers a record third consecutive world championship.

New York Yankees (AL), 4;
Chicago Cubs (NL), 0

NY (A)

PLAYER/POS	AVG	G	AB	R	H	2B	3B	HR	RB	BB	SO	SB
Frankie Crosetti, ss	.250	4	16	1	4	2	1	1	6	2	4	0
Bill Dickey, c	.400	4	15	2	6	0	0	1	2	1	0	1
Joe DiMaggio, of	.267	4	15	4	4	0	0	1	2	1	1	0
Lou Gehrig, 1b	.286	4	14	4	4	0	0	0	0	2	3	0
Lefty Gomez, p	.000	1	2	0	0	0	0	0	0	0	0	0
Joe Gordon, 2b	.400	4	15	3	6	2	0	1	6	1	3	1
Tommy Henrich, of	.250	4	16	3	4	1	0	1	1	0	1	0
Myril Hoag, of-1	.400	2	5	3	2	1	0	0	1	0	0	0
Johnny Murphy, p	.000	1	0	0	0	0	0	0	0	0	0	0
Monte Pearson, p	.333	1	3	1	1	0	0	0	0	1	0	0
Jake Powell, of	.000	1	0	0	0	0	0	0	0	0	0	0
Red Rolfe, 3b	.167	4	18	0	3	0	0	0	1	0	3	1
Red Ruffing, p	.167	2	6	1	1	0	0	0	1	1	0	0
George Selkirk, of	.200	3	10	0	2	0	0	0	1	2	1	0
TOTAL	.274		135	22	37	6	1	5	21	11	16	3

PITCHER	W	L	ERA	G	GS	CG	SV	SHO	IP	H	ER	BB	SO
Lefty Gomez	1	0	3.86	1	1	0	0	0	7.0	9	3	1	5
Johnny Murphy	0	0	0.00	1	0	0	1	0	2.0	2	0	1	1
Monte Pearson	1	0	1.00	1	1	1	0	0	9.0	5	1	2	9
Red Ruffing	2	0	1.50	2	2	2	0	0	18.0	17	3	2	11
TOTAL	4	0	1.75	5	4	3	1	0	36.0	33	7	6	26

CHI (N)

PLAYER/POS	AVG	G	AB	R	H	2B	3B	HR	RB	BB	SO	SB
Clay Bryant, p	.000	1	2	0	0	0	0	0	0	0	1	0
Tex Carleton, p	.000	1	0	0	0	0	0	0	0	0	0	0
Phil Cavaretta, of-3	.462	4	13	1	6	1	0	0	0	0	1	0
Ripper Collins, 1b	.133	4	15	1	2	0	0	0	0	0	3	0
Dizzy Dean, p	.667	2	3	0	2	0	0	0	0	0	0	0
Frank Demaree, of	.100	3	10	1	1	0	0	0	0	1	2	0
Larry French, p	.000	3	0	0	0	0	0	0	0	0	0	0
Augie Galan, ph	.000	2	2	0	0	0	0	0	0	0	1	0
Stan Hack, 3b	.471	4	17	3	8	1	0	0	1	1	2	0
Gabby Hartnett, c	.091	3	11	0	1	0	1	0	0	0	2	0
Billy Herman, 2b	.188	4	16	1	3	0	0	0	0	1	4	0
Billy Jurges, ss	.231	4	13	0	3	1	0	0	0	1	3	0
Tony Lazzeri, ph	.000	2	2	0	0	0	0	0	0	0	1	0
Bill Lee, p	.000	2	3	0	0	0	0	0	0	0	1	0
Joe Marty, of	.500	3	12	1	6	1	0	1	5	0	2	0
Ken O'Dea, c-1	.200	3	5	1	1	0	0	1	2	1	0	0
Vance Page, p	.000	1	0	0	0	0	0	0	0	0	0	0
Carl Reynolds, of-3	.000	4	12	0	0	0	0	0	0	1	3	0
Charlie Root, p	.000	1	0	0	0	0	0	0	0	0	0	0
Jack Russell, p	.000	2	0	0	0	0	0	0	0	0	0	0
TOTAL	.243		136	9	33	4	1	2	8	6	26	0

PITCHER	W	L	ERA	G	GS	CG	SV	SHO	IP	H	ER	BB	SO
Clay Bryant	0	1	6.75	1	1	0	0	0	5.1	6	4	5	3
Tex Carleton	0	0	INF	1	0	0	0	0	0.0	1	2	2	0
Dizzy Dean	0	1	6.48	2	1	0	0	0	8.1	8	6	1	2
Larry French	0	0	2.70	3	0	0	0	0	3.1	1	1	1	2
Bill Lee	0	2	2.45	2	2	0	0	0	11.0	15	3	1	8
Vance Page	0	0	13.50	1	0	0	0	0	1.1	2	2	0	0
Charlie Root	0	0	3.00	1	0	0	0	0	3.0	3	1	0	1
Jack Russell	0	0	0.00	2	0	0	0	0	1.2	1	0	1	0
TOTAL	0	4	5.03	13	4	0	0	0	34.0	37	19	11	16

GAME 1 AT CHI OCT 5

NY	020 000 100	3	12	1
CHI	001 000 000	1	9	1

Pitchers: RUFFING vs LEE, Russell (9)
Attendance: 43,642

GAME 2 AT CHI OCT 6

NY	020 000 022	6	7	2
CHI	102 000 000	3	11	0

Pitchers: GOMEZ, Murphy (8) vs J.DEAN, French (9)
Home Runs: Crosetti-NY, DiMaggio-NY
Attendance: 42,108

GAME 3 AT NY OCT 8

CHI	000 010 010	2	5	1
NY	000 022 01X	5	7	2

Pitchers: BRYANT, Russell (6), French (7) vs PEARSON
Home Runs: Dickey-NY, Gordon-NY, Marty-CHI
Attendance: 55,236

GAME 4 AT NY OCT 9

CHI	000 100 020	3	8	1
NY	030 001 04X	8	11	1

Pitchers: LEE, Root (4), Page (7), French (8), Carleton (8), J.Dean (8) vs RUFFING
Home Runs: Henrich-NY, O'Dea-CHI
Attendance: 59,847

The Yankees won their fourth consecutive World Series with their second sweep in a row. This time the victim was Cincinnati, in the Series for the first time since their tainted triumph over the Black Sox two decades earlier. New York had lost the power of Lou Gehrig (whose illness forced his retirement early in the season), but in the Series rookie outfielder Charlie Keller took up the slack. He led both clubs in batting, slugging, home runs, RBIs, hits, and runs, and hit one of the Series' two triples. His eight runs scored equalled those of the whole Cincinnati team.

The Yankees' Red Ruffing and Cincinnati's Paul Derringer hurled matching four-hitters through eight innings of Game One. With the score tied 1–1, Ruffing set the Reds down in order in the ninth. But in the bottom of the ninth Keller tripled off Derringer with one away, and scored the deciding run on catcher Bill Dickey's single.

Babe Dahlgren, Gehrig's replacement at first base, doubled in the third and later scored the Yankees' first run in Game Two, and homered in the next inning for New York's fourth and final run of the game. Red starter Bucky Walters stopped the Yankees after that, but they had more than enough runs for the win, as Monte Pearson held the Reds hitless through seven and wound up with a two-hit shutout.

Keller provided the margin of victory with a pair of two-run homers in the first and fifth innings of Game Three. Joe DiMaggio's two-run homer in the third and Bill Dickey's solo shot that followed Keller's homer in the fifth accounted for the rest of New York's runs in their 7–3 win.

No one scored through six innings of Game Four. Keller and Dickey then homered in the top of the seventh, but Red Rolfe's error at third in the last of the inning opened the way for the Reds to go ahead with three unearned runs. They earned a fourth run an inning later, but the Yankees tied it up with two in the ninth (one unearned) and took the lead in the tenth with three more runs (two unearned) on a walk, a single, and three more Red errors. Reliever Johnny Murphy held off a Red threat in the last of the tenth and the Series was over.

New York Yankees (AL), 4; Cincinnati Reds (NL), 0

NY (A)

PLAYER/POS	AVG	G	AB	R	H	2B	3B	HR	RB	BB	SO	SB
Frankie Crosetti, ss	.063	4	16	2	1	0	0	0	1	2	2	0
Babe Dahlgren, 1b	.214	4	14	2	3	2	0	1	2	0	4	0
Bill Dickey, c	.267	4	15	2	4	0	0	2	5	1	2	0
Joe DiMaggio, of	.313	4	16	3	5	0	0	1	3	1	1	0
Lefty Gomez, p	.000	1	1	0	0	0	0	0	0	0	1	0
Joe Gordon, 2b	.143	4	14	1	2	0	0	0	1	0	2	0
Bump Hadley, p	.000	1	3	0	0	0	0	0	0	0	0	0
Oral Hildebrand, p	.000	1	1	0	0	0	0	0	0	0	1	0
Charlie Keller, of	.438	4	16	8	7	1	1	3	6	1	2	0
Johnny Murphy, p	.000	1	2	0	0	0	0	0	0	0	1	0
Monte Pearson, p	.000	1	2	0	0	0	0	0	0	0	1	0
Red Rolfe, 3b	.125	4	16	2	2	0	0	0	0	0	0	0
Red Ruffing, p	.333	1	3	0	1	0	0	0	0	0	1	0
George Selkirk, of	.167	4	12	0	2	1	0	0	0	3	2	0
Steve Sundra, p	.000	1	0	0	0	0	0	0	0	0	1	0
TOTAL	.206		131	20	27	4	1	7	18	9	20	0

PITCHER	W	L	ERA	G	GS	CG	SV	SHO	IP	H	ER	BB	SO
Lefty Gomez	0	0	9.00	1	1	0	0	0	1.0	3	1	0	1
Bump Hadley	1	0	2.25	1	0	0	0	0	8.0	7	2	3	2
Oral Hildebrand	0	0	0.00	1	1	0	0	0	4.0	2	0	0	3
Johnny Murphy	1	0	2.70	1	0	0	0	0	3.1	5	1	0	2
Monte Pearson	1	0	0.00	1	1	1	0	1	9.0	2	0	1	8
Red Ruffing	1	0	1.00	1	1	1	0	0	9.0	4	1	1	4
Steve Sundra	0	0	0.00	1	0	0	0	0	2.2	4	0	1	2
TOTAL	4	0	1.22	7	4	2	0	1	37.0	27	5	6	22

CIN (N)

PLAYER/POS	AVG	G	AB	R	H	2B	3B	HR	RB	BB	SO	SB
Wally Berger, of	.000	4	15	0	0	0	0	0	0	1	0	4	0
Nino Bongiovanni, ph	.000	1	1	0	0	0	0	0	0	0	0	0
Frenchy Bordagaray, pr	.000	2	0	0	0	0	0	0	0	0	0	0
Harry Craft, of	.091	4	11	0	1	0	0	0	0	0	6	0
Paul Derringer, p	.200	2	5	0	1	0	0	0	0	0	0	0
Lonny Frey, 2b	.000	4	17	0	0	0	0	0	0	1	4	0
Lee Gamble, ph	.000	1	1	0	0	0	0	0	0	0	1	0
Ival Goodman, of	.333	4	15	3	5	1	0	0	1	1	2	1
Lee Grissom, p	.000	1	0	0	0	0	0	0	0	0	0	0
Willard Hershberger, c-2	.500	3	2	0	1	0	0	0	1	0	0	0
Ernie Lombardi, c	.214	4	14	0	3	0	0	0	2	0	1	0
Frank McCormick, 1b	.400	4	15	1	6	1	0	0	1	0	1	0
Whitey Moore, p	.000	1	1	0	0	0	0	0	0	0	0	0
Billy Myers, ss	.333	4	12	2	4	0	1	0	0	2	3	0
Al Simmons, of	.250	4	11	1	4	1	1	0	0	0	0	0
Junior Thompson, p	1.000	1	1	0	1	0	0	0	0	0	0	0
Bucky Walters, p	.000	2	3	0	0	0	0	0	0	0	0	0
Billy Werber, 3b	.250	4	16	1	4	0	0	0	2	2	0	0
TOTAL	.203		133	8	27	3	1	0	8	6	22	1

PITCHER	W	L	ERA	G	GS	CG	SV	SHO	IP	H	ER	BB	SO
Paul Derringer	0	1	2.35	2	2	1	0	0	15.1	9	4	3	9
Lee Grissom	0	0	0.00	1	0	0	0	0	1.1	0	0	1	0
Whitey Moore	0	0	0.00	1	0	0	0	0	3.0	0	0	0	2
Junior Thompson	0	1	13.50	1	1	0	0	0	4.2	5	7	4	3
Bucky Walters	0	2	4.91	2	1	1	0	0	11.0	13	6	1	6
TOTAL	0	4	4.33	7	4	2	0	0	35.1	27	17	9	20

GAME 1 AT NY OCT 4

CIN	000	100	000	1	4	0
NY	000	010	001	2	6	0

Pitchers: DERRINGER vs RUFFING
Attendance: 58,541

GAME 2 AT NY OCT 5

CIN	000	000	000	0	2	0
NY	003	100	00X	4	9	0

Pitchers: WALTERS vs PEARSON
Home Runs: Dalhgren-NY
Attendance: 59,791

GAME 3 AT CIN OCT 7

NY	202	030	000	7	5	1
CIN	120	000	000	3	10	0

Pitchers: Gomez, HADLEY (2) vs THOMPSON, Grissom (5), Moore (7)
Home Runs: Keller-NY (2), DiMaggio-NY, Dickey-NY
Attendance: 32,723

GAME 4 AT CIN OCT 8

NY	000	000	202	3	7	7	1
CIN	000	000	310	0	4	11	4

Pitchers: Hildebrand, Sundra, MURPHY (7) vs Derringer, WALTERS (8)
Home Runs: Keller-NY, Dickey-NY
Attendance: 32,794

The Tigers outpitched and outslugged the Reds, and scored six more runs than the Reds did. What they failed to do was win the Series.

Tiger ace Bobo Newsom, who had enjoyed what would be his finest season in a long career, carried his mastery into the Series opener. Detroit gave him an early lead, driving out Red starter Paul Derringer with five runs in the second inning, and added a pair of runs in the fifth on Bruce Campbell's home run. Newsom, meanwhile, held the Reds to single runs in the fourth and eighth.

Cincinnati's Bucky Walters walked the first two Tigers he faced in Game Two, and both scored. But two Red runs in the second tied the game, Jimmy Ripple's two-run homer an inning later gave them the lead, and pitcher Walters scored an insurance run in the fourth after doubling. Another Tiger walk in the sixth led to their third run, but Walters retired the remaining Tigers in order.

The Series moved to Detroit and the lead to the Tigers in Game Three. Detroit's Rocky Bridges yielded ten hits and four runs, but his teammates responded with 13 hits and seven runs, including a pair of two-run homers by Rudy York and Pinky Higgins in the seventh. Cincinnati again evened the Series the next day, though, with five runs to support Derringer's five-hit, two-run pitching. Although Newsom's father had suffered a fatal heart attack the day after seeing his son win the opener, the son pitched Game Five, and improved on his previous performance with a three-hit shutout. Hank Greenberg's homer in the third inning accounted for the first three of the Tigers' eight runs in their lopsided win.

The Reds returned home needing to win the final two games. Like Newsom, Bucky Walters bettered his earlier win with a shutout in Game Six, and drove in two of the Reds' four runs, one with a solo homer in the eighth. In the Series finale, Newsom and Derringer found themselves evenly matched. The Tigers scored a run in the third, while Newsom held Cincinnati scoreless through six. But in the seventh, leadoff doubles by Frank McCormick and Jimmy Ripple, plus a successful bunt and a fly to deep center, gave the Reds two runs—all they needed as Derringer stopped the Tigers through the final six innings for the victory.

Cincinnati Reds (NL), 4;
Detroit Tigers (AL), 3

CIN (N)

PLAYER/POS	AVG	G	AB	R	H	2B	3B	HR	RB	BB	SO	SB
Morrie Arnovich, of	.000	1	1	0	0	0	0	0	0	0	0	0
Bill Baker, c	.250	3	4	1	1	0	0	0	0	0	1	0
Joe Beggs, p	.000	1	0	0	0	0	0	0	0	0	0	0
Harry Craft, ph	.000	1	1	0	0	0	0	0	0	0	0	0
Paul Derringer, p	.000	3	7	0	0	0	0	0	0	0	1	0
Lonny Frey, ph	.000	3	2	0	0	0	0	0	0	0	0	0
Ival Goodman, of	.276	7	29	5	8	2	0	0	5	0	3	0
Johnny Hutchings, p	.000	1	0	0	0	0	0	0	0	0	0	0
Eddie Joost, 2b	.200	7	25	0	5	0	0	0	2	1	2	0
Ernie Lombardi, c-1	.333	2	3	0	1	1	0	0	0	1	0	0
Frank McCormick, 1b	.214	7	28	2	6	1	0	0	0	1	1	0
Mike McCormick, of	.310	7	29	1	9	3	0	0	2	1	6	0
Whitey Moore, p	.000	3	2	0	0	0	0	0	0	0	1	0
Billy Myers, ss	.130	7	23	0	3	0	0	0	2	2	5	0
Elmer Riddle, p	.000	1	0	0	0	0	0	0	0	0	0	0
Lew Riggs, ph	.000	3	3	1	0	0	0	0	0	0	2	0
Jimmy Ripple, of	.333	7	21	3	7	2	0	1	6	4	2	0
Junior Thompson, p	.000	1	1	0	0	0	0	0	0	0	1	0
Jim Turner, p	.000	1	2	0	0	0	0	0	0	0	0	0
Johnny Vander Meer, p	.000	1	0	0	0	0	0	0	0	0	0	0
Bucky Walters, p	.286	2	7	2	2	1	0	1	2	0	1	0
Billy Werber, 3b	.370	7	27	5	10	4	0	0	2	4	2	0
Jimmie Wilson, c	.353	6	17	2	6	0	0	0	0	1	2	1
TOTAL	.250		232	22	58	14	0	2	21	15	30	1

PITCHER	W	L	ERA	G	GS	CG	SV	SHO	IP	H	ER	BB	SO
Joe Beggs	0	0	9.00	1	0	0	0	0	1.0	3	1	0	1
Paul Derringer	2	1	2.79	3	3	2	0	0	19.1	17	6	10	6
Johnny Hutchings	0	0	9.00	1	0	0	0	0	1.0	2	1	1	0
Whitey Moore	0	0	3.24	3	0	0	0	0	8.1	8	3	6	7
Elmer Riddle	0	0	0.00	1	0	0	0	0	1.0	0	0	0	2
Junior Thompson	0	1	16.20	1	1	0	0	0	3.1	8	6	4	2
Jim Turner	0	1	7.50	1	1	0	0	0	6.0	8	5	0	4
Johnny Vander Meer	0	0	0.00	1	0	0	0	0	3.0	2	0	3	2
Bucky Walters	2	0	1.50	2	2	2	0	1	18.0	8	3	6	6
TOTAL	4	3	3.69	14	7	4	0	1	61.0	56	25	30	30

DET (A)

PLAYER/POS	AVG	G	AB	R	H	2B	3B	HR	RB	BB	SO	SB
Earl Averill, ph	.000	3	3	0	0	0	0	0	0	0	0	0
Dick Bartell, ss	.269	7	26	2	7	2	0	0	3	3	3	0
Tommy Bridges, p	.000	1	3	0	0	0	0	0	0	0	1	0
Bruce Campbell, of	.360	7	25	4	9	1	0	1	5	4	4	0
Frank Croucher, ss	.000	1	0	0	0	0	0	0	0	0	0	0
Pete Fox, ph	.000	1	1	0	0	0	0	0	0	0	0	0
Charlie Gehringer, 2b	.214	7	28	3	6	0	0	0	1	2	0	0
Johnny Gorsica, p	.000	2	4	0	0	0	0	0	0	0	2	0
Hank Greenberg, of	.357	7	28	5	10	2	1	1	6	2	5	0
Pinky Higgins, 3b	.333	7	24	2	8	3	1	1	6	3	3	0
Fred Hutchinson, p	.000	1	0	0	0	0	0	0	0	0	0	0
Barney McCosky, of	.304	7	23	5	7	1	0	0	1	7	0	0
Archie McKain, p	.000	1	0	0	0	0	0	0	0	0	0	0
Bobo Newsom, p	.100	3	10	1	1	0	0	0	0	0	1	0
Schoolboy Rowe, p	.000	2	1	0	0	0	0	0	0	0	1	0
Clay Smith, p	.000	1	1	0	0	0	0	0	0	0	1	0
Billy Sullivan, c-4	.154	5	13	3	2	0	0	0	0	5	2	0
Birdie Tebbetts, c-3	.000	4	11	0	0	0	0	0	0	0	0	0
Dizzy Trout, p	.000	1	1	0	0	0	0	0	0	0	0	0
Rudy York, 1b	.231	7	26	3	6	0	1	1	2	4	7	0
TOTAL	.246		228	28	56	9	3	4	24	30	30	0

PITCHER	W	L	ERA	G	GS	CG	SV	SHO	IP	H	ER	BB	SO
Tommy Bridges	1	0	3.00	1	1	1	0	0	9.0	10	3	1	5
Johnny Gorsica	0	0	0.79	2	0	0	0	0	11.1	6	1	4	4
Fred Hutchinson	0	0	9.00	1	0	0	0	0	1.0	1	1	1	1
Archie McKain	0	0	3.00	1	0	0	0	0	3.0	4	1	0	0
Bobo Newsom	2	1	1.38	3	3	3	0	1	26.0	18	4	4	17
Schoolboy Rowe	0	2	17.18	2	2	0	0	0	3.2	12	7	1	1
Clay Smith	0	0	2.25	1	0	0	0	0	4.0	1	1	3	1
Dizzy Trout	0	1	9.00	1	1	0	0	0	2.0	6	2	1	1
TOTAL	3	4	3.00	12	7	4	0	1	60.0	58	20	15	30

GAME 1 AT CIN OCT 2

DET	050 020 000	7 10 1
CIN	000 100 010	2 8 3

Pitchers: NEWSOM vs DERRINGER, Moore (2), Riddle (9)
Home Runs: Campbell-DET
Attendance: 31,793

GAME 2 AT CIN OCT 3

DET	200 001 000	3 3 1
CIN	022 100 00X	5 9 0

Pitchers: ROWE, Gorsica (4) vs WALTERS
Home Runs: Ripple-CIN
Attendance: 30,640

GAME 3 AT DET OCT 4

CIN	100 000 012	4 10 1
DET	000 100 42X	7 13 1

Pitchers: TURNER, Moore (7), Beggs (8) vs BRIDGES
Home Runs: York-DET, Higgins-DET
Attendance: 52,877

GAME 4 AT DET OCT 5

CIN	201 100 010	5 11 1
DET	001 001 000	2 5 1

Pitchers: DERRINGER vs TROUT, Smith (3), McKain (7)
Attendance: 54,093

GAME 5 AT DET OCT 6

CIN	000 000 000	0 3 0
DET	003 400 01X	8 13 0

Pitchers: THOMPSON, Moore (4), Vander Meer (5), Hutchings (8) vs NEWSOM
Home Runs: Greenberg-DET
Attendance: 55,189

GAME 6 AT CIN OCT 7

DET	000 000 000	0 5 0
CIN	200 001 01X	4 10 2

Pitchers: ROWE, Gorsica (1), Hutchinson (8) vs WALTERS
Home Runs: Walters-CIN
Attendance: 30,481

GAME 7 AT CIN OCT 8

DET	001 000 000	1 7 0
CIN	000 000 20X	2 7 1

Pitchers: NEWSOM vs DERRINGER
Attendance: 26,854

Dodger catcher Mickey Owen's dropped third strike in Game Four was the Series' memorable boner, but it was not the chief cause of Brooklyn's downfall. Yankee pitching was. Three Yankee starters hurled complete-game wins, with each giving the Dodgers only one earned run. And relief ace Johnny Murphy hurled two-hit shutout ball in six innings over two games, winning one.

Yankee Joe Gordon opened the Series scoring with a solo homer in the second inning of Game One, and the Yankees added runs in the fourth and sixth. Owen tripled in the Dodgers' first run in the fifth, and pinch hitter Lew Riggs singled in an unearned run in the seventh. But Yankee starter Red Ruffing held on to his slim lead through the final two innings for the win.

Dodger ace Whitlow Wyatt gave the Yankees single runs in the second and third innings of Game Two, but held them scoreless the rest of the way. Meanwhile, the Dodgers tied the game in the fifth, and scored an unearned run in the sixth to finish the scoring and give Brooklyn its only win of the Series.

Freddie Fitzsimmons, with the Dodgers' best pitching of the Series, dueled Yankee Marius Russo through seven scoreless innings in Game Three. But Fitzsimmons's final out of the seventh—a line drive by Russo that bounced off Fitzsimmons's leg into the glove of shortstop Pee Wee Reese—broke his kneecap. Hugh Casey, who replaced Fitzsimmons in the eighth, retired the first batter, but then gave up four straight singles for two runs before being removed. The Yankees scored no more, and Brooklyn came up with a run in the last of the eighth. But Russo stopped the Dodgers in order in the ninth to preserve his lead for the Yankees' second win.

In Game Four, for the first time in the Series, the margin of victory was more than one run, thanks to catcher Owen's famous boner. Brooklyn held the lead 4–3 with two out in the top of the ninth. Dodger reliever Casey, who had shut out the Yankees since coming on in the fifth inning, then struck out Tommy Henrich for what should have been the game-ending out. But Owen let the ball get by him, and before the third out was recorded Casey had given up a single, two doubles, and two walks—and four runs, for Brooklyn's third loss.

The Yankees scored twice off Wyatt in the second inning of Game Five, and once more in the fifth (on Henrich's home run), as Tiny Bonham held Brooklyn to four hits and a single run to clinch the ninth Yankee world title.

New York Yankees (AL), 4; Brooklyn Dodgers (NL), 1

NY (A)

PLAYER/POS	AVG	G	AB	R	H	2B	3B	HR	RB	BB	SO	SB
Tiny Bonham, p	.000	1	4	0	0	0	0	0	0	0	4	0
Frenchy Bordagaray, pr	.000	1	0	0	0	0	0	0	0	0	0	0
Marv Breuer, p	.000	1	1	0	0	0	0	0	0	0	0	0
Spud Chandler, p	.500	1	2	0	1	0	0	0	1	0	0	0
Bill Dickey, c	.167	5	18	3	3	1	0	0	1	3	1	0
Joe DiMaggio, of	.263	5	19	1	5	0	0	0	1	2	2	0
Atley Donald, p	.000	2	2	0	0	0	0	0	0	0	1	0
Joe Gordon, 2b	.500	5	14	2	7	1	1	1	5	7	0	0
Tommy Henrich, of	.167	5	18	4	3	1	0	1	1	3	3	0
Charlie Keller, of	.389	5	18	5	7	2	0	0	5	3	1	0
Johnny Murphy, p	.000	2	2	0	0	0	0	0	0	0	1	0
Phil Rizzuto, ss	.111	5	18	0	2	0	0	0	0	3	1	1
Red Rolfe, 3b	.300	5	20	2	6	0	0	0	0	2	1	0
Buddy Rosar, c	.000	1	0	0	0	0	0	0	0	0	0	0
Red Ruffing, p	.000	1	3	0	0	0	0	0	0	0	0	0
Marius Russo, p	.000	1	4	0	0	0	0	0	0	0	1	0
George Selkirk, ph	.500	2	2	0	1	0	0	0	0	0	0	0
Johnny Sturm, 1b	.286	5	21	0	6	0	0	0	2	0	2	1
TOTAL	.247		166	17	41	5	1	2	16	23	18	2

PITCHER	W	L	ERA	G	GS	CG	SV	SHO	IP	H	ER	BB	SO
Tiny Bonham	1	0	1.00	1	1	1	0	0	9.0	4	1	2	2
Marv Breuer	0	0	0.00	1	0	0	0	0	3.0	3	0	1	2
Spud Chandler	0	1	3.60	1	1	0	0	0	5.0	4	2	2	2
Atley Donald	0	0	9.00	1	1	0	0	0	4.0	6	4	3	2
Johnny Murphy	1	0	0.00	2	0	0	0	0	6.0	2	0	1	3
Red Ruffing	1	0	1.00	1	1	1	0	0	9.0	6	1	3	5
Marius Russo	1	0	1.00	1	1	1	0	0	9.0	4	1	2	5
TOTAL	4	1	1.80	8	5	3	0	0	45.0	29	9	14	21

BRO (N)

PLAYER/POS	AVG	G	AB	R	H	2B	3B	HR	RB	BB	SO	SB
Johnny Allen, p	.000	3	0	0	0	0	0	0	0	0	0	0
Dolph Camilli, 1b	.167	5	18	1	3	1	0	0	1	1	6	0
Hugh Casey, p	.500	3	2	0	1	0	0	0	0	0	1	0
Pete Coscarart, 2b	.000	3	7	1	0	0	0	0	0	1	2	0
Curt Davis, p	.000	1	2	0	0	0	0	0	0	0	0	0
Freddie Fitzsimmons, p	.000	1	2	0	0	0	0	0	0	0	0	0
Herman Franks, c	.000	1	1	0	0	0	0	0	0	0	0	0
Larry French, p	.000	2	0	0	0	0	0	0	0	0	0	0
Augie Galan, ph	.000	2	2	0	0	0	0	0	0	0	1	0
Billy Herman, 2b	.125	4	8	0	1	0	0	0	0	2	0	0
Kirby Higbe, p	1.000	1	1	0	1	0	0	0	0	0	0	0
Cookie Lavagetto, 3b	.100	3	10	1	1	0	0	0	0	2	0	0
Joe Medwick, of	.235	5	17	1	4	1	0	0	0	1	2	0
Mickey Owen, c	.167	5	12	1	2	0	1	0	2	3	0	0
Pee Wee Reese, ss	.200	5	20	1	4	0	0	0	2	0	0	0
Pete Reiser, of	.200	5	20	1	4	1	1	1	3	1	6	0
Lew Riggs, 3b-2	.250	3	8	0	2	0	0	0	1	1	1	0
Dixie Walker, of	.222	5	18	3	4	2	0	0	0	2	1	0
Jimmy Wasdell, of-1	.200	3	5	0	1	1	0	0	2	0	0	0
Whit Wyatt, p	.167	2	6	1	1	1	0	0	0	0	1	0
TOTAL	.182		159	11	29	7	2	1	11	14	21	0

PITCHER	W	L	ERA	G	GS	CG	SV	SHO	IP	H	ER	BB	SO
Johnny Allen	0	0	0.00	3	0	0	0	0	3.2	1	0	3	0
Hugh Casey	0	2	3.38	3	0	0	0	0	5.1	9	2	2	1
Curt Davis	0	1	5.06	1	1	0	0	0	5.1	6	3	3	1
Freddie Fitzsimmons	0	0	0.00	1	1	0	0	0	7.0	4	0	3	1
Larry French	0	0	0.00	2	0	0	0	0	1.0	0	0	0	0
Kirby Higbe	0	0	7.36	1	1	0	0	0	3.2	6	3	2	1
Whit Wyatt	1	1	2.50	2	2	2	0	0	18.0	15	5	10	14
TOTAL	1	4	2.66	13	5	2	0	0	44.0	41	13	23	18

GAME 1 AT NY OCT 1

BRO	000 010 100	2	6	0
NY	010 101 00X	3	6	1

Pitchers: DAVIS, Casey (6), Allen (7) vs RUFFING
Home Runs: Gordon-NY
Attendance: 68,540

GAME 2 AT NY OCT 2

BRO	000 021 000	3	6	2
NY	011 000 000	2	9	1

Pitchers: WYATT vs CHANDLER, Murphy (6)
Attendance: 66,248

GAME 3 AT BRO OCT 4

NY	000 000 020	2	8	0
BRO	000 000 010	1	4	0

Pitchers: RUSSO vs Fitzsimmons, CASEY (8), French (8), Allen (9)
Attendance: 33,100

GAME 4 AT BRO OCT 5

NY	100 200 004	7	12	0
BRO	000 220 000	4	9	1

Pitchers: Donald, Breuer (5), MURPHY (8) vs Higbe, French (4), Allen (5), CASEY (5)
Home Runs: Reiser-BRO
Attendance: 33,813

GAME 5 AT BRO OCT 6

NY	020 010 000	3	6	0
BRO	001 000 000	1	4	1

Pitchers: BONHAM vs WYATT
Home Runs: Henrich-NY
Attendance: 34,072

Cardinal rookies Stan Musial and Whitey Kurowski drove in game-winning runs for rookie-pitcher Johnny Beazley in Games Two and Five as the major leagues' youngest team upset the Yankees. New York won only the opener, building a seven-run lead for starter Red Ruffing, who shut out St. Louis on one hit through 8⅓ innings before giving up four hits and four harmless runs in the last of the ninth.

The Cardinals scored first in Game Two on catcher Walker Cooper's two-run double in the first inning. Kurowski tripled in a third Cardinal run in the seventh, but pitcher Beazley, after holding the Yankees scoreless through seven innings, gave up three runs in the eighth on two singles and Charlie Keller's two-run homer. St. Louis regained the lead a half-inning later when Musial singled home Enos Slaughter (who had doubled), and stifled a threat in the ninth as Slaughter's great throw from right field nailed a Yankee runner at third.

Second-year Cardinal pitcher Ernie White turned in the Series' top mound performance with a six-single, no-walk shutout in Game Three (aided by outfielders Musial and Slaughter, who hauled in a pair of potential home run blasts in the seventh inning). The Cards managed only five singles themselves, but they combined one with a walk, sacrifice, and ground out for a run in the third, and sandwiched a Yankee error with two hits in the nineth for an unearned insurance run.

Game Four saw the Series' heaviest hitting. New York scored once in the first, but the Cards exploded in the fourth for six runs on six hits and two walks. The Yankees tied it up two innings later, with Keller's three-run homer the feature of the five-run inning. St. Louis took the lead for good with two runs in the seventh, and added a ninth run in the ninth.

Beazley and Ruffing tangled in Game Five. Phil Rizzuto's solo homer put New York ahead in the first inning. Slaughter's fourth-inning home run tied the score, but the Yankees regained the lead with a run later in the inning. The Cards retied the game in the sixth, and took the final lead when Kurowski homered for two runs in the top of the ninth. The Yankees threatened in the last of the ninth, putting their first two men on with a single and error. But catcher Cooper picked a runner off second, second baseman Jimmy Brown redeemed his earlier error with a sparkling catch, then fielded a routine grounder for the final out and the Cardinal triumph.

St. Louis Cardinals (NL), 4;
New York Yankees (AL), 1

STL (N)

PLAYER/POS	AVG	G	AB	R	H	2B	3B	HR	RB	BB	SO	SB
Johnny Beazley, p	.143	2	7	0	1	0	0	0	0	0	5	0
Jimmy Brown, 2b	.300	5	20	2	6	0	0	0	1	3	0	0
Mort Cooper, p	.200	2	5	1	1	0	0	0	2	0	1	0
Walker Cooper, c	.286	5	21	3	6	1	0	0	4	0	1	0
Creepy Crespi, pr	.000	1	0	1	0	0	0	0	0	0	0	0
Harry Gumbert, p	.000	2	0	0	0	0	0	0	0	0	0	0
Johnny Hopp, 1b	.176	5	17	3	3	0	0	0	0	1	1	0
Whitey Kurowski, 3b	.267	5	15	3	4	0	1	1	5	2	3	0
Max Lanier, p	1.000	2	1	0	1	0	0	0	1	0	0	0
Marty Marion, ss	.111	5	18	2	2	0	1	0	3	1	2	0
Terry Moore, of	.294	5	17	2	5	1	0	0	2	2	3	0
Stan Musial, of	.222	5	18	2	4	1	0	0	2	4	0	0
Ken O'Dea, ph	1.000	1	1	0	1	0	0	0	1	0	0	0
Howie Pollet, p	.000	1	0	0	0	0	0	0	0	0	0	0
Ray Sanders, ph	.000	2	1	0	0	0	0	0	0	1	0	0
Enos Slaughter, of	.263	5	19	3	5	1	0	1	2	3	2	0
Harry Walker, ph	.000	1	1	0	0	0	0	0	0	0	1	0
Ernie White, p	.000	1	2	0	0	0	0	0	0	0	0	0
TOTAL	.239		163	23	39	4	2	2	23	17	19	0

PITCHER	W	L	ERA	G	GS	CG	SV	SHO	IP	H	ER	BB	SO
Johnny Beazley	2	0	2.50	2	2	2	0	0	18.0	17	5	3	6
Mort Cooper	0	1	5.54	2	2	0	0	0	13.0	17	8	4	9
Harry Gumbert	0	0	0.00	2	0	0	0	0	0.2	1	0	0	0
Max Lanier	1	0	0.00	2	0	0	0	0	4.0	3	0	1	1
Howie Pollet	0	0	0.00	1	0	0	0	0	0.1	0	0	0	0
Ernie White	1	0	0.00	1	1	1	0	1	9.0	6	0	0	6
TOTAL	4	1	2.60	10	5	3	0	1	45.0	44	13	8	22

NY (A)

PLAYER/POS	AVG	G	AB	R	H	2B	3B	HR	RB	BB	SO	SB
Tiny Bonham, p	.000	2	2	0	0	0	0	0	0	1	0	0
Hank Borowy, p	.000	1	1	0	0	0	0	0	0	0	1	0
Marv Breuer, p	.000	1	0	0	0	0	0	0	0	0	0	0
Spud Chandler, p	.000	2	2	0	0	0	0	0	0	0	1	0
Frankie Crosetti, 3b	.000	1	3	0	0	0	0	0	0	0	1	0
Roy Cullenbine, of	.263	5	19	3	5	1	0	0	2	1	2	1
Bill Dickey, c	.263	5	19	1	5	0	0	0	0	1	0	0
Joe DiMaggio, of	.333	5	21	3	7	0	0	0	3	0	1	0
Atley Donald, p	.000	1	2	0	0	0	0	0	0	0	0	0
Joe Gordon, 2b	.095	5	21	1	2	1	0	0	0	0	7	0
Buddy Hassett, 1b	.333	3	9	1	3	1	0	0	2	0	1	0
Charlie Keller, of	.200	5	20	2	4	0	0	2	5	1	3	0
Jerry Priddy, 1b-3,3b-1	.100	3	10	0	1	1	0	0	1	1	0	0
Phil Rizzuto, ss	.381	5	21	2	8	0	0	1	1	2	1	2
Red Rolfe, 3b	.353	4	17	5	6	2	0	0	0	1	2	0
Buddy Rosar, ph	1.000	1	1	0	1	0	0	0	0	0	0	0
Red Ruffing, p-2	.222	4	9	0	2	0	0	0	0	0	2	0
George Selkirk, ph	.000	1	1	0	0	0	0	0	0	0	0	0
Tuck Stainback, pr	.000	2	0	0	0	0	0	0	0	0	0	0
Jim Turner, p	.000	1	0	0	0	0	0	0	0	0	0	0
TOTAL	.247		178	18	44	6	0	3	14	8	22	3

PITCHER	W	L	ERA	G	GS	CG	SV	SHO	IP	H	ER	BB	SO
Tiny Bonham	0	1	4.09	2	1	1	0	0	11.0	9	5	3	3
Hank Borowy	0	0	18.00	1	1	0	0	0	3.0	6	6	3	1
Marv Breuer	0	0	INF	1	0	0	0	0	0.0	2	1	0	0
Spud Chandler	0	1	1.08	2	1	0	1	0	8.1	5	1	1	3
Atley Donald	0	1	6.00	1	0	0	0	0	3.0	3	2	2	1
Red Ruffing	1	1	4.08	2	2	1	0	0	17.2	14	8	7	11
Jim Turner	0	0	0.00	1	0	0	0	0	1.0	0	0	1	0
TOTAL	1	4	4.50	10	5	2	1	0	44.0	39	22	17	19

GAME 1 AT STL SEPT 30

NY	000 110 032	7 11 0
STL	000 000 004	4 7 4

Pitchers: RUFFING, Chandler (9) vs
  M.COOPER, Gumbert (8), Lanier (9)
Attendance: 34,769

GAME 2 AT STL OCT 1

NY	000 000 030	3 10 2
STL	200 000 11X	4 6 0

Pitchers: BONHAM vs BEAZLEY
Home Runs: Keller-NY
Attendance: 34,255

GAME 3 AT NY OCT 2

STL	001 000 001	2 5 1
NY	000 000 000	0 6 1

Pitchers: WHITE vs CHANDLER,
  Breuer (9), Turner (9)
Attendance: 69,123

GAME 4 AT NY OCT 4

STL	000 600 201	9 12 1
NY	100 005 000	6 10 1

Pitchers: M.Cooper, Gumbert (6),
  Pollet (6), LANIER (7) vs Borowy,
  DONALD (4), Bonham (7)
Home Runs: Keller-NY
Attendance: 69,902

GAME 5 AT NY OCT 5

STL	000 101 002	4 9 4
NY	100 100 000	2 7 1

Pitchers: BEAZLEY vs RUFFING
Home Runs: Rizzuto-NY,
  Slaughter-STL, Kurowski-STL
Attendance: 69,052

Although both clubs had lost players to military service since the previous World Series, history seemed to be repeating itself. The Cardinals lost to the Yankees in the opener and won the second game, as they had the previous year. But this year it was the Yankees who took the next three games and the Series, as fine Cardinal pitching gave way to even finer Yankee mound work.

Yankee pitcher Spurgeon (Spud) Chandler, coming off his finest season (20–4, 1.64 ERA), continued to overwhelm the opposition in the Series. He held the Cards to two runs (only one earned) in Game One, and the Yankees took advantage of a wild pitch to score two runs of their own in the sixth inning, breaking a 2–2 tie for a 4–2 win. Cardinal shortstop Marty Marion homered in the third inning for the first Cardinal run the next day, and first baseman Ray Sanders homered for two more runs in a three-run fourth. Cardinal ace Mort Cooper held New York to one run on four hits through eight innings, but he weakened in the last of the ninth, giving up a double and triple to the first two batters. But only two runs scored as he retired the next three men for St. Louis's only victory.

The Cardinals carried a 2–1 lead into the last of the eighth inning of Game Three, when a pair of errors, two walks, and five Yankee hits (including Billy Johnson's three-run triple) undid them. Yankee fireman Johnny Murphy retired the Cards in order in the ninth to save Hank Borowy's win. Max Lanier and Harry Brecheen held New York to just two runs (and six hits) in Game Four, but Yankee pitcher Marius Russo gave up only one run—and that was scored only because of two Yankee errors in the seventh inning.

In the fifth and (as it turned out) final game, St. Louis couldn't score even an unearned run, although they knocked Spud Chandler for ten hits. But they were all singles and were spaced harmlessly over eight of the nine innings. Three St. Louis pitchers held the Yankees to just seven hits, six of them singles. But in the sixth inning Bill Dickey followed one of the Yankee singles with the game's only extra-base hit—a home run—to produce the game's only scoring, and bring the Yankees yet another world championship, their tenth.

New York Yankees (AL), 4;
St. Louis Cardinals (NL), 1

NY (A)

PLAYER/POS	AVG	G	AB	R	H	2B	3B	HR	RB	BB	SO	SB
Tiny Bonham, p	.000	1	2	0	0	0	0	0	0	0	0	0
Hank Borowy, p	.500	1	2	1	1	1	0	0	0	0	1	0
Spud Chandler, p	.167	2	6	0	1	0	0	0	0	0	0	0
Frankie Crosetti, ss	.278	5	18	4	5	0	0	0	1	2	3	1
Bill Dickey, c	.278	5	18	1	5	0	0	1	4	2	2	0
Nick Etten, 1b	.105	5	19	0	2	0	0	0	2	1	2	0
Joe Gordon, 2b	.235	5	17	2	4	1	0	1	2	3	3	0
Billy Johnson, 3b	.300	5	20	3	6	1	1	0	3	0	3	0
Charlie Keller, of	.222	5	18	3	4	0	1	0	2	2	5	1
Johnny Lindell, of	.111	4	9	1	1	0	0	0	0	1	4	0
Bud Metheny, of	.125	2	8	0	1	0	0	0	0	0	2	0
Johnny Murphy, p	.000	2	0	0	0	0	0	0	0	0	0	0
Marius Russo, p	.667	1	3	1	2	2	0	0	0	1	1	0
Tuck Stainback, of	.176	5	17	0	3	0	0	0	0	0	2	0
Snuffy Stirnweiss, ph	.000	1	1	0	0	0	0	0	0	0	0	0
Roy Weatherly, ph	.000	1	1	0	0	0	0	0	0	0	0	0
TOTAL	.220		159	17	35	5	2	2	14	12	30	2

PITCHER	W	L	ERA	G	GS	CG	SV	SHO	IP	H	ER	BB	SO
Tiny Bonham	0	1	4.50	1	1	0	0	0	8.0	6	4	3	9
Hank Borowy	1	0	2.25	1	1	0	0	0	8.0	6	2	3	4
Spud Chandler	2	0	0.50	2	2	2	0	1	18.0	17	1	3	10
Johnny Murphy	0	0	0.00	2	0	0	1	0	2.0	1	0	1	1
Marius Russo	1	0	0.00	1	1	1	0	0	9.0	7	0	1	2
TOTAL	4	1	1.40	7	5	3	1	1	45.0	37	7	11	26

STL (N)

PLAYER/POS	AVG	G	AB	R	H	2B	3B	HR	RB	BB	SO	SB
Al Brazle, p	.000	1	3	0	0	0	0	0	0	0	1	0
Harry Brecheen, p	.000	3	0	0	0	0	0	0	0	0	0	0
Mort Cooper, p	.000	2	5	0	0	0	0	0	0	0	3	0
Walker Cooper, c	.294	5	17	1	5	0	0	0	0	0	1	0
Frank Demaree, ph	.000	1	1	0	0	0	0	0	0	0	0	0
Murry Dickson, p	.000	1	0	0	0	0	0	0	0	0	0	0
Debs Garms, of-1	.000	2	5	0	0	0	0	0	0	0	2	0
Johnny Hopp, of	.000	1	4	0	0	0	0	0	0	1	0	0
Lou Klein, 2b	.136	5	22	0	3	0	0	0	0	1	2	0
Howie Krist, p	.000	1	0	0	0	0	0	0	0	0	0	0
Whitey Kurowski, 3b	.222	5	18	2	4	1	0	0	1	0	3	0
Max Lanier, p	.250	3	4	0	1	0	0	0	1	0	0	0
Danny Litwhiler, of-4	.267	5	15	0	4	1	0	0	2	2	4	0
Marty Marion, ss	.357	5	14	1	5	2	0	1	2	3	1	1
Stan Musial, of	.278	5	18	2	5	0	0	0	0	2	2	0
Sam Narron, ph	.000	1	1	0	0	0	0	0	0	0	0	0
Ken O'Dea, c-1	.667	2	3	0	2	0	0	0	0	0	0	0
Ray Sanders, 1b	.294	5	17	3	5	0	0	1	2	3	4	0
Harry Walker, of	.167	5	18	0	3	1	0	0	0	0	2	0
Ernie White, pr	.000	1	0	0	0	0	0	0	0	0	0	0
TOTAL	.224		165	9	37	5	0	2	8	11	26	1

PITCHER	W	L	ERA	G	GS	CG	SV	SHO	IP	H	ER	BB	SO
Al Brazle	0	1	3.68	1	1	0	0	0	7.1	5	3	2	4
Harry Brecheen	0	1	2.45	3	0	0	0	0	3.2	5	1	3	3
Mort Cooper	1	1	2.81	2	2	1	0	0	16.0	11	5	3	10
Murry Dickson	0	0	0.00	1	0	0	0	0	0.2	0	0	1	0
Howie Krist	0	0	INF	1	0	0	0	0	0.0	1	0	0	0
Max Lanier	0	1	1.76	3	2	0	0	0	15.1	13	3	3	13
TOTAL	1	4	2.51	11	5	1	0	0	43.0	35	12	12	30

GAME 1 AT NY OCT 5

STL	010	010	000	2	7 2
NY	000	202	00X	4	8 2

Pitchers: LANIER, Brecheen (8) vs CHANDLER
Home Runs: Gordon-NY
Attendance: 68,676

GAME 2 AT NY OCT 6

STL	001	300	000	4	7 2
NY	000	100	002	3	6 0

Pitchers: M.COOPER vs BONHAM, Murphy (9)
Home Runs: Marion-STL, Sanders-STL
Attendance: 68,578

GAME 3 AT NY OCT 7

STL	000	200	000	2	6 4
NY	000	001	05X	6	8 0

Pitchers: BRAZLE, Krist (8), Brecheen (8) vs BOROWY, Murphy (9)
Attendance: 69,990

GAME 4 AT STL OCT 10

NY	000	100	010	2	6 2
STL	000	000	100	1	7 1

Pitchers: RUSSO vs Lanier, BRECHEEN (8)
Attendance: 36,196

GAME 5 AT STL OCT 11

NY	000	002	000	2	7 1
STL	000	000	000	0	10 1

Pitchers: CHANDLER vs M.COOPER, Lanier (8), Dickson (9)
Home Runs: Dickey-NY
Attendance: 33,872

The Cardinals—a much stronger team in the regular season—entered the World Series against their landlord Browns (who owned Sportsman's Park, where both teams played) as clear favorites. They won the Series in six games, but if the Browns' fielding had been as good as their pitching the outcome might have been different.

The Browns won the opener on Denny Galehouse's strong pitching. Galehouse gave up seven hits and four walks, but held the Cards scoreless for 8⅔ innings before yielding a run in the ninth. Cardinal ace Mort Cooper also pitched well in six of his seven innings. He allowed the Browns only two hits, but they came back to back in the fourth inning—a single followed by George McQuinn's home run—to give the Browns all the scoring they needed.

Brown pitcher Nelson Potter's two errors (a fumble and a wild throw) on a bunt in the third inning of Game Two led to an unearned run, and third baseman Mark Christman's fumble an inning later set up a second unearned run. The Browns tied the score with a pair of runs on three two-out hits in the seventh—enough to have won an error-free game—but lost when the Cardinals singled a run across in the last of the eleventh.

Two Brown errors led to a pair of unearned runs in Game Three, but Jack Kramer held the Cards scoreless apart from that, striking out ten. Meanwhile, Brown hitters tied together five singles with two out in the third inning for three runs, adding a fourth run on a wild pitch before the inning ended. In the seventh the Browns tacked on two more runs for a comfortable win and a 2–1 Series advantage.

The Cardinals came back to earn victory in Games Four and Five, knocking three Brown pitchers for 12 hits in Game Four (including Stan Musial's two-run homer in the first) and a 5–1 win for pitcher Harry Brecheen, then rapping Denny Galehouse for two solo homers in Game Five (by Danny Litwhiler and Ray Sanders) for the game's only scoring as Mort Cooper fanned 12 Browns while shutting them out.

Two of the Cardinals' three runs in the fourth inning of Game Six were made possible by Brown shortstop Vern Stephens's throwing error. They provided the margin of victory, as Cardinal pitchers Max Lanier and Ted Wilks held the Browns to three hits and a single run, and brought the Cards their second world title in three years.

St. Louis Cardinals (NL), 4;
St. Louis Browns (AL), 2

STL (N)

PLAYER/POS	AVG	G	AB	R	H	2B	3B	HR	RB	BB	SO	SB
Augie Bergamo, of-2	.000	3	6	0	0	0	0	0	0	1	2	3	0
Harry Brecheen, p	.000	1	4	0	0	0	0	0	0	0	1	0
Bud Byerly, p	.000	1	0	0	0	0	0	0	0	0	0	0
Mort Cooper, p	.000	2	4	0	0	0	0	0	0	0	2	0
Walker Cooper, c	.318	6	22	1	7	2	1	0	2	3	2	0
Blix Donnelly, p	.000	2	1	0	0	0	0	0	0	0	1	0
George Fallon, 2b	.000	2	2	0	0	0	0	0	0	0	1	0
Debs Garms, ph	.000	2	2	0	0	0	0	0	0	0	0	0
Johnny Hopp, of	.185	6	27	2	5	0	0	0	0	0	8	0
Al Jurisich, p	.000	1	0	0	0	0	0	0	0	0	0	0
Whitey Kurowski, 3b	.217	6	23	2	5	1	0	0	1	1	4	0
Max Lanier, p	.500	2	4	0	2	0	0	0	0	1	0	0
Danny Litwhiler, of	.200	5	20	2	4	1	0	1	1	2	7	0
Marty Marion, ss	.227	6	22	1	5	3	0	0	2	2	3	0
Stan Musial, of	.304	6	23	2	7	2	0	1	2	2	0	0
Ken O'Dea, ph	.333	3	3	0	1	0	0	0	2	0	0	0
Ray Sanders, 1b	.286	6	21	5	6	0	0	1	1	5	8	0
Freddy Schmidt, p	.000	1	1	0	0	0	0	0	0	0	1	0
Emil Verban, 2b	.412	6	17	1	7	0	0	0	2	2	0	0
Ted Wilks, p	.000	2	2	0	0	0	0	0	0	0	2	0
TOTAL	.240		204	16	49	9	1	3	15	19	43	0

PITCHER	W	L	ERA	G	GS	CG	SV	SHO	IP	H	ER	BB	SO
Harry Brecheen	1	0	1.00	1	1	1	0	0	9.0	9	1	4	4
Bud Byerly	0	0	0.00	1	0	0	0	0	1.1	0	0	0	1
Mort Cooper	1	1	1.13	2	2	1	0	1	16.0	9	2	5	16
Blix Donnelly	1	0	0.00	2	0	0	0	0	6.0	2	0	1	9
Al Jurisich	0	0	27.00	1	0	0	0	0	0.2	2	2	1	0
Max Lanier	1	0	2.19	2	2	0	0	0	12.1	8	3	8	11
Freddy Schmidt	0	0	0.00	1	0	0	0	0	3.1	1	0	1	1
Ted Wilks	0	1	5.68	2	1	0	1	0	6.1	5	4	3	7
TOTAL	4	2	1.96	12	6	2	1	1	55.0	36	12	23	49

STL (A)

PLAYER/POS	AVG	G	AB	R	H	2B	3B	HR	RB	BB	SO	SB
Floyd Baker, 2b	.000	2	2	0	0	0	0	0	0	0	2	0
Milt Byrnes, ph	.000	3	2	0	0	0	0	0	0	1	2	0
Mike Chartak, ph	.000	2	2	0	0	0	0	0	0	0	2	0
Mark Christman, 3b	.091	6	22	0	2	0	0	0	1	0	6	0
Ellis Clary, ph	.000	1	1	0	0	0	0	0	0	0	0	0
Denny Galehouse, p	.200	2	5	0	1	0	0	0	0	1	1	0
Don Gutteridge, 2b	.143	6	21	1	3	1	0	0	0	3	5	0
Red Hayworth, c	.118	6	17	1	2	1	0	0	1	3	1	0
Al Hollingsworth, p	.000	1	1	0	0	0	0	0	0	0	0	0
Sig Jakucki, p	.000	1	0	0	0	0	0	0	0	0	0	0
Jack Kramer, p	.000	2	4	0	0	0	0	0	0	0	2	0
Mike Kreevich, of	.231	6	26	0	6	3	0	0	0	0	5	0
Chet Laabs, of-4	.200	5	15	1	3	1	1	0	2	6	0	0
Frank Mancuso, c-1	.667	2	3	0	2	0	0	0	1	0	0	0
George McQuinn, 1b	.438	6	16	2	7	2	0	1	5	7	2	0
Gene Moore, of	.182	6	22	4	4	0	0	0	0	3	6	0
Bob Muncrief, p	.000	2	1	0	0	0	0	0	0	0	1	0
Nelson Potter, p	.000	2	4	0	0	0	0	0	0	0	1	0
Tex Shirley, p	.000	2	0	0	0	0	0	0	0	0	0	0
Vern Stephens, ss	.227	6	22	2	5	1	0	0	0	3	3	0
Tom Turner, ph	.000	1	1	0	0	0	0	0	0	0	0	0
Al Zarilla, of-3	.100	4	10	1	1	0	0	0	1	0	4	0
TOTAL	.183		197	12	36	9	1	1	9	23	49	0

PITCHER	W	L	ERA	G	GS	CG	SV	SHO	IP	H	ER	BB	SO
Denny Galehouse	1	1	1.50	2	2	2	0	0	18.0	13	3	5	15
Al Hollingsworth	0	0	2.25	1	0	0	0	0	4.0	5	1	2	1
Sig Jakucki	0	1	9.00	1	1	0	0	0	3.0	5	3	0	4
Jack Kramer	1	0	0.00	2	1	1	0	0	11.0	9	0	4	12
Bob Muncrief	0	1	1.35	2	0	0	0	0	6.2	5	1	4	4
Nelson Potter	0	1	0.93	2	2	0	0	0	9.2	10	1	3	6
Tex Shirley	0	0	0.00	1	0	0	0	0	2.0	2	0	1	1
TOTAL	2	4	1.49	11	6	3	0	0	54.1	49	9	19	43

As World War Two ended during the summer, military major leaguers began returning to their clubs. Hank Greenberg's return in July provided the spark needed for Detroit's narrow pennant victory, and his three-run homer in Game Two of the World Series proved to be the decisive blow in the Tigers' successful struggle for the world title.

Chicago started strong as Cub ace Hank Borowy shut out the Tigers on six singles while his teammates drove out Tiger ace Hal Newhouser with seven runs in the first three innings, to win 9–0. Chicago continued its assault the next day with a run in the top of the fourth, but in the fifth inning Tiger Doc Cramer—with two out and two on—singled in the tying run, and Greenberg followed with his tie-breaking homer for three additional runs. Detroit pitcher Virgil Trucks (who had returned from the Navy in time to pitch in the regular-season finale) held the Cubs scoreless after the fourth inning for the Tiger win.

Chicago's Claude Passeau moved the Cubs back into the Series lead with a one-hit shutout in Game Three, but Tiger Dizzy Trout's five-hitter in Game Four again evened the Series. The Tigers bunched four of their seven hits in the fourth inning for all four of their runs.

Detroit took the Series lead for the first time with an 8–4 win in Game Five. Borowy and Newhouser faced each other as they had in the opener, but this time Borowy was hit hard. Driven out when four Tigers opened the sixth inning with safe hits, he took the loss as Newhouser went the distance for the win.

In Game Six, Chicago concluded the seventh inning of a heavy-hitting game leading 7–3. Detroit tied the score with four runs in the top of the eighth (capped by Greenberg's home run), but in the last of the twelfth the Cubs' Stan Hack doubled home the winning run to keep Chicago's hopes alive.

Two days later in the finale, Cub manager Charlie Grimm started Borowy, who had relieved for four shutout innings to win Game Six. But this third appearance in four days proved too much. Removed after the first three batters to face him singled, he took the loss, as the Tigers went on to score nine runs to the Cubs' three.

Detroit Tigers (AL), 4; Chicago Cubs (NL), 3

DET (A)

PLAYER/POS	AVG	G	AB	R	H	2B	3B	HR	RB	BB	SO	SB
Al Benton, p	.000	3	0	0	0	0	0	0	0	0	0	0
Red Borom, ph	.000	2	1	0	0	0	0	0	0	0	0	0
Tommy Bridges, p	.000	1	0	0	0	0	0	0	0	0	0	0
George Caster, p	.000	1	0	0	0	0	0	0	0	0	0	0
Doc Cramer, of	.379	7	29	7	11	0	0	0	4	1	0	1
Roy Cullenbine, of	.227	7	22	5	5	2	0	0	4	8	2	1
Zeb Eaton, ph	.000	1	1	0	0	0	0	0	0	0	1	0
Hank Greenberg, of	.304	7	23	7	7	3	0	2	7	6	5	0
Joe Hoover, ss	.333	1	3	1	1	0	0	0	1	0	0	0
Chuck Hostetler, ph	.000	3	3	0	0	0	0	0	0	0	0	0
Bob Maier, ph	1.000	1	1	0	1	0	0	0	0	0	0	0
Eddie Mayo, 2b	.250	7	28	4	7	1	0	0	2	2	2	0
John McHale, ph	.000	3	3	0	0	0	0	0	0	0	1	0
Ed Mierkowicz, of	.000	1	0	0	0	0	0	0	0	0	0	0
Les Mueller, p	.000	1	0	0	0	0	0	0	0	0	0	0
Hal Newhouser, p	.000	3	8	0	0	0	0	0	0	1	1	0
Jimmy Outlaw, 3b	.179	7	28	1	5	0	0	0	3	2	1	1
Stubby Overmire, p	.000	1	1	0	0	0	0	0	0	0	0	0
Paul Richards, c	.211	7	19	0	4	2	0	0	6	4	3	0
Bob Swift, c	.250	3	4	1	1	0	0	0	0	2	0	0
Jim Tobin, p	.000	1	1	0	0	0	0	0	0	0	0	0
Dizzy Trout, p	.167	2	6	0	1	0	0	0	0	0	0	0
Virgil Trucks, p	.000	2	4	0	0	0	0	0	0	0	1	0
Hub Walker, ph	.500	2	2	1	1	1	0	0	0	0	0	0
Skeeter Webb, ss	.185	7	27	4	5	0	0	0	1	3	1	0
Rudy York, 1b	.179	7	28	1	5	1	0	0	3	3	4	0
TOTAL	.223		242	32	54	10	0	2	32	33	22	3

PITCHER	W	L	ERA	G	GS	CG	SV	SHO	IP	H	ER	BB	SO
Al Benton	0	0	1.93	3	0	0	0	0	4.2	6	1	0	5
Tommy Bridges	0	0	16.20	1	0	0	0	0	1.2	3	3	3	1
George Caster	0	0	0.00	1	0	0	0	0	0.2	0	0	0	1
Les Mueller	0	0	0.00	1	0	0	0	0	2.0	0	0	1	1
Hal Newhouser	2	1	6.10	3	3	2	0	0	20.2	25	14	4	22
Stubby Overmire	0	1	3.00	1	1	0	0	0	6.0	4	2	2	2
Jim Tobin	0	0	6.00	1	0	0	0	0	3.0	4	2	1	0
Dizzy Trout	1	1	0.66	2	1	1	0	0	13.2	9	1	3	9
Virgil Trucks	1	0	3.38	2	2	1	0	0	13.1	14	5	5	7
TOTAL	4	3	3.84	15	7	4	0	0	65.2	65	28	19	48

CHI (N)

PLAYER/POS	AVG	G	AB	R	H	2B	3B	HR	RB	BB	SO	SB
Heinz Becker, ph	.500	3	2	0	1	0	0	0	0	1	1	0
Cy Block, pr	.000	1	0	0	0	0	0	0	0	0	0	0
Hank Borowy, p	.167	4	6	1	1	1	0	0	0	0	3	0
Phil Cavaretta, 1b	.423	7	26	7	11	2	0	1	5	4	3	0
Bob Chipman, p	.000	2	0	0	0	0	0	0	0	0	0	0
Paul Derringer, p	.000	3	0	0	0	0	0	0	0	0	0	0
Paul Erickson, p	.000	4	0	0	0	0	0	0	0	0	0	0
Paul Gillespie, c-1	.000	3	6	0	0	0	0	0	0	0	0	0
Stan Hack, 3b	.367	7	30	1	11	3	0	0	4	4	2	0
Roy Hughes, ss	.294	6	17	1	5	1	0	0	3	4	5	0
Don Johnson, 2b	.172	7	29	4	5	2	1	0	0	8	1	0
Mickey Livingston, c	.364	6	22	3	8	3	0	0	4	1	1	0
Peanuts Lowrey, of	.310	7	29	4	9	1	0	0	0	1	2	0
Clyde McCullough, ph	.000	1	1	0	0	0	0	0	0	0	0	0
Lennie Merullo, ss	.000	3	2	0	0	0	0	0	0	0	1	0
Bill Nicholson, of	.214	7	28	1	6	1	1	0	8	2	5	0
Andy Pafko, of	.214	7	28	5	6	2	1	0	2	2	5	1
Claude Passeau, p	.000	3	7	1	0	0	0	0	1	0	4	0
Ray Prim, p	.000	2	0	0	0	0	0	0	0	0	0	0
Ed Sauer, ph	.000	2	2	0	0	0	0	0	0	0	2	0
Bill Schuster, ss-1	.000	2	1	1	0	0	0	0	0	0	0	0
Frank Secory, ph	.200	5	5	0	1	0	0	0	0	0	2	0
Hy Vandenberg, p	.000	3	1	0	0	0	0	0	0	0	0	0
Dewey Williams, c-1	.000	2	2	0	0	0	0	0	0	0	1	0
Hank Wyse, p	.000	3	3	0	0	0	0	0	0	0	0	0
TOTAL	.259		247	29	64	16	3	1	27	19	48	2

PITCHER	W	L	ERA	G	GS	CG	SV	SHO	IP	H	ER	BB	SO
Hank Borowy	2	2	4.00	4	3	1	0	1	18.0	21	8	6	8
Bob Chipman	0	0	0.00	1	0	0	0	0	0.1	0	0	1	0
Paul Derringer	0	0	6.75	3	0	0	0	0	5.1	5	4	7	1
Paul Erickson	0	0	3.86	4	0	0	0	0	7.0	8	3	3	5
Claude Passeau	1	0	2.70	3	2	1	0	1	16.2	7	5	8	3
Ray Prim	0	1	9.00	2	1	0	0	0	4.0	4	4	1	1
Hy Vandenberg	0	0	0.00	3	0	0	0	0	6.0	1	0	3	3
Hank Wyse	0	1	7.04	3	1	0	0	0	7.2	8	6	4	1
TOTAL	3	4	4.15	23	7	2	0	2	65.0	54	30	33	22

GAME 1 AT DET OCT 3

CHI	403	000	200	9	13	0
DET	000	000	000	0	6	0

Pitchers: BOROWY vs NEWHOUSER, Benton (3), Tobin (5), Mueller (8)
Home Runs: Cavaretta-CHI
Attendance: 54,637

GAME 2 AT DET OCT 4

CHI	000	100	000	1	7	0
DET	000	040	00X	4	7	0

Pitchers: WYSE, Erickson (7) vs TRUCKS
Home Runs: Greenberg-DET
Attendance: 53,636

GAME 3 AT DET OCT 5

CHI	000	200	100	3	8	0
DET	000	000	000	0	1	2

Pitchers: PASSEAU vs OVERMIRE, Benton (7)
Attendance: 55,500

GAME 4 AT CHI OCT 6

DET	000	400	000	4	7	1
CHI	000	001	000	1	5	1

Pitchers: TROUT vs PRIM, Derringer (4), Vandenberg (6), Erickson (8)
Attendance: 42,923

GAME 5 AT CHI OCT 7

DET	001	004	102	8	11	0
CHI	001	000	201	4	7	2

Pitchers: NEWHOUSER vs BOROWY, Vandenberg (6), Chipman (6), Derringer (7), Erickson (9)
Attendance: 43,463

GAME 6 AT CHI OCT 8

DET	010 000 240 000	7	13	1
CHI	000 041 200 001	8	15	3

Pitchers: Trucks, Caster (5), Bridges (6), Benton (7), TROUT (8) vs Passeau, Wyse (7), Prim (8), BOROWY (9)
Home Runs: Greenberg-DET
Attendance: 41,708

GAME 7 AT CHI OCT 10

DET	510	000	120	9	9	1
CHI	100	100	010	3	10	0

Pitchers: NEWHOUSER vs BOROWY, Derringer (1), Vandenberg (2), Erickson (6), Passeau (8), Wyse (9)
Attendance: 41,590

With World War Two over, the majors were at full strength for the first time in five years. Boston's big bats were back, and the Sox ran away with the American League pennant. St. Louis had Stan Musial back, but they struggled to their pennant, finishing the regular schedule tied with Brooklyn, and defeating them in the first major league tie-breaker playoff, two games to none.

Favored Boston edged St. Louis in the opener, but it took a home run by Rudy York in the top of the tenth to spoil Cardinal ace Howie Pollet's strong showing. Harry Brecheen brought the Cards back the next day with the first of his three Series wins—a four-hit shutout.

Boston regained the lead in Game Three. Sox ace Dave Ferriss spaced six hits and a walk, one per inning, in shutting out the Cardinals, and Rudy York hit his second game-winning homer, this time a three-run shot in the first inning. The next day, though, St. Louis exploded for a record-tying 20 hits—four apiece by Enos Slaughter, Joe Garagiola and Whitey Kurowski—to give Cardinal pitcher George Munger (who had completed only two of his seven regular-season starts) an easy complete-game 12–3 victory.

For the third time the Red Sox took the Series lead, winning Game Five 6–3 behind Joe Dobson's four-hit pitching (the Cards' three runs were unearned), but St. Louis tied the Series for the third time with a win in Game Six. Brecheen, in his second start, again pitched splendidly, holding Boston to a single run in the seventh inning, long after the Cards had driven out Sox starter Mickey Harris with three runs in the third.

The final game, like the Series itself, was a seesaw battle. Boston scored the first run in the top of the first, but St. Louis tied the score an inning later. The Cards took a two-run lead on three hits in the fifth, but the Sox came back in the eighth to tie it up as Dom DiMaggio doubled off reliever Brecheen to drive in a pair of pinch hitters who had singled and doubled off starter Murry Dickson. The Series' final run came a half inning later. Slaughter opened with a single, but moved no farther as the next two batters were retired. Then Harry Walker hit a liner over short. Slaughter, off with the crack of the bat, never paused and beat the relay to the plate with what proved the winning run, as Brecheen held the Sox in the ninth for his third win of the Series and the Cardinals' seventh world title.

St. Louis Cardinals (NL), 4; Boston Red Sox (AL), 3

STL (N)

PLAYER/POS	AVG	G	AB	R	H	2B	3B	HR	RB	BB	SO	SB
Johnny Beazley, p	.000	1	0	0	0	0	0	0	0	0	0	0
Al Brazle, p	.000	1	2	0	0	0	0	0	0	0	0	0
Harry Brecheen, p	.125	3	8	2	1	0	0	0	1	0	1	0
Murry Dickson, p	.400	2	5	1	2	2	0	0	1	0	1	0
Erv Dusak, of	.250	4	4	0	1	1	0	0	0	2	2	0
Joe Garagiola, c	.316	5	19	2	6	2	0	0	4	0	3	0
Nippy Jones, ph	.000	1	1	0	0	0	0	0	0	0	1	0
Whitey Kurowski, 3b	.296	7	27	5	8	3	0	0	2	0	3	0
Marty Marion, ss	.250	7	24	1	6	2	0	0	4	1	1	0
Terry Moore, of	.148	7	27	1	4	0	0	0	2	2	6	0
Red Munger, p	.250	1	4	0	1	0	0	0	0	0	2	0
Stan Musial, 1b	.222	7	27	3	6	4	1	0	4	4	2	1
Howie Pollet, p	.000	2	4	0	0	0	0	0	0	0	1	0
Del Rice, c	.500	3	6	2	3	1	0	0	0	0	2	0
Red Schoendienst, 2b	.233	7	30	3	7	1	0	0	1	0	2	1
Dick Sisler, ph	.000	2	2	0	0	0	0	0	0	0	0	0
Enos Slaughter, of	.320	7	25	5	8	1	1	1	2	4	3	1
Harry Walker, of	.412	7	17	3	7	2	0	0	6	4	2	0
Ted Wilks, p	.000	1	0	0	0	0	0	0	0	0	0	0
TOTAL	.259		232	28	60	19	2	1	27	19	30	3

PITCHER	W	L	ERA	G	GS	CG	SV	SHO	IP	H	ER	BB	SO
Johnny Beazley	0	0	0.00	1	0	0	0	0	1.0	1	0	0	1
Al Brazle	0	1	5.40	1	0	0	0	0	6.2	7	4	4	4
Harry Brecheen	3	0	0.45	3	2	2	0	1	20.0	14	1	5	11
Murry Dickson	0	1	3.86	2	2	0	0	0	14.0	11	6	4	7
Red Munger	1	0	1.00	1	1	1	0	0	9.0	9	1	3	2
Howie Pollet	0	1	3.48	2	2	1	0	0	10.1	12	4	4	3
Ted Wilks	0	0	0.00	1	0	0	0	0	1.0	2	0	0	0
TOTAL	4	3	2.32	11	7	4	0	1	62.0	56	16	22	28

BOS (A)

PLAYER/POS	AVG	G	AB	R	H	2B	3B	HR	RB	BB	SO	SB
Jim Bagby, p	.000	1	1	0	0	0	0	0	0	0	0	0
Mace Brown, p	.000	1	0	0	0	0	0	0	0	0	0	0
Paul Campbell, pr	.000	1	0	0	0	0	0	0	0	0	0	0
Leon Culberson, of-3	.222	5	9	1	2	0	0	1	1	1	2	1
Dom DiMaggio, of	.259	7	27	2	7	3	0	0	3	2	2	0
Joe Dobson, p	.000	3	3	0	0	0	0	0	0	0	2	0
Bobby Doerr, 2b	.409	6	22	1	9	1	0	1	3	2	2	0
Clem Dreisewerd, p	.000	1	0	0	0	0	0	0	0	0	0	0
Dave Ferriss, p	.000	2	6	0	0	0	0	0	0	0	1	0
Don Gutteridge, 2b-2	.400	3	5	1	2	0	0	0	1	0	0	0
Mickey Harris, p	.333	2	3	0	1	0	0	0	0	0	1	0
Pinky Higgins, 3b	.208	7	24	1	5	1	0	0	2	0	0	0
Tex Hughson, p	.333	3	3	0	1	0	0	0	0	0	0	0
Earl Johnson, p	.000	3	1	0	0	0	0	0	0	0	0	0
Bob Klinger, p	.000	1	0	0	0	0	0	0	0	0	0	0
Tom McBride, of-2	.167	5	12	0	2	0	0	0	1	0	1	0
Catfish Metkovich, ph	.500	2	2	1	1	1	0	0	0	0	0	0
Wally Moses, of	.417	4	12	1	5	0	0	0	0	1	2	0
Roy Partee, c	.100	5	10	1	1	0	0	0	0	1	2	0
Johnny Pesky, ss	.233	7	30	2	7	0	0	0	0	1	3	1
Rip Russell, 3b-1	1.000	2	2	1	2	0	0	0	0	0	0	0
Mike Ryba, p	.000	1	0	0	0	0	0	0	0	0	0	0
Hal Wagner, c	.000	5	13	0	0	0	0	0	0	0	1	0
Ted Williams, of	.200	7	25	2	5	0	0	0	1	5	5	0
Rudy York, 1b	.261	7	23	6	6	1	1	2	5	6	4	0
Bill Zuber, p	.000	1	0	0	0	0	0	0	0	0	0	0
TOTAL	.240		233	20	56	7	1	4	18	22	28	2

PITCHER	W	L	ERA	G	GS	CG	SV	SHO	IP	H	ER	BB	SO
Jim Bagby	0	0	3.00	1	0	0	0	0	3.0	6	1	1	1
Mace Brown	0	0	27.00	1	0	0	0	0	1.0	4	3	1	0
Joe Dobson	1	0	0.00	3	1	1	0	0	12.2	4	0	3	10
Clem Dreisewerd	0	0	0.00	1	0	0	0	0	0.1	0	0	0	0
Dave Ferriss	1	0	2.03	2	2	1	0	1	13.1	13	3	2	4
Mickey Harris	0	2	3.72	2	2	0	0	0	9.2	11	4	4	5
Tex Hughson	0	1	3.14	3	2	0	0	0	14.1	14	5	3	8
Earl Johnson	1	0	2.70	3	0	0	0	0	3.1	1	1	2	1
Bob Klinger	0	1	13.50	1	0	0	0	0	0.2	2	1	1	0
Mike Ryba	0	0	13.50	1	0	0	0	0	0.2	3	1	1	0
Bill Zuber	0	0	4.50	1	0	0	0	0	2.0	3	1	1	1
TOTAL	3	4	2.95	19	7	2	0	1	61.0	60	20	19	30

GAME 1 AT STL OCT 6

BOS 010 000 001 1   3 9 2
STL 000 000 010 0   2 7 0

Pitchers: Hughson, JOHNSON (9) vs POLLET
Home Runs: York-BOS
Attendance: 36,218

GAME 2 AT STL OCT 7

BOS 000 000 000   0 4 1
STL 001 020 00X   3 6 0

Pitchers: HARRIS, Dobson (8) vs BRECHEEN
Attendance: 35,815

GAME 3 AT BOS OCT 9

STL 000 000 000   0 6 1
BOS 300 000 01X   4 8 0

Pitchers: DICKSON, Wilks (8) vs FERRISS
Home Runs: York-BOS
Attendance: 34,500

GAME 4 AT BOS OCT 10

STL 033 010 104   12 20 1
BOS 000 100 020   3 9 4

Pitchers: MUNGER vs HUGHSON, Bagby (3), Zuber (6), Brown (8), Ryba (9), Dreisewerd (9)
Home Runs: Slaughter-STL, Doerr-BOS
Attendance: 35,645

GAME 5 AT BOS OCT 11

STL 010 000 002   3 4 1
BOS 110 001 30X   6 11 3

Pitchers: Pollet, BRAZLE (1), Beazley (8) vs DOBSON
Home Runs: Culberson-BOS
Attendance: 35,982

GAME 6 AT STL OCT 13

BOS 000 000 100   1 7 0
STL 003 000 01X   4 8 0

Pitchers: HARRIS, Hughson (3), Johnson (8) vs BRECHEEN
Attendance: 35,768

GAME 7 AT STL OCT 15

BOS 100 000 020   3 8 0
STL 010 020 01X   4 9 1

Pitchers: Ferriss, Dobson (5), KLINGER (8), Johnson (9) vs Dickson, BRECHEEN (8)
Attendance: 36,143

Two of the most memorable plays in World Series history brought Brooklyn victory in Games Four and Six, but when the Series had ended the Yankees were world champions for the eleventh time. Dodger ace Ralph Branca set New York down in order through the first four innings of Game One. But the first five batters to face him in the fifth inning reached base. Branca was lifted, but before the inning was over five Yankees had crossed the plate—more than enough for their first win.

The Yankees went two-up the next day, rocking four Brooklyn pitchers for 15 hits and an easy 10–3 win. Brooklyn finally made its presence felt in Game Three, another heavy-hitting affair, scoring six runs in the second inning to establish a lead the Yankees could not overcome. Both teams recorded 13 hits, but Dodger fireman Hugh Casey extinguished the last Yankee flame in the seventh inning, and preserved a narrow 9–8 Dodger lead the rest of the way.

Shortstop Pee Wee Reese's error and a bases-loaded walk gave the Yankees an unearned run in the first inning of Game Four, and they earned a second run in the fourth. Meanwhile, Yankee pitcher Bill Bevens, although he averaged a walk an inning, had allowed no Dodger hits and only one run as the game entered the last of the ninth. Bevens retired two in the ninth, but walked his ninth and tenth batters (one intentionally), then lost both his no-hitter and the game as Dodger pinch hitter Cookie Lavagetto doubled home the two baserunners to even the Series at two-all.

Yankee Spec Shea (the winning pitcher in Game One) held Brooklyn to four hits and one run in Game Five. Joe DiMaggio homered in the fifth inning for New York's second run, enough to put the Yankees back in the Series lead. The Dodgers rebounded in Game Six to build an early 4–0 lead. But the Yankees tied the score in the last of the third and took a lead in the fourth. Brooklyn regained the lead in the sixth with four runs, but when DiMaggio hit a long fly to left with two on in the Yankee half of the inning, it looked as if the score would be tied. But substitute left fielder Al Gionfriddo (in what turned out to be his last big league game) raced to the bullpen fence 415 feet out to rob DiMag of the home run. New York scored a run in the ninth, but thanks to Gionfriddo's catch it was not enough to win the game.

Brooklyn scored first in the finale with a pair of second-inning runs, but Yankee relievers Bill Bevens and Joe Page shut them out through the final seven innings as their teammates gradually built a Series-clinching 5–2 victory.

New York Yankees (AL), 4; Brooklyn Dodgers (NL), 3

NY (A)

PLAYER/POS	AVG	G	AB	R	H	2B	3B	HR	RB	BB	SO	SB
Yogi Berra, c-4,of-2	.158	6	19	2	3	0	0	1	2	1	2	0
Bill Bevens, p	.000	2	4	0	0	0	0	0	0	0	2	0
Bobby Brown, ph	1.000	4	3	2	3	2	0	0	3	1	0	0
Spud Chandler, p	.000	1	0	0	0	0	0	0	0	0	0	0
Allie Clark, of-1	.500	3	2	1	1	0	0	0	1	1	0	0
Joe DiMaggio, of	.231	7	26	4	6	0	0	2	5	6	2	0
Karl Drews, p	.000	2	2	0	0	0	0	0	0	0	2	0
Lonny Frey, ph	.000	1	1	0	0	0	0	0	0	1	0	0
Tommy Henrich, of	.323	7	31	2	10	2	0	1	5	2	3	0
Ralph Houk, ph	1.000	1	1	0	1	0	0	0	0	0	0	0
Billy Johnson, 3b	.269	7	26	8	7	0	3	0	2	3	4	0
Johnny Lindell, of	.500	6	18	3	9	3	1	0	7	5	2	0
Sherm Lollar, c	.750	2	4	3	3	2	0	0	1	0	0	0
George McQuinn, 1b	.130	7	23	3	3	0	0	0	1	5	8	0
Bobo Newsom, p	.000	2	0	0	0	0	0	0	0	0	0	0
Joe Page, p	.000	4	4	0	0	0	0	0	0	0	1	0
Jack Phillips, 1b-1	.000	2	2	0	0	0	0	0	0	0	0	0
Vic Raschi, p	.000	2	0	0	0	0	0	0	0	0	0	0
Allie Reynolds, p	.500	2	4	2	2	0	0	0	1	0	0	0
Phil Rizzuto, ss	.308	7	26	3	8	1	0	0	2	4	0	2
Aaron Robinson, c	.200	3	10	2	2	0	0	0	1	2	1	0
Spec Shea, p	.400	3	5	0	2	1	0	0	1	0	2	0
Snuffy Stirnweiss, 2b	.259	7	27	3	7	0	1	0	3	8	8	0
Butch Wensloff, p	.000	1	0	0	0	0	0	0	0	0	0	0
TOTAL	.282		238	38	67	11	5	4	36	38	37	2

PITCHER	W	L	ERA	G	GS	CG	SV	SHO	IP	H	ER	BB	SO
Bill Bevens	0	1	2.38	2	1	1	0	0	11.1	3	3	11	7
Spud Chandler	0	0	9.00	1	0	0	0	0	2.0	2	2	3	1
Karl Drews	0	0	3.00	2	0	0	0	0	3.0	2	1	1	0
Bobo Newsom	0	1	19.29	2	1	0	0	0	2.1	6	5	2	0
Joe Page	1	1	4.15	4	0	0	1	0	13.0	12	6	2	7
Vic Raschi	0	0	6.75	2	0	0	0	0	1.1	2	1	0	1
Allie Reynolds	1	0	4.76	2	2	1	0	0	11.1	15	6	3	6
Spec Shea	2	0	2.35	3	3	1	0	0	15.1	10	4	8	10
Butch Wensloff	0	0	0.00	1	0	0	0	0	2.0	0	0	0	0
TOTAL	4	3	4.09	19	7	3	1	0	61.2	52	28	30	32

BRO (N)

PLAYER/POS	AVG	G	AB	R	H	2B	3B	HR	RB	BB	SO	SB
Dan Bankhead, pr	.000	1	0	1	0	0	0	0	0	0	0	0
Rex Barney, p	.000	3	1	0	0	0	0	0	0	0	0	0
Hank Behrman, p	.000	5	1	0	0	0	0	0	0	0	0	0
Bobby Bragan, ph	1.000	1	1	0	1	1	0	0	1	0	0	0
Ralph Branca, p	.000	3	4	0	0	0	0	0	0	0	1	0
Hugh Casey, p	.000	6	1	0	0	0	0	0	0	0	1	0
Bruce Edwards, c	.222	7	27	3	6	1	0	0	2	2	7	0
Carl Furillo, of	.353	6	17	2	6	2	0	0	3	0	0	0
Al Gionfriddo, of-1	.000	4	3	2	0	0	0	0	0	1	0	1
Hal Gregg, p	.000	3	3	0	0	0	0	0	0	1	1	0
Joe Hatten, p	.333	4	3	1	1	0	0	0	0	0	0	0
Gene Hermanski, of	.158	7	19	4	3	0	1	0	1	3	3	0
Gil Hodges, ph	.000	1	1	0	0	0	0	0	0	0	0	0
Spider Jorgensen, 3b	.200	7	20	1	4	2	0	0	3	2	4	0
Cookie Lavagetto, 3b-3	.143	5	7	0	1	1	0	0	3	0	2	0
Vic Lombardi, p-2	.000	3	3	0	0	0	0	0	0	0	0	0
Eddie Miksis, 2b-1,of-1	.250	5	4	1	1	0	0	0	0	0	1	0
Pee Wee Reese, ss	.304	7	23	5	7	1	0	0	4	6	3	3
Pete Reiser, of-3	.250	5	8	1	2	0	0	0	3	3	1	0
Jackie Robinson, 1b	.259	7	27	3	7	2	0	0	3	2	4	2
Eddie Stanky, 2b	.240	7	25	4	6	1	0	0	2	3	2	0
Harry Taylor, p	.000	1	0	0	0	0	0	0	0	0	0	0
Arky Vaughan, ph	.500	3	2	0	1	0	0	0	0	1	0	0
Dixie Walker, of	.222	7	27	1	6	1	0	1	4	3	1	1
TOTAL	.230		226	29	52	13	1	1	26	30	32	7

PITCHER	W	L	ERA	G	GS	CG	SV	SHO	IP	H	ER	BB	SO
Rex Barney	0	1	2.70	3	1	0	0	0	6.2	4	2	10	3
Hank Behrman	0	0	7.11	5	0	0	0	0	6.1	9	5	5	3
Ralph Branca	1	1	8.64	3	1	0	0	0	8.1	12	8	5	8
Hugh Casey	2	0	0.87	6	0	0	1	0	10.1	5	1	1	3
Hal Gregg	0	1	3.55	3	1	0	0	0	12.2	9	5	8	10
Joe Hatten	0	0	7.00	4	1	0	0	0	9.0	12	7	7	5
Vic Lombardi	0	1	12.15	2	2	0	0	0	6.2	14	9	1	5
Harry Taylor	0	0	INF	1	1	0	0	0	0.0	2	0	1	0
TOTAL	3	4	5.55	27	7	0	1	0	60.0	67	37	38	37

GAME 1 AT NY SEPT 30

BRO	100	001	100	3	6	0
NY	000	050	00X	5	4	0

Pitchers: BRANCA, Behrman (5), Casey (7) vs SHEA, Page (6)
Attendance: 73,365

GAME 2 AT NY OCT 1

BRO	001	100	001	3	9	2
NY	101	121	40X	10	15	1

Pitchers: LOMBARDI, Gregg (5), Behrman (7), Barney (7) vs REYNOLDS
Home Runs: Walker-BRO, Henrich-NY
Attendance: 69,865

GAME 3 AT BRO OCT 2

NY	002	221	100	8	13	0
BRO	061	200	00X	9	13	1

Pitchers: NEWSOM, Raschi (2), Drews (3), Chandler (4), Page (6) vs Hatten, Branca (5), CASEY (7)
Home Runs: DiMaggio-NY, Berra-NY
Attendance: 33,098

GAME 4 AT BRO OCT 3

NY	100	100	000	2	8	1
BRO	000	010	002	3	1	3

Pitchers: BEVENS vs Taylor, Gregg (1), Behrman (8), CASEY (9)
Attendance: 33,443

GAME 5 AT BRO OCT 4

NY	000	110	000	2	5	0
BRO	000	001	000	1	4	1

Pitchers: SHEA vs BARNEY, Hatten (5), Behrman (7), Casey (8)
Home Runs: DiMaggio-NY
Attendance: 34,379

GAME 6 AT NY OCT 5

BRO	202	004	000	8	12	1
NY	004	100	001	6	15	2

Pitchers: Lombardi, BRANCA (3), Hatten (6), Casey (9) vs Reynolds, Drews (3), PAGE (5), Newsom (6), Raschi (7), Wensloff (8)
Attendance: 74,065

GAME 7 AT NY OCT 6

BRO	020	000	000	2	7	0
NY	010	201	10X	5	7	0

Pitchers: GREGG, Behrman (4), Hatten (6), Barney (6), Casey (7) vs Shea, Bevens (2), PAGE (5)
Attendance: 71,548

Boston outpitched and outhit Cleveland, and the clubs tied in runs scored. But the Braves scored most of their runs in one game, and the Indians, spreading theirs more evenly, took the Series. Boston ace Johnny Sain dueled Bob Feller in the opener. Feller gave up only two singles, but one of them followed a walk and a sacrifice (and a controversial pickoff play at second, in which the Boston runner was ruled safe although photos later showed him clearly out) and drove in the game's only run. Both teams registered eight hits in Game Two, but Cleveland's led to four runs, while Indian hurler Bob Lemon held Boston to just one—and that was unearned.

Cleveland's rookie sensation Gene Bearden shut out the Braves on five hits in Game Three as the Series moved to Cleveland's huge Municipal Stadium. Bearden himself, after doubling in the third, scored on a Boston error what proved to be the winning run. A record 81,897 fans saw Sain face Steve Gromek in Game Four. Only five Indians hit Sain safely, but a first-inning single and double put Cleveland on the board, and Larry Doby's home run two innings later made the score 2–0. Boston's Marv Rickert homered in the seventh to narrow Cleveland's lead, but that ended the scoring.

Another attendance record was set at Game Five as 86,288 fans gathered to watch Bob Feller sew up the title for Cleveland. They went home disappointed. In a game that featured five of the Series' eight home runs, Boston jumped ahead on Bob Elliott's three-run blast in the first. Dale Mitchell opened Cleveland's half of the inning with a home run, but Elliott neutralized it in the third with his second homer. The Indians drove out Boston starter Nelson Potter with four runs in the fourth inning (three coming on Jim Hegan's homer). But Warren Spahn (who had lost Game Two) hurled one-hit shutout relief over the final five frames as his Braves tied the game on Bill Salkeld's homer in the sixth, and blew out Feller and two relievers with six runs in the seventh. The fourth Indian pitcher, Satchel Paige (in his only World Series appearance), retired two batters to end the inning, but the damage had been done.

A day later though, back in Boston, Cleveland edged the Braves 4–3 for the title. Gene Bearden's relief pitching allowed two inherited baserunners to score in the eighth, but halted Boston's rally one run short of a tie.

Cleveland Indians (AL), 4; Boston Braves (NL), 2

CLE (A)

PLAYER/POS	AVG	G	AB	R	H	2B	3B	HR	RB	BB	SO	SB
Gene Bearden, p	.500	2	4	1	2	1	0	0	0	0	1	0
Ray Boone, ph	.000	1	1	0	0	0	0	0	0	0	1	0
Lou Boudreau, ss	.273	6	22	1	6	4	0	0	3	1	1	0
Russ Christopher, p	.000	1	0	0	0	0	0	0	0	0	0	0
Allie Clark, of	.000	1	3	0	0	0	0	0	0	0	1	0
Larry Doby, of	.318	6	22	1	7	1	0	1	2	2	4	0
Bob Feller, p	.000	2	4	0	0	0	0	0	0	0	2	0
Joe Gordon, 2b	.182	6	22	3	4	0	0	1	2	1	2	1
Steve Gromek, p	.000	1	3	0	0	0	0	0	0	0	1	0
Jim Hegan, c	.211	6	19	2	4	0	0	1	5	1	4	1
Wally Judnich, of	.077	4	13	1	1	0	0	0	1	1	4	0
Ken Keltner, 3b	.095	6	21	3	2	0	0	0	0	2	3	0
Bob Kennedy, of	.500	3	2	0	1	0	0	0	0	1	0	0
Ed Klieman, p	.000	1	0	0	0	0	0	0	0	0	0	0
Bob Lemon, p	.000	2	7	0	0	0	0	0	0	0	0	0
Dale Mitchell, of	.174	6	23	4	4	1	0	1	1	2	0	0
Bob Muncrief, p	.000	1	0	0	0	0	0	0	0	0	0	0
Satchel Paige, p	.000	1	0	0	0	0	0	0	0	0	0	0
Hal Peck, ph	.000	1	0	0	0	0	0	0	0	0	0	0
Eddie Robinson, 1b	.300	6	20	0	6	0	0	0	1	1	0	0
Al Rosen, ph	.000	1	1	0	0	0	0	0	0	0	0	0
Joe Tipton, ph	.000	1	1	0	0	0	0	0	0	0	1	0
Thurman Tucker, of	.333	1	3	1	1	0	0	0	0	0	0	0
TOTAL	.199		191	17	38	7	0	4	16	12	26	2

PITCHER	W	L	ERA	G	GS	CG	SV	SHO	IP	H	ER	BB	SO
Gene Bearden	1	0	0.00	2	1	1	1	1	10.2	6	0	1	4
Russ Christopher	0	0	INF	1	0	0	0	0	0.0	2	1	0	0
Bob Feller	0	2	5.02	2	2	1	0	0	14.1	10	8	5	7
Steve Gromek	1	0	1.00	1	1	1	0	0	9.0	7	1	1	2
Ed Klieman	0	0	INF	1	0	0	0	0	0.0	1	3	2	0
Bob Lemon	2	0	1.65	2	2	1	0	0	16.1	16	3	7	6
Bob Muncrief	0	0	0.00	1	0	0	0	0	2.0	1	0	0	0
Satchel Paige	0	0	0.00	1	0	0	0	0	0.2	0	0	0	0
TOTAL	4	2	2.72	11	6	4	1	1	53.0	43	16	16	19

BOS (N)

PLAYER/POS	AVG	G	AB	R	H	2B	3B	HR	RB	BB	SO	SB
Red Barrett, p	.000	2	0	0	0	0	0	0	0	0	0	0
Vern Bickford, p	.000	1	0	0	0	0	0	0	0	0	0	0
Clint Conatser, of	.000	2	4	0	0	0	0	0	1	0	0	0
Alvin Dark, ss	.167	6	24	2	4	1	0	0	0	0	2	0
Bob Elliott, 3b	.333	6	21	4	7	0	0	2	5	2	2	0
Tommy Holmes, of	.192	6	26	3	5	0	0	0	1	0	0	0
Phil Masi, c	.125	5	8	1	1	1	0	0	1	0	0	0
Frank McCormick, 1b-1	.200	3	5	0	1	0	0	0	0	0	2	0
Mike McCormick, of	.261	6	23	1	6	0	0	0	2	0	4	0
Nelson Potter, p	.500	2	2	0	1	0	0	0	0	0	1	0
Marv Rickert, of	.211	5	19	2	4	0	0	1	2	0	4	0
Connie Ryan, ph	.000	2	1	0	0	0	0	0	0	0	1	0
Johnny Sain, p	.200	2	5	0	1	0	0	0	0	0	0	0
Bill Salkeld, c	.222	5	9	2	2	0	0	1	1	5	1	0
Ray Sanders, ph	.000	1	1	0	0	0	0	0	0	0	0	0
Sibby Sisti, 2b	.000	2	1	0	0	0	0	0	0	0	0	0
Warren Spahn, p	.000	3	4	0	0	0	0	0	0	1	0	0
Eddie Stanky, 2b	.286	6	14	4	4	1	0	0	0	7	1	0
Earl Torgeson, 1b	.389	5	18	2	7	3	0	0	1	2	1	1
Bill Voiselle, p	.000	2	2	0	0	0	0	0	0	0	0	0
TOTAL	.230		187	17	43	6	0	4	16	16	19	1

PITCHER	W	L	ERA	G	GS	CG	SV	SHO	IP	H	ER	BB	SO
Red Barrett	0	0	0.00	2	0	0	0	0	3.2	1	0	0	1
Vern Bickford	0	1	2.70	1	1	0	0	0	3.1	4	1	5	1
Nelson Potter	0	0	8.44	2	1	0	0	0	5.1	6	5	2	1
Johnny Sain	1	1	1.06	2	2	2	0	1	17.0	9	2	0	9
Warren Spahn	1	1	3.00	3	1	0	0	0	12.0	10	4	3	12
Bill Voiselle	0	1	2.53	2	1	0	0	0	10.2	8	3	2	2
TOTAL	2	4	2.60	12	6	2	0	1	52.0	38	15	12	26

GAME 1 AT BOS OCT 6

CLE	000 000 000	0	4	0
BOS	000 000 01X	1	2	2

Pitchers: FELLER vs SAIN
Attendance: 40,135

GAME 2 AT BOS OCT 7

CLE	000 210 001	4	8	1
BOS	100 000 000	1	8	3

Pitchers: LEMON vs SPAHN, Barrett (5), Potter (8)
Attendance: 39,633

GAME 3 AT CLE OCT 8

BOS	000 000 000	0	5	1
CLE	001 100 00X	2	5	0

Pitchers: BICKFORD, Voiselle (4), Barrett (8) vs BEARDEN
Attendance: 70,306

GAME 4 AT CLE OCT 9

BOS	000 000 100	1	7	0
CLE	101 000 00X	2	5	0

Pitchers: SAIN vs GROMEK
Home Runs: Doby-CLE, Rickert-BOS
Attendance: 81,897

GAME 5 AT CLE OCT 10

BOS	301 001 600	11	12	0
CLE	100 400 000	5	6	2

Pitchers: Potter, SPAHN (4) vs FELLER, Klieman (7), Christopher (7), Paige (7), Muncrief (8)
Home Runs: Elliott-BOS (2), Mitchell-CLE, Hegan-CLE, Salkeld-BOS
Attendance: 86,288

GAME 6 AT BOS OCT 11

CLE	001 002 010	4	10	0
BOS	000 100 020	3	9	0

Pitchers: LEMON, Bearden (8) vs VOISELLE, Spahn (8)
Home Runs: Gordon-CLE
Attendance: 40,103

Casey Stengel, in the first of his twelve years as Yankee manager, edged his team past the Boston Red Sox for his first of ten American League pennants, then past the Dodgers for his first of seven world championships. New York and Brooklyn traded 1–0 wins to begin the Series. In Game One Yankee Allie Reynolds dueled Dodger rookie Don Newcombe scorelessly through 8½ innings—until Tommy Henrich led off the last of the ninth with a Yankee home run. Dodger Jackie Robinson scored after doubling off Vic Raschi in the second inning of Game Two for that game's only score, while Dodger ace Preacher Roe permitted the Yankees just six scattered hits—never more than one per inning.

The teams entered the ninth inning of Game Three tied 1–1. But in the top of the ninth, Dodger starter Ralph Branca, after loading the bases on two walks and a single, gave up another single to pinch hitter Johnny Mize for two runs. Jerry Coleman's single off reliever Jack Banta drove in another run before the third out was made. In the last of the ninth, Yankee fireman Joe Page (who had held Brooklyn scoreless since coming on with the bases loaded in the fourth) finally weakened. But after yielding solo homers to Luis Olmo and Roy Campanella, he struck out pinch hitter Bruce Edwards for New York's second win.

The Yankees' victory in Game Four came a little easier. They scored first, driving out starter Don Newcombe with three runs in the fourth, and rapping reliever Joe Hatten for three more runs an inning later. Brooklyn retaliated in the sixth, sending Yankee starter Ed Lopat to the showers with seven singles for four runs. But Allie Reynolds came on for 3⅓ innings of no-hit relief to preserve the Yankees lead—and his Series 0.00 earned run average.

After four closely contested games, the Yankees erupted in Game Five for ten runs in the first six innings as Brooklyn was held to just two. In the last of the seventh, the Dodgers came back, driving out starter Vic Raschi with a four-run rally, capped by Gil Hodges's three-run homer. But Joe Page came on to get the final out of the seventh, and held the Dodgers scoreless over the final two innings to bring the Yankees' world titles to an even dozen.

New York Yankees (AL), 4; Brooklyn Dodgers (NL), 1

NY (A)

PLAYER/POS	AVG	G	AB	R	H	2B	3B	HR	RBI	BB	SO	SB
Hank Bauer, of	.167	3	6	0	1	0	0	0	0	0	0	0
Yogi Berra, c	.063	4	16	2	1	0	0	0	1	1	3	0
Bobby Brown, 3b-3	.500	4	12	4	6	1	2	0	5	2	2	0
Tommy Byrne, p	1.000	1	1	0	1	0	0	0	0	0	0	0
Gerry Coleman, 2b	.250	5	20	0	5	3	0	0	4	0	4	0
Joe DiMaggio, of	.111	5	18	2	2	0	0	1	2	3	5	0
Tommy Henrich, 1b	.263	5	19	4	5	0	0	1	1	3	0	0
Billy Johnson, 3b	.143	2	7	0	1	0	0	0	0	0	2	1
Johnny Lindell, of	.143	2	7	0	1	0	0	0	0	0	2	0
Ed Lopat, p	.333	1	3	0	1	1	0	0	1	0	0	0
Cliff Mapes, of	.100	4	10	3	1	1	0	0	2	2	4	0
Johnny Mize, ph	1.000	2	2	0	2	0	0	0	2	0	0	0
Gus Niarhos, c	.000	1	0	0	0	0	0	0	0	0	0	0
Joe Page, p	.000	3	4	0	0	0	0	0	0	0	2	0
Vic Raschi, p	.200	2	5	0	1	0	0	0	1	1	1	0
Allie Reynolds, p	.500	2	4	0	2	1	0	0	0	0	1	0
Phil Rizzuto, ss	.167	5	18	2	3	0	0	0	1	3	1	1
Charlie Silvera, c	.000	1	2	0	0	0	0	0	0	0	0	0
Snuffy Stirnweiss, ph	.000	1	0	0	0	0	0	0	0	0	0	0
Gene Woodling, of	.400	3	10	4	4	3	0	0	0	3	0	0
TOTAL	.226		164	21	37	10	2	2	20	18	27	2

PITCHER	W	L	ERA	G	GS	CG	SV	SHO	IP	H	ER	BB	SO
Tommy Byrne	0	0	2.70	1	1	0	0	0	3.1	2	1	2	1
Ed Lopat	1	0	6.35	1	1	0	0	0	5.2	9	4	1	4
Joe Page	1	0	2.00	3	0	0	1	0	9.0	6	2	3	8
Vic Raschi	1	1	4.30	2	2	1	0	0	14.2	15	7	5	11
Allie Reynolds	1	0	0.00	2	1	1	1	1	12.1	2	0	4	14
TOTAL	4	1	2.80	9	5	1	2	1	45.0	34	14	15	38

BRO (N)

PLAYER/POS	AVG	G	AB	R	H	2B	3B	HR	RBI	BB	SO	SB
Jack Banta, p	.000	3	1	0	0	0	0	0	0	0	0	0
Rex Barney, p	.000	1	0	0	0	0	0	0	0	0	0	0
Ralph Branca, p	.000	1	3	0	0	0	0	0	0	0	3	0
Tommy Brown, ph	.000	2	2	0	0	0	0	0	0	0	1	0
Roy Campanella, c	.267	5	15	2	4	1	0	1	2	3	1	0
Billy Cox, 3b-1	.333	2	3	0	1	0	0	0	0	0	1	0
Bruce Edwards, ph	.500	2	2	0	1	0	0	0	0	0	1	0
Carl Erskine, p	.000	2	0	0	0	0	0	0	0	0	0	0
Carl Furillo, of-2	.125	3	8	0	1	0	0	0	0	1	0	0
Joe Hatten, p	.000	2	0	0	0	0	0	0	0	0	0	0
Gene Hermanski, of	.308	4	13	1	4	0	1	0	2	3	3	0
Gil Hodges, 1b	.235	5	17	2	4	0	0	1	4	1	4	0
Spider Jorgensen, 3b-3	.182	4	11	1	2	2	0	0	0	2	2	0
Mike McCormick, of	.000	1	0	0	0	0	0	0	0	0	0	0
Eddie Miksis, 3b-2	.286	3	7	0	2	1	0	0	0	0	1	0
Paul Minner, p	.000	1	0	0	0	0	0	0	0	0	0	0
Don Newcombe, p	.000	2	4	0	0	0	0	0	0	0	3	0
Luis Olmo, of	.273	4	11	2	3	0	0	1	2	0	2	0
Erv Palica, p	.000	1	0	0	0	0	0	0	0	0	0	0
Marv Rackley, of	.000	2	5	0	0	0	0	0	0	0	2	0
Pee Wee Reese, ss	.316	5	19	2	6	1	0	1	2	1	0	1
Jackie Robinson, 2b	.188	5	16	2	3	1	0	0	2	4	2	0
Preacher Roe, p	.000	1	3	0	0	0	0	0	0	0	3	0
Duke Snider, of	.143	5	21	2	3	1	0	0	0	0	8	0
Dick Whitman, ph	.000	1	1	0	0	0	0	0	0	0	1	0
TOTAL	.210		162	14	34	7	1	4	14	15	38	1

PITCHER	W	L	ERA	G	GS	CG	SV	SHO	IP	H	ER	BB	SO
Jack Banta	0	0	3.18	3	0	0	0	0	5.2	5	2	1	4
Rex Barney	0	1	16.88	1	1	0	0	0	2.2	3	5	6	2
Ralph Branca	0	1	4.15	1	1	0	0	0	8.2	4	4	4	6
Carl Erskine	0	0	16.20	2	0	0	0	0	1.2	3	3	1	0
Joe Hatten	0	0	16.20	2	0	0	0	0	1.2	4	3	2	0
Paul Minner	0	0	0.00	1	0	0	0	0	1.0	1	0	0	0
Don Newcombe	0	2	3.09	2	2	1	0	0	11.2	10	4	3	11
Erv Palica	0	0	0.00	1	0	0	0	0	2.0	1	0	1	0
Preacher Roe	1	0	0.00	1	1	1	0	1	9.0	6	0	0	3
TOTAL	1	4	4.30	14	5	2	0	1	44.0	37	21	18	27

GAME 1 AT NY OCT 5

BRO	000	000	000	0	2	0
NY	000	000	001	1	5	1

Pitchers: NEWCOMBE vs REYNOLDS
Home Runs: Henrich-NY
Attendance: 66,224

GAME 2 AT NY OCT 6

BRO	010	000	000	1	7	2
NY	000	000	000	0	6	1

Pitchers: ROE vs RASCHI, Page (9)
Attendance: 70,053

GAME 3 AT BRO OCT 7

NY	001	000	003	4	5	0
BRO	001	100	002	3	5	0

Pitchers: Byrne, PAGE (4) vs BRANCA, Banta (9)
Home Runs: Reese-BRO, Olmo-BRO, Campanella-BRO
Attendance: 32,788

GAME 4 AT BRO OCT 8

NY	000	330	000	6	10	0
BRO	000	004	000	4	9	1

Pitchers: LOPAT, Reynolds (6) vs NEWCOMBE, Hatten (4), Erskine (6), Banta (7)
Attendance: 33,934

GAME 5 AT BRO OCT 9

NY	203	113	000	10	11	1
BRO	001	001	400	6	11	2

Pitchers: RASCHI, Page (7) vs BARNEY, Banta (3), Erskine (6), Hatten (6), Palica (7), Minner (9)
Home Runs: DiMaggio-NY, Hodges-BRO
Attendance: 33,711

Philadelphia's Whiz Kids, who had capped an exciting pennant race with the Phillies' first flag in thirty-five years, carried the excitement into the World Series but couldn't quite catch up with the Yankees. New York scored only one run in the opener; Philadelphia didn't score any. The Phillies did score a run in the second game, but the Yankees scored two. In Game Three the Phillies scored two runs, the Yankees three.

Jim Konstanty, the National League's ace reliever (and MVP), started his first major league game in four years to lead off the Series, and held the Yankees to just four hits in eight innings of work. But Bobby Brown's double in the fourth was followed by two long flies which moved Brown around to the plate—all the scoring New York needed as Vic Raschi held the Phillies to two singles and a walk.

Robin Roberts and Allie Reynolds dueled in Game Two. New York scored first with a run on a walk and two singles in the second inning, but two Phillie singles and a fly to left tied the game in the last of the fifth. There matters stood until the top of the tenth, when Joe DiMaggio led off with a home run to the upper deck in left. Reynolds held the Phillies in the bottom of the tenth for the second Yankee win.

The Phillies took a lead for the only time in the Series when they broke a 1–1 tie with a run in the seventh inning of Game Three. But New York scored on a Phillie error to tie the game again in the eighth, and in the last of the ninth—with two outs—Yankees Gene Woodling, Phil Rizzuto, and Jerry Coleman singled to produce the winning run.

Rookie sensation Whitey Ford started Game Four and held Philadelphia scoreless into the ninth inning as his Yankees scored twice in the first and three more times in the sixth. He was taken out with two away in the ninth after two singles, a hit batsman, and a Yankee error had permitted two Phillies to score. But reliever Allie Reynolds struck out the final batter to secure for the Yankees a Series sweep.

New York Yankees (AL), 4;
Philadelphia Phillies (NL), 0

NY (A)

PLAYER/POS	AVG	G	AB	R	H	2B	3B	HR	RB	BB	SO	SB
Hank Bauer, of	.133	4	15	0	2	0	0	0	0	1	0	0
Yogi Berra, c	.200	4	15	2	3	0	0	1	2	2	1	0
Bobby Brown, 3b	.333	4	12	2	4	1	1	0	1	0	0	0
Gerry Coleman, 2b	.286	4	14	2	4	1	0	0	3	2	0	0
Joe Collins, 1b	.000	1	0	0	0	0	0	0	0	0	0	0
Joe DiMaggio, of	.308	4	13	2	4	1	0	1	2	3	1	0
Tom Ferrick, p	.000	1	0	0	0	0	0	0	0	0	0	0
Whitey Ford, p	.000	1	3	0	0	0	0	0	0	0	2	0
Johnny Hopp, 1b	.000	3	2	0	0	0	0	0	0	0	0	0
Jackie Jensen, pr	.000	1	0	0	0	0	0	0	0	0	0	0
Billy Johnson, 3b	.000	4	6	0	0	0	0	0	0	0	3	0
Ed Lopat, p	.500	1	2	0	1	0	0	0	0	0	1	0
Cliff Mapes, of	.000	1	4	0	0	0	0	0	0	0	1	0
Johnny Mize, 1b	.133	4	15	0	2	0	0	0	0	0	1	0
Vic Raschi, p	.333	1	3	0	1	0	0	0	0	0	0	0
Allie Reynolds, p	.333	2	3	0	1	0	0	0	0	1	2	0
Phil Rizzuto, ss	.143	4	14	1	2	0	0	0	0	3	0	1
Gene Woodling, of	.429	4	14	2	6	0	0	0	1	2	0	0
TOTAL	.222		135	11	30	3	1	2	10	13	12	1

PITCHER	W	L	ERA	G	GS	CG	SV	SHO	IP	H	ER	BB	SO
Tom Ferrick	1	0	0.00	1	0	0	0	0	1.0	1	0	1	0
Whitey Ford	1	0	0.00	1	1	0	0	0	8.2	7	0	1	7
Ed Lopat	0	0	2.25	1	1	0	0	0	8.0	9	2	0	5
Vic Raschi	1	0	0.00	1	1	1	0	1	9.0	2	0	1	5
Allie Reynolds	1	0	0.87	2	1	1	1	0	10.1	7	1	4	7
TOTAL	4	0	0.73	6	4	2	1	1	37.0	26	3	7	24

PHI (N)

PLAYER/POS	AVG	G	AB	R	H	2B	3B	HR	RB	BB	SO	SB
Richie Ashburn, of	.176	4	17	0	3	1	0	0	1	0	4	0
Jimmy Bloodworth, 2b	.000	1	0	0	0	0	0	0	0	0	0	0
Putsy Caballero, ph	.000	3	1	0	0	0	0	0	0	0	1	0
Del Ennis, of	.143	4	14	1	2	1	0	0	0	0	1	0
Mike Goliat, 2b	.214	4	14	1	3	0	0	0	1	1	2	0
Granny Hamner, ss	.429	4	14	1	6	2	1	0	0	1	2	1
Ken Heintzelman, p	.000	1	2	0	0	0	0	0	0	0	0	0
Ken Johnson, pr	.000	1	0	1	0	0	0	0	0	0	0	0
Willie Jones, 3b	.286	4	14	1	4	1	0	0	0	0	3	0
Jim Konstanty, p	.250	3	4	0	1	0	0	0	0	0	1	0
Stan Lopata, c-1	.000	2	1	0	0	0	0	0	0	0	1	0
Jackie Mayo, of-1	.000	3	0	0	0	0	0	0	0	1	0	0
Russ Meyer, p	.000	2	0	0	0	0	0	0	0	0	0	0
Bob Miller, p	.000	1	0	0	0	0	0	0	0	0	0	0
Robin Roberts, p	.000	2	2	0	0	0	0	0	0	0	1	0
Andy Seminick, c	.182	4	11	0	2	0	0	0	0	1	3	0
Ken Silvestri, c	.000	1	0	0	0	0	0	0	0	0	0	0
Dick Sisler, of	.059	4	17	0	1	0	0	0	1	0	5	0
Eddie Waitkus, 1b	.267	4	15	0	4	1	0	0	0	2	0	0
Dick Whitman, ph	.000	3	2	0	0	0	0	0	0	0	1	0
TOTAL	.203		128	5	26	6	1	0	3	7	24	1

PITCHER	W	L	ERA	G	GS	CG	SV	SHO	IP	H	ER	BB	SO
Ken Heintzelman	0	0	1.17	1	1	0	0	0	7.2	4	1	6	3
Jim Konstanty	0	1	2.40	3	1	0	0	0	15.0	9	4	4	3
Russ Meyer	0	1	5.40	2	0	0	0	0	1.2	4	1	0	1
Bob Miller	0	1	27.00	1	1	0	0	0	0.1	2	1	0	0
Robin Roberts	0	1	1.64	2	1	1	0	0	11.0	11	2	3	5
TOTAL	0	4	2.27	9	4	1	0	0	35.2	30	9	13	12

GAME 1 AT PHI OCT 4

NY	000	100	000	1	5	0
PHI	000	000	000	0	2	1

Pitchers: RASCHI vs KONSTANTY, Meyer (9)
Attendance: 30,746

GAME 2 AT PHI OCT 5

NY	010	000	000	1	2	10	0
PHI	000	010	000	0	1	7	0

Pitchers: REYNOLDS vs ROBERTS
Home Runs: DiMaggio-NY
Attendance: 32,660

GAME 3 AT NY OCT 6

PHI	000	001	100	2	10	2
NY	001	000	011	3	7	0

Pitchers: Heintzelman, Konstanty (8), MEYER (9) vs Lopat, FERRICK (9)
Attendance: 64,505

GAME 4 AT NY OCT 7

PHI	000	000	002	2	7	1
NY	200	003	00X	5	8	2

Pitchers: MILLER, Konstanty (1), Roberts (8) vs FORD, Reynolds (9)
Home Runs: Berra-NY
Attendance: 68,098

The Giants—who caught Brooklyn with a tremendous late-season drive, then defeated them for the pennant on Bobby Thomson's ninth-inning home run in Game Three of the tie-breaker playoff series—carried their momentum through Game Three of the World Series before bowing to the Yankees. Dave Koslo (the only Giant starter not to see action in the playoff) pitched the Series opener and held the Yankees to one run. Monte Irvin's steal of home for the Giants' second run in the top of the first was enough for the win, but Al Dark made Koslo's lead more secure with a three-run homer in the sixth.

The Yankees evened the Series in Game Two, scoring two early runs (one of them Joe Collins's home run) off Larry Jansen, and holding on for the win behind Ed Lopat's five-hit pitching. But the Giants regained the lead in Game Three with five unearned runs (three of them on Whitey Lockman's homer) in a fifth inning prolonged by two Yankee errors, as pitchers Jim Hearn and Sheldon Jones combined to hold the Bronx Bombers to five hits and a pair of runs (though Hearn issued eight walks).

But that was the end of the Giants' drive. Although they scored first in games Four and Five with first-inning runs, they couldn't hold the lead either time. In Game Four Allie Reynolds held the Giants to two runs as his Yankees scored six—including a two-run homer by Joe DiMaggio in the fifth inning that proved to be the last home run of his career. DiMag drove in three more Yankee runs in Game Five, as did Phil Rizzuto, and rookie infielder Gil McDougald contributed a grand slam as the Bombers earned their nickname in obliterating Giant pitching with 13 runs. Ed Lopat, meanwhile, hurled his second five-hitter of the Series for his second win.

Yankee Hank Bauer tripled with the bases full in the sixth inning of Game Six to break a tie and give the Yankees a 4–1 lead. The Giants loaded the bases with three straight singles to open the top of the ninth, and scored two runners on successive flies to left, to come within one run of a tie. But pinch hitter Sal Yvars (in his only Series at-bat) lined out to right and the Yankees had their fourteenth world title.

New York Yankees (AL), 4;
New York Giants (NL), 2

NY (A)

PLAYER/POS	AVG	G	AB	R	H	2B	3B	HR	RBI	BB	SO	SB
Hank Bauer, of	.167	6	18	3	0	1	0	3	1	1	0
Yogi Berra, c	.261	6	23	4	6	1	0	0	0	2	1	0
Bobby Brown, 3b-4	.357	5	14	1	5	1	0	0	0	2	1	0
Gerry Coleman, 2b	.250	5	8	2	2	0	0	0	0	1	2	0
Joe Collins, 1b-6,of-1	.222	6	18	2	4	0	0	1	3	2	1	0
Joe DiMaggio, of	.261	6	23	3	6	2	0	1	5	2	4	0
Bobby Hogue, p	.000	2	0	0	0	0	0	0	0	0	0	0
Johnny Hopp, ph	.000	1	0	0	0	0	0	0	0	1	0	0
Bob Kuzava, p	.000	1	0	0	0	0	0	0	0	0	0	0
Ed Lopat, p	.125	2	8	0	1	0	0	0	1	0	2	0
Mickey Mantle, of	.200	2	5	1	1	0	0	0	0	2	1	0
Billy Martin, pr	.000	1	0	1	0	0	0	0	0	0	0	0
Gil McDougald, 3b-5,2b-4	.261	6	23	2	6	1	0	1	7	2	2	0
Johnny Mize, 1b-2	.286	4	7	2	2	1	0	0	1	2	0	0
Tom Morgan, p	.000	1	0	0	0	0	0	0	0	0	0	0
Joe Ostrowski, p	.000	1	0	0	0	0	0	0	0	0	0	0
Vic Raschi, p	.000	2	2	0	0	0	0	0	0	2	1	0
Allie Reynolds, p	.333	2	6	0	2	0	0	0	1	0	1	0
Phil Rizzuto, ss	.320	6	25	5	8	0	0	1	3	2	3	0
Johnny Sain, p	.000	1	1	0	0	0	0	0	0	0	0	0
Gene Woodling, of-5	.167	6	18	6	3	1	1	1	1	5	3	0
TOTAL	.246		199	29	49	7	2	5	25	26	23	0

PITCHER	W	L	ERA	G	GS	CG	SV	SHO	IP	H	ER	BB	SO
Bobby Hogue	0	0	0.00	2	0	0	0	0	2.2	1	0	0	0
Bob Kuzava	0	0	0.00	1	0	0	1	0	1.0	0	0	0	0
Ed Lopat	2	0	0.50	2	2	2	0	0	18.0	10	1	3	4
Tom Morgan	0	0	0.00	1	0	0	0	0	2.0	2	0	1	3
Joe Ostrowski	0	0	0.00	1	0	0	0	0	2.0	1	0	0	1
Vic Raschi	1	1	0.87	2	2	0	0	0	10.1	12	1	8	4
Allie Reynolds	1	1	4.20	2	2	1	0	0	15.0	16	7	11	8
Johnny Sain	0	0	9.00	1	0	0	0	0	2.0	4	2	2	2
TOTAL	4	2	1.87	12	6	3	1	0	53.0	46	11	25	22

NY (N)

PLAYER/POS	AVG	G	AB	R	H	2B	3B	HR	RBI	BB	SO	SB
Al Corwin, p	.000	1	0	0	0	0	0	0	0	0	0	0
Alvin Dark, ss	.417	6	24	5	10	3	0	1	4	2	3	0
Clint Hartung, of	.000	2	4	0	0	0	0	0	0	0	0	0
Jim Hearn, p	.000	2	3	0	0	0	0	0	0	0	1	0
Monte Irvin, of	.458	6	24	3	11	0	1	0	2	2	1	2
Larry Jansen, p	.000	3	2	0	0	0	0	0	0	0	0	0
Sheldon Jones, p	.000	2	0	0	0	0	0	0	0	0	0	0
Monte Kennedy, p	.000	2	0	0	0	0	0	0	0	0	0	0
Alex Konikowski, p	.000	1	0	0	0	0	0	0	0	0	0	0
Dave Koslo, p	.000	2	5	0	0	0	0	0	0	0	2	0
Whitey Lockman, 1b	.240	6	25	1	6	2	0	1	4	1	2	0
Jack Lohrke, ph	.000	2	2	0	0	0	0	0	0	0	1	0
Sal Maglie, p	.000	1	1	0	0	0	0	0	0	0	0	0
Willie Mays, of	.182	6	22	1	4	0	0	0	1	2	2	0
Ray Noble, c	.000	2	2	0	0	0	0	0	0	0	1	0
Bill Rigney, ph	.250	4	4	0	1	0	0	0	1	0	1	0
Hank Schenz, pr	.000	1	0	0	0	0	0	0	0	0	0	0
George Spencer, p	.000	2	0	0	0	0	0	0	0	0	0	0
Eddie Stanky, 2b	.136	6	22	3	3	0	0	0	1	3	2	0
Hank Thompson, of	.143	5	14	2	2	0	0	0	0	5	2	0
Bobby Thomson, 3b	.238	6	21	5	5	1	0	0	2	5	0	0
Wes Westrum, c	.235	6	17	1	4	1	0	0	0	5	3	0
Davey Williams, ph	.000	2	1	0	0	0	0	0	0	0	0	0
Sal Yvars, ph	.000	1	1	0	0	0	0	0	0	0	0	0
TOTAL	.237		194	18	46	7	1	2	15	25	22	2

PITCHER	W	L	ERA	G	GS	CG	SV	SHO	IP	H	ER	BB	SO
Al Corwin	0	0	0.00	1	0	0	0	0	1.2	1	0	0	1
Jim Hearn	1	0	1.04	2	1	0	0	0	8.2	5	1	8	1
Larry Jansen	0	2	6.30	3	2	0	0	0	10.0	8	7	4	6
Sheldon Jones	0	0	2.08	2	0	0	1	0	4.1	5	1	2	2
Monte Kennedy	0	0	6.00	2	0	0	0	0	3.0	3	2	1	4
Alex Konikowski	0	0	0.00	1	0	0	0	0	1.0	1	0	0	0
Dave Koslo	1	1	3.00	2	2	1	0	0	15.0	12	5	7	6
Sal Maglie	0	1	7.20	1	1	0	0	0	5.0	8	4	2	3
George Spencer	0	0	18.90	2	0	0	0	0	3.1	6	7	3	0
TOTAL	2	4	4.67	16	6	1	1	0	52.0	49	27	26	23

GAME 1 AT NY-A OCT 4

NY-N	200 003 000	5	10	1
NY-A	010 000 000	1	7	1

Pitchers: KOSLO vs REYNOLDS, Hogue (7), Morgan (8)
Home Runs: Dark-NY(N)
Attendance: 65,673

GAME 2 AT NY-A OCT 5

NY-N	000 000 100	1	5	1
NY-A	110 000 01X	3	6	0

Pitchers: JANSEN, Spencer (7) vs LOPAT
Home Runs: Collins-NY(A)
Attendance: 66,018

GAME 3 AT NY-N OCT 6

NY-A	000 000 011	2	5	2
NY-N	010 050 00X	6	7	2

Pitchers: RASCHI, Hogue (5), Ostrowski (7) vs HEARN, Jones (8)
Home Runs: Lockman-NY(N), Woodling-NY(A)
Attendance: 52,035

GAME 4 AT NY-N OCT 8

NY-A	010 120 200	6	12	0
NY-N	100 000 001	2	8	2

Pitchers: REYNOLDS vs MAGLIE, Jones (6), Kennedy (9)
Home Runs: DiMaggio-NY(A)
Attendance: 49,010

GAME 5 AT NY-N OCT 9

NY-A	005 202 400	13	12	1
NY-N	100 000 000	1	5	3

Pitchers: LOPAT vs JANSEN, Kennedy (4), Spencer (6), Corwin (7), Konikowski (9)
Home Runs: McDougald-NY(A), Rizzuto-NY(A)
Attendance: 47,530

GAME 6 AT NY-A OCT 10

NY-N	000 010 002	3	11	1
NY-A	100 003 00X	4	7	0

Pitchers: KOSLO, Hearn (7), Jansen (8) vs RASCHI, Sain (7), Kuzava (9)
Attendance: 61,711

In four of the seven games, home runs provided the margin of victory. Homers accounted for five of the six runs scored in the opener, with Duke Snider's two-run blast in the sixth putting Brooklyn ahead to stay. Star Dodger reliever Joe Black, in only his third start of the year, held New York to six hits and two runs in defeating Yankee ace Allie Reynolds.

Four home runs enlivened the next three games but did not govern the outcomes. Billy Martin's three-run shot was the centerpiece of the Yankee assault in Game Two, but New York would have won without it behind Vic Raschi's one-run three-hitter. Brooklyn needed no homers to regain the Series advantage in Game Three. In the top of the ninth, with the Dodgers leading by a run, Pee Wee Reese and Jackie Robinson singled (driving out starter Ed Lopat) and pulled a double steal. Both then scored on a passed ball. Yankee pinch hitter Johnny Mize homered in the last of the ninth, but Preacher Roe escaped without further scoring for a complete-game 5–3 win.

Black opposed Reynolds again in Game Four and bettered his earlier performance, holding New York to three hits and one run (a Mize homer) in seven innings. But Reynolds improved even more, fanning ten as he shut the Dodgers out.

Snider hit his second homer of the Series and Mize his third in the fifth inning of Game Five. Mize's shot put New York ahead, but Brooklyn tied the game in the seventh and took a 6–5 lead when Snider doubled home a run in the eleventh. Dodger right fielder Carl Furillo's leaping catch in the last of the eleventh robbed Mize of another home run, and starter Carl Erskine held on for the win, giving Brooklyn a 3–2 Series lead.

Snider's home run in the last of the sixth ended Vic Raschi's shutout in Game Six, but Yogi Berra, the first Yankee up in the seventh, tied the game and spoiled Billy Loes's shutout with his home run, and pitcher Raschi singled home the go-ahead run two outs later. Yankee sophomore Mickey Mantle's blast in the eighth (the first of his record 18 World Series home runs) made the score 3–1. Snider's fourth homer of the Series gave the Dodgers a second run in the eighth, but Allie Reynolds relieved Raschi and prevented further scoring, sending the Series to a seventh game.

Joe Black traded three shutout innings with Yankee Ed Lopat in the finale before both clubs scored single runs in the fourth and fifth innings. Mantle homered off Black in the sixth for a third Yankee run that proved the Series winner, as

New York Yankees (AL), 4; Brooklyn Dodgers (NL), 3

NY (A)

PLAYER/POS	AVG	G	AB	R	H	2B	3B	HR	RB	BB	SO	SB
Hank Bauer, of	.056	7	18	2	1	0	0	0	1	4	3	0
Yogi Berra, c	.214	7	28	2	6	1	0	2	3	2	4	0
Ewell Blackwell, p	.000	1	1	0	0	0	0	0	0	0	0	0
Joe Collins, 1b	.000	6	12	1	0	0	0	0	0	1	3	0
Tom Gorman, p	.000	1	0	0	0	0	0	0	0	0	0	0
Ralph Houk, ph	.000	1	1	0	0	0	0	0	0	0	0	0
Bob Kuzava, p	.000	1	1	0	0	0	0	0	0	0	0	0
Ed Lopat, p	.333	2	3	0	1	0	0	0	0	1	1	0
Mickey Mantle, of	.345	7	29	5	10	1	1	2	3	3	4	0
Billy Martin, 2b	.217	7	23	2	5	0	0	1	4	2	2	0
Gil McDougald, 3b	.200	7	25	5	5	0	0	1	3	5	2	1
Johnny Mize, 1b-4	.400	5	15	3	6	1	0	3	6	3	1	0
Irv Noren, of-3	.300	4	10	0	3	0	0	0	1	1	3	0
Vic Raschi, p	.167	3	6	0	1	0	0	0	1	1	2	0
Allie Reynolds, p	.000	4	7	0	0	0	0	0	0	0	2	0
Phil Rizzuto, ss	.148	7	27	2	4	1	0	0	0	5	2	0
Johnny Sain, p-1	.000	2	3	0	0	0	0	0	0	0	0	0
Ray Scarborough, p	.000	1	0	0	0	0	0	0	0	0	0	0
Gene Woodling, of-6	.348	7	23	4	8	1	1	1	1	3	3	0
TOTAL	.216		232	26	50	5	2	10	24	31	32	1

PITCHER	W	L	ERA	G	GS	CG	SV	SHO	IP	H	ER	BB	SO
Ewell Blackwell	0	0	7.20	1	1	0	0	0	5.0	4	4	3	4
Tom Gorman	0	0	0.00	1	0	0	0	0	0.2	1	0	0	0
Bob Kuzava	0	0	0.00	1	0	0	1	0	2.2	0	0	0	2
Ed Lopat	0	1	4.76	2	2	0	0	0	11.1	14	6	4	3
Vic Raschi	2	0	1.59	3	2	1	0	0	17.0	12	3	8	18
Allie Reynolds	2	1	1.77	4	2	1	1	1	20.1	12	4	6	18
Johnny Sain	0	1	3.00	1	0	0	0	0	6.0	6	2	3	3
Ray Scarborough	0	0	9.00	1	0	0	0	0	1.0	1	1	0	1
TOTAL	4	3	2.81	14	7	2	2	1	64.0	50	20	24	49

BRO (N)

PLAYER/POS	AVG	G	AB	R	H	2B	3B	HR	RB	BB	SO	SB
Sandy Amoros, ph	.000	1	0	0	0	0	0	0	0	0	0	0
Joe Black, p	.000	3	6	0	0	0	0	0	0	1	6	0
Roy Campanella, c	.214	7	28	0	6	0	0	0	1	1	6	0
Billy Cox, 3b	.296	7	27	4	8	2	0	0	3	3	4	0
Carl Erskine, p	.000	3	6	1	0	0	0	0	0	0	1	0
Carl Furillo, of	.174	7	23	1	4	2	0	0	3	3	3	0
Gil Hodges, 1b	.000	7	21	1	0	0	0	0	1	5	6	0
Tommy Holmes, of	.000	3	1	0	0	0	0	0	0	0	0	0
Ken Lehman, p	.000	1	0	0	0	0	0	0	0	0	0	0
Billy Loes, p	.333	2	3	0	1	0	0	0	0	0	1	1
Bobby Morgan, 3b	.000	2	1	0	0	0	0	0	0	0	0	0
Rocky Nelson, ph	.000	4	5	0	0	0	0	0	0	1	2	0
Andy Pafko, of-3	.190	7	21	0	4	0	0	0	2	0	4	0
Pee Wee Reese, ss	.345	7	29	4	10	0	0	1	4	2	2	1
Jackie Robinson, 2b	.174	7	23	4	4	0	1	1	2	7	5	2
Preacher Roe, p	.000	3	2	0	0	0	0	0	0	0	0	0
Johnny Rutherford, p	.000	1	0	0	0	0	0	0	0	0	0	0
George Shuba, of-3	.300	4	10	0	3	1	0	0	0	0	4	0
Duke Snider, of	.345	7	29	5	10	2	0	4	8	1	5	1
TOTAL	.215		233	20	50	7	0	6	18	24	49	5

PITCHER	W	L	ERA	G	GS	CG	SV	SHO	IP	H	ER	BB	SO
Joe Black	1	2	2.53	3	3	1	0	0	21.1	15	6	8	9
Carl Erskine	1	1	4.50	3	2	1	0	0	18.0	12	9	10	10
Ken Lehman	0	0	0.00	1	0	0	0	0	2.0	2	0	1	0
Billy Loes	0	1	4.35	2	1	0	0	0	10.1	11	5	5	5
Preacher Roe	1	0	3.18	3	1	1	0	0	11.1	9	4	6	7
Johnny Rutherford	0	0	9.00	1	0	0	0	0	1.0	1	1	1	1
TOTAL	3	4	3.52	13	7	3	0	0	64.0	50	25	31	32

three Yankee relievers held Brooklyn scoreless through the final four frames.

GAME 1 AT BRO OCT 1

NY	010 000 010	2	6	2
BRO	010 002 01X	4	6	0

Pitchers: REYNOLDS, Scarborough (8) vs BLACK
Home Runs: Robinson-BRO, Snider-BRO, Reese-BRO, McDougald-NY
Attendance: 34,861

GAME 2 AT BRO OCT 2

NY	000 115 000	7	10	0
BRO	001 000 000	1	3	1

Pitchers: RASCHI vs ERSKINE, Loes (6), Lehman (8)
Home Runs: Martin-NY
Attendance: 33,792

GAME 3 AT NY OCT 3

BRO	001 010 012	5	11	0
NY	010 000 011	3	6	2

Pitchers: ROE vs LOPAT, Gorman (9)
Home Runs: Berra-NY, Mize-NY
Attendance: 66,698

GAME 4 AT NY OCT 4

BRO	000 000 000	0	4	1
NY	000 100 01X	2	4	1

Pitchers: BLACK, Rutherford (8) vs REYNOLDS
Home Runs: Mize-NY
Attendance: 71,787

GAME 5 AT NY OCT 5

BRO	010 030 100 01	6	10	0
NY	000 050 000 00	5	5	1

Pitchers: ERSKINE vs Blackwell, SAIN (6)
Home Runs: Snider-BRO, Mize-NY
Attendance: 70,536

GAME 6 AT BRO OCT 6

NY	000 000 210	3	9	0
BRO	000 001 010	2	8	1

Pitchers: RASCHI, Reynolds (8) vs LOES, Roe (9)
Home Runs: Snider-BRO (2), Berra-NY, Mantle-NY
Attendance: 30,037

GAME 7 AT BRO OCT 7

NY	000 111 100	4	10	4
BRO	000 110 000	2	8	1

Pitchers: Lopat, REYNOLDS (4), Raschi (7), Kuzava (7) vs BLACK, Roe (6), Erskine (8)
Home Runs: Woodling-NY, Mantle-NY
Attendance: 33,195

Although the Yankees easily won the American League pennant, the Dodgers seemed even more overwhelming, with a team batting average of .285 and a club-record 105 season wins. But when the Series was over, the Yankees had added a record fifth straight world championship to their record fifth straight pennant.

Dodger ace Carl Erskine lasted only one inning of the Series opener, giving up three walks and two triples for four Yankee runs. By the middle of the seventh inning, the Dodgers had tied the score at 5–5. But Yankee Joe Collins homered to break the tie in the last of the seventh, and reliever Johnny Sain ensured his own win with a two-run double an inning later. The Dodgers outhit New York in Game Two, and held a 2–1 lead entering the bottom of the seventh. But Billy Martin (who hit .500 and slugged .958 in the Series) tied the game with a leadoff homer in the seventh, and Mickey Mantle won it with a two-run blast in the eighth.

Down 0–2, Brooklyn evened the Series at home with victories in Games Three and Four. Erskine redeemed his poor start in Game One with a record-setting 14-strikeout performance in Game Three. But it was a narrow win, settled only when Roy Campanella homered in the last of the eighth to break a 2–2 tie. In Game Four, Duke Snider made Billy Loes's three-run pitching a winning performance, driving in four of the Dodgers' seven runs with two doubles and a homer.

But Brooklyn never even took the lead in the final two games. Four Yankee home runs (including a Mantle grand slam) rocked Dodger pitching in Game Five as the Bombers built a lead which Dodger home runs in the eighth and ninth were unable to overcome. In Game Six the Yankees built a 3–0 lead over Erskine in the first two innings. Brooklyn fought back with a run in the sixth, and tied the game on Carl Furillo's two-run homer in the top of the ninth. But with men on first and second in the last of the ninth, Yankee Billy Martin singled in the game-ending, Series-winning run. It was Martin's twelfth hit, a new record for a six-game Series.

New York Yankees (AL), 4; Brooklyn Dodgers (NL), 2

NY (A)

PLAYER/POS	AVG	G	AB	R	H	2B	3B	HR	RB	BB	SO	SB
Hank Bauer, of	.261	6	23	6	6	0	1	0	1	2	4	0
Yogi Berra, c	.429	6	21	3	9	1	0	1	4	3	3	0
Don Bollweg, 1b-1	.000	3	2	0	0	0	0	0	0	0	2	0
Joe Collins, 1b	.167	6	24	4	4	1	0	1	2	3	8	0
Whitey Ford, p	.333	2	3	0	1	0	0	0	0	0	0	0
Tom Gorman, p	.000	1	1	0	0	0	0	0	0	0	1	0
Bob Kuzava, p	.000	1	1	0	0	0	0	0	0	0	1	0
Ed Lopat, p	.000	1	3	0	0	0	0	0	0	0	2	0
Mickey Mantle, of	.208	6	24	3	5	0	0	2	7	3	8	0
Billy Martin, 2b	.500	6	24	5	12	1	2	2	8	1	2	1
Jim McDonald, p	.500	1	2	0	1	1	0	0	1	1	1	0
Gil McDougald, 3b	.167	6	24	2	4	0	1	2	4	1	3	0
Johnny Mize, ph	.000	3	3	0	0	0	0	0	0	0	1	0
Irv Noren, ph	.000	2	1	0	0	0	0	0	0	1	0	0
Vic Raschi, p	.000	1	2	0	0	0	0	0	0	0	1	0
Allie Reynolds, p	.500	3	2	0	1	0	0	0	0	1	1	0
Phil Rizzuto, ss	.316	6	19	4	6	1	0	0	0	3	2	1
Johnny Sain, p	.500	2	2	1	1	1	0	0	2	0	1	0
Art Schallock, p	.000	1	0	0	0	0	0	0	0	0	0	0
Gene Woodling, of	.300	6	20	5	6	0	0	1	3	6	2	0
TOTAL	.279		201	33	56	6	4	9	32	25	43	2

PITCHER	W	L	ERA	G	GS	CG	SV	SHO	IP	H	ER	BB	SO
Whitey Ford	0	1	4.50	2	2	0	0	0	8.0	9	4	2	7
Tom Gorman	0	0	3.00	1	0	0	0	0	3.0	4	1	0	1
Bob Kuzava	0	0	13.50	1	0	0	0	0	0.2	2	1	0	1
Ed Lopat	1	0	2.00	1	1	1	0	0	9.0	9	2	4	3
Jim McDonald	1	0	5.87	1	1	0	0	0	7.2	12	5	0	3
Vic Raschi	0	1	3.38	1	1	1	0	0	8.0	9	3	3	4
Allie Reynolds	1	0	6.75	3	0	0	1	0	8.0	9	6	4	9
Johnny Sain	1	0	4.76	2	0	0	0	0	5.2	8	3	1	1
Art Schallock	0	0	4.50	1	0	0	0	0	2.0	2	1	1	1
TOTAL	4	2	4.50	13	6	2	1	0	52.0	64	26	15	30

BRO (N)

PLAYER/POS	AVG	G	AB	R	H	2B	3B	HR	RB	BB	SO	SB
Wayne Belardi, ph	.000	2	2	0	0	0	0	0	0	0	1	0
Joe Black, p	.000	1	0	0	0	0	0	0	0	0	0	0
Roy Campanella, c	.273	6	22	6	6	0	0	1	2	2	3	0
Billy Cox, 3b	.304	6	23	3	7	3	0	1	6	1	4	0
Carl Erskine, p	.250	3	4	0	1	0	0	0	0	0	1	0
Carl Furillo, of	.333	6	24	4	8	2	0	1	4	1	3	0
Jim Gilliam, 2b	.296	6	27	4	8	3	0	2	4	0	2	0
Gil Hodges, 1b	.364	6	22	3	8	0	0	1	1	3	3	1
Jim Hughes, p	.000	1	1	0	0	0	0	0	0	0	1	0
Clem Labine, p	.000	3	2	0	0	0	0	0	0	0	1	0
Billy Loes, p	.667	1	3	0	2	0	0	0	0	0	0	0
Russ Meyer, p	.000	1	1	0	0	0	0	0	0	0	1	0
Bob Milliken, p	.000	1	1	0	0	0	0	0	0	0	0	0
Bobby Morgan, ph	.000	1	1	0	0	0	0	0	0	0	0	0
Johnny Podres, p	1.000	1	1	0	1	0	0	0	0	0	0	0
Pee Wee Reese, ss	.208	6	24	0	5	0	1	0	0	4	1	0
Jackie Robinson, of	.320	6	25	3	8	2	0	0	2	1	0	1
Preacher Roe, p	.000	1	3	0	0	0	0	0	0	0	2	0
George Shuba, ph	1.000	2	1	1	1	0	0	1	2	0	0	0
Duke Snider, of	.320	6	25	3	8	3	0	1	5	2	6	0
Don Thompson, of	.000	1	1	0	0	0	0	0	0	0	0	0
Ben Wade, p	.000	2	0	0	0	0	0	0	0	0	0	0
Dick Williams, ph	.500	3	2	0	1	0	0	0	0	1	1	0
TOTAL	.300		213	27	64	13	1	8	26	15	30	2

PITCHER	W	L	ERA	G	GS	CG	SV	SHO	IP	H	ER	BB	SO
Joe Black	0	0	9.00	1	0	0	0	0	1.0	1	1	0	2
Carl Erskine	1	0	5.79	3	3	1	0	0	14.0	14	9	9	16
Jim Hughes	0	0	2.25	1	0	0	0	0	4.0	3	1	1	3
Clem Labine	0	2	3.60	3	0	0	0	0	5.0	10	2	1	3
Billy Loes	1	0	3.38	1	1	0	0	0	8.0	8	3	2	8
Russ Meyer	0	0	6.23	1	0	0	0	0	4.1	8	3	4	5
Bob Milliken	0	0	0.00	1	0	0	0	0	2.0	2	0	1	0
Johnny Podres	0	1	3.38	1	1	0	0	0	2.2	1	1	2	0
Preacher Roe	0	1	4.50	1	1	1	0	0	8.0	5	4	4	4
Ben Wade	0	0	15.43	2	0	0	0	0	2.1	4	4	1	2
TOTAL	2	4	4.91	15	6	2	1	0	51.1	56	28	25	43

GAME 1 AT NY SEPT 30

BRO	000	013	100	5 12 2
NY	400	010	13X	9 12 0

Pitchers: Erskine, Hughes (2), LABINE (6), Wade (8) vs Reynolds, SAIN (6)
Home Runs: Gilliam-BRO, Hodges-BRO, Shuba-BRO, Berra-NY, Collins-NY
Attendance: 69,374

GAME 2 AT NY OCT 1

BRO	000	200	000	2 9 1
NY	100	000	12X	4 5 0

Pitchers: ROE vs LOPAT
Home Runs: Martin-NY, Mantle-NY
Attendance: 66,786

GAME 3 AT BRO OCT 2

NY	000	010	010	2 6 0
BRO	000	011	01X	3 9 0

Pitchers: RASCHI vs ERSKINE
Home Runs: Campanella-BRO
Attendance: 35,270

GAME 4 AT BRO OCT 3

NY	000	020	001	3 9 0
BRO	300	102	10X	7 12 0

Pitchers: FORD, Gorman (2), Sain (5), Schallock (7) vs LOES, Labine (9)
Home Runs: McDougald-NY, Snider-BRO
Attendance: 36,775

GAME 5 AT BRO OCT 4

NY	105	000	311	11 11 1
BRO	010	010	041	7 14 1

Pitchers: McDONALD, Kuzava (8), Reynolds (9) vs PODRES, Meyer (3), Wade (8), Black (9)
Home Runs: Woodling-NY, Mantle-NY, Martin-NY, McDougald-NY, Cox-BRO, Gilliam-BRO
Attendance: 36,775

GAME 6 AT NY OCT 5

BRO	000	001	002	3 8 3
NY	210	000	001	4 13 0

Pitchers: Erskine, Milliken (5), LABINE (7) vs Ford, REYNOLDS (8)
Home Runs: Furillo-BRO
Attendance: 62,370

The Indians, who had won a league-record 111 games to break the American League domination of the New York Yankees, entered the World Series as strong favorites to humble the Giants. It was not to be.

Cleveland would have won the opener had it not been played in New York's Polo Grounds, with their short foul lines and deep center field. Most of the game was a pitchers' duel. Vic Wertz (the only Indian to hit safely in all four games) tripled off Sal Maglie to give Cleveland a two-run lead in the top of the first, but three Giant singles and a walk in the third off Bob Lemon tied the score. Lemon then settled down to hold New York scoreless through the ninth. Cleveland threatened in the eighth when the first two batters reached base, bringing Wertz to the plate. As he had already hit Maglie safely three times, Don Liddle was brought in to pitch to him. Wertz responded with a fly to deep center that would have been a home run in Cleveland, but in New York turned into the most famous catch in World Series history as Willie Mays raced out and tracked down the ball about 425 feet from the plate. Marv Grissom replaced Liddle on the mound and issued a walk to load the bases, but he retired the next two batters and (despite Wertz's double in the top of the tenth) held Cleveland scoreless the rest of the way. In the last of the tenth, Lemon retired the first batter, but Mays walked and stole second, and Hank Thompson was walked intentionally to set up the double play. Pinch hitter Dusty Rhodes then entered the hall of heroes with a short fly to right that—though it would have been an out in Cleveland—fell into the Polo Grounds stands for three runs and a Giant victory.

The rest of the Series was anticlimax. In the second game Rhodes, with half the Giants' four hits, drove in two runs on a single and another homer, providing the margin of victory for Giant ace Johnny Antonelli, who allowed only one of Cleveland's 14 baserunners to score. Game Three was no contest. New York had scored all six of its runs before the Indians managed to come up with single runs in both the seventh and eighth. Pinch hitter Hank Majeski's three-run homer put Cleveland on the board in the fifth inning of Game Four. But as New York had already scored seven times, even a fourth Cleveland run in the seventh proved too little to prevent a Giant sweep.

New York Giants (NL), 4; Cleveland Indians (AL), 0

NY (N)

PLAYER/POS	AVG	G	AB	R	H	2B	3B	HR	RB	BB	SO	SB
Johnny Antonelli, p	.000	2	3	0	0	0	0	0	0	1	0	0
Alvin Dark, ss	.412	4	17	2	7	0	0	0	0	1	1	0
Ruben Gomez, p	.000	1	4	0	0	0	0	0	0	0	2	0
Marv Grissom, p	.000	1	1	0	0	0	0	0	0	0	1	0
Monte Irvin, of	.222	4	9	1	2	1	0	0	2	0	3	0
Don Liddle, p	.000	2	3	0	0	0	0	0	0	0	2	0
Whitey Lockman, 1b	.111	4	18	2	2	0	0	0	0	1	1	0
Sal Maglie, p	.000	1	3	0	0	0	0	0	0	0	0	0
Willie Mays, of	.286	4	14	4	4	1	0	0	3	4	1	1
Don Mueller, of	.389	4	18	4	7	0	0	0	1	0	1	0
Dusty Rhodes, of-2	.667	3	6	2	4	0	0	2	7	1	2	0
Hank Thompson, 3b	.364	4	11	6	4	1	0	0	2	7	1	0
Wes Westrum, c	.273	4	11	0	3	0	0	0	3	1	3	0
Hoyt Wilhelm, p	.000	2	1	0	0	0	0	0	0	0	1	0
Davey Williams, 2b	.000	4	11	0	0	0	0	0	1	2	2	0
TOTAL	.254		130	21	33	3	0	2	20	17	24	1

PITCHER	W	L	ERA	G	GS	CG	SV	SHO	IP	H	ER	BB	SO
Johnny Antonelli	1	0	0.84	2	1	1	1	0	10.2	8	1	7	12
Ruben Gomez	1	0	2.45	1	1	0	0	0	7.1	4	2	3	2
Marv Grissom	1	0	0.00	1	0	0	0	0	2.2	1	0	3	2
Don Liddle	1	0	1.29	2	1	0	0	0	7.0	5	1	1	2
Sal Maglie	0	0	2.57	1	1	0	0	0	7.0	7	2	2	2
Hoyt Wilhelm	0	0	0.00	2	0	0	1	0	2.1	1	0	0	3
TOTAL	4	0	1.46	9	4	1	2	0	37.0	26	6	16	23

CLE (A)

PLAYER/POS	AVG	G	AB	R	H	2B	3B	HR	RB	BB	SO	SB
Bobby Avila, 2b	.133	4	15	1	2	0	0	0	0	2	1	0
Sam Dente, ss	.000	3	3	1	0	0	0	0	0	1	0	0
Larry Doby, of	.125	4	16	0	2	0	0	0	0	2	4	0
Mike Garcia, p	.000	2	0	0	0	0	0	0	0	0	0	0
Bill Glynn, 1b-1	.500	2	2	1	1	1	0	0	0	0	1	0
Mickey Grasso, c	.000	1	0	0	0	0	0	0	0	0	0	0
Jim Hegan, c	.154	4	13	1	2	1	0	0	0	1	1	0
Art Houtteman, p	.000	1	0	0	0	0	0	0	0	0	0	0
Bob Lemon, p-2	.000	3	6	0	0	0	0	0	0	1	1	0
Hank Majeski, 3b-1	.167	4	6	1	1	0	0	1	3	0	1	0
Dale Mitchell, ph	.000	3	2	0	0	0	0	0	0	1	0	0
Don Mossi, p	.000	3	0	0	0	0	0	0	0	0	0	0
Hal Naragon, c	.000	1	0	0	0	0	0	0	0	0	0	0
Ray Narleski, p	.000	2	0	0	0	0	0	0	0	0	0	0
Hal Newhouser, p	.000	1	0	0	0	0	0	0	0	0	0	0
Dave Philley, of-2	.125	4	8	0	1	0	0	0	0	1	3	0
Dave Pope, of-2	.000	3	3	0	0	0	0	0	0	1	1	0
Rudy Regalado, 3b-1	.333	4	3	0	1	0	0	0	1	0	0	0
Al Rosen, 3b	.250	3	12	0	3	0	0	0	0	1	0	0
Al Smith, of	.214	4	14	2	3	0	0	1	2	2	2	0
George Strickland, ss	.000	3	9	0	0	0	0	0	0	2	0	0
Vic Wertz, 1b	.500	4	16	2	8	2	1	1	3	2	2	0
Wally Westlake, of	.143	2	7	0	1	0	0	0	0	1	3	0
Early Wynn, p	.500	1	2	0	1	0	0	0	0	0	1	0
TOTAL	.190		137	9	26	5	1	3	9	16	23	0

PITCHER	W	L	ERA	G	GS	CG	SV	SHO	IP	H	ER	BB	SO
Mike Garcia	0	1	5.40	2	1	0	0	0	5.0	6	3	4	4
Art Houtteman	0	0	4.50	1	0	0	0	0	2.0	2	1	1	1
Bob Lemon	0	2	6.75	2	2	1	0	0	13.1	16	10	8	11
Don Mossi	0	0	0.00	3	0	0	0	0	4.0	3	0	0	1
Ray Narleski	0	0	2.25	2	0	0	0	0	4.0	1	1	1	2
Hal Newhouser	0	0	INF	1	0	0	0	0	0.0	4	1	1	0
Early Wynn	0	1	3.86	1	1	0	0	0	7.0	4	3	2	5
TOTAL	0	4	4.84	12	4	1	0	0	35.1	33	19	17	24

GAME 1 AT NY SEPT 29

CLE 200 000 000 0   2 8 0
NY 002 000 000 3   5 9 3

Pitchers: LEMON vs Maglie, Liddle (8), GRISSOM (8)
Home Runs: Rhodes-NY
Attendance: 52,751

GAME 2 AT NY SEPT 30

CLE 100 000 000   1 8 0
NY 000 020 10X   3 4 0

Pitchers: WYNN, Mossi (8) vs ANTONELLI
Home Runs: Smith-CLE, Rhodes-NY
Attendance: 49,099

GAME 3 AT CLE OCT 1

NY 103 011 000   6 10 1
CLE 000 000 110   2 4 2

Pitchers: GOMEZ, Wilhelm (7) vs GARCIA, Houtteman (4), Narleski (6), Mossi (9)
Home Runs: Wertz-CLE
Attendance: 71,555

GAME 4 AT CLE OCT 2

NY 021 040 000   7 10 3
CLE 000 030 100   4 6 2

Pitchers: LIDDLE, Wilhelm (7), Antonelli (8) vs LEMON, Newhouser (5), Narleski (5), Mossi (6), Garcia (8)
Home Runs: Majeski-CLE
Attendance: 78,102

The Dodgers and Yankees, after a year's absence, faced each other again in the World Series—their sixth Series confrontation in fifteen years. And after Brooklyn had lost the first two games it began to look as though 1955 might also mark the Yankees' sixth Series triumph over the Dodgers. But this was Brooklyn's year.

The opener was a hitters' game, but closely contested. Both teams scored twice in the second inning and once in the third, but Yankee first baseman Joe Collins's leadoff homer in the last of the fourth gave New York its first lead of the game, and his two-run blast in the sixth made the score 6–3. Brooklyn clawed back in the eighth for two runs—including Jackie Robinson's steal of home—to pull within one run of a tie, but they came no closer. In Game Two, Yankee pitcher Tommy Byrne held the Dodgers to five hits and two runs, and won his own game at the bat with a two-run single that capped the Yankees' four-run fourth.

The Series turned around as the Dodgers captured the next three games in Brooklyn. Roy Campanella's two-run homer in the first inning of Game Three gave Brooklyn a quick lead. New York tied the game with a pair of runs in the second (one of them a homer by Mickey Mantle, who appeared in only three Series games because of a leg injury). But two more Dodger runs in the last of the second drove out Yankee starter Bob Turley and put them ahead to stay as Dodger hurler Johnny Podres held the Yankees to three runs. Home runs by Campanella, Gil Hodges, and Duke Snider accounted for six of Brooklyn's eight runs in Game Four as the Dodgers evened the Series at two-all. Sandy Amoros's second-inning homer initiated the scoring in Game Five, and Snider's blasts in the third and fifth (which made him the first player to hit four home runs in two different Series) gave Brooklyn a 4–1 lead, which even late-inning Yankee homers by Bob Cerv and Yogi Berra could not overcome.

New York bounced back in Game Six, scoring all five of their runs in the first inning (including three on Bill Skowron's homer) to give Whitey Ford a comfortable lead, which he held with a one-run four-hitter. But in the finale, Gil Hodges drove in two Brooklyn runs with a single in the fourth and a sacrifice fly in the sixth. They were all Brooklyn got, but they proved more than enough to carry the Dodgers to their first world title in fifty-five years, as left fielder Sandy Amoros stifled New York's only real scoring threat with a spectacular running catch in the sixth that started a double play and preserved Johnny Podres's second Series win.

Brooklyn Dodgers (NL), 4; New York Yankees (AL), 3

BRO (N)

PLAYER/POS	AVG	G	AB	R	H	2B	3B	HR	RB	BB	SO	SB
Sandy Amoros, of	.333	5	12	3	4	0	0	1	3	4	4	0
Don Bessent, p	.000	3	1	0	0	0	0	0	0	0	0	1	0
Roy Campanella, c	.259	7	27	4	7	3	0	2	4	3	3	0
Roger Craig, p	.000	1	0	0	0	0	0	0	0	1	0	0
Carl Erskine, p	.000	1	1	0	0	0	0	0	0	0	0	0
Carl Furillo, of	.296	7	27	4	8	1	0	1	3	3	5	0
Jim Gilliam, 2b-5,of-4	.292	7	24	2	7	1	0	0	3	8	1	1
Don Hoak, 3b-1	.333	3	3	0	1	0	0	0	0	2	0	0
Gil Hodges, 1b	.292	7	24	2	7	0	0	1	5	3	2	0
Frank Kellert, ph	.333	3	3	0	1	0	0	0	0	0	0	0
Clem Labine, p	.000	4	4	0	0	0	0	0	0	0	3	0
Billy Loes, p	.000	1	1	0	0	0	0	0	0	0	0	0
Russ Meyer, p	.000	1	2	0	0	0	0	0	0	0	1	0
Don Newcombe, p	.000	1	3	0	0	0	0	0	0	0	0	0
Johnny Podres, p	.143	2	7	1	1	0	0	0	0	0	1	0
Pee Wee Reese, ss	.296	7	27	5	8	1	0	0	2	3	5	0
Jackie Robinson, 3b	.182	6	22	5	4	1	1	0	1	2	1	1
Ed Roebuck, p	.000	1	0	0	0	0	0	0	0	0	0	0
George Shuba, ph	.000	1	1	0	0	0	0	0	0	0	0	0
Duke Snider, of	.320	7	25	5	8	1	0	4	7	2	6	0
Karl Spooner, p	.000	2	0	0	0	0	0	0	0	0	0	0
Don Zimmer, 2b	.222	4	9	0	2	0	0	0	0	2	2	5	0
TOTAL	.260		223	31	58	8	1	9	30	33	38	2

PITCHER	W	L	ERA	G	GS	CG	SV	SHO	IP	H	ER	BB	SO
Don Bessent	0	0	0.00	3	0	0	0	0	3.1	3	0	1	1
Roger Craig	1	0	3.00	1	1	0	0	0	6.0	4	2	5	4
Carl Erskine	0	0	9.00	1	1	0	0	0	3.0	3	3	2	3
Clem Labine	1	0	2.89	4	0	0	1	0	9.1	6	3	2	2
Billy Loes	0	1	9.82	1	1	0	0	0	3.2	7	4	1	5
Russ Meyer	0	0	0.00	1	0	0	0	0	5.2	4	0	2	4
Don Newcombe	0	1	9.53	1	1	0	0	0	5.2	8	6	2	4
Johnny Podres	2	0	1.00	2	2	2	0	1	18.0	15	2	4	10
Ed Roebuck	0	0	0.00	1	0	0	0	0	2.0	1	0	0	0
Karl Spooner	0	1	13.50	2	1	0	0	0	3.1	4	5	3	6
TOTAL	4	3	3.75	17	7	2	1	1	60.0	55	25	22	39

NY (A)

PLAYER/POS	AVG	G	AB	R	H	2B	3B	HR	RB	BB	SO	SB
Hank Bauer, of-5	.429	6	14	1	6	0	0	0	1	0	1	0
Yogi Berra, c	.417	7	24	5	10	1	0	1	2	3	1	0
Tommy Byrne, p-2	.167	3	6	0	1	0	0	0	2	0	2	0
Andy Carey, ph	.500	2	2	0	1	0	1	0	1	0	0	0
Tom Carroll, pr	.000	2	0	0	0	0	0	0	0	0	0	0
Bob Cerv, of-4	.125	5	16	2	2	0	0	1	1	0	4	0
Gerry Coleman, ss	.000	3	3	0	0	0	0	0	0	0	1	0
Rip Coleman, p	.000	1	0	0	0	0	0	0	0	0	0	0
Joe Collins, 1b-5,of-1	.167	5	12	6	2	0	0	2	3	6	4	1
Whitey Ford, p	.000	2	6	1	0	0	0	0	0	1	1	0
Bob Grim, p	.000	3	2	0	0	0	0	0	0	0	0	0
Elston Howard, of	.192	4	26	3	5	0	0	1	3	1	8	0
Johnny Kucks, p	.000	2	0	0	0	0	0	0	0	0	0	0
Don Larsen, p	.000	1	2	0	0	0	0	0	0	0	0	0
Mickey Mantle, of-2	.200	3	10	1	2	0	0	1	1	0	2	0
Billy Martin, 2b	.320	7	25	2	8	1	1	0	4	1	5	0
Gil McDougald, 3b	.259	7	27	2	7	0	0	1	1	2	6	0
Tom Morgan, p	.000	2	0	0	0	0	0	0	0	0	0	0
Irv Noren, of	.063	5	16	0	1	0	0	0	1	1	1	0
Phil Rizzuto, ss	.267	7	15	2	4	0	0	0	1	5	1	2
Eddie Robinson, 1b-1	.667	4	3	0	2	0	0	0	1	2	1	0
Bill Skowron, 1b-3	.333	5	12	4	4	2	0	1	3	0	1	0
Tom Sturdivant, p	.000	2	0	0	0	0	0	0	0	0	0	0
Bob Turley, p	.000	3	1	0	0	0	0	0	0	0	0	0
TOTAL	.248		222	26	55	4	2	8	25	22	39	3

PITCHER	W	L	ERA	G	GS	CG	SV	SHO	IP	H	ER	BB	SO
Tommy Byrne	1	1	1.88	2	2	1	0	0	14.1	8	3	8	8
Rip Coleman	0	0	9.00	1	0	0	0	0	1.0	5	1	0	1
Whitey Ford	2	0	2.12	2	2	1	0	0	17.0	13	4	8	10
Bob Grim	0	1	4.15	3	1	0	1	0	8.2	8	4	5	8
Johnny Kucks	0	0	6.00	2	0	0	0	0	3.0	4	2	1	1
Don Larsen	0	1	11.25	2	1	0	0	0	4.0	5	5	2	2
Tom Morgan	0	0	4.91	2	0	0	0	0	3.2	3	2	3	1
Tom Sturdivant	0	0	6.00	2	0	0	0	0	3.0	5	2	2	0
Bob Turley	0	1	8.44	3	1	0	0	0	5.1	7	5	4	7
TOTAL	3	4	4.20	18	7	2	1	0	60.0	58	28	33	38

GAME 1 AT NY SEPT 28

BRO	021	000	020	5	10	0
NY	021	102	00X	6	9	1

Pitchers: NEWCOMBE, Bessent (6), Labine (8) vs FORD, Grim (9)
Home Runs: Furillo-BRO, Snider-BRO, Howard-NY, Collins-NY (2)
Attendance: 63,869

GAME 2 AT NY SEPT 29

BRO	000	110	000	2	5	2
NY	000	400	00X	4	8	0

Pitchers: LOES, Bessent (4), Spooner (5), Labine (8) vs BYRNE
Attendance: 64,707

GAME 3 AT BRO SEPT 30

NY	020	000	100	3	7	0
BRO	220	200	20X	8	11	1

Pitchers: TURLEY, Morgan (2), Kucks (5), Sturdivant (7) vs PODRES
Home Runs: Campanella-BRO, Mantle-NY
Attendance: 34,209

GAME 4 AT BRO OCT 1

NY	110	102	000	5	9	0
BRO	001	330	10X	8	14	0

Pitchers: LARSEN, Kucks (5), R.Coleman (6), Morgan (7), Sturdivant (8) vs Erskine, Bessent (4), LABINE (5)
Home Runs: McDougald-NY, Campanella-BRO, Hodges-BRO, Snider-BRO
Attendance: 36,242

GAME 5 AT BRO OCT 2

NY	000	100	110	3	6	0
BRO	021	010	01X	5	9	2

Pitchers: GRIM, Turley (7) vs CRAIG, Labine (7)
Home Runs: Cerv-NY, Berra-NY, Amoros-BRO, Snider-BRO (2)
Attendance: 36,796

GAME 6 AT NY OCT 3

BRO	000	100	000	1	4	1
NY	500	000	00X	5	8	0

Pitchers: SPOONER, Meyer (1), Roebuck (7) vs FORD
Home Runs: Skowron-NY
Attendance: 64,022

GAME 7 AT NY OCT 4

BRO	000	101	000	2	5	0
NY	000	000	000	0	8	1

Pitchers: PODRES vs BYRNE, Grim (6), Turley (8)
Attendance: 62,465

The 1956 Series was a mirror image of 1955. With both teams repeaters as league champions, the Yankees this year followed Brooklyn's winning pattern of the previous Series: losing the first two games, winning the next three, then splitting the final pair.

Sal Maglie outlasted Yankee ace Whitey Ford in the opener. Maglie gave up nine hits and three runs (on homers by Mickey Mantle and Billy Martin), but struck out ten and took the win as Jackie Robinson and Gil Hodges contributed homers for four of Brooklyn's six runs. Dodger ace Don Newcombe was blown out by six Yankee runs (capped by Yogi Berra's grand slam) in the first two innings of Game Two. But Brooklyn came back with six unearned runs in their half of the second (three of them on Duke Snider's homer) and proceeded to run through seven Yankee pitchers for a 13–8 win and a two-game Series edge.

Whitey Ford tried again in Game Three, and this time held on for a complete-game 5–3 win, supported by Billy Martin's game-tying solo homer in the second and forty-year-old Enos Slaughter's go-ahead three-run shot in the sixth. Tom Sturdivant duplicated Ford's effectiveness and success the next day with a six-hit 6–2 win to even the Series.

Sal Maglie pitched Game Five for Brooklyn and improved on his winning performance of Game One, yielding only two runs and holding New York hitless until Mantle's two-out homer in the fourth inning. But no one was a match for Yankee pitcher Don Larsen that day. There was a close out on a deflected Dodger liner in the second inning, and center fielder Mantle made a fine running catch to prevent a hit in the fifth. But Larsen retired the rest routinely, and when Dale Mitchell fanned in the ninth Larsen had his perfect game—a feat still unique in World Series history.

Brooklyn reliever Clem Labine was started in Game Six against Yankee fastballer Bob Turley. No runner scored for either side until the last of the tenth inning when, with two out, Jackie Robinson lined a Turley pitch over the head of the left fielder, scoring Jim Gilliam from second and forcing New York into a seventh game.

The finale proved an anticlimactic disaster for Brooklyn. Once again Dodger starter Newcombe was driven out—this time by Yogi Berra's two two-run homers and Elston Howard's solo shot. By the time it was over, Bill Skowron had increased the Yankee run total to nine with a grand slam, and Yankee starter Johnny Kucks had shut Brooklyn out on three singles. For

New York Yankees (AL), 4; Brooklyn Dodgers (NL), 3

NY (A)

PLAYER/POS	AVG	G	AB	R	H	2B	3B	HR	RB	BB	SO	SB
Hank Bauer, of	.281	7	32	3	9	0	0	1	3	0	5	1
Yogi Berra, c	.360	7	25	5	9	2	0	3	10	4	1	0
Tommy Byrne, p-1	.000	2	1	0	0	0	0	0	0	0	0	0
Andy Carey, 3b	.158	7	19	2	3	0	0	0	0	1	6	0
Bob Cerv, ph	1.000	1	1	0	1	0	0	0	0	0	0	0
Gerry Coleman, 2b	.000	2	2	0	0	0	0	0	0	0	0	0
Joe Collins, 1b-5	.238	6	21	2	5	2	0	0	2	2	3	0
Whitey Ford, p	.000	2	4	0	0	0	0	0	0	0	3	0
Elston Howard, of	.400	1	5	1	2	1	0	1	1	0	0	0
Johnny Kucks, p	.000	3	3	0	0	0	0	0	0	0	1	0
Don Larsen, p	.333	2	3	1	1	0	0	0	1	0	1	0
Mickey Mantle, of	.250	7	24	6	6	1	0	3	4	6	5	1
Billy Martin, 2b-7,3b-1	.296	7	27	5	8	0	0	2	3	1	6	0
Maury McDermott, p	1.000	1	1	0	1	0	0	0	0	0	0	0
Gil McDougald, ss	.143	7	21	0	3	0	0	0	1	3	6	0
Tom Morgan, p	1.000	2	1	1	1	0	0	0	0	0	0	0
Norm Siebern, ph	.000	1	1	0	0	0	0	0	0	0	0	0
Bill Skowron, 1b-2	.100	3	10	1	1	0	0	1	4	0	3	0
Enos Slaughter, of	.350	6	20	6	7	0	0	1	4	4	0	0
Tom Sturdivant, p	.333	2	3	0	1	0	0	0	0	0	1	0
Bob Turley, p	.000	3	4	0	0	0	0	0	0	0	1	0
George Wilson, ph	.000	1	1	0	0	0	0	0	0	0	1	0
TOTAL	.253		229	33	58	6	0	12	33	21	43	2

PITCHER	W	L	ERA	G	GS	CG	SV	SHO	IP	H	ER	BB	SO
Tommy Byrne	0	0	0.00	1	0	0	0	0	0.1	1	0	0	1
Whitey Ford	1	1	5.25	2	2	1	0	0	12.0	14	7	2	8
Johnny Kucks	1	0	0.82	3	1	1	0	1	11.0	6	1	3	2
Don Larsen	1	0	0.00	2	2	1	0	1	10.2	1	0	4	7
Maury McDermott	0	0	3.00	1	0	0	0	0	3.0	2	1	3	3
Tom Morgan	0	1	9.00	2	0	0	0	0	4.0	6	4	4	3
Tom Sturdivant	1	0	2.79	2	1	1	0	0	9.2	8	3	8	9
Bob Turley	0	1	0.82	3	1	1	0	0	11.0	4	1	8	14
TOTAL	4	3	2.48	16	7	5	0	2	61.2	42	17	32	47

BRO (N)

PLAYER/POS	AVG	G	AB	R	H	2B	3B	HR	RB	BB	SO	SB
Sandy Amoros, of	.053	6	19	1	1	0	0	0	1	2	4	0
Don Bessent, p	.500	2	2	0	1	0	0	0	1	1	1	0
Roy Campanella, c	.182	7	22	2	4	1	0	0	3	3	7	0
Gino Cimoli, of	.000	1	0	0	0	0	0	0	0	0	0	0
Roger Craig, p	.500	2	2	0	1	0	0	0	0	0	0	0
Don Drysdale, p	.000	1	0	0	0	0	0	0	0	0	0	0
Carl Erskine, p	.000	2	1	0	0	0	0	0	0	0	1	0
Carl Furillo, of	.240	7	25	2	6	2	0	0	1	2	3	0
Jim Gilliam, 2b-6,of-1	.083	7	24	2	2	0	0	0	2	7	3	1
Gil Hodges, 1b	.304	7	23	5	7	2	0	1	8	4	4	0
Ransom Jackson, ph	.000	3	3	0	0	0	0	0	0	0	2	0
Clem Labine, p	.250	2	4	0	1	1	0	0	0	0	2	0
Sal Maglie, p	.000	2	5	0	0	0	0	0	0	0	2	0
Dale Mitchell, ph	.000	4	4	0	0	0	0	0	0	0	1	0
Charlie Neal, 2b	.000	1	4	0	0	0	0	0	0	0	1	0
Don Newcombe, p	.000	2	1	0	0	0	0	0	0	0	0	0
Pee Wee Reese, ss	.222	7	27	3	6	0	0	0	2	6	0	0
Jackie Robinson, 3b	.250	7	24	5	6	1	0	1	2	5	2	0
Ed Roebuck, p	.000	3	0	0	0	0	0	0	0	0	0	0
Duke Snider, of	.304	7	23	5	7	1	0	1	4	6	8	0
Rube Walker, ph	.000	2	2	0	0	0	0	0	0	0	0	0
TOTAL	.195		215	25	42	8	1	3	24	32	47	1

PITCHER	W	L	ERA	G	GS	CG	SV	SHO	IP	H	ER	BB	SO
Don Bessent	1	0	1.80	2	0	0	0	0	10.0	8	2	3	5
Roger Craig	0	1	12.00	2	1	0	0	0	6.0	10	8	3	4
Don Drysdale	0	0	9.00	2	0	0	0	0	2.0	2	2	1	1
Carl Erskine	0	1	5.40	2	1	0	0	0	5.0	4	3	2	2
Clem Labine	1	0	0.00	2	1	1	0	1	12.0	8	0	3	7
Sal Maglie	1	1	2.65	2	2	2	0	0	17.0	14	5	6	15
Don Newcombe	0	1	21.21	2	2	0	0	0	4.2	11	11	3	4
Ed Roebuck	0	0	2.08	3	0	0	0	0	4.1	1	1	0	5
TOTAL	3	4	4.72	16	7	3	0	1	61.0	58	32	21	43

New York it was world title number seventeen.

GAME 1 AT BRO OCT 3

NY	200 100 000	3 9 1
BRO	023 100 00X	6 9 0

Pitchers: FORD, Kucks (4), Morgan (6), Turley (8) vs MAGLIE
Home Runs: Mantle-NY, Robinson-BRO, Hodges-BRO, Martin-NY
Attendance: 34,479

GAME 2 AT BRO OCT 5

NY	150 100 001	8 12 2
BRO	061 220 02X	13 12 0

Pitchers: Larsen, Kucks (2), Byrne (2), Sturdivant (3), MORGAN (3), Turley (5), McDermott (6) vs Newcombe, Roebuck (2), BESSENT (3)
Home Runs: Berra-NY, Snider-BRO
Attendance: 36,217

GAME 3 AT NY OCT 6

BRO	010 001 100	3 8 1
NY	010 003 01X	5 8 1

Pitchers: CRAIG, Labine (7) vs FORD
Home Runs: Martin-NY, Slaughter-NY
Attendance: 73,977

GAME 4 AT NY OCT 7

BRO	000 100 001	2 6 0
NY	100 201 20X	6 7 2

Pitchers: ERSKINE, Roebuck (5), Drysdale (7) vs STURDIVANT
Home Runs: Mantle-NY, Bauer-NY
Attendance: 69,705

GAME 5 AT NY OCT 8

BRO	000 000 000	0 0 0
NY	000 101 00X	2 5 0

Pitchers: MAGLIE vs LARSEN
Home Runs: Mantle-NY
Attendance: 64,519

GAME 6 AT BRO OCT 9

NY	000 000 000 0	0 7 0
BRO	000 000 000 1	1 4 0

Pitchers: TURLEY vs LABINE
Attendance: 33,224

GAME 7 AT BRO OCT 10

NY	202 100 400	9 10 0
BRO	000 000 000	0 3 1

Pitchers: KUCKS vs NEWCOMBE, Bessent (4), Craig (7), Roebuck (7), Erskine (9)
Home Runs: Berra-NY (2), Howard-NY, Skowron-NY
Attendance: 33,782

Overall, the Yankees pitched better, hit oftener, and scored more runs than the Braves. But the Braves had Lew Burdette, and with him they won the Series.

The opener pitted the Braves' established great Warren Spahn against New York's emerging great Whitey Ford. Ford prevailed, with a five-hit 3–1 win as Spahn was chased in the sixth. Burdette, winner of 17 regular-season games, started Game Two against veteran Bobby Shantz, the American League ERA leader. After a scoreless first inning, both pitchers gave up a run in the second and another in the third. Two go-ahead runs in the top of the fourth ended the Braves' scoring, but they were enough, as Burdette blanked New York through the final six innings to even the Series. Before he was finished, Burdette would stretch his consecutive scoreless innings to 24.

The Yankees exploded in Game Three, in Milwaukee, running through six Brave pitchers for a 12–3 rout. Braves fans even ended up cheering Yankee second baseman Tony Kubek—a Milwaukee native—who opened the scoring with a solo homer in the first, scored again after singling in the fourth (on Mickey Mantle's home run), and concluded the Yankee scoring in the seventh with his second homer, with two aboard.

Warren Spahn carried a 4–1 Braves lead into the ninth inning of Game Four, but after retiring the first two batters in the ninth, he gave up singles to Yogi Berra and Gil McDougald, and a game-tying home run to Elston Howard. In the top of the tenth, Hank Bauer tripled in a go-ahead Yankee run, but Milwaukee's Johnny Logan doubled to tie it up in the last of the tenth, and Eddie Mathews homered to give Spahn a shaky victory.

Burdette faced Ford in Game Five. In the sixth inning the Braves put half their hits—three singles—back to back for a run. It was all they needed as Burdette spaced seven singles for the shutout. Back in New York the next day, all the scoring came on home runs. Each club hit a pair, but Berra's in the third was the only one with a man aboard. Brave blasts in the fifth (Frank Torre) and seventh (Hank Aaron) tied the score, but Bauer answered Aaron's homer in the last of the seventh with what proved the winning shot. Bob Turley, who yielded just four hits while fanning eight (the Series high) claimed the Yankee victory.

In the finale, Burdette, with only two days' rest, scattered four hits over the first eight innings as the Braves gave him a 5–0 lead. In the bottom of the ninth, though, three Yankee singles loaded the bases with two out. But third baseman

Milwaukee Braves (NL), 4; New York Yankees (AL), 3

MIL (N)

PLAYER/POS	AVG	G	AB	R	H	2B	3B	HR	RB	BB	SO	SB
Hank Aaron, of	.393	7	28	5	11	0	1	3	7	1	6	0
Joe Adcock, 1b	.200	5	15	1	3	0	0	0	2	0	2	0
Bob Buhl, p	.000	2	1	0	0	0	0	0	0	0	1	0
Lew Burdette, p	.000	3	8	0	0	0	0	0	0	1	2	0
Gene Conley, p	.000	1	0	0	0	0	0	0	0	0	0	0
Wes Covington, of	.208	7	24	1	5	1	0	0	1	2	6	1
Del Crandall, c	.211	6	19	1	4	0	0	1	1	1	1	0
John De Merit, pr	.000	1	0	0	0	0	0	0	0	0	0	0
Bob Hazle, of	.154	4	13	2	2	0	0	0	0	1	2	0
Ernie Johnson, p	.000	3	1	0	0	0	0	0	0	0	1	0
Nippy Jones, ph	.000	3	2	0	0	0	0	0	0	0	0	0
Johnny Logan, ss	.185	7	27	5	5	1	0	1	2	3	6	0
Felix Mantilla, 2b-3	.000	4	10	1	0	0	0	0	0	1	0	0
Eddie Mathews, 3b	.227	7	22	4	5	3	0	1	4	8	5	0
Don McMahon, p	.000	3	0	0	0	0	0	0	0	0	0	0
Andy Pafko, of-5	.214	6	14	1	3	0	0	0	0	0	1	0
Juan Pizarro, p	.000	1	1	0	0	0	0	0	0	0	0	0
Del Rice, c	.167	2	6	0	1	0	0	0	0	1	2	0
Carl Sawatski, ph	.000	2	2	0	0	0	0	0	0	0	2	0
Red Schoendienst, 2b	.278	5	18	0	5	1	0	0	2	0	1	0
Warren Spahn, p	.000	2	4	0	0	0	0	0	0	0	1	0
Frank Torre, 1b	.300	7	10	2	3	0	0	2	3	2	0	0
Bob Trowbridge, p	.000	1	0	0	0	0	0	0	0	0	0	0
TOTAL	.209		225	23	47	6	1	8	22	22	40	1

PITCHER	W	L	ERA	G	GS	CG	SV	SHO	IP	H	ER	BB	SO
Bob Buhl	0	1	10.80	2	2	0	0	0	3.1	6	4	6	4
Lew Burdette	3	0	0.67	3	3	3	0	2	27.0	21	2	4	13
Gene Conley	0	0	10.80	1	0	0	0	0	1.2	2	2	1	0
Ernie Johnson	0	1	1.29	3	0	0	0	0	7.0	2	1	1	8
Don McMahon	0	0	0.00	3	0	0	0	0	5.0	3	0	3	5
Juan Pizarro	0	0	10.80	1	0	0	0	0	1.2	3	2	2	1
Warren Spahn	1	1	4.70	2	2	1	0	0	15.1	18	8	2	2
Bob Trowbridge	0	0	45.00	1	0	0	0	0	1.0	2	5	3	1
TOTAL	4	3	3.48	16	7	4	0	2	62.0	57	24	22	34

NY (A)

PLAYER/POS	AVG	G	AB	R	H	2B	3B	HR	RB	BB	SO	SB
Hank Bauer, of	.258	7	31	3	8	2	1	2	6	1	6	0
Yogi Berra, c	.320	7	25	5	8	1	0	1	2	4	0	0
Tommy Byrne, p	.500	2	2	0	1	0	0	0	0	0	1	0
Andy Carey, 3b	.286	2	7	0	2	1	0	0	1	1	0	0
Gerry Coleman, 2b	.364	7	22	2	8	2	0	0	2	3	1	0
Joe Collins, 1b-5	.000	6	5	0	0	0	0	0	0	0	3	0
Art Ditmar, p	.000	2	1	0	0	0	0	0	0	0	1	0
Whitey Ford, p	.000	2	5	0	0	0	0	0	0	0	1	0
Bob Grim, p	.000	2	0	0	0	0	0	0	0	0	0	0
Elston Howard, 1b-3	.273	6	11	2	3	0	0	1	3	1	3	0
Tony Kubek, of-5,3b-2	.286	7	28	4	8	0	0	2	4	0	4	0
Johnny Kucks, p	.000	1	0	0	0	0	0	0	0	0	0	0
Don Larsen, p	.000	2	2	1	0	0	0	0	0	2	1	0
Jerry Lumpe, 3b-3	.286	6	14	0	4	0	0	0	2	1	1	0
Mickey Mantle, of-5	.263	6	19	3	5	0	0	1	2	3	1	0
Gil McDougald, ss	.250	7	24	3	6	0	0	0	2	3	3	1
Bobby Richardson, 2b-1	.000	2	0	0	0	0	0	0	0	0	0	0
Bobby Shantz, p	.000	3	1	0	0	0	0	0	0	0	0	0
Harry Simpson, 1b-4	.083	5	12	0	1	0	0	0	0	1	4	0
Bill Skowron, 1b	.000	2	4	0	0	0	0	0	0	0	0	0
Enos Slaughter, of	.250	5	12	3	3	1	0	0	0	3	2	0
Tom Sturdivant, p	.000	2	1	0	0	0	0	0	0	0	0	0
Bob Turley, p	.000	3	4	0	0	0	0	0	0	0	2	0
TOTAL	.248		230	25	57	7	1	7	25	22	34	1

PITCHER	W	L	ERA	G	GS	CG	SV	SHO	IP	H	ER	BB	SO
Tommy Byrne	0	0	5.40	2	0	0	0	0	3.1	1	2	2	1
Art Ditmar	0	0	0.00	2	0	0	0	0	6.0	2	0	0	2
Whitey Ford	1	1	1.13	2	2	1	0	0	16.0	11	2	5	7
Bob Grim	0	1	7.71	2	0	0	0	0	2.1	3	2	0	2
Johnny Kucks	0	0	0.00	1	0	0	0	0	0.2	1	0	1	1
Don Larsen	1	1	3.72	2	1	0	0	0	9.2	8	4	5	6
Bobby Shantz	0	1	4.05	3	1	0	0	0	6.2	8	3	2	7
Tom Sturdivant	0	0	6.00	2	1	0	0	0	6.0	6	4	1	2
Bob Turley	1	0	2.31	3	2	1	0	0	11.2	7	3	6	12
TOTAL	3	4	2.89	19	7	2	0	0	62.1	47	20	22	40

Eddie Mathews snared Bil Skowron's sharp grounder and stepped on the bag for a force out that preserved Burdette's second shutout and gave Milwaukee its first world championship.

GAME 1 AT NY OCT 2

MIL	000	000	100	1	5 0
NY	000	012	00X	3	9 1

Pitchers: SPAHN, Johnson (6), McMahon (7) vs FORD
Attendance: 69,476

GAME 2 AT NY OCT 3

MIL	011	200	000	4	8 0
NY	011	000	000	2	7 2

Pitchers: BURDETTE vs SHANTZ, Ditmar (4), Grim (8)
Home Runs: Logan-MIL, Bauer-NY
Attendance: 65,202

GAME 3 AT MIL OCT 5

NY	302	200	500	12	9 0
MIL	010	020	000	3	8 1

Pitchers: Turley, LARSEN (2) vs BUHL, Pizarro (1), Conley (3), Johnson (5), Trowbridge (7), McMahon (8)
Home Runs: Kubek-NY (2), Mantle-NY, Aaron-MIL
Attendance: 45,804

GAME 4 AT MIL OCT 6

NY	100	000	003 1	5	11 0
MIL	000	400	000 3	7	7 0

Pitchers: Sturdivant, Shantz (5), Kucks (8), Byrne (8), GRIM (10) vs SPAHN
Home Runs: Aaron-MIL, Torre-MIL, Howard-NY, Mathews-MIL
Attendance: 45,804

GAME 5 AT MIL OCT 7

NY	000	000	000	0	7 0
MIL	000	001	00X	1	6 1

Pitchers: FORD, Turley (8) vs BURDETTE
Attendance: 45,811

GAME 6 AT NY OCT 9

MIL	000	010	100	2	4 0
NY	002	000	10X	3	7 0

Pitchers: Buhl, JOHNSON (3), McMahon (8) vs TURLEY
Home Runs: Berra-NY, Torre-MIL, Aaron-MIL, Bauer-NY
Attendance: 61,408

GAME 7 AT NY OCT 10

MIL	004	000	010	5	9 1
NY	000	000	000	0	7 3

Pitchers: BURDETTE vs LARSEN, Shantz (3), Ditmar (4), Sturdivant (6), Byrne (8)
Home Runs: Crandall-MIL
Attendance: 61,207

After four games, Milwaukee held a 3–1 Series advantage, but New York rebounded to take the final three games and avenge their loss to the Braves the year before. As in the previous series, Warren Spahn faced Whitey Ford in the opener. The durable Spahn emerged the victor when Bill Bruton singled home the Braves' winning run off reliever Ryne Duren in the last of the tenth. In Game Two, home runs by Bruton and pitcher Lew Burdette (for three runs) helped put the Braves ahead 7–1 in the first inning. Milwaukee scored off five Yankee hurlers in their eventual 13–5 win.

Don Larsen and Ryne Duren combined for a shutout in Game Three to give New York its first victory. Hank Bauer drove in all four Yankee runs with a two-run single in the fifth and his third home run in three games in the seventh. Warren Spahn held Bauer hitless in Game Four, blanking New York on two hits to defeat Whitey Ford and bring Milwaukee within a win of the championship.

Yankee Bob Turley came up with a shutout of his own the next day, though, fanning ten men along the way. Gil McDougald's solo homer in the third inning was all the offense Turley needed, but as insurance the Yankees bunched six of their ten hits into the sixth inning for six more runs.

Spahn and Ford, with only two days' rest, confronted each other a third time in Game Six. Ford lasted less than two innings, but Spahn (despite Hank Bauer's fourth Series home run in the first inning) endured into extra innings, when McDougald put New York ahead with a leadoff homer in the tenth. Two outs and two hits later, Spahn was removed, and Bill Skowron's single off reliever Don McMahon drove home another Yankee run. Milwaukee scored once in the last of the tenth and threatened further damage with men on first and third. But Bob Turley came on to retire the final batter and send the Series to a seventh game.

In the sixth inning of the finale, the Braves' Del Crandall homered against Turley (who had relieved Don Larsen in the third) to tie the game 2–2. But four Yankee runs off starter Lew Burdette in the top of the eighth (including Skowron's three-run homer) made the score 6–2, where it remained, as Turley held on to bring Casey Stengel his seventh (and last) Series triumph— and the Yankees their eighteenth.

New York Yankees (AL), 4; Milwaukee Braves (NL), 3

NY (A)

PLAYER/POS	AVG	G	AB	R	H	2B	3B	HR	RB	BB	SO	SB
Hank Bauer, of	.323	7	31	6	10	0	0	4	8	0	5	0
Yogi Berra, c	.222	7	27	3	6	3	0	0	2	1	0	0
Andy Carey, 3b	.083	5	12	1	1	0	0	0	0	0	3	0
Murry Dickson, p	.000	2	0	0	0	0	0	0	0	0	0	0
Art Ditmar, p	.000	1	1	0	0	0	0	0	0	0	0	0
Ryne Duren, p	.000	3	3	0	0	0	0	0	0	0	2	0
Whitey Ford, p	.000	3	4	1	0	0	0	0	0	0	2	0
Elston Howard, of	.222	6	18	4	4	0	0	0	2	1	4	1
Tony Kubek, ss	.048	7	21	0	1	0	0	0	1	1	7	0
Johnny Kucks, p	1.000	2	1	0	1	0	0	0	0	0	0	0
Don Larsen, p	.000	2	2	0	0	0	0	0	0	1	0	0
Jerry Lumpe, 3b-3,ss-2	.167	6	12	0	2	0	0	0	0	1	2	0
Duke Maas, p	.000	1	0	0	0	0	0	0	0	0	0	0
Mickey Mantle, of	.250	7	24	4	6	0	1	2	3	7	4	0
Gil McDougald, 2b	.321	7	28	5	9	2	0	2	4	2	4	0
Zach Monroe, p	.000	1	0	0	0	0	0	0	0	0	0	0
Bobby Richardson, 3b	.000	4	5	0	0	0	0	0	0	0	0	0
Norm Siebern, of	.125	3	8	1	1	0	0	0	0	0	3	0
Bill Skowron, 1b	.259	7	27	3	7	0	0	2	7	1	4	0
Enos Slaughter, ph	.000	4	3	1	0	0	0	0	0	1	1	0
Marv Throneberry, ph	.000	1	1	0	0	0	0	0	0	0	1	0
Bob Turley, p	.200	4	5	0	1	0	0	0	2	0	1	0
TOTAL	.210		233	29	49	5	1	10	29	21	42	1

PITCHER	W	L	ERA	G	GS	CG	SV	SHO	IP	H	ER	BB	SO
Murry Dickson	0	0	4.50	2	0	0	0	0	4.0	4	2	0	1
Art Ditmar	0	0	0.00	1	0	0	0	0	3.2	2	0	0	2
Ryne Duren	1	1	1.93	3	0	0	1	0	9.1	7	2	6	14
Whitey Ford	0	1	4.11	3	3	0	0	0	15.1	19	7	5	16
Johnny Kucks	0	0	2.08	2	0	0	0	0	4.1	4	1	1	0
Don Larsen	1	0	0.96	2	2	0	0	0	9.1	9	1	6	9
Duke Maas	0	0	81.00	1	0	0	0	0	0.1	2	3	1	0
Zach Monroe	0	0	27.00	1	0	0	0	0	1.0	3	3	1	1
Bob Turley	2	1	2.76	4	2	1	1	1	16.1	10	5	7	13
TOTAL	4	3	3.39	19	7	1	2	1	63.2	60	24	27	56

MIL (N)

PLAYER/POS	AVG	G	AB	R	H	2B	3B	HR	RB	BB	SO	SB
Hank Aaron, of	.333	7	27	3	9	2	0	0	2	4	6	0
Joe Adcock, 1b	.308	4	13	1	4	0	0	0	0	1	3	0
Billy Bruton, of	.412	7	17	2	7	0	0	1	2	5	5	0
Lew Burdette, p	.111	3	9	1	1	0	0	1	3	0	3	0
Wes Covington, of	.269	7	26	2	7	0	0	0	4	2	4	0
Del Crandall, c	.240	7	25	4	6	0	0	1	3	3	10	0
Harry Hanebrink, ph	.000	2	2	0	0	0	0	0	0	0	0	0
Johnny Logan, ss	.120	7	25	3	3	2	0	0	2	2	4	0
Felix Mantilla, ss-1	.000	4	0	1	0	0	0	0	0	0	0	0
Eddie Mathews, 3b	.160	7	25	3	4	2	0	0	3	6	11	1
Don McMahon, p	.000	3	0	0	0	0	0	0	0	0	0	0
Andy Pafko, of	.333	4	9	0	3	1	0	0	1	0	0	0
Juan Pizarro, p	.000	1	0	0	0	0	0	0	0	0	0	0
Bob Rush, p	.000	1	2	0	0	0	0	0	0	0	2	0
Red Schoendienst, 2b	.300	7	30	5	9	3	1	0	0	2	1	0
Warren Spahn, p	.333	3	12	0	4	0	0	0	3	0	6	0
Frank Torre, 1b	.176	7	17	0	3	0	0	0	1	2	0	0
Carl Willey, p	.000	1	0	0	0	0	0	0	0	0	0	0
Casey Wise, ph	.000	2	1	0	0	0	0	0	0	0	1	0
TOTAL	.250		240	25	60	10	1	3	24	27	56	1

PITCHER	W	L	ERA	G	GS	CG	SV	SHO	IP	H	ER	BB	SO
Lew Burdette	1	2	5.64	3	3	1	0	0	22.1	22	14	4	12
Don McMahon	0	0	5.40	3	0	0	0	0	3.1	3	2	3	5
Juan Pizarro	0	0	5.40	1	0	0	0	0	1.2	2	1	1	3
Bob Rush	0	1	3.00	1	1	0	0	0	6.0	3	2	5	2
Warren Spahn	2	1	2.20	3	3	2	0	1	28.2	19	7	8	18
Carl Willey	0	0	0.00	1	0	0	0	0	1.0	0	0	0	2
TOTAL	3	4	3.71	12	7	3	0	1	63.0	49	26	21	42

GAME 1 AT MIL OCT 1

NY	000 120 000 0	3	8 1
MIL	000 200 010 1	4	10 0

Pitchers: Ford, DUREN (8) vs SPAHN
Home Runs: Skowron-NY, Bauer-NY
Attendance: 46,367

GAME 2 AT MIL OCT 2

NY	100 100 003	5	7 0
MIL	710 000 23X	13	15 1

Pitchers: TURLEY, Maas (1), Kucks (1), Dickson (5), Monroe (8) vs BURDETTE
Home Runs: Bruton-MIL, Burdette-MIL, Mantle-NY (2), Bauer-NY
Attendance: 46,367

GAME 3 AT NY OCT 4

MIL	000 000 000	0	6 0
NY	000 020 20X	4	4 0

Pitchers: RUSH, McMahon (7) vs LARSEN, Duren (8)
Home Runs: Bauer-NY
Attendance: 71,599

GAME 4 AT NY OCT 5

MIL	000 001 110	3	9 0
NY	000 000 000	0	2 1

Pitchers: SPAHN vs FORD, Kucks (8), Dickson (9)
Attendance: 71,563

GAME 5 AT NY OCT 6

MIL	000 000 000	0	5 0
NY	001 006 00X	7	10 0

Pitchers: BURDETTE, Pizarro (6), Willey (8) vs TURLEY
Home Runs: McDougald-NY
Attendance: 65,279

GAME 6 AT MIL OCT 8

NY	100 001 000 2	4	10 1
MIL	110 000 000 1	3	10 4

Pitchers: Ford, Ditmar (2), DUREN (6), Turley (10) vs SPAHN, McMahon (10)
Home Runs: Bauer-NY, McDougald-NY
Attendance: 46,367

GAME 7 AT MIL OCT 9

NY	020 000 040	6	8 0
MIL	100 001 000	2	5 2

Pitchers: Larsen, TURLEY (3) vs BURDETTE, McMahon (8)
Home Runs: Crandall-MIL, Skowron-NY
Attendance: 46,367

It took a nosedive from first to third by San Francisco and a Dodger playoff victory over Milwaukee (who had finished the season tied with the Dodgers), to bring Los Angeles the city's first major league pennant. But once they had made it to the Series, the Dodgers dispatched the White Sox in six games.

The opener, though, belonged to Chicago. In their first World Series in forty years, the White Sox overwhelmed Los Angeles with 11 runs in the first four innings as pitchers Early Wynn and Gerry Staley combined to blank the Dodgers. Chicago's big gun was veteran slugger Ted Kluszewski (acquired from Pittsburgh in late August), whose single and two homers drove in five runs. Chicago scored twice in the first inning the next day, but Dodger starter Johnny Podres settled down to blank the Sox over the next five innings as home runs by Charlie Neal in the fifth and pinch hitter Chuck Essegian and Neal (again) in the seventh put the Dodgers ahead by two. Rookie reliever Larry Sherry gave up a third Chicago run in the eighth on Al Smith's double, but a second runner was nailed at the plate, and Sherry set down the side in the ninth to save Podres's win.

When the Series moved to Los Angeles' cavernous Coliseum for the West Coast's first World Series games ever, fans turned out in record numbers, setting a new Series mark in each of the next three games. Dodger starter Don Drysdale yielded 11 hits and four walks in Game Three, but the only run scored against him came on a double-play after Larry Sherry had relieved him with two men on in the eighth. As Los Angeles had already scored twice, and added a third run in their half of the eighth, Drysdale emerged with the win and Sherry with his second save. In Game Four, the Sox's Sherm Lollar's three-run homer had tied the score by the time Sherry relieved Dodger starter Roger Craig in the eighth, so Gil Hodges's solo homer in the last of the eighth gave Sherry the win this time—and Los Angeles a 3–1 Series advantage.

Chicago's Bob Shaw dueled Dodger Sandy Koufax through seven innings of Game Five before 92,706 spectators (still a Series high). The Sox scored only once off Koufax, but one run was enough for their second win as a pair of Sox relievers continued Shaw's shutout through the final two innings.

Back in Chicago for Game Six, the Dodgers unloaded on Early Wynn and Dick Donovan for eight runs in the third and fourth innings. Ted Kluszewski's three-run homer in the last of the fourth led to Larry Sherry's fourth relief appear-

Los Angeles Dodgers (NL), 4;
Chicago White Sox (AL), 2

LA (N)

PLAYER/POS	AVG	G	AB	R	H	2B	3B	HR	RB	BB	SO	SB
Chuck Churn, p	.000	1	0	0	0	0	0	0	0	0	0	0
Roger Craig, p	.000	2	3	0	0	0	0	0	0	0	2	0
Don Demeter, of	.250	6	12	2	3	0	0	0	0	1	3	0
Don Drysdale, p	.000	1	2	0	0	0	0	0	0	0	2	0
Chuck Essegian, ph	.667	4	3	2	2	0	0	2	2	1	1	0
Ron Fairly, of-4	.000	6	3	0	0	0	0	0	0	0	1	0
Carl Furillo, of-1	.250	4	4	0	1	0	0	0	2	0	1	0
Jim Gilliam, 3b	.240	6	25	2	6	0	0	0	0	2	2	2
Gil Hodges, 1b	.391	6	23	2	9	0	1	1	2	1	2	0
Johnny Klippstein, p	.000	1	0	0	0	0	0	0	0	0	0	0
Sandy Koufax, p	.000	2	2	0	0	0	0	0	0	0	1	0
Clem Labine, p	.000	1	0	0	0	0	0	0	0	0	0	0
Norm Larker, of	.188	6	16	2	3	0	0	0	0	2	3	0
Wally Moon, of	.261	6	23	3	6	0	0	1	2	2	2	1
Charlie Neal, 2b	.370	6	27	4	10	2	0	2	6	0	1	1
Joe Pignatano, c	.000	1	0	0	0	0	0	0	0	0	0	0
Johnny Podres, p-2	.500	3	4	1	2	1	0	0	1	0	0	0
Rip Repulski, of	.000	1	0	0	0	0	0	0	0	1	0	0
Johnny Roseboro, c	.095	6	21	0	2	0	0	0	1	0	2	0
Larry Sherry, p-4	.500	5	4	0	2	0	0	0	0	0	1	0
Duke Snider, of-3	.200	4	10	1	2	0	0	1	2	2	0	0
Stan Williams, p	.000	1	0	0	0	0	0	0	0	0	0	0
Maury Wills, ss	.250	6	20	2	5	0	0	0	1	0	3	1
Don Zimmer, ss	.000	1	1	0	0	0	0	0	0	0	0	0
TOTAL	.261		203	21	53	3	1	7	19	12	27	5

PITCHER	W	L	ERA	G	GS	CG	SV	SHO	IP	H	ER	BB	SO
Chuck Churn	0	0	27.00	1	0	0	0	0	0.2	5	2	0	0
Roger Craig	0	1	8.68	2	2	0	0	0	9.1	15	9	5	8
Don Drysdale	1	0	1.29	1	1	0	0	0	7.0	11	1	4	5
Johnny Klippstein	0	0	0.00	1	0	0	0	0	2.0	1	0	0	2
Sandy Koufax	0	1	1.00	2	1	0	0	0	9.0	5	1	1	7
Clem Labine	0	0	0.00	1	0	0	0	0	1.0	0	0	0	1
Johnny Podres	1	0	4.82	2	2	0	0	0	9.1	7	5	6	4
Larry Sherry	2	0	0.71	4	0	0	2	0	12.2	8	1	2	5
Stan Williams	0	0	0.00	1	0	0	0	0	2.0	0	0	2	1
TOTAL	4	2	3.23	15	6	0	2	0	53.0	52	19	20	33

CHI (A)

PLAYER/POS	AVG	G	AB	R	H	2B	3B	HR	RB	BB	SO	SB
Luis Aparicio, ss	.308	6	26	1	8	1	0	0	0	2	3	1
Norm Cash, ph	.000	4	4	0	0	0	0	0	0	0	2	0
Dick Donovan, p	.333	3	3	0	1	0	0	0	0	0	1	0
Sammy Esposito, 3b	.000	2	2	0	0	0	0	0	0	0	1	0
Nellie Fox, 2b	.375	6	24	4	9	3	0	0	0	4	1	0
Billy Goodman, 3b	.231	5	13	1	3	0	0	0	1	0	5	0
Ted Kluszewski, 1b	.391	6	23	5	9	1	0	3	10	2	0	0
Jim Landis, of	.292	6	24	6	7	0	0	0	1	1	7	1
Sherm Lollar, c	.227	6	22	3	5	0	0	1	5	1	3	0
Turk Lown, p	.000	3	0	0	0	0	0	0	0	0	0	0
Jim McAnany, of	.000	3	5	0	0	0	0	0	0	1	0	0
Ray Moore, p	.000	1	0	0	0	0	0	0	0	0	0	0
Bubba Phillips, 3b-3,of-1	.300	3	10	0	3	1	0	0	0	0	0	0
Billy Pierce, p	.000	3	0	0	0	0	0	0	0	0	0	0
Jim Rivera, of	.000	5	11	1	0	0	0	0	0	3	1	0
Johnny Romano, ph	.000	1	1	0	0	0	0	0	0	0	0	0
Bob Shaw, p	.250	2	4	0	1	0	0	0	0	0	2	0
Al Smith, of	.250	6	20	1	5	3	0	0	1	4	4	0
Gerry Staley, p	.000	4	1	0	0	0	0	0	0	1	1	0
Earl Torgeson, 1b-1	.000	3	1	1	0	0	0	0	0	1	0	0
Early Wynn, p	.200	3	5	0	1	1	0	0	1	0	2	0
TOTAL	.261		199	23	52	10	0	4	19	20	33	4

PITCHER	W	L	ERA	G	GS	CG	SV	SHO	IP	H	ER	BB	SO
Dick Donovan	0	1	5.40	3	1	0	1	0	8.1	4	5	3	5
Turk Lown	0	0	0.00	3	0	0	0	0	3.1	2	0	1	3
Ray Moore	0	0	9.00	1	0	0	0	0	1.0	1	1	0	1
Billy Pierce	0	0	0.00	3	0	0	0	0	4.0	2	0	2	3
Bob Shaw	1	1	2.57	2	2	0	0	0	14.0	17	4	2	2
Gerry Staley	0	1	2.16	4	0	0	1	0	8.1	8	2	0	3
Early Wynn	1	1	5.54	3	3	0	0	0	13.0	19	8	4	10
TOTAL	2	4	3.46	19	6	0	2	0	52.0	53	20	12	27

ance—and his second Series win, as he held the Sox scoreless the rest of the game to bring the world championship to the West Coast for the first time.

GAME 1 AT CHI OCT 1

LA	000 000 000	0	8	3
CHI	207 200 00X	11	11	0

Pitchers: CRAIG, Churn (3), Labine (4), Koufax (5), Klippstein (7) vs WYNN, Staley (8)
Home Runs: Kluszewski-CHI (2)
Attendance: 48,013

GAME 2 AT CHI OCT 2

LA	000 010 300	4	9	1
CHI	200 000 010	3	8	0

Pitchers: PODRES, Sherry (7) vs SHAW, Lown (7)
Home Runs: Neal-LA (2), Essegian-LA
Attendance: 47,368

GAME 3 AT LA OCT 4

CHI	000 000 010	1	12	0
LA	000 000 21X	3	5	0

Pitchers: DONOVAN, Staley (7) vs DRYSDALE, Sherry (8)
Attendance: 92,394

GAME 4 AT LA OCT 5

CHI	000 000 400	4	10	3
LA	004 000 01X	5	9	0

Pitchers: Wynn, Lown (3), Pierce (4), STALEY (7) vs Craig, SHERRY (8)
Home Runs: Lollar-CHI, Hodges-LA
Attendance: 92,650

GAME 5 AT LA OCT 6

CHI	000 100 000	1	5	0
LA	000 000 000	0	9	0

Pitchers: SHAW, Pierce (7), Donovan (8) vs KOUFAX, Williams (8)
Attendance: 92,706

GAME 6 AT CHI OCT 8

LA	002 600 001	9	13	0
CHI	000 300 000	3	6	1

Pitchers: Podres, SHERRY (4) vs WYNN, Donovan (4), Staley (5), Pierce (8), Moore (9)
Home Runs: Snider-LA, Moon-LA, Kluszewski-CHI, Essegian-LA
Attendance: 47,653

Through six games and 8½ innings of the seventh, the Yankees had outscored the Pirates by 29 runs. But as Pirate second baseman Bill Mazeroski stepped to the plate to open the last of the ninth, the Series was even at three games apiece, and Game Seven was tied 9–9. The stage was set for Mazeroski to fulfill that ultimate baseball fantasy, and he did, on pitcher Ralph Terry's second pitch.

Yankee Roger Maris opened the Series scoring with a solo homer in the first inning of Game One, and Elston Howard added two more Yankee runs with a homer in the ninth. But between the home runs New York scored only one run to the Pirates' six (including a two-run homer by Mazeroski in the fourth).

The Yankees avenged their first-game loss with a blowout in Game Two—their first of three. Pittsburgh hit safely 13 times, but scored only three runs. New York, though, turned 19 hits (and a Pirate error) into 16 runs—five of them driven in by Mickey Mantle's two home runs. Continuing their assault in New York the next day, the Bronx Bombers scored six runs in the first inning and four in the fourth as Whitey Ford blanked the Pirates on four hits. Mantle homered again, and second baseman Bobby Richardson drove in a Series single-game record six runs with a grand slam and a single.

Pirate ace Vernon Law—the winner of Game One—started Game Four and, with relief help once again from Roy Face, held the Yankees to two runs to even the Series. Law's bat proved crucial, too, as he doubled in Pittsburgh's first run and scored the third in a three-run fifth that provided all the Pirate scoring. In Game Five, the Pirates' Mazeroski doubled in what proved the two decisive runs in a three-run second as Harvey Haddix and Roy Face (who recorded his third save of the Series) duplicated the previous day's achievement of limiting New York to two runs.

But once again the Yankees came back. Bobby Richardson drove in three of New York's 12 runs with two triples to establish a new Series record of 12 RBIs as the Yankees, behind Whitey Ford's second shutout, sent the Series into a seventh game.

Home runs dominated the finale. Rocky Nelson's two-run shot in the first opened the scoring, and Yankee homers by Bill Skowron in the fifth and Yogi Berra in the sixth contributed four of the five runs that put New York ahead 5–4. Pirate Hal Smith's three-run homer in the bottom of the eighth restored the lead to Pittsburgh, 9–7, and after the Yankees had tied the game

in the top of the ninth (on three singles and a ground out), Mazeroski's immortal shot over the wall in left gave Pittsburgh its first world championship in thirty-five years.

Pittsburgh Pirates (NL), 4; New York Yankees (AL), 3

PIT (N)

PLAYER/POS	AVG	G	AB	R	H	2B	3B	HR	RB	BB	SO	SB
Gene Baker, ph	.000	3	3	0	0	0	0	0	0	0	1	0
Smoky Burgess, c	.333	5	18	2	6	1	0	0	0	0	2	0
Tom Cheney, p	.000	3	0	0	0	0	0	0	0	0	0	0
Joe Christopher, ph	.000	3	0	2	0	0	0	0	0	0	0	0
Gino Cimoli, of-6	.250	7	20	4	5	0	0	0	1	2	4	0
Roberto Clemente, of	.310	7	29	1	9	0	0	0	3	0	4	0
Roy Face, p	.000	4	3	0	0	0	0	0	0	0	2	0
Bob Friend, p	.000	3	1	0	0	0	0	0	0	0	0	0
Joe Gibbon, p	.000	2	0	0	0	0	0	0	0	0	0	0
Fred Green, p	.000	3	1	0	0	0	0	0	0	0	0	0
Dick Groat, ss	.214	7	28	3	6	2	0	0	2	0	1	0
Harvey Haddix, p	.333	2	3	0	1	0	0	0	0	0	1	0
Don Hoak, 3b	.217	7	23	5	5	2	0	0	3	4	1	0
Clem Labine, p	.000	3	0	0	0	0	0	0	0	0	0	0
Vern Law, p	.333	3	6	1	2	1	0	0	1	0	1	0
Bill Mazeroski, 2b	.320	7	25	4	8	2	0	2	5	0	3	0
Vinegar Bend Mizell, p	.000	2	0	0	0	0	0	0	0	0	0	0
Rocky Nelson, 1b-3	.333	4	9	2	3	0	0	1	2	1	1	0
Bob Oldis, c	.000	2	0	0	0	0	0	0	0	0	0	0
Dick Schofield, ss-2	.333	3	3	0	1	0	0	0	0	1	0	0
Bob Skinner, of	.200	2	5	2	1	0	0	0	0	1	0	1
Hal Smith, c	.375	3	8	1	3	0	0	1	3	0	0	0
Dick Stuart, 1b	.150	5	20	0	3	0	0	0	0	0	3	0
Bill Virdon, of	.241	7	29	2	7	3	0	0	5	1	3	1
George Witt, p	.000	3	0	0	0	0	0	0	0	0	0	0
TOTAL	.256		234	27	60	11	0	4	26	12	26	2

PITCHER	W	L	ERA	G	GS	CG	SV	SHO	IP	H	ER	BB	SO
Tom Cheney	0	0	4.50	3	0	0	0	0	4.0	4	2	1	6
Roy Face	0	0	5.23	4	0	0	3	0	10.1	9	6	2	4
Bob Friend	0	2	13.50	3	2	0	0	0	6.0	13	9	3	7
Joe Gibbon	0	0	9.00	2	0	0	0	0	3.0	4	3	1	2
Fred Green	0	0	22.50	3	0	0	0	0	4.0	11	10	1	3
Harvey Haddix	2	0	2.45	2	1	0	0	0	7.1	6	2	2	6
Clem Labine	0	0	13.50	3	0	0	0	0	4.0	13	6	1	2
Vern Law	2	0	3.44	3	3	0	0	0	18.1	22	7	3	8
Vinegar Bend Mizell	0	1	15.43	2	1	0	0	0	2.1	4	4	2	1
George Witt	0	0	0.00	3	0	0	0	0	2.2	5	0	2	1
TOTAL	4	3	7.11	28	7	0	3	0	62.0	91	49	18	40

NY (A)

PLAYER/POS	AVG	G	AB	R	H	2B	3B	HR	RB	BB	SO	SB
Luis Arroyo, p	.000	1	1	0	0	0	0	0	0	0	0	0
Yogi Berra, of-4,c-3	.318	7	22	6	7	0	0	1	8	2	0	0
Johnny Blanchard, c-2	.455	5	11	2	5	2	0	0	2	0	0	0
Clete Boyer, 3b-4,ss-1	.250	4	12	1	3	2	1	0	1	0	1	0
Bob Cerv, of-3	.357	4	14	1	5	0	0	0	0	0	3	0
Jim Coates, p	.000	3	1	0	0	0	0	0	0	0	1	0
Joe De Maestri, ss-3	.500	4	2	1	1	0	0	0	0	0	0	0
Art Ditmar, p	.000	2	0	0	0	0	0	0	0	0	0	0
Ryne Duren, p	.000	2	0	0	0	0	0	0	0	0	0	0
Whitey Ford, p	.250	2	8	1	2	0	0	0	0	2	0	0
Eli Grba, pr	.000	2	0	0	0	0	0	0	0	0	0	0
Elston Howard, c-4	.462	5	13	4	6	1	1	1	4	1	4	0
Tony Kubek, ss-7,of-2	.333	7	30	6	10	1	0	0	3	2	2	0
Dale Long, ph	.333	3	3	0	1	0	0	0	0	0	0	0
Hector Lopez, of-1	.429	3	7	0	3	0	0	0	0	0	0	0
Duke Maas, p	.000	1	0	0	0	0	0	0	0	0	0	0
Mickey Mantle, of	.400	7	25	8	10	1	0	3	11	8	9	0
Roger Maris, of	.267	7	30	6	8	1	0	2	2	2	4	0
Gil McDougald, 3b	.278	6	18	4	5	1	0	0	2	2	3	0
Bobby Richardson, 2b	.367	7	30	8	11	2	2	1	12	1	1	0
Bobby Shantz, p	.333	3	3	0	1	0	0	0	0	0	0	0
Bill Skowron, 1b	.375	7	32	7	12	2	0	2	6	0	6	0
Bill Stafford, p	.000	2	1	0	0	0	0	0	0	0	1	0
Ralph Terry, p	.000	2	2	0	0	0	0	0	0	0	1	0
Bob Turley, p	.250	2	4	0	1	0	0	0	0	1	0	0
TOTAL	.338		269	55	91	13	4	10	54	18	40	0

PITCHER	W	L	ERA	G	GS	CG	SV	SHO	IP	H	ER	BB	SO
Luis Arroyo	0	0	13.50	1	0	0	0	0	0.2	2	1	0	1
Jim Coates	0	0	5.68	3	0	0	0	0	6.1	6	4	1	3
Art Ditmar	0	2	21.60	2	2	0	0	0	1.2	6	4	1	0
Ryne Duren	0	0	2.25	2	0	0	0	0	4.0	2	1	1	5
Whitey Ford	2	0	0.00	2	2	2	0	2	18.0	11	0	2	8
Duke Maas	0	0	4.50	1	0	0	0	0	2.0	2	1	0	1
Bobby Shantz	0	0	4.26	3	0	0	1	0	6.1	4	3	1	1
Bill Stafford	0	0	1.50	2	0	0	0	0	6.0	5	1	1	2
Ralph Terry	0	2	5.40	2	0	0	0	0	6.2	7	4	1	5
Bob Turley	1	0	4.82	2	2	0	0	0	9.1	15	5	4	0
TOTAL	3	4	3.54	20	7	2	1	2	61.0	60	24	12	26

GAME 1 AT PIT OCT 5

NY	100 100 002	4 13 2
PIT	300 201 00X	6 8 0

Pitchers: DITMAR, Coates (1), Maas (5), Duren (7) vs LAW, Face (8)
Home Runs: Maris-NY, Mazeroski-PIT, Howard-NY
Attendance: 36,676

GAME 2 AT PIT OCT 6

NY	002 127 301	16 19 1
PIT	000 100 002	3 13 1

Pitchers: TURLEY, Shantz (9) vs FRIEND, Green (5), Labine (6), WITT (6), Gibbon (7), Cheney (9)
Home Runs: Mantle-NY (2)
Attendance: 37,308

GAME 3 AT NY OCT 8

PIT	000 000 000	0 4 0
NY	600 400 00X	10 16 1

Pitchers: MIZELL, Labine (1), Green (1), Witt (4), Cheney (6), Gibbon (8) vs FORD
Home Runs: Richardson-NY, Mantle-NY
Attendance: 70,001

GAME 4 AT NY OCT 9

PIT	000 030 000	3 7 0
NY	000 100 100	2 8 0

Pitchers: LAW, Face (7) vs TERRY, Shantz (7), Coates (8)
Home Runs: Skowron-NY
Attendance: 67,812

GAME 5 AT NY OCT 10

PIT	031 000 001	5 10 2
NY	011 000 000	2 5 2

Pitchers: HADDIX, Face (7) vs DITMAR, Arroyo (2), Stafford (3), Duren (8)
Home Runs: Maris-NY
Attendance: 62,753

GAME 6 AT PIT OCT 12

NY	015 002 220	12 17 1
PIT	000 000 000	0 7 1

Pitchers: FORD vs FRIEND, Cheney (3), Mizell (4), Green (6), Labine (6), Witt (9)
Attendance: 38,580

GAME 7 AT PIT OCT 13

NY	000 014 022	9 13 1
PIT	220 000 051	10 11 0

Pitchers: Turley, Stafford (2), Shantz (3), Coates (8), TERRY (8) vs Law, Face (6), Friend (9), HADDIX (9)
Home Runs: Nelson-PIT, Skowron-NY, Berra-NY, Smith-PIT, Mazeroski-PIT
Attendance: 36,683

Slugger Mickey Mantle sat out most of the Series with a thigh infection, but rookie manager Ralph Houk enjoyed an otherwise splendid finish to a splendid season as his Yankees mauled the Reds, 27 runs to 13. Yankee ace Whitey Ford, coming off one of his finest seasons (25–4), carried his mound mastery into the Series opener, holding Cincinnati to two singles and a walk as he hurled his third straight World Series shutout. New York recorded only six hits, but two of them were home runs by Elston Howard and Bill Skowron.

Gordy Coleman's two-run homer the next day in the top of the fourth inning broke Cincinnati's scoring drought and gave the Reds a 2–0 lead. Yogi Berra tied the score half an inning later with a two-run blast for New York, but that was all they would get. Red starter Joey Jay blanked the Yankees the rest of the way as his teammates put across four more runs to even the Series. Bob Purkey pitched for the Reds in Game Three and blanked New York on one hit through the first six innings, taking a 1–0 lead into the top of the seventh. A pair of Yankee singles sandwiched around a passed ball evened the score, but the Reds regained the lead with a run in the last of the seventh. But Yankee pinch hitter Johnny Blanchard homered to re-tie the game in the eighth and—while Yankee relief ace Luis Arroyo stopped the Reds through the final two innings—Roger Maris hit his sixty-second home run of the year to win the game and regain the Series lead for New York.

Cincinnati never again threatened. In Game Four, Whitey Ford held the Reds to four harmless singles until he was removed in the sixth because of an ankle injury. (In the third inning he passed Babe Ruth's World Series record of 29⅔ consecutive scoreless innings.) Reliever Jim Coates continued Ford's shutout as the Yankees scored seven runs for the decisive win. The fifth and final game also was no contest. Cincinnati did score five runs—three on Frank Robinson's third-inning home run and two on Wally Post's shot in the fifth. But the Yankees ran through eight Red pitchers, scoring 13 times. Seven of their 15 hits went for extra bases, including Johnny Blanchard's second home run of the Series, and a triple and homer by utility outfielder Hector Lopez.

New York Yankees (AL), 4; Cincinnati Reds (NL), 1

NY (A)

PLAYER/POS	AVG	G	AB	R	H	2B	3B	HR	RB	BB	SO	SB
Luis Arroyo, p	.000	2	0	0	0	0	0	0	0	0	0	0
Yogi Berra, of	.273	4	11	2	3	0	0	1	3	5	1	0
Johnny Blanchard, of-2	.400	4	10	4	4	1	0	2	3	2	0	0
Clete Boyer, 3b	.267	5	15	0	4	2	0	0	3	4	0	0
Jim Coates, p	.000	1	1	0	0	0	0	0	0	0	1	0
Buddy Daley, p	.000	2	1	0	0	0	0	0	1	0	0	0
Whitey Ford, p	.000	2	5	1	0	0	0	0	0	1	0	0
Billy Gardner, ph	.000	1	1	0	0	0	0	0	0	0	0	0
Elston Howard, c	.250	5	20	5	5	3	0	1	1	2	3	0
Tony Kubek, ss	.227	5	22	3	5	0	0	0	1	1	4	0
Hector Lopez, of-3	.333	4	9	3	3	0	1	1	7	2	3	0
Mickey Mantle, of	.167	2	6	0	1	0	0	0	0	0	2	0
Roger Maris, of	.105	5	19	4	2	1	0	1	2	4	6	0
Jack Reed, of	.000	3	0	0	0	0	0	0	0	0	0	0
Bobby Richardson, 2b	.391	5	23	2	9	1	0	0	0	0	0	1
Bill Skowron, 1b	.353	5	17	3	6	0	0	1	5	3	4	0
Bill Stafford, p	.000	1	2	0	0	0	0	0	0	0	0	0
Ralph Terry, p	.000	2	3	0	0	0	0	0	0	0	1	0
TOTAL	.255		165	27	42	8	1	7	26	24	25	1

PITCHER	W	L	ERA	G	GS	CG	SV	SHO	IP	H	ER	BB	SO
Luis Arroyo	1	0	2.25	2	0	0	0	0	4.0	4	1	2	3
Jim Coates	0	0	0.00	1	0	0	1	0	4.0	1	0	1	2
Buddy Daley	1	0	0.00	2	0	0	0	0	7.0	5	0	0	3
Whitey Ford	2	0	0.00	2	2	1	0	1	14.0	6	0	1	7
Bill Stafford	0	0	2.70	1	1	0	0	0	6.2	7	2	2	5
Ralph Terry	0	1	4.82	2	2	0	0	0	9.1	12	5	2	7
TOTAL	4	1	1.60	10	5	1	1	1	45.0	35	8	8	27

CIN (N)

PLAYER/POS	AVG	G	AB	R	H	2B	3B	HR	RB	BB	SO	SB
Gus Bell, ph	.000	3	3	0	0	0	0	0	0	0	0	0
Don Blasingame, 2b	.143	3	7	1	1	0	0	0	0	0	3	0
Jim Brosnan, p	.000	3	0	0	0	0	0	0	0	0	0	0
Leo Cardenas, ph	.333	3	3	0	1	1	0	0	0	0	1	0
Elio Chacon, 2b-3	.250	4	12	2	3	0	0	0	0	1	2	0
Gordie Coleman, 1b	.250	5	20	2	5	0	0	1	2	0	1	0
Johnny Edwards, c	.364	3	11	1	4	2	0	0	2	0	0	0
Gene Freese, 3b	.063	5	16	0	1	1	0	0	0	3	4	0
Dick Gernert, ph	.000	4	4	0	0	0	0	0	0	0	1	0
Bill Henry, p	.000	2	0	0	0	0	0	0	0	0	0	0
Ken Hunt, p	.000	1	0	0	0	0	0	0	0	0	0	0
Joey Jay, p	.000	2	4	0	0	0	0	0	0	0	2	0
Darrell Johnson, c	.500	2	4	0	2	0	0	0	0	0	0	0
Ken Johnson, p	.000	1	0	0	0	0	0	0	0	0	0	0
Sherman Jones, p	.000	1	0	0	0	0	0	0	0	0	0	0
Eddie Kasko, ss	.318	5	22	1	7	0	0	0	1	0	2	0
Jerry Lynch, ph	.000	4	3	0	0	0	0	0	0	1	1	0
Jim Maloney, p	.000	1	0	0	0	0	0	0	0	0	0	0
Jim O'Toole, p	.000	2	3	0	0	0	0	0	0	0	1	0
Vada Pinson, of	.091	5	22	0	2	1	0	0	0	0	1	0
Wally Post, of	.333	5	18	3	6	1	0	1	2	0	1	0
Bob Purkey, p	.000	2	3	0	0	0	0	0	0	0	3	0
Frank Robinson, of	.200	5	15	3	3	2	0	1	4	3	4	0
Jerry Zimmerman, c	.000	2	0	0	0	0	0	0	0	0	0	0
TOTAL	.206		170	13	35	8	0	3	11	8	27	0

PITCHER	W	L	ERA	G	GS	CG	SV	SHO	IP	H	ER	BB	SO
Jim Brosnan	0	0	7.50	3	0	0	0	0	6.0	9	5	4	5
Bill Henry	0	0	19.29	2	0	0	0	0	2.1	4	5	2	3
Ken Hunt	0	0	0.00	1	0	0	0	0	1.0	0	0	1	1
Joey Jay	1	1	5.59	2	2	1	0	0	9.2	8	6	6	6
Ken Johnson	0	0	0.00	1	0	0	0	0	0.2	0	0	0	0
Sherman Jones	0	0	0.00	1	0	0	0	0	0.2	0	0	0	0
Jim Maloney	0	0	27.00	1	0	0	0	0	0.2	4	2	1	1
Jim O'Toole	0	2	3.00	2	2	0	0	0	12.0	11	4	7	4
Bob Purkey	0	1	1.64	2	1	1	0	0	11.0	6	2	3	5
TOTAL	1	4	4.91	15	5	2	0	0	44.0	42	24	24	25

GAME 1 AT NY OCT 4

CIN	000 000 000	0	2	0
NY	000 101 00X	2	6	0

Pitchers: O'TOOLE, Brosnan (8) vs FORD
Home Runs: Howard-NY, Skowron-NY
Attendance: 62,397

GAME 2 AT NY OCT 5

CIN	000 211 020	6	9	0
NY	000 200 000	2	4	3

Pitchers: JAY vs TERRY, Arroyo (8)
Home Runs: Coleman-CIN, Berra-NY
Attendance: 63,083

GAME 3 AT CIN OCT 7

NY	000 000 111	3	6	1
CIN	001 000 100	2	8	0

Pitchers: Stafford, Daley (7), ARROYO (8) vs PURKEY
Home Runs: Blanchard-NY, Maris-NY
Attendance: 32,589

GAME 4 AT CIN OCT 8

NY	000 112 300	7	11	0
CIN	000 000 000	0	5	1

Pitchers: FORD, Coates (6) vs O'TOOLE, Brosnan (6), Henry (9)
Attendance: 32,589

GAME 5 AT CIN OCT 9

NY	510 502 000	13	15	1
CIN	003 020 000	5	11	3

Pitchers: Terry, DALEY (3) vs JAY, Maloney (1), K.Johnson (2), Henry (3), Jones (4), Purkey (5), Brosnan (7), Hunt (9)
Home Runs: Blanchard-NY, Robinson-CIN, Lopez-NY, Post-CIN
Attendance: 32,589

After edging Los Angeles for the pennant in a three-game playoff to break a regular-season tie, San Francisco battled to the final out of Game Seven before falling to New York in the World Series. The teams alternated wins throughout the Series. In the opener Roger Maris doubled two runs home for a quick Yankee lead. Whitey Ford gave up a run in the second (ending his record streak for consecutive scoreless World Series innings pitched at 33⅔) and a tying run an inning later. But he blanked the Giants after that, and won the game on Clete Boyer's homer in the seventh.

Giant Jack Sanford blanked the Yankees on three hits in Game Two, but in Game Three Yankee Bill Stafford restored the Series edge to New York with a four-hit 3–2 win (a shutout until Giant Ed Bailey's ninth-inning home run). Both clubs hit safely nine times in Game Four. But one of the Giants' hits was Chuck Hiller's tie-breaking grand slam in the seventh—more than enough for a Giant win and another Series tie. In Game Five Sanford brought a three-hit 2–2 tie into the last of the eighth. But after he had notched his tenth strikeout, two singles and Tom Tresh's home run drove him out and gave Yankee pitcher Ralph Terry all the margin he needed to avenge his second-game loss to Sanford, and put the Yankees ahead in the Series for the third time.

When play resumed in San Francisco after several days of rain, Billy Pierce held New York to just three hits. One was Roger Maris's solo homer in the fifth, but Pierce's Giants unloaded on Whitey Ford for five runs, driving Ford out and keeping Giant hopes alive.

The finale pitted Terry against Sanford for the third time. Both pitched effectively, but Terry carried a 1–0 lead into the last of the ninth. Pinch hitter Matty Alou led off with a bunt single, but Terry fanned the next two batters. Then Willie Mays doubled to right, but Roger Maris's slick fielding stopped Alou at third. As Terry faced Willie McCovey (who had homered off him in Game Two), he pondered the home run he had given up to Bill Mazeroski two years earlier to lose the 1960 World Series to Pittsburgh. McCovey lined Terry's third pitch toward right—but right at second baseman Bobby Richardson, who grabbed it for the Yankees' twentieth world title. It would be fifteen years before they saw another.

New York Yankees (AL), 4;
San Francisco Giants (NL) 3

NY (A)

PLAYER/POS	AVG	G	AB	R	H	2B	3B	HR	RB	BB	SO	SB
Yogi Berra, c-1	.000	2	2	0	0	0	0	0	0	2	0	0
Johnny Blanchard, ph	.000	1	1	0	0	0	0	0	0	0	1	0
Clete Boyer, 3b	.318	7	22	2	7	1	0	1	4	1	3	0
Marshall Bridges, p	.000	2	0	0	0	0	0	0	0	0	0	0
Jim Coates, p	.000	2	0	0	0	0	0	0	0	0	0	0
Buddy Daley, p	.000	1	0	0	0	0	0	0	0	0	0	0
Whitey Ford, p	.000	3	7	0	0	0	0	0	0	1	3	0
Elston Howard, c	.143	6	21	1	3	1	0	0	1	1	4	0
Tony Kubek, ss	.276	7	29	2	8	1	0	0	1	1	3	0
Dale Long, 1b	.200	2	5	0	1	0	0	0	1	0	1	0
Hector Lopez, ph	.000	2	2	0	0	0	0	0	0	0	0	0
Mickey Mantle, of	.120	7	25	2	3	1	0	0	0	4	5	2
Roger Maris, of	.174	7	23	4	4	1	0	1	5	5	2	0
Bobby Richardson, 2b	.148	7	27	3	4	0	0	0	0	3	1	0
Bill Skowron, 1b	.222	6	18	1	4	0	1	0	1	1	5	0
Bill Stafford, p	.000	1	3	0	0	0	0	0	0	0	1	0
Ralph Terry, p	.125	3	8	0	1	0	0	0	0	1	6	0
Tom Tresh, of	.321	7	28	5	9	1	0	1	4	1	4	2
TOTAL	.199		221	20	44	6	1	3	17	21	39	4

PITCHER	W	L	ERA	G	GS	CG	SV	SHO	IP	H	ER	BB	SO
Marshall Bridges	0	0	4.91	2	0	0	0	0	3.2	4	2	2	3
Jim Coates	0	1	6.75	2	0	0	0	0	2.2	1	2	1	3
Buddy Daley	0	0	0.00	1	0	0	0	0	1.0	1	0	1	0
Whitey Ford	1	1	4.12	3	3	1	0	0	19.2	24	9	4	12
Bill Stafford	1	0	2.00	1	1	1	0	0	9.0	4	2	2	5
Ralph Terry	2	1	1.80	3	3	2	0	1	25.0	17	5	2	16
TOTAL	4	3	2.95	12	7	4	0	1	61.0	51	20	12	39

SF (N)

PLAYER/POS	AVG	G	AB	R	H	2B	3B	HR	RB	BB	SO	SB
Felipe Alou, of	.269	7	26	2	7	1	1	0	1	1	4	0
Matty Alou, of-4	.333	6	12	2	4	1	0	0	1	0	1	0
Ed Bailey, c-3	.071	6	14	1	1	0	0	1	2	0	3	0
Bobby Bolin, p	.000	2	0	0	0	0	0	0	0	0	0	0
Ernie Bowman, ss-1	.000	2	1	1	0	0	0	0	0	0	0	0
Orlando Cepeda, 1b	.158	5	19	1	3	1	0	0	2	0	4	0
Jim Davenport, 3b	.136	7	22	1	3	1	0	0	1	4	7	0
Tom Haller, c	.286	4	14	1	4	1	0	1	3	0	2	0
Chuck Hiller, 2b	.269	7	26	4	7	3	0	1	5	3	4	0
Harvey Kuenn, of	.083	4	12	1	1	0	0	0	0	1	1	0
Don Larsen, p	.000	3	0	0	0	0	0	0	0	0	0	0
Juan Marichal, p	.000	1	2	0	0	0	0	0	0	0	1	0
Willie Mays, of	.250	7	28	3	7	2	0	0	1	1	5	1
Willie McCovey, 1b-2,of-2	.200	4	15	2	3	0	1	1	1	1	3	0
Stu Miller, p	.000	2	0	0	0	0	0	0	0	0	0	0
Bob Nieman, ph	.000	1	0	0	0	0	0	0	0	1	0	0
Billy O'Dell, p	.333	3	3	0	1	0	0	0	0	0	0	0
John Orsino, c	.000	1	1	0	0	0	0	0	0	0	0	0
Jose Pagan, ss	.368	7	19	2	7	0	0	1	2	0	1	0
Billy Pierce, p	.000	2	5	0	0	0	0	0	0	0	1	0
Jack Sanford, p	.429	3	7	0	3	0	0	0	0	0	2	0
TOTAL	.226		226	21	51	10	2	5	19	12	39	1

PITCHER	W	L	ERA	G	GS	CG	SV	SHO	IP	H	ER	BB	SO
Bobby Bolin	0	0	6.75	2	0	0	0	0	2.2	4	2	2	2
Don Larsen	1	0	3.86	3	0	0	0	0	2.1	1	1	2	0
Juan Marichal	0	0	0.00	1	1	0	0	0	4.0	2	0	2	4
Stu Miller	0	0	0.00	2	0	0	0	0	1.1	1	0	2	0
Billy O'Dell	0	1	4.38	3	1	0	1	0	12.1	12	6	3	9
Billy Pierce	1	1	2.40	2	2	1	0	0	15.0	8	4	2	5
Jack Sanford	1	2	1.93	3	3	1	0	1	23.1	16	5	8	19
TOTAL	3	4	2.66	16	7	2	1	1	61.0	44	18	21	39

GAME 1 AT SF OCT 4

NY	200 000 121	6 11 0
SF	011 000 000	2 10 0

Pitchers: FORD vs O'DELL, Larsen (7), Miller (9)
Home Runs: Boyer-NY
Attendance: 43,852

GAME 2 AT SF OCT 5

NY	000 000 000	0 3 1
SF	100 000 10X	2 6 0

Pitchers: TERRY, Daley (8) vs SANFORD
Home Runs: McCovey-SF
Attendance: 43,910

GAME 3 AT NY OCT 7

SF	000 000 002	2 4 3
NY	000 000 30X	3 5 1

Pitchers: PIERCE, Larsen (7), Bolin (8) vs STAFFORD
Home Runs: Bailey-SF
Attendance: 71,434

GAME 4 AT NY OCT 8

SF	020 000 401	7 9 1
NY	000 002 001	3 9 1

Pitchers: Marichal, Bolin (5), LARSEN (6), O'Dell (7) vs Ford, COATES (7), Bridges (7)
Home Runs: Haller-SF, Hiller-SF
Attendance: 66,607

GAME 5 AT NY OCT 10

SF	001 010 001	3 8 2
NY	000 101 03X	5 6 0

Pitchers: SANFORD, Miller (8) vs TERRY
Home Runs: Pagan-SF, Tresh-NY
Attendance: 63,165

GAME 6 AT SF OCT 15

NY	000 010 010	2 3 2
SF	000 320 00X	5 10 1

Pitchers: FORD, Coates (5), Bridges (8) vs PIERCE
Home Runs: Maris-NY
Attendance: 43,948

GAME 7 AT SF OCT 16

NY	000 100 000	1 7 0
SF	000 000 000	0 4 1

Pitchers: TERRY vs SANFORD, O'Dell (8)
Attendance: 43,948

The Yankees won the American League pennant by 10½ games, but in the Series they were overwhelmed by Dodger pitching. The opener pitted two all-time greats against each other: Yankee Whitey Ford (24–7 that season) and Sandy Koufax (25–5). For an inning it was close. Ford fanned two of the first three batters to face him, and Koufax struck out the side. But in the top of the second the Dodgers' Frank Howard doubled with one out, and before Ford could record the second out, two singles and John Roseboro's home run had put four Dodger runs across. Koufax ran his consecutive Ks to five and had tied the Series single-game record of 14 by the time Tom Tresh tagged him for a two-run homer in the eighth. That was New York's only scoring, and Koufax ended the game with a new-record fifteenth strikeout an inning later.

Veteran Johnny Podres pitched shutout ball through 8⅓ innings of Game Two as his Dodgers built him a four-run lead (one of the runs a homer by ex-Yankee Bill Skowron). New York scored a run in the last of the ninth, but it was not enough to keep the Dodgers from returning to Los Angeles with a 2–0 Series advantage.

A first-inning walk, a wild pitch, and a single moved Dodger Jim Gilliam around the bases for the only scoring in Game Three as Yankee Jim Bouton hooked up in a duel with Don Drysdale. Bouton left after seven innings for Yankee relief ace Hal Reniff, who held Los Angeles hitless through the final frames. When Drysdale completed his shutout, only three singles had been hit against him, and he had struck out nine.

Ford and Koufax tangled again in the fourth game. Ford pitched much more impressively than he had in the opener, walking just one and yielding only two hits in seven innings. One of the Dodger hits was Frank Howard's solo homer in the fifth inning, but Mickey Mantle evened the score with a home run off Koufax in the seventh. But in the last of the seventh, Yankee first baseman Joe Pepitone lost sight of a throw from the third baseman for an error that sent batter Jim Gilliam all the way to third, and Willie Davis followed with a fly to center that scored Gilliam with the go-ahead run. No one else scored against Ford (or Reniff, who relieved him in the eighth), but no other Yankee scored against Koufax either, and the Dodgers, with just two hits, captured the game and the Series.

Los Angeles Dodgers (NL), 4; New York Yankees (AL), 0

LA (N)

PLAYER/POS	AVG	G	AB	R	H	2B	3B	HR	RB	BB	SO	SB
Tommy Davis, of	.400	4	15	0	6	0	2	0	2	0	2	1
Willie Davis, of	.167	4	12	2	2	2	0	0	3	0	6	0
Don Drysdale, p	.000	1	1	0	0	0	0	0	0	2	0	0
Ron Fairly, of	.000	4	1	0	0	0	0	0	0	3	0	0
Jim Gilliam, 3b	.154	4	13	3	2	0	0	0	0	3	1	0
Frank Howard, of	.300	3	10	2	3	1	0	1	1	0	2	0
Sandy Koufax, p	.000	2	6	0	0	0	0	0	0	0	2	0
Ron Perranoski, p	.000	1	0	0.	0	0	0	0	0	0	0	0
Johnny Podres, p	.250	1	4	0	1	0	0	0	0	0	0	0
Johnny Roseboro, c	.143	4	14	1	2	0	0	1	3	0	4	0
Bill Skowron, 1b	.385	4	13	2	5	0	0	1	3	1	3	0
Dick Tracewski, 2b	.154	4	13	1	2	0	0	0	0	1	2	0
Maury Wills, ss	.133	4	15	1	2	0	0	0	0	1	3	1
TOTAL	.214		117	12	25	3	2	3	12	11	25	2

PITCHER	W	L	ERA	G	GS	CG	SV	SHO	IP	H	ER	BB	SO
Don Drysdale	1	0	0.00	1	1	1	0	1	9.0	3	0	1	9
Sandy Koufax	2	0	1.50	2	2	2	0	0	18.0	12	3	3	23
Ron Perranoski	0	0	0.00	1	0	0	1	0	0.2	1	0	0	1
Johnny Podres	1	0	1.08	1	1	0	0	0	8.1	6	1	1	4
TOTAL	4	0	1.00	5	4	3	1	1	36.0	22	4	5	37

NY (A)

PLAYER/POS	AVG	G	AB	R	H	2B	3B	HR	RB	BB	SO	SB
Yogi Berra, ph	.000	1	1	0	0	0	0	0	0	0	0	0
Johnny Blanchard, of-1	.000	1	3	0	0	0	0	0	0	0	0	0
Jim Bouton, p	.000	1	2	0	0	0	0	0	0	0	2	0
Clete Boyer, 3b	.077	4	13	0	1	0	0	0	0	1	6	0
Harry Bright, ph	.000	2	2	0	0	0	0	0	0	0	2	0
Al Downing, p	.000	1	1	0	0	0	0	0	0	0	1	0
Whitey Ford, p	.000	2	3	0	0	0	0	0	0	0	0	0
Steve Hamilton, p	.000	1	0	0	0	0	0	0	0	0	0	0
Elston Howard, c	.333	4	15	0	5	0	0	0	1	0	3	0
Tony Kubek, ss	.188	4	16	1	3	0	0	0	0	0	3	0
Phil Linz, ph	.333	3	3	0	1	0	0	0	0	0	1	0
Hector Lopez, of-2	.250	3	8	1	2	2	0	0	0	0	1	0
Mickey Mantle, of	.133	4	15	1	2	0	0	1	1	1	5	0
Roger Maris, of	.000	2	5	0	0	0	0	0	0	0	1	0
Joe Pepitone, 1b	.154	4	13	0	2	0	0	0	0	1	3	0
Hal Reniff, p	.000	3	0	0	0	0	0	0	0	0	0	0
Bobby Richardson, 2b	.214	4	14	0	3	1	0	0	0	1	3	0
Ralph Terry, p	.000	1	0	0	0	0	0	0	0	0	0	0
Tom Tresh, of	.200	4	15	1	3	0	0	1	2	1	6	0
Stan Williams, p	.000	1	0	0	0	0	0	0	0	0	0	0
TOTAL	.171		129	4	22	3	0	2	4	5	37	0

PITCHER	W	L	ERA	G	GS	CG	SV	SHO	IP	H	ER	BB	SO
Jim Bouton	0	1	1.29	1	1	0	0	0	7.0	4	1	5	4
Al Downing	0	1	5.40	1	1	0	0	0	5.0	7	3	1	6
Whitey Ford	0	2	4.50	2	2	0	0	0	12.0	10	6	3	8
Steve Hamilton	0	0	0.00	1	0	0	0	0	1.0	0	0	0	1
Hal Reniff	0	0	0.00	3	0	0	0	0	3.0	0	0	1	1
Ralph Terry	0	0	3.00	1	0	0	0	0	3.0	3	1	1	0
Stan Williams	0	0	0.00	1	0	0	0	0	3.0	1	0	0	5
TOTAL	0	4	2.91	10	4	0	0	0	34.0	25	11	11	25

GAME 1 AT NY OCT 2

LA	041 000 000	5	9	0
NY	000 000 020	2	6	0

Pitchers: KOUFAX vs FORD, Williams (6), Hamilton (9)
Home Runs: Roseboro-LA, Tresh-NY
Attendance: 69,000

GAME 2 AT NY OCT 3

LA	200 100 010	4	10	1
NY	000 000 001	1	7	0

Pitchers: PODRES, Perranoski (9) vs DOWNING, Terry (6), Reniff (9)
Home Runs: Skowron-LA
Attendance: 66,455

GAME 3 AT LA OCT 5

NY	000 000 000	0	3	0
LA	100 000 00X	1	4	1

Pitchers: BOUTON, Reniff (8) vs DRYSDALE
Attendance: 55,912

GAME 4 AT LA OCT 6

NY	000 000 100	1	6	1
LA	000 010 10X	2	2	1

Pitchers: FORD, Reniff (8) vs KOUFAX
Home Runs: F.Howard-LA, Mantle-NY
Attendance: 55,912

With late-season spurts the Cardinals edged the Reds and Phillies for their first pennant in eighteen years and the Yankees overtook the White Sox and Orioles for their fifteenth in eighteen years and their twenty-ninth over all. But when the Series was over, the long era of Yankee dominance had come to an end.

St. Louis won the opener, a 24-hit slugfest in which Curt Flood's RBI triple in the sixth proved the decisive blow. But New York came back to take the next two games. Rookie Mel Stottlemyre won Game Two, holding the Cards to three runs as his Yankees scored eight. (Loser Bob Gibson struck out nine Yankees, though, on his way to a new Series record of 31.) Game Three, by contrast, featured a pitchers' duel between Jim Bouton and Cardinal veteran Curt Simmons. Cardinal reliever Barney Schultz, who replaced Simmons for the last of the ninth with the score 1–1, lost the game on his first pitch when Mickey Mantle homered to deep right (his sixteenth World Series home run, which moved him ahead of Babe Ruth into the all-time Series lead).

Cardinal Ray Sadecki (the winner in Game One) left with one out in the first inning of Game Four after four Yankee batters hit safely, but relievers Roger Craig and Ron Taylor stopped New York on just two singles the rest of the way. The Cards were also held to six hits, but one was Ken Boyer's grand slam in the sixth, which erased a 3–0 Yankee lead and gave St. Louis runs enough to even the Series at two games apiece.

Gibson and Stottlemyre faced off a second time in Game Five. Gibson carried a 2–0 lead into the last of the ninth, when with two out Tom Tresh tagged him for a game-tying home run. In the top of the tenth, though, the Cards regained the lead on Tim McCarver's three-run homer and held on for the win as Gibson notched his thirteenth K of the game.

Bouton and Simmons tangled again in Game Five. Another 1–1 duel was shattered this time in the top of the sixth when Roger Maris and Mantle tagged Simmons for back-to-back home runs. New York put the game away in the eighth with five runs off Cardinal relievers—four of them on Joe Pepitone's grand slam.

With the series tied 3–3, Gibson and Stottlemyre were called upon to settle the title. Gibson pitched the whole game, striking out nine. Mantle touched him for a three-run homer in the sixth inning, and Clete Boyer and Phil Linz hit solo shots in the ninth. But as St. Louis had scored six times off Stottlemyre and his replacement Al Downing before the Yankees

scored their first runs, the game ended with the Cards victors and world champions. Yogi Berra, New York's rookie manager, was fired the next day. The following season the Yankees finished sixth.

St. Louis Cardinals (NL), 4; New York Yankees (AL), 3

STL (N)

PLAYER/POS	AVG	G	AB	R	H	2B	3B	HR	RB	BB	SO	SB
Ken Boyer, 3b	.222	7	27	5	6	1	0	2	6	1	5	0
Lou Brock, of	.300	7	30	2	9	2	0	1	5	0	3	0
Gerry Buchek, 2b	1.000	4	1	1	1	0	0	0	0	0	0	0
Roger Craig, p	.000	2	1	0	0	0	0	0	0	0	0	0
Curt Flood, of	.200	7	30	5	6	0	1	0	3	3	1	0
Bob Gibson, p	.222	3	9	1	2	0	0	0	0	0	3	0
Dick Groat, ss	.192	7	26	3	5	1	1	0	1	4	3	0
Bob Humphreys, p	.000	1	0	0	0	0	0	0	0	0	0	0
Charlie James, ph	.000	3	3	0	0	0	0	0	0	0	1	0
Julian Javier, 2b	.000	1	0	1	0	0	0	0	0	0	0	0
Dal Maxvill, 2b	.200	7	20	0	4	1	0	0	1	1	4	0
Tim McCarver, c	.478	7	23	4	11	1	1	1	5	5	1	1
Gordie Richardson, p	.000	2	0	0	0	0	0	0	0	0	0	0
Ray Sadecki, p	.500	2	2	0	1	0	0	0	0	1	0	0
Barney Schultz, p	.000	4	1	0	0	0	0	0	0	0	0	0
Mike Shannon, of	.214	7	28	6	6	0	0	1	2	0	9	1
Curt Simmons, p	.500	2	4	0	2	0	0	0	1	0	1	0
Bob Skinner, ph	.667	4	3	0	2	1	0	0	1	1	0	0
Ron Taylor, p	.000	2	1	0	0	0	0	0	0	0	1	0
Carl Warwick, ph	.750	5	4	2	3	0	0	0	1	1	0	0
Bill White, 1b	.111	7	27	2	3	1	0	0	2	2	6	1
TOTAL	.254		240	32	61	8	3	5	29	18	39	3

PITCHER	W	L	ERA	G	GS	CG	SV	SHO	IP	H	ER	BB	SO
Roger Craig	1	0	0.00	2	0	0	0	0	5.0	2	0	3	9
Bob Gibson	2	1	3.00	3	3	2	0	0	27.0	23	9	8	31
Bob Humphreys	0	0	0.00	1	0	0	0	0	1.0	0	0	0	1
Gordie Richardson	0	0	40.50	2	0	0	0	0	0.2	3	3	2	0
Ray Sadecki	1	0	8.53	2	2	0	0	0	6.1	12	6	5	2
Barney Schultz	0	1	18.00	4	0	0	0	0	4.0	9	8	3	1
Curt Simmons	0	1	2.51	2	2	0	0	0	14.1	11	4	3	8
Ron Taylor	0	0	0.00	2	0	0	0	0	4.2	0	0	1	2
TOTAL	4	3	4.29	18	7	2	2	0	63.0	60	30	25	54

NY (A)

PLAYER/POS	AVG	G	AB	R	H	2B	3B	HR	RB	BB	SO	SB
Johnny Blanchard, ph	.250	4	4	0	1	1	0	0	0	0	1	0
Jim Bouton, p	.143	2	7	0	1	0	0	0	1	0	2	0
Clete Boyer, 3b	.208	7	24	2	5	1	0	1	3	1	5	1
Al Downing, p	.000	3	2	0	0	0	0	0	0	0	2	0
Whitey Ford, p	1.000	1	1	0	1	0	0	0	0	1	2	0
Pedro Gonzalez, 3b	.000	1	1	0	0	0	0	0	0	0	0	0
Steve Hamilton, p	.000	2	0	0	0	0	0	0	0	0	0	0
Mike Hegan, ph	.000	3	1	1	0	0	0	0	0	1	1	0
Elston Howard, c	.292	7	24	5	7	1	0	0	2	4	6	0
Phil Linz, ss	.226	7	31	5	7	1	0	2	2	2	5	0
Hector Lopez, of-1	.000	3	2	0	0	0	0	0	0	0	2	0
Mickey Mantle, of	.333	7	24	8	8	2	0	3	8	6	8	0
Roger Maris, of	.200	7	30	4	6	0	0	1	1	1	4	0
Pete Mikkelsen, p	.000	4	0	0	0	0	0	0	0	0	0	0
Joe Pepitone, 1b	.154	7	26	1	4	1	0	1	5	2	3	0
Hal Reniff, p	.000	1	0	0	0	0	0	0	0	0	0	0
Bobby Richardson, 2b	.406	7	32	3	13	2	0	0	3	0	2	1
Rollie Sheldon, p	.000	2	0	0	0	0	0	0	0	0	0	0
Mel Stottlemyre, p	.125	3	8	0	1	0	0	0	0	0	6	0
Ralph Terry, p	.000	1	0	0	0	0	0	0	0	0	0	0
Tom Tresh, of	.273	7	22	4	6	2	0	2	7	6	7	0
TOTAL	.251		239	33	60	11	0	10	33	25	54	2

PITCHER	W	L	ERA	G	GS	CG	SV	SHO	IP	H	ER	BB	SO
Jim Bouton	2	0	1.56	2	2	1	0	0	17.1	15	3	5	7
Al Downing	0	1	8.22	3	1	0	0	0	7.2	9	7	2	5
Whitey Ford	0	1	8.44	1	1	0	0	0	5.1	8	5	1	4
Steve Hamilton	0	0	4.50	2	0	0	0	1	2.0	3	1	0	2
Pete Mikkelsen	0	1	5.79	4	0	0	0	0	4.2	4	3	2	4
Hal Reniff	0	0	0.00	1	0	0	0	0	0.1	2	0	0	0
Rollie Sheldon	0	0	0.00	2	0	0	0	0	2.2	0	0	2	2
Mel Stottlemyre	1	1	3.15	3	3	1	0	0	20.0	18	7	6	12
Ralph Terry	0	0	0.00	1	0	0	0	0	2.0	2	0	0	3
TOTAL	3	4	3.77	19	7	2	1	0	62.0	61	26	18	39

GAME 1 AT STL OCT 7

NY	030 010 010	5	12	2
STL	110 004 03X	9	12	0

Pitchers: FORD, Downing (6), Sheldon (8), Mikkelsen (9) vs SADECKI, Schultz (7)
Home Runs: Tresh-NY, Shannon-STL
Attendance: 30,805

GAME 2 AT STL OCT 8

NY	000 101 204	8	12	0
STL	001 000 011	3	7	0

Pitchers: STOTTLEMYRE vs GIBSON, Schultz (9), Craig (9)
Home Runs: Linz-NY
Attendance: 30,805

GAME 3 AT NY OCT 10

STL	000 010 000	1	6	0
NY	010 000 001	2	5	2

Pitchers: Simmons, SCHULTZ (9) vs BOUTON
Home Runs: Mantle-NY
Attendance: 67,101

GAME 4 AT NY OCT 11

STL	000 004 000	4	6	1
NY	300 000 000	3	6	1

Pitchers: Sadecki, CRAIG (1), Taylor (6) vs DOWNING, Mikkelsen (7), Terry (8)
Home Runs: K.Boyer-STL
Attendance: 66,312

GAME 5 AT NY OCT 12

STL	000 020 000 3	5	10	1
NY	000 000 002 0	2	6	2

Pitchers: GIBSON vs Stottlemyre, Reniff (8), MIKKELSEN (8)
Home Runs: Tresh-NY, McCarver-STL
Attendance: 65,633

GAME 6 AT STL OCT 14

NY	000 012 050	8	10	0
STL	100 000 011	3	10	1

Pitchers: BOUTON, Hamilton (9) vs SIMMONS, Taylor (7), Schultz (8), Richardson (8), Humphreys (9)
Home Runs: Maris-NY, Mantle-NY, Pepitone-NY
Attendance: 30,805

GAME 7 AT STL OCT 15

NY	000 003 002	5	9	2
STL	000 330 10X	7	10	1

Pitchers: STOTTLEMYRE, Downing (5), Sheldon (5), Hamilton (7), Mikkelsen (8) vs GIBSON
Home Runs: Brock-STL, Mantle-NY, K.Boyer-STL, C.Boyer-NY, Linz-NY
Attendance: 30,346

The Twins (bringing the World Series to Minnesota for the first time ever) featured heavy hitting, while Dodger hopes rested on great pitching and speed on the bases. For a while it looked as if batting power would triumph as the Twins took the first two games at home. They drove out Dodger starter Don Drysdale with seven runs in the first three innings of the opener—including home runs by Don Mincher and Zoilo Versalles—on the way to a convincing 8–2 win, and followed up with a 5–1 triumph the next day over Dodger ace Sandy Koufax (who had declined to pitch Game One on Yom Kippur, the holiest day of the Jewish year) and star reliever Ron Perranoski, who was tagged for three of the Twins' runs.

But when the Series moved to Los Angeles, Dodger pitching began to assert itself. Claude Osteen held Minnesota to five hits and no runs, while Los Angeles bunched seven of their ten hits in the middle three innings for four runs. Drysdale evened the Series in Game Four, avenging his first-game pounding with a second Dodger five-hitter. Twins Harmon Killebrew and Tony Oliva tagged him for a pair of solo homers, but that was Minnesota's only scoring—more than balanced by seven Dodger runs, including homers by Wes Parker and Lou Johnson. In Game Five the next day, Koufax avenged his earlier loss, carrying Los Angeles to its first Series lead with a shutout in which he allowed only four singles and a walk, while fanning ten Twins. Speedster Willie Davis stole three bases and Maury Wills stole another as the Dodgers parlayed fourteen hits into a 7–0 victory.

Back in Minnesota for Game Six, the Twins rallied, using the long ball to even the Series again with a 5–1 win. Bob Allison opened the scoring with a two-run shot off Dodger starter Claude Osteen in the fourth, and Minnesota pitcher Mudcat Grant insured his own win with a three-run blast two innings later.

In the finale, though, the visiting team won for the only time in the Series. Koufax again struck out ten men, stopping the Twins on three hits for his second shutout. Lou Johnson's second Series homer (a fourth-inning solo shot to left off Twin starter Jim Kaat that was barely fair) was all the Dodgers needed for their fifth world championship, but Ron Fairly followed Johnson with a double and Wes Parker singled home an insurance run that drove Kaat out and concluded the Series scoring.

Los Angeles Dodgers (NL), 4; Minnesota Twins (AL), 3

LA (N)

PLAYER/POS	AVG	G	AB	R	H	2B	3B	HR	RB	BB	SO	SB
Jim Brewer, p	.000	1	0	0	0	0	0	0	0	0	0	0
Willie Crawford, ph	.500	2	2	0	1	0	0	0	0	0	1	0
Willie Davis, of	.231	7	26	3	6	0	0	0	0	0	2	3
Don Drysdale, p-2	.000	3	5	0	0	0	0	0	0	0	4	0
Ron Fairly, of	.379	7	29	7	11	3	0	2	6	0	1	0
Jim Gilliam, 3b	.214	7	28	2	6	1	0	0	2	1	0	0
Lou Johnson, of	.296	7	27	3	8	2	0	2	4	1	3	0
John Kennedy, 3b	.000	4	1	0	0	0	0	0	0	0	0	0
Sandy Koufax, p	.111	3	9	0	1	0	0	0	1	1	5	0
Jim Lefebvre, 2b	.400	3	10	2	4	0	0	0	0	0	0	0
Don LeJohn, ph	.000	1	1	0	0	0	0	0	0	0	1	0
Bob Miller, p	.000	2	0	0	0	0	0	0	0	0	0	0
Wally Moon, ph	.000	2	2	0	0	0	0	0	0	0	0	0
Claude Osteen, p	.333	2	3	0	1	0	0	0	0	0	0	0
Wes Parker, 1b	.304	7	23	3	7	0	1	1	2	3	3	2
Ron Perranoski, p	.000	2	0	0	0	0	0	0	0	0	0	0
Howie Reed, p	.000	2	0	0	0	0	0	0	0	0	0	0
Johnny Roseboro, c	.286	7	21	1	6	1	0	0	3	5	3	1
Dick Tracewski, 2b	.118	6	17	0	2	0	0	0	0	1	5	0
Maury Wills, ss	.367	7	30	3	11	3	0	0	3	1	3	3
TOTAL	.274		234	24	64	10	1	5	21	13	31	9

PITCHER	W	L	ERA	G	GS	CG	SV	SHO	IP	H	ER	BB	SO
Jim Brewer	0	0	4.50	1	0	0	0	0	2.0	3	1	0	1
Don Drysdale	1	1	3.86	2	2	1	0	0	11.2	12	5	3	15
Sandy Koufax	2	1	0.38	3	3	2	0	2	24.0	13	1	5	29
Bob Miller	0	0	0.00	2	0	0	0	0	1.1	0	0	0	0
Claude Osteen	1	1	0.64	2	2	1	0	1	14.0	9	1	5	4
Ron Perranoski	0	0	7.36	2	0	0	0	0	3.2	3	3	4	1
Howie Reed	0	0	8.10	2	0	0	0	0	3.1	2	3	2	4
TOTAL	4	3	2.10	14	7	4	0	3	60.0	42	14	19	54

MIN (A)

PLAYER/POS	AVG	G	AB	R	H	2B	3B	HR	RB	BB	SO	SB
Bob Allison, of	.125	5	16	3	2	1	0	1	2	2	9	1
Earl Battey, c	.120	7	25	1	3	0	1	0	2	0	5	0
Dave Boswell, p	.000	1	0	0	0	0	0	0	0	0	0	0
Mudcat Grant, p	.250	3	8	3	2	1	0	1	3	0	1	0
Jimmie Hall, of	.143	2	7	0	1	0	0	0	0	1	5	0
Jim Kaat, p	.167	3	6	0	1	0	0	0	2	0	5	0
Harmon Killebrew, 3b	.286	7	21	2	6	0	0	1	2	6	4	0
Johnny Klippstein, p	.000	2	0	0	0	0	0	0	0	0	0	0
Jim Merritt, p	.000	2	0	0	0	0	0	0	0	0	0	0
Don Mincher, 1b	.130	7	23	3	3	0	0	1	1	2	7	0
Joe Nossek, of-5	.200	6	20	0	4	0	0	0	0	0	1	0
Tony Oliva, of	.192	7	26	2	5	1	0	1	2	1	6	0
Camilo Pascual, p	.000	1	1	0	0	0	0	0	0	0	0	0
Jim Perry, p	.000	2	0	0	0	0	0	0	0	0	0	0
Bill Pleis, p	.000	1	0	0	0	0	0	0	0	0	0	0
Frank Quilici, 2b	.200	7	20	2	4	2	0	0	1	4	3	0
Rich Rollins, ph	.000	3	2	0	0	0	0	0	0	1	0	0
Sandy Valdespino, of-2	.273	5	11	1	3	1	0	0	0	0	1	0
Zoilo Versalles, ss	.286	7	28	3	8	1	1	1	4	2	7	1
Al Worthington, p	.000	2	0	0	0	0	0	0	0	0	0	0
Jerry Zimmerman, c	.000	2	1	0	0	0	0	0	0	0	0	0
TOTAL	.195		215	20	42	7	2	6	19	19	54	2

PITCHER	W	L	ERA	G	GS	CG	SV	SHO	IP	H	ER	BB	SO
Dave Boswell	1	0	3.38	1	0	0	0	0	2.2	3	1	2	3
Mudcat Grant	2	1	2.74	3	3	2	0	0	23.0	22	7	2	12
Jim Kaat	1	2	3.77	3	3	1	0	0	14.1	18	6	2	6
Johnny Klippstein	0	0	0.00	2	0	0	0	0	2.2	2	0	2	3
Jim Merritt	0	0	2.70	2	0	0	0	0	3.1	2	1	0	1
Camilo Pascual	0	1	5.40	1	1	0	0	0	5.0	8	3	1	0
Jim Perry	0	0	4.50	2	0	0	0	0	4.0	5	2	2	4
Bill Pleis	0	0	9.00	1	0	0	0	0	1.0	2	1	0	0
Al Worthington	0	0	0.00	2	0	0	0	0	4.0	2	0	2	2
TOTAL	4	4	3.15	17	7	3	0	0	60.0	64	21	13	31

GAME 1 AT MIN OCT 6

LA	010	000	001	2	10	1
MIN	016	001	00X	8	10	0

Pitchers: DRYSDALE, Reed (3), Brewer (5), Perranoski (7) vs GRANT
Home Runs: Fairly-LA, Mincher-MIN, Versalles-MIN
Attendance: 47,797

GAME 2 AT MIN OCT 7

LA	000	000	100	1	7	3
MIN	000	002	12X	5	9	0

Pitchers: KOUFAX, Perranoski (7), Miller (8) vs KAAT
Attendance: 48,700

GAME 3 AT LA OCT 9

MIN	000	000	000	0	5	0
LA	000	211	00X	4	10	1

Pitchers: PASCUAL, Merritt (6), Klippstein (8) vs OSTEEN
Attendance: 55,934

GAME 4 AT LA OCT 10

MIN	000	101	000	2	5	2
LA	110	103	01X	7	10	0

Pitchers: GRANT, Worthington (6), Pleis (8) vs DRYSDALE
Home Runs: Killebrew-MIN, Parker-LA, Oliva-MIN, Johnson-LA
Attendance: 55,920

GAME 5 AT LA OCT 11

MIN	000	000	000	0	4	1
LA	202	100	20X	7	14	0

Pitchers: KAAT, Boswell (3), Perry (6) vs KOUFAX
Attendance: 55,801

GAME 6 AT MIN OCT 13

LA	000	000	100	1	6	1
MIN	000	203	00X	5	6	1

Pitchers: OSTEEN, Reed (6), Miller (8) vs GRANT
Home Runs: Allison-MIN, Grant-MIN, Fairly-LA
Attendance: 49,578

GAME 7 AT MIN OCT 14

LA	000	200	000	2	7	0
MIN	000	000	000	0	3	1

Pitchers: KOUFAX vs KAAT, Worthington (4), Klippstein (6), Merritt (7), Perry (9)
Home Runs: Johnson-LA
Attendance: 50,596

The Orioles, with their first pennant since moving from St. Louis in 1954, won the franchise's first World Series ever, crushing NL repeater Los Angeles in four games. Back-to-back home runs by Frank and Brooks Robinson in the top of the first inning of the opener gave Baltimore a quick three-run lead, and the O's added a fourth run an inning later before the Dodgers attempted to come back with single runs in the second and third innings. But by then Oriole reliever Moe Drabowsky had come on to pitch, and he stopped the Dodgers on one hit the rest of the way, striking out eleven (including six in a row in the fourth and fifth innings). The Dodgers would not score again in the Series.

Sophomore Jim Palmer (a week shy of his twenty-first birthday) hurled a four-hit shutout at Los Angeles in Game Two, defeating the great—but critically sore-armed—Sandy Koufax, who, though only thirty years old himself, was pitching the final game of his career. Three errors by center fielder Willie Davis in the fifth (including a pair of flies lost in the sun) led to three unearned runs—the first scoring against Koufax. Frank Robinson's leadoff triple in the sixth and Boog Powell's single gave the Orioles an earned run before a double play ended the inning. Koufax was replaced after the inning by a succession of Dodger relievers as Baltimore went on to win 6–0.

Wally Bunker did the honors for the Orioles in Game Three, emerging the victor of a pitching duel with Dodger Claude Osteen on the strength of a fifth-inning home run by Paul Blair, a tremendous 430-foot shot to left. Osteen yielded only two other Orioles hits—both singles—in his seven innings, and Dodger reliever Phil Regan retired the side in the eighth. But one run was all Bunker needed for his shutout win.

Dave McNally, who had given up the Dodgers' only Series runs in Game One, mended his ways with a four-hit shutout in Game Four. He needed the shutout for the Oriole sweep, for Dodger Don Drysdale was also in top form. Drysdale, too, gave up only four hits. But one of them was Frank Robinson's second home run of the Series, a fourth-inning solo shot to left for the game's only scoring.

Baltimore Orioles (AL), 4;
Los Angeles Dodgers (NL) 0

BAL (A)

PLAYER/POS	AVG	G	AB	R	H	2B	3B	HR	RB	BB	SO	SB
Luis Aparicio, ss	.250	4	16	0	4	1	0	0	2	0	0	0
Paul Blair, of	.167	4	6	2	1	0	0	1	1	1	0	0
Curt Blefary, of	.077	4	13	0	1	0	0	0	0	2	3	0
Wally Bunker, p	.000	1	2	0	0	0	0	0	0	0	1	0
Moe Drabowsky, p	.000	1	2	0	0	0	0	0	0	1	1	0
Andy Etchebarren, c	.083	4	12	2	1	0	0	0	0	2	4	0
Davey Johnson, 2b	.286	4	14	1	4	1	0	0	1	0	1	0
Dave McNally, p	.000	2	3	0	0	0	0	0	0	0	1	0
Jim Palmer, p	.000	1	4	0	0	0	0	0	0	0	2	0
Boog Powell, 1b	.357	4	14	1	5	1	0	0	1	0	1	0
Brooks Robinson, 3b	.214	4	14	2	3	0	0	1	1	1	0	0
Frank Robinson, of	.286	4	14	4	4	0	1	2	3	2	3	0
Russ Snyder, of	.167	3	6	1	1	0	0	0	1	2	0	0
TOTAL	.200		120	13	24	3	1	4	10	11	17	0

PITCHER	W	L	ERA	G	GS	CG	SV	SHO	IP	H	ER	BB	SO
Wally Bunker	1	0	0.00	1	1	1	0	1	9.0	6	0	1	6
Moe Drabowsky	1	0	0.00	1	0	0	0	0	6.2	1	0	2	11
Dave McNally	1	0	1.59	2	2	1	0	1	11.1	6	2	7	5
Jim Palmer	1	0	0.00	1	1	1	0	1	9.0	4	0	3	6
TOTAL	4	0	0.50	5	4	3	0	3	36.0	17	2	13	28

LA (N)

PLAYER/POS	AVG	G	AB	R	H	2B	3B	HR	RB	BB	SO	SB
Jim Barbieri, ph	.000	1	1	0	0	0	0	0	0	0	1	0
Jim Brewer, p	.000	1	0	0	0	0	0	0	0	0	0	0
Wes Covington, ph	.000	1	1	0	0	0	0	0	0	0	1	0
Tommy Davis, of-3	.250	4	8	0	2	0	0	0	0	1	1	0
Willie Davis, of	.063	4	16	0	1	0	0	0	0	0	4	0
Don Drysdale, p	.000	2	2	0	0	0	0	0	0	0	1	0
Ron Fairly, of-2,1b-1	.143	3	7	0	1	0	0	0	0	2	4	0
Al Ferrara, ph	1.000	1	1	0	1	0	0	0	0	0	0	0
Jim Gilliam, 3b	.000	2	6	0	0	0	0	0	1	2	0	0
Lou Johnson, of	.267	4	15	1	4	1	0	0	0	1	1	0
John Kennedy, 3b	.200	2	5	0	1	0	0	0	0	0	0	0
Sandy Koufax, p	.000	1	2	0	0	0	0	0	0	0	0	0
Jim Lefebvre, 2b	.167	4	12	1	2	0	0	1	1	3	4	0
Bob Miller, p	.000	1	0	0	0	0	0	0	0	0	0	0
Joe Moeller, p	.000	1	0	0	0	0	0	0	0	0	0	0
Nate Oliver, pr	.000	1	0	0	0	0	0	0	0	0	0	0
Claude Osteen, p	.000	1	2	0	0	0	0	0	0	0	1	0
Wes Parker, 1b	.231	4	13	0	3	2	0	0	0	1	3	0
Ron Perranoski, p	.000	2	0	0	0	0	0	0	0	0	0	0
Phil Regan, p	.000	2	0	0	0	0	0	0	0	0	0	0
Johnny Roseboro, c	.071	4	14	0	1	0	0	0	0	0	3	0
Dick Stuart, ph	.000	2	2	0	0	0	0	0	0	0	1	0
Maury Wills, ss	.077	4	13	0	1	0	0	0	0	3	3	1
TOTAL	.142		120	2	17	3	0	1	2	13	28	1

PITCHER	W	L	ERA	G	GS	CG	SV	SHO	IP	H	ER	BB	SO
Jim Brewer	0	0	0.00	1	0	0	0	0	1.0	0	0	0	1
Don Drysdale	0	2	4.50	2	2	1	0	0	10.0	8	5	3	6
Sandy Koufax	0	1	1.50	1	1	0	0	0	6.0	6	1	2	2
Bob Miller	0	0	0.00	1	0	0	0	0	3.0	2	0	2	1
Joe Moeller	0	0	4.50	1	0	0	0	0	2.0	1	1	1	0
Claude Osteen	0	1	1.29	1	1	0	0	0	7.0	3	1	1	3
Ron Perranoski	0	0	5.40	2	0	0	0	0	3.1	4	2	1	2
Phil Regan	0	0	0.00	2	0	0	0	0	1.2	0	0	1	2
TOTAL	0	4	2.65	11	4	1	0	0	34.0	24	10	11	17

GAME 1 AT LA OCT 5

BAL	310 100 000	5	9 0
LA	011 000 000	2	3 0

Pitchers: McNally, DRABOWSKY (3) vs DRYSDALE, Moeller (3), Miller (5), Perranoski (8)
Home Runs: F.Robinson-BAL, B.Robinson-BAL, Lefebvre-LA
Attendance: 55,941

GAME 2 AT LA OCT 6

BAL	000 031 020	6	8 0
LA	000 000 000	0	4 6

Pitchers: PALMER vs KOUFAX, Perranoski (7), Regan (8), Brewer (9)
Attendance: 55,947

GAME 3 AT BAL OCT 8

LA	000 000 000	0	6 0
BAL	000 010 00X	1	3 0

Pitchers: OSTEEN, Regan (8) vs BUNKER
Home Runs: Blair-BAL
Attendance: 54,445

GAME 4 AT BAL OCT 9

LA	000 000 000	0	4 0
BAL	000 100 00X	1	4 0

Pitchers: DRYSDALE vs McNALLY
Home Runs: F.Robinson-BAL
Attendance: 54,458

The Cardinals cruised into the Series leading by 10½ games, whereas the Red Sox eked out their pennant over Minnesota and Detroit only by a dramatic win at season's end. The Sox continued to claw their way through six games of the Series before finally falling to superior pitching and hitting in the seventh game. Cardinal hurler Bob Gibson (who had missed a third of the season with a broken leg) edged Boston in the opener 2–1 with a six-hitter that included ten strikeouts. The only run against him came on a solo homer by opposing pitcher Jose Santiago in the third that tied the game. But Santiago was undone when Cardinal Lou Brock singled off him to open the seventh, then stole second, and moved around to score on a pair of ground outs.

Boston ace Jim Lonborg evened the Series the next day with a brilliant one-hit shutout. Sox Triple Crown winner Carl Yastrzemski accounted for four of Boston's five runs with homers in the fourth and seventh innings. Cardinal Nelson Briles outlasted a succession of Boston pitchers for a go-ahead 5–2 win in Game Three, and Gibson, with a five-hit shutout in Game Four, put St. Louis up three games to one.

But Boston's Lonborg kept Red Sox hopes alive with another pitching gem—a three-hitter in which the only extra-base hit was Roger Maris's harmless home run in the last of the ninth, after the Sox had already scored three runs (two of them unearned). Boston's bats came alive as the Series moved to Boston for Game Six, and the Sox evened the Series with an 8–4 win. The Cards used eight pitchers in a futile effort to hold off the Boston assault. Boston's score would have been greater had not all four Boston homers (including three in the fourth inning by Yastrzemski, Reggie Smith, and Rico Petrocelli—his second of the game) been solo shots.

With the Series tied at three-all, the Series' two-game winners, Gibson and Lonborg, faced off in the finale. It turned out to be no contest. Lonborg gave up ten hits and seven runs (including a homer by pitcher Gibson in the fifth and a three-run blast by Julian Javier an inning later) in six innings. Four Boston relievers held the Cards scoreless the rest of the game, but it was too late. Gibson's three-hitter included ten strikeouts and yielded only two Boston runs.

St. Louis Cardinals (NL), 4; Boston Red Sox (AL) 3

STL (N)

PLAYER/POS	AVG	G	AB	R	H	2B	3B	HR	RBI	BB	SO	SB
Eddie Bressoud, ss	.000	2	0	0	0	0	0	0	0	0	0	0
Nelson Briles, p	.000	2	3	0	0	0	0	0	0	0	0	0
Lou Brock, of	.414	7	29	8	12	2	1	1	3	2	3	7
Steve Carlton, p	.000	1	1	0	0	0	0	0	0	0	0	0
Orlando Cepeda, 1b	.103	7	29	1	3	2	0	0	1	0	4	0
Curt Flood, of	.179	7	28	2	5	1	0	0	3	3	3	0
Phil Gagliano, ph	.000	1	1	0	0	0	0	0	0	0	0	0
Bob Gibson, p	.091	3	11	1	1	0	0	1	1	1	2	0
Joe Hoerner, p	.000	2	0	0	0	0	0	0	0	0	0	0
Dick Hughes, p	.000	2	3	0	0	0	0	0	0	0	3	0
Larry Jaster, p	.000	1	0	0	0	0	0	0	0	0	0	0
Julian Javier, 2b	.360	7	25	2	9	3	0	1	4	0	6	0
Jack Lamabe, p	.000	3	0	0	0	0	0	0	0	0	0	0
Roger Maris, of	.385	7	26	3	10	1	0	1	7	3	1	0
Dal Maxvill, ss	.158	7	19	1	3	0	1	0	1	4	4	0
Tim McCarver, c	.125	7	24	3	3	1	0	0	2	2	2	0
Dave Ricketts, ph	.000	3	3	0	0	0	0	0	0	0	0	0
Mike Shannon, 3b	.208	7	24	3	5	1	0	1	2	1	4	0
Ed Spiezio, ph	.000	1	1	0	0	0	0	0	0	0	0	0
Bobby Tolan, ph	.000	3	2	1	0	0	0	0	0	1	1	0
Ray Washburn, p	.000	2	0	0	0	0	0	0	0	0	0	0
Ron Willis, p	.000	3	0	0	0	0	0	0	0	0	0	0
Hal Woodeshick, p	.000	1	0	0	0	0	0	0	0	0	0	0
TOTAL	.223		229	25	51	11	2	5	24	17	30	7

PITCHER	W	L	ERA	G	GS	CG	SV	SHO	IP	H	ER	BB	SO
Nelson Briles	1	0	1.64	2	1	1	0	0	11.0	7	2	1	4
Steve Carlton	0	1	0.00	1	1	0	0	0	6.0	3	0	2	5
Bob Gibson	3	0	1.00	3	3	3	0	1	27.0	14	3	5	26
Joe Hoerner	0	0	40.50	2	0	0	0	0	0.2	4	3	1	0
Dick Hughes	0	1	9.00	2	2	0	0	0	9.0	9	5	3	7
Larry Jaster	0	0	0.00	1	0	0	0	0	0.1	2	0	0	0
Jack Lamabe	0	1	6.75	3	0	0	0	0	2.2	5	2	0	4
Ray Washburn	0	0	0.00	2	1	0	0	0	2.1	1	0	1	2
Ron Willis	0	0	27.00	3	0	0	0	0	1.0	2	3	4	1
Hal Woodeshick	0	0	0.00	1	0	0	0	0	1.0	1	0	0	0
TOTAL	4	3	2.66	20	7	4	0	1	61.0	48	18	17	49

BOS (A)

PLAYER/POS	AVG	G	AB	R	H	2B	3B	HR	RBI	BB	SO	SB
Jerry Adair, 2b-4	.125	5	16	0	2	0	0	0	0	1	0	3	1
Mike Andrews, 2b-3	.308	5	13	2	4	0	0	0	1	0	1	0
Gary Bell, p	.000	3	0	0	0	0	0	0	0	0	0	0
Ken Brett, p	.000	2	0	0	0	0	0	0	0	0	0	0
Joe Foy, 3b-3	.133	6	15	2	2	1	0	0	1	1	5	0
Russ Gibson, c	.000	2	2	0	0	0	0	0	0	0	2	0
Ken Harrelson, of	.077	4	13	0	1	0	0	0	0	1	3	0
Elston Howard, c	.111	7	18	0	2	0	0	0	0	1	2	0
Dalton Jones, 3b-4	.389	6	18	2	7	0	0	0	1	1	3	0
Jim Lonborg, p	.000	3	9	0	0	0	0	0	0	0	7	0
Dave Morehead, p	.000	2	0	0	0	0	0	0	0	0	0	0
Dan Osinski, p	.000	2	0	0	0	0	0	0	0	0	0	0
Rico Petrocelli, ss	.200	7	20	3	4	1	0	2	3	3	8	0
Mike Ryan, c	.000	1	2	0	0	0	0	0	0	0	0	0
Jose Santiago, p	.500	3	2	1	1	0	0	1	1	0	1	0
George Scott, 1b	.231	7	26	3	6	1	1	0	0	3	6	0
Norm Siebern, of-1	.333	3	3	0	1	0	0	0	0	1	0	0
Reggie Smith, of	.250	7	24	3	6	1	0	2	3	2	2	0
Lee Stange, p	.000	1	0	0	0	0	0	0	0	0	0	0
Jerry Stephenson, p	.000	1	0	0	0	0	0	0	0	0	0	0
Jose Tartabull, of-6	.154	7	13	1	2	0	0	0	0	1	2	0
George Thomas, of-1	.000	2	2	0	0	0	0	0	0	0	1	0
Gary Waslewski, p	.000	2	1	0	0	0	0	0	0	0	1	0
John Wyatt, p	.000	2	0	0	0	0	0	0	0	0	0	0
Carl Yastrzemski, of	.400	7	25	4	10	2	0	3	5	4	1	0
TOTAL	.216		222	21	48	6	1	8	19	17	49	1

PITCHER	W	L	ERA	G	GS	CG	SV	SHO	IP	H	ER	BB	SO
Gary Bell	0	1	5.06	3	1	0	1	0	5.1	8	3	1	1
Ken Brett	0	0	0.00	2	0	0	0	0	1.1	0	0	1	1
Jim Lonborg	2	1	2.63	3	3	2	0	1	24.0	14	7	2	11
Dave Morehead	0	0	0.00	2	0	0	0	0	3.1	0	0	4	3
Dan Osinski	0	0	6.75	2	0	0	0	0	1.1	2	1	0	0
Jose Santiago	0	2	5.59	3	2	0	0	0	9.2	16	6	3	6
Lee Stange	0	0	0.00	1	0	0	0	0	2.0	3	0	0	0
Jerry Stephenson	0	0	9.00	1	0	0	0	0	2.0	3	2	1	0
Gary Waslewski	0	0	2.16	2	1	0	0	0	8.1	4	2	2	7
John Wyatt	1	0	4.91	2	0	0	0	0	3.2	1	2	3	1
TOTAL	3	4	3.39	21	7	2	1	1	61.0	51	23	17	30

GAME 1 AT BOS OCT 4

STL	001 000 100	2	10	0
BOS	001 000 000	1	6	0

Pitchers: GIBSON vs SANTIAGO, Wyatt (8)
Home Runs: Santiago-BOS
Attendance: 34,796

GAME 2 AT BOS OCT 5

STL	000 000 000	0	1	1
BOS	000 101 30X	5	9	0

Pitchers: HUGHES, Willis (6), Hoerner (7), Lamabe (7) vs LONBORG
Home Runs: Yastrzemski-BOS (2)
Attendance: 35,188

GAME 3 AT STL OCT 7

BOS	000 001 100	2	7	1
STL	120 001 01X	5	10	0

Pitchers: BELL, Waslewski (3), Stange (6), Osinski (8) vs BRILES
Home Runs: Shannon-STL, Smith-BOS
Attendance: 54,575

GAME 4 AT STL OCT 8

BOS	000 000 000	0	5	0
STL	402 000 00X	6	9	0

Pitchers: SANTIAGO, Bell (1), Stephenson (3), Morehead (5), Brett (8) vs GIBSON
Attendance: 54,575

GAME 5 AT STL OCT 9

BOS	001 000 002	3	6	1
STL	000 000 001	1	3	2

Pitchers: LONBORG vs CARLTON, Washburn (7), Willis (9), Lamabe (9)
Home Runs: Maris-STL
Attendance: 54,575

GAME 6 AT BOS OCT 11

STL	002 000 200	4	8	0
BOS	010 300 40X	8	12	1

Pitchers: Hughes, Willis (4), Briles (5), LAMABE (7), Hoerner (7), Jaster (7), Washburn (7), Woodeshick (8) vs Waslewski, WYATT (6), Bell (8)
Home Runs: Petrocelli-BOS (2), Yastrzemski-BOS, Smith-BOS, Brock-STL
Attendance: 35,188

GAME 7 AT BOS OCT 12

STL	002 023 000	7	10	1
BOS	000 010 010	2	3	1

Pitchers: GIBSON vs LONBORG, Santiago (7), Morehead (9), Osinski (9), Brett (9)
Home Runs: Gibson-STL, Javier-STL
Attendance: 35,188

In this "year of the pitcher," Tiger Denny McLain's 31 wins were the most for a major leaguer in thirty-seven years. Cardinal Bob Gibson's 1.12 ERA was the majors' best since Dutch Leonard's 1.01 in 1914, and his 13 season shutouts tied for third best of all time. In the Series, though, it was Detroit's second-best pitcher—Mickey Lolich—who emerged as the hero.

McLain came off second-best against Gibson in the opener. He yielded only three hits in his five innings, but two Cardinal singles in the fourth combined with a pair of walks and a Tiger error for three runs. Gibson, meanwhile, was in the process of striking out a Series-record 17 batters on the way to a five-hit shutout. But Lolich brought Detroit back in Game Two. He struck out nine, and his third-inning home run (the only one of his major league career) for the second Tiger run provided all the scoring needed for a Detroit victory, although the Tigers kept putting runs across for an eventual 8–1 win.

Home runs accounted for most of the scoring in Game Three. Veteran Al Kaline's two-run shot in the third gave Detroit the scoring, but Cardinal Tim McCarver's three-run blast in the fifth put St. Louis ahead. Tiger Dick McAuliffe's solo shot later in the inning brought Detroit within one run of a tie, but the Cardinals put the game away on Orlando Cepeda's three-run homer in the seventh.

McLain faced Gibson again in Game Four, and again came off second-best. Cardinal Lou Brock led off the game with a home run, and before the end of the third inning McLain was gone. Gibson gave up a solo homer to Tiger Jim Northrup in the fourth, but that was the only Detroit run he allowed. Gibson homered himself and struck out ten in an easy 10–1 win.

Down three games to one, the Tigers were saved from elimination by Lolich's arm. Although three Cardinal hits in the top of the first (including Orlando Cepeda's second homer of the Series) gave St. Louis a quick three runs, Lolich held the Cards scoreless the rest of the game as his Tigers fought back with two runs in the fourth and three more in the seventh (with a rally started by Lolich's single). McLain finally came through in Game Six, evening the Series with an easy 13–1 victory, in which Jim Northrup's grand slam provided the big blow of a ten-run third inning.

Lolich and Gibson—both 2–0 in the Series—faced off in the finale. Gibson broke his own World Series strikeout record in the third inning (finishing with 8 for the game and 35 for the Series), and both pitchers hurled shutout ball through six

innings. But four two-out Tiger hits in the top of the seventh—including a misplayed fly ball in center field—put three runs on the board, and another run in the ninth made the score 4–0. In the last of the ninth, Mike Shannon's solo homer spoiled Lolich's shutout, but not his third Series win—or the Tigers' comeback world title.

GAME 1 AT STL OCT 2

DET	000	000	000	0	5 3
STL	000	300	10X	4	6 0

Pitchers: McLAIN, Dobson (6), McMahon (8) vs GIBSON
Home Runs: Brock-STL
Attendance: 54,692

GAME 2 AT STL OCT 3

DET	011	003	102	8	13 1
STL	000	001	000	1	6 1

Pitchers: LOLICH vs BRILES, Carlton (6), Willis (7), Hoerner (9)
Home Runs: Horton-DET, Lolich-DET, Cash-DET
Attendance: 54,692

GAME 3 AT DET OCT 5

STL	000	040	300	7	13 0
DET	002	010	000	3	4 0

Pitchers: WASHBURN, Hoerner (6) vs WILSON, Dobson (5), McMahon (6), Patterson (7), Hiller (8)
Home Runs: Kaline-DET, McCarver-STL, McAuliffe-DET, Cepeda-STL
Attendance: 53,634

GAME 4 AT DET OCT 6

STL	202	200	040	10	13 0
DET	000	100	000	1	5 4

Pitchers: GIBSON vs McLAIN, Sparma (3), Patterson (4), Lasher (6), Hiller (8), Dobson (8)
Home Runs: Brock-STL, Gibson-STL, Northrup-DET
Attendance: 53,634

GAME 5 AT DET OCT 7

STL	300	000	000	3	9 0
DET	000	200	30X	5	9 1

Pitchers: Briles, HOERNER (7), Willis (7) vs LOLICH
Home Runs: Cepeda-STL
Attendance: 53,634

GAME 6 AT STL OCT 9

DET	0 210	010	000	13	12 1
STL	00 0	000	001	1	9 1

Pitchers: McLAIN vs WASHBURN, Jaster (3), Willis (3), Hughes (3), Carlton (4), Granger (7), Nelson (9)
Home Runs: Northrup-DET, Kaline-DET
Attendance: 54,692

GAME 7 AT STL OCT 10

DET	000	000	301	4	8 1
STL	000	000	001	1	5 0

Pitchers: LOLICH vs GIBSON
Home Runs: Shannon-STL
Attendance: 54,692

Detroit Tigers (AL), 4;
St. Louis Cardinals (NL) 3

DET (A)

PLAYER/POS	AVG	G	AB	R	H	2B	3B	HR	RB	BB	SO	SB
Gates Brown, ph	.000	1	1	0	0	0	0	0	0	0	0	0
Norm Cash, 1b	.385	7	26	5	10	0	0	1	5	3	5	0
Wayne Comer, ph	1.000	1	1	0	1	0	0	0	0	0	0	0
Pat Dobson, p	.000	3	0	0	0	0	0	0	0	0	0	0
Bill Freehan, c	.083	7	24	0	2	1	0	0	2	4	8	0
John Hiller, p	.000	2	0	0	0	0	0	0	0	0	0	0
Willie Horton, of	.304	7	23	6	7	1	1	1	3	5	6	0
Al Kaline, of	.379	7	29	6	11	2	0	2	8	0	7	0
Fred Lasher, p	.000	1	0	0	0	0	0	0	0	0	0	0
Mickey Lolich, p	.250	3	12	2	3	0	0	1	2	1	5	0
Tom Matchick, ph	.000	3	3	0	0	0	0	0	0	0	1	0
Eddie Mathews, 3b-1	.333	2	3	0	1	0	0	0	0	1	1	0
Dick McAuliffe, 2b	.222	7	27	5	6	0	0	1	3	4	6	0
Denny McLain, p	.000	3	6	0	0	0	0	0	0	0	4	0
Don McMahon, p	.000	2	0	0	0	0	0	0	0	0	0	0
Jim Northrup, of	.250	7	28	4	7	0	1	2	8	1	5	0
Ray Oyler, ss	.000	4	0	0	0	0	0	0	0	0	0	0
Daryl Patterson, p	.000	2	0	0	0	0	0	0	0	0	0	0
Jim Price, ph	.000	2	2	0	0	0	0	0	0	0	1	0
Joe Sparma, p	.000	1	0	0	0	0	0	0	0	0	0	0
Mickey Stanley, ss-7,of-4	.214	7	28	4	6	0	1	0	0	2	4	0
Dick Tracewski, 3b-1	.000	2	0	1	0	0	0	0	0	0	0	0
Don Wert, 3b	.118	6	17	1	2	0	0	0	2	6	5	0
Earl Wilson, p	.000	1	1	0	0	0	0	0	0	0	1	0
TOTAL	.242		231	34	56	4	3	8	33	27	59	0

PITCHER	W	L	ERA	G	GS	CG	SV	SHO	IP	H	ER	BB	SO
Pat Dobson	0	0	3.86	3	0	0	0	0	4.2	5	2	1	0
John Hiller	0	0	13.50	2	0	0	0	0	2.0	6	3	3	1
Fred Lasher	0	0	0.00	1	0	0	0	0	2.0	1	0	0	1
Mickey Lolich	3	0	1.67	3	3	3	0	0	27.0	20	5	6	21
Denny McLain	1	2	3.24	3	3	1	0	0	16.2	18	6	4	13
Don McMahon	0	0	13.50	2	0	0	0	0	2.0	4	3	0	1
Daryl Patterson	0	0	0.00	2	0	0	0	0	3.0	1	0	1	0
Joe Sparma	0	0	54.00	1	0	0	0	0	0.1	2	2	0	0
Earl Wilson	0	1	6.23	1	1	0	0	0	4.1	4	3	6	3
TOTAL	4	3	3.48	18	7	4	0	0	62.0	61	24	21	40

STL (N)

PLAYER/POS	AVG	G	AB	R	H	2B	3B	HR	RB	BB	SO	SB
Nelson Briles, p	.000	2	4	0	0	0	0	0	0	0	4	0
Lou Brock, of	.464	7	28	6	13	3	1	2	5	3	4	7
Steve Carlton, p	.000	2	0	0	0	0	0	0	0	0	0	0
Orlando Cepeda, 1b	.250	7	28	2	7	0	0	2	6	2	3	0
Ron Davis, of	.000	2	7	0	0	0	0	0	0	0	2	0
Johnny Edwards, ph	.000	1	1	0	0	0	0	0	0	0	1	0
Curt Flood, of	.286	7	28	4	8	1	0	0	2	2	2	3
Phil Gagliano, ph	.000	3	3	0	0	0	0	0	0	0	0	0
Bob Gibson, p	.125	3	8	2	1	0	0	1	2	1	2	0
Wayne Granger, p	.000	1	0	0	0	0	0	0	0	0	0	0
Joe Hoerner, p	.500	3	2	0	1	0	0	0	0	0	1	0
Dick Hughes, p	.000	1	0	0	0	0	0	0	0	0	0	0
Larry Jaster, p	.000	1	0	0	0	0	0	0	0	0	0	0
Julian Javier, 2b	.333	7	27	1	9	1	0	0	3	3	4	1
Roger Maris, of-5	.158	6	19	5	3	1	0	0	1	3	3	0
Dal Maxvill, ss	.000	7	22	1	0	0	0	0	0	3	5	0
Tim McCarver, c	.333	7	27	3	9	0	2	1	4	3	2	0
Mel Nelson, p	.000	1	0	0	0	0	0	0	0	0	0	0
Dave Ricketts, ph	1.000	2	1	0	1	0	0	0	0	0	0	0
Dick Schofield, ss-1	.000	2	0	0	0	0	0	0	0	0	0	0
Mike Shannon, 3b	.276	7	29	3	8	1	0	1	4	1	5	0
Ed Spiezio, ph	1.000	1	1	0	1	0	0	0	0	0	0	0
Bobby Tolan, ph	.000	1	1	0	0	0	0	0	0	0	1	0
Ray Washburn, p	.000	2	3	0	0	0	0	0	0	0	1	0
Ron Willis, p	.000	3	0	0	0	0	0	0	0	0	0	0
TOTAL	.255		239	27	61	7	3	7	27	21	40	11

PITCHER	W	L	ERA	G	GS	CG	SV	SHO	IP	H	ER	BB	SO
Nelson Briles	0	1	5.56	2	2	0	0	0	11.1	13	7	4	7
Steve Carlton	0	0	6.75	2	0	0	0	0	4.0	7	3	1	3
Bob Gibson	2	1	1.67	3	3	3	0	1	27.0	18	5	4	35
Wayne Granger	0	0	0.00	1	0	0	0	0	2.0	0	0	1	1
Joe Hoerner	0	1	3.86	3	0	0	1	0	4.2	5	2	5	3
Dick Hughes	0	0	0.00	1	0	0	0	0	0.1	2	0	0	0
Larry Jaster	0	0	INF	1	0	0	0	0	0.0	2	3	1	0
Mel Nelson	0	0	0.00	1	0	0	0	0	1.0	0	0	0	1
Ray Washburn	1	1	9.82	2	2	0	0	0	7.1	7	8	7	6
Ron Willis	0	0	8.31	3	0	0	0	0	4.1	2	4	4	3
TOTAL	3	4	4.65	19	7	3	1	1	62.0	56	32	27	59

Atlanta's Hank Aaron homered in each game and drove in a series-high seven runs. But the "Miracle Mets" as a team outhomered the Braves six to five, outhit them by seventy-two percentage points, and scored nearly twice as many runs.

Twice in the first game the Braves came from behind to lead by a run, but in the top of the eighth, five New York hits and poor Atlanta fielding buried starter Phil Niekro under five runs. In Game Two, home runs by Tommie Agee and Ken Boswell helped New York take an early 8–0 lead that even Aaron's three-run homer in the fifth couldn't damage.

In the third game the lead changed hands three times on home runs. Aaron began the barrage with a two-run shot in the first inning. Agee's homer in the third followed by Boswell's for two runs in the fourth put the Mets ahead—until Orlando Cepeda's two-run homer in the fifth gave Atlanta another lead. But in the bottom of the fifth, Met rookie Wayne Garrett's two-run blast reversed the lead one last time and, after four final shutout innings by twenty-two-year-old reliever Nolan Ryan, the Mets had swept to their first pennant.

New York Mets (East), 3;
Atlanta Braves (West) 0

NY (E)

PLAYER/POS	AVG	G	AB	R	H	2B	3B	HR	RB	BB	SO	SB
Tommie Agee, of	.357	3	14	4	5	1	0	2	4	2	5	2
Ken Boswell, 2b	.333	3	12	4	4	0	0	2	5	1	2	0
Wayne Garrett, 3b	.385	3	13	3	5	2	0	1	3	2	2	1
Rod Gaspar, of	.000	3	0	0	0	0	0	0	0	0	0	0
Gary Gentry, p	.000	1	0	0	0	0	0	0	0	0	0	0
Jerry Grote, c	.167	3	12	3	2	1	0	0	1	1	4	0
Bud Harrelson, ss	.182	3	11	2	2	1	1	0	3	1	2	0
Cleon Jones, of	.429	3	14	4	6	2	0	1	4	1	2	2
Jerry Koosman, p	.000	1	2	1	0	0	0	0	0	0	1	0
Ed Kranepool, 1b	.250	3	12	2	3	1	0	0	1	1	2	0
J. C. Martin, ph	.500	2	2	0	1	0	0	0	2	0	0	0
Tug McGraw, p	.000	1	0	0	0	0	0	0	0	0	0	0
Nolan Ryan, p	.500	1	4	1	2	0	0	0	0	0	1	0
Tom Seaver, p	.000	1	3	0	0	0	0	0	0	0	0	0
Art Shamsky, of	.538	3	13	3	7	0	0	0	1	0	3	0
Ron Taylor, p	.000	2	0	0	0	0	0	0	0	0	0	0
Al Weis, 2b	.000	3	1	0	0	0	0	0	0	0	0	0
TOTAL	.327		113	27	37	8	1	6	24	10	25	5

PITCHER	W	L	ERA	G	GS	CG	SV	SHO	IP	H	ER	BB	SO
Gary Gentry	0	0	9.00	1	1	0	0	0	2.0	5	2	1	1
Jerry Koosman	0	0	11.57	1	1	0	0	0	4.2	7	6	4	5
Tug McGraw	0	0	0.00	1	0	0	1	0	3.0	1	0	1	1
Nolan Ryan	1	0	2.57	1	0	0	0	0	7.0	3	2	2	7
Tom Seaver	1	0	6.43	1	1	0	0	0	7.0	8	5	3	2
Ron Taylor	1	0	0.00	2	0	0	1	0	3.1	3	0	0	4
TOTAL	3	0	5.00	7	3	0	2	0	27.0	27	15	11	20

ATL (W)

PLAYER/POS	AVG	G	AB	R	H	2B	3B	HR	RB	BB	SO	SB
Hank Aaron, of	.357	3	14	3	5	2	0	3	7	0	1	0
Tommie Aaron, ph	.000	1	1	0	0	0	0	0	0	0	0	0
Felipe Alou, ph	.000	1	1	0	0	0	0	0	0	0	0	0
Bob Aspromonte, ph	.000	3	3	0	0	0	0	0	0	0	0	0
Clete Boyer, 3b	.111	3	9	0	1	0	0	0	3	2	3	0
Jim Britton, p	.000	1	0	0	0	0	0	0	0	0	0	0
Rico Carty, of	.300	3	10	4	3	2	0	0	0	3	1	0
Orlando Cepeda, 1b	.455	3	11	2	5	2	0	1	3	1	2	1
Bob Didier, c	.000	3	11	0	0	0	0	0	0	0	2	0
Paul Doyle, p	.000	1	0	0	0	0	0	0	0	0	0	0
Gil Garrido, ss	.200	3	10	0	2	0	0	0	0	1	1	0
Tony Gonzalez, of	.357	3	14	4	5	1	0	1	2	1	4	0
Sonny Jackson, ss	.000	1	0	0	0	0	0	0	0	0	0	0
Pat Jarvis, p	.000	1	2	0	0	0	0	0	0	0	2	0
Mike Lum, of-1	1.000	2	2	0	2	1	0	0	0	0	0	0
Felix Millan, 2b	.333	3	12	2	4	1	0	0	0	3	0	0
Gary Neibauer, p	.000	1	0	0	0	0	0	0	0	0	0	0
Phil Niekro, p	.000	1	3	0	0	0	0	0	0	0	1	0
Milt Pappas, p	.000	1	1	0	0	0	0	0	0	0	1	0
Ron Reed, p	.000	1	0	0	0	0	0	0	0	0	0	0
George Stone, p	.000	1	1	0	0	0	0	0	0	0	1	0
Bob Tillman, c	.000	1	0	0	0	0	0	0	0	0	0	0
Cecil Upshaw, p	.000	3	1	0	0	0	0	0	0	0	1	0
TOTAL	.255		106	15	27	9	0	5	15	11	20	1

PITCHER	W	L	ERA	G	GS	CG	SV	SHO	IP	H	ER	BB	SO
Jim Britton	0	0	0.00	1	0	0	0	0	0.1	0	0	1	0
Paul Doyle	0	0	0.00	1	0	0	0	0	1.0	2	0	1	3
Pat Jarvis	0	1	12.46	1	1	0	0	0	4.1	10	6	0	6
Gary Neibauer	0	0	0.00	1	0	0	0	0	1.0	0	0	0	1
Phil Niekro	0	1	4.50	1	1	0	0	0	8.0	9	4	4	4
Milt Pappas	0	0	11.57	1	0	0	0	0	2.1	4	3	0	4
Ron Reed	0	1	21.60	1	1	0	0	0	1.2	5	4	3	3
George Stone	0	0	9.00	1	0	0	0	0	1.0	2	1	0	0
Cecil Upshaw	0	0	2.84	3	0	0	0	0	6.1	5	2	1	4
TOTAL	0	3	6.92	11	3	0	0	0	26.0	37	20	10	25

GAME 1 AT ATL OCT 4

NY	020 200 050	9	10	1
ATL	012 010 100	5	10	2

Pitchers: SEAVER, Taylor (8) vs NIEKRO, Upshaw (9)
Home Runs: Gonzalez-ATL, H.Aaron-ATL
Attendance: 50,122

GAME 2 AT ATL OCT 5

NY	132 210 200	11	13	1
ATL	000 150 000	6	9	3

Pitchers: Koosman, TAYLOR (5), McGraw (7) vs REED, Doyle (2), Pappas (3), Britton (6), Upshaw (6), Neibauer (9)
Home Runs: Agee-NY, Boswell-NY, H.Aaron-ATL, Jones-NY
Attendance: 50,270

GAME 3 AT NY OCT 6

ATL	200 020 000	4	8	1
NY	001 231 00X	7	14	0

Pitchers: JARVIS, Stone (5), Upshaw (6) vs Gentry, RYAN (3)
Home Runs: H.Aaron-ATL, Agee-NY, Boswell-NY, Cepeda-ATL, Garrett-NY
Attendance: 53,195

Minnesota led the league in batting, Baltimore in pitching. In the LCS, pitching prevailed as the Twins were held to a series batting average 113 points below their season mark.

Still, Minnesota nearly won the first game with three runs on only four hits. But the Orioles tied the score on Boog Powell's homer in the bottom of the ninth and won the game three innings later on Paul Blair's suicide squeeze bunt with two away. In Game Two, Minnesota's Dave Boswell scattered seven Baltimore hits over 10⅔ scoreless innings before giving way to Ron Perranoski in the eleventh. But Oriole pitcher Dave McNally was more than a match for Boswell. He gave up only three Twin hits—none in the final 7⅔ innings of the 11 he pitched—and took the win when Baltimore pinch hitter Curt Motton lined a single off Perranoski to score Powell from second with the game's only run.

In the third game, the Twins fell apart as the Orioles battered seven Minnesota pitchers for eighteen hits. Baltimore's Jim Palmer gave up more than a hit an inning himself, but coasted to the pennant 11–2.

Baltimore Orioles (East), 3; Minnesota Twins (West) 0

BAL (E)

PLAYER/POS	AVG	G	AB	R	H	2B	3B	HR	RB	BB	SO	SB
Mark Belanger, ss	.267	3	15	4	4	0	1	1	1	0	0	0
Paul Blair, of	.400	3	15	1	6	2	0	1	6	2	2	0
Don Buford, of	.286	3	14	3	4	1	0	0	1	3	0	0
Mike Cuellar, p	.000	1	2	0	0	0	0	0	0	0	1	0
Andy Etchebarren, c	.000	2	4	0	0	0	0	0	0	0	0	0
Dick Hall, p	.000	1	0	0	0	0	0	0	0	0	0	0
Elrod Hendricks, c	.250	3	8	2	2	2	0	0	3	1	2	0
Davey Johnson, 2b	.231	3	13	2	3	0	0	0	0	2	1	0
Marcelino Lopez, p	.000	1	0	0	0	0	0	0	0	0	0	0
Dave May, ph	.000	1	1	0	0	0	0	0	0	0	0	0
Dave McNally, p	.000	1	4	0	0	0	0	0	0	0	2	0
Curt Motton, ph	.500	2	2	0	1	0	0	0	1	0	0	0
Jim Palmer, p	.000	1	5	0	0	0	0	0	0	0	3	0
Boog Powell, 1b	.385	3	13	2	5	0	0	1	1	2	0	0
Merv Rettenmund, ph	.000	1	0	0	0	0	0	0	0	0	0	0
Pete Richert, p	.000	1	0	0	0	0	0	0	0	0	0	0
Brooks Robinson, 3b	.500	3	14	1	7	1	0	0	0	0	0	0
Frank Robinson, of	.333	3	12	1	4	2	0	1	2	3	3	0
Chico Salmon, ph	.000	1	1	0	0	0	0	0	0	0	0	0
Eddie Watt, p	.000	1	0	0	0	0	0	0	0	0	0	0
TOTAL	.293		123	16	36	8	1	4	15	13	14	0

PITCHER	W	L	ERA	G	GS	CG	SV	SHO	IP	H	ER	BB	SO
Mike Cuellar	0	0	2.25	1	1	0	0	0	8.0	3	2	1	7
Dick Hall	1	0	0.00	1	0	0	0	0	0.2	0	0	0	1
Marcelino Lopez	0	0	0.00	1	0	0	0	0	0.1	1	0	2	0
Dave McNally	1	0	0.00	1	1	1	0	1	11.0	3	0	5	11
Jim Palmer	1	0	2.00	1	1	1	0	0	9.0	10	2	2	4
Pete Richert	0	0	0.00	1	0	0	0	0	1.0	0	0	2	2
Eddie Watt	0	0	0.00	1	0	0	0	0	2.0	0	0	0	2
TOTAL	3	0	1.13	7	3	2	0	1	32.0	17	4	12	27

MIN (W)

PLAYER/POS	AVG	G	AB	R	H	2B	3B	HR	RB	BB	SO	SB
Bob Allison, of	.000	2	8	0	0	0	0	0	1	0	0	0
Dave Boswell, p	.000	1	4	0	0	0	0	0	0	0	4	0
Leo Cardenas, ss	.154	3	13	0	2	0	1	0	0	0	7	0
Rod Carew, 2b	.071	3	14	0	1	0	0	0	0	1	4	0
Dean Chance, p	.000	1	0	0	0	0	0	0	0	0	0	0
Joe Grzenda, p	.000	1	0	0	0	0	0	0	0	0	0	0
Tom Hall, p	.000	1	0	0	0	0	0	0	0	0	0	0
Harmon Killebrew, 3b	.125	3	8	2	1	1	0	0	0	6	2	0
Chuck Manuel, ph	.000	1	0	0	0	0	0	0	0	1	0	0
Bob Miller, p	.000	1	0	0	0	0	0	0	0	0	0	0
George Mitterwald, c	.143	2	7	0	1	0	0	0	0	1	3	0
Graig Nettles, ph	1.000	1	1	0	1	0	0	0	0	0	0	0
Tony Oliva, of	.385	3	13	3	5	2	0	1	2	1	3	1
Ron Perranoski, p	.000	3	1	0	0	0	0	0	0	0	1	0
Jim Perry, p	.000	1	3	0	0	0	0	0	0	0	0	0
Rich Reese, 1b	.167	3	12	0	2	0	0	0	2	1	1	0
Rich Renick, ph	.000	1	1	0	0	0	0	0	0	0	0	0
John Roseboro, c	.200	2	5	0	1	0	0	0	0	0	0	0
Cesar Tovar, of	.077	3	13	0	1	0	0	0	0	1	2	1
Ted Uhlaender, of	.167	2	6	0	1	0	0	0	0	0	0	0
Dick Woodson, p	1.000	1	1	0	1	0	0	0	0	0	0	0
Al Worthington, p	.000	1	0	0	0	0	0	0	0	0	0	0
TOTAL	.155		110	5	17	3	1	1	5	12	27	2

PITCHER	W	L	ERA	G	GS	CG	SV	SHO	IP	H	ER	BB	SO
Dave Boswell	0	1	0.84	1	1	0	0	0	10.2	7	1	7	4
Dean Chance	0	0	13.50	1	0	0	0	0	2.0	4	3	0	2
Joe Grzenda	0	0	0.00	1	0	0	0	0	0.2	0	0	0	0
Tom Hall	0	0	0.00	1	0	0	0	0	0.2	0	0	0	0
Bob Miller	0	1	5.40	1	1	0	0	0	1.2	5	1	0	0
Ron Perranoski	0	1	5.79	3	0	0	0	0	4.2	8	3	0	2
Jim Perry	0	0	3.38	1	1	0	0	0	8.0	6	3	3	3
Dick Woodson	0	0	10.80	1	0	0	0	0	1.2	3	2	3	2
Al Worthington	0	0	6.75	1	0	0	0	0	1.1	3	1	0	1
TOTAL	0	3	4.02	11	3	0	0	0	31.1	36	14	13	14

GAME 1 AT BAL OCT 4

MIN   000 010 200 000   3   4   2
BAL   000 110 001 001   4 10   1

Pitchers: Perry, PERRANOSKI (9) vs Cuellar, Richert (9), Watt (10), Lopez (12), HALL (12)
Home Runs: F.Robinson-BAL, Belanger-BAL, Oliva-MIN, Powell-BAL
Attendance: 39,324

GAME 2 AT BAL OCT 5

MIN   000 000 000 00   0   3   1
BAL   000 000 000 01   1   8   0

Pitchers: BOSWELL, Perranoski (11) vs McNALLY
Attendance: 41,704

GAME 3 AT MIN OCT 6

BAL   030 201 023   11 18   0
MIN   100 010 000   2 10   2

Pitchers: PALMER vs MILLER, Woodson (2), Hall (4), Worthington (5), Grzenda (6), Chance (7), Perranoski (9)
Home Runs: Blair-BAL
Attendance: 32,735

The heavy-hitting, slick-fielding Orioles, who also boasted the majors' top pitching staff, entered the Series clear favorites against the upstart Mets. But the "Miracle Mets," after losing the opener, polished off Baltimore with four straight wins.

The clubs' big winners, Met Tom Seaver (25–7) and Mike Cuellar (23–11) faced each other in the opener. Baltimore's leadoff batter, Don Buford, greeted Seaver with a home run, and a three-run Oriole rally with two out in the fourth made the score 4–0 before the Mets scored their first Series run in the seventh. Cuellar held New York to that one run for the victory.

No one scored for three innings of Game Two off Oriole Dave McNally or even hit Met Jerry Koosman safely. But Met Donn Clendenon led off the fourth with a home run as Koosman continued to no-hit Baltimore for three more innings. In the seventh, though, Baltimore's Paul Blair spoiled Koosman's no-hitter with a leadoff single, and after stealing second, scored the tying run on Brooks Robinson's single. But those were the only hits the O's would get, and in the top of the ninth three successive two-out Met singles produced what proved to be the winning run.

Met pitchers Gary Gentry and Nolan Ryan (with the assist of two spectacular catches by center fielder Tommie Agee that saved a total of five runs) combined for a shutout in Game Three. Agee's leadoff homer against Jim Palmer in the first was all the scoring the Mets would need, but they added four more runs before the game ended. Game Four was the Series' tightest. Seaver went the distance for the win, holding a 1–0 lead until a sacrifice fly scored the tying Baltimore run in the top of the ninth. In the bottom of the tenth, the Mets finally won it as a bunt thrown to first hit the runner and bounded away, allowing pinch runner Rod Gaspar to score all the way from second.

Dave McNally and Jerry Koosman tangled a second time in Game Five, and again Koosman and the Mets emerged victorious. McNally's two-run homer in the third gave him a lead which Frank Robinson expanded with a solo shot. But in an eerie sixth inning reprise of Game Four of the 1957 World Series featuring Nippy Jones, the Mets' Cleon Jones was struck by a pitch on the foot and awarded first base after inspection by the home plate umpire revealed tell-tale shoe polish on the ball. Each Jones produced a key run, Cleon coming home on Donn Clendenon's home run which followed immediately. Al Weis homered in the seventh for a 3–3 tie. With McNally now gone, two

doubles off Eddie Watt in the eighth brought in the go-ahead Met run, and a pair of errors let in a run for insurance. Koosman held Baltimore scoreless in the ninth and the Met miracle was complete.

New York Mets (NL), 4;
Baltimore Orioles (AL) 1

NY (N)

PLAYER/POS	AVG	G	AB	R	H	2B	3B	HR	RB	BB	SO	SB
Tommie Agee, of	.167	5	18	1	3	0	0	1	1	1	2	5	1
Ken Boswell, 2b	.333	1	3	1	1	0	0	0	0	0	0	0
Don Cardwell, p	.000	1	0	0	0	0	0	0	0	0	0	0
Ed Charles, 3b	.133	4	15	1	2	1	0	0	0	0	2	0
Donn Clendenon, 1b	.357	4	14	4	5	1	0	3	4	2	6	0
Duffy Dyer, ph	.000	1	1	0	0	0	0	0	0	0	0	0
Wayne Garrett, 3b	.000	2	1	0	0	0	0	0	0	2	1	0
Rod Gaspar, of-1	.000	3	2	1	0	0	0	0	0	0	0	0
Gary Gentry, p	.333	1	3	0	1	1	0	0	0	2	0	0
Jerry Grote, c	.211	5	19	1	4	2	0	0	1	1	3	0
Bud Harrelson, ss	.176	5	17	1	3	0	0	0	0	3	4	0
Cleon Jones, of	.158	5	19	2	3	1	0	0	0	0	1	0
Jerry Koosman, p	.143	2	7	0	1	1	0	0	0	0	4	0
Ed Kranepool, 1b	.250	1	4	1	1	0	0	1	1	0	0	0
J.C. Martin, ph	.000	1	0	0	0	0	0	0	0	0	0	0
Nolan Ryan, p	.000	1	0	0	0	0	0	0	0	0	0	0
Tom Seaver, p	.000	2	4	0	0	0	0	0	0	0	2	0
Art Shamsky, of-1	.000	3	6	0	0	0	0	0	0	0	0	0
Ron Swoboda, of	.400	4	15	1	6	1	0	0	1	1	3	0
Ron Taylor, p	.000	2	0	0	0	0	0	0	0	0	0	0
Al Weis, 2b	.455	5	11	1	5	0	0	1	3	4	2	0
TOTAL	.220		159	15	35	8	0	6	13	15	35	1

PITCHER	W	L	ERA	G	GS	CG	SV	SHO	IP	H	ER	BB	SO
Don Cardwell	0	0	0.00	1	0	0	0	0	1.0	0	0	0	0
Gary Gentry	1	0	0.00	1	1	0	0	0	6.2	3	0	5	4
Jerry Koosman	2	0	2.04	2	2	1	0	0	17.2	7	4	4	9
Nolan Ryan	0	0	0.00	1	0	0	1	0	2.1	1	0	2	3
Tom Seaver	1	1	3.00	2	2	1	0	0	15.0	12	5	3	9
Ron Taylor	0	0	0.00	2	0	0	1	0	2.1	0	0	1	3
TOTAL	4	1	1.80	9	5	2	2	0	45.0	23	9	15	28

BAL (A)

PLAYER/POS	AVG	G	AB	R	H	2B	3B	HR	RB	BB	SO	SB
Mark Belanger, ss	.200	5	15	2	3	0	0	0	0	1	2	1	0
Paul Blair, of	.100	5	20	1	2	0	0	0	0	2	5	1
Don Buford, of	.100	5	20	1	2	1	0	1	2	2	4	0
Mike Cuellar, p	.400	2	5	0	2	0	0	0	1	0	3	0
Clay Dalrymple, ph	1.000	2	2	0	2	0	0	0	0	0	0	0
Andy Etchebarren, c	.000	2	6	0	0	0	0	0	0	0	1	0
Dick Hall, p	.000	1	0	0	0	0	0	0	0	0	0	0
Elrod Hendricks, c	.100	3	10	1	1	0	0	0	0	1	0	0
Davey Johnson, 2b	.063	5	16	1	1	0	0	0	0	2	1	0
Dave Leonhard, p	.000	1	0	0	0	0	0	0	0	0	0	0
Dave May, ph	.000	2	1	0	0	0	0	0	0	1	1	0
Dave McNally, p	.200	2	5	1	1	0	0	1	2	0	2	0
Curt Motton, ph	.000	1	1	0	0	0	0	0	0	0	0	0
Jim Palmer, p	.000	1	2	0	0	0	0	0	0	0	0	0
Boog Powell, 1b	.263	5	19	0	5	0	0	0	0	1	4	0
Merv Rettenmund, pr	.000	1	0	0	0	0	0	0	0	0	0	0
Pete Richert, p	.000	1	0	0	0	0	0	0	0	0	0	0
Brooks Robinson, 3b	.053	5	19	0	1	0	0	0	2	0	3	0
Frank Robinson, of	.188	5	16	2	3	0	0	1	1	4	3	0
Chico Salmon, pr	.000	2	0	0	0	0	0	0	0	0	0	0
Eddie Watt, p	.000	2	0	0	0	0	0	0	0	0	0	0
TOTAL	.146		157	9	23	1	0	3	9	15	28	1

PITCHER	W	L	ERA	G	GS	CG	SV	SHO	IP	H	ER	BB	SO
Mike Cuellar	1	0	1.13	2	2	1	0	0	16.0	13	2	4	13
Dick Hall	0	1	INF	1	0	0	0	0	0.0	1	0	1	0
Dave Leonhard	0	0	4.50	1	0	0	0	0	2.0	1	1	1	1
Dave McNally	0	1	2.81	2	2	1	0	0	16.0	11	5	5	13
Jim Palmer	0	1	6.00	1	1	0	0	0	6.0	5	4	4	5
Pete Richert	0	0	INF	1	0	0	0	0	0.0	0	0	0	0
Eddie Watt	0	1	3.00	2	0	0	0	0	3.0	4	1	0	3
TOTAL	1	4	2.72	10	5	2	0	0	43.0	35	13	15	35

GAME 1 AT BAL OCT 11

						R	H	E
NY	000	000	100		1	6	1
BAL	100	300	00X		4	6	0

Pitchers: SEAVER, Cardwell (6), Taylor (7) vs CUELLAR
Home Runs: Buford-BAL
Attendance: 50,429

GAME 2 AT BAL OCT 12

					R	H	E
NY	000	100	001	2	6	0
BAL	000	000	100	1	2	0

Pitchers: KOOSMAN, Taylor (9) vs McNALLY
Home Runs: Clendenon-NY
Attendance: 50,850

GAME 3 AT NY OCT 14

					R	H	E
BAL	000	000	000	0	4	1
NY	120	001	01X	5	6	0

Pitchers: PALMER, Leonhard (7) vs GENTRY, Ryan (7)
Home Runs: Agee-NY, Kranepool-NY
Attendance: 56,335

GAME 4 AT NY OCT 15

					R	H	E
BAL	000	000	001	0	1	6	1
NY	010	000	000	1	2	10	1

Pitchers: Cuellar, Watt (8), HALL (10), Richert (10) vs SEAVER
Home Runs: Clendenon-NY
Attendance: 57,367

GAME 5 AT NY OCT 16

					R	H	E
BAL	003	000	000	3	5	2
NY	000	002	12X	5	7	0

Pitchers: McNally, WATT (8) vs KOOSMAN
Home Runs: McNally-BAL, F.Robinson-BAL, Clendenon-NY, Weis-NY
Attendance: 57,397

Pitching was the game and three the magic number, as Cincinnati swept Pittsburgh, scoring three runs in each game while holding the Pirates to just three runs for the whole series.

Pirate pitcher Dock Ellis matched the Reds' Gary Nolan for nine scoreless innings in Game One before a pinch-hit triple, a single, and a double undid him for three runs in the top of the tenth. In Game Two Pittsburgh scored its first series run, but Red center fielder Bobby Tolan scored three for Baltimore—including a home run—to give Cincinnati its second win.

The Pirates took a lead for the only time in the series with a run in the top of the first inning of Game Three. But Tony Perez and Johnny Bench homered in the bottom of the inning to put the Reds up 2–1. The Pirates tied the score in the fifth, but three Red relievers combined to shut them out over the final four innings, while Tolan sank the Pirate ship with his second game-winner in two days: a single in the eighth that drove in Cincinnati's third—and final—run.

Cincinnati Reds (West), 3; Pittsburgh Pirates (East) 0

CIN (W)

PLAYER/POS	AVG	G	AB	R	H	2B	3B	HR	RB	BB	SO	SB
Johnny Bench, c	.222	3	9	2	2	0	0	1	1	3	1	0
Angel Bravo, ph	.000	1	1	0	0	0	0	0	0	0	0	0
Bernie Carbo, of	.000	2	6	0	0	0	0	0	0	0	3	0
Clay Carroll, p	.000	2	0	0	0	0	0	0	0	0	0	0
Ty Cline, of-1	1.000	2	1	2	1	0	1	0	0	1	0	0
Tony Cloninger, p	.000	1	1	0	0	0	0	0	0	1	0	0
Dave Concepcion, ss	.000	3	0	0	0	0	0	0	0	0	0	0
Wayne Granger, p	.000	1	0	0	0	0	0	0	0	0	0	0
Don Gullett, p	.000	2	1	0	0	0	0	0	0	0	0	0
Tommy Helms, 2b	.273	3	11	0	3	0	0	0	0	0	1	0
Lee May, 1b	.167	3	12	0	2	1	0	0	2	0	2	0
Hal McRae, of-1	.000	2	4	0	0	0	0	0	0	0	1	0
Jim Merritt, p	.000	1	2	0	0	0	0	0	0	0	2	0
Gary Nolan, p	.333	1	3	0	1	0	0	0	0	0	0	0
Tony Perez, 3b-3,1b-1	.333	3	12	1	4	2	0	1	2	1	1	0
Pete Rose, of	.231	3	13	1	3	0	0	0	1	0	0	0
Jimmy Stewart, of	.000	1	2	0	0	0	0	0	0	0	0	0
Bobby Tolan, of	.417	3	12	3	5	0	0	1	2	1	1	1
Milt Wilcox, p	.000	1	0	0	0	0	0	0	0	0	0	0
Woody Woodward, ss-3,3b-3	.100	3	10	0	1	0	0	0	0	0	1	0
TOTAL	.220		100	9	22	3	1	3	8	8	12	1

PITCHER	W	L	ERA	G	GS	CG	SV	SHO	IP	H	ER	BB	SO
Clay Carroll	0	0	0.00	2	0	0	1	0	1.1	2	0	0	2
Tony Cloninger	0	0	5.40	1	1	0	0	0	5.0	7	3	4	1
Wayne Granger	0	0	0.00	1	0	0	0	0	0.2	1	0	0	0
Don Gullett	0	0	0.00	2	0	0	2	0	3.2	1	0	2	3
Jim Merritt	1	0	1.69	1	1	0	0	0	5.1	3	1	0	2
Gary Nolan	1	0	0.00	1	1	0	0	0	9.0	8	0	4	6
Milt Wilcox	1	0	0.00	1	0	0	0	0	3.0	1	0	2	5
TOTAL	3	0	1.29	9	3	0	3	0	28.0	23	4	12	19

PIT (E)

PLAYER/POS	AVG	G	AB	R	H	2B	3B	HR	RB	BB	SO	SB
Gene Alley, ss	.000	2	7	0	0	0	0	0	0	1	2	0
Matty Alou, of	.250	3	12	1	3	1	0	0	0	2	1	0
Dave Cash, 2b	.125	2	8	1	1	1	0	0	0	1	1	0
Roberto Clemente, of	.214	3	14	1	3	0	0	0	1	0	4	0
Dock Ellis, p	.000	1	2	0	0	0	0	0	0	0	1	0
Joe Gibbon, p	.000	2	0	0	0	0	0	0	0	0	0	0
Dave Giusti, p	.000	2	0	0	0	0	0	0	0	0	0	0
Richie Hebner, 3b	.667	2	6	0	4	2	0	0	0	2	1	0
Johnny Jeter, of-1	.000	3	2	0	0	0	0	0	0	0	2	0
Bill Mazeroski, 2b	.000	1	2	0	0	0	0	0	0	0	0	0
Bob Moose, p	.000	1	4	0	0	0	0	0	0	0	1	0
Al Oliver, 1b	.250	2	8	0	2	0	0	0	1	1	0	0
Jose Pagan, 3b	.333	1	3	0	1	0	0	0	0	1	1	0
Freddie Patek, ss	.000	3	3	0	0	0	0	0	0	1	2	0
Bob Robertson, 1b-1	.200	2	5	0	1	1	0	0	0	0	0	0
Manny Sanguillen, c	.167	3	12	0	2	0	0	0	0	0	1	0
Willie Stargell, of	.500	3	12	0	6	1	0	0	1	1	1	0
Luke Walker, p	.000	1	2	0	0	0	0	0	0	0	1	0
TOTAL	.225		102	3	23	6	0	0	3	12	19	0

PITCHER	W	L	ERA	G	GS	CG	SV	SHO	IP	H	ER	BB	SO
Dock Ellis	0	1	2.79	1	1	0	0	0	9.2	9	3	4	1
Joe Gibbon	0	0	0.00	2	0	0	0	0	0.1	1	0	0	1
Dave Giusti	0	0	3.86	2	0	0	0	0	2.1	3	1	1	1
Bob Moose	0	1	3.52	1	1	0	0	0	7.2	4	3	2	4
Luke Walker	0	1	1.29	1	1	0	0	0	7.0	5	1	1	5
TOTAL	0	3	2.67	7	3	0	0	0	27.0	22	8	8	12

GAME 1 AT PIT OCT 3

CIN	000 000 000 3	3	9	0
PIT	000 000 000 0	0	8	0

Pitchers: NOLAN, Carroll (10) vs ELLIS, Gibbon (10)
Attendance: 33,088

GAME 2 AT PIT OCT 4

CIN	001 010 010	3	8	1
PIT	000 001 000	1	5	2

Pitchers: MERRITT, Carroll (6), Gullett (6) vs WALKER, Giusti (8)
Home Runs: Tolan-CIN
Attendance: 39,317

GAME 3 AT CIN OCT 5

PIT	100 010 000	2	10	0
CIN	200 000 01X	3	5	0

Pitchers: MOOSE, Gibbon (8), Giusti (8) vs Cloninger, WILCOX (6), Granger (9), Gullett (9)
Home Runs: Perez-CIN, Bench-CIN
Attendance: 40,538

For the second year in a row, Baltimore swept Minnesota in the LCS. In the first two games the Orioles' attack featured the big inning. The score was tied 2–2 in the first game as the Orioles came to bat in the top of the fourth. But by the time the Twins came to bat in the inning, they were seven runs behind—thanks in part to a grand slam by Baltimore pitcher Mike Cuellar. Harmon Killebrew's two-run homer in the fifth helped bring the Twins within three, but they came no closer.

Except for home runs to Killebrew and Tony Oliva in the fourth inning, Oriole pitcher Dave McNally stopped the Twins in Game Two, and Baltimore held a close 4–3 lead after eight. If they had been playing at home, they wouldn't have needed to bat at all in the ninth. But they did come to bat in the top of the ninth, and they once again buried Minnesota under a seven-run inning.

In the third game, for the second year in a row, Oriole pitcher Jim Palmer breezed through the series clincher. Baltimore scored five runs for him in the first three innings, and another in the eighth—four more than he needed to carry his club to another pennant.

Baltimore Orioles (East), 3; Minnesota Twins (West) 0

BAL (E)

PLAYER/POS	AVG	G	AB	R	H	2B	3B	HR	RB	BB	SO	SB
Mark Belanger, ss	.333	3	12	5	4	0	0	0	1	1	0	0
Paul Blair, of	.077	3	13	0	1	0	0	0	0	1	4	0
Don Buford, of	.429	2	7	2	3	1	0	1	3	2	0	0
Mike Cuellar, p	.500	1	2	1	1	0	0	1	4	0	1	0
Andy Etchebarren, c	.111	2	9	1	1	0	0	0	0	0	3	0
Dick Hall, p	.500	1	2	0	1	0	0	0	0	0	1	0
Elrod Hendricks, c	.400	1	5	2	2	0	0	0	0	0	1	0
Davey Johnson, 2b	.364	3	11	4	4	0	0	2	4	1	1	0
Dave McNally, p	.400	1	5	1	2	1	0	0	1	0	1	0
Jim Palmer, p	.250	1	4	1	1	1	0	0	1	0	0	0
Boog Powell, 1b	.429	3	14	2	6	2	0	1	6	0	3	0
Merv Rettenmund, of	.333	1	3	1	1	0	0	0	1	2	1	1
Brooks Robinson, 3b	.583	3	12	4	7	2	0	0	1	0	1	0
Frank Robinson, of	.200	3	10	3	2	0	0	1	2	5	2	0
TOTAL	.330		109	27	36	7	0	6	24	12	19	1

PITCHER	W	L	ERA	G	GS	CG	SV	SHO	IP	H	ER	BB	SO
Mike Cuellar	0	0	12.46	1	1	0	0	0	4.1	10	6	1	2
Dick Hall	1	0	0.00	1	0	0	0	0	4.2	1	0	0	3
Dave McNally	1	0	3.00	1	1	1	0	0	9.0	6	3	5	5
Jim Palmer	1	0	1.00	1	1	1	0	0	9.0	7	1	3	12
TOTAL	3	0	3.33	4	3	2	0	0	27.0	24	10	9	22

MIN (W)

PLAYER/POS	AVG	G	AB	R	H	2B	3B	HR	RB	BB	SO	SB
Bob Allison, ph	.000	3	2	0	0	0	0	0	0	0	1	0
Brant Alyea, of-2	.000	3	7	1	0	0	0	0	0	2	3	0
Bert Blyleven, p	.000	1	0	0	0	0	0	0	0	0	0	0
Leo Cardenas, ss	.182	3	11	1	2	0	0	0	1	1	1	0
Rod Carew, ph	.000	2	2	0	0	0	0	0	0	0	1	0
Tom Hall, p	.000	2	1	0	0	0	0	0	0	0	1	0
Jim Holt, of	.000	3	5	0	0	0	0	0	0	0	2	0
Jim Kaat, p	.000	1	1	0	0	0	0	0	0	0	0	0
Harmon Killebrew, 3b-2,1b-1	.273	3	11	2	3	0	0	2	4	2	4	0
Chuck Manuel, ph	.000	1	1	0	0	0	0	0	0	0	1	0
George Mitterwald, c	.500	2	8	2	4	1	0	0	2	0	2	0
Tony Oliva, of	.500	3	12	2	6	2	0	1	1	0	1	0
Ron Perranoski, p	.000	2	0	0	0	0	0	0	0	0	0	0
Jim Perry, p	.000	2	1	0	0	0	0	0	1	0	1	0
Frank Quilici, 2b-2	.000	3	2	0	0	0	0	0	0	0	1	0
Paul Ratliff, c	.250	1	4	0	1	0	0	0	0	0	1	0
Rich Reese, 1b	.143	2	7	0	1	0	0	0	0	1	1	0
Rich Renick, 3b-1	.200	2	5	0	1	0	0	0	0	0	1	0
Danny Thompson, 2b	.125	3	8	0	1	1	0	0	0	1	0	0
Luis Tiant, p	.000	1	0	0	0	0	0	0	0	0	0	0
Cesar Tovar, of-3,2b-1	.385	3	13	2	5	0	1	0	1	0	0	0
Stan Williams, p	.000	2	0	0	0	0	0	0	0	0	1	0
Dick Woodson, p	.000	1	0	0	0	0	0	0	0	0	0	0
Bill Zepp, p	.000	2	0	0	0	0	0	0	0	0	0	0
TOTAL	.238		101	10	24	4	1	3	10	9	22	0

PITCHER	W	L	ERA	G	GS	CG	SV	SHO	IP	H	ER	BB	SO
Bert Blyleven	0	0	0.00	1	0	0	0	0	2.0	2	0	0	2
Tom Hall	0	1	6.75	2	1	0	0	0	5.1	6	4	4	6
Jim Kaat	0	1	9.00	1	1	0	0	0	2.0	6	2	2	1
Ron Perranoski	0	0	19.29	2	0	0	0	0	2.1	5	5	1	3
Jim Perry	0	1	13.50	2	1	0	0	0	5.1	10	8	1	3
Luis Tiant	0	0	13.50	1	0	0	0	0	0.2	1	1	0	0
Stan Williams	0	0	0.00	2	0	0	0	0	6.0	2	0	1	2
Dick Woodson	0	0	9.00	1	0	0	0	0	1.0	2	1	1	0
Bill Zepp	0	0	6.75	2	0	0	0	0	1.1	2	1	2	2
TOTAL	0	3	7.62	14	3	0	0	0	26.0	36	22	12	19

GAME 1 AT MIN OCT 3

BAL	020 701 000	10 13 0
MIN	110 130 000	6 11 2

Pitchers: Cuellar, HALL (5) vs PERRY, Zepp (4), Woodson (5), Williams (6), Perranoski (9)
Home Runs: Cuellar-BAL, Buford-BAL, Powell-BAL, Killebrew-MIN
Attendance: 26,847

GAME 2 AT MIN OCT 4

BAL	102 100 007	11 13 0
MIN	000 300 000	3 6 2

Pitchers: McNALLY vs HALL, Zepp (4), Williams (5), Perranoski (8), Tiant (9)
Home Runs: F.Robinson-BAL, Killebrew-MIN, Oliva-MIN, Johnson-BAL
Attendance: 27,490

GAME 3 AT BAL OCT 5

MIN	000 010 000	1 7 2
BAL	113 000 10X	6 10 0

Pitchers: KAAT, Blyleven (3), Hall (5), Perry (7) vs PALMER
Home Runs: Johnson-BAL
Attendance: 27,608

With a near-sweep of Cincinnati, the Orioles helped Baltimore fans forget their 1969 Series humiliation by the New York Mets. Baltimore's first two wins, though, were closely contested. In the opener in Cincinnati (the first World Series game played on artificial grass), a Red run in the first inning and Lee May's third-inning two-run homer off Oriole starter Jim Palmer gave Cincinnati a 3–0 lead. But Orioles Boog Powell and Elrod Hendricks tagged Red starter Gary Nolan for home runs in the fourth and fifth that evened the score, and Brooks Robinson—whose other-worldly defense at third gave Reds right-handed hitters nightmares throughout the Series—homered in the seventh for a one-run Baltimore lead that held up as Palmer settled down to pitch one-hit ball from the fourth inning until he was relieved for the final out of the ninth.

Game Two was just as close. The Reds scored four runs in the first three innings, but Baltimore came back with six in the fourth and fifth. Johnny Bench's leadoff homer in the last of the sixth brought the Reds within one, but that was the end of the scoring for either side. In Game Three Oriole Dave McNally gave up nine hits and three runs. But he himself hit a grand slam in the sixth inning to cement what became a 9–3 victory.

On the verge of a Series sweep, the Orioles scored three runs in the last of the third inning of Game Four to take a 4–2 lead. But the Reds' Pete Rose homered in the fifth, and although Baltimore got the run back in the sixth, Lee May's three-run blast in the eighth overcame the Oriole lead and gave the Reds a narrow 6–5 win as Red reliever Clay Carroll permitted only one Oriole to hit safely over the final 3⅔ innings.

Mike Cuellar, driven out of Game Two in the third inning, hurled the complete game for Baltimore in Game Five, even though Cincinnati hammered him for four hits (three of them doubles) and three runs in the top of the first inning. But as Oriole home runs by Frank Robinson and Merv Rettenmund highlighted a Baltimore onslaught that produced fifteen hits and nine runs, Cuellar settled down, holding Cincinnati to a walk and a pair of harmless singles over the final eight innings to bring Baltimore its second world title in five years.

Baltimore Orioles (AL), 4; Cincinnati Reds (NL) 1

BAL (A)

PLAYER/POS	AVG	G	AB	R	H	2B	3B	HR	RB	BB	SO	SB
Mark Belanger, ss	.105	5	19	0	2	0	0	0	1	1	2	0
Paul Blair, of	.474	5	19	5	9	1	0	0	3	2	4	0
Don Buford, of	.267	4	15	3	4	0	0	1	1	3	2	0
Terry Crowley, ph	.000	1	1	0	0	0	0	0	0	0	0	0
Mike Cuellar, p	.000	2	4	0	0	0	0	0	0	0	2	0
Moe Drabowsky, p	.000	2	1	0	0	0	0	0	0	0	1	0
Andy Etchebarren, c	.143	2	7	1	1	0	0	0	0	2	3	0
Dick Hall, p	.000	1	1	0	0	0	0	0	0	0	1	0
Elrod Hendricks, c	.364	3	11	1	4	1	0	1	4	1	2	0
Davy Johnson, 2b	.313	5	16	2	5	2	0	0	2	5	2	0
Marcelino Lopez, p	.000	1	0	0	0	0	0	0	0	0	0	0
Dave McNally, p	.250	1	4	1	1	0	0	1	4	0	2	0
Jim Palmer, p	.143	2	7	1	1	0	0	0	0	0	3	0
Tom Phoebus, p	.000	1	0	0	0	0	0	0	0	0	0	0
Boog Powell, 1b	.294	5	17	6	5	1	0	2	5	5	2	0
Merv Rettenmund, of-1	.400	2	5	2	2	0	0	1	2	1	0	0
Pete Richert, p	.000	1	0	0	0	0	0	0	0	0	0	0
Brooks Robinson, 3b	.429	5	21	5	9	2	0	2	6	0	2	0
Frank Robinson, of	.273	5	22	5	6	0	0	2	4	0	5	0
Chico Salmon, ph	1.000	1	1	1	1	0	0	0	0	0	0	0
Eddie Watt, p	.000	1	0	0	0	0	0	0	0	0	0	0
TOTAL	.292		171	33	50	7	0	10	32	20	33	0

PITCHER	W	L	ERA	G	GS	CG	SV	SHO	IP	H	ER	BB	SO
Mike Cuellar	1	0	3.18	2	2	1	0	0	11.1	10	4	2	5
Moe Drabowsky	0	0	2.70	2	0	0	0	0	3.1	2	1	1	1
Dick Hall	0	0	0.00	1	0	0	1	0	2.1	0	0	0	0
Marcelino Lopez	0	0	0.00	1	0	0	0	0	0.1	0	0	0	0
Dave McNally	1	0	3.00	1	1	1	0	0	9.0	9	3	2	5
Jim Palmer	1	0	4.60	2	2	0	0	0	15.2	11	8	9	9
Tom Phoebus	1	0	0.00	1	0	0	0	0	1.2	1	0	0	0
Pete Richert	0	0	0.00	1	0	0	1	0	0.1	0	0	0	0
Eddie Watt	0	1	9.00	1	0	0	0	0	1.0	2	1	1	3
TOTAL	4	1	3.40	12	5	2	2	0	45.0	35	17	15	23

CIN (N)

PLAYER/POS	AVG	G	AB	R	H	2B	3B	HR	RB	BB	SO	SB
Johnny Bench, c	.211	5	19	3	4	0	0	1	3	1	2	0
Angel Bravo, ph	.000	4	2	0	0	0	0	0	0	1	1	0
Bernie Carbo, of-2	.000	4	8	0	0	0	0	0	0	2	3	0
Clay Carroll, p	.000	4	1	0	0	0	0	0	0	0	1	0
Darrel Chaney, ss	.000	3	1	0	0	0	0	0	0	0	1	0
Ty Cline, ph	.333	3	3	0	1	0	0	0	0	0	0	0
Tony Cloninger, p	.000	2	2	0	0	0	0	0	0	0	1	0
Dave Concepcion, ss	.333	3	9	0	3	0	1	0	3	0	0	0
Pat Corrales, ph	.000	1	1	0	0	0	0	0	0	0	0	0
Wayne Granger, p	.000	2	0	0	0	0	0	0	0	0	0	0
Don Gullett, p	.000	3	1	0	0	0	0	0	0	0	1	0
Tommy Helms, 2b	.222	5	18	1	4	0	0	0	0	1	1	0
Lee May, 1b	.389	5	18	6	7	2	0	2	8	2	2	0
Jim McGlothlin, p	.000	1	2	0	0	0	0	0	0	0	1	0
Hal McRae, of	.455	3	11	1	5	2	0	0	3	0	1	0
Jim Merritt, p	.000	1	1	0	0	0	0	0	0	0	1	0
Gary Nolan, p	.000	2	3	0	0	0	0	0	0	0	0	0
Tony Perez, 3b	.056	5	18	2	1	0	0	0	0	3	4	0
Pete Rose, of	.250	5	20	2	5	1	0	1	2	2	0	0
Jimmy Stewart, ph	.000	2	2	0	0	0	0	0	0	0	1	0
Bobby Tolan, of	.211	5	19	5	4	1	0	1	1	3	2	1
Ray Washburn, p	.000	1	0	0	0	0	0	0	0	0	0	0
Milt Wilcox, p	.000	2	0	0	0	0	0	0	0	0	0	0
Woody Woodward, ss-3	.200	4	5	0	1	0	0	0	0	0	0	0
TOTAL	.213		164	20	35	6	1	5	20	15	23	1

PITCHER	W	L	ERA	G	GS	CG	SV	SHO	IP	H	ER	BB	SO
Clay Carroll	1	0	0.00	4	0	0	0	0	9.0	5	0	2	11
Tony Cloninger	0	1	7.36	2	1	0	0	0	7.1	10	6	5	4
Wayne Granger	0	0	33.75	2	0	0	0	0	1.1	7	5	1	1
Don Gullett	0	0	1.35	3	0	0	0	0	6.2	5	1	4	4
Jim McGlothlin	0	0	8.31	1	1	0	0	0	4.1	6	4	2	2
Jim Merritt	0	1	21.60	1	1	0	0	0	1.2	3	4	1	0
Gary Nolan	0	1	7.71	2	2	0	0	0	9.1	9	8	3	9
Ray Washburn	0	1	13.50	1	0	0	0	0	1.1	2	2	2	0
Milt Wilcox	0	1	9.00	2	0	0	0	0	2.0	3	2	2	2
TOTAL	1	4	6.70	18	5	0	0	0	43.0	50	32	20	33

GAME 1 AT CIN OCT 10

BAL	000 210 100	4	7	2
CIN	102 000 000	3	5	0

Pitchers: PALMER, Richert (9) vs NOLAN, Carroll (7)
Home Runs: May-CIN, Powell-BAL, Hendricks-BAL, B.Robinson-BAL
Attendance: 51,531

GAME 2 AT CIN OCT 11

BAL	000 150 000	6	10	2
CIN	301 001 000	5	7	0

Pitchers: Cuellar, PHOEBUS (3), Drabowsky (5), Lopez (7), Hall (7) vs McGlothlin, WILCOX (5), Carroll (5), Gullett (8)
Home Runs: Tolan-CIN, Powell-BAL, Bench-CIN
Attendance: 51,531

GAME 3 AT BAL OCT 13

CIN	010 000 200	3	9	0
BAL	201 014 10X	9	10	1

Pitchers: CLONINGER, Granger (6), Gullett (7) vs McNALLY
Home Runs: F.Robinson-BAL, Buford-BAL, McNally-BAL
Attendance: 51,773

GAME 4 AT BAL OCT 14

CIN	011 010 030	6	8	3
BAL	013 001 000	5	8	0

Pitchers: Nolan, Gullett (3), CARROLL (6) vs Palmer, WATT (8), Drabowsky (9)
Home Runs: B.Robinson-BAL, Rose-CIN, May-CIN
Attendance: 53,007

GAME 5 AT BAL OCT 15

CIN	300 000 000	3	6	0
BAL	222 010 02X	9	15	0

Pitchers: MERRITT, Granger (2), Wilcox (3), Cloninger (5), Washburn (7), Carroll (8) vs CUELLAR
Home Runs: F.Robinson-BAL, Rettenmund-BAL
Attendance: 45,341

For the first time, an LCS went more than the minimum three games, as Pittsburgh rebounded from a loss in the opener to take the next three from San Francisco.

The Pirates scored first, with two runs in the third inning of Game One, but the Giants came back with a run in the bottom of the inning and put the game away in the fifth as Tito Fuentes and Willie McCovey both hit two-out two-run homers. Pirate first baseman Bob Robertson avenged his club's opening-game defeat the next day, battering four of the Giants' six pitchers for three home runs and a double—and five RBIs—in the Pirates' 9–5 win. Robertson continued his assault in Game Three, homering off Juan Marichal in the second. The Giants came back with a run in the sixth, but third baseman Richie Hebner put the game away with a second Pirate home run off Marichal in the eighth.

Both clubs scored five times in the first two innings of Game Four. But Pirate relievers Bruce Kison and Dave Giusti then pinned the Giants down for the final seven innings, while Roberto Clemente and Al Oliver combined for four RBIs in the sixth to capture the flag.

Pittsburgh Pirates (East), 3;
San Francisco Giants (West), 1

PIT (E)

PLAYER/POS	AVG	G	AB	R	H	2B	3B	HR	RB	BB	SO	SB
Gene Alley, ss	.500	1	2	1	1	0	0	0	0	0	0	0
Steve Blass, p	.000	2	1	0	0	0	0	0	0	0	1	0
Dave Cash, 2b	.421	4	19	5	8	2	0	0	1	0	1	1
Roberto Clemente, of	.333	4	18	2	6	0	0	0	4	1	6	0
Gene Clines, of	.333	1	3	1	1	0	0	1	1	0	1	0
Vic Davalillo, ph	.000	2	2	0	0	0	0	0	0	0	1	0
Dock Ellis, p	.000	1	3	0	0	0	0	0	0	0	2	0
Dave Giusti, p	.000	4	1	0	0	0	0	0	0	0	0	0
Richie Hebner, 3b	.294	4	17	3	5	1	0	2	4	0	4	0
Jackie Hernandez, ss	.231	4	13	2	3	0	0	0	1	0	4	0
Bob Johnson, p	.000	1	2	0	0	0	0	0	0	0	1	0
Bruce Kison, p	.000	1	2	0	0	0	0	0	0	0	0	0
Milt May, ph	.000	1	1	0	0	0	0	0	0	0	0	0
Bill Mazeroski, ph	1.000	1	1	1	1	0	0	0	0	0	0	0
Bob Miller, p	.000	1	1	0	0	0	0	0	0	0	0	0
Bob Moose, p	.000	1	0	0	0	0	0	0	0	0	0	0
Al Oliver, of	.250	4	12	2	3	0	0	1	5	1	3	0
Jose Pagan, 3b	.000	1	1	0	0	0	0	0	0	0	0	0
Bob Robertson, 1b	.438	4	16	5	7	1	0	4	6	0	2	0
Manny Sanguillen, c	.267	4	15	1	4	0	0	0	1	1	1	1
Willie Stargell, of	.000	4	14	1	0	0	0	0	0	2	6	0
TOTAL	.271		144	24	39	4	0	8	23	5	33	2

PITCHER	W	L	ERA	G	GS	CG	SV	SHO	IP	H	ER	BB	SO
Steve Blass	0	1	11.57	2	2	0	0	0	7.0	14	9	2	11
Dock Ellis	1	0	3.60	1	1	0	0	0	5.0	6	2	4	1
Dave Giusti	0	0	0.00	4	0	0	3	0	5.1	1	0	2	3
Bob Johnson	1	0	0.00	1	1	0	0	0	8.0	5	0	3	7
Bruce Kison	1	0	0.00	1	0	0	0	0	4.2	2	0	2	3
Bob Miller	0	0	6.00	1	0	0	0	0	3.0	3	2	3	3
Bob Moose	0	0	0.00	1	0	0	0	0	2.0	0	0	0	0
TOTAL	3	1	3.34	11	4	0	3	0	35.0	31	13	16	28

SF (W)

PLAYER/POS	AVG	G	AB	R	H	2B	3B	HR	RB	BB	SO	SB
Jim Barr, p	.000	1	1	0	0	0	0	0	0	0	0	0
Bobby Bonds, of	.250	3	8	0	2	0	0	0	0	2	4	0
Ron Bryant, p	.000	1	0	0	0	0	0	0	0	0	0	0
Don Carrithers, p	.000	1	0	0	0	0	0	0	0	0	0	0
John Cumberland, p	.000	1	0	0	0	0	0	0	0	0	0	0
Dick Dietz, c	.067	4	15	0	1	0	0	0	0	2	5	0
Frank Duffy, ph	.000	1	1	0	0	0	0	0	0	0	1	0
Tito Fuentes, 2b	.313	4	16	4	5	1	0	1	2	1	3	0
Alan Gallagher, 3b	.100	4	10	0	1	0	0	0	0	0	2	0
Steve Hamilton, p	.000	1	0	0	0	0	0	0	0	0	0	0
Jim Ray Hart, 3b-1	.000	3	5	0	0	0	0	0	0	0	2	0
Ken Henderson, of	.313	4	16	3	5	1	0	0	2	2	1	1
Jerry Johnson, p	.000	1	0	0	0	0	0	0	0	0	0	0
Dave Kingman, of-2	.111	4	9	0	1	0	0	0	0	1	3	0
Hal Lanier, 3b	.000	1	1	0	0	0	0	0	0	0	0	0
Juan Marichal, p	.000	1	3	0	0	0	0	0	0	0	1	0
Willie Mays, of	.267	4	15	2	4	2	0	1	3	3	3	1
Willie McCovey, 1b	.429	4	14	2	6	0	0	2	6	4	2	0
Don McMahon, p	.000	2	0	0	0	0	0	0	0	0	0	0
Gaylord Perry, p	.250	2	4	0	1	0	0	0	0	0	0	0
Jimmy Rosario, pr	.000	1	0	0	0	0	0	0	0	0	0	0
Chris Speier, ss	.357	4	14	4	5	1	0	1	1	1	1	0
TOTAL	.235		132	15	31	5	0	5	14	16	28	2

PITCHER	W	L	ERA	G	GS	CG	SV	SHO	IP	H	ER	BB	SO
Jim Barr	0	0	9.00	1	0	0	0	0	1.0	3	1	0	2
Ron Bryant	0	0	4.50	1	0	0	0	0	2.0	1	1	1	2
Don Carrithers	0	0	INF	1	0	0	0	0	0.0	3	3	0	0
John Cumberland	0	1	9.00	1	1	0	0	0	3.0	7	3	0	4
Steve Hamilton	0	0	9.00	1	0	0	0	0	1.0	1	1	0	0
Jerry Johnson	0	0	13.50	1	0	0	0	0	1.1	1	2	1	2
Juan Marichal	0	1	2.25	1	1	1	0	0	8.0	4	2	0	6
Don McMahon	0	0	0.00	2	0	0	0	0	3.0	1	0	0	3
Gaylord Perry	1	1	6.14	2	2	1	0	0	14.2	19	10	3	11
TOTAL	1	3	6.09	11	4	2	0	0	34.0	39	23	5	33

GAME 1 AT SF OCT 2

PIT	002	000	200	4	9 0
SF	001	040	00X	5	7 2

Pitchers: BLASS, Moose (6), Giusti (8) vs PERRY
Home Runs: Fuentes-SF, McCovey-SF
Attendance: 40,977

GAME 2 AT SF OCT 3

PIT	010	210	401	9	15 0
SF	110	000	002	4	9 0

Pitchers: ELLIS, Miller (6), Giusti (9) vs CUMBERLAND, Barr (4), McMahon (5), Carrithers (7), Bryant (7), Hamilton (9)
Home Runs: Robertson-PIT (3), Clines-PIT, Mays-SF
Attendance: 42,562

GAME 3 AT PIT OCT 5

SF	000	001	000	1	5 2
PIT	010	000	01X	2	4 1

Pitchers: MARICHAL vs JOHNSON, Giusti (9)
Home Runs: Robertson-PIT, Hebner-PIT
Attendance: 38,322

GAME 4 AT PIT OCT 6

SF	140	000	000	5	10 0
PIT	230	004	00X	9	11 2

Pitchers: PERRY, Johnson (6), McMahon (8) vs Blass, KISON (3), Giusti (7)
Home Runs: Speier-SF, McCovey-SF, Hebner-PIT, Oliver-PIT
Attendance: 35,487

Baltimore, dividing its fifteen runs evenly among the three games, swept the ALCS for the third year in a row.

Oakland's Vida Blue took a 3–1 lead into the seventh inning of Game One, but with two away and men on first and third, an Oriole single and two doubles pushed across four runs to beat him 5–3, as Oriole starter Dave McNally and reliever Eddie Watt held the A's scoreless from the fifth inning on. In the second game Oakland managed only one run off Mike Cuellar, while the Orioles hammered Catfish Hunter for five runs on four homers—two of them by Boog Powell, including one in the eighth with a man aboard.

Reggie Jackson retaliated for the A's in Game Three with two home runs off Jim Palmer, and Sal Bando added a third. But Palmer permitted no other A's to score, and—supported by a Baltimore run in the first and two each in the fifth and seventh—preserved an Oriole lead throughout the game, for the third year in a row clinching the pennant for Baltimore with a complete-game victory.

Baltimore Orioles (East), 3; Oakland A's (West) 0

BAL (E)

PLAYER/POS	AVG	G	AB	R	H	2B	3B	HR	RB	BB	SO	SB
Mark Belanger, ss	.250	3	8	1	2	0	0	0	1	3	2	0
Paul Blair, of	.333	3	9	1	3	1	0	0	2	0	3	0
Don Buford, of	.429	2	7	1	3	0	1	0	0	2	1	0
Mike Cuellar, p	.333	1	3	0	1	0	0	0	0	0	2	0
Andy Etchebarren, c	.000	2	5	0	0	0	0	0	0	0	0	0
Elrod Hendricks, c	.500	2	4	1	2	0	0	1	2	1	1	0
Davey Johnson, 2b	.300	3	10	2	3	2	0	0	0	3	1	0
Dave McNally, p	.000	1	2	0	0	0	0	0	0	0	0	0
Curt Motton, ph	1.000	1	1	0	1	1	0	0	1	0	0	0
Jim Palmer, p-1	.200	2	5	1	1	0	0	0	0	0	1	0
Boog Powell, 1b	.300	3	10	4	3	0	0	2	3	3	3	0
Merv Rettenmund, of	.250	3	8	0	2	1	0	0	1	0	3	0
Brooks Robinson, 3b	.364	3	11	2	4	1	0	1	3	0	1	0
Frank Robinson, of	.083	3	12	2	1	1	0	0	1	1	4	0
Eddie Watt, p	.000	1	0	0	0	0	0	0	0	0	0	0
TOTAL	.274		95	15	26	7	1	4	14	13	22	0

PITCHER	W	L	ERA	G	GS	CG	SV	SHO	IP	H	ER	BB	SO
Mike Cuellar	1	0	1.00	1	1	1	0	0	9.0	6	1	1	2
Dave McNally	1	0	3.86	1	1	0	0	0	7.0	7	3	1	5
Jim Palmer	1	0	3.00	1	1	1	0	0	9.0	7	3	3	8
Eddie Watt	0	0	0.00	1	0	0	1	0	2.0	2	0	0	1
TOTAL	3	0	2.33	4	3	2	1	0	27.0	22	7	5	16

OAK (W)

PLAYER/POS	AVG	G	AB	R	H	2B	3B	HR	RB	BB	SO	SB
Sal Bando, 3b	.364	3	11	3	4	2	0	1	1	1	0	0
Curt Blefary, ph	.000	1	1	0	0	0	0	0	0	0	1	0
Vida Blue, p	.000	1	3	0	0	0	0	0	0	0	3	0
Bert Campaneris, ss	.167	3	12	0	2	1	0	0	0	0	1	0
Tommy Davis, 1b-2	.375	3	8	1	3	1	0	0	0	0	0	0
Dave Duncan, c	.500	2	6	0	3	1	0	0	2	0	0	0
Mike Epstein, 1b-1	.200	2	5	0	1	0	0	0	0	0	3	0
Rollie Fingers, p	.000	2	0	0	0	0	0	0	0	0	0	0
Mudcat Grant, p	.000	1	0	0	0	0	0	0	0	0	0	0
Dick Green, 2b	.286	3	7	0	2	0	0	0	0	1	1	0
Mike Hegan, ph	.000	1	1	0	0	0	0	0	0	0	1	0
Catfish Hunter, p	.000	1	3	0	0	0	0	0	0	0	1	0
Reggie Jackson, of	.333	3	12	2	4	1	0	2	2	0	1	0
Darold Knowles, p	.000	1	0	0	0	0	0	0	0	0	0	0
Bob Locker, p	.000	1	0	0	0	0	0	0	0	0	0	0
Angel Mangual, of	.167	3	12	1	2	1	1	0	2	0	1	0
Rick Monday, of	.000	1	3	0	0	0	0	0	0	1	2	0
Joe Rudi, of	.143	2	7	0	1	1	0	0	0	1	0	0
Diego Segui, p	.000	1	2	0	0	0	0	0	0	0	0	0
Gene Tenace, c	.000	1	3	0	0	0	0	0	0	1	1	0
TOTAL	.229		96	7	22	8	1	3	7	5	16	0

PITCHER	W	L	ERA	G	GS	CG	SV	SHO	IP	H	ER	BB	SO
Vida Blue	0	1	6.43	1	1	0	0	0	7.0	7	5	2	8
Rollie Fingers	0	0	7.71	2	0	0	0	0	2.1	2	2	1	2
Mudcat Grant	0	0	0.00	1	0	0	0	0	2.0	3	0	0	2
Catfish Hunter	0	1	5.63	1	1	1	0	0	8.0	7	5	2	6
Darold Knowles	0	0	0.00	1	0	0	0	0	0.1	1	0	0	0
Bob Locker	0	0	0.00	1	0	0	0	0	0.2	0	0	2	0
Diego Segui	0	1	5.79	1	1	0	0	0	4.2	6	3	6	4
TOTAL	0	3	5.40	8	3	1	0	0	25.0	26	15	13	22

GAME 1 AT BAL OCT 3

OAK	020	100	000	3	9	0
BAL	000	100	40X	5	7	1

Pitchers: BLUE, Fingers (8) vs McNALLY, Watt (8)
Attendance: 42,621

GAME 2 AT BAL OCT 4

OAK	000	100	000	1	6	0
BAL	000	100	40X	5	7	0

Pitchers: HUNTER vs CUELLAR
Home Runs: B.Robinson-BAL, Powell-BAL (2), Hendricks-BAL
Attendance: 35,003

GAME 3 AT OAK OCT 5

BAL	100	020	200	5	12	0
OAK	001	001	010	3	7	0

Pitchers: PALMER vs SEGUI, Fingers (5), Knowles (7), Locker (7), Grant (8)
Home Runs: Jackson-OAK (2), Bando-OAK
Attendance: 33,176

In its third successive Series, Baltimore faced its third different opponent and beat the Pirates in the first two games. A walk, a wild pitch, two Baltimore errors, and a single in the second inning of the opener gave Pittsburgh an early 3–0 lead. But Oriole pitcher Dave McNally shut out the Pirates on two hits the rest of the game as Frank Robinson, Merv Rettenmund and Don Buford homered to give Baltimore a 5–3 victory. Jim Palmer took the win in Game Two as Baltimore hammered Pirate pitching for fourteen hits and eleven runs before Palmer issued Richie Hebner a three-run homer—Pittsburgh's only scoring—in the eighth.

The Pirates overtook the Orioles when the Series moved to Pittsburgh. Steve Blass pitched a three-hitter in Game Three, and while Frank Robinson's solo homer in the seventh ended Blass's shutout, a three-run shot by Pirate Bob Robertson in the last of the inning cemented a 5–1 Pittsburgh win. The next evening (in the first World Series night game ever), Baltimore scored three times in the top of the first inning, but two Pirate runs later in the inning and another run in the third tied the game. It remained tied until Pirate pinch hitter Milt May singled home the game winner with two away in the seventh.

With the Series now even at two wins apiece, Pittsburgh's Nelson Briles stopped the Orioles in Game Five on a pair of singles. Bob Robertson's leadoff homer in the second proved all the Pirates needed for the win, but Briles himself drove in an insurance run later in the inning and Pittsburgh went on to win 4–0.

The Pirates tried to win it all in Game Six, scoring single runs against the O's Jim Palmer in the second inning and the third (Roberto Clemente's home run). But Pirate starter Bob Moose was replaced after giving up a solo homer to Don Buford in the sixth, and a tying Baltimore run came home an inning later. A ninth-inning pinch hitter for Palmer produced nothing, but Baltimore won in the last of the tenth, when Frank Robinson scored on Brooks Robinson's sacrifice fly to shallow center.

Steve Blass, who had defeated Oriole Mike Cuellar in Game Three, faced him again in the finale and again emerged the victor of a pitching duel. Clemente's two-out homer in the fourth inning provided the game's only run until the eighth, when both teams scored single runs. Blass retired Baltimore in order in the ninth and the Pirates were world champions.

Pittsburgh Pirates (NL), 4;
Baltimore Orioles (AL) 3

PIT (N)

PLAYER/POS	AVG	G	AB	R	H	2B	3B	HR	RB	BB	SO	SB
Gene Alley, ss	.000	2	2	0	0	0	0	0	0	1	0	0
Steve Blass, p	.000	2	7	0	0	0	0	0	0	0	1	0
Nelson Briles, p	.500	1	2	0	1	0	0	0	1	0	1	0
Dave Cash, 2b	.133	7	30	2	4	1	0	0	1	3	1	1
Roberto Clemente, of	.414	7	29	3	12	2	1	2	4	2	2	0
Gene Clines, of	.091	3	11	2	1	0	1	0	0	1	1	1
Vic Davalillo, of-2	.333	3	3	1	1	0	0	0	0	0	0	0
Dock Ellis, p	.000	1	1	0	0	0	0	0	0	0	1	0
Dave Giusti, p	.000	3	0	0	0	0	0	0	0	0	0	0
Richie Hebner, 3b	.167	3	12	2	2	0	0	1	3	3	3	0
Jackie Hernandez, ss	.222	7	18	2	4	0	0	0	1	2	5	1
Bob Johnson, p	.000	2	3	0	0	0	0	0	0	0	2	0
Bruce Kison, p	.000	2	2	0	0	0	0	0	0	1	2	0
Milt May, ph	.500	2	2	0	1	0	0	0	1	0	0	0
Bill Mazeroski, ph	.000	1	1	0	0	0	0	0	0	0	0	0
Bob Miller, p	.000	3	0	0	0	0	0	0	0	0	0	0
Bob Moose, p	.000	3	0	0	0	0	0	0	0	0	1	0
Al Oliver, of-4	.211	5	19	1	4	2	0	0	2	2	5	0
Jose Pagan, 3b	.267	4	15	0	4	2	0	0	2	0	1	0
Bob Robertson, 1b	.240	7	25	4	6	0	0	2	5	4	8	0
Charlie Sands, ph	.000	1	1	0	0	0	0	0	0	0	1	0
Manny Sanguillen, c	.379	7	29	3	11	1	0	0	0	0	3	2
Willie Stargell, of	.208	7	24	3	5	1	0	0	1	7	9	0
Bob Veale, p	.000	1	0	0	0	0	0	0	0	0	0	0
Luke Walker, p	.000	1	0	0	0	0	0	0	0	0	0	0
TOTAL	.235		238	23	56	9	2	5	21	26	47	5

PITCHER	W	L	ERA	G	GS	CG	SV	SHO	IP	H	ER	BB	SO
Steve Blass	2	0	1.00	2	2	2	0	0	18.0	7	2	4	13
Nelson Briles	1	0	0.00	1	1	1	0	1	9.0	2	0	2	2
Dock Ellis	0	1	15.43	1	1	0	0	0	2.1	4	4	1	1
Dave Giusti	0	0	0.00	3	0	0	1	0	5.1	3	0	2	4
Bob Johnson	0	1	9.00	2	1	0	0	0	5.0	5	5	3	3
Bruce Kison	1	0	0.00	2	0	0	0	0	6.1	1	0	2	3
Bob Miller	0	1	3.86	3	0	0	0	0	4.2	7	2	1	2
Bob Moose	0	0	6.52	3	1	0	0	0	9.2	12	7	2	7
Bob Veale	0	0	13.50	1	0	0	0	0	0.2	1	1	2	0
Luke Walker	0	0	40.50	1	1	0	0	0	0.2	3	3	1	0
TOTAL	4	3	3.50	19	7	3	1	1	61.2	45	24	20	35

BAL (A)

PLAYER/POS	AVG	G	AB	R	H	2B	3B	HR	RB	BB	SO	SB
Mark Belanger, ss	.238	7	21	4	5	0	1	0	0	5	2	1
Paul Blair, of-3	.333	4	9	2	3	1	0	0	0	0	1	0
Don Buford, of	.261	6	23	3	6	1	0	2	4	3	3	0
Mike Cuellar, p	.000	2	3	0	0	0	0	0	0	1	2	0
Pat Dobson, p	.000	3	2	0	0	0	0	0	0	0	2	0
Tom Dukes, p	.000	2	0	0	0	0	0	0	0	0	0	0
Andy Etchebarren, c	.000	1	2	0	0	0	0	0	0	0	0	0
Dick Hall, p	.000	1	0	0	0	0	0	0	0	0	0	0
Elrod Hendricks, c	.263	6	19	3	5	1	0	0	1	3	3	0
Grant Jackson, p	.000	1	0	0	0	0	0	0	0	0	0	0
Davy Johnson, 2b	.148	7	27	1	4	0	0	0	3	0	1	0
Dave Leonhard, p	.000	1	0	0	0	0	0	0	0	0	0	0
Dave McNally, p	.000	4	4	0	0	0	0	0	0	0	3	0
Jim Palmer, p	.000	2	4	0	0	0	0	0	0	2	2	0
Boog Powell, 1b	.111	7	27	1	3	0	0	0	1	1	3	0
Merv Rettenmund, of-6	.185	7	27	3	5	0	0	1	4	0	4	0
Pete Richert, p	.000	1	0	0	0	0	0	0	0	0	0	0
Brooks Robinson, 3b	.318	7	22	2	7	0	0	0	5	3	1	0
Frank Robinson, of	.280	7	25	5	7	0	0	2	2	2	8	0
Tom Shopay, ph	.000	5	4	0	0	0	0	0	0	0	0	0
Eddie Watt, p	.000	2	0	0	0	0	0	0	0	0	0	0
TOTAL	.205		219	24	45	3	1	5	22	20	35	1

PITCHER	W	L	ERA	G	GS	CG	SV	SHO	IP	H	ER	BB	SO
Mike Cuellar	0	2	3.86	2	2	0	0	0	14.0	11	6	6	10
Pat Dobson	0	0	4.05	3	1	0	0	0	6.2	13	3	4	6
Tom Dukes	0	0	0.00	2	0	0	0	0	4.0	2	0	0	1
Dick Hall	0	0	0.00	1	0	0	1	0	1.0	1	0	0	0
Grant Jackson	0	0	0.00	1	0	0	0	0	0.2	0	0	1	0
Dave Leonhard	0	0	0.00	1	0	0	0	0	1.0	0	0	1	0
Dave McNally	2	1	1.98	4	2	1	0	0	13.2	10	3	5	12
Jim Palmer	1	0	2.65	2	2	0	0	0	17.0	15	5	9	15
Pete Richert	0	0	0.00	1	0	0	0	0	0.2	0	0	0	1
Eddie Watt	0	1	3.86	2	0	0	0	0	2.1	4	1	0	2
TOTAL	3	4	2.66	19	7	1	1	0	61.0	56	18	26	47

GAME 1 AT BAL OCT 9

PIT	030 000 000	3 3 0
BAL	013 010 00X	5 10 3

Pitchers: ELLIS, Moose (3), Miller (7) vs McNALLY
Home Runs: F.Robinson-BAL, Rettenmund-BAL, Buford-BAL
Attendance: 53,229

GAME 2 AT BAL OCT 11

PIT	000 000 030	3 8 1
BAL	010 361 00X	11 14 1

Pitchers: R.JOHNSON, Kison (4), Moose (4), Veale (5), Miller (6), Giusti (8) vs PALMER, Hall (9)
Home Runs: Hebner-PIT
Attendance: 53,239

GAME 3 AT PIT OCT 12

BAL	000 000 100	1 3 3
PIT	100 001 30X	5 7 0

Pitchers: CUELLAR, Dukes (7), Watt (8) vs BLASS
Home Runs: F.Robinson-BAL, Robertson-PIT
Attendance: 50,403

GAME 4 AT PIT OCT 13

BAL	300 000 000	3 4 1
PIT	201 000 10X	4 14 0

Pitchers: Dobson, Jackson (6), WATT (7), Richert (8) vs Walker, KISON (1), Giusti (8)
Attendance: 51,378

GAME 5 AT PIT OCT 14

BAL	000 000 000	0 2 1
PIT	021 010 00X	4 9 0

Pitchers: McNALLY, Leonhard (5), Dukes (6) vs BRILES
Home Runs: Robertson-PIT
Attendance: 51,377

GAME 6 AT BAL OCT 16

PIT	011 000 000 0	2 9 1
BAL	000 001 100 1	3 8 0

Pitchers: Moose, R.Johnson (6), Giusti (7), MILLER (10) vs Palmer, Dobson (10), McNALLY (10)
Home Runs: Clemente-PIT, Buford-BAL
Attendance: 44,174

GAME 7 AT BAL OCT 17

PIT	000 100 010	2 6 1
BAL	000 000 001	1 4 0

Pitchers: BLASS vs CUELLAR, Dobson (9), McNally (9)
Home Runs: Clemente-PIT
Attendance: 47,291

Pittsburgh traded wins with Cincinnati through the first four games—winning the first and third—and took a lead into the ninth inning of the fifth game before a home run and a wild pitch undid them.

Cincinnati got eight hits in each of the first two games. In the first game, though, only Joe Morgan's first-inning homer produced a run, and the Reds lost 1–5. But the next day, five first-inning hits gave the Reds four runs and a lead the Pirates could not overcome.

Pirate catcher Manny Sanguillen brought Pittsburgh back in Game Three with a home run in the fifth and the game-winning RBI in the eighth. But Reds pitcher Ross Grimsley evened the series for Cincinnati the next day with a two-hitter, in the series' only complete-game performance.

Game Five was Pittsburgh's for 8½ innings. The Pirates scored first, and held the lead into the bottom of the ninth. But Johnny Bench opened the Reds' half of the ninth with a game-tying home run, and Tony Perez and Denis Menke followed him with singles. Bob Moose came in and retired the next two men, though George Foster (running for Perez) took third on a fly to right. Moose then threw away the pennant with a run-scoring, series-ending wild pitch.

Cincinnati Reds (West), 3;
Pittsburgh Pirates (East) 2

CIN (W)

PLAYER/POS	AVG	G	AB	R	H	2B	3B	HR	RB	BB	SO	SB
Johnny Bench, c	.333	5	18	3	6	1	1	1	2	1	3	2
Jack Billingham, p	.000	1	2	0	0	0	0	0	0	0	1	0
Pedro Borbon, p	.000	3	0	0	0	0	0	0	0	0	0	0
Clay Carroll, p	.000	2	0	0	0	0	0	0	0	0	0	0
Darrel Chaney, ss	.188	5	16	3	3	0	0	0	1	1	1	1
Dave Concepcion, ss-1	.000	3	2	0	0	0	0	0	0	0	0	0
George Foster, pr	.000	1	0	1	0	0	0	0	0	0	0	0
Cesar Geronimo, of	.100	5	20	2	2	0	0	1	1	0	2	0
Ross Grimsley, p	.500	1	4	0	2	1	0	0	1	0	1	0
Don Gullett, p	.500	2	2	0	1	0	0	0	0	0	0	0
Joe Hague, ph	.000	3	1	0	0	0	0	0	0	2	1	0
Tom Hall, p	.000	2	1	0	0	0	0	0	0	0	0	0
Jim McGlothlin, p	.000	1	0	0	0	0	0	0	0	0	0	0
Hal McRae, ph	.000	1	0	0	0	0	0	0	0	0	0	0
Denis Menke, 3b	.250	5	16	1	4	1	0	0	4	3	0	
Joe Morgan, 2b	.263	5	19	5	5	0	0	2	3	1	2	1
Gary Nolan, p	.000	1	2	0	0	0	0	0	0	0	1	0
Tony Perez, 1b	.200	5	20	0	4	1	0	0	2	0	7	0
Pete Rose, of	.450	5	20	1	9	4	0	0	2	1	2	0
Bobby Tolan, of	.238	5	21	3	5	1	1	0	4	0	4	0
Ted Uhlaender, ph	.500	2	2	0	1	0	0	0	0	0	0	0
TOTAL	.253		166	19	42	9	2	4	16	10	28	4

PITCHER	W	L	ERA	G	GS	CG	SV	SHO	IP	H	ER	BB	SO
Jack Billingham	0	0	3.86	1	1	0	0	0	4.2	5	2	2	4
Pedro Borbon	0	0	2.08	3	0	0	0	0	4.1	2	1	0	1
Clay Carroll	1	1	3.38	2	0	0	0	0	2.2	2	1	3	0
Ross Grimsley	1	0	1.00	1	1	1	0	0	9.0	2	1	0	5
Don Gullett	0	1	8.00	2	2	0	0	0	9.0	12	8	0	5
Tom Hall	1	0	1.23	2	0	0	0	0	7.1	3	1	3	8
Jim McGlothlin	0	0	0.00	1	0	0	0	0	1.0	0	0	0	0
Gary Nolan	0	0	1.50	1	1	0	0	0	6.0	4	1	1	4
TOTAL	3	2	3.07	13	5	1	0	0	44.0	30	15	9	27

PIT (E)

PLAYER/POS	AVG	G	AB	R	H	2B	3B	HR	RB	BB	SO	SB
Gene Alley, ss	.000	5	16	1	0	0	0	0	0	0	3	0
Steve Blass, p	.000	2	6	0	0	0	0	0	0	0	3	0
Nelson Briles, p	.000	1	2	0	0	0	0	0	0	0	1	0
Dave Cash, 2b	.211	5	19	0	4	0	0	0	3	0	0	0
Roberto Clemente, of	.235	5	17	1	4	1	0	1	2	3	5	0
Gene Clines, ph	.000	3	2	1	0	0	0	0	0	0	1	0
Vic Davalillo, ph	.000	1	0	0	0	0	0	0	0	1	0	0
Dock Ellis, p-1	.000	2	1	0	0	0	0	0	0	0	0	0
Dave Giusti, p	.000	3	1	0	0	0	0	0	0	0	0	0
Richie Hebner, 3b	.188	5	16	2	3	1	0	0	1	1	3	0
Ramon Hernandez, p	.000	3	0	0	0	0	0	0	0	0	0	0
Bob Johnson, p	.000	2	1	0	0	0	0	0	0	0	1	0
Bruce Kison, p	.000	2	0	0	0	0	0	0	0	0	0	0
Milt May, c	.500	1	2	0	1	0	0	0	1	0	0	0
Bill Mazeroski, ph	.500	2	2	0	1	0	0	0	0	1	0	0
Bob Miller, p	.000	1	0	0	0	0	0	0	0	0	0	0
Bob Moose, p	.000	2	0	0	0	0	0	0	0	0	0	0
Al Oliver, of	.250	5	20	3	5	2	1	1	3	0	4	0
Bob Robertson, 1b	.000	4	0	0	0	0	0	0	0	1	0	0
Manny Sanguillen, c	.313	5	16	4	5	1	0	1	2	0	0	0
Willie Stargell, 1b-5,of-1	.063	5	16	1	1	1	0	0	1	2	5	0
Rennie Stennett, of-5,2b-1	.286	5	21	2	6	0	0	0	1	1	0	0
Luke Walker, p	.000	1	0	0	0	0	0	0	0	0	0	0
TOTAL	.190		158	15	30	6	1	3	14	9	27	0

PITCHER	W	L	ERA	G	GS	CG	SV	SHO	IP	H	ER	BB	SO
Steve Blass	1	0	1.72	2	2	0	0	0	15.2	12	3	6	5
Nelson Briles	0	0	3.00	1	1	0	0	0	6.0	6	2	1	3
Dock Ellis	0	1	0.00	1	1	0	0	0	5.0	5	0	1	3
Dave Giusti	0	1	6.75	3	0	0	1	0	2.2	5	2	0	3
Ramon Hernandez	0	0	2.70	3	0	0	1	0	3.1	1	1	0	3
Bob Johnson	0	0	3.00	2	0	0	0	0	6.0	4	2	2	7
Bruce Kison	1	0	0.00	2	0	0	0	0	2.1	1	0	0	3
Bob Miller	0	0	0.00	1	0	0	0	0	1.0	0	0	0	1
Bob Moose	0	1	54.00	2	1	0	0	0	0.2	5	4	0	0
Luke Walker	0	0	18.00	1	0	0	0	0	1.0	3	2	0	0
TOTAL	2	3	3.30	18	5	0	2	0	43.2	42	16	10	28

GAME 1 AT PIT OCT 7

CIN	100	000	000	1	8	0
PIT	300	020	00X	5	6	0

Pitchers: GULLETT, Borbon (7) vs BLASS, R.Hernandez (9)
Home Runs: Morgan-CIN, Oliver-PIT
Attendance: 50,476

GAME 2 AT PIT OCT 8

CIN	400	000	010	5	8	1
PIT	000	111	000	3	7	1

Pitchers: Billingham, HALL (5) vs MOOSE, Johnson (1), Kison (6), R.Hernandez (7), Giusti (9)
Home Runs: Morgan-CIN
Attendance: 50,584

GAME 3 AT CIN OCT 9

PIT	000	010	110	3	7	0
CIN	002	000	000	2	8	1

Pitchers: Briles, KISON (7), Giusti (8) vs Nolan, Borbon (7), CARROLL (7), McGlothlin (9)
Home Runs: Sanguillen-PIT
Attendance: 52,420

GAME 4 AT CIN OCT 10

PIT	000	000	100	1	2	3
CIN	100	202	20X	7	11	1

Pitchers: ELLIS, Johnson (6), Walker (7), Miller (8) vs GRIMSLEY
Home Runs: Clemente-PIT
Attendance: 39,447

GAME 5 AT CIN OCT 11

PIT	020	100	000	3	8	0
CIN	001	010	002	4	7	1

Pitchers: Blass, R.Hernandez (8), GIUSTI (9), Moose (9) vs Gullett, Borbon (4), Hall (6), CARROLL (9)
Home Runs: Geronimo-CIN, Bench-CIN
Attendance: 41,887

Oakland turned back the Tigers in the first two games, but Detroit evened the series before succumbing in the fifth game.

In Game One, Tiger Al Kaline homered off Rollie Fingers in the eleventh to give starter Mickey Lolich a 2–1 lead. But in the last of the inning, pinch hitter Gonzalo Marquez singled off Tiger reliever Chuck Seelbach with two on to drive in the tying run, and Gene Tenace scored to win it on the same play as right fielder Kaline threw the ball away. Blue Moon Odom increased the A's series lead with a three-hit shutout in Game Two, but Detroit's Joe Coleman retaliated with 14 strikeouts and a shutout of his own to save the Tigers from elimination in Game Three.

In Game Four the A's pulled out of a 1–1 tie with two runs in the top of the tenth. But Detroit in its half of the inning went through three Oakland relievers for three runs and the win. In the finale, after Odom, the A's starter, had given Detroit a run and a brief lead in the first, he and Vida Blue divided eight shutout innings between them as the A's scored twice to capture their first pennant since Connie Mack won his last in Philadelphia forty-one years earlier.

Oakland A's (West), 3;
Detroit Tigers (East) 2

OAK (W)

PLAYER/POS	AVG	G	AB	R	H	2B	3B	HR	RB	BB	SO	SB
Matty Alou, of	.381	5	21	2	8	4	0	0	2	0	2	1
Sal Bando, 3b	.200	5	20	0	4	0	0	0	0	0	3	0
Vida Blue, p	.000	4	1	0	0	0	0	0	0	0	0	0
Bert Campaneris, ss	.429	2	7	3	3	0	0	0	0	1	0	2
Tim Cullen, ss	.000	2	1	0	0	0	0	0	0	0	0	0
Dave Duncan, c	.000	2	2	0	0	0	0	0	0	1	1	0
Mike Epstein, 1b	.188	5	16	1	3	0	0	1	1	4	5	1
Rollie Fingers, p	.000	3	1	0	0	0	0	0	0	0	0	0
Dick Green, 2b	.125	5	8	0	1	1	0	0	0	0	0	0
Dave Hamilton, p	.000	1	0	0	0	0	0	0	0	0	0	0
Mike Hegan, 1b-1	.000	3	1	1	0	0	0	0	0	0	0	0
George Hendrick, of-1	.143	5	7	2	1	0	0	0	0	0	1	0
Ken Holtzman, p	.000	1	1	0	0	0	0	0	0	0	1	0
Joe Horlen, p	.000	1	0	0	0	0	0	0	0	0	0	0
Catfish Hunter, p	.167	2	6	0	1	0	0	0	0	0	2	0
Reggie Jackson, of	.278	5	18	1	5	1	0	0	2	1	6	2
Ted Kubiak, 2b-3,ss-1	.500	4	4	0	2	0	0	0	1	0	0	0
Bob Locker, p	.000	2	0	0	0	0	0	0	0	0	0	0
Angel Mangual, ph	.000	3	3	0	0	0	0	0	0	0	1	0
Gonzalo Marquez, ph	.667	3	3	1	2	0	0	0	1	0	0	0
Dal Maxvill, ss-4,2b-1	.125	5	8	0	1	0	0	0	0	1	2	1
Don Mincher, ph	.000	1	1	0	0	0	0	0	0	0	0	0
Blue Moon Odom, p-2	.250	3	4	0	1	1	0	0	0	0	1	0
Joe Rudi, of	.250	5	20	1	5	1	0	0	2	1	4	0
Gene Tenace, c-5,2b-2	.059	5	17	1	1	0	0	0	1	3	5	0
TOTAL	.224		170	13	38	8	0	1	10	12	35	7

PITCHER	W	L	ERA	G	GS	CG	SV	SHO	IP	H	ER	BB	SO
Vida Blue	0	0	0.00	4	0	0	1	0	5.1	4	0	1	5
Rollie Fingers	1	0	1.69	3	0	0	0	0	5.1	4	1	1	3
Dave Hamilton	0	0	INF	1	0	0	0	0	0.0	1	0	1	0
Ken Holtzman	0	1	4.50	1	1	0	0	0	4.0	4	2	2	2
Joe Horlen	0	1	INF	1	0	0	0	0	0.0	0	1	1	0
Catfish Hunter	0	0	1.17	2	2	0	0	0	15.1	10	2	5	9
Bob Locker	0	0	13.50	2	0	0	0	0	2.0	4	3	0	1
Blue Moon Odom	2	0	0.00	2	2	1	0	1	14.0	5	0	2	5
TOTAL	3	2	1.76	16	5	1	1	1	46.0	32	9	13	25

DET (E)

PLAYER/POS	AVG	G	AB	R	H	2B	3B	HR	RB	BB	SO	SB
Ed Brinkman, ss	.250	1	4	0	1	1	0	0	0	0	0	0
Ike Brown, 1b	.500	1	2	0	1	0	0	0	2	0	1	0
Gates Brown, ph	.000	3	2	1	0	0	0	0	0	1	0	0
Norm Cash, 1b	.267	5	15	1	4	0	0	1	2	2	3	0
Joe Coleman, p	.500	1	2	0	1	0	0	0	0	1	0	0
Bill Freehan, c	.250	3	12	2	3	1	0	1	3	0	1	0
Woody Fryman, p	.000	2	3	0	0	0	0	0	0	0	0	0
Tom Haller, ph	.000	1	1	0	0	0	0	0	0	0	0	0
John Hiller, p	.000	3	0	0	0	0	0	0	0	0	0	0
Willie Horton, of-3	.100	5	10	0	1	0	0	0	0	1	3	0
Al Kaline, of	.263	5	19	3	5	0	0	1	1	2	2	0
John Knox, pr	.000	1	0	0	0	0	0	0	0	0	0	0
Lerrin La Grow, p	.000	1	0	0	0	0	0	0	0	0	0	0
Mickey Lolich, p	.000	2	7	0	0	0	0	0	0	0	2	0
Dick McAuliffe, ss-4,2b-1	.200	5	20	3	4	0	0	1	1	1	4	0
Jim Northrup, of	.357	5	14	0	5	0	0	0	1	2	3	0
Aurelio Rodriguez, 3b	.000	5	16	0	0	0	0	0	0	2	2	0
Fred Scherman, p	.000	1	0	0	0	0	0	0	0	0	0	0
Chuck Seelbach, p	.000	2	0	0	0	0	0	0	0	0	0	0
Duke Sims, c-2,of-2	.214	4	14	0	3	2	1	0	0	1	2	0
Mickey Stanley, of-3	.333	4	6	0	2	0	0	0	0	0	0	0
Tony Taylor, 2b	.133	4	15	0	2	2	0	0	0	0	2	0
Chris Zachary, p	.000	1	0	0	0	0	0	0	0	0	0	0
TOTAL	.198		162	10	32	6	1	4	10	13	25	0

PITCHER	W	L	ERA	G	GS	CG	SV	SHO	IP	H	ER	BB	SO
Joe Coleman	1	0	0.00	1	1	1	0	1	9.0	7	0	3	14
Woody Fryman	0	2	3.65	2	2	0	0	0	12.1	11	5	2	8
John Hiller	1	0	0.00	3	0	0	0	0	3.1	1	0	1	1
Lerrin La Grow	0	0	0.00	1	0	0	0	0	1.0	0	0	0	1
Mickey Lolich	0	1	1.42	2	2	0	0	0	19.0	14	3	5	10
Fred Scherman	0	0	0.00	1	0	0	0	0	0.2	1	0	0	1
Chuck Seelbach	0	0	18.00	2	0	0	0	0	1.0	4	2	0	0
Chris Zachary	0	0	INF	1	0	0	0	0	0.0	0	1	1	0
TOTAL	2	3	2.14	13	5	1	0	1	46.1	38	11	12	35

GAME 1 AT OAK OCT 7

DET	010	000	000	01	2 6 2
OAK	001	000	000	02	3 10 1

Pitchers: LOLICH, Seelbach (11) vs Hunter, Blue (9), FINGERS (9)
Home Runs: Cash-DET, Kaline-DET
Attendance: 29,536

GAME 2 AT OAK OCT 8

DET	000	000	000	0 3 1
OAK	100	040	00X	5 8 0

Pitchers: FRYMAN, Zachary (5), Scherman (5), LaGrow (6), Hiller (7) vs ODOM
Attendance: 31,088

GAME 3 AT DET OCT 10

OAK	000	000	000	0 7 0
DET	000	200	01X	3 8 1

Pitchers: HOLTZMAN, Fingers (5), Blue (6), Locker (7) vs COLEMAN
Home Runs: Freehan-DET
Attendance: 41,156

GAME 4 AT DET OCT 11

OAK	000	000	100	2 3 9 2
DET	001	000	000	3 4 10 1

Pitchers: Hunter, Fingers (8), Blue (9), Locker (10), HORLEN (10), Hamilton (10) vs Lolich, Seelbach (10), HILLER (10)
Home Runs: McAuliffe-DET, Epstein-OAK
Attendance: 37,615

GAME 5 AT DET OCT 12

OAK	010	100	000	2 4 0
DET	100	000	000	1 5 2

Pitchers: ODOM, Blue (6) vs FRYMAN, Hiller (9)
Attendance: 50,276

Oakland slugger Reggie Jackson missed the Series with a pulled hamstring, but Gene Tenace (the A's backup catcher during the season) took up the slack, hitting four of the club's five homers and driving in nine of their sixteen runs.

Six of the seven games were decided by a single run. Oakland won the first two in Cincinnati, 3–2 and 2–1. Tenace made the difference in the opener, driving in all the A's runs with a two-run homer in the second inning and a solo shot in the fifth. In the second game, A's starting pitcher Catfish Hunter singled in a run in the second inning which proved the margin of his victory. His 8⅔-inning performance was the longest mound outing in a Series which saw the two clubs together use nearly seven pitchers per game.

Cincinnati took the first game in Oakland, 1–0. The A's' Blue Moon Odom dueled the Reds' Jack Billingham scorelessly on one hit through six innings before giving up the game's only run on a single-sacrifice-single in the seventh. Billingham, too, yielded only three hits in eight-plus innings before yielding to ace reliever Clay Carroll, who retired the side in the ninth.

Oakland won Game Four, 3–2. Tenace opened the scoring with a solo homer in the fifth. The Reds' Bobby Tolan doubled in a pair in the eighth to put Cincinnati ahead, but in the last of the ninth four successive A's singles scored two runs, with Tenace scoring the game winner on pinch hitter Angel Mangual's hit. Tenace homered again in Game Five for three runs, but it wasn't enough as the Reds tied the score in the eighth and won on Pete Rose's RBI single in the ninth.

The Reds produced the Series' only blowout with five runs in the seventh inning of Game Six to make the score 8–1, where it remained. The finale saw Tenace drive in a run in the top of the first for a narrow Oakland lead which held until the Reds tied the game in the fifth. In the sixth the A's scored twice—Tenace doubling in the go-ahead run. Cincinnati scored once more in the eighth as a runner inherited by A's reliever Rollie Fingers came home on a sacrifice fly. But Fingers permitted no other runs to score, and the A's took the crown with their fourth one-run victory.

Oakland Athletics (AL), 4;
Cincinnati Reds (NL) 3

OAK (A)

PLAYER/POS	AVG	G	AB	R	H	2B	3B	HR	RB	BB	SO	SB
Matty Alou, of	.042	7	24	0	1	0	0	0	0	0	3	0	1
Sal Bando, 3b	.269	7	26	2	7	1	0	0	1	2	5	0
Vida Blue, p	.000	4	1	0	0	0	0	0	0	0	1	0
Bert Campaneris, ss	.179	7	28	1	5	0	0	0	0	1	4	0
Dave Duncan, c-1	.200	3	5	0	1	0	0	0	0	1	3	0
Mike Epstein, 1b	.000	6	16	1	0	0	0	0	0	5	3	0
Rollie Fingers, p	.000	6	1	0	0	0	0	0	0	0	0	0
Dick Green, 2b	.333	7	18	0	6	2	0	0	1	0	4	0
Dave Hamilton, p	.000	2	0	0	0	0	0	0	0	0	0	0
Mike Hegan, 1b-5	.200	6	5	0	1	0	0	0	0	0	2	0
George Hendrick, of	.133	5	15	3	2	0	0	0	0	1	2	0
Ken Holtzman, p	.000	3	5	0	0	0	0	0	0	0	0	0
Joe Horlen, p	.000	1	0	0	0	0	0	0	0	0	0	0
Catfish Hunter, p	.200	3	5	0	1	0	0	0	1	2	1	0
Ted Kubiak, 2b	.333	4	3	0	1	0	0	0	0	0	0	0
Allan Lewis, pr	.000	6	0	0	0	0	0	0	0	0	0	0
Bob Locker, p	.000	1	0	0	0	0	0	0	0	0	0	0
Angel Mangual, of-2	.300	4	10	1	3	0	0	0	1	0	0	0
Gonzalo Marquez, ph	.600	5	5	0	3	0	0	0	1	0	0	0
Don Mincher, ph	1.000	3	1	0	1	0	0	0	1	0	0	0
Blue Moon Odom, p-2	.000	4	4	0	0	0	0	0	0	0	3	0
Joe Rudi, of	.240	7	25	1	6	0	0	1	1	2	5	0
Gene Tenace, c-6,1b-1	.348	7	23	5	8	1	0	4	9	2	4	0
TOTAL	.209		220	16	46	4	0	5	16	21	37	1

PITCHER	W	L	ERA	G	GS	CG	SV	SHO	IP	H	ER	BB	SO
Vida Blue	0	1	4.15	4	1	0	1	0	8.2	8	4	5	5
Rollie Fingers	1	1	1.74	6	0	0	2	0	10.1	4	2	4	11
Dave Hamilton	0	0	6.75	2	0	0	0	0	1.1	2	1	2	1
Ken Holtzman	1	0	2.13	3	2	0	0	0	12.2	11	3	3	4
Joe Horlen	0	0	27.00	1	0	0	0	0	1.1	3	4	1	1
Catfish Hunter	2	0	2.81	3	2	0	0	0	16.0	12	5	6	11
Bob Locker	0	0	0.00	1	0	0	0	0	0.1	1	0	0	0
Blue Moon Odom	0	1	1.59	2	2	0	0	0	11.1	5	2	6	13
TOTAL	4	3	3.05	22	7	0	3	0	62.0	46	21	27	46

CIN (N)

PLAYER/POS	AVG	G	AB	R	H	2B	3B	HR	RB	BB	SO	SB
Johnny Bench, c	.261	7	23	4	6	1	0	1	1	5	5	2
Jack Billingham, p	.000	3	5	0	0	0	0	0	0	0	4	0
Pedro Borbon, p	.000	6	0	0	0	0	0	0	0	0	0	0
Clay Carroll, p	.000	5	0	0	0	0	0	0	0	0	0	0
Darrel Chaney, ss-3	.000	4	7	0	0	0	0	0	0	2	2	0
Dave Concepcion, ss-5	.308	6	13	2	4	0	1	0	2	2	2	1
George Foster, of-1	.000	2	0	0	0	0	0	0	0	0	0	0
Cesar Geronimo, of	.158	7	19	1	3	0	0	0	3	1	4	1
Ross Grimsley, p	.000	4	2	0	0	0	0	0	0	0	2	0
Don Gullett, p	.000	1	2	0	0	0	0	0	0	0	0	0
Joe Hague, of-1	.000	3	3	0	0	0	0	0	0	0	0	0
Tom Hall, p	.000	4	2	0	0	0	0	0	0	0	1	0
Julian Javier, ph	.000	4	2	0	0	0	0	0	0	0	0	0
Jim McGlothlin, p	.000	1	1	0	0	0	0	0	0	0	0	0
Hal McRae, of-2	.444	5	9	1	4	1	0	0	2	0	1	0
Denis Menke, 3b	.083	7	24	1	2	0	0	1	2	2	6	0
Joe Morgan, 2b	.125	7	24	4	3	2	0	0	1	6	3	2
Gary Nolan, p	.000	2	3	0	0	0	0	0	0	0	3	0
Tony Perez, 1b	.435	7	23	3	10	2	0	0	2	4	4	0
Pete Rose, of	.214	7	28	3	6	0	0	1	2	4	4	1
Bobby Tolan, of	.269	7	26	2	7	1	0	0	6	1	4	5
Ted Uhlaender, ph	.250	4	4	0	1	1	0	0	0	0	1	0
TOTAL	.209		220	21	46	8	1	3	21	27	46	12

PITCHER	W	L	ERA	G	GS	CG	SV	SHO	IP	H	ER	BB	SO
Jack Billingham	1	0	0.00	3	2	0	1	0	13.2	6	0	4	11
Pedro Borbon	0	1	3.86	6	0	0	0	0	7.0	7	3	2	4
Clay Carroll	0	1	1.59	5	0	0	1	0	5.2	6	1	4	3
Ross Grimsley	2	1	2.57	4	1	0	0	0	7.0	7	2	3	2
Don Gullett	0	0	1.29	1	1	0	0	0	7.0	5	1	2	4
Tom Hall	0	0	0.00	4	0	0	1	0	8.1	6	0	2	7
Jim McGlothlin	0	0	12.00	1	1	0	0	0	3.0	2	4	2	3
Gary Nolan	0	1	3.38	2	2	0	0	0	10.2	7	4	2	3
TOTAL	3	2	2.17	26	7	0	3	0	62.1	46	15	21	37

GAME 1 AT CIN OCT 14

OAK	020 010 000	3	4	0
CIN	010 100 000	2	7	0

Pitchers: HOLTZMAN, Fingers (6), Blue (7) vs NOLAN, Borbon (7), Carroll (8)
Home Runs: Tenace-OAK (2)
Attendance: 52,918

GAME 2 AT CIN OCT 15

OAK	011 000 000	2	9	2
CIN	000 000 001	1	6	0

Pitchers: HUNTER, Fingers (9) vs GRIMSLEY, Borbon (6), Hall (8)
Home Runs: Rudi-OAK
Attendance: 53,224

GAME 3 AT OAK OCT 18

CIN	000 000 100	1	4	2
OAK	000 000 000	0	3	2

Pitchers: BILLINGHAM, Carroll (9) vs ODOM, Blue (8), Fingers (8)
Attendance: 49,410

GAME 4 AT OAK OCT 19

CIN	000 000 020	2	7	1
OAK	000 010 002	3	10	1

Pitchers: Gullett, Borbon (8), CARROLL (9) vs Holtzman, Blue (8), FINGERS (9)
Home Runs: Tenace-OAK
Attendance: 49,410

GAME 5 AT OAK OCT 20

CIN	100 110 011	5	8	0
OAK	030 100 000	4	7	2

Pitchers: McGlothlin, Borbon (4), Hall (5), Carroll (7), GRIMSLEY (8), Billingham (9) vs Hunter, FINGERS (5), Hamilton (9)
Home Runs: Rose-CIN, Tenace-OAK, Menke-CIN
Attendance: 49,410

GAME 6 AT CIN OCT 21

OAK	000 010 000	1	7	1
CIN	000 111 50X	8	10	0

Pitchers: BLUE, Locker (6), Hamilton (7), Horlen (7) vs Nolan, GRIMSLEY (6), Borbon (6), Hall (8)
Home Runs: Bench-CIN
Attendance: 52,737

GAME 7 AT CIN OCT 22

OAK	100 002 000	3	6	1
CIN	000 010 010	2	4	2

Pitchers: Odom, HUNTER (5), Holtzman (8), Fingers (8) vs Billingham, BORBON (6), Carroll (6), Grimsley (7), Hall (8)
Attendance: 56,040

The Mets received strong pitching throughout the series, and their offense came through just often enough to defeat Cincinnati in five games.

Though three Reds pitchers held New York to three hits in Game One, the single Met run in the second seemed for a time enough for a win. But Tom Seaver gave up a home run to Pete Rose in the eighth and lost the game in the ninth when Johnny Bench homered. Not wanting another last-inning loss in Game Two, the Mets unloaded for four runs in the top of the ninth to add to their one in the fourth. But this time one would have been enough as Jon Matlack blanked the Reds on two hits.

The Mets made it easy for Jerry Koosman in Game Three in New York, scoring nine times in the first four innings. Things were more difficult for shortstop Bud Harrelson, who exchanged blows with Pete Rose following Rose's hard slide in the fifth inning. A bench-clearing melee ensued, and fans in the left field stands showered Rose with debris until a delegation of Tom Seaver, Willie Mays and Rusty Staub visited the area to calm nerves and eliminate the threat of a forfeit. In Game Four, though, Met bats were stifled once again as four Reds pitchers combined for a 12-inning three-hitter. The Reds won the game and tied the series on Rose's sweetly vengeful twelfth-inning homer.

In the finale the Mets took a quick two-run lead. Cincinnati tied the game in the top of the fifth, but New York retaliated with four more in the bottom of the inning. Seaver—and Tug McGraw in the ninth—held the Reds scoreless the rest of the way.

New York Mets (East), 3; Cincinnati Reds (West) 2

NY (E)

PLAYER/POS	AVG	G	AB	R	H	2B	3B	HR	RB	BB	SO	SB
Ken Boswell, ph	.000	1	1	0	0	0	0	0	0	0	0	0
Wayne Garrett, 3b	.087	5	23	1	2	1	0	1	1	0	5	0
Jerry Grote, c	.211	5	19	2	4	0	0	0	2	1	3	0
Don Hahn, of	.235	5	17	2	4	0	0	0	1	2	4	0
Bud Harrelson, ss	.167	5	18	1	3	0	0	0	2	1	1	0
Cleon Jones, of	.300	5	20	3	6	2	0	0	3	2	4	0
Jerry Koosman, p	.500	1	4	1	2	0	0	0	1	0	0	0
Ed Kranepool, of	.500	1	2	0	1	0	0	0	0	2	0	0
Jon Matlack, p	.000	1	2	0	0	0	0	0	0	1	2	0
Willie Mays, of	.333	1	3	1	1	0	0	0	1	0	0	0
Tug McGraw, p	.000	2	1	0	0	0	0	0	0	0	1	0
Felix Millan, 2b	.316	5	19	5	6	0	0	0	2	2	1	0
John Milner, 1b	.176	5	17	2	3	0	0	0	1	5	3	0
Harry Parker, p	.000	1	0	0	0	0	0	0	0	0	0	0
Tom Seaver, p	.333	2	6	1	2	2	0	0	1	1	1	0
Rusty Staub, of	.200	4	15	4	3	0	0	3	5	3	2	0
George Stone, p	.000	1	1	0	0	0	0	0	0	1	1	0
TOTAL	.220		168	23	37	5	0	3	22	19	28	0

PITCHER	W	L	ERA	G	GS	CG	SV	SHO	IP	H	ER	BB	SO
Jerry Koosman	1	0	2.00	1	1	1	0	0	9.0	8	2	0	9
Jon Matlack	1	0	0.00	1	1	1	0	1	9.0	2	0	3	9
Tug McGraw	0	0	0.00	2	0	0	1	0	5.0	4	0	3	3
Harry Parker	0	1	9.00	1	0	0	0	0	1.0	1	1	0	0
Tom Seaver	1	1	1.62	2	2	1	0	0	16.2	13	3	5	17
George Stone	0	0	1.35	1	1	0	0	0	6.2	3	1	2	4
TOTAL	3	2	1.33	8	5	3	1	1	47.1	31	7	13	42

CIN (W)

PLAYER/POS	AVG	G	AB	R	H	2B	3B	HR	RB	BB	SO	SB
Ed Armbrister, of-1	.167	3	6	0	1	0	0	0	0	0	5	0
Johnny Bench, c	.263	5	19	1	5	2	0	1	1	2	2	0
Jack Billingham, p	.000	2	3	0	0	0	0	0	0	0	1	0
Pedro Borbon, p	.000	4	0	0	0	0	0	0	0	0	0	0
Clay Carroll, p	.000	3	0	0	0	0	0	0	0	0	0	0
Darrel Chaney, ph	.000	5	9	0	0	0	0	0	0	3	4	0
Ed Crosby, ss	.500	2	2	0	1	0	0	0	0	0	1	0
Dan Driessen, 3b	.167	4	12	0	2	1	0	0	1	0	2	0
Phil Gagliano, ph	.000	3	3	0	0	0	0	0	0	0	2	0
Cesar Geronimo, of	.067	4	15	0	1	0	0	0	0	0	7	0
Ken Griffey, of-2	.143	3	7	0	1	1	0	0	0	0	1	0
Ross Grimsley, p	.000	2	0	0	0	0	0	0	0	0	0	0
Don Gullett, p	.000	3	1	0	0	0	0	0	0	0	0	0
Tom Hall, p	.000	3	0	0	0	0	0	0	0	0	0	0
Hal King, ph	.500	3	2	0	1	0	0	0	0	1	1	0
Andy Kosco, of	.300	3	10	0	3	0	0	0	0	2	3	0
Denis Menke, ss-2,3b-2	.222	3	9	1	2	0	0	1	1	1	2	0
Joe Morgan, 2b	.100	5	20	1	2	1	0	0	1	2	2	0
Roger Nelson, p	.000	1	1	0	0	0	0	0	0	0	1	0
Fred Norman, p	.000	1	1	0	0	0	0	0	0	0	1	0
Tony Perez, 1b	.091	5	22	1	2	0	0	1	2	0	4	0
Pete Rose, of	.381	5	21	3	8	1	0	2	2	2	2	0
Larry Stahl, ph	.500	4	4	1	2	0	0	0	0	0	1	0
Dave Tomlin, p	.000	1	0	0	0	0	0	0	0	0	0	0
TOTAL	.186		167	8	31	6	0	5	8	13	42	0

PITCHER	W	L	ERA	G	GS	CG	SV	SHO	IP	H	ER	BB	SO
Jack Billingham	0	1	4.50	2	2	0	0	0	12.0	9	6	4	9
Pedro Borbon	1	0	0.00	4	0	0	1	0	4.2	3	0	0	3
Clay Carroll	1	0	1.29	3	0	0	0	0	7.0	5	1	1	2
Ross Grimsley	0	1	12.27	2	1	0	0	0	3.2	7	5	2	3
Don Gullett	0	1	2.00	3	1	0	0	0	9.0	4	2	3	6
Tom Hall	0	0	67.50	3	0	0	0	0	0.2	3	5	4	1
Roger Nelson	0	0	0.00	1	0	0	0	0	2.1	0	0	1	0
Fred Norman	0	0	1.80	1	1	0	0	0	5.0	1	1	3	3
Dave Tomlin	0	0	16.20	1	0	0	0	0	1.2	5	3	1	1
TOTAL	2	3	4.50	20	5	0	1	0	46.0	37	23	19	28

GAME 1 AT CIN OCT 6

NY	010 000 000	1	3	0
CIN	000 000 011	2	6	0

Pitchers: SEAVER vs Billingham, Hall (9), BORBON (9)
Home Runs: Rose-CIN, Bench-CIN
Attendance: 53,431

GAME 2 AT CIN OCT 7

NY	000 100 004	5	7	0
CIN	000 000 000	0	2	0

Pitchers: MATLACK vs GULLETT, Carroll (6), Hall (9), Borbon (9)
Home Runs: Staub-NY
Attendance: 54,041

GAME 3 AT NY OCT 8

CIN	002 000 000	2	8	1
NY	151 200 00X	9	11	1

Pitchers: GRIMSLEY, Hall (2), Tomlin (3), Nelson (4), Borbon (7) vs KOOSMAN
Home Runs: Staub-NY (2), Menke-CIN
Attendance: 53,967

GAME 4 AT NY OCT 9

CIN	000 000 100 001	2	8	0
NY	001 000 000 000	1	3	2

Pitchers: Norman, Gullett (6), CARROLL (10), Borbon (12) vs Stone, McGraw (7), PARKER (12)
Home Runs: Perez-CIN, Rose-CIN
Attendance: 50,786

GAME 5 AT NY OCT 10

CIN	001 010 000	2	7	1
NY	200 041 00X	7	13	1

Pitchers: BILLINGHAM, Gullett (5), Carroll (5), Grimsley (7) vs SEAVER, McGraw (9)
Attendance: 50,323

The Orioles finally met their match in an LCS as Oakland took its second consecutive pennant. Baltimore started strong, chasing A's starter Vida Blue with four runs in the first inning as Jim Palmer—pitching the series opener for a change—blanked the A's on five hits. But Oakland snapped back in Game Two, with five of their six runs coming on homers by Sal Bando (two, for three runs), Joe Rudi, and Bert Campaneris.

Oriole Mike Cuellar and the A's Ken Holtzman cut down opposing batters for 10½ innings in Game Three before Oakland's Campaneris broke the 1–1 tie in the bottom of the eleventh with a leadoff home run. The next day Jim Palmer was driven out in the second inning by three Oakland runs, and the A's added to their lead with another run in the sixth. But Andy Etchebarren led a four-run Oriole comeback in the seventh with a three-run homer, and Bobby Grich's solo shot in the next inning gave the Orioles the margin they needed to win the game and tie the series.

The A's took it all in the finale, though, needing only one of their three runs as Catfish Hunter stopped Oakland cold on five scattered hits.

Oakland A's (West), 3;
Baltimore Orioles (East) 2

OAK (W)

PLAYER/POS	AVG	G	AB	R	H	2B	3B	HR	RB	BB	SO	SB
Jesus Alou, dh-1	.333	4	6	0	2	0	0	0	1	0	1	0
Mike Andrews, 1b-1,dh-1	.000	2	1	0	0	0	0	0	0	0	0	0
Sal Bando, 3b	.167	5	18	2	3	0	0	2	3	3	6	0
Vida Blue, p	.000	2	0	0	0	0	0	0	0	0	0	0
Pat Bourque, dh	.000	2	1	0	0	0	0	0	0	1	1	0
Bert Campaneris, ss	.333	5	21	3	7	1	0	2	3	2	2	3
Billy Conigliaro, of	.000	1	4	0	0	0	0	0	0	0	2	0
Vic Davalillo, 1b-2,of-2	.625	4	8	2	5	1	1	0	1	1	0	0
Rollie Fingers, p	.000	3	0	0	0	0	0	0	0	0	0	0
Ray Fosse, c	.091	5	11	2	1	1	0	0	3	2	2	0
Dick Green, 2b	.077	5	13	0	1	1	0	0	1	1	4	0
Ken Holtzman, p	.000	1	0	0	0	0	0	0	0	0	0	0
Catfish Hunter, p	.000	2	0	0	0	0	0	0	0	0	0	0
Reggie Jackson, of	.143	5	21	0	3	0	0	0	0	0	6	0
Deron Johnson, dh	.100	4	10	0	1	0	0	0	0	2	6	0
Ted Kubiak, 2b	.000	3	2	0	0	0	0	0	0	0	1	0
Allan Lewis, pr	.000	2	0	1	0	0	0	0	0	0	0	0
Angel Mangual, of	.111	3	9	1	1	0	0	0	0	0	3	0
Blue Moon Odom, p-2	.000	1	0	0	0	0	0	0	0	0	0	0
Horacio Pina, p	.000	1	0	0	0	0	0	0	0	0	0	0
Joe Rudi, of	.222	5	18	1	4	0	0	1	3	3	1	0
Gene Tenace, 1b-5,c-3	.235	5	17	3	4	1	0	0	0	2	4	0
TOTAL	.200		160	15	32	5	1	5	15	17	39	3

PITCHER	W	L	ERA	G	GS	CG	SV	SHO	IP	H	ER	BB	SO
Vida Blue	0	1	10.29	2	2	0	0	0	7.0	8	8	5	3
Rollie Fingers	0	1	1.93	3	0	0	1	0	4.2	4	1	2	4
Ken Holtzman	1	0	0.82	1	1	1	0	0	11.0	3	1	1	7
Catfish Hunter	2	0	1.65	2	2	1	0	0	16.1	12	3	5	6
Blue Moon Odom	0	0	1.80	2	0	0	0	0	5.0	6	1	2	4
Horacio Pina	0	0	0.00	1	0	0	0	0	2.0	3	0	1	1
TOTAL	3	2	2.74	11	5	2	1	0	46.0	36	14	16	25

BAL (E)

PLAYER/POS	AVG	G	AB	R	H	2B	3B	HR	RB	BB	SO	SB
Doyle Alexander, p	.000	1	0	0	0	0	0	0	0	0	0	0
Frank Baker, ss	.000	2	0	0	0	0	0	0	0	0	0	0
Don Baylor, of-3	.273	4	11	3	3	0	0	0	1	3	5	0
Mark Belanger, ss	.125	5	16	0	2	0	0	0	1	1	1	0
Paul Blair, of	.167	5	18	2	3	0	0	0	0	1	5	0
Larry Brown, 3b	.000	1	0	0	0	0	0	0	0	0	0	0
Al Bumbry, of	.000	2	7	1	0	0	0	0	0	2	2	1
Rich Coggins, of	.444	2	9	1	4	1	0	0	0	0	0	0
Terry Crowley, of-1	.000	2	2	0	0	0	0	0	0	0	0	0
Mike Cuellar, p	.000	1	0	0	0	0	0	0	0	0	0	0
Tommy Davis, dh	.286	5	21	1	6	1	0	0	2	1	0	0
Andy Etchebarren, c	.357	4	14	1	5	1	0	1	4	0	1	0
Bobby Grich, 2b	.100	5	20	1	2	0	0	1	1	2	5	0
Grant Jackson, p	.000	2	0	0	0	0	0	0	0	0	0	0
Dave McNally, p	.000	1	0	0	0	0	0	0	0	0	0	0
Jim Palmer, p	.000	3	0	0	0	0	0	0	0	0	0	0
Boog Powell, 1b	.000	1	4	1	0	0	0	0	0	0	1	0
Merv Rettenmund, of	.091	3	11	1	1	0	0	0	0	3	2	0
Bob Reynolds, p	.000	2	0	0	0	0	0	0	0	0	0	0
Brooks Robinson, 3b	.250	5	20	1	5	2	0	0	2	1	1	0
Eddie Watt, p	.000	1	0	0	0	0	0	0	0	0	0	0
Earl Williams, 1b-4,c-1	.278	5	18	2	5	2	0	1	4	2	2	0
TOTAL	.211		171	15	36	7	0	3	15	16	25	1

PITCHER	W	L	ERA	G	GS	CG	SV	SHO	IP	H	ER	BB	SO
Doyle Alexander	0	1	4.91	1	1	0	0	0	3.2	5	2	0	1
Mike Cuellar	0	1	1.80	1	1	1	0	0	10.0	4	2	3	11
Grant Jackson	1	0	0.00	2	0	0	0	0	3.0	0	0	1	0
Dave McNally	0	1	5.87	1	1	0	0	0	7.2	7	5	2	7
Jim Palmer	1	0	1.84	3	2	1	0	1	14.2	11	3	8	15
Bob Reynolds	0	0	3.18	2	0	0	0	0	5.2	5	2	3	5
Eddie Watt	0	0	0.00	1	0	0	0	0	0.1	0	0	0	0
TOTAL	2	3	2.80	11	5	2	0	1	45.0	32	14	17	39

GAME 1 AT BAL OCT 6

OAK	000	000	000	0	5	1
BAL	400	000	11X	6	12	0

Pitchers: BLUE, Pina (1), Odom (3), Fingers (8) vs PALMER
Attendance: 41,279

GAME 2 AT BAL OCT 7

OAK	100	002	021	6	9	0
BAL	100	001	010	3	8	0

Pitchers: HUNTER, Fingers (8) vs McNALLY, Reynolds (8), G.Jackson (9)
Home Runs: Campaneris-OAK, Rudi-OAK, Bando-OAK (2)
Attendance: 48,425

GAME 3 AT OAK OCT 9

BAL	010	000	000	00	1	3	0
OAK	000	000	010	01	2	4	3

Pitchers: CUELLAR vs HOLTZMAN
Home Runs: Williams-BAL, Campaneris-OAK
Attendance: 34,367

GAME 4 AT OAK OCT 10

BAL	000	000	410	5	8	0
OAK	030	001	000	4	7	0

Pitchers: Palmer, Reynolds (2), Watt (7), G.JACKSON (7) vs Blue, FINGERS (7)
Home Runs: Etchebarren-BAL, Grich-BAL
Attendance: 27,497

GAME 5 AT OAK OCT 11

BAL	000	000	000	0	5	2
OAK	001	200	00X	3	7	0

Pitchers: ALEXANDER, Palmer (4) vs HUNTER
Attendance: 24,265

For the second year in a row, the A's were outpitched and outscored by their Series opposition, and this time they were outhit as well. But again, when the dust of Game Seven had risen, they still wore the crown. A's starter Ken Holtzman, who because of the American League's new designated hitter rule had not batted all season, doubled for the A's first hit in the third inning of Game One and scored the first Oakland run on a Met error. The A's scored again in the inning, enough for the win as Holtzman and two relievers held New York to a single run.

The Mets evened things in a Game Two that lasted a record 4 hours 13 minutes, scoring four runs with two out in the top of the twelfth inning for a lead the A's were not able to overcome. (Three of the runs scored on a pair of errors by second-baseman Mike Andrews, prompting a flap that rocked the baseball world as A's owner Charlie Finley tried—unsuccessfully—to "fire" Andrews by declaring him injured.) Final score of the slugfest: 10–7.

In a somewhat more normal third game, the Mets grabbed an early lead on Wayne Garrett's lead-off homer in the bottom of the first and scored a second run on two singles and wild pitch for a 2–0 lead that held up until Oakland tied the game in the eighth. In the eleventh, the A's Ted Kubiak worked his way around the bases on a walk, passed ball, and single for a lead that reliever Rollie Fingers held in the bottom of the inning.

New York evened the Series on Rusty Staub's three-run homer in the first inning of Game Four (scoring three more times later for a 6–1 win). The Mets moved in front on a sparkling 2–0 three-hitter by Jerry Koosman and Tug McGraw in Game Five, but lost their edge as the Series returned to Oakland for Game Six, losing when Reggie Jackson's doubles in the first and third drove in two runs to give the A's a lead New York was unable to overtake.

Oakland made the finale look easy. Bert Campaneris and Jackson both hit two-run homers in the third inning, and Campaneris scored a fifth run two innings later before New York finally got on the board in the sixth. In the ninth inning the Mets scored a second run with two outs, but reliever Darold Knowles came on for a record seventh pitching appearance and retired the final batter for his second Series save.

Oakland Athletics (AL), 4; New York Mets (NL) 3

OAK (A)

PLAYER/POS	AVG	G	AB	R	H	2B	3B	HR	RB	BB	SO	SB
Jesus Alou, of-6	.158	7	19	0	3	1	0	0	0	3	0	0
Mike Andrews, 2b-1	.000	2	3	0	0	0	0	0	0	1	1	0
Sal Bando, 3b	.231	7	26	5	6	1	1	0	1	4	7	0
Vida Blue, p	.000	2	4	0	0	0	0	0	0	0	4	0
Pat Bourque, 1b	.500	2	2	0	1	0	0	0	0	0	0	0
Bert Campaneris, ss	.290	7	31	6	9	0	1	1	3	1	7	3
Billy Conigliaro, ph	.000	3	3	0	0	0	0	0	0	0	1	0
Vic Davalillo, of-4,1b-1	.091	6	11	0	1	0	0	0	0	2	1	0
Rollie Fingers, p	.333	6	3	0	1	0	0	0	0	0	1	0
Ray Fosse, c	.158	7	19	0	3	1	0	0	0	1	4	0
Dick Green, 2b	.063	7	16	0	1	0	0	0	0	1	6	0
Ken Holtzman, p	.667	3	3	2	2	2	0	0	0	0	0	0
Catfish Hunter, p	.000	2	5	0	0	0	0	0	0	0	3	0
Reggie Jackson, of	.310	7	29	3	9	3	1	1	6	2	7	0
Deron Johnson, 1b-2	.300	6	10	0	3	1	0	0	0	1	4	0
Darold Knowles, p	.000	7	0	0	0	0	0	0	0	0	0	0
Ted Kubiak, 2b	.000	4	3	1	0	0	0	0	0	1	1	0
Allan Lewis, pr	.000	3	0	1	0	0	0	0	0	0	0	0
Paul Lindblad, p	.000	3	1	0	0	0	0	0	0	0	0	0
Angel Mangual, of-1	.000	5	6	0	0	0	0	0	0	0	3	0
Blue Moon Odom, p-2	.000	3	1	0	0	0	0	0	0	0	1	0
Horacio Pina, p	.000	2	0	0	0	0	0	0	0	0	0	0
Joe Rudi, of	.333	7	27	3	9	2	0	0	4	3	4	0
Gene Tenace, 1b-7,c-3	.158	7	19	0	3	1	0	0	3	11	7	0
TOTAL	.212		241	21	51	12	3	2	20	28	62	3

PITCHER	W	L	ERA	G	GS	CG	SV	SHO	IP	H	ER	BB	SO
Vida Blue	0	1	4.91	2	2	0	0	0	11.0	10	6	3	8
Rollie Fingers	0	1	0.66	6	0	0	2	0	13.2	13	1	4	8
Ken Holtzman	2	1	4.22	3	3	0	0	0	10.2	13	5	5	6
Catfish Hunter	1	0	2.03	2	2	0	0	0	13.1	11	3	4	6
Darold Knowles	0	0	0.00	7	0	0	2	0	6.1	4	0	5	5
Paul Lindblad	1	0	0.00	3	0	0	0	0	3.1	4	0	1	1
Blue Moon Odom	0	0	3.86	2	0	0	0	0	4.2	5	2	2	2
Horacio Pina	0	0	0.00	2	0	0	0	0	3.0	6	0	2	0
TOTAL	4	3	2.32	27	7	0	4	0	66.0	66	17	26	36

NY (N)

PLAYER/POS	AVG	G	AB	R	H	2B	3B	HR	RB	BB	SO	SB
Jim Beauchamp, ph	.000	4	4	0	0	0	0	0	0	0	1	0
Ken Boswell, ph	1.000	3	3	1	3	0	0	0	0	0	0	0
Wayne Garrett, 3b	.167	7	30	4	5	0	0	2	2	5	11	0
Jerry Grote, c	.267	7	30	2	8	0	0	0	1	1	0	0
Don Hahn, of	.241	7	29	2	7	1	1	0	2	1	6	0
Bud Harrelson, ss	.250	7	24	2	6	1	0	0	1	5	3	0
Ron Hodges, ph	.000	1	0	0	0	0	0	0	0	1	0	0
Cleon Jones, of	.286	7	28	5	8	2	0	1	1	4	2	0
Jerry Koosman, p	.000	2	4	0	0	0	0	0	0	0	3	0
Ed Kranepool, ph	.000	4	3	0	0	0	0	0	0	0	0	0
Ted Martinez, pr	.000	2	0	0	0	0	0	0	0	0	0	0
Jon Matlack, p	.250	3	4	0	1	0	0	0	0	2	1	0
Willie Mays, of-2	.286	3	7	1	2	0	0	0	1	0	1	0
Tug McGraw, p	.333	5	3	1	1	0	0	0	0	0	1	0
Felix Millan, 2b	.188	7	32	3	6	1	1	0	1	1	1	0
John Milner, 1b	.296	7	27	2	8	0	0	0	2	5	1	0
Harry Parker, p	.000	3	0	0	0	0	0	0	0	0	0	0
Ray Sadecki, p	.000	4	0	0	0	0	0	0	0	0	0	0
Tom Seaver, p	.000	2	5	0	0	0	0	0	0	0	2	0
Rusty Staub, of	.423	7	26	1	11	2	0	1	6	2	2	0
George Stone, p	.000	2	0	0	0	0	0	0	0	0	0	0
George Theodore, of-1	.000	2	2	0	0	0	0	0	0	0	0	0
TOTAL	.253		261	24	66	7	2	4	16	26	36	0

PITCHER	W	L	ERA	G	GS	CG	SV	SHO	IP	H	ER	BB	SO
Jerry Koosman	1	0	3.12	2	2	0	0	0	8.2	9	3	7	8
Jon Matlack	1	2	2.16	3	3	0	0	0	16.2	10	4	5	11
Tug McGraw	1	0	2.63	5	0	0	1	0	13.2	8	4	9	14
Harry Parker	0	1	0.00	3	0	0	0	0	3.1	2	0	2	2
Ray Sadecki	0	0	1.93	4	0	0	1	0	4.2	5	1	1	6
Tom Seaver	0	1	2.40	2	2	0	0	0	15.0	13	4	3	18
George Stone	0	0	0.00	2	0	0	1	0	3.0	4	0	1	3
TOTAL	3	4	2.22	21	7	0	3	0	65.0	51	16	28	62

Dodger pitcher Don Sutton—who had brought his won-lost record from 10–9 to 19–9 with a nine-game winning streak in the regular season—continued his winning ways in the LCS, surrendering only seven hits and one run in seventeen innings and taking both the opener and clincher of the four-game series. Los Angeles's Andy Messersmith followed up Sutton's opening-game shutout with six shutout innings of his own in Game Two before Pittsburgh scored its first two runs of the series in the seventh. They tied the score, but the Dodgers countered with three more in the top of the eighth to assure their second win.

The Pirates captured their only victory in Game Three, as Richie Hebner and Willie Stargell homered for five of the Bucs' seven runs, while Bruce Kison and Ramon Hernandez shut out the Dodgers on four hits.

Pittsburgh finally got to Sutton for a run when Stargell homered in the seventh inning of Game Four. But it was too little, and too late to stem a twelve-run Dodger attack led by Steve Garvey's four hits (two of them home runs) and four RBIs.

Los Angeles Dodgers (West), 3; Pittsburgh Pirates (East) 1

LA (W)

PLAYER/POS	AVG	G	AB	R	H	2B	3B	HR	RB	BB	SO	SB
Rick Auerbach, ph	1.000	1	1	0	1	1	0	0	0	0	0	0
Bill Buckner, of	.167	4	18	0	3	1	0	0	0	0	2	0
Ron Cey, 3b	.313	4	16	2	5	3	0	1	1	3	2	0
Willie Crawford, of	.250	2	4	1	1	0	0	0	1	1	1	0
Al Downing, p	.000	1	1	0	0	0	0	0	0	0	0	0
Joe Ferguson, of-3,c-2	.231	4	13	3	3	0	0	0	2	5	1	0
Steve Garvey, 1b	.389	4	18	4	7	1	0	2	5	1	1	0
Charlie Hough, p	.000	1	0	0	0	0	0	0	0	0	0	0
Von Joshua, ph	.000	1	0	0	0	0	0	0	0	1	0	0
Lee Lacy, pr	.000	1	0	0	0	0	0	0	0	0	0	0
Davey Lopes, 2b	.267	4	15	4	4	0	1	0	3	5	1	3
Mike Marshall, p	.000	2	0	0	0	0	0	0	0	0	0	0
Ken McMullen, ph	.000	1	1	0	0	0	0	0	0	0	1	0
Andy Messersmith, p	.000	1	3	0	0	0	0	0	0	0	1	0
Manny Mota, of-1	.333	3	3	0	1	0	0	0	1	0	0	0
Tom Paciorek, of	1.000	1	1	0	1	0	0	0	0	0	0	0
Doug Rau, p	.000	1	0	0	0	0	0	0	0	0	0	0
Bill Russell, ss	.389	4	18	1	7	0	0	0	3	1	0	0
Eddie Solomon, p	.000	1	0	0	0	0	0	0	0	0	0	0
Don Sutton, p	.286	2	7	0	2	0	0	0	1	1	2	0
Jimmy Wynn, of	.200	4	10	4	2	2	0	0	2	9	1	1
Steve Yeager, c	.000	3	9	1	0	0	0	0	0	3	3	1
TOTAL	.268		138	20	37	8	1	3	19	30	16	5

PITCHER	W	L	ERA	G	GS	CG	SV	SHO	IP	H	ER	BB	SO
Al Downing	0	0	0.00	1	0	0	0	0	4.0	1	0	1	0
Charlie Hough	0	0	7.71	1	0	0	0	0	2.1	4	2	0	2
Mike Marshall	0	0	0.00	2	0	0	0	0	3.0	0	0	0	1
Andy Messersmith	1	0	2.57	1	1	0	0	0	7.0	8	2	3	0
Doug Rau	0	1	40.50	1	1	0	0	0	0.2	3	3	1	0
Eddie Solomon	0	0	0.00	1	0	0	0	0	2.0	2	0	1	1
Don Sutton	2	0	0.53	2	2	1	0	1	17.0	7	1	2	13
TOTAL	3	1	2.00	9	4	1	0	1	36.0	25	8	8	17

PIT (E)

PLAYER/POS	AVG	G	AB	R	H	2B	3B	HR	RB	BB	SO	SB
Ken Brett, p	.000	1	1	0	0	0	0	0	0	0	1	0
Gene Clines, of	.000	2	1	1	0	0	0	0	0	0	0	0
Larry Demery, p	.000	2	0	0	0	0	0	0	0	0	0	0
Dave Giusti, p	.000	3	0	0	0	0	0	0	0	0	0	0
Richie Hebner, 3b	.231	4	13	1	3	0	0	1	4	1	4	0
Ramon Hernandez, p	.000	2	1	0	0	0	0	0	0	0	1	0
Art Howe, ph	.000	1	1	0	0	0	0	0	0	0	0	0
Ed Kirkpatrick, 1b	.000	3	9	0	0	0	0	0	0	2	0	0
Bruce Kison, p	.000	1	3	0	0	0	0	0	0	0	2	0
Mario Mendoza, ss	.200	3	5	0	1	0	0	0	1	1	0	0
Al Oliver, of	.143	4	14	1	2	0	0	0	1	2	2	0
Dave Parker, of-2	.125	3	8	0	1	0	0	0	0	0	1	0
Juan Pizarro, p	.000	1	0	0	0	0	0	0	0	0	0	0
Paul Popovich, ss	.600	3	5	1	3	0	0	0	0	0	0	0
Jerry Reuss, p	.000	2	2	0	0	0	0	0	0	0	0	0
Bob Robertson, 1b	.000	1	5	1	0	0	0	0	0	0	0	0
Jim Rooker, p	.500	1	2	0	1	0	0	0	0	0	0	0
Manny Sanguillen, c	.250	4	16	0	4	1	0	0	0	0	0	0
Willie Stargell, of	.400	4	15	3	6	0	0	2	4	1	0	0
Rennie Stennett, 2b	.063	4	16	1	1	0	0	0	0	1	1	0
Frank Taveras, ss	.000	2	2	0	0	0	0	0	0	0	0	1
Richie Zisk, of-2	.300	3	10	1	3	0	0	0	0	0	3	0
TOTAL	.194		129	10	25	1	0	3	10	8	17	1

PITCHER	W	L	ERA	G	GS	CG	SV	SHO	IP	H	ER	BB	SO
Ken Brett	0	0	7.71	1	0	0	0	0	2.1	3	2	2	1
Larry Demery	0	0	27.00	2	0	0	0	0	1.0	3	3	2	0
Dave Giusti	0	1	21.60	3	0	0	0	0	3.1	13	8	5	1
Ramon Hernandez	0	0	0.00	2	0	0	0	0	4.1	3	0	1	2
Bruce Kison	1	0	0.00	1	1	0	0	0	6.2	2	0	6	5
Juan Pizarro	0	0	0.00	1	0	0	0	0	9.2	0	1	0	0
Jerry Reuss	0	2	3.72	2	2	0	0	0	9.2	7	4	8	3
Jim Rooker	0	0	2.57	1	1	0	0	0	7.0	6	2	5	4
TOTAL	1	3	4.89	13	4	0	0	0	35.0	37	19	30	16

GAME 1 AT PIT OCT 5

LA	010 000 002	3	9	2
PIT	000 000 000	0	4	0

Pitchers: SUTTON vs REUSS, Giusti (8)
Attendance: 40,638

GAME 2 AT PIT OCT 6

LA	100 100 030	5	12	1
PIT	000 000 200	2	8	3

Pitchers: MESSERSMITH, Marshall (8) vs Rooker, GIUSTI (8), Demery (8), Hernandez (8)
Home Runs: Cey-LA
Attendance: 49,247

GAME 3 AT LA OCT 8

PIT	502 000 000	7	10	0
LA	000 000 000	0	4	5

Pitchers: KISON, Hernandez (7) vs RAU, Hough (1), Downing (4), Solomon (8)
Home Runs: Stargell-PIT, Hebner-PIT
Attendance: 55,953

GAME 4 AT LA OCT 9

PIT	000 000 100	1	3	1
LA	102 022 23X	12	12	0

Pitchers: REUSS, Brett (3), Demery (6), Giusti (7), Pizarro (8) vs SUTTON, Marshall (9)
Home Runs: Garvey-LA (2), Stargell-PIT
Attendance: 54,424

After spotting Baltimore a win in the opener, Oakland took the next three games and their third consecutive pennant. Although the A's got nine hits in Game One—their series high—the Orioles hit harder, burying Oakland under home runs by Paul Blair, Brooks Robinson, and Bobby Grich. In Game Two, though, Ken Holtzman shut out Baltimore on five hits as Sal Bando and Ray Fosse homered. Bando homered again in the third game for the only Oakland run as Jim Palmer limited the A's to four hits. But one run was enough to defeat Baltimore, for Vida Blue shut them out on a masterly two-hitter.

Oriole starter Mike Cuellar walked nine men in 4⅔ innings of Game Four, including four in the fifth to force in Oakland's first run. Two innings later Reggie Jackson's double (the only Oakland hit of the game) off reliever Ross Grimsley drove in Oakland's second run, while starter Catfish Hunter was blanking the O's through seven-plus innings. After failing to score for thirty consecutive innings, the Orioles got to reliever Rollie Fingers for a run with two out in the bottom of the ninth. But Fingers then struck out Don Baylor, and the A's had their pennant.

Oakland A's (West), 3;
Baltimore Orioles (East) 1

OAK (W)

PLAYER/POS	AVG	G	AB	R	H	2B	3B	HR	RB	BB	SO	SB
Jesus Alou, ph	1.000	1	1	0	1	0	0	0	0	0	0	0
Sal Bando, 3b	.231	4	13	4	3	0	0	2	2	4	0	0
Vida Blue, p	.000	1	0	0	0	0	0	0	0	0	0	0
Bert Campaneris, ss	.176	4	17	0	3	0	0	0	3	0	3	1
Rollie Fingers, p	.000	2	0	0	0	0	0	0	0	0	0	0
Ray Fosse, c	.333	4	12	1	4	1	0	1	3	1	2	0
Dick Green, 2b	.222	4	9	0	2	0	0	0	0	2	1	0
Jim Holt, 1b-1	.000	2	0	0	0	0	0	0	0	1	0	0
Ken Holtzman, p	.000	1	0	0	0	0	0	0	0	0	0	0
Catfish Hunter, p	.000	2	0	0	0	0	0	0	0	0	0	0
Reggie Jackson, dh-3,of-1	.167	4	12	0	2	1	0	0	1	5	2	0
Angel Mangual, dh	.250	1	4	0	1	0	0	0	0	0	1	0
Dal Maxvill, 2b	.000	1	0	0	0	0	0	0	0	0	0	0
Billy North, of	.063	4	16	3	1	1	0	0	0	2	1	1
Blue Moon Odom, p-1	.000	3	0	0	0	0	0	0	0	0	0	0
Joe Rudi, of	.154	4	13	0	2	0	1	0	1	3	2	0
Gene Tenace, 1b	.000	4	11	0	0	0	0	0	0	1	4	1
Manny Trillo, pr	.000	1	0	1	0	0	0	0	0	0	0	0
Claudell Washington, of-3	.273	4	11	1	3	1	0	0	0	0	0	0
Herb Washington, pr	.000	2	0	0	0	0	0	0	0	0	0	0
TOTAL	.183		120	11	22	4	1	3	11	22	16	3

PITCHER	W	L	ERA	G	GS	CG	SV	SHO	IP	H	ER	BB	SO
Vida Blue	1	0	0.00	1	1	1	0	1	9.0	2	0	0	7
Rollie Fingers	0	0	3.00	2	0	0	1	0	3.0	3	1	1	3
Ken Holtzman	1	0	0.00	1	1	1	0	1	9.0	5	0	2	3
Catfish Hunter	1	1	4.63	2	2	0	0	0	11.2	11	6	2	6
Blue Moon Odom	0	0	0.00	1	0	0	0	0	3.1	1	0	0	1
TOTAL	3	1	1.75	7	4	2	1	2	36.0	22	7	5	20

BAL (E)

PLAYER/POS	AVG	G	AB	R	H	2B	3B	HR	RB	BB	SO	SB
Frank Baker, ss	.000	2	0	0	0	0	0	0	0	0	0	0
Don Baylor, of	.267	4	15	0	4	0	0	0	0	0	2	0
Mark Belanger, ss	.000	4	9	0	0	0	0	0	0	1	3	0
Paul Blair, of	.286	4	14	3	4	0	0	1	2	2	2	0
Al Bumbry, ph	.000	2	1	0	0	0	0	0	0	0	1	0
Enos Cabell, of-1	.250	3	4	0	1	0	0	0	0	0	2	0
Rich Coggins, of	.000	3	11	0	0	0	0	0	0	0	3	0
Mike Cuellar, p	.000	2	0	0	0	0	0	0	0	0	0	0
Tommy Davis, dh	.267	4	15	0	4	0	0	0	1	0	1	0
Andy Etchebarren, c	.333	2	6	2	2	0	0	0	0	0	1	0
Wayne Garland, p	.000	1	0	0	0	0	0	0	0	0	0	0
Bobby Grich, 2b	.250	4	16	2	4	1	0	1	2	0	1	0
Ross Grimsley, p	.000	2	0	0	0	0	0	0	0	0	0	0
Elrod Hendricks, c	.167	3	6	1	1	0	0	0	0	1	3	0
Grant Jackson, p	.000	1	0	0	0	0	0	0	0	0	0	0
Dave McNally, p	.000	1	0	0	0	0	0	0	0	0	0	0
Curt Motton, ph	.000	1	1	0	0	0	0	0	0	0	0	0
Jim Palmer, p-1	.000	2	0	0	0	0	0	0	0	0	0	0
Boog Powell, 1b	.125	2	8	0	1	0	0	0	1	0	0	0
Bob Reynolds, p	.000	1	0	0	0	0	0	0	0	0	0	0
Brooks Robinson, 3b	.083	4	12	1	1	0	0	1	1	1	0	0
Earl Williams, 1b	.000	2	6	0	0	0	0	0	0	0	2	0
TOTAL	.177		124	7	22	1	0	3	7	5	20	0

PITCHER	W	L	ERA	G	GS	CG	SV	SHO	IP	H	ER	BB	SO
Mike Cuellar	1	1	2.84	2	2	0	0	0	12.2	9	4	13	6
Wayne Garland	0	0	0.00	1	0	0	0	0	0.2	1	0	1	0
Ross Grimsley	0	0	1.69	2	0	0	0	0	5.1	1	1	2	2
Grant Jackson	0	0	0.00	1	0	0	0	0	0.1	1	0	0	1
Dave McNally	0	1	1.59	1	1	0	0	0	5.2	6	1	2	2
Jim Palmer	0	1	1.00	1	1	1	0	0	9.0	4	1	1	4
Bob Reynolds	0	0	0.00	1	0	0	0	0	1.1	0	0	3	1
TOTAL	1	3	1.80	9	4	1	0	0	35.0	22	7	22	16

GAME 1 AT OAK OCT 5

BAL	100 140 000	6	10	0
OAK	001 010 001	3	9	0

Pitchers: CUELLAR, Grimsley (9) vs HUNTER, Odom (5), Fingers (9)
Home Runs: Blair-BAL, Robinson-BAL, Grich-BAL
Attendance: 41,609

GAME 2 AT OAK OCT 6

BAL	000 000 000	0	5	2
OAK	000 101 03X	5	8	0

Pitchers: McNALLY, Garland (6), Reynolds (7), G.Jackson (8) vs HOLTZMAN
Home Runs: Bando-OAK, Fosse-OAK
Attendance: 42,810

GAME 3 AT BAL OCT 8

OAK	000 100 000	1	4	2
BAL	000 000 000	0	2	1

Pitchers: BLUE vs PALMER
Home Runs: Bando-OAK
Attendance: 32,060

GAME 4 AT BAL OCT 9

OAK	000 010 100	2	1	0
BAL	000 000 001	1	5	1

Pitchers: HUNTER, Fingers (8) vs CUELLAR, Grimsley (5)
Attendance: 28,136

Although the A's were in a turmoil of dislike for owner Charlie Finley—and for each other—they played well enough together to take their third consecutive world championship in just five games. Still, victory didn't come easily, as three of Oakland's wins came by identical 3–2 scores (as did the Dodgers' one victory), and their biggest winning margin was three runs in Game Four. It was the first World Series held entirely on the West Coast.

The A's and Dodgers split the first two games in Los Angeles. Oakland won the opener on the strength of Reggie Jackson's home run in the second inning, pitcher Ken Holtzman's double in the fifth (he moved around on a wild pitch and squeeze bunt), and a Dodger throwing error in the eighth. The Dodgers evened the Series on Joe Ferguson's two-run homer in the sixth inning of the second game, which gave Los Angeles a 3–0 lead that an Oakland rally in the ninth failed to catch.

Los Angeles outhit Oakland in Game Three, but two of the A's runs were unearned, coming after Dodger catcher Ferguson bobbled what should have been a third-out play in the third inning.

Pitcher Ken Holtzman, who had now gone two regular seasons without a time at bat, produced in Game Four his second hit of the Series, this one a homer in the third inning for the game's first run. The Dodgers' Bill Russell tripled off him for two runs a half inning later, but in the last of the sixth inning Oakland regained the lead on three walks interspersed with a pair of singles and an RBI grounder to short. Four runs scored—more in this one inning than either team scored in any of the other four games.

Oakland took an early 2–0 lead in Game Five, with single runs in the first and second innings (the latter a Ray Fosse home run). The Dodgers put together a pinch-hit double, a walk, a pair of sacrifices (bunt and fly), and a single to tie the score in the sixth. But Joe Rudi hit the first pitch of Oakland's half of the seventh into the stands in left for the run that decided the game and the Series.

Oakland Athletics (AL), 4;
Los Angeles Dodgers (NL) 1

OAK (A)

PLAYER/POS	AVG	G	AB	R	H	2B	3B	HR	RB	BB	SO	SB
Jesus Alou, ph	.000	1	1	0	0	0	0	0	0	0	1	0
Sal Bando, 3b	.063	5	16	3	1	0	0	0	2	2	5	0
Vida Blue, p	.000	2	4	0	0	0	0	0	0	0	4	0
Bert Campaneris, ss	.353	5	17	1	6	2	0	0	2	0	2	1
Rollie Fingers, p	.000	4	2	0	0	0	0	0	0	0	1	0
Ray Fosse, c	.143	5	14	1	2	0	0	1	1	1	5	0
Dick Green, 2b	.000	5	13	1	0	0	0	0	1	1	4	0
Larry Haney, c	.000	2	0	0	0	0	0	0	0	0	0	0
Jim Holt, 1b-1	.667	4	3	0	2	0	0	0	2	0	0	0
Ken Holtzman, p	.500	2	4	2	2	1	0	1	1	1	1	0
Catfish Hunter, p	.000	2	2	0	0	0	0	0	0	0	2	0
Reggie Jackson, of	.286	5	14	3	4	1	0	1	1	5	3	1
Angel Mangual, ph	.000	1	1	0	0	0	0	0	0	0	1	0
Dal Maxvill, 2b	.000	2	0	0	0	0	0	0	0	0	0	0
Billy North, of	.059	5	17	3	1	0	0	0	0	2	5	1
Blue Moon Odom, p	.000	2	0	0	0	0	0	0	0	0	0	0
Joe Rudi, of-5,1b-2	.333	5	18	1	6	0	0	1	4	0	3	0
Gene Tenace, 1b	.222	5	9	0	2	0	0	0	0	3	4	0
Claudell Washington, of	.571	5	7	1	4	0	0	0	0	1	1	0
Herb Washington, pr	.000	3	0	0	0	0	0	0	0	0	0	0
TOTAL	.211		142	16	30	4	0	4	14	16	42	3

PITCHER	W	L	ERA	G	GS	CG	SV	SHO	IP	H	ER	BB	SO
Vida Blue	0	1	3.29	2	2	0	0	0	13.2	10	5	7	9
Rollie Fingers	1	0	1.93	4	0	0	2	0	9.1	8	2	2	6
Ken Holtzman	1	0	1.50	2	2	0	0	0	12.0	13	2	4	10
Catfish Hunter	1	0	1.17	2	1	0	1	0	7.2	5	1	2	5
Blue Moon Odom	1	0	0.00	2	0	0	0	0	1.1	0	0	1	2
TOTAL	4	1	2.05	12	5	0	3	0	44.0	36	10	16	32

LA (N)

PLAYER/POS	AVG	G	AB	R	H	2B	3B	HR	RB	BB	SO	SB
Rick Auerbach, pr	.000	1	0	0	0	0	0	0	0	0	0	0
Jim Brewer, p	.000	1	0	0	0	0	0	0	0	0	0	0
Bill Buckner, of	.250	5	20	1	5	1	0	1	1	0	1	0
Ron Cey, 3b	.176	5	17	1	3	0	0	0	0	3	3	0
Willie Crawford, of-2	.333	3	6	1	2	0	0	1	1	0	0	0
Al Downing, p	.000	1	0	0	0	0	0	0	0	0	0	0
Joe Ferguson, of-4,c-2	.125	5	16	2	2	0	0	1	2	4	6	1
Steve Garvey, 1b	.381	5	21	2	8	0	0	0	1	0	3	0
Charlie Hough, p	.000	1	0	0	0	0	0	0	0	0	0	0
Von Joshua, ph	.000	1	4	0	0	0	0	0	0	0	0	0
Lee Lacy, ph	.000	1	1	0	0	0	0	0	0	0	1	0
Davey Lopes, 2b	.111	5	18	2	2	0	0	0	0	3	4	2
Mike Marshall, p	.000	5	0	0	0	0	0	0	0	1	0	0
Andy Messersmith, p	.500	2	4	0	2	0	0	0	0	0	2	0
Tom Paciorek, ph	.500	3	2	1	1	1	0	0	0	0	0	0
Bill Russell, ss	.222	5	18	0	4	0	1	0	2	0	2	0
Don Sutton, p	.000	2	3	0	0	0	0	0	0	0	2	0
Jimmy Wynn, of	.188	5	16	1	3	1	0	1	2	4	4	0
Steve Yeager, c	.364	4	11	0	4	1	0	0	1	1	4	0
TOTAL	.228		158	11	36	4	1	4	10	16	32	3

PITCHER	W	L	ERA	G	GS	CG	SV	SHO	IP	H	ER	BB	SO
Jim Brewer	0	0	0.00	1	0	0	0	0	0.1	0	0	0	1
Al Downing	0	1	2.45	1	1	0	0	0	3.2	4	1	4	3
Charlie Hough	0	0	0.00	1	0	0	0	0	2.0	0	0	1	4
Mike Marshall	0	1	1.00	5	0	0	1	0	9.0	6	1	1	10
Andy Messersmith	0	2	4.50	2	2	0	0	0	14.0	11	7	7	12
Don Sutton	1	0	2.77	2	2	0	0	0	13.0	9	4	3	12
TOTAL	1	4	2.79	12	5	0	1	0	42.0	30	13	16	42

The Reds, who had steamrolled the National League during the season, continued their roll in the LCS. Red pitcher Don Gullett gave up three Pirate runs in the first game, but he drove in three himself with a home run and a single. Pitching the series' only complete game, he won easily behind his club's twelve-hit, eight-run attack. The Reds won just as handily in Game Two, with Fred Norman and reliever Rawley Eastwick holding the Pirates to one run as Tony Perez drove in half the Reds' six runs—two of them with a first-inning homer.

In Game Three the Pirates struggled gamely against elimination. Cincinnati scored first in the second, but in the sixth Al Oliver put Pittsburgh ahead with a two-run homer. In the eighth, though, Pete Rose restored the Reds' lead (and nullified rookie John Candelaria's fourteen-strikeout effort over 7⅔ innings) with his two-run shot. The Pirates were granted a brief reprieve when Red reliever Eastwick walked in the tying run in the bottom of the ninth. But in the tenth the Reds scored twice on three hits, and when Eastwick's replacement Pedro Borbon shut the Pirates down in the bottom of the tenth, Cincinnati had its series sweep.

Cincinnati Reds (West), 3; Pittsburgh Pirates (East) 0

CIN (W)

PLAYER/POS	AVG	G	AB	R	H	2B	3B	HR	RB	BB	SO	SB
Ed Armbrister, ph	.000	2	0	0	0	0	0	0	0	1	0	0
Johnny Bench, c	.077	3	13	1	1	0	0	0	0	1	6	1
Pedro Borbon, p	.000	1	0	0	0	0	0	0	0	0	0	0
Clay Carroll, p	.000	1	0	0	0	0	0	0	0	0	0	0
Dave Concepcion, ss	.455	3	11	2	5	0	0	1	1	1	2	2
Terry Crowley, ph	.000	1	0	0	0	0	0	0	0	0	0	0
Rawly Eastwick, p	.000	2	0	0	0	0	0	0	0	0	0	0
George Foster, of	.364	3	11	3	4	0	0	0	0	1	2	1
Cesar Geronimo, of	.000	3	10	0	0	0	0	0	1	1	7	0
Ken Griffey, of	.333	3	12	4	4	1	0	0	4	0	3	3
Don Gullett, p	.500	1	4	1	2	0	0	1	3	0	0	0
Will McEnaney, p	.000	1	0	0	0	0	0	0	0	0	0	0
Joe Morgan, 2b	.273	3	11	2	3	3	0	0	1	3	2	4
Gary Nolan, p	.000	1	2	0	0	0	0	0	0	0	2	0
Fred Norman, p	.000	1	1	0	0	0	0	0	1	0	0	0
Tony Perez, 1b	.417	3	12	3	5	0	0	1	4	1	2	0
Merv Rettenmund, ph	.000	2	1	0	0	0	0	0	0	1	0	0
Pete Rose, 3b	.357	3	14	3	5	0	0	1	2	0	2	0
TOTAL	.284		102	19	29	4	0	4	18	9	28	11

PITCHER	W	L	ERA	G	GS	CG	SV	SHO	IP	H	ER	BB	SO
Pedro Borbon	0	0	0.00	1	0	0	1	0	1.0	0	0	0	1
Clay Carroll	0	0	0.00	1	0	0	0	0	1.0	0	0	1	1
Rawly Eastwick	0	0	0.00	2	0	0	1	0	3.2	2	0	2	1
Don Gullett	1	0	3.00	1	1	1	0	0	9.0	8	3	2	5
Will McEnaney	0	0	6.75	1	0	0	0	0	1.1	1	1	0	1
Gary Nolan	0	0	3.00	1	1	0	0	0	6.0	5	2	0	5
Fred Norman	1	0	1.50	1	1	0	0	0	6.0	4	1	5	4
TOTAL	3	0	2.25	8	3	1	2	0	28.0	20	7	10	18

PIT (E)

PLAYER/POS	AVG	G	AB	R	H	2B	3B	HR	RB	BB	SO	SB
Ken Brett, p	.000	2	0	0	0	0	0	0	0	0	0	0
John Candelaria, p	.000	1	3	0	0	0	0	0	0	0	3	0
Larry Demery, p	.000	1	0	0	0	0	0	0	0	0	0	0
Duffy Dyer, ph	.000	1	0	0	0	0	0	0	1	1	0	0
Dock Ellis, p	.000	1	0	0	0	0	0	0	0	0	0	0
Dave Giusti, p	.000	1	0	0	0	0	0	0	0	0	0	0
Richie Hebner, 3b	.333	3	12	2	4	1	0	0	2	1	1	0
Ramon Hernandez, p	.000	1	0	0	0	0	0	0	0	0	0	0
Ed Kirkpatrick, ph	.000	2	2	0	0	0	0	0	0	0	0	0
Bruce Kison, p	.000	1	0	0	0	0	0	0	0	0	0	0
Al Oliver, of	.182	3	11	1	2	0	0	1	2	2	0	0
Dave Parker, of	.000	3	10	2	0	0	0	0	0	1	3	0
Willie Randolph, 2b-1	.000	2	2	1	0	0	0	0	0	0	1	0
Jerry Reuss, p	.000	1	1	0	0	0	0	0	0	0	0	0
Craig Reynolds, ss-1	.000	2	1	0	0	0	0	0	0	0	0	0
Bob Robertson, 1b-1	.500	3	2	0	1	0	0	0	1	1	0	0
Bill Robinson, ph	.000	2	2	0	0	0	0	0	0	0	1	0
Jim Rooker, p	.000	1	1	0	0	0	0	0	0	0	1	0
Manny Sanguillen, c	.167	3	12	0	2	0	0	0	0	0	0	0
Willie Stargell, 1b	.182	3	11	1	2	1	0	0	0	1	3	0
Rennie Stennett, 2b-3,ss-1	.214	3	14	0	3	0	0	0	0	0	1	0
Frank Taveras, ss	.143	3	7	0	1	0	0	0	0	1	2	0
Kent Tekulve, p	.000	2	0	0	0	0	0	0	0	0	0	0
Richie Zisk, of	.500	3	10	0	5	1	0	0	0	2	2	0
TOTAL	.198		101	7	20	3	0	1	7	10	18	0

PITCHER	W	L	ERA	G	GS	CG	SV	SHO	IP	H	ER	BB	SO
Ken Brett	0	0	0.00	2	0	0	0	0	2.1	1	0	0	1
John Candelaria	0	0	3.52	1	1	0	0	0	7.2	3	3	2	14
Larry Demery	0	0	18.00	1	0	0	0	0	2.0	4	4	1	1
Dock Ellis	0	0	0.00	1	0	0	0	0	2.0	2	0	0	2
Dave Giusti	0	0	0.00	1	0	0	0	0	1.1	0	0	0	1
Ramon Hernandez	0	1	27.00	1	0	0	0	0	0.2	3	2	0	0
Bruce Kison	0	0	4.50	1	0	0	0	0	2.0	2	1	1	1
Jerry Reuss	0	1	13.50	1	1	0	0	0	2.2	4	4	4	1
Jim Rooker	0	1	9.00	1	1	0	0	0	4.0	7	4	0	5
Kent Tekulve	0	0	6.75	2	0	0	0	0	1.1	3	1	1	2
TOTAL	0	3	6.58	12	3	0	0	0	26.0	29	19	9	28

GAME 1 AT CIN OCT 4

PIT	020	000	001	3	8	0
CIN	013	040	00X	8	11	0

Pitchers: REUSS, Brett (3), Demery (5), Ellis (7) vs GULLETT
Home Runs: Gullett-CIN
Attendance: 54,633

GAME 2 AT CIN OCT 5

PIT	000	100	000	1	5	0
CIN	200	201	10X	6	12	1

Pitchers: ROOKER, Tekulve (5), Brett (6), Kison (7) vs NORMAN, Eastwick (7)
Home Runs: Perez-CIN
Attendance: 54,752

GAME 3 AT PIT OCT 7

CIN	010	000	020	2	5	6	0
PIT	000	002	001	0	3	7	2

Pitchers: NOLAN, C.Carroll (7), McEnaney (8), EASTWICK (9), Borbon (10) vs Candelaria, Giusti (8), HERNANDEZ (10), Tekulve (10)
Home Runs: Concepcion-CIN, Oliver-PIT, Rose-CIN
Attendance: 46,355

The Oakland A's ran their domination of the American League West to five years, but an aroused Boston team stifled their try for a fourth straight pennant.

In the first game Luis Tiant held Oakland to three hits as his teammates—aided by four Oakland errors—scored seven times before giving the A's an unearned run in the eighth. Oakland scored first in Game Two on Reggie Jackson's two-run homer in the first inning and added a run in the fourth. But Carl Yastrzemski's two-run shot in the last of the fourth, followed by a Carlton Fisk double and a Fred Lynn single, drove out A's starter Vida Blue, and the tying run scored on a double play. Single Boston runs in the sixth, seventh, and eighth put the game away.

The A's started Ken Holtzman for the second time in Game Three, after only two days of rest. He held the Sox scoreless for three innings, but was driven from the game in the fifth. Boston scored four times before Oakland put a run on the board, and retained the lead to the game's conclusion.

Boston Red Sox (East), 3;
Oakland A's (West) 0

BOS (E)

PLAYER/POS	AVG	G	AB	R	H	2B	3B	HR	RB	BB	SO	SB
Juan Beniquez, dh	.250	3	12	2	3	0	0	0	1	0	1	2
Rick Burleson, ss	.444	3	9	2	4	2	0	0	1	1	0	0
Reggie Cleveland, p	.000	1	0	0	0	0	0	0	0	0	0	0
Cecil Cooper, 1b	.400	3	10	0	4	2	0	0	1	0	2	0
Denny Doyle, 2b	.273	3	11	3	3	0	0	0	1	0	1	0
Dick Drago, p	.000	2	0	0	0	0	0	0	0	0	0	0
Dwight Evans, of	.100	3	10	1	1	1	0	0	1	1	2	0
Carlton Fisk, c	.417	3	12	4	5	1	0	0	2	0	2	1
Fred Lynn, of	.364	3	11	1	4	1	0	0	3	0	0	0
Roger Moret, p	.000	1	0	0	0	0	0	0	0	0	0	0
Rico Petrocelli, 3b	.167	3	12	1	2	0	0	1	2	0	3	0
Luis Tiant, p	.000	1	0	0	0	0	0	0	0	0	0	0
Rick Wise, p	.000	1	0	0	0	0	0	0	0	0	0	0
Carl Yastrzemski, of	.455	3	11	4	5	1	0	1	2	1	1	0
TOTAL	.316		98	18	31	8	0	2	14	3	12	3

PITCHER	W	L	ERA	G	GS	CG	SV	SHO	IP	H	ER	BB	SO
Reggie Cleveland	0	0	5.40	1	1	0	0	0	5.0	7	3	1	2
Dick Drago	0	0	0.00	2	0	0	2	0	4.2	2	0	1	2
Roger Moret	1	0	0.00	1	0	0	0	0	1.0	1	0	1	0
Luis Tiant	1	0	0.00	1	1	1	0	0	9.0	3	0	3	8
Rick Wise	1	0	2.45	1	1	0	0	0	7.1	6	2	3	2
TOTAL	3	0	1.67	6	3	1	2	0	27.0	19	5	9	14

OAK (W)

PLAYER/POS	AVG	G	AB	R	H	2B	3B	HR	RB	BB	SO	SB
Glenn Abbott, p	.000	1	0	0	0	0	0	0	0	0	0	0
Sal Bando, 3b	.500	3	12	1	6	2	0	0	2	0	3	0
Vida Blue, p	.000	1	0	0	0	0	0	0	0	0	0	0
Dick Bosman, p	.000	1	0	0	0	0	0	0	0	0	0	0
Bert Campaneris, ss	.000	3	11	1	0	0	0	0	0	1	1	0
Rollie Fingers, p	.000	1	0	0	0	0	0	0	0	0	0	0
Ray Fosse, c	.000	1	2	0	0	0	0	0	0	0	1	0
Phil Garner, 2b	.000	3	5	0	0	0	0	0	0	0	1	0
Tommy Harper, ph	.000	1	0	0	0	0	0	0	0	1	0	0
Jim Holt, 1b-1	.333	3	3	0	1	1	0	0	0	0	0	0
Ken Holtzman, p	.000	2	0	0	0	0	0	0	0	0	0	0
Don Hopkins, dh	.000	1	0	0	0	0	0	0	0	0	0	0
Reggie Jackson, of	.417	3	12	1	5	0	0	1	3	0	2	0
Paul Lindblad, p	.000	2	0	0	0	0	0	0	0	0	0	0
Ted Martinez, 2b	.000	3	0	0	0	0	0	0	0	0	0	0
Billy North, of	.000	3	10	0	0	0	0	0	1	2	0	0
Joe Rudi, 1b-2,of-1	.250	3	12	1	3	2	0	0	0	0	1	0
Gene Tenace, c-3,1b-1	.000	3	9	0	0	0	0	0	0	3	2	0
Jim Todd, p	.000	3	0	0	0	0	0	0	0	0	0	0
Cesar Tovar, 2b-1	.500	2	2	2	1	0	0	0	0	1	0	0
Claudell Washington, of-2,dh-1	.250	3	12	1	3	1	0	0	1	0	2	0
Billy Williams, dh-2	.000	3	8	0	0	0	0	0	0	1	1	0
TOTAL	.194		98	7	19	6	0	1	7	9	14	0

PITCHER	W	L	ERA	G	GS	CG	SV	SHO	IP	H	ER	BB	SO
Glenn Abbott	0	0	0.00	1	0	0	0	0	1.0	0	0	0	0
Vida Blue	0	0	9.00	1	1	0	0	0	3.0	6	3	0	2
Dick Bosman	0	0	0.00	1	0	0	0	0	0.1	0	0	0	0
Rollie Fingers	0	1	6.75	1	0	0	0	0	4.0	5	3	1	3
Ken Holtzman	0	2	4.09	2	2	0	0	0	11.0	12	5	1	7
Paul Lindblad	0	0	0.00	2	0	0	0	0	4.2	5	0	1	0
Jim Todd	0	0	9.00	3	0	0	0	0	1.0	3	1	0	0
TOTAL	0	3	4.32	11	3	0	0	0	25.0	31	12	3	12

The Red Sox entered the Series as underdogs to the mighty Reds, who had won 108 regular-season games. In the opening game, though, the Reds were surprised by veteran Sox starter Luis Tiant, who shut them out on five hits with the Series' first complete-game pitching effort in four years. Tiant also opened the Boston seventh with a single, starting a rally that ended only when he fouled out to end the inning after six runs had scored.

Boston took a 2–1 lead into the ninth inning of Game Two before Johnny Bench doubled to drive out starter Bill Lee, and Dave Concepcion and Ken Griffey drove in runs off reliever Dick Drago to turn the tide for Cincinnati. The Reds moved ahead in the Series with a tenth-inning victory in Game Three, a slugfest in which each club hit three home runs and used five pitchers. Boston tied the score on Dwight Evans's two-run homer in the ninth, but in the last of the tenth, the Reds' Joe Morgan drove one over the center fielder's head with the bases full to end the game.

Tiant pitched Game Four for Boston. Four of the nine hits against him went for extra bases, and each drove in a run. But the Sox bunched six of their eleven hits in the fourth inning for five runs—their only scoring, but enough for the win. Tiant himself scored the fifth run after singling. The Reds moved nearer the title in Game Five, though, as Tony Perez homered twice for four runs in a 6–2 win for a 3–2 Series advantage.

A day of travel to Boston and three days of rain between Games Five and Six brought Tiant back to the mound for a third time. Rookie standout Fred Lynn gave Tiant a three-run lead with a first-inning homer, but Ken Griffey's triple and Johnny Bench's long single drove in the tying Red runs in the fifth. Two more Red runs in the seventh and Cesar Geronimo's leadoff homer in the eighth drove out Tiant, but Boston pinch hitter Bernie Carbo homered to center in the last of the eighth for three runs that tied the score again. After a trio of Boston relievers had held Cincinnati in check through the top of the twelfth inning, the Sox lead-off hitter in the last of the twelfth, Carlton Fisk, ended the game dramatically with a home run to left on the first pitch that came within inches of being foul.

After the pyrotechnics of Game Six (ranked by some as the greatest World Series game ever), the seventh game, close as it was, came as an anticlimax. Boston scored three runs in the third inning, but the Reds began their comeback with

Cincinnati Reds (NL), 4; Boston Red Sox (AL) 3

CIN (N)

PLAYER/POS	AVG	G	AB	R	H	2B	3B	HR	RB	BB	SO	SB
Ed Armbrister, ph	.000	4	1	1	0	0	0	0	0	2	0	0
Johnny Bench, c	.207	7	29	5	6	2	0	1	4	2	4	0
Jack Billingham, p	.000	3	2	0	0	0	0	0	0	0	0	0
Pedro Borbon, p	.000	3	1	0	0	0	0	0	0	0	0	0
Clay Carroll, p	.000	5	0	0	0	0	0	0	0	0	0	0
Darrel Chaney, ph	.000	2	2	0	0	0	0	0	0	0	1	0
Dave Concepcion, ss	.179	7	28	3	5	1	0	1	4	0	1	3
Terry Crowley, ph	.500	2	2	0	1	0	0	0	0	0	1	0
Pat Darcy, p	.000	2	1	0	0	0	0	0	0	0	0	0
Dan Driessen, ph	.000	2	2	0	0	0	0	0	0	0	0	0
Rawly Eastwick, p	.000	5	1	0	0	0	0	0	0	0	0	0
George Foster, of	.276	7	29	1	8	1	0	0	2	1	1	1
Cesar Geronimo, of	.280	7	25	3	7	0	1	2	3	3	5	0
Ken Griffey, of	.269	7	26	4	7	3	1	0	4	4	2	2
Don Gullett, p	.286	3	7	1	2	0	0	0	0	0	2	0
Will McEnaney, p	1.000	5	1	0	1	0	0	0	0	0	0	0
Joe Morgan, 2b	.259	7	27	4	7	1	0	0	3	5	1	2
Gary Nolan, p	.000	2	1	0	0	0	0	0	0	0	0	0
Fred Norman, p	.000	2	1	0	0	0	0	0	0	0	0	0
Tony Perez, 1b	.179	7	28	4	5	0	0	3	7	3	9	1
Merv Rettenmund, ph	.000	3	3	0	0	0	0	0	0	0	1	0
Pete Rose, 3b	.370	7	27	3	10	1	1	0	2	5	1	0
TOTAL	.242		244	29	59	9	3	7	29	25	30	9

PITCHER	W	L	ERA	G	GS	CG	SV	SHO	IP	H	ER	BB	SO
Jack Billingham	0	0	1.00	3	1	0	0	0	9.0	8	1	5	7
Pedro Borbon	0	0	6.00	3	0	0	0	0	3.0	3	2	2	1
Clay Carroll	1	0	3.18	5	0	0	0	0	5.2	4	2	2	3
Pat Darcy	0	1	4.50	2	0	0	0	0	4.0	3	2	2	1
Rawly Eastwick	2	0	2.25	5	0	0	1	0	8.0	6	2	3	4
Don Gullett	1	1	4.34	3	3	0	0	0	18.2	19	9	10	15
Will McEnaney	0	0	2.70	5	0	0	1	0	6.2	3	2	2	5
Gary Nolan	0	0	6.00	2	2	0	0	0	6.0	6	4	1	2
Fred Norman	0	1	9.00	2	1	0	0	0	4.0	8	4	3	2
TOTAL	4	3	3.88	30	7	0	2	0	65.0	60	28	30	40

BOS (A)

PLAYER/POS	AVG	G	AB	R	H	2B	3B	HR	RB	BB	SO	SB
Juan Beniquez, of-2	.125	3	8	0	1	0	0	0	1	1	1	0
Rick Burleson, ss	.292	7	24	1	7	1	0	0	2	4	2	0
Jim Burton, p	.000	2	0	0	0	0	0	0	0	0	0	0
Bernie Carbo, of-2	.429	4	7	3	3	1	0	2	4	1	1	0
Reggie Cleveland, p	.000	3	2	0	0	0	0	0	0	0	0	0
Cecil Cooper, 1b	.053	5	19	0	1	1	0	0	1	0	3	0
Denny Doyle, 2b	.267	7	30	3	8	1	1	0	0	2	1	0
Dick Drago, p	.000	2	0	0	0	0	0	0	0	0	0	0
Dwight Evans, of	.292	7	24	3	7	1	1	1	5	3	4	0
Carlton Fisk, c	.240	7	25	5	6	0	0	2	4	7	7	0
Doug Griffin, ph	.000	1	1	0	0	0	0	0	0	0	0	0
Bill Lee, p	.167	2	6	0	1	0	0	0	0	0	0	0
Fred Lynn, of	.280	7	25	3	7	1	0	1	5	3	5	0
Rick Miller, of-2	.000	3	2	0	0	0	0	0	0	0	0	0
Bob Montgomery, ph	.000	1	1	0	0	0	0	0	0	0	0	0
Roger Moret, p	.000	3	0	0	0	0	0	0	0	0	0	0
Rico Petrocelli, 3b	.308	7	26	3	8	1	0	0	4	3	6	0
Dick Pole, p	.000	1	0	0	0	0	0	0	0	0	0	0
Diego Segui, p	.000	2	0	0	0	0	0	0	0	0	0	0
Luis Tiant, p	.250	3	8	2	2	0	0	0	0	2	4	0
Jim Willoughby, p	.000	3	0	0	0	0	0	0	0	0	0	0
Rick Wise, p	.000	2	2	0	0	0	0	0	0	0	0	0
Carl Yastrzemski, 1b-4,of-4	.310	7	29	7	9	0	0	0	4	4	1	0
TOTAL	.251		239	30	60	7	2	6	30	30	40	0

PITCHER	W	L	ERA	G	GS	CG	SV	SHO	IP	H	ER	BB	SO
Jim Burton	0	1	9.00	2	0	0	0	0	1.0	1	1	3	0
Reggie Cleveland	0	1	6.75	3	1	0	0	0	6.2	7	5	3	5
Dick Drago	0	1	2.25	2	0	0	0	0	4.0	3	1	1	1
Bill Lee	0	0	3.14	2	2	0	0	0	14.1	12	5	3	7
Roger Moret	0	0	0.00	3	0	0	0	0	1.2	2	0	3	1
Dick Pole	0	0	INF	1	0	0	0	0	0.0	0	1	2	0
Diego Segui	0	0	0.00	2	0	0	0	0	1.0	0	0	0	0
Luis Tiant	2	0	3.60	3	3	2	0	1	25.0	25	10	8	12
Jim Willoughby	0	1	0.00	3	0	0	0	0	6.1	3	0	0	2
Rick Wise	1	0	8.44	2	1	0	0	0	5.1	5	5	2	2
TOTAL	3	4	3.86	22	7	2	0	1	65.1	59	28	25	30

Tony Perez's two-run homer in the sixth, tied the game an inning later, and took a 4–3 lead on Joe Morgan's bloop RBI single in the ninth. Red reliever Will McEnaney came on to set the Sox down in order in the last of the ninth, and the Reds went home with their first world title in thirty-five years.

GAME 1 AT BOS OCT 11

CIN	000	000	000	0	5 0
BOS	000	000	60X	6	12 0

Pitchers: GULLETT, Carroll (7), McEnaney (7) vs TIANT
Attendance: 35,205

GAME 2 AT BOS OCT 12

CIN	000	100	002	3	7 1
BOS	100	001	000	2	7 0

Pitchers: Billingham, Borbon (6), McEnaney (7), EASTWICK (8) vs Lee, Drago (9)
Attendance: 35,205

GAME 3 AT CIN OCT 14

BOS	010	001	102 0	5	10 2
CIN	000	230	000 1	6	7 0

Pitchers: Wise, Burton (5), Cleveland (5), WILLOUGHBY (7), Moret (10) vs Nolan, Darcy (5), Carroll (7), McEnaney (7), EASTWICK (9)
Home Runs: Fisk-BOS, Bench-CIN, Concepcion-CIN, Geronimo-CIN, Carbo-BOS, Evans-BOS
Attendance: 55,392

GAME 4 AT CIN OCT 15

BOS	000	500	000	5	11 1
CIN	200	200	000	4	9 1

Pitchers: TIANT vs NORMAN, Borbon (4), Carroll (5), Eastwick (7)
Attendance: 55,667

GAME 5 AT CIN OCT 16

BOS	100	000	001	2	5 0
CIN	000	113	01X	6	8 0

Pitchers: CLEVELAND, Willoughby (6), Pole (8), Segui (8) vs GULLETT, Eastwick (9)
Home Runs: Perez-CIN (2)
Attendance: 56,393

GAME 6 AT BOS OCT 21

CIN	000	030	210	000	6	14 0
BOS	300	000	030	001	7	10 1

Pitchers: Nolan, Norman (3), Billingham (3), Carroll (5), Borbon (6), Eastwick (8), McEnaney (9), DARCY (10) vs Tiant, Moret (8), Drago (9), WISE (12)
Home Runs: Lynn-BOS, Geronimo-CIN, Carbo-BOS, Fisk-BOS
Attendance: 35,205

GAME 7 AT BOS OCT 22

CIN	000	002	101	4	9 0
BOS	003	000	000	3	5 2

Pitchers: Gullett, Billingham (5), CARROLL (7), McEnaney (9) vs Lee, Moret (7), Willoughby (7), BURTON (9), Cleveland (9)
Home Runs: Perez-CIN
Attendance: 35,205

Philadelphia outhit Cincinnati in two of the three games, but couldn't turn enough hits into runs, as the Reds for the second year in a row swept the LCS. The Phillies scored first in Game One with a run in the first inning. But pitcher Don Gullett held them scoreless for the next seven innings as his Reds caught up in the third, moved ahead in the sixth, and took a five-run lead into the last of the ninth. The Phillies scored twice in their half of the inning, but the rally fell short.

In the second game the Phillies outhit the Reds ten to six, scoring the game's first two runs while their starter Jim Lonborg threw a no-hitter for five innings. But in the sixth a walk and two singles drove Lonborg out and set the Reds off on a two-inning six-run spree for their second win.

Again in Game Three the Phillies outhit the Reds, this time going into the last of the ninth ahead by two runs. But George Foster and Johnny Bench hit back-to-back homers off Ron Reed to tie the score, and two relievers (and a single and two walks) later, the Reds brought home another pennant as Ken Griffey's high-bouncing chop glanced off first baseman Bobby Tolan's outstretched glove.

Cincinnati Reds (West), 3; Philadelphia Phillies (East) 0

CIN (W)

PLAYER/POS	AVG	G	AB	R	H	2B	3B	HR	RB	BB	SO	SB
Ed Armbrister, ph	.000	1	0	0	0	0	0	0	0	0	0	0
Johnny Bench, c	.333	3	12	3	4	1	0	1	1	1	2	1
Pedro Borbon, p	.000	2	2	1	0	0	0	0	0	0	2	0
Dave Concepcion, ss	.200	3	10	4	2	1	0	0	0	2	1	0
Dan Driessen, ph	.000	1	1	0	0	0	0	0	0	0	0	0
Rawly Eastwick, p	.000	2	0	0	0	0	0	0	0	0	0	0
Doug Flynn, 2b	.000	1	0	0	0	0	0	0	0	0	0	0
George Foster, of	.167	3	12	2	2	0	0	2	4	0	4	0
Cesar Geronimo, of	.182	3	11	0	2	0	1	0	2	1	3	0
Ken Griffey, of	.385	3	13	2	5	0	1	0	2	2	1	2
Don Gullett, p	.500	1	4	1	2	1	0	0	3	0	0	0
Mike Lum, ph	.000	1	1	0	0	0	0	0	0	0	0	0
Joe Morgan, 2b	.000	3	7	2	0	0	0	0	0	6	1	2
Gary Nolan, p	.000	1	0	0	0	0	0	0	0	1	0	0
Tony Perez, 1b	.200	3	10	1	2	0	0	0	3	1	2	0
Pete Rose, 3b	.429	3	14	3	6	2	1	0	2	1	0	0
Manny Sarmiento, p	.000	1	1	0	0	0	0	0	0	0	0	0
Pat Zachry, p	.000	1	1	0	0	0	0	0	0	0	0	0
TOTAL	.253		99	19	25	5	3	3	17	15	16	5

PITCHER	W	L	ERA	G	GS	CG	SV	SHO	IP	H	ER	BB	SO
Pedro Borbon	0	0	0.00	2	0	0	1	0	4.1	4	0	1	0
Rawly Eastwick	1	0	12.00	2	0	0	0	0	3.0	7	4	2	1
Don Gullett	1	0	1.13	1	1	0	0	0	8.0	2	1	3	4
Gary Nolan	0	0	1.59	1	1	0	0	0	5.2	6	1	2	1
Manny Sarmiento	0	0	18.00	1	0	0	0	0	1.0	2	2	1	0
Pat Zachry	1	0	3.60	1	1	0	0	0	5.0	6	2	3	3
TOTAL	3	0	3.33	8	3	0	1	0	27.0	27	10	12	9

PHI (E)

PLAYER/POS	AVG	G	AB	R	H	2B	3B	HR	RB	BB	SO	SB
Richie Allen, 1b	.222	3	9	1	2	0	0	0	0	3	2	0
Bob Boone, c	.286	3	7	0	2	0	0	0	1	1	0	0
Larry Bowa, ss	.125	3	8	1	1	1	0	0	1	3	0	0
Ollie Brown, of	.000	1	2	0	0	0	0	0	0	1	1	0
Steve Carlton, p	.000	1	2	0	0	0	0	0	0	0	0	0
Dave Cash, 2b	.308	3	13	1	4	1	0	0	1	0	0	0
Gene Garber, p	.000	2	0	0	0	0	0	0	0	0	0	0
Terry Harmon, pr	.000	1	0	1	0	0	0	0	0	0	0	0
Tom Hutton, ph	.000	1	1	0	0	0	0	0	0	0	0	0
Jay Johnstone, of-2	.778	3	9	1	7	1	1	0	2	1	0	0
Jim Kaat, p	.500	1	2	0	1	0	0	0	0	0	0	0
Jim Lonborg, p	.000	1	1	0	0	0	0	0	0	0	0	0
Greg Luzinski, of	.273	3	11	2	3	2	0	1	2	1	4	0
Garry Maddox, of	.231	3	13	2	3	1	0	0	2	2	0	0
Jerry Martin, of	.000	1	1	1	0	0	0	0	0	0	0	0
Tim McCarver, c-1	.000	2	4	0	0	0	0	0	0	0	1	0
Tug McGraw, p	.000	2	0	0	0	0	0	0	0	0	0	0
Johnny Oates, c	.000	1	1	0	0	0	0	0	0	0	0	0
Ron Reed, p	.000	2	1	0	0	0	0	0	0	0	0	0
Mike Schmidt, 3b	.308	3	13	1	4	2	0	0	2	0	1	0
Bobby Tolan, 1b-1,of-1	.000	3	2	0	0	0	0	0	0	0	0	0
Tom Underwood, p	.000	1	0	0	0	0	0	0	0	0	0	0
TOTAL	.270		100	11	27	8	1	1	11	12	9	0

PITCHER	W	L	ERA	G	GS	CG	SV	SHO	IP	H	ER	BB	SO
Steve Carlton	0	1	3.86	1	1	0	0	0	7.0	8	3	5	6
Gene Garber	0	1	40.50	2	0	0	0	0	0.2	2	3	1	0
Jim Kaat	0	0	3.00	1	1	0	0	0	6.0	2	2	2	1
Jim Lonborg	0	1	1.69	1	1	0	0	0	5.1	2	1	2	2
Tug McGraw	0	0	11.57	2	0	0	0	0	2.1	4	3	1	5
Ron Reed	0	0	7.71	2	0	0	0	0	4.2	6	4	2	2
Tom Underwood	0	0	0.00	1	0	0	0	0	0.1	1	0	2	0
TOTAL	0	3	5.47	10	3	0	0	0	26.1	25	16	15	16

GAME 1 AT PHI OCT 9

CIN	001	002	030	6	10	0
PHI	100	000	002	3	6	1

Pitchers: GULLETT, Eastwick (9) vs CARLTON, McGraw (8)
Home Runs: Foster-CIN
Attendance: 62,640

GAME 2 AT PHI OCT 10

CIN	000	004	200	6	6	0
PHI	010	010	000	2	10	1

Pitchers: ZACHRY, Borbon (6) vs LONBORG, Garber (6), McGraw (7), Reed (7)
Home Runs: Luzinski-PHI
Attendance: 62,651

GAME 3 AT CIN OCT 12

PHI	000	100	221	6	11	0
CIN	000	000	403	7	9	2

Pitchers: Kaat, Reed (7), GARBER (9), Underwood (9) vs Nolan, Sarmiento (6), Borbon (7), EASTWICK (8)
Home Runs: Foster-CIN, Bench-CIN
Attendance: 55,047

Returning to postseason play after a dozen years' absence, the Yankees found themselves evenly matched with the first-time-champion Royals. They didn't really need their two ninth-inning runs in the first game: the two they scored in the first inning proved cushion enough for Catfish Hunter's one-run five-hitter. But Kansas City came back the next day, scoring first, losing the lead in the third, then regaining it for good in the sixth.

The Royals again took a first-inning lead in Game Three, but this time the Yankees, once they went ahead in the sixth, didn't let go. Kansas City held on to its early lead in Game Four, building on it throughout the game for a second win, despite Yankee Graig Nettles' two home runs.

But Game Five—like the series itself—was a seesaw affair. For the fourth time the Royals scored first, with a pair in the first on John Mayberry's home run. But the Yankees tied the game when they came to bat, and K.C. retook the lead in the second. New York went ahead again in the third and increased its lead to 6–3 in the sixth. But in the top of the eighth, George Brett's three-run homer tied the score once again, setting the stage for Chris Chambliss to win for the Yankees their thirtieth American League pennant with his first-pitch home run in the bottom of the ninth.

New York Yankees (East), 3; Kansas City Royals (West) 2

NY (E)

PLAYER/POS	AVG	G	AB	R	H	2B	3B	HR	RB	BB	SO	SB
Sandy Alomar, dh-1	.000	2	1	0	0	0	0	0	0	0	0	0
Chris Chambliss, 1b	.524	5	21	5	11	1	1	2	8	0	1	2
Dock Ellis, p	.000	1	0	0	0	0	0	0	0	0	0	0
Ed Figueroa, p	.000	2	0	0	0	0	0	0	0	0	0	0
Oscar Gamble, of	.250	3	8	1	2	1	0	0	1	1	1	0
Ron Guidry, pr	.000	1	0	0	0	0	0	0	0	0	0	0
Elrod Hendricks, ph	1.000	1	1	0	1	0	0	0	0	0	0	0
Catfish Hunter, p	.000	2	0	0	0	0	0	0	0	0	0	0
Grant Jackson, p	.000	2	0	0	0	0	0	0	0	0	0	0
Sparky Lyle, p	.000	1	0	0	0	0	0	0	0	0	0	0
Elliott Maddox, of	.222	3	9	0	2	1	0	0	1	0	1	0
Jim Mason, ss	.000	2	0	0	0	0	0	0	0	0	0	0
Carlos May, dh	.200	3	10	1	2	1	0	0	0	1	4	0
Thurman Munson, c	.435	5	23	3	10	2	0	0	3	0	1	0
Graig Nettles, 3b	.235	5	17	2	4	1	0	2	4	3	3	0
Lou Piniella, dh-3	.273	4	11	1	3	1	0	0	0	0	1	0
Willie Randolph, 2b	.118	5	17	0	2	0	0	0	1	3	1	1
Mickey Rivers, of	.348	5	23	5	8	0	1	0	0	1	1	0
Fred Stanley, ss	.333	5	15	1	5	2	0	0	0	2	0	0
Dick Tidrow, p	.000	3	0	0	0	0	0	0	0	0	0	0
Otto Velez, ph	.000	1	1	0	0	0	0	0	0	0	0	0
Roy White, of	.294	5	17	4	5	3	0	0	3	5	1	1
TOTAL	.316		174	23	55	13	2	4	21	16	15	4

PITCHER	W	L	ERA	G	GS	CG	SV	SHO	IP	H	ER	BB	SO
Dock Ellis	1	0	3.38	1	1	0	0	0	8.0	6	3	2	5
Ed Figueroa	0	1	5.84	2	2	0	0	0	12.1	14	8	2	5
Catfish Hunter	1	1	4.50	2	2	1	0	0	12.0	10	6	1	5
Grant Jackson	0	0	8.10	2	0	0	0	0	3.1	4	3	1	3
Sparky Lyle	0	0	0.00	1	0	0	1	0	1.0	0	0	1	0
Dick Tidrow	1	0	3.68	3	0	0	0	0	7.1	6	3	4	0
TOTAL	3	2	4.70	11	5	1	1	0	44.0	40	23	11	18

KC (W)

PLAYER/POS	AVG	G	AB	R	H	2B	3B	HR	RB	BB	SO	SB
Doug Bird, p	.000	1	0	0	0	0	0	0	0	0	0	0
George Brett, 3b	.444	5	18	4	8	1	1	1	5	2	1	0
Al Cowens, of	.190	5	21	3	4	0	1	0	0	1	1	2
Larry Gura, p	.000	2	0	0	0	0	0	0	0	0	0	0
Tom Hall, p	.000	1	0	0	0	0	0	0	0	0	0	0
Andy Hassler, p	.000	2	0	0	0	0	0	0	0	0	0	0
Dennis Leonard, p	.000	2	0	0	0	0	0	0	0	0	0	0
Mark Littell, p	.000	3	0	0	0	0	0	0	0	0	0	0
Buck Martinez, c	.333	5	15	0	5	0	0	0	4	1	3	0
John Mayberry, 1b	.222	5	18	4	4	0	0	1	3	1	0	0
Hal McRae, dh-3,of-2	.118	5	17	2	2	1	1	0	1	1	4	0
Steve Mingori, p	.000	3	0	0	0	0	0	0	0	0	0	0
Dave Nelson, dh-1	.000	2	2	0	0	0	0	0	0	0	1	0
Amos Otis, of	.000	1	1	0	0	0	0	0	0	0	0	0
Freddie Patek, ss	.389	5	18	2	7	2	0	0	4	0	1	0
Marty Pattin, p	.000	2	0	0	0	0	0	0	0	0	0	0
Tom Poquette, of	.188	5	16	1	3	2	0	0	4	2	3	0
Jamie Quirk, dh-2	.143	4	7	1	1	0	1	0	2	0	2	0
Cookie Rojas, 2b	.333	4	9	2	3	0	0	0	1	0	0	1
Paul Splittorff, p	.000	2	0	0	0	0	0	0	0	0	0	0
Bob Stinson, c-1	.000	2	1	0	0	0	0	0	0	0	0	0
John Wathan, c	.000	1	0	0	0	0	0	0	0	0	0	0
Frank White, 2b	.125	4	8	2	1	0	0	0	0	0	1	0
Jim Wohlford, of	.182	5	11	3	2	0	0	0	0	3	1	2
TOTAL	.247		162	24	40	6	4	2	24	11	18	5

PITCHER	W	L	ERA	G	GS	CG	SV	SHO	IP	H	ER	BB	SO
Doug Bird	1	0	1.93	1	0	0	0	0	4.2	4	1	0	1
Larry Gura	0	1	4.22	2	2	0	0	0	10.2	18	5	1	4
Tom Hall	0	0	0.00	1	0	0	0	0	0.1	1	0	0	0
Andy Hassler	0	1	6.14	2	1	0	0	0	7.1	8	5	6	4
Dennis Leonard	0	0	19.29	2	2	0	0	0	2.1	9	5	2	0
Mark Littell	0	1	1.93	3	0	0	0	0	4.2	4	1	1	3
Steve Mingori	0	0	2.70	3	0	0	1	0	3.1	4	1	0	1
Marty Pattin	0	0	27.00	2	0	0	0	0	0.1	0	1	1	0
Paul Splittorff	1	0	1.93	2	0	0	0	0	9.1	7	2	5	2
TOTAL	2	3	4.40	18	5	0	1	0	43.0	55	21	16	15

GAME 1 AT KC OCT 9

NY	200 000 002	4	12	0
KC	000 000 010	1	5	2

Pitchers: HUNTER vs GURA, Littell (9)
Attendance: 41,077

GAME 2 AT KC OCT 10

NY	012 000 000	3	12	5
KC	200 002 03X	7	9	0

Pitchers: FIGUEROA, Tidrow (6) vs Leonard, SPLITTORFF (3), Mingori (9)
Attendance: 41,091

GAME 3 AT NY OCT 12

KC	300 000 000	3	6	0
NY	000 203 00X	5	9	0

Pitchers: HASSLER, Pattin (6), Hall (6), Mingori (6), Littell (6) vs ELLIS, Lyle (9)
Home Runs: Chambliss-NY
Attendance: 56,808

GAME 4 AT NY OCT 13

KC	030 201 010	7	9	1
NY	020 000 101	4	11	0

Pitchers: Gura, BIRD (3), Mingori (7) vs HUNTER, Tidrow (4), Jackson (7)
Home Runs: Nettles-NY (2)
Attendance: 56,355

GAME 5 AT NY OCT 14

KC	210 000 030	6	11	1
NY	202 002 001	7	11	1

Pitchers: Leonard, Splittorff (1), Pattin (4), Hassler (5), LITTELL (7) vs Figueroa, Jackson (8), TIDROW (9)
Home Runs: Mayberry-KC, Brett-KC, Chambliss-NY
Attendance: 56,821

The Reds led the National League in virtually every offensive category and in fielding as well. In the Series (which, incidentally, was the first to employ the designated hitter), the Big Red Machine continued its roll over the Yankees to become the first National League club in fifty-four years to repeat as world champions, as well as the first team to sweep both a League Championship and World Series. Red catcher Johnny Bench led the attack with eight hits, half of them for extra bases, for a batting average of .533 and a 1.133 average in slugging.

Joe Morgan's home run for Cincinnati in the first inning of Game One was the first hit of the Series, but New York pushed across a tying run half an inning later on a sacrifice fly. Red pitchers Don Gullett and Pedro Borbon held the Yankees scoreless after that as the Reds regained the lead with a run in the third and extended it in the sixth and seventh for a 5–1 win.

Game Two turned out to be the Reds' only narrow victory. They scored first, with three runs in the second inning. In the fourth the Yankees scored their first run, and they tied the score with two more runs in the seventh. But with two men out in the last of the ninth, a throwing error by Yankee shortstop Fred Stanley allowed the Reds' batter Ken Griffey to reach second, from where he scored the winning run on Tony Perez's line single to left.

In Game Three, four hits and a pair of stolen bases put Cincinnati ahead 3–0 in the second inning, and Dan Driessen homered in the fourth to make it 4–0 before the Yankees scored their first run. Another quartet of hits in the eighth gave the Reds two more runs and a 6–2 win.

New York took the lead for the only time in the Series when Chris Chambliss doubled in Thurman Munson in the first inning of Game Four. (Munson had singled with the third of what became six straight hits.) But the Reds' George Foster drove in a tying run in the fourth, and Johnny Bench followed him with a two-run homer. New York scored again an inning later to come close, but Bench's second home run, a three-run blast in the ninth, put the game out of reach, and a pair of ground-rule doubles touched by New York fans nailed the final run in the Yankee coffin.

Cincinnati Reds (NL), 4;
New York Yankees (AL) 0

CIN (N)

PLAYER/POS	AVG	G	AB	R	H	2B	3B	HR	RB	BB	SO	SB
Johnny Bench, c	.533	4	15	4	8	1	1	2	6	0	1	0
Jack Billingham, p	.000	1	0	0	0	0	0	0	0	0	0	0
Pedro Borbon, p	.000	1	0	0	0	0	0	0	0	0	0	0
Dave Concepcion, ss	.357	4	14	1	5	1	1	0	3	1	3	1
Dan Driessen, dh	.357	4	14	4	5	2	0	1	1	2	0	1
George Foster, of	.429	4	14	3	6	1	0	0	4	2	3	0
Cesar Geronimo, of	.308	4	13	3	4	2	0	0	1	2	2	2
Ken Griffey, of	.059	4	17	2	1	0	0	0	1	0	1	1
Don Gullett, p	.000	1	0	0	0	0	0	0	0	0	0	0
Will McEnaney, p	.000	2	0	0	0	0	0	0	0	0	0	0
Joe Morgan, 2b	.333	4	15	3	5	1	1	1	2	2	2	2
Gary Nolan, p	.000	1	0	0	0	0	0	0	0	0	0	0
Fred Norman, p	.000	1	0	0	0	0	0	0	0	0	0	0
Tony Perez, 1b	.313	4	16	1	5	1	0	0	2	1	2	0
Pete Rose, 3b	.188	4	16	1	3	1	0	0	1	2	2	0
Pat Zachry, p	.000	1	0	0	0	0	0	0	0	0	0	0
TOTAL	.313		134	22	42	10	3	4	21	12	16	7

PITCHER	W	L	ERA	G	GS	CG	SV	SHO	IP	H	ER	BB	SO
Jack Billingham	1	0	0.00	1	0	0	0	0	2.2	0	0	0	1
Pedro Borbon	0	0	0.00	1	0	0	0	0	1.2	0	0	0	0
Don Gullett	1	0	1.23	1	1	0	0	0	7.1	5	1	3	4
Will McEnaney	0	0	0.00	2	0	0	2	0	4.2	2	0	1	2
Gary Nolan	1	0	2.70	1	1	0	0	0	6.2	8	2	1	1
Fred Norman	0	0	4.26	1	1	0	0	0	6.1	9	3	2	2
Pat Zachry	1	0	2.70	1	1	0	0	0	6.2	6	2	5	6
TOTAL	4	0	2.00	8	4	0	2	0	36.0	30	8	12	16

NY (A)

PLAYER/POS	AVG	G	AB	R	H	2B	3B	HR	RB	BB	SO	SB
Doyle Alexander, p	.000	1	0	0	0	0	0	0	0	0	0	0
Chris Chambliss, 1b	.313	4	16	1	5	1	0	0	1	0	2	0
Dock Ellis, p	.000	1	0	0	0	0	0	0	0	0	0	0
Ed Figueroa, p	.000	1	0	0	0	0	0	0	0	0	0	0
Oscar Gamble, of-2	.125	3	8	0	1	0	0	0	1	0	0	0
Elrod Hendricks, ph	.000	2	2	0	0	0	0	0	0	0	0	0
Catfish Hunter, p	.000	1	0	0	0	0	0	0	0	0	0	0
Grant Jackson, p	.000	1	0	0	0	0	0	0	0	0	0	0
Sparky Lyle, p	.000	2	0	0	0	0	0	0	0	0	0	0
Elliott Maddox, of-1,dh-1	.200	2	5	0	1	0	1	0	0	1	2	0
Jim Mason, ss	1.000	3	1	1	1	0	0	1	1	0	0	0
Carlos May, dh	.000	4	9	0	0	0	0	0	0	0	1	0
Thurman Munson, c	.529	4	17	2	9	0	0	0	2	0	1	0
Graig Nettles, 3b	.250	4	12	0	3	0	0	0	2	3	1	0
Lou Piniella, of-2,dh-2	.333	4	9	1	3	1	0	0	0	0	0	0
Willie Randolph, 2b	.071	4	14	1	1	0	0	0	0	1	3	0
Mickey Rivers, of	.167	4	18	1	3	0	0	0	0	1	2	1
Fred Stanley, ss	.167	4	6	1	1	1	0	0	1	3	1	0
Dick Tidrow, p	.000	2	0	0	0	0	0	0	0	0	0	0
Otto Velez, ph	.000	3	3	0	0	0	0	0	0	0	3	0
Roy White, of	.133	4	15	0	2	0	0	0	0	3	0	0
TOTAL	.222		135	8	30	3	1	1	8	12	16	1

PITCHER	W	L	ERA	G	GS	CG	SV	SHO	IP	H	ER	BB	SO
Doyle Alexander	0	1	7.50	1	1	0	0	0	6.0	9	5	2	1
Dock Ellis	0	1	10.80	1	1	0	0	0	3.1	7	4	0	1
Ed Figueroa	0	1	5.63	1	1	0	0	0	8.0	6	5	5	2
Catfish Hunter	0	1	3.12	1	1	1	0	0	8.2	10	3	4	5
Grant Jackson	0	0	4.91	1	0	0	0	0	3.2	4	2	0	3
Sparky Lyle	0	0	0.00	2	0	0	0	0	2.2	1	0	0	3
Dick Tidrow	0	0	7.71	2	0	0	0	0	2.1	5	2	1	1
TOTAL	0	4	5.45	9	4	1	0	0	34.2	42	21	12	16

GAME 1 AT CIN OCT 16

NY	010 000 000	1	5	1
CIN	101 001 20X	5	10	1

Pitchers: ALEXANDER, Lyle (7) vs GULLETT, Borbon (8)
Home Runs: Morgan-CIN
Attendance: 54,826

GAME 2 AT CIN OCT 17

NY	000 100 200	3	9	1
CIN	030 000 001	4	10	0

Pitchers: HUNTER vs Norman, BILLINGHAM (7)
Attendance: 54,816

GAME 3 AT NY OCT 19

CIN	030 100 020	6	13	2
NY	000 100 100	2	8	0

Pitchers: ZACHRY, McEnaney (7) vs ELLIS, Jackson (4), Tidrow (8)
Home Runs: Driessen-CIN, Mason-NY
Attendance: 56,667

GAME 4 AT NY OCT 21

CIN	000 300 004	7	9	2
NY	100 010 000	2	8	0

Pitchers: NOLAN, McEnaney (7) vs FIGUEROA, Tidrow (9), Lyle (9)
Home Runs: Bench-CIN (2)
Attendance: 56,700

The Phillies took the first game, but the Dodgers proved better over all at turning hits into runs and swept the next three. Philadelphia jumped ahead in the first inning of Game One, and had built a 5–1 lead by the seventh, when Ron Cey tied the score with a Dodger grand slam. But the Phillies came back with two runs on three singles in the top of the ninth and held on for the win. As in Game One, both clubs again got nine hits apiece in Game Two, but this time Dodger pitcher Don Sutton scattered the Phillies' hits for a single run over nine innings, while Phillie starter Jim Lonborg—in the four innings he pitched—yielded five runs, including a grand slam to Dusty Baker.

In Game Three Los Angeles outhit the Phillies, but the Dodgers were nearly undone when starter Burt Hooton walked in three Phila-delphia runs in the second inning. The Phillies took a two-run lead into the ninth, but after two men were out the Dodgers rebounded, thanks largely to a couple of old pros. Pinch hitter Vic Davalillo, age 38, beat out a drag bunt on a disputed call, and 39-year-old Manny Mota doubled to deep left. Two more Dodger singles scored three runs that proved enough for the win.

The Dodgers didn't even need all of their five hits to take the final game behind Tommy John's one-run seven-hitter, for one of those hits was another Dusty Baker home run with a man aboard.

Los Angeles Dodgers (West), 3; Philadelphia Phillies (East) 1

LA (W)

PLAYER/POS	AVG	G	AB	R	H	2B	3B	HR	RB	BB	SO	SB
Dusty Baker, of	.357	4	14	4	5	1	0	2	8	2	3	0
Glenn Burke, of	.000	4	7	0	0	0	0	0	0	0	3	0
Ron Cey, 3b	.308	4	13	4	4	1	0	1	4	2	4	1
Vic Davalillo, ph	1.000	1	1	1	1	0	0	0	0	0	0	0
Mike Garman, p	.000	2	0	0	0	0	0	0	0	0	0	0
Steve Garvey, 1b	.308	4	13	2	4	0	0	0	0	2	1	1
Ed Goodson, ph	.000	1	1	0	0	0	0	0	0	0	0	0
Jerry Grote, c-1	.000	2	0	0	0	0	0	0	0	1	0	0
Burt Hooton, p	1.000	1	1	0	1	1	0	0	0	0	0	0
Charlie Hough, p	.000	1	0	0	0	0	0	0	0	0	0	0
Tommy John, p	.200	2	5	0	1	0	0	0	0	0	2	0
Lee Lacy, ph	1.000	1	1	1	1	0	0	0	0	0	0	0
Davey Lopes, 2b	.235	4	17	2	4	0	0	0	3	2	0	0
Rick Monday, of	.286	3	7	1	2	1	0	0	0	2	1	0
Manny Mota, ph	1.000	1	1	1	1	1	0	0	0	0	0	0
Doug Rau, p	.000	1	0	0	0	0	0	0	0	0	0	0
Lance Rautzhan, p	.000	1	0	0	0	0	0	0	0	0	0	0
Rick Rhoden, p	.000	1	1	0	0	0	0	0	0	0	0	0
Bill Russell, ss	.278	4	18	3	5	1	0	0	2	0	0	0
Reggie Smith, of	.188	4	16	2	3	0	1	0	1	2	5	1
Elias Sosa, p	.000	2	1	0	0	0	0	0	0	0	0	0
Don Sutton, p	.000	1	3	0	0	0	0	0	0	0	0	0
Steve Yeager, c	.231	4	13	1	3	0	0	0	2	1	3	0
TOTAL	.263		133	22	35	6	1	3	20	14	22	3

PITCHER	W	L	ERA	G	GS	CG	SV	SHO	IP	H	ER	BB	SO
Mike Garman	0	0	0.00	2	0	0	1	0	1.1	0	0	0	1
Burt Hooton	0	0	16.20	1	1	0	0	0	1.2	2	3	4	1
Charlie Hough	0	0	4.50	1	0	0	0	0	2.0	2	1	0	3
Tommy John	1	0	0.66	2	2	1	0	0	13.2	11	1	5	11
Doug Rau	0	0	0.00	1	0	0	0	0	1.0	0	0	0	1
Lance Rautzhan	1	0	0.00	1	0	0	0	0	0.1	0	0	0	0
Rick Rhoden	0	0	0.00	1	0	0	0	0	4.1	2	0	2	0
Elias Sosa	0	1	10.13	2	0	0	0	0	2.2	5	3	0	0
Don Sutton	1	0	1.00	1	1	1	0	0	9.0	9	1	0	4
TOTAL	3	1	2.25	12	4	2	1	0	36.0	31	9	11	21

PHI (E)

PLAYER/POS	AVG	G	AB	R	H	2B	3B	HR	RB	BB	SO	SB
Bob Boone, c	.400	4	10	1	4	0	0	0	0	0	0	0
Larry Bowa, ss	.118	4	17	2	2	0	0	0	1	1	0	0
Ollie Brown, ph	.000	2	2	0	0	0	0	0	0	0	1	0
Warren Brusstar, p	.000	2	0	0	0	0	0	0	0	0	0	0
Steve Carlton, p	.500	2	4	0	2	0	0	0	1	0	2	0
Larry Christenson, p	.000	1	0	0	0	0	0	0	0	1	1	0
Gene Garber, p	.000	3	0	0	0	0	0	0	0	0	0	0
Richie Hebner, 1b-3	.357	4	14	2	5	2	0	0	0	0	1	0
Tom Hutton, 1b-1	.000	3	3	0	0	0	0	0	0	0	0	0
Davey Johnson, 1b	.250	1	4	0	1	0	0	0	2	0	1	0
Jay Johnstone, of	.200	2	5	0	1	0	0	0	0	0	1	0
Jim Lonborg, p	.000	1	1	0	0	0	0	0	0	0	1	0
Greg Luzinski, of	.286	4	14	2	4	1	0	1	2	3	3	1
Garry Maddox, of	.429	2	7	1	3	0	0	0	2	0	1	0
Jerry Martin, of-1	.000	3	4	0	0	0	0	0	0	0	2	0
Bake McBride, of	.222	4	18	2	4	0	0	1	2	1	2	0
Tim McCarver, c-2	.167	3	6	1	1	0	0	0	0	1	3	0
Tug McGraw, p	.000	2	0	0	0	0	0	0	0	0	0	0
Ron Reed, p	.000	3	0	0	0	0	0	0	0	0	0	0
Mike Schmidt, 3b	.063	4	16	2	1	0	0	0	1	2	3	0
Ted Sizemore, 2b	.231	4	13	1	3	0	0	0	0	2	0	0
TOTAL	.225		138	14	31	3	0	2	12	11	21	1

PITCHER	W	L	ERA	G	GS	CG	SV	SHO	IP	H	ER	BB	SO
Warren Brusstar	0	0	3.38	2	0	0	0	0	2.2	2	1	1	2
Steve Carlton	0	1	6.94	2	2	0	0	0	11.2	13	9	8	6
Larry Christenson	0	0	8.10	1	1	0	0	0	3.1	7	3	0	2
Gene Garber	1	1	3.38	3	0	0	0	0	5.1	4	2	0	3
Jim Lonborg	0	1	11.25	1	1	0	0	0	4.0	5	5	1	1
Tug McGraw	0	0	0.00	2	0	0	1	0	3.0	1	0	2	3
Ron Reed	0	0	1.80	3	0	0	0	0	5.0	3	1	2	5
TOTAL	1	3	5.40	14	4	0	1	0	35.0	35	21	14	22

GAME 1 AT LA OCT 4

PHI   200 021 002   7 9 0
LA   000 010 400   5 9 2

Pitchers: Carlton, GARBER (7), McGraw (9) vs John, Garman (5), Hough (6), SOSA (8)
Home Runs: Luzinski-PHI, Cey-LA
Attendance: 55,968

GAME 2 AT LA OCT 5

PHI   001 000 000   1 9 1
LA   001 401 10X   7 9 1

Pitchers: LONBORG, Reed (5), Brusstar (7) vs SUTTON
Home Runs: McBride-PHI, Baker-LA
Attendance: 55,973

GAME 3 AT PHI OCT 7

LA   020 100 003   6 12 2
PHI   030 000 020   5 6 2

Pitchers: Hooton, Rhoden (2), Rau (7), Sosa (8), RAUTZHAN (8), Garman (9) vs Christensen, Brusstar (4), Reed (5), GARBER (7)
Attendance: 63,719

GAME 4 AT PHI OCT 8

LA   020 020 000   4 5 0
PHI   000 100 000   1 7 0

Pitchers: JOHN vs CARLTON, Reed (6), McGraw (7), Garber (9)
Home Runs: Baker-LA
Attendance: 64,924

As in 1976, the Royals met the Yankees in the LCS, and as in 1976 the series went five games, with the Royals outscoring New York by a single run. But this time Kansas City won the first game, and as the teams traded victories through the first four games and K.C. took a lead into the ninth inning of Game Five, it began to look as though this year the Royals might take the pennant.

Royal hitters began things with a bang, scoring six of their seven runs in Game One in the first three innings for an insurmountable lead. New York came back to take the second game 6–2 behind Ron Guidry's three-hitter, but the Royals reversed the score the next day as Dennis Leonard limited the Yankees to four hits. Yankee reliever Sparky Lyle shut K.C. down over the final five innings of Game Four after the Royals had drawn within a run of New York in the fourth inning, and the series was tied.

In the finale, Kansas City drew first blood with two runs in the bottom of the first and led by one run after eight. But with the pennant in sight, the Royals gave up three Yankee runs in the top of the ninth, scoring nothing themselves as reliever Lyle held them off to give the Yankees their thirty-first flag.

New York Yankees (East), 3;
Kansas City Royals (West) 2

NY (E)

PLAYER/POS	AVG	G	AB	R	H	2B	3B	HR	RB	BB	SO	SB
Paul Blair, of	.400	3	5	1	2	0	0	0	0	0	0	0
Chris Chambliss, 1b	.059	5	17	0	1	0	0	0	0	3	4	0
Bucky Dent, ss	.214	5	14	1	3	1	0	0	2	1	0	0
Ed Figueroa, p	.000	1	0	0	0	0	0	0	0	0	0	0
Ron Guidry, p	.000	2	0	0	0	0	0	0	0	0	0	0
Don Gullett, p	.000	1	0	0	0	0	0	0	0	0	0	0
Reggie Jackson, of-4,dh-1	.125	5	16	1	2	0	0	0	1	2	2	1
Cliff Johnson, dh-4	.400	5	15	2	6	2	0	1	2	1	2	0
Sparky Lyle, p	.000	4	0	0	0	0	0	0	0	0	0	0
Thurman Munson, c	.286	5	21	3	6	1	0	1	5	0	2	0
Graig Nettles, 3b	.150	5	20	1	3	0	0	0	1	0	3	0
Lou Piniella, of-4,dh-1	.333	5	21	1	7	3	0	0	2	0	1	0
Willie Randolph, 2b	.278	5	18	4	5	1	0	0	2	1	0	0
Mickey Rivers, of	.391	5	23	5	9	2	0	0	2	0	2	0
Fred Stanley, ss	.000	2	0	0	0	0	0	0	0	0	0	0
Dick Tidrow, p	.000	2	0	0	0	0	0	0	0	0	0	0
Mike Torrez, p	.000	2	0	0	0	0	0	0	0	0	0	0
Roy White, of-1,dh-1	.400	4	5	2	2	2	0	0	0	1	0	0
TOTAL	.263		175	21	46	12	0	2	17	9	16	2

PITCHER	W	L	ERA	G	GS	CG	SV	SHO	IP	H	ER	BB	SO
Ed Figueroa	0	0	10.80	1	1	0	0	0	3.1	5	4	2	3
Ron Guidry	1	0	3.97	2	2	1	0	0	11.1	9	5	3	8
Don Gullett	0	1	18.00	1	1	0	0	0	2.0	4	4	2	0
Sparky Lyle	2	0	0.96	4	0	0	0	0	9.1	7	1	0	3
Dick Tidrow	0	0	3.86	2	0	0	0	0	7.0	6	3	3	3
Mike Torrez	0	1	4.09	2	1	0	0	0	11.0	11	5	5	5
TOTAL	3	2	4.50	12	5	1	0	0	44.0	42	22	15	22

KC (W)

PLAYER/POS	AVG	G	AB	R	H	2B	3B	HR	RB	BB	SO	SB
Doug Bird, p	.000	3	0	0	0	0	0	0	0	0	0	0
George Brett, 3b	.300	5	20	2	6	0	2	0	2	1	0	0
Al Cowens, of	.263	5	19	2	5	0	0	1	5	1	3	0
Larry Gura, p	.000	2	0	0	0	0	0	0	0	0	0	0
Andy Hassler, p	.000	1	0	0	0	0	0	0	0	0	0	0
Pete LaCock, 1b	.000	1	1	0	0	0	0	0	0	1	1	0
Joe Lahoud, dh	.000	1	1	2	0	0	0	0	0	2	0	0
Dennis Leonard, p	.000	2	0	0	0	0	0	0	0	0	0	0
Mark Littell, p	.000	2	0	0	0	0	0	0	0	0	0	0
John Mayberry, 1b	.167	4	12	1	2	1	0	1	3	1	2	0
Hal McRae, dh-3,of-2	.444	5	18	6	8	3	0	1	2	3	1	0
Steve Mingori, p	.000	3	0	0	0	0	0	0	0	0	0	0
Amos Otis, of	.125	5	16	1	2	1	0	0	2	2	3	2
Freddie Patek, ss	.389	5	18	4	7	3	1	0	5	1	2	0
Marty Pattin, p	.000	1	0	0	0	0	0	0	0	0	0	0
Tom Poquette, of	.167	2	6	0	1	0	0	0	0	0	0	0
Darrell Porter, c	.333	5	15	3	5	0	0	0	0	3	0	0
Cookie Rojas, dh	.250	1	4	0	1	0	0	0	0	0	1	1
Paul Splittorff, p	.000	2	0	0	0	0	0	0	0	0	0	0
John Wathan, 1b-2,c-1,dh-1	.000	4	6	0	0	0	0	0	0	0	3	0
Frank White, 2b	.278	5	18	1	5	1	0	0	2	0	4	1
Joe Zdeb, of	.000	4	9	0	0	0	0	0	0	0	2	1
TOTAL	.258		163	22	42	9	3	3	21	15	22	5

PITCHER	W	L	ERA	G	GS	CG	SV	SHO	IP	H	ER	BB	SO
Doug Bird	0	0	0.00	3	0	0	0	0	2.0	4	0	0	1
Larry Gura	0	1	18.00	2	1	0	0	0	2.0	7	4	1	2
Andy Hassler	0	1	4.76	1	1	0	0	0	5.2	5	3	0	3
Dennis Leonard	1	1	3.00	2	1	1	0	0	9.0	5	3	2	4
Mark Littell	0	0	3.00	2	0	0	0	0	3.0	5	1	3	1
Steve Mingori	0	0	0.00	3	0	0	0	0	1.1	0	0	0	1
Marty Pattin	0	0	1.50	1	0	0	0	0	6.0	6	1	0	0
Paul Splittorff	1	0	2.40	2	2	0	0	0	15.0	14	4	3	4
TOTAL	2	3	3.27	16	5	1	0	0	44.0	46	16	9	16

GAME 1 AT NY OCT 5

KC	222 000 010	7	9	0
NY	002 000 000	2	9	0

Pitchers: SPLITTORFF, Bird (9) vs GULLETT. Tidrow (3), Lyle (9)
Home Runs: McRae-KC, Mayberry-KC, Munson-NY, Cowens-KC
Attendance: 54,930

GAME 2 AT NY OCT 6

KC	001 001 000	2	3	1
NY	000 023 01X	6	10	1

Pitchers: HASSLER, Littell (6), Mingori (8) vs GUIDRY
Home Runs: Johnson-NY
Attendance: 56,230

GAME 3 AT KC OCT 7

NY	000 010 001	2	4	1
KC	011 012 10X	6	12	1

Pitchers: TORREZ, Lyle (6) vs LEONARD
Attendance: 41,285

GAME 4 AT KC OCT 8

NY	121 100 001	6	13	0
KC	002 200 000	4	8	2

Pitchers: Figueroa, Tidrow (4), LYLE (4) vs GURA, Pattin (3), Mingori (9), Bird (9)
Attendance: 41,135

GAME 5 AT KC OCT 9

NY	001 000 013	5	10	0
KC	201 000 000	3	10	1

Pitchers: Guidry, Torrez (3), LYLE (8) vs Splittorff, Bird (8), Mingori (8), LEONARD (9), Gura (9), Littell (9)
Attendance: 41,133

This was the Series in which Yankee Reggie Jackson established his reputation as "Mr. October" with a record five home runs, including three in successive at-bats in the final game, and the Yankees showed that after a decade or so of decline they were once again the world's best. Los Angeles scored first in the opening game with a pair of first-inning runs. But New York gained back half the ground in the bottom of the first and tied the game on Willie Randolph's leadoff homer in the sixth. The clubs traded runs in the eighth and ninth to take the game into extra innings. The impasse was not breached until the last of the twelfth, when Randolph doubled and Paul Blair singled him home.

Game Two, by contrast, was a runaway Dodger victory. Home runs in the first three innings by Ron Cey, Steve Yeager, and Reggie Smith made the score 5–0 before New York scored its lone run in the fourth. Burt Hooton hurled the Dodger win, a five-hitter. And for good measure, Dodger Steve Garvey homered in the ninth inning. The Yankees returned to form two days later in Los Angeles, though, scoring three runs in the top of the first on pairs of doubles and singles (and a Dodger error). Dodger Dusty Baker's three-run homer tied the game in the third, but single Yankee runs in the next two innings provided pitcher Mike Torrez with runs enough for the win.

Two of the four hits yielded by emerging Yankee ace Ron Guidry in Game Four were pitcher Rick Rhoden's double followed by Davey Lopes's home run in the third inning. But the Yankees had already scored three times in the second, and Reggie Jackson homered in the sixth as Guidry held Los Angeles scoreless after the third for a 4–2 win. A Yankee assault against Dodger pitcher Don Sutton in Game Five included back-to-back home runs by Thurman Munson and Jackson in the eighth inning. But Los Angeles rocked Yankee pitching even harder, with homers by Steve Yeager and Reggie Smith producing five of the Dodgers' ten runs as the club evaded elimination with its second win.

The Dodgers scored first in the sixth game when Steve Garvey's first-inning triple drove in two runners. Yankee Chris Chambliss matched that an inning later with a two-run homer. Smith restored the lead to Los Angeles with a solo shot in the third inning, but Jackson put the Yankees back in front with the first of his three home runs, a two-run blast in the fourth. By the time he had homered again for two in the fifth and for the third time in the eighth, the Yankees' twenty-first world title was well in hand.

New York Yankees (AL), 4; Los Angeles Dodgers (NL) 2

NY (A)

PLAYER/POS	AVG	G	AB	R	H	2B	3B	HR	RB	BB	SO	SB
Paul Blair, of-3	.250	4	4	0	1	0	0	0	1	0	0	0
Chris Chambliss, 1b	.292	6	24	4	7	2	0	1	4	0	2	0
Ken Clay, p	.000	2	0	0	0	0	0	0	0	0	0	0
Bucky Dent, ss	.263	6	19	0	5	0	0	0	0	2	2	1
Ron Guidry, p	.000	1	2	0	0	0	0	0	0	0	1	0
Don Gullett, p	.000	2	0	0	0	0	0	0	0	0	2	0
Catfish Hunter, p	.000	2	0	0	0	0	0	0	0	0	0	0
Reggie Jackson, of	.450	6	20	10	9	1	0	5	8	3	4	0
Cliff Johnson, c-1	.000	2	1	0	0	0	0	0	0	0	0	0
Sparky Lyle, p	.000	2	2	0	0	0	0	0	0	0	2	0
Thurman Munson, c	.320	6	25	4	8	2	0	1	3	2	8	0
Graig Nettles, 3b	.190	6	21	1	4	1	0	0	2	2	3	0
Lou Piniella, of	.273	6	22	1	6	0	0	0	3	0	3	0
Willie Randolph, 2b	.160	6	25	5	4	2	0	1	1	1	2	0
Mickey Rivers, of	.222	6	27	1	6	2	0	0	1	0	2	1
Fred Stanley, ss	.000	1	0	0	0	0	0	0	0	0	0	0
Dick Tidrow, p	.000	2	1	0	0	0	0	0	0	0	1	0
Mike Torrez, p	.000	2	6	0	0	0	0	0	0	0	4	0
Roy White, ph	.000	2	2	0	0	0	0	0	0	0	0	0
George Zeber, ph	.000	2	2	0	0	0	0	0	0	0	2	0
TOTAL	.244		205	26	50	10	0	8	25	11	37	1

PITCHER	W	L	ERA	G	GS	CG	SV	SHO	IP	H	ER	BB	SO
Ken Clay	0	0	2.45	2	0	0	0	0	3.2	2	1	1	0
Ron Guidry	1	0	2.00	1	1	1	0	0	9.0	4	2	3	7
Don Gullett	0	1	6.39	2	2	0	0	0	12.2	13	9	7	10
Catfish Hunter	0	1	10.38	2	1	0	0	0	4.1	6	5	0	1
Sparky Lyle	1	0	1.93	2	0	0	0	0	4.2	2	1	0	2
Dick Tidrow	0	0	4.91	2	0	0	0	0	3.2	5	2	0	1
Mike Torrez	2	0	2.50	2	2	2	0	0	18.0	16	5	5	15
TOTAL	4	2	4.02	13	6	3	0	0	56.0	48	25	16	36

LA (N)

PLAYER/POS	AVG	G	AB	R	H	2B	3B	HR	RB	BB	SO	SB
Dusty Baker, of	.292	6	24	4	7	0	0	1	5	0	2	0
Glenn Burke, of	.200	3	5	0	1	0	0	0	0	0	1	0
Ron Cey, 3b	.190	6	21	2	4	1	0	1	3	3	5	0
Vic Davalillo, ph	.333	3	3	0	1	0	0	0	1	0	0	0
Mike Garman, p	.000	2	0	0	0	0	0	0	0	0	0	0
Steve Garvey, 1b	.375	6	24	5	9	1	1	1	3	1	4	0
Ed Goodson, ph	.000	1	1	0	0	0	0	0	0	0	1	0
Jerry Grote, c	.000	1	1	0	0	0	0	0	0	0	0	0
Burt Hooton, p	.000	2	5	0	0	0	0	0	0	0	2	0
Charlie Hough, p	.000	2	0	0	0	0	0	0	0	0	0	0
Tommy John, p	.000	1	2	0	0	0	0	0	0	0	2	0
Lee Lacy, of-2	.429	4	7	1	3	0	0	0	0	2	1	0
Rafael Landestoy, pr	.000	1	0	0	0	0	0	0	0	0	0	0
Davey Lopes, 2b	.167	6	24	3	4	0	1	1	2	4	3	2
Rick Monday, of	.167	4	12	0	2	0	0	0	0	0	3	0
Manny Mota, ph	.000	3	3	0	0	0	0	0	0	0	1	0
Johnny Oates, c	.000	1	1	0	0	0	0	0	0	0	0	0
Doug Rau, p	.000	2	0	0	0	0	0	0	0	0	0	0
Lance Rautzhan, p	.000	1	0	0	0	0	0	0	0	0	0	0
Rick Rhoden, p	.500	2	2	1	1	1	0	0	0	0	0	0
Bill Russell, ss	.154	6	26	3	4	0	1	0	2	1	3	0
Reggie Smith, of	.273	6	22	7	6	1	0	3	5	4	3	0
Elias Sosa, p	.000	2	0	0	0	0	0	0	0	0	0	0
Don Sutton, p	.000	2	6	0	0	0	0	0	0	1	4	0
Steve Yeager, c	.316	6	19	2	6	1	0	2	5	1	1	0
TOTAL	.231		208	28	48	5	3	9	28	16	36	2

PITCHER	W	L	ERA	G	GS	CG	SV	SHO	IP	H	ER	BB	SO
Mike Garman	0	0	0.00	2	0	0	0	0	4.0	2	0	1	3
Burt Hooton	1	1	3.75	2	2	1	0	0	12.0	8	5	2	9
Charlie Hough	0	0	1.80	2	0	0	0	0	5.0	3	1	0	5
Tommy John	0	1	6.00	1	1	0	0	0	6.0	9	4	3	7
Doug Rau	0	1	11.57	2	1	0	0	0	2.1	4	3	0	1
Lance Rautzhan	0	0	0.00	1	0	0	0	0	0.1	0	0	2	0
Rick Rhoden	0	1	2.57	2	2	0	0	0	7.0	4	2	1	5
Elias Sosa	0	0	11.57	2	0	0	0	0	2.1	3	3	1	1
Don Sutton	1	0	3.94	2	2	1	0	0	16.0	17	7	7	3
TOTAL	2	4	4.09	16	6	2	0	0	55.0	50	25	17	34

GAME 1 AT NY OCT 11

LA	200 000 001 000	3	6	0
NY	100 001 010 001	4	11	0

Pitchers: Sutton, Rautzhan (8), Sosa (8), Garman (9), RHODEN (12) vs Gullett, LYLE (9)
Home Runs: Randolph-NY
Attendance: 56,668

GAME 2 AT NY OCT 12

LA	212 000 001	6	9	0
NY	000 100 000	1	5	0

Pitchers: HOOTON vs HUNTER, Tidrow (3), Clay (6), Lyle (9)
Home Runs: Cey-LA, Yeager-LA, Smith-LA, Garvey-LA
Attendance: 56,691

GAME 3 AT LA OCT 14

NY	300 110 000	5	10	0
LA	003 000 000	3	7	1

Pitchers: TORREZ vs JOHN, Hough (7)
Home Runs: Baker-LA
Attendance: 55,992

GAME 4 AT LA OCT 15

NY	030 001 000	4	7	0
LA	002 000 000	2	4	0

Pitchers: GUIDRY vs RAU, Rhoden (2), Garman (9)
Home Runs: Lopes-LA, Jackson-NY
Attendance: 55,995

GAME 5 AT LA OCT 16

NY	000 000 220	4	9	2
LA	100 432 00X	10	13	0

Pitchers: GULLETT, Clay (5), Tidrow (6), Hunter (7) vs SUTTON
Home Runs: Yeager-LA, Smith-LA, Munson-NY, Jackson-NY
Attendance: 55,955

GAME 6 AT NY OCT 18

LA	201 000 001	4	9	0
NY	020 320 01X	8	8	1

Pitchers: HOOTON, Sosa (4), Rau (5), Hough (7) vs TORREZ
Home Runs: Chambliss-NY, Smith-LA, Jackson-NY (3)
Attendance: 56,407

Steve Garvey hit half the Dodgers' eight home runs and Tommy John hurled the first LCS shutout in four years as Los Angeles, for the second year in a row, defeated the Phillies for the pennant in four games. Philadelphia's five runs in Game One would have been enough to win any of the other games, but not this one as the Dodgers outhomered the Phillies four to one (including two by Garvey) and scored nine times. Dodger Davey Lopes hit the game's only home run the next day (with a man aboard), but it was more than enough support for John's four-hit shutout.

The series' most decisive win went to the Phillies in Game Three. Steve Carlton allowed four Dodger runs to score, but he made up for it by driving in his own four runs on a homer and sacrifice fly. His teammates added five more, rendering futile Garvey's third series home run.

But Garvey's fourth homer, in Game Four, helped carry the Dodgers into the tenth inning, when Bill Russell—capitalizing on Gary Maddox's muff of Ron Cey's fly to center—singled home Cey with the Dodgers' unearned pennant winner.

Los Angeles Dodgers (West), 3; Philadelphia Phillies (East), 1

LA (W)

PLAYER/POS	AVG	G	AB	R	H	2B	3B	HR	RB	BB	SO	SB
Dusty Baker, of	.467	4	15	1	7	2	0	0	1	3	0	0
Ron Cey, 3b	.313	4	16	4	5	1	0	1	3	2	4	0
Joe Ferguson, ph	.000	2	2	0	0	0	0	0	0	0	1	0
Terry Forster, p	.000	1	0	0	0	0	0	0	0	0	0	0
Steve Garvey, 1b	.389	4	18	6	7	1	1	4	7	0	1	0
Jerry Grote, c	.000	1	0	0	0	0	0	0	0	0	0	0
Burt Hooton, p	.000	1	2	0	0	0	0	0	0	0	1	0
Charlie Hough, p	.000	1	0	0	0	0	0	0	0	0	0	0
Tommy John, p	.000	1	3	0	0	0	0	0	0	0	0	0
Lee Lacy, ph	.000	2	2	0	0	0	0	0	0	0	0	0
Davey Lopes, 2b	.389	4	18	3	7	1	1	2	5	0	1	1
Rick Monday, of	.200	3	10	2	2	0	1	0	0	1	5	0
Manny Mota, ph	1.000	2	1	0	1	1	0	0	0	0	0	0
Billy North, of	.000	4	8	0	0	0	0	0	0	0	1	0
Doug Rau, p	.000	1	1	0	0	0	0	0	0	0	0	0
Lance Rautzhan, p	.000	1	0	0	0	0	0	0	0	0	0	0
Rick Rhoden, p	.000	1	1	0	0	0	0	0	0	0	0	0
Bill Russell, ss	.412	4	17	1	7	1	0	0	2	1	1	0
Reggie Smith, of	.188	4	16	2	3	1	0	1	1	0	2	0
Don Sutton, p	.000	1	2	0	0	0	0	0	0	0	2	0
Bob Welch, p	.000	1	2	0	0	0	0	0	0	0	1	0
Steve Yeager, c	.231	4	13	2	3	0	0	1	2	2	2	1
TOTAL	.286		147	21	42	8	3	8	21	9	22	2

PITCHER	W	L	ERA	G	GS	CG	SV	SHO	IP	H	ER	BB	SO
Terry Forster	1	0	0.00	1	0	0	0	0	1.0	1	0	0	2
Burt Hooton	0	0	7.71	1	1	0	0	0	4.2	10	4	0	5
Charlie Hough	0	0	4.50	1	0	0	0	0	2.0	1	1	0	1
Tommy John	1	0	0.00	1	1	1	0	1	9.0	4	0	2	4
Doug Rau	0	0	3.60	1	1	0	0	0	5.0	5	2	2	1
Lance Rautzhan	0	0	6.75	1	0	0	0	0	1.1	3	1	2	0
Rick Rhoden	0	0	2.25	1	0	0	0	0	4.0	2	1	1	3
Don Sutton	0	1	6.35	1	1	0	0	0	5.2	7	4	2	0
Bob Welch	1	0	2.08	1	0	0	0	0	4.1	2	1	0	5
TOTAL	3	1	3.41	9	4	1	0	1	37.0	35	14	9	21

PHI (E)

PLAYER/POS	AVG	G	AB	R	H	2B	3B	HR	RB	BB	SO	SB
Bob Boone, c	.182	3	11	0	2	0	0	0	0	0	1	0
Larry Bowa, ss	.333	4	18	2	6	0	0	0	0	1	2	0
Warren Brusstar, p	.000	3	0	0	0	0	0	0	0	0	0	0
Jose Cardenal, 1b	.167	2	6	0	1	0	0	0	0	1	1	0
Steve Carlton, p	.500	1	4	2	2	0	0	1	4	0	0	0
Larry Christenson, p	.000	1	1	0	0	0	0	0	0	0	1	0
Rawly Eastwick, p	.000	1	0	0	0	0	0	0	0	0	0	0
Barry Foote, ph	.000	1	1	0	0	0	0	0	0	0	1	0
Orlando Gonzalez, ph	.000	1	1	0	0	0	0	0	0	0	1	0
Richie Hebner, 1b-2	.111	3	9	0	1	0	0	0	1	0	0	0
Randy Lerch, p	.000	1	3	0	0	0	0	0	0	0	1	0
Greg Luzinski, of	.375	4	16	3	6	0	1	2	3	1	2	0
Garry Maddox, of	.263	4	19	1	5	0	0	0	2	0	3	0
Jerry Martin, of-3	.222	4	9	1	2	1	0	1	2	1	3	0
Bake McBride, of-2	.222	3	9	2	2	0	0	1	1	0	2	0
Tim McCarver, c-1	.000	2	4	2	0	0	0	0	1	2	0	0
Tug McGraw, p	.000	3	0	0	0	0	0	0	0	0	0	0
Jim Morrison, ph	.000	1	1	0	0	0	0	0	0	0	1	0
Ron Reed, p	.000	2	0	0	0	0	0	0	0	0	0	0
Dick Ruthven, p	.000	1	1	0	0	0	0	0	0	0	1	0
Mike Schmidt, 3b	.200	4	15	1	3	2	0	0	1	2	2	0
Ted Sizemore, 2b	.385	4	13	3	5	1	0	1	0	1	1	0
TOTAL	.250		140	17	35	3	2	5	16	9	21	0

PITCHER	W	L	ERA	G	GS	CG	SV	SHO	IP	H	ER	BB	SO
Warren Brusstar	0	0	0.00	3	0	0	0	0	2.2	2	0	1	0
Steve Carlton	1	0	4.00	1	1	1	0	0	9.0	8	4	2	8
Larry Christenson	0	1	12.46	1	1	0	0	0	4.1	7	6	1	3
Rawly Eastwick	0	0	9.00	1	0	0	0	0	1.0	3	1	0	1
Randy Lerch	0	0	5.06	1	1	0	0	0	5.1	7	3	0	0
Tug McGraw	0	1	1.59	3	0	0	0	0	5.2	3	1	5	5
Ron Reed	0	0	2.25	2	0	0	0	0	4.0	6	1	0	2
Dick Ruthven	0	1	5.79	1	1	0	0	0	4.2	6	3	0	3
TOTAL	1	3	4.66	13	4	1	0	0	36.2	42	19	9	22

GAME 1 AT PHI OCT 4

LA	004	211	001	9 13 1
PHI	010	030	001	5 12 1

Pitchers: Hooton, WELCH (5) vs CHRISTENSEN, Brusstar (5), Eastwick (6), McGraw (7)
Home Runs: Garvey-LA (2), Lopes-LA, Yeager-LA, Martin-PHI
Attendance: 63,460

GAME 2 AT PHI OCT 5

LA	000	120	100	4 8 0
PHI	000	000	000	0 4 0

Pitchers: JOHN vs RUTHVEN, Brusstar (5), Reed (7), McGraw (9)
Home Runs: Lopes-LA
Attendance: 60,642

GAME 3 AT LA OCT 6

PHI	040	003	101	9 11 1
LA	012	000	010	4 8 2

Pitchers: CARLTON vs SUTTON, Rautzhan (6), Hough (8)
Home Runs: Carlton-PHI, Luzinski-PHI, Garvey-LA
Attendance: 55,043

GAME 4 AT LA OCT 7

PHI	002	000	100	0	3 8 2
LA	010	101	000	1	4 13 0

Pitchers: Lerch, Brusstar (6), Reed (7), McGRAW (9) vs Rau, Rhoden (6), FORSTER (10)
Home Runs: Luzinski-PHI, Cey-LA, Garvey-LA, McBride-PHI
Attendance: 55,124

It took Bucky Dent's pop-fly home run against Boston in an Eastern Division tiebreaker to carry the Yankees into the LCS. But once there they took the pennant, downing the Royals for the third year in a row. Reggie Jackson's three-run homer in the eighth inning of Game One capped a sixteen-hit, seven-run Yankee attack, as pitchers Jim Beattie and Ken Clay combined to limit Kansas City to two hits and a single run. The Royals, though, made it look just as easy the next day as their own sixteen hits and ten runs evened the series.

Twice in Game Three George Brett gave the Royals a lead with a home run, and he tied the game with a third homer in the fifth. But Jackson's two-run homer in the fourth brought the Yankees back, and Thurman Munson's two-run shot in the eighth gave New York a close win. Game Four was just as close, but more of a pitcher's duel. Dennis Leonard, who went the distance, gave up only four hits, but two of them were home runs to Graig Nettles and Roy White. Yankee starter Ron Guidry allowed a run in the first, but shut out the Royals for the next seven innings. Goose Gossage preserved Guidry's good work—and the pennant—in the ninth.

New York Yankees (East), 3;
Kansas City Royals (West), 1

NY (E)

PLAYER/POS	AVG	G	AB	R	H	2B	3B	HR	RBI	BB	SO	SB
Jim Beattie, p	.000	1	0	0	0	0	0	0	0	0	0	0
Paul Blair, of-3,2b-1	.000	4	6	1	0	0	0	0	0	0	1	0
Chris Chambliss, 1b	.400	4	15	1	6	0	0	0	2	0	4	0
Ken Clay, p	.000	1	0	0	0	0	0	0	0	0	0	0
Bucky Dent, ss	.200	4	15	0	3	0	0	0	4	0	0	0
Brian Doyle, 2b	.286	3	7	0	2	0	0	0	1	1	1	0
Ed Figueroa, p	.000	1	0	0	0	0	0	0	0	0	0	0
Rich Gossage, p	.000	2	0	0	0	0	0	0	0	0	0	0
Ron Guidry, p	.000	1	0	0	0	0	0	0	0	0	0	0
Catfish Hunter, p	.000	1	0	0	0	0	0	0	0	0	0	0
Reggie Jackson, dh-3,of-1	.462	4	13	5	6	1	0	2	6	3	4	0
Cliff Johnson, ph	.000	1	1	0	0	0	0	0	0	0	0	0
Sparky Lyle, p	.000	1	0	0	0	0	0	0	0	0	0	0
Thurman Munson, c	.278	4	18	2	5	1	0	1	2	0	0	0
Graig Nettles, 3b	.333	4	15	3	5	0	1	1	2	0	1	0
Lou Piniella, of	.235	4	17	2	4	0	0	0	0	0	3	0
Mickey Rivers, of	.455	4	11	0	5	0	0	0	2	0	0	0
Fred Stanley, 2b	.200	2	5	0	1	0	0	0	0	0	2	0
Gary Thomasson, of	.000	3	1	0	0	0	0	0	0	0	0	0
Dick Tidrow, p	.000	1	0	0	0	0	0	0	0	0	0	0
Roy White, of-3,dh-1	.313	4	16	5	5	1	0	1	1	1	2	0
TOTAL	.300		140	19	42	3	1	5	18	7	18	0

PITCHER	W	L	ERA	G	GS	CG	SV	SHO	IP	H	ER	BB	SO
Jim Beattie	1	0	1.69	1	1	0	0	0	5.1	2	1	5	3
Ken Clay	0	0	0.00	1	0	0	1	0	3.2	0	0	3	2
Ed Figueroa	0	1	27.00	1	1	0	0	0	1.0	5	3	0	0
Rich Gossage	1	0	4.50	2	0	0	1	0	4.0	3	2	0	3
Ron Guidry	1	0	1.13	1	1	0	0	0	8.0	7	1	1	7
Catfish Hunter	0	0	4.50	1	1	0	0	0	6.0	7	3	3	5
Sparky Lyle	0	0	13.50	1	0	0	0	0	1.1	3	2	0	0
Dick Tidrow	0	0	4.76	1	0	0	0	0	5.2	8	3	2	1
TOTAL	3	1	3.86	9	4	0	2	0	35.0	35	15	14	21

KC (W)

PLAYER/POS	AVG	G	AB	R	H	2B	3B	HR	RBI	BB	SO	SB
Doug Bird, p	.000	2	0	0	0	0	0	0	0	0	0	0
Steve Braun, of-1	.000	2	5	0	0	0	0	0	0	1	1	0
George Brett, 3b	.389	4	18	7	7	1	1	3	3	0	1	0
Al Cowens, of	.133	4	15	2	2	0	0	0	1	0	2	0
Larry Gura, p	.000	1	0	0	0	0	0	0	0	0	0	0
Al Hrabosky, p	.000	3	0	0	0	0	0	0	0	0	0	0
Clint Hurdle, of-2	.375	4	8	1	3	0	1	0	1	2	3	0
Pete LaCock, 1b-3	.364	4	11	1	4	2	1	0	1	3	1	1
Dennis Leonard, p	.000	2	0	0	0	0	0	0	0	0	0	0
Hal McRae, dh	.214	4	14	0	3	0	0	0	2	2	2	1
Steve Mingori, p	.000	1	0	0	0	0	0	0	0	0	0	0
Amos Otis, of	.429	4	14	2	6	2	0	0	1	3	5	4
Freddie Patek, ss	.077	4	13	2	1	0	0	1	2	1	4	0
Marty Pattin, p	.000	1	0	0	0	0	0	0	0	0	0	0
Tom Poquette, ph	.000	1	1	0	0	0	0	0	0	0	0	0
Darrell Porter, c	.357	4	14	1	5	1	0	0	3	2	0	0
Paul Splittorff, p	.000	1	0	0	0	0	0	0	0	0	0	0
John Wathan, 1b	.000	1	3	0	0	0	0	0	0	0	0	0
Frank White, 2b	.231	4	13	1	3	0	0	0	2	0	0	0
Willie Wilson, of	.250	3	4	1	1	0	0	0	0	0	2	0
TOTAL	.263		133	17	35	6	3	4	16	14	21	6

PITCHER	W	L	ERA	G	GS	CG	SV	SHO	IP	H	ER	BB	SO
Doug Bird	0	1	9.00	2	0	0	0	0	1.0	2	1	0	1
Larry Gura	1	0	2.84	1	1	0	0	0	6.1	8	2	2	2
Al Hrabosky	0	0	3.00	3	0	0	0	0	3.0	3	1	0	2
Dennis Leonard	0	2	3.75	2	2	1	0	0	12.0	13	5	2	11
Steve Mingori	0	0	7.36	1	0	0	0	0	3.2	5	3	3	0
Marty Pattin	0	0	27.00	1	0	0	0	0	0.2	2	2	0	0
Paul Splittorff	0	0	4.91	1	1	0	0	0	7.1	9	4	0	2
TOTAL	1	3	4.76	11	4	1	0	0	34.0	42	18	7	18

GAME 1 AT KC OCT 3

NY	011 020 030	7 16 0
KC	000 001 000	1 2 2

Pitchers: BEATTIE, Clay (6) vs LEONARD, Mingori (5), Hrabosky (8), Bird (9)
Home Runs: Jackson-NY
Attendance: 41,143

GAME 2 AT KC OCT 4

NY	000 000 220	4 12 1
KC	140 000 32X	10 16 1

Pitchers: FIGUEROA, Tidrow (2), Lyle (7) vs GURA, Pattin (7), Hrabosky (8)
Home Runs: Patek-KC
Attendance: 41,158

GAME 3 AT NY OCT 6

KC	101 010 020	5 10 1
NY	010 201 02X	6 10 0

Pitchers: Splittorff, BIRD (8), Hrabosky (8) vs Hunter, GOSSAGE (7)
Home Runs: Brett-KC (3), Jackson-NY, Munson-NY
Attendance: 55,535

GAME 4 AT NY OCT 7

KC	100 000 000	1 7 0
NY	010 001 00X	2 4 0

Pitchers: LEONARD vs GUIDRY, Gossage (9)
Home Runs: Nettles-NY, R.White-NY
Attendance: 56,356

The outcome was the same as in 1977: the Yankees over the Dodgers in six games. But this year New York overcame a two-game deficit by sweeping the next four, a feat never before achieved in a World Series.

Los Angeles overwhelmed New York in the opener. Home runs in the second and fourth innings by Dusty Baker and Davey Lopes (two, for five RBIs), and another run in the fifth, gave the Dodgers a 7–0 lead before Reggie Jackson's leadoff homer in the seventh gave New York its first score. The Yankees scored four more times, but so did the Dodgers for an 11–5 win. Game Two was closer. The Yankees scored first and held a lead through the top of the sixth, but Ron Cey's three-run homer in the bottom of the sixth gave Los Angeles the runs they needed to win 4–3.

Yankee Ron Guidry, coming off a spectacular 25–3 regular season, pitched Game Three as the Series moved to New York. He gave up eight hits and issued seven walks. But only one baserunner scored, thanks in large part to several memorable stops and throws by third baseman Graig Nettles. Meanwhile, Roy White's home run in the first inning began Yankee scoring in what would become a 5–1 win.

It took ten innings for New York to win Game Four. Starters Tommy John and Ed Figueroa hurled shutout ball until Dodger Reggie Smith tagged Figueroa for a three-run homer in the top of the fifth. The Yankees clawed back in the sixth. Reggie Jackson singled in one run, then—in a play that stirred great controversy—got in the way (the Dodgers claimed intentionally) of a throw from second on an attempted double play, deflecting the ball to the outfield and permitting a second run to score. In the eighth, Thurman Munson doubled home the tying Yankee run, and in the last of the tenth Lou Piniella's two-out drive to center scored baserunner Roy White with the game winner.

Game Five was a Yankee blowout. No one hit home runs, but the Yankees hit sixteen singles (a Series record) and two doubles for twelve runs (five of them driven in by Munson's three hits) to give Yankee pitcher Jim Beattie (nine hits, two runs) an easy win. Back in Los Angeles for the sixth game, the Yankees won the crown on the hitting of two men at the bottom of the batting order: Denny Doyle and Bucky Dent. With three hits each, they combined for five RBIs in the 7–2 win. For good measure, Reggie Jackson concluded the Series scoring with a mighty two-run homer in the seventh.

New York Yankees (AL), 4; Los Angeles Dodgers (NL), 2

NY (A)

PLAYER/POS	AVG	G	AB	R	H	2B	3B	HR	RB	BB	SO	SB
Jim Beattie, p	.000	1	0	0	0	0	0	0	0	0	0	0
Paul Blair, of	.375	6	8	2	3	1	0	0	0	1	4	0
Chris Chambliss, 1b	.182	3	11	1	2	0	0	0	0	1	1	0
Ken Clay, p	.000	1	0	0	0	0	0	0	0	0	0	0
Bucky Dent, ss	.417	6	24	3	10	1	0	0	7	1	2	0
Brian Doyle, 2b	.438	6	16	4	7	1	0	0	2	0	0	0
Ed Figueroa, p	.000	2	0	0	0	0	0	0	0	0	0	0
Rich Gossage, p	.000	3	0	0	0	0	0	0	0	0	0	0
Ron Guidry, p	.000	1	0	0	0	0	0	0	0	0	0	0
Mike Heath, c	.000	1	0	0	0	0	0	0	0	0	0	0
Catfish Hunter, p	.000	2	0	0	0	0	0	0	0	0	0	0
Reggie Jackson, dh	.391	6	23	2	9	1	0	2	8	3	7	0
Cliff Johnson, ph	.000	2	2	0	0	0	0	0	0	0	1	0
Jay Johnstone, of	.000	2	0	0	0	0	0	0	0	0	0	0
Paul Lindblad, p	.000	1	0	0	0	0	0	0	0	0	0	0
Thurman Munson, c	.320	6	25	5	8	3	0	0	7	3	7	1
Graig Nettles, 3b	.160	6	25	2	4	0	0	0	1	0	6	0
Lou Piniella, of	.280	6	25	3	7	0	0	0	4	0	0	1
Mickey Rivers, of-4	.333	5	18	2	6	0	0	0	1	0	2	1
Jim Spencer, 1b-3	.167	4	12	3	2	0	0	0	0	2	4	0
Fred Stanley, 2b	.200	3	5	0	1	1	0	0	0	1	0	0
Gary Thomasson, of	.250	3	4	0	1	0	0	0	0	0	1	0
Dick Tidrow, p	.000	2	0	0	0	0	0	0	0	0	0	0
Roy White, of	.333	6	24	9	8	0	0	1	4	4	5	2
TOTAL	.306		222	36	68	8	0	3	34	16	40	5

PITCHER	W	L	ERA	G	GS	CG	SV	SHO	IP	H	ER	BB	SO
Jim Beattie	1	0	2.00	1	1	1	0	0	9.0	9	2	4	8
Ken Clay	0	0	11.57	1	0	0	0	0	2.1	4	3	2	2
Ed Figueroa	0	1	8.10	2	2	0	0	0	6.2	9	6	5	2
Rich Gossage	1	0	0.00	3	0	0	0	0	6.0	1	0	1	4
Ron Guidry	1	0	1.00	1	1	1	0	0	9.0	8	1	7	4
Catfish Hunter	1	1	4.15	2	2	0	0	0	13.0	13	6	1	5
Paul Lindblad	0	0	11.57	1	0	0	0	0	2.1	4	3	0	1
Dick Tidrow	0	0	1.93	2	0	0	0	0	4.2	4	1	0	5
TOTAL	4	2	3.74	13	6	2	0	0	53.0	52	22	20	31

LA (N)

PLAYER/POS	AVG	G	AB	R	H	2B	3B	HR	RB	BB	SO	SB
Dusty Baker, of	.238	6	21	2	5	0	0	1	1	1	3	0
Ron Cey, 3b	.286	6	21	2	6	0	0	1	4	3	3	0
Vic Davalillo, dh-1	.333	2	3	0	1	0	0	0	0	0	0	0
Joe Ferguson, c	.500	2	4	1	2	2	0	0	0	0	1	0
Terry Forster, p	.000	3	0	0	0	0	0	0	0	0	0	0
Steve Garvey, 1b	.208	6	24	1	5	1	0	0	0	1	7	1
Jerry Grote, c	.000	2	0	0	0	0	0	0	0	0	0	0
Burt Hooton, p	.000	2	0	0	0	0	0	0	0	0	0	0
Charlie Hough, p	.000	2	0	0	0	0	0	0	0	0	0	0
Tommy John, p	.000	2	0	0	0	0	0	0	0	0	0	0
Lee Lacy, dh	.143	4	14	0	2	0	0	0	1	1	3	0
Davey Lopes, 2b	.308	6	26	7	8	0	0	3	7	2	1	2
Rick Monday, of-4,dh-1	.154	5	13	2	2	1	0	0	0	4	3	0
Manny Mota, ph	.000	1	0	0	0	0	0	0	0	1	0	0
Billy North, of	.125	4	8	2	1	1	0	0	0	2	1	1
Johnny Oates, c	1.000	1	1	0	1	0	0	0	0	1	0	0
Doug Rau, p	.000	1	0	0	0	0	0	0	0	0	0	0
Lance Rautzhan, p	.000	2	0	0	0	0	0	0	0	0	0	0
Bill Russell, ss	.423	6	26	1	11	2	0	0	2	2	2	1
Reggie Smith, of	.200	6	25	3	5	0	0	1	5	2	6	0
Don Sutton, p	.000	2	0	0	0	0	0	0	0	0	0	0
Bob Welch, p	.000	3	0	0	0	0	0	0	0	0	0	0
Steve Yeager, c	.231	5	13	2	3	1	0	0	0	1	2	0
TOTAL	.261		199	23	52	8	0	6	22	20	31	5

PITCHER	W	L	ERA	G	GS	CG	SV	SHO	IP	H	ER	BB	SO
Terry Forster	0	0	0.00	3	0	0	0	0	4.0	5	0	1	6
Burt Hooton	1	1	6.48	2	2	0	0	0	8.1	13	6	3	6
Charlie Hough	0	0	8.44	2	0	0	0	0	5.1	10	5	2	5
Tommy John	1	0	3.07	2	2	0	0	0	14.2	14	5	4	6
Doug Rau	0	0	0.00	1	0	0	0	0	2.0	1	0	3	3
Lance Rautzhan	0	0	13.50	2	0	0	0	0	2.0	4	3	0	4
Don Sutton	0	2	7.50	2	2	0	0	0	12.0	17	10	4	8
Bob Welch	0	1	6.23	3	0	0	1	0	4.1	4	3	2	6
TOTAL	2	4	5.47	17	6	0	1	0	52.2	68	32	16	40

GAME 1 AT LA OCT 10

NY	000	000	320	5	9	1
LA	030	310	31X	11	15	2

Pitchers: FIGUEROA, Clay (2), Lindblad (5), Tidrow (7) vs JOHN, Forster (8)
Home Runs: Baker-LA, Lopes-LA (2), Jackson-NY
Attendance: 55,997

GAME 2 AT LA OCT 11

NY	002	000	100	3	11	0
LA	000	103	00X	4	7	0

Pitchers: HUNTER, Gossage (7) vs HOOTON, Forster (7), Welch (9)
Home Runs: Cey-LA
Attendance: 55,982

GAME 3 AT NY OCT 13

LA	001	000	000	1	8	0
NY	110	030	00X	5	10	1

Pitchers: SUTTON, Rautzhan (7), Hough (8) vs GUIDRY
Home Runs: White-NY
Attendance: 56,447

GAME 4 AT NY OCT 14

LA	000	030	000	0	3	6	1
NY	000	002	010	1	4	9	0

Pitchers: John, Forster (8), WELCH (8) vs Figueroa, Tidrow (6), GOSSAGE (9)
Home Runs: Smith-LA
Attendance: 56,445

GAME 5 AT NY OCT 15

LA	101	000	000	2	9	3
NY	004	300	41X	12	18	0

Pitchers: HOOTON, Rautzhan (3), Hough (4) vs BEATTIE
Attendance: 56,448

GAME 6 AT LA OCT 17

NY	030	002	200	7	11	0
LA	101	000	000	2	7	1

Pitchers: HUNTER, Gossage (8) vs SUTTON, Welch (7), Rau (8)
Home Runs: Lopes-LA, Jackson-NY
Attendance: 55,985

The Pirates—with a better season's record than Cincinnati and stronger hitting and pitching—proved their superiority in the LCS as well, dominating the statistics and sweeping the series. Yet the games were closer than the stats alone would suggest. Pittsburgh won the first game by three runs—but they didn't come until Willie Stargell's homer in the eleventh inning broke a 2–2 tie.

In Game Two, Cincinnati scored first. The Pirates tied the game with a run in the fourth and took a narrow lead with another in the fifth. But the Reds came back on a game-tying pair of doubles in the ninth, and it wasn't until the tenth that Pittsburgh eked out its victory with a run on two singles and Don Robinson's shutout relief.

Only in the third game did the Pirates take a commanding lead, with six runs in the first four innings (two of them on home runs by Stargell and Bill Madlock). The Reds outhit Pittsburgh eight to seven, but only Johnny Bench's homer brought them a run, as Bert Blyleven overcame them in the series' only complete-game pitching performance.

Pittsburgh Pirates (East), 3; Cincinnati Reds (West), 0

PIT (E)

PLAYER/POS	AVG	G	AB	R	H	2B	3B	HR	RB	BB	SO	SB
Matt Alexander, pr	.000	1	0	1	0	0	0	0	0	0	0	0
Jim Bibby, p	.000	1	0	0	0	0	0	0	0	1	0	0
Bert Blyleven, p	.333	1	3	1	1	0	0	0	0	0	1	0
John Candelaria, p	.000	1	3	0	0	0	0	0	0	0	2	0
Mike Easler, ph	.000	1	1	0	0	0	0	0	0	0	0	0
Tim Foli, ss	.333	3	12	1	4	1	0	0	3	0	0	0
Phil Garner, 2b-3,ss-1	.417	3	12	4	5	0	1	1	1	1	0	0
Grant Jackson, p	.000	2	1	0	0	0	0	0	0	0	0	0
Bill Madlock, 3b	.250	3	12	1	3	0	0	1	2	2	0	2
John Milner, of	.000	3	9	0	0	0	0	0	0	2	0	0
Omar Moreno, of	.250	3	12	3	3	0	1	0	0	2	2	1
Ed Ott, c	.231	3	13	0	3	0	0	0	0	0	2	0
Dave Parker, of	.333	3	12	2	4	0	0	0	2	2	3	1
Dave Roberts, p	.000	1	0	0	0	0	0	0	0	0	0	0
Don Robinson, p	.000	2	0	0	0	0	0	0	0	0	0	0
Bill Robinson, of	.000	3	3	0	0	0	0	0	0	0	0	0
Enrique Romo, p	.000	2	0	0	0	0	0	0	0	0	0	0
Willie Stargell, 1b	.455	3	11	2	5	2	0	2	6	3	2	0
Rennie Stennett, 2b	.000	1	0	0	0	0	0	0	0	0	0	0
Kent Tekulve, p	.000	2	1	0	0	0	0	0	0	0	1	0
TOTAL	.267		105	15	28	3	2	4	14	13	13	4

PITCHER	W	L	ERA	G	GS	CG	SV	SHO	IP	H	ER	BB	SO
Jim Bibby	0	0	1.29	1	1	0	0	0	7.0	4	1	4	5
Bert Blyleven	1	0	1.00	1	1	1	0	0	9.0	8	1	0	9
John Candelaria	0	0	2.57	1	1	0	0	0	7.0	5	2	2	4
Grant Jackson	1	0	0.00	2	0	0	0	0	2.0	1	0	1	2
Dave Roberts	0	0	INF	1	0	0	0	0	0.0	0	0	1	0
Don Robinson	1	0	0.00	2	0	0	1	0	2.0	0	0	1	3
Enrique Romo	0	0	0.00	2	0	0	0	0	0.1	3	0	1	1
Kent Tekulve	0	0	3.00	2	0	0	0	0	3.0	2	1	2	2
TOTAL	3	0	1.48	12	3	1	1	0	30.1	23	5	11	26

CIN (W)

PLAYER/POS	AVG	G	AB	R	H	2B	3B	HR	RB	BB	SO	SB
Rick Auerbach, ph	.000	2	2	0	0	0	0	0	0	0	1	0
Doug Bair, p	.000	1	0	0	0	0	0	0	0	0	0	0
Johnny Bench, c	.250	3	12	1	3	0	1	1	1	2	2	0
Dave Collins, of	.357	3	14	0	5	1	0	0	1	0	2	2
Dave Concepcion, ss	.429	3	14	0	6	1	0	0	0	0	3	0
Hector Cruz, of-1	.200	2	5	1	1	1	0	0	0	0	1	0
Dan Driessen, 1b	.083	3	12	1	1	0	0	0	0	0	3	0
George Foster, of	.200	3	10	1	2	0	0	1	2	4	3	0
Cesar Geronimo, of	.143	2	7	0	1	0	0	0	0	0	5	0
Tom Hume, p	.000	3	1	0	0	0	0	0	0	0	1	0
Ray Knight, 3b	.286	3	14	0	4	1	0	0	0	0	2	1
Mike LaCoss, p	.000	1	0	0	0	0	0	0	0	0	0	0
Charlie Leibrandt, p	.000	1	0	0	0	0	0	0	0	0	0	0
Joe Morgan, 2b	.000	3	11	0	0	0	0	0	0	3	1	1
Fred Norman, p	.000	1	1	0	0	0	0	0	0	0	1	0
Frank Pastore, p	.000	1	0	0	0	0	0	0	0	1	0	0
Tom Seaver, p	.000	1	2	0	0	0	0	0	0	0	1	0
Mario Soto, p	.000	1	0	0	0	0	0	0	0	0	0	0
Harry Spilman, ph	.000	2	2	0	0	0	0	0	0	0	0	0
Dave Tomlin, p	.000	3	0	0	0	0	0	0	0	0	0	0
TOTAL	.215		107	5	23	4	1	2	5	11	26	4

PITCHER	W	L	ERA	G	GS	CG	SV	SHO	IP	H	ER	BB	SO
Doug Bair	0	1	9.00	1	0	0	0	0	1.0	2	1	1	0
Tom Hume	0	1	6.75	3	0	0	0	0	4.0	6	3	0	2
Mike LaCoss	0	1	10.80	1	1	0	0	0	1.2	1	2	4	0
Charlie Leibrandt	0	0	0.00	1	0	0	0	0	0.1	0	0	0	0
Fred Norman	0	0	18.00	1	0	0	0	0	2.0	4	4	1	1
Frank Pastore	0	0	2.57	1	0	0	0	0	7.0	7	2	3	1
Tom Seaver	0	0	2.25	1	1	0	0	0	8.0	5	2	2	5
Mario Soto	0	0	0.00	1	0	0	0	0	2.0	0	0	0	1
Dave Tomlin	0	0	0.00	3	0	0	0	0	3.0	3	0	2	3
TOTAL	0	3	4.34	13	3	0	0	0	29.0	28	14	13	13

GAME 1 AT CIN OCT 2

PIT	002 000 000 03	5 10 0
CIN	000 000 000 00	2 7 0

Pitchers: Candelaria, Romo (8), Tekulve (8), JACKSON (10), D.Robinson (11) vs Seaver, HUME (9), Tomlin (11)
Home Runs: Garner-PIT, Foster-CIN, Stargell-PIT
Attendance: 55,006

GAME 2 AT CIN OCT 3

PIT	000 110 001 0	3 11 0
CIN	010 000 001 0	2 8 0

Pitchers: Bibby, Jackson (8), Romo (8), Tekulve (8), Roberts (9), D.ROBINSON (9) vs Pastore, Tomlin (8), Hume (8), BAIR (10)
Attendance: 55,000

GAME 3 AT PIT OCT 5

CIN	000 001 000	1 8 1
PIT	112 200 01X	7 7 0

Pitchers: LaCOSS, Norman (2), Leibrandt (4), Soto (5), Tomlin (7), Hume (8) vs BLYLEVEN
Home Runs: Stargell-PIT, Madlock-PIT, Bench-CIN
Attendance: 42,240

Baltimore, returning to postseason play after a four-year absence, struggled with first-timer California through three games before blowing them away in the fourth. Game One went into the last of the tenth, tied 3–3, when Oriole pinch hitter John Lowenstein, up with two men on, ended it with a two-out, two-strike shot that just cleared the left field wall.

Game Two looked like a blowout for Baltimore. Eddie Murray drove in four runs, and the rest of the team added five more to give the O's a 9–1 lead by the end of three. But California chipped away at the lead in the latter half of the game and drew within one in the ninth, before Brian Downing hit into a forceout with the bases full to end their scoring.

The Angels' late rally in Game Three was more successful. Down by a run in the bottom of the ninth, they scored twice, on a walk, a dropped outfield fly, and Larry Harlow's game-winning double. The final game, though, was all Baltimore's, as Scott McGregor—pitching the series' only complete game—blanked the Angels on six hits. The Orioles scored two in the third and another in the fourth, before Pat Kelly put Angel pennant hopes out of reach with a three-run homer in the O's five-run seventh.

Baltimore Orioles (East), 3;
California Angels (West), 1

BAL (E)

PLAYER/POS	AVG	G	AB	R	H	2B	3B	HR	RB	BB	SO	SB
Mark Belanger, ss	.200	3	5	0	1	0	0	0	0	1	0	2	0
Al Bumbry, of	.250	4	16	5	4	0	1	0	0	4	3	2
Terry Crowley, ph	.500	2	2	0	1	0	0	0	1	0	0	0
Rich Dauer, 2b	.182	4	11	0	2	0	0	0	0	0	1	0
Doug DeCinces, 3b	.308	4	13	4	4	1	0	0	3	1	1	0
Rick Dempsey, c	.400	3	10	3	4	2	0	0	2	1	0	1
Mike Flanagan, p	.000	1	0	0	0	0	0	0	0	0	0	0
Kiko Garcia, ss	.273	3	11	1	3	0	0	0	2	2	4	0
Pat Kelly, dh-2,of-1	.364	3	11	3	4	0	0	1	4	1	3	2
John Lowenstein, of-3	.167	4	6	2	1	0	0	1	3	2	2	0
Dennis Martinez, p	.000	1	0	0	0	0	0	0	0	0	0	0
Lee May, dh	.143	2	7	0	1	0	0	0	1	1	3	0
Scott McGregor, p	.000	1	0	0	0	0	0	0	0	0	0	0
Eddie Murray, 1b	.417	4	12	3	5	0	0	1	5	5	2	0
Jim Palmer, p	.000	1	0	0	0	0	0	0	0	0	0	0
Gary Roenicke, of	.200	2	5	1	1	0	0	0	1	0	0	0
Ken Singleton, of	.375	4	16	4	6	2	0	0	2	1	2	0
Dave Skaggs, c	.000	1	4	0	0	0	0	0	0	0	0	0
Billy Smith, 2b	.000	1	4	0	0	0	0	0	0	0	1	0
Don Stanhouse, p	.000	3	0	0	0	0	0	0	0	0	0	0
TOTAL	.278		133	26	37	5	1	3	25	18	24	5

PITCHER	W	L	ERA	G	GS	CG	SV	SHO	IP	H	ER	BB	SO
Mike Flanagan	1	0	5.14	1	1	0	0	0	7.0	6	4	1	2
Dennis Martinez	0	0	3.24	1	1	0	0	0	8.1	8	3	0	4
Scott McGregor	1	0	0.00	1	1	1	0	1	9.0	6	0	1	4
Jim Palmer	0	0	3.00	1	1	0	0	0	9.0	7	3	2	3
Don Stanhouse	1	1	6.00	3	0	0	0	0	3.0	5	2	3	0
TOTAL	3	1	2.97	7	4	1	0	1	36.1	32	12	7	13

CAL (W)

PLAYER/POS	AVG	G	AB	R	H	2B	3B	HR	RB	BB	SO	SB
Don Aase, p	.000	2	0	0	0	0	0	0	0	0	0	0
Jim Anderson, ss	.091	4	11	0	1	0	0	0	0	0	1	0
Mike Barlow, p	.000	1	0	0	0	0	0	0	0	0	0	0
Don Baylor, dh-3,of-1	.188	4	16	2	3	0	0	1	2	1	2	0
Bert Campaneris, ss	.000	1	0	0	0	0	0	0	0	0	0	0
Rod Carew, 1b	.412	4	17	4	7	3	0	0	1	0	0	1
Bobby Clark, of	.000	1	3	0	0	0	0	0	0	0	2	0
Mark Clear, p	.000	1	0	0	0	0	0	0	0	0	0	0
Willie Davis, ph	.500	2	2	1	1	1	0	0	0	0	0	0
Brian Downing, c	.200	4	15	1	3	0	0	0	1	1	1	0
Dan Ford, of	.294	4	17	2	5	1	0	2	4	0	0	0
Dave Frost, p	.000	2	0	0	0	0	0	0	0	0	0	0
Bobby Grich, 2b	.154	4	13	0	2	1	0	0	2	1	1	0
Larry Harlow, of-2	.125	3	8	0	1	1	0	0	1	1	2	0
Chris Knapp, p	.000	1	0	0	0	0	0	0	0	0	0	0
Carney Lansford, 3b	.294	4	17	2	5	0	0	0	3	1	2	1
Dave LaRoche, p	.000	1	0	0	0	0	0	0	0	0	0	0
Rick Miller, of	.250	4	16	2	4	0	0	0	0	0	1	0
John Montague, p	.000	2	0	0	0	0	0	0	0	0	0	0
Merv Rettenmund, dh	.000	2	2	0	0	0	0	0	0	2	1	0
Nolan Ryan, p	.000	1	0	0	0	0	0	0	0	0	0	0
Frank Tanana, p	.000	1	0	0	0	0	0	0	0	0	0	0
Dickie Thon, ss	.000	1	0	1	0	0	0	0	0	0	0	0
TOTAL	.234		137	15	32	7	0	3	14	7	13	2

PITCHER	W	L	ERA	G	GS	CG	SV	SHO	IP	H	ER	BB	SO
Don Aase	1	0	1.80	2	0	0	0	0	5.0	4	1	2	6
Mike Barlow	0	0	0.00	1	0	0	0	0	1.0	0	0	0	0
Mark Clear	0	0	4.76	1	0	0	0	0	5.2	4	3	2	3
Dave Frost	0	1	18.69	2	1	0	0	0	4.1	8	9	5	1
Chris Knapp	0	1	7.71	1	1	0	0	0	2.1	5	2	1	0
Dave LaRoche	0	0	6.75	1	0	0	0	0	1.1	2	1	1	1
John Montague	0	1	9.00	2	0	0	0	0	4.0	4	4	2	2
Nolan Ryan	0	0	1.29	1	1	0	0	0	7.0	4	1	3	8
Frank Tanana	0	0	3.60	1	1	0	0	0	5.0	6	2	2	3
TOTAL	1	3	5.80	12	4	0	0	0	35.2	37	23	18	24

GAME 1 AT BAL OCT 3

CAL	101 001 000 0	3	7	1
BAL	002 100 000 3	6	6	0

Pitchers: Ryan, MONTAGUE (8) vs Palmer, STANHOUSE (10)
Home Runs: Ford-CAL, Lowenstein-BAL
Attendance: 52,787

GAME 2 AT BAL OCT 4

CAL	100 001 132	8	10	1
BAL	441 000 00X	9	11	1

Pitchers: FROST, Clear (2), Aase (8) vs FLANAGAN, Stanhouse (8)
Home Runs: Ford-CAL, Murray-BAL
Attendance: 52,108

GAME 3 AT CAL OCT 5

BAL	000 101 100	3	8	3
CAL	100 100 002	4	9	0

Pitchers: D.Martinez, STANHOUSE (9) vs Tanana, AASE (6)
Home Runs: Baylor-CAL
Attendance: 43,199

GAME 4 AT CAL OCT 6

BAL	002 100 500	8	12	1
CAL	000 000 000	0	6	0

Pitchers: McGREGOR vs KNAPP, LaRoche (3), Frost (4), Montague (7), Barlow (9)
Home Runs: Kelly-BAL
Attendance: 43,199

Veteran Willie Stargell was "Pops," and in the Series he showed his Pirate "family" the way. Seven of his twelve hits went for extra bases, and he drove in a Series-high seven runs. What Stargell began, submarine reliever Kent Tekulve finished, appearing in five of the seven games and recording a record-tying three saves.

Stargell drove in a pair of runs in the opener—one of them with an eighth-inning homer—but Pittsburgh's four runs fell short of the five Baltimore had scored in the first inning. The only extra-base hits in Game Two came from the bat of Eddie Murray, who homered and doubled to drive in both Baltimore runs. But three singles and a sacrifice fly had already given Pittsburgh two runs in the second inning, and two more Pirate singles and a walk in the top of the ninth made the score 3–2. Tekulve came on in the last of the ninth to preserve the lead, fanning two as he retired the side in order.

Baltimore bounced back, though, to take the next two games in convincing fashion. The score favored the Orioles 8–4 when Tekulve came on to set the birds down in order over the final two innings. But Baltimore starter Scott McGregor had by then settled into his groove, retiring the final eleven Pirates with relative ease to preserve his lead and the Oriole win. It took four Orioles pitchers to hold the Pirates in Game Four. Stargell led the Bucs' seventeen-hit attack with a homer, double, and single, and the Pirates led 6–3 entering the eighth inning. But Baltimore loaded the bases in the top of the eighth, prompting Pirate manager Chuck Tanner to bring Tekulve in again. This one time the strategy failed, as Tekulve saw six runs score before he retired his first batter.

Down three games to one, the Pirates rebounded in Game Five, scoring seven times in the final three innings for a 7–1 victory. Baltimore starter Jim Palmer matched John Candelaria's shutout pitching through six innings of Game Six before the Pirates tagged him for pairs of runs in the seventh and eighth. Tekulve, meanwhile, continued Candelaria's shutout through the final three innings, retiring the last seven men in order, four by strikeout. Baltimore scored first in the finale on Rich Dauer's leadoff home run in the third inning, but Stargell put the Pirates ahead with a two-run homer in the sixth. Tekulve came in with two Orioles on base in the eighth to stifle the threat, and (after the Pirates had scored a pair of insurance runs in the top of the ninth) set Baltimore down in order to complete the Pirate comeback.

Pittsburgh Pirates (NL), 4;
Baltimore Orioles (AL), 3

PIT (N)

PLAYER/POS	AVG	G	AB	R	H	2B	3B	HR	RBI	BB	SO	SB
Matt Alexander, of	.000	1	0	0	0	0	0	0	0	0	0	0
Jim Bibby, p	.000	2	4	0	0	0	0	0	0	0	1	0
Bert Blyleven, p	.000	2	3	0	0	0	0	0	0	0	0	0
John Candelaria, p	.333	2	3	0	1	0	0	0	0	0	2	0
Mike Easler, ph	.000	2	1	0	0	0	0	0	0	1	0	0
Tim Foli, ss	.333	7	30	6	10	1	1	0	3	2	0	0
Phil Garner, 2b	.500	7	24	4	12	4	0	0	5	3	1	0
Grant Jackson, p	.000	4	1	0	0	0	0	0	0	0	0	0
Bruce Kison, p	.000	1	0	0	0	0	0	0	0	0	0	0
Lee Lacy, ph	.250	4	4	0	1	0	0	0	0	0	1	0
Bill Madlock, 3b	.375	7	24	2	9	1	0	0	3	5	1	0
John Milner, of	.333	3	9	2	3	1	0	0	1	2	0	0
Omar Moreno, of	.333	7	33	4	11	2	0	0	3	1	7	0
Steve Nicosia, c	.063	4	16	1	1	0	0	0	0	0	2	0
Ed Ott, c	.333	3	12	2	4	1	0	0	3	0	2	0
Dave Parker, of	.345	7	29	2	10	3	0	0	4	2	7	0
Don Robinson, p	.000	4	0	0	0	0	0	0	0	0	0	0
Bill Robinson, of-6	.263	7	19	2	5	1	0	0	2	0	4	0
Enrique Romo, p	.000	2	1	0	0	0	0	0	0	0	0	0
Jim Rooker, p	.000	2	2	0	0	0	0	0	0	0	1	0
Manny Sanguillen, ph	.333	3	3	0	1	0	0	0	1	0	0	0
Willie Stargell, 1b	.400	7	30	7	12	4	0	3	7	0	6	0
Rennie Stennett, ph	1.000	1	1	0	1	0	0	0	0	0	0	0
Kent Tekulve, p	.000	5	2	0	0	0	0	0	0	0	0	0
TOTAL	.323		251	32	81	18	1	3	32	16	35	0

PITCHER	W	L	ERA	G	GS	CG	SV	SHO	IP	H	ER	BB	SO
Jim Bibby	0	0	2.61	2	2	0	0	0	10.1	10	3	2	10
Bert Blyleven	1	0	1.80	2	1	0	0	0	10.0	8	2	3	4
John Candelaria	1	1	5.00	2	2	0	0	0	9.0	14	5	2	4
Grant Jackson	1	0	0.00	4	0	0	0	0	4.2	1	0	2	2
Bruce Kison	0	1	108.00	1	1	0	0	0	0.1	3	4	2	0
Don Robinson	1	0	5.40	4	0	0	0	0	5.0	4	3	6	3
Enrique Romo	0	0	3.86	2	0	0	0	0	4.2	5	2	3	4
Jim Rooker	0	0	1.04	2	1	0	0	0	8.2	5	1	3	4
Kent Tekulve	0	1	2.89	5	0	0	3	0	9.1	4	3	3	10
TOTAL	4	3	3.34	24	7	0	3	0	62.0	54	23	26	41

BAL (A)

PLAYER/POS	AVG	G	AB	R	H	2B	3B	HR	RBI	BB	SO	SB
Benny Ayala, of-3	.333	4	6	1	2	0	0	1	2	1	0	0
Mark Belanger, ss-4	.000	5	6	1	0	0	0	0	0	1	1	0
Al Bumbry, of	.143	7	21	3	3	0	0	0	1	2	1	0
Terry Crowley, ph	.250	5	4	0	1	1	0	0	2	1	0	0
Rich Dauer, 2b-5	.294	6	17	2	5	1	0	1	1	0	1	0
Doug DeCinces, 3b	.200	7	25	2	5	0	0	1	3	5	5	1
Rick Dempsey, c-6	.286	7	21	3	6	2	0	0	1	3	0	0
Mike Flanagan, p	.000	3	5	0	0	0	0	0	0	1	2	0
Kiko Garcia, ss	.400	6	20	4	8	2	1	0	6	1	3	0
Pat Kelly, ph	.250	5	4	0	1	0	0	0	0	1	1	0
John Lowenstein, of-3	.231	6	13	2	3	1	0	0	3	1	3	0
Tippy Martinez, p	.000	3	0	0	0	0	0	0	0	0	0	0
Dennis Martinez, p	.000	2	0	0	0	0	0	0	0	0	0	0
Lee May, ph	.000	2	1	0	0	0	0	0	0	1	1	0
Scott McGregor, p	.000	2	4	1	0	0	0	0	0	2	1	0
Eddie Murray, 1b	.154	7	26	3	4	1	0	1	2	4	4	1
Jim Palmer, p	.000	2	4	0	0	0	0	0	0	0	3	0
Gary Roenicke, of-5	.125	6	16	1	2	1	0	0	0	0	6	0
Ken Singleton, of	.357	7	28	1	10	1	0	0	2	2	5	0
Dave Skaggs, c	.333	1	3	1	1	0	0	0	0	0	0	0
Billy Smith, 2b-2	.286	4	7	1	2	0	0	0	0	2	0	0
Don Stanhouse, p	.000	3	0	0	0	0	0	0	0	0	0	0
Sammy Stewart, p	.000	1	1	0	0	0	0	0	0	0	1	0
Tim Stoddard, p	1.000	4	1	0	1	0	0	0	1	0	0	0
Steve Stone, p	.000	1	0	0	0	0	0	0	0	0	0	0
TOTAL	.232		233	26	54	10	1	4	23	26	41	2

PITCHER	W	L	ERA	G	GS	CG	SV	SHO	IP	H	ER	BB	SO
Mike Flanagan	1	1	3.00	3	2	1	0	0	15.0	18	5	2	13
Tippy Martinez	0	0	6.75	3	0	0	0	0	1.1	3	1	0	1
Dennis Martinez	0	0	18.00	2	1	0	0	0	2.0	6	4	0	0
Scott McGregor	1	1	3.18	2	2	1	0	0	17.0	16	6	2	8
Jim Palmer	0	1	3.60	2	2	0	0	0	15.0	18	6	5	8
Don Stanhouse	0	1	13.50	3	0	0	0	0	2.0	6	3	0	0
Sammy Stewart	0	0	0.00	1	0	0	0	0	2.2	4	0	1	0
Tim Stoddard	1	0	5.40	4	0	0	0	0	5.0	6	3	1	3
Steve Stone	0	0	9.00	1	0	0	0	0	2.0	4	2	2	2
TOTAL	3	4	4.35	21	7	2	0	0	62.0	81	30	16	35

GAME 1 AT BAL OCT 10

PIT	000	102	010	4	11 3
BAL	500	000	000	5	6 3

Pitchers: KISON, Rooker (1), Romo (5), D.Robinson (6), Jackson (8) vs FLANAGAN
Home Runs: Stargell-PIT, DeCinces-BAL
Attendance: 53,735

GAME 2 AT BAL OCT 11

PIT	020	000	001	3	11 2
BAL	010	001	000	2	6 1

Pitchers: Blyleven, D.ROBINSON (7), Tekulve (9) vs PALMER, T.Martinez (8), Stanhouse (8), T.Martinez (9)
Home Runs: Muuray-BAL
Attendance: 53,739

GAME 3 AT PIT OCT 12

BAL	002	500	100	8	13 0
PIT	120	001	000	4	9 2

Pitchers: McGREGOR vs CANDELARIA, Romo (4), Jackson (7), Tekulve (8)
Home Runs: Ayala-BAL
Attendance: 50,848

GAME 4 AT PIT OCT 13

BAL	003	000	060	9	12 0
PIT	040	011	000	6	17 1

Pitchers: D.Martinez, Stewart (2), Stone (5), STODDARD (7) vs Bibby, Jackson (6), D.Robinson (8), TEKULVE (8)
Home Runs: Stargell-PIT
Attendance: 50,883

GAME 5 AT PIT OCT 14

BAL	000	010	000	1	6 2
PIT	000	002	23X	7	13 1

Pitchers: FLANAGAN, Stoddard (7), T.Martinez (7), Stanhouse (8) vs Rooker, BLYLEVEN (6)
Attendance: 50,920

GAME 6 AT BAL OCT 16

PIT	000	000	220	4	10 0
BAL	000	000	000	0	7 1

Pitchers: CANDELARIA, Tekluve (7) vs PALMER, Stoddard (9)
Attendance: 53,739

GAME 7 AT BAL OCT 17

PIT	000	002	002	4	10 0
BAL	001	000	000	1	4 2

Pitchers: Bibby, D.Robinson (5), JACKSON (5), Tekulve (8) vs McGREGOR, Stoddard (9), Flanagan (9), Stanhouse (9), T.Martinez (9), D.Martinez (9)
Home Runs: Stargell-PIT, Dauer-BAL
Attendance: 53,733

In the tightest LCS yet, the Phillies took the opener 3–1 on the series' only home run—Greg Luzinski's two-run blast in the sixth inning. It was the only game not to go into extra innings.

The Astros evened the series in Game Two—demolishing a 3–3 tie with four runs in the tenth—and took the series lead in a Game Three pitchers' duel that saw Astro Joe Niekro hurl ten scoreless innings. Reliever Dave Smith continued the shutout and took the win as Joe Morgan's triple and Denny Walling's sacrifice fly off ace Phillie reliever Tug McGraw scored the game's only run in the bottom of the eleventh.

The Phillies rebounded, though, with their own set of extra-inning victories. In Game Four, a single and two doubles pushed across two go-ahead runs in the top of the tenth, and McGraw preserved the edge for his second series save. And in the finale—which saw the lead change hands three times—after Del Unser scored on Gary Maddox's tenth-inning double, Dick Ruthven held off Houston to bring the Phillies their first pennant in thirty years.

Philadelphia Phillies (East), 3; Houston Astros (West), 2

PHI (E)

PLAYER/POS	AVG	G	AB	R	H	2B	3B	HR	RB	BB	SO	SB
Ramon Aviles, pr	.000	1	0	1	0	0	0	0	0	0	0	0
Bob Boone, c	.222	5	18	1	4	0	0	0	2	1	2	0
Larry Bowa, ss	.316	5	19	2	6	0	0	0	0	3	3	1
Warren Brusstar, p	.000	2	1	0	0	0	0	0	0	0	1	0
Marty Bystrom, p	.000	1	2	0	0	0	0	0	0	0	1	0
Steve Carlton, p	.000	2	4	0	0	0	0	0	0	0	1	0
Larry Christenson, p	.000	1	2	0	0	0	0	0	0	0	1	0
Greg Gross, of-1	.750	4	4	2	3	0	0	0	1	0	0	0
Greg Luzinski, of	.294	5	17	3	5	2	0	1	4	0	6	0
Garry Maddox, of	.300	5	20	2	6	2	0	0	3	2	2	2
Bake McBride, of	.238	5	21	0	5	0	0	0	0	1	5	2
Tug McGraw, p	.000	5	1	0	0	0	0	0	0	0	0	0
Keith Moreland, c-1	.000	2	1	0	0	0	0	0	1	0	0	0
Dickie Noles, p	.000	2	0	0	0	0	0	0	0	0	0	0
Ron Reed, p	.000	3	0	0	0	0	0	0	0	0	0	0
Pete Rose, 1b	.400	5	20	3	8	0	0	0	2	5	3	0
Dick Ruthven, p	.000	2	3	0	0	0	0	0	0	0	2	0
Kevin Saucier, p	.000	2	0	0	0	0	0	0	0	0	0	0
Mike Schmidt, 3b	.208	5	24	1	5	1	0	0	1	1	6	1
Lonnie Smith, of-2	.600	3	5	2	3	0	0	0	0	0	0	1
Manny Trillo, 2b	.381	5	21	1	8	2	1	0	4	0	2	0
Del Unser, of-2	.400	5	5	2	2	1	0	0	1	0	2	0
George Vukovich, of-1	.000	4	3	0	0	0	0	0	0	0	0	0
TOTAL	.289		190	20	55	8	1	1	19	13	37	7

PITCHER	W	L	ERA	G	GS	CG	SV	SHO	IP	H	ER	BB	SO
Warren Brusstar	1	0	3.38	2	0	0	0	0	2.2	1	1	1	0
Marty Bystrom	0	0	1.69	1	1	0	0	0	5.1	7	1	2	1
Steve Carlton	1	0	2.19	2	2	0	0	0	12.1	11	3	8	6
Larry Christenson	0	0	4.05	1	1	0	0	0	6.2	5	3	5	2
Tug McGraw	0	1	4.50	5	0	0	2	0	8.0	8	4	4	5
Dickie Noles	0	0	0.00	2	0	0	0	0	2.2	1	0	3	0
Ron Reed	0	1	18.00	3	0	0	0	0	2.0	3	4	1	1
Dick Ruthven	1	0	2.00	2	1	0	0	0	9.0	3	2	5	4
Kevin Saucier	0	0	0.00	2	0	0	0	0	0.2	1	0	2	0
TOTAL	3	2	3.28	20	5	0	2	0	49.1	40	18	31	19

HOU (W)

PLAYER/POS	AVG	G	AB	R	H	2B	3B	HR	RB	BB	SO	SB
Joaquin Andujar, p	.000	1	0	0	0	0	0	0	0	0	0	0
Alan Ashby, c	.125	2	8	0	1	0	0	0	1	0	0	0
Dave Bergman, 1b	.333	4	3	0	1	0	1	0	2	0	0	0
Bruce Bochy, c	.000	1	0	0	0	0	0	0	0	0	0	0
Enos Cabell, 3b	.238	5	21	1	5	1	0	0	0	1	3	0
Cesar Cedeno, of	.182	3	11	1	2	0	0	0	1	1	0	0
Jose Cruz, of	.400	5	15	3	6	1	1	0	4	8	1	0
Ken Forsch, p	1.000	2	2	0	2	0	0	0	0	0	0	0
Danny Heep, ph	.000	1	1	0	0	0	0	0	0	0	0	0
Art Howe, 1b-4	.200	5	15	0	3	1	1	0	2	2	2	0
Frank LaCorte, p	.000	2	1	0	0	0	0	0	0	0	0	0
Rafael Landestoy, 2b-3,ss-1	.222	5	9	3	2	0	0	0	2	1	0	1
Jeffrey Leonard, of-1	.000	3	3	0	0	0	0	0	0	0	2	0
Joe Morgan, 2b	.154	4	13	1	2	1	1	0	0	6	1	0
Joe Niekro, p	.000	1	3	0	0	0	0	0	0	0	1	0
Terry Puhl, of-4	.526	5	19	4	10	2	0	0	3	3	2	2
Luis Pujols, c	.100	4	10	1	1	0	1	0	0	0	3	0
Craig Reynolds, ss	.154	4	13	2	2	1	0	0	0	3	1	0
Vern Ruhle, p	.000	1	3	0	0	0	0	0	0	0	1	0
Nolan Ryan, p	.000	2	4	1	0	0	0	0	0	0	2	0
Joe Sambito, p	.000	3	0	0	0	0	0	0	0	0	0	0
Dave Smith, p	.000	3	0	0	0	0	0	0	0	0	0	0
Denny Walling, of-2,1b-1	.111	3	9	2	1	0	0	0	2	1	1	0
Gary Woods, of-3	.250	4	8	0	2	0	0	0	1	1	3	1
TOTAL	.233		172	19	40	7	5	0	18	31	19	4

PITCHER	W	L	ERA	G	GS	CG	SV	SHO	IP	H	ER	BB	SO
Joaquin Andujar	0	0	0.00	1	0	0	1	0	1.0	0	0	1	0
Ken Forsch	0	0	4.15	2	1	1	0	0	8.2	10	4	1	6
Frank LaCorte	1	1	3.00	2	0	0	0	0	3.0	7	1	4	2
Joe Niekro	0	0	0.00	1	1	0	0	0	10.0	6	0	1	2
Vern Ruhle	0	0	3.86	1	1	0	0	0	7.0	8	3	1	3
Nolan Ryan	0	0	5.40	2	2	0	0	0	13.1	16	8	3	14
Joe Sambito	0	1	4.91	3	0	0	0	0	3.2	4	2	2	6
Dave Smith	1	0	3.86	3	0	0	0	0	2.1	4	1	2	4
TOTAL	2	3	3.49	15	5	1	1	0	49.0	55	19	13	37

GAME 1 AT PHI OCT 7

HOU	001 000 000	1	7	0
PHI	000 002 10X	3	8	1

Pitchers: FORSCH vs CARLTON, McGraw (8)
Home Runs: Luzinski-PHI
Attendance: 65,277

GAME 2 AT PHI OCT 8

HOU	001 000 110 4	7	8	1
PHI	000 200 010 1	4	14	2

Pitchers: Ryan, Sambito (7), D.Smith (7), LaCORTE (9), Andujar (10) vs Ruthven, McGraw (8), REED (9), Saucier (10)
Attendance: 65,476

GAME 3 AT HOU OCT 10

PHI	000 000 000 00	0	7	1
HOU	000 000 000 01	1	6	1

Pitchers: Christensen, Noles (7), McGRAW (8) vs Niekro, D.SMITH (11)
Attendance: 44,443

GAME 4 AT HOU OCT 11

PHI	000 000 030 2	5	13	0
HOU	000 110 001 0	3	5	1

Pitchers: Carlton, Noles (6), Saucier (7), Reed (7), BRUSSTAR (8), McGraw (10) vs Ruhle, D.Smith (8), SAMBITO (8)
Attendance: 44,952

GAME 5 AT HOU OCT 12

PHI	020 000 050 1	8	13	2
HOU	100 001 320 0	7	14	0

Pitchers: Bystrom, Brusstar (6), Christensen (7), Reed (7), McGraw (8), RUTHVEN (9) vs Ryan, Sambito (8), Forsch (8), LaCORTE (9)
Attendance: 44,802

Kansas City and New York met for the fourth time in the LCS, and this time the Royals swept to their first pennant. In the first game the Yankees scored first, with second-inning home runs by Rick Cerone and Lou Piniella, but the Royals' Frank White doubled in a pair later in the inning to tie it, and Willie Aikens's hit in the third gave K.C. the lead. They held it to the end as Larry Gura shut out New York the rest of the way.

The Royals scored three runs in the third inning of Game Two, on Willie Wilson's two-run triple and an RBI double by U. L. Washington. Yankee starter Rudy May stopped K.C. after that, but the Royals already had enough for the win as Dennis Leonard in eight innings held New York to two runs, and Dan Quisenberry kept the lid on in the ninth.

Game Three was decided by home runs. White scored first for the Royals with a solo shot in the fifth. New York took the lead briefly with a two-run sixth, but lost it—and the pennant—in the top of the seventh when Goose Gossage, relieving starter Tommy John with two out and a man on, gave up an infield single to Washington and a home run to George Brett.

Kansas City Royals (West), 3; New York Yankees (East), 0

KC (W)

PLAYER/POS	AVG	G	AB	R	H	2B	3B	HR	RB	BB	SO	SB
Willie Aikens, 1b	.364	3	11	0	4	0	0	0	2	0	1	0
George Brett, 3b	.273	3	11	3	3	1	0	2	4	1	0	0
Larry Gura, p	.000	1	0	0	0	0	0	0	0	0	0	0
Clint Hurdle, of	.000	3	2	0	0	0	0	0	0	0	1	0
Pete LaCock, 1b	.000	1	0	0	0	0	0	0	0	0	0	0
Dennis Leonard, p	.000	1	0	0	0	0	0	0	0	0	0	0
Hal McRae, dh	.200	3	10	0	2	0	0	0	0	1	3	0
Amos Otis, of	.333	3	12	2	4	1	0	0	0	0	3	2
Darrell Porter, c	.100	3	10	2	1	0	0	0	0	1	0	0
Dan Quisenberry, p	.000	2	0	0	0	0	0	0	0	0	0	0
Paul Splittorff, p	.000	1	0	0	0	0	0	0	0	0	0	0
U. L. Washington, ss	.364	3	11	1	4	1	0	0	1	2	3	0
John Wathan, of	.000	3	6	1	0	0	0	0	0	3	1	0
Frank White, 2b	.545	3	11	3	6	1	0	1	3	0	1	1
Willie Wilson, of	.308	3	13	2	4	2	1	0	4	1	2	0
TOTAL	.289		97	14	28	6	1	3	14	9	15	3

PITCHER	W	L	ERA	G	GS	CG	SV	SHO	IP	H	ER	BB	SO
Larry Gura	1	0	2.00	1	1	1	0	0	9.0	10	2	1	4
Dennis Leonard	1	0	2.25	1	1	0	0	0	8.0	7	2	1	8
Dan Quisenberry	1	0	0.00	2	0	0	1	0	4.2	4	0	2	1
Paul Splittorff	0	0	1.69	1	1	0	0	0	5.1	5	1	2	3
TOTAL	3	0	1.67	5	3	1	1	0	27.0	26	5	6	16

NY (E)

PLAYER/POS	AVG	G	AB	R	H	2B	3B	HR	RB	BB	SO	SB
Bobby Brown, of	.000	3	10	1	0	0	0	0	0	1	2	0
Rick Cerone, c	.333	3	12	1	4	0	0	1	2	0	1	0
Ron Davis, p	.000	1	0	0	0	0	0	0	0	0	0	0
Bucky Dent, ss	.182	3	11	0	2	0	0	0	0	0	1	0
Oscar Gamble, of-1,dh-1	.200	2	5	1	1	0	0	0	0	1	1	0
Rich Gossage, p	.000	1	0	0	0	0	0	0	0	0	0	0
Ron Guidry, p	.000	1	0	0	0	0	0	0	0	0	0	0
Reggie Jackson, of	.273	3	11	1	3	1	0	0	0	1	4	0
Tommy John, p	.000	1	0	0	0	0	0	0	0	0	0	0
Joe Lefebvre, of	.000	1	0	0	0	0	0	0	0	0	0	0
Rudy May, p	.000	1	0	0	0	0	0	0	0	0	0	0
Bobby Murcer, dh	.000	1	4	0	0	0	0	0	0	0	2	0
Graig Nettles, 3b	.167	2	6	1	1	0	0	1	1	0	1	0
Lou Piniella, of	.200	2	5	1	1	0	0	1	1	2	1	0
Willie Randolph, 2b	.385	3	13	0	5	2	0	0	1	1	3	0
Aurelio Rodriguez, 3b	.333	2	6	0	2	1	0	0	0	0	0	0
Eric Soderholm, dh	.167	2	6	0	1	0	0	0	0	0	0	0
Jim Spencer, ph	.000	1	1	0	0	0	0	0	0	0	0	0
Tom Underwood, p	.000	2	0	0	0	0	0	0	0	0	0	0
Bob Watson, 1b	.500	3	12	0	6	3	1	0	0	0	0	0
TOTAL	.255		102	6	26	7	1	3	5	6	16	0

PITCHER	W	L	ERA	G	GS	CG	SV	SHO	IP	H	ER	BB	SO
Ron Davis	0	0	2.25	1	0	0	0	0	4.0	3	1	1	3
Rich Gossage	0	1	54.00	1	0	0	0	0	0.1	3	2	0	0
Ron Guidry	0	1	12.00	1	1	0	0	0	3.0	5	4	4	2
Tommy John	0	0	2.70	1	1	0	0	0	6.2	8	2	1	3
Rudy May	0	1	3.38	1	1	1	0	0	8.0	6	3	3	4
Tom Underwood	0	0	0.00	2	0	0	0	0	3.0	3	0	0	3
TOTAL	0	3	4.32	7	3	1	0	0	25.0	28	12	9	15

GAME 1 AT KC OCT 8

NY	020	000	000	2	10	1
KC	022	000	12X	7	10	0

Pitchers: GUIDRY, Davis (4), Underwood (8) vs GURA
Home Runs: Cerone-NY, Piniella-NY, G.Brett-KC
Attendance: 42,598

GAME 2 AT KC OCT 9

NY	000	020	000	2	8	0
KC	003	000	00X	3	6	0

Pitchers: MAY vs LEONARD, Quisenberry (9)
Home Runs: Nettles-NY
Attendance: 42,633

GAME 3 AT NY OCT 10

KC	000	010	300	4	12	1
NY	000	002	000	2	8	0

Pitchers: Splittorff, QUISENBERRY (6) vs John, GOSSAGE (7), Underwood (8)
Home Runs: White-KC, G.Brett-KC
Attendance: 56,588

Both clubs had won divisional titles three years in a row—1976–1978—only to lose the League Championship Series. But both overcame the jinx in 1980 to face off in the World Series—the Phillies for the first time in thirty years, the Royals for the first time ever. Kansas City began with a rush in the opener, scoring two runs on Amos Otis's homer in the second inning and two more on Willie Aikens's blast an inning later. But the Phillies came back to take the lead in their half of the third with a five-run rally capped by Bake McBride's three-run homer. Single Phillie runs in each of the next two innings kept them out of reach of Aikens's second two-run shot in the eighth for a narrow 7–6 win. The Phillies extended their Series advantage with a 6–4 win in the second game, rebounding from a two-run deficit with four runs in the eighth inning.

The two clubs traded single runs throughout Game Three. Royal George Brett's first-inning homer began the scoring. The Phillies got the run back in the second inning, the Royals took the lead back in the fourth, Phillie Mike Schmidt homered to tie it again in the fifth, Amos Otis countered with a homer in the seventh, and Pete Rose singled in another tying Phillie run in the eighth. Phillie reliever Tug McGraw (who had a save in the opening game) came on to pitch the last of the tenth inning, but couldn't hold the tie, though two men were out before Willie Aikens singled in the Royals' winning run. The Royals evened the Series with their second victory the next day, scoring four times in the first inning and once in the second (with Willie Aikens for the second time in the Series hitting two home runs in a game), then holding on for a 5–3 win.

But the Phillies recovered to win the next two, and their first world crown. Mike Schmidt's fourth-inning two-run homer began the Phillies' scoring in Game Five. The Royals replied with one run in the fifth, and Amos Otis's home run an inning later tied the game. A second K.C. run in the inning put the Royals ahead until the top of the ninth, when pinch hitter Del Unser doubled home Schmidt to tie the game, and Manny Trillo drove home Unser with the go-ahead run. Tug McGraw, who had held K.C. scoreless through two innings of relief, loaded the bases in the last of the ninth with three walks, but at last fanned Jose Cardenal for the final out. In Game Six, with the Phillies ahead 4–0 in the eighth inning, McGraw relieved starter Steve Carlton with two men on, and loaded the bases with a walk. One Royal scored on a sacrifice fly before McGraw got his third out. In

the ninth, another McGraw walk and two singles again loaded the bases with only one away, but Frank White popped out foul, the ball bouncing off Bob Boone's catcher's mitt into Pete Rose's hand, and Willie Wilson struck out for the twelfth time to end the Series.

Philadelphia Phillies (NL), 4; Kansas City Royals (AL), 2

PHI (N)

PLAYER/POS	AVG	G	AB	R	H	2B	3B	HR	RB	BB	SO	SB
Bob Boone, c	.412	6	17	3	7	2	0	0	4	4	0	0
Larry Bowa, ss	.375	6	24	3	9	1	0	0	2	0	0	3
Warren Brusstar, p	.000	1	0	0	0	0	0	0	0	0	0	0
Marty Bystrom, p	.000	1	0	0	0	0	0	0	0	0	0	0
Steve Carlton, p	.000	2	0	0	0	0	0	0	0	0	0	0
Larry Christenson, p	.000	1	0	0	0	0	0	0	0	0	0	0
Greg Gross, of-3	.000	4	2	0	0	0	0	0	0	0	0	0
Greg Luzinski, dh-2,of-1	.000	3	9	0	0	0	0	0	0	1	5	0
Garry Maddox, of	.227	6	22	1	5	2	0	0	1	1	3	0
Bake McBride, of	.304	6	23	3	7	1	0	1	5	2	1	0
Tug McGraw, p	.000	4	0	0	0	0	0	0	0	0	0	0
Keith Moreland, dh	.333	3	12	1	4	0	0	0	1	0	1	0
Dickie Noles, p	.000	1	0	0	0	0	0	0	0	0	0	0
Ron Reed, p	.000	2	0	0	0	0	0	0	0	0	0	0
Pete Rose, 1b	.261	6	23	2	6	1	0	0	1	2	2	0
Dick Ruthven, p	.000	1	0	0	0	0	0	0	0	0	0	0
Kevin Saucier, p	.000	1	0	0	0	0	0	0	0	0	0	0
Mike Schmidt, 3b	.381	6	21	6	8	1	0	2	7	4	3	0
Lonnie Smith, of-5,dh-1	.263	6	19	2	5	1	0	0	1	1	1	0
Manny Trillo, 2b	.217	6	23	4	5	2	0	0	2	0	0	0
Del Unser, of	.500	3	6	2	3	2	0	0	2	0	1	0
Bob Walk, p	.000	1	0	0	0	0	0	0	0	0	0	0
TOTAL	.294		201	27	59	13	0	3	26	15	17	3

PITCHER	W	L	ERA	G	GS	CG	SV	SHO	IP	H	ER	BB	SO
Warren Brusstar	0	0	0.00	1	0	0	0	0	2.1	0	0	1	0
Marty Bystrom	0	0	5.40	1	1	0	0	0	5.0	10	3	1	4
Steve Carlton	2	0	2.40	2	2	0	0	0	15.0	14	4	9	17
Larry Christenson	0	1	108.00	1	1	0	0	0	0.1	5	4	1	0
Tug McGraw	1	1	1.17	4	0	0	2	0	7.2	7	1	8	10
Dickie Noles	0	0	1.93	1	0	0	0	0	4.2	5	1	2	6
Ron Reed	0	0	0.00	2	0	0	1	0	2.0	2	0	0	2
Dick Ruthven	0	0	3.00	1	1	0	0	0	9.0	9	3	0	7
Kevin Saucier	0	0	0.00	1	0	0	0	0	0.2	0	0	2	0
Bob Walk	1	0	7.71	1	1	0	0	0	7.0	8	6	3	3
TOTAL	4	2	3.69	15	6	0	3	0	53.2	60	22	27	49

KC (A)

PLAYER/POS	AVG	G	AB	R	H	2B	3B	HR	RB	BB	SO	SB
Willie Aikens, 1b	.400	6	20	5	8	0	1	4	8	6	8	0
George Brett, 3b	.375	6	24	3	9	2	1	1	3	2	4	1
Jose Cardenal, of	.200	4	10	0	2	0	0	0	0	0	3	0
Dave Chalk, 3b	.000	1	0	1	0	0	0	0	0	1	0	1
Onix Concepcion, pr	.000	3	0	0	0	0	0	0	0	0	0	0
Rich Gale, p	.000	2	0	0	0	0	0	0	0	0	0	0
Larry Gura, p	.000	2	0	0	0	0	0	0	0	0	0	0
Clint Hurdle, of	.417	4	12	1	5	1	0	0	2	1	1	0
Pete LaCock, 1b	.000	1	0	0	0	0	0	0	0	0	0	0
Dennis Leonard, p	.000	2	0	0	0	0	0	0	0	0	0	0
Renie Martin, p	.000	3	0	0	0	0	0	0	0	0	0	0
Hal McRae, dh	.375	6	24	3	9	3	0	0	1	2	2	0
Amos Otis, of	.478	6	23	4	11	2	0	3	7	3	3	0
Marty Pattin, p	.000	1	0	0	0	0	0	0	0	0	0	0
Darrell Porter, c-4	.143	5	14	1	2	0	0	0	3	4	0	0
Dan Quisenberry, p	.000	6	0	0	0	0	0	0	0	0	0	0
Paul Splittorff, p	.000	2	0	0	0	0	0	0	0	0	0	0
U L Washington, ss	.273	6	22	1	6	0	0	0	2	0	6	0
John Wathan, c-2,of-1	.286	3	7	1	2	0	0	0	1	2	1	0
Frank White, 2b	.080	6	25	0	2	0	0	0	0	1	5	1
Willie Wilson, of	.154	6	26	3	4	1	0	0	0	4	12	2
TOTAL	.290		207	23	60	9	2	8	22	26	49	6

PITCHER	W	L	ERA	G	GS	CG	SV	SHO	IP	H	ER	BB	SO
Rich Gale	0	1	4.26	2	2	0	0	0	6.1	11	3	4	4
Larry Gura	0	0	2.19	2	2	0	0	0	12.1	8	3	3	4
Dennis Leonard	1	1	6.75	2	2	0	0	0	10.2	15	8	2	5
Renie Martin	0	0	2.79	3	0	0	0	0	9.2	11	3	3	2
Marty Pattin	0	0	0.00	1	0	0	0	0	1.0	0	0	0	2
Dan Quisenberry	1	2	5.23	6	0	0	0	0	10.1	10	6	3	0
Paul Splittorff	0	0	5.40	1	0	0	0	0	1.2	4	1	0	0
TOTAL	2	4	4.15	17	6	0	1	0	52.0	59	24	15	17

GAME 1 AT PHI OCT 14

KC	022 000 020	6 9 1
PHI	005 110 00X	7 11 0

Pitchers: LEONARD, Martin (4), Quisenberry (8) vs WALK, McGraw (8)
Home Runs: Otis-KC, Aikens-KC (2), McBride-PHI
Attendance: 65,791

GAME 2 AT PHI OCT 15

KC	000 001 300	4 11 0
PHI	000 020 04X	6 8 1

Pitchers: Gura, QUISENBERRY (7) vs CARLTON, Reed (9)
Attendance: 65,775

GAME 3 AT KC OCT 17

PHI	010 010 010 0	3 14 0
KC	100 100 100 1	4 11 0

Pitchers: Ruthven, McGRAW (10) vs Gale, Martin (5), QUISENBERRY (8)
Home Runs: Schmidt-PHI, G.Brett-KC, Otis-KC
Attendance: 42,380

GAME 4 AT KC OCT 18

PHI	010 000 110	3 10 1
KC	410 000 00X	5 10 2

Pitchers: CHRISTENSEN, Noles (1), Saucier (6), Brusstar (6) vs LEONARD, Quisenberry (8)
Home Runs: Aikens-KC (2)
Attendance: 42,363

GAME 5 AT KC OCT 19

PHI	000 200 002	4 7 0
KC	000 012 000	3 12 2

Pitchers: Bystrom, Reed (6), McGRAW (7) vs Gura, QUISENBERRY (7)
Home Runs: Schmidt-PHI, Otis-KC
Attendance: 42,369

GAME 6 AT PHI OCT 21

KC	000 000 010	1 7 2
PHI	002 011 00X	4 9 0

Pitchers: GALE, Martin (3), Splittorff (5), Pattin (7), Quisenberry (8) vs CARLTON, McGraw (8)
Attendance: 65,838

The Expos, who triumphed over the NL East in the second half of the season, won the first two playoff games at home by identical 3–1 scores over the first-half champion Phillies. The Phillies rapped Expo ace Steve Rogers for ten hits in Game One, but Keith Moreland's solo home run in the second was the only hit to produce a run. The homer tied the score briefly, but the Expos regained the lead in the last of the second inning on Chris Speier's double and increased it to 3–1, two innings later. The Expos scored their three runs early in Game Two on Speier's second-inning single and Gary Carter's two-run homer an inning later. Expo starter Bill Gullickson blanked the Phillies on three hits through 7⅔ innings, but three two-out hits in the eighth scored a Phillie run and brought on reliever Jeff Reardon, who ended the threat for his second save in as many days.

When the Series moved to Philadelphia, the Phillies recovered to even things with a pair of wins. After an easy 13-hit 6–2 victory in Game Three, they took a 4–0 lead into the fourth inning of Game Four. Montreal fought back to tie the game, fell behind again, then re-tied the score at 5–5 in the top of the seventh. The final innings featured a duel between relievers Tug McGraw and Jeff Reardon. McGraw stopped the Expos on one hit through three innings, and took the win when Reardon, after retiring eight Phillies in a row, gave up a leadoff homer to pinch hitter George Vukovich in the bottom of the tenth.

Steve Rogers won the division title for Montreal in the finale, hurling a six-hit shutout against the Phillies and driving in the first two of the Expos' three runs with a bases-loaded single through the box in the fifth inning.

Montreal Expos, 3; Philadelphia Phillies, 2

MON (E)

PLAYER/POS	AVG	G	AB	R	H	2B	3B	HR	RB	BB	SO	SB
Stan Bahnsen, p	.000	1	0	0	0	0	0	0	0	0	0	0
Ray Burris, p	.000	1	2	0	0	0	0	0	0	0	2	0
Gary Carter, c	.421	5	19	3	8	3	0	2	6	1	1	0
Warren Cromartie, 1b	.227	5	22	1	5	2	0	0	1	0	9	0
Andre Dawson, of	.300	5	20	1	6	0	1	0	0	1	6	2
Terry Francona, of	.333	5	12	0	4	0	0	0	0	2	2	2
Woody Fryman, p	.000	1	0	0	0	0	0	0	0	0	0	0
Bill Gullickson, p	.000	1	3	0	0	0	0	0	0	0	1	0
Wallace Johnson, ph	.500	2	2	0	1	0	0	0	1	0	0	0
Bill Lee, p	.000	1	0	0	0	0	0	0	0	0	0	0
Jerry Manuel, 2b	.071	5	14	0	1	0	0	0	0	2	5	0
Brad Mills, ph	.000	1	0	0	0	0	0	0	0	1	0	0
John Milner, ph	.500	2	2	0	1	0	0	0	1	0	0	0
Larry Parrish, 3b	.150	5	20	3	3	1	0	0	1	1	3	0
Mike Phillips, 2b	.000	1	1	0	0	0	0	0	0	0	0	0
Jeff Reardon, p	.000	3	1	0	0	0	0	0	0	0	1	0
Steve Rogers, p	.400	2	5	0	2	0	0	0	2	0	1	0
Scott Sanderson, p	.000	1	1	0	0	0	0	0	0	0	1	0
Elias Sosa, p	.000	2	0	0	0	0	0	0	0	0	0	0
Chris Speier, ss	.400	5	15	4	6	2	0	0	3	4	2	0
Tim Wallach, of-3	.250	4	4	1	1	1	0	0	0	4	0	0
Jerry White, of	.167	5	18	3	3	1	0	0	1	2	2	3
TOTAL	.255		161	16	41	10	1	2	16	18	36	7

PITCHER	W	L	ERA	G	GS	CG	SV	SHO	IP	H	ER	BB	SO
Stan Bahnsen	0	0	0.00	1	0	0	0	0	1.1	1	0	1	1
Ray Burris	0	1	5.06	1	1	0	0	0	5.1	7	3	4	4
Woody Fryman	0	0	6.75	1	0	0	0	0	1.1	3	1	1	0
Bill Gullickson	1	0	1.17	1	1	0	0	0	7.2	6	1	1	3
Bill Lee	0	0	0.00	2	0	0	0	0	0.2	2	0	0	1
Jeff Reardon	0	1	2.08	3	0	0	2	0	4.1	1	1	1	2
Steve Rogers	2	0	0.51	2	2	1	0	1	17.2	16	1	3	5
Scott Sanderson	0	0	6.75	1	1	0	0	0	2.2	4	2	2	2
Elias Sosa	0	0	3.00	2	0	0	0	0	3.0	4	1	0	1
TOTAL	3	2	2.05	13	5	1	2	1	44.0	44	10	13	19

PHI (E)

PLAYER/POS	AVG	G	AB	R	H	2B	3B	HR	RB	BB	SO	SB
Luis Aguayo, pr	.000	2	0	1	0	0	0	0	0	0	0	0
Ramon Aviles, ph	.000	1	0	0	0	0	0	0	0	1	0	0
Bob Boone, c	.000	3	5	0	0	0	0	0	0	0	0	0
Larry Bowa, ss	.176	5	17	0	3	1	0	0	1	0	0	0
Warren Brusstar, p	.000	2	0	0	0	0	0	0	0	0	0	0
Steve Carlton, p	.250	2	4	0	1	0	0	0	0	0	1	0
Larry Christensen, p	.000	2	2	0	0	0	0	0	0	0	1	0
Dick Davis, of	.000	1	2	0	0	0	0	0	0	0	1	0
Greg Gross, of-2	.000	4	4	0	0	0	0	0	0	0	0	0
Sparky Lyle, p	.000	3	0	0	0	0	0	0	0	0	0	0
Garry Maddox, of	.333	2	3	0	1	1	0	0	0	0	0	0
Gary Matthews, of	.400	5	20	3	8	0	1	1	1	0	2	0
Bake McBride, of	.200	4	15	1	3	1	0	0	0	0	5	0
Tug McGraw, p	.000	2	0	0	0	0	0	0	0	0	0	0
Keith Moreland, c	.462	4	13	2	6	0	0	1	3	1	1	0
Dickie Noles, p	.000	1	0	0	0	0	0	0	0	1	0	0
Ron Reed, p	.000	4	0	0	0	0	0	0	0	0	0	0
Pete Rose, 1b	.300	5	20	1	6	1	0	0	0	2	0	0
Dick Ruthven, p	.000	1	1	0	0	0	0	0	0	0	0	0
Mike Schmidt, 3b	.250	5	16	3	4	1	0	1	2	4	2	0
Lonnie Smith, of	.263	5	19	1	5	1	0	0	0	0	4	0
Manny Trillo, 2b	.188	5	16	1	3	0	0	0	1	4	0	0
George Vukovich, of-3	.444	5	9	1	4	0	0	1	2	0	3	0
TOTAL	.265		166	14	44	6	1	4	12	13	19	0

PITCHER	W	L	ERA	G	GS	CG	SV	SHO	IP	H	ER	BB	SO
Warren Brusstar	0	0	4.91	2	0	0	0	0	3.2	5	2	1	3
Steve Carlton	0	2	3.86	2	2	0	0	0	14.0	14	6	8	13
Larry Christensen	1	0	1.50	1	1	0	0	0	6.0	4	1	1	8
Sparky Lyle	0	0	0.00	3	0	0	0	0	2.1	4	0	2	1
Tug McGraw	1	0	0.00	2	0	0	0	0	4.0	2	0	2	2
Dickie Noles	0	0	4.50	1	1	0	0	0	4.0	4	2	2	5
Ron Reed	0	0	3.00	4	0	0	0	0	6.0	5	2	3	4
Dick Ruthven	0	1	4.50	1	1	0	0	0	4.0	3	2	1	0
TOTAL	2	3	3.07	16	5	0	0	0	44.0	41	15	18	36

GAME 1 AT MON OCT 7

PHI	010	000	000	1	10	1
MON	110	100	00X	3	8	0

Pitchers: CARLTON, R.Reed (7) vs ROGERS, Reardon (9)
Home Runs: Moreland-PHI
Attendance: 34,327

GAME 2 AT MON OCT 8

PHI	000	000	010	1	6	2
MON	012	000	00X	3	7	0

Pitchers: RUTHVEN, Brusstar (5), Lyle (7), McGraw (8) vs GULLICKSON, Reardon (8)
Home Runs: Carter-MON
Attendance: 45,896

GAME 3 AT PHI OCT 9

MON	010	000	010	2	8	4
PHI	020	002	20X	6	13	0

Pitchers: BURRIS, Lee (6), Sosa (7) vs CHRISTENSON, Lyle (7), R.Reed (8)
Attendance: 36,835

GAME 4 AT PHI OCT 10

MON	000	112	100	0	5	10	1
PHI	202	001	000	1	6	9	0

Pitchers: Sanderson, Bahnsen (3), Sosa (5), Fryman (6), REARDON (7) vs Noles, Brusstar (5), Lyle (6), R.Reed (7), McGRAW (8)
Home Runs: Carter-MON, Schmidt-PHI, Matthews-PHI, G.Vukovich-PHI
Attendance: 38,818

GAME 5 AT PHI OCT 11

MON	000	021	000	3	8	1
PHI	000	000	000	0	6	0

Pitchers: ROGERS vs CARLTON, R.Reed (9)
Attendance: 47,384

Cincinnati, with the league's best overall season record, failed to win either half season in the NL West, and watched from the sidelines as first-half winner Los Angeles, down 0–2, recovered to win the final three games—and the division title—from second-half victor Houston. In the opener, Astro Alan Ashby's two-run homer in the last of the ninth broke a 1–1 tie and gave Nolan Ryan a two-hit victory. The next day, Astro Denny Walling's two-out bases-loaded single in the last of the eleventh scored Phil Garner with the game's only run.

When the clubs shifted to Los Angeles for the remainder of the series, the Dodgers came alive. In Game Three, a first-inning double by Dusty Baker and home run by Steve Garvey drove in three Dodger runs. Pitcher Burt Hooton and two relievers held Houston to three hits in what became a 6–1 Dodger victory. The next day, Dodger Fernando Valenzuela and Astro Vern Ruhle hurled matching four-hitters. But Pedro Guerrero's home run in the fifth inning and a pair of Dodger singles sandwiched around a sacrifice and intentional walk in the seventh gave Los Angeles two runs, while Valenzuela held Houston to a single run in the ninth. In the finale, Jerry Reuss blanked the Astros on five hits while his Dodgers blended three of their seven hits with a walk and Astro error for three runs in the sixth. Two more hits produced a final run an inning later.

Los Angeles Dodgers, 3; Houston Astros, 2

LA (W)

PLAYER/POS	AVG	G	AB	R	H	2B	3B	HR	RB	BB	SO	SB
Dusty Baker, of	.167	5	18	2	3	1	0	0	1	2	0	0
Terry Forster, p	.000	1	0	0	0	0	0	0	0	0	0	0
Steve Garvey, 1b	.368	5	19	4	7	0	1	2	4	0	2	0
Pedro Guerrero, 3b	.176	5	17	1	3	1	0	1	1	2	4	1
Burt Hooton, p	.000	1	3	0	0	0	0	0	0	0	0	0
Steve Howe, p	.000	2	0	0	0	0	0	0	0	0	0	0
Jay Johnstone, ph	.000	1	1	0	0	0	0	0	0	0	0	0
Ken Landreaux, of	.200	5	20	1	4	1	0	0	1	0	1	0
Davey Lopes, 2b	.200	5	20	1	4	1	0	0	0	3	7	1
Mike Marshall, ph	.000	1	1	0	0	0	0	0	0	0	1	0
Rick Monday, of	.214	5	14	1	3	0	0	0	1	2	4	0
Tom Niedenfuer, p	.000	1	0	0	0	0	0	0	0	0	0	0
Jerry Reuss, p	.000	2	8	0	0	0	0	0	0	0	8	0
Bill Russell, ss	.250	5	16	1	4	1	0	0	2	3	1	0
Steve Sax, 2b	.000	1	0	0	0	0	0	0	0	0	0	0
Mike Scioscia, c	.154	4	13	0	2	0	0	0	1	1	2	0
Reggie Smith, ph	.000	2	1	0	0	0	0	0	1	0	1	0
Dave Stewart, p	.000	2	0	0	0	0	0	0	0	0	0	0
Derrel Thomas, of	.000	4	2	1	0	0	0	0	0	0	1	0
Fernando Valenzuela, p	.000	2	4	0	0	0	0	0	0	0	1	0
Bob Welch, p	.000	1	0	0	0	0	0	0	0	0	0	0
Steve Yeager, c	.400	2	5	1	2	1	0	0	0	0	1	0
TOTAL	.198		162	13	32	6	1	3	12	13	34	2

PITCHER	W	L	ERA	G	GS	CG	SV	SHO	IP	H	ER	BB	SO
Terry Forster	0	0	0.00	1	0	0	0	0	0.1	0	0	0	0
Burt Hooton	1	0	1.29	1	1	0	0	0	7.0	3	1	3	2
Steve Howe	0	0	0.00	2	0	0	0	0	2.0	1	0	0	2
Tom Niedenfuer	0	0	0.00	1	0	0	0	0	0.1	1	0	1	1
Jerry Reuss	1	0	0.00	2	2	1	0	1	18.0	10	0	5	7
Dave Stewart	0	2	40.50	2	0	0	0	0	0.2	4	3	0	1
Fernando Valenzuela	1	0	1.06	2	2	1	0	0	17.0	10	2	3	10
Bob Welch	0	0	0.00	1	0	0	0	0	1.0	0	0	1	1
TOTAL	3	2	1.17	12	5	2	0	1	46.1	29	6	13	24

HOU (W)

PLAYER/POS	AVG	G	AB	R	H	2B	3B	HR	RB	BB	SO	SB
Alan Ashby, c	.111	3	9	1	1	0	0	1	2	2	0	0
Cesar Cedeno, 1b	.231	4	13	0	3	1	0	0	0	2	2	2
Jose Cruz, of	.300	5	20	0	6	1	0	0	0	1	3	1
Kiko Garcia, ss-1	.000	2	4	0	0	0	0	0	0	0	1	0
Phil Garner, 2b	.111	5	18	1	2	0	0	0	0	3	3	0
Art Howe, 3b	.235	5	17	1	4	0	0	1	1	2	1	0
Bob Knepper, p	.000	1	1	0	0	0	0	0	0	0	0	0
Frank LaCorte, p	.000	2	0	0	0	0	0	0	0	0	0	0
Joe Niekro, p	.000	1	2	0	0	0	0	0	0	0	0	0
Joe Pittman, ph	.000	2	2	0	0	0	0	0	0	0	0	0
Terry Puhl, of	.190	5	21	2	4	1	0	0	0	0	1	1
Luis Pujols, c	.000	2	6	0	0	0	0	0	0	0	1	0
Craig Reynolds, ss-1	.333	2	3	1	1	0	0	0	0	0	1	0
Dave Roberts, ph	.000	1	1	0	0	0	0	0	0	0	1	0
Vern Ruhle, p	.000	1	1	0	0	0	0	0	0	0	1	0
Nolan Ryan, p	.250	2	4	0	1	0	0	0	0	1	1	0
Joe Sambito, p	.000	2	0	0	0	0	0	0	0	0	0	0
Tony Scott, of	.150	5	20	0	3	0	0	0	2	1	6	0
Billy Smith, p	.000	1	0	0	0	0	0	0	0	0	0	0
Dave Smith, p	.000	2	0	0	0	0	0	0	0	0	0	0
Harry Spilman, ph	.000	1	1	0	0	0	0	0	0	0	0	0
Dickie Thon, ss	.182	4	11	0	2	0	0	0	0	1	0	0
Denny Walling, 1b-2	.333	3	6	0	2	0	0	0	1	0	1	0
Gary Woods, ph	.000	2	2	0	0	0	0	0	0	0	1	0
TOTAL	.179		162	6	29	3	0	2	6	13	24	4

PITCHER	W	L	ERA	G	GS	CG	SV	SHO	IP	H	ER	BB	SO
Bob Knepper	0	1	5.40	1	1	0	0	0	5.0	6	3	2	4
Frank LaCorte	0	0	0.00	2	0	0	0	0	3.2	2	0	1	5
Joe Niekro	0	0	0.00	1	1	0	0	0	8.0	7	0	3	4
Vern Ruhle	0	1	2.25	1	1	1	0	0	8.0	4	2	2	1
Nolan Ryan	1	1	1.80	2	2	1	0	0	15.0	6	3	3	14
Joe Sambito	1	0	16.20	2	0	0	0	0	1.2	5	3	2	2
Billy Smith	0	0	0.00	1	0	0	0	0	0.1	0	0	0	0
Dave Smith	0	0	3.86	2	0	0	0	0	2.1	2	1	0	4
TOTAL	2	3	2.45	12	5	2	0	0	44.0	32	12	13	34

GAME 1 AT HOU OCT 6

LA	000	000	100	1	2 0
HOU	000	001	002	3	8 0

Pitchers: Valenzuela, STEWART (9) vs RYAN
Home Runs: Garvey-LA, Ashby-HOU
Attendance: 44,836

GAME 2 AT HOU OCT 7

LA	000 000 000 00	0	9 1
HOU	000 000 000 01	1	9 0

Pitchers: Reuss, S.Howe (1), STEWART (11), Forster (11), Niedenfuer (11) vs Niekro, D.Smith (9), SAMBITO (11)
Attendance: 42,398

GAME 3 AT LA OCT 9

HOU	001	000	000	1	3 2
LA	300	000	03X	6	10 4

Pitchers: KNEPPER, LaCorte (6), Sambito (8), B.Smith (8) vs HOOTON, S.Howe (8), Welch (9)
Home Runs: Garvey-LA, A.Howe-HOU
Attendance: 46,820

GAME 4 AT LA OCT 10

HOU	000	000	001	1	4 0
LA	000	010	10X	2	4 0

Pitchers: RUHLE vs VALENZUELA
Home Runs: Guerrero-LA
Attendance: 55,983

GAME 5 AT LA OCT 11

HOU	000	000	000	0	5 3
LA	000	003	10X	4	7 2

Pitchers: RYAN, D.Smith (7), LaCorte (7) vs REUSS
Attendance: 55,979

Fine pitching characterized the series, with the losing team held to one run in four of the five games. In the exception Expo Ray Burris hurled a shutout.

Montreal put men on base in each inning of the opener. But the pitching of Burt Hooton and Bob Welch—plus some fine Dodger fielding—kept the Expos from scoring until the ninth, when their one run was too little to overcome the Dodger lead. Burris's shutout evened the series in Game Two as the Expos scored three times against rookie sensation Fernando Valenzuela. The Expos took the series lead in Game Three, overcoming a 0–1 deficit with a two-out four-run burst in the sixth (capped by Jerry White's three-run homer).

In the end, though, the Dodgers prevailed. Through seven innings of Game Four, Hooton and the Expos' Bill Gullickson dueled at 1–1. But in the top of the eighth, Steve Garvey homered with a man aboard, and four more Dodger runs in the ninth put the game away. The finale—Burris vs. Valenzuela again—featured another 1–1 duel, this one reaching into the top of the ninth when, with two out, Dodger Rick Monday homered off reliever Steve Rogers. In the bottom of the ninth, Valenzuela walked two batters after retiring two, but Welch came on to save the game and the pennant.

Los Angeles Dodgers (West), 3; Montreal Expos (East), 2

LA (W)

PLAYER/POS	AVG	G	AB	R	H	2B	3B	HR	RB	BB	SO	SB
Dusty Baker, of	.316	5	19	3	6	1	0	0	3	1	0	0
Bobby Castillo, p	.000	1	0	0	0	0	0	0	0	0	0	0
Ron Cey, 3b	.278	5	18	1	5	1	0	0	3	3	2	0
Terry Forster, p	.000	1	0	0	0	0	0	0	0	0	0	0
Steve Garvey, 1b	.286	5	21	2	6	0	0	1	2	0	4	0
Pedro Guerrero, of	.105	5	19	1	2	0	0	1	2	1	4	0
Burt Hooton, p	.000	2	5	0	0	0	0	0	0	0	2	0
Steve Howe, p	.000	2	0	0	0	0	0	0	0	0	0	0
Jay Johnstone, ph	.000	2	2	0	0	0	0	0	0	0	0	0
Ken Landreaux, of-3	.100	5	10	0	1	1	0	0	0	3	2	0
Davey Lopes, 2b	.278	5	18	0	5	0	0	0	0	1	3	5
Rick Monday, of-2	.333	3	9	2	3	0	0	1	1	0	4	0
Tom Niedenfuer, p	.000	1	0	0	0	0	0	0	0	0	0	0
Alejandro Pena, p	.000	2	0	0	0	0	0	0	0	0	0	0
Jerry Reuss, p	.000	1	2	0	0	0	0	0	0	0	0	0
Bill Russell, ss	.313	5	16	2	5	0	1	0	1	1	1	0
Steve Sax, 2b	.000	1	0	0	0	0	0	0	0	0	0	0
Mike Scioscia, c	.133	5	15	1	2	0	0	1	1	2	1	0
Reggie Smith, ph	1.000	1	1	0	1	0	0	0	1	0	0	0
Derrel Thomas, 3b-1,of-1	1.000	2	1	2	1	0	0	0	0	0	0	0
Fernando Valenzuela, p	.000	2	5	0	0	0	0	0	1	0	0	0
Bob Welch, p	.000	3	0	0	0	0	0	0	0	0	0	0
Steve Yeager, c	.500	1	2	1	1	0	0	0	0	0	0	0
TOTAL	.233		163	15	38	3	1	4	15	12	23	5

PITCHER	W	L	ERA	G	GS	CG	SV	SHO	IP	H	ER	BB	SO
Bobby Castillo	0	0	0.00	1	0	0	0	0	1.0	0	0	0	1
Terry Forster	0	0	0.00	1	0	0	0	0	1.0	0	0	0	1
Burt Hooton	2	0	0.00	2	2	0	0	0	14.2	11	0	6	7
Steve Howe	0	0	0.00	2	0	0	0	0	2.0	1	0	0	2
Tom Niedenfuer	0	0	0.00	1	0	0	0	0	0.1	2	0	0	0
Alejandro Pena	0	0	0.00	2	0	0	0	0	2.1	1	0	0	0
Jerry Reuss	0	1	5.14	1	1	0	0	0	7.0	7	4	1	2
Fernando Valenzuela	1	1	2.45	2	2	0	0	0	14.2	10	4	5	10
Bob Welch	0	0	5.40	3	0	0	1	0	1.2	2	1	0	2
TOTAL	3	2	1.84	15	5	0	1	0	44.0	34	9	12	25

MON (E)

PLAYER/POS	AVG	G	AB	R	H	2B	3B	HR	RB	BB	SO	SB
Ray Burris, p	.000	2	6	0	0	0	0	0	0	0	4	0
Gary Carter, c	.438	5	16	3	7	1	0	0	0	4	2	0
Warren Cromartie, 1b	.167	5	18	0	3	1	0	0	2	0	2	0
Andre Dawson, of	.150	5	20	2	3	0	0	0	0	0	4	0
Terry Francona, of-1	.000	2	1	0	0	0	0	0	0	0	1	0
Woody Fryman, p	.000	1	0	0	0	0	0	0	0	0	0	0
Bill Gullickson, p	.000	2	3	0	0	0	0	0	0	1	2	0
Bill Lee, p	.000	1	0	0	0	0	0	0	0	0	0	0
Jerry Manuel, pr	.000	1	0	0	0	0	0	0	0	0	0	0
John Milner, ph	.000	1	1	0	0	0	0	0	0	0	1	0
Larry Parrish, 3b	.263	5	19	2	5	2	0	0	2	1	1	0
Tim Raines, of	.238	5	21	1	5	2	0	0	1	0	3	0
Jeff Reardon, p	.000	1	0	0	0	0	0	0	0	0	0	0
Steve Rogers, p	.000	2	2	0	0	0	0	0	0	0	0	0
Rodney Scott, 2b	.167	5	18	0	3	0	0	0	0	1	3	1
Elias Sosa, p	.000	1	0	0	0	0	0	0	0	0	0	0
Chris Speier, ss	.188	5	16	0	3	0	0	0	0	2	0	0
Tim Wallach, ph	.000	1	1	0	0	0	0	0	0	0	0	0
Jerry White, of	.313	5	16	2	5	1	0	1	3	3	1	1
TOTAL	.215		158	10	34	7	0	1	8	12	25	2

PITCHER	W	L	ERA	G	GS	CG	SV	SHO	IP	H	ER	BB	SO
Ray Burris	1	0	0.53	2	2	1	0	1	17.0	10	1	3	4
Woody Fryman	0	0	36.00	1	0	0	0	0	1.0	3	4	1	1
Bill Gullickson	0	2	2.51	2	2	0	0	0	14.1	12	4	6	12
Bill Lee	0	0	0.00	1	0	0	0	0	0.1	1	0	0	0
Jeff Reardon	0	0	27.00	1	0	0	0	0	1.0	3	3	0	0
Steve Rogers	1	1	1.80	2	1	1	0	0	10.0	8	2	1	6
Elias Sosa	0	0	0.00	1	0	0	0	0	0.1	1	0	1	0
TOTAL	2	3	2.86	10	5	2	0	1	44.0	38	14	12	23

GAME 1 AT LA OCT 13

MON	000	000	001	1	9	0
LA	020	000	03X	5	8	0

Pitchers: GULLICKSON, Reardon (8) vs HOOTON, Welch (8), Howe (9)
Home Runs: Guerrero-LA, Scioscia-LA
Attendance: 51,273

GAME 2 AT LA OCT 14

MON	020	001	000	3	10	1
LA	000	000	000	0	5	1

Pitchers: BURRIS vs VALENZUELA, Niedenfuer (7), Forster (7), Pena (7), Castillo (9)
Attendance: 53,463

GAME 3 AT MON OCT 16

LA	000	100	000	1	7	0
MON	000	004	00X	4	7	1

Pitchers: REUSS, Pena (8) vs ROGERS
Home Runs: White-MON
Attendance: 54,372

GAME 4 AT MON OCT 17

LA	001	000	024	7	12	1
MON	000	100	000	1	5	1

Pitchers: HOOTON, Welch (8), Howe (9) vs GULLICKSON, Fryman (8), Sosa (9), Lee (9)
Home Runs: Garvey-LA
Attendance: 54,499

GAME 5 AT MON OCT 19

LA	000	010	001	2	6	0
MON	100	000	000	1	3	1

Pitchers: VALENZUELA, Welch (9) vs Burris, ROGERS (9)
Home Runs: Monday-LA
Attendance: 36,491

The home field didn't seem to offer any advantage. First-half winner New York captured both games played in Milwaukee, but when the Series moved to Yankee Stadium for the final three games, the second-half champion Brewers evened the series.

Milwaukee took a 2–0 lead early in the opener, but New York erupted for four runs in the fourth on Oscar Gamble's two-run homer and Rick Cerone's double, and held on to win 5–3. In Game Two, rookie starter Dave Righetti fanned ten Brewers in his six innings and Goose Gossage's brilliant relief earned him his second save in two days as the Yankees took a 3–0 win on homers by Lou Piniella and Reggie Jackson.

Milwaukee, struggling against elimination, took the lead in the seventh inning of Game Three on Ted Simmons' two-run homer. New York tied the score at 3–3 in their half of the inning, but Paul Molitor broke the tie in the eighth with a solo homer. Simmons doubled home an insurance run later in the inning for a 5–3 Brewer win. The Brewers tagged Yankee pitching for only four hits in Game Four, but three of them came in the fourth inning and combined with a sacrifice fly to produce the Brewers' two runs. New York scored once in the sixth, but baserunning errors an inning later ended their only other scoring threat.

In the finale Milwaukee scored two early runs, but the Yankees (as they had done in the opener) took the lead with a four-run fourth— this time on home runs by Reggie Jackson and Oscar Gamble, and Rick Cerone's single. Cerone later hit an insurance homer, as the home team finally won a game— and captured the division crown.

New York Yankees, 3;
Milwaukee Brewers, 2

NY (E)

PLAYER/POS	AVG	G	AB	R	H	2B	3B	HR	RB	BB	SO	SB
Bobby Brown, pr	.000	1	0	0	0	0	0	0	0	0	0	0
Rick Cerone, c	.333	5	18	1	6	2	0	1	5	0	2	0
Ron Davis, p	.000	3	0	0	0	0	0	0	0	0	0	0
Barry Foote, ph	.000	1	0	0	0	0	0	0	0	0	0	0
Oscar Gamble, dh	.556	4	9	2	5	1	0	2	3	1	2	0
Rich Gossage, p	.000	3	0	0	0	0	0	0	0	0	0	0
Ron Guidry, p	.000	2	0	0	0	0	0	0	0	0	0	0
Reggie Jackson, of	.300	5	20	4	6	0	0	2	4	1	5	0
Tommy John, p	.000	1	0	0	0	0	0	0	0	0	0	0
Rudy May, p	.000	1	0	0	0	0	0	0	0	0	0	0
Larry Milbourne, ss	.316	5	19	4	6	1	0	0	0	0	1	0
Jerry Mumphrey, of	.095	5	21	2	2	0	0	0	0	0	1	1
Bobby Murcer, ph	.000	2	1	0	0	0	0	0	0	1	0	0
Graig Nettles, 3b	.059	5	17	1	1	0	0	0	1	3	1	0
Lou Piniella, dh	.200	4	10	1	2	1	0	1	3	0	0	0
Willie Randolph, 2b	.200	5	20	0	4	0	0	0	1	1	4	0
Rick Reuschel, p	.000	1	0	0	0	0	0	0	0	0	0	0
Dave Revering, 1b	.000	2	0	0	0	0	0	0	0	0	0	0
Dave Righetti, p	.000	2	0	0	0	0	0	0	0	0	0	0
Bob Watson, 1b	.438	5	16	2	7	0	0	0	1	1	1	0
Dave Winfield, of	.350	5	20	2	7	3	0	0	0	1	5	0
TOTAL	.269		171	19	46	8	0	6	18	9	22	1

PITCHER	W	L	ERA	G	GS	CG	SV	SHO	IP	H	ER	BB	SO
Ron Davis	1	0	0.00	3	0	0	0	0	6.0	1	0	2	6
Rich Gossage	0	0	0.00	3	0	0	3	0	6.2	3	0	2	8
Ron Guidry	0	0	5.40	2	2	0	0	0	8.1	11	5	3	8
Tommy John	0	1	6.43	1	1	0	0	0	7.0	8	5	2	0
Rudy May	0	0	0.00	1	0	0	0	0	2.0	1	0	0	1
Rick Reuschel	0	1	3.00	1	1	0	0	0	6.0	4	2	1	3
Dave Righetti	2	0	1.00	2	1	0	0	0	9.0	8	1	3	13
TOTAL	3	2	2.60	13	5	0	3	0	45.0	36	13	13	39

MIL (E)

PLAYER/POS	AVG	G	AB	R	H	2B	3B	HR	RB	BB	SO	SB
Sal Bando, 3b	.294	5	17	1	5	3	0	0	1	2	3	0
Dwight Bernard, p	.000	2	0	0	0	0	0	0	0	0	0	0
Thad Bosley, dh	.000	1	0	0	0	0	0	0	0	0	0	0
Mike Caldwell, p	.000	2	0	0	0	0	0	0	0	0	0	0
Cecil Cooper, 1b	.222	5	18	1	4	0	0	0	3	1	3	0
Jamie Easterly, p	.000	2	0	0	0	0	0	0	0	0	0	0
Marshall Edwards, of	.000	2	1	0	0	0	0	0	0	0	1	0
Rollie Fingers, p	.000	3	0	0	0	0	0	0	0	0	0	0
Jim Gantner, 2b	.143	4	14	1	2	1	0	0	0	0	2	0
Moose Haas, p	.000	2	0	0	0	0	0	0	0	0	0	0
Roy Howell, dh-3	.400	4	5	2	2	0	0	0	0	2	2	0
Randy Lerch, p	.000	1	0	0	0	0	0	0	0	0	0	0
Bob McClure, p	.000	3	0	0	0	0	0	0	0	0	0	0
Paul Molitor, of	.250	5	20	2	5	0	0	1	1	2	5	0
Don Money, 2b-1,dh-1	.000	2	3	0	0	0	0	0	0	0	0	0
Charlie Moore, of-2,dh-2	.222	4	9	0	2	0	0	0	1	1	2	0
Ben Oglivie, of	.167	5	18	0	3	1	0	0	1	0	7	0
Ed Romero, 2b	.500	1	2	1	1	0	0	0	0	0	1	0
Ted Simmons, c	.211	5	19	1	4	1	0	1	4	2	2	0
Jim Slaton, p	.000	4	0	0	0	0	0	0	0	0	0	0
Gorman Thomas, of-3,dh-2	.118	5	17	2	2	0	0	1	1	1	9	0
Pete Vuckovich, p	.000	2	0	0	0	0	0	0	0	0	0	0
Robin Yount, ss	.316	5	19	4	6	0	1	0	1	2	2	1
TOTAL	.222		162	13	36	6	1	3	13	13	39	1

PITCHER	W	L	ERA	G	GS	CG	SV	SHO	IP	H	ER	BB	SO
Dwight Bernard	0	0	0.00	2	0	0	0	0	2.1	0	0	0	0
Mike Caldwell	0	1	4.32	2	1	0	0	0	8.1	9	4	0	4
Jamie Easterly	0	0	6.75	2	0	0	0	0	1.1	2	1	0	1
Rollie Fingers	1	0	3.86	3	0	0	1	0	4.2	7	2	1	5
Moose Haas	0	2	9.45	2	2	0	0	0	6.2	13	7	1	1
Randy Lerch	0	0	1.50	1	1	0	0	0	6.0	3	1	4	3
Bob McClure	0	0	0.00	3	0	0	0	0	3.1	4	0	0	2
Jim Slaton	0	0	3.00	4	0	0	0	0	6.0	6	2	0	2
Pete Vuckovich	1	0	0.00	2	1	0	0	0	5.1	2	0	3	4
TOTAL	2	3	3.48	21	5	0	1	0	44.0	46	17	9	22

First-half winner Oakland, with the league's best win-loss record over the full season, swept the division title from second-half champ Kansas City (who, with a full-season record of 50–53, had become the only club in major-league history to qualify for postseason play with a losing record). Twice in the opener the Royals loaded the bases against Mike Norris with fewer than two outs, but both times failed to score. Meanwhile, after a Royal error had prolonged the A's fourth inning, Wayne Gross homered for three unearned Oakland runs. Dwayne Murphy's eighth-inning solo shot gave the A's a fourth run. The game ended with Norris possessor of a four-hit shutout.

Game Two was closer. Oakland's Tony Armas doubled in a run in the top of the first, and doubled home another in the eighth (his fourth hit of the game) to break a 1–1 tie and provide the margin needed for pitcher Steve McCatty's six-hit win. The A's Rick Langford yielded ten hits in Game Three (including Kansas City's only extra-base hit of the series, a double), but only one Royal scored, meanwhile the A's were sending four runs across the plate—three of them by Rickey Henderson, who reached base four times on pairs of hits and walks.

Oakland Athletics, 3;
Kansas City Royals, 0

KC (W)

PLAYER/POS	AVG	G	AB	R	H	2B	3B	HR	RB	BB	SO	SB
Willie Aikens, 1b	.333	3	9	0	3	0	0	0	0	3	2	0
George Brett, 3b	.167	3	12	0	2	0	0	0	0	0	0	0
Cesar Geronimo, pr	.000	1	0	0	0	0	0	0	0	0	0	0
Larry Gura, p	.000	1	0	0	0	0	0	0	0	0	0	0
Clint Hurdle, of	.273	3	11	0	3	0	0	0	0	1	1	0
Mike Jones, p	.000	1	0	0	0	0	0	0	0	0	0	0
Dennis Leonard, p	.000	1	0	0	0	0	0	0	0	0	0	0
Renie Martin, p	.000	2	0	0	0	0	0	0	0	0	0	0
Lee May, 1b	.000	1	0	0	0	0	0	0	0	0	0	0
Hal McRae, dh	.091	3	11	0	1	1	0	0	0	1	1	0
Amos Otis, of	.000	3	12	0	0	0	0	0	1	0	4	0
Dan Quisenberry, p	.000	1	0	0	0	0	0	0	0	0	0	0
U. L. Washington, ss	.222	3	9	0	2	0	0	0	0	0	1	0
John Wathan, c	.300	3	10	1	3	0	0	0	0	1	1	0
Frank White, 2b	.182	3	11	1	2	0	0	0	0	1	1	0
Willie Wilson, of	.308	3	13	0	4	0	0	0	1	0	0	0
TOTAL	.204		98	2	20	1	0	0	2	7	11	0

PITCHER	W	L	ERA	G	GS	CG	SV	SHO	IP	H	ER	BB	SO
Larry Gura	0	1	7.36	1	1	0	0	0	3.2	7	3	3	3
Mike Jones	0	1	2.25	1	1	0	0	0	8.0	9	2	0	2
Dennis Leonard	0	1	1.13	1	1	0	0	0	8.0	7	1	1	3
Renie Martin	0	0	0.00	2	0	0	0	0	5.1	1	0	2	2
Dan Quisenberry	0	0	0.00	1	0	0	0	0	1.0	1	0	0	0
TOTAL	0	3	2.08	6	3	0	0	0	26.0	25	6	6	10

OAK (W)

PLAYER/POS	AVG	G	AB	R	H	2B	3B	HR	RB	BB	SO	SB
Tony Armas, of	.545	3	11	1	6	2	0	0	3	1	1	0
Dave Beard, p	.000	1	0	0	0	0	0	0	0	0	0	0
Rick Bosetti, of	.000	1	0	0	0	0	0	0	0	0	0	0
Keith Drumright, dh	.250	1	4	0	1	0	0	0	0	0	0	0
Wayne Gross, 3b-1	.400	2	5	1	2	0	0	1	3	0	0	0
Mike Heath, c	.000	2	8	0	0	0	0	0	0	0	1	0
Rickey Henderson, of	.182	3	11	3	2	0	0	0	0	2	0	2
Cliff Johnson, dh	.286	2	7	0	2	1	0	0	0	0	1	0
Mickey Klutts, 3b	.143	2	7	0	1	0	0	0	0	0	1	0
Rick Langford, p	.000	1	0	0	0	0	0	0	0	0	0	0
Steve McCatty, p	.000	1	0	0	0	0	0	0	0	0	0	0
Dave McKay, 2b	.273	3	11	1	3	0	0	1	1	1	1	0
Kelvin Moore, 1b	.000	2	8	0	0	0	0	0	0	0	2	0
Dwayne Murphy, of	.545	3	11	4	6	1	0	1	2	1	1	0
Jeff Newman, c	.000	1	3	0	0	0	0	0	0	0	1	0
Mike Norris, p	.000	1	0	0	0	0	0	0	0	0	0	0
Rob Picciolo, ss	.333	1	3	0	1	0	0	0	0	0	0	0
Jim Spencer, 1b	.250	1	4	0	1	1	0	0	0	0	0	0
Fred Stanley, ss	.000	3	6	0	0	0	0	0	0	1	1	0
Tom Underwood, p	.000	1	0	0	0	0	0	0	0	0	0	0
TOTAL	.253		99	10	25	5	0	3	9	6	10	2

PITCHER	W	L	ERA	G	GS	CG	SV	SHO	IP	H	ER	BB	SO
Dave Beard	0	0	0.00	1	0	0	1	0	1.1	0	0	0	2
Rick Langford	1	0	1.23	1	1	0	0	0	7.1	10	1	0	3
Steve McCatty	1	0	1.00	1	1	1	0	0	9.0	6	1	4	3
Mike Norris	1	0	0.00	1	1	1	0	1	9.0	4	0	3	2
Tom Underwood	0	0	0.00	1	0	0	0	0	0.1	0	0	0	1
TOTAL	3	0	0.67	5	3	2	1	1	27.0	20	2	7	11

The A's scored only four runs to their opponents' twenty as the Yankees swept the series. And only two of the six Yankee pitchers permitted an Oakland runner to score, while not one of Oakland's eight pitchers held New York scoreless. Even so, two of the three games were closely contested.

Oakland's Mike Norris gave up a bases-loaded double to Graig Nettles in the first inning of Game One before settling down to pitch shutout ball. But the three runs Nettles drove in were more than enough, as Tommy John and two relievers held the A's to a single run.

Game Two was the series' only blowout, and even it remained close for three innings. But, led by a pair of three-run homers from Nettles and Lou Piniella, the Yankees parlayed nineteen hits into thirteen runs as Yankee reliever George Frazier held the A's scoreless over the final five frames.

Game Three remained tight until the ninth. Through eight innings the only run came on Yankee Willie Randolph's homer off Oakland starter Matt Keough. But in the top of the ninth, Graig Nettles tagged reliever Tom Underwood for his second bases-clearing double of the series. The three runs weren't really needed, as Dave Righetti, Ron Davis, and Goose Gossage combined to shut out the A's for the full nine.

New York Yankees (East), 3;
Oakland A's (West), 0

NY (E)

PLAYER/POS	AVG	G	AB	R	H	2B	3B	HR	RB	BB	SO	SB
Bobby Brown, of-2	1.000	3	1	2	1	0	0	0	0	0	0	0
Rick Cerone, c	.100	3	10	1	1	0	0	0	0	0	0	0
Ron Davis, p	.000	2	0	0	0	0	0	0	0	0	0	0
Barry Foote, c-1	1.000	2	1	0	1	0	0	0	0	0	0	0
George Frazier, p	.000	1	0	0	0	0	0	0	0	0	0	0
Oscar Gamble, dh-2,of-1	.167	3	6	2	1	0	0	0	0	1	5	3	0
Rich Gossage, p	.000	2	0	0	0	0	0	0	0	0	0	0
Reggie Jackson, of	.000	2	4	1	0	0	0	0	0	1	1	0	1
Tommy John, p	.000	1	0	0	0	0	0	0	0	0	0	0
Rudy May, p	.000	1	0	0	0	0	0	0	0	0	0	0
Larry Milbourne, ss	.462	3	13	4	6	0	0	0	1	0	0	0
Jerry Mumphrey, of	.500	3	12	2	6	1	0	0	0	3	2	0
Bobby Murcer, dh	.333	1	3	0	1	0	0	0	0	1	1	0
Graig Nettles, 3b	.500	3	12	2	6	2	0	1	9	1	0	0
Lou Piniella, dh-2,of-1	.600	3	5	2	3	0	0	1	3	0	0	0
Willie Randolph, 2b	.333	3	12	2	4	0	0	1	2	0	1	0
Dave Revering, 1b	.500	2	2	0	1	0	0	0	0	0	0	0
Dave Righetti, p	.000	1	0	0	0	0	0	0	0	0	0	0
Andre Robertson, ss	.000	1	1	0	0	0	0	0	0	0	0	0
Aurelio Rodriguez, 3b	.000	1	0	0	0	0	0	0	0	0	0	0
Bob Watson, 1b	.250	3	12	0	3	0	0	0	1	0	1	0
Dave Winfield, of	.154	3	13	2	2	1	0	0	2	2	2	1
TOTAL	.336		107	20	36	4	0	3	20	13	10	2

PITCHER	W	L	ERA	G	GS	CG	SV	SHO	IP	H	ER	BB	SO
Ron Davis	0	0	0.00	2	0	0	0	0	3.1	0	0	2	4
George Frazier	1	0	0.00	1	0	0	0	0	5.2	5	0	1	5
Rich Gossage	0	0	0.00	2	0	0	1	0	2.2	1	0	0	2
Tommy John	1	0	1.50	1	1	0	0	0	6.0	6	1	1	3
Rudy May	0	0	8.10	1	0	0	0	0	3.1	6	3	0	5
Dave Righetti	1	0	0.00	1	1	0	0	0	6.0	4	0	2	4
TOTAL	3	0	1.33	8	2	0	1	0	27.0	22	4	6	23

OAK (W)

PLAYER/POS	AVG	G	AB	R	H	2B	3B	HR	RB	BB	SO	SB
Tony Armas, of	.167	3	12	0	2	0	0	0	0	0	5	0
Dave Beard, p	.000	1	0	0	0	0	0	0	0	0	0	0
Rick Bosetti, of-1,dh-1	.250	2	4	1	1	1	0	0	0	0	1	0
Mike Davis, ph	1.000	1	1	0	1	0	0	0	0	0	0	0
Keith Drumright, dh-1	.000	3	4	0	0	0	0	0	0	1	0	0
Wayne Gross, 3b	.000	3	5	0	0	0	0	0	0	0	0	0
Mike Heath, c-2,of-1	.333	3	6	1	2	0	0	0	0	0	1	0
Rickey Henderson, of	.364	3	11	0	4	2	1	0	1	1	2	2
Cliff Johnson, dh	.000	2	6	0	0	0	0	0	0	2	2	0
Jeff Jones, p	.000	1	0	0	0	0	0	0	0	0	0	0
Matt Keough, p	.000	1	0	0	0	0	0	0	0	0	0	0
Brian Kingman, p	.000	1	0	0	0	0	0	0	0	0	0	0
Mickey Klutts, 3b	.429	3	7	1	3	0	0	0	0	0	1	0
Steve McCatty, p	.000	1	0	0	0	0	0	0	0	0	0	0
Dave McKay, 2b	.273	3	11	0	3	0	0	0	1	0	2	0
Kelvin Moore, 1b	.222	3	9	0	2	0	0	0	0	0	1	0
Dwayne Murphy, of	.250	3	8	0	2	1	0	0	1	2	3	0
Jeff Newman, c	.000	2	5	0	0	0	0	0	0	0	2	0
Mike Norris, p	.000	1	0	0	0	0	0	0	0	0	0	0
Bob Owchinko, p	.000	1	0	0	0	0	0	0	0	0	0	0
Rob Picciolo, ss	.200	2	5	1	1	0	0	0	0	0	2	0
Jim Spencer, 1b	.000	2	2	0	0	0	0	0	0	0	0	0
Fred Stanley, ss	.333	2	3	0	1	0	0	0	0	1	1	0
Tom Underwood, p	.000	2	0	0	0	0	0	0	0	0	0	0
TOTAL	.222		99	4	22	4	1	0	4	6	23	2

PITCHER	W	L	ERA	G	GS	CG	SV	SHO	IP	H	ER	BB	SO
Dave Beard	0	0	40.50	1	0	0	0	0	0.2	5	3	0	0
Jeff Jones	0	0	4.50	1	0	0	0	0	2.0	2	1	1	0
Matt Keough	0	1	1.08	1	1	0	0	0	8.1	7	1	6	2
Brian Kingman	0	0	81.00	1	0	0	0	0	0.1	3	3	0	0
Steve McCatty	0	1	13.50	1	1	0	0	0	3.1	6	5	2	2
Mike Norris	0	1	3.68	1	1	0	0	0	7.1	6	3	2	4
Bob Owchinko	0	0	5.40	1	0	0	0	0	1.2	3	1	0	0
Tom Underwood	0	0	13.50	2	0	0	0	0	1.1	4	2	2	2
TOTAL	0	3	6.84	9	3	0	0	0	25.0	36	19	13	10

GAME 1 AT NY OCT 13

OAK	000	010	000	1	6	1
NY	300	000	00X	3	7	1

Pitchers: NORRIS, Underwood (8) vs JOHN, Davis (7), Gossage (8)
Attendance: 55,740

GAME 2 AT NY OCT 14

OAK	001	200	000	3	11	1
NY	100	701	40X	13	19	0

Pitchers: McCATTY, Beard (4), Jones (5), Kingman (7), Owchinko (7) vs May, FRAZIER (4)
Home Runs: Piniella-NY, Nettles-NY
Attendance: 48,497

GAME 3 AT OAK OCT 15

NY	000	001	003	4	10	0
OAK	000	000	000	0	5	2

Pitchers: RIGHETTI, Davis (7), Gossage (9) vs KEOUGH, Underwood (9)
Home Runs: Randolph-NY
Attendance: 47,302

What the Yankees had done to the Dodgers three years earlier, the Dodgers now did to the Yankees in this, their eleventh meeting in the Series: they took the crown with four straight wins after losing the first two games. In the opener Bob Watson's first-inning three-run homer gave New York an insurmountable lead. Yankee starter Ron Guidry pitched seven strong innings, yielding just one run on a Steve Yeager homer, but two eighth-inning Dodger runs charged to reliever Ron Davis made things exciting until Yankee third baseman Graig Nettles dampened the rally with a splendid diving catch of Steve Garvey's line drive. In Game Two, Tommy John (now a Yankee) shut out his old teammates on three hits for seven innings. Reliever Goose Gossage completed the shutout, earning his second save in two days in the 3–0 Yankee victory.

But as the Series moved to Los Angeles, the Dodgers took the upper hand. Rookie ace Fernando Valenzuela experienced rocky going in the early innings of Game Three, yielding six hits (including home runs to Bob Watson and Rick Cerone) and four runs in the second and third innings. But Ron Cey's first-inning home run had given Los Angeles three early runs, and Dodger hitters added two more in the fifth as Valenzuela settled down to blank New York on three hits over the final six innings. The next day the Dodgers evened the Series with another close win. New York scored four times before the Dodgers got their first runs, but L.A. tied the game at 6–6 in the sixth and took an 8–6 lead an inning later. Reggie Jackson homered in the eighth to bring New York within one run of a tie, but they came no closer.

In Game Five, for the third day in a row, the Dodgers ovecame a Yankee lead to claim a one-run victory. Dodger pitcher Jerry Reuss gave the Yankees a run on two hits in the second inning, but shut them out on just three additional hits the rest of the way. Yankee starter Ron Guidry, meanwhile, stopped the Dodgers on two hits through the first six innings, but then gave up back-to-back homers to Pedro Guerrero and Steve Yeager in the seventh—runs enough for a 2–1 Dodger win. The final game was close for four innings, but in the fifth and sixth the Dodgers broke it open in on seven runs and coasted in on Steve Howe's 3⅔ innings of shutout relief to a 9–2 win and, including 1900, their sixth world championship.

Los Angeles Dodgers (NL), 4; New York Yankees (AL), 2

LA (N)

PLAYER/POS	AVG	G	AB	R	H	2B	3B	HR	RB	BB	SO	SB
Dusty Baker, of	.167	6	24	3	4	0	0	0	0	1	6	0
Bobby Castillo, p	.000	1	0	0	0	0	0	0	0	0	0	0
Ron Cey, 3b	.350	6	20	3	7	0	0	1	6	3	3	0
Terry Forster, p	.000	2	0	0	0	0	0	0	0	0	0	0
Steve Garvey, 1b	.417	6	24	3	10	1	0	0	2	5	0
Dave Goltz, p	.000	2	0	0	0	0	0	0	0	0	0	0
Pedro Guerrero, of	.333	6	21	2	7	1	1	2	7	2	6	0
Burt Hooton, p	.000	2	4	1	0	0	0	0	0	1	3	0
Steve Howe, p	.000	3	2	0	0	0	0	0	0	0	2	0
Jay Johnstone, ph	.667	3	3	1	2	0	0	1	3	0	0	0
Ken Landreaux, of-3	.167	5	6	1	1	1	0	0	0	2	1
Davey Lopes, 2b	.227	6	22	6	5	1	0	0	2	4	3	4
Rick Monday, of-4	.231	5	13	1	3	1	0	0	0	3	6	0
Tom Niedenfuer, p	.000	2	0	0	0	0	0	0	0	0	0	0
Jerry Reuss, p	.000	2	3	0	0	0	0	0	0	1	2	0
Bill Russell, ss	.240	6	25	1	6	0	0	0	2	0	1	1
Steve Sax, 2b-1	.000	2	1	0	0	0	0	0	0	0	0	0
Mike Scioscia, c	.250	3	4	1	1	0	0	0	0	1	0	0
Reggie Smith, ph	.500	2	2	0	1	0	0	0	0	0	1	0
Dave Stewart, p	.000	2	0	0	0	0	0	0	0	0	0	0
Derrel Thomas, of-3,3b-2,ss-1	.000	5	7	2	0	0	0	0	0	1	2	0
Fernando Valenzuela, p	.000	1	3	0	0	0	0	0	0	1	0	0
Bob Welch, p	.000	1	0	0	0	0	0	0	0	0	0	0
Steve Yeager, c	.286	6	14	2	4	1	0	2	4	0	2	0
TOTAL	.258		198	27	51	6	1	6	26	20	44	6

PITCHER	W	L	ERA	G	GS	CG	SV	SHO	IP	H	ER	BB	SO
Bobby Castillo	0	0	9.00	1	0	0	0	0	1.0	0	1	5	0
Terry Forster	0	0	0.00	2	0	0	0	0	2.0	1	0	3	0
Dave Goltz	0	0	5.40	2	0	0	0	0	3.1	4	2	1	2
Burt Hooton	1	1	1.59	2	2	0	0	0	11.1	8	2	9	3
Steve Howe	1	0	3.86	3	0	0	1	0	7.0	7	3	1	4
Tom Niedenfuer	0	0	0.00	2	0	0	0	0	5.0	3	0	1	0
Jerry Reuss	1	1	3.86	2	2	1	0	0	11.2	10	5	3	8
Dave Stewart	0	0	0.00	2	0	0	0	0	1.2	1	0	2	1
Fernando Valenzuela	1	0	4.00	1	1	1	0	0	9.0	9	4	7	6
Bob Welch	0	0	INF	1	1	0	0	0	0.0	3	2	1	0
TOTAL	4	2	3.29	18	6	2	1	0	52.0	46	19	33	24

NY (A)

PLAYER/POS	AVG	G	AB	R	H	2B	3B	HR	RB	BB	SO	SB
Bobby Brown, of-2	.000	4	1	1	0	0	0	0	0	0	1	0
Rick Cerone, c	.190	6	21	2	4	1	0	1	3	4	2	0
Ron Davis, p	.000	4	0	0	0	0	0	0	0	0	0	0
Barry Foote, ph	.000	1	1	0	0	0	0	0	0	0	1	0
George Frazier, p	.000	3	2	0	0	0	0	0	0	0	1	0
Oscar Gamble, of-2	.333	3	6	1	2	0	0	0	1	1	0	0
Rich Gossage, p	.000	3	1	0	0	0	0	0	0	0	1	0
Ron Guidry, p	.000	2	5	0	0	0	0	0	0	0	3	0
Reggie Jackson, of	.333	3	12	3	4	1	0	1	1	2	3	0
Tommy John, p	.000	3	2	0	0	0	0	0	0	0	0	0
Dave LaRoche, p	.000	1	0	0	0	0	0	0	0	0	0	0
Rudy May, p	.000	3	1	0	0	0	0	0	0	0	0	0
Larry Milbourne, ss	.250	6	20	2	5	2	0	0	3	4	0	0
Jerry Mumphrey, of	.200	5	15	2	3	0	0	0	0	3	2	1
Bobby Murcer, ph	.000	4	3	0	0	0	0	0	0	0	0	0
Graig Nettles, 3b	.400	3	10	1	4	1	0	0	1	1	0	0
Lou Piniella, of-3	.438	6	16	2	7	1	0	0	3	0	1	1
Willie Randolph, 2b	.222	6	18	5	4	1	1	2	3	9	0	1
Rick Reuschel, p	.000	2	2	0	0	0	0	0	0	0	1	0
Dave Righetti, p	.000	1	1	0	0	0	0	0	0	0	1	0
Andre Robertson, pr	.000	1	0	0	0	0	0	0	0	0	0	0
Aurelio Rodriguez, 3b-3	.417	4	12	1	5	0	0	0	0	1	2	0
Bob Watson, 1b	.318	6	22	2	7	1	0	2	7	3	0	0
Dave Winfield, of	.045	6	22	0	1	0	0	0	1	5	4	1
TOTAL	.238		193	22	46	8	1	6	22	33	24	4

PITCHER	W	L	ERA	G	GS	CG	SV	SHO	IP	H	ER	BB	SO
Ron Davis	0	0	23.14	4	0	0	0	0	2.1	4	6	5	4
George Frazier	0	3	17.18	3	0	0	0	0	3.2	9	7	3	2
Rich Gossage	0	0	0.00	3	0	0	2	0	5.0	2	0	2	5
Ron Guidry	1	1	1.93	2	2	0	0	0	14.0	8	3	4	15
Tommy John	1	0	0.69	3	2	0	0	0	13.0	11	1	0	8
Dave LaRoche	0	0	0.00	1	0	0	0	0	1.0	0	0	0	2
Rudy May	0	0	2.84	3	0	0	0	0	6.1	5	2	1	5
Rick Reuschel	0	0	4.91	2	1	0	0	0	3.2	7	2	3	2
Dave Righetti	0	0	13.50	1	1	0	0	0	2.0	5	3	2	1
TOTAL	2	4	4.24	22	6	0	2	0	51.0	51	24	20	44

GAME 1 AT NY OCT 20

LA	000 010 020	3	5	0
NY	301 100 00X	5	6	0

Pitchers: REUSS, Castillo (3), Goltz (4), Niedenfuer (5), Stewart (8) vs GUIDRY, Davis (8), Gossage (8)
Home Runs: Watson-NY, Yeager-LA
Attendance: 56,470

GAME 2 AT NY OCT 21

LA	000 000 000	0	4	2
NY	000 010 02X	3	6	1

Pitchers: HOOTON, Forster (7), Howe (8), Stewart (8) vs JOHN, Gossage (8)
Attendance: 56,505

GAME 3 AT LA OCT 23

NY	022 000 000	4	9	0
LA	300 020 00X	5	11	1

Pitchers: Righetti, FRAZIER (3), May (5), Davis (8) vs VALENZUELA
Home Runs: Cey-LA, Watson-NY, Cerone-NY
Attendance: 56,236

GAME 4 AT LA OCT 24

NY	211 002 010	7	13	1
LA	002 013 20X	8	14	2

Pitchers: Reuschel, May (4), Davis (5), FRAZIER (5), John (7) vs Welch, Goltz (1), Forster (4), Niedenfuer (5), HOWE (7)
Home Runs: Johnstone-LA, Randolph-NY, Jackson-NY
Attendance: 56,242

GAME 5 AT LA OCT 25

NY	010 000 000	1	5	0
LA	000 000 20X	2	4	3

Pitchers: GUIDRY, Gossage (8) vs REUSS
Home Runs: Guerrero-LA, Yeager-LA
Attendance: 56,115

GAME 6 AT NY OCT 28

LA	000 134 010	9	13	1
NY	001 001 000	2	7	2

Pitchers: HOOTON, Howe (6) vs John, FRAZIER (5), Davis (6), Reuschel (6), May (7), LaRoche (9)
Home Runs: Guerrero-LA, Randolph-NY
Attendance: 56,513

The official records show Atlanta ahead and threatening only once in a three-game series swept by the Cardinals. But in the original Game One, Phil Niekro held a slim 1–0 Atlanta lead in the fifth inning when rain wiped out the game just before it could become official.

In the first official game, the Braves scored nothing at all as Bob Forsch held them to three hits. Atlanta's Pascual Perez gave up only one run through the first five innings, but the Cardinals exploded for five runs in the sixth to put the game away. Following another rainout, Niekro tried again in Game Two. He gave up a run in the first, but Atlanta came back with three before he yielded a second run in the sixth. Gene Garber, who relieved Niekro, gave up the tying run in the eighth and lost the game in the bottom of the ninth on Ken Oberkfell's RBI liner over the center fielder's head.

Joaquin Andujar shut out the Braves through six innings of Game Three before giving up two runs in the seventh. But by then St. Louis had scored five times. Bruce Sutter retired the last seven Braves in relief of Andujar, and the Cardinals had their pennant.

St. Louis Cardinals (East), 3;
Atlanta Braves (West), 0

STL (E)

PLAYER/POS	AVG	G	AB	R	H	2B	3B	HR	RB	BB	SO	SB
Joaquin Andujar, p	.000	1	1	0	0	0	0	0	0	0	1	0
Doug Bair, p	.000	1	0	0	0	0	0	0	0	0	0	0
Steve Braun, ph	.000	1	1	0	0	0	0	0	0	0	0	0
Bob Forsch, p	.667	1	3	1	2	0	0	0	1	0	0	0
David Green, of	1.000	2	1	1	1	0	0	0	0	0	0	0
George Hendrick, of	.308	3	13	2	4	0	0	0	2	1	2	0
Keith Hernandez, 1b	.333	3	12	3	4	0	0	0	1	2	3	0
Tommy Herr, 2b	.231	3	13	1	3	1	0	0	0	1	2	0
Willie McGee, of	.308	3	13	4	4	0	2	1	5	0	5	0
Ken Oberkfell, 3b	.200	3	15	1	3	0	0	0	2	0	0	0
Darrell Porter, c	.556	3	9	3	5	3	0	0	1	5	2	0
Lonnie Smith, of	.273	3	11	1	3	0	0	0	1	0	1	0
Ozzie Smith, ss	.556	3	9	0	5	0	0	0	3	3	0	1
John Stuper, p	.000	1	1	0	0	0	0	0	0	0	0	0
Bruce Sutter, p	.000	2	1	0	0	0	0	0	0	0	0	0
TOTAL	.330		103	17	34	4	2	1	16	12	16	1

PITCHER	W	L	ERA	G	GS	CG	SV	SHO	IP	H	ER	BB	SO
Joaquin Andujar	1	0	2.70	1	1	0	0	0	6.2	6	2	2	4
Doug Bair	0	0	0.00	1	0	0	0	0	1.0	2	0	3	0
Bob Forsch	1	0	0.00	1	1	1	0	1	9.0	3	0	0	6
John Stuper	0	0	3.00	1	1	0	0	0	6.0	4	2	1	4
Bruce Sutter	1	0	0.00	2	0	0	1	0	4.1	0	0	0	1
TOTAL	3	0	1.33	6	3	1	1	1	27.0	15	4	6	15

ATL (W)

PLAYER/POS	AVG	G	AB	R	H	2B	3B	HR	RB	BB	SO	SB
Steve Bedrosian, p	.000	2	0	0	0	0	0	0	0	0	0	0
Bruce Benedict, c	.250	3	8	1	2	1	0	0	0	2	1	0
Brett Butler, of-1	.000	2	1	0	0	0	0	0	0	0	0	0
Rick Camp, p	.000	1	0	0	0	0	0	0	0	0	0	0
Chris Chambliss, 1b	.000	3	10	0	0	0	0	0	0	1	0	0
Gene Garber, p	.000	2	1	0	0	0	0	0	0	0	0	0
Terry Harper, of	.000	1	1	1	0	0	0	0	0	0	0	0
Bob Horner, 3b	.091	3	11	0	1	0	0	0	0	0	2	0
Glenn Hubbard, 2b	.222	3	9	1	2	0	0	0	1	0	3	0
Rick Mahler, p	.000	1	0	0	0	0	0	0	0	0	0	0
Donnie Moore, p	.000	2	0	0	0	0	0	0	0	0	0	0
Dale Murphy, of	.273	3	11	1	3	0	0	0	0	0	2	1
Phil Niekro, p	.000	1	0	0	0	0	0	0	1	0	0	0
Pascual Perez, p	.000	2	3	0	0	0	0	0	0	0	1	0
Biff Pocoroba, ph	.000	1	1	0	0	0	0	0	0	0	0	0
Rafael Ramirez, ss	.182	3	11	1	2	0	0	0	1	1	1	0
Jerry Royster, of-3,3b-1	.182	3	11	0	2	0	0	0	0	0	2	0
Bob Walk, p	.000	1	0	0	0	0	0	0	0	0	0	0
Claudell Washington, of	.333	3	9	0	3	0	0	0	0	2	2	0
Larry Whisenton, ph	.000	2	2	0	0	0	0	0	0	0	1	0
TOTAL	.169		89	5	15	1	0	0	3	6	15	1

PITCHER	W	L	ERA	G	GS	CG	SV	SHO	IP	H	ER	BB	SO
Steve Bedrosian	0	0	18.00	2	0	0	0	0	1.0	3	2	1	2
Rick Camp	0	1	36.00	1	1	0	0	0	1.0	4	4	1	0
Gene Garber	0	1	8.10	2	0	0	0	0	3.1	4	3	1	3
Rick Mahler	0	0	0.00	1	0	0	0	0	1.2	3	0	2	0
Donnie Moore	0	0	0.00	2	0	0	0	0	2.2	2	0	0	1
Phil Niekro	0	0	3.00	1	1	0	0	0	6.0	6	2	4	5
Pascual Perez	0	1	5.19	2	1	0	0	0	8.2	10	5	2	4
Bob Walk	0	0	9.00	1	0	0	0	0	1.0	2	1	1	1
TOTAL	0	3	6.04	12	3	0	0	0	25.1	34	17	12	16

GAME 1 AT STL OCT 7

ATL	000 000 000	0 3 0
STL	001 005 01X	7 13 1

Pitchers: PEREZ, Bedrosian (6), Moore (6), Walk (8) vs FORSCH
Attendance: 53,008

GAME 2 AT STL OCT 9

ATL	002 010 000	3 6 0
STL	100 001 011	4 9 1

Pitchers: Niekro, GARBER (7) vs Stuper, Bair (7), SUTTER (8)
Attendance: 53,408

GAME 3 AT ATL OCT 10

STL	040 010 001	6 12 0
ATL	000 000 200	2 6 1

Pitchers: ANDUJAR, Sutter (7) vs CAMP, Perez (2), Moore (5), Mahler (7), Bedrosian (8), Garber (9)
Home Runs: McGee-STL
Attendance: 52,173

For the first time in LCS play, a club won the first two games but lost the series. The Angels overcame a 1–3 deficit to take Game One, with four runs in the third and three more later, while starter Tommy John settled down to stop the Brewers through the final six innings. In Game Two Bruce Kison prevailed, as the Angels built a 4–0 lead over Milwaukee and Pete Vuckovich before Kison gave up what proved to be a harmless two-run homer to Paul Molitor in the fifth.

With three chances to clinch the pennant, California three times fell short. In the third game, their three eighth-inning runs couldn't catch the Brewers, who already had five. In Game Four, Don Baylor's eighth-inning grand slam completed Angel scoring at five runs, but Milwaukee had already scored seven, and they added two more. In the finale, Kison held a 3–2 lead when he was relieved after five innings. But Cecil Cooper singled off Luis Sanchez in the seventh (with two out and the bases loaded) for two runs and a Brewer lead. Bob McClure and Pete Ladd held off the Angels through the final two innings, and the Brewers were on their way to their first World Series.

Milwaukee Brewers (East), 3; California Angels (West), 2

MIL (E)

PLAYER/POS	AVG	G	AB	R	H	2B	3B	HR	RB	BB	SO	SB
Dwight Bernard, p	.000	1	0	0	0	0	0	0	0	0	0	0
Mark Brouhard, of	.750	1	4	4	3	1	0	1	3	0	0	0
Mike Caldwell, p	.000	1	0	0	0	0	0	0	0	0	0	0
Cecil Cooper, 1b	.150	5	20	1	3	2	0	0	4	0	6	0
Marshall Edwards, dh-2,of-1	.000	3	1	2	0	0	0	0	0	0	0	1
Jim Gantner, 2b	.188	5	16	1	3	0	0	0	2	1	1	0
Moose Haas, p	.000	1	0	0	0	0	0	0	0	0	0	0
Roy Howell, dh	.000	1	3	0	0	0	0	0	0	0	1	0
Pete Ladd, p	.000	3	0	0	0	0	0	0	0	0	0	0
Bob McClure, p	.000	1	0	0	0	0	0	0	0	0	0	0
Paul Molitor, 3b	.316	5	19	4	6	1	0	2	5	2	3	1
Don Money, dh	.182	4	11	2	2	0	0	0	1	3	1	0
Charlie Moore, of	.462	5	13	3	6	0	0	0	0	1	2	0
Ben Oglivie, of	.133	4	15	1	2	0	0	1	1	0	3	0
Ted Simmons, c	.167	5	18	3	3	0	0	0	1	1	4	0
Jim Slaton, p	.000	2	0	0	0	0	0	0	0	0	0	0
Don Sutton, p	.000	1	0	0	0	0	0	0	0	0	0	0
Gorman Thomas, of	.067	5	15	1	1	0	0	1	3	2	7	0
Pete Vuckovich, p	.000	2	0	0	0	0	0	0	0	0	0	0
Robin Yount, ss	.250	5	16	1	4	0	0	0	0	5	0	0
TOTAL	.219		151	23	33	4	0	5	20	15	28	2

PITCHER	W	L	ERA	G	GS	CG	SV	SHO	IP	H	ER	BB	SO
Dwight Bernard	0	0	0.00	1	0	0	0	0	1.0	0	0	0	0
Mike Caldwell	0	1	15.00	1	1	0	0	0	3.0	7	5	1	2
Moose Haas	1	0	4.91	1	1	0	0	0	7.1	5	4	5	7
Pete Ladd	0	0	0.00	3	0	0	2	0	3.1	0	0	0	5
Bob McClure	1	0	0.00	1	0	0	0	0	1.2	2	0	0	0
Jim Slaton	0	0	1.93	2	0	0	1	0	4.2	3	1	1	3
Don Sutton	1	0	3.52	1	1	0	0	0	7.2	8	3	2	9
Pete Vuckovich	0	1	4.40	2	2	1	0	0	14.1	15	7	7	8
TOTAL	3	2	4.19	12	5	1	3	0	43.0	40	20	16	34

CAL (W)

PLAYER/POS	AVG	G	AB	R	H	2B	3B	HR	RB	BB	SO	SB
Don Baylor, dh	.294	5	17	2	5	1	1	1	10	2	0	0
Juan Beniquez, of	.000	2	0	0	0	0	0	0	0	0	0	0
Bob Boone, c	.250	5	16	3	4	0	0	1	4	0	2	0
Rod Carew, 1b	.176	5	17	2	3	1	0	0	0	4	4	1
Bobby Clark, of	.000	2	0	0	0	0	0	0	0	0	0	0
Doug De Cinces, 3b	.316	5	19	5	6	2	0	0	0	1	5	0
Brian Downing, of	.158	5	19	4	3	1	0	0	0	3	2	0
Tim Foli, ss	.125	5	16	0	2	0	0	0	0	1	0	3	0
Dave Goltz, p	.000	1	0	0	0	0	0	0	0	0	0	0
Bobby Grich, 2b	.200	5	15	1	3	1	0	0	1	2	7	0
Andy Hassler, p	.000	2	0	0	0	0	0	0	0	0	0	0
Reggie Jackson, of	.111	5	18	2	2	0	0	1	2	2	7	0
Ron Jackson, ph	1.000	1	1	0	1	0	0	0	0	0	0	0
Tommy John, p	.000	2	0	0	0	0	0	0	0	0	0	0
Bruce Kison, p	.000	2	0	0	0	0	0	0	0	0	0	0
Fred Lynn, of	.611	5	18	4	11	2	0	1	5	2	3	0
Luis Sanchez, p	.000	2	0	0	0	0	0	0	0	0	0	0
Rob Wilfong, ph	.000	2	1	0	0	0	0	0	0	0	1	0
Mike Witt, p	.000	1	0	0	0	0	0	0	0	0	0	0
Geoff Zahn, p	.000	1	0	0	0	0	0	0	0	0	0	0
TOTAL	.255		157	23	40	8	1	4	23	16	34	1

PITCHER	W	L	ERA	G	GS	CG	SV	SHO	IP	H	ER	BB	SO
Dave Goltz	0	0	7.36	1	0	0	0	0	3.2	4	3	2	2
Andy Hassler	0	0	0.00	2	0	0	0	0	2.2	0	0	0	2
Tommy John	1	1	5.11	2	2	1	0	0	12.1	11	7	6	6
Bruce Kison	1	0	1.93	2	2	1	0	0	14.0	8	3	3	12
Luis Sanchez	0	1	6.75	2	0	0	0	0	2.2	4	2	1	1
Mike Witt	0	0	6.00	1	0	0	0	0	3.0	2	2	2	3
Geoff Zahn	0	1	7.36	1	1	0	0	0	3.2	4	3	1	2
TOTAL	2	3	4.29	11	5	2	0	0	42.0	33	20	15	28

The Series was anticipated as a matchup of Cardinal speed and Brewer power. In the event, though, St. Louis outslugged the Brewers and wound up with their tenth world championship.

The Brewers, in their first World Series, looked unstoppable in the opening game. Hammering four Cardinal pitchers for seventeen hits (including a record five for Paul Molitor), they scored ten runs while pitcher Mike Caldwell was shutting out the Cards on three hits. In the second game Milwaukee continued the onslaught, building an early 3–0 lead. But St. Louis finally got on the scoreboard with two runs in the last of the third, and tied the game at 4–4 in the sixth on Darrell Porter's two-RBI double. And the Cards won the game on a bases-loaded walk in the eighth as relievers Doug Bair and Bruce Sutter held the Brewers scoreless over the final four innings.

St. Louis pushed into the Series lead in Game Three, thanks mostly to the 6⅓ shutout innings of starter Joaquin Andujar and the fielding and batting of center fielder Willie McGee. McGee drove in four of the six Cardinal runs with a pair of homers and prevented an extra-base hit and a two-run Brewer homer with leaping catches in the first and final innings. The Cards pressed their advantage in Game Four with four early runs. But in the last of the seventh (with the score now 5–1), an error by Cardinal pitcher Dave LaPoint opened the way for Milwaukee to win the game with six two-out runs on a barrage of hits (and the added assistance of a pair of walks and a wild pitch).

Brewer pitcher Mike Caldwell wasn't as effective in Game Five as he had been in the opener, yielding fourteen hits and four runs in 8⅓ innings of work. But he was never behind in the game as his teammates, with eleven hits of their own (four of them by Robin Yount, including a home run) and several fielding gems put Milwaukee ahead again in the Series with a 6–4 win.

The Cards had their backs to the wall as the Series moved to St. Louis for the final games. But in Game Six the Cards responded to their opening-game humiliation with a laugher of their own, 13–1, on John Stuper's four-hitter. And in the finale they rocked Brewer ace Pete Vuckovich and three relievers for fifteen hits and a 6–3 victory that gave starter Joaquin Andujar his second Series win and reliever Bruce Sutter his second save.

St. Louis Cardinals (NL), 4;
Milwaukee Brewers (AL), 3

STL (N)

PLAYER/POS	AVG	G	AB	R	H	2B	3B	HR	RB	BB	SO	SB
Joaquin Andujar, p	.000	2	0	0	0	0	0	0	0	0	0	0
Doug Bair, p	.000	3	0	0	0	0	0	0	0	0	0	0
Steve Braun, dh	.500	2	2	0	1	0	0	0	2	1	0	0
Glenn Brummer, c	.000	1	0	0	0	0	0	0	0	0	0	0
Bob Forsch, p	.000	2	0	0	0	0	0	0	0	0	0	0
David Green, of-4,dh-3	.200	7	10	3	2	1	1	0	0	1	3	0
George Hendrick, of	.321	7	28	5	9	0	0	0	5	2	2	0
Keith Hernandez, 1b	.259	7	27	4	7	2	0	1	8	4	2	0
Tommy Herr, 2b	.160	7	25	2	4	2	0	0	5	3	2	0
Dane Iorg, dh	.529	5	17	4	9	4	1	0	1	0	0	0
Jim Kaat, p	.000	4	0	0	0	0	0	0	0	0	0	0
Jeff Lahti, p	.000	2	0	0	0	0	0	0	0	0	0	0
Dave LaPoint, p	.000	2	0	0	0	0	0	0	0	0	0	0
Willie McGee, of	.240	6	25	6	6	0	0	2	5	1	3	2
Ken Oberkfell, 3b	.292	7	24	4	7	1	0	0	1	2	1	2
Darrell Porter, c	.286	7	28	1	8	2	0	1	5	1	4	0
Mike Ramsey, 3b-2	.000	3	1	1	0	0	0	0	0	0	1	0
Lonnie Smith, of-6,dh-1	.321	7	28	6	9	4	1	0	1	1	5	2
Ozzie Smith, ss	.208	7	24	3	5	0	0	0	1	3	0	1
John Stuper, p	.000	2	0	0	0	0	0	0	0	0	0	0
Bruce Sutter, p	.000	4	0	0	0	0	0	0	0	0	0	0
Gene Tenace, dh-1	.000	5	6	0	0	0	0	0	0	1	2	0
TOTAL	.273		245	39	67	16	3	4	34	20	26	7

PITCHER	W	L	ERA	G	GS	CG	SV	SHO	IP	H	ER	BB	SO
Joaquin Andujar	2	0	1.35	2	2	0	0	0	13.1	10	2	1	4
Doug Bair	0	1	9.00	3	0	0	0	0	2.0	2	2	2	3
Bob Forsch	0	2	4.97	2	2	0	0	0	12.2	18	7	3	4
Jim Kaat	0	0	3.86	4	0	0	0	0	2.1	4	1	2	2
Jeff Lahti	0	0	10.80	2	0	0	0	0	1.2	4	2	1	1
Dave LaPoint	0	0	3.24	2	1	0	0	0	8.1	10	3	2	3
John Stuper	1	0	3.46	2	2	1	0	0	13.0	10	5	5	5
Bruce Sutter	1	0	4.70	4	0	0	2	0	7.2	6	4	3	6
TOTAL	4	3	3.84	21	7	1	2	0	61.0	64	26	19	28

MIL (A)

PLAYER/POS	AVG	G	AB	R	H	2B	3B	HR	RB	BB	SO	SB
Dwight Bernard, p	.000	1	0	0	0	0	0	0	0	0	0	0
Mike Caldwell, p	.000	3	0	0	0	0	0	0	0	0	0	0
Cecil Cooper, 1b	.286	7	28	3	8	1	0	1	6	1	1	0
Marshall Edwards, of	.000	1	0	0	0	0	0	0	0	0	0	0
Jim Gantner, 2b	.333	7	24	5	8	4	1	0	4	1	1	0
Moose Haas, p	.000	2	0	0	0	0	0	0	0	0	0	0
Roy Howell, dh	.000	4	11	1	0	0	0	0	0	0	3	0
Pete Ladd, p	.000	1	0	0	0	0	0	0	0	0	0	0
Bob McClure, p	.000	5	0	0	0	0	0	0	0	0	0	0
Doc Medich, p	.000	1	0	0	0	0	0	0	0	0	0	0
Paul Molitor, 3b	.355	7	31	5	11	0	0	0	3	2	4	1
Don Money, dh-4	.231	5	13	4	3	1	0	0	1	2	3	0
Charlie Moore, of	.346	7	26	3	9	3	0	0	2	1	0	0
Ben Oglivie, of	.222	7	27	4	6	0	1	1	1	2	4	0
Ted Simmons, c	.174	7	23	2	4	0	0	2	3	5	3	0
Jim Slaton, p	.000	2	0	0	0	0	0	0	0	0	0	0
Don Sutton, p	.000	2	0	0	0	0	0	0	0	0	0	0
Gorman Thomas, of	.115	7	26	0	3	0	0	0	3	2	7	0
Pete Vuckovich, p	.000	2	0	0	0	0	0	0	0	0	0	0
Ned Yost, c	.000	1	0	0	0	0	0	0	0	1	0	0
Robin Yount, ss	.414	7	29	6	12	3	0	1	6	2	2	0
TOTAL	.269		238	33	64	12	2	5	29	19	28	1

PITCHER	W	L	ERA	G	GS	CG	SV	SHO	IP	H	ER	BB	SO
Dwight Bernard	0	0	0.00	1	0	0	0	0	1.0	0	0	0	1
Mike Caldwell	2	0	2.04	3	2	1	0	1	17.2	19	4	3	6
Moose Haas	0	0	7.36	2	1	0	0	0	7.1	8	6	3	4
Pete Ladd	0	0	0.00	1	0	0	0	0	0.2	1	0	2	0
Bob McClure	0	2	4.15	5	0	0	2	0	4.1	5	2	3	5
Doc Medich	0	0	18.00	1	0	0	0	0	2.0	5	4	1	0
Jim Slaton	1	0	0.00	2	0	0	0	0	2.2	1	0	2	1
Don Sutton	0	1	7.84	2	2	0	0	0	10.1	12	9	1	5
Pete Vuckovich	0	1	4.50	2	2	0	0	0	14.0	16	7	5	4
TOTAL	3	4	4.80	19	7	1	2	1	60.0	67	32	20	26

The Dodgers earned only four runs off Philadelphia pitching, and even though they doubled their run total to eight on unearned runs, the Phillies scored twice that number to take the pennant in four games.

Mike Schmidt homered off Jerry Reuss in the first inning of the opener for the game's only run. Phillie starter Steve Carlton loaded the bases in the eighth, but Al Holland came on to get the third out and preserve the shutout. The Phillies also scored only one run in the second game, on Gary Matthews's homer off Fernando Valenzuela in the second. But this time the run only tied the score, and in the fifth Pedro Guerrero tripled in two unearned runs to give Valenzuela the Dodgers' only win.

The Phillies' Charlie Hudson hurled the series' only complete game—a four-hitter—to win Game Three. Gary Matthews's four hits in Game Three and Four included his second and third series homers, and drove in half the Phillies' fourteen runs as they took the two games by identical 7–2 scores.

Philadelphia Phillies (East), 3;
Los Angeles Dodgers (West), 1

PHI (E)

PLAYER/POS	AVG	G	AB	R	H	2B	3B	HR	RB	BB	SO	SB
Steve Carlton, p	.200	2	5	0	1	0	0	0	0	0	3	0
Ivan DeJesus, ss	.250	4	12	0	3	0	0	0	1	3	3	0
John Denny, p	.000	1	1	0	0	0	0	0	0	0	0	0
Bob Dernier, of	.000	1	0	0	0	0	0	0	0	0	0	0
Bo Diaz, c	.154	4	13	0	2	1	0	0	0	2	1	0
Greg Gross, of-3	.000	4	5	1	0	0	0	0	0	2	2	0
Von Hayes, of-1	.000	2	2	0	0	0	0	0	0	0	0	0
Al Holland, p	.000	2	0	0	0	0	0	0	0	0	0	0
Charles Hudson, p	.000	1	4	0	0	0	0	0	0	0	3	0
Joe Lefebvre, of-1	.000	2	2	0	0	0	0	0	1	0	1	0
Sixto Lezcano, of	.308	4	13	2	4	0	0	1	2	1	1	0
Garry Maddox, of	.273	3	11	0	3	1	0	0	1	0	1	0
Gary Matthews, of	.429	4	14	4	6	0	0	3	8	2	1	1
Joe Morgan, 2b	.067	4	15	1	1	0	0	0	0	2	1	0
Tony Perez, ph	1.000	1	1	0	1	0	0	0	0	0	0	0
Ron Reed, p	.000	2	0	0	0	0	0	0	0	0	0	0
Pete Rose, 1b	.375	4	16	3	6	0	0	0	0	1	1	1
Juan Samuel, pr	.000	1	0	0	0	0	0	0	0	0	0	0
Mike Schmidt, 3b	.467	4	15	5	7	2	0	1	2	2	3	0
Ossie Virgil, ph	.000	1	1	0	0	0	0	0	0	0	1	0
TOTAL	.262		130	16	34	4	0	5	15	15	22	2

PITCHER	W	L	ERA	G	GS	CG	SV	SHO	IP	H	ER	BB	SO
Steve Carlton	2	0	0.66	2	2	0	0	0	13.2	13	1	5	13
John Denny	0	1	0.00	1	1	0	0	0	6.0	5	0	3	3
Al Holland	0	0	0.00	2	0	0	1	0	3.0	1	0	0	3
Charles Hudson	1	0	2.00	1	1	1	0	0	9.0	4	2	2	9
Ron Reed	0	0	2.70	2	0	0	0	0	3.1	4	1	1	3
TOTAL	3	1	1.03	8	4	1	1	0	35.0	27	4	11	31

LA (W)

PLAYER/POS	AVG	G	AB	R	H	2B	3B	HR	RB	BB	SO	SB
Dusty Baker, of	.357	4	14	4	5	1	0	1	1	2	0	0
Joe Beckwith, p	.000	2	0	0	0	0	0	0	0	0	0	0
Greg Brock, 1b	.000	3	9	1	0	0	0	0	0	0	3	0
Jack Fimple, c	.143	3	7	0	1	0	0	0	1	0	3	0
Pedro Guerrero, 3b	.250	4	12	1	3	1	1	0	2	3	3	0
Rick Honeycutt, p	.000	2	0	0	0	0	0	0	0	0	0	0
Rafael Landestoy, ph	.000	2	2	0	0	0	0	0	0	0	1	0
Ken Landreaux, of	.143	4	14	0	2	0	0	0	1	1	3	0
Candy Maldonado, ph	.000	2	2	0	0	0	0	0	0	0	1	0
Mike Marshall, 1b-3,of-2	.133	4	15	1	2	1	0	1	2	1	6	0
Rick Monday, ph	.000	1	0	0	0	0	0	0	0	0	0	0
Jose Morales, ph	.000	2	2	0	0	0	0	0	0	0	1	0
Tom Niedenfuer, p	.000	2	0	0	0	0	0	0	0	0	0	0
Alejandro Pena, p	1.000	1	1	0	1	0	0	0	0	0	0	0
Jerry Reuss, p	.000	2	3	0	0	0	0	0	0	0	3	0
Bill Russell, ss	.286	4	14	1	4	0	0	0	0	2	4	1
Steve Sax, 2b	.250	4	16	0	4	0	0	0	0	1	0	1
Derrel Thomas, of	.444	4	9	0	4	1	0	0	0	0	3	1
Fernando Valenzuela, p	.000	1	3	0	0	0	0	0	0	1	0	0
Bob Welch, p	.000	1	0	0	0	0	0	0	0	0	0	0
Steve Yeager, c	.167	2	6	0	1	1	0	0	0	0	0	0
Pat Zachry, p	.000	2	0	0	0	0	0	0	0	0	0	0
TOTAL	.209		129	8	27	5	1	2	7	11	31	3

PITCHER	W	L	ERA	G	GS	CG	SV	SHO	IP	H	ER	BB	SO
Joe Beckwith	0	0	0.00	2	0	0	0	0	2.1	1	0	2	3
Rick Honeycutt	0	0	21.60	2	0	0	0	0	1.2	4	4	0	2
Tom Niedenfuer	0	0	0.00	2	0	0	1	0	2.0	0	0	1	3
Alejandro Pena	0	0	6.75	1	0	0	0	0	2.2	4	2	1	3
Jerry Reuss	0	2	4.50	2	2	0	0	0	12.0	14	6	3	4
Fernando Valenzuela	1	0	1.13	1	1	0	0	0	8.0	7	1	4	5
Bob Welch	0	1	6.75	1	1	0	0	0	1.1	0	1	2	0
Pat Zachry	0	0	2.25	2	0	0	0	0	4.0	4	1	2	2
TOTAL	1	3	3.97	13	4	0	1	0	34.0	34	15	15	22

GAME 1 AT LA OCT 4

PHI	100 000 000	1 5 1
LA	000 000 000	0 7 0

Pitchers: CARLTON, Holland (8) vs REUSS, Niedenfuer (9)
Home Runs: Schmidt-PHI
Attendance: 49,963

GAME 2 AT LA OCT 5

PHI	010 000 000	1 7 2
LA	100 020 01X	4 6 1

Pitchers: DENNY, Reed (7) vs VALENZUELA, Niedenfuer (9)
Home Runs: Matthews-PHI
Attendance: 55,967

GAME 3 AT PHI OCT 7

LA	000 200 000	2 4 0
PHI	021 120 10X	7 9 1

Pitchers: WELCH, Pena (2), Honeycutt (5), Beckwith (5), Zachry (7) vs HUDSON
Home Runs: Marshall-LA, Matthews-PHI
Attendance: 53,490

GAME 4 AT PHI OCT 8

LA	000 100 010	2 10 0
PHI	300 022 00X	7 13 1

Pitchers: REUSS, Beckwith (5), Honeycutt (5), Zachry (7) vs CARLTON, Reed (7), Holland (8)
Home Runs: Matthews-PHI, Baker-LA, Lezcano-PHI
Attendance: 64,494

The White Sox and Orioles entered the LCS evenly matched, with similar season's records and stats. But in the LCS, Baltimore all but shut down Chicago's run production. Both teams had 28 hits, but the Sox, held to four for extra bases, found themselves outslugged by 116 percentage points and outscored by 16 runs.

Chicago won the first game, scoring two of their three series runs as LaMarr Hoyt shut Baltimore out for eight innings before letting in a run in the ninth. But the White Sox had concluded their effective scoring. In Game Two, Oriole rookie Mike Boddicker shut them out on five hits, striking out fourteen. In Game Three the Sox scored their final run. The Orioles got only two more hits than Chicago, but blended them with nine walks, a hit batsman, and a Sox error to score eleven runs. In the fourth game, Oriole pitchers Storm Davis and Tippy Martinez saw that ten Chicago hits scored no runs. Britt Burns held Baltimore scoreless, too, through nine innings. But Tito Landrum's solo homer in the top of the tenth drove Burns out, and two more Oriole runs provided more than enough scoring to win Baltimore the flag.

Baltimore Orioles (East), 3; Chicago White Sox (West), 1

BAL (E)

PLAYER/POS	AVG	G	AB	R	H	2B	3B	HR	RB	BB	SO	SB
Benny Ayala, dh	.000	1	0	0	0	0	0	0	0	1	0	0
Mike Boddicker, p	.000	1	0	0	0	0	0	0	0	0	0	0
Al Bumbry, of	.125	3	8	0	1	1	0	0	1	0	2	0
Todd Cruz, 3b	.133	4	15	0	2	0	0	0	1	0	5	0
Rich Dauer, 2b	.000	4	14	0	0	0	0	0	1	0	0	0
Storm Davis, p	.000	1	0	0	0	0	0	0	0	0	0	0
Rick Dempsey, c	.167	4	12	1	2	0	0	0	0	1	1	0
Jim Dwyer, of-1	.250	2	4	1	1	1	0	0	0	1	0	0
Mike Flanagan, p	.000	1	0	0	0	0	0	0	0	0	0	0
Dan Ford, of-1	.200	2	5	0	1	1	0	0	0	0	1	0
Tito Landrum, of-3	.200	4	10	2	2	0	0	1	1	0	2	0
John Lowenstein, of	.167	2	6	0	1	1	0	0	2	1	2	0
Tippy Martinez, p	.000	2	0	0	0	0	0	0	0	0	0	0
Scott McGregor, p	.000	1	0	0	0	0	0	0	0	0	0	0
Eddie Murray, 1b	.267	4	15	5	4	0	0	1	3	3	3	1
Joe Nolan, ph	.000	1	0	0	0	0	0	0	1	0	0	0
Jim Palmer, pr	.000	1	0	0	0	0	0	0	0	0	0	0
Cal Ripken, ss	.400	4	15	5	6	2	0	0	1	2	3	0
Gary Roenicke, of	.750	3	4	4	3	1	0	1	4	5	0	0
John Shelby, of-2	.222	3	9	1	2	0	0	0	0	1	3	1
Ken Singleton, dh	.250	4	12	0	3	2	0	0	1	2	2	0
Sammy Stewart, p	.000	2	0	0	0	0	0	0	0	0	0	0
TOTAL	.217		129	19	28	9	0	3	17	16	24	2

PITCHER	W	L	ERA	G	GS	CG	SV	SHO	IP	H	ER	BB	SO
Mike Boddicker	1	0	0.00	1	1	1	0	1	9.0	5	0	3	14
Storm Davis	0	0	0.00	1	1	0	0	0	6.0	5	0	2	2
Mike Flanagan	1	0	1.80	1	1	0	0	0	5.0	5	1	0	1
Tippy Martinez	1	0	0.00	2	0	0	0	0	6.0	5	0	3	5
Scott McGregor	0	1	1.35	1	1	0	0	0	6.2	6	1	3	2
Sammy Stewart	0	0	0.00	2	0	0	1	0	4.1	2	0	1	2
TOTAL	3	1	0.49	8	4	1	1	1	37.0	28	2	12	26

CHI (W)

PLAYER/POS	AVG	G	AB	R	H	2B	3B	HR	RB	BB	SO	SB
Juan Agosto, p	.000	1	0	0	0	0	0	0	0	0	0	0
Harold Baines, of	.125	4	16	0	2	0	0	0	0	1	3	0
Floyd Bannister, p	.000	1	0	0	0	0	0	0	0	0	0	0
Salome Barojas, p	.000	2	0	0	0	0	0	0	0	0	0	0
Britt Burns, p	.000	1	0	0	0	0	0	0	0	0	0	0
Julio Cruz, 2b	.333	4	12	0	4	0	0	0	0	3	4	2
Richard Dotson, p	.000	1	0	0	0	0	0	0	0	0	0	0
Jerry Dybzinski, ss	.250	2	4	0	1	0	0	0	0	0	0	0
Carlton Fisk, c	.176	4	17	0	3	1	0	0	0	1	3	0
Scott Fletcher, ss	.000	3	7	0	0	0	0	0	0	1	0	0
Jerry Hairston, of	.000	2	3	0	0	0	0	0	0	1	1	0
La Marr Hoyt, p	.000	1	0	0	0	0	0	0	0	0	0	0
Ron Kittle, of	.286	3	7	1	2	1	0	0	0	1	2	0
Jerry Koosman, p	.000	1	0	0	0	0	0	0	0	0	0	0
Dennis Lamp, p	.000	3	0	0	0	0	0	0	0	0	0	0
Rudy Law, of	.389	4	18	1	7	1	0	0	0	0	1	2
Vance Law, 3b	.182	4	11	0	2	0	0	0	1	1	3	0
Greg Luzinski, dh	.133	4	15	0	2	1	0	0	0	1	5	0
Tom Paciorek, 1b-3,of-2	.250	4	16	1	4	0	0	0	1	1	2	0
Aurelio Rodriguez, 3b	.000	2	0	0	0	0	0	0	0	0	0	0
Mike Squires, 1b-3	.000	4	4	0	0	0	0	0	0	0	0	0
Dick Tidrow, p	.000	1	0	0	0	0	0	0	0	0	0	0
Greg Walker, 1b-1	.333	2	3	0	1	0	0	0	0	1	2	0
TOTAL	.211		133	3	28	4	0	0	2	12	26	4

PITCHER	W	L	ERA	G	GS	CG	SV	SHO	IP	H	ER	BB	SO
Juan Agosto	0	0	0.00	1	0	0	0	0	0.1	0	0	0	0
Floyd Bannister	0	1	4.50	1	1	0	0	0	6.0	5	3	1	5
Salome Barojas	0	0	18.00	2	0	0	0	0	1.0	4	2	0	0
Britt Burns	0	1	0.96	1	1	0	0	0	9.1	6	1	5	8
Richard Dotson	0	1	10.80	1	1	0	0	0	5.0	6	6	3	3
La Marr Hoyt	1	0	1.00	1	1	1	0	0	9.0	5	1	0	4
Jerry Koosman	0	0	54.00	1	0	0	0	0	0.1	1	2	2	0
Dennis Lamp	0	0	0.00	3	0	0	0	0	2.0	0	0	2	1
Dick Tidrow	0	0	3.00	1	0	0	0	0	3.0	1	1	3	3
TOTAL	1	3	4.00	12	4	1	0	0	36.0	28	16	16	24

GAME 1 AT BAL OCT 5

CHI	001	001	000	2	7 0
BAL	000	000	001	1	5 1

Pitchers: HOYT vs McGREGOR, Stewart (7), T.Martinez (8)
Attendance: 51,289

GAME 2 AT BAL OCT 6

CHI	000	000	000	0	5 2
BAL	010	102	00X	4	6 0

Pitchers: BANNISTER, Barojas (7), Lamp (8) vs BODDICKER
Home Runs: Roenicke-BAL
Attendance: 52,347

GAME 3 AT CHI OCT 7

BAL	310	020	014	11	8 1
CHI	010	000	000	1	6 1

Pitchers: FLANAGAN, Stewart (6) vs DOTSON, Tidrow (6), Koosman (9), Lamp (9)
Home Runs: Murray-BAL
Attendance: 46,635

GAME 4 AT CHI OCT 8

BAL	000	000	000 3	3	9 0
CHI	000	000	000 0	0	10 0

Pitchers: Davis, T.MARTINEZ (7) vs BURNS, Barojas (10), Agosto (10), Lamp (10)
Home Runs: Landrum-BAL
Attendance: 45,477

Near neighbors Baltimore and Philadelphia met in a World Series for the first time. Both clubs were led by new managers: Baltimore by Joe Altobelli, who inherited a team built under longtime Oriole manager Earl Weaver; and the Phillies by general manager Paul Owens, who replaced Pat Corrales with himself in midseason. Both started their top game winners in the opener, and the result was a pitchers' duel, with all three runs scored on solo homers. Phillie John Denny gave up the first home run to Jim Dwyer in the first inning, but after that (with late-inning help from Al Holland) he blanked the Orioles, while Baltimore's Scott McGregor, after 5⅔ scoreless innings gave up home runs to Joe Morgan and (the game-loser two innings later) to Garry Maddox.

The Orioles swept the next four games. In Game Two, Mike Boddicker yielded just three singles (and no walks) to Phillie batters. Though one of the singles led to a run in the fourth inning, giving the Phillies a 1–0 lead, Oriole John Lowenstein tied the score with a home run in the fifth. Three more Oriole hits in the inning and a sacrifice fly made the score 3–1, and three two-out singles in the seventh inning brought in a fourth Baltimore run.

Philadelphia again scored first in Game Three, on leadoff home runs in the second and third innings by Gary Matthews and Joe Morgan. But the Orioles finally got to veteran starter Steve Carlton in the sixth for one run and drove him out after a second run scored an inning later. Carlton suffered the loss when the baserunner he left scored the tie-breaking run from second on an error by shortstop Ivan DeJesus.

The Phillies also lost Game Four by a single run. Baltimore scored first with two runs in the top of the fourth, but Philadelphia recovered with one run in the fourth and two an inning later. They would not lead again in the Series. Baltimore scored twice in the sixth to go ahead again, and once more in the seventh. The Phillies scored once more with two down in the last of the ninth to draw within one run of a tie, but Joe Morgan lined out to second to end the game.

Home runs by Rick Dempsey and Eddie Murray (who hit two) accounted for four of Baltimore's five runs in the final game—more than enough to support Scott Mc-Gregor's five-hit shutout pitching.

Baltimore Orioles (AL), 4; Philadelphia Phillies (NL), 1

BAL (A)

PLAYER/POS	AVG	G	AB	R	H	2B	3B	HR	RBI	BB	SO	SB
Benny Ayala, ph	1.000	1	1	1	1	0	0	0	1	0	0	0
Mike Boddicker, p	.000	1	3	0	0	0	0	0	0	1	0	1	0
Al Bumbry, of	.091	4	11	0	1	1	0	0	1	0	1	0
Todd Cruz, 3b	.125	6	16	1	2	0	0	0	0	1	3	0
Rich Dauer, 2b	.211	5	19	2	4	1	0	0	3	0	3	0
Storm Davis, p	.000	1	2	0	0	0	0	0	0	0	2	0
Rick Dempsey, c	.385	5	13	3	5	4	0	1	2	2	2	0
Jim Dwyer, of	.375	2	8	3	3	1	0	1	1	0	0	0
Mike Flanagan, p	.000	1	1	0	0	0	0	0	0	0	1	0
Dan Ford, of-4	.167	5	12	1	2	0	0	1	1	1	5	0
Tito Landrum, of	.000	3	0	0	0	0	0	0	0	0	0	1
John Lowenstein, of	.385	4	13	2	5	1	0	1	1	0	3	0
Tippy Martinez, p	.000	3	0	0	0	0	0	0	0	0	0	0
Scott McGregor, p	.000	2	5	0	0	0	0	0	0	0	0	0
Eddie Murray, 1b	.250	5	20	2	5	0	0	2	3	1	4	0
Joe Nolan, c	.000	2	2	0	0	0	0	0	0	1	0	0
Jim Palmer, p	.000	1	0	0	0	0	0	0	0	0	0	0
Cal Ripken, ss	.167	5	18	2	3	0	0	0	1	3	4	0
Gary Roenicke, of-2	.000	3	7	0	0	0	0	0	0	0	2	0
Len Sakata, 2b	.000	1	1	0	0	0	0	0	0	0	0	0
John Shelby, of	.444	5	9	1	4	0	0	0	1	0	4	0
Ken Singleton, ph	.000	2	1	0	0	0	0	0	0	1	1	0
Sammy Stewart, p	.000	3	2	0	0	0	0	0	0	0	1	0
TOTAL	.213		164	18	35	8	0	6	17	10	37	1

PITCHER	W	L	ERA	G	GS	CG	SV	SHO	IP	H	ER	BB	SO
Mike Boddicker	1	0	0.00	1	1	1	0	0	9.0	3	0	0	6
Storm Davis	1	0	5.40	1	1	0	0	0	5.0	6	3	1	3
Mike Flanagan	0	0	4.50	1	1	0	0	0	4.0	6	2	1	1
Tippy Martinez	0	0	3.00	3	0	0	2	0	3.0	3	1	0	0
Scott McGregor	1	1	1.06	2	2	1	0	1	17.0	9	2	2	12
Jim Palmer	1	0	0.00	1	0	0	0	0	2.0	2	0	1	1
Sammy Stewart	0	0	0.00	3	0	0	0	0	5.0	2	0	2	6
TOTAL	4	1	1.60	12	5	2	2	1	45.0	31	8	7	29

PHI (N)

PLAYER/POS	AVG	G	AB	R	H	2B	3B	HR	RBI	BB	SO	SB
Larry Andersen, p	.000	2	0	0	0	0	0	0	0	0	0	0
Marty Bystrom, p	.000	1	0	0	0	0	0	0	0	0	0	0
Steve Carlton, p	.000	1	3	0	0	0	0	0	0	0	1	0
Ivan DeJesus, ss	.125	5	16	0	2	0	0	0	0	1	2	0
John Denny, p	.200	2	5	1	1	0	0	0	1	0	1	0
Bob Dernier, pr	.000	3	0	1	0	0	0	0	0	0	0	0
Bo Diaz, c	.333	5	15	1	5	1	0	0	0	1	2	0
Greg Gross, of	.000	2	6	0	0	0	0	0	0	0	0	0
Von Hayes, of-1	.000	4	3	0	0	0	0	0	0	1	0	0
Willie Hernandez, p	.000	2	0	0	0	0	0	0	0	0	0	0
Al Holland, p	.000	2	0	0	0	0	0	0	0	0	0	0
Charles Hudson, p	.000	2	2	0	0	0	0	0	0	0	1	0
Joe Lefebvre, of-2	.200	3	5	0	1	1	0	0	0	2	1	0
Sixto Lezcano, of-3	.125	4	8	0	1	0	0	0	0	0	3	0
Garry Maddox, of-3	.250	4	12	1	3	1	0	1	1	0	2	0
Gary Matthews, of	.250	5	16	1	4	0	0	1	1	2	2	0
Joe Morgan, 2b	.263	5	19	3	5	0	1	2	2	2	3	1
Tony Perez, 1b-2	.200	4	10	0	2	0	0	0	0	0	2	0
Ron Reed, p	.000	3	0	0	0	0	0	0	0	0	0	0
Pete Rose, 1b-3,of-1	.313	5	16	1	5	1	0	0	1	1	3	0
Juan Samuel, ph	.000	3	1	0	0	0	0	0	0	0	0	0
Mike Schmidt, 3b	.050	5	20	0	1	0	0	0	0	0	6	0
Ossie Virgil, c-1	.500	3	2	0	1	0	0	0	1	0	0	0
TOTAL	.195		159	9	31	4	1	4	9	7	29	1

PITCHER	W	L	ERA	G	GS	CG	SV	SHO	IP	H	ER	BB	SO
Larry Andersen	0	0	2.25	2	0	0	0	0	4.0	4	1	0	1
Marty Bystrom	0	0	0.00	1	0	0	0	0	1.0	0	0	0	1
Steve Carlton	0	1	2.70	1	1	0	0	0	6.2	5	2	3	7
John Denny	1	1	3.46	2	2	0	0	0	13.0	12	5	3	9
Willie Hernandez	0	0	0.00	3	0	0	0	0	4.0	0	0	1	4
Al Holland	0	0	0.00	2	0	0	1	0	3.2	1	0	0	5
Charles Hudson	0	2	8.64	2	2	0	0	0	8.1	9	8	1	6
Ron Reed	0	0	2.70	3	0	0	0	0	3.1	4	1	2	4
TOTAL	1	4	3.48	16	5	0	1	0	44.0	35	17	10	37

GAME 1 AT BAL OCT 11

PHI	000	001	010	2	5	0
BAL	100	000	00	1	5	1

Pitchers: DENNY, Holland (8) vs McGREGOR, Stewart (9), T.Martinez (9)
Home Runs: Morgan-PHI, Maddox-PHI, Dwyer-BAL
Attendance: 52,204

GAME 2 AT BAL OCT 12

PHI	000	100	000	1	3	0
BAL	000	030	10X	4	9	1

Pitchers: HUDSON, Hernandez (5), Andersen (6), Reed (8) vs BODDICKER
Home Runs: Lowenstein-BAL
Attendance: 52,132

GAME 3 AT PHI OCT 14

BAL	000	001	200	3	6	1
PHI	011	000	000	2	8	2

Pitchers: Flanagan, PALMER (5), Stewart (7), T.Martinez (9) vs CARLTON, Holland (8)
Home Runs: Matthews-PHI, Morgan-PHI, Ford-BAL
Attendance: 65,792

GAME 4 AT PHI OCT 15

BAL	000	202	100	5	10	1
PHI	000	120	001	4	10	0

Pitchers: DAVIS, Stewart (6), T.Martinez (8) vs DENNY, Hernandez (6), Reed (6), Andersen (8)
Attendance: 66,947

GAME 5 AT PHI OCT 16

BAL	011	210	000	5	5	0
PHI	000	000	000	0	5	1

Pitchers: McGREGOR vs HUDSON, Bystrom (5), Hernandez (6), Reed (9)
Home Runs: Murray-BAL (2), Dempsey-BAL
Attendance: 67,064

After two games in Chicago, the Cubs appeared headed for their first pennant in thirty-nine years. Rick Sutcliffe and Warren Brusstar shut out the Padres 13–0 in an opener enlivened by five Cub home runs. In a quieter second game, the Cubs built a 4–1 lead over the first four innings and held on for the win.

When the series moved to San Diego, though, the Padres came to life. In the fifth and sixth innings of Game Three, they obliterated a 1–0 Cub lead with seven runs, as Ed Whitson and Goose Gossage held the Cubs scoreless after the second inning for what turned into an easy Padres win.

Game Four was not so easy. San Diego scored first in the third inning, lost their lead in the fourth, tied in the fifth, went ahead in the seventh, and fell back into a 5–5 tie in the eighth. But in the bottom of the ninth, Padre Steve Garvey's two-run homer sent the series into a fifth game.

Leon Durham put the Cubs ahead with a two-run homer in the first inning of the finale, and Jody Davis added to the lead with a solo shot in the second. Rick Sutcliffe, meanwhile, was setting down Padres as he added five shutout innings to his seven from Game One. But he gave up two runs in the sixth, and after first baseman Durham saw a grounder go through his legs to let in the tying run in the seventh, the Cubs watched the pennant slip away as Tony Gwynn's double and Garvey's single drove in the game's three final runs.

San Diego Padres (West), 3; Chicago Cubs (East), 2

SD (W)

PLAYER/POS	AVG	G	AB	R	H	2B	3B	HR	RB	BB	SO	SB
Kurt Bevacqua, ph	.000	2	2	0	0	0	0	0	0	0	0	0
Greg Booker, p	.000	1	0	0	0	0	0	0	0	0	0	0
Bobby Brown, of	.000	3	4	1	0	0	0	0	0	1	2	1
Dave Dravecky, p	.000	3	0	0	0	0	0	0	0	0	0	0
Tim Flannery, ph	.500	3	2	2	1	0	0	0	0	0	0	0
Steve Garvey, 1b	.400	5	20	1	8	1	0	1	7	1	2	0
Rich Gossage, p	.000	3	0	0	0	0	0	0	0	0	0	0
Tony Gwynn, of	.368	5	19	6	7	3	0	0	3	1	2	0
Greg Harris, p	.000	1	0	0	0	0	0	0	0	0	0	0
Andy Hawkins, p	.000	3	0	0	0	0	0	0	0	0	0	0
Terry Kennedy, c	.222	5	18	2	4	0	0	0	1	1	3	0
Craig Lefferts, p	.000	3	0	0	0	0	0	0	0	0	0	0
Tim Lollar, p	.000	1	1	0	0	0	0	0	0	0	1	0
Carmelo Martinez, of	.176	5	17	1	3	0	0	0	0	2	4	0
Kevin McReynolds, of	.300	4	10	2	3	0	0	1	4	3	1	0
Graig Nettles, 3b	.143	4	14	1	2	0	0	0	2	1	1	0
Mario Ramirez, ph	.000	2	2	0	0	0	0	0	0	0	0	0
Luis Salazar, of-2,3b-1	.200	3	5	0	1	0	1	0	0	0	1	0
Eric Show, p	.000	2	1	0	0	0	0	0	0	0	1	0
Champ Summers, ph	.000	2	2	0	0	0	0	0	0	0	1	0
Garry Templeton, ss	.333	5	15	2	5	1	0	0	2	2	0	1
Mark Thurmond, p	1.000	1	1	0	1	0	0	0	0	0	0	0
Ed Whitson, p	.000	2	3	0	0	0	0	0	0	0	1	0
Alan Wiggins, 2b	.316	5	19	4	6	0	0	0	1	2	2	0
TOTAL	.265		155	22	41	5	1	2	20	14	22	2

PITCHER	W	L	ERA	G	GS	CG	SV	SHO	IP	H	ER	BB	SO
Greg Booker	0	0	0.00	1	0	0	0	0	2.0	2	0	1	2
Dave Dravecky	0	0	0.00	3	0	0	0	0	6.0	2	0	0	5
Rich Gossage	0	0	4.50	3	0	0	1	0	4.0	5	2	1	5
Greg Harris	0	0	31.50	1	0	0	0	0	2.0	9	7	3	2
Andy Hawkins	0	0	0.00	3	0	0	0	0	3.2	0	0	2	1
Craig Lefferts	2	0	0.00	3	0	0	0	0	4.0	1	0	1	1
Tim Lollar	0	0	6.23	1	1	0	0	0	4.1	3	3	4	3
Eric Show	0	1	13.50	2	2	0	0	0	5.1	8	8	4	2
Mark Thurmond	0	1	9.82	1	1	0	0	0	3.2	7	4	2	1
Ed Whitson	1	0	1.13	1	1	0	0	0	8.0	5	1	2	6
TOTAL	3	2	5.23	19	5	0	1	0	43.0	42	25	20	28

CHI (E)

PLAYER/POS	AVG	G	AB	R	H	2B	3B	HR	RB	BB	SO	SB
Thad Bosley, ph	.000	2	2	0	0	0	0	0	0	0	2	0
Larry Bowa, ss	.200	5	15	1	3	1	0	0	1	1	0	0
Warren Brusstar, p	.000	3	1	0	0	0	0	0	0	0	0	0
Ron Cey, 3b	.158	5	19	3	3	1	0	1	3	3	3	0
Henry Cotto, of	1.000	3	1	1	1	0	0	0	0	0	0	0
Jody Davis, c	.389	5	18	3	7	0	0	2	6	0	3	0
Bob Dernier, of	.235	5	17	5	4	2	0	1	1	5	4	2
Leon Durham, 1b	.150	5	20	2	3	0	0	2	4	1	4	0
Dennis Eckersley, p	.000	1	2	0	0	0	0	0	0	0	1	0
George Frazier, p	.000	1	0	0	0	0	0	0	0	0	0	0
Richie Hebner, ph	.000	2	1	0	0	0	0	0	0	0	0	0
Steve Lake, c	1.000	1	1	0	1	1	0	0	0	0	0	0
Davey Lopes, of-1	.000	2	1	0	0	0	0	0	0	0	0	0
Gary Matthews, of	.200	5	15	4	3	0	0	2	5	6	4	1
Keith Moreland, of	.333	5	18	3	6	2	0	0	2	1	1	0
Ryne Sandberg, 2b	.368	5	19	3	7	2	0	0	2	3	2	3
Scott Sanderson, p	.000	1	2	0	0	0	0	0	0	0	1	0
Lee Smith, p	.000	2	0	0	0	0	0	0	0	0	0	0
Tim Stoddard, p	.000	2	0	0	0	0	0	0	0	0	0	0
Rick Sutcliffe, p	.500	2	6	1	3	0	0	1	1	0	2	0
Steve Trout, p	.500	2	2	0	1	0	0	0	0	0	0	0
Tom Veryzer, ss-2,3b-1	.000	3	1	0	0	0	0	0	0	0	0	0
Gary Woods, of	.000	1	1	0	0	0	0	0	0	0	1	0
TOTAL	.259		162	26	42	11	0	9	25	20	28	6

PITCHER	W	L	ERA	G	GS	CG	SV	SHO	IP	H	ER	BB	SO
Warren Brusstar	0	0	0.00	3	0	0	0	0	4.1	6	0	0	1
Dennis Eckersley	0	1	8.44	1	1	0	0	0	5.1	9	5	0	0
George Frazier	0	0	10.80	1	0	0	0	0	1.2	2	2	0	1
Scott Sanderson	0	0	5.79	1	1	0	0	0	4.2	6	3	1	2
Lee Smith	0	1	9.00	2	0	0	1	0	2.0	3	2	0	3
Tim Stoddard	0	0	4.50	2	0	0	0	0	2.0	1	1	2	2
Rick Sutcliffe	1	1	3.38	2	2	0	0	0	13.1	9	5	8	10
Steve Trout	1	0	2.00	2	1	0	0	0	9.0	5	2	3	3
TOTAL	2	3	4.25	14	5	0	1	0	42.1	41	20	14	22

GAME 1 AT CHI OCT 2

SD	000	000	000	0	6	1
CHI	203	062	00X	13	16	0

Pitchers: SHOW, Harris (5), Booker (7) vs SUTCLIFFE, Brusstar (8)
Home Runs: Dernier-CHI, Matthews-CHI (2), Sutcliffe-CHI, Cey-CHI
Attendance: 36,282

GAME 2 AT CHI OCT 3

SD	000	101	000	2	5	0
CHI	102	100	00X	4	8	1

Pitchers: THURMOND, Hawkins (4), Dravecky (6), Lefferts (8) vs TROUT, Smith (9)
Attendance: 36,282

GAME 3 AT SD OCT 4

CHI	010	000	000	1	5	0
SD	000	034	00X	7	11	0

Pitchers: ECKERSLEY, Frazier (6), Stoddard (8) vs WHITSON, Gossage (9)
Home Runs: McReynolds-SD
Attendance: 58,346

GAME 4 AT SD OCT 6

CHI	000	300	020	5	8	1
SD	002	010	202	7	11	0

Pitchers: Sanderson, Brusstar (5), Stoddard (7), SMITH (8) vs Lollar, Hawkins (5), Dravecky (6), Gossage (8), LEFFERTS (9)
Home Runs: Davis-CHI, Durham-CHI,Garvey-SD
Attendance: 58,354

GAME 5 AT SD OCT 7

CHI	210	000	000	3	5	1
SD	000	002	40X	6	8	0

Pitchers: SUTCLIFFE, Trout (7), Brusstar (8) vs Show, Hawkins (2), Dravecky (4), LEFFERTS (6), Gossage (8)
Home Runs: Durham-CHI, Davis-CHI
Attendance: 58,359

The heavily favored Tigers swept the series, but not without difficulty, despite a fourteen-hit, three-homer, 8–1 romp in the opener.

Games Two and Three were much tighter. In the second game, after Detroit had built a 3–0 lead over the first three innings, Royal rookie starter Bret Saberhagen settled down and blanked the Tigers for the next five innings as K.C. inched its way to a tie with runs in the fourth, seventh, and eighth. Through the ninth and tenth innings, Tiger reliever Aurelio Lopez and Royal Dan Quisenberry dueled scorelessly, but in the top of the eleventh Johnny Grubb doubled home two Tiger runs. Lopez struggled but held the Royals scoreless in the last of the eleventh for the win.

In Game Three, the Royals' Charlie Leibrandt and Tigers' Milt Wilcox and Willie Hernandez hurled matching three-hitters. But the Tigers secured the game—and the pennant—when Chet Lemon scored on a broken double play in the second inning for the game's only run.

Detroit Tigers (East), 3;
Kansas City Royals (West), 0

DET (E)

PLAYER/POS	AVG	G	AB	R	H	2B	3B	HR	RB	BB	SO	SB
Doug Baker, ss	.000	1	0	0	0	0	0	0	0	0	0	0
Dave Bergman, 1b-1	1.000	2	1	1	1	0	0	0	0	0	0	1
Tom Brookens, 2b-1,3b-1	.000	2	2	0	0	0	0	0	0	0	1	0
Marty Castillo, 3b	.250	3	8	0	2	0	0	0	2	0	3	1
Darrell Evans, 1b-3,3b-1	.300	3	10	1	3	1	0	0	1	1	0	1
Barbaro Garbey, dh-2	.333	3	9	1	3	0	0	0	0	0	1	0
Kirk Gibson, of	.417	3	12	2	5	1	0	1	2	2	1	1
Johnny Grubb, dh	.250	1	4	0	1	1	0	0	2	0	0	0
Willie Hernandez, p	.000	3	0	0	0	0	0	0	0	0	0	0
Larry Herndon, of	.200	2	5	1	1	0	0	1	1	1	2	0
Ruppert Jones, of	.000	2	5	1	0	0	0	0	0	1	1	0
Rusty Kuntz, of	.000	1	1	0	0	0	0	0	0	0	0	0
Chet Lemon, of	.000	3	13	1	0	0	0	0	0	0	1	0
Aurelio Lopez, p	.000	1	0	0	0	0	0	0	0	0	0	0
Jack Morris, p	.000	1	0	0	0	0	0	0	0	0	0	0
Lance Parrish, c	.250	3	12	1	3	1	0	1	3	0	3	0
Dan Petry, p	.000	1	0	0	0	0	0	0	0	0	0	0
Alan Trammell, ss	.364	3	11	2	4	0	1	1	3	3	1	0
Lou Whitaker, 2b	.143	3	14	3	2	0	0	0	0	0	3	0
Milt Wilcox, p	.000	1	0	0	0	0	0	0	0	0	0	0
TOTAL	.234		107	14	25	4	1	4	14	8	17	4

PITCHER	W	L	ERA	G	GS	CG	SV	SHO	IP	H	ER	BB	SO
Willie Hernandez	0	0	2.25	3	0	0	1	0	4.0	3	1	1	3
Aurelio Lopez	1	0	0.00	1	0	0	0	0	3.0	4	0	1	2
Jack Morris	1	0	1.29	1	1	0	0	0	7.0	5	1	1	4
Dan Petry	0	0	2.57	1	1	0	0	0	7.0	4	2	1	4
Milt Wilcox	1	0	0.00	1	1	0	0	0	8.0	2	0	2	8
TOTAL	3	0	1.24	7	3	0	1	0	29.0	18	4	6	21

KC (W)

PLAYER/POS	AVG	G	AB	R	H	2B	3B	HR	RB	BB	SO	SB
Steve Balboni, 1b	.100	3	10	0	1	0	0	0	0	0	1	4	0
Buddy Biancalana, ss	.000	2	1	0	0	0	0	0	0	0	1	0
Bud Black, p	.000	1	0	0	0	0	0	0	0	0	0	0
George Brett, 3b	.231	3	13	0	3	0	0	0	0	0	2	0
Onix Concepcion, ss	.000	3	7	0	0	0	0	0	0	0	0	0
Mark Huismann, p	.000	1	0	0	0	0	0	0	0	0	0	0
Dane Iorg, ph	.500	2	2	0	1	0	0	0	1	0	0	0
Lynn Jones, of-2	.200	3	5	1	1	0	0	0	0	0	0	0
Mike Jones, p	.000	1	0	0	0	0	0	0	0	0	0	0
Charlie Leibrandt, p	.000	1	0	0	0	0	0	0	0	0	0	0
Hal McRae, ph	1.000	2	2	0	2	1	0	0	1	0	0	0
Darryl Motley, of	.167	3	12	0	2	0	0	0	1	1	3	0
Jorge Orta, dh	.100	3	10	1	1	0	1	0	1	0	2	0
Greg Pryor, 3b	.000	1	0	0	0	0	0	0	0	0	0	0
Dan Quisenberry, p	.000	1	0	0	0	0	0	0	0	0	0	0
Bret Saberhagen, p	.000	1	0	0	0	0	0	0	0	0	0	0
Pat Sheridan, of	.000	3	6	1	0	0	0	0	0	3	3	0
Don Slaught, c	.364	3	11	0	4	0	0	0	0	0	0	0
U. L. Washington, ph	.000	2	1	0	0	0	0	0	0	0	1	0
John Wathan, dh	.000	1	1	0	0	0	0	0	0	0	0	0
Frank White, 2b	.083	3	12	1	1	0	0	0	0	0	3	0
Willie Wilson, of	.154	3	13	0	2	0	0	0	0	1	2	0
TOTAL	.170		106	4	18	1	1	0	4	6	21	0

PITCHER	W	L	ERA	G	GS	CG	SV	SHO	IP	H	ER	BB	SO
Bud Black	0	1	5.40	1	1	0	0	0	5.0	7	3	1	3
Mark Huismann	0	0	10.13	1	0	0	0	0	2.2	6	3	1	2
Mike Jones	0	0	6.75	1	0	0	0	0	1.1	1	1	0	0
Charlie Leibrandt	0	1	1.13	1	1	0	0	0	8.0	3	1	4	6
Dan Quisenberry	0	1	3.00	1	0	0	0	0	3.0	2	1	1	1
Bret Saberhagen	0	0	2.25	1	1	0	0	0	8.0	6	2	1	5
TOTAL	0	3	3.54	6	3	1	0	0	28.0	25	11	8	17

GAME 1 AT KC OCT 2

DET	200	110	121	8	14	0
KC	000	000	100	1	5	1

Pitchers: MORRIS, Hernandez (8) vs BLACK, Huismann (6), M.Jones (8)
Home Runs: Herndon-DET, Trammell-DET, Parrish-DET
Attendance: 41,973

GAME 2 AT KC OCT 3

DET	201	000	000	02	5	8	1
KC	000	100	110	00	3	10	3

Pitchers: Petry, Hernandez (8), LOPEZ (9) vs Saberhagen, QUISENBERRY (9)
Home Runs: Gibson-DET
Attendance: 42,019

GAME 3 AT DET OCT 5

KC	000	000	000	0	3	3
DET	010	000	00X	1	3	0

Pitchers: LEIBRANDT vs WILCOX, Hernandez (9)
Attendance: 52,168

Few objective observers expected the Padres (playing in their first World Series) to best the mighty Tigers—and they didn't. Detroit's first two batters in Game One hit safely to produce the Series' first scoring before an out had been recorded. San Diego countered with three two-out hits in their half of the first to go ahead 2–1. But Detroit starter Jack Morris settled down to shut out the Padres over the final eight innings, and his Tigers scored the tying and winning runs in the fifth on Larry Herndon's two-run homer. The Tigers scored again in Game Two before the first out was recorded and drove out Padre starter Ed Whitson with three first-inning runs on five singles. But this time Detroit was shut out (by relievers Andy Hawkins and Craig Lefferts) over the final eight, while San Diego scored single runs in the first and fourth and the winning runs in the fifth on a three-run homer by the normally light-hitting Kurt Bevacqua.

The Tigers won Game Three on walks—a Series-record eleven—as the Series moved to Detroit. After scoring their first two runs in the second on a single and Marty Castillo's home run, they continued on to put across two more in the inning on a pair of hits alternated with three walks (the last with the bases full). Three more walks an inning later, followed by a hit batsman, gave Detroit its final run in what became a 5–2 win.

Alan Trammell's two-run homer in the first inning of Game Four put the Tigers ahead to stay. Tiger pitcher Jack Morris gave up a solo home run to Terry Kennedy in the second, but Trammell swatted a second two-run shot an inning later for a 4–1 lead. Morris let a second Padre runner score on a wild pitch in the ninth, but then retired Kennedy for the third out and his second Series win. Kirk Gibson's two home runs framed Tiger scoring in the final game. His two-run shot in the first inning opened the game's scoring. San Diego tied it up with runs in the third and fourth, but Detroit took a 5–3 lead with runs in the fifth and seventh (the latter on Lance Parrish's homer). The unlikely Kurt Bevacqua brought the Padres within a run of tying the game with his second Series homer in the eighth (doubling his regular-season total), but Gibson ended the scoring—and Padre hopes—with a three-run blast half an inning later.

Detroit Tigers (AL), 4;
San Diego Padres (NL), 1

DET (A)

PLAYER/POS	AVG	G	AB	R	H	2B	3B	HR	RB	BB	SO	SB
Doug Bair, p	.000	1	0	0	0	0	0	0	0	0	0	0
Dave Bergman, 1b	.000	5	5	0	0	0	0	0	0	0	1	0
Tom Brookens, 3b	.000	3	3	0	0	0	0	0	0	0	1	0
Marty Castillo, 3b	.333	3	9	2	3	0	0	1	2	2	1	0
Darrell Evans, 1b-4,3b-2	.067	5	15	1	1	0	0	0	1	4	4	0
Barbaro Garbey, dh-3	.000	4	12	0	0	0	0	0	0	0	2	0
Kirk Gibson, of	.333	5	18	4	6	0	0	2	7	4	4	3
Johnny Grubb, dh-2	.333	4	3	0	1	0	0	0	0	0	0	0
Willie Hernandez, p	.000	3	0	0	0	0	0	0	0	0	0	0
Larry Herndon, of	.333	5	15	1	5	0	0	1	3	3	2	0
Howard Johnson, ph	.000	1	1	0	0	0	0	0	0	0	0	0
Ruppert Jones, of	.000	2	3	0	0	0	0	0	0	0	1	0
Rusty Kuntz, ph	.000	2	1	0	0	0	0	0	1	0	1	0
Chet Lemon, of	.294	5	17	1	5	0	0	0	1	2	2	2
Aurelio Lopez, p	.000	2	0	0	0	0	0	0	0	0	0	0
Jack Morris, p	.000	2	0	0	0	0	0	0	0	0	0	0
Lance Parrish, c	.278	5	18	3	5	1	0	1	2	3	2	1
Dan Petry, p	.000	2	0	0	0	0	0	0	0	0	0	0
Bill Scherrer, p	.000	3	0	0	0	0	0	0	0	0	0	0
Alan Trammell, ss	.450	5	20	5	9	1	0	2	6	2	1	0
Lou Whitaker, 2b	.278	5	18	6	5	2	0	0	0	4	4	0
Milt Wilcox, p	.000	1	0	0	0	0	0	0	0	0	0	0
TOTAL	.253		158	23	40	4	0	7	23	24	27	7

PITCHER	W	L	ERA	G	GS	CG	SV	SHO	IP	H	ER	BB	SO
Doug Bair	0	0	0.00	1	0	0	0	0	0.2	0	0	0	1
Willie Hernandez	0	0	1.69	3	0	0	2	0	5.1	4	1	0	0
Aurelio Lopez	1	0	0.00	2	0	0	0	0	3.0	1	0	1	4
Jack Morris	2	0	2.00	2	2	2	0	0	18.0	13	4	3	13
Dan Petry	0	1	9.00	2	2	0	0	0	8.0	14	8	5	4
Bill Scherrer	0	0	3.00	3	0	0	0	0	3.0	5	1	0	0
Milt Wilcox	1	0	1.50	1	1	0	0	0	6.0	7	1	2	4
TOTAL	4	1	3.07	14	5	2	2	0	44.0	44	15	11	26

SD (N)

PLAYER/POS	AVG	G	AB	R	H	2B	3B	HR	RB	BB	SO	SB
Kurt Bevacqua, dh	.412	5	17	4	7	2	0	2	4	1	2	0
Bruce Bochy, ph	1.000	1	1	0	1	0	0	0	0	0	0	0
Greg Booker, p	.000	1	0	0	0	0	0	0	0	0	0	0
Bobby Brown, of	.067	5	15	1	1	0	0	0	2	0	4	0
Dave Dravecky, p	.000	2	0	0	0	0	0	0	0	0	0	0
Tim Flannery, 2b	1.000	1	1	0	1	0	0	0	0	0	0	0
Steve Garvey, 1b	.200	5	20	2	4	2	0	0	2	0	2	0
Rich Gossage, p	.000	2	0	0	0	0	0	0	0	0	0	0
Tony Gwynn, of	.263	5	19	1	5	0	0	0	0	3	2	1
Greg Harris, p	.000	1	0	0	0	0	0	0	0	0	0	0
Andy Hawkins, p	.000	3	0	0	0	0	0	0	0	0	0	0
Terry Kennedy, c	.211	5	19	2	4	1	0	1	3	1	1	0
Craig Lefferts, p	.000	3	0	0	0	0	0	0	0	0	0	0
Tim Lollar, p	.000	1	0	0	0	0	0	0	0	0	0	0
Carmelo Martinez, of	.176	5	17	0	3	0	0	0	0	1	9	0
Graig Nettles, 3b	.250	5	12	2	3	0	0	0	2	5	0	0
Ron Roenicke, of-1	.000	2	0	0	0	0	0	0	0	0	0	0
Luis Salazar, of-2,3b-1	.333	4	3	0	1	0	0	0	0	0	0	0
Eric Show, p	.000	1	0	0	0	0	0	0	0	0	0	0
Champ Summers, ph	.000	1	1	0	0	0	0	0	0	0	1	0
Garry Templeton, ss	.316	5	19	1	6	1	0	0	0	0	3	0
Mark Thurmond, p	.000	2	0	0	0	0	0	0	0	0	0	0
Ed Whitson, p	.000	1	0	0	0	0	0	0	0	0	0	0
Alan Wiggins, 2b	.364	5	22	2	8	1	0	0	1	0	2	1
TOTAL	.265		166	15	44	7	0	3	14	11	26	2

PITCHER	W	L	ERA	G	GS	CG	SV	SHO	IP	H	ER	BB	SO
Greg Booker	0	0	9.00	1	0	0	0	0	1.0	0	1	4	0
Dave Dravecky	0	0	0.00	2	0	0	0	0	4.2	3	0	1	5
Rich Gossage	0	0	13.50	2	0	0	0	0	2.2	3	4	1	2
Greg Harris	0	0	0.00	1	0	0	0	0	5.1	3	0	3	5
Andy Hawkins	1	1	0.75	3	0	0	0	0	12.0	4	1	6	4
Craig Lefferts	0	0	0.00	3	0	0	1	0	6.0	2	0	1	7
Tim Lollar	0	1	21.60	1	1	0	0	0	1.2	4	4	4	0
Eric Show	0	1	10.13	1	1	0	0	0	2.2	4	3	1	2
Mark Thurmond	0	1	10.13	2	2	0	0	0	5.1	12	6	3	2
Ed Whitson	0	0	40.50	1	1	0	0	0	0.2	5	3	0	0
TOTAL	1	4	4.71	17	5	0	1	0	42.0	40	22	24	27

GAME 1 AT SD OCT 9

DET	100 020 000	3 8 0
SD	200 000 000	2 8 1

Pitchers: MORRIS vs THURMOND, Hawkins (6), Dravecky (8)
Home Runs: Herndon-DET
Attendance: 57,908

GAME 2 AT SD OCT 10

DET	300 000 000	3 7 3
SD	100 130 00X	5 11 0

Pitchers: PETRY, Lopez (5), Scherrer (6), Hernandez (8) vs Whitson, HAWKINS (1), Lefferts (7)
Home Runs: Bevacqua-SD
Attendance: 57,911

GAME 3 AT DET OCT 12

SD	001 000 100	2 5 0
DET	041 000 00X	5 7 0

Pitchers: LOLLAR, Booker (2), Harris (3) vs WILCOX, Scherrer (7), Hernandez (7)
Home Runs: Castillo-DET
Attendance: 51,970

GAME 4 AT DET OCT 13

SD	010 000 001	2 10 2
DET	202 000 00X	4 7 0

Pitchers: SHOW, Dravecky (3), Lefferts (7), Gossage (8) vs MORRIS
Home Runs: Trammell-DET (2), Kennedy-SD
Attendance: 52,130

GAME 5 AT DET OCT 14

SD	001 200 010	4 10 1
DET	300 010 13X	8 11 1

Pitchers: Thurmond, HAWKINS (1), Lefferts (5), Gossage (7) vs Petry, Scherrer (4), LOPEZ (5), Hernandez (8)
Home Runs: Gibson-DET (2), Parrish-DET, Bevacqua-SD
Attendance: 51,901

The Dodgers' league-leading pitchers held St. Louis to three runs over the first two games, even though the Cardinals recorded eight hits per game. But the Cards' league-leading hitters put their blows to better advantage in the next four games of the expanded LCS, scoring twenty-six times for four wins and the pennant.

Fernando Valenzuela captured Game One for the Dodgers, thanks in part to some ragged fielding by the usually sharp Cardinal infield. And as Orel Hershiser was holding St. Louis to two runs in Game Two, an errant Cardinal pickoff throw and heavy Dodger hitting gave him an increasingly comfortable lead.

When the series shifted to St. Louis for Game Three, the Cardinals revived, scoring twice in each of the first two innings for a quick lead, which they held for their first win. In Game Four they unloaded for nine runs in the second inning, and in Game Five—with the game and series tied in the bottom of the ninth—Ozzie Smith hit his first lefthanded home run ever to give St. Louis the series lead.

Back in Los Angeles, the Dodgers scored first in Game Six, and held a 4–1 lead after six innings. But three Cardinals scored on four hits in the seventh, and though Dodger Mike Marshall's eighth-inning home run restored the lead to Los Angeles, Cardinal Jack Clark settled things with a three-run homer in the ninth.

St. Louis Cardinals (East), 4; Los Angeles Dodgers (West), 2

STL (E)

PLAYER/POS	AVG	G	AB	R	H	2B	3B	HR	RB	BB	SO	SB
Joaquin Andujar, p	.250	2	4	1	1	1	0	0	0	0	1	0
Steve Braun, ph	.000	2	2	0	0	0	0	0	0	0	0	0
Bill Campbell, p	.000	3	0	0	0	0	0	0	0	0	0	0
Cesar Cedeno, of-4	.167	5	12	2	2	1	0	0	0	2	3	0
Jack Clark, 1b	.381	6	21	4	8	0	0	1	4	5	5	0
Vince Coleman, of	.286	3	14	2	4	0	0	0	1	0	2	1
Danny Cox, p	.000	1	2	0	0	0	0	0	0	1	1	0
Ken Dayley, p	.500	5	2	0	1	0	0	0	0	0	0	0
Bob Forsch, p	.000	1	0	0	0	0	0	0	0	0	0	0
Brian Harper, ph	.000	1	1	0	0	0	0	0	0	0	0	0
Tommy Herr, 2b	.333	6	21	2	7	4	0	1	6	5	2	1
Rick Horton, p	.000	3	0	0	0	0	0	0	0	0	0	0
Mike Jorgensen, ph	.000	2	2	0	0	0	0	0	0	0	1	0
Jeff Lahti, p	.000	2	0	0	0	0	0	0	0	0	0	0
Tito Landrum, of-4	.429	5	14	2	6	0	0	0	4	1	1	1
Willie McGee, of	.269	6	26	6	7	1	0	0	3	3	6	2
Tom Nieto, c	.000	1	3	1	0	0	0	0	0	1	2	0
Terry Pendleton, 3b	.208	6	24	2	5	1	0	0	4	1	3	0
Darrell Porter, c	.267	5	15	1	4	1	0	0	0	5	4	0
Ozzie Smith, ss	.435	6	23	4	10	1	1	1	3	3	1	1
John Tudor, p	.000	2	4	1	0	0	0	0	0	1	1	0
Andy Van Slyke, of	.091	5	11	1	1	0	0	0	1	2	1	0
Todd Worrell, p	.000	4	0	0	0	0	0	0	0	0	0	0
TOTAL	.279		201	29	56	10	1	3	26	30	34	6

PITCHER	W	L	ERA	G	GS	CG	SV	SHO	IP	H	ER	BB	SO
Joaquin Andujar	0	1	6.97	2	2	0	0	0	10.1	14	8	4	9
Bill Campbell	0	0	0.00	3	0	0	0	0	2.1	3	0	0	2
Danny Cox	1	0	3.00	1	1	0	0	0	6.0	4	2	5	4
Ken Dayley	0	0	0.00	5	0	0	2	0	6.0	2	0	1	3
Bob Forsch	0	0	5.40	1	1	0	0	0	3.1	3	2	2	0
Rick Horton	0	0	9.00	3	0	0	0	0	3.0	4	3	2	1
Jeff Lahti	1	0	0.00	2	0	0	0	0	2.0	2	0	0	1
John Tudor	1	1	2.84	2	2	0	0	0	12.2	10	4	3	8
Todd Worrell	1	0	1.42	4	0	0	0	0	6.1	4	1	2	3
TOTAL	4	2	3.46	23	6	0	2	0	52.0	46	20	19	31

LA (W)

PLAYER/POS	AVG	G	AB	R	H	2B	3B	HR	RB	BB	SO	SB
Dave Anderson, ss-3,3b-1	.000	4	5	1	0	0	0	0	0	3	1	0
Bob Bailor, 3b	.000	2	1	0	0	0	0	0	0	0	0	0
Greg Brock, 1b-4	.083	5	12	2	1	0	0	1	2	2	2	0
Enos Cabell, 1b-3	.077	5	13	1	1	0	0	0	0	0	3	0
Bobby Castillo, p	.000	1	2	0	0	0	0	0	0	0	0	0
Carlos Diaz, p	.000	2	0	0	0	0	0	0	0	0	0	0
Mariano Duncan, ss	.222	5	18	2	4	2	1	0	1	1	3	1
Pedro Guerrero, of	.250	6	20	2	5	1	0	0	4	5	2	2
Orel Hershiser, p	.286	2	7	1	2	0	0	0	0	1	2	0
Rick Honeycutt, p	.000	2	0	0	0	0	0	0	0	0	0	0
Ken Howell, p	.000	1	0	0	0	0	0	0	0	0	0	0
Jay Johnstone, ph	.000	1	1	0	0	0	0	0	0	0	0	0
Ken Landreaux, of	.389	5	18	4	7	3	0	0	2	1	1	0
Bill Madlock, 3b	.333	6	24	5	8	1	0	3	7	0	2	1
Candy Maldonado, of-3	.143	4	7	1	1	0	0	0	0	1	3	0
Mike Marshall, of	.217	6	23	1	5	2	0	1	3	1	3	0
Len Matuszek, 1b-1,of-1	1.000	3	1	1	1	0	0	0	0	0	0	0
Tom Niedenfuer, p	.000	3	1	0	0	0	0	0	0	0	1	0
Jerry Reuss, p	.000	1	0	0	0	0	0	0	0	0	0	0
Steve Sax, 2b	.300	6	20	1	6	3	0	0	1	1	5	0
Mike Scioscia, c	.250	6	16	2	4	0	0	0	1	4	0	0
Fernando Valenzuela, p	.200	2	5	0	1	0	0	0	0	0	0	0
Bob Welch, p	.000	1	1	0	0	0	0	0	0	0	1	0
Terry Whitfield, ph	.000	1	0	0	0	0	0	0	0	0	0	0
Steve Yeager, c	.000	1	2	0	0	0	0	0	0	0	1	0
TOTAL	.234		197	23	46	12	1	5	23	19	31	4

PITCHER	W	L	ERA	G	GS	CG	SV	SHO	IP	H	ER	BB	SO
Bobby Castillo	0	0	3.38	1	0	0	0	0	5.1	4	2	2	4
Carlos Diaz	0	0	3.00	2	0	0	0	0	3.0	5	1	1	2
Orel Hershiser	1	0	3.52	2	2	1	0	0	15.1	17	6	6	5
Rick Honeycutt	0	0	13.50	2	0	0	0	0	1.1	4	2	2	1
Ken Howell	0	0	0.00	1	0	0	0	0	2.0	0	0	0	2
Tom Niedenfuer	0	2	6.35	3	0	0	1	0	5.2	5	4	2	5
Jerry Reuss	0	1	10.80	1	1	0	0	0	1.2	5	2	1	0
F. Valenzuela	1	0	1.88	2	2	0	0	0	14.1	11	3	10	13
Bob Welch	0	1	6.75	1	1	0	0	0	2.2	5	2	6	2
TOTAL	2	4	3.86	15	6	1	1	0	51.1	56	22	30	34

GAME 1 AT LA OCT 9

STL	000 000 100	1 8 1
LA	000 103 00X	4 8 0

Pitchers: TUDOR, Dayley (6), Campbell (7), Worrell (8) vs VALENZUELA, Niedenfuer (7)
Attendance: 55,270

GAME 2 AT LA OCT 10

STL	001 000 001	2 8 1
LA	003 212 00X	8 13 1

Pitchers: ANDUJAR, Horton (5), Campbell (6), Dayley (7), Lahti (8) vs HERSHISER
Home Runs: Brock-LA
Attendance: 55,222

GAME 3 AT STL OCT 12

LA	000 100 100	2 7 2
STL	220 000 00X	4 8 0

Pitchers: WELCH, Honeycutt (3), Diaz (5), Howell (7), Horton (7), Worrell (7), Dayley (9)
Home Runs: Herr-STL
Attendance: 53,708

GAME 4 AT STL OCT 13

LA	000 000 110	2 5 2
STL	090 110 01X	12 15 0

Pitchers: REUSS, Honeycutt (2), Castillo (2), Diaz (8) vs TUDOR, Horton (8), Campbell (9)
Home Runs: Madlock-LA
Attendance: 53,708

GAME 5 AT STL OCT 14

LA	000 200 000	2 5 1
STL	200 000 001	3 5 1

Pitchers: Valenzuela, NIEDENFUER (9) vs Forsch, Dayley (4), Worrell (7), LAHTI (9)
Home Runs: Madlock-LA, Smith-STL
Attendance: 53,708

GAME 6 AT LA OCT 16

STL	001 000 303	7 12 1
LA	110 020 010	5 8 0

Pitchers: Andujar, WORRELL (7), Dayley (9) vs Hershiser, NIEDENFUER (7)
Home Runs: Madlock-LA, Marshall-LA, Clark-STL
Attendance: 55,208

Were it not for the expansion of the LCS to a best-of-seven series, the Blue Jays would have won the pennant. But after winning three of the first four games, the Jays lost their steam and K.C. swept to their second pennant.

The pitching of Toronto ace Dave Stieb proved a key to the club's fortunes. Three times he started for the Jays. In the opener he threw eight shutout innings as the Jays won easily. In Game Four he continued to dominate batters, though three walks in the sixth helped the Royals score a go-ahead run before Toronto pulled it out (for reliever Tom Henke) with a three-run ninth. Had the series ended there, Stieb would have been a hero. But it didn't, and he was called upon again for Game Seven—perhaps with inadequate rest. This time he faltered. After giving up single runs in the second and fourth innings, he loaded the bases in the sixth with two walks and a hit batsman. Jim Sundberg unloaded them with a wind-blown triple, later scoring himself, and the Royals were on the road to victory.

George Brett keyed Kansas City's triumph. His four hits in Game Three (including two home runs) gave the club its first victory, and his RBI ground out in Game Five and go-ahead homer in Game Six proved game-winners in contests the Royals had to win.

Kansas City Royals (West), 4;
Toronto Blue Jays (East), 3

KC (W)

PLAYER/POS	AVG	G	AB	R	H	2B	3B	HR	RB	BB	SO	SB
Steve Balboni, 1b	.120	7	25	1	3	0	0	0	0	1	2	8	0
Buddy Biancalana, ss	.222	7	18	2	4	1	0	0	1	1	6	0
Bud Black, p	.000	3	0	0	0	0	0	0	0	0	0	0
George Brett, 3b	.348	7	23	6	8	2	0	3	5	7	5	0
Onix Concepcion, ss	.000	4	1	0	0	0	0	0	0	0	0	0
Steve Farr, p	.000	2	0	0	0	0	0	0	0	0	0	0
Mark Gubicza, p	.000	2	0	0	0	0	0	0	0	0	0	0
Dane Iorg, ph	.500	4	2	0	1	1	0	0	0	2	0	0
Danny Jackson, p	.000	2	0	0	0	0	0	0	0	0	0	0
Lynn Jones, of	.000	5	0	0	0	0	0	0	0	0	0	0
Charlie Leibrandt, p	.000	3	0	0	0	0	0	0	0	0	0	0
Hal McRae, dh	.261	6	23	1	6	2	0	0	3	1	6	0
Darryl Motley, of	.333	2	3	1	1	0	0	0	1	1	2	0
Jorge Orta, dh-1	.000	2	5	0	0	0	0	0	0	0	1	0
Jamie Quirk, ph	.000	1	1	0	0	0	0	0	0	0	0	0
Dan Quisenberry, p	.000	4	0	0	0	0	0	0	0	0	0	0
Bret Saberhagen, p	.000	2	0	0	0	0	0	0	0	0	0	0
Pat Sheridan, of	.150	7	20	4	3	0	0	2	3	2	3	0
Lonnie Smith, of	.250	7	28	2	7	2	0	0	1	3	6	1
Jim Sundberg, c	.167	7	24	3	4	1	1	1	6	1	7	0
Frank White, 2b	.200	7	25	1	5	0	0	0	3	1	2	0
Willie Wilson, of	.310	7	29	5	9	0	0	1	2	1	5	1
TOTAL	.225		227	26	51	9	1	7	26	22	51	2

PITCHER	W	L	ERA	G	GS	CG	SV	SHO	IP	H	ER	BB	SO
Bud Black	0	0	1.69	3	1	0	0	0	10.2	11	2	4	8
Steve Farr	1	0	1.42	2	0	0	0	0	6.1	4	1	1	3
Mark Gubicza	1	0	3.24	2	1	0	0	0	8.1	4	3	4	4
Danny Jackson	1	0	0.00	2	1	1	0	1	10.0	10	0	1	7
Charlie Leibrandt	1	2	5.28	3	2	0	0	0	15.1	17	9	4	6
Dan Quisenberry	0	1	3.86	4	0	0	1	0	4.2	7	2	0	3
Bret Saberhagen	0	0	6.14	2	2	0	0	0	7.1	12	5	2	6
TOTAL	4	3	3.16	18	7	1	1	1	62.2	65	22	16	37

TOR (E)

PLAYER/POS	AVG	G	AB	R	H	2B	3B	HR	RB	BB	SO	SB
Jim Acker, p	.000	2	0	0	0	0	0	0	0	0	0	0
Doyle Alexander, p	.000	2	0	0	0	0	0	0	0	0	0	0
Jesse Barfield, of	.280	7	25	3	7	1	0	1	4	3	7	1
George Bell, of	.321	7	28	4	9	3	0	0	1	0	4	0
Jeff Burroughs, ph	.000	1	1	0	0	0	0	0	0	0	0	0
Jim Clancy, p	.000	1	0	0	0	0	0	0	0	0	0	0
Tony Fernandez, ss	.333	7	24	2	8	2	0	0	2	1	2	0
Cecil Fielder, ph	.333	3	3	0	1	1	0	0	0	0	1	0
Damaso Garcia, 2b	.233	7	30	4	7	4	0	1	3	3	0
Jeff Hearron, c	.000	2	0	0	0	0	0	0	0	0	0	0
Tom Henke, p	.000	3	0	0	0	0	0	0	0	0	0	0
Garth Iorg, 3b	.133	6	15	1	2	0	0	0	0	1	3	0
Cliff Johnson, dh	.368	7	19	1	7	2	0	0	2	1	4	0
Jimmy Key, p	.000	2	0	0	0	0	0	0	0	0	0	0
Dennis Lamp, p	.000	3	0	0	0	0	0	0	0	0	0	0
Gary Lavelle, p	.000	1	0	0	0	0	0	0	0	0	0	0
Manny Lee, 2b	.000	1	0	0	0	0	0	0	0	0	0	0
Lloyd Moseby, of	.226	7	31	5	7	1	0	0	4	2	3	1
Rance Mulliniks, 3b	.364	5	11	1	4	1	0	1	3	2	2	0
Al Oliver, dh	.375	5	8	0	3	1	0	0	3	0	0	0
Dave Stieb, p	.000	3	0	0	0	0	0	0	0	0	0	0
Lou Thornton, pr	.000	2	0	1	0	0	0	0	0	0	0	0
Willie Upshaw, 1b	.231	7	26	2	6	2	0	0	1	1	4	0
Ernie Whitt, c	.190	7	21	1	4	1	0	0	2	2	4	0
TOTAL	.269		242	25	65	19	0	2	23	16	37	2

PITCHER	W	L	ERA	G	GS	CG	SV	SHO	IP	H	ER	BB	SO
Jim Acker	0	0	0.00	2	0	0	0	0	6.0	2	0	0	5
Doyle Alexander	0	1	8.71	2	2	0	0	0	10.1	14	10	3	9
Jim Clancy	0	1	9.00	1	0	0	0	0	1.0	2	1	1	0
Tom Henke	2	0	4.26	3	0	0	0	0	6.1	5	3	4	4
Jimmy Key	0	1	5.19	2	2	0	0	0	8.2	15	5	2	5
Dennis Lamp	0	0	0.00	3	0	0	0	0	9.1	2	0	1	10
Gary Lavelle	0	0	INF	1	0	0	0	0	0.0	0	0	1	0
Dave Stieb	1	1	3.10	3	3	0	0	0	20.1	11	7	10	18
TOTAL	3	4	3.77	17	7	0	0	0	62.0	51	26	22	51

GAME 1 AT TOR OCT 8

KC	000 000 001	1	5	1
TOR	023 100 00X	6	11	0

Pitchers: LEIBRANDT, Farr (3), Gubicza (5), Jackson (8) vs STIEB, Henke (9)
Attendance: 39,115

GAME 2 AT TOR OCT 9

KC	002 100 001 1	5	10	3
TOR	000 102 010 2	6	10	0

Pitchers: Black, QUISENBERRY (8) vs Key, Lamp (4), Lavelle (8), HENKE (8)
Home Runs: Wilson-KC, Sheridan-KC
Attendance: 34,029

GAME 3 AT KC OCT 11

TOR	000 050 000	5	13	1
KC	100 112 01X	6	10	1

Pitchers: Alexander, Lamp (6), CLANCY (8) vs Saberhagen, Black (5), FARR (5)
Home Runs: Brett-KC (2), Barfield-TOR, Mulliniks-TOR, Sundberg-KC
Attendance: 40,224

GAME 4 AT KC OCT 12

TOR	000 000 003	3	7	0
KC	000 001 000	1	2	0

Pitchers: Stieb, HENKE (7) vs LEIBRANDT, Quisenberry (9)
Attendance: 41,112

GAME 5 AT KC OCT 13

TOR	000 000 000	0	8	0
KC	110 000 00X	2	8	0

Pitchers: KEY, Acker (6) vs JACKSON
Attendance: 40,046

GAME 6 AT TOR OCT 15

KC	101 012 000	5	8	1
TOR	101 001 000	3	8	2

Pitchers: GUBICZA, Black (6), Quisenberry (9) vs ALEXANDER, Lamp (6)
Home Runs: Brett-KC
Attendance: 37,557

GAME 7 AT TOR OCT 16

KC	010 104 000	6	8	0
TOR	000 010 001	2	8	1

Pitchers: Saberhagen, LEIBRANDT (4), Quisenberry (9) vs STIEB, Acker (6)
Home Runs: Sheridan-KC
Attendance: 32,084

The underdog Royals surprised St. Louis with superior hitting and pitching, and even outstole. the speedy Cards six bases to two. Still, had an umpire not muffed a call at first base in Game Six, St. Louis might have emerged from the fray wearing the world crown.

The Cardinals broke a 1–1 tie in the fourth inning of the opener with back-to-back doubles off Royal starter Danny Jackson, and held on behind the strong pitching of John Tudor and reliever Todd Worrell for a 3–1 win. In Game Two, except for the fourth inning, when he yielded a single and two doubles (for two runs) before retiring his first batter, Cardinal starter Danny Cox held the Royals in check. Royal starter Charlie Leibrandt hurled even more effectively, holding St. Louis to two hits—until the ninth inning, when four Cardinal hits (three of them doubles) produced four runs and a second Card victory.

Kansas City finally demonstrated its punch in Game Three. Frank White hit a two-run homer in the fifth, and the Royals scored four more times to win behind the six-hit hurling of sophomore sensation Bret Saberhagen. The next day, though, Royal bats died again against John Tudor, who shut them out on five hits. Three Royal pitchers yielded only six hits to Cardinal batters, but two were home runs to Tito Landrum and Willie McGee, and one was a triple to Terry Pendleton, who scored on a sacrifice squeeze.

Down three games to one, the Royals hammered eleven hits in Game Five for six runs to win behind Danny Jackson's five-hitter. Seven Royal hits in the first eight innings of Game Six, though, scored no runs against Cardinal starter Danny Cox and reliever Ken Dayley. But in the last of the ninth, with the Cards ahead 1–0 and Todd Worrell now pitching, Royal pinch hitter Jorge Orta was ruled safe at first on what the cameras showed clearly as an out. This miscall, followed by a pop foul that first baseman Jack Clark should have caught but didn't, opened the door to Cardinal disintegration. A single and passed ball put Royals at second and third, and after an intentional walk to set up the double play, pinch hitter Dane Iorg singled home the tying and winning Royal runs.

The Cardinals threw seven pitchers at Kansas City in the finale in a vain attempt to halt the Royals' fourteen-hit, eleven-run attack, while Bret Saberhagen stopped the Cards cold on five hits to bring the Royals their first world title.

Kansas City Royals (AL), 4; St. Louis Cardinals (NL), 3

KC (A)

PLAYER/POS	AVG	G	AB	R	H	2B	3B	HR	RB	BB	SO	SB
Steve Balboni, 1b	.320	7	25	2	8	0	0	0	3	5	4	0
Joe Beckwith, p	.000	1	0	0	0	0	0	0	0	0	0	0
Buddy Biancalana, ss	.278	7	18	2	5	0	0	0	2	5	4	0
Bud Black, p	.000	2	1	0	0	0	0	0	0	0	1	0
George Brett, 3b	.370	7	27	5	10	1	0	0	1	4	7	1
Onix Concepcion, ss-2	.000	3	0	1	0	0	0	0	0	0	0	0
Dane Iorg, ph	.500	2	2	0	1	0	0	0	2	0	0	0
Danny Jackson, p	.000	2	6	0	0	0	0	0	0	0	5	0
Lynn Jones, of-4	.667	6	3	0	2	1	1	0	0	0	0	0
Charlie Leibrandt, p	.000	2	4	0	0	0	0	0	0	0	2	0
Hal McRae, ph	.000	3	1	0	0	0	0	0	0	1	0	0
Darryl Motley, of-4	.364	5	11	1	4	0	0	1	3	0	1	0
Jorge Orta, ph	.333	3	3	0	1	0	0	0	0	0	0	0
Greg Pryor, 3b	.000	1	0	0	0	0	0	0	0	0	0	0
Dan Quisenberry, p	.000	4	0	0	0	0	0	0	0	0	0	0
Bret Saberhagen, p	.000	2	7	1	0	0	0	0	0	0	4	0
Pat Sheridan, of-4	.222	5	18	0	4	0	0	0	1	0	7	0
Lonnie Smith, of	.333	7	27	4	9	3	0	0	4	3	8	2
Jim Sundberg, c	.250	7	24	6	6	2	0	0	1	6	4	0
John Wathan, ph	.000	2	1	0	0	0	0	0	0	0	1	0
Frank White, 2b	.250	7	28	4	7	3	0	1	6	3	4	0
Willie Wilson, of	.367	7	30	2	11	0	1	0	3	1	4	3
TOTAL	.288		236	28	68	12	2	2	26	28	56	6

PITCHER	W	L	ERA	G	GS	CG	SV	SHO	IP	H	ER	BB	SO
Joe Beckwith	0	0	0.00	1	0	0	0	0	2.0	1	0	0	3
Bud Black	0	1	5.06	2	1	0	0	0	5.1	4	3	5	4
Danny Jackson	1	1	1.69	2	2	1	0	0	16.0	9	3	5	12
Charlie Leibrandt	0	1	2.76	2	2	0	0	0	16.1	10	5	4	10
Dan Quisenberry	1	0	2.08	4	0	0	0	0	4.1	5	1	3	3
Bret Saberhagen	2	0	0.50	2	2	2	0	1	18.0	11	1	1	10
TOTAL	4	3	1.89	13	7	3	0	1	62.0	40	13	18	42

STL (N)

PLAYER/POS	AVG	G	AB	R	H	2B	3B	HR	RB	BB	SO	SB
Joaquin Andujar, p	.000	2	1	0	0	0	0	0	0	0	1	0
Steve Braun, ph	.000	1	1	0	0	0	0	0	0	0	0	0
Bill Campbell, p	.000	3	0	0	0	0	0	0	0	0	0	0
Cesar Cedeno, of	.133	5	15	1	2	1	0	0	1	2	2	0
Jack Clark, 1b	.240	7	25	1	6	2	0	0	4	3	9	0
Danny Cox, p	.000	2	4	0	0	0	0	0	0	0	0	0
Ken Dayley, p	.000	4	0	0	0	0	0	0	0	0	0	0
Ivan DeJesus, ph	.000	1	1	0	0	0	0	0	0	0	0	0
Bob Forsch, p	.000	2	0	0	0	0	0	0	0	0	0	0
Brian Harper, ph	.250	4	4	0	1	0	0	0	1	0	1	0
Tommy Herr, 2b	.154	7	26	2	4	2	0	0	0	2	2	0
Rick Horton, p	.000	3	1	0	0	0	0	0	0	0	1	0
Mike Jorgensen, of-1	.000	2	3	0	0	0	0	0	0	0	0	0
Jeff Lahti, p	.000	3	0	0	0	0	0	0	0	0	0	0
Tito Landrum, of	.360	7	25	3	9	2	0	1	1	0	2	0
Tom Lawless, pr	.000	1	0	0	0	0	0	0	0	0	0	0
Willie McGee, of	.259	7	27	2	7	2	0	1	2	1	3	1
Tom Nieto, c	.000	2	5	0	0	0	0	0	0	1	2	0
Terry Pendleton, 3b	.261	7	23	2	6	1	1	0	3	3	2	0
Darrell Porter, c	.133	5	15	0	2	0	0	0	0	2	5	0
Ozzie Smith, ss	.087	7	23	1	2	0	0	0	0	4	0	1
John Tudor, p	.000	3	5	0	0	0	0	0	0	0	4	0
Andy Van Slyke, of	.091	6	11	0	1	0	0	0	0	0	5	0
Todd Worrell, p	.000	3	1	0	0	0	0	0	0	0	1	0
TOTAL	.185		216	13	40	10	1	2	13	18	42	2

PITCHER	W	L	ERA	G	GS	CG	SV	SHO	IP	H	ER	BB	SO
Joaquin Andujar	0	1	9.00	2	1	0	0	0	4.0	10	4	4	3
Bill Campbell	0	0	2.25	3	0	0	0	0	4.0	4	1	2	5
Danny Cox	0	0	1.29	2	2	0	0	0	14.0	14	2	4	13
Ken Dayley	1	0	0.00	4	0	0	0	0	6.0	1	0	3	5
Bob Forsch	0	1	12.00	2	1	0	0	0	3.0	6	4	1	3
Rick Horton	0	0	6.75	3	0	0	0	0	4.0	4	3	5	5
Jeff Lahti	0	0	12.27	3	0	0	1	0	3.2	10	5	0	2
John Tudor	2	1	3.00	3	3	1	0	1	18.0	15	6	7	14
Todd Worrell	0	1	3.86	3	0	0	1	0	4.2	4	2	2	6
TOTAL	3	4	3.96	25	7	1	2	1	61.1	68	27	28	56

Houston pitcher Mike Scott overwhelmed the Mets in Games One and Four, and would have faced them a third time in Game Seven if the Astros had won Game Six. They tried, scoring three runs in the first as Bob Knepper shut out the Mets on two hits through eight innings. But in the top of the ninth New York tied the game and held on into extra innings. No one scored again until the Mets put a run across in the fourteenth. Astro Billy Hatcher tied it up again later in the fourteenth with a home run just inside the left field foul pole. Two innings later the Mets (aided by a pair of wild pitches) scored three runs. Again the Astros came back, scoring twice, but fell just short as Jesse Orosco struck out Kevin Bass with two men on base to win his third game of the series and give New York the pennant.

In the series opener Houston scored just one run off Dwight Gooden, but it was enough, as Mike Scott, fanning fourteen, shut out the Mets on five hits. New York came back with five runs in Game Two to win behind Bob Ojeda, who gave up ten hits but only one run. In Game Three the Astros held the lead into the last of the sixth, when New York tied the score with four runs. Houston retook the lead in the seventh with a run, but Met Len Dykstra won it for New York with a two-run homer in the bottom of the ninth.

The Astros' win in Game Four evened the series. Houston had scored three runs by the time Scott (on his way to a three-hitter) gave the Mets their only run in the eighth. Houston's Nolan Ryan gave up only two hits in the first nine innings of Game Five (one of them Darryl Strawberry's game-tying solo homer in the fifth), striking out twelve. But New York's Gooden also yielded only one run in ten innings of work. Astro Charlie Kerfeld shut out the Mets in the tenth and eleventh, and the Mets' Orosco stopped Houston in the eleventh and twelfth. But in the last of the twelfth, Met catcher Gary Carter singled home a run off Kerfeld to end the game (and his series-long batting slump)—setting the stage for the sixteen-inning marathon the next day.

New York Mets (East), 4; Houston Astros (West), 2

NY (E)

PLAYER/POS	AVG	G	AB	R	H	2B	3B	HR	RB	BB	SO	SB
Rick Aguilera, p	.000	2	0	0	0	0	0	0	0	0	0	0
Wally Backman, 2b	.238	6	21	5	5	0	0	0	2	2	4	1
Gary Carter, c	.148	6	27	1	4	1	0	0	2	2	5	0
Ron Darling, p	.000	1	1	0	0	0	0	0	0	0	0	0
Lenny Dykstra, of	.304	6	23	3	7	1	1	1	3	2	4	1
Kevin Elster, ss	.000	4	3	0	0	0	0	0	0	0	1	0
Sid Fernandez, p	.000	1	1	0	0	0	0	0	0	0	0	0
Dwight Gooden, p	.000	2	5	0	0	0	0	0	0	0	2	0
Danny Heep, of-1	.250	5	4	0	1	0	0	0	1	0	2	0
Keith Hernandez, 1b	.269	6	26	3	7	1	1	0	3	3	6	0
Howard Johnson, ph	.000	2	2	0	0	0	0	0	0	0	0	0
Ray Knight, 3b	.167	6	24	1	4	0	0	0	2	1	5	0
Lee Mazzilli, ph	.200	5	5	0	1	0	0	0	0	0	3	0
Roger McDowell, p	.000	2	1	0	0	0	0	0	0	0	0	0
Kevin Mitchell, of	.250	2	8	1	2	0	0	0	0	0	1	0
Bob Ojeda, p	.000	2	5	1	0	0	0	0	0	0	2	0
Jesse Orosco, p	.000	4	0	0	0	0	0	0	0	0	0	0
Rafael Santana, ss	.176	6	17	0	3	0	0	0	0	0	3	0
Doug Sisk, p	.000	1	0	0	0	0	0	0	0	0	0	0
Darryl Strawberry, of	.227	6	22	4	5	1	0	2	5	3	12	1
Tim Teufel, 2b	.167	2	6	0	1	0	0	0	0	0	0	0
Mookie Wilson, of	.115	6	26	2	3	0	0	0	1	1	7	1
TOTAL	.189		227	21	43	4	2	3	19	14	57	4

PITCHER	W	L	ERA	G	GS	CG	SV	SHO	IP	H	ER	BB	SO
Rick Aguilera	0	0	0.00	2	0	0	0	0	5.0	2	0	2	2
Ron Darling	0	0	7.20	1	1	0	0	0	5.0	6	4	2	5
Sid Fernandez	0	1	4.50	1	1	0	0	0	6.0	3	3	1	5
Dwight Gooden	0	1	1.06	2	2	0	0	0	17.0	16	2	5	9
Roger McDowell	0	0	0.00	2	0	0	0	0	7.0	1	0	0	3
Bob Ojeda	1	0	2.57	2	2	1	0	0	14.0	15	4	4	6
Jesse Orosco	3	0	3.38	4	0	0	0	0	8.0	5	3	2	10
Doug Sisk	0	0	0.00	1	0	0	0	0	1.0	1	0	1	0
TOTAL	4	2	2.29	15	6	1	0		63.0	49	16	17	40

HOU (W)

PLAYER/POS	AVG	G	AB	R	H	2B	3B	HR	RB	BB	SO	SB
Larry Andersen, p	.000	2	0	0	0	0	0	0	0	0	0	0
Alan Ashby, c	.130	6	23	2	3	1	0	1	2	2	1	0
Kevin Bass, of	.292	6	24	0	7	2	0	0	0	4	4	2
Jeff Calhoun, p	.000	1	0	0	0	0	0	0	0	0	0	0
Jose Cruz, of	.192	6	26	0	5	0	0	0	2	1	8	0
Glenn Davis, 1b	.269	6	26	3	7	1	0	1	3	1	3	0
Bill Doran, 2b	.222	6	27	3	6	0	0	1	3	2	2	2
Phil Garner, 3b	.222	3	9	1	2	1	0	0	2	1	2	0
Billy Hatcher, of	.280	6	25	4	7	0	0	1	2	3	2	3
Charlie Kerfeld, p	.000	3	0	0	0	0	0	0	0	0	0	0
Bob Knepper, p	.000	2	5	0	0	0	0	0	0	1	2	0
Davey Lopes, ph	.000	3	2	1	0	0	0	0	0	1	0	0
Aurelio Lopez, p	.000	2	0	0	0	0	0	0	0	0	0	0
Jim Pankovits, ph	.000	2	2	0	0	0	0	0	0	0	1	0
Terry Puhl, ph	.667	3	3	0	2	0	0	0	0	0	0	1
Craig Reynolds, ss	.333	4	12	1	4	0	0	0	0	1	3	0
Nolan Ryan, p	.000	2	4	0	0	0	0	0	0	0	2	0
Mike Scott, p	.000	2	6	0	0	0	0	0	0	0	5	0
Dave Smith, p	.000	2	0	0	0	0	0	0	0	0	0	0
Dickie Thon, ss	.250	6	12	1	3	0	0	1	1	0	1	0
Denny Walling, 3b	.158	5	19	1	3	1	0	0	2	0	4	0
TOTAL	.218		225	17	49	6	0	5	17	17	40	8

PITCHER	W	L	ERA	G	GS	CG	SV	SHO	IP	H	ER	BB	SO
Larry Andersen	0	0	0.00	2	0	0	0	0	5.0	1	0	2	3
Jeff Calhoun	0	0	9.00	1	0	0	0	0	1.0	1	1	1	0
Charlie Kerfeld	0	1	2.25	3	0	0	0	0	4.0	2	1	1	4
Bob Knepper	0	0	3.52	2	2	0	0	0	15.1	13	6	1	9
Aurelio Lopez	0	1	8.10	2	0	0	0	0	3.1	7	3	4	3
Nolan Ryan	0	1	3.86	2	2	0	0	0	14.0	9	6	1	17
Mike Scott	2	0	0.50	2	2	2	0	1	18.0	8	1	1	19
Dave Smith	0	1	9.00	2	0	0	0	0	2.0	2	2	3	2
TOTAL	2	4	2.87	16	6	2	0	1	62.2	43	20	14	57

For the second time in the two years of the expanded LCS, a club that would have been eliminated in a five-game series came back to take the pennant in seven games. The first two games were one-sided. California scored five early runs off Roger Clemens and breezed to an easy 8–1 win in the opener. Boston retaliated in Game Two with nine runs, breaking the game open with six unanswered runs in the seventh and eighth innings.

Game Three was close until the Angels homered twice for three runs with two out in the seventh to break a 1–1 tie. In Game Four, the Angels were handed a tie in the last of the ninth when Boston reliever Calvin Schiraldi hit a batter with the bases loaded and won in the eleventh on Bobby Grich's RBI single.

The Red Sox, down three games to one, were on the brink of elimination in Game Five, with two out in the ninth, when Dave Henderson, after fouling off one third-strike pitch, hit the next for a two-run homer that gave Boston a one-run lead. The Angels tied the game in the last of the ninth, but Henderson's sacrifice fly in the eleventh put the Sox ahead for good.

Boston needed two more wins and got them with surprising ease, 10–4 and 8–1, as Oil Can Boyd and Clemens redeemed their earlier losses.

Boston Red Sox (East), 4;
California Angels (West), 3

BOS (E)

PLAYER/POS	AVG	G	AB	R	H	2B	3B	HR	RB	BB	SO	SB
Tony Armas, of	.125	5	16	1	2	1	0	0	0	0	2	0
Marty Barrett, 2b	.367	7	30	4	11	2	0	0	5	2	2	0
Don Baylor, dh	.346	7	26	6	9	3	0	1	2	4	5	0
Wade Boggs, 3b	.233	7	30	3	7	1	1	0	2	4	1	0
Oil Can Boyd, p	.000	2	0	0	0	0	0	0	0	0	0	0
Bill Buckner, 1b	.214	7	28	3	6	1	0	0	3	0	2	0
Roger Clemens, p	.000	3	0	0	0	0	0	0	0	0	0	0
Steve Crawford, p	.000	1	0	0	0	0	0	0	0	0	0	0
Dwight Evans, of	.214	7	28	2	6	1	0	1	4	3	3	0
Rich Gedman, c	.357	7	28	4	10	1	0	1	6	0	4	0
Mike Greenwell, ph	.500	2	2	0	1	0	0	0	0	0	0	0
Dave Henderson, of	.111	5	9	3	1	0	0	1	4	2	2	0
Bruce Hurst, p	.000	2	0	0	0	0	0	0	0	0	0	0
Spike Owen, ss	.429	7	21	5	9	0	1	0	3	2	2	1
Jim Rice, of	.161	7	31	8	5	1	0	2	6	1	8	0
Ed Romero, ss	.000	1	2	0	0	0	0	0	0	0	0	0
Joe Sambito, p	.000	3	0	0	0	0	0	0	0	0	0	0
Calvin Schiraldi, p	.000	4	0	0	0	0	0	0	0	0	0	0
Bob Stanley, p	.000	3	0	0	0	0	0	0	0	0	0	0
Dave Stapleton, 1b	.667	4	3	2	2	0	0	0	0	0	1	0
TOTAL	.272		254	41	69	11	2	6	35	19	31	1

PITCHER	W	L	ERA	G	GS	CG	SV	SHO	IP	H	ER	BB	SO
Oil Can Boyd	1	1	4.61	2	2	0	0	0	13.2	17	7	3	8
Roger Clemens	1	1	4.37	3	3	0	0	0	22.2	22	11	7	17
Steve Crawford	1	0	0.00	1	0	0	0	0	1.2	1	0	2	1
Bruce Hurst	1	0	2.40	2	2	1	0	0	15.0	18	4	1	8
Joe Sambito	0	0	13.50	3	0	0	0	0	0.2	1	1	1	0
Calvin Schiraldi	0	1	1.50	4	0	0	1	0	6.0	5	1	3	9
Bob Stanley	0	0	3.18	3	0	0	0	0	5.2	7	2	3	1
TOTAL	4	3	3.58	18	7	1	1	0	65.1	71	26	20	44

CAL (W)

PLAYER/POS	AVG	G	AB	R	H	2B	3B	HR	RB	BB	SO	SB
Bob Boone, c	.455	7	22	4	10	0	0	1	2	1	3	0
Rick Burleson, 2b-2,dh-1	.273	4	11	0	3	0	0	0	0	0	0	0
John Candelaria, p	.000	2	0	0	0	0	0	0	0	0	0	0
Doug Corbett, p	.000	3	0	0	0	0	0	0	0	0	0	0
Doug DeCinces, 3b	.281	7	32	2	9	3	0	1	3	0	2	0
Brian Downing, of	.222	7	27	2	6	0	0	1	7	4	5	0
Chuck Finley, p	.000	3	0	0	0	0	0	0	0	0	0	0
Bobby Grich, 2b-3,1b-3	.208	6	24	1	5	0	0	1	3	0	8	0
George Hendrick, of-2,1b-1	.083	3	12	0	1	0	0	0	0	0	2	0
Jack Howell, 3b	.000	2	1	0	0	0	0	0	0	1	1	0
Reggie Jackson, dh	.192	6	26	2	5	2	0	0	2	2	7	0
Ruppert Jones, of-5	.176	6	17	4	3	1	0	0	2	5	2	0
Wally Joyner, 1b	.455	3	11	3	5	2	0	1	2	2	0	0
Gary Lucas, p	.000	4	0	0	0	0	0	0	0	0	0	0
Kirk McCaskill, p	.000	2	0	0	0	0	0	0	0	0	0	0
Donnie Moore, p	.000	3	0	0	0	0	0	0	0	0	0	0
Jerry Narron, c-3	.500	4	2	1	1	0	0	0	0	0	1	0
Gary Pettis, of	.346	7	26	4	9	1	0	1	4	3	5	0
Vern Ruhle, p	.000	1	0	0	0	0	0	0	0	0	0	0
Dick Schofield, ss	.300	7	30	4	9	1	0	1	2	1	5	1
Don Sutton, p	.000	2	0	0	0	0	0	0	0	0	0	0
Devon White, of-3	.500	4	2	2	1	0	0	0	0	0	1	0
Rob Wilfong, 2b	.308	4	13	1	4	1	0	0	2	0	2	0
Mike Witt, p	.000	2	0	0	0	0	0	0	0	0	0	0
TOTAL	.277		256	30	71	11	0	7	29	20	44	1

PITCHER	W	L	ERA	G	GS	CG	SV	SHO	IP	H	ER	BB	SO
John Candelaria	1	1	0.84	2	2	0	0	0	10.2	11	1	6	7
Doug Corbett	1	0	5.40	3	0	0	0	0	6.2	9	4	2	2
Chuck Finley	0	0	0.00	3	0	0	0	0	2.0	1	0	0	1
Gary Lucas	0	0	11.57	4	0	0	0	0	2.1	3	3	1	2
Kirk McCaskill	0	2	7.71	2	2	0	0	0	9.1	16	8	5	7
Donnie Moore	0	1	7.20	3	0	0	1	0	5.0	8	4	2	0
Vern Ruhle	0	0	13.50	1	0	0	0	0	0.2	2	1	0	0
Don Sutton	0	0	1.86	2	1	0	0	0	9.2	6	2	1	4
Mike Witt	1	0	2.55	2	2	1	0	0	17.2	13	5	2	8
TOTAL	3	4	3.94	22	7	1	1	0	64.0	69	28	19	31

In their three most recent Series appearances—1946, 1967, and 1975—the Red Sox had battled to a seventh game, only to lose. This time they came within one strike of winning the crown in the sixth game—but wound up losing again in Game Seven.

Boston surprised the favored Mets by taking the first two games in New York. Bruce Hurst (with relief from Calvin Schiraldi in the ninth) pitched a four-hitter. New York's Ron Darling hurled just as well but lost when a seventh-inning walk, a wild pitch, and an error by second baseman Tim Teufel moved Jim Rice around the bases with the game's only run. Game Two, close for three innings, turned into a 9–3 Boston blowout as the Sox racked four of the five Met pitchers for eighteen hits, including home runs by Dave Henderson and Dwight Evans.

When the Series moved to Boston, though, the Mets revived to rap Sox starter Oil Can Boyd and two relievers for thirteen hits and seven runs (starting with Len Dykstra's leadoff home run in the first inning) as former Sox pitcher Bob Ojeda subdued his old teammates, giving up just one run on five hits in his seven innings of work. The next day Ron Darling redeemed his first-game loss with seven shutout innings as his teammates built him a 6–0 lead (five of the runs scoring on homers by Dykstra and a pair by Gary Carter). The game ended at 6–2, with the Series even at two wins apiece.

Boston recovered in its final home appearance, taking a 4–0 lead and holding it until Teufel spoiled Bruce Hurst's try for a second shutout by homering in the eighth inning. Hurst yielded a second run with two out in the ninth, but struck out Len Dykstra on three pitches to seal his second win.

The ninth inning of Game Six ended with the score tied 3–3. Boston's Dave Henderson led off the tenth with a home run and two more Sox hits made the score 5–3. Boston reliever Calvin Schiraldi retired the first two Mets in the last of the tenth on long flies, but then three Mets singled, driving in one run and driving out Schiraldi. Bob Stanley, his replacement, had two strikes on Mookie Wilson when a wild pitch let in the tying run, and then Wilson's grounder went through first baseman Bill Buckner's legs as the winning Met bounded across the plate.

The Red Sox nearly recovered in Game Seven. Second-inning home runs by Dwight Evans and Rich Gedman, a walk, sacrifice, and single gave Boston a 3–0 lead which they held into the sixth inning. But then starter Bruce Hurst lost his touch: four hits and a walk later the score was tied. A succession of five

New York Mets (NL), 4; Boston Red Sox (AL), 3

NY (N)

PLAYER/POS	AVG	G	AB	R	H	2B	3B	HR	RB	BB	SO	SB
Rick Aguilera, p	.000	1	0	0	0	0	0	0	0	0	0	0
Wally Backman, 2b	.333	6	18	4	6	0	0	0	1	3	2	1
Gary Carter, c	.276	7	29	4	8	2	0	2	9	0	4	0
Ron Darling, p	.000	3	3	0	0	0	0	0	0	0	1	0
Lenny Dykstra, of	.296	7	27	4	8	0	0	2	3	2	7	0
Kevin Elster, ss	.000	1	1	0	0	0	0	0	0	0	0	0
Sid Fernandez, p	.000	3	0	0	0	0	0	0	0	0	0	0
Dwight Gooden, p	.500	2	2	1	1	0	0	0	0	0	0	0
Danny Heep, dh-2,of-1	.091	5	11	0	1	0	0	0	2	1	1	0
Keith Hernandez, 1b	.231	7	26	1	6	0	0	0	4	5	1	0
Howard Johnson, 3b-1,ss-1	.000	2	5	0	0	0	0	0	0	0	2	0
Ray Knight, 3b	.391	6	23	4	9	1	0	1	5	2	2	0
Lee Mazzilli, of-1	.400	4	5	2	2	0	0	0	0	0	0	0
Roger McDowell, p	.000	5	0	0	0	0	0	0	0	0	0	0
Kevin Mitchell, of-2,dh-1	.250	5	8	1	2	0	0	0	0	0	3	0
Bob Ojeda, p	.000	2	2	0	0	0	0	0	0	0	1	0
Jesse Orosco, p	1.000	4	1	0	1	0	0	0	1	0	0	0
Rafael Santana, ss	.250	7	20	3	5	0	0	0	2	2	5	0
Doug Sisk, p	.000	1	0	0	0	0	0	0	0	0	0	0
Darryl Strawberry, of	.208	7	24	4	5	1	0	1	1	4	6	3
Tim Teufel, 2b	.444	3	9	1	4	1	0	1	1	1	2	0
Mookie Wilson, of	.269	7	26	3	7	1	0	0	0	1	6	3
TOTAL	.271		240	32	65	6	0	7	29	21	43	7

PITCHER	W	L	ERA	G	GS	CG	SV	SHO	IP	H	ER	BB	SO
Rick Aguilera	1	0	12.00	1	0	0	0	0	3.0	8	4	1	4
Ron Darling	1	1	1.53	3	3	0	0	0	17.2	13	3	10	12
Sid Fernandez	0	0	1.35	3	0	0	0	0	6.2	6	1	1	10
Dwight Gooden	0	2	8.00	2	2	0	0	0	9.0	17	8	4	9
Roger McDowell	1	0	4.91	5	0	0	0	0	7.1	10	4	6	2
Bob Ojeda	1	0	2.08	2	2	0	0	0	13.0	13	3	5	9
Jesse Orosco	0	0	0.00	4	0	0	2	0	5.2	2	0	0	6
Doug Sisk	0	0	0.00	1	0	0	0	0	0.2	0	0	1	1
TOTAL	4	3	3.29	21	7	0	2	0	63.0	69	23	28	53

BOS (A)

PLAYER/POS	AVG	G	AB	R	H	2B	3B	HR	RB	BB	SO	SB
Tony Armas, ph	.000	1	1	0	0	0	0	0	0	0	1	0
Marty Barrett, 2b	.433	7	30	1	13	2	0	0	4	5	2	0
Don Baylor, dh-3	.182	4	11	1	2	1	0	0	1	1	3	0
Wade Boggs, 3b	.290	7	31	3	9	3	0	0	3	4	2	0
Oil Can Boyd, p	.000	1	0	0	0	0	0	0	0	0	0	0
Bill Buckner, 1b	.188	7	32	2	6	0	0	0	1	0	3	0
Roger Clemens, p	.000	2	4	1	0	0	0	0	0	0	1	0
Steve Crawford, p	.000	3	1	0	0	0	0	0	0	0	0	0
Dwight Evans, of	.308	7	26	4	8	2	0	2	9	4	3	0
Rich Gedman, c	.200	7	30	1	6	1	0	1	1	0	10	0
Mike Greenwell, ph	.000	4	3	0	0	0	0	0	0	1	2	0
Dave Henderson, of	.400	7	25	6	10	1	1	2	5	2	6	0
Bruce Hurst, p	.000	3	3	0	0	0	0	0	0	0	3	0
Al Nipper, p	.000	2	0	0	0	0	0	0	0	0	0	0
Spike Owen, ss	.300	7	20	2	6	0	0	0	2	5	6	0
Jim Rice, of	.333	7	27	6	9	1	1	0	6	9	9	0
Ed Romero, ss	.000	3	1	0	0	0	0	0	0	0	0	0
Joe Sambito, p	.000	2	0	0	0	0	0	0	0	0	0	0
Calvin Schiraldi, p	.000	3	1	0	0	0	0	0	0	0	1	0
Bob Stanley, p	.000	5	1	0	0	0	0	0	0	0	0	0
Dave Stapleton, 1b	.000	3	1	0	0	0	0	0	0	0	0	0
TOTAL	.278		248	27	69	11	2	5	26	28	53	0

PITCHER	W	L	ERA	G	GS	CG	SV	SHO	IP	H	ER	BB	SO
Oil Can Boyd	0	1	7.71	1	1	0	0	0	7.0	9	6	1	3
Roger Clemens	0	0	3.18	2	2	0	0	0	11.1	9	4	6	11
Steve Crawford	1	0	6.23	3	0	0	0	0	4.1	5	3	0	4
Bruce Hurst	2	0	1.96	3	3	1	0	0	23.0	18	5	6	17
Al Nipper	0	1	7.11	2	1	0	0	0	6.1	10	5	2	2
Joe Sambito	0	0	27.00	2	0	0	0	0	0.1	2	1	2	0
Calvin Schiraldi	0	2	13.50	3	0	0	1	0	4.0	7	6	3	2
Bob Stanley	0	0	0.00	5	0	0	0	1	6.1	5	0	1	4
TOTAL	3	4	4.31	21	7	1	2	0	62.2	65	30	21	43

Sox relievers tried to hold the line, but the Mets scored five runs to Boston's two in the final innings for an 8–5 triumph.

GAME 1 AT NY OCT 18

BOS 000 000 100   1 5 0
NY 000 000 000   0 4 1

Pitchers: HURST, Schiraldi (9) vs DARLING, McDowell (8)
Attendance: 55,076

GAME 2 AT NY OCT 19

BOS 003 120 201   9 18 0
NY 002 010 000   3 8 1

Pitchers: Clemens, CRAWFORD (5), Stanley (7) vs GOODEN, Aguilera (6), Orosco (7), Fernandez (9), Sisk (9)
Home Runs: Henderson-BOS, Evans-BOS
Attendance: 55,063

GAME 3 AT BOS OCT 21

NY 400 000 210   7 13 0
BOS 001 000 000   1 5 0

Pitchers: OJEDA, McDowell (8) vs BOYD, Sambito (8), Stanley (8)
Home Runs: Dykstra-NY
Attendance: 33,595

GAME 4 AT BOS OCT 22

NY 000 300 210   6 12 0
BOS 000 000 020   2 7 1

Pitchers: DARLING, McDowell (7), Orosco (7) vs NIPPER, Crawford (7), Stanley (9)
Home Runs: Dykstra-NY, Carter-NY (2)
Attendance: 33,920

GAME 5 AT BOS OCT 23

NY 000 000 011   2 10 1
BOS 011 020 00X   4 12 0

Pitchers: GOODEN, Fernandez (5) vs HURST
Home Runs: Teufel-NY
Attendance: 34,010

GAME 6 AT NY OCT 25

BOS 110 000 100 2   5 13 3
NY 000 020 010 3   6 8 2

Pitchers: Clemens, SCHIRALDI (8), Stanley (10) vs Ojeda, McDowell (7), Orosco (8), AGUILERA (10)
Home Runs: Henderson-BOS
Attendance: 55,078

GAME 7 AT NY OCT 27

BOS 030 000 020   5 9 0
NY 000 003 32X   8 10 0

Pitchers: Hurst, SCHIRALDI (7), Sambito (7), Stanley (7), Nipper (8), Crawford (8) vs Darling, Fernandez (4), McDOWELL (8), Orosco (9)
Home Runs: Evans-BOS, Gedman-BOS, Knight-NY, Strawberry-NY
Attendance: 55,032

The Giants scored four times in the fourth inning of Game Five, winning the game and taking a 3–2 series advantage. But Cardinal pitchers shut them out the rest of the series (an NLCS record 22 innings) to capture the flag.

St. Louis won the opener 5–3, with pitcher Greg Mathews's two-run single in the sixth providing his margin of victory. The Giants came back in Game Two, supporting Dave Dravecky's two-hit shutout with home runs by Will Clark and Jeffrey Leonard. But the Cards retook the series lead in Game Three, overcoming a 0–4 deficit with two runs on Jim Lindeman's homer in the sixth and four more in the seventh (capped by Lindeman's sacrifice fly) for an eventual 6–5 win.

The Giants snapped back with a pair of wins, scoring four runs on three homers in Game Four (including Leonard's fourth in successive games—an LCS record), and six runs in Game Five. But Dravecky and the Giants lost a heartbreaker in Game Six when right fielder Candy Maldonado lost Tony Pena's fly in the lights for a triple. Pena scored on a sacrifice fly for the game's only run, as John Tudor and two late-inning relievers blanked the Giants. Danny Cox pitched an easier shutout in the finale as his Cardinals hammered seven Giant pitchers for twelve hits and six runs.

St. Louis Cardinals (East), 4; San Francisco Giants (West) 3

STL (E)

PLAYER/POS	AVG	G	AB	R	H	2B	3B	HR	RBI	BB	SO	SB
Jack Clark, ph	.000	1	1	0	0	0	0	0	0	0	1	0
Vince Coleman, of	.269	7	26	3	7	1	0	0	4	4	6	1
Danny Cox, p	.333	2	6	0	2	0	0	0	1	0	2	0
Ken Dayley, p	.000	3	0	0	0	0	0	0	0	0	0	0
Dan Driessen, 1b-4	.250	5	12	1	3	2	0	0	1	1	1	0
Curt Ford, of	.333	4	9	2	3	0	0	0	0	1	1	0
Bob Forsch, p	.000	3	0	0	0	0	0	0	0	0	0	0
Tommy Herr, 2b	.222	7	27	0	6	0	0	0	3	0	1	1
Rick Horton, p	.000	1	0	0	0	0	0	0	0	0	0	0
Lance Johnson, pr	.000	1	0	1	0	0	0	0	0	0	0	1
Tom Lawless, 3b-2,of-1	.333	3	6	0	2	0	0	0	0	0	1	0
Jim Lindeman, 1b	.308	5	13	1	4	0	0	1	3	0	3	0
Joe Magrane, p	.000	1	1	0	0	0	0	0	0	0	0	0
Greg Mathews, p	1.000	2	2	0	2	0	0	0	2	0	0	0
Willie McGee, of	.308	7	26	2	8	1	1	0	2	0	5	0
John Morris, of	.000	2	3	0	0	0	0	0	0	0	0	0
Jose Oquendo, of-5,3b-1	.167	5	12	3	2	0	0	1	4	3	2	0
Tom Pagnozzi, ph	.000	1	1	0	0	0	0	0	0	0	0	0
Tony Pena, c	.381	7	21	5	8	0	1	0	0	3	4	1
Terry Pendleton, 3b	.211	6	19	3	4	0	1	0	1	0	6	0
Ozzie Smith, ss	.200	7	25	2	5	0	1	0	1	3	4	0
John Tudor, p	.000	2	4	0	0	0	0	0	0	0	4	0
Todd Worrell, p-3,of-1	.000	3	1	0	0	0	0	0	0	0	1	0
TOTAL	.260		215	23	56	4	4	2	22	16	42	4

PITCHER	W	L	ERA	G	GS	CG	SV	SHO	IP	H	ER	BB	SO
Danny Cox	1	1	2.12	2	2	2	0	1	17.0	17	4	3	11
Ken Dayley	0	0	0.00	3	0	0	2	0	4.0	1	0	2	4
Bob Forsch	1	1	12.00	3	0	0	0	0	3.0	4	4	1	3
Rick Horton	0	0	0.00	1	0	0	0	0	3.0	2	0	0	2
Joe Magrane	0	0	9.00	1	1	0	0	0	4.0	4	4	2	3
Greg Mathews	1	0	3.48	2	2	0	0	0	10.1	6	4	3	10
John Tudor	1	1	1.76	2	2	0	0	0	15.1	16	3	5	12
Todd Worrell	0	0	2.08	3	0	0	1	0	4.1	4	1	1	6
TOTAL	4	3	2.95	17	7	2	3	1	61.0	54	20	17	51

SF (W)

PLAYER/POS	AVG	G	AB	R	H	2B	3B	HR	RBI	BB	SO	SB
Mike Aldrete, of-3	.100	5	10	0	1	0	0	0	0	1	2	0
Bob Brenly, c	.235	6	17	3	4	1	0	1	2	3	7	0
Will Clark, 1b	.360	7	25	3	9	2	0	1	3	3	6	1
Chili Davis, of	.150	6	20	2	3	1	0	0	0	1	4	0
Kelly Downs, p	.000	1	0	0	0	0	0	0	0	0	0	0
Dave Dravecky, p	.167	2	6	0	1	0	0	0	0	0	1	0
Scott Garrelts, p	.000	2	0	0	0	0	0	0	0	0	0	0
Atlee Hammaker, p	.000	2	3	0	0	0	0	0	0	0	2	0
Mike Krukow, p	.000	1	2	0	0	0	0	0	0	1	0	0
Mike LaCoss, p	.000	2	0	0	0	0	0	0	0	0	0	0
Craig Lefferts, p	.000	3	0	0	0	0	0	0	0	0	0	0
Jeffrey Leonard, of	.417	7	24	5	10	0	0	4	5	3	4	0
Candy Maldonado, of	.211	5	19	2	4	1	0	0	2	0	3	0
Bob Melvin, c-2	.429	3	7	0	3	0	0	0	0	1	1	0
Eddie Milner, of-4	.143	6	7	0	1	0	0	0	0	0	3	0
Kevin Mitchell, 3b	.267	7	30	2	8	1	0	1	2	0	3	1
Joe Price, p	.000	2	1	0	0	0	0	0	0	0	1	0
Rick Reuschel, p	.000	2	2	0	0	0	0	0	0	0	1	0
Don Robinson, p	.000	3	0	0	0	0	0	0	0	0	0	0
Chris Speier, 2b-1	.000	3	5	0	0	0	0	0	0	0	2	0
Harry Spilman, ph	.500	3	2	1	1	0	0	1	1	0	0	0
Rob Thompson, 2b-6	.100	7	20	4	2	0	1	1	1	2	5	2
Jose Uribe, ss	.269	7	26	1	7	1	0	0	0	2	4	1
TOTAL	.239		226	23	54	7	1	9	20	17	51	5

PITCHER	W	L	ERA	G	GS	CG	SV	SHO	IP	H	ER	BB	SO
Kelly Downs	0	0	0.00	1	0	0	0	0	1.1	1	0	0	0
Dave Dravecky	1	1	0.60	2	2	1	0	1	15.0	7	1	4	14
Scott Garrelts	0	0	6.75	2	0	0	0	0	2.2	2	2	4	4
Atlee Hammaker	0	1	7.87	2	2	0	0	0	8.0	12	7	0	7
Mike Krukow	1	0	2.00	1	1	1	0	0	9.0	9	2	1	3
Mike LaCoss	0	0	0.00	2	0	0	0	0	3.1	1	0	3	2
Craig Lefferts	0	0	0.00	3	0	0	0	0	2.0	3	0	1	0
Joe Price	1	0	0.00	2	0	0	0	0	5.2	3	0	1	7
Rick Reuschel	0	1	6.30	2	2	0	0	0	10.0	15	7	2	2
Don Robinson	0	1	9.00	3	0	0	0	0	3.0	3	3	0	3
TOTAL	3	4	3.30	20	7	2	0	1	60.0	56	22	16	42

GAME 1 AT STL OCT 6

SF	100 100 010	3	7	1
STL	001 103 00X	5	10	1

Pitchers: REUSCHEL, Lefferts (7), Garrelts (8) vs MATHEWS, Worrell (8), Dayley (8)
Home Runs: Leonard-SF
Attendance: 55,331

GAME 2 AT STL OCT 7

SF	020 100 020	5	10	0
STL	000 000 000	0	2	1

Pitchers: DRAVECKY vs TUDOR, Forsch (9)
Home Runs: Clark-SF, Leonard-SF
Attendance: 55,331

GAME 3 AT SF OCT 9

STL	000 002 400	6	11	1
SF	031 000 001	5	7	1

Pitchers: Magrane, FORSCH (5), Worrell (7) vs Hammaker, D.ROBINSON (7), Lefferts (7), LaCoss (8)
Home Runs: Lindeman-STL, Leonard-SF, Spilman-SF
Attendance: 57,913

GAME 4 AT SF OCT 10

STL	020 000 000	2	9	0
SF	000 120 01X	4	9	2

Pitchers: COX vs KRUKOW
Home Runs: Thompson-SF, Leonard-SF, Brenly-SF
Attendance: 57,997

GAME 5 AT SF OCT 11

STL	101 100 000	3	7	0
SF	101 400 00X	6	7	1

Pitchers: Mathews, FORSCH (4), Horton (4), Dayley (7) vs Reuschel, PRICE (5)
Home Runs: Mitchell-SF
Attendance: 59,363

GAME 6 AT STL OCT 13

SF	000 000 000	0	6	0
STL	010 000 00X	1	5	0

Pitchers: DRAVECKY, D.Robinson (7) vs TUDOR, Worrell (8), Dayley (9)
Attendance: 55,331

GAME 7 AT STL OCT 14

SF	000 000 000	0	8	1
STL	040 002 00X	6	12	0

Pitchers: HAMMAKER, Price (3), Downs (3), Garrelts (5), Lefferts (6), LaCoss (6), D.Robinson (8) vs COX
Home Runs: Oquendo-STL
Attendance: 55,331

The Tigers, with the best over-all won-lost record in the majors, were favored to defeat the ninth-ranked Twins, although Minnesota held the home field advantage and the major leagues' best record at home. Tiger pitcher Doyle Alexander—he had been 9–0 since joining Detroit in mid-August—took a 5–4 lead into the last of the eighth in Game One. But a single and double drove him out, and before the inning was over three more Twins had scored to sew up their first win. Detroit scored twice in the second inning the next day, but the Twins responded later in the inning with three runs, two on Tim Laudner's double off Tiger ace Jack Morris, and increased their lead in the fourth and fifth to seal Morris's first loss in Minnesota after eleven wins.

The Tigers won a game after the series moved to Detroit, when Pat Sheridan's two-run homer in the eighth inning of Game Three restored a lead they had squandered in the middle innings. But that was it for Detroit, as the Twins surprised everyone by subduing the Tigers in their den. In Game Four they took the lead for good on Greg Gagne's fourth-inning home run. And in Game Five, after initiating the scoring with four runs in the second, Minnesota pushed on to a 9–5 win and their first pennant in twenty-two years.

Minnesota Twins (West) 4; Detroit Tigers (East), 1

MIN (W)

PLAYER/POS	AVG	G	AB	R	H	2B	3B	HR	RB	BB	SO	SB
Keith Atherton, p	.000	1	0	0	0	0	0	0	0	0	0	0
Don Baylor, dh	.400	2	5	0	2	0	0	0	1	0	0	0
Juan Berenguer, p	.000	4	0	0	0	0	0	0	0	0	0	0
Bert Blyleven, p	.000	2	0	0	0	0	0	0	0	0	0	0
Tom Brunansky, of	.412	5	17	5	7	4	0	2	9	4	3	0
Randy Bush, dh	.250	4	12	4	3	0	1	0	2	3	2	3
Sal Butera, c	.667	1	3	0	2	0	0	0	0	0	0	0
Mark Davidson, pr	.000	1	0	0	0	0	0	0	0	0	0	0
Gary Gaetti, 3b	.300	5	20	5	6	1	0	2	5	1	3	0
Greg Gagne, ss	.278	5	18	5	5	3	0	2	3	3	4	0
Dan Gladden, of	.350	5	20	5	7	2	0	0	5	2	1	0
Kent Hrbek, 1b	.150	5	20	4	3	0	0	1	1	3	0	0
Gene Larkin, ph	1.000	1	1	0	1	1	0	0	1	0	0	0
Tim Laudner, c	.071	5	14	1	1	1	0	0	2	2	5	0
Steve Lombardozzi, 2b	.267	5	15	2	4	0	0	0	1	2	2	0
Al Newman, 2b	.000	1	2	0	0	0	0	0	0	0	0	0
Kirby Puckett, of	.208	5	24	3	5	1	0	1	3	0	5	1
Jeff Reardon, p	.000	4	0	0	0	0	0	0	0	0	0	0
Dan Schatzeder, p	.000	2	0	0	0	0	0	0	0	0	0	0
Les Straker, p	.000	1	0	0	0	0	0	0	0	0	0	0
Frank Viola, p	.000	2	0	0	0	0	0	0	0	0	0	0
TOTAL	.269		171	34	46	13	1	8	33	20	25	4

PITCHER	W	L	ERA	G	GS	CG	SV	SHO	IP	H	ER	BB	SO
Keith Atherton	0	0	0.00	1	0	0	0	0	0.1	1	0	0	0
Juan Berenguer	0	0	1.50	4	0	0	1	0	6.0	1	1	3	6
Bert Blyleven	2	0	4.05	2	2	0	0	0	13.1	12	6	3	9
Jeff Reardon	1	1	5.06	4	0	0	2	0	5.1	7	3	3	5
Dan Schatzeder	0	0	0.00	2	0	0	0	0	4.1	2	0	0	5
Les Straker	0	0	16.88	1	1	0	0	0	2.2	3	5	4	1
Frank Viola	1	0	5.25	2	2	0	0	0	12.0	14	7	5	9
TOTAL	4	1	4.50	16	5	0	3	0	44.0	40	22	18	35

DET (E)

PLAYER/POS	AVG	G	AB	R	H	2B	3B	HR	RB	BB	SO	SB
Doyle Alexander, p	.000	2	0	0	0	0	0	0	0	0	0	0
Dave Bergman, 1b-1,dh-1	.250	4	4	0	1	0	0	0	2	0	1	0
Tom Brookens, 3b	.000	5	13	0	0	0	0	0	0	0	3	0
Darrell Evans, 1b-5,3b-1	.294	5	17	0	5	0	0	0	0	4	2	0
Kirk Gibson, of	.286	5	21	4	6	1	0	1	4	3	8	3
Johnny Grubb, dh-1	.571	4	7	0	4	0	0	0	0	0	1	0
Mike Heath, c	.286	3	7	1	2	0	0	1	2	0	0	0
Mike Henneman, p	.000	3	0	0	0	0	0	0	0	0	0	0
Willie Hernandez, p	.000	1	0	0	0	0	0	0	0	0	0	0
Larry Herndon, of-2,dh-1	.333	3	9	1	3	1	0	0	2	1	1	0
Eric King, p	.000	2	0	0	0	0	0	0	0	0	0	0
Chet Lemon, of	.278	5	18	4	5	0	0	2	4	1	4	0
Bill Madlock, dh	.000	1	5	0	0	0	0	0	0	0	3	0
Jack Morris, p-1,dh-1	.000	2	0	1	0	0	0	0	0	0	0	0
Jim Morrison, 3b-1,dh-1	.400	2	5	1	2	0	0	0	0	0	1	0
Matt Nokes, c-3,dh-2	.143	5	14	2	2	0	0	1	2	1	4	0
Dan Petry, p	.000	1	0	0	0	0	0	0	0	0	0	0
Jeff Robinson, p	.000	1	0	0	0	0	0	0	0	0	0	0
Pat Sheridan, of-4	.300	5	10	2	3	1	0	1	2	0	2	1
Frank Tanana, p	.000	1	0	0	0	0	0	0	0	0	0	0
Walt Terrell, p	.000	1	0	0	0	0	0	0	0	0	0	0
Mark Thurmond, p	.000	1	0	0	0	0	0	0	0	0	0	0
Alan Trammell, ss	.200	5	20	3	4	1	0	0	2	1	2	0
Lou Whitaker, 2b	.176	5	17	4	3	0	0	1	1	7	3	1
TOTAL	.240		167	23	40	4	0	7	21	18	35	5

PITCHER	W	L	ERA	G	GS	CG	SV	SHO	IP	H	ER	BB	SO
Doyle Alexander	0	2	10.00	2	2	0	0	0	9.0	14	10	1	5
Mike Henneman	1	0	10.80	3	0	0	0	0	5.0	6	6	6	3
Willie Hernandez	0	0	0.00	1	0	0	0	0	0.1	2	0	0	0
Eric King	0	0	1.69	2	0	0	0	0	5.1	3	1	2	4
Jack Morris	0	1	6.75	1	1	1	0	0	8.0	6	6	3	7
Dan Petry	0	0	0.00	1	0	0	0	0	3.1	1	0	0	1
Jeff Robinson	0	0	0.00	1	0	0	0	0	0.1	1	0	0	0
Frank Tanana	0	1	5.06	1	1	0	0	0	5.1	6	3	4	1
Walt Terrell	0	0	9.00	1	1	0	0	0	6.0	7	6	4	4
Mark Thurmond	0	0	0.00	1	0	0	0	0	0.1	0	0	0	0
TOTAL	1	4	6.70	14	5	1	0	0	43.0	46	32	20	25

GAME 1 AT MIN OCT 7

DET	001	001	120	5	10	0
MIN	010	030	04X	8	10	0

Pitchers: ALEXANDER, Henneman (8), Hernandez (8), King (8) vs Viola, REARDON (8)
Home Runs: Heath-DET, Gibson-DET, Gaetti-MIN (2)
Attendance: 53,269

GAME 2 AT MIN OCT 8

DET	020	000	010	3	7	1
MIN	030	210	00X	6	6	0

Pitchers: MORRIS vs BLYLEVEN, Berenguer (8)
Home Runs: Lemon-DET, Whitaker-DET, Hrbek-MIN
Attendance: 55,245

GAME 3 AT DET OCT 10

MIN	000	202	200	6	8	1
DET	005	000	02X	7	7	0

Pitchers: Straker, Schatzeder (3), Berenguer (7), Reardon (8) vs Terrell, HENNEMAN (7)
Home Runs: Gagne-MIN, Brunansky-MIN, Sheridan-DET
Attendance: 49,730

GAME 4 AT DET OCT 11

MIN	001	111	010	5	7	1
DET	100	011	000	3	7	3

Pitchers: VIOLA, Atherton (6), Berenguer (6), Reardon (9) vs TANANA, Petry (6), Thurmond (9)
Home Runs: Puckett-MIN, Gagne-MIN
Attendance: 51,939

GAME 5 AT DET OCT 12

MIN	040	000	113	9	15	1
DET	000	300	011	5	9	1

Pitchers: BLYLEVEN, Schatzeder (7), Berenguer (8), Reardon (8) vs ALEXANDER, King (2), Henneman (7), Robinson (9)
Home Runs: Brunansky-MIN, Nokes-DET, Lemon-DET
Attendance: 47,448

Although the Twins compiled a dismal record on the road during the season (29–52), their play at home (56–25) topped the majors. In postseason play they won all six games played in their Metrodome, including the four that won them the world championship. They overwhelmed St. Louis in the Series opener, the first World Series game ever played indoors. The Cardinals scored first, in the second inning, but Twin ace Frank Viola (with relief from Keith Atherton in the ninth) stopped them after that as his teammates unloaded for seven runs in the fourth inning (capped by Dan Gladden's grand slam) on their way to a 10–1 win. The Cardinals scored four runs in Game Two, but again the Twins enjoyed a big fourth inning—bunching six of their ten hits together for six runs—and scored two other runs on homers by Gary Gaetti and Tim Laudner.

When the Series moved to St. Louis, the Cardinals grabbed the home advantage to post their three wins. In Game Three, Cardinal pitchers John Tudor and Todd Worrell combined for a five-hitter as the Cards came from behind with a three-run seventh to win 3–1. The next day St. Louis broke a 1–1 tie with their own fourth-inning explosion, for six runs. The big blow was a three-run homer by utility infielder Tom Lawless—only the second home run of his big league career. Final score: 7–2. After five scoreless innings in Game Five, St. Louis moved out to a 4–0 lead in the sixth and seventh innings. Gaetti's eighth-inning triple put two Minnesota runs across, but the Cards held on for a 4–2 win.

Back in Minneapolis, St. Louis built up a 5–2 lead in Game Six before the Twins retaliated with four runs in the fifth inning (with Don Baylor's three-run homer providing the tying runs) and four more an inning later on Kent Hrbek's grand slam. A final Twins run in the eighth ended the scoring at 11–5.

The Cardinals scored first in Game Seven, with a pair of runs in the second inning, but the Twins edged their way to a tie with single runs in the second and fifth, and an inning later took the lead on three walks and an infield single. As Twin starter Frank Viola held St. Louis scoreless on two hits after the second inning, Minnesota made the score 4–2 with a final run in the eighth, and ace reliever Jeff Reardon retired the Cards in order in the ninth to bring Minnesota its first world championship.

Minnesota Twins (AL) 4; St. Louis Cardinals (NL), 3

MIN (A)

PLAYER/POS	AVG	G	AB	R	H	2B	3B	HR	RB	BB	SO	SB
Keith Atherton, p	.000	2	0	0	0	0	0	0	0	0	0	0
Don Baylor, dh-3	.385	5	13	3	5	0	0	1	3	1	1	0
Juan Berenguer, p	.000	3	0	0	0	0	0	0	0	0	0	0
Bert Blyleven, p	.000	2	1	0	0	0	0	0	0	0	1	0
Tom Brunansky, of	.200	7	25	5	5	0	0	0	0	2	4	1
Randy Bush, dh-2	.167	4	6	1	1	1	0	0	2	0	1	0
Sal Butera, c	.000	1	0	0	0	0	0	0	0	0	0	0
Mark Davidson, of-1	.000	2	1	0	0	0	0	0	0	0	0	0
George Frazier, p	.000	1	0	0	0	0	0	0	0	0	0	0
Gary Gaetti, 3b	.259	7	27	4	7	2	1	1	4	2	5	2
Greg Gagne, ss	.200	7	30	5	6	1	0	1	3	1	6	0
Dan Gladden, of	.290	7	31	3	9	2	1	1	7	3	4	2
Kent Hrbek, 1b	.208	7	24	4	5	0	0	1	6	5	3	0
Gene Larkin, 1b-1,dh-1	.000	5	3	1	0	0	0	0	0	1	0	0
Tim Laudner, c	.318	7	22	4	7	1	0	1	4	5	3	0
Steve Lombardozzi, 2b	.412	6	17	3	7	1	0	1	4	2	3	0
Al Newman, 2b-3	.200	4	5	0	1	0	0	0	0	0	1	0
Joe Niekro, p	.000	1	0	0	0	0	0	0	0	0	0	0
Kirby Puckett, of	.357	7	28	5	10	1	1	0	3	2	1	1
Jeff Reardon, p	.000	4	0	0	0	0	0	0	0	0	0	0
Dan Schatzeder, p	.000	3	0	0	0	0	0	0	0	0	0	0
Roy Smalley, ph	.500	4	2	0	1	1	0	0	0	0	2	0
Les Straker, p	.000	2	2	0	0	0	0	0	0	0	2	0
Frank Viola, p	.000	3	1	0	0	0	0	0	0	0	1	0
TOTAL	.269		238	38	64	10	3	7	38	29	36	6

PITCHER	W	L	ERA	G	GS	CG	SV	SHO	IP	H	ER	BB	SO
Keith Atherton	0	0	6.75	2	0	0	0	0	1.1	0	1	1	0
Juan Berenguer	0	1	10.38	3	0	0	0	0	4.1	10	5	0	1
Bert Blyleven	1	1	2.77	2	2	0	0	0	13.0	13	4	2	12
George Frazier	0	0	0.00	1	0	0	0	0	2.0	1	0	0	2
Joe Niekro	0	0	0.00	1	0	0	0	0	2.0	1	0	1	1
Jeff Reardon	0	0	0.00	4	0	0	1	0	4.2	5	0	0	3
Dan Schatzeder	1	0	6.23	3	0	0	0	0	4.1	4	3	3	3
Les Straker	0	0	4.00	2	2	0	0	0	9.0	9	4	3	6
Frank Viola	2	1	3.72	3	3	0	0	0	19.1	17	8	3	16
TOTAL	4	3	3.75	21	7	0	1	0	60.0	60	25	13	44

STL (N)

PLAYER/POS	AVG	G	AB	R	H	2B	3B	HR	RB	BB	SO	SB
Vince Coleman, of	.143	7	28	5	4	2	0	0	2	2	10	6
Danny Cox, p	.000	3	2	0	0	0	0	0	0	0	1	0
Ken Dayley, p	.000	4	1	0	0	0	0	0	0	0	1	0
Dan Driessen, 1b	.231	4	13	3	3	2	0	0	1	1	1	0
Curt Ford, of-4	.308	5	13	1	4	0	0	0	2	1	1	0
Bob Forsch, p	.000	3	2	0	0	0	0	0	0	0	0	0
Tommy Herr, 2b	.250	7	28	2	7	0	0	1	1	2	2	0
Rick Horton, p	.000	2	0	0	0	0	0	0	0	0	0	0
Lance Johnson, pr	.000	1	0	0	0	0	0	0	0	0	0	1
Steve Lake, c	.333	3	3	0	1	0	0	0	0	0	0	0
Tom Lawless, 3b	.100	3	10	1	1	0	0	1	3	0	4	0
Jim Lindeman, 1b-6,of-1	.333	6	15	3	5	1	0	0	2	0	3	0
Joe Magrane, p	.000	2	0	0	0	0	0	0	0	0	0	0
Greg Mathews, p	.000	1	1	0	0	0	0	0	0	0	0	0
Willie McGee, of	.370	7	27	2	10	2	0	0	4	0	9	0
John Morris, of	.000	1	2	0	0	0	0	0	0	0	0	0
Jose Oquendo, 3b-4,of-3	.250	7	24	2	6	0	0	0	2	1	4	0
Tom Pagnozzi, dh-1	.250	2	4	0	1	0	0	0	0	0	0	0
Tony Pena, c-6,dh-1	.409	7	22	2	9	1	0	0	4	3	2	1
Terry Pendleton, dh-2	.429	3	7	2	3	0	0	0	1	1	1	2
Ozzie Smith, ss	.214	7	28	3	6	0	0	0	2	2	3	2
John Tudor, p	.000	2	2	0	0	0	0	0	0	0	2	0
Lee Tunnell, p	.000	2	0	0	0	0	0	0	0	0	0	0
Todd Worrell, p	.000	4	0	0	0	0	0	0	0	0	0	0
TOTAL	.259		232	26	60	8	0	2	25	13	44	12

PITCHER	W	L	ERA	G	GS	CG	SV	SHO	IP	H	ER	BB	SO
Danny Cox	1	2	7.71	3	2	0	0	0	11.2	13	10	8	9
Ken Dayley	0	0	1.93	4	0	0	1	0	4.2	2	1	0	3
Bob Forsch	1	0	9.95	3	0	0	0	0	6.1	8	7	5	3
Rick Horton	0	0	6.00	2	0	0	0	0	3.0	5	2	0	1
Joe Magrane	0	1	8.59	2	2	0	0	0	7.1	9	7	5	5
Greg Mathews	0	0	2.45	1	1	0	0	0	3.2	2	1	2	3
John Tudor	1	1	5.73	2	2	0	0	0	11.0	15	7	3	8
Lee Tunnell	0	0	2.08	2	0	0	0	0	4.1	4	1	2	1
Todd Worrell	0	0	1.29	4	0	0	2	0	7.0	6	1	4	3
TOTAL	3	4	5.64	23	7	0	3	0	59.0	64	37	29	36

GAME 1 AT MIN OCT 17

STL	010	000	000	1	5 1
MIN	000	720	10X	10	11 0

Pitchers: MAGRANE, Forsch (4), Horton (7) vs VIOLA, Atherton (9)
Home Runs: Gladden-MIN, Lombardozzi-MIN
Attendance: 55,171

GAME 2 AT MIN OCT 18

STL	000	010	120	4	9 0
MIN	010	601	00X	8	10 0

Pitchers: COX, Tunnell (4), Dayley (7), Worrell (8) vs BLYLEVEN, Berenguer (8), Reardon (9)
Home Runs: Gaetti-MIN, Laudner-MIN
Attendance: 55,257

GAME 3 AT STL OCT 20

MIN	000	001	000	1	5 1
STL	000	000	30X	3	9 1

Pitchers: Straker, BERENGUER (7), Schatzeder (7) vs TUDOR, Worrell (8)
Attendance: 55,347

GAME 4 AT STL OCT 21

MIN	001	010	000	2	7 1
STL	001	600	00X	7	10 1

Pitchers: VIOLA, Schatzeder (4), Niekro (5), Frazier (7) vs Mathews, FORSCH (4), Dayley (7)
Home Runs: Gagne-MIN, Lawless-STL
Attendance: 55,347

GAME 5 AT STL OCT 22

MIN	000	000	020	2	6 1
STL	000	003	10X	4	10 0

Pitchers: BLYLEVEN, Atherton (7), Reardon (7) vs COX, Dayley (8), Worrell (8)
Attendance: 55,347

GAME 6 AT MIN OCT 24

STL	110	210	000	5	11 2
MIN	200	044	01X	11	15 0

Pitchers: TUDOR, Horton (5), Forsch (6), Dayley (6), Tunnell (7) vs Straker, SCHATZEDER (4), Berenguer (6), Reardon (9)
Home Runs: Herr-STL, Baylor-MIN, Hrbek-MIN
Attendance: 55,293

GAME 7 AT MIN OCT 25

STL	020	000	000	2	6 1
MIN	010	011	01X	4	10 0

Pitchers: Magrane, COX (5), Worrell (6) vs VIOLA, Reardon (9)
Attendance: 55,376

The Mets had defeated the Dodgers in 10 of 11 regular season games, but in the LCS the pitching of Dodger ace Orel Hershiser and rookie Tim Belcher, and the timely hitting of Mike Scioscia and Kirk Gibson, propelled L.A. to the pennant. The Dodgers scored a first-inning run in the opener and carried a 2–0 lead into the ninth. But three Met runs in the top of the ninth (the final two scoring with two outs on a fly to short center that bounced off the glove of a diving John Shelby) gave New York the victory.

Dodger pitcher Tim Belcher singled with two away in the second inning of Game Two to start a four-run rally—the margin of victory in Belcher's 6–3 win. In Game Three (played in a steady downpour after a rainout the night before), the Mets overcame a 3–4 deficit, rapping four Dodger pitchers for five runs in the last of the eighth to take the series lead.

Kirk Gibson's twelfth-inning solo homer the next night put the Dodgers ahead 5–4, after Mike Scioscia's ninth-inning home run had pulled them into a tie. In the last of the twelfth, Orel Hershiser (who had pitched seven innings to no decision in the previous game) took the mound with two out and the bases full, and saved the game as center fielder Shelby, on the run, snared Kevin McReynolds' looping fly.

Gibson homered again in Game Four—for three runs that provided the winning margin in a 7–4 Dodger victory. One game from the pennant, as the series moved back to Los Angeles, the Dodgers for the first time failed to score first and saw the series evened a third time as David Cone held them to five hits and one run while the Mets scored five. But in the finale, the Dodgers unloaded on Ron Darling for six runs in the first two innings and Hershiser blanked the Mets on five hits.

Los Angeles Dodgers (West), 4; New York Mets (East), 3

LA (W)

PLAYER/POS	AVG	G	AB	R	H	2B	3B	HR	RB	BB	SO	SB
Tim Belcher, p	.125	2	8	1	1	0	0	0	0	0	3	0
Mike Davis, ph	.000	4	2	0	0	0	0	0	0	1	0	0
Rick Dempsey, c-3	.400	4	5	1	2	2	0	0	2	1	0	0
Kirk Gibson, of	.154	7	26	2	4	0	0	2	6	3	6	2
Jose Gonzalez, of-3	.000	4	0	2	0	0	0	0	0	0	0	0
Alfredo Griffin, ss	.160	7	25	1	4	1	0	0	3	0	5	0
Jeff Hamilton, 3b	.217	7	23	2	5	0	0	0	1	3	4	0
Mickey Hatcher, 1b-6,of-1	.238	6	21	4	5	2	0	0	3	3	0	0
Danny Heep, ph	.000	3	1	0	0	0	0	0	0	1	1	0
Orel Hershiser, p	.000	4	9	1	0	0	0	0	0	1	2	0
Brian Holton, p	1.000	3	1	1	1	0	0	0	0	0	0	0
Rick Horton, p	.000	4	0	0	0	0	0	0	0	0	0	0
Jay Howell, p	.000	2	0	0	0	0	0	0	0	0	0	0
Tim Leary, p	.000	2	1	0	0	0	0	0	0	0	0	0
Mike Marshall, of	.233	7	30	3	7	1	1	0	5	2	9	0
Jesse Orosco, p	.000	4	0	0	0	0	0	0	0	0	0	0
Alejandro Pena, p	.000	3	0	0	0	0	0	0	0	0	0	0
Steve Sax, 2b	.267	7	30	7	8	0	0	0	3	3	3	5
Mike Scioscia, c	.364	7	22	3	8	1	0	1	2	1	2	0
Mike Sharperson, ss-1,3b-1	.000	2	1	0	0	0	0	0	0	1	1	0
John Shelby, of	.167	7	24	3	4	0	0	0	3	5	12	2
Franklin Stubbs, 1b-3	.250	4	8	0	2	0	0	0	0	0	4	0
John Tudor, p	.000	1	2	0	0	0	0	0	0	0	2	0
Tracy Woodson, 1b	.250	3	4	0	1	0	0	0	0	0	1	0
TOTAL	.214		243	31	52	7	1	3	30	25	54	9

PITCHER	W	L	ERA	G	GS	CG	SV	SHO	IP	H	ER	BB	SO
Tim Belcher	2	0	4.11	2	2	0	0	0	15.1	12	7	4	16
Orel Hershiser	1	0	1.09	4	3	1	1	1	24.2	18	3	7	15
Brian Holton	0	0	2.25	3	0	0	1	0	4.0	2	1	1	2
Rick Horton	0	0	0.00	4	0	0	0	0	4.1	4	0	2	3
Jay Howell	0	1	27.00	2	0	0	0	0	0.2	1	2	2	1
Tim Leary	0	1	6.23	2	1	0	0	0	4.1	8	3	3	3
Jesse Orosco	0	0	7.71	4	0	0	0	0	2.1	4	2	3	0
Alejandro Pena	1	1	4.15	3	0	0	1	0	4.1	1	2	5	1
John Tudor	0	0	7.20	1	1	0	0	0	5.0	8	4	1	1
TOTAL	4	3	3.32	25	7	1	3	1	65.0	58	24	28	42

NY (E)

PLAYER/POS	AVG	G	AB	R	H	2B	3B	HR	RB	BB	SO	SB
Rick Aguilera, p	.000	3	1	0	0	0	0	0	0	0	1	0
Wally Backman, 2b	.273	7	22	2	6	1	0	0	2	2	5	1
Gary Carter, c	.222	7	27	0	6	1	1	0	4	1	3	0
David Cone, p	.000	3	4	0	0	0	0	0	0	0	0	0
Ron Darling, p-2	.000	2	3	0	0	0	0	0	0	0	2	0
Lennie Dykstra, of	.429	7	14	6	6	3	0	1	3	4	0	0
Kevin Elster, ss	.250	5	8	1	2	1	0	0	1	3	0	0
Sid Fernandez, p	.000	1	1	0	0	0	0	0	0	0	0	0
Dwight Gooden, p	.200	3	5	0	1	0	0	0	0	0	2	0
Keith Hernandez, 1b	.269	7	26	2	7	0	0	1	5	6	7	1
Gregg Jefferies, 3b	.333	7	27	2	9	2	0	0	1	4	0	0
Howard Johnson, ss-5,3b-1	.056	6	18	1	1	0	0	0	0	1	6	1
Terry Leach, p	.000	3	0	0	0	0	0	0	0	0	0	0
Dave Magadan, ph	.000	3	3	0	0	0	0	0	0	0	2	0
Lee Mazzilli, ph	.500	3	2	0	1	0	0	0	0	0	0	1
Roger McDowell, p	.000	4	0	0	0	0	0	0	0	0	0	0
Kevin McReynolds, of	.250	7	28	4	7	2	0	2	4	3	5	2
Randy Myers, p	.000	3	0	0	0	0	0	0	0	0	0	0
Mackey Sasser, c-1	.200	4	5	0	1	0	0	0	0	0	1	0
Darryl Strawberry, of	.300	7	30	5	9	2	0	1	6	2	5	0
Tim Teufel, 2b	.000	1	3	0	0	0	0	0	0	0	1	0
Mookie Wilson, of-3	.154	4	13	2	2	0	0	0	1	2	2	0
TOTAL	.242		240	27	58	12	1	5	27	28	42	6

PITCHER	W	L	ERA	G	GS	CG	SV	SHO	IP	H	ER	BB	SO
Rick Aguilera	0	0	1.29	3	0	0	0	0	7.0	3	1	2	4
David Cone	1	1	4.50	3	2	1	0	0	12.0	10	6	5	9
Ron Darling	0	1	7.71	2	2	0	0	0	7.0	11	6	4	7
Sid Fernandez	0	1	13.50	1	1	0	0	0	4.0	7	6	1	5
Dwight Gooden	0	0	2.95	3	2	0	0	0	18.1	10	6	8	20
Terry Leach	0	0	0.00	3	0	0	0	0	5.0	4	0	1	4
Roger McDowell	0	1	4.50	4	0	0	0	0	6.0	6	3	2	5
Randy Myers	2	0	0.00	3	0	0	0	0	4.2	1	0	2	0
TOTAL	3	4	3.94	22	7	1	0	0	64.0	52	28	25	54

GAME 1 AT LA OCT 4

NY	000 000 003	3	8 1
LA	100 000 100	2	4 0

Pitchers: Gooden, MYERS (8) vs Hershiser, J.HOWELL (9)
Attendance: 55,582

GAME 2 AT LA OCT 5

NY	000 200 001	3	6 0
LA	140 010 00X	6	7 0

Pitchers: CONE, Aguilera (3), Leach (6), McDowell (8) vs BELCHER, Orosco (9), Pena (9)
Home Runs: Hernandez-NY
Attendance: 55,780

GAME 3 AT NY OCT 8

LA	021 000 010	4	7 2
NY	001 002 05X	8	9 2

Pitchers: Hershiser, J.Howell (8), PENA (8), Orosco (8), Horton (8) vs Darling, McDowell (7), MYERS (8), Cone (9)
Attendance: 44,672

GAME 4 AT NY OCT 9

LA	200 000 002 001	5	7 1
NY	000 301 000 000	4	10 2

Pitchers: Tudor, Holton (6), Horton (7), PENA (9), Leary (12), Orosco (12), Hershiser (12) vs Gooden, Myers (9), McDOWELL (11)
Home Runs: Strawberry-NY, McReynolds-NY, Scioscia-LA, Gibson-LA
Attendance: 54,014

GAME 5 AT NY OCT 10

LA	000 330 001	7	12 0
NY	000 030 010	4	9 1

Pitchers: BELCHER, Horton (8), Holton (8) vs FERNANDEZ, Leach (5), Aguilera (6), McDowell (8)
Home Runs: Gibson-LA, Dykstra-NY
Attendance: 52,069

GAME 6 AT LA OCT 11

NY	101 021 000	5	11 0
LA	000 010 000	1	5 2

Pitchers: CONE vs LEARY, Holton (5), Horton (6), Orosco (8)
Home Runs: McReynolds-NY
Attendance: 55,885

GAME 7 AT LA OCT 12

NY	000 000 000	0	5 2
LA	150 000 00X	6	10 0

Pitchers: DARLING, Gooden (2), Leach (5), Aguilera (7) vs HERSHISER
Attendance: 55,693

Jose Canseco's three home runs and Dennis Eckersley's sparkling relief pitching highlighted Oakland's sweep to the pennant. In his six shutout innings, Eckersley gave up just one hit and a pair of walks while fanning five, to record an LCS record four saves.

Canseco's fourth-inning solo shot off the Sox' Bruce Hurst put the A's out in front in Game One. Boston tied it up in the seventh, but two former Boston players—Carney Lansford, who doubled, and Dave Henderson, who singled him home—put Oakland back in front in the eighth, and Eckersley (also an ex-Bostonian) held the Sox through the final two innings.

Oakland's Storm Davis and Boston's Roger Clemens dueled scorelessly through five innings of Game Two. The Sox took advantage of an Oakland error to score twice in the sixth, but four Oakland hits in the seventh (including a two-run homer by Canseco), a balk, and a wild pitch put the A's up 3–2. Rich Gedman's home run for Boston in the last of the seventh tied the score, but in the ninth Oakland's rookie shortstop Walt Weiss singled home what proved the game winner off Sox ace reliever Lee Smith.

Boston unloaded for five runs in the first two innings of Game Three. But Weiss's double and home runs by Mark McGwire and Carney Lansford in the last of the second brought the A's within one run of a tie, and Ron Hassey's two-run homer an inning later gave the A's a lead that they held to the end. Dave Henderson's two-run blast in the eighth capped the A's 10–6 victory.

Canseco's first-inning homer in Game Four put the A's ahead to stay, as starter Dave Stewart and relievers Rick Honeycutt and Eckersley combined for a four-hit, 4–1 pennant clincher.

Oakland Athletics (West), 4; Boston Red Sox (East), 0

OAK (W)

PLAYER/POS	AVG	G	AB	R	H	2B	3B	HR	RB	BB	SO	SB
Don Baylor, dh	.000	2	6	0	0	0	0	0	1	1	2	0
Greg Cadaret, p	.000	1	0	0	0	0	0	0	0	0	0	0
Jose Canseco, of	.313	4	16	4	5	1	0	3	4	1	2	1
Storm Davis, p	.000	1	0	0	0	0	0	0	0	0	0	0
Dennis Eckersley, p	.000	4	0	0	0	0	0	0	0	0	0	0
Mike Gallego, 2b	.083	4	12	1	1	0	0	0	0	0	3	0
Ron Hassey, c	.500	4	8	2	4	1	0	1	3	1	1	0
Dave Henderson, of	.375	4	16	2	6	1	0	1	4	1	7	0
Rick Honeycutt, p	.000	3	0	0	0	0	0	0	0	0	0	0
Stan Javier, of	.500	2	4	0	2	0	0	0	1	1	0	0
Carney Lansford, 3b	.294	4	17	4	5	1	0	1	2	0	2	0
Mark McGwire, 1b	.333	4	15	4	5	0	0	1	3	1	5	0
Gene Nelson, p	.000	2	0	0	0	0	0	0	0	0	0	0
Dave Parker, dh-2,of-1	.250	4	12	1	3	1	0	0	0	0	4	0
Tony Phillips, of-2,2b-1	.286	2	7	0	2	1	0	0	0	1	4	0
Eric Plunk, p	.000	1	0	0	0	0	0	0	0	0	0	0
Luis Polonia, of-1	.400	3	5	0	2	0	0	0	0	1	1	0
Terry Steinbach, c	.250	2	4	0	1	0	0	0	0	2	0	0
Dave Stewart, p	.000	2	0	0	0	0	0	0	0	0	0	0
Walt Weiss, ss	.333	4	15	2	5	2	0	0	2	0	4	0
Bob Welch, p	.000	1	0	0	0	0	0	0	0	0	0	0
Curt Young, p	.000	1	0	0	0	0	0	0	0	0	0	0
TOTAL	.299		137	20	41	8	0	7	20	10	35	1

PITCHER	W	L	ERA	G	GS	CG	SV	SHO	IP	H	ER	BB	SO
Greg Cadaret	0	0	27.00	1	0	0	0	0	0.1	1	1	0	0
Storm Davis	0	0	0.00	1	1	0	0	0	6.1	2	0	5	4
Dennis Eckersley	0	0	0.00	4	0	0	4	0	6.0	1	0	2	5
Rick Honeycutt	1	0	0.00	3	0	0	0	0	2.0	0	0	2	0
Gene Nelson	2	0	0.00	2	0	0	0	0	4.2	5	0	1	0
Eric Plunk	0	0	0.00	1	0	0	0	0	0.1	1	0	0	1
Dave Stewart	1	0	1.35	2	2	0	0	0	13.1	9	2	6	11
Bob Welch	0	0	27.00	1	1	0	0	0	1.2	6	5	2	0
Curt Young	0	0	0.00	1	0	0	0	0	1.1	1	0	0	2
TOTAL	4	0	2.00	16	4	0	4	0	36.0	26	8	18	23

BOS (E)

PLAYER/POS	AVG	G	AB	R	H	2B	3B	HR	RB	BB	SO	SB
Marty Barrett, 2b	.067	4	15	2	1	0	0	0	0	1	0	0
Todd Benzinger, 1b-3	.091	4	11	0	1	0	0	0	0	1	3	0
Mike Boddicker, p	.000	1	0	0	0	0	0	0	0	0	0	0
Wade Boggs, 3b	.385	4	13	2	5	0	0	0	3	3	4	0
Ellis Burks, of	.235	4	17	2	4	1	0	0	1	0	3	0
Roger Clemens, p	.000	1	0	0	0	0	0	0	0	0	0	0
Dwight Evans, of	.167	4	12	1	2	1	0	0	1	3	5	0
Wes Gardner, p	.000	1	0	0	0	0	0	0	0	0	0	0
Rich Gedman, c	.357	4	14	1	5	0	0	1	2	1	1	0
Mike Greenwell, of	.214	4	14	2	3	1	0	1	3	3	0	0
Bruce Hurst, p	.000	2	0	0	0	0	0	0	0	0	0	0
Spike Owen, dh	.000	1	0	0	0	0	0	0	0	1	0	0
Larry Parrish, 1b-2	.000	4	6	0	0	0	0	0	0	0	2	0
Jody Reed, ss	.273	4	11	0	3	1	0	0	0	2	1	0
Jim Rice, dh	.154	4	13	0	2	0	0	0	1	2	4	0
Ed Romero, pr	.000	1	0	0	0	0	0	0	0	0	0	0
Kevin Romine, pr	.000	2	0	1	0	0	0	0	0	0	0	0
Lee Smith, p	.000	2	0	0	0	0	0	0	0	0	0	0
Mike Smithson, p	.000	1	0	0	0	0	0	0	0	0	0	0
Bob Stanley, p	.000	2	0	0	0	0	0	0	0	0	0	0
TOTAL	.206		126	11	26	4	0	2	10	18	23	0

PITCHER	W	L	ERA	G	GS	CG	SV	SHO	IP	H	ER	BB	SO
Mike Boddicker	0	1	20.25	1	1	0	0	0	2.2	8	6	1	2
Roger Clemens	0	0	3.86	1	1	0	0	0	7.0	6	3	0	8
Wes Gardner	0	0	5.79	1	0	0	0	0	4.2	6	3	2	8
Bruce Hurst	0	2	2.77	2	2	1	0	0	13.0	10	4	5	12
Lee Smith	0	1	8.10	2	0	0	0	0	3.1	6	3	1	4
Mike Smithson	0	0	0.00	1	0	0	0	0	2.1	3	0	0	1
Bob Stanley	0	0	9.00	2	0	0	0	0	1.0	2	1	1	0
TOTAL	0	4	5.29	10	4	1	0	0	34.0	41	20	10	35

GAME 1 AT BOS OCT 5

OAK	000	100	010	2	6	0
BOS	000	000	100	1	6	0

Pitchers: Stewart, HONEYCUTT (7), Eckersley (8) vs HURST
Home Runs: Canseco-OAK
Attendance: 34,104

GAME 2 AT BOS OCT 6

OAK	000	000	301	4	10	1
BOS	000	002	100	3	4	1

Pitchers: Davis, Cadaret (7), NELSON (7), Eckersley (9) vs Clemens, Stanley (8), SMITH (8)
Home Runs: Canseco-OAK, Gedman-BOS
Attendance: 34,605

GAME 3 AT OAK OCT 8

BOS	320	000	100	6	12	0
OAK	042	010	12X	10	15	1

Pitchers: BODDICKER, Gardner (3), Stanley (8) vs Welch, NELSON (2), Young (6), Plunk (7), Honeycutt (7), Eckersley (8)
Home Runs: Greenwell-BOS, McGwire-OAK, Lansford-OAK, Hassey-OAK, Henderson-OAK
Attendance: 49,261

GAME 4 AT OAK OCT 9

BOS	000	001	000	1	4	0
OAK	101	000	02X	4	10	1

Pitchers: HURST, Smithson (5), Smith (7) vs STEWART, Honeycutt (8), Eckersley (9)
Home Runs: Canseco-OAK
Attendance: 49,406

Mickey Hatcher's home run in the first inning of Game One set the tone for the Dodgers' surprising triumph over Oakland's mighty A's. Hatcher, who homered only once during the season, initiated the Series scoring with a two-run blast to left center. Half an inning later the A's Jose Canseco—baseball's leading slugger, with 42 season homers—erased the Dodger lead with his first career grand slam. But while Hatcher went on to hit safely six more times in the Series—including another home run—Canseco's first hit was also his last, as he went 0 for 19 the rest of the way. The Dodgers scored once in the sixth inning to draw within one run of a tie, but remained behind until the last of the ninth when, with two out and one on, Kirk Gibson pinch hit for pitcher Alejandro Pena. Gibson, the Dodgers' top source of power during the season, was so hobbled by leg injuries that he had, till that moment, sat out the game in the training room. But with two strikes on him he belted a home run off baseball's premier reliever, Dennis Eckersley, to win the game. It was Gibson's only Series appearance.

Dodger ace Orel Hershiser blanked the A's on three hits in Game Two and led the offense with three hits of his own. His single in the third inning began a five-run Dodger rally (capped by Mike Marshall's three-run homer), and his fourth-inning double drove in the Dodgers' sixth and final run.

When the Series moved to Oakland, the A's recovered for a dramatic win in Game Three, as Mark McGwire (who had homered 32 times during the season) broke a 1–1 tie with his only Series hit, a solo homer in the last of the ninth. In Game Four, Dodger reliever Jay Howell, who had yielded the losing home run the day before, got McGwire to pop up with the bases full to end the seventh inning, and blanked the A's the rest of the way to preserve a narrow 4–3 Dodger victory.

Hershiser returned to pitch Game Five. He allowed two runs in his four-hitter, but Mickey Hatcher had given the Dodgers the lead with a two-run homer in the first inning, and Mike Davis (who had homered just twice during the season) drove a 3–0 pitch into the stands for two more runs in the fourth. Veteran catcher Rick Dempsey (substituting for injured first-stringer Mike Scioscia) doubled home a fifth Los Angeles run in the sixth, and the Dodgers were on their way to a seventh world title.

Los Angeles Dodgers (NL), 4; Oakland Athletics (AL), 1

LA (N)

PLAYER/POS	AVG	G	AB	R	H	2B	3B	HR	RB	BB	SO	SB
Dave Anderson, dh	.000	1	1	0	0	0	0	0	0	0	1	0
Tim Belcher, p	.000	2	0	0	0	0	0	0	0	0	0	0
Mike Davis, dh-2,of-1	.143	4	7	3	1	0	0	2	2	4	0	2
Rick Dempsey, c	.200	2	5	0	1	1	0	0	1	1	2	0
Kirk Gibson, ph	1.000	1	1	1	1	0	0	1	2	0	0	0
Jose Gonzalez, of-3	.000	4	2	0	0	0	0	0	0	0	2	0
Alfredo Griffin, ss	.188	5	16	2	3	0	0	0	0	2	4	0
Jeff Hamilton, 3b	.105	5	19	1	2	0	0	0	0	1	4	0
Mickey Hatcher, of	.368	5	19	5	7	1	0	2	5	1	3	0
Danny Heep, of-1,dh-1	.250	3	8	0	2	1	0	0	0	0	2	0
Orel Hershiser, p	1.000	2	3	1	3	2	0	0	1	0	0	0
Brian Holton, p	.000	1	0	0	0	0	0	0	0	0	0	0
Jay Howell, p	.000	2	0	0	0	0	0	0	0	0	0	0
Tim Leary, p	.000	2	0	0	0	0	0	0	0	0	0	0
Mike Marshall, of	.231	5	13	2	3	0	1	1	3	0	5	0
Alejandro Pena, p	.000	2	0	0	0	0	0	0	0	0	0	0
Steve Sax, 2b	.300	5	20	3	6	0	0	0	0	1	1	1
Mike Scioscia, c	.214	4	14	0	3	0	0	0	1	0	2	0
John Shelby, of	.222	5	18	0	4	1	0	0	1	2	7	1
Franklin Stubbs, 1b	.294	5	17	3	5	2	0	0	2	1	3	0
John Tudor, p	.000	1	0	0	0	0	0	0	0	0	0	0
Tracy Woodson, 1b-3	.000	4	4	0	0	0	0	0	0	1	0	0
TOTAL	.246		167	21	41	8	1	6	19	13	36	4

PITCHER	W	L	ERA	G	GS	CG	SV	SHO	IP	H	ER	BB	SO
Tim Belcher	1	0	6.23	2	2	0	0	0	8.2	10	6	6	10
Orel Hershiser	2	0	1.00	2	2	2	0	1	18.0	7	2	6	17
Brian Holton	0	0	0.00	1	0	0	0	0	2.0	0	0	0	0
Jay Howell	0	1	3.38	2	0	0	1	0	2.2	3	1	1	2
Tim Leary	0	0	1.35	2	0	0	0	0	6.2	6	1	2	4
Alejandro Pena	1	0	0.00	2	0	0	0	0	5.0	2	0	1	7
John Tudor	0	0	0.00	1	1	0	0	0	1.1	0	0	0	1
TOTAL	4	1	2.03	12	5	2	1	1	44.1	28	10	17	41

OAK (A)

PLAYER/POS	AVG	G	AB	R	H	2B	3B	HR	RB	BB	SO	SB
Don Baylor, ph	.000	1	1	0	0	0	0	0	0	0	1	0
Todd Burns, p	.000	1	0	0	0	0	0	0	0	0	0	0
Greg Cadaret, p	.000	3	0	0	0	0	0	0	0	0	0	0
Jose Canseco, of	.053	5	19	1	1	0	0	1	5	2	5	1
Storm Davis, p	.000	2	1	0	0	0	0	0	0	0	1	0
Dennis Eckersley, p	.000	2	0	0	0	0	0	0	0	0	0	0
Mike Gallego, 2b	.000	1	0	0	0	0	0	0	0	0	0	0
Ron Hassey, c-4	.250	5	8	0	2	0	0	0	1	3	3	0
Dave Henderson, of	.300	5	20	1	6	2	0	0	1	2	7	0
Rick Honeycutt, p	.000	3	0	0	0	0	0	0	0	0	0	0
Glenn Hubbard, 2b	.250	4	12	2	3	0	0	0	0	1	2	1
Stan Javier, of-2	.500	3	4	2	2	0	0	0	2	0	1	0
Carney Lansford, 3b	.167	5	18	2	3	0	0	0	1	2	2	0
Mark McGwire, 1b	.059	5	17	1	1	0	0	1	3	4	0	0
Gene Nelson, p	.000	3	0	0	0	0	0	0	0	0	0	0
Dave Parker, of-2,dh-2	.200	4	15	0	3	0	0	0	0	2	4	0
Tony Phillips, 2b-1,of-1	.250	3	4	1	1	0	0	0	0	1	2	0
Eric Plunk, p	.000	2	0	0	0	0	0	0	0	0	0	0
Luis Polonia, of-2	.111	3	9	1	1	0	0	0	0	0	2	0
Terry Steinbach, c-2,dh-1	.364	3	11	0	4	1	0	0	0	0	2	0
Dave Stewart, p	.000	2	3	1	0	0	0	0	0	1	3	0
Walt Weiss, ss	.063	5	16	1	1	0	0	0	0	0	2	1
Bob Welch, p	.000	1	0	0	0	0	0	0	0	0	0	0
Curt Young, p	.000	1	0	0	0	0	0	0	0	0	0	0
TOTAL	.177		158	11	28	3	0	2	11	17	41	3

PITCHER	W	L	ERA	G	GS	CG	SV	SHO	IP	H	ER	BB	SO
Todd Burns	0	0	0.00	1	0	0	0	0	0.1	0	0	0	0
Greg Cadaret	0	0	0.00	3	0	0	0	0	2.0	2	0	0	3
Storm Davis	0	2	11.25	2	2	0	0	0	8.0	14	10	1	7
Dennis Eckersley	0	1	10.80	2	0	0	0	0	1.2	2	2	1	2
Rick Honeycutt	1	0	0.00	3	0	0	0	0	3.1	0	0	0	5
Gene Nelson	0	0	1.42	3	0	0	0	0	6.1	4	1	3	3
Eric Plunk	0	0	0.00	2	0	0	0	0	1.2	0	0	3	3
Dave Stewart	0	1	3.14	2	2	0	0	0	14.1	12	5	5	5
Bob Welch	0	0	1.80	1	1	0	0	0	5.0	6	1	3	8
Curt Young	0	0	0.00	1	0	0	0	0	1.0	1	0	0	0
TOTAL	1	4	3.92	20	5	0	0	0	43.2	41	19	13	36

GAME 1 AT LA OCT 15

| OAK | 040 000 000 | 4 | 7 | 0 |
| LA | 200 001 002 | 5 | 7 | 0 |

Pitchers: Stewart, ECKERSLEY (9) vs Belcher, Leary (3), Holton (6), PENA (8) Home Runs: Hatcher-LA, Canseco-OAK, Gibson-LA
Attendance: 55,983

GAME 2 AT LA OCT 16

| OAK | 000 000 000 | 0 | 3 | 0 |
| LA | 005 100 00X | 6 | 10 | 1 |

Pitchers: DAVIS, Nelson (4), Young (6), Plunk (7), Honeycutt (8) vs HERSHISER
Home Runs: Marshall-LA
Attendance: 56,051

GAME 3 AT OAK OCT 18

| LA | 000 010 000 | 1 | 8 | 1 |
| OAK | 001 000 001 | 2 | 5 | 0 |

Pitchers: Tudor, Leary (2), Pena (6), J.HOWELL (9) vs Welch, Cadaret (6), Nelson (6), HONEYCUTT (8)
Home Runs: McGwire-OAK
Attendance: 49,316

GAME 4 AT OAK OCT 19

| LA | 201 000 100 | 4 | 8 | 1 |
| OAK | 100 001 100 | 3 | 9 | 2 |

Pitchers: BELCHER, J.Howell (7) vs STEWART, Cadaret (7), Eckersley (9)
Attendance: 49,317

GAME 5 AT OAK OCT 20

| LA | 200 201 000 | 5 | 8 | 0 |
| OAK | 001 000 010 | 2 | 4 | 0 |

Pitchers: HERSHISER vs DAVIS, Cadaret (5), Nelson (5), Honeycutt (8), Plunk (9), Burns (9)
Home Runs: Hatcher-LA, Davis-LA
Attendance: 49,317

From the first inning of Game 1 when they drove in their teams' first runs, first basemen Will Clark of the Giants and Mark Grace of the Cubs dominated the offense, finishing with eight RBIs apiece and LCS record-shattering BAs of .650 and .647. Although Grace homered for two Chicago runs in the opener, the game belonged to Clark, whose four hits—two of them home runs, one a grand slam—drove in six of the eleven Giant runs.

Grace led the Cubs' retaliation the next day with his second three-hit game, driving in four of Chicago's nine runs with doubles in the first and sixth innings. Kevin Mitchell, Matt Williams, and Rob Thompson—runners-up to Clark for Giant offensive honors in the series—all homered in the losing cause.

Chicago scored first in the next three games but narrowly lost them all. Thompson's two-run homer in the last of the seventh put the Giants ahead for good in Game 3. The next day, Williams's two-run single in the third inning overcame Chicago's lead, and his two-run homer in the fifth broke a 4–4 tie to conclude the scoring.

Cub starter Mike Bielecki stopped San Francisco on a pair of singles through six innings of Game 5, and carried a 1–0 lead into the seventh, when Clark's triple and Mitchell's sacrifice fly tied the score. An inning later, after Bielecki loaded the bases with three two-out walks, relief ace Mitch Williams was called on to face Clark and got two strikes on him. But after fouling off a slider and fastball, Clark lined a single up the middle for two go-ahead Giant runs. San Francisco closer Steve Bedrosian yielded Chicago a second run in the ninth on a trio of two-out singles, but Ryne Sandberg (until then batting .421 in the series) grounded out, and the Giants owned their first pennant in twenty-seven years.

San Francisco Giants (West), 4; Chicago Cubs (East), 1

SF (W)

PLAYER/POS	AVG	G	AB	R	H	2B	3B	HR	RBI	BB	SO	SB
Bill Bathe, ph	.000	2	1	0	0	0	0	0	0	0	1	0
Steve Bedrosian, p	.000	4	0	0	0	0	0	0	0	0	0	0
Jeff Brantley, p	.000	3	0	0	0	0	0	0	0	1	0	0
Brett Butler, of	.211	5	19	6	4	0	0	0	0	3	3	0
Will Clark, 1b	.650	5	20	8	13	3	1	2	8	2	2	0
Kelly Downs, p	.000	2	3	0	0	0	0	0	0	0	1	0
Scott Garrelts, p	.000	2	4	0	0	0	0	0	0	1	1	0
Atlee Hammaker, p	.000	1	0	0	0	0	0	0	0	0	0	0
Terry Kennedy, c	.188	5	16	0	3	1	0	0	0	1	4	0
Mike LaCoss, p	.000	1	1	0	0	0	0	0	0	0	0	0
Craig Lefferts, p	.000	2	0	0	0	0	0	0	0	0	0	0
Greg Litton, 3b	1.000	1	1	0	1	0	0	0	0	0	0	0
Candy Maldonado, of	.000	3	3	1	0	0	0	0	1	2	0	0
Kirt Manwaring, c	.000	3	2	0	0	0	0	0	0	0	0	0
Kevin Mitchell, of	.353	5	17	5	6	0	0	2	7	3	3	0
Donell Nixon, of-2	.000	3	0	0	0	0	0	0	0	0	1	1
Ken Oberkfell, 3b-1	.000	3	4	0	0	0	0	0	0	0	0	0
Rick Reuschel, p	.000	2	2	0	0	0	0	0	0	0	0	0
Ernest Riles, ph	.000	1	1	0	0	0	0	0	0	0	0	0
Don Robinson, p	.000	1	0	0	0	0	0	0	0	0	0	0
Pat Sheridan, of	.154	5	13	1	2	0	1	0	0	0	4	0
Robby Thompson, 2b	.278	5	18	5	5	0	0	2	3	3	2	0
Jose Uribe, ss	.235	5	17	2	4	1	0	1	1	1	5	1
Matt Williams, 3b-5,ss-1	.300	5	20	2	6	1	0	2	9	0	2	0
TOTAL	.267		165	30	44	6	2	8	29	17	29	2

PITCHER	W	L	ERA	G	GS	CG	SV	SHO	IP	H	ER	BB	SO
Steve Bedrosian	0	0	2.70	4	0	0	3	0	3.1	4	1	2	2
Jeff Brantley	0	0	0.00	3	0	0	0	0	5.0	1	0	2	3
Kelly Downs	1	0	3.12	2	0	0	0	0	8.2	8	3	6	6
Scott Garrelts	1	0	5.40	2	2	0	0	0	11.2	16	7	2	8
Atlee Hammaker	0	0	0.00	1	0	0	0	0	1.0	1	0	0	0
Mike LaCoss	0	0	9.00	1	1	0	0	0	3.0	7	3	0	2
Craig Lefferts	0	0	9.00	2	0	0	0	0	1.0	1	1	2	1
Rick Reuschel	1	1	5.19	2	2	0	0	0	8.2	12	5	2	5
Don Robinson	1	0	0.00	1	0	0	0	0	1.2	3	0	0	0
TOTAL	4	1	4.09	18	5	0	3	0	44.0	53	20	16	27

CHI (E)

PLAYER/POS	AVG	G	AB	R	H	2B	3B	HR	RBI	BB	SO	SB
Paul Assenmacher, p	.000	2	0	0	0	0	0	0	0	0	0	0
Mike Bielecki, p	.200	2	5	0	1	0	0	0	2	0	2	0
Andre Dawson, of	.105	5	19	0	2	1	0	0	3	2	6	0
Shawon Dunston, ss	.316	5	19	2	6	0	0	0	0	1	1	1
Joe Girardi, c	.100	4	10	1	1	0	0	0	0	1	2	0
Mark Grace, 1b	.647	5	17	3	11	3	1	1	8	4	1	1
Paul Kilgus, p	.000	1	0	0	0	0	0	0	0	0	0	0
Lester Lancaster, p	.000	3	1	0	0	0	0	0	0	0	1	0
Vance Law, 3b-1	.000	2	3	0	0	0	0	0	0	3	0	0
Greg Maddux, p-2	.000	3	3	1	0	0	0	0	0	0	0	0
L. McClendon, c-2,of-1	.667	3	3	0	2	0	0	0	1	0	0	0
Domingo Ramos, ph	.000	1	1	0	0	0	0	0	0	0	0	0
Luis Salazar, 3b	.368	5	19	2	7	0	1	1	2	0	0	0
Ryne Sandberg, 2b	.400	5	20	6	8	1	1	1	4	3	4	0
Scott Sanderson, p	.000	1	0	0	0	0	0	0	0	0	1	0
Dwight Smith, of	.200	4	15	2	3	1	0	0	0	2	2	1
Rick Sutcliffe, p	.500	1	2	0	1	1	0	0	0	0	0	0
Jerome Walton, of	.364	5	22	4	8	0	0	0	2	2	2	0
Mitch Webster, of-2	.333	3	3	0	1	0	0	0	0	0	0	0
Curtis Wilkerson, 3b-1	.500	2	2	1	1	0	0	0	0	0	0	0
Mitch Williams, p	.000	2	0	0	0	0	0	0	0	0	0	0
Steve Wilson, p	.000	2	0	0	0	0	0	0	0	0	0	0
Rick Wrona, c	.000	2	5	0	0	0	0	0	0	0	3	0
Marvell Wynne, of-2	.167	4	6	0	1	0	0	0	0	0	0	0
TOTAL	.303		175	22	53	9	3	3	21	16	27	3

PITCHER	W	L	ERA	G	GS	CG	SV	SHO	IP	H	ER	BB	SO
P. Assenmacher	0	0	13.50	2	0	0	0	0	0.2	3	1	0	0
Mike Bielecki	0	1	3.65	2	2	0	0	0	12.1	7	5	6	11
Paul Kilgus	0	0	0.00	1	0	0	0	0	3.0	4	0	1	1
Lester Lancaster	1	1	6.00	3	0	0	0	0	6.0	6	4	1	3
Greg Maddux	0	1	13.50	2	2	0	0	0	7.1	13	11	4	5
Scott Sanderson	0	0	0.00	1	0	0	0	0	2.0	2	0	0	1
Rick Sutcliffe	0	0	4.50	1	1	0	0	0	6.0	5	3	4	2
Mitch Williams	0	0	0.00	2	0	0	0	0	1.0	1	0	2	2
Steve Wilson	0	1	4.91	2	0	0	0	0	3.2	3	2	1	4
TOTAL	1	4	5.57	16	5	0	0	0	42.0	44	26	17	29

GAME 1 AT CHI OCT 4

SF	301 400 030	11	13	0
CHI	201 000 000	3	10	1

Pitchers: GARRELTS, Brantley (8), Hammaker (9) vs MADDUX, Kilgus (5), Wilson (8)
Home Runs: Grace-CHI, Clark-SF (2), Sandberg-CHI, Mitchell-SF
Attendance: 39,195

GAME 2 AT CHI OCT 5

SF	000 200 021	5	10	0
CHI	600 003 00X	9	11	0

Pitchers: REUSCHEL, Downs (1), Lefferts (6), Brantley (7), Bedrosian (8) vs Bielecki, Assenmacher (5), LANCASTER (6)
Home Runs: Mitchell-SF, Williams-SF, Thompson-SF
Attendance: 39,195

GAME 3 AT SF OCT 7

CHI	200 100 100	4	10	0
SF	300 000 20X	5	8	3

Pitchers: Sutcliffe, Assenmacher (7), LANCASTER (7) vs LaCoss, Brantley (4), ROBINSON (7), Lefferts (8), Bedrosian (9)
Home Runs: Thompson-SF
Attendance: 62,065

GAME 4 AT SF OCT 8

CHI	110 020 000	4	12	1
SF	102 120 00X	6	9	1

Pitchers: Maddux, WILSON (4), Sanderson (6), Williams (8) vs Garrelts, DOWNS (5), Bedrosian (9)
Home Runs: Salazar-CHI, Williams-SF
Attendance: 62,078

GAME 5 AT SF OCT 9

CHI	001 000 001	2	10	1
SF	000 000 12X	3	4	1

Pitchers: BIELECKI, Williams (8), Lancaster (8) vs REUSCHEL, Bedrosian (9)
Attendance: 62,084

The awesome A's produced their share of heroes. Jose Canseco powered a truly heroic home run into the top deck of Toronto's SkyDome in Game 4; Dave Parker, in his seventh postseason series, at last hit his first postseason homer (and later his second); closer Dennis Eckersley added three saves to his four from 1988 to establish a new LCS record; and Carney Lansford was batting .455, with four RBIs, when a hamstring pull in Game 3 ended his series play. But the hero of heroes was leadoff batter Rickey Henderson.

Oakland might have won the opener without Henderson, even though his hard slide into second in the sixth inning broke up a double play and forced a wide throw that gave the A's two runs and their first lead of the game. And the A's might also have won the next day even if Henderson had not rattled Toronto with four stolen bases. The A's suffered their loss in Game 3 despite an early 2–0 lead with Henderson scoring both runs—the first after walking, the second after a double and stolen base.

But in the final two games, Rickey Henderson's contribution made the difference between defeat and victory. A pair of two-run Henderson homers (together with Canseco's memorable blast and later RBI single) gave the A's their 6–5 win in Game 4. And in the first inning of Game 5, Henderson, after walking, stole his eighth base—a postseason series record—before Canseco singled him home with the A's first run. Two innings later Henderson tripled home the second Oakland run. The A's scored twice more in the seventh, but Toronto had narrowed Oakland's lead to one run when Eckersley fanned a final Blue Jay to secure the second straight Oakland pennant. Rickey Henderson was the unanimous choice for series MVP.

Oakland Athletics (West), 4; Toronto Blue Jays (East), 1

OAK (W)

PLAYER/POS	AVG	G	AB	R	H	2B	3B	HR	RB	BB	SO	SB
Lance Blankenship, 2b	.000	1	0	0	0	0	0	0	0	0	0	0
Jose Canseco, of	.294	5	17	1	5	0	0	1	3	3	7	0
Storm Davis, p	.000	1	0	0	0	0	0	0	0	0	0	0
Dennis Eckersley, p	.000	4	0	0	0	0	0	0	0	0	0	0
Mike Gallego, 2b-2,ss-2	.273	4	11	3	3	1	0	0	1	0	2	0
Ron Hassey, c	.167	2	6	0	1	0	0	0	1	1	2	0
Dave Henderson, of	.263	5	19	4	5	3	0	1	1	2	5	0
Rickey Henderson, of	.400	5	15	8	6	1	1	2	5	7	0	8
Rick Honeycutt, p	.000	3	0	0	0	0	0	0	0	0	0	0
Stan Javier, of	.000	1	2	0	0	0	0	0	0	0	1	0
Carney Lansford, 3b	.455	3	11	2	5	0	0	0	4	2	1	2
Mark McGwire, 1b	.389	5	18	3	7	1	0	1	3	1	4	0
Mike Moore, p	.000	1	0	0	0	0	0	0	0	0	0	0
Gene Nelson, p	.000	1	0	0	0	0	0	0	0	0	0	0
Dave Parker, dh	.188	4	16	2	3	0	0	2	3	0	0	0
Ken Phelps, ph	1.000	1	1	0	1	1	0	0	0	0	0	0
Tony Phillips, 2b-3,3b-3	.167	5	18	1	3	1	0	0	1	2	4	2
Terry Steinbach, c-3,dh-1	.200	4	15	0	3	0	0	0	1	1	5	0
Dave Stewart, p	.000	2	0	0	0	0	0	0	0	0	0	0
Walt Weiss, ss	.111	4	9	2	1	1	0	0	0	1	1	1
Bob Welch, p	.000	1	0	0	0	0	0	0	0	0	0	0
Matt Young, p	.000	1	0	0	0	0	0	0	0	0	0	0
TOTAL	.272		158	26	43	9	1	7	23	20	32	13

PITCHER	W	L	ERA	G	GS	CG	SV	SHO	IP	H	ER	BB	SO
Storm Davis	0	1	7.11	1	1	0	0	0	6.1	5	5	2	3
Dennis Eckersley	0	0	1.59	4	0	0	3	0	5.2	4	1	0	2
Rick Honeycutt	0	0	32.40	3	0	0	0	0	1.2	6	6	5	1
Mike Moore	1	0	0.00	1	1	0	0	0	7.0	4	0	2	3
Gene Nelson	0	0	0.00	1	0	0	0	0	1.1	1	0	0	2
Dave Stewart	2	0	2.81	2	2	0	0	0	16.0	13	5	3	9
Bob Welch	1	0	3.18	1	1	0	0	0	5.2	8	2	1	4
Matt Young	0	0	0.00	1	0	0	0	0	0.1	0	0	2	0
TOTAL	4	1	3.89	14	5	0	3	0	44.0	40	19	15	24

TOR (E)

PLAYER/POS	AVG	G	AB	R	H	2B	3B	HR	RB	BB	SO	SB
Jim Acker, p	.000	5	0	0	0	0	0	0	0	0	0	0
George Bell, dh-3,of-2	.200	5	20	2	4	0	0	1	2	0	3	0
Pat Borders, c	1.000	1	1	0	1	0	0	0	1	0	0	0
John Cerutti, p	.000	2	0	0	0	0	0	0	0	0	0	0
Junior Felix, of	.273	2	11	0	3	1	0	0	3	0	2	0
Tony Fernandez, ss	.350	5	20	6	7	3	0	0	1	1	2	5
Mike Flanagan, p	.000	1	0	0	0	0	0	0	0	0	0	0
Kelly Gruber, 3b	.294	5	17	2	5	1	0	0	1	3	2	1
Tom Henke, p	.000	3	0	0	0	0	0	0	0	0	0	0
Jimmy Key, p	.000	1	0	0	0	0	0	0	0	0	0	0
Manny Lee, 2b	.250	2	8	2	2	0	0	0	0	0	1	0
Nelson Liriano, 2b	.429	3	7	1	3	0	0	0	1	2	0	3
Lee Mazzilli, dh-2	.000	3	8	0	0	0	0	0	0	2	0	0
Fred McGriff, 1b	.143	5	21	1	3	0	0	0	3	0	4	0
Lloyd Moseby, of	.313	5	16	4	5	0	0	1	2	5	2	1
Rance Mulliniks, ph	.000	1	1	0	0	0	0	0	0	1	0	0
Dave Stieb, p	.000	2	0	0	0	0	0	0	0	0	0	0
Todd Stottlemyre, p	.000	1	0	0	0	0	0	0	0	0	0	0
Duane Ward, p	.000	2	0	0	0	0	0	0	0	0	0	0
David Wells, p	.000	1	0	0	0	0	0	0	0	0	0	0
Ernie Whitt, c	.125	5	16	1	2	0	0	1	3	2	3	0
Mookie Wilson, of	.263	5	19	2	5	0	0	0	2	2	2	1
TOTAL	.242		165	21	40	5	0	3	19	15	24	11

PITCHER	W	L	ERA	G	GS	CG	SV	SHO	IP	H	ER	BB	SO
Jim Acker	0	0	1.42	5	0	0	0	0	6.1	4	1	1	4
John Cerutti	0	0	0.00	2	0	0	0	0	2.2	0	0	3	1
Mike Flanagan	0	1	10.38	1	1	0	0	0	4.1	7	5	1	3
Tom Henke	0	0	0.00	3	0	0	0	0	2.2	0	0	0	3
Jimmy Key	1	0	4.50	1	1	0	0	0	6.0	7	3	2	2
Dave Stieb	0	2	6.35	2	2	0	0	0	11.1	12	8	6	10
Todd Stottlemyre	0	1	7.20	1	1	0	0	0	5.0	7	4	2	3
Duane Ward	0	0	7.36	2	0	0	0	0	3.2	6	3	3	5
David Wells	0	0	0.00	1	0	0	0	0	1.0	0	0	2	1
TOTAL	1	4	5.02	18	5	0	0	0	43.0	43	24	20	32

GAME 1 AT OAK OCT 3

TOR	020 100 000	3 5 1
OAK	010 013 02X	7 11 0

Pitchers: STIEB, Acker (6), Ward (8) vs STEWART, Eckersley (9)
Home Runs: D.Henderson-OAK, Whitt-TOR, McGwire-OAK
Attendance: 49,435

GAME 2 AT OAK OCT 4

TOR	001 000 020	3 5 1
OAK	000 203 10X	6 9 1

Pitchers: STOTTLEMYRE, Acker (6), Wells (6), Henke (7), Cerutti (8) vs MOORE, Honeycutt (8), Eckersley (8)
Home Runs: Parker-OAK
Attendance: 49,444

GAME 3 AT TOR OCT 6

OAK	101 100 000	3 8 1
TOR	000 400 30X	7 8 0

Pitchers: DAVIS, Honeycutt (7), Nelson (7), M.Young (7), Acker (7), Henke (9) vs KEY, Acker (7), Henke (9)
Home Runs: Parker-OAK
Attendance: 50,268

GAME 4 AT TOR OCT 7

OAK	003 020 100	6 11 1
TOR	000 101 120	5 13 0

Pitchers: WELCH, Honeycutt (6), Eckersley (8) vs FLANAGAN, Ward (5), Cerutti (8), Acker (9)
Home Runs: R.Henderson-OAK (2), Canseco-OAK
Attendance: 50,076

GAME 5 AT TOR OCT 8

OAK	101 000 200	4 4 0
TOR	000 000 012	3 9 0

Pitchers: STEWART, Eckersley (9) vs STIEB, Acker (7), Henke (9)
Home Runs: Moseby-TOR, Bell-TOR
Attendance: 50,024

Not even the devastating earthquake that blindsided baseball's first San Francisco Bay World Series could halt the Oakland juggernaut. The A's scored first in every game and, except for 1½ innings of Game 2 in which the score stood at 1–1, held their lead to the finish.

Athletic ace Dave Stewart shut out the Giants on five hits in the opener. Three second-inning Oakland runs initiated the Series scoring, and Dave Parker and Walt Weiss expanded Stewart's margin of comfort with solo homers in the third and fourth. In Game 2, doubles by Carney Lansford in the first inning and Parker in the fourth drove home the two runs the A's would need for victory; Terry Steinbach's three-run blast later in the fourth added frosting to Oakland's cake. A's starter Mike Moore yielded a pair of singles and the first Giant run of the Series in the third inning but held the Giants to just two more singles in his seven-plus innings of work. Relievers Rick Honeycutt and Dennis Eckersley hurled perfect ball in the eighth and ninth.

After a day off, the Series shifted eleven miles across the Bay to San Francisco for Game 3. But just as fans were settling into their seats, the earthquake struck, knocking out power to Candlestick Park and (as gradually became known) killing 67 people in scattered pockets of destruction throughout the Bay Area. The fans were sent home, but despite the pleas of a few Eastern reporters that the rest of the Series be cancelled, the overwhelming desire of Bay Area residents prevailed, and Game 3 came off at last, ten days late. Starter Dave Stewart gave up three Giant runs in seven innings, but by the time he was relieved, his A's had sent nine men across the plate. Four more runs in the eighth completed the Oakland scoring. The Giants put together their first big inning of the Series, scoring four runs in the last of the ninth. Although the Giants' effort fell far short of what was needed, pinch hitter Bill Bathe's home run—the game's seventh, including five by the A's—set a new World Series record.

Game 4 began as yet another Giant humiliation. Oakland's Rickey Henderson led off the game with a home run, and by the time Giant Kevin Mitchell homered in his team's first pair of runs in the sixth inning, the A's had scored eight times. The Giants struggled back, though, scoring four times in the seventh on a walk and a cycle of hits—home run, triple, double, and single—to draw within two runs of a tie. But they came no closer. Oakland scored a ninth run an inning later, and Todd Burns and Dennis Eckersley hurled the Series

Oakland Athletics (AL), 4; San Francisco Giants (NL), 0

OAK (A)

PLAYER/POS	AVG	G	AB	R	H	2B	3B	HR	RB	BB	SO	SB
Lance Blankenship, 2b	.500	1	2	1	1	0	0	0	0	0	0	0
Todd Burns, p	.000	2	0	0	0	0	0	0	0	0	0	0
Jose Canseco, of	.357	4	14	5	5	0	0	1	3	4	3	1
Dennis Eckersley, p	.000	2	0	0	0	0	0	0	0	0	0	0
Mike Gallego, 2b-1,3b-1	.000	2	1	0	0	0	0	0	0	0	0	0
Dave Henderson, of	.308	4	13	6	4	2	0	2	4	4	3	0
Rickey Henderson, of	.474	4	19	4	9	1	2	1	3	2	2	3
Rick Honeycutt, p	.000	3	0	0	0	0	0	0	0	0	0	0
Stan Javier, of	.000	1	0	0	0	0	0	0	0	0	0	0
Carney Lansford, 3b	.438	4	16	5	7	1	0	1	4	3	1	0
Mark McGwire, 1b	.294	4	17	0	5	1	0	0	1	1	3	0
Mike Moore, p	.333	2	3	1	1	1	0	0	2	0	1	0
Gene Nelson, p	.000	2	0	0	0	0	0	0	0	0	0	0
Dave Parker, dh-2	.222	3	9	2	2	1	0	1	2	0	2	0
Ken Phelps, ph	.000	1	1	0	0	0	0	0	0	0	0	0
Tony Phillips, 2b-3,3b-2,of-1	.235	4	17	2	4	1	0	1	3	0	3	0
Terry Steinbach, c	.250	4	16	3	4	0	1	1	7	2	1	0
Dave Stewart, p	.000	2	3	0	0	0	0	0	0	0	1	0
Walt Weiss, ss	.133	4	15	3	2	0	0	1	1	2	2	0
TOTAL	.301		146	32	44	8	3	9	30	18	22	4

PITCHER	W	L	ERA	G	GS	CG	SV	SHO	IP	H	ER	BB	SO
Todd Burns	0	0	0.00	2	0	0	0	0	1.2	1	0	1	0
Dennis Eckersley	0	0	0.00	2	0	0	1	0	1.2	0	0	0	0
Rick Honeycutt	0	0	6.75	3	0	0	0	0	2.2	4	2	0	2
Mike Moore	2	0	2.08	2	2	0	0	0	13.0	9	3	3	10
Gene Nelson	0	0	54.00	2	0	0	0	0	1.0	4	6	2	1
Dave Stewart	2	0	1.69	2	2	1	0	1	16.0	10	3	2	14
TOTAL	4	0	3.50	13	4	1	1	1	36.0	28	14	8	27

SF (N)

PLAYER/POS	AVG	G	AB	R	H	2B	3B	HR	RB	BB	SO	SB
Bill Bathe, ph	.500	2	2	1	1	0	0	1	3	0	0	0
Steve Bedrosian, p	.000	2	0	0	0	0	0	0	0	0	0	0
Jeff Brantley, p	.000	3	0	0	0	0	0	0	0	0	0	0
Brett Butler, of	.286	4	14	1	4	1	0	0	1	2	1	2
Will Clark, 1b	.250	4	16	2	4	1	0	0	1	3	0	0
Kelly Downs, p	.000	3	0	0	0	0	0	0	0	0	0	0
Scott Garrelts, p	.000	2	1	0	0	0	0	0	0	0	1	0
Atlee Hammaker, p	.000	2	0	0	0	0	0	0	0	0	0	0
Terry Kennedy, c	.167	4	12	1	2	0	0	0	2	1	3	0
Mike LaCoss, p	.000	2	1	0	0	0	0	0	0	0	0	0
Craig Lefferts, p	.000	3	0	0	0	0	0	0	0	0	0	0
Greg Litton, 2b-2,3b-1	.500	2	6	1	3	1	0	1	3	0	0	0
Candy Maldonado, of-3	.091	4	11	1	1	0	1	0	0	0	4	0
Kirt Manwaring, c	1.000	1	1	1	1	1	0	0	0	0	0	0
Kevin Mitchell, of	.294	4	17	2	5	0	0	1	2	0	3	0
Donell Nixon, of	.200	2	5	1	1	0	0	0	0	1	1	0
Ken Oberkfell, 3b	.333	4	6	1	2	0	0	0	0	3	0	0
Rick Reuschel, p	.000	1	0	0	0	0	0	0	0	0	0	0
Ernie Riles, dh-2	.000	3	8	0	0	0	0	0	0	0	1	0
Don Robinson, p	.000	1	0	0	0	0	0	0	0	0	0	0
Pat Sheridan, of	.000	1	2	0	0	0	0	0	0	0	0	0
Robby Thompson, 2b	.091	4	11	0	1	0	0	0	0	2	4	0
Jose Uribe, ss	.200	3	5	1	1	0	0	0	0	0	0	0
Matt Williams, ss-4,ss-3	.125	4	16	1	2	0	0	1	1	0	6	0
TOTAL	.209		134	14	28	4	1	4	14	8	27	2

PITCHER	W	L	ERA	G	GS	CG	SV	SHO	IP	H	ER	BB	SO
Steve Bedrosian	0	0	0.00	2	0	0	0	0	2.2	0	0	2	2
Jeff Brantley	0	0	4.15	3	0	0	0	0	4.1	5	2	3	1
Kelly Downs	0	0	7.71	3	0	0	0	0	4.2	3	4	2	4
Scott Garrelts	0	2	9.82	2	2	0	0	0	7.1	13	8	1	8
Atlee Hammaker	0	0	15.43	2	0	0	0	0	2.1	8	4	0	2
Mike LaCoss	0	0	6.23	2	0	0	0	0	4.1	4	3	3	2
Craig Lefferts	0	0	3.38	3	0	0	0	0	2.2	2	1	2	1
Rick Reuschel	0	1	11.25	1	1	0	0	0	4.0	5	5	4	2
Don Robinson	0	1	21.60	1	1	0	0	0	1.2	4	4	1	0
TOTAL	0	4	8.21	19	4	0	0	0	34.0	44	31	18	22

to its conclusion with 2⅓ innings of perfect relief.

GAME 1 AT OAK OCT 14

SF	000	000	000	0	5	1
OAK	031	100	00X	5	11	1

Pitchers: GARRELTS, Hammaker (5), Brantley (6), LaCoss (8) vs STEWART
Home Runs: Parker-OAK, Weiss-OAK
Attendance: 49,385

GAME 2 AT OAK OCT 15

SF	001	000	000	1	4	0
OAK	100	400	00X	5	7	0

Pitchers: REUSCHEL, Downs (5), Lefferts (7), Bedrosian (8) vs MOORE, Honeycutt (8), Eckersley (9)
Home Runs: Steinbach-OAK
Attendance: 49,388

GAME 3 AT SF OCT 27

OAK	200	241	040	13	14	0
SF	010	200	004	7	10	3

Pitchers: STEWART, Honeycutt (8), Nelson (9), Burns (9) vs GARRELTS, Downs (4), Brantley (5), Hammaker (8), Lefferts (9)
Home Runs: Williams-SF, D.Henderson-OAK (2), Phillips-OAK, Canseco-OAK, Lansford-OAK, Bathe-SF
Attendance: 62,038

GAME 4 AT SF OCT 28

OAK	130	031	010	9	12	0
SF	000	002	400	6	9	0

Pitchers: MOORE, Nelson (7), Honeycutt (7), Burns (7), Eckersley (9) vs ROBINSON, LaCoss (2), Brantley (6), Downs (6), Lefferts (8), Bedrosian (8)
Home Runs: R.Henderson-OAK, Mitchell-SF, Litton-SF
Attendance: 62,032

Fielding plays and misplays provided some of the most crucial moments of the series. After the Pirates had overcome a three-run deficit to tie the score in Game 1, for example, they won the game when Eric Davis misplayed Andy Van Slyke's fly to left field for a run-scoring double. Cincinnati right fielder Paul O'Neill evened the series in Game 2 by singling home the game's first run in the first inning, then (with the game tied 1–1 in the fifth) doubling in the go-ahead—and final—run on a fly Pirate left fielder Barry Bonds lost in the late afternoon sun. Finally, O'Neill gunned down Pittsburgh's potential tying run at third base when Van Slyke attempted to move up after Bonds's fly-out to right.

Two- and three-run homers by Reds Billy Hatcher and Mariano Duncan gave Cincinnati the series advantage in Game 3, and Chris Sabo's sacrifice fly and two-run blast proved the decisive blows a day later as the Reds pushed their series lead to 3–1. In that game left fielder Eric Davis, backing up Bobby Bonilla's double off the center field wall, prevented what would have become a game-tying run when, with a perfect throw to third, he nailed Bonilla trying for a triple.

The Pirates staved off elimination with a narrow 3–2 win in Game 5, a win preserved by a spectacular bases-loaded game-ending double play. But in Game 6, Pittsburgh's uncertain fielding in the first inning gave the Reds their first and, as it turned out, decisive run. In the ninth inning, with the Reds ahead 2–1, Reds right fielder Glen Braggs snared a deep fly with a leaping catch that prevented at least one, and perhaps two, Pirate runs from scoring. One strikeout later the Reds had snared the National League pennant.

Cincinnati Reds (West), 4; Pittsburgh Pirates (East), 2

CIN (W)

PLAYER/POS	AVG	G	AB	R	H	2B	3B	HR	RB	BB	SO	SB
Billy Bates, pr	.000	2	0	1	0	0	0	0	0	0	0	0
Todd Benzinger, 1b-2	.333	5	9	0	3	0	0	0	0	2	0	0
Glenn Braggs, of	.200	2	5	0	1	0	0	0	0	0	1	0
Tom Browning, p	.000	2	3	0	0	0	0	0	0	0	1	0
Norm Charlton, p	.000	4	0	0	0	0	0	0	0	0	0	0
Eric Davis, of	.174	6	23	2	4	1	0	0	2	1	9	0
Rob Dibble, p	.000	4	2	0	0	0	0	0	0	0	1	0
Mariano Duncan, 2b	.300	6	20	1	6	0	0	1	4	0	8	0
Billy Hatcher, of	.333	4	15	2	5	1	0	1	2	0	2	0
Danny Jackson, p	.000	2	3	0	0	0	0	0	0	0	2	0
Barry Larkin, ss	.261	6	23	5	6	2	0	0	1	3	1	3
Rick Mahler, p	.000	1	0	0	0	0	0	0	0	0	0	0
Hal Morris, 1b-4	.417	5	12	3	5	1	0	0	1	1	0	0
Randy Myers, p	.000	4	0	0	0	0	0	0	0	0	0	0
Ron Oester, 2b-2	.333	3	3	1	1	0	0	0	0	0	1	0
Joe Oliver, c	.143	5	14	1	2	0	0	0	0	0	2	0
Paul O'Neill, of	.471	5	17	1	8	3	0	1	4	1	1	1
Luis Quinones, ph	.500	3	2	1	1	0	0	0	2	0	0	1
Jeff Reed, c	.000	4	7	0	0	0	0	0	0	0	0	0
Jose Rijo, p	.000	2	5	0	0	0	0	0	0	0	1	0
Chris Sabo, 3b	.227	6	22	1	5	0	0	1	3	1	4	0
Scott Scudder, p	.000	1	0	0	0	0	0	0	0	0	0	0
Herm Winningham, of-2	.286	3	7	1	2	1	0	0	1	1	1	1
TOTAL	.255		192	20	49	9	0	4	20	10	37	6

PITCHER	W	L	ERA	G	GS	CG	SV	SHO	IP	H	ER	BB	SO
Tom Browning	1	1	3.27	2	2	0	0	0	11.0	9	4	6	5
Norm Charlton	1	1	1.80	4	0	0	0	0	5.0	4	1	3	3
Rob Dibble	0	0	0.00	4	0	0	1	0	5.0	0	0	1	10
Danny Jackson	1	0	2.38	2	2	0	0	0	11.1	8	3	7	8
Rick Mahler	0	0	0.00	1	0	0	0	0	1.2	2	0	0	0
Randy Myers	0	0	0.00	4	0	0	3	0	5.2	2	0	3	7
Jose Rijo	1	0	4.38	2	2	0	0	0	12.1	10	6	7	15
Scott Scudder	0	0	0.00	1	0	0	0	0	1.0	1	0	0	1
TOTAL	4	2	2.38	20	6	0	4	0	53.0	36	14	27	49

PIT (E)

PLAYER/POS	AVG	G	AB	R	H	2B	3B	HR	RB	BB	SO	SB
Wally Backman, 3b-2	.143	3	7	1	1	1	0	0	0	1	3	1
Stan Belinda, p	.000	3	0	0	0	0	0	0	0	0	0	0
Jay Bell, ss	.250	6	20	3	5	1	0	1	1	4	3	0
Barry Bonds, of	.167	6	18	4	3	0	0	0	1	6	6	2
Bobby Bonilla, of-5,3b-3	.190	6	21	0	4	1	0	0	1	3	1	0
Sid Bream, 1b	.500	4	8	1	4	1	0	1	3	2	3	0
Doug Drabek, p	.167	2	6	0	1	0	0	0	0	0	2	0
Jeff King, 3b-4	.100	5	10	0	1	0	0	0	0	1	5	0
Bill Landrum, p	.000	2	0	0	0	0	0	0	0	0	0	0
Mike LaValliere, c	.000	3	6	1	0	0	0	0	0	3	1	0
Jose Lind, 2b	.238	6	21	1	5	1	1	1	2	1	4	0
Carmelo Martinez, 1b	.250	2	8	0	2	0	0	0	2	0	1	0
Bob Patterson, p	.000	2	0	0	0	0	0	0	0	0	0	0
Ted Power, p	.000	2	1	0	0	0	0	0	0	0	1	0
Gary Redus, 1b-2	.250	5	8	1	2	0	0	0	0	1	3	1
R. J. Reynolds, of-3	.200	6	10	0	2	0	0	0	0	2	2	1
Don Slaught, c	.091	4	11	0	1	1	0	0	1	2	3	0
John Smiley, p	.000	1	0	0	0	0	0	0	0	0	0	0
Zane Smith, p	.000	2	3	0	0	0	0	0	0	0	1	0
Andy Van Slyke, of	.208	6	24	3	5	1	1	0	3	1	6	1
Bob Walk, p	.000	2	4	0	0	0	0	0	0	0	4	0
TOTAL	.194		186	15	36	9	2	3	14	27	49	6

PITCHER	W	L	ERA	G	GS	CG	SV	SHO	IP	H	ER	BB	SO
Stan Belinda	0	0	2.45	3	0	0	0	0	3.2	3	1	0	4
Doug Drabek	1	1	1.65	2	2	1	0	0	16.1	12	3	3	13
Bill Landrum	0	0	0.00	2	0	0	0	0	2.0	0	0	0	1
Bob Patterson	0	0	0.00	2	0	0	1	0	1.0	1	0	2	0
Ted Power	0	0	3.60	2	1	0	1	0	5.0	6	2	2	3
John Smiley	0	0	0.00	1	0	0	0	0	2.0	2	0	0	0
Zane Smith	0	2	6.00	2	1	0	0	0	9.0	14	6	1	8
Bob Walk	1	1	4.85	2	2	0	0	0	13.0	11	7	2	8
TOTAL	2	4	3.29	16	6	1	2	0	52.0	49	19	10	37

GAME 1 AT CIN OCT 4

PIT	001	200	100	4	7	1
CIN	300	000	000	3	5	0

Pitchers: WALK, Belinda (7), Patterson (9), Power (9) vs Rijo, CHARLTON (6), Dibble (9)
Home Runs: Bream-PIT
Attendance: 55,700

GAME 2 AT CIN OCT 5

PIT	000	010	000	1	6	0
CIN	100	010	00X	2	5	0

Pitchers: DRABEK vs BROWNING, Dibble (7), Myers (8)
Home Runs: Lind-PIT
Attendance: 54,456

GAME 3 AT PIT OCT 8

CIN	020	030	001	6	13	1
PIT	000	200	010	3	8	0

Pitchers: JACKSON, Dibble (6), Charlton (8), Myers (9) vs SMITH, Landrum (6), Smiley (7), Belinda (9)
Home Runs: Duncan-CIN, Hatcher-CIN
Attendance: 45,611

GAME 4 AT PIT OCT 9

CIN	000	200	201	5	10	1
PIT	100	100	010	3	8	0

Pitchers: RIJO, Myers (8), Dibble (9) vs WALK, Power (8)
Home Runs: O'Neill-CIN, Sabo-CIN, Bell-PIT
Attendance: 50,461

GAME 5 AT PIT OCT 10

CIN	100	000	010	2	7	0
PIT	200	100	00X	3	6	1

Pitchers: BROWNING, Mahler (6), Charlton (7), Scudder (8) vs DRABEK, Patterson (9)
Attendance: 48,221

GAME 6 AT CIN OCT 12

PIT	000	010	000	1	1	3
CIN	100	000	10X	2	9	0

Pitchers: Power, SMITH (3), Belinda (7), Landrum (8) vs Jackson, CHARLTON (7), Myers (8)
Attendance: 56,079

The ejection of Boston ace Roger Clemens from Game 4 for mouthing off to an umpire provided a moment of raucous counterpoint to the surgical precision with which Oakland dismembered the Red Sox. While the A's pitchers anesthetized Boston's hitters, parceling out just one run per game, their batters sliced up the Sox with singles, steals, and sacrifices.

In the fourth inning of Game 1, Boston's Wade Boggs interrupted a pitchers' duel between Clemens and Oakland's Dave Stewart with the series' only home run. But in the top of the seventh—after a tiring Clemens had been relieved—the A's evened the score with a walk, single, and sacrifice fly, took the lead an inning later with a pair of singles sandwiched around a bunt and stolen base, then buried the Sox with seven runs in the ninth. DH Harold Baines provided Oakland's most productive offense in the second game, singling home the tying run in the fourth inning, driving in the tiebreaker with a groundout in the seventh, and doubling home a third run in the ninth. In Game 3, a double steal by Baines and Jose Canseco set up the A's tying and tiebreaking runs, which scored on a sacrifice fly and a single.

The A's scored first for the only time in the series in Game 4, on a pair of singles and a grounder to short in the second inning. Following the shouting match between the Sox and umpires that erupted when pitcher Clemens was thrown out for disputing a walk to the next batter, Mike Gallego doubled home two more Oakland runs. A trio of Boston relievers stopped the Athletics the rest of the way, and a pair of Red Sox hits in the ninth ended Dave Stewart's shutout bid. But Rick Honeycutt came on to preserve Stewart's second win of the series and sew up Oakland's third successive American League championship.

Oakland Athletics (West), 4; Boston Red Sox (East), 0

OAK (W)

PLAYER/POS	AVG	G	AB	R	H	2B	3B	HR	RB	BB	SO	SB
Harold Baines, dh	.357	4	14	2	5	1	0	0	3	2	1	1
Lance Blankenship, dh	.000	3	0	1	0	0	0	0	0	0	0	1
Jose Canseco, of	.182	4	11	3	2	0	0	0	1	5	5	2
Dennis Eckersley, p	.000	3	0	0	0	0	0	0	0	0	0	0
Mike Gallego, ss-3,2b-2	.400	4	10	1	4	1	0	0	2	1	1	0
Ron Hassey, c-1,dh-1	.333	2	3	0	1	0	0	0	0	2	0	0
Dave Henderson, of	.167	2	6	0	1	0	0	0	1	0	2	1
Rickey Henderson, of	.294	4	17	1	5	0	0	0	3	1	2	2
Rick Honeycutt, p	.000	3	0	0	0	0	0	0	0	0	0	0
Doug Jennings, of	.000	1	1	0	0	0	0	0	0	0	0	0
Carney Lansford, 3b	.438	4	16	2	7	1	0	0	2	0	1	0
Willie McGee, of-2,dh-1	.222	3	9	3	2	1	0	0	0	1	2	2
Mark McGwire, 1b	.154	4	13	2	2	0	0	0	2	3	3	0
Mike Moore, p	.000	1	0	0	0	0	0	0	0	0	0	0
Gene Nelson, p	.000	1	0	0	0	0	0	0	0	0	0	0
Jamie Quirk, ph	1.000	1	1	0	1	0	0	0	0	0	0	0
Willie Randolph, 2b	.375	4	8	1	3	0	0	0	3	1	0	0
Terry Steinbach, c	.455	3	11	2	5	0	0	0	1	1	2	0
Dave Stewart, p	.000	2	0	0	0	0	0	0	0	0	0	0
Walt Weiss, ss	.000	2	7	2	0	0	0	0	0	2	2	0
Bob Welch, p	.000	1	0	0	0	0	0	0	0	0	0	0
TOTAL	.299		127	20	38	4	0	0	18	19	21	9

PITCHER	W	L	ERA	G	GS	CG	SV	SHO	IP	H	ER	BB	SO
Dennis Eckersley	0	0	0.00	3	0	0	2	0	3.1	2	0	0	3
Rick Honeycutt	0	0	0.00	3	0	0	1	0	1.2	0	0	0	0
Mike Moore	1	0	1.50	1	1	0	0	0	6.0	4	1	1	5
Gene Nelson	0	0	0.00	1	0	0	0	0	1.2	3	0	0	0
Dave Stewart	2	0	1.13	2	2	0	0	0	16.0	8	2	2	4
Bob Welch	1	0	1.23	1	1	0	0	0	7.1	6	1	3	4
TOTAL	4	0	1.00	11	4	0	3	0	36.0	23	4	6	16

BOS (E)

PLAYER/POS	AVG	G	AB	R	H	2B	3B	HR	RB	BB	SO	SB
Larry Andersen, p	.000	3	0	0	0	0	0	0	0	0	0	0
Marty Barrett, 2b	.000	3	0	0	0	0	0	0	0	0	0	0
Mike Boddicker, p	.000	1	0	0	0	0	0	0	0	0	0	0
Wade Boggs, 3b	.438	4	16	1	7	1	0	1	1	0	3	0
Tom Bolton, p	.000	2	0	0	0	0	0	0	0	0	0	0
Tom Brunansky, of	.083	4	12	0	1	0	0	0	1	1	3	0
Ellis Burks, of	.267	4	15	1	4	2	0	0	0	1	1	1
Roger Clemens, p	.000	2	0	0	0	0	0	0	0	0	0	0
Dwight Evans, dh	.231	4	13	0	3	1	0	0	0	1	3	0
Jeff Gray, p	.000	2	0	0	0	0	0	0	0	0	0	0
Mike Greenwell, of	.000	4	14	1	0	0	0	0	0	2	2	0
Greg Harris, p	.000	1	0	0	0	0	0	0	0	0	0	0
Danny Heep, ph	.000	2	2	0	0	0	0	0	0	0	0	0
Dana Kiecker, p	.000	1	0	0	0	0	0	0	0	0	0	0
Randy Kutcher, pr	.000	2	0	0	0	0	0	0	0	0	0	0
Dennis Lamp, p	.000	1	0	0	0	0	0	0	0	0	0	0
Mike Marshall, ph	.333	3	3	0	1	0	0	0	0	0	0	0
Rob Murphy, p	.000	1	0	0	0	0	0	0	0	0	0	0
Tony Pena, c	.214	4	14	0	3	0	0	0	0	0	0	0
Carlos Quintana, 1b	.000	4	13	0	0	0	0	0	0	1	1	0
Jeff Reardon, p	.000	1	0	0	0	0	0	0	0	0	0	0
Jody Reed, 2b-4,ss-3	.133	4	15	0	2	0	0	0	1	0	2	0
Luis Rivera, ss	.222	4	9	1	2	1	0	0	0	0	2	0
TOTAL	.183		126	4	23	5	0	1	4	6	16	1

PITCHER	W	L	ERA	G	GS	CG	SV	SHO	IP	H	ER	BB	SO
Larry Andersen	0	1	6.00	3	0	0	0	0	3.0	3	2	3	3
Mike Boddicker	0	1	2.25	1	1	1	0	0	8.0	6	2	3	7
Tom Bolton	0	0	0.00	2	0	0	0	0	3.0	2	0	2	3
Roger Clemens	0	1	3.52	2	2	0	0	0	7.2	7	3	5	4
Jeff Gray	0	0	2.70	2	0	0	0	0	3.1	4	1	1	2
Greg Harris	0	1	27.00	1	0	0	0	0	0.1	3	1	0	0
Dana Kiecker	0	0	1.59	1	1	0	0	0	5.2	6	1	1	2
Dennis Lamp	0	0	108.00	1	0	0	0	0	0.1	2	4	2	0
Rob Murphy	0	0	13.50	1	0	0	0	0	0.2	2	1	1	0
Jeff Reardon	0	0	9.00	1	0	0	0	0	2.0	3	2	1	0
TOTAL	0	4	4.50	15	4	1	0	0	34.0	38	17	19	21

GAME 1 AT BOS OCT 6

OAK	000	000	117	9	13 0
BOS	000	100	000	1	5 1

Pitchers: STEWART, Eckersley (9) vs Clemens, ANDERSEN (7), Bolton (8), Gray (8), Lamp (9), Murphy (9)
Home Runs: Boggs-BOS
Attendance: 35,192

GAME 2 AT BOS OCT 7

OAK	000	100	102	4	13 1
BOS	001	000	000	1	6 0

Pitchers: WELCH, Honeycutt (8), Eckersley (8) vs Kiecker, HARRIS (6), Andersen (7), Reardon (8)
Attendance: 35,070

GAME 3 AT OAK OCT 9

BOS	010	000	000	1	8 3
OAK	000	202	00X	4	6 0

Pitchers: BODDICKER vs MOORE, Nelson (7), Honeycutt (8), Eckersley (9)
Attendance: 49,026

GAME 4 AT OAK OCT 10

BOS	000	000	001	1	4 1
OAK	030	000	00X	3	6 0

Pitchers: CLEMENS, Bolton (2), Gray (5), Andersen (8) vs STEWART, Honeycutt (9)
Attendance: 49,052

In the most stunning World Series sweep since 1954, Cincinnati's fired-up Reds roasted the team many were proclaiming baseball's newest dynasty. Reds left fielder Eric Davis, playing despite shoulder and knee injuries, provided the A's their first hint of what was to come when—on the first pitch thrown to him in the first inning—he homered over the center field wall for two runs. Billy Hatcher, on base with a walk, scored ahead of Davis, the first of his Series-high six runs. Hatcher would not be retired at the plate until Game 3. Final score: 7–0. For Oakland starter Dave Stewart, the loss ended a personal postseason six-game win streak. For the club, the loss ended a streak of ten postseason wins.

The A's put up their best fight of the Series in Game 2, scoring first, then overcoming a 1–2 deficit in the third inning with three more runs for a 4–2 lead. Cincinnati narrowed the gap with a run in the fourth and tied the score in the eighth when Hatcher tripled—setting a World Series record with his seventh straight hit—and came home on a grounder to short. The A's held on until the tenth inning, when ace reliever Dennis Eckersley gave up three straight hits to lose the game.

Game 3 was another Cincinnati blowout, an 8–3 contest in which all eleven runs were scored in the second and third innings. Chris Sabo led the Reds assault with two home runs, and handled a Series-record ten chances at third base.

For seven innings of Game 4 the tide of battle seemed to be turning in Oakland's favor. Billy Hatcher —who was batting .750—left the game after a pitch hit his hand in the first inning. Later in the inning Eric Davis tore a kidney diving for a Willie McGee shot that went for a double. McGee went on to score, and Davis departed for the hospital. A renewed Dave Stewart, supported by sharp fielding, seemed capable of sustaining his 1–0 lead to the finish. But in the eighth the Reds, with just one solid hit, eked out the two runs they would need for victory. After loading the bases with a leadoff single, a third-strike bunt that went for a hit, and a sacrifice bunt that Stewart misplayed for an error, the Reds drove home the tying run with a grounder to short and took the lead on a sacrifice fly. Meanwhile Reds starter Jose Rijo held the A's hitless after the first inning, leveling twenty men in order from the second into the ninth, when ace closer Randy Myers relieved him for the final two outs of the splendid sweep.

Cincinnati Reds (NL), 4;
Oakland Athletics (AL), 0

CIN (N)

PLAYER/POS	AVG	G	AB	R	H	2B	3B	HR	RB	BB	SO	SB
Jack Armstrong, p	.000	1	0	0	0	0	0	0	0	0	0	0
Billy Bates, ph	1.000	1	1	1	1	0	0	0	0	0	0	0
Todd Benzinger, 1b-3	.182	4	11	1	2	0	0	0	0	0	0	0
Glenn Braggs, of-1	.000	2	4	0	0	0	0	0	0	2	1	0
Tom Browning, p	.000	1	0	0	0	0	0	0	0	0	0	0
Norm Charlton, p	.000	1	0	0	0	0	0	0	0	0	0	0
Eric Davis, of	.286	4	14	3	4	0	0	1	5	0	0	0
Rob Dibble, p	.000	3	0	0	0	0	0	0	0	0	0	0
Mariano Duncan, 2b	.143	4	14	1	2	0	0	0	1	2	2	1
Billy Hatcher, of	.750	4	12	6	9	4	1	0	2	2	0	0
Danny Jackson, p	.000	1	1	0	0	0	0	0	0	0	1	0
Barry Larkin, ss	.353	4	17	3	6	1	1	0	1	2	0	0
Hal Morris, 1b-2,dh-2	.071	4	14	0	1	0	0	0	2	1	1	0
Randy Myers, p	.000	3	0	0	0	0	0	0	0	0	0	0
Ron Oester, ph	1.000	1	1	0	1	0	0	0	0	1	0	0
Joe Oliver, c	.333	4	18	2	6	3	0	0	2	0	1	0
Paul O'Neill, of	.083	4	12	2	1	0	0	0	1	5	2	1
Jose Rijo, p	.333	2	3	0	1	0	0	0	0	0	0	0
Chris Sabo, 3b	.563	4	16	2	9	1	0	2	5	2	2	0
Scott Scudder, p	.000	1	0	0	0	0	0	0	0	0	0	0
Herm Winningham, of-1	.500	2	4	1	2	0	0	0	0	0	0	0
TOTAL	.317		142	22	45	9	2	3	22	15	9	2

PITCHER	W	L	ERA	G	GS	CG	SV	SHO	IP	H	ER	BB	SO
Jack Armstrong	0	0	0.00	1	0	0	0	0	3.0	1	0	0	3
Tom Browning	1	0	4.50	1	1	0	0	0	6.0	6	3	2	2
Norm Charlton	0	0	0.00	1	0	0	0	0	1.0	1	0	0	0
Rob Dibble	1	0	0.00	3	0	0	0	0	4.2	3	0	1	4
Danny Jackson	0	0	10.13	1	1	0	0	0	2.2	6	3	2	0
Randy Myers	0	0	0.00	3	0	0	1	0	3.0	2	0	0	3
Jose Rijo	2	0	0.59	2	2	0	0	0	15.1	9	1	5	14
Scott Scudder	0	0	0.00	1	0	0	0	0	1.1	0	0	2	2
TOTAL	4	0	1.70	13	4	0	1	0	37.0	28	7	12	28

OAK (A)

PLAYER/POS	AVG	G	AB	R	H	2B	3B	HR	RB	BB	SO	SB
Harold Baines, dh-2	.143	3	7	1	1	0	0	1	2	1	2	0
Lance Blankenship, ph	.000	1	1	0	0	0	0	0	0	0	1	0
Mike Bordick, ss	.000	3	0	0	0	0	0	0	0	0	0	0
Todd Burns, p	.000	2	0	0	0	0	0	0	0	0	0	0
Jose Canseco, of-3,dh-1	.083	4	12	1	1	0	0	1	2	2	3	0
Dennis Eckersley, p	.000	2	0	0	0	0	0	0	0	0	0	0
Mike Gallego, ss	.091	4	11	0	1	0	0	0	1	1	3	1
Ron Hassey, c-1	.333	3	6	0	2	0	0	0	1	0	0	0
Dave Henderson, of-3	.231	4	13	2	3	1	0	0	0	1	3	0
Rickey Henderson, of	.333	4	15	2	5	2	0	1	1	3	4	3
Rick Honeycutt, p	.000	1	0	0	0	0	0	0	0	0	0	0
Doug Jennings, ph	1.000	1	1	0	1	0	0	0	0	0	0	0
Joe Klink, p	.000	1	0	0	0	0	0	0	0	0	0	0
Carney Lansford, 3b	.267	4	15	0	4	0	0	0	1	1	0	1
Willie McGee, of-3	.200	4	10	1	2	1	0	0	0	0	2	1
Mark McGwire, 1b	.214	4	14	1	3	0	0	0	0	2	4	0
Mike Moore, p	.000	1	0	0	0	0	0	0	0	0	0	0
Gene Nelson, p	.000	2	0	0	0	0	0	0	0	0	0	0
Jamie Quirk, c	.000	1	3	0	0	0	0	0	0	0	2	0
Willie Randolph, 2b	.267	4	15	0	4	0	0	0	0	1	0	1
Scott Sanderson, p	.000	2	0	0	0	0	0	0	0	0	0	0
Terry Steinbach, c	.125	3	8	0	1	0	0	0	0	0	1	0
Dave Stewart, p	.000	2	1	0	0	0	0	0	0	0	0	0
Bob Welch, p	.000	1	3	0	0	0	0	0	0	0	2	0
Curt Young, p	.000	1	0	0	0	0	0	0	0	0	0	0
TOTAL	.207		135	8	28	4	0	3	8	12	28	7

PITCHER	W	L	ERA	G	GS	CG	SV	SHO	IP	H	ER	BB	SO
Todd Burns	0	0	16.20	2	0	0	0	0	1.2	5	3	2	0
Dennis Eckersley	0	1	6.75	2	0	0	0	0	1.1	3	1	0	1
Rick Honeycutt	0	0	0.00	1	0	0	0	0	1.2	2	0	1	0
Joe Klink	0	0	INF	1	0	0	0	0	0.0	0	0	1	0
Mike Moore	0	1	6.75	1	1	0	0	0	2.2	8	2	0	1
Gene Nelson	0	0	0.00	2	0	0	0	0	5.0	3	0	2	0
Scott Sanderson	0	0	10.80	2	0	0	0	0	1.2	4	2	1	0
Dave Stewart	0	2	3.46	2	2	1	0	0	13.0	10	5	6	5
Bob Welch	0	0	4.91	1	1	0	0	0	7.1	9	4	2	2
Curt Young	0	0	0.00	1	0	0	0	0	1.0	1	0	0	0
TOTAL	0	4	4.33	15	4	1	0	0	35.1	45	17	15	9

GAME 1 AT CIN OCT 16

OAK	000	000	000	0	9 1
CIN	202	030	00X	7	10 0

Pitchers: STEWART, Burns (5), Nelson (5), Sanderson (7), Eckersley (8) vs RIJO, Dibble (8), Myers (9)
Home Runs: Davis-CIN
Attendance: 55,830

GAME 2 AT CIN OCT 17

OAK	103	000	000	0	410
CIN	200	100	010	1	514

Pitchers: Welch, Honeycutt (8), ECKERSLEY (10) vs Jackson, Scudder (3), Armstrong (5), Charlton (8), DIBBLE (9)
Home Runs: Canseco-OAK
Attendance: 55,832

GAME 3 AT OAK OCT 19

CIN	017	000	000	8 14 1
OAK	021	000	000	3 7 1

Pitchers: BROWNING, Dibble (7), Myers (8) vs MOORE, Sanderson (3), Klink (4), Nelson (4), Burns (8), Young (9)
Home Runs: Sabo-CIN (2), Baines-OAK, R.Henderson-OAK
Attendance: 48,269

GAME 4 AT OAK OCT 20

CIN	000	000	020	2 7 1
OAK	100	000	000	1 2 1

Pitchers: RIJO, Myers (9) vs STEWART
Attendance: 48,613

Pitching dominated this back-and-forth series which featured four shutouts, including three 1–0 games. Three times Atlanta hurlers blanked Pittsburgh on the Pirates' home grounds, including a pair of must-win victories that brought the Braves back from the brink of defeat. Andy Van Slyke opened the series scoring with a first-inning Pirate home run. Pirate starter Doug Drabek held the Braves scoreless through six innings of the opener, before injuring himself on the basepath. By the time David Justice homered in the ninth for Atlanta's only score, the Pirates had the game well in hand.

Atlanta evened the series with its first of three shutouts in Game Two behind the pitching of young Steve Avery and (for the final ⅔ inning) Alejandro Pena, and the bat and glove of Mark Lemke. The Braves' second baseman doubled home that game's only run in the sixth inning and prevented a Pittsburgh run from scoring in the eighth with a diving stop of a grounder up the middle. In Atlanta for Game Three, the Braves took the series lead with a 10–3 route that featured home runs by Ron Gant, Greg Olson, and Sid Bream. (Orlando Merced and Derek Bell homered for Pittsburgh.)

Game Four was much closer; this time three Pirate runs brought them victory. The Braves took a quick lead with two first-inning runs, but Pittsburgh scored once in the second and tied the game in the fifth on a throwing error as Pirate pitching shut down Atlanta's offense. In the top of the tenth, Andy Van Slyke led off with a walk. With two away he stole second, and then scored what proved the winning run on Don Slaught's double. With the series even again, Atlanta lost a run in Game Five when David Justice was ruled out for missing third base as he dashed home from second. An inning later the Pirates parlayed a walk and a pair of singles into the only run they would need to carry the series advantage back to Pittsburgh.

In Game Six, though, the Braves returned the favor, tying the series once more with a gem of their own. Avery and Pena combined for their second 1–0 victory, holding Atlanta to just four singles. Drabek held the Braves scoreless into the ninth, when Olson doubled home the game's only run.

In the finale, Braves starter John Smoltz enjoyed a three-run lead when he took the mound in the bottom of the first inning. Rookie first baseman Brian Hunter (who had homered for two of the first-inning runs) doubled in an additional Atlanta run in the fifth. Meanwhile Smoltz stopped the Pirates on six hits to bring the Braves their first pennant since their move to Atlanta in 1966.

Atlanta Braves (West), 4; Pittsburgh Pirates (East), 3

ATL (W)

PLAYER/POS	AVG	G	AB	R	H	2B	3B	HR	RB	BB	SO	SB
Steve Avery, p	.143	2	7	0	1	0	0	0	0	0	4	0
Rafael Belliard, ss	.211	7	19	0	4	0	0	0	1	3	3	0
Jeff Blauser, ss	.000	2	2	0	0	0	0	0	0	0	0	0
Sid Bream, 1b	.300	4	10	1	3	0	0	1	3	0	1	0
Jim Clancy, p	.000	1	0	0	0	0	0	0	0	0	0	0
Ron Gant, of	.259	7	27	4	7	1	0	1	3	2	4	7
Tom Glavine, p	.250	2	4	0	1	0	0	0	0	0	2	0
Tommy Gregg, ph	.250	4	4	0	1	0	0	0	0	0	2	0
Brian Hunter, 1b	.333	5	18	2	6	2	0	1	4	0	2	0
David Justice, of	.200	7	25	4	5	1	0	1	2	3	7	0
Charlie Leibrandt, p	.000	1	1	0	0	0	0	0	0	0	0	0
Mark Lemke, 2b	.200	7	20	1	4	1	0	0	1	4	0	0
Kent Mercker, p	.000	5	0	0	0	0	0	0	0	0	0	0
Keith Mitchell, of	.000	5	4	0	0	0	0	0	0	0	1	0
Greg Olson, c	.333	7	24	3	8	0	0	1	4	4	3	1
Alejandro Pena, p	.000	4	0	0	0	0	0	0	0	0	0	0
Terry Pendleton, 3b	.167	7	30	1	5	1	1	0	1	1	3	0
Lonnie Smith, of	.250	7	24	3	6	3	0	0	0	4	5	2
John Smoltz, p	.200	2	5	0	1	0	0	0	0	1	4	1
Mike Stanton, p	.000	3	0	0	0	0	0	0	0	0	0	0
Jeff Treadway, 2b	.333	1	3	0	1	0	0	0	0	0	0	0
Jerry Willard, ph	.000	2	2	0	0	0	0	0	0	0	1	0
Mark Wohlers, p	.000	3	0	0	0	0	0	0	0	0	0	0
TOTAL	.231		229	19	53	10	1	5	19	22	42	11

PITCHER	W	L	ERA	G	GS	CG	SV	SHO	IP	H	ER	BB	SO
Steve Avery	2	0	0.00	2	2	0	0	0	16.1	9	0	4	17
Jim Clancy	0	0	0.00	1	0	0	0	0	0.1	0	0	0	0
Tom Glavine	0	2	3.21	2	2	0	0	0	14.0	12	5	6	11
Charlie Leibrandt	0	0	1.35	1	1	0	0	0	6.2	8	1	3	6
Kent Mercker	0	1	13.50	1	0	0	0	0	0.2	0	1	2	0
Alejandro Pena	0	0	0.00	4	0	0	3	0	4.1	1	0	0	4
John Smoltz	2	0	1.76	2	2	1	0	1	15.1	14	3	3	15
Mike Stanton	0	0	2.45	3	0	0	0	0	3.2	4	1	3	3
Mark Wohlers	0	0	0.00	3	0	0	0	0	1.2	3	0	1	1
TOTAL	4	3	1.57	19	7	1	3	1	63.0	51	11	22	57

PIT (E)

PLAYER/POS	AVG	G	AB	R	H	2B	3B	HR	RB	BB	SO	SB
Stan Belinda, p	.000	3	0	0	0	0	0	0	0	0	0	0
Jay Bell, ss	.414	7	29	2	12	2	0	1	1	0	10	0
Barry Bonds, of	.148	7	27	1	4	1	0	0	0	2	4	3
Bobby Bonilla, of	.304	7	23	2	7	2	0	0	1	6	2	0
Steve Buechele, 3b	.304	7	23	2	7	2	0	0	4	6	0	0
Doug Drabek, p	.200	2	5	0	1	1	0	0	1	0	2	0
Cecil Espy, ph	.000	2	2	0	0	0	0	0	0	0	2	0
Bob Kipper, p	.000	1	0	0	0	0	0	0	0	0	0	0
Bill Landrum, p	.000	1	0	0	0	0	0	0	0	0	0	0
Mike LaValliere, c	.333	3	6	0	2	0	0	0	1	2	0	0
Jose Lind, 2b	.160	7	25	0	4	0	0	0	3	0	6	0
Roger Mason, p	.000	3	1	0	0	0	0	0	0	0	1	0
Lloyd McClendon, 1b-1	.000	3	2	0	0	0	0	0	0	1	0	0
Orlando Merced, 1b-2	.222	3	9	1	2	0	0	1	1	0	1	0
Bob Patterson, p	.000	1	0	0	0	0	0	0	0	0	0	0
Gary Redus, 1b	.158	5	19	1	3	0	0	0	0	1	4	2
Rosario Rodriguez, p	.000	1	0	0	0	0	0	0	0	0	0	0
Don Slaught, c	.235	6	17	0	4	1	0	0	1	1	4	0
John Smiley, p	.000	2	0	0	0	0	0	0	0	0	0	0
Zane Smith, p	.000	2	5	0	0	0	0	0	0	0	4	0
Randy Tomlin, p	.000	1	2	0	0	0	0	0	0	0	0	0
Andy Van Slyke, of	.160	7	25	3	4	2	0	1	2	5	5	1
Gary Varsho, ph	.500	2	2	0	1	0	0	0	0	0	1	0
Bob Walk, p	.000	3	2	0	0	0	0	0	0	0	0	0
Curtis Wilkerson, ph	.000	4	4	0	0	0	0	0	0	0	3	0
TOTAL	.224		228	12	51	10	0	3	11	22	57	6

PITCHER	W	L	ERA	G	GS	CG	SV	SHO	IP	H	ER	BB	SO
Stan Belinda	1	0	0.00	3	0	0	0	0	5.0	0	0	3	4
Doug Drabek	1	1	0.60	2	2	1	0	0	15.0	10	1	5	10
Bob Kipper	0	0	4.50	1	0	0	0	0	2.0	2	1	0	1
Bill Landrum	0	0	9.00	1	0	0	0	0	1.0	2	1	2	2
Roger Mason	0	0	0.00	3	0	0	1	0	4.1	3	0	1	2
Bob Patterson	0	0	0.00	1	0	0	0	0	2.0	1	0	0	3
Rosario Rodriguez	0	0	27.00	1	0	0	0	0	1.0	1	3	2	1
John Smiley	0	2	23.63	2	2	0	0	0	2.2	8	7	1	3
Zane Smith	1	1	0.61	2	2	0	0	0	14.2	15	1	3	10
Randy Tomlin	0	0	3.00	1	1	0	0	0	6.0	6	2	2	1
Bob Walk	0	0	1.93	3	0	0	0	0	9.1	5	2	3	5
TOTAL	3	4	2.57	20	7	1	2	0	63.0	53	18	22	42

Minnesota struggled to achieve a 2–1 advantage in the first three games, then blew the Jays out of their SkyDome in the next two. Game One looked as though it would be an easy win for the Twins, who drove out starter Tom Candiotti with five runs on eight hits in the first 2⅔ innings. But Toronto scored once in the fourth and chased Twin starter Jack Morris in the sixth with five straight singles and three more runs. Relievers Carl Willis and Rick Aguilera, though, held Toronto to just one more single to preserve the victory for Minnesota.

The Jays scored three times in Game Two before Minnesota put its first run across in the last of the third, and scored twice more in the seventh, taking their first—and, as it turned out, only—win behind the strong pitching of rookie Juan Guzman and relievers Tom Henke and Duane Ward. Toronto again scored early in Game Three, with a pair of two-out runs (one of them Joe Carter's homer) in the first inning. Jays starter Jimmy Key held the Twins scoreless until they got to him for a run in the fifth, and another in the sixth which evened the score. Meanwhile a string of Minnesota pitchers stifled the Blue Jay bats from the second inning on. In the tenth, pinch hitter Mike Pagliarulo won it for the Twins with a home run to right.

For the third game in a row, Toronto scored first, with a run in the second inning of Game Four. But Minnesota's Kirby Puckett homered in the fourth to tie the score, and by the time Toronto scored again two innings later, the Twins had upped its run total to six. Puckett's home run in the first inning of Game Five gave the Twins the first of two early runs, but the Jays came back with three runs in the third and two more in the fourth to drive out starter Kevin Tapani. They scored no more, however, as three Twin relievers held them to one single in the final five frames. In the sixth inning, meanwhile, Minnesota reawakened to tie the game with a trio of runs, and salted it—and the pennant—away in the eighth: with two out, Puckett doubled home the go-ahead run, and Kent Hrbek singled in two more for insurance.

Minnesota Twins (West), 4;
Toronto Blue Jays (East), 1

MIN (W)

PLAYER/POS	AVG	G	AB	R	H	2B	3B	HR	RB	BB	SO	SB
Rick Aguilera, p	.000	3	0	0	0	0	0	0	0	0	0	0
Steve Bedrosian, p	.000	2	0	0	0	0	0	0	0	0	0	0
Jarvis Brown, dh	.000	1	0	1	0	0	0	0	0	0	0	0
Chili Davis, dh	.294	5	17	3	5	2	0	0	2	5	8	1
Scott Erickson, p	.000	1	0	0	0	0	0	0	0	0	0	0
Greg Gagne, ss	.235	5	17	1	4	0	0	0	1	1	5	0
Dan Gladden, of	.261	5	23	4	6	0	0	0	3	1	3	3
Mark Guthrie, p	.000	2	0	0	0	0	0	0	0	0	0	0
Brian Harper, c	.278	5	18	1	5	2	0	0	1	0	2	0
Kent Hrbek, 1b	.143	5	21	0	3	0	0	0	3	1	3	0
Chuck Knoblauch, 2b	.350	5	20	5	7	2	0	0	3	3	3	2
Gene Larkin, ph	.000	3	3	0	0	0	0	0	0	0	1	0
Scott Leius, 3b	.000	3	4	0	0	0	0	0	0	1	1	0
Shane Mack, of	.333	5	18	4	6	1	1	0	3	2	4	2
Jack Morris, p	.000	2	0	0	0	0	0	0	0	0	0	0
Al Newman, 2b-1,3b-1	.000	2	0	0	0	0	0	0	0	0	0	0
Junior Ortiz, c	.000	3	3	0	0	0	0	0	0	0	0	0
Mike Pagliarulo, 3b	.333	5	15	4	5	1	0	1	3	0	2	0
Kirby Puckett, of	.429	5	21	4	9	1	0	2	6	1	4	0
Paul Sorrento, ph	.000	1	1	0	0	0	0	0	0	0	1	0
Kevin Tapani, p	.000	2	0	0	0	0	0	0	0	0	0	0
David West, p	.000	2	0	0	0	0	0	0	0	0	0	0
Carl Willis, p	.000	3	0	0	0	0	0	0	0	0	0	0
TOTAL	.276		181	27	50	9	1	3	25	15	37	8

PITCHER	W	L	ERA	G	GS	CG	SV	SHO	IP	H	ER	BB	SO
Rick Aguilera	0	0	0.00	3	0	0	3	0	3.1	1	0	0	3
Steve Bedrosian	0	0	0.00	2	0	0	0	0	1.1	3	0	2	2
Scott Erickson	0	0	4.50	1	1	0	0	0	4.0	3	2	5	2
Mark Guthrie	1	0	0.00	2	0	0	0	0	2.2	2	0	0	0
Jack Morris	2	0	4.05	2	2	0	0	0	13.1	17	6	1	7
Kevin Tapani	0	1	7.84	2	2	0	0	0	10.1	16	9	3	9
David West	1	0	0.00	2	0	0	0	0	5.2	1	0	4	4
Carl Willis	0	0	0.00	3	0	0	0	0	5.1	2	0	0	3
TOTAL	4	1	3.33	17	5	0	3	0	46.0	43	17	15	30

TOR (E)

PLAYER/POS	AVG	G	AB	R	H	2B	3B	HR	RB	BB	SO	SB
Jim Acker, p	.000	1	0	0	0	0	0	0	0	0	0	0
Roberto Alomar, 2b	.474	5	19	3	9	0	0	0	4	2	3	2
Pat Borders, c	.263	5	19	0	5	1	0	0	2	0	0	0
Tom Candiotti, p	.000	2	0	0	0	0	0	0	0	0	0	0
Joe Carter, of-3,dh-2	.263	5	19	3	5	2	0	1	4	1	5	0
Rob Ducey, of	.000	1	1	0	0	0	0	0	0	0	0	0
Rene Gonzales, 1b-1,ss-1	.000	2	0	0	0	0	0	0	0	0	0	0
Kelly Gruber, 3b	.286	5	21	1	6	1	0	0	4	0	4	1
Juan Guzman, p	.000	1	0	0	0	0	0	0	0	0	0	0
Tom Henke, p	.000	2	0	0	0	0	0	0	0	0	0	0
Jimmy Key, p	.000	1	0	0	0	0	0	0	0	0	0	0
Manuel Lee, ss	.125	5	16	3	2	0	0	0	0	1	5	0
Rob MacDonald, p	.000	1	0	0	0	0	0	0	0	0	0	0
Candy Maldonado, of	.100	5	20	1	2	1	0	0	1	1	6	0
Rance Mulliniks, dh-3	.125	5	8	1	1	0	0	0	0	3	0	0
John Olerud, 1b	.153	5	19	1	3	0	0	0	3	3	1	0
Todd Stottlemyre, p	.000	1	0	0	0	0	0	0	0	0	0	0
Pat Tabler, dh	.000	2	1	0	0	0	0	0	0	1	0	0
Mike Timlin, p	.000	4	0	0	0	0	0	0	0	0	0	0
Duane Ward, p	.000	2	0	0	0	0	0	0	0	0	0	0
David Wells, p	.000	4	0	0	0	0	0	0	0	0	0	0
Devon White, of	.364	5	22	5	8	1	0	0	0	2	3	3
Mookie Wilson, of-2	.250	3	8	1	2	0	0	0	0	1	3	1
TOTAL	.249		173	19	43	6	0	1	18	15	30	7

PITCHER	W	L	ERA	G	GS	CG	SV	SHO	IP	H	ER	BB	SO
Jim Acker	0	0	0.00	1	0	0	0	0	0.2	1	0	0	1
Tom Candiotti	0	1	8.22	2	2	0	0	0	7.2	17	7	2	5
Juan Guzman	1	0	3.18	1	1	0	0	0	5.2	4	2	4	2
Tom Henke	0	0	0.00	2	0	0	0	0	2.2	0	0	1	5
Jimmy Key	0	0	3.00	1	1	0	0	0	6.0	5	2	1	1
Rob MacDonald	0	0	9.00	1	0	0	0	0	1.0	1	1	1	0
Todd Stottlemyre	0	1	9.82	1	1	0	0	0	3.2	7	4	1	3
Mike Timlin	0	1	3.18	4	0	0	0	0	5.2	5	2	2	5
Duane Ward	0	1	6.23	2	0	0	1	0	4.1	4	3	1	6
David Wells	0	0	2.35	4	0	0	0	0	7.2	6	2	2	9
TOTAL	1	4	4.60	19	5	0	1	0	45.0	50	23	15	37

GAME 1 AT MIN OCT 8

TOR	000	103	000	4	9	3
MIN	221	000	00X	5	11	0

Pitchers: CANDIOTTI, Wells (3), Timlin (6) vs MORRIS, Willis (6), Aguilera (8)
Attendance: 54,766

GAME 2 AT MIN OCT 9

TOR	102	000	200	5	9	0
MIN	001	001	000	2	5	1

Pitchers: GUZMAN, Henke (6), Ward (8) vs TAPANI, Bedrosian (7), Guthrie (7)
Attendance: 54,816

GAME 3 AT TOR OCT 11

MIN	000	011	000	1	3	7	0
TOR	200	000	000	0	2	5	1

Pitchers: Erickson, West (5), Willis (7), GUTHRIE (9), Aguilera (10) vs Key, Wells (7), Henke (8), TIMLIN (10)
Home Runs: Carter-TOR, Pagliarulo-MIN
Attendance: 51,454

GAME 4 AT TOR OCT 12

MIN	000	402	111	9	13	1
TOR	010	001	001	3	11	2

Pitchers: MORRIS, Bedrosian (9) vs STOTTLEMYRE, Wells (4), Acker (6), Timlin (7), MacDonald (9)
Home Runs: Puckett-MIN
Attendance: 51,526

GAME 5 AT TOR OCT 13

MIN	110	003	030	8	14	2
TOR	003	200	000	5	9	1

Pitchers: Tapani, WEST (5), Willis (8), Aguilera (9) vs Candiotti, Timlin (6), WARD (6), Wells (8)
Home Runs: Puckett-MIN
Attendance: 51,425

By any measure, this World Series was one of the great ones. Five of the seven games were decided by a single run, three of them—including Games Six and Seven—in extra innings.

The opener in Minnesota gave no indication of the suspense to come, as the Twins opened up a 4–0 lead in the fifth inning en route to a 5–2 win. Game Two proved more difficult. Chili Davis put the Twins in front with a two-run homer in the first inning, but in the fifth Atlanta tied the score. Braves hurler Tom Glavine but lost the game when the Twins' Scott Leius lofted a homer to lead off the eighth.

Minnesota took a quick lead in Game Three, but Atlanta tied the game an inning later, and went ahead on solo homers by David Justice in the fourth inning and Lonnie Smith in the fifth. Home runs by Kirby Puckett and Chili Davis in the fifth and sixth re-tied the score, which remained at 4–4 into the last of the eleventh inning, when Justice scored from second on Mark Lemke's two-out single. Lemke's heroics also made the difference in Game Four. Mike Pagliarulo drove in a pair of runs for Minnesota with a single in the second and a home run in the seventh, but Braves Terry Pendleton and Lonnie Smith neutralized the runs with solo homers in the third and seventh. Lemke came to bat in the bottom of the ninth with one out and the score still 2–2. He tripled, and scored in a tight play to even the Series.

In Game Five the Braves assaulted five Minnesota pitchers for fourteen runs and the Series lead, but when play returned to Minnesota for Game Six the Twins revived with two first-inning runs. In the third inning Puckett prevented two Atlanta runs with a leaping catch above the wall, but in the fifth, Atlanta's Terry Pendleton evened the score with a two-run homer. Later in the inning the Twins regained the lead on Puckett's sacrifice fly. Atlanta knotted the score again in the seventh, at 2–2. In the last of the eleventh, leadoff batter Puckett lined the ball over the wall near where he had earlier made his game-saving catch.

No one scored through 9½ innings of Game Seven as Minnesota's Jack Morris dueled John Smoltz, Mike Stanton, and Alejandro Pena. If the Braves had scored in the eighth as they could have, they would have won the game and the crown. Lonnie Smith singled to lead off the inning and could have come around on Terry Pendleton's double to the wall in left center. But, decoyed by the Twins' middle infielders into thinking there was a play at second, he paused just long enough after passing second to en-

able him to advance only to third. No one was out, but a grounder to first, an intentional walk to load the bases, and a smart 3–2–3 double play ended the Braves' threat.

Thus the game was still scoreless in the last of the tenth when Dan Gladden hustled his way into a broken-bat double and moved to third on Chuck Knoblauch's sacrifice bunt. Then, after the bases were loaded intentionally, pinch hitter Gene Larkin lobbed a hit over the head of the drawn-in left fielder. Gladden came home with the title for Minnesota.

Minnesota Twins (AL), 4; Atlanta Braves (NL), 3

MIN (A)

PLAYER/POS	AVG	G	AB	R	H	2B	3B	HR	RB	BB	SO	SB
Rick Aguilera, p	.000	4	1	0	0	0	0	0	0	0	0	0
Steve Bedrosian, p	.000	3	0	0	0	0	0	0	0	0	0	0
Jarvis Brown, of-2,dh-1	.000	3	2	0	0	0	0	0	0	0	0	0
Randy Bush, of-2	.250	3	4	0	1	0	0	0	0	0	1	0
Chili Davis, dh-4,of-1	.222	6	18	4	4	0	0	2	4	2	3	0
Scott Erickson, p	.000	2	1	0	0	0	0	0	0	0	1	0
Greg Gagne, ss	.167	7	24	1	4	1	0	1	3	0	7	0
Dan Gladden, of	.233	7	30	5	7	2	2	0	0	3	4	2
Mark Guthrie, p	.000	4	0	0	0	0	0	0	0	0	0	0
Brian Harper, c	.381	7	21	2	8	2	0	0	1	2	2	0
Kent Hrbek, 1b	.115	7	26	2	3	1	0	1	2	2	6	0
Chuck Knoblauch, 2b	.308	7	26	3	8	1	0	0	2	4	2	4
Gene Larkin, dh-1	.500	4	4	0	2	0	0	0	1	0	0	0
Terry Leach, p	.000	2	0	0	0	0	0	0	0	0	0	0
Scott Leius, 3b	.357	7	14	2	5	0	0	1	2	1	2	0
Shane Mack, of	.130	6	23	0	3	1	0	0	1	0	7	0
Jack Morris, p	.000	3	2	0	0	0	0	0	0	0	1	0
Al Newman, 3b-2,2b-1,ss-1	.500	4	2	0	1	0	1	0	1	0	0	0
Junior Ortiz, c	.200	3	5	0	1	0	0	0	1	0	1	0
Mike Pagliarulo, 3b	.273	6	11	1	3	0	0	1	2	1	2	0
Kirby Puckett, of	.250	7	24	4	6	0	1	2	4	5	7	1
Paul Sorrento, 1b-1	.000	3	2	0	0	0	0	0	0	1	2	0
Kevin Tapani, p	.000	2	1	0	0	0	0	0	0	0	0	0
David West, p	.000	2	0	0	0	0	0	0	0	0	0	0
Carl Willis, p	.000	4	0	0	0	0	0	0	0	0	0	0
TOTAL	.232		241	24	56	8	4	8	24	21	48	7

PITCHER	W	L	ERA	G	GS	CG	SV	SHO	IP	H	ER	BB	SO
Rick Aguilera	1	1	1.80	4	0	0	2	0	5.0	6	1	1	3
Steve Bedrosian	0	0	5.40	3	0	0	0	0	3.1	3	2	0	2
Scott Erickson	0	0	5.06	2	2	0	0	0	10.2	10	6	4	5
Mark Guthrie	0	1	2.25	4	0	0	0	0	4.0	3	1	4	3
Terry Leach	0	0	3.86	2	0	0	0	0	2.1	2	1	0	2
Jack Morris	2	0	1.17	3	3	1	0	1	23.0	18	3	9	15
Kevin Tapani	1	1	4.50	2	2	0	0	0	12.0	13	6	2	7
David West	0	0	INF	2	0	0	0	0	0.0	2	4	4	0
Carl Willis	0	0	5.14	4	0	0	0	0	7.0	6	4	2	2
TOTAL	4	3	3.74	26	7	1	2	1	67.1	63	28	26	39

ATL (N)

PLAYER/POS	AVG	G	AB	R	H	2B	3B	HR	RB	BB	SO	SB
Steve Avery, p	.000	2	3	0	0	0	0	0	0	0	2	0
Rafael Belliard, ss	.375	7	16	0	6	1	0	0	4	1	2	0
Jeff Blauser, ss	.167	5	6	0	1	0	0	0	0	1	1	0
Sid Bream, 1b	.125	7	24	0	3	2	0	0	0	3	4	0
Francisco Cabrera, c-1	.000	3	1	0	0	0	0	0	0	0	0	0
Jim Clancy, p	.000	3	1	0	0	0	0	0	0	0	1	0
Ron Gant, of	.267	7	30	3	8	0	1	0	4	2	3	1
Tom Glavine, p	.000	2	2	0	0	0	0	0	0	0	0	0
Tommy Gregg, ph	.000	4	3	0	0	0	0	0	0	0	2	0
Brian Hunter, 1b-4,of-4	.190	7	21	2	4	1	0	1	3	0	2	0
David Justice, of	.259	7	27	5	7	0	0	2	6	5	5	2
Charlie Leibrandt, p	.000	2	0	0	0	0	0	0	0	0	0	0
Mark Lemke, 2b	.417	6	24	4	10	1	3	0	4	2	4	0
Kent Mercker, p	.000	2	0	0	0	0	0	0	0	0	0	0
Keith Mitchell, of	.000	3	2	0	0	0	0	0	0	1	0	0
Greg Olson, c	.222	7	27	3	6	2	0	0	1	5	4	1
Alejandro Pena, p	.000	3	0	0	0	0	0	0	0	0	0	0
Terry Pendleton, 3b	.367	7	30	6	11	3	0	2	3	3	1	0
Randy St. Claire, p	.000	1	0	0	0	0	0	0	0	0	0	0
Lonnie Smith, dh-4,of-3	.231	7	26	5	6	0	0	3	3	4	1	0
John Smoltz, p	.000	2	2	0	0	0	0	0	0	0	1	0
Mike Stanton, p	.000	5	0	0	0	0	0	0	0	0	0	0
Jeff Treadway, 2b-1	.250	3	4	1	1	0	0	0	0	1	2	0
Jerry Willard, ph	.000	1	0	0	0	0	0	0	1	0	0	0
Mark Wohlers, p	.000	3	0	0	0	0	0	0	0	0	0	0
TOTAL	.253		249	29	63	10	4	8	29	26	39	5

PITCHER	W	L	ERA	G	GS	CG	SV	SHO	IP	H	ER	BB	SO
Steve Avery	0	0	3.46	2	2	0	0	0	13.0	10	5	1	8
Jim Clancy	1	0	4.15	3	0	0	0	0	4.1	3	2	4	2
Tom Glavine	1	1	2.70	2	2	1	0	0	13.1	8	4	7	8
Charlie Leibrandt	0	2	11.25	2	1	0	0	0	4.0	8	5	1	3
Kent Mercker	0	0	0.00	2	0	0	0	0	1.0	0	0	0	1
Alejandro Pena	0	1	3.38	3	0	0	0	0	5.1	6	2	3	7
Randy St. Claire	0	0	9.00	1	0	0	0	0	1.0	1	1	0	0
John Smoltz	0	0	1.26	2	2	0	0	0	14.1	13	2	1	11
Mike Stanton	1	0	0.00	5	0	0	0	0	7.1	5	0	2	7
Mark Wohlers	0	0	0.00	3	0	0	0	0	1.2	2	0	2	1
TOTAL	3	4	2.89	25	7	1	0	0	65.1	56	21	21	48

GAME 1 AT MIN OCT 19

```
ATL   000 001 010    2  6  1
MIN   001 031 00X    5  9  1
```
Pitchers: LEIBRANDT, Clancy (5), Wohlers (7), Stanton (8) vs MORRIS, Guthrie (8), Aguilera (8)
Home Runs: Gagne-MIN, Hrbek-MIN
Attendance: 55,108

GAME 2 AT MIN OCT 20

```
ATL   010 010 000    2  8  1
MIN   200 000 01X    3  4  1
```
Pitchers: GLAVINE vs TAPANI, Aguilera (9)
Home Runs: Davis-MIN, Leius-MIN
Attendance: 55,145

GAME 3 AT ATL OCT 22

```
MIN   100 000 120 000    4 10  1
ATL   010 120 000 001    5  8  2
```
Pitchers: Erickson, West (5), Leach (5), Bedrosian (6), Willis (8), Guthrie (10), AGUILERA (12) vs Avery, Pena (8), Stanton (10), Wohlers (12), Mercker (12), CLANCY (12)
Home Runs: Justice-ATL, Smith-ATL, Puckett-MIN, Davis-MIN
Attendance: 50,878

GAME 4 AT ATL OCT 23

```
MIN   010 000 100    2  7  0
ATL   001 000 101    3  8  0
```
Pitchers: Morris, Willis (7), GUTHRIE (8), Bedrosian (9) vs Smoltz, Wohlers (8), STANTON (8)
Home Runs: Pendleton-ATL, Pagliarulo-MIN, Smith-ATL
Attendance: 50,878

GAME 5 AT ATL OCT 24

```
MIN   000 003 011    5  7  1
ATL   000 410 63X   14 17  1
```
Pitchers: TAPANI, Leach (5), West (7), Bedrosian (7), Willis (8) vs GLAVINE, Mercker (6), Clancy (7), St. Claire (9)
Home Runs: Justice-ATL, Smith-ATL, Hunter-ATL
Attendance: 50,878

GAME 6 AT MIN OCT 26

```
ATL   000 020 100 00    3  9  1
MIN   200 010 000 01    4  9  0
```
Pitchers: Avery, Stanton (7), Pena (9), LEIBRANDT (11) vs Erickson, Guthrie (7), Willis (7), AGUILERA (10)
Home Runs: Pendleton-ATL, Puckett-MIN
Attendance: 55,155

GAME 7 AT MIN OCT 27

```
ATL   000 000 000 0    0  7  0
MIN   000 000 000 1    1 10  0
```
Pitchers: Smoltz, Stanton (8), PENA (9) vs MORRIS
Attendance: 55,118

Atlanta opened the series with a pair of one-sided wins but Pittsburgh pulled out a close victory in Game Three. After a third loss, the Piartes pummelled the Braves for two wins even more lopsided than their losses in the first two games. With the series now even, the stage was set for what turned out to be one of the most dramatic finishes in postseason history.

In Game One Pirate Jose Lind spoiled John Smoltz's shutout with his first home run of the season in the eighth inning. But by then the Braves had scored five times and held victory firmly in hand. Game Two was even easier. By the time the Pirates came up with four runs in the seventh inning (ending Steve Avery's LCS-record streak of scoreless innings at 22⅓), Atlanta had already compiled two four-run innings of their own (one of them on Ron Gant's grand slam). The Braves added five more runs in the last of the seventh to put the game out of reach.

At home for Game Three, the Pirates pulled themselves together behind the five-hit pitching of rookie knuckleballer Tim Wakefield. Sid Bream's solo homer in the fourth inning gave Atlanta a 1–0 lead, but Pirate Don Slaught homered to even the score an inning later and a pair of sixth-inning doubles put the Pirates ahead. Ron Gant's homer for Atlanta in the top of the seventh tied the score again, but a single, double, and sacrifice fly in the bottom of the inning put Pittsburgh on top to stay.

A 6–4 loss in Game Four brought the Pirates to the brink of elimination, but in Game Five they counterattacked, driving out Atlanta starter Steve Avery in the first inning with five hits (four of them doubles) and four runs, on their way to a 7–1 victory. With their feet still at the chasm's edge, the Pirates unloaded on Atlanta's Tom Glavine for eight runs in the second inning of Game Six before the first out was recorded, and pushed the assault to a 13–4 conclusion and a tied series.

While the Pirates scored single runs in the first and sixth innings of the final game, Pirate starter Doug Drabek (who had taken losses in Games One and Four) held Atlanta scoreless through eight innings. Then, in the last of the ninth, leadoff Brave Terry Pendleton doubled. He moved to third as David Justice reached on a grounder bobbled by the usually sure-handed second baseman Jose Lind. A walk to Sid Bream filled the bases. Stan Belinda replaced Drabek on the mound and retired Ron Gant on a fly to left, but Pendleton scored Atlanta's first run after the catch. Damon Berryhill walked to reload the bases, and pinch hitter Brian Hunter popped out. Had there been no error, the game would have

Atlanta Braves (West), 4; Pittsburgh Pirates (East), 3

ATL (W)

PLAYER/POS	AVG	G	AB	R	H	2B	3B	HR	RB	BB	SO	SB
Steve Avery, p	.000	3	2	0	0	0	0	0	0	1	0	1	0
R. Belliard, ss-3,2b-1	.000	4	2	1	0	0	0	0	0	1	0	0
Damon Berryhill, c	.167	7	24	1	4	1	0	0	1	3	2	0
Jeff Blauser, ss	.208	7	24	3	5	0	1	1	4	3	2	0
Sid Bream, 1b	.273	7	22	5	6	3	0	1	2	3	0	0
Francisco Cabrera, ph	.500	2	2	0	1	0	0	0	2	0	0	0
Marvin Freeman, p	.000	3	0	0	0	0	0	0	0	0	0	0
Ron Gant, of	.182	7	22	5	4	0	0	2	6	4	4	1
Tom Glavine, p	.000	2	2	0	0	0	0	0	0	0	0	0
Brian Hunter, 1b-2	.200	3	5	1	1	0	0	0	0	0	0	0
David Justice, of	.280	7	25	5	7	1	0	2	6	6	2	0
Charlie Leibrandt, p	.000	2	1	0	0	0	0	0	0	0	1	0
Mark Lemke, 2b-7,3b-1	.333	7	21	2	7	1	0	0	2	5	3	0
Javier Lopez, c	.000	1	1	0	0	0	0	0	0	0	0	0
Kent Mercker, p	.000	2	0	0	0	0	0	0	0	0	0	0
Otis Nixon, of	.286	7	28	5	8	2	0	0	0	2	4	3
Terry Pendleton, 3b	.233	7	30	2	7	2	0	0	3	0	2	0
Jeff Reardon, p	.000	3	0	0	0	0	0	0	0	0	0	0
Deion Sanders, of-3	.000	4	5	0	0	0	0	0	0	0	3	0
Lonnie Smith, ph	.333	6	6	1	2	0	1	0	1	0	0	0
Pete Smith, p	.000	2	1	0	0	0	0	0	0	0	0	0
John Smoltz, p	.286	3	7	1	2	0	0	0	1	0	2	1
Mike Stanton, p	1.000	5	1	1	1	1	0	0	1	0	0	0
Jeff Treadway, 2b-1	.667	3	3	1	2	0	0	0	0	0	1	0
Mark Wohlers, p	.000	3	0	0	0	0	0	0	0	0	0	0
TOTAL	.244		234	34	57	11	2	6	32	29	28	5

PITCHER	W	L	ERA	G	GS	CG	SV	SHO	IP	H	ER	BB	SO
Steve Avery	1	1	9.00	3	2	0	0	0	8.0	13	8	2	3
Marvin Freeman	0	0	14.73	3	0	0	0	0	3.2	8	6	2	1
Tom Glavine	0	2	12.27	2	2	0	0	0	7.1	13	10	3	2
Charlie Leibrandt	0	0	1.93	2	0	0	0	0	4.2	4	1	3	3
Kent Mercker	0	0	0.00	2	0	0	0	0	3.0	1	0	1	1
Jeff Reardon	1	0	0.00	3	0	0	1	0	3.0	0	0	2	3
Pete Smith	0	0	2.45	2	0	0	0	0	3.2	2	1	3	3
John Smoltz	2	0	2.66	3	3	0	0	0	20.1	14	6	10	19
Mike Stanton	0	0	0.00	5	0	0	0	0	4.1	2	0	2	5
Mark Wohlers	0	0	0.00	3	0	0	0	0	3.0	2	0	1	2
TOTAL	4	3	4.72	28	7	0	1	0	61.0	59	32	29	42

PIT (E)

PLAYER/POS	AVG	G	AB	R	H	2B	3B	HR	RB	BB	SO	SB
Stan Belinda, p	.000	2	0	0	0	0	0	0	0	0	0	0
Jay Bell, ss	.172	7	29	3	5	2	0	1	4	3	4	0
Barry Bonds, of	.261	7	23	5	6	1	0	1	2	6	4	1
Alex Cole, of	.200	4	10	2	2	0	0	0	1	3	2	0
Danny Cox, p	.000	2	0	0	0	0	0	0	0	0	0	0
Doug Drabek, p	.000	3	6	0	0	0	0	0	0	1	4	0
Cecil Espy, of-2	.667	4	3	0	2	0	0	0	0	0	1	0
Carlos Garcia, 2b	.000	1	1	0	0	0	0	0	0	0	0	0
Danny Jackson, p	.000	1	0	0	0	0	0	0	0	0	0	0
Jeff King, 3b	.241	7	29	4	7	4	0	0	2	0	1	0
Mike LaValliere, c	.200	3	10	1	2	0	0	0	0	0	3	0
Jose Lind, 2b	.222	7	27	5	6	2	1	1	5	1	4	0
Roger Mason, p	.000	2	0	0	0	0	0	0	0	0	0	0
Lloyd McClendon, of	.727	5	11	4	8	2	0	1	4	4	1	0
Orlando Merced, 1b	.100	4	10	0	1	1	0	0	2	2	4	0
Denny Neagle, p	.000	2	0	0	0	0	0	0	0	0	0	0
Bob Patterson, p	.000	2	0	0	0	0	0	0	0	0	0	0
Gary Redus, 1b	.438	5	16	4	7	4	1	0	3	2	3	0
Don Slaught, c	.333	5	12	5	4	1	0	1	5	6	3	0
Randy Tomlin, p	.000	2	0	0	0	0	0	0	0	0	0	0
Andy Van Slyke, of	.276	7	29	1	8	3	1	0	4	1	5	0
Gary Varsho, of-1	.500	2	2	0	1	0	0	0	0	0	0	0
Tim Wakefield, p	.000	2	6	1	0	0	0	0	0	0	0	0
Bob Walk, p	.000	2	5	0	0	0	0	0	0	0	1	0
John Wehner, ph	.000	2	2	0	0	0	0	0	0	0	0	0
TOTAL	.255		231	35	59	20	3	5	32	29	42	1

PITCHER	W	L	ERA	G	GS	CG	SV	SHO	IP	H	ER	BB	SO
Stan Belinda	0	0	0.00	2	0	0	0	0	1.2	2	0	0	2
Danny Cox	0	0	0.00	2	0	0	0	0	1.1	1	0	1	1
Doug Drabek	0	3	3.71	3	3	0	0	0	17.0	18	7	7	10
Danny Jackson	0	1	21.60	1	1	0	0	0	1.2	4	4	2	0
Roger Mason	0	0	0.00	2	0	0	0	0	3.1	0	0	2	1
Denny Neagle	0	0	27.00	2	0	0	0	0	1.2	4	5	3	0
Bob Patterson	0	0	5.40	2	0	0	0	0	1.2	3	1	1	1
Randy Tomlin	0	0	6.75	2	0	0	0	0	2.2	5	2	1	0
Tim Wakefield	2	0	3.00	2	2	2	0	0	18.0	14	6	5	7
Bob Walk	1	0	3.86	2	1	1	0	0	11.2	6	5	7	6
TOTAL	3	4	4.45	20	7	3	0	0	60.2	57	30	29	28

been over, with Pittsburgh waving the pennant. Instead, little-used pinch hitter Francisco Cabrera lined the ball safely to left, scoring Justice with the tying run and Bream with a repeat pennant for Atlanta.

GAME 1 AT ATL OCT 6

PIT	000	000	010		1	5	1
ATL	010	210	10X		5	8	0

Pitchers: DRABEK, Patterson (5), Neagle (7), Cox (8) vs SMOLTZ, Stanton (9)
Home Runs: Lind-PIT, Blauser-ATL
Attendance: 51,971

GAME 2 AT ATL OCT 7

PIT	000	000	410		5	7	0
ATL	040	040	50X		13	14	0

Pitchers: JACKSON, Mason (2), Walk (3), Tomlin (5), Neagle (7), Patterson (7), Belinda (8) vs AVERY, Freeman (7), Stanton (7), Wohlers (8), Reardon (9)
Home Runs: Gant-ATL
Attendance: 51,975

GAME 3 AT PIT OCT 9

ATL	000	100	100		2	5	0
PIT	000	011	10X		3	8	1

Pitchers: GLAVINE, Stanton (7), Wohlers (8) vs WAKEFIELD
Home Runs: Bream-ATL, Gant-ATL, Slaught-PIT
Attendance: 56,610

GAME 4 AT PIT OCT 10

ATL	020	022	000		6	11	1
PIT	021	000	100		4	6	1

Pitchers: SMOLTZ, Stanton (7), Reardon (9) vs DRABEK, Tomlin (5), Cox (6), Mason (7)
Attendance: 57,164

GAME 5 AT PIT OCT 11

ATL	000	000	010		1	3	0
PIT	401	001	10X		7	13	0

Pitchers: AVERY, Smith (1), Leibrandt (5), Freeman (6), Mercker (8) vs WALK
Attendance: 52,929

GAME 6 AT ATL OCT 13

PIT	080	041	000		13	13	1
ATL	000	100	102		4	9	1

Pitchers: WAKEFIELD vs GLAVINE, Leibrandt (2), Freeman (5), Mercker (7), Wohlers (9)
Home Runs: Bell-PIT, Bonds-PIT, McClendon-PIT, Justice-ATL (2)
Attendance: 51,975

GAME 7 AT ATL OCT 14

PIT	100	001	000		2	7	1
ATL	000	000	003		3	7	0

Pitchers: DRABEK, Belinda (9) vs Smoltz, Stanton (7), Smith (7), Avery (7), REARDON (9)
Attendance: 51,975

Oakland had competed in three League Championship Series in the previous four years and won them all. Toronto in its first fifteen seasons of existence had competed three times in the LCS and never won. In the first game of the 1992 matchup, the Athletics scored first on Mark McGwire's two-run homer and the next batter, Terry Steinbach, pushed the score to 3–0 with another home run. Toronto's Pat Borders and Dave Winfield retaliated with solo homers in the fifth and sixth innings to narrow the gap, and the Blue Jays tied the score in the eighth when Winfield, who had doubled with two outs, came home on John Olerud's single. But in the top of the ninth, Harold Baines led off with the game's fifth home run to put Oakland back into the lead, and A's reliever Dennis Eckersley preserved it for his tenth LCS save.

After this encouraging beginning, though, the A's went into a three-game decline. In Game Two, fireballer David Cone held Oakland scoreless through eight innings while the Jays built a 3–0 lead on Kelly Gruber's two-run homer in the fifth inning and a third score two innings later. Oakland finally touched Cone for a run in the ninth, but reliever Tom Henke smothered the threat. The A's recovered from an early deficit in Game Three to tie the score in the fourth inning, but fell behind on Candy Maldonado's leadoff homer in the sixth and never regained the lead. In Game Four the A's rocked Toronto starter Jack Morris for five runs in the fifth, and added another in the sixth to take a 6–1 lead. But in the eighth, reliever Eckersley, who came on with one run in and two on, yielded singles on his first two pitches to let in two more runs, and in the ninth gave up a leadoff single and a game-tying home run to Roberto Alomar. Toronto finally took the lead in the eleventh as Derek Bell fouled off several pitches before drawing a walk, took third on Maldonado's single, and scored on Pat Borders' fly to left. Reliever Tom Henke held the lead.

Down three games to one, Oakland came out slugging in Game Five. Ruben Sierra homered for a pair of runs in the first inning and the A's added a third run two innings later. Dave Winfield homered in the Toronto fourth, but the A's took advantage of two Toronto errors to score three more runs an inning later, putting the game out of the Blue Jays' reach. But they couldn't sustain their comeback. Joe Carter's two-run homer in the first inning of Game Six, and Candy Maldonado's three-run blast two innings later, highlighted a 9–2 Toronto romp

Toronto Blue Jays (East), 4
Oakland Athletics (West), 2

TOR (E)

PLAYER/POS	AVG	G	AB	R	H	2B	3B	HR	RB	BB	SO	SB
Roberto Alomar, 2b	.423	6	26	4	11	1	0	2	4	2	1	5
Derek Bell, of	.000	2	0	1	0	0	0	0	0	1	0	0
Pat Borders, c	.318	6	22	3	7	0	0	1	3	1	1	0
Joe Carter, of-6,1b-2	.192	6	26	2	5	0	0	1	3	2	4	2
David Cone, p	.000	2	0	0	0	0	0	0	0	0	0	0
Mark Eichhorn, p	.000	1	0	0	0	0	0	0	0	0	0	0
Alfredo Griffin, ss-1	.000	2	2	0	0	0	0	0	0	0	0	0
Kelly Gruber, 3b	.091	7	22	3	2	1	0	1	2	2	3	0
Juan Guzman, p	.000	2	0	0	0	0	0	0	0	0	0	0
Tom Henke, p	.000	4	0	0	0	0	0	0	0	0	0	0
Jimmy Key, p	.000	1	0	0	0	0	0	0	0	0	0	0
Manuel Lee, ss	.278	6	18	2	5	1	1	0	3	1	2	0
Candy Maldonado, of	.273	6	22	3	6	0	0	2	6	2	4	0
Jack Morris, p	.000	2	0	0	0	0	0	0	0	0	0	0
John Olerud, 1b	.348	6	23	4	8	2	0	1	4	2	5	0
Ed Sprague, ph	.500	2	2	0	1	0	0	0	0	0	1	0
Todd Stottlemyre, p	.000	1	0	0	0	0	0	0	0	0	0	0
Mike Timlin, p	.000	2	0	0	0	0	0	0	0	0	0	0
Duane Ward, p	.000	3	0	0	0	0	0	0	0	0	0	0
Devon White, of	.348	6	23	2	8	2	0	0	2	5	6	0
Dave Winfield, dh	.250	6	24	7	6	1	0	2	3	5	2	0
TOTAL	.281		210	31	59	8	1	10	30	23	29	7

PITCHER	W	L	ERA	G	GS	CG	SV	SHO	IP	H	ER	BB	SO
David Cone	1	1	3.00	2	2	0	0	0	12.0	11	4	5	9
Mark Eichhorn	0	0	0.00	1	0	0	0	0	1.0	0	0	0	0
Juan Guzman	2	0	2.08	2	2	0	0	0	13.0	12	3	5	11
Tom Henke	0	0	0.00	4	0	0	3	0	4.2	4	0	2	2
Jimmy Key	0	0	0.00	1	0	0	0	0	3.0	2	0	2	1
Jack Morris	0	1	6.57	2	2	1	0	0	12.1	11	9	9	6
Todd Stottlemyre	0	0	2.45	1	0	0	0	0	3.2	3	1	0	1
Mike Timlin	0	0	6.75	2	0	0	0	0	1.1	4	1	0	1
Duane Ward	1	0	6.75	3	0	0	0	0	4.0	5	3	1	2
TOTAL	4	2	3.44	18	6	1	3	0	55.0	52	21	24	33

OAK (W)

PLAYER/POS	AVG	G	AB	R	H	2B	3B	HR	RB	BB	SO	SB
Harold Baines, dh	.440	6	25	6	11	2	0	1	4	0	3	0
Lance Blankenship, 2b	.231	5	13	2	3	0	0	0	0	3	4	1
Mike Bordick, ss-4,2b-2	.053	6	19	1	1	0	0	0	0	1	2	1
Jerry Browne, 3b-2,of-1	.400	4	10	3	4	0	0	0	2	2	0	0
Jim Corsi, p	.000	3	0	0	0	0	0	0	0	0	0	0
Ron Darling, p	.000	1	0	0	0	0	0	0	0	0	0	0
Kelly Downs, p	.000	2	0	0	0	0	0	0	0	0	0	0
Dennis Eckersley, p	.000	3	0	0	0	0	0	0	0	0	0	0
Eric Fox, of-1,dh-1	.000	4	1	0	0	0	0	0	0	1	0	2
Rickey Henderson, of	.261	6	23	5	6	0	0	0	1	4	4	4
Rick Honeycutt, p	.000	2	0	0	0	0	0	0	0	0	0	0
Carney Lansford, 3b	.167	5	18	0	3	0	0	0	1	1	1	0
Mark McGwire, 1b	.150	6	20	1	3	0	0	1	3	5	4	0
Mike Moore, p	.000	2	0	0	0	0	0	0	0	0	0	0
Jeff Parrett, p	.000	3	0	0	0	0	0	0	0	0	0	0
Jamie Quirk, ph	.000	1	1	0	0	0	0	0	0	0	0	0
Randy Ready, ph	.000	1	1	0	0	0	0	0	0	0	1	0
Jeff Russell, p	.000	3	0	0	0	0	0	0	0	0	0	0
Ruben Sierra, of	.333	6	24	4	8	2	1	1	7	2	1	1
Terry Steinbach, c	.292	6	24	1	7	0	0	1	5	2	7	0
Dave Stewart, p	.000	2	0	0	0	0	0	0	0	0	0	0
Walt Weiss, ss	.167	3	6	1	1	0	0	0	0	2	1	2
Bob Welch, p	.000	1	0	0	0	0	0	0	0	0	0	0
Willie Wilson, of	.227	6	22	0	5	1	0	0	0	1	5	7
Bobby Witt, p	.000	1	0	0	0	0	0	0	0	0	0	0
TOTAL	.251		207	24	52	5	1	4	23	24	33	16

PITCHER	W	L	ERA	G	GS	CG	SV	SHO	IP	H	ER	BB	SO
Jim Corsi	0	0	0.00	3	0	0	0	0	2.0	2	0	3	0
Ron Darling	0	1	3.00	1	1	0	0	0	6.0	4	2	2	3
Kelly Downs	0	1	3.86	2	0	0	0	0	2.1	3	1	1	0
Dennis Eckersley	0	0	6.00	3	0	0	1	0	3.0	8	2	0	2
Rick Honeycutt	0	0	0.00	2	0	0	0	0	2.0	0	0	0	1
Mike Moore	0	2	7.45	2	2	0	0	0	9.2	11	8	5	7
Jeff Parrett	0	0	11.57	3	0	0	0	0	2.1	6	3	0	1
Jeff Russell	1	0	9.00	3	0	0	0	0	2.0	2	2	4	0
Dave Stewart	1	0	2.70	2	2	1	0	0	16.2	14	5	6	7
Bob Welch	0	0	2.57	1	1	0	0	0	7.0	7	2	1	7
Bobby Witt	0	0	18.00	1	0	0	0	0	1.0	2	2	1	1
TOTAL	2	4	4.50	23	6	1	1	0	54.0	59	27	23	29

that ended the team's string of failed opportunities and carried the American League pennant to Canada for the first time.

GAME 1 AT TOR OCT 7

OAK	030 000 001	4	6	1
TOR	000 011 010	3	9	0

Pitchers: Stewart, RUSSELL (8), Eckersley (9) vs MORRIS
Home Runs: Baines-OAK, McGwire-OAK, Steinbach-OAK, Winfield-TOR, Borders-TOR
Attendance: 51,039

GAME 2 AT TOR OCT 8

OAK	000 000 001	1	6	0
TOR	000 020 10X	3	4	0

Pitchers: MOORE, Corsi (8), Parrett (8) vs CONE, Henke (9)
Home Runs: Gruber-TOR
Attendance: 51,114

GAME 3 AT OAK OCT 10

TOR	010 110 211	7	9	1
OAK	000 200 210	5	13	3

Pitchers: GUZMAN, Ward (7), Timlin (8), Henke (8) vs DARLING, Downs (7), Corsi (8), Russell (8), Honeycutt (9), Eckersley (9)
Home Runs: Alomar-TOR, Maldonado-TOR
Attendance: 46,911

GAME 4 AT OAK OCT 11

TOR	010 000 032 01	7	17	4
OAK	005 001 000 00	6	12	2

Pitchers: Morris, Stottlemyre (4), Timlin (8), WARD (9), Henke (11) vs Welch, Parrett (8), Eckersley (8), Corsi (9), DOWNS (10)
Home Runs: Alomar-TOR, Olerud-TOR
Attendance: 47,732

GAME 5 AT OAK OCT 12

TOR	000 100 100	2	7	3
OAK	201 030 00X	6	8	0

Pitchers: CONE, Key (5), Eichhorn (8) vs STEWART
Home Runs: Winfield-TOR, Sierra-OAK
Attendance: 44,955

GAME 6 AT TOR OCT 14

OAK	000 001 010	2	7	1
TOR	204 010 02X	9	13	0

Pitchers: MOORE, Parrett (3), Honeycutt (5), Russell (7), Witt (8) vs GUZMAN, Ward (8), Henke (9)
Home Runs: Carter-TOR, Maldonado-TOR
Attendance: 51,335

Atlanta outscored Toronto in the Series 20 runs to 16, but the Blue Jays eked out four one-run victories to bring Canada its first world baseball championship. In the fourth inning of Game One, Atlanta's Tom Glavine gave up a leadoff homer to Joe Carter for the game's first run, but held the Jays to just one single the rest of the way. For five innings, meanwhile, Toronto starter Jack Morris shut out the Braves. But in the top of the sixth he gave up a deciding three-run homer to catcher Damon Berryhill. The next night, though, down 4–5 in the ninth inning, Toronto pinch hitter Derek Bell drew a walk from Braves closer Jeff Reardon, and pinch hitter Ed Sprague lined Reardon's first pitch over the left field wall.

Toronto moved ahead with another close victory in Game Three, the first World Series game ever played outside the United States. Atlanta threatened in the fourth inning when, with two on and none out, David Justice drove the ball to deep center. But in the defensive play of the Series, center fielder Devon White leaped high to snare the ball. Baserunner Terry Pendleton was ruled out for passing Deion Sanders on the basepath, and third baseman Kelly Gruber tagged Sanders, who was diving back into second base, to complete what seemed to be a triple play. The umpire didn't see the tag, however, and called Sanders safe. Still, no Brave scored, and Blue Jay Joe Carter homered for the game's first run in the last of the fourth. Atlanta tied the game in the sixth and took the lead in the top of the eighth. Gruber homered to re-tie it in the bottom of the inning, and after the Jays had filled the bases in the last of the ninth, Candy Maldonado tagged Reardon for a hit over the drawn-in outfield to bring home the winning run.

The Jays pushed their Series advantage to 3–1 in Game Four. Catcher Pat Borders opened the Toronto third with a home run, and Gruber scored from second on Devon White's seventh-inning single to push the Blue Jay lead to 2-0. The Braves got to Toronto starter Jimmy Key for a run in the eighth, but relievers Duane Ward and Tom Henke combined to stop them from scoring again.

In the fifth game the Blue Jays twice came from one run down to even the score. But in the fifth inning, after the Braves had once again built a one-run lead, Lonnie Smith extended it with a grand slam home run that sent the Series back to Atlanta.

Toronto Blue Jays (AL), 4; Atlanta Braves (NL), 2

TOR (A)

PLAYER/POS	AVG	G	AB	R	H	2B	3B	HR	RB	BB	SO	SB
Roberto Alomar, 2b	.208	6	24	3	5	1	0	0	0	3	3	2
Derek Bell, ph	.000	2	1	1	0	0	0	0	0	1	0	0
Pat Borders, c	.450	6	20	2	9	3	0	1	3	2	1	0
Joe Carter, of-4	.273	6	22	2	6	2	0	2	3	3	2	1
David Cone, p	.500	2	4	0	2	0	0	0	1	1	0	0
Mark Eichhorn, p	.000	1	0	0	0	0	0	0	0	0	0	0
Alfredo Griffin, ss	.000	2	0	0	0	0	0	0	0	0	0	0
Kelly Gruber, 3b	.105	6	19	2	2	0	0	1	1	2	5	1
Juan Guzman, p	.000	1	0	0	0	0	0	0	0	0	0	0
Tom Henke, p	.000	3	0	0	0	0	0	0	0	0	0	0
Jimmy Key, p	.000	2	1	0	0	0	0	0	0	0	0	0
Manuel Lee, ss	.105	6	19	1	2	0	0	0	0	1	2	0
Candy Maldonado, of-5	.158	6	19	1	3	0	0	1	2	2	5	0
Jack Morris, p	.000	2	2	0	0	0	0	0	0	0	2	0
John Olerud, 1b	.308	4	13	2	4	0	0	0	0	0	4	0
Ed Sprague, 1b-1	.500	3	2	1	1	0	0	1	2	1	0	0
Todd Stottlemyre, p	.000	4	0	0	0	0	0	0	0	0	0	0
Pat Tabler, ph	.000	2	2	0	0	0	0	0	0	0	0	0
Mike Timlin, p	.000	2	0	0	0	0	0	0	0	0	0	0
Duane Ward, p	.000	4	0	0	0	0	0	0	0	0	0	0
David Wells, p	.000	4	0	0	0	0	0	0	0	0	0	0
Devon White, of	.231	6	26	2	6	1	0	0	2	0	6	1
Dave Winfield, of-3,dh-3	.227	6	22	0	5	1	0	0	3	2	3	0
TOTAL	.230		196	17	45	8	0	6	17	18	33	5

PITCHER	W	L	ERA	G	GS	CG	SV	SHO	IP	H	ER	BB	SO
David Cone	0	0	3.48	2	2	0	0	0	10.1	9	4	8	8
Mark Eichhorn	0	0	0.00	1	0	0	0	0	1.0	0	0	0	1
Juan Guzman	0	0	1.13	1	1	0	0	0	8.0	8	1	1	7
Tom Henke	0	0	2.70	3	0	0	2	0	3.1	2	1	2	1
Jimmy Key	2	0	1.00	2	1	0	0	0	9.0	6	1	0	6
Jack Morris	0	2	8.71	2	2	0	0	0	10.1	13	10	6	12
Todd Stottlemyre	0	0	0.00	4	0	0	0	0	3.2	4	0	0	4
Mike Timlin	0	0	0.00	2	0	0	1	0	1.1	1	0	0	0
Duane Ward	2	0	0.00	4	0	0	0	0	3.1	1	0	1	6
David Wells	0	0	0.00	4	0	0	0	0	4.1	4	0	2	3
TOTAL	4	2	2.80	25	6	0	3	0	54.2	44	17	20	48

ATL (N)

PLAYER/POS	AVG	G	AB	R	H	2B	3B	HR	RB	BB	SO	SB
Steve Avery, p	.000	2	1	0	0	0	0	0	0	0	1	0
Rafael Belliard, ss-3,2b-1	.000	4	0	0	0	0	0	0	0	0	0	0
Damon Berryhill, c	.091	6	22	1	2	0	0	1	3	1	11	0
Jeff Blauser, ss	.250	6	24	2	6	0	0	0	0	1	9	2
Sid Bream, 1b	.200	5	15	1	3	0	0	0	4	0	0	0
Francisco Cabrera, ph	.000	1	1	0	0	0	0	0	0	0	0	0
Ron Gant, of-3	.125	4	8	2	1	1	0	0	0	1	2	2
Tom Glavine, p	.000	2	2	0	0	0	0	0	0	1	0	0
Brian Hunter, 1b-3	.200	4	5	0	1	0	0	0	2	0	1	0
David Justice, of	.158	6	19	4	3	0	0	1	3	6	5	1
Charlie Leibrandt, p	.000	1	0	0	0	0	0	0	0	0	0	0
Mark Lemke, 2b	.211	6	19	0	4	0	0	0	2	1	3	0
Otis Nixon, of	.296	6	27	3	8	1	0	0	1	1	3	5
Terry Pendleton, 3b	.240	6	25	2	6	2	0	0	2	1	5	0
Jeff Reardon, p	.000	2	0	0	0	0	0	0	0	0	0	0
Deion Sanders, of	.533	4	15	4	8	2	0	0	1	2	1	5
Lonnie Smith, dh-3	.167	5	12	1	2	0	0	1	5	1	4	0
Pete Smith, p	.000	1	1	0	0	0	0	0	0	0	1	0
John Smoltz, p-2	.000	3	3	0	0	0	0	0	0	0	2	0
Mike Stanton, p	.000	4	0	0	0	0	0	0	0	0	0	0
Jeff Treadway, ph	.000	1	1	0	0	0	0	0	0	0	0	0
Mark Wohlers, p	.000	2	0	0	0	0	0	0	0	0	0	0
TOTAL	.220		200	20	44	6	0	3	19	20	48	15

PITCHER	W	L	ERA	G	GS	CG	SV	SHO	IP	H	ER	BB	SO
Steve Avery	0	1	3.75	2	2	0	0	0	12.0	11	5	3	11
Tom Glavine	1	1	1.59	2	2	2	0	0	17.0	10	3	4	8
Charlie Leibrandt	0	1	9.00	1	0	0	0	0	2.0	3	2	0	0
Jeff Reardon	0	1	13.50	2	0	0	0	0	1.1	2	2	1	1
Pete Smith	0	0	0.00	1	0	0	0	0	3.0	3	0	0	0
John Smoltz	1	0	2.70	2	2	0	0	0	13.1	13	4	7	12
Mike Stanton	0	0	0.00	4	0	0	1	0	5.0	3	0	2	1
Mark Wohlers	0	0	0.00	2	0	0	0	0	0.2	0	0	0	0
TOTAL	2	4	2.65	16	6	2	1	0	54.1	45	16	18	33

Toronto scored a run in the first inning of Game Six. Atlanta tied the game in the third, but Candy Maldonado's leadoff homer in the fourth restored the advantage to Toronto. In the bottom of the ninth, the Braves scrabbled back to tie it up again. The score remained knotted at 2–2 until the top of the eleventh, when Toronto's Dave Winfield delivered runners from second and first with a two-out double into the left field corner. As it turned out, the Jays needed both runs, for Atlanta scored in the bottom of the eleventh. But with two out and the potential tying run on third, Otis Nixon, attempting a bunt single, just failed to reach safely, and the Series was over.

GAME 1 AT ATL OCT 17

TOR	000	100	000	1	4 0
ATL	000	003	00X	3	4 0

Pitchers: MORRIS, Stottlemyre (7), Wells (8) vs GLAVINE
Home Runs: Carter-TOR, Berryhill-ATL
Attendance: 51,763

GAME 2 AT ATL OCT 18

TOR	000	020	012	5	9 2
ATL	010	120	000	4	5 1

Pitchers: Cone, Wells (5), Stottlemyre (7), WARD (8), Henke (9) vs Smoltz, Stanton (8), REARDON (8)
Home Runs: Sprague-TOR
Attendance: 51,763

GAME 3 AT TOR OCT 20

ATL	000	001	010	2	9 0
TOR	000	100	011	3	6 1

Pitchers: AVERY, Wohlers (9), Stanton (9), Reardon (9) vs Guzman, WARD (9)
Home Runs: Carter-TOR, Gruber-TOR
Attendance: 51,813

GAME 4 AT TOR OCT 21

ATL	000	000	010	1	5 0
TOR	001	000	10X	2	6 0

Pitchers: GLAVINE vs KEY, Ward (8), Henke (9)
Home Runs: Borders-TOR
Attendance: 52,090

GAME 5 AT TOR OCT 22

ATL	100	150	000	7	13 0
TOR	010	100	000	2	6 0

Pitchers: SMOLTZ, Stanton (7) vs MORRIS, Wells (5), Timlin (7), Eichhorn (8), Stottlemyre (9)
Home Runs: Justice-ATL, L.Smith-ATL
Attendance: 52,268

GAME 6 AT ATL OCT 24

TOR	100	100	000 02	4	14 1
ATL	001	000	000 01	3	8 1

Pitchers: Cone, Stottlemyre (7), Wells (7), Ward (8), Henke (9), KEY (10), Timlin (11) vs Avery, P.Smith (5), Stanton (8), Wohlers (9), LEIBRANDT (10)
Home Runs: Maldonado-TOR
Attendance: 51,763

Atlanta outhit the Phillies by 47 percentage points, outscored them by ten runs, and yielded 1.6 fewer earned runs per game. But the Phillies won the pennant. In the opener, Philadelphia starter Curt Schilling fanned ten batters—including the first five he faced—and left the game after eight innings with a 3–2 lead. An errant throw by Phillie third baseman Kim Batiste (who had just entered the game to strengthen the defense) set up an unearned tying run in the ninth inning. But in the last of the tenth, after John Kruk had doubled, Batiste redeemed himself with a game-winning hit down the left field line, and was carried off the field on his teammates' shoulders.

While the Philadelphia offense remained steady over the next two games, the Braves erupted for 28 runs, quadrupling the Phillies' seven. By the time Philadelphia scored its first runs in the fourth inning of Game Two, Atlanta had already sent eight men across the plate. In Game Three the Phillies scored first, and held a 2–0 lead before the Braves destroyed them with five runs in the sixth inning and four more in the seventh.

Game Four featured only four fewer hits than Game Three, but ten fewer runs, as Philadelphia evened the series with its second close win. Phillie starter Danny Jackson yielded nine hits and a pair of walks in 7⅔ innings, but only one second-inning run. In the top of the fourth, Darren Daulton, who had reached on an infield error, took third on Milt Thompson's double and scored on Kevin Stocker's two-out single. Pitcher Jackson then singled home Thompson with what proved the winning run.

In the fifth game, Curt Schilling held Atlanta to four hits through eight innings, and carried a 3–0 lead into the bottom of the ninth. But when a walk and infield error put the first two men on, Mitch Williams relieved Schilling and gave up a trio of singles which tied the game. In the top of the tenth inning, though, Lenny Dykstra's solo homer restored the Phillies' lead, and veteran reliever Larry Andersen blanked the Braves in the bottom of the tenth—striking out the final two batters—to preserve the win.

After their two narrow wins on the road, the Phillies clinched the pennant with relative ease when the series returned to Philadelphia for Game Six. Darren Daulton's two-out double in the third inning put the Phillies up 2–0. Atlanta scored once in the fifth, but Dave Hollins' two-run homer in the last of the fifth increased the Phillies' lead to three runs, and Mickey Morandini's two-out two-run triple

an inning later pushed the score to 6–1, driving out Atlanta starter Greg Maddux. Atlanta's Jeff Blauser brought the score to 6–3 with a home run in the seventh inning, but Phillie relievers David West and Mitch Williams set the Braves down in order in the final two innings.

GAME 1 AT PHI OCT 6

ATL 001 100 001 0   3 9 0
PHI 100 101 000 1   4 9 1
Pitchers: Avery, Mercker (7), McMICHAEL (9) vs Schilling, WILLIAMS (9)
Home Runs: Incaviglia-PHI
Attendance: 62,012

GAME 2 AT PHI OCT 7

ATL 206 010 041   14 16 0
PHI 000 000 001   3 7 2
Pitchers: MADDUX, Stanton (8), Wohlers (9) vs GREENE, Thigpen (3), Rivera (4), Mason (6), West (8), Andersen (9)
Home Runs: Blauser-ATL, McGriff-ATL, Pendleton-ATL, Berryhill-ATL, Dykstra-PHI, Hollins-PHI
Attendance: 62,436

GAME 3 AT ATL OCT 9

PHI 000 101 011   4 10 1
ATL 000 005 40X   9 12 0
Pitchers: MULHOLLAND, Mason (6), Andersen (7), West (7), Thigpen (8) vs GLAVINE, Mercker (8), McMichael (9)
Home Runs: Kruk-PHI
Attendance: 52,032

GAME 4 AT ATL OCT 10

PHI 000 200 000   2 8 1
ATL 010 000 000   1 10 1
Pitchers: JACKSON, Williams (8) vs SMOLTZ, Mercker (7), Wohlers (8)
Attendance: 52,032

GAME 5 AT ATL OCT 11

PHI 100 100 001 1   4 6 1
ATL 000 000 003 0   3 7 1
Pitchers: Schilling, WILLIAMS (9), Andersen (10) vs Avery, Mercker (8), McMicahel (9), WOHLERS (10)
Home Runs: Dykstra-PHI, Daulton-PHI
Attendance: 52,032

GAME 6 AT PHI OCT 13

ATL 000 010 200   3 5 3
PHI 002 022 00X   6 7 1
Pitchers: MADDUX, Mercker (6), McMichael (7), Wohlers (7) vs GREENE, West (8), Williams (9)
Home Runs: Blauser-ATL, Hollins-PHI
Attendance: 62,502

Philadelphia Phillies (East), 4; Atlanta Braves (West), 2

PHI (E)

PLAYER/POS	AVG	G	AB	R	H	2B	3B	HR	RB	BB	SO	SB
Larry Andersen, p	.000	3	0	0	0	0	0	0	0	0	0	0
Kim Batiste, 3b	1.000	4	1	0	1	0	0	0	1	0	0	0
Wes Chamberlain, of-2	.364	4	11	1	4	3	0	0	1	1	3	0
Darren Daulton, c	.263	6	19	2	5	1	0	1	3	6	3	0
Mariano Duncan, 2b	.267	3	15	3	4	0	2	0	0	0	5	0
Lenny Dykstra, of	.280	6	25	5	7	1	0	2	2	5	8	0
Jim Eisenreich, of-5	.133	6	15	0	2	1	0	0	1	0	2	0
Tommy Greene, p	.000	2	0	1	0	0	0	0	0	1	0	0
Dave Hollins, 3b	.200	6	20	4	4	1	0	2	4	5	4	1
Pete Incaviglia, of	.167	3	12	2	2	0	0	1	1	0	3	0
Danny Jackson, p	.250	1	4	0	1	0	0	0	1	0	3	0
John Kruk, 1b	.250	6	24	4	6	2	1	1	5	4	5	0
Tony Longmire, ph	.000	2	1	0	0	0	0	0	0	0	1	0
Roger Mason, p	.000	2	0	0	0	0	0	0	0	0	0	0
Mickey Morandini, 2b	.250	4	16	1	4	1	1	0	2	0	3	1
Terry Mulholland, p	.000	1	2	0	0	0	0	0	0	0	1	0
Todd Pratt, c	.000	1	1	0	0	0	0	0	0	0	0	0
Ben Rivera, p	.000	1	0	0	0	0	0	0	0	0	0	0
Curt Schilling, p	.000	2	5	0	0	0	0	0	0	0	2	0
Kevin Stocker, ss	.182	6	22	0	4	1	0	0	1	2	5	0
Bobby Thigpen, p	.000	2	0	0	0	0	0	0	0	0	0	0
Milt Thompson, of-5	.231	6	13	2	3	1	0	0	0	1	2	0
David West, p	.000	3	0	0	0	0	0	0	0	0	0	0
Mitch Williams, p	.000	4	0	0	0	0	0	0	0	0	0	0
TOTAL	.227		207	23	47	11	4	7	22	26	51	2

PITCHER	W	L	ERA	G	GS	CG	SV	SHO	IP	H	ER	BB	SO
Larry Andersen	0	0	15.43	3	0	0	1	0	2.1	4	4	1	3
Tommy Greene	1	1	9.64	2	2	0	0	0	9.1	12	10	7	7
Danny Jackson	1	0	1.17	1	1	0	0	0	7.2	9	1	2	6
Roger Mason	0	0	0.00	2	0	0	0	0	3.0	1	0	0	2
Terry Mulholland	0	1	7.20	1	1	0	0	0	5.0	9	4	1	2
Ben Rivera	0	0	4.50	1	0	0	0	0	2.0	1	1	1	2
Curt Schilling	0	0	1.69	2	2	0	0	0	16.0	11	3	5	19
Bobby Thigpen	0	0	5.40	2	0	0	0	0	1.2	1	1	1	3
David West	0	0	13.50	3	0	0	0	0	2.2	5	4	2	5
Mitch Williams	2	0	1.69	4	0	0	2	0	5.1	6	1	2	5
TOTAL	4	2	4.75	21	6	0	3	0	55.0	59	29	22	54

ATL (W)

PLAYER/POS	AVG	G	AB	R	H	2B	3B	HR	RB	BB	SO	SB
Steve Avery, p	.500	2	4	1	2	1	0	0	0	0	1	0
Rafael Belliard, 2b-1,ss-1	.000	2	1	1	0	0	0	0	0	0	1	0
Damon Berryhill, c	.211	6	19	2	4	0	0	1	3	1	5	0
Jeff Blauser, ss	.280	6	25	5	7	1	0	2	4	4	7	0
Sid Bream, 1b	1.000	1	1	1	1	0	0	0	0	0	0	0
Francisco Cabrera, c-1	.667	3	3	0	2	0	0	0	1	0	1	0
Ron Gant, of	.185	6	27	4	5	3	0	0	3	2	9	0
Tom Glavine, p	.000	1	3	0	0	0	0	0	0	0	0	0
David Justice, of	.143	6	21	2	3	1	0	0	4	3	3	0
Mark Lemke, 2b	.208	6	24	2	5	2	0	0	4	1	6	0
Greg Maddux, p	.250	2	4	1	1	0	0	0	0	0	1	0
Fred McGriff, 1b	.435	6	23	6	10	2	0	1	4	4	7	0
Greg McMichael, p	.000	4	0	0	0	0	0	0	0	0	0	0
Kent Mercker, p	.000	5	0	0	0	0	0	0	0	0	0	0
Otis Nixon, of	.348	6	23	3	8	2	0	0	4	5	6	0
Greg Olson, c	.333	2	3	0	1	1	0	0	0	0	1	0
Bill Pecota, ph	.333	4	3	1	1	0	0	0	0	1	1	0
Terry Pendleton, 3b	.346	6	26	4	9	1	0	1	5	0	2	0
Deion Sanders, of-1	.000	3	0	0	0	0	0	0	0	0	0	0
John Smoltz, p	.000	1	1	0	0	0	0	0	0	0	1	0
Mike Stanton, p	.000	1	0	0	0	0	0	0	0	0	0	0
Tony Tarasco, of	.000	2	1	0	0	0	0	0	0	0	1	0
Mark Wohlers, p	.000	4	0	0	0	0	0	0	0	0	0	0
TOTAL	.274		215	33	59	14	0	5	32	22	54	0

PITCHER	W	L	ERA	G	GS	CG	SV	SHO	IP	H	ER	BB	SO
Steve Avery	0	0	2.77	2	2	0	0	0	13.0	9	4	6	10
Tom Glavine	1	0	2.57	1	1	0	0	0	7.0	6	2	0	5
Greg Maddux	1	1	4.97	2	2	0	0	0	12.2	11	7	7	11
Greg McMichael	0	1	6.75	4	0	0	0	0	4.0	7	3	2	1
Kent Mercker	0	0	1.80	5	0	0	0	0	5.0	3	1	2	4
John Smoltz	0	1	0.00	1	1	0	0	0	6.1	8	0	5	10
Mike Stanton	0	0	0.00	1	0	0	0	0	1.0	1	0	1	0
Mark Wohlers	0	1	3.38	4	0	0	0	0	5.1	2	2	3	10
TOTAL	2	4	3.15	20	6	0	0	0	54.1	47	19	26	51

The visiting team won the first four games of the series, but in Game Five, home team Toronto held off a ninth-inning White Sox rally to take a 3–2 series lead. Then, in Chicago two days later, the Jays put the Sox away with the series' fifth road victory in its six games.

In Chicago for the series opener, Toronto scored first when Ed Sprague tripled home a pair of runs in the fourth inning. The White Sox bounced ahead with three runs in the last of the fourth, but the Blue Jays regained the lead a half inning later on John Olerud's two-run double, then pulled away to a 17-hit 7–3 win. Toronto also scored first in Game Two, with an unearned run in the first inning. But in the last of the inning, Blue Jay pitcher Dave Stewart walked the bases full, then handed Chicago a tying run with a wild pitch. With two out in the fourth inning, though, back-to-back doubles by Paul Molitor and Tony Fernandez restored the lead to Toronto, and a walk, an infield hit and an error increased the Jays' lead to 3–1. This ended the scoring, although the White Sox loaded the bases in the sixth before Stewart retired the next three batters to stifle the threat.

The White Sox leaped to life when the series moved to Toronto for Game Three. After the first two men had been retired in the third inning, Sox batters combined five singles with a pair of walks for a 5–0 lead, which Chicago starter Wilson Alvarez held for a 6–1 complete game victory. Lance Johnson's two-run homer in the second inning of Game Four put Chicago ahead. The Jays overtook them with three runs an inning later, but in the sixth inning Frank Thomas homered to even the score at 3–3, and after two batters had been walked aboard, Johnson's two-out triple put the Sox ahead to stay.

In Game Five, the Blue Jays finally broke the visiting team's lock on victory, scoring single runs in each of the first four innings, and another in the seventh, while starter Juan Guzman held Chicago to three hits and a single run in his seven innings. Robin Ventura's two-run homer off Jays' reliever Duane Ward in the Chicago ninth narrowed Toronto's lead to 5–3, but Ward then retired Bo Jackson with his third swinging K of the inning to send the Jays back to Chicago with a 3–2 series advantage.

Errors ended the White Sox season in Game Six. With the score tied 2–2 in the fourth inning, a bobble by Chicago third baseman Robin Ventura put Paul Molitor on base. Molitor subsequently scored the go-ahead run when second baseman Joey Cora threw a ball

low to first into the dugout. Devon White homered in the ninth inning to stretch Toronto's lead to 4–2, and an error by Sox reliever Scott Radinsky on what should have been the third out set the stage for Molitor to triple home a pair of baserunners with the Jays' final runs. Warren Newson's leadoff homer against Toronto reliever Duane Ward in the bottom of the ninth narrowed the score to 6–3, but the White Sox came no closer. The win, starter Dave Stewart's second of the series, was his eighth triumph without a loss in LCS play.

Toronto Blue Jays (East), 4; Chicago White Sox (West), 2

TOR (E)

PLAYER/POS	AVG	G	AB	R	H	2B	3B	HR	RB	BB	SO	SB
Roberto Alomar, 2b	.292	6	24	3	7	1	0	0	4	4	3	4
Pat Borders, c	.250	6	24	1	6	1	0	0	3	0	6	1
Joe Carter, of	.259	6	27	2	7	0	0	0	2	1	5	0
Tony Castillo, p	.000	2	0	0	0	0	0	0	0	0	0	0
Danny Cox, p	.000	2	0	0	0	0	0	0	0	0	0	0
Mark Eichhorn, p	.000	1	0	0	0	0	0	0	0	0	0	0
Tony Fernandez, ss	.318	6	22	1	7	0	0	0	1	2	4	0
Juan Guzman, p	.000	2	0	0	0	0	0	0	0	0	0	0
Rickey Henderson, of	.120	6	25	4	3	2	0	0	0	4	5	2
Pat Hentgen, p	.000	1	0	0	0	0	0	0	0	0	0	0
Al Leiter, p	.000	2	0	0	0	0	0	0	0	0	0	0
Paul Molitor, dh	.391	6	23	7	9	2	1	1	5	3	3	0
John Olerud, 1b	.348	6	23	5	8	1	0	0	3	4	1	0
Ed Sprague, 3b	.286	6	21	0	6	0	1	0	4	2	4	0
Dave Stewart, p	.000	2	0	0	0	0	0	0	0	0	0	0
Todd Stottlemyre, p	.000	1	0	0	0	0	0	0	0	0	0	0
Mike Timlin, p	.000	1	0	0	0	0	0	0	0	0	0	0
Duane Ward, p	.000	4	0	0	0	0	0	0	0	0	0	0
Devon White, of	.444	6	27	3	12	1	1	1	2	1	5	0
TOTAL	.301		216	26	65	8	3	2	24	21	36	7

PITCHER	W	L	ERA	G	GS	CG	SV	SHO	IP	H	ER	BB	SO
Tony Castillo	0	0	0.00	2	0	0	0	0	2.0	0	0	1	1
Danny Cox	0	0	0.00	2	0	0	0	0	5.0	3	0	2	5
Mark Eichhorn	0	0	0.00	1	0	0	0	0	2.0	1	0	1	1
Juan Guzman	2	0	2.08	2	2	0	0	0	13.0	8	3	9	9
Pat Hentgen	0	1	18.00	1	1	0	0	0	3.0	9	6	2	3
Al Leiter	0	0	3.38	2	0	0	0	0	2.2	4	1	2	2
Dave Stewart	2	0	2.03	2	2	0	0	0	13.1	8	3	8	8
Todd Stottlemyre	0	1	7.50	1	1	0	0	0	6.0	6	5	4	4
Mike Timlin	0	0	3.86	1	0	0	0	0	2.1	3	1	0	2
Duane Ward	0	0	5.79	4	0	0	2	0	4.2	4	3	3	8
TOTAL	4	2	3.67	18	6	0	2	0	54.0	46	22	32	43

CHI (W)

PLAYER/POS	AVG	G	AB	R	H	2B	3B	HR	RB	BB	SO	SB
Wilson Alvarez, p	.000	1	0	0	0	0	0	0	0	0	0	0
Tim Belcher, p	.000	1	0	0	0	0	0	0	0	0	0	0
Jason Bere, p	.000	1	0	0	0	0	0	0	0	0	0	0
Ellis Burks, of	.304	6	23	4	7	1	0	1	3	3	5	0
Joey Cora, 2b	.136	6	22	1	3	0	0	0	1	3	6	0
Jose DeLeon, p	.000	2	0	0	0	0	0	0	0	0	0	0
Alex Fernandez, p	.000	2	0	0	0	0	0	0	0	0	0	0
Craig Grebeck, 3b	1.000	1	1	0	1	0	0	0	0	0	0	0
Ozzie Guillen, ss	.273	6	22	4	6	1	0	0	2	0	2	1
Roberto Hernandez, p	.000	4	0	0	0	0	0	0	0	0	0	0
Bo Jackson, dh	.000	3	10	0	0	0	0	0	0	3	6	0
Lance Johnson, of	.217	6	23	2	5	1	1	1	6	2	1	1
Ron Karkovice, c	.000	6	15	0	0	0	0	0	0	1	7	0
Mike LaValliere, c	.333	2	3	0	1	0	0	0	0	1	0	0
Kirk McCaskill, p	.000	3	0	0	0	0	0	0	0	0	0	0
Jack McDowell, p	.000	2	0	0	0	0	0	0	0	0	0	0
Warren Newson, dh-1	.200	2	5	1	1	0	0	1	1	0	1	0
Dan Pasqua, 1b	.000	2	6	0	0	0	0	0	0	1	2	0
Scott Radinsky, p	.000	4	0	0	0	0	0	0	0	0	0	0
Tim Raines, of	.444	6	27	5	12	3	0	0	1	2	2	1
Frank Thomas, 1b-4,dh-2	.353	6	17	2	6	0	0	1	3	10	5	0
Robin Ventura, 3b-6,1b-1	.200	6	20	2	4	0	0	1	5	6	6	0
TOTAL	.237		194	23	46	6	1	5	22	32	43	3

PITCHER	W	L	ERA	G	GS	CG	SV	SHO	IP	H	ER	BB	SO
Wilson Alvarez	1	0	1.00	1	1	0	0	0	9.0	7	1	2	6
Tim Belcher	0	0	2.45	1	0	0	0	0	3.2	3	1	3	1
Jason Bere	0	0	11.57	1	1	0	0	0	2.1	5	3	2	3
Jose DeLeon	0	0	1.93	2	0	0	0	0	4.2	7	1	6	6
Alex Fernandez	0	2	1.80	2	2	0	0	0	15.0	15	3	6	10
Roberto Hernandez	0	0	0.00	4	0	0	1	0	4.0	4	0	0	1
Kirk McCaskill	0	0	0.00	3	0	0	0	0	3.2	3	0	1	3
Jack McDowell	0	2	10.00	2	2	0	0	0	9.0	18	10	5	5
Scott Radinsky	0	0	10.80	4	0	0	0	0	1.2	3	2	1	1
TOTAL	1	4	3.57	20	6	0	1	0	53.0	65	21	21	36

GAME 1 AT CHI OCT 5

TOR	000 230 200	7	17	1
CHI	000 300 000	3	6	1

Pitchers: GUZMAN, Cox (7), Ward (9) vs McDOWELL, DeLeon (7), Radinsky (8), McCaskill (9)
Home Runs: Molitor-TOR
Attendance: 46,246

GAME 2 AT CHI OCT 6

TOR	100 200 000	3	8	0
CHI	100 000 000	1	7	2

Pitchers: STEWART, Leiter (7), Ward (9) vs FERNANDEZ, Hernandez (9)
Attendance: 46,101

GAME 3 AT TOR OCT 8

CHI	005 100 000	6	12	0
TOR	001 000 000	1	7	1

Pitchers: ALVAREZ vs HENTGEN, Cox (4), Eichhorn (7), Castillo (9)
Attendance: 51,783

GAME 4 AT TOR OCT 9

CHI	020 003 101	7	11	0
TOR	003 001 000	4	9	0

Pitchers: Bere, BELCHER (3), McCaskill (7), Radinsky (8), Hernandez (9) vs STOTTLEMYRE, Leiter (7), Timlin (7)
Home Runs: Thomas-CHI, Johnson-CHI
Attendance

GAME 5 AT TOR OCT 10

CHI	000 010 002	3	5	1
TOR	111 100 10X	5	14	0

Pitchers: McDOWELL, DeLeon (3), Radinsky (7), Hernandez (7) vs GUZMAN, Castillo (8), Ward (9)
Home Runs: Ventura-CHI, Burks-CHI
Attendance: 51,375

GAME 6 AT CHI OCT 12

TOR	020 100 003	6	10	0
CHI	002 000 001	3	5	3

Pitchers: STEWART, Ward (8) vs FERNANDEZ, McCaskill (8), Radinsky (9), Hernandez (9)
Home Runs: White-TOR, Newson-CHI
Attendance: 45,527

The Phillies and Blue Jays split the first two games, played in Toronto. But the defending champions captured the lead when play moved to Philadelphia for Game Three. In a contest delayed more than an hour by rain, Paul Molitor tripled home two Blue Jay runs before the first out had been recorded, and the Jays pushed on from there to an easy 10–3 win.

By just about any measure except pitching effectiveness, Game Four—played in a steady drizzle that for a time increased to a downpour—was one of the great ones. At 4 hours 14 minutes, it was the longest in World Series history, and its 29 total runs scored established a new record for major league postseason championship play, as did Philadelphia's 14 runs for a losing team. Toronto scored three times after two men had been retired in the top of the first inning, but Philadelphia retaliated immediately with four two-out runs in the bottom of the inning, as Jays' starter Todd Stottlemyre walked four batters, and Milt Thompson tripled over the center fielder's head. Lenny Dykstra's two-run homer an inning later pushed the Phillies' lead to 6–3, but Toronto scrambled back to regain a 7–6 advantage in the third inning on two walks and four singles. Philadelphia scored a tying run in the fourth inning, then scored five times an inning later with a barrage of hits highlighted by Darren Daulton's two-run homer and Dykstra's second two-run blast of the game. Toronto scored twice in the sixth inning, but single Phillie runs in the sixth and seventh restored their five-run lead. Then, in the top of the eighth, the Blue Jays parlayed two walks, two singles and a two-base error (later changed by the official scorer to a double) into a pair of runs and a diamond full of baserunners. Phillie reliever Mitch Williams fanned Ed Sprague for the second out of the inning, but Rickey Henderson lined a two-run single to center to bring the Jays within one run of a tie, and Devon White looped a triple to right center for the tying and go-ahead runs. Relievers Mike Timlin and Duane Ward retired the final six Phillie batters on five strikeouts and a pair of pop flies.

The Phillies salvaged their final home game, scoring single runs in the first two innings as Curt Schilling shut out the Blue Jays and forced the Series back to Toronto for a sixth game. Paul Molitor's RBI triple gave the Jays a first-inning lead, and his solo homer in the fifth stretched it to 5–1. Lenny Dykstra's three-run shot in the seventh (his fourth home run of the Series) brought Philadelphia to within a run of Toronto, however,

and Mariano Duncan scored the tying run on Dave Hollins' single. Pinch hitter Pete Incaviglia's sacrifice fly gave the Phillies their first lead of the game, 6–5. In the bottom of the ninth, Phillie reliever Mitch Williams walked Rickey Henderson and, with one away, gave up a single to Molitor (which raised his Series batting average to .500). Molitor scored the Series-winning run when Joe Carter, the next man up, lined Williams' would-be third strike over the left field fence for an 8–6 victory.

Toronto Blue Jays, 4; Philadelphia Phillies, 2

TOR (A)

PLAYER/POS	AVG	G	AB	R	H	2B	3B	HR	RB	BB	SO	SB
Roberto Alomar, 2b	.480	6	25	5	12	2	1	0	6	2	3	4
Pat Borders, c	.304	6	23	2	7	0	0	0	1	2	1	0
Rob Butler, ph	.500	2	2	1	1	0	0	0	0	0	0	0
Willie Canate, pr	.000	1	0	0	0	0	0	0	0	0	0	0
Joe Carter, of	.280	6	25	6	7	1	0	2	8	0	4	0
Tony Castillo, p	.000	2	1	0	0	0	0	0	0	0	1	0
Danny Cox, p	.000	3	1	0	0	0	0	0	0	0	0	0
Mark Eichhorn, p	.000	1	0	0	0	0	0	0	0	0	0	0
Tony Fernandez, ss	.333	6	21	2	7	1	0	0	9	3	3	0
Alfredo Griffin, 3b-2	.000	3	0	0	0	0	0	0	0	0	0	0
Juan Guzman, p	.000	2	2	0	0	0	0	0	0	0	1	0
Rickey Henderson, of	.227	6	22	6	5	2	0	0	2	5	2	1
Pat Hentgen, p	.000	1	3	0	0	0	0	0	0	0	1	0
Randy Knorr, c	.000	1	0	0	0	0	0	0	0	0	0	0
Al Leiter, p	1.000	3	1	0	1	1	0	0	0	0	0	0
Paul Molitor, dh-3	.500	6	24	10	12	2	2	2	8	3	0	1
John Olerud, 1b	.235	5	17	5	4	1	0	1	2	4	1	0
Ed Sprague, 3b-4,1b-1	.067	5	15	0	1	0	0	0	2	1	6	0
Dave Stewart, p	.000	2	0	0	0	0	0	0	0	0	0	0
Todd Stottlemyre, p	.000	1	0	0	0	0	0	0	0	0	1	0
Mike Timlin, p	.000	2	0	0	0	0	0	0	0	0	0	0
Duane Ward, p	.000	4	0	0	0	0	0	0	0	0	0	0
Devon White, of	.292	6	24	8	7	3	2	1	7	4	7	1
TOTAL	.311		206	45	64	13	5	6	45	25	30	7

PITCHER	W	L	ERA	G	GS	CG	SV	SHO	IP	H	ER	BB	SO
Tony Castillo	1	0	8.10	2	0	0	0	0	3.1	6	3	3	1
Danny Cox	0	0	8.10	3	0	0	0	0	3.1	6	3	5	6
Mark Eichhorn	0	0	0.00	1	0	0	0	0	0.1	1	0	1	0
Juan Guzman	0	1	3.75	2	2	0	0	0	12.0	10	5	8	12
Pat Hentgen	1	0	1.50	1	1	0	0	0	6.0	5	1	3	6
Al Leiter	1	0	7.71	3	0	0	0	0	7.0	12	6	2	5
Dave Stewart	0	1	6.75	2	2	0	0	0	12.0	10	9	8	8
Todd Stottlemyre	0	0	27.00	1	1	0	0	0	2.0	3	6	4	1
Mike Timlin	0	0	0.00	2	0	0	0	0	2.1	2	0	0	4
Duane Ward	1	0	1.93	4	0	0	2	0	4.2	3	1	0	7
TOTAL	4	2	5.77	21	6	0	2	0	53.0	58	34	34	50

PHI (N)

PLAYER/POS	AVG	G	AB	R	H	2B	3B	HR	RB	BB	SO	SB
Larry Andersen, p	.000	4	0	0	0	0	0	0	0	0	0	0
Kim Batiste, 3b	.000	2	0	0	0	0	0	0	0	0	0	0
Wes Chamberlain, ph	.000	2	2	0	0	0	0	0	0	0	1	0
Darren Daulton, c	.217	6	23	4	5	2	0	1	4	4	5	0
Mariano Duncan, 2b-5,dh-1	.345	6	29	5	10	0	0	1	0	2	1	7	3
Lenny Dykstra, of	.348	6	23	9	8	1	0	4	8	7	4	4
Jim Eisenreich, of	.231	6	26	3	6	0	0	1	7	2	4	0
Tommy Greene, p	1.000	1	1	1	1	0	0	0	0	0	0	0
Dave Hollins, 3b	.261	6	23	5	6	1	0	0	2	6	5	0
Pete Incaviglia, of	.125	4	8	0	1	0	0	0	1	0	4	0
Danny Jackson, p	.000	1	1	0	0	0	0	0	0	0	1	0
Ricky Jordan, dh-2	.200	3	10	0	2	0	0	0	0	0	2	0
John Kruk, 1b	.348	6	23	4	8	1	0	0	4	7	7	0
Roger Mason, p	.000	4	1	0	0	0	0	0	0	0	0	0
Mickey Morandini, 2b-1	.200	3	5	1	1	0	0	0	0	1	2	0
Terry Mulholland, p	.000	2	0	0	0	0	0	0	0	0	0	0
Ben Rivera, p	.000	1	0	0	0	0	0	0	0	0	0	0
Curt Schilling, p	.500	2	2	0	1	0	0	0	0	0	1	0
Kevin Stocker, ss	.211	6	19	1	4	1	0	0	1	5	5	0
Bobby Thigpen, p	.000	2	0	0	0	0	0	0	0	0	0	0
Milt Thompson, of	.313	5	16	3	5	1	1	1	6	1	2	0
David West, p	.000	3	0	0	0	0	0	0	0	0	0	0
Mitch Williams, p	.000	3	0	0	0	0	0	0	0	0	0	0
TOTAL	.274		212	36	58	7	2	7	35	34	50	7

PITCHER	W	L	ERA	G	GS	CG	SV	SHO	IP	H	ER	BB	SO
Larry Andersen	0	0	12.27	4	0	0	0	0	3.2	5	5	3	3
Tommy Greene	0	0	27.00	1	1	0	0	0	2.1	7	7	4	1
Danny Jackson	0	1	7.20	1	1	0	0	0	5.0	6	4	1	1
Roger Mason	0	0	1.17	4	0	0	0	0	7.2	4	1	1	7
Terry Mulholland	1	0	6.75	2	2	0	0	0	10.2	14	8	3	5
Ben Rivera	0	0	27.00	1	0	0	0	0	1.1	4	4	2	3
Curt Schilling	1	1	3.52	2	2	0	0	0	15.1	13	6	5	9
Bobby Thigpen	0	0	0.00	2	0	0	0	0	2.2	1	0	1	0
David West	0	0	27.00	3	0	0	0	0	1.0	5	3	1	0
Mitch Williams	0	2	20.25	3	0	0	1	0	2.2	5	6	4	1
TOTAL	2	4	7.57	23	6	0	1	0	52.1	64	44	25	30

GAME 1 AT TOR OCT 16

PHI	201	010	001	5	11	1
TOR	021	011	30X	8	10	3

Pitchers: SCHILLING, West (7), Andersen (7), Mason (8) vs Guzman, LEITER (6), Ward (8)
Home Runs: White-TOR, Olerud-TOR
Attendance: 52,011

GAME 2 AT TOR OCT 17

PHI	005	000	100	6	12	0
TOR	000	201	010	4	8	0

Pitchers: MULHOLLAND, Mason (6), Williams (7) vs STEWART, Castillo (7), Eichhorn (8), Timlin (8)
Home Runs: Dykstra-PHI, Eisenreich-PHI, Carter-TOR
Attendance: 52,062

GAME 3 AT PHI OCT 19

TOR	301	001	302	10	13	1
PHI	000	010	101	3	9	0

Pitchers: HENTGEN, Cox (7), Ward (9) vs JACKSON, Rivera (6), Thigpen (7), Andersen (9)
Home Runs: Molitor-TOR, Thompson-PHI
Attendance: 62,689

GAME 4 AT PHI OCT 20

TOR	304	002	060	15	18	0
PHI	420	151	100	14	14	0

Pitchers: Stottlemyre, Leiter (3), CASTILLO (5), Timlin (8), Ward (8) vs Greene, Mason (3), West (6), Andersen (7), WILLIAMS (8), Thigpen (9)
Home Runs: Dykstra-PHI (2), Daulton-PHI
Attendance: 62,731

GAME 5 AT PHI OCT 21

TOR	000	000	000	0	5	1
PHI	110	000	00X	2	5	1

Pitchers: GUZMAN, Cox (8) vs SCHILLING
Attendance: 62,706

GAME 6 AT TOR OCT 23

PHI	000	100	500	6	7	0
TOR	300	110	003	8	10	2

Pitchers: Mulholland, Mason (6), West (8), Andersen (8), WILLIAMS (9) vs Stewart, Cox (7), Leiter (7), WARD (9)
Home Runs: Molitor-TOR, Dykstra-PHI, Carter-TOR
Attendance: 52,195

## CHAPTER 16

The Postseason Registers

As detailed in the preceding section, major league postseason competition goes back to the dawn of professional league play, in 1871. The first such contest to determine the "champions of the world" dates from 1884, and it is from that date that we present the annual and cumulative batting/pitching records of every individual to have appeared in a World Series. (Sabermetric calculations have little value in such small samplings.)

In 1969 the National and American leagues each expanded to twelve teams and realigned into Eastern and Western divisions. This produced a new layer of postseason competition, the League Championship Series (LCS). Through 1984 the LCS was a best-of-five match,

but in the years since, it has been expanded to the best-of-seven format that has marked the World Series since 1922. Annual and cumulative records of every individual to have appeared in an LCS follow in discrete player and pitcher registers.

Also offered in separate player and pitcher registers are the records of the unique postseason competition of 1981, the divisional playoffs.

For more detail about a particular year's postseason competition, see the previous chapter. For an overview of that year's regular-season play, see The Annual Record. And for further details about a particular individual, refer to the Player and Pitcher Registers.

Player	YEAR TM/L	AVG	G	AB	R	H	2B	3B	HR	RBI	BB	SO	SB	POS
Luis Aguayo	1981 Phi-N	—	2	0	1	0	0	0	0	0	0	0	0	R
Willie Aikens	1981 KC-A	.333	3	9	0	3	0	0	0	0	3	2	0	1
Tony Armas	1981 Oak-A	.545	3	11	1	6	2	0	0	3	1	1	0	O
Alan Ashby	1981 Hou-N	.111	3	9	1	1	0	0	1	2	2	0	0	C
Ramon Aviles	1981 Phi-N	—	1	0	0	0	0	0	0	0	1	0	0	H
Dusty Baker	1981 LA-N	.167	5	18	2	3	1	0	0	1	2	0	0	O
Sal Bando	1981 Mil-A	.294	5	17	1	5	3	0	0	1	2	3	0	3
Bob Boone	1981 Phi-N	.000	3	5	0	0	0	0	0	0	0	0	0	C
Rick Bosetti	1981 Oak-A	—	1	0	0	0	0	0	0	0	0	0	0	O
Thad Bosley	1981 Mil-A	—	1	0	0	0	0	0	0	0	0	0	0	D
Larry Bowa	1981 Phi-N	.176	5	17	0	3	1	0	0	1	0	0	0	S
George Brett	1981 KC-A	.167	3	12	0	2	0	0	0	0	0	0	0	3
Bobby Brown	1981 NY-A	—	1	0	0	0	0	0	0	0	0	0	0	R
Gary Carter	1981 Mon-N	.421	5	19	3	8	3	0	2	6	1	1	0	C
Cesar Cedeno	1981 Hou-N	.231	4	13	0	3	1	0	0	2	2	2	1	
Rick Cerone	1981 NY-A	.333	5	18	1	6	2	0	1	5	0	2	0	C
Cecil Cooper	1981 Mil-A	.222	5	18	1	4	0	0	0	3	1	3	0	1
Warren Cromartie	1981 Mon-N	.227	5	22	1	5	2	0	0	1	0	9	0	1
Jose Cruz	1981 Hou-N	.300	5	20	0	6	1	0	0	0	1	3	1	O
Dick Davis	1981 Phi-N	.000	1	2	0	0	0	0	0	0	0	1	0	0
Andre Dawson	1981 Mon-N	.300	5	20	1	6	0	1	0	0	1	6	2	O
Keith Drumright	1981 Oak-A	.250	1	4	0	1	0	0	0	0	0	0	0	D
Marshall Edwards	1981 Mil-A	.000	2	1	0	0	0	0	0	0	0	1	0	O
Barry Foote	1981 NY-A	—	1	0	0	0	0	0	0	0	0	0	0	H
Terry Francona	1981 Mon-N	.333	5	12	0	4	0	0	0	2	2	2	0	O
Oscar Gamble	1981 NY-A	.556	4	9	2	5	1	0	2	3	1	2	0	D
Jim Gantner	1981 Mil-A	.143	4	14	1	2	1	0	0	0	0	2	0	2
Kiko Garcia	1981 Hou-N	.000	2	4	0	0	0	0	0	0	0	1	0	S*1
Phil Garner	1981 Hou-N	.111	5	18	1	2	0	0	0	0	3	3	0	2
Steve Garvey	1981 LA-N	.368	5	19	4	7	0	1	2	4	0	2	0	1
Cesar Geronimo	1981 KC-A	—	1	0	0	0	0	0	0	0	0	0	0	R
Greg Gross	1981 Phi-N	.000	4	4	0	0	0	0	0	0	0	0	0	O*2
Wayne Gross	1981 Oak-A	.400	2	5	1	2	0	0	1	3	0	0	0	3*1
Pedro Guerrero	1981 LA-N	.176	5	17	1	3	1	0	1	1	2	4	1	3
Mike Heath	1981 Oak-A	.000	2	8	0	0	0	0	0	0	0	1	0	C
Rickey Henderson	1981 Oak-A	.182	3	11	3	2	0	0	0	0	2	0	2	O
Art Howe	1981 Hou-N	.235	5	17	1	4	0	0	1	1	2	1	0	3
Roy Howell	1981 Mil-A	.400	4	5	0	2	0	0	0	0	2	2	0	D*3
Clint Hurdle	1981 KC-A	.273	3	11	0	3	0	0	0	0	1	1	0	O
Reggie Jackson	1981 NY-A	.300	5	20	4	6	0	0	2	4	1	5	0	O
Cliff Johnson	1981 Oak-A	.286	2	7	0	2	1	0	0	0	0	1	0	D
Wallace Johnson	1981 Mon-N	.500	2	2	0	1	0	0	0	0	1	0	0	H
Jay Johnstone	1981 LA-N	.000	1	1	0	0	0	0	0	0	0	0	0	H
Mickey Klutts	1981 Oak-A	.143	2	7	0	1	0	0	0	0	0	1	0	3
Ken Landreaux	1981 LA-N	.200	5	20	1	4	1	0	0	1	0	1	0	O
Davey Lopes	1981 LA-N	.200	5	20	1	4	1	0	0	0	3	7	1	2
Garry Maddox	1981 Phi-N	.333	2	3	0	1	1	0	0	0	0	0	0	O
Jerry Manuel	1981 Mon-N	.071	5	14	0	1	0	0	0	0	2	5	0	2
Mike Marshall	1981 LA-N	.000	1	1	0	0	0	0	0	0	0	1	0	H
Gary Matthews	1981 Phi-N	.400	5	20	3	8	0	1	1	1	0	2	0	O
Lee May	1981 KC-A	—	1	0	0	0	0	0	0	0	0	0	0	1
Bake McBride	1981 Phi-N	.200	4	15	1	3	1	0	0	0	0	5	0	O
Dave McKay	1981 Oak-A	.273	3	11	1	3	0	0	0	1	1	1	0	2
Hal McRae	1981 KC-A	.091	3	11	0	1	1	0	0	0	1	1	0	D
Larry Milbourne	1981 NY-A	.316	5	19	4	6	1	0	0	0	0	1	0	S
Brad Mills	1981 Mon-N	—	1	0	0	0	0	0	0	0	1	0	0	H
John Milner	1981 Mon-N	.500	2	2	0	1	0	0	0	0	1	0	0	H
Paul Molitor	1981 Mil-A	.250	5	20	2	5	0	0	1	1	2	5	0	O
Rick Monday	1981 LA-N	.214	5	14	1	3	0	0	0	1	2	4	0	O
Don Money	1981 Mil-A	.000	2	3	0	0	0	0	0	0	0	0	0	2*1,D*1
Charlie Moore	1981 Mil-A	.222	4	9	0	2	0	0	0	1	2	0		O*2,D*2
Kelvin Moore	1981 Oak-A	.000	2	8	0	0	0	0	0	0	0	2	0	1
Keith Moreland	1981 Phi-N	.462	4	13	2	6	0	0	1	3	1	1	0	C
Jerry Mumphrey	1981 NY-A	.095	5	21	2	2	0	0	0	0	0	1	1	O
Bobby Murcer	1981 NY-A	.000	2	1	0	0	0	0	0	0	0	1	0	H
Dwayne Murphy	1981 Oak-A	.545	3	11	4	6	1	0	1	2	1	1	0	O
Graig Nettles	1981 NY-A	.059	5	17	1	1	0	0	0	1	3	1	0	3
Jeff Newman	1981 Oak-A	.000	1	3	0	0	0	0	0	0	0	1	0	C
Ben Oglivie	1981 Mil-A	.167	5	18	0	3	1	0	0	1	0	7	0	O
Amos Otis	1981 KC-A	.000	3	12	0	0	0	0	0	0	1	4	0	O
Larry Parrish	1981 Mon-N	.150	5	20	3	3	1	0	0	1	1	3	0	3
Mike Phillips	1981 Mon-N	.000	1	1	0	0	0	0	0	0	0	0	0	2
Rob Picciolo	1981 Oak-A	.333	1	3	0	1	0	0	0	0	0	0	0	S
Lou Piniella	1981 NY-A	.200	4	10	1	2	1	0	1	3	0	0	0	D

YEAR	TM/L	AVG	G	AB	R	H	2B	3B	HR	RBI	BB	SO	SB	POS
Joe Pittman														
1981	Hou-N	.000	2	2	0	0	0	0	0	0	0	0	0	H
Terry Puhl														
1981	Hou-N	.190	5	21	2	4	1	0	0	0	0	1	1	O
Luis Pujols														
1981	Hou-N	.000	2	6	0	0	0	0	0	0	0	1	0	C
Willie Randolph														
1981	NY-A	.200	5	20	0	4	0	0	0	1	1	4	0	2
Dave Revering														
1981	NY-A	—	2	0	0	0	0	0	0	0	0	0	0	1
Craig Reynolds														
1981	Hou-N	.333	2	3	1	1	0	0	0	0	0	1	0	S*1
Dave Roberts														
1981	Hou-N	.000	1	1	0	0	0	0	0	0	0	1	0	H
Ed Romero														
1981	Mil-A	.500	1	2	1	1	0	0	0	0	0	1	0	2
Pete Rose														
1981	Phi-N	.300	5	20	1	6	1	0	0	2	2	0	0	1
Bill Russell														
1981	LA-N	.250	5	16	1	4	1	0	0	2	3	1	0	S
Steve Sax														
1981	LA-N	—	1	0	0	0	0	0	0	0	0	0	0	2
Mike Schmidt														
1981	Phi-N	.250	5	16	3	4	1	0	1	2	4	2	0	3
Mike Scioscia														
1981	LA-N	.154	4	13	0	2	0	0	0	1	1	2	0	C
Tony Scott														
1981	Hou-N	.150	5	20	0	3	0	0	0	2	1	6	0	O
Ted Simmons														
1981	Mil-A	.211	5	19	1	4	1	0	1	4	2	2	0	C
Reggie Smith														
1981	LA-N	.000	2	1	0	0	0	0	0	1	0	1	0	H
Lonnie Smith														
1981	Phi-N	.263	5	19	1	5	1	0	0	0	4	0	0	O
Chris Speier														
1981	Mon-N	.400	5	15	4	6	2	0	0	3	4	2	0	S
Jim Spencer														
1981	Oak-A	.250	1	4	0	1	1	0	0	0	0	0	1	

YEAR	TM/L	AVG	G	AB	R	H	2B	3B	HR	RBI	BB	SO	SB	POS
Harry Spilman														
1981	Hou-N	.000	1	1	0	0	0	0	0	0	0	0	0	H
Fred Stanley														
1981	Oak-A	.000	3	6	0	0	0	0	0	0	0	1	0	S
Derrel Thomas														
1981	LA-N	.000	4	2	1	0	0	0	0	0	0	0	1	O
Gorman Thomas														
1981	Mil-A	.118	5	17	2	2	0	0	1	1	1	9	0	O*3,D*2
Dickie Thon														
1981	Hou-N	.182	4	11	0	2	0	0	0	0	1	0	0	S
Manny Trillo														
1981	Phi-N	.188	5	16	1	3	0	0	0	1	4	0	0	2
George Vukovich														
1981	Phi-N	.444	5	9	1	4	0	0	1	2	0	3	0	O*3
Tim Wallach														
1981	Mon-N	.250	4	4	1	1	1	0	0	4	0	0	0	O*3
Denny Walling														
1981	Hou-N	.333	3	6	0	2	0	0	0	1	0	1	0	1*2
U L Washington														
1981	KC-A	.222	3	9	0	2	0	0	0	0	0	1	0	S
John Wathan														
1981	KC-A	.300	3	10	1	3	0	0	0	0	1	0	0	C
Bob Watson														
1981	NY-A	.438	5	16	2	7	0	0	1	1	1	0	1	1
Frank White														
1981	KC-A	.182	3	11	1	2	0	0	0	1	1	0	2	2
Jerry White														
1981	Mon-N	.167	5	18	3	3	1	0	0	1	2	2	3	O
Willie Wilson														
1981	KC-A	.308	3	13	0	4	0	0	0	1	0	0	0	O
Dave Winfield														
1981	NY-A	.350	5	20	2	7	3	0	0	1	5	0	0	O
Gary Woods														
1981	Hou-N	.000	2	2	0	0	0	0	0	0	0	0	1	H
Steve Yeager														
1981	LA-N	.400	2	5	1	2	1	0	0	0	0	1	0	C
Robin Yount														
1981	Mil-A	.316	5	19	4	6	0	1	0	1	2	2	1	S

YEAR	TM/L	W	L	ERA	G	GS	CG	SV	SHO	IP	H	ER	BB	SO
● Stan Bahnsen														
1981	Mon-N	0	0	0.00	1	0	0	0	0	1¹	1	0	1	1
● Dave Beard														
1981	Oak-A	0	0	0.00	1	0	0	1	0	1¹	0	0	0	2
● Dwight Bernard														
1981	Mil-A	0	0	0.00	2	0	0	0	0	2¹	0	0	0	0
● Warren Brusstar														
1981	Phi-N	0	0	4.91	2	0	0	0	0	3²	5	2	1	3
● Ray Burris														
1981	Mon-N	0	1	5.06	1	1	0	0	0	5¹	7	3	4	4
● Mike Caldwell														
1981	Mil-A	0	1	4.32	2	1	0	0	0	8¹	9	4	0	4
● Steve Carlton														
1981	Phi-N	0	2	3.86	2	2	0	0	0	14	14	6	8	13
● Larry Christenson														
1981	Phi-N	1	0	1.50	1	1	0	0	0	6	4	1	1	8
● Ron Davis														
1981	NY-A	1	0	0.00	3	0	0	0	0	6	1	0	2	6
● Jamie Easterly														
1981	Mil-A	0	0	6.75	2	0	0	0	0	1¹	2	1	0	1
● Rollie Fingers														
1981	Mil-A	1	0	3.86	3	0	0	1	0	4²	7	2	1	5
● Terry Forster														
1981	LA-N	0	0	0.00	1	0	0	0	0	0¹	0	0	0	0
● Woody Fryman														
1981	Mon-N	0	0	6.75	1	0	0	0	0	1¹	3	1	1	0
● Rich Gossage														
1981	NY-A	0	0	0.00	3	0	0	3	0	6²	3	0	2	8
● Ron Guidry														
1981	NY-A	0	0	5.40	2	2	0	0	0	8¹	11	5	3	8
● Bill Gullickson														
1981	Mon-N	1	0	1.17	1	1	0	0	0	7²	6	1	1	3
● Larry Gura														
1981	KC-A	0	1	7.36	1	1	0	0	0	3²	7	3	3	3
● Moose Haas														
1981	Mil-A	0	2	9.45	2	2	0	0	0	6²	13	7	1	1
● Burt Hooton														
1981	LA-N	1	0	1.29	1	1	0	0	0	7	3	1	3	2
● Steve Howe														
1981	LA-N	0	0	0.00	2	0	0	0	0	2	1	0	0	2
● Tommy John														
1981	NY-A	0	1	6.43	1	1	0	0	0	7	8	5	2	0
● Mike Jones														
1981	KC-A	0	1	2.25	1	1	0	0	0	8	9	2	0	2
● Bob Knepper														
1981	Hou-N	0	1	5.40	1	1	0	0	0	5	6	3	2	4
● Frank LaCorte														
1981	Hou-N	0	0	0.00	2	0	0	0	0	3²	2	0	1	5
● Rick Langford														
1981	Oak-A	1	0	1.23	1	1	0	0	0	7¹	10	1	0	3
● Bill Lee														
1981	Mon-N	0	0	0.00	1	0	0	0	0	0²	2	0	0	1
● Dennis Leonard														
1981	KC-A	0	1	1.13	1	1	0	0	0	8	7	1	1	3
● Randy Lerch														
1981	Mil-A	0	0	1.50	1	1	0	0	0	6	3	1	4	3
● Sparky Lyle														
1981	Phi-N	0	0	0.00	3	0	0	0	0	2¹	4	0	2	1
● Renie Martin														
1981	KC-A	0	0	0.00	2	0	0	0	0	5¹	1	0	2	2

YEAR	TM/L	W	L	ERA	G	GS	CG	SV	SHO	IP	H	ER	BB	SO
● Rudy May														
1981	NY-A	0	0	0.00	1	0	0	0	0	2	1	0	0	1
● Steve McCatty														
1981	Oak-A	1	0	1.00	1	1	1	0	0	9	6	1	4	3
● Bob McClure														
1981	Mil-A	0	0	0.00	3	0	0	0	0	3¹	4	0	0	2
● Tug McGraw														
1981	Phi-N	1	0	0.00	2	0	0	0	0	4	2	0	0	2
● Tom Niedenfuer														
1981	LA-N	0	0	0.00	1	0	0	0	0	0¹	1	0	1	1
● Joe Niekro														
1981	Hou-N	0	0	0.00	1	1	0	0	0	8	7	0	3	4
● Dickie Noles														
1981	Phi-N	0	0	4.50	1	1	0	0	0	4	4	2	2	5
● Mike Norris														
1981	Oak-A	1	0	0.00	1	1	1	0	1	9	4	0	3	2
● Dan Quisenberry														
1981	KC-A	0	0	0.00	1	0	0	0	0	1	1	0	0	0
● Jeff Reardon														
1981	Mon-N	0	1	2.08	3	0	0	2	0	4¹	1	1	1	2
● Ron Reed														
1981	Phi-N	0	0	3.00	4	0	0	0	0	6	5	2	3	4
● Rick Reuschel														
1981	NY-A	0	1	3.00	1	1	0	0	0	6	4	2	1	3
● Jerry Reuss														
1981	LA-N	1	0	0.00	2	2	1	0	1	18	10	0	5	7
● Dave Righetti														
1981	NY-A	2	0	1.00	2	1	0	0	0	9	8	1	3	13
● Steve Rogers														
1981	Mon-N	2	0	0.51	2	2	1	0	1	17²	16	1	3	5
● Vern Ruhle														
1981	Hou-N	0	1	2.25	1	1	1	0	0	8	4	2	2	1
● Dick Ruthven														
1981	Phi-N	0	1	4.50	1	1	0	0	0	4	3	2	1	0
● Nolan Ryan														
1981	Hou-N	1	1	1.80	2	2	1	0	0	15	6	3	3	14
● Joe Sambito														
1981	Hou-N	1	0	16.20	2	0	0	0	0	1²	5	3	2	2
● Scott Sanderson														
1981	Mon-N	0	0	6.75	1	1	0	0	0	2²	4	2	2	2
● Jim Slaton														
1981	Mil-A	0	0	3.00	4	0	0	0	0	6	6	2	0	2
● Billy Smith														
1981	Hou-N	0	0	0.00	1	0	0	0	0	0¹	0	0	0	0
● Dave Smith														
1981	Hou-N	0	0	3.86	2	0	0	0	0	2¹	2	1	0	4
● Elias Sosa														
1981	Mon-N	0	0	3.00	2	0	0	0	0	3	4	1	0	1
● Dave Stewart														
1981	LA-N	0	2	40.50	2	0	0	0	0	0²	4	3	0	1
● Tom Underwood														
1981	Oak-A	0	0	0.00	1	0	0	0	0	0¹	0	0	0	1
● Fernando Valenzuela														
1981	LA-N	1	0	1.06	2	2	1	0	0	17	10	2	3	10
● Pete Vuckovich														
1981	Mil-A	1	0	0.00	2	1	0	0	0	5¹	2	0	3	4
● Bob Welch														
1981	LA-N	0	0	0.00	1	0	0	0	0	1	0	0	1	1

YEAR	TM/L	AVG	G	AB	R	H	2B	3B	HR	RBI	BB	SO	SB	POS
Hank Aaron														
1969	Atl-N	.357	3	14	3	5	2	0	3	7	0	1	0	O
Tommie Aaron														
1969	Atl-N	.000	1	1	0	0	0	0	0	0	0	0	0	H
Tommie Agee														
1969	NY-N	.357	3	14	4	5	1	0	2	4	2	5	2	O
Willie Aikens														
1980	KC-A	.364	3	11	0	4	0	0	0	2	0	1	0	1
Mike Aldrete														
1987	SF-N	.100	5	10	0	1	0	0	0	1	0	2	0	O*3
Matt Alexander														
1979	Pit-N	—	1	0	1	0	0	0	0	0	0	0	0	R
Dick Allen														
1976	Phi-N	.222	3	9	1	2	0	0	0	3	2	0	1	
Gene Alley														
1970	Pit-N	.000	2	7	0	0	0	0	0	0	1	2	0	S
1971	Pit-N	.500	1	2	1	1	0	0	0	0	0	0	0	S
1972	Pit-N	.000	5	16	1	0	0	0	0	0	0	3	0	S
Total 3		.040	8	25	2	1	0	0	0	0	1	5	0	
Bob Allison														
1969	Min-A	.000	2	8	0	0	0	0	0	1	0	0	0	O
1970	Min-A	.000	3	2	0	0	0	0	0	0	1	1	0	H
Total 2		.000	5	10	0	0	0	0	0	1	1	1	0	
Roberto Alomar														
1991	Tor-A	.474	5	19	3	9	0	0	0	4	2	3	2	2
1992	Tor-A	.423	6	26	4	11	1	0	2	4	2	1	5	2
1993	Tor-A	.292	6	24	3	7	1	0	0	4	4	3	4	2
Total 3		.391	17	69	10	27	2	0	2	12	8	7	11	
Sandy Alomar														
1976	NY-A	.000	2	1	0	0	0	0	0	0	0	0	0	D*1
Felipe Alou														
1969	Atl-N	.000	1	1	0	0	0	0	0	0	0	0	0	H
Jesus Alou														
1973	Oak-A	.333	4	6	0	2	0	0	0	1	0	1	0	D*1
1974	Oak-A	1.000	1	1	0	1	0	0	0	0	0	0	0	H
Total 2		.429	5	7	0	3	0	0	0	1	0	1	0	
Matty Alou														
1970	Pit-N	.250	3	12	1	3	1	0	0	0	2	1	0	O
1972	Oak-A	.381	5	21	2	8	4	0	0	2	0	2	1	O
Total 2		.333	8	33	3	11	5	0	0	2	2	3	1	
Brant Alyea														
1970	Min-A	.000	3	7	1	0	0	0	0	2	3	0		O*2
Dave Anderson														
1985	LA-N	.000	4	5	1	0	0	0	0	0	3	1	0	S*3,3*1
Jim Anderson														
1979	Cal-A	.091	4	11	0	1	0	0	0	0	0	1	0	S
Mike Andrews														
1973	Oak-A	.000	2	1	0	0	0	0	0	0	0	0	0	1*1,D*1
Tony Armas														
1981	Oak-A	.167	3	12	0	2	0	0	0	0	0	5	0	O
1986	Bos-A	.125	5	16	1	2	1	0	0	0	0	2	0	O
Total 2		.143	8	28	1	4	1	0	0	0	0	7	0	
Ed Armbrister														
1973	Cin-N	.167	3	6	0	1	0	0	0	0	0	5	0	O*1
1975	Cin-N	—	2	0	0	0	0	0	0	1	0	0	0	H
1976	Cin-N	—	1	0	0	0	0	0	0	0	0	0	0	H
Total 3		.167	6	6	0	1	0	0	0	0	1	5	0	
Alan Ashby														
1980	Hou-N	.125	2	8	0	1	0	0	0	0	0	0	0	C
1986	Hou-N	.130	6	23	2	3	1	0	1	2	2	1	0	C
Total 2		.129	8	31	2	4	1	0	1	3	2	1	0	
Bob Aspromonte														
1969	Atl-N	.000	3	3	0	0	0	0	0	0	0	0	0	H
Rick Auerbach														
1974	LA-N	1.000	1	1	0	1	1	0	0	0	0	0	0	H
1979	Cin-N	.000	2	2	0	0	0	0	0	0	0	1	0	H
Total 2		.333	3	3	0	1	1	0	0	0	0	1	0	
Ramon Aviles														
1980	Phi-N	—	1	0	1	0	0	0	0	0	0	0	0	R
Benny Ayala														
1983	Bal-A	—	1	0	0	0	0	0	0	1	0	0	0	D
Wally Backman														
1986	NY-N	.238	6	21	5	5	0	0	0	2	2	4	1	2
1988	NY-N	.273	7	22	2	6	1	0	0	2	2	5	1	2
1990	Pit-N	.143	3	7	1	1	1	0	0	0	1	3	1	3*2
Total 3		.240	16	50	8	12	2	0	0	4	5	12	3	
Bob Bailor														
1985	LA-N	.000	2	1	0	0	0	0	0	0	0	0	0	3

YEAR	TM/L	AVG	G	AB	R	H	2B	3B	HR	RBI	BB	SO	SB	POS
Harold Baines														
1983	Chi-A	.125	4	16	0	2	0	0	0	0	0	3	0	O
1990	Oak-A	.357	4	14	2	5	1	0	0	3	2	1	1	D
1992	Oak-A	.440	6	25	6	11	2	0	1	4	1	3	0	D
Total 3		.327	14	55	8	18	3	0	1	7	3	7	1	
Doug Baker														
1984	Det-A	—	1	0	0	0	0	0	0	0	0	0	0	S
Frank Baker														
1973	Bal-A	—	2	0	0	0	0	0	0	0	0	0	0	S
1974	Bal-A	—	2	0	0	0	0	0	0	0	0	0	0	S
Total 2		—	4	0	0	0	0	0	0	0	0	0	0	
Dusty Baker														
1977	LA-N	.357	4	14	4	5	1	0	2	8	3	3	0	O
1978	LA-N	.467	4	15	1	7	2	0	1	3	0	0	0	O
1981	LA-N	.316	5	19	3	6	1	0	0	1	3	0	0	O
1983	LA-N	.357	4	14	4	5	1	0	0	1	2	0	0	O
Total 4		.371	17	62	12	23	5	0	3	13	8	3	0	
Steve Balboni														
1984	KC-A	.100	3	10	0	1	0	0	0	0	1	4	0	1
1985	KC-A	.120	7	25	1	3	0	0	0	1	2	8	0	1
Total 2		.114	10	35	1	4	0	0	0	1	3	12	0	
Sal Bando														
1971	Oak-A	.364	3	11	3	4	2	0	1	1	1	0	0	3
1972	Oak-A	.200	5	20	0	4	0	0	0	3	2	0	0	3
1973	Oak-A	.167	5	18	2	3	0	0	2	3	3	6	0	3
1974	Oak-A	.231	4	13	4	3	0	0	0	2	2	4	0	3
1975	Oak-A	.500	3	12	1	6	2	0	0	2	0	2	0	3
Total 5		.270	20	74	10	20	4	0	3	11	8	12	0	
Jesse Barfield														
1985	Tor-A	.280	7	25	3	7	1	0	1	4	3	7	1	O
Marty Barrett														
1986	Bos-A	.367	7	30	4	11	2	0	0	5	2	2	0	2
1988	Bos-A	.067	3	15	2	1	0	0	0	0	1	0	0	2
1990	Bos-A	—	3	0	0	0	0	0	0	0	0	0	0	2
Total 3		.267	14	45	6	12	2	0	0	5	3	2	0	
Kevin Bass														
1986	Hou-N	.292	6	24	0	7	2	0	0	0	4	4	2	O
Billy Bates														
1990	Cin-N	—	2	0	1	0	0	0	0	0	0	0	0	R
Bill Bathe														
1989	SF-N	.000	2	1	0	0	0	0	0	0	0	1	0	H
Kim Batiste														
1993	Phi-N	1.000	4	1	0	1	0	0	0	1	0	0	0	3
Don Baylor														
1973	Bal-A	.273	4	11	3	3	0	0	0	1	3	5	0	O*3
1974	Bal-A	.267	4	15	0	4	0	0	0	0	0	2	0	O
1979	Cal-A	.188	4	16	2	3	0	0	1	2	1	2	0	D*3,O*1
1982	Cal-A	.294	5	17	2	5	1	1	1	10	2	0	0	D
1986	Bos-A	.346	7	26	6	9	3	0	1	2	4	5	0	D
1987	Min-A	.400	2	5	0	2	0	0	0	1	0	0	0	D
1988	Oak-A	.000	2	6	0	0	0	0	0	1	1	2	0	D
Total 7		.271	28	96	13	26	4	1	3	17	11	16	0	
Mark Belanger														
1969	Bal-A	.267	3	15	4	4	0	1	1	1	0	0	0	S
1970	Bal-A	.333	3	12	5	4	0	0	0	1	1	0	0	S
1971	Bal-A	.250	3	8	1	2	0	0	0	1	3	2	0	S
1973	Bal-A	.125	5	16	0	2	0	0	0	1	1	1	0	S
1974	Bal-A	.000	4	9	0	0	0	0	0	0	1	3	0	S
1979	Bal-A	.200	3	5	0	1	0	0	0	1	0	2	0	S
Total 6		.200	21	65	10	13	0	1	1	5	6	8	0	
Derek Bell														
1992	Tor-A	—	2	0	1	0	0	0	0	0	1	0	0	O
Jay Bell														
1990	Pit-N	.250	6	20	3	5	1	0	1	1	4	3	0	S
1991	Pit-N	.414	7	29	2	12	2	0	1	1	0	10	0	S
1992	Pit-N	.172	7	29	3	5	2	0	1	4	3	4	0	S
Total 3		.282	20	78	8	22	5	0	3	6	7	17	0	
George Bell														
1985	Tor-A	.321	7	28	4	9	3	0	0	1	0	4	0	O
1989	Tor-A	.200	5	20	2	4	0	0	1	2	0	3	0	D*3,O*2
Total 2		.271	12	48	6	13	3	0	1	3	0	7	0	
Rafael Belliard														
1991	Atl-N	.211	7	19	0	4	0	0	0	1	3	3	0	S
1992	Atl-N	.000	4	2	1	0	0	0	0	0	1	0	0	S*3,2*1
1993	Atl-N	.000	2	1	1	0	0	0	0	0	0	1	0	2*1,S*1
Total 3		.182	13	22	2	4	0	0	0	1	4	4	0	
Johnny Bench														
1970	Cin-N	.222	3	9	2	2	0	0	1	3	1	3	0	C
1972	Cin-N	.333	5	18	3	6	1	1	1	2	1	3	2	C
1973	Cin-N	.263	5	19	1	5	2	0	0	1	2	2	0	C
1975	Cin-N	.077	3	13	1	1	0	0	0	0	1	6	1	C
1976	Cin-N	.333	3	12	3	4	1	0	1	1	1	2	0	C
1979	Cin-N	.250	3	12	1	3	0	0	1	1	1	2	0	C
Total 6		.253	22	83	11	21	4	2	5	6	10	16	4	

YEAR	TM/L	AVG	G	AB	R	H	2B	3B	HR	RBI	BB	SO	SB	POS
Bruce Benedict														
1982	Atl-N	.250	3	8	1	2	1	0	0	0	2	1	0	C
Juan Beniquez														
1975	Bos-A	.250	3	12	2	3	0	0	0	1	0	1	2	D
1982	Cal-A	—	2	0	0	0	0	0	0	0	0	0	0	O
Total 2		.250	5	12	2	3	0	0	0	1	0	1	2	
Todd Benzinger														
1988	Bos-A	.091	4	11	0	1	0	0	0	0	1	3	0	1*3
1990	Cin-N	.333	5	9	0	3	0	0	0	0	2	0	0	1*2
Total 2		.200	9	20	0	4	0	0	0	0	3	3	0	
Dave Bergman														
1980	Hou-N	.333	4	3	0	1	0	1	0	2	0	0	0	1
1984	Det-A	1.000	2	1	1	1	0	0	0	0	0	0	1	1*1
1987	Det-A	.250	4	4	0	1	0	0	0	2	0	1	0	1*1,D*1
Total 3		.375	10	8	1	3	0	1	0	4	0	1	1	
Damon Berryhill														
1992	Atl-N	.167	7	24	1	4	1	0	0	1	3	2	0	C
1993	Atl-N	.211	6	19	2	4	0	0	1	3	1	5	0	C
Total 2		.186	13	43	3	8	1	0	1	4	4	7	0	
Kurt Bevacqua														
1984	SD-N	.000	2	2	0	0	0	0	0	0	0	0	0	H
Buddy Biancalana														
1984	KC-A	.000	2	1	0	0	0	0	0	0	0	1	0	S
1985	KC-A	.222	7	18	2	4	1	0	0	1	1	6	0	S
Total 2		.211	9	19	2	4	1	0	0	1	1	7	0	
Paul Blair														
1969	Bal-A	.400	3	15	1	6	2	0	1	6	2	2	0	O
1970	Bal-A	.077	3	13	0	1	0	0	0	0	1	4	0	O
1971	Bal-A	.333	3	9	1	3	1	0	0	2	0	3	0	O
1973	Bal-A	.167	5	18	2	3	0	0	0	1	0	5	0	O
1974	Bal-A	.286	4	14	3	4	0	0	1	2	2	2	0	O
1977	NY-A	.400	3	5	1	2	0	0	0	0	0	0	0	O
1978	NY-A	.000	4	6	1	0	0	0	0	0	0	1	0	O*3,2*1
Total 7		.237	25	80	9	19	3	0	2	10	6	17	0	
Lance Blankenship														
1989	Oak-A	—	1	0	0	0	0	0	0	0	0	0	0	2
1990	Oak-A	—	3	0	1	0	0	0	0	0	0	0	1	D
1992	Oak-A	.231	5	13	2	3	0	0	0	0	3	4	1	2
Total 3		.231	9	13	3	3	0	0	0	0	3	4	2	
Jeff Blauser														
1991	Atl-N	.000	2	2	0	0	0	0	0	0	0	0	0	S
1992	Atl-N	.208	7	24	3	5	0	1	1	4	3	2	0	S
1993	Atl-N	.280	6	25	5	7	1	0	2	4	4	7	0	S
Total 3		.235	15	51	8	12	1	1	3	8	7	9	0	
Curt Blefary														
1971	Oak-A	.000	1	1	0	0	0	0	0	0	0	1	0	H
Bruce Bochy														
1980	Hou-N	.000	1	1	0	0	0	0	0	0	0	0	0	C
Wade Boggs														
1986	Bos-A	.233	7	30	3	7	1	0	2	4	1	0	3	3
1988	Bos-A	.385	4	13	2	5	0	0	0	3	3	4	0	3
1990	Bos-A	.438	4	16	1	7	1	0	1	1	0	3	0	3
Total 3		.322	15	59	6	19	2	1	1	6	7	8	0	
Barry Bonds														
1990	Pit-N	.167	6	18	4	3	0	0	0	1	6	6	2	O
1991	Pit-N	.148	7	27	1	4	1	0	0	0	2	4	3	O
1992	Pit-N	.261	7	23	5	6	1	0	1	2	6	4	1	O
Total 3		.191	20	68	10	13	2	0	1	3	14	14	6	
Bobby Bonds														
1971	SF-N	.250	3	8	0	2	0	0	0	0	0	2	4	0	O
Bobby Bonilla														
1990	Pit-N	.190	6	21	0	4	1	0	0	1	3	1	0	O*5,3*3
1991	Pit-N	.304	7	23	2	7	2	0	0	1	6	2	0	O
Total 2		.250	13	44	2	11	3	0	0	2	9	3	0	
Bob Boone														
1976	Phi-N	.286	3	7	0	2	0	0	0	1	1	0	0	C
1977	Phi-N	.400	4	10	1	4	0	0	0	0	0	0	0	C
1978	Phi-N	.182	3	11	0	2	0	0	0	0	0	1	0	C
1980	Phi-N	.222	5	18	1	4	0	0	0	1	2	0	0	C
1982	Cal-A	.250	5	16	3	4	0	0	1	4	0	2	0	C
1986	Cal-A	.455	7	22	4	10	0	0	1	2	1	3	0	C
Total 6		.310	27	84	9	26	0	0	2	9	3	8	0	
Pat Borders														
1989	Tor-A	1.000	1	1	0	1	0	0	0	1	0	0	0	C
1991	Tor-A	.263	5	19	0	5	1	0	0	2	0	0	0	C
1992	Tor-A	.318	6	22	3	7	0	0	1	3	1	1	0	C
1993	Tor-A	.250	6	24	1	6	1	0	0	3	0	6	1	C
Total 4		.288	18	66	4	19	2	0	1	9	1	7	1	
Mike Bordick														
1992	Oak-A	.053	6	19	1	1	0	0	0	0	1	2	1	S*4,2*2
Rick Bosetti														
1981	Oak-A	.250	2	4	1	1	1	0	0	0	0	0	1	0	O*1,D*1
Thad Bosley														
1984	Chi-N	.000	2	2	0	0	0	0	0	0	0	0	2	0	H
Ken Boswell														
1969	NY-N	.333	3	12	4	4	0	0	2	5	1	2	0	2
1973	NY-N	.000	1	1	0	0	0	0	0	0	0	0	0	H
Total 2		.308	4	13	4	4	0	0	2	5	1	2	0	
Pat Bourque														
1973	Oak-A	.000	2	1	0	0	0	0	0	0	0	1	1	0	D
Larry Bowa														
1976	Phi-N	.125	3	8	1	1	1	0	0	1	3	0	0	S
1977	Phi-N	.118	4	17	2	2	0	0	0	1	1	0	0	S
1978	Phi-N	.333	4	18	2	6	0	0	0	2	0	0	S
1980	Phi-N	.316	5	19	2	6	0	0	0	3	3	1	S
1984	Cal-A	.200	5	15	1	3	1	0	0	1	1	0	0	S
Total 5		.234	21	77	8	18	2	0	0	3	9	5	1	
Clete Boyer														
1969	Atl-N	.111	3	9	0	1	0	0	0	3	2	3	0	3
Glenn Braggs														
1990	Cin-N	.200	2	5	0	1	0	0	0	0	0	1	0	O
Steve Braun														
1978	KC-A	.000	2	5	0	0	0	0	0	0	1	1	0	O*1
1982	StL-N	.000	1	1	0	0	0	0	0	0	0	0	0	H
1985	StL-N	.000	2	2	0	0	0	0	0	0	0	0	0	H
Total 3		.000	5	8	0	0	0	0	0	0	1	1	0	
Angel Bravo														
1970	Cin-N	.000	1	1	0	0	0	0	0	0	0	0	0	H
Sid Bream														
1990	Pit-N	.500	4	8	1	4	1	0	1	3	2	3	0	1
1991	Atl-N	.300	4	10	1	3	0	0	1	3	0	1	0	1
1992	Atl-N	.273	7	22	5	6	3	0	1	2	3	0	0	1
1993	Atl-N	1.000	1	1	1	1	0	0	0	0	0	0	1	
Total 4		.341	16	41	8	14	4	0	3	8	5	4	0	
Bob Brenly														
1987	SF-N	.235	6	17	3	4	1	0	1	2	3	7	0	C
George Brett														
1976	KC-A	.444	5	18	4	8	1	1	1	5	2	1	0	3
1977	KC-A	.300	5	20	2	6	0	2	0	2	1	0	0	3
1978	KC-A	.389	4	18	7	7	1	0	3	3	0	1	0	3
1980	KC-A	.273	3	11	3	3	1	0	2	4	1	0	0	3
1984	KC-A	.231	3	13	0	3	0	0	0	0	0	2	0	3
1985	KC-A	.348	7	23	6	8	2	0	3	5	7	5	0	3
Total 6		.340	27	103	22	35	5	4	9	19	11	9	0	
Ed Brinkman														
1972	Det-A	.250	1	4	0	1	1	0	0	0	0	0	0	S
Greg Brock														
1983	LA-N	.000	3	9	1	0	0	0	0	0	0	3	0	1
1985	LA-N	.083	5	12	1	1	0	1	2	2	0	2	0	1*4
Total 2		.048	8	21	3	1	0	1	2	2	5	0		
Tom Brookens														
1984	Det-A	.000	2	2	0	0	0	0	0	0	0	1	0	2*1,3*1
1987	Det-A	.000	5	13	0	0	0	0	0	0	0	3	3	
Total 2		.000	7	15	0	0	0	0	0	0	0	4	0	
Mark Brouhard														
1982	Mil-A	.750	1	4	4	3	1	0	1	3	0	0	0	O
Ike Brown														
1972	Det-A	.500	1	2	0	1	0	0	0	2	0	1	0	1
Jarvis Brown														
1991	Min-A	—	1	0	1	0	0	0	0	0	0	0	0	D
Larry Brown														
1973	Bal-A	—	1	0	0	0	0	0	0	0	0	0	0	3
Ollie Brown														
1976	Phi-N	.000	1	2	0	0	0	0	0	0	0	1	0	O
1977	Phi-N	.000	2	2	0	0	0	0	0	0	0	1	0	H
Total 2		.000	3	4	0	0	0	0	0	0	0	2	0	
Bobby Brown														
1980	NY-A	.000	3	10	1	0	0	0	0	0	1	2	0	O
1981	NY-A	1.000	3	1	2	1	0	0	0	0	0	0	0	O*2
1984	SD-N	.000	3	4	1	0	0	0	0	0	1	2	1	O
Total 3		.067	9	15	4	1	0	0	0	0	2	4	1	
Gates Brown														
1972	Det-A	.000	3	2	1	0	0	0	0	0	1	0	0	H
Jerry Browne														
1992	Oak-A	.400	4	10	3	4	0	0	0	2	2	0	0	3*2,O*1
Tom Brunansky														
1987	Min-A	.412	5	17	5	7	4	0	2	9	4	3	0	O
1990	Bos-A	.083	5	12	0	1	0	0	0	1	3	0	0	O
Total 2		.276	9	29	5	8	4	0	2	10	5	6	0	
Bill Buckner														
1974	LA-N	.167	4	18	0	3	1	0	0	0	0	2	0	O
1986	Bos-A	.214	7	28	3	6	1	0	0	3	0	2	0	1
Total 2		.196	11	46	3	9	2	0	0	3	0	4	0	

YEAR	TM/L	AVG	G	AB	R	H	2B	3B	HR	RBI	BB	SO	SB	POS
Steve Buechele														
1991	Pit-N	.304	7	23	2	7	2	0	0	0	4	6	0	3
Don Buford														
1969	Bal-A	.286	3	14	3	4	1	0	0	1	3	0	0	O
1970	Bal-A	.429	2	7	2	3	1	0	1	3	2	0	0	O
1971	Bal-A	.429	2	7	1	3	0	1	0	0	2	1	0	O
Total 3		.357	7	28	6	10	2	1	1	4	7	1	0	
Al Bumbry														
1973	Bal-A	.000	2	7	1	0	0	0	0	0	2	2	1	O
1974	Bal-A	.000	2	1	0	0	0	0	0	0	0	0	1	H
1979	Bal-A	.250	4	16	5	4	0	1	0	0	4	3	2	O
1983	Bal-A	.125	3	8	0	1	1	0	0	1	0	2	0	O
Total 4		.156	11	32	6	5	1	1	0	1	6	8	3	
Glenn Burke														
1977	LA-N	.000	4	7	0	0	0	0	0	0	0	3	0	O
Ellis Burks														
1988	Bos-A	.235	4	17	2	4	1	0	0	1	0	3	0	O
1990	Bos-A	.267	4	15	1	4	2	0	0	0	1	1	1	O
1993	Chi-A	.304	6	23	4	7	1	0	1	3	3	5	0	O
Total 3		.273	14	55	7	15	4	0	1	4	4	9	1	
Rick Burleson														
1975	Bos-A	.444	3	9	2	4	2	0	0	1	1	0	0	S
1986	Cal-A	.273	4	11	0	3	0	0	0	0	0	0	1	2*2,D*1
Total 2		.350	7	20	2	7	2	0	0	1	1	0	0	
Jeff Burroughs														
1985	Tor-A	.000	1	1	0	0	0	0	0	0	0	0	0	H
Randy Bush														
1987	Min-A	.250	4	12	4	3	0	1	0	2	3	2	3	D
Sal Butera														
1987	Min-A	.667	1	3	0	2	0	0	0	0	0	0	0	C
Brett Butler														
1982	Atl-N	.000	2	1	0	0	0	0	0	0	0	0	0	O*1
1989	SF-N	.211	5	19	6	4	0	0	0	0	3	3	0	O
Total 2		.200	7	20	6	4	0	0	0	0	3	3	0	
Enos Cabell														
1974	Bal-A	.250	3	4	0	1	0	0	0	0	0	2	0	O*1
1980	Hou-N	.238	5	21	1	5	1	0	0	0	1	3	0	3
1985	LA-N	.077	5	13	1	1	0	0	0	0	0	3	0	1*3
Total 3		.184	13	38	2	7	1	0	0	0	1	8	0	
Francisco Cabrera														
1992	Atl-N	.500	2	2	0	1	0	0	0	2	0	0	0	H
1993	Atl-N	.667	3	3	0	2	0	0	0	1	0	1	0	C*1
Total 2		.600	5	5	0	3	0	0	0	3	0	1	0	
Bert Campaneris														
1971	Oak-A	.167	3	12	0	2	1	0	0	0	0	1	0	S
1972	Oak-A	.429	2	7	3	3	0	0	0	0	1	0	2	S
1973	Oak-A	.333	5	21	3	7	1	0	2	3	2	2	3	S
1974	Oak-A	.176	4	17	0	3	0	0	0	3	0	1	3	S
1975	Oak-A	.000	3	11	1	0	0	0	0	0	1	1	0	S
1979	Cal-A	—	1	0	0	0	0	0	0	0	0	0	0	S
Total 6		.221	18	68	7	15	2	0	2	6	4	7	6	
Jose Canseco														
1988	Oak-A	.313	4	16	4	5	1	0	3	4	1	2	1	O
1989	Oak-A	.294	5	17	1	5	0	0	1	3	3	7	0	O
1990	Oak-A	.182	4	11	3	2	0	0	0	1	5	5	2	O
Total 3		.273	13	44	8	12	1	0	4	8	9	14	3	
Bernie Carbo														
1970	Cin-N	.000	2	6	0	0	0	0	0	0	0	3	0	O
Jose Cardenal														
1978	Phi-N	.167	2	6	0	1	0	0	0	0	1	1	0	1
Leo Cardenas														
1969	Min-A	.154	3	13	0	2	0	1	0	0	0	7	0	S
1970	Min-A	.182	3	11	1	2	0	0	0	1	1	1	0	S
Total 2		.167	6	24	1	4	0	1	0	1	1	8	0	
Rod Carew														
1969	Min-A	.071	3	14	0	1	0	0	0	0	1	4	0	2
1970	Min-A	.000	2	2	0	0	0	0	0	0	1	0	0	H
1979	Cal-A	.412	4	17	4	7	3	0	0	1	0	1	1	
1982	Cal-A	.176	5	17	2	3	1	0	0	0	4	4	1	1
Total 4		.220	14	50	6	11	4	0	0	1	5	9	2	
Gary Carter														
1981	Mon-N	.438	5	16	7	7	1	0	0	4	2	0	0	C
1986	NY-N	.148	6	27	1	4	1	0	0	2	2	5	0	C
1988	NY-N	.222	7	27	0	6	1	1	0	4	1	3	0	C
Total 3		.243	18	70	4	17	3	1	0	6	7	10	0	
Joe Carter														
1991	Tor-A	.263	5	19	3	5	2	0	1	4	1	5	0	O*3,D*2
1992	Tor-A	.192	6	26	2	5	0	0	1	3	2	4	2	O*6,1*2
1993	Tor-A	.259	6	27	2	7	0	0	0	2	1	5	0	O
Total 3		.236	17	72	7	17	2	0	2	9	4	14	2	
Rico Carty														
1969	Atl-N	.300	3	10	4	3	2	0	0	0	3	1	0	O

YEAR	TM/L	AVG	G	AB	R	H	2B	3B	HR	RBI	BB	SO	SB	POS
Dave Cash														
1970	Pit-N	.125	2	8	1	1	1	0	0	0	1	1	0	2
1971	Pit-N	.421	4	19	5	8	2	0	0	1	0	1	1	2
1972	Pit-N	.211	5	19	0	4	0	0	0	3	0	0	0	2
1976	Phi-N	.308	3	13	1	4	1	0	0	1	0	0	0	2
Total 4		.288	14	59	7	17	4	0	0	5	1	2	1	
Norm Cash														
1972	Det-A	.267	5	15	1	4	0	0	1	2	2	3	0	1
Marty Castillo														
1984	Det-A	.250	3	8	0	2	0	0	0	2	0	3	1	3
Cesar Cedeno														
1980	Hou-N	.182	3	11	1	2	0	0	0	1	1	0	0	O
1985	StL-N	.167	5	12	2	2	1	0	0	0	2	3	0	O*4
Total 2		.174	8	23	3	4	1	0	0	1	3	3	0	
Orlando Cepeda														
1969	Atl-N	.455	3	11	2	5	2	0	1	3	1	2	1	1
Rick Cerone														
1980	NY-A	.333	3	12	1	4	0	0	1	2	0	1	0	C
1981	NY-A	.100	3	10	1	1	0	0	0	0	0	0	0	C
Total 2		.227	6	22	2	5	0	0	1	2	0	1	0	
Ron Cey														
1974	LA-N	.313	4	16	2	5	3	0	1	1	3	2	0	3
1977	LA-N	.308	4	13	4	4	1	0	1	4	2	4	0	3
1978	LA-N	.313	4	16	4	5	1	0	1	3	2	4	0	3
1981	LA-N	.278	5	18	1	5	1	0	0	3	3	2	0	3
1984	Chi-N	.158	5	19	3	3	1	0	1	3	3	3	0	3
Total 5		.268	22	82	14	22	7	0	4	14	13	15	1	
Wes Chamberlain														
1993	Phi-N	.364	4	11	1	4	3	0	0	1	1	3	0	O*2
Chris Chambliss														
1976	NY-A	.524	5	21	5	11	1	1	2	8	0	1	2	1
1977	NY-A	.059	5	17	0	1	0	0	0	3	4	0	1	
1978	NY-A	.400	4	15	1	6	0	0	0	2	0	4	0	1
1982	Atl-N	.000	3	10	0	0	0	0	0	0	1	0	0	1
Total 4		.286	17	63	6	18	1	1	2	10	4	9	2	
Darrel Chaney														
1972	Cin-N	.188	5	16	3	3	0	0	0	1	1	1	1	S
1973	Cin-N	.000	5	9	0	0	0	0	0	0	3	4	0	H
Total 2		.120	10	25	3	3	0	0	0	1	4	5	1	
Jack Clark														
1985	StL-N	.381	6	21	4	8	0	0	1	4	5	5	0	1
1987	StL-N	.000	1	1	0	0	0	0	0	0	0	1	0	H
Total 2		.364	7	22	4	8	0	0	1	4	5	6	0	
Bobby Clark														
1979	Cal-A	.000	1	3	0	0	0	0	0	0	0	0	2	O
1982	Cal-A	—	2	0	0	0	0	0	0	0	0	0	0	O
Total 2		.000	3	3	0	0	0	0	0	0	0	0	2	
Will Clark														
1987	SF-N	.360	7	25	3	9	2	0	1	3	3	6	1	1
1989	SF-N	.650	5	20	8	13	3	1	2	8	2	2	0	1
Total 2		.489	12	45	11	22	5	1	3	11	5	8	1	
Roberto Clemente														
1970	Pit-N	.214	3	14	1	3	0	0	0	1	0	4	0	O
1971	Pit-N	.333	4	18	2	6	0	0	0	4	1	6	0	O
1972	Pit-N	.235	5	17	1	4	1	0	0	2	3	5	0	O
Total 3		.265	12	49	4	13	1	0	0	7	4	15	0	
Ty Cline														
1970	Cin-N	1.000	2	1	2	1	0	1	0	0	1	0	0	O*1
Gene Clines														
1971	Pit-N	.333	3	3	1	1	0	0	1	1	0	1	0	O
1972	Pit-N	.000	3	2	1	0	0	0	0	0	0	1	0	H
1974	Pit-N	.000	2	1	1	0	0	0	0	0	0	0	0	O
Total 3		.167	6	6	3	1	0	0	1	1	0	2	0	
Rich Coggins														
1973	Bal-A	.444	2	9	1	4	0	0	0	0	0	0	0	O
1974	Bal-A	.000	3	11	0	0	0	0	0	0	0	3	0	O
Total 2		.200	5	20	1	4	1	0	0	0	0	3	0	
Alex Cole														
1992	Pit-N	.200	4	10	2	2	0	0	0	1	3	2	0	O
Vince Coleman														
1985	StL-N	.286	3	14	2	4	0	0	0	1	0	2	1	O
1987	StL-N	.269	7	26	3	7	1	0	0	4	4	6	1	O
Total 2		.275	10	40	5	11	1	0	0	5	4	8	2	
Dave Collins														
1979	Cin-N	.357	3	14	0	5	1	0	0	1	0	2	2	O
Dave Concepcion														
1970	Cin-N	—	3	0	0	0	0	0	0	0	0	0	0	S
1972	Cin-N	.000	3	2	0	0	0	0	0	0	0	0	0	S*1
1975	Cin-N	.455	3	11	2	5	0	0	1	1	1	2	2	S
1976	Cin-N	.200	3	10	4	2	0	0	0	0	2	1	0	S
1979	Cin-N	.429	3	14	1	6	1	0	0	0	0	3	0	S
Total 5		.351	15	37	7	13	2	0	1	1	3	6	2	

YEAR	TM/L	AVG	G	AB	R	H	2B	3B	HR	RBI	BB	SO	SB	POS
■ Onix Concepcion														
1984	KC-A	.000	3	7	0	0	0	0	0	0	0	0	0	S
1985	KC-A	.000	4	1	0	0	0	0	0	0	0	0	0	S
Total 2		.000	7	8	0	0	0	0	0	0	0	0	0	
■ Billy Conigliaro														
1973	Oak-A	.000	1	4	0	0	0	0	0	0	0	2	0	O
■ Cecil Cooper														
1975	Bos-A	.400	3	10	0	4	2	0	0	1	0	2	0	1
1982	Mil-A	.150	5	20	1	3	2	0	0	4	0	6	0	1
Total 2		.233	8	30	1	7	4	0	0	5	0	8	0	
■ Joey Cora														
1993	Chi-A	.136	6	22	1	3	0	0	0	1	3	6	0	2
■ Henry Cotto														
1984	Chi-N	1.000	3	1	1	1	0	0	0	0	0	0	0	0
■ Al Cowens														
1976	KC-A	.190	5	21	3	4	0	1	0	0	1	1	2	O
1977	KC-A	.263	5	19	2	5	0	0	1	5	1	3	0	O
1978	KC-A	.133	4	15	2	2	0	0	0	1	0	2	0	O
Total 3		.200	14	55	7	11	0	1	1	6	2	6	2	
■ Willie Crawford														
1974	LA-N	.250	2	4	1	1	0	0	0	1	1	1	0	O
■ Warren Cromartie														
1981	Mon-N	.167	5	18	0	3	1	0	0	2	0	2	0	1
■ Ed Crosby														
1973	Cin-N	.500	2	2	0	1	0	0	0	0	0	1	0	S
■ Terry Crowley														
1973	Bal-A	.000	2	2	0	0	0	0	0	0	0	0	0	O*1
1975	Cin-N	—	1	0	0	0	0	0	0	0	0	0	0	H
1979	Bal-A	.500	2	2	0	1	0	0	0	1	0	0	0	H
Total 3		.250	5	4	0	1	0	0	0	1	0	0	0	
■ Hector Cruz														
1979	Cin-N	.200	2	5	1	1	0	0	0	0	1	0		O*1
■ Jose Cruz														
1980	Hou-N	.400	5	15	3	6	1	1	0	4	8	1	0	O
1986	Hou-N	.192	6	26	0	5	0	0	0	2	1	8	0	O
Total 2		.268	11	41	3	11	1	1	0	6	9	9	0	
■ Julio Cruz														
1983	Chi-A	.333	4	12	0	4	0	0	0	0	3	4	2	2
■ Todd Cruz														
1983	Bal-A	.133	4	15	0	2	0	0	0	1	0	5	0	3
■ Tim Cullen														
1972	Oak-A	.000	2	1	0	0	0	0	0	0	0	0	0	S
■ Rich Dauer														
1979	Bal-A	.182	4	11	0	2	0	0	0	0	0	1	0	2
1983	Bal-A	.000	4	14	0	0	0	0	0	1	0	0	0	2
Total 2		.080	8	25	0	2	0	0	0	1	0	1	0	
■ Darren Daulton														
1993	Phi-N	.263	6	19	2	5	1	0	1	3	6	3	0	C
■ Vic Davalillo														
1971	Pit-N	.000	2	2	0	0	0	0	0	0	0	1	0	H
1972	Pit-N	—	1	0	0	0	0	0	0	0	1	0	0	H
1973	Oak-A	.625	4	8	2	5	1	1	0	1	1	0	0	1*2,O*2
1977	LA-N	1.000	1	1	1	1	0	0	0	0	0	0	0	H
Total 4		.545	8	11	3	6	1	1	0	1	2	1	0	
■ Mark Davidson														
1987	Min-A	—	1	0	0	0	0	0	0	0	0	0	0	R
■ Chili Davis														
1987	SF-N	.150	6	20	2	3	1	0	0	0	1	4	0	O
1991	Min-A	.294	5	17	3	5	2	0	0	2	5	8	1	D
Total 2		.216	11	37	5	8	3	0	0	2	6	12	1	
■ Eric Davis														
1990	Cin-N	.174	6	23	2	4	1	0	0	2	1	9	0	O
■ Glenn Davis														
1986	Hou-N	.269	6	26	3	7	1	0	1	3	1	3	0	1
■ Tommy Davis														
1971	Oak-A	.375	3	8	1	3	1	0	0	0	0	0	0	1*2
1973	Bal-A	.286	5	21	1	6	1	0	0	2	1	0	0	D
1974	Bal-A	.267	4	15	0	4	0	0	0	1	0	1	0	D
Total 3		.295	12	44	2	13	2	0	0	3	1	1	0	
■ Jody Davis														
1984	Chi-N	.389	5	18	3	7	2	0	2	6	0	3	0	C
■ Mike Davis														
1981	Oak-A	1.000	1	1	0	1	0	0	0	0	0	0	0	H
1988	LA-N	.000	4	2	0	0	0	0	0	0	0	1	0	H
Total 2		.333	5	3	0	1	0	0	0	0	0	1	0	
■ Willie Davis														
1979	Cal-A	.500	2	2	1	1	1	0	0	0	0	0	0	H
■ Andre Dawson														
1981	Mon-N	.150	5	20	2	3	0	0	0	0	0	4	0	O

YEAR	TM/L	AVG	G	AB	R	H	2B	3B	HR	RBI	BB	SO	SB	POS
1989	Chi-N	.105	5	19	0	2	1	0	0	3	2	6	0	O
Total 2		.128	10	39	2	5	1	0	0	3	2	10	0	
■ Doug DeCinces														
1979	Bal-A	.308	4	13	4	4	1	0	0	3	1	1	0	3
1982	Cal-A	.316	5	19	5	6	2	0	0	1	5	0		3
1986	Cal-A	.281	7	32	2	9	3	0	1	3	0	2	0	3
Total 3		.297	16	64	11	19	6	0	1	6	2	8	0	
■ Ivan DeJesus														
1983	Phi-N	.250	4	12	0	3	0	0	0	1	3	3	0	S
■ Rick Dempsey														
1979	Bal-A	.400	3	10	3	4	2	0	0	2	1	0	1	C
1983	Bal-A	.167	4	12	1	2	0	0	0	1	1	0		C
1988	LA-N	.400	4	5	1	2	2	0	0	4	1	0	0	C*3
Total 3		.296	11	27	5	8	4	0	0	4	3	1	1	
■ Bucky Dent														
1977	NY-A	.214	5	14	1	3	1	0	0	2	1	0	0	S
1978	NY-A	.200	4	15	0	3	0	0	0	4	0	0	0	S
1980	NY-A	.182	3	11	0	2	0	0	0	0	0	1	0	S
Total 3		.200	12	40	1	8	1	0	0	6	1	1	0	
■ Bob Dernier														
1983	Phi-N	—	1	0	0	0	0	0	0	0	0	0	0	O
1984	Chi-N	.235	5	17	5	4	2	0	1	5	4	2	0	O
Total 2		.235	6	17	5	4	2	0	1	5	4	2		
■ Bo Diaz														
1983	Phi-N	.154	4	13	0	2	1	0	0	0	2	1	0	C
■ Bob Didier														
1969	Atl-N	.000	3	11	0	0	0	0	0	0	0	2	0	C
■ Dick Dietz														
1971	SF-N	.067	4	15	0	1	0	0	0	0	2	5	0	C
■ Bill Doran														
1986	Hou-N	.222	6	27	3	6	0	0	1	3	2	2	2	2
■ Brian Downing														
1979	Cal-A	.200	4	15	1	3	0	0	0	1	1	0		C
1982	Cal-A	.158	5	19	4	3	1	0	0	0	3	2	0	O
1986	Cal-A	.222	7	27	2	6	0	0	1	7	4	5	0	O
Total 3		.197	16	61	7	12	1	0	1	8	8	8	0	
■ Brian Doyle														
1978	NY-A	.286	3	7	0	2	0	0	0	0	1	1	1	0	2
■ Denny Doyle														
1975	Bos-A	.273	3	11	3	3	0	0	0	2	0	1	0	2
■ Dan Driessen														
1973	Cin-N	.167	4	12	0	2	1	0	0	1	0	2	0	3
1976	Cin-N	.000	1	1	0	0	0	0	0	0	0	0	0	H
1979	Cin-N	.083	3	12	1	1	0	0	0	0	1	3	0	1
1987	StL-N	.250	5	12	1	3	2	0	0	1	1	1	0	1*4
Total 4		.162	13	37	2	6	3	0	0	2	2	6	0	
■ Keith Drumright														
1981	Oak-A	.000	3	4	0	0	0	0	0	0	0	1	0	0	D*1
■ Rob Ducey														
1991	Tor-A	.000	1	1	0	0	0	0	0	0	0	0	0	O
■ Frank Duffy														
1971	SF-N	.000	1	1	0	0	0	0	0	0	0	1	0	H
■ Dave Duncan														
1971	Oak-A	.500	2	6	0	3	1	0	0	0	0	0	0	C
1972	Oak-A	.000	2	2	0	0	0	0	0	0	1	1	0	C
Total 2		.375	4	8	0	3	1	0	0	2	1	1	0	
■ Mariano Duncan														
1985	LA-N	.222	5	18	2	4	2	1	0	1	1	3	1	S
1990	Cin-N	.300	6	20	1	6	0	0	1	4	0	8	0	2
1993	Phi-N	.267	3	15	3	4	0	2	0	0	0	5	0	2
Total 3		.264	14	53	6	14	2	3	1	5	1	16	1	
■ Shawon Dunston														
1989	Chi-N	.316	5	19	2	6	0	0	0	0	1	1	1	S
■ Leon Durham														
1984	Chi-N	.150	5	20	2	3	0	0	2	4	1	4	0	1
■ Jim Dwyer														
1983	Bal-A	.250	2	4	1	1	0	0	0	0	1	0	0	O*1
■ Jerry Dybzinski														
1983	Chi-A	.250	2	4	0	1	0	0	0	0	0	0	0	S
■ Duffy Dyer														
1975	Pit-N	—	1	0	0	0	0	0	0	0	1	1	0	0	H
■ Lenny Dykstra														
1986	NY-N	.304	6	23	3	7	1	1	1	3	2	4	1	O
1988	NY-N	.429	7	14	6	6	3	0	1	3	4	0	0	O
1993	Phi-N	.280	6	25	5	7	1	0	2	2	5	8	0	O
Total 3		.323	19	62	14	20	5	1	4	8	11	12	1	
■ Mike Easler														
1979	Pit-N	.000	1	1	0	0	0	0	0	0	0	0	0	H
■ Marshall Edwards														
1982	Mil-A	.000	3	1	2	0	0	0	0	0	0	0	1	D*2,O*1

YEAR	TM/L	AVG	G	AB	R	H	2B	3B	HR	RBI	BB	SO	SB	POS
Jim Eisenreich														
1993	Phi-N	.133	6	15	0	2	1	0	0	1	0	2	0	O*5
Kevin Elster														
1986	NY-N	.000	4	3	0	0	0	0	0	0	0	1	0	S
1988	NY-N	.250	5	8	1	2	1	0	0	1	3	0	0	S
Total 2		.182	9	11	1	2	1	0	0	1	3	1	0	
Mike Epstein														
1971	Oak-A	.200	2	5	0	1	0	0	0	0	0	3	0	1*1
1972	Oak-A	.188	5	16	1	3	0	0	1	1	4	5	1	1
Total 2		.190	7	21	1	4	0	0	1	1	4	8	1	
Cecil Espy														
1991	Pit-N	.000	2	2	0	0	0	0	0	0	0	2	0	H
1992	Pit-N	.667	4	3	0	2	0	0	0	0	0	1	0	O*2
Total 2		.400	6	5	0	2	0	0	0	0	0	3	0	
Andy Etchebarren														
1969	Bal-A	.000	2	4	0	0	0	0	0	0	0	0	0	C
1970	Bal-A	.111	2	9	1	1	0	0	0	0	0	3	0	C
1971	Bal-A	.000	2	5	0	0	0	0	0	0	0	0	0	C
1973	Bal-A	.357	4	14	1	5	1	0	1	4	0	1	0	C
1974	Bal-A	.333	2	6	0	2	0	0	0	0	0	0	0	C
Total 5		.211	12	38	2	8	1	0	1	4	0	4	0	
Darrell Evans														
1984	Det-A	.300	3	10	1	3	1	0	0	1	1	0	1	1*3,3*1
1987	Det-A	.294	5	17	0	5	0	0	0	0	4	2	0	1*5,3*1
Total 2		.296	8	27	1	8	1	0	0	1	5	2	1	
Dwight Evans														
1975	Bos-A	.100	3	10	1	1	1	0	0	0	1	2	0	O
1986	Bos-A	.214	7	28	2	6	1	0	4	3	3	0	0	O
1988	Bos-A	.167	4	12	1	2	1	0	0	1	3	5	0	O
1990	Bos-A	.231	4	13	0	3	1	0	0	1	0	3	0	D
Total 4		.190	18	63	4	12	4	0	1	5	8	13	0	
Junior Felix														
1989	Tor-A	.273	3	11	0	3	1	0	0	3	0	2	0	O
Joe Ferguson														
1974	LA-N	.231	4	13	3	3	0	0	0	2	5	1	0	O*3,C*2
1978	LA-N	.000	2	2	0	0	0	0	0	0	0	1	0	H
Total 2		.200	6	15	3	3	0	0	0	2	5	2	0	
Tony Fernandez														
1985	Tor-A	.333	7	24	2	8	2	0	0	2	1	2	0	S
1989	Tor-A	.350	5	20	6	7	3	0	0	1	1	2	5	S
1993	Tor-A	.318	6	22	1	7	0	0	0	1	2	4	0	S
Total 3		.333	18	66	9	22	5	0	0	4	4	8	5	
Cecil Fielder														
1985	Tor-A	.333	3	3	0	1	1	0	0	0	0	1	0	H
Jack Fimple														
1983	LA-N	.143	3	7	0	1	0	0	0	1	0	3	0	C
Carlton Fisk														
1975	Bos-A	.417	3	12	4	5	1	0	0	2	0	2	1	C
1983	Chi-A	.176	4	17	0	3	1	0	0	0	1	3	0	C
Total 2		.276	7	29	4	8	2	0	0	2	1	5	1	
Tim Flannery														
1984	SD-N	.500	3	2	1	1	0	0	0	0	0	0	0	H
Scott Fletcher														
1983	Chi-A	.000	3	7	0	0	0	0	0	0	0	1	0	S
Doug Flynn														
1976	Cin-N	—	1	0	0	0	0	0	0	0	0	0	0	2
Tim Foli														
1979	Pit-N	.333	3	12	1	4	1	0	0	3	0	0	0	S
1982	Cal-A	.125	5	16	0	2	0	0	0	1	0	3	0	S
Total 2		.214	8	28	1	6	1	0	0	4	0	3	0	
Barry Foote														
1978	Phi-N	.000	1	1	0	0	0	0	0	0	0	1	0	H
1981	NY-A	1.000	2	1	0	1	0	0	0	0	0	0	0	C*1
Total 2		.500	3	2	0	1	0	0	0	0	0	1	0	
Curt Ford														
1987	StL-N	.333	4	9	2	3	0	0	0	0	1	1	0	O
Dan Ford														
1979	Cal-A	.294	4	17	2	5	1	0	2	4	0	0	0	O
1983	Bal-A	.200	2	5	0	1	1	0	0	0	0	1	0	O*1
Total 2		.273	6	22	2	6	2	0	2	4	0	1	0	
Ray Fosse														
1973	Oak-A	.091	5	11	2	1	1	0	0	3	2	2	0	C
1974	Oak-A	.333	4	12	1	4	1	0	1	3	1	2	0	C
1975	Oak-A	.000	1	2	0	0	0	0	0	0	0	1	0	C
Total 3		.200	10	25	3	5	2	0	1	6	3	5	0	
George Foster														
1972	Cin-N	—	1	0	1	0	0	0	0	0	0	0	0	R
1975	Cin-N	.364	3	11	3	4	0	0	0	1	2	1	0	O
1976	Cin-N	.167	3	12	2	2	0	0	0	0	1	2	0	O
1979	Cin-N	.200	3	10	1	2	0	0	1	2	4	3	0	O
Total 4		.242	10	33	7	8	0	0	3	6	5	9	1	
Eric Fox														
1992	Oak-A	.000	4	1	0	0	0	0	0	0	1	0	2	O*1,D*1
Terry Francona														
1981	Mon-N	.000	2	1	0	0	0	0	0	0	0	1	0	O*1
Bill Freehan														
1972	Det-A	.250	3	12	2	3	1	0	1	3	0	1	0	C
Tito Fuentes														
1971	SF-N	.313	4	16	4	5	1	0	1	2	1	3	0	2
Gary Gaetti														
1987	Min-A	.300	5	20	5	6	1	0	2	5	1	3	0	3
Phil Gagliano														
1973	Cin-N	.000	3	3	0	0	0	0	0	0	0	2	0	H
Greg Gagne														
1987	Min-A	.278	5	18	5	5	3	0	2	3	3	4	0	S
1991	Min-A	.235	5	17	1	4	0	0	0	1	1	5	0	S
Total 2		.257	10	35	6	9	3	0	2	4	4	9	0	
Al Gallagher														
1971	SF-N	.100	4	10	0	1	0	0	0	0	0	2	0	3
Mike Gallego														
1988	Oak-A	.083	4	12	1	1	0	0	0	0	0	3	0	2
1989	Oak-A	.273	4	11	3	3	1	0	0	1	0	2	0	2*2,S*2
1990	Oak-A	.400	4	10	1	4	1	0	0	2	1	1	0	S*3,2*2
Total 3		.242	12	33	5	8	2	0	0	3	1	6	0	
Oscar Gamble														
1976	NY-A	.250	3	8	1	2	1	0	0	1	1	0	0	O
1980	NY-A	.200	2	5	1	1	0	0	0	1	1	0	0	O*1,D*1
1981	NY-A	.167	3	6	2	1	0	0	0	1	5	3	0	D*2,O*1
Total 3		.211	8	19	4	4	1	0	0	2	7	5	0	
Ron Gant														
1991	Atl-N	.259	7	27	4	7	1	0	1	3	2	4	7	O
1992	Atl-N	.182	7	22	5	4	0	0	2	6	4	4	1	O
1993	Atl-N	.185	6	27	4	5	3	0	0	3	2	9	0	O
Total 3		.211	20	76	13	16	4	0	3	12	8	17	8	
Jim Gantner														
1982	Mil-A	.188	5	16	1	3	0	0	0	2	1	1	0	2
Barbaro Garbey														
1984	Det-A	.333	3	9	1	3	0	0	0	0	0	1	0	D*2
Kiko Garcia														
1979	Bal-A	.273	3	11	1	3	0	0	0	2	2	4	0	S
Carlos Garcia														
1992	Pit-N	.000	1	1	0	0	0	0	0	0	0	0	0	2
Damaso Garcia														
1985	Tor-A	.233	7	30	4	7	4	0	0	1	3	3	0	2
Phil Garner														
1975	Oak-A	.000	3	5	0	0	0	0	0	0	0	1	0	2
1979	Pit-N	.417	3	12	4	5	0	1	1	1	1	0	0	2*3,S*1
1986	Hou-N	.222	3	9	1	2	1	0	0	2	1	2	0	3
Total 3		.269	9	26	5	7	1	1	1	3	2	3	0	
Wayne Garrett														
1969	NY-N	.385	3	13	3	5	2	0	1	3	2	2	1	3
1973	NY-N	.087	5	23	1	2	1	0	0	1	0	5	0	3
Total 2		.194	8	36	4	7	3	0	1	4	2	7	1	
Gil Garrido														
1969	Atl-N	.200	3	10	0	2	0	0	0	0	1	1	0	S
Steve Garvey														
1974	LA-N	.389	4	18	4	7	1	0	2	5	1	1	0	1
1977	LA-N	.308	4	13	2	4	0	0	0	0	2	1	1	1
1978	LA-N	.389	4	18	6	7	1	1	4	7	0	1	0	1
1981	LA-N	.286	5	21	0	6	1	0	0	1	2	0	0	1
1984	SD-N	.400	5	20	1	8	1	0	1	7	1	2	0	1
Total 5		.356	22	90	15	32	3	1	8	21	4	9	1	
Rod Gaspar														
1969	NY-N	—	3	0	0	0	0	0	0	0	0	0	0	O
Rich Gedman														
1986	Bos-A	.357	7	28	4	10	1	0	1	6	0	4	0	C
1988	Bos-A	.357	4	14	1	5	0	0	1	1	2	1	0	C
Total 2		.357	11	42	5	15	1	0	2	7	2	5	0	
Cesar Geronimo														
1972	Cin-N	.100	5	20	2	2	0	0	1	0	2	0	0	O
1973	Cin-N	.067	4	15	0	1	0	0	0	0	0	7	0	O
1975	Cin-N	.000	3	10	0	0	0	0	0	1	1	7	0	O
1976	Cin-N	.182	3	11	0	2	0	0	0	2	1	3	0	O
1979	Cin-N	.143	3	7	0	1	0	0	0	0	0	5	0	O
Total 5		.095	17	63	2	6	0	0	1	4	4	24	0	
Kirk Gibson														
1984	Det-A	.417	3	12	2	5	1	0	1	2	2	1	1	O
1987	Det-A	.286	5	21	4	6	1	1	0	4	3	8	3	O
1988	LA-N	.154	7	26	2	4	0	0	2	6	3	6	2	O
Total 3		.254	15	59	8	15	2	1	4	12	8	15	6	
Joe Girardi														
1989	Chi-N	.100	4	10	1	1	0	0	0	0	1	2	0	C

YEAR	TM/L	AVG	G	AB	R	H	2B	3B	HR	RBI	BB	SO	SB	POS
■ Dan Gladden														
1987	Min-A	.350	5	20	5	7	2	0	0	5	2	1	0	O
1991	Min-A	.261	5	23	4	6	0	0	0	3	1	3	3	O
Total 2		.302	10	43	9	13	2	0	0	8	3	4	3	
■ Rene Gonzales														
1991	Tor-A	—	2	0	0	0	0	0	0	0	0	0	0	1*1,S*1
■ Tony Gonzalez														
1969	Atl-N	.357	3	14	4	5	1	0	1	2	1	4	0	O
■ Jose Gonzalez														
1988	LA-N	—	4	0	2	0	0	0	0	0	0	0	0	O*3
■ Orlando Gonzalez														
1978	Phi-N	.000	1	1	0	0	0	0	0	0	0	1	0	H
■ Ed Goodson														
1977	LA-N	.000	1	1	0	0	0	0	0	0	0	0	0	H
■ Mark Grace														
1989	Chi-N	.647	5	17	3	11	3	1	1	8	4	1	1	1
■ Craig Grebeck														
1993	Chi-A	1.000	1	1	0	1	0	0	0	0	0	0	0	3
■ David Green														
1982	StL-N	1.000	2	1	1	1	0	0	0	0	0	0	0	O
■ Dick Green														
1971	Oak-A	.286	3	7	0	2	0	0	0	1	1	0	2	
1972	Oak-A	.125	5	8	0	1	1	0	0	0	0	0	2	
1973	Oak-A	.077	5	13	0	1	1	0	0	1	1	4	0	2
1974	Oak-A	.222	4	9	0	2	0	0	0	2	1	0	2	
Total 4		.162	17	37	0	6	2	0	0	1	4	6	0	
■ Mike Greenwell														
1986	Bos-A	.500	2	2	0	1	0	0	0	0	0	0	0	H
1988	Bos-A	.214	4	14	2	3	1	0	1	3	3	0	0	O
1990	Bos-A	.000	4	14	1	0	0	0	0	2	2	0	0	O
Total 3		.133	10	30	3	4	1	0	1	3	5	2	0	
■ Tommy Gregg														
1991	Atl-N	.250	4	4	0	1	0	0	0	0	0	2	0	H
■ Bobby Grich														
1973	Bal-A	.100	5	20	1	2	0	0	1	1	2	5	0	2
1974	Bal-A	.250	4	16	2	4	1	0	1	2	0	1	0	2
1979	Cal-A	.154	4	13	0	2	1	0	0	1	2	1	0	2
1982	Cal-A	.200	5	15	1	3	1	0	0	1	2	7	0	2
1986	Cal-A	.208	6	24	1	5	0	0	1	3	0	8	0	2*3,1*3
Total 5		.182	24	88	5	16	3	0	3	9	5	22	0	
■ Ken Griffey														
1973	Cin-N	.143	3	7	0	1	1	0	0	0	0	1	0	O*2
1975	Cin-N	.333	3	12	4	4	1	0	0	4	0	3	3	O
1976	Cin-N	.385	3	13	2	5	0	1	0	2	2	1	2	O
Total 3		.313	9	32	6	10	2	1	0	6	2	5	5	
■ Alfredo Griffin														
1988	LA-N	.160	7	25	1	4	1	0	0	3	0	5	0	S
1992	Tor-A	.000	2	2	0	0	0	0	0	0	0	0	0	S*1
Total 2		.148	9	27	1	4	1	0	0	3	0	5	0	
■ Greg Gross														
1980	Phi-N	.750	4	4	2	3	0	0	0	1	0	0	0	O*1
1983	Phi-N	.000	4	5	1	0	0	0	0	0	2	2	0	O*3
Total 2		.333	8	9	3	3	0	0	0	1	2	2	0	—
■ Wayne Gross														
1981	Oak-A	.000	3	5	0	0	0	0	0	0	0	0	3	
■ Jerry Grote														
1969	NY-N	.167	3	12	3	2	1	0	0	1	1	4	0	C
1973	NY-N	.211	5	19	2	4	0	0	0	2	1	3	0	C
1977	LA-N	—	2	0	0	0	0	0	0	0	1	0	0	C*1
1978	LA-N	—	1	0	0	0	0	0	0	0	0	0	0	C
Total 4		.194	11	31	5	6	1	0	0	3	3	7	0	
■ Johnny Grubb														
1984	Det-A	.250	1	4	0	1	1	0	0	2	0	0	0	D
1987	Det-A	.571	4	7	0	4	0	0	0	0	1	0	0	D*1
Total 2		.455	5	11	0	5	1	0	0	2	1	0	0	
■ Kelly Gruber														
1989	Tor-A	.294	5	17	2	5	1	0	0	1	3	2	1	3
1991	Tor-A	.286	5	21	1	6	1	0	0	4	0	4	1	3
1992	Tor-A	.091	7	22	3	2	1	0	1	2	2	3	0	3
Total 3		.217	17	60	6	13	3	0	1	7	5	9	2	
■ Pedro Guerrero														
1981	LA-N	.105	5	19	1	2	0	0	1	2	1	4	0	O
1983	LA-N	.250	4	12	1	3	1	1	0	2	3	3	0	3
1985	LA-N	.250	6	20	2	5	1	0	0	4	5	2	2	O
Total 3		.196	15	51	4	10	2	1	1	8	9	9	2	
■ Ron Guidry														
1976	NY-A	—	1	0	0	0	0	0	0	0	0	0	0	R
1977	NY-A	—	2	0	0	0	0	0	0	0	0	0	0	P
1978	NY-A	—	1	0	0	0	0	0	0	0	0	0	0	P
1980	NY-A	—	1	0	0	0	0	0	0	0	0	0	0	P
Total 4		—	5	0	0	0	0	0	0	0	0	0	0	

YEAR	TM/L	AVG	G	AB	R	H	2B	3B	HR	RBI	BB	SO	SB	POS
■ Ozzie Guillen														
1993	Chi-A	.273	6	22	4	6	1	0	0	2	0	2	1	S
■ Tony Gwynn														
1984	SD-N	.368	5	19	6	7	3	0	0	3	1	2	0	O
■ Joe Hague														
1972	Cin-N	.000	3	1	0	0	0	0	0	0	2	1	0	H
■ Don Hahn														
1973	NY-N	.235	5	17	2	4	0	0	0	1	2	4	0	O
■ Jerry Hairston														
1983	Chi-A	.000	2	3	0	0	0	0	0	0	1	1	0	O
■ Tom Haller														
1972	Det-A	.000	1	1	0	0	0	0	0	0	0	0	0	H
■ Jeff Hamilton														
1988	LA-N	.217	7	23	2	5	0	0	0	1	3	4	0	3
■ Larry Harlow														
1979	Cal-A	.125	3	8	0	1	1	0	0	1	1	2	0	O*2
■ Terry Harmon														
1976	Phi-N	—	1	0	1	0	0	0	0	0	0	0	0	R
■ Brian Harper														
1985	StL-N	.000	1	1	0	0	0	0	0	0	0	0	0	H
1991	Min-A	.278	5	18	1	5	2	0	0	1	0	2	0	C
Total 2		.263	6	19	1	5	2	0	0	1	0	2	0	
■ Terry Harper														
1982	Atl-N	.000	1	1	1	0	0	0	0	0	0	0	0	O
■ Tommy Harper														
1975	Oak-A	—	1	0	0	0	0	0	0	0	1	0	0	H
■ Bud Harrelson														
1969	NY-N	.182	3	11	2	2	1	1	0	3	1	2	0	S
1973	NY-N	.167	5	18	1	3	0	0	0	2	1	1	0	S
Total 2		.172	8	29	3	5	1	1	0	5	2	3	0	
■ Jim Ray Hart														
1971	SF-N	.000	3	5	0	0	0	0	0	0	0	2	0	3*1
■ Ron Hassey														
1988	Oak-A	.500	4	8	2	4	1	0	1	3	1	1	0	C
1989	Oak-A	.167	2	6	0	1	0	0	0	1	1	2	0	C
1990	Oak-A	.333	2	3	0	1	0	0	0	0	2	0	0	C*1,D*1
Total 3		.353	8	17	2	6	1	0	1	4	4	3	0	
■ Mickey Hatcher														
1988	LA-N	.238	6	21	4	5	2	0	0	3	3	0	0	1*6,O*1
■ Billy Hatcher														
1986	Hou-N	.280	6	25	4	7	0	0	1	2	3	2	3	O
1990	Cin-N	.333	4	15	2	5	1	0	1	2	0	2	0	O
Total 2		.300	10	40	6	12	1	0	2	4	3	4	3	
■ Von Hayes														
1983	Phi-N	.000	2	2	0	0	0	0	0	0	0	0	0	O*1
■ Jeff Hearron														
1985	Tor-A	—	2	0	0	0	0	0	0	0	0	0	0	C
■ Mike Heath														
1981	Oak-A	.333	3	6	1	2	0	0	0	0	0	1	0	C*2,O*1
1987	Det-A	.286	3	7	1	2	0	0	1	2	0	0	0	C
Total 2		.308	6	13	2	4	0	0	1	2	0	1	0	
■ Richie Hebner														
1970	Pit-N	.667	2	6	0	4	2	0	0	2	1	0	3	
1971	Pit-N	.294	4	17	3	5	1	0	2	4	0	4	0	3
1972	Pit-N	.188	5	16	2	3	1	0	0	1	1	3	0	3
1974	Pit-N	.231	4	13	1	3	0	0	1	4	1	4	0	3
1975	Pit-N	.333	3	12	2	4	1	0	0	2	1	1	0	3
1977	Phi-N	.357	4	14	2	5	2	0	0	0	1	0	0	1*3
1978	Phi-N	.111	3	9	0	1	0	0	0	0	0	0	0	1*2
1984	Chi-N	.000	2	1	0	0	0	0	0	0	0	2	0	H
Total 8		.284	27	88	10	25	7	0	3	12	5	14	0	
■ Danny Heep														
1980	Hou-N	.000	1	1	0	0	0	0	0	0	0	0	0	H
1986	NY-N	.250	5	4	0	1	0	0	0	1	0	2	0	O*1
1988	LA-N	.000	3	1	0	0	0	0	0	0	1	1	0	H
1990	Bos-A	.000	2	2	0	0	0	0	0	0	0	0	0	H
Total 4		.125	11	8	0	1	0	0	0	1	1	3	0	
■ Mike Hegan														
1971	Oak-A	.000	1	1	0	0	0	0	0	0	0	0	0	H
1972	Oak-A	.000	3	1	1	0	0	0	0	0	0	0	0	1*1
Total 2		.000	4	2	1	0	0	0	0	0	0	0	1	0
■ Tommy Helms														
1970	Cin-N	.273	3	11	0	3	0	0	0	0	0	1	0	2
■ Dave Henderson														
1986	Bos-A	.111	5	9	3	1	0	0	1	4	2	2	0	O
1988	Oak-A	.375	4	16	2	6	1	0	1	4	1	7	0	O
1989	Oak-A	.263	5	19	4	5	3	0	1	2	5	0	0	O
1990	Oak-A	.167	2	6	0	1	0	0	0	0	2	1	0	O
Total 4		.260	16	50	9	13	4	0	3	10	5	16	1	

Ken Henderson

YEAR	TM/L	AVG	G	AB	R	H	2B	3B	HR	RBI	BB	SO	SB	POS
1971	SF-N	.313	4	16	3	5	1	0	0	2	2	1	0	O

Rickey Henderson

YEAR	TM/L	AVG	G	AB	R	H	2B	3B	HR	RBI	BB	SO	SB	POS
1981	Oak-A	.364	3	11	0	4	2	1	0	1	1	2	2	O
1989	Oak-A	.400	5	15	8	6	1	1	2	5	7	0	8	O
1990	Oak-A	.294	4	17	1	5	0	0	0	3	1	2	2	O
1992	Oak-A	.261	6	23	5	6	0	0	0	1	4	4	2	O
1993	Tor-A	.120	6	25	4	3	2	0	0	0	4	5	2	O
Total 5		.264	24	91	18	24	5	2	2	10	17	13	16	

George Hendrick

YEAR	TM/L	AVG	G	AB	R	H	2B	3B	HR	RBI	BB	SO	SB	POS
1972	Oak-A	.143	5	7	2	1	0	0	0	0	0	1	0	O*1
1982	StL-N	.308	3	13	2	4	0	0	0	2	1	2	0	O
1986	Cal-A	.083	3	12	0	1	0	0	0	0	0	2	0	O*2,1*1
Total 3		.188	11	32	4	6	0	0	0	2	1	5	0	

Ellie Hendricks

YEAR	TM/L	AVG	G	AB	R	H	2B	3B	HR	RBI	BB	SO	SB	POS
1969	Bal-A	.250	3	8	2	2	2	0	0	3	1	2	0	C
1970	Bal-A	.400	1	5	2	2	0	0	0	0	1	0	0	C
1971	Bal-A	.500	2	4	1	2	0	0	1	2	1	1	0	C
1974	Bal-A	.167	3	6	1	1	0	0	0	0	1	3	0	C
1976	NY-A	1.000	1	1	0	1	0	0	0	0	0	0	0	H
Total 5		.333	10	24	6	8	2	0	1	5	3	7	0	

Jackie Hernandez

YEAR	TM/L	AVG	G	AB	R	H	2B	3B	HR	RBI	BB	SO	SB	POS
1971	Pit-N	.231	4	13	2	3	0	0	0	1	0	4	0	S

Keith Hernandez

YEAR	TM/L	AVG	G	AB	R	H	2B	3B	HR	RBI	BB	SO	SB	POS
1982	StL-N	.333	3	12	3	4	0	0	0	1	2	3	0	1
1986	NY-N	.269	6	26	3	7	1	1	0	3	3	6	0	1
1988	NY-N	.269	7	26	2	7	0	0	1	5	6	7	1	1
Total 3		.281	16	64	8	18	1	1	1	9	11	16	1	

Larry Herndon

YEAR	TM/L	AVG	G	AB	R	H	2B	3B	HR	RBI	BB	SO	SB	POS
1984	Det-A	.200	2	5	1	1	0	0	0	1	1	2	0	O
1987	Det-A	.333	3	9	1	3	1	0	0	2	1	1	0	O*2,D*1
Total 2		.286	5	14	2	4	1	0	1	3	2	3	0	

Tom Herr

YEAR	TM/L	AVG	G	AB	R	H	2B	3B	HR	RBI	BB	SO	SB	POS
1982	StL-N	.231	3	13	1	3	1	0	0	0	1	2	0	2
1985	StL-N	.333	6	21	2	7	4	0	1	6	5	2	1	2
1987	StL-N	.222	7	27	0	6	0	0	0	3	0	1	1	2
Total 3		.262	16	61	3	16	5	0	1	9	6	5	2	

Dave Hollins

YEAR	TM/L	AVG	G	AB	R	H	2B	3B	HR	RBI	BB	SO	SB	POS
1993	Phi-N	.200	6	20	2	4	1	0	2	4	5	4	1	3

Jim Holt

YEAR	TM/L	AVG	G	AB	R	H	2B	3B	HR	RBI	BB	SO	SB	POS
1970	Min-A	.000	3	5	0	0	0	0	0	0	0	2	0	O
1974	Oak-A	—	2	0	0	0	0	0	0	0	1	0	0	1*1
1975	Oak-A	.333	3	3	0	1	0	0	0	0	0	0	0	1*1
Total 3		.125	8	8	0	1	0	0	0	1	2	0		

Don Hopkins

YEAR	TM/L	AVG	G	AB	R	H	2B	3B	HR	RBI	BB	SO	SB	POS
1975	Oak-A	—	1	0	0	0	0	0	0	0	0	0	0	D

Bob Horner

YEAR	TM/L	AVG	G	AB	R	H	2B	3B	HR	RBI	BB	SO	SB	POS
1982	Atl-N	.091	3	11	0	1	0	0	0	0	0	2	0	3

Willie Horton

YEAR	TM/L	AVG	G	AB	R	H	2B	3B	HR	RBI	BB	SO	SB	POS
1972	Det-A	.100	5	10	0	1	0	0	0	0	1	3	0	O*3

Art Howe

YEAR	TM/L	AVG	G	AB	R	H	2B	3B	HR	RBI	BB	SO	SB	POS
1974	Pit-N	.000	1	1	0	0	0	0	0	0	0	0	0	H
1980	Hou-N	.200	5	15	0	3	1	1	0	2	2	2	0	1*4
Total 2		.188	6	16	0	3	1	1	0	2	2	2	0	

Jack Howell

YEAR	TM/L	AVG	G	AB	R	H	2B	3B	HR	RBI	BB	SO	SB	POS
1986	Cal-A	.000	2	1	0	0	0	0	0	0	1	1	0	H

Roy Howell

YEAR	TM/L	AVG	G	AB	R	H	2B	3B	HR	RBI	BB	SO	SB	POS
1982	Mil-A	.000	1	3	0	0	0	0	0	0	0	1	0	D

Kent Hrbek

YEAR	TM/L	AVG	G	AB	R	H	2B	3B	HR	RBI	BB	SO	SB	POS
1987	Min-A	.150	5	20	4	3	0	0	1	1	3	0	0	1
1991	Min-A	.143	5	21	0	3	0	0	0	3	1	3	0	1
Total 2		.146	10	41	4	6	0	0	1	4	4	3	0	

Glenn Hubbard

YEAR	TM/L	AVG	G	AB	R	H	2B	3B	HR	RBI	BB	SO	SB	POS
1982	Atl-N	.222	3	9	1	2	0	0	0	1	0	3	0	2

Brian Hunter

YEAR	TM/L	AVG	G	AB	R	H	2B	3B	HR	RBI	BB	SO	SB	POS
1991	Atl-N	.333	5	18	2	6	2	0	1	4	0	2	0	1
1992	Atl-N	.200	3	5	1	1	0	0	0	0	0	1	0	1*2
Total 2		.304	8	23	3	7	2	0	1	4	0	3	0	

Clint Hurdle

YEAR	TM/L	AVG	G	AB	R	H	2B	3B	HR	RBI	BB	SO	SB	POS
1978	KC-A	.375	4	8	1	3	0	1	0	1	2	3	0	O*2
1980	KC-A	.000	3	2	0	0	0	0	0	0	0	1	0	O
Total 2		.300	7	10	1	3	0	1	0	1	2	4	0	

Tom Hutton

YEAR	TM/L	AVG	G	AB	R	H	2B	3B	HR	RBI	BB	SO	SB	POS
1976	Phi-N	.000	1	1	0	0	0	0	0	0	0	0	0	H
1977	Phi-N	.000	3	3	0	0	0	0	0	0	0	0	0	1*1
Total 2		.000	4	4	0	0	0	0	0	0	0	0	0	

Pete Incaviglia

YEAR	TM/L	AVG	G	AB	R	H	2B	3B	HR	RBI	BB	SO	SB	POS
1993	Phi-N	.167	3	12	2	2	0	0	1	1	0	3	0	O

Dane Iorg

YEAR	TM/L	AVG	G	AB	R	H	2B	3B	HR	RBI	BB	SO	SB	POS
1984	KC-A	.500	2	2	0	1	0	0	0	1	0	0	0	H
1985	KC-A	.500	4	2	0	1	0	0	0	2	0	0	0	H
Total 2		.500	6	4	0	2	1	0	0	3	0	0	0	

Garth Iorg

YEAR	TM/L	AVG	G	AB	R	H	2B	3B	HR	RBI	BB	SO	SB	POS
1985	Tor-A	.133	6	15	1	2	0	0	0	0	1	3	0	3

Reggie Jackson

YEAR	TM/L	AVG	G	AB	R	H	2B	3B	HR	RBI	BB	SO	SB	POS
1971	Oak-A	.333	3	12	2	4	1	0	2	2	0	1	0	O
1972	Oak-A	.278	5	18	1	5	1	0	0	2	1	6	2	O
1973	Oak-A	.143	5	21	0	3	0	0	0	0	0	6	0	O
1974	Oak-A	.167	4	12	0	2	1	0	0	1	5	2	0	D*3,O*1
1975	Oak-A	.417	3	12	1	5	0	0	1	3	0	2	0	O
1977	NY-A	.125	5	16	1	2	0	0	0	1	2	1	1	O*4,D*1
1978	NY-A	.462	4	13	5	6	1	0	2	6	3	4	0	D*3,O*1
1980	NY-A	.273	3	11	1	3	1	0	0	1	4	0	0	O
1981	NY-A	.000	2	4	1	0	0	0	0	1	1	0	1	O
1982	Cal-A	.111	5	18	2	2	0	0	1	2	2	7	0	O
1986	Cal-A	.192	6	26	2	5	2	0	0	2	2	7	0	D
Total 11		.227	45	163	16	37	7	0	6	20	17	41	4	

Sonny Jackson

YEAR	TM/L	AVG	G	AB	R	H	2B	3B	HR	RBI	BB	SO	SB	POS
1969	Atl-N	—	1	0	0	0	0	0	0	0	0	0	0	S

Ron Jackson

YEAR	TM/L	AVG	G	AB	R	H	2B	3B	HR	RBI	BB	SO	SB	POS
1982	Cal-A	1.000	1	1	0	1	0	0	0	0	0	0	0	H

Bo Jackson

YEAR	TM/L	AVG	G	AB	R	H	2B	3B	HR	RBI	BB	SO	SB	POS
1993	Chi-A	.000	3	10	1	0	0	0	0	0	3	6	0	D

Stan Javier

YEAR	TM/L	AVG	G	AB	R	H	2B	3B	HR	RBI	BB	SO	SB	POS
1988	Oak-A	.500	2	4	0	2	0	0	0	1	1	0	0	O
1989	Oak-A	.000	1	2	0	0	0	0	0	0	0	1	0	O
Total 2		.333	3	6	0	2	0	0	0	1	1	1	0	

Gregg Jefferies

YEAR	TM/L	AVG	G	AB	R	H	2B	3B	HR	RBI	BB	SO	SB	POS
1988	NY-N	.333	7	27	2	9	2	0	0	1	4	0	0	3

Doug Jennings

YEAR	TM/L	AVG	G	AB	R	H	2B	3B	HR	RBI	BB	SO	SB	POS
1990	Oak-A	.000	1	1	0	0	0	0	0	0	0	0	0	O

Johnny Jeter

YEAR	TM/L	AVG	G	AB	R	H	2B	3B	HR	RBI	BB	SO	SB	POS
1970	Pit-N	.000	3	2	0	0	0	0	0	0	0	2	0	O*1

Cliff Johnson

YEAR	TM/L	AVG	G	AB	R	H	2B	3B	HR	RBI	BB	SO	SB	POS
1977	NY-A	.400	5	15	2	6	2	0	1	2	1	2	0	D*4
1978	NY-A	.000	1	1	0	0	0	0	0	0	0	0	0	H
1981	Oak-A	.000	2	6	0	0	0	0	0	0	2	2	0	H
1985	Tor-A	.368	7	19	1	7	2	0	0	2	1	4	0	D
Total 4		.317	15	41	3	13	4	0	1	4	4	8	0	

Davey Johnson

YEAR	TM/L	AVG	G	AB	R	H	2B	3B	HR	RBI	BB	SO	SB	POS
1969	Bal-A	.231	3	13	2	3	0	0	0	0	2	1	0	2
1970	Bal-A	.364	3	11	4	4	0	0	2	4	1	1	0	2
1971	Bal-A	.300	3	10	2	3	2	0	0	3	1	0	2	
1977	Phi-N	.250	1	4	0	1	0	0	0	0	2	0	1	1
Total 4		.289	10	38	8	11	2	0	2	6	6	4	0	

Deron Johnson

YEAR	TM/L	AVG	G	AB	R	H	2B	3B	HR	RBI	BB	SO	SB	POS
1973	Oak-A	.100	4	10	0	1	0	0	0	0	2	6	0	D

Howard Johnson

YEAR	TM/L	AVG	G	AB	R	H	2B	3B	HR	RBI	BB	SO	SB	POS
1986	NY-N	.000	2	2	0	0	0	0	0	0	0	0	0	H
1988	NY-N	.056	6	18	3	1	0	0	0	0	1	6	1	S*5,3*1
Total 2		.050	8	20	3	1	0	0	0	0	1	6	1	

Lance Johnson

YEAR	TM/L	AVG	G	AB	R	H	2B	3B	HR	RBI	BB	SO	SB	POS
1987	StL-N	—	1	0	1	0	0	0	0	0	0	0	1	R
1993	Chi-A	.217	6	23	2	5	1	1	1	6	2	1	1	O
Total 2		.217	7	23	3	5	1	1	1	6	2	1	2	

Jay Johnstone

YEAR	TM/L	AVG	G	AB	R	H	2B	3B	HR	RBI	BB	SO	SB	POS
1976	Phi-N	.778	3	9	1	7	1	1	0	2	1	0	0	O*2
1977	Phi-N	.200	2	5	0	1	0	0	0	0	0	1	0	O
1981	LA-N	.000	2	2	0	0	0	0	0	0	0	0	0	H
1985	LA-N	.000	1	1	0	0	0	0	0	0	0	0	0	H
Total 4		.471	8	17	1	8	1	1	0	2	1	1	0	

Cleon Jones

YEAR	TM/L	AVG	G	AB	R	H	2B	3B	HR	RBI	BB	SO	SB	POS
1969	NY-N	.429	3	14	4	6	2	0	1	4	1	2	0	O
1973	NY-N	.300	5	20	3	6	2	0	0	3	2	4	0	O
Total 2		.353	8	34	7	12	4	0	1	7	3	6	2	

Lynn Jones

YEAR	TM/L	AVG	G	AB	R	H	2B	3B	HR	RBI	BB	SO	SB	POS
1984	KC-A	.200	3	5	1	1	0	0	0	0	0	0	0	O*2
1985	KC-A	—	5	0	0	0	0	0	0	0	0	0	0	O
Total 2		.200	8	5	1	1	0	0	0	0	0	0	0	

Ruppert Jones

YEAR	TM/L	AVG	G	AB	R	H	2B	3B	HR	RBI	BB	SO	SB	POS
1984	Det-A	.000	2	5	1	0	0	0	0	0	1	1	0	O
1986	Cal-A	.176	6	17	4	3	1	0	0	2	5	2	0	O*5
Total 2		.136	8	22	5	3	1	0	0	2	6	3	0	

Ricky Jordan

YEAR	TM/L	AVG	G	AB	R	H	2B	3B	HR	RBI	BB	SO	SB	POS
1993	Phi-N	.000	2	1	0	0	0	0	0	0	1	0	0	H

Mike Jorgensen

YEAR	TM/L	AVG	G	AB	R	H	2B	3B	HR	RBI	BB	SO	SB	POS
1985	StL-N	.000	2	2	0	0	0	0	0	0	0	1	0	H

Von Joshua

YEAR	TM/L	AVG	G	AB	R	H	2B	3B	HR	RBI	BB	SO	SB	POS
1974	LA-N	—	1	0	0	0	0	0	0	0	1	0	0	H

Wally Joyner

YEAR	TM/L	AVG	G	AB	R	H	2B	3B	HR	RBI	BB	SO	SB	POS
1986	Cal-A	.455	3	11	3	5	2	0	1	2	2	0	1	

David Justice

YEAR	TM/L	AVG	G	AB	R	H	2B	3B	HR	RBI	BB	SO	SB	POS
1991	Atl-N	.200	7	25	4	5	1	0	1	2	3	7	0	O
1992	Atl-N	.280	7	25	5	7	1	0	2	6	6	2	0	O

YEAR	TM/L	AVG	G	AB	R	H	2B	3B	HR	RBI	BB	SO	SB	POS
1993	Atl-N	.143	6	21	2	3	1	0	0	4	3	3	0	O
Total 3		.211	20	71	11	15	3	0	3	12	12	12	0	

■ Al Kaline

YEAR	TM/L	AVG	G	AB	R	H	2B	3B	HR	RBI	BB	SO	SB	POS
1972	Det-A	.263	5	19	3	5	0	0	1	1	2	2	0	O

■ Ron Karkovice

| 1993 | Chi-A | .000 | 6 | 15 | 0 | 0 | 0 | 0 | 0 | 0 | 1 | 7 | 0 | C |

■ Pat Kelly

| 1979 | Bal-A | .364 | 3 | 11 | 3 | 4 | 0 | 1 | 4 | 1 | 4 | 3 | 2 | D*2,O*1 |

■ Terry Kennedy

1984	SD-N	.222	5	18	2	4	0	0	0	1	1	3	0	C
1989	SF-N	.188	5	16	0	3	1	0	0	1	1	4	0	C
Total 2		.206	10	34	2	7	1	0	0	1	2	7	0	

■ Harmon Killebrew

1969	Min-A	.125	3	8	2	1	1	0	0	0	6	2	0	3
1970	Min-A	.273	3	11	2	3	0	0	2	4	2	4	0	3*2,1*1
Total 2		.211	6	19	4	4	1	0	2	4	8	6	0	

■ Hal King

| 1973 | Cin-N | .500 | 3 | 2 | 0 | 1 | 0 | 0 | 0 | 0 | 1 | 1 | 0 | H |

■ Jeff King

1990	Pit-N	.100	5	10	0	1	0	0	0	0	1	5	0	3*4
1992	Pit-N	.241	7	29	4	7	4	0	0	2	0	1	0	3
Total 2		.205	12	39	4	8	4	0	0	2	1	6	0	

■ Dave Kingman

| 1971 | SF-N | .111 | 4 | 9 | 0 | 1 | 0 | 0 | 0 | 1 | 3 | 3 | 0 | O*2 |

■ Ed Kirkpatrick

1974	Pit-N	.000	3	9	0	0	0	0	0	0	2	0	0	1
1975	Pit-N	.000	2	2	0	0	0	0	0	0	0	0	0	H
Total 2		.000	5	11	0	0	0	0	0	0	2	0	0	

■ Ron Kittle

| 1983 | Chi-A | .286 | 3 | 7 | 1 | 2 | 1 | 0 | 0 | 0 | 1 | 2 | 0 | O |

■ Mickey Klutts

| 1981 | Oak-A | .429 | 3 | 7 | 1 | 3 | 0 | 0 | 0 | 0 | 0 | 1 | 0 | 3 |

■ Ray Knight

1979	Cin-N	.286	3	14	0	4	1	0	0	0	0	2	1	3
1986	NY-N	.167	6	24	1	4	0	0	0	2	1	5	0	3
Total 2		.211	9	38	1	8	1	0	0	2	1	7	1	

■ Chuck Knoblauch

| 1991 | Min-A | .350 | 5 | 20 | 5 | 7 | 2 | 0 | 0 | 3 | 3 | 3 | 2 | 2 |

■ John Knox

| 1972 | Det-A | — | 1 | 0 | 0 | 0 | 0 | 0 | 0 | 0 | 0 | 0 | 0 | R |

■ Andy Kosco

| 1973 | Cin-N | .300 | 3 | 10 | 0 | 3 | 0 | 0 | 0 | 0 | 2 | 3 | 0 | O |

■ Ed Kranepool

1969	NY-N	.250	3	12	2	3	1	0	0	1	1	2	0	1
1973	NY-N	.500	1	2	0	1	0	0	0	2	0	0	0	O
Total 2		.286	4	14	2	4	1	0	0	3	1	2	0	

■ John Kruk

| 1993 | Phi-N | .250 | 6 | 24 | 4 | 6 | 2 | 1 | 1 | 5 | 4 | 5 | 0 | 1 |

■ Ted Kubiak

1972	Oak-A	.500	4	4	0	2	0	0	0	1	0	0	0	2*3,S*1
1973	Oak-A	.000	3	2	0	0	0	0	0	0	0	1	0	2
Total 2		.333	7	6	0	2	0	0	0	1	0	1	0	

■ Rusty Kuntz

| 1984 | Det-A | .000 | 1 | 1 | 0 | 0 | 0 | 0 | 0 | 0 | 0 | 0 | 0 | O |

■ Randy Kutcher

| 1990 | Bos-A | — | 2 | 0 | 0 | 0 | 0 | 0 | 0 | 0 | 0 | 0 | 0 | R |

■ Pete LaCock

1977	KC-A	.000	1	1	0	0	0	0	0	0	0	1	0	1
1978	KC-A	.364	4	11	1	4	2	1	0	1	3	1	1	1*3
1980	KC-A	—	1	0	0	0	0	0	0	0	0	0	1	1
Total 3		.333	6	12	1	4	2	1	0	1	4	2	1	

■ Lee Lacy

1974	LA-N	—	1	0	0	0	0	0	0	0	0	0	0	R
1977	LA-N	1.000	1	1	1	1	0	0	0	0	0	0	0	H
1978	LA-N	.000	2	2	0	0	0	0	0	0	0	0	0	H
Total 3		.333	4	3	1	1	0	0	0	0	0	0	0	

■ Joe Lahoud

| 1977 | KC-A | .000 | 1 | 1 | 2 | 0 | 0 | 0 | 0 | 0 | 2 | 0 | 0 | D |

■ Steve Lake

| 1984 | Chi-N | 1.000 | 1 | 1 | 0 | 1 | 1 | 0 | 0 | 0 | 0 | 0 | 0 | C |

■ Rafael Landestoy

1980	Hou-N	.222	5	9	3	2	0	0	0	2	1	0	1	2*3,S*1
1983	LA-N	.000	2	2	0	0	0	0	0	0	0	1	0	H
Total 2		.182	7	11	3	2	0	0	0	2	1	1	1	

■ Ken Landreaux

1981	LA-N	.100	5	10	1	1	0	0	0	0	3	2	0	O*3
1983	LA-N	.143	4	14	0	2	0	0	0	1	1	3	0	O
1985	LA-N	.389	5	18	4	7	3	0	0	2	1	1	0	O
Total 3		.238	14	42	4	10	4	0	0	3	5	6	0	

■ Tito Landrum

YEAR	TM/L	AVG	G	AB	R	H	2B	3B	HR	RBI	BB	SO	SB	POS
1983	Bal-A	.200	4	10	2	2	0	0	1	1	0	2	0	O*3
1985	StL-N	.429	5	14	2	6	0	0	0	4	1	1	1	O*4
Total 2		.333	9	24	4	8	0	0	1	5	1	3	1	

■ Hal Lanier

| 1971 | SF-N | .000 | 1 | 1 | 0 | 0 | 0 | 0 | 0 | 0 | 0 | 0 | 0 | 3 |

■ Carney Lansford

1979	Cal-A	.294	4	17	2	5	0	0	0	3	1	2	1	3
1988	Oak-A	.294	4	17	4	5	1	0	1	2	0	2	0	3
1989	Oak-A	.455	3	11	2	5	0	0	0	4	2	1	2	3
1990	Oak-A	.438	4	16	2	7	1	0	0	2	0	1	0	3
1992	Oak-A	.167	5	18	0	3	0	0	0	1	1	1	0	3
Total 5		.316	20	79	10	25	2	0	1	12	4	7	3	

■ Barry Larkin

| 1990 | Cin-N | .261 | 6 | 23 | 5 | 6 | 2 | 0 | 0 | 1 | 3 | 1 | 3 | S |

■ Gene Larkin

1987	Min-A	1.000	1	1	0	1	1	0	0	1	0	0	0	H
1991	Min-A	.000	3	3	0	0	0	0	0	0	0	1	0	H
Total 2		.250	4	4	0	1	1	0	0	1	0	1	0	

■ Tim Laudner

| 1987 | Min-A | .071 | 5 | 14 | 1 | 1 | 1 | 0 | 0 | 2 | 2 | 5 | 0 | C |

■ Mike LaValliere

1990	Pit-N	.000	3	6	1	0	0	0	0	0	3	1	0	C
1991	Pit-N	.333	3	6	0	2	0	0	0	1	2	0	0	C
1992	Pit-N	.200	3	10	1	2	0	0	0	0	0	3	0	C
1993	Chi-A	.333	2	3	0	1	0	0	0	0	1	0	0	C
Total 4		.200	11	25	2	5	0	0	0	1	6	4	0	

■ Rudy Law

| 1983 | Chi-A | .389 | 4 | 18 | 1 | 7 | 1 | 0 | 0 | 0 | 0 | 1 | 2 | O |

■ Vance Law

1983	Chi-A	.182	4	11	0	2	0	0	0	1	1	3	0	3
1989	Chi-N	.000	2	3	0	0	0	0	0	0	0	3	0	3*1
Total 2		.143	6	14	0	2	0	0	0	1	1	6	0	

■ Tom Lawless

| 1987 | StL-N | .333 | 3 | 6 | 0 | 2 | 0 | 0 | 0 | 1 | 1 | 0 | 0 | 3*2,O*1 |

■ Manuel Lee

1985	Tor-A	—	1	0	0	0	0	0	0	0	0	0	0	2
1989	Tor-A	.250	2	8	2	2	0	0	0	0	0	1	0	2
1991	Tor-A	.125	5	16	3	2	0	0	0	1	5	5	0	S
1992	Tor-A	.278	6	18	2	5	1	1	0	3	1	2	0	S
Total 4		.214	14	42	7	9	1	1	0	3	2	8	0	

■ Joe Lefebvre

1980	NY-A	—	1	0	0	0	0	0	0	0	0	0	0	O
1983	Phi-N	.000	2	2	0	0	0	0	0	0	1	0	1	O*1
Total 2		.000	3	2	0	0	0	0	0	0	1	0	1	

■ Scott Leius

| 1991 | Min-A | .000 | 3 | 4 | 0 | 0 | 0 | 0 | 0 | 0 | 1 | 1 | 0 | 3 |

■ Mark Lemke

1991	Atl-N	.200	7	20	1	4	1	0	0	1	4	0	0	2
1992	Atl-N	.333	7	21	2	7	1	0	0	2	5	3	0	2*7,3*1
1993	Atl-N	.208	6	24	2	5	2	0	0	4	1	6	0	2
Total 3		.246	20	65	5	16	4	0	0	7	10	9	0	

■ Chet Lemon

1984	Det-A	.000	3	13	1	0	0	0	0	0	0	1	0	O
1987	Det-A	.278	5	18	4	5	0	0	0	2	4	4	0	O
Total 2		.161	8	31	5	5	0	0	0	2	4	5	0	

■ Jeffrey Leonard

1980	Hou-N	.000	3	3	0	0	0	0	0	0	0	2	0	O*1
1987	SF-N	.417	7	24	5	10	0	0	4	5	3	4	0	O
Total 2		.370	10	27	5	10	0	0	4	5	3	6	0	

■ Allan Lewis

| 1973 | Oak-A | — | 2 | 0 | 1 | 0 | 0 | 0 | 0 | 0 | 0 | 0 | 0 | R |

■ Sixto Lezcano

| 1983 | Phi-N | .308 | 4 | 13 | 2 | 4 | 0 | 0 | 1 | 2 | 1 | 1 | 0 | O |

■ Jose Lind

1990	Pit-N	.238	6	21	1	5	1	1	1	2	1	4	0	2
1991	Pit-N	.160	7	25	0	4	0	0	0	3	0	6	0	2
1992	Pit-N	.222	7	27	5	6	2	1	1	5	1	4	0	2
Total 3		.205	20	73	6	15	3	2	2	10	2	14	0	

■ Jim Lindeman

| 1987 | StL-N | .308 | 5 | 13 | 1 | 4 | 0 | 0 | 1 | 3 | 0 | 3 | 0 | 1 |

■ Nelson Liriano

| 1989 | Tor-A | .429 | 3 | 7 | 1 | 3 | 0 | 0 | 0 | 1 | 2 | 0 | 3 | 2 |

■ Greg Litton

| 1989 | SF-N | 1.000 | 1 | 1 | 0 | 1 | 0 | 0 | 0 | 0 | 0 | 0 | 0 | 3 |

■ Steve Lombardozzi

| 1987 | Min-A | .267 | 5 | 15 | 2 | 4 | 0 | 0 | 1 | 2 | 2 | 0 | 2 | |

■ Tony Longmire

| 1993 | Phi-N | .000 | 1 | 1 | 0 | 0 | 0 | 0 | 0 | 0 | 0 | 0 | 1 | 0 | H |

■ Davey Lopes

| 1974 | LA-N | .267 | 4 | 15 | 4 | 4 | 0 | 1 | 0 | 3 | 5 | 1 | 3 | 2 |

YEAR	TM/L	AVG	G	AB	R	H	2B	3B	HR	RBI	BB	SO	SB	POS
1977	LA-N	.235	4	17	2	4	0	0	0	3	2	0	0	2
1978	LA-N	.389	4	18	3	7	1	1	2	5	0	1	1	2
1981	LA-N	.278	5	18	0	5	0	0	0	0	1	3	5	2
1984	Chi-N	.000	2	1	0	0	0	0	0	0	0	0	0	O*1
1986	Hou-N	.000	3	2	1	0	0	0	0	0	1	0	0	H
Total 6		.282	22	71	10	20	1	2	2	11	9	5	9	

■ Javier Lopez

YEAR	TM/L	AVG	G	AB	R	H	2B	3B	HR	RBI	BB	SO	SB	POS
1992	Atl-N	.000	1	1	0	0	0	0	0	0	0	0	0	C

■ John Lowenstein

YEAR	TM/L	AVG	G	AB	R	H	2B	3B	HR	RBI	BB	SO	SB	POS
1979	Bal-A	.167	4	6	2	1	0	0	1	3	2	2	0	O*3
1983	Bal-A	.167	2	6	0	1	1	0	0	2	1	2	0	O
Total 2		.167	6	12	2	2	1	0	1	5	3	4	0	

■ Mike Lum

YEAR	TM/L	AVG	G	AB	R	H	2B	3B	HR	RBI	BB	SO	SB	POS
1969	Atl-N	1.000	2	2	0	2	1	0	0	0	0	0	0	O*1
1976	Cin-N	.000	1	1	0	0	0	0	0	0	0	0	0	H
Total 2		.667	3	3	0	2	1	0	0	0	0	0	0	

■ Greg Luzinski

YEAR	TM/L	AVG	G	AB	R	H	2B	3B	HR	RBI	BB	SO	SB	POS
1976	Phi-N	.273	3	11	2	3	2	0	1	2	1	4	0	O
1977	Phi-N	.286	4	14	2	4	1	0	1	2	3	3	1	O
1978	Phi-N	.375	4	16	3	6	0	1	2	3	1	2	0	O
1980	Phi-N	.294	5	17	3	5	2	0	1	4	0	6	0	O
1983	Chi-A	.133	4	15	0	2	1	0	0	1	5	0	0	D
Total 5		.274	20	73	10	20	6	1	5	11	6	20	1	

■ Fred Lynn

YEAR	TM/L	AVG	G	AB	R	H	2B	3B	HR	RBI	BB	SO	SB	POS
1975	Bos-A	.364	3	11	1	4	1	0	0	3	0	0	0	O
1982	Cal-A	.611	5	18	4	11	2	0	1	5	2	3	0	O
Total 2		.517	8	29	5	15	3	0	1	8	2	3	0	

■ Shane Mack

YEAR	TM/L	AVG	G	AB	R	H	2B	3B	HR	RBI	BB	SO	SB	POS
1991	Min-A	.333	5	18	4	6	1	1	0	3	2	4	2	O

■ Elliott Maddox

YEAR	TM/L	AVG	G	AB	R	H	2B	3B	HR	RBI	BB	SO	SB	POS
1976	NY-A	.222	3	9	0	2	1	0	0	1	0	1	0	O

■ Garry Maddox

YEAR	TM/L	AVG	G	AB	R	H	2B	3B	HR	RBI	BB	SO	SB	POS
1976	Phi-N	.231	3	13	2	3	1	0	0	2	2	0	0	O
1977	Phi-N	.429	2	7	1	3	0	0	0	2	0	1	0	O
1978	Phi-N	.263	4	19	1	5	0	0	0	2	0	3	0	O
1980	Phi-N	.300	5	20	2	6	2	0	0	3	2	2	2	O
1983	Phi-N	.273	3	11	0	3	1	0	0	1	0	1	0	O
Total 5		.286	17	70	6	20	4	0	0	10	4	7	2	

■ Bill Madlock

YEAR	TM/L	AVG	G	AB	R	H	2B	3B	HR	RBI	BB	SO	SB	POS
1979	Pit-N	.250	3	12	1	3	0	0	1	2	2	0	2	3
1985	LA-N	.333	6	24	5	8	1	0	3	7	0	2	1	3
1987	Det-A	.000	1	5	0	0	0	0	0	0	0	3	0	D
Total 3		.268	10	41	6	11	1	0	4	9	2	5	3	

■ Dave Magadan

YEAR	TM/L	AVG	G	AB	R	H	2B	3B	HR	RBI	BB	SO	SB	POS
1988	NY-N	.000	3	3	0	0	0	0	0	0	0	2	0	H

■ Candy Maldonado

YEAR	TM/L	AVG	G	AB	R	H	2B	3B	HR	RBI	BB	SO	SB	POS
1983	LA-N	.000	2	2	0	0	0	0	0	0	0	1	0	H
1985	LA-N	.143	4	7	0	1	0	0	0	1	0	3	0	O*3
1987	SF-N	.211	5	19	2	4	1	0	0	2	0	3	0	O
1989	SF-N	.000	3	3	1	0	0	0	0	1	2	0	0	O
1991	Tor-A	.100	5	20	1	2	1	0	0	1	1	6	0	O
1992	Tor-A	.273	6	22	3	6	0	0	2	6	2	4	0	O
Total 6		.178	25	73	7	13	2	0	2	11	5	17	0	

■ Angel Mangual

YEAR	TM/L	AVG	G	AB	R	H	2B	3B	HR	RBI	BB	SO	SB	POS
1971	Oak-A	.167	3	12	1	2	1	1	0	2	0	1	0	O
1972	Oak-A	.000	3	3	0	0	0	0	0	0	1	0	0	H
1973	Oak-A	.111	3	9	1	1	0	0	0	0	3	0	0	O
1974	Oak-A	.250	1	4	0	1	0	0	0	0	0	0	0	D
Total 4		.143	10	28	2	4	1	1	0	2	0	5	0	

■ Chuck Manuel

YEAR	TM/L	AVG	G	AB	R	H	2B	3B	HR	RBI	BB	SO	SB	POS
1969	Min-A	.000	1	0	0	0	0	0	0	0	1	0	0	H
1970	Min-A	.000	1	1	0	0	0	0	0	0	0	1	0	H
Total 2		.000	2	1	0	0	0	0	0	0	1	1	0	

■ Jerry Manuel

YEAR	TM/L	AVG	G	AB	R	H	2B	3B	HR	RBI	BB	SO	SB	POS
1981	Mon-N	—	1	0	0	0	0	0	0	0	0	0	0	R

■ Kirt Manwaring

YEAR	TM/L	AVG	G	AB	R	H	2B	3B	HR	RBI	BB	SO	SB	POS
1989	SF-N	.000	3	2	0	0	0	0	0	0	0	0	0	C

■ Gonzalo Marquez

YEAR	TM/L	AVG	G	AB	R	H	2B	3B	HR	RBI	BB	SO	SB	POS
1972	Oak-A	.667	3	3	1	2	0	0	0	1	0	0	0	H

■ Mike Marshall

YEAR	TM/L	AVG	G	AB	R	H	2B	3B	HR	RBI	BB	SO	SB	POS
1983	LA-N	.133	4	15	1	2	1	0	1	2	1	6	0	1*3,O*2
1985	LA-N	.217	6	23	1	5	2	0	1	3	1	3	0	O
1988	LA-N	.233	7	30	3	7	1	1	0	5	2	9	0	O
1990	Bos-A	.333	3	3	0	1	0	0	0	0	0	0	0	H
Total 4		.211	20	71	5	15	4	1	2	10	4	18	0	

■ Jerry Martin

YEAR	TM/L	AVG	G	AB	R	H	2B	3B	HR	RBI	BB	SO	SB	POS
1976	Phi-N	.000	1	1	0	0	0	0	0	0	0	0	0	O
1977	Phi-N	.000	3	4	1	0	0	0	0	0	0	2	0	O*1
1978	Phi-N	.222	4	9	1	2	1	0	0	1	2	1	3	O*3
Total 3		.143	8	14	2	2	1	0	1	2	1	5	0	

■ J. C. Martin

YEAR	TM/L	AVG	G	AB	R	H	2B	3B	HR	RBI	BB	SO	SB	POS
1969	NY-N	.500	2	2	0	1	0	0	0	2	0	0	0	H

■ Carmelo Martinez

YEAR	TM/L	AVG	G	AB	R	H	2B	3B	HR	RBI	BB	SO	SB	POS
1984	SD-N	.176	5	17	1	3	0	0	0	0	2	4	0	O
1990	Pit-N	.250	2	8	0	2	2	0	0	2	0	1	0	1
Total 2		.200	7	25	1	5	2	0	0	2	2	5	0	

■ Buck Martinez

YEAR	TM/L	AVG	G	AB	R	H	2B	3B	HR	RBI	BB	SO	SB	POS
1976	KC-A	.333	5	15	0	5	0	0	0	4	1	3	0	C

■ Ted Martinez

YEAR	TM/L	AVG	G	AB	R	H	2B	3B	HR	RBI	BB	SO	SB	POS
1975	Oak-A	—	3	0	0	0	0	0	0	0	0	0	0	2

■ Jim Mason

YEAR	TM/L	AVG	G	AB	R	H	2B	3B	HR	RBI	BB	SO	SB	POS
1976	NY-A	—	2	0	0	0	0	0	0	0	0	0	0	S

■ Gary Matthews

YEAR	TM/L	AVG	G	AB	R	H	2B	3B	HR	RBI	BB	SO	SB	POS
1983	Phi-N	.429	4	14	4	6	0	0	3	8	2	1	0	O
1984	Chi-N	.200	5	15	4	3	0	0	2	5	6	4	1	O
Total 2		.310	9	29	8	9	0	0	5	13	8	5	2	

■ Len Matuszek

YEAR	TM/L	AVG	G	AB	R	H	2B	3B	HR	RBI	BB	SO	SB	POS
1985	LA-N	1.000	3	1	1	1	0	0	0	0	0	0	0	1*1,O*1

■ Dal Maxvill

YEAR	TM/L	AVG	G	AB	R	H	2B	3B	HR	RBI	BB	SO	SB	POS
1972	Oak-A	.125	5	8	0	1	0	0	0	0	0	2	1	S*4,2*1
1974	Oak-A	.000	1	1	0	0	0	0	0	0	0	1	0	2
Total 2		.111	6	9	0	1	0	0	0	0	0	3	1	

■ Carlos May

YEAR	TM/L	AVG	G	AB	R	H	2B	3B	HR	RBI	BB	SO	SB	POS
1976	NY-A	.200	3	10	1	2	1	0	0	0	1	4	0	D

■ Dave May

YEAR	TM/L	AVG	G	AB	R	H	2B	3B	HR	RBI	BB	SO	SB	POS
1969	Bal-A	.000	1	1	0	0	0	0	0	0	0	0	0	H

■ Lee May

YEAR	TM/L	AVG	G	AB	R	H	2B	3B	HR	RBI	BB	SO	SB	POS
1970	Cin-N	.167	3	12	0	2	1	0	0	2	0	2	0	1
1979	Bal-A	.143	2	7	0	1	0	0	0	1	1	3	0	D
Total 2		.158	5	19	0	3	1	0	0	3	1	5	0	

■ Milt May

YEAR	TM/L	AVG	G	AB	R	H	2B	3B	HR	RBI	BB	SO	SB	POS
1971	Pit-N	.000	1	1	0	0	0	0	0	0	0	0	0	H
1972	Pit-N	.500	1	2	0	1	0	0	0	1	0	0	0	C
Total 2		.333	2	3	0	1	0	0	0	1	0	0	0	

■ John Mayberry

YEAR	TM/L	AVG	G	AB	R	H	2B	3B	HR	RBI	BB	SO	SB	POS
1976	KC-A	.222	5	18	4	4	0	0	1	3	1	0	0	1
1977	KC-A	.167	4	12	1	2	1	0	1	3	1	2	0	1
Total 2		.200	9	30	5	6	1	0	2	6	2	2	0	

■ Willie Mays

YEAR	TM/L	AVG	G	AB	R	H	2B	3B	HR	RBI	BB	SO	SB	POS
1971	SF-N	.267	4	15	2	4	2	0	1	3	3	3	1	O
1973	NY-N	.333	1	3	1	1	0	0	0	1	0	0	0	O
Total 2		.278	5	18	3	5	2	0	1	4	3	3	1	

■ Bill Mazeroski

YEAR	TM/L	AVG	G	AB	R	H	2B	3B	HR	RBI	BB	SO	SB	POS
1970	Pit-N	.000	1	2	0	0	0	0	0	0	2	0	0	2
1971	Pit-N	1.000	1	1	1	1	0	0	0	0	0	0	0	H
1972	Pit-N	.500	2	2	0	1	0	0	0	0	0	1	0	H
Total 3		.400	4	5	1	2	0	0	0	0	2	1	0	

■ Lee Mazzilli

YEAR	TM/L	AVG	G	AB	R	H	2B	3B	HR	RBI	BB	SO	SB	POS
1986	NY-N	.200	5	5	0	1	0	0	0	0	0	3	0	H
1988	NY-N	.500	3	2	0	1	0	0	0	0	0	0	1	H
1989	Tor-A	.000	3	8	0	0	0	0	0	0	0	2	0	D*2
Total 3		.133	11	15	0	2	0	0	0	0	0	5	1	

■ Dick McAuliffe

YEAR	TM/L	AVG	G	AB	R	H	2B	3B	HR	RBI	BB	SO	SB	POS
1972	Det-A	.200	5	20	3	4	0	0	1	1	1	4	0	S*4,2*1

■ Bake McBride

YEAR	TM/L	AVG	G	AB	R	H	2B	3B	HR	RBI	BB	SO	SB	POS
1977	Phi-N	.222	4	18	2	4	0	0	1	2	1	2	0	O
1978	Phi-N	.222	3	9	2	2	0	0	1	1	0	2	0	O*2
1980	Phi-N	.238	5	21	0	5	0	0	0	0	1	5	2	O
Total 3		.229	12	48	4	11	0	0	2	3	2	9	2	

■ Tim McCarver

YEAR	TM/L	AVG	G	AB	R	H	2B	3B	HR	RBI	BB	SO	SB	POS
1976	Phi-N	.000	2	4	0	0	0	0	0	0	0	1	0	C*1
1977	Phi-N	.167	3	6	1	1	0	0	0	0	1	3	0	C*2
1978	Phi-N	.000	2	4	2	0	0	0	0	0	2	0	0	C*1
Total 3		.071	7	14	3	1	0	0	0	1	3	4	0	

■ Lloyd McClendon

YEAR	TM/L	AVG	G	AB	R	H	2B	3B	HR	RBI	BB	SO	SB	POS
1989	Chi-N	.667	3	3	0	2	0	0	0	0	1	0	0	C*2,O*1
1991	Pit-N	.000	3	2	0	0	0	0	0	0	1	0	0	1*1
1992	Pit-N	.727	5	11	4	8	2	0	1	4	4	1	0	O
Total 3		.625	11	16	4	10	2	0	1	4	6	1	0	

■ Willie McCovey

YEAR	TM/L	AVG	G	AB	R	H	2B	3B	HR	RBI	BB	SO	SB	POS
1971	SF-N	.429	4	14	2	6	0	0	2	6	4	2	0	1

■ Willie McGee

YEAR	TM/L	AVG	G	AB	R	H	2B	3B	HR	RBI	BB	SO	SB	POS
1982	StL-N	.308	3	13	4	4	0	0	1	5	0	5	0	O
1985	StL-N	.269	6	26	6	7	1	0	0	3	3	6	2	O
1987	StL-N	.308	7	26	2	8	1	1	0	2	0	5	0	O
1990	Oak-A	.222	3	9	3	2	1	0	0	0	1	2	2	O*2,D*1
Total 4		.284	19	74	15	21	3	1	1	10	4	18	4	

■ Fred McGriff

YEAR	TM/L	AVG	G	AB	R	H	2B	3B	HR	RBI	BB	SO	SB	POS
1989	Tor-A	.143	5	21	1	3	0	0	3	3	0	4	0	1
1993	Atl-N	.435	6	23	6	10	2	0	1	4	4	7	0	1
Total 2		.295	11	44	7	13	2	0	1	7	4	11	0	

■ Mark McGwire

YEAR	TM/L	AVG	G	AB	R	H	2B	3B	HR	RBI	BB	SO	SB	POS
1988	Oak-A	.333	4	15	4	5	0	0	1	3	1	5	0	1
1989	Oak-A	.389	5	18	3	7	1	0	1	3	1	4	0	1

YEAR	TM/L	AVG	G	AB	R	H	2B	3B	HR	RBI	BB	SO	SB	POS
1990	Oak-A	.154	4	13	2	2	0	0	0	2	3	3	0	1
1992	Oak-A	.150	6	20	1	3	0	0	1	3	5	4	0	1
Total 4		.258	19	66	10	17	1	0	3	11	10	16	0	
■ Dave McKay														
1981	Oak-A	.273	3	11	0	3	0	0	0	1	0	2	0	2
■ Ken McMullen														
1974	LA-N	.000	1	1	0	0	0	0	0	0	0	1	0	H
■ Hal McRae														
1970	Cin-N	.000	2	4	0	0	0	0	0	0	0	1	0	O*1
1972	Cin-N	—	1	0	0	0	0	0	0	0	0	0	0	H
1976	KC-A	.118	5	17	2	2	1	1	0	1	1	4	0	D*3,O*2
1977	KC-A	.444	5	18	6	8	3	0	1	2	3	1	0	D*3,O*2
1978	KC-A	.214	4	14	0	3	0	0	0	2	2	2	1	D
1980	KC-A	.200	3	10	0	2	0	0	0	0	1	3	0	D
1984	KC-A	1.000	2	2	0	2	1	0	0	1	0	0	0	H
1985	KC-A	.261	6	23	1	6	2	0	0	3	1	6	0	D
Total 8		.261	28	88	9	23	7	1	1	9	8	17	1	
■ Kevin McReynolds														
1984	SD-N	.300	4	10	2	3	0	0	1	4	3	1	0	O
1988	NY-N	.250	7	28	4	7	2	0	2	4	3	5	2	O
Total 2		.263	11	38	6	10	2	0	3	8	6	6	2	
■ Bob Melvin														
1987	SF-N	.429	3	7	0	3	0	0	0	0	1	1	0	C*2
■ Mario Mendoza														
1974	Pit-N	.200	3	5	0	1	0	0	0	1	1	0	0	S
■ Denis Menke														
1972	Cin-N	.250	5	16	1	4	1	0	0	0	4	3	3	
1973	Cin-N	.222	3	9	1	2	0	0	1	1	1	2	0	S*2,3*2
Total 2		.240	8	25	2	6	1	0	1	1	5	5	0	
■ Orlando Merced														
1991	Pit-N	.222	3	9	1	2	0	0	1	1	0	1	0	1*2
1992	Pit-N	.100	4	10	0	1	1	0	0	2	2	4	0	1
Total 2		.158	7	19	1	3	1	0	1	3	2	5	0	
■ Larry Milbourne														
1981	NY-A	.462	3	13	4	6	0	0	0	1	0	0	0	S
■ Felix Millan														
1969	Atl-N	.333	3	12	2	4	1	0	0	0	3	0	0	2
1973	NY-N	.316	5	19	5	6	0	0	0	2	2	1	0	2
Total 2		.323	8	31	7	10	1	0	0	2	5	1	0	
■ Rick Miller														
1979	Cal-A	.250	4	16	2	4	0	0	0	0	0	1	0	O
■ Eddie Milner														
1987	SF-N	.143	6	7	0	1	0	0	0	0	0	3	0	O*4
■ John Milner														
1973	NY-N	.176	5	17	2	3	0	0	0	1	5	3	0	1
1979	Pit-N	.000	3	9	0	0	0	0	0	0	2	0	0	O
1981	Mon-N	.000	1	1	0	0	0	0	0	0	0	1	0	H
Total 3		.111	9	27	2	3	0	0	0	1	7	4	0	
■ Don Mincher														
1972	Oak-A	.000	1	1	0	0	0	0	0	0	0	1	0	H
■ Keith Mitchell														
1991	Atl-N	.000	5	4	0	0	0	0	0	0	0	1	0	O
■ Kevin Mitchell														
1986	NY-N	.250	2	8	1	2	0	0	0	0	0	1	0	O
1987	SF-N	.267	7	30	2	8	1	0	1	2	0	3	1	3
1989	SF-N	.353	5	17	5	6	0	0	2	7	3	3	0	O
Total 3		.291	14	55	8	16	1	0	3	9	3	7	1	
■ George Mitterwald														
1969	Min-A	.143	2	7	0	1	0	0	0	0	1	3	0	C
1970	Min-A	.500	2	8	2	4	1	0	0	2	0	2	0	C
Total 2		.333	4	15	2	5	1	0	0	2	1	5	0	
■ Paul Molitor														
1982	Mil-A	.316	5	19	4	6	1	0	2	5	2	3	1	3
1993	Tor-A	.391	6	23	7	9	2	1	1	5	3	3	0	D
Total 2		.357	11	42	11	15	3	1	3	10	5	6	1	
■ Rick Monday														
1971	Oak-A	.000	1	3	0	0	0	0	0	0	1	2	0	O
1977	LA-N	.286	3	7	1	2	1	0	0	0	2	1	0	O
1978	LA-N	.200	3	10	2	2	0	1	0	0	1	5	0	O
1981	LA-N	.333	3	9	2	3	0	0	1	5	0	4	0	O*2
1983	LA-N	—	1	0	0	0	0	0	0	0	0	0	0	H
Total 5		.241	11	29	5	7	1	1	1	1	4	12	0	
■ Don Money														
1982	Mil-A	.182	4	11	2	2	0	0	0	1	3	1	0	D
■ Charlie Moore														
1982	Mil-A	.462	5	13	3	6	0	0	0	1	2	0	0	O
■ Kelvin Moore														
1981	Oak-A	.222	3	9	0	2	0	0	0	0	1	0	0	O
■ Jose Morales														
1983	LA-N	.000	2	2	0	0	0	0	0	0	0	1	0	H
■ Mickey Morandini														
1993	Phi-N	.250	4	16	1	4	0	1	0	2	0	3	1	2
■ Keith Moreland														
1980	Phi-N	.000	2	1	0	0	0	0	0	1	0	0	0	C*1
1984	Chi-N	.333	5	18	3	6	2	0	0	3	1	1	0	O
Total 2		.316	7	19	3	6	2	0	0	3	1	1	0	
■ Omar Moreno														
1979	Pit-N	.250	3	12	3	3	0	1	0	0	2	2	1	O
■ Joe Morgan														
1972	Cin-N	.263	5	19	5	5	0	0	2	3	1	2	1	2
1973	Cin-N	.100	5	20	1	2	1	0	0	1	2	2	0	2
1975	Cin-N	.273	3	11	2	3	3	0	0	1	3	2	4	2
1976	Cin-N	.000	3	7	2	0	0	0	0	0	6	1	2	2
1979	Cin-N	.000	3	11	0	0	0	0	0	0	3	1	1	2
1980	Hou-N	.154	4	13	1	2	1	1	0	0	6	1	0	2
1983	Phi-N	.067	4	15	1	1	0	0	0	0	2	1	0	2
Total 7		.135	27	96	12	13	5	2	2	5	23	10	8	
■ John Morris														
1987	StL-N	.000	2	3	0	0	0	0	0	0	0	0	0	O
■ Hal Morris														
1990	Cin-N	.417	5	12	3	5	1	0	0	1	1	0	0	1*4
■ Jim Morrison														
1978	Phi-N	.000	1	1	0	0	0	0	0	0	0	1	0	H
1987	Det-A	.400	2	5	1	2	0	0	0	0	0	1	0	3*1,D*1
Total 2		.333	3	6	1	2	0	0	0	0	0	2	0	
■ Lloyd Moseby														
1985	Tor-A	.226	7	31	5	7	1	0	0	4	2	3	1	O
1989	Tor-A	.313	5	16	4	5	0	0	1	2	5	2	1	O
Total 2		.255	12	47	9	12	1	0	1	6	7	5	2	
■ Manny Mota														
1974	LA-N	.333	3	3	0	1	0	0	0	1	0	0	0	O*1
1977	LA-N	1.000	1	1	1	1	1	0	0	0	0	0	0	H
1978	LA-N	1.000	2	1	0	1	1	0	0	0	0	0	0	H
Total 3		.600	6	5	1	3	2	0	0	1	0	0	0	
■ Darryl Motley														
1984	KC-A	.167	3	12	0	2	0	0	0	1	1	3	0	O
1985	KC-A	.333	2	3	1	1	0	0	0	1	1	2	0	O
Total 2		.200	5	15	1	3	0	0	0	2	2	5	0	
■ Curt Motton														
1969	Bal-A	.500	2	2	0	1	0	0	0	1	0	0	0	H
1971	Bal-A	1.000	1	1	0	1	1	0	0	0	0	0	0	H
1974	Bal-A	.000	1	1	0	0	0	0	0	0	0	0	0	H
Total 3		.500	4	4	0	2	1	0	0	2	0	0	0	
■ Rance Mulliniks														
1985	Tor-A	.364	5	11	1	4	1	0	1	3	2	2	0	3
1989	Tor-A	.000	1	1	0	0	0	0	0	0	0	1	0	H
1991	Tor-A	.125	5	8	1	1	0	0	0	0	3	0	0	D*3
Total 3		.250	11	20	2	5	1	0	1	3	5	3	0	
■ Jerry Mumphrey														
1981	NY-A	.500	3	12	2	6	1	0	0	0	3	2	0	O
■ Thurman Munson														
1976	NY-A	.435	5	23	3	10	2	0	0	3	0	1	0	C
1977	NY-A	.286	5	21	3	6	1	0	1	5	0	2	0	C
1978	NY-A	.278	4	18	2	5	1	0	1	2	0	0	0	C
Total 3		.339	14	62	8	21	4	0	2	10	0	3	0	
■ Bobby Murcer														
1980	NY-A	.000	1	4	0	0	0	0	0	0	0	2	0	D
1981	NY-A	.333	1	3	0	1	0	0	0	0	1	1	0	D
Total 2		.143	2	7	0	1	0	0	0	0	1	3	0	
■ Dale Murphy														
1982	Atl-N	.273	3	11	1	3	0	0	0	0	0	2	1	O
■ Dwayne Murphy														
1981	Oak-A	.250	3	8	0	2	1	0	0	1	2	3	0	O
■ Eddie Murray														
1979	Bal-A	.417	4	12	3	5	0	0	1	5	5	2	0	1
1983	Bal-A	.267	4	15	4	4	0	0	1	3	3	3	1	1
Total 2		.333	8	27	8	9	0	0	2	8	8	5	1	
■ Jerry Narron														
1986	Cal-A	.500	4	2	1	1	0	0	0	0	1	1	0	C*3
■ Dave Nelson														
1976	KC-A	.000	2	2	0	0	0	0	0	0	0	1	0	D*1
■ Graig Nettles														
1969	Min-A	1.000	1	1	0	1	0	0	0	0	0	0	0	H
1976	NY-A	.235	5	17	2	4	1	0	2	4	3	3	0	3
1977	NY-A	.150	5	20	1	3	0	0	0	0	1	0	0	3
1978	NY-A	.333	4	15	3	5	1	0	1	2	0	1	0	3
1980	NY-A	.167	2	6	1	1	0	0	1	0	1	3	0	3
1981	NY-A	.500	3	12	2	6	2	0	1	9	1	0	0	3
1984	SD-N	.143	4	14	1	2	0	0	0	2	1	1	0	3
Total 7		.259	24	85	10	22	3	1	5	19	5	9	0	
■ Al Newman														
1987	Min-A	.000	1	2	0	0	0	0	0	0	0	0	0	2

YEAR	TM/L	AVG	G	AB	R	H	2B	3B	HR	RBI	BB	SO	SB	POS
1991	Min-A	—	2	0	0	0	0	0	0	0	0	0	0	2*1,3*1
Total 2		.000	3	2	0	0	0	0	0	0	0	0	0	
■ Jeff Newman														
1981	Oak-A	.000	2	5	0	0	0	0	0	0	0	2	0	C
■ Warren Newson														
1993	Chi-A	.200	2	5	1	1	0	0	1	1	0	1	0	D*1
■ Tom Nieto														
1985	StL-N	.000	1	3	1	0	0	0	0	0	1	2	0	C
■ Otis Nixon														
1992	Atl-N	.286	7	28	5	8	2	0	0	2	4	4	3	O
1993	Atl-N	.348	6	23	3	8	2	0	0	4	5	6	0	O
Total 2		.314	13	51	8	16	4	0	0	6	9	10	3	
■ Donell Nixon														
1989	SF-N	.000	3	3	0	0	0	0	0	0	0	1	1	O*2
■ Matt Nokes														
1987	Det-A	.143	5	14	2	2	0	0	1	2	1	4	0	C*3,D*2
■ Joe Nolan														
1983	Bal-A	—	1	0	0	0	0	0	0	1	0	0	0	H
■ Billy North														
1974	Oak-A	.063	4	16	3	1	0	0	0	0	2	1	1	O
1975	Oak-A	.000	3	10	0	0	0	0	0	1	2	0	0	O
1978	LA-N	.000	4	8	0	0	0	0	0	0	0	1	0	O
Total 3		.029	11	34	3	1	1	0	0	1	4	2	1	
■ Jim Northrup														
1972	Det-A	.357	5	14	0	5	0	0	1	2	3	0	0	O
■ Johnny Oates														
1976	Phi-N	.000	1	1	0	0	0	0	0	0	0	0	0	C
■ Ken Oberkfell														
1982	StL-N	.200	3	15	1	3	0	0	0	2	0	0	0	3
1989	SF-N	.000	3	4	0	0	0	0	0	0	0	0	0	3*1
Total 2		.158	6	19	1	3	0	0	0	2	0	0	0	
■ Ron Oester														
1990	Cin-N	.333	3	3	1	1	0	0	0	0	0	1	0	2*2
■ Ben Oglivie														
1982	Mil-A	.133	4	15	1	2	0	0	1	1	0	3	0	O
■ John Olerud														
1991	Tor-A	.158	5	19	1	3	0	0	0	3	3	1	0	1
1992	Tor-A	.348	6	23	4	8	2	0	1	4	2	5	0	1
1993	Tor-A	.348	6	23	5	8	1	0	0	3	4	1	0	1
Total 3		.292	17	65	10	19	3	0	1	10	9	7	0	
■ Tony Oliva														
1969	Min-A	.385	3	13	3	5	2	0	1	2	1	3	1	O
1970	Min-A	.500	3	12	2	6	2	0	1	1	0	1	0	O
Total 2		.440	6	25	5	11	4	0	2	3	1	4	1	
■ Al Oliver														
1970	Pit-N	.250	2	8	0	2	0	0	0	1	1	0	0	1
1971	Pit-N	.250	4	12	2	3	0	0	1	5	1	3	0	O
1972	Pit-N	.250	5	20	3	5	2	1	1	3	0	4	0	O
1974	Pit-N	.143	4	14	1	2	0	0	0	1	2	2	0	O
1975	Pit-N	.182	3	11	1	2	0	0	1	2	2	0	0	O
1985	Tor-A	.375	5	8	0	3	1	0	0	3	0	0	0	D
Total 6		.233	23	73	7	17	3	1	3	15	6	9	0	
■ Joe Oliver														
1990	Cin-N	.143	5	14	1	2	0	0	0	0	0	2	0	C
■ Greg Olson														
1991	Atl-N	.333	7	24	3	8	1	0	1	4	4	3	1	C
1993	Atl-N	.333	2	3	0	1	1	0	0	0	0	1	0	C
Total 2		.333	9	27	3	9	2	0	1	4	4	4	1	
■ Paul O'Neill														
1990	Cin-N	.471	5	17	1	8	3	0	1	4	1	1	0	O
■ Jose Oquendo														
1987	StL-N	.167	5	12	3	2	0	0	1	4	3	2	0	O*5,3*1
■ Jorge Orta														
1984	KC-A	.100	3	10	1	1	0	1	0	1	0	2	0	D
1985	KC-A	.000	2	5	0	0	0	0	0	0	0	1	0	D*1
Total 2		.067	5	15	1	1	0	1	0	1	0	3	0	
■ Junior Ortiz														
1991	Min-A	.000	3	3	0	0	0	0	0	0	0	0	0	C
■ Amos Otis														
1976	KC-A	.000	1	0	1	0	0	0	0	0	0	0	0	O
1977	KC-A	.125	5	16	1	2	1	0	0	2	2	3	2	O
1978	KC-A	.429	4	14	2	6	0	0	1	3	5	4	0	O
1980	KC-A	.333	3	12	2	4	1	0	0	0	3	2	0	O
Total 4		.279	13	43	5	12	4	0	3	5	11	8		
■ Ed Ott														
1979	Pit-N	.231	3	13	0	3	0	0	0	0	0	2	0	C
■ Spike Owen														
1986	Bos-A	.429	7	21	5	9	0	1	0	3	2	2	1	S
1988	Bos-A	—	1	0	0	0	0	0	0	0	1	0	0	D
Total 2		.429	8	21	5	9	0	1	0	3	3	2	1	

YEAR	TM/L	AVG	G	AB	R	H	2B	3B	HR	RBI	BB	SO	SB	POS
■ Tom Paciorek														
1974	LA-N	1.000	1	1	0	1	0	0	0	0	0	0	0	O
1983	Chi-A	.250	4	16	1	4	0	0	0	1	1	2	0	1*3,O*2
Total 2		.294	5	17	1	5	0	0	0	1	1	2	0	
■ Jose Pagan														
1970	Pit-N	.333	1	3	0	1	0	0	0	0	1	1	0	3
1971	Pit-N	.000	1	1	0	0	0	0	0	0	0	0	0	3
Total 2		.250	2	4	0	1	0	0	0	0	1	1	0	
■ Mike Pagliarulo														
1991	Min-A	.333	5	15	4	5	1	0	1	3	0	2	0	3
■ Tom Pagnozzi														
1987	StL-N	.000	1	1	0	0	0	0	0	0	0	0	0	H
■ Jim Palmer														
1969	Bal-A	.000	1	5	0	0	0	0	0	0	0	3	0	P
1970	Bal-A	.250	1	4	1	1	0	0	0	1	0	0	0	P
1971	Bal-A	.200	2	5	1	1	0	0	0	0	0	1	0	P*1
1973	Bal-A	—	3	0	0	0	0	0	0	0	0	0	0	P
1974	Bal-A	—	2	0	0	0	0	0	0	0	0	0	0	P*1
1979	Bal-A	—	1	0	0	0	0	0	0	0	0	0	0	P
1983	Bal-A	—	1	0	0	0	0	0	0	0	0	0	0	R
Total 7		.143	11	14	2	2	1	0	0	1	0	4	0	
■ Jim Pankovits														
1986	Hou-N	.000	2	2	0	0	0	0	0	0	0	1	0	H
■ Dave Parker														
1974	Pit-N	.125	3	8	0	1	0	0	0	0	1	0		O*2
1975	Pit-N	.000	3	10	2	0	0	0	0	0	1	3	0	O
1979	Pit-N	.333	3	12	2	4	0	0	0	2	2	3	1	O
1988	Oak-A	.250	4	12	1	3	1	0	0	0	4	0		D*2,O*1
1989	Oak-A	.188	4	16	2	3	0	0	2	3	0	0	0	D
Total 5		.190	17	58	7	11	1	0	2	5	3	11	1	
■ Lance Parrish														
1984	Det-A	.250	3	12	1	3	1	0	1	3	0	3	0	C
■ Larry Parrish														
1981	Mon-N	.263	5	19	2	5	2	0	0	2	1	1	0	3
1988	Bos-A	.000	4	6	0	0	0	0	0	0	0	2	0	1*2
Total 2		.200	9	25	2	5	2	0	0	2	1	3	0	
■ Dan Pasqua														
1993	Chi-A	.000	2	6	1	0	0	0	0	0	1	2	0	1
■ Freddie Patek														
1970	Pit-N	.000	1	3	0	0	0	0	0	0	1	2	0	S
1976	KC-A	.389	5	18	2	7	2	0	0	4	0	1	0	S
1977	KC-A	.389	5	18	4	7	3	1	0	5	1	2	0	S
1978	KC-A	.077	4	13	2	1	0	0	1	2	1	4	0	S
Total 4		.288	15	52	8	15	5	1	1	11	3	9	0	
■ Bill Pecota														
1993	Atl-N	.333	4	3	1	1	0	0	0	0	1	1	0	H
■ Tony Pena														
1987	StL-N	.381	7	21	5	8	0	1	0	3	4	1		C
1990	Bos-A	.214	4	14	0	3	0	0	0	0	0	0	0	C
Total 2		.314	11	35	5	11	0	1	0	3	4	1		
■ Terry Pendleton														
1985	StL-N	.208	6	24	2	5	1	0	0	4	1	3	0	3
1987	StL-N	.211	6	19	3	4	0	1	0	1	0	6	0	3
1991	Atl-N	.167	7	30	1	5	1	1	0	1	1	3	0	3
1992	Atl-N	.233	7	30	2	7	2	0	0	3	0	2	0	3
1993	Atl-N	.346	6	26	4	9	1	0	1	5	0	2	0	3
Total 5		.233	32	129	12	30	5	2	1	14	2	16	0	
■ Tony Perez														
1970	Cin-N	.333	3	12	1	4	2	0	1	2	1	1	0	3*3,1*1
1972	Cin-N	.200	5	20	0	4	1	0	0	2	0	7	0	1
1973	Cin-N	.091	5	22	1	2	0	0	1	2	0	4	0	1
1975	Cin-N	.417	3	12	3	5	0	0	1	4	1	2	0	1
1976	Cin-N	.200	3	10	1	2	0	0	0	3	1	2	0	1
1983	Phi-N	1.000	1	1	0	1	0	0	0	0	0	0	0	H
Total 6		.234	20	77	6	18	3	0	3	13	3	16	0	
■ Rico Petrocelli														
1975	Bos-A	.167	3	12	1	2	0	0	1	2	0	3	0	3
■ Gary Pettis														
1986	Cal-A	.346	7	26	4	9	1	0	1	4	3	5	0	O
■ Ken Phelps														
1989	Oak-A	1.000	1	1	0	1	1	0	0	0	0	0	0	H
■ Tony Phillips														
1988	Oak-A	.286	2	7	0	2	1	0	0	0	1	4	0	O*2,2*1
1989	Oak-A	.167	5	18	1	3	1	0	0	1	2	4	2	2*3,3*3
Total 2		.200	7	25	1	5	2	0	0	1	3	8	2	
■ Rob Picciolo														
1981	Oak-A	.200	2	5	1	1	0	0	0	0	0	2	0	S
■ Lou Piniella														
1976	NY-A	.273	4	11	1	3	1	0	0	0	0	1	0	D*3
1977	NY-A	.333	5	21	1	7	3	0	0	2	0	1	0	O*4,D*1
1978	NY-A	.235	4	17	2	4	0	0	0	1	0	3	0	O
1980	NY-A	.200	2	5	1	1	0	0	1	1	2	1	0	O

YEAR	TM/L	AVG	G	AB	R	H	2B	3B	HR	RBI	BB	SO	SB	POS
1981	NY-A	.600	3	5	2	3	0	0	1	3	0	0	0	D*2,O*1
Total 5		.305	18	59	7	18	4	0	2	6	2	6	0	

■ Biff Pocoroba

YEAR	TM/L	AVG	G	AB	R	H	2B	3B	HR	RBI	BB	SO	SB	POS
1982	Atl-N	.000	1	1	0	0	0	0	0	0	0	0	0	H

■ Luis Polonia

YEAR	TM/L	AVG	G	AB	R	H	2B	3B	HR	RBI	BB	SO	SB	POS
1988	Oak-A	.400	3	5	0	2	0	0	0	0	1	1	0	O*1

■ Paul Popovich

YEAR	TM/L	AVG	G	AB	R	H	2B	3B	HR	RBI	BB	SO	SB	POS
1974	Pit-N	.600	3	5	1	3	0	0	0	0	0	0	0	S

■ Tom Poquette

YEAR	TM/L	AVG	G	AB	R	H	2B	3B	HR	RBI	BB	SO	SB	POS
1976	KC-A	.188	5	16	1	3	2	0	0	4	2	3	0	O
1977	KC-A	.167	2	6	0	1	0	0	0	0	0	0	0	O
1978	KC-A	.000	1	1	0	0	0	0	0	0	0	0	0	H
Total 3		.174	8	23	1	4	2	0	0	4	2	3	0	

■ Darrell Porter

YEAR	TM/L	AVG	G	AB	R	H	2B	3B	HR	RBI	BB	SO	SB	POS
1977	KC-A	.333	5	15	3	5	0	0	0	0	3	0	0	C
1978	KC-A	.357	4	14	1	5	1	0	0	3	2	0	0	C
1980	KC-A	.100	3	10	2	1	0	0	0	0	1	0	0	C
1982	StL-N	.556	3	9	3	5	3	0	0	1	5	2	0	C
1985	StL-N	.267	5	15	1	4	1	0	0	0	5	4	0	C
Total 5		.317	20	63	10	20	5	0	0	4	16	6	0	

■ Boog Powell

YEAR	TM/L	AVG	G	AB	R	H	2B	3B	HR	RBI	BB	SO	SB	POS
1969	Bal-A	.385	3	13	2	5	0	0	1	3	0	3	0	1
1970	Bal-A	.429	3	14	2	6	2	0	1	6	0	3	0	1
1971	Bal-A	.300	3	10	4	3	0	0	2	3	3	3	0	1
1973	Bal-A	.000	1	4	1	0	0	0	0	0	0	1	0	1
1974	Bal-A	.125	2	8	0	1	0	0	0	1	4	0	0	1
Total 5		.306	12	49	9	15	2	0	4	11	5	7	0	

■ Todd Pratt

YEAR	TM/L	AVG	G	AB	R	H	2B	3B	HR	RBI	BB	SO	SB	POS
1993	Phi-N	.000	1	1	0	0	0	0	0	0	0	1	0	C

■ Greg Pryor

YEAR	TM/L	AVG	G	AB	R	H	2B	3B	HR	RBI	BB	SO	SB	POS
1984	KC-A	—	1	0	0	0	0	0	0	0	0	0	0	3

■ Kirby Puckett

YEAR	TM/L	AVG	G	AB	R	H	2B	3B	HR	RBI	BB	SO	SB	POS
1987	Min-A	.208	5	24	3	5	1	0	1	3	0	5	1	O
1991	Min-A	.429	5	21	4	9	1	0	2	6	1	4	0	O
Total 2		.311	10	45	7	14	2	0	3	9	1	9	1	

■ Terry Puhl

YEAR	TM/L	AVG	G	AB	R	H	2B	3B	HR	RBI	BB	SO	SB	POS
1980	Hou-N	.526	5	19	4	10	2	0	0	3	3	2	2	O*4
1986	Hou-N	.667	3	3	0	2	0	0	0	0	0	0	1	H
Total 2		.545	8	22	4	12	2	0	0	3	3	2	3	

■ Luis Pujols

YEAR	TM/L	AVG	G	AB	R	H	2B	3B	HR	RBI	BB	SO	SB	POS
1980	Hou-N	.100	4	10	1	1	0	1	0	0	3	0	0	C

■ Frank Quilici

YEAR	TM/L	AVG	G	AB	R	H	2B	3B	HR	RBI	BB	SO	SB	POS
1970	Min-A	.000	3	2	0	0	0	0	0	0	1	0	2	2*2

■ Luis Quinones

YEAR	TM/L	AVG	G	AB	R	H	2B	3B	HR	RBI	BB	SO	SB	POS
1990	Cin-N	.500	3	2	1	1	0	0	0	2	0	0	1	H

■ Carlos Quintana

YEAR	TM/L	AVG	G	AB	R	H	2B	3B	HR	RBI	BB	SO	SB	POS
1990	Bos-A	.000	4	13	0	0	0	0	0	1	1	0	0	1

■ Jamie Quirk

YEAR	TM/L	AVG	G	AB	R	H	2B	3B	HR	RBI	BB	SO	SB	POS
1976	KC-A	.143	4	7	1	1	0	1	0	2	0	2	0	D*2
1985	KC-A	.000	1	1	0	0	0	0	0	0	0	0	0	H
1990	Oak-A	1.000	1	1	0	1	0	0	0	0	0	0	0	H
1992	Oak-A	.000	1	1	0	0	0	0	0	0	0	0	0	H
Total 4		.200	7	10	1	2	0	1	0	2	0	2	0	

■ Tim Raines

YEAR	TM/L	AVG	G	AB	R	H	2B	3B	HR	RBI	BB	SO	SB	POS
1981	Mon-N	.238	5	21	1	5	2	0	0	1	0	3	0	O
1993	Chi-A	.444	6	27	5	12	3	0	0	1	2	2	1	O
Total 2		.354	11	48	6	17	5	0	0	2	2	5	1	

■ Mario Ramirez

YEAR	TM/L	AVG	G	AB	R	H	2B	3B	HR	RBI	BB	SO	SB	POS
1984	SD-N	.000	2	2	0	0	0	0	0	0	0	0	0	H

■ Rafael Ramirez

YEAR	TM/L	AVG	G	AB	R	H	2B	3B	HR	RBI	BB	SO	SB	POS
1982	Atl-N	.182	3	11	1	2	0	0	0	1	1	1	0	S

■ Domingo Ramos

YEAR	TM/L	AVG	G	AB	R	H	2B	3B	HR	RBI	BB	SO	SB	POS
1989	Chi-N	.000	1	1	0	0	0	0	0	0	0	0	0	H

■ Willie Randolph

YEAR	TM/L	AVG	G	AB	R	H	2B	3B	HR	RBI	BB	SO	SB	POS
1975	Pit-N	.000	2	2	1	0	0	0	0	0	0	1	0	2*1
1976	NY-A	.118	5	17	0	2	0	0	0	1	3	1	1	2
1977	NY-A	.278	5	18	4	5	1	0	0	2	1	0	0	2
1980	NY-A	.385	3	13	0	5	2	0	0	1	3	0	2	2
1981	NY-A	.333	3	12	2	4	0	0	1	2	0	1	0	2
1990	Oak-A	.375	4	8	1	3	0	0	0	0	3	1	0	2
Total 6		.271	22	70	8	19	3	0	1	9	6	6	1	

■ Paul Ratliff

YEAR	TM/L	AVG	G	AB	R	H	2B	3B	HR	RBI	BB	SO	SB	POS
1970	Min-A	.250	1	4	0	1	0	0	0	0	0	1	0	C

■ Randy Ready

YEAR	TM/L	AVG	G	AB	R	H	2B	3B	HR	RBI	BB	SO	SB	POS
1992	Oak-A	.000	1	1	0	0	0	0	0	0	0	1	0	H

■ Gary Redus

YEAR	TM/L	AVG	G	AB	R	H	2B	3B	HR	RBI	BB	SO	SB	POS
1990	Pit-N	.250	5	8	1	2	0	0	0	1	3	1	1*2
1991	Pit-N	.158	5	19	1	3	0	0	0	1	4	2	1	O
1992	Pit-N	.438	5	16	4	7	4	1	0	3	2	3	1	O
Total 3		.279	15	43	6	12	4	1	0	3	4	10	3	

■ Jeff Reed

YEAR	TM/L	AVG	G	AB	R	H	2B	3B	HR	RBI	BB	SO	SB	POS
1990	Cin-N	.000	4	7	0	0	0	0	0	0	0	2	0	C

■ Jody Reed

YEAR	TM/L	AVG	G	AB	R	H	2B	3B	HR	RBI	BB	SO	SB	POS
1988	Bos-A	.273	4	11	0	3	1	0	0	0	2	1	0	S
1990	Bos-A	.133	4	15	0	2	0	0	1	0	2	0	2*4,S*3
Total 2		.192	8	26	0	5	1	0	1	2	3	0	

■ Rich Reese

YEAR	TM/L	AVG	G	AB	R	H	2B	3B	HR	RBI	BB	SO	SB	POS
1969	Min-A	.167	3	12	0	2	0	0	0	2	1	1	0	1
1970	Min-A	.143	2	7	0	1	0	0	0	0	1	1	0	1
Total 2		.158	5	19	0	3	0	0	0	2	2	2	0	

■ Rick Renick

YEAR	TM/L	AVG	G	AB	R	H	2B	3B	HR	RBI	BB	SO	SB	POS
1969	Min-A	.000	1	1	0	0	0	0	0	0	0	0	0	H
1970	Min-A	.200	2	5	0	1	0	0	0	0	0	1	0	3*1
Total 2		.167	3	6	0	1	0	0	0	0	0	1	0	

■ Merv Rettenmund

YEAR	TM/L	AVG	G	AB	R	H	2B	3B	HR	RBI	BB	SO	SB	POS
1969	Bal-A	—	1	0	0	0	0	0	0	0	0	0	0	H
1970	Bal-A	.333	1	3	1	1	0	0	0	1	2	1	1	O
1971	Bal-A	.250	3	8	0	2	1	0	0	1	0	3	0	O
1973	Bal-A	.091	3	11	1	1	0	0	0	0	3	2	0	O
1975	Cin-N	.000	2	1	0	0	0	0	0	0	1	0	0	H
1979	Cal-A	.000	2	2	0	0	0	0	0	0	2	1	0	D
Total 6		.160	12	25	2	4	1	0	0	2	8	7	1	

■ Dave Revering

YEAR	TM/L	AVG	G	AB	R	H	2B	3B	HR	RBI	BB	SO	SB	POS
1981	NY-A	.500	2	2	0	1	0	0	0	0	0	0	0	1

■ Craig Reynolds

YEAR	TM/L	AVG	G	AB	R	H	2B	3B	HR	RBI	BB	SO	SB	POS
1975	Pit-N	.000	2	1	0	0	0	0	0	0	0	0	0	S*1
1980	Hou-N	.154	4	13	2	2	1	0	0	0	3	1	0	S
1986	Hou-N	.333	4	12	1	4	0	0	0	1	3	0	0	S
Total 3		.231	10	26	3	6	1	0	0	4	4	0	

■ R. J. Reynolds

YEAR	TM/L	AVG	G	AB	R	H	2B	3B	HR	RBI	BB	SO	SB	POS
1990	Pit-N	.200	6	10	0	2	0	0	0	0	2	2	1	O*3

■ Jim Rice

YEAR	TM/L	AVG	G	AB	R	H	2B	3B	HR	RBI	BB	SO	SB	POS
1986	Bos-A	.161	7	31	8	5	1	0	2	6	1	8	0	O
1988	Bos-A	.154	4	13	0	2	0	0	0	1	2	4	0	D
Total 2		.159	11	44	8	7	1	0	2	7	3	12	0	

■ Ernest Riles

YEAR	TM/L	AVG	G	AB	R	H	2B	3B	HR	RBI	BB	SO	SB	POS
1989	SF-N	.000	1	1	0	0	0	0	0	0	0	0	0	H

■ Cal Ripken

YEAR	TM/L	AVG	G	AB	R	H	2B	3B	HR	RBI	BB	SO	SB	POS
1983	Bal-A	.400	4	15	5	6	2	0	0	1	2	3	0	S

■ Luis Rivera

YEAR	TM/L	AVG	G	AB	R	H	2B	3B	HR	RBI	BB	SO	SB	POS
1990	Bos-A	.222	4	9	1	2	1	0	0	0	0	2	0	S

■ Mickey Rivers

YEAR	TM/L	AVG	G	AB	R	H	2B	3B	HR	RBI	BB	SO	SB	POS
1976	NY-A	.348	5	23	5	8	0	1	0	1	1	1	0	O
1977	NY-A	.391	5	23	5	9	2	0	0	2	0	2	1	O
1978	NY-A	.455	4	11	0	5	0	0	0	0	2	0	0	O
Total 3		.386	14	57	10	22	2	1	0	2	3	3	1	

■ Andre Robertson

YEAR	TM/L	AVG	G	AB	R	H	2B	3B	HR	RBI	BB	SO	SB	POS
1981	NY-A	.000	1	1	0	0	0	0	0	0	0	0	0	S

■ Bob Robertson

YEAR	TM/L	AVG	G	AB	R	H	2B	3B	HR	RBI	BB	SO	SB	POS
1970	Pit-N	.200	2	5	0	1	0	0	0	0	0	0	0	1*1
1971	Pit-N	.438	4	16	5	7	1	0	4	6	0	2	0	1
1972	Pit-N	—	4	0	0	0	0	0	0	0	1	0	0	1
1974	Pit-N	.000	1	5	1	0	0	0	0	0	0	0	0	1
1975	Pit-N	.500	3	2	0	1	0	0	0	1	1	0	0	1*1
Total 5		.321	14	28	6	9	2	0	4	7	2	2	0	

■ Brooks Robinson

YEAR	TM/L	AVG	G	AB	R	H	2B	3B	HR	RBI	BB	SO	SB	POS
1969	Bal-A	.500	3	14	1	7	1	0	0	0	0	0	0	3
1970	Bal-A	.583	3	12	4	7	2	0	0	0	1	0	0	3
1971	Bal-A	.364	3	11	2	4	1	0	1	3	0	1	0	3
1973	Bal-A	.250	5	20	1	5	2	0	0	2	1	1	0	3
1974	Bal-A	.083	4	12	1	1	0	0	0	0	1	0	0	3
Total 5		.348	18	69	9	24	6	0	2	7	3	3	0	

■ Frank Robinson

YEAR	TM/L	AVG	G	AB	R	H	2B	3B	HR	RBI	BB	SO	SB	POS
1969	Bal-A	.333	3	12	1	4	2	0	1	2	3	3	0	O
1970	Bal-A	.200	3	10	3	2	0	0	1	2	5	2	0	O
1971	Bal-A	.083	3	12	2	1	0	0	1	1	4	0	0	O
Total 3		.206	9	34	6	7	3	0	2	5	9	9	0	

■ Bill Robinson

YEAR	TM/L	AVG	G	AB	R	H	2B	3B	HR	RBI	BB	SO	SB	POS
1975	Pit-N	.000	2	2	0	0	0	0	0	0	0	1	0	H
1979	Pit-N	.000	3	3	0	0	0	0	0	0	0	0	0	O
Total 2		.000	5	5	0	0	0	0	0	0	0	1	0	

■ Aurelio Rodriguez

YEAR	TM/L	AVG	G	AB	R	H	2B	3B	HR	RBI	BB	SO	SB	POS
1972	Det-A	.000	5	16	0	0	0	0	0	0	2	2	0	3
1980	NY-A	.333	2	6	0	2	1	0	0	0	0	0	0	3
1981	NY-A	—	2	0	0	0	0	0	0	0	0	0	0	3
1983	Chi-A	—	1	2	0	0	0	0	0	0	0	0	0	3
Total 4		.091	10	22	0	2	1	0	0	0	2	2	0	

■ Gary Roenicke

YEAR	TM/L	AVG	G	AB	R	H	2B	3B	HR	RBI	BB	SO	SB	POS
1979	Bal-A	.200	2	5	1	1	0	0	0	0	1	0	0	O
1983	Bal-A	.750	3	4	4	3	1	0	1	5	4	5	0	O
Total 2		.444	5	9	5	4	1	0	1	5	5	5	0	

■ Cookie Rojas

YEAR	TM/L	AVG	G	AB	R	H	2B	3B	HR	RBI	BB	SO	SB	POS
1976	KC-A	.333	4	9	2	3	0	0	0	1	0	0	1	2

YEAR	TM/L	AVG	G	AB	R	H	2B	3B	HR	RBI	BB	SO	SB	POS
1977	KC-A	.250	1	4	0	1	0	0	0	0	0	1	1	D
Total 2		.308	5	13	2	4	0	0	0	1	0	1	2	

■ Ed Romero

1986	Bos-A	.000	1	2	0	0	0	0	0	0	0	0	0	S
1988	Bos-A	—	1	0	0	0	0	0	0	0	0	0	0	R
Total 2		.000	2	2	0	0	0	0	0	0	0	0	0	

■ Kevin Romine

1988	Bos-A	—	2	0	1	0	0	0	0	0	0	0	0	R

■ Jimmy Rosario

1971	SF-N	—	1	0	0	0	0	0	0	0	0	0	0	R

■ Pete Rose

1970	Cin-N	.231	3	13	1	3	0	0	0	1	0	0	0	O
1972	Cin-N	.450	5	20	1	9	4	0	0	2	1	2	0	O
1973	Cin-N	.381	5	21	3	8	1	0	2	2	2	2	0	O
1975	Cin-N	.357	3	14	5	5	0	0	1	2	0	2	3	O
1976	Cin-N	.429	3	14	3	6	2	1	0	2	1	0	3	O
1980	Phi-N	.400	5	20	3	8	0	0	0	2	5	3	1	O
1983	Phi-N	.375	4	16	3	6	0	0	0	0	1	1	1	1
Total 7		.381	28	118	17	45	7	1	3	11	10	10	1	

■ John Roseboro

1969	Min-A	.200	2	5	0	1	0	0	0	0	0	0	0	C

■ Jerry Royster

1982	Atl-N	.182	3	11	0	2	0	0	0	0	0	2	0	O*3,3*1

■ Joe Rudi

1971	Oak-A	.143	2	7	0	1	1	0	0	0	1	0	0	O
1972	Oak-A	.250	5	20	1	5	1	0	0	2	1	4	0	O
1973	Oak-A	.222	5	18	1	4	0	0	1	3	3	1	0	O
1974	Oak-A	.154	4	13	0	2	0	1	0	1	3	2	0	O
1975	Oak-A	.250	3	12	1	3	2	0	0	0	1	0	0	1*2,O*1
Total 5		.214	19	70	3	15	4	1	1	6	8	8	0	

■ Bill Russell

1974	LA-N	.389	4	18	1	7	0	0	0	3	1	0	0	S
1977	LA-N	.278	4	18	3	5	1	0	0	2	0	0	0	S
1978	LA-N	.412	4	17	1	7	1	0	0	2	1	1	0	S
1981	LA-N	.313	5	16	2	5	0	1	0	1	1	1	0	S
1983	LA-N	.286	4	14	1	4	0	0	0	0	2	4	1	S
Total 5		.337	21	83	8	28	2	1	0	8	5	6	1	

■ Chris Sabo

1990	Cin-N	.227	6	22	1	5	0	0	1	3	1	4	0	3

■ Luis Salazar

1984	SD-N	.200	3	5	0	1	0	1	0	0	0	1	0	O*2,3*1
1989	Chi-N	.368	5	19	2	7	0	1	1	2	0	0	0	3
Total 2		.333	8	24	2	8	0	2	1	2	0	1	0	

■ Chico Salmon

1969	Bal-A	.000	1	1	0	0	0	0	0	0	0	0	0	H

■ Juan Samuel

1983	Phi-N	—	1	0	0	0	0	0	0	0	0	0	0	R

■ Ryne Sandberg

1984	Chi-N	.368	5	19	3	7	2	0	0	2	3	2	3	2
1989	Chi-N	.400	5	20	6	8	3	1	1	4	3	4	0	2
Total 2		.385	10	39	9	15	5	1	1	6	6	6	3	

■ Deion Sanders

1992	Atl-N	.000	4	5	0	0	0	0	0	0	0	0	0	O*3
1993	Atl-N	.000	5	3	0	0	0	0	0	0	0	1	0	O*1
Total 2		.000	9	8	0	0	0	0	0	0	0	4	0	

■ Manny Sanguillen

1970	Pit-N	.167	3	12	0	2	0	0	0	0	0	1	0	C
1971	Pit-N	.267	4	15	1	4	0	0	0	1	1	1	1	C
1972	Pit-N	.313	5	16	4	5	1	0	1	2	0	0	0	C
1974	Pit-N	.250	4	16	0	4	1	0	0	0	0	0	0	C
1975	Pit-N	.167	3	12	0	2	0	0	0	0	0	0	0	C
Total 5		.239	19	71	5	17	2	0	1	3	1	2	1	

■ Rafael Santana

1986	NY-N	.176	6	17	0	3	0	0	0	0	3	0	S

■ Mackey Sasser

1988	NY-N	.200	4	5	0	1	0	0	0	0	1	0	C*1

■ Steve Sax

1981	LA-N	—	1	0	0	0	0	0	0	0	0	0	0	2
1983	LA-N	.250	4	16	0	4	0	0	0	1	0	1	2	
1985	LA-N	.300	6	20	1	6	3	0	0	1	1	5	0	2
1988	LA-N	.267	7	30	7	8	0	0	0	3	3	3	5	2
Total 4		.273	18	66	8	18	3	0	0	4	5	8	6	

■ Mike Schmidt

1976	Phi-N	.308	3	13	1	4	2	0	0	2	0	1	0	3
1977	Phi-N	.063	4	16	2	1	0	0	0	1	2	3	0	3
1978	Phi-N	.200	4	15	1	3	2	0	0	1	2	2	0	3
1980	Phi-N	.208	5	24	1	5	0	0	1	1	6	3	1	3
1983	Phi-N	.467	4	15	5	7	2	0	1	2	2	3	0	3
Total 5		.241	20	83	10	20	7	0	1	7	12	11	1	

■ Dick Schofield

1986	Cal-A	.300	7	30	4	9	1	0	1	2	1	5	1	S

■ Mike Scioscia

1981	LA-N	.133	5	15	1	2	0	0	1	1	2	1	0	C
1985	LA-N	.250	6	16	2	4	0	0	0	1	4	0	0	C
1988	LA-N	.364	7	22	3	8	1	0	1	2	1	2	0	C
Total 3		.264	18	53	6	14	1	0	2	4	7	3	0	

■ Rodney Scott

1981	Mon-N	.167	5	18	0	3	0	0	0	0	1	3	1	2

■ Art Shamsky

1969	NY-N	.538	3	13	3	7	0	0	0	1	0	3	0	O

■ Mike Sharperson

1988	LA-N	.000	2	1	0	0	0	0	0	1	1	0	0	S*1,3*1

■ John Shelby

1983	Bal-A	.222	3	9	1	2	0	0	0	0	1	3	1	O*2
1988	LA-N	.167	7	24	3	4	0	0	0	3	5	12	2	O
Total 2		.182	10	33	4	6	0	0	0	3	6	15	3	

■ Pat Sheridan

1984	KC-A	.000	3	6	1	0	0	0	0	0	3	3	0	O
1985	KC-A	.150	7	20	4	3	0	0	2	3	2	3	0	O
1987	Det-A	.300	5	10	2	3	1	0	1	2	0	2	1	O*4
1989	SF-N	.154	5	13	1	2	0	1	0	0	0	4	0	O
Total 4		.163	20	49	8	8	1	1	3	5	5	12	1	

■ Ruben Sierra

1992	Oak-A	.333	6	24	4	8	2	1	1	7	2	1	0	O

■ Ted Simmons

1982	Mil-A	.167	5	18	3	3	0	0	1	1	1	4	0	C

■ Duke Sims

1972	Det-A	.214	4	14	0	3	2	1	0	0	1	2	0	C*2,O*2

■ Ken Singleton

1979	Bal-A	.375	4	16	4	6	2	0	0	2	1	2	0	O
1983	Bal-A	.250	4	12	0	3	2	0	0	1	2	2	0	D
Total 2		.321	8	28	4	9	4	0	0	3	3	4	0	

■ Ted Sizemore

1977	Phi-N	.231	4	13	1	3	0	0	0	0	2	0	0	2
1978	Phi-N	.385	4	13	3	5	0	1	0	1	1	0	0	2
Total 2		.308	8	26	4	8	0	1	0	1	3	0	0	

■ Dave Skaggs

1979	Bal-A	.000	1	4	0	0	0	0	0	0	0	0	0	C

■ Don Slaught

1984	KC-A	.364	3	11	0	4	0	0	0	0	0	0	0	C
1990	Pit-N	.091	4	11	0	1	1	0	0	1	2	3	0	C
1991	Pit-N	.235	6	17	0	4	0	0	0	1	1	4	0	C
1992	Pit-N	.333	5	12	5	4	1	0	1	5	6	3	0	C
Total 4		.255	18	51	5	13	2	0	1	7	9	10	0	

■ Billy Smith

1979	Bal-A	.000	1	4	0	0	0	0	0	0	0	1	0	2

■ Reggie Smith

1977	LA-N	.188	4	16	2	3	0	1	0	1	2	5	1	O
1978	LA-N	.188	4	16	2	3	1	0	0	1	0	2	0	O
1981	LA-N	1.000	1	1	0	1	0	0	0	1	0	0	0	H
Total 3		.212	9	33	4	7	1	1	0	3	2	7	1	

■ Dwight Smith

1989	Chi-N	.200	4	15	2	3	1	0	0	0	2	2	1	O

■ Lonnie Smith

1980	Phi-N	.600	3	5	2	3	0	0	0	0	0	1	0	O*2
1982	StL-N	.273	3	11	1	3	0	0	0	1	0	1	0	O
1985	KC-A	.250	7	28	2	7	2	0	0	1	3	6	1	O
1991	Atl-N	.250	7	24	3	6	3	0	0	0	4	5	2	O
1992	Atl-N	.333	6	6	1	2	0	1	0	1	0	0	0	H
Total 5		.284	26	74	9	21	5	1	0	3	7	12	4	

■ Ozzie Smith

1982	StL-N	.556	3	9	0	5	0	0	0	3	3	0	1	S
1985	StL-N	.435	6	23	4	10	1	1	1	3	3	1	1	S
1987	StL-N	.200	7	25	2	5	0	1	0	1	3	4	0	S
Total 3		.351	16	57	6	20	1	2	1	7	9	5	2	

■ Eric Soderholm

1980	NY-A	.167	2	6	0	1	0	0	0	0	0	0	0	D

■ Paul Sorrento

1991	Min-A	.000	1	1	0	0	0	0	0	0	0	1	0	H

■ Chris Speier

1971	SF-N	.357	4	14	4	5	1	0	1	1	1	0	S
1981	Mon-N	.188	5	16	0	3	0	0	0	0	2	0	0	S
1987	SF-N	.000	3	5	0	0	0	0	0	0	0	2	0	2*1
Total 3		.229	12	35	4	8	1	0	1	1	3	3	0	

■ Jim Spencer

1980	NY-A	—	1	1	0	0	0	0	0	0	0	0	0	H
1981	Oak-A	.000	2	2	0	0	0	0	0	0	0	0	1	
Total 2		.000	3	3	0	0	0	0	0	0	0	0	1	

■ Harry Spilman

1979	Cin-N	.000	2	2	0	0	0	0	0	0	0	0	0	H
1987	SF-N	.500	3	2	1	1	0	0	1	1	0	0	0	H
Total 2		.250	5	4	1	1	0	0	1	1	0	0	0	

Ed Sprague

YEAR	TM/L	AVG	G	AB	R	H	2B	3B	HR	RBI	BB	SO	SB	POS
1992	Tor-A	.500	2	2	0	1	0	0	0	0	0	1	0	H
1993	Tor-A	.286	6	21	0	6	0	1	0	4	2	4	0	3
Total 2		.304	8	23	0	7	0	1	0	4	2	5	0	

Mike Squires

YEAR	TM/L	AVG	G	AB	R	H	2B	3B	HR	RBI	BB	SO	SB	POS
1983	Chi-A	.000	4	4	0	0	0	0	0	0	0	0	0	1*3

Larry Stahl

YEAR	TM/L	AVG	G	AB	R	H	2B	3B	HR	RBI	BB	SO	SB	POS
1973	Cin-N	.500	4	4	1	2	0	0	0	0	0	1	0	H

Fred Stanley

YEAR	TM/L	AVG	G	AB	R	H	2B	3B	HR	RBI	BB	SO	SB	POS
1976	NY-A	.333	5	15	1	5	2	0	0	0	2	0	0	S
1977	NY-A	—	2	0	0	0	0	0	0	0	0	0	0	S
1978	NY-A	.200	2	5	0	1	0	0	0	0	0	2	0	2
1981	Oak-A	.333	2	3	0	1	0	0	0	1	0	1	0	S
Total 4		.304	11	23	1	7	2	0	0	1	2	3	0	

Mickey Stanley

YEAR	TM/L	AVG	G	AB	R	H	2B	3B	HR	RBI	BB	SO	SB	POS
1972	Det-A	.333	4	6	0	2	0	0	0	0	0	0	0	O*3

Dave Stapleton

YEAR	TM/L	AVG	G	AB	R	H	2B	3B	HR	RBI	BB	SO	SB	POS
1986	Bos-A	.667	4	3	2	2	0	0	0	0	0	1	0	0	1

Willie Stargell

YEAR	TM/L	AVG	G	AB	R	H	2B	3B	HR	RBI	BB	SO	SB	POS
1970	Pit-N	.500	3	12	0	6	1	0	0	1	1	1	0	O
1971	Pit-N	.000	4	14	1	0	0	0	0	0	2	6	0	0
1972	Pit-N	.063	5	16	1	1	0	0	1	2	5	0		1*5,O*1
1974	Pit-N	.400	4	15	3	6	0	0	2	4	1	2	0	O
1975	Pit-N	.182	3	11	1	2	1	0	0	0	1	3	0	1
1979	Pit-N	.455	3	11	2	5	2	0	2	6	3	2	0	1
Total 6		.253	22	79	8	20	5	0	4	12	10	19	0	

Rusty Staub

YEAR	TM/L	AVG	G	AB	R	H	2B	3B	HR	RBI	BB	SO	SB	POS
1973	NY-N	.200	4	15	4	3	0	0	3	5	3	2	0	O

Terry Steinbach

YEAR	TM/L	AVG	G	AB	R	H	2B	3B	HR	RBI	BB	SO	SB	POS
1988	Oak-A	.250	2	4	0	1	0	0	0	0	2	0	0	C
1989	Oak-A	.200	4	15	0	3	0	0	0	1	1	5	0	C*3,D*1
1990	Oak-A	.455	3	11	2	5	0	0	0	1	1	2	0	C
1992	Oak-A	.292	6	24	1	7	0	0	1	5	2	7	0	C
Total 4		.296	15	54	3	16	0	0	1	7	6	14	0	

Rennie Stennett

YEAR	TM/L	AVG	G	AB	R	H	2B	3B	HR	RBI	BB	SO	SB	POS
1972	Pit-N	.286	5	21	2	6	0	0	0	1	1	0		O*5,2*1
1974	Pit-N	.063	4	16	1	1	0	0	0	0	1	1	0	2
1975	Pit-N	.214	3	14	0	3	0	0	0	0	0	1	0	2*3,S*1
1979	Pit-N	—	1	0	0	0	0	0	0	0	0	0	0	2
Total 4		.196	13	51	3	10	0	0	0	1	2	2	0	

Jimmy Stewart

YEAR	TM/L	AVG	G	AB	R	H	2B	3B	HR	RBI	BB	SO	SB	POS
1970	Cin-N	.000	1	2	0	0	0	0	0	0	0	0	0	O

Bob Stinson

YEAR	TM/L	AVG	G	AB	R	H	2B	3B	HR	RBI	BB	SO	SB	POS
1976	KC-A	.000	2	1	0	0	0	0	0	0	0	0	0	C*1

Kevin Stocker

YEAR	TM/L	AVG	G	AB	R	H	2B	3B	HR	RBI	BB	SO	SB	POS
1993	Phi-N	.182	6	22	0	4	1	0	0	1	2	5	0	S

Darryl Strawberry

YEAR	TM/L	AVG	G	AB	R	H	2B	3B	HR	RBI	BB	SO	SB	POS
1986	NY-N	.227	6	22	4	5	1	0	2	5	3	12	1	O
1988	NY-N	.300	7	30	5	9	2	0	1	6	2	5	0	O
Total 2		.269	13	52	9	14	3	0	3	11	5	17	1	

Franklin Stubbs

YEAR	TM/L	AVG	G	AB	R	H	2B	3B	HR	RBI	BB	SO	SB	POS
1988	LA-N	.250	4	8	0	2	0	0	0	0	0	4	0	1*3

Champ Summers

YEAR	TM/L	AVG	G	AB	R	H	2B	3B	HR	RBI	BB	SO	SB	POS
1984	SD-N	.000	2	2	0	0	0	0	0	0	0	1	0	H

Jim Sundberg

YEAR	TM/L	AVG	G	AB	R	H	2B	3B	HR	RBI	BB	SO	SB	POS
1985	KC-A	.167	7	24	3	4	1	1	1	6	1	7	0	C

Pat Tabler

YEAR	TM/L	AVG	G	AB	R	H	2B	3B	HR	RBI	BB	SO	SB	POS
1991	Tor-A	.000	2	1	0	0	0	0	0	0	0	1	0	0	D

Tony Tarasco

YEAR	TM/L	AVG	G	AB	R	H	2B	3B	HR	RBI	BB	SO	SB	POS
1993	Atl-N	.000	2	1	0	0	0	0	0	0	0	1	0	0	O

Frank Taveras

YEAR	TM/L	AVG	G	AB	R	H	2B	3B	HR	RBI	BB	SO	SB	POS
1974	Pit-N	.000	2	2	0	0	0	0	0	0	0	0	1	S
1975	Pit-N	.143	3	7	0	1	0	0	0	1	1	2	0	S
Total 2		.111	5	9	0	1	0	0	0	1	1	2	1	

Tony Taylor

YEAR	TM/L	AVG	G	AB	R	H	2B	3B	HR	RBI	BB	SO	SB	POS
1972	Det-A	.133	4	15	0	2	2	0	0	0	0	2	0	2

Garry Templeton

YEAR	TM/L	AVG	G	AB	R	H	2B	3B	HR	RBI	BB	SO	SB	POS
1984	SD-N	.333	5	15	2	5	1	0	0	2	2	0	1	S

Gene Tenace

YEAR	TM/L	AVG	G	AB	R	H	2B	3B	HR	RBI	BB	SO	SB	POS
1971	Oak-A	.000	1	3	0	0	0	0	0	0	0	1	1	0	C
1972	Oak-A	.059	5	17	1	1	0	0	0	1	3	5	0	C*5,2*2
1973	Oak-A	.235	5	17	3	4	1	0	0	2	4	0		1*5,C*3
1974	Oak-A	.000	4	11	1	0	0	0	0	1	4	4	1	1
1975	Oak-A	.000	3	9	0	0	0	0	0	0	3	2	0	C*3,1*1
Total 5		.088	18	57	5	5	1	0	0	2	13	16	1	

Tim Teufel

YEAR	TM/L	AVG	G	AB	R	H	2B	3B	HR	RBI	BB	SO	SB	POS
1986	NY-N	.167	2	6	0	1	0	0	0	0	0	0	0	2
1988	NY-N	.000	1	3	0	0	0	0	0	0	0	0	0	2
Total 2		.111	3	9	0	1	0	0	0	0	0	0	1	

Derrel Thomas

YEAR	TM/L	AVG	G	AB	R	H	2B	3B	HR	RBI	BB	SO	SB	POS
1981	LA-N	1.000	2	1	2	1	0	0	0	0	0	0	0	3*1,O*1
1983	LA-N	.444	4	9	0	4	1	0	0	0	0	3	1	O
Total 2		.500	6	10	2	5	1	0	0	0	0	3	1	

Frank Thomas

YEAR	TM/L	AVG	G	AB	R	H	2B	3B	HR	RBI	BB	SO	SB	POS
1993	Chi-A	.353	6	17	2	6	0	0	1	3	10	5	0	1*4,D*2

Gorman Thomas

YEAR	TM/L	AVG	G	AB	R	H	2B	3B	HR	RBI	BB	SO	SB	POS
1982	Mil-A	.067	5	15	1	1	0	0	1	3	2	7	0	O

Gary Thomasson

YEAR	TM/L	AVG	G	AB	R	H	2B	3B	HR	RBI	BB	SO	SB	POS
1978	NY-A	.000	3	1	0	0	0	0	0	0	0	0	0	O

Danny Thompson

YEAR	TM/L	AVG	G	AB	R	H	2B	3B	HR	RBI	BB	SO	SB	POS
1970	Min-A	.125	3	8	0	1	1	0	0	0	0	1	1	0	2

Milt Thompson

YEAR	TM/L	AVG	G	AB	R	H	2B	3B	HR	RBI	BB	SO	SB	POS
1993	Phi-N	.231	6	13	2	3	1	0	0	0	1	2	0	O*5

Robby Thompson

YEAR	TM/L	AVG	G	AB	R	H	2B	3B	HR	RBI	BB	SO	SB	POS
1987	SF-N	.100	7	20	4	2	0	1	1	2	5	7	2	2*6
1989	SF-N	.278	5	18	5	5	0	0	2	3	3	2	0	2
Total 2		.184	12	38	9	7	0	1	3	5	8	9	2	

Dickie Thon

YEAR	TM/L	AVG	G	AB	R	H	2B	3B	HR	RBI	BB	SO	SB	POS
1979	Cal-A	—	1	0	1	0	0	0	0	0	0	0	0	S
1986	Hou-N	.250	6	12	1	3	0	0	1	1	0	1	0	S
Total 2		.250	7	12	2	3	0	0	1	1	0	1	0	

Lou Thornton

YEAR	TM/L	AVG	G	AB	R	H	2B	3B	HR	RBI	BB	SO	SB	POS
1985	Tor-A	—	2	0	1	0	0	0	0	0	0	0	0	R

Bob Tillman

YEAR	TM/L	AVG	G	AB	R	H	2B	3B	HR	RBI	BB	SO	SB	POS
1969	Atl-N	—	1	0	0	0	0	0	0	0	0	0	0	C

Bobby Tolan

YEAR	TM/L	AVG	G	AB	R	H	2B	3B	HR	RBI	BB	SO	SB	POS
1970	Cin-N	.417	3	12	3	5	0	0	0	1	2	1	1	O
1972	Cin-N	.238	5	21	3	5	1	1	0	4	0	4	0	O
1976	Phi-N	.000	3	2	0	0	0	0	0	0	0	0	0	1*1,O*1
Total 3		.286	11	35	6	10	1	1	1	6	1	5	1	

Cesar Tovar

YEAR	TM/L	AVG	G	AB	R	H	2B	3B	HR	RBI	BB	SO	SB	POS
1969	Min-A	.077	3	13	0	1	0	0	0	0	1	2	0	O
1970	Min-A	.385	3	13	2	5	0	1	0	1	0	0	0	O*3,2*1
1975	Oak-A	.500	2	2	2	1	0	0	0	0	1	0	0	2*1
Total 3		.250	8	28	4	7	0	1	0	1	2	2	1	

Alan Trammell

YEAR	TM/L	AVG	G	AB	R	H	2B	3B	HR	RBI	BB	SO	SB	POS
1984	Det-A	.364	3	11	2	4	0	1	1	3	3	1	0	S
1987	Det-A	.200	5	20	3	4	1	0	0	2	1	2	0	S
Total 2		.258	8	31	5	8	1	1	1	5	4	3	0	

Jeff Treadway

YEAR	TM/L	AVG	G	AB	R	H	2B	3B	HR	RBI	BB	SO	SB	POS
1991	Atl-N	.333	1	3	0	1	0	0	0	0	0	0	0	2
1992	Atl-N	.667	3	3	1	2	0	0	0	0	0	1	0	2*1
Total 2		.500	4	6	1	3	0	0	0	0	0	1	0	

Manny Trillo

YEAR	TM/L	AVG	G	AB	R	H	2B	3B	HR	RBI	BB	SO	SB	POS
1974	Oak-A	—	1	0	1	0	0	0	0	0	0	0	0	R
1980	Phi-N	.381	5	21	1	8	2	1	0	4	0	2	0	2
Total 2		.381	6	21	2	8	2	1	0	4	0	2	0	

Ted Uhlaender

YEAR	TM/L	AVG	G	AB	R	H	2B	3B	HR	RBI	BB	SO	SB	POS
1969	Min-A	.167	2	6	0	1	0	0	0	0	0	0	0	O
1972	Cin-N	.500	2	2	0	1	0	0	0	0	0	0	0	H
Total 2		.250	4	8	0	2	0	0	0	0	0	0	0	

Del Unser

YEAR	TM/L	AVG	G	AB	R	H	2B	3B	HR	RBI	BB	SO	SB	POS
1980	Phi-N	.400	5	5	2	2	1	0	0	1	0	2	0	O*2

Willie Upshaw

YEAR	TM/L	AVG	G	AB	R	H	2B	3B	HR	RBI	BB	SO	SB	POS
1985	Tor-A	.231	7	26	2	6	2	0	0	1	1	4	0	1

Jose Uribe

YEAR	TM/L	AVG	G	AB	R	H	2B	3B	HR	RBI	BB	SO	SB	POS
1987	SF-N	.269	7	26	1	7	1	0	0	2	0	4	1	S
1989	SF-N	.235	5	17	2	4	1	0	0	1	1	5	1	S
Total 2		.256	12	43	3	11	2	0	0	3	1	9	2	

Andy Van Slyke

YEAR	TM/L	AVG	G	AB	R	H	2B	3B	HR	RBI	BB	SO	SB	POS
1985	StL-N	.091	5	11	1	1	0	0	0	1	2	1	0	O
1990	Pit-N	.208	6	24	3	5	1	1	0	3	1	6	1	O
1991	Pit-N	.160	7	25	3	4	2	0	1	2	5	5	1	O
1992	Pit-N	.276	7	29	1	8	3	1	0	4	1	5	0	O
Total 4		.202	25	89	8	18	6	2	1	10	9	17	2	

Gary Varsho

YEAR	TM/L	AVG	G	AB	R	H	2B	3B	HR	RBI	BB	SO	SB	POS
1991	Pit-N	.500	2	2	0	1	0	0	0	0	0	1	0	H
1992	Pit-N	.500	2	2	0	1	0	0	0	0	0	0	0	O*1
Total 2		.500	4	4	0	2	0	0	0	0	0	1	0	

Otto Velez

YEAR	TM/L	AVG	G	AB	R	H	2B	3B	HR	RBI	BB	SO	SB	POS
1976	NY-A	.000	1	1	0	0	0	0	0	0	0	0	0	H

Robin Ventura

YEAR	TM/L	AVG	G	AB	R	H	2B	3B	HR	RBI	BB	SO	SB	POS
1993	Chi-A	.200	6	20	2	4	0	0	1	5	6	6	0	3*6,1*1

Tom Veryzer

YEAR	TM/L	AVG	G	AB	R	H	2B	3B	HR	RBI	BB	SO	SB	POS
1984	Chi-N	.000	3	1	0	0	0	0	0	0	0	0	0	S*2,3*1

Ozzie Virgil

YEAR	TM/L	AVG	G	AB	R	H	2B	3B	HR	RBI	BB	SO	SB	POS
1983	Phi-N	.000	1	1	0	0	0	0	0	0	0	1	0	H

George Vukovich

YEAR	TM/L	AVG	G	AB	R	H	2B	3B	HR	RBI	BB	SO	SB	POS
1980	Phi-N	.000	4	3	0	0	0	0	0	0	0	0	0	O*1

Greg Walker

YEAR	TM/L	AVG	G	AB	R	H	2B	3B	HR	RBI	BB	SO	SB	POS
1983	Chi-A	.333	2	3	0	1	0	0	0	0	1	2	0	1*1

YEAR	TM/L	AVG	G	AB	R	H	2B	3B	HR	RBI	BB	SO	SB	POS
■ Tim Wallach														
1981	Mon-N	.000	1	1	0	0	0	0	0	0	0	0	0	H
■ Denny Walling														
1980	Hou-N	.111	3	9	2	1	0	0	0	2	1	0	0	O*2,1*1
1986	Hou-N	.158	5	19	1	3	1	0	0	2	0	4	0	3
Total 2		.143	8	28	3	4	1	0	0	4	1	4	0	
■ Jerome Walton														
1989	Chi-N	.364	5	22	4	8	0	0	0	2	2	2	0	O
■ Claudell Washington														
1974	Oak-A	.273	4	11	1	3	1	0	0	0	0	0	0	O*3
1975	Oak-A	.250	3	12	1	3	1	0	0	1	0	2	0	O*2,D*1
1982	Atl-N	.333	3	9	0	3	0	0	0	0	2	2	0	O
Total 3		.281	10	32	2	9	2	0	0	1	2	4	0	
■ Herb Washington														
1974	Oak-A	—	2	0	0	0	0	0	0	0	0	0	0	R
■ U L Washington														
1980	KC-A	.364	3	11	1	4	1	0	0	1	2	3	0	S
1984	KC-A	.000	2	1	0	0	0	0	0	0	0	1	0	H
Total 2		.333	5	12	1	4	1	0	0	1	2	4	0	
■ John Wathan														
1976	KC-A	—	1	0	0	0	0	0	0	0	0	0	0	C
1977	KC-A	.000	4	6	0	0	0	0	0	0	0	3	0	1*2,C*1,D*1
1978	KC-A	.000	1	3	0	0	0	0	0	0	0	0		1
1980	KC-A	.000	3	6	1	0	0	0	0	0	3	1	0	O
1984	KC-A	.000	1	1	0	0	0	0	0	0	0	0	0	D
Total 5		.000	10	16	1	0	0	0	0	0	3	4	0	
■ Bob Watson														
1980	NY-A	.500	3	12	0	6	3	1	0	0	0	0	1	1
1981	NY-A	.250	3	12	0	3	0	0	0	1	0	1	0	1
Total 2		.375	6	24	0	9	3	1	0	1	0	1	0	
■ Mitch Webster														
1989	Chi-N	.333	3	3	0	1	0	0	0	0	0	0	0	O*2
■ John Wehner														
1992	Pit-N	.000	2	2	0	0	0	0	0	0	0	2	0	H
■ Al Weis														
1969	NY-N	.000	3	1	0	0	0	0	0	0	0	0	0	2
■ Walt Weiss														
1988	Oak-A	.333	4	15	2	5	2	0	0	2	0	4	0	S
1989	Oak-A	.111	4	9	2	1	1	0	0	0	1	1	1	S
1990	Oak-A	.000	2	7	2	0	0	0	0	0	2	2	0	S
1992	Oak-A	.167	3	6	1	1	0	0	0	0	2	1	2	S
Total 4		.189	13	37	7	7	3	0	0	2	5	8	3	
■ Larry Whisenton														
1982	Atl-N	.000	2	2	0	0	0	0	0	0	0	1	0	H
■ Lou Whitaker														
1984	Det-A	.143	3	14	3	2	0	0	0	0	0	3	0	2
1987	Det-A	.176	5	17	4	3	0	0	1	1	7	3	1	2
Total 2		.161	8	31	7	5	0	0	1	1	7	6	1	
■ Devon White														
1986	Cal-A	.500	4	2	2	1	0	0	0	0	0	1	0	O*3
1991	Tor-A	.364	5	22	5	8	1	0	0	2	3	3	0	O
1992	Tor-A	.348	6	23	2	8	2	0	0	2	5	6	0	O
1993	Tor-A	.444	6	27	3	12	1	1	1	2	1	5	0	O
Total 4		.392	21	74	12	29	4	1	1	4	8	15	3	
■ Frank White														
1976	KC-A	.125	4	8	2	1	0	0	0	0	0	1	0	2
1977	KC-A	.278	5	18	1	5	1	0	0	2	0	4	1	2
1978	KC-A	.231	4	13	1	3	0	0	0	2	1	0	0	2
1980	KC-A	.545	3	11	3	6	1	0	1	3	0	1	1	2
1984	KC-A	.083	3	12	1	1	0	0	0	0	0	3	0	2
1985	KC-A	.200	7	25	1	5	0	0	0	3	0	2	0	2
Total 6		.241	26	87	9	21	2	0	1	10	1	11	2	
■ Jerry White														
1981	Mon-N	.313	5	16	2	5	1	0	1	3	3	1	1	O
■ Roy White														
1976	NY-A	.294	5	17	4	5	3	0	0	3	5	1	1	O
1977	NY-A	.400	4	5	2	2	0	0	0	1	0	0	0	O*1,D*1
1978	NY-A	.313	4	16	5	5	1	0	1	1	1	2	0	O*3,D*1
Total 3		.316	13	38	11	12	6	0	1	4	7	3	1	
■ Terry Whitfield														
1985	LA-N	—	1	0	0	0	0	0	0	0	0	0	0	H
■ Ernie Whitt														
1985	Tor-A	.190	7	21	1	4	1	0	0	2	2	4	0	C
1989	Tor-A	.125	5	16	1	2	0	0	1	3	2	3	0	C
Total 2		.162	12	37	2	6	1	0	1	5	4	7	0	
■ Alan Wiggins														
1984	SD-N	.316	5	19	4	6	0	0	0	1	2	2	2	2
■ Rob Wilfong														
1982	Cal-A	.000	2	1	0	0	0	0	0	0	0	1	0	H
1986	Cal-A	.308	4	13	1	4	1	0	0	2	0	2	0	2
Total 2		.286	6	14	1	4	1	0	0	2	0	3	0	
■ Curtis Wilkerson														
1989	Chi-N	.500	2	2	1	1	0	0	0	0	0	0	0	3*1
1991	Pit-N	.000	4	4	0	0	0	0	0	0	0	3	0	H
Total 2		.167	6	6	1	1	0	0	0	0	0	3	0	
■ Jerry Willard														
1991	Atl-N	.000	2	2	0	0	0	0	0	0	0	1	0	H
■ Billy Williams														
1975	Oak-A	.000	3	8	0	0	0	0	0	0	1	1	0	D*2
■ Earl Williams														
1973	Bal-A	.278	5	18	2	5	2	0	1	4	2	2	0	1*4,C*1
1974	Bal-A	.000	2	6	0	0	0	0	0	0	0	2	0	1
Total 2		.208	7	24	2	5	2	0	1	4	2	4	0	
■ Matt Williams														
1989	SF-N	.300	5	20	2	6	1	0	2	9	0	2	0	3*5,S*1
■ Mookie Wilson														
1986	NY-N	.115	6	26	2	3	0	0	0	1	1	7	1	O
1988	NY-N	.154	4	13	2	2	0	0	0	1	2	2	0	O*3
1989	Tor-A	.263	5	19	2	5	0	0	0	2	2	2	1	O
1991	Tor-A	.250	3	8	1	2	0	0	0	0	1	3	1	O*2
Total 4		.182	18	66	7	12	0	0	0	4	6	14	3	
■ Willie Wilson														
1978	KC-A	.250	3	4	0	1	0	0	0	0	0	2	0	O
1980	KC-A	.308	3	13	2	4	2	1	0	4	1	2	0	O
1984	KC-A	.154	3	13	0	2	0	0	0	0	1	2	0	O
1985	KC-A	.310	7	29	5	9	0	0	1	2	1	5	1	O
1992	Oak-A	.227	6	22	0	5	1	0	0	0	1	5	7	O
Total 5		.259	22	81	7	21	3	1	1	6	4	16	8	
■ Dave Winfield														
1981	NY-A	.154	3	13	2	2	1	0	0	2	2	2	1	O
1992	Tor-A	.250	6	24	7	6	1	0	2	3	5	2	0	D
Total 2		.216	9	37	9	8	2	0	2	5	7	4	1	
■ Herm Winningham														
1990	Cin-N	.286	3	7	1	2	1	0	0	1	1	1	1	O*2
■ Jim Wohlford														
1976	KC-A	.182	5	11	3	2	0	0	0	0	3	1	2	O
■ Gary Woods														
1980	Hou-N	.250	4	8	2	2	0	0	0	1	1	3	1	O*3
1984	Chi-N	.000	1	1	0	0	0	0	0	0	0	1	0	O
Total 2		.222	5	9	2	2	0	0	0	1	1	4	1	
■ Tracy Woodson														
1988	LA-N	.250	3	4	0	1	0	0	0	0	0	1	0	1
■ Woody Woodward														
1970	Cin-N	.100	3	10	1	1	0	0	0	0	1	0	0	S*3,3*3
■ Rick Wrona														
1989	Chi-N	.000	2	5	0	0	0	0	0	0	0	3	0	C
■ Jim Wynn														
1974	LA-N	.200	4	10	4	2	0	0	0	2	9	1	0	O
■ Marvell Wynne														
1989	Chi-N	.167	4	6	0	1	0	0	0	0	0	0	0	O*2
■ Carl Yastrzemski														
1975	Bos-A	.455	3	11	4	5	0	1	2	1	1	1	0	O
■ Steve Yeager														
1974	LA-N	.000	3	9	1	0	0	0	0	0	3	3	1	C
1977	LA-N	.231	4	13	1	3	0	0	0	1	1	3	0	C
1978	LA-N	.231	4	13	2	3	0	0	1	2	2	2	1	C
1981	LA-N	.500	1	2	1	1	1	0	0	1	0	0	0	C
1983	LA-N	.167	2	6	0	1	0	0	0	0	0	0	0	C
1985	LA-N	.000	1	2	0	0	0	0	0	0	1	1	0	C
Total 6		.178	15	45	5	8	1	0	1	4	7	9	2	
■ Robin Yount														
1982	Mil-A	.250	5	16	1	4	0	0	0	0	5	0	0	S
■ Joe Zdeb														
1977	KC-A	.000	4	9	0	0	0	0	0	0	0	2	1	0
■ Richie Zisk														
1974	Pit-N	.300	3	10	1	3	0	0	0	0	0	3	0	O*2
1975	Pit-N	.500	3	10	0	5	1	0	0	0	2	2	0	O
Total 2		.400	6	20	1	8	1	0	0	0	2	5	0	

YEAR	TM/L	W	L	ERA	G	GS	CG	SV	SHO	IP	H	ER	BB	SO
● Don Aase														
1979	Cal-A	1	0	1.80	2	0	0	0	0	5	4	1	2	6
● Glenn Abbott														
1975	Oak-A	0	0	0.00	1	0	0	0	0	1	0	0	0	0
● Jim Acker														
1985	Tor-A	0	0	0.00	2	0	0	0	0	6	2	0	0	5
1989	Tor-A	0	0	1.42	5	0	0	0	0	6^1	4	1	1	4
1991	Tor-A	0	0	0.00	1	0	0	0	0	0^2	1	0	0	1
Total 3		0	0	0.69	8	0	0	0	0	13	7	1	1	10
● Juan Agosto														
1983	Chi-A	0	0	0.00	1	0	0	0	0	0^1	0	0	0	0
● Rick Aguilera														
1986	NY-N	0	0	0.00	2	0	0	0	0	5	2	0	2	2
1988	NY-N	0	0	1.29	3	0	0	0	0	7	3	1	2	4
1991	Min-A	0	0	0.00	3	0	0	3	0	3^1	1	0	0	3
Total 3		0	0	0.59	8	0	0	3	0	15^1	6	1	4	9
● Doyle Alexander														
1973	Bal-A	0	1	4.91	1	1	0	0	0	3^2	5	2	0	1
1985	Tor-A	0	1	8.71	2	2	0	0	0	10^1	14	10	3	9
1987	Det-A	0	2	10.00	2	2	0	0	0	9	14	10	1	5
Total 3		0	4	8.61	5	5	0	0	0	23	33	22	4	15
● Wilson Alvarez														
1993	Chi-A	1	0	1.00	1	1	0	0	0	9	7	1	2	6
● Larry Andersen														
1986	Hou-N	0	0	0.00	2	0	0	0	0	5	1	0	2	3
1990	Bos-A	0	1	6.00	3	0	0	0	0	3	3	2	3	3
1993	Phi-N	0	0	15.43	3	0	0	1	0	2^1	4	4	1	3
Total 3		0	1	5.23	8	0	0	1	0	10^1	8	6	6	9
● Joaquin Andujar														
1980	Hou-N	0	0	0.00	1	0	0	0	0	1	0	0	1	0
1982	StL-N	1	0	2.70	1	1	0	0	0	6^2	6	2	2	4
1985	StL-N	0	1	6.97	2	2	0	0	0	10^1	14	8	4	9
Total 3		1	1	5.00	4	3	0	1	0	18	20	10	7	13
● Paul Assenmacher														
1989	Chi-N	0	0	13.50	2	0	0	0	0	0^2	3	1	0	0
● Keith Atherton														
1987	Min-A	0	0	0.00	1	0	0	0	0	0^1	1	0	0	0
● Steve Avery														
1991	Atl-N	2	0	0.00	2	2	0	0	0	16^1	9	0	4	17
1992	Atl-N	1	1	9.00	3	2	0	0	0	8	13	8	2	3
1993	Atl-N	0	0	2.77	2	2	0	0	0	13	9	4	6	10
Total 3		3	1	2.89	7	6	0	0	0	37^1	31	12	12	30
● Doug Bair														
1979	Cin-N	0	1	9.00	1	0	0	0	0	1	2	1	1	0
1982	StL-N	0	0	0.00	1	0	0	0	0	1	2	0	3	0
Total 2		0	1	4.50	2	0	0	0	0	2	4	1	4	0
● Floyd Bannister														
1983	Chi-A	0	1	4.50	1	1	0	0	0	6	5	3	1	5
● Mike Barlow														
1979	Cal-A	0	0	0.00	1	0	0	0	0	1	0	0	0	0
● Salome Barojas														
1983	Chi-A	0	0	18.00	2	0	0	0	0	1	4	2	0	0
● Jim Barr														
1971	SF-N	0	0	9.00	1	0	0	0	0	1	3	1	0	2
● Dave Beard														
1981	Oak-A	0	0	40.50	1	0	0	0	0	0^2	5	3	0	0
● Jim Beattie														
1978	NY-A	1	0	1.69	1	1	0	0	0	5^1	2	1	5	3
● Joe Beckwith														
1983	LA-N	0	0	0.00	2	0	0	0	0	2^1	1	0	2	3
● Steve Bedrosian														
1982	Atl-N	0	0	18.00	2	0	0	0	0	1	3	2	1	2
1989	SF-N	0	0	2.70	4	0	0	3	0	3^1	4	1	2	2
1991	Min-A	0	0	0.00	2	0	0	0	0	1^1	3	0	2	2
Total 3		0	0	4.76	8	0	0	3	0	5^2	10	3	5	6
● Tim Belcher														
1988	LA-N	2	0	4.11	2	2	0	0	0	15^1	12	7	4	16
1993	Chi-A	1	0	2.45	1	0	0	0	0	3^2	3	1	3	1
Total 2		3	0	3.79	3	2	0	0	0	19	15	8	7	17
● Stan Belinda														
1990	Pit-N	0	0	2.45	3	0	0	0	0	3^2	3	1	0	4
1991	Pit-N	1	0	0.00	3	0	0	0	0	5	0	0	3	4
1992	Pit-N	0	0	0.00	2	0	0	0	0	1^2	2	0	0	2
Total 3		1	0	0.87	8	0	0	0	0	10^1	5	1	3	10
● Jason Bere														
1993	Chi-A	0	0	11.57	1	1	0	0	0	2^1	5	3	2	3
● Juan Berenguer														
1987	Min-A	0	0	1.50	4	0	0	0	0	6	1	1	3	6
● Dwight Bernard														
1982	Mil-A	0	0	0.00	1	0	0	0	0	1	0	0	0	0

YEAR	TM/L	W	L	ERA	G	GS	CG	SV	SHO	IP	H	ER	BB	SO
● Jim Bibby														
1979	Pit-N	0	0	1.29	1	1	0	0	0	7	4	1	4	5
● Mike Bielecki														
1989	Chi-N	0	1	3.65	2	2	0	0	0	12^1	7	5	6	11
● Jack Billingham														
1972	Cin-N	0	0	3.86	1	1	0	0	0	4^2	5	2	4	4
1973	Cin-N	0	1	4.50	2	2	0	0	0	12	9	6	4	9
Total 2		0	1	4.32	3	3	0	0	0	16^2	14	8	6	13
● Doug Bird														
1976	KC-A	1	0	1.93	1	0	0	0	0	4^2	4	1	0	1
1977	KC-A	0	0	0.00	3	0	0	0	0	2	4	0	0	1
1978	KC-A	0	1	9.00	2	0	0	0	0	1	2	1	0	1
Total 3		1	1	2.35	6	0	0	0	0	7^2	10	2	0	3
● Bud Black														
1984	KC-A	0	1	5.40	1	1	0	0	0	5	7	3	1	3
1985	KC-A	0	0	1.69	3	1	0	0	0	10^2	11	2	4	8
Total 2		0	1	2.87	4	2	0	0	0	15^2	18	5	5	11
● Steve Blass														
1971	Pit-N	0	1	11.57	2	2	0	0	0	7	14	9	2	11
1972	Pit-N	1	0	1.72	2	2	0	0	0	15^2	12	3	6	5
Total 2		1	1	4.76	4	4	0	0	0	22^2	26	12	8	16
● Vida Blue														
1971	Oak-A	0	1	6.43	1	1	0	0	0	7	7	5	2	8
1972	Oak-A	0	0	0.00	4	0	0	1	0	5^1	4	0	1	5
1973	Oak-A	0	1	10.29	2	2	0	0	0	7	8	8	5	3
1974	Oak-A	1	0	0.00	1	1	1	0	1	9	2	0	0	7
1975	Oak-A	0	0	9.00	1	1	0	0	0	3	6	3	0	2
Total 5		1	2	4.60	9	5	1	1	1	31^1	27	16	8	25
● Bert Blyleven														
1970	Min-A	0	0	0.00	1	0	0	0	0	2	0	0	0	2
1979	Pit-N	1	0	1.00	1	1	1	0	0	9	8	1	0	9
1987	Min-A	2	0	4.05	2	2	0	0	0	13^1	12	6	3	9
Total 3		3	0	2.59	4	3	1	0	0	24^1	22	7	3	20
● Mike Boddicker														
1983	Bal-A	1	0	0.00	1	1	1	0	1	9	5	0	3	14
1988	Bos-A	0	1	20.25	1	1	0	0	0	2^2	8	6	1	2
1990	Bos-A	0	1	2.25	1	1	1	0	0	8	6	2	3	7
Total 3		1	2	3.66	3	3	2	0	1	19^2	19	8	7	23
● Tom Bolton														
1990	Bos-A	0	0	0.00	2	0	0	0	0	3	2	0	2	3
● Greg Booker														
1984	SD-N	0	0	0.00	1	0	0	0	0	2	2	0	1	2
● Pedro Borbon														
1972	Cin-N	0	0	2.08	3	0	0	0	0	4^1	2	1	0	1
1973	Cin-N	1	0	0.00	4	0	0	1	0	4^2	3	0	0	3
1975	Cin-N	0	0	0.00	1	0	0	1	0	1	0	0	0	1
1976	Cin-N	0	0	0.00	2	0	0	1	0	4^1	4	0	1	0
Total 4		1	0	0.63	10	0	0	3	0	14^1	9	1	1	5
● Dick Bosman														
1975	Oak-A	0	0	0.00	1	0	0	0	0	0^1	0	0	0	0
● Dave Boswell														
1969	Min-A	0	1	0.84	1	1	0	0	0	10^2	7	1	7	4
● Oil Can Boyd														
1986	Bos-A	1	1	4.61	2	2	0	0	0	13^2	17	7	3	8
● Jeff Brantley														
1989	SF-N	0	0	0.00	3	0	0	0	0	5	1	0	2	3
● Ken Brett														
1974	Pit-N	0	0	7.71	1	0	0	0	0	2^1	3	2	2	1
1975	Pit-N	0	0	0.00	2	0	0	0	0	2^1	1	0	0	1
Total 2		0	0	3.86	3	0	0	0	0	4^2	4	2	2	2
● Nelson Briles														
1972	Pit-N	0	0	3.00	1	1	0	0	0	6	6	2	1	3
● Jim Britton														
1969	Atl-N	0	0	0.00	1	0	0	0	0	0^1	0	0	1	0
● Tom Browning														
1990	Cin-N	1	1	3.27	2	2	0	0	0	11	9	4	6	5
● Warren Brusstar														
1977	Phi-N	0	0	3.38	2	0	0	0	0	2^2	2	1	1	2
1978	Phi-N	0	0	0.00	3	0	0	0	0	2^2	2	0	1	0
1980	Phi-N	1	0	3.38	2	0	0	0	0	2^2	1	1	1	0
1984	Chi-N	0	0	0.00	3	0	0	0	0	4^1	6	0	0	1
Total 4		1	0	1.46	10	0	0	0	0	12^1	11	2	3	3
● Ron Bryant														
1971	SF-N	0	0	4.50	1	0	0	0	0	2	1	1	1	2
● Britt Burns														
1983	Chi-A	0	1	0.96	1	1	0	0	0	9^1	7	1	5	8
● Ray Burris														
1981	Mon-N	1	0	0.53	2	2	0	0	1	17	10	1	3	4
● Marty Bystrom														
1980	Phi-N	0	0	1.69	1	1	0	0	0	5^1	7	1	2	1

YEAR TM/L	W	L	ERA	G	GS	CG	SV	SHO	IP	H	ER	BB	SO
Greg Cadaret													
1988 Oak-A	0	0	27.00	1	0	0	0	0	0¹	1	1	0	0
Mike Caldwell													
1982 Mil-A	0	1	15.00	1	1	0	0	0	3	7	5	1	2
Jeff Calhoun													
1986 Hou-N	0	0	9.00	1	0	0	0	0	1	1	1	1	0
Rick Camp													
1982 Atl-N	0	1	36.00	1	1	0	0	0	1	4	4	1	0
Bill Campbell													
1985 StL-N	0	0	0.00	3	0	0	0	0	2¹	3	0	0	2
John Candelaria													
1975 Pit-N	0	0	3.52	1	1	0	0	0	7²	3	3	2	14
1979 Pit-N	0	0	2.57	1	1	0	0	0	7	5	2	1	4
1986 Cal-A	1	1	0.84	2	2	0	0	0	10²	11	1	6	7
Total 3	1	1	2.13	4	4	0	0	0	25¹	19	6	9	25
Tom Candiotti													
1991 Tor-A	0	1	8.22	2	2	0	0	0	7²	17	7	2	5
Steve Carlton													
1976 Phi-N	0	1	3.86	1	1	0	0	0	7	8	3	5	6
1977 Phi-N	0	1	6.94	2	2	0	0	0	11²	13	9	8	6
1978 Phi-N	1	0	4.00	1	1	1	0	0	9	8	4	2	8
1980 Phi-N	1	0	2.19	2	2	0	0	0	12¹	11	3	8	6
1983 Phi-N	2	0	0.66	2	2	0	0	0	13²	13	1	5	13
Total 5	4	2	3.35	8	8	1	0	0	53²	53	20	28	39
Don Carrithers													
1971 SF-N	0	0	∞	1	0	0	0	0	0	3	3	0	0
Clay Carroll													
1970 Cin-N	0	0	0.00	2	0	0	1	0	1¹	2	0	0	2
1972 Cin-N	1	1	3.38	2	0	0	0	0	2²	1	3	0	0
1973 Cin-N	1	0	1.29	3	0	0	0	0	7	5	1	1	2
1975 Cin-N	0	0	0.00	1	0	0	0	0	1	0	0	1	1
Total 4	2	1	1.50	8	0	0	1	0	12	9	2	5	5
Tony Castillo													
1993 Tor-A	0	0	0.00	2	0	0	0	0	2	0	0	1	1
Bobby Castillo													
1981 LA-N	0	0	0.00	1	0	0	0	0	1	0	0	0	1
1985 LA-N	0	0	3.38	1	0	0	0	0	5¹	4	2	2	4
Total 2	0	0	2.84	2	0	0	0	0	6¹	4	2	2	5
John Cerutti													
1989 Tor-A	0	0	0.00	1	0	0	0	0	2²	0	0	3	1
Dean Chance													
1969 Min-A	0	0	13.50	1	0	0	0	0	2	4	3	0	2
Norm Charlton													
1990 Cin-N	1	1	1.80	4	0	0	0	0	5	4	1	3	3
Larry Christenson													
1977 Phi-N	0	0	8.10	1	1	0	0	0	3¹	7	3	0	2
1978 Phi-N	0	1	12.46	1	1	0	0	0	4¹	7	6	1	3
1980 Phi-N	0	0	4.05	1	1	0	0	0	6²	5	3	5	2
Total 3	0	1	7.53	3	3	0	0	0	14¹	19	12	6	7
Jim Clancy													
1985 Tor-A	0	1	9.00	1	0	0	0	0	1	2	1	1	0
1991 Atl-N	0	0	0.00	1	0	0	0	0	0¹	0	0	0	0
Total 2	0	1	6.75	2	0	0	0	0	1¹	2	1	1	0
Ken Clay													
1978 NY-A	0	0	0.00	1	0	0	1	0	3²	0	0	3	2
Mark Clear													
1979 Cal-A	0	0	4.76	1	0	0	0	0	5²	4	3	2	3
Roger Clemens													
1986 Bos-A	1	1	4.37	3	3	0	0	0	22²	22	11	7	17
1988 Bos-A	0	0	3.86	1	1	0	0	0	7	6	3	0	8
1990 Bos-A	0	1	3.52	2	2	0	0	0	7²	7	3	5	4
Total 3	1	2	4.10	6	6	0	0	0	37¹	35	17	12	29
Reggie Cleveland													
1975 Bos-A	0	0	5.40	1	1	0	0	0	5	7	3	1	2
Tony Cloninger													
1970 Cin-N	0	0	5.40	1	1	0	0	0	5	7	3	4	1
Joe Coleman													
1972 Det-A	1	0	0.00	1	1	1	0	1	9	7	0	3	14
David Cone													
1988 NY-N	1	1	4.50	3	2	1	0	0	12	10	6	5	9
1992 Tor-A	1	1	3.00	2	2	0	0	0	12	11	4	5	9
Total 2	2	2	3.75	5	4	1	0	0	24	21	10	10	18
Doug Corbett													
1986 Cal-A	1	0	5.40	3	0	0	0	0	6²	9	4	2	2
Jim Corsi													
1992 Oak-A	0	0	0.00	3	0	0	0	0	2	2	0	3	0
Danny Cox													
1985 StL-N	1	0	3.00	1	1	0	0	0	6	4	2	5	4
1987 StL-N	1	1	2.12	2	2	2	0	1	17	17	4	3	11
1992 Pit-N	0	0	0.00	2	0	0	0	0	1¹	1	0	1	1
1993 Tor-A	0	0	0.00	2	0	0	0	0	5	3	0	2	5
Total 4	2	1	1.84	7	3	2	0	1	29¹	25	6	11	21
Steve Crawford													
1986 Bos-A	1	0	0.00	1	0	0	0	0	1²	1	0	2	1
Mike Cuellar													
1969 Bal-A	0	0	2.25	1	1	0	0	0	8	3	2	1	7
1970 Bal-A	0	0	12.46	1	1	0	0	0	4¹	10	6	1	2
1971 Bal-A	1	0	1.00	1	1	1	0	0	9	6	1	1	2
1973 Bal-A	0	1	1.80	1	1	1	0	0	10	4	2	3	11
1974 Bal-A	1	1	2.84	2	2	0	0	0	12²	9	4	13	6
Total 5	2	2	3.07	6	6	2	0	0	44	32	15	19	28
John Cumberland													
1971 SF-N	0	1	9.00	1	1	0	0	0	3	7	3	0	4
Ron Darling													
1986 NY-N	0	0	7.20	1	1	0	0	0	5	6	4	2	5
1988 NY-N	0	1	7.71	2	2	0	0	0	7	11	6	4	7
1992 Oak-A	0	1	3.00	1	1	0	0	0	6	4	2	2	3
Total 3	0	2	6.00	4	4	0	0	0	18	21	12	8	15
Storm Davis													
1983 Bal-A	0	0	0.00	1	1	0	0	0	6	5	0	2	2
1988 Oak-A	0	0	0.00	1	1	0	0	0	6¹	2	0	5	4
1989 Oak-A	0	1	7.11	1	1	0	0	0	6¹	5	5	2	3
Total 3	0	1	2.41	3	3	0	0	0	18²	12	5	9	9
Ron Davis													
1980 NY-A	0	0	2.25	1	0	0	0	0	4	3	1	1	3
1981 NY-A	0	0	0.00	2	0	0	0	0	3¹	0	0	2	4
Total 2	0	0	1.23	3	0	0	0	0	7¹	3	1	3	7
Ken Dayley													
1985 StL-N	0	0	0.00	5	0	0	2	0	6	2	0	1	3
1987 StL-N	0	0	0.00	3	0	0	2	0	4	1	0	2	4
Total 2	0	0	0.00	8	0	0	4	0	10	3	0	3	7
Jose DeLeon													
1993 Chi-A	0	0	1.93	2	0	0	0	0	4²	7	1	1	6
Larry Demery													
1974 Pit-N	0	0	27.00	2	0	0	0	0	1	3	3	2	0
1975 Pit-N	0	0	18.00	1	0	0	0	0	2	4	4	1	1
Total 2	0	0	21.00	3	0	0	0	0	3	7	7	3	1
John Denny													
1983 Phi-N	0	1	0.00	1	1	0	0	0	6	5	0	3	3
Carlos Diaz													
1985 LA-N	0	0	3.00	2	0	0	0	0	3	5	1	1	2
Rob Dibble													
1990 Cin-N	0	0	0.00	4	0	0	1	0	5	0	0	1	10
Richard Dotson													
1983 Chi-A	0	1	10.80	1	1	0	0	0	5	6	6	3	3
Al Downing													
1974 LA-N	0	0	0.00	1	0	0	0	0	4	1	0	1	0
Kelly Downs													
1987 SF-N	0	0	0.00	1	0	0	0	0	1¹	1	0	0	0
1989 SF-N	1	0	3.12	2	0	0	0	0	8²	8	3	6	6
1992 Oak-A	0	1	3.86	2	0	0	0	0	2¹	3	1	1	0
Total 3	1	1	2.92	5	0	0	0	0	12¹	12	4	7	6
Paul Doyle													
1969 Atl-N	0	0	0.00	1	0	0	0	0	1	2	0	1	3
Doug Drabek													
1990 Pit-N	1	1	1.65	2	2	1	0	0	16¹	12	3	3	13
1991 Pit-N	1	1	0.60	2	2	1	0	0	15	10	1	5	10
1992 Pit-N	0	3	3.71	3	3	0	0	0	17	18	7	7	10
Total 3	2	5	2.05	7	7	2	0	0	48¹	40	11	15	33
Dick Drago													
1975 Bos-A	0	0	0.00	2	0	0	0	0	4²	2	0	1	2
Dave Dravecky													
1984 SD-N	0	0	0.00	3	0	0	0	0	6	2	0	0	5
1987 SF-N	1	1	0.60	2	2	1	0	1	15	7	1	4	14
Total 2	1	1	0.43	5	2	1	0	1	21	9	1	4	19
Rawly Eastwick													
1975 Cin-N	1	0	0.00	2	0	0	1	0	3²	2	0	2	1
1976 Cin-N	1	0	12.00	2	0	0	0	0	3	7	4	2	1
1978 Phi-N	0	0	9.00	1	0	0	0	0	1	3	1	0	1
Total 3	2	0	5.87	5	0	0	1	0	7²	12	5	4	3
Dennis Eckersley													
1984 Chi-N	0	1	8.44	1	1	0	0	0	5¹	9	5	0	0
1988 Oak-A	0	0	0.00	4	0	0	4	0	6	1	0	0	5
1989 Oak-A	0	0	1.59	4	0	0	3	0	5²	4	1	0	2
1990 Oak-A	0	0	0.00	3	0	0	2	0	3¹	2	0	0	3
1992 Oak-A	0	0	6.00	3	0	0	1	0	3	8	2	0	2
Total 5	0	1	3.09	15	1	0	10	0	23¹	24	8	2	12
Mark Eichhorn													
1992 Tor-A	0	0	0.00	1	0	0	0	0	1	0	0	0	0
1993 Tor-A	0	0	0.00	1	0	0	0	0	2	1	0	1	1
Total 2	0	0	0.00	2	0	0	0	0	3	1	0	1	1

YEAR	TM/L	W	L	ERA	G	GS	CG	SV	SHO	IP	H	ER	BB	SO
● **Dock Ellis**														
1970	Pit-N	0	1	2.79	1	1	0	0	0	9²	9	3	4	1
1971	Pit-N	1	0	3.60	1	1	0	0	0	5	6	2	4	1
1972	Pit-N	0	1	0.00	1	1	0	0	0	5	5	0	1	3
1975	Pit-N	0	0	0.00	1	0	0	0	0	2	2	0	0	2
1976	NY-A	1	0	3.38	1	1	0	0	0	8	6	3	2	5
Total 5		2	2	2.43	5	4	0	0	0	29²	28	8	11	12
● **Scott Erickson**														
1991	Min-A	0	0	4.50	1	1	0	0	0	4	3	2	5	2
● **Steve Farr**														
1985	KC-A	1	0	1.42	2	0	0	0	0	6¹	4	1	1	3
● **Alex Fernandez**														
1993	Chi-A	0	2	1.80	2	2	0	0	0	15	15	3	6	10
● **Sid Fernandez**														
1986	NY-N	0	1	4.50	1	1	0	0	0	6	3	3	1	5
1988	NY-N	0	1	13.50	1	1	0	0	0	4	7	6	1	5
Total 2		0	2	8.10	2	2	0	0	0	10	10	9	2	10
● **Ed Figueroa**														
1976	NY-A	0	1	5.84	2	2	0	0	0	12¹	14	8	2	5
1977	NY-A	0	0	10.80	1	1	0	0	0	3¹	5	4	2	3
1978	NY-A	0	1	27.00	1	1	0	0	0	1	5	3	0	0
Total 3		0	2	8.10	4	4	0	0	0	16²	24	15	4	8
● **Rollie Fingers**														
1971	Oak-A	0	0	7.71	2	0	0	0	0	2¹	2	2	1	2
1972	Oak-A	1	0	1.69	3	0	0	0	0	5¹	4	1	1	3
1973	Oak-A	0	1	1.93	3	0	0	1	0	4²	4	1	2	4
1974	Oak-A	0	0	3.00	2	0	0	1	0	3	3	1	1	3
1975	Oak-A	0	1	6.75	1	0	0	0	0	4	5	3	1	3
Total 5		1	2	3.72	11	0	0	2	0	19¹	18	8	6	15
● **Chuck Finley**														
1986	Cal-A	0	0	0.00	3	0	0	0	0	2	1	0	0	1
● **Mike Flanagan**														
1979	Bal-A	1	0	5.14	1	1	0	0	0	7	6	4	1	2
1983	Bal-A	1	0	1.80	1	1	0	0	0	5	5	1	0	1
1989	Tor-A	0	1	10.38	1	1	0	0	0	4¹	7	5	1	3
Total 3		2	1	5.51	3	3	0	0	0	16¹	18	10	2	6
● **Ken Forsch**														
1980	Hou-N	0	1	4.15	2	1	0	0	0	8²	10	4	1	6
● **Bob Forsch**														
1982	StL-N	1	0	0.00	1	1	0	1	0	9	3	0	0	6
1985	StL-N	0	0	5.40	1	1	0	0	0	3¹	3	2	2	0
1987	StL-N	1	1	12.00	3	0	0	0	0	3	4	4	1	3
Total 3		2	1	3.52	5	2	1	0	1	15¹	10	6	3	9
● **Terry Forster**														
1978	LA-N	1	0	0.00	1	0	0	0	0	1	1	0	0	2
1981	LA-N	0	0	0.00	1	0	0	0	0	0¹	0	0	0	1
Total 2		1	0	0.00	2	0	0	0	0	1¹	1	0	0	3
● **George Frazier**														
1981	NY-A	1	0	0.00	1	0	0	0	0	5²	5	0	1	5
1984	Chi-N	0	0	10.80	1	0	0	0	0	1²	2	2	0	1
Total 2		1	0	2.45	2	0	0	0	0	7¹	7	2	1	6
● **Marvin Freeman**														
1992	Atl-N	0	0	14.73	3	0	0	0	0	3²	8	6	2	1
● **Dave Frost**														
1979	Cal-A	0	1	18.69	2	1	0	0	0	4¹	8	9	5	1
● **Woodie Fryman**														
1972	Det-A	0	2	3.65	2	2	0	0	0	12¹	11	5	2	8
1981	Mon-N	0	0	36.00	1	0	0	0	0	1	3	4	1	1
Total 2		0	2	6.07	3	2	0	0	0	13¹	14	9	3	9
● **Gene Garber**														
1976	Phi-N	0	1	40.50	2	0	0	0	0	0²	2	3	1	0
1977	Phi-N	1	1	3.38	3	0	0	0	0	5¹	4	2	0	3
1982	Atl-N	0	1	8.10	2	0	0	0	0	3¹	4	3	1	3
Total 3		1	3	7.71	7	0	0	0	0	9¹	10	8	2	6
● **Wes Gardner**														
1988	Bos-A	0	0	5.79	2	0	0	0	0	4²	6	3	2	8
● **Wayne Garland**														
1974	Bal-A	0	0	0.00	1	0	0	0	0	0²	1	0	1	0
● **Mike Garman**														
1977	LA-N	0	0	0.00	2	0	0	1	0	1¹	0	0	0	1
● **Scott Garrelts**														
1987	SF-N	0	0	6.75	2	0	0	0	0	2²	2	2	4	4
1989	SF-N	1	0	5.40	2	2	0	0	0	11²	16	7	2	8
Total 2		1	0	5.65	4	2	0	0	0	14¹	18	9	6	12
● **Gary Gentry**														
1969	NY-N	0	0	9.00	1	1	0	0	0	2	5	2	1	1
● **Joe Gibbon**														
1970	Pit-N	0	0	0.00	2	0	0	0	0	0¹	1	0	0	1
● **Dave Giusti**														
1970	Pit-N	0	0	3.86	2	0	0	0	0	2¹	3	1	1	1
1971	Pit-N	0	0	0.00	4	0	0	3	0	5¹	1	0	2	3
1972	Pit-N	0	1	6.75	3	0	0	1	0	2²	5	2	0	3
1974	Pit-N	0	1	21.60	3	0	0	0	0	3¹	13	8	5	1
1975	Pit-N	0	0	0.00	1	0	0	0	0	1¹	0	0	0	1
Total 5		0	2	6.60	13	0	0	4	0	15	22	11	8	9
● **Tom Glavine**														
1991	Atl-N	0	2	3.21	2	2	0	0	0	14	12	5	6	11
1992	Atl-N	0	2	12.27	2	2	0	0	0	7¹	13	10	3	2
1993	Atl-N	1	0	2.57	1	1	0	0	0	7	6	2	0	5
Total 3		1	4	5.40	5	5	0	0	0	28¹	31	17	9	18
● **Dave Goltz**														
1982	Cal-A	0	0	7.36	1	0	0	0	0	3²	4	3	2	2
● **Dwight Gooden**														
1986	NY-N	0	1	1.06	2	2	0	0	0	17	16	2	5	9
1988	NY-N	0	0	2.95	3	2	0	0	0	18¹	10	6	8	20
Total 2		0	1	2.04	5	4	0	0	0	35¹	26	8	13	29
● **Rich Gossage**														
1978	NY-A	1	0	4.50	2	0	0	1	0	4	3	2	0	3
1980	NY-A	0	1	54.00	1	0	0	0	0	0¹	3	2	0	0
1981	NY-A	0	0	0.00	2	0	0	1	0	2²	1	0	0	2
1984	SD-N	0	0	4.50	3	0	0	1	0	4	5	2	1	5
Total 4		1	1	4.91	8	0	0	3	0	11	12	6	1	10
● **Wayne Granger**														
1970	Cin-N	0	0	0.00	1	0	0	0	0	0²	1	0	0	0
● **Mudcat Grant**														
1971	Oak-A	0	0	0.00	1	0	0	0	0	2	3	0	0	2
● **Jeff Gray**														
1990	Bos-A	0	0	2.70	2	0	0	0	0	3¹	4	1	1	2
● **Tommy Greene**														
1993	Phi-N	1	1	9.64	2	2	0	0	0	9¹	12	10	7	7
● **Ross Grimsley**														
1972	Cin-N	1	0	1.00	1	1	1	0	0	9	2	1	0	5
1973	Cin-N	0	1	12.27	2	1	0	0	0	3²	7	5	2	3
1974	Bal-A	0	0	1.69	2	0	0	0	0	5¹	1	1	2	2
Total 3		1	1	3.50	5	2	1	0	0	18	10	7	4	10
● **Joe Grzenda**														
1969	Min-A	0	0	0.00	1	0	0	0	0	0²	0	0	0	0
● **Mark Gubicza**														
1985	KC-A	1	0	3.24	2	1	0	0	0	8¹	4	3	4	4
● **Ron Guidry**														
1977	NY-A	1	0	3.97	2	2	1	0	0	11¹	9	5	3	8
1978	NY-A	1	0	1.13	1	1	0	0	0	8	7	1	1	7
1980	NY-A	0	1	12.00	1	1	0	0	0	3	5	4	4	2
Total 3		2	1	4.03	4	4	1	0	0	22¹	21	10	8	17
● **Don Gullett**														
1970	Cin-N	0	0	0.00	2	0	0	0	0	3²	1	0	2	3
1972	Cin-N	0	1	8.00	2	2	0	0	0	9	12	8	0	5
1973	Cin-N	0	1	2.00	3	1	0	0	0	9	4	2	3	6
1975	Cin-N	1	0	3.00	1	1	0	0	0	9	8	3	2	5
1976	Cin-N	1	0	1.13	1	1	0	0	0	8	2	1	3	4
1977	NY-A	0	1	18.00	1	1	0	0	0	2	4	4	2	0
Total 6		2	3	3.98	10	6	1	2	0	40²	31	18	12	23
● **Bill Gullickson**														
1981	Mon-N	0	2	2.51	2	2	0	0	0	14¹	12	4	6	12
● **Larry Gura**														
1976	KC-A	0	1	4.22	2	2	0	0	0	10²	18	5	1	4
1977	KC-A	0	1	18.00	2	1	0	0	0	2	7	4	1	2
1978	KC-A	1	0	2.84	1	1	0	0	0	6¹	8	2	2	2
1980	KC-A	1	0	2.00	1	1	0	0	0	9	10	2	1	4
Total 4		2	2	4.18	6	5	1	0	0	28	43	13	5	12
● **Mark Guthrie**														
1991	Min-A	1	0	0.00	2	0	0	0	0	2²	0	0	0	0
● **Juan Guzman**														
1991	Tor-A	1	0	3.18	1	1	0	0	0	5²	4	2	4	2
1992	Tor-A	2	0	2.08	2	2	0	0	0	13	12	3	5	11
1993	Tor-A	2	0	2.08	2	2	0	0	0	13	8	3	9	9
Total 3		5	0	2.27	5	5	0	0	0	31²	24	8	18	22
● **Moose Haas**														
1982	Mil-A	1	0	4.91	1	1	0	0	0	7¹	5	4	5	7
● **Dick Hall**														
1969	Bal-A	1	0	0.00	1	0	0	0	0	0²	0	0	0	1
1970	Bal-A	1	0	0.00	1	0	0	0	0	4²	1	0	0	3
Total 2		2	0	0.00	2	0	0	0	0	5¹	1	0	0	4
● **Tom Hall**														
1969	Min-A	0	0	0.00	1	0	0	0	0	0²	0	0	0	0
1970	Min-A	0	1	6.75	2	1	0	0	0	5¹	6	4	4	6
1972	Cin-N	1	0	1.23	2	0	0	0	0	7¹	3	1	3	8
1973	Cin-N	0	0	67.50	3	0	0	0	0	0²	3	5	4	1
1976	KC-A	0	0	0.00	1	0	0	0	0	0¹	1	0	0	0
Total 5		1	1	6.28	9	1	0	0	0	14¹	13	10	11	15
● **Dave Hamilton**														
1972	Oak-A	0	0	—	1	0	0	0	0	0	1	0	1	0

YEAR TM/L	W	L	ERA	G	GS	CG	SV	SHO	IP	H	ER	BB	SO
● **Steve Hamilton**													
1971 SF-N	0	0	9.00	1	0	0	0	0	1	1	1	0	3
● **Atlee Hammaker**													
1987 SF-N	0	1	7.87	2	2	0	0	0	8	12	7	0	7
1989 SF-N	0	0	0.00	1	0	0	0	0	1	1	0	0	0
Total 2	0	1	7.00	3	2	0	0	0	9	13	7	0	7
● **Greg Harris**													
1984 SD-N	0	0	31.50	1	0	0	0	0	2	9	7	3	2
1990 Bos-A	0	1	27.00	1	0	0	0	0	0^1	3	1	0	0
Total 2	0	1	30.86	2	0	0	0	0	2^1	12	8	3	2
● **Andy Hassler**													
1976 KC-A	0	1	6.14	2	1	0	0	0	7^1	8	5	6	4
1977 KC-A	0	1	4.76	1	1	0	0	0	5^2	5	3	0	3
1982 Cal-A	0	0	0.00	2	0	0	0	0	2^2	0	0	0	2
Total 3	0	2	4.60	5	2	0	0	0	15^2	13	8	6	9
● **Andy Hawkins**													
1984 SD-N	0	0	0.00	3	0	0	0	0	3^2	0	0	2	1
● **Tom Henke**													
1985 Tor-A	2	0	4.26	3	0	0	0	0	6^1	5	3	4	4
1989 Tor-A	0	0	0.00	3	0	0	0	0	2^2	0	0	0	3
1991 Tor-A	0	0	0.00	2	0	0	0	0	2^2	0	0	1	5
1992 Tor-A	0	0	0.00	4	0	0	3	0	4^2	4	0	2	2
Total 4	2	0	1.65	12	0	0	3	0	16^1	9	3	7	14
● **Mike Henneman**													
1987 Det-A	1	0	10.80	3	0	0	0	0	5	6	6	6	3
● **Pat Hentgen**													
1993 Tor-A	0	1	18.00	1	1	0	0	0	3	9	6	2	3
● **Willie Hernandez**													
1984 Det-A	0	0	2.25	3	0	0	1	0	4	3	1	1	3
1987 Det-A	0	0	0.00	1	0	0	0	0	0^1	2	0	0	0
Total 2	0	0	2.08	4	0	0	1	0	4^1	5	1	1	3
● **Ramon Hernandez**													
1972 Pit-N	0	0	2.70	3	0	0	1	0	3^1	1	1	0	3
1974 Pit-N	0	0	0.00	2	0	0	0	0	4^1	3	0	1	2
1975 Pit-N	0	1	27.00	1	0	0	0	0	0^2	3	2	0	0
Total 3	0	1	3.24	6	0	0	1	0	8^1	7	3	1	5
● **Roberto Hernandez**													
1993 Chi-A	0	0	0.00	4	0	0	1	0	4	4	0	0	1
● **Orel Hershiser**													
1985 LA-N	1	0	3.52	2	2	1	0	0	15^1	17	6	6	5
1988 LA-N	1	0	1.09	4	3	1	1	0	24^2	18	3	7	15
Total 2	2	0	2.03	6	5	2	1	1	40	35	9	13	20
● **John Hiller**													
1972 Det-A	1	0	0.00	3	0	0	0	0	3^1	1	0	1	1
● **Al Holland**													
1983 Phi-N	0	0	0.00	2	0	0	1	0	3	1	0	0	3
● **Brian Holton**													
1988 LA-N	0	0	2.25	3	0	0	1	0	4	2	1	1	2
● **Ken Holtzman**													
1972 Oak-A	0	1	4.50	1	1	0	0	0	4	4	2	2	2
1973 Oak-A	1	0	0.82	1	1	1	0	0	11	3	1	1	7
1974 Oak-A	1	0	0.00	1	1	1	0	1	9	5	0	2	3
1975 Oak-A	0	2	4.09	2	2	0	0	0	11	12	5	1	7
Total 4	2	3	2.06	5	5	2	0	1	35	24	8	6	19
● **Rick Honeycutt**													
1983 LA-N	0	0	21.60	2	0	0	0	0	1^2	4	4	0	2
1985 LA-N	0	0	13.50	2	0	0	0	0	1^1	4	2	2	1
1988 Oak-A	1	0	0.00	3	0	0	0	0	2	0	0	2	0
1989 Oak-A	0	0	32.40	2	0	0	0	0	1^2	6	6	5	1
1990 Oak-A	0	0	0.00	3	0	0	1	0	1^2	0	0	0	0
1992 Oak-A	0	0	0.00	2	0	0	0	0	2	0	0	0	1
Total 6	1	0	10.45	15	0	0	1	0	10^1	14	12	9	5
● **Burt Hooton**													
1977 LA-N	0	1	16.20	1	1	0	0	0	1^2	2	3	4	1
1978 LA-N	0	0	7.71	1	1	0	0	0	4^2	10	4	0	5
1981 LA-N	2	0	0.00	2	2	0	0	0	14^2	11	0	6	7
Total 3	2	0	3.00	4	4	0	0	0	21	23	7	10	13
● **Joe Horlen**													
1972 Oak-A	0	1	∞	1	0	0	0	0	0	1	1	1	0
● **Ricky Horton**													
1985 StL-N	0	0	9.00	3	0	0	0	0	3	4	3	2	1
1987 StL-N	0	0	0.00	1	0	0	0	0	3	2	0	0	2
1988 LA-N	0	0	0.00	4	0	0	0	0	4^1	4	0	2	3
Total 3	0	0	2.61	8	0	0	0	0	10^1	10	3	4	6
● **Charlie Hough**													
1974 LA-N	0	0	7.71	1	0	0	0	0	2^1	4	2	0	2
1977 LA-N	0	0	4.50	1	0	0	0	0	2	2	1	0	3
1978 LA-N	0	0	4.50	1	0	0	0	0	2	1	1	0	1
Total 3	0	0	5.68	3	0	0	0	0	6^1	7	4	0	6
● **Steve Howe**													
1981 LA-N	0	0	0.00	2	0	0	0	0	2	1	0	0	2
● **Jay Howell**													
1988 LA-N	0	1	27.00	2	0	0	0	0	0^2	1	2	2	1
● **Ken Howell**													
1985 LA-N	0	0	0.00	1	0	0	0	0	2	0	0	0	2
● **La Marr Hoyt**													
1983 Chi-A	1	0	1.00	1	1	1	0	0	9	5	1	0	4
● **Al Hrabosky**													
1978 KC-A	0	0	3.00	3	0	0	0	0	3	3	1	0	2
● **Charles Hudson**													
1983 Phi-N	1	0	2.00	1	1	1	0	0	9	4	2	2	9
● **Mark Huismann**													
1984 KC-A	0	0	10.13	1	0	0	0	0	2^2	6	3	1	2
● **Tom Hume**													
1979 Cin-N	0	1	6.75	3	0	0	0	0	4	6	3	0	2
● **Catfish Hunter**													
1971 Oak-A	0	1	5.63	1	1	1	0	0	8	7	5	2	6
1972 Oak-A	0	0	1.17	2	2	0	0	0	15^1	10	2	5	9
1973 Oak-A	2	0	1.65	2	2	1	0	0	16^1	12	3	5	6
1974 Oak-A	1	1	4.63	2	2	0	0	0	11^2	11	6	2	6
1976 NY-A	1	1	4.50	2	2	1	0	0	12	10	6	1	5
1978 NY-A	0	0	4.50	1	1	0	0	0	6	7	3	3	5
Total 6	4	3	3.25	10	10	3	0	0	69^1	57	25	18	37
● **Bruce Hurst**													
1986 Bos-A	1	0	2.40	2	2	1	0	0	15	18	4	1	8
1988 Bos-A	0	2	2.77	2	2	1	0	0	13	10	4	5	12
Total 2	1	2	2.57	4	4	2	0	0	28	28	8	6	20
● **Danny Jackson**													
1985 KC-A	1	0	0.00	2	1	1	0	1	10	10	0	1	7
1990 Cin-N	1	0	2.38	2	2	0	0	0	11^1	8	3	7	8
1992 Pit-N	0	1	21.60	1	1	0	0	0	1^2	4	4	2	0
1993 Phi-N	1	0	1.17	1	1	0	0	0	7^2	9	1	2	6
Total 4	3	1	2.35	6	5	1	0	1	30^2	31	8	12	21
● **Grant Jackson**													
1973 Bal-A	1	0	0.00	2	0	0	0	0	3	0	0	1	0
1974 Bal-A	0	0	0.00	1	0	0	0	0	0^1	1	0	0	1
1976 NY-A	0	0	8.10	2	0	0	0	0	3^1	4	3	1	3
1979 Pit-N	1	0	0.00	2	0	0	0	0	2	1	0	1	2
Total 4	2	0	3.12	7	0	0	0	0	8^2	6	3	3	6
● **Pat Jarvis**													
1969 Atl-N	0	1	12.46	1	1	0	0	0	4^1	10	6	0	6
● **Tommy John**													
1977 LA-N	1	0	0.66	2	2	1	0	0	13^2	11	1	5	11
1978 LA-N	1	0	0.00	1	1	1	0	1	9	4	0	2	4
1980 NY-A	0	0	2.70	1	1	0	0	0	6^2	8	2	1	3
1981 NY-A	1	0	1.50	1	1	0	0	0	6	6	1	1	3
1982 Cal-A	1	1	5.11	2	2	1	0	0	12^1	11	7	6	6
Total 5	4	1	2.08	7	7	3	0	1	47^2	40	11	15	27
● **Jerry Johnson**													
1971 SF-N	0	0	13.50	1	0	0	0	0	1^1	1	2	1	2
● **Bob Johnson**													
1971 Pit-N	1	0	0.00	1	1	0	0	0	8	5	0	3	7
1972 Pit-N	0	0	3.00	2	0	0	0	0	6	4	2	2	7
Total 2	1	0	1.29	3	1	0	0	0	14	9	2	5	14
● **Jeff Jones**													
1981 Oak-A	0	0	4.50	1	0	0	0	0	2	2	1	1	0
● **Mike Jones**													
1984 KC-A	0	0	6.75	1	0	0	0	0	1^1	1	1	0	0
● **Jim Kaat**													
1970 Min-A	0	1	9.00	1	1	0	0	0	2	6	2	2	1
1976 Phi-N	0	0	3.00	1	1	0	0	0	6	2	2	2	1
Total 2	0	1	4.50	2	2	0	0	0	8	8	4	4	2
● **Matt Keough**													
1981 Oak-A	0	1	1.08	1	1	0	0	0	8^1	7	1	6	2
● **Charlie Kerfeld**													
1986 Hou-N	0	1	2.25	3	0	0	0	0	4	2	1	1	4
● **Jimmy Key**													
1985 Tor-A	0	1	5.19	2	2	0	0	0	8^2	15	5	2	5
1989 Tor-A	1	0	4.50	1	1	0	0	0	6	7	3	2	2
1991 Tor-A	0	0	3.00	1	1	0	0	0	6	5	2	1	1
1992 Tor-A	0	0	0.00	1	0	0	0	0	3	2	0	2	1
Total 4	1	1	3.80	5	4	0	0	0	23^2	29	10	7	9
● **Dana Kiecker**													
1990 Bos-A	0	0	1.59	1	1	0	0	0	5^2	6	1	1	2
● **Paul Kilgus**													
1989 Chi-N	0	0	0.00	1	0	0	0	0	3	4	0	1	1
● **Eric King**													
1987 Det-A	0	0	1.69	1	0	0	0	0	5^1	3	1	2	4
● **Brian Kingman**													
1981 Oak-A	0	0	81.00	1	0	0	0	0	0^1	3	3	0	0

Bob Kipper

YEAR	TM/L	W	L	ERA	G	GS	CG	SV	SHO	IP	H	ER	BB	SO
1991	Pit-N	0	0	4.50	1	0	0	0	0	2	2	1	0	1

Bruce Kison

YEAR	TM/L	W	L	ERA	G	GS	CG	SV	SHO	IP	H	ER	BB	SO
1971	Pit-N	1	0	0.00	1	0	0	0	0	4^2	2	0	2	3
1972	Pit-N	1	0	0.00	2	0	0	0	0	2^1	1	0	0	3
1974	Pit-N	1	0	0.00	1	1	0	0	0	6^2	2	0	6	5
1975	Pit-N	0	0	4.50	1	0	0	0	0	2	2	1	1	1
1982	Cal-A	1	0	1.93	2	2	1	0	0	14	8	3	3	12
Total 5		4	0	1.21	7	3	1	0	0	29^2	15	4	12	24

Chris Knapp

YEAR	TM/L	W	L	ERA	G	GS	CG	SV	SHO	IP	H	ER	BB	SO
1979	Cal-A	0	1	7.71	1	1	0	0	0	2^1	5	2	1	0

Bob Knepper

YEAR	TM/L	W	L	ERA	G	GS	CG	SV	SHO	IP	H	ER	BB	SO
1986	Hou-N	0	0	3.52	2	2	0	0	0	15^1	13	6	1	9

Darold Knowles

YEAR	TM/L	W	L	ERA	G	GS	CG	SV	SHO	IP	H	ER	BB	SO
1971	Oak-A	0	0	0.00	1	0	0	0	0	0^1	1	0	0	0

Jerry Koosman

YEAR	TM/L	W	L	ERA	G	GS	CG	SV	SHO	IP	H	ER	BB	SO
1969	NY-N	0	0	11.57	1	1	0	0	0	4^2	7	6	4	5
1973	NY-N	1	0	2.00	1	1	1	0	0	9	8	2	0	9
1983	Chi-A	0	0	54.00	1	0	0	0	0	0^1	1	2	2	0
Total 3		1	0	6.43	3	2	1	0	0	14	16	10	6	14

Mike Krukow

YEAR	TM/L	W	L	ERA	G	GS	CG	SV	SHO	IP	H	ER	BB	SO
1987	SF-N	0	1	2.00	1	1	0	0	0	9	9	2	1	3

Frank LaCorte

YEAR	TM/L	W	L	ERA	G	GS	CG	SV	SHO	IP	H	ER	BB	SO
1980	Hou-N	1	1	3.00	2	0	0	0	0	3	7	1	2	2

Mike LaCoss

YEAR	TM/L	W	L	ERA	G	GS	CG	SV	SHO	IP	H	ER	BB	SO
1979	Cin-N	0	1	10.80	1	1	0	0	0	1^2	1	2	4	0
1987	SF-N	0	0	0.00	2	0	0	0	0	3^1	1	0	3	2
1989	SF-N	0	0	9.00	1	1	0	0	0	3	7	3	0	2
Total 3		0	1	5.63	4	2	0	0	0	8	9	5	7	4

Pete Ladd

YEAR	TM/L	W	L	ERA	G	GS	CG	SV	SHO	IP	H	ER	BB	SO
1982	Mil-A	0	0	0.00	3	0	0	2	0	3^1	0	0	0	5

Lerrin LaGrow

YEAR	TM/L	W	L	ERA	G	GS	CG	SV	SHO	IP	H	ER	BB	SO
1972	Det-A	0	0	0.00	1	0	0	0	0	1	0	0	0	1

Jeff Lahti

YEAR	TM/L	W	L	ERA	G	GS	CG	SV	SHO	IP	H	ER	BB	SO
1985	StL-N	1	0	0.00	2	0	0	0	0	2	2	0	0	1

Dennis Lamp

YEAR	TM/L	W	L	ERA	G	GS	CG	SV	SHO	IP	H	ER	BB	SO
1983	Chi-A	0	0	0.00	3	0	0	0	0	2	0	0	2	1
1985	Tor-A	0	0	0.00	3	0	0	0	0	9^1	2	0	1	10
1990	Bos-A	0	0	108.00	1	0	0	0	0	0^1	2	4	2	0
Total 3		0	0	3.09	7	0	0	0	0	11^2	4	4	5	11

Les Lancaster

YEAR	TM/L	W	L	ERA	G	GS	CG	SV	SHO	IP	H	ER	BB	SO
1989	Chi-N	1	1	6.00	3	0	0	0	0	6	6	4	1	3

Bill Landrum

YEAR	TM/L	W	L	ERA	G	GS	CG	SV	SHO	IP	H	ER	BB	SO
1990	Pit-N	0	0	0.00	2	0	0	0	0	2	0	0	0	1
1991	Pit-N	0	0	9.00	1	0	0	0	0	1	2	1	2	2
Total 2		0	0	3.00	3	0	0	0	0	3	2	1	2	3

Dave LaRoche

YEAR	TM/L	W	L	ERA	G	GS	CG	SV	SHO	IP	H	ER	BB	SO
1979	Cal-A	0	0	6.75	1	0	0	0	0	1^1	2	1	1	1

Gary Lavelle

YEAR	TM/L	W	L	ERA	G	GS	CG	SV	SHO	IP	H	ER	BB	SO
1985	Tor-A	0	0	—	1	0	0	0	0	0	0	0	0	1	0

Terry Leach

YEAR	TM/L	W	L	ERA	G	GS	CG	SV	SHO	IP	H	ER	BB	SO
1988	NY-N	0	0	0.00	3	0	0	0	0	5	4	0	1	4

Tim Leary

YEAR	TM/L	W	L	ERA	G	GS	CG	SV	SHO	IP	H	ER	BB	SO
1988	LA-N	0	1	6.23	2	1	0	0	0	4^1	8	3	3	3

Bill Lee

YEAR	TM/L	W	L	ERA	G	GS	CG	SV	SHO	IP	H	ER	BB	SO
1981	Mon-N	0	0	0.00	1	0	0	0	0	0^1	1	0	0	0

Craig Lefferts

YEAR	TM/L	W	L	ERA	G	GS	CG	SV	SHO	IP	H	ER	BB	SO
1984	SD-N	2	0	0.00	3	0	0	0	0	4	1	0	1	1
1987	SF-N	0	0	0.00	3	0	0	0	0	2	3	0	1	0
1989	SF-N	0	0	9.00	2	0	0	0	0	1	1	1	2	1
Total 3		2	0	1.29	8	0	0	0	0	7	5	1	4	2

Charlie Leibrandt

YEAR	TM/L	W	L	ERA	G	GS	CG	SV	SHO	IP	H	ER	BB	SO
1979	Cin-N	0	0	0.00	1	0	0	0	0	0^1	0	0	0	0
1984	KC-A	0	1	1.13	1	1	1	0	0	8	3	1	4	6
1985	KC-A	1	2	5.28	3	2	0	0	0	15^1	17	9	4	6
1991	Atl-N	0	0	1.35	1	1	0	0	0	6^2	8	1	3	6
1992	Atl-N	0	0	1.93	2	0	0	0	0	4^2	4	1	3	3
Total 5		1	3	3.09	8	4	1	0	0	35	32	12	14	21

Al Leiter

YEAR	TM/L	W	L	ERA	G	GS	CG	SV	SHO	IP	H	ER	BB	SO
1993	Tor-A	0	0	3.38	2	0	0	0	0	2^2	4	1	2	2

Dennis Leonard

YEAR	TM/L	W	L	ERA	G	GS	CG	SV	SHO	IP	H	ER	BB	SO
1976	KC-A	0	0	19.29	2	2	0	0	0	2^1	9	5	2	0
1977	KC-A	1	1	3.00	2	1	1	0	0	9	5	3	2	4
1978	KC-A	0	2	3.75	2	2	1	0	0	12	13	5	2	11
1980	KC-A	1	0	2.25	1	1	0	0	0	8	7	2	1	8
Total 4		2	3	4.31	7	6	2	0	0	31^1	34	15	7	23

Randy Lerch

YEAR	TM/L	W	L	ERA	G	GS	CG	SV	SHO	IP	H	ER	BB	SO
1978	Phi-N	0	0	5.06	1	1	0	0	0	5^1	7	3	0	0

Paul Lindblad

YEAR	TM/L	W	L	ERA	G	GS	CG	SV	SHO	IP	H	ER	BB	SO
1975	Oak-A	0	0	0.00	2	0	0	0	0	4^2	5	0	1	0

Mark Littell

YEAR	TM/L	W	L	ERA	G	GS	CG	SV	SHO	IP	H	ER	BB	SO
1976	KC-A	0	1	1.93	3	0	0	0	0	4^2	4	1	1	3
1977	KC-A	0	0	3.00	2	0	0	0	0	3	5	1	3	1
Total 2		0	1	2.35	5	0	0	0	0	7^2	9	2	4	4

Bob Locker

YEAR	TM/L	W	L	ERA	G	GS	CG	SV	SHO	IP	H	ER	BB	SO
1971	Oak-A	0	0	0.00	1	0	0	0	0	0^2	0	0	2	0
1972	Oak-A	0	0	13.50	2	0	0	0	0	2	4	3	0	1
Total 2		0	0	10.13	3	0	0	0	0	2^2	4	3	2	1

Mickey Lolich

YEAR	TM/L	W	L	ERA	G	GS	CG	SV	SHO	IP	H	ER	BB	SO
1972	Det-A	0	1	1.42	2	2	0	0	0	19	14	3	5	10

Tim Lollar

YEAR	TM/L	W	L	ERA	G	GS	CG	SV	SHO	IP	H	ER	BB	SO
1984	SD-N	0	0	6.23	1	1	0	0	0	4^1	3	3	4	3

Jim Lonborg

YEAR	TM/L	W	L	ERA	G	GS	CG	SV	SHO	IP	H	ER	BB	SO
1976	Phi-N	0	1	1.69	1	1	0	0	0	5^1	2	1	2	2
1977	Phi-N	0	1	11.25	1	1	0	0	0	4	5	5	1	1
Total 2		0	2	5.79	2	2	0	0	0	9^1	7	6	3	3

Aurelio Lopez

YEAR	TM/L	W	L	ERA	G	GS	CG	SV	SHO	IP	H	ER	BB	SO
1984	Det-A	1	0	0.00	1	0	0	0	0	3	4	0	1	2
1986	Hou-N	0	1	8.10	2	0	0	0	0	3^1	7	3	4	3
Total 2		1	1	4.26	3	0	0	0	0	6^1	11	3	5	5

Marcelino Lopez

YEAR	TM/L	W	L	ERA	G	GS	CG	SV	SHO	IP	H	ER	BB	SO
1969	Bal-A	0	0	0.00	1	0	0	0	0	0^1	1	0	2	0

Gary Lucas

YEAR	TM/L	W	L	ERA	G	GS	CG	SV	SHO	IP	H	ER	BB	SO
1986	Cal-A	0	0	11.57	4	0	0	0	0	2^1	3	3	1	2

Sparky Lyle

YEAR	TM/L	W	L	ERA	G	GS	CG	SV	SHO	IP	H	ER	BB	SO
1976	NY-A	0	0	0.00	1	0	0	1	0	1	0	0	1	0
1977	NY-A	2	0	0.96	4	0	0	1	0	9^1	7	1	0	3
1978	NY-A	0	0	13.50	1	0	0	0	0	1^1	3	2	0	0
Total 3		2	0	2.31	6	0	0	1	0	11^2	10	3	1	3

Rob Mac Donald

YEAR	TM/L	W	L	ERA	G	GS	CG	SV	SHO	IP	H	ER	BB	SO
1991	Tor-A	0	0	9.00	1	0	0	0	0	1	1	1	1	0

Greg Maddux

YEAR	TM/L	W	L	ERA	G	GS	CG	SV	SHO	IP	H	ER	BB	SO
1989	Chi-N	0	1	13.50	2	2	0	0	0	7^1	13	11	4	5
1993	Atl-N	1	1	4.97	2	2	0	0	0	12^2	11	7	7	11
Total 2		1	2	8.10	4	4	0	0	0	20	24	18	11	16

Joe Magrane

YEAR	TM/L	W	L	ERA	G	GS	CG	SV	SHO	IP	H	ER	BB	SO
1987	StL-N	0	0	9.00	1	1	0	0	0	4	4	4	2	3

Rick Mahler

YEAR	TM/L	W	L	ERA	G	GS	CG	SV	SHO	IP	H	ER	BB	SO
1982	Atl-N	0	0	0.00	1	0	0	0	0	1^2	3	0	2	0
1990	Cin-N	0	0	0.00	1	0	0	0	0	1^2	2	0	0	0
Total 2		0	0	0.00	2	0	0	0	0	3^1	5	0	2	0

Juan Marichal

YEAR	TM/L	W	L	ERA	G	GS	CG	SV	SHO	IP	H	ER	BB	SO
1971	SF-N	0	1	2.25	1	1	1	0	0	8	4	2	0	6

Mike Marshall

YEAR	TM/L	W	L	ERA	G	GS	CG	SV	SHO	IP	H	ER	BB	SO
1974	LA-N	0	0	0.00	2	0	0	0	0	3	0	0	0	1

Tippy Martinez

YEAR	TM/L	W	L	ERA	G	GS	CG	SV	SHO	IP	H	ER	BB	SO
1983	Bal-A	1	0	0.00	2	0	0	0	0	6	5	0	3	5

Dennis Martinez

YEAR	TM/L	W	L	ERA	G	GS	CG	SV	SHO	IP	H	ER	BB	SO
1979	Bal-A	0	0	3.24	1	1	0	0	0	8^1	8	3	0	4

Roger Mason

YEAR	TM/L	W	L	ERA	G	GS	CG	SV	SHO	IP	H	ER	BB	SO
1991	Pit-N	0	0	0.00	3	0	0	1	0	4^1	3	0	1	2
1992	Pit-N	0	0	0.00	2	0	0	0	0	3^1	0	0	2	1
1993	Phi-N	0	0	0.00	2	0	0	0	0	3	1	0	0	2
Total 3		0	0	0.00	7	0	0	1	0	10^2	4	0	3	5

Greg Mathews

YEAR	TM/L	W	L	ERA	G	GS	CG	SV	SHO	IP	H	ER	BB	SO
1987	StL-N	1	0	3.48	2	2	0	0	0	10^1	6	4	3	10

Jon Matlack

YEAR	TM/L	W	L	ERA	G	GS	CG	SV	SHO	IP	H	ER	BB	SO
1973	NY-N	1	0	0.00	1	1	1	0	1	9	2	0	3	9

Rudy May

YEAR	TM/L	W	L	ERA	G	GS	CG	SV	SHO	IP	H	ER	BB	SO
1980	NY-A	0	1	3.38	1	1	0	0	0	8	6	3	3	4
1981	NY-A	0	0	8.10	1	1	0	0	0	3^1	6	3	0	5
Total 2		0	1	4.76	2	2	1	0	0	11^1	12	6	3	9

Kirk McCaskill

YEAR	TM/L	W	L	ERA	G	GS	CG	SV	SHO	IP	H	ER	BB	SO
1986	Cal-A	0	2	7.71	2	2	0	0	0	9^1	16	8	5	7
1993	Chi-A	0	0	0.00	3	0	0	0	0	3^2	3	0	1	3
Total 2		0	2	5.54	5	2	0	0	0	13	19	8	6	10

Steve McCatty

YEAR	TM/L	W	L	ERA	G	GS	CG	SV	SHO	IP	H	ER	BB	SO
1981	Oak-A	0	1	13.50	1	1	0	0	0	3^1	6	5	2	2

Bob McClure

YEAR	TM/L	W	L	ERA	G	GS	CG	SV	SHO	IP	H	ER	BB	SO
1982	Mil-A	1	0	0.00	1	0	0	0	0	1^2	2	0	0	0

Jack McDowell

YEAR	TM/L	W	L	ERA	G	GS	CG	SV	SHO	IP	H	ER	BB	SO
1993	Chi-A	0	2	10.00	2	2	0	0	0	9	18	10	5	5

Roger McDowell

YEAR	TM/L	W	L	ERA	G	GS	CG	SV	SHO	IP	H	ER	BB	SO
1986	NY-N	0	0	0.00	2	0	0	0	0	7	1	0	0	3
1988	NY-N	0	1	4.50	4	0	0	0	0	6	6	3	2	5
Total 2		0	1	2.08	6	0	0	0	0	13	7	3	2	8

Will McEnaney

YEAR	TM/L	W	L	ERA	G	GS	CG	SV	SHO	IP	H	ER	BB	SO
1975	Cin-N	0	0	6.75	1	0	0	0	0	1^1	1	1	0	1

YEAR	TM/L	W	L	ERA	G	GS	CG	SV	SHO	IP	H	ER	BB	SO
● Jim McGlothlin														
1972	Cin-N	0	0	0.00	1	0	0	0	0	1	0	0	0	0
● Tug McGraw														
1969	NY-N	0	0	0.00	1	0	0	1	0	3	1	0	1	1
1973	NY-N	0	0	0.00	2	0	0	1	0	5	4	0	3	3
1976	Phi-N	0	0	11.57	2	0	0	0	0	2¹	4	3	1	5
1977	Phi-N	0	0	0.00	2	0	0	1	0	3	1	0	2	3
1978	Phi-N	0	1	1.59	3	0	0	0	0	5²	3	1	5	5
1980	Phi-N	0	1	4.50	5	0	0	2	0	8	8	4	4	5
Total 6		0	2	2.67	15	0	0	5	0	27	21	8	16	22
● Scott McGregor														
1979	Bal-A	1	0	0.00	1	1	1	0	1	9	6	0	1	4
1983	Bal-A	0	1	1.35	1	1	0	0	0	6²	6	1	3	2
Total 2		1	1	0.57	2	2	1	0	1	15²	12	1	4	6
● Don McMahon														
1971	SF-N	0	0	0.00	2	0	0	0	0	3	0	0	0	3
● Greg McMichael														
1993	Atl-N	0	1	6.75	4	0	0	0	0	4	7	3	2	1
● Dave McNally														
1969	Bal-A	1	0	0.00	1	1	1	0	1	11	3	0	5	11
1970	Bal-A	1	0	3.00	1	1	1	0	0	9	6	3	5	5
1971	Bal-A	1	0	3.86	1	1	0	0	0	7	7	3	1	5
1973	Bal-A	0	1	5.87	1	1	0	0	0	7²	7	5	2	7
1974	Bal-A	0	1	1.59	1	1	0	0	0	5²	6	1	2	2
Total 5		3	2	2.68	5	5	2	0	1	40¹	29	12	15	30
● Kent Mercker														
1991	Atl-N	0	1	13.50	1	0	0	0	0	0²	0	1	2	0
1992	Atl-N	0	0	0.00	2	0	0	0	0	3	1	0	1	1
1993	Atl-N	0	0	1.80	5	0	0	0	0	5	3	1	2	4
Total 3		0	1	2.08	8	0	0	0	0	8²	4	2	5	5
● Jim Merritt														
1970	Cin-N	1	0	1.69	1	1	0	0	0	5¹	3	1	0	2
● Andy Messersmith														
1974	LA-N	1	0	2.57	1	1	0	0	0	7	8	2	3	0
● Bob Miller														
1969	Min-A	0	1	5.40	1	0	0	0	0	1²	5	1	0	0
1971	Pit-N	0	0	6.00	1	0	0	0	0	3	3	2	3	3
1972	Pit-N	0	0	0.00	1	0	0	0	0	1	0	0	0	1
Total 3		0	1	4.76	3	1	0	0	0	5²	8	3	3	4
● Steve Mingori														
1976	KC-A	0	0	2.70	3	0	0	1	0	3¹	4	1	0	1
1977	KC-A	0	0	0.00	3	0	0	0	0	1¹	0	0	0	1
1978	KC-A	0	0	7.36	1	0	0	0	0	3²	5	3	3	0
Total 3		0	0	4.32	7	0	0	1	0	8¹	9	4	3	2
● John Montague														
1979	Cal-A	0	1	9.00	2	0	0	0	0	4	4	4	2	2
● Donnie Moore														
1982	Atl-N	0	0	0.00	2	0	0	0	0	2²	2	0	0	1
1986	Cal-A	0	1	7.20	3	0	0	1	0	5	8	4	2	0
Total 2		0	1	4.70	5	0	0	1	0	7²	10	4	2	1
● Mike Moore														
1989	Oak-A	1	0	0.00	1	1	0	0	0	7	3	0	2	3
1990	Oak-A	1	0	1.50	1	1	0	0	0	6	4	1	1	5
1992	Oak-A	0	2	7.45	2	2	0	0	0	9²	11	8	5	7
Total 3		2	2	3.57	4	4	0	0	0	22²	18	9	8	15
● Bob Moose														
1970	Pit-N	0	1	3.52	1	1	0	0	0	7²	4	3	2	4
1971	Pit-N	0	0	0.00	1	0	0	0	0	2	0	0	0	0
1972	Pit-N	0	1	54.00	2	1	0	0	0	0²	5	4	0	0
Total 3		0	2	6.10	4	2	0	0	0	10¹	9	7	2	4
● Roger Moret														
1975	Bos-A	1	0	0.00	1	0	0	0	0	1	1	0	1	0
● Jack Morris														
1984	Det-A	1	0	1.29	1	1	0	0	0	7	5	1	1	4
1987	Det-A	0	1	6.75	1	1	1	0	0	8	6	6	3	7
1991	Min-A	2	0	4.05	2	2	0	0	0	13¹	17	6	1	7
1992	Tor-A	0	1	6.57	2	2	1	0	0	12¹	11	9	9	6
Total 4		3	2	4.87	6	6	2	0	0	40²	39	22	14	24
● Terry Mulholland														
1993	Phi-N	0	1	7.20	1	1	0	0	0	5	9	4	1	2
● Rob Murphy														
1990	Bos-A	0	0	13.50	1	0	0	0	0	0²	2	1	1	0
● Randy Myers														
1988	NY-N	2	0	0.00	3	0	0	0	0	4²	1	0	2	0
1990	Cin-N	0	0	0.00	4	0	0	3	0	5²	2	0	3	7
Total 2		2	0	0.00	7	0	0	3	0	10¹	3	0	5	7
● Denny Neagle														
1992	Pit-N	0	0	27.00	2	0	0	0	0	1²	4	5	3	0
● Gary Neibauer														
1969	Atl-N	0	0	0.00	1	0	0	0	0	1	0	0	0	1
● Roger Nelson														
1973	Cin-N	0	0	0.00	1	0	0	0	0	2¹	0	0	1	0

YEAR	TM/L	W	L	ERA	G	GS	CG	SV	SHO	IP	H	ER	BB	SO
● Gene Nelson														
1988	Oak-A	2	0	0.00	2	0	0	0	0	4²	5	0	1	0
1989	Oak-A	0	0	0.00	1	0	0	0	0	1¹	1	0	0	2
1990	Oak-A	0	0	0.00	1	0	0	0	0	1²	3	0	0	0
Total 3		2	0	0.00	4	0	0	0	0	7²	9	0	1	2
● Tom Niedenfuer														
1981	LA-N	0	0	0.00	1	0	0	0	0	0¹	2	0	0	0
1983	LA-N	0	0	0.00	2	0	0	1	0	2	0	0	1	3
1985	LA-N	0	2	6.35	3	0	0	1	0	5²	5	4	2	5
Total 3		0	2	4.50	6	0	0	2	0	8	7	4	3	8
● Joe Niekro														
1980	Hou-N	0	0	0.00	1	1	0	0	0	10	6	0	1	2
● Phil Niekro														
1969	Atl-N	0	1	4.50	1	1	0	0	0	8	9	4	4	4
1982	Atl-N	0	0	3.00	1	1	0	0	0	6	6	2	4	5
Total 2		0	1	3.86	2	2	0	0	0	14	15	6	8	9
● Gary Nolan														
1970	Cin-N	1	0	0.00	1	1	0	0	0	9	8	0	4	6
1972	Cin-N	0	0	1.50	1	1	0	0	0	6	4	1	1	4
1975	Cin-N	0	0	3.00	1	1	0	0	0	6	5	2	0	5
1976	Cin-N	0	0	1.59	1	1	0	0	0	5²	6	1	2	1
Total 4		1	0	1.35	4	4	0	0	0	26²	23	4	7	16
● Dickie Noles														
1980	Phi-N	0	0	0.00	2	0	0	0	0	2²	1	0	3	0
● Fred Norman														
1973	Cin-N	0	0	1.80	1	1	0	0	0	5	1	1	3	3
1975	Cin-N	1	0	1.50	1	1	0	0	0	6	4	1	5	4
1979	Cin-N	0	0	18.00	1	0	0	0	0	2	4	4	1	1
Total 3		1	0	4.15	3	2	0	0	0	13	9	6	9	8
● Mike Norris														
1981	Oak-A	0	1	3.68	1	1	0	0	0	7¹	6	3	2	4
● Blue Moon Odom														
1972	Oak-A	2	0	0.00	2	2	1	0	1	14	5	0	2	5
1973	Oak-A	0	0	1.80	2	0	0	0	0	5	6	1	2	4
1974	Oak-A	0	0	0.00	1	0	0	0	0	3¹	1	0	0	1
Total 3		2	0	0.40	5	2	1	0	1	22¹	12	1	4	10
● Bob Ojeda														
1986	NY-N	1	0	2.57	2	2	1	0	0	14	15	4	4	6
● Jesse Orosco														
1986	NY-N	3	0	3.38	4	0	0	0	0	8	5	3	2	10
1988	LA-N	0	0	7.71	4	0	0	0	0	2¹	4	2	3	0
Total 2		3	0	4.35	8	0	0	0	0	10¹	9	5	5	10
● Bob Owchinko														
1981	Oak-A	0	0	5.40	1	0	0	0	0	1²	3	1	0	0
● Jim Palmer														
1969	Bal-A	1	0	2.00	1	1	1	0	0	9	10	2	4	4
1970	Bal-A	1	0	1.00	1	1	1	0	0	9	7	1	3	12
1971	Bal-A	1	0	3.00	1	1	1	0	0	9	7	3	3	8
1973	Bal-A	1	0	1.84	3	2	1	0	1	14²	11	3	8	15
1974	Bal-A	0	1	1.00	1	1	0	0	0	9	4	1	1	4
1979	Bal-A	0	0	3.00	1	1	0	0	0	9	7	3	2	3
Total 6		4	1	1.96	8	7	5	0	1	59²	46	13	19	46
● Milt Pappas														
1969	Atl-N	0	0	11.57	1	0	0	0	0	2¹	4	3	0	4
● Harry Parker														
1973	NY-N	0	1	9.00	1	0	0	0	0	1	1	1	0	0
● Jeff Parrett														
1992	Oak-A	0	0	11.57	3	0	0	0	0	2¹	6	3	0	1
● Frank Pastore														
1979	Cin-N	0	0	2.57	1	1	0	0	0	7	7	2	3	1
● Bob Patterson														
1990	Pit-N	0	0	0.00	2	0	0	1	0	1	1	0	2	0
1991	Pit-N	0	0	0.00	1	0	0	0	0	2	1	0	0	3
1992	Pit-N	0	0	5.40	2	0	0	0	0	1²	3	1	1	1
Total 3		0	0	1.93	5	0	0	1	0	4²	5	1	3	4
● Marty Pattin														
1976	KC-A	0	0	27.00	2	0	0	0	0	0¹	0	1	1	0
1977	KC-A	0	0	1.50	1	0	0	0	0	6	6	1	0	0
1978	KC-A	0	0	27.00	1	0	0	0	0	0²	2	2	0	0
Total 3		0	0	5.14	4	0	0	0	0	7	8	4	1	0
● Alejandro Pena														
1981	LA-N	0	0	0.00	2	0	0	0	0	2¹	1	0	0	0
1983	LA-N	0	0	6.75	1	0	0	0	0	2²	4	2	1	3
1988	LA-N	1	1	4.15	3	0	0	1	0	4¹	1	2	5	1
1991	Atl-N	0	0	0.00	4	0	0	3	0	4¹	1	0	0	4
Total 4		1	1	2.63	10	0	0	4	0	13²	7	4	6	8
● Pascual Perez														
1982	Atl-N	0	1	5.19	2	1	0	0	0	8²	10	5	2	2
● Ron Perranoski														
1969	Min-A	0	1	5.79	3	0	0	0	0	4²	8	3	0	2
1970	Min-A	0	0	19.29	2	0	0	0	0	2¹	5	5	1	3
Total 2		0	1	10.29	5	0	0	0	0	7	13	8	1	5

Gaylord Perry

YEAR	TM/L	W	L	ERA	G	GS	CG	SV	SHO	IP	H	ER	BB	SO
1971	SF-N	1	1	6.14	2	2	1	0	0	14²	19	10	3	11

Jim Perry

YEAR	TM/L	W	L	ERA	G	GS	CG	SV	SHO	IP	H	ER	BB	SO
1969	Min-A	0	0	3.38	1	1	0	0	0	8	6	3	3	3
1970	Min-A	0	1	13.50	2	1	0	0	0	5¹	10	8	1	3
Total 2		0	1	7.43	3	2	0	0	0	13¹	16	11	4	6

Dan Petry

YEAR	TM/L	W	L	ERA	G	GS	CG	SV	SHO	IP	H	ER	BB	SO
1984	Det-A	0	0	2.57	1	1	0	0	0	7	4	2	1	4
1987	Det-A	0	0	0.00	1	0	0	0	0	3¹	1	0	0	1
Total 2		0	0	1.74	2	1	0	0	0	10¹	5	2	1	5

Horacio Pina

YEAR	TM/L	W	L	ERA	G	GS	CG	SV	SHO	IP	H	ER	BB	SO
1973	Oak-A	0	0	0.00	1	0	0	0	0	2	3	0	1	1

Juan Pizarro

YEAR	TM/L	W	L	ERA	G	GS	CG	SV	SHO	IP	H	ER	BB	SO
1974	Pit-N	0	0	0.00	1	0	0	0	0	0²	0	0	1	0

Eric Plunk

YEAR	TM/L	W	L	ERA	G	GS	CG	SV	SHO	IP	H	ER	BB	SO
1988	Oak-A	0	0	0.00	1	0	0	0	0	0¹	1	0	0	1

Ted Power

YEAR	TM/L	W	L	ERA	G	GS	CG	SV	SHO	IP	H	ER	BB	SO
1990	Pit-N	0	0	3.60	2	1	0	1	0	5	6	2	2	3

Joe Price

YEAR	TM/L	W	L	ERA	G	GS	CG	SV	SHO	IP	H	ER	BB	SO
1987	SF-N	1	0	0.00	2	0	0	0	0	5²	3	0	1	7

Dan Quisenberry

YEAR	TM/L	W	L	ERA	G	GS	CG	SV	SHO	IP	H	ER	BB	SO
1980	KC-A	1	0	0.00	2	0	0	1	0	4²	4	0	2	1
1984	KC-A	0	1	3.00	1	0	0	0	0	3	2	1	1	1
1985	KC-A	0	1	3.86	4	0	0	1	0	4²	7	2	0	3
Total 3		1	2	2.19	7	0	0	2	0	12¹	13	3	3	5

Scott Radinsky

YEAR	TM/L	W	L	ERA	G	GS	CG	SV	SHO	IP	H	ER	BB	SO
1993	Chi-A	0	0	10.80	4	0	0	0	0	1²	3	2	1	1

Doug Rau

YEAR	TM/L	W	L	ERA	G	GS	CG	SV	SHO	IP	H	ER	BB	SO
1974	LA-N	0	1	40.50	1	1	0	0	0	0²	3	3	1	0
1977	LA-N	0	0	0.00	1	0	0	0	0	1	0	0	0	1
1978	LA-N	0	0	3.60	1	1	0	0	0	5	5	2	2	1
Total 3		0	1	6.75	3	2	0	0	0	6²	8	5	3	2

Lance Rautzhan

YEAR	TM/L	W	L	ERA	G	GS	CG	SV	SHO	IP	H	ER	BB	SO
1977	LA-N	1	0	0.00	1	0	0	0	0	0¹	0	0	0	0
1978	LA-N	0	0	6.75	1	0	0	0	0	1¹	3	1	2	0
Total 2		1	0	5.40	2	0	0	0	0	1²	3	1	2	0

Jeff Reardon

YEAR	TM/L	W	L	ERA	G	GS	CG	SV	SHO	IP	H	ER	BB	SO
1981	Mon-N	0	0	27.00	1	0	0	0	0	1	3	3	0	0
1987	Min-A	1	1	5.06	4	0	0	2	0	5¹	7	3	3	5
1990	Bos-A	0	0	9.00	1	0	0	0	0	2	3	2	1	0
1992	Atl-N	1	0	0.00	3	0	0	1	0	3	0	0	2	3
Total 4		2	1	6.35	9	0	0	3	0	11¹	13	8	6	8

Ron Reed

YEAR	TM/L	W	L	ERA	G	GS	CG	SV	SHO	IP	H	ER	BB	SO
1969	Atl-N	0	1	21.60	1	1	0	0	0	1²	5	4	3	3
1976	Phi-N	0	0	7.71	2	0	0	0	0	4²	6	4	2	2
1977	Phi-N	0	0	1.80	3	0	0	0	0	5	3	1	2	5
1978	Phi-N	0	0	2.25	2	0	0	0	0	4	6	1	0	2
1980	Phi-N	0	1	18.00	3	0	0	0	0	2	3	4	1	1
1983	Phi-N	0	0	2.70	2	0	0	0	0	3¹	4	1	1	3
Total 6		0	2	6.53	13	1	0	0	0	20²	27	15	9	16

Rick Reuschel

YEAR	TM/L	W	L	ERA	G	GS	CG	SV	SHO	IP	H	ER	BB	SO
1987	SF-N	0	1	6.30	2	2	0	0	0	10	15	7	2	2
1989	SF-N	1	1	5.19	2	2	0	0	0	8²	12	5	2	5
Total 2		1	2	5.79	4	4	0	0	0	18²	27	12	4	7

Jerry Reuss

YEAR	TM/L	W	L	ERA	G	GS	CG	SV	SHO	IP	H	ER	BB	SO
1974	Pit-N	0	2	3.72	2	2	0	0	0	9²	7	4	8	3
1975	Pit-N	0	1	13.50	1	1	0	0	0	2²	4	4	4	1
1981	LA-N	0	1	5.14	1	1	0	0	0	7	7	4	1	2
1983	LA-N	0	2	4.50	2	2	0	0	0	12	14	6	3	4
1985	LA-N	0	1	10.80	1	1	0	0	0	1²	5	2	1	0
Total 5		0	7	5.45	7	7	0	0	0	33	37	20	17	10

Bob Reynolds

YEAR	TM/L	W	L	ERA	G	GS	CG	SV	SHO	IP	H	ER	BB	SO
1973	Bal-A	0	0	3.18	2	0	0	0	0	5²	5	2	3	5
1974	Bal-A	0	0	0.00	1	0	0	0	0	1¹	0	0	3	1
Total 2		0	0	2.57	3	0	0	0	0	7	5	2	6	6

Rick Rhoden

YEAR	TM/L	W	L	ERA	G	GS	CG	SV	SHO	IP	H	ER	BB	SO
1977	LA-N	0	0	0.00	1	0	0	0	0	4¹	2	0	2	0
1978	LA-N	0	0	2.25	1	0	0	0	0	4	2	1	1	3
Total 2		0	0	1.08	2	0	0	0	0	8¹	4	1	3	3

Pete Richert

YEAR	TM/L	W	L	ERA	G	GS	CG	SV	SHO	IP	H	ER	BB	SO
1969	Bal-A	0	0	0.00	2	0	0	0	0	2	2	0	2	2

Dave Righetti

YEAR	TM/L	W	L	ERA	G	GS	CG	SV	SHO	IP	H	ER	BB	SO
1981	NY-A	1	0	0.00	1	1	0	0	0	6	4	0	4	4

Jose Rijo

YEAR	TM/L	W	L	ERA	G	GS	CG	SV	SHO	IP	H	ER	BB	SO
1990	Cin-N	1	0	4.38	2	2	0	0	0	12¹	10	6	7	15

Ben Rivera

YEAR	TM/L	W	L	ERA	G	GS	CG	SV	SHO	IP	H	ER	BB	SO
1993	Phi-N	0	0	4.50	1	0	0	0	0	2	1	1	1	2

Dave Roberts

YEAR	TM/L	W	L	ERA	G	GS	CG	SV	SHO	IP	H	ER	BB	SO
1979	Pit-N	0	0	—	1	0	0	0	0	0	0	0	1	0

Don Robinson

YEAR	TM/L	W	L	ERA	G	GS	CG	SV	SHO	IP	H	ER	BB	SO
1979	Pit-N	0	0	0.00	2	0	0	1	0	2	0	0	1	3

YEAR	TM/L	W	L	ERA	G	GS	CG	SV	SHO	IP	H	ER	BB	SO
1987	SF-N	0	1	9.00	3	0	0	0	0	3	3	3	0	3
1989	SF-N	1	0	0.00	1	0	0	0	0	1²	3	0	0	0
Total 3		2	1	4.05	6	0	0	1	0	6²	6	3	1	6

Jeff Robinson

YEAR	TM/L	W	L	ERA	G	GS	CG	SV	SHO	IP	H	ER	BB	SO
1987	Det-A	0	0	0.00	1	0	0	0	0	0¹	1	0	0	0

Rosario Rodriguez

YEAR	TM/L	W	L	ERA	G	GS	CG	SV	SHO	IP	H	ER	BB	SO
1991	Pit-N	0	0	27.00	1	0	0	0	0	1	1	3	2	1

Steve Rogers

YEAR	TM/L	W	L	ERA	G	GS	CG	SV	SHO	IP	H	ER	BB	SO
1981	Mon-N	1	1	1.80	2	1	1	0	0	10	8	2	1	6

Enrique Romo

YEAR	TM/L	W	L	ERA	G	GS	CG	SV	SHO	IP	H	ER	BB	SO
1979	Pit-N	0	0	0.00	2	0	0	0	0	0¹	3	0	1	1

Jim Rooker

YEAR	TM/L	W	L	ERA	G	GS	CG	SV	SHO	IP	H	ER	BB	SO
1974	Pit-N	0	0	2.57	1	1	0	0	0	7	6	2	5	4
1975	Pit-N	0	1	9.00	1	1	0	0	0	4	7	4	0	5
Total 2		0	1	4.91	2	2	0	0	0	11	13	6	5	9

Vern Ruhle

YEAR	TM/L	W	L	ERA	G	GS	CG	SV	SHO	IP	H	ER	BB	SO
1980	Hou-N	0	0	3.86	1	1	0	0	0	7	8	3	1	3
1986	Cal-A	0	0	13.50	1	0	0	0	0	0²	2	1	0	0
Total 2		0	0	4.70	2	1	0	0	0	7²	10	4	1	3

Jeff Russell

YEAR	TM/L	W	L	ERA	G	GS	CG	SV	SHO	IP	H	ER	BB	SO
1992	Oak-A	1	0	9.00	3	0	0	0	0	2	2	2	4	0

Dick Ruthven

YEAR	TM/L	W	L	ERA	G	GS	CG	SV	SHO	IP	H	ER	BB	SO
1978	Phi-N	0	1	5.79	1	1	0	0	0	4²	6	3	0	3
1980	Phi-N	1	0	2.00	2	1	0	0	0	9	3	2	5	4
Total 2		1	1	3.29	3	2	0	0	0	13²	9	5	5	7

Nolan Ryan

YEAR	TM/L	W	L	ERA	G	GS	CG	SV	SHO	IP	H	ER	BB	SO
1969	NY-N	1	0	2.57	1	0	0	0	0	7	3	2	2	7
1979	Cal-A	0	0	1.29	1	1	0	0	0	7	4	1	3	8
1980	Hou-N	0	0	5.40	2	2	0	0	0	13¹	16	8	3	14
1986	Hou-N	0	1	3.86	2	2	0	0	0	14	9	6	1	17
Total 4		1	1	3.70	6	5	0	0	0	41¹	32	17	9	46

Bret Saberhagen

YEAR	TM/L	W	L	ERA	G	GS	CG	SV	SHO	IP	H	ER	BB	SO
1984	KC-A	0	0	2.25	1	1	0	0	0	8	6	2	1	5
1985	KC-A	0	0	6.14	2	2	0	0	0	7¹	12	5	2	6
Total 2		0	0	4.11	3	3	0	0	0	15¹	18	7	3	11

Joe Sambito

YEAR	TM/L	W	L	ERA	G	GS	CG	SV	SHO	IP	H	ER	BB	SO
1980	Hou-N	0	1	4.91	3	0	0	0	0	3²	4	2	2	6
1986	Bos-A	0	0	13.50	3	0	0	0	0	0²	1	1	1	0
Total 2		0	1	6.23	6	0	0	0	0	4¹	5	3	3	6

Luis Sanchez

YEAR	TM/L	W	L	ERA	G	GS	CG	SV	SHO	IP	H	ER	BB	SO
1982	Cal-A	0	1	6.75	2	0	0	0	0	2²	4	2	1	1

Scott Sanderson

YEAR	TM/L	W	L	ERA	G	GS	CG	SV	SHO	IP	H	ER	BB	SO
1984	Chi-N	0	0	5.79	1	1	0	0	0	4²	6	3	1	2
1989	Chi-N	0	0	0.00	1	0	0	0	0	2	2	0	0	1
Total 2		0	0	4.05	2	1	0	0	0	6²	8	3	1	3

Manny Sarmiento

YEAR	TM/L	W	L	ERA	G	GS	CG	SV	SHO	IP	H	ER	BB	SO
1976	Cin-N	0	0	18.00	1	0	0	0	0	1	2	2	1	0

Kevin Saucier

YEAR	TM/L	W	L	ERA	G	GS	CG	SV	SHO	IP	H	ER	BB	SO
1980	Phi-N	0	0	0.00	2	0	0	0	0	0²	1	0	2	0

Dan Schatzeder

YEAR	TM/L	W	L	ERA	G	GS	CG	SV	SHO	IP	H	ER	BB	SO
1987	Min-A	0	0	0.00	1	0	0	0	0	4¹	2	0	0	5

Fred Scherman

YEAR	TM/L	W	L	ERA	G	GS	CG	SV	SHO	IP	H	ER	BB	SO
1972	Det-A	0	0	0.00	1	0	0	0	0	0²	1	0	0	1

Curt Schilling

YEAR	TM/L	W	L	ERA	G	GS	CG	SV	SHO	IP	H	ER	BB	SO
1993	Phi-N	0	0	1.69	2	2	0	0	0	16	11	3	5	19

Calvin Schiraldi

YEAR	TM/L	W	L	ERA	G	GS	CG	SV	SHO	IP	H	ER	BB	SO
1986	Bos-A	0	1	1.50	4	0	0	1	0	6	5	1	3	9

Mike Scott

YEAR	TM/L	W	L	ERA	G	GS	CG	SV	SHO	IP	H	ER	BB	SO
1986	Hou-N	2	0	0.50	2	2	0	0	1	18	8	1	1	19

Scott Scudder

YEAR	TM/L	W	L	ERA	G	GS	CG	SV	SHO	IP	H	ER	BB	SO
1990	Cin-N	0	0	0.00	1	0	0	0	0	1	1	0	0	1

Tom Seaver

YEAR	TM/L	W	L	ERA	G	GS	CG	SV	SHO	IP	H	ER	BB	SO
1969	NY-N	1	0	6.43	1	1	0	0	0	7	8	5	3	2
1973	NY-N	1	1	1.62	2	2	1	0	0	16²	13	3	5	17
1979	Cin-N	0	0	2.25	1	1	0	0	0	8	5	2	2	5
Total 3		2	1	2.84	4	4	1	0	0	31²	26	10	10	24

Chuck Seelbach

YEAR	TM/L	W	L	ERA	G	GS	CG	SV	SHO	IP	H	ER	BB	SO
1972	Det-A	0	0	18.00	2	0	0	0	0	1	4	2	0	0

Diego Segui

YEAR	TM/L	W	L	ERA	G	GS	CG	SV	SHO	IP	H	ER	BB	SO
1971	Oak-A	0	1	5.79	1	1	0	0	0	4²	6	3	6	4

Eric Show

YEAR	TM/L	W	L	ERA	G	GS	CG	SV	SHO	IP	H	ER	BB	SO
1984	SD-N	0	1	13.50	2	2	0	0	0	5¹	8	8	4	2

Doug Sisk

YEAR	TM/L	W	L	ERA	G	GS	CG	SV	SHO	IP	H	ER	BB	SO
1986	NY-N	0	0	0.00	1	0	0	0	0	1	0	1	0	0

Jim Slaton

YEAR	TM/L	W	L	ERA	G	GS	CG	SV	SHO	IP	H	ER	BB	SO
1982	Mil-A	0	0	1.93	2	0	0	1	0	4²	3	1	1	3

John Smiley

YEAR	TM/L	W	L	ERA	G	GS	CG	SV	SHO	IP	H	ER	BB	SO
1990	Pit-N	0	0	0.00	1	0	0	0	0	2	2	0	0	0

YEAR TM/L	W	L	ERA	G	GS	CG	SV	SHO	IP	H	ER	BB	SO
1991 Pit-N	0	2	23.63	2	2	0	0	0	2²	8	7	1	3
Total 2	0	2	13.50	3	2	0	0	0	4²	10	7	1	3
● Dave Smith													
1980 Hou-N	1	0	3.86	3	0	0	0	0	2¹	4	1	2	4
1986 Hou-N	0	1	9.00	2	0	0	0	0	2	2	2	3	2
Total 2	1	1	6.23	5	0	0	0	0	4¹	6	3	5	6
● Lee Smith													
1984 Chi-N	0	1	9.00	2	0	0	1	0	2	3	2	0	3
1988 Bos-A	0	1	8.10	2	0	0	0	0	3¹	6	3	1	4
Total 2	0	2	8.44	4	0	0	1	0	5¹	9	5	1	7
● Pete Smith													
1992 Atl-N	0	0	2.45	2	0	0	0	0	3²	2	1	3	3
● Zane Smith													
1990 Pit-N	0	2	6.00	2	1	0	0	0	9	14	6	1	8
1991 Pit-N	1	1	0.61	2	2	0	0	0	14²	15	1	3	10
Total 2	1	3	2.66	4	3	0	0	0	23²	29	7	4	18
● Mike Smithson													
1988 Bos-A	0	0	0.00	1	0	0	0	0	2¹	3	0	0	1
● John Smoltz													
1991 Atl-N	2	0	1.76	2	2	0	0	1	15¹	14	3	3	15
1992 Atl-N	2	0	2.66	3	3	0	0	0	20¹	14	6	10	19
1993 Atl-N	0	1	0.00	1	1	0	0	0	6¹	8	0	5	10
Total 3	4	1	1.93	6	6	1	0	1	42	36	9	18	44
● Eddie Solomon													
1974 LA-N	0	0	0.00	1	0	0	0	0	2	2	0	1	1
● Elias Sosa													
1977 LA-N	0	1	10.13	2	0	0	0	0	2²	5	3	0	0
1981 Mon-N	0	0	0.00	1	0	0	0	0	0¹	1	0	1	0
Total 2	0	1	9.00	3	0	0	0	0	3	6	3	1	0
● Mario Soto													
1979 Cin-N	0	0	0.00	1	0	0	0	0	2	0	0	0	1
● Paul Splittorff													
1976 KC-A	1	0	1.93	2	0	0	0	0	9¹	7	2	5	2
1977 KC-A	1	0	2.40	2	2	0	0	0	15	14	4	3	4
1978 KC-A	0	0	4.91	1	1	0	0	0	7¹	9	4	0	2
1980 KC-A	0	0	1.69	1	1	0	0	0	5¹	5	1	2	3
Total 4	2	0	2.68	6	4	0	0	0	37	35	11	10	11
● Don Stanhouse													
1979 Bal-A	1	1	6.00	3	0	0	0	0	3	5	2	3	0
● Bob Stanley													
1986 Bos-A	0	0	3.18	3	0	0	0	0	5²	7	2	3	1
1988 Bos-A	0	0	9.00	2	0	0	0	0	1	2	1	1	0
Total 2	0	0	4.05	5	0	0	0	0	6²	9	3	4	1
● Mike Stanton													
1991 Atl-N	0	0	2.45	3	0	0	0	0	3²	4	1	3	3
1992 Atl-N	0	0	0.00	5	0	0	0	0	4¹	2	0	2	5
1993 Atl-N	0	0	0.00	1	0	0	0	0	1	1	0	1	0
Total 3	0	0	1.00	9	0	0	0	0	9	7	1	6	8
● Dave Stewart													
1988 Oak-A	1	0	1.35	2	2	0	0	0	13¹	9	2	6	11
1989 Oak-A	2	0	2.81	2	2	0	0	0	16	13	5	3	9
1990 Oak-A	2	0	1.13	2	2	0	0	0	16	8	2	2	4
1992 Oak-A	1	0	2.70	2	2	1	0	0	16²	14	5	6	7
1993 Tor-A	2	0	2.03	2	2	0	0	0	13¹	8	3	8	8
Total 5	8	0	2.03	10	10	1	0	0	75¹	52	17	25	39
● Sammy Stewart													
1983 Bal-A	0	0	0.00	2	0	0	1	0	4¹	2	0	1	2
● Dave Stieb													
1985 Tor-A	1	1	3.10	3	3	0	0	0	20¹	11	7	10	18
1989 Tor-A	0	2	6.35	2	2	0	0	0	11¹	12	8	6	10
Total 2	1	3	4.26	5	5	0	0	0	31²	23	15	16	28
● Tim Stoddard													
1984 Chi-N	0	0	4.50	2	0	0	0	0	2	1	1	2	2
● George Stone													
1969 Atl-N	0	0	9.00	1	0	0	0	0	1	2	1	0	0
1973 NY-N	0	0	1.35	1	1	0	0	0	6²	3	1	2	4
Total 2	0	0	2.35	2	1	0	0	0	7²	5	2	2	4
● Todd Stottlemyre													
1989 Tor-A	0	1	7.20	1	1	0	0	0	5	7	4	2	3
1991 Tor-A	0	1	9.82	1	1	0	0	0	3²	7	4	1	3
1992 Tor-A	0	0	2.45	1	1	0	0	0	3²	3	1	0	1
1993 Tor-A	0	1	7.50	1	1	0	0	0	6	6	5	4	4
Total 4	0	3	6.87	4	3	0	0	0	18¹	23	14	7	11
● Les Straker													
1987 Min-A	0	0	16.88	1	1	0	0	0	2²	3	5	4	1
● John Stuper													
1982 StL-N	0	0	3.00	1	1	0	0	0	6	6	2	1	4
● Rick Sutcliffe													
1984 Chi-N	1	1	3.38	2	2	0	0	0	13¹	9	5	8	10
1989 Chi-N	0	0	4.50	1	1	0	0	0	6	5	3	4	2
Total 2	1	1	3.72	3	3	0	0	0	19¹	14	8	12	12

YEAR TM/L	W	L	ERA	G	GS	CG	SV	SHO	IP	H	ER	BB	SO
● Bruce Sutter													
1982 StL-N	1	0	0.00	2	0	0	1	0	4¹	0	0	0	1
● Don Sutton													
1974 LA-N	2	0	0.53	2	2	1	0	1	17	7	1	2	13
1977 LA-N	1	0	1.00	1	1	1	0	0	9	9	1	0	4
1978 LA-N	0	1	6.35	1	1	0	0	0	5²	7	4	2	0
1982 Mil-A	1	0	3.52	1	1	0	0	0	7²	8	3	2	9
1986 Cal-A	0	0	1.86	2	1	0	0	0	9²	6	2	1	4
Total 5	4	1	2.02	7	6	2	0	1	49	37	11	7	30
● Frank Tanana													
1979 Cal-A	0	0	3.60	1	1	0	0	0	5	6	2	2	3
1987 Det-A	0	1	5.06	1	1	0	0	0	5¹	6	3	4	1
Total 2	0	1	4.35	2	2	0	0	0	10¹	12	5	6	4
● Kevin Tapani													
1991 Min-A	0	1	7.84	2	2	0	0	0	10¹	16	9	3	9
● Ron Taylor													
1969 NY-N	1	0	0.00	2	0	0	1	0	3¹	3	0	0	4
● Kent Tekulve													
1975 Pit-N	0	0	6.75	2	0	0	0	0	1¹	3	1	1	2
1979 Pit-N	0	0	3.00	2	0	0	0	0	3	2	1	2	2
Total 2	0	0	4.15	4	0	0	0	0	4¹	5	2	3	4
● Walt Terrell													
1987 Det-A	0	0	9.00	1	1	0	0	0	6	7	6	4	4
● Bobby Thigpen													
1993 Phi-N	0	0	5.40	1	0	0	0	0	1²	1	1	1	3
● Mark Thurmond													
1984 SD-N	0	1	9.82	1	1	0	0	0	3²	7	4	2	1
1987 Det-A	0	0	—	1	0	0	0	0	0¹	0	0	0	0
Total 2	0	1	9.00	2	1	0	0	0	4	7	4	2	1
● Luis Tiant													
1970 Min-A	0	0	13.50	1	0	0	0	0	0²	1	1	0	0
1975 Bos-A	1	0	0.00	1	1	1	0	0	9	3	0	3	8
Total 2	1	0	0.93	2	1	1	0	0	9²	4	1	3	8
● Dick Tidrow													
1976 NY-A	1	0	3.68	2	0	0	0	0	7¹	6	3	4	0
1977 NY-A	0	0	3.86	2	0	0	0	0	7	6	3	3	3
1978 NY-A	0	0	4.76	1	0	0	0	0	5²	8	3	2	1
1983 Chi-A	0	0	3.00	1	0	0	0	0	3	1	1	3	3
Total 4	1	0	3.91	7	0	0	0	0	23	21	10	12	7
● Mike Timlin													
1991 Tor-A	0	1	3.18	4	0	0	0	0	5²	5	2	2	5
1992 Tor-A	0	0	6.75	2	0	0	0	0	1¹	4	1	0	1
1993 Tor-A	0	0	3.86	1	0	0	0	0	2¹	3	1	0	2
Total 3	0	1	3.86	7	0	0	0	0	9¹	12	4	2	8
● Jim Todd													
1975 Oak-A	0	0	9.00	3	0	0	0	0	1	3	1	0	0
● Dave Tomlin													
1973 Cin-N	0	0	16.20	1	0	0	0	0	1²	5	3	1	1
1979 Cin-N	0	0	0.00	3	0	0	0	0	3	3	0	2	3
Total 2	0	0	5.79	4	0	0	0	0	4²	8	3	3	4
● Randy Tomlin													
1991 Pit-N	0	0	3.00	1	1	0	0	0	6	6	2	2	1
1992 Pit-N	0	0	6.75	2	0	0	0	0	2²	5	2	1	0
Total 2	0	0	4.15	3	1	0	0	0	8²	11	4	3	1
● Mike Torrez													
1977 NY-A	0	1	4.09	2	1	0	0	0	11	11	5	5	5
● Steve Trout													
1984 Chi-N	1	0	2.00	2	1	0	0	0	9	5	2	3	3
● John Tudor													
1985 StL-N	1	1	2.84	2	2	0	0	0	12²	10	4	3	8
1987 StL-N	1	1	1.76	2	2	0	0	0	15¹	16	3	5	12
1988 LA-N	0	0	7.20	1	1	0	0	0	5	8	4	1	1
Total 3	2	2	3.00	5	5	0	0	0	33	34	11	9	21
● Tom Underwood													
1976 Phi-N	0	0	0.00	1	0	0	0	0	0¹	1	0	2	0
1980 NY-A	0	0	0.00	2	0	0	0	0	3	3	0	0	3
1981 Oak-A	0	0	13.50	2	0	0	0	0	1¹	4	2	2	2
Total 3	0	0	3.86	5	0	0	0	0	4²	8	2	4	5
● Cecil Upshaw													
1969 Atl-N	0	0	2.84	3	0	0	0	0	6¹	5	2	1	4
● Fernando Valenzuela													
1981 LA-N	1	1	2.45	2	2	0	0	0	14²	10	4	5	10
1983 LA-N	0	1	1.13	1	1	0	0	0	8	7	1	4	5
1985 LA-N	1	0	1.88	2	2	0	0	0	14¹	11	3	10	13
Total 3	3	1	1.95	5	5	0	0	0	37	28	8	19	28
● Frank Viola													
1987 Min-A	0	0	5.25	2	0	0	0	0	12	14	7	5	9
● Pete Vuckovich													
1982 Mil-A	0	1	4.40	2	1	0	0	0	14¹	15	7	7	8
● Tim Wakefield													
1992 Pit-N	2	0	3.00	2	2	2	0	0	18	14	6	5	7

YEAR	TM/L	W	L	ERA	G	GS	CG	SV	SHO	IP	H	ER	BB	SO
● Bob Walk														
1982	Atl-N	0	0	9.00	1	0	0	0	0	1	2	1	1	1
1990	Pit-N	1	1	4.85	2	2	0	0	0	13	11	7	2	8
1991	Pit-N	0	0	1.93	3	0	0	1	0	9^1	5	2	3	5
1992	Pit-N	1	0	3.86	2	1	1	0	0	11^2	6	5	7	6
Total 4		2	1	3.86	8	3	1	1	0	35	24	15	13	20
● Luke Walker														
1970	Pit-N	0	1	1.29	1	1	0	0	0	7	5	1	1	5
1972	Pit-N	0	0	18.00	1	0	0	0	0	1	3	2	0	0
Total 2		0	1	3.38	2	1	0	0	0	8	8	3	1	5
● Duane Ward														
1989	Tor-A	0	0	7.36	2	0	0	0	0	3^2	6	3	3	5
1991	Tor-A	0	1	6.23	2	0	0	1	0	4^1	4	3	1	6
1992	Tor-A	1	0	6.75	3	0	0	0	0	4	5	3	1	2
1993	Tor-A	0	0	5.79	4	0	0	2	0	4^2	4	3	3	8
Total 4		1	1	6.48	11	0	0	3	0	16^2	19	12	8	21
● Eddie Watt														
1969	Bal-A	0	0	0.00	1	0	0	0	0	2	0	0	0	2
1971	Bal-A	0	0	0.00	1	0	0	1	0	2	2	0	0	1
1973	Bal-A	0	0	0.00	1	0	0	0	0	0^1	0	0	0	0
Total 3		0	0	0.00	3	0	0	1	0	4^1	2	0	0	3
● Bob Welch														
1978	LA-N	1	0	2.08	1	0	0	0	0	4^1	2	1	0	5
1981	LA-N	0	0	5.40	3	0	0	1	0	1^2	2	1	0	2
1983	LA-N	0	1	6.75	1	1	0	0	0	1^1	0	1	2	0
1985	LA-N	0	1	6.75	1	1	0	0	0	2^2	5	2	6	2
1988	Oak-A	0	0	27.00	1	1	0	0	0	1^2	6	5	2	0
1989	Oak-A	1	0	3.18	1	1	0	0	0	5^2	8	2	1	4
1990	Oak-A	1	0	1.23	1	1	0	0	0	7^1	6	1	3	4
1992	Oak-A	0	0	2.57	1	1	0	0	0	7	7	2	1	7
Total 8		3	2	4.26	10	6	0	1	0	31^2	36	15	15	24
● David Wells														
1989	Tor-A	0	0	0.00	1	0	0	0	0	1	0	0	2	1
1991	Tor-A	0	0	2.35	4	0	0	0	0	7^2	6	2	2	9
Total 2		0	0	2.08	5	0	0	0	0	8^2	6	2	4	10
● David West														
1991	Min-A	1	0	0.00	2	0	0	0	0	5^2	1	0	4	4
1993	Phi-N	0	0	13.50	3	0	0	0	0	2^2	5	4	2	5
Total 2		1	0	4.32	5	0	0	0	0	8^1	6	4	6	9
● Ed Whitson														
1984	SD-N	1	0	1.13	1	1	0	0	0	8	5	1	2	6
● Milt Wilcox														
1970	Cin-N	1	0	0.00	1	0	0	0	0	3	1	0	2	5
1984	Det-A	1	0	0.00	1	1	0	0	0	8	2	0	2	8
Total 2		2	0	0.00	2	1	0	0	0	11	3	0	4	13
● Mitch Williams														
1989	Chi-N	0	0	0.00	2	0	0	0	0	1	1	0	0	2
1993	Phi-N	2	0	1.69	4	0	0	2	0	5^1	6	1	2	5
Total 2		2	0	1.42	6	0	0	2	0	6^1	7	1	2	7

YEAR	TM/L	W	L	ERA	G	GS	CG	SV	SHO	IP	H	ER	BB	SO
● Stan Williams														
1970	Min-A	0	0	0.00	2	0	0	0	0	6	2	0	1	2
● Carl Willis														
1991	Min-A	0	0	0.00	3	0	0	0	0	5^1	2	0	0	3
● Steve Wilson														
1989	Chi-N	0	1	4.91	2	0	0	0	0	3^2	3	2	1	4
● Rick Wise														
1975	Bos-A	1	0	2.45	1	1	0	0	0	7^1	6	2	3	2
● Mike Witt														
1982	Cal-A	0	0	6.00	1	0	0	0	0	3	2	2	2	3
1986	Cal-A	1	0	2.55	2	2	1	0	0	17^2	13	5	2	8
Total 2		1	0	3.05	3	2	1	0	0	20^2	15	7	4	11
● Bobby Witt														
1992	Oak-A	0	0	18.00	1	0	0	0	0	1	2	2	1	1
● Mark Wohlers														
1991	Atl-N	0	0	0.00	3	0	0	0	0	1^2	3	0	1	1
1992	Atl-N	0	0	0.00	3	0	0	0	0	3	2	0	1	2
1993	Atl-N	0	1	3.38	4	0	0	0	0	5^1	2	2	3	10
Total 3		0	1	1.80	10	0	0	0	0	10	7	2	5	13
● Dick Woodson														
1969	Min-A	0	0	10.80	1	0	0	0	0	1^2	3	2	3	2
1970	Min-A	0	0	9.00	1	0	0	0	0	1	2	1	1	0
Total 2		0	0	10.13	2	0	0	0	0	2^2	5	3	4	2
● Todd Worrell														
1985	StL-N	1	0	1.42	4	0	0	0	0	6^1	4	1	2	3
1987	StL-N	0	0	2.08	3	0	0	1	0	4^1	4	1	1	6
Total 2		1	0	1.69	7	0	0	1	0	10^2	8	2	3	9
● Al Worthington														
1969	Min-A	0	0	6.75	1	0	0	0	0	1^1	3	1	0	1
● Curt Young														
1988	Oak-A	0	0	0.00	1	0	0	0	0	1^1	1	0	0	2
● Matt Young														
1989	Oak-A	0	0	0.00	1	0	0	0	0	0^1	0	0	2	0
● Chris Zachary														
1972	Det-A	0	0	∞	1	0	0	0	0	0	1	1	1	0
● Pat Zachry														
1976	Cin-N	1	0	3.60	1	1	0	0	0	5	6	2	3	3
1983	LA-N	0	0	2.25	2	0	0	0	0	4	4	1	2	2
Total 2		1	0	3.00	3	1	0	0	0	9	10	3	5	5
● Geoff Zahn														
1982	Cal-A	0	1	7.36	1	1	0	0	0	3^2	4	3	1	2
● Bill Zepp														
1970	Min-A	0	0	6.75	2	0	0	0	0	1^1	2	1	2	2

YEAR	TM/L	AVG	G	AB	R	H	2B	3B	HR	RBI	BB	SO	SB	POS
Hank Aaron														
1957	Mil-N	.393	7	28	5	11	0	1	3	7	1	6	0	O
1958	Mil-N	.333	7	27	3	9	2	0	0	2	4	6	0	O
Total 2		.364	14	55	8	20	2	1	3	9	5	12	0	
Ed Abbaticchio														
1909	Pit-N	.000	1	1	0	0	0	0	0	0	0	0	0	H
Bill Abstein														
1909	Pit-N	.231	7	26	3	6	2	0	0	2	3	10	1	1
Jerry Adair														
1967	Bos-A	.125	5	16	0	2	0	0	0	1	0	3	1	2*4
Sparky Adams														
1930	StL-N	.143	6	21	0	3	0	0	0	1	0	4	0	3
1931	StL-N	.250	2	4	0	1	0	0	0	0	0	1	0	3
Total 2		.160	8	25	0	4	0	0	0	1	0	5	0	
Spencer Adams														
1925	Was-A	.000	2	1	0	0	0	0	0	0	0	0	0	2*1
1926	NY-A	—	2	0	0	0	0	0	0	0	0	0	0	H
Total 2		.000	4	1	0	0	0	0	0	0	0	0	0	
Joe Adcock														
1957	Mil-N	.200	5	15	1	3	0	0	0	2	0	2	0	1
1958	Mil-N	.308	4	13	1	4	0	0	0	0	1	3	0	1
Total 2		.250	9	28	2	7	0	0	0	2	1	5	0	
Tommie Agee														
1969	NY-N	.167	5	18	1	3	0	0	1	1	2	5	1	O
Sam Agnew														
1918	Bos-A	.000	4	9	0	0	0	0	0	0	0	0	0	C
Willie Aikens														
1980	KC-A	.400	6	20	5	8	0	1	4	8	6	0	1	
Matt Alexander														
1979	Pit-N	—	1	0	0	0	0	0	0	0	0	0	0	O
Gene Alley														
1971	Pit-N	.000	2	2	0	0	0	0	0	0	1	0	0	S
Bob Allison														
1965	Min-A	.125	5	16	3	2	1	0	1	2	2	9	1	O
Roberto Alomar														
1992	Tor-A	.208	6	24	3	5	1	0	0	3	3	2	2	
1993	Tor-A	.480	6	25	5	12	2	1	0	6	2	3	4	2
Total 2		.347	12	49	8	17	3	1	0	6	5	6	6	
Felipe Alou														
1962	SF-N	.269	7	26	2	7	1	1	0	1	1	4	0	O
Jesus Alou														
1973	Oak-A	.158	7	19	0	3	1	0	0	3	0	0	0	O*6
1974	Oak-A	.000	1	1	0	0	0	0	0	0	0	1	0	H
Total 2		.150	8	20	0	3	1	0	0	3	0	1	0	
Matty Alou														
1962	SF-N	.333	6	12	2	4	1	0	0	1	0	1	0	O*4
1972	Oak-A	.042	7	24	0	1	0	0	0	0	3	0	1	O
Total 2		.139	13	36	2	5	1	0	0	1	3	1	1	
Sandy Amoros														
1952	Bro-N	—	1	0	0	0	0	0	0	0	0	0	0	H
1955	Bro-N	.333	5	12	3	4	0	0	1	3	4	4	0	O
1956	Bro-N	.053	6	19	1	1	0	0	0	1	2	4	0	O
Total 3		.161	12	31	4	5	0	0	1	4	6	8	0	
Dave Anderson														
1988	LA-N	.000	1	1	0	0	0	0	0	0	0	1	0	D
Mike Andrews														
1967	Bos-A	.308	5	13	2	4	0	0	0	1	0	1	0	2*3
1973	Oak-A	.000	2	3	0	0	0	0	0	0	1	1	0	2*1
Total 2		.250	7	16	2	4	0	0	0	1	1	2	0	
Cap Anson														
1885	Chi-N	.423	7	26	8	11	1	1	0	0	2	0	0	1
1886	Chi-N	.238	6	21	3	5	1	0	0	1	4	0	1	1*6,C*2
Total 2		.340	13	47	11	16	2	1	0	1	6	0	1	
Luis Aparicio														
1959	Chi-A	.308	6	26	1	8	1	0	0	0	2	3	1	S
1966	Bal-A	.250	4	16	0	4	1	0	0	2	0	0	0	S
Total 2		.286	10	42	1	12	2	0	0	2	2	3	1	
Jimmy Archer														
1907	Det-N	.000	1	3	0	0	0	0	0	0	0	1	0	C
1910	Chi-N	.182	3	11	1	2	1	0	0	0	0	3	0	C*2,1*1
Total 2		.143	4	14	1	2	1	0	0	0	0	4	0	
Tony Armas														
1986	Bos-A	.000	1	1	0	0	0	0	0	0	0	1	0	H
Ed Armbrister														
1975	Cin-N	.000	4	1	0	0	0	0	0	0	2	0	0	H
Morrie Arnovich														
1940	Cin-N	.000	1	1	0	0	0	0	0	0	0	0	0	O
Richie Ashburn														
1950	Phi-N	.176	4	17	0	3	1	0	0	1	0	4	0	O

YEAR	TM/L	AVG	G	AB	R	H	2B	3B	HR	RBI	BB	SO	SB	POS
Rick Auerbach														
1974	LA-N	—	1	0	0	0	0	0	0	0	0	0	0	R
Earl Averill														
1940	Det-A	.000	3	3	0	0	0	0	0	0	0	0	0	H
Bobby Avila														
1954	Cle-A	.133	4	15	1	2	0	0	0	0	2	1	0	2
Benny Ayala														
1979	Bal-A	.333	4	6	1	2	0	0	1	2	1	0	0	O*3
1983	Bal-A	1.000	1	1	1	1	0	0	0	1	0	0	0	H
Total 2		.429	5	7	2	3	0	0	1	3	1	0	0	
Wally Backman														
1986	NY-N	.333	6	18	4	6	0	0	0	1	3	2	1	2
Ed Bailey														
1962	SF-N	.071	6	14	1	1	0	0	1	2	0	3	0	C*3
Harold Baines														
1990	Oak-A	.143	3	7	1	1	0	0	1	2	1	2	0	D*2
Gene Baker														
1960	Pit-N	.000	3	3	0	0	0	0	0	0	0	1	0	H
Floyd Baker														
1944	StL-A	.000	2	2	0	0	0	0	0	0	0	2	0	2
Frank Baker														
1910	Phi-A	.409	5	22	6	9	3	0	0	4	2	1	0	3
1911	Phi-A	.375	6	24	7	9	2	0	2	5	1	5	0	3
1913	Phi-A	.450	5	20	2	9	0	0	1	7	0	2	1	3
1914	Phi-A	.250	4	16	0	4	2	0	0	2	1	3	0	3
1921	NY-A	.250	4	8	0	2	0	0	0	1	0	1	0	3*2
1922	NY-A	.000	1	1	0	0	0	0	0	0	0	0	0	H
Total 6		.363	25	91	15	33	7	0	3	18	5	11	1	
Dusty Baker														
1977	LA-N	.292	6	24	4	7	0	0	1	5	0	2	0	O
1978	LA-N	.238	6	21	2	5	0	0	1	1	1	3	0	O
1981	LA-N	.167	6	24	3	4	0	0	0	1	1	6	0	O
Total 3		.232	18	69	9	16	0	0	2	7	2	11	0	
Bill Baker														
1940	Cin-N	.250	3	4	1	1	0	0	0	0	0	1	0	C
Steve Balboni														
1985	KC-A	.320	7	25	2	8	0	0	0	3	5	4	0	1
Neal Ball														
1912	Bos-A	.000	1	1	0	0	0	0	0	0	0	1	0	H
Dave Bancroft														
1915	Phi-N	.294	5	17	2	5	0	0	0	1	2	2	0	S
1921	NY-N	.152	8	33	3	5	1	0	0	3	1	5	0	S
1922	NY-N	.211	5	19	4	4	0	0	0	2	2	1	0	S
1923	NY-N	.083	6	24	1	2	0	0	0	1	1	2	1	S
Total 4		.172	24	93	10	16	1	0	0	7	6	10	1	
Sal Bando														
1972	Oak-A	.269	7	26	2	7	1	0	0	1	2	5	0	3
1973	Oak-A	.231	7	26	5	6	1	1	0	1	4	7	0	3
1974	Oak-A	.063	5	16	3	1	0	0	0	2	2	5	0	3
Total 3		.206	19	68	10	14	2	1	0	4	8	17	0	
Dan Bankhead														
1947	Bro-N	—	1	0	1	0	0	0	0	0	0	0	0	R
Turner Barber														
1918	Chi-N	.000	3	2	0	0	0	0	0	0	0	0	0	H
Jim Barbieri														
1966	LA-N	.000	1	1	0	0	0	0	0	0	0	1	0	H
Sam Barkley														
1885	StL-A	.087	7	23	3	2	0	0	0	0	2	0	0	2
Clyde Barnhart														
1925	Pit-N	.250	7	28	1	7	1	0	0	5	3	5	1	O
1927	Pit-N	.313	4	16	0	5	1	0	0	4	0	0	0	O
Total 2		.273	11	44	1	12	2	0	0	9	3	5	1	
Marty Barrett														
1986	Bos-A	.433	7	30	1	13	2	0	0	4	5	2	0	2
Jack Barry														
1910	Phi-A	.235	5	17	3	4	2	0	0	3	1	3	0	S
1911	Phi-A	.368	6	19	2	7	4	0	0	2	0	2	2	S
1913	Phi-A	.300	5	20	3	6	3	0	0	2	0	0	0	S
1914	Phi-A	.071	4	14	1	1	0	0	0	0	1	3	1	S
1915	Bos-A	.176	5	17	1	3	0	0	0	1	1	2	0	2
Total 5		.241	25	87	10	21	9	0	0	8	3	10	3	
Dick Bartell														
1936	NY-N	.381	6	21	5	8	3	0	1	3	4	4	0	S
1937	NY-N	.238	5	21	3	5	1	0	0	1	0	3	0	S
1940	Det-A	.269	7	26	2	7	2	0	0	3	3	3	0	S
Total 3		.294	18	68	10	20	6	0	1	7	7	10	0	
Billy Bates														
1990	Cin-N	1.000	1	1	1	1	0	0	0	0	0	0	0	H
Bill Bathe														
1989	SF-N	.500	2	2	1	1	0	0	1	3	0	0	0	H

Kim Batiste

YEAR	TM/L	AVG	G	AB	R	H	2B	3B	HR	RBI	BB	SO	SB	POS
1993	Phi-N	—	2	0	0	0	0	0	0	0	0	0	0	3

Earl Battey

YEAR	TM/L	AVG	G	AB	R	H	2B	3B	HR	RBI	BB	SO	SB	POS
1965	Min-A	.120	7	25	1	3	0	1	0	2	0	5	0	C

Hank Bauer

YEAR	TM/L	AVG	G	AB	R	H	2B	3B	HR	RBI	BB	SO	SB	POS
1949	NY-A	.167	3	6	0	1	0	0	0	0	0	0	0	O
1950	NY-A	.133	4	15	0	2	0	0	0	1	0	0	0	O
1951	NY-A	.167	6	18	0	3	0	1	0	3	1	1	0	O
1952	NY-A	.056	7	18	2	1	0	0	0	1	4	3	0	O
1953	NY-A	.261	6	23	6	6	0	1	0	1	2	4	0	O
1955	NY-A	.429	6	14	1	6	0	0	0	1	0	1	0	O*5
1956	NY-A	.281	7	32	3	9	0	0	1	3	0	5	1	O
1957	NY-A	.258	7	31	8	8	2	1	2	6	1	6	0	O
1958	NY-A	.323	7	31	6	10	0	0	4	8	0	5	0	O
Total 9		.245	53	188	21	46	2	3	7	24	8	25	1	

Don Baylor

YEAR	TM/L	AVG	G	AB	R	H	2B	3B	HR	RBI	BB	SO	SB	POS
1986	Bos-A	.182	4	11	1	2	1	0	0	1	1	3	0	D*3
1987	Min-A	.385	5	13	3	5	0	0	1	3	1	1	0	D*3
1988	Oak-A	.000	1	1	0	0	0	0	0	0	0	1	0	H
Total 3		.280	10	25	4	7	1	0	1	4	2	5	0	

Jim Beauchamp

YEAR	TM/L	AVG	G	AB	R	H	2B	3B	HR	RBI	BB	SO	SB	POS
1973	NY-N	.000	4	4	0	0	0	0	0	0	0	1	0	H

Ginger Beaumont

YEAR	TM/L	AVG	G	AB	R	H	2B	3B	HR	RBI	BB	SO	SB	POS
1900	Pit-N	.267	4	15	2	4	0	0	0	1	1	0	1	O
1903	Pit-N	.265	8	34	6	9	0	1	0	1	2	4	2	O
1910	Chi-N	.000	3	2	1	0	0	0	0	0	1	1	0	H
Total 3		.255	15	51	9	13	0	1	0	2	4	5	3	

Beals Becker

YEAR	TM/L	AVG	G	AB	R	H	2B	3B	HR	RBI	BB	SO	SB	POS
1911	NY-N	.000	3	3	0	0	0	0	0	0	0	0	0	H
1912	NY-N	.000	2	4	1	0	0	0	0	0	2	0	0	O*1
1915	Phi-N	—	2	0	0	0	0	0	0	0	0	0	0	O
Total 3		.000	7	7	1	0	0	0	0	0	2	0	0	

Heinz Becker

YEAR	TM/L	AVG	G	AB	R	H	2B	3B	HR	RBI	BB	SO	SB	POS
1945	Chi-N	.500	3	2	0	1	0	0	0	0	1	1	0	H

Mark Belanger

YEAR	TM/L	AVG	G	AB	R	H	2B	3B	HR	RBI	BB	SO	SB	POS
1969	Bal-A	.200	5	15	2	3	0	0	0	0	2	1	0	S
1970	Bal-A	.105	5	19	2	0	0	0	0	1	1	2	0	S
1971	Bal-A	.238	7	21	4	5	0	1	0	0	5	2	1	S
1979	Bal-A	.000	5	6	1	0	0	0	0	0	1	1	0	S*4
Total 4		.164	22	61	7	10	0	1	0	2	9	6	1	

Wayne Belardi

YEAR	TM/L	AVG	G	AB	R	H	2B	3B	HR	RBI	BB	SO	SB	POS
1953	Bro-N	.000	2	2	0	0	0	0	0	0	0	1	0	H

Gus Bell

YEAR	TM/L	AVG	G	AB	R	H	2B	3B	HR	RBI	BB	SO	SB	POS
1961	Cin-N	.000	3	3	0	0	0	0	0	0	0	0	0	H

Derek Bell

YEAR	TM/L	AVG	G	AB	R	H	2B	3B	HR	RBI	BB	SO	SB	POS
1992	Tor-A	.000	2	1	1	0	0	0	0	0	1	0	0	H

Les Bell

YEAR	TM/L	AVG	G	AB	R	H	2B	3B	HR	RBI	BB	SO	SB	POS
1926	StL-N	.259	7	27	4	7	1	0	1	6	2	5	0	3

Rafael Belliard

YEAR	TM/L	AVG	G	AB	R	H	2B	3B	HR	RBI	BB	SO	SB	POS
1991	Atl-N	.375	7	16	0	6	1	0	0	4	1	2	0	S
1992	Atl-N	—	4	0	0	0	0	0	0	0	0	0	0	S*3,2*1
Total 2		.375	11	16	0	6	1	0	0	4	1	2	0	

Johnny Bench

YEAR	TM/L	AVG	G	AB	R	H	2B	3B	HR	RBI	BB	SO	SB	POS
1970	Cin-N	.211	5	19	3	4	0	0	1	3	1	2	0	C
1972	Cin-N	.261	7	23	4	6	1	0	1	1	5	5	2	C
1975	Cin-N	.207	7	29	5	6	2	0	1	4	2	4	0	C
1976	Cin-N	.533	4	15	4	8	1	1	2	6	0	1	0	C
Total 4		.279	23	86	16	24	4	1	5	14	8	12	2	

Benny Bengough

YEAR	TM/L	AVG	G	AB	R	H	2B	3B	HR	RBI	BB	SO	SB	POS
1927	NY-A	.000	2	4	1	0	0	0	0	0	0	1	0	C
1928	NY-A	.231	4	13	1	3	0	0	0	1	1	1	0	C
Total 2		.176	6	17	2	3	0	0	0	1	2	1	0	

Juan Beniquez

YEAR	TM/L	AVG	G	AB	R	H	2B	3B	HR	RBI	BB	SO	SB	POS
1975	Bos-A	.125	3	8	0	1	0	0	0	0	1	1	0	O*2

Charlie Bennett

YEAR	TM/L	AVG	G	AB	R	H	2B	3B	HR	RBI	BB	SO	SB	POS
1887	Det-N	.262	11	42	6	11	2	1	0	9	3	5	5	C*10,1*3
1892	Bos-N	.286	2	7	2	2	0	0	1	1	0	2	1	C
Total 2		.265	13	49	8	13	2	1	1	10	3	7	6	

Todd Benzinger

YEAR	TM/L	AVG	G	AB	R	H	2B	3B	HR	RBI	BB	SO	SB	POS
1990	Cin-N	.182	4	11	2	2	0	0	0	0	0	0	0	1*3

Augie Bergamo

YEAR	TM/L	AVG	G	AB	R	H	2B	3B	HR	RBI	BB	SO	SB	POS
1944	StL-N	.000	3	6	0	0	0	0	0	1	2	3	0	O*2

Marty Bergen

YEAR	TM/L	AVG	G	AB	R	H	2B	3B	HR	RBI	BB	SO	SB	POS
1897	Bos-N	.500	1	4	0	2	0	0	0	1	0	1	1	C

Wally Berger

YEAR	TM/L	AVG	G	AB	R	H	2B	3B	HR	RBI	BB	SO	SB	POS
1937	NY-N	.000	3	3	0	0	0	0	0	0	0	1	0	H
1939	Cin-N	.000	4	15	0	0	0	0	0	1	0	5	0	H
Total 2		.000	7	18	0	0	0	0	0	1	0	5	0	

Dave Bergman

YEAR	TM/L	AVG	G	AB	R	H	2B	3B	HR	RBI	BB	SO	SB	POS
1984	Det-A	.000	5	5	0	0	0	0	0	0	0	1	0	1

Yogi Berra

YEAR	TM/L	AVG	G	AB	R	H	2B	3B	HR	RBI	BB	SO	SB	POS
1947	NY-A	.158	6	19	2	3	0	0	1	2	1	2	0	C*4,O*2
1949	NY-A	.063	4	16	2	1	0	0	0	1	1	3	0	C
1950	NY-A	.200	4	15	2	3	0	0	1	2	2	1	0	C
1951	NY-A	.261	6	23	4	6	1	0	0	0	2	1	0	C
1952	NY-A	.214	7	28	2	6	1	0	2	3	2	4	0	C
1953	NY-A	.429	6	21	3	9	1	0	1	4	3	3	0	C
1955	NY-A	.417	7	24	5	10	1	0	1	2	3	1	0	C
1956	NY-A	.360	7	25	5	9	2	0	3	10	4	1	0	C
1957	NY-A	.320	7	25	5	8	1	0	1	2	4	0	0	C
1958	NY-A	.222	7	27	3	6	3	0	0	2	1	0	0	C
1960	NY-A	.318	7	22	6	7	0	0	1	8	2	0	0	O*4,C*3
1961	NY-A	.273	4	11	2	3	0	0	1	3	5	1	0	O
1962	NY-A	.000	2	2	0	0	0	0	0	0	2	0	0	C*1
1963	NY-A	.000	1	1	0	0	0	0	0	0	0	0	0	H
Total 14		.274	75	259	41	71	10	0	12	39	32	17	0	

Damon Berryhill

YEAR	TM/L	AVG	G	AB	R	H	2B	3B	HR	RBI	BB	SO	SB	POS
1992	Atl-N	.091	6	22	1	2	0	0	1	3	1	11	0	C

Kurt Bevacqua

YEAR	TM/L	AVG	G	AB	R	H	2B	3B	HR	RBI	BB	SO	SB	POS
1984	SD-N	.412	5	17	4	7	2	0	2	4	1	2	0	D

Buddy Biancalana

YEAR	TM/L	AVG	G	AB	R	H	2B	3B	HR	RBI	BB	SO	SB	POS
1985	KC-A	.278	7	18	2	5	0	0	0	2	5	4	0	S

Carson Bigbee

YEAR	TM/L	AVG	G	AB	R	H	2B	3B	HR	RBI	BB	SO	SB	POS
1925	Pit-N	.333	4	3	1	1	1	0	0	1	0	0	1	O*1

Max Bishop

YEAR	TM/L	AVG	G	AB	R	H	2B	3B	HR	RBI	BB	SO	SB	POS
1929	Phi-A	.190	5	21	2	4	0	0	0	1	2	3	0	2
1930	Phi-A	.222	6	18	5	4	0	0	0	0	7	3	0	2
1931	Phi-A	.148	7	27	4	4	0	0	0	0	3	5	0	2
Total 3		.182	18	66	11	12	0	0	0	1	12	11	0	

Ray Blades

YEAR	TM/L	AVG	G	AB	R	H	2B	3B	HR	RBI	BB	SO	SB	POS
1928	StL-N	.000	1	1	0	0	0	0	0	0	0	1	0	H
1930	StL-N	.111	5	9	2	1	0	0	0	0	2	2	0	O*3
1931	StL-N	.000	2	2	0	0	0	0	0	0	0	2	0	H
Total 3		.083	8	12	2	1	0	0	0	0	2	5	0	

Footsie Blair

YEAR	TM/L	AVG	G	AB	R	H	2B	3B	HR	RBI	BB	SO	SB	POS
1929	Chi-N	.000	1	1	0	0	0	0	0	0	0	0	0	H

Paul Blair

YEAR	TM/L	AVG	G	AB	R	H	2B	3B	HR	RBI	BB	SO	SB	POS
1966	Bal-A	.167	4	6	2	1	0	0	1	1	1	0	0	O
1969	Bal-A	.100	5	20	1	2	0	0	0	0	2	5	1	O
1970	Bal-A	.474	5	19	5	9	1	0	0	3	2	4	0	O
1971	Bal-A	.333	4	9	2	3	1	0	0	0	0	1	0	O*3
1977	NY-A	.250	4	4	0	1	0	0	0	1	0	0	0	O*3
1978	NY-A	.375	6	8	2	3	1	0	0	0	1	4	0	O
Total 6		.288	28	66	12	19	3	0	1	5	6	14	1	

Harry Blake

YEAR	TM/L	AVG	G	AB	R	H	2B	3B	HR	RBI	BB	SO	SB	POS
1895	Cle-N	.250	5	20	1	5	3	0	0	2	0	2	0	O
1896	Cle-N	.071	4	14	1	1	0	0	0	0	1	1	1	O
Total 2		.176	9	34	2	6	3	0	0	2	1	3	1	

Johnny Blanchard

YEAR	TM/L	AVG	G	AB	R	H	2B	3B	HR	RBI	BB	SO	SB	POS
1960	NY-A	.455	5	11	2	5	2	0	0	2	0	0	0	C*2
1961	NY-A	.400	4	10	4	4	1	0	2	3	2	0	0	O*2
1962	NY-A	.000	1	1	0	0	0	0	0	0	0	1	0	H
1963	NY-A	.000	1	3	0	0	0	0	0	0	0	0	0	O*1
1964	NY-A	.250	4	4	0	1	1	0	0	0	0	1	0	H
Total 5		.345	15	29	6	10	4	0	2	5	2	2	0	

Lance Blankenship

YEAR	TM/L	AVG	G	AB	R	H	2B	3B	HR	RBI	BB	SO	SB	POS
1989	Oak-A	.500	1	2	1	1	0	0	0	0	0	0	0	2
1990	Oak-A	.000	1	1	0	0	0	0	0	0	0	1	0	H
Total 2		.333	2	3	1	1	0	0	0	0	0	1	0	

Don Blasingame

YEAR	TM/L	AVG	G	AB	R	H	2B	3B	HR	RBI	BB	SO	SB	POS
1961	Cin-N	.143	3	7	1	1	0	0	0	0	0	3	0	2

Jeff Blauser

YEAR	TM/L	AVG	G	AB	R	H	2B	3B	HR	RBI	BB	SO	SB	POS
1991	Atl-N	.167	5	6	0	1	0	0	0	0	1	1	0	S
1992	Atl-N	.250	6	24	2	6	0	0	0	1	1	9	2	S
Total 2		.233	11	30	2	7	0	0	0	1	2	10	2	

Curt Blefary

YEAR	TM/L	AVG	G	AB	R	H	2B	3B	HR	RBI	BB	SO	SB	POS
1966	Bal-A	.077	4	13	0	1	0	0	0	0	0	2	0	O

Ned Bligh

YEAR	TM/L	AVG	G	AB	R	H	2B	3B	HR	RBI	BB	SO	SB	POS
1890	Lou-A	.000	2	3	0	0	0	0	0	0	0	1	0	C

Cy Block

YEAR	TM/L	AVG	G	AB	R	H	2B	3B	HR	RBI	BB	SO	SB	POS
1945	Chi-N	—	1	0	0	0	0	0	0	0	0	0	0	R

Jimmy Bloodworth

YEAR	TM/L	AVG	G	AB	R	H	2B	3B	HR	RBI	BB	SO	SB	POS
1950	Phi-N	—	1	0	0	0	0	0	0	0	0	0	0	2

Ossie Bluege

YEAR	TM/L	AVG	G	AB	R	H	2B	3B	HR	RBI	BB	SO	SB	POS
1924	Was-A	.192	7	26	2	5	0	0	0	2	3	4	1	S*5,3*4
1925	Was-A	.278	5	18	2	5	1	0	0	2	1	4	0	3
1933	Was-A	.125	5	16	1	2	1	0	0	1	6	6	0	3
Total 3		.200	17	60	5	12	2	0	0	4	5	14	1	

Bruce Bochy

YEAR	TM/L	AVG	G	AB	R	H	2B	3B	HR	RBI	BB	SO	SB	POS
1984	SD-N	1.000	1	1	0	1	0	0	0	0	0	0	0	H

Wade Boggs

YEAR	TM/L	AVG	G	AB	R	H	2B	3B	HR	RBI	BB	SO	SB	POS
1986	Bos-A	.290	7	31	3	9	3	0	0	3	4	2	0	3

YEAR	TM/L	AVG	G	AB	R	H	2B	3B	HR	RBI	BB	SO	SB	POS
■ **Joe Boley**														
1929	Phi-A	.235	5	17	1	4	0	0	0	1	0	3	0	S
1930	Phi-A	.095	6	21	1	2	0	0	0	1	0	1	0	S
1931	Phi-A	.000	1	1	0	0	0	0	0	0	0	1	0	H
Total 3		.154	12	39	2	6	0	0	0	2	0	5	0	
■ **Don Bollweg**														
1953	NY-A	.000	3	2	0	0	0	0	0	0	0	2	0	1*1
■ **Cliff Bolton**														
1933	Was-A	.000	2	2	0	0	0	0	0	0	0	0	0	H
■ **Nino Bongiovanni**														
1939	Cin-N	.000	1	1	0	0	0	0	0	0	0	0	0	H
■ **Frank Bonner**														
1894	Bal-N	.000	2	5	0	0	0	0	0	0	0	2	0	S*1,O*1
■ **Ray Boone**														
1948	Cle-A	.000	1	1	0	0	0	0	0	0	0	1	0	H
■ **Bob Boone**														
1980	Phi-N	.412	6	17	3	7	2	0	0	4	4	0	0	C
■ **Frenchy Bordagaray**														
1939	Cin-N	—	2	0	0	0	0	0	0	0	0	0	0	R
1941	NY-A	—	1	0	0	0	0	0	0	0	0	0	0	R
Total 2		—	3	0	0	0	0	0	0	0	0	0	0	
■ **Pat Borders**														
1992	Tor-A	.450	6	20	2	9	3	0	1	3	2	1	0	C
1993	Tor-A	.304	6	23	2	7	0	0	0	1	2	1	0	C
Total 2		.372	12	43	4	16	3	0	1	4	4	2	0	
◨ **Mike Bordick**														
1990	Oak-A	—	3	0	0	0	0	0	0	0	0	0	0	S
■ **Red Borom**														
1945	Det-A	.000	2	1	0	0	0	0	0	0	0	0	0	H
■ **Ken Boswell**														
1969	NY-N	.333	1	3	1	1	0	0	0	0	0	0	0	2
1973	NY-N	1.000	3	3	1	3	0	0	0	0	0	0	0	H
Total 2		.667	4	6	2	4	0	0	0	0	0	0	0	
■ **Jim Bottomley**														
1926	StL-N	.345	7	29	4	10	3	0	0	5	1	2	0	1
1928	StL-N	.214	4	14	1	3	0	1	1	3	2	6	0	1
1930	StL-N	.045	6	22	1	1	0	0	0	2	9	0	1	1
1931	StL-N	.160	7	25	2	4	1	0	0	2	2	5	0	1
Total 4		.200	24	90	8	18	5	1	1	10	7	22	0	
■ **Lou Boudreau**														
1948	Cle-A	.273	6	22	1	6	4	0	0	3	1	1	0	S
■ **Pat Bourque**														
1973	Oak-A	.500	2	2	0	1	0	0	0	0	0	0	0	1
■ **Larry Bowa**														
1980	Phi-N	.375	6	24	3	9	1	0	0	2	0	0	3	S
■ **Frank Bowerman**														
1897	Bal-N	.500	2	8	2	4	0	1	0	4	0	0	0	C*1,1*1
■ **Ernie Bowman**														
1962	SF-N	.000	2	1	1	0	0	0	0	0	0	0	0	S*1
■ **Clete Boyer**														
1960	NY-A	.250	4	12	1	3	2	1	0	1	0	1	0	3*4,S*1
1961	NY-A	.267	5	15	0	4	2	0	0	3	4	0	0	3
1962	NY-A	.318	7	22	2	7	1	0	1	4	1	3	0	3
1963	NY-A	.077	4	13	0	1	0	0	0	0	1	6	0	3
1964	NY-A	.208	7	24	2	5	1	0	1	3	1	5	1	3
Total 5		.233	27	86	5	20	6	1	2	11	7	15	1	
■ **Ken Boyer**														
1964	StL-N	.222	7	27	5	6	1	0	2	6	1	5	0	3
■ **Jack Boyle**														
1887	StL-A	.208	6	24	1	5	0	0	0	2	0	4	0	C
1888	StL-A	.438	4	16	4	7	0	1	0	4	2	2	3	C*4,O*1
Total 2		.300	10	40	5	12	0	1	0	6	2	6	3	
■ **Steve Brady**														
1884	NY-A	.000	3	10	1	0	0	0	0	0	0	0	0	O
■ **Bobby Bragan**														
1947	Bro-N	1.000	1	1	0	1	0	0	0	0	0	0	0	H
■ **Glenn Braggs**														
1990	Cin-N	.000	2	4	0	0	0	0	0	2	1	0	0	O*1
■ **Kitty Bransfield**														
1903	Pit-N	.207	8	29	3	6	0	2	0	1	1	6	1	1
■ **Steve Braun**														
1982	StL-N	.500	2	2	0	1	0	0	0	2	1	0	0	D
1985	StL-N	.000	1	1	0	0	0	0	0	0	0	0	0	H
Total 2		.333	3	3	0	1	0	0	0	2	1	0	0	
■ **Angel Bravo**														
1970	Cin-N	.000	4	2	0	0	0	0	0	0	1	0	0	O
■ **Sid Bream**														
1991	Atl-N	.125	7	24	0	3	2	0	0	0	3	4	0	1

YEAR	TM/L	AVG	G	AB	R	H	2B	3B	HR	RBI	BB	SO	SB	POS
1992	Atl-N	.200	5	15	1	3	0	0	0	0	4	0	0	1
Total 2		.154	12	39	1	6	2	0	0	0	7	4	0	
■ **Roger Bresnahan**														
1905	NY-N	.313	5	16	3	5	2	0	0	1	4	0	1	C
■ **Eddie Bressoud**														
1967	StL-N	—	2	0	0	0	0	0	0	0	0	0	0	S
■ **George Brett**														
1980	KC-A	.375	6	24	3	9	2	1	1	3	2	4	1	3
1985	KC-A	.370	7	27	5	10	1	0	0	1	4	7	1	3
Total 2		.373	13	51	8	19	3	1	1	4	6	11	2	
■ **Fred Brickell**														
1927	Pit-N	.000	2	2	1	0	0	0	0	0	0	0	0	H
■ **Harry Bright**														
1963	NY-A	.000	2	2	0	0	0	0	0	0	0	2	0	H
■ **Lou Brock**														
1964	StL-N	.300	7	30	2	9	2	0	1	5	0	3	0	O
1967	StL-N	.414	7	29	8	12	2	1	1	3	2	3	7	O
1968	StL-N	.464	7	28	6	13	3	1	2	5	3	4	7	O
Total 3		.391	21	87	16	34	7	2	4	13	5	10	14	
■ **Steve Brodie**														
1894	Bal-N	.000	4	15	2	0	0	0	0	0	2	1	1	O
1895	Bal-N	.200	5	20	1	4	0	0	0	2	0	0	0	O
1896	Bal-N	.067	4	15	1	1	0	0	0	3	0	0	1	O
Total 3		.100	13	50	4	5	0	0	0	5	2	1	2	
■ **Tom Brookens**														
1984	Det-A	.000	3	3	0	0	0	0	0	0	0	1	0	3
■ **Dan Brouthers**														
1887	Det-N	.667	1	3	0	2	0	0	0	0	0	0	1	
1894	Bal-N	.188	4	16	2	3	0	0	0	0	1	0	3	1
Total 2		.263	5	19	2	5	0	0	0	0	1	0	3	
■ **Jimmy Brown**														
1942	StL-N	.300	5	20	2	6	0	0	0	1	3	0	0	2
■ **Jarvis Brown**														
1991	Min-A	.000	3	2	0	0	0	0	0	0	0	0	0	O*2,D*1
■ **Bobby Brown**														
1947	NY-A	1.000	4	3	2	3	2	0	0	3	1	0	0	H
1949	NY-A	.500	4	12	4	6	1	2	0	5	2	2	0	3*3
1950	NY-A	.333	4	12	2	4	1	1	0	1	0	0	0	3
1951	NY-A	.357	5	14	1	5	1	0	0	0	2	1	0	3*4
Total 4		.439	17	41	9	18	5	3	0	9	5	3	0	
■ **Bobby Brown**														
1981	NY-A	.000	4	1	1	0	0	0	0	0	0	1	0	O*2
1984	SD-N	.067	5	15	1	1	0	0	0	2	0	4	0	O
Total 2		.063	9	16	2	1	0	0	0	2	0	5	0	
■ **Tommy Brown**														
1949	Bro-N	.000	2	2	0	0	0	0	0	0	0	1	0	H
■ **Willard Brown**														
1888	NY-N	.375	2	8	1	3	1	0	0	0	0	0	0	C
1889	NY-N	.600	1	5	3	3	0	1	0	2	0	0	0	C
Total 2		.462	3	13	4	6	1	1	0	2	0	0	0	
■ **Gates Brown**														
1968	Det-A	.000	1	1	0	0	0	0	0	0	0	0	0	H
■ **George Browne**														
1905	NY-N	.182	5	22	2	4	0	0	0	1	0	2	2	O
■ **Glenn Brummer**														
1982	StL-N	—	1	0	0	0	0	0	0	0	0	0	0	C
■ **Tom Brunansky**														
1987	Min-A	.200	7	25	5	5	0	0	0	2	4	4	1	O
■ **Bill Bruton**														
1958	Mil-N	.412	7	17	2	7	0	0	1	2	5	5	0	O
■ **Jerry Buchek**														
1964	StL-N	1.000	4	1	1	1	0	0	0	0	0	0	0	2
■ **Bill Buckner**														
1974	LA-N	.250	5	20	1	5	1	0	1	1	0	1	0	O
1986	Bos-A	.188	7	32	2	6	0	0	0	3	0	3	0	1
Total 2		.212	12	52	3	11	1	0	1	2	0	4	0	
■ **Don Buford**														
1969	Bal-A	.100	5	20	1	2	1	0	1	2	2	4	0	O
1970	Bal-A	.267	4	15	3	4	0	0	1	1	3	2	0	O
1971	Bal-A	.261	6	23	3	6	1	0	2	4	3	3	0	O
Total 3		.207	15	58	7	12	2	0	4	7	8	9	0	
■ **Al Bumbry**														
1979	Bal-A	.143	7	21	3	3	0	0	0	1	2	1	0	O
1983	Bal-A	.091	4	11	0	1	0	0	0	1	0	1	0	O
Total 2		.125	11	32	3	4	1	0	0	2	2	2	0	
■ **Smoky Burgess**														
1960	Pit-N	.333	5	18	2	6	1	0	0	0	2	1	0	C
■ **Eddie Burke**														
1894	NY-N	.389	4	18	3	7	1	0	0	2	1	0	1	O

Glenn Burke

YEAR	TM/L	AVG	G	AB	R	H	2B	3B	HR	RBI	BB	SO	SB	POS
1977	LA-N	.200	3	5	0	1	0	0	0	0	0	1	0	O

Jesse Burkett

YEAR	TM/L	AVG	G	AB	R	H	2B	3B	HR	RBI	BB	SO	SB	POS
1892	Cle-N	.320	6	25	3	8	1	0	0	1	0	2	4	O
1895	Cle-N	.429	5	21	3	9	2	0	0	2	0	0	1	O
1896	Cle-N	.333	4	15	1	5	0	0	0	0	2	3	0	O
Total 3		.361	15	61	7	22	3	0	0	3	2	5	5	

Rick Burleson

YEAR	TM/L	AVG	G	AB	R	H	2B	3B	HR	RBI	BB	SO	SB	POS
1975	Bos-A	.292	7	24	1	7	1	0	0	2	4	2	0	S

Ed Burns

YEAR	TM/L	AVG	G	AB	R	H	2B	3B	HR	RBI	BB	SO	SB	POS
1915	Phi-N	.188	5	16	1	3	0	0	0	0	1	2	0	C

George Burns

YEAR	TM/L	AVG	G	AB	R	H	2B	3B	HR	RBI	BB	SO	SB	POS
1920	Cle-A	.300	5	10	1	3	1	0	0	2	3	3	0	1*4
1929	Phi-A	.000	1	2	0	0	0	0	0	0	0	1	0	H
Total 2		.250	6	12	1	3	1	0	0	2	3	4	0	

George Burns

YEAR	TM/L	AVG	G	AB	R	H	2B	3B	HR	RBI	BB	SO	SB	POS
1913	NY-N	.158	5	19	2	3	2	0	0	1	1	5	1	O
1917	NY-N	.227	6	22	3	5	0	0	0	2	2	6	1	O
1921	NY-N	.333	8	33	2	11	4	1	0	2	3	5	1	O
Total 3		.257	19	74	7	19	6	1	0	5	6	16	3	

Tom Burns

YEAR	TM/L	AVG	G	AB	R	H	2B	3B	HR	RBI	BB	SO	SB	POS
1885	Chi-N	.080	7	25	3	2	0	1	0	0	0	0	0	S*4,3*3
1886	Chi-N	.286	6	21	2	6	2	1	0	1	0	2	0	3*6,O*1
Total 2		.174	13	46	5	8	2	2	0	1	0	2	0	

Oyster Burns

YEAR	TM/L	AVG	G	AB	R	H	2B	3B	HR	RBI	BB	SO	SB	POS
1889	Bro-A	.229	9	35	8	8	3	0	2	11	5	6	0	O
1890	Bro-A	.222	7	27	6	6	2	0	1	5	3	4	0	O*4,3*3
Total 2		.226	16	62	14	14	5	0	3	16	8	10	0	

Donie Bush

YEAR	TM/L	AVG	G	AB	R	H	2B	3B	HR	RBI	BB	SO	SB	POS
1909	Det-A	.261	7	23	5	6	1	0	0	3	5	3	1	S

Randy Bush

YEAR	TM/L	AVG	G	AB	R	H	2B	3B	HR	RBI	BB	SO	SB	POS
1987	Min-A	.167	4	6	1	1	1	0	0	2	0	1	0	D*2
1991	Min-A	.250	3	4	0	1	0	0	0	0	0	1	0	O*2
Total 2		.200	7	10	1	2	1	0	0	2	0	2	0	

Doc Bushong

YEAR	TM/L	AVG	G	AB	R	H	2B	3B	HR	RBI	BB	SO	SB	POS
1885	StL-A	.154	4	13	1	2	0	0	0	0	0	0	0	C
1886	StL-A	.188	6	16	4	3	1	0	0	2	4	5	0	C
1887	StL-A	.241	9	29	3	7	0	0	0	1	4	1	0	C
1889	Bro-A	.000	3	8	0	0	0	0	0	0	1	0	0	C
1890	Bro-N	.000	2	6	0	0	0	0	0	0	0	1	0	C
Total 5		.167	24	72	8	12	1	0	0	3	9	7	0	

Sal Butera

YEAR	TM/L	AVG	G	AB	R	H	2B	3B	HR	RBI	BB	SO	SB	POS
1987	Min-A	—	1	0	0	0	0	0	0	0	0	0	0	C

Brett Butler

YEAR	TM/L	AVG	G	AB	R	H	2B	3B	HR	RBI	BB	SO	SB	POS
1989	SF-N	.286	4	14	1	4	1	0	0	1	2	1	2	O

Rob Butler

YEAR	TM/L	AVG	G	AB	R	H	2B	3B	HR	RBI	BB	SO	SB	POS
1993	Tor-A	.500	2	2	1	1	0	0	0	0	0	0	0	H

Sammy Byrd

YEAR	TM/L	AVG	G	AB	R	H	2B	3B	HR	RBI	BB	SO	SB	POS
1932	NY-A	—	1	0	0	0	0	0	0	0	0	0	0	O

Bobby Byrne

YEAR	TM/L	AVG	G	AB	R	H	2B	3B	HR	RBI	BB	SO	SB	POS
1909	Pit-N	.250	7	24	5	6	1	0	0	0	1	4	1	3
1915	Phi-N	.000	1	1	0	0	0	0	0	0	0	0	0	H
Total 2		.240	8	25	5	6	1	0	0	0	1	4	1	

Milt Byrnes

YEAR	TM/L	AVG	G	AB	R	H	2B	3B	HR	RBI	BB	SO	SB	POS
1944	StL-A	.000	3	2	0	0	0	0	0	0	1	2	0	H

Putsy Caballero

YEAR	TM/L	AVG	G	AB	R	H	2B	3B	HR	RBI	BB	SO	SB	POS
1950	Phi-N	.000	3	1	0	0	0	0	0	0	0	1	0	H

Francisco Cabrera

YEAR	TM/L	AVG	G	AB	R	H	2B	3B	HR	RBI	BB	SO	SB	POS
1991	Atl-N	.000	3	1	0	0	0	0	0	0	0	0	0	C*1
1992	Atl-N	.000	1	1	0	0	0	0	0	0	0	0	0	H
Total 2		.000	4	2	0	0	0	0	0	0	0	0	0	

Hick Cady

YEAR	TM/L	AVG	G	AB	R	H	2B	3B	HR	RBI	BB	SO	SB	POS
1912	Bos-A	.136	7	22	1	3	0	0	0	1	0	3	0	C
1915	Bos-A	.333	4	6	1	2	0	0	0	0	1	2	0	C
1916	Bos-A	.250	2	4	1	1	0	0	0	0	3	0	0	C
Total 3		.188	13	32	3	6	0	0	0	1	4	5	0	

Dolph Camilli

YEAR	TM/L	AVG	G	AB	R	H	2B	3B	HR	RBI	BB	SO	SB	POS
1941	Bro-N	.167	5	18	1	3	1	0	0	1	6	0	1	

Roy Campanella

YEAR	TM/L	AVG	G	AB	R	H	2B	3B	HR	RBI	BB	SO	SB	POS
1949	Bro-N	.267	5	15	2	4	1	0	1	2	3	1	0	C
1952	Bro-N	.214	7	28	0	6	0	0	0	1	1	6	0	C
1953	Bro-N	.273	6	22	6	6	0	0	1	2	2	3	0	C
1955	Bro-N	.259	7	27	4	7	3	0	2	4	3	3	0	C
1956	Bro-N	.182	7	22	2	4	1	0	0	3	3	7	0	C
Total 5		.237	32	114	14	27	5	0	4	12	12	20	0	

Bert Campaneris

YEAR	TM/L	AVG	G	AB	R	H	2B	3B	HR	RBI	BB	SO	SB	POS
1972	Oak-A	.179	7	28	1	5	0	0	0	0	1	3	0	S
1973	Oak-A	.290	7	31	6	9	0	1	1	3	1	7	3	S
1974	Oak-A	.353	5	17	1	6	2	0	0	2	0	3	1	S
Total 3		.263	19	76	8	20	2	1	1	5	2	13	4	

Bruce Campbell

YEAR	TM/L	AVG	G	AB	R	H	2B	3B	HR	RBI	BB	SO	SB	POS
1940	Det-A	.360	7	25	4	9	1	0	1	5	4	4	0	O

Paul Campbell

YEAR	TM/L	AVG	G	AB	R	H	2B	3B	HR	RBI	BB	SO	SB	POS
1946	Bos-A	—	1	0	0	0	0	0	0	0	0	0	0	R

Willie Canate

YEAR	TM/L	AVG	G	AB	R	H	2B	3B	HR	RBI	BB	SO	SB	POS
1993	Tor-A	—	1	0	0	0	0	0	0	0	0	0	0	R

Jose Canseco

YEAR	TM/L	AVG	G	AB	R	H	2B	3B	HR	RBI	BB	SO	SB	POS
1988	Oak-A	.053	5	19	1	1	0	0	1	5	2	5	1	O
1989	Oak-A	.357	4	14	5	5	0	0	1	3	4	3	1	O
1990	Oak-A	.083	4	12	1	1	0	0	1	2	2	3	0	O*3,D*1
Total 3		.156	13	45	7	7	0	0	3	10	8	11	2	

Bernie Carbo

YEAR	TM/L	AVG	G	AB	R	H	2B	3B	HR	RBI	BB	SO	SB	POS
1970	Cin-N	.000	4	8	0	0	0	0	0	0	2	3	0	O*2
1975	Bos-A	.429	4	7	3	3	1	0	2	4	1	1	0	O*2
Total 2		.200	8	15	3	3	1	0	2	4	3	4	0	

Jose Cardenal

YEAR	TM/L	AVG	G	AB	R	H	2B	3B	HR	RBI	BB	SO	SB	POS
1980	KC-A	.200	4	10	0	2	0	0	0	0	0	3	0	O

Leo Cardenas

YEAR	TM/L	AVG	G	AB	R	H	2B	3B	HR	RBI	BB	SO	SB	POS
1961	Cin-N	.333	3	3	0	1	1	0	0	0	0	1	0	H

Andy Carey

YEAR	TM/L	AVG	G	AB	R	H	2B	3B	HR	RBI	BB	SO	SB	POS
1955	NY-A	.500	2	2	0	1	0	1	0	1	0	0	0	H
1956	NY-A	.158	7	19	2	3	0	0	0	1	6	0	3	
1957	NY-A	.286	2	7	0	2	1	0	0	1	1	0	0	3
1958	NY-A	.083	5	12	1	1	0	0	0	0	0	3	0	3
Total 4		.175	16	40	3	7	1	1	0	2	2	9	0	

Scoops Carey

YEAR	TM/L	AVG	G	AB	R	H	2B	3B	HR	RBI	BB	SO	SB	POS
1895	Bal-N	.263	5	19	0	5	1	0	0	1	0	0	0	1

Max Carey

YEAR	TM/L	AVG	G	AB	R	H	2B	3B	HR	RBI	BB	SO	SB	POS
1925	Pit-N	.458	7	24	6	11	4	0	0	2	2	3	0	O

Bill Carrigan

YEAR	TM/L	AVG	G	AB	R	H	2B	3B	HR	RBI	BB	SO	SB	POS
1912	Bos-A	.000	2	7	0	0	0	0	0	0	0	0	0	C
1915	Bos-A	.000	1	2	0	0	0	0	0	0	1	1	0	C
1916	Bos-A	.667	1	3	0	2	0	0	0	1	0	1	0	C
Total 3		.167	4	12	0	2	0	0	0	1	1	2	0	

Cliff Carroll

YEAR	TM/L	AVG	G	AB	R	H	2B	3B	HR	RBI	BB	SO	SB	POS
1884	Pro-N	.100	3	10	2	1	0	0	0	1	1	1	0	O

Tom Carroll

YEAR	TM/L	AVG	G	AB	R	H	2B	3B	HR	RBI	BB	SO	SB	POS
1955	NY-A	—	2	0	0	0	0	0	0	0	0	0	0	R

Gary Carter

YEAR	TM/L	AVG	G	AB	R	H	2B	3B	HR	RBI	BB	SO	SB	POS
1986	NY-N	.276	7	29	4	8	2	0	2	9	4	4	0	C

Joe Carter

YEAR	TM/L	AVG	G	AB	R	H	2B	3B	HR	RBI	BB	SO	SB	POS
1992	Tor-A	.273	6	22	2	6	2	0	2	3	3	2	1	O*4,1-2
1993	Tor-A	.280	6	25	6	7	1	0	2	8	0	4	0	O
Total 2		.277	12	47	8	13	3	0	4	11	3	6	1	

Bob Caruthers

YEAR	TM/L	AVG	G	AB	R	H	2B	3B	HR	RBI	BB	SO	SB	POS
1885	StL-A	.200	5	15	1	3	0	0	1	0	1	0		P*3,O*2
1886	StL-A	.250	6	24	6	6	1	2	0	5	1	4	1	P*3,O*3
1887	StL-A	.239	10	46	2	11	0	0	0	3	1	1	3	P*8,O*3
1889	Bro-A	.250	4	8	1	2	0	0	0	1	3	3	0	P
1890	Bro-N	.000	2	6	0	0	0	0	0	0	2	0	0	P
Total 5		.222	27	99	10	22	1	3	0	9	8	8	4	

Dave Cash

YEAR	TM/L	AVG	G	AB	R	H	2B	3B	HR	RBI	BB	SO	SB	POS
1971	Pit-N	.133	7	30	2	4	1	0	0	1	3	1	2	

Norm Cash

YEAR	TM/L	AVG	G	AB	R	H	2B	3B	HR	RBI	BB	SO	SB	POS
1959	Chi-A	.000	4	4	0	0	0	0	0	0	0	2	0	H
1968	Det-A	.385	7	26	5	10	0	0	1	5	3	5	0	1
Total 2		.333	11	30	5	10	0	0	1	5	3	7	0	

Marty Castillo

YEAR	TM/L	AVG	G	AB	R	H	2B	3B	HR	RBI	BB	SO	SB	POS
1984	Det-A	.333	3	9	2	3	0	0	1	2	1	2	1	3

Ted Cather

YEAR	TM/L	AVG	G	AB	R	H	2B	3B	HR	RBI	BB	SO	SB	POS
1914	Bos-N	.000	1	5	0	0	0	0	0	0	0	1	0	O

Phil Cavarretta

YEAR	TM/L	AVG	G	AB	R	H	2B	3B	HR	RBI	BB	SO	SB	POS
1935	Chi-N	.125	6	24	1	3	0	0	0	0	0	5	0	1
1938	Chi-N	.462	4	13	1	6	1	0	0	0	0	1	0	O*3
1945	Chi-N	.423	7	26	7	11	2	0	1	5	4	3	0	1
Total 3		.317	17	63	9	20	3	0	1	5	4	9	0	

Cesar Cedeno

YEAR	TM/L	AVG	G	AB	R	H	2B	3B	HR	RBI	BB	SO	SB	POS
1985	StL-N	.133	5	15	1	2	1	0	0	1	2	2	0	O

Orlando Cepeda

YEAR	TM/L	AVG	G	AB	R	H	2B	3B	HR	RBI	BB	SO	SB	POS
1962	SF-N	.158	5	19	1	3	1	0	0	2	0	4	0	1
1967	StL-N	.103	7	29	1	3	2	0	0	1	0	4	0	1
1968	StL-N	.250	7	28	2	7	0	0	2	6	2	3	0	1
Total 3		.171	19	76	4	13	3	0	2	9	2	11	0	

Rick Cerone

YEAR	TM/L	AVG	G	AB	R	H	2B	3B	HR	RBI	BB	SO	SB	POS
1981	NY-A	.190	6	21	2	4	1	0	1	3	4	2	0	C

Bob Cerv

YEAR	TM/L	AVG	G	AB	R	H	2B	3B	HR	RBI	BB	SO	SB	POS
1955	NY-A	.125	5	16	1	2	0	0	0	1	0	4	0	O*4
1956	NY-A	1.000	1	1	0	1	0	0	0	0	0	0	0	H
1960	NY-A	.357	4	14	1	5	0	0	0	0	0	3	0	O*3
Total 3		.258	10	31	2	8	0	0	1	1	0	7	0	

YEAR	TM/L	AVG	G	AB	R	H	2B	3B	HR	RBI	BB	SO	SB	POS
■ Ron Cey														
1974	LA-N	.176	5	17	1	3	0	0	0	0	3	3	0	3
1977	LA-N	.190	6	21	2	4	1	0	1	3	3	5	0	3
1978	LA-N	.286	6	21	2	6	0	0	1	4	3	3	0	3
1981	LA-N	.350	6	20	3	7	0	0	1	6	3	3	0	3
Total 4		.253	23	79	8	20	1	0	3	13	12	14	0	
■ Elio Chacon														
1961	Cin-N	.250	4	12	2	3	0	0	0	0	1	2	0	2*3
■ Dave Chalk														
1980	KC-A	—	1	0	1	0	0	0	0	0	1	0	1	3
■ Wes Chamberlain														
1993	Phi-N	.000	2	2	0	0	0	0	0	0	0	1	0	H
■ Chris Chambliss														
1976	NY-A	.313	4	16	1	5	1	0	0	1	0	2	0	1
1977	NY-A	.292	6	24	4	7	2	0	1	4	0	2	0	1
1978	NY-A	.182	3	11	1	2	0	0	0	0	1	1	0	1
Total 3		.275	13	51	6	14	3	0	1	5	1	5	0	
■ Frank Chance														
1906	Chi-N	.238	6	21	3	5	1	0	0	0	2	1	2	1
1907	Chi-N	.214	4	14	3	3	1	0	0	0	3	2	3	1
1908	Chi-N	.421	5	19	4	8	0	0	0	2	3	1	5	1
1910	Chi-N	.353	5	17	1	6	1	1	0	4	0	3	0	1
Total 4		.310	20	71	11	22	3	1	0	6	8	7	10	
■ Darrel Chaney														
1970	Cin-N	.000	3	1	0	0	0	0	0	0	0	1	0	S
1972	Cin-N	.000	4	7	0	0	0	0	0	0	2	2	0	S*3
1975	Cin-N	.000	2	2	0	0	0	0	0	0	0	1	0	H
Total 3		.000	9	10	0	0	0	0	0	0	2	4	0	
■ Ben Chapman														
1932	NY-A	.294	4	17	1	5	2	0	0	6	2	4	0	O
■ Ed Charles														
1969	NY-N	.133	4	15	1	2	1	0	0	0	0	2	0	3
■ Mike Chartak														
1944	StL-A	.000	2	2	0	0	0	0	0	0	0	2	0	H
■ Cupid Childs														
1892	Cle-N	.409	6	22	3	9	0	0	0	5	1	0	2	
1895	Cle-N	.200	5	20	4	4	1	0	0	2	1	0	1	2
1896	Cle-N	.231	4	13	2	3	0	0	0	0	4	0	1	2
Total 3		.291	15	55	9	16	1	2	0	2	10	1	2	
■ Lou Chiozza														
1937	NY-N	.286	2	7	0	2	0	0	0	0	1	1	0	O
■ Mark Christman														
1944	StL-A	.091	6	22	0	2	0	0	0	1	0	6	0	3
■ Joe Christopher														
1960	Pit-N	—	3	0	2	0	0	0	0	0	0	0	0	H
■ Gino Cimoli														
1956	Bro-N	—	1	0	0	0	0	0	0	0	0	0	0	0
1960	Pit-N	.250	7	20	4	5	0	0	0	1	2	4	0	O*6
Total 2		.250	8	20	4	5	0	0	0	1	2	4	0	
■ Allie Clark														
1947	NY-A	.500	3	2	1	1	0	0	0	1	1	0	0	O*1
1948	Cle-A		1	3	0	0	0	0	0	0	0	1	0	O
Total 2		.200	4	5	1	1	0	0	0	1	1	1	0	
■ Jack Clark														
1985	StL-N	.240	7	25	1	6	2	0	0	4	3	9	0	1
■ Bob Clark														
1889	Bro-A	.417	4	12	3	5	2	0	0	3	2	2	0	C
1890	Bro-N	.667	1	3	2	2	0	1	0	1	0	0	0	C
Total 2		.467	5	15	5	7	2	1	0	4	2	2	0	
■ Will Clark														
1989	SF-N	.250	4	16	2	4	1	0	0	0	1	3	0	1
■ Fred Clarke														
1903	Pit-N	.265	8	34	3	9	2	1	0	2	1	5	1	O
1909	Pit-N	.211	7	19	7	4	0	0	2	7	5	3	3	O
Total 2		.245	15	53	10	13	2	1	2	9	6	8	4	
■ Boileryard Clarke														
1895	Bal-N	.286	2	7	1	2	0	0	0	0	0	0	2	C
1897	Bal-N	.563	4	16	5	9	1	1	1	4	1	0	0	C
Total 2		.478	6	23	6	11	1	1	1	4	1	0	2	
■ Ellis Clary														
1944	StL-A	.000	1	1	0	0	0	0	0	0	0	0	0	H
■ Roberto Clemente														
1960	Pit-N	.310	7	29	1	9	0	0	0	3	0	4	0	O
1971	Pit-N	.414	7	29	3	12	2	1	2	4	2	2	0	O
Total 2		.362	14	58	4	21	2	1	2	7	2	6	0	
■ Donn Clendenon														
1969	NY-N	.357	4	14	4	5	1	0	3	4	2	6	0	1
■ Flea Clifton														
1935	Det-A	.000	4	16	1	0	0	0	0	0	0	2	4	0	3

YEAR	TM/L	AVG	G	AB	R	H	2B	3B	HR	RBI	BB	SO	SB	POS
■ Ty Cline														
1970	Cin-N	.333	3	3	0	1	0	0	0	0	0	0	0	H
■ Gene Clines														
1971	Pit-N	.091	3	11	2	1	0	1	0	0	1	1	0	O
■ Ty Cobb														
1907	Det-A	.200	5	20	1	4	0	1	0	0	0	3	0	O
1908	Det-A	.368	5	19	3	7	1	0	0	4	1	2	2	O
1909	Det-A	.231	7	26	3	6	3	0	0	5	2	2	2	O
Total 3		.262	17	65	7	17	4	1	0	9	3	7	4	
■ Mickey Cochrane														
1929	Phi-A	.400	5	15	5	6	1	0	0	0	7	0	0	C
1930	Phi-A	.222	6	18	5	4	1	0	2	4	5	2	0	C
1931	Phi-A	.160	7	25	2	4	0	0	0	1	5	2	0	C
1934	Det-A	.214	7	28	2	6	1	0	0	1	4	3	0	C
1935	Det-A	.292	6	24	3	7	1	0	0	1	4	1	0	C
Total 5		.245	31	110	17	27	4	0	2	7	25	8	0	
■ Jerry Coleman														
1949	NY-A	.250	5	20	0	5	0	0	0	4	0	4	0	2
1950	NY-A	.286	4	14	2	4	1	0	0	3	2	0	0	2
1951	NY-A	.250	5	8	2	2	0	0	0	0	1	2	0	2
1955	NY-A	.000	3	3	0	0	0	0	0	0	0	1	0	S
1956	NY-A	.000	2	2	0	0	0	0	0	0	0	0	0	2
1957	NY-A	.364	7	22	2	8	2	0	0	2	3	1	0	2
Total 6		.275	26	69	6	19	6	0	0	9	6	8	0	
■ Gordy Coleman														
1961	Cin-N	.250	5	20	2	5	0	0	1	2	0	1	0	1
■ Vince Coleman														
1987	StL-N	.143	7	28	5	4	2	0	0	2	2	10	6	O
■ Eddie Collins														
1910	Phi-A	.429	5	21	5	9	4	0	0	3	2	0	4	2
1911	Phi-A	.286	6	21	4	6	1	0	0	1	2	2	2	2
1913	Phi-A	.421	5	19	5	8	0	2	0	3	1	2	3	2
1914	Phi-A	.214	4	14	0	3	0	0	0	1	2	1	1	2
1917	Chi-A	.409	6	22	4	9	1	0	0	2	2	3	3	2
1919	Chi-A	.226	8	31	2	7	1	0	0	1	1	2	1	2
Total 6		.328	34	128	20	42	7	2	0	11	10	10	14	
■ Hub Collins														
1889	Bro-A	.371	9	35	13	13	3	0	1	2	7	5	6	2
1890	Bro-N	.310	7	29	7	9	0	1	0	1	3	0	2	2
Total 2		.344	16	64	20	22	3	1	1	3	10	5	8	
■ Ripper Collins														
1931	StL-N	.000	2	2	0	0	0	0	0	0	0	1	0	H
1934	StL-N	.367	7	30	4	11	1	0	0	3	1	2	0	1
1938	Chi-N	.133	4	15	1	2	0	0	0	0	0	3	0	1
Total 3		.277	13	47	5	13	1	0	0	3	1	6	0	
■ Jimmy Collins														
1897	Bos-N	.182	5	22	2	4	0	0	0	4	1	0	0	3
1903	Bos-A	.250	8	36	5	9	1	2	0	1	1	1	3	3
Total 2		.224	13	58	7	13	1	2	0	5	2	1	3	
■ Shano Collins														
1917	Chi-A	.286	6	21	2	6	1	0	0	0	0	0	0	O
1919	Chi-A	.250	4	16	2	4	1	0	0	0	0	0	0	O
Total 2		.270	10	37	4	10	2	0	0	0	0	2	0	
■ Joe Collins														
1950	NY-A	—	1	0	0	0	0	0	0	0	0	0	0	1
1951	NY-A	.222	6	18	2	4	0	0	1	3	2	1	0	1*6,O*1
1952	NY-A	.000	6	12	1	0	0	0	0	0	1	3	0	1
1953	NY-A	.167	6	24	4	4	1	0	1	2	3	8	0	1
1955	NY-A	.167	5	12	6	2	0	0	2	3	6	4	1	1*5,O*1
1956	NY-A	.238	6	21	2	5	2	0	0	2	2	3	0	1*5
1957	NY-A	.000	6	5	0	0	0	0	0	0	0	3	0	1*5
Total 7		.163	36	92	15	15	3	0	4	10	14	22	1	
■ Pat Collins														
1926	NY-A	.000	3	2	0	0	0	0	0	0	0	1	0	C
1927	NY-A	.600	2	5	0	3	1	0	0	0	3	0	0	C
1928	NY-A	1.000	1	1	0	1	1	0	0	0	0	0	0	C
Total 3		.500	6	8	0	4	2	0	0	3	1	0		
■ Earle Combs														
1926	NY-A	.357	7	28	3	10	0	0	0	2	5	2	0	O
1927	NY-A	.313	4	16	6	5	0	0	0	2	1	2	0	O
1928	NY-A	—	1	0	0	0	0	0	0	1	0	0	0	H
1932	NY-A	.375	4	16	8	6	1	0	0	1	4	4	3	0	O
Total 4		.350	16	60	17	21	3	0	1	9	10	7	0	
■ Wayne Comer														
1968	Det-A	1.000	1	1	0	1	0	0	0	0	0	0	0	H
■ Charlie Comiskey														
1885	StL-A	.292	7	24	6	7	0	0	0	0	0	0	1	1
1886	StL-A	.292	6	24	2	7	1	0	0	2	0	4	0	1
1887	StL-A	.306	15	62	8	19	2	0	0	5	1	1	4	1*14,O*1
1888	StL-A	.268	10	41	6	11	1	1	0	3	1	1	4	1*10,O*1
Total 4		.291	38	151	22	44	4	1	0	10	2	6	8	
■ Clint Conatser														
1948	Bos-N	.000	2	4	0	0	0	0	0	0	1	0	0	O

YEAR	TM/L	AVG	G	AB	R	H	2B	3B	HR	RBI	BB	SO	SB	POS
Dave Concepcion														
1970	Cin-N	.333	3	9	0	3	0	1	0	3	0	0	0	S
1972	Cin-N	.308	6	13	2	4	0	1	0	2	2	2	1	S*5
1975	Cin-N	.179	7	28	3	5	1	0	1	4	0	1	3	S
1976	Cin-N	.357	4	14	1	5	1	1	0	3	1	3	1	S
Total 4		.266	20	64	6	17	2	3	1	12	3	6	5	
Onix Concepcion														
1980	KC-A	—	3	0	0	0	0	0	0	0	0	0	0	R
1985	KC-A	—	3	0	1	0	0	0	0	0	0	0	0	S*2
Total 2		—	6	0	1	0	0	0	0	0	0	0	0	
Billy Conigliaro														
1973	Oak-A	.000	3	3	0	0	0	0	0	0	0	1	0	H
Joe Connolly														
1914	Bos-N	.111	3	9	1	1	0	0	0	1	1	1	0	O
Roger Connor														
1888	NY-N	.304	7	23	7	7	1	2	0	3	4	0	4	1
1889	NY-N	.343	9	35	9	12	2	2	0	12	3	2	8	1
Total 2		.328	16	58	16	19	3	4	0	15	7	2	12	
Cecil Cooper														
1975	Bos-A	.053	5	19	0	1	0	0	1	0	0	3	0	1
1982	Mil-A	.286	7	28	3	8	1	0	1	6	1	1	0	1
Total 2		.191	12	47	3	9	2	0	1	7	1	4	0	
Claude Cooper														
1913	NY-N	—	2	0	0	0	0	0	0	0	0	0	1	R
Walker Cooper														
1942	StL-N	.286	5	21	3	6	1	0	0	4	0	1	0	C
1943	StL-N	.294	5	17	1	5	0	0	0	0	1	0	0	C
1944	StL-N	.318	6	22	1	7	2	1	0	2	3	2	0	C
Total 3		.300	16	60	5	18	3	1	0	6	3	4	0	
Pop Corkhill														
1889	Bro-A	.208	9	24	4	5	1	0	1	5	6	2	1	O
Pat Corrales														
1970	Cin-N	.000	1	1	0	0	0	0	0	0	0	0	0	H
Pete Coscarart														
1941	Bro-N	.000	3	7	1	0	0	0	0	0	1	2	0	2
Bill Coughlin														
1907	Det-A	.250	5	20	0	5	0	0	0	1	1	4	1	3
1908	Det-A	.125	3	8	0	1	0	0	0	1	0	1	0	3
Total 2		.214	8	28	0	6	0	0	0	1	1	5	1	
Wes Covington														
1957	Mil-N	.208	7	24	1	5	1	0	0	1	2	6	1	O
1958	Mil-N	.269	7	26	2	7	0	0	0	4	2	4	0	O
1966	LA-N	.000	1	1	0	0	0	0	0	0	0	1	0	H
Total 3		.235	15	51	3	12	1	0	0	5	4	11	1	
Billy Cox														
1949	Bro-N	.333	2	3	0	1	0	0	0	0	0	1	0	3*1
1952	Bro-N	.296	7	27	4	8	2	0	0	3	4	0	3	3
1953	Bro-N	.304	6	23	3	7	3	0	1	6	1	4	0	3
Total 3		.302	15	53	7	16	5	0	1	6	4	9	0	
Harry Craft														
1939	Cin-N	.091	4	11	0	1	0	0	0	0	0	6	0	O
1940	Cin-N	.000	1	1	0	0	0	0	0	0	0	0	0	H
Total 2		.083	5	12	0	1	0	0	0	0	0	6	0	
Doc Cramer														
1931	Phi-A	.500	2	2	0	1	0	0	0	2	0	0	0	H
1945	Det-A	.379	7	29	7	11	0	0	0	4	1	0	1	O
Total 2		.387	9	31	7	12	0	0	0	6	1	0	1	
Del Crandall														
1957	Mil-N	.211	6	19	1	4	0	0	1	1	1	1	0	C
1958	Mil-N	.240	7	25	4	6	0	0	1	3	3	10	0	C
Total 2		.227	13	44	5	10	0	0	2	4	4	11	0	
Gavvy Cravath														
1915	Phi-N	.125	5	16	2	2	1	1	0	1	2	6	0	O
Pat Crawford														
1934	StL-N	.000	2	2	0	0	0	0	0	0	0	0	0	H
Sam Crawford														
1907	Det-A	.238	5	21	1	5	1	0	0	3	0	3	0	O
1908	Det-A	.238	5	21	2	5	1	0	0	1	1	2	0	O
1909	Det-A	.250	7	28	4	7	3	0	1	4	1	1	1	O*7,1*1
Total 3		.243	17	70	7	17	5	0	1	8	2	6	1	
Willie Crawford														
1965	LA-N	.500	2	2	0	1	0	0	0	0	0	1	0	H
1974	LA-N	.333	3	6	1	2	0	0	1	1	0	0	0	O*2
Total 2		.375	5	8	1	3	0	0	1	1	0	1	0	
Creepy Crespi														
1942	StL-N	—	1	0	1	0	0	0	0	0	0	0	0	R
Lou Criger														
1903	Bos-A	.231	8	26	1	6	0	0	0	4	2	3	0	C
Hughie Critz														
1933	NY-N	.136	5	22	2	3	0	0	0	1	0	0	2	2

YEAR	TM/L	AVG	G	AB	R	H	2B	3B	HR	RBI	BB	SO	SB	POS
Joe Cronin														
1933	Was-A	.318	5	22	1	7	0	0	0	2	0	2	0	S
Frankie Crosetti														
1932	NY-A	.133	4	15	2	2	1	0	0	0	2	3	0	S
1936	NY-A	.269	6	26	5	7	2	0	0	3	3	5	0	S
1937	NY-A	.048	5	21	2	1	0	0	0	0	3	2	0	S
1938	NY-A	.250	4	16	1	4	2	1	1	6	2	4	0	S
1939	NY-A	.063	4	16	2	1	0	0	0	1	2	2	0	S
1942	NY-A	.000	1	3	0	0	0	0	0	0	0	1	0	3
1943	NY-A	.278	5	18	4	5	0	0	0	1	2	3	1	S
Total 7		.174	29	115	16	20	5	1	1	11	14	20	1	
Lave Cross														
1900	Bro-N	.278	4	18	2	5	0	1	0	1	0	0	1	3
1905	Phi-A	.105	5	19	0	2	0	0	0	0	1	1	0	3
Total 2		.189	9	37	2	7	0	1	0	1	1	1	1	
Monte Cross														
1905	Phi-A	.176	5	17	0	3	0	0	0	0	0	7	0	S
Frank Croucher														
1940	Det-A	—	1	0	0	0	0	0	0	0	0	0	0	S
Terry Crowley														
1970	Bal-A	.000	1	1	0	0	0	0	0	0	0	0	0	H
1975	Cin-N	.500	2	2	0	1	0	0	0	0	0	1	0	H
1979	Bal-A	.250	5	4	0	1	1	0	0	2	1	0	0	H
Total 3		.286	8	7	0	2	1	0	0	2	1	1	0	
Todd Cruz														
1983	Bal-A	.125	6	16	1	2	0	0	0	1	0	3	0	3
Leon Culberson														
1946	Bos-A	.222	5	9	1	2	0	0	1	1	1	2	1	O*3
Roy Cullenbine														
1942	NY-A	.263	5	19	3	5	1	0	0	2	1	2	1	O
1945	Det-A	.227	7	22	5	5	2	0	0	4	8	2	1	O
Total 2		.244	12	41	8	10	3	0	0	6	9	4	2	
Bill Cunningham														
1922	NY-N	.200	4	10	0	2	0	0	0	2	2	1	0	O
1923	NY-N	.143	4	7	0	1	0	0	0	1	0	1	0	O*3
Total 2		.176	8	17	0	3	0	0	0	3	2	2	0	
George Cutshaw														
1916	Bro-N	.105	5	19	2	2	1	0	0	2	1	1	0	2
Kiki Cuyler														
1925	Pit-N	.269	7	26	3	7	3	0	1	6	1	4	0	O
1929	Chi-N	.300	5	20	4	6	1	0	0	4	1	7	0	O
1932	Chi-N	.278	4	18	2	5	1	1	1	2	0	3	1	O
Total 3		.281	16	64	9	18	5	1	2	12	2	14	1	
Bill Dahlen														
1900	Bro-N	.176	4	17	3	3	0	1	0	2	0	3	1	S
1905	NY-N	.000	5	15	1	0	0	0	0	1	3	2	3	S
Total 2		.094	9	32	4	3	0	1	0	3	3	5	4	
Babe Dahlgren														
1939	NY-A	.214	4	14	2	3	2	0	1	2	0	4	0	1
Ed Daily														
1890	Lou-A	.136	6	22	1	3	1	1	0	3	1	2	2	O*4,P*2
Abner Dalrymple														
1885	Chi-N	.269	7	26	4	7	2	0	1	2	0	0	0	O
1886	Chi-N	.190	6	21	2	4	1	0	0	2	0	5	1	O
Total 2		.234	13	47	6	11	3	1	1	2	2	5	1	
Clay Dalrymple														
1969	Bal-A	1.000	2	2	0	2	0	0	0	0	0	0	0	H
Tom Daly														
1890	Bro-N	.182	6	22	1	4	2	0	0	3	0	4	2	C*6,1*1
1900	Bro-N	.154	4	13	2	2	1	0	0	1	3	1	0	2
Total 2		.171	10	35	3	6	3	0	0	4	3	5	2	
Harry Danning														
1936	NY-N	.000	2	2	0	0	0	0	0	0	0	1	0	C*1
1937	NY-N	.250	3	12	0	3	1	0	0	2	0	2	0	C
Total 2		.214	5	14	0	3	1	0	0	2	0	3	0	
Alvin Dark														
1948	Bos-N	.167	6	24	2	4	1	0	0	0	0	2	0	S
1951	NY-N	.417	6	24	5	10	3	0	1	4	2	3	0	S
1954	NY-N	.412	4	17	2	7	0	0	0	0	1	1	0	S
Total 3		.323	16	65	9	21	4	0	1	4	3	6	0	
Jake Daubert														
1916	Bro-N	.176	4	17	1	3	0	1	0	0	2	3	0	1
1919	Cin-N	.241	8	29	4	7	0	1	0	1	1	2	1	1
Total 2		.217	12	46	5	10	0	2	0	1	3	5	1	
Rich Dauer														
1979	Bal-A	.294	6	17	2	5	1	0	1	1	0	1	0	2*5
1983	Bal-A	.211	5	19	2	4	1	0	0	3	0	3	0	2
Total 2		.250	11	36	4	9	2	0	1	4	0	4	0	
Darren Daulton														
1993	Phi-N	.217	6	23	4	5	2	0	1	4	4	5	0	C

Vic Davalillo

YEAR	TM/L	AVG	G	AB	R	H	2B	3B	HR	RBI	BB	SO	SB	POS
1971	Pit-N	.333	3	3	1	1	0	0	0	0	0	0	0	O*2
1973	Oak-A	.091	6	11	0	1	0	0	0	0	2	1	0	O*4,1*1
1977	LA-N	.333	3	3	0	1	0	0	0	0	1	0	0	H
1978	LA-N	.333	2	3	0	1	0	0	0	0	0	0	0	D*1
Total 4		.200	14	20	1	4	0	0	0	1	2	1	0	

Jim Davenport

YEAR	TM/L	AVG	G	AB	R	H	2B	3B	HR	RBI	BB	SO	SB	POS
1962	SF-N	.136	7	22	1	3	1	0	0	1	4	7	0	3

Mark Davidson

1987	Min-A	.000	2	1	0	0	0	0	0	0	0	0	0	O*1

Chili Davis

1991	Min-A	.222	6	18	4	4	0	0	2	4	2	3	0	D*4,O*1

Eric Davis

1990	Cin-N	.286	4	14	3	4	0	1	5	0	0	0	0	O

George Davis

1892	Cle-N	.167	3	6	0	1	0	0	0	0	1	0		3*2
1894	NY-N	.313	4	16	5	5	2	2	0	5	2	0	2	S
1906	Chi-A	.308	3	13	4	4	3	0	0	6	0	1	1	S
Total 3		.286	10	35	9	10	5	2	0	11	2	2	3	

Kiddo Davis

1933	NY-N	.368	5	19	1	7	1	0	0	0	0	3	0	O
1936	NY-N	.500	4	2	2	1	0	0	0	0	0	0	0	H
Total 2		.381	9	21	3	8	1	0	0	0	0	3	0	

Harry Davis

1905	Phi-A	.200	5	20	0	4	1	0	0	0	0	1	0	1
1910	Phi-A	.353	5	17	5	6	3	0	0	2	3	4	0	1
1911	Phi-A	.208	6	24	3	5	1	0	0	5	0	3	0	1
Total 3		.246	16	61	8	15	5	0	0	7	3	8	0	

Tommy Davis

1963	LA-N	.400	4	15	0	6	0	2	0	2	0	2	1	0
1966	LA-N	.250	4	8	0	2	0	0	0	0	1	1	0	O*3
Total 2		.348	8	23	0	8	0	2	0	2	1	3	1	

Jumbo Davis

1889	Bro-A	.000	1	4	0	0	0	0	0	0	0	0	0	S

Mike Davis

1988	LA-N	.143	4	7	3	1	0	0	2	2	4	0	2	D*2,O*1

Ron Davis

1968	StL-N	.000	2	7	0	0	0	0	0	0	0	2	0	O

Spud Davis

1934	StL-N	1.000	2	2	0	2	0	0	0	1	0	0	0	H

Willie Davis

1963	LA-N	.167	4	12	2	2	2	0	0	3	0	6	0	O
1965	LA-N	.231	7	26	3	6	0	0	0	0	2	3	0	O
1966	LA-N	.063	4	16	0	1	0	0	0	0	0	4	0	O
Total 3		.167	15	54	5	9	2	0	0	3	0	12	3	

Charlie Deal

1914	Bos-N	.125	4	16	1	2	0	0	0	0	0	0	2	3
1918	Chi-N	.176	6	17	0	3	0	0	0	0	1	0	3	
Total 2		.152	10	33	1	5	2	0	0	0	1	2		

Doug DeCinces

1979	Bal-A	.200	7	25	2	5	0	0	1	3	5	5	1	3

Ivan DeJesus

1983	Phi-N	.125	5	16	0	2	0	0	0	0	1	2	0	S
1985	StL-N	.000	1	1	0	0	0	0	0	0	0	0	0	H
Total 2		.118	6	17	0	2	0	0	0	0	1	2	0	

Jim Delahanty

1909	Det-A	.346	7	26	2	9	4	0	0	4	2	5	0	2

Bill DeLancey

1934	StL-N	.172	7	29	3	5	3	0	1	4	2	8	0	C

Joe DeMaestri

1960	NY-A	.500	4	2	1	1	0	0	0	0	0	0	1	S*3

Frank Demaree

1932	Chi-N	.286	2	7	1	2	0	0	1	4	1	0	0	O
1935	Chi-N	.250	6	24	2	6	1	0	2	2	1	4	0	O
1938	Chi-N	.100	3	10	1	1	0	0	0	0	1	2	0	O
1943	StL-N	.000	1	1	0	0	0	0	0	0	0	0	0	H
Total 4		.214	12	42	4	9	1	0	3	6	3	6	0	

John DeMerit

1957	Mil-N	—	1	0	0	0	0	0	0	0	0	0	0	R

Don Demeter

1959	LA-N	.250	6	12	2	3	0	0	0	0	1	3	0	O

Rick Dempsey

1979	Bal-A	.286	7	21	3	6	2	0	0	1	3	0		C*6
1983	Bal-A	.385	5	13	3	5	4	0	1	2	2	2	0	C
1988	LA-N	.200	2	5	0	1	1	0	0	1	1	2	0	C
Total 3		.308	14	39	6	12	7	0	1	3	4	7	0	

Jerry Denny

1884	Pro-N	.444	3	9	3	4	0	1	1	2	0	3	0	3

Bucky Dent

1977	NY-A	.263	6	19	0	5	0	0	0	2	2	1	0	S
1978	NY-A	.417	6	24	3	10	1	0	0	7	1	2	0	S
Total 2		.349	12	43	3	15	1	0	0	9	3	3	0	

Sam Dente

1954	Cle-A	.000	3	3	1	0	0	0	0	0	0	1	0	0	S

Bob Dernier

1983	Phi-N	—	1	0	1	0	0	0	0	0	0	0	0	0	R

Art Devlin

1905	NY-N	.250	5	16	0	4	1	0	0	1	1	3	3	3

Josh Devore

1911	NY-N	.167	6	24	1	4	1	0	0	3	1	8	0	O
1912	NY-N	.250	7	24	4	6	0	0	0	0	7	5	4	O
1914	Bos-N	.000	1	1	0	0	0	0	0	0	0	1	0	H
Total 3		.204	14	49	5	10	1	0	0	3	8	14	4	

Al DeVormer

1921	NY-A	.000	2	1	0	0	0	0	0	0	0	0	0	C*1

Bo Diaz

1983	Phi-N	.333	5	15	1	5	0	0	0	1	2	0		C

Bill Dickey

1932	NY-A	.438	4	16	2	7	0	0	0	4	2	1	0	C
1936	NY-A	.120	6	25	5	3	0	0	1	5	3	4	0	C
1937	NY-A	.211	5	19	3	4	0	1	0	3	2	2	0	C
1938	NY-A	.400	4	15	2	6	0	0	1	2	1	0	1	C
1939	NY-A	.267	4	15	2	4	0	0	2	5	1	2	0	C
1941	NY-A	.167	5	18	3	3	1	0	0	1	3	1	0	C
1942	NY-A	.263	5	19	1	5	0	0	0	1	0	0	0	C
1943	NY-A	.278	5	18	1	5	0	0	1	4	2	2	0	C
Total 8		.255	38	145	19	37	1	1	5	24	15	12	1	

Dom DiMaggio

1946	Bos-A	.259	7	27	2	7	3	0	0	3	2	2	0	O

Joe DiMaggio

1936	NY-A	.346	6	26	3	9	3	0	0	3	1	3	0	O
1937	NY-A	.273	5	22	2	6	0	0	1	4	0	3	0	O
1938	NY-A	.267	4	15	4	4	0	0	1	2	1	1	0	O
1939	NY-A	.313	4	16	3	5	0	0	1	3	1	1	0	O
1941	NY-A	.263	5	19	1	5	0	0	0	1	2	2	0	O
1942	NY-A	.333	5	21	3	7	0	0	0	3	0	1	0	O
1947	NY-A	.231	7	26	4	6	0	0	2	5	6	2	0	O
1949	NY-A	.111	5	18	2	2	0	0	1	2	3	5	0	O
1950	NY-A	.308	4	13	2	4	1	0	1	2	3	1	0	O
1951	NY-A	.261	6	23	3	6	2	0	1	5	2	4	0	O
Total 10		.271	51	199	27	54	6	0	8	30	19	23	0	

Larry Doby

1948	Cle-A	.318	6	22	1	7	1	0	1	2	2	4	0	O
1954	Cle-A	.125	4	16	0	2	0	0	0	0	2	4	0	O
Total 2		.237	10	38	1	9	1	0	1	2	4	8	0	

Bobby Doerr

1946	Bos-A	.409	6	22	1	9	1	0	1	3	2	2	0	2

Frank Doljack

1934	Det-A	.000	2	2	0	0	0	0	0	0	0	0	0	O*1

Jiggs Donahue

1906	Chi-A	.333	6	18	0	6	2	1	0	4	3	3	0	1

Mike Donlin

1905	NY-N	.263	5	19	4	5	1	0	0	1	2	1	2	O

Patsy Donovan

1890	Bro-N	.471	5	17	5	8	1	0	0	3	2	1	3	O

Patsy Dougherty

1903	Bos-A	.235	8	34	3	8	0	2	2	5	2	6	0	O
1906	Chi-A	.100	6	20	1	2	0	0	0	1	3	4	2	O
Total 2		.185	14	54	4	10	0	2	2	6	5	10	2	

Taylor Douthit

1926	StL-N	.267	4	15	3	4	2	0	0	1	3	2	0	O
1928	StL-N	.091	3	11	1	1	0	0	0	0	1	1	0	O
1930	StL-N	.083	6	24	1	2	0	0	1	2	0	2	0	O
Total 3		.140	13	50	5	7	2	0	1	4	4	5	0	

Red Downs

1908	Det-A	.167	2	6	1	1	1	0	0	1	1	2	0	2

Brian Doyle

1978	NY-A	.438	6	16	4	7	1	0	0	2	0	0	0	2

Jack Doyle

1894	NY-N	.588	4	17	4	10	1	1	0	6	1	1	6	1
1896	Bal-N	.294	4	17	3	5	1	0	0	4	0	0	2	1
1897	Bal-N	.526	5	19	7	10	2	0	0	9	0	1	2	1
Total 3		.472	13	53	14	25	4	1	0	19	1	2	10	

Larry Doyle

1911	NY-N	.304	6	23	3	7	3	1	0	1	2	1	2	2
1912	NY-N	.242	8	33	5	8	1	0	1	2	3	2	2	2
1913	NY-N	.150	5	20	1	3	0	0	0	2	0	1	0	2
Total 3		.237	19	76	9	18	4	1	1	5	5	4	4	

Denny Doyle

1975	Bos-A	.267	7	30	3	8	1	1	0	0	2	1	0	2

YEAR	TM/L	AVG	G	AB	R	H	2B	3B	HR	RBI	BB	SO	SB	POS
Dan Driessen														
1975	Cin-N	.000	2	2	0	0	0	0	0	0	0	0	0	H
1976	Cin-N	.357	4	14	4	5	2	0	1	1	2	0	1	D
1987	StL-N	.231	4	13	3	3	2	0	0	1	1	1	0	1
Total 3		.276	10	29	7	8	4	0	1	2	3	1	1	
Jean Dubuc														
1918	Bos-A	.000	1	1	0	0	0	0	0	0	0	1	0	H
Hugh Duffy														
1892	Bos-N	.462	6	26	3	12	3	2	1	9	1	0	3	O
1897	Bos-N	.524	5	21	6	11	2	0	0	7	1	0	0	O
Total 2		.489	11	47	9	23	5	2	1	16	2	0	3	
Joe Dugan														
1922	NY-A	.250	5	20	4	5	1	0	0	0	1	0	3	
1923	NY-A	.280	6	25	5	7	2	1	1	5	3	1	0	3
1926	NY-A	.333	7	24	2	8	1	0	0	2	1	1	0	3
1927	NY-A	.200	4	15	2	3	0	0	0	0	0	1	0	3
1928	NY-A	.167	3	6	0	1	0	0	0	1	0	0	0	3
Total 5		.267	25	90	13	24	4	1	1	8	4	2	0	
Oscar Dugey														
1915	Phi-N	—	2	0	0	0	0	0	0	0	0	0	1	R
Dave Duncan														
1972	Oak-A	.200	3	5	0	1	0	0	0	0	1	3	0	C*1
Pat Duncan														
1919	Cin-N	.269	8	26	3	7	2	0	0	8	2	2	0	O
Mariano Duncan														
1990	Cin-N	.143	4	14	1	2	0	0	0	1	2	2	1	2
1993	Phi-N	.345	6	29	5	10	0	1	0	2	1	7	3	2*5,D*1
Total 2		.279	10	43	6	12	0	1	0	3	3	9	4	
Fred Dunlap														
1887	Det-N	.150	11	40	5	6	0	1	0	1	0	4	4	2
Leo Durocher														
1928	NY-A	.000	4	2	0	0	0	0	0	0	0	1	0	2
1934	StL-N	.259	7	27	4	7	1	0	0	0	0	0	0	S
Total 2		.241	11	29	4	7	1	1	0	0	0	1	0	
Cedric Durst														
1927	NY-A	.000	1	1	0	0	0	0	0	0	0	0	0	H
1928	NY-A	.375	4	8	3	3	0	0	1	2	0	1	0	O
Total 2		.333	5	9	3	3	0	0	1	2	0	1	0	
Erv Dusak														
1946	StL-N	.250	4	4	0	1	1	0	0	0	2	2	0	O
Jim Dwyer														
1983	Bal-A	.375	2	8	3	3	1	0	1	1	0	0	0	O
Duffy Dyer														
1969	NY-N	.000	1	1	0	0	0	0	0	0	0	0	0	H
Jimmy Dykes														
1929	Phi-A	.421	5	19	2	8	1	0	0	4	1	1	0	3
1930	Phi-A	.222	6	18	2	4	3	0	1	5	5	3	0	3
1931	Phi-A	.227	7	22	2	5	0	0	0	2	5	1	0	3
Total 3		.288	18	59	6	17	4	0	1	11	11	5	0	
Lenny Dykstra														
1986	NY-N	.296	7	27	4	8	0	0	2	3	2	7	0	O
1993	Phi-N	.348	6	23	9	8	1	0	4	8	7	4	4	O
Total 2		.320	13	50	13	16	1	0	6	11	9	11	4	
Mike Easler														
1979	Pit-N	.000	2	1	0	0	0	0	0	0	1	0	0	H
Zeb Eaton														
1945	Det-A	.000	1	1	0	0	0	0	0	0	0	1	0	H
Bruce Edwards														
1947	Bro-N	.222	7	27	3	6	1	0	0	2	2	7	0	C
1949	Bro-N	.500	2	2	0	1	0	0	0	0	0	1	0	H
Total 2		.241	9	29	3	7	1	0	0	2	2	8	0	
Johnny Edwards														
1961	Cin-N	.364	3	11	1	4	3	0	0	2	0	0	0	C
1968	StL-N	.000	1	1	0	0	0	0	0	0	0	1	0	H
Total 2		.333	4	12	1	4	2	0	0	2	0	1	0	
Marshall Edwards														
1982	Mil-A	—	1	0	0	0	0	0	0	0	0	0	0	O
Jim Eisenreich														
1993	Phi-N	.231	6	26	3	6	0	0	1	7	2	4	0	O
Bob Elliott														
1948	Bos-N	.333	6	21	4	7	0	0	2	5	2	2	0	3
Kevin Elster														
1986	NY-N	.000	1	1	0	0	0	0	0	0	0	0	0	S
Fred Ely														
1900	Pit-N	.286	4	14	1	4	1	0	0	0	1	1	2	S
Clyde Engle														
1912	Bos-A	.333	3	3	1	1	1	0	0	2	0	0	0	H
Woody English														
1929	Chi-N	.190	5	21	1	4	2	0	0	0	1	6	0	S
1932	Chi-N	.176	4	17	2	3	0	0	0	1	2	2	0	3
Total 2		.184	9	38	3	7	2	0	0	1	3	8	0	
Del Ennis														
1950	Phi-N	.143	4	14	1	2	1	0	0	0	0	0	1	O
Mike Epstein														
1972	Oak-A	.000	6	16	1	0	0	0	0	0	0	5	3	0	1
Sammy Esposito														
1959	Chi-A	.000	2	2	0	0	0	0	0	0	0	1	0	3
Chuck Essegian														
1959	LA-N	.667	4	3	2	2	0	0	2	2	1	1	0	H
Dude Esterbrook														
1884	NY-A	.300	3	10	0	3	1	0	0	0	0	3	1	3
Andy Etchebarren														
1966	Bal-A	.083	4	12	2	1	0	0	0	0	2	4	0	C
1969	Bal-A	.000	2	6	0	0	0	0	0	0	0	1	0	C
1970	Bal-A	.143	2	7	1	1	0	0	0	0	2	3	0	C
1971	Bal-A	.000	1	2	0	0	0	0	0	0	0	0	0	C
Total 4		.074	9	27	3	2	0	0	0	0	4	8	0	
Nick Etten														
1943	NY-A	.105	5	19	0	2	0	0	0	2	1	2	0	1
Darrell Evans														
1984	Det-A	.067	5	15	1	1	0	0	0	1	4	4	0	1*4,3*2
Dwight Evans														
1975	Bos-A	.292	7	24	3	7	1	1	1	5	3	4	0	O
1986	Bos-A	.308	7	26	4	8	2	0	2	9	4	3	0	O
Total 2		.300	14	50	7	15	3	1	3	14	7	7	0	
Joe Evans														
1920	Cle-A	.308	4	13	0	4	0	0	0	0	1	0	0	O
Johnny Evers														
1906	Chi-N	.150	6	20	2	3	1	0	0	1	1	3	2	2
1907	Chi-N	.350	5	20	2	7	2	0	0	1	0	1	3	2*5,S*1
1908	Chi-N	.350	5	20	5	7	1	0	0	2	1	2	2	2
1914	Bos-N	.438	4	16	2	7	0	0	0	2	2	2	1	2
Total 4		.316	20	76	11	24	4	0	0	6	4	8	8	
Buck Ewing														
1888	NY-N	.346	7	26	5	9	0	2	1	6	1	3	5	C*6,1*1
1889	NY-N	.250	8	36	5	9	4	0	0	7	2	5	1	C
Total 2		.290	15	62	10	18	4	2	1	13	3	8	6	
Ron Fairly														
1959	LA-N	.000	6	3	0	0	0	0	0	0	0	0	1	O*4
1963	LA-N	.000	4	1	0	0	0	0	0	0	3	0	0	O
1965	LA-N	.379	7	29	7	11	3	0	2	6	0	1	0	O
1966	LA-N	.143	3	7	0	1	0	0	0	0	2	4	0	O*2,1*1
Total 4		.300	20	40	7	12	3	0	2	6	5	6	0	
George Fallon														
1944	StL-N	.000	2	2	0	0	0	0	0	0	0	1	0	2
Duke Farrell														
1894	NY-N	.400	4	15	5	6	0	0	0	2	1	1	1	C
1900	Bro-N	.375	2	8	0	3	0	0	0	1	0	0	1	C
1903	Bos-A	.000	2	2	0	0	0	0	0	0	1	0	0	H
Total 3		.360	8	25	5	9	0	0	0	4	1	1	2	
Jack Farrell														
1884	Pro-N	.444	3	9	3	4	2	0	0	0	0	0	1	2
Happy Felsch														
1917	Chi-A	.273	6	22	4	6	1	0	1	3	1	5	0	O
1919	Chi-A	.192	8	26	2	5	1	0	0	3	1	4	0	O
Total 2		.229	14	48	6	11	2	0	1	6	2	9	0	
Joe Ferguson														
1974	LA-N	.125	5	16	2	2	0	0	1	2	4	6	1	O*4,C*2
1978	LA-N	.500	2	4	1	2	0	0	0	0	0	1	0	C
Total 2		.200	7	20	3	4	2	0	1	2	4	7	1	
Tony Fernandez														
1993	Tor-A	.333	6	21	2	7	1	0	0	9	3	3	0	S
Al Ferrara														
1966	LA-N	1.000	1	1	0	1	0	0	0	0	0	0	0	H
Hobe Ferris														
1903	Bos-A	.290	8	31	3	9	0	1	0	5	0	6	0	2
Chick Fewster														
1921	NY-A	.200	4	10	3	2	0	0	0	1	2	3	0	O
Showboat Fisher														
1930	StL-N	.500	2	2	0	1	1	0	0	0	0	1	0	H
Carlton Fisk														
1975	Bos-A	.240	7	25	5	6	0	0	2	4	7	7	0	C
Max Flack														
1918	Chi-N	.263	6	19	2	5	0	0	0	4	1	1	0	O
Tim Flannery														
1984	SD-N	1.000	1	1	0	1	0	0	0	0	0	0	0	2
Art Fletcher														
1911	NY-N	.130	6	23	1	3	1	0	0	1	0	4	0	S

YEAR	TM/L	AVG	G	AB	R	H	2B	3B	HR	RBI	BB	SO	SB	POS
1912	NY-N	.179	8	28	1	5	1	0	0	3	1	4	1	S
1913	NY-N	.278	5	18	1	5	0	0	0	4	1	1	1	S
1917	NY-N	.200	6	25	2	5	1	0	0	0	0	2	0	S
Total 4		.191	25	94	5	18	3	0	0	8	2	11	2	
■ Silver Flint														
1885	Chi-N	.143	4	14	0	2	0	0	0	0	0	0	0	C
1886	Chi-N	.000	1	3	0	0	0	0	0	1	0	1	0	C
Total 2		.118	5	17	0	2	0	0	0	1	0	1	0	
■ Curt Flood														
1964	StL-N	.200	7	30	5	6	1	0	0	3	3	1	0	O
1967	StL-N	.179	7	28	2	5	1	0	0	3	3	3	0	O
1968	StL-N	.286	7	28	4	8	1	0	0	2	2	2	3	O
Total 3		.221	21	86	11	19	2	1	0	8	8	6	3	
■ Jake Flowers														
1926	StL-N	.000	3	3	0	0	0	0	0	0	0	1	0	H
1931	StL-N	.091	5	11	1	1	1	0	0	0	1	0	0	3*4
Total 2		.071	8	14	1	1	1	0	0	0	1	1	0	
■ Tim Foli														
1979	Pit-N	.333	7	30	6	10	1	1	0	3	2	0	0	S
■ Barry Foote														
1981	NY-A	.000	1	1	0	0	0	0	0	0	0	1	0	H
■ Curt Ford														
1987	StL-N	.308	5	13	1	4	0	0	0	2	1	0	0	O*4
■ Dan Ford														
1983	Bal-A	.167	5	12	1	2	0	0	1	1	5	0	0	O*4
■ Tom Forster														
1884	NY-A	.000	1	3	0	0	0	0	0	0	0	1	0	2
■ Ray Fosse														
1973	Oak-A	.158	7	19	0	3	1	0	0	0	1	4	0	C
1974	Oak-A	.143	5	14	1	2	0	0	1	1	1	5	0	C
Total 2		.152	12	33	1	5	1	0	1	1	2	9	0	
■ George Foster														
1972	Cin-N	—	2	0	0	0	0	0	0	0	0	0	0	O*1
1975	Cin-N	.276	7	29	1	8	1	0	0	2	1	1	1	O
1976	Cin-N	.429	4	14	3	6	1	0	0	4	2	3	0	O
Total 3		.326	13	43	4	14	2	0	0	6	3	4	1	
■ Dave Foutz														
1885	StL-A	.167	4	12	1	2	0	0	0	0	0	0	0	P
1886	StL-A	.200	4	15	2	3	1	0	3	0	3	0		P*2,O*2
1887	StL-A	.169	15	59	4	10	2	1	0	3	2	3	0	O*11,P*3,1*1
1889	Bro-A	.286	9	35	7	10	2	0	1	9	4	2	3	1*9,P*1
1890	Bro-N	.300	7	30	6	9	2	1	0	4	0	1	1	1*7,O*1
Total 5		.225	39	151	20	34	7	3	1	19	6	9	4	
■ Pete Fox														
1934	Det-A	.286	7	28	1	8	6	0	2	1	4	0	0	O
1935	Det-A	.385	6	26	1	10	3	1	0	4	0	1	0	O
1940	Det-A	.000	1	1	0	0	0	0	0	0	0	0	0	H
Total 3		.327	14	55	2	18	9	1	0	6	1	5	0	
■ Nellie Fox														
1959	Chi-A	.375	6	24	4	9	3	0	0	0	4	1	0	2
■ Jimmie Foxx														
1929	Phi-A	.350	5	20	5	7	1	0	2	5	1	1	0	1
1930	Phi-A	.333	6	21	3	7	2	1	1	3	2	4	0	1
1931	Phi-A	.348	7	23	3	8	0	0	1	3	6	5	0	1
Total 3		.344	18	64	11	22	3	1	4	11	9	10	0	
■ Joe Foy														
1967	Bos-A	.133	6	15	2	2	1	0	0	1	5	0		3*3
■ Herman Franks														
1941	Bro-N	.000	1	1	0	0	0	0	0	0	0	0	0	C
■ Bill Freehan														
1968	Det-A	.083	7	24	0	2	1	0	0	2	4	8	0	C
■ Buck Freeman														
1903	Bos-A	.281	8	32	6	9	0	3	0	4	2	2	0	O
■ Gene Freese														
1961	Cin-N	.063	5	16	0	1	1	0	0	0	3	4	0	3
■ Walter French														
1929	Phi-A	.000	1	1	0	0	0	0	0	0	0	1	0	H
■ Lonny Frey														
1939	Cin-N	.000	4	17	0	0	0	0	0	0	1	4	0	2
1940	Cin-N	.000	3	2	0	0	0	0	0	0	0	0	0	H
1947	NY-A	.000	1	1	0	0	0	0	0	0	1	0	0	H
Total 3		.000	8	20	0	0	0	0	0	0	1	4	0	
■ Frankie Frisch														
1921	NY-N	.300	8	30	5	9	0	1	0	1	4	3	3	3
1922	NY-N	.471	5	17	3	8	1	0	0	2	1	0	1	2
1923	NY-N	.400	6	25	2	10	1	0	1	1	0	0	2	2
1924	NY-N	.333	7	30	1	10	4	1	0	0	4	1	1	2*7,3*1
1928	StL-N	.231	4	13	1	3	0	0	0	1	2	2	2	2
1930	StL-N	.208	6	24	0	5	2	0	0	0	0	1	2	2
1931	StL-N	.259	7	27	2	7	2	0	0	1	1	2	1	2
1934	StL-N	.194	7	31	2	6	1	0	0	4	0	1	0	2
Total 8		.294	50	197	16	58	10	3	0	10	12	9	9	

YEAR	TM/L	AVG	G	AB	R	H	2B	3B	HR	RBI	BB	SO	SB	POS
■ Shorty Fuller														
1894	NY-N	.286	4	14	4	4	0	0	0	2	2	0	1	S
■ Chick Fullis														
1934	StL-N	.400	3	5	0	2	0	0	0	0	0	0	0	O
■ Carl Furillo														
1947	Bro-N	.353	6	17	2	6	2	0	0	3	3	0	0	O
1949	Bro-N	.125	3	8	0	1	0	0	0	0	1	0	0	O*2
1952	Bro-N	.174	7	23	1	4	2	0	0	3	3	0	0	O
1953	Bro-N	.333	6	24	0	8	0	1	4	1	3	0		O
1955	Bro-N	.296	7	27	4	8	1	0	1	3	3	5	0	O
1956	Bro-N	.240	7	25	2	6	0	0	1	2	3	0	0	O
1959	LA-N	.250	4	10	0	1	0	0	0	2	0	1	0	O*1
Total 7		.266	40	128	13	34	9	0	2	13	13	15	0	
■ Gary Gaetti														
1987	Min-A	.259	7	27	4	7	2	1	1	4	2	5	2	3
■ Phil Gagliano														
1967	StL-N	.000	1	1	0	0	0	0	0	0	0	0	0	H
1968	StL-N	.000	3	3	0	0	0	0	0	0	0	0	0	H
Total 2		.000	4	4	0	0	0	0	0	0	0	0	0	
■ Greg Gagne														
1987	Min-A	.200	7	30	5	6	1	0	1	3	1	6	0	S
1991	Min-A	.167	7	24	1	4	1	0	1	3	0	7	0	S
Total 2		.185	14	54	6	10	2	0	2	6	1	13	0	
■ Del Gainer														
1915	Bos-A	.333	1	3	1	1	0	0	0	0	0	0	0	1
1916	Bos-A	1.000	1	1	0	1	0	0	0	1	0	0	0	H
Total 2		.500	2	4	1	2	0	0	0	1	0	0	0	
■ Augie Galan														
1935	Chi-N	.160	6	25	2	4	1	0	0	2	2	0	0	O
1938	Chi-N	.000	2	2	0	0	0	0	0	0	0	1	0	H
1941	Bro-N	.000	2	2	0	0	0	0	0	0	0	1	0	H
Total 3		.138	10	29	2	4	1	0	0	2	2	4	0	
■ Mike Gallego														
1988	Oak-A	—	1	0	0	0	0	0	0	0	0	0	0	2
1989	Oak-A	.000	2	1	0	0	0	0	0	0	0	0	0	2*1,3*1
1990	Oak-A	.091	4	11	0	1	0	0	0	0	1	3	1	S
Total 3		.083	7	12	0	1	0	0	0	0	1	3	1	
■ Lee Gamble														
1939	Cin-N	.000	1	1	0	0	0	0	0	0	0	1	0	H
■ Oscar Gamble														
1976	NY-A	.125	3	8	0	1	0	0	0	1	0	0	0	O*2
1981	NY-A	.333	3	6	1	2	0	0	0	1	1	0	0	O*2
Total 2		.214	6	14	1	3	0	0	0	2	1	0	0	
■ Chick Gandil														
1917	Chi-A	.261	6	23	1	6	1	0	0	5	0	2	1	1
1919	Chi-A	.233	8	30	1	7	0	1	0	5	1	3	1	1
Total 2		.245	14	53	2	13	1	1	0	10	1	5	2	
■ Ron Gant														
1991	Atl-N	.267	7	30	3	8	0	1	0	4	2	3	1	O
1992	Atl-N	.125	4	8	2	1	1	0	0	1	2	2	2	O*3
Total 2		.237	11	38	5	9	1	1	0	4	3	5	3	
■ Jim Gantner														
1982	Mil-A	.333	7	24	5	8	4	1	0	4	1	0	2	
■ Charlie Ganzel														
1887	Det-N	.224	14	58	5	13	1	0	0	3	1	2	3	1*10,C*7
1892	Bos-N	.500	2	8	1	4	0	0	0	2	1	0	0	C
Total 2		.258	16	66	6	17	1	0	0	5	2	2	3	
■ Joe Garagiola														
1946	StL-N	.316	5	19	2	6	2	0	0	4	0	3	0	C
■ Barbaro Garbey														
1984	Det-A	.000	4	12	0	0	0	0	0	0	0	2	0	D*3
■ Kiko Garcia														
1979	Bal-A	.400	6	20	4	8	2	1	0	6	1	3	0	S
■ Billy Gardner														
1961	NY-A	.000	1	1	0	0	0	0	0	0	0	0	0	H
■ Larry Gardner														
1912	Bos-A	.179	8	28	4	5	2	1	1	4	2	5	0	3
1915	Bos-A	.235	5	17	2	4	0	1	0	1	0	0	3	3
1916	Bos-A	.176	5	17	2	3	0	0	0	2	6	0	2	3
1920	Cle-A	.208	7	24	1	5	1	0	0	2	1	1	0	3
Total 4		.198	25	86	9	17	3	2	3	12	4	8	0	
■ Debs Garms														
1943	StL-N	.000	2	5	0	0	0	0	0	0	0	2	0	O*1
1944	StL-N	.000	2	2	0	0	0	0	0	0	0	0	0	H
Total 2		.000	4	7	0	0	0	0	0	0	0	2	0	
■ Phil Garner														
1979	Pit-N	.500	7	24	4	12	4	0	0	5	3	1	0	2
■ Wayne Garrett														
1969	NY-N	.000	2	1	0	0	0	0	0	0	2	1	0	3
1973	NY-N	.167	7	30	4	5	0	0	2	2	5	11	0	3
Total 2		.161	9	31	4	5	0	0	2	2	7	12	0	

Steve Garvey

YEAR	TM/L	AVG	G	AB	R	H	2B	3B	HR	RBI	BB	SO	SB	POS
1974	LA-N	.381	5	21	2	8	0	0	0	1	0	3	0	1
1977	LA-N	.375	6	24	5	9	1	1	1	3	1	4	0	1
1978	LA-N	.208	6	24	1	5	1	0	0	0	1	7	1	1
1981	LA-N	.417	6	24	3	10	1	0	0	0	2	5	0	1
1984	SD-N	.200	5	20	2	4	2	0	0	2	0	2	0	1
Total 5		.319	28	113	13	36	5	1	1	6	4	21	1	

Rod Gaspar

YEAR	TM/L	AVG	G	AB	R	H	2B	3B	HR	RBI	BB	SO	SB	POS
1969	NY-N	.000	3	2	1	0	0	0	0	0	0	0	0	O*1

Mike Gazella

YEAR	TM/L	AVG	G	AB	R	H	2B	3B	HR	RBI	BB	SO	SB	POS
1926	NY-A	—	1	0	0	0	0	0	0	0	0	0	0	3

Dinty Gearin

YEAR	TM/L	AVG	G	AB	R	H	2B	3B	HR	RBI	BB	SO	SB	POS
1923	NY-N	—	1	0	0	0	0	0	0	0	0	0	0	R

Rich Gedman

YEAR	TM/L	AVG	G	AB	R	H	2B	3B	HR	RBI	BB	SO	SB	POS
1986	Bos-A	.200	7	30	1	6	1	0	1	1	0	10	0	C

Lou Gehrig

YEAR	TM/L	AVG	G	AB	R	H	2B	3B	HR	RBI	BB	SO	SB	POS
1926	NY-A	.348	7	23	1	8	2	0	0	4	5	4	0	1
1927	NY-A	.308	4	13	2	4	2	2	0	4	3	3	0	1
1928	NY-A	.545	4	11	5	6	1	0	4	9	6	0	0	1
1932	NY-A	.529	4	17	9	9	1	0	3	8	2	1	0	1
1936	NY-A	.292	6	24	5	7	1	0	2	7	3	2	0	1
1937	NY-A	.294	5	17	4	5	1	1	1	3	5	4	0	1
1938	NY-A	.286	4	14	4	4	0	0	0	0	2	3	0	1
Total 7		.361	34	119	30	43	8	3	10	35	26	17	0	

Charlie Gehringer

YEAR	TM/L	AVG	G	AB	R	H	2B	3B	HR	RBI	BB	SO	SB	POS
1934	Det-A	.379	7	29	5	11	1	0	1	2	3	0	1	2
1935	Det-A	.375	6	24	4	9	3	0	0	4	2	1	1	2
1940	Det-A	.214	7	28	3	6	0	0	0	1	7	7	0	2
Total 3		.321	20	81	12	26	4	0	1	7	7	1	2	

Charlie Gelbert

YEAR	TM/L	AVG	G	AB	R	H	2B	3B	HR	RBI	BB	SO	SB	POS
1930	StL-N	.353	6	17	2	6	0	1	0	2	3	3	0	S
1931	StL-N	.261	7	23	0	6	1	0	0	3	0	4	0	S
Total 2		.300	13	40	2	12	1	1	0	5	3	7	0	

Dick Gernert

YEAR	TM/L	AVG	G	AB	R	H	2B	3B	HR	RBI	BB	SO	SB	POS
1961	Cin-N	.000	4	4	0	0	0	0	0	0	0	1	0	H

Cesar Geronimo

YEAR	TM/L	AVG	G	AB	R	H	2B	3B	HR	RBI	BB	SO	SB	POS
1972	Cin-N	.158	7	19	1	3	0	0	0	3	1	4	1	O
1975	Cin-N	.280	7	25	3	7	0	1	2	3	3	5	0	O
1976	Cin-N	.308	4	13	3	4	2	0	0	1	2	2	0	O
Total 3		.246	18	57	7	14	2	1	2	7	6	11	3	

Doc Gessler

YEAR	TM/L	AVG	G	AB	R	H	2B	3B	HR	RBI	BB	SO	SB	POS
1906	Chi-N	.000	2	1	0	0	0	0	0	0	1	0	0	H

Gus Getz

YEAR	TM/L	AVG	G	AB	R	H	2B	3B	HR	RBI	BB	SO	SB	POS
1916	Bro-N	.000	1	1	0	0	0	0	0	0	0	0	0	H

George Gibson

YEAR	TM/L	AVG	G	AB	R	H	2B	3B	HR	RBI	BB	SO	SB	POS
1909	Pit-N	.240	7	25	2	6	2	0	0	2	1	1	2	C

Russ Gibson

YEAR	TM/L	AVG	G	AB	R	H	2B	3B	HR	RBI	BB	SO	SB	POS
1967	Bos-A	.000	2	2	0	0	0	0	0	0	0	2	0	C

Kirk Gibson

YEAR	TM/L	AVG	G	AB	R	H	2B	3B	HR	RBI	BB	SO	SB	POS
1984	Det-A	.333	5	18	4	6	0	0	2	7	4	4	3	O
1988	LA-N	1.000	1	1	1	1	0	0	1	2	0	0	0	H
Total 2		.368	6	19	5	7	0	0	3	9	4	4	3	

Larry Gilbert

YEAR	TM/L	AVG	G	AB	R	H	2B	3B	HR	RBI	BB	SO	SB	POS
1914	Bos-N	—	1	0	0	0	0	0	0	0	1	0	0	H

Billy Gilbert

YEAR	TM/L	AVG	G	AB	R	H	2B	3B	HR	RBI	BB	SO	SB	POS
1905	NY-N	.235	5	17	1	4	0	0	0	2	0	2	1	2

Paul Gillespie

YEAR	TM/L	AVG	G	AB	R	H	2B	3B	HR	RBI	BB	SO	SB	POS
1945	Chi-N	.000	3	6	0	0	0	0	0	0	0	0	0	C*1

Jim Gilliam

YEAR	TM/L	AVG	G	AB	R	H	2B	3B	HR	RBI	BB	SO	SB	POS
1953	Bro-N	.296	6	27	4	8	3	0	2	4	0	2	0	2
1955	Bro-N	.292	7	24	2	7	1	0	0	3	8	1	1	2*5,O*4
1956	Bro-N	.083	7	24	2	2	0	0	0	2	7	3	1	2*6,O*1
1959	LA-N	.240	6	25	2	6	0	0	0	0	2	2	3	3
1963	LA-N	.154	4	13	3	2	0	0	0	0	3	1	0	3
1965	LA-N	.214	7	28	2	6	1	0	0	2	1	0	0	3
1966	LA-N	.000	2	6	0	0	0	0	0	1	2	0	0	3
Total 7		.211	39	147	15	31	5	0	2	12	23	9	4	

Barney Gilligan

YEAR	TM/L	AVG	G	AB	R	H	2B	3B	HR	RBI	BB	SO	SB	POS
1884	Pro-N	.444	3	9	3	4	2	0	0	2	0	1	0	C

Al Gionfriddo

YEAR	TM/L	AVG	G	AB	R	H	2B	3B	HR	RBI	BB	SO	SB	POS
1947	Bro-N	.000	4	3	2	0	0	0	0	0	1	0	1	O*1

Dan Gladden

YEAR	TM/L	AVG	G	AB	R	H	2B	3B	HR	RBI	BB	SO	SB	POS
1987	Min-A	.290	7	31	3	9	2	1	1	7	3	4	2	O
1991	Min-A	.233	7	30	5	7	2	2	0	3	4	2	0	O
Total 2		.262	14	61	8	16	4	3	1	7	6	8	4	

Bill Gleason

YEAR	TM/L	AVG	G	AB	R	H	2B	3B	HR	RBI	BB	SO	SB	POS
1885	StL-A	.231	7	26	5	6	2	0	0	0	1	0	0	S
1886	StL-A	.208	6	24	3	5	0	0	0	0	5	1	3	S
1887	StL-A	.163	13	49	3	8	0	0	0	1	3	2	1	S
Total 3		.192	26	99	11	19	2	0	0	6	5	5	1	

Kid Gleason

YEAR	TM/L	AVG	G	AB	R	H	2B	3B	HR	RBI	BB	SO	SB	POS
1894	Bal-N	.200	2	5	0	1	0	1	0	1	0	1	0	P
1895	Bal-N	.105	5	19	0	2	0	0	0	0	0	1	0	2
Total 2		.125	7	24	0	3	0	1	0	1	0	2	0	

Bill Glynn

YEAR	TM/L	AVG	G	AB	R	H	2B	3B	HR	RBI	BB	SO	SB	POS
1954	Cle-A	.500	2	2	1	1	1	0	0	0	0	1	0	1*1

Mike Goliat

YEAR	TM/L	AVG	G	AB	R	H	2B	3B	HR	RBI	BB	SO	SB	POS
1950	Phi-N	.214	4	14	1	3	0	0	0	1	1	2	0	2

Jose Gonzalez

YEAR	TM/L	AVG	G	AB	R	H	2B	3B	HR	RBI	BB	SO	SB	POS
1988	LA-N	.000	4	2	0	0	0	0	0	0	0	2	0	O*3

Mike Gonzalez

YEAR	TM/L	AVG	G	AB	R	H	2B	3B	HR	RBI	BB	SO	SB	POS
1929	Chi-N	.000	2	1	0	0	0	0	0	0	0	1	0	C*1

Pedro Gonzalez

YEAR	TM/L	AVG	G	AB	R	H	2B	3B	HR	RBI	BB	SO	SB	POS
1964	NY-A	.000	1	1	0	0	0	0	0	0	0	0	0	3

Johnny Gooch

YEAR	TM/L	AVG	G	AB	R	H	2B	3B	HR	RBI	BB	SO	SB	POS
1925	Pit-N	.000	3	3	0	0	0	0	0	0	0	0	0	C
1927	Pit-N	.000	3	5	0	0	0	0	0	0	1	1	0	C
Total 2		.000	6	8	0	0	0	0	0	0	1	1	0	

Ival Goodman

YEAR	TM/L	AVG	G	AB	R	H	2B	3B	HR	RBI	BB	SO	SB	POS
1939	Cin-N	.333	4	15	3	5	1	0	0	1	1	2	1	O
1940	Cin-N	.276	7	29	5	8	2	0	0	5	0	3	0	O
Total 2		.295	11	44	8	13	3	0	0	6	1	5	1	

Billy Goodman

YEAR	TM/L	AVG	G	AB	R	H	2B	3B	HR	RBI	BB	SO	SB	POS
1959	Chi-A	.231	5	13	1	3	0	0	0	1	0	5	0	3

Ed Goodson

YEAR	TM/L	AVG	G	AB	R	H	2B	3B	HR	RBI	BB	SO	SB	POS
1977	LA-N	.000	1	1	0	0	0	0	0	0	0	1	0	H

Joe Gordon

YEAR	TM/L	AVG	G	AB	R	H	2B	3B	HR	RBI	BB	SO	SB	POS
1938	NY-A	.400	4	15	3	6	2	0	1	6	1	3	1	2
1939	NY-A	.143	4	14	1	2	0	0	0	1	0	2	0	2
1941	NY-A	.500	5	14	2	7	1	1	1	5	7	0	0	2
1942	NY-A	.095	5	21	1	2	0	0	0	0	7	2	0	2
1943	NY-A	.235	5	17	2	4	1	0	1	2	3	3	0	2
1948	Cle-A	.182	6	22	3	4	0	0	1	2	1	2	1	2
Total 6		.243	29	103	12	25	5	1	4	16	12	17	2	

George Gore

YEAR	TM/L	AVG	G	AB	R	H	2B	3B	HR	RBI	BB	SO	SB	POS
1885	Chi-N	.000	1	3	1	0	0	0	0	0	1	0	0	O
1886	Chi-N	.174	6	23	4	4	0	0	1	2	3	0	0	O
1888	NY-N	.455	3	11	5	5	1	0	0	0	2	2	2	O*2,3*1
1889	NY-N	.333	5	21	5	7	1	1	0	1	3	0	2	O
Total 4		.276	15	58	15	16	2	1	1	3	9	5	4	

Goose Goslin

YEAR	TM/L	AVG	G	AB	R	H	2B	3B	HR	RBI	BB	SO	SB	POS
1924	Was-A	.344	7	32	4	11	1	0	3	7	0	7	0	O
1925	Was-A	.308	7	26	6	8	1	0	3	6	3	3	0	O
1933	Was-A	.250	5	20	2	5	1	0	1	1	3	0	0	O
1934	Det-A	.241	7	29	2	7	1	0	0	2	3	1	0	O
1935	Det-A	.273	6	22	2	6	1	0	0	3	5	0	0	O
Total 5		.287	32	129	16	37	5	0	7	19	12	14	0	

Hank Gowdy

YEAR	TM/L	AVG	G	AB	R	H	2B	3B	HR	RBI	BB	SO	SB	POS
1914	Bos-N	.545	4	11	3	6	3	1	1	3	5	1	1	C
1923	NY-N	.000	3	4	0	0	0	0	0	0	1	0	0	C*2
1924	NY-N	.259	7	27	4	7	0	0	0	1	2	2	0	C
Total 3		.310	14	42	7	13	3	1	1	4	8	3	1	

Johnny Grabowski

YEAR	TM/L	AVG	G	AB	R	H	2B	3B	HR	RBI	BB	SO	SB	POS
1927	NY-A	.000	1	2	0	0	0	0	0	0	0	0	0	C

Jack Graney

YEAR	TM/L	AVG	G	AB	R	H	2B	3B	HR	RBI	BB	SO	SB	POS
1920	Cle-A	.000	3	3	0	0	0	0	0	0	2	2	0	O*2

Eddie Grant

YEAR	TM/L	AVG	G	AB	R	H	2B	3B	HR	RBI	BB	SO	SB	POS
1913	NY-N	.000	2	1	0	0	0	0	0	0	0	0	0	H

George Grantham

YEAR	TM/L	AVG	G	AB	R	H	2B	3B	HR	RBI	BB	SO	SB	POS
1925	Pit-N	.133	5	15	0	2	0	0	0	0	0	3	1	1*4
1927	Pit-N	.364	3	11	0	4	1	0	0	0	1	1	0	2
Total 2		.231	8	26	0	6	1	0	0	0	1	4	1	

Mickey Grasso

YEAR	TM/L	AVG	G	AB	R	H	2B	3B	HR	RBI	BB	SO	SB	POS
1954	Cle-A	—	1	0	0	0	0	0	0	0	0	0	0	C

Eli Grba

YEAR	TM/L	AVG	G	AB	R	H	2B	3B	HR	RBI	BB	SO	SB	POS
1960	NY-A	—	1	0	0	0	0	0	0	0	0	0	0	R

David Green

YEAR	TM/L	AVG	G	AB	R	H	2B	3B	HR	RBI	BB	SO	SB	POS
1982	StL-N	.200	7	10	3	2	1	1	0	0	1	3	0	O*4,D*3

Dick Green

YEAR	TM/L	AVG	G	AB	R	H	2B	3B	HR	RBI	BB	SO	SB	POS
1972	Oak-A	.333	7	18	0	6	2	0	0	1	0	4	0	2
1973	Oak-A	.063	7	16	0	1	0	0	0	0	1	6	0	2
1974	Oak-A	.000	5	13	1	0	0	0	0	1	1	4	0	2
Total 3		.149	19	47	1	7	2	0	0	2	2	14	0	

Hank Greenberg

YEAR	TM/L	AVG	G	AB	R	H	2B	3B	HR	RBI	BB	SO	SB	POS
1934	Det-A	.321	7	28	4	9	2	1	1	7	4	9	1	1
1935	Det-A	.167	2	6	1	1	0	0	0	1	2	0	0	1
1940	Det-A	.357	7	28	5	10	2	1	1	6	2	5	0	O
1945	Det-A	.304	7	23	7	7	3	0	2	7	6	5	0	O
Total 4		.318	23	85	17	27	7	2	5	22	13	19	1	

Mike Greenwell

YEAR	TM/L	AVG	G	AB	R	H	2B	3B	HR	RBI	BB	SO	SB	POS
1986	Bos-A	.000	4	3	0	0	0	0	0	0	0	1	2	0	H

YEAR	TM/L	AVG	G	AB	R	H	2B	3B	HR	RBI	BB	SO	SB	POS
■ Tommy Gregg														
1991	Atl-N	.000	4	3	0	0	0	0	0	0	0	2	0	H
■ Ken Griffey														
1975	Cin-N	.269	7	26	4	7	3	1	0	4	4	2	2	0	O
1976	Cin-N	.059	4	17	2	1	0	0	0	1	0	1	1	0	O
Total 2		.186	11	43	6	8	3	1	0	5	4	3	3	0	
■ Alfredo Griffin														
1988	LA-N	.188	5	16	2	3	0	0	0	0	2	4	0	S
1992	Tor-A	—	2	0	0	0	0	0	0	0	0	0	0	S
1993	Tor-A	—	3	0	0	0	0	0	0	0	0	0	0	3*2
Total 3		.188	10	16	2	3	0	0	0	0	2	4	0	
■ Doug Griffin														
1975	Bos-A	.000	1	1	0	0	0	0	0	0	0	0	0	H
■ Tommy Griffith														
1920	Bro-N	.190	7	21	1	4	2	0	0	3	0	2	0	O
■ Charlie Grimm														
1929	Chi-N	.389	5	18	2	7	0	0	1	4	1	2	0	1
1932	Chi-N	.333	4	15	2	5	2	0	0	1	2	2	0	1
Total 2		.364	9	33	4	12	2	0	1	5	3	4	0	
■ Dick Groat														
1960	Pit-N	.214	7	28	3	6	2	0	0	2	0	1	0	S
1964	StL-N	.192	7	26	3	5	1	1	0	1	4	3	0	S
Total 2		.204	14	54	6	11	3	1	0	3	4	4	0	
■ Heinie Groh														
1919	Cin-N	.172	8	29	6	5	2	0	0	2	6	4	0	3
1922	NY-N	.474	5	19	4	9	0	1	0	0	2	1	0	3
1923	NY-N	.182	6	22	3	4	0	1	0	2	3	1	0	3
1924	NY-N	1.000	1	1	0	1	0	0	0	0	0	0	0	H
1927	Pit-N	.000	1	1	0	0	0	0	0	0	0	0	0	H
Total 5		.264	21	72	13	19	2	2	0	4	11	6	0	
■ Greg Gross														
1980	Phi-N	.000	4	2	0	0	0	0	0	0	0	0	0	O*3
1983	Phi-N	.000	2	6	0	0	0	0	0	0	0	0	0	O
Total 2		.000	6	8	0	0	0	0	0	0	0	0	0	
■ Jerry Grote														
1969	NY-N	.211	5	19	1	4	2	0	0	1	1	3	0	C
1973	NY-N	.267	7	30	2	8	0	0	0	0	0	1	0	C
1977	LA-N	.000	1	1	0	0	0	0	0	0	0	0	0	C
1978	LA-N	—	2	0	0	0	0	0	0	0	0	0	0	C
Total 4		.240	15	50	3	12	2	0	0	1	1	4	0	
■ Johnny Grubb														
1984	Det-A	.333	4	3	0	1	0	0	0	0	0	0	0	D*2
■ Kelly Gruber														
1992	Tor-A	.105	6	19	2	2	0	0	1	1	2	5	1	3
■ Marv Gudat														
1932	Chi-N	.000	2	2	0	0	0	0	0	0	0	1	0	H
■ Pedro Guerrero														
1981	LA-N	.333	6	21	2	7	1	1	2	7	2	6	0	O
■ Don Gutteridge														
1944	StL-A	.143	6	21	1	3	1	0	0	0	3	5	0	2
1946	Bos-A	.400	3	5	1	2	0	0	0	1	0	0	0	2*2
Total 2		.192	9	26	2	5	1	0	0	1	3	5	0	
■ Tony Gwynn														
1984	SD-N	.263	5	19	1	5	0	0	0	0	3	2	1	0
■ Mule Haas														
1929	Phi-A	.238	5	21	3	5	0	0	2	6	1	3	0	O
1930	Phi-A	.111	6	18	1	2	0	1	0	1	1	3	0	O
1931	Phi-A	.130	7	23	1	3	1	0	0	2	3	5	0	O
Total 3		.161	18	62	5	10	1	1	2	9	5	11	0	
■ Stan Hack														
1932	Chi-N	—	1	0	0	0	0	0	0	0	0	0	0	H
1935	Chi-N	.227	6	22	2	5	1	1	0	0	2	2	1	3*6,S*1
1938	Chi-N	.471	4	17	3	8	1	0	0	1	1	2	0	3
1945	Chi-N	.367	7	30	1	11	3	0	0	4	4	2	0	3
Total 4		.348	18	69	6	24	5	1	0	5	7	6	1	
■ Chick Hafey														
1926	StL-N	.185	7	27	2	5	2	0	0	0	7	0	0	O
1928	StL-N	.200	4	15	0	3	0	0	0	0	1	4	0	O
1930	StL-N	.273	6	22	2	6	5	0	0	2	1	3	0	O
1931	StL-N	.167	6	24	1	4	0	0	0	0	5	1	0	O
Total 4		.205	23	88	5	18	7	0	0	2	2	19	1	
■ Joe Hague														
1972	Cin-N	.000	3	3	0	0	0	0	0	0	0	0	0	O*1
■ Don Hahn														
1973	NY-N	.241	7	29	2	7	1	1	0	2	1	6	0	O
■ Ed Hahn														
1906	Chi-A	.273	6	22	4	6	0	0	0	1	1	1	0	O
■ Hinkey Haines														
1923	NY-A	.000	2	1	1	0	0	0	0	0	0	0	0	O
■ Jimmie Hall														
1965	Min-A	.143	2	7	0	1	0	0	0	0	0	1	5	0	O

YEAR	TM/L	AVG	G	AB	R	H	2B	3B	HR	RBI	BB	SO	SB	POS
■ Tom Haller														
1962	SF-N	.286	4	14	1	4	1	0	1	3	0	2	0	C
■ Charlie Hamburg														
1890	Lou-A	.269	7	26	3	7	1	0	0	2	0	3	0	O
■ Jeff Hamilton														
1988	LA-N	.105	5	19	1	2	0	0	0	0	1	4	0	3
■ Billy Hamilton														
1897	Bos-N	.500	4	16	6	8	1	0	0	2	5	3	2	O
■ Granny Hamner														
1950	Phi-N	.429	4	14	1	6	2	1	0	0	1	2	1	S
■ Harry Hanebrink														
1958	Mil-N	.000	2	2	0	0	0	0	0	0	0	0	0	H
■ Larry Haney														
1974	Oak-A	—	2	0	0	0	0	0	0	0	0	0	0	C
■ Ned Hanlon														
1887	Det-N	.220	15	50	5	11	1	1	0	4	5	1	7	O
■ Brian Harper														
1985	StL-N	.250	4	4	0	1	0	0	0	1	0	1	0	H
1991	Min-A	.381	7	21	2	8	2	0	0	1	2	2	0	C
Total 2		.360	11	25	2	9	2	0	0	2	2	3	0	
■ George Harper														
1928	StL-N	.111	3	9	1	1	0	0	0	0	0	2	0	O
■ Bud Harrelson														
1969	NY-N	.176	5	17	1	3	0	0	0	0	3	4	0	S
1973	NY-N	.250	7	24	2	6	1	0	0	1	5	3	0	S
Total 2		.220	12	41	3	9	1	0	0	1	8	7	0	
■ Ken Harrelson														
1967	Bos-A	.077	4	13	0	1	0	0	0	1	1	3	0	O
■ Dave Harris														
1933	Was-A	.000	3	2	0	0	0	0	0	0	2	0	0	O*1
■ Joe Harris														
1925	Was-A	.440	7	25	5	11	2	0	3	6	3	4	0	O
1927	Pit-N	.200	4	15	0	3	0	0	0	1	0	0	0	1
Total 2		.350	11	40	5	14	2	0	3	7	3	4	0	
■ Bucky Harris														
1924	Was-A	.333	7	33	5	11	0	0	2	7	1	4	0	2
1925	Was-A	.087	7	23	2	2	0	0	0	0	1	3	0	2
Total 2		.232	14	56	7	13	0	0	2	7	2	7	0	
■ Gabby Hartnett														
1929	Chi-N	.000	3	3	0	0	0	0	0	0	0	3	0	H
1932	Chi-N	.313	4	16	2	5	2	0	1	1	1	3	0	C
1935	Chi-N	.292	6	24	1	7	0	0	1	2	0	3	0	C
1938	Chi-N	.091	3	11	0	1	0	1	0	0	2	2	0	C
Total 4		.241	16	54	3	13	2	1	2	3	3	11	0	
■ Topsy Hartsel														
1905	Phi-A	.294	5	17	1	5	1	0	0	0	2	1	2	O
1910	Phi-A	.200	1	5	2	1	0	0	0	0	0	1	2	O
Total 2		.273	6	22	3	6	1	0	0	0	2	2	4	
■ Clint Hartung														
1951	NY-N	.000	2	4	0	0	0	0	0	0	0	0	0	0
■ Buddy Hassett														
1942	NY-A	.333	3	9	1	3	1	0	0	2	0	1	0	1
■ Ron Hassey														
1988	Oak-A	.250	5	8	0	2	0	0	0	1	3	3	0	C*4
1990	Oak-A	.333	3	6	0	2	0	0	0	1	0	0	0	C*1
Total 2		.286	8	14	0	4	0	0	0	2	3	3	0	
■ Mickey Hatcher														
1988	LA-N	.368	5	19	5	7	1	0	2	5	1	3	0	O
■ Billy Hatcher														
1990	Cin-N	.750	4	12	6	9	4	1	0	2	2	0	0	O
■ Von Hayes														
1983	Phi-N	.000	4	3	0	0	0	0	0	0	0	1	0	O*1
■ Red Hayworth														
1944	StL-A	.118	6	17	1	2	1	0	0	1	3	1	0	C
■ Ray Hayworth														
1934	Det-A	—	1	0	0	0	0	0	0	0	0	0	0	C
■ Bob Hazle														
1957	Mil-N	.154	4	13	2	2	0	0	0	0	1	2	0	O
■ Mike Heath														
1978	NY-A	—	1	0	0	0	0	0	0	0	0	0	0	C
■ Cliff Heathcote														
1929	Chi-N	.000	2	1	0	0	0	0	0	0	0	0	0	H
■ Richie Hebner														
1971	Pit-N	.167	3	12	2	2	0	0	1	3	3	3	0	3
■ Danny Heep														
1986	NY-N	.091	5	11	0	1	0	0	0	2	1	1	0	D*2,O*1
1988	LA-N	.250	3	8	0	2	1	0	0	0	0	2	0	O*1,D*1
Total 2		.158	8	19	0	3	1	0	0	2	1	3	0	

YEAR	TM/L	AVG	G	AB	R	H	2B	3B	HR	RBI	BB	SO	SB	POS
■ Jim Hegan														
1948	Cle-A	.211	6	19	2	4	0	0	1	5	1	4	1	C
1954	Cle-A	.154	4	13	1	2	1	0	0	0	1	1	0	C
Total 2		.188	10	32	3	6	1	0	1	5	2	5	1	
■ Mike Hegan														
1964	NY-A	.000	3	1	1	0	0	0	0	0	1	1	0	H
1972	Oak-A	.200	6	5	0	1	0	0	0	0	0	2	0	1*5
Total 2		.167	9	6	1	1	0	0	0	0	1	3	0	
■ Tommy Helms														
1970	Cin-N	.222	5	18	1	4	0	0	0	0	1	1	0	2
■ Rollie Hemsley														
1932	Chi-N	.000	3	3	0	0	0	0	0	0	0	3	0	C*1
■ Dave Henderson														
1986	Bos-A	.400	7	25	6	10	1	1	2	5	2	6	0	O
1988	Oak-A	.300	5	20	1	6	2	0	0	1	2	7	0	O
1989	Oak-A	.308	4	13	6	4	2	0	2	4	4	3	0	O
1990	Oak-A	.231	4	13	2	3	1	0	0	0	1	3	0	O*3
Total 4		.324	20	71	15	23	6	1	4	10	9	19	0	
■ Rickey Henderson														
1989	Oak-A	.474	4	19	4	9	1	2	1	3	2	2	3	O
1990	Oak-A	.333	4	15	2	5	2	0	1	1	3	4	3	O
1993	Tor-A	.227	6	22	6	5	2	0	0	2	5	2	1	O
Total 3		.339	14	56	12	19	5	2	2	6	10	8	7	
■ George Hendrick														
1972	Oak-A	.133	5	15	3	2	0	0	0	0	1	2	0	O
1982	StL-N	.321	7	28	5	9	0	0	0	5	2	2	0	O
Total 2		.256	12	43	8	11	0	0	0	5	3	4	0	
■ Harvey Hendrick														
1923	NY-A	.000	1	1	0	0	0	0	0	0	0	0	0	H
■ Ellie Hendricks														
1969	Bal-A	.100	3	10	1	1	0	0	0	0	1	0	0	C
1970	Bal-A	.364	3	11	1	4	1	0	1	4	1	2	0	C
1971	Bal-A	.263	6	19	3	5	1	0	0	1	3	3	0	C
1976	NY-A	.000	2	2	0	0	0	0	0	0	0	0	0	H
Total 4		.238	14	42	5	10	2	0	1	5	5	5	0	
■ Tommy Henrich														
1938	NY-A	.250	4	16	3	4	1	0	1	1	0	1	0	O
1941	NY-A	.167	5	18	4	3	1	0	1	1	3	3	0	O
1947	NY-A	.323	7	31	2	10	2	0	1	5	2	3	0	O
1949	NY-A	.263	5	19	4	5	0	0	1	1	3	0	0	1
Total 4		.262	21	84	13	22	4	0	4	8	8	7	0	
■ Olaf Henriksen														
1912	Bos-A	1.000	2	1	0	1	1	0	0	1	0	0	0	H
1915	Bos-A	.000	2	2	0	0	0	0	0	0	0	0	0	H
1916	Bos-A	—	1	0	1	0	0	0	0	0	1	0	0	H
Total 3		.333	5	3	1	1	1	0	0	1	1	0	0	
■ Billy Herman														
1932	Chi-N	.222	4	18	5	4	1	0	0	1	1	3	0	2
1935	Chi-N	.333	6	24	3	8	2	1	1	6	0	2	0	2
1938	Chi-N	.188	4	16	1	3	0	0	0	1	1	4	0	2
1941	Bro-N	.125	4	8	0	1	0	0	0	0	2	0	0	2
Total 4		.242	18	66	9	16	3	1	1	7	4	9	0	
■ Gene Hermanski														
1947	Bro-N	.158	7	19	4	3	0	1	0	1	3	3	0	O
1949	Bro-N	.308	4	13	1	4	0	1	0	2	3	3	0	O
Total 2		.219	11	32	5	7	0	2	0	3	6	6	0	
■ Jackie Hernandez														
1971	Pit-N	.222	7	18	2	4	0	0	0	1	2	5	1	S
■ Keith Hernandez														
1982	StL-N	.259	7	27	4	7	2	0	1	8	4	2	0	1
1986	NY-N	.231	7	26	1	6	0	0	0	4	5	1	0	1
Total 2		.245	14	53	5	13	2	0	1	12	9	3	0	
■ Larry Herndon														
1984	Det-A	.333	5	15	1	5	0	0	1	3	3	2	0	O
■ Ed Herr														
1888	StL-A	.091	3	11	2	1	0	0	0	0	0	5	1	O
■ Tom Herr														
1982	StL-N	.160	7	25	2	4	2	0	0	5	3	3	0	2
1985	StL-N	.154	7	26	2	4	2	0	0	0	2	2	0	2
1987	StL-N	.250	7	28	2	7	0	0	1	1	2	2	0	2
Total 3		.190	21	79	6	15	4	0	1	6	7	7	0	
■ Willard Hershberger														
1939	Cin-N	.500	3	2	0	1	0	0	0	1	0	0	0	C*2
■ Buck Herzog														
1911	NY-N	.190	6	21	3	4	2	0	0	0	2	3	2	3
1912	NY-N	.400	8	30	6	12	4	1	0	4	1	3	2	3
1913	NY-N	.053	5	19	1	1	0	0	0	0	0	1	0	3
1917	NY-N	.250	6	24	1	6	0	1	0	2	1	4	0	3
Total 4		.245	25	94	11	23	6	2	0	6	4	11	4	
■ Johnnie Heving														
1931	Phi-A	.000	1	1	0	0	0	0	0	0	0	0	0	H

YEAR	TM/L	AVG	G	AB	R	H	2B	3B	HR	RBI	BB	SO	SB	POS
■ Pinky Higgins														
1940	Det-A	.333	7	24	2	8	3	1	1	6	3	3	0	3
1946	Bos-A	.208	7	24	1	5	1	0	0	2	2	0	0	3
Total 2		.271	14	48	3	13	4	1	1	8	5	3	0	
■ Andy High														
1928	StL-N	.294	4	17	1	5	2	0	0	1	1	3	0	3
1930	StL-N	.500	2	1	1	1	0	0	0	0	0	0	0	3
1931	StL-N	.267	4	15	3	4	0	0	0	0	0	2	0	3
Total 3		.294	9	34	5	10	2	0	0	1	1	5	0	
■ Chuck Hiller														
1962	SF-N	.269	7	26	4	7	3	0	1	5	3	4	0	2
■ Paul Hines														
1884	Pro-N	.250	3	8	5	2	0	0	0	1	3	0	2	O
■ Myril Hoag														
1932	NY-A	—	1	0	1	0	0	0	0	0	0	0	0	R
1937	NY-A	.300	5	20	4	6	1	0	1	2	0	1	0	O
1938	NY-A	.400	2	5	3	2	1	0	0	1	0	0	0	O*1
Total 3		.320	8	25	8	8	2	0	1	3	0	1	0	
■ Don Hoak														
1955	Bro-N	.333	3	3	0	1	0	0	0	0	2	0	0	3*1
1960	Pit-N	.217	7	23	3	5	2	0	0	3	4	1	0	3
Total 2		.231	10	26	3	6	2	0	0	3	6	1	0	
■ Dick Hoblitzel														
1915	Bos-A	.313	5	16	1	5	0	0	0	1	0	1	1	1
1916	Bos-A	.235	5	17	3	4	1	0	0	2	6	0	0	1
Total 2		.273	10	33	4	9	1	0	0	3	6	1	1	
■ Gil Hodges														
1947	Bro-N	.000	1	1	0	0	0	0	0	0	0	0	0	H
1949	Bro-N	.235	5	17	2	4	0	0	1	4	1	4	0	1
1952	Bro-N	.000	7	21	1	0	0	0	0	1	5	6	0	1
1953	Bro-N	.364	6	22	3	8	0	0	1	1	3	3	1	1
1955	Bro-N	.292	7	24	2	7	0	0	1	5	3	2	0	1
1956	Bro-N	.304	7	23	5	7	2	0	1	8	4	4	0	1
1959	LA-N	.391	6	23	2	9	0	1	1	2	1	2	0	1
Total 7		.267	39	131	15	35	2	1	5	21	17	22	1	
■ Ron Hodges														
1973	NY-N	—	1	0	0	0	0	0	0	0	0	1	0	H
■ Danny Hoffman														
1905	Phi-A	.000	1	1	0	0	0	0	0	0	0	1	0	H
■ Solly Hofman														
1906	Chi-N	.304	6	23	3	7	1	0	0	2	3	5	1	O
1908	Chi-N	.316	5	19	2	6	0	1	0	4	1	4	2	O
1910	Chi-N	.267	5	15	2	4	0	0	0	2	4	3	0	O
Total 3		.298	16	57	7	17	1	1	0	8	8	12	3	
■ Fred Hofmann														
1923	NY-A	.000	2	1	0	0	0	0	0	0	1	0	0	H
■ Bill Holbert														
1884	NY-A	.000	1	2	0	0	0	0	0	0	0	1	0	C
■ Walter Holke														
1917	NY-N	.286	6	21	2	6	2	0	0	1	0	6	0	1
■ Bug Holliday														
1885	Chi-N	.000	1	4	0	0	0	0	0	0	0	0	0	0
■ Dave Hollins														
1993	Phi-N	.261	6	23	5	6	1	0	0	2	6	5	0	3
■ Charlie Hollocher														
1918	Chi-N	.190	6	21	2	4	0	1	0	1	1	1	1	S
■ Wattie Holm														
1926	StL-N	.125	5	16	1	2	0	0	0	1	1	2	0	O*4
1928	StL-N	.167	3	6	0	1	0	0	0	1	0	1	0	O*1
Total 2		.136	8	22	1	3	0	0	0	2	1	3	0	
■ Tommy Holmes														
1948	Bos-N	.192	6	26	3	5	0	0	0	1	0	0	0	O
1952	Bro-N	.000	3	1	0	0	0	0	0	0	0	0	0	O
Total 2		.185	9	27	3	5	0	0	0	1	0	0	0	
■ Jim Holt														
1974	Oak-A	.667	4	3	0	2	0	0	0	2	0	0	0	1*1
■ Harry Hooper														
1912	Bos-A	.290	8	31	3	9	2	1	0	2	4	4	2	O
1915	Bos-A	.350	5	20	4	7	0	0	2	3	2	4	0	O
1916	Bos-A	.333	5	21	6	7	1	1	0	3	1	3	1	O
1918	Bos-A	.200	6	20	0	4	0	0	0	0	2	2	0	O
Total 4		.293	24	92	13	27	3	2	2	6	11	13	3	
■ Joe Hoover														
1945	Det-A	.333	1	3	1	1	0	0	0	1	0	0	0	S
■ Johnny Hopp														
1942	StL-N	.176	5	17	3	3	0	0	0	0	1	1	0	1
1943	StL-N	.000	1	4	0	0	0	0	0	0	0	1	0	O
1944	StL-N	.185	6	27	2	5	0	0	0	0	0	8	0	O
1950	NY-A	.000	3	2	0	0	0	0	0	0	0	0	0	1
1951	NY-A	—	1	0	0	0	0	0	0	0	1	0	0	H
Total 5		.160	16	50	5	8	0	0	0	0	2	10	0	

YEAR	TM/L	AVG	G	AB	R	H	2B	3B	HR	RBI	BB	SO	SB	POS
■ Rogers Hornsby														
1926	StL-N	.250	7	28	2	7	1	0	0	4	2	2	1	2
1929	Chi-N	.238	5	21	4	5	1	1	0	1	1	8	0	2
Total 2		.245	12	49	6	12	2	1	0	5	3	10	1	
■ Willie Horton														
1968	Det-A	.304	7	23	6	7	1	1	1	3	5	6	0	O
■ Chuck Hostetler														
1945	Det-A	.000	3	3	0	0	0	0	0	0	0	0	0	H
■ Ralph Houk														
1947	NY-A	1.000	1	1	0	1	0	0	0	0	0	0	0	H
1952	NY-A	.000	1	1	0	0	0	0	0	0	0	0	0	H
Total 2		.500	2	2	0	1	0	0	0	0	0	0	0	
■ Elston Howard														
1955	NY-A	.192	7	26	3	5	0	0	1	3	1	8	0	O
1956	NY-A	.400	1	5	1	2	1	0	1	1	0	0	0	O
1957	NY-A	.273	6	11	2	3	0	0	1	3	1	3	0	1*3
1958	NY-A	.222	6	18	4	4	0	0	0	2	1	4	1	O
1960	NY-A	.462	5	13	4	6	1	1	1	4	1	4	0	C*4
1961	NY-A	.250	5	20	5	5	3	0	1	1	2	3	0	C
1962	NY-A	.143	6	21	1	3	1	0	0	1	1	4	0	C
1963	NY-A	.333	4	15	0	5	0	0	0	1	0	3	0	C
1964	NY-A	.292	7	24	5	7	1	0	0	2	4	6	0	C
1967	Bos-A	.111	7	18	0	2	0	0	0	1	1	2	0	C
Total 10		.246	54	171	25	42	7	1	5	19	12	37	1	
■ Frank Howard														
1963	LA-N	.300	3	10	2	3	1	0	1	1	0	2	0	O
■ Del Howard														
1907	Chi-N	.200	2	5	0	1	0	0	0	0	0	2	1	1*1
1908	Chi-N	.000	1	1	0	0	0	0	0	0	0	0	0	H
Total 2		.167	3	6	0	1	0	0	0	0	0	2	1	
■ Roy Howell														
1982	Mil-A	.000	4	11	1	0	0	0	0	0	0	3	0	D
■ Kent Hrbek														
1987	Min-A	.208	7	24	4	5	0	0	1	6	5	3	0	1
1991	Min-A	.115	7	26	2	3	1	0	1	2	2	6	0	1
Total 2		.160	14	50	6	8	1	0	2	8	7	9	0	
■ Glenn Hubbard														
1988	Oak-A	.250	4	12	2	3	0	0	0	0	1	2	1	2
■ Roy Hughes														
1945	Chi-N	.294	6	17	1	5	1	0	0	3	4	5	0	S
■ Brian Hunter														
1991	Atl-N	.190	7	21	2	4	1	0	1	3	0	2	0	1*4,O*4
1992	Atl-N	.200	4	5	0	1	0	0	0	2	0	1	0	1*3
Total 2		.192	11	26	2	5	1	0	1	5	0	3	0	
■ Clint Hurdle														
1980	KC-A	.417	4	12	1	5	1	0	0	0	2	1	1	O
■ Ham Hyatt														
1909	Pit-N	.000	2	4	1	0	0	0	0	0	1	0	0	O*1
■ Pete Incaviglia														
1993	Phi-N	.125	4	8	0	1	0	0	0	1	0	4	0	O
■ Dane Iorg														
1982	StL-N	.529	5	17	4	9	4	1	0	1	0	0	0	D
1985	KC-A	.500	2	2	0	1	0	0	0	2	0	0	0	H
Total 2		.526	7	19	4	10	4	1	0	3	0	0	0	
■ Monte Irvin														
1951	NY-N	.458	6	24	3	11	0	1	0	2	2	1	2	O
1954	NY-N	.222	4	9	1	2	1	0	0	2	0	3	0	O
Total 2		.394	10	33	4	13	1	1	0	4	2	4	2	
■ Arthur Irwin														
1884	Pro-N	.222	3	9	3	2	0	1	0	2	0	2	0	S
■ Frank Isbell														
1906	Chi-A	.308	6	26	4	8	4	0	0	4	0	6	1	2
■ Joe Jackson														
1917	Chi-A	.304	6	23	4	7	0	0	0	2	1	0	1	O
1919	Chi-A	.375	8	32	5	12	3	0	1	6	1	2	0	O
Total 2		.345	14	55	9	19	3	0	1	8	2	2	1	
■ Randy Jackson														
1956	Bro-N	.000	3	3	0	0	0	0	0	0	0	2	0	H
■ Reggie Jackson														
1973	Oak-A	.310	7	29	3	9	3	1	1	6	2	7	0	O
1974	Oak-A	.286	5	14	3	4	1	0	1	1	5	3	1	O
1977	NY-A	.450	6	20	10	9	1	0	5	8	3	4	0	O
1978	NY-A	.391	6	23	2	9	1	0	2	8	3	7	0	D
1981	NY-A	.333	3	12	3	4	1	0	1	1	2	3	0	O
Total 5		.357	27	98	21	35	7	1	10	24	15	24	1	
■ Travis Jackson														
1923	NY-N	.000	1	1	0	0	0	0	0	0	0	0	0	H
1924	NY-N	.074	7	27	3	2	0	0	0	1	1	4	1	S
1933	NY-N	.222	5	18	3	4	1	0	0	2	1	3	0	3
1936	NY-N	.190	6	21	1	4	0	0	0	1	1	3	0	3
Total 4		.149	19	67	7	10	1	0	0	4	3	10	1	
■ Charlie James														
1964	StL-N	.000	3	3	0	0	0	0	0	0	0	1	0	H
■ Charlie Jamieson														
1920	Cle-A	.333	6	15	2	5	1	0	0	1	1	0	1	O*5
■ Hal Janvrin														
1915	Bos-A	.000	1	1	0	0	0	0	0	0	0	0	0	S
1916	Bos-A	.217	5	23	2	5	3	0	0	1	0	6	0	2
Total 2		.208	6	24	2	5	3	0	0	1	0	6	0	
■ Julian Javier														
1964	StL-N	—	1	0	1	0	0	0	0	0	0	0	0	2
1967	StL-N	.360	7	25	2	9	3	0	1	4	0	6	0	2
1968	StL-N	.333	7	27	1	9	1	0	0	3	3	4	1	2
1972	Cin-N	.000	4	2	0	0	0	0	0	0	0	0	0	H
Total 4		.333	19	54	4	18	4	0	1	7	3	10	1	
■ Stan Javier														
1988	Oak-A	.500	3	4	0	2	0	0	0	2	0	1	0	O*2
1989	Oak-A	—	1	0	0	0	0	0	0	0	0	0	0	0
Total 2		.500	4	4	0	2	0	0	0	2	0	1	0	
■ Hughie Jennings														
1894	Bal-N	.143	4	14	0	2	0	0	0	1	0	2	0	S
1895	Bal-N	.368	5	19	3	7	2	0	0	2	1	0	1	S
1896	Bal-N	.333	4	15	5	5	2	0	0	3	1	2	1	S
1897	Bal-N	.318	5	22	5	7	2	0	0	3	4	0	0	S
1900	Bro-N	.167	4	18	1	3	1	0	0	2	1	1	0	1
Total 5		.273	22	88	14	24	7	0	0	11	7	5	2	
■ Doug Jennings														
1990	Oak-A	1.000	1	1	0	1	0	0	0	0	0	0	0	H
■ Jackie Jensen														
1950	NY-A	—	1	0	0	0	0	0	0	0	0	0	0	R
■ Cliff Johnson														
1977	NY-A	.000	2	1	0	0	0	0	0	0	0	0	0	C*1
1978	NY-A	.000	2	2	0	0	0	0	0	0	0	1	0	H
Total 2		.000	4	3	0	0	0	0	0	0	0	1	0	
■ Darrell Johnson														
1961	Cin-N	.500	2	4	0	2	0	0	0	0	0	0	0	C
■ Davey Johnson														
1966	Bal-A	.286	4	14	1	4	1	0	0	1	0	1	0	2
1969	Bal-A	.063	5	16	1	1	0	0	0	0	2	1	0	2
1970	Bal-A	.313	5	16	2	5	0	0	0	2	5	2	0	2
1971	Bal-A	.148	7	27	1	4	0	0	0	3	0	1	0	2
Total 4		.192	21	73	5	14	3	0	0	6	7	5	0	
☑ Deron Johnson														
1973	Oak-A	.300	6	10	0	3	1	0	0	0	1	4	0	1*2
⬛ Don Johnson														
1945	Chi-N	.172	7	29	4	5	2	1	0	0	0	8	1	2
⬛ Ernie Johnson														
1923	NY-A	—	2	0	1	0	0	0	0	0	0	0	0	S*1
■ Howard Johnson														
1984	Det-A	.000	1	1	0	0	0	0	0	0	0	0	0	H
1986	NY-N	.000	2	5	0	0	0	0	0	0	0	2	0	3*1,S*1
Total 2		.000	3	6	0	0	0	0	0	0	0	2	0	
■ Lance Johnson														
1987	StL-N	—	1	0	0	0	0	0	0	0	0	0	1	R
■ Ken Johnson														
1950	Phi-N	—	1	0	1	0	0	0	0	0	0	0	0	R
■ Lou Johnson														
1965	LA-N	.296	7	27	3	8	2	0	2	4	1	3	0	O
1966	LA-N	.267	4	15	1	4	1	0	0	0	1	1	0	O
Total 2		.286	11	42	4	12	3	0	2	4	2	4	0	
■ Roy Johnson														
1936	NY-A	.000	2	1	0	0	0	0	0	0	0	0	1	H
■ Billy Johnson														
1943	NY-A	.300	5	20	3	6	1	1	0	3	0	3	0	3
1947	NY-A	.269	7	26	8	7	0	3	0	2	3	4	0	3
1949	NY-A	.143	2	7	0	1	0	0	0	0	0	2	1	3
1950	NY-A	.000	4	6	0	0	0	0	0	0	0	3	0	3
Total 4		.237	18	59	11	14	1	4	0	5	3	12	1	
■ Jimmy Johnston														
1916	Bro-N	.300	3	10	1	3	0	1	0	0	1	0	0	O*2
1920	Bro-N	.214	4	14	2	3	0	0	0	0	0	2	1	3
Total 2		.250	7	24	3	6	0	1	0	0	1	2	1	
■ Doc Johnston														
1920	Cle-A	.273	5	11	1	3	0	0	0	0	0	2	1	1
■ Jay Johnstone														
1978	NY-A	—	2	0	0	0	0	0	0	0	0	0	0	O
1981	LA-N	.667	3	3	1	2	0	0	1	3	0	0	0	O
Total 2		.667	5	3	1	2	0	0	1	3	0	0	0	
■ Cleon Jones														
1969	NY-N	.158	5	19	2	3	1	0	0	0	0	1	0	O
1973	NY-N	.286	7	28	5	8	2	0	1	4	4	2	0	O
Total 2		.234	12	47	7	11	3	0	1	4	4	3	0	

YEAR	TM/L	AVG	G	AB	R	H	2B	3B	HR	RBI	BB	SO	SB	POS
Davy Jones														
1907	Det-A	.353	5	17	1	6	0	0	0	0	4	0	3	O
1908	Det-A	.000	3	2	1	0	0	0	0	0	1	1	0	H
1909	Det-A	.233	7	30	6	7	0	0	1	1	2	1	1	O
Total 3		.265	15	49	8	13	0	0	1	1	7	2	4	
Fielder Jones														
1900	Bro-N	.278	4	18	3	5	0	0	0	4	1	1	1	O
1906	Chi-A	.095	6	21	4	2	0	0	0	0	3	3	0	O
Total 2		.179	10	39	7	7	0	0	0	4	4	4	1	
Dalton Jones														
1967	Bos-A	.389	6	18	2	7	0	0	0	1	1	3	0	3*4
Lynn Jones														
1985	KC-A	.667	6	3	0	2	1	1	0	0	0	0	0	O*4
Ruppert Jones														
1984	Det-A	.000	2	3	0	0	0	0	0	0	0	1	0	O
Tom Jones														
1909	Det-A	.250	7	24	3	6	1	0	0	2	2	0	1	1
Nippy Jones														
1946	StL-N	.000	1	1	0	0	0	0	0	0	0	0	0	H
1957	Mil-N	.000	3	2	0	0	0	0	0	0	0	0	0	H
Total 2		.000	4	3	0	0	0	0	0	0	0	1	0	
Willie Jones														
1950	Phi-N	.286	4	14	1	4	1	0	0	0	0	3	0	3
Eddie Joost														
1940	Cin-N	.200	7	25	0	5	0	0	0	2	1	2	0	2
Ricky Jordan														
1993	Phi-N	.200	3	10	0	2	0	0	0	0	0	2	0	D*2
Spider Jorgensen														
1947	Bro-N	.200	7	20	1	4	2	0	0	3	2	4	0	3
1949	Bro-N	.182	4	11	1	2	2	0	0	0	2	2	0	3*3
Total 2		.194	11	31	2	6	4	0	0	3	4	6	0	
Mike Jorgensen														
1985	StL-N	.000	2	3	0	0	0	0	0	0	0	0	0	O*1
Von Joshua														
1974	LA-N	.000	4	4	0	0	0	0	0	0	0	0	0	H
Joe Judge														
1924	Was-A	.385	7	26	4	10	1	0	0	0	5	2	0	1
1925	Was-A	.174	7	23	2	4	1	0	1	3	3	2	0	1
Total 2		.286	14	49	6	14	2	0	1	3	8	4	0	
Wally Judnich														
1948	Cle-A	.077	4	13	1	1	0	0	0	1	1	4	0	O
Billy Jurges														
1932	Chi-N	.364	3	11	1	4	1	0	0	1	0	2		S
1935	Chi-N	.250	6	16	3	4	0	0	1	4	4	0		S
1938	Chi-N	.231	4	13	0	3	1	0	0	1	3	0		S
Total 3		.275	13	40	4	11	2	0	2	5	8	2		
David Justice														
1991	Atl-N	.259	7	27	5	7	0	0	2	6	5	5	2	O
1992	Atl-N	.158	6	19	4	3	0	0	1	3	6	5	1	O
Total 2		.217	13	46	9	10	0	0	3	9	11	10	3	
Al Kaline														
1968	Det-A	.379	7	29	6	11	2	0	2	8	0	7	0	O
John Kane														
1910	Chi-N	—	1	0	0	0	0	0	0	0	0	0	0	R
Eddie Kasko														
1961	Cin-N	.318	5	22	1	7	0	0	0	1	0	2	0	S
Benny Kauff														
1917	NY-N	.160	6	25	2	4	1	0	2	5	0	2	1	O
Willie Keeler														
1894	Bal-N	.250	3	12	1	3	0	0	0	1	1	0	0	O
1895	Bal-N	.235	5	17	3	4	0	0	0	1	3	1	0	O
1896	Bal-N	.471	4	17	4	8	1	2	0	4	0	0	1	O
1897	Bal-N	.391	5	23	5	9	2	0	0	2	4	0	0	O
1900	Bro-N	.353	4	17	0	6	0	0	0	0	1	0	0	O
Total 5		.349	21	86	13	30	3	2	0	8	9	1	1	
Charlie Keller														
1939	NY-A	.438	4	16	8	7	1	1	3	6	1	2	0	O
1941	NY-A	.389	5	18	5	7	2	0	0	5	3	1	0	O
1942	NY-A	.200	5	20	2	4	0	0	2	5	1	3	0	O
1943	NY-A	.222	5	18	3	4	0	0	1	2	2	5	1	O
Total 4		.306	19	72	18	22	3	2	5	18	7	11	1	
Frank Kellert														
1955	Bro-N	.333	3	3	0	1	0	0	0	0	0	0	0	H
Joe Kelley														
1894	Bal-N	.333	4	15	2	5	1	0	0	3	2	1	0	O
1895	Bal-N	.368	5	19	1	7	0	0	0	5	1	1	0	O
1896	Bal-N	.471	4	17	3	8	1	0	0	4	0	1	0	O
1897	Bal-N	.313	4	16	7	5	3	0	0	5	5	0	0	O
1900	Bro-N	.176	4	17	2	3	0	0	1	2	3	0	0	O
Total 5		.333	21	84	15	28	5	1	0	15	11	7	4	

YEAR	TM/L	AVG	G	AB	R	H	2B	3B	HR	RBI	BB	SO	SB	POS
George Kelly														
1921	NY-N	.233	8	30	3	7	1	0	0	4	3	10	0	1
1922	NY-N	.278	5	18	0	5	0	0	0	2	0	3	0	1
1923	NY-N	.182	6	22	1	4	0	0	1	1	2	0		1
1924	NY-N	.290	7	31	9	9	1	0	1	4	1	8	0	1*4,O*4,2*1
Total 4		.248	26	101	11	25	2	0	1	11	5	23	0	
Pat Kelly														
1979	Bal-A	.250	5	4	0	1	0	0	0	0	1	1	0	H
King Kelly														
1885	Chi-N	.346	7	26	9	9	3	1	0	0	2	0	0	O*4,C*3
1886	Chi-N	.208	6	24	4	5	0	0	1	1	2	2	1	C*5,S*2,3,1
1892	Bos-N	.000	2	8	0	0	0	0	0	0	0	2	1	C
Total 3		.241	15	58	13	14	3	1	1	1	4	4	2	
Ken Keltner														
1948	Cle-A	.095	6	21	3	2	0	0	0	2	3	0		3
Ed Kennedy														
1884	NY-A	.000	3	7	0	0	0	0	0	0	0	2	0	O
John Kennedy														
1965	LA-N	.000	4	1	0	0	0	0	0	0	0	0	0	3
1966	LA-N	.200	2	5	0	1	0	0	0	0	0	0	0	3
Total 2		.167	6	6	0	1	0	0	0	0	0	0	0	
Bob Kennedy														
1948	Cle-A	.500	3	2	0	1	0	0	0	1	0	1	0	O
Terry Kennedy														
1984	SD-N	.211	5	19	2	4	1	0	1	3	1	1	0	C
1989	SF-N	.167	4	12	1	2	0	0	0	2	1	3	0	C
Total 2		.194	9	31	3	6	1	0	1	5	2	4	0	
John Kerr														
1933	Was-A	—	1	0	0	0	0	0	0	0	0	0	0	R
Pete Kilduff														
1920	Bro-N	.095	7	21	0	2	0	0	0	0	1	4	0	2
Harmon Killebrew														
1965	Min-A	.286	7	21	2	6	0	0	1	2	6	4	0	3
Bill Killefer														
1915	Phi-N	.000	1	1	0	0	0	0	0	0	0	0	0	H
1918	Chi-N	.118	6	17	2	2	1	0	0	2	2	0	0	C
Total 2		.111	7	18	2	2	1	0	0	2	2	0	0	
Lee King														
1922	NY-N	1.000	2	1	0	1	0	0	0	1	0	0	0	O
Chuck Klein														
1935	Chi-N	.333	5	12	2	4	0	0	1	2	0	2	0	O*3
Lou Klein														
1943	StL-N	.136	5	22	0	3	0	0	0	0	1	2	0	2
Johnny Kling														
1906	Chi-N	.176	6	17	2	3	1	0	0	0	4	3	0	C
1907	Chi-N	.211	5	19	2	4	0	0	0	1	1	4	0	C
1908	Chi-N	.250	5	16	2	4	0	0	0	2	2	2	0	C
1910	Chi-N	.077	5	13	0	1	0	0	0	1	1	2	0	C*3
Total 4		.185	21	65	6	12	2	0	0	4	8	11	0	
Ted Kluszewski														
1959	Chi-A	.391	6	23	5	9	1	0	3	10	2	0	0	1
Ray Knight														
1986	NY-N	.391	6	23	4	9	1	0	1	5	2	2	0	3
Chuck Knoblauch														
1991	Min-A	.308	7	26	3	8	1	0	0	2	4	2	4	2
Randy Knorr														
1993	Tor-A	—	1	0	0	0	0	0	0	0	0	0	0	C
Mark Koenig														
1926	NY-A	.125	7	32	2	4	1	0	0	2	0	6	0	S
1927	NY-A	.500	4	18	5	9	2	0	0	2	0	2	0	S
1928	NY-A	.158	4	19	3	3	0	0	0	0	0	1	0	S
1932	Chi-N	.250	2	4	1	1	0	1	0	1	1	0		S*1
1936	NY-N	.333	3	3	0	1	0	0	0	0	0	1	0	2*1
Total 5		.237	20	76	9	18	3	1	0	5	1	10	0	
Ed Konetchy														
1920	Bro-N	.174	7	23	0	4	0	0	0	2	3	2	0	1
Larry Kopf														
1919	Cin-N	.222	8	27	3	6	0	2	0	3	3	2	0	S
Ed Kranepool														
1969	NY-N	.250	1	4	1	1	0	0	1	1	0	0	0	1
1973	NY-N	.000	4	3	0	0	0	0	0	0	0	0	0	H
Total 2		.143	5	7	1	1	0	0	1	1	0	0	0	
Mike Kreevich														
1944	StL-A	.231	6	26	0	6	3	0	0	0	0	5	0	O
Ernie Krueger														
1920	Bro-N	.167	4	6	0	1	0	0	0	0	0	0	0	C*3
John Kruk														
1993	Phi-N	.348	6	23	4	8	1	0	0	4	7	7	0	1

YEAR TM/L	AVG	G	AB	R	H	2B	3B	HR	RBI	BB	SO	SB	POS
Tony Kubek													
1957 NY-A	.286	7	28	4	8	0	0	2	4	0	4	0	O*5,3*2
1958 NY-A	.048	7	21	0	1	0	0	0	1	1	7	0	S
1960 NY-A	.333	7	30	6	10	1	0	0	3	2	2	0	S*7,O*2
1961 NY-A	.227	5	22	3	5	0	0	0	1	1	4	0	S
1962 NY-A	.276	7	29	2	8	1	0	0	1	1	3	0	S
1963 NY-A	.188	4	16	1	3	0	0	0	0	0	3	0	S
Total 6	.240	37	146	16	35	2	0	2	10	5	23	0	
Ted Kubiak													
1972 Oak-A	.333	4	3	0	1	0	0	0	0	0	0	0	2
1973 Oak-A	.000	4	3	1	0	0	0	0	0	1	1	0	2
Total 2	.167	8	6	1	1	0	0	0	0	1	1	0	
Harvey Kuenn													
1962 SF-N	.083	4	12	1	1	0	0	0	0	1	1	0	O
Joe Kuhel													
1933 Was-A	.150	5	20	1	3	0	0	0	0	1	4	0	1
Rusty Kuntz													
1984 Det-A	.000	2	1	0	0	0	0	0	0	1	0	1	H
Whitey Kurowski													
1942 StL-N	.267	5	15	3	4	0	1	1	5	2	3	0	3
1943 StL-N	.222	5	18	2	4	1	0	0	1	0	3	0	3
1944 StL-N	.217	6	23	2	5	1	0	0	1	1	4	0	3
1946 StL-N	.296	7	27	5	8	3	0	0	2	0	3	0	3
Total 4	.253	23	83	12	21	5	1	1	9	3	13	0	
Chet Laabs													
1944 StL-A	.200	5	15	1	3	1	1	0	0	2	6	0	O*4
Candy LaChance													
1903 Bos-A	.222	8	27	5	6	2	1	0	4	3	2	0	1
Pete LaCock													
1980 KC-A	—	1	0	0	0	0	0	0	0	0	0	0	1
Lee Lacy													
1974 LA-N	.000	1	1	0	0	0	0	0	0	0	1	0	H
1977 LA-N	.429	4	7	1	3	0	0	0	2	1	1	0	O*2
1978 LA-N	.143	4	14	0	2	0	0	0	1	1	3	0	D
1979 Pit-N	.250	4	4	0	1	0	0	0	0	0	1	0	H
Total 4	.231	13	26	1	6	0	0	0	3	2	6	0	
Fred Lake													
1897 Bos-N	.000	1	3	0	0	0	0	0	0	0	1	0	C
Steve Lake													
1987 StL-N	.333	3	3	0	1	0	0	0	0	1	0	0	C
Bill Lamar													
1920 Bro-N	.000	3	3	0	0	0	0	0	0	0	0	0	H
Rafael Landestoy													
1977 LA-N	—	1	0	0	0	0	0	0	0	0	0	0	R
Jim Landis													
1959 Chi-A	.292	6	24	6	7	0	0	0	1	7	1	0	O
Ken Landreaux													
1981 LA-N	.167	5	6	1	1	1	0	0	0	0	2	1	O*3
Tito Landrum													
1983 Bal-A	—	3	0	0	0	0	0	0	0	0	0	1	O
1985 StL-N	.360	7	25	3	9	2	0	1	1	0	2	0	O
Total 2	.360	10	25	3	9	2	0	1	1	0	2	1	
Carney Lansford													
1988 Oak-A	.167	5	18	2	3	0	0	0	1	2	0	3	3
1989 Oak-A	.438	4	16	5	7	1	0	1	4	3	1	0	3
1990 Oak-A	.267	4	15	0	4	0	0	0	1	1	0	1	3
Total 3	.286	13	49	7	14	1	0	1	6	6	3	1	
Jack Lapp													
1910 Phi-A	.250	1	4	0	1	0	0	0	0	1	0	2	C
1911 Phi-A	.250	2	8	1	2	0	0	0	0	0	0	1	C
1913 Phi-A	.250	1	4	0	1	0	0	0	0	0	0	1	C
1914 Phi-A	.000	1	1	0	0	0	0	0	0	0	0	0	C
Total 4	.235	5	17	1	4	0	0	0	1	0	4	0	
Norm Larker													
1959 LA-N	.188	6	16	2	3	0	0	0	0	2	3	0	O
Barry Larkin													
1990 Cin-N	.353	4	17	3	6	1	1	0	1	2	0	0	S
Gene Larkin													
1987 Min-A	.000	5	3	1	0	0	0	0	0	1	0	0	1*1,D*1
1991 Min-A	.500	4	4	0	2	0	0	0	1	0	0	0	D*1
Total 2	.286	9	7	1	2	0	0	0	1	1	0	0	
Arlie Latham													
1885 StL-A	.318	7	22	5	7	3	0	0	2	0	3	0	3
1886 StL-A	.174	6	23	4	4	0	1	0	3	3	4	2	3*6,C*1
1887 StL-A	.293	15	58	12	17	1	0	0	2	9	2	15	3
1888 StL-A	.250	10	40	10	10	0	0	0	3	5	6	11	3
Total 4	.266	38	143	31	38	4	1	0	8	19	12	28	
Tim Laudner													
1987 Min-A	.318	7	22	4	7	1	0	1	4	5	3	0	C
Cookie Lavagetto													
1941 Bro-N	.100	3	10	1	1	0	0	0	0	0	2	0	3

YEAR TM/L	AVG	G	AB	R	H	2B	3B	HR	RBI	BB	SO	SB	POS
1947 Bro-N	.143	5	7	0	1	1	0	0	3	0	2	0	3*3
Total 2	.118	8	17	1	2	1	0	0	3	2	2	0	
Tom Lawless													
1985 StL-N	—	1	0	0	0	0	0	0	0	0	0	0	R
1987 StL-N	.100	3	10	1	1	0	0	1	3	0	4	0	3
Total 2	.100	4	10	1	1	0	0	1	3	0	4	0	
Tony Lazzeri													
1926 NY-A	.192	7	26	2	5	1	0	0	3	1	6	0	2
1927 NY-A	.267	4	15	1	4	1	0	0	2	1	4	0	2
1928 NY-A	.250	4	12	2	3	1	0	0	0	1	0	2	2
1932 NY-A	.294	4	17	4	5	0	0	2	5	2	1	0	2
1936 NY-A	.250	6	20	4	5	0	0	1	7	4	4	0	2
1937 NY-A	.400	5	15	3	6	0	1	1	2	3	3	0	2
1938 Chi-N	.000	2	2	0	0	0	0	0	0	0	1	0	H
Total 7	.262	32	107	16	28	3	1	4	19	12	19	2	
Tommy Leach													
1900 Pit-N	.176	4	17	4	3	0	0	0	1	1	2	0	O
1903 Pit-N	.273	8	33	3	9	0	4	0	7	1	4	1	3
1909 Pit-N	.360	7	25	8	9	4	0	0	2	2	1	1	O*7,3*1
Total 3	.280	19	75	15	21	4	4	0	10	4	7	2	
Manuel Lee													
1992 Tor-A	.105	6	19	1	2	0	0	0	0	1	2	0	S
Jim Lefebvre													
1965 LA-N	.400	3	10	2	4	0	0	0	0	0	0	0	2
1966 LA-N	.167	4	12	1	2	0	0	0	1	3	4	0	2
Total 2	.273	7	22	3	6	0	0	0	1	3	4	0	
Joe Lefebvre													
1983 Phi-N	.200	3	5	0	1	1	0	0	2	0	1	0	O*2
Hank Leiber													
1936 NY-N	.000	2	6	0	0	0	0	0	0	2	2	0	O
1937 NY-N	.364	3	11	2	4	0	0	0	2	1	1	0	O
Total 2	.235	5	17	2	4	0	0	0	2	3	3	0	
Nemo Leibold													
1917 Chi-A	.400	2	5	1	2	0	0	0	2	1	1	0	O
1919 Chi-A	.056	5	18	0	1	0	0	0	0	2	3	1	O
1924 Was-A	.167	3	6	1	1	0	0	0	0	1	0	0	O*1
1925 Was-A	.500	3	2	1	1	1	0	0	0	1	0	0	H
Total 4	.161	13	31	3	5	2	0	0	2	5	4	1	
Scott Leius													
1991 Min-A	.357	7	14	2	5	0	0	1	2	1	2	0	3
Don LeJohn													
1965 LA-N	.000	1	1	0	0	0	0	0	0	0	1	0	H
Mark Lemke													
1991 Atl-N	.417	6	24	4	10	1	3	0	4	2	4	0	2
1992 Atl-N	.211	6	19	0	4	0	0	0	2	1	3	0	2
Total 2	.326	12	43	4	14	1	3	0	6	3	7	0	
Chet Lemon													
1984 Det-A	.294	5	17	1	5	0	0	0	1	2	2	0	O
Sam Leslie													
1936 NY-N	.667	3	3	0	2	0	0	0	0	0	0	0	H
1937 NY-N	.000	2	1	0	0	0	0	0	0	1	0	0	H
Total 2	.500	5	4	0	2	0	0	0	0	1	0	0	
Allan Lewis													
1972 Oak-A	—	6	0	2	0	0	0	0	0	0	0	0	R
1973 Oak-A	—	3	0	1	0	0	0	0	0	0	0	0	R
Total 2	—	9	0	3	0	0	0	0	0	0	0	0	
Duffy Lewis													
1912 Bos-A	.156	8	32	4	5	3	0	0	2	2	2	0	O
1915 Bos-A	.444	5	18	1	8	1	0	1	5	1	4	0	O
1916 Bos-A	.353	5	17	3	6	2	1	0	1	2	1	0	O
Total 3	.284	18	67	8	19	6	1	1	8	5	7	0	
Sixto Lezcano													
1983 Phi-N	.125	4	8	0	1	0	0	0	0	0	2	0	O*3
Johnny Lindell													
1943 NY-A	.111	4	9	1	1	0	0	0	0	1	4	0	O
1947 NY-A	.500	6	18	3	9	3	1	0	7	5	2	0	O
1949 NY-A	.143	2	7	0	1	0	0	0	0	0	2	0	O
Total 3	.324	12	34	4	11	3	1	0	7	6	8	0	
Jim Lindeman													
1987 StL-N	.333	6	15	3	5	1	0	0	2	0	3	0	1*6,O*1
Freddie Lindstrom													
1924 NY-N	.333	7	30	1	10	2	0	0	4	3	6	0	3
1935 Chi-N	.200	4	15	0	3	1	0	0	1	1	1	0	O*4,3*1
Total 2	.289	11	45	1	13	3	0	0	5	4	7	0	
Phil Linz													
1963 NY-A	.333	3	3	1	1	0	0	0	0	0	1	0	H
1964 NY-A	.226	7	31	5	7	1	0	2	2	5	5	0	S
Total 2	.235	10	34	5	8	1	0	2	2	5	6	0	
Greg Litton													
1989 SF-N	.500	2	6	1	3	1	0	1	3	0	0	0	2*2,3*1
Danny Litwhiler													
1943 StL-N	.267	5	15	0	4	1	0	0	2	2	4	0	O*4

YEAR	TM/L	AVG	G	AB	R	H	2B	3B	HR	RBI	BB	SO	SB	POS
1944 StL-N		.200	5	20	2	4	1	0	1	1	2	7	0	O
Total 2		.229	10	35	2	8	2	0	1	3	4	11	0	
■ Mickey Livingston														
1945 Chi-N		.364	6	22	3	8	3	0	0	4	1	1	0	C
■ Whitey Lockman														
1951 NY-N		.240	6	25	1	6	2	0	1	4	1	2	0	1
1954 NY-N		.111	4	18	2	2	0	0	0	0	1	2	0	1
Total 2		.186	10	43	3	8	2	0	1	4	2	4	0	
■ Johnny Logan														
1957 Mil-N		.185	7	27	5	5	1	0	1	2	3	6	0	S
1958 Mil-N		.120	7	25	3	3	2	0	0	2	2	4	0	S
Total 2		.154	14	52	8	8	3	0	1	4	5	10	0	
■ Jack Lohrke														
1951 NY-N		.000	2	2	0	0	0	0	0	0	0	1	0	H
■ Sherm Lollar														
1947 NY-A		.750	2	4	3	3	2	0	0	0	0	0	0	C
1959 Chi-A		.227	6	22	3	5	0	0	1	5	1	3	0	C
Total 2		.308	8	26	6	8	2	0	1	6	1	3	0	
■ Ernie Lombardi														
1939 Cin-N		.214	4	14	0	3	0	0	0	2	0	1	0	C
1940 Cin-N		.333	2	3	0	1	1	0	0	0	1	0	0	C*1
Total 2		.235	6	17	0	4	1	0	0	2	1	1	0	
■ Steve Lombardozzi														
1987 Min-A		.412	6	17	3	7	1	0	1	4	2	3	0	2
■ Herman Long														
1892 Bos-N		.222	6	27	4	6	0	0	0	1	0	0	2	S
1897 Bos-N		.286	5	21	4	6	1	1	1	5	2	2	1	S
Total 2		.250	11	48	8	12	1	1	1	6	2	2	3	
■ Dale Long														
1960 NY-A		.333	3	3	0	1	0	0	0	0	0	0	0	H
1962 NY-A		.200	2	5	0	1	0	0	0	1	0	1	0	1
Total 2		.250	5	8	0	2	0	0	0	1	0	1	0	
■ Stan Lopata														
1950 Phi-N		.000	2	1	0	0	0	0	0	0	0	1	0	C*1
■ Davey Lopes														
1974 LA-N		.111	5	18	2	2	0	0	0	0	3	4	2	2
1977 LA-N		.167	6	24	3	4	0	1	2	4	3	2	2	
1978 LA-N		.308	6	26	7	8	0	0	3	7	2	1	2	2
1981 LA-N		.227	6	22	6	5	1	0	2	4	3	4	2	
Total 4		.211	23	90	18	19	1	1	4	11	13	11	10	
■ Hector Lopez														
1960 NY-A		.429	3	7	0	3	0	0	0	0	0	0	0	O*1
1961 NY-A		.333	4	9	3	3	0	1	1	7	3	0	0	O*3
1962 NY-A		.000	2	2	0	0	0	0	0	0	0	0	0	H
1963 NY-A		.250	3	8	1	2	2	0	0	0	1	0	0	O*2
1964 NY-A		.000	3	2	0	0	0	0	0	0	0	2	0	O*1
Total 5		.286	15	28	4	8	2	1	1	7	2	6	0	
■ Bris Lord														
1905 Phi-A		.100	5	20	0	2	0	0	0	2	0	5	0	O
1910 Phi-A		.182	5	22	3	4	2	0	0	1	1	3	0	O
1911 Phi-A		.185	6	27	2	5	2	0	0	1	0	5	0	O
Total 3		.159	16	69	5	11	4	0	0	4	1	13	0	
■ Bobby Lowe														
1892 Bos-N		.130	6	23	2	3	0	0	0	0	1	2	1	O
1897 Bos-N		.391	5	23	6	9	2	0	0	6	1	0	1	2
Total 2		.261	11	46	8	12	2	0	0	6	2	2	2	
■ John Lowenstein														
1979 Bal-A		.231	6	13	2	3	1	0	0	3	1	3	0	O*3
1983 Bal-A		.385	4	13	2	5	1	0	1	1	0	3	0	O
Total 2		.308	10	26	4	8	2	0	1	4	1	6	0	
■ Peanuts Lowrey														
1945 Chi-N		.310	7	29	4	9	1	0	0	0	1	2	0	O
■ Fred Luderus														
1915 Phi-N		.438	5	16	1	7	2	0	1	6	1	4	0	1
■ Jerry Lumpe														
1957 NY-A		.286	6	14	0	4	0	0	0	2	1	1	0	3*3
1958 NY-A		.167	6	12	0	2	0	0	0	0	1	2	0	3*3,S*2
Total 2		.231	12	26	0	6	0	0	0	2	2	3	0	
■ Harry Lunte														
1920 Cle-A		—	1	0	0	0	0	0	0	0	0	0	0	2
■ Greg Luzinski														
1980 Phi-N		.000	3	9	0	0	0	0	0	0	1	5	0	D*2,O*1
■ Jerry Lynch														
1961 Cin-N		.000	4	3	0	0	0	0	0	0	0	1	0	H
■ Byrd Lynn														
1917 Chi-A		.000	1	1	0	0	0	0	0	0	0	0	0	H
1919 Chi-A		.000	1	1	0	0	0	0	0	0	0	0	0	C
Total 2		.000	2	2	0	0	0	0	0	0	0	0	0	
■ Fred Lynn														
1975 Bos-A		.280	7	25	3	7	1	0	1	5	3	5	0	O

YEAR	TM/L	AVG	G	AB	R	H	2B	3B	HR	RBI	BB	SO	SB	POS
■ Harry Lyons														
1887 StL-A		.286	2	7	3	2	0	0	0	2	1	0	0	S
1888 StL-A		.118	5	17	0	2	0	0	0	1	1	5	0	O
Total 2		.167	7	24	3	4	0	0	0	3	2	5	0	
■ Shane Mack														
1991 Min-A		.130	6	23	0	3	1	0	0	1	0	7	0	O
■ Elliott Maddox														
1976 NY-A		.200	2	5	0	1	0	1	0	0	1	2	0	O*1,D*1
■ Garry Maddox														
1980 Phi-N		.227	6	22	1	5	2	0	0	1	1	3	0	O
1983 Phi-N		.250	4	12	1	3	1	0	1	1	0	2	0	O*3
Total 2		.235	10	34	2	8	3	0	1	2	1	5	0	
■ Bill Madlock														
1979 Pit-N		.375	7	24	2	9	1	0	0	3	5	1	0	3
■ Sherry Magee														
1919 Cin-N		.500	2	2	0	1	0	0	0	0	0	0	0	H
■ Freddie Maguire														
1923 NY-N		—	2	0	1	0	0	0	0	0	0	0	0	R
■ Bob Maier														
1945 Det-A		1.000	1	1	0	1	0	0	0	0	0	0	0	H
■ Hank Majeski														
1954 Cle-A		.167	4	6	1	1	0	0	1	3	0	1	0	3*1
■ Candy Maldonado														
1989 SF-N		.091	4	11	1	1	0	1	0	0	0	4	0	O*3
1992 Tor-A		.158	6	19	1	3	0	0	1	2	2	5	0	O*5
Total 2		.133	10	30	2	4	0	1	1	2	2	9	0	
■ Gus Mancuso														
1930 StL-N		.286	2	7	1	2	0	0	0	1	2	0		C
1931 StL-N		.000	2	1	0	0	0	0	0	0	0	0	0	C*1
1933 NY-N		.118	5	17	2	2	1	0	0	2	3	0	0	C
1936 NY-N		.263	6	19	3	5	2	0	0	1	3	3	0	C
1937 NY-N		.000	3	8	0	0	0	0	0	1	0	1	0	C*2
Total 5		.173	18	52	6	9	3	0	0	4	7	6	0	
■ Frank Mancuso														
1944 StL-A		.667	2	3	0	2	0	0	0	0	0	0	0	C*1
■ Angel Mangual														
1972 Oak-A		.300	4	10	1	3	0	0	0	1	0	0	0	O*2
1973 Oak-A		.000	5	6	0	0	0	0	0	0	0	3	0	O*1
1974 Oak-A		.000	1	1	0	0	0	0	0	0	0	1	0	H
Total 3		.176	10	17	1	3	0	0	0	1	0	4	0	
■ Les Mann														
1914 Bos-N		.286	3	7	1	2	0	0	0	1	0	1	0	O*2
1918 Chi-N		.227	6	22	0	5	2	0	0	2	0	0	0	O
Total 2		.241	9	29	1	7	2	0	0	3	0	1	0	
■ Felix Mantilla														
1957 Mil-N		.000	4	10	1	0	0	0	0	0	1	0	0	2*3
1958 Mil-N		—	4	0	1	0	0	0	0	0	0	0	0	S*1
Total 2		.000	8	10	2	0	0	0	0	0	1	0	0	
■ Mickey Mantle														
1951 NY-A		.200	2	5	1	1	0	0	0	0	2	1	0	O
1952 NY-A		.345	7	29	5	10	1	1	2	3	3	4	0	O
1953 NY-A		.208	6	24	3	5	0	0	2	7	3	8	0	O
1955 NY-A		.200	3	10	1	2	0	0	1	1	0	2	0	O*2
1956 NY-A		.250	7	24	6	6	1	0	3	4	6	5	1	O
1957 NY-A		.263	6	19	3	5	0	0	1	2	3	1	0	O*5
1958 NY-A		.250	7	24	4	6	0	1	2	3	7	4	0	O
1960 NY-A		.400	7	25	8	10	1	0	3	11	8	9	0	O
1961 NY-A		.167	2	6	0	1	0	0	0	0	0	2	0	O
1962 NY-A		.120	7	25	2	3	1	0	0	0	4	5	2	O
1963 NY-A		.133	4	15	1	2	0	0	1	1	1	5	0	O
1964 NY-A		.333	7	24	8	8	2	0	3	8	6	8	0	O
Total 12		.257	65	230	42	59	6	2	18	40	43	54	3	
■ Heinie Manush														
1933 Was-A		.111	5	18	2	2	0	0	0	0	2	1	0	O
■ Kirt Manwaring														
1989 SF-N		1.000	1	1	1	1	1	0	0	0	0	0	0	C
■ Cliff Mapes														
1949 NY-A		.100	4	10	3	1	1	0	0	2	2	4	0	O
1950 NY-A		.000	1	4	0	0	0	0	0	0	0	1	0	O
Total 2		.071	5	14	3	1	1	0	0	2	2	5	0	
■ Rabbit Maranville														
1914 Bos-N		.308	4	13	1	4	0	0	0	3	1	1	2	S
1928 StL-N		.308	4	13	2	4	1	0	0	0	1	1	1	S
Total 2		.308	8	26	3	8	1	0	0	3	2	2	3	
■ Marty Marion														
1942 StL-N		.111	5	18	2	2	0	1	0	3	1	2	0	S
1943 StL-N		.357	5	14	1	5	2	0	1	2	3	1	1	S
1944 StL-N		.227	6	22	1	5	3	0	0	2	2	3	0	S
1946 StL-N		.250	7	24	1	6	2	0	0	4	1	1	0	S
Total 4		.231	23	78	5	18	7	1	1	11	7	7	1	
■ Roger Maris														
1960 NY-A		.267	7	30	6	8	1	0	2	2	2	4	0	O

YEAR	TM/L	AVG	G	AB	R	H	2B	3B	HR	RBI	BB	SO	SB	POS
1961	NY-A	.105	5	19	4	2	1	0	1	2	4	6	0	O
1962	NY-A	.174	7	23	4	4	1	0	1	5	5	2	0	O
1963	NY-A	.000	2	5	0	0	0	0	0	0	0	1	0	O
1964	NY-A	.200	7	30	4	6	0	0	1	1	1	4	0	O
1967	StL-N	.385	7	26	3	10	1	0	1	7	3	1	0	O
1968	StL-N	.158	6	19	5	3	1	0	1	3	3	3	0	O*5
Total 7		.217	41	152	26	33	5	0	6	18	18	21	0	

■ Gonzalo Marquez

1972	Oak-A	.600	5	5	0	3	0	0	0	1	0	0	0	H

■ Mike Marshall

1988	LA-N	.231	5	13	2	3	0	1	1	3	0	5	0	O

■ Billy Martin

1951	NY-A	—	1	0	1	0	0	0	0	0	0	0	0	R
1952	NY-A	.217	7	23	2	5	0	0	1	4	2	2	0	2
1953	NY-A	.500	6	24	5	12	1	2	2	8	1	2	1	2
1955	NY-A	.320	7	25	2	8	1	1	0	4	1	5	0	2
1956	NY-A	.296	7	27	5	8	0	0	2	3	1	6	0	2*7,3*1
Total 5		.333	28	99	15	33	2	3	5	19	5	15	1	

■ Pepper Martin

1928	StL-N	—	1	0	1	0	0	0	0	0	0	0	0	R
1931	StL-N	.500	7	24	5	12	4	0	1	5	2	3	5	O
1934	StL-N	.355	7	31	8	11	3	1	0	4	3	3	2	3
Total 3		.418	15	55	14	23	7	1	1	9	5	6	7	

■ J.C. Martin

1969	NY-N	—	1	0	0	0	0	0	0	0	0	0	0	H

■ Carmelo Martinez

1984	SD-N	.176	5	17	0	3	0	0	0	1	9	0	0	O

■ Ted Martinez

1973	NY-N	—	2	0	0	0	0	0	0	0	0	0	0	R

■ Joe Marty

1938	Chi-N	.500	3	12	1	6	1	0	1	5	0	2	0	O

■ Phil Masi

1948	Bos-N	.125	5	8	1	1	1	0	0	1	0	0	0	C

■ Jim Mason

1976	NY-A	1.000	3	1	1	1	0	0	1	1	0	0	0	S

■ Tom Matchick

1968	Det-A	.000	3	3	0	0	0	0	0	0	0	1	0	H

■ Eddie Mathews

1957	Mil-N	.227	7	22	4	5	3	0	1	4	8	5	0	3
1958	Mil-N	.160	7	25	3	4	2	0	0	3	6	11	1	3
1968	Det-A	.333	2	3	0	1	0	0	0	0	1	1	0	3*1
Total 3		.200	16	50	7	10	5	0	1	7	15	17	1	

■ Gary Matthews

1983	Phi-N	.250	5	16	1	4	0	0	1	1	2	2	0	O

■ Dal Maxvill

1964	StL-N	.200	7	20	0	4	1	0	0	1	1	4	0	2
1967	StL-N	.158	7	19	1	3	0	1	0	1	4	1	0	S
1968	StL-N	.000	7	22	1	0	0	0	0	0	3	5	0	S
1974	Oak-A	—	2	0	0	0	0	0	0	0	0	0	0	2
Total 4		.115	23	61	2	7	1	1	0	2	8	10	0	

■ Carlos May

1976	NY-A	.000	4	9	0	0	0	0	0	0	0	0	1	0	D

■ Dave May

1969	Bal-A	.000	2	1	0	0	0	0	0	0	1	1	0	H

■ Lee May

1970	Cin-N	.389	5	18	6	7	0	0	2	8	2	2	0	1
1979	Bal-A	.000	2	1	0	0	0	0	0	0	1	1	0	H
Total 2		.368	7	19	6	7	2	0	2	8	3	3	0	

■ Milt May

1971	Pit-N	.500	2	2	0	1	0	0	0	1	0	0	0	H

■ Eddie Mayo

1936	NY-N	.000	1	1	0	0	0	0	0	0	0	0	0	3
1945	Det-A	.250	7	28	4	7	1	0	0	2	2	2	0	2
Total 2		.241	8	29	4	7	1	0	0	2	2	2	0	

■ Jackie Mayo

1950	Phi-N	—	3	0	0	0	0	0	0	0	1	0	0	O*1

■ Willie Mays

1951	NY-N	.182	6	22	1	4	0	0	0	1	2	2	0	O
1954	NY-N	.286	4	14	4	4	1	0	0	3	4	1	1	O
1962	SF-N	.250	7	28	3	7	2	0	0	1	1	5	1	O
1973	NY-N	.286	3	7	1	2	0	0	0	0	1	0	0	O*2
Total 4		.239	20	71	9	17	3	0	0	6	7	9	2	

■ Bill Mazeroski

1960	Pit-N	.320	7	25	4	8	2	0	2	5	0	3	0	2
1971	Pit-N	.000	1	1	0	0	0	0	0	0	0	0	0	H
Total 2		.308	8	26	4	8	2	0	2	5	0	3	0	

■ Lee Mazzilli

1986	NY-N	.400	4	5	2	2	0	0	0	0	0	0	0	O*1

■ Jimmy McAleer

1892	Cle-N	.182	6	22	0	4	0	0	0	1	2	2	1	O
1895	Cle-N	.286	5	21	2	6	0	0	0	2	0	0	1	O
1896	Cle-N	.133	4	15	0	2	0	0	0	1	1	2	1	O
Total 3		.207	15	58	2	12	0	0	0	4	3	4	3	

■ Jim McAnany

1959	Chi-A	.000	3	5	0	0	0	0	0	0	1	0	0	O

■ Dick McAuliffe

1968	Det-A	.222	7	27	5	6	0	0	1	3	4	6	0	2

■ Bake McBride

1980	Phi-N	.304	6	23	3	7	1	0	1	5	2	1	0	O

■ Tom McBride

1946	Bos-A	.167	5	12	0	2	0	0	0	1	0	1	0	O*2

■ Bill McCabe

1918	Chi-N	.000	3	1	1	0	0	0	0	0	0	0	0	H
1920	Bro-N	—	1	0	0	0	0	0	0	0	0	0	0	R
Total 2		.000	4	1	1	0	0	0	0	0	0	0	0	

■ Johnny McCarthy

1937	NY-N	.211	5	19	1	4	1	0	0	1	1	2	0	1

■ Tommy McCarthy

1888	StL-A	.244	10	41	10	10	1	0	1	9	0	0	6	O
1892	Bos-N	.381	6	21	8	8	2	0	0	2	6	1	3	O
Total 2		.290	16	62	18	18	3	0	1	11	6	1	9	

■ Lew McCarty

1917	NY-N	.400	3	5	1	2	0	1	0	1	0	0	0	C*2

■ Tim McCarver

1964	StL-N	.478	7	23	4	11	1	1	1	5	5	1	1	C
1967	StL-N	.125	7	24	3	3	1	0	0	2	2	2	0	C
1968	StL-N	.333	7	27	3	9	0	2	1	4	3	2	0	C
Total 3		.311	21	74	10	23	2	3	2	11	10	5	1	

■ Frank McCormick

1939	Cin-N	.400	4	15	1	6	1	0	0	1	0	1	0	1
1940	Cin-N	.214	7	28	2	6	1	0	0	1	1	1	0	1
1948	Bos-N	.200	3	5	0	1	0	0	0	0	0	2	0	1*1
Total 3		.271	14	48	3	13	2	0	0	1	1	4	0	

■ Moose McCormick

1912	NY-N	.250	5	4	0	1	0	0	0	1	0	0	0	H
1913	NY-N	.500	2	2	1	1	0	0	0	0	0	0	0	H
Total 2		.333	7	6	1	2	0	0	0	1	0	0	0	

■ Mike McCormick

1940	Cin-N	.310	7	29	1	9	3	0	0	2	1	6	0	O
1948	Bos-N	.261	6	23	1	6	0	0	0	2	0	4	0	O
1949	Bro-N	—	1	0	0	0	0	0	0	0	0	0	0	O
Total 3		.288	14	52	2	15	3	0	0	4	1	10	0	

■ Barney McCosky

1940	Det-A	.304	7	23	5	7	1	0	0	1	7	0	0	O

■ Willie McCovey

1962	SF-N	.200	4	15	2	3	0	1	1	1	1	3	0	1*2,O*2

■ Clyde McCullough

1945	Chi-N	.000	1	1	0	0	0	0	0	0	0	1	0	H

■ Gil McDougald

1951	NY-A	.261	6	23	2	6	1	0	1	7	2	2	0	3*5,2*4
1952	NY-A	.200	7	25	5	5	0	0	1	3	5	2	1	3
1953	NY-A	.167	6	24	2	4	0	1	2	4	1	3	0	3
1955	NY-A	.259	7	27	2	7	0	0	1	1	2	6	0	3
1956	NY-A	.143	7	21	0	3	0	0	0	1	3	6	0	S
1957	NY-A	.250	7	24	3	6	0	0	0	2	3	3	1	S
1958	NY-A	.321	7	28	6	9	0	0	2	4	2	4	0	2
1960	NY-A	.278	6	18	4	5	1	0	0	2	2	3	0	3
Total 8		.237	53	190	23	45	4	1	7	24	20	29	2	

■ Ed McFarland

1906	Chi-A	.000	1	1	0	0	0	0	0	0	0	0	0	H

■ Dan McGann

1905	NY-N	.235	5	17	1	4	2	0	0	4	2	7	0	1

■ Chippy McGarr

1895	Cle-N	.368	5	19	3	7	2	0	0	1	1	1	2	3
1896	Cle-N	.063	4	16	0	1	0	0	0	0	0	3	2	3
Total 2		.229	9	35	3	8	2	0	0	1	1	4	4	

■ Willie McGee

1982	StL-N	.240	6	25	6	6	0	0	2	5	1	3	2	O
1985	StL-N	.259	7	27	2	7	2	0	1	2	1	3	1	O
1987	StL-N	.370	7	27	2	10	2	0	0	4	0	9	0	O
1990	Oak-A	.200	4	10	1	2	1	0	0	0	0	2	1	O*3
Total 4		.281	24	89	11	25	5	0	3	11	2	17	4	

■ John McGraw

1894	Bal-N	.250	4	16	2	4	0	0	0	2	0	0	1	3
1895	Bal-N	.400	5	20	4	8	2	0	0	1	2	0	2	3
1896	Bal-N	.267	4	15	4	4	0	0	0	1	5	0	4	3
1897	Bal-N	.300	5	20	6	6	1	1	0	6	1	0	3	3
Total 4		.310	18	71	16	22	3	1	0	10	9	0	7	

■ Deacon McGuire

1900	Bro-N	.375	2	8	1	3	1	0	0	0	0	1	0	C

■ Mark McGwire

1988	Oak-A	.059	5	17	1	1	0	0	1	1	3	4	0	1

YEAR	TM/L	AVG	G	AB	R	H	2B	3B	HR	RBI	BB	SO	SB	POS
1989	Oak-A	.294	4	17	0	5	1	0	0	1	1	3	0	1
1990	Oak-A	.214	4	14	1	3	0	0	0	0	2	4	0	1
Total 3		.188	13	48	2	9	1	0	1	2	6	11	0	

■ John McHale

| 1945 | Det-A | .000 | 3 | 3 | 0 | 0 | 0 | 0 | 0 | 0 | 0 | 1 | 0 | H |

■ Stuffy McInnis

1911	Phi-A	—	1	0	0	0	0	0	0	0	0	0	0	1
1913	Phi-A	.118	5	17	1	2	1	0	0	2	0	2	0	1
1914	Phi-A	.143	4	14	2	2	1	0	0	0	3	3	0	1
1918	Bos-A	.250	6	20	2	5	0	0	0	1	1	1	0	1
1925	Pit-N	.286	4	14	0	4	0	0	0	1	0	2	0	1*3
Total 5		.200	20	65	5	13	2	0	0	4	4	8	0	

■ Matty McIntyre

1908	Det-A	.222	5	18	2	4	1	0	0	0	3	2	1	O
1909	Det-A	.000	4	3	0	0	0	0	0	0	0	1	0	O*1
Total 2		.190	9	21	2	4	1	0	0	0	3	3	1	

■ Ed McKean

1892	Cle-N	.440	6	25	2	11	0	0	0	6	1	3	0	S
1895	Cle-N	.300	5	20	2	6	1	1	0	4	3	0	1	S
1896	Cle-N	.313	4	16	0	5	1	1	0	1	1	2	1	S
Total 3		.361	15	61	4	22	2	2	0	11	5	5	2	

■ Larry McLean

| 1913 | NY-N | .500 | 5 | 12 | 0 | 6 | 0 | 0 | 0 | 2 | 0 | 0 | 0 | C*4 |

■ Norm McMillan

1922	NY-A	.000	1	2	0	0	0	0	0	0	0	0	0	O
1929	Chi-N	.100	5	20	0	2	0	0	0	0	2	6	1	3
Total 2		.091	6	22	0	2	0	0	0	0	2	6	1	

■ Fred McMullin

1917	Chi-A	.125	6	24	1	3	1	0	0	2	1	6	0	3
1919	Chi-A	.500	2	2	0	1	0	0	0	0	0	0	0	H
Total 2		.154	8	26	1	4	1	0	0	2	1	6	0	

■ Eric McNair

1930	Phi-A	.000	1	1	0	0	0	0	0	0	0	0	0	H
1931	Phi-A	.000	2	2	1	0	0	0	0	0	0	1	0	2*1
Total 2		.000	3	3	1	0	0	0	0	0	0	1	0	

■ Mike McNally

1916	Bos-A	—	1	0	1	0	0	0	0	0	0	0	0	R
1921	NY-A	.200	7	20	3	4	1	0	0	1	1	3	2	3
1922	NY-A	—	1	0	0	0	0	0	0	0	0	0	0	2
Total 3		.200	9	20	4	4	1	0	0	1	1	3	2	

■ Earl McNeely

1924	Was-A	.222	7	27	4	6	3	0	0	1	4	4	1	O
1925	Was-A	—	4	0	2	0	0	0	0	0	0	0	1	O*2
Total 2		.222	11	27	6	6	3	0	0	1	4	4	2	

■ George McQuinn

1944	StL-A	.438	6	16	2	7	2	0	1	5	7	2	0	1
1947	NY-A	.130	7	23	3	3	0	0	0	1	5	8	0	1
Total 2		.256	13	39	5	10	2	0	1	6	12	10	0	

■ Hal McRae

1970	Cin-N	.455	3	11	1	5	2	0	0	3	0	1	0	O
1972	Cin-N	.444	5	9	1	4	1	0	0	2	0	1	0	O*2
1980	KC-A	.375	6	24	3	9	3	0	0	1	2	2	0	D
1985	KC-A	.000	3	1	0	0	0	0	0	0	0	1	0	H
Total 4		.400	17	45	5	18	6	0	0	6	3	4	0	

■ Joe Medwick

1934	StL-N	.379	7	29	4	11	0	1	1	5	1	7	0	O
1941	Bro-N	.235	5	17	1	4	1	0	0	0	1	2	0	O
Total 2		.326	12	46	5	15	1	1	1	5	2	9	0	

■ Denis Menke

| 1972 | Cin-N | .083 | 7 | 24 | 1 | 2 | 0 | 0 | 1 | 2 | 2 | 6 | 0 | 3 |

■ Fred Merkle

1911	NY-N	.150	6	20	1	3	1	0	0	1	2	6	0	1
1912	NY-N	.273	8	33	5	9	2	1	0	3	0	7	1	1
1913	NY-N	.231	4	13	3	3	0	0	1	3	1	2	0	1
1916	Bro-N	.250	3	4	0	1	0	0	0	0	1	2	0	1*1
1918	Chi-N	.278	6	18	1	5	0	0	0	1	4	3	0	1
Total 5		.239	27	88	10	21	3	1	1	9	9	18	1	

■ Sam Mertes

| 1905 | NY-N | .176 | 5 | 17 | 2 | 3 | 1 | 0 | 0 | 2 | 2 | 5 | 0 | O |

■ Lennie Merullo

| 1945 | Chi-N | .000 | 3 | 2 | 0 | 0 | 0 | 0 | 0 | 0 | 0 | 1 | 0 | S |

■ Bud Metheny

| 1943 | NY-A | .125 | 2 | 8 | 0 | 1 | 0 | 0 | 0 | 0 | 0 | 2 | 0 | O |

■ Catfish Metkovich

| 1946 | Bos-A | .500 | 2 | 2 | 1 | 1 | 1 | 0 | 0 | 0 | 0 | 0 | 0 | H |

■ Irish Meusel

1921	NY-N	.345	8	29	4	10	2	1	1	7	2	3	1	O
1922	NY-N	.250	5	20	3	5	0	0	1	7	0	1	0	O
1923	NY-N	.280	6	25	3	7	1	1	1	2	0	2	0	O
1924	NY-N	.154	4	13	0	2	0	0	0	1	2	0	0	O
Total 4		.276	23	87	10	24	3	2	3	17	4	6	1	

■ Bob Meusel

YEAR	TM/L	AVG	G	AB	R	H	2B	3B	HR	RBI	BB	SO	SB	POS
1921	NY-A	.200	8	30	3	6	2	0	0	3	2	5	1	O
1922	NY-A	.300	5	20	2	6	1	0	0	2	1	3	1	O
1923	NY-A	.269	6	26	1	7	1	2	0	8	0	3	0	O
1926	NY-A	.238	7	21	3	5	1	0	0	6	1	0	0	O
1927	NY-A	.118	4	17	1	2	0	0	0	1	1	7	1	O
1928	NY-A	.200	4	15	5	3	1	0	1	3	2	5	2	O
Total 6		.225	34	129	15	29	6	3	1	17	12	24	5	

■ Chief Meyers

1911	NY-N	.300	6	20	2	6	0	0	0	2	0	3	0	C
1912	NY-N	.357	8	28	2	10	0	1	0	3	2	3	1	C
1913	NY-N	.000	1	4	0	0	0	0	0	0	0	0	0	C
1916	Bro-N	.200	3	10	0	2	1	0	0	1	0	0	0	C
Total 4		.290	18	62	4	18	2	2	0	5	3	6	1	

■ Ed Mierkowicz

| 1945 | Det-A | — | 1 | 0 | 0 | 0 | 0 | 0 | 0 | 0 | 0 | 0 | 0 | 0 | O |

■ Eddie Miksis

1947	Bro-N	.250	5	4	1	1	0	0	0	0	0	1	0	2*1,O*1
1949	Bro-N	.286	3	7	0	2	1	0	0	0	0	1	0	3*2
Total 2		.273	8	11	1	3	1	0	0	0	0	2	0	

■ Larry Milbourne

| 1981 | NY-A | .250 | 6 | 20 | 2 | 5 | 2 | 0 | 0 | 3 | 4 | 0 | 0 | S |

■ Felix Millan

| 1973 | NY-N | .188 | 7 | 32 | 3 | 6 | 1 | 1 | 0 | 1 | 1 | 1 | 0 | 2 |

■ Bing Miller

1929	Phi-A	.368	5	19	1	7	1	0	0	4	0	2	0	O
1930	Phi-A	.143	6	21	0	3	2	0	0	3	0	4	0	O
1931	Phi-A	.269	7	26	3	7	1	0	0	1	0	4	0	O
Total 3		.258	18	66	4	17	4	0	0	8	0	10	0	

■ Elmer Miller

| 1921 | NY-A | .161 | 8 | 31 | 3 | 5 | 1 | 0 | 0 | 2 | 2 | 5 | 0 | O |

■ Dots Miller

| 1909 | Pit-N | .250 | 7 | 28 | 2 | 7 | 1 | 0 | 0 | 4 | 2 | 5 | 3 | 2 |

■ Hack Miller

| 1918 | Bos-A | .000 | 1 | 1 | 0 | 0 | 0 | 0 | 0 | 0 | 0 | 0 | 0 | H |

■ Otto Miller

1916	Bro-N	.125	2	8	0	1	0	0	0	0	0	1	0	C
1920	Bro-N	.143	6	14	0	2	0	0	0	0	1	2	0	C
Total 2		.136	8	22	0	3	0	0	0	0	1	3	0	

■ Ralph Miller

| 1924 | Was-A | .182 | 4 | 11 | 0 | 2 | 0 | 0 | 0 | 2 | 1 | 0 | 0 | 3 |

■ Rick Miller

| 1975 | Bos-A | .000 | 3 | 2 | 0 | 0 | 0 | 0 | 0 | 0 | 0 | 0 | 0 | O*2 |

■ Jocko Milligan

| 1888 | StL-A | .400 | 8 | 25 | 5 | 10 | 2 | 1 | 0 | 4 | 3 | 3 | 0 | C*8,1*1 |

■ John Milner

1973	NY-N	.296	7	27	2	8	0	0	0	2	5	1	0	1
1979	Pit-N	.333	3	9	2	3	1	0	0	1	2	0	0	O
Total 2		.306	10	36	4	11	1	0	0	3	7	1	0	

■ Don Mincher

1965	Min-A	.130	7	23	3	3	0	0	1	1	2	7	0	1
1972	Oak-A	1.000	3	1	0	1	0	0	0	1	0	0	0	H
Total 2		.167	10	24	3	4	0	0	1	2	2	7	0	

■ Keith Mitchell

| 1991 | Atl-N | .000 | 3 | 2 | 0 | 0 | 0 | 0 | 0 | 0 | 0 | 0 | 1 | 0 | O |

■ Kevin Mitchell

1986	NY-N	.250	5	8	1	2	0	0	0	0	3	3	0	O*2,D*1
1989	SF-N	.294	4	17	2	5	0	0	1	2	0	3	0	O
Total 2		.280	9	25	3	7	0	0	1	2	0	6	0	

■ Dale Mitchell

1948	Cle-A	.174	6	23	4	4	1	0	1	1	2	0	0	O
1954	Cle-A	.000	3	2	0	0	0	0	0	0	1	0	0	H
1956	Bro-N	.000	4	4	0	0	0	0	0	0	0	1	0	H
Total 3		.138	13	29	4	4	1	0	1	1	3	1	0	

■ Johnny Mize

1949	NY-A	1.000	2	2	0	2	0	0	0	2	0	0	0	H
1950	NY-A	.133	4	15	0	2	0	0	0	0	0	1	0	1
1951	NY-A	.286	4	7	2	2	1	0	0	1	2	0	0	1*2
1952	NY-A	.400	5	15	3	6	1	0	3	6	3	1	0	1*4
1953	NY-A	.000	3	3	0	0	0	0	0	0	1	0	0	H
Total 5		.286	18	42	5	12	2	0	3	9	5	3	0	

■ Paul Molitor

1982	Mil-A	.355	7	31	5	11	0	0	0	3	2	4	1	3 D*3,3-2,1-1
1993	Tor-A	.500	6	24	10	12	2	2	2	8	3	0	1	
Total 2		.418	13	55	15	23	2	2	2	11	5	4	2	

■ Rick Monday

1977	LA-N	.167	4	12	0	2	0	0	0	0	0	3	0	O
1978	LA-N	.154	5	13	2	2	1	0	0	0	4	3	0	O*4,D*1
1981	LA-N	.231	5	13	1	3	1	0	0	0	3	6	0	O*4
Total 3		.184	14	38	3	7	2	0	0	0	7	12	0	

Don Money

YEAR	TM/L	AVG	G	AB	R	H	2B	3B	HR	RBI	BB	SO	SB	POS
1982	Mil-A	.231	5	13	4	3	1	0	0	1	2	3	0	D*4

Bob Montgomery

YEAR	TM/L	AVG	G	AB	R	H	2B	3B	HR	RBI	BB	SO	SB	POS
1975	Bos-A	.000	1	1	0	0	0	0	0	0	0	0	0	H

Wally Moon

YEAR	TM/L	AVG	G	AB	R	H	2B	3B	HR	RBI	BB	SO	SB	POS
1959	LA-N	.261	6	23	3	6	0	0	1	2	2	2	1	O
1965	LA-N	.000	2	2	0	0	0	0	0	0	0	0	0	H
Total 2		.240	8	25	3	6	0	0	1	2	2	2	1	

Charlie Moore

YEAR	TM/L	AVG	G	AB	R	H	2B	3B	HR	RBI	BB	SO	SB	POS
1982	Mil-A	.346	7	26	3	9	3	0	0	2	1	0	0	O

Gene Moore

YEAR	TM/L	AVG	G	AB	R	H	2B	3B	HR	RBI	BB	SO	SB	POS
1944	StL-A	.182	6	22	4	4	0	0	0	3	6	0	0	O

Eddie Moore

YEAR	TM/L	AVG	G	AB	R	H	2B	3B	HR	RBI	BB	SO	SB	POS
1925	Pit-N	.231	7	26	7	6	1	0	1	2	5	2	0	2

Jimmy Moore

YEAR	TM/L	AVG	G	AB	R	H	2B	3B	HR	RBI	BB	SO	SB	POS
1930	Phi-A	.333	3	3	0	1	0	0	0	0	1	1	0	O*1
1931	Phi-A	.333	2	3	0	1	0	0	0	0	0	1	0	O*1
Total 2		.333	5	6	0	2	0	0	0	0	1	2	0	

Johnny Moore

YEAR	TM/L	AVG	G	AB	R	H	2B	3B	HR	RBI	BB	SO	SB	POS
1932	Chi-N	.000	2	7	1	0	0	0	0	0	2	1	0	O

Jo-Jo Moore

YEAR	TM/L	AVG	G	AB	R	H	2B	3B	HR	RBI	BB	SO	SB	POS
1933	NY-N	.227	5	22	1	5	0	0	0	1	1	3	0	O
1936	NY-N	.214	6	28	4	6	2	0	1	1	1	4	0	O
1937	NY-N	.391	5	23	1	9	1	0	0	1	0	1	0	O
Total 3		.274	16	73	6	20	4	0	1	3	2	8	0	

Terry Moore

YEAR	TM/L	AVG	G	AB	R	H	2B	3B	HR	RBI	BB	SO	SB	POS
1942	StL-N	.294	5	17	2	5	1	0	0	2	2	3	0	O
1946	StL-N	.148	7	27	1	4	0	0	0	2	2	6	0	O
Total 2		.205	12	44	3	9	1	0	0	4	4	9	0	

Herbie Moran

YEAR	TM/L	AVG	G	AB	R	H	2B	3B	HR	RBI	BB	SO	SB	POS
1914	Bos-N	.077	3	13	2	1	1	0	0	0	1	1	0	O

Pat Moran

YEAR	TM/L	AVG	G	AB	R	H	2B	3B	HR	RBI	BB	SO	SB	POS
1906	Chi-N	.000	2	2	0	0	0	0	0	0	0	0	0	H
1907	Chi-N	—	1	0	0	0	0	0	0	0	0	0	0	H
Total 2		.000	3	2	0	0	0	0	0	0	0	0	0	

Mickey Morandini

YEAR	TM/L	AVG	G	AB	R	H	2B	3B	HR	RBI	BB	SO	SB	POS
1993	Phi-N	.200	3	5	1	1	0	0	0	0	1	2	0	2*1

Keith Moreland

YEAR	TM/L	AVG	G	AB	R	H	2B	3B	HR	RBI	BB	SO	SB	POS
1980	Phi-N	.333	3	12	1	4	0	0	0	1	0	1	0	D

Omar Moreno

YEAR	TM/L	AVG	G	AB	R	H	2B	3B	HR	RBI	BB	SO	SB	POS
1979	Pit-N	.333	7	33	4	11	2	0	0	3	1	7	0	O

Joe Morgan

YEAR	TM/L	AVG	G	AB	R	H	2B	3B	HR	RBI	BB	SO	SB	POS
1972	Cin-N	.125	7	24	4	3	2	0	0	1	6	3	2	2
1975	Cin-N	.259	7	27	4	7	1	0	0	3	5	1	2	2
1976	Cin-N	.333	4	15	3	5	1	1	1	2	2	2	2	2
1983	Phi-N	.263	5	19	3	5	0	1	2	2	2	3	1	2
Total 4		.235	23	85	14	20	4	2	3	8	15	9	7	

Bobby Morgan

YEAR	TM/L	AVG	G	AB	R	H	2B	3B	HR	RBI	BB	SO	SB	POS
1952	Bro-N	.000	2	1	0	0	0	0	0	0	0	0	0	3
1953	Bro-N	.000	1	1	0	0	0	0	0	0	0	0	0	H
Total 2		.000	3	2	0	0	0	0	0	0	0	0	0	

George Moriarty

YEAR	TM/L	AVG	G	AB	R	H	2B	3B	HR	RBI	BB	SO	SB	POS
1909	Det-A	.273	7	22	4	6	1	0	0	1	3	1	0	3

John Morris

YEAR	TM/L	AVG	G	AB	R	H	2B	3B	HR	RBI	BB	SO	SB	POS
1987	StL-N	.000	1	2	0	0	0	0	0	0	0	0	0	O

Hal Morris

YEAR	TM/L	AVG	G	AB	R	H	2B	3B	HR	RBI	BB	SO	SB	POS
1990	Cin-N	.071	4	14	0	1	0	0	0	2	1	1	0	1*2,D*2

Wally Moses

YEAR	TM/L	AVG	G	AB	R	H	2B	3B	HR	RBI	BB	SO	SB	POS
1946	Bos-A	.417	4	12	1	5	0	0	0	0	1	2	0	O

Manny Mota

YEAR	TM/L	AVG	G	AB	R	H	2B	3B	HR	RBI	BB	SO	SB	POS
1977	LA-N	.000	3	3	0	0	0	0	0	0	0	1	0	H
1978	LA-N	—	1	0	0	0	0	0	0	0	0	1	0	H
Total 2		.000	4	3	0	0	0	0	0	0	0	1	1	0

Darryl Motley

YEAR	TM/L	AVG	G	AB	R	H	2B	3B	HR	RBI	BB	SO	SB	POS
1985	KC-A	.364	5	11	1	4	0	0	1	3	0	1	0	O*4

Curt Motton

YEAR	TM/L	AVG	G	AB	R	H	2B	3B	HR	RBI	BB	SO	SB	POS
1969	Bal-A	.000	1	1	0	0	0	0	0	0	0	0	0	H

Mike Mowrey

YEAR	TM/L	AVG	G	AB	R	H	2B	3B	HR	RBI	BB	SO	SB	POS
1916	Bro-N	.176	5	17	2	3	0	0	0	1	3	2	0	3

Don Mueller

YEAR	TM/L	AVG	G	AB	R	H	2B	3B	HR	RBI	BB	SO	SB	POS
1954	NY-N	.389	4	18	4	7	0	0	0	1	0	1	0	O

Jerry Mumphrey

YEAR	TM/L	AVG	G	AB	R	H	2B	3B	HR	RBI	BB	SO	SB	POS
1981	NY-A	.200	5	15	2	3	0	0	0	0	3	2	1	O

Thurman Munson

YEAR	TM/L	AVG	G	AB	R	H	2B	3B	HR	RBI	BB	SO	SB	POS
1976	NY-A	.529	4	17	2	9	0	0	0	2	0	1	0	C
1977	NY-A	.320	6	25	4	8	2	0	1	3	2	8	0	C
1978	NY-A	.320	6	25	5	8	3	0	0	7	3	7	1	C
Total 3		.373	16	67	11	25	5	0	1	12	5	16	1	

Bobby Murcer

YEAR	TM/L	AVG	G	AB	R	H	2B	3B	HR	RBI	BB	SO	SB	POS
1981	NY-A	.000	4	3	0	0	0	0	0	0	0	0	0	H

Danny Murphy

YEAR	TM/L	AVG	G	AB	R	H	2B	3B	HR	RBI	BB	SO	SB	POS
1905	Phi-A	.188	5	16	0	3	1	0	0	0	0	2	0	2
1910	Phi-A	.350	5	20	6	7	3	0	1	9	1	0	1	O
1911	Phi-A	.304	6	23	4	7	3	0	0	3	0	3	0	O
Total 3		.288	16	59	10	17	7	0	1	12	1	5	1	

Eddie Murphy

YEAR	TM/L	AVG	G	AB	R	H	2B	3B	HR	RBI	BB	SO	SB	POS
1913	Phi-A	.227	5	22	2	5	0	0	0	0	2	0	0	O
1914	Phi-A	.188	4	16	2	3	2	0	0	0	2	2	0	O
1919	Chi-A	.000	3	2	0	0	0	0	0	0	0	1	0	H
Total 3		.200	12	40	4	8	2	0	0	0	4	3	0	

Pat Murphy

YEAR	TM/L	AVG	G	AB	R	H	2B	3B	HR	RBI	BB	SO	SB	POS
1888	NY-N	.100	3	10	1	1	0	0	0	0	1	0	0	C

Yale Murphy

YEAR	TM/L	AVG	G	AB	R	H	2B	3B	HR	RBI	BB	SO	SB	POS
1894	NY-N	.000	1	1	0	0	0	0	0	0	0	0	0	

Eddie Murray

YEAR	TM/L	AVG	G	AB	R	H	2B	3B	HR	RBI	BB	SO	SB	POS
1979	Bal-A	.154	7	26	3	4	1	0	1	2	4	4	1	1
1983	Bal-A	.250	5	20	2	5	0	0	2	3	1	4	0	1
Total 2		.196	12	46	5	9	1	0	3	5	5	8	1	

Red Murray

YEAR	TM/L	AVG	G	AB	R	H	2B	3B	HR	RBI	BB	SO	SB	POS
1911	NY-N	.000	6	21	0	0	0	0	0	0	2	5	0	O
1912	NY-N	.323	8	31	5	10	4	1	0	5	2	2	0	O
1913	NY-N	.250	5	16	2	4	0	0	0	1	2	2	2	O
Total 3		.206	19	68	7	14	4	1	0	6	6	9	2	

Stan Musial

YEAR	TM/L	AVG	G	AB	R	H	2B	3B	HR	RBI	BB	SO	SB	POS
1942	StL-N	.222	5	18	2	4	1	0	0	2	4	0	0	O
1943	StL-N	.278	5	18	2	5	0	0	0	2	2	0	0	O
1944	StL-N	.304	6	23	2	7	2	0	1	2	2	0	0	O
1946	StL-N	.222	7	27	3	6	4	1	0	4	4	2	1	1
Total 4		.256	23	86	9	22	7	1	1	8	12	4	1	

Buddy Myer

YEAR	TM/L	AVG	G	AB	R	H	2B	3B	HR	RBI	BB	SO	SB	POS
1925	Was-A	.250	3	8	0	2	0	0	0	0	1	2	0	3
1933	Was-A	.300	5	20	2	6	1	0	0	2	2	3	0	2
Total 2		.286	8	28	2	8	1	0	0	2	3	5	0	

Hy Myers

YEAR	TM/L	AVG	G	AB	R	H	2B	3B	HR	RBI	BB	SO	SB	POS
1916	Bro-N	.182	5	22	2	4	0	0	1	3	0	3	0	O
1920	Bro-N	.231	7	26	0	6	0	0	0	1	0	1	0	O
Total 2		.208	12	48	2	10	0	0	1	4	0	4	0	

Billy Myers

YEAR	TM/L	AVG	G	AB	R	H	2B	3B	HR	RBI	BB	SO	SB	POS
1939	Cin-N	.333	4	12	2	4	0	1	0	0	2	3	0	S
1940	Cin-N	.130	7	23	0	3	0	0	0	2	2	5	0	S
Total 2		.200	11	35	2	7	0	1	0	2	4	8	0	

Hal Naragon

YEAR	TM/L	AVG	G	AB	R	H	2B	3B	HR	RBI	BB	SO	SB	POS
1954	Cle-A	—	1	0	0	0	0	0	0	0	0	0	0	C

Sam Narron

YEAR	TM/L	AVG	G	AB	R	H	2B	3B	HR	RBI	BB	SO	SB	POS
1943	StL-N	.000	1	1	0	0	0	0	0	0	0	0	0	H

Billy Nash

YEAR	TM/L	AVG	G	AB	R	H	2B	3B	HR	RBI	BB	SO	SB	POS
1892	Bos-N	.167	6	24	3	4	0	0	0	4	2	3	2	3

Charlie Neal

YEAR	TM/L	AVG	G	AB	R	H	2B	3B	HR	RBI	BB	SO	SB	POS
1956	Bro-N	.000	1	4	0	0	0	0	0	0	0	1	0	2
1959	LA-N	.370	6	27	4	10	2	0	2	6	0	1	1	2
Total 2		.323	7	31	4	10	2	0	2	6	0	2	1	

Greasy Neale

YEAR	TM/L	AVG	G	AB	R	H	2B	3B	HR	RBI	BB	SO	SB	POS
1919	Cin-N	.357	8	28	3	10	1	1	0	4	2	5	1	O

Tom Needham

YEAR	TM/L	AVG	G	AB	R	H	2B	3B	HR	RBI	BB	SO	SB	POS
1910	Chi-N	.000	1	1	0	0	0	0	0	0	0	0	0	H

Bernie Neis

YEAR	TM/L	AVG	G	AB	R	H	2B	3B	HR	RBI	BB	SO	SB	POS
1920	Bro-N	.000	4	5	0	0	0	0	0	0	1	0	0	O*2

Rocky Nelson

YEAR	TM/L	AVG	G	AB	R	H	2B	3B	HR	RBI	BB	SO	SB	POS
1952	Bro-N	.000	4	3	0	0	0	0	0	0	1	2	0	H
1960	Pit-N	.333	4	9	2	3	0	0	1	2	1	1	0	1*3
Total 2		.250	8	12	2	3	0	0	1	2	2	3	0	

Candy Nelson

YEAR	TM/L	AVG	G	AB	R	H	2B	3B	HR	RBI	BB	SO	SB	POS
1884	NY-A	.100	3	10	0	1	0	0	0	0	0	1	0	S

Graig Nettles

YEAR	TM/L	AVG	G	AB	R	H	2B	3B	HR	RBI	BB	SO	SB	POS
1976	NY-A	.250	4	12	0	3	0	0	0	2	3	1	0	3
1977	NY-A	.190	6	21	1	4	1	0	0	2	2	6	0	3
1978	NY-A	.160	6	25	2	4	0	0	0	1	0	6	0	3
1981	NY-A	.400	3	10	1	4	1	0	0	0	1	1	0	3
1984	SD-N	.250	5	12	2	3	0	0	0	2	5	0	0	3
Total 5		.225	24	80	6	18	2	0	0	7	11	11	0	

Al Newman

YEAR	TM/L	AVG	G	AB	R	H	2B	3B	HR	RBI	BB	SO	SB	POS
1987	Min-A	.200	4	5	0	1	0	0	0	0	1	1	0	2*3
1991	Min-A	.500	4	2	0	1	0	1	0	1	0	0	0	3*2,2*1,S*1
Total 2		.286	8	7	0	2	0	1	0	1	1	1	0	

Gus Niarhos

YEAR	TM/L	AVG	G	AB	R	H	2B	3B	HR	RBI	BB	SO	SB	POS
1949	NY-A	—	1	0	0	0	0	0	0	0	0	0	0	C

Bill Nicholson

YEAR	TM/L	AVG	G	AB	R	H	2B	3B	HR	RBI	BB	SO	SB	POS
1945	Chi-N	.214	7	28	1	6	1	1	0	8	2	5	0	O

YEAR	TM/L	AVG	G	AB	R	H	2B	3B	HR	RBI	BB	SO	SB	POS
Hugh Nicol														
1885	StL-A	.000	1	2	0	0	0	0	0	0	0	0	0	O
Steve Nicosia														
1979	Pit-N	.063	4	16	1	1	0	0	0	0	0	2	0	C
Bert Niehoff														
1915	Phi-N	.063	5	16	1	1	0	0	0	0	1	5	0	2
Bob Nieman														
1962	SF-N	—	1	0	0	0	0	0	0	0	0	1	0	0 H
Tom Nieto														
1985	StL-N	.000	2	5	0	0	0	0	0	1	1	2	0	C
Otis Nixon														
1992	Atl-N	.296	6	27	3	8	1	0	0	1	1	3	5	O
Donell Nixon														
1989	SF-N	.200	2	5	1	1	0	0	0	0	1	1	0	O
Ray Noble														
1951	NY-N	.000	2	2	0	0	0	0	0	0	0	1	0	C
Joe Nolan														
1983	Bal-A	.000	2	2	0	0	0	0	0	0	1	0	0	C
Irv Noren														
1952	NY-A	.300	4	10	0	3	0	0	0	1	1	3	0	O*3
1953	NY-A	.000	2	1	0	0	0	0	0	0	0	1	0	0 H
1955	NY-A	.063	5	16	0	1	0	0	0	1	1	1	0	O
Total 3		.148	11	27	0	4	0	0	0	2	3	4	0	
Billy North														
1974	Oak-A	.059	5	17	3	1	0	0	0	0	2	5	1	O
1978	LA-N	.125	4	8	2	1	1	0	0	2	1	0	1	O
Total 2		.080	9	25	5	2	1	0	0	2	3	5	2	
Jim Northrup														
1968	Det-A	.250	7	28	4	7	0	1	2	8	1	5	0	O
Joe Nossek														
1965	Min-A	.200	6	20	0	4	0	0	0	0	0	1	0	O*5
Les Nunamaker														
1920	Cle-A	.500	2	2	0	1	0	0	0	0	0	0	0	C*1
Tom O'Brien														
1897	Bal-N	.400	1	5	2	2	1	0	0	0	0	0	0	O
1900	Pit-N	.125	4	16	1	2	1	0	0	2	0	1	0	1
Total 2		.190	5	21	3	4	2	0	0	2	0	1	0	
Darby O'Brien														
1889	Bro-A	.161	8	31	8	5	0	1	0	4	12	6	6	O
1890	Bro-N	.125	6	24	3	3	0	1	0	3	1	5	3	O
Total 2		.145	15	55	11	8	0	2	0	7	13	11	9	
Jack O'Connor														
1892	Cle-N	.136	6	22	1	3	0	0	0	0	2	3	0	O
1896	Cle-N	.286	4	14	1	4	0	0	0	1	1	2	0	1
1900	Pit-N	.250	2	4	0	1	0	0	0	1	0	0	0	C
Total 3		.200	12	40	2	8	0	0	0	2	3	5	0	
Tip O'Neill														
1885	StL-A	.208	7	24	4	5	0	0	0	0	0	0	0	O
1886	StL-A	.400	6	20	4	8	0	2	2	5	4	5	2	O
1887	StL-A	.200	15	65	7	13	2	1	1	9	0	2	0	O
1888	StL-A	.243	10	37	8	9	1	0	2	11	6	3	0	O
Total 4		.240	38	146	23	35	3	3	5	25	10	10	2	
Jim O'Rourke														
1888	NY-N	.222	10	36	4	8	0	0	0	1	4	2	3	O*7,1*2,S*1
1889	NY-N	.389	9	36	7	14	2	2	2	7	2	2	3	O
Total 2		.306	19	72	11	22	2	2	2	8	6	4	6	
Johnny Oates														
1977	LA-N	.000	1	1	0	0	0	0	0	0	0	0	0	C
1978	LA-N	1.000	1	1	0	1	0	0	0	0	1	0	0	C
Total 2		.500	2	2	0	1	0	0	0	0	1	0	0	
Ken Oberkfell														
1982	StL-N	.292	7	24	4	7	1	0	0	1	2	1	2	3
1989	SF-N	.333	4	6	1	2	0	0	0	0	3	0	0	3
Total 2		.300	11	30	5	9	1	0	0	1	5	1	2	
Jack O'Brien														
1903	Bos-A	.000	2	2	0	0	0	0	0	0	0	1	0	H
Jimmy O'Connell														
1923	NY-N	.000	2	1	0	0	0	0	0	0	0	1	0	H
Paddy O'Connor														
1909	Pit-N	.000	1	1	0	0	0	0	0	0	1	0	0	H
Ken O'Dea														
1935	Chi-N	1.000	1	1	0	1	0	0	0	1	0	0	0	H
1938	Chi-N	.200	3	5	1	1	0	0	1	2	1	0	0	C*1
1942	StL-N	1.000	1	1	0	1	0	0	0	1	0	0	0	H
1943	StL-N	.667	2	3	0	2	0	0	0	3	0	0	0	C*1
1944	StL-N	.333	3	3	0	1	0	0	0	2	0	0	0	H
Total 5		.462	10	13	1	6	0	0	1	6	1	0	0	
Lefty O'Doul														
1933	NY-N	1.000	1	1	1	1	0	0	0	2	0	0	0	H

YEAR	TM/L	AVG	G	AB	R	H	2B	3B	HR	RBI	BB	SO	SB	POS
Ron Oester														
1990	Cin-N	1.000	1	1	0	1	0	0	0	0	1	0	0	H
Bob O'Farrell														
1918	Chi-N	.000	3	3	0	0	0	0	0	0	0	0	0	C*1
1926	StL-N	.304	7	23	2	7	1	0	0	2	2	2	0	C
Total 2		.269	10	26	2	7	1	0	0	2	2	2	0	
Ben Oglivie														
1982	Mil-A	.222	7	27	4	6	0	1	1	1	2	4	0	O
Bob Oldis														
1960	Pit-N	—	2	0	0	0	0	0	0	0	0	0	0	C
Rube Oldring														
1911	Phi-A	.200	6	25	2	5	2	0	1	3	0	5	0	O
1913	Phi-A	.273	5	22	5	6	0	1	0	0	0	1	0	O
1914	Phi-A	.067	4	15	0	1	0	0	0	0	0	5	0	O
Total 3		.194	15	62	7	12	2	1	1	3	0	11	1	
Charley O'Leary														
1907	Det-A	.059	5	17	0	1	0	0	0	0	1	3	0	S
1908	Det-A	.158	5	19	2	3	0	0	0	0	0	3	0	S
1909	Det-A	.000	1	3	0	0	0	0	0	0	0	0	0	3
Total 3		.103	11	39	2	4	0	0	0	0	1	6	0	
John Olerud														
1992	Tor-A	.308	4	13	2	4	0	0	0	0	0	4	0	1
1993	Tor-A	.235	5	17	5	4	1	0	1	2	4	1	0	1
Total 2		.267	9	30	7	8	1	0	1	2	4	5	0	
Tony Oliva														
1965	Min-A	.192	7	26	2	5	1	0	1	2	1	6	0	O
Al Oliver														
1971	Pit-N	.211	5	19	1	4	2	0	0	2	2	5	0	O*4
Joe Oliver														
1990	Cin-N	.333	4	18	2	6	3	0	0	2	0	1	0	C
Nate Oliver														
1966	LA-N	—	1	0	0	0	0	0	0	0	0	0	0	R
Luis Olmo														
1949	Bro-N	.273	4	11	2	3	0	0	1	2	0	2	0	O
Greg Olson														
1991	Atl-N	.222	7	27	3	6	2	0	0	1	5	4	1	C
Ivy Olson														
1916	Bro-N	.250	5	16	1	4	0	1	0	2	2	2	0	S
1920	Bro-N	.320	7	25	2	8	1	0	0	3	1	3	0	S
Total 2		.293	12	41	3	12	1	1	0	2	5	3	0	
Ollie O'Mara														
1916	Bro-N	.000	1	1	0	0	0	0	0	0	0	1	0	H
Paul O'Neill														
1990	Cin-N	.083	4	12	2	1	0	0	0	1	5	2	1	O
Steve O'Neill														
1920	Cle-A	.333	7	21	1	7	3	0	0	2	4	3	0	C
Bill O'Neill														
1906	Chi-A	.000	1	1	1	0	0	0	0	0	0	0	0	O
Jose Oquendo														
1987	StL-N	.250	7	24	2	6	0	0	0	2	1	4	0	3*4,O*3
Dave Orr														
1884	NY-A	.111	3	9	0	1	0	0	0	0	0	0	1	1
Ernie Orsatti														
1928	StL-N	.286	4	7	1	2	1	0	0	0	1	3	0	O*1
1930	StL-N	.000	1	1	0	0	0	0	0	0	0	0	0	H
1931	StL-N		1	3	0	0	0	0	0	0	0	3	0	0	O
1934	StL-N	.318	7	22	3	7	0	1	0	2	3	1	0	O
Total 4		.273	13	33	4	9	1	1	0	2	4	7	0	
John Orsino														
1962	SF-N	.000	1	1	0	0	0	0	0	0	0	0	0	C
Jorge Orta														
1985	KC-A	.333	3	3	0	1	0	0	0	0	0	1	0	H
Junior Ortiz														
1991	Min-A	.200	3	5	0	1	0	0	0	1	0	1	0	C
Amos Otis														
1980	KC-A	.478	6	23	4	11	2	0	3	7	3	3	0	O
Mel Ott														
1933	NY-N	.389	5	18	3	7	0	0	2	4	4	4	0	O
1936	NY-N	.304	6	23	4	7	2	0	1	3	3	1	0	O
1937	NY-N	.200	5	20	1	4	0	0	1	3	3	4	0	3
Total 3		.295	16	61	8	18	2	0	4	10	8	9	0	
Ed Ott														
1979	Pit-N	.333	3	12	2	4	1	0	0	3	0	2	0	C
Jimmy Outlaw														
1945	Det-A	.179	7	28	1	5	0	0	0	0	3	2	1	3
Mickey Owen														
1941	Bro-N	.167	5	12	1	2	0	1	0	2	3	0	0	C

YEAR	TM/L	AVG	G	AB	R	H	2B	3B	HR	RBI	BB	SO	SB	POS
■ Marv Owen														
1934	Det-A	.069	7	29	0	2	0	0	0	0	1	0	5	1 3
1935	Det-A	.050	6	20	2	1	0	0	0	1	2	3	0	1*4,3*2
Total 2		.061	13	49	2	3	0	0	0	2	2	8	1	
■ Spike Owen														
1986	Bos-A	.300	7	20	2	6	0	0	0	2	5	6	0	S
■ Ray Oyler														
1968	Det-A	—	4	0	0	0	0	0	0	0	0	0	0	S
■ Tom Paciorek														
1974	LA-N	.500	3	2	1	1	1	0	0	0	0	0	0	H
■ Andy Pafko														
1945	Chi-N	.214	7	28	5	6	2	1	0	2	2	5	1	O
1952	Bro-N	.190	7	21	0	4	0	0	0	2	0	4	0	O*5
1957	Mil-N	.214	6	14	1	3	0	0	0	0	0	1	0	O*5
1958	Mil-N	.333	4	9	0	3	1	0	0	1	0	0	0	O
Total 4		.222	24	72	6	16	3	1	0	5	2	10	1	
■ Jose Pagan														
1962	SF-N	.368	7	19	2	7	0	0	1	2	0	1	0	S
1971	Pit-N	.267	4	15	0	4	2	0	0	2	0	1	0	3
Total 2		.324	11	34	2	11	2	0	1	4	0	2	0	
■ Mike Pagliarulo														
1991	Min-A	.273	6	11	1	3	0	0	1	2	1	2	0	3
■ Tom Pagnozzi														
1987	StL-N	.250	2	4	0	1	0	0	0	0	0	0	0	D*1
■ Freddy Parent														
1903	Bos-A	.281	8	32	8	9	0	3	0	4	1	1	0	S
■ Dave Parker														
1979	Pit-N	.345	7	29	2	10	3	0	0	4	2	7	0	O
1988	Oak-A	.200	4	15	0	3	0	0	0	2	4	0		O*2,D*2
1989	Oak-A	.222	3	9	2	2	1	0	1	0	2	0		D*2
Total 3		.283	14	53	4	15	4	0	1	6	4	13	0	
■ Wes Parker														
1965	LA-N	.304	7	23	3	7	0	1	1	2	3	3	2	1
1966	LA-N	.231	4	13	0	3	2	0	0	0	1	3	0	1
Total 2		.278	11	36	3	10	2	1	1	2	4	6	2	
■ Lance Parrish														
1984	Det-A	.278	5	18	3	5	1	0	1	2	3	2	1	C
■ Roy Partee														
1946	Bos-A	.100	5	10	1	1	0	0	0	1	1	2	0	C
■ Ben Paschal														
1926	NY-A	.250	5	4	0	1	0	0	0	1	1	2	0	H
1928	NY-A	.200	3	10	0	2	0	0	0	1	1	0	0	O
Total 2		.214	8	14	0	3	0	0	0	2	2	2	0	
■ Dode Paskert														
1915	Phi-N	.158	5	19	2	3	0	0	0	0	1	2	0	O
1918	Chi-N	.190	6	21	0	4	1	0	0	2	2	2	0	O
Total 2		.175	11	40	2	7	1	0	0	2	3	4	0	
■ Fred Payne														
1907	Det-A	.250	2	4	0	1	0	0	0	1	0	0	1	C*1
■ Hal Peck														
1948	Cle-A	—	1	0	0	0	0	0	0	0	0	0	0	
■ Roger Peckinpaugh														
1921	NY-A	.179	8	28	2	5	1	0	0	0	4	3	0	S
1924	Was-A	.417	4	12	1	5	2	0	0	2	1	0	1	S
1925	Was-A	.250	7	24	1	6	1	0	1	3	1	2	1	S
Total 3		.250	19	64	4	16	4	0	1	5	6	5	2	
■ Homer Peel														
1933	NY-N	.500	2	2	0	1	0	0	0	0	0	0	0	O*1
■ Tony Pena														
1987	StL-N	.409	7	22	2	9	1	0	0	4	3	2	1	C*6,D*1
■ Terry Pendleton														
1985	StL-N	.261	7	23	3	6	1	1	0	3	3	2	0	3
1987	StL-N	.429	3	7	2	3	0	0	0	1	1	2		D*2
1991	Atl-N	.367	7	30	6	11	3	0	2	3	3	1	0	3
1992	Atl-N	.240	6	25	2	6	2	0	0	2	1	5	0	3
Total 4		.306	23	85	13	26	6	1	2	9	8	9	2	
■ Joe Pepitone														
1963	NY-A	.154	4	13	0	2	0	0	0	0	1	3	0	1
1964	NY-A	.154	7	26	1	4	1	0	1	5	2	3	0	1
Total 2		.154	11	39	1	6	1	0	1	5	3	6	0	
■ Tony Perez														
1970	Cin-N	.056	5	18	2	1	0	0	0		3	4	0	3
1972	Cin-N	.435	7	23	3	10	2	0	0	2	4	4	0	1
1975	Cin-N	.179	7	28	4	5	0	0	3	7	3	9	1	1
1976	Cin-N	.313	4	16	1	5	1	0	0	2	1	2	0	1
1983	Phi-N	.200	4	10	0	2	0	0	0	0	0	2	0	1*2
Total 5		.242	27	95	10	23	3	0	3	11	11	21	1	
■ Johnny Pesky														
1946	Bos-A	.233	7	30	2	7	0	0	0	0	1	3	1	S
■ Rico Petrocelli														
1967	Bos-A	.200	7	20	3	4	1	0	2	3	3	8	0	S

YEAR	TM/L	AVG	G	AB	R	H	2B	3B	HR	RBI	BB	SO	SB	POS
1975	Bos-A	.308	7	26	3	8	1	0	0	4	3	6	0	3
Total 2		.261	14	46	6	12	2	0	2	7	6	14	0	
■ Fred Pfeffer														
1885	Chi-N	.407	7	27	5	11	2	0	1	0	0	0	0	2
1886	Chi-N	.286	6	21	7	6	0	0	1	4	2	1	2	
Total 2		.354	13	48	12	17	2	0	2	4	2	1	2	
■ Ed Phelps														
1903	Pit-N	.231	8	26	1	6	2	0	0	1	1	6	0	C*7
■ Ken Phelps														
1989	Oak-A	.000	1	1	0	0	0	0	0	0	0	0	0	H
■ Dave Philley														
1954	Cle-A	.125	4	8	0	1	0	0	0	0	0	1	3	O*2
■ Jack Phillips														
1947	NY-A	.000	2	2	0	0	0	0	0	0	0	0	0	1*1
■ Bubba Phillips														
1959	Chi-A	.300	3	10	0	3	1	0	0	0	0	0	0	3*3,O*1
■ Tony Phillips														
1988	Oak-A	.250	2	4	1	1	0	0	0	0	1	2	0	2*1,O*1
1989	Oak-A	.235	4	17	2	4	1	0	1	3	0	3	0	2*4,3*2,O*1
Total 2		.238	6	21	3	5	1	0	1	3	1	5	0	
■ Charlie Pick														
1918	Chi-N	.389	6	18	2	7	1	0	0	0	1	1	2	
■ Joe Pignatano														
1959	LA-N	—	1	0	0	0	0	0	0	0	0	0	0	C
■ Lou Piniella														
1976	NY-A	.333	4	9	1	3	1	0	0	0	0	0	0	O*2,D*2
1977	NY-A	.273	6	22	1	6	0	0	0	3	0	3	0	O
1978	NY-A	.280	6	25	3	7	0	0	0	4	0	1	0	O
1981	NY-A	.438	6	16	2	7	1	0	0	3	0	1	1	O*3
Total 4		.319	22	72	7	23	2	0	0	10	0	4	2	
■ George Pinkney														
1889	Bro-A	.258	9	31	2	8	2	0	0	3	4	2	3	
1890	Bro-N	.357	4	14	4	5	0	0	0	3	2	1	3	
Total 2		.289	13	45	6	13	2	2	0	6	6	3	3	
■ Vada Pinson														
1961	Cin-N	.091	5	22	0	2	1	0	0	0	0	1	0	O
■ Wally Pipp														
1921	NY-A	.154	8	26	1	4	1	0	0	2	2	3	1	1
1922	NY-A	.286	5	21	0	6	1	0	0	3	0	2	1	1
1923	NY-A	.250	6	20	2	5	0	0	0	2	4	1	0	1
Total 3		.224	19	67	3	15	2	0	0	7	6	6	2	
■ Luis Polonia														
1988	Oak-A	.111	3	9	1	1	0	0	0	0	0	2	0	O*2
■ Dave Pope														
1954	Cle-A	.000	3	3	0	0	0	0	0	0	1	1	0	O*2
■ Darrell Porter														
1980	KC-A	.143	5	14	1	2	0	0	0		3	4	0	C*4
1982	StL-N	.286	7	28	1	8	2	0	1	5	1	4	0	C
1985	StL-N	.133	5	15	0	2	0	0	0	0	2	5	0	C
Total 3		.211	17	57	2	12	2	0	1	5	6	13	0	
■ Wally Post														
1961	Cin-N	.333	5	18	3	6	1	0	2	1	2	0	1	O
■ Jake Powell														
1936	NY-A	.455	6	22	8	10	1	0	1	5	4	4	1	O
1937	NY-A	.000	1	1	0	0	0	0	0	0	0	1	0	H
1938	NY-A	—	1	0	0	0	0	0	0	0	0	0	0	O
Total 3		.435	8	23	8	10	1	0	1	5	4	5	1	
■ Boog Powell														
1966	Bal-A	.357	4	14	1	5	1	0	0	1	0	1	0	1
1969	Bal-A	.263	5	19	0	5	0	0	0	0	4	0	1	1
1970	Bal-A	.294	5	17	6	5	1	0	2	5	5	2	0	1
1971	Bal-A	.111	7	27	1	3	0	0	0	1	1	3	0	1
Total 4		.234	21	77	8	18	2	0	2	7	7	10	0	
■ Mike Powers														
1905	Phi-A	.143	3	7	0	1	1	0	0	0	0	0	0	C
■ Jim Price														
1968	Det-A	.000	2	2	0	0	0	0	0	0	0	1	0	H
■ Jerry Priddy														
1942	NY-A	.100	3	10	0	1	1	0	0	1	1	0	0	1*3,3*1
■ Greg Pryor														
1985	KC-A	—	1	0	0	0	0	0	0	0	0	0	0	3
■ George Puccinelli														
1930	StL-N	.000	1	1	0	0	0	0	0	0	0	0	0	H
■ Kirby Puckett														
1987	Min-A	.357	7	28	5	10	1	0	3	2	1	1	0	O
1991	Min-A	.250	7	24	4	6	0	1	2	4	5	7	1	O
Total 2		.308	14	52	9	16	1	2	2	7	7	8	2	
■ Frank Quilici														
1965	Min-A	.200	7	20	2	4	2	0	0	1	4	3	0	2

Joe Quinn

YEAR	TM/L	AVG	G	AB	R	H	2B	3B	HR	RBI	BB	SO	SB	POS
1892	Bos-N	.286	6	21	2	6	1	1	0	4	1	2	0	2
1896	Bal-N	.000	1	3	1	0	0	0	0	0	0	0	0	3
Total 2		.250	7	24	3	6	1	1	0	4	1	2	0	

Jamie Quirk

YEAR	TM/L	AVG	G	AB	R	H	2B	3B	HR	RBI	BB	SO	SB	POS
1990	Oak-A	.000	1	3	0	0	0	0	0	0	0	2	0	C

Marv Rackley

YEAR	TM/L	AVG	G	AB	R	H	2B	3B	HR	RBI	BB	SO	SB	POS
1949	Bro-N	.000	2	5	0	0	0	0	0	0	0	2	0	O

Paul Radford

YEAR	TM/L	AVG	G	AB	R	H	2B	3B	HR	RBI	BB	SO	SB	POS
1884	Pro-N	.000	3	7	1	0	0	0	0	0	1	0	1	0 O

Mike Ramsey

YEAR	TM/L	AVG	G	AB	R	H	2B	3B	HR	RBI	BB	SO	SB	POS
1982	StL-N	.000	3	1	1	0	0	0	0	0	0	1	0	3*2

Willie Randolph

YEAR	TM/L	AVG	G	AB	R	H	2B	3B	HR	RBI	BB	SO	SB	POS
1976	NY-A	.071	4	14	1	1	0	0	0	0	1	3	0	2
1977	NY-A	.160	6	25	5	4	2	0	1	1	2	2	0	2
1981	NY-A	.222	6	18	5	4	1	1	2	3	9	0	1	2
1990	Oak-A	.267	4	15	0	4	0	0	0	1	0	1	0	2
Total 4		.181	20	72	11	13	3	1	3	4	13	5	2	

Bill Rariden

YEAR	TM/L	AVG	G	AB	R	H	2B	3B	HR	RBI	BB	SO	SB	POS
1917	NY-N	.385	5	13	2	5	0	0	0	2	2	1	0	C
1919	Cin-N	.211	5	19	0	4	0	0	0	2	0	0	1	C
Total 2		.281	10	32	2	9	0	0	0	4	2	1	1	

Morrie Rath

YEAR	TM/L	AVG	G	AB	R	H	2B	3B	HR	RBI	BB	SO	SB	POS
1919	Cin-N	.226	8	31	5	7	1	0	0	2	4	1	2	

Johnny Rawlings

YEAR	TM/L	AVG	G	AB	R	H	2B	3B	HR	RBI	BB	SO	SB	POS
1921	NY-N	.333	8	30	2	10	3	0	0	4	0	3	0	2

Harry Raymond

YEAR	TM/L	AVG	G	AB	R	H	2B	3B	HR	RBI	BB	SO	SB	POS
1890	Lou-A	.148	7	27	5	4	1	1	0	1	2	5	1	S*5,S*3

Jack Reed

YEAR	TM/L	AVG	G	AB	R	H	2B	3B	HR	RBI	BB	SO	SB	POS
1961	NY-A	—	3	0	0	0	0	0	0	0	0	0	0	O

Pee Wee Reese

YEAR	TM/L	AVG	G	AB	R	H	2B	3B	HR	RBI	BB	SO	SB	POS
1941	Bro-N	.200	5	20	1	4	0	0	0	2	0	0	0	S
1947	Bro-N	.304	7	23	5	7	1	0	0	4	6	3	3	S
1949	Bro-N	.316	5	19	2	6	1	0	1	2	1	0	1	S
1952	Bro-N	.345	7	29	4	10	0	0	1	4	2	2	1	S
1953	Bro-N	.208	6	24	0	5	0	1	0	4	4	1	0	S
1955	Bro-N	.296	7	27	5	8	1	0	0	2	3	5	0	S
1956	Bro-N	.222	7	27	3	6	0	1	0	2	2	6	0	S
Total 7		.272	44	169	20	46	3	2	2	16	18	17	5	

Rudy Regalado

YEAR	TM/L	AVG	G	AB	R	H	2B	3B	HR	RBI	BB	SO	SB	POS
1954	Cle-A	.333	4	3	0	1	0	0	0	1	0	0	0	3*1

Charlie Reipschlager

YEAR	TM/L	AVG	G	AB	R	H	2B	3B	HR	RBI	BB	SO	SB	POS
1884	NY-A	.000	2	5	1	0	0	0	0	0	0	1	0	C

Pete Reiser

YEAR	TM/L	AVG	G	AB	R	H	2B	3B	HR	RBI	BB	SO	SB	POS
1941	Bro-N	.200	5	20	1	4	1	1	1	3	1	6	0	O
1947	Bro-N	.250	5	8	1	2	0	0	0	3	1	0		O*3
Total 2		.214	10	28	2	6	1	1	1	3	4	7	0	

Heinie Reitz

YEAR	TM/L	AVG	G	AB	R	H	2B	3B	HR	RBI	BB	SO	SB	POS
1894	Bal-N	.333	4	15	1	5	0	0	0	4	1	3	1	2
1896	Bal-N	.133	4	15	1	2	0	0	0	2	1	0	0	2
1897	Bal-N	.250	5	20	4	5	1	0	1	4	2	0	0	2
Total 3		.240	13	50	6	12	1	0	1	10	4	3	1	

Rip Repulski

YEAR	TM/L	AVG	G	AB	R	H	2B	3B	HR	RBI	BB	SO	SB	POS
1959	LA-N	—	1	0	0	0	0	0	0	0	0	1	0	O

Merv Rettenmund

YEAR	TM/L	AVG	G	AB	R	H	2B	3B	HR	RBI	BB	SO	SB	POS
1969	Bal-A	—	1	0	0	0	0	0	0	0	0	0	0	R
1970	Bal-A	.400	2	5	2	2	0	0	1	2	1	0	0	O*1
1971	Bal-A	.185	7	27	3	5	0	0	1	4	0	4	0	O*6
1975	Cin-N	.000	3	0	0	0	0	0	0	0	0	1	0	H
Total 4		.200	13	35	5	7	0	0	2	6	1	5	0	

Carl Reynolds

YEAR	TM/L	AVG	G	AB	R	H	2B	3B	HR	RBI	BB	SO	SB	POS
1938	Chi-A	.000	4	12	0	0	0	0	0	0	1	3	0	O*3

Dusty Rhodes

YEAR	TM/L	AVG	G	AB	R	H	2B	3B	HR	RBI	BB	SO	SB	POS
1954	NY-N	.667	3	6	2	4	0	0	2	7	1	2	0	O*2

Hal Rhyne

YEAR	TM/L	AVG	G	AB	R	H	2B	3B	HR	RBI	BB	SO	SB	POS
1927	Pit-N	.000	1	4	0	0	0	0	0	0	0	0		2

Del Rice

YEAR	TM/L	AVG	G	AB	R	H	2B	3B	HR	RBI	BB	SO	SB	POS
1946	StL-N	.500	3	6	2	3	1	0	0	0	2	0	0	C
1957	Mil-N	.167	2	6	0	1	0	0	0	0	1	2	0	C
Total 2		.333	5	12	2	4	1	0	0	0	3	2	0	

Sam Rice

YEAR	TM/L	AVG	G	AB	R	H	2B	3B	HR	RBI	BB	SO	SB	POS
1924	Was-A	.207	7	29	2	6	0	0	0	1	3	2	0	O
1925	Was-A	.364	7	33	5	12	0	0	0	3	0	1	0	O
1933	Was-A	1.000	1	1	0	1	0	0	0	0	0	0	0	H
Total 3		.302	15	63	7	19	0	0	0	4	3	3	2	

Jim Rice

YEAR	TM/L	AVG	G	AB	R	H	2B	3B	HR	RBI	BB	SO	SB	POS
1986	Bos-A	.333	7	27	6	9	1	1	0	6	9	0	0	

Paul Richards

YEAR	TM/L	AVG	G	AB	R	H	2B	3B	HR	RBI	BB	SO	SB	POS
1945	Det-A	.211	7	19	0	4	2	0	0	6	4	3	0	C

Hardy Richardson

YEAR	TM/L	AVG	G	AB	R	H	2B	3B	HR	RBI	BB	SO	SB	POS
1887	Det-N	.197	15	66	12	13	5	2	1	4	1	9	7	O*10,2*5,3*1

Danny Richardson

YEAR	TM/L	AVG	G	AB	R	H	2B	3B	HR	RBI	BB	SO	SB	POS
1888	NY-N	.167	9	36	6	6	2	0	0	6	3	5	3	2
1889	NY-N	.314	9	35	8	11	1	1	3	8	3	5	3	2
Total 2		.239	18	71	14	17	3	1	3	14	6	10	6	

Bobby Richardson

YEAR	TM/L	AVG	G	AB	R	H	2B	3B	HR	RBI	BB	SO	SB	POS
1957	NY-A	—	2	0	0	0	0	0	0	0	0	0	0	2*1
1958	NY-A	.000	4	5	0	0	0	0	0	0	0	0	0	3
1960	NY-A	.367	7	30	8	11	2	2	1	12	1	1	0	2
1961	NY-A	.391	5	23	2	9	1	0	0	0	0	1	2	2
1962	NY-A	.148	7	27	3	4	0	0	0	0	3	1	0	2
1963	NY-A	.214	4	14	0	3	1	0	0	1	0	3	0	2
1964	NY-A	.406	7	32	3	13	2	0	0	3	0	2	1	2
Total 7		.305	36	131	16	40	6	2	1	15	5	7	2	

Marv Rickert

YEAR	TM/L	AVG	G	AB	R	H	2B	3B	HR	RBI	BB	SO	SB	POS
1948	Bos-N	.211	5	19	2	4	0	0	1	2	0	4	0	O

Dave Ricketts

YEAR	TM/L	AVG	G	AB	R	H	2B	3B	HR	RBI	BB	SO	SB	POS
1967	StL-N	.000	3	3	0	0	0	0	0	0	0	0	0	H
1968	StL-N	1.000	1	1	0	1	0	0	0	0	0	0	0	H
Total 2		.250	4	4	0	1	0	0	0	0	0	0	0	

Lew Riggs

YEAR	TM/L	AVG	G	AB	R	H	2B	3B	HR	RBI	BB	SO	SB	POS
1940	Cin-N	.000	3	3	1	0	0	0	0	0	0	2	0	H
1941	Bro-N	.250	3	8	0	2	0	0	0	1	1	1	0	3*2
Total 2		.182	6	11	1	2	0	0	0	1	1	3	0	

Bill Rigney

YEAR	TM/L	AVG	G	AB	R	H	2B	3B	HR	RBI	BB	SO	SB	POS
1951	NY-N	.250	4	4	0	1	0	0	0	1	0	1	0	H

Ernest Riles

YEAR	TM/L	AVG	G	AB	R	H	2B	3B	HR	RBI	BB	SO	SB	POS
1989	SF-N	.000	3	8	0	0	0	0	0	0	0	1	0	D*2

Cal Ripken

YEAR	TM/L	AVG	G	AB	R	H	2B	3B	HR	RBI	BB	SO	SB	POS
1983	Bal-A	.167	5	18	2	3	0	0	0	1	3	4	0	S

Jimmy Ripple

YEAR	TM/L	AVG	G	AB	R	H	2B	3B	HR	RBI	BB	SO	SB	POS
1936	NY-N	.333	5	12	2	4	0	0	1	3	3	3	0	O
1937	NY-N	.294	5	17	2	5	0	0	0	3	1	0	0	O
1940	Cin-N	.333	7	21	3	7	2	0	1	6	4	2	0	O
Total 3		.320	17	50	7	16	2	0	2	9	10	6	0	

Swede Risberg

YEAR	TM/L	AVG	G	AB	R	H	2B	3B	HR	RBI	BB	SO	SB	POS
1917	Chi-A	.500	2	2	0	1	0	0	0	1	0	0	0	H
1919	Chi-A	.080	8	25	3	2	0	1	0	0	5	3	1	S
Total 2		.111	10	27	3	3	0	1	0	1	5	3	1	

Claude Ritchey

YEAR	TM/L	AVG	G	AB	R	H	2B	3B	HR	RBI	BB	SO	SB	POS
1900	Pit-N	.333	4	15	3	5	1	0	0	1	1	0	0	2
1903	Pit-N	.111	8	27	2	3	1	0	0	2	4	7	1	2
Total 2		.190	12	42	5	8	2	0	0	3	5	7	1	

Jim Rivera

YEAR	TM/L	AVG	G	AB	R	H	2B	3B	HR	RBI	BB	SO	SB	POS
1959	Chi-A	.000	5	11	1	0	0	0	0	0	3	1	0	O

Mickey Rivers

YEAR	TM/L	AVG	G	AB	R	H	2B	3B	HR	RBI	BB	SO	SB	POS
1976	NY-A	.167	4	18	1	3	0	0	0	0	1	2	1	O
1977	NY-A	.222	6	27	1	6	2	0	0	1	0	2	1	O
1978	NY-A	.333	5	18	2	6	0	0	0	1	0	2	1	O*4
Total 3		.238	15	63	4	15	2	0	0	2	1	6	3	

Phil Rizzuto

YEAR	TM/L	AVG	G	AB	R	H	2B	3B	HR	RBI	BB	SO	SB	POS
1941	NY-A	.111	5	18	0	2	0	0	0	0	3	1	1	S
1942	NY-A	.381	5	21	2	8	0	0	1	1	2	1	2	S
1947	NY-A	.308	7	26	3	8	1	0	0	2	4	0	2	S
1949	NY-A	.167	5	18	2	3	0	0	0	0	3	1	1	S
1950	NY-A	.143	4	14	1	2	0	0	0	0	3	0	1	S
1951	NY-A	.320	6	25	5	8	0	0	1	3	2	3	0	S
1952	NY-A	.148	7	27	2	4	1	0	0	0	5	2	0	S
1953	NY-A	.316	6	19	4	6	0	0	0	0	3	2	1	S
1955	NY-A	.267	7	15	2	4	0	0	0	1	5	1	2	S
Total 9		.246	52	183	21	45	3	0	2	8	30	11	10	

Andre Robertson

YEAR	TM/L	AVG	G	AB	R	H	2B	3B	HR	RBI	BB	SO	SB	POS
1981	NY-A	—	1	0	0	0	0	0	0	0	0	0	0	R

Dave Robertson

YEAR	TM/L	AVG	G	AB	R	H	2B	3B	HR	RBI	BB	SO	SB	POS
1917	NY-N	.500	6	22	3	11	1	1	0	1	0	0	2	O

Gene Robertson

YEAR	TM/L	AVG	G	AB	R	H	2B	3B	HR	RBI	BB	SO	SB	POS
1928	NY-A	.125	3	8	1	1	0	0	0	2	1	0		3

Bob Robertson

YEAR	TM/L	AVG	G	AB	R	H	2B	3B	HR	RBI	BB	SO	SB	POS
1971	Pit-N	.240	7	25	4	6	0	0	2	5	4	8	0	1

Aaron Robinson

YEAR	TM/L	AVG	G	AB	R	H	2B	3B	HR	RBI	BB	SO	SB	POS
1947	NY-A	.200	3	10	2	2	0	0	0	1	2	1	0	C

Brooks Robinson

YEAR	TM/L	AVG	G	AB	R	H	2B	3B	HR	RBI	BB	SO	SB	POS
1966	Bal-A	.214	4	14	2	3	0	0	1	1	1	0	0	3
1969	Bal-A	.053	5	19	0	1	0	0	0	2	0	3	0	3
1970	Bal-A	.429	5	21	5	9	2	0	2	6	2	0		3
1971	Bal-A	.318	7	22	3	7	0	0	1	5	4	6	0	
Total 4		.263	21	76	9	20	2	0	3	14	4	6	0	

Frank Robinson

YEAR	TM/L	AVG	G	AB	R	H	2B	3B	HR	RBI	BB	SO	SB	POS
1961	Cin-N	.200	5	15	3	3	2	0	1	4	3	4	0	O
1966	Bal-A	.286	4	14	4	4	0	1	2	3	2	3	0	O
1969	Bal-A	.188	5	16	2	3	0	0	1	1	4	3	0	O

YEAR	TM/L	AVG	G	AB	R	H	2B	3B	HR	RBI	BB	SO	SB	POS
1970	Bal-A	.273	5	22	5	6	0	0	0	2	4	0	5	O
1971	Bal-A	.280	7	25	5	7	0	0	2	2	2	8	0	O
Total 5		.250	26	92	19	23	2	1	8	14	11	23	0	
■ Jackie Robinson														
1947	Bro-N	.259	7	27	3	7	2	0	0	3	2	4	2	1
1949	Bro-N	.188	5	16	2	3	1	0	0	2	4	2	0	2
1952	Bro-N	.174	7	23	4	4	0	0	1	2	7	5	2	2
1953	Bro-N	.320	6	25	3	8	2	0	0	2	1	0	1	O
1955	Bro-N	.182	6	22	5	4	1	0	1	2	1	1	3	
1956	Bro-N	.250	7	24	5	6	1	0	1	2	5	2	0	3
Total 6		.234	38	137	22	32	7	1	2	12	21	14	6	
■ Wilbert Robinson														
1894	Bal-N	.267	4	15	1	4	0	0	0	1	1	1	1	C
1895	Bal-N	.250	3	12	1	3	1	0	0	0	0	1	0	C
1896	Bal-N	.267	4	15	1	4	1	0	0	2	0	3	0	C
Total 3		.262	11	42	3	11	2	0	0	3	1	5	1	
■ Eddie Robinson														
1948	Cle-A	.300	6	20	0	6	0	0	0	1	1	0	0	1
1955	NY-A	.667	4	3	0	2	0	0	0	1	2	1	0	1*1
Total 2		.348	10	23	0	8	0	0	0	2	3	1	0	
■ Yank Robinson														
1885	StL-A	.174	7	23	5	4	1	0	0	1	0	0	0	O*4,C*3
1886	StL-A	.316	6	19	5	6	1	1	0	3	2	3	2	2
1887	StL-A	.326	15	46	5	15	5	1	0	4	10	6	4	2
1888	StL-A	.250	10	36	7	9	2	1	0	7	6	12	2	2
Total 4		.274	38	124	22	34	8	4	0	14	19	21	8	
■ Bill Robinson														
1979	Pit-N	.263	7	19	2	5	1	0	0	2	0	4	0	O*6
■ Aurelio Rodriguez														
1981	NY-A	.417	4	12	1	5	0	0	0	0	1	2	0	3*3
■ Gary Roenicke														
1979	Bal-A	.125	6	16	1	2	1	0	0	0	0	6	0	O*5
1983	Bal-A	.000	3	7	0	0	0	0	0	0	0	2	0	O*2
Total 2		.087	9	23	1	2	1	0	0	0	0	8	0	
■ Ron Roenicke														
1984	SD-N	—	2	0	0	0	0	0	0	0	0	0	0	O*1
■ Wally Roettger														
1931	StL-N	.286	3	14	1	4	1	0	0	0	0	3	0	O
■ Billy Rogell														
1934	Det-A	.276	7	29	3	8	1	0	0	4	1	4	1	S
1935	Det-A	.292	6	24	1	7	2	0	0	1	2	5	0	S
Total 2		.283	13	53	4	15	3	0	0	5	3	9	1	
■ George Rohe														
1906	Chi-A	.333	6	21	2	7	1	2	0	4	3	1	2	3
■ Red Rolfe														
1936	NY-A	.400	6	25	5	10	0	0	0	4	3	1	0	3
1937	NY-A	.300	5	20	3	6	2	1	0	1	3	2	0	3
1938	NY-A	.167	4	18	0	3	0	0	0	1	0	3	1	3
1939	NY-A	.125	4	16	2	2	0	0	0	0	0	0	0	3
1941	NY-A	.300	5	20	2	6	0	0	0	0	2	1	0	3
1942	NY-A	.353	4	17	5	6	2	0	0	0	1	2	0	3
Total 6		.284	28	116	17	33	4	1	0	6	9	9	1	
■ Rich Rollins														
1965	Min-A	.000	3	2	0	0	0	0	0	0	1	0	0	H
■ Johnny Romano														
1959	Chi-A	.000	1	1	0	0	0	0	0	0	0	0	0	H
■ Ed Romero														
1986	Bos-A	.000	3	1	0	0	0	0	0	0	0	0	0	S
■ Buddy Rosar														
1941	NY-A	—	1	0	0	0	0	0	0	0	0	0	0	C
1942	NY-A	1.000	1	1	0	1	0	0	0	0	0	0	0	H
Total 2		1.000	2	1	0	1	0	0	0	0	0	0	0	
■ Pete Rose														
1970	Cin-N	.250	5	20	2	5	1	0	1	2	2	0	0	O
1972	Cin-N	.214	7	28	3	6	0	0	1	2	4	4	1	O
1975	Cin-N	.370	7	27	3	10	1	1	0	2	5	1	0	3
1976	Cin-N	.188	4	16	1	3	1	0	0	1	2	2	0	3
1980	Phi-N	.261	6	23	4	6	1	0	0	1	2	2	0	1
1983	Phi-N	.313	5	16	1	5	1	0	0	1	1	3	0	1*3,O*1
Total 6		.269	34	130	12	35	5	1	2	9	16	12	1	
■ Johnny Roseboro														
1959	LA-N	.095	6	21	0	2	0	0	0	1	0	2	0	C
1963	LA-N	.143	4	14	1	2	0	0	1	3	0	4	0	C
1965	LA-N	.286	7	21	1	6	1	0	0	3	5	3	1	C
1966	LA-N	.071	4	14	0	1	0	0	0	0	0	3	0	C
Total 4		.157	21	70	2	11	1	0	1	7	5	12	1	
■ Chief Roseman														
1884	NY-A	.333	3	9	1	3	0	0	0	1	0	1	0	O
■ Al Rosen														
1948	Cle-A	.000	1	1	0	0	0	0	0	0	0	0	0	H
1954	Cle-A	.250	3	12	0	3	0	0	0	0	1	0	0	3
Total 2		.231	4	13	0	3	0	0	0	0	1	0	0	
■ Claude Rossman														
1907	Det-A	.400	5	20	1	8	0	1	0	2	1	0	1	1
1908	Det-A	.211	5	19	3	4	0	0	0	3	1	4	1	1
Total 2		.308	10	39	4	12	0	1	0	5	2	4	2	
■ Jack Rothrock														
1934	StL-N	.233	7	30	3	7	3	1	0	6	1	2	0	O
■ Edd Roush														
1919	Cin-N	.214	8	28	6	6	2	1	0	7	3	0	2	O
■ Jack Rowe														
1887	Det-N	.333	15	63	12	21	1	1	0	7	2	1	5	S
■ Joe Rudi														
1972	Oak-A	.240	7	25	1	6	0	0	1	1	2	5	0	O
1973	Oak-A	.333	7	27	3	9	2	0	0	4	3	4	0	O
1974	Oak-A	.333	5	18	1	6	0	0	1	4	0	3	0	O*5,1*2
Total 3		.300	19	70	5	21	2	0	2	9	5	12	0	
■ Muddy Ruel														
1924	Was-A	.095	7	21	2	2	1	0	0	0	6	1	0	C
1925	Was-A	.316	7	19	0	6	1	0	0	1	3	2	0	C
Total 2		.200	14	40	2	8	2	0	0	1	9	3	0	
■ Dutch Ruether														
1919	Cin-N	.667	3	6	2	4	1	2	0	4	1	0	0	P*2
1925	Was-A	.000	1	1	0	0	0	0	0	0	0	1	0	H
1926	NY-A	.000	3	4	0	0	0	0	0	0	0	1	0	P*1
Total 3		.364	7	11	2	4	1	2	0	4	1	1	0	
■ Rip Russell														
1946	Bos-A	1.000	2	2	1	2	0	0	0	0	0	0	0	3*1
■ Bill Russell														
1974	LA-N	.222	5	18	0	4	0	1	0	2	0	2	0	S
1977	LA-N	.154	6	26	3	4	0	1	0	2	1	3	0	S
1978	LA-N	.423	6	26	1	11	2	0	0	2	2	2	1	S
1981	LA-N	.240	6	25	1	6	0	0	0	2	0	1	1	S
Total 4		.263	23	95	5	25	2	2	0	8	3	8	2	
■ Babe Ruth														
1915	Bos-A	.000	1	1	0	0	0	0	0	0	0	0	0	H
1916	Bos-A	.000	1	5	0	0	0	0	0	1	0	2	0	P
1918	Bos-A	.200	3	5	0	1	0	1	0	2	0	2	0	P*2,O*2
1921	NY-A	.313	6	16	3	5	0	0	1	4	5	8	2	O
1922	NY-A	.118	5	17	1	2	1	0	0	1	2	3	0	O
1923	NY-A	.368	6	19	8	7	1	1	3	3	8	6	0	O*6,1*1
1926	NY-A	.300	7	20	6	6	0	0	4	5	11	2	1	O
1927	NY-A	.400	4	15	4	6	0	0	2	7	2	2	1	O
1928	NY-A	.625	4	16	9	10	3	0	3	4	1	2	0	O
1932	NY-A	.333	4	15	6	5	0	0	2	6	4	3	0	—
Total 10		.326	41	129	37	42	5	2	15	33	33	30	4	
■ Connie Ryan														
1948	Bos-N	.000	2	1	0	0	0	0	0	0	0	1	0	H
■ Jimmy Ryan														
1886	Chi-N	.250	6	20	4	5	1	0	0	2	0	1	1	O*6,P*1,S*1
■ John Ryan														
1890	Lou-A	.053	6	19	0	1	0	0	0	2	0	1	1	C
■ Blondy Ryan														
1933	NY-N	.278	5	18	0	5	0	0	0	1	1	5	0	S
1937	NY-N	.000	1	1	0	0	0	0	0	0	0	1	0	H
Total 2		.263	6	19	0	5	0	0	0	1	1	6	0	
■ Mike Ryan														
1967	Bos-A	.000	1	2	0	0	0	0	0	0	0	1	0	C
■ Chris Sabo														
1990	Cin-N	.563	4	16	2	9	1	0	2	5	2	2	0	3
■ Pop Schriver														
1900	Pit-N	.000	1	1	0	0	0	0	0	0	0	0	0	H
■ Tim Shinnick														
1890	Lou-A	.292	7	24	3	7	1	1	0	3	2	2	2	2
■ Mike Slattery														
1888	NY-N	.205	10	39	6	8	2	0	0	5	0	5	6	O*10,2*1
1889	NY-N	.188	4	16	6	3	0	0	0	1	3	1	1	O
Total 2		.200	14	55	12	11	2	0	0	6	3	6	7	
■ Germany Smith														
1889	Bro-A	.172	8	29	2	5	2	1	0	2	3	2	2	S
1890	Bro-N	.276	7	29	3	8	0	2	0	7	0	3	1	S
Total 2		.224	15	58	5	13	2	3	0	9	3	5	3	
■ Lenn Sakata														
1983	Bal-A	.000	1	1	0	0	0	0	0	0	0	0	0	2
■ Luis Salazar														
1984	SD-N	.333	4	3	0	1	0	0	0	0	0	0	0	O*2,3*1
■ Bill Salkeld														
1948	Bos-N	.222	5	9	2	2	0	0	1	1	5	1	0	C
■ Chico Salmon														
1969	Bal-A	—	2	0	0	0	0	0	0	0	0	0	0	R
1970	Bal-A	1.000	1	1	1	1	0	0	0	0	0	0	0	H
Total 2		1.000	3	1	1	1	0	0	0	0	0	0	0	

YEAR	TM/L	AVG	G	AB	R	H	2B	3B	HR	RBI	BB	SO	SB	POS
Juan Samuel														
1983	Phi-N	.000	3	1	0	0	0	0	0	0	0	0	0	H
Deion Sanders														
1992	Atl-N	.533	4	15	4	8	2	0	0	1	2	1	5	O
Ray Sanders														
1942	StL-N	.000	2	1	1	0	0	0	0	0	0	1	0	H
1943	StL-N	.294	5	17	3	5	0	0	1	2	3	4	0	1
1944	StL-N	.286	6	21	5	6	0	0	1	1	5	8	0	1
1948	Bos-N	.000	1	1	0	0	0	0	0	0	0	0	0	H
Total 4		.275	14	40	9	11	0	0	2	3	9	12	0	
Charlie Sands														
1971	Pit-N	.000	1	1	0	0	0	0	0	0	0	0	1	0 H
Manny Sanguillen														
1971	Pit-N	.379	7	29	3	11	1	0	0	0	0	3	2	C
1979	Pit-N	.333	3	3	0	1	0	0	0	1	0	0	0	H
Total 2		.375	10	32	3	12	1	0	0	1	0	3	2	
Rafael Santana														
1986	NY-N	.250	7	20	3	5	0	0	0	2	2	5	0	S
Ed Sauer														
1945	Chi-N	.000	2	2	0	0	0	0	0	0	0	0	2	0 H
Carl Sawatski														
1957	Mil-N	.000	2	2	0	0	0	0	0	0	0	0	2	0 H
Steve Sax														
1981	LA-N	.000	2	1	0	0	0	0	0	0	0	0	0	2*1
1988	LA-N	.300	5	20	3	6	0	0	0	0	1	1	2	
Total 2		.286	7	21	3	6	0	0	0	0	1	1	1	
Germany Schaefer														
1907	Det-A	.143	5	21	1	3	0	0	0	0	0	3	0	2
1908	Det-A	.125	5	16	0	2	0	0	0	0	1	4	1	2*3,3*2
Total 2		.135	10	37	1	5	0	0	0	1	0	7	1	
Ray Schalk														
1917	Chi-A	.263	6	19	1	5	0	0	0	0	2	1	1	C
1919	Chi-A	.304	8	23	1	7	0	0	0	2	4	2	1	C
Total 2		.286	14	42	2	12	0	0	0	2	6	3	2	
Wally Schang														
1913	Phi-A	.357	4	14	2	5	0	1	1	6	2	4	0	C
1914	Phi-A	.167	4	12	1	2	1	0	0	0	1	4	0	C
1918	Bos-A	.444	5	9	1	4	0	0	0	1	2	3	1	C
1921	NY-A	.286	8	21	1	6	1	1	0	1	5	4	0	C
1922	NY-A	.188	5	16	0	3	1	0	0	0	0	3	0	C
1923	NY-A	.318	6	22	3	7	1	0	0	0	1	2	0	C
Total 6		.287	32	94	8	27	4	2	1	8	11	20	1	
Hank Schenz														
1951	NY-N	—	1	0	0	0	0	0	0	0	0	0	0	R
Ray Schmandt														
1920	Bro-N	.000	1	1	0	0	0	0	0	0	0	0	0	H
Boss Schmidt														
1907	Det-A	.167	4	12	0	2	0	0	0	0	2	1	0	C*3
1908	Det-A	.071	4	14	0	1	0	0	0	1	0	2	0	C
1909	Det-A	.222	6	18	0	4	2	0	0	4	2	0	0	C
Total 3		.159	14	44	0	7	2	0	0	5	4	3	0	
Butch Schmidt														
1914	Bos-N	.294	4	17	2	5	0	0	0	2	0	2	1	1
Mike Schmidt														
1980	Phi-N	.381	6	21	6	8	1	0	2	7	4	3	0	3
1983	Phi-N	.050	5	20	0	1	0	0	0	0	0	6	0	3
Total 2		.220	11	41	6	9	1	0	2	7	4	9	0	
Red Schoendienst														
1946	StL-N	.233	7	30	3	7	1	0	0	1	0	2	1	2
1957	Mil-N	.278	5	18	0	5	1	0	0	2	0	1	0	2
1958	Mil-N	.300	7	30	5	9	3	1	0	0	2	1	0	2
Total 3		.269	19	78	8	21	5	1	0	3	2	4	1	
Dick Schofield														
1960	Pit-N	.333	3	3	0	1	0	0	0	0	1	0	0	S*2
1968	StL-N	—	2	0	0	0	0	0	0	0	0	0	0	S*1
Total 2		.333	5	3	0	1	0	0	0	0	1	0	0	
Ossee Schreckengost														
1905	Phi-A	.222	3	9	2	2	1	0	0	0	0	0	0	C
Frank Schulte														
1906	Chi-N	.269	6	26	1	7	3	0	0	3	1	3	0	O
1907	Chi-N	.250	5	20	3	5	0	0	0	2	1	2	0	O
1908	Chi-N	.389	5	18	4	7	0	1	0	2	2	1	0	O
1910	Chi-N	.353	5	17	3	6	3	0	0	2	2	3	0	O
Total 4		.309	21	81	11	25	6	1	0	9	6	9	2	
Fred Schulte														
1933	Was-A	.333	5	21	1	7	1	0	1	4	1	1	0	O
Bill Schuster														
1945	Chi-N	.000	2	1	1	0	0	0	0	0	0	0	0	S*1
Mike Scioscia														
1981	LA-N	.250	3	4	1	1	0	0	0	0	1	0	0	C
1988	LA-N	.214	4	14	0	3	0	0	0	1	0	2	0	C
Total 2		.222	7	18	1	4	0	0	0	1	1	2	0	
George Scott														
1967	Bos-A	.231	7	26	3	6	1	1	0	0	3	6	0	1
Everett Scott														
1915	Bos-A	.056	5	18	0	1	0	0	0	0	0	3	0	S
1916	Bos-A	.125	5	16	1	2	0	1	0	1	1	1	0	S
1918	Bos-A	.095	6	21	0	2	0	0	0	1	1	1	0	S
1922	NY-A	.143	5	14	0	2	0	0	0	1	1	0	0	S
1923	NY-A	.318	6	22	2	7	0	0	0	3	0	1	0	S
Total 5		.154	27	91	3	14	0	1	0	6	3	6	0	
Jimmy Sebring														
1903	Pit-N	.367	8	30	3	11	0	1	1	3	1	4	0	O
Frank Secory														
1945	Chi-N	.200	5	5	0	1	0	0	0	0	0	2	0	H
Bob Seeds														
1936	NY-A	—	1	0	0	0	0	0	0	0	0	0	0	R
George Selkirk														
1936	NY-A	.333	6	24	6	8	0	1	2	3	4	4	0	O
1937	NY-A	.263	5	19	5	5	1	0	0	6	2	0	0	O
1938	NY-A	.200	3	10	0	2	0	0	0	1	2	1	0	O
1939	NY-A	.167	4	12	0	2	1	0	0	3	2	0	0	O
1941	NY-A	.500	2	2	0	1	0	0	0	0	0	0	0	H
1942	NY-A	.000	1	1	0	0	0	0	0	0	0	0	0	H
Total 6		.265	21	68	11	18	2	1	2	10	11	7	0	
Andy Seminick														
1950	Phi-N	.182	4	11	0	2	0	0	0	1	3	0		C
Hank Severeid														
1925	Was-A	.333	1	3	0	1	0	0	0	0	0	0	0	C
1926	NY-A	.273	7	22	1	6	1	0	0	1	1	2	0	C
Total 2		.280	8	25	1	7	1	0	0	1	1	2	0	
Luke Sewell														
1933	Was-A	.176	5	17	1	3	0	0	0	1	2	0	1	C
Joe Sewell														
1920	Cle-A	.174	7	23	0	4	0	0	0	0	2	1	0	S
1932	NY-A	.333	4	15	4	5	1	0	0	3	4	0	0	3
Total 2		.237	11	38	4	9	1	0	0	3	6	1	0	
Socks Seybold														
1905	Phi-A	.125	5	16	0	2	0	0	0	0	0	3	0	O
Tillie Shafer														
1912	NY-N	—	3	0	0	0	0	0	0	0	0	0	0	S
1913	NY-N	.158	5	19	2	3	1	1	0	1	2	3	0	O*5,3*1
Total 2		.158	8	19	2	3	1	1	0	1	2	3	0	
Art Shamsky														
1969	NY-N	.000	3	6	0	0	0	0	0	0	0	0	0	O*1
Mike Shannon														
1964	StL-N	.214	7	28	6	6	0	0	1	2	0	9	1	O
1967	StL-N	.208	7	24	3	5	1	0	1	2	1	4	0	3
1968	StL-N	.276	7	29	3	8	1	0	1	4	1	5	0	3
Total 3		.235	21	81	12	19	2	0	3	8	2	18	1	
Dave Shean														
1918	Bos-A	.211	6	19	2	4	1	0	0	0	4	3	1	2
Jimmy Sheckard														
1906	Chi-N	.000	6	21	0	0	0	0	0	1	2	4	1	O
1907	Chi-N	.238	5	21	0	5	2	0	0	2	0	4	1	O
1908	Chi-N	.238	5	21	2	5	2	0	0	1	2	3	1	O
1910	Chi-N	.286	5	14	5	4	2	0	0	1	7	2	1	O
Total 4		.182	21	77	7	14	6	0	0	5	11	13	4	
Jack Sheehan														
1920	Bro-N	.182	3	11	0	2	0	0	0	0	0	1	0	3
John Shelby														
1983	Bal-A	.444	5	9	1	4	0	0	0	1	0	4	0	O
1988	LA-N	.222	5	18	0	4	1	0	0	1	2	7	1	O
Total 2		.296	10	27	1	8	1	0	0	2	2	11	1	
Pat Sheridan														
1985	KC-A	.222	5	18	0	4	2	0	0	1	0	7	0	O*4
1989	SF-N	.000	1	2	0	0	0	0	0	0	0	0	0	O
Total 2		.200	6	20	0	4	2	0	0	1	0	7	0	
Mule Shirley														
1924	Was-A	.500	3	2	1	1	0	0	0	0	1	0	0	H
Tom Shopay														
1971	Bal-A	.000	5	4	0	0	0	0	0	0	0	2	0	H
Chick Shorten														
1916	Bos-A	.571	2	7	0	4	0	0	0	2	0	1	0	O
George Shuba														
1952	Bro-N	.300	4	10	0	3	1	0	0	0	0	4	0	O*3
1953	Bro-N	1.000	2	1	1	1	0	0	1	2	0	0	0	H
1955	Bro-N	.000	1	1	0	0	0	0	0	0	0	0	0	H
Total 3		.333	7	12	1	4	1	0	1	2	0	4	0	
Norm Siebern														
1956	NY-A	.000	1	1	0	0	0	0	0	0	0	0	0	H

YEAR	TM/L	AVG	G	AB	R	H	2B	3B	HR	RBI	BB	SO	SB	POS
1958	NY-A	.125	3	8	1	1	0	0	0	0	3	2	0	
1967	Bos-A	.333	3	3	0	1	0	0	0	1	0	0	0	O*1
Total 3		.167	7	12	1	2	0	0	0	1	3	2	0	
Charlie Silvera														
1949	NY-A	.000	1	2	0	0	0	0	0	0	0	0	0	C
Ken Silvestri														
1950	Phi-N	—	1	0	0	0	0	0	0	0	0	0	0	C
Al Simmons														
1929	Phi-A	.300	5	20	6	6	1	0	2	5	1	4	0	O
1930	Phi-A	.364	6	22	4	8	2	0	2	4	2	2	0	O
1931	Phi-A	.333	7	27	4	9	2	0	2	8	3	3	0	O
1939	Cin-N	.250	1	4	1	1	1	0	0	0	0	0	0	O
Total 4		.329	19	73	15	24	6	0	6	17	6	9	0	
Ted Simmons														
1982	Mil-A	.174	7	23	2	4	0	0	2	3	5	3	0	C
Harry Simpson														
1957	NY-A	.083	5	12	0	1	0	0	0	1	0	4	0	1*4
Ken Singleton														
1979	Bal-A	.357	7	28	1	10	1	0	0	2	2	5	0	O
1983	Bal-A	.000	2	1	0	0	0	0	0	1	1	1	0	H
Total 2		.345	9	29	1	10	1	0	0	3	3	6	0	
Dick Sisler														
1946	StL-N	.000	2	2	0	0	0	0	0	0	0	0	0	H
1950	Phi-N	.059	4	17	0	1	0	0	0	1	0	5	0	O
Total 2		.053	6	19	0	1	0	0	0	1	0	5	0	
Sibby Sisti														
1948	Bos-N	.000	2	1	0	0	0	0	0	0	0	0	0	2
Dave Skaggs														
1979	Bal-A	.333	1	3	1	1	0	0	0	0	0	0	0	C
Bob Skinner														
1960	Pit-N	.200	2	5	2	1	0	0	0	1	1	0	1	O
1964	StL-N	.667	4	3	0	2	1	0	0	1	1	0	0	H
Total 2		.375	6	8	2	3	1	0	0	2	2	0	1	
Bill Skowron														
1955	NY-A	.333	5	12	2	4	2	0	1	3	0	1	0	1*3
1956	NY-A	.100	3	10	1	1	0	0	1	4	0	3	0	1*2
1957	NY-A	.000	2	4	0	0	0	0	0	0	0	0	0	1
1958	NY-A	.259	7	27	3	7	0	0	2	7	1	4	0	1
1960	NY-A	.375	7	32	7	12	2	0	2	6	0	6	0	1
1961	NY-A	.353	5	17	3	6	0	0	1	5	3	4	0	1
1962	NY-A	.222	6	18	1	4	0	1	0	1	1	5	0	1
1963	LA-N	.385	4	13	2	5	0	0	1	3	1	3	0	1
Total 8		.293	39	133	19	39	4	1	8	29	6	26	0	
Jimmy Slagle														
1907	Chi-N	.273	5	22	3	6	0	0	0	4	2	3	6	O
Enos Slaughter														
1942	StL-N	.263	5	19	3	5	1	0	1	2	3	2	0	O
1946	StL-N	.320	7	25	5	8	1	1	1	2	4	3	1	O
1956	NY-A	.350	6	20	6	7	0	0	1	4	4	0	0	O
1957	NY-A	.250	5	12	2	3	1	0	0	0	3	2	0	O
1958	NY-A	.000	4	3	1	0	0	0	0	0	1	1	0	H
Total 5		.291	27	79	17	23	3	1	3	8	15	8	1	
Roy Smalley														
1987	Min-A	.500	4	2	0	1	1	0	0	0	2	0	0	H
Al Smith														
1954	Cle-A	.214	4	14	2	3	0	0	1	2	2	2	0	O
1959	Chi-A	.250	6	20	1	5	3	0	0	1	4	4	0	O
Total 2		.235	10	34	3	8	3	0	1	3	6	6	0	
Billy Smith														
1979	Bal-A	.286	4	7	1	2	0	0	0	0	2	0	0	2*2
Reggie Smith														
1967	Bos-A	.250	7	24	3	6	1	0	2	3	2	2	0	O
1977	LA-N	.273	6	22	7	6	1	0	3	5	4	3	0	O
1978	LA-N	.200	6	25	3	5	0	0	1	5	2	6	0	O
1981	LA-N	.500	2	2	0	1	0	0	0	0	0	1	0	H
Total 4		.247	21	73	13	18	2	0	6	13	8	12	0	
Earl Smith														
1921	NY-N	.000	3	7	0	0	0	0	0	0	1	0	0	C*2
1922	NY-N	.143	4	7	0	1	0	0	0	0	2	0	0	C*1
1925	Pit-N	.350	6	20	0	7	1	0	0	1	2	0	0	C
1927	Pit-N	.000	3	8	0	0	0	0	0	0	0	0	0	C*2
1928	Pit-N	.750	1	4	0	3	0	0	0	0	0	0	0	C
Total 5		.239	17	46	0	11	1	0	0	2	4	0	0	
Elmer Smith														
1920	Cle-A	.308	5	13	1	4	0	1	1	5	1	1	0	O
1922	NY-A	.000	2	2	0	0	0	0	0	0	0	2	0	H
Total 2		.267	7	15	1	4	0	1	1	5	1	3	0	
Hal Smith														
1960	Pit-N	.375	3	8	1	3	0	0	1	3	0	0	0	C
Harry Smith														
1903	Pit-N	.000	1	3	0	0	0	0	0	0	0	0	0	C
Jimmy Smith														
1919	Cin-N	—	1	0	0	0	0	0	0	0	0	0	0	R
Lonnie Smith														
1980	Phi-N	.263	6	19	2	5	1	0	0	1	1	1	0	O*5,D*1
1982	StL-N	.321	7	28	6	9	4	1	0	1	1	5	2	O*6,D*1
1985	KC-A	.333	7	27	4	9	3	0	0	4	3	8	2	O
1991	Atl-N	.231	7	26	5	6	0	0	3	3	3	4	1	D*4,O*3
1992	Atl-N	.167	5	12	1	2	0	0	1	5	1	4	0	D*3
Total 5		.277	32	112	18	31	8	1	4	14	9	22	5	
Ozzie Smith														
1982	StL-N	.208	7	24	3	5	0	0	0	1	3	0	1	S
1985	StL-N	.087	7	23	1	2	0	0	0	0	4	0	1	S
1987	StL-N	.214	7	28	3	6	0	0	0	2	2	3	2	S
Total 3		.173	21	75	7	13	0	0	0	3	9	3	4	
Duke Snider														
1949	Bro-N	.143	5	21	2	3	1	0	0	0	0	8	0	O
1952	Bro-N	.345	7	29	5	10	2	0	4	8	1	5	1	O
1953	Bro-N	.320	6	25	3	8	3	0	1	5	2	6	0	O
1955	Bro-N	.320	7	25	5	8	1	0	4	7	2	6	0	O
1956	Bro-N	.304	7	23	5	7	1	0	1	4	6	8	0	O
1959	LA-N	.200	4	10	1	2	0	0	1	2	2	0	0	O*3
Total 6		.286	36	133	21	38	8	0	11	26	13	33	1	
Fred Snodgrass														
1911	NY-N	.105	6	19	1	2	0	0	0	1	2	7	0	O
1912	NY-N	.212	8	33	2	7	2	0	0	2	2	5	1	O
1913	NY-N	.333	2	3	0	1	0	0	0	0	0	0	0	1*1,O*1
Total 3		.182	16	55	3	10	2	0	0	3	4	12	1	
Frank Snyder														
1921	NY-N	.364	7	22	4	8	1	0	1	3	0	2	0	C*6
1922	NY-N	.333	4	15	1	5	0	0	0	0	1	1	0	C
1923	NY-N	.118	5	17	1	2	0	0	1	2	0	2	0	C
1924	NY-N	.000	1	1	0	0	0	0	0	0	0	0	0	H
Total 4		.273	17	55	6	15	1	0	2	5	0	5	0	
Russ Snyder														
1966	Bal-A	.167	3	6	1	1	0	0	0	1	2	0	0	O
Paul Sorrento														
1991	Min-A	.000	3	2	0	0	0	0	0	0	1	2	0	1*1
Billy Southworth														
1924	NY-N	.000	5	1	1	0	0	0	0	0	0	0	0	O*2
1926	StL-N	.345	7	29	6	10	1	1	1	4	0	0	1	O
Total 2		.333	12	30	7	10	1	1	1	4	0	0	1	
Tris Speaker														
1912	Bos-A	.300	8	30	4	9	1	2	0	2	4	2	1	O
1915	Bos-A	.294	5	17	2	5	0	1	0	0	4	1	0	O
1920	Cle-A	.320	7	25	6	8	2	1	0	1	3	1	0	O
Total 3		.306	20	72	12	22	3	4	0	3	11	4	1	
Jim Spencer														
1978	NY-A	.167	4	12	3	2	0	0	0	0	2	4	0	1*3
Roy Spencer														
1927	Pit-N	.000	1	1	0	0	0	0	0	0	0	0	0	C
Ed Spiezio														
1967	StL-N	.000	1	1	0	0	0	0	0	0	0	0	0	H
1968	StL-N	1.000	1	1	0	1	0	0	0	0	0	0	0	H
Total 2		.500	2	2	0	1	0	0	0	0	0	0	0	
Ed Sprague														
1992	Tor-A	.500	3	2	1	1	0	0	1	2	1	0	0	1*1
1993	Tor-A	.067	5	15	0	1	0	0	0	2	1	6	0	3*4,1*1
Total 2		.118	8	17	1	2	0	0	1	4	2	6	0	
Chick Stahl														
1897	Bos-N	.400	5	20	6	8	1	0	0	6	3	2	2	O
1903	Bos-A	.303	8	33	6	10	1	3	0	3	1	2	2	O
Total 2		.340	13	53	12	18	2	3	0	9	4	4	4	
Jake Stahl														
1912	Bos-A	.281	8	32	3	9	2	0	0	2	0	6	2	1
Tuck Stainback														
1942	NY-A	—	2	0	0	0	0	0	0	0	0	0	0	R
1943	NY-A	.176	5	17	0	3	0	0	0	0	0	2	0	O
Total 2		.176	7	17	0	3	0	0	0	0	0	2	0	
Oscar Stanage														
1909	Det-A	.200	2	5	0	1	0	0	0	2	0	2	0	C
Eddie Stanky														
1947	Bro-N	.240	7	25	4	6	1	0	0	2	3	2	0	2
1948	Bos-N	.286	6	14	0	4	1	0	0	1	7	1	0	2
1951	NY-N	.136	6	22	3	3	0	0	0	1	3	2	0	2
Total 3		.213	19	61	7	13	2	0	0	4	13	5	0	
Fred Stanley														
1976	NY-A	.167	4	6	1	1	1	0	0	1	3	1	0	S
1977	NY-A	—	1	0	0	0	0	0	0	0	0	0	0	S
1978	NY-A	.200	3	5	0	1	0	0	0	2	0	3	0	2
Total 3		.182	8	11	1	2	2	0	0	1	4	1	0	
Mickey Stanley														
1968	Det-A	.214	7	28	4	6	0	1	0	0	2	4	0	S*7,O*4

YEAR	TM/L	AVG	G	AB	R	H	2B	3B	HR	RBI	BB	SO	SB	POS
Dave Stapleton														
1986	Bos-A	.000	3	1	0	0	0	0	0	0	0	0	1	1
Willie Stargell														
1971	Pit-N	.208	7	24	3	5	1	0	0	1	7	9	0	O
1979	Pit-N	.400	7	30	7	12	4	0	3	7	0	6	0	1
Total 2		.315	14	54	10	17	5	0	3	8	7	15	0	
Joe Start														
1884	Pro-N	.100	3	10	0	1	0	0	0	1	0	2	0	1
Rusty Staub														
1973	NY-N	.423	7	26	1	11	2	0	1	6	2	2	0	O
Terry Steinbach														
1988	Oak-A	.364	3	11	0	4	1	0	0	0	2	0	C*2,D*1
1989	Oak-A	.250	4	16	3	4	0	1	1	7	2	1	0	C
1990	Oak-A	.125	3	8	0	1	0	0	0	0	0	1	0	C
Total 3		.257	10	35	3	9	1	1	1	7	2	4	0	
Harry Steinfeldt														
1906	Chi-N	.250	6	20	2	5	1	0	0	2	1	0	3	
1907	Chi-N	.471	5	17	2	8	1	1	0	2	1	2	1	3
1908	Chi-N	.250	5	16	3	4	0	0	0	3	2	5	1	3
1910	Chi-N	.100	5	20	0	2	1	0	0	1	0	4	0	3
Total 4		.260	21	73	7	19	3	1	0	8	4	11	2	
Casey Stengel														
1916	Bro-N	.364	4	11	2	4	0	0	0	0	0	1	0	O*3
1922	NY-N	.400	2	5	0	2	0	0	0	0	0	1	0	O
1923	NY-N	.417	6	12	3	5	0	0	2	4	4	0	0	O
Total 3		.393	12	28	5	11	0	0	2	4	4	2	0	
Rennie Stennett														
1979	Pit-N	1.000	1	1	0	1	0	0	0	0	0	0	0	H
Jake Stenzel														
1897	Bal-N	.381	5	21	7	8	1	1	0	3	2	0	2	O
Vern Stephens														
1944	StL-A	.227	6	22	2	5	1	0	0	3	3	0	S
Riggs Stephenson														
1929	Chi-N	.316	5	19	3	6	1	0	0	3	2	2	0	O
1932	Chi-N	.444	4	18	2	8	1	0	0	4	0	0	0	O
Total 2		.378	9	37	5	14	2	0	0	7	2	2	0	
Walter Stephenson														
1935	Chi-N	.000	1	1	0	0	0	0	0	0	0	1	0	H
Jimmy Stewart														
1970	Cin-N	.000	2	2	0	0	0	0	0	0	0	1	0	H
Snuffy Stirnweiss														
1943	NY-A	.000	1	1	1	0	0	0	0	0	0	0	0	H
1947	NY-A	.259	7	27	3	7	0	1	0	3	8	8	0	2
1949	NY-A	—	1	0	0	0	0	0	0	0	0	0	0	H
Total 3		.250	9	28	4	7	0	1	0	3	8	8	0	
Milt Stock														
1915	Phi-N	.118	5	17	1	2	1	0	0	1	0	0	3	
Kevin Stocker														
1993	Phi-N	.211	6	19	1	4	1	0	0	1	5	5	0	S
Sammy Strang														
1905	NY-N	.000	1	1	0	0	0	0	0	0	0	1	0	H
Darryl Strawberry														
1986	NY-N	.208	7	24	4	5	1	0	1	4	6	3	0	O
George Strickland														
1954	Cle-A	.000	3	9	0	0	0	0	0	0	2	0	S
Amos Strunk														
1910	Phi-A	.278	4	18	2	5	1	1	0	2	2	5	0	O
1911	Phi-A	—	1	0	0	0	0	0	0	0	0	0	0	R
1913	Phi-A	.118	5	17	3	2	0	0	0	0	2	2	0	O
1914	Phi-A	.286	2	7	0	2	0	0	0	0	0	2	0	O
1918	Bos-A	.174	6	23	1	4	1	1	0	0	0	5	0	O
Total 5		.200	18	65	6	13	2	2	0	2	4	14	0	
Dick Stuart														
1960	Pit-N	.150	5	20	0	3	0	0	0	0	3	0	1	
1966	LA-N	.000	2	2	0	0	0	0	0	0	0	1	0	H
Total 2		.136	7	22	0	3	0	0	0	0	0	4	0	
Franklin Stubbs														
1988	LA-N	.294	5	17	3	5	2	0	0	2	1	3	0	1
Johnny Sturm														
1941	NY-A	.286	5	21	0	6	0	0	0	2	0	2	1	1
Billy Sullivan														
1940	Det-A	.154	5	13	3	2	0	0	0	0	5	2	0	C*4
Billy Sullivan														
1906	Chi-A	.000	6	21	0	0	0	0	0	0	0	9	0	C
Homer Summa														
1929	Phi-A	.000	1	1	0	0	0	0	0	0	0	1	0	H
Champ Summers														
1984	SD-N	.000	1	1	0	0	0	0	0	0	0	1	0	H

YEAR	TM/L	AVG	G	AB	R	H	2B	3B	HR	RBI	BB	SO	SB	POS
Billy Sunday														
1885	Chi-N	.273	6	22	5	6	2	0	0	0	2	0	0	O
Jim Sundberg														
1985	KC-A	.250	7	24	6	6	2	0	0	1	6	4	0	C
Cy Sutcliffe														
1887	Det-N	.091	4	11	1	1	0	0	0	1	1	1	1	1*3,C*1
Bob Swift														
1945	Det-A	.250	3	4	1	1	0	0	0	0	2	0	0	C
Ron Swoboda														
1969	NY-N	.400	4	15	1	6	1	0	0	1	1	3	0	O
Pat Tabler														
1992	Tor-A	.000	2	2	0	0	0	0	0	0	0	0	0	H
Lee Tannehill														
1906	Chi-A	.111	3	9	1	1	0	0	0	0	0	2	0	S
Jose Tartabull														
1967	Bos-A	.154	7	13	1	2	0	0	0	1	2	0	O*6
Bennie Tate														
1924	Was-A	—	3	0	0	0	0	0	0	1	3	0	0	H
Harry Taylor														
1890	Lou-A	.300	7	30	6	9	1	0	0	2	2	3	3	1
Zack Taylor														
1929	Chi-N	.176	5	17	0	3	0	0	0	3	0	3	0	C
Tommy Taylor														
1924	Was-A	.000	3	2	0	0	0	0	0	0	0	2	0	3
Birdie Tebbetts														
1940	Det-A	.000	4	11	0	0	0	0	0	0	0	0	0	C*3
Patsy Tebeau														
1892	Cle-N	.000	5	18	1	0	0	0	0	0	0	2	1	3
1895	Cle-N	.286	5	21	3	6	1	0	0	3	1	0	1	
1896	Cle-N	.000	1	1	0	0	0	0	0	0	0	0	0	1
Total 3		.150	11	40	4	6	1	0	0	3	1	2	1	
Garry Templeton														
1984	SD-N	.316	5	19	1	6	1	0	0	0	0	3	0	S
Gene Tenace														
1972	Oak-A	.348	7	23	5	8	1	0	4	9	2	4	0	C*6,1*1
1973	Oak-A	.158	7	19	0	3	1	0	0	3	11	7	0	1*7,C*3
1974	Oak-A	.222	5	9	0	2	0	0	0	0	3	4	0	1
1982	StL-N	.000	5	6	0	0	0	0	0	0	1	2	0	D*1
Total 4		.228	24	57	5	13	2	0	4	12	17	17	0	
Fred Tenney														
1897	Bos-N	.286	5	21	4	6	0	0	0	2	4	1	2	1
Bill Terry														
1924	NY-N	.429	5	14	3	6	0	1	1	1	3	1	0	1*4
1933	NY-N	.273	5	22	3	6	1	0	1	1	0	0	1	1
1936	NY-N	.240	6	25	1	6	0	0	0	5	1	4	0	1
Total 3		.295	16	61	7	18	1	1	2	7	4	5	0	
Tim Teufel														
1986	NY-N	.444	3	9	1	4	1	0	1	1	1	2	0	2
George Theodore														
1973	NY-N	.000	2	2	0	0	0	0	0	0	0	0	0	O*1
Tommy Thevenow														
1926	StL-N	.417	7	24	5	10	1	0	1	4	0	1	0	S
1928	StL-N	—	1	0	0	0	0	0	0	0	0	0	0	S
Total 2		.417	8	24	5	10	1	0	1	4	0	1	0	
Pinch Thomas														
1915	Bos-A	.200	2	5	0	1	0	0	0	0	0	0	0	C
1916	Bos-A	.143	3	7	0	1	0	1	0	0	0	1	0	C
1920	Cle-A	—	1	0	0	0	0	0	0	0	0	0	0	C
Total 3		.167	6	12	0	2	0	1	0	0	0	1	0	
Derrel Thomas														
1981	LA-N	.000	5	7	2	0	0	0	0	1	1	2	0	O*3,3*2,S*1
Fred Thomas														
1918	Bos-A	.125	6	16	0	2	0	0	0	0	1	2	0	3
George Thomas														
1967	Bos-A	.000	2	2	0	0	0	0	0	0	0	1	0	O*1
Ira Thomas														
1908	Det-A	.500	2	4	0	2	1	0	0	1	1	0	0	C*1
1910	Phi-A	.250	4	12	2	3	0	0	0	1	4	1	0	C
1911	Phi-A	.083	4	12	1	1	0	0	0	1	1	2	0	C
Total 3		.214	10	28	3	6	1	0	0	3	6	3	0	
Gorman Thomas														
1982	Mil-A	.115	7	26	0	3	0	0	0	3	2	7	0	O
Gary Thomasson														
1978	NY-A	.250	3	4	0	1	0	0	0	0	1	0	0	O
Don Thompson														
1953	Bro-N	—	2	0	0	0	0	0	0	0	0	0	0	O
Hank Thompson														
1951	NY-N	.143	5	14	3	2	0	0	0	0	5	2	0	O

YEAR	TM/L	AVG	G	AB	R	H	2B	3B	HR	RBI	BB	SO	SB	POS
1954	NY-N	.364	4	11	6	4	1	0	0	2	7	1	0	3
Total 2		.240	9	25	9	6	1	0	0	2	12	3	0	

■ Milt Thompson

| 1993 | Phi-N | .313 | 5 | 16 | 3 | 5 | 1 | 1 | 1 | 6 | 1 | 2 | 0 | O |

■ Robby Thompson

| 1989 | SF-N | .091 | 4 | 11 | 0 | 1 | 0 | 0 | 0 | 2 | 0 | 4 | 0 | 2 |

■ Sam Thompson

| 1887 | Det-N | .362 | 15 | 58 | 8 | 21 | 2 | 0 | 2 | 8 | 3 | 3 | 5 | O |

■ Bobby Thomson

| 1951 | NY-N | .238 | 6 | 21 | 1 | 5 | 1 | 0 | 0 | 2 | 5 | 0 | 0 | 3 |

■ Jim Thorpe

| 1917 | NY-N | — | 1 | 0 | 0 | 0 | 0 | 0 | 0 | 0 | 0 | 0 | 0 | O |

■ Marv Throneberry

| 1958 | NY-A | .000 | 1 | 1 | 0 | 0 | 0 | 0 | 0 | 0 | 0 | 1 | 0 | H |

■ Mike Tiernan

1888	NY-N	.342	10	38	8	13	0	0	1	6	8	2	5	O
1889	NY-N	.289	9	38	12	11	1	1	1	5	5	3	3	O
1894	NY-N	.294	4	17	5	5	0	1	0	3	2	2	0	O
Total 3		.312	23	93	25	29	1	2	2	14	15	7	8	

■ Joe Tinker

1906	Chi-N	.167	6	18	4	3	0	0	0	1	2	2	3	S
1907	Chi-N	.154	5	13	4	2	0	0	0	1	3	3	1	S
1908	Chi-N	.263	5	19	2	5	0	0	1	4	0	2	2	S
1910	Chi-N	.333	5	18	2	6	2	0	0	0	2	2	1	S
Total 4		.235	21	68	12	16	2	0	1	6	7	9	7	

■ Joe Tipton

| 1948 | Cle-A | .000 | 1 | 1 | 0 | 0 | 0 | 0 | 0 | 0 | 0 | 1 | 0 | H |

■ Phil Todt

| 1931 | Phi-A | — | 1 | 0 | 0 | 0 | 0 | 0 | 0 | 0 | 1 | 0 | 0 | H |

■ Bobby Tolan

1967	StL-N	.000	3	2	1	0	0	0	0	0	1	1	0	H
1968	StL-N	.000	1	1	0	0	0	0	0	0	0	1	0	H
1970	Cin-N	.211	5	19	5	4	1	0	1	1	3	2	1	O
1972	Cin-N	.269	7	26	2	7	1	0	0	6	1	4	5	O
Total 4		.229	16	48	8	11	2	0	1	7	5	8	6	

■ Chick Tolson

| 1929 | Chi-N | .000 | 1 | 1 | 0 | 0 | 0 | 0 | 0 | 0 | 0 | 1 | 0 | H |

■ Phil Tomney

| 1890 | Lou-A | .200 | 3 | 5 | 1 | 1 | 0 | 0 | 0 | 0 | 3 | 1 | 0 | S |

■ Specs Toporcer

| 1926 | StL-N | — | 1 | 0 | 0 | 0 | 0 | 0 | 0 | 1 | 0 | 0 | 0 | H |

■ Earl Torgeson

1948	Bos-N	.389	5	18	2	7	3	0	0	1	2	1	1	1
1959	Chi-A	.000	3	1	1	0	0	0	0	0	1	0	0	1*1
Total 2		.368	8	19	3	7	3	0	0	1	3	1	1	

■ Frank Torre

1957	Mil-N	.300	7	10	2	3	0	0	2	3	2	0	0	1
1958	Mil-N	.176	7	17	0	3	0	0	0	1	2	0	0	1
Total 2		.222	14	27	2	6	0	0	2	4	4	0	0	

■ Babe Towne

| 1906 | Chi-A | .000 | 1 | 1 | 0 | 0 | 0 | 0 | 0 | 0 | 0 | 0 | 0 | H |

■ Dick Tracewski

1963	LA-N	.154	4	13	1	2	0	0	0	0	1	2	0	2
1965	LA-N	.118	6	17	0	2	0	0	0	1	5	0	2	
1968	Det-A	—	2	0	1	0	0	0	0	0	0	0	0	3*1
Total 3		.133	12	30	2	4	0	0	0	2	7	0		

■ Alan Trammell

| 1984 | Det-A | .450 | 5 | 20 | 5 | 9 | 1 | 0 | 2 | 6 | 2 | 2 | 1 | S |

■ Pie Traynor

1925	Pit-N	.346	7	26	2	9	0	2	1	4	3	1	3	
1927	Pit-N	.200	4	15	1	3	1	0	0	0	0	1	0	3
Total 2		.293	11	41	3	12	1	2	1	4	3	2	1	

■ Jeff Treadway

1991	Atl-N	.250	3	4	1	1	0	0	0	0	1	2	0	2*1
1992	Atl-N	.000	1	1	0	0	0	0	0	0	0	0	0	H
Total 2		.200	4	5	1	1	0	0	0	0	1	2	0	

■ Tom Tresh

1962	NY-A	.321	7	28	5	9	1	0	1	4	1	4	2	O
1963	NY-A	.200	4	15	1	3	0	0	1	2	1	6	0	O
1964	NY-A	.273	7	22	4	6	2	0	2	7	6	7	0	O
Total 3		.277	18	65	10	18	3	0	4	13	8	17	2	

■ Manny Trillo

| 1980 | Phi-N | .217 | 6 | 23 | 4 | 5 | 2 | 0 | 0 | 2 | 0 | 0 | 0 | 2 |

■ Dasher Troy

| 1884 | NY-A | .200 | 2 | 5 | 0 | 1 | 0 | 0 | 0 | 0 | 1 | 0 | 1 | 0 2 |

■ Tommy Tucker

| 1892 | Bos-N | .261 | 6 | 23 | 2 | 6 | 0 | 0 | 1 | 2 | 0 | 1 | 0 | 1 |

■ Thurman Tucker

| 1948 | Cle-A | .333 | 1 | 3 | 1 | 1 | 0 | 0 | 0 | 0 | 1 | 0 | 0 | O |

■ Tom Turner

| 1944 | StL-A | .000 | 1 | 1 | 0 | 0 | 0 | 0 | 0 | 0 | 0 | 0 | 0 | 0 | H |

■ Larry Twitchell

| 1887 | Det-N | .250 | 6 | 20 | 5 | 5 | 1 | 0 | 1 | 3 | 0 | 1 | 1 | O |

■ Ted Uhlaender

| 1972 | Cin-N | .250 | 4 | 4 | 0 | 1 | 1 | 0 | 0 | 0 | 0 | 1 | 0 | H |

■ Del Unser

| 1980 | Phi-N | .500 | 3 | 6 | 2 | 3 | 0 | 0 | 0 | 2 | 0 | 1 | 0 | 0 |

■ Jose Uribe

| 1989 | SF-N | .200 | 3 | 5 | 1 | 1 | 0 | 0 | 0 | 0 | 0 | 0 | 0 | S |

■ Sandy Valdespino

| 1965 | Min-A | .273 | 5 | 11 | 1 | 3 | 1 | 0 | 0 | 0 | 0 | 1 | 0 | O*2 |

■ George Van Haltren

| 1894 | NY-N | .500 | 4 | 14 | 3 | 7 | 1 | 1 | 0 | 0 | 2 | 2 | 2 | O |

■ Andy Van Slyke

| 1985 | StL-N | .091 | 6 | 11 | 0 | 1 | 0 | 0 | 0 | 0 | 0 | 5 | 0 | O |

■ Arky Vaughan

| 1947 | Bro-N | .500 | 3 | 2 | 0 | 1 | 1 | 0 | 0 | 0 | 1 | 0 | 0 | H |

■ Bobby Veach

| 1925 | Was-A | .000 | 2 | 1 | 0 | 0 | 0 | 0 | 0 | 1 | 0 | 0 | 0 | H |

■ Otto Velez

| 1976 | NY-A | .000 | 3 | 3 | 0 | 0 | 0 | 0 | 0 | 0 | 0 | 3 | 0 | H |

■ Emil Verban

| 1944 | StL-N | .412 | 6 | 17 | 1 | 7 | 0 | 0 | 0 | 2 | 2 | 0 | 0 | 2 |

■ Zoilo Versalles

| 1965 | Min-A | .286 | 7 | 28 | 3 | 8 | 1 | 1 | 1 | 4 | 2 | 7 | 1 | S |

■ Bill Virdon

| 1960 | Pit-N | .241 | 7 | 29 | 2 | 7 | 3 | 0 | 0 | 5 | 1 | 3 | 1 | O |

■ Ozzie Virgil

| 1983 | Phi-N | .500 | 3 | 2 | 0 | 1 | 0 | 0 | 0 | 1 | 0 | 0 | 0 | C*1 |

■ Jake Virtue

| 1892 | Cle-N | .125 | 6 | 24 | 1 | 3 | 0 | 0 | 0 | 0 | 2 | 5 | 1 | 1 |

■ Joe Visner

| 1889 | Bro-N | .125 | 5 | 16 | 2 | 2 | 1 | 0 | 0 | 2 | 3 | 0 | | C*3,O*2 |

■ Heinie Wagner

| 1912 | Bos-A | .167 | 8 | 30 | 1 | 5 | 1 | 0 | 0 | 0 | 3 | 6 | 1 | S |

■ Hal Wagner

| 1946 | Bos-A | .000 | 5 | 13 | 0 | 0 | 0 | 0 | 0 | 0 | 0 | 1 | 0 | C |

■ Honus Wagner

1900	Pit-N	.400	4	15	2	6	1	0	0	3	0	1	2	O
1903	Pit-N	.222	8	27	2	6	1	0	0	3	3	4	3	S
1909	Pit-N	.333	7	24	4	8	2	1	0	6	4	2	6	S
Total 3		.303	19	66	8	20	4	1	0	12	7	7	11	

■ Eddie Waitkus

| 1950 | Phi-N | .267 | 4 | 15 | 0 | 4 | 1 | 0 | 0 | 0 | 2 | 0 | 0 | 1 |

■ Rube Walker

| 1956 | Bro-N | .000 | 2 | 2 | 0 | 0 | 0 | 0 | 0 | 0 | 0 | 0 | 0 | H |

■ Tilly Walker

| 1916 | Bos-A | .273 | 3 | 11 | 1 | 3 | 0 | 1 | 0 | 1 | 1 | 2 | 0 | O |

■ Dixie Walker

1941	Bro-N	.222	5	18	3	4	2	0	0	0	2	1	0	O
1947	Bro-N	.222	7	27	1	6	1	0	1	4	3	1	1	O
Total 2		.222	12	45	4	10	3	0	1	4	5	2	1	

■ Gee Walker

1934	Det-A	.333	3	3	0	1	0	0	0	1	0	1	0	H
1935	Det-A	.250	3	4	1	1	0	0	0	0	1	0	0	O*1
Total 2		.286	6	7	1	2	0	0	0	1	1	1	0	

■ Harry Walker

1942	StL-N	.000	1	1	0	0	0	0	0	0	0	1	0	H
1943	StL-N	.167	5	18	0	3	1	0	0	0	0	2	0	O
1946	StL-N	.412	7	17	3	7	2	0	0	6	4	2	0	O
Total 3		.278	13	36	3	10	3	0	0	6	4	5	0	

■ Hub Walker

| 1945 | Det-A | .500 | 2 | 2 | 1 | 1 | 1 | 0 | 0 | 0 | 0 | 0 | 0 | H |

■ Jimmy Walsh

1914	Phi-A	.333	3	6	0	2	1	0	0	1	3	1	0	O*2
1916	Bos-A	.000	1	3	0	0	0	0	0	0	0	0	0	0
Total 2		.222	4	9	0	2	1	0	0	1	3	1	0	

■ Bill Wambsganss

| 1920 | Cle-A | .154 | 7 | 26 | 3 | 4 | 0 | 0 | 0 | 1 | 2 | 1 | 0 | 2 |

■ Lloyd Waner

| 1927 | Pit-N | .400 | 4 | 15 | 5 | 6 | 1 | 1 | 0 | 0 | 1 | 0 | 0 | O |

■ Paul Waner

| 1927 | Pit-N | .333 | 4 | 15 | 0 | 5 | 1 | 0 | 0 | 3 | 0 | 1 | 0 | O |

■ Aaron Ward

| 1921 | NY-A | .231 | 8 | 26 | 1 | 6 | 0 | 0 | 0 | 4 | 2 | 6 | 0 | 2 |
| 1922 | NY-A | .154 | 5 | 13 | 3 | 2 | 0 | 0 | 2 | 3 | 3 | 3 | 0 | 2 |

YEAR	TM/L	AVG	G	AB	R	H	2B	3B	HR	RBI	BB	SO	SB	POS
1923	NY-A	.417	6	24	4	10	0	0	1	2	1	3	1	2
Total 3		.286	19	63	8	18	0	0	3	9	6	12	1	

■ Monte Ward

1888	NY-N	.379	8	29	4	11	1	0	0	6	1	0	6	S
1889	NY-N	.417	9	36	10	15	0	1	0	7	5	2	10	S
1894	NY-N	.294	4	17	1	5	0	0	0	6	0	0	0	2
Total 3		.378	21	82	15	31	1	1	0	19	6	2	16	

■ Carl Warwick

1964	StL-N	.750	5	4	2	3	0	0	0	1	1	0	0	H

■ Jimmy Wasdell

1941	Bro-N	.200	3	5	0	1	1	0	0	2	0	0	0	O*1

■ Claudell Washington

1974	Oak-A	.571	5	7	1	4	0	0	0	0	1	1	0	O

■ Herb Washington

1974	Oak-A	—	3	0	0	0	0	0	0	0	0	0	0	R

■ U L Washington

1980	KC-A	.273	6	22	1	6	0	0	0	2	0	6	0	S

■ John Wathan

1980	KC-A	.286	3	7	1	2	0	0	0	1	2	1	0	C*2,O*1
1985	KC-A	.000	2	1	0	0	0	0	0	0	0	1	0	H
Total 2		.250	5	8	1	2	0	0	0	1	2	2	0	

■ George Watkins

1930	StL-N	.167	4	12	2	2	0	0	1	1	1	3	0	O
1931	StL-N	.286	5	14	4	4	1	0	1	2	2	1	1	O
Total 2		.231	9	26	6	6	1	0	2	3	3	4	1	

■ Bob Watson

1981	NY-A	.318	6	22	2	7	1	0	2	7	3	0	0	1

■ Roy Weatherly

1943	NY-A	.000	1	1	0	0	0	0	0	0	0	0	0	H

■ Buck Weaver

1917	Chi-A	.333	6	21	3	7	1	0	0	1	0	2	0	S
1919	Chi-A	.324	8	34	4	11	4	1	0	0	0	2	0	3
Total 2		.327	14	55	7	18	5	1	0	1	0	4	0	

■ Farmer Weaver

1890	Lou-A	.259	7	27	4	7	1	0	0	4	1	2	5	O

■ Skeeter Webb

1945	Det-A	.185	7	27	4	5	0	0	0	1	3	1	0	S

■ Pete Weckbecker

1890	Lou-A	.000	1	4	0	0	0	0	0	0	0	1	0	C

■ Al Weis

1969	NY-N	.455	5	11	1	5	0	0	1	3	4	2	0	2

■ Walt Weiss

1988	Oak-A	.063	5	16	1	1	0	0	0	0	0	2	1	S
1989	Oak-A	.133	4	15	3	2	0	0	1	1	2	2	0	S
Total 2		.097	9	31	4	3	0	0	1	1	2	4	1	

■ Curt Welch

1885	StL-A	.148	7	27	5	4	1	1	0	0	0	0	0	O
1886	StL-A	.350	6	20	7	7	2	0	0	1	3	4	2	O
1887	StL-A	.207	15	58	6	12	3	1	1	8	0	2	1	O
Total 3		.219	28	105	18	23	6	2	1	9	3	6	3	

■ Billy Werber

1939	Cin-N	.250	4	16	1	4	0	0	0	2	2	0	0	3
1940	Cin-N	.370	7	27	5	10	4	0	0	2	4	2	0	3
Total 2		.326	11	43	6	14	4	0	0	4	6	2	0	

■ Don Wert

1968	Det-A	.118	6	17	1	2	0	0	0	2	6	5	0	3

■ Vic Wertz

1954	Cle-A	.500	4	16	2	8	2	1	1	3	2	2	0	1

■ Wally Westlake

1954	Cle-A	.143	2	7	0	1	0	0	0	0	1	3	0	O

■ Wes Westrum

1951	NY-N	.235	6	17	1	4	1	0	0	0	5	3	0	C
1954	NY-N	.273	4	11	0	3	0	0	0	3	1	3	0	C
Total 2		.250	10	28	1	7	1	0	0	3	6	6	0	

■ Zack Wheat

1916	Bro-N	.211	5	19	2	4	0	1	0	1	2	2	1	O
1920	Bro-N	.333	7	27	2	9	2	0	0	2	1	2	0	O
Total 2		.283	12	46	4	13	2	1	0	3	3	4	1	

■ Lou Whitaker

1984	Det-A	.278	5	18	6	5	2	0	0	4	4	0	2	

■ Devon White

1992	Tor-A	.231	6	26	2	6	1	0	0	2	0	6	1	O
1993	Tor-A	.292	6	24	8	7	3	1	1	7	4	7	1	O
Total 2		.260	12	50	10	13	4	2	1	9	4	13	2	

■ Ernie White

1942	StL-N	.000	1	2	0	0	0	0	0	0	0	0	0	P
1943	StL-N	—	1	0	0	0	0	0	0	0	0	0	0	R
Total 2		.000	2	2	0	0	0	0	0	0	0	0	0	

■ Frank White

1980	KC-A	.080	6	25	0	2	0	0	0	0	1	5	1	2
1985	KC-A	.250	7	28	4	7	3	0	1	6	3	4	0	2
Total 2		.170	13	53	4	9	3	0	1	6	4	9	1	

■ Deacon White

1887	Det-N	.207	15	58	8	12	1	0	5	2	0	2	3*14,1*1

■ Jo-Jo White

1934	Det-A	.130	7	23	6	3	0	0	0	0	8	4	1	O
1935	Det-A	.263	5	19	3	5	0	0	0	1	5	7	0	O
Total 2		.190	12	42	9	8	0	0	0	1	13	11	1	

■ Roy White

1976	NY-A	.133	4	15	0	2	0	0	0	0	3	0	0	O
1977	NY-A	.000	2	2	0	0	0	0	0	0	0	0	0	H
1978	NY-A	.333	6	24	9	8	0	0	1	4	4	5	2	O
Total 3		.244	12	41	9	10	0	0	1	4	7	5	2	

■ Bill White

1964	StL-N	.111	7	27	2	3	1	0	0	2	6	1	1	

■ Bill White

1888	StL-A	.143	10	35	4	5	1	0	0	4	3	6	1	S

■ Burgess Whitehead

1934	StL-N	—	1	0	0	0	0	0	0	0	0	0	0	S
1936	NY-N	.048	6	21	1	1	0	0	0	2	1	3	0	2
1937	NY-N	.250	5	16	1	4	2	0	0	2	0	1	2	2
Total 3		.135	12	37	2	5	2	0	0	3	3	3	1	

■ George Whiteman

1918	Bos-A	.250	6	20	2	5	0	1	0	1	2	1	0	O

■ Dick Whitman

1949	Bro-N	.000	1	1	0	0	0	0	0	0	0	1	0	H
1950	Phi-N	.000	3	2	0	0	0	0	0	0	1	0	0	H
Total 2		.000	4	3	0	0	0	0	0	0	1	1	0	

■ Art Whitney

1888	NY-N	.324	10	37	7	12	0	1	0	12	1	4	2	3*9,O*1
1889	NY-N	.229	9	35	4	8	2	1	0	3	1	0	0	3
Total 2		.278	19	72	11	20	2	2	0	15	2	4	2	

■ Possum Whitted

1914	Bos-N	.214	4	14	2	3	0	1	0	2	3	1	1	O
1915	Phi-N	.067	5	15	0	1	0	0	0	1	1	0	1	O*5,1*1
Total 2		.138	9	29	2	4	0	1	0	3	4	1	2	

■ Alan Wiggins

1984	SD-N	.364	5	22	2	8	1	0	0	1	0	2	1	2

■ Joe Wilhoit

1917	NY-N	.000	2	1	0	0	0	0	0	0	1	0	0	H

■ Jerry Willard

1991	Atl-N	—	1	0	0	0	0	0	0	1	0	0	0	H

■ Davey Williams

1951	NY-N	.000	1	0	0	0	0	0	0	0	0	0	0	H
1954	NY-N	.000	4	11	0	0	0	0	0	1	2	2	0	2
Total 2		.000	6	12	0	0	0	0	0	1	2	2	0	

■ Dewey Williams

1945	Chi-N	.000	2	2	0	0	0	0	0	0	0	1	0	C*1

■ Dib Williams

1931	Phi-A	.320	7	25	2	8	1	0	0	1	2	9	0	S

■ Jimmy Williams

1900	Pit-N	.214	4	14	0	3	0	0	0	0	1	0	0	3

■ Matt Williams

1989	SF-N	.125	4	16	1	2	0	0	1	1	0	6	0	S*4,3*3

■ Dick Williams

1953	Bro-N	.500	3	2	0	1	0	0	0	0	1	1	0	H

■ Ted Williams

1946	Bos-A	.200	7	25	2	5	0	0	0	1	5	5	0	O

■ Ned Williamson

1885	Chi-N	.087	7	23	1	2	0	0	0	4	0	0	3*4,S*3
1886	Chi-N	.056	6	18	2	1	0	1	0	3	4	5	1	S*6,P*2,C,O
Total 2		.073	13	41	3	3	0	1	0	3	8	5	1	

■ Maury Wills

1959	LA-N	.250	6	20	2	5	0	0	0	1	0	3	1	S
1963	LA-N	.133	4	15	1	2	0	0	0	0	1	3	1	S
1965	LA-N	.367	7	30	3	11	3	0	0	3	1	3	3	S
1966	LA-N	.077	4	13	0	1	0	0	0	0	3	3	1	S
Total 4		.244	21	78	6	19	3	0	0	4	5	12	6	

■ Art Wilson

1911	NY-N	.000	1	1	0	0	0	0	0	0	0	0	0	C
1912	NY-N	1.000	2	1	0	1	0	0	0	0	0	0	0	C
1913	NY-N	.000	3	3	0	0	0	0	0	0	2	0	0	C
Total 3		.200	6	5	0	1	0	0	0	0	2	0	0	

■ George Wilson

1956	NY-A	.000	1	1	0	0	0	0	0	0	0	1	0	H

■ Jimmie Wilson

1928	StL-N	.091	3	11	1	1	1	0	0	1	0	3	0	C
1930	StL-N	.267	4	15	0	4	1	0	0	2	0	1	0	C

YEAR	TM/L	AVG	G	AB	R	H	2B	3B	HR	RBI	BB	SO	SB	POS
1931	StL-N	.217	7	23	0	5	0	0	0	2	1	1	0	C
1940	Cin-N	.353	6	17	2	6	0	0	0	0	1	2	1	C
Total 4		.242	20	66	3	16	2	0	0	5	2	7	1	

■ Chief Wilson

YEAR	TM/L	AVG	G	AB	R	H	2B	3B	HR	RBI	BB	SO	SB	POS
1909	Pit-N	.154	7	26	2	4	1	0	0	1	0	2	1	O

■ Hack Wilson

YEAR	TM/L	AVG	G	AB	R	H	2B	3B	HR	RBI	BB	SO	SB	POS
1924	NY-N	.233	7	30	1	7	1	0	0	3	1	9	0	O
1929	Chi-N	.471	5	17	2	8	0	1	0	0	4	3	0	O
Total 2		.319	12	47	3	15	1	1	0	3	5	12	0	

■ Mookie Wilson

YEAR	TM/L	AVG	G	AB	R	H	2B	3B	HR	RBI	BB	SO	SB	POS
1986	NY-N	.269	7	26	3	7	1	0	0	0	1	6	3	O

■ Willie Wilson

YEAR	TM/L	AVG	G	AB	R	H	2B	3B	HR	RBI	BB	SO	SB	POS
1980	KC-A	.154	6	26	3	4	1	0	0	0	4	12	2	O
1985	KC-A	.367	7	30	2	11	0	1	0	3	1	4	3	O
Total 2		.268	13	56	5	15	1	1	0	3	5	16	5	

■ Hooks Wiltse

YEAR	TM/L	AVG	G	AB	R	H	2B	3B	HR	RBI	BB	SO	SB	POS
1911	NY-N	.000	2	1	0	0	0	0	0	0	0	1	0	P
1913	NY-N	.000	2	2	0	0	0	0	0	0	0	1	0	1
Total 2		.000	4	3	0	0	0	0	0	0	0	2	0	

■ Dave Winfield

YEAR	TM/L	AVG	G	AB	R	H	2B	3B	HR	RBI	BB	SO	SB	POS
1981	NY-A	.045	6	22	0	1	0	0	0	1	5	4	1	O
1992	Tor-A	.227	6	22	0	5	1	0	0	3	2	3	0	O*3,D*3
Total 2		.136	12	44	0	6	1	0	0	4	7	7	1	

■ Ivey Wingo

YEAR	TM/L	AVG	G	AB	R	H	2B	3B	HR	RBI	BB	SO	SB	POS
1919	Cin-N	.571	3	7	1	4	0	0	0	1	3	1	0	C

■ Herm Winningham

YEAR	TM/L	AVG	G	AB	R	H	2B	3B	HR	RBI	BB	SO	SB	POS
1990	Cin-N	.500	2	4	1	2	0	0	0	0	0	0	0	O*1

■ Casey Wise

YEAR	TM/L	AVG	G	AB	R	H	2B	3B	HR	RBI	BB	SO	SB	POS
1958	Mil-N	.000	2	1	0	0	0	0	0	0	0	1	0	H

■ Whitey Witt

YEAR	TM/L	AVG	G	AB	R	H	2B	3B	HR	RBI	BB	SO	SB	POS
1922	NY-A	.222	5	18	1	4	1	1	0	0	1	2	0	O
1923	NY-A	.240	6	25	1	6	2	0	0	4	1	1	0	O
Total 2		.233	11	43	2	10	3	1	0	4	2	3	0	

■ Chicken Wolf

YEAR	TM/L	AVG	G	AB	R	H	2B	3B	HR	RBI	BB	SO	SB	POS
1890	Lou-A	.360	7	25	4	9	3	1	0	8	3	0	2	3*5,O*3

■ Joe Wood

YEAR	TM/L	AVG	G	AB	R	H	2B	3B	HR	RBI	BB	SO	SB	POS
1912	Bos-A	.286	4	7	1	2	0	0	0	1	1	0	0	P
1920	Cle-A	.200	4	10	2	2	1	0	0	0	1	2	0	O
Total 2		.235	8	17	3	4	1	0	0	1	2	2	0	

■ Gene Woodling

YEAR	TM/L	AVG	G	AB	R	H	2B	3B	HR	RBI	BB	SO	SB	POS
1949	NY-A	.400	3	10	4	4	3	0	0	0	3	0	0	O
1950	NY-A	.429	4	14	2	6	0	0	0	1	2	0	0	O
1951	NY-A	.167	6	18	6	3	1	1	1	1	5	3	0	O*5
1952	NY-A	.348	7	23	4	8	1	1	1	1	3	3	0	O*6
1953	NY-A	.300	6	20	5	6	0	0	1	3	6	2	0	O
Total 5		.318	26	85	21	27	5	2	3	6	19	8	0	

■ Tracy Woodson

YEAR	TM/L	AVG	G	AB	R	H	2B	3B	HR	RBI	BB	SO	SB	POS
1988	LA-N	.000	4	4	0	0	0	0	0	1	0	0	0	1*3

■ Woody Woodward

YEAR	TM/L	AVG	G	AB	R	H	2B	3B	HR	RBI	BB	SO	SB	POS
1970	Cin-N	.200	4	5	0	1	0	0	0	0	0	0	0	S*3

■ Chuck Wortman

YEAR	TM/L	AVG	G	AB	R	H	2B	3B	HR	RBI	BB	SO	SB	POS
1918	Chi-N	.000	1	1	0	0	0	0	0	0	0	0	2	

■ Glenn Wright

YEAR	TM/L	AVG	G	AB	R	H	2B	3B	HR	RBI	BB	SO	SB	POS
1925	Pit-N	.185	7	27	3	5	1	0	1	3	1	4	0	S
1927	Pit-N	.154	4	13	1	2	0	0	0	2	0	0	0	S
Total 2		.175	11	40	4	7	1	0	1	5	1	4	0	

■ Jim Wynn

YEAR	TM/L	AVG	G	AB	R	H	2B	3B	HR	RBI	BB	SO	SB	POS
1974	LA-N	.188	5	16	1	3	1	0	1	2	4	4	0	O

■ Carl Yastrzemski

YEAR	TM/L	AVG	G	AB	R	H	2B	3B	HR	RBI	BB	SO	SB	POS
1967	Bos-A	.400	7	25	4	10	2	0	3	5	4	1	0	O
1975	Bos-A	.310	7	29	7	9	0	0	0	4	4	1	0	1*4,O*4
Total 2		.352	14	54	11	19	2	0	3	9	8	2	0	

■ Emil Yde

YEAR	TM/L	AVG	G	AB	R	H	2B	3B	HR	RBI	BB	SO	SB	POS
1925	Pit-N	.000	2	1	1	0	0	0	0	0	0	0	0	P*1
1927	Pit-N	—	1	0	1	0	0	0	0	0	0	0	0	R
Total 2		.000	3	1	2	0	0	0	0	0	0	0	0	

■ George Yeager

YEAR	TM/L	AVG	G	AB	R	H	2B	3B	HR	RBI	BB	SO	SB	POS
1897	Bos-N	.500	3	12	2	6	1	1	0	2	2	0	0	C

■ Steve Yeager

YEAR	TM/L	AVG	G	AB	R	H	2B	3B	HR	RBI	BB	SO	SB	POS
1974	LA-N	.364	4	11	0	4	1	0	0	1	1	4	0	C
1977	LA-N	.316	6	19	2	6	1	0	2	5	1	1	0	C
1978	LA-N	.231	5	13	2	3	1	0	0	0	1	2	0	C
1981	LA-N	.286	6	14	2	4	1	0	2	4	0	2	0	C
Total 4		.298	21	57	6	17	4	0	4	10	3	9	0	

■ Steve Yerkes

YEAR	TM/L	AVG	G	AB	R	H	2B	3B	HR	RBI	BB	SO	SB	POS
1912	Bos-A	.250	8	32	3	8	0	2	0	4	2	3	0	2

■ Rudy York

YEAR	TM/L	AVG	G	AB	R	H	2B	3B	HR	RBI	BB	SO	SB	POS
1940	Det-A	.231	7	26	3	6	0	1	1	2	4	7	0	1
1945	Det-A	.179	7	28	1	5	1	0	0	3	3	4	0	1
1946	Bos-A	.261	7	23	6	6	1	1	2	5	6	4	0	1
Total 3		.221	21	77	10	17	2	2	3	10	13	15	0	

■ Ned Yost

YEAR	TM/L	AVG	G	AB	R	H	2B	3B	HR	RBI	BB	SO	SB	POS
1982	Mil-A	—	1	0	0	0	0	0	0	0	0	1	0	C

■ Ross Youngs

YEAR	TM/L	AVG	G	AB	R	H	2B	3B	HR	RBI	BB	SO	SB	POS
1921	NY-N	.280	8	25	3	7	1	1	0	4	7	2	2	O
1922	NY-N	.375	5	16	2	6	0	0	0	2	3	1	0	O
1923	NY-N	.348	6	23	2	8	0	0	1	3	2	0	0	O
1924	NY-N	.185	7	27	3	5	1	0	0	2	5	6	1	O
Total 4		.286	26	91	10	26	2	1	1	11	17	9	3	

■ Robin Yount

YEAR	TM/L	AVG	G	AB	R	H	2B	3B	HR	RBI	BB	SO	SB	POS
1982	Mil-A	.414	7	29	6	12	3	0	1	6	2	2	0	S

■ Sal Yvars

YEAR	TM/L	AVG	G	AB	R	H	2B	3B	HR	RBI	BB	SO	SB	POS
1951	NY-N	.000	1	1	0	0	0	0	0	0	0	0	0	H

■ Al Zarilla

YEAR	TM/L	AVG	G	AB	R	H	2B	3B	HR	RBI	BB	SO	SB	POS
1944	StL-A	.100	4	10	1	1	0	0	0	1	0	4	0	O*3

■ George Zeber

YEAR	TM/L	AVG	G	AB	R	H	2B	3B	HR	RBI	BB	SO	SB	POS
1977	NY-A	.000	2	2	0	0	0	0	0	0	0	2	0	H

■ Rollie Zeider

YEAR	TM/L	AVG	G	AB	R	H	2B	3B	HR	RBI	BB	SO	SB	POS
1918	Chi-N	—	2	0	0	0	0	0	0	0	2	0	0	3

■ Chief Zimmer

YEAR	TM/L	AVG	G	AB	R	H	2B	3B	HR	RBI	BB	SO	SB	POS
1892	Cle-N	.261	6	23	2	6	1	1	0	2	0	3	0	C
1895	Cle-N	.333	4	18	2	6	2	0	0	3	3	5	0	C
1896	Cle-N	.214	4	14	0	3	1	0	0	1	2	6	0	C
1900	Pit-N	.111	3	9	1	1	0	0	0	1	1	2	1	C
Total 4		.250	17	64	5	16	4	1	0	7	6	16	1	

■ Don Zimmer

YEAR	TM/L	AVG	G	AB	R	H	2B	3B	HR	RBI	BB	SO	SB	POS
1955	Bro-N	.222	4	9	0	2	0	0	0	2	2	5	0	2
1959	LA-N	.000	1	1	0	0	0	0	0	0	0	0	0	S
Total 2		.200	5	10	0	2	0	0	0	2	2	5	0	

■ Jerry Zimmerman

YEAR	TM/L	AVG	G	AB	R	H	2B	3B	HR	RBI	BB	SO	SB	POS
1961	Cin-N	—	2	0	0	0	0	0	0	0	0	0	0	C
1965	Min-A	.000	2	1	0	0	0	0	0	0	0	0	0	C
Total 2		.000	4	1	0	0	0	0	0	0	0	0	0	

■ Heinie Zimmerman

YEAR	TM/L	AVG	G	AB	R	H	2B	3B	HR	RBI	BB	SO	SB	POS
1907	Chi-N	.000	1	1	0	0	0	0	0	0	0	0	0	2
1910	Chi-N	.235	5	17	0	4	1	0	0	2	1	3	1	2
1917	NY-N	.120	6	25	1	3	0	1	0	0	0	0	3	
Total 3		.163	12	43	1	7	1	1	0	2	1	4	1	

YEAR	TM/L	W	L	ERA	G	GS	CG	SV	SHO	IP	H	ER	BB	SO
● Babe Adams														
1909	Pit-N	3	0	1.33	3	3	3	0	1	27	18	4	6	11
1925	Pit-N	0	0	0.00	1	0	0	0	0	1	2	0	0	0
Total 2		3	0	1.29	4	3	3	0	1	28	20	4	6	11
● Rick Aguilera														
1986	NY-N	1	0	12.00	1	0	0	0	0	3	8	4	1	4
1991	Min-A	1	1	1.80	4	0	0	2	0	5	6	1	1	3
Total 2		2	1	5.63	5	0	0	2	0	8	14	5	2	7
● Vic Aldridge														
1925	Pit-N	2	0	4.42	3	3	2	0	0	18¹	18	9	9	9
1927	Pit-N	0	1	7.36	1	1	0	0	0	7¹	10	6	4	4
Total 2		2	1	5.26	4	4	2	0	0	25²	28	15	13	13
● Doyle Alexander														
1976	NY-A	0	1	7.50	1	1	0	0	0	6	9	5	2	1
● Pete Alexander														
1915	Phi-N	1	1	1.53	2	2	2	0	0	17²	14	3	4	10
1926	StL-N	2	0	1.33	3	2	2	1	0	20¹	12	3	4	17
1928	StL-N	0	1	19.80	2	1	0	0	0	5	10	11	4	2
Total 3		3	2	3.56	7	5	4	1	0	43	36	17	12	29
● Johnny Allen														
1932	NY-A	0	0	40.50	1	1	0	0	0	0²	5	3	0	0
1941	Bro-N	0	0	0.00	3	0	0	0	0	3²	1	0	3	0
Total 2		0	0	6.23	4	1	0	0	0	4¹	6	3	3	0
● Nick Altrock														
1906	Chi-A	1	1	1.00	2	2	2	0	0	18	11	2	2	5
● Red Ames														
1905	NY-N	0	0	0.00	1	0	0	0	0	1	1	0	1	1
1911	NY-N	0	1	2.25	2	1	0	0	0	8	6	2	1	6
1912	NY-N	0	0	4.50	1	0	0	0	0	2	3	1	1	0
Total 3		0	1	2.45	4	1	0	0	0	11	10	3	3	7
● Larry Andersen														
1983	Phi-N	0	0	2.25	2	0	0	0	0	4	4	1	0	1
1993	Phi-N	0	0	12.27	4	0	0	0	0	3²	5	5	3	3
Total 2		0	0	7.04	6	0	0	0	0	7²	9	6	3	4
● Fred Anderson														
1917	NY-N	0	1	18.00	1	0	0	0	0	2	5	4	0	3
● Ivy Andrews														
1937	NY-A	0	0	3.18	1	0	0	0	0	5²	6	2	4	1
● Joaquin Andujar														
1982	StL-N	2	0	1.35	2	2	0	0	0	13¹	10	2	1	4
1985	StL-N	0	1	9.00	2	1	0	0	0	4	10	4	4	3
Total 2		2	1	3.12	4	3	0	0	0	17¹	20	6	5	7
● Johnny Antonelli														
1954	NY-N	1	0	0.84	2	1	1	1	0	10²	8	1	7	12
● Jack Armstrong														
1990	Cin-N	0	0	0.00	1	0	0	0	0	3	1	0	0	3
● Luis Arroyo														
1960	NY-A	0	0	13.50	1	0	0	0	0	0²	2	1	0	1
1961	NY-A	1	0	2.25	2	0	0	0	0	4	4	1	2	3
Total 2		1	0	3.86	3	0	0	0	0	4²	6	2	2	4
● Keith Atherton														
1987	Min-A	0	0	6.75	2	0	0	0	0	1¹	0	1	1	0
● Eldon Auker														
1934	Det-A	1	1	5.56	2	2	1	0	0	11¹	16	7	5	2
1935	Det-A	0	0	3.00	1	1	0	0	0	6	6	2	2	1
Total 2		1	1	4.67	3	3	1	0	0	17¹	22	9	7	3
● Steve Avery														
1991	Atl-N	0	0	3.46	2	2	0	0	0	13	10	5	1	8
1992	Atl-N	0	1	3.75	2	2	0	0	0	12	11	5	3	11
Total 2		0	1	3.60	4	4	0	0	0	25	21	10	4	19
● Jim Bagby														
1946	Bos-A	0	0	3.00	1	0	0	0	0	3	6	1	1	1
● Jim Bagby														
1920	Cle-A	1	1	1.80	2	2	1	0	0	15	20	3	1	3
● Doug Bair														
1982	StL-N	0	1	9.00	3	0	0	0	0	2	2	2	2	3
1984	Det-A	0	0	0.00	1	0	0	0	0	0²	0	0	0	1
Total 2		0	1	6.75	4	0	0	0	0	2²	2	2	2	4
● Lady Baldwin														
1887	Det-N	4	1	1.50	5	5	5	0	1	42	28	7	10	4
● Harry Baldwin														
1924	NY-N	0	0	0.00	1	0	0	0	0	2	1	0	0	1
● Win Ballou														
1925	Was-A	0	0	0.00	2	0	0	0	0	1²	0	0	1	1
● Jack Banta														
1949	Bro-N	0	0	3.18	3	0	0	0	0	5²	5	2	1	4
● Jesse Barnes														
1921	NY-N	2	0	1.65	3	0	0	0	0	16¹	10	3	6	18
1922	NY-N	0	0	1.80	1	1	1	0	0	10	8	2	2	6
Total 2		2	0	1.71	4	1	1	0	0	26¹	18	5	8	24

YEAR	TM/L	W	L	ERA	G	GS	CG	SV	SHO	IP	H	ER	BB	SO
● Virgil Barnes														
1923	NY-N	0	0	0.00	2	0	0	0	0	4²	4	0	0	4
1924	NY-N	0	1	5.68	2	2	0	0	0	12²	15	8	1	9
Total 2		0	1	4.15	4	2	0	0	0	17¹	19	8	1	13
● Rex Barney														
1947	Bro-N	0	1	2.70	3	1	0	0	0	6²	4	2	10	3
1949	Bro-N	0	1	16.88	1	1	0	0	0	2²	3	5	6	2
Total 2		0	2	6.75	4	2	0	0	0	9¹	7	7	16	5
● Red Barrett														
1948	Bos-N	0	0	0.00	2	0	0	0	0	3²	1	0	0	1
● Gene Bearden														
1948	Cle-A	1	0	0.00	2	1	1	1	1	10²	6	0	1	4
● Jim Beattie														
1978	NY-A	1	0	2.00	1	1	1	0	0	9	9	2	4	8
● Johnny Beazley														
1942	StL-N	2	0	2.50	2	2	2	0	0	18	17	5	3	6
1946	StL-N	0	0	0.00	1	0	0	0	0	1	1	0	0	1
Total 2		2	0	2.37	3	2	2	0	0	19	18	5	3	7
● Buck Becannon														
1884	NY-A	0	1	10.50	1	1	1	0	0	6	9	7	2	1
● Joe Beckwith														
1985	KC-A	0	0	0.00	2	0	0	0	0	2	1	0	0	3
● Hugh Bedient														
1912	Bos-A	1	0	1.00	4	2	1	0	0	18	10	2	7	7
● Steve Bedrosian														
1989	SF-N	0	0	0.00	2	0	0	0	0	2²	0	0	2	2
1991	Min-A	0	0	5.40	3	0	0	0	0	3¹	3	2	0	2
Total 2		0	0	3.00	5	0	0	0	0	6	3	2	2	4
● Joe Beggs														
1940	Cin-N	0	0	9.00	1	0	0	0	0	1	3	1	0	1
● Hank Behrman														
1947	Bro-N	0	0	7.11	5	0	0	0	0	6¹	9	5	5	3
● Tim Belcher														
1988	LA-N	1	0	6.23	2	2	0	0	0	8²	10	6	6	10
● Gary Bell														
1967	Bos-A	0	1	5.06	3	1	0	1	0	5¹	8	3	1	1
● Hi Bell														
1926	StL-N	0	0	9.00	1	0	0	0	0	2	4	2	1	1
1930	StL-N	0	0	0.00	1	0	0	0	0	1	0	0	0	0
1933	NY-N	0	0	0.00	1	0	0	0	0	1	0	0	0	0
Total 3		0	0	4.50	3	0	0	0	0	4	4	2	1	1
● Chief Bender														
1905	Phi-A	1	1	1.06	2	2	2	0	1	17	9	2	6	13
1910	Phi-A	1	1	1.93	2	2	2	0	0	18²	12	4	4	14
1911	Phi-A	2	1	1.04	3	3	3	0	0	26	16	3	8	20
1913	Phi-A	2	0	4.00	2	2	2	0	0	18	19	8	1	9
1914	Phi-A	0	1	10.13	1	1	0	0	0	5¹	8	6	2	3
Total 5		6	4	2.44	10	10	9	0	1	85	64	23	21	59
● Jack Bentley														
1923	NY-N	0	1	9.45	2	1	0	0	0	6²	10	7	4	1
1924	NY-N	1	2	3.71	3	2	1	0	0	17	18	7	8	10
Total 2		1	3	5.32	5	3	1	0	0	23²	28	14	12	11
● Al Benton														
1945	Det-A	0	0	1.93	3	0	0	0	0	4²	6	1	0	5
● Rube Benton														
1917	NY-N	1	1	0.00	2	2	1	0	1	14	9	0	1	8
● Juan Berenguer														
1987	Min-A	0	1	10.38	3	0	0	0	0	4¹	10	5	0	1
● Dwight Bernard														
1982	Mil-A	0	0	0.00	1	0	0	0	0	1	0	0	0	1
● Don Bessent														
1955	Bro-N	0	0	0.00	3	0	0	0	0	3¹	3	0	1	1
1956	Bro-N	1	0	1.80	2	0	0	0	0	10	8	2	3	5
Total 2		1	0	1.35	5	0	0	0	0	13¹	11	2	4	6
● Bill Bevens														
1947	NY-A	0	1	2.38	2	1	1	0	0	11¹	3	3	11	1
● Jim Bibby														
1979	Pit-N	0	0	2.61	2	2	0	0	0	10¹	10	3	2	10
● Vern Bickford														
1948	Bos-N	0	1	2.70	1	1	0	0	0	3¹	4	1	5	1
● Jack Billingham														
1972	Cin-N	1	0	0.00	3	2	0	1	0	13²	6	0	4	11
1975	Cin-N	0	0	1.00	3	1	0	0	0	9	8	1	5	7
1976	Cin-N	1	0	0.00	1	0	0	0	0	2²	0	0	0	1
Total 3		2	0	0.36	7	3	0	1	0	25¹	14	1	9	19
● Bud Black														
1985	KC-A	0	1	5.06	2	1	0	0	0	5¹	4	3	5	4
● Joe Black														
1952	Bro-N	1	2	2.53	3	3	1	0	0	21¹	15	6	8	9

YEAR	TM/L	W	L	ERA	G	GS	CG	SV	SHO	IP	H	ER	BB	SO
1953	Bro-N	0	0	9.00	1	0	0	0	0	1	1	1	0	2
Total 2		1	2	2.82	4	3	1	0	0	22¹	16	7	8	11

● Ewell Blackwell

| 1952 | NY-A | 0 | 0 | 7.20 | 1 | 1 | 0 | 0 | 0 | 5 | 4 | 4 | 3 | 4 |

● Sheriff Blake

| 1929 | Chi-N | 0 | 1 | 13.50 | 2 | 0 | 0 | 0 | 0 | 1¹ | 4 | 2 | 0 | 1 |

● Steve Blass

| 1971 | Pit-N | 2 | 0 | 1.00 | 2 | 2 | 2 | 0 | 0 | 18 | 7 | 2 | 4 | 13 |

● Vida Blue

1972	Oak-A	0	1	4.15	4	1	0	1	0	8²	8	4	5	5
1973	Oak-A	0	1	4.91	2	2	0	0	0	11	10	6	3	8
1974	Oak-A	0	1	3.29	2	2	0	0	0	13²	10	5	7	9
Total 3		0	3	4.05	8	5	0	1	0	33¹	28	15	15	22

● Bert Blyleven

1979	Pit-N	1	0	1.80	2	1	0	0	0	10	8	2	3	4
1987	Min-A	1	1	2.77	2	2	0	0	0	13	13	4	2	12
Total 2		2	1	2.35	4	3	0	0	0	23	21	6	5	16

● Mike Boddicker

| 1983 | Bal-A | 1 | 0 | 0.00 | 1 | 1 | 1 | 0 | 0 | 9 | 3 | 0 | 0 | 6 |

● Bobby Bolin

| 1962 | SF-N | 0 | 0 | 6.75 | 2 | 0 | 0 | 0 | 0 | 2² | 4 | 2 | 2 | 2 |

● Tiny Bonham

1941	NY-A	1	0	1.00	1	1	1	0	0	9	4	1	2	2
1942	NY-A	0	1	4.09	2	1	1	0	0	11	9	5	3	3
1943	NY-A	0	1	4.50	1	1	0	0	0	8	6	4	3	9
Total 3		1	2	3.21	4	3	2	0	0	28	19	10	8	14

● Greg Booker

| 1984 | SD-N | 0 | 0 | 9.00 | 1 | 0 | 0 | 0 | 0 | 1 | 0 | 1 | 4 | 0 |

● Pedro Borbon

1972	Cin-N	0	1	3.86	6	0	0	0	0	7	7	3	2	4
1975	Cin-N	0	0	6.00	3	0	0	0	0	3	3	2	2	1
1976	Cin-N	0	0	0.00	1	0	0	0	0	1²	0	0	0	0
Total 3		0	1	3.86	10	0	0	0	0	11²	10	5	4	5

● Hank Borowy

1942	NY-A	0	0	18.00	1	1	0	0	0	3	6	6	3	1
1943	NY-A	1	0	2.25	1	1	0	0	0	8	6	2	3	4
1945	Chi-N	2	2	4.00	4	3	1	0	1	18	21	8	6	8
Total 3		3	2	4.97	6	5	1	0	1	29	33	16	12	13

● Dave Boswell

| 1965 | Min-A | 1 | 0 | 3.38 | 1 | 0 | 0 | 0 | 0 | 2² | 3 | 1 | 2 | 3 |

● Jim Bouton

1963	NY-A	0	1	1.29	1	1	0	0	0	7	4	1	5	4
1964	NY-A	2	0	1.56	2	2	1	0	0	17¹	15	3	5	7
Total 2		2	1	1.48	3	3	1	0	0	24¹	19	4	10	11

● Oil Can Boyd

| 1986 | Bos-A | 0 | 1 | 7.71 | 1 | 1 | 0 | 0 | 0 | 7 | 9 | 6 | 1 | 3 |

● Ralph Branca

1947	Bro-N	1	1	8.64	3	1	0	0	0	8¹	12	8	5	8
1949	Bro-N	0	1	4.15	1	1	0	0	0	8²	4	4	4	6
Total 2		1	2	6.35	4	2	0	0	0	17	16	12	9	14

● Jeff Brantley

| 1989 | SF-N | 0 | 0 | 4.15 | 3 | 0 | 0 | 0 | 0 | 4¹ | 5 | 2 | 3 | 1 |

● Al Brazle

1943	StL-N	0	1	3.68	1	1	0	0	0	7¹	5	3	2	4
1946	StL-N	0	1	5.40	1	0	0	0	0	6²	7	4	6	4
Total 2		0	2	4.50	2	1	0	0	0	14	12	7	8	8

● Harry Brecheen

1943	StL-N	0	1	2.45	3	0	0	0	0	3²	5	1	3	3
1944	StL-N	1	0	1.00	1	1	1	0	0	9	9	1	4	4
1946	StL-N	3	0	0.45	3	2	2	0	0	20	14	1	5	11
Total 3		4	1	0.83	7	3	3	0	1	32²	28	3	12	18

● Don Brennan

| 1937 | NY-N | 0 | 0 | 0.00 | 2 | 0 | 0 | 0 | 0 | 3 | 1 | 0 | 1 | 1 |

● Ken Brett

| 1967 | Bos-A | 0 | 0 | 0.00 | 2 | 0 | 0 | 0 | 0 | 1¹ | 0 | 0 | 1 | 1 |

● Marv Breuer

1941	NY-A	0	0	0.00	1	0	0	0	0	3	3	0	1	2
1942	NY-A	0	0	—	1	0	0	0	0	0	2	0	0	0
Total 2		0	0	0.00	2	0	0	0	0	3	5	0	1	2

● Jim Brewer

1965	LA-N	0	0	4.50	1	0	0	0	0	2	3	1	0	1
1966	LA-N	0	0	0.00	1	0	0	0	0	1	0	0	0	1
1974	LA-N	0	0	0.00	1	0	0	0	0	0¹	0	0	0	1
Total 3		0	0	2.70	3	0	0	0	0	3¹	3	1	0	3

● Marshall Bridges

| 1962 | NY-A | 0 | 0 | 4.91 | 2 | 0 | 0 | 0 | 0 | 3² | 4 | 2 | 4 | 3 |

● Tommy Bridges

1934	Det-A	1	1	3.63	3	2	1	0	0	17¹	21	7	1	12
1935	Det-A	2	0	2.50	2	2	2	0	0	18	18	5	4	9
1940	Det-A	1	0	3.00	1	1	0	0	0	9	10	3	1	5

YEAR	TM/L	W	L	ERA	G	GS	CG	SV	SHO	IP	H	ER	BB	SO
1945	Det-A	0	0	16.20	1	0	0	0	0	1²	3	3	3	1
Total 4		4	1	3.52	7	5	4	0	0	46	52	18	9	27

● Nelson Briles

1967	StL-N	1	0	1.64	2	1	1	0	0	11	7	2	1	4
1968	StL-N	0	1	5.56	2	2	0	0	0	11¹	13	7	4	7
1971	Pit-N	1	0	0.00	1	1	1	0	1	9	2	0	2	2
Total 3		2	1	2.59	5	4	2	0	1	31¹	22	9	7	13

● Jim Brosnan

| 1961 | Cin-N | 0 | 0 | 7.50 | 3 | 0 | 0 | 0 | 0 | 6 | 9 | 5 | 4 | 5 |

● Mace Brown

| 1946 | Bos-A | 0 | 0 | 27.00 | 1 | 0 | 0 | 0 | 0 | 1 | 4 | 3 | 1 | 0 |

● Mordecai Brown

1906	Chi-N	1	2	3.20	3	3	2	0	1	19²	14	7	4	12
1907	Chi-N	1	0	0.00	1	1	1	0	1	9	7	0	1	4
1908	Chi-N	2	0	0.00	2	1	1	0	0	11	6	0	1	5
1910	Chi-N	1	2	5.50	3	2	1	0	0	18	23	11	7	14
Total 4		5	4	2.81	9	7	5	0	3	57²	50	18	13	35

● Tom Browning

| 1990 | Cin-N | 0 | 0 | 4.50 | 1 | 1 | 0 | 0 | 0 | 6 | 6 | 3 | 2 | 2 |

● Warren Brusstar

| 1980 | Phi-N | 0 | 0 | 0.00 | 1 | 0 | 0 | 0 | 0 | 2¹ | 0 | 0 | 1 | 0 |

● Clay Bryant

| 1938 | Chi-N | 0 | 1 | 6.75 | 1 | 1 | 0 | 0 | 0 | 5¹ | 6 | 4 | 5 | 3 |

● Bob Buhl

| 1957 | Mil-N | 0 | 1 | 10.80 | 2 | 2 | 0 | 0 | 0 | 3¹ | 6 | 4 | 6 | 4 |

● Wally Bunker

| 1966 | Bal-A | 1 | 0 | 0.00 | 1 | 1 | 1 | 0 | 1 | 9 | 6 | 0 | 1 | 6 |

● Lew Burdette

1957	Mil-N	3	0	0.67	3	3	3	0	2	27	21	2	4	13
1958	Mil-N	1	2	5.64	3	3	1	0	0	22¹	22	14	4	12
Total 2		4	2	2.92	6	6	4	0	2	49¹	43	16	8	25

● Todd Burns

1988	Oak-A	0	0	0.00	1	0	0	0	0	0¹	0	0	0	0
1989	Oak-A	0	0	0.00	2	0	0	0	0	1²	1	0	1	0
1990	Oak-A	0	0	16.20	2	0	0	0	0	1²	5	3	2	0
Total 3		0	0	7.36	5	0	0	0	0	3²	6	3	3	0

● Jim Burton

| 1975 | Bos-A | 0 | 1 | 9.00 | 1 | 0 | 0 | 0 | 0 | 1 | 1 | 1 | 3 | 0 |

● Guy Bush

1929	Chi-N	1	0	0.82	2	1	1	0	0	11	12	1	2	4
1932	Chi-N	0	1	14.29	2	2	0	0	0	5²	5	9	6	2
Total 2		1	1	5.40	4	3	1	0	0	16²	17	10	8	6

● Joe Bush

1913	Phi-A	1	0	1.00	1	1	1	0	0	9	5	1	4	3
1914	Phi-A	0	1	3.27	1	1	1	0	0	11	9	4	4	4
1918	Bos-A	0	1	3.00	2	1	1	0	0	9	7	3	3	0
1922	NY-A	0	2	4.80	2	2	1	0	0	15	21	8	5	6
1923	NY-A	1	1	1.08	3	1	1	0	0	16²	7	2	4	5
Total 5		2	5	2.67	9	6	5	1	0	60²	49	18	20	18

● Bud Byerly

| 1944 | StL-N | 0 | 0 | 0.00 | 1 | 0 | 0 | 0 | 0 | 1¹ | 0 | 0 | 0 | 1 |

● Tommy Byrne

1949	NY-A	0	0	2.70	1	1	0	0	0	3¹	2	1	2	1
1955	NY-A	1	1	1.88	2	2	1	0	0	14¹	8	3	8	8
1956	NY-A	0	0	0.00	1	0	0	0	0	0¹	1	0	0	1
1957	NY-A	0	0	5.40	2	0	0	0	0	3¹	1	2	2	1
Total 4		1	1	2.53	6	3	1	0	0	21¹	12	6	12	11

● Marty Bystrom

1980	Phi-N	0	0	5.40	1	1	0	0	0	5	10	3	1	4
1983	Phi-N	0	0	0.00	1	0	0	0	0	1	0	0	0	1
Total 2		0	0	4.50	2	1	0	0	0	6	10	3	1	5

● Greg Cadaret

| 1988 | Oak-A | 0 | 0 | 0.00 | 3 | 0 | 0 | 0 | 0 | 2 | 0 | 0 | 0 | 3 |

● Leon Cadore

| 1920 | Bro-N | 0 | 1 | 9.00 | 2 | 1 | 0 | 0 | 0 | 4 | 2 | 1 | 1 | 1 |

● Mike Caldwell

| 1982 | Mil-A | 2 | 0 | 2.04 | 3 | 2 | 1 | 0 | 1 | 17² | 19 | 4 | 3 | 6 |

● Ray Caldwell

| 1920 | Cle-A | 0 | 1 | 27.00 | 1 | 1 | 0 | 0 | 0 | 0¹ | 2 | 1 | 1 | 0 |

● Howie Camnitz

| 1909 | Pit-N | 0 | 1 | 9.82 | 2 | 1 | 0 | 0 | 0 | 3² | 8 | 4 | 2 | 2 |

● Bill Campbell

| 1985 | StL-N | 0 | 0 | 2.25 | 3 | 0 | 0 | 0 | 0 | 4 | 4 | 1 | 2 | 5 |

● John Candelaria

| 1979 | Pit-N | 1 | 1 | 5.00 | 2 | 2 | 0 | 0 | 0 | 9 | 14 | 5 | 2 | 4 |

● Don Cardwell

| 1969 | NY-N | 0 | 0 | 0.00 | 1 | 0 | 0 | 0 | 0 | 1 | 0 | 0 | 0 | 0 |

● Tex Carleton

| 1934 | StL-N | 0 | 0 | 7.36 | 2 | 1 | 0 | 0 | 0 | 3² | 5 | 3 | 2 | 2 |
| 1935 | Chi-N | 0 | 1 | 1.29 | 1 | 1 | 0 | 0 | 0 | 7 | 6 | 1 | 7 | 4 |

YEAR	TM/L	W	L	ERA	G	GS	CG	SV	SHO	IP	H	ER	BB	SO
1938	Chi-N	0	0	∞	1	0	0	0	0	0	1	2	2	0
Total 3		0	1	5.06	4	2	0	0	0	10²	12	6	11	6

● Hal Carlson

YEAR	TM/L	W	L	ERA	G	GS	CG	SV	SHO	IP	H	ER	BB	SO
1929	Chi-N	0	0	6.75	2	0	0	0	0	4	7	3	1	3

● Steve Carlton

YEAR	TM/L	W	L	ERA	G	GS	CG	SV	SHO	IP	H	ER	BB	SO
1967	StL-N	0	1	0.00	1	1	0	0	0	6	3	0	2	5
1968	StL-N	0	0	6.75	2	0	0	0	0	4	7	3	1	3
1980	Phi-N	2	0	2.40	2	2	0	0	0	15	14	4	9	17
1983	Phi-N	0	1	2.70	1	1	0	0	0	6²	5	2	3	7
Total 4		2	2	2.56	6	4	0	0	0	31²	29	9	15	32

● Clay Carroll

YEAR	TM/L	W	L	ERA	G	GS	CG	SV	SHO	IP	H	ER	BB	SO
1970	Cin-N	1	0	0.00	4	0	0	0	0	9	5	0	2	11
1972	Cin-N	0	1	1.59	5	0	0	1	0	5²	6	1	4	3
1975	Cin-N	1	0	3.18	5	0	0	0	0	5²	4	2	2	3
Total 3		2	1	1.33	14	0	0	1	0	20¹	15	3	8	17

● Bob Caruthers

YEAR	TM/L	W	L	ERA	G	GS	CG	SV	SHO	IP	H	ER	BB	SO
1885	StL-A	1	1	2.42	3	3	3	0	0	26	25	7	4	16
1886	StL-A	2	1	2.42	3	3	3	0	1	26	18	7	6	12
1887	StL-A	4	4	2.13	8	8	8	0	0	71²	64	17	12	19
1889	Bro-A	0	2	3.75	4	2	2	1	0	24	28	10	6	6
Total 4		7	8	2.50	18	16	16	1	1	147²	135	41	28	53

● Hugh Casey

YEAR	TM/L	W	L	ERA	G	GS	CG	SV	SHO	IP	H	ER	BB	SO
1941	Bro-N	0	2	3.38	3	0	0	0	0	5¹	9	2	2	1
1947	Bro-N	2	0	0.87	6	0	0	1	0	10¹	5	1	1	3
Total 2		2	2	1.72	9	0	0	1	0	15²	14	3	3	4

● George Caster

YEAR	TM/L	W	L	ERA	G	GS	CG	SV	SHO	IP	H	ER	BB	SO
1945	Det-A	0	0	0.00	1	0	0	0	0	0²	0	0	0	1

● Tony Castillo

YEAR	TM/L	W	L	ERA	G	GS	CG	SV	SHO	IP	H	ER	BB	SO
1993	Tor-A	1	0	8.10	2	0	0	0	0	3¹	6	3	3	1

● Bobby Castillo

YEAR	TM/L	W	L	ERA	G	GS	CG	SV	SHO	IP	H	ER	BB	SO
1981	LA-N	0	0	9.00	1	0	0	0	0	1	0	1	5	0

● Slick Castleman

YEAR	TM/L	W	L	ERA	G	GS	CG	SV	SHO	IP	H	ER	BB	SO
1936	NY-N	0	0	2.08	1	0	0	0	0	4¹	3	1	2	5

● George Chalmers

YEAR	TM/L	W	L	ERA	G	GS	CG	SV	SHO	IP	H	ER	BB	SO
1915	Phi-N	0	1	2.25	1	1	1	0	0	8	8	2	3	6

● Icebox Chamberlain

YEAR	TM/L	W	L	ERA	G	GS	CG	SV	SHO	IP	H	ER	BB	SO
1888	StL-A	2	3	5.32	5	5	5	0	1	44	52	26	16	13

● Spud Chandler

YEAR	TM/L	W	L	ERA	G	GS	CG	SV	SHO	IP	H	ER	BB	SO
1941	NY-A	0	1	3.60	1	1	0	0	0	5	4	2	2	2
1942	NY-A	0	1	1.08	2	1	0	1	0	8¹	5	1	1	3
1943	NY-A	2	0	0.50	2	2	2	0	1	18	17	1	3	10
1947	NY-A	0	0	9.00	1	0	0	0	0	2	2	2	3	1
Total 4		2	2	1.62	6	4	2	1	1	33¹	28	6	9	16

● Norm Charlton

YEAR	TM/L	W	L	ERA	G	GS	CG	SV	SHO	IP	H	ER	BB	SO
1990	Cin-N	0	0	0.00	1	0	0	0	0	1	1	0	0	0

● Larry Cheney

YEAR	TM/L	W	L	ERA	G	GS	CG	SV	SHO	IP	H	ER	BB	SO
1916	Bro-N	0	0	3.00	1	0	0	0	0	3	4	1	1	5

● Tom Cheney

YEAR	TM/L	W	L	ERA	G	GS	CG	SV	SHO	IP	H	ER	BB	SO
1960	Pit-N	0	0	4.50	3	0	0	0	0	4	4	2	1	6

● Bob Chipman

YEAR	TM/L	W	L	ERA	G	GS	CG	SV	SHO	IP	H	ER	BB	SO
1945	Chi-N	0	0	0.00	1	0	0	0	0	0¹	0	0	1	0

● Larry Christenson

YEAR	TM/L	W	L	ERA	G	GS	CG	SV	SHO	IP	H	ER	BB	SO
1980	Phi-N	0	1	108.00	1	1	0	0	0	0¹	5	4	1	0

● Russ Christopher

YEAR	TM/L	W	L	ERA	G	GS	CG	SV	SHO	IP	H	ER	BB	SO
1948	Cle-A	0	0	∞	1	0	0	0	0	2	1	0	0	

● Chuck Churn

YEAR	TM/L	W	L	ERA	G	GS	CG	SV	SHO	IP	H	ER	BB	SO
1959	LA-N	0	0	27.00	1	0	0	0	0	0²	5	2	0	0

● Eddie Cicotte

YEAR	TM/L	W	L	ERA	G	GS	CG	SV	SHO	IP	H	ER	BB	SO
1917	Chi-A	1	1	1.96	3	2	2	0	0	23	23	5	2	13
1919	Chi-A	1	2	2.91	3	3	2	0	0	21²	19	7	5	7
Total 2		2	3	2.42	6	5	4	0	0	44²	42	12	7	20

● Jim Clancy

YEAR	TM/L	W	L	ERA	G	GS	CG	SV	SHO	IP	H	ER	BB	SO
1991	Atl-N	1	0	4.15	3	0	0	0	0	4¹	3	2	4	2

● John Clarkson

YEAR	TM/L	W	L	ERA	G	GS	CG	SV	SHO	IP	H	ER	BB	SO
1885	Chi-N	0	1	1.13	2	2	2	0	0	16	15	2	1	15
1886	Chi-N	2	2	2.01	4	4	3	0	1	31¹	25	7	12	28
1892	Cle-N	0	2	5.29	2	2	2	0	0	17	24	10	5	9
Total 3		2	5	2.66	8	8	7	0	1	64¹	64	19	18	52

● Ken Clay

YEAR	TM/L	W	L	ERA	G	GS	CG	SV	SHO	IP	H	ER	BB	SO
1977	NY-A	0	0	2.45	2	0	0	0	0	3²	3	1	1	0
1978	NY-A	0	0	11.57	1	0	0	0	0	2¹	4	3	2	2
Total 2		0	0	6.00	3	0	0	0	0	6	6	4	3	2

● Roger Clemens

YEAR	TM/L	W	L	ERA	G	GS	CG	SV	SHO	IP	H	ER	BB	SO
1986	Bos-A	0	0	3.18	2	2	0	0	0	11¹	9	4	6	11

● Reggie Cleveland

YEAR	TM/L	W	L	ERA	G	GS	CG	SV	SHO	IP	H	ER	BB	SO
1975	Bos-A	0	1	6.75	3	1	0	0	0	6²	7	5	3	5

● Tony Cloninger

YEAR	TM/L	W	L	ERA	G	GS	CG	SV	SHO	IP	H	ER	BB	SO
1970	Cin-N	0	1	7.36	2	1	0	0	0	7¹	10	6	5	4

● Andy Coakley

YEAR	TM/L	W	L	ERA	G	GS	CG	SV	SHO	IP	H	ER	BB	SO
1905	Phi-A	0	1	2.00	1	1	1	0	0	9	8	2	5	2

● Jim Coates

YEAR	TM/L	W	L	ERA	G	GS	CG	SV	SHO	IP	H	ER	BB	SO
1960	NY-A	0	0	5.68	3	0	0	0	0	6¹	6	4	1	3
1961	NY-A	0	0	0.00	1	0	0	1	0	4	1	0	1	2
1962	NY-A	0	1	6.75	2	0	0	0	0	2²	1	2	1	3
Total 3		0	1	4.15	6	0	0	1	0	13	8	6	3	8

● Dick Coffman

YEAR	TM/L	W	L	ERA	G	GS	CG	SV	SHO	IP	H	ER	BB	SO
1936	NY-N	0	0	32.40	2	0	0	0	0	1²	5	6	1	1
1937	NY-N	0	0	4.15	2	0	0	0	0	4¹	2	2	5	1
Total 2		0	0	12.00	4	0	0	0	0	6	7	8	6	2

● King Cole

YEAR	TM/L	W	L	ERA	G	GS	CG	SV	SHO	IP	H	ER	BB	SO
1910	Chi-N	0	0	3.38	1	1	0	0	0	8	10	3	3	5

● Rip Coleman

YEAR	TM/L	W	L	ERA	G	GS	CG	SV	SHO	IP	H	ER	BB	SO
1955	NY-A	0	0	9.00	1	0	0	0	0	1	5	1	0	1

● Rip Collins

YEAR	TM/L	W	L	ERA	G	GS	CG	SV	SHO	IP	H	ER	BB	SO
1921	NY-A	0	0	54.00	1	0	0	0	0	0²	4	4	1	0

● Ray Collins

YEAR	TM/L	W	L	ERA	G	GS	CG	SV	SHO	IP	H	ER	BB	SO
1912	Bos-A	0	0	1.88	2	1	0	0	0	14¹	14	3	0	6

● David Cone

YEAR	TM/L	W	L	ERA	G	GS	CG	SV	SHO	IP	H	ER	BB	SO
1992	Tor-A	0	0	3.48	2	2	0	0	0	10¹	9	4	8	8

● Gene Conley

YEAR	TM/L	W	L	ERA	G	GS	CG	SV	SHO	IP	H	ER	BB	SO
1957	Mil-N	0	0	10.80	1	0	0	0	0	1²	2	2	1	0

● Pete Conway

YEAR	TM/L	W	L	ERA	G	GS	CG	SV	SHO	IP	H	ER	BB	SO
1887	Det-N	2	2	3.00	4	4	4	0	0	33	31	11	6	10

● Jack Coombs

YEAR	TM/L	W	L	ERA	G	GS	CG	SV	SHO	IP	H	ER	BB	SO
1910	Phi-A	3	0	3.33	3	3	3	0	0	27	23	10	14	17
1911	Phi-A	1	0	1.35	2	2	1	0	0	20	11	3	6	16
1916	Bro-N	1	0	4.26	1	1	0	0	0	6¹	7	3	1	1
Total 3		5	0	2.70	6	6	4	0	0	53¹	41	16	21	34

● Mort Cooper

YEAR	TM/L	W	L	ERA	G	GS	CG	SV	SHO	IP	H	ER	BB	SO
1942	StL-N	0	1	5.54	2	2	0	0	0	13	17	8	4	9
1943	StL-N	1	1	2.81	2	2	1	0	0	16	11	5	3	10
1944	StL-N	1	1	1.13	2	2	1	0	1	16	9	2	5	16
Total 3		2	3	3.00	6	6	2	0	1	45	37	15	12	35

● Joe Corbett

YEAR	TM/L	W	L	ERA	G	GS	CG	SV	SHO	IP	H	ER	BB	SO
1896	Bal-N	2	0	0.50	2	2	2	0	1	18	11	1	7	10
1897	Bal-N	1	0	9.00	2	1	1	0	0	12	21	12	8	5
Total 2		3	0	3.90	4	3	3	0	1	30	32	13	15	15

● Al Corwin

YEAR	TM/L	W	L	ERA	G	GS	CG	SV	SHO	IP	H	ER	BB	SO
1951	NY-N	0	0	0.00	1	0	0	0	0	1²	1	0	0	1

● Stan Coveleski

YEAR	TM/L	W	L	ERA	G	GS	CG	SV	SHO	IP	H	ER	BB	SO
1920	Cle-A	3	0	0.67	3	3	3	0	1	27	15	2	2	8
1925	Was-A	0	2	3.77	2	2	1	0	0	14¹	16	6	5	3
Total 2		3	2	1.74	5	5	4	0	1	41²	31	8	7	11

● Danny Cox

YEAR	TM/L	W	L	ERA	G	GS	CG	SV	SHO	IP	H	ER	BB	SO
1985	StL-N	0	0	1.29	2	2	0	0	0	14	14	2	4	13
1987	StL-N	1	2	7.71	3	2	0	0	0	11²	13	10	8	9
1993	Tor-A	0	0	8.10	3	0	0	0	0	3¹	6	3	5	6
Total 3		1	2	4.66	8	4	0	0	0	29	33	15	17	28

● Roger Craig

YEAR	TM/L	W	L	ERA	G	GS	CG	SV	SHO	IP	H	ER	BB	SO
1955	Bro-N	1	0	3.00	1	1	0	0	0	6	4	2	5	4
1956	Bro-N	0	1	12.00	2	1	0	0	0	6	10	8	3	4
1959	LA-N	0	1	8.68	2	2	0	0	0	9¹	15	9	5	8
1964	StL-N	1	0	0.00	2	0	0	0	0	5	2	0	3	9
Total 4		2	2	6.49	7	4	0	0	0	26¹	31	19	16	25

● Doc Crandall

YEAR	TM/L	W	L	ERA	G	GS	CG	SV	SHO	IP	H	ER	BB	SO
1911	NY-N	1	0	0.00	2	0	0	0	0	4	2	0	0	2
1912	NY-N	0	0	0.00	1	0	0	0	0	2	1	0	0	2
1913	NY-N	0	0	3.86	2	0	0	0	0	4²	4	2	0	2
Total 3		1	0	1.69	5	0	0	0	0	10²	7	2	0	6

● Ed Crane

YEAR	TM/L	W	L	ERA	G	GS	CG	SV	SHO	IP	H	ER	BB	SO
1888	NY-N	1	1	2.12	2	2	2	0	0	17	15	4	6	12
1889	NY-N	4	1	3.72	5	5	4	0	0	38²	29	16	32	19
Total 2		5	2	3.23	7	7	6	0	0	55²	44	20	38	31

● Steve Crawford

YEAR	TM/L	W	L	ERA	G	GS	CG	SV	SHO	IP	H	ER	BB	SO
1986	Bos-A	1	0	6.23	3	0	0	0	0	4¹	5	3	0	4

● General Crowder

YEAR	TM/L	W	L	ERA	G	GS	CG	SV	SHO	IP	H	ER	BB	SO
1933	Was-A	0	1	7.36	2	2	0	0	0	11	16	9	5	7
1934	Det-A	0	1	1.50	2	1	0	0	0	6	6	1	1	2
1935	Det-A	1	0	1.00	1	1	1	0	0	9	5	1	3	5
Total 3		1	2	3.81	5	4	1	0	0	26	27	11	9	14

● Mike Cuellar

YEAR	TM/L	W	L	ERA	G	GS	CG	SV	SHO	IP	H	ER	BB	SO
1969	Bal-A	1	0	1.13	2	2	1	0	0	16	13	2	4	13
1970	Bal-A	1	0	3.18	2	2	1	0	0	11¹	10	4	2	5
1971	Bal-A	0	2	3.86	2	2	0	0	0	14	11	6	6	10
Total 3		2	2	2.61	6	6	2	0	0	41¹	34	12	12	28

● Nig Cuppy

YEAR	TM/L	W	L	ERA	G	GS	CG	SV	SHO	IP	H	ER	BB	SO
1892	Cle-N	0	1	1.13	1	1	1	0	0	8	6	1	4	1
1895	Cle-N	1	1	3.18	2	2	2	0	0	17	14	6	4	6
1896	Cle-N	0	2	4.76	2	2	2	0	0	17	19	9	0	4
Total 3		1	4	3.43	5	5	5	0	0	42	39	16	8	11

YEAR	TM/L	W	L	ERA	G	GS	CG	SV	SHO	IP	H	ER	BB	SO
● Mike Cvengros														
1927	Pit-N	0	0	3.86	2	0	0	0	0	2¹	3	1	0	2
● Ed Daily														
1890	Lou-A	0	2	2.65	2	2	2	0	0	17	12	5	8	5
● Bud Daley														
1961	NY-A	1	0	0.00	2	0	0	0	0	7	5	0	0	3
1962	NY-A	0	0	0.00	1	0	0	0	0	1	1	0	1	0
Total 2		1	0	0.00	3	0	0	0	0	8	6	0	1	3
● Dave Danforth														
1917	Chi-A	0	0	18.00	1	0	0	0	0	1	3	2	0	2
● Pat Darcy														
1975	Cin-N	0	1	4.50	1	0	0	0	0	4	3	2	2	1
● Ron Darling														
1986	NY-N	1	1	1.53	3	3	0	0	0	17²	13	3	10	12
● Curt Davis														
1941	Bro-N	0	1	5.06	1	1	0	0	0	5¹	6	3	3	1
● Storm Davis														
1983	Bal-A	1	0	5.40	1	1	0	0	0	5	6	3	1	3
1988	Oak-A	0	2	11.25	2	2	0	0	0	8	14	10	1	7
Total 2		1	2	9.00	3	3	0	0	0	13	20	13	2	10
● Ron Davis														
1981	NY-A	0	0	23.14	4	0	0	0	0	2¹	4	6	5	4
● Joe Dawson														
1927	Pit-N	0	0	0.00	1	0	0	0	0	1	0	0	0	0
● Ken Dayley														
1985	StL-N	1	0	0.00	4	0	0	0	0	6	1	0	3	5
1987	StL-N	0	0	1.93	4	0	0	1	0	4²	2	1	0	3
Total 2		1	0	0.84	8	0	0	1	0	10²	3	1	3	8
● Dizzy Dean														
1934	StL-N	2	1	1.73	3	3	2	0	1	26	20	5	5	17
1938	Chi-N	0	1	6.48	2	1	0	0	0	8¹	8	6	1	2
Total 2		2	2	2.88	5	4	2	0	1	34¹	28	11	6	19
● Paul Dean														
1934	StL-N	2	0	1.00	2	2	2	0	0	18	15	2	7	11
● Wayland Dean														
1924	NY-N	0	0	4.50	1	0	0	0	0	2	3	1	0	2
● Wheezer Dell														
1916	Bro-N	0	0	0.00	1	0	0	0	0	1	1	0	0	0
● Al Demaree														
1913	NY-N	0	1	4.50	1	1	0	0	0	4	7	2	1	0
● John Denny														
1983	Phi-N	1	1	3.46	2	2	0	0	0	13	12	5	3	9
● Paul Derringer														
1931	StL-N	0	2	4.26	3	2	0	0	0	12²	14	6	7	14
1939	Cin-N	0	1	2.35	2	2	1	0	0	15¹	9	4	3	9
1940	Cin-N	2	1	2.79	3	3	2	0	0	19¹	17	6	10	6
1945	Chi-N	0	0	6.75	3	0	0	0	0	5¹	5	4	7	1
Total 4		2	4	3.42	11	7	3	0	0	52²	45	20	27	30
● Jim Devlin														
1888	StL-A	1	0	2.57	1	0	0	0	0	7	5	2	2	5
● Rob Dibble														
1990	Cin-N	1	0	0.00	3	0	0	0	0	4²	3	0	1	4
● Murry Dickson														
1943	StL-N	0	0	0.00	1	0	0	0	0	0²	0	0	1	0
1946	StL-N	0	1	3.86	2	2	0	0	0	14	11	6	4	7
1958	NY-A	0	0	4.50	2	0	0	0	0	4	4	2	0	1
Total 3		0	1	3.86	5	2	0	0	0	18²	15	8	5	8
● Bill Dinneen														
1903	Bos-A	3	1	2.06	4	4	4	0	2	35	29	8	8	28
● Art Ditmar														
1957	NY-A	0	0	0.00	2	0	0	0	0	6	2	0	0	2
1958	NY-A	0	0	0.00	1	0	0	0	0	3²	2	0	0	2
1960	NY-A	0	2	21.60	2	2	0	0	0	1²	6	4	1	0
Total 3		0	2	3.18	5	2	0	0	0	11¹	10	4	1	4
● Joe Dobson														
1946	Bos-A	1	0	0.00	3	1	1	0	0	12²	4	0	3	10
● Pat Dobson														
1968	Det-A	0	0	3.86	3	0	0	0	0	4²	5	2	1	0
1971	Bal-A	0	0	4.05	3	1	0	0	0	6²	13	3	4	6
Total 2		0	0	3.97	6	1	0	0	0	11¹	18	5	5	6
● Atley Donald														
1941	NY-A	0	0	9.00	1	1	0	0	0	4	6	4	3	2
1942	NY-A	0	1	6.00	1	0	0	0	0	3	3	2	2	1
Total 2		0	1	7.71	2	1	0	0	0	7	9	6	5	3
● Blix Donnelly														
1944	StL-N	1	0	0.00	2	0	0	0	0	6	2	0	1	9
● Dick Donovan														
1959	Chi-A	0	1	5.40	3	1	0	1	0	8¹	4	5	3	5

YEAR	TM/L	W	L	ERA	G	GS	CG	SV	SHO	IP	H	ER	BB	SO
● Bill Donovan														
1907	Det-A	0	1	1.71	2	2	2	0	0	21	17	4	5	16
1908	Det-A	0	2	4.24	2	2	2	0	0	17	17	8	4	10
1909	Det-A	1	1	3.00	2	2	1	0	0	12	7	4	8	7
Total 3		1	4	2.88	6	6	5	0	0	50	41	16	17	33
● Phil Douglas														
1918	Chi-N	0	1	0.00	1	0	0	0	0	1	1	0	0	0
1921	NY-N	2	1	2.08	3	3	2	0	0	26	20	6	5	17
Total 2		2	2	2.00	4	3	2	0	0	27	21	6	5	17
● Al Downing														
1963	NY-A	0	1	5.40	1	1	0	0	0	5	7	3	1	6
1964	NY-A	0	1	8.22	3	1	0	0	0	7²	9	7	2	5
1974	LA-N	0	1	2.45	1	1	0	0	0	3²	4	1	4	3
Total 3		0	3	6.06	5	3	0	0	0	16¹	20	11	7	14
● Kelly Downs														
1989	SF-N	0	0	7.71	3	0	0	0	0	4²	3	4	2	4
● Moe Drabowsky														
1966	Bal-A	1	0	0.00	1	0	0	0	0	6²	1	0	2	11
1970	Bal-A	0	0	2.70	2	0	0	0	0	3¹	2	1	1	1
Total 2		1	0	0.90	3	0	0	0	0	10	3	1	3	12
● Dick Drago														
1975	Bos-A	0	1	2.25	2	0	0	0	0	4	3	1	1	1
● Dave Dravecky														
1984	SD-N	0	0	0.00	2	0	0	0	0	4²	3	0	1	5
● Clem Dreisewerd														
1946	Bos-A	0	0	0.00	1	0	0	0	0	0¹	0	0	0	0
● Karl Drews														
1947	NY-A	0	0	3.00	2	0	0	0	0	3	2	1	0	0
● Don Drysdale														
1956	Bro-N	0	0	9.00	1	0	0	0	0	2	2	2	1	1
1959	LA-N	1	0	1.29	1	1	0	0	0	7	11	1	4	5
1963	LA-N	1	0	0.00	1	1	1	0	1	9	3	0	1	9
1965	LA-N	1	1	3.86	2	2	1	0	0	11²	12	5	3	15
1966	LA-N	0	2	4.50	2	2	1	0	0	10	8	5	3	6
Total 5		3	3	2.95	7	6	3	0	1	39²	36	13	12	36
● Tom Dukes														
1971	Bal-A	0	0	0.00	2	0	0	0	0	4	2	0	0	1
● Ryne Duren														
1958	NY-A	1	1	1.93	3	0	0	1	0	9¹	7	2	6	14
1960	NY-A	0	0	2.25	2	0	0	0	0	4	2	1	1	5
Total 2		1	1	2.03	5	0	0	1	0	13¹	9	3	7	19
● George Earnshaw														
1929	Phi-A	1	1	2.63	2	2	1	0	0	13²	14	4	6	17
1930	Phi-A	2	0	0.72	3	3	2	0	0	25	13	2	7	19
1931	Phi-A	1	2	1.88	3	3	2	0	1	24	12	5	4	20
Total 3		4	3	1.58	8	8	5	0	1	62²	39	11	17	56
● Rawly Eastwick														
1975	Cin-N	2	0	2.25	5	0	0	1	0	8	6	2	3	4
● Dennis Eckersley														
1988	Oak-A	0	1	10.80	2	0	0	0	0	1²	2	2	1	2
1989	Oak-A	0	0	0.00	2	0	0	1	0	1²	0	0	0	0
1990	Oak-A	0	1	6.75	2	0	0	0	0	1¹	3	1	0	1
Total 3		0	2	5.79	6	0	0	1	0	4²	5	3	1	3
● Howard Ehmke														
1929	Phi-A	1	0	1.42	2	2	1	0	0	12²	14	2	3	13
● Red Ehret														
1890	Lou-A	2	0	1.35	3	2	2	1	0	20	12	3	6	13
● Mark Eichhorn														
1992	Tor-A	0	0	0.00	1	0	0	0	0	1	0	0	0	1
1993	Tor-A	0	0	0.00	1	0	0	0	0	0¹	1	0	1	0
Total 2		0	0	0.00	2	0	0	0	0	1¹	1	0	1	1
● Hod Eller														
1919	Cin-N	2	0	2.00	2	2	2	0	1	18	13	4	2	15
● Dock Ellis														
1971	Pit-N	0	1	15.43	1	1	0	0	0	2¹	4	4	1	1
1976	NY-A	0	1	10.80	1	1	0	0	0	3¹	7	4	0	1
Total 2		0	2	12.71	2	2	0	0	0	5²	11	8	1	2
● Paul Erickson														
1945	Chi-N	0	0	3.86	4	0	0	0	0	7	8	3	3	5
● Scott Erickson														
1991	Min-A	0	0	5.06	2	2	0	0	0	10²	10	6	4	5
● Carl Erskine														
1949	Bro-N	0	0	16.20	1	0	0	0	0	1²	3	3	1	0
1952	Bro-N	1	1	4.50	3	2	1	0	0	18	12	9	10	10
1953	Bro-N	1	0	5.79	3	3	1	0	0	14	14	9	9	16
1955	Bro-N	0	0	9.00	1	1	0	0	0	3	3	3	2	3
1956	Bro-N	0	1	5.40	2	1	0	0	0	5	4	3	2	2
Total 8		2	2	5.83	11	7	2	0	0	41²	36	27	24	31
● Duke Esper														
1894	Bal-N	0	1	4.00	1	1	1	0	0	9	13	4	1	3

YEAR TM/L	W	L	ERA	G	GS	CG	SV	SHO	IP	H	ER	BB	SO
1895 Bal-N	1	0	0.00	1	1	1	0	1	9	5	0	0	3
Total 2	1	1	2.00	2	2	2	0	1	18	18	4	1	6
● Red Faber													
1917 Chi-A	3	1	2.33	4	3	2	0	0	27	21	7	3	9
● Roy Face													
1960 Pit-N	0	0	5.23	4	0	0	3	0	10¹	9	6	2	4
● Bob Feller													
1948 Cle-A	0	2	5.02	2	2	1	0	0	14¹	10	8	5	7
● Alex Ferguson													
1925 Was-A	1	1	3.21	2	2	1	0	0	14	13	5	6	11
● Sid Fernandez													
1986 NY-N	0	0	1.35	3	0	0	0	0	6²	6	1	1	10
● Tom Ferrick													
1950 NY-A	1	0	0.00	1	0	0	0	0	1	1	0	1	0
● Dave Ferriss													
1946 Bos-A	1	0	2.03	2	2	1	0	0	13¹	13	3	2	4
● Ed Figueroa													
1976 NY-A	0	1	5.63	1	1	0	0	0	8	6	5	5	2
1978 NY-A	0	1	8.10	2	2	0	0	0	6²	9	6	5	2
Total 2	0	2	6.75	3	3	0	0	0	14²	15	11	10	4
● Rollie Fingers													
1972 Oak-A	1	1	1.74	6	0	0	2	0	10¹	4	2	4	11
1973 Oak-A	0	1	0.66	6	0	0	2	0	13²	13	1	4	8
1974 Oak-A	1	0	1.93	4	0	0	2	0	9¹	8	2	2	6
Total 3	2	2	1.35	16	0	0	6	0	33¹	25	5	10	25
● Ray Fisher													
1919 Cin-N	0	1	2.35	2	1	0	0	0	7²	7	2	2	2
● Freddie Fitzsimmons													
1933 NY-N	0	1	5.14	1	1	0	0	0	7	9	4	0	2
1936 NY-N	0	2	5.40	2	2	1	0	0	11²	13	7	2	6
1941 Bro-N	0	0	0.00	1	1	0	0	0	7	4	0	3	1
Total 3	0	3	3.86	4	4	1	0	0	25²	26	11	5	9
● Mike Flanagan													
1979 Bal-A	1	1	3.00	3	2	1	0	0	15	18	5	2	13
1983 Bal-A	0	0	4.50	1	1	0	0	0	4	6	2	1	1
Total 2	1	1	3.32	4	3	1	0	0	19	24	7	3	14
● Whitey Ford													
1950 NY-A	1	0	0.00	1	1	0	0	0	8²	7	0	1	7
1953 NY-A	0	1	4.50	2	2	0	0	0	8	9	4	2	7
1955 NY-A	2	0	2.12	2	2	1	0	0	17	13	4	8	10
1956 NY-A	1	1	5.25	2	2	1	0	0	12	14	7	2	8
1957 NY-A	1	1	1.13	2	2	1	0	0	16	11	2	5	7
1958 NY-A	0	1	4.11	3	3	0	0	0	15¹	19	7	5	16
1960 NY-A	2	0	0.00	2	2	2	0	2	18	11	0	2	8
1961 NY-A	2	0	0.00	2	2	1	0	1	14	6	0	1	7
1962 NY-A	1	1	4.12	3	3	1	0	0	19²	24	9	4	12
1963 NY-A	0	2	4.50	2	2	0	0	0	12	10	6	3	8
1964 NY-A	0	1	8.44	1	1	0	0	0	5¹	8	5	1	4
Total 11	10	8	2.71	22	22	7	0	3	146	132	44	34	94
● Bob Forsch													
1982 StL-N	0	2	4.97	2	2	0	0	0	12²	18	7	3	4
1985 StL-N	0	1	12.00	2	1	0	0	0	3	6	4	1	3
1987 StL-N	1	0	9.95	3	0	0	0	0	6¹	8	7	5	3
Total 3	1	3	7.36	7	3	0	0	0	22	32	18	9	10
● Terry Forster													
1978 LA-N	0	0	0.00	3	0	0	0	0	4	5	0	1	6
1981 LA-N	0	0	0.00	2	0	0	0	0	2	1	0	3	0
Total 2	0	0	0.00	5	0	0	0	0	6	6	0	4	6
● Rube Foster													
1915 Bos-A	2	0	2.00	2	2	2	0	0	18	12	4	2	13
1916 Bos-A	0	0	0.00	1	0	0	0	0	3	3	0	0	1
Total 2	2	0	1.71	3	2	2	0	0	21	15	4	2	14
● Dave Foutz													
1885 StL-A	2	2	0.61	4	4	4	0	0	29¹	30	2	9	14
1886 StL-A	1	1	3.60	2	2	2	0	0	15	16	6	6	7
1887 StL-A	0	3	3.46	3	3	3	0	0	26	36	10	9	6
1889 Bro-A	0	0	7.20	1	0	0	0	0	5	5	4	2	2
Total 4	3	6	2.63	10	9	9	0	0	75¹	87	22	26	29
● George Frazier													
1981 NY-A	0	3	17.18	3	0	0	0	0	3²	9	7	3	2
1987 Min-A	0	0	0.00	1	0	0	0	0	2	1	0	0	2
Total 2	0	3	11.12	4	0	0	0	0	5²	10	7	3	4
● Larry French													
1935 Chi-N	0	2	3.38	2	1	1	0	0	10²	15	4	2	8
1938 Chi-N	0	0	2.70	3	0	0	0	0	3¹	1	1	1	2
1941 Bro-N	0	0	0.00	2	0	0	0	0	1	0	0	0	0
Total 3	0	2	3.00	7	1	1	0	0	15	16	5	3	10
● Bob Friend													
1960 Pit-N	0	2	13.50	3	2	0	0	0	6	13	9	3	7
● Frank Gabler													
1936 NY-N	0	0	7.20	2	0	0	0	0	5	7	4	4	0

YEAR TM/L	W	L	ERA	G	GS	CG	SV	SHO	IP	H	ER	BB	SO
● Rich Gale													
1980 KC-A	0	1	4.26	2	2	0	0	0	6¹	11	3	4	4
● Denny Galehouse													
1944 StL-A	1	1	1.50	2	2	2	0	0	18	13	3	5	15
● Mike Garcia													
1954 Cle-A	0	1	5.40	2	1	0	0	0	5	6	3	4	4
● Mike Garman													
1977 LA-N	0	0	0.00	2	0	0	0	0	4	2	0	1	3
● Scott Garrelts													
1989 SF-N	0	2	9.82	2	2	0	0	0	7¹	13	8	1	8
● Gary Gentry													
1969 NY-N	1	0	0.00	1	1	0	0	0	6²	3	0	5	4
● Bill George													
1888 NY-N	0	1	7.20	1	1	1	0	0	10	15	8	3	4
● Charlie Getzien													
1887 Det-N	4	2	2.48	6	6	6	0	1	58	61	16	15	17
● Joe Gibbon													
1960 Pit-N	0	0	9.00	2	0	0	0	0	3	4	3	1	2
● Bob Gibson													
1964 StL-N	2	1	3.00	3	3	2	0	0	27	23	9	8	31
1967 StL-N	3	0	1.00	3	3	3	0	1	27	14	3	5	26
1968 StL-N	2	1	1.67	3	3	3	0	2	27	18	5	4	35
Total 3	7	2	1.89	9	9	8	0	2	81	55	17	17	92
● Dave Giusti													
1971 Pit-N	0	0	0.00	3	0	0	1	0	5¹	3	0	2	4
● Tom Glavine													
1991 Atl-N	1	1	2.70	2	2	1	0	0	13¹	8	4	7	8
1992 Atl-N	1	1	1.59	2	2	2	0	0	17	10	3	4	8
Total 2	2	2	2.08	4	4	3	0	0	30¹	18	7	11	16
● Kid Gleason													
1894 Bal-N	0	1	9.69	2	1	1	0	0	13	25	14	6	3
● Dave Goltz													
1981 LA-N	0	0	5.40	2	0	0	0	0	3¹	4	2	1	2
● Ruben Gomez													
1954 NY-N	1	0	2.45	1	1	0	0	0	7¹	4	2	3	2
● Lefty Gomez													
1932 NY-A	1	0	1.00	1	1	1	0	0	9	9	1	1	8
1936 NY-A	2	0	4.70	2	2	1	0	0	15¹	14	8	11	9
1937 NY-A	2	0	1.50	2	2	2	0	0	18	16	3	2	8
1938 NY-A	1	0	3.86	1	1	0	0	0	7	9	3	1	5
1939 NY-A	0	0	9.00	1	1	0	0	0	1	3	1	0	1
Total 5	6	0	2.86	7	7	4	0	0	50¹	51	16	15	31
● Dwight Gooden													
1986 NY-N	0	2	8.00	2	2	0	0	0	9	17	8	4	9
● Tom Gorman													
1952 NY-A	0	0	0.00	1	0	0	0	0	0²	1	0	0	0
1953 NY-A	0	0	3.00	1	0	0	0	0	3	4	1	0	1
Total 2	0	0	2.45	2	0	0	0	0	3²	5	1	0	1
● Johnny Gorsica													
1940 Det-A	0	0	0.79	2	0	0	0	0	11¹	6	1	4	4
● Rich Gossage													
1978 NY-A	1	0	0.00	3	0	0	0	0	6	1	0	1	4
1981 NY-A	0	0	0.00	3	0	0	2	0	5	2	0	2	5
1984 SD-N	0	0	13.50	2	0	0	0	0	2²	3	4	1	2
Total 3	1	0	2.63	8	0	0	2	0	13²	6	4	4	11
● Wayne Granger													
1968 StL-N	0	0	0.00	1	0	0	0	0	2	0	0	1	1
1970 Cin-N	0	0	33.75	2	0	0	0	0	1¹	7	5	1	1
Total 2	0	0	13.50	3	0	0	0	0	3¹	7	5	2	2
● Mudcat Grant													
1965 Min-A	2	1	2.74	3	3	2	0	0	23	22	7	2	12
● Fred Green													
1960 Pit-N	0	0	22.50	3	0	0	0	0	4	11	10	1	3
● Tommy Greene													
1993 Phi-N	0	0	27.00	1	1	0	0	0	2¹	7	7	4	1
● Hal Gregg													
1947 Bro-N	0	1	3.55	3	1	0	0	0	12²	9	5	8	10
● Bob Grim													
1955 NY-A	0	1	4.15	3	1	0	1	0	8²	8	4	5	8
1957 NY-A	0	1	7.71	2	0	0	0	0	2¹	3	2	0	2
Total 2	0	2	4.91	5	1	0	1	0	11	11	6	5	10
● Burleigh Grimes													
1920 Bro-N	1	2	4.19	3	3	3	0	0	19¹	23	9	9	4
1930 StL-N	0	2	3.71	2	2	2	0	0	17	10	7	6	13
1931 StL-N	2	0	2.04	2	2	1	0	0	17²	9	4	9	11
1932 Chi-N	0	0	23.63	2	0	0	0	0	2²	7	7	2	0
Total 4	3	4	4.29	9	7	4	0	1	56²	49	27	26	28
● Ross Grimsley													
1972 Cin-N	2	1	2.57	4	1	0	0	0	7	7	2	3	2

YEAR	TM/L	W	L	ERA	G	GS	CG	SV	SHO	IP	H	ER	BB	SO
● Lee Grissom														
1939	Cin-N	0	0	0.00	1	0	0	0	0	1¹	0	0	1	0
● Marv Grissom														
1954	NY-N	1	0	0.00	1	0	0	0	0	2²	1	0	3	2
● Steve Gromek														
1948	Cle-A	1	0	1.00	1	1	1	0	0	9	7	1	1	2
● Lefty Grove														
1929	Phi-A	0	0	0.00	2	0	0	2	0	6¹	3	0	1	10
1930	Phi-A	2	1	1.42	3	2	2	0	0	19	15	3	3	10
1931	Phi-A	2	1	2.42	3	3	2	0	0	26	28	7	2	16
Total 3		4	2	1.75	8	5	4	2	0	51¹	46	10	6	36
● Ron Guidry														
1977	NY-A	1	0	2.00	1	1	1	0	0	9	4	2	3	7
1978	NY-A	1	0	1.00	1	1	1	0	0	9	8	1	7	4
1981	NY-A	1	1	1.93	2	2	0	0	0	14	8	3	4	15
Total 3		3	1	1.69	4	4	2	0	0	32	20	6	14	26
● Don Gullett														
1970	Cin-N	0	0	1.35	3	0	0	0	0	6²	5	1	4	4
1972	Cin-N	0	0	1.29	1	1	0	0	0	7	5	1	2	4
1975	Cin-N	1	1	4.34	3	3	0	0	0	18²	19	9	10	15
1976	Cin-N	1	0	1.23	1	1	0	0	0	7¹	5	1	3	4
1977	NY-A	0	1	6.39	2	2	0	0	0	12²	13	9	7	10
Total 5		2	2	3.61	10	7	0	0	0	52¹	47	21	26	37
● Harry Gumbert														
1936	NY-N	0	0	36.00	2	0	0	0	0	2	7	8	4	2
1937	NY-N	0	0	27.00	2	0	0	0	0	1¹	4	4	1	1
1942	StL-N	0	0	0.00	2	0	0	0	0	0²	1	0	0	0
Total 3		0	0	27.00	6	0	0	0	0	4	12	12	5	3
● Larry Gura														
1980	KC-A	0	0	2.19	2	2	0	0	0	12¹	8	3	3	4
● Mark Guthrie														
1991	Min-A	0	1	2.25	4	0	0	0	0	4	3	1	4	3
● Juan Guzman														
1992	Tor-A	0	0	1.13	1	1	0	0	0	8	8	1	1	7
1993	Tor-A	0	1	3.75	2	2	0	0	0	12	10	5	8	12
Total 2		0	1	2.70	3	3	0	0	0	20	18	6	9	19
● Moose Haas														
1982	Mil-A	0	0	7.36	2	1	0	0	0	7¹	8	6	3	4
● Harvey Haddix														
1960	Pit-N	2	0	2.45	2	1	0	0	0	7¹	6	2	2	6
● Bump Hadley														
1936	NY-A	1	0	1.13	1	1	0	0	0	8	10	1	1	2
1937	NY-A	0	1	33.75	1	1	0	0	0	1¹	6	5	0	0
1939	NY-A	1	0	2.25	1	0	0	0	0	8	7	2	3	2
Total 3		2	1	4.15	3	2	0	0	0	17¹	23	8	4	4
● Jesse Haines														
1926	StL-N	2	0	1.08	3	2	1	0	1	16²	13	2	9	5
1928	StL-N	0	1	4.50	1	1	0	0	0	6	6	3	3	3
1930	StL-N	1	0	1.00	1	1	1	0	0	9	4	1	4	2
1934	StL-N	0	0	0.00	1	0	0	0	0	0²	1	0	0	2
Total 4		3	1	1.67	6	4	2	0	1	32¹	24	6	16	12
● Charley Hall														
1912	Bos-A	0	0	3.38	2	0	0	0	0	10²	11	4	9	1
● Dick Hall														
1969	Bal-A	0	1	—	1	0	0	0	0	0	1	0	1	0
1970	Bal-A	0	0	0.00	1	0	0	1	0	2¹	0	0	0	0
1971	Bal-A	0	0	0.00	1	0	0	1	0	1	1	0	0	0
Total 3		0	1	0.00	3	0	0	2	0	3¹	2	0	1	0
● Tom Hall														
1972	Cin-N	0	0	0.00	4	0	0	1	0	8¹	6	0	2	7
● Bill Hallahan														
1926	StL-N	0	0	4.50	1	0	0	0	0	2	2	1	3	1
1930	StL-N	1	1	1.64	2	2	1	0	1	11	9	2	8	8
1931	StL-N	2	0	0.49	3	2	2	1	1	18¹	12	1	8	12
1934	StL-N	0	0	2.16	1	1	0	0	0	8¹	6	2	4	6
Total 4		3	1	1.36	7	5	3	1	2	39²	29	6	23	27
● Dave Hamilton														
1972	Oak-A	0	0	6.75	2	0	0	0	0	1¹	2	1	2	1
● Steve Hamilton														
1963	NY-A	0	0	0.00	1	0	0	0	0	1	0	0	0	1
1964	NY-A	0	0	4.50	2	0	0	1	0	2	3	1	0	2
Total 2		0	0	3.00	3	0	0	1	0	3	3	1	0	3
● Atlee Hammaker														
1989	SF-N	0	0	15.43	2	0	0	0	0	2¹	8	4	0	2
● Harry Harper														
1921	NY-A	0	0	20.25	1	1	0	0	0	1¹	3	3	2	1
● Greg Harris														
1984	SD-N	0	0	0.00	1	0	0	0	0	5¹	3	0	3	5
● Mickey Harris														
1946	Bos-A	0	2	3.72	2	2	0	0	0	9²	11	4	4	5

YEAR	TM/L	W	L	ERA	G	GS	CG	SV	SHO	IP	H	ER	BB	SO
● Gil Hatfield														
1888	NY-N	0	0	12.60	1	0	0	0	0	5	12	7	3	2
● Joe Hatten														
1947	Bro-N	0	0	7.00	4	1	0	0	0	9	12	7	7	5
1949	Bro-N	0	0	16.20	2	0	0	0	0	1²	4	3	2	0
Total 2		0	0	8.44	6	1	0	0	0	10²	16	10	9	5
● Bill Hawke														
1894	Bal-N	0	1	9.00	1	1	0	0	0	4	9	4	1	0
● Andy Hawkins														
1984	SD-N	1	1	0.75	3	0	0	0	0	12	4	1	6	4
● Jim Hearn														
1951	NY-N	1	0	1.04	2	1	0	0	0	8²	5	1	8	1
● Ken Heintzelman														
1950	Phi-N	0	0	1.17	1	1	0	0	0	7²	4	1	6	3
● George Hemming														
1894	Bal-N	0	1	1.13	1	1	1	0	0	8	10	1	3	2
● Claude Hendrix														
1918	Chi-N	0	0	0.00	1	0	0	0	0	1	0	0	0	0
● Tom Henke														
1992	Tor-A	0	0	2.70	3	0	0	2	0	3¹	2	1	2	1
● Bill Henry														
1961	Cin-N	0	0	19.29	2	0	0	0	0	2¹	4	5	2	3
● Roy Henshaw														
1935	Chi-N	0	0	7.36	1	0	0	0	0	3²	2	3	5	2
● Pat Hentgen														
1993	Tor-A	1	0	1.50	1	1	0	0	0	6	5	1	3	6
● Willie Hernandez														
1983	Phi-N	0	0	0.00	3	0	0	0	0	4	0	0	1	4
1984	Det-A	0	0	1.69	3	0	0	2	0	5¹	4	1	0	0
Total 2		0	0	0.96	6	0	0	2	0	9¹	4	1	1	4
● Orel Hershiser														
1988	LA-N	2	0	1.00	2	2	2	0	1	18	7	2	6	17
● Charlie Hickman														
1897	Bos-N	0	1	3.60	1	1	0	0	0	5	7	2	2	0
● Kirby Higbe														
1941	Bro-N	0	0	7.36	1	1	0	0	0	3²	6	3	2	1
● Oral Hildebrand														
1939	NY-A	0	0	0.00	1	1	0	0	0	4	2	0	0	3
● Carmen Hill														
1927	Pit-N	0	0	4.50	1	1	0	0	0	6	9	3	1	6
● John Hiller														
1968	Det-A	0	0	13.50	2	0	0	0	0	2	6	3	3	1
● Joe Hoerner														
1967	StL-N	0	0	40.50	2	0	0	0	0	0²	4	3	1	0
1968	StL-N	0	1	3.86	3	0	0	1	0	4²	5	2	5	3
Total 2		0	1	8.44	5	0	0	1	0	5¹	9	5	6	3
● Bill Hoffer														
1895	Bal-N	0	2	4.24	2	2	2	0	0	17	21	8	6	4
1896	Bal-N	2	0	1.50	2	2	2	0	0	18	15	3	5	10
1897	Bal-N	2	0	3.38	2	2	2	0	0	16	25	6	4	2
Total 3		4	2	3.00	6	6	6	0	0	51	61	17	15	16
● Chief Hogsett														
1934	Det-A	0	0	1.23	3	0	0	0	0	7¹	6	1	3	3
1935	Det-A	0	0	0.00	1	0	0	0	0	1	0	0	1	0
Total 2		0	0	1.08	4	0	0	0	0	8¹	6	1	4	3
● Bobby Hogue														
1951	NY-A	0	0	0.00	2	0	0	0	0	2²	1	0	0	0
● Al Holland														
1983	Phi-N	0	0	0.00	2	0	0	1	0	3²	1	0	0	5
● Al Hollingsworth														
1944	StL-A	0	0	2.25	1	0	0	0	0	4	5	1	2	1
● Brian Holton														
1988	LA-N	0	0	0.00	1	0	0	0	0	2	0	0	1	0
● Ken Holtzman														
1972	Oak-A	1	0	2.13	3	2	0	0	0	12²	11	3	3	4
1973	Oak-A	2	1	4.22	3	3	0	0	0	10²	13	5	5	6
1974	Oak-A	1	0	1.50	2	2	0	0	0	12	13	2	4	10
Total 3		4	1	2.55	8	7	0	0	0	35¹	37	10	12	20
● Rick Honeycutt														
1988	Oak-A	1	0	0.00	3	0	0	0	0	3¹	0	0	0	5
1989	Oak-A	0	0	6.75	3	0	0	0	0	2²	4	2	0	2
1990	Oak-A	0	0	0.00	1	0	0	0	0	1²	2	0	1	0
Total 3		1	0	2.35	7	0	0	0	0	7²	6	2	1	7
● Burt Hooton														
1977	LA-N	1	1	3.75	2	2	1	0	0	12	8	5	2	9
1978	LA-N	1	1	6.48	2	2	0	0	0	8¹	13	6	3	6
1981	LA-N	1	1	1.59	2	2	0	0	0	11¹	8	2	9	3
Total 3		3	3	3.69	6	6	1	0	0	31²	29	13	14	18

Joe Horlen

YEAR TM/L	W	L	ERA	G	GS	CG	SV	SHO	IP	H	ER	BB	SO
1972 Oak-A	0	0	27.00	1	0	0	0	0	1¹	3	4	1	1

Ricky Horton

YEAR TM/L	W	L	ERA	G	GS	CG	SV	SHO	IP	H	ER	BB	SO
1985 StL-N	0	0	6.75	3	0	0	0	0	4	4	3	5	5
1987 StL-N	0	0	6.00	2	0	0	0	0	3	5	2	0	1
Total 2	0	0	6.43	5	0	0	0	0	7	9	5	5	6

Charlie Hough

YEAR TM/L	W	L	ERA	G	GS	CG	SV	SHO	IP	H	ER	BB	SO
1974 LA-N	0	0	0.00	1	0	0	0	0	2	0	0	1	4
1977 LA-N	0	0	1.80	2	0	0	0	0	5	3	1	0	5
1978 LA-N	0	0	8.44	2	0	0	0	0	5¹	10	5	2	5
Total 3	0	0	4.38	5	0	0	0	0	12¹	13	6	3	14

Art Houtteman

YEAR TM/L	W	L	ERA	G	GS	CG	SV	SHO	IP	H	ER	BB	SO
1954 Cle-A	0	0	4.50	1	0	0	0	0	2	2	1	1	1

Steve Howe

YEAR TM/L	W	L	ERA	G	GS	CG	SV	SHO	IP	H	ER	BB	SO
1981 LA-N	1	0	3.86	3	0	0	1	0	7	7	3	1	4

Harry Howell

YEAR TM/L	W	L	ERA	G	GS	CG	SV	SHO	IP	H	ER	BB	SO
1900 Bro-N	0	1	3.38	1	1	1	0	0	8	13	3	2	3

Jay Howell

YEAR TM/L	W	L	ERA	G	GS	CG	SV	SHO	IP	H	ER	BB	SO
1988 LA-N	0	1	3.38	2	0	0	1	0	2²	3	1	1	2

Waite Hoyt

YEAR TM/L	W	L	ERA	G	GS	CG	SV	SHO	IP	H	ER	BB	SO
1921 NY-A	2	1	0.00	3	3	3	0	1	27	18	0	11	18
1922 NY-A	0	1	1.13	2	1	0	0	0	8	11	1	2	4
1923 NY-A	0	0	15.43	1	1	0	0	0	2¹	4	4	1	0
1926 NY-A	1	1	1.20	2	2	1	0	0	15	19	2	1	10
1927 NY-A	1	0	4.91	1	1	0	0	0	7¹	8	4	1	2
1928 NY-A	2	0	1.50	2	2	2	0	0	18	14	3	6	14
1931 Phi-A	0	1	4.50	1	1	0	0	0	6	7	3	0	1
Total 7	6	4	1.83	12	11	6	0	1	83²	81	17	22	49

Carl Hubbell

YEAR TM/L	W	L	ERA	G	GS	CG	SV	SHO	IP	H	ER	BB	SO
1933 NY-N	2	0	0.00	2	2	2	0	0	20	13	0	6	15
1936 NY-N	1	1	2.25	2	2	1	0	0	16	15	4	2	10
1937 NY-N	1	1	3.77	2	2	1	0	0	14¹	12	6	4	7
Total 3	4	2	1.79	6	6	4	0	0	50¹	40	10	12	32

Charles Hudson

YEAR TM/L	W	L	ERA	G	GS	CG	SV	SHO	IP	H	ER	BB	SO
1983 Phi-N	0	2	8.64	2	2	0	0	0	8¹	9	8	1	6

Nat Hudson

YEAR TM/L	W	L	ERA	G	GS	CG	SV	SHO	IP	H	ER	BB	SO
1886 StL-A	1	0	2.57	1	1	1	0	0	7	3	2	3	3

Jim Hughes

YEAR TM/L	W	L	ERA	G	GS	CG	SV	SHO	IP	H	ER	BB	SO
1953 Bro-N	0	0	2.25	1	0	0	0	0	4	3	1	1	3

Mickey Hughes

YEAR TM/L	W	L	ERA	G	GS	CG	SV	SHO	IP	H	ER	BB	SO
1889 Bro-A	1	1	7.71	1	1	0	0	0	7	14	6	3	3

Dick Hughes

YEAR TM/L	W	L	ERA	G	GS	CG	SV	SHO	IP	H	ER	BB	SO
1967 StL-N	0	1	5.00	2	2	0	0	0	9	9	5	3	7
1968 StL-N	0	0	0.00	1	0	0	0	0	0¹	2	0	0	0
Total 2	0	1	4.82	3	2	0	0	0	9¹	11	5	3	7

Tom Hughes

YEAR TM/L	W	L	ERA	G	GS	CG	SV	SHO	IP	H	ER	BB	SO
1903 Bos-A	0	1	9.00	1	1	0	0	0	2	4	2	2	0

Tex Hughson

YEAR TM/L	W	L	ERA	G	GS	CG	SV	SHO	IP	H	ER	BB	SO
1946 Bos-A	0	1	3.14	3	2	0	0	0	14¹	14	5	3	8

Bob Humphreys

YEAR TM/L	W	L	ERA	G	GS	CG	SV	SHO	IP	H	ER	BB	SO
1964 StL-N	0	0	0.00	1	0	0	0	0	1	0	0	0	1

Ken Hunt

YEAR TM/L	W	L	ERA	G	GS	CG	SV	SHO	IP	H	ER	BB	SO
1961 Cin-N	0	0	0.00	1	0	0	0	0	1	0	0	1	1

Catfish Hunter

YEAR TM/L	W	L	ERA	G	GS	CG	SV	SHO	IP	H	ER	BB	SO
1972 Oak-A	2	0	2.81	3	2	0	0	0	16	12	5	6	11
1973 Oak-A	1	0	2.03	2	2	0	0	0	13¹	11	3	4	6
1974 Oak-A	1	0	1.17	2	1	0	1	0	7²	5	1	2	5
1976 NY-A	0	1	3.12	1	1	1	0	0	8²	10	3	4	5
1977 NY-A	0	1	10.38	2	1	0	0	0	4¹	6	5	0	1
1978 NY-A	1	1	4.15	2	2	0	0	0	13	13	6	1	5
Total 6	5	3	3.29	12	9	1	1	0	63	57	23	17	33

Bruce Hurst

YEAR TM/L	W	L	ERA	G	GS	CG	SV	SHO	IP	H	ER	BB	SO
1986 Bos-A	2	0	1.96	3	3	1	0	0	23	18	5	6	17

Johnny Hutchings

YEAR TM/L	W	L	ERA	G	GS	CG	SV	SHO	IP	H	ER	BB	SO
1940 Cin-N	0	0	9.00	1	0	0	0	0	1	2	1	1	0

Fred Hutchinson

YEAR TM/L	W	L	ERA	G	GS	CG	SV	SHO	IP	H	ER	BB	SO
1940 Det-A	0	0	9.00	1	0	0	0	0	1	1	1	1	1

Danny Jackson

YEAR TM/L	W	L	ERA	G	GS	CG	SV	SHO	IP	H	ER	BB	SO
1985 KC-A	1	1	1.69	2	2	1	0	0	16	9	3	5	12
1990 Cin-N	0	0	10.13	1	1	0	0	0	2²	6	3	2	0
1993 Phi-N	0	1	7.20	1	1	0	0	0	5	6	4	1	1
Total 3	1	2	3.80	4	4	1	0	0	23²	21	10	8	13

Grant Jackson

YEAR TM/L	W	L	ERA	G	GS	CG	SV	SHO	IP	H	ER	BB	SO
1971 Bal-A	0	0	0.00	1	0	0	0	0	0²	0	0	1	0
1976 NY-A	0	0	4.91	1	0	0	0	0	3²	4	2	0	3
1979 Pit-N	1	0	0.00	4	0	0	0	0	4²	1	0	2	2
Total 3	1	0	2.00	6	0	0	0	0	9	5	2	3	5

Sig Jakucki

YEAR TM/L	W	L	ERA	G	GS	CG	SV	SHO	IP	H	ER	BB	SO
1944 StL-A	0	1	9.00	1	1	0	0	0	3	5	3	0	4

Bill James

YEAR TM/L	W	L	ERA	G	GS	CG	SV	SHO	IP	H	ER	BB	SO
1919 Chi-A	0	0	5.79	1	0	0	0	0	4²	8	3	3	2

Bill James

YEAR TM/L	W	L	ERA	G	GS	CG	SV	SHO	IP	H	ER	BB	SO
1914 Bos-N	2	0	0.00	2	1	1	0	1	11	2	0	6	9

Larry Jansen

YEAR TM/L	W	L	ERA	G	GS	CG	SV	SHO	IP	H	ER	BB	SO
1951 NY-N	0	2	6.30	3	2	0	0	0	10	8	7	4	6

Larry Jaster

YEAR TM/L	W	L	ERA	G	GS	CG	SV	SHO	IP	H	ER	BB	SO
1967 StL-N	0	0	0.00	1	0	0	0	0	0¹	2	0	0	0
1968 StL-N	0	0	∞	1	0	0	0	0	0	2	3	1	0
Total 2	0	0	81.00	2	0	0	0	0	0¹	4	3	1	0

Joey Jay

YEAR TM/L	W	L	ERA	G	GS	CG	SV	SHO	IP	H	ER	BB	SO
1961 Cin-N	1	1	5.59	2	2	1	0	0	9²	8	6	6	6

Tommy John

YEAR TM/L	W	L	ERA	G	GS	CG	SV	SHO	IP	H	ER	BB	SO
1977 LA-N	0	1	6.00	1	1	0	0	0	6	9	4	3	7
1978 LA-N	1	0	3.07	2	2	0	0	0	14²	14	5	4	6
1981 NY-A	1	0	0.69	3	2	0	0	0	13	11	1	0	8
Total 3	2	1	2.67	6	5	0	0	0	33²	34	10	7	21

Earl Johnson

YEAR TM/L	W	L	ERA	G	GS	CG	SV	SHO	IP	H	ER	BB	SO
1946 Bos-A	1	0	2.70	3	0	0	0	0	3¹	1	1	2	1

Ernie Johnson

YEAR TM/L	W	L	ERA	G	GS	CG	SV	SHO	IP	H	ER	BB	SO
1957 Mil-N	0	1	1.29	3	0	0	0	0	7	2	1	1	8

Ken Johnson

YEAR TM/L	W	L	ERA	G	GS	CG	SV	SHO	IP	H	ER	BB	SO
1961 Cin-N	0	0	0.00	1	0	0	0	0	0²	0	0	0	0

Bob Johnson

YEAR TM/L	W	L	ERA	G	GS	CG	SV	SHO	IP	H	ER	BB	SO
1971 Pit-N	0	1	9.00	2	1	0	0	0	5	5	5	3	3

Syl Johnson

YEAR TM/L	W	L	ERA	G	GS	CG	SV	SHO	IP	H	ER	BB	SO
1928 StL-N	0	0	4.50	2	0	0	0	0	2	4	1	1	1
1930 StL-N	0	0	7.20	2	0	0	0	0	5	4	4	3	4
1931 StL-N	0	1	3.00	3	1	0	0	0	9	10	3	1	6
Total 3	0	1	4.50	7	1	0	0	0	16	18	8	5	11

Walter Johnson

YEAR TM/L	W	L	ERA	G	GS	CG	SV	SHO	IP	H	ER	BB	SO
1924 Was-A	1	2	2.25	3	2	2	0	0	24	30	6	11	20
1925 Was-A	2	1	2.08	3	3	3	0	1	26	26	6	4	15
Total 2	3	3	2.16	6	5	5	0	1	50	56	12	15	35

Sam Jones

YEAR TM/L	W	L	ERA	G	GS	CG	SV	SHO	IP	H	ER	BB	SO
1918 Bos-A	0	1	3.00	1	1	1	0	0	9	7	3	5	5
1922 NY-A	0	0	0.00	2	0	0	0	0	2	1	0	1	0
1923 NY-A	0	1	0.90	2	1	0	1	0	10	5	1	2	3
1926 NY-A	0	0	9.00	1	0	0	0	0	1	2	1	2	1
Total 4	0	2	2.05	6	2	1	1	0	22	15	5	10	9

Sheldon Jones

YEAR TM/L	W	L	ERA	G	GS	CG	SV	SHO	IP	H	ER	BB	SO
1951 NY-N	0	0	2.08	2	0	0	1	0	4¹	5	1	1	2

Sherman Jones

YEAR TM/L	W	L	ERA	G	GS	CG	SV	SHO	IP	H	ER	BB	SO
1961 Cin-N	0	0	0.00	1	0	0	0	0	0²	0	0	0	0

Claude Jonnard

YEAR TM/L	W	L	ERA	G	GS	CG	SV	SHO	IP	H	ER	BB	SO
1923 NY-N	0	0	0.00	2	0	0	0	0	2	1	0	1	1
1924 NY-N	0	0	—	1	0	0	0	0	0	0	0	1	0
Total 2	0	0	0.00	3	0	0	0	0	2	1	0	2	1

Al Jurisich

YEAR TM/L	W	L	ERA	G	GS	CG	SV	SHO	IP	H	ER	BB	SO
1944 StL-N	0	0	27.00	1	0	0	0	0	0²	2	2	1	0

Jim Kaat

YEAR TM/L	W	L	ERA	G	GS	CG	SV	SHO	IP	H	ER	BB	SO
1965 Min-A	1	2	3.77	3	3	1	0	0	14¹	18	6	2	6
1982 StL-N	0	0	3.86	4	0	0	0	0	2¹	4	1	2	2
Total 2	1	2	3.78	7	3	1	0	0	16²	22	7	4	8

Tim Keefe

YEAR TM/L	W	L	ERA	G	GS	CG	SV	SHO	IP	H	ER	BB	SO
1884 NY-N	0	2	3.60	2	2	2	0	0	15	10	6	3	12
1888 NY-N	4	0	0.51	4	4	4	0	0	35	18	2	9	30
1889 NY-N	0	1	8.18	2	1	1	1	0	11	17	10	2	4
Total 3	4	3	2.66	8	7	7	1	0	61	45	18	14	46

Vic Keen

YEAR TM/L	W	L	ERA	G	GS	CG	SV	SHO	IP	H	ER	BB	SO
1926 StL-N	0	0	0.00	1	0	0	0	0	1	0	0	0	0

Monte Kennedy

YEAR TM/L	W	L	ERA	G	GS	CG	SV	SHO	IP	H	ER	BB	SO
1951 NY-N	0	0	6.00	2	0	0	0	0	3	3	2	1	4

Brickyard Kennedy

YEAR TM/L	W	L	ERA	G	GS	CG	SV	SHO	IP	H	ER	BB	SO
1903 Pit-N	0	1	5.14	1	1	0	0	0	7	11	4	3	3

Dickie Kerr

YEAR TM/L	W	L	ERA	G	GS	CG	SV	SHO	IP	H	ER	BB	SO
1919 Chi-A	2	0	1.42	2	2	2	0	1	19	14	3	3	6

Jimmy Key

YEAR TM/L	W	L	ERA	G	GS	CG	SV	SHO	IP	H	ER	BB	SO
1992 Tor-A	2	0	1.00	2	1	0	0	0	9	6	1	0	6

Ed Killian

YEAR TM/L	W	L	ERA	G	GS	CG	SV	SHO	IP	H	ER	BB	SO
1907 Det-A	0	0	2.25	1	0	0	0	0	4	3	1	1	1
1908 Det-A	0	0	11.57	1	1	0	0	0	2¹	5	3	3	1
Total 2	0	0	5.68	2	1	0	0	0	6¹	8	4	4	2

Silver King

YEAR TM/L	W	L	ERA	G	GS	CG	SV	SHO	IP	H	ER	BB	SO
1887 StL-A	1	3	2.03	4	4	3	0	0	31	26	7	2	21
1888 StL-A	1	3	2.31	5	5	4	0	0	35	37	9	9	12
Total 2	2	6	2.18	9	9	8	0	0	66	63	16	11	33

Bruce Kison

YEAR TM/L	W	L	ERA	G	GS	CG	SV	SHO	IP	H	ER	BB	SO
1971 Pit-N	1	0	0.00	2	0	0	0	0	6¹	1	0	2	3

YEAR	TM/L	W	L	ERA	G	GS	CG	SV	SHO	IP	H	ER	BB	SO
1979	Pit-N	0	1	108.00	1	1	0	0	0	0¹	3	4	2	0
Total 2		1	1	5.40	3	1	0	0	0	6²	4	4	4	3

● Frank Kitson

YEAR	TM/L	W	L	ERA	G	GS	CG	SV	SHO	IP	H	ER	BB	SO
1900	Bro-N	1	0	1.00	1	1	1	0	0	9	4	1	1	2

● Ed Klieman

1948	Cle-A	0	0	∞	1	0	0	0	0	0	1	3	2	0

● Bob Klinger

1946	Bos-A	0	1	13.50	1	0	0	0	0	0²	2	1	1	0

● Joe Klink

1990	Oak-A	0	0	—	1	0	0	0	0	0	0	0	1	0

● Johnny Klippstein

1959	LA-N	0	0	0.00	1	0	0	0	0	2	1	0	0	2
1965	Min-A	0	0	0.00	2	0	0	0	0	2²	2	0	2	3
Total 2		0	0	0.00	3	0	0	0	0	4²	3	0	2	5

● Fred Klobedanz

1897	Bos-N	0	1	9.35	2	1	0	0	0	8²	12	9	8	0

● Darold Knowles

1973	Oak-A	0	0	0.00	7	0	0	2	0	6¹	4	0	5	5

● Alex Konikowski

1951	NY-N	0	0	0.00	1	0	0	0	0	1	1	0	0	0

● Jim Konstanty

1950	Phi-N	0	1	2.40	3	1	0	0	0	15	9	4	4	3

● Jerry Koosman

1969	NY-N	2	0	2.04	2	2	1	0	0	17²	7	4	4	9
1973	NY-N	1	0	3.12	2	2	0	0	0	8²	9	3	7	8
Total 2		3	0	2.39	4	4	1	0	0	26¹	16	7	11	17

● Dave Koslo

1951	NY-N	1	1	3.00	2	2	1	0	0	15	12	5	7	6

● Sandy Koufax

1959	LA-N	0	1	1.00	2	1	0	0	0	9	5	1	1	7
1963	LA-N	2	0	1.50	2	2	2	0	0	18	12	3	3	23
1965	LA-N	2	1	0.38	3	3	2	0	2	24	13	1	5	29
1966	LA-N	0	1	1.50	1	1	0	0	0	6	6	1	2	2
Total 4		4	3	0.95	8	7	4	0	2	57	36	6	11	61

● Fabian Kowalik

1935	Chi-N	0	0	2.08	1	0	0	0	0	4¹	3	1	1	1

● Jack Kramer

1944	StL-A	1	0	0.00	2	1	1	0	0	11	9	0	4	12

● Ray Kremer

1925	Pit-N	2	1	3.00	3	2	2	0	0	21	17	7	4	9
1927	Pit-N	0	1	3.60	1	1	0	0	0	5	5	2	3	1
Total 2		2	2	3.12	4	3	2	0	0	26	22	9	7	10

● Howie Krist

1943	StL-N	0	0	—	1	0	0	0	0	0	1	0	0	0

● Johnny Kucks

1955	NY-A	0	0	6.00	2	0	0	0	0	3	4	2	1	1
1956	NY-A	1	0	0.82	3	1	1	0	1	11	6	1	3	2
1957	NY-A	0	0	0.00	1	0	0	0	0	0²	1	0	1	1
1958	NY-A	0	0	2.08	2	0	0	0	0	4¹	4	1	1	0
Total 4		1	0	1.89	8	1	1	0	1	19	15	4	6	4

● Bob Kuzava

1951	NY-A	0	0	0.00	1	0	0	1	0	1	0	0	0	0
1952	NY-A	0	0	0.00	1	0	0	1	0	2²	0	0	0	2
1953	NY-A	0	0	13.50	1	0	0	0	0	0²	2	1	0	1
Total 3		0	0	2.08	3	0	0	2	0	4¹	2	1	0	3

● Clem Labine

1953	Bro-N	0	2	3.60	3	0	0	0	0	5	10	2	1	3
1955	Bro-N	1	0	2.89	4	0	0	1	0	9¹	6	3	2	2
1956	Bro-N	1	0	0.00	2	1	1	0	1	12	8	0	3	7
1959	LA-N	0	0	0.00	1	0	0	0	0	1	0	0	0	1
1960	Pit-N	0	0	13.50	3	0	0	0	0	4	13	6	1	2
Total 5		2	2	3.16	13	1	1	2	1	31¹	37	11	7	15

● Mike LaCoss

1989	SF-N	0	0	6.23	2	0	0	0	0	4¹	4	3	3	2

● Pete Ladd

1982	Mil-A	0	0	0.00	1	0	0	0	0	0²	1	0	2	0

● Jeff Lahti

1982	StL-N	0	0	10.80	2	0	0	0	0	1²	4	2	1	1
1985	StL-N	0	0	12.27	3	0	0	1	0	3²	10	5	0	2
Total 2		0	0	11.81	5	0	0	1	0	5¹	14	7	1	3

● Jack Lamabe

1967	StL-N	0	1	6.75	3	0	0	0	0	2²	5	2	0	4

● Max Lanier

1942	StL-N	1	0	0.00	2	0	0	0	0	4	3	0	1	1
1943	StL-N	0	1	1.76	3	2	0	0	0	15¹	13	3	3	13
1944	StL-N	1	0	2.19	2	2	0	0	0	12¹	8	3	8	11
Total 3		2	1	1.71	7	4	0	0	0	31²	24	6	12	25

● Dave LaPoint

1982	StL-N	0	0	3.24	2	1	0	0	0	8¹	10	3	2	3

● Dave LaRoche

YEAR	TM/L	W	L	ERA	G	GS	CG	SV	SHO	IP	H	ER	BB	SO
1981	NY-A	0	0	0.00	1	0	0	0	0	1	0	0	0	2

● Don Larsen

1955	NY-A	0	1	11.25	1	1	0	0	0	4	5	5	2	2
1956	NY-A	1	0	0.00	2	2	1	0	1	10²	1	0	4	7
1957	NY-A	1	1	3.72	2	1	0	0	0	9²	8	4	5	6
1958	NY-A	1	0	0.96	2	2	0	0	0	9¹	9	1	6	9
1962	SF-N	1	0	3.86	3	0	0	0	0	2¹	1	1	2	0
Total 5		4	2	2.75	10	6	1	0	1	36	24	11	19	24

● Fred Lasher

1968	Det-A	0	0	0.00	1	0	0	0	0	2	1	0	0	1

● Vern Law

1960	Pit-N	2	0	3.44	3	3	0	0	0	18¹	22	7	3	8

● Terry Leach

1991	Min-A	0	0	3.86	2	0	0	0	0	2¹	2	1	0	2

● Tim Leary

1988	LA-N	0	0	1.35	2	0	0	0	0	6²	6	1	2	4

● Bill Lee

1935	Chi-N	0	0	3.48	2	1	0	1	0	10¹	11	4	5	5
1938	Chi-N	0	2	2.45	2	2	0	0	0	11	15	3	1	8
Total 2		0	2	2.95	4	3	0	1	0	21¹	26	7	6	13

● Bill Lee

1975	Bos-A	0	0	3.14	2	2	0	0	0	14¹	12	5	3	7

● Sam Leever

1900	Pit-N	0	2	1.38	2	2	1	0	0	13	13	2	4	4
1903	Pit-N	0	2	5.40	2	2	1	0	0	10	13	6	3	2
Total 2		0	4	3.13	4	4	2	0	0	23	26	8	7	6

● Craig Lefferts

1984	SD-N	0	0	0.00	3	0	0	0	0	6	2	0	1	7
1989	SF-N	0	0	3.38	3	0	0	0	0	2²	2	1	2	1
Total 2		0	0	1.04	6	0	0	0	0	8²	4	1	3	8

● Ken Lehman

1952	Bro-N	0	0	0.00	1	0	0	0	0	2	2	0	1	0

● Charlie Leibrandt

1985	KC-A	0	1	2.76	2	2	0	0	0	16¹	10	5	4	10
1991	Atl-N	0	2	11.25	2	1	0	0	0	4	8	5	1	3
1992	Atl-N	0	1	9.00	1	0	0	0	0	2	3	2	0	0
Total 3		0	4	4.84	5	3	0	0	0	22¹	21	12	5	13

● Lefty Leifield

1909	Pit-N	0	1	11.25	1	1	0	0	0	4	7	5	1	0

● Al Leiter

1993	Tor-A	1	0	7.71	3	0	0	0	0	7	12	6	2	5

● Bob Lemon

1948	Cle-A	2	0	1.65	2	2	1	0	0	16¹	16	3	7	6
1954	Cle-A	0	2	6.75	2	2	0	0	0	13¹	16	10	8	11
Total 2		2	2	3.94	4	4	2	0	0	29²	32	13	15	17

● Dennis Leonard

1980	KC-A	1	1	6.75	2	2	0	0	0	10²	15	8	2	5

● Dutch Leonard

1915	Bos-A	1	0	1.00	1	1	1	0	0	9	3	1	0	6
1916	Bos-A	1	0	1.00	1	1	1	0	0	9	5	1	4	3
Total 2		2	0	1.00	2	2	2	0	0	18	8	2	4	9

● Dave Leonhard

1969	Bal-A	0	0	4.50	1	0	0	0	0	2	1	1	1	1
1971	Bal-A	0	0	0.00	1	0	0	0	0	1	0	0	1	0
Total 2		0	0	3.00	2	0	0	0	0	3	1	1	2	1

● Ted Lewis

1897	Bos-N	1	1	6.00	3	1	0	0	0	12	18	8	9	4

● Don Liddle

1954	NY-N	1	0	1.29	2	1	0	0	0	7	5	1	1	2

● Paul Lindblad

1973	Oak-A	1	0	0.00	3	0	0	0	0	3¹	4	0	1	1
1978	NY-A	0	0	11.57	1	0	0	0	0	2¹	4	3	0	1
Total 2		1	0	4.76	4	0	0	0	0	5²	8	3	1	2

● Jim Lindsey

1930	StL-N	0	0	1.93	2	0	0	0	0	4²	1	1	1	2
1931	StL-N	0	0	5.40	2	0	0	0	0	3¹	4	2	3	2
Total 2		0	0	3.38	4	0	0	0	0	8	5	3	4	4

● Bob Locker

1972	Oak-A	0	0	0.00	1	0	0	0	0	0¹	1	0	0	0

● Billy Loes

1952	Bro-N	0	1	4.35	2	1	0	0	0	10¹	11	5	5	5
1953	Bro-N	1	0	3.38	2	1	0	0	0	8	8	3	2	8
1955	Bro-N	0	1	9.82	1	0	0	0	0	3²	7	4	1	5
Total 3		1	2	4.91	4	3	0	0	0	22	26	12	8	18

● Mickey Lolich

1968	Det-A	3	0	1.67	3	3	3	0	0	27	20	5	6	21

● Tim Lollar

1984	SD-N	0	1	21.60	1	1	0	0	0	1²	4	4	4	0

YEAR TM/L	W	L	ERA	G	GS	CG	SV	SHO	IP	H	ER	BB	SO
● Vic Lombardi													
1947 Bro-N	0	1	12.15	2	2	0	0	0	6²	14	9	1	5
● Jim Lonborg													
1967 Bos-A	2	1	2.63	3	3	2	0	1	24	14	7	2	11
● Ed Lopat													
1949 NY-A	1	0	6.35	1	1	0	0	0	5²	9	4	1	4
1950 NY-A	0	0	2.25	1	1	0	0	0	8	9	2	0	5
1951 NY-A	2	0	0.50	2	2	2	0	0	18	10	1	3	4
1952 NY-A	0	1	4.76	2	2	0	0	0	11¹	14	6	4	3
1953 NY-A	1	0	2.00	1	1	1	0	0	9	9	2	4	3
Total 8	4	1	2.60	7	7	3	0	0	52	51	15	12	19
● Aurelio Lopez													
1984 Det-A	1	0	0.00	2	0	0	0	0	3	1	0	1	4
● Marcelino Lopez													
1970 Bal-A	0	0	0.00	1	0	0	0	0	0¹	0	0	0	0
● Tom Lovett													
1889 Bro-A	0	1	24.00	1	1	0	0	0	3	8	8	2	1
1890 Bro-N	2	2	2.83	4	4	4	0	0	35	29	11	6	14
Total 2	2	3	4.50	5	5	4	0	0	38	37	19	8	15
● Grover Lowdermilk													
1919 Chi-A	0	0	9.00	1	0	0	0	0	1	2	1	1	0
● Turk Lown													
1959 Chi-A	0	0	0.00	3	0	0	0	0	3¹	2	0	1	3
● Dolf Luque													
1919 Cin-N	0	0	0.00	2	0	0	0	0	5	1	0	0	6
1933 NY-N	1	0	0.00	1	0	0	0	0	4¹	2	0	2	5
Total 2	1	0	0.00	3	0	0	0	0	9¹	3	0	2	11
● Sparky Lyle													
1976 NY-A	0	0	0.00	2	0	0	0	0	2²	1	0	0	3
1977 NY-A	1	0	1.93	2	0	0	0	0	4²	2	1	0	2
Total 2	1	0	1.23	4	0	0	0	0	7¹	3	1	0	5
● Duke Maas													
1958 NY-A	0	0	81.00	1	0	0	0	0	0¹	2	3	1	0
1960 NY-A	0	0	4.50	1	0	0	0	0	2	2	1	0	1
Total 2	0	0	15.43	2	0	0	0	0	2¹	4	4	1	1
● Nick Maddox													
1909 Pit-N	1	0	1.00	1	1	1	0	0	9	10	1	2	4
● Sal Maglie													
1951 NY-N	0	1	7.20	1	1	0	0	0	5	8	4	2	3
1954 NY-N	0	0	2.57	1	1	0	0	0	7	7	2	2	2
1956 Bro-N	1	1	2.65	2	2	2	0	0	17	14	5	6	15
Total 3	1	2	3.41	4	4	2	0	0	29	29	11	10	20
● Joe Magrane													
1987 StL-N	0	1	8.59	2	2	0	0	0	7¹	9	7	5	5
● Roy Mahaffey													
1931 Phi-A	0	0	9.00	1	0	0	0	0	1	1	1	1	0
● Duster Mails													
1920 Cle-A	1	0	0.00	2	1	1	0	1	15²	6	0	6	6
● Pat Malone													
1929 Chi-N	0	2	4.15	3	2	1	0	0	13	12	6	7	11
1932 Chi-N	0	0	0.00	1	0	0	0	0	2²	1	0	4	4
1936 NY-A	0	1	1.80	2	0	0	1	0	5	2	1	1	2
Total 3	0	3	3.05	6	2	1	1	0	20²	15	7	12	17
● Jim Maloney													
1961 Cin-N	0	0	27.00	1	0	0	0	0	0²	4	2	1	1
● Al Mamaux													
1920 Bro-N	0	0	4.50	3	0	0	0	0	4	2	2	0	5
● Firpo Marberry													
1924 Was-A	0	1	1.13	4	1	0	2	0	8	9	1	4	10
1925 Was-A	0	0	0.00	2	0	0	1	0	2¹	3	0	0	2
1934 Det-A	0	0	21.60	2	0	0	0	0	1²	5	4	1	0
Total 3	0	1	3.75	8	1	0	3	0	12	17	5	5	12
● Juan Marichal													
1962 SF-N	0	0	0.00	1	1	0	0	0	4	2	0	2	4
● Rube Marquard													
1911 NY-N	0	1	1.54	3	2	0	0	0	11²	9	2	1	8
1912 NY-N	2	0	0.50	2	2	2	0	0	18	14	1	2	9
1913 NY-N	0	1	7.00	2	1	0	0	0	9	10	7	3	3
1916 Bro-N	0	2	6.55	2	2	0	0	0	11	12	8	6	9
1920 Bro-N	0	1	1.00	2	1	0	0	0	9	7	1	3	6
Total 5	2	5	2.91	11	8	2	0	0	58²	52	19	15	35
● Mike Marshall													
1974 LA-N	0	1	1.00	5	0	0	1	0	9	6	1	1	10
● Renie Martin													
1980 KC-A	0	0	2.79	3	0	0	0	0	9²	11	3	3	2
● Joe Martina													
1924 Was-A	0	0	0.00	1	0	0	0	0	1	0	0	0	1
● Tippy Martinez													
1979 Bal-A	0	0	6.75	3	0	0	0	0	1¹	3	1	0	1
1983 Bal-A	0	0	3.00	3	0	0	2	0	3	3	1	0	0
Total 2	0	0	4.15	6	0	0	2	0	4¹	6	2	0	1
● Dennis Martinez													
1979 Bal-A	0	0	18.00	2	1	0	0	0	2	6	4	0	0
● Roger Mason													
1993 Phi-N	0	0	1.17	4	0	0	0	0	7²	4	1	1	7
● Greg Mathews													
1987 StL-N	0	0	2.45	1	1	0	0	0	3²	1	2	1	3
● Christy Mathewson													
1905 NY-N	3	0	0.00	3	3	3	0	3	27	14	0	1	18
1911 NY-N	1	2	2.00	3	3	2	0	0	27	25	6	2	13
1912 NY-N	0	2	1.26	3	3	3	0	0	28²	23	4	5	10
1913 NY-N	1	1	0.95	2	2	2	0	1	19	14	2	2	7
Total 4	5	5	1.06	11	11	10	0	4	101²	76	12	10	48
● Jon Matlack													
1973 NY-N	1	2	2.16	3	3	0	0	0	16²	10	4	5	11
● Jakie May													
1932 Chi-N	0	1	11.57	2	0	0	0	0	4²	9	6	3	4
● Rudy May													
1981 NY-A	0	0	2.84	3	0	0	0	0	6¹	5	2	1	5
● Erskine Mayer													
1915 Phi-N	0	1	2.38	2	2	1	0	0	11¹	16	3	2	7
1919 Chi-A	0	0	0.00	1	0	0	0	0	1	0	0	1	0
Total 2	0	1	2.19	3	2	1	0	0	12¹	16	3	3	7
● Carl Mays													
1916 Bos-A	0	1	5.06	2	1	0	1	0	5¹	8	3	3	2
1918 Bos-A	2	0	1.00	2	2	2	0	0	18	10	2	3	5
1921 NY-A	1	2	1.73	3	3	3	0	1	26	20	5	0	9
1922 NY-A	0	1	4.50	1	1	0	0	0	8	9	4	2	1
Total 4	3	4	2.20	8	7	5	1	1	57¹	47	14	8	17
● Bob McClure													
1982 Mil-A	0	2	4.15	5	0	0	2	0	4¹	5	2	3	5
● Alex McColl													
1933 Was-A	0	0	0.00	1	0	0	0	0	2	0	0	0	0
● Jim McCormick													
1885 Chi-N	3	2	2.00	5	5	5	0	0	36	27	8	6	19
1886 Chi-N	0	1	6.75	1	1	1	0	0	8	13	6	2	4
Total 2	3	3	2.86	6	6	6	0	0	44	40	14	8	23
● Mickey McDermott													
1956 NY-A	0	0	3.00	1	0	0	0	0	3	2	1	3	3
● Jim McDonald													
1953 NY-A	1	0	5.87	1	1	0	0	0	7²	12	5	0	3
● Roger McDowell													
1986 NY-N	0	0	4.91	5	0	0	0	0	7¹	10	4	6	2
● Will McEnaney													
1975 Cin-N	0	0	2.70	5	0	0	1	0	6²	3	2	2	5
1976 Cin-N	0	0	0.00	2	0	0	2	0	4²	2	0	1	2
Total 2	0	0	1.59	7	0	0	3	0	11¹	5	2	3	7
● Joe McGinnity													
1900 Bro-N	2	0	0.00	2	2	2	0	0	18	14	0	3	5
1905 NY-N	1	1	0.00	2	2	1	0	1	17	10	0	3	6
Total 2	3	1	0.00	4	4	3	0	1	35	24	0	6	11
● Jim McGlothlin													
1970 Cin-N	0	0	8.31	1	1	0	0	0	4¹	4	4	2	2
1972 Cin-N	0	0	12.00	1	1	0	0	0	3	4	4	2	3
Total 2	0	0	9.82	2	2	0	0	0	7¹	8	8	4	5
● Tug McGraw													
1973 NY-N	1	0	2.63	5	0	0	1	0	13²	8	4	9	14
1980 Phi-N	1	1	1.17	4	0	0	2	0	7²	7	1	8	10
Total 2	2	1	2.11	9	0	0	3	0	21¹	15	5	17	24
● Scott McGregor													
1979 Bal-A	1	1	3.18	2	2	1	0	0	17	16	6	2	8
1983 Bal-A	1	1	1.06	2	2	1	0	1	17	9	2	2	12
Total 2	2	2	2.12	4	4	2	0	1	34	25	8	4	20
● Harry McIntire													
1910 Chi-N	0	1	6.75	2	0	0	0	0	5¹	4	4	3	3
● Archie McKain													
1940 Det-A	0	0	3.00	1	0	0	0	0	3	4	1	0	0
● Denny McLain													
1968 Det-A	1	2	3.24	3	3	1	0	0	16²	18	6	4	13
● Don McMahon													
1957 Mil-N	0	0	0.00	3	0	0	0	0	5	3	0	3	5
1958 Mil-N	0	0	5.40	3	0	0	0	0	3¹	3	2	3	5
1968 Det-A	0	0	13.50	2	0	0	0	0	2	4	3	0	1
Total 3	0	0	4.35	8	0	0	0	0	10¹	10	5	6	11
● Sadie McMahon													
1895 Bal-N	0	2	5.94	2	2	2	0	0	16²	27	11	3	2
● Dave McNally													
1966 Bal-A	1	0	1.59	2	2	1	0	1	11¹	6	2	7	5
1969 Bal-A	0	1	2.81	2	2	1	0	0	16	11	5	5	13

YEAR	TM/L	W	L	ERA	G	GS	CG	SV	SHO	IP	H	ER	BB	SO
1970	Bal-A	1	0	3.00	1	1	1	0	0	9	9	3	2	5
1971	Bal-A	2	1	1.98	4	2	1	0	0	13²	10	3	5	12
Total 4		4	2	2.34	9	7	4	0	1	50	36	13	19	35

● Hugh McQuillan

YEAR	TM/L	W	L	ERA	G	GS	CG	SV	SHO	IP	H	ER	BB	SO
1922	NY-N	1	0	3.00	1	1	1	0	0	9	8	3	2	4
1923	NY-N	0	1	5.00	2	1	0	0	0	9	11	5	4	3
1924	NY-N	0	0	2.57	3	1	0	1	0	7	2	2	6	2
Total 3		1	1	3.60	6	3	1	1	0	25	21	10	12	9

● Lee Meadows

1925	Pit-N	0	1	3.38	1	1	0	0	0	8	6	3	0	4
1927	Pit-N	0	1	9.95	1	1	0	0	0	6¹	7	7	1	6
Total 2		0	2	6.28	2	2	0	0	0	14¹	13	10	1	10

● George Meakim

1890	Lou-A	0	0	0.00	1	0	0	0	0	4	6	0	1	1

● Doc Medich

1982	Mil-A	0	0	18.00	1	0	0	0	0	2	5	4	1	0

● Jouett Meekin

1894	NY-N	2	0	1.59	2	2	2	0	0	17	13	3	8	6

● Cliff Melton

1937	NY-N	0	2	4.91	3	2	0	0	0	11	12	6	6	7

● Kent Mercker

1991	Atl-N	0	0	0.00	2	0	0	0	0	1	0	0	0	1

● Jim Merritt

1965	Min-A	0	0	2.70	2	0	0	0	0	3¹	2	1	0	1
1970	Cin-N	0	1	21.60	1	1	0	0	0	1²	3	4	1	0
Total 2		0	1	9.00	3	1	0	0	0	5	5	5	1	1

● Andy Messersmith

1974	LA-N	0	2	4.50	2	2	0	0	0	14	11	7	7	12

● Russ Meyer

1950	Phi-N	0	1	5.40	2	0	0	0	0	1²	4	1	0	1
1953	Bro-N	0	0	6.23	1	0	0	0	0	4¹	8	3	4	5
1955	Bro-N	0	0	0.00	1	0	0	0	0	5²	4	0	2	4
Total 3		0	1	3.09	4	0	0	0	0	11²	16	4	6	10

● Pete Mikkelsen

1964	NY-A	0	1	5.79	4	0	0	0	0	4²	4	3	2	4

● Johnny Miljus

1927	Pit-N	0	1	1.35	2	0	0	0	0	6²	4	1	4	6

● Bob Miller

1950	Phi-N	0	1	27.00	1	1	0	0	0	0¹	2	1	0	0

● Bob Miller

1965	LA-N	0	0	0.00	2	0	0	0	0	1¹	0	0	0	0
1966	LA-N	0	0	0.00	1	0	0	0	0	3	2	0	2	0
1971	Pit-N	0	1	3.86	3	0	0	0	0	4²	7	2	1	2
Total 3		0	1	2.00	6	0	0	0	0	9	9	2	3	3

● Stu Miller

1962	SF-N	0	0	0.00	2	0	0	0	0	1¹	1	0	2	0

● Bob Milliken

1953	Bro-N	0	0	0.00	1	0	0	0	0	2	2	0	1	0

● Paul Minner

1949	Bro-N	0	0	0.00	1	0	0	0	0	1	1	0	0	0

● Clarence Mitchell

1920	Bro-N	0	0	0.00	1	0	0	0	0	4²	3	0	3	1
1928	StL-N	0	0	1.59	1	0	0	0	0	5²	2	1	2	2
Total 2		0	0	0.87	2	0	0	0	0	10¹	5	1	5	3

● Vinegar Bend Mizell

1960	Pit-N	0	1	15.43	2	1	0	0	0	2¹	4	4	2	1

● Joe Moeller

1966	LA-N	0	0	4.50	1	0	0	0	0	2	1	1	1	0

● George Mogridge

1924	Was-A	1	0	2.25	2	1	0	0	0	12	7	3	6	5

● Zach Monroe

1958	NY-A	0	0	27.00	1	0	0	0	0	1	3	3	1	1

● Jim Mooney

1934	StL-N	0	0	0.00	1	0	0	0	0	1	1	0	0	0

● Whitey Moore

1939	Cin-N	0	0	0.00	1	0	0	0	0	3	0	0	0	2
1940	Cin-N	0	0	3.24	3	0	0	0	0	8¹	8	3	6	7
Total 2		0	0	2.38	4	0	0	0	0	11¹	8	3	6	9

● Mike Moore

1989	Oak-A	2	0	2.08	2	2	0	0	0	13	9	3	3	10
1990	Oak-A	0	1	0.00	1	1	0	0	0	2²	8	0	0	1
Total 2		2	1	1.72	3	3	0	0	0	15²	17	3	3	11

● Ray Moore

1959	Chi-A	0	0	9.00	1	0	0	0	0	1	1	1	0	1

● Wilcy Moore

1927	NY-A	1	0	0.84	2	1	1	0	0	10²	11	1	2	2
1932	NY-A	1	0	0.00	1	0	0	0	0	5¹	2	0	0	1
Total 2		2	0	0.56	3	1	1	1	0	16	13	1	2	3

● Bob Moose

YEAR	TM/L	W	L	ERA	G	GS	CG	SV	SHO	IP	H	ER	BB	SO
1971	Pit-N	0	0	6.52	3	1	0	0	0	9²	12	7	2	7

● Dave Morehead

1967	Bos-A	0	0	0.00	2	0	0	0	0	3¹	0	0	4	3

● Roger Moret

1975	Bos-A	0	0	0.00	3	0	0	0	0	1²	2	0	3	1

● Tom Morgan

1951	NY-A	0	0	0.00	1	0	0	0	0	2	2	0	1	3
1955	NY-A	0	0	4.91	2	0	0	0	0	3²	3	2	3	1
1956	NY-A	0	1	9.00	2	0	0	0	0	4	6	4	4	3
Total 3		0	1	5.59	5	0	0	0	0	9²	11	6	8	7

● Jack Morris

1984	Det-A	2	0	2.00	2	2	2	0	0	18	13	4	3	13
1991	Min-A	2	0	1.17	3	3	1	0	1	23	18	3	9	15
1992	Tor-A	0	2	8.71	2	2	0	0	0	10¹	13	10	6	12
Total 3		4	2	2.98	7	7	3	0	1	51¹	44	17	18	40

● Johnny Morrison

1925	Pit-N	0	0	2.89	3	0	0	0	0	9¹	11	3	1	7

● Don Mossi

1954	Cle-A	0	0	0.00	3	0	0	0	0	4	3	0	0	1

● Les Mueller

1945	Det-A	0	0	0.00	1	0	0	0	0	2	0	0	1	1

● Terry Mulholland

1993	Phi-N	1	0	6.75	2	2	0	0	0	10²	14	8	3	5

● George Mullin

1907	Det-A	0	2	2.12	2	2	2	0	0	17	16	4	6	8
1908	Det-A	1	0	0.00	1	1	1	0	0	9	7	0	1	8
1909	Det-A	2	1	2.25	4	3	3	0	1	32	23	8	8	20
Total 3		3	3	1.86	7	6	6	0	1	58	46	12	15	36

● Bob Muncrief

1944	StL-A	0	1	1.35	2	0	0	0	0	6²	5	1	4	4
1948	Cle-A	0	0	0.00	1	0	0	0	0	2	1	0	0	0
Total 2		0	1	1.04	3	0	0	0	0	8²	6	1	4	4

● Red Munger

1946	StL-N	1	0	1.00	1	1	1	0	0	9	9	1	3	2

● Johnny Murphy

1936	NY-A	0	0	3.38	1	0	0	1	0	2²	1	1	1	1
1937	NY-A	0	0	0.00	1	0	0	1	0	0¹	0	0	0	0
1938	NY-A	0	0	0.00	1	0	0	1	0	2	2	0	1	1
1939	NY-A	1	0	2.70	1	0	0	0	0	3¹	5	1	0	2
1941	NY-A	1	0	0.00	2	0	0	0	0	6	2	0	1	3
1943	NY-A	0	0	0.00	2	0	0	1	0	2	1	0	1	1
Total 6		2	0	1.10	8	0	0	4	0	16¹	11	2	4	8

● Randy Myers

1990	Cin-N	0	0	0.00	3	0	0	1	0	3	2	0	0	3

● Ray Narleski

1954	Cle-A	0	0	2.25	2	0	0	0	0	4	1	1	1	2

● Art Nehf

1921	NY-N	1	2	1.38	3	3	3	0	1	26	13	4	13	8
1922	NY-N	1	0	2.25	2	2	1	0	0	16	11	4	3	6
1923	NY-N	1	1	2.76	2	2	1	0	1	16¹	10	5	6	7
1924	NY-N	1	1	1.83	3	2	1	0	0	19²	15	4	9	7
1929	Chi-N	0	0	18.00	2	0	0	0	0	1	1	2	1	0
Total 5		4	4	2.16	12	9	6	0	2	79	50	19	32	28

● Mel Nelson

1968	StL-N	0	0	0.00	1	0	0	0	0	1	0	0	0	1

● Gene Nelson

1988	Oak-A	0	0	1.42	3	0	0	0	0	6¹	4	1	3	3
1989	Oak-A	0	0	54.00	2	0	0	0	0	1	4	6	2	1
1990	Oak-A	0	0	0.00	2	0	0	0	0	5	3	0	2	0
Total 3		0	0	5.11	7	0	0	0	0	12¹	11	7	7	4

● Don Newcombe

1949	Bro-N	0	2	3.09	2	2	1	0	0	11²	10	4	3	11
1955	Bro-N	0	1	9.53	1	1	0	0	0	5²	8	6	2	4
1956	Bro-N	0	1	21.21	2	2	0	0	0	4²	11	11	3	4
Total 3		0	4	8.59	5	5	1	0	0	22	29	21	8	19

● Hal Newhouser

1945	Det-A	2	1	6.10	3	3	2	0	0	20²	25	14	4	22
1954	Cle-A	0	0	∞	1	0	0	0	0	0	1	1	1	0
Total 2		2	1	6.53	4	3	2	0	0	20²	26	15	5	22

● Bobo Newsom

1940	Det-A	2	1	1.38	3	3	3	0	1	26	18	4	4	17
1947	NY-A	0	1	19.29	2	1	0	0	0	2¹	6	5	2	0
Total 2		2	2	2.86	5	4	3	0	1	28¹	24	9	6	17

● Kid Nichols

1892	Bos-N	2	0	1.00	2	2	2	0	1	18	17	2	4	13
1897	Bos-N	0	0	12.00	1	1	0	0	0	6	14	8	0	3
Total 2		2	0	3.75	3	3	2	0	1	24	31	10	4	16

● Tom Niedenfuer

1981	LA-N	0	0	0.00	2	0	0	0	0	5	3	0	1	0

YEAR	TM/L	W	L	ERA	G	GS	CG	SV	SHO	IP	H	ER	BB	SO

● Joe Niekro

| 1987 | Min-A | 0 | 0 | 0.00 | 1 | 0 | 0 | 0 | 0 | 2 | 1 | 0 | 1 | 1 |

● Al Nipper

| 1986 | Bos-A | 0 | 1 | 7.11 | 2 | 1 | 0 | 0 | 0 | 6¹ | 10 | 5 | 2 | 2 |

● Gary Nolan

1970	Cin-N	0	1	7.71	2	2	0	0	0	9¹	9	8	3	9
1972	Cin-N	0	1	3.38	2	2	0	0	0	10²	7	4	2	3
1975	Cin-N	0	0	6.00	2	2	0	0	0	6	6	4	1	2
1976	Cin-N	1	0	2.70	1	1	0	0	0	6²	8	2	1	1
Total 4		1	2	4.96	7	7	0	0	0	32²	30	18	7	15

● Dickie Noles

| 1980 | Phi-N | 0 | 0 | 1.93 | 1 | 0 | 0 | 0 | 0 | 4² | 5 | 1 | 2 | 6 |

● Jerry Nops

| 1897 | Bal-N | 1 | 1 | 12.86 | 2 | 2 | 1 | 0 | 0 | 14 | 23 | 20 | 9 | 3 |

● Fred Norman

1975	Cin-N	0	1	9.00	2	1	0	0	0	4	8	4	3	2
1976	Cin-N	0	0	4.26	1	1	0	0	0	6¹	9	3	2	2
Total 2		0	1	6.10	3	2	0	0	0	10¹	17	7	5	4

● Hank O'Day

| 1889 | NY-N | 2 | 0 | 1.17 | 3 | 2 | 2 | 0 | 0 | 23 | 10 | 3 | 14 | 12 |

● Buck O'Brien

| 1912 | Bos-A | 0 | 2 | 5.00 | 2 | 2 | 0 | 0 | 0 | 9 | 12 | 5 | 3 | 4 |

● Billy O'Dell

| 1962 | SF-N | 0 | 1 | 4.38 | 3 | 1 | 0 | 1 | 0 | 12¹ | 12 | 6 | 3 | 9 |

● Blue Moon Odom

1972	Oak-A	0	1	1.59	2	2	0	0	0	11¹	5	2	6	13
1973	Oak-A	0	0	3.86	2	0	0	0	0	4²	5	2	2	2
1974	Oak-A	1	0	0.00	2	0	0	0	0	1¹	0	0	1	2
Total 3		1	1	2.08	6	2	0	0	0	17¹	10	4	9	17

● Curly Ogden

| 1924 | Was-A | 0 | 0 | 0.00 | 1 | 1 | 0 | 0 | 0 | 0¹ | 0 | 0 | 1 | 1 |

● Bob Ojeda

| 1986 | NY-N | 1 | 0 | 2.08 | 2 | 2 | 0 | 0 | 0 | 13 | 13 | 3 | 5 | 9 |

● Red Oldham

| 1925 | Pit-N | 0 | 0 | 0.00 | 1 | 0 | 0 | 1 | 0 | 1 | 0 | 0 | 0 | 2 |

● Jesse Orosco

| 1986 | NY-N | 0 | 0 | 0.00 | 4 | 0 | 0 | 2 | 0 | 5² | 2 | 0 | 0 | 6 |

● Dan Osinski

| 1967 | Bos-A | 0 | 0 | 6.75 | 2 | 0 | 0 | 0 | 0 | 1¹ | 2 | 1 | 0 | 0 |

● Claude Osteen

1965	LA-N	1	1	0.64	2	2	1	0	1	14	9	1	5	4
1966	LA-N	0	1	1.29	1	1	0	0	0	7	3	1	1	3
Total 2		1	2	0.86	3	3	1	0	1	21	12	2	6	7

● Joe Ostrowski

| 1951 | NY-A | 0 | 0 | 0.00 | 1 | 0 | 0 | 0 | 0 | 4 | 1 | 0 | 0 | 1 |

● Jim O'Toole

| 1961 | Cin-N | 0 | 2 | 3.00 | 2 | 0 | 0 | 0 | 0 | 12 | 11 | 4 | 7 | 4 |

● Orval Overall

1906	Chi-N	0	0	2.25	2	0	0	0	0	12	10	3	3	8
1907	Chi-N	1	0	1.00	2	2	1	0	0	18	14	2	4	11
1908	Chi-N	2	0	0.98	3	2	2	0	1	18¹	7	2	7	15
1910	Chi-N	0	1	9.00	1	1	0	0	0	3	6	3	1	1
Total 4		3	1	1.75	8	5	3	0	1	51¹	37	10	15	35

● Stubby Overmire

| 1945 | Det-A | 0 | 1 | 3.00 | 1 | 1 | 0 | 0 | 0 | 6 | 4 | 2 | 2 | 2 |

● Frank Owen

| 1906 | Chi-A | 0 | 0 | 0.00 | 1 | 0 | 0 | 0 | 0 | 6 | 4 | 0 | 2 | 1 |

● Joe Page

1947	NY-A	1	1	4.15	4	0	0	1	0	13	12	6	2	7
1949	NY-A	1	0	2.00	3	0	0	1	0	9	6	2	3	8
Total 2		2	1	3.27	7	0	0	2	0	22	18	8	5	15

● Vance Page

| 1938 | Chi-N | 0 | 0 | 13.50 | 1 | 0 | 0 | 0 | 0 | 1¹ | 2 | 2 | 0 | 0 |

● Satchel Paige

| 1948 | Cle-A | 0 | 0 | 0.00 | 1 | 0 | 0 | 0 | 0 | 0² | 0 | 0 | 0 | 0 |

● Erv Palica

| 1949 | Bro-N | 0 | 0 | 0.00 | 1 | 0 | 0 | 0 | 0 | 2 | 1 | 0 | 1 | 1 |

● Jim Palmer

1966	Bal-A	1	0	0.00	1	1	1	0	1	9	4	0	3	6
1969	Bal-A	0	1	6.00	1	1	0	0	0	6	5	4	4	5
1970	Bal-A	1	0	4.60	2	2	0	0	0	15²	11	8	9	9
1971	Bal-A	1	0	2.65	2	2	0	0	0	17	15	5	9	15
1979	Bal-A	0	1	3.60	2	2	0	0	0	15	18	6	5	8
1983	Bal-A	1	0	0.00	1	0	0	1	0	2	2	0	1	1
Total 6		4	2	3.20	9	8	1	0	1	64²	55	23	31	44

● Harry Parker

| 1973 | NY-N | 0 | 1 | 0.00 | 3 | 0 | 0 | 0 | 0 | 3¹ | 2 | 0 | 2 | 2 |

● Camilo Pascual

| 1965 | Min-A | 0 | 1 | 5.40 | 1 | 1 | 0 | 0 | 0 | 5 | 8 | 3 | 1 | 0 |

● Claude Passeau

| 1945 | Chi-N | 1 | 0 | 2.70 | 3 | 2 | 1 | 0 | 1 | 16² | 7 | 5 | 8 | 3 |

● Daryl Patterson

| 1968 | Det-A | 0 | 0 | 0.00 | 2 | 0 | 0 | 0 | 0 | 3 | 1 | 0 | 1 | 0 |

● Marty Pattin

| 1980 | KC-A | 0 | 0 | 0.00 | 1 | 0 | 0 | 0 | 0 | 1 | 0 | 0 | 0 | 2 |

● Monte Pearson

1936	NY-A	1	0	2.00	1	1	0	0	0	9	7	2	2	7
1937	NY-A	1	0	1.04	1	1	0	0	0	8²	5	1	2	4
1938	NY-A	1	0	1.00	1	1	1	0	0	9	5	1	2	9
1939	NY-A	1	0	0.00	1	1	1	0	1	9	2	0	1	8
Total 4		4	0	1.01	4	4	3	0	1	35²	19	4	7	28

● Alejandro Pena

1988	LA-N	1	0	0.00	2	0	0	0	0	5	2	0	1	7
1991	Atl-N	0	1	3.38	3	0	0	0	0	5¹	6	2	3	7
Total 2		1	1	1.74	5	0	0	0	0	10¹	8	2	4	14

● Herb Pennock

1914	Phi-A	0	0	0.00	1	0	0	0	0	3	2	0	2	3
1923	NY-A	2	0	3.63	3	2	1	1	0	17¹	19	7	1	8
1926	NY-A	2	0	1.23	3	2	2	0	0	22	13	3	4	8
1927	NY-A	1	0	1.00	1	1	1	0	0	9	3	1	0	1
1932	NY-A	0	0	2.25	2	0	0	2	0	4	2	1	1	4
Total 5		5	0	1.95	10	5	4	3	0	55¹	39	12	8	24

● Ron Perranoski

1963	LA-N	0	0	0.00	1	0	0	1	0	0²	1	0	0	1
1965	LA-N	0	0	7.36	2	0	0	0	0	3²	3	3	4	1
1966	LA-N	0	0	5.40	2	0	0	0	0	3¹	4	2	1	2
Total 3		0	0	5.87	5	0	0	1	0	7²	8	5	5	4

● Pol Perritt

| 1917 | NY-N | 0 | 0 | 2.16 | 3 | 0 | 0 | 0 | 0 | 8¹ | 9 | 2 | 3 | 3 |

● Jim Perry

| 1965 | Min-A | 0 | 0 | 4.50 | 2 | 0 | 0 | 0 | 0 | 4 | 5 | 2 | 2 | 4 |

● Dan Petry

| 1984 | Det-A | 0 | 1 | 9.00 | 2 | 2 | 0 | 0 | 0 | 8 | 14 | 8 | 5 | 4 |

● Jeff Pfeffer

1916	Bro-N	0	1	1.69	3	1	0	0	0	10²	7	2	4	5
1920	Bro-N	0	0	3.00	1	0	0	0	0	3	4	1	2	1
Total 2		0	1	1.98	4	1	0	0	0	13²	11	3	6	6

● Jack Pfiester

1906	Chi-N	0	2	6.10	2	1	1	0	0	10¹	7	7	3	11
1907	Chi-N	1	0	1.00	1	1	1	0	0	9	9	1	1	3
1908	Chi-N	0	1	7.87	1	1	0	0	0	8	10	7	3	1
1910	Chi-N	0	0	0.00	1	0	0	0	0	6²	9	0	1	1
Total 4		1	3	3.97	5	3	2	0	0	34	35	15	8	16

● Deacon Phillippe

1900	Pit-N	1	0	0.00	1	1	1	0	1	9	6	0	2	5
1903	Pit-N	3	2	2.86	5	5	5	0	0	44	38	14	3	22
1909	Pit-N	0	0	0.00	2	0	0	0	0	6	2	0	1	2
Total 3		4	2	2.14	8	6	6	0	1	59	46	14	6	29

● Tom Phoebus

| 1970 | Bal-A | 1 | 0 | 0.00 | 1 | 0 | 0 | 0 | 0 | 1² | 1 | 0 | 0 | 0 |

● Billy Pierce

1959	Chi-A	0	0	0.00	3	0	0	0	0	4	2	0	2	3
1962	SF-N	1	1	2.40	2	2	1	0	0	15	8	4	2	5
Total 2		1	1	1.89	5	2	1	0	0	19	10	4	4	8

● Bill Piercy

| 1921 | NY-A | 0 | 0 | 0.00 | 1 | 0 | 0 | 0 | 0 | 1 | 2 | 0 | 0 | 2 |

● Horacio Pina

| 1973 | Oak-A | 0 | 0 | 0.00 | 2 | 0 | 0 | 0 | 0 | 3 | 1 | 0 | 0 | 0 |

● George Pipgras

1927	NY-A	1	0	2.00	1	1	1	0	0	9	7	2	1	2
1928	NY-A	1	0	2.00	1	1	1	0	0	9	4	2	4	8
1932	NY-A	1	0	4.50	1	1	0	0	0	8	9	4	3	1
Total 3		3	0	2.77	3	3	2	0	0	26	20	8	8	11

● Juan Pizarro

1957	Mil-N	0	0	10.80	1	0	0	0	0	1²	3	2	2	1
1958	Mil-N	0	0	5.40	1	0	0	0	0	1²	2	1	1	3
Total 2		0	0	8.10	2	0	0	0	0	3¹	5	3	3	4

● Eddie Plank

1905	Phi-A	0	2	1.59	2	2	2	0	0	17	14	3	4	11
1911	Phi-A	1	1	1.86	2	1	1	0	0	9²	6	2	0	8
1913	Phi-A	1	1	0.95	2	2	2	0	0	19	9	2	3	7
1914	Phi-A	0	1	1.00	1	1	1	0	0	9	7	1	4	6
Total 4		2	5	1.32	7	6	6	0	0	54²	36	8	11	32

● Bill Pleis

| 1965 | Min-A | 0 | 0 | 9.00 | 1 | 0 | 0 | 0 | 0 | 1 | 2 | 1 | 0 | 0 |

● Eric Plunk

| 1988 | Oak-A | 0 | 0 | 0.00 | 2 | 0 | 0 | 0 | 0 | 1² | 0 | 0 | 0 | 3 |

● Johnny Podres

1953	Bro-N	0	1	3.38	2	1	1	0	0	2²	1	1	2	0
1955	Bro-N	2	0	1.00	2	2	2	0	1	18	15	2	4	10
1959	LA-N	1	0	4.82	2	2	0	0	0	9¹	7	5	6	4

YEAR TM/L	W	L	ERA	G	GS	CG	SV	SHO	IP	H	ER	BB	SO
1963 LA-N	1	0	1.08	1	1	0	0	0	8¹	6	1	1	4
Total 4	4	1	2.11	6	6	2	0	1	38¹	29	9	13	18
● Dick Pole													
1975 Bos-A	0	0	∞	1	0	0	0	0	0	0	0	1	2	0
● Howie Pollet													
1942 StL-N	0	0	0.00	1	0	0	0	0	0¹	0	0	0	0
1946 StL-N	0	1	3.48	2	2	1	0	0	10¹	12	4	4	3
Total 2	0	1	3.38	3	2	1	0	0	10²	12	4	4	3
● Nels Potter													
1944 StL-A	0	1	0.93	2	2	0	0	0	9²	10	1	3	6
1948 Bos-N	0	0	8.44	2	1	0	0	0	5¹	6	5	2	1
Total 2	0	1	3.60	4	3	0	0	0	15	16	6	5	7
● Ray Prim													
1945 Chi-N	0	1	9.00	2	1	0	0	0	4	4	4	1	1
● Bob Purkey													
1961 Cin-N	0	1	1.64	2	1	1	0	0	11	6	2	3	5
● Jack Quinn													
1921 NY-A	0	1	9.82	1	0	0	0	0	3²	8	4	2	2
1929 Phi-A	0	0	9.00	1	1	0	0	0	5	7	5	2	2
1930 Phi-A	0	0	4.50	1	0	0	0	0	2	3	1	0	1
Total 3	0	1	8.44	3	1	0	0	0	10²	18	10	4	5
● Dan Quisenberry													
1980 KC-A	1	2	5.23	6	0	0	1	0	10¹	10	6	3	0
1985 KC-A	1	0	2.08	4	0	0	0	0	4¹	5	1	3	3
Total 2	2	2	4.30	10	0	0	1	0	14²	15	7	6	3
● Charlie Radbourn													
1884 Pro-N	3	0	0.00	3	3	3	0	1	22	11	0	0	17
● Vic Raschi													
1947 NY-A	0	0	6.75	2	0	0	0	0	1¹	2	1	0	1
1949 NY-A	1	1	4.30	2	2	0	0	0	14²	15	7	5	11
1950 NY-A	1	0	0.00	1	1	1	0	1	9	2	0	1	5
1951 NY-A	1	1	0.87	2	2	0	0	0	10¹	12	1	8	4
1952 NY-A	2	0	1.59	3	2	1	0	0	17	12	3	8	18
1953 NY-A	0	1	3.38	1	1	1	0	0	8	9	3	3	4
Total 6	5	3	2.24	11	8	3	0	1	60¹	52	15	25	43
● Doug Rau													
1977 LA-N	0	1	11.57	2	1	0	0	0	2¹	4	3	0	1
1978 LA-N	0	0	0.00	1	0	0	0	0	2	1	0	0	3
Total 2	0	1	6.23	3	1	0	0	0	4¹	5	3	0	4
● Lance Rautzhan													
1977 LA-N	0	0	0.00	1	0	0	0	0	0¹	0	0	2	0
1978 LA-N	0	0	13.50	2	0	0	0	0	2	4	3	0	0
Total 2	0	0	11.57	3	0	0	0	0	2¹	4	3	2	0
● Jeff Reardon													
1987 Min-A	0	0	0.00	4	0	0	1	0	4²	5	0	0	3
1992 Atl-N	0	1	13.50	2	0	0	0	0	1¹	2	2	1	1
Total 2	0	1	3.00	6	0	0	1	0	6	7	2	1	4
● Howie Reed													
1965 LA-N	0	0	8.10	2	0	0	0	0	3¹	2	3	2	4
● Ron Reed													
1980 Phi-N	0	0	0.00	2	0	0	1	0	2	2	0	0	2
1983 Phi-N	0	0	2.70	3	0	0	0	0	3¹	4	1	2	4
Total 2	0	0	1.69	5	0	0	1	0	5¹	6	1	2	6
● Phil Regan													
1966 LA-N	0	0	0.00	2	0	0	0	0	1²	0	0	1	2
● Art Reinhart													
1926 StL-N	0	1	∞	1	0	0	0	0	0	1	4	4	0
● Hal Reniff													
1963 NY-A	0	0	0.00	3	0	0	0	0	3	0	0	1	1
1964 NY-A	0	0	0.00	1	0	0	0	0	0¹	2	0	0	0
Total 2	0	0	0.00	4	0	0	0	0	3¹	2	0	1	1
● Ed Reulbach													
1906 Chi-N	1	0	2.45	2	2	1	0	0	11	6	3	8	4
1907 Chi-N	1	0	0.75	2	1	1	0	0	12	6	1	3	4
1908 Chi-N	0	0	4.70	2	1	0	0	0	7²	9	4	1	5
1910 Chi-N	0	0	9.00	1	1	0	0	0	2	3	2	2	0
Total 4	2	0	2.76	7	5	2	0	0	32²	24	10	14	13
● Rick Reuschel													
1981 NY-A	0	0	4.91	2	1	0	0	0	3²	7	2	3	2
1989 SF-N	0	1	11.25	1	1	0	0	0	4	5	5	4	2
Total 2	0	1	8.22	3	2	0	0	0	7²	12	7	7	4
● Jerry Reuss													
1981 LA-N	1	1	3.86	2	2	1	0	0	11²	10	5	3	8
● Allie Reynolds													
1947 NY-A	1	0	4.76	2	2	1	0	0	11¹	15	6	3	6
1949 NY-A	1	0	0.00	2	1	1	1	1	12¹	2	0	4	14
1950 NY-A	1	0	0.87	2	1	1	0	0	10¹	7	1	4	7
1951 NY-A	1	1	4.20	2	2	1	0	0	15	16	7	11	8
1952 NY-A	2	1	1.77	4	2	1	1	1	20¹	12	4	6	18
1953 NY-A	1	0	6.75	3	1	0	1	0	8	9	6	4	9
Total 6	7	2	2.79	15	9	5	4	2	77¹	61	24	32	62
● Flint Rhem													
1926 StL-N	0	0	6.75	1	1	0	0	0	4	7	3	2	4
1928 StL-N	0	0	0.00	1	0	0	0	0	2	0	0	0	1
1930 StL-N	0	1	10.80	1	1	0	0	0	3¹	7	4	2	3
1931 StL-N	0	0	0.00	1	0	0	0	0	1	1	0	0	1
Total 4	0	1	6.10	4	2	0	0	0	10¹	15	7	4	9
● Rick Rhoden													
1977 LA-N	0	1	2.57	2	0	0	0	0	7	4	2	1	5
● Gordie Richardson													
1964 StL-N	0	0	40.50	2	0	0	0	0	0²	3	3	2	0
● Pete Richert													
1969 Bal-A	0	0	—	1	0	0	0	0	0	0	0	0	0
1970 Bal-A	0	0	0.00	1	0	0	1	0	0¹	0	0	0	0
1971 Bal-A	0	0	0.00	1	0	0	0	0	0²	0	0	0	1
Total 3	0	0	0.00	3	0	0	1	0	1	0	0	0	1
● Lew Richie													
1910 Chi-N	0	0	0.00	1	0	0	0	0	1	1	0	0	0
● Elmer Riddle													
1940 Cin-N	0	0	0.00	1	0	0	0	0	1	0	0	0	2
● Dave Righetti													
1981 NY-A	0	0	13.50	1	1	0	0	0	2	5	3	2	1
● Jose Rijo													
1990 Cin-N	2	0	0.59	2	2	0	0	0	15¹	9	1	5	14
● Jimmy Ring													
1919 Cin-N	1	1	0.64	2	1	1	0	1	14	7	1	6	4
● Ben Rivera													
1993 Phi-N	0	0	27.00	1	0	0	0	0	1¹	4	4	2	3
● Eppa Rixey													
1915 Phi-N	0	1	4.05	1	0	0	0	0	6²	4	3	2	2
● Robin Roberts													
1950 Phi-N	0	1	1.64	2	1	1	0	0	11	11	2	3	5
● Don Robinson													
1979 Pit-N	1	0	5.40	4	0	0	0	0	5	4	3	6	3
1989 SF-N	0	1	21.60	1	1	0	0	0	1²	4	4	1	0
Total 2	1	1	9.45	5	1	0	0	0	6²	8	7	7	3
● Preacher Roe													
1949 Bro-N	1	0	0.00	1	1	1	0	1	9	6	0	0	3
1952 Bro-N	1	0	3.18	3	1	1	0	0	11¹	9	4	6	7
1953 Bro-N	0	1	4.50	1	1	1	0	0	8	5	4	4	4
Total 3	2	1	2.54	5	3	3	0	1	28¹	20	8	10	14
● Ed Roebuck													
1955 Bro-N	0	0	0.00	1	0	0	0	0	2	1	0	0	0
1956 Bro-N	0	0	2.08	3	0	0	0	0	4¹	1	1	0	5
Total 2	0	0	1.42	4	0	0	0	0	6¹	2	1	0	5
● Tom Rogers													
1921 NY-A	0	0	6.75	1	0	0	0	0	1¹	3	1	0	1
● Eddie Rommel													
1929 Phi-A	1	0	9.00	1	0	0	0	0	1	2	1	0	0
1931 Phi-A	0	0	9.00	1	0	0	0	0	1	3	1	0	0
Total 2	1	0	9.00	2	0	0	0	0	2	5	2	1	0
● Enrique Romo													
1979 Pit-N	0	0	3.86	2	0	0	0	0	4²	5	2	3	4
● Jim Rooker													
1979 Pit-N	0	0	1.04	2	1	0	0	0	8²	5	1	3	4
● Charlie Root													
1929 Chi-N	0	1	4.72	2	2	0	0	0	13¹	12	7	2	8
1932 Chi-N	0	1	10.38	1	1	0	0	0	4¹	6	5	3	4
1935 Chi-N	0	1	18.00	2	1	0	0	0	2	5	4	1	2
1938 Chi-N	0	0	3.00	1	0	0	0	0	3	3	1	0	1
Total 4	0	3	6.75	6	4	0	0	0	22²	26	17	6	15
● Schoolboy Rowe													
1934 Det-A	1	1	2.95	3	2	2	0	0	21¹	19	7	0	12
1935 Det-A	1	2	2.57	3	2	2	0	0	21	19	6	1	14
1940 Det-A	0	2	17.18	2	2	0	0	0	3²	12	7	1	1
Total 3	2	5	3.91	8	6	4	0	0	46	50	20	2	27
● Nap Rucker													
1916 Bro-N	0	0	0.00	1	0	0	0	0	2	1	0	0	3
● Dick Rudolph													
1914 Bos-N	2	0	0.50	2	2	2	0	0	18	12	1	4	15
● Dutch Ruether													
1919 Cin-N	1	0	2.57	2	2	1	0	0	14	12	4	4	1
1926 NY-A	0	1	4.15	1	1	0	0	0	4¹	7	2	2	1
Total 2	1	1	2.95	3	3	1	0	0	18¹	19	6	6	2
● Red Ruffing													
1932 NY-A	1	0	4.00	1	1	1	0	0	9	10	4	6	10
1936 NY-A	0	1	4.50	2	2	1	0	0	14	16	7	5	12
1937 NY-A	1	0	1.00	1	1	1	0	0	9	7	1	3	8
1938 NY-A	2	0	1.50	2	2	2	0	0	18	17	3	2	11
1939 NY-A	1	0	1.00	1	1	1	0	0	9	4	1	1	4
1941 NY-A	1	0	1.00	1	1	1	0	0	9	6	1	3	5

YEAR TM/L	W	L	ERA	G	GS	CG	SV	SHO	IP	H	ER	BB	SO
1942 NY-A	1	1	4.08	2	2	1	0	0	17²	14	8	7	11
Total 7	7	2	2.63	10	10	7	0	0	85²	74	25	27	61
● Bob Rush													
1958 Mil-N	0	1	3.00	1	1	0	0	0	6	3	2	5	2
● Amos Rusie													
1894 NY-N	2	0	0.50	2	2	2	0	0	18	14	1	3	9
● Allan Russell													
1924 Was-A	0	0	3.00	1	0	0	0	0	3	4	1	0	0
● Reb Russell													
1917 Chi-A	0	0	∞	1	1	0	0	0	0	2	1	1	0
● Jack Russell													
1933 Was-A	0	1	0.87	3	0	0	0	0	10¹	8	1	0	7
1938 Chi-N	0	0	0.00	2	0	0	0	0	1²	1	0	1	0
Total 2	0	1	0.75	5	0	0	0	0	12	9	1	1	7
● Marius Russo													
1941 NY-A	1	0	1.00	1	1	1	0	0	9	4	1	2	5
1943 NY-A	1	0	0.00	1	1	1	0	0	9	7	0	1	2
Total 2	2	0	0.50	2	2	2	0	0	18	11	1	3	7
● Babe Ruth													
1916 Bos-A	1	0	0.64	1	1	1	0	0	14	6	1	3	4
1918 Bos-A	2	0	1.06	2	2	1	0	1	17	13	2	7	4
Total 2	3	0	0.87	3	3	2	0	1	31	19	3	10	8
● Johnny Rutherford													
1952 Bro-N	0	0	9.00	1	0	0	0	0	1	1	1	1	1
● Dick Ruthven													
1980 Phi-N	0	0	3.00	1	1	0	0	0	9	9	3	0	7
● Jimmy Ryan													
1886 Chi-N	0	0	9.00	1	0	0	0	0	5	8	5	4	4
● Nolan Ryan													
1969 NY-N	0	0	0.00	1	0	0	1	0	2¹	1	0	2	3
● Rosy Ryan													
1922 NY-N	0	0	0.00	1	0	0	0	0	2	1	0	0	2
1923 NY-N	1	0	0.96	3	0	0	0	0	9¹	11	1	3	3
1924 NY-N	1	0	3.18	2	0	0	0	0	5²	7	2	4	3
Total 3	3	0	1.59	6	0	0	0	0	17	19	3	7	8
● Mike Ryba													
1946 Bos-A	0	0	13.50	1	0	0	0	0	0²	2	1	1	0
● Bret Saberhagen													
1985 KC-A	2	0	0.50	2	2	2	0	1	18	11	1	1	10
● Ray Sadecki													
1964 StL-N	1	0	8.53	2	2	0	0	0	6¹	12	6	5	2
1973 NY-N	0	0	1.93	4	0	0	1	0	4²	5	1	1	6
Total 2	1	0	5.73	6	2	0	1	0	11	17	7	6	8
● Johnny Sain													
1948 Bos-N	1	1	1.06	2	2	2	0	1	17	9	2	0	9
1951 NY-A	0	0	9.00	1	0	0	0	0	2	4	2	2	2
1952 NY-A	0	1	3.00	1	0	0	0	0	6	6	2	3	3
1953 NY-A	1	0	4.76	2	0	0	0	0	5²	8	3	1	1
Total 4	2	2	2.64	6	2	2	0	1	30²	27	9	6	15
● Randy St.Claire													
1991 Atl-N	0	0	9.00	1	0	0	0	0	1	1	1	0	0
● Slim Sallee													
1917 NY-N	0	2	5.28	2	2	1	0	0	15¹	20	9	4	4
1919 Cin-N	1	1	1.35	2	2	1	0	0	13¹	19	2	1	2
Total 2	1	3	3.45	4	4	2	0	0	28²	39	11	5	6
● Joe Sambito													
1986 Bos-A	0	0	27.00	2	0	0	0	0	0¹	2	1	2	0
● Scott Sanderson													
1990 Oak-A	0	0	10.80	2	0	0	0	0	1²	4	2	1	0
● Jack Sanford													
1962 SF-N	1	2	1.93	3	3	1	0	1	23¹	16	5	8	19
● Jose Santiago													
1967 Bos-A	0	2	5.59	3	2	0	0	0	9²	16	6	3	6
● Kevin Saucier													
1980 Phi-N	0	0	0.00	1	0	0	0	0	0²	0	0	2	0
● Ray Scarborough													
1952 NY-A	0	0	9.00	1	0	0	0	0	1	1	1	0	1
● Art Schallock													
1953 NY-A	0	0	4.50	1	0	0	0	0	2	2	1	1	1
● Dan Schatzeder													
1987 Min-A	1	0	6.23	3	0	0	0	0	4¹	4	3	3	3
● Bill Scherrer													
1984 Det-A	0	0	3.00	3	0	0	0	0	3	5	1	0	0
● Curt Schilling													
1993 Phi-N	1	1	3.52	2	2	0	0	0	15¹	13	6	5	9
● Calvin Schiraldi													
1986 Bos-A	0	2	13.50	3	0	0	1	0	4	7	6	3	2

YEAR TM/L	W	L	ERA	G	GS	CG	SV	SHO	IP	H	ER	BB	SO
● Freddy Schmidt													
1944 StL-N	0	0	0.00	1	0	0	0	0	3¹	1	0	1	1
● Barney Schultz													
1964 StL-N	0	1	18.00	4	0	0	1	0	4	9	8	3	1
● Hal Schumacher													
1933 NY-N	1	0	2.45	2	2	1	0	0	14²	13	4	5	3
1936 NY-N	1	1	5.25	2	2	1	0	0	12	13	7	10	11
1937 NY-N	0	1	6.00	1	1	0	0	0	6	9	4	4	3
Total 3	2	2	4.13	5	5	2	0	0	32²	35	15	19	17
● Ferdie Schupp													
1917 NY-N	1	0	1.74	2	2	1	0	1	10¹	11	2	2	9
● Jack Scott													
1922 NY-N	1	0	0.00	1	1	1	0	1	9	4	0	1	2
1923 NY-N	0	1	12.00	2	1	0	0	0	3	9	4	1	2
Total 2	1	1	3.00	3	2	1	0	1	12	13	4	2	4
● Scott Scudder													
1990 Cin-N	0	0	0.00	1	0	0	0	0	1¹	0	0	2	2
● Tom Seaver													
1969 NY-N	1	1	3.00	2	2	1	0	0	15	12	5	3	9
1973 NY-N	0	1	2.40	2	2	0	0	0	15	13	4	3	18
Total 2	1	2	2.70	4	4	1	0	0	30	25	9	6	27
● Diego Segui													
1975 Bos-A	0	0	0.00	1	0	0	0	0	1	0	0	0	0
● Bobby Shantz													
1957 NY-A	0	1	4.05	3	1	0	0	0	6²	8	3	2	7
1960 NY-A	0	0	4.26	3	0	0	1	0	6¹	4	3	1	1
Total 2	0	1	4.15	6	1	0	1	0	13	12	6	3	8
● Bob Shaw													
1959 Chi-A	1	1	2.57	2	2	0	0	0	14	17	4	2	2
● Bob Shawkey													
1914 Phi-A	0	1	3.60	1	1	0	0	0	5	4	2	2	0
1921 NY-A	0	1	7.00	2	1	0	0	0	9	13	7	6	5
1922 NY-A	0	0	2.70	1	1	1	0	0	10	8	3	2	4
1923 NY-A	1	0	3.52	1	1	0	0	0	7²	12	3	4	2
1926 NY-A	0	1	5.40	3	1	0	0	0	10	8	6	2	7
Total 8	1	3	4.54	8	5	1	0	0	41²	45	21	16	18
● Spec Shea													
1947 NY-A	2	0	2.35	3	3	1	0	0	15¹	10	4	8	10
● Rollie Sheldon													
1964 NY-A	0	0	0.00	2	0	0	0	0	2²	0	0	2	2
● Bill Sherdel													
1926 StL-N	0	2	2.12	2	2	1	0	0	17	15	4	8	3
1928 StL-N	0	2	4.72	2	2	0	0	0	13¹	15	7	3	3
Total 2	0	4	3.26	4	4	1	0	0	30¹	30	11	11	6
● Larry Sherry													
1959 LA-N	2	0	0.71	4	0	0	2	0	12²	8	1	2	5
● Tex Shirley													
1944 StL-A	0	0	0.00	1	0	0	0	0	2	2	0	1	1
● Urban Shocker													
1926 NY-A	0	1	5.87	2	1	0	0	0	7²	13	5	0	3
● Ernie Shore													
1915 Bos-A	1	1	2.12	2	2	2	0	0	17	12	4	8	6
1916 Bos-A	2	0	1.53	2	1	1	0	0	17²	12	3	4	9
Total 2	3	1	1.82	4	3	3	0	0	34²	24	7	12	15
● Bill Shores													
1930 Phi-A	0	0	13.50	1	0	0	0	0	1¹	3	2	0	0
● Eric Show													
1984 SD-N	0	1	10.13	1	1	0	0	0	2²	4	3	1	2
● Ed Siever													
1907 Det-A	0	1	4.50	1	1	0	0	0	4	7	2	0	1
● Curt Simmons													
1964 StL-N	0	1	2.51	2	2	0	0	0	14¹	11	4	3	8
● Doug Sisk													
1986 NY-N	0	0	0.00	1	0	0	0	0	0²	0	0	1	1
● Jim Slaton													
1982 Mil-A	1	0	0.00	2	0	0	0	0	2²	1	0	2	1
● Al Smith													
1936 NY-N	0	0	81.00	1	0	0	0	0	0¹	2	3	1	0
1937 NY-N	0	0	3.00	2	0	0	0	0	3	2	1	0	1
Total 2	0	0	10.80	3	0	0	0	0	3¹	4	4	1	1
● Clay Smith													
1940 Det-A	0	0	2.25	1	0	0	0	0	4	1	1	3	1
● Pete Smith													
1992 Atl-N	0	0	0.00	1	0	0	0	0	3	3	0	0	0
● Bob Smith													
1932 Chi-N	0	0	9.00	1	0	0	0	0	2	1	2	1	0
● Sherry Smith													
1916 Bro-N	0	1	1.35	1	1	1	0	0	13¹	7	2	6	2

YEAR	TM/L	W	L	ERA	G	GS	CG	SV	SHO	IP	H	ER	BB	SO
1920	Bro-N	1	1	0.53	2	2	2	0	0	17	10	1	3	3
Total 2		1	2	0.89	3	3	3	0	0	30¹	17	3	9	5
● **John Smoltz**														
1991	Atl-N	0	0	1.26	2	2	0	0	0	14¹	13	2	1	11
1992	Atl-N	1	0	2.70	2	2	0	0	0	13¹	13	4	7	12
Total 2		1	0	1.95	4	4	0	0	0	27²	26	6	8	23
● **Elias Sosa**														
1977	LA-N	0	0	11.57	2	0	0	0	0	2¹	3	3	1	1
● **Warren Spahn**														
1948	Bos-N	1	1	3.00	3	1	0	0	0	12	10	4	3	12
1957	Mil-N	1	1	4.70	2	2	1	0	0	15¹	18	8	2	18
1958	Mil-N	2	1	2.20	3	3	2	0	1	28²	19	7	8	18
Total 3		4	3	3.05	8	6	3	0	1	56	47	19	13	32
● **Joe Sparma**														
1968	Det-A	0	0	54.00	1	0	0	0	0	0¹	2	2	0	0
● **By Speece**														
1924	Was-A	0	0	9.00	1	0	0	0	0	1	3	1	0	0
● **George Spencer**														
1951	NY-N	0	0	18.90	2	0	0	0	0	3¹	6	7	3	0
● **Paul Splittorff**														
1980	KC-A	0	0	5.40	1	0	0	0	0	1²	4	1	0	0
● **Karl Spooner**														
1955	Bro-N	0	1	13.50	2	1	0	0	0	3¹	4	5	3	6
● **Bill Stafford**														
1960	NY-A	0	0	1.50	2	0	0	0	0	6	5	1	1	2
1961	NY-A	0	0	2.70	1	1	0	0	0	6²	7	2	2	5
1962	NY-A	1	0	2.00	1	1	1	0	0	9	4	2	2	5
Total 3		1	0	2.08	4	2	1	0	0	21²	16	5	5	12
● **Gerry Staley**														
1959	Chi-A	0	1	2.16	4	0	0	1	0	8¹	8	2	0	3
● **Harry Staley**														
1892	Bos-N	1	0	3.00	1	1	1	0	0	9	10	3	1	0
● **Lee Stange**														
1967	Bos-A	0	0	0.00	1	0	0	0	0	2	3	0	0	0
● **Don Stanhouse**														
1979	Bal-A	0	1	13.50	3	0	0	0	0	2	6	3	3	0
● **Bob Stanley**														
1986	Bos-A	0	0	0.00	5	0	0	1	0	6¹	5	0	1	4
● **Mike Stanton**														
1991	Atl-N	1	0	0.00	5	0	0	0	0	7¹	5	0	2	7
1992	Atl-N	0	0	0.00	4	0	0	1	0	5	3	0	2	1
Total 2		1	0	0.00	9	0	0	1	0	12¹	8	0	4	8
● **Jerry Stephenson**														
1967	Bos-A	0	0	9.00	1	0	0	0	0	2	3	2	1	0
● **Dave Stewart**														
1981	LA-N	0	0	0.00	2	0	0	0	0	1²	1	0	2	1
1988	Oak-A	0	1	3.14	2	2	0	0	0	14¹	12	5	5	5
1989	Oak-A	2	0	1.69	2	2	1	0	1	16	10	3	2	14
1990	Oak-A	0	2	3.46	2	2	1	0	0	13	10	5	6	5
1993	Tor-A	0	1	6.75	2	2	0	0	0	12	10	9	8	8
Total 5		2	4	3.47	10	8	2	0	1	57	43	22	23	33
● **Sammy Stewart**														
1979	Bal-A	0	0	0.00	1	0	0	0	0	2²	4	0	1	0
1983	Bal-A	0	0	0.00	3	0	0	0	0	5	2	0	2	6
Total 2		0	0	0.00	4	0	0	0	0	7²	6	0	3	6
● **Lefty Stewart**														
1933	Was-A	0	1	9.00	1	1	0	0	0	2	6	2	0	0
● **Jack Stivetts**														
1892	Bos-N	2	0	0.93	3	3	3	0	1	29	21	3	7	17
1897	Bos-N	0	1	18.47	2	1	0	0	0	6¹	16	13	7	0
Total 2		2	1	4.08	5	4	3	0	1	35¹	37	16	14	17
● **Tim Stoddard**														
1979	Bal-A	1	0	5.40	4	0	0	0	0	5	6	3	1	3
● **George Stone**														
1973	NY-N	0	0	0.00	2	0	0	1	0	3	4	0	1	3
● **Steve Stone**														
1979	Bal-A	0	0	9.00	1	0	0	0	0	2	4	2	2	2
● **Mel Stottlemyre**														
1964	NY-A	1	1	3.15	3	3	1	0	0	20	18	7	6	12
● **Todd Stottlemyre**														
1992	Tor-A	0	0	0.00	4	0	0	0	0	3²	4	0	0	4
1993	Tor-A	0	0	27.00	1	1	0	0	0	2	3	6	4	1
Total 2		0	0	9.53	5	1	0	0	0	5²	7	6	4	5
● **Les Straker**														
1987	Min-A	0	0	4.00	2	2	0	0	0	9	9	4	3	6
● **Scott Stratton**														
1890	Lou-A	1	1	2.37	3	3	1	0	0	19	26	5	4	8
● **John Stuper**														
1982	StL-N	1	0	3.46	2	2	1	0	0	13	10	5	5	5

YEAR	TM/L	W	L	ERA	G	GS	CG	SV	SHO	IP	H	ER	BB	SO
● **Tom Sturdivant**														
1955	NY-A	0	0	6.00	2	0	0	0	0	3	5	2	2	0
1956	NY-A	1	0	2.79	2	1	1	0	0	9²	8	3	8	9
1957	NY-A	0	0	6.00	2	1	0	0	0	6	6	4	1	2
Total 3		1	0	4.34	6	2	1	0	0	18²	19	9	11	11
● **Jim Sullivan**														
1897	Bos-N	0	0	3.00	1	0	0	0	0	3	6	1	0	0
● **Ed Summers**														
1908	Det-A	0	2	4.30	2	1	0	0	0	14²	18	7	4	7
1909	Det-A	0	2	8.59	2	2	0	0	0	7¹	13	7	4	4
Total 2		0	4	5.73	4	3	0	0	0	22	31	14	8	11
● **Steve Sundra**														
1939	NY-A	0	0	0.00	1	0	0	0	0	2²	4	0	1	2
● **Bruce Sutter**														
1982	StL-N	1	0	4.70	4	0	0	2	0	7²	6	4	3	6
● **Don Sutton**														
1974	LA-N	1	0	2.77	2	2	0	0	0	13	9	4	3	12
1977	LA-N	1	0	3.94	2	2	1	0	0	16	17	7	7	3
1978	LA-N	0	2	7.50	2	2	0	0	0	12	17	10	4	8
1982	Mil-A	0	1	7.84	2	2	0	0	0	10¹	12	9	1	5
Total 4		2	3	5.26	8	8	1	0	0	51¹	55	30	15	28
● **Kevin Tapani**														
1991	Min-A	1	1	4.50	2	2	0	0	0	12	13	6	2	7
● **Harry Taylor**														
1947	Bro-N	0	0	—	1	1	0	0	0	2	0		1	0
● **Ron Taylor**														
1964	StL-N	0	0	0.00	2	0	0	1	0	4²	0	0	1	2
1969	NY-N	0	0	0.00	2	0	0	1	0	2¹	0	0	1	3
Total 2		0	0	0.00	4	0	0	2	0	7	0	0	2	5
● **Kent Tekulve**														
1979	Pit-N	0	1	2.89	5	0	0	3	0	9¹	4	3	3	10
● **Ralph Terry**														
1960	NY-A	0	2	5.40	2	2	0	0	0	6²	7	4	1	5
1961	NY-A	0	1	4.82	2	2	0	0	0	9¹	12	5	2	7
1962	NY-A	2	1	1.80	3	3	2	0	1	25	17	5	2	16
1963	NY-A	0	0	3.00	1	0	0	0	0	3	3	1	1	0
1964	NY-A	0	0	0.00	1	0	0	0	0	2	2	0	0	3
Total 5		2	4	2.93	9	6	2	0	1	46	41	15	6	31
● **Adonis Terry**														
1889	Bro-A	2	3	5.97	5	5	4	0	0	37²	47	25	18	14
1890	Bro-N	1	1	3.60	3	3	3	0	1	25	25	10	10	8
Total 2		3	4	5.03	8	8	7	0	1	62²	72	35	28	22
● **Jeff Tesreau**														
1912	NY-N	1	2	3.13	3	3	1	0	0	23	19	8	11	15
1913	NY-N	0	1	6.48	2	1	0	0	0	8¹	11	6	1	4
1917	NY-N	0	0	0.00	1	0	0	0	0	1	0	0	1	1
Total 3		1	3	3.90	6	4	1	0	0	32¹	30	14	13	20
● **Bobby Thigpen**														
1993	Phi-N	0	0	0.00	2	0	0	0	0	2²	1	0	1	0
● **Tommy Thomas**														
1933	Was-A	0	0	0.00	2	0	0	0	0	1¹	1	0	0	2
● **Myles Thomas**														
1926	NY-A	0	0	3.00	2	0	0	0	0	3	3	1	0	0
● **Junior Thompson**														
1939	Cin-N	0	1	13.50	1	1	0	0	0	4²	5	7	4	3
1940	Cin-N	0	1	16.20	1	1	0	0	0	3¹	8	6	4	2
Total 2		0	2	14.63	2	2	0	0	0	8	13	13	8	5
● **Gus Thompson**														
1903	Pit-N	0	0	4.50	1	0	0	0	0	2	3	1	0	1
● **Mark Thurmond**														
1984	SD-N	0	1	10.13	2	2	0	0	0	5¹	12	6	3	2
● **Luis Tiant**														
1975	Bos-A	2	0	3.60	3	3	2	0	1	25	25	10	8	12
● **Dick Tidrow**														
1976	NY-A	0	0	7.71	2	0	0	0	0	2¹	5	2	1	1
1977	NY-A	0	0	4.91	2	0	0	0	0	3²	5	2	0	1
1978	NY-A	0	0	1.93	2	0	0	0	0	4²	4	1	0	5
Total 3		0	0	4.22	6	0	0	0	0	10²	14	5	1	7
● **Mike Timlin**														
1992	Tor-A	0	0	0.00	2	0	0	1	0	1¹	0	0	0	0
1993	Tor-A	0	0	0.00	2	0	0	0	0	2¹	2	0	0	4
Total 2		0	0	0.00	4	0	0	1	0	3²	2	0	0	4
● **Bud Tinning**														
1932	Chi-N	0	0	0.00	2	0	0	0	0	2¹	0	0	0	3
● **Ledell Titcomb**														
1888	NY-N	0	1	6.75	1	1	0	0	0	4	5	3	2	2
● **Jim Tobin**														
1945	Det-A	0	0	6.00	1	0	0	0	0	3	4	2	1	0
● **Fred Toney**														
1921	NY-N	0	0	23.63	2	2	0	0	0	2²	7	7	3	1

Mike Torrez

YEAR TM/L	W	L	ERA	G	GS	CG	SV	SHO	IP	H	ER	BB	SO
1977 NY-A	2	0	2.50	2	2	2	0	0	18	16	5	5	15

Dizzy Trout

YEAR TM/L	W	L	ERA	G	GS	CG	SV	SHO	IP	H	ER	BB	SO
1940 Det-A	0	1	9.00	1	1	0	0	0	2	6	2	1	1
1945 Det-A	1	1	0.66	2	1	1	0	0	13^2	9	1	3	9
Total 2	1	2	1.72	3	2	1	0	0	15^2	15	3	4	10

Bob Trowbridge

YEAR TM/L	W	L	ERA	G	GS	CG	SV	SHO	IP	H	ER	BB	SO
1957 Mil-N	0	0	45.00	1	0	0	0	0	1	2	5	3	1

Virgil Trucks

YEAR TM/L	W	L	ERA	G	GS	CG	SV	SHO	IP	H	ER	BB	SO
1945 Det-A	1	0	3.38	2	1	0	0	0	13^1	14	5	5	7

John Tudor

YEAR TM/L	W	L	ERA	G	GS	CG	SV	SHO	IP	H	ER	BB	SO
1985 StL-N	2	1	3.00	3	3	1	0	1	18	15	6	7	14
1987 StL-N	1	1	5.73	2	2	0	0	0	11	15	7	3	8
1988 LA-N	0	0	0.00	1	1	0	0	0	1^1	0	0	0	1
Total 3	3	2	3.86	6	6	1	0	1	30^1	30	13	10	23

Lee Tunnell

YEAR TM/L	W	L	ERA	G	GS	CG	SV	SHO	IP	H	ER	BB	SO
1987 StL-N	0	0	2.08	2	0	0	0	0	4^1	4	1	2	1

Bob Turley

YEAR TM/L	W	L	ERA	G	GS	CG	SV	SHO	IP	H	ER	BB	SO
1955 NY-A	0	1	8.44	3	1	0	0	0	5^1	7	5	4	7
1956 NY-A	0	1	0.82	3	1	1	0	0	11	4	1	8	14
1957 NY-A	1	0	2.31	3	2	1	0	0	11^2	7	3	6	12
1958 NY-A	2	1	2.76	4	2	1	1	1	16^1	10	5	7	13
1960 NY-A	1	0	4.82	2	2	0	0	0	9^1	15	5	4	0
Total 5	4	3	3.19	15	8	3	1	1	53^2	43	19	29	46

Jim Turner

YEAR TM/L	W	L	ERA	G	GS	CG	SV	SHO	IP	H	ER	BB	SO
1940 Cin-N	0	1	7.50	1	1	0	0	0	6	8	5	0	4
1942 NY-A	0	0	0.00	1	0	0	0	0	1	0	0	1	0
Total 2	0	1	6.43	2	1	0	0	0	7	8	5	1	4

Lefty Tyler

YEAR TM/L	W	L	ERA	G	GS	CG	SV	SHO	IP	H	ER	BB	SO
1914 Bos-N	0	0	3.60	1	1	0	0	0	10	8	4	3	4
1918 Chi-N	1	1	1.17	3	3	1	0	0	23	14	3	11	4
Total 2	1	1	1.91	4	4	1	0	0	33	22	7	14	8

George Uhle

YEAR TM/L	W	L	ERA	G	GS	CG	SV	SHO	IP	H	ER	BB	SO
1920 Cle-A	0	0	0.00	2	0	0	0	0	3	1	0	0	3

Fernando Valenzuela

YEAR TM/L	W	L	ERA	G	GS	CG	SV	SHO	IP	H	ER	BB	SO
1981 LA-N	1	0	4.00	1	1	1	0	0	9	9	4	7	6

Dazzy Vance

YEAR TM/L	W	L	ERA	G	GS	CG	SV	SHO	IP	H	ER	BB	SO
1934 StL-N	0	0	0.00	1	0	0	0	0	1^1	2	0	1	3

Hy Vandenberg

YEAR TM/L	W	L	ERA	G	GS	CG	SV	SHO	IP	H	ER	BB	SO
1945 Chi-N	0	0	0.00	3	0	0	0	0	6	1	0	3	3

Johnny Vander Meer

YEAR TM/L	W	L	ERA	G	GS	CG	SV	SHO	IP	H	ER	BB	SO
1940 Cin-N	0	0	0.00	1	0	0	0	0	3	2	0	3	2

Hippo Vaughn

YEAR TM/L	W	L	ERA	G	GS	CG	SV	SHO	IP	H	ER	BB	SO
1918 Chi-N	1	2	1.00	3	3	3	0	1	27	17	3	5	17

Bob Veale

YEAR TM/L	W	L	ERA	G	GS	CG	SV	SHO	IP	H	ER	BB	SO
1971 Pit-N	0	0	13.50	1	0	0	0	0	0^2	1	1	2	0

Bucky Veil

YEAR TM/L	W	L	ERA	G	GS	CG	SV	SHO	IP	H	ER	BB	SO
1903 Pit-N	0	0	1.29	1	0	0	0	0	7	6	1	5	1

Frank Viola

YEAR TM/L	W	L	ERA	G	GS	CG	SV	SHO	IP	H	ER	BB	SO
1987 Min-A	2	1	3.72	3	3	0	0	0	19^1	17	8	3	16

Bill Voiselle

YEAR TM/L	W	L	ERA	G	GS	CG	SV	SHO	IP	H	ER	BB	SO
1948 Bos-N	0	1	2.53	2	1	0	0	0	10^2	8	3	2	2

Pete Vuckovich

YEAR TM/L	W	L	ERA	G	GS	CG	SV	SHO	IP	H	ER	BB	SO
1982 Mil-A	0	1	4.50	2	2	0	0	0	14	16	7	5	4

Rube Waddell

YEAR TM/L	W	L	ERA	G	GS	CG	SV	SHO	IP	H	ER	BB	SO
1900 Pit-N	0	1	1.93	2	1	1	0	0	14	15	3	3	7

Ben Wade

YEAR TM/L	W	L	ERA	G	GS	CG	SV	SHO	IP	H	ER	BB	SO
1953 Bro-N	0	0	15.43	2	0	0	0	0	2^1	4	4	1	2

Rube Walberg

YEAR TM/L	W	L	ERA	G	GS	CG	SV	SHO	IP	H	ER	BB	SO
1929 Phi-A	1	0	0.00	2	0	0	0	0	6^1	3	0	0	8
1930 Phi-A	0	1	3.86	1	1	0	0	0	4^2	4	2	1	3
1931 Phi-A	0	0	3.00	2	0	0	0	0	3	3	1	2	4
Total 3	1	1	1.93	5	1	0	0	0	14	10	3	3	15

Bob Walk

YEAR TM/L	W	L	ERA	G	GS	CG	SV	SHO	IP	H	ER	BB	SO
1980 Phi-N	1	0	7.71	1	1	0	0	0	7	8	6	3	3

Luke Walker

YEAR TM/L	W	L	ERA	G	GS	CG	SV	SHO	IP	H	ER	BB	SO
1971 Pit-N	0	0	40.50	1	1	0	0	0	0^2	3	3	1	0

Bill Walker

YEAR TM/L	W	L	ERA	G	GS	CG	SV	SHO	IP	H	ER	BB	SO
1934 StL-N	0	2	7.11	2	0	0	0	0	6^1	6	5	6	2

Bobby Wallace

YEAR TM/L	W	L	ERA	G	GS	CG	SV	SHO	IP	H	ER	BB	SO
1896 Cle-N	0	1	4.50	1	1	1	0	0	8	10	4	2	4

Ed Walsh

YEAR TM/L	W	L	ERA	G	GS	CG	SV	SHO	IP	H	ER	BB	SO
1906 Chi-A	2	0	1.20	2	2	1	0	1	15	7	2	6	17

Bucky Walters

YEAR TM/L	W	L	ERA	G	GS	CG	SV	SHO	IP	H	ER	BB	SO
1939 Cin-N	0	2	4.91	2	2	2	0	0	11	13	6	1	6
1940 Cin-N	2	0	1.50	2	2	2	0	1	18	8	3	6	6
Total 2	2	2	2.79	4	4	4	0	1	29	21	9	7	12

Duane Ward

YEAR TM/L	W	L	ERA	G	GS	CG	SV	SHO	IP	H	ER	BB	SO
1992 Tor-A	2	0	0.00	4	0	0	0	0	3^1	1	0	1	6
1993 Tor-A	1	0	1.93	4	0	0	2	0	4^2	3	1	0	7
Total 2	3	0	1.13	8	0	0	2	0	8	4	1	1	13

Lon Warneke

YEAR TM/L	W	L	ERA	G	GS	CG	SV	SHO	IP	H	ER	BB	SO
1932 Chi-N	0	1	5.91	2	1	1	0	0	10^2	15	7	5	8
1935 Chi-N	2	0	0.54	3	2	1	0	1	16^2	9	1	4	5
Total 2	2	1	2.63	5	3	2	0	1	27^1	24	8	9	13

Ray Washburn

YEAR TM/L	W	L	ERA	G	GS	CG	SV	SHO	IP	H	ER	BB	SO
1967 StL-N	0	0	0.00	2	0	0	0	0	2^1	1	0	1	2
1968 StL-N	1	1	9.82	2	2	0	0	0	7^1	7	8	7	6
1970 Cin-N	0	0	13.50	1	0	0	0	0	1^1	2	2	2	0
Total 3	1	1	8.18	5	2	0	0	0	11	10	10	10	8

Gary Waslewski

YEAR TM/L	W	L	ERA	G	GS	CG	SV	SHO	IP	H	ER	BB	SO
1967 Bos-A	0	0	2.16	2	1	0	0	0	8^1	4	2	2	7

Mule Watson

YEAR TM/L	W	L	ERA	G	GS	CG	SV	SHO	IP	H	ER	BB	SO
1923 NY-N	0	0	13.50	1	1	0	0	0	2	4	3	1	1
1924 NY-N	0	0	0.00	1	0	0	1	0	0^2	0	0	0	0
Total 2	0	0	10.13	2	1	0	1	0	2^2	4	3	1	1

Eddie Watt

YEAR TM/L	W	L	ERA	G	GS	CG	SV	SHO	IP	H	ER	BB	SO
1969 Bal-A	0	1	3.00	2	0	0	0	0	3	4	1	0	3
1970 Bal-A	0	1	9.00	1	0	0	0	0	1	2	1	1	3
1971 Bal-A	0	1	3.86	2	0	0	0	0	2^1	4	1	0	2
Total 3	0	3	4.26	5	0	0	0	0	6^1	10	3	1	8

Monte Weaver

YEAR TM/L	W	L	ERA	G	GS	CG	SV	SHO	IP	H	ER	BB	SO
1933 Was-A	0	1	1.74	1	1	0	0	0	10^1	11	2	4	3

Mickey Welch

YEAR TM/L	W	L	ERA	G	GS	CG	SV	SHO	IP	H	ER	BB	SO
1888 NY-N	1	1	2.65	2	2	2	0	0	17	10	5	9	2
1889 NY-N	0	1	9.00	1	1	0	0	0	5	11	5	3	1
Total 2	1	2	4.09	3	3	2	0	0	22	21	10	12	3

Bob Welch

YEAR TM/L	W	L	ERA	G	GS	CG	SV	SHO	IP	H	ER	BB	SO
1978 LA-N	0	1	6.23	3	0	0	1	0	4^1	4	3	2	6
1981 LA-N	0	0	∞	1	1	0	0	0	0	3	2	1	0
1988 Oak-A	0	0	1.80	1	1	0	0	0	5	6	1	3	8
1990 Oak-A	0	0	4.91	1	1	0	0	0	7^1	9	4	2	2
Total 4	0	1	5.40	6	3	0	1	0	16^2	22	10	8	16

David Wells

YEAR TM/L	W	L	ERA	G	GS	CG	SV	SHO	IP	H	ER	BB	SO
1992 Tor-A	0	0	0.00	4	0	0	0	0	4^1	1	0	2	3

Butch Wensloff

YEAR TM/L	W	L	ERA	G	GS	CG	SV	SHO	IP	H	ER	BB	SO
1947 NY-A	0	0	0.00	1	0	0	0	0	2	0	0	0	0

David West

YEAR TM/L	W	L	ERA	G	GS	CG	SV	SHO	IP	H	ER	BB	SO
1991 Min-A	0	0	∞	2	0	0	0	0	0	2	4	4	0
1993 Phi-N	0	0	27.00	3	0	0	0	0	1	5	3	1	0
Total 2	0	0	63.00	5	0	0	0	0	1	7	7	5	0

Ernie White

YEAR TM/L	W	L	ERA	G	GS	CG	SV	SHO	IP	H	ER	BB	SO
1942 StL-N	1	0	0.00	1	1	1	0	1	9	6	0	0	6

Doc White

YEAR TM/L	W	L	ERA	G	GS	CG	SV	SHO	IP	H	ER	BB	SO
1906 Chi-A	1	1	1.80	3	2	1	1	0	15	12	3	7	4

Earl Whitehill

YEAR TM/L	W	L	ERA	G	GS	CG	SV	SHO	IP	H	ER	BB	SO
1933 Was-A	1	0	0.00	1	1	1	0	1	9	5	0	2	2

Ed Whitson

YEAR TM/L	W	L	ERA	G	GS	CG	SV	SHO	IP	H	ER	BB	SO
1984 SD-N	0	0	40.50	1	1	0	0	0	0^2	5	3	0	0

Kemp Wicker

YEAR TM/L	W	L	ERA	G	GS	CG	SV	SHO	IP	H	ER	BB	SO
1937 NY-A	0	0	0.00	1	0	0	0	0	1	0	0	0	0

Milt Wilcox

YEAR TM/L	W	L	ERA	G	GS	CG	SV	SHO	IP	H	ER	BB	SO
1970 Cin-N	0	1	9.00	2	0	0	0	0	2	3	2	0	2
1984 Det-A	1	0	1.50	1	1	0	0	0	6	7	1	2	4
Total 2	1	1	3.38	3	1	0	0	0	8	10	3	2	6

Hoyt Wilhelm

YEAR TM/L	W	L	ERA	G	GS	CG	SV	SHO	IP	H	ER	BB	SO
1954 NY-N	0	0	0.00	2	0	0	1	0	2^1	1	0	0	3

Roy Wilkinson

YEAR TM/L	W	L	ERA	G	GS	CG	SV	SHO	IP	H	ER	BB	SO
1919 Chi-A	0	0	1.23	2	0	0	0	0	7^1	9	1	4	3

Ted Wilks

YEAR TM/L	W	L	ERA	G	GS	CG	SV	SHO	IP	H	ER	BB	SO
1944 StL-N	0	1	5.68	2	1	0	1	0	6^1	5	4	3	7
1946 StL-N	0	0	0.00	1	0	0	0	0	1	2	0	0	0
Total 2	0	1	4.91	3	1	0	1	0	7^1	7	4	3	7

Ed Willett

YEAR TM/L	W	L	ERA	G	GS	CG	SV	SHO	IP	H	ER	BB	SO
1909 Det-A	0	0	0.00	2	0	0	0	0	7^2	3	0	0	1

Carl Willey

YEAR TM/L	W	L	ERA	G	GS	CG	SV	SHO	IP	H	ER	BB	SO
1958 Mil-N	0	0	0.00	1	0	0	0	0	1	0	0	0	2

Lefty Williams

YEAR TM/L	W	L	ERA	G	GS	CG	SV	SHO	IP	H	ER	BB	SO
1917 Chi-A	0	0	9.00	1	0	0	0	0	1	2	1	0	3
1919 Chi-A	0	3	6.61	3	3	1	0	0	16^1	12	12	8	4
Total 2	0	3	6.75	4	3	1	0	0	17^1	14	13	8	7

Mitch Williams

YEAR TM/L	W	L	ERA	G	GS	CG	SV	SHO	IP	H	ER	BB	SO
1993 Phi-N	0	2	20.25	3	0	0	1	0	2^2	5	6	4	1

Stan Williams

YEAR TM/L	W	L	ERA	G	GS	CG	SV	SHO	IP	H	ER	BB	SO
1959 LA-N	0	0	0.00	1	0	0	0	0	2	0	0	2	1
1963 NY-A	0	0	0.00	1	0	0	0	0	3	1	0	0	5
Total 2	0	0	0.00	2	0	0	0	0	5	1	0	2	6

YEAR TM/L	W	L	ERA	G	GS	CG	SV	SHO	IP	H	ER	BB	SO
● **Ned Williamson**													
1886 Chi-N	0	1	4.50	2	1	0	0	0	2	4	1	1	2
● **Carl Willis**													
1991 Min-A	0	0	5.14	4	0	0	0	0	7	6	4	2	2
● **Ron Willis**													
1967 StL-N	0	0	27.00	3	0	0	0	0	1	2	3	4	1
1968 StL-N	0	0	8.31	3	0	0	0	0	4¹	2	4	4	3
Total 2	0	0	11.81	6	0	0	0	0	5¹	4	7	8	4
● **Vic Willis**													
1909 Pit-N	0	1	3.97	2	1	0	0	0	11¹	10	5	8	3
● **Jim Willoughby**													
1975 Bos-A	0	1	0.00	3	0	0	0	0	6¹	3	0	0	2
● **Earl Wilson**													
1968 Det-A	0	1	6.23	1	1	0	0	0	4¹	4	3	6	3
● **Hooks Wiltse**													
1911 NY-N	0	0	18.90	2	0	0	0	0	3¹	8	7	0	2
● **George Winter**													
1908 Det-A	0	0	0.00	1	0	0	0	0	1	1	0	1	0
● **Rick Wise**													
1975 Bos-A	1	0	8.44	2	1	0	0	0	5¹	6	5	2	2
● **George Witt**													
1960 Pit-N	0	0	0.00	3	0	0	0	0	2²	5	0	2	1
● **Mark Wohlers**													
1991 Atl-N	0	0	0.00	3	0	0	0	0	1²	2	0	2	1
1992 Atl-N	0	0	0.00	2	0	0	0	0	0²	0	0	1	0
Total 2	0	0	0.00	5	0	0	0	0	2¹	2	0	3	1
● **Joe Wood**													
1912 Bos-A	3	1	3.68	4	3	2	0	0	22	27	9	3	21
● **Hal Woodeshick**													
1967 StL-N	0	0	0.00	1	0	0	0	0	1	1	0	0	0
● **Ralph Works**													
1909 Det-A	0	0	9.00	1	0	0	0	0	2	4	2	0	2
● **Todd Worrell**													
1985 StL-N	0	1	3.86	3	0	0	1	0	4²	4	2	2	6
1987 StL-N	0	0	1.29	4	0	0	2	0	7	6	1	4	3
Total 2	0	1	2.31	7	0	0	3	0	11²	10	3	6	9

YEAR TM/L	W	L	ERA	G	GS	CG	SV	SHO	IP	H	ER	BB	SO
● **Al Worthington**													
1965 Min-A	0	0	0.00	2	0	0	0	0	4	2	0	2	2
● **John Wyatt**													
1967 Bos-A	1	0	4.91	2	0	0	0	0	3²	1	2	3	1
● **Whit Wyatt**													
1941 Bro-N	1	1	2.50	2	2	2	0	0	18	15	5	10	14
● **Weldon Wyckoff**													
1914 Phi-A	0	0	2.45	1	0	0	0	0	3²	3	1	1	2
● **Early Wynn**													
1954 Cle-A	0	1	3.86	1	1	0	0	0	7	4	3	2	5
1959 Chi-A	1	1	5.54	3	3	0	0	0	13	19	8	4	10
Total 2	1	2	4.95	4	4	0	0	0	20	23	11	6	15
● **Hank Wyse**													
1945 Chi-N	0	1	7.04	3	1	0	0	0	7²	8	6	4	1
● **Emil Yde**													
1925 Pit-N	0	1	11.57	1	1	0	0	0	2¹	5	3	3	1
● **Curt Young**													
1988 Oak-A	0	0	0.00	1	0	0	0	0	1	1	0	0	0
1990 Oak-A	0	0	0.00	1	0	0	0	0	1	1	0	0	0
Total 2	0	0	0.00	2	0	0	0	0	2	2	0	0	0
● **Cy Young**													
1892 Cle-N	0	2	3.00	3	3	3	0	1	27	26	9	3	9
1895 Cle-N	3	0	2.33	3	3	3	0	0	27	28	7	4	2
1896 Cle-N	0	1	6.00	1	1	1	0	0	9	13	6	1	0
1903 Bos-A	2	1	1.85	4	3	3	0	0	34	31	7	4	17
Total 4	5	4	2.69	11	10	10	0	1	97	98	29	12	28
● **Tom Zachary**													
1924 Was-A	2	0	2.04	2	2	1	0	0	17²	13	4	3	3
1925 Was-A	0	0	10.80	1	0	0	0	0	1²	3	2	1	0
1928 NY-A	1	0	3.00	1	1	1	0	0	9	9	3	1	7
Total 3	3	0	2.86	4	3	2	0	0	28¹	25	9	5	10
● **Pat Zachry**													
1976 Cin-N	1	0	2.70	1	1	0	0	0	6²	6	2	5	6
● **Bill Zuber**													
1946 Bos-A	0	0	4.50	1	0	0	0	0	2	3	1	1	1

No player/pitcher records are included for 1994 postseason competition.

National League Divisional Playoffs, canceled.

American League Divisional Playoffs, canceled.

National League Championship Series, canceled.

American League Championship Series, canceled.

World Series, canceled.

OTHER LEAGUES

## CHAPTER 17

Black Ball

Jules Tygiel

In 1987, Major League Baseball, amidst much fanfare and publicity, celebrated the 40th anniversary of the finest moment in the history of the national pastime—Jackie Robinson's heroic shattering of the color barrier. But baseball might also have commemorated the centennial of a related, but far less auspicious event—the banishment of blacks from the International League in 1887 which ushered in six disgraceful decades of Jim Crow baseball. During this era, some of America's greatest ballplayers plied their trade on all-black teams, in Negro Leagues, on the playing fields of Latin America, and along the barnstorming frontier of the cities and towns of the United States, but never within the major and minor league realm of "organized baseball." When slowly and grudgingly given their chance in the years after 1947, blacks conclusively proved their competitive abilities on the diamond, but discrimination persisted as baseball executives continued to deny them the opportunity to display their talents in managerial and front office positions.

Scattered evidence exists of blacks playing baseball in the antebellum period, but the first recorded black teams surfaced in Northern cities in the aftermath of the Civil War. In October 1867, the Uniques of Brooklyn hosted the Excelsiors of Philadelphia in a contest billed as the "championship of colored clubs." Before a large crowd of black and white spectators, the Excelsiors marched around the field behind a fife and drum corps before defeating the Uniques, 37–24. Two months later, a second Philadelphia squad, the Pythians, dispatched a representative to the inaugural meetings of the National Association of Base Ball Players, the first organized league. The nominating committee unanimously rejected the Pythian's application, barring "any club which may be composed of one or more colored persons.". Using the impeccable logic of a racist society, the committee proclaimed, "If colored clubs were admitted there would be in all probability some division of feeling, whereas, by excluding them no injury could result to anyone." The Philadelphia Pythians, however, continued their quest for interracial competition. In 1869, they became the first black team to face an all-white squad, defeating the crosstown City Items, 27–17.

In 1876, athletic entrepreneurs in the nation's metropolitan centers established the National League which quickly came to represent the pinnacle of the sport. The new entity had no written policy regarding blacks, but precluded them nonetheless through a "gentleman's agreement" among the owners. In the smaller cities and towns of America, however, where under-funded teams

and fragile minor league coalitions quickly appeared and faded, individual blacks found scattered opportunities to pursue baseball careers. During the next decade, at least two dozen black ballplayers sought to earn a living in this erratic professional baseball world.

Bud Fowler ranked among the best and most persistent of these trailblazers. Born John Jackson in upstate New York in 1858 and raised, ironically, in Cooperstown, Fowler first achieved recognition as a 20-year-old pitcher for a local team in Chelsea, Massachusetts. In April 1878, Fowler defeated the National League's Boston club, which included future Hall of Famers George Wright and Jim O' Rourke, 2–1, in an exhibition game, besting 40-game winner Tommy Bond. Later that season, Fowler hurled three games for the Lynn Live Oaks of the International Association, the nation's first minor league, and another for Worcester in the New England League. For the next six years, he toiled for a variety of independent and semi-professional teams in the United States and Canada. Despite a reputation as "one of the best pitchers on the continent," he failed to catch on with any major or minor league squads. In 1884, now appearing regularly as a second baseman, as well as a pitcher, Fowler joined Stillwater, Minnesota, in the Northwestern League. Over the next seven seasons, Fowler played for fourteen teams in nine leagues, seldom batting less than .300 for a season. In 1886, he led the Western League in triples. "He is one of the best general players in the country," reported *Sporting Life* in 1885, "and if he had a white face he would be playing with the best of them. . . Those who know, say there is no better second baseman in the country."

In 1886, however, a better second baseman did appear in the form of Frank Grant, perhaps the greatest black player of the nineteenth century. The light-skinned Grant, described as a "Spaniard" in the *Buffalo Express*, batted .325 for Meriden in the Eastern League. When that squad folded he joined Buffalo in the prestigious International Association and improved his average to .340, third best in the league.

Although not as talented as Fowler and Grant, barehand-catcher Moses Fleetwood Walker achieved the highest level of play of blacks of this era. The son of an Ohio physician, Fleet Walker had studied at Oberlin College, where in 1881 he and his younger brother Welday helped launch a varsity baseball team. For the next two years, the elder Walker played for the University of Michigan and in 1883 he appeared in 60 games for the pennant-winning Toledo squad in the Northwestern League. In 1884, Toledo entered the American Association, the National

League's primary rival, and Walker became the first black major leaguer. In an age when many catchers caught barehanded and lacked chest protectors, Walker suffered frequent injuries and played little after a foul tip broke his rib in mid-July. Nonetheless, he batted .263 and pitcher Tony Mullane later called him "the best catcher I ever worked with." In July, Toledo briefly signed Walker's brother, Welday, who appeared in six games batting .182. The following year, Toledo dropped from the league, ending the Walkers' major league careers.

These early black players found limited acceptance among teammates, fans, and opponents. In Ontario, in 1881, Fowler's teammates forced him off the club. Walker found that Mullane and other pitchers preferred not to pitch to him. Although he acknowledged Walker's skills, Mullane confessed, "I disliked a Negro and whenever I had to pitch to him I used anything I wanted without looking at his signals." At Louisville in 1884, insults from Kentucky fans so rattled Walker that he made five errors in a game. In Richmond, after Walker had actually left the team due to injuries, the Toledo manager received a letter from "75 determined men" threatening "to mob Walker" and cause "much bloodshed" if the black catcher appeared. On August 10, 1883, Chicago White Stockings star and manager Cap Anson had threatened to cancel an exhibition game with Toledo if Walker played. The injured catcher had not been slated to start, but Toledo manager Charlie Morton defied Anson and inserted Walker into the lineup. The game proceeded without incident.

In 1887, Walker, Fowler, Grant, Higgins, Stovey, and three other blacks converged on the International League, a newly reorganized circuit in Canada and upstate New York, one notch below the major league level. At the same time, a new six-team entity, the League of Colored Baseball Clubs, won recognition under baseball's National Agreement, a mutual pact to honor player contracts among team owners. Thus, an air of optimism pervaded the start of the season. But 1887 would prove a fateful year for the future of blacks in baseball.

On May 6, the Colored League made its debut in Pittsburgh with "a grand street parade and a brass band concert." Twelve hundred spectators watched the hometown Keystones lose to the Gorhams of New York, 11–8. Within days, however, the new league began to flounder. The Boston franchise disbanded in Louisville on May 8, stranding its players in the Southern city. Three weeks later, league-founder Walter Brown formally announced the demise of the infant circuit.

Meanwhile, in the International League, black players found their numbers growing, but their status increasingly uncertain. Six of the 10 teams fielded blacks, prompting *Sporting Life* to wonder, "How far will this mania for engaging colored players go?" In Newark, fans marveled at the "colored battery" of Fleet Walker, dubbed the "coon catcher" by one Canadian newspaper, and "headstrong" pitcher George Stovey. Stovey, one of the greatest black pitchers of the nineteenth century, won 35 games, still an International League record. Frank Grant, in his second season as the Buffalo second baseman, led the league in batting average and home runs. Bud Fowler, one of two blacks on the Binghamton squad, compiled a .350 average through early July and stole 23 bases.

These athletes compiled their impressive statistics under the most adverse conditions. "I could not help pitying some of the poor black fellows that played in the International League," reported a white player. "Fowler used to play second base with the lower part of his legs encased in wooden guards. He knew that about every player that came down to second base on a steal had it in for him." Both Fowler and Grant, "would muff balls intentionally, so that [they] would not have to touch runners, fearing that they might injure [them]." In addition, "About half the pitchers try their best to hit these colored players when [they are] at bat." Grant, whose Buffalo teammates had refused to sit with him for a team portrait in 1886, reportedly saved himself from a "drubbing" at their hands in 1887, only by "the effective use of a club." In Toronto, fans chanted, "Kill the Nigger," at Grant, and a local newspaper headline declared, "THE COLORED PLAYERS DISTASTEFUL." In late June, Bud Fowler's Binghamton teammates refused to take the field unless the club removed him from the lineup. Soon after, on July 7, the Binghamton club submitted to the players' demands, releasing Fowler and a black teammate, a pitcher named Renfroe.

The most dramatic confrontations between black and white players occurred on the Syracuse squad, where a clique of refugees from the Southern League exacerbated racial tensions. In spring training, the club included a catcher named Dick Male, who, rumors had it, was a light-skinned black named Richard Johnson. Male charged "that the man calling him a Negro is himself a black liar," but when released after a poor preseason performance, he returned to his old club, Zanesville in the Ohio State League, and resumed his true identity as Richard Johnson. In May, Syracuse signed 19-year-old black pitcher Robert Higgins, angering the Southern clique. On May 25, Higgins appeared in his first International League game in Toronto. "THE SYRACUSE PLOTTERS," as a *Sporting News* headline called his teammates, undermined his debut. According to one account, they "seemed to want the Toronto team to knock Higgins out of the box, and time and again they fielded so badly that the home team were enabled to secure many hits after the side had been retired." "A disgusting exhibition," admonished *The Toronto World*. "They succeeded in running Male out of the club," reported a Newark paper, "and they will do the same with Higgins." One week later, two Syracuse players refused to pose for a team picture with Higgins. When manager "Ice Water" Joe Simmons suspended pitcher Doug Crothers for this incident, Crothers slugged the manager. Higgins miraculously recovered from his early travails and lack of support to post a 20–7 record.

On July 14, as the directors of the International League discussed the racial situation in Buffalo, the Newark Little Giants planned to send Stovey, their ace, to the mound in an exhibition game against the National League Chicago White Stockings. Once again manager Anson refused to field his squad if either Stovey or Walker appeared. Unlike 1883, Anson's will prevailed. On the same day, team owners, stating that "Many of the best players in the league are anxious to leave on account of the colored element," allowed current black players to remain, but voted by a six-to-four margin to reject all future contracts with blacks. The teams with black players all voted against the measure, but Binghamton, which had just released Fowler and Renfroe, swung the vote in favor of exclusion.

Events in 1887 continued to conspire against black players. On September 11, the St. Louis Browns of the American Association refused to play a scheduled contest against the all-black Cuban Giants. "We are only doing what is right," they proclaimed. In November, the Buffalo and Syracuse teams unsuccessfully attempted to lift the International League ban on blacks. The Ohio State League, which had fielded three black players, also adopted a rule barring additional contracts with blacks, prompting Welday Walker, who had appeared in the league, to protest, "The law is a disgrace to the present age. . . There should be some broader cause—such as lack of ability, behavior and intelligence—for barring a player, rather than his color."

After 1887, only a handful of blacks appeared on integrated squads. Grant and Higgins returned to their original teams in 1888. Walker jumped from Newark to Syracuse. The following year, only Walker remained for one final season, the last black in the International League until 1946. Richard Johnson, the erstwhile Dick Male, reappeared in the Ohio State League in 1888 and in 1889 joined Springfield in the Central Interstate League, where he hit 14 triples, stole 45 bases, and scored 100 runs in 100 games. In 1890, Harrisburg in the Eastern Interstate League fielded two blacks, while Jamestown in the New York Penn League featured another. Bud Fowler and several other black players appeared in the Nebraska State League in 1892. Three years later, Adrian in the Michigan State League signed five blacks, including Fowler and pitcher George Wilson who posted a 29–4 record. Meanwhile Sol White, who later chronicled these events in his 1906 book, *The History of Colored Baseball*, played for Fort Wayne in the Western State League. In 1896, pitcher-outfielder Bert Jones joined Atchison in the Kansas State League where he played for three seasons before being forced out in 1898. Almost 50 years would pass before another black would appear on an interracial club in organized baseball.

While integrated teams grew rare, several leagues allowed entry to all black squads. In 1889, the Middle States League included the New York Gorhams and the Cuban Giants, the most famous black team of the age. The Giants posted a 55–17 record. In 1890, the alliance reorganized as the Eastern Interstate League and again included the Cuban Giants. Giants' star George Williams paced the circuit with a .391 batting average, while teammate Arthur Thomas slugged 26 doubles and 10 triples, both league-leading totals. The Eastern Interstate League folded in midseason, and in 1891 the Giants made one final minor league appearance in the Connecticut State League. When this circuit also disbanded, the brief entry of the Cuban Giants in organized baseball came to an end. In 1898, a team calling itself the Acme Colored Giants affiliated with Pennsylvania's Iron and Oil League, but won only eight of 49 games before dropping out, marking an ignoble conclusion to these early experiments in interracial play.

Overall, at least 70 blacks appeared in organized baseball in the late 19th century. About half played for all-black teams, the remainder for integrated clubs. Few lasted more than one season with the same team. By the 1890s, the pattern for black baseball that would prevail for the next half century had emerged. Blacks were relegated to "colored" teams playing most of their games on the barnstorming circuit, outside of any organized league structure. While exhibition contests allowed them to pit their skills against whites, they remained on the outskirts of baseball's mainstream, unheralded and unknown to most Americans.

As early as the 1880s and 1890s several all-black traveling squads had gained national reputations. The Cuban Giants, formed among the waiters of the Argyle Hotel to entertain guests in 1885, set the pattern and provided the recurrent nickname for these teams. Passing as Cubans, so as not to offend their white clientele, the Giants toured the East in a private railroad car playing amateur and professional opponents. In the 1890s, rivals like the Lincoln Giants from Nebraska, the Page Fence Giants from Michigan, and the Cuban X Giants in New York emerged. From the beginning these teams combined entertainment with their baseball to attract crowds. The Page Fence Giants, founded by Bud Fowler in 1895, would ride through the streets on bicycles to attract attention. In 1899, Fowler organized the All-American Black Tourists, who would arrive in full dress suits with opera hats and silk umbrellas. Their showmanship notwithstanding, the black teams of the 1890s included some of the best players in the nation. The Page Fence Giants won 118 of 154 games in 1895, with two of their losses coming against the major league Cincinnati Reds.

During the early years of the 20th century many blacks still harbored hopes of regaining access to organized baseball. Sol White wrote in 1906 that baseball, "should be taken seriously by the colored player. An honest effort of his great ability will open the avenue in the near future wherein he may walk hand-in-hand with the opposite race in the greatest of all American games—baseball." Rube Foster, the outstanding figure in black baseball from 1910-1926, stressed excellence because "we have to be ready when the time comes for integration."

But even clandestine efforts to bring in blacks met a harsh fate. In 1901, Baltimore Orioles Manager John McGraw attempted to pass second baseman Charlie Grant of the Columbia Giants off as an Indian named Chief Tokohama, until Chicago White Sox President Charles Comiskey exposed the ruse. In 1911, the Cincinnati Reds raised black hopes by signing two light-skinned Cubans, Armando Marsans and Rafael Almeida, prompting the *New York Age* to speculate, "Now that the first shock is over it would not be surprising to see a Cuban a few shades darker. . .breaking into the professional ranks. . .it would then be easier for colored players who are citizens of this country to get into fast company." But the Reds rushed to certify that Marsans and Almeida were "genuine Caucasians," and while light-skinned Cubans became a fixture in the majors, their darker brethren remained unwelcome. Over the years, tales circulated of United States blacks passing as Indians or Cubans, but no documented cases exist.

Although most blacks lived in the South, during the first two decades of the 20th century, the great black teams and players congregated in the metropolises and industrial cities of the North. Chicago emerged as the primary center of black baseball with teams like the Leland Giants and the Chicago American Giants. In New York, the Lincoln Giants, which boasted pitching stars Smokey Joe Williams and Cannonball Dick Redding, shortstop John Henry Lloyd and catcher Louis Santop, reigned supreme. Other top clubs of the era included the Philadelphia Giants, the Hilldale Club (also of Philadelphia), the Indianapolis ABC's and the Bacharach Giants of Atlantic City. Player contracts were nonexistent or nonbinding and stars jumped frequently from team to team. "Wherever the money was," recalled John Henry Lloyd, "that's where I was."

Fans and writers often compared the great black players of this era to their white counterparts. Lloyd, one of the outstanding shortstops and hitters of that or any era, came to be known as "The Black Wagner," after his white contemporary Honus Wagner, who called it an "honor" and a "privilege" to be compared to the gangling black infielder. A St. Louis sportswriter once said when asked who was the best player in baseball history, "If you mean in organized baseball, the answer would be Babe Ruth; but if you mean in all baseball. . .the answer would have to be a colored man named John Henry Lloyd." Pitcher "Rube" Foster earned his nickname by outpitching future Hall of Famer Rube Waddell, and Cuban Jose Mendez was called "The Black Matty" after Christy Mathewson.

The talents of Foster and Mendez notwithstanding, the greatest black pitcher of the early twentieth century was 6'5" Smokey Joe Williams. Born in 1886, Williams spent a good part of his career pitching in his native Texas, unheralded until he joined the Leland Giants in 1909 at the age of 24. From 1912-1923 he won renown as a strikeout artist for Harlem's Lincoln Giants. Against major league competition Williams won six games, lost four, and tied two, including a three-hit 1–0 victory over the National League champion Philadelphia Phillies in 1915. In 1925, he signed with the Homestead Grays and although approaching his fortieth birthday, starred for seven more seasons. A 1952 poll to name the outstanding black pitcher of the half-century, placed Williams in first place, ahead of the legendary Satchel Paige.

Oscar Charleston ranks as the greatest outfielder of the 1910s and 1920s. With tremendous speed and a strong, accurate arm, Charleston was the quintessential centerfielder. During his 15-year career starting in 1915, Charleston hit for both power and average and may have been the most popular player of the 1920s. After he retired he managed the Philadelphia Stars, Brooklyn Brown Dodgers, and other clubs.

Several major stars of this era labored outside the usual channels of black baseball. In 1914, white Kansas City promoter J. L. Wilkinson organized the All-Nations team, which included whites, blacks, Indians, Asians, and Latin Americans. Pitchers John Donaldson, Jose Mendez, and Bill Drake and outfielder Cristobel Torriente played for the All-Nations team, described by one observer as "strong enough to give any major league team a nip-and-tuck battle." A black Army team from the 25th Infantry Unit in Nogales, Arizona, featured pitcher Bullet Joe Rogan and shortstop Dobie Moore. In 1920, when Wilkinson formed the famed Kansas City Monarchs, the players from the All-Nations and 25th Infantry teams formed the nucleus of his club. In 1921, the Monarchs

challenged the minor league Kansas City Blues to a tournament for the city championship. The Blues won the series five games to three. In 1922, however, the Monarchs won five of six games to claim boasting honors in Kansas City. One week later, they swept a doubleheader from the touring Babe Ruth All-Stars.

In the years after 1910, Andrew "Rube" Foster emerged as the dominant figure in black baseball. Like many of his white contemporaries, Foster rose through the ranks of the national pastime from star player to field manager to club owner. Born in Texas in 1879, Foster accepted an invitation to pitch for Chicago's Union Giants in 1902. "If you play the best clubs in the land, white clubs as you say," he told owner Frank Leland, "it will be a case of Greek meeting Greek. I fear nobody." By 1903, he was hurling for the Cuban X Giants against the Philadelphia Giants in a series billed as the "Colored Championship of the World." His four victories in a best of nine series clinched the title. The following year, he had switched sides and registered two of three wins for the Philadelphia Giants in a similar matchup, striking out 18 batters in one game and tossing a two-hitter in another. In 1907, he rejoined the Leland Giants and, in 1910, pitched for and managed a reconstituted team of that name to a 123–6 record.

As a pitcher, Foster had ranked among the nation's best; as a manager, his skills achieved legendary proportions. A master strategist and motivator, Foster's teams specialized in the bunt, the steal, and the hit-and-run, which came to characterize black baseball. Fans came to watch him sit on the bench giving signs with a wave of his ever-present pipe. He became the friend and confidant of major league managers like John McGraw. Over the years, Foster trained a generation of black managers, like Dave Malarcher, Biz Mackey, and Oscar Charleston in the subtleties of the game.

In 1911, Foster entered the ownership ranks, uniting with white saloon keeper John Schorling (the son-in-law of White Sox owner Charles Comiskey) to form the Chicago American Giants. With Schorling's financial backing, Foster's managerial acumen, a regular home field in Chicago, and high salaries, the American Giants attracted the best black players in the nation. Throughout the decade, whether barnstorming or hosting opponents in Chicago, the American Giants came to represent the pinnacle of black baseball.

By World War One, Foster dominated black baseball in Chicago and parts of the Midwest. In most other areas, however, white booking agents controlled access to stadiums, and as one newspaperman charged in 1917, "used circus methods to drag a bunch of our best citizens out, only to undergo humiliation . . . while [they sat] back and [grew] rich off a percentage of the proceeds." In the East, Nat Strong, the part owner of the Brooklyn Royal Giants, Philadelphia Giants, Cuban Stars, Cuban Giants, New York Black Yankees, and the renowned white semi-pro team, the Bushwicks, held a stranglehold on black competition. To break this monopoly and place the game more firmly under black control, Foster created the National Association of Professional Baseball Clubs, better known as the Negro National League, in 1920.

Foster's new organization marked the third attempt of the century to meld black teams into a viable league. In

1906, the International League of Independent Baseball Clubs, which had four black and two white teams, struggled through one season characterized by shifting and collapsing franchises. Four years later, Beauregard Moseley, secretary of Chicago's Leland Giants attempted to form a National Negro Baseball League, but the association folded before a single game had been played.

The new Negro National League, which included the top teams from Chicago, St. Louis, Detroit, and other Midwestern cities, fared far better. At Foster's insistence, all clubs, with the exception of the Kansas City Monarchs, whom Foster reluctantly accepted, were controlled by blacks. J. L. Wilkinson, who owned the Monarchs, a major drawing card, had won the respect of his fellow owners and soon overcame Foster's reservations. He became the league secretary and Foster's trusted ally. Operating under the able guidance of Foster and Wilkinson, the league flourished during its early years. In 1923, it attracted 400,000 fans and accumulated $200,000 in gate receipts.

The success of the Negro National League inspired competitors. In 1923, booking agent Nat Strong formed an Eastern Colored League, with teams in New York, Brooklyn, Baltimore, New Jersey, and Philadelphia. With four of the six teams owned by whites, and Strong controlling an erratic schedule, the league had somewhat less legitimacy than Foster's circuit. Playing in larger population centers, however, the more affluent Eastern clubs successfully raided some of the top players of the Negro National League before the circuits negotiated an uneasy truce in 1924. Throughout the remainder of the decade, however, acrimony rather than harmony characterized interleague relations. A third association emerged in the South, where the stronger independent teams in major cities formed the Southern Negro League. While this group became a breeding ground for top players, the impoverished nature of its clientele, and the inability of clubs to bolster revenues with games against white squads, rendered them unable to prevent their best players from jumping to the higher paying Northern teams.

At their best the Negro Leagues of the 1920s were haphazard affairs. Since most clubs continued to rely on barnstorming for their primary livelihood, scheduling proved difficult. Teams played uneven numbers of games and especially in the Eastern circuit skipped official contests for more lucrative nonleague matchups. Several of the stronger independent teams, like the Homestead Grays, remained unaffiliated. Umpires were often incompetent and lacked authority to control conditions. Finally, players frequently jumped from one franchise to another, peddling their services to the highest bidder. In 1926, Foster grew ill, stripping the Negro National League of his vital leadership. Two years later, the Eastern Colored League disbanded and in 1931, less than a year after Foster's death, the Negro National League departed the scene, once again leaving black baseball with no organized structure.

With the collapse of Foster's Negro National League and the onset of the Great Depression, the always-borderline economics of operating a black baseball club grew more precarious. White booking agents, like Philadelphia's Eddie Gottlieb or Abe Saperstein of the Midwest, again reigned supreme. In the early 1930s, only the stronger independent clubs like the Homestead Grays or Kansas City Monarchs, novelty acts like the Cincinnati Clowns, or those teams backed by the "numbers kings" of the black ghettos could survive.

The Kansas City Monarchs emerged as the healthiest holdover from the old Negro National League. In 1929, owner Wilkinson had commissioned an Omaha, Nebraska, company to design a portable lighting system for night games. The equipment, consisting of a 250-horsepower motor and a 100-kilowatt generator, which illuminated lights atop telescoping poles 50 feet above the field, took about two hours to assemble. To pay for the innovation, Wilkinson mortgaged everything he owned and took in Kansas City businessman Tom Baird as a partner. But the gamble paid off. The novelty of night baseball allowed the Monarchs to play two and three games a day and made them the most popular touring club in the nation.

Meanwhile, in Pittsburgh, former basketball star Cumberland Posey, Jr. had forged the Homestead Grays into one of the best teams in America. Posey, the son of one of Pittsburgh's wealthiest black businessmen, had joined the Grays, then a sandlot team, as an outfielder in 1911. By the early 1920s he owned the club and began recruiting top national players to supplement local talent. In 1925, he signed 39-year-old Smokey Joe Williams, and the following year he lured Oscar Charleston, whom many consider the top black player of that era. Over the next several seasons Posey recruited Judy Johnson, Martin Dihigo, and Cool Papa Bell. In 1930, he added a catcher from the Pittsburgh sandlots named Josh Gibson, and in 1934 brought in first baseman Buck Leonard from North Carolina. Unwilling to subject himself to outside control, Posey preferred to remain free from league affiliations. Yet for two decades, the Homestead Grays reigned as one of the strongest teams in black baseball.

In the 1930s, Posey faced competition from crosstown rival Gus Greenlee, "Mr. Big" of Pittsburgh's North Side numbers rackets. Greenlee took over the Pittsburgh Crawfords, a local team, in 1930. Greenlee spent $100,000 to build a new stadium, and wooed established ballplayers with lavish salary offers. In 1931, he landed the colorful Satchel Paige, the hottest young pitcher in the land, and the following year raided the Grays, outbidding Posey for the services of Charleston, Johnson, and Gibson. In 1934, James "Cool Papa" Bell jumped the St. Louis Stars and brought his legendary speed to the Crawfords. With five future Hall of Famers, Greenlee had assembled one of the great squads of baseball history.

The emergence of Gus Greenlee marked a new era for black baseball, the reign of the numbers men. In an age of limited opportunities for blacks, many of the most talented northern black entrepreneurs turned to gambling and other illegal operations for their livelihood. Novelist Richard Wright explained, "They would have been steel tycoons, Wall Street brokers, auto moguls, had they been white." Like the political bosses of nineteenth century urban America, numbers operators provided an informal assistance network for needy patrons in the impoverished black communities and represented a major source of capital for black businesses. In city after city, the numbers barons, seeking an element of respectability or an outlet to shield gambling profits from the Internal Revenue Service or merely the thrill of sports ownership, came to dominate black baseball. In Harlem, second-generation Cuban immigrant Alex Pompez, a powerful figure in the Dutch Schultz mob, ran the Cuban Stars, while Ed "Soldier Boy" Semler controlled the Black Yankees. Abe Manley of the Newark Eagles, Ed Bolden of the Philadelphia Stars, and Tom Wilson of the Baltimore Elite Giants all garnered their fortunes from the numbers game. Even Cum Posey, who had no connection with the rackets, had to bring in Homestead numbers banker Rufus "Sonnyman" Jackson as a partner and financier to stave off Greenlee's challenge.

In 1933, Greenlee unified the franchises owned by the numbers kings into a rejuvenated Negro National League. Under his leadership, writes Donn Rogosin, "The Negro National League meetings were enclaves of the most powerful black gangsters in the nation." This "unholy alliance" sustained black baseball in the Northeast through depression and war. Even the collapse of the Crawfords and demolition of Greenlee Stadium in 1939, failed to weaken the league which survived until the onset of integration. In 1937 a second circuit, the Negro American League was formed in the Midwest and South. Dominated by Wilkinson and the Kansas City Monarchs, the Negro American League relied less on numbers brokers, but more on white ownership for their financing.

The formation of the Negro American League encouraged the rejuvenation of an annual World Series, matching the champions of the two leagues. But the Negro League World Series never achieved the prominence of its white counterpart. The fact that league standings were often determined among teams playing uneven numbers of games, diluted the notion of a champion. Furthermore, impoverished urban blacks could not sustain attendance at a prolonged series. As a result, the Negro League World Series always took a back seat to the annual East-West All-Star Game played in Chicago. The East-West Game, originated by Greenlee in 1933, quickly emerged as the centerpiece of black baseball. Fans chose the players in polls conducted by black newspapers. By 1939, leading candidates received as many as 500,000 votes. Large crowds of blacks and whites watched the finest Negro League stars, and the revenues divided among the teams often spelled the difference between profit and loss at the season's end.

By the 1930s and 1940s, black baseball had become an integral part of Northern ghetto life. With hundreds of employees and millions of dollars in revenue, the Negro Leagues, as Donn Rogosin notes, "may rank among the highest achievements of black enterprise during segregation." In addition, baseball provided an economic ripple effect, boosting business in hotels, cafes, restaurants and bars. In Kansas City and other towns, games became social events, as black citizens, recalls manager Buck O'Neil, "wore their finery." The Monarch Booster Club was a leading civic organization and the "Miss Monarch Bathing Beauty" pageant a popular event.

Black baseball also represented a source of pride for the black community. "The Monarchs was Kansas City's team," boasted bartender Jesse Fisher. "They made Kansas City the talk of the town all over the world." In several cities, white politicians routinely appeared at Opening Day games to curry favor with their often neglected black constituents. When Greenlee Field launched its opera-

tions in Pittsburgh, the mayor, city council, and county commissioners lined the field boxes. Negro League owners also played a role in the fight against segregation. In Newark, Effa Manley, who ran the Eagles with her husband Abe, served as treasurer of the New Jersey NAACP and belonged to the Citizen's League for Fair Play which fought for black employment opportunities. Manley sponsored a "Stop Lynching" fundraiser at one Eagles home game.

The impact of the Negro Leagues, however, ranged beyond the communities whose names the teams bore. Throughout the age of Jim Crow baseball, even in those years when a substantial league structure existed, official league games accounted for a relatively small part of the black baseball experience. Black teams would typically play over 200 games a year, only a third of which counted in the league standings. The vast majority of contests occurred on the "barnstorming" circuit, pitting black athletes against a broad array of professional and semi-professional competition, white and black, throughout the nation. In the pre-television era, traveling teams brought a higher level of baseball to fans in the towns and cities of America and allowed local talent to test their skills against the professionals. While some all-white teams, like the "House of David" also trod the barnstorming trail, itinerancy was the key to survival for black squads. The capital needed to finance a Negro League team existed primarily in Northern cities, but the overwhelming majority of blacks lived in the South.

"The schedule was a rugged one," recalled Roy Campanella of the Baltimore Elite Giants. "Rarely were we in the same city two days in a row. Mostly we played by day and traveled by night." After the Monarchs introduced night baseball, teams played both day and night appearing in two and sometimes three different ballparks on the same day. Teams traveled in buses—"our home, dressing room, dining room, and hotel"—or sandwiched into touring cars. "We had little time to waste on the road," states Quincy Trouppe, "so it was a rare treat when the cars would stop at times to let us stretch out and exercise for a few minutes." Most major hotels barred black guests, so even when the schedule allowed overnight stays, the athletes found themselves in less than comfortable accommodations. Large cities usually had better black hotels where ballplayers, entertainers, and other members of the black bourgeoisie congregated. On the road, however, Negro Leaguers more frequently were relegated to Jim Crow roadhouses, "continually under attack by bedbugs."

The black baseball experience extended beyond the confines of the United States and into Central America and the Caribbean. Negro Leaguers appeared regularly in the Cuban, Puerto Rican, Venezuelan, and Dominican winter leagues where they competed against black and white Latin stars and major leaguers as well. Some blacks, like Willie Wells and Ray Dandridge, jumped permanently to the Mexican League, where several also became successful managers of interracial teams. As Wells explained, "I am not faced by the racial problem. . . I've found freedom and democracy here, something I never found in the United States. . . In Mexico, I am a man."

In the United States, however, blacks often found themselves in more distasteful roles. To attract crowds throughout the nation and to keep fans interested in the frequently one-sided contests against amateur competition, some black clubs injected elements of clowning and showmanship into their pre-game and competitive performances. As early as the 1880s, comedy had characterized many barnstorming teams. Black baseball, even in its most serious form, tended to be flashier and less formal than white play. Against inferior teams, players often showboated and flaunted their superior skills. Pitcher Satchel Paige would call in his outfielders or guarantee to strike out the first six or nine batters to face him against semi-professional squads. In the late 1930s, Olympic star Jesse Owens traveled with the Monarchs, racing against horses in pre-game exhibitions.

Black teams, like the Tennessee Rats and Zulu Cannibals, thrived on their minstrel show reputations. The most famous of these franchises were the "Ethiopian Clowns." Originating in Miami in the 1930s, the Clowns later operated out of Cincinnati and then Indianapolis. Their antics included a "pepperball and shadowball" performance (later emulated by basketball's Harlem Globetrotters), and mid-game vaudeville routines by comics Spec Bebop, a dwarf, and King Tut. Players like Pepper Bassett, "the Rocking Chair Catcher" and "Goose" Tatum, a talented first baseman and natural comedian, enlivened the festivities. By the 1940s, the Clowns, through the effort of booking agent Syd Pollack, dominated the baseball comedy market. In 1943, their popularity won the Clowns entrance into the Negro Leagues, although other owners demanded they drop the demeaning "Ethiopian" nickname. Although never one of the better black teams, the Clowns greatly bolstered Negro League attendance.

Their popularity notwithstanding, the comedy teams reflected one of the worst elements of black baseball. The Clowns and Zulus perpetuated stereotypes drawn from Stepin Fetchit and Tarzan movies. "Negroes must realize the danger in insisting that ballplayers paint their faces and go through minstrel show revues before each ballgame," protested sportswriter Wendell Smith. Many black players resented the image that all were clowns. "Didn't nobody clown in our league but the Indianapolis Clowns," objected Piper Davis. "We played baseball."

Even without the clowning, black baseball offered a more freewheeling and, in many respects, more exciting brand of baseball than the major leagues. Since the 1920s, when Babe Ruth had revolutionized the game, the majors had pursued power strategies, emphasizing the home run above all else. Although the great sluggers of the Negro Leagues rivaled those in the National and American Leagues, they comprised but one element in the speed-dominated universe of "tricky baseball." Black teams emphasized the bunt, the stolen base, and the hit-and-run. "We played by the 'coonsbury' rules," boasted second baseman Newt Allen. "That's just any way you think you can win, any kind of play you think you could get by on." In games between white and black all-star teams, this style of play often confounded the major leaguers. Centerfielder James "Cool Papa" Bell personified this approach. Bell was so fast, marveled rival third baseman Judy Johnson, "You couldn't play back in your regular position or you'd never throw him out." In one game against a major league All-Star squad, Bell scored from

first base on a sacrifice bunt! In center field, his great speed allowed him to lurk in the shallow reaches of the outfield, ranging great distances to make spectacular catches.

Negro League pitching also took on a peculiar caste. "Anything went in the Negro League," reported catcher Roy Campanella, "Spitballs, shineballs, emery balls; pitchers used any and all of them." Since league officials could not afford to replace the balls as frequently as in organized ball, scuffed and nicked baseballs remained in the game, giving pitchers great latitude for creative efforts. "I never knew what the ball would do once it left the pitcher's hand," recalled Campanella.

Since most rosters included only 14 to 18 men, Negro League players demonstrated a wide range of versatility. Each was required to fill in at a variety of positions. Star pitchers often found themselves in the outfield when not on the mound. Some won renown at more than one position. Ted "Double-Duty" Radcliffe often pitched in the first game of a doubleheader and caught in the second. Cuban Martin Dihigo, whom many rank as the greatest player of all time, excelled at every position. In 1938, in the Mexican League he led the league's pitchers with an 18–2 record and the league's hitters with a .387 average.

The manpower shortage offered opportunities for individuals to display their all-around talents, but it also limited the competitiveness of the black teams. While on a given day a Negro League franchise, featuring one of its top pitchers, might defeat a major league squad, most teams lacked the depth to compete on a regular basis. "The big leagues were strong in every position," remarks Radcliffe. "Most of the colored teams had a few stars but they weren't strong in every position."

While black teams may not have matched the top clubs in organized baseball, the individual stars of the 1930s and 1940s clearly ranked among the best of any age. Homestead Gray teammates Josh Gibson and Buck Leonard won renown as the Babe Ruth and Lou Gehrig of the Negro Leagues. The Grays discovered Gibson in 1929 as an 18-year-old catcher on the sandlots of Pittsburgh, where he had already earned a reputation for 500-foot home runs. For 17 years, he launched prodigious blasts off pitchers in the Negro Leagues, on the barnstorming tour, and in Latin America. As talented as any major league star, Gibson died in January 1947, at age 35, just three months before Jackie Robinson joined the Brooklyn Dodgers. Leonard, four-years older than Gibson, starred in both the Negro and Mexican Leagues as a sure-handed, power-hitting first baseman. The Newark Eagles in the early 1940s, boasted the "million dollar infield" of first baseman Mule Suttles, second baseman Dick Seay, shortstop Willie Wells, and third baseman Ray Dandridge. The acrobatic fielding skills of Seay, Wells and Dandridge led Roy Campanella to call this the greatest infield he ever saw.

Amidst the many talented Negro Leaguers of 1930s and 1940s, however, one long, lean figure came to personify black baseball to blacks and whites alike. Leroy "Satchel" Paige began his prolonged athletic odyssey in his hometown in 1924 as a 17-year-old pitcher with the semi-professional Mobile Tigers. He joined the Chattanooga Black Lookouts of the Negro Southern League in 1926. Two years later, the Lookouts sold his contract to the Birmingham Black Barons. By 1930, his explosive fastball, impeccable control, and eccentric mannerisms had made him a legend in the South. In 1932, Gus Greenlee brought Paige to the Pittsburgh Crawfords where the colorful pitcher embellished his reputation by winning 54 games in his first two years. Greenlee also began the practice of hiring out Paige to semi-professional clubs that needed a one-day box office boost.

For seven years Paige feuded with Greenlee, jumping the club when a better offer appeared, being banished "for life," and then returning. In the mid-1930s, in addition to his stints with the Crawfords, Paige won fame by boosting Bismarck, North Dakota, to the national semi-professional championships, hurling for the Dominican Republic at the behest of dictator Rafael Trujillo, in the Mexican League, and especially on the postseason barnstorming trail pitted against Dizzy Dean's Major League All-Stars. "That skinny old Satchel Paige with those long arms is my idea of the pitcher with the greatest stuff I ever saw," claimed the unusually immodest Dean.

Paige's appeal stemmed as much from his unusual persona as his pitching prowess. A born showman, Paige's lanky, lackadaisical presence evoked popular racial stereotypes of the age. "As undependable as a pair of second-hand suspenders," Paige often arrived late or failed to show. His names for his pitches (the "bee ball" which buzzed and all of a sudden, "be there"; the "jump ball"; and the "trouble ball") and his minstrel show one-liners enhanced the image. But on the mound, Paige invariably rose to the occasion against top competition or challenged inferior opponents by calling in the outfield or promising to strike out the side.

In 1938, a sore arm threatened to curtail Paige's career but the Kansas City Monarchs, hoping his reputation alone would draw fans, signed him for their traveling second team. On the road, Paige perfected a repertoire of curves and off-speed pitches, including his famous "hesitation" pitch. When his fastball returned in 1939, he became a better pitcher than ever. Promoted to the main Monarch club, Paige pitched the team to four consecutive Negro American League pennants. From 1941-1947, although officially still a Monarch, Paige spent far more time as an independent performer, hired out by Monarchs' owner J. L. Wilkinson to semi-pro and Negro League clubs. "He kept our league going," recalls Othello Renfroe. "Anytime a team got into trouble, it sent for Satchel to pitch." Paige also continued to hurl against major league All-Star teams. In the 1940s, the example of Satchel Paige, whose legend had spread into the white community, offered the most compelling argument for the desegregation of the National Pastime.

Paige's exploits against white players revealed a fundamental irony about baseball in the Jim Crow era. While organized baseball rigidly enforced its ban on black players within the major and minor leagues, opportunities abounded for black athletes to prove themselves against white competition along the unpoliced boundaries of the national pastime. During the 1930s, Western promoters sponsored tournaments for the best semi-professional teams in the nation. These squads often featured former and future major leaguers as well as top local talent. In 1934, the *Denver Post* tourney, "the little World Series of the West," invited the Kansas City Monarchs to compete for the $7,500 first prize. The Monarchs fought their way into the finals against the House of David team (also owned by J. L. Wilkinson) only to find themselves confronted on the mound by Paige, rented out to pitch this one game. Paige outdueled Monarchs ace, Chet Brewer, 2–1. Black teams became a fixture in the Post series, emerging victorious for several consecutive years.

In 1935, the National Baseball Congress began an annual tournament in Wichita, Kansas. The competition attracted community squads heartily bankrolled by local business leaders. Neil Churchill, an auto dealer from Bismarck, North Dakota, recruited a half-dozen black stars, including Paige and Brewer, to represent the town in the Wichita competition. Bismarck naturally swept the series, and thereafter teams that were either integrated or all black routinely appeared in the National Baseball Congress invitational each year.

In an age in which the major leagues were confined to the East and Midwest, and television had yet to bring baseball into people's homes, postseason tours by big league stars offered yet another opportunity for black players to prove their equality on the diamond. Games pitting blacks against whites were popular features of the barnstorming circuit. Until the late 1920s, when Commissioner Kenesaw Mountain Landis limited postseason play to all-star squads, black teams frequently met and defeated major league clubs in postseason competition. During the next decade, matchups between the Babe Ruth or Dizzy Dean "All-Stars" and black players became frequent. In the autumns of 1934 and 1935, Dean's team traveled the nation accompanied by the "Satchel Paige All-Stars." In one memorable 1934 game, called by baseball executive Bill Veeck, "the greatest pitching battle I have ever seen," Paige bested Dean 1–0. Surviving records of interracial contests during the 1930s reveal that blacks won two-thirds of the games. "That's when we played the hardest," asserted Judy Johnson, "to let them know, and to let the public know, that we had the same talent they did and probably a little better at times."

The rivalries proved particularly keen on the West Coast where Monarchs co-owner Tom Baird organized the California Winter League, which included black teams, white major and minor league stars, and some of Mexico's top players. In 1940, pitcher Chet Brewer formed the Kansas City Royals, which each year fielded one of the best clubs on the coast. One year the Royals defeated the Hollywood Stars, who had won the Pacific Coast League championship, six straight times. In 1945, Brewer's team, including Jackie Robinson and Satchel Paige, regularly defeated major league competition.

The most famous of the interracial barnstorming tours occurred in 1946, when Cleveland Indian pitcher Bob Feller organized a major league All-Star Team, rented two Flying Tiger aircraft and hopped the nation accompanied by the Satchel Paige All-Stars. With Feller and Paige each pitching a few innings a day, the tour proved extremely lucrative for promoters and players alike and gave widespread publicity to the skills of the black athletes.

The World War Two years marked the heyday of the Negro Leagues. With black and white workers flooding into Northern industrial centers, relatively full employment, and a scarcity of available consumer goods, attendance at all sorts of entertainment events increased dramatically. In 1942, three million fans saw Negro League teams play, while the East-West game in 1943 attracted over 51,000 fans. "Even the white folks was coming out big," recalled Satchel Paige.

But World War Two also generated forces which would challenge the foundations of Jim Crow baseball. In the armed forces, baseball teams like the Black Bluejackets of the Great Lakes Naval Station team posted outstanding records against teams featuring white major leaguers. In 1945, a well-publicized tournament of teams in the European theatre featured top black players like Leon Day, Joe Green, and Willard Brown in the championship round. More significantly, the hypocrisy of blacks fighting for their country but unable to participate in the national pastime grew steadily more apparent. As wartime manpower shortages forced major league teams to rely on a 15-year-old pitcher, over-the-hill veterans, and one-armed Pete Gray, their refusal to sign black players seemed increasingly irrational. "How do you think I felt when I saw a one-armed outfielder?" moaned Chet Brewer. Pitcher Nate Moreland protested, "I can play in Mexico, but I have to fight for America where I can't play." Pickets at Yankee Stadium carried placards asking, "If we are able to stop bullets, why not balls?"

Amidst this heightened awareness, organized baseball repeatedly walked to the precipice of integration, but always failed to take the final leap. In 1942, Moreland and All-American football star Jackie Robinson requested a tryout at a White Sox training camp in Pasadena, California. Robinson, in particular, impressed White Sox Jimmy Dykes but nothing came of the event. Brooklyn Dodger manager Leo Durocher publicly stated his willingness to sign blacks, only to receive a stinging rebuke from Commissioner Landis. Landis again short-circuited integration talk the following year. At the annual baseball meetings, black leaders led by actor Paul Robeson gained the opportunity to address major league owners on the issue, but Landis ruled all further discussion out of order.

In 1943, several minor and major league teams were rumored close to signing black players. In California, where winter league play had demonstrated the potential of black players, several clubs considered integration. The Los Angeles Angels of the Pacific Coast League announced tryouts for three black players, but pressure from other league owners doomed the plan. Oakland owner Vince DeVicenzi ordered Manager Johnny Vergez to consider pitcher Chet Brewer, the most popular black player on the West Coast, for the Oaks. Vergez refused and the issue died. Two years later, Bakersfield, a Cleveland Indian farm team in the California League, offered Brewer a position as player-coach, but the parent club vetoed the plan.

At the major league level, Washington Senators owner Clark Griffith called sluggers Josh Gibson and Buck Leonard into his office and asked if they would like to play in the major leagues. They answered affirmatively, but never heard from Griffith again. In Pittsburgh, *Daily Worker* sports editor Nat Low pressured Pirate owner William Benswanger to arrange a tryout for catcher Roy Campanella and pitcher Dave Barnhill. At the last minute, Benswanger canceled the audition, citing "unnamed pressures." The most promising situation occurred in Philadelphia where young Bill Veeck had arranged to buy the

Phillies. Veeck planned to stock the team with Negro League stars, whom he felt sure would guarantee Philadelphia the pennant. When Commissioner Landis learned of his plans, however, Veeck suddenly found his purchase blocked.

For more than two decades, the imperial Landis had reigned over baseball as an implacable foe of integration. While hypocritically denying the existence of any "rule, formal or informal, or any understanding—unwritten, subterranean, or sub-anything—against the signing of Negro players," Landis had stringently policed the color line. His death in 1944 removed a major barrier for integration advocates.

In April 1945, with World War Two entering its final months, the integration crusade gained momentum. On April 6, *People's Voice* sportswriter Joe Bostic appeared at the Brooklyn Dodger training camp at Bear Mountain, New York, with two Negro League players, Terris McDuffie and Dave "Showboat" Thomas, and demanded a tryout. An outraged, but outmaneuvered Dodger President Branch Rickey, allowed the pair to work out with the club. One week later, a more serious confrontation occurred in Boston. The Red Sox, under pressure from popular columnist Dave Egan and city councilman Isidore Muchnick, agreed to audition Sam Jethroe, the Negro League's leading hitter in 1944, second baseman Marvin Williams, and Kansas City Monarch shortstop Jackie Robinson, all top prospects in their mid-twenties. The Fenway Park tryout, however, proved little more than a formality and the players never again heard from the Red Sox.

The publicity surrounding these events, however, forced the major leagues to address the issue at its April meetings. At the urging of black sportswriter Sam Lacy, Leslie O'Connor, Landis's interim successor, established a Major League Committee on Baseball Integration in April 1945, to review the problem. In addition, the racial views of newly appointed Commissioner A. B. "Happy" Chandler came under close scrutiny. A former governor of the segregated state of Kentucky, Chandler nonetheless offered at least verbal support to the entry of blacks into organized ball. "If a black boy can make it on Okinawa and Guadalcanal, hell, he can make it in baseball," Chandler told black reporter Rick Roberts. Whether Chandler, however, unlike Landis, would reinforce his rhetoric with positive actions remained uncertain.

Unbeknownst to the integration advocates, baseball officials, and local politicians sand-dancing around the race issue, Branch Rickey, the president of the Brooklyn Dodgers, had already set in motion the events which would lead to the historic breakthrough.

Raised in rural Ohio in a strict Methodist family, Rickey, nicknamed by sportwriters "The Deacon" and "The Mahatma," had financed his way through college and law school playing and coaching baseball. His skills as a catcher merited two years in the major leagues. In 1913, he abandoned a fledgling law career to manage the St. Louis Browns, and in 1917 he began a 25-year relationship with the St. Louis Cardinals. Rickey served as the field manager of the Cardinals from 1919–1925, after which he became the club's vice-president and business manager. In the 1920s and 1930s, Rickey perfected the farm system, whereby a major league team controlled young, undeveloped players through a chain of minor league franchises. This innovation allowed the Cardinals to compete equally with richer teams in larger cities, generating pennants for the "Gas House Gang" and allowing the team to profitably sell off surplus talent.

Although Rickey later claimed that his desire to integrate baseball dated from 1904, when an Indiana hotel had denied lodgings to a black player on his college squad, he gave no indication of any interest in the race issue during his years in St. Louis. Perhaps this stemmed from the fact that St. Louis was a Southern city with firmly entrenched segregationist traditions. Throughout Rickey's reign with the Cardinals, blacks sat in Jim Crow sections at Sportsman's Park, a policy which he never openly challenged.

Nonetheless, in 1942, when Rickey left the Cardinals and assumed control of the Brooklyn Dodgers, he informed the Dodger ownership of his intentions to recruit black players in the near future. Rickey never clearly explained the motivations for this dramatic turnaround. At times Rickey cited moral considerations, stating, "I couldn't face my God much longer knowing that His black creatures are held separate and distinct from His white creatures in the game that has given me all I own." On other occasions, he eschewed the role of "crusader," proclaiming, "My selfish objective is to win baseball games. . .The Negroes will make us winners for years to come." Some observers saw financial reasons behind Rickey's actions, citing the lure of the growing black population in Northern cities and the prospects of increased attendance. Certainly, Brooklyn offered a more congenial atmosphere for integration than St. Louis. In all probability, a combination of these factors—geographic, moral, competitive, and financial—coupled with Rickey's desire for a broader role in history, impelled him to seek black players.

From 1942–1945, Rickey, a conservative, cautious, and conspiratorial man, moved slowly, studying the philosophical and sociological ramifications of integration and taking few people into his confidence. During the spring and summer of 1945, under the guise of creating a new black baseball circuit, the United States League, Rickey's scouts combed the nation and the Caribbean for black players. Rickey sought one player who would spearhead the breakthrough and several other potential stars who would follow in his wake. By August 1945, scouting reports and Rickey's own investigations pointed to one man as the ideal candidate for the struggle ahead—Kansas City Monarch shortstop Jackie Robinson.

In Robinson, Rickey had found a rare combination of athletic ability, competitive fire, intelligence, maturity, and poise. Born in Georgia and raised in Pasadena, California, Robinson had won fame at UCLA as the nation's greatest all-around athlete, earning All-America honors in football, establishing broad-jump records, and leading his basketball conference in scoring, all in addition to his baseball exploits. In 1942, he enlisted in the army where he attended officer's candidate school and became a lieutenant. Two years later, while stationed in Texas, Robinson's refusal to move to the back of a bus resulted in a court martial and ultimate acquittal. This incident demonstrated his commitment to the cause of equal rights. After his discharge from the army, Robinson joined the

Monarchs and earned a starting spot in the 1945 East-West All-Star Game. Robinson's college education, experience in interracial athletics, and army career complemented his playing talents. But his fiery pride and temper seemed a potential obstacle to his success.

On August 28, 1945, Robinson met with Rickey at the latter's Brooklyn offices. Rickey revealed his bold plan to integrate organized baseball and challenged Robinson to accept the primary role. The Mahatma flamboyantly play-acted, assuming the role of racist players, fans and hotel clerks, impressing upon Robinson the need to "turn the other cheek" in the event of racial confrontations. By the end of the session, Robinson had signed a contract to play for the Montreal Royals in the International League, the top farm team in the Brooklyn system. Rickey promised that if Robinson's performance merited it, he would be promoted to the Dodgers.

Rickey intended to announce the Robinson signing along with that of several other black players, but political pressures stemming from the New York City fall elections forced him to abandon his original plans and, on October 23, 1945, to reveal the signing of Robinson alone. The announcement sent shock waves through the baseball establishment and placed Robinson into a spotlight that he would never relinquish. Numerous sports figures, from players to executives to reporters, predicted the ultimate failure of Rickey's "great experiment."

Robinson's first test came at spring training in Florida in 1946. Thrust into the deep South where Jim Crow reigned supreme, Robinson and black pitcher John Wright, whom Rickey had recruited to room with Robinson, were unable to room with their teammates and barred from playing in Jacksonville and other Florida cities. In addition, a shoulder injury hindered Robinson's performance, raising doubts about his abilities.

On April 18, 1946, at Roosevelt Stadium in Jersey City, Robinson became the first black to appear in modern Organized Baseball (excepting Jimmy Claxton, who passed as white in 1916 for the Oakland Oaks of the Pacific Coast League). In the process he staged one of the most remarkable performances under pressure in the history of the game. In Robinson's second at-bat, he hit a three-run home run. He followed this with three singles and two stolen bases, scoring a total of four runs. As the *New York Times* reported, "This would have been a big day for any man, but under the circumstances, it was a tremendous feat."

In many respects, 1946 proved a nightmare season for Robinson. Fans jeered him in Baltimore, and opposing players tormented him with insults. Pitchers made him a frequent target of brushback pitches and baserunners attempted to spike and maim him at second base. As the season drew to a close, Robinson hovered on the brink of a nervous breakdown. Through it all, however, Robinson remained a dominant force on the field. His .349 batting average and 113 runs-scored led the league and paced the Royals to the International League pennant. His presence inspired new attendance records throughout the circuit. In the Little World Series, which pitted Montreal against the Louisville Colonels of the American Association, Robinson braved the hostility of Kentucky fans and stroked game-winning hits in the final two games to give the Royals the championship.

Rickey's initiative and Robinson's dramatic success failed to inspire other team owners. In August, major league executives debated a controversial report discussing the "Race Question" which argued that integration would "lessen the value of several major league franchises." No other clubs moved to sign black players. Only four blacks, all in the Brooklyn system, joined Robinson in organized baseball in 1946. At Nashua, New Hampshire, in the New England League, the Dodger farm club fielded catcher Roy Campanella and pitcher Don Newcombe. The Nashua Dodgers won the league championship largely due to Campanella's hitting and Newcombe's hurling. In the small town of Trois Rivières in Quebec, pitchers John Wright and Roy Partlow, both of whom had appeared briefly with Robinson at Montreal, led a third Dodger farm team to the Canadian-American league crown. Nonetheless, at the start of the 1947 season, no additional black players appeared on major or minor league rosters.

Although Robinson's performance at Montreal merited promotion to the Dodgers, Robinson remained a Royal when he reported to spring training in 1947. Rickey hoped that the Brooklyn players themselves, when exposed to Robinson's talents, would request his addition to the team. He switched Robinson to first base, a weak spot on the Dodger squad, to make his case more compelling. Robinson compiled a .519 batting average against the major leaguers, but several Dodger players, instead of demanding his promotion, rebelled. Led by "Dixie" Walker, a group of mostly Southern Dodgers circulated a petition against Robinson. Rickey moved quickly to short-circuit the dissension, threatening to trade any athletes who opposed Robinson. In addition, the refusal of Pete Reiser, "Pee Wee" Reese and other Dodger stars to support the protestors, effectively squelched the petition drive. Finally, on April 10, just five days before the start of the 1947 season, Rickey officially announced that Robinson would join the Dodgers.

Throughout the early months of the 1947 campaign Robinson stoically endured crises and challenges. The Philadelphia Phillies, led by manager Ben Chapman, unleashed a barrage of verbal abuse against Robinson which horrified Dodger players and fans. The Benjamin Franklin Hotel in Philadelphia refused lodgings for Robinson and death threats appeared among his voluminous daily mail. In early May, rumors that the St. Louis Cardinals planned to strike rather than compete against Robinson prompted National League President Ford Frick to warn the players, "If you do this you will be suspended from the league." Opposing pitchers targeted Robinson's body at a record setting pace and an early season 0 for 20 batting drought led many to question his qualifications as a professional baseball player. "But for the fact that he is the first acknowledged Negro in major league history," observed a Cincinnati sportswriter, "he would have been benched a week ago."

Yet, as the season unfolded, Robinson converted doubters and enemies into admirers. By the end of June, a 21-game hitting streak had raised his batting average to .315 and propelled the Dodgers into first place. Robinson's daring baserunning, typical of Negro League play, evoked images of an "Ebony Ty Cobb." In city after city, record crowds flocked to experience Robinson's charismatic dy-

namism as five teams set new all-time season attendance marks. While periodic controversies erupted over baserunners who used their spikes "to make a pincushion out of Robinson" at first base, Robinson won the acceptance and respect of teammates and opponents alike. In September, as the Dodgers coasted to the pennant, *The Sporting News* named Robinson the major league Rookie of the Year. To cap his triumphant season, Robinson became the first black player to appear in the World Series.

Robinson's success on the field and at the box office stimulated some movement on the part of other clubs to hire black players. In Cleveland Bill Veeck recruited 23-year-old Larry Doby, who jumped straight from the Negro League Newark Eagles to the Indians in July. Used sparingly, Doby batted a meager .156, casting doubts upon his future. The St. Louis Browns, seeking to boost flagging attendance, signed Willard Brown and Hank Thompson of the Kansas City Monarchs. When the turnstiles failed to respond, the Browns released both Brown and Thompson, although the latter had established himself as a top prospect. In the National League, the Dodgers signed Dan Bankhead to bolster the club's pitching down the stretch. On August 25, Bankhead, the first black pitcher to appear in the major leagues, surrendered eight runs in three innings but also slammed a home run in his initial at bat.

In addition to the five athletes who appeared in the major leagues, a handful of blacks surfaced in the minors. Campanella succeeded Robinson at Montreal, earning accolades as "the best catcher in the business." Newcombe returned to Nashua where he won 19 games. The independent Stamford Bombers of the Colonial League fielded six black players, and two blacks, including future major leaguer Chuck Harmon, played in the Canadian-American League. Veteran Negro League hurler Nate Moreland won 20 games in California's Class C Sunset League. For the most part, however, organized baseball continued to ignore the treasure trove of black talent submerged in the Negro Leagues. A full year would pass before additional major league teams would add black players to their chains.

In 1948, the integration focus shifted from the Dodgers, where Robinson now reigned at second base, to the Cleveland Indians. In spring training, Larry Doby, who had performed so dismally in 1947, unexpectedly won a starting berth in the Cleveland outfield. After an erratic early season stretch in which Doby alternated errors and strikeouts with tape-measure home runs, he batted .301 and became a key performer for the American League champion Indians. In July, Cleveland owner Bill Veeck added the legendary Satchel Paige to the team. Amidst charges that his signing had been a publicity stunt, the 42-year-old Paige won six out of seven decisions, including back-to-back shutouts, and posted a 2.47 earned run average. Standing-room-only crowds greeted him in Washington, Chicago, Boston, and even in Cleveland's mammoth Municipal Stadium. The Indians, after defeating the Boston Red Sox in a pennant playoff, won the World Series in six games with Doby's .318 average leading the club.

In 1947, the Dodgers had integrated and reached the World Series; in 1948, the Indians had duplicated and surpassed this achievement. Both teams had set all-time attendance records. Remarkably, as the 1948 season drew to a close, no other franchise had followed their lead. In the minor leagues, Roy Campanella became the first black in the American Association, stopping at St. Paul before permanently joining Robinson on the Dodgers. Newcombe and Bankhead each won more than 20 games for Brooklyn affiliates. The Dodgers also added fleet-footed Sam Jethroe to the Montreal roster, where he batted .322. The Indians also began to stockpile black talent, signing future major leaguers Al Smith, Dave Hoskins, and Orestes "Minnie" Minoso to minor league contracts. Several other blacks, including San Diego catcher John Ritchey, who broke the Pacific Coast League color line, played for independent teams.

In the interregnum between the 1948 and 1949 seasons four more teams—the Giants, Yankees, Braves, and Cubs—signed blacks to play in their farm systems, and 1949 would herald the beginning of widespread integration in the minor leagues. Blacks starred in all three Triple A leagues. In the Pacific Coast League, Luke Easter won acclaim as the "greatest natural hitter . . . since Ted Williams," amassing 25 home runs and 92 runs-batted-in in just 80 games before succumbing to a knee injury. Oakland's Artie Wilson led the league in hits, stolen bases, and batting average. In the International League, Jethroe scored 151 runs and stole 89 bases while Montreal teammate Dan Bankhead won 20 games for the second straight year. At Jersey City, Monte Irvin batted .373. The outstanding performer in the American Association was Ray Dandridge. Considered by many the greatest third baseman of all time, the acrobatic Dandridge, now in his late 30s, thrilled Minneapolis fans with his spectacular fielding, batting .364 in the process. Former Negro Leaguers turned in equally stellar performances at lower minor league levels as well.

In the major leagues, the spotlight again returned to Jackie Robinson. For three years, Robinson had honored his pledge to Branch Rickey "to turn the other cheek" and avoid confrontations. With his position in the majors firmly established, Robinson announced, "They better be prepared to be rough this year, because I'm going to be rough on them." The more combative Robinson produced his finest year, batting .342 and earning the Most Valuable Player Award. Complemented by teammates Newcombe and Campanella, Robinson led the Dodgers to another pennant.

By the end of the 1949 season, integration had achieved spectacular success at both the major and minor league level, but most teams moved "with all deliberate speed" in signing black players. The New York Giants joined the interracial ranks in 1949 when they promoted Monte Irvin and Hank Thompson. The following year, the Boston Braves purchased Jethroe from the Dodgers for $100,000 and installed him in the starting lineup. In 1951, the Chicago White Sox acquired Minnie Minoso in a trade with Cleveland, and Bill Veeck, who had acquired the hapless St. Louis Browns, brought back Satchel Paige for another major league stint. Yet, as late as August 1953, out of sixteen major league teams only these six fielded black players. Several teams displayed an interest in signing blacks but bypassed established Negro League stars who might have jumped directly to the majors, concentrating instead on younger prospects for the minor leagues. Still others like the Red Sox, Phillies, Cardinals, and Tigers continued to pursue a whites-only policy.

This failure to hire and promote blacks occurred amidst a continuing backdrop of outstanding performances by black players. The first generation of players from the Negro Leagues proved an extraordinary group. Jackie Robinson quickly established himself as one of the dominant stars in the national pastime, compiling a .311 batting average over his 10-year career while thrilling fans with his baserunning and clutch-hitting talents. Sportswriters called him, "the most dangerous man in baseball today." Campanella won accolades as the best catcher in the National League and won the Most Valuable Player Award in 1951, 1953, and 1955. Both Campanella and Robinson later won election to the Baseball Hall of Fame. Pitcher Don Newcombe averaged better than 20 wins a season during his first five full years with the Dodgers. In addition, from 1950-1953 Negro League graduates Sam Jethroe, Willie Mays, Joe Black, and Jim Gilliam each won the National League Rookie of the Year Award.

In the American League, where integration proceeded at a slower pace, several players compiled outstanding records. Larry Doby, while never achieving the superstar status many expected, nonetheless became a steady producer, twice leading the league in home runs and five times driving in more than 100 runs. His Cleveland teammate Luke Easter, who reached the majors in his mid-30s, slugged 86 home runs and drove in 300 runs in his brief three-season career. Satchel Paige, after a two-year stint with the Indians, joined the hapless St. Louis Browns from 1951-1953 and became one of the American League's best relief pitchers. On the Chicago White Sox, Minnie Minoso proved himself a consistent .300 hitter. Despite their relatively small numbers, teams with black players in both major leagues regularly finished high in the standings and only in 1950 did both pennant winners field all-white squads. In addition, the more aggressive stance of National League teams in recruiting black players gave that circuit a clear superiority in World Series and All-Star contests for more than two decades.

By the end of the 1953 season, the benefits of integration had grown apparent to all but the most recalcitrant of major league owners. In September, the Chicago Cubs purchased shortstop Ernie Banks from the Kansas City Monarchs and finally elevated longtime minor league standout Gene Baker. Connie Mack's Philadelphia Athletics ended their Jim Crow era by acquiring pitcher Bob Trice. At the start of the 1954 season, the Washington Senators, St. Louis Cardinals, Pittsburgh Pirates, and Cincinnati Reds all joined the interracial ranks. The sudden integration of six more clubs left only the Yankees, Tigers, Phillies, and Red Sox with all-white personnel. In addition, 1954 marked the debut of young Henry Aaron with the Braves and the return of Willie Mays, who had sparkled for the Giants in 1951, from military service.

The desegregation of organized baseball opened the way not only to blacks in the United States but to those in other parts of the Americas as well. Throughout the 20th century, baseball had imposed a curious double standard on Latin players, accepting those with light complexions but rejecting their darker countrymen. With the color barrier down, major league clubs found a wealth of talent in the Carribbean. Minnie Minoso, the "Cuban Comet" who integrated the Chicago White Sox, became the first of the great Latin stars. Over a 15-year career, Minoso compiled a .298 batting average. In 1954, slick-fielding Puerto Rican Vic Power launched his career with the Athletics. The following year, Roberto Clemente, the greatest of the Latin stars, debuted with the Pittsburgh Pirates. The proud Puerto Rican won four batting championships and amassed 3,000 hits en route to a .317 lifetime batting average. In the late 1950s, the San Francisco Giants revealed the previously ignored treasure trove that existed in the Dominican Republic. In 1958, Felipe Alou became the first of three Alou brothers to play for the Giants, and in 1960 the Giants unveiled pitcher Juan Marichal, "the Dominican Dandy," who won 243 games en route to the Hall of Fame.

Among the early Latin players were two sons of stars of the Jim Crow age. Perucho Cepeda, who had won renown as "The Bull" in his native Puerto Rico, had refused to play in the segregated Negro leagues. His son Orlando, dubbed "The Baby Bull," went on to star for the Giants and Cardinals. Luis Tiant, Sr., a standout performer in both Cuba and the Negro Leagues, lived to see Luis, Jr. win over 200 major league games and excel in the 1975 World Series.

As the major leagues moved slowly toward complete desegregation, throughout the nation blacks invaded the minor leagues. In the Northern and Western states, these athletes, a combination of youthful prospects and Negro League veterans, were greeted by a storm of insults, beanballs, and discrimination. "I learned more names than I thought we had," states Piper Davis of his treatment by fans in the Pacific Coast League. At least a half-dozen blacks had to be carried off the field on stretchers after being hit by pitches between 1949 and 1951. In city after city, blacks found hotels and restaurants unwilling to serve them. "At the same time when they signed blacks and Latins," argues John Roseboro about his Dodger employers, "they should have made sure they would be welcome." But neither the Dodgers nor other clubs provided any special assistance for their black farmhands. Despite these conditions, blacks compiled remarkable records in league after league. In the early 1950s, blacks overcame adversity and dominated the lists of batting leaders at the Triple A level and in many of the lower circuits as well.

In 1952, blacks began to appear on minor league clubs in the Jim Crow South. The Dallas Eagles of the Texas League, hoping to boost sagging attendance, signed former Homestead Gray pitcher Dave Hoskins to become the "Jackie Robinson of the Texas League." Hoskins took the Lone Star State by storm, attracting record crowds en route to a 22–10 record. The black pitcher posted a 2.12 earned run average and also finished third in the league in batting with a .328 mark. By 1955, every Texas League club except Shreveport fielded black players.

Hoskins' performance inspired other teams throughout the South to scramble for black players. In 1953, 19-year-old Henry Aaron desegregated the South Atlantic League, which included clubs in Florida, Atlanta, and Georgia, while Bill White appeared in the Carolina League. Playing for Jacksonville (a city which seven years earlier had barred Jackie Robinson), Aaron "led the league in every-

thing but hotel accommodations." By 1954, when the United States Supreme Court issued its historic *Brown* v. *Board of Education* decision ordering school desegregation, blacks had appeared in most Southern minor leagues.

The integration of the South, however, did not proceed without incidents. Black players recall these years as "an ordeal" or a "sentence" and described the South as "enemy country" or a "hellhole." In 1953, the Cotton States League barred brothers Jim and Leander Tugerson from competing. The following year, Nat Peeples broke the color line in the Southern Association, but lasted only two weeks. For the remainder of the decade, the league adhered to a whites-only policy, a strategy which contributed to the collapse of the Southern Association in 1961. As resistance to the civil rights movement mounted in the 1950s, black players found themselves in increasingly hostile territory. Even in the pioneering Texas League, teams visiting Shreveport, Louisiana, in 1956 had to leave their black players at home due to stricter segregation laws.

In the face of these obstacles, young black stars like Aaron, Curt Flood, Frank Robinson, Bill White, and Leon Wagner overcame their frustrations "by taking it out on the ball." "What had started as a chance to test my baseball ability in a professional setting," wrote Curt Flood, "had become an obligation to test myself as a man." Throughout the 1950s, blacks appeared regularly among the league leaders of the Texas, South Atlantic, Carolina, and other circuits, advancing both their own careers and the cause of integration.

As these events unfolded in the South, the major leagues completed their long overdue integration process. In 1955, the Yankees, after denying charges of racism for almost a decade, finally promoted Elston Howard to the parent club. Two more years passed before the Phillies integrated, and not until 1958 did a black player don a Tiger uniform. Thus, at the start of the 1959 season, only the Boston Red Sox, who had yet to hire either black scouts or representatives in the Caribbean, retained their Jim Crow heritage. A storm of protest arose when the Red Sox cut black infielder Elijah "Pumpsie" Green just before Opening Day, but on July 21, 1959, 12 years and 107 days after Jackie Robinson's Dodger debut, Green won promotion to the Boston club, completing the cycle of major league integration.

While integration became a reality in organized baseball, the Negro Leagues gradually faded into oblivion. As early as 1947, Negro League attendance, especially in cities close to National League parks, dropped precipitously. "People wanted to go Brooklynites," recalls Monarch pitcher Hilton Smith. "Even if we were playing here in Kansas City, people wanted to go over to St. Louis to see Jackie." Negro League owners hoped to offset declining attendance by selling players to organized baseball, but major league teams paid what Effa Manley called "bargain basement" prices for all-star talent. In 1948, the Manleys' Newark Eagles and New York Black Yankees disbanded. The Homestead Grays severed all league connections and returned to its roots as a barnstorming unit. Without these teams, the Negro National League collapsed. A reorganized 10-team Negro American League, most of whose franchises were located in minor league cities, vowed to go on, but the spread of integration quickly thinned its ranks. By 1951, the league had dwindled to six teams. Two years later, only the Birmingham Black Barons, Memphis Red Sox, Kansas City Monarchs, and Indianapolis Clowns remained.

For several years in the early 1950s, the Negro Leagues remained a breeding ground for young black talent. The New York Giants plucked Willie Mays from the roster of the Birmingham Black Barons, while the Boston Braves discovered Hank Aaron on the Indianapolis Clowns. The Kansas City Monarchs produced more than two dozen major leaguers, including Robinson, Paige, Banks, and Howard. But for most black players, the demise of the Negro Leagues had disastrous effects. "The livelihoods, the careers, the families of 400 Negro ballplayers are in jeopardy," complained Effa Manley in 1948, "because four players were successful in getting into the major leagues." The slow pace of integration left most in a state of limbo set adrift by their former teams, but still unwelcomed in organized baseball. Some players like Buck Leonard and Cool Papa Bell were too old to be considered, while others like Ray Dandridge and Piper Davis found themselves relegated to the minor leagues, where outstanding records failed to win them promotion.

Throughout the 1950s the Negro American League struggled to survive, recruiting teenagers and second-rate talent for the modest four-team loop. In 1963, Kansas City hosted the 30th and last East-West All-Star Game and the following year the famed Monarchs ceased touring the nation. By 1965, the Indianapolis Clowns remained as a last vestige of Jim Crow baseball. Utilizing white as well as black players, the Clowns continued for another decade. "We are all show now," explained their owner. "We clown, clown, clown."

But the legacy of the Negro Leagues remained. Robinson and other early black players introduced new elements of speed and "tricky baseball" into the major leagues, transforming and improving the quality of play. Since 1947, blacks have led the National League in stolen bases in all but two seasons. In the American League, a black or Latin baserunner has topped the league every year since 1951 with only two exceptions. Nor did this injection of speed come at the expense of power. In the 1950s and 1960s, Hank Aaron, Willie Mays, and Frank Robinson reigned as the greatest power hitters in baseball. Thus, by the 1960s, the national pastime more closely resembled the well-balanced offensive structure of the Negro Leagues than the unidimensional power-oriented attack that had typified the all-white majors.

The demise of the Negro Leagues and the decline of segregation in the majors, however, did not end discrimination. Conditions on and off the field, in spring training and in the executive suites, repeatedly reminded the black athletes of their second-class status. In the early 1950s, all-white teams taunted their black opponents with racial insults. Blacks like Jackie and Frank Robinson, Minnie Minoso and Luke Easter repeatedly appeared among the league leaders in being hit by pitches. While black superstars like Willie Mays had little difficulty ascending to the major leagues, players of only slightly above average talent found themselves buried for years in the minors. Many observers charged that teams had imposed quotas on the number of blacks they would field at one time.

In cities like St. Louis, Washington, D. C., and, later, Baltimore, black ballplayers could not stay at hotels with their teammates. In 1954, they achieved a breakthrough of sorts when the luxury Chase Hotel in St. Louis informed Jackie Robinson and other Dodger players that they could room there, but had to refrain from using the dining room or swimming pool or loitering in the lobby. Ten years later, the hotel had removed these restrictions, but still relegated black players, according to Hank Aaron, to rooms "looking out over some old building or some green pastures or a blank wall, so nobody can see us through a window."

Blacks faced even greater discrimination each year in spring training in Florida. While all spring training sites now accepted blacks, segregation statutes and local traditions forced them to live in all-black boarding houses far from the luxury air-conditioned hotels which accommodated white players. "The whole set-up is wrong," protested Jackie Robinson. "There is no reason why we shouldn't be able to live with our teammates." When teams traveled from place to place, blacks could not join their fellow players in restaurants. Instead they had to wait on the bus until someone brought their food out to them. Some teams attempted to reduce the problems faced by blacks. Several clubs moved to Arizona, where conditions were only moderately improved. The Dodgers built a special spring training camp at Vero Beach where players could live together. Most organizations, however, did very little to assist their black employees.

By the time that Jackie Robinson retired in 1956, conditions had barely improved. "After 10 years of traveling in the South," he charged, " I don't think advances have been fast enough. It's my belief that baseball itself hasn't done all it can to remedy the problems faced by . . . players." Over the next decade, a new generation of black players militantly demanded change. Cardinal stars Bill White, Curt Flood, and Bob Gibson protested against conditions in St. Petersburg, while Aaron and other black Braves demanded changes in Bradenton. In many instances, however, significant changes awaited passage of the Civil Rights Act of 1965 barring segregation in public facilities.

By 1960, Robinson, Campanella, Doby, and the cadre of Negro League veterans who had formed the vanguard of baseball integration had retired. In their wake, a second generation of black players, most of whom had never appeared in the Negro Leagues, made most Americans forget that Jim Crow baseball had ever existed, as they shattered longstanding "unbreakable" records. In 1962, black shortstop Maury Wills stole 104 bases, eclipsing Ty Cobb's 47-year-old stolen base mark. Twelve years later, outfielder Lou Brock stole 118 bases en route to breaking Cobb's career stolen-base record as well. In 1966, Frank Robinson, who had won the National League Most Valuable Player Award in 1961, became the first player to win that honor in both leagues when he led the Baltimore Orioles to the American League pennant. By the end of his career, Robinson had slugged 586 home runs; only Babe Ruth among players of the Jim Crow era had hit more. Both Ernie Banks and Willie McCovey also amassed more than 500 home runs during this era. On the pitcher's mound, the indomitable Bob Gibson proved himself one of the greatest strikeout pitchers in the game's history. Upon retirement, Gibson had amassed more strikeouts than anyone except Walter Johnson. Brock, Frank Robinson, Banks, McCovey, and Gibson all won election to the Hall of Fame in their first year of eligibility.

The greatness of these players notwithstanding, two other black players, Willie Mays and Hank Aaron, both of whom ironically had begun their careers in the Negro Leagues, reigned as the dominant stars of baseball in the 1950s and 1960s. Originally signed by the Birmingham Black Barons of the Negro American League, Mays had joined the New York Giants in midseason 1951, sparking their triumph in the most famous pennant race in history and winning the Rookie of the Year Award. After two years in the military, he returned in 1954 to bat a league-leading .345 and hit 41 home runs. The following year, he pounded 51 homers. A spectacular center fielder, Mays won widespread acclaim as the greatest all-around player in the history of the game. In 1969, he became only the second player in major league history to hit 600 home runs and took aim at Babe Ruth's legendary lifetime total of 714. Over the next four seasons, the aging Mays added 60 more homers before retiring, still well short of Ruth's record.

Unlike Mays, who had begun his career amidst the glare of the New York media, Hank Aaron had spent his career first in Milwaukee and later in Atlanta, far distant from the center of national publicity. Nonetheless, he steadily compiled record- threatening statistics in almost every offensive category. In 1972, at age 38, he surpassed Mays's home run total and set his sights on Ruth. Entering the 1973 season, he needed just 41 home runs to catch the Babe. Performing under tremendous pressure and fanfare, Aaron stroked 40 homers, leaving him just one shy of the record. He tied Ruth's mark with his first swing of the 1974 season. Three days later, on April 8, 1974, a nationwide television audience watched Aaron stroke home run number 715. Babe Ruth's "unreachable" record thus fell to a man whose career had started with the Indianapolis Clowns of the Negro Leagues. When Aaron retired in 1976, he boasted 755 home runs and held major league records for games played, at-bats, runs batted in and extra-base hits. He also ranked second to Ty Cobb in hits and runs scored.

By the 1970s, black players had become an accepted part of the baseball scene and regularly ranked among the most well-known symbols of the sport. Reggie Jackson, Willie Stargell, and Joe Morgan had succeeded Aaron, Mays, and the Robinsons as Hall of Fame caliber superstars. Yet three decades after Jackie Robinson had broken the color barrier, racism and discrimination remained a persistent problem for baseball. Several studies demonstrated that baseball management channeled blacks into positions thought to require less thinking and fewer leadership qualities. In 1968, blacks accounted for more than half of the major league outfielders, but only 20 percent of other position players. Black catchers were rare and fewer than one in 10 pitchers were black. By 1986, the disparity had grown greater. American-born blacks comprised 70 percent of all outfield positions but only 7 percent of all pitcher, second basemen, and third basemen positions. There were no American-born black catchers in the major leagues at the start of the 1986 season.

While superior black players had open access to the major leagues, those of average or slightly above average skills often found their paths blocked. "The Negro player may have to be better qualified than a white player to win the same position," argued Aaron Rosenblatt in 1967. "The undistinguished Negro player is less likely to play in the major leagues than the equally undistinguished white player." Rosenblatt demonstrated that black major leaguers on the whole batted 20 points higher than whites. As batting averages dropped, so did the proportion of blacks. This trend continued into the 1980s. A 1982 study revealed that 70 percent of all black non-pitchers were everyday starters, indicating a substantial bias against blacks who filled utility or pinch-hitting roles. Statistics compiled in 1986 showed a strikingly similar pattern.

The subtle nature of this on-the-field discrimination obscured it from public controversy. The failure of baseball to provide jobs for blacks in managerial and front office positions, however, became an increasing embarrassment. In the early years of integration, baseball executives bypassed the substantial pool of experienced Negro Leaguers from consideration for managerial and coaching positions. A handful of blacks, including Sam Bankhead, Nate Moreland, Marvin Williams, and Chet Brewer managed independent, predominantly all-black teams in the minor leagues. The first generation of black major leaguers fared no better. "We bring dollars into club treasuries when we play," exclaimed Larry Doby, "but when we stop playing, our dollars stop." No major league organization hired a black pilot at any level until 1961 when the Pittsburgh Pirates placed Gene Baker at the helm of their Batavia franchise. By the mid-1960s no blacks had managed in the majors and only two had held full-time major league coaching positions. The first black umpire did not appear in the majors until 1966, when Emmett Ashford appeared in the American League.

In the final years of his life, Jackie Robinson made repeated pleas for baseball to eliminate these lingering vestiges of Jim Crow. "I'd like to live to see a black manager," he stated before a national television audience at the 1972 World Series. Nine days later he died, his dream unfulfilled. In 1975, the Cleveland Indians hired Frank Robinson to be the first black major league manager. This precedent, however, opened few new doors. Robinson lasted two-and-a-half seasons with the Indians, later managed the San Francisco Giants for four years, and in 1988 was made manager of the Baltimore Orioles. Maury Wills and Larry Doby each had brief half-season stints as managers. After four decades of integration, only these three men had received major league managerial opportunities.

A similar situation existed in major league front offices. Only one black man, Bill Lucas of the Atlanta Braves, had served as a general manager. As late as 1982, a survey of 24 clubs (the Yankees and Red Sox refused to provide information) found that of 913 available white-collar baseball jobs, blacks held just 32 positions. Among 568 full-time major league scouts, only 15 were black. While many teams hired former players as announcers, few employed blacks in these roles. Five years later, conditions had not improved. Of the top 879 administrative positions in baseball only 17 were filled by blacks and 15 by Hispanics. Four teams in California—the Dodgers,

Giants, Athletics, and Angels—accounted for almost two-thirds of the minority hiring. Ten out of 14 American League teams, and five of 12 National League franchises had no blacks in management positions.

These shortcomings came to haunt baseball in 1987. Commissioner Peter Ueberroth had dedicated the season to the commemoration of the fortieth anniversary of Jackie Robinson's major league debut. As the celebration began, Los Angeles Dodger general manager Al Campanis, who had played with Robinson at Montreal, appeared on ABC-TV's *Nightline*. When asked about the dearth of black managers, Campanis explained that blacks "may not have some of the necessities to be, let's say, a field manager or general manager." Campanis's statement, which surely reflected the thinking of many baseball executives, evoked a storm of protest, and precipitated his resignation. An embarrassed Ueberroth pledged to take action to bring more blacks into leadership positions and hired University of California sociologist Harry Edwards to facilitate the process. Fifty blacks and Latins with past or present connections to baseball created their own Minority Baseball Network to apprise blacks of employment opportunities and to lobby clubs to recruit more minorities for front office jobs.

When the controversy of 1987 had subsided, few franchises had taken significant steps to increase minority hiring. Several clubs added blacks to administrative positions, but none offered field or general manager positions to nonwhite candidates (although Bill White was named National League president). In 1988 Frank Robinson received his third chance to manage in the major leagues, this time with the Baltimore Orioles. At midseason 1989 Cito Gaston assumed the reins of the Toronto Blue Jays. When the squads managed by Robinson and Gaston had their initial confrontation, it marked, after 40 years of integration, the first time that two teams managed by black men had competed in a major league game. Fittingly, on the final weekend of the season, the Orioles and Blue Jays met face-to-face in a series to decide the championship of the American League Eastern Division. The spectacle offered a resounding rebuke to the short-sightedness and discrimination that continue to plague the national pastime.

By the 1993 season baseball seemed to have finally made some real progress in including minorities in its managerial ranks. The season saw five black and Hispanic field managers: Gaston, who after five years at the helm of the Blue Jays ranks as one of the most successful managers in baseball history, winning four divisional championships, two pennants and two world championships; Felipe Alou, who led the Montreal Expos to consecutive second place finishes; Dusty Baker, who became the winningest rookie manager ever, when his San Francisco Giants won 103 games (after winning only 72 games the year before); Don Baylor, who piloted the expansion Colorado Rockies; and Tony Perez, who started the season as the manager of the Cincinnati Reds. At the season's end, the Houston Astros named Bob Watson their general manager, making him the second black man to assume these responsibilities. In 1994 Leonard Coleman succeeded Bill White as National League president.

These undeniable gains, however, occurred against a backdrop of continuing racial controversy. During preceding seasons, several of the game's top black stars had complained about unequal treatment of black players; and many observers voiced concern about the miniscule level of black attendance and the declining numbers of United States-born blacks in the game.

Allegations that Cincinnati Reds owner Marge Schott had repeatedly used racial slurs (and that other owners had ignored these offenses) led to her suspension in 1993. When the Reds first hired, then unceremoniously fired, Perez as manager after a poor start, it appeared to some that the team had shamefully manipulated a local hero to evade charges of discrimination.

During the early 1990s baseball undertook several initiatives to improve its image among minorities. The major leagues embraced John Young's RBI ("Reviving Baseball in the Inner Cities") program, an effort to entice black youth away from other sports and back to the diamond. Attempts were also made to secure health benefits for surviving Negro League players and to gain Hall of Fame recognition for more stars from the Jim Crow era. Nonetheless, as baseball neared the fiftieth anniversary of the signing of Jackie Robinson, issues of race and discrimination remained as a persistent reminder of the legacy of the past and challenges of the present.

## CHAPTER 18

The Minor Leagues

Bob Hoie

The International Association, founded in 1877, is frequently described as the first minor league. For two major reasons it shouldn't be so regarded. First, it was barely a league. Structurally it resembled the old National Association—there was virtually no central authority, no limitation on the number or location of member teams, no set schedule, and haphazard umpire selection. The league was so loosely assembled in fact that some member teams competed at the same time for the championships of other organizations like the New England Association and the League Alliance. Second, the International Association was originally established as a rival to the National League and never officially recognized itself as being subordinate. It was generally acknowledged that several of its teams were as good as or better than some in the National League. Various off-the-field problems, administrative weaknesses, and a lack of solidarity and resolve on the part of the member clubs assured its subordinate status.

A strong case could be made for the 1879 Northwestern League as the first minor league—it had a preset schedule and had no pretensions of rivaling the National League, but the absence of league-appointed umpires led to frequent forfeits due to charges of biased "hometown" umpiring, and the league folded after only two months.

The Eastern Association was founded in 1881, but this was another loose alliance with no set schedule.

The first recognized minor league was another Northwestern League, this one organized on October 27, 1882. At that time they requested of the National League cooperation and reciprocity in protecting player contracts. This was necessary because independent clubs frequently lost their best players during the course of the season to the National League and later to the American Association clubs. In response to this request, the National League, American Association, and Northwestern League signed a "Tripartite Agreement" in March 1883. This agreement bound the clubs to honor the contracts of players on reserve lists, assured mutual recognition of expulsions and suspensions, established territorial rights, and created an arbitration committee to settle disputes. Minimum salaries were established and pegged at a higher level in the National League and American Association than in the Northwestern League or "any other parties to the agreement," thus by implication assigning a "major" and "minor" status to the leagues.

The Interstate Association was established early in 1883 and was quickly accepted as an "alliance" league by the American Association, becoming a junior partner of the Tripartite Agreement. Both the Northwestern and the Interstate opened their seasons on May 1, 1883. Each had a formal league organization, a schedule that was preset before the season opening, and a complement of umpires appointed and paid for by the league. Both leagues recognized and accepted their status as subordinate to the two "majors." In 1884 the Interstate Association reorganized as the Eastern League and became a fourth member of what now became known as the National Agreement.

In October 1885 a new National Agreement was adopted which made the National League and American Association the principal parties and removed from minor league clubs the protection of the reserve clause. Two years later the reserve clause was reinstated for the minors, but the major-minor league distinction had been formalized. Following the collapse of the American Association in 1892, another National Agreement for the first time established minor league classifications and gave major league clubs the right to draft minor league players at fixed prices.

While these events were taking place, organized baseball expanded dramatically, going from two minor leagues in 1883 to seventeen by 1888. Baseball was played throughout the country, of course, but organized ball was confined to the northeast quadrant of the United States in 1884; it expanded to the South in 1885, to Colorado and the upper Midwest in 1886, California in 1887, Texas in 1888, and the Pacific Northwest in 1890. So in the year that the American frontier was officially declared closed, organized baseball had extended to all corners of the country.

In 1887 an organization called the Negro Baseball League, fearing player raids by the still moderately integrated minors, sought and received protection under the National Agreement. The league was to play in eight cities that also had major league teams, but it folded in less than two weeks. This was unfortunately characteristic of the era. Many teams and leagues were underfinanced and were ultrasensitive to changes in the national or local economy. In addition, being unable or unwilling to pay the required fees for reserving their players, they lost their better ones at the close of the season—and those teams that even managed to finish the season could usually consider themselves lucky. During the nineteenth century, more than 40 percent of the leagues that started a season failed to finish it. There was, however, a solid core of support for minor league baseball. Regardless of how many leagues started each season—usually about fifteen but often as many as twenty—only eight to ten usually finished; the rest failed. The 1890s were not a period of expansion nor of stability as throughout the decade nearly half of the leagues that started a season failed to finish it.

A depression in 1892–1893 and the Spanish-American War in 1898 were significant factors, but a proliferation of "fly-by-night" operators played a role as well.

At the close of the 1900 season, the still minor American League withdrew from the National Agreement, announcing through that action its intention not to allow its players to be drafted and not to respect the reserve clause or territorial rights any longer.

In September 1901 the National League announced its intention to abrogate the National Agreement, contending that with the American League invading its cities and raiding its players the National League could not be expected to sit back and abide by restrictions which did not hinder its rival. Essentially this meant that the National, like the American, considered the players on minor league rosters "fair game."

In immediate reaction to this, the presidents of seven minor leagues met in Chicago on September 5, 1901, and in an act of self-protection they organized the National Association of Professional Baseball Leagues. On October 25 representatives of nine minor leagues met in New York and adopted a new "National Agreement." This new agreement established league classifications, roster and salary limits, and a draft system; it recognized reserve lists and created a Board of Arbitration which was given the power to suspend players, clubs, or officials for violations of the agreement. By the beginning of the 1902 season, the National Association included fifteen member leagues.

The American and National Leagues ratified a peace agreement early in 1903, and in late August the presidents of the two major leagues and the National Association drafted a National Agreement which was initially rejected by the minors. After some concessions were made by the majors, such as a prohibition on "farming," the plan was adopted in September. The agreement formalized relations between the majors and minors and established a National Commission to serve as a Board of Arbitration.

These agreements were necessary because the majors and minors were mutually dependent on each other. The majors needed the minors as a reliable source of talent, while the minors, many of whom relied on player sales to stay in business, needed assurances from the majors that they would recognize their property rights in players.

Despite this mutual dependence there was a basic buyer-seller conflict. The majors wanted to acquire players as cheaply as possible, while the minors wanted to sell them for as much as possible. This same conflict existed within the minors as well, with the highest-classification clubs wanting to buy cheaply from the lower minors and sell at high prices to the majors. Thus the National Agreement, the major-minor agreement, and the National Association itself were uneasy alliances of clubs and leagues with competing and often conflicting objectives, and the nearly annual revisions in draft rules and prices and limits on optional player assignments were required to maintain the equilibrium necessary to keep the alliance intact.

The majors favored an unlimited draft—i.e., any player on a minor league roster could be purchased for a fixed rate. As early as 1896, when Minneapolis of the Western League was decimated through what were in effect forced sales, it became clear that some limitations were necessary, so by 1905 only one player could be drafted from a club per year. The draft prices of top-classification minor leaguers went from $750 to $1,000 in 1905 and then to $2,500 in 1911. While these prices were not particularly low for average prospects in that era, they were well below the value of the best prospects in the minors; thus the draft or the threat of it served as an incentive for minor league clubs at all levels to sell their better players to major or higher-classification minor league clubs at competitive market prices. From the players' standpoint, the draft had the positive effect of allowing them eventually to advance to whatever levels their ability would take them. The lower-classification minor league clubs received lower draft prices for their players but seemed relatively satisfied with the system—after all, this was an era when the contracts of Tris Speaker, Rogers Hornsby, and Ty Cobb were sold to major league clubs for $400, $500, and $700 respectively.

On the other hand, many of the higher-classification minor league clubs had never really been satisfied with the draft. As early as 1908, this dissatisfaction nearly caused the two top minor leagues at that time—the American Association and the Eastern League—to go independent. Several of the top minor league clubs drew more fans annually than some major league clubs and represented substantial investments; their owners were understandably not happy with a system that forced the sale of their top players for below-market prices to the majors; in addition to the challenge to club stability and autonomy caused by the draft, the gap between the market value of the top prospects and the draft price widened throughout the 1910s.

Despite the rumblings of discontent, the establishment of the National Association ushered in a period of minor league expansion to a fairly stable core of thirty leagues. While there were still leagues that failed to finish the season, the failure rate was down to 10–15 percent. For some reason, in 1910 the minors reached a level never to be topped until the post–World War Two boom era—fifty-two leagues started the season and forty-six finished it. For the next five years more leagues folded, but each season generally closed with forty leagues operating. Then, for reasons that ranged from the automobile, movies, the war in Europe, and the Federal League War, the bottom started to drop out. Forty-four leagues started in the 1914 season, and by the end of the 1918 season only one was operating (ten leagues had started that year—one folded and eight suspended operations due to the war).

After the 1918 season, with most of the lower minors driven out of business, the National Association, for the first time dominated by the higher minors, adopted a resolution demanding that the majors relinquish the right of the draft and end the practice of "farming out" players. When the majors as expected rejected these demands, the National Association withdrew from the National Agreement. Pending a new major agreement, the majors and minors reached general agreement on property rights in players and territorial rights, and the National Commission ruled that the major league draft would be suspended. In addition the minors would not accept major league players on option, meaning that any players owned or controlled by major league clubs in excess of the active player roster limit would have to be sold or released to minor league clubs.

A. R. Tierney, president of two minor leagues and a leader in the fight to end the draft, said, "This means that the minor leagues will be able to build fences for themselves instead of for the major leagues." He predicted expansion of the minors and higher sale prices for the players. He was correct on both counts. With no players on option, the majors needed to buy more players from the minors, some of whom they had been forced to sell but now had to buy back at higher prices, and without the draft the minor league clubs could virtually name their own price. The minors expanded, as the leagues that had been driven out of business during the war now reentered the fold.

The reappearance of the low minors again shifted the balance of power within the minors. The higher minors had never been happy with the one-league, one-vote system in the National Association. Club owners were wary of having their investments affected by the vote of what they perceived as little more than "fly-by-night" operators, and on occasion they tried to change the arrangement. But just as the majors needed the minors, so the high minors needed the low minors. Thus the high minors always stopped short of enacting measures that might drive their underlings out of the Association.

As noted previously, many of the low minors needed the revenues they received from the draft to survive, and although the minor league draft still existed, it had ceased to be a dependable source of revenue as the combination of numerous prewar minor league failures and returning military veterans yielded more than enough talent to fill the higher minors' rosters. In addition, many of the low-minor clubs did not have the resources to scout for and sign enough players to remain competitive on the field and/or at the box office; thus they were dependent on receiving some players on option.

So while most of the higher minor leagues were prospering as never before under the new independence, by 1920 the low minors were ready to withdraw from the National Association if a new agreement with the majors restoring the draft was not adopted. In addition, some of the higher minor league clubs were upset that the "no-farming" rules were being circumvented by "gentleman's agreements" which enabled the major league clubs to "sell" a player to a minor league club and "buy" him back at the end of the season with little or no money actually changing hands.

On January 10, 1921, a new major-minor league agreement was signed which restored the major league draft with a top price of $5,000 but as a compromise gave individual minor leagues the right to be exempt from the draft; in addition major league clubs could option up to eight players for no more than two consecutive years, and a tax on player sales was instituted to help reduce the fake player transfers. Quickly the top three minors—the International League, Pacific Coast League, and the American Association—together with the Western and Three-I Leagues declared their exemption from the draft; this in turn prohibited them from drafting from the lower minors.

The prices the majors paid for top minor league players nearly doubled between 1919 and 1920, but they skyrocketed during the draft-exemption era. In 1921 the Giants paid $75,000 to San Francisco for Jimmy O'Connell; in 1922 the Giants paid $72,000 to Baltimore for Jack Bent-

ley and the White Sox paid $100,000 to San Francisco for Willie Kamm. The majors clearly were not happy with this situation, and in 1922 they offered to raise the draft price to $7,500, but this failed to lure back the draft-exempt leagues. In early 1923 the majors, after considering but eventually rejecting the idea of a maximum purchase price of $25,000 for any minor league player and/or a boycott of draft-exempt leagues, declared that all players sent to the minors either by sale or option would be subject to the draft and increased the number of players who could be optioned to fifteen. Western League clubs immediately began accepting players on option under these conditions.

The prices for ballplayers remained high in 1923. Baltimore of the International League was reportedly offered $100,000 by Brooklyn for Joe Boley and sold Max Bishop to the Philadelphia A's for $50,000. Salt Lake sold Paul Strand to the A's for a reported $70,000, Louisville sold Earle Combs to the Yankees for $50,000, Toronto sold Red Wingo to the Tigers for $50,000 and Rochester sold Maurice Archdeacon to the White Sox for $50,000, but these were isolated cases. Baltimore, aided by five years of draft exemption, had built a powerhouse, but many of the higher-classification minor league clubs had not been nearly as successful and found that they needed to receive players on option to fill holes and remain competitive. Therefore at the close of the 1923 season all exempt leagues but the International agreed to the modified draft which exempted only those players who had come up through the minors. In 1924, after Baltimore sold Lefty Grove for $100,000 to the A's, the International League also fell into line.

The modified draft did nothing to reduce the prices paid for top minor league stars: Louisville sold Wayland Dean to the Giants for $72,000 in 1924, San Francisco sold Paul Waner and Hal Rhyne to Pittsburgh for $100,000 in 1925, and Baltimore continued selling star players to the majors for big prices—Tommy Thomas to the White Sox in 1925, Joe Boley to the A's in 1926, John Ogden to the Browns and George Earnshaw to the A's in 1927. In 1927 Portland (of the PCL) sold Billy Cissel to the White Sox for a package of cash and players worth over $100,000 and Oakland sold Lyn Lary and Jimmy Reese to the Yankees for $100,000. With prices like these, clubs could afford to lose an occasional Lefty O'Doul or Hack Wilson in the modified draft.

The major-minor agreement expired at the end of the 1927 season, with the National Association members deadlocked on the issue of the draft. The majors and minors were also at an impasse, so the modified draft continued and many of the higher minor league clubs continued to prosper, both through player sales and at the gate. The Los Angeles franchise and ballpark were valued at $2 million, but in the lower minors all was not well through the 1920s. There were generally twenty-five or thirty leagues starting each year, and an average of three or four of these would fold during the season. Leagues were operating that never should have been admitted to the National Association—for example, one of the four leagues that not unexpectedly failed in 1924 was the West Arkansas, which included six towns within a 750-square-mile area with a combined population of 16,000.

In 1929 the rift between the high and low minors widened as the low minors, rebuffed in their efforts to nullify the modified draft agreement, now attempted to impose their own draft exemption—essentially exempting from the draft any player with fewer than two seasons of organized baseball.

Early in 1931 the majors and minors finally adopted a new National Agreement, including a provision which eliminated the modified draft and granted to major league clubs greater control of talent through revised option and draft rules. The higher minors had originally objected, but the majors told them to accept the universal draft or they would no longer have any relations with them—in other words, major league teams would not sell or option players to or buy players from the American Association, the International League, or the Pacific Coast League. While such threats had been taken relatively lightly by the minors in the early days of the draft-exempt leagues, they were now taken seriously enough that in less than a month the three recalcitrant leagues capitulated to the majors' terms. In exchange for all this and largely to secure the support of the low minors, the majors agreed to sign only collegian amateurs, leaving all high-schoolers and sandlotters to the minors. Of course, by this time farm systems had developed to the point that most major league clubs could still sign noncollegian amateurs through their farm clubs.

Milwaukee had sold Fred Schulte to the Browns for a reported $100,000 in 1928, but this was the end of an era. There would be no more $100,000 minor leaguers; in fact there would be few if any minor leaguers sold for as much as $50,000 again. At the 1928 National Association Convention, president Mike Sexton wondered when the majors would own enough clubs to control the National Association. The farm system, an old idea now in the process of being perfected by Branch Rickey, had clearly begun to alter the way the minors operated, and despite the efforts of some—most notably Judge Landis—the trend couldn't be reversed.

The Great Depression caused a contraction of the minors in the early 1930s, but even though a near-record low of fourteen leagues opened the 1933 season, none of them folded. The minors then entered an era of unprecedented growth and stability, reaching forty-four leagues in 1940, with only two leagues failing to finish the season between 1933 and 1941. This can be attributed in part to the substantial involvement of the major leagues through outright ownership or regular infusions of money through working agreements, but there were obviously other factors at work. Judge Bramham, on becoming president of the National Association, instituted a number of reforms, many of which were aimed at getting rid of "fly-by-night" or "shoestring" operators. Minor league baseball was better promoted—they had established a public relations department in 1934—and the advent of night baseball was of incalculable value in generating attendance, which reached 20 million in 1940. Interestingly, that year 54 percent of the minor league clubs were not affiliated with any major league clubs compared to just 37 percent that operated independently in 1936.

World War Two caused the minors to drop to just ten leagues in 1944, but in the first postwar year it was up to forty-three, increasing to an all-time high of fifty-nine in 1949, and during that time no leagues folded. (In 1946 the

Mexican National League, set up by organized baseball to compete with the outlaw Mexican League, is listed by the National Association as having folded during the season, but actually it only withdrew from the Association and continued to operate independently.)

According to a general consensus, it was the coming of television that caused the minors to begin to disintegrate. Between 1949 and 1963 the number of minor leagues dropped from fifty-nine to eighteen. Attendance decreased even more sharply, going from 42 million to less than 10 million over the same time period.

By 1963, the minors had become nothing more than a training ground for the majors—90 percent of the clubs were major league affiliates, and most of those that weren't were in the largely autonomous Mexican League. While television was commonly cited as the cause of the minors' contraction, some contended it was a natural response to overexpansion. Gerry Hirn, in an April 1954 *Baseball Digest* article, contended that while the number of minor leagues had dropped from fifty-nine to thirty-six, that was still too many and the minors would be stronger and more efficient if only sixteen to twenty leagues operated. Interestingly, in 1954 three leagues failed to finish the season, the most failures in peacetime since 1932; they remain the last United States–based minor leagues that failed to finish a season (the Inter-American League, which had a team in Miami but was largely based in the Caribbean, failed to finish the 1979 season—the only year it operated).

For reasons that aren't entirely clear, minor league baseball exploded in popularity in the 1980s. Attendance, which had remained stuck at 10–11 million through the 1960s and most of the 1970s, took off in the late 1970s, topping 20 million in 1987 for the first time since 1953. Louisville, which dropped out of organized ball after drawing just 116,000 in 1972, topped a million in 1983. Nashville, which dropped out in 1963 after drawing just 54,000 for the season, drew over half a million in 1980. Buffalo, which drew only 78,000 in 1969 and saw its franchise shifted to Winnipeg the following year, came back to set an all-time minor league attendance record with 1.1 million in 1988. The Louisville franchise, which didn't exist in 1981 (what became the Louisville franchise was at that time in Springfield, Illinois, drawing 120,000), sold for more than $4 million in 1987. In 1990 the far less successful Vancouver franchise sold to Japanese interests for $5.5 million. Minor league franchises that could be picked up in the early 1970s by anyone who would pay the outstanding debts were selling for several million dollars.

The high prices being paid for franchises may have precipitated the major-minor-league crisis of 1990, reminiscent of the battles earlier in the century. The Professional Baseball Agreement which binds the majors and minors was set to expire at the end of 1990. The majors, who under that agreement provided substantial financial support for the minors, proposed a reduction in those subsidies. The majors believed that the now financially healthy minor league clubs should assume a greater share of operational expenses. In addition, the majors wanted the Commissioner's office to have greater control over minor league affairs. The minors felt the majors were trying to usurp their autonomy and, to add injury to insult, charge them for the privilege. If there was no agreement, the majors threatened to place their entire farm systems in spring training complexes in Arizona and Florida. Some minor league operators threatened to go independent and even form a third major league.

In the end, however, the majority of minor league clubs capitulated, believing that they could not afford to operate without players supplied by the majors. The majors would still pick up most of the expenses, but the new agreement (a) eliminated the minors' share of big-league TV revenue, (b) required that the minors pay a share of their ticket revenues to the majors, and (c) established minimum standards that must be met by minor league facilities by 1994 (subsequently extended to 1995). It was generally believed that these changes, by reducing minor league clubs' profits, might stabilize or reduce the value of franchises. However, in 1992 the Las Vegas franchise sold for a record $7 million and some unsuccessful Class A franchises were sold for well over a million dollars each. And the fans kept coming—in 1993 minor league attendance topped 30 million for the first time since 1950, and in 1993 Buffalo went over 1 million in attendance for the sixth consecutive year. In 1994 the Bisons just missed a seventh million-fan season due to two rainouts.

The positive trend of the past fifteen years is not unprecedented, but the minors have been riding a rollercoaster of success and failure over the past century—the Newark franchise which sold for a reported $600,000 during the depths of the Depression didn't even exist twenty years later. Even today the picture is not all positive: between 1987 and 1992 more than two dozen franchises were shifted, usually due to poor attendance; more than one quarter of the clubs still draw less than a thousand a game; and it is generally believed that many clubs substantially pad their attendance totals. So the current wave of success is somewhat deceptive and history tells us it won't last forever. However, regardless of fluctuations in popularity and economic viability, the minors have been and one can safely assume will continue to be the primary training ground for major league players.

The Players

Great players have passed through the minors, their careers frequently going in opposite directions and occasionally teaming up or crossing in unlikely locations such as Easton, Maryland, where in 1924 Jimmie Foxx broke into organized baseball as a catcher and the player-manager was Home Run Baker in his last season as an active player. There were many others: Rube Waddell and Red Faber with Minneapolis in 1911, young Waite Hoyt and ancient Jesse Burkett with Hartford in 1916, Dazzy Vance and Roger Bresnahan with Toledo in 1917, Chief Bender and Lefty Grove with Baltimore in 1923, and more recently Enos Slaughter and Billy Williams with Houston in 1960.

Former Negro Leaguers, their careers going in opposite directions, Ray Dandridge and Willie Mays were teammates at Minneapolis in 1951 where another teammate was a seven-year minor league veteran, Hoyt Wilhelm. Wilhelm, a twenty-eight-year-old knuckleballer with a background that included three years in Class D ball and three more in the military service, at that time appeared to

be a member of what in that era was a vast army of career minor leaguers, the best of whom held their own with the acknowledged major league greats passing through the minors, but who for a variety of reasons—some good, some not—would themselves spend the bulk of their careers in the minors.

For some of these players who were left behind, the DH rule came fifty years too late, because while they could hit both for average and power, they generally lacked speed or had defensive shortcomings. For others it is less clear what, if any, deficiencies kept them in the minors, but from these groups a few players emerged as true minor league greats whose impact on fans in minor league cities—Buzz Arlett in Oakland, Joe Hauser in Minneapolis, and Bunny Brief in Kansas City, to name a few—was as great as that of more renowned players in major league cities.

The greatest of the minor league players is generally acknowledged to be Buzz Arlett.

Arlett started his career as a right-handed spitball pitcher with the hometown Oakland Oaks in 1918 and went on to win 108 games, twice going over 25 wins in a season. The Detroit Tigers looked at him, but without the spitball, which he wouldn't be able to use in the majors, they did not consider him a prospect. After suffering arm trouble early in 1923, Buzz switched to the outfield. Although he had been nothing more than a fair-hitting pitcher, once becoming a regular he annually averaged nearly .360 with 30 homers and 140 RBIs through the rest of the 1920s, but early in his career as an outfielder a Cardinal scout labeled him "good hit, no field," and it stuck. Finally in 1931 he was purchased by the Phillies. The thirty-two-year-old switch-hitter batted .313 with 18 homers and 73 RBIs in a season when the National League introduced a "dead ball" in reaction to the hitting orgies of 1929–1930. However, at the end of the year Arlett was sent to Baltimore, where in 1932 he hit 4 homers in a game twice within a five-week period and led the league with 54 homers for the season, but he would never return to the majors. He spent another year with Baltimore, when he again won the home run title, a little over a month with Birmingham, and nearly three years with Minneapolis, where he had another home run championship. After a few games with Syracuse in 1937, Arlett's career was over.

In addition to his 108 wins, he hit 432 homers, a minor league record that held up until Hector Espino topped it in 1977. Arlett walked a lot, didn't strike out much, ran pretty well early in his career, had a .341 lifetime batting average—.350 after he became an outfielder—and was the only player to finish in the top five in home runs and slugging percentage in his only season in the majors. In addition, modern statistical analysis, including range factors, suggests he was nowhere near the defensive liability he was portrayed as being. He was big (6-4, 230) and gave the appearance of being lackadaisical, which apparently irritated some of his managers, but the evidence is strong that Arlett, despite nearly two decades spent in the minors, was a major-league-caliber player.

Ike Boone was another player whose hitting feats were not limited to the minors. Boone was a college teammate (at the University of Alabama) of Joe Sewell and Riggs Stephenson; his lifetime major league batting average was

.319, and in his only two full seasons in the majors—1924-1925 with the Boston Red Sox—he hit .333 and .330, but due to alleged defensive deficiencies most of his career was spent in the minors. In 1929 with the Missions of San Francisco, Boone probably had the finest season any player has had in the minors. On the all-time minor league list of single-season accomplishments, his 553 total bases that year are first, his 323 hits are second, his 195 runs scored are tied for third, and his 218 RBIs are fourth. On the all-time Pacific Coast League list, his .407 average is second, and his 55 home runs are tied for fourth.

Boone's greatness wasn't confined to a single season; in four of his first eight years in the minors he hit over .400 (he was on his way to perhaps his greatest season in 1930, batting .448 with 22 homers and 96 RBIs when he was sold to Brooklyn in late June). His .402 average with San Antonio in 1923 is the highest in twentieth-century Texas League history; his .389 with New Orleans in 1921 is the fifth highest in the Southern Association; he also led the International League in batting twice. His .370 lifetime average is the minor league record for players with ten or more seasons. He had an exceptional arm, but limited range in the outfield. Although he hit 77 home runs in a season and a half with the Missions, he was not generally regarded as a power hitter. He was, however, a great pure hitter; in eleven of his fourteen seasons in the minors, he hit over .350, and there is no evidence that he couldn't hit major league pitching.

Smead Jolley was an atrocious outfielder. Stories of his defensive lapses are legion, and the statistical evidence suggests those stories are more than isolated anecdotes. Like Boone, Jolley had a powerful arm but no speed; like Arlett, he was big and awkward; and like both, he could hit—majors or minors. In the equivalent of three full major league seasons with the White Sox and Red Sox, he hit .305 and averaged 15 homers and 105 RBIs. He won six minor league batting championships—leading the Pacific Coast League in hitting three times (winning the Triple Crown with San Francisco in 1928) and the International League once. Twice he had over 300 hits in a season, and twice he drove in more than 180 runs. In the thirteen minor league seasons in which he played over 100 games, he had this run: .370, .372, .346, .397, .404, .387, .360, .372, .373, .350, .309, .373, .345. Perhaps because he spent nearly six years in the low minors, the first four as a pitcher, and had a somewhat nomadic career (he was with thirteen minor league teams), he has not always been ranked in the top echelon of minor league greats, yet he may have been the finest hitter of them all.

Minor league stars generally fit two stereotypes: one-dimensional players who could hit but could do nothing else well enough to stay in the majors—justly or not, Arlett, Boone, and Jolley were consigned to this group. Then there are those who excelled in the minors but couldn't produce in the majors. Perhaps the classic example is Bunny Brief.

Brief, born Antonio Bordetski, may have been the most dominant power hitter in the minor leagues. In major league trials with the Browns, White Sox, and Pirates between 1912 and 1917, he was consistently unimpressive—in a combined 569 at-bats, he hit .223 with 5 homers, 59 RBIs, and nearly 100 strikeouts. In the minors,

however, it was a different story. Although he hit 40 or more homers only twice and never had more than 42, he had eight league home run championships. Before going up to the majors, he led the Michigan State League twice; later he led the Pacific Coast League once and the American Association five times. He also led the Association in RBIs five times (four in succession), including a league-record 191 in 1921. He had a six-year stretch (1921–1926) with Kansas City and Milwaukee, where he averaged 90 extra-base hits, 151 RBIs, and a .351 average per season. Brief also drew a lot of walks. Early in his career he had excellent speed, and although he played most of his career at first base, he was the best defensive outfielder of the big minor league sluggers, with good range and an excellent arm—yet for reasons that remain unclear, Brief never played in a major league game after his twenty-fifth birthday.

Nick Cullop was another minor league great who never produced in the majors. He, like many of the great minor league sluggers, began his career as a pitcher. In trials with the Yankees, Senators, Indians, Dodgers, and Reds between 1926 and 1931 he totaled 490 at-bats, hit 11 homers, drove in 67 runs, hit .249, and struck out 128 times. He was the first farm-system minor league star, playing 1,450 games in the Cardinal chain from 1932 to 1944. In the minors, he hit 420 home runs and drove in 1,857 runs, ten times exceeding 100 in a season.

Cullop had good speed early in his career and was a good enough outfielder to play center field into the late 1920s, but he slowed up considerably in the 1930s. While it is not clear why Brief never did well in the majors, Cullop struck out a lot even in the minors and didn't walk much—suggesting that he had holes which could be and were pitched to effectively in the majors.

Ox Eckhardt was a great football star at the University of Texas who after graduation signed with both Austin of the Texas Association and the Cleveland Indians. The resulting dispute delayed his real professional debut for three years until he was twenty-six years old. Ox quickly made up for lost time, hitting .376 with a league leading 27 triples for Wichita and Amarillo in the Western League in 1928. That fall he played for the New York Giants of the NFL. His baseball contract had been acquired by the Detroit Tigers and although he was on their spring roster in 1929, 1930, and 1931 he never got into a game with the big club. In 1929 he was sent to Seattle, where he hit .354 and again led the league in triples. In 1930 he went to Beaumont, where he led the Texas League with a .379 average. In 1931 he was sold to the Missions, for whom he led the PCL with a .369 average. In the spring of 1932 he was with the Boston Braves—he played 8 games at the start of the season as a pinch hitter and was then sent back to the Missions, where over the next four seasons he hit .371, .414, .378, and .399, winning the batting title three times. He went to the Dodgers in 1936, lasted 16 games batting just .182, and was sent to Indianapolis, where he hit .353 and .341 over the next two years. He hit .321 with Toledo and Beaumont in 1938, .361 with Memphis in 1939, and after hitting .293 with Dallas in 1940, he retired with a minor league career batting average of .367 and the highest career average in organized baseball—.365. (Ty Cobb's minor league record drops his overall average to .3630; Ike Boone's major league record drops his organized-baseball average to .3629.) Eckhardt has the highest single-season and career batting average in the PCL, and ten times he hit over .350.

Unlike many of the minor league stars, Eckhardt did not want for opportunities to play in the majors—counting a trial with the Indians in 1925, he had six shots, but they resulted in his playing in just 24 major league games. The reasons for his failure to make it in the majors are not obscure. Despite being an exceptional athlete with good speed early in his career, he was a poor fielder with a weak arm and no power. Although he was 6-1, 190, the left-handed-hitting Eckhardt slapped the ball to left field. Reportedly managers tried to get him to pull the ball—an idea that should certainly have advanced his career in Detroit or Brooklyn—but it only served to foul up his swing, which he would rediscover after being returned to the minors.

A few minor league greats don't fit the stereotypes: Jigger Statz was the opposite of most—his strengths were speed and defense. Joe Hauser appeared to be on his way to a successful career in the majors, broke his leg, never regained his past form, and went to the minors, where he became the only player to have two 60-home-run seasons. Hector Espino spent virtually his entire career in Mexico, and while major league scouts believed he could hit in the majors, he apparently had no desire to leave his homeland.

Of the great minor league stars, Statz spent the most time in the majors—683 games—and the most time with one club: all of his eighteen minor league seasons were with Los Angeles. His 3,473 games in organized baseball were a record until broken by Hank Aaron in 1976.

Statz was a great fielder; virtually all of his contemporaries considered him the best or one of the best they had seen. Playing very shallow, he reminded many of Tris Speaker. The statistics offer strong support for his claim to greatness. In four full seasons in the majors, he led the league in chances-per-game once and was second the other three years. Between 1922 and 1932 in the majors and minors he had a stretch of ten seasons in which he played in at least 100 games and never finished lower than second in chances-per-game. He had excellent speed, but during most of his career with the Angels they were a hard-hitting club that did not feature the running game, but that changed in the mid-1930s, and in the three seasons following his thirty-sixth birthday he stole 157 bases. His game was not just limited to speed and defense. A classic leadoff man of his era—a good contact hitter, small and fast—he hit .285 in the majors and .315 in the minors, collecting over 2,300 runs, 4,000 hits, 700 doubles, and 500 stolen bases in his organized-baseball career.

On April 7, 1925, the day of Babe Ruth's "big belly-ache," Joe Hauser a twenty-six-year-old first baseman beginning his fourth season with the Athletics, broke his leg in a non-contact play while fielding during a preseason game against the Phillies at Baker Bowl. He had a .304 average for his first three major league seasons and had hit 27 homers with 115 RBIs in 1924. The injury kept him out for the entire 1925 season. In 1926 he tried to come back but hit only .192. After an excellent season with Kansas City, he went back to the majors but didn't do much in stints with the Philadelphia A's and Indians.

He went back to the minors and had 4½ remarkable seasons. In 1930 with Baltimore he set a professional record with 63 homers; then he dropped to 31 in 1931 but still led the league. In 1932 he went to Minneapolis, where he led the American Association in homers with 49. In 1933 he broke his own home run record with 69, and he was off to a great start in 1934—33 homers, 88 RBIs in 82 games—when he broke his kneecap, knocking him out for the season. He continued to play until 1942 but never came close to achieving the success he had in the early 1930s.

Hauser did not hit for a high average, and it has been suggested that he took enormous advantage of short right field fences in Baltimore and Minneapolis—no one would argue that point, since 50 of his 69 homers in 1933 came at home—but many greats played in Oriole and Nicollet Parks, and none came close to Hauser's two record-breaking seasons, which remain the two highest home run seasons in the high minors.

Hector Espino holds the minor league career home run record with 484, and all but 3 of those were hit in Mexico. At the end of the 1964 Mexican League season, the twenty-five-year-old first baseman, who had led the league with 46 homers and a .371 batting average, was sold by Monterrey to the St. Louis Cardinals' Jacksonville farm club. He hit .300 with those 3 homers in 100 at-bats and was invited to spring training by the Cards for 1965, but he never reported and was eventually returned to Monterrey. In the late 1960s, the California Angels coveted Espino, who had led the Mexican League in hitting in 1966–1968, but they were never able to consummate a deal. Espino was a legend in Mexico, but it has never been clear why he didn't try the majors—he has given conflicting answers. Possibly he enjoyed being a big fish in a small pond—it wasn't the money, since he never made more than $18,000 a year in Mexico. He was notorious for marching to his own drummer, occasionally leaving clubs for a midseason vacation, and perhaps he was unwilling to sacrifice that independence.

Espino could hit for power and average—he led the Mexican League in batting five times and home runs four times—and scouts said he could have done the same in the majors, but like many players he played too long. His power started a sharp decline after his thirty-third birthday, and he was virtually helpless at the plate during his last two or three seasons. Nevertheless he ranks as perhaps the greatest minor league player who never played in the majors.

Great players do not have to be distributed evenly among all positions or across all eras, but the emphasis being on great hitters, the result is a number of outfielder-first baseman-designated hitter types, most of whom played in the high-scoring 1920s and 1930s.

Ray French was perhaps the best middle infielder in the minors. He spent twenty-eight years in the minors, most of it in the Pacific Coast League. He played 2,736 games at shortstop and was a brilliant fielder. In the fourteen seasons that he played more than 100 games at short, he led the league in chances-per-game seven times. He was not an outstanding hitter, but his fielding kept him around long enough for him to collect 3,254 hits—seventh on the all-time minor league list.

The two best nineteenth-century minor leaguers were

first baseman Perry Werden and pitcher Willie Mains. Werden had good speed and power. He had several good years in the majors (twice leading the league in triples), won six minor league home run titles, including two seasons when he went over 40, and his .341 lifetime average was exceptionally high for that era.

Mains was the first minor league pitcher to win 300 games, reaching that figure early in 1905. A seven-time twenty-game winner, he was also an excellent hitter in an era when pitchers were frequently expected to take a shift in the outfield. Most of his career was in the New York State League, but in an interesting example of the mobility of players even in the game's early years, in 1892–1893 Mains had back-to-back seasons in Portland, Oregon, and Portland, Maine.

A highly productive but not great player who deserves mention is Spencer Harris, a little lefthanded-hitting outfielder who holds the minor league career records for runs, hits, doubles, total bases, and walks. He reached those levels primarily because he kept playing until he was forty-eight years old. He did lead the American Association in homers in 1928 while at Minneapolis, but he was aided enormously by the friendly right field fence at Nicollet Park. (He averaged 17 homers a year in ten seasons with Minneapolis but only 6 a year in his sixteen other minor league seasons.) He was never thought of as the top player on his many minor league clubs—just as a good solid player of the type that formed the backbone of the minors for so many years.

There have been few minor league pitching stars of the magnitude of the great hitters. Perhaps this is because pitching is a one-dimensional skill—no pitchers were kept in the minors because they couldn't hit or field. Many of the outstanding minor league pitchers stayed there because they didn't have great stuff. Bill Thomas, who won 383 games, and Hal Turpin, who won 271 without ever getting shots at the majors, had the same statistical profile—they struck out few, walked even less, and allowed a lot of hits.

Two pitchers that didn't fit that profile, however, were Joe Martina and Dick Barrett. Martina was a power pitcher who spent most of his career with Beaumont and with his hometown New Orleans Pelicans. He held the minor league career strikeout record until ageless George Brunet broke it while toiling in the Mexican League in 1981. Martina was a workhorse, pitching over 250 innings thirteen times and was a seven-time twenty-game winner. He got his first and only big league opportunity at age thirty-five with the world champion Washington Senators in 1924.

Kewpie Dick Barrett didn't really find himself until he joined Seattle of the PCL in 1935, ten years into his professional career. A little lefthander with less than pinpoint control (he holds the minor league record for career bases on balls), he had good stuff and eight 20-win seasons.

Frank Shellenback is most frequently named as the greatest minor league pitcher. The Pacific Coast League career leader in wins with 295, Shellenback won 10 games with the White Sox as a nineteen-year-old rookie spitballer in 1918. After a poor start the following season, he was sent to Minneapolis. In February 1920 the baseball rules committee outlawed the spitball and other trick pitches. Each major league team was allowed to designate two spitball pitchers who would be able to continue using the pitch in the majors. Unfortunately for Shellenback, he was on the Vernon roster by this time and at age twenty-one would be consigned forever to pitching in the minors if he couldn't get by without the spitball. Throughout much of his career, articles would be written that usually declared that Shellenback would be a major league star if he was eligible to play there. He did have a great six-year stretch with Hollywood (1928–1933) when he went 142–59. He was a very popular player with the Stars as well as Vernon and a fine hitter with good power, but a review of his record suggests he was never as good as everyone thought he was—he led the PCL in wins twice but never led in another category. He had only five 20-win seasons.

Because of the spitball ban, Shellenback was viewed as a tragic figure, but he wasn't alone. Spitballer Paul Wachtel won 203 games in the Texas League after the ban, including five 20-win seasons. Rube Robinson won 148 games in the Southern Association, including two league-leading 26-win seasons. Wheeler Fuller, who never pitched in the majors, won 156 in the Eastern League after the ban.

Perhaps the greatest minor league pitcher was Tony Freitas, a little lefthander who spent all or part of fifteen seasons with Sacramento. He had great control, could get the strikeout, and had nine 20-win seasons (plus two 19-win seasons). If he hadn't lost three years to the military, he probably would have won 400 games in the minors. Freitas had an impressive major league debut, going 12–5 in less than a full season with the 1932 Philadelphia A's, but that was the last success he would have in the majors.

Four other pitchers worthy of mention are Sam Gibson, George Boehler, Bill Bailey, and George Brunet.

Gibson was an underappreciated pitcher who spent most of his career in the PCL—twelve years with San Francisco. He didn't make his organized-baseball debut until he was twenty-three years old. After two promising seasons with Detroit, he never had much success in the majors, but he was extremely effective in the minors. He had six 20-win seasons (plus three 19-win seasons) and, pitching in a high-scoring era, he had eight seasons where his ERA was below 3.00.

Boehler was a hard-throwing workhorse who spent most of his career in the Western League. Twice he pitched over 400 innings, six times over 300. Unfortunately he was terribly inconsistent: with Tulsa in 1921–1923 his seasonal win totals were 4–38–7. He was consistently ineffective in a number of major league trials.

Bailey had seven league-leading strikeout seasons in four different leagues (International, Texas, Southern, Western) but only three 20-win seasons. After a promising September debut with the Browns in 1907, he pitched over 200 games in the majors with five teams spread over fifteen years with no success.

Brunet pitched in organized ball for thirty-three years (1953-1985), and astonishingly he was a regular-rotation pitcher for all but the last year. When he was forty-eight years old, he had a 1.94 ERA pitching regularly in the Mexican League. He never won more than 17 games in a season, had only two 200-strikeout seasons (they were twenty-one years apart), but he had a credible major league career and holds the minor league career strikeout record.

The Teams

There have been a number of debates about the greatest minor league teams. The 1937 Newark Bears, the 1934 Los Angeles Angels, the 1920-1925 Ft. Worth Panthers, and the 1919-1925 Baltimore Orioles usually draw the most support. All were dominant teams with good players.

The Bears included Charlie Keller, Joe Gordon, George McQuinn, Atley Donald, and five other players who would go to the majors the following year. They won the International League pennant by 25½ games with a 109–41 record. The Angels included Frank Demaree, Jigger Statz, Gene Lillard, and Fay Thomas, and they compiled an astounding 137–50 record. The Panthers (or Cats) won six straight pennants and five Dixie Series. They were led by the home run hitting of Big Boy Kraft and a fine pitching staff that included spitballer Paul Wachtel and Joe Pate.

It is doubtful that any of the three could have competed successfully in the majors. It is occasionally claimed that the 1937 Newark Bears were the Yankee B team and could have finished second in the American League, or at least in the first division. But that ignores the talent that was in the majors. The Red Sox finished fifth in 1937 with a club that included Jimmie Foxx, Joe Cronin, Lefty Grove, Pinky Higgins, Doc Cramer, Ben Chapman, Jack Wilson, and Bobo Newsom, all of whom, it is safe to say, would have started for the Bears. The same is true of the Angels, whose pitching staff chose 1934 to have career years, and of the Cats, who played well as a team but had few players that were even considered minor league standouts.

The Orioles were a different story. Thanks to the draft exemption, Jack Dunn was able to assemble a powerhouse comprised of players ready and capable of playing in the majors. The 1922 team was probably the best minor league club ever assembled. It had Jack Bentley, Max Bishop, Fritz Maisel, and Joe Boley in the infield, and Otis Lawry, Merwyn Jacobson, and Jimmy Walsh in the outfield. The catcher was Lena Styles, and the pitchers were Lefty Grove, John Ogden, Tommy Thomas, Rube Parnham, and Harry Frank with Bentley occasionally seeing action on the mound.

Grove, Ogden, and Thomas combined for 60 wins and six years later would win a combined 56 games in the majors. Parnham, a free spirit who pitched when he wanted, was around long enough to win 16 (the following year he won 33). Frank won 22, but his career would soon be cut short by illness. Bentley hit .350 and won 13 games; he went to the Giants in 1923 as a pitcher but hit .427. Bishop and Boley, who hit .261 and .343 respectively, went on to become the double-play combo with the 1929-1930 world champion Philadelphia A's. Styles was just twenty-two years old and hit .315, but that was his peak. Maisel (.306), Walsh (.327), Jacobson (.304), and Lawry (.333) had all played briefly and/or ineffectively in the majors but would all go on to have great careers in the International League. A twenty-year-old rookie utility player on the team was Dick Porter, who hit .279 and

would have seven excellent seasons with the Orioles before going on to have several good years with the Indians.

As good as the Orioles were and as good as some of their players became, it is doubtful that even they could have finished in the first division of the American or National Leagues in 1922. Yet the strongest evidence of the attraction of minor league baseball and the hold it has long held on fans who were exposed to it is that those great Oriole, Bear, and Angel teams are far better known and more fondly remembered than hundreds of more talented second-division and higher major league clubs.

The Farm System

Farm teams are nearly as old as organized baseball. In 1884 the Boston Beaneaters of the National League owned a team called the Boston Reserves in the Massachusetts State Association. The Reserves, also called the Colts, were apparently intended to serve as a source of replacements for disabled members of the major league club. It has also been suggested that the farm team was a device to keep more players under contract and out of the hands of the Union Association that year. Whatever the origins of the idea, during the next decade a number of major league clubs operated such reserve teams, but they usually competed in local semipro leagues rather than in organized baseball and were viewed more as quick sources of replacements rather than as training grounds for players.

With John B. Day's joint ownership of the New York Gothams of the National League and the New York Metropolitans of the American Association as early as 1883 and with the proliferation of interlocking ownerships of major league clubs in the 1890s, it was only natural that some major and minor league clubs would come under joint ownership as well. The first instance of any significance, however, occurred when John T. Brush, owner of Cincinnati in the National League, entered the Indianapolis club in the newly formed Western League in 1894. While this was not the first case of joint major-minor league club ownership, Brush appears to have been the first to grasp the potential of such an arrangement. Indianapolis served as a place to develop talent that was not quite ready for the majors. The team gave Cincinnati an expanded roster as players were frequently shuffled to and from Indianapolis during the season; it also served as a source of profit because Indianapolis drew well at the gate, having become the dominant club in the Western League, with three pennants and two second-place finishes in five seasons (1895–1899). Indianapolis's success was aided in no small part by Brush's practice of drafting players from other Western League clubs and sending them to Indianapolis, thus simultaneously weakening the opposition and strengthening the Hoosiers. Efforts were made by the other Western League club owners to control "farming" or to modify the draft rules to stop Brush, but none were successful.

Perhaps copying Brush's strategy, in 1896 several National League clubs obtained minor league affiliates: Pittsburgh had Toronto, Boston had Wilkes-Barre, and Cleveland had Ft. Wayne. Philadelphia had a Philadelphia farm club in the Pennsylvania State League, and when that league folded, they shifted the junior club to the Atlantic Association. The New York Giants had the first farm "system," with the New York Mets in the Atlantic Association and Syracuse in the Eastern League.

When the National Agreement was adopted in 1903, it banned the "farming out" of players, but "farming" as defined in the agreement referred only to those efforts by major league clubs to exceed the limits on players who could be optioned through subterfuge—"fake transfers" such as loans or sell/buy-back arrangements with minor league clubs where title to a player was never actually surrendered.

The independent minor league operators saw farming as a curse for two reasons. First, it reduced their autonomy and potential revenue by placing more players under major league ownership, thus reducing the majors' need to buy or draft players from the minors. Second, clubs accepting players from the majors, either openly through options or secretly, might gain an unfair competitive advantage on the field. So while in 1905 the New York Giants' request to establish a working agreement with Bridgeport was validated by the National Commission, most of the legislation was focused on restricting farming, normally by limiting the number of players who could be optioned and the number of times each player could be optioned. For example, in 1904 a rule was adopted which required a player sent out on option to stay with the minor league club for the remainder of that season. In 1907 the rule was relaxed so that a major league club could option a player and recall him, but only once in a season. In 1911 a team could have no more than eight players out on option at one time.

Working agreements became quite common during this period. The major league club furnished the minor league club with its surplus players—youngsters in need of more experience or veterans past their prime who could still strengthen a minor league club—and/or cash. In return the major league club could obtain promising players from the minor league club. During this era the formal working agreement between major and minor league clubs was usually of short duration—a year or two at most—suggesting that major league clubs targeted certain minor league clubs that had two or three players they might be interested in and established a working agreement in order to get first claim on those that developed satisfactorily. There were also informal working agreements, generally based on friendships between major and minor league club operators, and it was usually through such arrangements that the "fake transfers" banned by the National Agreement took place. In the early 1900s, for example, there was substantial traffic in players between the White Sox and Milwaukee of the American Association and between the Dodgers and Baltimore in the Eastern League. (Brewer manager Joe Cantillon was a longtime friend of Charles Comiskey, and Brooklyn manager Ned Hanlon was also a minority owner of the Orioles.)

The most efficient and only legal method of circumventing the rules relating to major league control of players was through joint ownership of major and minor league clubs. By 1912 Charles W. Somers owned Cleveland and Toledo, and Charles Ebbets owned both Brooklyn and Newark. This enabled the Indians to hold title to sixty players and the Dodgers to sixty-one. In 1913 a National Commission confidential bulletin directed major league clubs to divest their interest in minor league clubs by January 1, 1914, but neither Somers nor Ebbets complied until several years later (in fact, Somers secretly acquired New Orleans in 1913). In 1921 the joint ownership of major and minor league clubs was again permitted, and the New National Agreement, although retaining option limits, dropped the antifarming provisions that had been in it since 1903.

In 1921 the Cardinals, who had already acquired an interest in Ft. Smith of the Western Association and Houston of the Texas League, acquired a half interest in Syracuse of the International League. This was the beginning of Branch Rickey's farm system, but initially it attracted little attention as it didn't appear to represent anything particularly new. Major league clubs had long been signing young talent directly off the sandlots and developing it in the minors. In 1910, for example, Cleveland signed Roger Peckinpaugh out of the Cleveland City League, gave him a brief trial, and then optioned him to New Haven and Portland in successive seasons before recalling him when he was deemed ready for the majors. This practice had developed to the point that Mike Sexton, president of the National Association, in 1921 spoke out against the fact that the majors and higher minors had preempted the low minors' traditional role of discovering and signing young talent.

As we have seen, major league clubs had occasionally owned minor league clubs, primarily to expand the number of players under their control, but these were always higher-classification clubs, where talent was refined rather than developed. Rickey's approach was original because he was the first to assemble a system of teams at various levels or classifications. This enabled him to sign young talent and, through a hierarchy of minor league clubs, to develop and retain continuous title to a large number of players, his theory being that out of quantity comes quality. It didn't take long for the system to begin producing talent—the Cards, who had never finished higher than third in this century, won the World Series in 1926 with a team that included future Hall of Famers Jim Bottomley and Chick Hafey as well as regulars Taylor Douthit, Tommy Thevenow, Les Bell, Ray Blades, Flint Rhem, and Art Reinhardt plus reserves Watty Holm, Jake Flowers, Spec Toporcher, Ernie Vick, and Bill Hallahan—all of whom were products of a farm system that was less than seven years old. In addition, Billy Southworth was acquired from the Giants for Heinie Mueller, another product of the Cardinal farm system.

During those seven years when the Cardinals were discovering, signing, and developing unprecedented quantities of players at little expense, the other major league clubs were essentially operating as they always had, signing some players out of the amateur ranks, optioning them out for seasoning, and buying top prospects from minor league clubs, even though the new draft rules were driving the prices of such players to unprecedented levels. For example, the Yankee team the Cardinals defeated in the 1926 World Series had just one home-grown player—Lou Gehrig, who was signed out of Columbia University in 1923 and optioned to Hartford until ready. Although this had been an inexpensive acquisition, the Yankees subsequently had purchased, for $50,000 each,

Earle Combs from Louisville, Mark Koenig from St. Paul (with whom the Yankees had a working agreement), and Tony Lazzeri from Salt Lake. In 1925, the year the Pirates won the World Series, they acquired Paul Waner and Hal Rhyne from the San Francisco Seals for $100,000 and also signed Joe Cronin off the San Francisco sandlots for little more than train fare to his first assignment—Johnstown, Pennsylvania.

But the escalating prices of players and the success of the Cardinals finally encouraged other clubs to begin acquiring minor league clubs. Shortly after the Cardinals acquired the half interest in Syracuse in 1921, William Wrigley, owner of the Cubs, acquired Los Angeles of the Pacific Coast League, but he treated them virtually as separate investments. By 1927, however, major league acquisition of minor league clubs was causing concern in the minors. The first formal notice came late that year, when the American Association adopted a new Constitution which effectively prohibited major league ownership of its clubs (excluding Columbus, which was already owned by Cincinnati). At the National Association meeting in December 1928, Mike Sexton wondered aloud when the majors would own enough clubs to control the National Association. Early in 1929 major league clubs owned or controlled twenty-seven minor league clubs. At that point Judge Landis, who until then had been remarkably quiet on the issue of farm systems, opened fire. He began granting free agency to minor leaguers "covered up" by various major league organizations. Later in 1929, Landis denounced the farm system, and announced his intention of destroying it. In response, Sam Breadon, owner of the Cardinals, cited letters from seven minor leagues saying the farm system was beneficial to them. Interestingly, in 1921 Landis had said, "The object of organized baseball is to facilitate the development of skill among ball players." No one could seriously argue that this wasn't the purpose of the farm system, but by 1929 Landis was accusing Rickey and Breadon of "raping the minors," robbing smalltown America of its precious heritage of independent minor league baseball.

Through the 1930s Landis tried to make good on his threat to destroy the farm system, but since it was not contrary to baseball law, he had to pick at the edges—by levying fines against teams having an interest in more than one team in a minor league or by granting free agency to players who were "covered up" through violations of the option rules or "secret agreements." Attracting much attention in Landis's crusade was his granting of free agency to seventy-four Cardinal farmhands in 1938, and to ninety-one Detroit minor leaguers in 1940, but these shots were fired after the war was lost.

More important than the fireworks that erupted between Landis and Breadon at the 1929 major league meeting was Yankees owner Jacob Ruppert's declaration at the same meetings that no ball club could afford the prices being paid for minor league players; Ruppert added that he was "going to be forced into owning minor league clubs, and so is every other major league owner in this room." At the time he spoke, the Yankees had already purchased the Chambersburg club of the Class D Blue Ridge League. In November 1931 Ruppert purchased Newark of the International League for a reported $600,000 and soon thereafter hired Baltimore general manager George Weiss to develop a farm system. Thus the farm system, a concept that had been created largely out of necessity by Branch Rickey because the Cardinals didn't have the financial resources to compete with other clubs for top minor league prospects, had in less than a decade been embraced by the wealthiest club in baseball as being the most efficient method of acquiring talent. There would still be an occasional Joe DiMaggio or Ted Williams, signed by a minor league club and sold to the majors, but the major league club that didn't establish a farm system did so at its own peril—it cannot be coincidental that the eight teams which were the slowest to get on the bandwagon and had the thinnest farm systems in the 1930s—the Phillies, Athletics, Senators, White Sox, Giants, Cubs, Braves, and Pirates—were, aside from the Browns, the eight least successful teams in the 1940s. (The Browns and Reds established extensive farm systems in the 1930s, and overall they were the two most improved clubs of the 1940s.)

While several clubs caught on to what the Cardinals were doing, none could catch up as Rickey, taking advantage of the Depression, which had created a large pool of young men with few career options, signed players by the hundreds at tryout camps. Whereas during the 1920s the Cardinal system had only increased from three clubs to five, by 1936 it had expanded to twenty-eight teams—remarkable considering that there were only twenty-six minor leagues that year (the Cardinals had two teams each in the Nebraska State, Georgia-Florida, and Arkansas-Missouri Leagues). The Cardinal system finally topped out with thirty-three clubs in 1937—more than the two next-largest farm systems combined. Rickey's belief that out of quantity comes quality was proven on the field by the 1942 world champion Cardinals. Every player on the active roster, except for second-line pitchers Harry Gumbert and Whitey Moore, was a product of the Cardinal farm system, and Gumbert had been acquired in exchange for Cardinal farm graduate Bill McGee. In addition, the sale of players developed by the Cardinals kept the coffers full—in 1940–1941 alone, Johnny Mize, Joe Medwick, and Mickey Owen were exchanged to other clubs for $240,000 and nine players.

Thus from the perspective of the majors the farm system was a success, and the minors seemed to be flourishing—going from fourteen leagues in 1933 to forty-four by 1940. Sam Breadon, responding to another barrage of attacks by Landis in the late 1930s, claimed that the farm system had brought stability and strength to the minors, but there were other factors at work—the proliferation of night games, better promotion, and an influx of good young talent resulted in a per-club increase in attendance of 40 percent from 1937 to 1940. During that same period the portion of minor league clubs affiliated with the majors actually dropped from 61 to 46 percent. Rickey's theory that out of quantity comes quality might have had practical merit during a depression, or again immediately following World War Two when there was an influx of returning veterans. However, under normal circumstances huge farm systems were not cost-effective. While the minors were still expanding in the late 1930s, the Cardinals began pruning back their farm system of more than thirty teams; again while the minors were expanding in the late 1940s, farm systems were contracting—in

1948 there were six farm systems of twenty or more teams; by 1951 there were none. The portion of minor league teams affiliated with major league teams dropped from 62 percent in 1946 to 47 percent in 1951 as major league farm systems collectively dropped from 280 to 175 clubs and outright major league ownership of minor league clubs dropped from 125 to 75.

In 1950 there were 232 minor league teams not affiliated with the majors. This was the highest number of independent teams in organized baseball since the early teens. Nine of the fifty-eight leagues had no teams with major league affiliations, and more than a dozen others had only one or two affiliates. These leagues operated virtually outside the player-development chain, existing much as a semipro team or league does—to provide entertainment and reflect civic pride. Their only source of revenue was through the turnstiles, and just as forty years earlier automobiles and the movies helped drive out the marginal teams and leagues, now TV did the same. This can be clearly seen as the heavily populated Northeast, the first region to be heavily penetrated by television, suffered the first wave of league failures.

Over the next few years, attendance declined sharply, most of the independent clubs folded, and farm systems continued to contract. In 1956 the majors established a "stabilization fund" of $500,000 to aid clubs and leagues in lower classifications, but the free-fall of leagues, clubs, and attendance continued. In 1959 the majors discontinued the stabilization fund and established a fund of $1 million to finance a player-development and promotional program for the minors. In 1962 the majors and minors adopted the Player Development Plan that, by requiring each major league club to have five farm teams, would guarantee the operation of at least one-hundred minor league teams, which the majors felt was adequate for their player-development purposes. The plan also included the Player Development Contract under the terms of which the parent major league club became responsible for all spring training costs and all or most of the salaries of players, managers, and coaches. After major league expansion in 1969, major league clubs were only required to support four farm clubs each, but their financial support

of each was increased. By 1976 there were only 106 minor league teams with major league affiliations, the lowest peacetime total since 1935. American League expansion the following year created the need for additional minor league affiliates, and in subsequent years major league clubs expanded their farm systems—all of them back up to a minimum of five clubs by 1984. With the dramatic increase in minor league attendance and the resulting increase in the value of franchises in the 1980s, a new Professional Baseball Agreement was ratified by the majors and minors in 1990 that required the minors to assume a greater share of operational expenses but the majors continued to pay the salaries and meal money of all uniformed personnel (including umpires). And farm systems continued to grow—by 1994 each major league club had at least six farm clubs and the number of minor league teams with major league affiliations was up to 195 (including 21 in the Dominican Rookie League), the highest total since 1950.

In 1928 Mike Sexton had asked how long it would be before the majors owned enough minor league clubs to control the National Association. Other than during World War Two, when the minors were severely constricted, major league clubs never have "owned" more than 28 percent of the minor league clubs; however, possibly as early as 1934, probably by 1935, and certainly by 1936, the majors through outright ownership, working agreements, or other interlocking devices "controlled" the National Association, and this situation was generally acknowledged throughout baseball by 1938.

Until about 1960 there was still some room in the National Association for independent clubs and career minor league players, but since then the minors have existed almost exclusively to develop talent for the majors. While this has dismayed many minor league fans and traditionalists, it should be remembered that the principal role of the minors within organized baseball has always been to develop talent for the majors, and to receive money in exchange. The farm system, which owed its success in no small part to the greed of some minor league operators, was merely a different device by which talent moved to the majors and money moved to the minors.

Minor Leagues

Year	Leagues Started	Didn't Finish	Year	Leagues Started	Didn't Finish	Year	Leagues Started	Didn't Finish	Year	Leagues Started	Didn't Finish	Year	Leagues Started	Didn't Finish	Year	Leagues Started	Didn't Finish
1883	2		1902	17	2	1921	26		1940	44	1	1959	21		1977	19	
1884	7	3	1903	20		1922	30	2	1941	41		1960	22		1978	18	
1885	8	3	1904	24	2	1923	31	3	1942	31	5	1961	22		1979	18	1
1886	11	3	1905	32	5	1924	29	4	1943	10	1	1962	20		1980	17	
1887	15	6	1906	33	3	1925	25	3	1944	10		1963	18		1981	17	
1888	17	9	1907	37	4	1926	30	4	1945	12		1964	20		1982	17	
1889	15	5	1908	40	11	1927	24		1946	43	1	1965	19		1983	17	
1890	18	9	1909	34	4	1928	31	3	1947	52		1966	19		1984	17	
1891	13	5	1910	51	6	1929	26	2	1948	58		1967	19		1985	18	
1892	14	10	1911	51	10	1930	23	2	1949	59		1968	20		1986	17	
1893	7	4	1912	47	11	1931	19	3	1950	58	1	1969	21		1987	18	
1894	8	2	1913	42	4	1932	19	4	1951	50	1	1970	21		1988	19	
1895	17	9	1914	43	6	1933	14		1952	43		1971	20		1989	19	
1896	15	8	1915	33	8	1934	20	1	1953	38		1972	19		1990	19	
1897	20	8	1916	27	6	1935	21		1954	36	3	1973	18		1991	19	
1898	20	11	1917	21	9	1936	26		1955	33		1974	18		1992	19	
1899	14	5	1918	10	9	1937	37		1956	28		1975	18		1993	19	
1900	15	6	1919	15	1	1938	37		1957	28		1976	20		1994	19	
1901	13	2	1920	22	1	1939	41		1958	24							

Minor League Career Records

Batters	Years	G	AB	R	H	2B	3B	HR	RBI	SB	AVG
Buzz Arlett	1918–37	2390	8001	1610	2726	598	107	432	1786	200	.341
Ike Boone	1920–37	1857	6807	1362	2521	477	128	215	1334	120	.370
Bunny Brief	1910–28	2426	8945	1776	2963	594	152	340	1776	247	.331
Nick Cullop	1920–44	2484	8571	1607	2670	523	147	420	1857	154	.312
Ox Eckhardt	1925–40	1926	7563	1275	2773	455	146	66	1037	140	.367
Hector Espino	1960–84	2500	8605	1597	2898	403	49	484	1678	54	.337
Ray French	1914–41	3278	12174	1769	3254	590	129	46	1029	363	.267
Spencer Harris	1921–48	3258	11377	2287	3617	743	150	258	1769	241	.318
Joe Hauser	1918–42	1854	6426	1430	1923	340	116	399	1353	109	.299
Smead Jolley	1922–41	2231	8298	1455	3037	633	78	336	1593	61	.366
Jigger Statz	1920–42	2790	10657	1996	3356	595	137	66	1044	466	.315
Perry Werden	1884–1908	1539	6233	1214	2124	392	87	169	—	350	.341

Pitchers	Years	G	IP	W	L	H	R	ER	BB	SO	ERA
Bill Bailey	1906–25	578	3730	242	219	3452	1572	612	1565	2375	2.87
Dick Barrett	1925–53	790	4961	325	257	4572	2170	1747	2096	2512	3.34
George Boehler	1911–30	562	3711	248	202	3421	1745	874	1464	2319	3.74
George Brunet	1953–85	668	4041	244	242	3761	1832	1466	1754	3175	3.27
Tony Freitas	1928–53	736	4905	342	238	5090	2073	1694	932	2324	3.11
Sam Gibson	1923–49	661	4469	307	200	4460	1860	1413	1073	2195	3.08
Willie Mains	1887–1906	545	4014	318	179	4399	2417	—	1280	1669	
Joe Martina	1910–31	833	5417	349	277	4950	2307	1355	1868	2770	3.22
Frank Shellenback	1917–38	638	4514	315	192	4922	2110	1775	1021	1742	3.55
Bill Thomas	1926–52	1016	5995	383	347	6721	3098	2211	1230	2204	3.71
Hal Turpin	1927–46	635	4084	271	203	4512	1917	1367	807	1254	3.28

Major League Farm Systems
1936–1969

	36	37	38	39	40	41	42	43	44	45	46	47	48	49	50	51	52	53	54	55	56	57	58	59	60	61	62	63	64	65	66	67	68	69
Boston, AL	9	10	7	8	6	7	6	3	5	4	12	15	15	11	8	8	6	6	6	6	5	7	7	6	6	6	5	5	5	6	5	6	6	
Chicago, AL	5	4	10	8	6	5	5	0	0	0	17	12	15	9	8	8	8	6	8	6	6	5	6	6	6	6	6	5	5	5	6	6	6	6
Cleveland, AL	5	7	13	16	8	9	8	3	3	3	11	18	20	20	16	12	10	8	8	9	9	8	8	7	5	6	5	4	4	4	4	5	5	
Detroit, AL	11	8	12	7	5	11	8	2	3	2	7	11	16	14	9	8	7	7	8	10	9	8	10	7	8	8	6	6	5	5	5	5	6	6
New York, AL	11	15	15	15	14	12	9	5	5	5	15	22	24	22	15	14	10	11	9	10	11	10	10	8	8	7	7	6	5	7	7	6	6	
Phila.-K.C.- Oakland, AL	5	3	3	3	4	5	3	2	2	4	7	15	10	11	9	8	8	6	7	9	8	8	8	8	6	5	5	6	6	6	6	6	5	
St. Louis- Baltimore, AL	3	15	16	12	11	11	6	1	3	3	11	15	20	18	13	10	12	10	12	8	9	8	9	7	7	9	6	6	7	6	6	6	
Wash.-Minnesota, AL	1	5	2	8	4	6	3	1	2	2	5	7	12	9	10	6	8	7	8	7	6	8	8	7	6	7	7	7	6	8	8	8	8	8
Milwaukee- Atlanta, NL	4	6	6	6	5	4	4	1	1	2	13	15	11	8	8	12	11	10	10	12	15	14	12	10	9	8	7	6	5	6	7	5	4	
Brklyn.-Los Angeles, NL	5	14	14	11	18	14	10	4	7	9	21	25	26	26	22	19	17	15	15	16	14	13	12	12	12	11	9	7	8	6	6	6	6	
Chicago, NL	5	6	5	2	2	9	11	4	6	7	18	23	19	16	15	14	10	9	9	8	8	10	8	6	6	6	5	5	5	6	6	5	5	
Cincinnati, NL	16	10	10	10	8	8	5	2	1	3	4	8	11	10	7	4	9	9	9	11	11	8	8	6	5	5	5	4	5	5	5	
N.Y.-San Francisco, NL	2	11	4	5	6	7	7	3	5	8	16	19	22	19	18	14	13	9	9	10	10	10	8	9	7	7	6	6	6	5	6		
Philadelphia, NL	1	2	3	3	8	3	2	1	3	5	9	11	15	14	12	11	11	9	9	8	8	9	9	7	10	8	7	6	6	7	7	6	6	
Pittsburgh, NL	4	5	7	7	9	8	7	4	4	4	13	14	19	13	13	11	15	11	10	13	13	10	11	9	7	7	7	6	6	6	6	6	6	
St. Louis, NL	28	33	32	28	29	25	22	6	7	7	18	19	22	20	21	16	15	16	22	18	15	11	14	12	9	8	6	5	5	6	7	7	
L.A.-California, AL																										2	4	6	6	5	5	5	5	
Washington, AL																										2	4	4	4	4	4	5	5	
Houston, NL																										2	4	5	5	6	6	5	6	
New York, NL																										3	4	5	4	4	6	6	5	
Kansas City, AL																																	7	
Seattle, AL																																	4	
Montreal, NL																																	3	
San Diego, NL																																	4	

Annual Overall Minor League Pitching Percentage Leader (20 or more decisions)

Year	Player	Team (League)	W–L	Pct.	Overall W–L	Pct.	Year	Player	Team (League)	W–L	Pct.	Overall W–L	Pct.
1900	Willie Mains	Rome (N.Y. St.)	27–5	.844			1915	Booth Hopper	Minneapolis (A.A.)	18–3	.857		
1901	Henry Allemang	Little Rock (So. Assn.)	20–4	.833			1916	Howard Ehmke	Syracuse (N.Y. St.)	31–7	.816		
1902	Louis Bruce	Toronto (Eastern)	18–2	.900			1917	John Verbout	Wilkes-Barre (N.Y. St.)	26–7	.788		
1903	Ernest Nichols	Spokane (Pac. Nat.)	20–4	.833			1918	John Beckvermit	Binghamton (Int.)	17–4	.810		
1904	Ed Craig	Springfield (Mo. Valley)	19–4	.826			1919	C. A. (Chief) Bender	Richmond (Va.)	29–2	.935		
1905	Fred Steele	Oskaloosa (Iowa St.)	18–3	.857									
1906	Frank Dick	Marshalltown (Iowa St.)	18–3	.857			1920	George Carmen	London (Mich.,-Ont.)	26–2	.926		
1907	Harley Young	Wichita (West. Assn.)	29–4	.879			1921	Earl Keiser	Mitchell (Dakota)	20–2			
1908	Harry Gaspar	Waterloo (Cent. Assn.)	32–4	.889					Oakland (PCL)	3–0		23–2	.920
1909	Ray Fisher	Hartford (Conn.)	24–5	.828			1922	Byrd Hodges	Joplin (West. Assn.)	26–3	.897		
1910	Cyrus Dahlgren	Superior (Minn.-Wis.)	22–3	.880			1923	Emil Levsen	Cedar Rapids (Miss. Val.)	19–4	.826		
1911	Howard Northrop	Reading (Inter.-St.)	27–4	.871			1924	Carl Dunagan	Dyersburg (Kitty)	19–2	.905		
1912	Larue Kirby	Traverse City (Mich. St.)	18–3	.857			1925	Lloyd Brown	Ardmore-Western Assn.	17–1	.944*		
1913	Ralph Bell	Winona (Northern)	28–6	.824			1926	Frank Tubbs	Port Huron (Mich.-Ont.)	8–1			
1914	Joe Chabek	Harrisburg (Tri-St.)	28–3	.903					Port Huron (Mich. St.)	8–0			

	Oklahoma City (Western)	9–2	25–3	.893
1927 Ben Cantwell	Jacksonville (So'east.)	25–5	.833	
1928 Paul Fittery	Carrollton (Ga.-Ala.)	21–2	.913	
1929 Andrew Bednar	McCook (Neb. St.)	21–4	.840	
1930 Jim Cameron	McCook (Neb. St.)	19–2	.905	
1931 Lyle (Bud) Tinning	Minneapolis (A.A.)	1–2		
	Des Moines (West. Assn.)	24–2	25–4	.862
1932 Marvin Duke	Erie (Central)	23–4	.852	
1933 Al Piechota	Davenport (Miss. Val.)	19–4	.826	
1934 Fay Thomas	Los Angeles (PCL)	28–4	.875	
1935 Lloyd Sterling	Winnipeg (Northern)	24–2	.923	
1936 Bill Yocke	Akron (Mid. Atl.)	1–2		
	Norfolk (Piedmont)	18–1	19–3	.864
1937 Joe Kohlman	Salisbury (E. Shore)	25–1	.962	
1938 Paige Dennis	Thomasville (N.C. St.)	28–2	.933	
1939 Charles Wensloff	Joplin (West. Assn.)	26–4	.867	
1940 Arthur Cyrolewski	Johnson City (App.)	20–3	.870	
Mervin Hensley	La Crosse (Wis. St.)	20–3	.870	
1941 Frank Marino	Macon (Sally)	19–1	.950	
1942 Paul Minner	Elizabethton (App.)	18–2		
	Knoxville (So. Assn.)	1–0	19–2	.905
1943 Irvin Stein	Portsmouth (Piedmont)	24–6	.800	
1944 Pete Naktenis	Hartford (Eastern)	18–3	.857	
1945 Lewis Carpenter	Atlanta (So. Assn.)	22–2	.917	
1946 Bill Kennedy	Rocky Mount (C. Plain)	28–3	.903	
1947 Chris VanCuyk	Cambridge (E. Shore)	25–2	.926	
1948 Albert Tefft	Blackstone (Va.)	20–1	.952	
1949 Lynn Southworth	Thomasville (N.C. St.)	21–1	.955	
1950 Mike Hudak	Big Stone Gap (Mt. St.)	19–2	.905	
1951 Anderson Bush	Hagerstown (Int. St.)	22–3	.880	
1952 Russell Harris	Ozark (Ala.-Fla.)	27–3	.900	
1953 Steve Kraly	Binghamton (Eastern)	19–2	.905	
1954 Don Vaughn	Merryville-Morristown (Mt. St.)	11–1	20–2	.909
	Highpoint-Thomasville (Carolina)	0–0		
	Vidalia (Ga. St.)	9–1		
1955 Jim Grant	Keokuk (I-I-I)	19–3	.864	
1956 Francisco Ramirez	Mexico City Reds (Mex.)	20–3	.870	
1957 Bob Riesner	Alexandria (Evang.)	20–0		
	New Orleans (So. Assn.)	0–2	20–2	.909
1958 Jerry Walker	Knoxville (Sally)	18–4	.818	
Art Henriksen	St. Petersburg (Fla. St.)	17–3		
	New Orleans (So. Assn.)	0–1	18–4	.818
1959 Les Bass	Boise (Pioneer)	21–3	.875	
1960 Tom Haake	Grand Forks (Northern)	0–1		
	Dubuque (Midwest)	19–3	19–4	.826
1961 David Seeman	Selma (Ala.-Fla.)	17–3		
	Burlington (Carolina)	7–0	24–3	.889
1962 Bob Schmidt	Modesto (Calif.)	0–0		
	Jamestown (NYP)	17–3	17–3	.850
1963 Bob Lee	Batavia (NYP)	20–2		

	Asheville (Sally)	1–1	21–3	.875
1964 Ed Watt	Aberdeen (Northern)	14–1		
	Elmira (Eastern)	3–1	17–2	.895**
1965 Billy MacLeod	Pittsfield (Eastern)	18–0	1.000†	
1966 Bob Snow	Winston-Salem (Carolina)	20–2	.909	
1967 John Parker	Spartanburg (W. Car.)	17–3	.850	
1968 Pablo Montes De Oca	Campeche (Mex. S.E.)	21–4	.840	
1969 Don Eddy	Appleton (Midwest)	18–3	.857	
1970 Jim Flynn	Albuquerque (Texas)	19–4	.826	
1971 Rich Gossage	Appleton (Midwest)	18–2	.900	
1972 Andres Ayon	Saltillo (Mexican)	22–3	.880	
1973 Silvano Quezada	Tampico (Mexican)	22–2	.917	
1974 Bob Knepper	Fresno (Calif.)	20–5	.800	
1975 Jerry Garvin	Reno (Calif.)	17–5	.773	
1976 Enrique Romo	Mexico City Reds (Mexican)	20–4	.833	
1977 Mike Chris	Lakeland (Fla. St.)	18–5	.783	
1978 Tomas Armas	Saltillo (Mexican)	22–4	.846	
1979 Miguel Solis	Saltillo (Mexican)	25–5	.833	
1980 Gene Nelson	Ft. Lauderdale (Fla. St.)	18–3	.870	
1981 Ted Power	Albuquerque (PCL)	18–3	.857	
1982 Mike Warren	Stockton-Modesto (Calif.)	19–4	.826	
1983 Alfonso Pulido	Mexico City Reds (Mexican)	17–3	.850	
1984 Mike Bielecki	Hawaii (PCL)	19–3	.864	
1985 Eleazar Beltran	Tampico (Mexican)	18–3	.857	
1986 George Ferran	Shreveport (Texas)	16–1	.941‡	
1987 Bob Faron	Springfield (Midwest)	19–2	.905	
1988 Jimmy Rodgers	Myrtle Beach (So. Atl.)	18–4	.818	
1989 Royal Clayton	Albany (Eastern)	16–4	.800	
1989 Mercedes Esquer	Yucatan (Mexican)	16–4	.800	
1989 Walt Trice	Osceola (Fla. St.)	16–4	.800	
1990 Randy Marshall	Fayetteville (So. Atl.)	13–0	1.000	
	Lakeland (Fla. St.)	7–2	20–2	.909
1991 Jose Martinez	Columbus (So. Atl.)	20–4	.833	
1992 John Fritz	Quad Cities (Midwest)	20–4	.833	
1993 John Dettmer	Charlotte (Fla. St.)	16–3	.842	
Ryan Karp	Albany (Eastern)	0–0		
	Prince William (Carolina)	3–2		
	Greensboro (So. Atl.)	13–1	.842	
1994 Francisco Montana	Monclova (Mexican)	19–1	.950	

*Adding 2 losses to Brown's record giving him 20 decisions yields a .850 percent, better than John Schmutte, Johnstown Middle Atlantic, 19–4, .822
**Adding 1 loss to Watt's record, giving him 20 decisions, yields an .850 percentage, better than Dave Leonhard, Aberdeen (Northern), 16–4 .800
†Adding 2 losses to MacLeod's record, giving him 20 decisions, yields a .900 percentage, better than Dave Leonhard, Elmira (Eastern), 20–5 .800
‡Adding 3 losses to Ferran's record, giving him 20 decisions, yields an .800 percentage, better than Kevin Armstrong, Columbia (Sally), 17–5 .773

Annual Overall Minor League Batting Leader (400 or more at-bats)

Year	Player	Team (League)	G	AB	R	H	2B	3B	HR	RBI	SB	AVG.
1900	Kitty Bransfield	Worcester (Eastern)	122	501	115*	186*	30	8	17	—	40	.371*
1901	Frank Huelsman	Shreveport (So. Assn.)	121*	487	98	191*	31	10	9	—	15	.392*
1902	Emil Frisk	Denver (Western)	123	450	89	168	22	22	14*	—	20	.373*
1903	Frank Huelsman	Spokane (Pac. Int.)	98	418	89	160	35	11	6	—	14	.392*
1904	Billy Hamilton	Haverhill (New Eng.)	113	408	113*	168*	32	8	0	—	74*	.412*
1905	Charlie Hemphill	St. Paul (A. A.)	145	560	122	204*	38	12	5	—	40	.364*
1906	Mike Welday	Des Moines (Western)	129	549	93	197	—	—	—	—	31	.359
1907	Ed Householder	Aberdeen (Northwest)	127	499	64	173	30*	19	9	—	19	.347*
1908	Ward Miller	Wausau (Wis.-Ill.)	124	408	91*	156*	—	—	—	—	—	.382*
1909	Harry Welch	Omaha (Western)	151	527	81	196*	41	15	7	—	51	.372*
1910	Dave Callahan	Eau Claire (Minn.-Wis.)	126	460	92*	168*	25	17*	2	—	52	.365*
1911	Frank Huelsman	Great Falls (U.A.)	135	516	117	212	48	15	17*	125*	25	.411*
1912	Charlie Johnson	Trenton (Tri-State)	109	400	86	161	31	5	14	—	22	.403*
1913	Frank Huelsman	Salt Lake City (U.A.)	122	473	123*	200*	36*	20*	22*	126*	16	.423*
1914	Joe Harris	Bay City (So. Michigan)	139	510	135	197*	39	22*	10	—	42	.386*
1915	Big Bill Kay	Binghamton (N.Y. St.)	125	447	98*	169*	22	25*	7	—	35	.378*
1916	Hank Butcher	Denver (Western)	145	541	116	204	31	20*	15	—	32	.377*
1917	Nap Lajoie	Toronto (Int.)	151	581	83	221*	39*	4	5	—	4	.380*
1918	Polly McLarry	Shreveport (Texas)	29	84	12	24	3	1	1	—	6	.286
		Binghamton (Int.)	103	335	51	129	26	7	4	—	15	.385*
											overall	.365
1919	Joe Wilhoit	Seattle (PCL)	17	67	8	11	1	0	0	—	3	.164
		Wichita (Western)	128	526	126*	222*	41	10	7	—	13	.422*
											overall	.393
1920	Merwyn Jacobson	Baltimore (Int.)	154*	581	161*	235*	35	16*	7	—	18	.404*
1921	Jack Lelivelt	Omaha (Western)	166	659	149	274*	70*	9	14	—	24	.416*
1922	Jack Schaefer	London (Mich.-Ont.)	100	407	79	167	27	21	9	—	9	.410*
1923	Moses Solomon	Hutchinson (So'west.)	134	527	143*	222*	40*	15	49*	—	12	.421*
1924	T. P. Osborne	Mt. Pleasant (E. Tex.)	101	396	93	171*	48	3	23	—	46*	.432*[1]
1925	Paul Waner	San Francisco (PCL)	174	599	167	280	75*	7	11	130	8	.401*
1926	Bill Diester	Salina (So'west.)	106	428	110*	190*	33*	4	27	—	10	.444*
		Tulsa (Western)	11	44	5	15	4	0	0	—	0	.341
											overall	.434
1927	Elton Langford	Des Moines (Western)	149	611	132	250	47	28*	8	—	31	.409*

Year	Player	Team (League)	G	AB	R	H	2B	3B	HR	RBI	SB	AVG
1928	Danny Boone	High Point (Piedmont)	128	468	123	**196***	40	11	**38***	**131***	11	**.419***
1929	Ed Kallina	Midland(W. Tex.)	94	367	126	159	28	7	**44***	—	16	**.433***
		Sherman (Lone Star)	17	64	22	22	—	—	6	—	1	.344
		overall										.420
1930	Tony Antista	Bisbee (Arizona St.)	**109***	444	**127***	**191***	36	**16***	17	100	18	**.430***
1931	Babe Phelps	Youngstown (Mid-Atl.)	115	436	71	178	29	9	15	88	9	**.408***
1932	George Puccinelli	Rochester (Int.)	133	478	102	187	34	8	28	115	2	**.391***
1933	Ox Eckhardt	Mission (PCL)	**189***	760	145	**315***	56	16	12	143	15	**.414***
1934	Frank Demaree	Los Angeles (PCL)	186	702	**190***	**269***	**51***	4	**45***	**173***	41	**.383***
1935	Ox Eckhardt	Mission (PCL)	172	710	149	**283***	40	11	2	114	8	**.399***
1936	Cal Lahman	Jamestown (Northern)	127	466	**154***	**182***	30	9	**48***	**162***	20	**.391***
1937	Earl (Red) Martin	Beckley (Mt. St.)	91	360	80	144	**39***	**14***	8	**96***	7	**.400***
		Scranton (NYP)	11	41	7	10	1	0	0	4	1	.244
		overall										.384
1938	Murray Franklin	Beckley (Mt. St.)	94	385	91	169	31	**13***	**26***	110	13	**.439***[2]
1939	Joe Schmidt	Duluth (Northern)	120	440	**114***	**194***	29	9	**31***	**133***	17	**.441***
1940	Ed Schweda	Lubbock (W. Tex.-N.M.)	114	469	142	198	39	15	11	118	7	**.422***
1941	Lew Flick	Elizabethton (App.)	117	**502***	**127***	**210***	**37***	13	5	**116***	20	**.418***
1942	Don Manno	Welch (Mt. St.)	117	457	**136***	**174***	32	**14***	**34***	**122***	23	**.381***
1943	George Kell	Lancaster (Inter-St.)	138	555	**120***	**220***	33	**23***	5	79	14	**.396***
1944	Roland Gladu	Hartford (Eastern)	119	417	92	155	28	14	7	102	8	.372
1945	Arden (Cotton) McCaskey	Bristol (App.)	106	437	72	**164***	**26***	**14***	2	96	5	**.375***
1946	Walt Forwood	Carbondale (N. Atl.)	111	419	98	**170***	**43***	7	3	101	22	**.406***
1947	Jim Prince	Midland (Longhorn)	108	415	111	178	31	6	34	141	4	**.429***
		Lubbock (W. Tex.-N.M.)	12	37	7	10	3	0	1	12	0	.270
		overall										.416
1948	Hershel Martin	Albuquerque (W. Tex.-N.M.)	132	447	133	190	**61***	6	18	128	5	**.425***
1949	Bob Montag	Pawtucket (New Eng.)	125	454	**139***	**192***	36	**18***	**21***	91	**43***	**.423***
1950	Oscar Sierra	Hornell (Pony)	93	358	99	151	28	2	21	114	12	**.422***
		Newport News (Piedmont)	15	45	5	13	1	0	0	5	0	.289
		overall										.407
1951	D. C. (Pud) Miller	Hickory (N.C. St.)	119	426	115	181	32	1	**40***	**136***	2	**.425***
1952	Don Stafford	Salisbury (N.C. St.)	105	392	99	160	31	3	18	90	1	**.408***[3]
1953	Russ Snyder	McAlester (Sooner St.)	138	556	137	**240***	32	16	2	84	**74***	**.432***
1954	Neal Cobb	Crestview (Ala.-Fla.)	115	435	108	188	27	8	5	124	3	**.432***
1955	Tom Jordan	Artesia (Longhorn)	136	543	116	**221***	**69***	2	28	**159***	4	**.407***
1956	Len Tucker	Pampa (So'west)	140	565	**181***	228	40	13	51	181	**47***	**404***
1957	Fran Boniar	Reno (Calif.)	110	443	102	193	33	15	11	**138***	4	**.436***
		Pueblo (Western)	11	37	5	9	1	0	0	7	3	.243
		overall										.421
1958	Neb Wilson	Ft. Walton Beach-Pensacola (Ala.-Fla.)	119	409	**102***	162	**38***	3	**24***	**106***	3	**.396***
1959	Tom Hamilton	St. Petersburg (Fla. St.)	125	401	109	155	20	3	**20***	96	3	**.387***
1960	Al Pinkston	Mexico City Reds (Mexican)	138	567	110	**225***	41	11	26	**144***	4	**.397***
1961	Al Pinkston	Vera Cruz (Mexican)	109	406	79	152	**26***	4	13	86	4	**.374***
1962	Ramiro Caballero	Guanajuato (Mex. Center)	113	423	123	**175***	25	0	**59***	170	3	**.414***
1963	Vinicio Garcia	Monterrey (Mexican)	122	475	**107***	175	**36***	5	21	88	3	**.368***
1964	Ramiro Caballero	Leon (Mex. Center)	121	460	**135***	**175***	29	1	**35***	**145***	3	**.380***
1965	Alfonso Peciado	Guanajuato (Mex. Center)	130	529	103	**224***	**48***	**14***	11	147	11	**.423***
1966	Heriberto Vargas	Vera Cruz (Mexican)	7	14	0	3	0	0	0	0	0	.214
		Guanajuato (Mex. Center)	127	481	**168***	214	33	1	**55***	**174***	3	**.445***
		overall										.438
1967	Hilario Pena	Campeche (Mex. S.E.)	102	404	60	159	61	3	1	49	9	**.394***
1968	Jim Hicks	Tulsa (PCL)	117	407	**100***	149	32	7	23	85	14	**.366***
1969	Bernie Carbo	Indianapolis (A.A.)	111	404	83	145	37	2	21	76	7	**.359***
1970	Miguel Suarez	Tampico (Mex. Center)	126	460	105	**181***	**37***	4	14	101	15	**.393***
1971	Téolindo Acosta	Puebla (Mexican)	133	441	75	173	22	11	7	71	17	**.392***
1972	Don Anderson	Jalisco (Mexican)	130	445	76	161	31	2	8	68	0	**.362***
1973	Hector Espino	Tampico (Mexican)	116	422	82	159	20	2	22	**107***	3	**.377***
1974	Téolindo Acosta	Puebla (Mexican)	122	464	**93***	**170***	17	6	2	43	20	**.366***
1975	Gene Richards	Reno (Calif.)	134	**501***	**148***	**191***	29	10	12	58	**85***	**.381***
1976	Pat Putnam	Asheville (W. Car.)	138	538	100	**194***	**33***	3	**24***	**142***	8	**.361***
1977	Rudy Law	Lodi (California)	122	451	124	174	22	5	9	88	37	**.386***
1978	Champ Summers	Indianapolis (A.A.)	132	462	98	**170***	25	5	**34***	**124***	11	.368
1979	Jimmie Collins	Chihuahua (Mexican)	124	470	95	**206***	35	10	6	60	33	**.438***
1980	Jimmie Collins	Chihuahua (Mex. #1)	91	346	62	131	19	13	4	52	19	.379
		Saltillo (Mex. #2)	39	137	25	**52***	8	**3***	2	**31***	5	.380
		overall										.379
1981	Kent Hrbek	Visalia (Calif.)	121	462	119	175	25	5	27	111	12	**.379***
1982	Randy Ready	El Paso (Texas)	132	475	**122***	**178***	33	5	20	99	13	**.375***
1983	Chris Smith	Phoenix (PCL)	123	449	88	170	31	5	21	102	4	**379***
1984	Jimmie Collins	Mexico City Reds-Cordoba (Mexican)	109	403	81	166	35	4	6	59	12	**.412***
1985	Oswaldo Olivares	Aguas.-Campeche (Mexican)	110	441	85	**175***	22	**14***	5	49	20	**.397***
1986	Willie Aikens	Puebla (Mexican)	129	445	134	**202***	38	3	46	**154***	0	**.454***
1987	Orlando Sanchez	Puebla (Mexican)	123	439	95	182	34	1	25	115	6	**.415***
1988	Nelson Barrera	Mexico City Reds (Mexican)	129	460	90	171	26	0	31	**124***	7	**.372***
1989	Willie Aikens	León (Mexican)	128	423	**108***	167	40	1	37	**131***	1	**.395***
1990	Trench Davis	Saltillo (Mexican)	127	498	84	**189***	33	4	5	50	20	.380
1991	Rich Renteria	Jalisco (Mexican)	104	382	90	169	30	6	24	106	17	**.442***
		Indianapolis (A.A.)	20	72	6	17	5	0	1	5	0	.236
		overall										.410
1992	Raul Perez Tovar	Monclova (Mexican)	129	483	83	201	32	5	8	93	14	**.416***
1993	Nelson Simmons	Jalisco (Mexican)	109	369	81	141	27	0	34	95	1	.382
		Palm Springs (California)	20	76	13	25	8	0	5	23	0	.329
1994	Brian Hunter	Tucson (PCL)	128	513	113	191	28	9	10	51	49	.372

*Led league in category

[1]If charged with 400 at-bats, Osborne's average would be .428, higher than any player with 400 or more at-bats.
(George Rhinehardt, Greenville (Sally) G: 120, AB: 495, R: 110*, H: 200*, 2B: 45*, 3B: 18, HR: 8, RBI: 92, SB: 32*, AVG: .404*)

[2]If charged with 400 at-bats, Franklin's average would be .423, higher than any player with 400 or more at-bats.
(Butch Moran, Rogers (Ark.-Mo.) G: 105, AB: 406, R: 107, H: 159, 2B: 43*, 3B: 12, HR: 22*, RBI: 114, SB: 8, AVG: .392*)

[3]If charged with 400 at-bats, Stafford's average would be .400, higher than any player with 400 or more at-bats.
(Clint McCord, Clinton (Miss. Ohio Val.) G:119, AB: 482, R: 123, H: 189*, 2B: 40, 3B: 15, HR: 15, RBI: 109, SB: 20, AVG: .392*)

## CHAPTER 19

Japanese Baseball

Yoichi Nagata and John B. Holway

Just when baseball arrived in Japan, and who introduced it, is not clear. Horace Wilson, a professor in Tokyo in the 1870s, is one of those credited with being the Abner Doubleday of Japan, teaching baseball to students who ran bases and flagged grounders in *geta,* or wooden clogs. They named it *yakyu* (yok-yoo')—field ball—or *beisu boru*. In 1908, the University of Washington team, the first American college team to visit Japan, won six games but lost four games to Japanese colleges.

In 1913 the Chicago White Sox and New York Giants stopped in Japan on a round-the-world tour, playing three games with Japanese college teams. In 1922 a big league All-Star team, including Casey Stengel, also sailed into Yokohama harbor. And in 1928 Ty Cobb himself went over to teach the Japanese his batting secrets.

By 1930 *yakyu* began to rival *sumo* as the Japanese national pastime. The two games still tug in opposite directions at the nation's sports psyche, the one traditional and native, the other newer and outward-looking, but baseball has far outdistanced *sumo* as the nation's most popular sport.

The game thrived in schools and colleges. In fact, scholastic baseball still has a grip on the fans, like college football in America, high school basketball in Indiana, or the Final Four of the NCAA basketball tourney. Japan's annual national high school tournaments in Osaka every March and August fill huge Koshien Stadium for two weeks and command dawn-to-dusk TV coverage.

Japan's first professional team, the Nihon Undo Kyokai (Japan Athletic Association), was formed in 1920, which was followed by a second club, somewhat like the U.S. Harlem Globetrotters. When the great earthquake of 1923 hit the Tokyo metropolitan area, the NUK was forced to disband. The next year the Hankyu Railway reorganized former NUK players into a third pro club, the Takarazuka Kyokai. However, those teams couldn't survive because of a lack of competition.

In the fall of 1931, Lou Gehrig, Lefty Grove, Frankie Frisch, and Lefty O'Doul arrived for a tour. Several black teams visited Japan in the 1920s and in 1932, with stars such as Bullet Joe Rogan and Biz Mackey, who later became Roy Campanella's mentor.

Japanese baseball reached a watershed in 1934 with the arrival of Babe Ruth, Gehrig, Jimmy Foxx, Al Simmons, Charlie Gehringer, and Lefty Gomez. Matsutaro Shoriki, owner of the Yomiuri newspapers, sponsored the tour and would become the great genius–father figure of professional baseball there. Ruth and the others, soon to receive plaques in Cooperstown, played sixteen games and easily won fifteen of them. Ruth hit thirteen home runs and

clowned in right field, holding an umbrella, while Gehrig played first base in galoshes. But they weren't clowning when a high school boy, Eiji Sawamura, almost shut them out, whiffing Gehringer, Ruth, Gehrig, and Foxx in succession before losing 1–0. Sawamura became, and still is, a national hero, especially on his death, at twenty-six, in World War Two.

Shoriki signed a professional, Osamu Mihara (later famous as the "Magic Manager"), to his All-Japan team to oppose Ruth, although the Japanese looked down on professional sports as "unpure." At the end of the year he formed an all-pro team, Dai-Nippon (Greater Japan), with Sawamura, Mihara, the White Russian Vic Starffin, and others. They toured the United States the next year and would become the present-day Yomiuri (Tokyo) Giants (*Kyojin*), a nickname hung on them by O'Doul. Shoriki urged other businesses to form pro teams and by 1936 formed the country's first professional league, the Japan Pro-Baseball League.

World War Two interrupted baseball. American words, such as *out* and *safe*, became *hi-ké* (withdraw) and *yoshi* (good), etc., and Japanese soldiers shouted, "To hell with Beibu Rusu." The league succumbed completely in 1945, and the Giants' proud stadium became an ammo dump.

After the war General MacArthur ordered the stadium cleared and encouraged the rebirth of the game. O'Doul, a veteran of the 1931 and 1934 tours, brought his San Francisco Seals of the PCL in 1949 and won all seven games. He returned with Joe DiMaggio and other big leaguers in 1951.

The big league tours continued every other year or so, and, *mirabile dictu*, in 1953 the Americans even lost one game with two ties. In 1956 the champion Dodgers lost four games, and in 1966 they lost eight and won nine. Of course the players considered the tours as vacations for shopping and partying, but they were learning that unless they played their best, they could no longer waltz to easy victories.

In 1950 the JPBL split into two leagues, which now have six teams apiece. The Central League, dominated by the Giants, is by far the more popular, with the benefit of the nationwide publicity the Yomiuri empire gives its club. The Giants have drawn 3.5 million fans in a 65-game home schedule. That's nearly 53,000 per game, or 4.2 million for a U.S. schedule of 81 games. Even when they finished last in 1975, they drew 2.8 million. The Pacific League, struggling to break even, in 1973 instituted a split season (since abandoned) and the DH (still in effect). It now averages about 24,400 attendance per game, compared to 35,300 for the Central League. The average Japanese player's salary in 1994 was $235,000, compared to $1.2 million for US major leaguers. However, the Japanese figure includes both farm team members and players on the twelve big league teams, but does not include foreigners. The figure is up 20 percent from 1993 as a result of Japan's new free agency rule for ten-year veterans.

Oddly, of sixty players eligible for free agency in 1994, only five declared. The biggest name was Hiromitsu Ochiai, who was signed by the Tokyo Giants for $3.6 million, compared to the $2.7 million he had received from the Nagoya Dragons in '93. He rewarded the Giants by helping lead them to the pennant.

Of course every Japanese kid wants to grow up to play for the Giants, leaving the other eleven clubs talent-poor. A draft system, begun in 1966, has helped give the other teams a better chance to compete.

Every night a Japanese *sarariman* (salaried man, or wage earner) who is *kichigai* (crazy) about *yakyu* can switch on nationwide TV to watch the Giants. Where America has two weekly sports papers, *The Sporting News* and the *USA Today Baseball Weekly*, Japan has seven sports *dailies*, which concentrate mostly on baseball. Now Japan's sports dailies give their readers baseball, soccer, horse racing, and bicycle racing, as well as titillating nude photos and scandal stories.

Most teams are owned by large companies and operated as advertising write-offs. For years Hiroshima was the only club owned by a city, but it is now owned by the Mazda company. Nine of the twelve clubs play in the two metropolitan centers, Tokyo-Yokohama and Osaka-Kobe-Kyoto.

In the early 1950s, it was a shock for Tokyo fans when the American big leaguers arrived, standing a head taller than the Japanese. Today it is a shock for the same fan to visit a U.S. spring training camp and see visiting Japanese dressing at lockers next to the Americans: There isn't that much difference anymore. Sadaharu Oh and Hank Aaron could almost trade uniforms.

The Japanese began talking of a real World Series. Their victory over America in the 1984 Los Angeles Olympics stirred the fantasy even more.

In general, American observers say, Japanese outfielders and catchers don't have the arms of Americans and Latins. But their infielders are among the best in the world, many of their pitchers are outstanding, and their batters are beginning to hit with big league power.

Americans also say the draconian training methods leave the players burned out in the second half of the season. And especially the Japanese attitude that "the future is now" has led to sacrificing many a great young pitcher to brutal overwork until his arm is ruined forever. In 1961 Hiroshi Gondo won 35 games in 429 innings. The next year he won 30 in 362. The next year he was down to 10, then 6, then 1; then he was out. This, however, is changing, as the Japanese are beginning to adopt the American pitching rotation.

About half the teams play on artificial turf. Following the Tokyo dome ("the Big Egg") and the retractable Fukuoka Dome, two more domes are under construction, in Osaka and Nagoya. Contrary to the U.S. trend toward nostalgic parks, Japan is emphasizing multipurpose domes because of the many rain days in the Japanese season and the high cost of real estate.

The domes will all have bigger playing fields, making them closer to U.S. parks in size. Thus the 280-foot foul lines may soon become a thing of the past.

Japanese teams also play league games in neutral parks all over the country. In 1994 fifty-two local parks were used.

A Gallery of Stars

Tetsuharu Kawakami "The God of Batting," he has also been called "Japan's Lou Gehrig." Wearing glasses and swinging his famous red bat, Kawakami hit cleanup on the great Tokyo Giant teams of 1938–1958 and hit a high of .377 in 1951. His lifetime .313 is fifth highest in Japanese annals. Against the Dodgers in 1956, he batted .364 with two home runs. His concentration was so intense, he said he could visually "stop" a pitch in midflight.

But Kawakami's hitting paled compared to his managing—11 pennants in fourteen years. He was the man at the helm as the Giants won nine straight Japan Series, a feat accomplished by no other professional team in any sport. The Negro League Homestead Grays won nine straight pennants 1937–1945, but they lost several Black World Series and one playoff.

The Grays had Josh Gibson and Buck Leonard. Kawakami had Sadaharu Oh and Shigeo Nagashima. And he did it without using a single foreign player, desiring to prove the superiority of a "pure" Japanese team with fighting spirit.

Hiroshi Oshita (O'-shta) A three-time batting champ and three-time home run leader, Oshita was the postwar hero who dueled with his blue bat against Kawakami's red bat and helped lift the nation's spirit after World War Two. He was popular with the fans and with visiting Americans, who nicknamed him "Oyster."

With a soft and graceful swing, he lofted balls that left lofty, graceful traces in the sky. His 20 homers in 1946 seem a modest total, but they were 10 percent of all the homers hit in the Japanese majors that year. He hit cleanup on the Lions' "H-Bomb Row" of the 1950s.

Futoshi Nakanishi A Japanese Hack Wilson, in Leo Durocher's phrase, Nakanishi hit the second-longest tape-measure home run in Japanese history—530 feet—as a sophomore in 1953. He led the league in homers five out of the six years 1953–1958 and, with Oshita and pitcher Kazuhisa Inao, helped the Nishitetsu Lions win three successive Japan championships, all over the hated Giants.

Nakanishi helped spark the Lions to an amazing comeback in 1958, beginning from eleven games behind the Hawks. In one September stretch, they won seventeen out of eighteen games, and Nakanishi's homer vanquished the Hawks in their final meeting.

Nakanishi's career was cut short by an injury to his left hand after 244 home runs and a .307 average.

Katsuya Nomura (Kot'-su-ya) The slugging catcher Nomura was the first home run king Oh had to catch before he could go after Ruth and Aaron. Nomura played in Japan's smallest park, with 280-foot foul lines, but he was a legitimate star, with a high of 52 homers in 150 games in 1963, when he almost batted the Hawks to the pennant over the Lions. Nomura's lifetime homer total, 1954–1980, was 657. He led the Pacific League eight straight times—nine in all.

Nomura was the most enduring catcher of all time. His 2,921 games behind the plate are almost 1,000 more than the U.S. record, by Carlton Fisk. Six years Nomura played every game on the schedule. Once he caught every inning in 150 games, including 16 doubleheaders.

In 1965 he won the Triple Crown, with a little help from the league's pitchers, who walked American Daryl Spencer to prevent him from winning the home run title.

Shigeo Nagashima (She-gay'-o) The most popular star ever to play in Japan, Nagashima came to the Yomiuri Giants in 1958 and led the league in homers and RBIs his rookie year. He went on to win another HR crown, four more RBI titles, six batting crowns, and five MVPs—pretty good for a man whose main rival for all these honors was Sadaharu Oh.

In fact, Oh joined the team the year after Nagashima, and the two of them gave the Giants the dreaded "O-N Cannons" that propelled them to nine straight Japan championships. With Nagashima hitting cleanup behind Oh, pitchers couldn't pitch around Sadaharu. In the first year of Nagashima's retirement, 1975, Oh lost his HR crown after thirteen straight years as king.

Nagashima was considered the greater clutch hitter. He was nicknamed "Mr. Giant" and "the burning man" for the intensity of his play. His years of greatness coincided with Japan's dramatic economic surge, a period of national pride that he seemed to symbolize.

In 1959 Nagashima won the most famous game ever played in Japan, before the Emperor and Empress, with a ninth-inning homer. Seven years later, in 1966, His Majesty attended his second game, against the L.A. Dodgers. Nagashima homered off Alan Foster in the first, singled in the fourth after a brushback pitch, and singled again in the seventh, as the Japanese won 11–3. He was the first baseball player to receive an audience at the Imperial Palace.

At third base, Nagashima was compared to Ron Santo by Americans who saw him. Dodger G.M. Fresco Thompson said Los Angeles could have won two extra pennants with Nagashima on third.

When Oh won a then unprecedented second straight Triple Crown in 1974, he as usual had to take a back seat to Nagashima, whose retirement was the biggest story of the year. In true Ted Williams fashion, Nagashima hit his 444th, and last, home run on his final day, then tearfully toured the field, while his fans wept with him and implored him not to go.

The next year Nagashima succeeded Kawakami as manager. The Giants came in last, a national shock. Nagashima led the team in a formal bow of apology to the fans on the final day. But they bounced back to first the next two years.

Nagashima returned as Giants manager in 1993 after a twelve-year absence and in 1994 took the team to its first pennant in four years, beating the Dragons on the last day of the season.

Sadaharu Oh The world home-run king, Oh smashed 868 to pass Ruth and Aaron by more than 100 and put the record out of sight for at least the rest of the twentieth century and probably for several generations into the twenty-first. Clete Boyer, who played and coached for many years in Japan, said Oh had the strength of Aaron and the eyes of Williams. Oh's homers were the result of his samurai dedication, his mastery of the martial arts of *aikido* and *kendo* (swordsmanship), and thousands of hours of work with his devoted coach, Hiroshi Arakawa.

Sadaharu hit .161 as a Yomiuri Giant rookie pitcher (!) in 1959. Then Oh and Arakawa began their search for The Way. Oh gave up late-night drinking bouts on the Ginza and studied with masters of martial arts to attain physical, mental, and spiritual mastery. From the legend of the swordsman Miyamoto Musashi, Oh learned that superior spirit conquers superior technique.

But a hitch in his swing still kept Oh back until Arakawa made him stand on one leg before the pitch. If he hitched, he'd topple over. Thus the famous dog-at-the-hydrant stance, which no one before or since has attempted. (Mel Ott's raised foot was entirely different.) The bat angle, with the barrel pointing toward the pitcher, was an integral part of the balance.

Aikido taught Oh patience at the plate. *Kendo* taught him hip action, a downward swing (the fastest path to the ball), and focusing *ki*, or energy, from the shoulders to the "sweet" part of the bat.

Oh put it together in 1962, and the home runs began to explode. For 14 of the next 15 years he hit 40–55 homers a year. True, Japanese fences are shorter, 300 feet down the line. But so is the Japanese season—130 games. And Oh saw a lot more junkball pitchers than American hitters do. In addition, they walked him as many as 166 times a year—he never came to bat 500 times in one year in his life. The result: home run totals that ranged up to 67 per 550 at-bats. The 67 came in 1974 with 49 homers in only 385 AB.

After leaving as Giants manager in 1988, Oh embarked with Hank Aaron on a campaign to extend baseball's popularity by working with kids worldwide.

He is due to return to Japan in 1995 as manager of the Hawks of Fukuoka. With Oh at the helm, the fans in southern Japan look forward to ending the Lions' dynasty.

Isao Harimoto (E'-sow) The only member of Japan's 3,000-hit club, Harimoto set the then Japanese batting record with .383 in 1970, and many thought he could go on to become the country's first .400 hitter. He didn't, partly because he refused to bunt, but he did win two more titles, for a total of seven, slugged 504 home runs, and batted .319, fourth-highest lifetime average in Japan.

A Korean born in Hiroshima, he was being carried by his mother outside the city when the atom bomb went off. She shielded him, but a sister was killed. At the age of four, two fingers on his right hand were severely burned, making it difficult for him to swing a bat.

Harimoto used a "level-up" swing—the bat was level until it met the ball, then went sharply up on the follow-through. Harimoto was active in establishing pro ball in Korea.

Koichi Tabuchi Big (six-three, 210 pounds), handsome Tabuchi is the man who ended Oh's home run reign in

1975 after thirteen straight titles. Tabuchi slugged 43 that year, in spite of playing in the country's largest park. He had done even better the year before with 45 to Oh's 49. The Japanese call him their Johnny Bench.

Japanese connoisseurs consider Tabuchi's homers even more beautiful than Oh's—long and high, with a lot of "hang time." He accumulated 474 in a career that stretched from 1969 to 1984.

Yutaka Fukumoto   This fleet little (five-seven) Braves outfielder was the world's stolen base champ (1,065) until Rickey Henderson broke his record.

Did he run against weak-armed Japanese catchers? In 1978 he stole second twice in one game against a battery of Tom Seaver and Johnny Bench.

With a tip from Daryl Spencer on how to read the pitchers, Fukumoto led the league thirteen years in a row, 1970-1982. His high, 106 in 122 games in 1972, broke Maury Wills's then record of 104 in 148 games. Brock stole 118 in 1974, but he had many more opportunities:

Player	Year	1B	BB	OB*	SB	SB/OB
Wills	1962	150	59	209	104	.498
Brock	1974	159	61	220	118	.536
Cobb	1915	161	118	279	96	.344
Fukumoto	1972	97	65	163	106	.650

*Times reached first base

Fukumoto stole 95 more in 1973 and 94 in 1974.

In that thirteen-year span, the Braves won six pennants. No wonder they took out a half-million-dollar insurance policy on his legs.

Sachio Kinugasa (Sah′-chio Ke-nu-ga′-sa)   Kinugasa passed Lou Gehrig's consecutive-game record in 1987 (2,215 games to Gehrig's 2,130) and topped him in lifetime homers as well, 504–493.

Breaking in with the doormat Hiroshima Carp in 1965, he teamed with college star Koji Yamamoto to lift the Carp to their first pennant in 1975. They won again in 1979 and 1980.

A "GI baby" (his father was black), Kinugasa played in Yamamoto's shadow, often taking practice swings in his hotel room until two A.M. It paid off in 1984, his twentieth season, when he hit .300 for the only time in his life, led in RBI, and won the MVP.

Hiromitsu Ochiai (O′-che-aye)   Ochiai has stepped into the shoes of Oh and Nomura as Japan's top slugger, as well as the highest paid: his $3.6 million salary is far more than that of any other Japanese player. Before the 1991 season Ochiai went to arbitration, the first such case in Japanese history. He said he did it "for the coming generation" to make baseball careers popular in the face of the new popularity of soccer.

With his bat, his big mouth, and his hot-dog character, he is dubbed "the Japanese *gaijin*."

From 1981 through 1993, Ochiai won three triple crowns (1982, 1985, 1986), five batting titles, and five RBI crowns for the Lotte Orions and the Chunichi Dragons.

At the age of forty, Ochiai's skills have fallen off (he batted .280 with 15 home runs), but when he signed with the Giants for the 1994 campaign, he promised that by season's end "we'll toss Nagashima in the air." (This is the traditional Japanese celebration on clinching the pennant, a way to let the fans savor the victory.) He kept his promise with a dramatic homer on the final day.

Koji Akiyama (Ah′-ke-yama)   Considered the best all-around athlete in Japanese pro ball today, center fielder Akiyama is the man the Americans always point to as the best and a sure major leaguer. He can run, field, throw, hit, and hit with power. At the age of thirty he had hit 328 homers in nine full years, 1985-93, and was Japan's first 30-50 man (35 homers and 51 stolen bases in 1990).

One of the "young Lions" who received his training in the U.S. minors in 1982-83, Akiyama jump-started the Seibu Lions' winning streak in his first full season, when he hit 41 homers. In 1986 he was joined by Kazuhiro Kiyohara and in 1989 by Orestes Destrade to power the team's dynasty.

Akiyama would be even better if he did not suffer from hay fever every April. He comes to life when the pollen is gone and thus is nicknamed "Mr. May."

Kazuhiro Kiyohara (Kazu-he′ro Ke-o-ha′ra))   In his nine seasons through 1994, Kiyohara has slugged 273 home runs, compared to 307 by Oh at the same age, and has led the Lions to their seventh pennant over the span. His slugging teammate, Koji Akiyama, was traded away after the '93 season, so Kiyohara took over the main burden alone, though he was unable to win any major batting titles.

Ichiro Suzuki   Not even Oh or Harimoto can match the record of this skinny twenty-year-old outfielder, who in 1994 threatened to become the first Japanese to break .400. He finished at .385, only four points below the Japanese record, .389 by Randy Bass in 1986.

Suzuki uses a unique, one-legged "pendulum swing," bringing his front (right) foot back behind his left before striding into the ball.

In his two previous seasons, his manager had ordered him to stop using the swing; Suzuki's average fell to .188, and he was sent to Hawaii to change his style. But a new manager in '94 let him keep his swing, and his batting average soared.

Despite his unorthodox stance, Suzuki's stroke seems effortless. Years of swinging a heavy coal shovel have given him an extraordinarily fast bat, which allows him to adjust for breaking pitches and hit to all fields.

Swift on his feet (he runs 100 meters in 11.1 seconds), Suzuki can beat out ground balls (he hit a record 151 singles) and stretch line drives into doubles (he hit 41 two-baggers). He also stole 29 bases and hit 13 home runs.

Suzuki set a Japan record by getting on base in 69 straight games. He's the first Japanese to reach 200 hits in the 130-game season.

Pitchers

Eiji Sawamura   A true folk hero, in 1934 the eighteen-year-old Sawamura whiffed four of America's greatest Hall of Famers in a row—Gehringer, Ruth, Gehrig, and Foxx. In all, the kid gave five hits, struck out nine, and walked one. Connie Mack was so impressed, he offered the boy a contract.

The next year Sawamura toured the States with Shoriki's Dai Nippon nine (later tagged the Tokyo Giants by Lefty O'Doul), playing PCL and semipro clubs. American fans crowded around for autographs, and one asked him to sign in English, not Japanese. Sawamura obliged, only to discover later that he had signed a contract! It took some fast talking, and perhaps some yen, to get Sawamura out of the scout's clutches.

Sawamura went on to lead the new pro league in 1936 with a 13–3 record. In the postseason playoff against the Osaka Tigers, he pitched all three games, holding them to a .116 batting average and a 0.19 ERA, as the Giants won, two games to one.

The next year he was 33–10.

In his brief five-year career, he pitched three no-hitters.

Sawamura was called away to military service in 1938–1939, and again in 1942 and 1944. In December 1944 his troop ship was torpedoed by a submarine off Formosa, and he went down with the ship.

Masaichi Kaneda (Masa-ichi Ka-nay'-da)

Only Cy Young and Walter Johnson have surpassed Kaneda's 400 victories. Akin to Johnson's experience, he won most of his with one of the weakest teams in Japan, the Kokutetsu Swallows, who finished in the first division only once in his fifteen years with them, 1950–1964.

In 1958 the Swallows were last in homers and near last in batting. But Kaneda was 31–14 with a 1.30 ERA. The Swallows were 27–54 without him.

In all, he won 43 percent of the Swallows' victories. He won and lost more 1–0 games than anyone—21 victories, 23 defeats.

The lefthanded Kaneda was the first man to break Walter Johnson's lifetime strikeout record, as well as the first to break his scoreless innings streak. Nolan Ryan broke Kaneda's strikeout mark, 4,490, but no one has touched his mark of $64\frac{1}{3}$ straight shutout innings.

Takumi Otomo (Ta-ku'-me O'-to-mo)

The little submarine-baller beat the New York Giants and Hoyt Wilhelm 2–1 in 1953 in one of the ten greatest games in Japan's history. With Lefty O'Doul urging him to keep the ball high, Otomo stayed ahead in the count, then fed them bad balls until they popped up or rolled out.

He won the MVP that year with a 27–6 record, plus two wins in the Japan Series. His ERA, 1.85, was the highest he posted in a four-year period. The lowest: 1.63 in 1956. In 1955 he was 30–6.

Kazuhisa Inao (Ka-zu-hee'-sa E-now')

Until his arm finally weakened from overwork, Inao was one of the world's most amazing pitchers.

His record of pitching six Japan Series games in 1958 and winning the last four of them will probably never be done again by any pitcher in any country. He won 42 games in 1961, 35 in 1957, and 33 in 1958. He was voted best pitcher in the league five times.

A poor fisherman's son, he reported as an unknown rookie to the Nishitetsu Lions' camp, with muscles bulging from rowing his father's boat in rough seas. He threw as many as 300 pitches a day, posted a 21–6 record with a 1.06 ERA, and lifted the Lions to the pennant. In 262 innings, he gave up two home runs. He won three more games in the Japan Series.

Nicknamed *"Tetsu Wan"*—Iron Arm—in 1957 Inao won a record 20 straight at the end of the year to lift the Lions from third to another pennant.

In 1961 he tied Vic Starffin's record of 42 wins and lost his bid for his forty-third, 1–0, in the first game of two on the final day. He considered coming back in Game Two and going for the record but at last decided to rest on his laurels.

Tadashi Sugiura (Su-ghee-u'-ra)

One year after Inao won four straight games in the Japan Series, the bespectacled Sugiura won four straight too. But he won all four games he pitched.

Nagashima's teammate in college, Sugiura had spurned the Yomiuri Giants after Nankai Hawk manager Tsuruoka bowed to him and said, "We need you to beat the Giants."

As a rookie Sugiura was 27–12, 2.05 with the second-place Hawks, though Inao (33–10) and the Lions won their third straight flag.

Then in 1959 it was Sugiura's turn. He pitched 371 innings, held enemy hitters to a 1.40 ERA, and posted a 38–4 record. He pitched 29 games in the last eight weeks, or virtually every other day. He was 17–1 after August 1 and won his last 13 in a row. The stretch included 54 straight shutout innings, an ERA of 0.10, 95 strikeouts, and only 4 walks! His final victory clinched the flag.

Then came the Japan Series against the Giants, who had just won their fifth straight flag. The Hawks had never beaten them.

In spite of a painful elbow, Sugiura went eight innings in Game One, gave up nine hits, but won 10–7. The next day Sugiura pitched five innings of relief, gave three hits and one run, and got the victory 6-3.

After travel days Sugiura started Game Three in Tokyo. Midway through, a corn came off his pitching hand, and catcher Nomura suddenly found himself catching a bloody ball. In the samurai spirit, however, Sugiura refused to come out. He lost a 2–1 lead on a homer in the ninth, and the Giants put two more men on second and third with one out. "My God, I'm done for," he says he thought, desperately looking into the dugout for relief. Tsuruoka kept his eyes averted, however, sending a coach out with a good luck amulet instead. Sugiura buckled down and got the last two outs and won in the tenth 3–2. He gave up only one walk.

Rain gave Sugiura a day of rest. Would the Hawks give him another in Game Four? The finger still pained him. "Can you go?" Tsuruoka asked. "I can go," Sugiura answered. He went nine more innings and shut the Giants out on five hits.

In his first three years, he had won 96 games:

Year	Rank	G	IP	BB	SO	W–L	ERA	Series	Awards
1958	2	53	299	85	215	27–12	2.05		
1959	1	69	371	46	336	38–4	1.40*	4–0	MVP
1960	2	57	333	49	317	31–11	2.05		

But then the overwork finally told. After an operation on his arm, he fell to 20–9 in 1961. He dropped to 14–15, then 14–16, made a brief comeback in 1964 with 20–15, and then was sent to the bullpen. He was all pitched out.

His final totals: 187–106.

Tetsuya Yoneda (Tet'-su-ya Yo-nay-da)   Like Kaneda or Phil Niekro, Yoneda slaved for a doormat team, the Braves. Yet he posted the second-highest winning total in Japan—350–285, second only to Kaneda's 400 wins.

In 1966 Yoneda led the league with 25–17, while his team finished next to last. His biggest year was 1968, when he went 29–13 as the Braves won the pennant. He was voted the MVP of the league.

Yoneda is second to Kaneda in hitting too, with 33 homers to Kaneda's 36. Yoneda might have passed his rival, but the coming of the DH rule stopped his bid.

He did pass Kaneda, and everyone, including Cy Young, in one department, total games—949.

Keishi Suzuki   For six straight years, 1967–1972—eight years in all—the lefty Suzuki led the Pacific League in strikeouts. As a sophomore lefty in 1967, he was 21–13 for the last-place Kintetsu Buffaloes.

Like Robin Roberts, another fastballing control pitcher, Suzuki gave up a lot of homers—560.

He was a natural righthander, but his father had tied his right hand to force him to pitch as a lefty.

His final figures: 317–238, and 3,061 strikeouts.

Minoru Murayama   In 1959 rookie fastballer Murayama faced Japan's best player, Nagashima, in the greatest game ever played in Japan, a contest before 50,000 fans, including the Emperor himself.

Murayama, as famous for his forkball as his fastball, pitched for the Yomiuri Giants' biggest rivals, the Hanshin Tigers. An Osaka native and boyhood Tiger fan, he spurned a Giant bonus in order to stay home and pitch for the Tigers for half the amount the Giants offered.

The night before the big game, Murayama had come in in the ninth inning against the Giants and struck out the side, Nagashima included.

The next night, before their majesties, Koyama started for the Tigers and they took an early lead. Nagashima ripped a home run to tie the score. The Tigers went back into the lead, and in the seventh Nagashima struck out, but a rookie named Sadaharu Oh pumped a two-run home run to tie it again.

That brought in Murayama, who got the Giants out to end the seventh, then shut them out in the eighth, as the scoreboard clock inched toward nine-thirty, the time when the imperial couple would have to leave. They stayed in their seats, however, to see Nagashima and Murayama duel each other in the last of the ninth.

This was a classic Japanese showdown, or *shobu*. Under the unwritten rule, there could be no nibbling the corners or dirty tricks; it had to be a head-on challenge, strength against strength.

Murayama's first pitch was a forkball, for a ball. Next another forkball, for a strike. Then a fastball, which Nagashima fouled back.

Another fastball was outside, making the count 2–2. Then he uncorked still another fastball on the inside. Nagashima swung and parked it ten rows into the left field stands. To this day Murayama insists it was foul. But Nagashima circled the bases before the royal box, to be mobbed by his teammates waiting at the plate.

Nagashima went on to win the batting championship. Murayama went on to strike out 294 men in 295 innings;

he won 18 and lost 10, with a 1.19 ERA, and won the Sawamura Award.

But nothing could erase the memory of that one fateful home run.

His final stats: 222–147, 2.09.

Yutaka Enatsu   One of the most amazing athletes in Japanese baseball, in 1968 Enatsu struck out 401 men in 329 innings—that's eleven every nine innings. He was only twenty years old and just two years out of high school.

The lefty was one of the few pitchers who could get Nagashima and Oh out consistently. As a result his pennant-hungry managers worked him like a slave in every series against the Giants. Enatsu pitched the first and third games of a three-game series, and sometimes relieved in the middle game as well.

In 1970 he shut the Giants out twice in three days, then pitched the final game of the season with no rest and lost it 2–1 in ten innings. The Giants won by two games.

In 1971 Enatsu had elbow trouble and won only 15 games—but six of them were against the Giants, including 34 straight scoreless innings. And in the All-Star Game that summer he pitched three innings and struck out all nine men he faced.

Enatsu was a free spirit who rebelled against the strict samurai-style workouts, saying he wanted to save himself for the season—the way they worked him, he was probably right. To dramatize his revolt one spring, he lay down in the outfield and went to sleep while the other pitchers ran. The Tigers finished last that year. They fired the manager and kept Enatsu.

In 1973 the Tigers were making a hard run at ending the Giants' pennant streak. On August 30, with one day of rest, Enatsu tossed an eleven-inning no-hitter, winning it himself 1–0 with a home run. In September he pitched a fourteen-inning one-hitter, retiring thirty-three straight batters in a row—the equal of eleven perfect innings—then lost 1–0.

When the Giants arrived for the climactic series, Enatsu faced them with two days rest and lost. As usual manager Murayama put him in to pitch the third game. The exhausted pitcher was leading 3–1 in the seventh, when he loaded the bases on a walk, a single, and a bunt, with Oh at bat. Enatsu got two strikes on Oh, then walked him on four straight pitches. Nagashima followed with a single to win the game and, eventually, the pennant. Enatsu ended with 24–13. It was his last great year as a starter.

He became Japan's greatest relief ace and bounced to the Hawks, Carp, and Lions, fighting with most of his managers. Finally, at the age of thirty-eight, he came to America to try out with the Brewers. It was too late; his arm was gone.

Enatsu's final record: 206–158, plus 193 saves. And 2,987 strikeouts.

Hideo Nomo (He-day'o)   Japan's "Doctor K," Nomo is the modern strikeout king. His fans raise "K" cards for every strikeout he records—and they raised 1,078 cards in 937 innings over his first four seasons, 1990-93.

Mixing a fastball and forkball, the former Olympian righthander whiffed 17 men in his first pro game to tie the

Japanese record. He went on to strike out 287 men in 235 innings and lead the Pacific League in just about every category.

It took Nomo only three years to break the record for double-digit strikeout games, 43, set by Suzuki over a twenty-year span.

Like oldtime U.S. pitcher Freddie Fitzsimmons or Luis Tiant, Nomo turns his back on the hitter, as if coiling a spring, then turns and unwinds, with his whole body behind the pitch. His nickname is "the Tornado," or twister. Nomo's father taught the four-year-old Hideo to emulate Muyayama, who also put his whole body into the pitch. His mother fed him lots of eel to make him loose on the mound.

For the first time in his five-year career, Nomo had a bad season in 1994 with an 8–7 record in 17 games.

Gaijin—*Foreigners*

"East is East, and west is West, and never the twain shall meet."—Rudyard Kipling

Next to trade policy, no area of U.S.-Japanese relations contains the seeds of more controversy than baseball. The two games may appear the same from the left field stands, but the two nations actually play two quite different games. The differences can sometimes lead to bitter misunderstanding.

According to U.S. observers, among the differences are:

Japanese managers . . .
- Conduct spring training like marine boot camp.
- Overwork their pitchers.
- Bench players in midgame for one error or one strikeout.
- Overemphasize home runs.
- Resent advice.
- Are too conservative.
- Won't let Americans excel.

Japanese players . . .
- Take half an hour batting practice every day.
- Don't miss signs.
- Don't dive for fly balls.
- Won't break up double plays.
- Don't block the plate.
- Don't backhand grounders.
- Don't chew tobacco.

Japanese pitchers . . .
- Throw sidearm and underhand more than in the States.
- Have good curves but mediocre fastballs.
- Throw brushback pitches to American hard hitters.
- Throw 300–500 pitches a day—just to stay in shape.
- Burn out early.

Japanese fans . . .
- Eat sushi instead of hotdogs at the game.
- Throw foul balls back.
- Never stop cheering with drums and trumpets throughout the game (big noise).

According to the Japanese, among the differences are:

American players . . .
- Are overpaid, stuck up, and out of shape.
- Won't work hard.
- Don't follow orders.
- Play dirty baseball.
- Bait the umpires.
- Are quick to punch opponents.
- Look down on the Japanese.
- Won't learn the language.
- Don't like Japanese food.

Still, like lovers having a quarrel, the two nations can't stay away from each other on the ballfield.

The Japanese have used 400 foreigners—in Japanese, *gaijin*, which means "outside people." There is an ambivalence toward these aliens. On the one hand, teams are tempted to use them to gain a competitive advantage (there's a cap of three per team). On the other hand, the Japanese yearn for the day that an all-Japanese team will win a *real* world series and reign as kings of the baseball world.

Although the Japanese regularly import players, they are paranoid about exporting any to the U.S. majors. America has a very favorable "balance-of-baseball" trade. And the currently devalued dollar means Japan can afford even more Yanks for the yen.

In 1987 they gave Bob Horner of the Braves $1.4 million dollars. He rewarded them with six homers in his first four games and put an estimated quarter of a million more people in the park. But he spurned a $3 million offer to stay, preferring to go home to the Cards for $1 million rather than play "something like baseball."

The Japanese offered Dave Righetti a reported $8 million for two years and Reggie Jackson $2 million for one. They turned it down. But the Japanese teams landed Bill Madlock for $1 million, Bill Gullickson for $1.1 million, and Doug DeCinces for $1.5 million—this only four years after Japan's commissioner had announced a plan to ban all *gaijin*.

Here are some of the best foreigners to play in Japan.

Victor Starffin Now that baseball is an Olympic sport, the Russians have set themselves the goal of winning a gold medal some day. A preview of what the future may hold was big (six-four) Victor Starffin, the White Russian whose parents brought him to Japan fleeing the Bolshevik Revolution. He took to baseball like Khrushchev to vodka and became the greatest Russian baseball player ever.

Joining the Dai-Nippon team, Starffin towered over the Japanese and opened a rivalry with teammate Sawamura. Vic was 28–11 in 1937, 33–5 in 1938, 42–15 in 1939 (two-thirds of the team's wins), and 38–12 (1.09) in 1940. Those 42 wins remained the record until Inao tied it in 1961.

Excused from military service as a stateless person, Starffin served as a Russian translator at the Tokyo war crimes trials. He spent his postwar years with some tailend teams but finished at 303–176, Japan's first 300-game winner.

He was killed soon afterward when he was driving his car home while drunk and hit a train. His plaque in Japan's Hall of Fame is inscribed in both Japanese and Russian.

Henry "Bozo" Wakabayashi (Wa-ka-bah-yah'-shee)
The son of a Japanese immigrant to Hawaii, Wakabayashi first played in Japan in 1928, graduated from one of Tokyo's "Big Six" universities, and pitched for the Osaka Tigers from the beginning of pro ball in 1936. A finesse pitcher, Wakabayashi threw seven different pitches ("seven-color magic pitches"). In 1939 he was 30–7 with a 1.25 ERA. For six years in a row, 1939–1944, he had ERAs of under 1.81; his best was 1.06 in 1943.

Twice MVP, his most famous game came in the first Japan Series in 1950 at the age of forty-two, when he was the surprise starter in Game One against the Robins, who boasted a batting average of .287. Bozo beat them 3–2.

Wakabayashi retired at 240–141 and 1.99 and remained a baseball ambassador for decades.

Bucky Harris Bucky Harris, another American (no, not the Senators' manager), was the Japanese home run king in the spring season of 1938 and the first foreigner to win the MVP. A veteran catcher from the American PCL, he had a good throwing arm and repeatedly won exhibitions throwing through a barrel at second base.

He studied hard to learn the language and, honored at his retirement, made a *sayonara* speech in Japanese.

Wally Yonamine (Yo-na'-mi-nay) The Jackie Robinson of Japan, Yonamine introduced a slashing, running game and blazed the way for American players there. This Hawaiian-born Nisei didn't know a word of Japanese when he left the San Francisco 49ers' backfield to join the Yomiuri Giants in 1951. (He'd played some baseball in the low U.S. minors; Brooklyn's Billy Loes, who pitched against him, said he was the toughest out he ever faced.)

Wally carried a double stigma. Not only was he an American, when the wounds of the war were still fresh, he was a Nisei (son of a Japanese who chooses another country), who was regarded by the Japanese in about the same way as Americans would regard a fellow countryman who had defected to Russia.

The Giants put him in center field and batted him leadoff, and he promptly hit .354. He also ran out sacrifice bunts, which surprised the Japanese, and threw rolling blocks into second basemen on the double play, which horrified them. And he played center like his stateside contemporary, Dom DiMaggio, who also wore glasses.

A Yonamine single, a hit-and-run, and a base hit by Kawakami was the usual Giant formula. They rose from third to first in Wally's first season and won the flag every year he was with them except one. Wally and Kawakami were rivals for hitting honors, and a jealousy arose. Yonamine was much the better fielder and won three batting titles and one MVP, made seven All-Star teams, and ended with a .311 average, one of the highest in Japan. Against the Dodgers in 1956 Wally hit .347. The Japanese hailed him as the greatest leadoff man in their history, and he's probably still the biggest American star to play in Japan.

Attendance

In 1994 Japan smashed all attendance records, even outdrawing the U.S. major leagues in average attendance per game.

The Giants pulled in a record 3.5 million fans to the Tokyo Dome, an average of over 54,000 per game for 65 home games, surpassing the western hemisphere leaders, Toronto (49,300) and Atlanta (47,000).

In the Pacific League, the Fukuoka Hawks, playing in their new domed stadium, drew over 2.5 million fans, a league record.

In all, almost 23 million people saw the twelve teams play in a 130-game schedule. The Central League, starring the popular Giants, averaged over 33,000 fans per game, topping the U.S. National League's average of 32,500. Average attendance figures for Japan and the big leagues were:

Central League	33,700	National League	32,500
Pacific League	24,500	American League	30,700
Japan average	29,100	Big league average	31,600

Japanese in America

Mashi Murakami Many Japanese have played in the U.S. minors but to date, only one has played American major league baseball.

The big leaguer was Masanori "Mashi" Murakami, who almost caused a complete rupture in U.S.-Japan diamond relations. Murakami was one of three members of the Nankai Hawks sent over to gain experience with the San Francisco Giants' farm teams in Fresno and Magic Valley in 1964. The twenty-year-old did so well (11–7) and was so well liked (bowing to teammates who made good plays behind him) that he was promoted to the Giants. He made his debut against the last-place Mets before 50,000 fans at Shea Stadium and pitched one inning of shutout relief. That year he won one and saved one with a 1.80 ERA. He struck out 15 men in 15 innings and walked only 1.

At this point the Giants invoked the fine print in their contract—the paragraph giving them the right to buy any of the three who made the parent club. The Japanese had never anticipated this development! They said Murakami had only been on loan. Besides, they said, he was homesick and didn't want to go back to the States. The boy dutifully agreed. The Hawks even charged that the contract was a forgery, thus enraging the Giants. Who did they think Murakami was, club president Chub Feeney demanded—Christy Mathewson?

U.S. Commissioner Ford Frick threatened to break relations with Japan if they didn't honor the contract. This could have cut off all further U.S. players going there to play. At last a compromise broke the impasse. Murakami would play one more year in the States, then would be free to choose his own destiny. Mashi flew back to San Francisco, won 4 games, lost 1, saved 8, and struck out 85 men in 74 innings. He was a darling of the San Francisco Nisei community.

In 1966 the Hawks enticed him home with a $40,000 contract, twice what the Giants had offered. The Hawks rubbed their hands in anticipation of seeing Murakami obliterate every pitching record in the book. Alas, he never lived up to his promise. He won a total of 9 games his first two years. He had only one good year, 1968, when he was 18–4. He was the first and last Japanese to play in the U.S. majors.

The Young Lions

In a second experiment, the Taiheiyo Lions bought a U.S. minor league team in Lodi, California, and stocked it with nine of their rookies plus a coach, along with U.S. players.

But the Japanese players, like some Americans in Japan, couldn't adjust to the food and the language. After two years the Lions sold their Lodi club and brought their players home.

Undaunted, in 1982 the Seibu Lions (bought by Seibu Railway Co. after the 1978 season) signed a working agreement with the Baltimore Orioles' Class A farm team at San Jose and each year have sent several rookies there for experience. The plan paid off big. The Lions won the pennant five of the next six years, and experts attributed it in part to their San Jose graduates. Most famous of the group was Koji Akiyama, the 1987 home run king.

The young Lions are now the seasoned veteran Lions. They've won nine pennants in eleven years, 1983-93. They built their empire with strong administration on the U.S. model—good scouting, a strong farm system, and a huge wallet.

In spring 1990, American baseball fans were irritated when a Japanese whiskey company, Suntory, bought the Birmingham Barons (AA). Further inflaming nativist feeling was acquisition of the major league Seattle Mariners by Japanese interests.

Before the '94 season began, hopes were high that Makoto "Mac" Suzuki would be the first Japanese in the U.S. majors since Murakami in 1965. Suzuki, on the Mariners' roster in spring training, was assigned to their Jacksonville AA team, where he pitched only 13 innings due to tendinitis. He struck out ten, won one, saved one, and had a 2.84 ERA.

Olympics

Japan stunned the Americans at the 1984 Los Angeles Games (where baseball was still a demonstration sport) by taking the gold medal over a team headed by Will Clark, Mark McGwire, and Shane Mack.

At Seoul in 1988, again in a demonstration, the Americans extracted revenge as hurler Jim Abbott beat Japan in the Gold Medal finals 5–3.

Cuba beat everyone at Barcelona in 1992, and a surprising Taiwan knocked both Japan and the United States out of the running for the silver medal. Taiwan's Chien-fu Kuo Lee made the Japanese hitters look foolish with his breaking pitches—so they signed him to a Hanshin Tiger contract. Japan and America had to settle for the playoff for the bronze, which the Japanese won.

A Real World Series

Matsutaro Shoriki died in 1969 with one dream still unfulfilled—a real World Series between his Giants and the winner of the American World Series. It's a goal every Japanese fan keeps before his eyes.

In frequent series against U.S. big league teams, the Japanese have already established one thing: the Americans can still win, but they have to field strong teams and play hard to do it.

In 1966 the Giants played seven games against the NL champion Dodgers and won four of them. Overall, the Dodgers were 9–8–1 in Japan. Of course, Sandy Koufax and Don Drysdale didn't make the trip. But their number three pitcher, Claude Osteen (17–14), did and was bombed out of the box five times.

In 1968 the NL champion Cards (Bob Gibson, Lou Brock, Orlando Cepeda, etc.) arrived fresh from the World Series. Beset by jet lag, they lost two of their first three games but came back to win 12 of their last 15 for a 13–5 record overall. The Japanese might have done better if Nagashima had not missed the series with an injury. Oh hit .356 with six homers.

In 1971, after a 9–6 spring training record against U.S. teams, Kawakami announced that "the Americans have nothing more to teach us." The nation looked confidently forward to the arrival that fall of the AL champ Orioles for what the Japanese were hailing as the long awaited "world series." Bowie Kuhn even threw out the first ball.

The Japanese knocked Jim Palmer (20–9) out three times, but Pat Dobson (20–8) pitched three shutouts, including a no-hitter. The O's held Oh to a .111 average. Nagashima hit .258, and the Orioles won 12 games to two, with four ties. But when the Americans sent subpar teams—the fifth-place Mets in 1974 and the fifth-place Orioles in 1984, the competition was closer.

The U.S.–Japan Series

Satellite TV brings U.S. major league games to fans in Japan, and as a result major league caps, jackets, and T-shirts sell well there.

In 1990 Japan stunned a visiting U.S. all star team, winning 4 games against 3 losses and a tie. The major leaguers included Barry Bonds, Cecil Fielder, Roberto Alomar, Kelly Gruber, Bobby Thigpen, Ramon Martinez, Dave Stewart, and others. Following Japan's 1984 Olympic gold medal, the results started speculation that the Japanese were approaching U.S. major league caliber.

However, in 1992 Roger Clemens led another all star squad to Japan, and they won handily, 7 games to 1 with a tie. It seemed clear that Japan has not produced the formidable players it did in the 1960s, such as Oh, Nagashima, Nakanishi, Inao, Kaneda, etc. The biannual U.S.-Japan series scheduled for 1994 was canceled due to the U.S. players' strike.

There is still about a twenty-pound difference between the average U.S. and Japanese big leaguer, which means that today's Japanese player is about as big as a major leaguer of Babe Ruth's day.

Some Japanese doubt that Japan can ever catch up with the U.S. majors. They say the Olympics are a better arena for competition.

Pennant Winners: Japan Pro-Baseball League

YEAR		TEAM	WON	LOST	PCT.	YEAR		TEAM	WON	LOST	PCT.
1936	FALL	TOKYO GIANTS	18	9	—	1942		TOKYO GIANTS	73	27	.730
1937	SPRING	TOKYO GIANTS	41	13	.759	1943		TOKYO GIANTS	54	27	.667
	FALL	OSAKA TIGERS	39	9	.813	1944		HANSHIN	27	6	.818
1938	SPRING	OSAKA TIGERS	29	6	.829	1945		PLAY SUSPENDED			
	FALL	TOKYO GIANTS	30	9	.769	1946		KINKI GREATRING	65	38	.631
1939		TOKYO GIANTS	66	26	.717	1947		OSAKA TIGERS	79	37	.681
1940		TOKYO GIANTS	76	28	.731	1948		NANKAI HAWKS	87	49	.640
1941		TOKYO GIANTS	62	22	.738	1949		YOMIURI GIANTS	85	48	.639

Pennant Winners: Central League

YEAR	TEAM	WON	LOST	PCT.	YEAR	TEAM	WON	LOST	PCT.
1950	SHOCHIKU ROBINS	98	35	.737	1973	YOMIURI GIANTS	66	60	.524
1951	YOMIURI GIANTS	79	29	.731	1974	CHUNICHI DRAGONS	70	49	.588
1952	YOMIURI GIANTS	83	37	.692	1975	HIROSHIMA CARP	72	47	.605
1953	YOMIURI GIANTS	87	37	.702	1976	YOMIURI GIANTS	76	45	.628
1954	CHUNICHI DRAGONS	86	40	.683	1977	YOMIURI GIANTS	80	46	.635
1955	YOMIURI GIANTS	92	37	.713	1978	YAKULT SWALLOWS	68	46	.596
1956	YOMIURI GIANTS	82	44	.646	1979	HIROSHIMA CARP	67	50	.573
1957	YOMIURI GIANTS	74	53	.581	1980	HIROSHIMA CARP	73	44	.624
1958	YOMIURI GIANTS	77	52	.596	1981	YOMIURI GIANTS	73	48	.603
1959	YOMIURI GIANTS	77	48	.612	1982	CHUNICHI DRAGONS	64	47	.577
1960	TAIYO WHALES	70	56	.554	1983	YOMIURI GIANTS	72	50	.590
1961	YOMIURI GIANTS	71	53	.569	1984	HIROSHIMA CARP	75	45	.625
1962	HANSHIN TIGERS	75	55	.577	1985	HANSHIN TIGERS	74	49	.602
1963	YOMIURI GIANTS	83	55	.601	1986	HIROSHIMA CARP	73	46	.613
1964	HANSHIN TIGERS	80	56	.588	1987	YOMIURI GIANTS	76	43	.639
1965	YOMIURI GIANTS	91	47	.659	1988	CHUNICHI DRAGONS	79	46	.632
1966	YOMIURI GIANTS	89	41	.685	1989	YOMIURI GIANTS	84	44	.656
1967	YOMIURI GIANTS	84	46	.646	1990	YOMIURI GIANTS	88	42	.677
1968	YOMIURI GIANTS	77	53	.592	1991	HIROSHIMA CARP	74	56	.569
1969	YOMIURI GIANTS	73	51	.589	1992	YAKULT SWALLOWS	69	61	.531
1970	YOMIURI GIANTS	79	47	.627	1993	YAKULT SWALLOWS	80	50	.615
1971	YOMIURI GIANTS	70	52	.574	1994	YOMIURI GIANTS	70	60	.538
1972	YOMIURI GIANTS	74	52	.587					

Pennant Winners: Pacific League

YEAR		TEAM	WON	LOST	PCT.	YEAR		TEAM	WON	LOST	PCT.
1950		MAINICHI ORIONS	81	34	.704		2nd HALF	KINTETSU BUFFALOES	40	20	.667
1951		NANKAI HAWKS	72	24	.750	1976	1st HALF	HANKYU BRAVES	42	21	.667
1952		NANKAI HAWKS	76	44	.633		2nd HALF	HANKYU BRAVES	37	24	.607
1953		NANKAI HAWKS	71	48	.597	1977	1st HALF	*HANKYU BRAVES	35	25	.583
1954		NISHITETSU LIONS	90	47	.657		2nd HALF	LOTTE ORIONS	33	24	.579
1955		NANKAI HAWKS	99	41	.707	1978	1st HALF	HANKYU BRAVES	44	20	.688
1956		NISHITETSU LIONS	96	51	.646		2nd HALF	HANKYU BRAVES	38	19	.667
1957		NISHITETSU LIONS	83	44	.648	1979	1st HALF	*KINTETSU BUFFALOES	39	19	.672
1958		NISHITETSU LIONS	78	47	.619		2nd HALF	HANKYU BRAVES	36	23	.610
1959		NANKAI HAWKS	88	42	.677	1980	1st HALF	LOTTE ORIONS	33	25	.569
1960		DAIMAI ORIONS	82	48	.631		2nd HALF	*KINTETSU BUFFALOES	35	26	.574
1961		NANKAI HAWKS	85	49	.629	1981	1st HALF	LOTTE ORIONS	35	26	.574
1962		TOEI FLYERS	78	52	.600		2nd HALF	*NIPPON HAM FIGHTERS	37	23	.617
1963		NISHITETSU LIONS	86	60	.589	1982	1st HALF	*SEIBU LIONS	36	27	.571
1964		NANKAI HAWKS	84	63	.571		2nd HALF	NIPPON HAM FIGHTERS	35	23	.603
1965		NANKAI HAWKS	88	49	.642	1983		SEIBU LIONS	86	40	.683
1966		NANKAI HAWKS	79	51	.608	1984		HANKYU BRAVES	75	45	.625
1967		HANKYU BRAVES	75	55	.577	1985		SEIBU LIONS	79	45	.637
1968		HANKYU BRAVES	80	50	.615	1986		SEIBU LIONS	68	49	.581
1969		HANKYU BRAVES	76	50	.603	1987		SEIBU LIONS	71	45	.612
1970		LOTTE ORIONS	80	47	.630	1988		SEIBU LIONS	73	51	.589
1971		HANKYU BRAVES	80	39	.672	1989		KINTETSU BUFFALOES	71	54	.568
1972		HANKYU BRAVES	80	48	.625	1990		SEIBU LIONS	81	45	.643
1973	1st HALF	*NANKAI HAWKS	38	26	.594	1991		SEIBU LIONS	81	43	.653
	2nd HALF	HANKYU BRAVES	43	19	.694	1992		SEIBU LIONS	80	47	.630
1974	1st HALF	HANKYU BRAVES	36	23	.610	1993		SEIBU LIONS	74	53	.581
	2nd HALF	*LOTTE ORIONS	38	23	.623	1994		SEIBU LIONS	76	52	.594
1975	1st HALF	*HANKYU BRAVES	38	25	.603						

*playoff winner

Japan Series

YEAR	TEAM/LEAGUE	WON	TEAM/LEAGUE	WON		YEAR	TEAM/LEAGUE	WON	TEAM/LEAGUE	WON	
1950	MAINICHI ORIONS, PL	4	SHOCHIKU ROBINS, CL	2		1960	TAIYO WHALES, CL	4	DAIMAI ORIONS, PL	0	
1951	YOMIURI GIANTS, CL	4	NANKAI HAWKS, PL	1		1961	YOMIURI GIANTS, CL	4	NANKAI HAWKS, PL	2	
1952	YOMIURI GIANTS, CL	4	NANKAI HAWKS, PL	2		1962	TOEI FLYERS, PL	4	HANSHIN TIGERS, CL	2	1 TIE
1953	YOMIURI GIANTS, CL	4	NANKAI HAWKS, PL	2	1 TIE	1963	YOMIURI GIANTS, CL	4	NISHITETSU LIONS, PL	3	
1954	CHUNICHI DRAGONS, CL	4	NISHITETSU LIONS, PL	3		1964	NANKAI HAWKS, PL	4	HANSHIN TIGERS	3	
1955	YOMIURI GIANTS, CL	4	NANKAI HAWKS, PL	3		1965	YOMIURI GIANTS, CL	4	NANKAI HAWKS, PL	1	
1956	NISHITETSU LIONS, PL	4	YOMIURI GIANTS, CL	2		1966	YOMIURI GIANTS, CL	4	NANKAI HAWKS, PL	2	
1957	NISHITETSU LIONS, PL	4	YOMIURI GIANTS, CL	0	1 TIE	1967	YOMIURI GIANTS, CL	4	HANKYU BRAVES, PL	2	
1958	NISHITETSU LIONS, PL	4	YOMIURI GIANTS, CL	3		1968	YOMIURI GIANTS, CL	4	HANKYU BRAVES, PL	2	
1959	NANKAI HAWKS, PL	4	YOMIURI GIANTS, CL	0		1969	YOMIURI GIANTS, CL	4	HANKYU BRAVES, PL	2	
						1970	YOMIURI GIANTS, CL	4	LOTTE ORIONS, PL	1	

Year	PL/CL Winner		G	Runner-up		G	
1971	YOMIURI GIANTS, CL	4		HANKYU BRAVES, PL	1		
1972	YOMIURI GIANTS, CL	4		HANKYU BRAVES, PL	1		
1973	YOMIURI GIANTS, CL	4		NANKAI HAWKS, PL	1		
1974	LOTTE ORIONS, PL	4		CHUNICHI DRAGONS, CL	2		
1975	HANKYU BRAVES, PL	4		HIROSHIMA CARP, CL	0	2 TIES	
1976	HANKYU BRAVES, PL	4		YOMIURI GIANTS, CL	3		
1977	HANKYU BRAVES, PL	4		YOMIURI GIANTS, CL	1		
1978	YAKULT SWALLOWS, CL	4		HANKYU BRAVES, PL	3		
1979	HIROSHIMA CARP, CL	4		KINTETSU BUFFALOES, PL	3		
1980	HIROSHIMA CARP, CL	4		KINTETSU BUFFALOES, PL	3		
1981	YOMIURI GIANTS, CL	4		NIPPON HAM FIGHTERS, PL	2		
1982	SEIBU LIONS, PL	4		CHUNICHI DRAGONS, CL	2		
1983	SEIBU LIONS, PL	4		YOMIURI GIANTS, CL	3		
1984	HIROSHIMA CARP, CL	4		HANKYU BRAVES, PL	3		
1985	HANSHIN TIGERS, CL	4		SEIBU LIONS, PL	2		
1986	SEIBU LIONS, PL	4		HIROSHIMA CARP, CL	3	1 TIE	
1987	SEIBU LIONS, PL	4		YOMIURI GIANTS, CL	2		
1988	SEIBU LIONS, PL	4		CHUNICHI DRAGONS, CL	1		
1989	YOMIURI GIANTS, CL	4		KINTETSU BUFFALOES, PL	3		
1990	SEIBU LIONS, PL	4		YOMIURI GIANTS, CL	0		
1991	SEIBU LIONS, PL	4		HIROSHIMA CARP, CL	3		
1992	SEIBU LIONS, PL	4		YAKULT SWALLOWS, CL	3		
1993	YAKULT SWALLOWS, CL	4		SEIBU LIONS, PL	3		
1994	YOMIURI GIANTS, CL	4		SEIBU LIONS, PL	2		

U.S. Major League Batters in Japan

Name	Yrs		G	HR	BA	Titles Won
Adair, Jerry	1	1971	90	7	.300	
Adduci, Jim	1	1987	82	13	.268	
Allen, Kim	2	1982-83	125	5	.265	
Allen, Rod	3	1989-91	245	45	.288	
Alou, Matty	3	1974-76	262	14	.283	
Altman, George	8	1968-75	935	205	.309	68 rbi, 71 ba
Andrews, Mike	1	1975-76	123	12	.231	
Arnold, Chris	3	1978-81	330	43	.274	
Aspromonte, Ken	3	1964-66	295	31	.273	
Ault, Doug	1	1981	102	18	.307	
Barbieri, Jim	1	1970	93	9	.188	
Barfield, Jesse	1	1993	104	26	.215	
Bass, Randy	6	1983-88	614	202	.337	85-86 hr-ba-rbi, 83-84 ba, 85 MVP
Bathe, Bill	2	1991-92	156	16	.236	
Batista, Rafael	1	1975	48	3	.204	
Baumer, Jim	5	1963-67	690	82	.251	
Bean, Billy	1	1992	7	0	.208	
Bernazard, Tony	3	1988-90	308	67	.289	
Bertoia, Reno	1	1964	20	1	.175	
Blasingame, Don	3	1967-69	366	15	.274	
Boisclair, Bruce	1	1980	80	1	.249	
Boles, Carl	6	1966-71	577	117	.265	
Boyer, Clete	4	1972-75	419	71	.257	
Bradford, Buddy	1	1977	56	4	.192	
Bradley, Phil	1	1991	121	21	.282	
Braggs, Glenn	2	1993-94	194	54	.326	
Brant, Marshall	2	1984-85	118	25	.244	
Brantley, Mickey	1	1993	13	0	.182	
Breeden, Hal	3	1976-78	260	79	.251	
Brewer, Rod	1	1994	74	8	.232	
Brewer, Tony	3	1986-89	389	82	.310	
Briggs, Dan	2	1982-83	176	18	.258	
Briggs, John	1	1976	47	7	.227	
Brouhard, Mark	2	1986-87	140	23	.265	
Brown, Marty	3	1992-94	229	50	.256	
Brown, Mike	1	1990	70	7	.282	
Bryant, Ralph	7	1988-94	725	249	.266	89 hr-MVP, 93 hr-rbi, 94 hr
Budaska, Mark	1	1982	86	3	.208	
Buford, Don	4	1973-76	490	65	.270	
Cabrera, Francisco	1	1994	95	11	.237	
Cage, Wayne	2	1981-82	252	62	.235	
Chance, Bob	2	1969-70	143	22	.271	
Christian, Bob	2	1971-72	232	27	.263	
Clark, Jerald	1	1994	99	20	.293	
Coggins, Frank	1	1973	13	2	.125	
Corey, Mark	1	1984	31	3	.215	
Cosey, Ray	1	1981	120	15	.251	
Cotto, Henry	1	1994	107	18	.251	
Cromartie, Warren	7	1984-90	779	171	.321	89 ba-MVP
Cruz, Hector	1	1983	58	4	.240	
Cruz, Tommy	6	1980-85	712	120	.310	
Dade, Paul	1	1981	37	1	.219	
Davis, Alvin	1	1992	40	5	.275	
Davis, Dick	5	1984-88	461	117	.331	
Davis, Willie	2	1977-78	199	43	.297	
Dayett, Brian	4	1988-91	145	121	.268	
DeCinces, Doug	1	1989	84	19	.244	
Deer, Rob	1	1994	70	8	.151	
Destrade, Orestes	4	1989-92	471	154	.264	90-92 hr, 90-91 rbi
Diaz, Mike	4	1989-92	350	114	.281	
Distefano, Benny	1	1990	56	39	.215	
Doby, Larry	1	1962	72	10	.225	
Dodson, Pat	1	1989	6	0	.313	
Doyle, Jeff	2	1984-85	243	29	.263	
Duncan, Taylor	1	1980	64	14	.235	
Dupree, Mike	1	1980	127	10	.266	
Easler, Mike	2	1988-89	142	26	.302	
Edwards, Mike	1	1983	53	1	.291	
Emery, Calvin	1	1970	94	8	.213	
Essegian, Chuck	1	1964	110	15	.263	
Ewing, Sam	1	1979	119	15	.286	
Fernandez, Chico	1	1965	52	1	.144	
Fielder, Cecil	1	1989	106	38	.302	
Gaines, Joe	1	1969	51	3	.205	
Gainey, Ty	2	1993-94	176	33	.270	
Gardner, Art	2	1981-82	218	30	.272	
Garrett, Adrian	3	1977-79	384	102	.260	
Garrett, Wayne	2	1979-80	192	28	.241	
Gentile, Jim	1	1969	65	8	.256	
Gladden, Dan	1	1994	98	15	.267	
Gonzales, Dan	1	1981	9	1	.174	
Gonzalez, Denny	2	1991-92	41	9	.248	
Gonzalez, Tony	1	1972	31	0	.297	
Goodwin, Danny	1	1986	83	8	.231	
Green, David	1	1986	67	10	.270	
Grunwald, Alfred	1	1962	70	3	.211	
Hadley, Kent	6	1962-67	781	131	.260	
Hall, Mel	2	1993-94	248	52	.286	
Hammond, Steve	1	1987	115	9	.274	
Hampton, Ike	1	1981	72	15	.230	
Hansen, Bob	2	1977-78	232	31	.271	
Harlow, Larry	1	1982	42	4	.164	
Harper, Terry	1	1988	10	2	.143	
Harris, Vic	3	1981-83	280	35	.253	
Hengel, Dave	2	1990-91	21	4	.183	
Hicks, Jim	2	1973-74	183	33	.247	
Hilton, Dave	3	1978-80	251	38	.284	
Hinshaw, George	1	1989	53	8	.294	
Hopkins, Gail	3	1975-77	360	69	.282	
Horner, Bob	1	1987	93	31	.327	
Hostetler, Dave	2	1986-87	254	42	.270	
Howard, Frank	1	1974	1	0	.000	
Howell, Jack	3	1992-94	339	86	.293	92 hr-ba-MVP
Hudler, Rex	1	1993	120	14	.300	
Ireland, Tim	2	1983-84	204	18	.275	
Jackson, Lou	3	1966-68	329	68	.257	
Jacoby, Brook	1	1993	18	2	.183	
James, Dion	1	1994	100	8	.263	
James, Skip	1	1980	111	21	.269	
Jestadt, Garry	2	1975-76	256	27	.239	
Johnson, Davey	2	1975-76	199	39	.241	
Johnson, Frank	1	1972	101	13	.232	
Johnson, Randy	2	1987-88	142	9	.306	
Johnson, Stan	1	1969	96	5	.242	
Johnston, Greg	1	1982	104	10	.256	
Jones, Bobby	2	1979-80	174	20	.284	
Jones, Clarence	8	1970-77	961	246	.239	74, 76 hr
Jones, Ruppert	1	1988	52	8	.254	
Keough, Marty	1	1968	134	17	.231	
Kirkland, Willie	6	1968-73	723	126	.246	
Klaus, Billy	1	1963	62	3	.257	
Kostro, Frank	1	1970	37	1	.200	
Krsnich, Mike	5	1963-67	506	90	.265	
LaCock, Pete	1	1981	90	10	.269	
Laga, Mike	2	1991-2	136	35	.231	
Lancellotti, Rich	2	1987-88	200	55	.207	87 hr
Larker, Norm	2	1965-66	224	14	.267	
Law, Vance	1	1990	122	29	.313	
Lee, Leron	11	1977-87	1315	283	.320	80 ba, 77 hr-rbi
Lefebvre, Jim	4	1973-76	330	60	.263	
Lezcano, Sixto	1	1987	20	3	.217	
Lind, Jack	1	1977	65	7	.237	
Lis, Joe	1	1978	95	6	.206	
Llenas, Winston	1	1976	101	6	.227	
Locklear, Gene	1	1978	108	8	.240	
Logan, Johnny	1	1964	96	7	.189	
Lolich, Ron	3	1974-76	272	56	.238	
Lopez, Arturo	6	1968-73	750	116	.290	

Name	Yrs		G	HR	BA	Titles Won
Loman, Doug	1	1986	126	14	.291	
Lum, Mike	1	1982	117	12	.269	
Lyttle, Jim	7	1977-83	876	166	.285	
Macha, Ken	4	1982-85	473	82	.304	
Madlock, Bill	1	1988	123	19	.263	
Manuel, Charlie	6	1976-81	621	189	.303	79-80 hr, 80 rbi, 79 MVP
Marshall, Jim	3	1963-65	408	78	.268	
Marshall, Mike	1	1992	67	9	.246	
Martin, Gene	6	1974-79	746	189	.272	
Martinez, Carmelo	1	1992	42	6	.227	
May, Carlos	4	1978-81	415	70	.309	
McFadden, Leon	1	1972	54	2	.283	
McGuire, Mickey	2	1973-74	207	11	.265	
McManus, Jim	2	1962-63	190	20	.236	
McNulty, Bill	1	1975	64	13	.190	
Medina, Luis	2	1993-94	109	14	.272	
Mejias, Roman	1	1966	30	0	.288	
Meyer, Joey	1	1990	42	26	.275	
Millan, Felix	3	1978-80	325	12	.306	79 ba
Miller, John	3	1970-72	382	79	.245	
Mitchell, Bobby	4	1976-79	474	113	.250	78 hr
Money, Don	1	1984	29	8	.260	
Morton, Bubba	1	1970	48	3	.173	
Moseby, Lloyd	2	1992-93	133	29	.289	
Motley, Darryl	2	1992-93	44	7	.222	
Muelens, Hensley	1	1994	122	23	.248	
Murphy, Dwayne	1	1990	34	5	.229	
Muser, Tony	1	1979	65	2	.196	
Nettles, Jim	1	1975	84	3	.234	
Newcombe, Don	1	1962	81	12	.262	
Nieman, Bob	1	1963	110	13	.301	
Nyman, Chris	2	1984-85	246	55	.276	
Oglivie, Ben	2	1987-88	224	46	.306	
O'Malley, Tom	4	1991-94	490	74	.318	93 ba
Ontiveros, Steve	6	1980-85	686	82	.312	
Ortenzio, Frank	2	1979-80	149	30	.250	
Paciorek, Jim	6	1988-93	698	86	.315	90 ba
Pagliarulo, Mike	1	1994	80	7	.263	
Palys, Stan	4	1964-67	446	66	.275	
Paredes, Johnny	1	1992	53	3	.242	
Parker, Wes	1	1974	127	14	.301	
Parrish, Larry	1	1989-90	235	70	.260	89 hr
Patterson, Mike	1	1985	88	16	.225	
Pepitone, Joe	1	1973	14	1	.163	
Perlozzo, Sam	1	1980	118	15	.281	
Peterson, Carl	3	1961-63	357	58	.272	
Pierce, Jack	1	1977	95	13	.227	
Pointer, Aaron	3	1970-72	302	40	.230	
Ponce, Carlos	5	1986-90	533	119	.296	87 rbi, 88 hr-rbi
Powell, Alonzo	3	1992-94	295	60	.317	94 ba
Putnam, Pat	2	1986-87	243	37	.266	
Qualls, Jimmy	2	1972-73	162	15	.252	
Raines, Larry	3	1953-55	330	31	.302	54 ba, 53 sb
Rajsich, Gary	3	1986-88	317	76	.283	
Rawdon, Wade	2	1989-90	149	24	.289	
Ray, Johnny	2	1991-92	159	13	.269	
Reid, Jessie	2	1991-92	128	20	.250	
Reimer, Kevin	1	1994	127	26	.298	
Reinback, Mike	5	1976-80	565	94	.296	
Repoz, Roger	5	1974-77	526	122	.262	
Reynolds, R.J.	3	1991-93	335	52	.288	
Rivera, Bombo	2	1985-86	158	37	.240	
Rivera, German	1	1989	123	25	.260	
Roberts, Dave	7	1967-73	814	183	.275	
Robson, Tom	1	1976	37	3	.209	

Name	Yrs		G	HR	BA	Titles Won
Rodgers, Andre	1	1969	49	4	.210	
Roig, Tony	6	1963-78	779	126	.255	
Rosario, Jim	2	1975-76	131	5	.215	
Rose, Bobby	2	1993-94	260	34	.310	93 rbi
Ryal, Mark	2	1991-92	124	24	.286	
Scheinblum, Rich	2	1975-76	239	33	.295	
Schu, Rick	2	1993-94	257	38	.257	
Scott, John	3	1979-81	279	48	.262	
Sheets, Larry	1	1992	131	26	.308	92
Shirley, Bart	2	1971-72	246	15	.183	
Sipin, John	9	1972-80	1036	218	.297	
Smith, Chris	2	1984-85	68	5	.202	
Smith, Reggie	2	1983-84	186	45	.271	
Smith, Willie	2	1972-73	170	29	.259	
Solaita, Tony	4	1980-83	510	155	.268	81 hr-rbi
Sorrell, Bill	2	1972-73	183	20	.278	
Spencer, Daryl	7	1964-70	731	152	.275	64, 65 ba
Spikes, Charlie	1	1981	26	1	.122	
Stairs, Matt	1	1993	60	6	.250	
Stanton, Leroy	1	1979	121	23	.225	
Stephens, Gene	1	1966	109	5	.224	
Stevens, Lee	1	1994	93	20	.288	
Strougther, Steve	1	1983	28	5	.276	
Stuart, Dick	2	1967-68	208	49	.257	
Tatum, Jarvis	1	1971	31	1	.192	
Taylor, Robert	3	1973-75	358	30	.259	
Testa, Nick	1	1962	57	0	.136	
Thomas, Lee	1	1969	109	12	.263	
Thomasson, Gary	2	1981-82	167	20	.249	
Tolan, Bobby	1	1978	98	6	.267	
Tolentino, Jose	1	1993	30	1	.152	
Torve, Kelvin	2	1992-93	192	20	.271	
Traber, Jim	2	1990-91	247	53	.287	
Tracy, Jim	2	1983-84	128	20	.301	
Traxler, Brian	1	1994	129	15	.263	
Tyrone, Jim	3	1979-82	435	74	.287	
Upshaw, Willie	2	1989-90	174	39	.245	
Valentine, Fred	1	1970	123	11	.246	
Venable, Max	2	1992-93	214	20	.270	
Versalles, Zoilo	1	1972	48	4	.189	
Vidal, Jose	1	1971	39	2	.221	
Vukovich, George	2	1986-87	222	32	.256	
Walls, Lee	1	1965	108	14	.239	
Walton, Danny	1	1978	75	9	.215	
Ward, Jay	1	1966	104	14	.238	
Wells, Greg	10	1983-92	1148	277	.317	84 hr-ba-rbi-MVP, 87 rbi, 89 ba-rbi
Werhas, Johnny	1	1971	100	8	.214	
White, Jerry	2	1984-85	218	37	.251	
White, Roy	3	1980-82	362	54	.283	
Whitfield, Terry	3	1981-83	374	85	.289	
Williams, Bernie	6	1975-80	718	96	.258	
Williams, Dallas	1	1988	100	10	.242	
Williams, Eddie	1	1991	49	5	.252	
Williams, Walt	2	1976-77	239	44	.277	
Wills, Bump	2	1983-84	203	16	.259	
Wilson, George	2	1963-64	225	27	.258	
Wilson, Jim	1	1990	6	1	.059	
Windhorn, Gordon	6	1964-69	641	86	.255	
Winters, Matt	5	1990-94	637	160	.271	
Wolfe, Larry	1	1982	88	14	.224	
Woods, Ron	2	1975-76	192	19	.263	
Wright, George	2	1988&93	183	20	.247	
Wynne, Marvell	1	1991	123	13	.230	
Young, Mike	1	1990	69	11	.234	
Zimmer, Don	1	1966	87	9	.182	

U.S. Major League Pitchers in Japan*

Name	Yrs		Won-Lost	ERA	Name	Yrs		Won-Lost	ERA
Abbott, Kyle	1	1994	0-0	7.71	Krueger, Rich	1	1979	2-1	4.66
Alexander, Bob	1	1959	2-5	4.67	Kuhaulua, Fred	1	1978	3-4	4.32
Anderson, Scott	2	1991-92	18-21	4.00	Lesley, Brad	2	1986-87	7-5	3.00
Austin, Rick	1	1974	1-1	2.33	Ley, Richard	2	1974-75	5-5	4.09
Baller, Jay	1	1994	0-0	4.15	Mickens, Glenn	5	1959-63	45-51	2.50
Bannister, Floyd	1	1990	3-2	4.04	Newcombe, Don	1	1962	0-0	4.50
Beene, Andy	1	1985	2-2	7.25	Paine, Phil	1	1953	4-3	1.77
Birtsas, Tim	1	1991	3-5	5.61	Palmquist, Ed	1	1963	0-1	3.00
Burnside, Pete	2	1964-65	10-22	3.10	Perez, Yorkis	1	1992	0-1	7.11
Cary, Chuck	1	1992	3-5	3.61	Rajsich, David	1	1984	0-1	3.18
Castillo, Bobby	1	1987	1-1	7.84	Reynolds, Bob	1	1977	0-0	9.00
Comstock, Keith	2	1985	8-10	4.47	Rochford, Mike	1	1990	0-3	8.61
Culver, George	1	1975	1-4	6.50	Sanchez, Luis	2	1986-87	4-4	2.54
Davis, Ron	1	1989	4-5	3.97	Schulze, Don	3	1990-92	12-11	4.94
Eichelberger, Juan	1	1989	0-3	7.04	Scott, Darril	1	1994	0-1	2.51
Foytack, Paul	1	1965	2-3	3.16	Shirley, Steve	2	1983-84	5-7	4.17
Gail, Rich	2	1985-86	18-18	4.42	Smith, Willie	1	1972	0-1	81.00
Gibson, Bob	1	1988	7-11	4.87	Stanka, Joe	7	1960-66	100-72	3.03
Gossage, Goose	1	1990	2-3	4.40	Stone, Dean	1	1964	0-0	3.75
Gross, Kip	1	1994	6-12	4.29	Thigpin, Bobby	1	1994	2-2	1.93
Grunwald, Alfred	1	1962	2-8	4.50	Tillotson, Thad	1	1971	3-4	6.40
Gullickson, Bill	2	1988-89	21-14	3.29	Tunnell, Lee	3	1991-93	10-19	4.90
Hartley, Mike	1	1994	1-6	4.29	Wright, Clyde	3	1976-78	22-18	3.97
Henry, Dwayne	1	1994	3-7	6.69	TOTALS			433-452	
Hoffman, Guy	3	1989-91	20-19	4.33					
Jones, Jimmy	1	1994	7-2	4.11					
Kekich, Mike	1	1974	5-11	4.13					
Keough, Matt	4	1987-90	45-44	3.73					
Kiely, Leo	1	1953	6-0	1.80					

* Lists compiled from Wayne Graczyk, *Americans in Japan 1950-1986*, and Isao Chiba, "Kiroku no Techo (Record Notes)," *Shukan Baseball*, March 28, 1988, and April 4, 1988.

## CHAPTER 20

Baseball in the Caribbean

Rob Ruck

Soon after the World Series marks the season's end in the United States, baseball springs back to life in and around the Caribbean. There, to the beat of *salsa* and *merengue* and against a backdrop of palm trees and seasonal labor, some of the best baseball in the world is played each winter. While most of South America follows football and the British West Indies follows cricket, the rest of the Caribbean basin plays baseball—and has for the better part of a century.

Since baseball fever first infected Cuba in the 1870s, the game has infiltrated the sporting psyches of Mexico, Nicaragua, the Dominican Republic, Venezuela, Puerto Rico, Panama, and Colombia. Although tied to major league baseball in four of these countries through a set of winter leagues and as a source of fresh talent, Caribbean baseball is not simply an appendage of the game that is played in the United States. Rather, baseball has acquired an autonomous persona as the peoples of the region have made the game into their own national pastimes.

More than simply recreation or a display of grace and competence, baseball has catalyzed national consciousness and cohesion in the Caribbean basin. A critical part of the fabric of everyday life, the sport has also influenced how these societies have come to define themselves, their relations with each other, and their ties to the United States. "It's more than a game," Dominican winter league general manager Winston Llenas once remarked. "It's our passion. It's almost our way of life."

Pedro Julio Santana stands at his office window in what was once the colonial zone of Santo Domingo. A sportsman at the center of Dominican baseball's evolution earlier this century, he searches for words to describe how the game penetrated his country and the rest of the basin. Glancing below to the hulking walls of the first Catholic cathedral in the western hemisphere, Santana finds his metaphor. "It is much the same as that which happened with Christianity. Jesus could be compared to the North Americans, but the apostles were the ones that spread the faith, and the apostles of baseball were Cubans. Even though the Dominican Republic and Puerto Rico were occupied by the North Americans, the Cubans first brought baseball here, and to Mexico and Venezuela, too."

Caribbean baseball's first epicenter was Cuba, which had fallen into orbit around the United States by the late nineteenth century. Baseball arrived there last century, brought by sailors, students, and businessmen from the United States as well as by Cubans who had traveled

north. The U.S. military occupations that followed the 1898 conflict with Spain stimulated baseball's expansion there and across the basin. By the time the Good Neighbor Policy had supplanted the Big Stick in the 1930s, baseball was entrenched. Moreover, Cuban baseball had become the focal point of an international network that stretched from the Caribbean basin through the Negro Leagues.

What was likely the first ballgame in Cuba with local participation occurred in June 1866, when sailors of a U.S. ship taking on sugar invited Cuban longshoremen to play. *El Club Habana* (Havana) began two years later, crushing a team from Matanzas in the first organized contest of two Cuban teams.

Havana's victory over Matanzas featured two of Cuba's sporting pioneers, Esteban Bellan and Emilio Sabourín. Bellan became the first Latino in U.S. organized baseball, playing three seasons in the National Association (1871–1873). Sabourín, the A. G. Spalding of Cuban baseball, was the motivating force behind the *Liga de Beisbol Profesional Cubana,* whose inaugural tournament was won by Sabourín's reconstituted Havana club in 1878. Sabourín proselytized for his sport as well as for the cause of Cuban independence from Spain until his contribution of baseball revenues to the independence movement incurred the wrath of Spanish officials. They imprisoned Sabourín until his death and banned baseball in parts of their colony.

While initially a game of the more affluent and those with contact with the United States, baseball soon spread to all classes of Cuban society, both urban and rural. U.S. military occupations, support by companies and businessmen, and close ties to political elites would shape its subsequent development, much as these forces would elsewhere in the basin.

The game was organized on three overlapping levels in its early years. The first was an ad hoc player-organized, self-directed network of teams. The second involved clubs sponsored by businessmen, companies, and politicians who sought the promotional advantages of such patronage. The third level was that of professional (sometimes semiprofessional) baseball, which organized championships from 1878 until 1961, with a changing cast of teams and format. In some years, no tournaments were held, while in others both a summer and winter season took place. Havana, Almendares, Santa Clara, Cienfuegos, and Marianao were the league's mainstays.

Until the 1959 Cuban Revolution and the ensuing U.S. blockade, Cuba set the standard for Caribbean baseball. It sent the most players to the major and Negro leagues while its winter and summer tournaments featured the highest caliber of Latin ball and attracted players from both the States and the basin. Cuban players, radio broadcasts, and emigrants, in turn, became baseball's emissaries to the rest of the region.

In the Dominican Republic, Cubans who had migrated to escape the turmoil of the Ten Years' War (1868–1878) were the first to form teams. Young Dominicans emulated them and joined with compatriots who had studied in the United States to establish a self-organized matrix of teams and tournaments well in place before the U.S. Marines arrived in 1916 for their eight-year occupation. Santo Domingo's *Licey,* the oldest of the six professional Dominican clubs, formed in 1907, while the forerunners of San Pedro de Macoris's *Estrellas Orientales,* Santiago's *Aguilas Cibaeñas,* and Santo Domingo's other club, *Escogido,* took to the field soon afterward.

While Dominicans refer to these early decades as the romantic epoch of baseball, commercial forces were already at work there and across the basin. Teams occasionally recruited players with the lure of financial reward and soon began importing Cubans and Puerto Ricans for championship tournaments. Moreover, local clubs often induced talented players with payment in cash or work. North American oil companies in Venezuela, rum distilleries and tobacco manufacturers in Cuba, and sugar cane companies in Nicaragua, Puerto Rico, Cuba, and the Dominican Republic sponsored or assisted workplace teams for recreation and community entertainment, but with an industrial agenda, too — winning their workers' hearts and minds.

During these "Yankee years," between 1898 and 1933, when the Marines hit the beaches thirty-four times in ten different basin countries, they found baseball already implanted in Cuba, Puerto Rico, Nicaragua, Mexico, and the Dominican Republic. They never made it to Venezuela, but would have found baseball there, too, as early as the organization of the Caracas club in 1895. The occupations, though, helped to push the sport along. While Nicaraguans had played on their Atlantic coast since 1888, the nation's longest-running pro team, *Boer,* was founded by the U.S. consul in Managua. In the Dominican Republic, U.S. marines and sailors played ball to bolster morale; they were frequently challenged by Dominican teams, for whom these contests were both a test of sporting abilities and national character. Far more baseball was in evidence by the end of the U.S. stay on the island.

While Cubans and some other basin natives had broken into baseball in the States during the first half of the century, the center of gravity for Caribbean baseball remained a regional one. A "Have Glove—Will Travel" mentality soon took hold of basin baseball and its ablest practitioners made the rounds of national tournaments. A core of the finest black players from the States—then barred from major league play by the color line, as were most Latinos—joined them in Cuba, the Dominican Republic, Puerto Rico, Venezuela, and Mexico.

Caribbean baseball's apogee was probably reached in the summer of 1937 in the Dominican Republic during a national championship dedicated to the re-election of the then state-of-the-art dictator Rafael Trujillo. Top Dominican players were joined by the best Cuban, Puerto Rican, and Negro league talent that the Dominican peso could buy to form a three-team league. Santiago boasted the services of Martín Dihigo, Luís Tiant Sr., and Horacio Martínez; San Pedro de Macoris countered with Tetelo Vargas, Ramón Bragaña, and Cocaína García, while the eventual victor, *Ciudad Trujillo* (a merger of *Licey* and *Escogido* that represented the city Trujillo had renamed in his own honor) relied on future Hall of Famers Josh Gibson, Cool Papa Bell, and Satchel Paige, as well as Silvío García, Perucho Cepeda, and Sam Bankhead. Baseball on the island was the equal of that played anywhere that summer. These players barnstormed yearround, and many of them later played together as *Santa Clara* in Cuba and as *La Concordia* in Venezuela.

The proprietary interest taken by caudillos such as Trujillo or Nicaragua's Anastasio Somoza ensured baseball of its most-favored sport status and contributed to the growth of strong regional rivalries. Caribbean participation in the *Mundiales,* the world amateur baseball championships that began in 1938, and later the Caribbean Series of pro circuits, which started in 1949, reinforced the game's hegemony.

Latin ball was an opportunity for North American players to supplement their income and hone their skills in encounters that sometimes surpassed the caliber of major league play. However, it was also a threat to organized baseball in the States. Major league teams had played in Cuba before the turn of the century, and afterward Negro league squads as well as individual black and white pros journeyed south. The 1937 raids on the Negro leagues by Dominican teams destroyed the Pittsburgh Crawfords, and other Negro league squads frequently lost their best players and gate attractions to basin teams. From 1939 until the demise of independent black baseball a decade later, Venezuelan and Mexican franchises vied for Negro leaguers during the summer months, enticing Josh Gibson, Ray Dandridge, and other stars to jump their Negro league teams. They offered better pay and a different atmosphere. "Not only do I get more money playing here, but I live like a king," Willie Wells wrote to *Pittsburgh Courier* sportswriter Wendell Smith in 1939 to explain his switch from the Newark Eagles to Vera Cruz. "I am not faced with the racial problem. . . . I've found freedom and democracy here, something I never found in the United States. . . . Here, in Mexico, I am a man."

The major leagues were less vulnerable to such competition, but even they blanched when Mexican liquor mogul Jorge Pasquel sought major leaguers in addition to Negro leaguers to bolster the six-team summer Mexican League in 1946. Railroad workers from the States taught the game to their Mexican colleagues as early as the 1880s and a strong semipro league formed in the 1920s. In Sonora and Mexico City, the game felt the pull of baseball across the northern border, which Mexican and black teams frequently crossed. In the Yucatan, baseball pointed more toward the Caribbean, especially Cuba. Pasquel, pumping new capital into the league, persuaded Mickey Owen, Sal Maglie, and Max Lanier to desert their major league teams, prompting the latter to ban them. Pasquel also pursued Stan Musial, reportedly placing $50,000 on the bed in his spring training hotel room at a time when the Cardinals' outfielder was making but $13,000 a season. Other basin leagues also lost top players in the Mexican effort to upgrade. Pasquel's challenge, however, was blunted by organized baseball in the States, which tried to limit any competition for its players, and by the Mexican League's own logistical and financial difficulties. The challenge faded after the 1948 season. In the aftermath of the Mexican raids and with integration imminent, major league baseball began to sign accords with professional leagues throughout the basin, formalizing player movement and institutionalizing winter play.

That was especially important, for with the end of the color line in 1947 Latinos soon renewed their assault on major league ball. By the 1970s, the basin would constitute the freshest source of talent in the majors, especially important as the black community turned away from baseball as part of a general shift toward other sports in the United States. But Latin players—black and white—had played pro ball in the United States long before Jackie Robinson's historic debut.

Colombia's Luis Castro broke ground in baseball's modern era, after the creation of the National and American Leagues, but Cubans for the most part led the way. While Castro played only part of the 1902 season, Rafael Almeida and Armando Marsans spearheaded a Cuban invasion in 1911 that left its imprimatur on the game and numbered over thirty players before integration. Another ninety or so Cubans played major league ball after that divide.

The crucial factor controlling the entry of Cubans and other basin players into the major leagues was skin color. Barnstorming their way through black communities from the early century on, Cuban teams had become a mainstay of the Negro leagues that began in 1920. Popular draws, the Cuban Stars and the New York Cubans featured Latinos too dark to pass the color line into the majors. Playing most of their contests on the road, these Caribbean squads injected talent and a tropical allure to the game. Cubans Martín Dihigo, Alejandro Oms, Luís Tiant Sr., Orestes "Minnie" Miñoso, and Silvío García were joined by Dominicans Horacio Martínez and Tetelo Vargas, Puerto Rican Peruchin Cepeda, Panamanian Pat Scantlebury, and sometimes several black North Americans who passed for Cubans, on these pan-Caribbean aggregations. A few Cubans, such as Cristóbal Torriente, a powerful outfielder, and José de la Caridad Méndez, *"El Diamante Negro,"* who took a no-hitter into the ninth inning the first time he faced the barnstorming Cincinnati Reds, became mainstays of other Negro league franchises.

Lighter-skinned Cubans from that predominantly mixed island played on the other side of sport's racial boundary in the States, in the major leagues. Perhaps the greatest pre–Jackie Robinson Cuban major leaguer was Adolfo Luque, a pitcher whose twenty big league seasons were capped by a brilliant 27–8 record in 1923 and a winning relief stint of shutout ball in the seventh game of the 1933 World Series. Following that game, Clark Griffith, whose Washington Senators had lost the Series, decided to back a scouting exhibition to Cuba. He sent Joe Cambria.

"Papa Joe," as many still refer to Cambria, stocked the Senators with Cubans. Among his first signees was Roberto Estalella, from the sugarcane milltown that Hershey Chocolate operated in Cárdenas. The *Cincinnati Enquirer* had greeted the signings of Almeida and Marsans in 1911 with relief, introducing them as "two of the purest bars of

Castilian soap to ever wash upon our shores," but the darker-hued Estalella was more controversial. No one challenged this indirect breaching of the color line, although it prompted Red Smith to write his classic column in which he suspected that "there was a Senegambian somewhere in the Cuban batpile where Senatorial lumber was seasoned."

The player regarded in the Caribbean as the best Cuban ever, and arguably the finest ballplayer of all time, never played major league ball. Martín Dihigo displayed his talents in Cuba, the United States, Mexico, Venezuela, and the Dominican Republic, and is enshrined in the Hall of Fame of three of these nations. Dihigo excelled at the plate, on the mound, and as a manager, but integration came too late for him. His bust at Havana's *Estadio Latinoamericano* reads simply, *El Immortal.*

The contradiction that some Cubans played in the majors and others in the Negro leagues was not lost upon blacks in the States or on Latin ballplayers. As early as Almeida's and Marsans' 1911 debut, the black press began to hope that black ballplayers would soon follow them into baseball's most exclusive league. And while Negro leaguers went south to adulation and greater pay, dark-skinned Latinos who came north encountered prejudice based on both skin color and nationality. As major leaguers such as Ty Cobb, Tris Speaker, and Carl Hubbell traveled south to play in winter ball, black North Americans and Latinos found that they could more than hold their own. These symbolic victories were appreciated both in the States and throughout the basin. North American blacks and the peoples of the region shared each other's athletes and appropriated each other's sporting heroes and symbols. If a proving ground was necessary to show that blacks could compete with whites, that the two could coexist on the same squad, or to dispel any other racial shibboleth, Caribbean baseball was just that.

Following integration, the more farsighted owners began scouring the islands for prospects. Soon a fresh wave of Latinos arrived in the majors, including three future Hall of Famers: Venezuela's Luís Aparicio, Puerto Rico's Roberto Clemente, and the Dominican Republic's Juan Marichal. They signaled, moreover, a shift away from Cuba as the primary spawning waters for Caribbean players.

With the 1959 Cuban Revolution and the subsequent deterioration of relations with the United States, Cuba fell out of organized baseball's system. The Havana Sugar Kings, an International League franchise affiliated with the Reds since 1954, were on their way to winning the Little World Series of the AAA minor leagues in 1959, just months after Fidel Castro came to power. The revolutionary government offered to underwrite the Sugar Kings' debts, and Castro sought to keep the franchise there, "even if I have to pitch," but the International League shipped the club to Jersey City during the 1960 season. Baseball in Cuba was cut off completely from baseball in the United States, and the movement of players and equipment halted. Cuba developed its own sporting goods industry and relied on the repatriated Dihigo, a political exile during the 1950s who had given money to Che Guevara and who now returned to help teach the game. Cuban baseball soon shed its commercial skin and sought instead to advance the social and political aims of the revolution. Cuba has remained *the* powerhouse in world amateur baseball ever since, but the island stopped producing new major leaguers. After the Zoilo Versalles, Tony Oliva, Tony Pérez generations passed out of baseball, the next set of Cubans to reach the majors were those who, while born on the island, had grown up in the United States.

The fulcrum of baseball power, meanwhile, shifted one island to the east, where the Dominican Republic shared Hispaniola with French-speaking, soccer-playing Haiti. After the star-studded 1937 season, pro ball in the Dominican Republic entered a fourteen-year hiatus. While an occasional tournament celebrated an event such as the nation's centennial, Dominican pros Horacio Martínez and Tetelo Vargas plied their trade in Cuba, Venezuela, or the United States. But several forces revitalized Dominican baseball in the 1940s, and after the reappearance of a professional league in 1951, these dynamics propelled over a hundred players to the major leagues.

The first catalyst was the birth of the *Mundial,* an international championship tournament for amateur baseball. After its inauguration in England in 1938, the *Mundial* moved to the Caribbean. Held in the basin throughout the 1940s, with Cuba hosting five consecutive tournaments, the *Mundial* had a decidedly Latin flavor and became the most important sporting competition in which these nations competed on something approximating equal footing, both with each other and with the United States. Basin nations won every championship from 1940 through 1972, with Cuba winning eleven out of eighteen times.

National aspirations and international rivalries sometimes were injected into the *Mundial.* An irate Anastasio Somoza fired the Nicaraguan manager in the midst of one and took to the dugout to direct the team himself. Nicaraguan national honor was restored by a victory over Cuba in the final game of the 1972 series, an event still celebrated as one of the Central American nation's greatest sporting exploits. The Dominican victory in 1948, coming just months after virtually the entire national championship team perished in a plane crash by the Río Verde, captivated the Republic and lent impetus to pro ball's rebirth there.

A second factor in Dominican baseball's rejuvenation was the creation of the *Dirección General de Deportes.* Modeled in part after the comparable Cuban agency, this government body organized regional and then national tournaments for amateur baseball (often with semiprofessional overtones) that gave further purpose to local, company, and armed forces support. Many of the Dominicans that entered the majors from the late 1950s on, including Marichal, Manuel Mota, and the three Rojas Alou brothers, played on these squads.

The final catalysts to Dominican ascendancy were bananas and sugarcane, and the concentrations of baseball fervor and expertise which they fostered. While the sugarcane milltowns of the southeast produce the most prospects today, the banana region along the northwest border with Haiti was instrumental in cultivating the first contingent of pros in the late 1950s. There the Grenada Company, a United Fruit Company subsidiary, began two teams for its workers and their sons in the 1940s. The squad won three national championships, and Juan

Marichal and Guayubín Olivo passed through its ranks to the majors.

Dominican sugarcane milltowns, like those in Cuba, had long spawned ballclubs. The six-month long *tiempo muerto,* or dead season, when the cane required minimal attention and most workers were unemployed, contributed to an intense sporting environment, first for cricket and ultimately for baseball. In the 1920s and '30s, *Central La Romana's Papagayo* team was an amateur powerhouse, and in the 1940s the milltowns in and around San Pedro de Macoris made their play. There the descendants of cricket-playing migrants from the British West Indies brought to cut cane and work in the mills displayed an aptitude for playing baseball and an approach to organizing the game that made San Pedro baseball's Mecca. Since Rico Carty's breakthrough in the 1960s, San Pedro has contributed about one-third of the Dominicans to play in the big leagues. The town currently sends more of its native sons to the majors on a per-capita basis than any town ever has. There is probably no other place on earth where the game is played as well and as widely.

Since the end of the color line, ballplayers from Cuba, the Dominican Republic, Venezuela, Puerto Rico, Panama, Nicaragua, Mexico, Colombia, and even the Bahamas have played major league ball. Although the Dominican Republic leads this basin contingent, substantial numbers of Puerto Ricans and Venezuelans are present, too. Mexico, despite a population that dwarfs the rest of the region combined and its well-developed pro leagues, sends few players to the majors. Unlike the other basin leagues, Mexican teams retain first rights to sign any native amateur. A major league club, therefore, must buy the contract from a player's Mexican club, usually for more than it costs to sign a prospect elsewhere in the region. This relationship, the summer Mexican league, and perhaps cultural factors, too, persuade native ballplayers to remain in Mexico.

Cuba opted out of this network after its revolution, and Nicaragua, whose eleven-year fling with the pro winter leagues ended in 1967, followed suit after its 1979 revolution. Panama and Colombia have also tried winter ball, but financial pressures made play sporadic.

The flow of players continues to run both north and south. Minor and major leaguers from the United States still play in the winter leagues, which presently operate in Venezuela, Puerto Rico, the Dominican Republic, and Mexico. In their heyday during the 1950s and '60s, these winter leagues featured major leaguers like Tommy Lasorda, Whitey Ford, and Willie Stargell. But as major league salaries soared in the 1970s and unfavorable rates of exchanges weakened basin economies, the winter leagues restricted the number of North American imports. Minor leaguers and inexperienced major leaguers have replaced them. For them, these leagues provide the chance to play in the winter months, developing the potential that might allow them to crack a big league roster. They also earn higher pay than they do in the minors, encounter competition from top Latino players, and are treated as demigods by the impassioned *fanáticos* of the winter game.

The winners of the winter leagues have met in a *Serie del Caribe* since 1949. Between 1949 and 1960, the pennant-winning squads of Cuba, Panama, Puerto Rico, and

Venezuela played in early February to determine a champion of the Caribbean. Cuba won over half of these tournaments, but after the revolution, the series was discontinued. When it resumed in 1970, Mexico and the Dominican Republic replaced Cuba and Panama. The current round-robin format sends the teams that win their postseason tournaments to the *Serie del Caribe* along with a number of reinforcements, including North Americans, from their defeated opponents. Willie Mays, Monte Irvin, Camilo Pasqual, Rico Carty, and Vic Pellot Power are among those who have starred in these postseason celebrations.

Winter ball has descended from its zenith of the 1950s and '60s largely due to economic dynamics beyond the control of the Caribbean franchises. Rising player and fuel costs, devalued currencies, and underdevelopment pushed many into deficits, with government subsidies often vital to their continuation. Government support, long a feature of basin baseball, helps to keep current the Dominican saying that there will never be political trouble during the baseball season, only afterward. But by the middle of the 1980s, fewer of the established Latin major leaguers suited up for the October-through-January campaign. The demands of the regular season, the threat of injury, and the relatively inconsequential pay of winter ball suggest that this trend will continue. The pattern, however, has given younger Latin ballplayers the chance to play before knowledgeable fans and against competition that is often at a major league level.

While winter ball in the late 1980s was troubled and other sports were making inroads, baseball remains *el rey de deportes* (the king of sports) throughout the basin. From the rocky hillsides and arid plains of northern Mexico through the canefields of the islands to the basin's southernmost flank in the Andes, baseball commands a fascination approaching reverence.

Baseball's significance derives from the role that it has played in the coming together of these societies in the twentieth century. Knitting a common cultural fabric, serving as a vent to social and political tensions, and offering a vehicle not only for individual mobility but collective social affirmation, baseball indeed has been more than a game. It has offered the citizens of the basin a chance to enter a ritual kinship embracing all fans and players. And while reflecting the progressive penetration of the United States in the region, baseball has been more than a cultural transmission belt for North American values. Beating each other and excelling in the major leagues and international competitions at a time when the Caribbean basin has encountered difficulties in asserting either its political or economic autonomy have been tremendous sources of pride. And that symbolic recognition has become a catalyst to national cohesion and consciousness for the region in its troubled evolution this century.

First Major Leaguers from Caribbean Basin Countries

Country	Player	Year	Team
Belize	Chito Martinez	1991	Baltimore Orioles
Colombia	Luis "Jud" Castro	1902	Philadelphia Athletics
Cuba	Esteban Bellan	1871	Troy Haymakers
	Rafael Almeida	1911	Cincinnati Reds
	Armando Marsans	1911	Cincinnati Reds
Mexico	Baldomero "Mel" Almada	1933	Boston Red Sox
Venezuela	Alejandro Carrasquel	1939	Washington Senators
Puerto Rico	Hiram Bithorn	1942	Chicago Cubs
Panama	Héctor López	1955	Kansas City Athletics
	Humberto Robinson	1955	Milwaukee Braves
Dominican Republic	Osvaldo Virgil	1956	New York Giants
Virgin Islands	Joe Christopher	1959	Pittsburgh Pirates
Nicaragua	Dennis Martínez	1976	Baltimore Orioles
Honduras	Gerald Young	1987	Houston Astros
Curacao	Hensley Meulens	1990	New York Yankees

Serie del Caribe

Series	Year	Site	Winning Team/Country
I	1949	Cuba	Almendares/Cuba
II	1950	Puerto Rico	Carta Vieja/Panama
III	1951	Venezuela	Santurce/Puerto Rico
IV	1952	Panama	La Habana/Cuba
V	1953	Cuba	Santurce/Puerto Rico
VI	1954	Puerto Rico	Caguas/Puerto Rico
VII	1955	Venezuela	Santurce/Puerto Rico
VIII	1956	Panama	Cienfuegos/Cuba
IX	1957	Cuba	Marianao/Cuba
X	1958	Puerto Rico	Marianao/Cuba
XI	1959	Venezuela	Almendares/Cuba
XII	1960	Panama	Cienfuegos/Cuba
	1961–69	Not Held	
XIII	1970	Venezuela	Magallanes/Venezuela
XIV	1971	Puerto Rico	Licey/Dominican Republic
XV	1972	Dominican Republic	Ponce/Puerto Rico
XVI	1973	Venezuela	Licey/Dominican Republic
XVII	1974	Mexico	Caguas/Puerto Rico
XVIII	1975	Puerto Rico	Bayamón/Puerto Rico
XIX	1976	Dominican Republic	Hermosillo/Mexico
XX	1977	Venezuela	Licey/Dominican Republic
XXI	1978	Mexico	Mayagüez/Puerto Rico
XXII	1979	Puerto Rico	Magallanes/Venezuela
XXIII	1980	Dominican Republic	Licey/Dominican Republic
	1981	Not Held	
XXIV	1982	Mexico	Caracas/Venezuela
XXV	1983	Venezuela	Arecibo/Puerto Rico
XXVI	1984	Puerto Rico	Zulia/Venezuela
XXVII	1985	Mexico	Licey/Dominican Republic
XXVIII	1986	Venezuela	Mexicali/Mexico
XXIX	1987	Mexico	Caguas/Venezuela
XXX	1988	Dominican Republic	Escogido/Dominican Republic
XXXI	1989	Mazatlan	Zulia/Venezuela
XXXII	1990	Miami	Escogido/Dominican Republic
XXXIII	1991	Miami	Licey/Dominican Republic
XXXIV	1992	Mexico	Mayagüez/Puerto Rico
XXXV	1993	Mexico	Mayagüez/Puerto Rico
XXXVI	1994	Mexico	Licey/Dominican Republic

Dominican League Statistics

Year	Champion	BA Leader	HR Leader	Most Games Won
1951	Licey	Luis Villodas .346	Pedro Formental 13	Guayuabín Olivo 10
1952	Aguilas	Luis Olmo .344	Alonzo Perry 11	Terry McDuffie 14
1953	Licey	Tetelo Vargas .355	Alonzo Perry 11	Emilio Cueche 13
1954	Estrellas Orientales	Alonzo Perry .326	Bob Thurman 11	Carrao Bracho G. Olivo 8
1955–56	Escogido*	Bob Wilson .333	Willie Kirkland 9	Fred Waters 11
1956–57	Escogido	Osvaldo Virgil .312	Danny Kravitz 4	Pete Burnside 11
1957–58	Escogido	Alonzo Perry .332	Dick Stuart 14	Fred Kipp 11
1958–59	Licey	Felipe Alou .351	Jim McDaniels 12	Bennie Daniels 12
1959–60	Escogido	Felipe Alou .359	Frank Howard 9	Stan Williams 12
1960–61	Escogido	Manuel Mota .344	Manuel Jiménez J.V. Nicolás Victor Ramirez Felipe Alou N. Saviñón Tied with 4	Danilo Riva 13
1961–62	Incomplete Season			
1962–63	Not Held			
1963–64	Licey	Manuel Mota .379	O. McFarlane 10	G. Olivo Steve Blass 9
1964–65	Aguilas	Manuel Mota .364	O. McFarlane 8	Dick LeMay 8
1965–66	Season not organized by league			
1966–67	Aguilas	Mateo Alou .363	Winston Llenas Bob Robertson 10	Dock Ellis 9
1967–68	Estrellas Orientales	Ricardo Carty .350	Bob Robertson 9	Silvano Quezada 11
1968–69	Escogido	Mateo Alou .390	Nate Colbert 8	Jay Ritchie 9
1969–70	Licey	Ralph Garr .387	Winston Llenas Byron Browne 9	G. Rounsaville 8
1970–71	Licey	Ralph Garr .457	César Cedeño 8	Rollie Fingers 9
1971–72	Aguilas	Ralph Garr .388	Charlie Sands 10	Gene Garber 9
1972–73	Licey	Von Joshua .358	Adrian Garrett 9	Pedro Borbón 9
1973–74	Licey	Dave Parker .345	Ricardo Carty 9	Rick Waits 8
1974–75	Aguilas	Bruce Bochte .352	Rafael Batista Bobby Darwin 8	James Richards 8
1975–76	Aguilas	Wilbur Howard .341	Wilbur Howard John Hale Gary Alexander Larry Parrish G. Thomasson Bill Nahorodny Andre Thornton Tied with 4	Nino Espinosa Tom Dettore 8
1976–77	Licey	Mario Guerrero .365	Pedro Guerrero Ike Hampton 6	Angel Torres 10
1977–78	Aguilas	Omar Moreno .345	Dick Davis 8	Odell Jones Al Holland Mickey Mahler 7
1978–79	Aguilas	Ted Cox .319	Bob Beall Dick Davis 7	Bo McLaughlin Mike Proly 9
1979–80	Licey	Tony Peña .317	A. De Freitas Alberto Lois Leon Durham Samuel Mejía Pedro Guerrero Tied with 3	Jerry Hannahs 9
1980–81	Escogido	Ken Landreaux .394	Tony Peña 7	Mario Soto M. Mahler 7
1981–82	Escogido	Pedro Hernandez .408	Dave Hostetler 9	Pasqual Pérez 10
1982–83	Licey	César Geronimo .341	Howard Johnson 8	Pasqual Pérez 9
1983–84	Licey	Miguel Diloné .343	Reggie Whittemore 12	Orel Hershiser Frank Wills 8
1984–85	Licey	Junior Noboa .327	Ralph Bryant 9	Tom Filer 8
1985–86	Aguilas	Tony Fernández .364	Tony Peña 9	Mickey Mahler 8
1986–87	Aguilas	Stanley Javier .374	Ralph Bryant 13	Gibson Alba José Nuñez Eric Plunk Tied with 5
1987–88	Escogido	Stanley Javier .363	Mark Parent 10	José Bautista 8
1988–89	Licey	Julio Peguero .327	Domingo Michel 9	Melido Perez 8–3
1989–90	Escogido	Angel González .403	Denny González 5	Mel Rojas Jeff Shaw Kevin Wicklander Darren Holmes Tied with 6
1990–91	Licey	Hensley Meulens .338	Francisco Cabrera 8	Francesco De la Rosa 7
1991–92	Escogido	Luis Mercedes .333	Francisco Cabrera, Sammy Sosa, Geronimo Berroa, Kevin Koslofski, and Julian Yan tied with 4	José Nuñez 6
1992–93	Aguilas	Tom Marsh .318	Domingo Martinez 6	Efrain Valdez, Jose Martinez, Howard Farmer, ans Rafael Valdez 5
1993–94	Licey	Alex Arias .371	Henry Rodriguez 6	Apolinar Garcia 6

* First year held in winter

Cuban League Statistics

Year	Champion	BA Leader	HR Leader	Most Games Won
1878–79	Habana Undefeated			
1879–80	Habana			
1880–81	Not held			
1882	Disputed: Fe and Habana			
1882–83	Habana			
1885	Habana	Pablo Ronquilla .350		
1885–86	Habana Undefeated	Wenceslao Gálvez .345		Adolfo Luján 5–0
1887	Habana	R. Martínez .439		Adolfo Luján 5–0
1888	Fe	Antonio García .448		Francisco Hernández 10–2
1889	Habana	Francisco Salabarria .305		Adolfo Luján 10–3
1889–90	Habana	Antonio García .364		Miguel Prats 11–2

Year	Champion	BA Leader	HR Leader	Most Games Won
1890–91	Fe	Alfredo Crespo .375		Miguel Prats 9–4
1892	Habana	Antonio García .362		E. Hernández 4–1
1892–93	Matanzas	Antonio García .385		Francisco Hernández 4–1
1893–94	Almendares	Miguel Pratts .394		José Pastoriza 16–7
1894–95	Suspended due to War of Independence	Alfredo Arcaño .430		Enrique García 12–4
1897–98	Not finished			
1898	Habanista	Valentín González .394		José Romero 5–2
1900	San Francisco	Esteban Pratts .333		Luis Padrón 13–4
1901	Habana	Julián Castillo .454		Carlos Royer 12–3
1902	Habana Undefeated	Luis Padrón .463		Carlos Royer 17–0
1903	Habana	Julián Castillo .330		Cándido Fontanals 14–6
1904	Habana	Regino García .397		Carlos Royer 13–3
1905	Almendares	Regino García .305		Angel D'Meza 10–4
1905–6	Fe	Regino García .304		José Muñoz 8–1
1907	Almendares	Regino García .324		George Mack 4–2
1908	Almendares	Emilio Palomino .350		José Méndez 9–0
1908–9	Habana	Julián Castillo .315		L. Haggerman 15–6
1910	Almendares	Emilio Palomino .408		José Méndez 7–0
1910–11	Almendares	Preston Hill .365		José Méndez 11–2
1912	Habana	Emilio Palomino .440		José Junco 6–1
1913	Fe	Armando Marsans .400		Red Redding 7–2
1913–14	Almendares	Manuel Villa .351		José Méndez 10–0
1914–15	Habana	Cristóbal Torriente .387		José Acosta 5–1
1915–16	Almendares	Eustaquio Pedrosos .413		José Acosta 8–3
1917	Orientales	Adolfo Luque .355		José Acosta 2–1
1918–19	Habana	Manuel Cueto .344		José Acosta 16–10
1919–20	Almendares	Cristóbal Torriente .360		Emilio Palmero 5–1
1920–21	Habana	Pelayo Chacon .344	Cristóbal Torriente M. González B. Jiménez M. Guerra Tied with 1	José "Cheo" Hernández 4–1
1921*	Habana	Bienvenido Jiménez .619	Manuel Cueto 1	Julio Leblanc 2–0
1922–23	Marianao	Bernardo Baró .401	Cristóbal Torriente 4	Lucas Boada 10–4
1923–24	Santa Clara	Oliver Marcells .393	Bienvenido Jiménez 4	Bill Holland 10–2
1924–25	Almendares	Manuel Cueto .364	Esteban Mantalvo 5	José Acosta 4–1
1925–26	Almendares	Johnny Wilson .430	J. H. Lloyd Jud Wilson 3	César Alvarez 10–2
1926–27	Habana	Manuel Cueto .404	J. Hernández 3	Juan Olmo 3–0
1927–28	Habana	Johnny Wilson .424	Oscar Charleston 5	Oscar Levis 7–2
1928–29	Habana	Alejandro Oms .432	Cool Papa Bell 5	Adolfo Luque 9–2
1929–30	Cienfuegos	Alejandro Oms .380	Mule Suttles 7	Heliodoro "Yoyo" Diaz 13–3

Year	Champion	BA Leader	HR Leader	Most Games Won
1930–31*	Not finished	O. Charleston .373	Ernest Smith José Fernández 1	Martin Dihigo 2–0
1931–32	Almendares	Rámon Cueto .400	Alejandro Oms Ismael Morales 3	Juan Eckelson 5–1
1932–33	Tie: Habana Almendares	M. González .432	R. Estalella 3	Jésus Lorenzo 3–0
1933–34	No championship held			
1934–35	Almendares	Lázaro Salazar .407	Eleven tied with 1	Lázaro Salazar 6–1
1935–36	Santa Clara	Martín Dihigo .358	Willie Wells Jacinto Roque 5	Martín Dihigo 11–2
1936–37	Marianao	Harry Williams .349	H. Andrews R. Estalella 5	Raymond Brown 21–4
1937–38	Santa Clara	Sam Bankhead .366	Willie Wells R. Estalella Raymond Brown 4	Raymond Brown 12–5
1938–39	Santa Clara	Tony Castaños .371	Josh Gibson 11	Martín Dihigo 14–2
1939–40	Almendares	Tony Castaños .340	Mule Suttles 4	Rodolfo Fernández 7–4
1940–41	Habana	Lázaro Salazar .316	A. Crespo 3	Gilberto Torres 10–3
1941–42	Almendares	Silvío García .351		Macon Mayor Agapito Mayor 6–2
1942–43	Almendares	A. Crespo .337	Roberto Ortiz Saguita Hernández 2	Cocaina García 10–3
1943–44	Habana	Roberto Ortiz .337	Saguita Hernández 3	Martín Dihigo 8–1
1944–45	Almendares	Claro Duany .340	Claro Duany 3	Oliverio Ortiz 10–4
1945–46	Cienfuegos	L. Davenport .333	Dick Sisler 9	Adrián Zabala 9–3
1946–47	Almendares	Lou Klein .330	Roberto Ortiz 11	Cocaina García 10–3
1947–48	Habana	Harry Kimbro .346	Jesús Chanquilon Díaz 7	C. Marrero 12–2
1948–49	Almendares	A. Crespo .326	Monte Irvin 10	Octavio Rubert 8–1
1949–50	Almendares	P. Formental .336	Roberto Ortiz Don Lenhardt 15	Octavio Rubert 5–1
1950–51	Habana	Silvío García .347	P. Formental, Bert Hass Ed Mierkowitz Charles Grant Tied with 8	Vincente López]7–3
1951–52	Habana	Bert Hass .323	P. Formental James Basso 9	Joe Black 15–6
1952–53	Habana	Edmundo Amorós .373	Louis Klein 16	R. Alexander 10–3
1953–54	Almendares	Rocky Nelson .352	Earl Rapp Rafael Noble 10	Cliff Fanning 13–4
1954–55	Almendares	Angel Scull .370	Rocky Nelson 13	Joe Hatten 13–5
1955–56	Cienfuegos	Forrest Jacobs .321	Ultus Alvarez 10	Pedro Ramos 13–5
1956–57	Marianao	Orestes Miñoso .312	Archie Wilson 11	Camilo Pascual 15–5
1957–58	Marianao	Milton Smith .320	Daniel Morejon Norman Laker B. Robinson Frank Herrera 9	Billy O'Dell 7–2
1958–59	Almendares	Tony Taylor .303	Jim Baxes 9	Orlando Peña 13–5
1959–60	Cienfuegos	Octavio Rojas .322		
1960–61	Cienfuegos			

* Short season

Latin American Halls of Fame
Compiled by Eduardo Valero

Cooperstown's National Baseball Hall of Fame and the Canadian Baseball Hall of Fame are not the game's only Valhallas. Halls of Fame exist throughout Latin America, most notably in Cuba, Mexico, the Dominican Republic and Venezuela. They enshrine not only local favorites but also such major league Hall of Famers as Roberto Cle-mente, Juan Marichal, and Luis Aparicio and Negro League immortals such as Josh Gibson, Monte Irvin, Raymond Dandridge, and Martin Dihigo. Some Latin halls date back to 1939, the first year that the Baseball Hall of Fame opened in Cooperstown. Others are more recent, but all hold players worthy of our admiration.

Players Selected for Cuban Baseball Hall of Fame
Selected in Cuba:

1939
Rafael Almeida
Luis (Anguilla) Bustamante
Antonio Maria (el Ingles) Garcia
Gervasio (Strike) Gonzalez
Adolfo Lujan
Armando Marsans
Jose de la Caridad Mendez
Carlos (Bebe) Royer
Cristobal Torriente

1940
Alfredo Arcano
Jose (Joseito) Munoz

1941
Regino (Mamelo) Garcia
Emilio Sabourin

1942
Alfredo (Pajaro) Cabrera
Agustin (Tinti) Molina

1943
Julian Castillo
Heliodoro (Jabuco) Hidalgo
Luis (Mulo) Padron

1944
Carlos Macia
Alejandro Oms

1945
Bernardo Baro
Roman Calzadilla

Valentin Dreke
Carlos (Chino) Moran
Juan Manuel Pastoriza

1946
Ricardo Cabaleiro
Wenceslao Galvez
Francisco A. Poyo
Arturo Valdes
Rogelio Valdes

1948
Juan Antiga
Jacinto Calvo
Nemesio Guillo
Rafael Hernandez
Antonio (Antonico) Mesa
Tomas (Italiano) Romanach

1949
Pelayo Chacon
Julio (El Cartero) Lopez
Eduardo Machado
Gonzalo Sanchez
Manuel Villa

1950
Manuel (Patato) Cueto
Rafael Figarola
Eustaquio Gutierrez
Eugenio Jimenez
Ricardo Martinez

1951
Alfredo Arango

Martin Dihigo
Bienvenido (Pata Joroba) Jiminez
Jose (Joseito) Rodriguez
Jose Maria Teuma

1953
Moises Quintero
Juan Viola
Carlos Zaldo

1954
Emilio Palmero
Pablo Ronquillo

1955
Baldomero (Merito) Acosta
Miguel Angel Gonzalez

1956
Isidro Fabre
Emilio Palomino

1957
Adolfo Luque

1958
Jose (Acostica) Acosta
Lazaro Salazar

1959
Ramon Bragana
Armando Cabanas

1960

Tomas De la Cruz
Oscar Rodriguez

Selected in Miami in 1983:
Eustaquio (Bombin) Pedroso
Rogelio Crespo
Agustin Parpetti
Pedro Dibut
Ramon (Paito) Herrera
Estaban (Mayari) Montalvo
Pablo (Champion) Mesa
Heliodoro (Yoyo) Diaz
Jose Maria Fernandez
Luis Tiant Sr.
Rodolfo Fernandez
Antonio (Tony) Castano
Santos Amaro
Roberto Estalella
Manuel (Cocaina) Garcia
Fermin Guerra
Agapito Mayor
Regino Otero
Andres Fleitas
Pedro Formental
Alejandro Crespo
Napoleon Reyes
Hector Rodriguez
Silvio Garcia
Roberto Ortiz
Julio Moreno
Sandalio Consuegra
Conrado Marrero
Edmundo Amoros
Guillermo (Willy) Mirando
Leonardo Cardenas

Zoilo Versalles
Pedro Ramos
Antonio (Tony) Taylor
Pedro (Tony) Oliva
Octavio (Cuqui) Rojas
Camilo Pascual
Orestes Minoso

Selected in Miami in 1984:
Esteban Bellan
Justo (Cando) Lopez
Julio Rojo
Miguel (Mike) Cuellar
Pedro (Preston) Gomez
Adrian Zabala

Selected in Miami in 1985
Bartolo Portuondo
Basilio (Brujo) Rosell
Jose (Cheo) Olivares
Rafael Noble
Lorenzo (Chiguitin) Cabrera
Miguel (Mike) Fornieles
Antonio (Tony) Gonzalez

Selected in Miami in 1986
Francisco (Cuco) Correa
Jose (Cheo) Ramos
Pedro Arango
Marcelino Guerra
Jorge Comellas
Renée Monteagudo
Orlando Pena

The following executives, league presidents, umpires and journalists have also been elected to the Cuban Baseball Hall of Fame:

Executives:
Alfredo Suarez
Emilio de Armas
Mario Mendoza
Julio Sanguily
Roberto (Bobby) Maduro
Abel Linares
Julio Blanco Herrera
Miguel Suarez de Cardenas
Antonio (Tony) Pacheco
Rafael Inclan

Cuban League Presidents:
Leopoldo de Sola
Jose Antonio Lopez del Valle

Umpires:
Amado Maestri

Journalists:
Jose (Joe) Massaguer
Rafael Conte
Pedro Galiana
Bernardo (Llillo) Jimenez

Negro Leaguers Who Performed in Cuba:
Andrew (Rube) Foster – Pitcher
Preston Hill – Outfielder
John Henry Lloyd (Sam) – Infielder
Oscar Charleston – Outfielder
Oscar Lewis – Pitcher
William Julius (Judy) Johnson – Infielder
John (Jorocon) Wilson – Infielder
Charles (El Chino) Smith – Outfielder
Chaney Whitte – Outfielder

Baseball Players in the Dominican Republic Sports Hall of Fame

Andres J. (Grillo B) Baez	p–of
Luis A. (Grillo C) Baez	of
Rafael A. (Sonlly) Alvarado	of
Pedro A. (Grillo A) Baez	if
Rafael Batista*	1b
Pedro Borbon*	p
Manuel (Manolete) Caceres	p–of
Pedro J. Caratini	ss (Puerto Rican mgr.)
Ricardo (Rico) Carty*	if–of
Luis (Nino el Zurdo) Castro	p
Alcibiades Colon	of
Ramon (Sijo) del Monte Consuegr	p
Ventura (Loro) Escalante	p
Juan Delfin (Braganita) Garcia	2b
Cesar Geronimo*	of

Rafael Emilio (Sijo) Gomez	p
Pedro Gonzalez*	if
Rafael A. (Fellito) Guerra	p
Manuel Henriquez	c
Enrique (Indio Bravo) Hernandez	p
Julian Javier*	2b
Enrique Lantingua	c
Diogenes Lara	2b
Winston Llenas*	if
Gustavo Lluvera	p
Manuel Mallens (Lico)	p
Juan Marichal*	p
Aquiles Martinez	2b
Horacio Martinez	ss
Fernando (Pita) Miranda	of

Manuel (Manny) Mota*	of		Mateo Rojas Alou*	of
Diomedes (Guayubin) Olivo*	p		Mateo de la Rosa	1b
Federico (Chichi) Olivo*	p		Miguel (Abejita) Ruiz	p
Juan Manuel Ortiz Pina	c		Pedro Alejandro San	p
Juan Buatista Perdomo	p–of		Jose (Pepe Lucas) St. Clair	if
Julio H. Pina	p		Luis (Guigui Lucas) St. Clair	c
Miguel (Turco Pinto) Penales	p		Joaquien Suncar	p
Rafael (Mellizo) Puesan	p–if		Baldomero (Mero) Urena	p
Silvano Quesada	p		Juan E. (Tetelo) Vargas	of–if
Danilo Rivas	p		Rafael A. (Papito) Vargas	if
Fernando (Minin) Rodriguez	of–if		Rafael (Guagua) Vargas	c
Juan Bautista Rodriguez Cuevas	of		Rene Velazquez	ss
Luis Ernesto (Burrolote) Rodriguéz	p–c–if–of		Osvaldo (Ossie) Virgil Sr.*	if–of–c
Felipe Rojas Alou*	of–if			
Jesus Rojas Alou*	of		*Played in Major Leagues	

Members of the Hall of Fame of Mexican Professional Baseball

1939
Lucas Juarez
Antonio Delfin "Laniza"
Julio Molina
Leonardo "Najo" Alanis
Fernando Barradas

1964
Angel Castro
Martin Dihigo
Epitacio "La Mala" Torres
Lazaro Salázar
Ramon Bragana
Genaro Casas

1972
Roberto "Beto" Avila
Jose Luis "Chige" Gomez
Baldomero "Melo" Almada
Alberto Romo Chavez
Jesus "Cochihuila" Valenzuela
Alejandro Aguilar Reyes
Jorge Pasqual
Ernesto Carmona
Roy Campanella
Joshua Gibson
Monte Irvin

1973
Daniel "La Coyota" Rios
Roberto Ortiz
Agustin Bejerano
Anuar Canavati

Lazaro Penagos
Manuel Oliveros

1974
No Members Elected

1975
Guilermo "Huevito" Alvarez
Luis Montes De Oca "Molinero"
Fernando M. Campos "Fray Kempis"

1976
Alfred Pinkston
Ramiro Cuevas
Agustin Verdo

1977
Santos Amaro
Guillermo "Memo" Garibay

1978
Felipe Montufar

1979
Basilio "Brujo" Rosell
Jesus "Chanquilon" Diaz

1980
Leonardo "Leo" Rodriguez
Eduardo "Lalo" Orvananos
Carlos Alberto Gonzalez
Ramon Montes De Oca

1981
Vinicio Garcia
Tomas Arroyo
Salvador Castro
Apolinar Pulido "Polin"

1982
Manuel Echevarria
Burnis "Wild Bill" Wright
Francisco "Panchillo" Ramirez
Horacio Lopez Diaz
Mario Ariosa

1983
Claudio Solano
Jose Bache
Ronaldo Camacho
Felipe Montemayor
Ing. Elejo Peralta Y D.C.
Rafael Reyes Najera "Kid Alto"

1984
Alfonso "La Tuza" Ramirez
Miguel "Becerril" Fernandez
Guillermo "Memo" Lopez
Manuel Gonzalez Caballero
Gabriel Atristain

1985
Porfirio "Chio" Martinez
Adolfo Luque
Miguel Sotelo

1986
Ruben Amaro
Moises "Moi" Camacho
Benjamin Valenzuela
Marcos Valdez "Bugarini"

1987
Manuel "Moro" Chavez
Jesus "Jessie" Flores
Guillermo "Memo" Luna
Raul Mendoza
Antonio Ramirez Muro
Juan Ley Fong

1988
Lino Donoso Galata
Horacio Pina
Arnulfo Rodriguez
Abel Francisco Cano
Hector Espino Gonzalez
Pedro Septien Orozco

1989
Raymond "Mamerto" Dandrige
Jose "Zacatillo" Guerrero
Teodoro Marical
Oscal "Rapido" Esquivel

1990
Alfredo "Yaqui" Rios
Ramon "Diablo" Montaya
Alfonso Robinson Bours

Amado Maestri
Tomas Morales

1991
Jaime Corella
Antonio Pollorena
Chara Mansur Julian
Agustin D. Valdez
Juan Lima Hernandez

1992
Benjamin "Cananea" Reyes
Vicente "Huevo" Romo
Jose Pena
Armando Rodriguez
Jorge Blanco

1993
Ramon Arano
Aurelio Lopez
Alfredo Ortiz
Rene Gonzalez
Oscar Rodriguez
Homobono Marquez
Humberto Galaz

1994
Celerino Sanchez
Miguel Suarez
Miguel Gaspar
Carlos Galina
Jaime Perez a Vella

Puerto Rico Professional Baseball Hall of Fame

Jose (Pito) Alvarez de la Vega	p–if–of		Luis R. Olmo*	if–of
Luis (Tite) Arroyo*	p		Rafael Ortiz	p
Carlos Bernier*	of		Demetrio (Menchin) Pesante	if
Pedro M. Caratini	if		Juan (Terin) Pizarro*	p
Orlando Cepeda*	if–of		Victor (Pellot) Power*	if–of
Pedro Cepeda	if–of		Carlos M. Santiago	if
Francisco Coimbre	p–of		Jose G. (Pantalones) Santiago*	p
Roberto Clemente*	of		Jorge (Griffin) Tirado	c
Ceferino (Cefo) Conde	p		Robert (Bob) Thurman	p–of
Leon Day	p–of		Juan E. (Tetelo) Vargas	if–of
Saturnino (Nino) Escalera*	if–of		Luis Villodas	c
Jose A. Figueroa	p–of		Artie Wilson*	ss
Ruben Gomez*	p–of			
Juan Guilbe	p–if–of		*Played in Major Leagues	
Emilio (Millito) Navarro	if–of			

Venezuela Sports Hall of Fame

Luis Aparicio, Jr.*	ss		Luis (Camaleon) Garcia	if
Luis Aparicio Sr.	ss		Manuel (Cocaina) Garcia	p–of
Jose (Carrao) Bracho	p		Vidal Lopez	p–of
Daniel Canonico	p		Ramon Monzant*	p
Alejandro Carrasquel*	p		Andres Quintero	if–of
Alfonso Carrasquel*	ss		Jesus (Chucho) Ramos*	if–of
Emilio Cueche	p		Benito (Juey) Torrens	if–of
Buadilio Diaz*	c			
Victor Davalillo*	of–if		* Played in Major Leagues	

## CHAPTER 21

Baseball in Canada

Bruce L. Prentice and Merritt Clifton

Baseball as we know it—with three bases and home, nine players to a side, and three outs to an inning—has been played in Canada at least since 1860, when the existing teams in London, Hamilton, St. Thomas, and Woodstock, Ontario, all accepted the rules of the New York Game popularized by Henry Chadwick. This was the game played on June 19, 1846 between the New York and Knickerbocker clubs on the Elysian Fields of Hoboken, New Jersey.

But a game differing from early baseball mainly in having five bases was played in Beechville, Ontario, as early as June 4, 1838, according to witness Adam Ford, who described it in a letter to *Sporting Life* published on May 5, 1886. The game included at least two "greyheaded men" who "used to play when they were boys."

Thus the Canadian baseball tradition certainly predates Abner Doubleday's apocryphal invention of the game at Cooperstown in 1839, and may go back as far as the U.S. tradition. Indeed, in both nations, ancestors of baseball including cricket and rounders had been played since the early 1700s, and determining exactly where their derivatives ended and baseball began may be impossible.

Before the arrival of the New York Game, the southwestern Ontario teams played the Canadian Game, with five bases and eleven fielders. All eleven batters had to be retired to end an inning. Only after the New York rules were adopted did the game spread to the other provinces. By 1865 baseball had become so popular in Montreal that an ordinance was passed forbidding games in city parks as a menace to other users.

Baseball reached Manitoba no later than 1874, supplanting a local ancestor game called "bat," which had been played around the Red River Settlement as early as the 1840s. A professional three-team Manitoba League failed in 1886, but the game had firmly caught on by 1902, when the Great Northern Railway sponsored a Winnipeg entry in the professional North Dakota League.

Saskatchewan had semiprofessional baseball by 1887, when future provincial prime minister Walter Scott led a Regina team to two successive regional championships. Amateur baseball emerged in Alberta at about the same time, with games recorded as early as 1886.

By 1903 baseball was even played in the Yukon, where games attracted heavy gambling. Professional baseball debuted the same year in British Columbia, as twenty-year-old Hal Chase—"Prince Hal," the slick-fielding first baseman—starred for a Victoria entry in an otherwise Washington-based league.

While major league baseball came late to Canada, Canadian entries in U.S.-based professional leagues won pennants as early as 1877, when the Tecumsehs of London, Ontario, led the International Association. The Tecumsehs reputedly declined a chance to join the two-year-old National League later that year, and disbanded from lack of fan support in early 1878. Ontario acquired another pennant winner in 1887, as Toronto began an only briefly interrupted eighty-year run as a mainstay of the International League, then called the Eastern League. Toronto either finished first during the regular season or won four-team playoffs fifteen times, with back-to-back winners in 1917–1918, 1956–1957, and 1965–1966.

Montreal's first Eastern League entry folded within weeks in 1890. While another Montreal club won the 1898 championship, the by then renamed International League didn't become lastingly situated there until 1928. Even then, Montreal's third entry struggled until it was acquired in 1935 by gas station magnate Charlie Trudeau, father of future Canadian prime minister Pierre Elliot Trudeau. Trudeau anchored the lineup with French-speaking Del Bissonnette and Quebec native Gus Dugas, who hit .327 with 191 homers in thirteen minor league seasons. Under manager Frank Shaughnessy, who became International League president in 1936 and originated the four-club playoff format many experts credit with saving minor league baseball, the Montreal Royals won the 1935 pennant.

Bought by the Brooklyn Dodgers in 1940, the Royals won either pennant or playoffs in ten of the next twenty years. Led by Quebecois Roland Gladu (12 homers, 105 RBIs, .338 batting average) and pitcher Jean Pierre Roy (25–11), the 1945 club was probably Montreal's favorite, but the 1946 Royals are best remembered: with them, second baseman Jackie Robinson (.349) broke the Organized Baseball color line that had prevailed since 1899, when Bill "Hippo" Galloway was released after playing five games for Woodstock, Ontario.

The color line had already been broken in Quebec by .392-hitting pitcher/outfielder Fred Wilson, who joined Granby of the then-outlaw Provincial League for the 1935 stretch run. The Provincial League had included a Montreal-based all-black entry, the Black Panthers, in 1936 and 1937; was all white again in 1940, during a one-year fling at Organized Baseball; and was reintegrated in 1946 by minor league hockey star Manny McIntyre, who signed with Sherbrooke only days after the Dodgers had signed Robinson and optioned him to Montreal.

The Provincial League was the longest-running of numerous native Canadian circuits, many of which owed ancestry to the work of longtime Canadian Pacific Railway sports representative Joseph Page, who helped set up teams and leagues wherever the trains stopped. A former semipro teammate of Tip O'Neill, Page was involved with O'Neill in assembling Montreal's 1898 International League pennant winner. He later enlisted former major league pitcher Jean Dubuc to help him organize the Eastern Canada League, a.k.a. the Ontario-Quebec-Vermont League, of 1922–1924. This was an ancestor of three leagues of note, each of which sent over 100 players to the majors—the Provincial, which had already come together for single seasons in 1894 and 1900; the Canadian-American League, which could claim descent from the short lived, Ontario-based Canadian League of 1885; and the outlaw Northern League that flourished in New York and Vermont from 1935 to 1952.

Reorganized a fourth time, the Provincial League grew steadily from 1935 to 1940, was interrupted by World War II, resumed play in 1944, collapsed in 1956 after a disastrous six-year return to Organized Baseball, and struggled on as an outlaw circuit in 1958–1971. Stars were plentiful, from Quebec native Sam LaRoque (1900) to Felix Mantilla (1969), but the zenith came in 1948–1949, as the league attracted black greats who were hoping to prove themselves against whites, displaced wartime major leaguers, and the so-called Mexican League Jumpers, who were barred from Organized Baseball in 1946–1950 after breaking their major league contracts in an ill-fated stand against the reserve clause. At least twenty-five major leaguers played in the Provincial League during those two years, among them Sal Maglie, Max Lanier, Vic Power, Gladu and Roy, and Negro League stars Dave Pope, Bus Clarkson, and Quincy Trouppe.

The less colorful Can-Am belonged to Organized Baseball from 1936 through 1951. Several of the Ontario teams continued as an outlaw league into the 1960s.

Page also helped promote the Western Canada League, which began play in 1907, continuing with frequent interruptions and occasional name changes into the late 1940s, when Edmonton and Calgary anchored the Big Four League. The Western Canada League's best year was probably 1921, when its stars included Babe Herman and Heinie Manush.

Canadian teams have also been part of the bygone Northern Copper Country League, which later became the Northern League; the Northwestern League and Western International League, which evolved into today's Northwest League; the Pacific Coast League; the American Association; the Eastern League; the New York–Pennsylvania League; and the Pioneer League.

As well as helping return blacks to Organized Baseball, Canada played a part in popularizing baseball in Japan, through the Asahis (Rising Suns), a team of Vancouver teenagers of Japanese descent (Niseis) formed in 1914. In 1921, twelve years after the first visit by a U.S. collegiate team and thirteen years before the first visit by U.S. major leaguers, the Asahis and a touring team from Seattle barnstormed Japan, playing both Japanese clubs and each other. The Asahis remained a power in Vancouver-area amateur baseball and heroes to the substantial British Columbia Nisei population for over twenty years.

Despite the many major leaguers who have played for Canadian teams, relatively few Canadian natives have made the majors—a reflection of short summers and a paucity of places to play since television killed the old town teams and outlaw leagues in the 1950s. (Only one high school baseball team exists in Quebec; none in several other provinces.) Of the ten Canadian provinces, only Newfoundland hasn't produced a major leaguer.

High school baseball programs have flourished in the Metro Toronto area since 1979, when four schools experimented with a short schedule. There are now close to seventy schools playing a spring schedule that culminates in a championship game played at the SkyDome, prior to a regular-season Blue Jays game. The winning team receives the "Blue Jays Cup."

College baseball was started in 1978, when Seneca College (near Toronto) joined the NJCAA, New York-Penn Conference, for five seasons and was the forerunner to the National Baseball Institute (NBI) located in British Columbia. This college program has produced Canadian major leaguers including outfielders Kevin Reimer and Larry Walker, plus lefthanded pitchers Steve Wilson and Dennis Boucher.

Seven players from the late 1800s are listed by most record books as having been born in the U.S., but are believed to have altered their birth records for various reasons, including the 1894 Alien Exemption Act, which barred Canadian athletes from U.S. employment. In addition, several players who were born abroad actually grew up in Canada, e.g., Hank Biasatti and Reno Bertoia, natives of Italy but raised in Windsor, Ontario, and Jimmy Archer, born in Ireland, raised in Toronto, and signed into Organized Baseball from an independent team in Manitoba.

Many of the best Canadian players actually grew up in the U.S., among them infielder Pete Ward, son of former Montreal hockey great Jim Ward, who learned baseball in Oregon; pitcher Dick Lines, born in Montreal but raised in Florida; pitcher Kirk McCaskill, born in Kapuskasing, Ontario, who grew up in Burlington, Vermont; and infielder Sherry Robertson, born in Montreal but raised in Washington, D.C. (as the nephew of Senators and Twins club owner Calvin Griffith, who was also born in Montreal but was brought to Washington in 1921 by Senators owner Clark Griffith, who married Calvin's aunt).

Pitcher Sheldon Burnside reversed that pattern. Born in South Bend, Indiana, Burnside grew up in Toronto.

The first Canadian-born major leaguer was first baseman Bill Phillips, who played for Cleveland, Brooklyn, and Kansas City, from 1879 to 1888. Born in St. John, New Brunswick, Phillips actually grew up in Chicago.

Among the 150 to follow Phillips are active players Rob Ducey, Larry Walker, Kevin Reimer, and Matt Stairs, as well as pitchers Steve Wilson, Kirk McCaskill, Dennis Boucher, Mike Gardiner, Vince Horsman, Paul Quantrill, and Rheal Cormier. While the number of players by position is roughly proportional to the numbers on major league rosters, pitchers have won the most distinction, perhaps because pitching skills can be developed more readily in short amateur seasons. Bob Emslie of Guelph, Ontario, was the first Canadian pitcher of note, and won more games in a big league season than any other Canadian, posting a 32–17 mark for the 1884 Baltimore Orioles. A poor start in 1885 sent him back to the minors, with a career major league record of just 44–44. Emslie returned to the majors, however, as an umpire, serving thirty-five years before retiring in 1926.

O'Neill, born at either Woodstock or Springfield, Ontario, in 1858, was the best Canadian hitter of his time or ever, batting .326 in a big-league career that ran from 1883 to 1892. Breaking into the majors with New York as a pitcher, O'Neill soon switched to the outfield. In 1886 he led the then-major league American Association in hits, doubles, triples, homers, runs scored, batting, and slugging. His batting average, at the time, was actually listed as .492, but 50 walks were counted as hits. Subtracting them, he still hit .435. Though O'Neill fell to .335 in 1887, he repeated as batting champion.

The best Canadian player of all was probably Ferguson Jenkins, a 6′5″ righthander from Chatham, Ontario, who compiled a 284–226 record over nineteen seasons from 1965 to 1983. At his peak, Jenkins won 20 games or more seven times in eight years. Noted for control, Jenkins fanned over three times as many batters as he walked— and led the NL with 273 whiffs in 1969, retiring ninth on the all-time strikeout list. He earned the 1971 NL Cy Young Award by leading the league in wins (24), innings pitched, and, for the third time each, starts and complete games. He also hit 6 homers that year, one behind the NL record for home runs by a pitcher.

Other Canadian pitchers of note include Russ Ford, John Hiller, Reggie Cleveland, Phil Marchildon, Dick Fowler, Claude Raymond, and Ron Taylor. Ford, whose older brother also made the big leagues briefly, won 26 games for the New York Highlanders in 1910, his first full season. Hiller saved a then-record 38 games in 1973 and won an AL record 17 games in relief the next year, but is best known for his comeback from a 1971 heart attack. Marchildon and Fowler were half of the Athletics' rotation during the 1940s. On September 9, 1945, Fowler became the only Canadian to hurl a no-hitter, beating the Browns 1–0 for his only victory that year after coming back from military service. Marchildon peaked with 19 wins in 1947. Raymond is remembered as the first native Quebecois to play for the Expos. Taylor relieved for two World Champions, the 1964 Cardinals and the 1969 Mets, then became team physician for the Toronto Blue Jays.

Other top Canadian hitters were George Selkirk and Jeff Heath. Selkirk, who replaced Babe Ruth in the Yankees' lineup in 1934, hit .290 over nine seasons, topping .300 five times and twice driving in more than 100 runs. He later served for ten years as general manager of the Washington Senators. Heath, who reputedly never lived up to his potential, averaged .293 over fourteen years, beginning in 1936, with 194 homers. His best years were 1938 (21–112–.343) and 1941 (24–123–.340.) In between he led a player revolt against Indians manager Oscar Vitt. In his final full year, Heath hit .319 with twenty-four homers, pacing the Braves to the 1948 NL pennant, but broke his leg sliding during the last week of the season, missing his only chance at a World Series.

Canadian managers have included Art Irwin, Freddie Lake, Moon Gibson, and Bill Watkins, who led the Detroit Wolverines to the 1887 NL pennant.

Catcher Nig Clarke, from Amhurstburg, Ontario, won a spot in the minor league record books on June 15, 1902, hitting eight homers for Corsicana of the Texas League in a 51–3 rout of Texarkana. Outfielder Jack Graney, of St.

Thomas, Ontario, was reputedly the first major leaguer to wear a number, and was also both the first hitter to face Babe Ruth when the latter debuted as a pitcher, and the first ex-player to become a baseball broadcaster. Outfielder Glen Gorbous, of Drumheller, Alberta, made the *Guinness Book of Records* with the longest measured throw on record. Black pitcher Jimmy Claxton, of New Westminster, British Columbia, briefly broke the color line by passing as an alleged Native American with Oakland of the Pacific Coast League in 1916.

National League baseball finally came to Canada with the expansion Montreal Expos in 1969. Hoping to get off to a good start, the Expos drafted mainly veterans, including Maury Wills, who became the only player to appear with Montreal in both the majors and the minors. Wills was soon traded for another veteran, Ron Fairly, who had led the University of Edmonton into the 1957 College World Series. A preseason swap of sluggers Donn Clendenon and Rusty Staub had to be rearranged when Clendenon quit rather than join the Astros. Clendenon eventually unretired and was swapped to the Mets. The affair was a milestone in the series of events that led to overturning the reserve clause in 1975. Although the Expos won both their first game and their home opener (on a home run by pitcher Dan McGinn), they finished last. No-hitters by Bill Stoneman in 1969 and 1972 were the club high points until 1973. Then, despite a 79–83 record, the Expos were in contention into the final week, paced by Ken Singleton, Ron Hunt, who set an all-time record by getting hit with pitches 50 times, rookie Steve Rogers, and reliever Mike Marshall, who saved 31 games and won 14 in 92 appearances.

Marshall was promptly traded to the Dodgers for Willie Davis, who staged a sit-down strike in center field before moving on. Singleton and pitcher Mike Torrez were sent to the Orioles a year later for former Cy Young Award winner Dave McNally and outfielder Rich Coggins. A thyroid ailment ended Coggins's career at age 25, while McNally played the 1975 season without a contract, then filed one of the two lawsuits that finally broke the reserve clause (Andy Messersmith of the Dodgers filed the other).

The Expos regrouped under new manager Dick Williams to win a club record 95 games in 1979. The arrival of young stars including Rogers, Andre Dawson, Gary Carter, Larry Parrish, Tim Raines, and Tim Wallach led management to bill the Expos as "The Team of the Eighties." The promise seemed real when the Expos won a playoff against the Phillies for the NL East title during the strike-shortened split season of 1981, and were leading the Dodgers 1–0 in the fifth inning of the final game of the NL Championship Series. But Rick Monday singled and scored the tying run, then won the game 2–1 with a two-out ninth inning homer off Rogers.

Toronto appeared ready to enter the National League in 1976 by purchasing the San Francisco Giants. When that deal fell through at the last minute, the American League admitted the Blue Jays as an expansion team in 1977. The Blue Jays drafted for the future, enduring six years in the cellar before winning 89 games to place fourth in 1983.

Good trades and a strong farm system loaded the lineup with sluggers George Bell, Jesse Barfield, Lloyd Moseby, and Willie Upshaw, plus hard-hitting infielders Tony Fernandez and Damaso Garcia, and produced a perennially strong pitching staff led by Dave Stieb and Jimmy Key. Ernie Whitt, an expansion draft selection, supplied power behind the plate through 1989. Winning 99 games and the AL East title in 1985, the Jays took a 3–1 lead in the Championship Series against Kansas City, but then dropped three games in a row to lose. The Jays disappointed their fans by dropping the ALCS again in 1989 and 1991, and losing the AL East lead in the last week of 1987 and 1990.

Perhaps those disappointments built character in Toronto. Then again, general manager Pat Gillick, nicknamed "Stand Pat" for his previous conservatism, might have turned the team around with the biggest trade of his career, sending first baseman Fred McGriff and shortstop Tony Fernandez to the San Diego Padres for outfielder Joe Carter and second baseman Roberto Alomar. McGriff was the Jays' top slugger, but Carter virtually duplicated his numbers; Fernandez, a former All Star, was the Jays' senior position player, but Alomar hit with more power, stole more bases, and was equally flashy on defense. Two costly free agent additions—Jack Morris, the pitching ace of the World Championship Minnesota club, and veteran designated hitter Dave Winfield—completed a $41 million roster, the most expensive in Canadian baseball history. Morris won 21 games; Winfield, at age forty-one, became the oldest player to knock in 100 runs.

A six-game victory over the Oakland Athletics in the Championship Series set up the first-ever genuinely international World Series, as Toronto met Atlanta. The Blue Jays split the first two games in Atlanta, took a pair at home, and then appeared to choke again, dropping the last game in Toronto and losing a 2-1 lead in the sixth Series game in the bottom of the ninth. But with the score still tied in the top of the eleventh, Winfield doubled home two runs. Reliever Mike Timlin held off one last Atlanta rally to preserve a 4-3 win. For the first time the World Championship of baseball belonged to a team from outside the U.S.—though to be sure, the Blue Jays had no native Canadian players, having unloaded reserve outfielder Rob Ducey midway through the season.

The 1993 team, shaken up by more Gillick moves, nonetheless picked up where the 1992 edition left off, leading the AL East virtually from start to finish as first baseman John Olerud, a .269 lifetime hitter, averaged .400 for more than half the season. Rolling over the Chicago White Sox in the ALCS, the Blue Jays took the World Championship for the second consecutive year on Joe Carter's bottom-of-the-ninth home run off the Phillies' Mitch Williams in the decisive sixth game.

While the Blue Jays struggled to turn near-success into glorious triumph, drawing more than 4 million fans a year, the Expos entered the 1990s just struggling. Discouraged by twenty-two years without a pennant, and by dropping fan support as the advertised "Team of the Eighties" aged and departed, founding owner Charles Bronfman sold the franchise—after a prolonged hunt for takers—to a group headed by club president Claude Brochu.

The 1991 Expos finished dead last, ending the unpromising campaign with a long unscheduled road trip after a fifty-ton block of concrete fell from the Olympic Stadium roof. The fifteen-year-old ballpark was closed for extensive repairs, while Brochu et al. contemplated relocating to either Buffalo or St. Petersburg.

But Felipe Alou, the first former Montreal player to manage the team, turned everything around after taking over in early 1992, leading the Expos to a 70-55 record in the last four months of the season. In 1993 Alou brought Montreal a club record of 97 victories. And 1994 promised to be Montreal's year, as the Expos held a six-game lead over Atlanta, the second-best team in baseball, when the August 12 strike stopped play. For the first time in several years, fans in other cities began to recognize the Expo regulars, notably the outfield of Moises Alou, Marquis Grissom, and Larry Walker, as well as All Star shortstop Wil Cordero and top starter Ken Hill.

[Thanks for research help to Eves Raja; Bill Humber; Donald Guay; and the Brome County Historical Society.]

## CHAPTER 22

Spring Training

Myles E. Friedman

Like the origins of baseball itself, the beginnings of spring training are veiled behind the mists of myth and legend. Throughout the 1930s and 1940s, baseball writers generally identified Cap Anson as the father of spring training. As evidence, reporters cited his Chicago White Stockings' 1886 trip to Hot Springs, Arkansas, as the crystallizing moment. Since Anson has been credited (incorrectly) by several writers as the greatest innovator of baseball in the nineteenth century, it may have been easy to overlook the journey Harry Wright's Philadelphia nine took that same year to Charleston and New Orleans.

In 1951, *The Sporting News* reported that the Boston Beaneaters, Honest John Morrill's National League outfit of 1884, should earn credit for a jaunt that year to New Orleans. Lee Allen's 1955 book, *The Hot Stove League,* reached even farther back, to 1870, and unearthed a preseason trip by Jimmy Wood's newly formed Chicago White Stockings. (Wood's men journeyed to New Orleans in an effort to steel themselves for a run at the Cincinnati Red Stockings, undefeated champions in 1869.) "The plan," wrote Allen, "worked so well that Chicago beat the Red Stockings not once, but twice. So in the years that immediately followed, many of the old National Association teams would winter at New Orleans and play games there."

Later, it was asserted that the Red Stockings themselves trained at New Orleans in 1870, though strictly speaking, they were into their season by the time they reached New Orleans, having already trounced the Louisville Eagle nine, 94-7, in Kentucky. Finally, some historians assert that in 1869 and possibly even before that, the New York Mutuals, who had recently come under the control of a new president, William "Boss" Tweed of Tammany Hall, put in a training session at New Orleans.

In fact, before the first major league was organized in 1871, baseball clubs often packed up in February for southern tours, though at the beginning with less emphasis on training and more on barnstorming. The famous Excelsior Base Ball Club of Brooklyn, led by Jim Creighton, made a "grand tour" in 1860, playing games as far south as Baltimore.

During the early years of major league baseball, the 1870s and '80s, it was hard enough to turn a profit without the additional burden of cold and ice. Weather played the largest role in directing itineraries southward, and big league squads leased locales in Charleston, Mobile, Macon, Savannah, Atlanta, Pensacola, and Jacksonville.

The outlays for training were incredibly modest by today's standards. In 1892, Wright's Phillies ran a spring training season from February 28 through March 29. Included were two weeks in Gainesville, Florida, and two weeks of barnstorming on the way back north; gate receipts for the whole exercise totaled nearly $700, leaving a net loss of $469.

In 1888 the Washington Nationals became the first club to train in Florida. It was not until 1914, however, that more than two teams would train in Florida during the same year. The idea of concentrating clubs in close proximity to each other for the purpose of exhibition play came not from the minds of baseball men, but from civic leaders and promoters of the sun belt.

Al Lang, a Pittsburgh businessman who had moved to St. Petersburg and later became its mayor, began wooing major league clubs in 1913. At first, Lang made the mistake of promising Barney Dreyfuss and his Pittsburgh Pirates beautiful scenery and excellent fishing if they were to shift to Florida from their long-time home in Hot Springs. Dreyfuss replied scornfully that he wasn't interested in giving his boys a good time for fishing and sitting; they were at training camp for hard work and the rougher environs of Arkansas were just fine for that.

Lang did entice Branch Rickey's St. Louis Browns to St. Petersburg for the 1914 season. A Browns' official had persuaded several of the town's citizens into agreeing to pay all the expenses for the Browns' retinue of fifty. Later, when Lang learned of the deal, he and public officials refused to pay any of the $6,500 bill. The Browns did not return the following spring.

Soon Lang drew the Boston Braves and New York Yankees to St. Petersburg. The Braves' requirement for relocating in 1922 was a new ballpark. Lang accommodated them with Waterfront Park and in 1925 lured the Yankees by extolling St. Petersburg's relatively chaste society—at least in comparison to New Orleans, the Bombers' long-time preseason home. (It didn't hurt Lang's pitch that manager Miller Huggins had recently bought a home in St. Pete.)

There were several semipermanent training sites before the 1920s, but they were the exceptions. The Pirates lasted at Hot Springs from the turn of the century until 1917, and John McGraw established a Giants camp at Marlin, Texas, that lasted eleven seasons. Marlin, the site of purportedly curative mineral baths like those at Hot Springs, was sufficiently remote for McGraw to keep his men in line. However, when spring training was delayed until mid-March in 1919 in the aftermath of World War I, McGraw opted for the convenience of Gainesville, Florida.

The land boom in the Sunshine State in the 1920s was

accompanied by a full-scale rush of baseball clubs. The Athletics, Braves, Browns, Dodgers, Yankees, Senators, Reds, and Phillies all set up long-term residences during the decade and most never left except during World War II, when long-distance travel was curtailed. One club that did leave was the Giants. In 1924, McGraw moved his outfit to Sarasota, but, after losing $100,000 in a land deal, he said goodbye to Florida; the Giants returned only after McGraw surrendered the reins.

Spring training sites were often determined by the personal holdings of owners or managers. The Cubs only became fixtures on Santa Catalina Island, twenty miles off the coast of Los Angeles, after Phil Wrigley, who owned Catalina, bought the Cubs in 1921. When the Tigers moved to Augusta, Georgia, in 1922, it was at the behest of their new manager, Ty Cobb, the Georgia Peach, who was part owner of the ballpark.

Bill Veeck, who bought the Indians in 1946, owned an Arizona ranch; hence the Indians' move to Tucson, where they stayed for forty-six years. The Yankees might still be in St. Petersburg but for owner Dan Topping's yacht and his desire to sail from a Fort Lauderdale mooring (though a promise to provide integrated housing in Fort Lauderdale may have been an equally forceful motivation).

The new congregation of clubs in Florida coincided with an unrelated phenomenon that changed spring training forever: Babe Ruth. When Ruth joined New York in 1920, his arrival had two immediate effects: (1) a nineteen-game barnstorming trip by the Giants and Red Sox—now without Ruth—became one of the worst spring training fiascoes of all time; and (2) Ruth generated tremendous interest for Yankee exhibitions. When the Yankees finally set up shop in St. Petersburg, spring training reached its zenith for ticket sales. In the spring after Ruth's record-setting 1927 season, 270,000 fans paid to see Yankee exhibition games, enabling Jacob Ruppert to clear an amazing profit of $60,000.

Naturally, other clubs wanted a piece of that action. By the mid-1930s only the Pirates, White Sox, Cubs, and Indians regularly trained outside Florida. Several teams split their spring between Florida and sites off-shore— Havana, San Juan, Bermuda, and the Dominican Republic; however, each returned to the mainland for games in Florida and a barnstorming jaunt north. Clubs sometimes scheduled more than 40 games before opening the regular season in mid-April.

World War II travel restrictions forced teams to train nearer home—north of the Potomac River and east of St. Louis. Clubs opened camps later and, from 1943 to 1945, lengthy barnstorming ventures were dropped.

After the War, the major leagues' passion for Florida continued, though with a harsh new aspect. In 1946 Branch Rickey brought Jackie Robinson to camp as a member of the Dodgers' Class AAA Montreal club, thus beginning a twenty-year campaign to reverse racism. The Dodgers trained at Daytona Beach, a city which, though allowing Robinson to play in games, still enforced segregationist housing, dining, and travel codes. Robinson was barred from games in Sanford, Jacksonville, and Deland and other games were canceled. In 1947 Rickey moved his club to Cuba and Panama and only returned to Florida after making an inspired decision, one that would have an enduring impact on the game.

Rickey wanted to insulate his club from the hateful Jim Crow racial policies that prevailed in Florida and found the answer in a decommissioned naval base at Vero Beach. In 1948, the Dodgers would live, eat, train, and play at the club's new Dodgertown complex. In addition, the camp would encompass Brooklyn's entire minor league system, more than 400 players, giving Rickey the "baseball college" he had long wanted.

Other clubs encountered similar problems as they tried to integrate the game and, by 1953, five of the seven teams with black players on their rosters trained out west. Gradually most Florida communities, fearful of losing their lucrative spring showpiece, accepted the presence of blacks. But towns which played host to an occasional barnstorming game (and as such, were unaffected by the economic imperatives that worked on training camp cities), were slow to change.

In the spring of 1950, with fans eager to see Robinson, the Dodgers drew 232,000 on a tour north from Florida. But incidents of bigotry only worsened. By the late 1950s, racism throughout the region helped end the barnstorming circuits that had operated for nearly a century.

Like Florida, California offered great weather for training, and several teams had sampled West Coast training early in the century. Until 1924, however, there was never more than one per year. By 1932 four clubs trained in California (the Cubs, Pirates, Tigers, and Giants) and, for most of the next twenty years, the Orange League would remain four strong.

The directors of the Pacific Coast League ended spring training by major league teams in California by prohibiting games in PCL cities the week before the PCL season opened (about April 1). That meant that big-league teams had nearly three weeks to kill before their seasons opened. The last major league teams ensconced in California, the Orioles and the White Sox, pulled out after the 1953 season.

Arizona had had a spring training as early as 1929 when the Tigers trained in Phoenix, but eighteen years passed before another club trained in Arizona. In 1947, Horace Stoneham of the Giants and Bill Veeck of the Indians agreed to take their teams to Phoenix and Tucson, respectively. Those clubs, which had or would soon have black players on their rosters, may have stayed in Arizona because of eased race relations. Until 1993, when they moved to Winter Haven, Florida, the Indians (along with the Cubs, who arrived in 1952) formed the backbone of the Cactus League. By the 1969 expansion, seven teams were training in Arizona.

In 1951, the Giants and the Yankees engineered one of baseball's great trades. Yankee partner Del Webb was a Phoenix resident and was anxious to give his home town a close look at his championship squad. He prevailed upon Stoneham to switch training sites for one year and, for the last time, the Yankees trained away from Florida. Incidentally, the two met in the World Series that fall.

The next decisive stage in the evolution of spring training was a consequence of baseball's renaissance following the 1975 World Series. After struggling to compete with America's expanding entertainment marketplace in the 1960s and 1970s, baseball surged in popularity. Attendance in the two years following Carlton Fisk's World Series body-English homer jumped 19 percent, more than twice the growth during all the years since 1950. Then baseball really took off, reaching in 1994 a per-game figure (31,609) nearly twice that of 1975.

By 1977, renewed devotion to the game was evident throughout the Cactus League (eight teams) and Grapefruit Leagues (eighteen teams). Games which were once casual diversions became characterized by sold-out signs, scalpers, and ever-rising ticket prices. In 1990, *USA Today* began running box scores of spring games, providing a level of national coverage beyond the imaginings of earlier fans. Clubs began training in "complexes," following the example of Branch Rickey thirty years later.

By the late 1980s most teams played their spring training games in municipal ballparks or were seeking new ones, complete with practice fields for minor league camps and amenities rivaling major league ballparks. Even as the costs of luring a team to town or keeping it there escalated, cities in Arizona and Florida continued to compete for big league tenants. In 1937, $5,000 in cash was enough to lure Sam Breadon's St. Louis Cardinals to

Daytona Beach. In 1994, Peoria, Arizona, invested $32 million into a stadium and compound for the Mariners and Padres.

Much of spring training remains unchanged. Scribes and savants continue to debate the necessity of the six-week regimen of calisthenics and infield drills. Though professional to a fault, some ballplayers still arrive needing a concentrated cycle of weight reduction. And, despite it all, fans still look to the lengthening days of March for the renewal of hope and a new season in which past promises are at last fulfilled.

Spring Training Sites by Team Nickname

Records of spring training prior to 1900 are incomplete and unclear. While some teams went south as early as the 1860s, it is difficult to separate clubs that were barnstorming from clubs that were training. Future editions of *Total Baseball* will attempt to sort out the facts.

NATIONAL LEAGUE

Astros
1962-63 Apache Junction, Ariz.
1964-84 Cocoa Beach, Fla.
1985 Kissimmee, Fla.

Braves
1901 Norfolk, Va.
1902-04 Thomasville, Ga.
1905 Charleston, S.C.
1906 Jacksonville, Fla.
1907 Thomasville, Ga.
1908-12 Augusta, Ga.
1913 Athens, Ga.
1914-15 Macon, Ga.
1916-18 Miami, Fla.
1919-20 Columbus, Ga.
1921 Galveston, Tex.
1922-37 St. Petersburg, Fla.
1938-40 Bradenton, Fla.
1941 San Antonio, Tex.
1942 Sanford, Fla.
1943-44 Wallingford, Conn.
1945 Washington, D.C.
1946-47 Fort Lauderdale, Fla.
1948-62 Bradenton, Fla.
1963- West Palm Beach, Fla.

Cardinals
1901-02 St. Louis, Mo.
1903 Dallas, Tex.
1904 Houston, Tex.
1905 Marlin Springs, Tex.
1906-08 Houston, Tex.
1909-10 Little Rock, Ark.
1911 West Baden, Ind.
1912 Jackson, Miss.
1913 Columbus, Ga.
1914 St. Augustine, Fla.
1915-17 Hot Wells, Tex.
1918 San Antonio, Tex.
1919 St. Louis, Mo.
1920 Brownsville, Tex.
1921-22 Orange, Tex.
1923-24 Bradenton, Fla.
1925 Stockton, Cal.
1926 San Antonio, Tex.
1927-29 Avon Park, Fla.
1930-36 Bradenton, Fla.
1937 Daytona Beach, Fla.
1938-42 St. Petersburg, Fla.
1943-45 Cairo, Ill.
1946- St. Petersburg, Fla.

Cubs
1901-02 Champaign, Ill.
1903-04 Los Angeles, Cal.
1905 Santa Monica, Cal.
1906 Champaign, Ill.
1907 New Orleans, La.
1908 Vicksburg, Miss.

1909-10 Hot Springs, Ark.
1911-12 New Orleans, La.
1913-16 Tampa, Fla.
1917-21 Pasadena, Cal.
1922-42 Catalina Island, Cal.
1943-45 French Lick, Ind.
1946-47 Catalina Island, Cal.
1948-49 Los Angeles, Cal.
1950-51 Catalina Island, Cal.
1952-65 Mesa, Ariz.
1966 Long Beach, Cal.
1967-78 Scottsdale, Ariz.
1979- Mesa, Ariz.

Dodgers
1901 Charlotte, N.C.
1902-06 Columbia, S.C.
1907-09 Jacksonville, Fla.
1910-12 Hot Springs, Ark.
1913-14 Augusta, Ga.
1915-16 Daytona Beach, Fla.
1917-18 Hot Springs, Ark.
1919-20 Jacksonville, Fla.
1921 New Orleans, La.
1922 Jacksonville, Fla.
1923-32 Clearwater, Fla.
1933 Miami, Fla.
1934-35 Orlando, Fla.
1936-40 Clearwater, Fla.
1941-42 Havana, Cuba
1943-45 Bear Mountain, N.Y.
1946 Daytona Beach, Fla.
1947 Havana, Cuba
1948 Ciudad Trujillo, D.R.
1949- Vero Beach, Fla.

Expos
1969-72 West Palm Beach, Fla.
1973-80 Daytona Beach, Fla.
1981- West Palm Beach, Fla.

Giants
1901-02 N.Y., N.Y.
1903-05 Savannah, Ga.
1906 Memphis, Tenn.
1907 Los Angeles, Cal.
1908-18 Marlin Springs, Tex.
1919 Gainesville, Fla.
1920-23 San Antonio, Tex.
1924-27 Sarasota, Fla.
1928 Augusta, Ga.
1929-31 San Antonio, Tex.
1932-33 Los Angeles, Cal.
1934-35 Miami Beach, Fla.
1936 Pensacola, Fla.
1937 Havana, Cuba
1938-39 Baton Rouge, La.
1940 Winter Haven, Fla.
1941-42 Miami, Fla.
1943-45 Lakewood, N.J.
1946 Miami, Fla.
1947-50 Phoenix, Ariz.

1951 St. Petersburg, Fla.
1952-83 Phoenix, Ariz.
1984- Scottsdale, Ariz.

Marlins
1993 Cocoa, Fla.
1994- Melbourne, Fla.

Mets
1962-87 St. Petersburg, Fla.
1988- Port St. Lucie, Fla.

Padres
1969-93 Yuma, Ariz.
1994- Peoria, Ariz.

Phillies
1901 Philadelphia, Pa.
1902 Washington, N.C.
1903 Richmond, Va.
1904 Savannah, Ga.
1905 Augusta, Ga.
1906-08 Savannah, Ga.
1909-10 Southern Pines, N.C.
1911 Birmingham, Al.
1912 Hot Springs, Ark.
1913 Southern Pines, N.C.
1914 Wilmington, N.C.
1915-18 St. Petersburg, Fla.
1919 Charlotte, N.C.
1920 Birmingham, Al.
1921 Gainesville, Fla.
1922-24 Leesburg, Fla.
1925-27 Bradenton, Fla.
1928-37 Winter Haven, Fla.
1938 Biloxi, Miss.
1939 New Braunfels, Tex.
1940-42 Miami Beach, Fla.
1943 Hershey, Pa.
1944-45 Wilmington, Del.
1946 Miami Beach, Fla.
1947- Clearwater, Fla.

Pirates
1901-16 Hot Springs, Ark.
1917 Columbus, Ga.
1918 Jacksonville, Fla.
1919 Birmingham, Al.
1920-23 Hot Springs, Ark.
1924-34 Paso Robles, Cal.
1935 San Bernardino, Cal.
1936 San Antonio, Tex.
1937-42 San Bernardino, Cal.
1943-45 Muncie, Ind.
1946 San Bernardino, Cal.
1947 Miami Beach, Fla.
1948 Hollywood, Cal.
1949-52 San Bernardino, Cal.
1953 Havana, Cuba
1954 Fort Pierce, Fla.
1955-68 Fort Myers, Fla.

1969- Bradenton, Fla.

Reds
1901-02 Cincinnati, Oh.
1903 Augusta, Ga.
1904 Dallas, Tex.
1905 Jacksonville, Fla.
1906 San Antonio, Tex.
1907 Marlin Springs, Tex.
1908 St. Augustine, Tex.
1909 Atlanta, Ga.
1910-11 Hot Springs, Ark.
1912 Columbus, Ga.
1913 Mobile, Al.
1914-15 Alexandria, La.
1916-17 Shreveport, La.
1918 Montgomery, Al.
1919 Waxahachie, Tex.
1920 Miami, Fla.
1921 Cisco, Tex.
1922 Mineral Wells, Tex.
1923-30 Orlando, Fla.
1931-42 Tampa, Fla.
1943-45 Bloomington, Ind.
1946-87 Tampa, Fla.
1988- Plant City, Fla.

Rockies
1993- Tucson, Ariz.

AMERICAN LEAGUE

Angels
1961-92 Mesa/Palm Springs, Ariz.
1993 Mesa/Tempe, Ariz.

Athletics
1901 Philadelphia, Pa.
1902 Charlotte, N.C.
1903 Jacksonville, Fla.
1904 Spartanburg, S.C.
1905 Shreveport, La.
1906 Montgomery, Al.
1907 Dallas, Tex.
1908-09 New Orleans, La.
1910 Atlanta, Ga.
1911 Savannah, Ga.
1912-13 San Antonio, Tex.
1914-18 Jacksonville, Fla.
1919 Philadelphia, Pa.
1920-21 Lake Charles, La.
1922 Eagle Pass, Tex.
1923-24 Montgomery, Al.
1925-36 Fort Myers, Fla.
1937 Mexico City, Mex.
1938-39 Lake Charles, La.
1940-42 Anaheim, Cal.
1943 Wilmington, Del.
1944-45 Frederick, Md.
1946-62 West Palm Beach, Fla.
1963-68 Bradenton, Fla.
1969-78 Mesa, Ariz.

1979-83 Scottsdale, Ariz.
1984- Phoenix, Ariz.

Blue Jays
1977- Dunedin, Fla.

Brewers (Pilots)
1969-72 Tempe, Ariz.
1973-85 Sun City, Ariz.
1986- Chandler, Ariz.

Indians
1901 Cleveland, Oh.
1902-03 New Orleans, La.
1904 San Antonio, Tex.
1905-06 Atlanta, Ga.
1907-08 Macon, Ga.
1909 Mobile, Al.
1910-11 Alexandria, La.
1912 Mobile, Al.
1913 Pensacola, Fla.
1914 Athens, Ga.
1915 San Antonio, Tex.
1916-20 New Orleans, La.
1921-22 Dallas, Tex.
1923-27 Lakeland, Fla.
1928-39 New Orleans, La.
1940-41 Fort Myers, Fla.
1942 Clearwater, Fla.
1943-45 Lafayette, Ind.
1946 Clearwater, Fla.
1947-92 Tucson, Ariz.
1993- Winter Haven, Fla.

Mariners
1977-92 Tempe, Ariz.
1993- Peoria, Ariz.

Orioles (Browns)
1901 St. Louis, Mo.
1902 French Lick, Ind.
1903 Baton Rouge, La.
1904 Corsicana, Tex.
1905-06 Dallas, Tex.
1907 San Antonio, Tex.
1908 Shreveport, La.
1909-10 Houston, Tex.
1911 Hot Springs, Ark.
1912 Montgomery, Al.
1913 Waco, Tex.
1914 St. Petersburg, Fla.

1915 Houston, Tex.
1916-17 Palestine, Tex.
1918 Shreveport, La.
1919 San Antonio, Tex.
1920 Taylor, Al.
1921 Bogalusa, Al.
1922-24 Mobile, Al.
1925-27 Tarpon Springs, Fla.
1928-36 West Palm Beach, Fla.
1937-41 San Antonio, Tex.
1942 Deland, Fla.
1943-45 Cape Girardeau, Mo.
1946 Anaheim, Cal.
1947 Miami, Fla.
1948 San Bernardino, Cal.
1949-52 Burbank, Cal.
1953 San Bernardino, Cal.
1954 Yuma, Ariz.
1955 Daytona Beach, Fla.
1956-58 Scottsdale, Ariz.
1959-88 Miami, Fla.
1989-90 Miami/Sarasota, Fla.
1991 Sarasota, Fla.
1993- St. Petersburg/Sarasota, Fla.

Rangers (Senators)
1961-86 Pompano Beach, Fla.
1987- Port Charlotte, Fla.

Red Sox
1901 Charlottesville, Va.
1902 Augusta, Ga.
1903-06 Macon, Ga.
1907-08 Little Rock, Ark.
1909-10 Hot Springs, Ark.
1911 Redondo Beach, Cal.
1912-18 Hot Springs, Ark.
1919 Tampa, Fla.
1920-23 Hot Springs, Ark.
1924 San Antonio, Tex.
1925-27 New Orleans, La.
1928-29 Bradenton, Fla.
1930-31 Pensacola, Fla.
1932 Savannah, Ga.
1933-42 Sarasota, Fla.
1943-44 Medford, Mass.
1945 Atlantic City, N.J.
1946-58 Sarasota, Fla.
1959-65 Scottsdale, Ariz.
1966-92 Winter Haven, Fla.

1993- Fort Myers, Fla.

Royals
1969-87 Fort Myers, Fla.
1988- Baseball City, Fla.

Tigers
1901 Detroit, Mich.
1902 Ypsilanti, Mich.
1903-04 Shreveport, La.
1905-07 Augusta, Ga.
1908 Hot Springs, Ark.
1909-10 San Antonio, Tex.
1911-12 Monroe, La.
1913-15 Gulfport, Miss.
1916-18 Waxahachie, Tex.
1919-20 Macon, Ga.
1921 San Antonio, Tex.
1922-26 Augusta, Ga.
1927-28 San Antonio, Tex.
1929 Phoenix, Ariz.
1930 Tampa, Fla.
1931 Sacramento, Cal.
1932 Palo Alto, Cal.
1933 San Antonio, Tex.
1934-42 Lakeland, Fla.
1943-45 Evansville, Ind.
1946- Lakeland, Fla.

Twins (Senators)
1901 Phoebus, Va.
1902-04 Washington, D.C.
1905 Hampton, Va.
1906 Charlottesville, Va.
1907-09 Galveston, Tex.
1910 Norfolk, Va.
1911 Atlanta, Ga.
1912-16 Charlottesville, Va.
1917 Atlanta, Ga.
1918-19 Augusta, Ga.
1920-29 Tampa, Fla.
1930-35 Biloxi, Miss.
1936-42 Orlando, Fla.
1943-45 College Park, Md.
1946-90 Orlando, Fla.
1991 Fort Myers, Fla.

White Sox
1901-02 Excelsior Springs, Mo.
1903 Mobile, Al.

1904 Marlin Springs, Tex.
1905-06 New Orleans, La.
1907 Mexico City, Mex.
1908 Los Angeles, Cal.
1909-10 San Francisco, Cal.
1911 Mineral Wells, Tex.
1912 Waco, Tex.
1913-15 Paso Robles, Cal.
1916-19 Mineral Wells, Tex.
1920 Waco, Tex.
1921 Waxahachie, Tex.
1922-23 Seguin, Tex.
1924 Winter Haven, Fla.
1925-28 Shreveport, La.
1929 Dallas, Tex.
1930-32 San Antonio, Tex.
1933-42 Pasadena, Cal.
1943-44 French Lick, Ind.
1945 Terre Haute, Ind.
1946-50 Pasadena, Cal.
1951 Pasadena/Palm Springs, Cal.
1952 Pasadena/El Centro, Cal.
1953 El Centro, Cal.
1954-59 Tampa, Fla.
1960- Sarasota, Fla.

Yankees
1901 Baltimore, Md.
1902 Savannah, Ga.
1903-04 Atlanta, Ga.
1905 Montgomery, Al.
1906 Birmingham, Al.
1907-08 Atlanta, Ga.
1909 Macon, Ga.
1910-11 Athens, Ga.
1912 Atlanta, Ga.
1913 Hamilton, Berm.
1914 Houston, Tex.
1915 Savannah, Ga.
1916-18 Macon, Ga.
1919-20 Jacksonville, Fla.
1921 Shreveport, La.
1922-24 New Orleans, La.
1925-42 St. Petersburg, Fla.
1943 Asbury Park, N.J.
1944-45 Atlantic City, N.J.
1946-50 St Petersburg, Fla.
1951 Phoenix, Ariz.
1952-61 St. Petersburg, Fla.
1962- Fort Lauderdale, Fla.

## CHAPTER 23

College Baseball

Cappy Gagnon

Intercollegiate baseball has come a long way since July 1, 1859, when the first match was played between Amherst and Williams Colleges, at Pittsfield, Massachusetts. Amherst won by a 73–32 score, on a playing field unrecognizable today. The pitcher was twenty-five feet closer to the batter, and the diamond was only sixty feet on a side. In keeping more with the academic orientation of the times, the two schools engaged in a chess match on the following day. The baseball game was played under the "Massachusetts rules," which eventually gave way to "New York rules," the forerunner of the game we know today. At the time of this game, Abraham Lincoln was not yet President. After the game there were rumors of some "ringers" being used by each team. This was a problem which haunted college sports for the next six decades.

Early college baseball thus preceded the National League by seventeen years. The colleges also provided one very significant equipment innovation. It was a Harvard man named Fred W. Thayer who invented the catcher's mask. Thayer gave his homemade creation to Harry Thatcher, the Crimson backstop (though several sources credit instead Harvard's star, James Tyng). After overcoming taunts about his "babyish and cowardly" act, Thatcher adjusted to wearing the mask. A short while later, Thayer saw the potential of this invention, and on February 12, 1878, he obtained a patent for it.

From the founding of the National Association in 1871 to the present there has been a collegiate influence on the national pastime. There is little evidence that this influence has raised the level of scholarship in the dugout, but unquestionably college baseball has provided an important feeder system for the majors. Initially, this role was important because major league teams of the pre-Rickey era did not have their own farm systems and competed vigorously with each other for raw playing talent. Colleges were an additional place for youngsters to develop.

The majors became more closely aligned with the campuses beginning in the 1890s, when veteran players began to serve as coaches of college teams. Until about 1910, college teams did not have full-time baseball field coaches. During February and March of each year, teams practiced in gymnasiums until weather permitted outside play. These practices were often supervised by a big leaguer, or other pro, limbering up for his own spring training to follow. He might have been a player from the neighboring area, as when Lou Criger of Elkhart, Indiana, or Harry Arndt of South Bend coached the Notre Dame teams. Or he might have been a recent graduate of the school, as when Jesse Burkett coached Holy Cross. Such

coaches usually retained an entrée with the college when his big league team was looking for prospects. Norwood Gibson and Red Morgan followed Criger to the Red Sox, Red Murray followed Arndt to the Cardinals, and Lou Sockalexis followed Burkett to the Cleveland Spiders.

Once the intercollegiate season began, there would be little or no involvement from university staff in the conduct of play. The team captain, a player, would function as the manager. Another student, a nonplayer, would function as the athletic director, scheduling games with other colleges and with independent and professional teams. George Huff, of Illinois, was probably the first paid full-time "coacher." His knowledge of the game helped make the Illini a "western" power, while at the same time developing future pros. Huff scouted for the Cubs and recruited players from his own teams and neighboring colleges for the Northsiders. In the former group were pitchers Carl Lundgren, Big Jeff Pfeffer, and Fred Beebe. Pitcher Ed Reulbach, of Notre Dame, was an example of the latter.

With a few exceptions in California (notably St. Mary's), college baseball until after World War Two was primarily a northeastern and midwestern sport. Because of travel difficulties and the location of all sixteen major league teams within a handful of eastern and midwestern states, college baseball became dominated by the eastern athletic powers (Harvard, Yale, Princeton, and Brown). "Western" upstarts like Illinois, Michigan, Chicago, and Notre Dame were lightly regarded by them. Because intersectional play did not occur until around 1910, however, there was no way to evaluate the competing claims of superiority. Catholic schools Boston College, Fordham, and Manhattan and the Ivy League were strong at the turn of the century, as were many small eastern colleges like Amherst. Harvard had such a strong team, they were able to defeat the defending and soon to repeat world champion Boston Red Sox, 1–0, on April 10, 1916.

Early collegians showed their cleverness in choosing pseudonyms. The two great Columbia players were known as "Sullivan" (Eddie Collins) and "Lewis" (Lou Gehrig). John Mohardt of Notre Dame had an interesting story as a result of his baseball alias: Mohardt became "Cavanaugh" when the entire Notre Dame team went to New Hampton, Iowa, for the summer of 1920. Mohardt picked up a girlfriend during that summer. He confided to her what the "ND" on the team caps stood for (his teammates claimed they were from North Dakota), but did not divulge his real name. Later that fall, when she sent a love note to "Johnny Cavanaugh, c/o Notre Dame," it was delivered to the Reverend John Cavanaugh, C.S.C., president of the university, who was not amused.

Early "tramp athletes" went from school to school and played on semipro teams under various aliases. Some "collegiate" players were not even enrolled in the colleges they represented.

Perhaps the most flagrant use of a "ringer" was by Volant College, of Butler, Pennsylvania. In 1896, Volant hired the great Rube Waddell, reportedly for $3 per week, to pitch for their baseball team. Waddell was hardly college material; he may have been retarded; but he led Volant to an undefeated season.

Bert Daniels was one of a number of itinerant collegians. He played at Villanova, Notre Dame, and Bucknell—all under his own name, while playing minor league ball during the summers, using five different aliases. As "Ayres," at Altoona in 1910, he was called the "next Ty Cobb." Unfortunately, he was already twenty-seven years old and had already played ten years of college and semipro football. All this had taken its toll on his legs. Daniels did make good use of his schooling, however, becoming an engineer.

Big leaguers came from virtually every college, including small and lesser-known colleges. Mathewson of Bucknell, Coombs of Colby, Plank of Gettysburg, Thorpe of Carlisle, and Beaumont of Beloit were good examples of why the majors scouted even the small schools. Although college teams played fewer than thirty games at this time, due to cold weather and travel difficulties and perhaps an occasional class or two, the top collegiate players seemed to get in sufficient playing time to impress big league scouts. Semipro, Industrial League, and town-team leagues were three of the types of ball for which a skilled collegian could pick up a little money for tuition and supporting his family.

The rise of college programs in the South and Far West came much later. The first major leaguer from the University of Southern California was Fay Thomas in 1927. Rod Dedeaux of the 1935 Dodgers was the fourth. Notre Dame had at least forty men reach the big leagues by 1920. Brown had fourteen in the majors by 1900. Georgetown was another early producer of big leaguers.

Once there was full-time college baseball, the relationship between the majors and the colleges became even more pronounced. In 1909 Connie Mack installed Jack Barry, a Holy Cross collegian as the shortstop in his $100,000 infield. During his forty years as coach of the Crusaders (1921–1961), Barry sent at least twenty-three players to the majors, including Gene Desautels and Mike Hegan. Connie Mack sent his son Earle to Niagara and Notre Dame.

According to Ellery Clark in *Red Sox Forever,* the early Bosox team featured many collegians, including two stars from St. Mary's (Duffy Lewis and Harry Hooper) who formed two-thirds of the best outfield of its day and the two best players from Vermont's 1908 team (Ray Collins and Larry Gardner).

One factor which may have encouraged many players to matriculate instead of trying out with the majors was the number of them who were multiple-sports stars. Christy Mathewson played football and basketball; Robin Roberts played basketball at Michigan State; Alvin Dark was a football star at Louisiana State University; Ted Kluszewski and Moose Skowron were football players at Indiana and Purdue respectively; Joe Adcock was a scoring star in basketball at Louisiana State University; Lou Boudreau, Frank Baumholtz, and Dick Groat were All-Americans in basketball at Illinois, Ohio, and Duke; and Jackie Robinson starred in football and track at U.C.L.A.

Many players better known for football were major leaguers too: George Halas, Ernie Nevers, Jim Thorpe, Sam Chapman, Red Badgro, Ace Parker, etc. Similarly, many collegiate baseball players achieved fame in other professional sports, like NFL quarterbacks Joe Theismann (ND) and John Elway (Stanford). The legendary George Gipp played a little baseball at Notre Dame. The Cubs allegedly offered him a contract after watching him play semipro baseball with Kiki Cuyler in Michigan.

College men were not always warmly received into the majors. Veteran players had a natural reluctance to accept anyone who was out to win a scarce job, in the days of sixteen teams and eighteen-man rosters. Secondly, the crude, often ill-educated pros were more than a little resentful of the more-cultured and better-educated collegians. Writing just before the turn of the century, sportswriter George E. Stackhouse quoted "a well-known professional catcher . . . [whose manager] . . . was beginning to get the college baseball fever." The player approached a collegian and asked him if he were thinking of becoming a professional. When the collegian said he had no idea of becoming a pro, the catcher replied, "with much warmth: "Now that's square, old man. You know Greek, Latin, and something about the world. You can make a good living anywhere. Don't interfere with us fellows, because you don't have to.' "

While the above writer may have exaggerated the collegian's knowledge of classical languages, there was a grain of truth in his observation. More than fifty major leaguers, mostly pre-WW I, later became physicians. Another forty were dentists. The number with law degrees was also significant.

Bobby Brown served baseball as a Yankee third sacker, Ranger President, and American League President. While earning his medical degree, he started for the baseball teams at Stanford, U.C.L.A., and Tulane.

Henry Edwards of the Major League Service Bureau estimated this percentage of collegians in the majors at almost one-third in 1932. This is a big jump from 1909, when only fifty-seven big leaguers—or approximately 14 percent—had college backgrounds.

Because of the harsh conditions they faced, many star baseballers took their schooling seriously and skipped the majors. Another factor is that player salaries, in an era long before Marvin Miller, were often not attractive enough to persuade a bright college man to give up a career in a profession.

According to the 1900 U.S. Census, fewer than 2 percent of twenty-three-year-old men were college graduates. The average annual earnings of a working man from 1900 through World War One ranged from a little more than $400 to a little less than $1,000. A college man stood a much better chance to earn more than his counterpart. Similarly, professional players did not earn much more than average, and their short careers and unpleasant travel conditions made it difficult to develop either a nest egg or a head start on a post-playing career.

The Notre Dame baseball captain in 1900 was probably as good a player as Peaches O'Neill, Red Morgan, Bob

Bescher, Henry Thielman, Norwood Gibson, Bert Keeley, Frank Shaughnessy, and several other of his teammates who went on to the majors. Instead, first baseman Angus MacDonald, a four-letter winner, took his business degree to New York City, where he went to work for the Southern Pacific Railroad, later becoming president of the railroad.

Despite the closer relationship, considerable hostility remained between organized ball and the colleges. An editorial in *The Sporting News* on March 14, 1946, defended major league baseball's plantation treatment of the colleges.

Referring to the case of Gale Bishop of Washington State, who was signed early and made ineligible for further collegiate play, "University authorities have complained about this and similar practices, but few have shown any disposition to give the game an adequate place in their athletic programs, because of the emphasis placed on football and basketball." The fact that Bishop had no major league career to show for the disruption of his college athletics only exacerbated the problem.

On July 2, 1947, *The Sporting News* reported that a foundation was being laid for a truce between organized ball and the colleges. Earlier, Branch Rickey, himself a college man from Ohio Wesleyan and later George Sisler's baseball coach at Michigan when he was the country's top college pitcher, said that he felt the colleges had "dirty skirts" themselves and were in no position to lecture the majors. Rickey said he would continue to scout and sign collegians because he felt that some college teams had relationships with major league teams that were akin to their being farmclubs. And we know that Branch Rickey was not going to be "out-farmclubbed" by anyone.

When the Mahatma was looking for the ideal candidate to integrate major league baseball, he turned to a collegian, UCLA's Jackie Robinson. Education was undoubtedly an important part of the makeup Rickey was seeking. Ironically, some have argued that baseball was Jackie's fourth best college sport, after football, track, and basketball.

One of the committee members representing organized baseball in its deliberations with the colleges was Frank "Shag" Shaughnessy, president of the International League. He said, "The player should not be compelled to wait to play professional ball if he needs the money to complete his education."

Shag was a star baseball and football player at Notre Dame who paid for his college education by playing semipro (as "Shannon") and professional ball.

Once the minor league teams were no longer able to sign and develop their own players, but were dependent upon "working agreements" with big league teams, long-term player development became a function of college baseball programs. Major league teams could avoid signing hundreds of players and maintaining ten or more minor league affiliates by simply letting the colleges do their work for them. College facilities and coaching were at least as good as the low minors. Players were "signed" to a scholarship and nurtured by the colleges. Big league scouts could watch their playing and learn something about their competitive abilities, injury history, and maturity. After two or three years, the best players would be drafted and sent to Rookie Ball or higher. Some think that a good college program might be the equivalent of Double-A baseball.

From the 1950s on, the major leagues changed their relationship with the minors dramatically, thereby thrusting the college game into an even more prominent role. Schools such as Arizona, Arizona State, and Texas began to produce big leaguers by the gross. When Dedeaux returned to his alma mater as coach, he increased their big league output dramatically while winning ten collegiate championships from 1958 to 1978.

Top-flight college programs also began to attract fans in large numbers. Texas drew more than a quarter of a million fans during its 1993 48-game home season. Miami, Fresno State, Mississippi State, Hawaii, L.S.U., and Texas A & M are other top-drawing college programs.

From 1954 through 1980, there were only three years when U.S.C. did not send at least one player to the majors—forty-five players in twenty-seven years. Tom Seaver, Dave Kingman, Fred Lynn, Ron Fairly, and Don Buford were among this invasion. Commissioner Bowie Kuhn estimated in 1978 that more than two-thirds of major leaguers were college men.

There are also advantages for the collegians in this relationship. If an aspiring major leaguer's baseball apprenticeship does not work out, he can concentrate on his studies and find another vocation. He is in an environment where he has more opportunity for enrichment, for overall personal development, than would result from his being thrown into the minors at age seventeen or eighteen, as so often occurred during baseball's early days.

Great collegiate baseball teams can be evaluated in terms of two measures: the number of games won and the number of major league players produced. It is hard to argue with those who regard the University of Southern California as the greatest school on both counts. Since the inception of the Division I NCAA baseball championship in 1947, the U.S.C. Trojans have won eleven times and have finished as runner-up once. Next closest are Arizona State, with five firsts and three seconds; Texas with four firsts and one second; Arizona with three of each; and Minnesota with three titles. Oklahoma State, Cal State Fullerton, Florida State, Wichita State, and Miami are other schools with baseball programs that have been very strong during the past decade.

Oklahoma's 1994 championship kept the trophy in the South or Sun Belt for the twenty-fourth year in the past twenty-seven. Only Wichita State's 1989 title interrupted the run which began after Ohio State University's win in 1966.

Besides Barry and Dedeaux, former big leaguers coaching these NCAA championship teams have included Bibb Falk (at Texas), Ray Fisher and Don Lund (Michigan), Dick Siebert (Minnesota), and Jerry Kindall (Arizona).

The Trojans of USC, Texas Longhorns and Arizona Sun Devils are the three top schools in producing major leaguers. The next echelon, in order, includes Michigan, Holy Cross, Illinois, and Notre Dame. The Michigan Wolverines are the only school to have produced a major leaguer in every decade since the founding of the National Association in 1871.

Texas has provided the majors with Roger Clemens, Greg Swindell, Burt Hooten, Calvin Schiraldi, and Keith Moreland among recent stars. Alabama claims Frank Lary, Riggs Stephenson, Joe Sewell, Del Pratt, and Butch Hobson. Michigan has sent an all-world infield combo which will be hard to top: George Sisler, Charlie Gehringer, Bill Freehan, Barry Larkin, and Chris Sabo. Brigham Young has been strong recently with Jack Morris, Wally Joyner, and Cory Snyder.

In 1973, the California Angels thought so much of the coaching of Bobby Winkles of the Arizona State Sun Devils that they hired him as their manager, the first time the majors had ever hired a college coach with no prior big league experience. Winkles managed two years each with the Angels and the A's. At Arizona State Winkles had coached Rick Monday, Reggie Jackson, and Sal Bando.

The NCAA has selected a championship Series Most Valuable Player since 1949. Winners of this award have included future big leaguers Tom Yewcic (C, Michigan State), Tom Borland (P, Oklahoma State), Cal Emery (P-1B, Penn State), Bob Garibaldi (P, Santa Clara), Sal Bando (3B, Arizona State), Steve Arlin (P, Ohio State), Jerry Tabb (1B, Tulsa), Dave Winfield (P-OF, Minnesota), Bob Horner (3B, Arizona State), Terry Francona (LF, Arizona), and Calvin Schiraldi (P, Texas).

The first two college championships were played in Kalamazoo, Michigan; the third in Wichita, Kansas. Since 1950, the annual event has been held in Omaha, Nebraska, where game attendance frequently exceeds 20,000.

As President of the United States, George Bush was known for having a strong defense. As the captain and first baseman for the Yale team which finished runner-up to California in the inaugural 1947 College World Series, Bush was a good defensive player with a weak bat.

The list of single game seasonal and career record holders in NCAA baseball contains many recognizable future big leaguers. Among these are:

Robin Ventura, Oklahoma State, 58 game batting streak (1987) Pete Incaviglia, Oklahoma State, 48 home runs (75 game season, 1985, and 100 home runs, 213-game career, 1983-85) Greg Swindell, Texas, 14 career shutouts (1984-86) Floyd Bannister, Arizona State, 186 innings pitched (1976) Ralph Garr, Grambling (Division II), .582 season B.A. (1967) Gary Varsho, Wisconsin-Oshkosh (Division III), 56 consecutive stolen bases (1980-82)

Determining the number of players who have attended each college is a difficult job, especially for pre-World War I players. Most sports information directors have very little information prior to the 1920s. Many have little before World War II. Several other colleges have become defunct or merged out of their previous identity. Some "colleges" were actually prep schools, but with college in their name, such as Girard College of Philadelphia. Early "collegians" may not have been enrolled as students. Many colleges have been unresponsive to research requests. The ranking lists change frequently as new players reach the majors and as the college affiliation of oldtimers gets uncovered.

As of this publication, this is the ranking of colleges attended by major leaguers:

U.S.C. | Arizona | Missouri | Washington State | Harvard | San Diego State
Texas | Georgetown | Florida State | Penn State | Maryland | South Carolina
Arizona State | U.C.L.A. | Villanova | Mississippi State | Oregon | Virginia
Michigan | Santa Clara | Duke | Texas A & M | Northwestern | Wisconsin
Holy Cross | Alabama | Michigan State | L.S.U. | Georgia | Cal State Fullerton
Illinois | Brown | Florida | Clemson | Mississippi | Iowa
Notre Dame | Oklahoma | Tennessee | Yale | Dartmouth | Princeton
Pennsylvania | Stanford | Western Michigan | Georgia Tech | Southern Illinois | Brigham Young
St. Mary's | North Carolina | Baylor | Manhattan | Boston College | Indiana
Ohio State | California

College and Major League Register, through 1900
National Association 1871-1875

1871
Cap Anson
Attended on-campus prep programs at Iowa and Notre Dame. Helped found campus baseball program at Notre Dame in 1866

Steve Bellan
Unconfirmed matriculation at Fordham, then known as Rose Hill; played for college team
Denny Mack
Attended Villanova 1866-70

1872
Tim Murnane
Prep Division at Holy Cross, 1868-70
Jim O'Rourke
Received LL.B. from Yale, 1887

1873
Alexander Nevins
Graduated from Yale, 1874
1875
Albert Bushong
Received D.D.S. from Penn in 1882

George Knight
Received B.A. from Yale in 1877

Beginning of the National League and All Other Major Leaguers (1876)

1877
John Haldeman
Attended Washington and Lee, 1872-75
Leonidas Lee
Received A.B. from Princeton, 1878. Unconfirmed Medical work at "Missouri Medical"
Lawrence Reis
Attended Chicago University (now defunct)
1878
Frank Bliss
Attended Michigan
Russell McKelvy
Attended Allegheny

Monte Ward
Attended Penn State and Columbia
1879
Cyrus Allen
Received D.D.S. from Penn, 1882
Pat McManus
Unconfirmed at Manhattan
J. Lee Richmond
Oberlin College Prep Department, 1873-76; Brown, 1876-80; A.B. A.M., 1883; College of Physicians and Surgeons (now Columbia), 1881-82; University of the City of New York, (now N.Y.U.), 1882-83, M.D.

Henry Salisbury
Unconfirmed at Brown
Dennis Sullivan
Uncertain conformation at Boston College and Holy Cross
James Tyng
Class of 1876 at Harvard
William White
Class of 1883 at Brown
1880
Frank Mountain
Attended Union (Schenectady, N.Y.), Class of 1884
1881
Asa Stratton
A.B., Brown, 1873; LL.B., Boston University, 1875

Jerry Denny
Attended St. Mary's (California), 1877-79
1882
Hal McClure
Unconfirmed at Penn State, Bucknell Grad, 1877
Ren Wylie
Confirmed at Geneva
1883
Ben Guiney
Unconfirmed at Assumption (Canada)
Allen Hubbard
Received Ph.B. from Yale, 1883
John Humphries
Cornell Grad, 1883 (Law)

Daniel James
B.A., Yale, 1884; D.D.S., Harvard, 1889
Willard Sawyer
Graduated from Adalbert College (Case-Western), 1883
Albert Smith
Attended Yale, 1879-82
Billy Sunday
Attended Northwestern, 1884
George Andrews
At Western Reserve (Case-Western), 1 year, Class of 1884
Charles Bassett
Attended Brown 3 years, Class of 1885

Fred Carroll
Attended St. Mary's (California), 1883

Edward Conley
Unconfirmed at Holy Cross, Class of 1897

Jim Fogarty
Attended St. Mary's (California), 1883

Charlie Gagus
Attended St. Mary's (California), 1875-77

Thomas Gunning
Attended Holy Cross, 1886-87; M.D., Penn, 1891

John Harkins
Unconfirmed at Rutgers

John Hibbard
Lettered at Michigan, 1885-87

William Hutchison
A.B., Yale, 1880

Milo Lockwood
Unconfirmed at Hiram

William Loughran
Attended Columbia Law School, 1887

Thomas Lynch
Diploma from Gallaudet, 1886

James McCauley
Attended Union (Schenectady, NY), Class of 1885

Ed Morris
At St. Mary's (California), 1883

Hank O'Day
At St. Mary's (California), 1882

Frank Olin
Attended Cornell, 1881-86 Studying Chemical Engineering

John Smith
Unconfirmed at St. Anselm's

Fred Clay Tenney
Attended Brown, Class of 1880

William Vinton
Attended Yale, Class of 1888

Moses Walker
Oberlin Prep & College (1877-81); Michigan Letters (1882)

Weldy Walker
Oberlin Prep (1881-83); Michigan Letters (1883-84)

1885

Peter Wood
Western University of London (Ontario), M.D.; 1893

1886

Daniel Bickham
A.B., Princeton; 1886

William Finley
Attended Columbia Law School, 1887

William Irwin
Unconfirmed at Ohio Wesleyan

George Winkleman
Attended Georgetown

1887

Mark Baldwin
Prep Class at Penn State, (1887); M.D., Baltimore Medical College (now University of Maryland), 1900

Doc Hall
M.D., Rush Medical (Chicago), 1887

Doc Leitner
Unconfirmed at Fordham; M.D., Bellevue Medical (N.Y.)

George Townsend
M.D., Bellevue Medical (NY)

1888

Count Campau
Prep Program at Notre Dame

Frank Dwyer
Attended Hobart, Class of 1890

Hartman Oberlander
Attended Syracuse

Ben Sanders
Received Bachelor of Engineering from Vanderbilt, 1892

Leon Viau
Attended Dartmouth, 1884-87

Woodie Wagenhurst
A.B. (1888) & A.M. (1892), Princeton; Also attended Penn Law School

1889

William Garfield
At Oberlin Prep & College (1882-89), A.B., 1889

Mike Sullivan
Received LL. B. from Boston University, 1896 1890

Sumner Bowman
Penn LL. B., 1891

Hiram Church
At Syracuse, 1886-87

Archie Clark
At Brown, 1885-86; A.B., Williams, 1889

Ed Eiteljorg
Played football at DePauw two years after majors debut

Robert Gibson
Penn State, Class of 1889, Washington and Jefferson, B.S.

John Keefe
Attended Holy Cross, 1889

Willie McGill
Pitched first varsity game at Notre Dame while in third big league season. May have previously attended Notre Dame while in third big league season. May have previously attended Notre Dame's prep program.

Harry Taylor
Repeatedly attended Cornell, 1891

Tom Cahill
Holy Cross Prep, 1882-4, A.B.; 1888, Penn Medical, 1888-90

Jim Darragh
D.D.S., Penn 1891

Tom Dowd
Brown, Class of 1893; also attended Georgetown

George Fox
Unconfirmed at Georgetown

Bert Inks
Attended Notre Dame

Hugh Jennings
St. Bonaventure, 1894-97; Cornell, 1901-04

John McGraw
St. Bonaventure, 1892-95

John Merritt
Holy Cross Prep, 1890-91

John O'Connell
Attended Northwestern

Phil Saylor
Attended Ohio Wesleyan 1892

Bert Abbey
Attended Vermont, 1887-1891

Daniel Daub
Attended Granville Academy and Denison, 1890-96

John Hollison
Attended Dunham Medical College

Mark McGrillis
Unconfirmed at Penn

John Shannon
Lawrence Scientific School at Harvard, 1897-99; Unconfirmed at Holy Cross

William Thompson
D.D.S., Penn, 1897

Fred Woodcock
Dartmouth Class of 1891; A.B., Brown, 1891

1893

Jesse Allen
B.A., Amherst, 1893; M.D., Penn, 1897; Ursinus, 1904

James Bannon
Attended Holy Cross, 1892-94

Dick Brown
Unconfirmed at Johns Hopkins

Red Donahue
Attended Villanova, 1890-93

Jack McCarthy
Attended Holy Cross, 1892

Frank O'Connor
Attended Dartmouth; M.D. Long Island Medical, 1898

Dennis O'Neil
A.B., Holy Cross, 1892; Yale Law 1892-93

Doc Parker
M.D., Herring Medical College

John Stafford
Holy Cross Prep, 1890-93

Otis Stocksdale
Unconfirmed at Johns Hopkins 1894

Alva Burris
Unconfirmed at Washington College; M.D., Hanneman Medical, 1909

Frank Griffith
Attended Northwestern

Yale Murphy
B.A., Yale 1893

Tom Smith
At Fordham (St. John's College) 1891-92; Holy Cross, 1893-94

Andy Sommerville
M.D., Tulane; Brown, Class of 1898; Attended Virginia Medical 1897-1900; Unconfirmed at Vermont

Fred Steere
Brown, Class of 1894, A.B., 1909

Frederick Tenney
Brown, Class of 1894

Bill Wynne
Unconfirmed at Wake Forest

1895

Henry Adkinson
A.M. (1898) & A.B. (1897), Chicago

Andrew Boswell
Penn, Class of 1897

Frank Bowerman
Attended Michigan

Daniel Coogan
Penn, Class of 1895; A.B., Georgetown, 1895

Joe Corbett
Attended St. Mary's, 1889-93

James Gannon
Unconfirmed at Allegheny

James Gardner
Unconfirmed at Allegheny

Thomas McCreery
Unconfirmed at Georgetown

Andy McFarland
Washington and Lee, Class of 1896

James McJames
Unconfirmed at South Carolina Medical College

Al Orth
Unconfirmed at DePauw

Arlie Pond
M.D. (1894) & Ph.B. (1889), Vermont; Unconfirmed at Maryland

Frank Sexton
Brown, Class of 1893; Attended Michigan; M.D. Penn, 1898

Frank Shannon
Attended Holy Cross "Special Classes," 1892-94

William Stuart
Penn State, Class of 1896

Walter Thornton
Attended Cornell College (Iowa) and Prep Department, 1894-96

1896

Charlie Dexter
Unconfirmed at the University of the South

Dale Gear
Attended Kansas, 1893-95

Edward Lewis
Attended Marietta, 1892-93; A.B. (1896) & A.M. (1899)

Elisha Norton
Attended Ohio State

Harvey Smith
Ph.B., Bucknell, 1894; M.D., Penn, 1897

1897

Ed Abbaticchio
Unconfirmed at St. Mary's (N.C)

Henry Clarke
Attended Williams, 1892-94; Ph.B., Chicago, 1896

Roy Evans
Attended Emporia

William Fox
Holy Cross Prep (1894-96) & College (1896-97)

Richard Harley
Georgetown graduate

Charles Hickman
Unconfirmed as D.C.-area collegian

Tom Leahy
Played at Holy Cross, 1891-93, "Special Student"

John Pappalau
At Holy Cross Prep, 1895-97

Lou Sockalexis
At Holy Cross Prep, 1894-97; at Notre Dame, February and March 1897. Borrowed train fare to Cleveland from University to sign with Spiders.

Cy Swaim
Unconfirmed at Scio (Ohio) 1898

Charles Carr
Attended Lehigh, 1904, in Engineering

James Casey
Attended Baltimore Medical College

David Fultz
Ph.B., 1898

William Lauder
Ph.B., Brown, 1898; Harvard

George Mahoney
Unconfirmed at Georgetown

Peter McBride
Attended Manhattan

Wiley Piatt
Unconfirmed at Ohio University

Mike Powers
Attended Holy Cross Prep (1893-94) & College (1894-97); Litt. B., Notre Dame, 1898; M.D., Louisville Medical

Walter Williams
Bowdoin Class of 1896

Vic Willis
Unconfirmed at Delaware

Harry Wolverton
Attended Kenyon, 1892-95

1899

Charles Atherton
Attended Penn State, 1891-95

Ginger Beaumont
Unconfirmed matriculation at Beloit; played for college team

John Burke
Attended St. Bonaventure, 1897-1908; Ordained as a priest

Walter Curley
Attended U. Mass., 1896; A.B., Holy Cross, 1898; Virginia Medical, 1898-99; M.D., Jefferson Medical, 1902.

Clayton Fauver
Attended Oberlin Prep (1891-95) & College (1894-97, Ph.B., LL.B., Western Reserve, 1900

Leo Fishel
LL.B. Columbia, 1900

Charles Frisbee
Attended Grinnell College Academy, 1896-97; Unconfirmed at Iowa State University

William Goeckel
B.A., Canisius, 1892; LL.B., Penn, 1896

Charles Harris
Attended Mercer, 1897-99

Mike Hickey
Attended Holy Cross, 1893-94

Skel Roach
LL.B., Northwestern, 1909

Roy Thomas
B.S., Penn, 1894

Harry Wilhelm
Unconfirmed at Westminster College

Davis Wills
Attended Virginia Medical College, 1897-1900

1900

Jerome Chambers
Unconfirmed at Lenoir Rhyne

Charles Husting
Attended Wisconsin, 1897-1900

Christy Mathewson
Bucknell, Class of 1902

Eustace Newton
Unconfirmed at Morris Hale College

Archibald Stimmel
Unconfirmed at Gettysburg

The above listings were developed with the invaluable assistance of Tom Shea and Dick Thompson.

## CHAPTER 24

Baseball and the Olympics

David Osinski

Even though it became the twenty-fifth sport in the Summer Olympiad as recently as October 13, 1986, Olympic baseball is increasingly facing the kind of hardball that has been played in international political circles for years. After its inclusion in the 1992 Barcelona Olympics, baseball seemed ready to take a prominent position in the Games. At the same time, within the Olympic movement, century-old barriers to professionals participating in the Olympics were crumbling, signaling the need for adjustment in all sports.

The International Baseball Association (IBA), a scant eleven years old as of 1986, had been the driving force in achieving Olympic medal status for its 50 million players from some ninety baseball-playing countries. (Only thirty-six countries were playing baseball when the IBA was formed in 1975 as an amalgamation of two separate international baseball organizations.). In 1995 the IBA member countries find themselves enjoying the warmth of the Olympic family, yet at the same time chafing at some of the family's demands, most particularly the inclusion of professional athletes in the Summer Olympiads. To understand the challenges posed to the international baseball community by this mandate. one requires a review of Olympic baseball history.

Baseball Competition in the Twentieth Century

Ever since the turn of the century, baseball enthusiasts and administrators had lobbied for the sport's inclusion in the Olympics. But it was not until 1984, at the final press conference following the 1984 Summer Olympiad in Los Angeles, that their labors were rewarded, as Juan Antonio Samaranch, International Olympic Committee president, proclaimed his belief that baseball deserved to be the next sport added to the Olympics.

Although there is little corroborative documentation, the report of James E. Sullivan, Olympic Director of the 1904 Olympics held in St. Louis, notes that a baseball competition among amateurs was held in June of that year. Because many other local or regional events were also part of the Olympiad, the competition most probably did not include athletes from any of the other twelve countries which came to the Midwest, and thus did not further international baseball's growth.

The morning of Monday, July 15, 1912, witnessed the first "international" baseball game under aegis of the Games of the Fifth Olympiad as a team of host Swedes locked horns with members of the U.S. track and field delegation to play the exhibition sport. The six-inning affair ended with the hosts, whose nation had begun to play baseball only two summers before the Stockholm Olympics, on the short end of a 13–3 score.

The following day, an all-U.S. exhibition was held as the U.S. delegation members from the western part of the country bowed to their eastern counterparts by a score of 6–3. Jim Thorpe, the celebrated U.S. amateur athlete and future major leaguer, played right field for the eastern team.

Despite being passed over as a possible exhibition sport during the Olympiads held in Europe during the 1920s, baseball had acquired an international champion by 1936 (it was part of the Central American Championships of 1926). In the 1932 Los Angeles Olympics, baseball lost out to football and lacrosse, but American Leslie Mann, a former major league outfielder, lobbied successfully to stage an exhibition baseball game during the 1936 Berlin Olympics.

While the original intent was to have a U.S. team face a team from Japan, both teams were formed from the Americans who had tried out for the team in Baltimore. The nighttime affair, staged in front of over 90,000 German fans in the principal Olympic venue, saw the "World Champions" edge the "Olympics" by virtue of a seventh inning blast by Les McNeese breaking a 5–5 tie. Mann had sealed his name in Olympic history as the manager of the teams.

Two years after the Berlin Olympics, the first "World Championship" was held in Great Britain between a team from the U.S. and one from the host country, but the Olympics and baseball parted ways with the world at war, precluding the inclusion of baseball in the scheduled Games in Tokyo for 1940 and London for 1944, neither of which took place.

The U.S. soccer team provided the manpower in the first exhibition baseball game in the 1950s as the U.S. defeated host Finland before some 4,000 enthusiasts in Helsinki. The fact that Finnish baseball, a traditional bat and ball game with the name of *pesapallo,* possesses a pitcher who merely tosses the ball to the batter figured largely in the first inning as the North Americans scored seven runs, on their way to a 19-1 verdict.

By 1956, when the Melbourne Olympiad was held during the start of Southern Hemisphere summer, baseball was over sixty years old in several parts of Australia, although it was usually played at local clubs only by adults. An exhibition started before track and field events on December 1. A team made up of U.S. military men brought to Australia for the exhibition managed an 11–5 spanking of the hosts as more than 114,000 people filled the stands at the MCG (Melbourne Cricket Ground) for the track and field meet. The attendance record for one baseball game stands to the present (although it was a hybrid doubleheader, with racing rather than another ballgame concluding the twin bill).

In the winter of 1964, for the first time in Olympic baseball history, representative teams were recruited and prepared to compete. For the U.S., Rod Dedeaux of the University of Southern California, the all-time winningest college coach, created a team of college stars from as far away as Florida, eight of whom eventually played in the majors. On October 11, more than 50,000 baseball fans cheered the host Japanese team. Shawn Fitzmaurice of the University of Notre Dame homered on the first pitch of the game, and the U.S. prevailed, 6–2.

The success in 1964 died aborning after the IOC voted in 1972 to discontinue demonstration sports during the Summer Olympiad. However, once the 1984 Games were awarded to Los Angeles, the international baseball community rallied with leadership from Dodgers owner Peter O'Malley and future commissioner Peter Ueberroth. With the Dodgers agreeing to host baseball in their stadium and international baseball unified under Dr. Robert E. Smith, who also headed the U.S. Baseball Federation, baseball managed to become a demonstration sport and proved to the IOC members that its contribution was significant.

Ironically the first real baseball series proved disappointing to American fans primed for an easy victory. Although the U.S. had by far the most formidable amateur team ever assembled for an Olympic event and its leader, Rod Dedeaux, once again tutored such future stars such as Will Clark, Mark McGwire, and Barry Larkin, Japan's first baseman, Katsumi Hirosawa, broke open a 3–1 game with a three-run home run that insured a 6–3 victory and the gold medal for his team.

Cuba, defending Pan American champion and winner of eight of eleven Pan American titles dating to 1951, boycotted the Games, leaving the Republic of Korea, Italy, Nicaragua, Chinese Taipei, the Dominican Repub-

lic, and Canada to round out the two-group competition. For the first time, the Olympic baseball event reflected the sport's essence of daily competition, allowing the best team to surface and compete for medal-round rewards.

Four years later, real baseball competition returned to the Olympics as Smith and the Korean baseball leader Jong Nak Kim lobbied successfully to have the sport played at Chamsil Stadium, directly across the quad from the Olympic track and field venue. Defending champion Japan returned to face the U.S., Puerto Rico, the Netherlands, Chinese Taipei, Canada, and Australia. (Cuba repeated its boycott.)

The U.S.A.'s Jim Abbott turned back the Japanese as he pitched his team to a 5–3 win and the gold medal. Korean fans responded to the competition, but, because of baseball's status as a demonstration sport, ticket sales and national media coverage lagged behind those of the medal sports.

Realization of the Goal

Official status in the Summer Olympiad brings designation of the International Olympics Committee as the sole world governing body for the sport; a seat in ASOIF, the twenty-five-member organization of the summer Olympic sports; and revenues from the Olympiad. Baseball's official inclusion in 1986 allowed the sport to point toward the first tournament that would bring gold medals at the end of the competition.

Barcelona built a cozy stadium seating 7,000 fans in a country with 6,000 registered baseball players, and Cuba couldn't find a reason not to visit the *madre patria* and compete. The islanders blitzed the competition to capture the gold and remained undefeated in the field made up of host Spain, Puerto Rico, Italy, the Dominican Republic, U.S.A., Japan, and Chinese Taipei. All activity in Cuba ceased as the population stopped to watch their heroes turn back Chinese Taipei, 13–3, in the final game.

CHAPTER 25

Women in Baseball

Debra A. Shattuck

omen have been associated with baseball, either as players or spectators, since the game's dawn in the early nineteenth century. Even before baseball emerged in its final form, girls and young women sometimes played precursors of the game like One Old Cat, Town Ball, and Stoolball in Colonial America. As time passed, and the boys' amusement became serious business for grown men, baseball's reputation as a masculine domain was established. In 1865, one year before Charles Peverelly observed that baseball "has now become beyond question the leading feature of the outdoor sports of the United States," *Harper's Weekly* proclaimed: "There is no nobler or manlier game than base-ball." During the latter half of the nineteenth century, women's presence as spectators at baseball games was tolerated and sometimes encouraged. Eventually promoters of the game hosted regular "Ladies Days" to attract women fans who would bring in added gate receipts and, hopefully, have a calming effect on the sometimes unruly crowds. Many women were content with their role as spectators and moral uplifters, but others yearned for the opportunity to try their hand at the national pastime. Those who lived out their fantasy often had to endure verbal and written derision from observers anxious to preserve the baseball status quo.

For the most part, the negative attitude toward women baseball players continues to this day. Many still share the opinion of an editorialist who noted in The St. Louis *Globe-Democrat* in 1885 that "The female has no place in base ball, except to the degradation of the game." The criticisms notwithstanding, uncounted women have pursued their own field of dreams, contributing their unique chapter to baseball's rich heritage.

Many of the first women baseball players were college students. The secluded atmosphere of all-girl's schools enabled women to play the game without attracting too much attention. Students at Vassar College organized two baseball clubs as early as 1866. In 1879, according to Vassar alumna Sophia Foster Richardson, the Vassar girls organized at least seven baseball clubs. The private grounds of college campuses did not always protect female players from public criticism, however. In a speech to an alumnae association in 1896, Richardson recalled, "The public, so far as it knew of our playing, was shocked, but in our retired grounds, and protected from observation even in these grounds by sheltering trees, we continued to play in spite of a censorious public." Within a few years, however, the "censorious public" and "disapproving mothers" had succeeded in stifling the game at Vassar.

But Vassar was not the only college where women tried their hand at baseball. In a letter to her former classmates at Smith College, Minnie Stephens (class of 1883) reminisced about the baseball clubs they had organized at the school in 1880. Stephens described the enthusiasm of the players and the keen competition at games. She also related how the Victorian-style clothing of the day, generally a hindrance to sporting endeavors, had actually benefited one of the players during a heated contest, "One vicious batter drove a ball directly into the belt line of her opponent, and had it not been for the rigid steel corset clasp worn in those days, she would have been knocked out completely." Like the women at Vassar, baseball players at Smith College faced opposition which eventually forced them to give up the game for a number of years.

Women baseball players were not limited to college campuses. In Springfield, Illinois, three men organized a women's baseball club in 1875. They were confident that the novelty of women playing baseball would attract large crowds and fatten their bankroll. On September 11, 1875, the club's teams, labeled the "Blondes" and "Brunettes," played their first match. Newspapers heralded the event as the "first game of baseball ever played in public for gate money between feminine ball-tossers." The concept evidently caught on, for numerous other male entrepreneurs copied the idea and organized women's baseball teams. One group started the "Young Ladies' Baseball Club" in Philadelphia in 1883. These owners billed their team's games as entertainment spectacles, not serious competition, and they continually stressed the femininity and moral respectability of their players. A newspaper account of one of the club's first games relayed the management's claim that players were "selected with tender solicitude from 200 applicants, variety actresses and ballet girls being positively barred." Furthermore the article noted, "Only three of the lot had ever been on the stage, and they were in the strictly legitimate business."

The Young Ladies Baseball Club played its first game on August 18, 1883, at Pastime Park in Philadelphia. Despite the supposed "200 applicants," only sixteen girls were mustered to form the two teams for the contest; two young men rounded out the rosters. The game was played on a regulation-size diamond, but, as one observer wrote, it was too large for the women. "A ball thrown from pitcher to second base almost invariably fell short and was stopped on the roll. The throw from first to third base was an utter impossibility." Five hundred spectators witnessed the club's debut and were caught up in "uncontrollable laughter" much of the time. From a financial standpoint, however, the venture was a success. More than 1,500 fans turned out for the club's match at the Manhattan Athletic Club on September 23, 1883, where they "laughed themselves hungry and thirsty." Though one observer conceded that "four of the girls had become expert—for girls," it is obvious that "novelty" and not "ability" was the hallmark of women's baseball at the time.

Another novel group of women baseball players was the Bloomer Girls. Actually "Bloomer Girls" was a misnomer, since Bloomer Girls teams were composed of both men and women. Kansas City Bloomer Girls, New York Bloomer Girls, Texas Bloomer Girls, and Boston Bloomer Girls were just a few of the teams traveling from diamond to diamond in the late nineteenth and early twentieth centuries in search of fame and fortune. Despite the number of Bloomer Girl teams, they did not play each other and no formal league was set up. Instead, they journeyed from town to town, challenging men's amateur and semiprofessional teams. The Bloomer Girls teams relied on sideshow style appeal to draw fans and, not surprisingly, the bottom line was money. The manager of the Texas Bloomer Girls wrote to one prospective promoter in 1913, assuring him that the team's seven girls and four boys, "including the one-armed boy who plays center field," would draw enough fans to ensure the backer "three hundred dollars clear money" each week. A few of the male Bloomer Girls players like "Smoky Joe" Wood and Hall of Famer Rogers Hornsby went on to become successful big league ballplayers, but the future was not as bright for the female players who could not aspire to anything higher in the baseball world.

The Bloomer Girls teams were not the only option available to baseball-playing females around the turn of the century. Women's teams and mixed teams competed occasionally in "pickup" games. One such game took place in Kearsarge, New Hampshire, on August 7, 1903. An article in the *Boston Herald* the following day noted, "The teams were made up of young ladies gowned in white and young men decked out in girls' clothes, all New Englanders, guests at the hotel." On August 31, the newspaper announced an upcoming game at Forest Hills between the "Hickey and Clover clubs," each composed of five women and four men. One year later, in Flat Rock, Indiana, a group of women organized two baseball clubs, one consisting only of married players, the other only of single players.

While some women played on all-female or coed teams, others challenged social constraints of the day by playing on otherwise all-male teams. On June 12, 1903, the *Cincinnati Enquirer* printed an article about the efforts of a local woman, Miss M. E. Phelan, to get a job as center fielder with the all-male Flora Baseball Club of Indiana. Phelan wrote to the club's manager informing him, "I have played with a number of lady ball clubs and am considered the equal of the average country player." Whether the Flora club took Phelan up on her offer to play for them for "$60 per month and expenses" is unknown, but only four years later another Ohioan, Alta Weiss, became an overnight female baseball-playing sensation and, as one article put it, "perhaps the only girl in the United States to obtain [a] college education through skill as a baseball player."

Weiss, a native of Ragersville, Ohio, became a celebrity in the Cleveland area when she made her pitching debut with the all-male, semiprofessional Vermilion Independents on September 2, 1907. More than 1,200 fans attended the game in which Weiss pitched 5 innings, giving up only 4 hits and 1 run. By the time Weiss made her second appearance on September 8, she was already being heralded as the "Girl Wonder" in the press. According to the *Vermilion News,* so many fans wanted to see Weiss play that special trains had to be run to Vermilion from Cleveland and surrounding towns.

Weiss pitched 8 games for the Independents during their 1907 season. More than 13,000 fans saw the games, including a season high of 3,182, who witnessed her debut at Cleveland's League Park on October 2, 1907. At least a dozen newspapers covered her exploits. The following year her father bought a half-interest in a men's semiprofessional team which was known thereafter as the Weiss All-Stars. It was based in Cleveland and, with Alta as a drawing card, played for large crowds throughout Ohio and Kentucky.

Though Weiss was far and away the best-known woman baseball player in northern Ohio at this time, she was not the only one. On June 22, 1908, the *Cleveland Press* introduced fourteen-year-old Carita Masteller to the public. The paper reported that she had been playing baseball for eight or nine years and was as good as Weiss. That same month Weiss pitched against another female pitcher, Irma Gribble. The two dueled again in August. In another unique game, two sisters from Bellevue, Ohio, Irene and Ruth Basford, pitched for opposing men's teams.

Another well-known woman baseball player who played on men's teams was Rhode Islander Elizabeth Murphy. "Lizzie," as she liked to be called, played amateur and semiprofessional baseball from about 1915 to 1935 and was known as the "Queen of Baseball" throughout New England and eastern Canada. After playing for a number of amateur teams in Rhode Island, Murphy signed with the semiprofessional Providence Independents in 1918. A few years later she joined Ed Carr's All-Stars of Boston and earned quite a reputation for her skills as a first baseman.

In 1928, while Murphy was still impressing the fans in New England, fourteen-year-old Margaret Gisolo helped her Blanford, Indiana, American Legion boys' baseball team win county, district, sectional, and state championships. In seven tournament games she had 9 hits in 21 at-bats. She scored 10 putouts and 28 assists in the field, with no errors charged against her. A protest against her participation filed by opposing teams went all the way to the American Legion's National Americanism Commission, which referred it to the major league baseball commissioner, Judge Kenesaw Mountain Landis. Landis determined that American Legion rules did not specifically ban the participation of women and disallowed the protest.

Landis had to address a similar situation three years later when the "Barnum of Baseball," Chattanooga Lookouts manager Joe Engel, signed seventeen-year-old Jackie Mitchell to a contract with his Class AA minor league team, thus making her the first female professional baseball player. Mitchell had been taught to pitch by major leaguer Dazzy Vance and had once struck out nine men in a row in an amateur game. She became an overnight celebrity on April 2, 1931, when she pitched in an exhibition game against the visiting New York Yankees—and struck out Babe Ruth and Lou Gehrig, back to back. Speculation continues as to whether Ruth and Gehrig were merely putting on a show or really trying to hit Mitchell's pitches. Mitchell contended that it was not a setup and that the only instructions to the Yankee players had been to try not to hit the ball straight through the pitcher's box. A number of Yankee players confirmed her story. Unfortunately Mitchell never had a chance to repeat her performance as a professional baseball player. A few days after her debut, Landis informed Engel that he had disallowed Mitchell's contract on the grounds that life in baseball was too strenuous for women. Organized baseball formalized the ban against women signing professional baseball contracts with men's teams on June 21, 1952; the ruling still stands.

The restriction on women playing professional baseball on men's teams did not prevent the formation of a women's professional baseball league, however. In 1943, with wartime manpower shortages threatening major league baseball, Chicago Cubs' owner Philip K. Wrigley decided to form a women's professional softball league which would play its games in the major league stadiums while the men were away at war. Within a year of its founding, the league modified its rules and the All-American Girls *Baseball* League (AAGBL) was born. The AAGBL made its debut in 1943, when four teams—the Rockford [Illinois] Peaches, the South Bend [Indiana] Blue Sox, the Racine [Wisconsin] Belles, and the Kenosha [Wisconsin] Comets—squared off during the League's 108-game schedule. Attendance that year was 176,000 fans, which, according to one contemporary, meant that the League was "drawing a higher percentage of the population [in league cities] than major league baseball ever did in its greatest attendance years." Attendance figures continued to rise year after year, reaching a peak in 1948, when the League's ten teams drew almost 1,000,000 fans. That same year, AAGBL teams drew more than 100,000 fans for a series of nine games in Puerto Rico.

Unlike women's teams of the past, the AAGBL relied on players' skills, not just their gender, to draw fans to the ballpark. The more than 500 women who played in the AAGBL during its twelve-year existence were top-notch athletes. Many were veterans of championship school, community, or industrial softball teams, and a few had even played on boys' or men's baseball teams. In addition, many of the AAGBL managers were experienced professional baseball players—some, like Bill Wambsganss (the only player ever to achieve an unassisted triple play in a World Series), Max Carey, Jimmie Foxx, and Dave Bancroft, were legends.

The AAGBL represented one of the only times in history that women baseball players received widespread moral and financial support. Once World War II ended, however, social pressures for women to leave nontraditional jobs and return to household duties resumed. This fact, coupled with organizational problems and the rise of televised major league games, led to the demise of the AAGBL. Interest in the league all but disappeared until the 1980s, when a group of former players organized a

players association and began lobbying to have the league honored in the National Baseball Hall of Fame. The popular media and serious scholars rediscovered the league and hundreds of articles about the AAGBL appeared in newspapers and magazines across the country. In October 1988, the Hall of Fame unveiled a permanent exhibit of AAGBL league memorabilia. In the summer of 1992, the AAGBL was further memorialized when it became the subject of the feature film, *A League of Their Own.*

Despite the newfound popularity of the AAGBL, modern-day women baseball players still face the same obstacles and criticisms endured by nineteenth century players. For the most part, organized teams and leagues remain closed to women. When Commissioner Ford Frick issued his ban against women players in 1952, his purpose was to prevent teams from using women players as publicity stunts. The end result of his edict was that even highly skilled women players (like those on the all-female team that tried, unsuccessfully, to gain admission to the men's Class A Florida State League in 1984) lost an important avenue for upward mobility and legitimacy in baseball. Women who challenge baseball's "men only" reputation rarely escape the experience unscathed. Julie Croteau, who gained notoriety in the late 1980s by playing first base for the St. Mary's (Maryland) College men's baseball team, earned school and conference honors yet still had to endure derisive comments from teammates. She left school in the middle of her junior year disillusioned with a system she believed treated women as inferior to men.

There is some indication, however, that the 1990s will see the gradual transformation of baseball from a strictly masculine pastime to a truly "national" pastime. Thanks to a series of court battles in the 1970s, generations of young girls have had the opportunity to play baseball on Little League teams. Many have resisted abandoning the game of their youth. A growing number of girls and women are finding opportunities to play baseball on newly organized municipal and professional teams. At least half a dozen cities, including Fort Wayne and Chicago, currently sponsor girls baseball leagues. In 1994, the Coors Brewing Company fielded the Colorado Silver Bullets, a professional women's baseball team that plays men's teams.

In June 1995 the All-American Women's Professional Baseball League will debut in the Midwest. The AAWPBL, which bears similarities to Philip Wrigley's All-American Girls Baseball League, is the brainchild of Global Sports Marketing, Inc., a company run by Alan Levin and Eric Margenau. Two of the new league's four teams will be located in former AAGBL cities—Fort Wayne and South Bend. A third is slated for Kane County, Illinois, and the fourth site was to have been announced before the end of 1994.

If girls and women continue to enjoy opportunities to play baseball, the sport will undoubtedly lose its masculine reputation. The question is whether or not current opportunities for female players will last. If they don't, today's female baseball players may find themselves sidelined, once again, with "a league of their own," watching rather than directly experiencing the national pastime.

THE GAME OFF THE FIELD

## CHAPTER 26

The Business of Baseball

David Pietrusza

Baseball has been a business almost from its outset. When it was *not* a business, it was barely recognizable as baseball. And even before players received compensation and owners charged admissions, the games were played for money—in the form of widespread fan gambling.

While Harry Wright's 1869 Cincinnati Red Stockings were baseball's first *fully* professional team, players had been compensated both openly and covertly for at least ten years before that. In May 1862 William H. Cammeyer had charged admissions at his enclosed field, Brooklyn's Union Grounds, thus, as Michael Gershman pointed out in *Diamonds*, commencing "the true beginning of professional baseball as a spectator sport."

In 1870 the governing body of baseball, the National Association of Base Ball Players, heard a resolution ("That this Association regard the custom of hiring men to play the game of baseball as reprehensible and injurious to the best interests of the game.") proposed by a Mr. Cantwell of Albany, New York, which would ban professionalism in the sport. It was the last gasp of the "gentleman's game." The resolution failed to pass; the old amateur association soon collapsed, and the National Association of *Professional* Base Ball Players, the first major league, formed for the following year.

This new National Association, a jerrybuilt league, collapsed in 1876 and was replaced by William Hulbert's more structured National League of Professional Baseball Clubs. That circuit quickly moved to elevate baseball's organization as well as its tone. Gambling, Sunday ball, and the sale of alcohol on the grounds were banned. The new league created territorial rights (i.e., geographic monopolies) and imposed minimum ticket prices of fifty cents. "A good game is worth 50 cts, a poor one is dear at 25," contended Harry Wright.

But soon the American Association, "The Beer and Whiskey League," challenged the National League, and, for competitive reasons, alcohol would again be sold at National League parks. Attendance increased as the range of concessions widened and moralistic restrictions eased (Sunday ball took hold in a few cities and by the turn of the century became the norm). At the Polo Grounds, around the turn of the century, English-born Harry Mosely Stevens, the inventor of the scorecard, also gave the world the hot dog. Harry Payne Whitney once remarked that Stevens had "parlayed a bag of peanuts into millions." (The concessions business was so good for Stevens that, when the Polo Grounds burnt in 1911, owner John T. Brush turned to him for a loan to rebuild it.)

As money came in, it also flowed out. Players had to eat, and being the best in their profession, were not going to be satisfied with hot dogs. From the earliest days of the game, players sold—or, more precisely, rented—their services to the highest bidder. The inflation of players' salaries as they moved from club to club ("revolving") helped collapse the National Association. The National League would not follow the same path. "It is ridiculous to pay ballplayers $2,000 a year," complained William Hulbert in the 1870s, "when the $800 boys often do just as well."

The Reserve Clause

Before long the National League was "reserving" players' services. On September 29, 1879, it created a secret "reserve list" of five players per club with whom other teams would not "contract with, employ, engage or negotiate." At first players did not mind being reserved, for it signified their stature and guaranteed employment for the upcoming season.

Before long entire rosters were reserved, and the basis of major league labor relations was set for a century. Even in an age of few labor rights, management, however, knew the reserve clause stood on woefully weak legal ground. When players revolted in 1890 and formed their own Players National League, management went to court to compel their return. Their efforts failed. During the birth of the American League and, during the Federal League war of 1914-15, similar judgments went against the reserve clause.

As the Federal League collapsed, however, the outlaw circuit's Baltimore Terrapins were unhappy with the terms of the settlement that terminated their league. In 1917 they sued in Federal Court, charging Organized Baseball with violation of the Clayton Antitrust Act. The United States Supreme Court, however, not only ruled against Baltimore, but surprisingly provided Organized Baseball with legal protection far beyond what it could have realistically hoped: antitrust exemption.

On May 22, 1922, speaking for the court's majority, Justice Oliver Wendell Holmes held that baseball was not interstate commerce. He further held that the reserve clause, "intended to protect the rights of clubs . . . to retain the services of sufficient players," was legal.

With the exception of gradually increasing revenues from radio, and then from television, baseball's business practices remained remarkably static for the next few decades. Not until after the Second World War II was there a significant legal challenge to the reserve clause, and that was settled out of court. In the 1950s, however, the pace of change quickened. Franchise shifts moved teams into Milwaukee, Kansas City, Baltimore, Los Angeles and San Francisco. And New York City's abandonment of the National League led to the Continental League challenge and then to expansion.

A Peculiar Institution

Baseball, indeed any sports league, operates in a universe far different from that of normal commerce. On the one hand there is fierce competition—for fans, labor, advertising, etc. On the other hand there must be a balance between competing entities.

This is not the case with baseball, and never has been. The New York Yankees or Los Angeles Dodgers *need* competition. On the most basic level, both clubs require opponents in order to play games, and baseball needs *healthy* rivalries to attract crowds both at home and away. (Of the several reasons for the collapse of the old National Association, an important one was the overwhelming dominance of the Boston Red Stockings.)

On a deeper level, however, a national network of clubs is necessary to create a national base of fans as opposed to a local or regional one, as Hulbert recognized from the dawn of professional league play. Such a need for a national fan base now mandates expansion into areas of growing population, while striving to protect existing franchises in older cities.

This need to succeed at the cost of one's competitor without crushing him entirely forms some of the basis of the current "big market-small market" controversy. In fact, though, the paradox is decades old and produced such implausible results as the continued existence of chronically impoverished franchises like the St. Louis Browns. It also led to the imposition of the amateur free agent draft in the 1960s, which aimed at equalizing the talent pool as it first came into Organized Baseball (and also to stop the upward spiral of bonuses).

As television contracts, particularly cable contracts, grew larger so did the disparity in club resources. Once free agency came upon the scene such disparity would help fuel bidding wars for talent not seen since Federal League days.

The MLBPA

In 1946 an abortive attempt at a player's union, the American Baseball Guild, failed. Nevertheless, the group did obtain a $5,000 minimum salary for ballplayers. In 1954 big league players, led by Allie Reynolds and Ralph Kiner, formed the Major League Baseball Players' Association (MLBPA). Although not originally a union in the true sense of the word, the MLBPA secured 60 percent of television revenues from both the World Series and the All-Star Game for player pensions. Not until 1966, when the MLBPA selected as its chief Marvin Miller—a veteran of the U.S. Department of Labor, the International Association of Machinists, the United Auto Workers and the United Steelworkers of America—did baseball labor-

management negotiations enter the modern era.

The following season ownership responded by creating the Player Relations Committee (PRC), consisting of both league presidents and three owners from each league. Named as the PRC's first head was John J. Gaherin, former president of the New York City Newspapers Association.

By February 1968 the MLBPA and the PRC had hammered out Major League Baseball's first Basic Agreement. It raised the minimum major league salary from $6,000 to $10,000 but, more significantly for the future, created a grievance procedure and promised a review of the reserve clause.

Events rapidly accelerated. In 1969 the MLBPA threatened to strike, but was dissuaded from that course of action when management conceded to Miller increases in the pension fund and in the minimum major league salary along with the right of players to employ agents. Key to reaching that settlement was the National League's attorney, Bowie Kuhn. Six months later management rewarded Kuhn for his efforts by tendering him an eight-year contract as Commissioner.

A new Basic Agreement was arrived at in 1970. It raised the minimum player salary from $10,000 to $15,000, restricted salary cuts to 20 percent, and—most importantly—set up a system of impartial arbitration.

Strike One

In 1972 the Players Association staged the first general work stoppage in baseball history, delaying the start of the season for thirteen days and forcing the cancellation of eighty-six regular season games.

Prior to the 1972 season opening, players requested a 25 percent raise in pension benefits, but then reduced their demand to 17 percent. This lower amount created an $800,000 cost to ownership, but represented only the amount necessary to keep pace with the cost of living since enactment of the last Basic Agreement in 1969. The Players Association also wanted $400,000 to cover increased medical and health care benefits.

The owners agreed to pick up this latter cost, but later produced a lower bid of $250,000 from Blue Cross-Blue Shield. Miller charged that management had not bargained in "good faith" and had decreased the amount of money previously offered. This issue galvanized player support for a work stoppage, with the MLBPA voting 663-10 (with two abstentions) to authorize a strike. Finally the MLBPA's Executive Board authorized a strike by a vote of 47-0.

Major League Baseball (MLB) suffered its first general strike on April 1, 1972, five days before the start of the regular season. As the stoppage unfolded, Miller developed a compromise solution that eventually led to a return to work, although management's Player Relations Committee at first dismissed the idea as "imprudent."

At this point President Richard Nixon suggested that both parties be brought together by the Federal Mediation and Reconciliation Service.

Miller eventually won an increased management contribution of $490,000 to the players' benefit plan, plus a transfer of $400,000 in surplus pension funds to improve players' retirement benefits and maintain their health benefits. However, the players did lose 4.9 percent in their salaries for the season because of the strike. Management wanted lost games to be made up, but Miller rejected the idea unless that 4.9 percent salary loss was likewise recovered.

And so baseball's first player strike came to an end at 4:15 p.m. on April 13, with play to resume two days later. Players lost $600,000 in salaries. Owners lost an estimated $5.2 in revenue from eighty-six canceled games over the thirteen days of the stoppage.

Lost amid the dollar figures in the newspaper stories was a very important concession granted labor—the right to arbitrate grievances. In just a few years that right would turn baseball on its head.

Curt Flood Tests the Waters

Coming hard on the heels of these events was the United States Supreme Court's June 19, 1972, ruling in the Curt Flood case. By a 5–3 majority the high court reluctantly reaffirmed both the game's antitrust exemption and the reserve clause. (See "Baseball and The Law" by Gary Hailey & Doug Pappas, in this volume.)

A third Basic Agreement was negotiated following the 1972 season. The MLBPA accepted management's proposal that players with two years plus one day of major league service could have their salary disputes arbitrated. The MLBPA also gained the so-called five-and-ten year rule. Any player with ten years of service in the major leagues and five years of service with his current club could veto a proposed trade. Had that rule been in effect in 1970 Curt Flood would not have sought recourse in the courts.

The Seitz Decisions

Since the signing of Basic Agreement of 1972, players had had the right to arbitration of grievances before a three-person panel, consisting of labor, management, and an impartial arbitrator. In practice, since the labor representative would always uphold the labor view, and management that of its side, the impartial arbitrator held immense power.

In 1974 Peter Seitz, a graduate of New York University and a man with decades of experience in the arbitration field but "only a passing interest in spectator sports," was named baseball's fourth arbitrator. He replaced Gabriel Alexander of Detroit.

Wrote Bowie Kuhn: "There were some misgivings on the PRC in selecting Seitz because he was thought to favor the labor side of issues. But he had served in the same role for the NBA with no disastrous results."

However, Marvin Miller had detected something else in Seitz's record. In one NBA opinion Seitz cited a 1969 California Court of Appeals ruling allowing San Francisco's Rick Barry to sign with an American Basketball Association team after finishing his NBA option year. MLB and NBA option clauses were identical. If a similar case were to come before Seitz would he rule in the same way?

On December 13, 1973, Seitz gave a hint of the changes he would unleash, when he found that A's owner Charles Finley had failed to comply with the terms of pitcher Catfish Hunter's 1973 contract. It was "pellucidly clear," Seitz stated, that under article 7A of the Standard Player Contract a player could terminate his contract—including the reserve clause—if management failed to live up to its terms. Seitz's decision set off an unprecedented bidding war by fifteen major league clubs which resulted in Hunter's signing an estimated $3.75 million, five-year contract with the Yankees.

The following year the Expos' Dave McNally and the Dodgers' Andy Messersmith, dissatisfied with their contracts, refused to sign new ones. Their respective clubs exercised their rights to renew their agreements for an additional year without the player's signature. At season's end both pitchers claimed free agency.

On December 23, 1975, Seitz ruled for McNally and Messersmith, and the very basis of the reserve clause—to bind a player in perpetuity to a single club—was overturned. Organized Baseball reacted with anger. Seitz was immediately dismissed by the owners, as was their right, although it was the first time either management or labor had exercised that privilege.

The owners appealed Seitz's decision regarding McNally and Messersmith, but it was affirmed in Federal District Court on February 4, 1976, and on appeal one month later.

The Fourth Basic Agreement

By this time the Third Basic Agreement had expired. In the spring of 1976, it was ownership's turn to bring play to a halt, locking players out of the spring training camps. After twenty-four days of the shutdown, Commissioner Bowie Kuhn ordered the camps reopened. Even though no Basic Agreement existed, the season began anyway. It was not until July that an agreement was reached. The Fourth Basic Agreement granted free agency to all players with six or more seasons of major league service. Under the Fourth Basic Agreement, the average player salary increased nearly threefold from 1976 ($51,501) to 1980 ($143,756).

Two factors fueled the increase: bidding wars for established stars and salary arbitration. The pivotal arbitration case involved Cubs relief ace Bruce Sutter. Following the 1979 season, Sutter (who then had only four years of major league service) went to arbitration. The Cubs offered him $350,000. Sutter wanted $700,000, then a staggering amount for a player with such relatively limited service. In February an arbitrator ruled in Sutter's favor. Previously, only long-time (and often somewhat past their prime) stars had reaped the really big salaries, but now the floodgates were opening.

Strike Two

The strike of 1972 was replayed with greater volume in 1981, when the Players Association staged baseball's first midseason work stoppage. A strike had been narrowly averted in May 1980 but was not to be halted in 1981.

The Fourth Basic Agreement expired on December 31, 1979. Despite—or perhaps because of—numerous owners' measures to protect themselves from a work stoppage (including $50 million in Lloyds of London strike insurance, purchased at a cost of $2.2 million in premiums, and a $15 million strike fund), no strike occurred in 1980.

The issue now at stake was free agent compensation. Miller staked out a position that he wanted to expand free agency, cutting its threshold from six years of service to four. Ownership (represented by PRC head Ray Grebey) pressed for increased compensation for clubs losing free agents. Management wanted clubs which had lost such players to receive major league players in return, instead of extra selections in the June amateur draft.

In February 1981 management invoked its right to unilaterally implement this plan. Less than a week later labor indicated a strike was possible if they did. In May 1981 Miller filed a brief with the National Labor Relations Board asking that club financial data be turned over to the union, to validate management's claim that free agency was causing financial havoc. His request was refused.

In June ownership proposed a variant on the idea of free-agent compensation, but Miller again rejected it. On June 11 Miller removed himself from the bargaining process, and the next day the strike began. Unlike the clubs, the Players Association had no strike insurance. Miller, himself, forswore his estimated $160,000 salary during the work stoppage.

Miller personally returned to the bargaining table on July 1. The strike ended on July 31, and the settlement involved complex compensation formulas, an increase in the minimum major league salary to $40,000, and a myriad of provisions involving the strike-shortened season itself, including the use of a split-season format for 1981 and an extra round of postseason play.

The settlement's key provision provided for clubs to receive a player in compensation for better talent (so called "Class A" free agents) lost. Clubs could protect up to twenty-four players from being chosen as compensation. Clubs eligible for compensation need not select a player from the club that had signed their free agent, but clubs could exempt themselves from the risk of losing players in this fashion by voluntarily electing not to sign Class A free agents themselves for the term of this Basic Agreement.

Players ratified the settlement by a vote of 627 to 37; clubs approved it, 21-2, with St. Louis and Cincinnati casting negative votes and three franchises abstaining.

The strike cost players (now earning a minimum of $32,000 per season and an average of $193,000 annually) between $28 million and $34 million in lost salaries. Estimates for management losses ranged from a low of $1.6 million to a high of $7.6 million in revenues, although in many cases losses were offset by the aforementioned $50 million in strike insurance.

The Ueberroth Era

This new Basic Agreement was set to expire on December 31, 1984. As it did, major league finances strained to the breaking point.

Former Olympics organizer Peter V. Ueberroth replaced Bowie Kuhn as Commissioner in October 1984 and was soon faced with the crisis. At the Los Angeles Olympics Ueberroth had turned an impressive $215 million profit. Major League Baseball, on the other hand, seemed headed for bankruptcy. It turned to Ueberroth for salvation and significantly strengthened the Commissioner's powers to lure him to the job.

In early 1985 Major League Baseball opened its books and revealed the full dimensions of the situation. Twenty-two of the twenty-six big league clubs had lost money in 1984, totaling an aggregate deficit of $42 million. If the trend continued, MLB's accounting firm of Ernst & Whinney warned, the red ink would total $58 million in 1985, $94 million in 1986, $113 million in 1987 and $155 million in 1988. Management figures also contended that, as a whole, MLB had enjoyed a positive balance sheet just once in the previous nine seasons—in 1978, and that was only a mere $4,586.

The MLBPA disputed these figures, contending that MLB had actually turned a $9.3 million profit in 1984. Figures reported a full decade later by the Associated Press, however, largely reiterated Ernst & Whinney's claims.

Several other events of 1984 served to emphasize management's claim that the game was financially unsound. In June the Mariners' George Argyros, reportedly seeking bankruptcy protection, renegotiated his lease on the Kingdome. In September the A's received similar concessions at the Oakland-Alameda County Coliseum and even obtained a $15 million loan from Coliseum authorities to deal with existing debt. Across the Bay, Bob Lurie's Giants faced defeat in efforts to secure a new ballpark and mulled playing at the Coliseum. That October the Galbreath family sold the Pittsburgh Pirates. They sought $35-$40 million for the club; they received just $22 million.

Greatly aggravating management's financial woes was the huge increase in player salaries following the institution of free agency and arbitration. In 1976 the average major league salary was $51,501. It jumped to $76,066 in 1977 and had grown to $371,571 by 1985.

Ueberroth swung into action and recreated his Olympic strategy of securing lucrative corporate sponsorships, such as designating IBM the official computer of Major League Baseball or Chevrolet the official car.

Successful marketing and a terrific pennant race (fifteen clubs were still contenders on September 1) caused attendance to skyrocket in 1986. For the first time every major league club exceeded the million mark in paid attendance. The result was the end of red ink. In 1986 MLB turned a net operating profit of $11.5 million. It was a modest profit, but it presaged far greater ones, peaking at a 1989 level of $214 million.

In the Reagan boom years baseball also succeeded in negotiating a lucrative six-season (1984-89) television contract with NBC and ABC generating $1.125 billion in revenue for MLB. That translated into $8 million per year per club and tripled the revenue flow from the previous TV contract.

Aiding Ueberroth was a turnaround in baseball's popularity that had been building for some time. Starting back in 1968, the Harris poll had identified football as the nation's most popular spectator sport. In the late 1970s baseball began climbing back, overtaking the NFL in the polls. Attendance steadily climbed and so did telecasting of individual team broadcasts. In 1982 the Los Angeles Dodgers had been the first major league club to attract 3 million fans. In 1987 they were joined by the Cards and Mets; in 1988 by the Twins (who had drawn just 469,000 paying customers in the strike-shortened 1981 season); and in 1989 by Toronto. In 1991, aided by SkyDome, the Blue Jays smashed through the 4 million fan level. In 1993 the expansion Rockies set the major league attendance record.

At work was the new technology of cable television. "Superstations" such as Ted Turner's WTBS (Braves), WGN (Cubs), WPIX (Yankees), WOR (Mets), and WKTV (Rangers) brought baseball into millions of homes on a daily basis, strengthening fan loyalties. A positive development in making baseball more widely available, superstations, which are based in major markets, increased the historical disparity between "have" and "have not" teams.

The Strikes of 1984-85

As Ueberroth took office, major league umpires threatened to strike during the 1984 postseason. Ueberroth stepped in, appointed himself sole mediator and avoided a work stoppage, but he faced a far more difficult challenge as baseball's Basic Agreement expired on December 31, 1984. Three issues dominated events: pension plan contributions, free agent compensation, and salary arbitration. As the agreement expired, players were receiving $15.5 million annually toward their pension plan. Donald Fehr wanted one-third of Ueberroth's new television contract, a sum equivalent to $62.5 million annually.

The MLBPA also desired elimination of the free agent compensation plan adopted back in 1981, but counterbalancing that was management's agenda for curtailing salary arbitration. As negotiations continued in 1985, ownership proposed a freeze in both salaries and pension levels, as they opened their books to display red ink.

As negotiations progressed, the union set an August 6, 1985, strike deadline. Management countered with an increase in pension contributions to $25 million annually but tied its offer to stability in salary levels (i.e. pension contributions would rise to that level only if salaries increased by no more than $13 million). For example, if salaries rose by $14 million, only $24 million in pension contributions would result. Some projected that this method would produce an actual *reduction* in pension contributions.

On August 2 Ueberroth proposed a compromise settlement but players went out on strike as threatened. Despite tough talk from both sides, a settlement was reached just two days later. Only twenty-five games were lost, fourteen in the American League, eleven in the National. All contests were eventually rescheduled.

On the larger issues, both sides received some satisfaction. Management obtained gains on the arbitration front. Instead of going to arbitration after two seasons, players would now wait three years before exercising that option. This provision would translate into major savings for

management, most notably in the case of 1986 Cy Young Award winner Roger Clemens. Ownership also received concessions regarding arbitration mechanisms.

On the other hand, the MLBPA received what it wanted in regard to free agency. Limitations on the number of clubs eligible to negotiate with a free agent were now lifted. Compensation for signing a free agent was no longer to be in the form of major league players. Instead, teams signing free agents would now forfeit amateur draft picks.

On a more basic level, the major league minimum salary was raised from $40,000 to $60,000 with cost of living adjustments promised for 1987 and 1989. Players also gained in regard to pensions and World Series shares. Owners would retroactively contribute $25 million toward 1984 pension accounts, with payments rising to $39 million by 1989. In terms of what an average player would net from this settlement, a ten-year veteran could now collect $91,000 per year starting at age 62. The previous Basic Agreement called for such players to receive $57,000 at age 65.

A little-noted provision of the Sixth Basic Agreement provided for what prove to be an increasingly debated concept: revenue sharing. Of the ABC-NBC television contract money, $20 million dollars would be set aside for financially troubled franchises.

Collusion or Fiscal Restraint?

As the smoke cleared from the August 1985 strike, ownership looked for ways to control labor costs. In September 1984 Ueberroth had personally addressed ownership and urged fiscal restraint. Salaries had continued to escalate. The average major league salary rose from $329,408 in 1984 to $371,157 in 1985. Forty-three players now had million dollar contracts, headed by Mike Schmidt at $2,130,000 and Gary Carter at $2,028,571. Ueberroth's message was simple: "It is not smart to sign long-term contracts."

That advice soon translated into a far more controversial outcome. As the 1985 season ended, sixty-two major league players (including Detroit's All-Star outfielder Kirk Gibson) filed for arbitration. Few of them received offers from new clubs. Gibson did not receive contract offers from any club other than Detroit. Hoping to receive an $8 million, five-year pact, he instead agreed to a three-year, $4 million contract. Only five players changed clubs, and all five had been virtually cut loose by their previous teams.

The MLBPA charged "collusion" and filed grievances against all twenty-six big league clubs, noting that the Basic Agreement included a clause stating that "Players shall not act in concert with other Players and Clubs shall not act in concert with the other Clubs" in regard to player signings. Oddly enough, that clause had been inserted at ownership's behest to prevent dual holdouts, such as the celebrated one staged by Don Drysdale and Sandy Koufax in 1966.

In the middle of the case, the PRC fired arbitrator Thomas Tuttle Roberts because of its displeasure over Roberts' decision voiding player drug testing. The dismissal was hardly unprecedented; the MLBPA had four times dismissed arbitrators and the PRC had exercised that option once previously. But no dismissal had ever occurred while a decision was ongoing. The union grieved once more, and Roberts was reinstated.

Before Roberts reached a decision, another crop of free agents emerged at the close of the 1986 season. Unlike the largely lackluster contingent of the previous season, this crop of seventy-nine free agents included such stars as Jack Morris, Ron Guidry, Dale Murphy, Lance Parrish, Tim Raines, Bob Horner, and Andre Dawson. Again, only players unwanted by their original team received offers from competing clubs. Parrish, Horner and Knight signed with new clubs; Dawson signed a blank contract to join the Cubs. Parrish and Knight went to new teams for less than their old clubs had offered. Horner fled to Japan, taking a job with Japan's Yakult Swallows. Again the MLBPA filed grievances.

One player, Tiger pitcher Jack Morris, beat the system. Seeing he would receive no other offers besides Detroit's, Morris and his agent Richard Moss withdrew their bid for free agency and instead submitted to salary arbitration. Morris was awarded $1,850,000 for 1987.

On September 22, 1987, Roberts finally issued his decision in the case, ruling in favor of the union. On January 22, 1988, Roberts also allowed seven players to exercise what became known as "new look free agency." Of the seven, only Kirk Gibson signed with a new club, reaching agreement with Los Angeles on a three-year $4.5 million contract. Still unsettled was the issue of financial compensation. The MLBPA wanted anywhere between $7.2 and $15 million. The owners argued the total should be between $2.2 and $4.4 million. On August 31, 1989, Roberts awarded $10,528,086.71 in damages to 139 players.

The decision in the second case was equally disappointing to management. After reviewing 8,346 pages of testimony, arbitrator George Nicolau found owners guilty once more of collusion, this time in the case of the free agent crop of 1986. On October 24—Nicolau had delayed his action to avoid disrupting the pennant races—"new look" free agency was granted to twelve more players, including Bob Boone, Jim Clancy, and Willie Randolph, all of whom signed with new teams. Others such as Rich Gedman and Ken Dayley gained lucrative new contracts from their old clubs. The first of the damage awards involved Yankees pitcher Ron Guidry, who in June 1989 received $91,758.24 in compensation.

A third case was filed by the union in January 1989 regarding those who had become free agents after the 1987 campaign. In July 1990 Nicolau again found for labor. Seventy-six players, including such stars as Jack Clark, Gary Gaetti, Jack Morris, Dave Righetti, Mike Witt, and Paul Molitor were involved in the case, which revolved around management's creation of an "information bank" in the winter of 1986-87. This data bank reported all salary offers made to free agents. Nicolau found it a "quiet" form of cooperation between supposed rivals, endeavoring to keep tabs on what each competitor was offering on the supposedly free market. By the time damages were finally determined, they exceeded the $100 million mark.

In the midst of this series of reverses, management did win one battle. The Sixth Basic Agreement had given clubs the option of reducing rosters to twenty-five men. As a cost-costing measure, all clubs used the lower number in 1986 and 1987. The union again charged collusion, but in this instance Nicolau ruled in favor of management.

New Sources of Revenue

Reports of the demise of television's profitability proved premature. Toward the end of Ueberroth's tenure, a series of blockbuster broadcasting deals were negotiated. The biggest was a four-year deal with CBS in December 1988 for $1.06 billion. The network received rights to the All-Star Game, League Championship Series, World Series, and twelve regular-season weekend games. Criticism surrounded the cutback in regular-season broadcasts, but Ueberroth answered with an unprecedented deal with the cable industry. ESPN outbid such rivals as TNT and USA in January 1989 for a four-year, $400-million pact, featuring 175 regular-season games, including groundbreaking Sunday-night cablecasts. No one knew how successful the package would be, but even ESPN officials admitted they would lose money for at least the first two years. At the same time a $50-million, four-year agreement with CBS Radio for the Game of the Week, All-Star Game, and postseason contests was finalized.

While Organized Baseball as a whole was cashing in, so were individual clubs. Perhaps the best example was George Steinbrenner obtaining a $500-million, twelve-year agreement with the Madison Square Garden cable network.

The Franchise Game

By 1987 twenty-two out of twenty-six major league clubs either broke even or were profitable on industry-wide revenues of $910.9 million and profits of $103 million. There had always been an interest in ballclubs as rich men's toys, but when it appeared once again that money could be made at the national pastime, bidding went through the roof for franchises.

Even the most moribund franchises sold for big bucks. Somewhat understandably the New York Mets changed hands for $100 million, and Baltimore sold for $70 million, but when the woeful Seattle Mariners were peddled for $77 million (George Argyros had paid $13.1 million for these latter-day St. Louis Browns in 1981), it was clear that the economic balance had been tilted.

Back in the early 1980s Commissioner Ueberroth announced that the majors would feature two new AL and four new NL clubs by 2000. However, by the late 1980s the game faced increased pressure from a number of sources for expansion. The Players Association wished to open up more jobs for its members. The U.S. Senate formed a fourteen-member panel on the subject. A new league was announced by agent Dick Moss in 1989, backed by Donald Trump's ephemeral billions.

Baseball now announced a willingness to add two more National League franchises. The NL would announce its two newest members in September 1991, who would draft entry-level minor-league players in late 1991, and actually operate farm systems in 1992. During that season, they would draft college and high school players. Major league expansion drafts occurred after the 1992 World Series. An interesting—and definitely different—aspect of this draft was that the newest senior-circuit clubs selected personnel (thirty-six for each club) from both major leagues, and the AL and NL clubs alike divided the $95 million franchise fee from each rookie owner.

Frontrunners for the new franchises included Denver (where voters in 1990 approved a new 40,000-seat stadium); St. Petersburg (which nearly attracted the White Sox in 1988 and the Giants in 1992); Miami; Buffalo (where the Rich family ran a big league operation at the AAA level); and Washington (a two-time loser, but a loser with political connections). The huge franchise fees plus a projected $65 million in startup costs (a figure that ultimately reached $95 million) did not dissuade prospective backers.

Major league expansion also triggered minor league expansion, as the new clubs would require new farm teams. With such franchises as Oklahoma City going for $4.5 million, the price tag at the AAA level wasn't cheap. Most observers estimated it would be $5 million per club (consider that the Mets had cost $1.8 million in 1962 and the Kansas City Royals just $5.5 million in 1969). Even applying for a minor league club required a $5,000 nonrefundable deposit, but in September 1990 eighteen groups mailed in their checks.

As minor league franchises were bought and sold for record prices, the major league clubs took notice. Claiming they no longer saw the wisdom of subsidizing such "profitable" ventures (in all too many cases the only profit came from selling to the next party willing to take operating losses), in 1990 the big leaguers started to place pressure on their farm clubs.

The Lockout of 1990

Baseball's Basic Agreement expired on December 31, 1989, and despite the prosperity both sides now enjoyed, open warfare was imminent. The Players Association was hardly blind to the marvelously round figures Ueberroth had pried out of the networks. Beyond that they were particularly irritated by the year of arbitration they had given away in the last settlement.

Club owners, on the other hand, were tired of forking over millions through the arbitration process. The problem for management was not simply the cost of losing specific arbitration cases. Winning could also be costly. In the winter of 1989-90 the ten "losers" in the process received average raises of $477,050. Average salaries doubled for only the second time in the fifteen-year history of the process. First-year arbitration players saw paychecks skyrocket by 166 percent. While the vast majority of disputes were settled before they reached arbitration, they still involved huge increases, such as Teddy Higuera's $2,125,000 stipend and Tom Browning's pact for the same figure. Fred McGriff saw his income rise from $325,000 to $1,450,000 in a prearbitration settlement. A showdown had to occur.

Negotiations dragged on during the winter of 1989-90, and it was widely believed that the players would collect their checks for a few months and then strike at mid-season, when the owners were gearing up for large crowds and were most vulnerable. To thwart this plan, management struck first, engaging in yet another lockout of spring training camps.

The owners' strategy was to hold firm on the third-year threshold for arbitration. The PRC tendered a number of alternatives to the Players Association, including one granting 48 percent of club profits to players and another offering a cumbersome $4 million bonus-pool scheme to be shared by two-year players.

After thirty-two bitter days, the MLBPA's Donald Fehr and Charles O'Connor, the new PRC negotiator, hammered out a compromise. Seventeen percent of the second-year players would now become eligible for arbitration. The minimum salary would rise from $68,000 to $100,000, the largest percentage increase ever. Management would contribute $55 million to the players' pension fund, up from $39 million. To the casual observer this seemed a victory for labor, but the players had wanted $80 million and the settlement was a giant step back from the traditional one-third of national TV revenues that players had contended was their right. Additionally, it was written into the agreement that baseball would announce its long-stalled expansion plans within ninety days. Another change in the contract involved collusion. Henceforth, only clubs actively found guilty of the process would be fined—but they would be assessed triple damages. Twenty-four-man rosters were again allowed in 1990, but the traditional twenty-five-man roster would be mandated again, starting in 1991.

It was not a settlement that established any great principles, and most fans were no doubt just as puzzled as ever as to what all the shouting had been about, but it appeared that the process had cooled some tempers.

Baseball Enters the Nineties

In the 1991 season, salaries, arbitration settlements, and attendance continued their seemingly inexorable climb. The average player salary soared an astonishing 42.5 percent to $851,383. The highest stipend was accorded to Los Angeles' Darryl Strawberry—$3,800,000—while the average Oakland paycheck was a handsome $1,394,119. Yet major league attendance continued to climb along with salary expenses, hitting an all-time high of 56,813,760, paced by Toronto's exceeding the 4 million mark.

Long-stalled National League expansion finally occurred in June 1991 with $95 million franchises being granted for the 1993 season to the Colorado Rockies, headed by John Antonucci, and the Florida Marlins, led by Blockbuster Video tycoon Wayne Huizenga. Commissioner Fay Vincent ruled that American League teams would receive $42 million of the franchise fees.

Issues such as disparities in television revenue still festered. Local television, cable, and radio rights generated $200 million for Major League Baseball, but just four teams—the Yanks, Mets, Phils, and Dodgers—garnered more than 35 percent of the total. The Yankees' $41.5 million per year deal towered over the funding available to such small market franchises as Pittsburgh ($5.8 million), Kansas City ($5 million), and Seattle ($4 million). In September 1991 the American League voted to channel 20 percent of local broadcasting "net revenues" into a pool which would be shared equally (the NL formula, on the other hand, now calls for sharing 25 percent). Controversy was expected over what revenue would be considered "net."

As the 1991 season ended, another round of free agent signings ensued with the New York Mets snagging Pittsburgh's Bobby Bonilla with a five-year, $29 million pact. This largesse was soon eclipsed by the Cubs signing thirty-two-year old Ryne Sandberg to a four-year $28.4 million agreement. At the lower end of the spectrum, the big league minimum wage inched up to $109,000—an almost meaningless figure with the average major league salary now at $1,043,156.

Big losers in the free agent-big salary game were the 1992 Mets, Dodgers, and Red Sox. These teams spent $130.5 million in finishing a collective 82 games out of first as their attendance plummeted by a total of 1.5 million paying customers.

Despite another 4-million-plus season in Toronto and the million-fan boost given to the Orioles by the opening of the new park at Camden Yards, major league attendance dropped by 1.6 percent in 1992. Major league profits plummeted from $143 million in 1990 to just $8.7 million in 1991 to virtually nothing in 1992. Nervousness increased over the coming end of the lucrative CBS television contract after the 1993 campaign. Given these alarming indicators, it was mistakenly anticipated that the extraordinarily large number of free agents testing the market after the 1992 World Series—including such stars as Barry Bonds, David Cone, Kirby Puckett, and Greg Maddux—would find few takers.

As the World Series ended, a bombshell struck Major League Baseball when ESPN announced it would not exercise its option for 1994-95 television coverage. Claiming that so far it had lost more than half of its investment in the deal, the decision makers at ESPN chose a $13 million buyout rather than further payments of $250 million for the two seasons available to them. The cable network left the door open for negotiations, but obviously at a much lower starting point. Among other factors, baseball was losing its popularity with American youth: Nielsen ratings revealed a disconcerting 24 percent drop in viewership of regular season games by twelve-to-seventeen-year-olds from 1989 to 1992 even though overall ballpark attendance had increased during that period.

Meanwhile the saga of Bob Lurie and the San Francisco Giants went on and on. In June 1990 he had received permission to shift the club thirty-five miles south to Santa Clara County, California. But that November, voters in fifteen Santa Clara County cities turned thumbs down on a 1 percent utility tax to pay for a new stadium—the third year in a row such a referendum had failed. In January 1992 Lurie announced plans to move to San Jose if a new $155 million, 48,000-seat stadium could be constructed. The plan foundered on the shoals of a projected 2 percent increase in the city's utility tax. On August 7, 1992, Lurie (who had paid $8 million for the franchise in 1976) announced the Giants' sale for $115 million to a group headed by Vincent J. Naimoli bent on relocating the club to St. Petersburg, Florida. That triggered a $100 million counteroffer from local investors

headed by Safeway magnate Peter Magowan and stockbroker Charles Schwab, who were intent on keeping the team in the Bay area. The National League, by a 9-4 vote on November 10, 1992, rejected the St. Petersburg offer, leaving the status of the Magowan offer up in the air, although the issue was ultimately settled in Magowan's favor. The maneuvering sparked new Congressional interest (particularly that of the Senate Judiciary Committee) in baseball's antitrust status.

Several other franchises changed hands in 1991-1992. On November 2, 1991, John Labatt Ltd. paid $67.5 million (Canadian) to acquire majority control (going from 45 percent to 90 percent ownership) of the Blue Jays. In a controversial move that sparked xenophobic responses, Jeff Smulyan turned the woeful Seattle Mariners over to Japanese interests connected to the Nintendo corporation for $106 million. John McMullen unloaded the Astros to Texas business executive Drayton McLane, Jr., for $115 million. Finally, Domino's Pizza baron Tom Monaghan peddled the club to fellow pizza magnate Mike Ilitch (a former Tiger farmhand) for a relatively paltry $85 million. The Orioles were rumored to be on the block for $200 million.

The biggest casualty of the 1992 season was Commissioner Fay Vincent, who resigned under pressure on September 7, 1992. Brewers owner Bud Selig stepped in as Commissioner Pro Tem. The first tangible result of Vincent's departure was rescission of his controversial National League realignment plan, which would have placed the Cardinals and the Cubs in the NL West and the Reds and Braves in the NL East.

Some observers felt that Vincent's downfall was foreshadowed in December 1991 when owners hired Richard Ravitch, a one-time candidate for mayor of New York City, to the post of President of the PRC at a salary $100,000 greater than Vincent's. The owners did not want Vincent interfering in labor relations as he had when he intervened in the 1990 spring training lockout. Vincent's dismissal only fueled the false rumors, already rampant, of an owner-generated lockout for 1993.

Sales of Major League Baseball licensed products continued to soar—from $200 million in 1987 to $1.5 billion in 1990 to $2 billion in 1992. Despite the fact that items with Mets and Yankees logos account for 20 percent of all sales, revenues were split equally among the twenty-eight franchises. To compete with the rival NBA and NFL in an increasingly global struggle for fan dollars, MLB started to promote overseas sales and by 1991 was doing $20 million a year in foreign sales.

In 1992 even the minors got into the act with a similar centralized licensing approach (under the control of Major League Baseball Properties, which can keep up to 30 percent of the royalties). National Association licensed sales in 1992 were an estimated $12 to $15 million.

1993: A Season of Fear—and Profits

Early in 1993 it was fashionable to write baseball off as a sport that was finished. Newspapers, magazines, and even entire books purported that the game's long-awaited crash (proclaimed regularly ever since the 1860s) had finally occurred.

Attendance figures proved otherwise. Major League Baseball set an all-time record of 70,257,938—a figure 23.7 percent above the record set in 1991. Even taking into consideration the two expansion teams, the Rockies and the Marlins, and factoring out the National League's new method of counting attendance (the same method employed by the American League, based on tickets sold, not on actual bodies in the park), attendance was estimated to be 5.2 percent above the 1991 record and 7 percent over 1992.

The Giants, on the ropes in 1992, drew 2.6 million in 1993. Montreal, another moribund franchise, also showed signs of life. "The amazing thing is not simply that our crowds have been good," said Expos owner Claude Brochu. "What's really significant are the demographics. We're getting a very young, vibrant audience."

The lackluster Reds were estimating a $12 million profit for the season. The Rockies, who had projected a debut season attendance of 2.5 million, attracted nearly 4.5 million customers and suddenly were looking at ways to increase the size of their new Coors Field.

A new record was set for the value of a franchise. The Orioles sold for a record $173 million at bankruptcy court auction. The club's new owners were led by Baltimore attorney Peter Angelos and Cincinnati businessman William DeWitt. Minority partners included movie director Barry Levinson, author Tom Clancy, broadcaster Jim McKay, and tennis star Pam Shriver.

The minors topped 30 million fans for the first time since 1950, when there were 446 clubs. Average 1993 per-game attendance in the National Association was 3,316—the highest in history. Eight leagues (the International, Eastern, Southern, California, Carolina, South Atlantic, Northwest, and Appalachian) posted attendance records. The International League set an all-time minor league attendance record, drawing 4.6 million customers.

In the Courts and in the halls of Congress, rumblings continued regarding removal of baseball's special legal status. On August 4, 1993, U.S. District Court Judge John Padova of Philadelphia, in a move many interpreted as a distinct restriction of baseball's antitrust exemption, denied Organized Baseball's request to dismiss a suit brought by disgruntled St. Petersburg interests. Padova ruled that the 1922 Supreme Court decision exempted O.B. from antitrust legislation only in those things that were unique to baseball, such as players' contracts. Thus, the buying and selling of clubs was not covered.

Hearings were scheduled for September 30, 1993 (but delayed until 1994) in the Senate Judiciary Committee on a measure sponsored by Howard Metzenbaum (D-Ohio) revoking baseball's antitrust exemption. Judiciary Chairman Joseph Biden (D-Del.) threatened: "Unless baseball gets its act together in a way that is monumentally different from where they are now, this committee will be back with the votes that will change the status of baseball."

A meeting took place in Kohler, Wisconsin on August 11-13, 1993, under the leadership of Richard Ravitch. While a widely anticipated agreement on revenue-sharing failed to come about, owners did pledge to refrain from a threatened lockout of players in spring training and throughout the 1994 season.

By 1993 about one-third of major league revenues was shared; in the National Football League the figure was roughly 75 percent. How Major League Baseball would divide its spoils between "big market" teams and "small market" franchises was anybody's guess, but it was correctly theorized that a new revenue-sharing formula would go hand-in-hand with some sort of salary cap. Complicating the situation were threats by small market clubs to veto televising of games from their parks by visiting clubs. The small market clubs would have the power to do this except for games covered by the various national TV contracts.

Salaries continued to escalate in 1993, and the grossly underachieving Mets started the year with an average salary of $1,534,007. But some teams featured relatively low average salaries: the expansion Rockies ($327,000) and Marlins ($649,876) for example, and the more established Expos ($513,149) and Indians ($541,989).

The Padres angered many fans by trimming salaries and talent in the 1993 season. Star performers such as Fred McGriff, Tony Fernandez, Darrin Jackson, Gary Sheffield, and Bruce Hurst were all sent packing. General Manager Joe McIlvaine abandoned ship as owner Tom Werner successfully pursued a course of lowering the payroll from the $30 million level in 1992 to a goal of $18 million in 1993.

"They have been losing money ever since the purchase," explained Richard Ravitch. "They lost $12 million the last two years . . . . And they're going to do what Milwaukee is doing, what Houston did under its prior ownership, what Pittsburgh is doing in order to be able to operate within their resources."

The most significant event of the year was the change from a two-division to a three-division league setup, a concept favored by both the Players Association and the owners. Formal approval occurred on September 9, 1993, by a 27-1 vote, with only Texas' George W. Bush dissenting. Playoffs would involve the three division winners, plus a so-called wild card team, i.e., the non-division winner with the best won-lost record. The first round would be a best-of-five format; the second, a best of seven. A potential ramification regarding the realignment is an accelerated expansion schedule, perhaps as early as 1996.

Also causing controversy were fears that a team with a regular-season losing record could conceivably win a World Series. However, that possibility had already existed under the two-division system, as witnessed by the barely over-.500 Mets lasting until the seventh game of the 1973 World Series.

Meanwhile, television was becoming a problem. CBS, which claimed it had lost $500 million on its last deal, was reluctant to renew at the same rate. In May 1993 a joint venture known as The Baseball Network was created between MLB and two TV networks, NBC and ABC. Unlike prior arrangements in which MLB sold national TV rights for a fee, this new relationship gave The Baseball Network responsibility for advertising sales and production of the telecasts and established a mechanism for splitting the profits.

Signs of fiscal retrenchment were visible in scouting and the minors. A cutback in the Major League Scouting Bureau was announced in the late summer of 1993. All twenty-one part-time scouts employed by the Bureau were laid off September 1, 1993.

Facing opposition from minor league clubs and financially strapped local communities, the Major Leagues relented on the ballpark improvement provisions of the Professional Baseball Agreement, delaying the deadline for its provisions to April 1, 1995. The minors on their part agreed to put off reopening the entire PBA until September 1994 (a reopening that was delayed because of the 1994 strike).

The minors in 1993 also featured the creation of three independent circuits. Two of them, the Texas-Louisiana and the Frontier Leagues, were unmitigated flops, but the Northern League showed that, under the right circumstances, such entities could succeed.

1994: The Best of Times, The Worst of Times

The 1994 season saw an explosion of offense and fan interest in the game. The initially controversial three-division structure created new races and excitement. Ken Griffey, Jr., Matt Williams, Tony Gwynn, Greg Maddux, and Jeff Bagwell were on track for monster—perhaps even historic—seasons. Minor league attendance (helped along by attractive new parks, clever marketing and promotions, and Michael Jordan's presence in the Southern League) continued its steady growth. The National Association attracted 33,355,199 fans, up 11 percent from 1993, with the Eastern, Southern, Texas, California, Midwest, Southern, New-York Penn, and Northwest leagues all setting attendance records. While the Buffalo Bisons (hampered by two rainouts) narrowly missed achieving the million fan mark for only the first time since 1988, most other clubs had no reason to complain. Totals of a million were growing commonplace at the Triple-A level with the PCL's new Salt Lake City Buzz drawing 713,224. In independent play, both the Northern League and the newly invigorated Texas-Louisiana League did well at the gate.

Despite widespread media grousing about MLB ticket and concession prices, *Money Magazine*'s survey indicated that baseball pricing was more than competitive. The average MLB ticket cost just $10.62 compared to $27.17 in the NBA and $31 in the NFL. And while the average cost for parking, two tickets, two sodas and two hot dogs to a Knicks game was an astronomical $108.32, equivalent MLB packages ranged from a low of just $28.87 to a high of $50.74. The magazine also polled fans regarding what teams' games they considered the best "sports values" for their money. Out of the eighty-three major league sports team, MLB teams (led by the San Francisco Giants) captured ten of the survey's first dozen spots and sixteen of the top twenty-five.

Despite the loss of baseball's once-lucrative TV contract, there were signs of hope on the broadcast front. MLB's first televised night opener drew the second highest rating for an ESPN baseball telecast. The All-Star Game was exciting and well-watched, seen by an estimated 50 million viewers, its highest Nielsen rating in three years. Even the Seattle Mariners, one of only three MLB clubs without a cable television contract (the Royals and the Brewers were the other two) secured a modest $3.8 million, 2.5 year agreement with Prime Sports Northwest.

Expansion, Again

On March 2, 1994 Major League Baseball, facing ever tougher competition from other sports, established a six-man committee headed by Boston's John Harrington to deal once again with the issue of expansion. The committee eventually set August 12, 1994 as the deadline for bidders for two additional expansion franchises to submit their proposals. In all, twenty-seven groups, representing nine cities—Buffalo, Mexico City, Monterrey, Nashville, Northern Virginia, Orlando, Phoenix, Tampa-St. Petersburg, and Vancouver—requested proposals for new franchises, which many thought would go for $150 million each. Nine groups finally sent in bids, and five groups (representing Phoenix, Orlando, St. Petersburg, and two from Northern Virginia) met with MLB's expansion committee. Virtually all observers saw no actual expansion taking place until the 1998 season at the earliest.

In Phoenix, the Maricopa County Board of Supervisors had already authorized spending up to $238 million on a new domed stadium, to be paid for in part by a one-quarter-cent increase in the local sales tax. In Tampa-St. Petersburg 32,079 local fans left $50 deposits for season tickets. In Orlando the Orange County Commission granted conceptual approval for a new $150 million stadium near the Florida Citrus Bowl. Not among the groups represented was that headed by Buffalo's Robert Rich, Jr., operator of that city's flourishing American Association franchise, who feared his area could not compete with larger ones. "It has been very apparent to us that salary caps and revenue sharing have to be in place for small-market teams to survive," said Rich. "Pittsburgh lost $9 million last year. That's hard dollars. We know. They have 2.5 million people in their metropolitan area. We have less than 1.2 million people."

The Strike

Baseball's Basic Agreement expired on December 31, 1993. Baseball beat writers certainly expected a strike, but few thought it would destroy utterly what President Bill Clinton described as "the most exciting baseball season in forty years."

The year began with ownership initially divided on the issue of revenue sharing, but on January 18, 1994, owners agreed by a vote of 28-0 to increase it. That agreement, however, was contingent on labor accepting a salary cap. It was not until June 13 that the PRC's Richard Ravitch put forward a complicated package:

- Revenue sharing between management and labor;
- A salary cap in which no club could have a payroll of more than 110 percent of the major league average nor less than 84 percent of that average;
- Elimination of salary arbitration;
- Lowering the threshold for free agency from six years to four years, but allowing current clubs to match best offers until players reach their sixth year of service;
- An escalating (but unspecified) scale of minimum salaries for players with less than four years of service.

Ravitch proposed that this Basic Agreement extend for seven years. He estimated that if MLB revenues expanded by 7 percent, player salaries would grow from a base of $1.2 at the start of the 1994 season to $1.6 million by 2001. With a 10 percent growth, players would receive a $2 million average salary, and a revenue growth of 14 percent would yield an average player salary of a $2.6 million.

Financial Pressures

Despite a $50.3 million industry-wide operating profit in 1993, management felt compelled to press such sweeping changes in view of certain financial realities. While at first glance a $50.3 million profit seemed comforting, it was a sharp drop from the peak of $214.5 million in black ink achieved in 1989. Based on club financial projections, nineteen clubs reportedly faced the possibility of losing money in 1994. Later, when Bud Selig was asked how many clubs would lose money in 1994, he estimated twelve to fourteen.

One of the most distressed franchises was Pittsburgh. Despite drastically cutting their payroll, the Pirates had lost an estimated $40 million over the preceding five seasons. They owed $20 million to CitiBank, with $5 million of that due in August 1994. The situation grew so desperate that during the 1994 season, an emergency $8 million loan was engineered, with ownership anteing up $4 million and the City of Pittsburgh coming up with the remainder. Still, another $8 million might prove necessary in January 1995.

Plaguing Pittsburgh was not only its small market status but an outdated "cookie-cutter" stadium. However, the Pirates suffering was not merely aesthetic, for they were also saddled with one of the worst leases in the majors. The club surrendered 10 percent of ticket revenues to the city, plus another 10 percent in amusement taxes. Retaining just 28 percent of concession revenues, they secured nothing from either stadium parking or advertising.

Even among still-profitable franchises there were difficulties. New Orioles owner Peter G. Angelos contended that Baltimore would suffer a $25.5 million drop in net profits in 1994. Some $10 million of that resulted from higher player salaries (including that for expensive free agents), while another $8 million came in decreases from national television revenues.

The MLBPA Response

On the other hand, players saw that MLB revenues had reached a historic high of $1.88 billion in 1993. They contended that no one was forcing ownership to pay exorbitant free agent salaries to often overvalued players. They were not about to make concessions without receiving significant concessions in return. Basically, they were satisfied with the status quo. And even outside union ranks political and economic conservatives likened the idea of a salary cap to such notions as wage-and-price controls.

On July 18, 1994 Donald Fehr presented this list of demands to Ravitch:

• Ending the ban on so-called repeat free agency within a five-year span if the player's club offered arbitration at contract's end;

• Reducing the threshold for arbitration from three years to two years, plus the top 17 percent of the players with between two and three years of major league service (this former threshold had existed from 1974 to 1986);
• Increasing the MLB minimum salary from $109,000 to $175,000 $200,000;
• Increasing pension benefits for players who had retired before 1970.

There was no give between the two positions. The situation was further exacerbated on August 1, 1994, when management withheld a $7.8 million payment to the players' pension and benefit fund.

On August 12, 1994 (ironically, the deadline set for the delivery of expansion proposals), the players struck. They could have walked out at any point earlier in the year, but, by striking later in the season, they were able to collect a good portion (an estimated 75 percent on August 14) of their salaries and signing bonuses; at the same time, management would not yet have collected any significant portion of their $140 million due from national television contracts. Plus, with the postseason and World Series in jeopardy, Fehr and the MLBPA theorized they could force Ravitch and the PRC to a relatively quick capitulation.

It didn't happen that way.

Counteroffers and Cancellation

The costs of the strike—both direct and indirect—were immense. The average major league player lost $6,496 per day, with the stoppage costing Bobby Bonilla, the majors' highest-paid player, $31,148 daily. Players at the ML minimum lost $596 per diem. The strike cost management an estimated $8.5 million in revenues per day, although this was offset by the $4.4 million they no longer had to pay each day in player salaries.

As the strike dragged on, meetings—some open, some secret—were held, but no movement occurred. On September 8, 1994, the MLBPA proposed a variant on the salary cap and revenue sharing ideas. Under their counterproposal, the richest sixteen franchises would pay a 1.5 percent penalty on their payrolls. The sum would then be distributed among the remaining twelve clubs. In terms of revenue sharing, visiting teams in both leagues would receive 25 percent of all gate receipts. Under the present system visiting American League teams receive 20 percent of ticket sales, while in the National League visitors receive only 43 cents on each ticket, a sum equivalent to only about 4 percent of gate receipts. The union proposed no concessions on either arbitration or free agency.

Management did not consider this an answer to their problems. It also appeared that the PRC's salary cap proposal may have been only one of a number of ways to relieve its problem of cost containment.

Also aggravating owner sensibilities was a report on MLB finances generated by Stanford University economist Roger Noll, which ownership derided as "theatrical." Some said Noll's report merely solidified ownership resolve. The MLBPA and many observers had expected management to quickly fold, but the owners (tied together by a rule mandating 75 percent approval of any settlement) held firm.

With anxieties from the networks and fans building,

and difficulties in scheduling a meaningful postseason looming, a determination had to be reached on continuation of major league baseball for 1994. On September 14, Bud Selig canceled the remainder of the regular season play, both the playoffs and the World Series. Only two owners, Baltimore's Peter Angelos and Cincinnati's Marge Schott, dissented from the determination. Selig's fateful announcement read:

Due to the player strike that began on August 12, 1994, the Office of the Commissioner of Baseball, acting pursuant to a resolution of the major league clubs, reluctantly concluded today that the remainder of the 1994 season, the Division Series, the League Championship Series, and the World Series will not be played.

This is a sad day. Nobody wanted this to happen, but the continuing player strike leaves us no choice but to take this action. We have reached the point where it is no longer practical to complete the remainder of the season or to preserve the integrity of postseason play.

On June 14, the clubs proposed a reasonable offer to the players' union which included a guarantee of $1 billion in salary and benefits for the players—the largest players' payroll ever. Since that time the clubs have asked the players to negotiate some reasonable division of revenues between players and clubs or some other method of controlling the growth in salaries and ensuring competitive balance.

The union refused to bargain with us over costs and took a hard-line position that the clubs would fold as they had in past negotiations. That was a terrible mistake, one for which all of us must pay.

## CHAPTER 27

Baseball and the Law

Gary D. Hailey and Douglas R. Pappas

Like many other members of our litigation-happy society, baseball players and team owners have spent their fair share of time in the courtroom. Judges have been asked to decide lawsuits involving everything from a team's liability for fan injuries from foul balls and thrown bats to the legality of the decision to resume the infamous Yankees-Royals "Pine Tar Game" nearly a month after George Brett's home run had been ruled a game-ending out.

But the most significant baseball-related court cases were a series of mostly unsuccessful challenges to Organized Baseball's attempts to limit competition—especially from rivals like the Players League and the Federal League—for players' services. That litigation has reached the United States Supreme Court three times, and all three times that Court has ruled that baseball is not governed by the antitrust laws. The reasoning behind this holding may have been perfectly logical when the first of those cases was decided in 1922, but today it seems anachronistic.

From the game's earliest days, baseball owners have struggled to keep their expenses down by maintaining control over the players, who often decide that the grass (and the money) is greener in someone else's ballpark. In 1870 the National Association of Base Ball Players tried to stop "revolving," or contract jumping, by adopting a rule requiring players to give 60 days' notice before leaving one club for another. Tougher controls were agreed to after word leaked that A. G. Spalding and three other Boston Red Stockings stars had signed contracts in the middle of the 1875 season to play for Chicago in 1876. In 1879 the National League secretly agreed to allow each team owner to "reserve" his five best players at the end of the season; other owners were prohibited from bidding for the services of the reserved players. The owners also agreed not to sign any player who refused to play for the team that reserved him.

Forty-seven National Leaguers jumped to the American Association when that rival league commenced play in 1882, but virtually none of them were reserved players. During the 1882 season, the AA induced other NL players to promise to jump leagues in 1883, but the NL fought back to prevent these impending desertions. Charles Bennett, Detroit's star catcher, accepted $100 in exchange for his written promise to sign a contract with the AA's Pittsburgh team in 1883. Before Bennett signed that contract, Detroit offered him more money to stay in the NL. Pittsburgh got wind of what was happening and immediately filed suit in federal court, seeking an injunction ordering Bennett to sign the Pittsburgh contract.

Bennett's lawyers offered a number of legal defenses, some rather narrow and technical. The court ruled in Bennett's favor[1] but did not issue a written opinion, so it is unclear just which of his attorneys' arguments were persuasive. But the court may have refused to enjoin Bennett's jump to Detroit simply because of the timing of the lawsuit. The Pittsburgh club would have suffered no real harm from Bennett's refusal to sign an 1883 contract until it had to play a game without him in the lineup. Its October 1882 lawsuit was, in a sense, premature because Bennett might have changed his mind and returned to Pittsburgh before the opening day of the 1883 season.

Shortstop Sam Wise followed in Bennett's footsteps, signing with the Cincinnati AA team but eventually jumping back to his NL team, the Boston Red Stockings, when they promised to increase his salary. Cincinnati persuaded an Ohio judge to order Wise not to play for Boston. But Cincinnati was unable to enforce the Ohio order in other states. Wise had to stay at home when the Red Stockings came to Cleveland, but was otherwise free to play for Boston.

The National League and American Association made peace in 1883 and signed the "National Agreement," which contained a strengthened reserve rule. The promoters of the Union Association hoped to capitalize on the players' resentment of the one-sided terms of their contracts with organized baseball, but the established leagues fought back hard by adopting the "Day Resolution," an agreement to blacklist any reserved player who jumped to a Union club. Star pitcher Tony Mullane, who jumped from the St. Louis Browns to the St. Louis Maroons of the new league, tried to return to the Browns after hearing about the Day Resolution. The Browns refused to welcome their prodigal back because they knew the Maroons would haul them into court if they did. The Toledo AA club wanted Mullane, but the National Agreement did not provide for player trades or sales. The Browns simply released Mullane outright, and Toledo signed him. The Union Association failed to persuade an Ohio federal judge to order Mullane back to the Maroons.[2] After the demise of the upstart league at the end of the 1884 season, Toledo agreed to send Mullane back to the Browns, but the Cincinnati AA club—in flagrant violation of the National Agreement—signed the 35-game winner to a lucrative bonus contract. The Association's powers-that-be ultimately awarded Mullane to Cincinnati, but ordered him to sit out the 1885 season and give back part of his bonus.

Once the Union Association was dead and buried, Organized Baseball established a maximum annual player salary of $2,000. Owners soon found ways around this provision—in 1887, Boston paid superstar Mike "King" Kelly an additional $3,000 "for use of his picture." Their reduced bargaining leverage caused the players to form the National Brotherhood of Professional Base Ball Players under the leadership of John Montgomery Ward, the New York Giants shortstop who attended Columbia University law school in the off-season. Ward claimed that the reserve clause, the blacklist, and other intimidating provisions of the standard player contract were legally unenforceable. When the owners refused to scrap the salary cap or to agree not to sell or trade players without their consent, the brotherhood went on to form the Players League, which fielded eight teams in 1890. Over 80 National League players and almost 30 from the American Association—including future Hall of Famers Ward, Jake Beckley, Dan Brouthers, John Clarkson, Charles Comiskey, Roger Connor, Hugh Duffy, "Buck" Ewing, Tim Keefe, "King" Kelly, Connie Mack, "Orator Jim" O'Rourke, and "Old Hoss" Radbourn—signed up with the Players League.

Organized Baseball used every weapon at its disposal to strike back at this new rival. The owners told fans that the players were aligned with radical unionists. Boston reportedly gave pitcher Clarkson $10,000—five times the average 1889 salary—to desert the brotherhood, while Spalding offered King Kelly a blank check to play for the White Stockings. When propaganda and bankrolls failed, the established league fielded a team of lawyers at courthouses around the country.

The reserve rule was originally adopted by the parties to the National Agreement as a sort of gentlemen's agreement not to compete for their fellow owners' players. When the National League tried to enforce the reserve clause against the Players League, it got nowhere. A federal court in New York City held that the Giants could not keep catcher Ewing from playing for their brotherhood rival because the reserve provisions in his 1889 contract were "merely a contract to make a contract" for 1890 "if the parties agree."[3] The reserve clause was valuable because it gave the Giants a "prior and exclusive" right to negotiate with Ewing that was enforceable against other clubs in Organized Baseball. But as a basis for an injunction preventing a player from taking the field for a Players League team, Ewing's contract was held "wholly nugatory" because it did not set forth in detail contract terms and conditions (including salary) for 1890. A party who seeks enforcement of a contract with vague or indefinite terms is really asking the court to fill in the blank spaces in that contract, which is something that courts are reluctant to do.

Other courts objected not only to the indefiniteness of player contracts but also to their one-sidedness, which they referred to as a "lack of mutuality." Owners could release players on ten days' notice, but the reserve clause purported to bind a player to one team for as long as the team wanted him. A New York state court judge expressed disgust at "the spectacle" of the Giants' attempt to enforce "a contract which binds [the player] for a series of years and [the team] for 10 days."[4] The National League spent $15,000 on lawyers' fees in New York alone fighting the Players League, but came away with nothing to show for it.

The Players League won the legal battles, but not the war—in fact, everyone lost money. Both sides agreed to Spalding's suggestion that some Players League teams be merged with existing NL and AA franchises and the rest be dissolved. After a bit of skirmishing over the rights to sign some of the returning Players League stars, the NL and AA merged their sixteen clubs into twelve after the 1891 season, and then signed a new National Agreement with the minor leagues. Players had little choice but to accept the terms offered by the "Baseball Trust," but a few rebelled. Amos Rusie won 22 games in 1895 and led the league in strikeouts, but Giants owner Andrew Freedman rewarded him by withholding $600 in fines from his paycheck. Rusie sat out 1896 and then sued the Giants when they invoked their reserve for 1897 as well. The case was settled before trial, with all the National League owners reportedly kicking in a portion of Rusie's $5,000 claim.

As usual the next baseball war set off a spate of contract jumping and legal skirmishes. Over half of the players who suited up for the American League's first season of play were ex-National Leaguers. The older league went to court to try to wrest back a number of their players, most notably Napoleon Lajoie. Lajoie signed a contract with the Phillies in 1900, but refused to be bound by the reserve clause and jumped to the Athletics before the 1901 season. The Pennsylvania Supreme Court held that the Phillies were entitled to an injunction barring the batting champ from playing for the A's.[5]

But that decision turned in part on two unusual factors. First, the Phillies' contract reserved Lajoie for only three years and stated what salary would be paid in each of those three years, so it was not simply "a contract to make a contract." Second, Lajoie was a star of the very highest order. Courts are reluctant to order someone to perform a contract for personal services, although they are not at all reluctant to order the defendant to pay monetary damages equal to the harm caused by his nonperformance. Only when the harm cannot be measured in dollars or the contract involves something unique or irreplaceable are injunctions or other nonmonetary remedies granted by a court. The Phillies may have been able to find equally talented replacements for many of their players, but Lajoie—who led the AL in hits, doubles, home runs, runs, RBIs, batting average, and slugging average in 1901—was a unique talent.

The Phillies' legal victory proved hollow. The A's quickly dealt Lajoie to Cleveland. Whenever Cleveland was scheduled to play in Philadelphia, Lajoie stayed far away. His old team's attempts to obtain an injunction from an Ohio court were not successful.

Other National League efforts to hold on to players also failed. Citing a Supreme Court case holding that a contract that could be abandoned on one year's notice was not enforceable, a federal judge dismissed Brooklyn's suit against veteran catcher Deacon McGuire because the team could terminate his contract on only ten days' notice.[6] The judge also questioned whether McGuire's talents were so "unique and peculiar" that Brooklyn could not replace him. McGuire was a fine player, but he was no Nap Lajoie. A state judge in St. Louis went further in a case involving pitcher Jack Harper. Not only was the standard NL player contract lacking in mutuality, according to the court, but it also unreasonably restrained competition in violation of the Sherman Antitrust Act.[7]

After two years of rivalry, the National League agreed to recognize the American League as an equal. The two major leagues used blacklists and boycotts to bring "outlaw" minor leagues to their knees and keep control of players who had the audacity to hold out for higher salaries. When Ty Cobb refused to accept Detroit's 1913 salary offer, the Tigers suspended him. The impasse was broken only when two Georgia congressmen called for a federal investigation. The threat of government action got Ty Cobb a raise, but the players in general benefited much more from Organized Baseball's war with the Federal League, which no doubt had the National and American Leagues muttering "Two's company, three's a crowd" when the 1914 season opened.

The established leagues didn't even try to use the courts to stop reserve jumpers from playing for the Federal League, but they did seek injunctions against a number of players who jumped, even though they had signed contracts for the upcoming season. The irrepressible Hal Chase signed a 1914 contract with the White Sox, but then moved on to the new league. Teams could release players they didn't want on ten days' notice, so Chase gave Chicago ten days' warning and shuffled off to the Buffalo Federals. A New York state judge agreed with Chase's reasoning and turned down Chicago's request that he order Chase to return.[8] Not only did the contract lack mutuality, said the judge, but Organized Baseball placed so many limits on the freedom of players that they were left in a state of "*quasi* peonage" that was "contrary to the spirit of American institutions and . . . contrary to the spirit of the Constitution of the United States." The court's opinion did contain some good news for Organized Baseball: while implying that baseball may have violated the common-law prohibition against monopolies, it ruled that baseball did not involve interstate commerce and, therefore, did not violate the Sherman Act.

The judges who heard cases involving contract jumpers occasionally showed real distaste for the whole nasty business. Phillies catcher Bill Killefer signed with the Chicago Federal League club for a substantial increase in salary, but re-signed with the Phillies only 12 days later when they topped Chicago's offer. When the Federals asked a Michigan federal judge to order Killefer not to play for Philadelphia, they were rudely received. Citing the opinions in the Ewing, Ward, and McGuire cases, Judge Sessions noted that the right of reservation in the Phillies' 1913 contract with Killefer did not bind him for the 1914 season because it was indefinite and lacked mutuality.[9] But he refused to enforce Chicago's contract because it came into court with "unclean hands." Killefer was under a moral, although not a legal obligation to play for Philadelphia in 1914, but Chicago persuaded him to repudiate that obligation. Both teams had "acted wrongfully and in bad faith," and the judge refused to lift a finger to help either one of them. He also let Killefer know what he thought of him, calling him "a person upon whose pledged word little or no reliance can be placed, and who, for gain to himself, neither scruples nor hesitates to disregard and violate his express engagements and agreements." Chicago appealed the decision but was unsuccessful. The Sixth Circuit Court of Appeals agreed with Judge Sessions that none of the parties to these underhanded dealings was deserving of any assistance from the courts.[10]

Knowing that they could not outlast their better-financed rivals, the Federal League owners filed an antitrust suit against Organized Baseball in Chicago on January 5, 1915. They asked federal Judge Kenesaw Mountain Landis, who had a reputation as a committed trustbuster, to declare the National Agreement's reserve and blacklisting provisions to be unreasonable and illegal restraints on competition. The trial was completed that month, but the Federal League's hopes for a quick verdict in their favor were in vain. The future baseball commissioner pondered the evidence all through the 1915 season, which resulted in another healthy dose of red ink for team owners. After waiting almost a year for Judge Landis to make up his mind, the rival leagues cut a deal. Organized Baseball bought some of the Federal League's player contracts and stadiums—in reality, they were buying peace—and the Federals dropped the antitrust suit.

The final deal satisfied everyone except AL president Ban Johnson, who preferred to fight to the death rather than pay his enemies a nickel of tribute, and the Baltimore Federal League club, which wanted to buy an existing major league franchise and move it to Baltimore. Angered by Brooklyn owner Ebbets's scornful description of their city as "one of the worst minor league towns in this country," the Baltimore owners pledged $50,000 to finance a new antitrust suit against Organized Baseball and the Federal League owners who had sold the league out for a few pieces of silver. When the Department of Justice refused to investigate, Baltimore filed its complaint in federal district court in Washington, D.C., in 1917.

The testimony given at the trial, which didn't begin until March 1919, left little doubt that Organized Baseball's team owners had agreed to use the reserve clause and blacklisting to maintain tight control over the supply of players and paid the Federal League to go out of business in order to protect their monopoly over professional baseball. The judge's directions to the jury virtually directed a verdict for the plaintiffs. The Baltimore club won $254,000 in damages.

Organized Baseball's lawyers immediately appealed the decision. They contended that baseball was not commerce because it involved "personal effort not related to [the] production" of material goods. If baseball did not involve interstate commerce, it was not subject to the Sherman Act or any other federal law. The court of appeals heard oral arguments on October 15, 1920, only three days after the final game of the World Series was played between the Cleveland Indians and the Brooklyn Dodgers. Only a few weeks later, it overturned the lower court's decision in favor of Baltimore.[11] The appellate court first noted that

The transportation in interstate commerce of the players and the paraphernalia used by them was but an incident to the main purpose of the appellants, namely the production of the game. It was for it they were in business—not for the purpose of transferring players, balls, and uniforms . . .

. . . So here, baseball is not commerce, though some of its incidents may be. Suppose a law firm in the city of Washington sends its members to points in different states to try

lawsuits; they would travel, and probably carry briefs and records, in interstate commerce. Could it be correctly said that the firm, in the trial of the lawsuits, was engaged in trade and commerce? Or, take the case of a lecture bureau, which employs persons to deliver lectures before Chautauqua gatherings at points in different states. It would be necessary for the lecturers to travel in interstate commerce, in order that they might fulfill their engagements; but would it not be an unreasonable stretch of the ordinary meaning of the words to say that the bureau was engaged in trade or commerce?

The court of appeals then cited with approval cases holding that those who produce theatrical exhibitions, practice medicine, or launder clothes are not engaged in commerce.

The Baltimore club tried to persuade the United States Supreme Court to reinstate the original verdict in its favor. But Justice Oliver Wendell Holmes, writing for a unanimous Court, upheld the decision of the court of appeals.[12]

Exhibitions of base ball . . . are purely state affairs. It is true that, in order to attain for the exhibitions the great popularity that they have achieved, competitions must be arranged between clubs from different cities and States. But the fact that in order to give the exhibitions the League must induce free persons to cross state lines and arrange and pay for their doing so is not enough to change the character of the business. . . . [T]he transport is a mere incident, not the essential thing. That to which it is incident, the exhibition, although made for money would not be called trade or commerce in the commonly accepted use of those words. As it is put by the defendants, personal effort, not related to production, is not a subject of commerce. That which in its consummation is not commerce does not become commerce among the States because the transportation that we have mentioned takes place. To repeat the illustrations given by the Court below, a firm of lawyers sending out a member to argue a case, or the Chautauqua lecture bureau sending out lecturers, does not engage in such commerce because the lawyer or lecturer goes to another State.

Only a year later, the Court ruled that a company that presented vaudeville shows in cities around the country was, unlike major league baseball, engaged in interstate commerce.[13] Justice Holmes explained the different outcomes in the two cases by pointing to the difference in "the degree of interstate activity" in baseball games and vaudeville shows.

The next challenge to Organized Baseball's hegemony came a quarter century later from Don Jorge Pasqual, the millionaire organizer of the Mexican League, who lured eighteen major leaguers south of the border in 1946. In August of that year, the owners amended their Rule 15 to provide that any player who jumped to the new league would be ineligible to return to Organized Baseball for five years. The Cubs' general manager, who proposed the amendment, said that the prospect of being blacklisted for five years "will do a lot more to discourage Stan Musial from going to Mexico next winter than any suits we may file on the reserve clause."

The Rule 15 blacklist stemmed the southward flow of players. Commissioner A. B. "Happy" Chandler refused to reinstate the players who returned to the states in 1947. Catcher Mickey Owen was reduced to managing a semi-pro club in Winner, South Dakota, while several other Mexican League refugees signed with Cuban and Canadian clubs.

When blacklisted outfielder Danny Gardella filed an antitrust complaint against Organized Baseball, a federal district judge in New York noted the "clear trend toward a broader conception of what constitutes interstate commerce" than had existed when *Federal Baseball Club of Baltimore* was decided over twenty-five years earlier, but felt bound to follow the Supreme Court's decision in that case.[14] But in February 1949 a federal court of appeals voted 2–1 to reverse the district court's dismissal of Gardella's complaint.[15] Judge Learned Hand distinguished *Federal Baseball* by emphasizing the importance to modern-day baseball of interstate radio and television broadcasts of major league games. Judge Frank's separate opinion strongly condemned the reserve system.

For the "reserve clause," as has been observed, results in something resembling peonage of the baseball player. . . . Although many courts have refused to enforce the "reserve" clause, yet severe and practically efficacious extra-legal penalties are imposed for violation. The most extreme of these penalties is the blacklisting of the player so that no club in Organized Baseball will hire him. . . . The violator may perhaps become a . . . bartender or a street-sweeper, but his chances of ever again playing baseball are exceedingly slim.

Gardella's victory was not a final one; it simply allowed him the opportunity to prove his allegations in a trial. Former Cardinals Fred Martin, Max Lanier, and Lou Klein filed a separate suit, and all four players asked the district court to order their immediate reinstatement pending the outcome of the trials, but the court declined to do so.[16] Faced with the prospect of spending the 1949 season in a courtroom rather than on a baseball field, the players were receptive to baseball's offer to settle the case. Commissioner Chandler later characterized his reinstatement of the four "good kids" who had "said they were sorry" for jumping their reserves as inspired by his desire to "temper justice with mercy." But the court of appeals decision—and Judge Frank's sentiments in particular—no doubt had an effect too. Gardella, who had been working as a hospital orderly after returning from Mexico, was reportedly given $60,000 to drop his case.

Subsequent litigation and congressional inquiries kept baseball's attorneys busy in the 1950s. Organized Baseball was the defendant in eight pending antitrust suits when it sought relief from Congress in 1951. At its behest three separate bills that would have granted all professional sports leagues a complete exemption from the antitrust laws were introduced in the House of Representatives that year. After lengthy hearings, Congressman Emanuel Celler's Subcommittee on the Study of Monopoly Power recommended that the bills not be passed, and none of them were. The Celler Subcommittee did not favor blanket antitrust immunity, but it did conclude that professional baseball could not operate successfully without some form of the reserve clause.[17]

After the Gardella decision, Organized Baseball's lawyers and the Subcommittee assumed that *Federal Baseball* was no longer good law. But the Supreme Court surprised them in 1953 in *Toolson* v. *New York Yankees*.[18] When Yankee farmhand George Toolson was placed on the ineligible list for refusing to accept a demotion to a lower-classification team, he sued the Yankees. A California federal judge dismissed the case before trial on the basis of *Federal Baseball*. "If [that] case is, as Judge Frank intimates [in his *Gardella* opinion], an 'impotent zombi,'" the judge wrote, "I feel that it is not my duty to so find but that the Supreme Court should so declare."[19] The Ninth Circuit Court of Appeals agreed,[20] and the Supreme Court reaffirmed *Federal Baseball* with two Justices dissenting, in a one-paragraph opinion.

In Federal Baseball . . . *this Court held that . . . professional baseball . . . was not within the scope of the federal antitrust laws. Congress has had the ruling under consideration but has not seen fit to bring such business under these laws by legislation having prospective effect. . . . The present cases ask us to overrule the prior decision, and, with retrospective effect, hold the [antitrust laws] applicable. We think that if there are evils in this field which now warrant application to it of the antitrust laws it should be by legislation. Without re-examination of the underlying issues, the judgments below are affirmed on the authority of* Federal Baseball . . .

The Court's conclusion that "Congress has had the ruling under consideration but has not seen fit to bring [baseball] under [the antitrust] laws by legislation" is questionable. The Celler Subcommittee report concluded that given the *Gardella* decision and cases subsequent to *Federal Baseball*, which took a broader view of what constituted interstate commerce, "it may be seriously doubted whether baseball should now be regarded as exempt from the antitrust laws." If Congress assumed that baseball was subject to the antitrust laws, its failure to act on bills granting an antitrust exemption was evidence that it did not intend baseball to be exempt—which was just the opposite of what the Court said in *Toolson*.

The next few years saw the Supreme Court hold that professional boxing and football did not share baseball's antitrust immunity. In *Radovich* v. *National Football League*,[21] the Court expressly limited the reach of the *Federal Baseball* precedent to baseball. Three justices dissented from this decision "to put baseball in a class by itself."

Another flurry of congressional activity followed. In 1957 the House Antitrust Subcommittee held fifteen days of hearings on seven different bills, some of which would have exempted all professional sports from antitrust liability. Congressman Celler introduced a bill exempting only those acts that were "reasonably necessary" to maintaining competitive balance and the integrity of sports, but the full House voted to give professional sports leagues a broader although not unlimited exemption. A Senate committee held more hearings in 1958—Casey Stengel, Mickey Mantle, Ted Williams, and Stan Musial testified the day after the All-Star Game was played in nearby Baltimore—but the full Senate never considered the bill. In a 1959 report to the membership, the Major League Baseball Players Association's lawyers said, "There does not seem any doubt that Congress will eventually pass a law concerning Baseball's right to continue its reserve clause," but Congress never came any closer to passing comprehensive sports antitrust legislation. Bills were introduced year after year—attempts to organize a third major league, franchise moves, and the CBS purchase of the Yankees inspired some of the legislative proposals—but none was enacted.

In 1972 the U.S. Supreme Court upheld *Federal Baseball* once more in *Flood* v. *Kuhn*.[22] When the Cardinals traded Curt Flood to the Phillies after the 1969 season, Flood refused to go. "I am [not] a piece of property to be bought and sold irrespective of my wishes," he wrote to Commissioner Bowie Kuhn. Although Flood had not signed a contract for the 1970 season, Kuhn refused to declare him a free agent, so Flood filed suit, hiring former Supreme Court Justice and Secretary of Labor Arthur Goldberg to represent him. The lower court dismissed his case, and, by a 5-3 vote, the Supreme Court upheld its dismissal.

After opening with an overview of baseball history so effusively unjudicial that two members of the majority refused to join it, Justice Harry Blackmun's opinion recognized that, *Federal Baseball* notwithstanding, "Professional baseball is a business and it is engaged in interstate commerce," and that subsequent decisions had applied the antitrust laws to the NFL and professional boxing. Justice Blackmun referred to baseball's antitrust immunity as an "exception," an "anomaly," and an "aberration," but concluded that after fifty years, any change must come from Congress:

The Court has emphasized that since 1922 baseball, with full and continuing congressional awareness, has been allowed to develop and to expand unhindered by federal legislative action. Remedial legislation has been introduced repeatedly in Congress but none has ever been enacted. The Court, accordingly, has concluded that Congress as yet has had no intention to subject baseball's reserve system to the reach of the antitrust statutes. . . . If there is any inconsistency or illogic in all this, it is an inconsistency and illogic of long standing that is to be remedied by the Congress and not by this Court.

The dissenting Justices responded that "[t]he unbroken silence of Congress should not prevent us from correcting our own mistakes," but to date neither the Court nor Congress has done so. Major League Baseball has relied upon *Federal Baseball* and *Flood* to rebuff a variety of antitrust claims, including umpires' allegations that they were illegally dismissed for union activity[23] and a minor league team's challenge to the rules governing player assignment and franchise location.[24] After *Flood*, however, baseball's antitrust status faded into the background for two decades as free agency created new legal problems.

On December 23, 1975, an arbitration panel issued a decision which shook baseball to its foundations by rejecting the owners' interpretation of the reserve clause. The reserve clause, contained in every player's contract, stated that if the player and club hadn't agreed to terms by

March 1, "the Club shall have the right by written notice to the Player ... to renew this contract for one year on the same terms."[25] The owners read the reserve clause as creating another identical contract with the same right of renewal, thereby giving the club a perpetual option on the player's services. However, arbitrator Peter Seitz agreed with the players that this language created only a one-year right of renewal, after which the club had no further claim to the player. The arbitrator's decision allowed pitcher Andy Messersmith, who had played without a written contract in 1975, to sell his services to the highest bidder: Messersmith, who had earned $115,000 with the Dodgers in 1975, soon signed a three- year, $1 million contract with the Atlanta Braves.

The owners attacked the panel's decision in court but could not overcome the strong federal policy favoring arbitration of labor disputes. The courts "do not sit as an appellate tribunal to review the merits of the arbitrator's decision"; rather, they ask only whether a reasonable arbitrator could have reached that result. A century of owners' control over the labor market ended when the Court of Appeals affirmed the arbitrators' decision with the words, "We cannot say that [the reserve clause and related provisions] are not susceptible of the construction given them by the panel. Accordingly, the award must be sustained."[26] The era of free agency had begun.

In 1976, as players and owners adjusted to the new rules, Braves owner Ted Turner ran afoul of Commissioner Kuhn by announcing he would outbid anyone for the Giants' Gary Matthews when Matthews became a free agent. Kuhn suspended Turner for one year for tampering and revoked the Braves' first-round choice in the 1977 amateur draft. A federal court upheld Turner's suspension, citing a clause in the Major League Agreement which empowered the Commissioner "to investigate . . . any act . . . not in the best interests of the national game of Baseball" and "to determine . . . what punitive action is appropriate . . . ."[27] However, the court restored the Braves' draft pick, limiting the Commissioner to those punitive sanctions expressly made available to him by the Major League Agreement.[28] Although the Commissioner had "all the attributes of a benevolent but absolute despot and all the disciplinary powers of the proverbial pater familias,"[29] the Major League Agreement which established his authority also limited its exercise.

No team was more affected by free agency than the Oakland A's, whose talented roster had won three of the past four World Series and five straight division championships. Concluding that he couldn't afford the enormous salaries his stars would command in the open market, A's owner Charles O. Finley decided to sell their contracts to wealthier clubs before they could leave as free agents. In June 1976, Finley sold Joe Rudi and Rollie Fingers to the Boston Red Sox for $2 million and Vida Blue to the New York Yankees for $1.5 million, but Commissioner Bowie Kuhn quickly nullified the transactions as "inconsistent with the best interests of baseball, the integrity of the game, and the maintenance of public confidence in it."

A federal judge rejected Finley's argument that Kuhn had exceeded his authority, pointing to the Commissioner's power to invalidate acts "not in the best interests of Baseball" and a provision in the Major League Agreement through which the club owners agreed to be bound by the Commissioner's decisions and to "waive such right of recourse to the courts as would otherwise have existed in their favor."[30] This decision was upheld on appeal,[31] the appeals court noting that the "waiver of recourse" provision quoted above kept Finley from going to court to challenge Kuhn's ruling unless he could show that the Major League Agreement was inconsistent with state or federal law or that the procedures followed by Kuhn "failed to follow the basic rudiments of due process of law."[32]

Pete Rose's 1989 lawsuit against A. Bartlett Giamatti relied on just that argument—that Rose was being denied the right to a fair hearing by an unbiased decisionmaker. When Rose asked a state court judge in his home town of Cincinnati to enjoin the Commissioner from holding a hearing on charges that Rose had bet on baseball games, he claimed that Giamatti had already decided he was guilty. Giamatti's lawyers filed a motion to remove the case to federal court. In most cases, state courts have jurisdiction if one or both of the parties to the lawsuit are citizens of that state; if the plaintiff and defendant are citizens of different states, federal courts usually have jurisdiction to hear the case. Because Rose was a citizen of Ohio and Giamatti was a citizen of New York, Giamatti was able to remove the case from the Ohio court—which might favor Ohioans over New Yorkers—to a federal court.[33] After losing that legal skirmish, Rose withdrew his lawsuit and agreed to be suspended indefinitely from baseball, so the courts never ruled on the merits of Rose's claim that the Commissioner was not treating him fairly.

Twenty years after Flood, baseball's antitrust exemption came under renewed attack in Congress and the courts. The judicial challenge arose in the context of a thwarted franchise sale. In August 1992, a group headed by Vincent Piazza (father of Dodger catcher Mike) signed an agreement to purchase the San Francisco Giants for $115 million with the intention of moving the club to St. Petersburg, Florida. The sale was subject to approval by Major League Baseball's Ownership Committee. After two of its members publicly implied that background checks had uncovered serious problems about two members of the Piazza group, the Committee rejected Piazza's bid. The Giants were ultimately sold, for $15 million less, to a group which pledged to keep the team in San Francisco. Piazza and his fellow investor Vincent Tirendi sued Major League Baseball in a Pennsylvania federal court, alleging that the Committee's comments falsely linked them to organized crime and asserting that the Committee's rejection of their higher bid violated the antitrust laws.

The district judge ruled against Major League Baseball, rejecting its claim to an antitrust exemption.[34] Seizing on language in Flood v. Kuhn that "Congress as yet has had no intention to subject baseball's reserve system to the reach of the antitrust statutes," the judge held that baseball's antitrust exemption extended only to the reserve system and did not allow owners arbitrarily to block franchise sales or engage in other types of anticompetitive activity. The Court of Appeals rejected Major League Baseball's request for immediate, emergency review of this ruling. While the case subsequently settled on the eve of trial, with Piazza receiving an apology and a reported $6 million from Major League Baseball, the court's ruling remains the first crack in baseball's antitrust armor.

While *Piazza* would limit the antitrust exemption to labor issues, the labor troubles which culminated in the strike- shortened 1994 season have caused Congress to consider removing the exemption altogether in the context of collective bargaining. The exemption first came under attack following the forced resignation of Commissioner Fay Vincent on September 7, 1992, amidst widespread speculation that Vincent's ouster was designed to prevent a Commissioner from invoking his "best interests" power to end a lockout or alter the owners' collective bargaining proposal. While the Commissioner was selected and paid by the owners, many Congressmen considered him an intermediary between owners and players whose authority and nominal independence made repeal of the antitrust exemption unnecessary. When Congress held hearings on a bill to repeal the exemption in early 1993, Major League Baseball pledged it would name a new Commissioner by the end of 1993.

But 1994 arrived with no Commissioner and no labor agreement. Senator Howard Metzenbaum (D-Ohio), a former minority owner of the Cleveland Indians, introduced a bill to repeal baseball's antitrust exemption as applied to labor matters. (Few people appreciate the fact that there are really *two* antitrust exemptions that affect baseball. First, there is the broad exemption created by *Federal Baseball*. Second, there is the "labor exemption," which exempts from antitrust laws collective bargaining agreements in all industries. That is why repealing *Federal Baseball* would not have prevented the strike of 1994; when there is a collective bargaining relationship, the employees can't bring an antitrust suit against their employers. Interestingly, some of the proposed 1994 bills would have given the MLBPA—which is really a union in name only—the ability to use the antitrust laws as both a sword and a shield.)

Metzenbaum's efforts were supported by Senator Connie Mack III (R-Florida), grandson of the legendary owner/manager, and Representative Jim Bunning (R-Kentucky), a 224-game winner and former player representative, who had hailed Marvin Miller's appointment as the first independent director of the Players' Association. In June, the Senate Judiciary Committee rejected Metzenbaum's bill by a vote of 10-7.

The players struck on August 12. On September 14, following a month of fruitless negotiations, the owners formally cancelled the remainder of the 1994 season and the playoffs. The following week, the House Judiciary Committee considered chairman Jack Brooks' (D-Texas) proposal to limit the exemption. Donald Fehr, Executive Director of the Players' Association, testified that if Congress lifted the antitrust exemption and barred the owners from unilaterally imposing a salary cap while litigation was pending, he would recommend the players immediately return to work. While some legislators did not think Congress should interject itself into a private labor dispute, the House Judiciary Committee voted on September 29 to repeal baseball's antitrust exemption in the context of collective bargaining. The Committee's bill did not, however, go so far as Fehr wanted by forbidding the owners from imposing their own terms during an impasse. While the bill was not considered by the full House or the Senate before their October adjournment, many Congressmen and Senators strongly cautioned Major League Baseball that a similar measure would likely become law unless the parties reached agreement before spring training, 1995.

What would happen if Major League Baseball's antitrust exemption were repealed? For antitrust purposes, Major League Baseball, like other sports leagues, is considered 28 separate, independently owned and managed businesses (although the final word on the "single entity" defense to antitrust violations has not yet been uttered). The antitrust laws limit the ways in which such businesses can control one another's business decisions. For example, antitrust cases involving other professional sports leagues have held that the NFL could not require the Oakland Raiders to obtain the unanimous consent of all other clubs before moving to Los Angeles[35] and that the NBA could not prohibit the Chicago Bulls from broadcasting more than 20 games per season on a cable "superstation."[36] While the Sports Broadcasting Act of 1961[37] expressly authorizes Organized Baseball's member clubs to pool their television rights to sell a national "Game of the Week"-style package to broadcast television networks without violating the antitrust laws, one lower court and the Department of Justice have concluded that this exemption does not apply to leaguewide contracts with cable networks such as ESPN.[38]

Most importantly, if Major League Baseball's antitrust exemption, won through *Federal Baseball* in 1922, were repealed, its labor relations would be subject to the same antitrust principles applicable to other professional team sports. Under ordinary circumstances, the antitrust laws forbid businesses from colluding to fix the terms on which they will hire workers; such practices are legal only in the context of a multi-employer collective bargaining agreement ("CBA"). But what happens when, as in 1994, the CBA expires and the parties are unable to agree on a new CBA? May Major League Baseball's clubs then restrict free agency, eliminate salary arbitration, or impose a salary cap over the objections of the Players' Association?

When the NFL faced a similar situation, the Eighth Circuit Court of Appeals allowed its owners to adopt "unilateral changes that are reasonably comprehended within [their] pre-impasse proposals."[39] The NFLPA could strike, continue negotiating, or file a grievance with the National Labor Relations Board which would take years to resolve; until then, the salary game would be played under the owners' rules. But with running back Freeman McNeil carrying the ball in court, the NFL players swept around the labor exemption. They decertified the NFL Players' Association, thereby ending the collective bargaining relationship which had allowed the owners to impose their system, and filed individual antitrust claims. After a jury hearing McNeil's case condemned the NFL's free-agent compensation system as an illegal restraint of trade, the NFL was forced to liberalize its rules governing free agency.[40] Within days the NFLPA was back in its customary seat at the bargaining table, and the parties soon negotiated another CBA.

Unless the MLBPA likewise opts for decertification, an implausible scenario, a repeal of the Federal Baseball exemption will have little impact on labor relations, though it may be powerfully influential in such matters as franchise relocation and expansion decisions. In any event, many observers believe the NFLPA won its labor battle but lost the salary war. The NBA and its players are embroiled in a similar court battle over the players' desire to eliminate the league's existing salary cap; so far, the courts have allowed the cap to remain in effect during negotiations over a new CBA.

As the 1995 season approached, Major League Baseball's unique antitrust exemption was challenged as never before. Yet, it was only one of many issues that Major League Baseball and the Players Association had to resolve, most of which were unrelated to the antitrust exemption.

[1]*Allegheny Base-ball Club* v. *Bennett,* 14 Fed. 257 (C.C.W.D. Pa., 1882).

[2]*St. Louis Athletic Ass'n* v. *Mullane,* No. 3642 (C.C.S.D. Ohio, May 13, 1884). Reprinted in *Sporting Life,* May 21, 1884, p.2, col.1.

[3]*Metropolitan Exhibition Co.* v. *Ewing,* 42 Fed. 198 (C.C.S.D. N.Y. 1890).

[4]*Metropolitan Exhibition Co.* v. *Ward,* 9 N.Y.S. 779 (Sup. Ct., New York Co. 1890).

[5]*Philadelphia Base Ball Club* v. *Lajoie,* 51 Atl. 973 (Pa. S. Ct. 1902).

[6]*Brooklyn Baseball Club* v. *McGuire,* 116 Fed. 783 (C.C.E.D. Pa. 1902).

[7]*American Base Ball & Athletic Exhibition Co. of St. Louis* v. *Harper,* 54 Cent. L.J. 449 (St. Louis Cir. Ct. 1902).

[8]*American League Baseball Club of Chicago* v. *Chase,* 86 Misc. 441, 149 N.Y. Supp. 6 (Sup. Ct. 1914).

[9]*Weeghman* v. *Killefer,* 214 Fed. 168 (W.D. Mich. 1914).

[10]*Weeghman* v. *Killefer,* 215 Fed. 289 (6th Cir. 1914).

[11]*National League of Professional Baseball Clubs* v. *Federal Baseball Club of Baltimore,* 269 Fed. 681 (D.C. Cir. 1921).

[12]*Federal Baseball Club of Baltimore* v. *National League of Professional Baseball Clubs,* 259 U.S. 200 (1922).

[13]*Hart* v. *Keith Vaudeville Exchange,* 262 U.S. 271 (1923).

[14]*Gardella* v. *Chandler,* 79 F.Supp. 260 (S.D.N.Y. 1948).

[15]*Gardella* v. *Chandler,* 172 F.2d 402 (2d Cir. 1949).

[16]*Martin* v. *Chandler,* 174 F.2d 917 (2d. Cir. 1949); *Gardella* v. *Chandler,* 174 F.2d 919 (2d. Cir. 1949).

[17]H.R. Rep. 2002, 82d Cong., 2d Sess. 228–32 (1952).

[18]346 U.S. 356 (1953).

[19]*Toolson* v. *New York Yankees,* 101 F.Supp. 93 (S.D. Cal. 1951).

[20]200 F.2d 198 (9th Cir. 1952).

[21]358 U.S. 445 (1957).

[22]407 U.S. 258 (1972).

[23]*Salerno* v. *American League,* 429 F.2d 1003 (2d Cir. 1970).

[24]*Professional Baseball Schools and Clubs, Inc.* v. *Kuhn,* 693 F.2d 1085 (11th Cir. 1982).

[25]Player Contract, P 10(a).

[26]*Kansas City Royals Baseball Corp.* v. *Major League Baseball Players Association,* 532 F.2d 615 (8th Cir. 1976).

[27]Major League Agreement, Art. I, Sec. 2.

[28]*Atlanta National League Baseball Club* v. *Kuhn,* 432 F. Supp. 1213 (N.D. Ga. 1977).

[29]*Milwaukee American Ass'n* v. *Landis,* 49 F.2d 298 (N.D. Ill. 1931).

[30]Id. at Art. VII, Sec. 2.

[31]*Charles O. Finley & Co.* v. *Kuhn,* 569 F.2d 527 (7th Cir. 1978).

[32]Id. at 544.

[33]*Rose* v. *Giamatti,* 721 F. Supp. 906 (1989).

[34]*Piazza* v. *Major League Baseball,* 831 F Supp. 420 (E.D. Pa. 1993).

[35]*Los Angeles Memorial Coliseum Commission* v. *National Football League,* 726 F.2d 1381 (9th Cir.), cert. denied, 469 U.S. 990 (1984).

[36]*Chicago Professional Sports Ltd. Partnership* v. *National Basketball Association,* 961 F.2d 667 (7th Cir.), cert. denied, 113 S.Ct. 409 (1992).

[37]15 U.S.C. S 1291.

[38]*Chicago Professional Sports Limited Partnership* v. *National Basketball Association,* 808 F. Supp. 646, 650 (N.D. Ill. 1992), quoting March 30, 1988 letter from the Antitrust Division of the Department of Justice to the Senate Judiciary Committee.

[39]*Powell* v. *National Football League,* 930 F.2d 1293, 1302 (8th Cir. 1989), cert. denied, 111 S.Ct. 711 (1991).

[40]*See White* v. *National Football League,* 836 F. Supp. 1458 (D. Minn. 1993).

## CHAPTER 28

The Amateur Draft

Allan Simpson

It was 1964, and major league baseball was at a crossroads. By buying up the best amateur talent, the Yankees and other wealthy clubs were threatening to make a mockery of competitive balance, one of the game's time-honored virtues. The more these clubs spent on talent, it seemed, the more successful they became.

To keep pace with the Yankees, who had won nine of the last ten American League pennants and fourteen of the last sixteen, some smaller-market teams were paying steep prices for players and committing financial suicide. The fledgling Los Angeles Angels, for instance, paid untested outfielder Rick Reichardt a record $205,000; at the time, that signing bonus was far higher than the annual salary of any major leaguer.

The more money every club misspent on raw, unproven amateur prospects, the less there was to invest in a sagging player-development system. Vibrant and self-sustaining in 1949 with 461 teams, the minor leagues had decayed fifteen years later to just 136 clubs, nearly all of which were dependent on major league subsidies for survival. By overspending for amateur talent and underspending to develop it, baseball was undercutting its investment.

On January 15, 1964, baseball's high-ranking officers instituted a much-debated, much-awaited draft of amateur players which would become effective in 1965 as the primary means by which amateurs would infiltrate the professional ranks. Created in reaction to the Reichardt signing and the Yankees' decade of dominance, the draft's purpose was twofold: to stop the upward spiral of bonuses and to distribute talent more evenly.

In 1936, the year the National Football League adopted its annual player draft, the Cleveland Indians had signed seventeen-year-old farmboy Bob Feller to a contract for one dollar. Players then yearned for the opportunity to play professional baseball, and there was little competition among clubs for players' services.

By 1942, World War II had siphoned off much of the available talent. Competition drove the Detroit Tigers to sign untested outfielder Dick Wakefield to an unprecedented $52,000 bonus. By the end of the War, baseball had entered a new era, a golden era. Interest in the game spread like wildfire; minor league teams sprung up all over, and competition for players became fierce, forcing teams to offer bonuses.

At the 1946 winter meetings, baseball made its first effort to curtail escalating bonuses. An agreement between the two major leagues and the National Association (the governing body for the minor leagues) designated a bonus player as anyone signed to a contract that exceeded a fixed amount which varied by the level of the league. The figure was $6,000 for major league teams, $4,000 for Triple-A teams, and so on down to $800 for Class D and E clubs. Teams were fined if they exceeded the imposed limit.

For the next two decades, major league officials wrestled with problems stemming from reckless spending and the competition for new recruits. Baseball's bosses tried several variations of the bonus rule, but none worked because teams found ways around them. Detroit general manager Jim Campbell said, "We'd pass a bonus rule and, by the time we got out of the room, we'd already figured out how to skin the cat."

It also didn't help that few high-priced bonus babies ever established themselves in the major leagues. In 1950 Pittsburgh made eighteen-year-old lefthander Paul Pettit the game's first $100,000 bonus player; the victim of a sore arm, he went on to win only one game in the big leagues.

Beginning in 1958, baseball tried a first-year rule that required teams to retain bonus babies on major league rosters in each of their first two full seasons or expose them to waivers; that didn't work either. Opponents said it was counterproductive, that too many young players were forced to play in the big leagues before they were ready.

Meanwhile bonuses continued to escalate. In 1960, the Cubs organization signed pitcher-outfielder Danny Murphy, seventeen, to a record $130,000 bonus and immediately placed him with the parent club. He played and pitched for both the Cubs and White Sox without distinction. A year later, shortstop Bob Bailey was awarded $175,000 by Pittsburgh, and enjoyed a long career, mostly at third base.

In 1961 six other teams shelled out the largest bonuses in their clubs' histories, and the heavy spending sent ripples throughout baseball. Braves general manager John McHale said, "A club like ours must be competitive . . . if you're not prepared to pay, well, you just stand by and watch somebody else sign 'em."

In 1958-63, an estimated $45 million was spent on bonuses and first-year player salaries. In 1964, $7 million was paid out to amateur players—more than was spent on major league salaries.

By 1964, the three other major American team sports used a draft to distribute amateur talent. Football introduced the concept in 1936, basketball followed in 1947, and hockey adopted a draft in 1963; baseball officials were reluctant to follow suit, because a draft would penalize industrious teams and constitute a form of socialism.

Others opposed the draft for legal reasons, concerned that a draft, which would restrict a player's freedom and bargaining power, might jeopardize baseball's antitrust exemption. Some feared that Congress might take an adverse stance on the premise that a baseball draft would deal primarily with high school players, who were not legally of age.

Teams like the Dodgers and Yankees opposed the draft not on legal principle, but for more selfish reasons. Lee MacPhail, mastermind of the powerful Yankees teams of the '50s and early '60s, said, "We won the World Series five years in a row. Kids wanted to sign with the Yankees, the most glamorous team in baseball at the time. If two or three teams were after them, and one was the Yankees, we generally had the inside track."

That changed when Major League Baseball adopted its draft at the 1964 winter meetings. All eligible talent would be placed in a common pool with every team selecting from it in turn. When a team picked a player, it would gain exclusive rights to negotiate with him.

The baseball draft introduced several notable innovations. First, three drafts would be held each year instead of one. A summer meeting would be held around June 1, a winter session around January 15. A third draft, limited to American Legion players not eligible to sign until September 1, would be held in late summer. (The Legion draft lasted only one year. and the winter session was also phased out, in 1986.)

This new amateur draft, officially the Rule IV draft, was open to permanent residents of the U.S. only, with a focus on high school graduates and college players who had attained sophomore standing or had reached the age of twenty-one. The college rule was amended two years later to include players of junior class standing. By 1990, players from Canada and the U.S. territories, including Puerto Rico, had also become subject to selection.

Whereas a football team retained permanent negotiating rights to a draftee, a baseball club's rights terminated fifteen days before the next draft session. If a player didn't sign by then, he went back into a special "secondary" pool for the next time he was eligible to be selected. (The secondary phase of the draft was eliminated in 1987.)

One of the immediate benefits of a free-agent draft, most clubs agreed, would be an improved game at the major league level. No longer would clubs be forced to clutter their twenty-five-man rosters with green, untested youngsters. (In 1964, major league teams had been forced to protect seventy-seven first-year players on their winter rosters.)

While most of the emphasis in the early years of the draft was on raw high school talent, a gradual transition took place in the mid-'70s. College players became more and more attractive to scouts as college programs around the country took on a new commitment to fielding competitive teams.

In 1977, for the first time, more college players than high school players were selected, a trend that has never been reversed. By 1981, the swing to college talent was so pronounced that the ratio of players entering the professional ranks from college programs compared to high schools was nearly five to one.

No matter what the source of talent, the baseball draft remained, at best, an inexact science. Unlike football and basketball, whose drafts deal with more nearly finished products, the best baseball players drafted invariably need to develop and refine their skills for several seasons in the minor leagues. In the draft's first thirty years, only eighteen players went directly to the major leagues, and fourteen of them had to return to the minors for further seasoning.

Boston Red Sox scout Joe Stephenson described how unpredictable the draft can be. "We belong to the 4-H club," Stephenson said. "You hope you find a prospect. You hope you get him in the draft. You hope you can sign him. And you hope he can play."

The 1979 draft provided evidence of what a crap shoot the selection process can be. Seattle made outfielder Al Chambers number one overall, and he only enjoyed a cup of coffee in the big leagues. Outfielder Kevin Brandt, Minnesota's first-round pick, played in just 40 minor league games. Meanwhile, the Dodgers got Orel Hershiser in the seventeenth round, and the Yanks picked Don Mattingly in the nineteenth.

Several other potential Hall of Famers were late-round finds. Ryne Sandberg went to Philadelphia in the twentieth round in 1978. Mike Piazza, National League Rookie of the Year in 1993, was a sixty-second-round pick of Los Angeles in 1988. Impact players such as Kevin Mitchell and Bobby Bonilla weren't drafted at all.

Astute drafting was largely responsible for a series of minidynasties in the 1970s, 1980s, and 1990s. Oakland laid the foundation for World Series championship teams from 1972 to 1974 by selecting Rick Monday, Sal Bando, Gene Tenace, and Reggie Jackson in 1965 and 1966, the first two drafts. The Dodgers contended for much of the 1970s due to a 1968 draft that produced Bill Buckner, Ron Cey, Steve Garvey, and Davey Lopes. The Mets became a force in the mid-1980s because of accurate drafting earlier in the decade, landing Darryl Strawberry (1980) and Dwight Gooden (1982) with first-round picks.

The White Sox designed a contending team in the 1987-90 period by choosing pitcher Jack McDowell, third baseman Robin Ventura, first baseman Frank Thomas, and pitcher Alex Fernandez with consecutive first-round picks; in those same years, the corresponding first-round picks for the Dodgers were pitchers Dan Opperman, Bill Bene, Kiki Jones, and Ron Walden—none of whom reached the big leagues.

Since its inception, the draft has largely achieved its two underlying goals. Payments to untried amateur players were kept in line until the late 1980s, while new meaning has been given to competitive balance. Monday, the number one selection in the first draft, received a signing bonus from Kansas City of $104,000, about half of what Reichardt received in his landmark deal of 1964. As late as 1987, Seattle paid a mere $160,000 to sign Ken Griffey, Jr., the first overall pick.

It was only in 1988 when Baltimore signed No. 1 overall pick Ben McDonald to an $800,000 three-year major league contract that provided for a $350,000 bonus, and Toronto later went to $575,000 for first baseman John Olerud in 1989, that players regularly topped the $200,000 mark.

Atlanta refused to select Arlington, Texas, high school pitcher Todd Van Poppel with the first selection in 1990 because of his insistence on attending the University of

Texas. Undeterred, Oakland drafted Van Poppel with its first-round pick and signed him to a $1.2 million, three-year major league contract that provided for a $500,000 bonus.

A year later, the Yankees stunned the baseball world by signing pitcher Brien Taylor to a whopping $1.55 million bonus—more than double the previous record. Average bonus payments to first-round picks began to escalate appreciably, rising from $355,000 in 1991 to $482,000 in 1992 to $611,000 in 1993.

In 1994, with a player strike looming, the average first-round bonus reached $796,000 with five players receiving bonuses of $1 million or more. Number one pick Paul

Wilson tied Taylor's record bonus by signing with the Mets for $1.55 million. Within weeks, that record was broken when the Florida Marlins paid $1.6 million to entice shortstop Josh Booty away from a promising football career at Louisiana State University.

In the last thirty years, some 38,000 players have been selected in baseball's annual draft. Despite the spending frenzy of the late 1980s, during the draft era no team would ever dominate the game as the Yankees had. From 1978 to 1987 ten different teams won the World Series, making the adoption of the draft in 1964 a blessing for baseball.

Top 10 Draft Picks 1965-1994

Players are listed in the order in which they were drafted. Those who did not reach the major leagues are listed with the highest minor league classification they attained as of October 1994. DNP signifies that the draft pick did not play in Organized Baseball.

Year/ Selection Number	Player	Team	Position — Highest Minor League Reached	Year/ Selection Number	Player	Team	Position — Highest Minor League Reached	Year/ Selection Number	Player	Team	Position — Highest Minor League Reached
1965				**1969**				**1973**			
1	Rick Monday	A's	OF	1	Jeff Burroughs	Senators	OF	1	David Clyde	Rangers	P
2	Les Rohr	Mets	P	2	J.R. Richard	Astros	P	2	John Stearns	Phillies	C
3	Joe Coleman	Senators	P	3	Ted Nicholson	White Sox	3B - A	3	Robin Yount	Brewers	SS
4	Alex Barrett	Astros	SS - AAA	4	Randy Sterling	Mets	P	4	Dave Winfield	Padres	P-OF
5	Billy Conigliaro	Red Sox	OF	5	Alan Bannister	Angels	SS	5	Glenn Tufts	Indians	1B-P - AA
6	Rick James	Cubs	P	6	Mike Anderson	Phillies	1B	6	Johnnie LeMaster	Giants	SS
7	Ray Fosse	Indians	C	7	Paul Ray Powell	Twins	OF	7	Billy Taylor	Angels	OF - A
8	John Wyatt	Dodgers	SS - A	8	Terry McDermot	Dodgers	C	8	Gary Roenicke	Expos	SS
9	Eddie Leon	Twins	SS	9	Don Stanhouse	A's	SS	9	Lew Olsen	Royals	P-AAA
10	Doug Dickerson	Pirates	OF - A	10	Bob May	Pirates	P - A	10	Pat Rockett	Braves	SS
1966				**1970**				**1974**			
1	Steve Chilcott	Mets	C - AAA	1	Mike Ivie	Padres	C	1	Bill Almon	Padres	SS
2	Reggie Jackson	A's	OF	2	Steve Dunning	Indians	P	2	Tommy Boggs	Rangers	P
3	Wayne Twitchell	Astros	P	3	Barry Foote	Expos	C	3	Lonnie Smith	Phillies	OF
4	Ken Brett	Red Sox	P-OF	4	Darrell Porter	Brewers	C	4	Tom Brennan	Indians	P
5	Dean Burk	Cubs	P - AAA	5	Mike Martin	Phillies	P - AAA	5	Dale Murphy	Braves	C
6	Tom Grieve	Senators	OF	6	Lee Richard	White Sox	SS	6	Butch Edge	Brewers	P
7	Leron Lee	Cardinals	OF	7	Randy Scarberry	Astros	P	7	Scot Thompson	Cubs	OF
8	Jim De Neff	Angels	SS - AAA	8	Rex Goodson	Royals	C - AA	8	Larry Monroe	White Sox	P
9	Mike Biko	Phillies	P - A	9	Jim Haller	Dodgers	P - AAA	9	Ron Sorey	Expos	3B - A
10	Jim Lyttle	Yankees	OF	10	Paul Dade	Angels	3B-OF	10	Mike Miley	Angels	SS
1967				**1971**				**1975**			
1	Ron Blomberg	Yankees	1B	1	Denny Goodwin	White Sox	C	1	Danny Goodwin	Angels	C
2	Terry Hughes	Cubs	SS	2	Jay Franklin	Padres	P	2	Mike Lentz	Padres	P
3	Mike Garman	Red Sox	P	3	Tom Bianco	Brewers	SS	3	Les Filkins	Tigers	OF - AAA
4	Jon Matlack	Mets	P	4	Condredge Holloway	Expos	SS - DNP	4	Brian Rosinski	Cubs	OF - AAA
5	John Jones	Senators	C - A	5	Roy Branch	Royals	P	5	Rich O'Keefe	Brewers	OF- AAA
6	John Mayberry	Astros	1B	6	Roy Thomas	Phillies	P	6	Butch Benton	Mets	C - AAA
7	Brian Bickerton	A's	P - AAA	7	Roger Quiroga	Senators	P - A	7	Rick Cerone	Indians	C
8	Wayne Simpson	Reds	P	8	Ed Kurpiel	Cardinals	1B-P - AAA	8	Ted Barnickle	Giants	P - AAA
9	Mike Nunn	Angel	C - AAA	9	David Sloan	Indians	P - AA	9	Clint Hurdle	Royals	OF
10	Ted Simmons	Cardinals	C	10	Taylor Duncan	Braves	SS	10	Art Miles	Expos	SS - A
1968				**1972**				**1976**			
1	Tim Foli	Mets	SS	1	Dave Roberts	Padres	3B	1	Floyd Bannister	Astros	P
2	Pete Broberg	A's	P	2	Rick Manning	Indians	SS	2	Pat Underwood	Tigers	P
3	Marty Cott	Astros	C - AAA	3	Larry Christenson	Phillies	P	3	Ken Smith	Braves	3B
4	Thurman Munson	Yankees	C	4	Roy Howell	Rangers	3B	4	Bill Bordley	Brewers	P
5	Bobby Valentine	Dodgers	OF	5	Bobby Goodman	Expos	C - AAA	5	Bob Owchinko	Padres	P
6	Robert Weaver	Indians	SS - AA	6	Danny Thomas	Brewers	1B	6	Ken Landreaux	Angels	OF
7	Curtis Moore	Braves	OF - AAA	7	Larry Payne	Reds	P - AAA	7	Herm Segelke	Cubs	P
8	Donnie Castle	Senators	P-OF	8	Dick Ruthven	Twins	P	8	Steve Trout	White Sox	P
9	Dick Sharon	Pirates	OF	9	Steve Englishbey	Astros	OF - AA	9	Bob James	Expos	P
10	Junior Kennedy	Orioles	SS	10	Dave Chalk	Angels	3B	10	Jamie Allen	Twins	P

Year/ Selection Number	Player	Team	Position — Highest Minor League Reached
1977			
1	Harold Baines	White Sox	1B-OF
2	Bill Gullikson	Expos	P
3	Paul Molitor	Brewers	SS
4	Tim Cole	Braves	P - AAA
5	Kevin Richards	Tigers	P - AA
6	Terry Kennedy	Cardinals	C
7	Richard Dotson	Angels	P
8	Brian Greer	Padres	OF
9	David Hibner	Rangers	SS - A
10	Craig Landis	Giants	SS - AAA
1978			
1	Bob Horner	Braves	3B
2	Lloyd Moseby	Blue Jays	1B
3	Hubie Brooks	Mets	SS
4	Mike Morgan	A's	P
5	Andy Hawkins	Padres	P
6	Tito Nanni	Mariners	OF-1B - AAA
7	Bob Cummings	Giants	C - AA
8	Nick Hernandez	Brewers	C - A
9	Glen Franklin	Expos	SS - AAA
10	Phil Lansford	Indians	SS - A
1979			
1	Al Chambers	Mariners	OF
2	Tim Leary	Mets	P
3	Jay Schroeder	Blue Jays	C - A
4	Brad Komminsk	Braves	OF
5	Juan Bustabad	A's	SS - AAA
6	Andy Van Slyke	Cardinals	OF
7	Jon Bohnet	Indians	P
8	John Mizerock	Astros	C
9	Steve Buechele	White Sox	SS
10	Tim Wallach	Expos	1B
1980			
1	Darryl Strawberry	Mets	OF
2	Gary Harris	Blue Jays	SS - AA
3	Ken Dayley	Braves	P
4	Mike King	A's	P - AAA
5	Jeff Pyburn	Padres	OF - AAA
6	Darnell Coles	Mariners	SS
7	Jay Reid	Giants	1B
8	Cecil Espy	White Sox	OF
9	Ross Jones	Dodgers	SS
10	Kelly Gruber	Indians	SS
1981			
1	Mike Moore	Mariners	P
2	Joe Carter	Cubs	OF
3	Dick Schofield	Angels	SS
4	Terry Blocker	Mets	OF
5	Matt Williams	Blue Jays	P
6	Kevin McReynolds	Padres	OF
7	Daryl Boston	White Sox	OF
8	Bobby Meacham	Cardinals	SS
9	Ron Darling	Rangers	P
10	Mark Grant	Giants	P
1982			
1	Shawon Dunston	Cubs	SS
2	Augie Schmidt	Blue Jays	SS - AAA
3	Jimmy Jones	Padres	P
4	Bryan Oelkers	Twins	P
5	Dwight Gooden	Mets	P
6	Spike Owen	Mariners	SS
7	Sam Khalifa	Pirates	SS
8	Bob Kipper	Angels	P
9	Duane Ward	Braves	P
10	John Morris	Royals	OF

Year/ Selection Number	Player	Team	Position — Highest Minor League Reached
1983			
1	Tim Belcher	Twins	P
2	Kurt Stillwell	Reds	SS
3	Jeff Kunkel	Rangers	SS
4	Eddie Williams	Mets	3B
5	Stan Hilton	A's	P - AAA
6	Jackie Davidson	Cubs	P - AAA
7	Darrel Ackerfields	Mariners	P
8	Robbie Wine	Astros	C
9	Matt Stark	Blue Jays	C
10	Ray Hayward	Padres	P
1984			
1	Shawn Abner	Mets	OF
2	Billy Swift	Mariners	P
3	Drew Hall	Cubs	P
4	Cory Snyder	Indians	AA
5	Pat Pacillo	Reds	P
6	Erik Pappas	Angels	C - AA
7	Mike Dunne	Cardinals	P
8	Jay Bell	Twins	SS
9	Alan Cockrell	Giants	OF - AAA
10	Mark McGwire	A's	1B
1985			
1	B.J. Surhoff	Brewers	SS
2	Will Clark	Giants	1B
3	Bobby Witt	Rangers	P
4	Barry Larkin	Reds	SS
5	Kurt Brown	White Sox	C - AA
6	Barry Bonds	Pirates	OF
7	Mike Campbell	Mariners	P
8	Pete Incaviglia	Expos	OF
9	Mike Poehl	Indians	P - AA
10	Chris Gwynn	Dodgers	OF
1986			
1	Jeff King	Pirates	3B
2	Greg Swindell	Indians	P
3	Matt Williams	Giants	SS
4	Kevin Brown	Rangers	P
5	Kent Mercker	Braves	P
6	Gary Sheffield	Brewers	SS
7	Brad Brink	Phillies	P - AAA
8	Patrick Lennon	Mariners	SS - AA
9	Derrick May	Cubs	OF
10	Derek Parks	Twins	C - AA
1987			
1	Ken Griffey, Jr.	Mariners	OF
2	Mark Merchant	Pirates	OF - A
3	Willie Banks	Twins	P
4	Mike Harkey	Cubs	P
5	Jack McDowell	White Sox	P
6	Derek Lilliquist	Braves	P
7	Chris Myers	Orioles	P - AA
8	Dan Opperman	Dodgers	P - A
9	Kevin Appier	Royals	P
10	Kevin Garner	Padres	P-OF - AA
1988			
1	Andy Benes	Padres	P
2	Mark Lewis	Indians	SS
3	Steve Avery	Braves	P
4	Greg Olson	Orioles	P
5	Bill Bene	Dodgers	P - A
6	Monty Fariss	Rangers	SS
7	Willie Ansley	Astros	OF - AA
8	Jim Abbott	Angels	P
9	Ty Griffin	Cubs	2B - AA
10	Robin Ventura	White Sox	3B

Year/ Selection Number	Player	Team	Position — Highest Minor League Reached
1989			
1	Ben McDonald	Orioles	P
2	Tyler Houston	Braves	C - AAA
3	Roger Salkeld	Mariners	P
4	Jeff Jackson	Phillies	OF - AA
5	Donald Harris	Rangers	OF
6	Paul Coleman	Cardinals	OF - AA
7	Frank Thomas	White Sox	1B
8	Earl Cunningham	Cubs	OF - A
9	Kyle Abbott	Angels	P
10	Charles Johnson	Expos	C
1990			
1	Chipper Jones	Braves	SS
2	Tony Clark	Tigers	1B - AAA
3	Mike Lieberthal	Phillies	C
4	Alex Fernandez	White Sox	P
5	Kurt Miller	Pirates	P
6	Marc Newfield	Mariners	1B-OF
7	Dan Wilson	Reds	C
8	Tim Costo	Indians	SS
9	Ron Walden	Dodgers	P - A
10	Carl Everett	Yankees	OF
1991			
1	Brien Taylor	Yankees	P - AA
2	Mike Kelly	Braves	OF
3	David McCarty	Twins	1B
4	Dmitri Young	Cardinals	3B - AA
5	Kenny Henderson	Brewers	P - DNP
6	John Burke	Astros	P - AAA
7	Joe Vitiello	Royals	1B - AAA
8	Joey Hamilton	Padres	P
9	Mark Smith	Orioles	OF
10	Tyler Green	Phillies	P
1992			
1	Phil Nevin	Astros	3B - AAA
2	Paul Shuey	Indians	P
3	B.J. Wallace	Expos	P - AAA
4	Jeffrey Hammonds	Orioles	OF
5	Chad Mottola	Reds	OF - AA
6	Derek Jeter	Yankees	SS - AAA
7	Calvin Murray	Giants	OF - AA
8	Pete Janicki	Angels	P - A
9	Preston Wilson	Mets	3B - A
10	Michael Tucker	Royals	SS - AAA
1993			
1	Alex Rodriguez	Mariners	SS
2	Darren Dreifort	Dodgers	P
3	Brian Anderson	Angels	P
4	Wayne Gomes	Phillies	P - A
5	Jeff Granger	Royals	P
6	Steve Soderstrom	Giants	P - A
7	Trot Nixon	Red Sox	OF - A
8	Kirk Presley	Mets	P
9	Matt Brunson	Tigers	SS - A
10	Brooks Kieschnick	Cubs	1B-OF - AA
1994			
1	Paul Wilson	Mets	P - A
2	Ben Grieve	A's	OF - A
3	Dustin Hermanson	Padres	P - AAA
4	Antone Williamson	Brewers	3B - AA
5	Josh Booty	Marlins	SS - A
6	McKay Christensen	Angels	OF - DNP
7	Doug Million	Rockies	P - A
8	Todd Walker	Twins	2B - A
9	C.J. Nitkowski	Reds	P - AA
10	Jaret Wright	Indians	P - Rookie

## CHAPTER 29

Baseball Reporting

Jack Lang

If baseball really was invented by Abner Doubleday at Cooperstown, N.Y., in 1839, we have only the findings of the Mills Commission to support the theory. That commission, formed in 1905, relied heavily on the rambling recollections of an old mining engineer named Abner Graves to reach the conclusion that Doubleday indeed "devised the first scheme for playing baseball." Graves's testimonies were later found to be chock full of inaccuracies.

There can be no dispute, however, as to when the art of writing about baseball began. In the mid-1850s William Trotter Porter gave a decided lift to the game with extensive coverage in his publication *Spirit of the Times.* Until Porter's reports began appearing regularly, baseball in America was ignored in most publications.

John Rickards Betts of Tulane University, in his American Quarterly paper "Sporting Journalism in Nineteenth-Century America," credits Porter with being the greatest "antebellum sports editor" in America. On December 10, 1831, he published the first copy of *Spirit of the Times.* It was, for a time, the country's leading sports journal. But while it reported on racing, prize fighting, and even cricket, it did not devote space to baseball until the 1850s.

When he did start reporting on baseball, Porter is credited with having given it the title of "the national game" and also with having printed the first box scores (although this claim is questionable) and "dope" stories.

Shortly thereafter, Frank Queen and Harrison Trent founded the *New York Clipper,* which devoted even more space to baseball. One reason was the addition to the staff of Henry Chadwick, who had begun his career as a journalist in 1844 by contributing to the *Long Island Star.* Chadwick, who had played baseball briefly in his youth, was a devotee of the game and wrote of it voluminously.

Alfred H. Spink, in his book *The National Game,* published in 1910, credits William Cauldwell, editor of the *New York Mercury,* as being the first man to write about baseball for a daily newspaper. Spink's authority for this assertion is a gentleman named William M. Rankin, one of the nation's leading reporters on sports in the late 1880s. Rankin, who was the official scorer for the Mutual Club, also wrote extensively for such New York papers as the *Times, Tribune, World, Mail, and Express.* He was considered one of the game's leading authorities. According to Rankin, Cauldwell was writing about baseball by 1853. But Cauldwell found the work of editing his newspaper and writing about baseball too exhausting, and he soon hired Chadwick to write on baseball for the *Mercury.* It was not long before Henry Chadwick became the leading baseball authority in America.

If weekly and daily publications were slow to catch on to the popularity of baseball, they caught up in the late 1880s. Magazines like *The Police Gazette* and *Sporting Life* devoted considerable space to the game. Soon editors of daily newspapers recognized the interest in baseball. James Gordon Bennett, one of the world's most respected newspapermen, who was editor of the *New York Tribune,* was one of the first to increase coverage of the game.

In time every newspaper in America devoted a full page to sports . . . focusing on baseball. Charles Dana of the *New York Sun* and Joseph Pulitzer of the *New York World* are recognized as pioneers in the creation of entire sports departments. By the 1890s, most newspapers in America had created a sports staff. It was in the final decade of the nineteenth century that sports writing began to develop as a full-time occupation on the nation's newspapers.

At the time of his death in 1908, Chadwick was clearly established as the nation's leading baseball authority. Chadwick, who even in his youth had been honored with the nickname "Father Chadwick" for his role in the development of baseball, was such a busy writer that the history of his various affiliations is in conflict. He is credited in some publications as having worked for the *Brooklyn Eagle* in 1856 and the *New York Clipper* in 1857. In others, Chadwick is reported to have written for the *Mercury* before any of the others, or for both at the same time.

Whatever his affiliations, Chadwick was the most prolific of the early-day baseball writers, and eventually he abandoned daily reporting of the game to concentrate on weekly roundups and books about the game.

Chadwick originated what is known today as *The Baseball Guide,* published by *The Sporting News.* He wrote and edited the first baseball guide in 1860, the *Beadle's Dime Base Ball Player.* Later he edited the *DeWitt's Guide* from 1869 to 1880 and, finally, *Spalding's Baseball Guide* from 1881 until his death.

Chadwick's involvement in the game was more than just writing of it. He was instrumental in changing several rules, is credited with having perfected the box score, and was most concerned about drinking, gambling, and rowdyism at ballparks. He led campaigns to clean up the game. Baseball officials of the day heeded his advice.

As early as 1868, Chadwick wrote the first hardcover book in America devoted strictly to baseball. Appropriately, it was titled: *The Game of Base Ball.*

Chadwick's writings on the game led to honors that would be unheard of in the modern era. In 1894, the National League elected Henry an honorary member and two years later voted him a lifetime pension of $600 a year. If a major league today awarded a baseball writer a pension, it would result in an investigation.

Honors continued for Chadwick thirty years after his death. In 1938, one year before the Hall of Fame opened, Chadwick was elected to the Cooperstown shrine as one of the great contributors to the game along with Alexander Cartwright. It was the same year that Grover Cleveland Alexander was elected. Although baseball writers are now honored with the J.G. Taylor Spink Award and scrolls in their honor are mounted in the Hall of Fame Library, Chadwick is the only former baseball writer with a bronze plaque in the main hall, alongside those of Babe Ruth, Ty Cobb, Joe DiMaggio, Cy Young, Mickey Mantle, Ted Williams, and others.

Another early-day baseball writer who earned great respect from the leaders of the game was Timothy H. Murnane, known as the Silver King. When Murnane died in 1917, he was so highly regarded that the American League paid for and erected a huge marble tombstone over his grave in Old Calvary Cemetery in Roslindale, Massachusetts.

The tombstone cites Murnane as a "pioneer of baseball . . . champion of its integrity . . . gifted and fearless writer."

Murnane was a baseball player who turned to writing after his playing days were over. He founded the *Boston Referee* in 1885, and his writings attracted the editors of the *Boston Globe,* who in 1888 hired him as their baseball writer, a job he held until his death. In his thirty years as baseball editor of the *Globe,* he was one of the most influential writers in the country and even found time to serve as president of the New England League for twenty-four years.

Upon his death, it was learned that Murnane left only a small estate to his widow. Immediately, a benefit all-star game was scheduled between great players of the American League and the Boston Red Sox with all proceeds to go to Murnane's widow.

On September 17, 1917, 17,119 Boston fans attended the game which included a pregame show featuring Ziegfeld Follies stars Will Rogers and Fanny Brice. The all-star team included such names as Grover Cleveland Alexander, Walter Johnson, Johnny Evers, Wally Schang, Shoeless Joe Jackson, Buck Weaver, Stuffy McInnis, Eddie Collins, Ty Cobb, and Tris Speaker. Heavyweight boxing champion John L. Sullivan coached first base and Babe Ruth pitched the first six innings for Boston.

All appeared without pay. That was evidence of the esteem in which Murnane was held.

Until the creation of full-time sports staffs in the late 1890s, writing about baseball was, in many cities, a hit-and-miss affair. In many areas, the reports of games were turned in by club secretaries or part-time correspondents. It was often less-than-objective reporting.

With the advent of full-time sports reporters and sports editors in the early 1890s, especially in New York, other major cities suddenly followed suit. This resulted in localized styles of writing and language familiar to the areas. John Rickards Betts describes it in his *American Quarterly* article on nineteenth-century journalism: "The most important developments in sporting journalism outside New York were taking place on the Chicago newspapers. Charles Seymour of the *Herald,* Finley Peter Dunne of the *News* and a reporter for the *Times* were creators of a novel style among baseball writers, a style based on picturesque jargon, lively humor and grotesque exaggeration."

Hugh Fullerton, who was one of the great turn-of-the-century baseball writers in Chicago, noted that "the style of reporting baseball changed all over the country."

In New York and Boston the style of baseball writing emphasized expert knowledge of the game. In Chicago and other western cities, the style involved more humor and cynicism. Often the final score of the game was secondary. Reporters described games with a great flourish and seemed intent on capturing readers' interest with their individual writing styles. Here is the way one *Chicago Times* writer reported a Chicago Cubs game on September 26, 1888:

"The ninth inning of yesterday's ball game was a marvel of beauty. To describe it one needs a big stretch of canvas, a white-wash brush, a pan of green paint, and an artist's hand. Words are hardly expressive enough . . . Mr. Schoeneck is a large secretion of fat around considerable bone and muscle, and he knocked the ball out of the diamond and puffed down to first base . . . Immediately after which Mr. Buckley bunted the ball and went to first, his fatness moving to second.

"The inning had not been particularly gorgeous up to this moment, but with the hitting of a fly by Mr. Hines it took on a resplendent and glorious aspect, for Mr. Van Altren [Van Haltren] got under the fly, gauged it with his blue eye, and muffed it beautifully. When the ball reached Capt. Anson it had lost much of its virulence and was bounding gently long, smiling the while. But if it had not been for a chunk of lava fresh from the earth it could not have had more fun with Capt. Anson, for it rollicked out of his hands and into them again and all over his person, blithely tapped him in the face, and danced away. Indeed, it was a beautiful error, that one of Anson's—a regular sunset error flushed and radiant with shadings of purple and a mellow border.

"Mr. Van Altren picked it up and looked about irresolutely. He was debating whether he should sacrifice skill to art, and being a young man of no high culture in this respect, he esteemed art as naught, but hurled the ball to the plate to catch Mr. Hines. But art was triumphant for all, for Mr. Van Altren's irresolution had been fatal. The ball came to the plate a second after Mr. Hines crossed safe, and Mr. Raphael, Mr. M. Angelo, and Mr. Turner will have to take a seat near the door."

A reporter describing a game in that manner today would not be assigned to cover the next day's game. But it was in that style that games were recorded around the turn of the century. A baseball writer, covering a game at three o'clock in the afternoon, had until three o'clock in the morning to write his story. This enabled many to write what some journalists later referred to as "fabulous narratives." Writers were bent on influencing the readers with their imaginative use of the language in long, descriptive phrases. Space in newspapers was plentiful, and baseball writers frequently used two and three columns to describe a single game. It gave writers an opportunity to develop their own style in an effort to capture the imagination of the readers.

Nowhere was this more evident than in Chicago, where such writers as Sy Sanborn, Ring Lardner, Hugh Fullerton, and Charles Dryden were winning over readers with their often humorous accounts of baseball games. Lardner came out of South Bend, Indiana, and covered the Chicago Cubs for the *Inter-Ocean,* the *Examiner* and later the *Tribune.* Eventually he abandoned daily baseball writing and made his mark as an author of short stories, many with a baseball theme. *You Know Me Al* and "Alibi Ike" are two of his baseball classics.

Fullerton was considered the most remarkable forecaster of his day, and his predictions on the outcome of games were sought in every major league city. When he died at age seventy-two in 1946, he was hailed in his obituaries as "the game's original dopester." But for all the expertise and humor that he brought to his readers, Fullerton is best remembered in journalistic circles as the writer most responsible for exposing the Chicago White Sox for throwing the 1919 World Series.

Prior to the 1919 Series, the fearless forecaster had predicted an easy victory for the Sox against Cincinnati. But early in the Series Fullerton was convinced that the Sox were not giving it their best effort. In his summary of the Series after Chicago lost, Fullerton suggested as much. But he was not about to let go of it there. Fullerton went to New York, where he followed up leads that tied some of the White Sox to gamblers. The *New York Evening World* published a toned-down version of his theory, and Fullerton was criticized by members of his own craft. But his persistence continued until he convinced American League president Ban Johnson to investigate the matter. Using much of the information Fullerton supplied, Johnson brought the investigation to a head late in the 1920 season. The result was a trial in which eight players were found innocent. But the same eight were later banned from organized baseball for life by Judge Kenesaw Mountain Landis, the newly appointed commissioner of baseball. Fullerton's investigative reporting was responsible for the findings of the commissioner.

Fullerton was a baseball purist, and his Ten Commandments of Sports were widely published. They read:

1. *Thou shalt not quit.*
2. *Thou shalt not alibi.*
3. *Thou shalt not gloat over winning.*
4. *Thou shalt not sulk over losing.*
5. *Thou shalt not take unfair advantage.*
6. *Thou shalt not ask odds thou art not willing to give.*
7. *Thou shalt always be willing to give the benefit of doubt.*
8. *Thou shalt not underestimate an opponent or overestimate thyself.*
9. *Remember that the game is the thing and he who thinks otherwise is no true sportsman.*
10. *Honor the game thou playest; he who plays the game straight and hard wins even when he loses.*

It was common at the turn of the century for baseball writers to begin their stories with a few lines of verse. Grantland Rice, who came out of Nashville, where he had been sports editor of the *Tennessean,* to join the staff of the *Cleveland Plain Dealer,* was perhaps the most widely known writer in this style. His poetic jingles were read throughout the American League and many attempted to copy his style.

Rice did not remain long in Cleveland. He longed for the South and returned there. But then he returned North to New York, where his syndicated column appeared throughout the country. Rice actually was better known for his football writing than he was for his baseball work.

Besides Rice, another leading baseball writer of the early twentieth century who frequently began his stories with a few lines of verse was Franklin Pierce Adams, who wrote under the byline of "F.P.A." He wrote what is known as "Baseball's Sad Lexicon" during a New York Giants-Chicago Cubs series in 1908. Quoted to this day, it read in part:

Ruthlessly pricking our gonfalon bubble,
Making a Giant hit into a double,
Words that are weighty with nothing but trouble,
Tinker to Evers to Chance.

That verse, as much as their actual records on the field, is credited with leading to the induction of the Chicago Cubs' infield trio into the Hall of Fame.

Charles Dryden, born in 1857, moved about as much as any baseball writer in the late 1890s and into the 1900s. He covered the California League for the *San Francisco Examiner* and then moved to the *New York American* and on again to Philadelphia with the *North American.* But in 1905 he was offered what was then considered the highest salary paid a baseball writer and moved to the *Chicago Examiner.* The salary was reported to be $100 weekly.

It was in Chicago that Dryden gained fame with his nicknames for the baseball people he wrote about. He called Charles Comiskey, the White Sox owner, "the Old Roman". He termed the light-hitting White Sox the "Hitless Wonders." Chicago Cubs' manager Frank Chance was dubbed "the Peerless Leader." It was also Dryden who coined the phrase about the hapless Washington Senators: "Washington . . . first in war, first in peace and last in the American League."

Dryden was a charter member of the Baseball Writers Association of America (BBWAA), which was formed officially in 1908. It was an association born of necessity when baseball writing in the early years of the twentieth century was attracting some of the nation's outstanding young writers and baseball itself was dominating the sports pages. Only the baseball owners failed to recognize the importance of this feisty band of scribes. They were treated—or mistreated—as a necessary evil.

At the 1908 playoff game between the Chicago Cubs and the New York Giants at New York's Polo Grounds, Hugh Fullerton arrived to find actor Louis Mann in his seat. This was not uncommon. Giants manager John McGraw loved to hobnob with Broadway actors and often told them to sit in the press box. When Fullerton asked Mann to vacate the seat, Mann refused. No Giants official would order him to move. At first Fullerton attempted to write his story sitting on Mann's lap, but eventually he sat on a box in the aisle next to him and covered the entire game from that seat.

Baseball writers continued to suffer mistreatment during the Chicago Cubs-Detroit Tigers World Series that followed. The writers covering the Series were outraged at the treatment accorded them. In Chicago, out-of-town writers were placed in the back row of the grandstand. In

Detroit, the writers were compelled to climb a ladder to the roof of the first base pavilion, where they were forced to write in the rain and snow that hampered the Series. Finally, unwilling to endure these conditions another year, the writers decided to organize. At the request of Jack Ryder of Cincinnati and Henry Edwards of Cleveland, Joseph S. Jackson, sports editor of the *Detroit Free Press,* arranged a meeting room in the Hotel Ponchartrain on the morning of the final game. That was October 14, 1908. Present at that first meeting, the founding fathers of the Baseball Writers Association of America, were: Tim Murnane and Paul Shannon, Boston; Charles Hughes, Hugh Keough, Malcolm McLean, Hugh Fullerton, Bill Phelon, and Sy Sanborn, Chicago; Ed Bang and Henry Edwards, Cleveland; Jack Ryder and Charles Zuber, Cincinnati; J.W. McConaughy and Sid Mercer, New York; William Weart, Philadelphia; George Moreland, Pittsburgh; Joseph Jackson and Joseph Smith, Detroit; James Crusinberry, Hal Lanigan, W.G. Murphy, and J.B. Sheridan, St. Louis; and Ed Grillo, Washington.

Joseph Jackson was appointed temporary chairman and Sy Sanborn, secretary. Tim Murnane was appointed treasurer, and he passed the hat to collect $1 dues from each of the founding fathers.

A more formal meeting was held in New York in December 1908 at the annual winter meetings of the two leagues. Fullerton, Edwards, and Weart, who had been appointed in Detroit to draw up a constitution, listed four items as the main objective of the BBWAA. They were:

1. *To encourage a square deal in baseball.*
2. *To simplify the rules in scoring baseball games and promote uniformity in scoring.*
3. *To secure better facilities for reporting baseball games and better regulation of the scorers' boxes during both championship seasons and World Series at the parks of the American and National League Clubs, hereinafter to be designated the major leagues.*
4. *To bring together into a closer bond of friendship the writers of baseball throughout the United States and Canada.*

The organization was enthusiastically endorsed from the start by both leagues. Promise of full support was received by league presidents, who appointed the local representatives of chapters in each city to serve as custodians of the league press boxes.

Immediately conditions improved throughout baseball. No longer did writers have the problem of outsiders occupying seats in the press box. Interlopers were immediately escorted out by park security men upon orders of the local BBWAA representative. The writers had the backing of the league to police their own work area.

By 1910-11, the baseball writing fraternity was accepting into its ranks some of the bright young writers of that era—men who would go on to greater heights in the field of literature. Covering the Giants in New York that year were men like Grantland Rice, Damon Runyon, Heywood Broun, and Fred Lieb. Rice later became recognized as the dean of America's sportswriters; Runyon became the chronicler of Broadway night life and the characters who inhabited the Great White Way, while

Broun went on to the editorial side of newspapers and founded the Newspaper Guild of America. Lieb was a prolific writer who was one of baseball's leading biographers.

Elsewhere in the country, other fine young writers were honing their skills covering baseball. Some of the greats who were regular beat writers in those days were Red Smith, Frank Graham, John Kieran, J. Roy Stockton, Warren Brown, John Carmichael, Shirley Povich, John Drebinger, and Tom Meany.

There was a coterie of writers in that era whose names were synonymous with baseball for the simple reason that they covered baseball from the first day of spring training until the final out of the World Series. A writer assigned to the Tigers or Cardinals or Pirates or any other club stayed with that team the entire season, traveled to the cities in each league, and made every road trip. Writers associated with one club were almost as well known as the players they wrote about.

Baseball coverage did not vary until after World War II. It was standard practice up to then for the writers on morning newspapers to wait until the end of the game and write on who won or lost, and how. The final score might not appear until well down into the story, but the reporter was writing up the details of the game. Writers for afternoon papers also often sat in the press box after the game and wrote their versions, with considerable editorial opinion and second-guessing. Talking to ballplayers after the game was not considered a necessity. Occasionally, but not always, writers did visit the clubhouses after games for some conversation and verification with ballplayers.

The style of writing changed after World War II. The need to know was of primary importance, and reporters for afternoon papers made it a habit to get down to the clubhouse after a game for what was then known as "the second-day angle." The afternoon papers of the next day had to offer the readers something they had not learned in their morning paper.

But starting in 1946 and in the years that followed, a change in the style of covering a baseball game was evident—especially in New York. No longer did the writers on afternoon papers have the ballplayers to themselves after a game. Dick Young was an enterprising young baseball writer for the *New York Daily News,* a morning newspaper. Because of the multiple editions of his newspaper, he had the time to visit the clubhouse and "pick up quotes" or find out why certain plays had occurred.

Young changed the style of baseball reporting with his hustle, and ever since he arrived, the work of the morning newspaper reporter has not been the same. No beat reporter nowadays would dare turn in a story unless it had clubhouse quotes. Editors demand it.

Along with the enterprise of Dick Young came radio and the television age. Fans were now able to listen to and watch games at home. What they wanted in their papers the next day was inside stuff from the players and managers. For reporters working night games with deadlines approaching, the job of writing baseball was no longer the sinecure it had been in the first four decades of the century.

Picture the baseball writer of the 1930s. All games started around 3 PM. There was no need for a pregame story, since most newspapers did not go to press until around midnight. A baseball writer in that era was finished working around 6 or 7 PM and was free again until game time the next day.

The baseball beat writer's job was always considered the glamour assignment on any sports staff. Baseball writers were envied for what was considered an easy lifestyle: spring training in some warm climate around the middle of February and then a ballgame every afternoon for six months followed by the World Series. From mid-October until mid-February, the baseball writer had a relative vacation, covering only signings, trades, and trivial matters.

Today's baseball writer, what with virtually every game being played at night and early editions at all papers, finds himself working around the clock. The average writer covering baseball today, especially for a morning newspaper, will find himself writing three or four stories in a single day. He also works year-round, covering labor-management issues.

Night games and travel have also made it difficult for the modern-day writer. Before plane travel, all clubs moved from city to city by train, and the writers traveled with them. Trains left around midnight and arrived early the next morning in the team's next city. At least there was a night of rest and time to fraternize with the ballplayers. Today, teams fly out right after a game, and writers find it impossible to catch the team plane. They most often travel alone.

The result is that fewer writers remain on the baseball beat for any length of time. The travel, the long hours, and the night games have made it an arduous task. Before the age of television, it was quite common for a writer to remain on the beat for twenty to thirty years. Today, a writer feels "burned out" after just a few years.

Despite the changes in baseball writing, the BBWAA retains the prestige it earned shortly after being founded in 1908. Much of this is due to the organization's annual awards and its responsibility for voting on the Hall of Fame.

The major awards the BBWAA votes on each year are the Most Valuable Player, the Cy Young Award, the Rookie of the Year, the Manager of the Year, and the Hall of Fame, since the Cooperstown shrine's creation in 1936. (For a detailed discussion and the annual balloting for these awards, see Bill Deane's essay in this volume.)

Of all the responsibilities of the Baseball Writers Association, none is taken more seriously than voting for the Hall of Fame. The idea for a baseball Hall of Fame was first discussed in 1935 to celebrate the hundredth anniversary of baseball in 1939. The National Baseball Centennial Commission was formed. Ford Frick, then the National League president, was the moving force behind the creation of the Hall of Fame and the decision to name Cooperstown as the site for the museum. That same year,

the Baseball Writers Association was asked by the Commission to vote for players to be elected to the Hall of Fame and inducted officially when the Hall opened in 1939.

The BBWAA has been charged with that responsibility ever since. Another group, known as the Veterans Committee, also votes on players, former executives, managers, and umpires.

Baseball, especially in recent years, has been the most written-about sport in America. No longer is it a sport covered solely by the beat writers for newspapers. It is a game that captures the imagination of authors, a fact born out by the Hall of Fame Library. By the middle of 1990, the library contained approximately 25,000 books about baseball.

By the end of 1990 the library was unable to handle the volume of books and magazine and newspaper articles that were being written about the game. Under the directorship of Hall of Fame President Edward Stack, an expansion to the library was undertaken. The completely refurbished library opened late in 1993 and included over 30,000 books. In addition, the written words of the game on file at the library include copies of the *New York Clipper* from the 1850s, *Sporting Life,* and *The Sporting News.*

So important have the contributions of the Baseball Writers Association of America been to the Hall of Fame that in 1962, the Hall decided to honor the outstanding writers with an award and a place of honor in the library. The award was named in honor of J. G. Taylor Spink, former publisher of *The Sporting News.* Since 1962, over 40 writers have had their names enshrined in the writers' wing of the Hall, among them Damon Runyon, Ring Lardner, Grantland Rice, and Dick Young.

Leonard Koppett, the 1993 honoree, noted in his Cooperstown acceptance speech: "The daily baseball writer has played an indispensable role in the creation, growth and maintenance of baseball's popularity. Its commercial success, as well as its place in American culture, have been based on daily newspaper accounts, from Henry B. Chadwick down through Red Smith.

"Even today, when radio and television have surpassed newspapers in impact, it is the daily baseball coverage from which all other media get their information about what they decide to emphasize. And even the call-in talk shows, which set so much of the news agenda, exist only because callers form opinions from what they read about that they cannot see."

It is a sport that has inspired political columnists like George Will and Pulitzer Prize-winning authors such as James Michener and David Halberstam to publish books about the game. No sport in America is covered more extensively or comprehensively than baseball. It all begins with the game and the beat writers who cover it.

## CHAPTER 30

Phantom Ballplayers

Clifford S. Kachline

arbage in, garbage out is an expression that gained currency with the advent of the computer age. The logic behind the catch phrase, however, prevailed long before the electronic marvels came into being. Baseball, in fact, has had its own version of the maxim almost since the game's earliest days, largely as a consequence of recordkeepers who sometimes unwittingly entered erroneous data into the record books.

Numerous examples of the *garbage in, garbage out* principle have been discovered in baseball's statistical archives through the years. But statistics aren't the only area where the phenomenon has shown up. Another involves what researchers of the sport refer to as "phantoms"—players credited with having performed in the major leagues but who in reality never did appear in a big league game.

Phantoms are hardly a recent phenomenon. They have existed almost as long as boxscores have been published. Some were the product of misunderstandings by—or misinformation given to—official scorers or the parties who compiled the boxscores. A few of these crept into the leagues' official records. Others were created by mistakes on the part of telegraph operators or by typographical errors and appeared only in newspaper boxscores.

Little if any attention was paid to the situation until the 1950s. The original edition of *The Official Encyclopedia of Baseball,* published by A. S. Barnes and Co. in 1951, provided fans for the first time with a supposedly complete alphabetical tabulation of every man who ever played in the majors, together with his basic yearly big league stats. The publication stimulated the interest of the sport's researchers. When editors Hy Turkin and S. C. Thompson deleted the names of some players—most of whom were previously shown as having a one-game career—from subsequent revised editions, the matter of phantoms started to become a source of fascination.

Who really were the "impostors" that were listed in earlier editions? What had prompted the editors to include them in the first place? And what evidence had been found to prove conclusively that they never played in the big leagues?

The introduction of *The Baseball Encyclopedia* by the Macmillan Publishing Company in 1969 focused additional attention on the subject. In compiling data for that publication, David Neft and his crew of Information Concepts, Inc. researchers continued the process of purging phantoms from the records. Since then, further investigation by Neft, Pete Palmer, Bill Haber, Al Kermisch, and others has led to the expunging of several more players.

In many instances confirming the status of a phantom was a complicated chore. The task sometimes was made more difficult because the player's name was included in the official league statistics. In other cases, especially those involving nineteenth-century performers, the fact that official league records no longer exist compounded the problem because it made it impossible to determine who was credited by the official scorer and/or league statistician with appearing in the game or games in question. (The American League's official game-by-game player sheets of 1901–1904 reportedly were destroyed by fire decades ago, while the official National League data also vanished for the pre-1902 period except for the 1899 season.)

An example of a phantom who appears in the league records is Albert W. Olsen. For thirty-five years he was carried in the *Encyclopedias* and shown as participating in one game—as a pinch hitter—for the Boston Red Sox in 1943. Olsen did train with the Red Sox that spring, but he was shipped to San Diego of the Pacific Coast League before opening day and spent the entire season in the minors. In addition, it was his exploits as a lefthanded pitcher, not as a hitter, that originally attracted the Red Sox.

Nevertheless, American League records list Olsen as playing for Boston in a game in Chicago on May 16, 1943. Newspaper boxscores credited him with drawing a walk while batting for pitcher Dick Newsome and subsequently stealing a base. However, research has confirmed that the Red Sox pinch-hitter on that occasion definitely was not Olsen. Instead, it may have been outfielder Leon Culberson, who had just been called up from Louisville of the American Association, or possibly another Boston rookie outfielder, Johnny Lazor.

And why is there still uncertainty as to who the pinch-hitter really was? How could this mistake have occurred? First off, the exchange of roster data among major league teams during that period was quite limited. Consequently scorecards often contained the same player names and uniform numbers for the visiting team, especially early in the season, as the team listed in spring training. For example, the scorecard for a Red Sox–Senators game in Washington approximately a week before the incident in question showed Olsen on Boston's roster with uniform number 14, even though he was pitching for San Diego. Second, it's unlikely there were phone lines from the pressbox to the dugouts in those days, and in the absence of being able to call down to check on the identity of a player, the media and official scorers relied on outdated roster information.

Several years ago researchers felt they had cleared up the Olsen mystery upon discovering that one Boston newspaper identified the pinch-hitter as "Culbeson." This seemed to settle the matter. After all, Culberson had joined the team that day and was installed as the Red Sox' leadoff batter in the second half of the afternoon doubleheader, collecting a single and triple in five at-bats. But the mystery was revived when Ed Walton, a Red Sox historian, discussed the situation with Culberson at a Red Sox Old Timers affair in 1986. According to Walton, Culberson contended he did not pinch-hit in the twin-bill opener, but rather made his debut in the second game. He added that manager Joe Cronin said he wanted the young newcomer to sit beside him (Cronin) through the first game to get a feel of the big leagues. However, the records reveal Cronin played third base during the entire first game. All of which raises the questions: Was Culberson's memory playing tricks on him and was he indeed the pinch-hitter listed as Olsen? Or was it Lazor, who is shown as wearing uniform number 14 later in the year but who was batting a mere .136 (3 for 22) at the time? Because the passage of time makes memories hazy and also because the incident was of no particular significance, the mystery may never be solved.

A manager's pique led to a phantom known as J. A. Costello getting into the early Encyclopedias. Curiously, the incident also took place in Chicago and likewise involved a player's big league debut. It occurred in the morning half of a holiday bill between Cleveland and the White Sox on July 4, 1912. Late in the contest, Indians' Manager Harry Davis, still burning over an umpire's decision, sent the newcomer into the game to replace center fielder Joe Birmingham and instructed him to announce himself to umpire Gene Hart as "Costello."

In reality, the player was Kenneth Nash, who had only recently joined Cleveland from Boston University law school. He subsequently appeared in ten additional games with Cleveland that season under his correct surname, mostly as a shortstop, and then played with the St. Louis Cardinals for part of 1914. Nash later became a prominent state representative, state senator, and judge in his home state of Massachusetts.

The 1903 official National League records contain a phantom who long baffled researchers. Among the Pittsburgh player sheets is one headed "George Gray" with entries for two games as an outfielder—on May 28 and May 31. Four years earlier the Pirates had a pitcher named George "Chummy" Gray, and it's possible the scorer or league statistician remembered him while filling in the player's first name. When the first Official Encyclopedia appeared in 1951, the player was identified as William (rather than George) Gray, a native of Pittsburgh.

It turns out that the two George (or William) Gray entries properly belonged to not one, but two different players. The Pirates' left fielder in the May 28 game really was Romer Carl "Reddy" Grey, younger brother of novelist Zane Grey. He had been obtained on loan from the Worcester club of the Eastern League to fill in that afternoon in the final game of a series in Boston.

On the other hand, while boxscores in Cincinnati newspapers listed the Pittsburgh left fielder for the May 31 game in Cincinnati as "Gray," the player actually was Ernest Diehl, a Cincinnati sandlotter who had been re-

cruited by the injury-riddled Pirates. The game represented Diehl's first appearance in the major leagues and his only game that season, but he played 12 more games with Pittsburgh the following year. It should be noted that ever since the original Turkin/Thompson tome, the Encyclopedias have credited Diehl with playing one game with Pittsburgh in 1903, but until recent years they also carried William Gray with two games.

A majority of baseball's phantoms were the product of typographical errors—instances where a linotypist or a typesetter mistakenly included one or more incorrect letters in a name, or where a printer inserted a correction line in the wrong place. In compiling data for the Encyclopedias, the authors/researchers relied not only on the so-called official league records but also combed boxscores published in The Sporting News, Sporting Life, The New York Clipper, and various local newspapers. In the process they occasionally came upon what appeared to be a previously unlisted "new" player who, in the final analysis, proved to be someone else. Even today, misspellings of this type in newspapers can cause great befuddlement.

A classic illustration of a phantom who was created by a typographical error is the player carried in the early Encyclopedias as John P. Morgan. He was listed as appearing in one game as a third baseman with the Philadelphia Athletics in 1916. A study of A's boxscores for the season disclosed the source of the mix-up: It was The Sporting News's boxscore of the August 3 game at Cleveland. (Sporting Life had dropped boxscores by this time.) The Philadelphia half of TSN's box has "Morgan, 2b," while on the same line in Cleveland's half is "Gandil, 1b."

Careful examination reveals the Morgan/Gandil type slug was a correction line that the printer inserted in the wrong place. It was intended for the Washington-at-Cleveland boxscore of the previous day (August 2) in which the Senators' second baseman, Harry Morgan, appeared on the same line as Chick Gandil and contained the identical AB-H-PO-A-E figures given for each player in the misaligned August 2 line.

This explanation may well leave you, the reader, with several questions, to wit: (1) Who did play third for the A's that day, and was he properly credited in the official records? (2) Why did the Encyclopedia compilers show Morgan as a third baseman instead of a second baseman? (3) How did they come up with "John P." for the impostor's name?

The answers are: (1) Lee McElwee and, yes, he was credited with this game; (2) because veteran Nap Lajoie played the entire game at his usual second base position for the A's, the researcher who made this "discovery" apparently assumed it should have read "Morgan, 3b" rather than "2b"; (3) an infielder named John P. Morgan was active in the minor leagues that season, and the Encyclopedia editors probably figured the A's had given him a trial. Numerous other phantoms were similarly tagged with the first names of then-current minor leaguers.

Typos involving misspelled names led to a number of one-game phantoms. Two examples will serve to demonstrate the point. They are John H. Carlock (1912, Cleveland) and a player listed simply as Deniens (no first name given) with the 1914 Chicago Federals. Sporting Life had "Carlock, ph" for Cleveland in an August 24, 1912, game at Boston, but Cleveland newspapers and *The Sporting News* reported the pinch-hitter was Fred Carisch, a reserve catcher with the Indians. Official AL records also credit Carisch with that appearance. "Deniens, c" turned out to be Clem Clemens, a catcher in 13 games with the 1914 ChiFeds. One can readily visualize how handwritten names "Carisch" and "Clemens" could have been misinterpreted by a telegrapher or linotypist for "Carlock" and "Deniens."

The origins of some other phantoms are more mysterious. Take the case of Lou Proctor. The *Encyclopedias* credited him with one appearance with the 1912 St. Louis Browns. *The Sporting News* and *Sporting Life,* which may have obtained their boxscores from the same source, show "Proctor, ph" and "Procter, pi," respectively, in a May 13 game at Boston. However, a Boston newspaper referred to the pinch hitter as Albert "Pete" Compton, a catcher with the Browns that season (whose real first name was, of all things, Anna). While AL records contain no reference to Proctor, they unfortunately also fail to include the May 13 appearance among Compton's 100 games. Rumor has it that Proctor was a prankish Western Union telegrapher who inserted his own name as a pinch hitter.

The presence on one team of two players with the same or an almost similar surname can lead to problems. The Washington Senators figured in three such mixups. Ironically, in one instance research by Kermisch has established that a player long labeled a phantom was, in fact, the real McCoy. The player in question was Charles C. Conway. In 1911 the Senators had both Conway, a rookie outfielder up from Youngstown (Ohio-Pennsylvania League), and William "Wid" Conroy, veteran infielder-outfielder, on their spring roster. When the season began, Conroy was idled by a stone bruise of the foot. Meantime, Conway appeared in two games during opening week, finishing up in right field on April 15 and starting at that position three days later, before the Senators returned him to Youngstown. Unfortunately, *Sporting Life* and *The Sporting News* each showed "Conroy" as the replacement in the first contest, but both had "Conway, rf" in their April 18 boxscore. Although the early *Encyclopedias* listed Conway and credited him with playing two games, the Macmillan compilers dropped his name 20 years ago on the erroneous premise that it was the veteran Conroy who participated in the April 15-18 games. Actually, Conroy didn't make the first of his 106 appearances that year until April 27.

An equally confusing puzzle centered on a 1914 Washington pitcher known as Barron or Barton. The early *Encyclopedias* carried both John J. Barron (later changed to Frank John Barron) and Carroll R. "Buck" Barton and credited each with pitching in one game for the '14 Senators. Actually only one pitcher was involved (and just one appearance), but which pitcher was it? Player contract data of the period reveal that Washington signed Carroll R. Barton in 1913 and retained rights to him while he pitched for Newport News (Virginia League) that season and again in 1914. During the same two years John J. Barron was pitching in the New England League. To complicate matters further, Washington signed Frank J. Barron in 1914 and shipped him to Newport News, where he became a teammate of Barton. While Barron posted a dismal 1-3 record, Barton was a 16-game winner.

So who was the 1914 Washington pitcher? The American League player records contain an entry headed "Barron" with data for an August 18 game, and boxscores of the contest likewise have "Barron" pitching one inning—the ninth—for the Senators against the visiting St. Louis Browns. The player's correct identity was confirmed when, shortly before his death in 1964, Frank Barron disclosed in an interview that while still studying for his law degree at West Virginia University he was signed by Clark Griffith in 1914, was assigned to Newport News and later pitched one inning for Washington before resuming his law studies.

The third Washington mix-up relates to a 1944 player identified in the *Encyclopedias* as Armando Viera Valdes. Official AL records contain a sheet for Armand (without the final "o") Valdes and note that he made a pinch-hitting appearance for the Senators in a May 3 game at Boston, but Richard Topp's research has disclosed that the pinch hitter was Rogelio "Roy" Valdes, a fellow Cuban but no relative of Armando.

With many major leaguers lost to military service in 1944, scout Joe Cambria lined up several Cubans to fill voids on the Senators' roster. Early in the year he signed an outfielder who was listed in the 1944 *American League Red Book* as Armand (without the "o") Valdes. Several weeks thereafter—too late for inclusion in the *Red Book*—Cambria signed Rogelio Valdes, a catcher. Both spent the early weeks of the season with Washington (each was later optioned to Williamsport of the Eastern League), and presumably the official scorer and/or league statistician picked up the incorrect first name from the Senator roster in the *AL Red Book*.

As in the case of Charles Conway, another player once regarded as a phantom has turned out to be a legitimate athlete after all. The Turkin-Thompson tomes listed him as William Krouse, a second baseman in one game with Cincinnati in 1901. Compilers of the Macmillan encyclopedia decided he was an imposter and dropped him, crediting his appearance to Bill Fox, the Reds' regular keystoner. However, research has revealed that the "Krouse, 2b" for Cincinnati in the July 27, 1901 game at Chicago was a recently-released minor leaguer whose correct name was Charles "Famous" Krause. Krause, who was on his way home to Detroit at the time, was given a chance with the Reds because Fox was sidelined with a split finger, but the "famous" newcomer performed so poorly that, not only was his name misspelled in the record, he was dumped after that one appearance.

Recent research has revealed that one player long listed as a phantom—Ivan Bigler, who was shown in one boxscore at first base with the 1917 St. Louis Browns when George Sisler actually played there that day—really did make an appearance with the Browns as a pinch runner on May 6 that season, and thus he's been restored to the all-time list of major leaguers.

The accompanying table lists the phantoms who have been eliminated from the all-time roster of major league players since the first Turkin/Thompson *Official Encyclopedia* of 1951. In the absence of an official clearinghouse for such data, no claim is made that the list is complete. Where it is available, brief information on the reason for the deletion of the player is given. Unfortunately, documentation by Turkin/Thompson and the ICI group that compiled the 1969 *Encyclopedia* disappeared years ago.

With today's sophisticated technology and record-keeping procedures, the margin for error in the identification of players—and in the official statistics—has been reduced considerably. Still, a slipup that occurred in the 1984 official American League averages (Alvaro Espinoza was omitted completely, even though he appeared in one game with Minnesota) emphasizes that mistakes still are possible.

A factor that poses the potential for error is the increasing frequency in recent years of teams having two or more players with an identical surname—and who often perform at the same position. In 1992 and 1993, for instance, the Los Angeles pitching staff included brothers Ramon and Pedro J. Martinez as well as Kip and Kevin Gross, who are not related. Meantime, San Diego unveiled pitcher Pedro A. Martinez in '93. Following that season, the Dodgers swapped Pedro J. Martinez to Montreal, where he succeeded another Martinez—Dennis—on the Expos' pitching staff when the latter signed with Cleveland as a free agent. But lo and behold, the situation was further muddied in 1994 when San Diego added a second pitching Martinez—Jose. This meant there were five Martinezes pitching in the majors at the same time, including Pedro J. with Montreal and Pedro A. with San Diego.

Besides the Dodgers, four other teams had a pair of pitchers of the same surname in 1993. They were: Houston—Todd and Doug Jones; Philadelphia— Mitch and Mike Williams; Cleveland—Matt and Curt Young; and San Diego—Gene and Greg W. Harris (not to be confused with Boston pitcher Greg A. Harris). In addition, Philadelphia also had Tommy Greene and Tyler Green on its staff at one point.

To add to the confusion, the Phillies swapped relief ace Mitch Williams to Houston after the '93 World Series, and he teamed on the Astros' mound corps briefly in 1994 with Brian Williams. The '94 season also found several other teams fielding players with the identical surname who played the same position. The most confusing situation involved Baltimore. At one time or another the Orioles had three outfielders named Smith—Lonnie, Mark, and Dwight—as well as relief ace Lee Smith. An early-season Atlanta-Cincinnati trade sent Roberto Kelly to the Braves, where he joined Mike Kelly, likewise an outfielder, while Deion Sanders went to the Reds and teamed in the outfield with Reggie Sanders. Other 1993-94 teammates sharing a common surname and position included Bernie and Gerald Williams, outfielders with the New York Yankees, and infielders Edgar and Tino Martinez of Seattle, who normally man third base and first base, respectively, but on occasion in the past performed at the opposite corner.

Couple these potential mixups with the typographical errors that still show up in newspaper boxscores, and you can see that the days of *"garbage in, garbage out"* are likely to continue.

Tabulation of Phantoms

Allen, Robert. 1919 Philadelphia AL, 9 games as OF. Pseudonym used by Alvah C. "Rowdy" Elliott, long-time minor leaguer.

Baldwin,——. 1907 Boston NL, 1 game as C. One of James C. Ball's 10 games.

Barton, Carroll R. 1914 Washington AL, 1 game as P. Same as game credited to Frank J. Barron.

Boylan,——. 1887 Philadelphia NL, 1 game as 2B. One of Charles J. Bastian's 60 games.

Carlock, John H. 1912 Cleveland AL, 1 game as PH. Typographical error; one of Frederick B. Carisch's 25 games.

Christman, H. B. 1888 Kansas City AA, 1 game as C. Documentation behind deletion no longer available.

Costello, J. A. 1912 Cleveland AL, 1 game as OF. One of 11 games played by Kenneth L. Nash, who used pseudonym in debut.

Davis, Thomas J. 1890 Cleveland NL, 1 game as OF. One of George Stacey Davis' 136 games.

Davis,——. 1903 Chicago NL, 1 game as OF. Documentation behind deletion no longer available.

Deniens,——. 1914 Chicago FL, 1 game as C. Typographical error; one of Clement L. Clemens' 13 games.

Drennan, K. John. 1904 Detroit AL, 1 game as 1B. Typographical error; one of William "Wild Bill" Donovan's 46 games.

Dresser, Edward. 1898 Brooklyn NL, 1 game as SS. Typographical error; one of Jack Dunn's 51 games.

Dugan, E. 1884 Kansas City UA, 3 games as OF. Same player as William H. Dugan, who played 9 games with Richmond AA the same year.

Gray, William. 1903 Pittsburgh NL, 2 games as OF. One game belongs to Romer C. Grey; other game belongs to Ernest G. Diehl.

Kerns, Daniel P. 1920 Philadelphia AL, 1 game as PH. Pseudonym used by Edward "Ted" Kearns, later a 1B with 1924–25 Chicago NL.

King, Frederick. 1901 Milwaukee AL, 1 game as C. Game belongs to John A. Butler, later with St. Louis and Brooklyn NL, who used pseudonym in debut.

Lane,——. 1901 Boston NL, 1 game as 3B. Typographical error; one of Bobby Lowe's 129 games.

Mares,——. 1894 Louisville NL, 1 games as OF. Documentation behind deletion no longer available.

McCauley, William. 1884 St. Louis AA, 1 game as C. Game belongs to James A. McCauley, who also played in 1885–1886.

Meddlebrook,——. 1884 Baltimore UA, 1 game as OF. Documentation behind deletion no longer available.

Merson,——. 1914 Brooklyn FL, 1 game as PH. Typographical error; one of George J. Anderson's 98 games.

Miller, Bert. 1897 Philadelphia NL, 3 games as 2B. Games belong to Frank A. Miller, formerly listed as Frederick Miller, who also played one game each with Washington NL and St. Louis NL in 1892.

Miller, Henry D. 1892 Chicago NL, 4 games as P. Games belong to Harry DeMiller, who was erroneously listed for 1 game as 3B with 1892 St. Louis NL.

Moore, Guy W. 1922 St. Louis NL, 1 game as OF. Documentation behind deletion no longer available.

Morgan, John P. 1916 Philadelphia AL, 1 game as 3B. Typographical error; one of Leland S. McElwee's 54 games.

Olsen, Albert W. 1943 Boston AL, 1 game as PH. Appearance apparently belongs to either Leon Culberson or Johnny Lazor.

Pratt, Thomas J. 1884 Baltimore AA, 1 game as OF. Documentation behind deletion no longer available.

Proctor, Lou. 1912 St. Louis AL, 1 game as PH. Game belongs to Anna S. "Pete" Compton, who played in 103 games that season.

Ritchie,——. 1910 St. Louis NL, 1 game as PH. Documentation behind deletion no longer available.

Schauer,——. 1890 Columbus AA, 1 game as 1B. Documentation behind deletion no longer available.

Seymour, Thomas. 1882 Pittsburgh AA, 1 game as P. Player's correct name was Jacob Semer.

Sheehan, Timothy. 1884 Washington UA, 1 game as OF. One of seven games belonging to player known as John A. Ryan, whose real name was Daniel Sheehan.

Smith, Charles H. "Pacer." 1877 Chicago/Cincinnati NL, 34 games as 2B-OF-C. Record belongs to Harry W. Smith, who also played 1 game with 1889 Louisville AA.

Smith, E. J. 1890 Buffalo PL, 1 game as 1B. One of John Irwin's 77 games.

Strands, Lewis. 1915 Chicago FL, 1 game as 2B. One of John J. Farrell's 70 games.

Thayer, Edward L. 1876 New York NL, 1 game as 2B. Player's correct name was George T. Fair.

Turbot,——. 1902 St. Louis NL, 1 game as OF. Documentation behind deletion no longer available.

Valdes, Armando V. 1944 Washington AL, 1 game as PH. Game belongs to a different player, Rogelio "Roy" Valdes.

Young, David. 1895 St. Louis NL, 1 game as 3B. Documentation behind deletion no longer available.

## CHAPTER 31

Casey at the Bat:
A Ballad of the Republic

Donald Hall

A century ago, on June 3, 1888, a twenty-five-year-old Harvard graduate, one-poem poet Ernest Lawrence Thayer, published "Casey at the Bat" in the pages of the San Francisco *Examiner*. I suppose it's the most popular poem in our country's history, if not exactly in its literature. Martin Gardner collected twenty-five sequels and parodies to print in his prodigy of scholarship, *The Annotated Casey at the Bat* (1967; rev. 1984). Will the next Casey bat clean-up in a St. Petersburg Over-Ninety Softball League? Perhaps, instead, we will hear of a transparent Casey on an Elysian diamond, shade swinging the shadow of a bat while wraith pitcher uncoils phantom ball—or spheroid, I should say.

The author of this people's poem was raised in Worcester, Massachusetts: gentleman and scholar, son of a mill owner. At Harvard he combined scholastic and social eminence, not always feasible on the banks of the Charles. A bright student of William James in philosophy, he graduated magna cum laude and delivered the Ivy Oration at graduation. On the other hand, he was editor of the *Lampoon*, for which traditional requirements are more social than literary; he belonged to Fly, a club of decent majesty. It is perhaps not coincidence, considering Victorian Boston's social prejudices, that Thayer's vainglorious mock hero carries an Irish name.

After his lofty graduation, Thayer drifted about in Europe. One of his Harvard acquaintances had been young William Randolph Hearst, business manager of the *Lampoon*, expelled from Harvard for various pranks while Thayer was pulling a magna. The disgraced young Hearst was rewarded by his father with editorship of the San Francisco *Examiner*, where he offered Thayer work as humorous columnist. By the time "Casey" appeared, Thayer had left California to return to Worcester, where he later managed a mill for his father and studied philosophy in his spare time.

He received five dollars for "Casey" and never claimed reward for its hundreds of further printings. By all accounts, "Casey's" author found his notoriety problematic. As with all famous nineteenth-century recitation pieces—"The Night Before Christmas," "Backward Turn Backward O Time in Thy Flight"—other poets claimed authorship, which annoyed Thayer first because he *did* write it, and second because he wasn't especially proud of it. There was the additional annoyance that old ballplayers continually asserted themselves the *original* Casey of the ballad: Thayer insisted that he made the poem up. The author of "Casey at the Bat" died in Santa Barbara in 1940 without ever doing another notable thing.

The poem's biography is richer than the poet's: At first "Casey" blushed unseen, wasting its sweetness on the desert air, until an accident blossomed it into eminence. In New York, DeWolf Hopper, a young star of comic opera, was acting in *Prince Methusalem*. On August 15, 1888, management invited players from the New York Giants and the Chicago White Stockings to attend a performance, and Hopper gave thought to finding a special bit that he might perform in the ballplayers' honor. His friend the novelist Archibald Clavering Gunter, recently returned from San Francisco, showed him a clipping from the San Francisco *Examiner*.

In Hopper's autobiography, he noted that when "[I] dropped my voice to B-flat, below low C, at the 'multitude was awed,' I remember seeing Buck Ewing's gallant mustachios give a single nervous twitch." Apparently Hopper's recitation left everyone in the house twitching with joy, and not only the Giants' hirsute catcher. For the rest of his life, Hopper repeated his performance by demand, no matter what part he sang or played, doomed to recite the poem (five minutes and forty seconds) an estimated ten thousand times before his death in 1935. As word spread from Broadway, the poem was reprinted in newspapers across the country, clipped out, memorized, and performed for the millions who would never hear De Wolf Hopper. Eventually the ballad was set to music, made into silent movies, and animated into cartoons; radio broadcast it, there were recordings by Hopper and others, and William Schuman wrote an opera called *The Mighty Casey* [premiere 1953].

When he first recited the poem, Hopper had no notion who had written it. Thayer had signed it "Phin.," abbreviating his college nickname of Phinny. Editors reprinted the poem anonymously or made up a name that sounded reasonable. When Hopper played Worcester early in the 1890s, he met the retiring Thayer—and poet recited poem for actor, as Hopper later reported, without a trace of elocutionary ability.

There are things in any society that *we always knew*. We do not remember when we first heard about Ground Hog Day or Thirty Days Hath September. Who remembers first hearing "Casey at the Bat"? Although I cannot remember my original exposure, I remember many splendid renditions from early in my life by the great ham actor of my childhood. My New Hampshire grandfather, Wesley Wells, was locally renowned for his powers of recitation—for speaking pieces, as we called it. He farmed bad soil in central New Hampshire: eight Holsteins, fifty sheep, a hundred chickens. In the tie-up for milking, morning and night, he leaned his bald head into warm Holstein ribs and recited poems with me for audience; he kept time as his hands pulled blue milk from long teats. When he got to the best part, he let go the nozzles, leaned back in his milking chair, spread his arms wide and opened his mouth in a great O, the taught gestures of elocution. He spellbound me as he set the line out on the warm cowy air: "But there is no joy in Mudville—mighty Casey has struck out!" The old barn (with its whitewash over rough boards, with its spider webs and straw, with its patched harness and homemade ladders and pitchforks shiny from decades of hand labor) paused in its shadowy hugeness and applauded again the ringing failure of the hero.

If he had not recited it for me lately, I reminded him. He recited a hundred other poems also, a few from Whittier and Longfellow, but mostly from newspapers by poets without names. I don't suppose he knew "Ernest Lawrence Thayer" or the history of the poem, but "Casey" itself was as solid as the rocks of his fields. The word that left Broadway and traveled was: *This poem is good to say out loud.* Earlier, the same news traveled about Edgar Allan Poe's "The Raven" and Bret Harte's "The Heathen Chinee." Public schooling once consisted largely of group memorization and recitation. The New England Primer taught theology and the alphabet together: "In Adam's fall / We sinnèd all" through "Zacchaeus he / Did climb a tree / His Lord to see." Less obviously the Primer instilled pleasures of rhyme and oral performance. When we decided fifty and sixty years ago that rote memorization was bad teaching, we threw out not only the multiplication table but also "Barbara Frietchie." Recitation of verse was turned over to experts.

Earlier, for two hundred years at least, recitation and performance took center stage in the one-room schools; but it did not end there. At schools, recitation as performance—not merely to retain information—climbed toward competitive speaking, elimination and reward on Prize Speaking Day, when the athletes of elocution recited in contest before judges. The same athletes did not stop when school stopped, and recitation exfoliated into the adult world as a major form of entertainment. Hamlets and cities alike formed clubs meeting weekly for mutual entertainment that variously included singing, playing the violin and the piano, recitation, and political debate. In the country towns and villages, which couldn't afford to hire Mr. Hopper to entertain them (nor earlier Mr. Emerson to instruct and inspire them), citizens made their own Lyceums and Chautauquas. In my grandfather's South Danbury, New Hampshire, young people founded the South Danbury Debating and Oratorical Society. Twice a month they met for programs that began with musical offerings and recitations, paused for coffee and doughnuts, and concluded with a political debate. "Resolved:

That the United States should Cease from Territorial Expansion."

While recitation thrived, the recitable poem became a way of entertaining ideas and each other, of exposing or exercising public concerns. Poetry in the United States was briefly a public art. But after the Great War came cars, radios, and John Dewey; recitation departed, and poets have been blamed ever since for losing their audience. The blame is unfair, because the connection between poetry and a mass audience was brief, nor did it work for all poetry. John Donne never had a great audience; neither did George Herbert nor Andrew Marvell, nor in America Walt Whitman or Emily Dickinson. These poets made poems with a fineness of language that required sophisticated reading.

All the same, *some* nineteenth-century poets wrote poems both popular and fine—without being as popular as baseball or as fine as Gerard Manley Hopkins. This moment was the fragile age of elocution. Many poets turned in one direction to talk to the people, and in another to talk to the ages. Longfellow's best work—the *Divine Comedy* sonnets, "The Jewish Cemetery at Newport"—is dense, sophisticated, adult poetry of the second order. But in his nationalistic fervor he also wrote epics of the Republic's prehistory like *Evangeline*, or lyrics of the common life like "The Village Blacksmith." Making these poems, he made recitation pieces; without intending to, he wrote poems for children and for entertainment. When Whittier made "Barbara Frietchie" in his abolitionist passion, he made willy-nilly a patriotic poem for schoolkids to recite. Meantime Walt Whitman—who had notions about poetry for the people—went relatively unread as he went unrecited. Mind you, he showed he could turn his hand to the recitation piece: "O Captain My Captain" is poetically inferior to "Casey."

The twin phenomena of recitation and the popular poem thrived in England at the same time, and Macaulay's *The Lays of Ancient Rome* turned up in American school readers and on prize-speaking days. The public Tennyson, laureate not melancholic, wrote verses often memorized for performance; lyrical Wordsworth and bouncy Browning served as well. There were many English sources, even for "Casey at the Bat": Thayer remembered reading W.S. Gilbert's *Bab Ballads* before composing "Casey."

At my school in the 1930s we memorized American poets: Whitman for "O Captain My Captain," Joaquin Miller's "Columbus," something by James Whitcomb Riley. The trajectory of the recitation piece, of which "Casey" is a late honorable example, began its descent early. James Whitcomb Riley scored hits with "Little Orphant Annie" and others, but Riley was mostly hokum. Then there was Eugene Field, whose "Little Boy Blue" is gross sentimentality accomplished with skill; then there is Ella Wheeler Wilcox; then there is Edgar Lee Guest. [The Canadian Robert Service is a late recitable anomaly.] Vachel Lindsay and Carl Sandburg were themselves performers who did not give rise to performance in others; they led from recitation toward the poetry reading. There are poets today as sentimental and popular as Edgar Guest, but they write free verse and no one recites them.

The tradition of recitation survives only in backwaters, like Danbury, New Hampshire. If you come on Prize

Speaking Day and sit in the school cafeteria-gymnasium-assembly, a miniature elocutionist may break your heart reciting "Little Boy Blue," or you may watch a rawboned young outfielder, straight out of central casting, begin: "The outlook wasn't brilliant for the Mudville nine that day. . ."

Among the thousands of pieces memorized and recited, few survive. Why "Casey at the Bat"? For a hundred years this mock heroic ballad has lurked alive at the edges of American consciousness. It has endured past the culture that spawned it. When an artifact like this old clownish poem persists for a century, surviving not only its moment but its natural elocutionary habitat, there must be reasons. There must be public reasons for public endurance.

We might as well ask: Why has baseball survived? Neither the Black Sox scandal nor the Crash nor two World Wars nor the National Football League have ended the game of baseball. Every year more people buy tickets to sit in wooden seats over a diamond of grass—or in plastic seats over plastic grass, as may be. We need to ask: *Has* baseball survived? Casey's game pitted town against town with five thousand neighbors watching. Maybe the descendant of Casey's game is industrial league softball played under the lights by teams wearing rainbow acrylics. These days when we speak of baseball we mostly mean the Major Leagues, millionaire's hardball, where our box seats place us half a mile from the symmetrical petro-chemical field. Do we watch the game that Mudville watched?

Yes.

As "Casey at the Bat" survives the culture of recitation, the game's shape and import survive its intimate origins. Not without *change*: If the five thousand ghosts of the Mudville crowd, drinking a Mississippi of blood to turn solid, reconstituted themselves on a Friday night at Three Rivers Stadium to witness combat between Cincinnati's team and Pittsburgh's, they would gape in spiritual astonishment at the zircon light of a distant diamond under the velvet darkness, at the pool-table green of imitation grass, at amenities of Lite, at the wave, at the skin color of many players, at tight uniforms, and at a scoreboard that shows moving pictures of what just happened.

But in their ectoplasmic witness they would also observe the template of an unaltered game. They would watch a third baseman move to his right, a second baseman flip underhand to a shortstop pivoting toward first for the double play, and an outfielder charge a line drive while setting himself to throw. Above all, they would see a pitcher facing a batter late in the game with men on base. They would see a cleanup man approaching the batter's box with defiance curling his lip. "Casey at the Bat" survives—to begin with—because it crystallizes baseball's moment, the medallion carved at the center of the game, where pitcher and batter confront each other.

There are other reasons, literary and historical. When a poem is so popular, one needs to quote Mallarmé again, and observe that poems are made of words. "Casey's" language is a small, consistent, comic triumph of irony. The diction is mock heroic, big words for small occasions: When a few fans go home in the ninth inning, they depart not in discouragement but "in deep despair." The

remaining five thousand illustrate a learned illusion: In his *Essay on Man*, Alexander Pope wrote that, "Hope springs eternal in the human breast. . ." and Thayer of course knew the source of his saw; but Pope, like Shakespeare, is largely composed of book titles and proverbs: Thayer uses Pope not as literary allusion but as appeal to common knowledge by way of common elevated sentiment.

Elevation is fundamental: Despite the flicker of hope, the crowd is a "grim multitude"—a language appropriate to Milton's hell—and if the hero is mocked, hero worshippers are twice mocked. Thayer's poetic similes are Homeric—as if Achilles faced Hector instead of Casey the pitcher; or if Casey is not quite Achilles, at least he is Ajax. Imagery of noise, loud in Homer and his echo Virgil, rouses Thayer to exalted moments: A yell "rumbled through the valley, it rattled in the dell; / It knocked upon the mountain and recoiled upon the flat. . ." This yell is cousin to the "roar / Like the beating of the stormwaves on a stern and distant shore." It is noise again when Thayer's crowd reacts to a called strike: "'Fraud!' cried the maddened thousands, and echo answered fraud. . ." These days at Fenway Park the bleacherites divide themselves for a rhythmic double chant, but they do not say "Fraud." When they feel polite they cry "less filling" and echo answers "tastes great."

Possibly crowds were not chanting "Fraud" in the late 1880s either. It was a major form of Victorian humor to elevate diction over circumstance. Mr. Micawber soared with paraphrastic euphemism to admit that he was in debt; W. C. Fields was an orotund low-comedy grandson. For a hundred years it was witty or amusing to call kissing osculation, and to refer to a house as a domicile. If somebody missed our tone, we sounded pompous, but usually people understood us: When we enjoyed something common or vulgar (like baseball) we could show a humorous affection for it, yet retain our superiority by calling the ball a spheroid.

This habit of language has not entirely disappeared, but more and more it looks like an anglophile or academic *tic*. The late poet and renowned advocate of baseball, Marianne Moore, always talked this way, never more than when she spoke of the game. When she identified the Giants' pitcher, "Mr. Mathewson," she noted: "I've read his instructive book on the art of pitching, and it's a pleasure to note how unerringly his execution supports his theories." Another St. Louis poet was T. S. Eliot, born the same year as "Casey," and, like Moore, expert in the humor of a polysyllabic synonym. Eliot is the most eminent poet influenced by "Casey at the Bat." *Old Possum's Book of Practical Cats* includes "Growltiger's Last Stand," conflation of Custer and Casey, written in metrical homage and in allusion: "Oh there was joy in Wapping when the news flew through the land. . ." Growltiger is a vicious fellow, racist or at least nationalist ("But most to Cats of foreign race his hatred has been vowed"), and loathed by felines of an Asian provenance. Absorbed in romantic adventure he is surrounded by a "fierce Mongolian horde," captured, and made to walk the plank.

The author of *Four Quartets* and "The Love Song of J. Alfred Prufrock" grew up in the age of recitation; we could be certain that he knew "Casey" even if "Growltiger" were not written in homage. Like many poets he could write high or low, wide or narrow; unlike some poets, when he wrote for children he recognized that he was doing it.

Mockery is "Casey's" point, with humor to soften it. After the crowd (which is us), the great Casey himself takes the brunt of our laughter. His name is the poem's mantra, repeated twenty-two times, often twice in a line: As he puffs with vainglory, "Defiance gleamed in Casey's eye, a sneer curled Casey's lip." The hero's role is written in the script of gesture. After five stanzas of requisite exposition, we catch sight of the rumored Casey in the sixth stanza: "There was ease in Casey's manner. . ." By this phrase we are captured and the double-naming locks us in: "There was pride in Casey's bearing and a smile on Casey's face." We know the smile's message, and we know how Casey doffs his cap. Casey is Godlike: "With a smile of Christian charity. . ." he "stilled the rising tumult"; if we remember that this metaphoric storm occurs at sea ("the beating of the stormwaves"), we may understand that Casey's charity earns its adjective.

And every time we hear "Casey at the Bat," the hero strikes out. We require this failure.

Not all of us. My grandfather, who was sanguine, always regretted that Casey struck out. He memorized the sequels and tried them all, especially "The Volunteer." In Clarence P. MacDonald's poem, printed in the San Francisco *Examiner* in 1908, the home team plays with no bench; behind in the game, it loses its catcher to an injury, and the captain calls for a substitute from the stands: A gray-headed volunteer finishes the game as catcher and his home run wins the game in the ninth. Besieged by teammates and fans to reveal his identity, the weeping stranger proclaims: "I'm mighty Casey who struck out just twenty years ago."

Wonderful.

But it won't do. None of the triumphant sequels will do. None show the flair of Thayer's ballad, its vigorous bumpety septameter and mostly well-earned rhymes, or its consistently overplayed language. Most important, none celebrate failure: Casey must strike out: Casey's failure makes the poem.

When Thayer first published "Casey at the Bat" in 1888, it bore a subtitle seldom reprinted: "A Ballad of the Republic." Once we lived in heroic times: once—and then again. When we suffer wars and undertake explorations we require heroes, and Jeb Stuart must gallop behind Union lines, Lindbergh fly the Atlantic, Davey Crockett enter the wilderness alone, Washington endure Valley Forge, the *Merrimack* attack the *Monitor*, Neil Armstrong step on the moon, and U.S. stand for Ulysses S., Unconditional Surrender, *and* the United States.

The Civil War, which ripped the country apart, began the work of stitching it together again. (One small agent of integrity was baseball, as blue and gray troops played the game at rest and even in prison camps, even North against South, as legend tells us.) For five years North and South lived through the triumphs and disasters of heroes. Although nameless boys charged stone walls blazing with rifle fire, we concentrated our attention on heroic leaders, from dandified cavalrymen to dignified generals. Sons born to veterans, late in the sixties and early in the seventies, were christened Forrest, Jackson, Sherman, Grant, Lee, Bedford, Beauregard. . .

But hero worship is dangerous and needs correction, especially in a democracy if we will remain democratic. To survive hero worship we mock our heroes; if we don't, we become their victims. Odysseus came home to slay the suitors; Ulysses S. allowed them to fatten on our larder: Heroic governance became disaster as the triumphant General Grant turned into the ruinous President. Many other heroes struck out. When the romantic vainglorious George Custer, with his shoulder-length hair, made combat with Crazy Horse and Sitting Bull in 1876, Growltiger walked the plank. Affluence and corruption, defeat and corruption bred irony. Violence of reconstruction and violence of anti-reconstruction eventually encouraged detachment from crowd passion.

Whatever young Thayer had in mind as he wrote his "Ballad of the Republic," 1888 was of course a Presidential year. We elected the mighty Benjamin Harrison President, a former officer of the Union Army, who took the job in a deal and installed as Secretary of State the notorious James G. Blaine. De Tocqueville stands behind this poem as much as Homer does. Democracies choose figures to vote in and out of office—to argue over, to ridicule: We do not want gods or kings—that's why we crossed the ocean west—but human beings, fallible like us.

We pretend to forgive failure; really we celebrate it. Bonehead Merkle lives forever and Bill Mazeroski's home run fades in memory. We fail, we all fail, we fail all our lives. The best hitters fail, two out of three at bats. If from time to time we succeed, our success is only prelude to further failure—and success's light makes failure darker still. Triumph's pleasures are intense but brief; failure remains with us forever, a featherbed, a mothering nurturing common humanity. With Casey we all strike out. Although Bill Buckner won a thousand games with his line drives and brilliant fielding, he will endure in our memories in the ninth inning of the sixth game of a World Series, one out to go, as the ball inexplicably, ineluctably, and eternally rolls between his legs.

Casey at the Bat

A Ballad of the Republic, Sung in the Year 1888

The outlook wasn't brilliant for the Mudville nine that
day;
The score stood four to two with but one inning more to
play.
And then when Cooney died at first, and Barrows did the
same,
A sickly silence fell upon the patrons of the game.

A straggling few got up to go in deep despair. The rest
Clung to that hope which springs eternal in the human
breast;
They thought if only Casey could but get a whack at
that—
We'd put up even money now with Casey at the bat.

But Flynn preceded Casey, as did also Jimmy Blake,
And the former was a lulu and the latter was a cake;
So upon that stricken multitude grim melancholy sat,
For there seemed but little chance of Casey's getting to
the bat.

But Flynn let drive a single, to the wonderment of all,
And Blake, the much despis-ed, tore the cover off the ball;
And when the dust had lifted, and the men saw what had
occurred,
There was Johnnie safe at second and Flynn a-hugging
third.

Then from 5,000 throats and more there rose a lusty yell;
It rumbled through the valley, it rattled in the dell;
It knocked upon the mountain and recoiled upon the flat,
For Casey, mighty Casey, was advancing to the bat.

There was ease in Casey's manner as he stepped into his
place;
There was pride in Casey's bearing and a smile on
Casey's face.
And when, responding to the cheers, he lightly doffed his
hat,
No stranger in the crowd could doubt 'twas Casey at the
bat.

Ten thousand eyes were on him as he rubbed his hands
with dirt;
Five thousand tongues applauded when he wiped them on
his shirt.
Then while the writhing pitcher ground the ball into his
hip,

Defiance gleamed in Casey's eye, a sneer curled Casey's
lip.

And now the leather-covered sphere came hurtling
through the air,
And Casey stood a-watching it in haughty grandeur there.
Close by the sturdy batsman the ball unheeded sped—
"That ain't my style," said Casey. "Strike one," the um-
pire said.

From the benches, black with people, there went up a
muffled roar,
Like the beating of the storm-waves on a stern and distant
shore.
"Kill him! Kill the umpire!" shouted some one on the
stand;
And it's likely they'd have killed him had not Casey
raised his hand.

With a smile of Christian charity great Casey's visage
shone;
He stilled the rising tumult; he bade the game go on;
He signaled to the pitcher, and once more the spheroid
flew;
But Casey still ignored it, and the umpire said, "Strike
two."

"Fraud!" cried the maddened thousands, and echo answered fraud;
But one scornful look from Casey and the audience was
awed.
They saw his face grow stern and cold, they saw his
muscles strain,
And they knew that Casey wouldn't let that ball go by
again.

The sneer is gone from Casey's lip, his teeth are clenched
in hate;
He pounds with cruel violence his bat upon the plate.
And now the pitcher holds the ball, and now he lets it go,
And now the air is shattered by the force of Casey's blow.

Oh, somewhere in this favored land the sun is shining
bright;
The band is playing somewhere, and somewhere hearts
are light,
And somewhere men are laughing, and somewhere children shout;
But there is no joy in Mudville—mighty Casey has struck
out.

Ernest Lawrence Thayer

## CHAPTER 32

Take Me Out to the Ball Game

Warner Fusselle

On a sunshiny September Saturday in Chicago, around 4 o'clock, a portly, grandfatherly man with white hair and thick, dark-rimmed glasses, wearing a light-colored, short-sleeved shirt with buttoned-down collar, beige sweater vest, and tan trousers, stood up, grabbed a microphone, and started to sway.

"All right! Let me hear you. A one, a two, a three! *Take me out to the ball game. Take me out with the crowd. Buy me some peanuts and Cracker Jack. I don't care if I never get back. Oh, it's root, root, root, for the [what's the name of that team?] . . . If they don't win it's a shame. For it's one, two, three strikes you're out, at the old ball game.* Hey!"

Harry Caray, the voice of the Chicago Cubs, had just led a gathering of 32,043 people at Wrigley Field in the singing of baseball's greatest song—"Take Me Out to the Ball Game." It was the seventh-inning stretch, and the Cubs led the Cardinals, 6-4, in a meaningless late-season game in 1988. Both teams were 20 games out of first place; nevertheless, everyone stood, waved, and cheered as they eyed the WGN broadcast booth overlooking the Friendly Confines.

The Chicago Pied Piper led the singing of those wearing Cubs blue and Cardinals red. There were young, and there were old, all waving their baseball caps. There were toddlers hanging on to their fathers. There were mothers who glowed, holding up their babies who cooed in wonderment.

Harry worked the crowd, holding a microphone with a blue wind screen in his left hand, while waving and encouraging the world of baseball fans standing below with his right hand. It was a special moment. From the first chord on the ballpark organ to Harry's exclamatory "Hey" at the end, "Take Me Out to the Ball Game" took less than a minute—only fifty-one seconds to be exact. However, it was an eventful minute, a happy minute, the happiest minute in all of sports.

Harry Caray has sung "Take Me Out to the Ballgame" to hometown fans during the seventh-inning stretch since 1976. That was the year Bill Veeck bought the White Sox. Harry had been the voice of the Sox since 1971 and had always sung baseball's beloved chorus whenever the organist played it. He had the perfect explanation, "I would always sing it, because I think it's the only song I knew the words to." However, no one except Harry's broadcast partner and a couple of others had heard it.

When Harry broadcast the White Sox games on TV, Bill Veeck noticed that the fans within earshot of Caray's booth would always sing along. One day Veeck had a microphone secretly installed in the broadcast booth, and the rest is history.

Harry joined the Cubs in 1982, where "Take Me Out to the Ball Game" elevated the word "Cubbies" into modern, respectable usage. Harry needed two syllables to replace "home team," so it just had to be "root, root, root for the Cub-bies" instead of Cubs. Lifelong Cub fan Mike Royko, Chicago's most famous columnist, had detested the term "Cubbies" for years, but Harry Caray and "Take Me Out to the Ball Game" prevailed.

In the Beginning

"Take Me Out to the Ball Game" was neither the first baseball song nor the first hit baseball song. Fifty years earlier, in 1858, "The Base Ball Polka" was written by an amateur player on the Niagara Base Ball Club of Buffalo, and the "Home Run Polka" followed nine years later. Neither song had words, nor were they recorded since sound recording wouldn't become a reality until 1877; however, they were available to the public in the form of sheet music.

Baseball's first hit song was "Slide, Kelly, Slide," published in 1889. The Kelly in verse spoofed the baseball star of the day, Michael "King" Kelly. King Kelly stole 208 bases for Boston of the National League from 1887 to 1889. He was King of the Diamond, a nineteenth century combination of Babe Ruth and Ty Cobb. Kelly even batted with a Cobb-like split grip and had once hit .388. His speed and daring made him the darling of the day. He developed the hook slide, and his base-stealing prowess encouraged the cheers of "Slide, Kelly, Slide." In 1893, "Slide, Kelly, Slide" became the first known baseball recording when it was issued on an Edison cylinder.

"Slide, Kelly, Slide" actually lampooned King Kelly and made fun of another buffoonish Kelly, but the two were linked in comedic fun. Even though "Slide, Kelly, Slide" remained a baseball standard even after the King's premature death in 1894, its success was scant compared with that of a sensational new song written in 1908.

Manhattan Transfer

"Take Me Out to the Ball Game" was written in fifteen minutes on a piece of scrap paper by vaudeville entertainer and songwriter Jack Norworth as he rode the (oxymoronic) elevated subway train toward the tip of Manhattan in New York City.

Norworth, who wrote 2,500 songs including "Shine On, Harvest Moon," had never seen a big league baseball game. His inspiration was a poster, prominently displayed on the brand new subway, which invited fans to take in a baseball game at the Polo Grounds. After he wrote the lyrics, his longtime friend, Albert Von Tilzer (who had also never attended a baseball game) composed the music. Von Tilzer was also the manager of the York Music Company, which published "Take Me Out to the Ball Game."

Norworth decided to debut "Take Me Out to the Ball Game" on stage at the Amphion Theater in Brooklyn. "It didn't go over," he later said, "because I was fumbling for the lyrics, and I did it deadpanned."

Three weeks later, Norworth, who had conceived the song as a romantic ballad, decided to try again. Booked as the closing act at Hammerstein's Victoria Theater in New York, the top vaudeville house in the country, he decided to liven up "Take Me Out to the Ball Game" in hopes of better results.

When the day came for the big show, Norworth was forced to change his plans. "I couldn't sing my own song, because every act ahead of me used it." The song was already on its way to becoming a nationwide hit thanks to the nickelodeon, an early-day movie house that charged a nickel for admission. Some of the more popular nickelodeons had started using illustrated songs, pictured on a set of slides, between the several short silent films that made up a typical program in the first decade of the century. "Take Me Out to the Ball Game" was played by the resident pianist and accompanied by pictorial slides that also displayed the words, for the audience to sing along.

A slide at the outset pictured the cover of the sheet music (on which "Take Me Out to the Ball Game" was prophetically named "The Sensational Base Ball Song") and other slides told the story of one afternoon in the life of Katie Casey, the heroine of "Take Me Out to the Ball Game." She and her beau, portrayed by models, were photographed going to the ball game at the Polo Grounds, and a final slide showed the lyrics of the chorus and invited the audience to "All join in."

The song caught on in the midst of one of baseball's greatest two-league pennant races; six teams were battling for the 1908 pennants a mere two days before the season ended. The effect of these races, which involved both Chicago teams as well as clubs in Cleveland, Detroit, New York, and Pittsburgh, was to make baseball front-page news across the country and promote Norworth's song.

Several recordings of "Take Me Out to the Ball Game" were made in 1908. Edward Meeker performed it on an Edison two-minute roll, an early phonograph record shaped like a cylinder. Frank Lambert's 1908 recording was available on a ten-inch, single-faced Zon-O-Phone record, and the Haydn Quartet recorded "Take Me Out to the Ball Game" on a Victor ten-inch single-faced record.

The Denver Nightingale

Harry MacDonough sang with the Haydn Quartet at first, but later the quartet re-recorded the song with vaudevil-lian and baseball fanatic Billy Murray. Murray, who was the number one recording artist of all time in terms of records made, was known as "The Denver Nightingale." He made more than 6,000 recordings between 1897 and 1943. Moreover, he knew and befriended all the Yankees (known as the Highlanders until 1913) and even practiced with them.

In 1906, Murray had recorded "It's Great at a Base Ball Game." On October 24, 1908, he performed "Take Me Out to the Ball Game" and immediately became identified with the song. His recorded version was easily the most popular of his many recordings.

Norworth's success encouraged many other songwriters to try their hand at diamond ditties. George M. Cohan wrote "Take Your Girl to the Ball Game" and the "Connie Mack Song." Cohan's failure, after Jack Norworth's success, caused him to alibi, "I didn't write mine soon enough." Norworth's response? "Or good enough."

In 1913, Irving Berlin composed the music to the baseball novelty song "Jake! Jake! The Yiddisher Ball Player." Then in 1925, he wrote "I Know a Foul Ball." John Philip Sousa penned "The National Game March," but none of the big names came close to the success that Norworth enjoyed. Yet, while "Take Me Out to the Ball Game" is one of the three most frequently sung compositions in the United States (only "Happy Birthday" and "The Star Spangled Banner" top it), the song everyone sings today is just the chorus of the tune.

Katie Casey to Nelly Kelly

The song actually begins, "Katie Casey was baseball mad." Katie Casey was such a big baseball fan that when her beau suggested they take in a show, Miss Kate expressed her preference for baseball.

Katie Casey was base ball mad,
Had the fever and had it bad;
Just to root for the home town crew,
Ev'ry sou Katie blew.
On a Saturday, her young beau
Called to see if she'd like to go,
To see a show but Miss Kate said,
"No, I'll tell you what you can do."

"Take me out to the ball game,
Take me out with the crowd.
Buy me some peanuts and cracker jack,
I don't care if I never get back,
Let me root, root, root, for the home team,
If they don't win it's a shame.
For it's one, two, three strikes, you're out,
At the old ball game."

Katie Casey saw all the games,
Knew the players by their first names;
Told the umpire he was wrong,
All along good and strong.
When the score was just two to two,
Katie Casey knew what to do,
Just to cheer up the boys she knew,
She made the gang sing this song:
(REPEAT CHORUS)

Despite the song's success, Jack Norworth decided to change some of the words. In 1927, he changed Katie Casey to Nelly Kelly (and thus secured a new copyright).

Nelly Kelly loved baseball games,
Knew the players, knew all their names,
You could see her there ev'ry day,
Shout "Hurray," when they'd play.
Her boy friend by the name of Joe
Said, "To Coney Isle, dear, let's go,"
Then Nelly started to fret and pout,
And to him I heard her shout.

"Take me out to the ball game,
Take me out with the crowd,
Buy me some peanuts and crackerjack,
I don't care if I never get back.
Let me root root root for the home team,
If they don't win it's a shame,
For it's one two three strikes, you're out
At the old ball game."

Nelly Kelly was sure some fan,
She would root just like any man,
Told the umpire he was wrong,
All along, good and strong.
When the score was just two to two,
Nelly Kelly knew what to do,
Just to cheer up the boys she knew,
She made the gang sing this song.
(REPEAT CHORUS)

The original copyright of "Take Me Out to the Ball Game" expired in 1936. The renewed copyright had a new subtitle, "The Famous Baseball Song." Not only had the word "baseball" become one word instead of two, "sensational" was updated to "famous." That would change again in 1949 to "Official," as in "The Official Baseball Song."

The Aftermath of the Hit

After his success with "Take Me Out to the Ball Game," Von Tilzer, previously known as Albert Gumm, tried again but failed with other baseball tunes. In 1909 he wrote the music for "Did He Run?" This song satirized Fred Merkle's Boner in the famous 1908 pennant race involving the Giants and Cubs. The chorus began,

Did he run?
Did he run to second,
As he should that day.
Or did Mr. Merkle semi-circle away?

Albert also wrote "Back to the Bleachers for Mine" and "I Want to Go to the Ball Game." His brother Harry, who wrote "Wait Till the Sun Shines, Nellie," also tried to write a baseball hit without success. He was 0-for-2 with "My Old Man Is Baseball Mad" in 1910 and "The Baseball Glide" in 1911.

Norworth, too, tried his hand at more baseball music but failed. With his wife Nora Bayes, a musical comedy star, he wrote "Let's Get the Umpire's Goat." Often criticized for writing a baseball song even though he had never seen a game, he had the perfect response: "A friend of mine, Harry Williams, wrote 'In the Shade of the Old Apple Tree,' and he never saw an apple tree."

Finally, however, Jack did get to see his first major league game. Some say he saw his first game in 1916 at Ebbets Field in Brooklyn where he root, root, rooted like crazy for the hometown, pennant-winning Robins. Other historians push the date to somewhere in the 1940s, when the Robins-turned-Dodgers supposedly had a special day for Jack at Ebbets Field on June 27, 1940.

Whenever it was, Norworth became fascinated with what he saw and later pioneered Little League Baseball in California. The Cracker Jack Company even honored him with a trophy, the Jack Norworth Award, which was given to deserving Little Leaguers. In 1958, on the fiftieth anniversary of his creation of "Take Me Out to the Ball Game," Norworth was honored in Los Angeles and was presented with a gold lifetime pass which would enable him to see any major league game. Norworth, proud of his accomplishment, said, "It has kept me eating for fifty years."

He died September 1, 1959, at age eighty, but almost every ballpark features "Take Me Out to the Ball Game" during the seventh-inning stretch. One notable exception is the Toronto Blue Jays, who have used a fan-participation song since 1979 called "OK Blue Jays," which has become the team's theme song. At Busch Stadium in St. Louis, Norworth's composition is replaced by the Budweiser beer jingle, "Here Comes the King."

Oriole Park at Camden Yards in Baltimore is also an exception, but only sometimes. There, the fans get to choose their favorite song for that day's game from a list of four choices; however, the fans' applause usually selects "Take Me Out to the Ball Game," with John Denver's "Thank God I'm a Country Boy" a close second.

"Take Me Out to the Ball Game" has been called by some an American folk song. Children learn it right after their nursery rhymes, and soldiers sing it during world wars. Music boxes play it, and so do doorbell chimes. Baseball's most popular song has even been played in wedding processions, and, in 1955, *Variety* gave the song its stamp of approval by naming "Take Me Out to the Ball Game" one of the ten greatest popular songs of the last fifty years.

## CHAPTER 33

Fantasy Baseball

Don L. Daglow and Jack Kavanagh

Young baseball fans lie in bed at night and dream of playing baseball in the big leagues. Old boys—that is, grownups—imagine that they may yet manage their hometown teams. Table-top board games, dice baseball, and the computer have allowed us to live out both fantasies by recreating game situations and allowing us to experiment, rewarding us with different results based on the strategic wisdom of our decisions.

Table Baseball — A World Apart

Baseball simulations have been around longer than organized baseball. The first professional league, the National Association, was formed in 1871. The first table baseball game had been patented in 1868. In 1994, baseball simulations took the place of the real thing when major league baseball shut down. "Rotisserie" type leagues—for which team owners drafted and traded major-league players and conducted their season's play based on real-life performances—could not feed off daily boxscores. However, table gamers rolled dice, shuffled cards, flicked spinners or, in the digital simulations, tapped keyboards or clicked mouse buttons.

The undisputed Father of Table Baseball was Francis C. Sebring, whose board game, *Parlour Baseball,* was described in an 1866 issue of *Frank Leslie's Illustrated Newspaper.* The game was patented in 1868 (patent No. 74154). The diagram shows it was a mechanical game. One player sent a coin plateward by a spring mechanism while another swung a swiveled bat. The coin, when struck, would end up in a slot, designated an out or a hit. This simple approach was continued in dozens of mechanical games, on tabletops and in pinball arcades, which miniaturized the real game.

However, games played with dice, cards, or spinners have dominated the home baseball game area. These approaches provide greater options and more variable outcomes. Thousands of such games were invented. Most probably remained the private passion of a fan who created his own game to play on his own table. "Inventing" a simulation of baseball is simple. Baseball itself can be viewed as being transferred from a board game to a playing field. The ancient Hindu game of *Pachesi* ("parcheesi") starts the player at home base and returns him there after he has circled the bases. That's what the play action of baseball amounts to. As in more complicated board games, the trip around the bases can be made more elaborate and difficult, but the goal is the same: to score more times than your opponents.

However, for the first sixty-plus years of table baseball, a problem existed. The players in the lineup did not perform the way they did in actual baseball play. Babe Ruth was no more likely to hit a home run than the weakest hitting infielder. Even worse, the good glove work of the infielder was not reflected in the play of the table game. Pitchers had no traits of superiority nor were any of them easier to hit than others. You could write Walter Johnson's name in the lineup but a pitcher with any other name was as likely to strike out batters.

The first breakthrough to "real life" came when Clifford A. Van Beek of Green Bay, Wisconsin, marketed *National Pastime* in 1931. He had patented his game in 1923 and was issued No. 1,536,639 in 1925. Although it was advertised in the 1931 issues of *Baseball Magazine,* the fledgling game succumbed to the Great Depression and was not seen again until *APBA* was marketed in 1951. The *APBA* game imitated *National Pastime* and, as its followers grew into cultlike devotees, its "inventor," J. Richard Seitz, allowed them to believe he was the one who had mastered a way to imitate the baseball performances of actual players.

Actually, a game with a different approach, *All-Star Baseball,* marketed by CADACO and designed by a real-life baseball player, Ethan Allen, had appeared in 1941. Seitz had contributed a primitive method of ranking pitchers to his upgrading of the *National Pastime* game. Allen, a .300 hitting outfielder in the National League, did not bother (all pitchers might have looked alike to him). At any rate, in *All-Star Baseball,* the spinner was influenced only by the batter's tendencies. Babe Ruth would hit more home runs than the weak-hitting shortstop because the space for HRs was larger on his player disc. Alas, Allen had not built in a way for the glove man to justify his place on the team. Seitz had tackled that with a grading system. Seitz also widened the play variations by borrowing another idea from the past. Although it was not a "real life" game, like the one that appeared in the early 1930s, purportedly the brainstorm of pitcher Danny MacFayden, it provided different play charts according to the base/out situation.

The *APBA* game was challenged by *Strat-O-Matic,* also using dice and cards, and its own closely guarded method of rating players. Both games found acceptance and survive to the present. Many other games came and went, but a few had enduring value beyond their playability because, unlike *APBA* and *Strat-O-Matic,* they did not conceal their codes. They revealed the process of rating players for batting, for power factors, for defense, and for pitching effectiveness as well as strikeout and walks. At least one of these, *Extra Innings,* by Big League Game Company of Duluth, Minnesota, is still marketed.

The market for fantasy baseball games in the home has expanded, but largely through the rise of computer and cartridge games. This has been a fairly recent development in fantasy baseball. There were no video games as late as the early 1970s, when Pong was not a word—unless preceded by Ping—and Pac Man had yet to munch his first dot.

In 1971, I *(D.D. speaking here)* was a freshman at Pomona College, and I spent many evenings with a set of dice and the 1954 *Who's Who in Baseball,* trying to invent a better baseball board game. My goal was to weigh batters and pitchers accurately, not only over a long season (as paper games like *Strat-O-Matic* and *APBA* did well), but also in a short best-of-seven series. I failed miserably; the math was too complex to be fun.

That fall I joined a computer programming course on the Digital Equipment Corp. (DEC) PDP-10 computer and immediately realized that the computer made my too-complex formulas simple to calculate. The sky-blue machines had 32,000 bytes (32 kilobytes, or 32K) of RAM (random access memory), shared among over thirty users at a time, quickly "swapping" one program into memory for a few tenths of a second before kicking it out and bringing in the next one. It was the technical equivalent of watching thirty-five students recite thirty-five different poems over thirty-five different telephones, with each poet speaking one word before yielding to the next person. Under such a system no one could finish his or her poem quickly, and to search a list of 200 names took almost a minute during peak usage. (Searching through 200 names now appears to be instantaneous.)

By Christmas, I could simulate the entire 1953 American League season, and, by the following year, make basic decisions such as inserting a pinch hitter, walking the batter, or warming up a reliever. I didn't know it at the time, but this was the first computer baseball simulation game, the first time a human could match wits against a computer in a mathematically defined environment.

The pioneering work of such computer simulation innovators as R.E. Trueman, Allen Freeze, George Lindsey, Dick Cramer, Bill James, and Pete Palmer focused on the scientific analysis of baseball strategy (and the debunking of some myths); that first game in 1971-72 emphasized a different power of the computer—interaction.

The First Great Video Game War

In the early and mid-1970s, a series of arcade machines entertained people by showing squares and lines on a TV screen, then allowing users to move the lines or squares to play a game. The most famous was *Pong,* in which two lines controlled by plastic knobs knocked a square "ball" back and forth across the screen. Atari improved on this concept by creating a console that played different games on interchangeable cartridges. By the late 1970s the Atari VCS (video cartridge system) was a huge hit.

Baseball games of that era were arcade contests. The screen showed the outline of a field, and single-color player silhouettes were drawn at each position. Everything was controlled by humans. One user (the pitcher) pressed a button to choose a fast or slow pitch and decided whether the pitch would be straight or would curve. The other (the batter) pressed a button to swing the bat. (This was not so very different from Francis Sebring's baseball game of 1868.) Once the ball was in play, each player used a joystick or "control disk" to direct the lead runner and the fielder closest to the ball. (Some of these primitive-sounding games sold over 2 million copies.)

Atari's success inspired competition from two toy manufacturers, Coleco (Colecovision) and Mattel (Intellivision), for the latter of whom I was one of five in-house video game programmers. By that time we no longer needed to show simply an outline of a baseball field on the user's TV screen. We could show the game on their TV set the same way broadcasts showed it, from a center field camera, with insets in the corners to show the runner on first dancing off the bag.

With this level of realism, it became practical for the first time in video games to spend the extra money to license the names and statistics of real major league players, so that a computer figure that represented Dale Murphy or Andre Dawson really would hit more home runs than an Alfredo Griffin. In turn, this assignment of an identity to each player allowed us to have pitchers tire, pinch hitters enter the game, and use more strategy.

World Series Baseball by Mattel marked two important firsts in the history of baseball cartridges: (1) the first baseball simulation in a video game and (2) the first use of television camera angles in a game. It was so striking visually that, for Christmas 1982, Mattel created a television campaign with George Plimpton to preview it.

Software publishers built a $5 billion market in the U.S. by 1982, but, when Mattel's *World Series Baseball* shipped in 1983, too many games crowded the stores. Many game publishers went bankrupt. Unable to return games to defunct manufacturers, toy stores sold them at bargain prices. Parents and kids soon balked at paying $35 for one new game when they could buy seven $5 games. The final blow was the arrival of inexpensive computers such as the Commodore 64 and Atari 800, which not only played games but could also be used for word processing and educational software.

One by one, the major firms folded their video game divisions, laid off their staffs and struggled to save what was left of their companies. Atari split into two separate units that were sold to different investors. Mattel Electronics went from 1,800 people to five in fifteen months; Coleco ultimately disappeared into bankruptcy.

1982-94: The Home Computer Comes of Age

When the Apple II home computer was first introduced in 1977, it seemed to be yet another device computer nerds sold to techie wizards. Instead it proved to be the defining moment of home computer technology, when the prior generation of machines (led by the 1975 MITS Altair 8800) slipped into obscurity, while the next wave—the Tandy TRS-80, Commodore PET—pushed on to a whole new level of public acceptance.

The earliest baseball simulation on home computers was Apple II's *Computer Baseball,* published by Strategic Simulations Inc. (SSI) in 1981. A reasonably accurate simulation, it pitted great teams from history against each other and allowed the user to manage. Taking advantage of the 48K of memory in the Apple (versus the 4K-8K for video game cartridges of the time), *Computer Baseball* ignored flashy graphics, displaying an outline of a stadium and a ball while describing the action in text.

By 1982 the Commodore 64 home computer had challenged the Apple II, offering many of the same capabilities for much less money ($850 for a complete system versus about twice that much for a somewhat more powerful contemporary Apple IIe). To the layman, only the much-slower disk drives represented a clear difference between the two; the Commodores sold millions.

Apple focused on the new Macintosh, eventually discontinuing the Apple II line, and Mattel and Atari were very slow to introduce their planned new computers. In 1983-84, the height of the Commodore 64's success, its sales wave helped push the first-generation video games over the brink of disaster.

Ironically, these less expensive home computers often turned out to be used primarily as game machines, and the computer game business grew into a real industry as more and more Commodores were sold. Manufacturers like Electronic Arts Inc., founded in 1982 by Trip Hawkins, pushed lasting play value, simple interfaces, and graphic quality; arcade games looked simplistic by comparison, and began a slow fade from prominence.

In 1984 this trend caught up with *Computer Baseball.* Micro League Sports Inc., creators of *Micro League Baseball,* featured better graphics than earlier games. Pictures now told the story so well that text narration was omitted, and only the names and stats of the batter and the pitcher were displayed.

Action-only games, which ignored stats and played as arcade-style contests, also flourished. Scott Orr's Gamestar Inc. produced *Star League Baseball,* and no other baseball game of that era, including the simulations, sold as well. In the mid-1980's Gamestar was sold to Activision, while Accolade introduced the first *Hardball* game. Although Intellivision *World Series Baseball* was the first game to show the pitches from one angle and the fielding action from another, *Hardball* was the first to do so on home computers, and its graphics were larger and its textures more detailed than prior games. Replacing *Star League* as the leading action baseball game, *Hardball* and its sequels have been major products for almost a decade.

In 1985, while working at Electronic Arts, I began discussing a new kind of game with Hawkins, who had played in board game baseball leagues for years. We believed the newest computers (then the Amiga and the IBM PC) could support a hybrid game, one which was both an accurate simulation and a competitive graphic display of baseball. Our idea was to imitate the strategy of an individual manager, and Earl Weaver, then newly retired as Orioles manager, was our choice. Over the next several years EA published versions of *Earl Weaver Baseball* for the Amiga, the PC, and the Macintosh.

Utilizing a split screen that showed a closeup of batter and pitcher next to a picture of the field, *Weaver* changed the face of simulations by creating an electronic version of Weaver's strategy. We met with him several times, trying to distill his "God bless the three-run homer" philosophy into the key factors he used to make decisions.

Once the "electronic Earl Weaver" had been built, we compared its tendencies against those that Weaver himself showed in real games and fine-tuned the model.

That game allowed players to schedule and simulate a complete season of 162 games and keep records of the simulated stats, although to play such a full schedule game by game (at half an hour per) would take several months. Earlier games had required the user to plan a schedule, play games, keep stats, and figure out who were the league leaders. Weaver automated the process, a huge improvement over paper-and-pencil recordkeeping.

The introduction of *Weaver* put pressure on *Hardball* and *Micro League Baseball,* and the late 1980s saw a "battle of the versions" as all three games maneuvered for position. Activision's *Pete Rose Baseball* and Epyx's *Sporting News Baseball,* each of which combined stats with graphics, lasted one season each, but the venerable board games *Strat-O-Matic Baseball, Pursue the Pennant,* and *APBA* all introduced text-only, then text-with-graphics versions of their bestselling products. By 1990 baseball fans had a broad choice of computer games.

Not wanting to be typecast as "all action and no simulation," *Hardball II* included a core of basic baseball stats to add simulation to the game. In *Hardball III* Accolade introduced the first "VGA" baseball game to PCs. The visual graphics adapter showed the power of a new graphic format with higher resolution graphics.

Micro League Baseball II and *III* added more stats to refine the simulation plus a "draft," and *Micro League IV* added miniature videos to its display to keep up on the graphics front. *Weaver II* experimented with a "multiple camera" TV-style display that showed the action from behind the fielders and allowed users to choose between different angles for the display. Although the game was not as popular as its predecessor, *Weaver II* (and *Pete Rose Baseball*) broke new ground in 3-D displays.

I ultimately left Electronic Arts, founded Stormfront Studios, and created *Tony La Russa Baseball.* La Russa, who lived near our office, reviewed version after version for errors in strategy. We designed La Russa specifically to balance sabermetrics and traditional stats.

Ultimately, a 486 PC replayed every play from a full 162-game season for twenty-eight teams in less than fifteen minutes. Where the room-sized PDP-10 in 1971 replayed a season at the rate of five seconds per game, the desk-sized PC in 1993 used ten times as many variables for every batter and pitcher, yet still played each complete game in less than half a second.

For years, games that allowed users to control the fielding had suffered from a basic problem: it was hard to catch a fly or popup on the TV screen just by watching the tiny white circle that was the ball and the tiny black circle that was its shadow. Even experienced players missed routine flies, undermining the enjoyment of many games.

Knowing that computers are good at quickly drawing basic geometric shapes, I asked a programmer to create a shaded circle on the field to show where the ball was going to land. When the ball was high in the air the circle would be large, and as it fell the circle would shrink and then disappear as the ball hit the ground. This single innovation drew more attention from the press than all the work that went into perfecting the baseball simulation.

1989-94: The Second Great Video Game War

Japanese gamemakers Nintendo and Sega first started showing their new video game consoles at trade shows in the United States in 1987, and by 1988 Nintendo's NES unit in particular was selling well to its young audience, although many buyers from toy store chains were careful to keep game inventories small.

Some of the first baseball games for Nintendo, Japanese-designed by companies such as Jaleco, already included the stats of American major leaguers and used batter power ratings, runners' speed, and pitchers' control abilities to influence play. Although very simple by comparison with PC simulations, these cartridges hooked video game-playing kids who wanted to see the names and stats of real players in the game.

The next year the Sega Genesis, more powerful than the original Nintendo, also began to sell. One of the first Genesis games was Sega's *Tommy Lasorda Baseball,* which featured a unique "blimp view," looking straight down on the players' heads. Stores began to believe that video games were really back, and stocked Sega and Nintendo cartridges as their popularity kept growing.

These 1990s cartridges were very different from those we had programmed only a decade before. *Utopia,* an Intellivision video game of the mid-1980s, had contained 4,000 characters of computer code and graphics. *La Russa Baseball '95* for the Sega Genesis held the equivalent of 2 million characters of information, an increase of 500 times.

That size, of course, made these new video game platforms potential battlegrounds for the creators of baseball simulations. Some games, like *Cal Ripken Baseball, Ken Griffey Baseball, Nolan Ryan Baseball,* and *Roger Clemens Baseball* used famous players and flashy graphics to appeal to the younger audiences who buy video games, while also including basic player stats and baseball simulation. Sega's *1992 Sports Talk Baseball* featured the voice of veteran broadcaster Lon Simmons, and Accolade's *Hardball III* for Sega and PC featured network broadcaster Al Michaels, but the digitized voices used too much precious cartridge space and were dropped from later incarnations.

What We Cannot Simulate

The compact disk has already impacted the market through products such as Microsoft's *Complete Baseball* (a multimedia reference work whose basis is *Total Baseball*) and *La Russa Baseball for CD.* Increasingly, more and more games are offering modem play, allowing users in different cities to play against each other over telephone lines. Fantasy baseball is now also on-line; Prodigy has debuted *Baseball Manager,* a fantasy game in which the computer actually plays every game between teams whose rosters subscribers build via drafting and trades.

For all our new technology, there are different schools of thought on what "baseball simulations" ought to be. One designer who was not himself a fan tried to develop a game by listening carefully to co-workers who were baseball experts. He concluded that he could create the best baseball simulation ever . . . by making sure all the statistics from the simulated games came out exactly the same as those from real life!

If a player had a .280 batting average in real life, and his simulated average was below .280, he would get a hit the next time up, guaranteed, whether the pitcher was Roger Clemens or a recently converted peanut vendor. If a player who hit 30 homers in real life had 30 home runs on August 20 of the simulated season, he couldn't hit another the rest of the season lest he make the game "inaccurate." Fortunately, management listened to customer complaints, and the design was altered to allow reasonable results.

The interaction that makes games fun to play on the computer can also create havoc with the simulation. At the simplest level, the user might change the 1994 Tigers' usual lineup, batting Kirk Gibson, Alan Trammell and Cecil Fielder 1-2-3 to see if this would work better than Sparky Anderson's alignment; however, after users make such changes they can be expected to make complaints to game companies about the resulting inaccuracy of the final standings.

For those games in which the user can control the pitching, hitting, and fielding, even greater chaos can occur. You can pitch fastball after fastball down the pipe to Willie Mays or Babe Ruth and watch the home run totals mount. Simulation sometimes takes a back seat to fun, and fun is the reason people buy the games.

At one national SABR Convention, I attended a presentation where a researcher had replayed a recent season ten times with a leading simulation to see how often the real-life pennant winners came out ahead. The average was about six times out of ten, but one pennant winner only won two of the ten simulated seasons, while the second-place team won five times. Although even the best baseball simulation can't predict the future or precisely duplicate the past, these results seemed intuitively reasonable to me. Yet several members of the audience politely indicated their skepticism as to the scholar's methodology.

The skeptics missed one key point about real baseball in their assumption. After a 162-game season, very often the records of the pennant contending teams are so close as to be almost identical. The decade from 1970-79, for example, is remembered for pennant races that were over in July as teams ran away from the competition. Nevertheless, in that ten-year span, 22.5 percent of the division races were decided by two games or less, 30 percent of the League Championship Series went what was then the complete five games, and five out of the ten World Series went the full seven games.

The difference between the performance of the champion and that of the second place team in baseball is often perilously thin, one that no simulation can ever seriously address. Similarly, we can get close to predicting behavior, but human beings are ultimately unpredictable. Will John Doe's new baby keep him up at night and reduce his performance, or will his sense of satisfaction and happiness at being a daddy raise his average to new heights?

These are not studies for statistical experts but rather for psychologists, and our inscrutable human individuality should keep that part of baseball sacrosanct for the foreseeable future. When it's the top of the seventh of a close contest on a beautiful sunny day, it's time to forget the analysis and just enjoy the game.

## CHAPTER 34

Reel Baseball

Bob Carroll

Thomas Alva Edison barely had the final sprocket in place on his film before he put baseball in the movies. In 1898, only four years after his motion picture, *Fred Ott's Sneeze*, proved pictures could move, the great inventor released *The Ball Game*, showing an amateur New Jersey nine performing against an unnamed opponent. A paper print of the film was deposited at the Library of Congress for copyright purposes. And, because the paper has held up much better than the quickly decomposing nitrate-stock film that became the norm a dozen years later, *The Ball Game* and several other early baseball films can still be viewed today.

Alas! Because of nitrate's peculiar qualities, most baseball films shot between 1912 and 1939 are not gathering dust on some studio shelf but have become dust themselves. We can know about them only through contemporary reviews. And, to be honest, many of the descriptions of stale plots, wooden acting, and creaky humor might lead a modern fan to conclude that the loss of most of these epics is a blessing.

Nevertheless, although we cannot view all the potboilers, we can safely say that baseball, for better or for worse, has been a staple of the cinema down through the years. On somewhat shakier ground, we can also assert that most of the films worth watching have been made in our own era. It's likely that even Ty Cobb himself would prefer sitting through the pedestrian *Major League II* rather than be subjected to *Somewhere in Georgia*, a 1916 atrocity in which he starred. (What he would think of *Cobb*, released in the fall of 1994, is another matter entirely.)

"Baseball movie" is actually an inclusive term that covers three broad categories of films (or videos)—historicals, instructionals, and "movie" movies—each with its own set of subspecies:

1. The first category involves real ballplayers *being* real ballplayers playing real baseball. *Golden Decade of Baseball, 1947-1957* (Norman Baer Productions, 1991), focusing on New York's great teams of the period, is obviously historical.

2. The second employs real ballplayers to explain to the uninitiated how real ballplayers ply their trade. *Tony Gwynn's King of Swing* (Premier Home Video, 1991) is designed to improve your batting stroke or your Little Leaguer's.

3. A movie in the third category, the one that most often comes to mind as a "baseball movie," may sometimes be taken from a novel, such as *The Natural* or *Bang the Drum Slowly*, and may also feature real ballplayers.

Historicals

Historical baseball films run the gamut from World Series and All-Star Game recapitulations through teams' season highlights to paeans to individual star players. Most of them are available on video so you can sit in your own living room and watch Willie Mays catch Vic Wertz's drive in the 1954 World Series over and over again.

The World Series went on film as long ago as 1905, but those pre-1940s prints that exist at all are not available to the general public. You can see some bits and pieces in *75 Years of World Series Memories*, made in 1979 by Major League Baseball.

For those who want to brush up on a particular World Series of yesteryear, through Blockbuster Video, Major League Baseball has a separate entry available for every year back to 1943, when the New York Yankees whipped the St. Louis Cardinals. That film is in black and white and runs 30 minutes. In 1958, when the Yankees beat the Milwaukee Braves, Major League Baseball began shooting the Series in color. (It wasn't until 1984 that the Series highlights were expanded to a full 60 minutes.)

The excitement factor for any of these films depends on the events portrayed; 1975 is a gem but there's not much suspense in 1950. Yankee-haters are advised to skip 1949 through 1953, but they should enjoy 1955, 1960, 1963, and 1964. Any Red Sox rooter who can watch the sixth game of the 1986 classic and not cry out in agony is made of sterner stuff than the stone face of Abraham Lincoln on Mount Rushmore.

Team highlights have been available on video for the past decade or so. The purpose of these 30-minute promos is, of course, not so much to relive last season as to help sell tickets for next season. Therefore, the story line is always upbeat with the local heroes showing gameness against overwhelming odds and, while they may have finished last for the third season in a row, they exhibited signs that better days are definitely just around the corner. Fortunately for the makers of highlight films, even the most inept of teams will produce enough stellar plays over its approximately 500 hours of game time to fill a 30-minute video.

For star-watchers, the videos of All-Star Games are available from 1962 on. Again, snippets from earlier games can be seen in other films. *Fifty Years of Baseball Memories* (MLB, 1980) is a fun trip into the past. One of the most enjoyable films featuring interviews with players from the distant past is *The Glory of Their Times* (PBS, 1977), based on Lawrence Ritter's book. In interviewing players from the 1898-1916 era, Ritter started a whole genre of oral history, and many of the men he interviewed were still alive when this film was made. Another excellent film along similar lines is *The Boys of Summer* (VCA Programs Inc., 1983). Based on Roger Kahn's book, the interviews here are with Brooklyn Dodgers stars of the 1950s.

Just about every top star of the past dozen years as well as a number of earlier stars has a personal-highlight video out there someplace. You may have to weed through some collectors' lists to find videos on retired stars, but *Nolan Ryan: Feel the Heat* (HPG Home Video, 1992) is still a top seller.

Ken Burns's film, *Baseball*, is the king of the historical baseball movies. While some quibbled about its pace and wondered if the national pastime merited an 18-hour epic, *Baseball* is certain to be the standard by which all subsequent baseball historicals are judged.

Instructionals

Technically, *Babe Ruth, How He Makes His Home Runs*, a 1920 one-reeler, qualifies as an instructional; the Bambino is shown swinging a bat in practice and in game action. The real point, however, was to give fans who couldn't get to the Polo Grounds (where the Yankees played then) or any other American League ballpark a chance to see baseball's newest hero "up close and personal." If any major leaguers owed their subsequent batting success to watching this film, it has not been recorded.

Lew Fonseca, the 1929 American League batting champion, became interested in film after acting in a 1927 Joe E. Brown movie. While serving as manager of the Chicago White Sox (1932-34), Fonseca experimented with using film to detect flaws in his players' techniques. (Considering that the Sox never rose above sixth place under his tutelage, he must have shot a lot of film.)

Despite such worthy efforts as *Play Ball, Son*, a 1946 three-reeler with sound that showed viewers how to play the game position by position, instructionals were not an important part of baseball films until recently. The home market was tiny for the obvious reason that film projectors were not "must" items for most American families.

Videotape changed all that. Today, a Little Leaguer can relax in his own living room and be tutored in batting by Charley Lau, baserunning by Maury Wills, fielding by Ozzie Smith, or pitching by Tom Seaver. Any number of other stars, along with numerous college coaches, are available to give out tips on tape, and more are cranked out every year.

A proud parent seeking to improve his son's or daughter's play will find plenty of instructionals, but he must select the *right* instructional. The trick is to find a video that teaches at the proper level for the student. Just as a fourth grader would be overwhelmed by a course in algebra, a baseball beginner won't be ready for a video meant to fine-tune the skills of a more advanced player. At the same time, that already skilled player will quickly become bored with a video dealing only in basics he learned years ago. Most instructionals list a range of ages that they are designed for, but the buyer should still ask if his or her youngster plays above or below others in that age range.

For example, *Baseball Tips for All Ages*, with Mickey Mantle, Whitey Ford, and Phil Rizzuto, is one of many excellent instructionals for beginners. It includes instruction on proper equipment, warming up, and safety. On the other hand, *Play Ball with Mickey Mantle*, featuring Gary Carter and Tom Seaver, is designed for more advanced students and contains tips that a beginner won't use for several years.

One other thing proud parents should keep in mind is that kids are more impressed with current players than with greats of the past. No matter how much you may worship Al Kaline, your kid is more likely to pay attention to Ken Griffey, Jr.

Movie Movies

Of course, when we use the term "baseball movie," most of us immediately think of something along the lines of *The Natural* or *The Bad News Bears in Breaking Training*, to go from the sublime to the ridiculous, movies with fictional plots and real actors. Baseball plays a significant part in these movies but most of the time we're really supposed to worry more whether or not the hero will get the girl than whether he'll hit a home run. Like any other dramatic presentation, the characters must engage our interest. That they play out their stories in a baseball milieu is just an added fillip for the baseball fan.

Trivia buffs can go on endlessly about various *faux pas* in baseball films—Shoeless Joe Jackson batting right-handed in *Field of Dreams* or Crash Davis's spurious home run record in *Bull Durham*. It's certainly true that such errors can distract a true baseball fan from the main plot for a few seconds. But only a confirmed nitpicker would let an occasional lapse ruin an otherwise enjoyable film. After all, correct statistics can't make *The Babe Ruth Story* into a winner. When one spots a gaffe in a baseball movie, perhaps it is best to take solace in the simple knowledge that one knows more about baseball than some high-paid Hollywood scriptwriter.

Starting with pre-World War I silents right up through the talkies of the 1930s, the standard baseball movie plot began with a nice young man from a small town who has a wonderful talent for baseball. Although he's as green as Barney's belly, he soon becomes the star of a big city team fighting for a pennant.

Then conflict seems to doom him and his team. Often he's confronted by gamblers who may go so far as to kidnap him on the eve of the big game; sometimes his problem is his own swelled head. Or he may have dumped his loyal fiancee back home for a fancier lady. Fortunately, by the final reel, he escapes the gamblers, learns humility, or returns to his true love just in time to hit the home run that wins the pennant. To add visual excitement, the homer is usually an inside-the-park job.

This all-purpose plot with only slight variations could be played as light melodrama, as in *Headin' Home* (1920), with Babe Ruth as the young, clean-living lad, or as comedy as in *Hot Curves* (1930), with veteran vaudeville comic Benny Rubin. Among the most watchable examples are three comedies from the 1930s starring Joe E. Brown, the wide-mouthed comic: *Fireman, Save My Child* (1932), *Elmer the Great* (1933), and *Alibi Ike*

(1935). The latter two had the benefit of being based loosely on the stories of sportswriter Ring Lardner; however, the real plus was Brown, an excellent athlete with a likable screen presence, who could actually look like a ballplayer even when winding up to pitch like some lunatic windmill.

A departure from the usual was *Death on the Diamond* (1934), a totally implausible murder mystery starring Robert Young. The team struggles on toward a pennant even as its best hitter, top pitcher, and star catcher get knocked off in bizarre fashion. Young finally unmasks the murderer with a beanball tossed from the mound. None of it is believable, but it's still great fun.

In 1942, Hollywood at long last made a baseball movie for grownups—*The Pride of the Yankees*, starring Gary Cooper as doomed superstar Lou Gehrig. The rangy Cooper was an awkward athlete and reportedly batted lefthanded so ineptly that batting scenes were shot with him swinging righty and heading for third base with the film later flipped. Nevertheless, he and Teresa Wright as his wife gave such winning performances that even Yankee-haters made an exception for the Gehrigs. Few baseball fans realized that what they were really watching was a love story rather than a baseball movie. In fact, a TV retelling of the Gehrig story in 1979 was titled *A Love Affair: The Eleanor and Lou Gehrig Story* and had not a single scene of baseball action.

Angels, Bums, and "Biopics"

After World War II, it took Hollywood some time to remember baseball. When it did, the first effort was probably the worst baseball movie ever made—*The Babe Ruth Story* (1948), with William Bendix as the Babe. Ex-football player Paul Douglas was originally slated for the role but, when that fell through, poor Bendix was sent up to bat.

Bendix had practically made a career of playing the marine from Brooklyn who loved "Dem Bums" in countless wartime flicks. He should have stayed in the service. As written, the role of Ruth is so honorable, heroic and downright nice as to be unplayable. Whether leaving a game to take an injured puppy to the hospital, promising a sick child to hit two homers, passing on a manager job so another man won't be fired, or volunteering to take an experimental treatment to help mankind, St. Babe is a wonder to behold. Furthermore, Bendix swings a baseball bat so ludicrously he makes Gary Cooper look like Ted Williams. (Ruth, who was dying of cancer at the time, reportedly sat through about half of this mess before getting up and stomping out of the theater.)

Two years later, Bendix found his niche in the occasionally funny *Kill the Umpire* (1950).

A much better example of what *Variety* would call a "biopic," was *The Stratton Story* (1949). The film starred James Stewart as pitcher Monte Stratton, who lost his leg in a hunting accident but came back to pitch in the Texas League. As in the Gehrig movies, the emphasis was on romance. And why not? June Allyson played the ever-supportive, girl-next-door, loving wife that every jock dreams about.

No baseball movie ever had a lead more believable on the diamond than *The Jackie Robinson Story* (1950) simply because Jackie played himself. He did okay in the straight scenes too, helped by Ruby Dee as his wife. Purists might quibble that Branch Rickey comes off a bit too noble, but Robinson's struggle to face down racism and become the first twentieth century African American to play in the major leagues makes compelling watching.

Three other biopics from the 1950s are worth mentioning. *The Pride of St. Louis* (1952) with Dan Dailey is a sometimes entertaining, sometime accurate retelling of Dizzy Dean's career. Less successful is *The Winning Team* (1952), whose producers made the unfortunate decision to use Mrs. Grover Cleveland Alexander as technical advisor. The result was a textbook movie on how Mrs. Alex made Mr. Alex into a great pitcher. Doris Day inspires as Mrs. Alexander; Ronald Reagan plays the pitcher.

Another largely unbelievable movie, *Fear Strikes Out* (1957), was based on Jim Piersall's battle to overcome mental illness. It's a fine movie—if one shuts one's eyes during the baseball scenes. Anthony Perkins in his pre-Norman Bates period makes a believable Piersall except when he's throwing the ball.

Fantasy baseball pictures were all the rage during this period. The best was *It Happens Every Spring* (1949), in which Ray Milland plays a chemistry professor who comes up with a concoction that has the peculiar ability to avoid wood. By rubbing it on a baseball, he becomes an unhittable pitcher. For once, an actor's awkward throwing style worked to the movie's advantage; this guy wasn't really a pitcher and he looked it. Paul Douglas, who had a real knack for these things, practically stole the movie as Milland's catcher.

A review of the 1994 remake of *Angels in the Outfield* described the original, made in 1951 as a "classic." It was so only by comparison. In the original, Douglas is quite funny as the hard-headed, hard-hearted, hard-cursing manager of an inept team that is helped to a pennant by angels. There's a nice whimsical quality here. In the remake, Danny Glover is not funny and the angels are offensive.

Other gimmick pictures are *Rhubarb*; *The Kid from Left Field* (1953), in which a nine-year-old becomes the manager of a major league team; and *Roogie's Bump* (1954), in which a mysterious bump on his arm allows a little boy to throw a fearsome fastball. *Rhubarb* (1951), in which a cat inherits a ballclub, is the only one worth catching as entertainment on the Late Show. Ray Milland plays the cat's keeper and Jan Sterling is his fiancee who is apparently allergic to cats.

Nevertheless, the other two gimmick movies were later remade. In the 1979, made-for-TV version, Gary Coleman is terminally cute as *The Kid from Left Field*. At least the original had Dan Dailey as the brains behind the kid (proving there was life after Dizzy Dean). *Rookie of the Year* (1993) is superior to *Roogie's Bump*, which is like saying having a tooth drilled is more fun than a root canal operation. Here the kid gets his fantastic fastball when his broken arm heals strangely. Actually, the movie might have survived if director Daniel Stern had not put himself in an embarrassingly unfunny role as the Chicago Cubs' pitching coach. Everytime he does a three minute "bit," it can seem like three hours.

The two best (and only) baseball musicals were made during this period. In *Take Me Out to the Ball Game* (1949), Gene Kelly, Frank Sinatra, and Jules Munshin sing and dance as a turn-of-the-century Tinker-to-Evers-to-Chance who double as vaudevillians in the offseason. Esther Williams swims as the team owner, proving incontrovertibly that she does more for a bathing suit than George Steinbrenner.

Even better is *Damn Yankees* (1958), the film version of the long-running Broadway show. A middle-aged Washington fan sells his soul to the devil to become a superstar (Tab Hunter) and lead the Senators (remember the Senators?) to the pennant. Of course, the devil (Ray Walston before he became our favorite Martian) is a Yankees fan with a dastardly plot, aided by the beautiful Lola (Gwen Verdon). Whatever Lola wants Lola gets but you've got to have heart and in the end one of these two lost souls comes out on top.

Big Leaguer (1953), with Edward G. Robinson running a tryout camp, and *The Great American Pastime* (1956), with Tom Ewell as a Little League coach, are pleasant and forgettable. However, the period is flanked by two of the most memorable baseball movie clunkers of all time. In *The Kid from Cleveland* (1949), the previous year's World Champion Indians save the title character (Russ Tamblyn) from juvenile delinquency. Had they played as well as they acted, the Indians would have finished below the St. Louis Browns. Despite appearing in this career jeopardizer, Indian utility infielder John Berardino went on to become a successful actor playing Dr. Steve Hardy for decades on the TV soap opera *General Hospital*.

In 1962, Mickey Mantle and Roger Maris came off their greatest home run season to prove they could still strike out in *Safe at Home*, some nonsense that saw M & M come to the rescue of a Little Leaguer who'd bragged he could get them for his team banquet. As actors both sluggers are well below the Mendoza line, but Olivier in his prime couldn't save this turkey.

The Golden Age of Baseball Movies

It's heretical to say that these are the best of times for anything, but for baseball movies, it's true. After a fallow 1960s in which Hollywood considered any movie with a baseball theme sure death at the box office, things picked up considerably in the 1970s and reached a high point in the 1980s that shows signs of continuing. That's not to say that bad baseball movies aren't available. There's no excuse for either of the Bad News Bears sequels or the remake of *Angels in the Outfield*, and anyone who can get a laugh out of Neil Simon's *The Slugger's Wife* (1985) should take an ink-blot test. But, by and large, even the second-rate efforts of the last few years have some watchable qualities.

For example, *The Babe* (1992) is essentially a linear, warts-and-all retelling of a lot of things we already knew about Ruth that manages to make even baseball, gluttony, and sex a bit boring. On the other hand, John Goodman is an agreeable actor and, compared with Bill Bendix's *The Babe Ruth Story*, this one is *Citizen Kane*. A 1991 NBC production for television, *Babe Ruth*, with Stephen Lang as the Bambino, is similar to *The Babe* in its tell-all approach and got higher marks from some TV critics.

Five made-for-TV biopics are worth a look:

It's Good to Be Alive (1974), the story of Roy Campanella's struggle after a near-fatal accident left him paralyzed, benefits from a remarkable performance by Paul Winfield as the former Dodger catcher.

One in a Million: The Ron LeFlore Story (1978) casts LeVar Burton in the title role of the outfielder who went from prison to the Tigers.

Aunt Mary (1979) gives us Jean Stapleton as Mary Dobkin, a woman who coached Little League teams in Baltimore.

Don't Look Back: The Story of Leroy "Satchel" Paige (1981) is an acceptable biography starring Louis Gossett, Jr.

A Winner Never Quits (1986) stars Keith Carradine as Pete Gray, the one-armed outfielder who played for the St. Louis Browns during World War II.

All five movies are of the inspirational, feel-good mode but for the most part avoid maudlin sentimentality. Tom Selleck's *Mr. Baseball* (1992) turned out to be a disappointment both at the box office and critically. Reportedly, most of the sharp edges about an American playing in Japan were sanded off when Matsushita Electrical Industrial Company bought MCA, Inc., the owner of the movie studio. Much funnier, though sillier, is *Major League* (1989), with its traditional bad-players-pull-together-and-win plot. Most of the same cast—Tom Berenger, Corbin Bernsen, and Charlie Sheen—disdained free agency to win again for Cleveland, though with many fewer laughs, in *Major League II* (1993).

There are also two little-known movies about life in the minor leagues in the 1950s: *Pastime* (1991), with William Russ as an aging pitcher who befriends a young African-American rookie, and *Long Gone* (HBO 1987), with William L. Peterson as a grizzled player-manager. Both work right up to the last reel but could benefit from different endings. The finale of *Long Gone* is too hokey even for what is basically a comedy; *Pastime*'s finish comes out of left field (to use a baseball cliché) and leaves a sour taste.

The Golden Age of Baseball Movies really dawned with *Bang the Drum Slowly* (1973), based on Mark Harris's novel. This is a touching story about a star pitcher and journeyman catcher with nothing in common who nevertheless become close friends when the catcher is diagnosed with Hodgkin's Disease. The movie helped make stars of Michael Moriarty and Robert De Niro, who are excellent as, respectively, the pitcher and catcher.

The Bad News Bears (1976) with Walter Matthau as a grumpy, beer-guzzling Little League coach and Tatum O'Neal as the team's star pitcher was flat-out funny but never slipped into caricature. Some critics objected to all the profanity spouted by the Bears; then again, some critics have never listened to modern youngsters.

The Bingo Long Traveling All-Stars & Motor Kings (1976) starred Billy Dee Williams and James Earl Jones as African-American baseball stars on the road during the Depression. Though highly entertaining, the film was not popular with purists who would have preferred a somber piece about the tragedy of excluding African Americans from the major leagues at this time.

The Natural (1984) was a break-out baseball movie in that it was adult, serious, and made money. The Robert

Redford vehicle tells the story of Roy Hobbs, who would have been a great star had he not been shot and nearly killed by a mysterious lady in black. Eventually, he makes a marvelous comeback at an age when most players are ready to retire. Heavy on symbolism, the movie departs from the Bernard Malamud novel which has a "down" ending. All the better—the film winds up with a home run even more spectacular than Bill Mazeroski's.

Bull Durham (1988) ranks first among baseball movies with many critics and certainly among the top three with most. Although it's a wonderful comedy, it always treats baseball with respect and honesty. The cast is headed by Kevin Costner as a career minor league catcher, Tim Robbins as a young pitcher with a million dollar arm and five-cent head, and Susan Sarandon as the ultimate Baseball Annie.

John Sayles's *Eight Men Out* (1988), though decidedly different in content, is no less a quality movie. The story of the 1919 Black Sox is retold with great attention to period detail. The movie's only weakness is that it tries to tell too many stories—the players, the gamblers, the owners, and the media's—so that the tragedy inherent in eight players destroying their careers for thirty pieces of silver is somewhat diffused.

Field of Dreams (1989) tells the story of an Iowa farmer (Kevin Costner) who builds a baseball field in his cornfield after receiving instructions from a mysterious voice—"If you build it, they will come." Sure enough, Joe Jackson and other ghosts are soon cavorting around the infield. There's endless blab about how glorious baseball is and the whimsy level is often in the red zone; regardless, the movie was a critical and box office success.

A League of Their Own (1992), tells—with fictional flourishes—the story of the All American Girls Baseball League that began during World War II when many of the men were away. Tom Hanks is the irascible ex-big leaguer and manager who comes to believe in his players; Geena Davis is the team's star catcher.

The baseball movies of the next few years may well be mostly gimmicky entertainments like *Rookie of the Year* or unconvincing biopics like *The Babe*. But the high quality of such films as *Bull Durham*, *Eight Men Out*, and *Field of Dreams* allows the moviegoing baseball fan to hope the best is yet to come.

A Baseball Film Chronology

The list below is not all-inclusive; many silent films, particularly those for which no print has survived, are omitted.

The Ball Game (1898) Thomas A. Edison, B&W, one reel. First outdoor baseball action ever filmed.

Casey at the Bat (1899) Thomas A. Edison, B&W, one reel. Comic bit which concludes with batter pummeling umpire.

How the Office Boy Saw the Game (1906) Thomas A. Edison, B&W, one reel. Comedy short.

Christy Mathewson, New York National League Baseball Team (1907) The Winthrop Moving Picture Co., B&W, one reel. Early action footage.

World Championship Baseball (1908) Essanay, B&W, one reel. First World Series film.

His Last Game (1909) Independent Motion Picture Co., B&W, one reel. First feature film with baseball action.

Hal Chase's Home Run (1911) Kalem, B&W, one reel. Cast: Hal Chase. (Not a newsreel; homer by Chase wins teammate his lady love.)

Breaking into the Big League 1913 Kalem, B&W, two-part story over two reels. Cast: Christy Mathewson, John J. McGraw, other New York Giants.

1915 World's Championship Baseball Series (1915) World Series Film Co., B&W, one reel.

Right Off the Bat (1915) Arrow Film Corp., B&W, 5 reels. Dir.: Hugh Reticker. Cast: Mike Donlin, John J. McGraw, Claire Mesereau.

Casey at the Bat (1916) Fine Arts Film Co., B&W, 5 reels. Dir.: Lloyd Ingraham. Cast: DeWolf Hopper, Kate Toncray.

Somewhere in Georgia (1916) Sunbeam Motion Picture Corp., B&W, 6 reels. Dir.: George Ridgwell. Cast: Ty Cobb, Elsie MacLeod.

The Pinch Hitter (1917) New York Motion Picture Corp., B&W 5 reels. Dir.: Victor L. Schertzinger. Cast: Charles Ray, Sylvia Bremer.

One Touch of Nature (1917) Thomas A. Edison, Inc., B&W, 5 reels. Dir.: Edward H. Griffith. Cast: John Drew Bennett, Viola Cain, John J. McGraw.

The Busher (1919) Thomas H. Ince Corp., B&W, 5 reels. Dir.: Jerome Storm. Cast: Charles Ray, Colleen Moore, John Gilbert.

Babe Ruth, How He Makes His Home Runs (1920) Educational Pictures, B&W, one reel. One of the earliest instructional films.

Headin' Home (1920) Kessel & Baumann Yankee Film Corp., B&W, 5 reels. Dir.: Lawrence Windom. Cast: Babe Ruth, Ruth Taylor.

As the World Turns (1921) Andlauer Productions Elk Photo Plays, B&W, 7 reels. Dir.: W.A. Andlauer. Cast: Jack Johnson, Blanche Thompson.

Trifling with Honor (1923) Universal Pictures, B&W, 8 reels. Dir.: Harry A. Pollard. Cast: Rockliffe Fellowes, Fritzi Ridgeway.

The Battling Orioles (1924) Hal E. Roach Studios, B&W, 6 reels. Dir.: Ted Wilde, Fred Guiol. Cast: Glenn Tryon, Blanche Mahaffey.

Hit and Run (1924) Universal Pictures, B&W, 6 reels. Dir.: Edward Sedgwick. Cast: Hoot Gibson, Marion Harlan, Mike Donlin.

Life's Greatest Game (1924) Emory Johnson Productions, B&W, 8 reels. Dir.: Emory Johnson. Cast: Tom Santschi, Johnnie Walker.

The Pinch Hitter (1925) Associated Exhibitors, B&W, 7 reels. Dir.: Joseph Henabery. Cast: Glenn Hunter, Constance Bennett.

Play Ball (1925) Pathe Exchange, B&W, 10 chapter serial, 2 reels per chapter. Dir.: Spencer G. Bennett. Cast: Allene Ray, Walter Miller, John McGraw and the New York Giants.

The New Klondike (1926) Famous Players-Lasky Paramount Pictures, B&W, 8 reels. Dir.: Lewis Milestone. Cast: Thomas Meighan, Lila Lee, Paul Kelly.

Out of the West (1926) R-C Pictures, B&W, 5 reels. Dir.: Robert De Lacy. Cast: Tom Tyler, Bernice Welch.

The Babe Comes Home (1927) First National Pictures, B&W. Dir.: Ted Wilde. Cast: Babe Ruth, Anna Q. Nilsson.

The Bush Leaguer (1927) Warner Bros., B&W. Dir.: Howard Bretherton. Cast: Monte Blue, Clyde Cook, William Demarest.

Casey at the Bat (1927) Famous Players-Lasky Paramount Pictures, B&W. Dir.: Monte Brice. Cast: Wallace Beery, Ford Sterling, ZaSu Pitts, Sterling Holloway.

Catch-as-Catch-Can (1927) Gotham Productions, B&W. Dir.: Charles Hutchinson. Cast: William Fairbanks, Jack Richardson.

College (1927) Buster Keaton Productions United Artists, B&W. Dir.: James W. Horne. Cast: Buster Keaton, Anne Cornwall, U. of Southern California Baseball Team.

Slide, Kelly, Slide (1927) Metro-Goldwyn-Mayer, B&W, 8 reels. Dir.: Edward Sedgwick. Cast: William Haines, Sally O'Neil, Harry Carey, Mike Donlin, Bob Meusel, Irish Meusel, Tony Lazerri.

The Cameraman (1928) Metro-Goldwyn-Mayer, B&W, 8 reels. Dir.: Edward Sedgwick. Cast: Buster Keaton, Marceline Day.

Speedy (1928) Harold Lloyd Corp. Paramount Famous Lasky Corp., B&W. Dir.: Ted Wilde. Cast: Harlod Lloyd, Ann Christy, Babe Ruth.

Warming Up (1928) Paramount Famous Lasky Corp., B&W. Dir.: Fred Newmeyer. Cast: Richard Dix, Jean Arthur, Roscoe Karns, Mike Donlin.

Fast Company (1929) Paramount Famous Lasky Corp., B&W, 8 reels. Dir.: A. Edward Sutherland. Cast: Jack Oakie, Evelyn Brent.

Hot Curves (1930) Tiffany Productions, B&W, 9 reels. Dir.: Norman Taurog. Cast: Benny Rubin, Rex Lease, Pert Kelton, Mike Donlin.

They Learned About Women (1930) Metro-Goldwyn-Mayer, B&W, 11 reels. Dir.: Jack Conway, Sam Wood. Cast: Joseph T. Schenck, Gus Van, Bessie Love, Benny Rubin.

Fireman, Save My Child (1932) First National and Vitaphone, B&W, 67 min. Dir.: Lloyd Bacon. Cast: Joe E. Brown, Evalyn Knapp, Guy Kibbee.

Elmer the Great (1933) First National and Vitaphone, B&W, 74 min. Dir.: Mervyn LeRoy. Cast: Joe E. Brown, Patricia Ellis, Frank McHugh, Preston Foster.

Death on the Diamond (1934) Metro-Goldwyn-Mayer, B&W, 69 min. Dir.: Edward Sedgwick. Cast: Robert Young, Madge Evans, Nat Pendleton, Ted Healy.

Alibi Ike (1935) Warner Brothers and Vitaphone, B&W, 73 min. Dir.: Ray Enright. Cast: Joe E. Brown, Olivia de Havilland, Roscoe Karns, William Frawley.

Swell-Head (1935) Columbia Pictures, B&W, 62 min. Dir.: Ben Stoloff. Cast: Wallace Ford, Dickie Moore, Barbara Kent.

The Adventures of Frank Merriwell (1936) Universal Pictures, B&W, 12-chapter serial, 2 reels per chapter. Dir.: Cliff Smith. Cast: Don Briggs, Jean Rogers, John King.

Girls Can Play (1937) Columbia Pictures, B&W, 6 reels. Dir.: Lambert Hillyer. Cast: Jacqueline Wells, Charles Quigley, Rita Hayworth.

The Pride of the Yankees (1942) The Samuel Goldwyn Company RKO-Radio, B&W, 128 min. Dir.: Sam Wood. Cast: Gary Cooper, Teresa Wright, Walter Brennan, Dan Duryea, Babe Ruth.

Ladies' Day (1943) RKO-Radio, B&W, 62 min. Dir.: Leslie Goodwins. Cast: Lupe Velez, Eddie Albert, Patsy Kelly, Max Baer.

The Naughty Nineties (1945) Universal Pictures, B&W, 76 min. Dir.: Jean Yarbrough. Cast: But Abbott, Lou Costello. Includes Abbott and Costello's fames "Who's on first?" routine.

Make Mine Music (1946) Walt Disney Productions RKO-Radio, Color, 75 min. Casey at the Bat sequence directed by Clyde Geronimi and narrated by Jerry Colonna.

The Babe Ruth Story (1948) Allied Artists, B&W, 106 min. Dir.: Roy Del Ruth. Cast: William Bendix, Claire Trevor, Charles Bickford, Sam Levene, William Frawley.

It Happens Every Spring (1949) Twentieth Century-Fox, B&W, 87 min. Dir.: Lloyd Bacon. Cast: Ray Milland, Jean Peters, Paul Douglas, Ed Begley.

The Kid from Cleveland (1949) Republic Pictures, B&W, 89 min. Dir.: Herbert Kline. Cast: George Brent, Lynn Bari, Rusty Tamblyn, Bill Veeck, The Cleveland Indians.

The Stratton Story (1949) Metro-Goldwyn-Mayer, B&W, 106 min. Dir.: Sam Wood. Cast: James Stewart, June Allyson, Frank Morgan, Agnes Moorehead.

Take Me Out to the Ball Game (1949) Metro-Goldwyn-Mayer, Color, 93 min. Dir.: Busby Berkeley. Cast: Gene Kelly, Frank Sinatra, Esther Williams, Jules Munshin, Betty Garrett.

The Jackie Robinson Story (1950) Jewell Pictures Corp. Eagle-Lion Films, B&W, 77 min. Dir.: Alfred E. Green. Cast: Jackie Robinson, Ruby Dee, Minor Watson.

Kill the Umpire (1950) Columbia Pictures, B&W, 78 min. Dir.: William Bendix, Una Merkel, Ray Collins, William Frawley.

Angels in the Outfield (1951) Metro-Goldwyn-Mayer, B&W, 99 min. Dir.: Clarence Brown. Cast: Paul Douglas, Janet Leigh, Donna Corcoran, Keenan Wynn.

Rhubarb (1951) Paramount Pictures, B&W, 94 min. Dir.: Arthur Lubin. Cast: Ray Milland, Jan Sterling, Gene Lockhart, William Frawley.

The Pride of St. Louis (1952) Twentieth Century-Fox, B&W, 93 min. Dir.: Harmon Jones. Cast: Dan Dailey, Joanne Dru, Richard Hylton, Richard Crenna.

The Winning Team (1952) Warner Bros., B&W, 98 min. Dir.: Lewis Seiler. Cast: Doris Day, Ronald Reagan, Frank Lovejoy.

Big Leaguer (1953) Metro-Goldwyn-Mayer, B&W, 70 min. Dir.: Robert Aldrich. Cast: Edward G. Robinson, Vera Ellen, Jeff Richards.

The Kid from Left Field (1953) Twentieth Century-Fox, B&W, 80 min. Dir.: Harmon Jones. Cast: Dan Dailey, Anne Bancroft, Billy Chapin, Lloyd Bridges.

Roogie's Bump (1954) Republic Pictures, B&W, 71 min. Dir.: Harold Young. Cast: Robert Marriot, Ruth Warrick, Olive Blackeney.

The Great American Pastime (1956) Metro-Goldwyn-Mayer, B7W, 89 min. Dir.: Herman Hoffman. Cast: Tom Ewell, Anne Francis, Ann Miller, Dean Jones.

I'll Buy You (1956) Shochiku, B&W, 113 min. Dir.: Masaki Kobayashi. Cast: Keiji Sata, Keiko Kishi, Minoru Oki.

Fear Strikes Out (1957) Paramount Pictures, B&W, 100 min. Dir.: Robert Mulligan. Cast: Anthony Perkins, Karl Malden, Norma Moore.

Damn Yankees (1958) Warner Bros., Color, 110 min. Dir.: George Abbott, Stanley Donen. Cast: Tab Hunter, Gwen Verdon, Ray Walston.

Safe at Home (1962) Maud-Hamilburg Productions Columbia Pictures, B&W, 83 min. Dir.: Walter Doniger. Cast: Mickey

Mantle, Roger Maris, William Frawley, Patricia Barry, Bryan Russell.

Bang the Drum Slowly (1973) Paramount Pictures, Color, 97 min. Dir.: John Hancock. Cast: Michael Moriarty, Robert De Niro, Vincent Gardenia, Phil Foster.

It's Good to Be Alive (1974, made for TV) Metromedia Producers Corporation/ Larry Harman Pictures, Color, 100 min. Dir.: Michael Landon. Cast: Paul Winfield, Louis Gossett Jr., Ruby Dee, Ramon Bieri.

The Bad News Bears (1976) Paramount Pictures, Color, 102 min. Dir.: Michael Ritchie. Cast: Walter Matthau, Tatum O'Neal, Vic Morrow.

The Bingo Long Traveling All-Stars & Motor Kings (1976) Motown Production/Pan Arts Enterprises Universal Pictures, Color, 110 minutes. Dir.: Jon Badham. Cast: Billy Dee Williams, James Earl Jones, Richard Pryor, Stan Shaw.

The Bad News Bears in Breaking Training (1977) Paramount Pictures, Color, 100 min. Dir.: Michael Pressman. Cast: William Devane, Clifton James, Jackie Earle Haley, Jimmy Baio.

The Glory of Their Times (1977, documentary made for TV) PBS, 60 min. Interviews with early twentieth century players.

Just the Beginning (1977) Yung Bang Films, Color, 105 min. Dir.: Jung in Yup. Cast: Jin Yoo Young, Ha Myoung Jung.

Murder at the World Series (1977, made for TV) ABC Circle Films, Color, 100 min. Dir.: Andrew V. McLaglen. Cast: Lynda Day George, Murray Hamilton, Karen Valentine, Gerald S. O'Loughlin, Michael Parks, Janet Leigh.

The Bad News Bears Go to Japan (1978) Paramount Pictures, Color, 91 min. Dir.: John Berry. Cast: Tony Curtis, Jackie Earle Haley, Tomasaburo Wakayama.

A Boy Called Third Base (1978) Gentosha and ATG, Color, 102 min. Dir.: Yoichi Higashi. Cast: Toshiyuki Nagashima, Tsuguaki Yoshida, Aiko Morishita.

Goodbye, Franklin High (1978) Cal-Am Productions, Color, 94 min. Dir.: Mike MacFarland. Cast: Lan Caudell, Julie Adams, William Windom.

Here Come the Tigers (1978) Filmways Pictures American International, Color, 90 min. Dir.: Sean S. Cunningham. Cast: Richard Lincoln, James Zvanut, Samanth Grey.

A Love Affair: The Eleanor and Lou Gehrig Story (1978, made for TV) Charles Fries Productions/Stonehenge Productions ABC, Color, 100 min. Dir.: Fielder Cook. Cast: Blythe Danner, Edward Herrmann, Patricia Neal, Gerald S. O'Laughlin, Ramon Bieri.

One in a Million: The Ron LeFlore Story (1978, made for TV) Roger Gimbel Productions/EMI Television CBS, Color, 100 min. Dir.: William A. Grahame. Cast: LeVar Burton, Madge Sinclair, Billy Martin.

Aunt Mary (1979, made for TV) Henry Jaffe Enterprises CBS, Color, 100 min. Dir.: Peter Werner. Cast: Jean Stapleton, Martin Balsam, Harold Gould, Dolph Sweet.

The Kid from Left Field (1979, made for TV) Gary Coleman Productions/Deena Silver Kramer's Movie Company NBC, Color, 100 min. Dir.: Adell Aldrich. Cast: Gary Coleman, Robert Guillaume, Gary Collins, Ed McMahon.

The Comeback Kid (1980, made for TV) ABC Circle Films ABC, Color, 100 min. Dir.: Peter Levin. Cast: John Ritter, Susan Dey, Doug McKeon, James Gregory.

Squeeze Play (1980) Troma, Color, 92 minutes. Dir.: Samuel Weil. Cast: Jim Harris, Jenni Hetrick, Rick Gitlin.

Don't Look Back: The Story of Leroy "Satchel" Paige (1981, made for TV) TBA Productions; Satie Productions; Triseme ABC, Color, 100 min. Dir.: Richard A. Colla. Cast: Louis Gossett Jr., Beverly Todd, Cleavon Little, Ernie Barnes, Clifton Davis.

Only the Ball Was White (1981, documentary made for TV) Chicago Public Television PBS, 30 min. Dir.: Ken Solarz. Life in the Negro Leagues.

Chasing Dreams (1982) Nascent Productions Prism Entertainment Corp., Color, 96 min. Dir.: Therese Conte. Cast: David G. Brown, John Fife, Jim Shane.

Million Dollar Infield (1982, made for TV) CBS Entertainment CBS, Color, 100 min. Dir.: Hal Cooper. Cast: Bonnie Bedelia, Robert Costanzo, Rob Reiner, Christopher Guest.

Zapped (1982) Embassy Pictures, Color, 96 min. Dir.: Robert J. Rosenthal. Cast: Scott Baio, Willie Aames, Heather Thomas.

Blue Skies Again (1983) Lantana Production Warner Bros., Color, 96 min. Dir.: Richard Michaels. Cast: Harry Hamlin, Mimi Rogers, Robyn Barto.

The Boys of Summer (1993) VidAmerica VCA Programs, Inc, 90 min. Interviews with 1950s Brooklyn Dodgers.

Tiger Town (1983, made for TV) Walt Disney Productions The Disney Channel, Color, 76 min. Dir.: Alan Shapiro. Cast: Roy Scheider, Justin Henry, Sparky Anderson.

The Natural (1984) Tri-Star-Delphi II Tri-Star Pictures, Color, 134 min. Dir.: Barry Levinson. Cast: Robert Redford, Robert Duvall, Glenn Close, Kim Basinger, Wilford Brimley.

The Slugger's Wife (1985) Rastar Columbia Pictures, Color, 105 min. Dir.: Hal Ashby. Cast: Michael O'Keefe, Rebecca De Mornay, Martin Ritt, Randy Quaid.

A Winner Never Quits (1986, made for TV) Blatt/Singer Production Columbia Pictures ABC, Color, 100 min. Dir.: Mel Damski. Cast: Keith Carradine, Huckleberry Fox, Mare Winningham, Dennis Weaver.

A League of Their Own (1987, documentary made for TV) PBS, 30 min. Dir.: Mary Wallace. About 1940s all-women league.

Long Gone (1987, made for TV) Landsburg Company HBO, Color, 110 min. Dir.: Martin Davidson. Cast: William L. Peterson, Virginia Madsen, Dermot Mulroney, Larry Riley.

Bull Durham (1988) Mount Company Orion Pictures, Color, 115 min. Dir,: Ron Shelton. Cast: Kevin Costner, Susan Sarandon, Tim Robbins.

Eight Men Out (1988) Orion Pictures, Color, 115 min. Dir.: John Sayles. Cast: John Cusack, David Strathairn, D.B. Sweeney, Michael Rooker, Charlie Sheen.

Stealing Home (1988) Orion Pictures, Color, 115 min. Dir.: John Sayles. Cast: Mark Harmon, Jodie Foster, Blair Brown.

Field of Dreams (1989) Gordon Company Production Universal Pictures, Color, 107 min. Dir.: Phil Alden Robinson. Cast: Kevin Costner, Any Madigan, Gaby Hoffman, James Earl Jones, Ray Liotta, Burt Lancaster.

Major League (1989) Morgan Creek/Mirage Production Paramount Pictures, Color, 106 min. Dir.: David Ward. Cast: Tom Berenger, Charlie Sheen, Corbin Bernsen.

The Court-Martial of Jackie Robinson (1990, made for TV) Von Zerneck-Sertner Films; Turner Pictures TNT, Color, 100 min. Dir.: Larry Peerce. Cast: Andre Braugher, Ruby Dee, Stan Shaw, Bruce Dern, Paul Dooley.

Babe Ruth (1991, made for TV) Lyttle Productions NBC, Color, 100 min. Dir.: Mark Tinker. Cast: Stephan Lang, Bruce Weitz, Donald Moffat, Lisa Zane, Pete Rose.

Pastime (1991) Bullpen Ltd./Open Road Productions Miramax, Color, 95 min. Dir.: Robin B. Armstrong. Cast: William Russ, Glenn Plummer, Noble Willingham, Jeffrey Tambor.

Talent for the Game (1991) Paramount Pictures, Color, 91 min. Dir.: Robert M. Young. Cast: Edward James Olmos, Lorraine Bracco, Jeffrey Corbett.

The Babe (1992) Waterhorse/Finnegan-Pinchuk Universal Pictures, Color, 113 min. Dir.: Arthur Hiller. Cast: John Goodman, Kelly McGillis, Trini Alvarado, Bruce Boxleitner.

The Comrades of Summer (1992, made for TV) Grossbart Barnett Productions HBO, Color, 108 min. Dir.: Tommy Lee Wallace. Cast: Joe Mantegna, Natalya Negoda, Mark Rolston.

A League of Their Own (1992) Parkway Production Columbia Pictures, Color, 124 min. Dir.: Penny Marshall. Cast: Tom Hanks, Geena Davis, Lori Petty, Madonna, Rosie O'Donnell.

Mr. Baseball (1992) Outlaw Production Universal Pictures, Color, 100 min. Dir.: Fred Schepisi. Cast: Tom Selleck, Ken Takakura, Aya Takanashi.

Cooperstown (1993, made for TV) Brandman Productions, Inc./Ambler Television TNT Screenworks, Color, 90 min. Dir.: Charles Haid. Cast: Alan Arkin, Graham Greene, Hope Lange, Josh Charles, Ed Begley Jr.

Rookie of the Year (1993) Twentieth Century-Fox, Color, 103 min. Dir.: Daniel Stern. Cast: Thomas Ian Nicholas, Gary Busey, Albert Hall, Amy Morton.

The Sandlot (1993) Island World Twentieth Century-Fox, Color, 101 min. Dir.: David Mickey Evans. Cast: Tom Guiry, Mike Vitar, Patrick Renna, Chauncy Leopardi.

Cobb (1994) Warner Bros. in association with Regency Enterprises and Alcor Film, Color, 126 min. Dir.: Ron Shelton. Cast: Tommy Lee Jones, Robert Wuhl, Lolita Davidovich.

THE REGISTERS, LEADERS & ROSTERS

The History of Major League Baseball Statistics

John Thorn, Pete Palmer, and Joseph M. Wayman

Part Two, the statistical section of *Total Baseball*, presents the record of major league contests played from 1871 through 1994—all 160,582 of them. It details the accomplishments of the game's 2,181 teams and 14,166 players so completely and accurately that Major League Baseball has, with publication of this volume, authorized *Total Baseball* to be the official encyclopedia of the game, its authentic historical record.

In its previous three editions, *Total Baseball* won critical acclaim and a devoted following not only for its breadth and depth of information but also for its pioneering "sabermetric" stats that offered alternative, unofficial measures of player performance. Yet for all the innovation of its previous three editions, *Total Baseball* has stood squarely in the tradition of baseball record keeping; it is—like each new spring of our national pastime—a link in a long, long chain. As the New York Knickerbockers' game of 150 years ago lives on in the game of today, so is this volume enriched by the labors of statisticians from Henry Chadwick to Ernie Lanigan, from S.C. Thompson and Seymour Siwoff to David Neft and Bill James.

How we came from the Knickerbockers' primitive accounting of outs and runs to the vast array of statistics available today is an interesting process, in which Major League Baseball's role has been central. Through its evolving scoring rules and procedures, its judicious endorsement of new measures, and its continuing mission to set the record straight, the Commissioner's Office and its official scorers have provided fans with a wealth of statistical data unmatched by any other sport—perhaps any other human activity—on earth.

Here is how we who love baseball came to this fortunate estate, and how we at *Total Baseball* created what is now the official historical record.

The Origins, 1845-1875

Baseball and stats were a tandem from the very Eden of the game. The first box score appeared in the *New York Morning News* on October 22, 1845, less than a month after Alexander Cartwright and his Knickerbocker teammates codified the first set of rules. Why did these early players and scribes measure individual performance rather than simply count the score? In part to imitate the custom of cricket; yet the larger explanation is that the numbers served to legitimize men's concern with a boys' pastime. The pioneers of baseball reporting—William Cauldwell of the *Sunday Mercury*, William Porter of *Spirit of the Times*, the unknown annalist at the *News*, and later Henry Chadwick—may indeed have reflected that if they did not cloak the game in the "importance" of statistics, it might not seem worthwhile for adults to read about, let alone play. Statistics elevated baseball from other boys' field games of the 1840s and '50s to make it somehow systematic and serious, like business; despite baseball's essential simplicity, it was laced with intricate detail that suited it perfectly to quantification.

In the development of baseball statistics, no man is more important than Father Chadwick. Born in England in 1824, he came to these shores at age thirteen steeped in the tradition of cricket. In his teens he played the English game and in his twenties he reported on it for a variety of newspapers, including the *Long Island Star* and the *New York Times*. In the early 1840s, before the Knickerbocker rules eliminated the practice of retiring a base runner by throwing the ball at him rather than to the base, Chadwick occasionally played baseball too, but he was not favorably impressed, having received "some hard hits in the ribs." Not until 1856, by which time he had been a cricket reporter for a decade, were Chadwick's eyes opened to the possibilities in the American game, which had improved dramatically since his youth. In 1868 he recalled, "On returning from the early close of a cricket match on Fox Hill, I chanced to go through the Elysian Fields during the progress of a contest between the noted Eagle and Gotham clubs. The game was being sharply played on both sides, and I watched it with deeper interest than any previous ball game between clubs that I had seen. It was not long before I was struck with the idea that baseball was just the game for a national sport for Americans . . . as much so as cricket in England. At the time I refer to I had been reporting cricket for years, and, in my method of taking notes of contests, I had a plan peculiarly my own. It was not long, therefore, after I had become interested in baseball, before I began to invent a method of giving detailed reports of leading contests at baseball . . . ."

Thus Chadwick's cricket background was largely the impetus to his method of scoring a baseball game, the format of his early box scores, and the copious if primitive statistics that appeared in his year-end summaries in the

New York Clipper, Beadle's *Dime Base-Ball Player*, and other publications.

Actually, cricket had begun to shape baseball statistics even before Chadwick's conversion. The first box score reported on two categories, outs and runs: outs, or "hands out," counted both unsuccessful times at bat and outs run into on the basepaths; "runs" were runs scored, not those driven in. The reason for not recording hits in the early years, when coverage of baseball matches appeared alongside reports of cricket matches, was that, unlike baseball, cricket had no such category as the successful hit which did not produce a run. To reach "base" in cricket is to run to the opposite wicket, which tallies a run; if you hit the ball and do not score a run, you have been put out.

Cricket box scores were virtual play-by-plays, a fact made possible by the lesser number of possible events. This play-by-play aspect was applied to a baseball box score as early as 1856; interestingly, despite the abundance of detail, hits were not accounted, nor did they appear in Chadwick's own box scores until 1867. The batting champion as declared by Chadwick, whose computations were immediately and universally accepted as "official," was the man with the highest average of runs per game. An inverse though imprecise measure of batting quality was outs per game. After 1863, when a fair ball caught on one bounce was no longer an out, fielding leaders were those with the greatest total of fly catches, assists, and "foul bounds" (fouls caught on one bounce). Pitching effectiveness was based purely on control, with the leader recognized as the one whose delivery offered the most opportunities for outs at first base and led to the fewest passed balls.

In a sense, Chadwick's measuring of baseball as if it were cricket can be viewed as correct: when you strip the game to its basic elements, those that determine victory or defeat, outs and runs are indeed all that count in the end. No individual statistic is meaningful to the team unless it relates directly to the scoring of runs.

Early player stats were of the most primitive kind, the counting kind. They'd tell you how many runs, or outs, or fly catches had occurred—later, how many hits or total bases. Counting is the most basic of all statistical processes; the next step up is averaging, and Chadwick was the first to put this into practice.

As professionalism infiltrated the game, teams began to bid for star-caliber players. Stars were known not by their stats but by their style until 1865, when Chadwick began to record in the *Clipper* a form of batting average taken from the cricket pages—runs per game. Two years later, in his newly founded baseball weekly, *The Ball Players' Chronicle*, he began to record not only average runs and outs per game, but also home runs, total bases, total bases per game—and hits per game. The averages were expressed not with decimal places but in the standard cricket format of the "average and over." Thus a batter with 23 hits in 6 games would have an average expressed not as 3.83 but as "3–5"—an average of 3 with an overage, or remainder, of 5. Another innovation was to remove from the individual accounting all bases gained through errors. Runs scored by a team, beginning in 1867, were divided between those scored after a man reached base on a clean hit and those arising from a runner's having reached base on an error. This was a clear precursor of the modern earned run average.

By the end of the decade Chadwick was recording total bases and home runs, but he placed little stock in either, as conscious attempts at slugging violated his cricket-bred image of "form." Just as cricket aficionados watch the game for the many opportunities for fine fielding it affords, so was baseball from its inception perceived as a fielders' sport. The original Knickerbocker rules of 1845, in fact, specified that a ball hit out of the field—in fair territory or foul—was a foul ball! "Long hits are showy," Chadwick wrote in the *Clipper* in 1868, "but they do not pay in the long run. Sharp grounders insuring the first-base certain, and sometimes the second-base easily, are worth all the hits made for home-runs which players strive for."

Chadwick prevailed, and the batting average used from that year on is the same as that used today except in its denominator, where at bats replaced games in 1876. Moreover, Chadwick created a measure in the 1860s that divided total bases by games played; change that denominator to at bats and you have today's slugging average—which, incidentally, was not accepted by the National League as an official statistic until 1923 and by the American until 1946.

Chadwick's "total bases average" represent the game's first attempt at a weighted average—an average in which the elements collected together in the numerator or the denominator are recognized numerically as being unequal. In this instance, a single is the unweighted unit, the double is weighted by a factor of two, the triple by three, and the home run by four. Statistically, this is a distinct leap forward from, first, counting, and next, averaging. The weighted average is in fact the cornerstone of today's statistical innovations, or sabermetrics.

The 1870s gave rise to some new batting stats and to the first attempt to quantify thoroughly the other principal facets of the game, pitching and fielding. Although the *Clipper* recorded base hits and total bases as early as 1868, a significant wrinkle was added in 1870 when at bats were listed as well. This was a critical introduction because it permitted the improvement of the batting average, first introduced in its current form by H.A. Dobson of Washington, D.C., in the *Dime Base-Ball Player* of 1872, and first computed "officially"—that is, for the newly created National League—in 1876, the lone year in which bases on balls were figured as outs. Since then the batting average has not changed, except for 1887, when bases on balls were counted as *hits*. In accord with previously created Major League Baseball policy, *Total Baseball* counts a walk as neither an out nor a hit for all years since 1871.

The objections to the batting average are well known, but to date have not disturbed its place as the most popular measure of hitting ability. First of all, the batting average makes no distinction between the single, the double, the triple, and the home run, treating all as the same unit. This objection had been addressed in 1868 by Chadwick's total bases average. Second, the batting average gives no indication of the effect of that base hit—that is, its value to the team. Third, the batting average does not take into account those occasions when first base is reached via a walk, hit batsman, or error. This last point was addressed at a surprisingly early date, too: in 1879 the National

League adopted as an official statistic a forerunner of the on base percentage; it was called "reached first base," which included times reached by error as well as base on balls and base hits. (Being hit by a pitch did not give the batter first base until the ensuing decade.)

The Flowering, 1876-1920

Ever since the Civil War, serial guides like *Beadle* and *DeWitt* and sporting columns like those in the *Clipper* had carried year-end tabulations of batting, fielding, and pitching exploits, varying from year to year with the brainstorms of Chadwick or other demon compilers like New York's M.J. Kelly or Philadelphia's Al Wright. But the year 1876 was special. It was significant not only for the founding of the National League and the official debut of the batting average in its current form, it was also the Centennial of the United States, which was marked by a giant exposition in Philadelphia celebrating the mechanical marvels of the day. American ingenuity reigned, and technology was seen as the new handmaiden of democracy. Baseball, that mirror of American life, reflected the fervor for things scientific with an explosion of statistics far more complex than those seen before, particularly in the previously neglected areas of pitching and fielding. The increasingly minute statistical examination of the game met a responsive audience, one primed to view complexity as a measure of worth.

In 1876 the number of "official" offensive stats tabulated at season's end—i.e., in any of the publications inspired by Chadwick or Albert Spalding—was six: games, at bats, runs, hits, runs per game, and batting average. (And as with all the various guides until 1941, the stats of men who played in fewer than a specified minimum number of games were not noted.) Of these six, only runs and runs per game were common in the 1860s, while that decade's tabulation of total bases vanished. The number of official offensive stats a hundred years later? Twenty. (Today the number is twenty-one, with the addition of on base percentage).

The number of "official" pitching categories in 1876 was eleven, and there were some modernistic surprises, such as earned run average, hits allowed, hits per game, and opponents' batting average. Strikeouts were not recorded, for Chadwick saw them strictly as a sign of poor batting rather than good pitching (his view had such an impact that pitcher strikeouts were not kept officially until 1889). The number of official pitching stats today? Twenty-four.

The number of fielding categories in 1876 was six. One hundred years later it was still six (with the exception of the catcher, who gets a seventh: passed balls), dramatizing how the game, which originated as a showcase for fielders, had changed. The fielding stats of 1876 lumped "battery errors" with fielding errors, so that wild pitches and passed balls—in some years, even walks—diminished one's fielding percentage. This practice continued until 1887, but in *Total Baseball* battery errors are not included in fielding stats. Battery-mates' fielding stats were boosted by the awarding of an assist to the pitcher on strikeouts. This practice lasted until 1889, but is not reflected in *Total Baseball*.

The custom in 1876, as it is now, was to combine putouts, assists, and errors to form a "percentage of chances accepted," or what is today known as fielding average or fielding percentage. A "missing link" variant, devised by Al Wright in 1875, was to form averages by dividing the putouts by the number of games to yield a "putout average"; dividing the assists similarly to arrive at an "assist average"; and dividing putouts plus assists by games to get "fielding average." These averages took no account of errors. (Wright's "fielding average" was reborn a century later as Bill James's "range factor.")

The public's appetite for new statistics was not sated by the outburst of 1876. New measures were introduced in dizzying profusion in the remaining years of the century. Some of these did not catch on and were soon dropped for all time, like the meaningless "total bases run," while others fizzled only to reappear with new vigor in the twentieth century. These include (a) the above-mentioned "reached first base," which resurfaced in the early 1950s in an unofficial, improved form called on base percentage and became an official stat more than thirty years later, and (b) an 1860s stat, earned run average, which was periodically revived before dropping from sight in the 1880s, only to return triumphant to the NL in 1912 and the AL in 1913. (In 1913 Ban Johnson not only proclaimed the ERA official but became so enamored with it that he also instructed American League scorers to compile no official won-lost records. This state of affairs lasted for seven years, 1913-1919, but *Total Baseball* does record wins and losses by pitchers in those years, in accordance with the understood scoring practices of the time.)

Another stat that was "sent back to the minors" before its eventual adoption as an official stat in 1920 was the run batted in. Introduced by a Buffalo newspaper in 1879, the stat was picked up the following year by the *Chicago Tribune* and even became an official NL stat for the opening months of 1891. By season's end it had faded as most NL scorers declined to account for it in their summaries (the American Association, however, recorded it all year long). Ernie Lanigan picked up the RBI baton with his reports to the *New York Press* from 1907 through 1919, and he did not figure RBIs for men who played in fewer than ten games, or club totals for traded players. For *Total Baseball* we have placed much reliance upon the source material donated by Information Concepts, Inc. (ICI) to the National Baseball Library in Cooperstown following publication of *The Baseball Encyclopedia* which it developed for publication by Macmillan in 1969. David Neft also kindly supplied us with his unpublished RBI data for the previously missing National League seasons of 1880-1885. The John Tattersall collection of nineteenth century game accounts and box scores was valuable for uncovering RBIs as well. (For a detailed accounting of the sources employed for this official historical record of Major League Baseball, see the conclusion of the essay.)

Other statistics introduced officially before the turn of the century were stolen bases (though not caught stealing); doubles, triples, and homers; and sacrifice bunts (though an at-bat was charged from 1889 through 1893). Pitcher strikeouts, bases on balls, and the hit-by-pitch also appeared before 1900, but hit-by-pitch stats were not kept for batters on a systematic basis until 1917 in the NL and 1920 in the AL. Through newspaper research, we have filled in HBP data from 1884 through 1916 in the National League; the Players League of 1890; the American Association of 1882-1891; from 1901 through 1919 in the American League, and the 1914-1915 Federal League.

Hit into double play—including line outs as well as an groundouts—was an erratically recorded stat in the nineteenth century, but separate stats for groundouts into double plays have been kept by the leagues only since 1933 in the NL and 1939 in the AL. Batters' strikeouts were reported unofficially in 1891, but not as a league stat until 1910 in the NL and 1913 in the AL. Innings pitched were not kept until 1908 in the AL and 1903 in the NL. You can see what a patchwork quilt the records of Major League Baseball were in its early years.

Stolen bases were awarded not only for clean steals but also for extra bases taken through daring, from the first year in which totals were kept, 1886, until 1898. Because the figures reported in the guides were grossly inflated (such as Harry Stovey's ostensible 156 steals in 1888), the figures in *Total Baseball* reflect game-by-game research and refiguring. Caught-stealing (CS) figures are available on a very sketchy basis in some of the later years of the century, as some newspapers carried the data in the box scores of hometown games. From 1912 on, Lanigan recorded CS in box scores of the *New York Press*, but the leagues did not keep the figure officially until 1920. The AL has tabulated CS from that year to the present, excepting 1927, which members of the Society for American Baseball Research reconstructed from newspaper box scores. National League caught-stealing data exists for 1920-1925, and for 1951 to the present.

The new century added little in the way of new official statistics—ERA, RBI, and slugging average are better regarded as revivals despite their respective adoption dates of 1912, 1920, and 1923. But back in 1908 there was a classic case of a statistic rushing in to fill a void, as Phillies' manager Billy Murray observed that his outfielder Sherry Magee had the happy facility of providing a long fly ball whenever presented with a situation of a man on third and fewer than two outs. Taking up the cudgels on his player's behalf, Murray protested to the National League office that it was unfair to charge Magee with an unsuccessful time at bat when he was in fact succeeding, doing precisely what the situation demanded. (More recent stats—the save and the late lamented game-winning run batted in, or GWRBI—have followed from this sort of perception that something important was occurring on the field yet had no verifiable reality because it was not being measured.)

A signal event took place in 1912: the publication by *Baseball Magazine* editor John Lawres of *Who's Who in Baseball,* a small book that became the first to provide career statistics and personal facts for a group of players. Although thoroughly inadequate by today's standards—its only tabulations were games, batting average, and fielding average (even for pitchers, who were given no pitching records!)—*Who's Who* was a groundbreaking work. It gave rise to a much-expanded format in 1916 and inspired two other significant encyclopedic works: in 1914, George Moreland's self-published opus called *Balldom* (grandiosely subtitled "The Britannica of Baseball,") and Ernest J. Lanigan's *Baseball Cyclopedia*, also sponsored by *Baseball Magazine*, which debuted in 1922 and was updated annually through 1933.

The Golden Age, 1920-1968

There have been other new statistical tabulations in this century, but generally of the counting sort: complete games (NL 1910, AL 1922), games started (AL 1926, NL 1938), games finished (NL 1920, AL 1926). And there were sacrifice bunts allowed (NL 1913, AL 1921), intentional bases on balls (only since 1955), and, in the next period, saves (1969) and game-winning RBIs (1980). The only new average since slugging average was adopted in 1923 has been the on base percentage, adopted in 1985. The ICI group computed saves for prior years. Another such stat that failed to survive, alas, was stolen bases off pitchers, which the American League recorded only in 1920-1924; it has been recorded on an unofficial basis since the 1980s by the Elias Sports Bureau and Baseball Workshop. The only new fielding measure was team double plays, added to the AL list in 1912 and the NL in 1919. Other new and more interesting stats appeared in the 1940s and '50s but have not yet gained the official stamp of approval, such as Ted Oliver's Weighted Rating System, Alfred P. Berry's Average Bases Allowed (opponents' slugging average), and Branch Rickey and Allan Roth's Isolated Power. (See the ensuing essay, "Sabermetrics" for more about these unorthodox measures, some of which have gained wide acceptance and may, like the on base percentage, one day be embraced by Major League Baseball.)

This period of baseball's history may have fielded its most dazzling array of stars, but strategically and statistically it was rather dim. There was some excitement, however, in baseball record keeping. First came *Daguerreotypes*, issued by *The Sporting News* in 1934, featuring the playing records of many retired players both celebrated and obscure; most if not all of these statistical and biographical profiles originally appeared in the pages of TSN. Although its number of statistical categories was fewer than one might have wished, *Daguerreotypes* was very useful and, through its several editions ably edited by Paul MacFarlane, long-lived.

In 1940 came *The Sporting News's Baseball Register*, which supplied full records for active players, managers, coaches, and umpires, plus a grab bag of former stars. Since the expansion of the major leagues from sixteen teams to twenty-eight, the Register has only accommodated contemporary players and managers, but it remains a valuable source.

Then in 1951 came the first true encyclopedia of baseball, the claims of Moreland and Lanigan notwithstanding. Compiled by Hy Turkin and S.C. Thompson, *The Official Encyclopedia of Baseball* was published by the A.S. Barnes Company. Its 620 pages contained a wealth of features such as manager and umpire rosters, historical essays, playing tips, a bibliography, and much more. But the heart of the volume and the key to its subsequent success was a register of nearly nine thousand men who had played one or more games at the major league level from 1871 through 1949 (the 1950 record of players appearing in ten games or more was tacked on to the end). In this register, Turkin/Thompson also offered birth and death data and what today seems fairly limited statistical information but by previous standards was a veritable cornucopia: year, club, league, position, games, and batting average or won-lost record. A landmark volume that did much to inspire this one, the Barnes encyclopedia endured through ten revised editions, the last being published in 1979, ten years after the initial appearance of Macmillan's *The Baseball Encyclopedia.*

The Barnes encyclopedia went a long way toward making the study of baseball history and records a respectable pursuit, just as a century earlier the statistical accounting of a boys' game had helped to make baseball a sport for grown men. The researchers' ranks expanded to include such men as Bob Davids, who in 1971, aided by other experts like Cliff Kachline, Bill Haber, Ray Nemec, John Pardon, and Joe Simenic, would create SABR, the Society for American Baseball Research (pronounced "saber"). Formerly the lonely pursuit of a handful of "nuts" like S.C. Thompson, baseball research and sabermetrics—a neologism coined in honor of SABR, signifying the statistical analysis of the game's records—would become the pastime of thousands.

An article in *Life* magazine by Branch Rickey on August 2, 1954, gave further impetus to the study of baseball statistics, but not just to set the historical record straight. Indeed, this article may be viewed as the opening shot of the sabermetric assault of the 1980s. In "Goodby to Some Old Baseball Ideas," Rickey, with the aid of some new mathematical tools supplied by Dodger statistician Allan Roth, sought to puncture some long-held conceptions about how the game was divided among its elements (batting, baserunning, pitching, fielding), who was best at playing it, and what caused one team to win and another to lose. This is a pretty fair statement of what sabermetrics is about.

Rickey attacked the batting average and proposed in its place the on base percentage, but the most important thing Rickey did for baseball statistics was to strip the game and its stats to their pre-1876 essentials and start again, this time remembering that individual stats came into being as an attempt to apportion the players' contributions to achieving a team victory.

Rickey and Roth devised a formula to measure a team's efficiency in turning its offensive and defensive statistics into runs, and thus wins. They realized, and had confirmed for them by mathematicians at the Massachusetts Institute of Technology, that just as the team which scores more runs in a game gets the win, so a team which over the course of a season scores more runs than it allows should win more games than it loses—and by an extent correlated to its run differential. From this startlingly simple (or rather, seemingly simple) observation of 1954 flowed: first, the trailblazing but little noted work of George Lindsey in the 1950s and early 1960s, when he developed a model for run-scoring probability from the twenty-four combinations of outs and bases occupied; the development of "percentage baseball" stats and strategies by Earnshaw Cook in the 1960s; the play-by-play analysis of complete seasons by the Mills brothers, Eldon and Harlan, in 1969–1970; the recording and analysis of situational statistics by the Elias Sports Bureau for use by

Major League Baseball and its clubs; and, over the next two decades, the statistical and historical works of many sabermetricians.

The Computer Age, 1969-

Despite the death of Turkin in 1957 and Thompson ten years later, their encyclopedia remained the dominant book of baseball statistics, although many fans were frustrated with the fragmentary records it presented. As Frank V. Phelps wrote in the 1987 edition of *The National Pastime,* "Gaps and obvious errors in official averages, the lack of many early records, difficulty in securing the records of players who appeared in only a few games, and frustrating discrepancies among existing guides and registers had long since created a desire for an ultimate, complete, correct set of major league records. But it wasn't until the mid-1960s that the development of sophisticated computers which could absorb, retain, order, and output huge amounts of data finally made a project feasible."

Beginning in 1967, a battalion of researchers commanded by David Neft foraged through the official records and newspaper box scores to provide freshly compiled figures for those who had no ERAs, RBIs, slugging averages, saves, and all manner of wonderful things. The material which finally appeared in the tome was entered into a data bank, and the book was the first to be typeset entirely by computer, now a common practice. Published in 1969, *The Baseball Encyclopedia* was a milestone in computer technology, but as indispensable as the computer were the old-fashioned scrapbooks and files of Lee Allen and John Tattersall. The result was a mammoth ledger book of the major leagues more thorough than any that had appeared before.

The ICI group not only found new data to correct old inaccuracies but also applied new yardsticks to men who had gone to their graves never having heard of an RBI or a save. The ICI research that went into *The Baseball Encyclopedia* of 1969 created new stars, launching several previously underappreciated heroes of old into the Hall of Fame. Sam Thompson, Addie Joss, Roger Connor, Amos Rusie—their phenomenal level of play was hidden simply because statisticians back then were not recording the particular numbers which would show them off to best advantage. If sabermetrics consists of finding things in the existing data that were not seen before, or in collecting that data which makes possible the application of new statistics to old performances, the first edition of *The Baseball Encyclopedia* was a monument in the course of sabermetrics.

However, its subsequent editions declined from that standard, dropping valuable data, altering figures for star players in a misguided homage to tradition, and making a shambles of individual/team balance in the totals. As Phelps wrote of the second edition, supervised by the Macmillan Company after the ICI group broke up:

"Players' batting statistics were changed without compensating for changes in the records of other players on the same teams or in the corresponding team and league totals. Later editions included even more unbalanced adjustments . . .

"Quite apart from the problem of record-balancing, the numerous changes in players' totals and averages has caused serious misapprehensions and confusions for fans, writers, and researchers. The records of Fred Clarke and Cy Young differ in all six editions [to 1987] even without counting Clarke's astronomical 1899 BA [in the third edition, Clarke was credited with a batting average of .986 that boosted his lifetime mark by 15 points]. The figures for Burkett, Chesbro, Duffy, Hornsby, Walter Johnson, Radbourn, Speaker, and Waddell differ in five of the six books. The same is so in four of six for at least twenty-three other Hall of Famers, and many more less gifted players."

The seventh edition was issued in 1988 and, like the five that preceded it, was less accurate than the classic first issue. The eighth edition, published in 1990, corrected many of the errors in the seventh but retained many once-contested errors that historians had long since expunged from the record, while changing other statistics in a manner at variance with Major League Baseball's standards and with a rationale that remains unclear. For the ninth edition, Major League Baseball distanced itself from the both the product and its database.

Even when *The Baseball Encyclopedia* had been launched back in 1969, the ICI findings raised the hackles of traditionalists, prompting the formation by Major League Baseball of a Special Baseball Records Committee. Its members ruled upon such matters as whether, for the historical record, bases on balls should be counted as hits (as they were in 1887), outs (as they were in 1876), or neither (as has been the practice in all other years); or whether "sudden-death" home runs—thirty-seven game-winning blows with men on base that they identified as having occurred in the bottom half of the ninth or an extra inning—would be credited as homers or, in the practice before 1920, would count for only as many bases as were needed to push across the winning run. In the latter controversy, committee members first decided to count the disputed blows as homers, but then, when complaints arose that Babe Ruth's famous total of 714 would change to 715, they reversed themselves. They also decided that the National Association of 1871-1875 was not a major league, while the Federal League, Union Association, and Players League were; and they ruled on several other issues, all of which were published in the Appendix to *The Baseball Encyclopedia.*

Because earlier editions of *Total Baseball* enjoyed neither the privilege nor the responsibility of official Major League Baseball status, the editors committed themselves to the *process* of history—its research, reporting, and interpretation—rather than to its product. History is not static and unchanging. Our course then as now seemed unassailable: publish the best-documented data and remain humbly amenable to subsequent revision in the light of new evidence. (This is not very different from the placard in the Baseball Hall of Fame, which states that although later studies have called into question the accuracy of information on the plaques, the facts as engraved were believed to be accurate at the time.)

However, it must be acknowledged that we paid little mind to the consequences of our findings and reasoned judgments, such as the stripping of a batting championship from Ty Cobb in 1910 or Bobby Avila in 1954. For

this fourth, landmark edition of *Total Baseball,* our challenge was to devise a more historically sensitive framework that would permit us to incorporate the best modern research while continuing to honor the judgments of the past.

Total Baseball has abided by the Special Baseball Records Committee's decision on game-ending homers—not to preserve Ruth's total, but because there were many more such homers before 1920 than the thirty-seven the committee identified, and the disputes surrounding some of them are now beyond settling.

Like Turkin/Thompson and all previous record books, and in accordance with the view of most historians, we rejected the committee's position that the National Association was not a major league. We committed fully to the creation of a full statistical record of that trailblazing circuit, and hope one day soon to integrate the NA and NL records of such players as Al Spalding, Cap Anson, George Wright, and all the others who played in the professional league between 1871 and 1875. For now, we provide NA stats within the Player and Pitcher Registers, but total them separately from those of the NL (or, in a rare case, the American Association, a major league from 1882 through 1891).

We also differed from the committee's ruling on awarding pitchers wins and losses in the years before 1920. Not finding any official scoring rule or practice for that time, they chose to apply 1950 guidelines to decisions awarded in 1876-1920. This well-intentioned decision produced substantial alterations in the records of such hurlers as Cy Young, Christy Mathewson, Grover Alexander, and others. In the ensuing years, the notable research of Frank Williams (reported in "All the Record Books Are Wrong," *The National Pastime*, 1982) revealed that there was indeed a pattern and a rationale for the way decisions were awarded in those days; the data in *Total Baseball* conforms with his meticulously substantiated findings.

More involved, and perhaps of most direct interest to fans and media, are the subjects of (a) statistical discrepancies between the official record presented in *Total Baseball* and the figures published in other reference works, or memorialized on Hall of Fame plaques, and (b) the implications of corrected data for the awarding of batting championships. We will address those questions, as well as the larger ones of transcription accuracy and ledger balance, in the "Issues and Answers" section of this essay.

Let's resume our chronicle of how Major League Baseball and others have kept the record of the game. Besides the debut of *The Baseball Encyclopedia* (and the Miracle Mets and the centennial of professional baseball), there were two other interesting baseball developments in 1969. The first and less celebrated was a research project launched by Eldon and Harlan Mills that, like the ICI effort, could not have been contemplated without the computer. The Mills brothers tracked the entire major league seasons of 1969 and 1970 on a play-by-play basis. Then they applied to that record the probabilities of winning which derived from each possible outcome of a plate appearance, as determined by a computer simulation incorporating nearly eight thousand possibilities. What, for example, was the visiting team's chance of winning the game before the first pitch was thrown? Fifty percent, if we are pitting two theoretical teams of equal or unknown ability on a neutral site. If the first man fails to get on base, the chances of the visiting team winning are reduced to 49.8 percent; should he hit a double, the visiting team's chance of victory is raised to 55.9 percent, as determined by the probabilistic simulation. Every possible situation—combining half-inning, score, men on base, and men out—was tested by the simulator to arrive at "Win Points."

The Millses' purpose was to determine the clutch value of, say, hitting a homer with two men on and one man out in the bottom of the ninth, with the team trailing by two runs, the situation Bobby Thomson faced in the climactic National League game of 1951—oddly, the rookie year of the first modern computer. (That home run gained for him 1,472 Win Points; had it come with no one on in the eighth inning of a game in which his team led 4-0, the homer would have been worth only 12 Win Points.) What the Mills brothers were attempting to do was to evaluate not only the *what* of a performance, which traditional statistics indicate, but the *when*, or clutch factor, which no measure to that time could provide.

This project, detailed in a small book issued in 1970 called *Player Win Averages*, proceeded from the same impulse that led to other measures of clutch performance: the game winning RBI, introduced as an official Major League Baseball stat in 1980 and scrapped in 1989; the measures of batting performance in late-inning and men-on-base situations first published by Seymour Siwoff, Steve Hirdt, and Peter Hirdt of the Elias Sports Bureau in 1985; and the historically complete indexes of clutch hitting and clutch pitching developed for the first edition of this book.

The other noteworthy baseball event of 1969 was the official adoption by the major leagues of the save, the stat associated with relief pitching, the game's most significant strategic development since the advent of the gopher ball. Now shown in the papers on a daily basis, saves were not officially recorded at all until 1960; it was at the instigation of Jerome Holtzman of the *Chicago Sun-Times*, with the cooperation of *The Sporting News*, that this statistic was finally accepted. (Although Pat McDonough, a founding member of SABR, had developed a similar stat in 1924 which he called "games finished by relief hurlers"; its first appearance in print came in the *New York Telegram* three years later.) The need for the save arose because relievers operated at a disadvantage when it came to picking up wins. The bullpen specialists were a new breed, and as their role increased, the need emerged to identify excellence, as it had long ago for batters, starting pitchers, and fielders.

The save's prime statistical drawback is that there is no negative to counteract the positive, no stat for saves blown (except, all too often, a victory for the "fireman"); unofficial attempts to develop such a stat have accelerated in recent years, and now are part of the formula for the Fireman of the Year award.

August 10, 1971, marked another milestone, the founding in Cooperstown of SABR, the group in whose annual publications most of today's sabermetricians cut their analytical teeth. Its statistical analysis research committee, headed for more than a decade by Pete Palmer, has served as a sounding board for the inventive approaches of such men as Dallas Adams, Dick Cramer, Steve Mann, Craig Wright, Gary Gillette, and Bill James.

Developments of the ensuing decade include the previously mentioned adoption of the game-winning RBI (GWRBI) in 1980; it rewarded the batter who drove in a run to give his club a lead that it never relinquished. This stat was pilloried in the press from its introduction; Major League Baseball finally gave up on it before the 1989 season. In 1985 on base percentage was made official, thirty-one years after its introduction to the general baseball public by Rickey and Roth.

Situational stats, unofficial but widely reported and employed, have been the specialty of the Elias Sports Bureau, the Baseball Workshop, and Stats, Inc.—performance in day games vs. night, grass vs. artificial turf, lefty vs. righty, day game following night, bases-loaded situations, and so on. When the data is drawn from a large enough sample, these stats can be provocative and meaningful; they represent the wave of the future in baseball, and are fast becoming useful analytical tools for review of the past—Elias has recorded situational data systematically since 1975, Baseball Workshop since 1984.

Total Baseball

The next major event in the history of baseball record keeping has been *Total Baseball*. Founded upon a unique historical database that Pete Palmer has cultivated for decades—in the tradition of baseball archivists like S.C. Thompson, Bradshaw Swales, Leonard Gettelson, and John Tattersall—*Total Baseball* is the third-generation encyclopedia of the game. Just as the advent of the Macmillan/ICI encyclopedia supplanted Turkin/ Thompson, the standard for two decades, *Total Baseball* has taken advantage of new technology and new research, notably by members of the Society for American Baseball Research, to present data more accurate than ever before, and more of it. There are, of course, the traditional stats one would expect in a baseball reference work; there are many of the more revealing sabermetric stats (discussed in detail in the essay that follows this); there are stats never published before their appearance in this book. And as you have seen in Part One, there is a recognition that baseball history and knowledge resides not only in its numbers.

Issues and Answers: Sources of Baseball Statistics

There are six major sources for baseball statistical research, and thus for the official statistics that comprise *Total Baseball*. By far the most significant one is the official Major League Baseball records kept by the leagues, published in the baseball guides, and maintained on microfilm at the Baseball Hall of Fame in Cooperstown and in the league offices. These records cover the years since 1903 for the National League and 1905 for the American League. Any source data before these years were lost.

The second major source is the computer printouts prepared by ICI for *The Baseball Encyclopedia* in 1969.

These cover the NL for 1891-1902, the AL for 1901-05, the Federal League for 1914-15, plus all the nineteenth-century leagues (1882-91 American Association, 1884 Union Association, and the 1890 Players League). These records, obtained from newspaper box scores, were turned over to the Baseball Hall of Fame and made public by agreement with its resident historian Lee Allen, who permitted ICI to use his voluminous player demographic files.

The third source is John Tattersall's newspaper box-score research for the NL of 1876-90. Since Tattersall had done such careful work, day-by-day computer printouts were never generated for this period. Any day-by-day records created by John have been lost, but what has survived is a batting and fielding summary and a pitching summary for each club each year listing many categories. This collection, now owned by SABR, also includes the home run log, which lists every home run ever hit from 1871 to date, the date, teams, game location, batter, pitcher, inning, men on base, and other notes. This has been computerized by SABR and is maintained by David Vincent. John Tattersall, Bob McConnell, and Pete Palmer have discovered over a hundred errors in the homer data from the various accepted sources, either ICI research or guide data.

The fourth source for baseball statistics is a box score collection accumulated by Michael Stagno, covering the National Association of 1871-1875, which was also purchased by SABR. Preliminary basic data was calculated by Stagno. Currently Bob Richardson of Boston and Bob Tiemann of St. Louis are working on getting complete totals in most categories from this data.

The fifth source is additional work done by the ICI researchers for the 1969 edition, covering data that were not kept officially during the years since 1903 for the NL and 1905 for the AL. Examples of this data are runs batted in before 1920, extra base hits in the AL for 1905 and 1906, double plays by fielders before 1920 NL and 1923 AL, pitching data except wins and losses for the AL for 1905-07, earned runs for pitchers before 1912 NL and 1913 AL, complete games before 1913 NL and 1926 AL, games started before 1926 AL and 1938 NL, and saves before 1969. Any day-by-day records from this source have been lost, but the season totals have survived.

The sixth source is newspaper box score research to pick up additional categories not covered by the first five sources. Examples of this are hit by pitch for batters before 1917 NL and 1920 AL (by Alex Haas, Tattersall, Palmer, and many others), triple plays by fielders before 1928 AL and 1930 NL (mainly by Jim Smith), home runs allowed by pitchers before 1950 AL and 1952 NL (again by Tattersall). Frank Williams carefully researched AL pitching records for 1901-1919, when the league records were particularly sloppy. *Total Baseball* has day-by-day sheets for most of this data, with the rest residing in the Tattersall collection.

Issues and Answers: Discrepancies

The original data for record books and Hall of Fame plaques, before the 1969 ICI research, were mostly obtained from two sources, the Spalding and Reach annual guides and two Sporting News publications: the *Baseball Register* (published yearly 1940-date), which often contained records of oldtimers, and *Daguerreotypes* (published every so often from 1951-date), which had records of all Hall of Famers and many other notable players. This research was done from guides and newspapers by Paul Rickart, Leonard Gettelson, and Paul MacFarlane.

When the 1969 encyclopedia came out, there were many small differences in player stats when compared to the traditional data. However, since any records used to generate guide data in the early years were lost, the new data appeared to be more reliable. In addition, many more categories were given, like extra base hits, runs batted in, pitcher innings, hits and earned runs allowed, and fielder double plays. Also included in the new data were club splits for traded players and information on those who played in fewer than fifteen games.

In addition to the previously mentioned retroactive scoring decisions of the Special Baseball Records Committee, it ruled to include in the averages many games that were thrown out before, particularly in 1877, 1879, and 1899. Also included were the NL's tie games of five or more innings in 1878 through 1884 (thirty-eight of them) previously uncounted. Before 1912 in the NL pinch hitters and defensive replacements were included in the official game sheets, but the players were not credited with a game played. The committee decided to add these in, too.

Our research has uncovered a great many small errors and a few major ones in the official statistics. This was done by comparing individual totals to team totals, and by rechecking the addition on the player sheets. Most of these errors were in the American League, particularly before 1920, for which the record keeping was very sloppy. The NL has been much better over the years. For example, from 1910 to date, they took the sum of all the batter and fielder stats for each team, compared them to the sum of the team stats, and resolved almost all the differences. The AL did not start doing this until 1973 when the record keeping was first computerized. The NL went to computers in 1981.

For example, up through 1935, most AL clubs are not in agreement in player sums and team figures for at bats and hits. The differences are usually small, less than 10. (We have corrected the larger discrepancies of those years, but the smaller ones are yet to be resolved.) For 1905 to 1920, the team totals are further removed from the sum of the players, so that *The Baseball Encyclopedia* and *Total Baseball* have replaced the team totals with the sum of the players. We corrected all the post-1935 cases of team at-bat and hit totals not agreeing, but have not yet begun work on the previous years.

An interesting quirk in the way records are kept—and another reminder, as if one needed it, that baseball record keeping remains subject to error and controversy—occurred as recently as the strike-shortened season of 1981. The American League rule was to round off the innings pitched at the end of the season, although the weekly reports showed thirds of innings. Baltimore's Sammy Stewart had 29 earned runs in 112⅓ innings, while Oakland's Steve McCatty had 48 in 185⅔ innings. This gave Stewart the ERA title, 2.323 to 2.327. But when the innings were rounded off, McCatty won, 2.32 to 2.33.

McCatty got the title, but the next year both leagues decided to count thirds of innings.

Issues and Answers: Hall of Famers

The data reported by the ICI group in the first edition of *The Baseball Encyclopedia* upset many people in baseball, for their numbers were different from those traditionally accepted; in subsequent editions, many of the prominent players' statistics were fudged back to their traditional values. Yet 1969 had hardly been the first time corrections had been made to official data. In 1929 Grover Cleveland Alexander won his 373rd game, breaking Christy Mathewson's National League record, then thought to be 372. He never won another game. A number of years later, Joseph Reichler found a game in which, by the rules of that time, Matty should have gotten the win, this game taking place on May 21, 1902. The official record was changed and Matty pulled into a tie with Alex. The problem was that no one checked all of Mathewson's other games to see how many times he received a win under the old rules that wouldn't have been credited that way today. When ICI did its original research in 1968, it found Matty had only 367 wins total by today's rules, while Alexander had 374. (Further research, notably by Frank Williams, has restored Alexander and Mathewson to a tie at 373 wins.)

In another celebrated example of record-book flip-flops, when the American League was formed in 1901, Nap Lajoie was credited with a .422 average, with 220 hits in 543 at bats. After a number of years, someone noticed that if you take these at bats and hits, the average comes out only to .405, so his average was changed. (Turkin/Thompson gave Nap a mark of .409 in its first edition.) Later in the 1950s, John Tattersall had his doubts and decided to go through his newspaper collection of box scores. He found 229 hits for Lajoie, not 220—the error had been in the figure for hits, not in the figure for batting average. Thus his average was restored to .422, which happened to be the highest in American League history. Then ICI research in this area came up with a .426 mark (232 for 544, based on newspaper accounts), which was published in the first edition, then trimmed back to .422 in subsequent editions. The .426 figure is the one this book uses, because the day-by-day source data for the American League of 1901 has been lost.

Lajoie seemed to be involved in a number of controversies. ICI research found four more hits for him in 1902, raising his average from .369 to .378. Later editions of *The Baseball Encyclopedia* have changed Lajoie's stats back to the old values; we have not.

In 1910 there was a very close batting race between Cobb and Lajoie. At the end of the season, most people thought Nap had won, based on his getting seven hits in a doubleheader on the final day of the season. There was talk that the opposing Browns had let him get a number of bunts by playing back, so that the hated Cobb would lose. However, the AL office went over their figures and gave Cobb the title, .385 to .384. Nearly eighty years later, Palmer discovered a critical error: a game in which Cobb had two hits in three at bats had been entered twice. This was found because Sam Crawford had 14 games on his

official sheet for the homestand yet the Tigers had only played 13. It turned out that Detroit played a doubleheader on September 24, but the second game inadvertently was inserted in the official sheets as being played on September 25. Later, this second game of the 24th, which appeared to have been missing, was put in the scoresheets again. The League Office discovered this mistake soon after its official announcement that Cobb had won the batting title, because the double entry was corrected for all the other Detroit players. However, Ban Johnson had made a big deal out of how carefully his people had checked the figures in order to settle the controversy, so the AL kept quiet about the gaffe, leaving Cobb the winner.

Appeals to Commissioner Kuhn in 1981 to set the matter straight officially were to no avail, because that would not only have changed the outcome of the 1910 batting race, it would also have altered Cobb's lifetime hit total, then being pursued to massive media attention by Pete Rose. Kuhn's statement read, in part, "The passage of seventy years, in our judgment . . . constitutes a certain statute of limitation as to recognizing any changes in the records with confidence of the accuracy of such changes . . . . Since a variety of questions have been raised through the years about the accuracy of the statistics of that period, the only way to make changes with confidence would be for a complete and thorough review of all team and individual statistics. That is not practical." It may not have not been practical, but we have embarked upon such a course, and Major League Baseball has dedicated itself to that ongoing process.

Asked at the time how we would have resolved the dispute over the 1910 batting race, we responded in this way: remove Cobb's two redundant hits and alter his batting average accordingly, effectively dropping it beneath Lajoie's, and correct his lifetime hit total as well; however, retain Cobb's batting championship, for two reasons—one, because Lajoie's flurry of bunt hits were highly suspect, and two, because Cobb was awarded the title *in his day*, and awards should be permanent, not contingent. Furthermore, a reasonable case can be made that Ban Johnson, if he had believed that Lajoie's tainted hits would have been sufficient to produce a batting championship, would have nullified them; after all, he did banish from baseball the Browns' manager who had instructed his rookie third baseman to play exceptionally deep.

It is this singular event in baseball history that supplied a model for how *Total Baseball* and Major League Baseball developed a policy for incorporating new research finds into the historical record without revoking long-held personal championships. Player records may be changed upon the evidence of historical error, but league awards and titles are forever.

Here is what happened in the now celebrated Honus Wagner case in the 1990 edition of *The Baseball Encyclopedia*, over which Major League Baseball and the Macmillan publishing firm became estranged. The Macmillan editor noticed that previous edition figures for Wagner did not agree with the data presented in the first edition in 1969. He assumed that the data had been corrupted over the years, and thus returned the 1897-1900 data to the original figures, costing Wagner 12 hits. However, the editor did not restore the 1901-02 data, which would have resulted in Wagner losing three more hits. The outcome was that Wagner had a total of 3415 hits in the 1969 edition, 3430 in the 1988 edition (the traditional figure) and 3418 in the 1990 edition (also in 1993). One of the problems with the Macmillan newspaper research was that it did not count protested games in the player data. Although the games were thrown out of the standings, the player stats *did* count in the league compilations at the time, which should be the criterion for inclusion. (Protested games were included in the official records through 1909, then omitted 1910-1919, and were made once again part of the official records in 1920. When our review of these protested games prior to 1909 is completed, the individual stats will be added to our figures.)

Wagner was involved in three of these protested games. There were about twenty-five of them altogether in the nineteenth century. However, the newspaper research did show up additional differences in player stats beyond those from the protested games.

When checking the plaques for the Hall of Fame players, we found about forty players with differences from the *Total Baseball* data. Most were nineteenth century players with small differences due to discrepancies between the old guide figures and the later newspaper research. Some had to do with rule changes from the 1969 Special Baseball Records Committee, such as not counting walks as hits in 1887. For the twentieth century, there were a number of differences due to official errors, mostly in the area of pitcher won-lost marks in the 1901-1919 American League period. There were only a few outright errors on the plaques (see below for Anson, Clarkson, Hamilton, McCarthy, McGinnity, and Nichols). Exact differences can be found by comparing *Daguerreotypes* (which often agrees with the plaques) with *Total Baseball*.

Below is a guide to variances between the plaques and the official record of Major League Baseball embodied in *Total Baseball* (TB).

Nineteenth Century Hall of Famers:

Cap Anson   *Plaque, four batting titles;* **TB**, *three*
In 1879, Anson appears to have been the beneficiary of 20 extra hits, either by error or, as is commonly believed, a civic-minded Chicago official scorer. This error was found by John Tattersall in his review of newspaper box scores. In addition he (and we) incorporated the player records of four Chicago tie games, of which Anson played in two. His traditional mark of .407 was really only .317, and is so recorded in this volume; however, although a modern accounting would result in an 1879 batting title for Paul Hines, with .357, we credit the *championship* that year to Anson, as an instance of the official Major League Baseball policy cited above.

The singular season of 1887 presents a different case. Following the long-standing directive of the Special Baseball Records Committee, we do not count walks as hits, the practice which had been the sole basis of Anson's fourth batting championship. The modern computation reveals Sam Thompson to have had the highest batting average, and in this instance we withdraw the

fourth batting title from Anson. Note that only for this year, in which walks were aberrationally recorded as hits, and 1876, when they were aberrationally recorded as outs, will we overturn the scoring practice of the time in favor of a modern reinterpretation of who was the batting leader.

Jake Beckley   *Plaque, .309 lifetime, also for fielding at first base, 2368 games, 23696 putouts, 25000 chances;* **TB**, *.308, 2377, 23709, 25024*
These are about as close as you can get when comparing several sources prior to 1900.

Dan Brouthers   *Plaque, .419 average in 1887;* **TB**, *.338*
This average is inflated by the aforementioned scoring practice of 1887; even if we elected to keep that practice in effect, Brouthers' walks would have lifted him to .426.

John Clarkson   *Plaque, 175 losses, 2013 strikeouts, 4514 innings;* **TB**, *178, 1978, 4536*
The major difference in strikeouts occurred in 1886, where the guide had 340 and we counted only 313. We recorded two additional losses in 1894, in accordance with the scoring rules of the day. Reviewing our sources, we counted 27 more innings in 1887. His plaque bore a clear error concerning his wins in 1888. He had 33 and did not lead the league, although the plaque says 49. This was a confusion with the 49 Clarkson did win in 1889, which was also listed.

Roger Connor   *Plaque, hit .300 twelve times;* **TB**, *eleven*
If we counted walks as hits in 1887, we would also have twelve times.

Ed Delahanty   *Plaque, hit .408 in 1899;* **TB**, *.410*
The discrepancy is a product of newspaper research.

Hugh Duffy   *Plaque, hit .438 in 1894;* **TB**, *.440*
This was the highest average all-time. The 1895 guide has 236 hits while the newspaper count is 237; both had 539 at bats. Since no backup data has survived for the guide, there is no way to determine where the difference might be.

Jim Galvin   *Plaque, 365-311 won-lost;* **TB**, *360-308*
The plaque data includes a 4-2 mark in the 1875 NA, which has been denied major league status by the Special Baseball Records Committee. There are other smaller differences.

Billy Hamilton   *Plaque, 196 runs in 1894, 115 stolen bases and .338 batting average in 1891, 937 stolen bases total, 1893-1895 batting averages of .395, .399 .393, ten times scoring 100 runs;* **TB**, *192 runs in '94, 111 steals and .340 batting average in '91, 912 lifetime steals, 1893-1895 batting averages of .380, .404, .389, eleven times scoring 100 runs*
Whether Hamilton scored 196 runs or 192, he still holds the all-time record. There were small differences in stolen bases in several years. We speculate that when the folks at Cooperstown counted Hamilton's seasons of scoring 100 or more runs, they overlooked his 1889 A.A. accomplishment.

Hughie Jennings *Plaque, once hit .397;* **TB**, *.401 in 1896*
The guide had 208 hits in 523 at bats, which actually computes to .398, although .397 was shown. The newspaper research showed 209 for 521.

Tim Keefe *Plaque, 346 wins;* **TB**, *342*
Daguerreotypes currently also has 342.

Joe Kelley *Plaque, .391 in 1894;* **TB**, *.393*
Newspaper box score research pointed up discrepancies in the figures recorded in the guides.

King Kelly *Plaque, .394 average in 1887;* **TB**, *.322*
We do not count walks as hits; if we did, Kelly would have a mark of .393.

Tommy McCarthy *Plaque, 1268 games, 109 stolen bases in 1888, 53 assists in 1893;* **TB**, *1275 games, 93 steals, 28 assists*
Newspaper research found the early stolen base figures to be inflated, especially for the American Association. His 53 assists in 1893 included many at second base and shortstop. However, he did have 44 in the outfield in 1888, fourth best all-time.

Kid Nichols *Plaque, 360-202 won-lost, 30 wins in 1895;* **TB** *361-208, 26*
Daguerreotypes now has 361-208 as we do, including 26 wins in 1895. Nichols for years had been credited with winning 30 or more games from 1891 through 1897, but it has been conclusively shown that he had only 26 in 1895. The Spalding guide showed games pitched (which was usually interpreted to be decisions) and percentage. They had 44 and .681 which would give a mark of 30-14. The 1942 *Baseball Register* showed him 30-15. ICI's *The Baseball Encyclopedia* had him at 26-16 in 42 complete games and 0-0 in 5 relief appearances. Ironically, the corrected figures give him 30 wins in 1898, for seven seasons of 30 victories or more—total, but not consecutive.

Amos Rusie *Plaque, led in shutouts five times;* **TB**, *4*
Rusie pitched 7 innings of a 9-inning shutout on July 5, 1897. Taking this shutout away, in accordance with current scoring rules (there were no official rules for crediting shutouts until 1951), gave him 2 shutouts instead of 3 that year.

Sam Thompson *Plaque, .336 lifetime, hit .400 twice;* **TB**, *.331, once*
If walks counted as hits, we would have him at .407 in 1887 and .334 lifetime.

John Ward *Plaque, 158-102 won-lost, 2151 hits;* **TB**, *164-102, 2105*
Walks in 1887 accounted for 29 of the now "missing" hits. An additional 18 came from the 1890 Players League, for which newspaper research offered a lower total than the league figures. Other discrepancies were spread out over several years. We spotted 3 extra wins in 1879 and again in 1883.

Twentieth Century Hall of Famers

Luke Appling *Plaque, 11,569 chances accepted at shortstop;* **TB**, *11,616*
There was an addition error for his putouts in 1940. He had 307, not 257. *Daguerreotypes* had 11,566, not 11,569.

Jack Chesbro *Plaque, 192-128 won-lost;* **TB**, *198-132*
Daguerreotypes now has 198-128. The 1947 *Baseball Register*—only one year after Jack's election and the creation of his plaque—had 197-127. Still under review are two other games for which it has been argued that Chesbro should have received wins.

Ty Cobb *Plaque, 4191 hits;* **TB**, *4189*
See above for discussion of the doubly entered 2-for-3 game. But that is not the whole story of how Cobb's lifetime hit total fell by two, nor of how he comes to retain his twelve batting titles. Modern research of the official day-by-day sheets revealed that Cobb had two games in 1906—on April 22 and 23—in which he went 1-for-8 that were not entered on his sheet. Additionally, there was a game on July 12, 1912 (the first game of a doubleheader) in which Cobb had a run which was entered in his hit column. (If this had indeed been a hit, he would have had a 34-game hitting streak. It was really only 23 games.) Finally, under today's rules, Cobb would not have won the batting title in 1914, because he didn't have enough plate appearances (or at bats). However, he did win it under the rules of the day, as he won the 1910 title, and that is what counts.

Eddie Collins *Plaque, 3313 hits;* **TB**, *3312*
Collins picked up two hits in 1920 in a game for which his stats were switched with those of Buck Weaver. But he lost a hit in 1907 in a mixup with Jimmy Collins, giving Eddie a net loss of one hit.

Stan Coveleski *Plaque, 214-141 won-lost, 2.88 ERA;* **TB**, *215-142, 2.89 Daguerreotypes* has 215-141. The 1942 Baseball Register has 216-142. Our ERA includes 1912, when Stan had a 3.43 era in 21 innings. The beginning of official status for ERA in the AL was 1913.

Sam Crawford *Plaque, 2505 games, 2964 hits, 312 triples;* **TB**, *2517, 2961, 309*
Crawford's games played vary from the plaque largely because of the practice of not counting pinch-hit apperaances as games played. His ICI sheets reveal 5 additional games in 1900 and 7 in 1901. Also, he loses a triple in each of three seasons (1899, 1902, 1904) before the survival of official sheets; newspaper research does not support the Guide figures. And finally, Crawford lost 3 hits in 1900 through a recount of box score data, and 5 more in 1901. He gained back 3 in 1903 and 2 in 1904.

Red Faber *Plaque, 253-211 won-lost, 3.13 era;* **TB**, *254-213, 3.*
15 Faber was credited with one win less than he actually recorded in 1916, one of the years in which the American League, at Ban Johnson's behest, posted no official data in this category. For 1915, we add a loss that clearly was

overlooked on the official AL sheet, and for 1926 we add another loss that somehow was not posted when the Guide figures were released. The ERA variance is purely mathematical; it had been computed incorrectly.

Elmer Flick   *Plaque, .378 in 1900;* **TB**, *.367*
The guide had 207 hits in 547 at bats, while the newspaper research showed 200 in 545.

Harry Heilmann   *Plaque, 2146 games;* **TB**, *2148*
Daguerreotypes has 2145 games. Heilmann appeared in 69 games in 1914, not 66. For 1912-14 the official AL averages did not count a game for any player who had all zeros in his entry. These would be pinch-runners or late-inning defensive replacements. There were a total of over 400 such uncounted appearances in this category altogether.

Walter Johnson   *Plaque, 414 wins;* **TB**, *417*
This research was done by Frank Williams and detailed minutely in his previously cited essay in *The National Pastime* of 1982. Walter had a 16-game winning streak in 1912, but one of the games (August 5) was not marked as a win on his sheet. In 1911, wins were incorrectly marked as losses on June 27 and July 9. For the AL before 1920, there were about twenty or thirty errors in awarding wins and losses in the official statistics each year.

Heinie Manush   *Plaque, 2009 games;* **TB**, *2008*
His games were added incorrectly on the 1927 American League official sheet.

Joe McGinnity   *Plaque, won 20 seven times;* **TB**, *eight*
This looks like an error made by the Hall of Fame. He won 20 in 1902 between two leagues, as shown in the 1941 *Baseball Register* (McGinnity was elected in 1946).

Herb Pennock   *Plaque, 161 losses;* **TB**, *162*
Daguerreotypes agrees with 162 losses. The 1941 Baseball Register had 161.

Eppa Rixey   *Plaque, 4494 innings;* **TB**, *4494 2/3*
Official stats rounded innings pitched until 1982. *Total Baseball* records thirds of innings pitched in all seasons.

Red Ruffing   *Plaque, led in shutouts 1938 and 1939;* **TB**, *1939 only*
Lefty Gomez had 4 shutouts in 1938, not 3. This included a rain-shortened complete game on July 15. Ruffing had 3. Also, the comment on the plaque about making the all-star team in 1937-38-39 applies to the Sporting News All-Star team, not the All-Star Game team.

Tris Speaker   *Plaque, .344 lifetime;* **TB**, *.345*
There was an addition error on his official sheet for 1911. He had 500 at bats, not 510.

Pie Traynor   *Plaque, one of few players with 200 hits in a season;* **TB**, *of course, many players have had 200 or more hits in a season*

Zack Wheat   *Plaque, 2318 games for Brooklyn, 2406 total;* **TB**, *2322 for Brooklyn, 2410 total*

There were four unrecorded games in 1911 in which Wheat appeared only as a pinch hitter.

Issues and Answers: League Batting Leaders

Until this edition of *Total Baseball*, Major League Baseball had established no official historical record, despite its product endorsement of several statistical compendiums over the years. As a result, writers, historians, statisticians, and fans were offered a choice amongst differing annual league batting leaders, depending on the major record book favored. Those most favored by recent chroniclers have been *Total Baseball* and *The Baseball Encyclopedia* because they had all player and club records.

There are two recognized record summary tomes which feature leaders in various statistical categories, lifetime or single-season: *The Book of Baseball Records* (Elias Sports Bureau Inc.) and *The Complete Baseball Record Book* (The Sporting News). Though both are respected works, and both organizations have had long, and often times official, relationships with Organized Baseball, neither record book enjoys official status, and discrepancies exist between the two.

There was *no* official batting championship rule until 1950. *Total Baseball* and *The Baseball Encyclopedia* remedied this oversight by formulating—independently—their own guidelines for the many years of omission, each based on their own concepts of fairness and equality.

In previous editions, *Total Baseball* established the following criteria for batting championships: 1876-1956, qualification by having plate appearances equal to 3.1 per game times the number of scheduled games, thus conforming to the Major League Baseball practice since 1957. The batting championship criteria for *The Baseball Encyclopedia* over the years have been: 1876-1919, games played equal to at least 60 percent of games the team scheduled; 1920-1949, at least 100 games played, based on acceptance of the unofficial but universally assumed rule requiring appearance in at least 100 games; and 1950-present, the various changing official rule definitions.

In a policy shift endorsed by Major League Baseball, *Total Baseball* will now identify league batting champions according to the practice of the time, in each league, and each champion will have his seasonal batting average recorded in boldface in his entry in the Player Register. However, as noted above in the discussion of the 1910 AL batting race, in the Annual Record section of this volume, we record the highest batting averages in each league season as correctly calculated, although not necessarily in descending order.

The history of the official batting championship rule is as follows: (1) 1950-1951, 400 official times at bat; (2) 1952-1954, 400 official times at bat or, if less than 400 times at bat and by adding enough imaginary hitless at bats so as to total 400, "he still would have the highest batting average in his league, he shall be the champion batter"; (3) 1955-1956, 400 official times at bat; (4) 1957-1966, 3.1 plate appearances per game times number of scheduled games, equaling 477 in a 154-game schedule and 502 in a 162-game schedule; and it's 502 plate appearances; and (5) 1967-present, 3.1 plate appearances per scheduled game, except that "if there is any player whose average would be the highest if he were charged with the required number of plate appearances or official at bats, then that player shall be awarded the batting championship."

In the strike-shortened season of 1972, a 156-game standard prevailed instead of the 162 scheduled games. In the strike seasons of 1981 and 1994, the rule of 3.1 plate appearances per game was applied to the number of games played by each team, rather than to those scheduled.

The early record tomes, the *Spalding Record Book* and *The Sporting News Record Book*, placed Jake Stenzel (NL) in the lead for 1893 and Nap Lajoie (AL) on top in 1905. Both Stenzel and Lajoie were the leaders during the life of the Spalding volumes, 1908-1924, and in the Sporting News volume from its debut in 1921 until 1929, when Hugh Duffy replaced Stenzel and 1930, when Elmer Flick supplanted Lajoie. The reasoning behind the Sporting News switches was that both Stenzel and Lajoie failed to meet the unwritten criterion of a representative number of games—Stenzel had played in only 60 games and Lajoie in 65, not even half of their club's scheduled games. Otherwise the early record books' leaders were those endorsed by the leagues.

The Spalding Record Book in its 1917 edition made two important batting championship changes, both on the basis of mathematical errors which their editors had noted. To that time, Dan Brouthers had been tied with Cupid Childs for the highest batting average in 1892, but had been awarded the title based on his having played in more games, which was the tie-breaking guideline of the day. In 1917, however, Childs went to the front on the basis of extended batting average (calculating to extra decimal places beyond the thousandths that comprise conventional reporting of batting averages). Next, Lajoie's average of .422 in 1901 was reduced in 1917 because of a *Reach Guide* typo in the hit column to a .405 figure. The Spalding management (the once independent Reach company had long since been acquired by Spalding) should have known that in 1892, the criterion for awarding a batting championship was indeed games played, not extended batting average, and that in 1901 they would have found Lajoie's correct (as then calculated) average in any number of newspapers. Lajoie's .422 average was restored in 1954 in response to John Tattersall's research, but Childs remained, until this writing, ahead of Brouthers in the NL's *Green Book*. (In this fourth, now official, edition of *Total Baseball*, Brouthers is credited as the champion because he played in more games, which was the criterion of the time—not because modern research has lowered Childs' batting average from .335 to .317.)

During its formative years, 1876-1919, the National League omitted any mention of batting championship criteria in its published rules. Certainly, this should have been addressed before 1920. Still, batting championships were tacitly acknowledged by the league, with guidelines drawn primarily from the comments of Henry Chadwick.

From 1876 to ca. 1888, the criterion was understood to be the best seasonal performance; as expressed by Chadwick in the *Spalding Guide* of 1887, "an average rating of a player should be on a season's work." Seasonal leadership may be deduced when the league's recognized champion was not listed first in the official averages. His preeminence was based on a representative number of games played over the season in which he excelled, as opposed to the nominal leader's handful of games.

The yardstick between 1889 and 1919 was playing in at least 100 games. In the 1890 *Spalding Guide* Chadwick wrote: "With the object in view of equalizing the averages and placing the names of the batsmen who have played in 100 games or over, are given the front rank, while those who have played in 50 games and over occupy second place, and those in 25 games and over third place, and so on."

The American League rules in its early years, 1901-1919, omitted any batting championship language. In honoring Cobb as its 1914 bat champ, the AL was undoubtedly proceeding from the guideline of best seasonal performance.

As discussed in the "Sources of Baseball Statistics" section of this essay, *Total Baseball* relies upon newspaper research and other data for the years before 1903 in the NL and 1905 in the AL. For subsequent seasons, the official league day-by-day sheets are available for study. The record summary books issued by Elias and Sporting News accept all the batting leaders recognized in the yearly Guides (Spalding, Reach, etc.). These champions are also accepted in today's league publications (AL *Red Book* and NL *Green Book*). Henceforward, *Total Baseball* recognizes the same champions, with the exception of 1892, discussed above, and 1887, when walks were counted as hits.

For students of the game, Joe Wayman documented the variances among the record books and encyclopedias and highlighted particularly those traditional batting champions whom previous editions of *Total Baseball* had toppled from the pinnacle. Even though most of these champions have been rethroned, the following thumbnail account of the debatable batting leaders will serve to explain the seeming anomaly of a batting champion whose average is lower than that of a rival.

OFFICIAL   TB (eds. 1-3)

			G	AB	H	BA		G	AB	H	BA
1878	NL	Dalrymple	60	267	95	.356	Hines	62	257	92	.358
1879	NL	Anson	49	221	90	.407	Hines	85	409	146	.357
1884	NL	O'Rourke	104	448	197	.350	Kelly	108	452	160	.354
1887	NL	Anson	122	532	224	.421	Thompson	127	545	203	.372
1892	NL	Brouthers	152	588	197	.335	Brouthers	152	588	197	.335
1892	NL	Childs	144	552	185	.335					
1893	NL	Duffy	131	537	203	.378	Hamilton	82	355	135	.380
1910	AL	Cobb	140	509	196	.385	Lajoie	159	591	227	.384
1914	AL	Cobb	97	345	127	.368	Collins	152	526	181	.344
1926	NL	Hargrave	105	326	115	.353	Waner,P.	144	536	180	.336
1932	AL	Alexander	124	392	144	.367	Foxx	154	585	213	.364
1938	AL	Foxx	149	565	197	.349	Foxx	149	565	197	.349
1940	NL	Garms	103	358	127	.355	Hack	149	603	191	.317
1942	NL	Lombardi	105	309	102	.330	Slaughter	152	591	188	.318
1954	AL	Avila	143	555	189	.341	Williams	117	386	133	.345
1981	NL	Madlock	83	279	95	.341	Rose	107	431	140	.325

*Thompson becomes the official batting champion with a .372 average in accordance with e decision of the Special Baseball Records Committee not to count walks as hits. Anson would be a .347 hitter without the benefit of his walks.

1878: Abner Dalrymple captured the NL's batting title. Modern record tomes (*The Baseball Encyclopedia* and

Total Baseball) list Paul Hines in the top spot. The NL in 1878 did not include tie games in its official averages, while today's record tomes count them. Thus, by counting tie games, Hines emerges with the higher average, but does not take away Dalrymple's championship.

1879: Cap Anson, the day's recognized batting champion, has been challenged by the moderns (*The Baseball Encyclopedia*, *Total Baseball*, *The Sports Encyclopedia: Baseball*, and *The National League Story*, Lee Allen) as to whether his .407 average is legitimate. In fact, the average was disputed as early as the 1880 DeWitt Guide, the averages for which were compiled by William Stevens of the *Boston Herald*, and *Balldom* (1914), compiled by George Moreland. *Total Baseball* keeps the title with Anson in recognition of the league action at the time, but reports his batting average correctly in the Player Register and in the Annual Record's listing of top batting averages in the 1879 NL.

1884: The official batting champion remains Orator Jim O'Rourke. Newspaper box scores, game accounts, and the results of tie games elevate King Kelly to a higher average. Tie games were not included in the official averages at the time, and how to handle them today remains a matter of controversy. No matter how we treat Kelly's 2-for-4 in his only tie-game appearance (August 11), his average is higher than O'Rourke's.

1887: In only this season, bases on balls counted as hits. One month into the season, the American Association wanted to scrap the absurd rule, but the NL would not consent. *Total Baseball* gives the championship to Sam Thompson. Without his 60 walks registering as hits, Anson batted .347.

1892: Brouthers and Childs were honored as co-champions at .335, as discussed above. Childs had the higher extended average, .3351, against Brouthers' .3350 mark. By the day's reasoning, however, Brouthers is the leader. As Chadwick noted in the *Spalding Guide*, "the lead in all cases of tie scores in base hits belongs by right to the batsman who has played in the greatest number of games, and in this case Brouthers batted in 152 games to Child's 144." Childs's statistics, as compiled by ICI from newspapers, yield a batting average of .317, placing him third.

1893: Billy Hamilton's average was higher than Duffy's, and he would have met modern criteria for plate appearances. The NL, however, honored Duffy because he appeared in at least 100 games, which was expected of the leading players of that day. The title is thus accorded to him.

1910: Cobb is the champion, for reasons discussed amply above.

1914: Cobb, due to his proven hitting excellence, was awarded the championship because, in all reasoned probability, he would have been the leader over the full season. Consider, also, that the batting championship for the Chalmers car in 1910 for position players was based on 350 at bats. Cobb would have easily captured the hit crown on a mythical 100 game requirement, even though he was three games shy.

1926: Bubbles Hargrave topped three other questionable contenders—those not credited with at least 400 at bats. All qualified for the title, though, based on the period's acceptance of appearance in at least 100 games. In Hargrave's favor was his position—catcher. Over the years,

catchers were considered somewhat differently when it came to handing out awards, because of the demands of their position. In fact, in order for a catcher to qualify for the fielding championship at his position, he need only have appeared in at least 77 games. Hargrave caught in 93 games.

1932: Dale Alexander had the games and at bats to satisfy the AL as to his claim. If the 400 at bat rule had been on the books, Alexander no doubt would have been inserted into the lineup until he secured eight additional at bats. If Jimmie Foxx were today recognized as champion, he would have the first of two consecutive Triple Crowns.

1938: Foxx was the AL leader—no ifs, ands, or buts about it. The AL had a rule in 1938 requiring the batting " . . . winner to be at least 400 times at bat." (*Reach Guide*, 1939) Taffy Wright is the trivia-question champion, batting .350 in 100 games.

1940: Debs Garms raised a few eyebrows as a come-from-nowhere champion. If enough imaginary at bats to reach 400 were to be added to Garms' total, his adjusted average would still be one point higher than that of Stan Hack, the runnerup.

1942: Ernie Lombardi was the recognized NL batting king. As a *Sporting News* headline advised, "Ernie's 105 contests suffice to qualify him for a second title." The announcement called attention to the "inquiries" which had been made regarding a Lombardi award since the AL had put in place a 400 at bat requirement. Bill James noted that the NL announced a "meritorious 400 at bat" requirement after the problematic Garms award two years earlier. NL President Frick, however, contended there was no specific bat rule and catchers, because of their demanding position, deserved special consideration. The catcher's fielding championship by this time was based on 100 games, lessening the Frick contention. Frick may have had in mind the prior, 77-game catching requirement for fielding leadership. Thus, Frick's reasoning could have been to create a proportion: 77 games for catchers is to 100 games for position players what 77 percent of 400 at bats (308) for catchers is to 400 at bats for position players.

1954: Ted Williams, the batter with the highest average in the AL, did not meet the official qualifications to claim the title. The 1954 official Rule 10.17 spelled out the champion as one who, with at least 400 at bats, or with fewer than 400 at bats plus enough imaginary ones to equal 400, has the higher average. Under the official rules definition, Bobby Avila is the batting leader. During the closing weeks of the campaign, Williams was aware of the rule but continued to be selective of pitches, rather than swing at those outside the strike zone simply in order to reach the required 400 at bats. Williams' extended average based on adding imaginary at bats to his 386 is a .331 figure.

1981: Bill Madlock is the official batting champion by the rules of the day. Due to the strike-shortened season, the games a team played, rather than the scheduled games, were the basis for individual championships. Pittsburgh, Madlock's club, played 103 games. Thus, 103 × 3.1 = 319 plate appearances to qualify for the batting championship. Madlock topped the required 319 PA's by one, with 279 at bats, 4 sacrifice flies, 34 bases on balls, 3 hit by pitch, and no sacrifice hits or interference calls. *Total*

Baseball awarded the title to Pete Rose in editions 1 and 2, based on average games played per team, then corrected the procedure in its third edition.

The record of the four defunct major leagues show only the American Association had batting champions not agreeing with *Total Baseball* champions. This happened twice: in the 1884 AA, the official winner was Dude Esterbrook though his teammate Dave Orr actually batted 50 points higher; and in 1886 AA, the champ was officially Orr though Guy Hecker's recomputed average nips him by a point. (Pete Browning also surpassed Orr and was listed as champion in earlier editions of *Total Baseball*, for which a guideline of 3.1 plate appearances per game was employed throughout.)

A Little Help from Our Friends

The computer has made possible the rapid analysis of mountains of raw baseball data. But as invaluable as the computer has been in producing and cross-checking the statistical data for *Total Baseball*, the editors owe more to the people who have contributed their time, their expertise, their love of the game, and their passion for getting things right. These individuals are listed below, or in the Acknowledgements, or in the table at the end of the book that enumerates those readers of the first three editions who helped us improve the accuracy of *Total Baseball* this time around. A collective debt is owed to the Society for American Baseball Research and the National Baseball Library.

The six principal sources of the statistics herein were discussed earlier. Supplemental sources were:

- For work on the Stagno Collection of NA data, 1871-75, SABR's nineteenth-century research committee, headed successively by John Thorn and Mark Rucker, Bob Tiemann, Bob Richardson, and Fred Ivor-Campbell.
- For batters hit by pitch, 1884-1896 AA/NL/PL, 1909-1916 NL, 1909-1919 AL, research from newspapers by Alex Haas, Pete Palmer, John Schwartz, Bob Davids, John Tattersall, Lyle Spatz, Herb Goldman, Keith Carlson, Tom Chase, Ed Luteran, Frank Phelps, and others. (Note: research continues for the 1897-1908 period, but the data is, at this writing, about 95 percent complete.)
- For home runs allowed by pitchers, 1876-1950 AL/NL, the Tattersall Collection, aided by Bob McConnell.

- For runs batted in, 1903-1919 NL, 1905-1919 AL, ICI research.
- For runs batted in, 1880-1885 NL, David Neft.
- For pitcher saves (except 1901-1919 AL) 1876-1968 NL/AA/UA/PL/AL, ICI research.
- For stolen bases, 1886 NL, Spalding *Baseball Guide*.
- For wins and losses for pitchers, 1876-1900 NL/AA/PL, and for wins, losses, games started, complete games, shutouts, saves, 1901-1919 AL, and complete pitching data, 1892, research from newspapers and official sheets by Frank Williams.
- For shutouts, 1876-1939, Joe Wayman.
- For biographical data, the biographical research committee of SABR, notably Richard Topp, Bill Carle.
- For caught-stealing data, 1914-1916 AL, 1915-1916 NL, Ernie Lanigan, courtesy of Bob Davids.
- For home/away data, 1876-1891 NL/AA/UA/PL, Bob McConnell.
- For game scores, 1876-1884 NL/AA/UA, Bob Tiemann.
- For game scores, 1885-1891 NL/AA/PL, Richard Topp.
- For runs and homers home/away, 1980s NL/AL, Bill Carr.

Missing data includes:

- Hit batters: 1897-1908, scattered data, especially for New York and Cincinnati.
- Caught stealing: 1886-1914, 1916 (players with fewer than 20 steals), 1917-1919, 1926-1950 NL; 1886-1891 AA; 1890 PL; 1901-1913, 1916 (players with fewer than 20 steals), 1917-1919, 1914-15 FL.
- Sacrifice hits: 1927-1930 (fly balls advancing runners to any base counted as sacrifice hits).
- Sacrifice flies: 1908-1930, 1939.
- Runs batted in, 1882-1887, 1890 AA; 1884 UA.
- Strikeouts for batters: 1882-1888, 1890 AA; 1884 UA; 1897-1909 NL; 1901-1912 AL. (Team batting strikeouts are presented for 1897-1902 NL and 1901-1904 AL.)

Incomplete data for those years up to 1903 NL and 1905 AL are available from the ICI computer printouts at the National Baseball Library. Additional research could turn up more data. If your research or sharp eye should detect errors or gaps in *Total Baseball*, please write us in care of the publisher and we'll be delighted to improve our data and credit your catch in the next edition.

Sabermetrics

Pete Palmer and John Thorn

Sabermetrics may be a new coinage for the statistical analysis of baseball but it is not a new phenomenon. Henry Chadwick, in the antebellum period, was as much a sabermetrician as Allan Roth or Bill James: he saw as clearly as they that because the object of the game is to win, runs are the best measure of player performance, just as they are of team performance at the end of a game.

After many decades in which this fundamental truth was lost (amid the general worship of false idols like batting average and pitcher won-lost percentage), today's sabermetricians have come around full circle to the game as it was originally understood. And what's remarkable about this is that in order to return to the primordial simplicity of the 1840s, '50s, and '60s, when runs and outs were all that went into the box score, they have relied upon computer simulations and higher mathematics. In other words, with the new statistics, simplicity emerges from complexity; what baseball statistics have offered for the last hundred years or so has been, despite the appearance of simplicity, in fact extremely complex.

For the veteran fan as well as for Major League Baseball, new ideas, new statistics, and new discoveries that dispute long-held verities (Ty Cobb's hit total, Hoss Radbourn's number of victories in 1884, etc.) may represent a challenge to tradition and thus a threat to the very soul of baseball, its pride in anachronism. Bernard Malamud wrote, "The whole history of baseball has the quality of mythology." The editors of *Total Baseball* relish the game's myths, from Abner Doubleday to the sacrifice bunt, and believe that in setting the record straight or turning conventional wisdom on its head, they are adding to the fan's enjoyment of the rich texture of the game. If you are one of the skeptics—like Earl Weaver, who once said, "There's no such thing as a new statistic"—please permit us to make the case for sabermetrics. (Much of the material in this section is adapted from our 1984 study, *The Hidden Game of Baseball*.)

What's in a Number?

On April 27, 1983, the Montreal Expos came to bat in the bottom of the eighth inning trailing the Houston Astros 4-2. First up to face pitcher Nolan Ryan was Tim Blackwell, a lifetime .228 hitter who had struck out in his first time at bat. At this routine juncture of this commonplace game, Ryan stared down at Blackwell, but his invisible—yet, for all that, more substantial—opponent was a man who had died the month before Ryan was born, a man about whom

Ryan knew nothing, he confessed, except his statistical line. For at this moment of his glorious big-league career, Ryan had accumulated a total of 3,507 strikeouts, only one short of the mark Walter Johnson had set over twenty-one seasons, from 1907 to 1927. Long thought invulnerable, Johnson's record was in imminent danger of falling, in 1983, not only to Ryan but also to Steve Carlton and Gaylord Perry.

Ryan fanned Blackwell and then froze the next batter, pinch hitter Brad Mills, with a 1-and-2 curveball. The pinnacle was his. Johnson had been baseball's all-time strikeout leader since 1921, when he surpassed Cy Young. Ryan would hold that title for just a few weeks, then would be overtaken by Carlton, only to display an incredible finishing kick and finish at 5,714 in 1994. But at the time that Ryan topped Johnson, baseball savants scurried to assess the meaning of 3,509 for both the deposed King of K and the new.

In the aftermath of Ryan's feat, some writers pointed out that he only needed sixteen full seasons, plus fractions of two others, in which to record 3,509 strikeouts while Johnson needed twenty-one, or that Johnson pitched over 2,500 more innings than Ryan. Coming into the 1983 season, Ryan had fanned 9.44 men per nine innings, while Johnson was way down the list at 5.33. And Ryan had allowed fewer hits per nine innings than Johnson, or, for that matter, anyone in the history of the game. So, it would seem 3,509 was not just one batter better than Johnson, but rather was mere confirmation for the masses of a superiority that was clear to the cognoscenti years before.

However, other writers introduced mitigating factors on Johnson's behalf, much as Ruth found supporters as the home run king even after Aaron hit number 715. These champions of the old order cited Johnson's won-lost record of 417-279 and earned run average of 2.17 while scoffing at Ryan's mark, entering 1983, of 205-186 with an ERA of 3.11. This tack led to further argument in print, bringing in the quality of the teams each man pitched for and against, the resiliency of the ball, the attitudes of the batters in each era toward the strikeout, the advent of night ball, integration, expansion, the designated hitter, the overall talent pool, competition from other professional sports . . . and on down into the black hole of subjectivism.

Why were so many things dragged into that discussion? Because the underlying question about 3,509 was: does this total make Ryan better than Johnson, or even a better strikeout pitcher than Johnson? At the least, does it make him a great pitcher? In our drive to identify excellence on the baseball field (or off it), we inevitably look to the numbers as a means of encapsulating and comprehending experience. This quantifying habit is at the heart of baseball's hidden game, the one ceaselessly played by Ryan and Johnson and Ruth and Aaron—and, thanks to baseball's voluminous records, more than 14,000 other players—in a stadium bounded only by the imagination.

What's in a number? The answer to "How Many?" and sometimes a great deal more. In this case, 3,509 men had come to the plate against Ryan and failed to put the ball in play, one more man than Johnson had returned to the dugout, cursing. So what's the big deal? That Ryan was .0002849 faster, scarier, tougher—better—than Johnson? An absolute number like 3,509, or 714 (the home-run record once thought invulnerable, too), or 4,191 (the erroneous hit total of Ty Cobb that Pete Rose finally surpassed) does not resound with meaning unless it is placed into some context that will give it life.

Baseball statistics are not the instruments of vivisection, taking the life out of the game in order to examine it; rather, statistics are themselves the vital part of baseball, the only tangible and imperishable remains of contests played yesterday or a hundred years ago. Baseball may be loved without statistics, but it cannot be understood without them. As the statistics reflect more accurately the reality of what happened on the field, greater understanding leads to a deeper love and appreciation of this great game—which is, essentially, the case for sabermetrics and the reason for *Total Baseball*.

The Linear Weights System

In 1982, Milwaukee's Robin Yount had the year of his life, batting .331 with 29 homers, 114 RBIs and 129 runs scored; he led the American League in hits, doubles, total bases, and slugging percentage, while finishing just one point behind the league leader in batting average. First of the two times in his career, he was voted the Most Valuable Player in the American League, being named first on all but one of the twenty-eight ballots cast by the baseball writers.

Over in the other league, Mike Schmidt of the Phillies was having an off year, batting only .280 with 35 homers and 87 RBIs; the previous year, when he was awarded the MVP, in only 102 games played he had totaled 31 homers and 91 RBIs. He did lead the league once again in 1982 in slugging percentage, and he did win the Gold Glove at third base for the seventh straight year, yet in the MVP balloting none of the ballots listed him higher than fourth; ten ballots were cast without listing him at all.

For Yount, 1982 was a crowning achievement; for Schmidt, a disappointment: that was the verdict reached by the baseball writers and conventional baseball statistics. Yet in terms of actual performance, as determined by the number of runs contributed, Schmidt's "off year" was scarcely different from Yount's. With the bat, Yount accounted for 59 park-adjusted runs beyond what an average batter might have contributed; Schmidt, 45. Through base stealing, Yount added 2; Schmidt none. With the glove, Yount was 4 runs below league average at his position, shortstop; Schmidt was 19 above average at third base. Total runs contributed: Yount 57, Schmidt 64.

(Because Yount's batting so far exceeded that of other shortstops, while third base provided several heavy hitters, Yount contributed 7.0 extra wins to his Brewers; Schmidt contributed 6.1 to the Phillies.) Both men had outstanding seasons, the best in their respective leagues, and both outstripped the second-best player by about the same margin.

Viewing player (and team) performance through this sort of prism frequently produces such illuminating results. Cecil Fielder had a wonderful year in 1990, with his 51 homers, 132 RBIs, and league-leading figures in slugging average and extra-base hits. But how did he convince any writer voting for MVP that he had a better year than Rickey Henderson? In *Total Baseball,* you could look it up: Fielder contributed 4.2 extra wins to his team (wins that an average player would not), which was the fourth-best figure in the American League that year; Henderson was responsible for a whopping 8.2, not only the top mark in 1990 but also, at the time, the second-best mark in the AL since Mickey Mantle's epic seasons of 1956-57!

This is the kind of analysis of player performance possible with a variety of sabermetric measures, not just the Linear Weights System. The common ingredient of most of the new, as yet unofficial statistics is their creators' recognition of the relationship between runs and wins. These newly calculated measures are not official statistics of Major League Baseball, but they are constructed from the raw data of the official record. Some of the new measures may one day be officially embraced, as the on base percentage became an official stat three decades after its introduction. Because of fan interest, we include them in the Player and Pitcher Registers that follow, alongside the officially tabulated numbers.

Runs and Wins

George Lindsey, in an article in *Operations Research* in 1963, was the first to assign run values to the various offensive events which lead to runs: Runs = (.41)1B + (.82)2B + (1.06)3B + (1.42)HR. He based these values on recorded play-by-play data and basic probability theory. Unlike Earnshaw Cook, who in the following year assigned run values on the basis of the sum of the individual scoring probabilities—that is, the *direct* run potential of the hit or walk plus those of the baserunners set in motion—Lindsey recognized that a substantial part of the run value of any non-out is that it *brings another man to the plate*. This additional batter has a one-in-three chance of reaching base and thus bringing another man to the plate with the same chance, as do the batters to follow. The *indirect* run potential of these batters cannot be ignored.

Steve Mann's Run Productivity Average (RPA) assigned these values based on observation of some 12,000 plate appearances: RPA = (.51)1B + (.82)2B + (1.38)3B + (2.63)HR + (.25)BB + (.15)SB − (.25)CS, all divided by plate appearances, then plus .016. His values were denominated in terms of the number of runs and RBIs each event produced. Bill James, at about the same time, came up with a similar formula, since shunned, with values based on runs plus RBIs *minus home runs*. The drawbacks to the approaches of Mann and James were the drawbacks of the RBI, which gives the entire credit for producing a run to the man who plates it, and of the run scored, which gives credit only to the man who touches home, no matter how he came to do so. For example, with no outs, a man reaches first on an error; the next batter hits a double, placing runners on second and third; the following batter taps a roller to short and is thrown out at first, with the run scoring from third. The man who produced the out is given the credit for producing a run, while the man who started the sequence by reaching first on an error is likewise credited with a run. The man who hit the double, which was surely the key event in the sequence which produced the run, and the only one reflecting batting skill, receives no credit whatsoever. In this regard, any formula based on "Runs Produced" (whether R + RBI or R + RBI − HR) is philosophically inferior to the formula Lindsey proposed, despite his failure to account for walks, steals, and other events.

The run values in the Linear Weights formula for identifying batters' real contribution are derived from Pete Palmer's 1978 computer simulation of all major-league games played since 1901. All the data available concerning the frequencies of the various events was collected; following a test run, these were tabulated. Unmeasured quantities, such as the probability of a man going from first to third on a single vs. that of his advancing only one base, were assigned values based on play-by-play analysis of over 100 World Series contests. The goal was to get all the measured quantities very nearly equal to the league statistics; then the simulation would provide run values of each event in terms of net runs produced above average. Expressing the values in those terms would give a meaningful base line to individual performances, because if you are told that a player contributed 87 runs you don't know what that signifies unless you know the average level of run contribution in that year: 87 may sound like a lot, but if the norm was 80, then you know the player contributed only 7 runs beyond average.

The values obtained from the simulation are remarkably similar from one era to the next, confounding expectations that the home run would prove more valuable today than in the dead-ball era, or that the steal was once a primary offensive weapon. These values are expressed in beyond-average runs.

Run Values of Various Events, by Periods

Event	Period			
	1901–20	1921–40	1941–60	1961–77
home run	1.36	1.40	1.42	1.42
triple	1.02	1.05	1.03	1.00
double	.82	.83	.80	.77
single	.46	.50	.47	.45
walk/HBP	.32	.35	.35	.33
stolen base	.20	.22	.19	.19
caught stealing	−.33	−.39	−.36	−.32
out*	−.24	−.30	−.27	−.25

*An out is considered to be a hitless at bat and its value is set so that the sum of all events times their frequency is zero, thus establishing zero as the base line, or norm, for performance.

In the years since this simulation was conducted, statistician Dave Smith ("Maury Wills and the Value of the Stolen Base," *Baseball Research Journal,* 1980) convinced Pete to adjust the values of the stolen base and caught stealing because of their situation-dependent,

elective nature: attempts are apt to occur more frequently in close games, where they would be worth more than if they were distributed randomly the way an event like a single or a home run would be. Pete revised the value for the steal upward to .30 runs, while for the caught stealing it becomes -.60 runs.

Just as these run values change marginally with changing conditions of play, they differ slightly up and down the batting order (a homer is not worth as much to the leadoff hitter as it is to the fifth-place batter; a walk is worth more for the man batting second than for the man batting eighth); however, these differences have been averaged out in the figures above. For evaluating runs contributed by any batter at any time, there is no better method than Batting Runs, the Linear Weights formula derived from the computer simulation which is the basis of the table above.

The Formula

Runs = (.47)1B + (.78)2B + (1.09)3B + (1.40)HR + (.33)(BB + HB) + (.30)SB − (.60)CS − (.25)(AB − H) − .50(OOB).

The events not included in the formula that you might have thought to see are sacrifices, sacrifice hits, grounded into double plays, and reached on error. The last is not known for most years and in the official statistics is indistinguishable from outs on base (OOB). The sacrifice has essentially canceling values, trading an out for an advanced base which, often as not, leaves the team in a situation with poorer run potential than it had before the sacrifice. The sacrifice fly has dubious run value because it is entirely dependent upon a situation not under the batter's control: while a single or a walk always has a potential run value, a long fly does not, unless a man happens to be poised at third base (whether it is achieved by accident or design is open to question, as well, but that is beside the point—getting hit by a pitch is not a product of intent, either). Last, the grounded into double play is to a far greater extent a function of one's place in the batting order than it is of poor speed or failure in the clutch, and thus it does not find a home in a formula applicable to all batters. It is no accident that Henry Aaron, who ran well for most of his long career and wasn't too bad in the clutch, hit into more DP's than anyone else, nor that Roberto Clemente, Al Kaline, and Frank Robinson, who fit the same description, are also among the ten "worst" in this department. If a .230-hitting American League shortstop doesn't hit into many twin killings, it's not because of adept bat handling or blazing speed but because he bats ninth.

The Linear Weights formula for batters may be long, but it calls for only addition, subtraction, and multiplication and thus is as simple as the slugging average, whose incorrect weights (1, 2, 3, and 4) it revises and expands upon. Each event has a value and a frequency, just as in slugging average, yet—as in no batting statistic you have ever seen—outs are treated as offensive events with a run value of their own (albeit a negative one), a truth so obvious it somehow escaped notice. Just as the run potential for a team in a given half inning is boosted by a man reaching base, it is diminished by a man being retired; not only has he failed to change the situation on the bases but he has deprived his team of the services of a man further down the order who might have come up in this half inning, either with men on base and/or with scores already in.

What Batting Runs does is to take every offensive event and treat it in terms of its impact upon the team—an average team, so that a man does not benefit in his individual record for having the good fortune to bat cleanup with the Giants or suffer for batting seventh with the Marlins. The relationship of individual performance to team play is stated poorly or not at all in conventional baseball statistics. In Batting Runs it is crystal clear: the linear progression, the sum of the various offensive events, when weighted by their accurately predicted run values, will total the runs contributed by that batter or that team beyond the league average.

Recognizing that some dedicated readers of *Total Baseball* will wish to keep track of batting performance by computing Batting Runs themselves over the course of a season, and that they may be frustrated by the difficulty of calculating the "At Bats-Hits" factor for the league, which is necessary to determine the negative value of an out, we advise that using a fixed value of -.25 for outs will tend to work quite well if you wish to include pitcher batting performance, and a fixed value of -.27 will serve if you wish to delete it. Actually, any fixed value will suffice in midseason; it's only when all the numbers are in and you care to compare this year's results with last year's (or with those of the 1927 Yankees) that more precision is desirable. At that point the value of the out may be calculated by the ambitious among you, but ideally, the sporting press will provide accurate Batting Runs figures. Who, after all, calculates ERA for himself?

Batting Runs and Production

For those to whom calculation is anathema, or at the least no pleasure, Batting Runs has a "shadow stat" that tracks its accuracy to a remarkable degree and is a breeze to calculate: Production, which consists simply of On Base Percentage plus Slugging Average. While it is not expressed in runs and thus lacks the philosophical appeal of Batting Runs, the standard deviation of its most complete version is 20.4 runs compared to the 19.8 of Batting Runs. In other words, the correlation between Batting Runs and Production over the course of an average team season is 99.7 percent.

However, as an average or ratio, Production measures the *rate* of batting success (efficiency), while Batting Runs measures the *amount* of success. For example, a batter who goes 2-for-5 with a walk in one game, those 2 hits being doubles, will have an On Base Percentage of .500 and a Slugging Average of .800; his Production will be 1.30 or, as stated for convenience in *Total Baseball*, 130. Another batter, who in 162 games gets 200 hits and 100 walks in 500 at bats, with 400 total bases, will have an identical OBP, SLG, and PRO. Which player has contributed more to his team? Clearly, longevity, or amount of production, is no less important than rate of production.

To cite a specific instance in which Production and Batting Runs differ, take George Brett's remarkable 1980

season in which he batted .390, had 298 total bases, 75 bases through walks or HBP, and 118 RBIs—all in only 117 games played. In the table of all-time single-season leaders in Production, the Kansas City third baseman ranks 48th when his PRO of 1.124 is normalized to the league average and adjusted for home-park effects. Yet in the table of park adjusted Batting Runs, Brett's season ranks only 96th all-time because he missed 45 games, in which his team derived no benefit from his high rate of performance. (Had Brett played 162 games and continued to perform at the same level, his Batting Runs would have been not 64 but 88.6, the 21st best mark in history.)

Because PRO is not expressed in runs, it is less versatile than Batting Runs. For just as runs are proportional to the events that form them, so are they proportional to wins and losses. This statement, a truism today, was a novelty in 1954 when Rickey and Roth first stated the correlation between run differentials and team standings. But they did not take the next step, to recognize that not only a team's standing but even its won-lost record could be predicted from the run totals.

"The initial published attempt on this subject," Palmer wrote in the 1982 issue of the SABR annual *The National Pastime,* "was Earnshaw Cook's *Percentage Baseball,* in 1964. Examining major-league results from 1950 through 1960 he found winning percentage equal to .484 times runs scored divided by runs allowed. . . . Arnold Soolman, in an unpublished paper which received some media attention, looked at results from 1901 through 1970 and came up with winning percentage equal to .102 times runs scored per game minus .103 times runs allowed per game plus .505. . . . Bill James, in the *Baseball Abstract,* developed winning percentage equal to runs scored raised to the power *x,* divided by the sum of runs scored and runs allowed, each raised to the power *x.* Originally, *x* was equal to two but then better results were obtained when a value of 1.83 was used. . . .

"My work showed that as a rough rule of thumb, each additional ten runs scored (or ten less runs allowed) produced one extra win, essentially the same as the Soolman study. However, breaking the teams into groups showed that high-scoring teams needed more runs to produce a win. This runs-per-win factor I determined to be ten times the square root of the average number of runs scored per inning by both teams. Thus in normal play, when 4.5 runs per game are scored by each club, each team scores .5 runs per inning—totaling one run, the square root of which is one, times ten."

Note that when we refer to the need for approximately ten additional runs scored (or ten fewer allowed) to provide a team with an additional win, we do not mean that it takes ten runs to win any given game. Obviously, in a specific case, a one-run margin is all that is required; but statistics are designed for the long haul, not the short.

What does this have to do with Batting Runs? Remembering that Batting Runs are expressed not simply in runs but in beyond-average runs, the conversion from a batter's Linear Weights runs to his wins is a snap: simply divide Batting Runs by the number of runs it takes to gain an extra win in a given year. Taking the exploits of Babe Ruth in 1927, we see that through batting alone he contributed 100.7 runs, or 9.56 wins, since in the American League in 1927 it took 10.53 runs to produce an additional win. If every other player on the Yankees had performed at the league average, the New York record should have been 87-67; if each of the seven other batters had performed only half as well as Ruth and had added five extra wins (discounting reserves, pitchers, fielders, and stealers, whom we shall presume for this discussion to have been average), the Yankees would have gained another 35 wins (7 × 5) to finish with a won-lost mark of 122-32.

Stolen Base Runs

The Linear Weights formula for batters contains a factor for base stealers, expressed in runs. How do you judge the effectiveness of a base stealer? Conventional baseball statistics will lead you to the conclusion that whoever has the most steals is the best thief; that is the sole criterion for *The Sporting News* annual "Golden Shoe Award" in each league. How often the man with the most steals may have been thrown out is of no concern.

An article in the 1981 *Baseball Research Journal* by Bob Davids offered something more sophisticated yet utterly simple: a stolen base percentage, which is simply stolen bases divided by attempts. The best stolen base average of all time, insofar as we know and based on a minimum of 30 attempts, is Max Carey's in 1922 when he stole 51 bases in 53 attempts. The most times caught stealing in the course of a season was Ty Cobb's 38 in 1915, until 1982 when Rickey Henderson was nabbed 42 times. But the best method yet devised, and the one that is pleasingly simple, is to apply the Linear Weights method to get Stolen Base Runs. One multiplies the steals by their run value of .30 and the failed attempts by -.60, and adds the two products. The implication for such men as Ty Cobb, Rickey Henderson, and Vince Coleman is clear: it takes a fabulous stealing performance to produce as many as ten extra runs—i.e., one extra win—for the team.

In 1915 Ty Cobb, when he established the modern stolen base record of 96, can be seen to have contributed to his team 28.8 runs, while his 38 foiled larcenies cost 22.8. Thus Cobb, for all his whirling-dervish activity, accounted for only 6 non-par runs—not even a single win. Whoa! You mean that not a single one of Cobb's steals produced a victory? That is not what is being said: the fact is that while the gain from the stolen base is entirely visible—an extra base which may be followed by a hit that would otherwise not have produced a run—the cost of the caught stealing is entirely invisible, or conjectural, except with the aid of statistics. How many big innings did Cobb run his team out of? How many batters reached base in ensuing innings who might, in an earlier inning, have had their contributions count for runs? What Stolen Base Runs indicate are that, on balance, not on a specific-case basis, the stolen base is at best a dubious method of increasing a team's run production.

Now let's take a look at what Henderson did. His record 130 stolen bases in 1982 produced 39 runs for his team. His 42 failed attempts took away 25.2 possible runs. Net effect: approximately 14 runs, or one and a half wins, a performance nearly three times as good as Cobb's. In 1983, stealing 22 fewer bases, he was even better, accounting for 21.0 runs. However, the all-time best stealing record is that of Maury Wills in 1962, when he stole 104 bases and was caught only 13 times. Wills's 104 stolen bases produced 31.2 runs; his 13 failed attempts cost only 7.8. So, his baserunning contribution was 23.4, or a little over two wins.

Fielding Runs

In 1954 when Branch Rickey and Allan Roth came up with their "efficiency formula" for run scoring and run prevention, the defensive half of the equation was divided into five segments, the last of which was fielding, to which they assigned a mathematical value of zero. "There is nothing on earth," Rickey declared, "anyone can do with fielding."

Since then many have tried, with mixed results, to improve upon the mere toting up of raw data—putouts, assists, errors, double plays. In the second edition of *Total Baseball,* we improved upon the Fielding Runs formula by calculating innings played at each position, plate appearances for all players on the team, and then rating each fielder based on his chances per inning. Where previously all outfield positions had been grouped together, we now rate left fielders against left fielders, center fielders against center fielders, and right fielders against right fielders; we also revised thoroughly the formula for catchers, which retains the highest degree of subjectivism because their primary defensive contribution comes not with the glove but through calling the pitches.

More on this complex subject in the Glossary.

Pitching Runs

Determining the run contributions of pitchers is much easier than determining those of fielders or batters, though not quite so simple as that of base stealers. Actual runs allowed are known, as are innings pitched. Let's assume that a pitcher is responsible only for earned runs. Then why, we hear some of you asking, is the ERA not measure enough of his ability? Because it tells only the pitcher's *rate* of efficiency, not his actual benefit to the team. In a league with an ERA of 3.50, a starter who throws 300 innings with an ERA of 2.50 must be worth twice as much to his team as a starter with the same ERA who appears in only 150 innings. Through Pitching Runs, we seek to determine the number of beyond-average runs a pitcher saved—the number he prevented from scoring that an average pitcher would have allowed.

The formula for Earned Run Average is:

$$\text{ERA} = (\text{Earned Runs} \times 9)/\text{Innings Pitched}$$

The number of average, or par, runs for a pitcher, which is represented by a Pitching Runs figure of zero, is equal to:

$$(\text{League ERA} \times \text{IP})/9$$

If the league ERA is 4.21 (as the National League's was in 1994) and a pitcher's ERA is also 4.21, he will by definition have held batters in check at the league average no matter how many innings he pitched. If, however, his ERA was 1.56 and he hurled 202 innings (as Greg Maddux did for the Braves in '94), he will have saved a certain number of runs that an average pitcher might have allowed in his place; to find that number we employ the Pitching Runs formula:

Pitcher's Runs = Innings Pitched × (League ERA/9) − ER

This represents the difference between the number of earned runs allowed at the league average for the innings pitched and the actual earned runs allowed. For the case of Maddux, we get

$$Runs = 202 \times (4.21/9) - 35 = 59.5$$

Maddux was 59.5 runs better than the average National League pitcher in 1994, and had he been transported to an average NL team—that mythical entity that scores as many runs as it allows while winning 81 and losing 81—he would have made that team's mark 87-75. (Actually, in the strike shortened 112 game season of 1994, an average team would have been 56-56, and the addition of Maddux would have made that team's record 62-50.) An alternative way to calculate pitchers' Linear Weights, useful with oldtimers for whom you may have the ERA but not the number of earned runs allowed, is to use the pitcher's ERA, subtracted from the league's ERA, multiplying by the innings pitched, then dividing by nine. In Maddux's case, this approach would look like:

$$(4.21 - 1.56) \times 202/9 = 59.5$$

The two parts of performance—efficiency and durability—are incorporated into all Linear Weights measures. If you are performing at a better than average clip, the more regularly you do so, the more your team will benefit and thus the higher your Linear Weights measure. If you are stealing bases nine times out of ten, your team will benefit more from sixty attempts than from forty; if you are batting at an above average clip, it's better to play in 160 games than 110; if you're allowing one earned run per game less than the average pitcher, your LWTS will increase with innings pitched.

Linear Weights in Practice

Having formulas for pitching, fielding, baserunning, and batting, we can assess the run-scoring contribution of every individual who has ever played the game, and thus the number of wins that he has contributed in a given season or over his career. The number of runs required to produce an additional win has varied over the years between 9 and 11 runs, with a very few league seasons outside those parameters.

Limited by conventional baseball statistics, one might, in 1990, have uttered something like, "Barry Bonds hit .293 with 33 homers and 114 RBIs—the guy must have been worth 10 extra wins to Pittsburgh all by himself!" Or: "The White Sox are only one pitcher away from winning the division." Or: "The Yankees are only three players away from being a contender." Or, "Letting Darryl Strawberry get away was the worst thing the Mets ever did; they'll be a second-division club for a decade." With Linear Weights, these statements, or rather the concerns they reflect, can be approached with some data and with some degree of objectivity. First: Barry Bonds had a fine year in 1990, but to have contributed 10 wins by himself

he would have had to account for nearly 100 Linear Weights runs, a mark that up till then had been attained by only three men in major-league history. In fact, Bonds contributed 6.5 wins in '90, though he did post 9.0 wins in 1992.

As to the White Sox, they finished 94-68 in 1990, while their Linear Weights projected them to finish at 81-81. The Athletics, who won the AL West at 103-59, actually projected to finish 96-66. So, the Sox management might have asked, how to close ground on the Athletics? Could one pitcher—like Bob Welch, for whom they bid in the free-agent bazaar—make the difference? To do so, he would have to contribute about 150 Pitching Runs, a feat no pitcher has ever accomplished. In 1990, pitching for Oakland—and remember, the Linear Weights formula is divorced from considerations of batter support—Welch contributed 20.7 park-adjusted Pitching Runs. So presuming that he pitched as well for the White Sox as he did for the Athletics, or even slightly better, he would not be enough to "win" Chicago the flag on paper; Chicago would need help from other quarters.

Regarding the other statements, you get the picture: sabermetric analyses like the ones above will tend to puncture fantasies.

Park Factor

A central issue for sabermetricians is the network of illusion created by home-park dimensions, atmospheric conditions, and visibility for batters. How many home runs would Matt Williams hit if he played half his games in Fenway Park? Will the Boston Red Sox and Chicago Cubs keep "failing" to put together solid pitching staffs—or has their pitching been adequate all along? Why have the American League leaders in triples so often worn a Royals uniform? One's home park has a powerful effect on a player or pitcher's record, elevating some good players to greatness and denying the spotlight to some outstanding performers.

It should be understood that the average player does better at home regardless of the park—familiarity breeds success. Individuals bat and pitch at a rate 10 percent higher at home, on average. But parks don't create performance; they only affect it. For example, a lefthanded hitter at Fenway can do very well indeed, as Wade Boggs did, by learning to take the outside pitch to left field. Likewise, a righthanded batter can make the friendly Green Monster into his nemesis by trying to pull every pitch.

If we desire to remove the silver spoon or the millstone that a home park can be, and measure individual ability alone, we must create a statistical balancer that diminishes the individual batting marks created in parks like Fenway and augments those created in San Diego. We developed an adjustment that enables us, for the first time, to measure a player's accomplishments apart from the influence of his home park.

Parks differ in so many ways that it may be hard to imagine how their differences can be quantified. The most obvious way in which they differ is in their dimensions, from home plate to the outfield walls, and from the base lines to the stands. The older arenas—Fenway Park,

Wrigley Field, Tiger Stadium—tend to favor hitters in both regards, with reachable fences and little room to pursue a foul pop. Yet two parks can have nearly equal dimensions, like Pittsburgh's Three Rivers Stadium and Atlanta's Fulton County Stadium, yet have highly dissimilar impacts upon hitters because of climate (balls travel farther in hot weather), elevation (travel farther as altitude increases), and playing surface (travel faster and truer on artificial turf). Still another factor is how well batters think they see the ball; Shea Stadium is notorious as a cause of complaints.

And perhaps more important than any of the objective park characteristics, suggested Robert Kingsley in a 1980 study of why so many homers were hit in Atlanta, is the attitude of the players, the way that the park changes their view of how the game must be played in order to win. Every team that comes into Atlanta in August knows that the ball is going to fly and, whether it is a team designed for power or not, it plays ball there as if it were the 1927 Yankees. In their own home park the Astros might peck and scratch for runs, but in Atlanta they will put the steal and hit-and-run in mothballs. Conversely, a team which comes into the Astrodome and plays for the big inning will generally get what it deserves—a loss. The successful team is one that can play its game at home—the game for which the team was constructed—yet is flexible enough to adapt when on the road. How to quantify attitude?

Rather than try to assign a numerical value to each of the six or more variables that might go into establishing an estimator of home park impact, we looked to the single measure in which all these variables are reflected—runs. After all, why would we assign one value to dimensions, another to climate, and so on, except to identify their impact on scoring? If a stadium is a "hitters' park," it stands to reason that more runs would be scored there than in a park perceived as neutral, just as a "pitchers' park" could be expected to depress scoring.

The full and lengthy explanation for the computation of the Park Factor is left to the Glossary, where hardy readers might consider taking a peek right now. For most of us, though, it will be enough to understand that the Park Factor consists mainly of the team's home-road ratio of runs allowed, compared to the league's home-road ratio.

Relativity

Sabermetric statistics can be marvelous tools for cross-era comparisons, enabling us to determine if baseball's history is truly a seamless web or if its seams are real enough, but are camouflaged by traditional statistics.

If Batter A presented himself to you for approval with these statistics—.330 batting average, 16 home runs, 107 RBIs—what would your reaction be? You'd like to have him on your team, right? And what to make of Batter B, who presents these numbers—.257 batting average, 14 home runs, 53 RBIs? Not bad for a middle infielder with a good glove, you say, but otherwise undistinguished? In fact, the "impressive" figures of Batter A represent the average performance of a National League outfielder in 1930, while the "blah" figures of Batter B are those of the average American League outfielder of 1968: the former

has more than twice the RBIs of the latter, along with a batting average 73 points higher, yet the two performed at identical levels, and an argument could be made that Batter B was superior.

In a similar comparison involving those two years of extremes, Bill Terry led the National League in 1930 with a BA of .401, a mark surpassed by Ted Williams in 1941 but not equaled since; Carl Yastrzemski led the American League of 1968 with a performance that oldtimers held to be a disgrace, a lowly BA of .301, the worst ever to win a batting championship. Terry's mark was achieved at a time when most pitchers had only two pitches, a fastball and a curve, and not enough confidence in the latter to throw it when behind in the count at 2-0 or 3-1. The parks were smaller; there was no night ball; the game was segregated racially; and a team played 22 games with each of its seven rivals, none farther west of the Mississippi than St. Louis. Moreover, 1930 was the year in which National League officials, attempting to match the popularity of the slugging American League, juiced the ball to such an extent that the entire league batted .312 (if you remove pitcher batting). In other words, the average nonpitcher in the NL of 1930 batted higher than the AL leader in 1968! When Yaz hit .301, pitchers dominated the game and the average American League nonpitcher hit .238. How to compare Terry and Yaz, who played under such different conditions thirty-eight years apart?

You could view Terry's .401 in relation to his league's BA of .312, concluding that Memphis Bill was a better hitter (by BA alone, which despite its previously cited deficiencies remains the most comfortable stat by which to introduce this technique) by 28.5 percent. You could compare Yaz's .301 to his league's BA of .238 and conclude that he was a better than average hitter by 26.5 percent. A mere 2 percentage points separate the men— had they both played in the National League of 1983, when the league average was .255, the Terry of 1930 might have hit .328, the Yaz of 1968, .323. (A further refinement of this method would be to delete Terry's at bats and hits from his league's, and those of Yastrzemski from his league's, so that the batters are not in effect compared with themselves. This, however, necessitates the use of at bats and hits rather than simply the averages and does not significantly alter the results.)

Why do we need relative measures? Basically, for the same reason we need statistics altogether, to compare, to interpret, and to comprehend, but in a more reasonable and accurate manner when the disparity of the data sources makes the use of absolute, unadjusted numbers illogical. If the analysis involves data produced under widely varying conditions, such as a sample including performances twenty, fifty, or a hundred years apart, any comparison will be meaningless without dragging in a series of rather complex historical understandings to modify the analysis—and in a highly subjective, unreliable manner.

Until the 1970s, when David Shoebotham ("Relative Batting Averages," *Baseball Research Journal,* 1976) and Merritt Clifton ("Relative Baseball," *Samisdat,* 1979) introduced the relativist approach, all baseball stats were absolute. And for cross-era comparison, that favorite Hot Stove League activity, absolute stats were absolutely useless, generating plenty of heat and precious little light.

What the theory of relativity, baseball-style, does beautifully is to eliminate the need for bringing historical baggage to statistical analysis. The normalized or relative versions of any statistic—batting average, Production, ERA, slugging average, you name it; even homers or strikeouts, though there are problems with these—will be greater than 1.00 for all above-average performers (1.41, for example, means 41 percent better than average in the given category) while relative statistics less than 1.00 will indicate a below average level of play (0.88 means 12 percent below the norm).

It is as simple as can be. So Early Wynn had a 3.20 ERA in 1950? What does that mean? Well, the league ERA was 4.58, so Wynn did very well indeed. His normalized ERA thus was 143, a mark better than that earned by Tom Seaver in 1968, when he had an absolute ERA a full run lower at 2.20.

We cannot employ a Relative Won-Lost record, for the league average is every year the same: .500. (A logical corollary is that one cannot fruitfully use relative measures of any sort for a single season's analysis, as all like figures will be compared to the same league average. The numbers may be changed into normalized form, but the players' rankings will be unchanged.

Relativism in baseball echoes not only Einstein but also Shakespeare, whose words in *Hamlet* might be modified to read "There is nothing either good or bad, but context makes it so." No longer must we accept arbitrary assessments of performance or regard with awe such old-time figures as Hugh Duffy's BA of .440 in 1894 (not the accomplishment that Rod Carew's .388 was in 1977) or George Sisler's .407 in 1920 (not as good as Roberto Clemente's .357 in 1967). Conversely, a "mediocre" performance of recent years, such as Bobby Murcer's .292 of 1972, for instance, stacks up as the equal of Eddie Collins' .360 in 1923, while Charlie Grimm's seemingly solid .298 in 1929 compares unfavorably to Mike Cubbage's .260 in 1976.

Relativism redefines our understanding not only of particular accomplishments but also of baseball history it-self. We see that the men who batted .400 with numbing regularity in the 1890s and 1920s were not supermen (would you swap Wade Boggs for Tuck Turner? Tony Gwynn for Tip O'Neill?) anymore than the sub-2.00 ERA pitchers of the late 1960s were superhuman (Gary Peters, Bob Bolin, Dave McNally, et al.). Absolute figures lie. Are hitters today worse because none has hit .400 since 1941? Or are they superior because a Dave Kingman can average nearly 30 homers a year while Cap Anson only averaged 4? Are infielders better today because they make fewer errors than their counterparts of 50, 75, or 100 years ago? Do modern outfielders have limp-noodle arms because their assist totals pale before those registered in the early decades of the 1900s? Is baseball improving or declining, and has its rise or fall been steady? One can spit absolute stats on the hot stove all winter long and get no closer to the answer, but with relative statistics, the issues are clarified.

The Future

The most exciting frontier for sabermetrics is in situational stats, the type employed by The Elias Sports Bureau, The Baseball Workshop, and Stats, Inc. As the years go by and their data bases grow, the sampling sizes of the data will enlarge and their figures for day vs. night, left vs. right, and so on, will be statistically meaningful as well as statistically correct. Cross-era comparison remains a subject of intense interest, and the debate over average-player skill rages on. Fielding stats, as discussed, also provide fertile ground for invention.

Fantasy baseball aficionados seem caught up in the competition and dealmaking (as well as player evaluation), but some of the newsletters provide sound analysis and trend-spotting tips. It would not be surprising if Rotisserie-type leagues and digital game designers compete with SABR to furnish the best sabermetricians of the 1990s.

The Player Register

The Player Register consists of the central batting, baserunning, and fielding statistics of every man who has batted in major league play since 1871, excepting those men who were primarily pitchers. A pitcher's complete batting record, however, is included for those pitchers who also, over the course of their careers, played in 100 or more games at another position—including pinch hitter—or played in more than half of their total major league games at a position other than pitcher, or played more games at a position other than pitcher in at least one year. (Pitcher batting is also expressed in Batting Wins in the Pitcher Batting column of the Pitcher Register.)

The players are listed alphabetically by surname and, when more than one player bears the name, alphabetically by *given* name—not by "use name," by which we mean the name that may have been applied to him during his playing career. This is the standard method of alphabetizing used in other biographical reference works, and in the case of baseball it makes it easier to find a lesser-known player with a common surname like Smith or Johnson. This method also jibes with that employed in the Annual Record where, for example, Charles "Old Hoss" Radbourn is shown not as the puzzling O. Radbourn or H. Radbourn, as some reference books have it, but as C. Radbourn. On the whole, we have been conservative in ascribing nicknames, doing so only when the player was in fact known by that name during his playing days.

Each page of the Player Register is topped at the corner by a finding aid: in capital letters, the surname of, first, the player whose entry heads up the page and, second, the player whose entry concludes it. Another finding aid is the use of boldface numerals to indicate a league-leading total in those categories in which a player is truly attempting to excel (no boldface is given to the "leaders" in batter strikeouts, times caught stealing, at bats, or games played). An additional finding aid is an asterisk alongside the team for which a player appeared in postseason competition, thus making for easy cross-reference to the earlier section on postseason play and the Postseason Register. Additional symbols denote All Star Game selection and/or play; these appear to the right of the team/league column. Condensed type appears occasionally throughout this section; it has no special significance but is designed simply to accommodate unusually wide figures, such as the 4.000 slugging average of a man who, in his only at bat of the year, hit a home run.

The record for each man who played in more than one season is given in a line for each season, plus a career total line. If he played for more than one team in a given year, his totals for each team are stated on separate lines. And if the teams for which he played in his "traded year" are in the same league, then his full record is stated in both separate and combined fashion. (In the odd case of a man playing for three or more clubs in one year, with some of these clubs being in the same league, the combined total line will reflect only his play in that one league.) Also in this edition, we include position data in the "Yr" line for traded players. A man who played in only one year will have no additional career total line, since it would be identical to his seasonal listing.

Batting records for the National Association are included in The Player Register because the editors, like most baseball historians, regard it as a major league, inasmuch as it was the only professional league of its day and supplied the National League of 1876 with most of its players. In this edition of *Total Baseball*, we benefit from the SABR research project referred to in the Introduction to the Annual Record—which to date has produced extra-base hits, corrected averages, walks, and some stolen bases, strikeouts, and other data heretofore unavailable; fielding data for the NA may be available for *Total Baseball 5*. Unless Major League Baseball reverses the position it adopted in 1969 and restores the NA to offical major-league status, we will continue the practice of carrying separate totals lines for the National Association years rather than integrating them into the career marks of those players whose major league tenures began before 1876 and concluded in that year or later.

Gaps remain elsewhere in the official record of baseball and in the ongoing process of sabermetric reconstruction. The reader will note occasional blank elements in biographical lines, or in single-season columns; these are not typographical lapses but signs that the information does not exist or has not yet been found. In the totals lines of many players, an underlined figure indicates that the total reflects partial data, such as caught stealing for a man whose career covers the National League of 1918–1930 (during which this data was available only for 1920–1925), or batter strikeouts for a man whose career spanned both sides of the year 1909.

For a discussion of which data is missing for particular years, see "The History of Major League Baseball Statistics." Here is a quick summation of the missing data:

Hit batters, 1897–1908 NL/AL, 5 percent missing;
Caught stealing, 1886–1914, 1916 for players with fewer than 20 stolen bases, 1917–1919, 1926–1950 NL; 1886–1891 AA; 1890 PL; 1901–1913, 1916 for players with fewer than 20 stolen bases, 1917–1919 AL (1927 data, missing from the first edition, is now 90 percent complete); 1914–15 FL;

Sacrifice hit, 1908–1930, 1939 (in these years fly balls scoring runners counted as sacrifice hits, and in 1927–1930 fly balls advancing runners to any base counted as sacrifices);

Sacrifice fly, 1908–1930, 1939 (counted but inseparable from sacrifice hits), 1940–1953 (not counted);

Runs batted in, 1882–1887, 1890 AA; 1884 UA;

Strikeouts for batters, 1882–1888, 1890 AA; 1884 UA; 1897–1909 NL; 1901-1912 AL.

For a key to the team and league abbreviations used in the Player Register, flip to the last page of this volume. For a guide to the other procedures and abbreviations employed in the Player Register, review the comments on the prodigiously extended playing record below.

Looking at the biographical line for any player, we see first his use name in full capitals, then his given name and nickname (and any other name he may have used or been born with, such as the matronymic of a Latin American

YEAR	TM/L	G	AB	R	H	2B	3B	HR	RBI	BB	SO	AVG	OBP	SLG	PRO+	BR/A	SB	CS	SBR	FA	FR	G/POS	TPR

■ KID DE LEON Ponce de Leon, Juan "Castilian Kid" (also played in 1874 as Kid Madrid)
b: 3/13/1460, Madrid, Spain d: 2/25/1963, St. Augustine, Fl. BR/TR, 5'11", 173 lbs. Deb: 5/21/1874 FMUCH

YEAR	TM/L	G	AB	R	H	2B	3B	HR	RBI	BB	SO	AVG	OBP	SLG	PRO+	BR/A	SB	CS	SBR	FA	FR	G/POS	TPR
1874	Bos-n	52	277	73	94	7	4	1	14	2		.339	.342	.400	111	4						*2-52	0.2
1875	Wes-n	2	3	1	1	0	0	0	0			.333	.333	.333	95	0						/S-2	0.0
1883	Bal-a	28	121	12	33	2	1	1			8	.273	.318	.331	101	1				.901	0	C-16,O-10/S	0.0
1884	Was-U	86	371	75	107	12	5	1			11	.288	.309	.356	127	5	0			.913	0	1-62,O-15/C	0.9
	KC-U	1	4	1	0	0	0	0			0	.000	.000	.000	97	0				1.000	0	/1-1	0.0
	Yr	87	375	76	107	12	5	1			11	.287	.308	.355	126	-0	0			.914	0	1-63,O-15/C	0.9
1890	Cin-P	1	1	1	1	0	0	1	1	0		1.000	1.000	4.000	700	1	0			.000	0	/2-1	0.0
1908	Phi-N	1	0	0	0	0	0	0	0	0		—	—	—			0	0		.000	0	/R-1	0.0
	Phi-A	9	31	5	9	3	0	2		0		.290	.290	.387	113	0	0			.899	-1	/3-8	0.0
1909	Phi-A	148	541	73	165	27	19	4	85	26		.305	.343	.447	146	26	20			.920	-5	*3-141	3.0
1910	Phi-A	146	561	83	159	25	15	2	74	34		.283	.329	.392	123	13	21			.934	3	*3-144	2.4
1911	Phi-A	148	592	96	198	40	4	11	115	50		.334	.379	.505	157	38	38			.912	-8	*3-147	3.3
1912	Phi-A	149	577	116	200	40	21	10	130	50		.347	.404	.541	171	50	40			.930	9	*3-149	5.4
1913	Phi-A	149	564	116	190	34	9	12	117	63	31	.337	.413	.493	171	48	34			.927	7	*3-148	6.1
1914	Phi-A	150	570	84	182	23	10	9	89	53	37	.319	.380	.442	151	33	19	20	-6	.929	8	*3-150	4.1
1915	Nwk-F	2	8	5	4	2	1	1	4	0	2	.500	.500	1.38	304	3	0			.977	1	/3-2	0.1
1916	NY-A	100	360	46	97	23	2	10	52	36	30	.269	.344	.428	130	12	15			.931	3	3-98	2.1
1917	NY-A	146	553	57	156	24	2	6	71	48	27	.282	.345	.365	109	6	18			.940	11	*3-145	2.7
1918	NY-A	126	504	65	154	24	5	6	62	38	13	.306	.357	.409	138	20	8			.943	11	*3-122	3.4
1939	*NY-A☆	141	567	70	166	22	1	10	83	44	18	.293	.346	.388	100	-0	13			.944	-2	*3-140	0.9
1941	*NY-A★	94	330	46	97	16	2	9	71	26	12	.294	.353	.436	98	-2	8	5	-1	.955	13	3-92	1.6
1942	*NY-A†	69	234	30	65	12	3	7	36	15	14	.278	.327	.444	98	-2	1	3	-2	.940	-8	3-67	-0.4
Total	2 n	54	280	74	95	7	4	1	14	2		.339	.348	.404	110	4						*2-52/S-2	0.2
Total	17	1694	6489	981	1983	329	100	100	992	502	184	.306	.354	.446	130	246	235	28		.938	41	*3-1409,1-126/CSO2R	35.6

player). His date and place of birth follow "b" and his date and place of death follow "d." Years through 1900 are expressed fully, in four digits, and years after 1900 are expressed in their last two digits.

Then comes the player's manner of batting and throwing, abbreviated for a lefthanded batter who throws right as BL/TR (a switch-hitter would be shown as BB for "bats both" and a switch thrower as TB for "throws both").

Next, and for most players last, is the player's debut date in the major leagues, all of which are reported now.

Some players continue in major league baseball after their playing days are through, as managers, coaches, or even umpires. A player whose biographical line concludes with an M can be located in the Manager Roster; one whose line bears a C will be listed in the Coach Roster; and one with a U occupies a place in the Umpire Roster. (In the last case we have placed a U on the biographical line only for those players who umpired in at least six games in a year, for in the nineteenth century—and especially in the years of the National Association—literally hundreds of players were pressed into service as umpires for a game or two. It would be misleading to accord such players the same code we give to Bob Emslie or Babe Pinelli.) The select few who have been enshrined in the Baseball Hall of Fame at Cooperstown, NY, are noted with an H. They are also listed in the Hall of Fame Roster found toward the end of Bill Deane's "Awards and Honors" essay. Also in this edition is an F on this line to denote family connection—father-son-grandson or brother.

The explanations for the statistical column heads follow; for more technical information about formulas and calculations, see the Glossary. The vertical rules in the

column-header line separate the stats into seven logical groupings: year, team, league; fundamental counting stats for batters; hits and plate appearances broken out into their component counting stats; basic calculated averages; sabermetric figures of more complex calculation; base-running stats; fielding stats and Total Player Rating.

Absent from the Player Register in this edition are some statistics present in the original: production as a raw, unadjusted figure (still available by simply adding OBP plus SLG, as well as in the Annual Record and Leaders sections); Park Factor for batters (still available from the Annual Record); Clutch Hitting Index, newly developed for *Total Baseball* but which we have judged to be of lesser interest and value than the more established sabermetric measures (like PRO, however, it is still present in the Annual Record and Leaders sections); and Total Average, a popular stat but one that is mirrored by Runs Created and Batting Runs, both of which are more accurate (TA is present in the Annual Record and Leaders sections). By deleting these statistics from the Register we have improved legibility, particularly by adding to the margin in the gutter of the book, and reduced some redundancy.

New to this edition are additional hit-by-pitch data for batters in the 1897-1908 period, which is reflected in their on base percentages. We have also made an upward adjustment to overall league performance in the Federal League of 1914-15 and the Union Association of 1884 (thus lowering individual ratings), because while both leagues are regarded as major leagues, there can be no doubt that their caliber of play was not equivalent to that in the rival leagues of those years. Suffice it to say here that league at bats were reduced to 80 percent for the UA and 90 percent for the FL. A full explanation of the adjustment procedure may be found in the Glossary, under "League Performance."

YEAR   Year of play (when a space in the column is blank, this indicates that the man has played for two or more clubs in the last year stated in the column; if those clubs were in the same league, then the man will also have a combined total line, beginning with the abbreviation "Yr" placed in the TEAM/L column)

Yr   Year's totals for play with two or more clubs in same league (see comments for YEAR)

*   Denotes postseason play, World Series or League Championship Series

TM/L   Team and League (see comments for YEAR)

★   Named to All Star Game, played

☆   Named to All Star Game, did not play

†   Named to All Star Game, replaced because of injury

G   Games

AB   At-bats

R   Runs

H   Hits (Bases on balls were counted as hits by scorers in 1887, but in *Total Baseball* they are not figured as times at bat, nor as hits.)

2B   Doubles

3B   Triples

HR   Home Runs

RBI   Runs Batted In

BB   Bases on Balls (Bases on balls were counted as outs by scorers in 1876, but in *Total Baseball* they are not figured as times at bat nor as outs.)

SO   Strikeouts

AVG   Batting Average (Figured as hits over at-bats; mathematically meaningless averages created through a division by zero are rendered as dashes; see Kid De Leon's entry for 1908 with Pit-N. League leaders in this category, as in others in the Player Register, are noted by bold type. However, some boldface leaders in batting average will have lower marks than other batters who are not credited with having won a championship; for a full explanation of the reasoning for this anomaly, see "The History of Major League Baseball Statistics."

OBP   On Base Percentage (See comments for AVG)

SLG   Slugging Average (See comments for AVG, and note the use of condensed type to express Kid De Leon's maximum SLG in 1890.)

PRO+   Production Plus, or Adjusted Production (On Base Percentage plus Slugging Average, normalized to league average and adjusted for home-park factor.) See comments for /A.

BR/A   Batting Runs (Linear Weights measure of runs contributed beyond what a league-average batter or team might have contributed, defined as zero. Occasionally the curious figure of -0 will appear in this column, or in the columns of other Linear Weights measures of batting, baserunning, fielding, and the TPR. This "negative zero" figure signifies a run contribution that falls below the league average, but to so small a degree that it cannot be said to have cost the team a run. The "/A" signifies that the measure has been adjusted for home-park factor and normalized to league average. A mark of 100 is a league-average performance. Pitcher batting is removed from all league batting statistics before normalization, for a variety of reasons expanded upon in the Glossary. Three-year averages are employed for batting park factors. If a team moved or the park changed dramatically, then two-year averages are employed; if the park was used for only one year, then of course only that run-scoring data is used.)

SB   Stolen Bases (for 1886 to the present, plus partial data for the NA years, 1871-75.)

CS   Caught Stealing (Available 1915, 1916 for players with 20 or more stolen bases, 1920–1925, 1951–date NL; 1914–1915, 1916 for players with 20 or more stolen bases, 1920 to date AL with scattered data still missing from 1927.)

SBA   Stolen Base Average (Stolen bases divided by attempts; availability dependent upon CS as shown above.)

SBR   Stolen Base Runs (This is a Linear Weights measure of runs contributed beyond what a league-average base stealer might have gained, defined as zero and calculated on the basis of a 66.7 percent success rate, which computer simulations have shown to be the break-even point beyond which stolen bases have positive run value to the team; see the general introduction to Part Two and the Glossary. The presence of a figure in the SBR column in the Player Register is dependent upon the availability of CS as shown above. Lifetime Stolen Base Runs are not totaled where data is incomplete, but seasonal SBRs are reflected in the seasonal Total Player Ratings, which in turn are added to form the lifetime Total Player Rating.)

FA   Fielding Average, often called Fielding Percentage as well (putouts plus assists divided by putouts plus assists plus errors, here calculated only for the position at which a man played the most games in a season or career.)

FR   Fielding Runs (The Linear Weights measure of runs saved beyond what a league-average player at that position might have saved, defined as zero; this stat is calculated to take account of the particular demands of the different positions; see Glossary for formulas, and note new method for the positional adjustment.)

G/POS Positions played (This is a ranking from left to right by frequency of the positions played in the field or at designated hitter. An asterisk to the left of the position indicates, generally, that in a given year the man played about two-thirds of his team's scheduled games at that position; more precisely, it is figured at 20 games in 1871, 30 in 1872, 35 in 1873, 40 in 1874, and 50 in 1875; two-thirds of the scheduled games in 1876-1900, and 100 or more games since. When a slash separates positions, the man played those positions listed to the left of the slash in 10 or more games and the positions to the right of the slash in fewer than 10 games. If there is no slash, he played all positions listed in 10 or more games. For the lifetime line, the asterisk signifies 1,000 games and the slash marks a dividing point of 100 games. A player's POS column will list him as a pinch runner or pinch hitter in only those years in which he appeared at no other position. New to this edition are listings of the number of games played at the individual's two most common positions. The positions and their abbreviations are)

1: First base	P: Pitcher
2: Second base	D: Designated hitter
S: Shortstop	R: Runner (pinch)
3: Third base	H: Hitter (pinch)
O: Outfield	M: Manager (playing)
C: Catcher	

TPR Total Player Rating (This is the sum of a player's Adjusted Batting Runs, Fielding Runs, and Base Stealing Runs, minus his positional adjustment, all divided by the Runs Per Win factor for that year—generally around 10, historically in the 9–11 range. For more information on the formula and the Runs Per Win concept, see the general introduction to the statistical section and the Glossary. In the lifetime line, the TPR is the sum of the seasonal TPRs. For men who were primarily pitchers but whose extent of play at other positions warrants a listing in the Player Register as well as the Pitcher Register, the TPR may be listed as 0.0; this signifies that their batting records are summed up in the Total Pitcher Index [TPI] column of the Pitcher Register.) Note that the TPR (and the TPI, Total Pitcher Index) in this fourth edition will differ from those in earlier volumes, for four reasons which are explained in greater detail in the Glossary. (1) A broader and more sophisticated computation of the positional adjustment to Batting Runs has improved the accuracy and reasonableness of the method, by which the TPR of those who play skill positions like shortstop and second base tend to be boosted and the TPR of the sluggers who customarily play first base and left field are generally diminished. (2) Because games in left, center, and right fields are now available for all outfielders, center fielders no longer need be compared to an average of the regular center fielders and now may be set against all the men who played center, thus tending to elevate their Fielding Runs. (3) Because Hit Batsmen data is now available for the 1903–1908 period, plus considerable data for the years 1897–1902, men like Frank Chance, who was hit over 100 times in his career, increase their Batter Ratings perceptibly. (4) And for players who were both batters and pitchers, the method of allocating Wins between TPR and TPI (Total Pitcher Index) was improved. Previously, if a pitcher pitched in over half his games, all his batting was included with his pitcher rating (TPI); if he pitched in less than half his games, his Batting Wins were thrown over to his batter rating (TPR), with his TPI including only his Pitching Wins and Pitcher Defense. The new method prorates batting proportionally with the number of games pitched. In addition, fielding ratings at nonpitching positions for players who pitched in over half their games, previously omitted, are now part of the Total Baseball Ranking. In any case, the TPR values of batter-pitchers should remain about the same. Thus in 1918, Babe Ruth now has a batter rating of 2.6 Wins and a pitcher rating of 2.9 (total 5.5). In previous editions his marks used to be 4.1 and 1.0, respectively, or 5.1 overall, with none of his batting counted in with his pitching record even though he pitched 20 of 95 games. The large jump in his pitcher rating is because now his pitcher batting is compared against average batting for pitchers.

Total For players whose careers include play in the National Association as well as other major leagues, two totals are given, as described above and as illustrated in Kid De Leon's record, where the record of his years in the National Association is shown alongside the notation "Total 2 n," where 2 stands for the number of years totaled and n stands for National Association. For players whose careers began in 1876 or later, the lifetime record is shown alongside the notation "Total x," where x stands for the number of post-1875 years totaled. Note the underlined entries in the record for Kid De Leon, reflecting the partial data for RBI, batter strikeouts, stolen bases, and times caught stealing.

YEAR	TM/L	G	AB	R	H	2B	3B	HR	RBI	BB	SO	AVG	OBP	SLG	PRO+	BR/A	SB	CS	SBR	FA	FR	G/POS	TPR

■ HANK AARON   Aaron, Henry Louis "Hammerin' Hank" b: 2/5/34, Mobile, Ala.   BR/TR, 6', 180 lbs.   Deb: 4/13/54   FH

YEAR	TM/L	G	AB	R	H	2B	3B	HR	RBI	BB	SO	AVG	OBP	SLG	PRO+	BR/A	SB	CS	SBR	FA	FR	G/POS	TPR
1954	Mil-N	122	468	58	131	27	6	13	69	28	39	.280	.325	.447	105	1	2	2	-1	.970	-2	*O-116	-0.6
1955	Mil-N★	153	602	105	189	**37**	9	27	106	49	61	.314	.369	.540	144	36	3	1	0	.967	6	*O-126,2-27	3.8
1956	Mil-N★	153	609	106	**200**	34	14	26	92	37	54	**.328**	.369	.558	154	43	2	4	-2	.962	10	*O-152	4.4
1957	*Mil-N★	151	615	**118**	198	27	6	**44**	**132**	57	58	.322	.379	.600	170	58	1	1	-0	.983	2	*O-150	5.0
1958	*Mil-N★	153	601	109	196	34	4	30	95	59	49	.326	.387	.546	157	47	4	1	1	.984	2	*O-153	4.1
1959	Mil-N★	154	629	116	**223**	46	7	39	123	51	54	**.355**	.406	**.636**	**188**	75	8	0	2	.982	-2	*O-152/3-5	**6.6**
1960	Mil-N★	153	590	102	172	20	11	40	126	60	63	.292	.359	.566	160	46	16	7	1	.982	9	*O-153/2-2	4.8
1961	Mil-N★	155	603	115	197	**39**	10	34	120	56	64	.327	.386	.594	165	54	21	9	1	.982	12	*O-154/3-2	5.6
1962	Mil-N★	156	592	127	191	28	6	45	128	66	73	.323	.393	.618	171	58	15	7	0	.980	8	*O-153/1-1	5.5
1963	Mil-N★	161	631	**121**	201	29	4	**44**	**130**	78	94	.319	.391	**.586**	180	64	31	5	**6**	.979	-1	*O-161	6.5
1964	Mil-N★	145	570	103	187	30	2	24	95	62	46	.328	.394	.514	152	40	22	4	4	.983	11	*O-139,2-11	5.1
1965	Mil-N★	150	570	109	181	**40**	1	32	89	60	81	.318	.384	.560	161	45	24	4	5	.987	10	*O-148	5.5
1966	Atl-N★	158	603	117	168	23	1	**44**	**127**	76	96	.279	.360	.539	144	35	21	3	5	.988	9	*O-158/2-2	4.3
1967	Atl-N★	155	600	**113**	184	37	3	**39**	109	63	97	.307	.373	**.573**	169	52	17	6	2	.979	12	*O-152/2-1	6.1
1968	Atl-N★	160	606	84	174	33	4	29	86	64	62	.287	.356	.498	154	39	28	5	5	.991	14	*O-151,1-14	**5.5**
1969	*Atl-N★	147	547	100	164	30	3	44	97	87	47	.300	.398	.607	177	56	9	10	-3	.982	6	*O-144/1-4	5.2
1970	Atl-N★	150	516	103	154	26	1	38	118	74	63	.298	.389	.574	146	33	9	0	3	.977	5	*O-125,1-11	3.2
1971	Atl-N★	139	495	95	162	22	3	47	118	71	58	.327	.414	**.669**	**190**	58	1	1	-0	.996	-8	1-71,O-60	4.2
1972	Atl-N★	129	449	75	119	10	0	34	77	92	55	.265	.391	.514	142	27	4	0	1	.987	1	*1-109,O-15	1.9
1973	Atl-N★	120	392	84	118	12	1	40	96	68	51	.301	.406	.643	173	39	1	1	-0	.977	2	*O-105	3.7
1974	Atl-N	112	340	47	91	16	0	20	69	39	29	.268	.343	.491	126	11	1	0	0	.986	-4	O-89	0.3
1975	Mil-A★	137	465	45	109	16	2	12	60	70	51	.234	.336	.355	95	-2	0	1	-1	1.000	-1	*D-128/O-3	-0.7
1976	Mil-A	85	271	22	62	8	0	10	35	35	38	.229	.317	.369	102	1	0	1	-1	1.000	-0	D-74/O-1	-0.2
Total	23	3298	12364	2174	3771	624	98	755	2297	1402	1383	.305	.377	.555	156	914	240	73	28	.980	101	*O-2760,1-210,D/23	89.8

■ TOMMIE AARON   Aaron, Tommie Lee b: 8/5/39, Mobile, Ala.   d: 8/16/84, Atlanta, Ga.   BR/TR, 6'1", 200 lbs.   Deb: 4/10/62   FC

YEAR	TM/L	G	AB	R	H	2B	3B	HR	RBI	BB	SO	AVG	OBP	SLG	PRO+	BR/A	SB	CS	SBR	FA	FR	G/POS	TPR
1962	Mil-N	141	334	54	77	20	2	8	38	41	58	.231	.315	.374	86	-7	6	0	2	.989	2	*1-110,O-42/23	-0.8
1963	Mil-N	72	135	6	27	6	1	1	15	11	27	.200	.260	.281	57	-8	0	3	-2	1.000	-6	1-45,O-14/23	-1.8
1965	Mil-N	8	16	1	3	0	0	0	1	1	2	.188	.235	.188	21	-2	0	0		.961	0	/1-6	-0.2
1968	Atl-N	98	283	21	69	10	3	1	25	21	37	.244	.296	.311	82	-6	3	4	-2	.942	-4	O-62,1-28/3	-1.9
1969	*Atl-N	49	60	13	15	2	0	1	5	6	6	.250	.318	.333	82	-1	0	1	-1	1.000	1	1-16/O-8	-0.2
1970	Atl-N	44	63	3	13	2	0	2	7	3	10	.206	.242	.333	50	-5	0	0		.955	-2	1-16,O-12	-0.2
1971	Atl-N	25	53	4	12	2	0	0	3	3	5	.226	.268	.264	48	-4	0	0		.974	2	1-11/3-7	-0.2
Total	7	437	944	102	216	42	6	13	94	86	145	.229	.293	.327	75	-31	9	8	-2	.990	-7	1-232,O-138/32	-5.9

■ JOHN ABADIE   Abadie, John b: 11/4/1854, Philadelphia, Pa.   d: 5/17/05, Pemberton, N.J.   BR/TR, 6', 192 lbs.   Deb: 6/10/1875

YEAR	TM/L	G	AB	R	H	2B	3B	HR	RBI	BB	SO	AVG	OBP	SLG	PRO+	BR/A	SB	CS	SBR	FA	FR	G/POS	TPR
1875	Cen-n	11	45	3	10	0	0	0		0		.222	.222	.222	59	-2						1-11	-0.1
	Atl-n	1	4	1	1	0	0	0		0		.250	.250	.250	84	-0						/1-1	0.0
	Yr	12	49	4	11	0	0	0		0		.224	.224	.224	61	-2						1-12	-0.1

■ ED ABBATICCHIO   Abbaticchio, Edward James "Batty" b: 4/15/1877, Latrobe, Pa.   d: 1/6/57, Ft.Lauderdale, Fla.   BR/TR, 5'11", 170 lbs.   Deb: 9/4/1897

YEAR	TM/L	G	AB	R	H	2B	3B	HR	RBI	BB	SO	AVG	OBP	SLG	PRO+	BR/A	SB	CS	SBR	FA	FR	G/POS	TPR
1897	Phi-N	3	10	0	3	0	0	0		0	1	.300	.364	.300	78	-0				.875	-2	/2-3	-0.2
1898	Phi-N	25	92	9	21	4	0	0	14	7		.228	.290	.272	64	-4	4			.818	-13	3-20/2-4,O	-1.6
1903	Bos-N	136	489	61	111	18	5	1	46	52		.227	.306	.290	73	-16	23			.934	3	*2-116,S-17	-0.8
1904	Bos-N	154	579	76	148	18	10	3	54	40		.256	.309	.337	103	2	24			.915	2	*S-154	0.9
1905	Bos-N	153	610	70	170	25	12	3	41	35		.279	.326	.374	111	7	30			.919	-12	*S-152/O-1	-0.2
1907	Pit-N	147	496	63	130	14	7	2	82	65		.262	.357	.331	114	10	35			.951	-23	*2-147	-1.6
1908	Pit-N	146	500	43	125	16	7	1	61	58		.250	.336	.316	108	7	22			**.969**	-12	*2-144	-0.8
1909	*Pit-N	36	87	13	20	0	0	0	16	19		.230	.368	.264	89	-0	2			.966	2	S-18/2-4,O	0.2
1910	Pit-N	3	3	0	0	0	0	0	0	0	0	.000	.000	.000	-95	-1	0			.500	-1	/S-1	-0.1
	Bos-N	52	178	20	44	4	2	0	10	12	16	.247	.295	.292	68	-7	2			.910	-3	S-46/2-1	-0.9
	Yr	55	181	20	44	4	2	0	10	12	16	.243	.290	.287	66	-8	2			.907	-4	S-47/2-1	-1.0
Total	9	855	3044	355	772	99	43	11	324	289	16	.254	.325	.325	98	-4	142			.949	-59	2-419,S-388/3O	-5.1

■ CHARLIE ABBEY   Abbey, Charles S. b: 10/14/1866, Falls City, Neb.   d: 4/27/26, San Francisco, Cal.   BL, 5'8.5", 169 lbs.   Deb: 8/16/1893

YEAR	TM/L	G	AB	R	H	2B	3B	HR	RBI	BB	SO	AVG	OBP	SLG	PRO+	BR/A	SB	CS	SBR	FA	FR	G/POS	TPR
1893	Was-N	31	116	11	30	1	4	0	12	12	6	.259	.333	.336	80	-3	9			.937	3	O-31	-0.2
1894	Was-N	129	523	95	164	26	18	7	101	58	38	.314	.389	.472	110	9	31			.909	14	*O-129	1.0
1895	Was-N	132	511	102	141	14	10	8	84	43	41	.276	.340	.389	89	-9	28			.903	10	*O-132	-0.8
1896	Was-N	79	301	47	79	12	6	1	49	27	20	.262	.331	.352	80	-9	16			.879	-6	O-78/P-1	-1.8
1897	Was-N	80	300	52	78	14	8	3	34	27		.260	.329	.390	90	-5	9			.946	2	O-80	-0.8
Total	5	451	1751	307	492	67	46	19	280	167	105	.281	.351	.404	94	-17	93			.910	21	O-450/P-1	-2.6

■ FRED ABBOTT   Abbott, Harry Frederick (b: Harry Frederick Winbigler)   b: 10/22/1874, Versailles, Ohio   d: 6/11/35, Los Angeles, Cal.   BR/TR, 5'10", 180 lbs.   Deb: 4/25/03

YEAR	TM/L	G	AB	R	H	2B	3B	HR	RBI	BB	SO	AVG	OBP	SLG	PRO+	BR/A	SB	CS	SBR	FA	FR	G/POS	TPR
1903	Cle-A	77	255	25	60	11	3	1	25	7		.235	.270	.314	76	-8	8			.958	9	C-71/1-3	0.8
1904	Cle-A	41	130	14	22	4	2	0	12	6		.169	.206	.231	38	-9	2			.953	-3	C-33/1-7	-1.0
1905	Phi-N	42	128	9	25	6	1	0	12	6		.195	.248	.258	53	-8	4			.954	-0	C-34/1-5	-0.5
Total	3	160	513	48	107	21	6	1	49	19		.209	.248	.279	61	-24	14			.956	6	C-138/1-15	-0.7

■ KURT ABBOTT   Abbott, Kurt Thomas b: 6/2/69, Zanesville, Ohio   BR/TR, 6', 170 lbs.   Deb: 9/8/93

YEAR	TM/L	G	AB	R	H	2B	3B	HR	RBI	BB	SO	AVG	OBP	SLG	PRO+	BR/A	SB	CS	SBR	FA	FR	G/POS	TPR
1993	Oak-A	20	61	11	15	1	0	3	9	3	20	.246	.281	.410	89	-1	2	0	1	.971	1	O-13/S-6,2	0.1
1994	Fla-N	101	345	41	86	17	3	9	33	16	98	.249	.292	.394	73	-14	3	0	1	.966	-8	S-99	-1.4
Total	2	121	406	52	101	18	3	12	42	19	118	.249	.291	.397	75	-16	5	0	2	.965	-7	S-105/O-13,2	-1.3

■ ODY ABBOTT   Abbott, Ody Cleon b: 9/5/1888, New Eagle, Pa.   d: 4/13/33, Washington, D.C.   BR/TR, 6'2", 180 lbs.   Deb: 9/10/10

YEAR	TM/L	G	AB	R	H	2B	3B	HR	RBI	BB	SO	AVG	OBP	SLG	PRO+	BR/A	SB	CS	SBR	FA	FR	G/POS	TPR
1910	StL-N	22	70	2	13	2	1	0	6	6		.186	.250	.243	46	-5	3			.982	1	O-21	-0.5

■ DAVE ABERCROMBIE   Abercrombie, David b: 5/6/1840, Falkirk, Scotland   d: 9/2/16, Baltimore, Md.   Deb: 10/21/1871

YEAR	TM/L	G	AB	R	H	2B	3B	HR	RBI	BB	SO	AVG	OBP	SLG	PRO+	BR/A	SB	CS	SBR	FA	FR	G/POS	TPR
1871	Tro-n	1	4	0	0	0	0	0	0	0	0	.000	.000	.000	-99	-1	0					/S-1	-0.1

■ CLIFF ABERSON   Aberson, Clifford Alexander "Kif" b: 8/28/21, Chicago, Ill.   d: 6/23/73, Vallejo, Cal.   BR/TR, 6', 200 lbs.   Deb: 7/18/47

YEAR	TM/L	G	AB	R	H	2B	3B	HR	RBI	BB	SO	AVG	OBP	SLG	PRO+	BR/A	SB	CS	SBR	FA	FR	G/POS	TPR
1947	Chi-N	47	140	24	39	6	3	4	20	20	32	.279	.369	.450	121	4	0			.920	-1	O-40	0.1
1948	Chi-N	12	32	1	6	1	0	1	6	5	10	.188	.297	.313	68	-1	0			.867	-1	/O-8	-0.3
1949	Chi-N	4	7	0	0	0	0	0	0	0	2	.000	.000	.000	-99	-2	0			1.000	0	/O-1	-0.2
Total	3	63	179	25	45	7	3	5	26	25	44	.251	.343	.408	103	1	0			.913	-2	/O-49	-0.4

■ SHAWN ABNER   Abner, Shawn Wesley b: 6/17/66, Hamilton, Ohio   BR/TR, 6'1", 190 lbs.   Deb: 9/8/87

YEAR	TM/L	G	AB	R	H	2B	3B	HR	RBI	BB	SO	AVG	OBP	SLG	PRO+	BR/A	SB	CS	SBR	FA	FR	G/POS	TPR
1987	SD-N	16	47	5	13	3	1	2	7	2	8	.277	.306	.511	116	1	1	0	0	.926	1	O-14	0.1
1988	SD-N	37	83	6	15	3	0	2	5	4	19	.181	.227	.289	48	-6	0	1	-1	.982	-4	O-35	-1.2
1989	SD-N	57	102	13	18	4	0	2	14	5	20	.176	.215	.275	39	-8	1	0	0	1.000	-9	O-51	-1.9
1990	SD-N	91	184	13	45	9	1	1	15	9	28	.245	.287	.310	64	-9	2	3	-1	.991	-7	O-62	-1.9
1991	SD-N	53	115	15	19	4	1	1	5	7	25	.165	.220	.243	29	-11	0	0	0	1.000	-5	O-39	-1.1
	Cal-A	41	101	12	23	6	1	2	9	4	18	.228	.257	.366	71	-4	1	2	-1	1.000	-1	O-38/D-3	-0.7

YEAR	TM/L	G	AB	R	H	2B	3B	HR	RBI	BB	SO	AVG	OBP	SLG	PRO+	BR/A	SB	CS	SBR	FA	FR	G/POS	TPR
1992	Chi-A	97	208	21	58	10	1	1	16	12	35	.279	.327	.351	91	-2	1	2	-1	1.000	-13	O-94/D-1	-1.8
Total	6	392	840	89	191	39	4	11	71	43	153	.227	.271	.323	65	-40	6	8	-3	.993	-32	O-333/D-4	-8.5

■ CAL ABRAMS Abrams, Calvin Ross b: 3/2/24, Philadelphia, Pa. BL/TL, 5'11", 195 lbs. Deb: 4/20/49

YEAR	TM/L	G	AB	R	H	2B	3B	HR	RBI	BB	SO	AVG	OBP	SLG	PRO+	BR/A	SB	CS	SBR	FA	FR	G/POS	TPR
1949	Bro-N	8	24	6	2	1	0	0	0	7	6	.083	.290	.125	15	-3	1			.833	-1	/O-7	-0.4
1950	Bro-N	38	44	5	9	1	0	0	4	9	13	.205	.340	.227	51	-3	0			1.000	-0	O-15	-0.6
1951	Bro-N	67	150	27	42	8	0	3	19	36	26	.280	.419	.393	118	6	3	2	-0	.944	-1	O-34	0.3
1952	Bro-N	10	10	1	2	0	0	0	0	2	4	.200	.333	.200	51	-1	0	0	0	.000	-0	/O-1	-0.1
	Cin-N	71	158	23	44	9	2	2	13	19	25	.278	.356	.399	109	2	1	0	0	1.000	-5	O-46	-0.4
	Yr	81	168	24	46	9	2	2	13	21	29	.274	.354	.387	106	2	1	0	0	1.000	-5	O-47	-0.5
1953	Pit-N	119	448	66	128	10	6	15	43	58	70	.286	.368	.435	109	7	4	4	-1	.973	5	*O-112	0.6
1954	Pit-N	17	42	6	6	1	1	0	2	10	9	.143	.308	.214	39	-4	0	0	0	1.000	0	O-13	-0.4
	Bal-A	115	423	67	124	22	7	6	25	72	67	.293	.401	.421	135	23	1	4	-2	.977	4	*O-115	2.0
1955	Bal-A	118	309	56	75	12	3	6	32	89	69	.243	.416	.359	118	14	2	8	-4	.985	-13	O-96/1-4	-0.8
1956	Chi-A	4	3	0	1	0	0	0	0	2	1	.333	.600	.333	150	1	0	0	0	1.000	-0	/O-2	-0.1
Total	8	567	1611	257	433	64	19	32	138	304	290	.269	.387	.392	113	42	12	18		.977	-14	O-441/1-4	0.2

■ JOE ABREU Abreu, Joseph Lawrence b: 5/24/13, Oakland, Cal. d: 3/17/93, Hayward, Cal. BR/TR, 5'8", 160 lbs. Deb: 4/23/42

YEAR	TM/L	G	AB	R	H	2B	3B	HR	RBI	BB	SO	AVG	OBP	SLG	PRO+	BR/A	SB	CS	SBR	FA	FR	G/POS	TPR
1942	Cin-N	9	28	4	6	1	0	1	3	4	4	.214	.313	.357	96	-0	0			.941	-1	/3-6,2-2	-0.1

■ BILL ABSTEIN Abstein, William Henry "Big Bill" b: 2/2/1883, St.Louis, Mo. d: 4/8/40, St.Louis, Mo. BR/TR, 6', 185 lbs. Deb: 9/25/06

YEAR	TM/L	G	AB	R	H	2B	3B	HR	RBI	BB	SO	AVG	OBP	SLG	PRO+	BR/A	SB	CS	SBR	FA	FR	G/POS	TPR
1906	Pit-N	8	20	2	4	0	0	0	3	0		.200	.200	.200	24	-2	2			.769	-2	/2-3,O-2	-0.4
1909	*Pit-N	137	512	51	133	20	10	1	70	27		.260	.302	.344	93	-6	16			.982	-5	*1-135	-1.4
1910	StL-A	25	87	1	13	2	0	0	3	2		.149	.169	.172	7	-9	3			.963	2	1-23	-0.9
Total	3	170	619	54	150	22	10	1	76	29		.242	.281	.315	80	-18	21			.979	-5	1-158/2-3,O	-2.7

■ MERITO ACOSTA Acosta, Balmodero Pedro (Fernandez) b: 5/19/1896, Bauta, Cuba d: 11/17/63, Miami, Fla. BL/TL, 5'7", 140 lbs. Deb: 6/15/13 F

YEAR	TM/L	G	AB	R	H	2B	3B	HR	RBI	BB	SO	AVG	OBP	SLG	PRO+	BR/A	SB	CS	SBR	FA	FR	G/POS	TPR
1913	Was-A	12	20	3	6	0	1	0	1	4	2	.300	.417	.400	136	1	2			.714	-3	/O-9	-0.2
1914	Was-A	39	74	10	19	2	2	0	4	11	18	.257	.353	.338	104	1	3	4	-2	.857	-2	O-25	-0.4
1915	Was-A	72	163	20	34	4	1	0	18	28	15	.209	.338	.245	73	-4	8	4	0	.963	-4	O-53	-1.1
1916	Was-A	5	8	0	1	0	0	0	0	2	0	.125	.300	.125	28	-1	0			1.000	1	/O-4	0.0
1918	Was-A	3	2	0	0	0	0	0	0	0	1	.000	.000	.000	-99	-0	0			.000	0	H	-0.1
	Phi-A	49	169	23	51	3	3	0	14	18	10	.302	.369	.355	117	4	4			.944	-3	O-45	-0.2
	Yr	52	171	23	51	3	3	0	14	18	11	.298	.365	.351	115	3	4			.944	-3	O-45	-0.3
Total	5	180	436	56	111	9	7	0	37	63	46	.255	.354	.307	97	0	17	8		.933	-11	O-136	-2.0

■ JIMMY ADAIR Adair, James Aubrey "Choppy" b: 1/25/07, Waxahachie, Tex. d: 12/9/82, Dallas, Tex. BR/TR, 5'10.5", 154 lbs. Deb: 8/24/31 C

YEAR	TM/L	G	AB	R	H	2B	3B	HR	RBI	BB	SO	AVG	OBP	SLG	PRO+	BR/A	SB	CS	SBR	FA	FR	G/POS	TPR
1931	Chi-N	18	76	9	21	3	1	0	3	1	8	.276	.286	.342	67	-4	1			.948	-1	S-18	-0.3

■ JERRY ADAIR Adair, Kenneth Jerry b: 12/17/36, Sand Springs, Okla. d: 5/31/87, Tulsa, Okla. BR/TR, 6', 175 lbs. Deb: 9/2/58 C

YEAR	TM/L	G	AB	R	H	2B	3B	HR	RBI	BB	SO	AVG	OBP	SLG	PRO+	BR/A	SB	CS	SBR	FA	FR	G/POS	TPR
1958	Bal-A	11	19	1	2	0	0	0	0	1	7	.105	.150	.105	-30	-3	0	0	0	.967	2	S-10/2-1	-0.1
1959	Bal-A	12	35	3	11	0	1	0	2	1	5	.314	.333	.371	95	-0	0	0	0	.932	-4	2-11/S-1	-0.3
1960	Bal-A	3	5	1	1	0	0	1	1	0	0	.200	.200	.800	159	0	0	0	0	1.000	-2	/2-3	0.1
1961	Bal-A	133	386	41	102	21	1	9	37	35	51	.264	.329	.394	95	-3	5	2	0	.987	-1	*2-107,S-27/3	0.8
1962	Bal-A	139	538	67	153	29	4	11	48	27	77	.284	.321	.414	103	-0	7	7	-2	.969	-10	*S-113,2-34/3	0.1
1963	Bal-A	109	382	34	87	21	3	6	30	9	51	.228	.249	.346	67	-18	3	3	-1	.985	-0	*2-103	-1.0
1964	Bal-A	155	569	56	141	20	3	9	47	28	72	.248	.284	.341	73	-21	3	2	-0	.994	9	*2-153	0.0
1965	Bal-A	157	582	51	151	26	3	7	66	35	65	.259	.304	.351	84	-13	6	4	-1	.986	12	*2-157	1.4
1966	Bal-A	17	52	3	15	1	0	0	3	4	8	.288	.339	.308	89	-1	0	0	0	.969	-1	2-13	-0.1
	Chi-A	105	370	27	90	18	2	4	36	17	44	.243	.278	.335	81	-10	3	2	0	.975	-2	S-75,2-50	-0.4
	Yr	122	422	30	105	19	2	4	39	21	52	.249	.286	.332	82	-11	3	2	-0	.975	-3	S-75,2-63	-0.5
1967	Chi-A	28	98	6	20	4	0	0	9	4	17	.204	.243	.245	46	-7	0	1	-1	.985	-0	2-27	-0.6
	*Bos-A	89	316	41	92	13	1	3	26	13	35	.291	.323	.367	96	-2	1	4	-2	.952	-8	3-35,S-30,2	-1.0
	Yr	117	414	47	112	17	1	3	35	17	52	.271	.304	.338	85	-8	1	5	-3	.976	-9	2-50,3-35,S	-1.6
1968	Bos-A	74	208	18	45	1	0	2	12	9	28	.216	.252	.250	49	-13	0	0	0	.976	-5	S-46,2-12/31	-1.6
1969	KC-A	126	432	29	108	9	1	5	48	20	36	.250	.288	.310	67	-20	1	3	-2	.984	-22	*2-109/S-8,3	-3.6
1970	KC-A	7	27	0	4	0	0	0	1	5	3	.148	.281	.148	22	-3	0	1	-1	1.000	2	2-7	-0.1
Total	13	1165	4019	378	1022	163	19	57	366	208	499	.254	.294	.347	80	-112	29	29		.985	-30	2-810,S-310/31	-6.4

■ SPARKY ADAMS Adams, Earl John b: 8/26/1894, Zerbe, Pa. d: 2/24/89, Pottsville, Pa. BR/TR, 5'5.5", 151 lbs. Deb: 9/18/22

YEAR	TM/L	G	AB	R	H	2B	3B	HR	RBI	BB	SO	AVG	OBP	SLG	PRO+	BR/A	SB	CS	SBR	FA	FR	G/POS	TPR
1922	Chi-N	11	44	5	11	0	1	0	3	4	3	.250	.313	.295	56	-3	1	2	-1	.914	-4	2-11	-0.7
1923	Chi-N	95	311	40	90	12	0	4	35	26	10	.289	.346	.367	88	-5	20	19	-5	.935	-6	S-79/O-1	-0.9
1924	Chi-N	117	418	66	117	11	5	2	27	40	20	.280	.344	.337	83	-9	15	17	-6	.941	-8	S-88,2-19	-1.3
1925	Chi-N	149	627	95	180	29	8	2	48	44	15	.287	.341	.368	80	-18	26	12		.983	28	*2-144/S-5	1.3
1926	Chi-N	154	624	95	193	35	3	0	39	52	27	.309	.367	.375	99	1	27			.965	17	*2-136,3-19/S	2.2
1927	Chi-N	146	647	100	189	17	7	0	49	42	26	.292	.335	.340	81	-17	26			.994	-1	2-60,3-53,S	-0.8
1928	Pit-N	135	539	91	149	14	6	0	38	64	18	.276	.357	.325	76	-16	8			.971	-11	*2-107,S-27/O	-2.1
1929	Pit-N	74	196	37	51	8	1	0	11	15	5	.260	.316	.311	55	-14	3			.901	-15	S-30,2-20,3/O	-2.3
1930	*StL-N	137	570	98	179	36	9	0	55	45	27	.314	.365	.409	84	-14	7			.966	-11	*3-104,2-25/S	-1.7
1931	*StL-N	143	608	97	178	46	5	1	40	42	24	.293	.340	.390	92	-7	16			.963	-12	*3-138/S-6	-1.0
1932	StL-N	31	127	22	35	3	1	0	13	14	5	.276	.352	.315	79	-3	1			.931	-4	3-30	-0.5
1933	StL-N	8	30	1	5	1	0	0	0	1	3	.167	.219	.200	19	-3	0			.955	-2	/S-5,3-3	-0.5
	Cin-N	137	538	59	141	21	1	0	22	44	30	.262	.320	.310	82	-12	3			.963	-3	*3-132/S-8	-0.6
	Yr	145	568	60	146	22	1	0	22	45	33	.257	.315	.305	78	-15	3			.959	-5	*3-135,S-13	-1.1
1934	Cin-N	87	278	38	70	16	1	0	14	20	10	.252	.307	.317	69	-12	3			.955	-3	3-38,2-29	-1.1
Total	13	1424	5557	844	1588	249	48	9	394	453	223	.286	.343	.353	82	-131	154	50		.974	-37	2-551,3-532,S/O	-10.0

■ BUSTER ADAMS Adams, Elvin Clark b: 6/24/15, Trinidad, Col. d: 9/1/90, Rancho Mirage, Cal. BR/TR, 6', 180 lbs. Deb: 4/27/39

YEAR	TM/L	G	AB	R	H	2B	3B	HR	RBI	BB	SO	AVG	OBP	SLG	PRO+	BR/A	SB	CS	SBR	FA	FR	G/POS	TPR
1939	StL-N	2	1	1	0	0	0	0	0	0	0	.000	.000	.000	-94	-0	0			.000	0	H	0.0
1943	StL-N	8	11	1	1	1	0	0	1	4	4	.091	.333	.182	48	-1	0			1.000	-1	/O-6	-0.2
	Phi-N	111	418	48	107	14	7	4	38	39	67	.256	.319	.352	98	-2	2			.984	3	*O-107	-0.5
	Yr	119	429	49	108	15	7	4	39	43	71	.252	.320	.347	96	-3	2			.984	2	*O-113	-0.7
1944	Phi-N	151	584	86	165	35	3	17	64	74	74	.283	.370	.440	132	25	2			.979	11	*O-151	2.8
1945	Phi-N	14	56	6	13	3	1	2	8	5	5	.232	.295	.429	103	-0	0			1.000	-1	O-14	-0.2
	StL-N	140	578	98	169	26	0	20	101	57	75	.292	.359	.441	119	14	3			.978	1	*O-140	0.7
	Yr	154	634	104	182	29	1	22	109	62	80	.287	.353	.440	117	14	3			.979	0	*O-154	0.5
1946	StL-N	81	173	21	32	6	0	5	22	29	27	.185	.312	.306	73	-6	3			.990	-9	O-58	-1.8
1947	Phi-N	69	182	21	45	11	1	2	15	26	29	.247	.341	.352	88	-3	2			.954	-4	O-51	-0.9
Total	6	576	2003	282	532	96	12	50	249	234	281	.266	.346	.400	110	27	12			.979	0	O-527	-0.1

■ GEORGE ADAMS Adams, George b: Grafton, Mass. BR/TR, 5'6", 175 lbs. Deb: 6/14/1879

YEAR	TM/L	G	AB	R	H	2B	3B	HR	RBI	BB	SO	AVG	OBP	SLG	PRO+	BR/A	SB	CS	SBR	FA	FR	G/POS	TPR
1879	Syr-N	4	13	0	3	0	0	0		1	1	.231	.286	.231	82	-0				1.000	-1	/O-2,1-2	-0.1

■ GLENN ADAMS Adams, Glenn Charles b: 10/4/47, Northbridge, Mass. BL/TR, 6', 185 lbs. Deb: 5/4/75

YEAR	TM/L	G	AB	R	H	2B	3B	HR	RBI	BB	SO	AVG	OBP	SLG	PRO+	BR/A	SB	CS	SBR	FA	FR	G/POS	TPR
1975	SF-N	61	90	10	27	2	1	4	15	11	25	.300	.382	.478	132	4	1	0	0	.941	-3	O-25	0.1

YEAR	TM/L	G	AB	R	H	2B	3B	HR	RBI	BB	SO	AVG	OBP	SLG	PRO+	BR/A	SB	CS	SBR	FA	FR	G/POS	TPR
1976	SF-N	69	74	2	18	4	0	0	3	1	12	.243	.253	.297	54	-5	1	0	0	1.000	-2	/O-6	-0.7
1977	Min-A	95	269	32	91	17	0	6	49	18	30	.338	.380	.468	132	12	0	2	-1	.969	-4	D-47,O-44	0.4
1978	Min-A	116	310	27	80	18	1	7	35	17	32	.258	.297	.390	90	-5	0	1	-1	1.000	-1	*D-101/O-5	-1.0
1979	Min-A	119	326	34	98	13	1	8	50	25	27	.301	.356	.420	104	2	2	2	-1	.958	-6	D-55,O-53	-1.0
1980	Min-A	99	262	32	75	11	2	6	38	15	26	.286	.325	.412	94	-3	2	4	-2	.947	-2	D-81,O-12	-1.0
1981	Min-A	72	220	13	46	10	0	2	24	20	26	.209	.275	.282	57	-12	0	1	-1	.000	0	D-62	-1.6
1982	Tor-A	30	66	2	17	4	0	1	11	4	5	.258	.300	.364	74	-2	0	0	0	.000	0	D-27	-0.3
Total	8	661	1617	152	452	79	5	34	225	111	183	.280	.327	.398	96	-9	6	10	-4	.959	-20	D-373,O-145	-5.1

■ DOUG ADAMS

Adams, Harold Douglas   b: 1/27/43, Blue River, Wis.   BL/TR, 6'3", 185 lbs.   Deb: 9/8/69

YEAR	TM/L	G	AB	R	H	2B	3B	HR	RBI	BB	SO	AVG	OBP	SLG	PRO+	BR/A	SB	CS	SBR	FA	FR	G/POS	TPR
1969	Chi-A	8	14	1	3	0	0	0	1	1	3	.214	.267	.214	34	-1	0	0	0	1.000	-1	/C-4	-0.2

■ HERB ADAMS

Adams, Herbert Loren   b: 4/14/28, Hollywood, Cal.   BL/TL, 5'9", 160 lbs.   Deb: 9/17/48

YEAR	TM/L	G	AB	R	H	2B	3B	HR	RBI	BB	SO	AVG	OBP	SLG	PRO+	BR/A	SB	CS	SBR	FA	FR	G/POS	TPR
1948	Chi-A	5	11	1	3	1	0	0	0	1	1	.273	.333	.364	88	-0	0	0	0	1.000	2	/O-4	0.1
1949	Chi-A	56	208	26	61	5	3	0	16	9	16	.293	.323	.346	79	-7	1	2	-1	.975	-0	O-48	-1.0
1950	Chi-A	34	118	12	24	2	3	0	2	12	7	.203	.288	.271	45	-10	3	0	1	.978	-1	O-33	-1.1
Total	3	95	337	39	88	8	6	0	18	22	24	.261	.310	.320	67	-17	4	2	0	.978	0	/O-85	-2.0

■ JIM ADAMS

Adams, James J.   b: 1868, E.St.Louis, Ill.   TR   Deb: 4/21/1890

YEAR	TM/L	G	AB	R	H	2B	3B	HR	RBI	BB	SO	AVG	OBP	SLG	PRO+	BR/A	SB	CS	SBR	FA	FR	G/POS	TPR
1890	StL-a	1	4	0	1	0	0	0		0		.250	.250	.250	42	-0	0			1.000	-1	/C-1	-0.1

■ BERT ADAMS

Adams, John Bertram   b: 6/21/1891, Wharton, Tex.   d: 6/24/40, Los Angeles, Cal.   BB/TR, 6'1", 185 lbs.   Deb: 8/30/10

YEAR	TM/L	G	AB	R	H	2B	3B	HR	RBI	BB	SO	AVG	OBP	SLG	PRO+	BR/A	SB	CS	SBR	FA	FR	G/POS	TPR
1910	Cle-A	5	13	1	3	0	0	0	0	0		.231	.231	.231	44	-1	0			.964	3	/C-5	0.3
1911	Cle-A	2	5	0	1	0	0	0	0	1		.200	.333	.200	50	-0	0			.900	-1	/C-2	-0.1
1912	Cle-A	20	54	5	11	2	1	0	6	4		.204	.259	.278	52	-4	0			.942	2	C-20	0.0
1915	Phi-N	24	27	1	3	0	0	0	2	2	3	.111	.172	.111	-13	-4	0			.974	-4	C-23/1-1	-0.8
1916	Phi-N	11	13	2	3	0	0	0	1	0	3	.231	.231	.231	40	-1	0			.929	1	C-11	-0.4
1917	Phi-N	43	107	4	22	4	1	1	7	0	20	.206	.206	.290	49	-7	0			.994	1	C-38/1-1	-0.4
1918	Phi-N	84	227	10	40	4	0	0	12	10	26	.176	.214	.194	23	-21	5			.976	-2	C-76	-1.8
1919	Phi-N	78	232	14	54	7	2	1	17	6	27	.233	.252	.293	59	-12	4			.966	-2	C-73/1-1	-0.2
Total	8	267	678	37	137	17	4	2	45	23	79	.202	.229	.248	42	-48	9			.970	-2	C-248/1-3	-3.7

■ DICK ADAMS

Adams, Richard Leroy   b: 4/8/20, Tuolumne, Cal.   BR/TL, 6', 185 lbs.   Deb: 5/20/47   F

YEAR	TM/L	G	AB	R	H	2B	3B	HR	RBI	BB	SO	AVG	OBP	SLG	PRO+	BR/A	SB	CS	SBR	FA	FR	G/POS	TPR
1947	Phi-A	37	89	9	18	2	3	2	11	2	18	.202	.220	.360	58	-6	0	0	0	.995	0	1-24/O-3	-0.6

■ RICKY ADAMS

Adams, Ricky Lee   b: 1/21/59, Upland, Cal.   BR/TR, 6'2", 180 lbs.   Deb: 9/15/82

YEAR	TM/L	G	AB	R	H	2B	3B	HR	RBI	BB	SO	AVG	OBP	SLG	PRO+	BR/A	SB	CS	SBR	FA	FR	G/POS	TPR
1982	Cal-A	8	14	1	2	0	0	0	0	0	2	.143	.200	.143	-4	-2	1	0	0	.947	-1	/S-8	-0.2
1983	Cal-A	58	112	22	28	2	0	2	6	5	12	.250	.300	.321	72	-4	1	1	-0	.960	22	S-38,3-16/2	1.9
1985	SF-N	54	121	12	23	3	1	2	10	5	23	.190	.228	.281	44	-9	1	1	-0	.964	3	S-25,3-16/2	-0.5
Total	3	120	247	35	53	5	1	4	16	10	37	.215	.260	.291	54	-16	3	2	-0	.961	24	/S-71,3-32,2	1.2

■ BOBBY ADAMS

Adams, Robert Henry   b: 12/14/21, Tuolumne, Cal.   BR/TR, 5'10", 170 lbs.   Deb: 4/16/46   FC

YEAR	TM/L	G	AB	R	H	2B	3B	HR	RBI	BB	SO	AVG	OBP	SLG	PRO+	BR/A	SB	CS	SBR	FA	FR	G/POS	TPR
1946	Cin-N	94	311	35	76	13	6	4	24	18	32	.244	.292	.344	83	-8	16			.967	24	2-74/O-2,3	2.2
1947	Cin-N	81	217	39	59	11	2	4	20	25	23	.272	.358	.396	101	1	9			.967	14	2-69	1.8
1948	Cin-N	87	262	33	78	20	3	1	21	25	23	.298	.361	.408	112	4	6			.965	-12	2-64/3-7	-0.4
1949	Cin-N	107	277	32	70	16	2	0	25	26	36	.253	.317	.325	72	-11	4			.984	-9	2-63,3-14	-1.7
1950	Cin-N	115	348	57	98	21	8	3	25	43	29	.282	.361	.414	103	2	7			.981	-9	2-53,3-42	-0.6
1951	Cin-N	125	403	57	107	12	5	5	24	44	40	.266	.338	.357	86	-7	4	10	-5	.956	-10	3-60,2-42/O	-2.1
1952	Cin-N	154	637	85	180	25	4	6	48	49	67	.283	.334	.363	93	-6	11	9	-2	.962	9	*3-154	-0.2
1953	Cin-N	150	607	99	167	14	6	8	49	58	67	.275	.338	.357	81	-16	3	2	-0	.951	8	*3-150	-1.1
1954	Cin-N	110	390	69	105	25	6	3	23	55	46	.269	.364	.387	93	-3	2	5	-2	.951	1	3-93/2-2	-0.6
1955	Cin-N	64	150	23	41	11	2	2	20	20	21	.273	.370	.413	102	1	2	0	1	.969	3	3-42/2-5	0.5
	Chi-N	28	21	8	2	0	1	0	3	4	4	.095	.240	.190	16	-3	0	0	0	.933	5	/3-9,2-1	0.3
1956	Bal-A	41	111	19	25	6	1	0	7	25	15	.225	.368	.297	84	-2	1	1	-0	.984	-6	3-24,2-18	-0.6
1957	Chi-N	60	187	21	47	10	2	1	10	17	28	.251	.320	.342	79	-5	0	3	-2	.949	-8	3-47/2-1	-1.4
1958	Chi-N	62	96	14	27	4	0	4	6	15	15	.281	.324	.406	93	-1	2	0	1	.961	-2	1-11/3-9,2	-0.2
1959	Chi-N	3	2	0	0	0	0	0	0	0	1	.000	.000	.000	-99	-1	0	0	0	.667	-0	/1-1	-0.1
Total	14	1281	4019	591	1082	188	49	37	303	414	447	.269	.340	.368	90	-54	67	30		.955	10	3-652,2-399/1O	-4.2

■ BOB ADAMS

Adams, Robert Melvin   b: 1/6/52, Pittsburgh, Pa.   BR/TR, 6'2", 200 lbs.   Deb: 7/10/77

YEAR	TM/L	G	AB	R	H	2B	3B	HR	RBI	BB	SO	AVG	OBP	SLG	PRO+	BR/A	SB	CS	SBR	FA	FR	G/POS	TPR
1977	Det-A	15	24	2	6	1	0	2	5	0	5	.250	.250	.542	103	-0	0	0	0	1.000	-0	/1-2,C-1	0.0

■ MIKE ADAMS

Adams, Robert Michael   b: 7/24/48, Cincinnati, Ohio   BR/TR, 5'9", 180 lbs.   Deb: 9/10/72   F

YEAR	TM/L	G	AB	R	H	2B	3B	HR	RBI	BB	SO	AVG	OBP	SLG	PRO+	BR/A	SB	CS	SBR	FA	FR	G/POS	TPR
1972	Min-A	3	6	0	2	0	0	0	0	0	1	.333	.333	.333	94	-0	0	0	0	1.000	-0	/O-1	0.0
1973	Min-A	55	66	21	14	2	0	3	6	17	18	.212	.381	.379	110	2	2	1	0	.978	-4	O-24/D-2	-0.5
1976	Chi-N	25	29	1	4	2	0	0	2	8	7	.138	.342	.207	54	-1	0	0	0	1.000	-3	/O-4,3-2	-0.1
1977	Chi-N	2	2	0	0	0	0	0	0	0	0	.000	.000	.000	-90	-1	0	0	0	.000	-1	/O-2	-0.1
1978	Oak-A	15	15	5	3	1	0	0	1	7	2	.200	.455	.267	113	1	0	0	0	1.000	-1	/2-6,3-3,D	0.1
Total	5	100	118	27	23	5	0	3	9	32	29	.195	.375	.314	93	1	2	1	0	.980	-5	/O-31,2-7,3D	-0.5

■ SPENCER ADAMS

Adams, Spencer Dewey   b: 6/21/1898, Layton, Utah   d: 11/24/70, Salt Lake City, Ut   BL/TR, 5'9", 158 lbs.   Deb: 5/8/23

YEAR	TM/L	G	AB	R	H	2B	3B	HR	RBI	BB	SO	AVG	OBP	SLG	PRO+	BR/A	SB	CS	SBR	FA	FR	G/POS	TPR
1923	Pit-N	25	56	11	14	0	1	0	4	6	6	.250	.323	.286	60	-3	2	1	0	.879	-6	2-11/S-6	-0.8
1925	*Was-A	39	55	11	15	4	1	0	4	5	4	.273	.333	.382	83	-2	1	1	-0	.941	-2	2-15/S-8,3	-0.3
1926	*NY-A	28	25	7	3	1	0	0	1	3	7	.120	.214	.160	-1	-4	1	0	0	1.000	4	/2-4,3-1	0.1
1927	StL-A	88	259	32	69	11	3	0	29	24	33	.266	.333	.332	71	-11	1	8	-5	.948	1	2-54,3-28	-1.1
Total	4	180	395	61	101	16	5	0	38	38	50	.256	.324	.324	66	-19	5	10	-5	.944	-3	/2-84,3-32,S	-2.1

■ JOE ADCOCK

Adcock, Joseph Wilbur   b: 10/30/27, Coushatta, La.   BR/TR, 6'4", 220 lbs.   Deb: 4/23/50   M

YEAR	TM/L	G	AB	R	H	2B	3B	HR	RBI	BB	SO	AVG	OBP	SLG	PRO+	BR/A	SB	CS	SBR	FA	FR	G/POS	TPR
1950	Cin-N	102	372	46	109	16	6	8	55	24	24	.293	.336	.406	94	-4	2			.968	6	O-75,1-24	-0.2
1951	Cin-N	113	395	40	96	16	4	10	47	24	29	.243	.288	.380	77	-14	1	2	-1	.983	1	*O-107	-1.8
1952	Cin-N	117	378	43	105	22	4	13	52	23	38	.278	.321	.460	115	6	1	4	-2	.985	4	O-85,1-17	0.4
1953	Mil-N	157	590	71	168	33	6	18	80	42	82	.285	.334	.453	110	6	3	2	-0	.991	-4	*1-157	-0.5
1954	Mil-N	133	500	73	154	27	5	23	87	44	58	.308	.367	.520	137	25	1	4	-2	.995	-11	*1-133	0.5
1955	Mil-N	84	288	40	76	14	0	15	45	31	44	.264	.340	.469	118	7	0	2	-1	.990	-5	1-78	-0.4
1956	Mil-N	137	454	76	132	23	1	38	103	36	86	.291	.339	.597	154	31	1	0	0	.995	-3	*1-129	1.8
1957	*Mil-N	65	209	31	60	13	2	12	38	20	51	.287	.352	.541	146	13	0	0	0	.996	1	1-56	0.6
1958	*Mil-N	105	320	40	88	15	1	19	54	21	63	.275	.322	.506	125	9	0	1	-1	.989	-1	1-71,O-22	0.3
1959	Mil-N	115	404	53	118	19	2	25	76	32	77	.292	.344	.535	141	17	2	5	-2	.998	10	1-89,O-21	2.5
1960	Mil-N★	138	514	55	153	21	4	25	91	46	86	.298	.357	.500	142	28	2	2	-1	.993	3	*1-136	1.9
1961	Mil-N	152	562	77	160	20	0	35	108	59	94	.285	.355	.507	133	25	2	2	-1	.993	-5	*1-148	0.8
1962	Mil-N	121	391	48	97	11	1	29	78	50	91	.248	.335	.506	126	13	2	4	-2	.997	-4	*1-112	0.3
1963	Cle-A	97	283	28	71	7	1	13	49	30	53	.251	.323	.420	107	3	1	2	-1	.995	-4	1-78	-0.6
1964	LA-A	118	366	39	98	13	0	21	64	48	61	.268	.353	.475	142	20	0	2	-1	.993	-4	*1-105	1.0
1965	Cal-A	122	349	30	84	14	0	14	47	37	74	.241	.315	.401	104	2	2	2	-1	.996	-4	1-97	-0.9

YEAR	TM/L	G	AB	R	H	2B	3B	HR	RBI	BB	SO	AVG	OBP	SLG	PRO+	BR/A	SB	CS	SBR	FA	FR	G/POS	TPR
1966	Cal-A	83	231	33	63	10	3	18	48	31	48	.273	.359	.576	168	20	2	2	-1	.997	-0	1-71	1.6
Total	17	1959	6606	823	1832	295	35	336	1122	594	1059	.277	.339	.485	125	210	20	25		.994	-28	*1-1501,O-310	7.3

■ BOB ADDIS
Addis, Robert Gordon b: 11/6/25, Mineral, Ohio BL/TR, 6', 175 lbs. Deb: 9/1/50

YEAR	TM/L	G	AB	R	H	2B	3B	HR	RBI	BB	SO	AVG	OBP	SLG	PRO+	BR/A	SB	CS	SBR	FA	FR	G/POS	TPR
1950	Bos-N	16	28	7	7	1	0	0	2	3	5	.250	.323	.286	66	-1	1			1.000	-2	/O-7	-0.3
1951	Bos-N	85	199	23	55	7	0	1	24	9	10	.276	.308	.327	76	-7	3	2	-0	.982	-0	O-46	-0.9
1952	Chi-N	93	292	38	86	13	2	1	20	23	30	.295	.346	.363	96	-1	4	4	-1	.988	-2	O-79	-0.8
1953	Chi-N	10	12	2	2	1	0	0	1	2	0	.167	.286	.250	40	-1	0	0	0	1.000	1	/O-3	0.0
	Pit-N	4	3	0	0	0	0	0	0	0	2	.000	.000	.000	-99	-1	0	0	0	.000	0	H	-0.1
	Yr	14	15	2	2	1	0	0	1	2	2	.133	.235	.200	15	-2	0	0	0	1.000	1	/O-3	-0.1
Total	4	208	534	70	150	22	2	2	47	37	47	.281	.327	.341	84	-12	8	6		.986	-3	O-135	-2.1

■ JIM ADDUCI
Adduci, James David b: 8/9/59, Chicago, Ill. BL/TL, 6'5", 200 lbs. Deb: 9/12/83

YEAR	TM/L	G	AB	R	H	2B	3B	HR	RBI	BB	SO	AVG	OBP	SLG	PRO+	BR/A	SB	CS	SBR	FA	FR	G/POS	TPR
1983	StL-N	10	20	0	1	0	0	0	0	1	6	.050	.095	.050	-59	-4	0	0	0	1.000	0	/1-6,O-1	-0.5
1986	Mil-A	3	11	2	1	1	0	0	0	1	2	.091	.167	.182	-5	-2	0	0	0	1.000	0	/1-3	-0.2
1988	Mil-A	44	94	8	25	6	1	1	15	0	15	.266	.266	.383	79	-3	0	1	-1	.969	-4	O-24,D-10/1	-0.8
1989	Phi-N	13	19	1	7	1	0	0	0	0	4	.368	.368	.421	125	1	0	0	0	1.000	0	/1-4,O-1	0.1
Total	4	70	144	11	34	8	1	1	15	2	27	.236	.247	.326	58	-8	0	1	-1	.969	-3	/O-26,1-16,D	-1.4

■ BOB ADDY
Addy, Robert Edward "Magnet" b: 2/1845, Rochester, N.Y. d: 4/9/10, Pocatello, Idaho BL/TL, 5'8", 160 lbs. Deb: 5/6/1871 M

YEAR	TM/L	G	AB	R	H	2B	3B	HR	RBI	BB	SO	AVG	OBP	SLG	PRO+	BR/A	SB	CS	SBR	FA	FR	G/POS	TPR
1871	Rok-n	25	118	30	32	6	0	0	13	4	0	.271	.295	.322	81	-2	8					*2-22/S-3	-0.3
1873	Phi-n	10	51	12	16	1	0	0	9	2	0	.314	.340	.333	95	-0						2-10	-0.1
	Bos-n	31	152	37	54	6	2	1	36	1	0	.355	.359	.441	124	3						*O-31	0.2
	Yr	41	203	49	70	7	2	1	45	3	0	.345	.354	.414	117	3						O-31,2-10	0.1
1874	Har-n	50	211	25	50	9	2	0		2		.237	.244	.299	68	-8						*2-45/3-4,S	-0.8
1875	Phi-n	69	311	60	79	11	4	0		0		.254	.254	.315	92	-3						*O-66/2-3M	-0.2
1876	Chi-N	32	142	36	40	4	1	0	16	5	0	.282	.306	.324	98	-1				.800	0	O-32	-0.1
1877	Cin-N	57	245	27	68	2	3	0	31	6	5	.278	.295	.310	102	1				.805	5	*O-57/M	0.3
Total	4 n	185	843	164	231	33	8	1	58	9		.274	.282	.336	91	-11						/O-97,2-80,3S	-1.2
Total	2	89	387	63	108	6	4	0	47	11	5	.279	.299	.315	100	0				.803	5	/O-89	0.2

■ MORRIE ADERHOLT
Aderholt, Morris Woodrow b: 9/13/15, Mt.Olive, N.C. d: 3/18/55, Sarasota, Fla. BL/TR, 6'1", 188 lbs. Deb: 9/13/39

YEAR	TM/L	G	AB	R	H	2B	3B	HR	RBI	BB	SO	AVG	OBP	SLG	PRO+	BR/A	SB	CS	SBR	FA	FR	G/POS	TPR
1939	Was-A	7	25	5	5	0	0	1	4	2	6	.200	.259	.320	51	-2	0	1	-1	.872	0	/2-7	-0.2
1940	Was-A	1	2	0	0	0	0	0	0	0	0	.000	.000	.000	-99	-1	0	0	0	1.000	0	/2-1	0.0
1941	Was-A	11	14	3	2	0	0	0	1	1	3	.143	.200	.143	-8	-2	0	0	0	.818	1	/2-2,3-1	-0.2
1944	Bro-N	17	59	9	16	2	3	0	10	4	4	.271	.317	.407	105	0	0			.871	-1	O-13	-0.1
1945	Bro-N	39	60	4	13	1	0	0	6	3	10	.217	.254	.233	36	-5	0			1.000	-2	/O-8	-0.8
	Bos-N	31	102	15	34	4	0	2	11	9	6	.333	.387	.431	127	4	3			.984	-1	O-24/2-1	0.3
	Yr	70	162	19	47	5	0	2	17	12	16	.290	.339	.358	94	-1	3			.985	-2	O-32/2-1	-0.5
Total	5	106	262	36	70	7	3	3	32	19	29	.267	.317	.351	85	-6	3	1		.949	-2	/O-45,2-11,3	-1.0

■ DICK ADKINS
Adkins, Richard Earl b: 3/3/20, Electra, Tex. d: 9/12/55, Electra, Tex. BR/TR, 5'10", 165 lbs. Deb: 9/19/42

YEAR	TM/L	G	AB	R	H	2B	3B	HR	RBI	BB	SO	AVG	OBP	SLG	PRO+	BR/A	SB	CS	SBR	FA	FR	G/POS	TPR
1942	Phi-A	3	7	2	1	0	0	0	0	0	2	.143	.333	.143	37	-0	0	0	0	.875	-1	/S-3	-0.2

■ HENRY ADKINSON
Adkinson, Henry Magee b: 9/1/1874, Chicago, Ill. d: 5/1/23, Salt Lake City, Ut. Deb: 9/25/1895

YEAR	TM/L	G	AB	R	H	2B	3B	HR	RBI	BB	SO	AVG	OBP	SLG	PRO+	BR/A	SB	CS	SBR	FA	FR	G/POS	TPR
1895	StL-N	1	5	1	2	0	0	0	0	0	2	.400	.400	.400	108	0				.667	-0	/O-1	0.0

■ DAVE ADLESH
Adlesh, David George b: 7/15/43, Long Beach, Cal. BR/TR, 6', 187 lbs. Deb: 5/12/63

YEAR	TM/L	G	AB	R	H	2B	3B	HR	RBI	BB	SO	AVG	OBP	SLG	PRO+	BR/A	SB	CS	SBR	FA	FR	G/POS	TPR
1963	Hou-N	6	8	0	0	0	0	0	0	0	4	.000	.000	.000	-99	-2	0	0	0	.889	-2	/C-6	-0.4
1964	Hou-N	3	10	0	2	0	0	0	0	0	5	.200	.200	.200	14	-2	0	0	0	1.000	-1	/C-3	-0.2
1965	Hou-N	15	34	2	5	1	0	0	3	2	12	.147	.216	.176	13	-4	0	0	0	1.000	-1	C-13	-0.5
1966	Hou-N	3	6	0	0	0	0	0	0	0	4	.000	.000	.000	-99	-2	0	0	0	1.000	1	/C-1	-0.1
1967	Hou-N	39	94	4	17	1	0	1	4	11	28	.181	.267	.223	43	-7	0	0	0	.995	-3	C-31	-0.9
1968	Hou-N	40	104	3	19	1	1	0	4	5	27	.183	.227	.212	33	-8	0	0	0	.990	-3	C-36	-1.0
Total	6	106	256	9	43	3	1	1	11	18	80	.168	.228	.199	26	-24	0	0	0	.992	-8	/C-90	-3.1

■ TROY AFENIR
Afenir, Michael Troy b: 9/21/63, Escondido, Cal. BR/TR, 6'4", 185 lbs. Deb: 9/14/87

YEAR	TM/L	G	AB	R	H	2B	3B	HR	RBI	BB	SO	AVG	OBP	SLG	PRO+	BR/A	SB	CS	SBR	FA	FR	G/POS	TPR
1987	Hou-N	10	20	1	6	1	0	0	1	0	12	.300	.300	.350	74	-1	0	0	0	.974	-1	C-10	-0.1
1990	Oak-A	14	14	0	2	0	0	0	2	0	6	.143	.143	.143	-21	-2	0	0	0	1.000	0	C-12/D-1	-0.3
1991	Oak-A	5	11	0	1	0	0	0	0	0	2	.091	.091	.091	-53	-2	0	0	0	1.000	1	/C-4,D-1	-0.1
1992	Cin-N	16	34	3	6	1	2	0	4	5	12	.176	.282	.324	69	-1	0	0	0	1.000	-3	/C-15	-0.4
Total	4	45	79	4	15	2	2	0	7	5	32	.190	.238	.266	40	-7	0	0	0	.992	-4	/C-41,D-2	-0.9

■ TOMMIE AGEE
Agee, Tommie Lee b: 8/9/42, Magnolia, Ala. BR/TR, 5'11", 195 lbs. Deb: 9/14/62

YEAR	TM/L	G	AB	R	H	2B	3B	HR	RBI	BB	SO	AVG	OBP	SLG	PRO+	BR/A	SB	CS	SBR	FA	FR	G/POS	TPR
1962	Cle-A	5	14	0	3	0	0	0	2	0	4	.214	.214	.214	16	-2	0	0	0	1.000	-0	/O-3	-0.2
1963	Cle-A	13	27	3	4	1	0	1	3	2	9	.148	.207	.296	39	-2	0	0	0	1.000	-1	O-13	-0.4
1964	Cle-A	10	12	0	2	0	0	0	0	0	3	.167	.167	.167	-7	-2	0	0	0	1.000	-4	O-12	-0.6
1965	Chi-A	14	19	2	3	1	0	0	3	2	6	.158	.238	.211	30	-2	0	1	-1	1.000	-2	/O-9	-0.5
1966	Chi-A★	160	629	98	172	27	8	22	86	41	127	.273	.328	.447	129	21	44	18	2	.982	11	*O-159	2.9
1967	Chi-A★	158	529	73	124	26	2	14	52	44	129	.234	.303	.371	102	0	28	10	2	.969	-2	*O-152	-0.3
1968	NY-N	132	368	30	80	12	3	5	17	15	103	.217	.256	.307	68	-15	13	8	-1	.978	-10	*O-127	-3.6
1969	*NY-N	149	565	97	153	23	4	26	76	59	137	.271	.343	.464	121	15	12	9	-2	.986	6	*O-146	1.1
1970	NY-N	153	636	107	182	30	7	24	75	55	156	.286	.345	.469	115	12	31	15	0	.967	13	*O-150	1.7
1971	NY-N	113	425	58	121	19	0	14	50	50	84	.285	.363	.428	125	14	28	6	5	.978	5	*O-107	1.9
1972	NY-N	114	422	52	96	23	0	13	47	53	92	.227	.319	.374	99	-0	8	9	-3	.962	6	*O-109	-0.3
1973	Hou-N	83	204	30	48	5	2	8	15	16	55	.235	.294	.397	90	-2	2	5	-2	.983	-4	O-67	-1.3
	StL-N	26	62	8	11	3	1	3	7	5	13	.177	.239	.403	75	-2	1	0	0	.981	1	O-19	-0.2
	Yr	109	266	38	59	8	3	11	22	21	68	.222	.281	.398	87	-6	3	5	-2	.982	-3	O-86	-1.5
Total	12	1129	3912	558	999	170	27	130	433	342	918	.255	.321	.412	108	35	167	81	2	.975	22	*O-1073	0.2

■ HARRY AGGANIS
Agganis, Harry "The Golden Greek" b: 4/20/29, Lynn, Mass. d: 6/27/55, Cambridge, Mass. BL/TL, 6'2", 200 lbs. Deb: 4/13/54

YEAR	TM/L	G	AB	R	H	2B	3B	HR	RBI	BB	SO	AVG	OBP	SLG	PRO+	BR/A	SB	CS	SBR	FA	FR	G/POS	TPR
1954	Bos-A	132	434	54	109	18	8	11	57	47	57	.251	.324	.394	86	-9	6	3	0	.990	7	*1-119	-0.8
1955	Bos-A	25	83	11	26	10	1	0	10	10	10	.313	.387	.458	116	2	2	0	1	.987	0	1-20	0.1
Total	2	157	517	65	135	23	9	11	67	57	67	.261	.334	.404	91	-7	8	3	1	.989	7	1-139	-0.7

■ JOE AGLER
Agler, Joseph Abram b: 6/12/1887, Coshocton, Ohio d: 4/26/71, Massillon, Ohio BL/TL, 5'11", 165 lbs. Deb: 10/1/12

YEAR	TM/L	G	AB	R	H	2B	3B	HR	RBI	BB	SO	AVG	OBP	SLG	PRO+	BR/A	SB	CS	SBR	FA	FR	G/POS	TPR
1912	Was-A	2	1	0	0	0	0	0	0	0		.000	.000	.000	-99	-0	0			.000	0	/1-1	0.0
1914	Buf-F	135	463	82	126	17	6	0	20	77	78	.272	.376	.335	83	-8	21			.985	5	1-76,O-54	-0.8
1915	Buf-F	25	73	11	13	1	2	0	2	20	14	.178	.355	.247	61	-3	2			.973	-2	O-20/1-1	-0.8
	Bal-F	72	214	28	46	4	2	0	14	34	38	.215	.325	.252	54	-13	15			.981	5	1-58/O-4,2	-1.1
	Yr	97	287	39	59	5	4	0	16	54	52	.206	.333	.251	56	-16	17			.981	3	1-59/O-24,2	-1.8
Total	3	234	751	121	185	22	10	0	36	131	130	.246	.359	.302	73	-25	38			.983	7	1-136/O-78,2	-2.6

■ SAM AGNEW
Agnew, Samuel Lester "Slam" b: 4/12/1887, Farmington, Mo. d: 7/19/51, Sonoma, Cal. BR/TR, 5'11", 185 lbs. Deb: 4/10/13

YEAR	TM/L	G	AB	R	H	2B	3B	HR	RBI	BB	SO	AVG	OBP	SLG	PRO+	BR/A	SB	CS	SBR	FA	FR	G/POS	TPR
1913	StL-A	105	307	27	64	9	5	2	24	20	49	.208	.272	.290	66	-14	11			.952	2	*C-103	-0.3
1914	StL-A	115	311	22	66	5	4	0	16	24	63	.212	.279	.254	63	-14	10	8	-2	.961	3	*C-115	-0.5

YEAR	TM/L	G	AB	R	H	2B	3B	HR	RBI	BB	SO	AVG	OBP	SLG	PRO+	BR/A	SB	CS	SBR	FA	FR	G/POS	TPR
1915	StL-A	104	295	18	60	4	2	0	19	12	36	.203	.247	.231	45	-21	5	2	0	.934	5	*C-102	-0.8
1916	Bos-A	40	67	4	14	2	1	0	7	6	4	.209	.293	.269	69	-3	0			.952	8	C-38	0.8
1917	Bos-A	85	260	17	54	6	2	0	16	19	30	.208	.267	.246	57	-13	2			.965	-10	C-85	-1.9
1918	*Bos-A	72	199	11	33	8	0	0	6	11	26	.166	.221	.206	29	-17	0			.965	11	C-72	-0.2
1919	Was-A	42	98	6	23	7	0	0	10	10	8	.235	.312	.306	74	-3	1			.974	8	C-36	0.7
Total	7	563	1537	105	314	41	14	2	98	102	216	.204	.265	.253	56	-85	29	10		.955	26	C-551	-2.2

■ LUIS AGUAYO

Aguayo, Luis (Muriel) b: 3/13/59, Vega Baja, P.R. BR/TR, 5'9", 185 lbs. Deb: 4/19/80

YEAR	TM/L	G	AB	R	H	2B	3B	HR	RBI	BB	SO	AVG	OBP	SLG	PRO+	BR/A	SB	CS	SBR	FA	FR	G/POS	TPR
1980	Phi-N	20	47	7	13	1	2	1	8	2	3	.277	.306	.447	102	-0	1	1	-0	.962	1	2-14/S-5	0.2
1981	*Phi-N	45	84	11	18	4	0	1	7	6	15	.214	.283	.298	62	-4	1	0	0	.938	-4	2-21,S-21/3	-0.7
1982	Phi-N	50	56	11	15	1	2	3	7	5	7	.268	.339	.518	133	2	1	1	0	.966	3	2-21,S-15/3	0.6
1983	Phi-N	2	4	1	1	0	0	0	0	1	2	.250	.400	.250	85	-0	0	0	0	1.000	-2	/S-2	-0.2
1984	Phi-N	58	72	15	20	4	0	3	11	8	16	.278	.350	.458	123	2	0	0	0	.909	8	3-14,2-12,S	1.0
1985	Phi-N	91	165	27	46	7	3	6	21	22	26	.279	.383	.467	133	8	1	0	0	.957	3	S-60,2-17/3	1.6
1986	Phi-N	62	133	17	28	6	1	4	19	8	26	.211	.271	.361	70	-6	1	1	0	.967	-7	2-31,S-20/3	-1.1
1987	Phi-N	94	209	25	43	9	1	12	21	15	56	.206	.275	.431	81	-7	0	0	0	.971	-9	S-78/2-6,3	-1.1
1988	Phi-N	49	97	9	24	3	0	3	5	13	17	.247	.336	.371	101	0	2	0	1	.967	2	S-27,3-13/2	0.5
	NY-A	50	140	12	35	4	0	3	8	7	33	.250	.291	.343	77	-4	0	2	-1	.961	-2	3-33,2-13/S	-0.7
1989	Cle-A	47	97	7	17	4	1	1	8	7	19	.175	.245	.268	44	-7	0	0	0	.950	5	3-19,S-15,2/D	-0.1
Total	10	568	1104	142	260	43	10	37	109	94	220	.236	.307	.393	91	-16	7	5	-2	.960	-2	S-259,2-147/3D	-0.0

■ CHARLIE AHEARN

Ahearn, Charles b: Troy, N.Y. Deb: 6/19/1880

YEAR	TM/L	G	AB	R	H	2B	3B	HR	RBI	BB	SO	AVG	OBP	SLG	PRO+	BR/A	SB	CS	SBR	FA	FR	G/POS	TPR
1880	Tro-N	1	4	1	1	0	0	0	0	0	0	.250	.250	.250	67	-0				.778	-0	/C-1	0.0

■ WILLIE AIKENS

Aikens, Willie Mays b: 10/14/54, Seneca, S.C. BL/TR, 6'3", 220 lbs. Deb: 5/17/77

YEAR	TM/L	G	AB	R	H	2B	3B	HR	RBI	BB	SO	AVG	OBP	SLG	PRO+	BR/A	SB	CS	SBR	FA	FR	G/POS	TPR
1977	Cal-A	42	91	5	18	4	0	0	6	10	23	.198	.277	.242	45	-7	1	2	-1	.971	0	1-13,D-13	-0.9
1979	Cal-A	116	379	59	106	18	0	21	81	61	79	.280	.381	.493	138	21	1	3	-2	.996	-2	1-55,D-51	1.3
1980	*KC-A	151	543	70	151	24	0	20	98	64	88	.278	.362	.433	116	13	1	0	0	.990	-9	*1-138,D-13	-0.4
1981	*KC-A	101	349	45	93	16	0	17	53	62	47	.266	.382	.458	142	21	0	0	0	.992	-5	1-99	1.0
1982	KC-A	134	466	50	131	29	1	17	74	45	70	.281	.348	.457	119	12	0	1	-1	.994	-3	*1-128	0.1
1983	KC-A	125	410	49	124	26	1	23	72	45	75	.302	.374	.539	148	26	0	0	0	.989	-5	*1-112/D-6	1.5
1984	Tor-A	93	234	21	48	7	0	11	26	29	56	.205	.298	.376	82	-6	0	0	0	1.000	0	D-81/1-2	-0.8
1985	Tor-A	12	20	2	4	1	0	1	5	3	6	.200	.304	.400	89	-0	0	0	0	.000	0	D-11	-0.1
Total	8	774	2492	301	675	125	2	110	415	319	444	.271	.358	.455	123	80	3	6	-3	.991	-24	1-547,D-175	1.7

■ DANNY AINGE

Ainge, Daniel Ray b: 3/17/59, Eugene, Ore. BR/TR, 6'4", 175 lbs. Deb: 5/21/79

YEAR	TM/L	G	AB	R	H	2B	3B	HR	RBI	BB	SO	AVG	OBP	SLG	PRO+	BR/A	SB	CS	SBR	FA	FR	G/POS	TPR
1979	Tor-A	87	308	26	73	7	1	2	19	12	58	.237	.270	.286	50	-22	1	0	0	.977	-4	2-86	-1.9
1980	Tor-A	38	111	11	27	6	1	0	4	2	29	.243	.263	.315	55	-7	3	0	1	.986	2	O-29/3-3,2D	-0.5
1981	Tor-A	86	246	20	46	6	2	0	14	23	41	.187	.259	.228	39	-19	8	5	-1	.949	1	3-77/S-6,02D	-2.1
Total	3	211	665	57	146	19	4	2	37	37	128	.220	.265	.269	47	-48	12	5	1	.977	-1	/2-89,3-80,OSD	-4.5

■ EDDIE AINSMITH

Ainsmith, Edward Wilbur "Dorf" b: 2/4/1892, Cambridge, Mass. d: 9/6/81, Ft.Lauderdale, Fla BR/TR, 5'11", 180 lbs. Deb: 8/9/10

YEAR	TM/L	G	AB	R	H	2B	3B	HR	RBI	BB	SO	AVG	OBP	SLG	PRO+	BR/A	SB	CS	SBR	FA	FR	G/POS	TPR
1910	Was-A	33	104	4	20	1	2	0	9	6		.192	.236	.240	52	-6	0			.963	-4	C-30	-0.8
1911	Was-A	61	149	12	33	2	3	0	14	10		.221	.275	.275	55	-9	5			.952	0	C-47	-0.4
1912	Was-A	61	186	22	42	7	2	0	22	14		.226	.280	.285	61	-10	4			.958	15	C-59	1.1
1913	Was-A	84	229	26	49	4	4	2	20	12	41	.214	.262	.293	61	-12	17			.967	6	C-79/P-1	0.0
1914	Was-A	62	151	11	34	7	0	0	13	9	20	.225	.273	.272	61	-7	8	5	-1	.969	8	C-51	0.4
1915	Was-A	47	120	13	24	4	2	0	6	10	18	.200	.267	.267	59	-6	7	4	-0	.988	6	C-42	0.2
1916	Was-A	51	100	11	17	4	0	0	8	8	14	.170	.231	.210	33	-8	3			.959	13	C-46	0.7
1917	Was-A	125	350	38	67	17	4	0	42	40	48	.191	.280	.263	66	-14	16			.971	15	*C-119	1.1
1918	Was-A	96	292	22	62	10	9	0	20	29	44	.212	.283	.308	80	-8	6			.975	8	C-89	0.8
1919	Det-A	114	364	42	99	17	12	3	32	45	30	.272	.354	.409	117	8	9			.962	-11	*C-106	0.7
1920	Det-A	69	186	19	43	5	3	1	19	14	19	.231	.285	.306	58	-11	4	3	-0	.955	-3	C-61/1-1	-1.1
1921	Det-A	35	98	6	27	5	2	0	12	13	7	.276	.360	.367	87	-2	1	0	0	.947	-4	C-34	-0.3
	StL-N	27	62	5	18	0	1	0	5	3	4	.290	.323	.323	73	-2	0	0	0	.956	1	C-23/1-1	0.0
1922	StL-N	119	379	46	111	14	4	13	59	24	43	.293	.343	.454	109	2	4	2	3	.963	-2	*C-116	0.6
1923	StL-N	82	263	22	56	11	6	3	34	22	19	.213	.276	.335	62	-15	4	0	1	.980	-8	C-80	-1.8
	Bro-N	2	10	0	2	0	0	0	0	0	0	.200	.200	.200	6	-1	0	0	-1	1.000	1	/C-2	-0.1
	Yr	84	273	22	58	11	6	3	36	22	19	.212	.274	.330	60	-17	4	1	1	.981	-7	C-82	-1.9
1924	NY-N	10	5	0	3	0	0	0	0	0	0	.600	.600	.600	229	-1	0	0	0	1.000	-0	/C-9	0.1
Total	15	1078	3048	299	707	108	54	22	317	263	315	.232	.296	.324	76	-100	86	16		.966	41	C-993/1-2,P	1.2

■ GEORGE AITON

Aiton, George Wilson b: 12/29/1890, Kingman, Kan. d: 8/16/76, Van Nuys, Cal. BB/TR, 5'11.5", 175 lbs. Deb: 6/29/12

YEAR	TM/L	G	AB	R	H	2B	3B	HR	RBI	BB	SO	AVG	OBP	SLG	PRO+	BR/A	SB	CS	SBR	FA	FR	G/POS	TPR
1912	StL-A	10	17	1	4	0	0	0	0	1	4	.235	.381	.235	80	-0	0			.917	-0	/O-7	-0.1

■ JOHN AKE

Ake, John Leckie b: 8/29/1861, Altoona, Pa. d: 5/11/1887, LaCrosse, Wis. BR/TR, 6'1", 180 lbs. Deb: 5/12/1884

YEAR	TM/L	G	AB	R	H	2B	3B	HR	RBI	BB	SO	AVG	OBP	SLG	PRO+	BR/A	SB	CS	SBR	FA	FR	G/POS	TPR
1884	Bal-a	13	52	1	10	0	1	0		0	0	.192	.208	.231	41	-3				.677	-3	/3-9,O-3,S	-0.6

■ BILL AKERS

Akers, William G. "Bump" b: 12/25/04, Chattanooga, Tenn. d: 4/13/62, Chattanooga, Tenn. BR/TR, 5'11", 178 lbs. Deb: 9/8/29

YEAR	TM/L	G	AB	R	H	2B	3B	HR	RBI	BB	SO	AVG	OBP	SLG	PRO+	BR/A	SB	CS	SBR	FA	FR	G/POS	TPR
1929	Det-A	24	83	15	22	4	1	1	9	10	9	.265	.351	.373	86	-2	2	0	1	.935	-9	S-24	-0.6
1930	Det-A	85	233	36	65	8	5	9	40	36	34	.279	.375	.472	111	4	5	5	-2	.944	9	S-49,3-26	1.6
1931	Det-A	29	66	5	13	2	2	0	3	7	6	.197	.274	.288	46	-5	0	1	-1	.935	-2	3-20/2-5,S	-0.6
1932	Bos-N	36	93	8	24	3	1	1	17	10	15	.258	.330	.344	85	-2	0			.927	-5	3-20/2-5,S	-0.5
Total	4	174	475	64	124	17	9	11	69	63	64	.261	.349	.404	93	-4	7	6		.936	-6	/S-99,3-46,2	-0.1

■ GUS ALBERTS

Alberts, Augustus Peter b: 1861, Reading, Pa. d: 5/7/12, Idaho Springs, Colo BR/TR, 5'6.5", 180 lbs. Deb: 5/1/1884

YEAR	TM/L	G	AB	R	H	2B	3B	HR	RBI	BB	SO	AVG	OBP	SLG	PRO+	BR/A	SB	CS	SBR	FA	FR	G/POS	TPR
1884	Pit-a	2	5	1	1	0	0	0		0	0	.200	.200	.200	30	-0				.500	-1	/S-2	-0.2
	Was-U	4	16	4	4	0	0	0		0	4	.250	.400	.250	83	-0				.870	2	/S-4	0.2
1888	Cle-a	102	364	51	75	10	6	1	48	41		.206	.299	.275	87	-4	26			.862	9	S-53,3-49	0.3
1891	Mil-a	12	41	6	4	0	0	0	2	7	5	.098	.260	.098	2	-6	1			.814	-3	3-12	-0.7
Total	3	120	426	62	84	10	6	1	50	52	5	.197	.298	.256	75	-10	27			.880	2	/3-61,S-59	-0.4

■ BUTCH ALBERTS

Alberts, Francis Burt b: 5/4/50, Williamsport, Pa. BR/TR, 6'2", 205 lbs. Deb: 9/7/78

YEAR	TM/L	G	AB	R	H	2B	3B	HR	RBI	BB	SO	AVG	OBP	SLG	PRO+	BR/A	SB	CS	SBR	FA	FR	G/POS	TPR
1978	Tor-A	6	18	1	5	1	0	0	0	0	2	.278	.278	.333	70	-1	0	0	0	.000	0	/D-4	-0.1

■ JACK ALBRIGHT

Albright, Harold John b: 6/30/21, St.Petersburg, Fl d: 7/22/91, San Diego, Cal. BR/TR, 5'9", 175 lbs. Deb: 5/19/47

YEAR	TM/L	G	AB	R	H	2B	3B	HR	RBI	BB	SO	AVG	OBP	SLG	PRO+	BR/A	SB	CS	SBR	FA	FR	G/POS	TPR
1947	Phi-N	41	99	9	23	4	0	2	5	10	11	.232	.303	.333	71	-4				.943	3	S-33	0.0

■ LUIS ALCARAZ

Alcaraz, Angel Luis (Acosta) b: 6/20/41, Humacao, P.R. BR/TR, 5'9", 165 lbs. Deb: 9/13/67

YEAR	TM/L	G	AB	R	H	2B	3B	HR	RBI	BB	SO	AVG	OBP	SLG	PRO+	BR/A	SB	CS	SBR	FA	FR	G/POS	TPR
1967	LA-N	17	60	1	14	0	0	0	3	1	13	.233	.246	.250	46	-4	1	1	-0	.990	9	2-17	0.5
1968	LA-N	41	106	4	16	1	0	2	5	9	23	.151	.217	.217	33	-9	1	1	-0	.979	3	2-20,3-13/S	-0.5
1969	KC-A	22	79	15	20	2	1	1	7	7	9	.253	.314	.342	83	-2	0	0	0	.988	-5	2-19/3-2,S	-0.5
1970	KC-A	35	120	10	20	5	1	1	14	4	13	.167	.194	.250	21	-13	0	0	0	.993	-8	2-31	-2.0
Total	4	115	365	30	70	9	2	4	29	21	58	.192	.236	.260	43	-28	2	2	-0	.988	-1	/2-87,3-15,S	-2.5

YEAR	TM/L	G	AB	R	H	2B	3B	HR	RBI	BB	SO	AVG	OBP	SLG	PRO+	BR/A	SB	CS	SBR	FA	FR	G/POS	TPR

■ SCOTTY ALCOCK
Alcock, John Forbes b: 11/29/1885, Wooster, Ohio d: 1/30/73, Wooster, Ohio BR/TR, 5'9.5", 160 lbs. Deb: 4/19/14

YEAR	TM/L	G	AB	R	H	2B	3B	HR	RBI	BB	SO	AVG	OBP	SLG	PRO+	BR/A	SB	CS	SBR	FA	FR	G/POS	TPR
1914	Chi-A	54	156	12	27	4	2	0	7	7	14	.173	.213	.224	32	-13	4	2	0	.905	4	3-48/2-1	-0.9

■ MIKE ALDRETE
Aldrete, Michael Peter b: 1/29/61, Carmel, Cal. BL/TL, 5'11", 185 lbs. Deb: 5/28/86

YEAR	TM/L	G	AB	R	H	2B	3B	HR	RBI	BB	SO	AVG	OBP	SLG	PRO+	BR/A	SB	CS	SBR	FA	FR	G/POS	TPR
1986	SF-N	84	216	27	54	18	3	2	25	33	34	.250	.355	.389	110	4	1	3	-2	1.000	3	1-37,O-31	0.2
1987	*SF-N	126	357	50	116	18	2	9	51	43	50	.325	.398	.462	133	18	6	0	2	.986	-2	O-79,1-33	1.4
1988	SF-N	139	389	44	104	15	0	3	50	56	65	.267	.360	.329	103	4	6	5	-1	.982	-7	*O-115,1-10	-0.9
1989	Mon-N	76	136	12	30	8	1	1	12	19	30	.221	.321	.316	81	-3	1	3	-2	.980	-3	O-37,1-10	-0.9
1990	Mon-N	96	161	22	39	7	1	1	18	37	31	.242	.387	.317	100	1	2	1	-1	.982	-4	O-38,1-18	-0.4
1991	SD-N	12	15	2	0	0	0	0	1	3	4	.000	.167	.000	-48	-3	0	1	-1	1.000	0	/O-5	-0.4
	Cle-A	85	183	22	48	6	1	1	19	36	37	.262	.384	.322	97	1	1	2	-1	.994	-3	1-47,O-16/D	-0.5
1993	Oak-A	95	255	40	68	13	1	10	33	34	45	.267	.353	.443	120	7	1	1	-0	.995	-3	1-59,O-20/D	0.0
1994	Oak-A	76	178	23	43	5	0	4	18	20	35	.242	.318	.337	75	-7	2	0	1	1.000	-8	O-35,1-27/D	-1.5
Total	8	789	1890	242	502	90	9	31	227	281	331	.266	.362	.372	106	23	19	17	-5	.985	-25	O-376,1-241/D	-3.0

■ CHUCK ALENO
Aleno, Charles b: 2/19/17, St.Louis, Mo. BR/TR, 6'1.5", 215 lbs. Deb: 5/15/41

YEAR	TM/L	G	AB	R	H	2B	3B	HR	RBI	BB	SO	AVG	OBP	SLG	PRO+	BR/A	SB	CS	SBR	FA	FR	G/POS	TPR
1941	Cin-N	54	169	23	41	7	3	1	18	11	16	.243	.289	.337	76	-6	3			.975	-4	3-40/1-2	-0.9
1942	Cin-N	7	14	1	2	1	0	0	0	3	3	.143	.294	.214	50	-1	0			.727	1	/3-2,2-1	0.1
1943	Cin-N	7	10	0	3	0	0	0	1	1	1	.300	.417	.300	110	0	0			1.000	-1	/O-2	0.0
1944	Cin-N	50	127	10	21	3	0	1	15	15	15	.165	.259	.213	35	-11	0			.952	-4	3-42/1-3,S	-1.5
Total	4	118	320	34	67	11	3	2	34	31	35	.209	.281	.281	60	-17	0			.954	-7	/3-84,1-5,SO2	-2.3

■ DALE ALEXANDER
Alexander, David Dale "Moose" b: 4/26/03, Greeneville, Tenn. d: 3/2/79, Greeneville, Tenn. BR/TR, 6'3", 210 lbs. Deb: 4/16/29

YEAR	TM/L	G	AB	R	H	2B	3B	HR	RBI	BB	SO	AVG	OBP	SLG	PRO+	BR/A	SB	CS	SBR	FA	FR	G/POS	TPR
1929	Det-A	155	626	110	215	43	15	25	137	56	63	.343	.397	.580	148	42	5	9	-4	.988	-4	*1-155	1.7
1930	Det-A	154	602	86	196	33	8	20	135	42	56	.326	.372	.507	118	15	6	5	-1	.985	-8	*1-154	-0.7
1931	Det-A	135	517	75	168	47	3	3	87	64	35	.325	.401	.445	118	15	5	8	-3	.987	-8	*1-126/O-4	-0.8
1932	Det-A	23	16	0	4	0	0	0	4	6	2	.250	.455	.250	84	0	0	0	0	1.000	-0	/1-2	0.0
	Bos-A	101	376	58	140	27	3	8	56	55	19	.372	.454	.524	157	34	4	5	-2	.992	2	*1-101	2.4
	Yr	124	392	58	144	27	3	8	60	61	21	.367	.454	.513	152	33	4	5	-2	.992	2	*1-103	2.4
1933	Bos-A	94	313	40	88	14	1	5	40	25	22	.281	.336	.380	90	-5	0	1	-1	.992	3	1-79	-0.9
Total	5	662	2450	369	811	164	30	61	459	248	197	.331	.394	.497	128	102	20	28	-11	.988	-14	1-617/O-4	1.7

■ GARY ALEXANDER
Alexander, Gary Wayne b: 3/27/53, Los Angeles, Cal. BR/TR, 6'2", 200 lbs. Deb: 9/12/75

YEAR	TM/L	G	AB	R	H	2B	3B	HR	RBI	BB	SO	AVG	OBP	SLG	PRO+	BR/A	SB	CS	SBR	FA	FR	G/POS	TPR
1975	SF-N	3	3	1	0	0	0	0	0	1	2	.000	.250	.000	-25	-0	0	0	0	1.000	-1	/C-2	-0.1
1976	SF-N	23	73	12	13	1	1	2	7	10	14	.178	.277	.301	62	-4	1	0	0	.964	-4	C-23	-0.7
1977	SF-N	51	119	17	36	4	2	5	20	20	33	.303	.411	.496	143	8	3	1	0	.968	-8	C-33/O-1	0.1
1978	Oak-A	58	174	18	36	6	1	10	22	22	66	.207	.299	.425	107	1	0	3	-2	1.000	-6	D-45/O-6,C1	-0.2
	Cle-A	90	324	39	76	14	3	17	62	35	100	.235	.311	.454	114	5	0	2	-1	.983	-9	C-66,D-25	-0.5
	Yr	148	498	57	112	20	4	27	84	57	166	.225	.307	.444	112	6	0	5	-3	.983	-9	D-70,C-67/O1	-0.7
1979	Cle-A	110	358	54	82	9	2	15	54	46	100	.229	.319	.391	90	-5	4	2	0	.961	-20	C-91,D-13/O	-2.2
1980	Cle-A	76	178	22	40	7	1	5	31	17	52	.225	.292	.360	77	-6	0	4	-2	.971	-2	D-40,C-13/O	-1.1
1981	Pit-N	21	47	6	10	4	1	1	6	3	12	.213	.260	.404	84	-1	0	0	0	.964	1	/1-9,O-8	-0.1
Total	7	432	1276	169	293	45	11	55	202	154	381	.230	.315	.411	99	-3	8	12	-5	.969	-42	C-229,D-123/O1	-4.8

■ HUGH ALEXANDER
Alexander, Hugh b: 7/10/17, Buffalo, Mo. BR/TR, 6', 190 lbs. Deb: 8/15/37

YEAR	TM/L	G	AB	R	H	2B	3B	HR	RBI	BB	SO	AVG	OBP	SLG	PRO+	BR/A	SB	CS	SBR	FA	FR	G/POS	TPR
1937	Cle-A	7	11	0	1	0	0	0	0	0	5	.091	.091	.091	-54	-3	1	0	0	.667	-2	/O-3	-0.4

■ MANNY ALEXANDER
Alexander, Manuel De Jesus (b: Manuel De Jesus (Alexander)) b: 3/20/71, San Pedro De Macoris, D.R. BR/TR, 5'10", 150 lbs. Deb: 9/18/92

YEAR	TM/L	G	AB	R	H	2B	3B	HR	RBI	BB	SO	AVG	OBP	SLG	PRO+	BR/A	SB	CS	SBR	FA	FR	G/POS	TPR
1992	Bal-A	4	5	1	1	0	0	0	0	0	3	.200	.200	.200	12	-1	0	0	0	1.000	1	/S-3	0.0
1993	Bal-A	3	0	1	0	0	0	0	0	0	0	—	—	—		0	0	0	0	.000	0	/R	0.0
Total	2	7	5	2	1	0	0	0	0	0	3	.200	.200	.200	12	-1	0	0	0	1.000	1	/S-3	0.0

■ MATT ALEXANDER
Alexander, Matthew b: 1/30/47, Shreveport, La. BB/TR, 5'11", 169 lbs. Deb: 8/23/73

YEAR	TM/L	G	AB	R	H	2B	3B	HR	RBI	BB	SO	AVG	OBP	SLG	PRO+	BR/A	SB	CS	SBR	FA	FR	G/POS	TPR
1973	Chi-N	12	5	4	1	0	0	0	1	1	1	.200	.333	.200	48	-0	2	0	1	1.000	-1	/O-3	-0.1
1974	Chi-N	45	54	15	11	2	1	0	0	12	12	.204	.358	.278	76	-1	8	4	0	.921	-2	3-19/O-4,2	-0.3
1975	Oak-A	63	10	16	1	0	0	0	0	0	1	.100	.182	.100	-19	-2	17	10	-1	1.000	-3	D-17,O-11/23	-0.6
1976	Oak-A	61	30	16	1	1	0	0	2	4	5	.033	.033	.033	-84	-7	20	7	0	1.000	-3	O-23,D-19	-1.4
1977	Oak-A	90	42	24	10	1	0	0	2	4	6	.238	.304	.262	57	-2	26	14	-1	1.000	-11	O-31,S-12/23D	-1.4
1978	Pit-N	7	0	2	0	0	0	0	0	0	0	—	—	—		0	4	1	1	.000	0	R	0.0
1979	*Pit-N	44	13	16	7	1	0	0	1	0	0	.538	.538	.692	223	2	13	1	3	1.000	-1	O-11/S-1	0.2
1980	Pit-N	37	3	13	1	1	0	0	0	0	0	.333	.333	.667	170	0	10	3	1	1.000	-1	/O-4,2-1	0.1
1981	Pit-N	15	11	5	4	0	1	0	1	0	2	.364	.364	.364	104	0	3	2	-0	1.000	-1	/O-6	-0.2
Total	9	374	168	111	36	4	2	0	4	18	26	.214	.294	.262	56	-10	103	42	6	1.000	-29	/O-93,D-37,3S2	-3.7

■ WALT ALEXANDER
Alexander, Walter Ernest b: 3/5/1891, Atlanta, Ga. d: 12/29/78, Fort Worth, Tex. BR/TR, 5'10.5", 165 lbs. Deb: 6/21/12

YEAR	TM/L	G	AB	R	H	2B	3B	HR	RBI	BB	SO	AVG	OBP	SLG	PRO+	BR/A	SB	CS	SBR	FA	FR	G/POS	TPR
1912	StL-A	37	97	5	17	4	0	0	5	8		.175	.245	.216	34	-8	1			.969	-3	C-37	-0.8
1913	StL-A	43	110	5	15	2	1	0	7	4	36	.136	.174	.173	2	-14	1			.947	3	C-43	-0.8
1915	StL-A	1	1	0	0	0	0	0	0	0	0	.000	.000	.000	-99	-0	0			.000	0	/C-1	0.0
	NY-A	25	68	7	17	4	0	1	5	13	16	.250	.370	.353	117	2	2	1	0	.967	9	C-24	1.3
	Yr	26	69	7	17	4	0	1	5	13	16	.246	.366	.348	114	2	2	1	0	.967	9	C-25	1.3
1916	NY-A	36	78	8	20	6	1	0	3	13	20	.256	.376	.359	118	2				.960	2	C-27	0.6
1917	NY-A	20	51	1	7	2	1	0	4	4	11	.137	.200	.216	27	-5	1			.951	0	C-20	-0.4
Total	5	162	405	26	76	18	3	1	24	42	83	.188	.271	.254	56	-23	5	1		.959	11	C-152	-0.1

■ NIN ALEXANDER
Alexander, William Henry b: 11/24/1858, Pana, Ill. d: 12/22/33, Pana, Ill. BR/TR, 5'4.5", 163 lbs. Deb: 6/7/1884

YEAR	TM/L	G	AB	R	H	2B	3B	HR	RBI	BB	SO	AVG	OBP	SLG	PRO+	BR/A	SB	CS	SBR	FA	FR	G/POS	TPR
1884	KC-U	19	65	2	9	0	0	0		1		.138	.152	.138	-24	-11				.907	-2	C-17/S-2,O	-1.0
	StL-a	1	4	0	0	0	0	0		0		.000	.000	.000	-97	-1				.667	-0	/C-1,O-1	-0.1
Total	1	20	69	2	9	0	0	0		1		.130	.143	.130	-28	-12				.895	-2	/C-18,O-3,S	-1.1

■ LUIS ALICEA
Alicea, Luis Rene (De Jesus) b: 7/29/65, Santurce, P.R. BB/TR, 5'9", 165 lbs. Deb: 4/23/88

YEAR	TM/L	G	AB	R	H	2B	3B	HR	RBI	BB	SO	AVG	OBP	SLG	PRO+	BR/A	SB	CS	SBR	FA	FR	G/POS	TPR
1988	StL-N	93	297	20	63	10	4	1	24	25	32	.212	.278	.283	61	-15	1	1	-0	.970	4	2-91	-0.9
1991	StL-N	56	68	5	13	3	0	0	0	8	19	.191	.276	.235	45	-5	0	1	-1	1.000	-1	2-11/3-2,S	-0.7
1992	StL-N	85	265	26	65	9	11	2	32	27	40	.245	.324	.385	103	1	2	5	-2	.989	2	2-75/S-4	0.2
1993	StL-N	115	362	50	101	19	3	3	46	47	54	.279	.368	.373	101	2	11	1	3	.978	2	2-96/O-4,3	0.9
1994	StL-N	88	205	32	57	12	5	5	29	30	38	.278	.378	.459	121	7	4	5	-2	.986	4	2-53/O-2	1.0
Total	5	437	1197	133	299	53	23	11	131	137	183	.250	.333	.360	92	-10	18	13	-2	.980	10	2-326/O-6,S3	0.5

■ ANDY ALLANSON
Allanson, Andrew Neal b: 12/22/61, Richmond, Va. BR/TR, 6'5", 225 lbs. Deb: 4/7/86

YEAR	TM/L	G	AB	R	H	2B	3B	HR	RBI	BB	SO	AVG	OBP	SLG	PRO+	BR/A	SB	CS	SBR	FA	FR	G/POS	TPR
1986	Cle-A	101	293	30	66	7	3	1	29	14	36	.225	.263	.280	49	-21	10	1	2	.960	-7	C-99	-2.0
1987	Cle-A	50	154	17	41	6	0	3	16	9	30	.266	.307	.364	76	-5	1	1	-0	.986	-7	C-50	-0.9
1988	Cle-A	133	434	44	114	11	0	5	50	25	63	.263	.307	.323	75	-14	5	9	-4	.986	1	*C-133	-0.8
1989	Cle-A	111	323	30	75	9	1	3	17	23	47	.232	.291	.294	64	-15	4	4	-1	.986	4	*C-111	-0.8
1991	Det-A	60	151	10	35	10	1	0	16	7	31	.232	.266	.318	60	-8	2	1	-1	.979	6	C-56/1-2,D	-0.1
1992	Mil-A	9	25	6	8	1	0	0	1	2	5	.320	.346	.360	100	-0	3	1	0	.943	-2	/C-9	-0.1

YEAR	TM/L	G	AB	R	H	2B	3B	HR	RBI	BB	SO	AVG	OBP	SLG	PRO+	BR/A	SB	CS	SBR	FA	FR	G/POS	TPR
1993	SF-N	13	24	3	4	1	0	0	2	1	2	.167	.200	.208	10	-3	0	0	0	1.000	-1	/C-8,1-2	-0.4
Total	7	477	1404	140	343	45	4	13	130	80	211	.244	.289	.310	65	-67	23	17	-3	.979	-7	C-466/1-4,D	-5.0

■ NICK ALLEN
Allen, Artemus Ward b: 9/14/1888, Norton, Kan. d: 10/16/39, Hines, Ill. BR/TR, 6', 180 lbs. Deb: 5/1/14

YEAR	TM/L	G	AB	R	H	2B	3B	HR	RBI	BB	SO	AVG	OBP	SLG	PRO+	BR/A	SB	CS	SBR	FA	FR	G/POS	TPR
1914	Buf-F	32	63	3	15	1	0	0	4	3	12	.238	.273	.254	36	-6	4			.969	2	C-26	-0.3
1915	Buf-F	84	215	14	44	7	1	0	17	18	34	.205	.269	.247	38	-19	4			.956	7	C-80	-0.7
1916	Chi-N	5	16	1	1	0	0	0	1	0	3	.063	.063	.063	-56	-3	0			.958	-1	/C-4	-0.4
1918	Cin-N	37	96	6	25	2	2	0	5	4	7	.260	.297	.323	91	-1	0			.950	8	C-31	0.9
1919	Cin-N	15	25	7	8	0	1	0	5	2	6	.320	.393	.400	142	1	0			.958	3	C-12	0.5
1920	Cin-N	43	85	10	23	3	1	0	4	6	11	.271	.340	.329	94	-0	0	0	0	.961	6	C-36	0.8
Total	6	216	500	41	116	13	5	0	36	33	73	.232	.288	.278	58	-28	8	0		.958	25	C-189	0.8

■ BERNIE ALLEN
Allen, Bernard Keith b: 4/16/39, E.Liverpool, O. BL/TR, 6', 185 lbs. Deb: 4/10/62

YEAR	TM/L	G	AB	R	H	2B	3B	HR	RBI	BB	SO	AVG	OBP	SLG	PRO+	BR/A	SB	CS	SBR	FA	FR	G/POS	TPR
1962	Min-A	159	573	79	154	27	7	12	64	62	82	.269	.340	.403	96	-3	0	1	-1	.983	-17	*2-158	-0.4
1963	Min-A	139	421	52	101	20	1	9	43	38	52	.240	.304	.356	83	-10	0	0	0	.976	-24	*2-128	-2.5
1964	Min-A	74	243	28	52	8	1	6	20	33	30	.214	.310	.329	78	-7	1	2	-1	.979	-11	2-71	-1.4
1965	Min-A	19	39	2	9	2	0	0	6	6	8	.231	.333	.282	73	-1	0	0	0	1.000	-2	2-10/3-1	-0.2
1966	Min-A	101	319	34	76	18	1	5	30	26	40	.238	.300	.348	80	-8	2	3	-1	.974	-7	2-89/3-2	-1.1
1967	Was-A	87	254	13	49	5	1	3	18	18	43	.193	.246	.256	51	-16	1	2	-1	.990	19	2-75	0.7
1968	Was-A	120	373	31	90	12	4	6	40	28	35	.241	.301	.343	98	-1	2	0	1	**.991**	5	*2-110/3-2	1.1
1969	Was-A	122	365	33	90	17	4	9	45	50	35	.247	.337	.389	108	4	5	4	-1	.974	3	*2-110/3-6	1.5
1970	Was-A	104	261	31	61	7	1	8	29	43	21	.234	.342	.360	99	0	2	0	-1	.969	-0	2-80,3-12	0.4
1971	Was-A	97	229	18	61	11	1	4	22	33	27	.266	.359	.376	115	5	2	1	0	.961	-11	2-41,3-34	-0.4
1972	NY-A	84	220	26	50	9	0	9	21	23	42	.227	.300	.391	108	2	0	1	-1	.940	-2	3-44,2-20	0.1
1973	NY-A	17	57	5	13	3	0	0	4	5	5	.228	.290	.281	64	-3	0	0	0	.985	-2	2-13/D-2	-0.2
	Mon-N	16	50	5	9	1	0	2	9	4	5	.180	.255	.320	56	-3	0	0	0	.970	-1	/2-9,3-8	-0.4
Total	12	1139	3404	357	815	140	21	73	351	370	424	.239	.315	.357	91	-41	13	16	-6	.980	-47	2-914,3-109/D	-2.8

■ JACK ALLEN
Allen, Cyrus Alban b: 10/2/1855, Woodstock, Ill. d: 4/21/15, Girard, Pa. BR/TR, 160 lbs. Deb: 5/1/1879

YEAR	TM/L	G	AB	R	H	2B	3B	HR	RBI	BB	SO	AVG	OBP	SLG	PRO+	BR/A	SB	CS	SBR	FA	FR	G/POS	TPR
1879	Syr-N	11	48	7	9	2	1	0	3	1	5	.188	.204	.271	62	-2				.655	-6	/3-8,O-3	-0.7
	Cle-N	16	60	7	7	1	1	0	4	1	9	.117	.131	.167	-3	-6				.845	3	3-14/O-4	-0.3
	Yr	27	108	14	16	3	2	0	7	2	14	.148	.164	.213	24	-8				.790	-3	3-22/O-5	-1.0

■ ETHAN ALLEN
Allen, Ethan Nathan b: 1/1/04, Cincinnati, Ohio d: 9/15/93, Brookings, Ore. BR/TR, 6'1", 180 lbs. Deb: 6/21/26

YEAR	TM/L	G	AB	R	H	2B	3B	HR	RBI	BB	SO	AVG	OBP	SLG	PRO+	BR/A	SB	CS	SBR	FA	FR	G/POS	TPR
1926	Cin-N	18	13	3	4	1	0	0	0	0	3	.308	.308	.385	88	-0	0			1.000	-3	/O-9	-0.3
1927	Cin-N	111	359	54	106	26	4	2	20	14	23	.295	.325	.407	98	-2	12			.988	2	O-98	-1.0
1928	Cin-N	129	485	55	148	30	7	1	62	27	29	.305	.343	.402	96	-4	6			.981	3	*O-129	-1.0
1929	Cin-N	143	538	69	157	27	11	6	64	20	21	.292	.317	.416	84	-16	21			**.988**	-10	*O-137	-3.2
1930	Cin-N	21	46	10	10	1	0	3	7	5	2	.217	.294	.435	77	-2	1			.969	-2	O-15	-0.4
	NY-N	76	238	48	73	9	2	7	31	12	23	.307	.340	.450	91	-4	5			.985	-4	O-62	-1.1
	Yr	97	284	58	83	10	2	10	38	17	25	.292	.332	.447	89	-6	6			.981	-6	O-77	-1.5
1931	NY-N	94	298	58	98	18	2	5	43	15	15	.329	.363	.453	121	8	6			.975	-7	O-77	-0.3
1932	NY-N	54	103	13	18	6	2	1	7	1	12	.175	.198	.301	33	-10	0			.957	-4	O-24	-1.5
1933	StL-N	91	261	25	63	7	3	0	36	13	22	.241	.280	.291	60	-13	3			.984	8	O-67	-0.9
1934	Phi-N	145	581	87	192	**42**	4	10	85	33	47	.330	.370	.468	108	6	6			.978	9	*O-145	0.8
1935	Phi-N	156	645	90	198	46	1	8	63	43	54	.307	.351	.419	96	-4	5			.980	17	*O-156	0.6
1936	Phi-N	30	125	21	37	3	1	1	9	4	8	.296	.318	.360	75	-5	4			.954	-0	O-30	-0.6
	Chi-N	91	373	47	110	18	6	3	39	13	30	.295	.322	.399	91	-5	12			.980	-2	O-89	-1.1
	Yr	121	498	68	147	21	7	4	48	17	38	.295	.321	.390	87	-10	16			.972	-3	*O-119	-1.7
1937	StL-A	103	320	39	101	18	1	0	31	21	17	.316	.360	.378	86	-7	3	4	-2	1.000	-1	/O-7	-1.1
1938	StL-A	19	33	4	10	3	1	0	4	2	4	.303	.343	.455	98	-0	0	0	0	1.000	-1	/O-7	-0.2
Total	13	1281	4418	623	1325	255	45	47	501	223	310	.300	.336	.410	92	-58	84	4		.981	-0	*O-1123	-11.3

■ SLED ALLEN
Allen, Fletcher Manson b: 8/23/1886, West Plains, Mo. d: 10/16/59, Lubbock, Tex. BR/TR, 6'1", 180 lbs. Deb: 5/4/10

YEAR	TM/L	G	AB	R	H	2B	3B	HR	RBI	BB	SO	AVG	OBP	SLG	PRO+	BR/A	SB	CS	SBR	FA	FR	G/POS	TPR
1910	StL-A	14	23	3	3	1	0	0	1	1		.130	.231	.174	29	-2				.903	-6	C-12/1-1	-0.8

■ HANK ALLEN
Allen, Harold Andrew b: 7/23/40, Wampum, Pa. BR/TR, 6', 190 lbs. Deb: 9/9/66 F

YEAR	TM/L	G	AB	R	H	2B	3B	HR	RBI	BB	SO	AVG	OBP	SLG	PRO+	BR/A	SB	CS	SBR	FA	FR	G/POS	TPR
1966	Was-A	9	31	2	12	0	0	1	6	3	6	.387	.441	.484	167	3	0	0	0	.917	0	/O-9	0.2
1967	Was-A	116	292	34	68	8	4	3	17	13	53	.233	.266	.318	75	-10	3	4	-2	.980	-21	O-99	-4.1
1968	Was-A	68	128	16	28	2	2	1	9	7	16	.219	.265	.289	70	-5	0	0	0	.895	-8	O-25,3-16,2	-1.5
1969	Was-A	109	271	42	75	9	3	1	17	19	28	.277	.312	.343	88	-5	12	3	2	.933	-17	O-91/3-6,2	-2.5
1970	Was-A	22	38	3	8	2	0	0	4	5	9	.211	.302	.263	60	-2	0	0	0	1.000	-3	O-17	-0.6
	Mil-A	28	61	4	14	4	0	0	4	7	5	.230	.309	.295	67	-3	0	1	-1	1.000	-4	O-14/2-5,1	-0.5
	Yr	50	99	7	22	6	0	0	8	12	14	.222	.306	.283	65	-5	0	1	-1	1.000	-4	O-31/2-5,1	-1.1
1972	Chi-A	9	21	1	3	0	0	0	0	0	2	.143	.143	.143	-15	-3	0	0	0	.905	3	/3-6	0.0
1973	Chi-A	28	39	2	4	2	0	0	0	1	9	.103	.125	.154	-21	-6	0	1	0	1.000	-8	/3-9,1-8,0C2	-0.8
Total	7	389	881	104	212	27	9	6	57	49	128	.241	.282	.312	74	-31	15	9	-1	.957	-48	O-260/3-37,21C	-9.8

■ HEZEKIAH ALLEN
Allen, Hezekiah "Ki" b: 2/25/1863, Westport, Conn. d: 9/21/16, Saugatuck, Conn. 5'11", 160 lbs. Deb: 5/16/1884

YEAR	TM/L	G	AB	R	H	2B	3B	HR	RBI	BB	SO	AVG	OBP	SLG	PRO+	BR/A	SB	CS	SBR	FA	FR	G/POS	TPR
1884	Phi-N	1	3	0	2	0	0	0	0	0	0	.667	.667	.667	337	1				1.000	-1	/C-1	0.0

■ HAM ALLEN
Allen, Homer S. b: 8/1854, Hamden, Conn. d: 1/7/1892, Hamden, Conn. Deb: 4/27/1872

YEAR	TM/L	G	AB	R	H	2B	3B	HR	RBI	BB	SO	AVG	OBP	SLG	PRO+	BR/A	SB	CS	SBR	FA	FR	G/POS	TPR
1872	Man-n	15	59	8	15	2	0	0	1	0	1	.254	.254	.288	71	-2						O-10/S-6	-0.1

■ HORACE ALLEN
Allen, Horace Tanner "Pug" b: 6/11/1899, DeLand, Fla. d: 7/5/81, Canton, N.C. BL/TR, 6', 187 lbs. Deb: 6/15/19

YEAR	TM/L	G	AB	R	H	2B	3B	HR	RBI	BB	SO	AVG	OBP	SLG	PRO+	BR/A	SB	CS	SBR	FA	FR	G/POS	TPR
1919	Bro-N	4	7	0	0	0	0	0	0	0	0	.000	.000	.000	-98	-2	0			1.000	-0	/O-2	-0.2

■ JAMIE ALLEN
Allen, James Bradley b: 5/29/58, Yakima, Wash. BR/TR, 6', 205 lbs. Deb: 5/1/83

YEAR	TM/L	G	AB	R	H	2B	3B	HR	RBI	BB	SO	AVG	OBP	SLG	PRO+	BR/A	SB	CS	SBR	FA	FR	G/POS	TPR
1983	Sea-A	86	273	23	61	10	0	4	21	33	52	.223	.309	.304	67	-12	6	5	-1	.959	-6	3-82/D-2	-2.0

■ PETE ALLEN
Allen, Jesse Hall b: 5/1/1868, Columbiana, Ohio d: 4/16/46, Philadelphia, Pa. BR/TR, 5'8.5", 185 lbs. Deb: 8/4/1893

YEAR	TM/L	G	AB	R	H	2B	3B	HR	RBI	BB	SO	AVG	OBP	SLG	PRO+	BR/A	SB	CS	SBR	FA	FR	G/POS	TPR
1893	Cle-N	1	4	0	0	0	0	0	0	0	0	.000	.000	.000	-94	-1	0			1.000	-1	/C-1	-0.2

■ KIM ALLEN
Allen, Kim Bryant b: 4/5/53, Fontana, Cal. BR/TR, 5'11", 175 lbs. Deb: 9/2/80

YEAR	TM/L	G	AB	R	H	2B	3B	HR	RBI	BB	SO	AVG	OBP	SLG	PRO+	BR/A	SB	CS	SBR	FA	FR	G/POS	TPR
1980	Sea-A	23	51	9	12	3	0	0	3	8	3	.235	.350	.294	78	-1	10	3	1	.970	-2	2-15/O-4,S	-0.2
1981	Sea-A	19	3	1	0	0	0	0	0	0	2	.000	.000	.000	-96	-1	2	1	0	.000	-1	/2-2,O-2,D	-0.2
Total	2	42	54	10	12	3	0	0	3	8	5	.222	.333	.278	69	-2	12	4	1	.970	-4	/2-17,O-6,DS	-0.4

■ MYRON ALLEN
Allen, Myron Smith "Zeke" b: 3/22/1854, Kingston, N.Y. d: 3/8/24, Kingston, N.Y. BR/TR, 5'8", 150 lbs. Deb: 7/19/1883

YEAR	TM/L	G	AB	R	H	2B	3B	HR	RBI	BB	SO	AVG	OBP	SLG	PRO+	BR/A	SB	CS	SBR	FA	FR	G/POS	TPR
1883	NY-N	1	4	0	0	0	0	0	0	1	0	.000	.000	.000	-99	-1				1.000	-0	/P-1	0.0
1886	Bos-N	1	3	0	0	0	0	0	0	0	1	.000	.000	.000	-99	-1				1.000	-0	/2-1	-0.1
1887	Cle-a	117	463	66	128	22	10	4		36		.276	.335	.393	106	3	26			.894	8	*O-115/3-3,SP	0.8
1888	KC-a	37	136	23	29	6	4	0	10	9		.213	.267	.316	81	-3	4			.931	7	O-35/P-2	0.2
Total	4	156	606	89	157	28	14	4	_11_	45	_3_	.259	.317	.371	98	-2	30			.903	15	O-150/P-5,3S2	0.9

DICK ALLEN
Allen, Richard Anthony b: 3/8/42, Wampum, Pa. BR/TR, 5'11", 190 lbs. Deb: 9/3/63 F

YEAR	TM/L	G	AB	R	H	2B	3B	HR	RBI	BB	SO	AVG	OBP	SLG	PRO+	BR/A	SB	CS	SBR	FA	FR	G/POS	TPR
1963	Phi-N	10	24	6	7	2	1	0	2	0	5	.292	.292	.458	114	0	0	0	0	.833	-1	/O-7,3-1	-0.1
1964	Phi-N	162	632	**125**	201	38	**13**	29	91	67	138	.318	.383	.557	163	52	3	4	-2	.921	7	*3-162	5.8
1965	Phi-N★	161	619	93	187	31	14	20	85	74	150	.302	.378	.494	146	38	15	3	3	.943	-2	*3-160/S-2	3.7
1966	Phi-N★	141	524	112	166	25	10	40	110	68	136	.317	.398	**.632**	**181**	57	10	6	-1	.967	-2	3-91,O-47	4.5
1967	Phi-N★	122	463	89	142	31	10	23	77	75	117	.307	**.404**	.566	173	45	20	5	3	.908	-6	*3-121/2-1,S	4.4
1968	Phi-N	152	521	87	137	17	9	33	90	74	161	.263	.356	.520	160	38	7	7	-2	.973	-5	*O-139,3-10	2.7
1969	Phi-N	118	438	79	126	23	3	32	89	64	144	.288	.378	.573	168	38	9	3	1	.985	-9	*1-117	2.1
1970	StL-N★	122	459	88	128	17	5	34	101	71	118	.279	.378	.560	145	28	5	4	-1	.993	-12	1-79,3-38/O	0.9
1971	LA-N	155	549	82	162	24	1	23	90	93	113	.295	.398	.468	154	41	8	1	2	.918	-8	3-67,O-60,1	3.1
1972	Chi-A★	148	506	90	156	28	5	**37**	**113**	**99**	126	.308	**.422**	.603	**199**	64	19	8	1	.995	-4	*1-143/3-2	5.4
1973	Chi-A†	72	250	39	79	20	3	16	41	33	51	.316	.398	.612	175	24	7	1	2	.994	0	1-67/2-2,D	2.0
1974	Chi-A★	128	462	84	139	23	1	**32**	88	57	89	.301	.379	**.563**	164	37	7	1	2	.986	-11	*1-125/2-1,D	2.0
1975	Phi-N	119	416	54	97	21	3	12	62	58	109	.233	.330	.385	94	-3	11	2	2	.982	-1	*1-113	-1.0
1976	*Phi-N	85	298	52	80	16	1	15	49	37	63	.268	.349	.480	130	11	11	4	1	.989	-3	1-85	0.3
1977	Oak-A	54	171	19	41	4	0	5	31	24	36	.240	.337	.351	89	-2	1	3	-2	.984	2	1-50/D-1	-0.5
Total	15	1749	6332	1099	1848	320	79	351	1119	894	1556	.292	.381	.534	156	469	133	52	9	.989	-62	1-807,3-652,O/2DS	35.3

BOB ALLEN
Allen, Robert (b: Alvah Charles Elliott) b: 10/13/1894, Muscoda, Wis. d: 12/18/75, Naperville, Ill. BR/TR, 5'10", 180 lbs. Deb: 8/20/19

YEAR	TM/L	G	AB	R	H	2B	3B	HR	RBI	BB	SO	AVG	OBP	SLG	PRO+	BR/A	SB	CS	SBR	FA	FR	G/POS	TPR
1919	Phi-A	9	22	3	3	1	0	0	0	3	7	.136	.269	.182	27	-2	0			.889	-2	/O-6	-0.5

BOB ALLEN
Allen, Robert Gilman b: 7/10/1867, Marion, Ohio d: 5/14/43, Little Rock, Ark. BR/TR, 5'11", 175 lbs. Deb: 4/19/1890 M

YEAR	TM/L	G	AB	R	H	2B	3B	HR	RBI	BB	SO	AVG	OBP	SLG	PRO+	BR/A	SB	CS	SBR	FA	FR	G/POS	TPR
1890	Phi-N	133	456	69	103	15	11	2	57	87	54	.226	.356	.320	95	-5	13			.924	**39**	*S-133/M	4.0
1891	Phi-N	118	438	46	97	7	4	1	51	43	44	.221	.291	.263	60	-22	12			.896	13	*S-118	-0.2
1892	Phi-N	152	563	77	128	20	14	2	64	61	60	.227	.304	.323	90	-7	15			.919	18	*S-152	1.6
1893	Phi-N	124	471	86	126	19	12	8	90	71	40	.268	.369	.410	107	5	8			.919	18	*S-124	2.4
1894	Phi-N	40	149	26	38	10	3	0	19	17	11	.255	.335	.362	70	-7	4			.915	-2	S-40	-0.6
1897	Bos-N	34	119	33	38	5	0	1	24	18		.319	.408	.387	104	1	1			.924	8	S-32/O-1,2	0.8
1900	Cin-N	5	15	0	2	1	0	0	1	0		.133	.188	.200	7	-2	0			.864	-0	/S-5,M	-0.2
Total	7	606	2211	337	532	77	44	14	306	297	209	.241	.334	.334	88	-32	53			.915	93	S-604/2-1,O	7.8

ROD ALLEN
Allen, Roderick Bernet b: 10/5/59, Los Angeles, Cal. BR/TR, 6'1", 185 lbs. Deb: 4/7/83

YEAR	TM/L	G	AB	R	H	2B	3B	HR	RBI	BB	SO	AVG	OBP	SLG	PRO+	BR/A	SB	CS	SBR	FA	FR	G/POS	TPR
1983	Sea-A	11	12	1	2	0	0	0	0	0	1	.167	.167	.167	-8	-2	0	0	0	1.000	0	/O-2,D-3	-0.2
1984	Det-A	15	27	6	8	1	0	0	3	2	8	.296	.367	.333	96	-0	1	0	0	1.000	-0	D-11/O-2	0.0
1988	Cle-A	5	11	1	1	1	0	0	0	0	2	.091	.091	.182	-25	-2	0	0	0	.000	0	/D-4	-0.2
Total	3	31	50	8	11	2	0	0	3	2	11	.220	.264	.260	45	-4	1	0	0	1.000	-0	/D-18,O-4	-0.4

RON ALLEN
Allen, Ronald Frederick b: 12/23/43, Wampum, Pa. BB/TR, 6'3", 205 lbs. Deb: 8/11/72 F

YEAR	TM/L	G	AB	R	H	2B	3B	HR	RBI	BB	SO	AVG	OBP	SLG	PRO+	BR/A	SB	CS	SBR	FA	FR	G/POS	TPR
1972	StL-N	7	11	2	1	0	0	1	1	3	5	.091	.286	.364	84	-0	0	0	0	.968	-0	/1-5	-0.1

GARY ALLENSON
Allenson, Gary Martin b: 2/4/55, Culver City, Cal. BR/TR, 5'11", 185 lbs. Deb: 4/8/79 C

YEAR	TM/L	G	AB	R	H	2B	3B	HR	RBI	BB	SO	AVG	OBP	SLG	PRO+	BR/A	SB	CS	SBR	FA	FR	G/POS	TPR
1979	Bos-A	108	241	27	49	10	2	3	22	20	42	.203	.267	.299	50	-17	1	1	-0	.980	9	*C-104/3-3	-0.6
1980	Bos-A	36	70	9	25	6	0	0	10	13	11	.357	.458	.443	141	5	2	2	-1	.981	4	C-24/3-5,D	0.9
1981	Bos-A	47	139	23	31	8	0	5	25	23	33	.223	.337	.388	102	1	0	0	0	.969	1	C-47	0.3
1982	Bos-A	92	264	25	54	11	0	6	33	38	39	.205	.307	.314	67	-11	0	3	-2	.992	8	C-91	-0.2
1983	Bos-A	84	230	19	53	11	0	3	30	27	43	.230	.317	.317	70	-9	0	1	-1	.984	4	C-84	-0.2
1984	Bos-A	35	83	9	19	2	0	2	8	9	14	.229	.304	.325	71	-3	0	0	0	.987	0	C-35	-0.2
1985	Tor-A	14	34	2	4	1	0	0	3	0	10	.118	.118	.147	-27	-6	0	0	0	1.000	-2	C-14	-0.7
Total	7	416	1061	114	235	49	2	19	131	130	192	.221	.309	.325	71	-41	3	7	-3	.984	25	C-399/3-8,D	-0.7

GENE ALLEY
Alley, Leonard Eugene b: 7/10/40, Richmond, Va. BR/TR, 6', 165 lbs. Deb: 9/4/63

YEAR	TM/L	G	AB	R	H	2B	3B	HR	RBI	BB	SO	AVG	OBP	SLG	PRO+	BR/A	SB	CS	SBR	FA	FR	G/POS	TPR
1963	Pit-N	17	51	3	11	1	0	0	0	2	12	.216	.245	.235	39	-4	0	1	-1	.947	1	/3-7,2-4,S	-0.3
1964	Pit-N	81	209	30	44	3	1	6	13	21	56	.211	.289	.321	72	-8	0	1	-1	.966	24	S-61/3-3,2	2.0
1965	Pit-N	153	500	47	126	21	6	5	47	32	82	.252	.302	.348	82	-12	7	2	1	.968	**30**	*S-110,2-40/3	3.0
1966	Pit-N	147	579	88	173	28	10	3	43	27	83	.299	.336	.418	108	6	8	8	-2	.979	13	*S-143	3.1
1967	Pit-N★	152	550	59	158	25	7	6	55	36	70	.287	.339	.391	108	6	10	5	0	.967	8	*S-146	3.0
1968	Pit-N†	133	474	48	116	20	2	4	39	39	78	.245	.309	.321	91	-5	13	5	1	.974	26	*S-109,2-24	3.8
1969	Pit-N	82	285	28	70	3	2	8	32	19	48	.246	.295	.354	83	-7	4	0	1	.977	7	2-53,S-25/3	0.8
1970	*Pit-N	121	426	46	104	16	5	8	41	31	70	.244	.300	.362	78	-14	7	3	0	.975	34	*S-108/2-8,3	3.2
1971	*Pit-N	114	348	38	79	8	7	6	28	35	63	.227	.298	.342	81	-9	9	2	2	.958	-16	*S-108/3-1	-1.1
1972	*Pit-N	119	347	30	86	12	2	3	36	38	52	.248	.322	.320	85	-6	3	4	-1	.970	-5	*S-114/3-4	0.3
1973	Pit-N	76	158	25	32	3	2	2	8	20	28	.203	.292	.285	62	-8	1	0	0	.981	5	S-49/3-8	0.2
Total	11	1195	3927	442	999	140	44	55	342	300	622	.254	.312	.354	88	-62	63	30	1	.970	125	S-977,2-130/3	18.0

GAIR ALLIE
Allie, Gair Roosevelt b: 10/28/31, Statesville, N.C. BR/TR, 6'1", 190 lbs. Deb: 4/13/54

YEAR	TM/L	G	AB	R	H	2B	3B	HR	RBI	BB	SO	AVG	OBP	SLG	PRO+	BR/A	SB	CS	SBR	FA	FR	G/POS	TPR
1954	Pit-N	121	418	38	83	8	6	3	30	56	84	.199	.296	.268	49	-31	1	1	-0	.952	-16	S-95,3-19	-4.0

BOB ALLIETTA
Allietta, Robert George b: 5/1/52, New Bedford, Mass. BR/TR, 6', 190 lbs. Deb: 5/6/75

YEAR	TM/L	G	AB	R	H	2B	3B	HR	RBI	BB	SO	AVG	OBP	SLG	PRO+	BR/A	SB	CS	SBR	FA	FR	G/POS	TPR
1975	Cal-A	21	45	4	8	1	0	1	2	1	6	.178	.196	.267	32	-4	0	0	0	1.000	2	C-21	-0.2

ANDY ALLISON
Allison, Andrew K. b: 1848, New York, N.Y. 5'10", 150 lbs. Deb: 5/7/1872

YEAR	TM/L	G	AB	R	H	2B	3B	HR	RBI	BB	SO	AVG	OBP	SLG	PRO+	BR/A	SB	CS	SBR	FA	FR	G/POS	TPR
1872	Eck-n	24	99	15	15	2	0	0	7	0	3	.152	.152	.172	-1	-10						1-23/O-2	-0.6

ART ALLISON
Allison, Arthur Algernon b: 1/29/1849, Philadelphia, Pa. d: 2/25/16, Washington, D.C. 5'8", 150 lbs. Deb: 5/4/1871 F

YEAR	TM/L	G	AB	R	H	2B	3B	HR	RBI	BB	SO	AVG	OBP	SLG	PRO+	BR/A	SB	CS	SBR	FA	FR	G/POS	TPR
1871	Cle-n	29	137	28	40	4	5	0	19	2	5	.292	.302	.394	104	1	3					*O-29	0.2
1872	Cle-n	19	85	13	23	6	0	0	8	0	2	.271	.271	.341	92	-0						O-18	0.0
1873	Res-n	23	99	12	32	5	0	0	11	0		.323	.323	.374	113	2						O-21/1-3,C	0.2
1875	Was-n	26	110	18	24	3	1	0			1	.218	.225	.264	71	-3						1-24/O-2,C	-0.3
	Har-n	40	173	26	41	6	0	1			1	.237	.237	.289	77	-4						O-34/2-1	-0.3
	Yr	66	283	44	65	9	1	1			1	.230	.232	.279	75	-7						O-36,1-24/C2	-0.7
1876	Lou-N	31	130	9	27	4	0	1	10	2	6	.208	.220	.238	45	-9				.789	6	O-23/1-8	-0.3
Total	4 n	137	604	97	160	24	6	1	38	3	7	.265	.269	.329	90	-4						O-104/1-27,C2	-0.3

DOUG ALLISON
Allison, Douglas L. b: 7/1845, Philadelphia, Pa. d: 12/19/16, Washington, D.C. BR/TR, 5'10.5", 160 lbs. Deb: 5/5/1871 F

YEAR	TM/L	G	AB	R	H	2B	3B	HR	RBI	BB	SO	AVG	OBP	SLG	PRO+	BR/A	SB	CS	SBR	FA	FR	G/POS	TPR
1871	Oly-n	27	133	28	44	10	2	2	27	0	2	.331	.331	.481	137	7	1					*C-27	0.4
1872	Tro-n	23	118	23	34	5	2	0	20	1	0	.288	.294	.364	100	1						C-22/S-1	-0.1
	Eck-n	18	79	18	27	1	0	0	6	1	2	.342	.350	.392	151	6						C-18	0.4
	Yr	41	197	41	61	7	3	0	26	2	5	.310	.317	.376	119	5						C-40/S-1	0.3
1873	Res-n	18	84	11	24	2	0	0	8	0		.286	.286	.345	92	-0						C-18/O-3	0.0
	Mut-n	11	49	6	11	3	1	0	3	1	0	.224	.240	.245	43	-3						C-11/O-1	-0.2
	Yr	29	133	17	35	6	2	0			0	.263	.269	.308	73	-4						C-29/O-4	-0.2
1874	Mut-n	65	316	69	88	8	5	0			6	.278	.292	.335	96	-2						*O-41,C-24	0.0
1875	Har-n	61	267	38	67	7	0	0			7	.251	.270	.277	85	-5						*C-59/1-3	-0.2
1876	Har-N	44	163	19	43	4	0	0	15	3	9	.264	.277	.288	82	-4				.881	11	C-40/O-6	0.7
1877	Har-N	29	115	14	17	2	0	0	6	3	7	.148	.169	.165	7	-11				.896	2	C-29	-0.8

YEAR	TM/L	G	AB	R	H	2B	3B	HR	RBI	BB	SO	AVG	OBP	SLG	PRO+	BR/A	SB	CS	SBR	FA	FR	G/POS	TPR
1878	Pro-N	19	76	9	22	2	0	0	7	1	8	.289	.299	.316	102	0				.911	-0	C-19/P-1	0.0
1879	Pro-N	1	5	0	0	0	0	0	0	0	1	.000	.000	.000	-99	-1				.833	0	/C-1	-0.1
1883	Bal-a	1	3	2	2	0	0	0		0		.667	.667	.667	321	1				.000	-1	/O-1,C-1	0.3
Total	5 n	223	1046	193	295	38	10	2	64	16	7	.282	.293	.343	100	2						C-179/O-45,1S	0.3
Total	5	94	362	44	84	8	0	0	28	7	25	.232	.247	.254	63	-15				.892	12	/C-90,O-7,P	-0.2

■ MILO ALLISON
Allison, Milo Henry b: 10/16/1890, Elk Rapids, Mich. d: 6/18/57, Kenosha, Wis. BL/TR, 6', 163 lbs. Deb: 9/26/13

YEAR	TM/L	G	AB	R	H	2B	3B	HR	RBI	BB	SO	AVG	OBP	SLG	PRO+	BR/A	SB	CS	SBR	FA	FR	G/POS	TPR
1913	Chi-N	2	6	1	2	0	0	0	0	0	1	.333	.333	.333	90	-0	1			1.000	0	/O-1	0.0
1914	Chi-N	1	1	0	1	0	0	0	0	0	0	1.000	1.000	1.000	497	0	0			.000	0	H	0.0
1916	Cle-A	14	18	10	5	0	0	0	0	6	1	.278	.458	.278	115	1	0			1.000	-1	/O-5	0.0
1917	Cle-A	32	35	4	5	0	0	0	0	9	7	.143	.318	.143	38	-2	3			1.000	-3	O-11	-0.6
Total	4	49	60	15	13	0	0	0	0	15	9	.217	.373	.217	74	-1	4			1.000	-4	/O-17	-0.6

■ BILL ALLISON
Allison, William Andrew b: 9/18/1848, Philadelphia, Pa. d: 6/12/23, Deb: 5/21/1872

YEAR	TM/L	G	AB	R	H	2B	3B	HR	RBI	BB	SO	AVG	OBP	SLG	PRO+	BR/A	SB	CS	SBR	FA	FR	G/POS	TPR
1872	Eck-n	3	10	3	2	0	0	0	1	0	1	.200	.200	.200	28	-1						/O-2,2-1	0.0

■ BOB ALLISON
Allison, William Robert b: 7/11/34, Raytown, Mo. BR/TR, 6'4", 220 lbs. Deb: 9/16/58

YEAR	TM/L	G	AB	R	H	2B	3B	HR	RBI	BB	SO	AVG	OBP	SLG	PRO+	BR/A	SB	CS	SBR	FA	FR	G/POS	TPR
1958	Was-A	11	35	1	7	1	0	0	2	5		.200	.243	.229	31	-3	0	2	-1	1.000	-0	O-11	-0.5
1959	Was-A☆	150	570	83	149	18	9	30	85	60	92	.261	.334	.482	122	15	13	8	-1	.974	-2	*O-149	0.5
1960	Was-A	144	501	79	126	30	3	15	69	92	94	.251	.370	.413	113	11	11	9	-2	.965	9	*O-140/1-4	1.1
1961	Min-A	159	556	83	136	21	3	29	105	103	100	.245	.367	.450	111	10	2	7	-4	.975	7	*O-150,1-18	0.4
1962	Min-A	149	519	102	138	24	8	29	102	84	115	.266	.372	.511	130	22	8	5	-1	.977	7	*O-147	2.1
1963	Min-A★	148	527	99	143	25	4	35	91	90	109	.271	.381	.533	150	37	6	1	1	.971	11	*O-147	4.2
1964	Min-A★	149	492	90	141	27	4	32	86	92	99	.287	.406	.553	163	44	10	1	2	.986	-4	1-93,O-61	3.8
1965	*Min-A	135	438	71	102	14	5	23	78	73	114	.233	.345	.445	118	11	10	2	2	.972	11	*O-122/1-3	1.9
1966	Min-A	70	168	34	37	6	1	8	19	30	34	.220	.348	.411	110	3	6	0	2	.967	-1	O-56	0.2
1967	Min-A	153	496	73	128	21	6	24	75	74	114	.258	.357	.470	132	20	4	-1		.978	-4	*O-145	1.3
1968	Min-A	145	469	63	116	16	8	22	52	52	98	.247	.325	.456	128	15	9	7	-2	.966	-4	*O-117,1-17	0.4
1969	*Min-A	81	189	18	43	8	2	8	27	19	39	.228	.333	.418	107	2	2	4	-2	1.000	-3	O-58/1-3	-0.6
1970	*Min-A	47	72	15	15	5	0	1	7	14	20	.208	.345	.319	83	-1	1	0	0	1.000	-3	O-17/1-7	-0.5
Total	13	1541	5032	811	1281	216	53	256	796	795	1033	.255	.360	.471	126	186	84	50	-5	.975	27	*O-1320,1-145	14.3

■ BEAU ALLRED
Allred, Dale Le Beau b: 6/4/65, Mesa, Ariz. BL/TL, 6', 190 lbs. Deb: 9/7/89

YEAR	TM/L	G	AB	R	H	2B	3B	HR	RBI	BB	SO	AVG	OBP	SLG	PRO+	BR/A	SB	CS	SBR	FA	FR	G/POS	TPR
1989	Cle-A	13	24	0	6	3	0	0	1	2	10	.250	.308	.375	90	-0	0	0	0	1.000	1	/O-5,D-2	0.1
1990	Cle-A	4	16	2	3	1	0	1	2	3	2	.188	.278	.438	98	-0	0	0	0	.833	-1	/O-4	-0.1
1991	Cle-A	48	125	17	29	3	0	3	12	25	35	.232	.364	.328	92	-0	2	2	-1	.972	2	O-42/D-1	0.0
Total	3	65	165	19	38	7	0	4	15	29	48	.230	.349	.345	93	-1	2	2	-1	.969	2	/O-51,D-3	0.0

■ MEL ALMADA
Almada, Baldomero Melo b: 2/7/13, Hwatabampo, Mexico d: 8/13/88, Hermosillo, Mexico BL/TL, 6', 170 lbs. Deb: 9/8/33

YEAR	TM/L	G	AB	R	H	2B	3B	HR	RBI	BB	SO	AVG	OBP	SLG	PRO+	BR/A	SB	CS	SBR	FA	FR	G/POS	TPR
1933	Bos-A	14	44	11	15	0	0	1	3	11	3	.341	.473	.409	137	3	3	1	0	1.000	-0	O-13	0.2
1934	Bos-A	23	90	7	21	2	1	0	10	6	8	.233	.281	.278	42	-8	3	2	-0	.985	4	O-23	-0.5
1935	Bos-A	151	607	85	176	27	9	3	59	55	34	.290	.350	.379	83	-15	20	9	1	.968	-2	*O-149/1-3	-2.0
1936	Bos-A	96	320	40	81	16	4	1	21	24	15	.253	.305	.338	55	-23	2	4	-2	.987	-2	O-81	-2.7
1937	Bos-A	32	110	17	26	6	2	1	9	15	6	.236	.328	.355	69	-5	0	1	-1	.927	-6	O-27/1-4	-1.2
	Was-A	100	433	74	134	21	4	0	33	38	21	.309	.365	.404	98	-1	12	4	1	.964	14	*O-100	1.0
	Yr	132	543	91	160	27	6	1	42	53	27	.295	.357	.394	91	-7	12	5	1	.960	2	*O-127/1-4	-0.2
1938	Was-A	47	197	24	48	7	4	1	15	8	16	.244	.277	.335	56	-14	4	1	1	.968	5	O-47	-0.9
	StL-A	102	436	77	149	22	2	3	37	38	22	.342	.398	.422	106	5	9	5	-0	.966	-1	*O-101	0.1
	Yr	149	633	101	197	29	6	4	52	46	38	.311	.362	.395	92	-8	13	6	1	.967	4	*O-148	-0.8
1939	StL-A	42	134	17	32	2	1	1	7	10	8	.239	.292	.291	48	-10	1	0	0	.987	-3	O-34	-1.3
	Bro-N	39	112	11	24	4	0	0	3	9	17	.214	.273	.250	40	-9	2			.977	2	O-32	-0.9
Total	7	646	2483	363	706	107	27	15	197	214	150	.284	.342	.367	79	-78	56	27		.970	13	O-607/1-7	-8.2

■ RAFAEL ALMEIDA
Almeida, Rafael D. "Mike" b: 7/30/1887, Havana, Cuba d: 3/68, Havana, Cuba BR/TR, 5'9", 164 lbs. Deb: 7/4/11

YEAR	TM/L	G	AB	R	H	2B	3B	HR	RBI	BB	SO	AVG	OBP	SLG	PRO+	BR/A	SB	CS	SBR	FA	FR	G/POS	TPR
1911	Cin-N	36	96	9	30	5	1	0	15	9	16	.313	.383	.385	120	3	3			.890	-2	3-27/2-1,S	0.1
1912	Cin-N	16	59	9	13	4	3	0	10	5	8	.220	.281	.390	85	-2	0			.891	-2	3-15	-0.3
1913	Cin-N	50	130	14	34	4	2	3	21	11	16	.262	.324	.392	104	0	4			.919	4	3-37/O-3,S2	0.5
Total	3	102	285	32	77	13	6	3	46	25	40	.270	.335	.389	106	2				.904	0	/3-79,O-3,S2	0.3

■ BILL ALMON
Almon, William Francis b: 11/21/52, Providence, R.I. BR/TR, 6'3", 190 lbs. Deb: 9/2/74

YEAR	TM/L	G	AB	R	H	2B	3B	HR	RBI	BB	SO	AVG	OBP	SLG	PRO+	BR/A	SB	CS	SBR	FA	FR	G/POS	TPR
1974	SD-N	16	38	4	12	1	0	0	3	2	9	.316	.350	.342	98	-0	1	0	0	.915	-2	S-14	0.0
1975	SD-N	6	10	0	4	0	0	0	0	0	1	.400	.400	.400	131	0	0	0	0	1.000	1	/S-2	0.1
1976	SD-N	14	57	6	14	3	0	1	6	2	9	.246	.271	.351	82	-2	3	1	0	.962	1	S-14	0.2
1977	SD-N	155	613	75	160	18	11	2	43	37	114	.261	.303	.336	79	-20	20	9	1	.954	18	*S-155	1.6
1978	SD-N	138	405	39	102	19	2	0	21	33	74	.252	.308	.309	79	-12	17	5	2	.933	4	*3-114,S-15/2	-1.1
1979	SD-N	100	198	20	45	3	0	1	8	21	48	.227	.301	.258	57	-11	6	5	-1	.985	16	2-61,S-25/O	0.8
1980	Mon-N	18	38	2	10	1	1	0	3	1	5	.263	.282	.342	73	-1	0	0	0	.911	-2	S-12/2-1	-0.3
	NY-N	48	112	13	19	3	0	2	4	8	27	.170	.225	.232	29	-11	2	0	1	.967	9	S-22,2-18/3	0.1
	Yr	66	150	15	29	4	3	2	7	9	32	.193	.239	.260	40	-12	2	0	1	.948	6	S-34,2-19/3	-0.2
1981	Chi-A	103	349	46	105	10	2	4	41	21	60	.301	.344	.375	109	4	16	6	1	.969	14	*S-103	3.1
1982	Chi-A	111	308	40	79	10	4	4	26	25	49	.256	.314	.354	83	-7	10	8	-2	.949	20	S-108/D-1	1.9
1983	Oak-A	143	451	45	120	29	1	4	63	26	67	.266	.309	.361	89	-7	26	8	3	.941	-31	S-52,3-40,10/2D	-3.5
1984	Oak-A	106	211	24	47	11	0	7	16	10	42	.223	.258	.374	78	-7	5	7	-3	1.000	-9	O-48,1-44,D/3CS	-2.2
1985	Pit-N	88	244	33	66	17	0	6	29	22	61	.270	.333	.414	109	3	10	7	-1	.987	-22	S-43,O-32/13	-1.9
1986	Pit-N	102	196	29	43	7	2	7	27	30	38	.219	.323	.383	92	-2	11	4	3	.983	-13	O-54,3-28,S/1	-1.5
1987	Pit-N	19	20	5	4	1	0	0	1	1	5	.200	.238	.250	29	-2	0	0	0	.944	1	/S-4,O-2,3	-0.1
	NY-N	49	54	8	13	3	0	0	4	8	16	.241	.339	.296	74	-2	0	0	0	.972	-3	S-22,2-10/1O	-0.4
	Yr	68	74	13	17	4	0	0	5	9	21	.230	.313	.284	62	-4	0	0	0	.963	-2	S-26,2-10/013	-0.5
1988	Phi-N	20	26	1	3	2	0	0	1	3	11	.115	.207	.192	15	-3	0	0	0	.944	1	/3-9,S-5,1	-0.2
Total	15	1236	3330	390	846	138	25	36	296	250	636	.254	.307	.343	83	-81	128	60	2	.956	-2	S-616,3-212,O2/1DC	-3.4

■ ROBERTO ALOMAR
Alomar, Roberto (Velazquez) b: 2/5/68, Ponce, P.R. BB/TR, 6', 184 lbs. Deb: 4/22/88 F

YEAR	TM/L	G	AB	R	H	2B	3B	HR	RBI	BB	SO	AVG	OBP	SLG	PRO+	BR/A	SB	CS	SBR	FA	FR	G/POS	TPR
1988	SD-N	143	545	84	145	24	6	9	41	47	83	.266	.328	.382	105	3	24	6	4	.980	17	*2-143	3.1
1989	SD-N	158	623	82	184	27	1	7	56	53	76	.295	.352	.376	108	7	42	17	2	.967	6	*2-157	2.1
1990	SD-N★	147	586	80	168	27	5	6	60	48	72	.287	.343	.381	98	-1	24	7	3	.976	6	*2-137/S-5	0.4
1991	*Tor-A★	161	637	88	188	41	11	9	69	57	86	.295	.357	.436	114	12	53	11	9	.981	-22	*2-160	1.3
1992	*Tor-A★	152	571	105	177	27	8	8	76	87	52	.310	.406	.427	128	25	49	9	8	.993	-24	*2-150/D-1	4.0
1993	*Tor-A★	153	589	109	192	35	6	17	93	80	67	.326	.411	.492	141	36	55	15	8	.980	-6	*2-150	0.9
1994	Tor-A★	107	392	78	120	25	4	8	38	51	41	.306	.389	.452	115	10	19	8	1	.991	-4	*2-106	12.0
Total	7	1021	3943	626	1174	206	41	64	433	423	477	.298	.369	.419	116	91	266	73	36	.980	-36	2-1003/S-5,D	12.0

■ SANDY ALOMAR
Alomar, Santos Jr. (Velazquez) b: 6/18/66, Salinas, P.R. BR/TR, 6'5", 200 lbs. Deb: 9/30/88 F

YEAR	TM/L	G	AB	R	H	2B	3B	HR	RBI	BB	SO	AVG	OBP	SLG	PRO+	BR/A	SB	CS	SBR	FA	FR	G/POS	TPR
1988	SD-N	1	1	0	0	0	0	0	0	0	0	.000	.000	.000	-99	-0	0	0	0	.000	0	H	0.0
1989	SD-N	7	19	1	4	1	0	1	6	3	3	.211	.318	.421	110	0	0	0	0	1.000	-0	/C-6	0.0
1990	Cle-A★	132	445	60	129	26	2	9	66	25	46	.290	.331	.418	109	4	4	1	1	.981	-13	*C-129	0.0

YEAR	TM/L	G	AB	R	H	2B	3B	HR	RBI	BB	SO	AVG	OBP	SLG	PRO+	BR/A	SB	CS	SBR	FA	FR	G/POS	TPR
1991	Cle-A★	51	184	10	40	9	0	0	7	8	24	.217	.265	.266	47	-13	0	4	-2	.987	2	C-46/D-4	-1.1
1992	Cle-A★	89	299	22	75	16	0	2	26	13	32	.251	.293	.324	74	-11	3	3	-1	.996	-4	C-88/D-1	-1.1
1993	Cle-A	64	215	24	58	7	1	6	32	11	28	.270	.323	.395	92	-3	3	1	0	.984	-12	C-64	-1.0
1994	Cle-A	80	292	44	84	15	1	14	43	25	31	.288	.348	.490	108	3	8	4	0	.996	1	C-78	0.8
Total	7	424	1455	161	390	74	4	32	180	85	165	.268	.317	.390	92	-19	18	13	-2	.989	-26	C-411/D-5	-2.4

■ SANDY ALOMAR

Alomar, Santos Sr. (Conde) b: 10/19/43, Salinas, P.R.   BB/TR, 5'9", 155 lbs.   Deb: 9/15/64   FC

YEAR	TM/L	G	AB	R	H	2B	3B	HR	RBI	BB	SO	AVG	OBP	SLG	PRO+	BR/A	SB	CS	SBR	FA	FR	G/POS	TPR
1964	Mil-N	19	53	3	13	1	0	0	6	0	11	.245	.245	.264	43	-4	1	0	0	.967	8	S-19	0.6
1965	Mil-N	67	108	16	26	1	1	0	8	4	12	.241	.268	.269	51	-7	12	5	1	.964	14	S-39,2-19	1.0
1966	Atl-N	31	44	4	4	1	0	0	2	1	10	.091	.111	.114	-37	-8	0	0	0	.981	3	2-21/S-5	-0.4
1967	NY-N	15	22	1	0	0	0	0	0	0	6	.000	.000	.000	-99	-6	0	0	0	1.000	1	S-10/3-3,2	-0.3
	Chi-A	12	15	4	3	0	0	0	0	2	0	.200	.294	.200	50	-1	2	0	1	.952	2	/S-8,2-2	0.2
1968	Chi-A	133	363	41	92	8	2	0	12	20	42	.253	.294	.287	76	-11	21	8	2	.958	-16	2-99,3-27/SO	-2.2
1969	Chi-A	22	58	8	13	2	0	0	4	4	6	.224	.274	.259	47	-4	2	0	1	.980	3	2-22	0.1
	Cal-A	134	559	60	140	10	2	1	30	36	48	.250	.296	.281	65	-26	18	3	4	.969	-10	*2-134	-2.2
	Yr	156	617	68	153	12	2	1	34	40	54	.248	.294	.279	63	-31	20	3	4	.970	-7	*2-156	-2.1
1970	Cal-A★	162	672	82	169	18	2	3	36	49	65	.251	.303	.293	68	-30	35	12	3	.979	9	*2-153,S-10/3	-0.3
1971	Cal-A	162	689	77	179	24	3	4	42	41	60	.260	.301	.321	82	-18	39	10	6	.989	21	*2-137,S-28	2.6
1972	Cal-A	155	610	65	146	20	3	1	25	47	55	.239	.294	.287	78	-17	20	12	-1	.977	-3	*2-154/S-4	-0.7
1973	Cal-A	136	470	45	112	7	1	0	28	34	44	.238	.290	.257	60	-25	25	10	2	.979	-8	*2-110,S-31	-2.2
1974	Cal-A	46	54	12	12	0	0	1	2	8	2	.222	.250	.259	49	-4	2	0	1	.977	9	S-19,2-15/3OD	0.7
	NY-A	76	279	35	75	8	1	0	27	14	25	.269	.304	.308	79	-8	6	4	-1	.977	-12	2-76	-1.8
	Yr	122	333	47	87	8	1	1	28	16	33	.261	.295	.300	74	-11	8	4	0	.976	-3	2-91,S-19/3OD	-1.1
1975	NY-A	151	489	61	117	18	4	2	39	26	58	.239	.286	.305	66	-22	28	6	5	**.985**	-12	*2-150/S-1	-2.3
1976	*NY-A	67	163	20	39	4	0	1	10	13	12	.239	.295	.282	70	-6	12	7	-1	.970	-5	2-38/S-6,310	-1.0
1977	Tex-A	69	83	21	22	3	0	1	11	8	13	.265	.337	.337	84	-2	4	3	-1	.973	13	D-26,2-18/SO13	1.0
1978	Tex-A	24	29	3	6	1	0	0	1	1	7	.207	.233	.241	34	-3	0	0	0	.975	5	/1-9,2-6,3SD	0.3
Total	15	1481	4760	558	1168	126	19	13	282	302	482	.245	.291	.288	68	-200	227	80	20	.977	31	*2-1156,S-197/3D10	-6.9

■ FELIPE ALOU

Alou, Felipe Rojas (b: Felipe Rojas (Alou))   b: 5/12/35, Haina, D.R.   BR/TR, 6', 195 lbs.   Deb: 6/8/58   FMC

YEAR	TM/L	G	AB	R	H	2B	3B	HR	RBI	BB	SO	AVG	OBP	SLG	PRO+	BR/A	SB	CS	SBR	FA	FR	G/POS	TPR
1958	SF-N	75	182	21	46	9	2	4	16	19	34	.253	.327	.390	91	-2	4	2	0	.985	-3	O-70	-0.8
1959	SF-N	95	247	38	68	13	2	10	33	17	38	.275	.322	.466	109	2	5	3	-0	.974	-6	O-69	-0.7
1960	SF-N	106	322	48	85	17	3	8	44	16	42	.264	.303	.410	99	-2	10	2	2	.958	-4	O-95	-0.8
1961	SF-N	132	415	59	120	19	0	18	52	26	41	.289	.334	.465	113	7	11	4	1	.990	-4	*O-122	-0.2
1962	*SF-N★	154	561	96	177	30	3	25	98	33	66	.316	.359	.513	133	24	10	7	-1	.971	-2	*O-150	1.3
1963	SF-N	157	565	75	159	31	9	20	82	27	87	.281	.321	.474	127	18	11	2	2	.986	0	*O-153	1.3
1964	Mil-N	121	415	60	105	26	3	9	51	30	41	.253	.310	.395	96	-2	5	2	0	.975	-1	O-92,1-18	-0.9
1965	Mil-N	143	555	80	165	29	2	23	78	31	63	.297	.340	.481	128	19	8	4	0	.980	-1	O-91,1-69/3S	0.8
1966	Atl-N☆	154	666	**122**	**218**	32	6	31	74	24	51	.327	.362	.533	143	36	5	7	-3	.988	1	1-90,O-79/3S	2.7
1967	Atl-N	140	574	76	157	26	3	15	43	32	50	.274	.320	.408	108	5	6	5	-1	.993	-11	1-85,O-56	-1.7
1968	Atl-N★	160	662	72	**210**	37	5	11	57	48	56	.317	.367	.438	140	32	12	11	-3	.980	8	*O-158	3.2
1969	*Atl-N	123	476	54	134	13	1	5	32	23	23	.282	.320	.345	86	-9	4	2	0	.989	3	*O-116	-1.6
1970	Oak-A	154	575	70	156	25	3	8	55	32	31	.271	.311	.367	89	-10	10	5	0	.977	-3	*O-145/1-1	-2.1
1971	Oak-A	2	8	0	2	1	0	0	0	0	1	.250	.250	.375	77	-0	0	0	0	1.000	1	/O-2	0.0
	NY-A	131	461	52	133	20	6	8	69	32	24	.289	.337	.410	118	9	5	5	-2	.985	-12	O-80,1-42	-1.3
	Yr	133	469	52	135	21	6	8	69	32	25	.288	.336	.409	117	9	5	5	-2	.986	-11	O-82,1-42	-1.3
1972	NY-A	120	324	33	90	18	1	6	37	22	27	.278	.328	.395	118	6	1	0	0	.990	1	1-95,O-15	0.1
1973	NY-A	93	280	25	66	12	0	4	27	9	25	.236	.260	.321	65	-14	0	1	-1	.988	-1	1-67,O-22	-2.1
	Mon-N	19	48	4	10	1	0	1	4	2	4	.208	.240	.292	45	-4	0	0	0	1.000	1	O-15/1-1	-0.4
1974	Mil-A	3	3	0	0	0	0	0	0	0	2	.000	.000	.000	-99	-1	0	0	0	1.000	-1	/O-1	-0.2
Total	17	2082	7339	985	2101	359	49	206	852	423	706	.286	.330	.433	114	114	107	67	-8	.979	-37	*O-1531,1-468/3S	-3.4

■ JESUS ALOU

Alou, Jesus Maria Rojas (b: Jesus Maria Rojas (Alou))   b: 3/24/42, Haina, D.R.   BR/TR, 6'2", 195 lbs.   Deb: 9/10/63   FC

YEAR	TM/L	G	AB	R	H	2B	3B	HR	RBI	BB	SO	AVG	OBP	SLG	PRO+	BR/A	SB	CS	SBR	FA	FR	G/POS	TPR
1963	SF-N	16	24	3	6	1	0	0	5	0	3	.250	.280	.292	66	-1	0	1	-1	.875	-4	O-12	-0.6
1964	SF-N	115	376	42	103	11	4	3	28	14	35	.274	.305	.327	77	-11	6	6	-2	.973	-1	*O-108	-1.9
1965	SF-N	143	543	76	162	19	4	9	52	13	40	.298	.318	.398	98	-3	5	5	-1	.980	1	*O-136	-0.9
1966	SF-N	110	370	41	96	13	1	1	20	9	22	.259	.281	.308	62	-19	5	5	-1	.967	-5	*O-100	-3.2
1967	SF-N	129	510	55	149	15	4	5	30	14	39	.292	.316	.367	96	-3	1	7	-4	.948	-6	*O-123	-2.1
1968	SF-N	120	419	26	110	15	4	0	39	9	23	.263	.280	.317	79	-11	4	4	-0	.989	0	*O-105	-2.1
1969	Hou-N	115	452	49	112	19	4	5	34	15	30	.248	.278	.341	74	-17	4	6	-2	.928	-0	*O-112	-2.8
1970	Hou-N	117	458	59	140	27	3	1	44	21	15	.306	.338	.384	97	-3	3	2	-0	.962	-7	*O-108	-1.5
1971	Hou-N	122	433	41	121	21	4	2	40	13	17	.279	.307	.360	91	-6	3	7	-3	.983	6	*O-109	-0.9
1972	Hou-N	52	93	8	29	4	1	0	11	7	5	.312	.366	.376	114	2	0	2	-1	.970	-3	O-23	-0.3
1973	Hou-N	28	55	7	13	2	0	1	8	1	6	.236	.276	.327	67	-2	0	0	0	.941	-3	O-14	-0.6
	*Oak-A	36	108	10	33	4	0	1	11	2	6	.306	.318	.361	96	-1	0	0	0	1.000	-0	O-21/D-6	-0.2
1974	*Oak-A	96	220	13	59	8	0	2	15	5	9	.268	.291	.332	84	-5	0	0	0	1.000	-1	D-41,O-25	-0.8
1975	NY-N	62	102	8	27	3	0	0	11	4	5	.265	.299	.294	68	-5	0	1	-1	.963	-1	O-20	-0.7
1978	Hou-N	77	139	7	45	5	1	2	19	6	6	.324	.352	.417	123	4	0	0	0	.976	-2	O-28	0.1
1979	Hou-N	42	43	3	11	4	0	0	10	6	12	.256	.347	.349	96	-0	0	1	-1	1.000	-1	/O-6,1-1	-0.1
Total	15	1380	4345	448	1216	170	26	32	377	138	267	.280	.307	.353	87	-83	31	46	-18	.968	-26	*O-1050/D-47,1	-18.6

■ MATTY ALOU

Alou, Mateo Rojas (b: Mateo Rojas (Alou))   b: 12/22/38, Haina, D.R.   BL/TL, 5'9", 160 lbs.   Deb: 9/26/60   F

YEAR	TM/L	G	AB	R	H	2B	3B	HR	RBI	BB	SO	AVG	OBP	SLG	PRO+	BR/A	SB	CS	SBR	FA	FR	G/POS	TPR
1960	SF-N	4	3	1	1	0	0	0	0	0	0	.333	.333	.333	88	-0	0	0	0	1.000	-0	/O-1	0.0
1961	SF-N	81	200	38	62	7	2	6	24	15	18	.310	.358	.455	118	5	3	2	-0	.978	-4	O-58	-0.2
1962	*SF-N	78	195	28	57	8	1	3	14	14	17	.292	.349	.390	100	0	3	1	0	.976	-6	O-57	-0.8
1963	SF-N	63	76	4	11	1	0	0	2	3	13	.145	.177	.158	-3	-10	0	0	0	.952	-3	O-20	-1.6
1964	SF-N	110	250	28	66	4	2	1	14	11	25	.264	.303	.308	71	-9	5	3	-0	.976	-9	O-80	-2.2
1965	SF-N	117	324	37	75	12	2	2	18	17	28	.231	.274	.299	60	-17	10	2	3	.986	4	*O-103/P-1	-1.6
1966	Pit-N	141	535	86	183	18	9	2	27	24	44	**.342**	.375	.421	121	15	23	15	-2	.972	-1	*O-136	0.6
1967	Pit-N	139	550	87	186	21	7	2	28	24	42	.338	.372	.413	124	17	16	10	-1	.989	-3	*O-134/1-1	0.7
1968	Pit-N★	146	558	59	185	28	4	0	52	27	26	.332	.365	.396	130	20	18	10	-1	.984	-0	*O-144	1.1
1969	Pit-N★	162	698	105	**231**	**41**	6	1	48	42	35	.331	.371	.411	121	19	24	11	1	.977	5	*O-162	1.7
1970	*Pit-N	155	677	97	201	21	8	1	47	30	18	.297	.331	.356	86	-14	19	11	-1	.975	-5	*O-153	-1.8
1971	StL-N	149	609	85	192	28	6	7	74	34	27	.315	.355	.415	113	10	19	10	-0	.981	-0	O-94,1-57	-0.1
1972	StL-N	108	404	46	127	17	2	3	31	24	23	.314	.354	.389	112	6	11	4	1	.988	-2	1-66,O-39	-0.2
	*Oak-A	32	121	11	34	5	0	1	16	11	12	.281	.346	.347	112	2	2	1	0	1.000	-2	O-32/1-1	-0.2
1973	NY-A	123	497	59	147	22	1	2	28	30	43	.296	.340	.356	100	-0	5	2	0	.974	-4	O-85,1-40/D	-1.1
	StL-N	11	11	1	3	0	0	0	1	0	1	.273	.333	.273	70	-0	0	1	-1	1.000	-0	/O-1,1-1	0.0
1974	SD-N	48	81	8	16	3	0	0	3	5	6	.198	.244	.222	36	-7	0	0	0	.947	-2	O-13/1-2	-0.7
Total	15	1667	5789	780	1777	236	50	31	427	311	377	.307	.346	.381	105	35	156	80	-1	.979	-23	*O-1312,1-168/DP	-6.7

■ MOISES ALOU

Alou, Moises Rojas (b: Moises Rojas)   b: 7/3/66, Atlanta, Ga.   BR/TR, 6'3", 185 lbs.   Deb: 7/26/90   F

YEAR	TM/L	G	AB	R	H	2B	3B	HR	RBI	BB	SO	AVG	OBP	SLG	PRO+	BR/A	SB	CS	SBR	FA	FR	G/POS	TPR
1990	Pit-N	2	5	0	1	0	0	0	0	0	0	.200	.200	.200	11	-1	0	0	0	1.000	-0	/O-2	-0.1
	Mon-N	14	15	4	3	0	1	0	0	0	3	.200	.200	.333	46	-1	0	0	0	1.000	-0	/O-5	-0.1

YEAR	TM/L	G	AB	R	H	2B	3B	HR	RBI	BB	SO	AVG	OBP	SLG	PRO+	BR/A	SB	CS	SBR	FA	FR	G/POS	TPR
	Yr	16	20	4	4	0	1	0	0	0	3	.200	.200	.300	37	-2	0	0	0	1.000	-0	/O-7	-0.2
1992	Mon-N	115	341	53	96	28	2	9	56	25	46	.282	.332	.455	122	9	16	2	4	.978	-3	*O-100	0.8
1993	Mon-N	136	482	70	138	29	6	18	85	38	53	.286	.345	.483	114	9	17	6	2	.985	-1	*O-136	0.7
1994	Mon-N★	107	422	81	143	31	5	22	78	42	63	.339	.401	.592	152	32	7	6	-2	.986	4	*O-106	3.1
Total	4	374	1265	208	381	88	14	49	219	105	165	.301	.358	.509	128	47	40	14	4	.984	-0	O-349	4.4

■ WHITEY ALPERMAN
Alperman, Charles Augustus b: 11/11/1879, Etna, Pa. d: 12/25/42, Pittsburgh, Pa. BR/TR, 5'10", 180 lbs. Deb: 4/13/06

YEAR	TM/L	G	AB	R	H	2B	3B	HR	RBI	BB	SO	AVG	OBP	SLG	PRO+	BR/A	SB	CS	SBR	FA	FR	G/POS	TPR
1906	Bro-N	128	441	38	111	15	7	3	46	6		.252	.284	.338	102	-2	13			.940	2	*2-103,S-24/3	0.2
1907	Bro-N	141	558	44	130	23	16	2	39	13		.233	.266	.342	98	-5	5			.953	14	*2-115,3-14,S	0.9
1908	Bro-N	70	213	17	42	3	1	1	15	9		.197	.253	.235	58	-10	2			.934	-5	2-42/3-9,OS	-1.8
1909	Bro-N	111	420	35	104	19	12	1	41	2		.248	.262	.357	95	-6	7			.931	9	*2-108	0.1
Total	4	450	1632	134	387	60	36	7	141	30		.237	.268	.331	93	-23	27			.941	20	2-368/S-38,3O	-0.6

■ TOM ALSTON
Alston, Thomas Edison b: 1/31/26, Greensboro, N.C. d: 12/30/93, Winston-Salem, N.C. BL/TR, 6'5", 210 lbs. Deb: 4/13/54

YEAR	TM/L	G	AB	R	H	2B	3B	HR	RBI	BB	SO	AVG	OBP	SLG	PRO+	BR/A	SB	CS	SBR	FA	FR	G/POS	TPR
1954	StL-N	66	244	28	60	14	2	4	34	24	41	.246	.319	.369	78	-8	3	5	-2	.989	10	1-65	-0.3
1955	StL-N	13	8	0	1	0	0	0	0	0	0	.125	.125	.125	-33	-2	0	0	0	1.000	0	/1-7	-0.1
1956	StL-N	3	2	0	0	0	0	0	0	0	0	.000	.000	.000	-99	-1	0	0	0	1.000	0	/1-3	-0.0
1957	StL-N	9	17	2	5	1	0	0	2	1	5	.294	.333	.353	83	-0	0	0	0	.947	-1	/1-6	-0.2
Total	4	91	271	30	66	15	2	4	36	25	46	.244	.312	.358	74	-10	3	5	-2	.987	9	/1-81	-0.6

■ WALTER ALSTON
Alston, Walter Emmons "Smokey" b: 12/1/11, Venice, Ohio d: 10/1/84, Oxford, Ohio BR/TR, 6'2", 195 lbs. Deb: 9/27/36 MH

YEAR	TM/L	G	AB	R	H	2B	3B	HR	RBI	BB	SO	AVG	OBP	SLG	PRO+	BR/A	SB	CS	SBR	FA	FR	G/POS	TPR
1936	StL-N	1	1	0	0	0	0	0	0	0	1	.000	.000	.000	-99	-0				.500	-0	/1-1	-0.1

■ DELL ALSTON
Alston, Wendell b: 9/22/52, Valhalla, N.Y. BL/TR, 6', 180 lbs. Deb: 5/17/77

YEAR	TM/L	G	AB	R	H	2B	3B	HR	RBI	BB	SO	AVG	OBP	SLG	PRO+	BR/A	SB	CS	SBR	FA	FR	G/POS	TPR
1977	NY-A	22	40	10	13	4	0	1	4	3	4	.325	.372	.500	137	2	3	3	-1	1.000	0	D-10/O-2	0.1
1978	NY-A	3	3	0	0	0	0	0	0	0	2	.000	.000	.000	-99	-1	0	0	0	.000	0	H	-0.1
	Oak-A	58	173	17	36	2	0	1	10	10	21	.208	.251	.237	40	-14	11	10	-3	.956	-5	O-50/1-9,D	-2.5
	Yr	61	176	17	36	2	0	1	10	10	23	.205	.247	.233	38	-15	11	10	-3	.956	-5	O-50/1-9,D	-2.6
1979	Cle-A	54	62	10	18	0	2	1	12	10	10	.290	.389	.403	114	2	4	4	-1	.969	-5	O-30	-0.5
1980	Cle-A	52	54	11	12	1	2	0	9	5	7	.222	.311	.315	72	-2	2	4	-2	.947	-4	O-26/D-6	-0.8
Total	4	189	332	48	79	7	4	3	35	28	44	.238	.301	.310	71	-13	20	21	-7	.957	-14	O-108/D-19,1	-3.8

■ JESSE ALTENBURG
Altenburg, Jesse Howard b: 1/2/1893, Ashley, Mich. d: 3/12/73, Lansing, Mich. BL/TR, 5'9", 158 lbs. Deb: 9/19/16

YEAR	TM/L	G	AB	R	H	2B	3B	HR	RBI	BB	SO	AVG	OBP	SLG	PRO+	BR/A	SB	CS	SBR	FA	FR	G/POS	TPR
1916	Pit-N	8	14	2	6	1	1	0	1	0	1	.429	.467	.643	237	2	0			1.000	-2	/O-8	0.0
1917	Pit-N	11	17	1	3	0	0	0	3	0	4	.176	.176	.176	8	-2	0			1.000	-1	/O-4	-0.3
Total	2	19	31	3	9	1	1	0	3	1	5	.290	.313	.387	112	0	0			1.000	-3	/O-12	-0.3

■ DAVE ALTIZER
Altizer, David Tilden "Filipino" b: 11/6/1876, Pearl, Ill. d: 5/14/64, Pleasant Hill, Ill. BL/TR, 5'10.5", 160 lbs. Deb: 5/29/06

YEAR	TM/L	G	AB	R	H	2B	3B	HR	RBI	BB	SO	AVG	OBP	SLG	PRO+	BR/A	SB	CS	SBR	FA	FR	G/POS	TPR
1906	Was-A	115	433	56	111	9	5	1	27	35		.256	.324	.307	103	2	37			.931	-21	*S-113/O-2	-1.7
1907	Was-A	147	540	60	145	15	5	2	42	34		.269	.319	.326	115	8	38			.927	-10	S-78,1-50,O	-0.2
1908	Was-A	67	205	19	46	1	1	0	18	13		.224	.274	.239	73	-6	8			.959	-2	2-38,3-16/1S	-0.9
	Cle-A	29	89	11	19	1	2	0	5	7		.213	.278	.270	78	-2	7			.952	4	O-24/S-3	0.1
	Yr	96	294	30	65	2	3	0	23	20		.221	.275	.248	75	-8	15			.959	1	2-38,O-24,3/1S	-0.8
1909	Chi-A	116	382	47	89	6	7	1	20	39		.233	.330	.293	101	2	27			.949	8	O-61,1-46	0.8
1910	Cin-N	3	10	3	6	0	0	0	0	3	0	.600	.692	.600	290	3	0			.933	-2	/S-3	0.2
1911	Cin-N	37	75	8	17	4	1	0	4	9	5	.227	.318	.307	78	-2	2			.907	1	S-23/1-1,2O	0.0
Total	6	514	1734	204	433	36	21	4	116	140	5	.250	.318	.302	101	6	119			.926	-22	S-221,O-107,1/23	-1.7

■ GEORGE ALTMAN
Altman, George Lee b: 3/20/33, Goldsboro, N.C. BL/TR, 6'4", 200 lbs. Deb: 4/11/59

YEAR	TM/L	G	AB	R	H	2B	3B	HR	RBI	BB	SO	AVG	OBP	SLG	PRO+	BR/A	SB	CS	SBR	FA	FR	G/POS	TPR
1959	Chi-N	135	420	54	103	14	4	12	47	34	80	.245	.312	.383	85	-9	1	0	0	.990	4	*O-121	-1.1
1960	Chi-N	119	334	50	89	16	4	13	51	42	67	.266	.332	.455	114	6	4	3	-1	.993	-5	O-79,1-21	-0.4
1961	Chi-N★	138	518	77	157	28	12	27	96	40	92	.303	.358	.560	137	26	6	2	1	.978	-0	*O-130/1-3	1.9
1962	Chi-N★	147	534	74	170	27	5	22	74	62	89	.318	.394	.511	136	28	19	7	2	.972	-0	*O-129,1-16	2.0
1963	StL-N	135	464	62	127	18	7	9	47	47	93	.274	.343	.401	104	3	13	4	2	.979	2	*O-124	0.0
1964	NY-N	124	422	48	97	14	1	9	47	18	70	.230	.263	.332	68	-19	4	4	0	.968	13	*O-109	-1.2
1965	Chi-N	90	196	24	46	7	1	4	23	19	36	.235	.302	.342	79	-5	3	2	-0	.943	-3	O-45/1-2	-1.1
1966	Chi-N	88	185	19	41	6	0	5	17	14	27	.222	.276	.335	68	-8	2	2	-1	.958	-1	/O-4,1-1	-1.4
1967	Chi-N	15	18	1	2	2	0	0	1	2	8	.111	.200	.222	20	-2	0	0	0	1.000	-0	/O-9	-0.4
Total	9	991	3091	409	832	132	34	101	403	268	572	.269	.331	.432	105	19	52	22	6	.977	7	O-783/1-47	-1.7

■ JOE ALTOBELLI
Altobelli, Joseph Salvatore b: 5/26/32, Detroit, Mich. BL/TL, 6', 185 lbs. Deb: 4/14/55 MC

YEAR	TM/L	G	AB	R	H	2B	3B	HR	RBI	BB	SO	AVG	OBP	SLG	PRO+	BR/A	SB	CS	SBR	FA	FR	G/POS	TPR
1955	Cle-A	42	75	8	15	3	0	2	5	5	14	.200	.259	.320	53	-5			-1	.992	-1	1-40	-0.8
1957	Cle-A	83	87	9	18	3	2	0	9	5	14	.207	.258	.287	49	-6	3	2	-0	.994	-0	1-56/O-7	-0.8
1961	Min-A	41	95	10	21	2	1	3	14	13	14	.221	.315	.358	75	-3	0	0	0	.951	-2	O-25/1-2	-0.7
Total	3	166	257	27	54	8	3	5	28	23	42	.210	.280	.323	60	-15	3	3	-1	.993	-3	/1-98,O-32	-2.3

■ NICK ALTROCK
Altrock, Nicholas b: 9/15/1876, Cincinnati, Ohio d: 1/20/65, Washington, D.C. BB/TL, 5'10", 197 lbs. Deb: 7/14/1898 C

YEAR	TM/L	G	AB	R	H	2B	3B	HR	RBI	BB	SO	AVG	OBP	SLG	PRO+	BR/A	SB	CS	SBR	FA	FR	G/POS	TPR
1898	Lou-N	11	29	4	7	0	0	0	2	2		.241	.313	.241	60	-1	1			1.000	2	P-11	0.0
1902	Bos-A	3	8	0	0	0	0	0	0	0		.000	.000	.000	-97	-2	0			.818	1	/P-3	0.0
1903	Bos-A	1	3	0	2	0	0	0	0	1		.667	.750	.667	311	1	0			1.000	3	/P-1	0.0
	Chi-A	13	30	6	9	0	0	0	3	3		.300	.364	.300	105	0	1			.935	3	P-12	0.0
	Yr	14	33	6	11	0	0	0	3	4		.333	.405	.333	128	1	1			.944	4	P-13	0.0
1904	Chi-A	41	111	13	22	1	0	1	8	4		.198	.239	.234	52	-6	0			.969	4	P-38/1-1	0.0
1905	Chi-A	40	112	8	14	1	0	0	5	6		.125	.190	.134	3	-12	0			.988	8	P-38/1-1	0.0
1906	*Chi-A	38	100	4	16	2	0	0	8	0		.160	.222	.180	27	-8	2			.970	4	P-38/1-1	0.0
1907	Chi-A	30	72	7	13	2	0	0	2	3		.181	.234	.222	47	-4	0			.958	5	P-30	0.0
1908	Chi-A	23	49	6	10	2	0	0	3	0		.204	.235	.245	57	-2	1			.967	5	P-23	0.0
1909	Chi-A	1	3	0	0	0	0	0	0	0		.000	.000	.000	-99	-1	0			1.000	0	/P-1	0.0
	Was-A	12	19	2	1	0	0	0	0	1		.053	.143	.053	-40	-3	0			.905	-0	/P-9,O-3	-0.2
	Yr	13	22	2	1	0	0	0	0	1		.045	.125	.045	-48	-4	0			.920	-0	P-10/O-3	-0.2
1912	Was-A	1	1	0	0	0	0	0	0	0		.000	.000	.000	-99	-0	0			.000	-0	/P-1,1-1	0.0
1913	Was-A	4	1	0	0	0	0	0	0	0		.000	.000	.000	-98	-0	0			.833	-0	/P-4	0.0
1914	Was-A	1	0	0	0	0	0	0	0	0		—	—	—			0			.000	-0	/P-1	0.0
1915	Was-A	1	1	0	0	0	0	0	0	0		.000	.000	.000	-98	-0	0			.917	-0	/P-5,1-1	0.0
1918	Was-A	5	8	1	1	0	0	0	0	0		.125	.125	.500	90	-0	0			.000	-0	/P-1	0.0
1919	Was-A	1	0	0	0	0	0	0	0	0		—	1.000	—	182	-0	0			.000	-0	/P-1	0.0
1924	Was-A	1	1	1	1	0	0	0	0	0		1.000	1.000	3.000	935	1	0		-1	.667	-0	/P-1	0.0
1929	Was-A	1	1	0	1	0	0	0	0	0		1.000	1.000	1.000	413	0	0			1.000	-0	/O-1	0.0
1931	Was-A	1	1	0	0	0	0	0	0	0		.000	.000	.000	-99	-0	0			.000	-0	H	0.0
1933	Was-A	230	550	52	97	9	0	2	27	29	0	.176	.232	.207	39	-38	5	1		.964	33	P-218/1-5,O	-0.2
Total	19																						

■ GEORGE ALUSIK
Alusik, George Joseph b: 2/11/35, Ashley, Pa. BR/TR, 6'3.5", 175 lbs. Deb: 9/11/58

YEAR	TM/L	G	AB	R	H	2B	3B	HR	RBI	BB	SO	AVG	OBP	SLG	PRO+	BR/A	SB	CS	SBR	FA	FR	G/POS	TPR
1958	Det-A	2	2	0	0	0	0	0	0	0	1	.000	.000	.000	-93	-1	0	0	0	1.000	-0	/O-1	-0.1
1961	Det-A	15	14	0	2	0	0	0	2	1	4	.143	.200	.143	-6	-2	0	0	0	.000	-0	/O-1	-0.3

YEAR	TM/L	G	AB	R	H	2B	3B	HR	RBI	BB	SO	AVG	OBP	SLG	PRO+	BR/A	SB	CS	SBR	FA	FR	G/POS	TPR
1962	Det-A	2	2	0	0	0	0	0	0	0	0	.000	.000	.000	-97	-1	0	0	-0	.000	0	H	-0.1
	KC-A	90	209	29	57	10	1	11	35	16	29	.273	.327	.488	111	3	1	1	-0	.968	-3	O-50/1-1	-0.3
	Yr	92	211	29	57	10	1	11	35	16	29	.270	.325	.483	109	2	1	1	-0	.968	-3	O-50/1-1	-0.4
1963	KC-A	87	221	28	59	11	0	9	37	26	33	.267	.347	.439	112	4	0	1	-1	1.000	-3	O-63	-0.3
1964	KC-A	102	204	18	49	10	1	3	19	30	36	.240	.343	.343	89	-2	0	0	0	.984	-4	O-44,1-12	-0.9
Total	5	298	652	75	167	31	2	23	93	73	103	.256	.335	.416	101	1	1	2	-1	.985	-10	O-159/1-13	-2.0

■ LUIS ALVARADO

Alvarado, Luis Cesar (Martinez) b: 1/15/49, Lajas, P.R. BR/TR, 5'9", 162 lbs. Deb: 9/13/68

YEAR	TM/L	G	AB	R	H	2B	3B	HR	RBI	BB	SO	AVG	OBP	SLG	PRO+	BR/A	SB	CS	SBR	FA	FR	G/POS	TPR
1968	Bos-A	11	46	3	6	2	0	0	1	1	11	.130	.167	.174	3	-5	0	0	0	.976	-4	S-11	-0.9
1969	Bos-A	6	5	0	0	0	0	0	0	0	2	.000	.000	.000	-95	-1	0	1	-1	1.000	2	/S-5	0.0
1970	Bos-A	59	183	19	41	11	0	1	10	9	30	.224	.260	.301	51	-12	1	2	-1	.929	5	3-29,S-27	-0.6
1971	Chi-A	99	264	22	57	14	1	0	8	11	34	.216	.247	.277	47	-19	1	2	-1	.959	15	S-71,2-16	0.4
1972	Chi-A	103	254	30	54	4	1	4	29	13	36	.213	.254	.283	58	-13	2	2	-1	.957	2	S-81,2-16/3	-0.3
1973	Chi-A	80	203	21	47	7	2	0	20	4	20	.232	.250	.286	49	-14	6	2	1	.980	5	2-45,S-18,3/D	-0.5
1974	Chi-A	8	10	1	1	0	0	0	0	0	1	.100	.100	.100	-41	-2	0	0	0	.667	-1	/S-4,2-1,3	-0.3
	StL-N	17	36	3	5	2	0	0	1	2	6	.139	.184	.194	6	-5	0	0	0	.980	-2	S-17	-0.5
	Cle-A	61	114	12	25	2	0	0	12	6	14	.219	.258	.237	44	-8	1	1	-0	.972	11	2-46/S-7,D	0.4
1976	StL-N	16	42	5	12	1	0	0	3	3	6	.286	.333	.310	82	-1	0	0	0	.936	-9	2-16	-1.0
1977	NY-N	1	2	0	0	0	0	0	0	0	0	.000	.000	.000	-99	-1	0	0	0	1.000	0	/2-1	0.0
	Det-A	2	1	0	0	0	0	0	0	0	0	.000	.000	.000	-95	-0	0	0	0	.000	0	/3-2	0.0
Total	9	463	1160	116	248	43	4	5	84	49	160	.214	.248	.271	47	-81	11	10	-3	.957	26	S-241,2-141/3D	-3.3

■ ORLANDO ALVAREZ

Alvarez, Jesus Manuel Orlando (Monge) b: 2/28/52, Rio Grande, P.R. BR/TR, 6', 165 lbs. Deb: 9/1/73

YEAR	TM/L	G	AB	R	H	2B	3B	HR	RBI	BB	SO	AVG	OBP	SLG	PRO+	BR/A	SB	CS	SBR	FA	FR	G/POS	TPR
1973	LA-N	4	4	0	1	1	0	0	0	0	1	.250	.250	.500	108	-0	0	0	0	.000	0	H	0.0
1974	LA-N	2	1	0	0	0	0	0	0	0	0	.000	.000	.000	-99	-0	0	0	0	1.000	-0	/O-1	0.0
1975	LA-N	4	4	0	0	0	0	0	0	0	1	.000	.000	.000	-99	-1	0	0	0	.000	0	H	-0.1
1976	Cal-A	15	42	4	7	1	0	2	8	0	3	.167	.167	.333	47	-3	0	0	0	1.000	-1	O-11/D-2	-0.5
Total	4	25	51	4	8	2	0	2	8	0	5	.157	.157	.314	36	-4	0	0	0	1.000	-2	/O-12,D-2	-0.6

■ OSSIE ALVAREZ

Alvarez, Oswaldo (Gonzalez) b: 10/19/33, Matanzas, Cuba BR/TR, 5'10", 165 lbs. Deb: 4/19/58

YEAR	TM/L	G	AB	R	H	2B	3B	HR	RBI	BB	SO	AVG	OBP	SLG	PRO+	BR/A	SB	CS	SBR	FA	FR	G/POS	TPR
1958	Was-A	87	196	20	41	3	0	0	5	16	26	.209	.269	.224	38	-16	1	1	-0	.968	12	S-64,2-14/3	0.0
1959	Det-A	8	2	0	1	0	0	0	0	0	1	.500	.500	.500	166	0	0	0	0	.000	0	H	0.0
Total	2	95	198	20	42	3	0	0	5	16	27	.212	.271	.227	39	-16	1	1	-0	.968	12	/S-64,2-14,3	0.0

■ ROGELIO ALVAREZ

Alvarez, Rogelio (Hernandez) b: 4/18/38, Pinar Del Rio, Cuba BR/TR, 5'11", 183 lbs. Deb: 9/18/60

YEAR	TM/L	G	AB	R	H	2B	3B	HR	RBI	BB	SO	AVG	OBP	SLG	PRO+	BR/A	SB	CS	SBR	FA	FR	G/POS	TPR
1960	Cin-N	3	9	1	1	0	0	0	0	0	3	.111	.111	.111	-38	-2	0	0	0	1.000	-1	/1-2	-0.3
1962	Cin-N	14	28	1	6	0	0	0	2	1	10	.214	.241	.214	23	-3	0	0	0	.973	-1	1-13	-0.4
Total	2	17	37	2	7	0	0	0	2	1	13	.189	.211	.189	8	-5	0	0	0	.979	-1	/1-15	-0.7

■ MAX ALVIS

Alvis, Roy Maxwell b: 2/2/38, Jasper, Tex. BR/TR, 5'11", 187 lbs. Deb: 9/11/62

YEAR	TM/L	G	AB	R	H	2B	3B	HR	RBI	BB	SO	AVG	OBP	SLG	PRO+	BR/A	SB	CS	SBR	FA	FR	G/POS	TPR
1962	Cle-A	12	51	1	11	2	0	0	3	2	13	.216	.245	.255	36	-5	3	1	0	.935	-4	3-12	-0.8
1963	Cle-A	158	602	81	165	32	7	22	67	36	109	.274	.326	.460	118	13	9	7	-2	.942	-5	*3-158	0.7
1964	Cle-A	107	381	51	96	14	3	18	53	29	77	.252	.315	.446	110	4	5	5	-2	.955	-7	*3-105	-0.6
1965	Cle-A★	159	604	88	149	24	2	21	61	47	121	.247	.311	.397	99	-2	12	8	-1	.958	-19	*3-156	-2.7
1966	Cle-A	157	596	67	146	22	3	17	55	50	98	.245	.306	.378	95	-4	4	7	-3	.958	-6	*3-157	-1.8
1967	Cle-A★	161	637	66	163	23	4	21	70	38	107	.256	.302	.403	106	3	3	10	-5	.965	-8	*3-161	-1.3
1968	Cle-A	131	452	38	101	17	3	8	37	41	91	.223	.294	.327	89	-6	5	5	-2	.960	-17	*3-128	-2.8
1969	Cle-A	66	191	13	43	6	0	1	15	14	64	.225	.278	.272	53	-12	1	1	-0	.973	-2	3-58/S-1	-1.5
1970	Mil-A	62	115	16	21	2	0	3	12	5	22	.183	.217	.278	35	-10	1	2	-1	.909	2	3-36	-1.0
Total	9	1013	3629	421	895	142	22	111	373	262	662	.247	.304	.390	97	-19	43	46	-15	.956	-64	3-971/S-1	-11.8

■ BILLY ALVORD

Alvord, William Charles "Uncle Bill" b: 8/1863, St.Louis, Mo. 5'10", 187 lbs. Deb: 4/30/1885

YEAR	TM/L	G	AB	R	H	2B	3B	HR	RBI	BB	SO	AVG	OBP	SLG	PRO+	BR/A	SB	CS	SBR	FA	FR	G/POS	TPR
1885	StL-N	2	5	0	0	0	0	0	0	1	2	.000	.167	.000	-45	-1				.714	-1	/3-2	-0.1
1889	KC-a	50	186	23	43	8	9	0	18	10	35	.231	.270	.371	77	-7	3			.877	5	3-34/S-8,2	0.0
1890	Tol-a	116	495	69	135	13	16	2		22		.273	.304	.376	97	-5	21			.872	4	*3-116	0.3
1891	Cle-N	13	59	7	17	2	1	0	7	0	7	.288	.300	.441	110	0	0			.814	-2	3-13	-0.1
	Was-a	81	312	28	73	8	3	0	30	11	38	.234	.260	.279	57	-19	3			.862	17	3-81	0.2
1893	Cle-N	3	12	2	2	0	0	0	2	0	1	.167	.167	.167	-11	-2	0			.875	-2	/3-3	-0.3
Total	5	265	1069	129	270	31	30	3	57	44	83	.253	.283	.346	81	-33	27			.865	22	3-249/2-8,S	0.0

■ BRANT ALYEA

Alyea, Garrabrant Ryerson b: 12/8/40, Passaic, N.J. BR/TR, 6'3", 215 lbs. Deb: 9/11/65

YEAR	TM/L	G	AB	R	H	2B	3B	HR	RBI	BB	SO	AVG	OBP	SLG	PRO+	BR/A	SB	CS	SBR	FA	FR	G/POS	TPR
1965	Was-A	8	13	3	3	0	0	2	6	1	4	.231	.286	.692	171	1	0	0	0	1.000	-1	/1-3,O-1	0.0
1968	Was-A	53	150	18	40	11	1	6	23	10	39	.267	.317	.473	141	7	0	0	0	1.000	1	O-39	0.6
1969	Was-A	104	237	29	59	4	0	11	40	34	67	.249	.346	.405	115	5	1	3	-2	.938	-7	O-69/1-3	-0.8
1970	*Min-A	94	258	34	75	12	1	16	61	28	51	.291	.367	.531	143	14	3	3	-1	.980	-5	O-75	0.5
1971	Min-A	79	158	13	28	4	0	2	15	24	38	.177	.290	.241	50	-10	1	1	-0	.962	-6	O-48	-2.0
1972	Oak-A	20	31	2	6	1	0	1	2	3	5	.194	.265	.323	78	-1	0	0	0	1.000	3	/O-8	0.2
	StL-N	13	19	0	3	1	0	0	1	0	6	.158	.158	.211	4	-2	0	0	0	1.000	1	/O-3	-0.2
Total	6	371	866	100	214	33	2	38	148	100	210	.247	.329	.421	113	14	5	7	-3	.972	-15	O-243/1-6	-1.7

■ JOEY AMALFITANO

Amalfitano, John Joseph b: 1/23/34, San Pedro, Cal. BR/TR, 5'11", 180 lbs. Deb: 5/3/54 MC

YEAR	TM/L	G	AB	R	H	2B	3B	HR	RBI	BB	SO	AVG	OBP	SLG	PRO+	BR/A	SB	CS	SBR	FA	FR	G/POS	TPR
1954	NY-N	9	5	2	0	0	0	0	0	0	4	.000	.000	.000	-99	-1	0	0	0	1.000	2	/3-4,2-1	0.1
1955	NY-N	36	22	8	5	1	1	0	1	2	4	.227	.292	.364	72	-1	0	0	0	.957	10	/S-5,3-2	0.9
1960	SF-N	106	328	47	91	15	3	1	27	26	31	.277	.336	.351	94	-3	2	3	-1	.935	3	3-63,2-33/SO	0.1
1961	SF-N	109	384	64	98	11	4	2	23	44	59	.255	.332	.320	77	-12	7	4	-0	.970	-22	2-95/3-6	-2.4
1962	Hou-N	117	380	44	90	12	5	1	27	45	43	.237	.319	.303	73	-14	4	4	-1	.967	2	*2-110/3-5	-0.3
1963	SF-N	54	137	11	24	3	0	1	7	12	18	.175	.247	.219	36	-11	2	6	-3	.980	-3	2-37/3-7	-1.6
1964	Chi-N	100	324	51	78	19	6	4	27	40	42	.241	.333	.373	95	-1	2	7	-4	.964	1	2-86/1-1,S	0.4
1965	Chi-N	67	96	13	26	4	0	0	8	12	14	.271	.364	.313	90	-1	2	2	-1	.989	5	2-24/S-4	0.5
1966	Chi-N	41	38	8	6	2	0	0	3	4	10	.158	.238	.211	26	-4	0	0	0	.977	1	2-12/3-3,S	-0.2
1967	Chi-N	4	1	0	0	0	0	0	0	0	1	.000	.000	.000	-96	-0	0	0	0	.000	0	H	0.0
Total	10	643	1715	248	418	67	19	9	123	185	224	.244	.322	.321	78	-48	19	26	-10	.970	2	2-398/3-90,S10	-2.5

■ RICH AMARAL

Amaral, Richard Louis b: 4/1/62, Visalia, Cal. BR/TR, 6', 175 lbs. Deb: 5/27/91

YEAR	TM/L	G	AB	R	H	2B	3B	HR	RBI	BB	SO	AVG	OBP	SLG	PRO+	BR/A	SB	CS	SBR	FA	FR	G/POS	TPR
1991	Sea-A	14	16	2	1	0	0	0	0	1	5	.063	.167	.063	-34	-3				1.000	4	/2-5,3-2,S1D	0.1
1992	Sea-A	35	100	9	24	3	0	1	7	5	16	.240	.276	.300	61	-5	4	2	0	.955	2	3-17,S-17/O12	0.1
1993	Sea-A	110	373	53	108	24	1	1	44	33	54	.290	.352	.367	92	-3	19	11	-1	.975	10	2-77,3-19,S/1D	0.8
1994	Sea-A	77	228	37	60	10	2	4	18	24	28	.263	.332	.377	82	-6	5	1	1	.943	-12	2-42,O-16/S1D	-1.5
Total	4	236	717	101	193	37	3	6	69	63	103	.269	.332	.354	82	-17	28	14	0	.965	3	2-125/S-40,3OD1	-0.9

■ RUBEN AMARO

Amaro, Ruben Jr. b: 2/12/65, Philadelphia, Pa. BB/TR, 5'10", 170 lbs. Deb: 6/8/91 F

YEAR	TM/L	G	AB	R	H	2B	3B	HR	RBI	BB	SO	AVG	OBP	SLG	PRO+	BR/A	SB	CS	SBR	FA	FR	G/POS	TPR
1991	Cal-A	10	23	0	5	1	0	2	3	3	.217	.308	.261	59	-2	0	0	0	1.000	-2	/O-5,2-4,D	-0.4
1992	Phi-N	126	374	43	82	15	6	7	34	37	54	.219	.305	.348	85	-7	11	5	0	.992	0	*O-113	-1.0
1993	Phi-N	25	48	7	16	2	1	0	6	6	5	.333	.407	.521	149	3	0	0	0	.963	-2	O-16	0.2

YEAR	TM/L	G	AB	R	H	2B	3B	HR	RBI	BB	SO	AVG	OBP	SLG	PRO+	BR/A	SB	CS	SBR	FA	FR	G/POS	TPR
1994	Cle-A	26	23	5	5	1	0	2	5	2	3	.217	.280	.522	96	-0	2	1	0	.909	-4	O-12/D-3	-0.4
Total	4	187	468	55	108	19	8	10	47	48	65	.231	.314	.370	91	-6	13	6	0	.986	-8	O-146/D-4,2	-1.6

■ RUBEN AMARO
Amaro, Ruben Sr. (Mora) b: 1/6/36, Veracruz, Mexico   BR/TR, 5'11", 170 lbs.   Deb: 6/29/58 FC

YEAR	TM/L	G	AB	R	H	2B	3B	HR	RBI	BB	SO	AVG	OBP	SLG	PRO+	BR/A	SB	CS	SBR	FA	FR	G/POS	TPR
1958	StL-N	40	76	8	17	2	1	0	0	5	8	.224	.272	.276	44	-6	0	1	-1	.948	3	S-36/2-1	-0.2
1960	Phi-N	92	264	25	61	9	1	0	16	21	32	.231	.293	.273	56	-16	0	1	-1	.965	-8	S-92	-1.9
1961	Phi-N	135	381	34	98	14	9	1	32	53	59	.257	.351	.349	88	-5	1	0	0	.970	14	*S-132/1-3,2	1.9
1962	Phi-N	79	226	24	55	10	0	0	19	30	28	.243	.335	.288	71	-8	5	2	0	.968	6	S-78/1-1	0.5
1963	Phi-N	115	217	25	47	9	2	2	19	19	31	.217	.280	.304	69	-9	0	1	-1	.950	2	S-63,3-45/1	-0.5
1964	Phi-N	129	299	31	79	11	0	4	34	16	37	.264	.308	.341	84	-6	1	6	-3	.971	-4	S-79,1-58/230	-1.0
1965	Phi-N	118	184	26	39	7	0	0	15	27	22	.212	.316	.250	63	-8	1	1	0	.990	-3	1-60,S-60/2	-0.9
1966	NY-A	14	23	0	5	0	0	0	3	0	2	.217	.217	.217	26	-2	0	0	0	.977	5	S-14	0.4
1967	NY-A	130	417	31	93	12	1	1	17	43	49	.223	.297	.259	68	-16	3	2	0	.973	9	*S-123/3-3,1	0.5
1968	NY-A	47	41	3	5	1	0	0	0	9	6	.122	.280	.146	33	-3	0	0	0	.962	-1	S-23,1-22	-0.3
1969	Cal-A	41	27	4	6	0	0	0	1	4	6	.222	.323	.222	58	-1	0	0	0	1.000	0	1-18/2-9,S3	-0.1
Total	11	940	2155	211	505	75	13	8	156	227	280	.234	.310	.292	70	-81	11	14	-5	.967	24	S-705,1-169/32O	-1.6

■ WAYNE AMBLER
Ambler, Wayne Harper b: 11/8/15, Abington, Pa.   BR/TR, 5'8.5", 165 lbs.   Deb: 6/4/37

YEAR	TM/L	G	AB	R	H	2B	3B	HR	RBI	BB	SO	AVG	OBP	SLG	PRO+	BR/A	SB	CS	SBR	FA	FR	G/POS	TPR
1937	Phi-A	56	162	3	35	5	0	0	11	13	8	.216	.274	.247	33	-17	1	0	0	.955	-4	2-56	-1.6
1938	Phi-A	120	393	42	92	21	2	0	38	48	31	.234	.317	.298	56	-26	2	1	0	.942	-19	*S-116/2-4	-3.3
1939	Phi-A	95	227	15	48	13	0	0	24	22	25	.211	.281	.269	42	-20	1	0	0	.954	-3	S-77,2-19	-1.5
Total	3	271	782	60	175	39	2	0	73	83	64	.224	.298	.279	47	-63	4	1	0	.946	-26	S-193/2-79	-6.4

■ ED AMELUNG
Amelung, Edward Allen b: 4/13/59, Fullerton, Cal.   BL/TL, 5'11", 180 lbs.   Deb: 7/28/84

YEAR	TM/L	G	AB	R	H	2B	3B	HR	RBI	BB	SO	AVG	OBP	SLG	PRO+	BR/A	SB	CS	SBR	FA	FR	G/POS	TPR
1984	LA-N	34	46	7	10	0	0	0	4	2	4	.217	.250	.217	33	-4	3	2	-0	1.000	-3	O-23	-0.8
1986	LA-N	8	11	0	1	0	0	0	0	0	4	.091	.091	.091	-53	-2	0	0	0	1.000	-1	/O-4	-0.3
Total	2	42	57	7	11	0	0	0	4	2	8	.193	.220	.193	17	-6	3	2	-0	1.000	-4	/O-27	-1.1

■ SANDY AMOROS
Amoros, Edmundo (Isasi) b: 1/30/30, Havana, Cuba   d: 6/27/92, Miami, Fla.   BL/TL, 5'7.5", 170 lbs.   Deb: 8/22/52

YEAR	TM/L	G	AB	R	H	2B	3B	HR	RBI	BB	SO	AVG	OBP	SLG	PRO+	BR/A	SB	CS	SBR	FA	FR	G/POS	TPR
1952	*Bro-N	20	44	10	11	3	1	0	3	5	14	.250	.327	.364	90	-1	1	0	0	1.000	-3	O-10	-0.4
1954	Bro-N	79	263	44	72	18	6	9	34	31	24	.274	.353	.490	113	5	1	4	-2	.987	5	O-70	0.4
1955	*Bro-N	119	388	59	96	16	7	10	51	55	45	.247	.350	.402	96	-1	10	5	0	.972	-1	*O-109	-0.7
1956	*Bro-N	114	292	53	76	11	8	16	58	59	51	.260	.386	.517	120	13	3	4	-2	.955	-10	O-86	-0.3
1957	Bro-N	106	238	40	66	7	1	7	26	46	42	.277	.401	.403	107	4	3	2	0	.984	-1	O-66	0.0
1959	LA-N	5	5	1	1	0	0	0	1	0	1	.200	.200	.200	6	-1	0	0	0	.000	0	H	-0.1
1960	LA-N	9	14	1	2	0	0	0	0	3	2	.143	.294	.143	23	-1	0	0	0	1.000	0	/O-3	-0.1
	Det-A	65	67	7	10	0	0	1	7	12	10	.149	.278	.194	29	-6	0	0	0	1.000	-1	O-10	-0.8
Total	7	517	1311	215	334	55	23	43	180	211	189	.255	.363	.430	105	12	18	15	-4	.976	-11	O-354	-2.0

■ ALF ANDERSON
Anderson, Alfred Walton b: 1/28/14, Gainesville, Ga.   d: 6/23/85, Albany, Ga.   BR/TR, 5'11", 165 lbs.   Deb: 4/20/41

YEAR	TM/L	G	AB	R	H	2B	3B	HR	RBI	BB	SO	AVG	OBP	SLG	PRO+	BR/A	SB	CS	SBR	FA	FR	G/POS	TPR
1941	Pit-N	70	223	32	48	7	2	1	10	14	30	.215	.265	.278	53	-14	2			.931	-6	S-58	-1.7
1942	Pit-N	54	166	24	45	4	1	0	7	18	19	.271	.342	.307	89	-2	4			.942	-15	S-48	-1.6
1946	Pit-N	2	1	0	0	0	0	0	0	1	0	.000	.500	.000	47	0	0			.000	0	H	0.0
Total	3	126	390	56	93	11	3	1	17	33	49	.238	.300	.290	68	-16	6			.936	-21	S-106	-3.3

■ ANDY ANDERSON
Anderson, Andy Holm b: 11/13/22, Bremerton, Wash.   d: 7/18/82, Seattle, Wash.   BR/TR, 5'11", 172 lbs.   Deb: 5/10/48

YEAR	TM/L	G	AB	R	H	2B	3B	HR	RBI	BB	SO	AVG	OBP	SLG	PRO+	BR/A	SB	CS	SBR	FA	FR	G/POS	TPR
1948	StL-A	51	87	13	24	5	1	1	12	8	15	.276	.337	.391	91	-1	0	0	0	.917	-2	2-21,S-10/1	-0.2
1949	StL-A	71	136	10	17	3	0	1	5	14	21	.125	.207	.169	-0	-20	0	1	-1	.957	-7	S-44/2-8,3	-2.5
Total	2	122	223	23	41	8	1	2	17	22	36	.184	.257	.256	35	-21	0	1	-1	.946	-9	/S-54,2-29,31	-2.7

■ BRADY ANDERSON
Anderson, Brady Kevin b: 1/18/64, Silver Spring, Md.   BL/TL, 6'1", 170 lbs.   Deb: 4/4/88

YEAR	TM/L	G	AB	R	H	2B	3B	HR	RBI	BB	SO	AVG	OBP	SLG	PRO+	BR/A	SB	CS	SBR	FA	FR	G/POS	TPR
1988	Bos-A	41	148	14	34	5	3	0	12	15	35	.230	.317	.304	72	-5	4	2	0	.989	2	O-41	-0.5
	Bal-A	53	177	17	35	8	1	1	9	8	40	.198	.232	.271	42	-14	6	4	-1	.981	5	O-49	-1.1
	Yr	94	325	31	69	13	4	1	21	23	75	.212	.273	.286	57	-19	10	6	-1	.984	7	O-90	-1.6
1989	Bal-A	94	266	44	55	12	2	4	16	43	45	.207	.324	.312	82	-5	16	4	2	.985	-2	O-79/D-8	-0.7
1990	Bal-A	89	234	24	54	5	2	3	24	31	46	.231	.333	.308	83	-4	15	2	3	.987	6	O-63,D-11	0.0
1991	Bal-A	113	256	40	59	12	3	2	27	38	44	.230	.341	.324	89	-3	12	5	1	.981	-15	*O-101/D-2	-1.9
1992	Bal-A★	159	623	100	169	28	10	21	80	98	98	.271	.378	.449	128	25	53	16	6	.980	14	*O-158	4.2
1993	Bal-A	142	560	87	147	36	8	13	66	82	99	.262	.361	.425	108	7	24	12	0	.993	2	*O-140/D-2	0.7
1994	Bal-A	111	453	78	119	25	5	12	48	57	75	.263	.358	.419	93	-4	31	1	9	**.996**	-0	*O-109	0.2
Total	7	802	2717	404	672	131	34	56	282	372	482	.247	.348	.382	98	-3	161	46	21	.987	8	O-740/D-23	0.9

■ DAVE ANDERSON
Anderson, David Carter b: 8/1/60, Louisville, Ky.   BR/TR, 6'2", 185 lbs.   Deb: 5/8/83

YEAR	TM/L	G	AB	R	H	2B	3B	HR	RBI	BB	SO	AVG	OBP	SLG	PRO+	BR/A	SB	CS	SBR	FA	FR	G/POS	TPR
1983	LA-N	61	115	12	19	4	2	1	2	12	15	.165	.244	.261	40	-9	6	3	0	.969	3	S-53/3-1	-0.3
1984	LA-N	121	374	51	94	16	2	3	34	45	55	.251	.335	.329	88	-5	15	5	2	.965	19	*S-111,3-11	2.6
1985	*LA-N	77	221	24	44	6	0	4	18	35	42	.199	.311	.281	69	-8	5	4	-1	.957	17	3-51,S-25/2	1.0
1986	LA-N	92	216	31	53	9	0	1	15	22	39	.245	.315	.301	76	-7	5	1	1	.976	9	3-51,S-34/2	0.5
1987	LA-N	108	265	32	62	12	3	1	13	24	43	.234	.300	.313	64	-13	9	5	-0	.977	6	S-82,3-12,2	-0.4
1988	*LA-N	116	285	31	71	10	2	2	20	32	45	.249	.327	.319	89	-3	4	4	0	.986	14	S-82,3-12,2	1.8
1989	LA-N	87	140	15	32	2	0	1	14	17	26	.229	.312	.264	67	-5	2	0	1	.990	5	S-33,3-18/2	-0.3
1990	SF-N	60	100	14	35	5	1	1	6	9	20	.350	.369	.450	129	4	2	2	-1	1.000	-6	S-29,2-13/13	-0.2
1991	SF-N	100	226	24	56	5	2	2	13	12	35	.248	.286	.314	71	-9	2	4	-2	.956	-10	S-63,1-16,3/2	-1.9
1992	LA-N	51	84	10	24	4	0	3	8	8	11	.286	.318	.440	115	1	0	4	-2	.974	2	3-26/S-7	0.1
Total	10	873	2026	244	490	73	12	19	143	206	331	.242	.313	.318	79	-56	49	30	-3	.970	54	S-502,3-218/21	2.9

■ DWAIN ANDERSON
Anderson, Dwain Cleaven b: 11/23/47, Oakland, Cal.   BR/TR, 5'11", 165 lbs.   Deb: 9/3/71

YEAR	TM/L	G	AB	R	H	2B	3B	HR	RBI	BB	SO	AVG	OBP	SLG	PRO+	BR/A	SB	CS	SBR	FA	FR	G/POS	TPR
1971	Oak-A	16	37	3	10	2	1	0	3	5	9	.270	.372	.378	115	1	0	1	-1	.968	-1	S-10/2-5,3	0.1
1972	Oak-A	3	7	2	0	0	0	0	0	1	4	.000	.125	.000	-64	-1	0	0	0	1.000	-0	/S-1,3-1	-0.2
	StL-N	57	135	12	36	4	1	1	8	8	23	.267	.313	.333	85	-3	0	0	0	.952	-3	S-43,3-13/2	-0.3
1973	StL-N	18	17	5	2	0	0	0	0	4	4	.118	.286	.118	16	-2	0	0	0	.500	-3	/S-3,O-2	-0.4
	SD-N	53	107	11	13	0	0	0	3	14	29	.121	.223	.121	-2	-15	2	0	1	.932	3	S-39/3-6	-0.8
	Yr	71	124	16	15	0	0	0	3	18	33	.121	.232	.121	1	-16	2	0	1	.919	1	S-42/3-6,O	-1.2
1974	Cle-A	2	3	0	1	0	0	0	0	0	1	.333	.333	.333	93	-0	0	0	0	1.000	-1	/2-1	-0.1
Total	4	149	306	33	62	6	2	1	14	32	70	.203	.282	.245	52	-20	2	1	0	.940	-4	/S-96,3-21,2O	-1.7

■ GOAT ANDERSON
Anderson, Edward John b: 1/13/1880, Cleveland, Ohio   d: 3/15/23, South Bend, Ind.   BL/TR, Deb: 4/11/07

YEAR	TM/L	G	AB	R	H	2B	3B	HR	RBI	BB	SO	AVG	OBP	SLG	PRO+	BR/A	SB	CS	SBR	FA	FR	G/POS	TPR
1907	Pit-N	127	413	73	85	3	1	1	12	80		.206	.343	.225	77	-6	27			.953	-1	*O-117/2-5	-1.3

■ FERRELL ANDERSON
Anderson, Ferrell Jack "Andy" b: 1/9/18, Maple City, Kan.   d: 3/12/78, Joplin, Mo.   BR/TR, 6'1", 200 lbs.   Deb: 4/16/46

YEAR	TM/L	G	AB	R	H	2B	3B	HR	RBI	BB	SO	AVG	OBP	SLG	PRO+	BR/A	SB	CS	SBR	FA	FR	G/POS	TPR
1946	Bro-N	79	199	19	51	10	0	2	14	18	21	.256	.330	.337	89	-3	1			.964	-2	C-70	-0.2
1953	StL-N	18	35	1	10	2	0	0	1	0	4	.286	.286	.343	63	-2	0			1.000	-1	C-12	-0.3
Total	2	97	234	20	61	12	0	2	15	18	25	.261	.324	.338	85	-5	1	0		.968	-3	/C-82	-0.5

■ GARRET ANDERSON
Anderson, Garret Joseph b: 6/30/72, Los Angeles, Cal.   BL/TL, 6'3", 190 lbs.   Deb: 7/27/94

YEAR	TM/L	G	AB	R	H	2B	3B	HR	RBI	BB	SO	AVG	OBP	SLG	PRO+	BR/A	SB	CS	SBR	FA	FR	G/POS	TPR
1994	Cal-A	5	13	0	5	0	0	0	1	0	2	.385	.385	.385	96	-0	0	0	0	1.000	0	/O-4	0.0

YEAR	TM/L	G	AB	R	H	2B	3B	HR	RBI	BB	SO	AVG	OBP	SLG	PRO+	BR/A	SB	CS	SBR	FA	FR	G/POS	TPR

■ GEORGE ANDERSON Anderson, George Jendrus "Andy" (Born George Andrew Jendrus) b: 9/26/1889, Cleveland, Ohio d: 5/28/62, Cleveland, Ohio BL/TR, 5'8.5", 160 lbs. Deb: 5/26/14

1914	Bro-F	98	364	58	115	13	3	3	24	31	50	.316	.376	.393	100	1	16			.946	4	O-92	0.0
1915	Bro-F	136	511	70	135	23	9	2	39	52	54	.264	.342	.356	87	-9	20			.956	-8	*O-134	-2.5
1918	StL-N	35	132	20	39	4	5	0	6	15	7	.295	.380	.402	143	7	0			.956	-1	O-35	0.4
Total	3	269	1007	148	289	40	17	5	69	98	111	.287	.359	.375	99	-1	36			.952	-5	O-261	-2.1

■ SPARKY ANDERSON Anderson, George Lee b: 2/22/34, Bridgewater, S.Dak BR/TR, 5'9", 170 lbs. Deb: 4/10/59 MC

1959	Phi-N	152	477	42	104	9	3	0	34	42	53	.218	.283	.249	43	-38	6	9	-4	.984	3	*2-152	-2.9

■ HAL ANDERSON Anderson, Harold b: 2/10/04, St.Louis, Mo. d: 5/1/74, St.Louis, Mo. BR/TR, 5'11", 160 lbs. Deb: 4/12/32

1932	Chi-A	9	32	4	8	0	0	0	2	0	1	.250	.250	.250	32	-3	0	1	-1	1.000	0	/O-9	-0.4

■ HARRY ANDERSON Anderson, Harry Walter b: 9/10/31, North East, Md. BL/TR, 6'3", 210 lbs. Deb: 4/18/57

1957	Phi-N	118	400	53	107	15	4	17	61	36	61	.268	.337	.452	113	7	2	3	-1	.986	4	*O-109	0.4
1958	Phi-N	140	515	80	155	34	6	23	97	59	95	.301	.376	.524	137	27	0	2	-1	.975	-2	O-87,1-49	1.7
1959	Phi-N	142	508	50	122	28	6	14	63	43	95	.240	.306	.402	85	-12	1	1	-0	.980	18	*O-137	-0.2
1960	Phi-N	38	93	10	23	2	0	5	12	10	19	.247	.333	.430	107	1	0	0	0	1.000	-1	O-16,1-12	-0.2
	Cin-N	42	66	6	11	3	0	1	9	11	20	.167	.286	.258	49	-4	0	0	0	.990	-1	1-15/O-4	-0.7
	Yr	80	159	16	34	5	0	6	21	21	39	.214	.313	.358	82	-4	0	0	0	.989	-2	1-27,O-20	-0.9
1961	Cin-N	4	4	0	1	0	0	0	0	0	1	.250	.250	.250	33	-0	0	0	0	.000	0	H	-0.0
Total	5	484	1586	199	419	82	16	60	242	159	291	.264	.337	.450	109	18	3	6	-3	.982	19	O-353/1-76	1.2

■ JIM ANDERSON Anderson, James Lea b: 2/23/57, Los Angeles, Cal. BR/TR, 6', 170 lbs. Deb: 7/2/78

1978	Cal-A	48	108	6	21	7	0	0	7	11	16	.194	.269	.259	51	-7	0	0	0	.955	3	S-47/2-1	0.0
1979	*Cal-A	96	234	33	58	13	1	3	23	17	31	.248	.302	.350	78	-7	3	2	-0	.949	-1	S-82,3-10/2C	-0.1
1980	Sea-A	116	317	46	72	7	0	8	30	27	39	.227	.294	.325	69	-14	2	4	-2	.958	4	S-65,3-33/2CD	-0.6
1981	Sea-A	70	162	12	33	7	0	2	19	17	29	.204	.283	.284	61	-8	3	5	-2	.947	4	S-68/3-2	-0.1
1983	Tex-A	50	102	8	22	1	1	0	6	5	8	.216	.252	.245	38	-9	1	2	-1	.962	5	S-27,2-17/3OCD	-0.2
1984	Tex-A	39	47	2	5	0	0	0	1	4	7	.106	.176	.106	-19	-8	0	0	0	.989	10	S-31/3-6,2	0.4
Total	6	419	970	107	211	35	2	13	86	81	130	.218	.281	.298	60	-52	9	13	-5	.955	25	S-320/3-54,2DCO	-0.6

■ JOHN ANDERSON Anderson, John Joseph "Honest John" b: 12/14/1873, Sarpsborg, Norway d: 7/23/49, Worcester, Mass. BB/TR, 6'2", 180 lbs. Deb: 9/8/1894

1894	Bro-N	17	63	14	19	1	3	1	19	3	3	.302	.333	.460	97	-1	7			.778	-5	O-16/3-1	-0.5
1895	Bro-N	102	419	76	120	11	14	9	87	12	29	.286	.314	.444	102	-1	24			.882	-6	*O-101	-1.2
1896	Bro-N	108	430	70	135	23	17	1	55	18	23	.314	.344	.453	116	8	37			.942	-3	O-68,1-42	0.0
1897	Bro-N	117	492	93	160	28	12	4	85	17		.325	.357	.455	120	12	29			.936	0	*O-115/1-3	0.3
1898	Bro-N	6	21	1	3	2	0	0	2	1		.143	.217	.238	31	-2	0			1.000	0	/O-5	-0.2
	Was-N	110	430	70	131	28	18	9	71	23		.305	.344	.516	150	24	18			.948	9	O-93,1-17	2.4
	Bro-N	19	69	11	19	3	4	0	8	5		.275	.333	.435	120	1	2			.966	-1	O-17/1-2	0.0
	Yr	135	520	82	153	33	**22**	9	81	29		.294	.348	**.494**	141	24	20			.952	8	*O-115,1-19	2.2
1899	Bro-N	117	439	65	118	18	7	4	92	27		.269	.317	.369	86	-10	25			.933	-4	O-76,1-41	-1.7
1901	Mil-A	138	576	90	190	46	7	8	99	24		.330	.360	.476	137	26	35			**.982**	-5	*1-125,O-13	2.6
1902	StL-A	126	524	60	149	29	6	4	85	21		.284	.316	.385	95	-5	15			.985	-9	*1-126/O-3	-1.6
1903	StL-A	138	550	65	156	34	8	2	78	23		.284	.312	.385	111	6	16			.986	4	*1-133/O-7	0.8
1904	NY-A	143	558	62	155	27	12	3	82	23		.278	.313	.385	115	8	20			.956	-0	*O-112,1-33	0.1
1905	NY-A	32	99	12	23	3	1	0	14	8		.232	.296	.283	75	-3	9			.900	-2	O-22/1-3	-0.7
	Was-A	101	400	50	116	21	6	1	38	22		.290	.330	.380	130	12	22			.960	-0	O-97/1-4	0.8
	Yr	133	499	62	139	24	7	1	52	30		.279	.323	.361	117	9	31			.949	-2	O-119/1-7	0.1
1906	Was-A	151	583	62	158	25	4	3	70	19		.271	.296	.343	105	1	**39**			.953	5	*O-151	-0.2
1907	Was-A	87	333	33	96	12	4	0	44	34		.288	.359	.348	136	14	19			.983	-1	1-61,O-26	1.2
1908	Chi-A	123	355	36	93	17	1	0	47	30		.262	.321	.315	109	4	21			.963	-6	O-87/1-9	-0.6
Total	14	1635	6341	870	1841	328	124	49	976	310	55	.290	.329	.404	114	96	338			.939	-14	*O-1009,1-599/3	1.5

■ KENT ANDERSON Anderson, Kent McKay b: 8/12/63, Florence, S.C. BR/TR, 6'1", 180 lbs. Deb: 4/15/89 F

1989	Cal-A	86	223	27	51	6	1	0	17	17	42	.229	.286	.265	57	-12	1	2	-1	.972	14	S-70/2-7,3OD	0.6
1990	Cal-A	49	143	16	44	6	1	1	5	13	19	.308	.369	.385	113	3	0	2	-1	.964	13	S-28,3-16/2	1.6
Total	2	135	366	43	95	12	2	1	22	30	61	.260	.319	.311	79	-9	1	4	-2	.969	27	/S-98,3-21,2OD	2.2

■ MIKE ANDERSON Anderson, Michael Allen b: 6/22/51, Florence, S.C. BR/TR, 6'2", 200 lbs. Deb: 9/2/71 F

1971	Phi-N	26	89	11	22	5	1	2	5	13	28	.247	.343	.393	108	1	0	0	0	.986	2	O-26	0.2
1972	Phi-N	36	103	8	20	5	1	2	5	19	36	.194	.320	.320	80	-2	1	0	0	.987	4	O-35	0.0
1973	Phi-N	87	193	32	49	9	1	9	28	19	53	.254	.324	.451	110	2	3	-2		.981	-6	O-67	-0.8
1974	Phi-N	145	395	35	99	22	2	5	34	37	75	.251	.315	.354	83	-9	2	1	0	.980	4	*O-133/1-1	-1.0
1975	Phi-N	115	247	24	64	10	3	4	28	17	66	.259	.312	.372	86	-5	1	2	-1	.977	-10	*O-105/1-3	-1.9
1976	StL-N	86	199	17	58	8	1	1	12	26	30	.291	.376	.357	108	3	1	1	-0	.982	0	O-58/1-5	0.1
1977	StL-N	94	154	18	34	4	1	4	17	14	31	.221	.286	.338	68	-7	2	3	-1	.980	-10	O-77	-2.0
1978	Bal-A	53	32	2	3	0	0	0	3	3	10	.094	.171	.156	-8	-5	0	0	0	.962	-15	O-47	-2.1
1979	Phi-N	79	78	12	18	7	1	1	13	12	14	.231	.341	.321	79	-2	1	2	-1	.973	-13	O-70/P-1	-1.8
Total	9	721	1490	159	367	67	11	28	134	161	343	.246	.321	.362	88	-24	8	12	-5	.980	-44	O-618/1-9,P	-9.3

■ ERNIE ANDRES Andres, Ernest Henry "Junie" b: 1/11/18, Jeffersonville, Ind. BR/TR, 6'1", 200 lbs. Deb: 4/16/46

1946	Bos-A	15	41	0	4	2	0	0	1	3	5	.098	.159	.146	-14	-6	0	0	0	1.000	1	3-15	-0.5

■ KIM ANDREW Andrew, Kim Darrell b: 11/14/53, Glendale, Cal. BR/TR, 5'10", 160 lbs. Deb: 4/16/75

1975	Bos-A	2	2	0	1	0	0	0	0	0	0	.500	.500	.500	169	0	0	0	0	1.000	-0	/2-2	0.0

■ FRED ANDREWS Andrews, Fred b: 5/4/52, Lafayette, La. BR/TR, 5'8", 163 lbs. Deb: 9/26/76

1976	Phi-N	4	6	1	4	0	0	0	0	0	0	.667	.778	.667	304	2	1	1	-0	1.000	-1	/2-4	0.2
1977	Phi-N	12	23	3	4	0	1	0	2	1	5	.174	.208	.261	24	-2	1	0	0	1.000	3	/2-7	0.1
Total	2	16	29	4	8	0	1	0	2	1	5	.276	.364	.345	90	-0	2	1	0	1.000	2	/2-11	0.3

■ ED ANDREWS Andrews, George Edward b: 4/5/1859, Painesville, Ohio d: 8/12/34, W.Palm Beach, Fla. BR/TR, 5'8", 160 lbs. Deb: 5/1/1884 U

1884	Phi-N	109	420	74	93	21	2	0	23	9	42	.221	.238	.281	66	-16				.891	-22	*2-109	-3.2
1885	Phi-N	103	421	77	112	15	3	0	23	22	25	.266	.318	.316	108	4				.921	-0	*O-99/2-5	0.2
1886	Phi-N	107	437	93	109	15	4	2	28	31	35	.249	.299	.316	86	-7	**56**			.903	4	O-104/2-3	-0.5
1887	Phi-N	104	464	110	151	19	7	4	67	21	21	.325	.359	.422	110	5	57			.902	-4	*O-99/2-7,1	-0.1
1888	Phi-N	124	528	75	126	14	4	3	44	21	41	.239	.272	.297	77	-14	35			.903	-4	*O-124	-2.2
1889	Phi-N	10	39	10	11	1	0	0	7	2	4	.282	.317	.308	69	-2	7			.808	-1	/O-9,2-1	-0.2
	Ind-N	40	173	32	53	11	0	2	22	5	10	.306	.330	.370	94	-2	7			.885	-3	O-40/2-1	-0.5
	Yr	50	212	42	64	12	0	2	29	7	14	.302	.327	.358	89	-4	14			.867	-4	O-49/2-2	-0.7
1890	Bro-P	94	395	84	100	14	2	3	38	40	32	.253	.323	.322	68	-19	21			.912	1	*O-94	-1.7
1891	Cin-a	83	356	47	75	7	4	0	26	33	25	.211	.279	.253	48	-26	22			.961	17	O-83	-1.0
Total	8	774	3233	602	830	117	26	14	278	194	245	.257	.301	.320	82	-76	205			.912	-13	O-652,2-126/1	-9.2

YEAR	TM/L	G	AB	R	H	2B	3B	HR	RBI	BB	SO	AVG	OBP	SLG	PRO+	BR/A	SB	CS	SBR	FA	FR	G/POS	TPR

■ JIM ANDREWS Andrews, James Pratt b: 6/5/1865, Shelburne Falls, Mass. d: 12/27/07, Chicago, Ill. Deb: 4/19/1890

| 1890 | Chi-N | 53 | 202 | 32 | 38 | 4 | 2 | 3 | 17 | 23 | 41 | .188 | .278 | .272 | 58 | -11 | 11 | | | .900 | 1 | O-53 | -1.1 |

■ MIKE ANDREWS Andrews, Michael Jay b: 7/9/43, Los Angeles, Cal. BR/TR, 6'3", 195 lbs. Deb: 9/18/66 F

1966	Bos-A	5	18	1	3	0	0	0	0	0	2	.167	.167	.167	-4	-2	0	0	0	1.000	2	/2-5	0.0
1967	*Bos-A	142	494	79	130	20	0	8	40	62	72	.263	.348	.352	99	1	7	7	-2	.976	-6	*2-139/S-6	0.2
1968	Bos-A	147	536	77	145	22	1	7	45	81	57	.271	.369	.354	113	11	3	8	-4	.976	1	*2-139/S-4,3	2.0
1969	Bos-A★	121	464	79	136	26	2	15	59	71	53	.293	.393	.455	129	20	1	1	-0	.972	5	*2-120	3.6
1970	Bos-A	151	589	91	149	28	1	17	65	81	63	.253	.346	.390	96	-2	2	1	-0	.973	-30	*2-148	-2.0
1971	Chi-A	109	330	45	93	16	0	12	47	67	36	.282	.405	.439	135	18	3	5	-2	.956	-3	2-76,1-25	1.8
1972	Chi-A	148	505	58	111	18	0	7	50	70	78	.220	.317	.297	82	-9	2	2	-1	.973	-14	*2-145/1-5	-1.9
1973	Chi-A	52	159	10	32	9	0	0	10	23	28	.201	.302	.258	57	-9	0	1	-1	1.000	-3	D-30/1-9,23	-1.4
	*Oak-A	18	21	1	4	1	0	0	0	3	1	.190	.292	.238	53	-1	0	0	0	.944	-1	/2-9,D-2	-0.2
	Yr	70	180	11	36	10	0	0	10	26	29	.200	.301	.256	57	-10	0	1	-1	.974	-4	D-32,2-15/13	-1.6
Total	8	893	3116	441	803	140	4	66	316	458	390	.258	.356	.369	104	26	18	25	-10	.973	-49	2-787/1-39,DS3	2.1

■ ROB ANDREWS Andrews, Robert Patrick b: 12/11/52, Santa Monica, Cal. BR/TR, 6', 185 lbs. Deb: 4/7/75 F

1975	Hou-N	103	277	29	66	5	4	0	19	31	34	.238	.315	.285	73	-10	12	5	1	.982	7	2-94/S-6	0.2
1976	Hou-N	109	410	42	105	8	5	0	23	33	27	.256	.312	.300	81	-11	7	3	0	.977	8	*2-107/S-3	0.5
1977	SF-N	127	436	60	115	11	3	0	25	56	33	.264	.348	.303	76	-12	5	6	-2	.964	-12	*2-115	-1.9
1978	SF-N	79	177	21	39	3	3	1	11	20	18	.220	.299	.288	67	-8	5	1	1	.977	9	2-62/S-1	0.6
1979	SF-N	75	154	22	40	3	0	2	13	8	9	.260	.296	.318	73	-6	4	1	1	.956	4	2-53/3-3	0.1
Total	5	493	1454	174	365	30	15	3	91	148	121	.251	.320	.298	76	-47	33	16	0	.972	15	2-431/S-10,3	-0.5

■ STAN ANDREWS Andrews, Stanley Joseph "Polo" (b: Stanley Joseph Andruskewicz) b: 4/17/17, Lynn, Mass. BR/TR, 5'11", 178 lbs. Deb: 6/11/39

1939	Bos-N	13	26	1	6	0	0	0	1	1	2	.231	.259	.231	35	-2	0			.857	-2	C-10	-0.4
1940	Bos-N	19	33	1	6	0	0	0	2	0	3	.182	.182	.182	1	-4	1			.944	-1	C-14	-0.5
1944	Bro-N	4	8	1	1	0	0	0	1	1	2	.125	.222	.125	-1	-1	0			1.000	0	/C-4	-0.1
1945	Bro-N	21	49	5	8	0	1	0	2	5	4	.163	.255	.204	29	-5	0			.948	2	C-21	-0.2
	Phi-N	13	33	3	11	2	0	1	6	1	5	.333	.353	.485	135	1	1			.950	-1	C-12	0.1
	Yr	34	82	8	19	2	1	1	8	6	9	.232	.292	.317	70	-3	1			.949	1	C-33	-0.1
Total	4	70	149	11	32	2	1	1	12	8	16	.215	.259	.262	46	-11	2			.938	-1	/C-61	-1.1

■ WALLY ANDREWS Andrews, William Walter b: 9/18/1859, Philadelphia, Pa. d: 1/20/40, Indianapolis, Ind. BR/TR, 6'3", 170 lbs. Deb: 5/22/1884

1884	Lou-a	14	49	10	10	5	1	0		4		.204	.264	.347	102	0				.950	-1	/1-9,3-3,OS	-0.1
1888	Lou-a	26	93	12	18	6	3	0	6	13		.194	.292	.323	99	0	5			.997	2	1-26	-0.1
Total	2	40	142	22	28	11	4	0	6	17		.197	.283	.331	100	0	5			.985	1	/1-35,3-3,SO	-0.2

■ FRED ANDRUS Andrus, Frederick Hotham b: 8/23/1850, Washington, Mich. d: 11/10/37, Detroit, Mich. BR/TR, 6'2", 185 lbs. Deb: 7/25/1876

1876	Chi-N	8	36	6	11	3	0	0	2	0	5	.306	.306	.389	116	-3				.714	-3	/O-8	-0.3
1884	Chi-N	1	5	3	1	0	0	0	0	1	0	.200	.333	.200	67	-0				1.000	0	/P-1	0.0
Total	2	9	41	9	12	3	0	0	2	1	5	.293	.310	.366	110	0				.714	-3	/O-8,P-1	-0.3

■ BILL ANDRUS Andrus, William Morgan "Andy" b: 7/25/07, Beaumont, Tex. d: 3/12/82, Washington, D.C. BR/TR, 6', 185 lbs. Deb: 9/19/31

1931	Was-A	3	7	0	0	0	0	0	1	0	1	.000	.000	.000	-99	-2	0	0	0	.750	-0	/3-2	-0.2
1937	Phi-N	3	2	0	0	0	0	0	0	0	2	.000	.000	.000	-93	-1	0			.000	0	/3-1	-0.1
Total	2	6	9	0	0	0	0	0	1	0	3	.000	.000	.000	-98	-3	0	0		.750	0	/3-3	-0.3

■ WIMAN ANDRUS Andrus, William Wiman b: 10/14/1858, Orono, Ontario, Can d: 6/17/35, Miles City, Mont. Deb: 9/15/1885

| 1885 | Pro-N | 1 | 4 | 0 | 0 | 0 | 0 | 0 | 0 | 0 | 0 | .000 | .000 | .000 | -99 | 0 | | | | 1.000 | 1 | /3-1 | 0.0 |

■ TOM ANGLEY Angley, Thomas Samuel b: 10/2/04, Baltimore, Md. d: 10/26/52, Wichita, Kan. BL/TR, 5'8", 190 lbs. Deb: 4/23/29

| 1929 | Chi-N | 5 | 16 | 1 | 4 | 1 | 0 | 0 | 6 | 2 | 2 | .250 | .333 | .313 | 61 | -1 | 0 | | | .968 | 1 | /C-5 | 0.1 |

■ PAT ANKENMAN Ankenman, Frederick Norman b: 12/23/12, Houston, Tex. d: 1/13/89, Houston, Tex. BR/TR, 5'4", 125 lbs. Deb: 4/16/36

1936	StL-N	1	3	0	0	0	0	0	0	0	0	.000	.000	.000	-99	-1	0			.600	-1	/S-1	-0.2
1943	Bro-N	1	2	1	1	0	0	0	0	0	0	.500	.500	.500	189	0	0			1.000	1	/S-1	0.1
1944	Bro-N	13	24	1	6	1	0	0	2	0	2	.250	.250	.292	53	-2	0			.971	0	2-11/S-2	-0.1
Total	3	15	29	2	7	1	0	0	2	0	5	.241	.241	.276	46	-2	0			.800	-1	/2-11,S-4	-0.2

■ BILL ANNIS Annis, William Perley b: 3/8/1857, Stoneham, Mass. d: 6/10/23, Kennebunkport, Me. BR, 5'7", 150 lbs. Deb: 5/1/1884

| 1884 | Bos-N | 27 | 96 | 17 | 17 | 2 | 0 | 0 | 3 | 0 | 8 | .177 | .177 | .198 | 18 | -9 | | | | .897 | -3 | O-27 | -1.2 |

■ CAP ANSON Anson, Adrian Constantine b: 4/11/1852, Marshalltown, Iowa d: 4/14/22, Chicago, Ill. BR/TR, 6', 227 lbs. Deb: 5/6/1871 MH

1871	Rok-n	25	120	29	39	11	3	0	16	2	1	.325	.336	.467	134	6	6					*3-20/C-3,2O	0.2
1872	Ath-n	46	215	60	89	9	7	0	50	16	3	.414	.455	.521	199	25						*3-45	1.4
1873	Ath-n	52	254	53	101	9	2	0	36	5	1	.398	.409	.449	142	11						*1-36,3-11/C2O	0.8
1874	Ath-n	55	260	51	86	8	3	0			3	.331	.338	.385	119	4						1-22,3-20/OS	0.3
1875	Ath-n	69	324	84	105	17	4	1			6	.324	.336	.410	141	10						1-32,O-22,C/3M	0.9
1876	Chi-N	66	309	63	110	9	7	2	59	12	6	.356	.380	.450	157	16				.849	13	*3-66/C-2	2.6
1877	Chi-N	59	255	52	86	19	1	0	32	9	3	.337	.360	.420	129	7				.883	8	*3-40,C-31	1.5
1878	Chi-N	60	261	55	89	12	2	0	40	13	1	.341	.372	.402	145	12				.825	-8	*O-48/2-9,3C	0.2
1879	Chi-N	51	227	40	72	20	1	0	34	2	2	.317	.323	.414	133	7				.975	0	1-51/M	0.5
1880	Chi-N	86	356	54	120	24	1	1	74	14	12	.337	.362	.419	154	19				.978	0	*1-81/3-9,S2M	1.2
1881	Chi-N	84	343	67	137	21	7	1	82	26	4	.399	.442	.510	189	35				.975	0	*1-84/C-2,SM	3.1
1882	Chi-N	82	348	69	126	29	8	1	83	20	7	.362	.397	.500	177	29				.949	-1	*1-82/C-1M	1.7
1883	Chi-N	98	413	70	127	36	5	0	68	18	9	.308	.336	.419	121	9				.964	3	*1-98/P-2,OCM	0.1
1884	Chi-N	112	475	108	159	30	3	21	102	29	13	.335	.373	.543	170	35				.956	-1	*1-112/C-3,SPM	2.0
1885	*Chi-N	112	464	100	144	35	7	7	108	34	13	.310	.357	.461	142	18				.958	-4	*1-112/C-1M	0.0
1886	*Chi-N	125	504	117	187	35	11	10	147	55	19	.371	.433	.544	170	39	29			.963	8	*1-125,C-12M	3.0
1887	Chi-N	122	472	107	164	33	13	7	102	60	18	.347	.422	.517	141	24	27			.973	10	*1-122/C-1M	1.8
1888	Chi-N	134	515	101	177	20	12	12	84	47	24	.344	.400	.499	173	41	28			.986	9	*1-134/M	3.6
1889	Chi-N	134	518	100	161	32	7	7	117	86	19	.311	.414	.440	132	24	27			.982	9	*1-134/M	2.1
1890	Chi-N	139	504	95	157	14	5	7	107	113	23	.312	.443	.401	141	33	29			.978	0	*1-135/C-3,2M	2.3
1891	Chi-N	136	540	81	157	24	8	8	120	75	29	.291	.378	.409	129	21	17			.981	3	*1-136/C-2M	2.0
1892	Chi-N	146	559	62	152	25	9	1	74	67	30	.272	.354	.354	113	10	13			.973	-5	*1-146/M	-0.2
1893	Chi-N	103	398	70	125	24	2	0	91	68	12	.314	.415	.384	115	12	13			.981	-4	*1-101/M	0.4
1894	Chi-N	83	340	82	132	28	4	5	99	40	15	.388	.457	.538	142	18	17			.990	3	1-82/2-1M	1.6
1895	Chi-N	122	474	87	159	23	6	2	91	55	23	.335	.408	.422	107	6	12			.985	-1	*1-122/M	0.6
1896	Chi-N	108	402	72	133	18	2	2	90	49	10	.331	.407	.400	109	7	24			.983	-1	*1-98,C-10/M	0.7
1897	Chi-N	114	424	67	121	17	3	3	75	60		.285	.379	.361	92	-3	11			.975	-1	*1-103,C-11/M	-0.1
Total	5 n	247	1173	277	420	54	19	1	102	32	5	.358	.375	.439	146	56	12					3-100/1-90,OCS2	3.6
Total	22	2276	9101	1719	2995	528	124	97	1879	952	294	.329	.395	.446	128	417	247			.974	57	*1-2058,3-118/CO2PS	30.7

YEAR	TM/L	G	AB	R	H	2B	3B	HR	RBI	BB	SO	AVG	OBP	SLG	PRO+	BR/A	SB	CS	SBR	FA	FR	G/POS	TPR

■ ERIC ANTHONY
Anthony, Eric Todd b: 11/8/67, San Diego, Cal. BL/TL, 6'2", 195 lbs. Deb: 7/29/89

1989	Hou-N	25	61	7	11	2	0	4	7	9	16	.180	.286	.410	100	-0	0	0	0	1.000	-1	O-21	-0.1
1990	Hou-N	84	239	26	46	8	0	10	29	29	78	.192	.285	.351	76	-8	5	0	2	.970	-2	O-71	-1.1
1991	Hou-N	39	118	11	18	6	0	1	7	12	41	.153	.231	.229	31	-11	1	0	0	.986	3	O-37	-0.9
1992	Hou-N	137	440	45	105	15	1	19	80	38	98	.239	.301	.407	103	0	5	4	-1	.973	-6	*O-115	-1.0
1993	Hou-N	145	486	70	121	19	4	15	66	49	88	.249	.320	.397	94	-5	3	5	-2	.988	-7	*O-131	-1.7
1994	Sea-A	79	262	31	62	14	1	10	30	23	66	.237	.298	.412	79	-9	6	2	1	.985	-2	O-71/D-4	-1.1
Total	6	509	1606	190	363	64	6	59	219	160	387	.226	.298	.384	87	-33	20	11	-1	.981	-16	O-446/D-4	-5.9

■ JOE ANTOLICK
Antolick, Joseph b: 4/11/16, Hokendauqua, Pa. BR/TR, 6', 185 lbs. Deb: 9/20/44

| 1944 | Phi-N | 4 | 6 | 1 | 2 | 0 | 0 | 0 | 0 | 1 | 0 | .333 | .429 | .333 | 120 | 0 | 0 | | | 1.000 | 1 | /C-3 | 0.1 |

■ JOHN ANTONELLI
Antonelli, John Lawrence b: 7/15/15, Memphis, Tenn. d: 4/18/90, Memphis, Tenn. BR/TR, 5'10.5", 165 lbs. Deb: 9/16/44

1944	StL-N	8	21	0	4	1	0	0	1	0	4	.190	.190	.238	20	-2	0			1.000	1	/1-3,3-3,2	-0.1
1945	StL-N	2	3	0	0	0	0	0	0	0	1	.000	.000	.000	-98	-1	0			.667	-0	/3-1	-0.1
	Phi-N	125	504	50	129	27	2	1	28	24	24	.256	.292	.323	73	-19	1			.959	-9	*3-108,2-23/1S	-2.5
	Yr	127	507	50	129	27	2	1	28	24	25	.254	.291	.321	72	-20	1			.957	-9	*3-109,2-23/1S	-2.6
Total	2	135	528	50	133	28	2	1	29	24	29	.252	.287	.318	70	-22	1			.958	-8	3-112/2-25,1S	-2.7

■ BILL ANTONELLO
Antonello, William James b: 5/19/27, Brooklyn, N.Y. d: 3/4/93, Fridley, Minn. BR/TR, 5'11", 185 lbs. Deb: 4/30/53

| 1953 | Bro-N | 40 | 43 | 9 | 7 | 1 | 1 | 1 | 4 | 2 | 11 | .163 | .200 | .302 | 28 | -5 | 0 | 0 | 0 | .964 | -6 | O-25 | -1.0 |

■ LUIS APARICIO
Aparicio, Luis Ernesto (Montiel) b: 4/29/34, Maracaibo, Venez. BR/TR, 5'9", 160 lbs. Deb: 4/17/56 H

1956	Chi-A	152	533	69	142	19	6	3	56	34	63	.266	.312	.341	71	-23	21	4	4	.954	-9	*S-152	-0.6
1957	Chi-A	143	575	82	148	22	6	3	41	52	55	.257	.319	.332	78	-17	28	8	4	.972	-13	*S-142	-1.4
1958	Chi-A★	145	557	76	148	20	9	2	40	35	38	.266	.310	.345	82	-14	29	6	5	.973	9	*S-145	1.3
1959	*Chi-A★	152	612	98	157	18	5	6	51	53	40	.257	.319	.332	80	-16	56	13	9	.970	-4	*S-152	0.2
1960	Chi-A★	153	600	86	166	20	7	2	61	43	39	.277	.326	.343	82	-15	51	8	11	.979	30	*S-153	3.8
1961	Chi-A★	156	625	90	170	24	4	6	45	38	33	.272	.315	.352	79	-19	53	13	8	.962	6	*S-156	0.8
1962	Chi-A★	153	581	72	140	23	5	7	40	32	36	.241	.282	.334	65	-29	31	12	2	.973	10	*S-152	-0.4
1963	Bal-A	146	601	73	150	18	8	5	45	36	55	.250	.294	.331	78	-18	40	6	8	.983	-5	*S-145	-0.5
1964	Bal-A†	146	578	93	154	20	3	10	37	49	51	.266	.327	.363	92	-6	57	17	7	.979	3	*S-145	1.5
1965	Bal-A	144	564	67	127	20	10	8	40	46	56	.225	.287	.339	76	-18	26	7	4	.971	3	*S-141	-0.2
1966	*Bal-A	151	659	97	182	25	8	6	41	33	42	.276	.312	.366	95	-5	25	11	1	.978	10	*S-151	2.2
1967	Bal-A	134	546	55	127	22	5	4	31	29	44	.233	.273	.313	73	-19	18	5	2	.957	-20	*S-131	-2.6
1968	Chi-A	155	622	55	164	24	4	4	36	33	43	.264	.303	.334	92	-7	17	11	-2	.977	25	*S-154	3.7
1969	Chi-A	156	599	77	168	24	5	5	51	66	29	.280	.354	.362	96	-2	24	4	5	.976	29	*S-154	5.1
1970	Chi-A★	146	552	86	173	29	3	5	43	53	34	.313	.375	.404	110	9	8	3	1	.976	18	*S-146	4.6
1971	Bos-A★	125	491	56	114	23	0	4	45	35	43	.232	.286	.303	63	-24	6	4	-1	.971	-18	*S-121	-2.9
1972	Bos-A†	110	436	47	112	26	3	3	39	26	28	.257	.302	.351	89	-6	3	3	-1	.968	-17	*S-109	-1.0
1973	Bos-A	132	499	56	135	17	1	0	49	43	33	.271	.328	.309	76	-15	13	1	3	.966	-17	*S-132	-1.2
Total	18	2599	10230	1335	2677	394	92	83	791	736	742	.262	.313	.343	82	-245	506	136	70	.972	51	*S-2581	12.4

■ LUKE APPLING
Appling, Lucius Benjamin b: 4/2/07, High Point, N.C. d: 1/3/91, Cumming, Ga. BR/TR, 5'10", 183 lbs. Deb: 9/10/30 MCH

1930	Chi-A	6	26	2	8	2	0	0	2	0	0	.308	.308	.385	77	-1	2	0	1	.879	-1	/S-6	-0.1
1931	Chi-A	96	297	36	69	13	4	1	28	29	27	.232	.303	.313	66	-15	9	2	2	.900	-6	S-76/2-1	-1.1
1932	Chi-A	139	489	66	134	20	10	3	63	40	36	.274	.329	.374	87	-10	9	8	-2	.929	18	S-85,2-30,3	1.4
1933	Chi-A	151	612	90	197	36	10	6	85	56	29	.322	.379	.443	122	19	6	11	-5	.939	11	*S-151	3.4
1934	Chi-A	118	452	75	137	28	6	2	61	59	27	.303	.384	.405	100	2	3	1	0	.945	-9	*S-110/2-8	-0.3
1935	Chi-A	153	525	94	161	28	6	1	71	122	40	.307	.437	.389	112	17	12	6	0	.958	21	*S-153	4.3
1936	Chi-A★	138	526	111	204	31	7	6	128	85	25	.388	.474	.508	137	36	10	6	-1	.951	15	*S-137	5.1
1937	Chi-A	154	574	98	182	42	8	4	77	86	28	.317	.407	.439	113	15	18	10	-1	.944	14	*S-154	3.5
1938	Chi-A	81	294	41	89	14	0	0	44	42	17	.303	.392	.350	85	-5	1	3	-2	.953	1	S-78	0.1
1939	Chi-A☆	148	516	82	162	16	6	0	56	105	37	.314	.430	.368	103	9	16	9	-1	.951	-2	*S-148	1.8
1940	Chi-A☆	150	566	96	197	27	13	0	79	69	35	.348	.420	.442	122	22	3	5	-2	.953	-2	*S-150	2.9
1941	Chi-A☆	154	592	93	186	26	8	1	57	82	32	.314	.399	.390	111	13	12	8	-1	.948	13	*S-154	2.2
1942	Chi-A	142	543	78	142	26	4	3	53	63	23	.262	.342	.341	94	-3	17	5	2	.948	-7	*S-141	0.1
1943	Chi-A☆	155	585	63	192	33	2	3	80	90	29	.328	.419	.407	142	35	27	8	1	.957	7	*S-155	6.0
1945	Chi-A	18	57	12	21	2	1	1	10	12	7	.368	.478	.526	197	8	1	0	0	.930	-1	S-17	0.9
1946	Chi-A★	149	582	59	180	27	5	1	55	71	41	.309	.384	.378	118	16	6	4	-1	.951	7	*S-149	3.2
1947	Chi-A★	139	503	67	154	29	0	8	49	64	28	.306	.386	.412	126	19	8	6	-1	.949	-7	*S-129/3-2	1.8
1948	Chi-A	139	497	63	156	16	2	0	47	94	35	.314	.423	.354	112	14	10	4	1	.943	12	3-72,S-64	2.9
1949	Chi-A	142	492	82	148	21	5	5	58	121	24	.301	.439	.394	125	25	7	12	-5	.964	-1	*S-141	2.8
1950	Chi-A	50	128	11	30	3	4	0	13	12	8	.234	.300	.320	61	-8	2	0	1	.967	0	S-20,1-13/2	-0.5
Total	20	2422	8856	1319	2749	440	102	45	1116	1302	528	.310	.399	.398	113	207	179	108	-11	.948	73	*S-2218/3-88,21	40.7

■ JACK ARAGON
Aragon, Angel Valdes (Reyes) b: 11/20/15, Havana, Cuba d: 4/4/88, Clearwater, Fla. BR/TR, 5'10", 176 lbs. Deb: 8/13/41 F

| 1941 | NY-N | 1 | 0 | 0 | 0 | 0 | 0 | 0 | 0 | 0 | 0 | — | — | — | | 0 | 0 | | | .000 | 0 | R | 0.0 |

■ ANGEL ARAGON
Aragon, Angel (Valdes) "Pete" b: 8/2/1890, Havana, Cuba d: 1/24/52, New York, N.Y. BR/TR, 5'5", 150 lbs. Deb: 8/20/14 F

1914	NY-A	6	7	1	1	0	0	0	0	1	2	.143	.333	.143	44	-0	0			.000	-1	/O-1	-0.1
1916	NY-A	12	24	1	5	0	0	0	3	2	2	.208	.269	.208	43	-2	2			.864	1	/3-8,O-2	-0.1
1917	NY-A	14	45	2	3	1	0	0	2	2	2	.067	.106	.089	-40	-8	0			.933	1	/O-6,3-4,S	-0.8
Total	3	32	76	4	9	1	0	0	5	5	6	.118	.183	.132	-4	-10	2			.921	2	/3-12,O-9,S	-0.9

■ MAURICE ARCHDEACON
Archdeacon, Maurice John "Flash" b: 12/14/1898, St.Louis, Mo. d: 9/5/54, St.Louis, Mo. BL/TL, 5'8", 153 lbs. Deb: 9/17/23

1923	Chi-A	22	87	23	35	5	1	0	4	6	8	.402	.441	.448	145	6	2	3	-1	.918	-2	O-20	0.1
1924	Chi-A	95	288	59	92	9	3	0	25	40	30	.319	.410	.372	106	5	11	7	-1	.958	-5	O-77	-0.5
1925	Chi-A	10	9	2	1	0	0	0	0	2	1	.111	.273	.111	0	-1	0	0	0	1.000	0	/O-1	-0.1
Total	3	127	384	84	128	14	4	0	29	48	39	.333	.413	.391	112	9	13	10	-2	.950	-7	/O-98	-0.5

■ JIMMY ARCHER
Archer, James Patrick b: 5/13/1883, Dublin, Ireland d: 3/29/58, Milwaukee, Wis. BR/TR, 5'10", 168 lbs. Deb: 9/6/04

1904	Pit-N	7	20	1	3	0	0	0	1	0		.150	.150	.150	-7	-2	0			.919	0	/C-7,O-1	-0.2
1907	*Det-A	18	42	6	5	0	0	0	4	1		.119	.136	.119	1	-5	0			.975	2	C-17/2-1	-0.1
1909	Chi-N	80	261	31	60	9	2	1	30	12		.230	.266	.291	71	-10	5			.960	-4	C-80	-0.7
1910	*Chi-N	98	313	36	81	17	6	2	41	14	49	.259	.293	.371	94	-4	6			.970	3	C-49,1-40	0.4
1911	Chi-N	116	387	41	98	18	5	4	41	18	43	.253	.288	.357	80	-12	5			.977	-1	*C-102,1-10/2	-0.3
1912	Chi-N	120	385	35	109	20	1	6	58	22	36	.283	.330	.387	96	-3	7			.966	-5	*C-118	0.3
1913	Chi-N	111	368	38	98	14	7	2	44	19	27	.266	.311	.359	91	-5	4			.969	-3	*C-103/1-8	0.1
1914	Chi-N	79	248	17	64	9	2	0	19	9	9	.258	.284	.310	77	-8	1			.973	5	C-76	0.4
1915	Chi-N	97	309	21	75	11	5	1	27	11	38	.243	.273	.320	79	-9	5	6	-2	.977	-2	C-88/1-4	-0.6
1916	Chi-N	77	205	11	45	6	2	1	30	12	24	.220	.269	.283	63	-9	3			.979	-3	C-61/3-1	-0.9
1917	Chi-N	2	2	0	0	0	0	0	0	0	1	.000	.000	.000	-93	-0	0			.000	0	H	-0.1
1918	Pit-N	24	58	4	9	1	0	0	3	1	6	.155	.197	.241	32	-5	0			.989	5	C-21/1-1	0.1
	Bro-N	9	22	3	6	1	0	0	1	0	5	.273	.304	.364	104	0	0			.968	1	/C-7	0.1

YEAR	TM/L	G	AB	R	H	2B	3B	HR	RBI	BB	SO	AVG	OBP	SLG	PRO+	BR/A	SB	CS	SBR	FA	FR	G/POS	TPR
	Cin-N	9	26	2	7	1	0	0	2	1	3	.269	.296	.308	86	-0	0			1.000	1	/C-7,1-1	0.1
	Yr	42	106	9	22	2	3	0	5	3	14	.208	.243	.283	59	-5	0			.987	7	C-35/1-2	0.3
Total	12	847	2646	246	660	106	33	17	296	124	241	.249	.288	.334	80	-72	36	6		.971	-0	C-736/1-64,230	-1.4

■ GEORGE ARCHIE   Archie, George Albert b: 4/27/14, Nashville, Tenn. BR/TR, 6', 170 lbs. Deb: 9/14/38

YEAR	TM/L	G	AB	R	H	2B	3B	HR	RBI	BB	SO	AVG	OBP	SLG	PRO+	BR/A	SB	CS	SBR	FA	FR	G/POS	TPR
1938	Det-A	3	2	1	0	0	0	0	0	0	1	.000	.000	.000	-95	-1	0	0	0	.000	0	H	-0.1
1941	Was-A	105	379	45	102	20	4	3	48	30	42	.269	.324	.367	87	-8	8	4	0	.936	-4	3-73,1-23	-1.2
	StL-A	9	29	3	11	3	0	0	5	7	3	.379	.500	.483	156	3	2	0	1	.975	0	/1-8	0.3
	Yr	114	408	48	113	23	4	3	53	37	45	.277	.339	.375	92	-5	10	4	1	.936	-4	3-73,1-31	-0.9
1946	StL-A	4	11	1	2	1	0	0	0	0	0	.182	.182	.273	25	-1	0	0	0	1.000	0	/1-3	0.1
Total	3	121	421	50	115	24	4	3	53	37	47	.273	.333	.357	90	-7	10	4	1	.988	-2	/3-73,1-34	-0.9

■ JOSE ARCIA   Arcia, Jose Raimundo (Orta) b: 8/22/43, Havana, Cuba BR/TR, 6'3", 170 lbs. Deb: 4/10/68

YEAR	TM/L	G	AB	R	H	2B	3B	HR	RBI	BB	SO	AVG	OBP	SLG	PRO+	BR/A	SB	CS	SBR	FA	FR	G/POS	TPR
1968	Chi-N	59	84	15	16	4	0	1	8	3	24	.190	.218	.274	44	-6	0	0	0	1.000	-2	O-17,2-10/S3	-0.9
1969	SD-N	120	302	35	65	11	3	0	10	14	47	.215	.255	.272	49	-21	14	7	0	.977	5	2-68,S-37/3O1	-1.0
1970	SD-N	114	229	28	51	9	3	0	17	12	36	.223	.282	.288	55	-15	3	6	-3	.955	10	S-67,2-20/3O	-0.1
Total	3	293	615	78	132	24	6	1	35	29	107	.215	.260	.278	51	-41	17	13	-3	.950	13	S-111/2-98,031	-2.0

■ DAN ARDELL   Ardell, Daniel Miers b: 5/27/41, Seattle, Wash. BL/TL, 6'2", 190 lbs. Deb: 9/14/61

YEAR	TM/L	G	AB	R	H	2B	3B	HR	RBI	BB	SO	AVG	OBP	SLG	PRO+	BR/A	SB	CS	SBR	FA	FR	G/POS	TPR
1961	LA-A	7	4	1	1	0	0	0	0	1	2	.250	.400	.250	70	-0	0	0	0	1.000	-0	/1-1	0.0

■ JOE ARDNER   Ardner, Joseph A. "Old Hoss" b: 2/27/1858, Mt.Vernon, Ohio d: 9/15/35, Cleveland, Ohio BR/TR, 160 lbs. Deb: 5/1/1884

YEAR	TM/L	G	AB	R	H	2B	3B	HR	RBI	BB	SO	AVG	OBP	SLG	PRO+	BR/A	SB	CS	SBR	FA	FR	G/POS	TPR
1884	Cle-N	26	92	6	16	1	1	0	4	1	24	.174	.183	.207	21	-8				.866	-5	2-25/3-1	-1.1
1890	Cle-N	84	323	28	72	13	1	0	35	17	40	.223	.266	.269	57	-18	9			.920	-6	2-84	-1.7
Total	2	110	415	34	88	14	2	0	39	18	64	.212	.248	.255	50	-26	9			.908	-11	2-109/3-1	-2.8

■ HANK ARFT   Arft, Henry Irven "Bow Wow" b: 1/28/22, Manchester, Mo. BL/TL, 5'10.5", 190 lbs. Deb: 7/27/48

YEAR	TM/L	G	AB	R	H	2B	3B	HR	RBI	BB	SO	AVG	OBP	SLG	PRO+	BR/A	SB	CS	SBR	FA	FR	G/POS	TPR
1948	StL-A	69	248	25	59	10	3	5	38	45	43	.238	.355	.363	89	-3	1	2	-1	.995	-1	1-69	-0.5
1949	StL-A	6	5	1	1	1	0	0	2	0	1	.200	.200	.400	55	-0	0	0	0	.000	0	H	0.0
1950	StL-A	98	280	45	75	16	4	1	32	46	48	.268	.375	.364	87	-5	3	2	-0	.995	-1	1-84	-0.5
1951	StL-A	112	345	44	90	16	5	7	42	41	34	.261	.339	.397	96	-2	4	6	-2	.989	8	1-97	-0.1
1952	StL-A	15	28	1	4	3	1	0	4	5	7	.143	.273	.321	63	-1	0	0	0	.985	0	1-10	-0.2
Total	5	300	906	116	229	46	13	13	118	137	133	.253	.352	.375	90	-12	8	10	-3	.992	8	1-260	-1.3

■ ALEX ARIAS   Arias, Alejandro b: 11/20/67, New York, N.Y. BR/TR, 6'3", 185 lbs. Deb: 5/12/92

YEAR	TM/L	G	AB	R	H	2B	3B	HR	RBI	BB	SO	AVG	OBP	SLG	PRO+	BR/A	SB	CS	SBR	FA	FR	G/POS	TPR
1992	Chi-N	32	99	14	29	6	0	0	7	11	13	.293	.375	.354	105	1	0	0	0	.967	-4	S-30	-0.1
1993	Fla-N	96	249	27	67	5	1	2	20	27	18	.269	.348	.321	76	-7	1	1	-0	.987	-9	2-30,3-22,S	-1.4
1994	Fla-N	59	113	4	27	5	0	0	15	9	19	.239	.301	.283	51	-8	0	1	-1	.985	-5	S-20,3-15	-1.2
Total	3	187	461	45	123	16	1	2	42	47	50	.267	.342	.319	75	-14	1	2	-1	.967	-17	/S-68,3-37,2	-2.7

■ BUZZ ARLETT   Arlett, Russell Loris b: 1/3/1899, Elmhurst, Cal. d: 5/16/64, Minneapolis, Minn. BB/BR, 6'3.5", 225 lbs. Deb: 4/14/31

YEAR	TM/L	G	AB	R	H	2B	3B	HR	RBI	BB	SO	AVG	OBP	SLG	PRO+	BR/A	SB	CS	SBR	FA	FR	G/POS	TPR
1931	Phi-N	121	418	65	131	26	7	18	72	45	39	.313	.387	.538	135	20	3			.955	1	O-94,1-13	1.4

■ TONY ARMAS   Armas, Antonio Rafael (Machado) b: 7/2/53, Anzoategui, Venez. BR/TR, 6'1", 200 lbs. Deb: 9/6/76 F

YEAR	TM/L	G	AB	R	H	2B	3B	HR	RBI	BB	SO	AVG	OBP	SLG	PRO+	BR/A	SB	CS	SBR	FA	FR	G/POS	TPR
1976	Pit-N	4	6	0	2	0	0	0	1	0	2	.333	.333	.333	89	-0	0	0	0	1.000	-0	/O-2	0.0
1977	Oak-A	118	363	26	87	8	2	13	53	20	99	.240	.279	.380	79	-12	1	2	-1	.981	9	*O-112/S-1	-0.7
1978	Oak-A	91	239	17	51	6	1	2	13	10	62	.213	.251	.272	50	-16	1	2	-1	.991	3	O-85/D-3	-1.8
1979	Oak-A	80	278	29	69	9	3	11	34	16	67	.248	.292	.421	95	-3	1	0	0	.976	7	O-80	0.1
1980	Oak-A	158	628	87	175	18	8	35	109	29	128	.279	.313	.500	128	19	5	3	-0	.975	18	*O-158	3.1
1981	*Oak-A★	109	440	51	115	24	3	**22**	76	19	115	.261	.295	.480	126	11	5	1	1	.993	12	*O-109	2.1
1982	Oak-A	138	536	58	125	19	2	28	89	33	128	.233	.279	.433	96	-5	2	2	-1	.983	12	*O-135/D-1	0.2
1983	Bos-A	145	574	77	125	23	2	36	107	29	131	.218	.258	.453	85	-14	0	1	-1	.985	7	*O-116,D-27	-1.3
1984	Bos-A☆	157	639	107	171	29	5	**43**	**123**	32	156	.268	.304	.531	120	14	1	3	-2	.974	2	*O-126,D-31	0.9
1985	Bos-A	103	385	50	102	17	5	23	64	18	90	.265	.301	.514	114	5	0	0	0	.983	-7	O-79,D-19	-0.5
1986	*Bos-A	121	425	40	112	21	4	11	58	24	77	.264	.306	.409	92	-5	0	2	-1	.969	-13	*O-117/D-1	-2.4
1987	Cal-A	28	81	8	16	3	1	3	9	1	11	.198	.207	.370	51	-4	1	0	0	1.000	-4	O-27	-1.0
1988	Cal-A	120	368	42	100	20	2	13	49	22	87	.272	.313	.443	112	5	3	4	-2	.986	-5	*O-113/D-5	-0.9
1989	Cal-A	60	202	22	52	7	1	11	30	7	48	.257	.282	.465	109	1	0	0	0	.990	2	O-47/1-2,D	0.2
Total	14	1432	5164	614	1302	204	39	251	815	260	1201	.252	.290	.453	103	-7	18	20	-7	.981	38	*O-1306/D-93,1S	-2.0

■ MARCOS ARMAS   Armas, Marcos Rafael (Ruiz) b: 8/5/69, Puerto Piritu, Venez. BR/TR, 6'5", 195 lbs. Deb: 5/25/93 F

YEAR	TM/L	G	AB	R	H	2B	3B	HR	RBI	BB	SO	AVG	OBP	SLG	PRO+	BR/A	SB	CS	SBR	FA	FR	G/POS	TPR
1993	Oak-A	15	31	7	6	2	0	1	1	1	12	.194	.242	.355	62	-2	1	0	0	1.000	0	1-12/O-1,D	-0.2

■ ED ARMBRISTER   Armbrister, Edison Rosanda b: 7/4/48, Nassau, Bahamas BR/TR, 5'11", 160 lbs. Deb: 8/31/73

YEAR	TM/L	G	AB	R	H	2B	3B	HR	RBI	BB	SO	AVG	OBP	SLG	PRO+	BR/A	SB	CS	SBR	FA	FR	G/POS	TPR
1973	*Cin-N	18	37	5	8	3	1	1	5	2	8	.216	.256	.432	92	-1	0	0	0	.917	-2	O-14	-0.3
1974	Cin-N	9	7	0	2	0	0	0	0	1	1	.286	.375	.286	88	-0	0	0	0	1.000	-1	/O-4	-0.2
1975	*Cin-N	59	65	9	12	1	0	0	2	5	19	.185	.254	.200	27	-6	3	1	0	.867	-7	O-19	-1.4
1976	*Cin-N	73	78	20	23	3	2	2	7	6	22	.295	.345	.462	124	2	7	3	0	.972	-4	O-32	-0.2
1977	Cin-N	65	78	12	20	4	3	1	5	10	21	.256	.341	.423	102	0	5	6	-2	.903	-3	O-27	-0.5
Total	5	224	265	46	65	11	6	4	19	24	71	.245	.310	.377	88	-5	15	10	-2	.925	-17	/O-96	-2.6

■ CHARLIE ARMBRUSTER   Armbruster, Charles A. b: 8/30/1880, Cincinnati, Ohio d: 10/7/64, Grants Pass, Ore. BR/TR, 5'9", 180 lbs. Deb: 7/17/05

YEAR	TM/L	G	AB	R	H	2B	3B	HR	RBI	BB	SO	AVG	OBP	SLG	PRO+	BR/A	SB	CS	SBR	FA	FR	G/POS	TPR
1905	Bos-A	35	91	13	18	4	0	0	6	18		.198	.336	.242	83	-1	3			.944	-6	C-35	-0.4
1906	Bos-A	72	201	9	29	6	1	0	6	25		.144	.242	.184	34	-15	2			.955	1	C-66/1-1	-0.8
1907	Bos-A	23	60	2	6	1	0	0	0	8		.100	.206	.117	3	-6	1			.935	2	C-21	-0.2
	Chi-A	1	3	0	0	0	0	0	0	1		.000	.250	.000	-20	-0	0			1.000	1	/C-1	0.0
	Yr	24	63	2	6	1	0	0	0	9		.095	.208	.111	2	-7	1			.940	3	C-22	-0.2
Total	3	131	355	24	53	11	1	0	12	52		.149	.262	.186	42	-22	6			.949	-2	C-123/1-1	-1.4

■ HARRY ARMBRUSTER   Armbruster, Henry "Army" b: 3/20/1882, Cincinnati, Ohio d: 12/10/53, Cincinnati, Ohio BL/TL, 5'10", 190 lbs. Deb: 4/30/06

YEAR	TM/L	G	AB	R	H	2B	3B	HR	RBI	BB	SO	AVG	OBP	SLG	PRO+	BR/A	SB	CS	SBR	FA	FR	G/POS	TPR
1906	Phi-A	91	265	40	63	6	3	2	24	43		.238	.353	.306	103	3	13			.971	0	O-74	-0.3

■ GEORGE ARMSTRONG   Armstrong, Noble George "Dodo" b: 6/3/24, Orange, N.J. d: 7/24/93, Orange, N.J. BR/TR, 5'10", 190 lbs. Deb: 4/26/46

YEAR	TM/L	G	AB	R	H	2B	3B	HR	RBI	BB	SO	AVG	OBP	SLG	PRO+	BR/A	SB	CS	SBR	FA	FR	G/POS	TPR
1946	Phi-A	8	6	0	1	1	0	0	0	1		.167	.286	.333	73	-0	0	0	0	1.000	0	/C-4	0.0

■ SAM ARMSTRONG   Armstrong, Samuel b: 1850, Baltimore, Md. 6'2", 160 lbs. Deb: 6/26/1871

YEAR	TM/L	G	AB	R	H	2B	3B	HR	RBI	BB	SO	AVG	OBP	SLG	PRO+	BR/A	SB	CS	SBR	FA	FR	G/POS	TPR
1871	Kek-n	12	49	9	11	2	1	0	5	0	1	.224	.224	.306	50	-3	0					O-12	-0.2

■ HARRY ARNDT   Arndt, Harry J. b: 2/12/1879, South Bend, Ind. d: 3/25/21, South Bend, Ind. TR Deb: 7/2/02

YEAR	TM/L	G	AB	R	H	2B	3B	HR	RBI	BB	SO	AVG	OBP	SLG	PRO+	BR/A	SB	CS	SBR	FA	FR	G/POS	TPR
1902	Det-A	10	34	4	5	1	0		7	6		.147	.275	.206	34	-4	0			.958	0	O-10/1-1	-0.3
	Bal-A	68	248	41	63	7	4	2	28	35		.254	.355	.339	89	-3	9			.872	1	O-62/2-4,3S	-0.6
	Yr	78	282	45	68	7	5	2	35	41		.241	.346	.323	83	-5	9			.885	0	O-72/2-4,31S	-0.9
1905	StL-N	113	415	40	101	11	6	2	36	24		.243	.290	.313	82	-10	13			.951	-14	2-90/O-9,3S	-2.4
1906	StL-N	69	256	30	69	7	9	2	26	19		.270	.320	.391	127	7	5			.965	13	3-65/1-1,O	2.2
1907	StL-N	11	32	5	6	1	0	0	2	1		.188	.212	.219	36	-2	0			1.000	0	/1-4,3-3	-0.3
Total	4	271	985	118	244	26	20	6	99	85		.248	.312	.333	91	-11	27			.952	-1	/2-94,0-82,3S1	-1.4

YEAR	TM/L	G	AB	R	H	2B	3B	HR	RBI	BB	SO	AVG	OBP	SLG	PRO+	BR/A	SB	CS	SBR	FA	FR	G/POS	TPR

■ LARRY ARNDT
Arndt, Larry Wayne   b: 2/25/63, Fremont, Ohio   BR/TR, 6'1", 195 lbs.   Deb: 6/6/89

YEAR	TM/L	G	AB	R	H	2B	3B	HR	RBI	BB	SO	AVG	OBP	SLG	PRO+	BR/A	SB	CS	SBR	FA	FR	G/POS	TPR
1989	Oak-A	2	6	1	1	0	0	0	0	0	1	.167	.167	.167	-6	-1	0	0	0	1.000	0	/1-1,3-1	-0.1

■ CHRIS ARNOLD
Arnold, Christopher Paul   b: 11/6/47, Long Beach, Cal.   BR/TR, 5'10", 160 lbs.   Deb: 9/7/71

YEAR	TM/L	G	AB	R	H	2B	3B	HR	RBI	BB	SO	AVG	OBP	SLG	PRO+	BR/A	SB	CS	SBR	FA	FR	G/POS	TPR
1971	SF-N	6	13	2	3	0	0	1	3	1	2	.231	.286	.462	110	0	0	0	0	.917	-3	/2-3	-0.1
1972	SF-N	51	84	8	19	3	1	1	4	8	12	.226	.293	.321	74	-3	0	1	-1	.970	-3	3-17/2-7,S	0.0
1973	SF-N	49	54	7	16	2	0	1	13	8	11	.296	.387	.389	111	1	0	0	0	.944	-5	/C-9,2-1,3	-0.4
1974	SF-N	78	174	22	42	7	3	1	26	15	27	.241	.305	.333	75	-6	1	1	-0	.974	-6	2-31/3-7,S	-1.1
1975	SF-N	29	41	4	8	0	0	0	0	4	1	.195	.267	.195	28	-4	0	0	0	.923	1	/2-4,O-4	-0.4
1976	SF-N	60	69	4	15	0	1	0	5	6	16	.217	.280	.246	49	-4	0	0	0	1.000	3	/2-8,3-4,1S	-0.1
Total	6	273	435	47	103	12	5	4	51	42	76	.237	.305	.315	72	-16	1	2	-1	.971	-5	/2-54,3-29,CSO1	-2.1

■ BILLY ARNOLD
Arnold, Willis S.   b: 3/2/1851, Middletown, Conn.   d: 1/17/1899, Albany, N.Y.   Deb: 4/26/1872

YEAR	TM/L	G	AB	R	H	2B	3B	HR	RBI	BB	SO	AVG	OBP	SLG	PRO+	BR/A	SB	CS	SBR	FA	FR	G/POS	TPR
1872	Man-n	2	8	2	1	0	0	0	0	0	0	.125	.125	.125	-24	-1						/O-2	-0.1

■ MORRIE ARNOVICH
Arnovich, Morris "Snooker"   b: 11/16/10, Superior, Wis.   d: 7/20/59, Superior, Wis.   BR/TR, 5'10", 168 lbs.   Deb: 9/14/36

YEAR	TM/L	G	AB	R	H	2B	3B	HR	RBI	BB	SO	AVG	OBP	SLG	PRO+	BR/A	SB	CS	SBR	FA	FR	G/POS	TPR
1936	Phi-N	13	48	4	15	3	0	1	7	1	3	.313	.353	.438	102	0	0			1.000	2	O-13	0.2
1937	Phi-N	117	410	60	119	27	4	10	60	34	32	.290	.349	.449	107	3	5			.972	7	*O-107	0.7
1938	Phi-N	139	502	47	138	29	0	4	72	42	37	.275	.333	.357	92	-5	2			.983	17	*O-133	0.8
1939	Phi-N☆	134	491	68	159	25	2	5	67	58	28	.324	.397	.413	122	17	7			.983	15	*O-132	2.7
1940	Phi-N	39	141	13	28	2	1	0	12	14	15	.199	.276	.242	42	-11	0			.959	3	O-37	-1.0
	*Cin-N	62	211	17	60	10	2	0	21	13	10	.284	.326	.351	86	-4	1			1.000	2	O-60	-0.5
	Yr	101	352	30	88	12	3	0	33	27	25	.250	.305	.301	68	-15	1			.983	5	O-97	-1.5
1941	NY-N	85	207	25	58	8	3	2	22	23	14	.280	.352	.377	103	1	2			.982	-4	O-61	-0.6
1946	NY-N	1	3	0	0	0	0	0	0	0	0	.000	.000	.000	-99	-1	0			1.000	-0	/O-1	-0.1
Total	7	590	2013	234	577	104	12	22	261	185	139	.287	.350	.383	100	0	17			.981	42	O-544	2.2

■ TUG ARUNDEL
Arundel, John Thomas   b: 6/30/1862, Romulus, N.Y.   d: 9/5/12, Auburn, N.Y.   Deb: 5/23/1882

YEAR	TM/L	G	AB	R	H	2B	3B	HR	RBI	BB	SO	AVG	OBP	SLG	PRO+	BR/A	SB	CS	SBR	FA	FR	G/POS	TPR
1882	Phi-a	1	5	0	0	0	0	0		0		.000	.000	.000	-90	-1				.800	-0	/C-1	-0.1
1884	Tol-a	15	47	6	4	0	0	0		0	3	.085	.140	.085	-24	-6				.946	8	C-15	0.3
1887	Ind-N	43	157	13	31	4	0	0	13	8	12	.197	.241	.223	31	-14	8			.865	-5	C-42/O-2,1	-1.4
1888	Was-N	17	51	2	10	0	1	0	3	5	10	.196	.268	.235	65	-2	1			.840	-7	C-17	-0.8
Total	4	76	260	21	45	4	1	0	16	16	22	.173	.224	.196	25	-23	9			.882	-4	/C-75,O-2,1	-2.0

■ RANDY ASADOOR
Asadoor, Randall Carl   b: 10/20/62, Fresno, Cal.   BR/TR, 6'1", 185 lbs.   Deb: 9/14/86

YEAR	TM/L	G	AB	R	H	2B	3B	HR	RBI	BB	SO	AVG	OBP	SLG	PRO+	BR/A	SB	CS	SBR	FA	FR	G/POS	TPR
1986	SD-N	15	55	9	20	5	0	0	7	3	13	.364	.397	.455	137	3	1	2	-1	.889	0	3-15/2-2	0.2

■ JIM ASBELL
Asbell, James Marion "Big Train"   b: 6/22/14, Dallas, Tex.   d: 7/6/67, San Mateo, Cal.   BR/TR, 6', 195 lbs.   Deb: 5/8/38

YEAR	TM/L	G	AB	R	H	2B	3B	HR	RBI	BB	SO	AVG	OBP	SLG	PRO+	BR/A	SB	CS	SBR	FA	FR	G/POS	TPR
1938	Chi-N	17	33	6	6	2	0	0	3	3	9	.182	.250	.242	35	-3	0			1.000	-1	O-10	-0.4

■ CASPER ASBJORNSON
Asbjornson, Robert Anthony (Name Changed To Asby)
b: 6/19/09, Concord, Mass.   d: 1/21/70, Williamsport, Pa.   BR/TR, 6'1", 196 lbs.   Deb: 9/17/28

YEAR	TM/L	G	AB	R	H	2B	3B	HR	RBI	BB	SO	AVG	OBP	SLG	PRO+	BR/A	SB	CS	SBR	FA	FR	G/POS	TPR
1928	Bos-A	6	16	0	3	1	0	0	1	1	1	.188	.235	.250	28	-2	0	0	0	.917	-2	/C-6	-0.3
1929	Bos-A	17	29	1	3	0	0	0	0	1	6	.103	.133	.103	-39	-6	0	0	0	.897	-3	C-15	-0.7
1931	Cin-N	45	118	13	36	7	1	0	22	7	23	.305	.349	.381	102	0	0			.981	-0	C-31	0.2
1932	Cin-N	29	58	5	10	2	0	1	4	0	15	.172	.186	.259	19	-7	0			.961	0	C-16	-0.6
Total	4	97	221	19	52	10	1	1	27	9	45	.235	.272	.303	56	-14	0	0		.960	-5	/C-68	-1.4

■ RICHIE ASHBURN
Ashburn, Rich "Whitey"   b: 3/19/27, Tilden, Neb.   BL/TR, 5'10", 170 lbs.   Deb: 4/20/48

YEAR	TM/L	G	AB	R	H	2B	3B	HR	RBI	BB	SO	AVG	OBP	SLG	PRO+	BR/A	SB	CS	SBR	FA	FR	G/POS	TPR
1948	Phi-N★	117	463	78	154	17	4	2	40	60	22	.333	.410	.400	122	17	32			.981	18	*O-116	2.8
1949	Phi-N	154	662	84	188	18	11	1	37	58	38	.284	.343	.349	88	-10	9			.980	25	*O-154	0.6
1950	*Phi-N	151	594	84	180	25	14	2	41	63	32	.303	.372	.402	105	6	14			.988	8	*O-147	0.7
1951	Phi-N★	154	643	92	221	31	5	4	63	50	37	.344	.393	.426	122	21	29	6	5	.988	32	*O-154	5.2
1952	Phi-N	154	613	93	173	31	6	1	42	75	30	.282	.362	.357	101	3	16	11	-2	.980	15	*O-154	1.1
1953	Phi-N★	156	622	110	205	25	9	2	57	61	35	.330	.394	.408	110	12	14	6	1	.990	26	*O-156	3.1
1954	Phi-N	153	559	111	175	16	8	1	41	125	46	.313	.442	.376	116	22	11	8	-2	.984	17	*O-153	3.0
1955	Phi-N	140	533	91	180	32	9	3	42	105	36	.338	.449	.448	142	39	12	10	-2	.983	11	*O-140	4.0
1956	Phi-N	154	628	94	190	26	8	3	50	79	45	.303	.385	.384	110	12	10	1	2	.983	25	*O-154	3.2
1957	Phi-N	156	626	93	186	26	8	0	33	94	44	.297	.392	.364	108	12	13	10	-2	.987	32	*O-156	3.3
1958	Phi-N☆	152	615	98	215	24	13	2	33	97	48	.350	.441	.441	136	38	30	12	2	.984	22	*O-152	5.3
1959	Phi-N	153	564	86	150	16	2	1	20	79	42	.266	.362	.307	79	-13	9	11	-4	.971	5	*O-149	-2.0
1960	Chi-N	151	547	99	159	16	5	0	40	116	50	.291	.416	.338	110	15	16	4	2	.976	1	*O-146	1.2
1961	Chi-N	109	307	49	79	7	4	0	19	55	27	.257	.375	.306	83	-5	7	6	-2	.978	-7	O-76	-1.8
1962	NY-N★	135	389	60	119	7	3	7	28	81	39	.306	.426	.393	119	15	12	7	-1	.975	-4	O-97/2-2	0.5
Total	15	2189	8365	1322	2574	317	109	29	586	1198	571	.308	.397	.382	111	184	234	92		.983	227	*O-2104/2-2	30.2

■ ALAN ASHBY
Ashby, Alan Dean   b: 7/8/51, Long Beach, Cal.   BB/TR, 6'2", 190 lbs.   Deb: 7/3/73

YEAR	TM/L	G	AB	R	H	2B	3B	HR	RBI	BB	SO	AVG	OBP	SLG	PRO+	BR/A	SB	CS	SBR	FA	FR	G/POS	TPR
1973	Cle-A	11	29	4	5	1	0	1	3	2	11	.172	.226	.310	49	-2	0	0	0	.978	-2	C-11	-0.4
1974	Cle-A	10	7	1	1	0	0	0	1	2	1	.143	.250	.143	15	-1	0	0	0	1.000	0	/C-9	0.0
1975	Cle-A	90	254	32	57	10	1	5	32	30	42	.224	.309	.331	81	-6	3	2	-0	.990	3	C-87/1-2,3D	0.0
1976	Cle-A	89	247	26	59	5	1	4	32	27	49	.239	.314	.316	86	-4	0	2	-1	.987	6	C-86/1-2,3	0.3
1977	Tor-A	124	396	25	83	16	3	2	29	50	51	.210	.301	.280	59	-22	0	2	-1	.984	-7	*C-124	-2.6
1978	Tor-A	81	264	27	69	15	0	9	29	28	32	.261	.344	.420	109	3	1	1	-0	.986	-7	*C-81	-0.3
1979	Hou-N	108	336	25	68	15	2	2	35	26	70	.202	.264	.277	51	-24	0	0	0	.987	-1	*C-105	-2.2
1980	*Hou-N	116	352	30	90	19	2	3	48	35	40	.256	.323	.347	94	-3	0	0	0	.991	2	*C-114	0.3
1981	*Hou-N	83	255	20	69	13	0	4	33	35	33	.271	.359	.369	112	5	0	2	-1	.982	7	C-81	1.4
1982	Hou-N	100	339	40	87	14	2	12	49	27	53	.257	.313	.416	111	2	0	0	0	.977	-5	C-95	0.3
1983	Hou-N	87	275	21	63	18	1	8	34	31	38	.229	.307	.389	98	-2	2	0	1	.974	-13	C-85	-1.1
1984	Hou-N	66	191	16	50	7	2	4	27	20	22	.262	.335	.361	103	1	0	0	0	.986	-6	C-63	0.3
1985	Hou-N	65	189	20	53	8	0	8	25	24	27	.280	.364	.450	130	8	0	0	0	.978	-0	C-60	1.1
1986	*Hou-N	120	315	24	81	15	0	7	38	39	56	.257	.339	.371	98	-0	1	0	0	.985	-4	*C-103	1.1
1987	Hou-N	125	386	53	111	16	0	14	63	50	52	.288	.371	.438	118	10	0	0	0	.993	-4	*C-110	1.4
1988	Hou-N	73	227	19	54	10	0	7	33	29	36	.238	.324	.374	104	1	0	0	1	.991	-10	C-66	-0.4
1989	Hou-N	22	61	4	10	1	1	0	3	7	8	.164	.261	.213	38	-5	0	0	0	1.000	-3	C-19	-0.7
Total	17	1370	4123	397	1010	183	13	90	513	461	622	.245	.323	.361	93	-37	7	10	-4	.986	-41	*C-1299/1-4,3D	-2.6

■ TUCKER ASHFORD
Ashford, Thomas Steven   b: 12/4/54, Memphis, Tenn.   BR/TR, 6'1", 195 lbs.   Deb: 9/21/76

YEAR	TM/L	G	AB	R	H	2B	3B	HR	RBI	BB	SO	AVG	OBP	SLG	PRO+	BR/A	SB	CS	SBR	FA	FR	G/POS	TPR
1976	SD-N	4	5	0	3	1	0	0	1	0	0	.600	.667	.800	343	2	0	0	0	1.000	0	/3-1	0.3
1977	SD-N	81	249	25	54	18	0	3	24	21	35	.217	.280	.325	69	-12	2	3	-1	.937	-4	3-74,S-10/2	-1.1
1978	SD-N	75	155	11	38	11	0	3	26	14	31	.245	.308	.374	97	-1	1	0	0	.917	-16	3-32,2-18,1	-1.8
1980	Tex-A	15	32	2	4	0	0	0	3	3	3	.125	.200	.125	-9	-5	0	0	0	.943	4	3-12/S-2	-0.2
1981	NY-A	3	0	0	0	0	0	0	0	0	0						0	0	0	.000	0	/2-2	0.0
1983	NY-N	35	56	3	10	0	1	0	1	5	4	.179	.270	.214	36	-5	0	0	0	.957	-1	3-15,2-13/C	-0.6
1984	KC-A	9	13	1	2	1	0	0	0	4	2	.154	.214	.231	42	-2	0	0	0	.909	3	/3-9	-0.1
Total	7	222	510	42	111	31	1	6	55	47	75	.218	.285	.318	70	-22	5	3	-0	.936	-12	3-143/2-37,1SC	-3.5

YEAR	TM/L	G	AB	R	H	2B	3B	HR	RBI	BB	SO	AVG	OBP	SLG	PRO+	BR/A	SB	CS	SBR	FA	FR	G/POS	TPR

■ BILLY ASHLEY   Ashley, Billy Manual   b: 7/11/70, Trenton, Mich.   BR/TR, 6'7", 220 lbs.   Deb: 9/1/92

1992	LA-N	29	95	6	21	5	0	2	6	5	34	.221	.260	.337	69	-4	0	0	0	.857	-3	O-27	-0.8
1993	LA-N	14	37	0	9	0	0	0	0	2	11	.243	.282	.243	45	-3	0	0	0	1.000	0	O-11	-0.3
1994	LA-N	2	6	0	2	1	0	0	0	0	2	.333	.333	.500	121	0	0	0	0	1.000	-0	/O-2	0.0
Total	3	45	138	6	32	6	0	2	6	7	47	.232	.269	.319	65	-7	0	0	0	.898	-3	/O-40	-1.1

■ TOM ASMUSSEN   Asmussen, Thomas William   b: 9/26/1876, Chicago, Ill.   d: 8/21/63, Arlington Heights, Ill.   TR ,   Deb: 8/10/07

1907	Bos-N	2	5	0	0	0	0	0	0	0	0	.000	.000	.000	-99	-1	0			1.000	-1	/C-2	-0.3

■ KEN ASPROMONTE   Aspromonte, Kenneth Joseph   b: 9/22/31, Brooklyn, N.Y.   BR/TR, 6', 180 lbs.   Deb: 9/2/57   FM

1957	Bos-A	24	78	9	21	5	0	0	4	17	10	.269	.400	.333	97	1	0	1	-1	.965	-3	2-24	-0.1
1958	Bos-A	6	16	0	2	0	0	0	0	3	1	.125	.263	.125	10	-2	0	0	-0	.952	-3	/2-6	-0.5
	Was-A	92	253	15	57	9	1	5	27	25	28	.225	.297	.328	73	-9	1	1	-0	.964	3	2-72,3-11/S	-0.2
	Yr	98	269	15	59	9	1	5	27	28	29	.219	.295	.316	69	-11	1	1	-0	.963	-0	2-78,3-11/S	-0.7
1959	Was-A	70	225	31	55	12	0	2	14	26	39	.244	.323	.324	79	-6	2	1	0	.960	-10	2-52,S-12/1O	-1.1
1960	Was-A	4	3	0	0	0	0	0	0	0	1	.000	.000	.000	-99	-1	0	0	0	.000	0	H	-0.1
	Cle-A	117	459	65	133	20	1	10	48	53	32	.290	.366	.403	111	8	4	1	1	.976	-12	2-80,3-36	0.4
	Yr	121	462	65	133	20	1	10	48	53	33	.288	.364	.400	110	7	4	1	1	.976	-12	2-80,3-36	0.3
1961	LA-A	66	238	29	53	10	0	2	14	33	21	.223	.322	.290	58	-14	0	0	0	.970	18	2-62	1.1
	Cle-A	22	70	5	16	6	1	0	5	6	3	.229	.289	.343	70	-3	0	0	0	.963	-2	2-21	-0.3
	Yr	88	308	34	69	16	1	2	19	39	24	.224	.315	.302	61	-17	0	0	0	.969	16	2-83	0.8
1962	Cle-A	20	28	4	4	2	0	0	1	6	5	.143	.294	.214	41	-2	0	0	0	1.000	-1	/2-6,3-3	-0.3
	Mil-N	34	79	11	23	2	0	0	7	6	5	.291	.349	.316	82	-2	0	1	-1	1.000	-0	2-12/3-6	-0.1
1963	Chi-N	20	34	2	5	3	0	0	4	4	4	.147	.237	.235	35	-3	0	0	0	.951	3	/2-7,1-2	0.1
Total	7	475	1483	171	369	69	3	19	124	179	149	.249	.332	.338	82	-33	7	5	-1	.969	-7	2-342/3-56,S10	-1.1

■ BOB ASPROMONTE   Aspromonte, Robert Thomas   b: 6/19/38, Brooklyn, N.Y.   BR/TR, 6'2", 185 lbs.   Deb: 9/19/56   F

1956	Bro-N	1	1	0	0	0	0	0	0	0	1	.000	.000	.000	-93	-0	0	0	0	.000	0	H	0.0
1960	LA-N	21	55	1	10	1	0	1	6	0	6	.182	.196	.255	21	-6	1	0	0	.933	-2	S-15/3-4	-0.7
1961	LA-N	47	58	7	14	3	0	0	2	4	12	.241	.290	.293	51	-4	0	0	0	.917	0	/3-9,S-4,2	-0.3
1962	Hou-N	149	534	59	142	18	4	11	59	46	54	.266	.333	.376	97	-2	4	5	-2	.967	1	*3-142,S-11/2	-0.1
1963	Hou-N	136	468	42	100	9	5	8	49	40	57	.214	.277	.306	72	-17	3	1	0	.938	-16	*3-131/1-1	-3.6
1964	Hou-N	157	553	51	155	20	3	12	69	35	54	.280	.332	.392	109	6	6	7	-2	**.973**	-15	*3-155	-1.4
1965	Hou-N	152	578	53	152	15	2	5	52	38	54	.263	.312	.322	85	-12	2	2	-1	.962	0	*3-146/1-6,S	-1.7
1966	Hou-N	152	560	55	141	16	3	8	52	35	63	.252	.298	.334	81	-15	0	4	-2	**.962**	-11	*3-149/1-2,S	-3.3
1967	Hou-N	137	486	51	143	24	5	6	58	45	44	.294	.356	.401	121	13	2	2	-1	.963	-4	*3-133	0.8
1968	Hou-N	124	409	25	92	9	2	1	46	35	57	.225	.289	.264	68	-15	1	0	0	.973	-6	3-75,O-36/1S	-1.9
1969	*Atl-N	82	198	16	50	8	1	3	24	13	19	.253	.305	.348	82	-5	0	1	-1	.975	-6	O-24,3-23,S/2	-1.3
1970	Atl-N	62	127	5	27	3	0	0	7	13	13	.213	.286	.236	39	-11	0	0	0	.938	-1	3-30/S-4,1O	-1.1
1971	NY-N	104	342	21	77	9	1	5	33	29	25	.225	.286	.301	67	-15	0	0	0	.965	-5	3-97	-2.3
Total	13	1324	4369	386	1103	135	26	60	457	333	459	.252	.310	.336	86	-84	19	24	-9	.960	-57	*3-1094/O-61,S12	-16.9

■ BRIAN ASSELSTINE   Asselstine, Brian Hanly   b: 9/23/53, Santa Barbara, Cal   BL/TR, 6'1", 175 lbs.   Deb: 9/14/76

1976	Atl-N	11	33	2	7	0	0	1	3	1	2	.212	.235	.303	49	-2	0	0	0	1.000	-1	/O-9	-0.3
1977	Atl-N	83	124	12	26	6	0	4	19	9	10	.210	.263	.355	57	-8	1	0	0	.983	-2	O-35	-1.1
1978	Atl-N	39	103	11	28	3	3	2	13	11	16	.272	.353	.417	103	0	2	1	0	.968	-5	O-35	-0.7
1979	Atl-N	8	10	1	1	0	0	0	0	1	2	.100	.182	.100	-20	-2	0	0	0	1.000	-0	/O-1	-0.2
1980	Atl-N	87	218	18	62	13	1	3	25	11	37	.284	.322	.394	96	-2	1	3	-2	.962	-9	O-61	-1.5
1981	Atl-N	56	86	8	22	5	0	2	10	5	7	.256	.297	.384	90	-1	1	0	0	.958	-1	O-16	-0.3
Total	6	284	574	52	146	27	4	12	68	38	74	.254	.304	.378	83	-14	5	4	-1	.971	-19	O-157	-4.1

■ JOE ASTROTH   Astroth, Joseph Henry   b: 9/1/22, East Alton, Ill.   BR/TR, 5'9", 187 lbs.   Deb: 8/13/45

1945	Phi-A	10	17	1	1	0	0	0	1	0	1	.059	.111	.059	-50	-3	0	0	0	.857	-0	/C-8	-0.3
1946	Phi-A	4	7	0	1	0	0	0	0	0	2	.143	.143	.143	-20	-1	0	0	0	.889	-0	/C-4	-0.1
1949	Phi-A	55	148	18	36	4	1	0	12	21	13	.243	.337	.284	67	-7	1	0	0	.979	2	C-44	-0.2
1950	Phi-A	39	110	11	36	3	1	1	18	18	3	.327	.422	.400	113	3	0	0	0	.985	-6	C-38	-0.1
1951	Phi-A	64	187	30	46	10	2	2	19	18	13	.246	.312	.353	78	-6	0	1	-1	.992	4	C-57	-0.1
1952	Phi-A	104	337	24	84	7	1	1	36	25	27	.249	.305	.291	62	-17	2	2	0	.992	-5	*C-102	-1.8
1953	Phi-A	82	260	28	77	15	2	3	24	27	12	.296	.367	.404	104	2	1	0	0	.987	7	C-79	1.2
1954	Phi-A	77	226	22	50	8	1	1	23	21	19	.221	.296	.279	58	-13	0	0	0	.988	-2	C-71	-1.2
1955	KC-A	101	274	29	69	4	1	5	23	47	33	.252	.373	.328	89	-2	2	3	-1	.989	-4	*C-100	-0.4
1956	KC-A	8	13	0	1	0	0	0	0	0	0	.077	.077	.077	-59	-3	0	0	0	1.000	-1	/C-8	-0.1
Total	10	544	1579	163	401	51	10	13	156	177	124	.254	.334	.324	77	-47	6	6	-2	.987	-2	C-511	-3.1

■ CHARLIE ATHERTON   Atherton, Charles Morgan Herbert "Prexy"   b: 10/19/1873, New Brunswick, N.J   d: 12/19/34, Vienna, Austria   BR/TR, 5'10", 160 lbs.   Deb: 5/30/1899

1899	Was-N	65	242	28	60	5	6	0	23	21		.248	.313	.318	74	-9	2			.890	-6	3-63/O-1	-1.3

■ ED ATKINSON   Atkinson, Edward   b: 1851, Baltimore, Md.   Deb: 10/22/1873

1873	Was-n	2	8	2	0	0	0	0	0	0	0	.000	.000	.000	-99	-2						/O-2	-0.1

■ LEFTY ATKINSON   Atkinson, Hubert Burley   b: 6/4/04, Chicago, Ill.   d: 2/12/61, Chicago, Ill.   BL/TL, 5'6.5", 149 lbs.   Deb: 8/5/27

1927	Was-A	1	1	0	0	0	0	0	0	0	0	.000	.000	.000	-99	-0	0	0	0	.000	0	H	0.0

■ DICK ATTREAU   Attreau, Richard Gilbert   b: 4/8/1897, Chicago, Ill.   d: 7/5/64, Chicago, Ill.   BL/TL, 6', 160 lbs.   Deb: 9/14/26

1926	Phi-N	17	61	9	14	1	1	0	5	6	5	.230	.299	.279	53	-4	0			.989	-1	1-17	-0.6
1927	Phi-N	44	83	17	17	1	1	2	11	14	18	.205	.320	.277	60	-4	1			.989	-2	1-26	-0.7
Total	2	61	144	26	31	2	2	2	16	20	23	.215	.311	.278	57	-8	1			.989	-3	/1-43	-1.3

■ TOBY ATWELL   Atwell, Maurice Dailey   b: 3/8/24, Leesburg, Va.   BL/TR, 5'9.5", 185 lbs.   Deb: 4/15/52

1952	Chi-N☆	107	362	36	105	16	3	2	31	40	22	.290	.362	.367	102	2	2	1	0	.977	-7	*C-101	0.0
1953	Chi-N	24	74	10	17	2	0	1	8	13	7	.230	.345	.297	68	-3	0	0	0	.940	1	C-24	-0.1
	Pit-N	53	139	11	34	6	0	0	17	20	12	.245	.352	.288	70	-5	0	0	0	.967	-3	C-45	-0.6
	Yr	77	213	21	51	8	0	1	25	33	19	.239	.349	.291	69	-8	0	0	0	.957	-2	C-69	-0.7
1954	Pit-N	96	287	36	83	8	4	3	26	43	21	.289	.387	.376	101	2	2	3	-1	.990	-2	C-88	0.3
1955	Pit-N	71	207	21	44	5	0	1	18	40	16	.213	.343	.266	65	-9	0	1	-1	.992	6	C-67	-0.2
1956	Pit-N	12	18	0	2	0	0	0	3	1	5	.111	.158	.111	-27	-3	0	0	0	1.000	1	/C-9	-0.2
	Mil-N	15	30	2	5	1	0	1	4	7	4	.167	.265	.400	80	-1	0	0	0	1.000	-1	C-10	-0.1
	Yr	27	48	2	7	1	0	1	7	8	9	.146	.226	.292	40	-4	0	0	0	1.000	0	C-19	-0.3
Total	5	378	1117	116	290	41	7	9	110	161	84	.260	.357	.333	86	-17	4	5	-2	.980	-5	C-344	-0.9

■ BILL ATWOOD   Atwood, William Franklin   b: 9/25/11, Rome, Ga.   d: 9/14/93, Snyder, Tex.   BR/TR, 5'11.5", 190 lbs.   Deb: 4/15/36

1936	Phi-N	71	192	21	58	9	2	2	29	11	15	.302	.346	.401	92	-2	0			.972	-1	C-53	-0.1
1937	Phi-N	87	279	27	68	15	1	2	32	30	27	.244	.317	.326	69	-12	3			.968	-14	C-80	-2.2
1938	Phi-N	102	281	27	55	8	1	3	28	25	26	.196	.261	.263	46	-21	0			.969	0	C-94	-1.6

YEAR	TM/L	G	AB	R	H	2B	3B	HR	RBI	BB	SO	AVG	OBP	SLG	PRO+	BR/A	SB	CS	SBR	FA	FR	G/POS	TPR
1939	Phi-N	4	6	0	0	0	0	0	1	2	3	.000	.250	.000	-29	-1	1			1.000	-0	/C-2	-0.1
1940	Phi-N	78	203	7	39	9	0	0	22	25	18	.192	.284	.236	47	-14		1		.989	1	C-69	-0.9
Total	5	342	961	82	220	41	4	7	112	93	89	.229	.299	.302	63	-50	4			.974	-14	C-298	-4.9

■ JAKE ATZ
Atz, John Jacob (b: John Jacob Zimmerman) b: 7/1/1879, Washington, D.C. d: 5/22/45, New Orleans, La. BR/TR, 5'9.5", 160 lbs. Deb: 9/24/02

YEAR	TM/L	G	AB	R	H	2B	3B	HR	RBI	BB	SO	AVG	OBP	SLG	PRO+	BR/A	SB	CS	SBR	FA	FR	G/POS	TPR
1902	Was-A	3	10	1	1	0	0	0	0	0		.100	.100	.100	-44	-2	0			1.000	0	/2-3	-0.1
1907	Chi-A	4	8	0	1	0	0	0	0	0		.125	.125	.125	-21	-1	0			1.000	1	/3-2,O-1	-0.1
1908	Chi-A	83	206	24	40	3	0	0	27	31		.194	.311	.209	71	-5	9			.936	-3	2-46,S-18/3	-0.9
1909	Chi-A	119	381	39	90	18	3	0	22	38		.236	.309	.299	96	-1	14			.954	-7	*2-114/O-3,S	-1.2
Total	4	209	605	64	132	21	3	0	49	69		.218	.304	.263	83	-9	23			.949	-9	2-163/S-19,O3	-2.2

■ HARRY AUBREY
Aubrey, Harry Herbert "Chub" b: 7/5/1880, St.Joseph, Mo. d: 9/18/53, Baltimore, Md. TR , Deb: 4/22/03

YEAR	TM/L	G	AB	R	H	2B	3B	HR	RBI	BB	SO	AVG	OBP	SLG	PRO+	BR/A	SB	CS	SBR	FA	FR	G/POS	TPR
1903	Bos-N	96	325	26	69	8	2	0	27	18		.212	.264	.249	49	-22	7			.868	-10	S-94/2-1,O	-2.7

■ RICH AUDE
Aude, Richard Thomas b: 7/13/71, Van Nuys, Cal. BR/TR, 6'5", 180 lbs. Deb: 9/9/93

YEAR	TM/L	G	AB	R	H	2B	3B	HR	RBI	BB	SO	AVG	OBP	SLG	PRO+	BR/A	SB	CS	SBR	FA	FR	G/POS	TPR
1993	Pit-N	13	26	1	3	1	0	0	4	1	7	.115	.148	.154	-19	-4	0	0	0	1.000	-1	/1-7,O-1	-0.6

■ RICK AUERBACH
Auerbach, Frederick Steven b: 2/15/50, Woodland Hills, Cal BR/TR, 6', 165 lbs. Deb: 4/13/71

YEAR	TM/L	G	AB	R	H	2B	3B	HR	RBI	BB	SO	AVG	OBP	SLG	PRO+	BR/A	SB	CS	SBR	FA	FR	G/POS	TPR
1971	Mil-A	79	236	22	48	10	0	1	9	20	40	.203	.271	.258	51	-15	3	2	-0	.963	-10	S-78	-1.7
1972	Mil-A	153	554	50	121	16	3	2	30	43	62	.218	.277	.269	64	-24	24	8	2	.959	-21	*S-153	-2.5
1973	Mil-A	6	10	2	1	1	0	0	0	0	1	.100	.100	.200	-18	-2	0	1	-1	.833	0	/S-2	-0.2
1974	*LA-N	45	73	12	25	0	0	1	4	8	9	.342	.407	.384	127	3	4	2	0	.950	2	S-19,2-16/3	0.6
1975	LA-N	85	170	18	38	9	0	0	12	18	22	.224	.298	.276	63	-8	3	2	-0	.960	-17	S-81/2-1,3	-2.1
1976	LA-N	36	47	7	6	0	0	0	1	6	6	.128	.226	.128	2	-6	0	1	-1	.943	11	S-12/3-8,2	0.6
1977	Cin-N	33	45	5	7	2	0	0	3	4	7	.156	.224	.200	15	-5	0	0	0	.976	6	2-19,S-12	0.2
1978	Cin-N	63	55	17	18	6	0	2	5	7	12	.327	.413	.545	166	5	1	0	0	.971	10	S-26,2-10/3	1.7
1979	*Cin-N	62	100	17	21	8	1	1	12	14	19	.210	.307	.340	76	-3	0	1	-1	.933	-1	3-18,S-16/2	-0.3
1980	Cin-N	24	33	5	11	1	1	1	4	3	5	.333	.389	.515	150	2	0	3	-2	1.000	-1	/S-3,3-3,2	-0.3
1981	Sea-A	38	84	12	13	3	0	1	6	4	15	.155	.202	.226	22	-8	1	1	-0	.979	3	S-38	-0.3
Total	11	624	1407	167	309	56	5	9	86	127	198	.220	.287	.286	65	-62	36	21		.960	-16	S-440/2-57,3	-4.0

■ DAVE AUGUSTINE
Augustine, David Ralph b: 11/28/49, Follansbee, W.Va. BR/TR, 6'2", 174 lbs. Deb: 9/3/73

YEAR	TM/L	G	AB	R	H	2B	3B	HR	RBI	BB	SO	AVG	OBP	SLG	PRO+	BR/A	SB	CS	SBR	FA	FR	G/POS	TPR
1973	Pit-N	11	7	1	2	1	0	0	0	0	1	.286	.286	.429	98	-0	0	0	0	1.000	-2	/O-9	-0.2
1974	Pit-N	18	22	3	4	0	0	0	0	0	5	.182	.182	.182	2	-3	0	1	-1	1.000	1	O-11	-0.3
Total	2	29	29	4	6	1	0	0	0	0	6	.207	.207	.241	26	-3	0	1	-1	1.000	-2	/O-20	-0.5

■ TEX AULDS
Aulds, Leycester Doyle b: 12/28/20, Farmerville, La. BR/TR, 6'2", 185 lbs. Deb: 5/25/47

YEAR	TM/L	G	AB	R	H	2B	3B	HR	RBI	BB	SO	AVG	OBP	SLG	PRO+	BR/A	SB	CS	SBR	FA	FR	G/POS	TPR
1947	Bos-A	3	4	0	1	0	0	0	0	0	1	.250	.250	.250	37	-0	0	0	0	1.000	0	/C-3	0.0

■ DOUG AULT
Ault, Douglas Reagan b: 3/9/50, Beaumont, Tex. BR/TL, 6'3", 200 lbs. Deb: 9/9/76

YEAR	TM/L	G	AB	R	H	2B	3B	HR	RBI	BB	SO	AVG	OBP	SLG	PRO+	BR/A	SB	CS	SBR	FA	FR	G/POS	TPR
1976	Tex-A	9	20	0	6	1	0	0	1	0	3	.300	.333	.350	98	-0	0	0	0	1.000	-1	/1-4,D-3	-0.1
1977	Tor-A	129	445	44	109	22	3	11	64	39	68	.245	.311	.382	87	-8	4	4	-1	.987	7	*1-122/D-4	-1.0
1978	Tor-A	54	104	10	25	1	1	3	7	17	14	.240	.352	.356	98	-0	0	1	-0	.979	-2	1-25/O-7,D	-0.3
1980	Tor-A	64	144	12	28	5	1	3	15	14	23	.194	.275	.306	56	-9	0	1	-1	1.000	2	1-32,D-21/O	-0.8
Total	4	256	713	66	168	29	5	17	86	71	108	.236	.311	.362	82	-17	4	5	-2	.988	8	1-183/D-33,O	-2.2

■ BRAD AUSMUS
Ausmus, Bradley David b: 4/14/69, New Haven, Conn. BR/TR, 5'11", 185 lbs. Deb: 7/28/93

YEAR	TM/L	G	AB	R	H	2B	3B	HR	RBI	BB	SO	AVG	OBP	SLG	PRO+	BR/A	SB	CS	SBR	FA	FR	G/POS	TPR
1993	SD-N	49	160	18	41	8	1	5	12	6	28	.256	.283	.412	82	-5	2	0	1	.975	6	C-49	0.4
1994	SD-N	101	327	45	82	12	1	7	24	30	63	.251	.316	.358	76	-12	5	1	1	.991	3	C-99/1-1	-0.3
Total	2	150	487	63	123	20	2	12	36	36	91	.253	.305	.376	78	-16	7	1	2	.986	8	C-148/1-1	0.1

■ HENRY AUSTIN
Austin, Henry C. b: 1844, Brooklyn, N.Y. d: 9/3/1895, Amityville, N.Y. Deb: 4/28/1873

YEAR	TM/L	G	AB	R	H	2B	3B	HR	RBI	BB	SO	AVG	OBP	SLG	PRO+	BR/A	SB	CS	SBR	FA	FR	G/POS	TPR
1873	Res-n	23	101	10	25	3	3	0	11	0	4	.248	.248	.337	76	-2						O-23	-0.1

■ JIMMY AUSTIN
Austin, James Philip "Pepper" b: 12/8/1879, Swansea, Wales d: 3/6/65, Laguna Beach, Cal. BB/TR, 5'7.5", 155 lbs. Deb: 4/19/09 MC

YEAR	TM/L	G	AB	R	H	2B	3B	HR	RBI	BB	SO	AVG	OBP	SLG	PRO+	BR/A	SB	CS	SBR	FA	FR	G/POS	TPR
1909	NY-A	136	437	37	101	11	5	1	39	32		.231	.285	.286	80	-10	30			.928	13	*3-111,S-23/2	0.8
1910	NY-A	133	432	46	94	11	4	2	36	47		.218	.305	.275	77	-11	22			.942	4	*3-133	-0.4
1911	StL-A	148	541	84	141	25	11	2	45	69		.261	.351	.359	102	3	26			.931	16	*3-148	2.0
1912	StL-A	149	536	57	135	14	8	2	44	38		.252	.306	.319	82	-13	28			.911	-1	*3-149	-1.4
1913	StL-A	142	489	56	130	18	6	2	42	45	51	.266	.338	.339	101	1	37			.944	7	*3-142,M	1.0
1914	StL-A	130	466	55	111	16	4	0	30	40	59	.238	.300	.290	80	-12	20	23	-8	.935	1	*3-127	-1.5
1915	StL-A	141	477	61	127	6	6	1	30	64	60	.266	.355	.310	103	3	18	15	-4	.917	10	*3-141	1.7
1916	StL-A	129	411	55	85	15	6	1	28	74	59	.207	.333	.280	89	-3	19			.939	-7	*3-124	-0.6
1917	StL-A	127	455	61	109	18	8	0	19	50	46	.240	.319	.314	97	-1	13			.947	3	*3-121/S-6	0.4
1918	StL-A	110	367	42	97	14	4	0	20	53	32	.264	.359	.324	109	6	18			.939	-17	S-57,3-48M	-0.8
1919	StL-A	106	396	54	94	9	9	1	21	42	31	.237	.314	.313	74	-13	8			.939	7	3-98	-0.3
1920	StL-A	83	280	38	76	11	3	1	32	31	15	.271	.352	.343	82	-6	2	4	-2	.943	2	3-75	-0.2
1921	StL-A	27	66	8	18	2	1	0	2	4	7	.273	.324	.333	64	-4	2	1	0	.938	-3	S-14/2-6,3	-0.5
1922	StL-A	15	31	6	9	3	1	0	1	3	2	.290	.353	.452	105	0	0	0	0	.957	-3	/3-9,2-2	-0.2
1923	StL-A	1	0	0	0	0	0	0	0	0	0	—	—	—			0			.000	0	/M	0.0
1925	StL-A	1	1	0	0	0	0	0	0	0	0	.000	.000	.000	-95	-0	0			1.000	0	/3-1	0.0
1926	StL-A	1	2	1	1	0	0	0	1	0	0	.500	.500	1.000	272	0	1	0		1.000	0	/3-1	0.1
1929	StL-A	1	1	0	0	0	0	0	0	0	1	.000	.000	.000	-96	-0	0	0		1.000	1	/3-1	0.0
Total	18	1580	5388	661	1328	174	76	13	390	592	363	.246	.326	.314	90	-60	244	43		.933	33	*3-1431,S-100/2	0.1

■ CHICK AUTRY
Autry, Martin Gordon b: 3/5/03, Martindale, Tex. d: 1/26/50, Savannah, Ga. BR/TR, 6', 180 lbs. Deb: 4/20/24

YEAR	TM/L	G	AB	R	H	2B	3B	HR	RBI	BB	SO	AVG	OBP	SLG	PRO+	BR/A	SB	CS	SBR	FA	FR	G/POS	TPR
1924	NY-A	2	0	1	0	0	0	0	0	0	0	—	1.000	—	172	0	0	0	0	1.000	-0	/C-2	0.0
1926	Cle-A	3	7	1	1	0	0	0	0	1	0	.143	.250	.143	4	-1	0	0	0	1.000	-0	/C-3	-0.1
1927	Cle-A	16	43	5	11	4	1	0	7	0	6	.256	.256	.395	66	-2	0	0	0	.933	2	C-14	0.1
1928	Cle-A	22	60	6	18	6	1	1	9	1	7	.300	.311	.483	105	0	0	0	0	.972	0	C-18	0.2
1929	Chi-A	43	96	7	20	6	0	1	12	1	8	.208	.224	.302	45	-10	0	0	0	.940	-4	C-30	-1.1
1930	Chi-A	34	71	1	18	1	1	0	5	4	8	.254	.293	.296	52	-5	0	0	0	.992	8	C-29	0.4
Total	6	120	277	21	68	17	3	2	33	7	29	.245	.269	.350	59	-18	0	0	0	.965	5	/C-96	-0.5

■ CHICK AUTRY
Autry, William Askew b: 1/2/1885, Humboldt, Tenn. d: 1/16/76, Santa Rosa, Cal. BL/TL, 5'11", 168 lbs. Deb: 9/18/07

YEAR	TM/L	G	AB	R	H	2B	3B	HR	RBI	BB	SO	AVG	OBP	SLG	PRO+	BR/A	SB	CS	SBR	FA	FR	G/POS	TPR
1907	Cin-N	7	25	3	5	0	0	0	0	0	1	.200	.231	.200	34	-2	0			.929	-1	/O-7	-0.4
1909	Cin-N	9	33	3	6	2	0	0	4	2		.182	.229	.242	46	-2	1			.956	0	/1-9	-0.2
	Bos-N	65	199	16	39	4	0	0	13	21		.196	.279	.216	51	-11	5			.994	5	1-61/O-4	-0.8
	Yr	74	232	19	45	6	0	0	17	23		.194	.272	.220	51	-13	6			.989	5	1-70/O-4	-1.0
Total	2	81	257	22	50	6	0	0	17	24		.195	.269	.218	49	-15	6			.968	4	/1-70,O-11	-1.4

■ EARL AVERILL
Averill, Earl Douglas b: 9/9/31, Cleveland, Ohio BR/TR, 5'10", 190 lbs. Deb: 4/19/56 F

YEAR	TM/L	G	AB	R	H	2B	3B	HR	RBI	BB	SO	AVG	OBP	SLG	PRO+	BR/A	SB	CS	SBR	FA	FR	G/POS	TPR
1956	Cle-A	42	93	12	22	6	0	3	14	14	25	.237	.343	.398	93	-1	0	1	-1	.994	3	C-34	0.2
1958	Cle-A	17	55	2	10	1	0	2	5	2	10	.182	.207	.309	54	-2	0	1	-0	.863	3	3-17	-0.3
1959	Chi-N	74	186	22	44	10	0	10	34	15	39	.237	.300	.452	98	-1	0	1	-0	.963	3	C-32,3-13/O2	0.3
1960	Chi-N	52	102	14	24	4	0	1	13	11	16	.235	.316	.304	71	-4	1	1	-0	.979	-9	C-34/3-1,O	-1.2

YEAR	TM/L	G	AB	R	H	2B	3B	HR	RBI	BB	SO	AVG	OBP	SLG	PRO+	BR/A	SB	CS	SBR	FA	FR	G/POS	TPR
	Chi-A	10	14	2	3	0	0	0	2	4	2	.214	.389	.214	68	-0	0	0	0	1.000	2	/C-5	0.2
1961	LA-A	115	323	56	86	9	0	21	59	62	70	.266	.388	.489	119	9	1	0	0	.991	-7	C-88/O-9,2	0.7
1962	LA-A	92	187	21	41	9	0	4	22	43	47	.219	.368	.332	93	-0	0	0	0	1.000	-4	O-49/C-6	-0.6
1963	Phi-N	47	71	8	19	2	0	3	8	9	14	.268	.350	.423	123	2	0	0	0	.966	1	C-20/O-8,13	0.3
Total	7	449	1031	137	249	41	0	44	159	162	220	.242	.349	.409	101	1	3	3	-1	.984	-11	C-219/O-72,321	-0.4

■ EARL AVERILL
Averill, Howard Earl "Rock" b: 5/21/02, Snohomish, Wash. d: 8/16/83, Everett, Wash. BL/TR, 5'9.5", 172 lbs. Deb: 4/16/29 FH

YEAR	TM/L	G	AB	R	H	2B	3B	HR	RBI	BB	SO	AVG	OBP	SLG	PRO+	BR/A	SB	CS	SBR	FA	FR	G/POS	TPR
1929	Cle-A	151	597	110	198	43	13	18	96	63	53	.332	.398	.538	134	29	13	13	-4	.966	-4	*O-151	1.1
1930	Cle-A	139	534	102	181	33	8	19	119	56	48	.339	.404	.537	131	25	10	7	-1	.949	2	*O-134	1.5
1931	Cle-A	155	627	140	209	36	10	32	143	68	38	.333	.404	.576	147	41	9	9	-3	.976	0	*O-155	2.5
1932	Cle-A	153	631	116	198	37	14	32	124	75	40	.314	.392	.569	137	33	5	8	-3	.964	2	*O-153	1.9
1933	Cle-A★	151	599	83	180	39	16	11	92	54	29	.301	.363	.474	115	12	3	1	0	.971	2	*O-149	0.6
1934	Cle-A★	154	598	128	187	48	6	31	113	99	44	.313	.414	.569	149	44	5	3	-0	.970	9	*O-154	4.2
1935	Cle-A†	140	563	109	162	34	13	19	79	70	58	.288	.368	.496	119	15	8	4	0	.982	-2	*O-139	0.7
1936	Cle-A★	152	614	136	**232**	39	**15**	28	126	65	35	.378	.438	.627	159	55	3	3	-1	.969	-4	*O-150	3.9
1937	Cle-A★	156	609	121	182	33	11	21	92	88	65	.299	.387	.493	119	18	5	4	-1	.976	-8	*O-156	0.4
1938	Cle-A★	134	482	101	159	27	15	14	93	81	48	.330	.429	.535	143	34	5	2	0	.975	5	*O-131	3.2
1939		24	55	8	15	8	0	1	7	6	12	.273	.344	.473	111	1	0	1	-1	1.000	-0	O-11	-0.3
	Det-A	87	309	58	81	20	6	10	58	43	30	.262	.354	.463	100	-1	4	2	0	.976	-5	O-80	-0.8
	Yr	111	364	66	96	28	6	11	65	49	42	.264	.353	.464	102	0	4	3	-1	.977	-7	O-91	-1.1
1940	*Det-A	64	118	10	33	4	1	2	20	5	14	.280	.309	.381	71	-5	0	0	0	.962	-5	O-22	-1.1
1941	Bos-N	8	17	2	2	0	0	0	2	1	4	.118	.211	.118	-6	-2	0			1.000	1	/O-4	-0.2
Total	13	1668	6353	1224	2019	401	128	238	1164	774	518	.318	.395	.534	132	296	70	57		.970	-8	*O-1589	17.6

■ BOBBY AVILA
Avila, Roberto Francisco (Gonzalez) b: 4/2/24, Veracruz, Mexico BR/TR, 5'10", 175 lbs. Deb: 4/30/49

YEAR	TM/L	G	AB	R	H	2B	3B	HR	RBI	BB	SO	AVG	OBP	SLG	PRO+	BR/A	SB	CS	SBR	FA	FR	G/POS	TPR
1949	Cle-A	31	14	3	3	0	0	0	3	1	3	.214	.267	.214	29	-1	0	0	0	1.000	4	/2-5	0.2
1950	Cle-A	80	201	39	60	10	2	1	21	29	17	.299	.390	.383	102	1	5	0	2	.983	-5	2-62/S-2	0.0
1951	Cle-A	141	542	76	165	21	3	10	58	60	31	.304	.374	.410	118	14	14	8	-1	.982	-1	*2-136	1.9
1952	Cle-A★	150	597	102	179	26	**11**	7	45	67	36	.300	.371	.415	127	21	12	10	-2	.966	-18	2-149	0.9
1953	Cle-A	141	559	85	160	22	3	8	55	58	27	.286	.355	.379	101	1	10	8	-2	**.986**	13	*2-140	2.1
1954	*Cle-A★	143	555	112	189	27	2	15	67	59	31	**.341**	.405	.477	139	30	9	7	-2	.976	8	*2-141/S-7	4.7
1955	Cle-A★	141	537	83	146	22	4	13	61	82	47	.272	.370	.400	103	4	1	4	-2	.982	-3	*2-141	1.0
1956	Cle-A	138	513	74	115	14	2	10	54	70	68	.224	.323	.318	68	-23	17	4	3	.977	-10	*2-135	-1.8
1957	Cle-A	129	463	60	124	19	3	5	48	44	47	.268	.335	.354	89	-6	2	4	-2	.983	-15	*2-107,3-16	-1.5
1958	Cle-A	113	375	54	95	21	3	5	30	55	45	.253	.350	.365	100	1	5	7	-3	.986	-21	2-82,3-33	-1.7
1959	Bal-A	20	47	1	8	0	0	0	0	4	5	.170	.235	.170	14	-6	0	0	0	1.000	-4	O-10/2-8,3	-1.0
	Bos-A	22	45	7	11	0	0	3	6	6	11	.244	.333	.444	107	0	3	0	1	.975	-2	2-11	-0.1
	Yr	42	92	8	19	0	0	3	6	10	16	.207	.284	.304	61	-5	0	0	0	.967	-6	2-19,O-10/3	-1.1
	Mil-N	51	172	29	41	3	2	3	19	24	31	.238	.332	.331	84	-4	3	0	1	.967	-12	2-51	-1.1
Total	11	1300	4620	725	1296	185	35	80	467	561	399	.281	.360	.388	104	34	78	52	-8	.979	-64	*2-1168/3-50,OS	3.6

■ RAMON AVILES
Aviles, Ramon Antonio (Miranda) b: 1/22/52, Manati, P.R. BR/TR, 5'9", 155 lbs. Deb: 7/10/77

YEAR	TM/L	G	AB	R	H	2B	3B	HR	RBI	BB	SO	AVG	OBP	SLG	PRO+	BR/A	SB	CS	SBR	FA	FR	G/POS	TPR
1977	Bos-A	1	0	0	0	0	0	0	0	0	0	—	—	—	—	-0	0	0	0	1.000	0	/2-1	0.0
1979	Phi-N	27	61	7	17	2	0	0	12	8	8	.279	.371	.311	86	-1	0	0	0	.977	-7	2-27	-0.7
1980	*Phi-N	51	101	12	28	6	0	2	9	10	9	.277	.342	.396	100	0	0	0	0	.944	-7	S-29,2-15	-0.4
1981	*Phi-N	38	28	2	6	1	0	0	3	3	5	.214	.290	.250	52	-2	0	0	0	1.000	4	2-20,3-13/S	0.3
Total	4	117	190	21	51	9	0	2	24	21	22	.268	.344	.347	88	-2	0	0	0	.971	-10	/2-63,S-34,3	-0.8

■ BENNY AYALA
Ayala, Benigno (Felix) b: 2/7/51, Yauco, P.R. BR/TR, 6'1", 185 lbs. Deb: 8/27/74

YEAR	TM/L	G	AB	R	H	2B	3B	HR	RBI	BB	SO	AVG	OBP	SLG	PRO+	BR/A	SB	CS	SBR	FA	FR	G/POS	TPR
1974	NY-N	23	68	9	16	1	0	2	7	8	17	.235	.316	.338	84	-1	0	0	0	.927	0	O-20	-0.2
1976	NY-N	22	26	2	3	0	0	1	2	2	6	.115	.179	.231	16	-3	0	1	-1	.889	-1	/O-7	-0.5
1977	StL-N	1	3	0	1	0	0	0	0	0	1	.333	.333	.333	81	-0	0	0	0	1.000	0	/O-1	0.2
1979	*Bal-A	42	86	15	22	5	0	6	13	6	9	.256	.304	.523	123	2	0	0	0	.974	-3	O-24,D-10	-0.2
1980	Bal-A	76	170	28	45	8	1	10	33	19	21	.265	.339	.500	128	6	0	0	0	1.000	-2	D-41,O-19	0.2
1981	Bal-A	44	86	12	24	2	0	3	13	11	9	.279	.367	.407	123	3	0	1	-1	1.000	0	D-27/O-4	0.2
1982	Bal-A	64	128	17	39	6	0	6	24	5	14	.305	.331	.492	123	3	1	1	-0	.972	-5	O-25,D-17/1	-0.3
1983	*Bal-A	47	104	12	23	7	0	4	13	9	18	.221	.283	.404	88	-2	0	0	0	.953	-3	O-24,D-11	-0.6
1984	Bal-A	60	118	9	25	6	0	4	24	8	24	.212	.262	.364	73	-5	1	1	-0	1.000	-4	D-34,O-13	-1.0
1985	Cle-A	46	76	10	19	7	0	2	15	4	17	.250	.287	.421	92	-1	0	0	0	.917	-4	O-20/D-3	-0.5
Total	10	425	865	114	217	42	1	38	145	71	136	.251	.309	.434	104	2	2	4	-2	.958	-19	O-157,D-143/1	-2.7

■ DICK AYLWARD
Aylward, Richard John "Dandy" b: 6/4/25, Baltimore, Md. d: 6/11/83, Spring Valley, Cal. BR/TR, 6', 190 lbs. Deb: 5/1/53

YEAR	TM/L	G	AB	R	H	2B	3B	HR	RBI	BB	SO	AVG	OBP	SLG	PRO+	BR/A	SB	CS	SBR	FA	FR	G/POS	TPR
1953	Cle-A	4	3	0	0	0	0	0	0	0	1	.000	.000	.000	-99	-1	0	0	0	1.000	-0	/C-4	-0.1

■ JOE AZCUE
Azcue, Jose Joaquin (Lopez) b: 8/18/39, Cienfuegos, Cuba BR/TR, 6', 200 lbs. Deb: 8/3/60

YEAR	TM/L	G	AB	R	H	2B	3B	HR	RBI	BB	SO	AVG	OBP	SLG	PRO+	BR/A	SB	CS	SBR	FA	FR	G/POS	TPR
1960	Cin-N	14	31	1	3	0	0	0	3	2	6	.097	.152	.097	-30	-5	0	1	-1	1.000	5	C-14	0.0
1962	KC-A	72	223	18	51	9	1	2	25	17	27	.229	.292	.305	58	-13	1	0	0	.985	3	C-70	-0.8
1963	KC-A	2	4	0	0	0	0	0	0	0	0	.000	.000	.000	-95	-1	0	0	0	1.000	0	C-1	-0.1
	Cle-A	94	320	26	91	16	0	14	46	15	46	.284	.316	.466	117	6	1	1	-0	.992	5	C-91	1.4
	Yr	96	324	26	91	16	0	14	46	15	47	.281	.313	.460	114	5	1	1	-0	.992	5	C-92	1.3
1964	Cle-A	83	271	20	74	9	1	4	34	16	38	.273	.318	.358	88	-4	0	2	-1	.993	-0	C-76	-0.2
1965	Cle-A	111	335	16	77	7	0	2	35	27	54	.230	.293	.269	60	-17	2	1	0	.994	-1	*C-108	-1.3
1966	Cle-A	98	302	22	83	10	1	9	37	20	22	.275	.324	.404	108	3	0	2	-1	.989	-8	C-97	-0.1
1967	Cle-A	86	295	33	74	12	5	11	34	22	35	.251	.309	.437	117	5	0	3	-2	**.999**	5	C-86	1.5
1968	Cle-A★	115	357	23	100	10	4	4	42	28	33	.280	.332	.342	106	3	1	1	-0	**.996**	11	C-97	2.2
1969	Cle-A	7	24	1	7	0	0	1	1	4	3	.292	.393	.417	122	1	0	0	0	.980	2	/C-6	0.3
	Bos-A	19	51	7	11	2	0	0	3	4	5	.216	.273	.255	46	-4	0	0	0	.981	3	C-19	0.0
	Cal-A	80	248	15	54	6	0	1	19	27	28	.218	.300	.254	59	-13	0	1	-1	.992	5	C-80	-0.5
	Yr	106	323	23	72	8	0	2	23	35	36	.223	.303	.266	62	-16	0	1	-1	.989	9	*C-105	-0.2
1970	Cal-A	114	351	19	85	13	1	2	25	24	40	.242	.294	.302	67	-16	0	0	0	.991	-5	*C-112	-1.7
1972	Cal-A	3	2	0	0	0	0	0	0	0	1	.000	.000	.000	-99	-1	0	0	0	1.000	1	/C-2	0.0
	Mil-A	11	14	0	2	0	0	0	0	1	9	.143	.200	.143	3	-2	0	0	0	1.000	-0	C-9	0.0
	Yr	14	16	0	2	0	0	0	0	1	10	.125	.176	.125	-10	-2	0	0	0	1.000	0	C-11	0.0
Total	11	909	2828	201	712	94	6	50	304	207	344	.252	.307	.344	85	-58	5	12	-6	.992	25	C-868	0.7

■ OSCAR AZOCAR
Azocar, Oscar Gregorio (Azocar) b: 2/21/65, Soro, Venez. BL/TL, 6'1", 170 lbs. Deb: 7/17/90

YEAR	TM/L	G	AB	R	H	2B	3B	HR	RBI	BB	SO	AVG	OBP	SLG	PRO+	BR/A	SB	CS	SBR	FA	FR	G/POS	TPR
1990	NY-N	65	214	18	53	8	0	5	19	2	15	.248	.258	.355	70	-9	7	0	2	.991	0	O-57/D-1	-0.9
1991	SD-N	38	57	5	14	2	0	0	9	1	9	.246	.271	.281	54	-3	2	0	1	.875	-3	O-13/1-1	-0.6
1992	SD-N	99	168	15	32	6	0	0	9	9	12	.190	.232	.226	30	-15	1	0	0	.942	-1	O-37	-1.8
Total	3	202	439	38	99	16	0	5	36	12	36	.226	.249	.296	52	-28	10	0	3	.964	-4	O-107/1-1,D	-3.3

■ CHARLIE BABB
Babb, Charles Amos b: 2/20/1873, Milwaukie, Ore. d: 3/20/54, Portland, Ore. BB/TR, 5'10", 165 lbs. Deb: 4/17/03

YEAR	TM/L	G	AB	R	H	2B	3B	HR	RBI	BB	SO	AVG	OBP	SLG	PRO+	BR/A	SB	CS	SBR	FA	FR	G/POS	TPR
1903	NY-N	121	424	68	105	15	8	0	46	45		.248	.350	.321	88	-5	22			.912	-2	*S-113/3-8	-0.1
1904	Bro-N	151	521	49	138	18	3	0	53	53		.265	.345	.311	106	6	34			.927	-3	*S-151	0.7

YEAR	TM/L	G	AB	R	H	2B	3B	HR	RBI	BB	SO	AVG	OBP	SLG	PRO+	BR/A	SB	CS	SBR	FA	FR	G/POS	TPR
1905	Bro-N	75	235	27	44	8	2	0	17	27		.187	.303	.238	67	-8	10			.923	-2	S-36,1-31/32	-1.1
Total	3	347	1180	144	287	41	13	0	116	125		.243	.339	.300	92	-7	66			.921	-7	S-300/1-31,32	-0.5

■ LOREN BABE
Babe, Loren Rolland "Bee Bee" b: 1/11/28, Pisgah, Iowa   d: 2/14/84, Omaha, Neb.   BL/TR, 5'10", 180 lbs.   Deb: 8/19/52   C

YEAR	TM/L	G	AB	R	H	2B	3B	HR	RBI	BB	SO	AVG	OBP	SLG	PRO+	BR/A	SB	CS	SBR	FA	FR	G/POS	TPR
1952	NY-A	12	21	1	2	1	0	0	0	4	4	.095	.240	.143	9	-3	1	0	0	.909	2	/3-9	-0.1
1953	NY-A	5	18	2	6	1	0	2	6	0	2	.333	.333	.722	185	2	0	0	0	.920	3	/3-5	0.5
	Phi-A	103	343	34	77	16	2	0	20	35	20	.224	.300	.283	56	-21	0	1	-1	.950	1	3-93/S-1	-2.2
	Yr	108	361	36	83	17	2	2	26	35	22	.230	.302	.305	62	-19	0	1	-1	.948	5	3-98/S-1	-1.7
Total	2	120	382	37	85	18	2	2	26	39	26	.223	.298	.296	59	-21	1	1	-0	.946	6	3-107/S-1	-1.8

■ CHARLIE BABINGTON
Babington, Charles Percy b: 5/4/1895, Cranston, R.I.   d: 3/22/57, Providence, R.I.   BR/TR, 6', 170 lbs.   Deb: 7/20/15

YEAR	TM/L	G	AB	R	H	2B	3B	HR	RBI	BB	SO	AVG	OBP	SLG	PRO+	BR/A	SB	CS	SBR	FA	FR	G/POS	TPR
1915	NY-N	28	33	5	8	3	1	0	2	0	4	.242	.265	.394	104	-0	1			.909	-5	O-12/1-1	-0.6

■ SHOOTY BABITT
Babitt, Mack Neal b: 3/9/59, Oakland, Cal.   BR/TR, 5'8", 174 lbs.   Deb: 4/9/81

YEAR	TM/L	G	AB	R	H	2B	3B	HR	RBI	BB	SO	AVG	OBP	SLG	PRO+	BR/A	SB	CS	SBR	FA	FR	G/POS	TPR
1981	Oak-A	54	156	10	40	1	3	0	14	13	13	.256	.314	.301	82	-4	5	4	-1	.972	-17	2-52	-2.0

■ WALLY BACKMAN
Backman, Walter Wayne b: 9/22/59, Hillsboro, Ore.   BB/TR, 5'9", 160 lbs.   Deb: 9/2/80

YEAR	TM/L	G	AB	R	H	2B	3B	HR	RBI	BB	SO	AVG	OBP	SLG	PRO+	BR/A	SB	CS	SBR	FA	FR	G/POS	TPR
1980	NY-N	27	93	12	30	1	1	0	9	11	14	.323	.400	.355	115	3	2	3	-1	1.000	-10	2-20/S-8	-0.7
1981	NY-N	26	36	5	10	2	0	0	0	4	7	.278	.350	.333	96	-0	1	0	0	.946	-3	2-11/3-1	-0.3
1982	NY-N	96	261	37	71	13	2	3	22	49	47	.272	.387	.372	114	7	8	7	-2	.964	-13	2-88/3-6,S	-0.5
1983	NY-N	26	42	6	7	0	1	0	3	2	8	.167	.205	.214	16	-5	0	0	0	1.000	-2	2-14/3-2	-0.7
1984	NY-N	128	436	68	122	19	2	1	26	56	63	.280	.362	.339	99	2	32	9	4	.981	-12	*2-115/S-8	-0.2
1985	NY-N	145	520	77	142	24	5	1	38	36	72	.273	.320	.344	88	-8	30	12	2	.989	-9	*2-140/S-1	-1.2
1986	*NY-N	124	387	67	124	18	2	1	27	36	32	.320	.378	.385	114	8	13	7	-0	.966	-3	*2-113	0.9
1987	NY-N	94	300	43	75	6	1	1	23	25	43	.250	.308	.287	62	-16	11	3	2	.983	-7	2-87	-1.8
1988	*NY-N	99	294	44	89	12	0	0	17	41	49	.303	.388	.394	118	9	9	5	-0	.989	-9	2-92	0.3
1989	Min-A	87	299	33	69	9	1	1	26	32	45	.231	.307	.284	63	-14	1	1	-0	.982	-22	2-84/D-1	-3.5
1990	*Pit-N	104	315	62	92	21	3	2	28	42	53	.292	.377	.397	118	9	6	3	0	.920	-19	3-71,2-15	-1.0
1991	Phi-N	94	185	20	45	12	0	0	15	30	30	.243	.349	.308	87	-2	3	2	-0	.981	-15	2-36,3-20	-1.7
1992	Phi-N	42	48	6	13	1	0	0	6	6	9	.271	.352	.292	84	-1	1	0	-0	.968	0	2-10/3-2	0.0
1993	Sea-A	10	29	2	4	0	0	0	0	1	8	.138	.167	.138	-17	-5	0	0	0	.857	-1	/3-9,2-1	-0.5
Total	14	1102	3245	482	893	138	19	10	240	371	480	.275	.350	.339	94	-13	117	52	4	.980	-125	2-826,3-111/SD	-10.9

■ EDDIE BACON
Bacon, Edgar Suter b: 4/8/1895, Franklin Co., Ky.   d: 10/2/63, Louisville, Ky.   Deb: 8/13/17

YEAR	TM/L	G	AB	R	H	2B	3B	HR	RBI	BB	SO	AVG	OBP	SLG	PRO+	BR/A	SB	CS	SBR	FA	FR	G/POS	TPR
1917	Phi-A	4	6	1	3	1	0	0	2	0	0	.500	.500	.667	259	1	1			1.000	1	/P-1	0.0

■ ART BADER
Bader, Arthur Herman b: 9/21/1886, St.Louis, Mo.   d: 4/5/57, St.Louis, Mo.   BR/TR, 5'10", 170 lbs.   Deb: 8/2/04

YEAR	TM/L	G	AB	R	H	2B	3B	HR	RBI	BB	SO	AVG	OBP	SLG	PRO+	BR/A	SB	CS	SBR	FA	FR	G/POS	TPR
1904	StL-A	2	3	0	0	0	0	0	0	0	1	.000	.250	.000	-19	-0	0			1.000	1	/O-1	0.0

■ RED BADGRO
Badgro, Morris Hiram b: 12/1/02, Orilla, Wash.   BL/TR, 6', 190 lbs.   Deb: 6/20/29

YEAR	TM/L	G	AB	R	H	2B	3B	HR	RBI	BB	SO	AVG	OBP	SLG	PRO+	BR/A	SB	CS	SBR	FA	FR	G/POS	TPR
1929	StL-A	54	148	27	42	12	0	1	18	11	15	.284	.342	.385	84	-4	1	0	0	.983	-4	O-37	-0.9
1930	StL-A	89	234	30	56	18	3	1	27	13	27	.239	.285	.355	59	-15	3	5	-2	.952	0	O-61	-1.9
Total	2	143	382	57	98	30	3	2	45	24	42	.257	.307	.366	69	-19	4	5	-2	.962	-4	/O-98	-2.8

■ CARLOS BAERGA
Baerga, Carlos Obed (Ortiz) b: 11/4/68, Santurce, P.R.   BB/TR, 5'11", 165 lbs.   Deb: 4/14/90

YEAR	TM/L	G	AB	R	H	2B	3B	HR	RBI	BB	SO	AVG	OBP	SLG	PRO+	BR/A	SB	CS	SBR	FA	FR	G/POS	TPR
1990	Cle-A	108	312	46	81	17	2	7	47	16	57	.260	.304	.394	94	-3	0	2	-1	.944	-9	3-50,S-48/2	-1.2
1991	Cle-A	158	593	80	171	28	2	11	69	48	74	.288	.348	.398	105	4	3	2	-0	.944	11	3-89,2-75/S	1.7
1992	Cle-A★	161	657	92	205	32	1	20	105	35	76	.312	.359	.455	129	24	10	2	2	.979	8	*2-160/D-1	3.8
1993	Cle-A★	154	624	105	200	28	6	21	114	34	68	.321	.361	.486	126	21	15	4	2	.979	8	*2-150/D-4	3.4
1994	Cle-A	103	442	81	139	32	2	19	80	10	45	.314	.338	.525	113	7	8	2	1	.973	9	*2-102/D-1	1.8
Total	5	684	2628	404	796	137	13	78	415	143	320	.303	.347	.454	116	53	36	12	4	.975	27	2-495,3-139/SD	9.5

■ JOSE BAEZ
Baez, Jose Antonio (b: Jose Antonio Mota (Baez)) b: 12/31/53, San Cristobal, D.R.   BR/TR, 5'8", 160 lbs.   Deb: 4/6/77

YEAR	TM/L	G	AB	R	H	2B	3B	HR	RBI	BB	SO	AVG	OBP	SLG	PRO+	BR/A	SB	CS	SBR	FA	FR	G/POS	TPR
1977	Sea-A	91	305	39	79	14	1	1	17	19	20	.259	.305	.321	71	-12	6	1	1	.973	9	2-77/3-1,D	0.3
1978	Sea-A	23	50	8	8	0	1	0	2	6	7	.160	.250	.200	28	-5	1	0	0	.978	12	2-14/3-3,D	0.9
Total	2	114	355	47	87	14	2	1	19	25	27	.245	.297	.304	65	-17	7	1	1	.974	21	/2-91,D-4,3	1.2

■ KEVIN BAEZ
Baez, Kevin Richard b: 1/10/67, Brooklyn, N.Y.   BR/TR, 6', 160 lbs.   Deb: 9/3/90

YEAR	TM/L	G	AB	R	H	2B	3B	HR	RBI	BB	SO	AVG	OBP	SLG	PRO+	BR/A	SB	CS	SBR	FA	FR	G/POS	TPR
1990	NY-N	5	12	0	2	1	0	0	0	0	0	.167	.167	.250	13	-1	0	0	0	1.000	0	/S-4	-0.1
1992	NY-N	6	13	0	2	0	0	0	0	0	0	.154	.154	.154	-13	-2	0	0	0	.889	1	/S-5	-0.1
1993	NY-N	52	126	10	23	9	0	0	7	13	17	.183	.259	.254	38	-11	0	0	0	.967	-4	S-52	-1.2
Total	3	63	151	10	27	10	0	0	7	13	17	.179	.244	.245	33	-14	0	0	0	.962	-4	/S-61	-1.4

■ JEFF BAGWELL
Bagwell, Jeffery Robert b: 5/27/68, Boston, Mass.   BR/TR, 6', 195 lbs.   Deb: 4/8/91

YEAR	TM/L	G	AB	R	H	2B	3B	HR	RBI	BB	SO	AVG	OBP	SLG	PRO+	BR/A	SB	CS	SBR	FA	FR	G/POS	TPR
1991	Hou-N	156	554	79	163	26	4	15	82	75	116	.294	.391	.437	141	32	7	4	-0	.991	-1	*1-155	2.1
1992	Hou-N	162	586	87	160	34	6	18	96	84	97	.273	.375	.444	137	31	10	6	-1	.995	7	*1-159	2.7
1993	Hou-N	142	535	76	171	37	4	20	88	62	73	.320	.393	.516	146	35	13	4	2	.993	6	*1-140	3.1
1994	Hou-N★	110	400	104	147	32	2	39	116	65	65	.368	**.461**	**.750**	213	68	15	4	2	.991	17	*1-109/O-1	**7.4**
Total	4	570	2075	346	641	129	16	92	382	286	351	.309	.401	.520	157	166	45	18	3	.993	29	1-563/O-1	15.3

■ BILL BAGWELL
Bagwell, William Mallory "Big Bill" b: 2/24/1896, Choudrant, La.   d: 10/5/76, Choudrant, La.   BL/TL, 6'1", 175 lbs.   Deb: 4/17/23

YEAR	TM/L	G	AB	R	H	2B	3B	HR	RBI	BB	SO	AVG	OBP	SLG	PRO+	BR/A	SB	CS	SBR	FA	FR	G/POS	TPR
1923	Bos-N	56	93	8	27	4	2	0	10	6	12	.290	.333	.441	107	1	0	0	0	1.000	-3	O-22	-0.3
1925	Phi-A	36	50	4	15	2	1	0	10	2	2	.300	.327	.380	74	-2	0	0	0	.667	-2	/O-4	-0.4
Total	2	92	143	12	42	6	3	2	20	8	14	.294	.331	.420	95	-2	0	0	0	.973	-5	/O-26	-0.7

■ FRANK BAHRET
Bahret, Frank J. b: Poughkeepsie, N.Y.   6'1", 184 lbs.   Deb: 4/17/1884

YEAR	TM/L	G	AB	R	H	2B	3B	HR	RBI	BB	SO	AVG	OBP	SLG	PRO+	BR/A	SB	CS	SBR	FA	FR	G/POS	TPR
1884	Bal-U	2	8	0	0	0	0	0	0	0	0	.000	.000	.000	-91	-2				1.000	0	/O-2	-0.2

■ GENE BAILEY
Bailey, Arthur Eugene b: 11/25/1893, Pearsall, Tex.   d: 11/14/73, Houston, Tex.   BR/TR, 5'8", 160 lbs.   Deb: 9/10/17

YEAR	TM/L	G	AB	R	H	2B	3B	HR	RBI	BB	SO	AVG	OBP	SLG	PRO+	BR/A	SB	CS	SBR	FA	FR	G/POS	TPR
1917	Phi-A	5	12	1	1	0	0	0	0	1	1	.083	.154	.083	-28	-2	1			.833	-1	/O-4	-0.4
1919	Bos-N	4	6	0	2	0	0	0	1	0	0	.333	.333	.333	105	-0	1			1.000	-1	/O-3	0.0
1920	Bos-N	13	24	2	2	0	0	0	0	3	3	.083	.185	.083	-22	-4	0	1	-1	.929	-2	/O-8	-0.8
	Bos-A	46	135	14	31	2	0	5	9	15	20	.230	.288	.244	42	-11	2	7	-4	.986	-4	O-40	-2.1
1923	Bro-N	127	411	71	109	11	7	1	42	43	34	.265	.343	.333	81	-10	9	7	-2	.959	2	*O-100/1-5	-1.5
1924	Bro-N	18	46	7	11	3	1	0	4	7	6	.239	.340	.370	93	-0	1			1.000	1	O-17	0.0
Total	5	213	634	95	156	16	8	7	52	63	64	.246	.321	.303	69	-27	13	<u>15</u>		.965	-5	O-172/1-5	-4.8

■ FRED BAILEY
Bailey, Frederick Middleton "Penny" b: 8/16/1895, Mt.Hope, W.Va.   d: 8/16/72, Huntington, W.Va.   BL/TL, 5'11", 150 lbs.   Deb: 8/19/16

YEAR	TM/L	G	AB	R	H	2B	3B	HR	RBI	BB	SO	AVG	OBP	SLG	PRO+	BR/A	SB	CS	SBR	FA	FR	G/POS	TPR
1916	Bos-N	6	10	0	1	0	0	0	1	0	3	.100	.100	.100	-40	-2	0			1.000	-0	/O-2	-0.2
1917	Bos-N	50	110	9	21	2	1	1	5	9	25	.191	.270	.255	65	-4	3			.962	-1	/O-27	-0.8
1918	Bos-N	4	4	1	1	0	0	0	0	0	1	.250	.250	.250	55	-0	0			.000	0	H	-0.1
Total	3	60	124	10	23	2	1	1	6	9	29	.185	.257	.242	57	-6	3			.963	-2	/O-29	-1.0

■ BILL BAILEY
Bailey, Harry Lewis b: 11/19/1881, Shawnee, Ohio   d: 10/27/67, Seattle, Wash.   BL/TR, 5'10.5", 170 lbs.   Deb: 4/21/11

YEAR	TM/L	G	AB	R	H	2B	3B	HR	RBI	BB	SO	AVG	OBP	SLG	PRO+	BR/A	SB	CS	SBR	FA	FR	G/POS	TPR
1911	NY-A	5	9	1	1	0	0	0	0	0	0	.111	.111	.111	-36	-2	0			.000	0	/O-2,3-1	-0.1

■ MARK BAILEY

Bailey, John Mark b: 11/4/61, Springfield, Mo. BB/TR, 6'5", 195 lbs. Deb: 4/27/84

YEAR	TM/L	G	AB	R	H	2B	3B	HR	RBI	BB	SO	AVG	OBP	SLG	PRO+	BR/A	SB	CS	SBR	FA	FR	G/POS	TPR
1984	Hou-N	108	344	38	73	16	1	9	34	53	71	.212	.321	.343	93	-3	0	1	-1	.983	-2	*C-108	0.0
1985	Hou-N	114	332	47	88	14	0	10	45	67	70	.265	.390	.398	124	14	0	2	-1	.979	-10	*C-110/1-2	0.8
1986	Hou-N	57	153	9	27	5	0	4	15	28	45	.176	.304	.288	66	-7	1	1	-0	.989	2	C-53/1-1	-0.3
1987	Hou-N	35	64	5	13	1	0	0	3	10	21	.203	.311	.219	45	-5	1	0	0	.985	-0	C-27	-0.4
1988	Hou-N	8	23	1	3	0	0	0	0	5	6	.130	.286	.130	24	-2	0	1	-1	.981	-1	/C-8	-0.3
1990	SF-N	5	7	1	1	0	0	1	3	0	2	.143	.143	.571	90	-0	0	0	0	1.000	-0	/C-1	-0.1
1992	SF-N	13	26	0	4	1	0	0	1	3	7	.154	.241	.192	26	-3	0	0	0	1.000	-1	/C-7	-0.3
Total	7	340	949	101	209	37	1	24	101	166	222	.220	.338	.337	93	-5	2	5	-2	.983	-13	C-314/1-3	-0.6

■ ED BAILEY

Bailey, Lonas Edgar b: 4/15/31, Strawberry Plains, Tenn. BL/TR, 6'2", 205 lbs. Deb: 9/26/53 F

YEAR	TM/L	G	AB	R	H	2B	3B	HR	RBI	BB	SO	AVG	OBP	SLG	PRO+	BR/A	SB	CS	SBR	FA	FR	G/POS	TPR
1953	Cin-N	2	8	1	3	1	0	0	1	1	3	.375	.444	.500	145	1	0	0	0	1.000	-1	/C-2	0.0
1954	Cin-N	73	183	21	36	2	3	9	20	35	34	.197	.326	.388	83	-5	1	0	0	.973	-12	C-61	-1.4
1955	Cin-N	21	39	3	8	1	1	1	4	4	10	.205	.326	.359	77	-1	0	0	0	.962	3	C-11	0.2
1956	Cin-N★	118	383	59	115	8	2	28	75	52	50	.300	.388	.551	140	22	2	0	1	.984	-4	*C-106	3.1
1957	Cin-N★	122	391	54	102	15	2	20	48	73	69	.261	.380	.463	117	11	5	3	-0	.991	-12	*C-115	0.3
1958	Cin-N	112	360	39	90	23	1	11	59	47	61	.250	.338	.411	92	-4	2	2	-1	.988	-4	C-99	-0.3
1959	Cin-N	121	379	43	100	13	0	12	40	62	53	.264	.370	.393	101	2	2	0	1	.990	2	*C-117	1.1
1960	Cin-N★	133	441	52	115	19	3	13	67	59	70	.261	.351	.406	105	4	0	0	0	.990	-13	C-129	-0.1
1961	Cin-N	12	43	4	13	4	0	0	2	3	5	.302	.348	.395	95	-0	0	0	0	.967	-4	C-12	-0.4
	SF-N☆	107	340	39	81	9	1	13	51	42	41	.238	.329	.385	92	-4	1	5	-3	.985	-1	*C-103/O-1	-0.2
	Yr	119	383	43	94	13	1	13	53	45	46	.245	.331	.386	93	-4	1	5	-3	.984	-5	*C-115/O-1	-0.6
1962	*SF-N	96	254	32	59	9	1	17	45	42	42	.232	.354	.476	123	8	1	1	0	.987	-5	C-75	0.6
1963	SF-N★	105	308	41	81	8	0	21	68	50	64	.263	.368	.494	147	19	0	6	-4	.987	-0	C-88	2.0
1964	Mil-N	95	271	30	71	10	1	5	34	34	39	.262	.346	.362	99	1	2	0	1	.982	-10	C-80	-0.5
1965	SF-N	24	28	1	3	0	0	0	3	6	7	.107	.265	.107	9	-3	0	0	0	1.000	-0	C-12/1-2	0.0
	Chi-N	66	150	13	38	6	0	5	23	34	28	.253	.391	.393	119	5	0	1	-1	.981	-5	C-54/1-3	0.2
	Yr	90	178	14	41	6	0	5	26	40	35	.230	.372	.348	102	2	0	1	-1	.984	-2	C-66/1-5	0.2
1966	Cal-A	5	3	0	0	0	0	0	0	1	1	.000	.250	.000	-22	-0	0	0	0	.000	0	H	0.0
Total	14	1212	3581	432	915	128	15	155	540	545	577	.256	.358	.429	110	56	17	18	-6	.986	-54	*C-1064/1-5,O	4.6

■ BOB BAILEY

Bailey, Robert Sherwood b: 10/13/42, Long Beach, Cal. BR/TR, 6', 188 lbs. Deb: 9/14/62

YEAR	TM/L	G	AB	R	H	2B	3B	HR	RBI	BB	SO	AVG	OBP	SLG	PRO+	BR/A	SB	CS	SBR	FA	FR	G/POS	TPR
1962	Pit-N	14	42	6	7	2	1	0	6	6	10	.167	.271	.262	44	-3	1	1	-0	.921	0	3-12	-0.3
1963	Pit-N	154	570	60	130	15	3	12	45	58	98	.228	.305	.328	82	-13	10	9	-2	.933	6	*3-153/S-3	-1.0
1964	Pit-N	143	530	73	149	26	3	11	51	44	78	.281	.337	.404	108	6	10	8	-2	.943	6	*3-105,O-35/S	0.8
1965	Pit-N	159	626	87	160	28	3	11	49	70	93	.256	.330	.363	95	-3	10	14	-5	.939	-18	*3-142,O-28	-3.2
1966	Pit-N	126	380	51	106	19	3	13	46	47	65	.279	.361	.447	123	13	5	3	-0	.956	-0	3-96,O-20	1.0
1967	LA-N	116	322	21	73	8	2	4	28	40	50	.227	.314	.301	84	-6	5	5	-2	.941	0	3-65,O-27/1S	-1.0
1968	LA-N	105	322	24	73	9	3	8	39	38	69	.227	.310	.348	105	2	1	2	-1	.953	-3	3-90/S-1,O	-0.2
1969	Mon-N	111	358	46	95	16	6	9	53	40	76	.265	.341	.419	111	5	3	3	-1	.992	4	1-85,O-12/3	0.1
1970	Mon-N	131	352	77	101	19	3	28	84	72	70	.287	.409	.597	166	34	5	3	-0	.953	-13	3-48,O-44,1	1.7
1971	Mon-N	157	545	65	137	21	4	14	83	97	105	.251	.364	.382	111	11	13	7	-0	.960	-15	*3-120,O-51/1	-0.8
1972	Mon-N	143	489	55	114	10	4	16	57	59	112	.233	.317	.368	92	-5	6	7	-2	.938	-8	*3-134/O-5,1	-1.7
1973	Mon-N	151	513	77	140	25	4	26	86	88	99	.273	.380	.489	134	25	5	8	-3	.956	-5	*3-146/O-2	1.7
1974	Mon-N	152	507	69	142	20	2	20	73	100	107	.280	.400	.446	129	23	4	7	-3	.974	-16	O-78,3-68	0.0
1975	Mon-N	106	227	23	62	5	0	5	30	46	38	.273	.398	.361	107	4	4	4	-1	.979	-5	O-61/3-3	-0.4
1976	Cin-N	69	124	17	37	6	1	6	23	16	26	.298	.379	.508	146	7	0	0	0	.974	-5	O-31,3-10	0.2
1977	Cin-N	49	79	9	20	2	1	2	11	12	10	.253	.352	.380	94	-0	1	1	0	.975	-1	1-19/O-3	-0.2
	Bos-A	2	2	0	0	0	0	0	0	0	1	.000	.000	.000	-90	-1	0	0	0	.000	0	H	-0.1
1978	Bos-A	43	94	12	18	3	0	4	9	19	19	.191	.333	.351	84	-2	2	1	0	1.000	0	D-34/3-1,O	-0.3
Total	17	1931	6082	772	1564	234	43	189	773	852	1126	.257	.350	.403	111	97	85	83	-24	.946	-71	*3-1194,O-399,1/DS	-3.7

■ BOB BAILOR

Bailor, Robert Michael b: 7/10/51, Connellsville, Pa. BR/TR, 5'11", 170 lbs. Deb: 9/6/75 C

YEAR	TM/L	G	AB	R	H	2B	3B	HR	RBI	BB	SO	AVG	OBP	SLG	PRO+	BR/A	SB	CS	SBR	FA	FR	G/POS	TPR
1975	Bal-A	5	7	0	1	0	0	0	0	1	0	.143	.250	.143	14	-1	0	0	0	1.000	2	/S-2,2-1	0.1
1976	Bal-A	9	6	2	2	0	1	0	0	0	0	.333	.333	.667	200	1	0	1	-1	.000	-0	/S-1,D-1	0.0
1977	Tor-A	122	496	62	154	21	5	5	32	17	26	.310	.336	.403	99	-1	15	6	1	.988	0	O-63,S-53/D	0.4
1978	Tor-A	154	621	74	164	29	7	1	52	38	21	.264	.312	.338	81	-16	5	6	-2	.964	15	*O-125,3-28/S	-0.8
1979	Tor-A	130	414	50	95	11	5	1	38	36	27	.229	.300	.287	59	-23	14	8	-1	.987	1	*O-118/3-9	-2.7
1980	Tor-A	117	347	44	82	14	2	1	16	36	33	.236	.312	.297	65	-16	12	8	-1	.991	12	O-98,S-12,3/P2D	-0.8
1981	NY-N	51	81	11	23	3	1	0	8	8	11	.284	.356	.346	101	0	2	0	1	.955	-5	S-22,2-13,O/3	-0.2
1982	NY-N	110	376	44	104	14	1	0	31	20	17	.277	.317	.319	79	-10	20	3	4	.984	-19	S-60,2-56,3/O	-2.1
1983	NY-N	118	340	33	85	8	0	1	30	20	23	.250	.294	.282	61	-18	18	3	4	.969	-6	S-75,2-50,3/O	-1.4
1984	LA-N	65	131	11	36	4	0	0	8	8	1	.275	.317	.305	76	-4	3	1	0	.944	10	2-23,3-17,S	0.8
1985	*LA-N	74	118	8	29	3	1	0	7	3	5	.246	.270	.288	58	-7	1	0	0	.962	15	3-45,2-16/SO	0.9
Total	11	955	2937	339	775	107	23	9	222	187	164	.264	.312	.325	76	-95	90	36	5	.980	26	O-425,S-250,23/DP	-5.8

■ HAROLD BAINES

Baines, Harold Douglass b: 3/15/59, Easton, Md. BL/TL, 6'2", 195 lbs. Deb: 4/10/80

YEAR	TM/L	G	AB	R	H	2B	3B	HR	RBI	BB	SO	AVG	OBP	SLG	PRO+	BR/A	SB	CS	SBR	FA	FR	G/POS	TPR
1980	Chi-A	141	491	55	125	23	6	13	49	19	65	.255	.284	.405	87	-11	2	4	-2	.963	-7	*O-137/D-1	-2.4
1981	Chi-A	82	280	42	80	11	7	10	41	12	41	.286	.320	.482	131	10	6	2	1	.985	-0	O-80/D-1	0.8
1982	Chi-A	161	608	89	165	29	8	25	105	49	95	.271	.326	.469	115	11	10	3	1	.980	2	*O-161	1.0
1983	*Chi-A	156	596	76	167	33	2	20	99	49	85	.280	.336	.443	108	6	7	5	-1	.973	0	*O-155	0.1
1984	Chi-A	147	569	72	173	28	10	29	94	54	75	.304	.364	.541	141	30	1	2	-1	.981	0	*O-147	2.5
1985	Chi-A★	160	640	86	198	29	3	22	113	42	89	.309	.345	.467	118	15	1	1	-0	.994	7	*O-159/D-1	1.6
1986	Chi-A★	145	570	72	169	29	2	21	88	38	89	.296	.343	.465	114	10	2	1	0	.984	12	*O-141/D-3	1.7
1987	Chi-A★	132	505	59	148	26	4	20	93	46	82	.293	.353	.479	115	11	0	0	0	1.000	-1	*D-117/O-8	0.6
1988	Chi-A	158	599	55	166	39	1	13	81	67	109	.277	.351	.411	113	11	0	0	0	.882	-1	*D-147/O-9	0.6
1989	Chi-A★	96	333	55	107	20	1	13	56	60	52	.321	.426	.505	165	31	0	1	-1	.981	-0	D-70,O-25	2.8
	Tex-A	50	172	18	49	9	0	3	16	13	27	.285	.335	.390	102	0	0	2	-1	.667	-0	D-46/O-1	-0.2
	Yr	146	505	73	156	29	1	16	72	73	79	.309	.397	.465	144	31	0	3	-2	.964	-1	*D-116/O-26	2.6
1990	Tex-A	103	321	41	93	10	1	13	44	47	63	.290	.380	.449	131	14	0	1	-1	.833	0	D-95/O-2	1.1
	*Oak-A	32	94	11	25	5	0	3	21	20	17	.266	.395	.415	132	5	0	0	0	.000	0	D-30	0.3
	Yr	135	415	52	118	15	1	16	65	67	80	.284	.384	.441	131	19	0	1	-1	.851	0	*D-125/O-2	1.4
1991	Oak-A★	141	488	76	144	25	1	20	90	72	67	.295	.387	.453	145	31	0	4	-3	.923	-2	*D-125,O-12	2.3
1992	*Oak-A	140	478	58	121	18	0	16	76	59	61	.253	.335	.391	109	5	1	3	-2	.964	-5	*D-116/O-23	-0.5
1993	Bal-A	118	416	64	130	22	0	20	78	57	52	.313	.395	.510	136	21	0	0	0	.000	0	*D-116	1.6
1994	Bal-A	94	326	44	96	12	1	16	54	30	49	.294	.356	.485	107	3	0	0	0	.000	0	D-91	1.3
Total	15	2056	7486	973	2156	368	47	277	1198	734	1118	.288	.353	.461	120	203	30	28	-8	.978	6	*O-1060,D-959	13.8

■ AL BAIRD

Baird, Albert Wells b: 6/2/1895, Cleburne, Tex. d: 11/27/76, Shreveport, La. BR/TR, 5'9", 160 lbs. Deb: 9/10/17

YEAR	TM/L	G	AB	R	H	2B	3B	HR	RBI	BB	SO	AVG	OBP	SLG	PRO+	BR/A	SB	CS	SBR	FA	FR	G/POS	TPR
1917	NY-N	10	24	1	7	0	0	0	4	2	2	.292	.346	.292	100	0	2			1.000	2	/2-7,S-3	0.2
1919	NY-N	38	83	8	20	1	0	0	5	5	9	.241	.284	.253	63	-4	3			.898	8	2-24/S-9,3	0.6
Total	2	48	107	9	27	1	0	0	9	7	11	.252	.298	.262	71	-4	5			.921	10	/2-31,S-12,3	0.8

YEAR	TM/L	G	AB	R	H	2B	3B	HR	RBI	BB	SO	AVG	OBP	SLG	PRO+	BR/A	SB	CS	SBR	FA	FR	G/POS	TPR

■ DOUG BAIRD
Baird, Howard Douglas b: 9/27/1891, St.Charles, Mo. d: 6/13/67, Thomasville, Ga. BR/TR, 5'9.5", 148 lbs. Deb: 4/18/15

1915	Pit-N	145	512	49	112	26	12	1	53	37	88	.219	.277	.322	82	-12	29	12	2	.939	-1	*3-120,O-20/2	-0.8
1916	Pit-N	128	430	41	93	10	7	1	28	24	49	.216	.263	.279	66	-18	20	16	-4	.933	-5	3-80,2-29,O	-2.7
1917	Pit-N	43	135	17	35	6	1	0	18	20	19	.259	.355	.319	104	1	8			.935	-4	3-41/2-2	-0.2
	StL-N	104	364	38	92	19	12	0	24	23	52	.253	.301	.371	108	3	18			.941	13	*3-103/O-2	2.0
	Yr	147	499	55	127	25	13	0	42	43	71	.255	.316	.357	107	4	26			.940	9	*3-144/2-2,O	1.8
1918	StL-N	82	316	41	78	12	8	2	25	25	42	.247	.304	.354	104	1	25			.967	16	3-81/S-1,O	2.0
1919	Phi-N	66	242	33	61	13	3	2	30	22	28	.252	.317	.355	95	-1	13			.950	11	3-66	1.3
	StL-N	16	33	4	7	0	1	0	4	2	3	.212	.257	.273	63	-2	2			.773	-4	/3-8,2-1,O	-0.6
	Bro-N	20	60	6	11	0	1	0	8	1	10	.183	.197	.217	24	-6	3			1.000	1	3-17	-0.4
	Yr	102	335	43	79	13	5	2	42	25	41	.236	.291	.322	81	-8	18			.946	8	3-91/2-1,O	0.3
1920	Bro-N	6	6	1	2	0	0	0	1	2	1	.333	.556	.333	154	1	0	0	0	.800	-0	/3-2	0.1
	NY-N	7	8	0	1	0	0	0	0	1	2	.125	.222	.125	1	-1	0	0	0	1.000	2	/3-4	0.1
	Yr	13	14	1	3	0	0	0	1	3	3	.214	.389	.214	76	-0	0	0	0	.929	1	/3-6	0.2
Total	6	617	2106	230	492	86	45	6	191	157	295	.234	.291	.326	88	-33	118	28		.944	28	3-522/O-40,2S	0.8

■ CHARLIE BAKER
Baker, Charles A. b: 1/15/1857, Westborough, Mass. d: 1/15/37, Manchester, N.H. Deb: 8/1/1884

1884	CP-U	15	57	5	8	2	0	1		0		.140	.140	.228	-2	-8				.722	-1	O-11/S-3,2	-0.8

■ CHUCK BAKER
Baker, Charles Joseph b: 12/6/52, Seattle, Wash. BR/TR, 5'11", 180 lbs. Deb: 4/7/78

1978	SD-N	44	58	8	12	1	0	0	3	2	15	.207	.233	.224	31	-5	0	0	0	.952	14	2-24,S-12	1.0
1980	SD-N	9	22	0	3	1	0	0	0	0	4	.136	.136	.182	-13	-3	0	0	0	.963	2	/S-8	-0.1
1981	Min-A	40	66	6	12	0	3	0	6	1	8	.182	.194	.273	31	-6	0	0	0	.969	7	S-31/2-3,3D	0.3
Total	3	93	146	14	27	2	3	0	9	3	27	.185	.201	.240	25	-15	0	0	0	.962	22	/S-51,2-27,D3	1.2

■ DAVE BAKER
Baker, David Glenn b: 11/25/57, Lacona, Iowa BL/TR, 6', 185 lbs. Deb: 9/12/82 F

1982	Tor-A	9	20	3	5	1	0	0	2	3	2	.250	.400	.300	88	-0	0	0	0	.808	1	/3-8	0.0

■ DEL BAKER
Baker, Delmer David b: 5/3/1892, Sherwood, Ore. d: 9/11/73, San Antonio, Tex. BR/TR, 5'11.5", 176 lbs. Deb: 4/16/14 MC

1914	Det-A	44	70	4	15	2	1	0	1	6	9	.214	.276	.271	63	-2	0	2	-1	.920	-6	C-38	-0.9
1915	Det-A	68	134	16	33	3	3	0	15	15	15	.246	.327	.313	87	-2	3	1	0	.940	-5	C-61	-0.3
1916	Det-A	61	98	7	15	4	0	0	6	11	8	.153	.245	.194	31	-8	2			.975	-2	C-59	-0.9
Total	3	173	302	27	63	9	4	0	22	32	32	.209	.289	.265	63	-13	5	3		.948	-12	C-158	-2.1

■ DOUG BAKER
Baker, Douglas Lee b: 4/3/61, Fullerton, Cal. BB/TR, 5'9", 165 lbs. Deb: 7/2/84 F

1984	*Det-A	43	108	15	20	4	1	0	12	7	22	.185	.241	.241	34	-10	3	0	1	.969	2	S-39/2-5,D	-0.4
1985	Det-A	15	27	4	5	1	0	0	1	0	9	.185	.185	.222	11	-3	0	0	0	.960	-3	S-12/2-1	-0.5
1986	Det-A	13	24	1	3	1	0	0	0	2	7	.125	.192	.167	-1	-3	0	0	0	.970	-2	S-10/2-2,D	-0.1
1987	Det-A	8	1	0	0	0	0	0	0	0	1	.000	.000	.000	-99	-0	0	0	0	1.000	3	/S-6,2-1,3	0.2
1988	Min-A	11	7	1	0	0	0	0	0	0	1	.000	.000	.000	-97	-2	0	0	0	1.000	1	/S-9,2-1,3	0.0
1989	Min-A	43	78	17	23	5	1	0	9	9	18	.295	.382	.385	109	1	0	0	0	.982	-2	2-25,S-19/D	0.1
1990	Min-A	3	1	0	0	0	0	0	0	0	0	.000	.000	.000	-94	-0	0	0	0	1.000	1	/2-3	0.0
Total	7	136	246	38	51	11	2	0	22	18	62	.207	.270	.268	49	-17	3	0	1	.973	5	/S-95,2-38,D3	-0.7

■ GENE BAKER
Baker, Eugene Walter b: 6/15/25, Davenport, Iowa BR/TR, 6'1", 170 lbs. Deb: 9/20/53 C

1953	Chi-N	7	22	1	5	1	0	0	1	4	.227	.261	.273	39	-2	1	0		.917	-3	/2-6	-0.4
1954	Chi-N	135	541	68	149	32	5	13	61	47	55	.275	.336	.425	96	-4	4	5	-2	.967	-3	*2-134	0.0
1955	Chi-N★	154	609	82	163	29	7	11	52	49	57	.268	.324	.392	89	-10	9	7	-2	.967	7	*2-154	0.8
1956	Chi-N	140	546	65	141	23	3	12	57	39	54	.258	.311	.377	85	-12	4	3	-1	.969	17	*2-140	1.7
1957	Chi-N	12	44	4	11	3	1	1	10	6	3	.250	.353	.432	111	1	0	0	0	.867	1	3-12	-0.3
	Pit-N	111	365	36	97	19	4	2	36	29	29	.266	.322	.356	84	-8	3	2	-0	.955	-4	3-60,S-28,2	-0.8
	Yr	123	409	40	108	22	5	3	46	35	32	.264	.325	.364	87	-7	3	2	-0	.942	-7	3-72,S-28,2	-1.1
1958	Pit-N	29	56	3	14	2	1	0	7	8	6	.250	.344	.321	80	-1	0	0	0	1.000	-1	3-11/2-3	-0.2
1960	*Pit-N	33	37	5	9	0	0	0	4	2	9	.243	.282	.243	45	-3	0	0	0	1.000	2	/3-7,2-1	-0.1
1961	Pit-N	9	10	1	1	0	0	0	0	3	2	.100	.308	.100	15	-1	0	0	0	1.000	1	/3-3	0.0
Total	8	630	2230	265	590	109	21	39	227	184	219	.265	.323	.385	88	-40	21	17	-4	.968	12	2-451/3-93,S	0.7

■ FLOYD BAKER
Baker, Floyd Wilson b: 10/10/16, Luray, Va. BL/TR, 5'9", 160 lbs. Deb: 5/4/43 C

1943	StL-A	22	46	5	8	2	0	0	4	6	4	.174	.269	.217	42	-3	0	1	-1	.961	0	S-10/3-1	-0.3
1944	*StL-A	44	97	10	17	3	0	0	5	11	5	.175	.259	.206	32	-8	2	0	1	.979	-3	2-17,S-16	-1.0
1945	Chi-A	82	208	22	52	8	0	0	19	23	12	.250	.325	.288	81	-5	3	2	-0	.971	2	3-58,2-11	-0.2
1946	Chi-A	9	24	2	6	1	0	0	3	2	3	.250	.308	.292	71	-1	0	0	0	.962	1	/3-6	0.1
1947	Chi-A	105	371	61	98	12	3	0	22	66	28	.264	.375	.313	96	1	9	7	-2	.980	18	*3-101/2-1,S	1.9
1948	Chi-A	104	335	47	72	8	3	0	18	73	26	.215	.359	.257	68	-12	4	10	-5	.961	13	3-71,2-18/S	-0.4
1949	Chi-A	125	388	38	101	15	4	1	40	84	32	.260	.392	.327	94	1	3	1	0	**.977**	12	*3-122/S-3,2	1.1
1950	Chi-A	83	186	26	59	7	0	0	11	32	10	.317	.417	.355	102	3	1	1	-0	.987	3	3-53/2-3,O	0.4
1951	Chi-A	82	133	24	35	6	1	0	14	25	12	.263	.380	.323	93	-0	0	1	-1	.924	1	3-44/2-5,S	-0.2
1952	Was-A	79	263	27	69	8	0	0	33	30	17	.262	.342	.293	81	-6	1	0	0	.994	-16	2-68/S-7,3	-1.9
1953	Was-A	9	7	0	0	0	0	0	0	1	0	.000	.222	.000	-37	-1	0	0	0	.000	-0	/3-1	-0.2
	Bos-A	81	172	22	47	4	2	0	24	24	10	.273	.365	.320	82	-3	0	2	-1	.963	1	3-37,2-16	-0.4
	Yr	90	179	22	47	4	2	0	24	25	10	.263	.359	.307	78	-5	0	2	-1	.952	1	3-38,2-16	-0.6
1954	Bos-A	21	20	1	4	2	0	0	3	0	1	.200	.200	.300	32	-1	0	0	0	.889	-2	/3-7,2-1	-0.1
	Phi-N	23	22	0	5	0	0	0	0	5	4	.227	.370	.227	60	-1	0	0	0	1.000	4	/3-7,2-2	0.3
1955	Phi-N	5	8	0	0	0	0	0	0	1	0	.000	.000	.000	-99	-2	0	0	0	1.000	1	/3-1	-0.1
Total	13	874	2280	285	573	76	13	1	196	382	165	.251	.360	.297	82	-41	23	25	-8	.971	34	3-510,2-143/SO	-1.0

■ FRANK BAKER
Baker, Frank b: 1/11/44, Bartow, Fla. BL/TR, 5'10", 180 lbs. Deb: 7/27/69

1969	Cle-A	52	172	21	44	5	3	3	15	14	34	.256	.316	.372	89	-3	2	1	0	.950	1	O-46	-0.5
1971	Cle-A	73	181	18	38	12	1	1	23	12	34	.210	.269	.304	55	-11	1	3	-2	.985	-6	O-51	-2.3
Total	2	125	353	39	82	17	4	4	38	26	68	.232	.289	.337	71	-14	3	4	-2	.966	-6	/O-97	-2.8

■ FRANK BAKER
Baker, Frank Watts b: 10/29/46, Meridian, Miss. BL/TR, 6'2", 178 lbs. Deb: 8/9/70

1970	NY-A	35	117	6	27	4	1	0	11	14	26	.231	.323	.282	72	-4	1	2	-1	.973	4	S-35	0.3
1971	NY-A	43	79	9	11	2	0	0	2	16	22	.139	.284	.165	32	-7	3	0	1	.949	11	S-38	0.9
1973	*Bal-A	44	63	10	12	1	2	1	11	7	7	.190	.271	.317	66	-2	0	0	0	.964	1	S-32/2-7,13	0.3
1974	*Bal-A	24	29	3	5	1	0	0	0	3	5	.172	.250	.207	34	-2	0	0	0	.842	2	S-17/2-3,3	-0.1
Total	4	146	288	28	55	8	3	2	24	40	60	.191	.294	.250	56	-16	4	2	0	.953	20	S-122/2-10,31	1.5

■ GEORGE BAKER
Baker, George F. b: 1859, St.Louis, Mo. Deb: 5/24/1883

1883	Bal-a	7	22	0	5	0	0	0		0		.227	.227	.227	45	-1				.667	-3	/S-4,C-3,O	-0.3
1884	StL-U	80	317	39	52	6	0	0		5		.164	.177	.183	-2	-44				**.897**	16	C-68/2-4,O3S	-1.9
1885	StL-N	38	131	5	16	0	0	0	3	9	28	.122	.179	.122	-8	-14				.865	-11	C-32/3-3,O2	-2.1
1886	KC-N	1	4	1	1	0	0	0	0	0	1	.250	.250	.250	49	-0	0			.889	-0	/C-1	0.0
Total	4	126	474	45	74	6	0	0	5	14	29	.156	.180	.169	1	-60	0			.887	3	C-104/O-7,3S2	-4.3

YEAR	TM/L	G	AB	R	H	2B	3B	HR	RBI	BB	SO	AVG	OBP	SLG	PRO+	BR/A	SB	CS	SBR	FA	FR	G/POS	TPR

■ HOWARD BAKER
Baker, Howard Francis   b: 3/1/1888, Bridgeport, Conn.   d: 1/16/64, Bridgeport, Conn.   BR/TR, 5'11", 175 lbs.   Deb: 8/11/12

YEAR	TM/L	G	AB	R	H	2B	3B	HR	RBI	BB	SO	AVG	OBP	SLG	PRO+	BR/A	SB	CS	SBR	FA	FR	G/POS	TPR
1912	Cle-A	11	30	1	5	0	0	0	2	5		.167	.286	.167	29	-3	0			.964	-1	3-10	-0.4
1914	Chi-A	15	47	4	13	1	1	0	5	3	8	.277	.320	.340	100	-0	2	1	0	.879	-4	3-15	-0.5
1915	Chi-A	2	2	0	0	0	0	0	0	0	2	.000	.000	.000	-97	-0	0			.000	0	H	-0.1
	NY-N	1	3	0	0	0	0	0	0	0	0	.000	.000	.000	-99	-1	0			1.000	0	/3-1	-0.1
Total	3	29	82	5	18	1	1	0	7	8	10	.220	.289	.256	61	-4	2	1		.922	-6	/3-26	-1.1

■ JACK BAKER
Baker, Jack Edward   b: 5/4/50, Birmingham, Ala.   BR/TR, 6'5", 225 lbs.   Deb: 9/11/76

YEAR	TM/L	G	AB	R	H	2B	3B	HR	RBI	BB	SO	AVG	OBP	SLG	PRO+	BR/A	SB	CS	SBR	FA	FR	G/POS	TPR
1976	Bos-A	12	23	1	3	0	0	1	2	1	5	.130	.167	.261	21	-2	0	0	0	.981	-0	/1-8,D-1	-0.3
1977	Bos-A	2	3	0	0	0	0	0	0	0	1	.000	.000	.000	-90	-1	0	0	0	.857	0	/1-1	-0.1
Total	2	14	26	1	3	0	0	1	2	1	6	.115	.148	.231	8	-3	0	0	0	.966	-0	/1-9,D-1	-0.4

■ JESSE BAKER
Baker, Jesse (b: Michael Myron Silverman)   b: 3/4/1895, Cleveland, Ohio   d: 7/29/76, W.Los Angeles, Cal.   BR/TR, 5'4", 140 lbs.   Deb: 9/14/19

YEAR	TM/L	G	AB	R	H	2B	3B	HR	RBI	BB	SO	AVG	OBP	SLG	PRO+	BR/A	SB	CS	SBR	FA	FR	G/POS	TPR
1919	Was-A	1	0	0	0	0	0	0	1	0	0	—	—	—	—		0	0		1.000	0	/S-1	0.0

■ FRANK BAKER
Baker, John Franklin "Home Run"   b: 3/13/1886, Trappe, Md.   d: 6/28/63, Trappe, Md.   BL/TR, 5'11", 173 lbs.   Deb: 9/21/08   H

YEAR	TM/L	G	AB	R	H	2B	3B	HR	RBI	BB	SO	AVG	OBP	SLG	PRO+	BR/A	SB	CS	SBR	FA	FR	G/POS	TPR
1908	Phi-A	9	31	5	9	3	0	0	2	0		.290	.290	.387	112	0	0			1.000	2	/3-9	0.3
1909	Phi-A	148	541	73	165	27	**19**	4	85	26		.305	.343	.447	146	25	20			.920	-8	*3-146	2.5
1910	*Phi-A	146	561	83	159	25	15	2	74	34		.283	.329	.392	127	15	21			.920	6	*3-146	2.7
1911	*Phi-A	148	592	96	198	42	14	**11**	115	40		.334	.379	.508	149	35	38			**.942**	-1	*3-148	3.6
1912	Phi-A	149	577	116	200	40	21	**10**	**130**	50		.347	.404	.541	176	54	40			.941	10	*3-149	6.3
1913	*Phi-A	149	564	116	190	34	9	**12**	**117**	63	31	.337	.413	.493	169	48	34			.921	3	*3-149	6.1
1914	*Phi-A	150	570	84	182	23	10	**9**	89	53	37	.319	.380	.442	153	35	19	20	-6	.955	10	*3-149	4.7
1916	NY-A	100	360	46	97	23	2	10	52	36	30	.269	.344	.428	129	11	15			.940	2	3-96	1.8
1917	NY-A	146	553	57	156	24	2	6	71	48	27	.282	.345	.365	116	10	18			.949	11	*3-146	2.6
1918	NY-A	126	504	65	154	24	5	6	62	38	13	.306	.357	.409	128	15	8			**.972**	11	*3-126	3.2
1919	NY-A	141	567	70	166	22	1	10	83	44	18	.293	.346	.388	105	3	13			.955	-2	*3-141	0.7
1921	*NY-A	94	330	46	97	16	2	9	71	26	12	.294	.353	.436	98	-2	8	5	-1	.959	-2	3-83	0.2
1922	*NY-A	69	234	30	65	12	3	7	36	15	14	.278	.327	.444	97	-2	1	3	-2	.962	-10	3-60	-0.9
Total	13	1575	5984	887	1838	315	103	96	987	473	182	.307	.363	.442	136	250	235	28		.943	37	*3-1548	33.8

■ DUSTY BAKER
Baker, Johnnie B   b: 6/15/49, Riverside, Cal.   BR/TR, 6'2", 187 lbs.   Deb: 9/7/68   CM

YEAR	TM/L	G	AB	R	H	2B	3B	HR	RBI	BB	SO	AVG	OBP	SLG	PRO+	BR/A	SB	CS	SBR	FA	FR	G/POS	TPR
1968	Atl-N	6	5	0	2	0	0	0	0	0	1	.400	.400	.400	140	0	0	0	0	.000	-1	/O-3	-0.1
1969	Atl-N	3	7	0	0	0	0	0	0	0	3	.000	.000	.000	-99	-2	0	0	0	1.000	-0	/O-3	-0.3
1970	Atl-N	13	24	3	7	0	0	0	4	2	4	.292	.346	.292	69	-1	0	0	0	.800	-2	O-11	-0.3
1971	Atl-N	29	62	2	14	2	0	0	4	1	14	.226	.238	.258	38	-5	0	1	-1	1.000	-2	O-18	-0.9
1972	Atl-N	127	446	62	143	27	2	17	76	45	68	.321	.388	.504	139	23	4	7	-3	.989	-2	*O-123	1.7
1973	Atl-N	159	604	101	174	29	4	21	99	67	72	.288	.364	.454	116	14	24	3	5	.983	10	*O-156	2.3
1974	Atl-N	149	574	80	147	35	0	20	69	71	87	.256	.339	.422	107	5	18	7	1	.981	-18	*O-148	-1.9
1975	Atl-N	142	494	63	129	18	2	19	72	67	57	.261	.349	.421	109	6	12	7	-1	.990	7	*O-136	0.7
1976	LA-N	112	384	36	93	13	0	4	39	31	54	.242	.300	.307	74	-13	2	4	-2	.996	-1	*O-106	-2.1
1977	*LA-N	153	533	86	155	26	1	30	86	58	89	.291	.367	.512	134	25	2	6	-3	.987	-4	*O-152	1.2
1978	*LA-N	149	522	62	137	24	1	11	66	47	66	.262	.327	.375	96	-3	12	3	2	.985	5	*O-145	-0.2
1979	LA-N	151	554	86	152	29	1	23	88	56	62	.274	.342	.455	117	12	11	4	1	.990	13	*O-150	2.0
1980	LA-N	153	579	80	170	26	4	29	97	43	66	.294	.346	.503	137	26	12	10	-2	.991	-6	*O-151	2.5
1981	*LA-N★	103	400	48	128	17	3	9	49	29	43	.320	.367	.445	134	17	10	7	-1	.990	1	*O-101	1.5
1982	LA-N★	147	570	80	171	19	1	23	88	56	62	.300	.362	.458	132	24	17	10	-1	.975	-7	*O-144	1.3
1983	*LA-N	149	531	71	138	25	1	15	73	72	59	.260	.350	.395	107	6	7	1	2	.981	-1	*O-143	0.2
1984	SF-N	100	243	31	71	7	2	3	32	40	27	.292	.392	.374	120	8	4	1	1	.974	-1	O-62	0.7
1985	Oak-A	111	343	48	92	15	1	14	52	50	47	.268	.361	.440	128	14	2	1	0	.993	-5	1-58,O-35,D	0.4
1986	Oak-A	83	242	25	58	8	0	4	19	27	37	.240	.316	.322	80	-6	0	1	-1	1.000	-3	O-55,D-15/1	-1.2
Total	19	2039	7117	964	1981	320	23	242	1013	762	926	.278	.351	.432	116	149	137	73	-3	.985	-0	*O-1842/1-61,D	7.5

■ KIRTLEY BAKER
Baker, Kirtley "Whitey"   b: 6/24/1869, Aurora, Ind.   d: 4/15/27, Covington, Ky.   BR/TR, 5'9", 160 lbs.   Deb: 5/7/1890

YEAR	TM/L	G	AB	R	H	2B	3B	HR	RBI	BB	SO	AVG	OBP	SLG	PRO+	BR/A	SB	CS	SBR	FA	FR	G/POS	TPR
1890	Pit-N	26	68	6	10	0	0	0	10	6		.147	.275	.147	27	-6	1			.878	-0	P-25	0.0
1893	Bal-N	19	57	9	17	1	1	0	6	8	6	.298	.385	.351	94	-0	1			.930	5	P-15/O-3	0.2
1894	Bal-N	2	4	0	0	0	0	0	0	0	1	.000	.000	.000	-96	-1	0			1.000	1	/O-1,P-1	0.0
1898	Was-N	6	18	3	5	0	1	0	3	3		.278	.381	.389	121	1	0			1.000	-1	/P-6	0.0
1899	Was-N	12	19	1	3	0	0	0	1	1		.158	.200	.158	-1	-3	0			.862	2	P-11	0.0
Total	5	65	166	19	35	1	2	0	10	22	13	.211	.311	.241	57	-9	2			.895	7	/P-58,O-4	0.2

■ PHIL BAKER
Baker, Philip   b: 9/19/1856, Philadelphia, Pa.   d: 6/4/40, Washington, D.C.   BL/TL, 5'8", 152 lbs.   Deb: 5/1/1883

YEAR	TM/L	G	AB	R	H	2B	3B	HR	RBI	BB	SO	AVG	OBP	SLG	PRO+	BR/A	SB	CS	SBR	FA	FR	G/POS	TPR
1883	Bal-a	28	121	22	33	2	1	1		8		.273	.318	.331	106	1				.883	-7	C-19,O-14/S	-0.4
1884	Was-U	86	371	75	107	12	5	1		19		.288	.309	.356	83	-9				.955	-7	1-39,O-32,C	-1.9
1886	Was-N	81	325	37	72	6	5	1	34	20	32	.222	.267	.280	70	-11	16			.967	-7	1-56,O-21/C	-2.3
Total	3	195	817	134	212	20	11	3	34	39	32	.259	.293	.322	82	-19	16			.963	-24	/1-95,O-67,CS	-4.6

■ TRACY BAKER
Baker, Tracy Lee   b: 11/7/1891, Pendleton, Ore.   d: 3/14/75, Placerville, Cal.   BR/TR, 6'1", 180 lbs.   Deb: 6/19/11

YEAR	TM/L	G	AB	R	H	2B	3B	HR	RBI	BB	SO	AVG	OBP	SLG	PRO+	BR/A	SB	CS	SBR	FA	FR	G/POS	TPR
1911	Bos-A	1	0	0	0	0	0	0	0	0	0	—	—	—	—		0	0		1.000	-0	/1-1	0.0

■ BILL BAKER
Baker, William Presley   b: 2/22/11, Paw Creek, N.C.   BR/TR, 6', 200 lbs.   Deb: 5/4/40   C

YEAR	TM/L	G	AB	R	H	2B	3B	HR	RBI	BB	SO	AVG	OBP	SLG	PRO+	BR/A	SB	CS	SBR	FA	FR	G/POS	TPR
1940	*Cin-N	27	69	5	15	1	1	0	7	4	8	.217	.260	.261	44	-5	2			1.000	4	C-24	0.0
1941	Cin-N	2	1	0	0	0	0	0	0	1	1	.000	.500	.000	49	0	0			1.000	0	/C-1	0.0
	Pit-N	35	67	5	15	3	0	0	6	11	0	.224	.333	.269	71	-2	0			.967	0	C-33	0.0
	Yr	37	68	5	15	3	0	0	6	12	1	.221	.338	.265	71	-2	0			.967	0	C-34	0.0
1942	Pit-N	18	17	1	2	0	0	0	2	1	0	.118	.167	.118	-16	-2	0			1.000	1	C-11	-0.1
1943	Pit-N	63	172	12	47	6	3	1	26	22	6	.273	.365	.360	106	2	3			.979	0	C-56	0.6
1946	Pit-N	53	113	7	27	4	0	1	8	12	6	.239	.312	.301	72	-4	0			.965	-6	C-41/1-1	-0.9
1948	StL-N	45	119	13	35	10	1	0	15	15	7	.294	.373	.395	102	1	1			.994	-1	C-36	0.2
1949	StL-N	20	30	2	4	1	0	0	4	2	2	.133	.188	.167	-4	-4	0			1.000	-2	C-10	-0.6
Total	7	263	588	45	145	25	5	2	68	68	30	.247	.328	.316	79	-15	6			.983	-3	C-212/1-1	-0.8

■ JOHN BALAZ
Balaz, John Lawrence   b: 11/24/50, Toronto, Ont., Can.   BR/TR, 6'3", 180 lbs.   Deb: 9/10/74

YEAR	TM/L	G	AB	R	H	2B	3B	HR	RBI	BB	SO	AVG	OBP	SLG	PRO+	BR/A	SB	CS	SBR	FA	FR	G/POS	TPR
1974	Cal-A	14	42	4	10	0	0	1	5	2	10	.238	.289	.310	76	-1	0	0	0	1.000	-1	O-12	-0.3
1975	Cal-A	45	120	10	29	8	1	1	10	5	25	.242	.272	.350	80	-4	0	0	0	1.000	-0	O-27,D-11	-0.5
Total	2	59	162	14	39	8	1	2	15	7	35	.241	.276	.340	79	-5	0	0	0	1.000	-1	/O-39,D-11	-0.8

■ STEVE BALBONI
Balboni, Stephen Charles   b: 1/16/57, Brockton, Mass.   BR/TR, 6'3", 225 lbs.   Deb: 4/22/81

YEAR	TM/L	G	AB	R	H	2B	3B	HR	RBI	BB	SO	AVG	OBP	SLG	PRO+	BR/A	SB	CS	SBR	FA	FR	G/POS	TPR
1981	NY-A	4	7	2	2	1	0	2	1	4		.286	.375	.714	211		0	0	0	1.000	-0	/1-3,D-1	0.1
1982	NY-A	33	107	8	20	2	1	2	4	6	34	.187	.230	.280	40	-9	0	0	0	.990	-1	1-26/D-1	-0.2
1983	NY-A	32	86	8	20	2	0	5	17	8	23	.233	.298	.430	101	-0	0	0	0	.984	-1	1-23/D-4	-0.2
1984	*KC-A	126	438	58	107	23	2	28	77	45	139	.244	.320	.498	122	11	0	0	0	.987	-5	*1-125/D-1	-0.1
1985	*KC-A	160	600	74	146	28	2	36	88	52	166	.243	.309	.477	111	7	1	0	0	.993	-8	*1-160	-1.1
1986	KC-A	138	512	54	117	25	0	29	88	43	146	.229	.290	.451	96	-5	0	0	0	.987	-6	*1-137	-2.0
1987	KC-A	121	386	44	80	11	1	24	60	34	97	.207	.275	.427	80	-12	1			.989	1	1-55,D-52	-1.6

YEAR	TM/L	G	AB	R	H	2B	3B	HR	RBI	BB	SO	AVG	OBP	SLG	PRO+	BR/A	SB	CS	SBR	FA	FR	G/POS	TPR
1988	KC-A	21	63	2	9	2	0	2	5	1	20	.143	.156	.270	17	-7	0	0	0	.980	-1	1-13/D-6	-0.9
	Sea-A	97	350	44	88	15	1	21	61	23	67	.251	.299	.480	110	3	0	1	-1	.994	-1	D-56,1-40	-0.4
	Yr	118	413	46	97	17	1	23	66	24	87	.235	.279	.448	96	-4	0	1	-1	.991	-2	D-62,1-53	-1.3
1989	NY-A	110	300	33	71	12	2	17	59	25	67	.237	.302	.460	113	4	0	0	0	.994	-2	D-82,1-20	-0.1
1990	NY-A	116	266	24	51	6	0	17	34	35	91	.192	.293	.406	93	-3	0	0	0	.984	-3	D-72,1-28	-1.0
1993	Tex-A	2	5	0	3	0	0	0	0	0	2	.600	.600	.600	233	1	0	0	0	.000	0	/D-2	0.1
Total	11	960	3120	351	714	127	11	181	495	273	856	.229	.295	.451	100	-9	1	2	-1	.989	-26	1-630,D-281	-8.3

■ BOBBY BALCENA
Balcena, Robert Rudolph   b: 8/1/25, San Pedro, Cal.   d: 1/4/90, San Pedro, Cal.   BR/TL, 5'7", 160 lbs.   Deb: 9/16/56

YEAR	TM/L	G	AB	R	H	2B	3B	HR	RBI	BB	SO	AVG	OBP	SLG	PRO+	BR/A	SB	CS	SBR	FA	FR	G/POS	TPR
1956	Cin-N	7	2	2	0	0	0	0	0	0	1	.000	.000	.000	-94	-1	0	0	0	1.000	-1	/O-2	-0.1

■ LADY BALDWIN
Baldwin, Charles Busted   b: 4/8/1859, Oramel, N.Y.   d: 3/7/37, Hastings, Mich.   BL/TL, 5'11", 160 lbs.   Deb: 9/30/1884

YEAR	TM/L	G	AB	R	H	2B	3B	HR	RBI	BB	SO	AVG	OBP	SLG	PRO+	BR/A	SB	CS	SBR	FA	FR	G/POS	TPR
1884	Mil-U	7	27	6	6	3	0	0				.222	.222	.333	90	-2				.778	0	/O-5,P-2	-0.1
1885	Det-N	31	124	12	30	6	3	0	18	6	22	.242	.277	.339	98	-0				.879	1	P-21,O-12	-0.1
1886	Det-N	57	204	25	41	6	3	0	25	18	44	.201	.266	.260	59	-10	3			.969	5	P-56/O-2	0.0
1887	*Det-N	24	85	15	23	0	1	0	7	10	6	.271	.354	.294	79	-2	4			.926	3	P-24	0.0
1888	Det-N	6	23	5	6	0	0	0	3	3	3	.261	.346	.261	96	0	0			1.000	-0	/P-6,O-1	0.0
1890	Bro-N	2	3	1	0	0	0	0	0	1	1	.000	.250	.000	-25	-0	0			.625	0	/P-2	0.0
	Buf-P	7	28	4	8	1	0	0	2	2	1	.286	.333	.321	82	-1	0			1.000	-0	/P-7	0.0
Total	6	134	494	68	114	16	7	0	55	40	77	.231	.290	.291	75	-15	7			.934	6	P-118/O-20	-0.2

■ KID BALDWIN
Baldwin, Clarence Geoghan   b: 11/1/1864, Newport, Ky.   d: 7/10/1897, Cincinnati, Ohio   BR/TR, 5'6", 147 lbs.   Deb: 7/27/1884

YEAR	TM/L	G	AB	R	H	2B	3B	HR	RBI	BB	SO	AVG	OBP	SLG	PRO+	BR/A	SB	CS	SBR	FA	FR	G/POS	TPR
1884	KC-U	50	191	19	37	6	3	0			4	.194	.210	.257	30	-18				.885	1	C-44,O-10/23	-1.3
	CP-U	1	1	0	1	0	0	0			0	1.000	1.000	1.000	448	0				1.000	-0	/C-1	0.0
	Yr	51	192	19	38	6	3	0			4	.198	.214	.260	33	-18				.885	1	C-45,O-10/23	-1.3
1885	Cin-a	34	126	9	17	1	0	1			3	.135	.155	.167	2	-14				.863	-2	C-25/O-6,2P3	-1.3
1886	Cin-a	87	315	41	72	8	7	3			6	.229	.252	.327	78	-9	12			.891	-6	C-71,3-13/O	-0.7
1887	Cin-a	96	388	46	98	15	10	1			6	.253	.271	.351	71	-17	13			.874	-2	*C-96/O-2	-0.8
1888	Cin-a	67	271	27	59	11	3	1	25		3	.218	.235	.292	65	-12	4			.918	-2	C-65/O-2,1	-0.7
1889	Cin-a	60	223	34	55	14	2	1	34	5	32	.247	.273	.341	72	-9	7			.912	2	C-55/O-4,31	-0.2
1890	Cin-N	22	72	5	11	0	0	0	10	3	6	.153	.187	.153	-1	-9	2			.902	3	C-20/O-2	-0.4
	Phi-a	24	90	5	21	1	2	0			4	.233	.274	.289	67	-4	2			.887	1	C-19/3-5	-0.1
Total	7	441	1677	186	371	56	27	7	69	36	38	.221	.243	.299	59	-93	40			.893	-6	C-396/O-32,321P	-5.5

■ FRANK BALDWIN
Baldwin, Frank De Witt   b: 12/25/28, High Bridge, N.J.   BR/TR, 5'11", 195 lbs.   Deb: 4/22/53

YEAR	TM/L	G	AB	R	H	2B	3B	HR	RBI	BB	SO	AVG	OBP	SLG	PRO+	BR/A	SB	CS	SBR	FA	FR	G/POS	TPR
1953	Cin-N	16	20	0	2	0	0	0	0	1	9	.100	.143	.100	-35	-4	0	0	0	1.000	-1	/C-6	-0.5

■ HENRY BALDWIN
Baldwin, Henry Clay "Ted"   b: 6/13/1894, Chadds Ford, Pa.   d: 2/24/64, West Chester, Pa.   BR/TR, 5'11", 180 lbs.   Deb: 5/22/27

YEAR	TM/L	G	AB	R	H	2B	3B	HR	RBI	BB	SO	AVG	OBP	SLG	PRO+	BR/A	SB	CS	SBR	FA	FR	G/POS	TPR
1927	Phi-N	6	16	1	5	0	0	0	1	1	2	.313	.353	.313	78	-0		0		.857	-2	/S-3,3-2	-0.2

■ JEFF BALDWIN
Baldwin, Jeffrey Allen   b: 9/5/65, Milford, Del.   BL/TL, 6'1", 180 lbs.   Deb: 5/22/90

YEAR	TM/L	G	AB	R	H	2B	3B	HR	RBI	BB	SO	AVG	OBP	SLG	PRO+	BR/A	SB	CS	SBR	FA	FR	G/POS	TPR
1990	Hou-N	7	8	1	0	0	0	0	0	1	2	.000	.111	.000	-69	-2	0	0	0	1.000	-1	/O-3	-0.3

■ REGGIE BALDWIN
Baldwin, Reginald Conrad   b: 8/19/54, River Rouge, Mich.   BR/TR, 6'1", 195 lbs.   Deb: 5/25/78

YEAR	TM/L	G	AB	R	H	2B	3B	HR	RBI	BB	SO	AVG	OBP	SLG	PRO+	BR/A	SB	CS	SBR	FA	FR	G/POS	TPR
1978	Hou-N	38	67	5	17	5	0	1	11	3	3	.254	.286	.373	89	-1	0	0	0	.955	-1	C-17	-0.2
1979	Hou-N	14	20	0	4	1	0	0	1	0	1	.200	.200	.250	23	-2	0	0	0	1.000	-1	/C-3,1-1	-0.3
Total	2	52	87	5	21	6	0	1	12	3	4	.241	.267	.345	74	-4	0	0	0	.956	-2	/C-20,1-1	-0.5

■ BILLY BALDWIN
Baldwin, Robert Harvey   b: 6/9/51, Tazewell, Va.   BL/TL, 6', 175 lbs.   Deb: 7/29/75

YEAR	TM/L	G	AB	R	H	2B	3B	HR	RBI	BB	SO	AVG	OBP	SLG	PRO+	BR/A	SB	CS	SBR	FA	FR	G/POS	TPR
1975	Det-A	30	95	8	21	3	0	4	8	5	14	.221	.260	.379	75	-3	2	1	0	.983	2	O-25/D-1	-0.3
1976	NY-N	9	22	4	6	1	1	1	5	1	2	.273	.304	.545	146	1	0	0	0	.929	1	/O-5	0.2
Total	2	39	117	12	27	4	1	5	13	6	16	.231	.268	.410	87	-2	2	1	0	.972	3	/O-30,D-1	-0.1

■ MIKE BALENTI
Balenti, Michael Richard   b: 7/3/1886, Calumet, Okla.   d: 8/4/55, Altus, Okla.   BR/TR, 5'11", 175 lbs.   Deb: 7/19/11

YEAR	TM/L	G	AB	R	H	2B	3B	HR	RBI	BB	SO	AVG	OBP	SLG	PRO+	BR/A	SB	CS	SBR	FA	FR	G/POS	TPR
1911	Cin-N	8	8	2	2	0	0	0	0		1	.250	.250	.250	42	-1	3			.857	0	/S-2,O-1	0.0
1913	StL-A	70	211	17	38	2	4	0	11	6	32	.180	.206	.227	28	-20	3			.923	1	S-56/O-8	-1.6
Total	2	78	219	19	40	2	4	0	11	6	33	.183	.208	.228	28	-21	6			.922	1	/S-58,O-9	-1.6

■ LEE BALES
Bales, Wesley Owen   b: 12/4/44, Los Angeles, Cal.   BB/TR, 5'10.5", 165 lbs.   Deb: 8/7/66

YEAR	TM/L	G	AB	R	H	2B	3B	HR	RBI	BB	SO	AVG	OBP	SLG	PRO+	BR/A	SB	CS	SBR	FA	FR	G/POS	TPR
1966	Atl-N	12	16	4	1	0	0	0	0	0	5	.063	.063	.063	-64	-3	0	0	0	1.000	3	/2-7,3-3	0.0
1967	Hou-N	19	27	4	3	0	0	0	2	8	7	.111	.314	.111	28	-2	1	1	-0	.944	-2	/2-6,S-1	-0.4
Total	2	31	43	8	4	0	0	0	2	8	12	.093	.235	.093	-3	-6	1	1	-0	.978	1	/2-13,3-3,S	-0.4

■ ART BALL
Ball, Arthur Clark   b: 4/1876, Kentucky   d: 12/26/15, Chicago, Ill.   TR,   Deb: 8/1/1894

YEAR	TM/L	G	AB	R	H	2B	3B	HR	RBI	BB	SO	AVG	OBP	SLG	PRO+	BR/A	SB	CS	SBR	FA	FR	G/POS	TPR
1894	StL-N	1	3	0	1	0	0	0	0	0	1	.333	.333	.333	61	-0	0			.667	-1	/2-1	-0.1
1898	Bal-N	32	81	7	15	2	0	0	8	7		.185	.258	.210	34	-7	2			.906	9	3-15,S-14/2O	0.2
Total	2	33	84	7	16	2	0	0	8	7	1	.190	.261	.214	35	-7	2			.929	8	/3-15,S-14,2O	0.1

■ NEAL BALL
Ball, Cornelius   b: 4/22/1881, Grand Haven, Mich.   d: 10/15/57, Bridgeport, Conn.   BR/TR, 5'7", 145 lbs.   Deb: 9/12/07

YEAR	TM/L	G	AB	R	H	2B	3B	HR	RBI	BB	SO	AVG	OBP	SLG	PRO+	BR/A	SB	CS	SBR	FA	FR	G/POS	TPR
1907	NY-A	15	44	5	9	1	1	0	4	1		.205	.222	.273	53	-2	1			.817	-3	S-11/2-5	-0.6
1908	NY-A	132	446	34	110	16	2	0	38	21		.247	.284	.291	86	-7	32			.898	-3	*S-130/2-1	-1.3
1909	NY-A	8	29	5	6	1	1	0	3	3		.207	.281	.310	86	-0	2			.917	-3	/2-8	-0.5
	Cle-A	96	324	29	83	13	2	1	25	17		.256	.295	.318	90	-4	17			.914	-11	S-95	-1.6
	Yr	104	353	34	89	14	3	1	28	20		.252	.294	.317	90	-5	19			.914	-14	S-95/2-8	-2.1
1910	Cle-A	53	119	13	25	3	1	0	12	9		.210	.266	.252	61	-5	4			.927	-4	S-27/2-6,O3	-0.7
1911	Cle-A	116	412	45	122	14	9	4	45	27		.296	.339	.396	104	1	21			.945	6	2-94,3-17/S	0.5
1912	Cle-A	40	132	12	30	4	1	0	14	9		.227	.277	.273	55	-8	7			.938	0	2-37	-0.8
	*Bos-A	18	45	10	9	2	0	0	6	3		.200	.250	.244	40	-4	5			.927	-4	2-17	-0.7
	Yr	58	177	22	39	6	1	0	20	12		.220	.270	.266	51	-11	12			.936	-3	2-54	-1.5
1913	Bos-A	23	58	9	10	2	0	0	4	9	13	.172	.294	.207	46	-4	3			.902	-2	2-10/S-7,3	-0.5
Total	7	501	1609	162	404	56	17	4	151	99	13	.251	.296	.314	83	-34	92			.902	-25	S-271,2-178/3O	-6.2

■ JIM BALL
Ball, James Chandler   b: 2/22/1884, Harford Co., Md.   d: 4/7/63, Glendale, Cal.   BR/TR, 5'11", 175 lbs.   Deb: 9/21/07

YEAR	TM/L	G	AB	R	H	2B	3B	HR	RBI	BB	SO	AVG	OBP	SLG	PRO+	BR/A	SB	CS	SBR	FA	FR	G/POS	TPR
1907	Bos-N	10	36	3	6	2	0	0			3	.167	.211	.222	36	-3	0			.963	-2	C-10	-0.4
1908	Bos-N	6	15	1	1	0	0	0		1	2	.067	.125	.067	-39	-2	0			.917	-1	/C-6	-0.3
Total	2	16	51	4	7	2	0	0		3	3	.137	.185	.176	14	-5	0			.949	-2	/C-16	-0.7

■ PELHAM BALLENGER
Ballenger, Pelham Ashby   b: 2/6/1894, Gilreath Mill, S.C.   d: 12/8/48, Greenville County, S.C.   BR/TR, 5'11", 160 lbs.   Deb: 5/7/28

YEAR	TM/L	G	AB	R	H	2B	3B	HR	RBI	BB	SO	AVG	OBP	SLG	PRO+	BR/A	SB	CS	SBR	FA	FR	G/POS	TPR
1928	Was-A	3	9	0	1	0	0	0	0	0	1	.111	.111	.111	-42	-2	0	0	0	1.000	1	/3-3	0.0

■ HAL BAMBERGER
Bamberger, Harold Earl "Dutch"   b: 10/29/24, Lebanon, Pa.   BL/TR, 6', 173 lbs.   Deb: 9/15/48

YEAR	TM/L	G	AB	R	H	2B	3B	HR	RBI	BB	SO	AVG	OBP	SLG	PRO+	BR/A	SB	CS	SBR	FA	FR	G/POS	TPR
1948	NY-N	7	12	0	1	0	0	0	0	1	2	.083	.154	.083	-34	-2				1.000	-0	/O-3	-0.3

■ STUD BANCKER
Bancker, John   b: Philadelphia, Pa.   Deb: 4/21/1875

YEAR	TM/L	G	AB	R	H	2B	3B	HR	RBI	BB	SO	AVG	OBP	SLG	PRO+	BR/A	SB	CS	SBR	FA	FR	G/POS	TPR
1875	NH-n	19	72	3	11	0	0	0		0		.153	.153	.153	7	-6						C-12/2-3,S3	-0.5

■ DAVE BANCROFT
Bancroft, David James "Beauty" b: 4/20/1891, Sioux City, Iowa d: 10/9/72, Superior, Wis. BB/TR, 5'9.5", 160 lbs. Deb: 4/14/15 MCH

YEAR	TM/L	G	AB	R	H	2B	3B	HR	RBI	BB	SO	AVG	OBP	SLG	PRO+	BR/A	SB	CS	SBR	FA	FR	G/POS	TPR
1915	*Phi-N	153	563	85	143	18	2	7	30	77	62	.254	.346	.330	104	5	15	27	-12	.928	5	*S-153	1.2
1916	Phi-N	142	477	53	101	10	0	3	33	74	57	.212	.323	.252	75	-11	15			.933	25	*S-142	2.4
1917	Phi-N	127	478	56	116	22	5	4	43	44	42	.243	.307	.335	93	-4	14			.936	28	*S-120/2-3,O	3.3
1918	Phi-N	125	499	69	132	19	4	0	26	54	36	.265	.338	.319	94	-2	11			.928	18	*S-125	2.4
1919	Phi-N	92	335	45	91	13	7	0	25	31	30	.272	.333	.352	99	0	8			.951	10	S-88	1.7
1920	Phi-N	42	171	23	51	7	2	0	5	9	12	.298	.337	.363	96	-1	1	7	-4	.981	9	S-42	0.9
	NY-N	108	442	79	132	29	7	0	31	33	32	.299	.349	.396	115	8	7	5	-1	.946	30	*S-108	4.8
	Yr	150	613	102	183	36	9	0	36	42	44	.299	.346	.387	109	7	8	12	-5	.955	39	*S-150	5.7
1921	*NY-N	153	606	121	193	26	15	6	67	66	23	.318	.389	.441	119	18	17	10	-1	.960	17	*S-153	4.8
1922	*NY-N	156	651	117	209	41	5	4	60	79	23	.321	.397	.418	109	12	16	11	-2	.941	22	*S-156	4.5
1923	*NY-N	107	444	80	135	33	3	1	31	62	23	.304	.391	.399	110	9	8	7	-2	.936	21	S-96,2-11	3.6
1924	Bos-N	79	319	49	89	11	1	2	21	37	24	.279	.356	.339	91	-3	4	4	-1	.961	-5	S-79,M	-0.1
1925	Bos-N	128	479	75	153	29	8	2	49	64	22	.319	.400	.426	122	18	7	4	-0	.945	10	*S-125,M	3.8
1926	Bos-N	127	453	70	141	18	6	1	44	64	29	.311	.399	.384	122	17	3			.956	-3	*S-123/3-2M	2.7
1927	Bos-N	111	375	44	91	13	4	1	31	43	36	.243	.322	.307	75	-13	5			.939	6	*S-104/3-1M	0.4
1928	Bro-N	149	515	47	127	19	5	0	51	59	20	.247	.326	.303	66	-24	7			.948	4	*S-149	-0.3
1929	Bro-N	104	358	35	99	11	3	1	44	29	11	.277	.331	.332	66	-19	7			.955	-0	*S-102	-0.6
1930	NY-N	10	17	0	1	1	0	0	0	2	1	.059	.158	.118	-33	-4	0			.966	1	/S-8	-0.6
Total	16	1913	7182	1048	2004	320	77	32	591	827	487	.279	.355	.358	98	8	145	75		.944	198	*S-1873/2-14,3O	35.3

■ CHRIS BANDO
Bando, Christopher Michael b: 2/4/56, Cleveland, Ohio BB/TR, 6', 195 lbs. Deb: 8/13/81 F

YEAR	TM/L	G	AB	R	H	2B	3B	HR	RBI	BB	SO	AVG	OBP	SLG	PRO+	BR/A	SB	CS	SBR	FA	FR	G/POS	TPR
1981	Cle-A	21	47	3	10	3	0	0	6	2	2	.213	.245	.277	51	-3	0	0	0	.967	-2	C-15/D-2	-0.5
1982	Cle-A	66	184	13	39	6	1	3	16	24	30	.212	.303	.304	68	-8	0	0	0	.990	-6	C-63/3-2	-1.2
1983	Cle-A	48	121	15	31	3	0	4	15	15	19	.256	.348	.380	94	-1	0	1	-1	.995	-2	C-43	-0.2
1984	Cle-A	75	220	38	64	11	0	12	41	33	35	.291	.383	.505	141	13	0	2	-1	.982	-4	C-63/1-1,3D	1.1
1985	Cle-A	73	173	11	24	4	1	0	13	22	21	.139	.236	.173	14	-20	0	1	-1	.986	-3	C-67	-2.1
1986	Cle-A	92	254	28	68	9	0	2	26	22	49	.268	.329	.327	81	-6	0	1	-1	.990	-10	C-86	-1.2
1987	Cle-A	89	211	20	46	9	0	5	16	12	28	.218	.260	.332	55	-14	0	0	-1	.990	-2	C-86	-1.1
1988	Cle-A	32	72	6	9	1	0	1	8	8	12	.125	.222	.181	14	-8	0	0	0	.979	1	C-32	-0.6
	Det-A	1	0	0	0	0	0	0	0	0	0	—	—	—			0	0	0	.000	0	/C-1	0.0
	Yr	33	72	6	9	1	0	1	8	8	12	.125	.222	.181	14	-8	0	0	0	.979	1	C-33	-0.6
1989	Oak-A	1	2	0	1	0	0	0	1	0	1	.500	.500	.500	189	0	0	0	0	1.000	0	/C-1	0.1
Total	9	498	1284	134	292	46	2	27	142	138	197	.227	.303	.329	73	-47	1	5	-3	.987	-28	C-457/3-3,D1	-5.7

■ SAL BANDO
Bando, Salvatore Leonard b: 2/13/44, Cleveland, O. BR/TR, 6', 205 lbs. Deb: 9/3/66 FC

YEAR	TM/L	G	AB	R	H	2B	3B	HR	RBI	BB	SO	AVG	OBP	SLG	PRO+	BR/A	SB	CS	SBR	FA	FR	G/POS	TPR
1966	KC-A	11	24	1	7	1	0	0	1	1	3	.292	.320	.417	113	0	0	0	0	.933	4	/3-7	0.5
1967	KC-A	47	130	11	25	3	2	0	6	16	24	.192	.295	.246	64	-5	1	0	0	.959	8	3-44	0.3
1968	Oak-A	162	605	67	152	25	5	9	67	51	78	.251	.317	.354	108	5	13	4	2	.964	-13	*3-162/O-1	-0.5
1969	Oak-A★	162	609	106	171	25	3	31	113	111	84	.281	.401	.484	153	47	1	4	-2	.954	-13	*3-162	3.3
1970	Oak-A	155	502	93	132	20	2	20	75	118	88	.263	.409	.430	137	31	6	10	-4	.954	-22	*3-152	0.4
1971	*Oak-A	153	538	75	146	23	1	24	94	86	55	.271	.380	.452	137	28	3	7	-3	.971	-17	*3-153	0.8
1972	*Oak-A★	152	535	64	126	20	3	15	77	78	55	.236	.342	.368	118	13	3	1	0	.960	6	*3-151/2-1	2.0
1973	*Oak-A★	162	592	97	170	**32**	3	29	98	82	84	.287	.378	.498	153	41	4	2	0	.949	-23	*3-159/D-3	1.8
1974	*Oak-A†	146	498	84	121	21	2	22	103	86	79	.243	.360	.426	134	24	2	3	-1	.946	-13	*3-141/D-3	0.8
1975	*Oak-A	160	562	64	129	24	1	15	78	87	80	.230	.338	.356	98	1	7	1	2	.967	-16	*3-160	-1.4
1976	Oak-A	158	550	75	132	18	2	27	84	76	74	.240	.337	.427	128	19	20	6	2	.962	-5	*3-155/S-5,D	1.7
1977	Mil-A	159	580	65	145	27	3	17	82	75	89	.250	.339	.395	99	0	4	2	0	.966	-2	*3-135,D-24/2S	-0.3
1978	Mil-A	152	540	85	154	20	6	17	78	72	52	.285	.375	.439	124	22	3	2	-0	.968	12	*3-134,D-12/1	3.1
1979	Mil-A	130	476	57	117	14	3	9	43	57	42	.246	.330	.345	82	-11	2	0	1	.963	9	*3-109,D-19/1P2	-2.0
1980	Mil-A	78	254	28	50	12	1	5	31	29	35	.197	.282	.311	64	-13	5	3	0	.934	-4	3-57,D-15/1	-1.9
1981	*Mil-A	32	65	10	13	2	0	2	9	6	3	.200	.268	.354	82	-2	1	1	-0	.967	0	3-15/1-9,D	-0.2
Total	16	2019	7060	982	1790	289	38	242	1039	1031	923	.254	.355	.408	120	200	75	46	-5	.959	-104	*3-1896/D-80,1S2PO	8.4

■ JEFF BANISTER
Banister, Jeffery Todd b: 1/15/65, Weatherford, Okla. BR/TR, 6'2", 200 lbs. Deb: 7/23/91

YEAR	TM/L	G	AB	R	H	2B	3B	HR	RBI	BB	SO	AVG	OBP	SLG	PRO+	BR/A	SB	CS	SBR	FA	FR	G/POS	TPR
1991	Pit-N	1	1	0	1	0	0	0	0	0	0	1.000	1.000	1.000	471	0	0	0	0	.000	0	/H	0.0

■ ERNIE BANKS
Banks, Ernest b: 1/31/31, Dallas, Tex. BR/TR, 6'1", 180 lbs. Deb: 9/17/53 CH

YEAR	TM/L	G	AB	R	H	2B	3B	HR	RBI	BB	SO	AVG	OBP	SLG	PRO+	BR/A	SB	CS	SBR	FA	FR	G/POS	TPR
1953	Chi-N	10	35	3	11	1	1	2	6	4	5	.314	.385	.571	142	2	0	0	0	.981	3	S-10	0.5
1954	Chi-N	154	593	70	163	19	7	19	79	40	50	.275	.328	.427	94	-6	6	10	-4	.959	-1	*S-154	0.1
1955	Chi-N★	154	596	98	176	29	9	44	117	45	72	.295	.347	.596	145	35	9	3	1	**.972**	5	*S-154	5.3
1956	Chi-N☆	139	538	82	160	25	8	28	85	52	62	.297	.359	.530	137	27	6	9	-4	.962	-16	*S-139	2.0
1957	Chi-N	156	594	113	169	34	6	43	102	70	85	.285	.363	.579	150	40	8	4	0	.975	-17	*S-100,3-58	3.5
1958	Chi-N★	154	617	119	193	23	11	**47**	**129**	52	87	.313	.370	**.614**	157	48	4	4	-1	.960	-2	*S-154	5.7
1959	Chi-N★	155	589	97	179	25	6	45	**143**	64	72	.304	.379	.596	146	46	2	4	-2	**.985**	4	*S-154	6.2
1960	Chi-N★	156	597	94	162	32	7	**41**	117	71	69	.271	.353	.554	145	36	1	3	-2	**.977**	11	*S-156	5.8
1961	Chi-N★	138	511	75	142	22	4	29	80	54	75	.278	.349	.507	122	15	1	2	-1	.965	13	*S-104,O-23/1	3.3
1962	Chi-N★	154	610	87	164	20	6	37	104	30	71	.269	.311	.503	110	6	5	1	1	.993	0	*1-149/3-3	-0.3
1963	Chi-N	130	432	41	98	20	1	18	64	39	73	.227	.297	.403	94	-4	0	3	-2	.993	-2	*1-125	-1.4
1964	Chi-N	157	591	67	156	29	6	23	95	36	84	.264	.310	.450	107	4	1	2	-1	.994	11	*1-157	0.8
1965	Chi-N★	163	612	79	162	25	3	28	106	55	64	.265	.331	.453	116	12	3	5	-2	.992	-7	*1-162	-0.7
1966	Chi-N	141	511	52	139	23	7	15	75	29	59	.272	.317	.432	105	-1	0	1	-1	.992	2	*1-130/3-8	-0.5
1967	Chi-N★	151	573	68	158	26	4	23	95	27	93	.276	.312	.455	112	7	2	2	-1	.993	-1	*1-147	-0.5
1968	Chi-N	150	552	71	136	27	0	32	83	27	67	.246	.288	.469	116	9	2	0	1	.996	-1	*1-147	-0.4
1969	Chi-N★	155	565	60	143	19	2	23	106	42	101	.253	.313	.416	91	-8	0	0	0	**.997**	1	*1-153	-2.1
1970	Chi-N	72	222	25	56	6	2	12	44	20	33	.252	.317	.459	94	-3	0	0	0	.993	-2	1-62	-1.0
1971	Chi-N	39	83	4	16	2	0	3	6	6	14	.193	.247	.325	53	-5	0	0	0	1.000	1	1-20	-0.7
Total	19	2528	9421	1305	2583	407	90	512	1636	763	1236	.274	.333	.500	122	262	50	53	-17	.994	4	*1-1259,S-1125/3O	25.9

■ GEORGE BANKS
Banks, George Edward b: 9/24/38, Pacolet Mills, S.C. d: 3/1/85, Spartanburg, S.C. BR/TR, 5'11", 185 lbs. Deb: 4/15/62

YEAR	TM/L	G	AB	R	H	2B	3B	HR	RBI	BB	SO	AVG	OBP	SLG	PRO+	BR/A	SB	CS	SBR	FA	FR	G/POS	TPR
1962	Min-A	63	103	22	26	0	2	4	15	21	27	.252	.384	.408	109	2	0	0	0	.962	-3	O-17/3-6	-0.1
1963	Min-A	25	71	5	11	4	0	3	8	9	21	.155	.259	.338	65	-3	0	0	0	.910	2	3-21	-0.2
1964	Min-A	1	1	0	0	0	0	0	0	0	0	.000	.000	.000	-99	-0	0	0	0	.000	0	H	0.0
	Cle-A	9	17	6	5	1	0	2	3	6	6	.294	.478	.706	226	3	0	0	-1	1.000	-1	/O-3,2-1,3	0.3
	Yr	10	18	6	5	1	0	2	3	6	7	.278	.458	.667	210	3	0	0	-1	1.000	-1	/O-3,2-1,3	0.3
1965	Cle-A	4	5	0	1	1	0	0	1	0	1	.200	.333	.400	107	0	0	1	-1	1.000	0	/3-1	0.0
1966	Cle-A	4	4	0	1	0	0	0	1	0	1	.250	.250	.250	44	-0	0	0	0	.000	0	H	0.0
Total	5	106	201	33	44	6	2	9	27	37	59	.219	.346	.403	102	1	0	1	-1	.919	-1	/3-29,O-20,2	0.0

■ BILL BANKSTON
Bankston, Wilborn Everett b: 5/25/1893, Barnesville, Ga. d: 2/26/70, Griffin, Ga. BL/TR, 5'11", 180 lbs. Deb: 8/15/15

YEAR	TM/L	G	AB	R	H	2B	3B	HR	RBI	BB	SO	AVG	OBP	SLG	PRO+	BR/A	SB	CS	SBR	FA	FR	G/POS	TPR
1915	Phi-A	11	36	6	5	1	1	1	2	2	5	.139	.205	.306	55	-2	1			.882	-1	/O-8	-0.3

■ JIM BANNING
Banning, James M. b: 1866, New York, N.Y. BL/TR, 5'6", 150 lbs. Deb: 9/27/1888

YEAR	TM/L	G	AB	R	H	2B	3B	HR	RBI	BB	SO	AVG	OBP	SLG	PRO+	BR/A	SB	CS	SBR	FA	FR	G/POS	TPR
1888	Was-N	1	0	0	0	0	0	0	0	0	0	—	—	—			0			1.000	-0	/C-1	0.0

YEAR	TM/L	G	AB	R	H	2B	3B	HR	RBI	BB	SO	AVG	OBP	SLG	PRO+	BR/A	SB	CS	SBR	FA	FR	G/POS	TPR
1889	Was-N	2	1	0	0	0	0	0	0	0	0	.000	.000	.000	-99	-0	0			1.000	1	/C-2	0.1
Total	2	3	1	0	0	0	0	0	0	0	0	.000	.000	.000	-99	-0				1.000	1	/C-3	0.1

■ ALAN BANNISTER
Bannister, Alan b: 9/3/51, Montebello, Cal. BR/TR, 5'11", 175 lbs. Deb: 7/13/74

YEAR	TM/L	G	AB	R	H	2B	3B	HR	RBI	BB	SO	AVG	OBP	SLG	PRO+	BR/A	SB	CS	SBR	FA	FR	G/POS	TPR
1974	Phi-N	26	25	4	3	0	0	0	1	3	7	.120	.241	.120	3	-3	0	0	0	1.000	-2	/O-8,S-2	-0.6
1975	Phi-N	24	61	10	16	3	1	0	0	1	9	.262	.274	.344	68	-3	2	2	-1	1.000	1	O-18/2-1,S	-0.3
1976	Chi-A	73	145	19	36	6	2	0	8	14	23	.248	.319	.317	86	-2	12	4	1	.988	-2	O-43,S-14/23D	-0.4
1977	Chi-A	139	560	87	154	20	3	3	57	54	49	.275	.341	.338	86	-10	4	3	-1	.936	-34	*S-133/2-3,O	-2.9
1978	Chi-A	49	107	16	24	3	2	0	8	11	12	.224	.303	.290	67	-5	3	3	-1	1.000	-3	D-19,O-15/S2	-0.9
1979	Chi-A	136	506	71	144	28	8	2	55	43	40	.285	.344	.383	96	-2	22	6	3	.963	-24	2-65,O-47,3/1D	-2.1
1980	Chi-A	45	130	16	25	6	0	0	9	12	16	.192	.261	.238	38	-11	5	2	0	1.000	-2	O-23,3-17	-1.4
	Cle-A	81	262	41	86	17	4	1	32	28	25	.328	.393	.435	126	10	9	2	2	.968	-17	2-41,O-40/3S	-0.4
	Yr	126	392	57	111	23	4	1	41	40	41	.283	.350	.370	97	-1	14	4	2	.981	-19	O-63,2-41,3/S	-1.8
1981	Cle-A	68	232	36	61	11	1	1	17	16	19	.263	.310	.332	86	-4	16	2	4	.986	-14	O-35,2-30/1S	-1.4
1982	Cle-A	101	348	40	93	16	1	4	41	42	41	.267	.348	.353	94	-2	18	5	2	.991	-11	O-55,2-48/S3D	-1.0
1983	Cle-A	117	377	51	100	25	4	5	45	31	43	.265	.326	.393	93	-4	6	6	-2	.969	-14	O-91,2-27/1D	-2.1
1984	Hou-N	9	20	2	4	2	0	0	0	2	1	.200	.273	.300	65	-1	0	0	0	.947	-1	/S-4,O-1	-0.2
	Tex-A	47	112	20	33	2	1	2	9	21	17	.295	.410	.384	118	4	3	0	1	.959	-12	2-25/O-3,13D	-0.7
1985	Tex-A	57	122	17	32	4	1	1	6	14	17	.262	.338	.336	84	-2	8	2	1	1.000	-1	D-21,O-14,2/31	-0.4
Total	12	972	3007	430	811	143	28	19	288	292	318	.270	.337	.355	90	-35	108	37	10	.983	-138	O-396,2-256,S/D31	-14.8

■ JIMMY BANNON
Bannon, James Henry "Foxy Grandpa" b: 5/5/1871, Amesbury, Mass. d: 3/24/48, Glen Rock, N.J. BR/TR, 5'5", 160 lbs. Deb: 6/15/1893 F

YEAR	TM/L	G	AB	R	H	2B	3B	HR	RBI	BB	SO	AVG	OBP	SLG	PRO+	BR/A	SB	CS	SBR	FA	FR	G/POS	TPR
1893	StL-N	26	107	9	36	3	4	0	15	4	5	.336	.366	.439	113	2	8			.795	-6	O-24/S-2,P	-0.4
1894	Bos-N	128	494	130	166	29	14	13	114	62	42	.336	.414	.514	114	9	47			.873	18	*O-128/P-1	1.4
1895	Bos-N	123	489	101	171	35	5	6	74	54	31	.350	.420	.479	122	15	28			.879	10	*O-122/P-1	1.3
1896	Bos-N	89	343	52	86	9	5	0	50	32	23	.251	.316	.306	61	-20	16			.901	-1	O-76/2-6,S3	-2.2
Total	4	366	1433	292	459	76	24	19	253	152	101	.320	.390	.447	105	5	99			.877	22	O-350/S-7,23P	0.1

■ TOM BANNON
Bannon, Thomas Edward "Ward Six" b: 5/8/1869, Amesbury, Mass. d: 1/26/50, Lynn, Mass. BR/TR, 5'8", 175 lbs. Deb: 5/10/1895 F

YEAR	TM/L	G	AB	R	H	2B	3B	HR	RBI	BB	SO	AVG	OBP	SLG	PRO+	BR/A	SB	CS	SBR	FA	FR	G/POS	TPR
1895	NY-N	37	159	33	43	6	2	0	8	7	8	.270	.301	.333	65	-9	20			.894	2	O-21,1-16	-0.7
1896	NY-N	2	7	1	1	1	0	0	0	1	1	.143	.250	.286	42	-1	0			.500	-1	/O-2	-0.2
Total	2	39	166	34	44	7	2	0	8	8	9	.265	.299	.331	64	-9	20			.878	1	/O-23,1-16	-0.9

■ WALTER BARBARE
Barbare, Walter Lawrence "Dinty" b: 8/11/1891, Greenville, S.C. d: 10/28/65, Greenville, S.C. BR/TR, 6', 162 lbs. Deb: 9/17/14

YEAR	TM/L	G	AB	R	H	2B	3B	HR	RBI	BB	SO	AVG	OBP	SLG	PRO+	BR/A	SB	CS	SBR	FA	FR	G/POS	TPR
1914	Cle-A	15	52	6	16	2	2	0	5	2	5	.308	.345	.423	126	1	1	4	-2	.933	0	3-14/S-1	0.0
1915	Cle-A	77	246	15	47	3	1	0	11	10	27	.191	.235	.211	33	-21	6	5	-1	.960	7	3-68/1-1	-1.3
1916	Cle-A	13	48	3	11	1	0	0	3	4	9	.229	.288	.250	58	-2	0			.977	1	3-12	-0.1
1918	Bos-A	13	29	2	5	3	0	0	2	0	1	.172	.172	.276	36	-2	1			.826	-4	3-11/S-1	-0.7
1919	Pit-N	85	293	34	80	11	5	1	34	18	18	.273	.317	.355	98	-1	11			.961	-7	3-80/2-1	-0.5
1920	Pit-N	57	186	9	51	5	2	0	12	9	11	.274	.308	.323	79	-5	5	3	-0	.923	-5	S-34,2-12/3	-0.8
1921	Bos-N	134	550	66	166	22	7	0	49	24	28	.302	.331	.367	89	-9	11	4	1	.957	-17	*S-121/2-8,3	-1.3
1922	Bos-N	106	373	38	86	5	4	0	40	21	22	.231	.272	.265	41	-33	2	0	1	.966	2	2-45,3-38,1	-2.5
Total	8	500	1777	173	462	52	21	1	156	88	121	.260	.297	.315	71	-72	37	16		.959	-21	3-230,S-157/21	-7.2

■ RED BARBARY
Barbary, Donald Odell b: 6/20/20, Simpsonville, S.C BR/TR, 6'3", 190 lbs. Deb: 5/22/43

YEAR	TM/L	G	AB	R	H	2B	3B	HR	RBI	BB	SO	AVG	OBP	SLG	PRO+	BR/A	SB	CS	SBR	FA	FR	G/POS	TPR
1943	Was-A	1	1	0	0	0	0	0	0	0	0	.000	.000	.000	-99	-0	0	0	0	.000	0	H	0.0

■ JAP BARBEAU
Barbeau, William Joseph b: 6/10/1882, New York, N.Y. d: 9/10/69, Milwaukee, Wis. BR/TR, 5'5", 140 lbs. Deb: 9/27/05

YEAR	TM/L	G	AB	R	H	2B	3B	HR	RBI	BB	SO	AVG	OBP	SLG	PRO+	BR/A	SB	CS	SBR	FA	FR	G/POS	TPR
1905	Cle-A	11	37	1	10	1	1	0	2	1		.270	.289	.351	102	-0	1			.905	1	2-11	0.1
1906	Cle-A	42	129	8	25	5	3	0	12	9		.194	.257	.279	69	-5	5			.830	-7	3-32/S-6	-1.2
1909	Pit-N	91	350	60	77	16	3	0	25	37		.220	.302	.283	75	-10	19			.891	-19	3-85	-3.0
	StL-N	48	175	23	44	3	0	0	5	28		.251	.370	.269	105	3	14			.901	-10	3-47	-0.6
	Yr	139	525	83	121	19	3	0	30	65		.230	.326	.278	85	-7	33			.895	-29	*3-132	-3.6
1910	StL-N	7	21	4	4	0	1	0	2	3	3	.190	.292	.286	71	-1	0			.917	2	/3-6,2-1	-0.2
Total	4	199	712	96	160	25	8	0	46	78	3	.225	.311	.282	82	-12	39			.884	-33	3-170/2-12,S	-4.5

■ DAVE BARBEE
Barbee, David Monroe b: 5/7/05, Greensboro, N.C. d: 7/1/68, Albemarle, N.C. BR/TR, 5'11.5", 178 lbs. Deb: 7/29/26

YEAR	TM/L	G	AB	R	H	2B	3B	HR	RBI	BB	SO	AVG	OBP	SLG	PRO+	BR/A	SB	CS	SBR	FA	FR	G/POS	TPR
1926	Phi-A	19	47	7	8	1	1	1	5	2	4	.170	.220	.298	32	-5	0	0	0	1.000	0	O-10	-0.5
1932	Pit-N	97	327	37	84	22	6	5	55	18	38	.257	.300	.407	89	-6	1			.975	4	O-78	-0.7
Total	2	116	374	44	92	23	7	6	60	20	42	.246	.290	.393	82	-11	1	0		.977	4	/O-88	-1.2

■ CHARLIE BARBER
Barber, Charles D. b: 1854, Philadelphia, Pa. d: 11/23/10, Philadelphia, Pa. BR/TR, Deb: 4/17/1884

YEAR	TM/L	G	AB	R	H	2B	3B	HR	RBI	BB	SO	AVG	OBP	SLG	PRO+	BR/A	SB	CS	SBR	FA	FR	G/POS	TPR
1884	Cin-U	55	204	38	41	1	4	0		1	16	.201	.242	.245	30	-10				.837	4	3-55	-1.4

■ TURNER BARBER
Barber, Tyrus Turner b: 7/9/1893, Lavinia, Tenn. d: 10/20/68, Milan, Tenn. BL/TR, 5'11", 170 lbs. Deb: 8/19/15

YEAR	TM/L	G	AB	R	H	2B	3B	HR	RBI	BB	SO	AVG	OBP	SLG	PRO+	BR/A	SB	CS	SBR	FA	FR	G/POS	TPR
1915	Was-A	20	53	9	16	1	1	0	6	6	7	.302	.383	.358	120	1	0	3	-2	.952	-2	O-19	-0.3
1916	Was-A	15	33	3	7	0	1	1	5	2	6	.212	.257	.364	87	-1	0			.833	-3	O-10	-0.4
1917	Chi-N	7	28	2	6	1	0	0	2	2	8	.214	.267	.250	55	-1	1			1.000	1	/O-7	-0.1
1918	*Chi-N	55	121	19	29	3	2	0	10	9	16	.236	.293	.293	77	-3	3			.940	-8	O-27/1-4	-1.4
1919	Chi-N	76	230	26	72	9	4	0	21	14	17	.313	.355	.387	122	6	7			.949	-4	O-68	-0.3
1920	Chi-N	94	340	27	90	10	6	0	50	9	26	.265	.290	.324	74	-12	5	6	-2	.988	-7	1-69,O-17/2	-2.5
1921	Chi-N	127	452	73	142	14	4	1	54	41	24	.314	.379	.369	99	1	5	9	-4	.970	2	*O-123	-1.0
1922	Chi-N	84	226	35	70	7	4	0	29	30	9	.310	.391	.376	97	0	7	4	-0	.953	-6	O-47,1-16	-0.9
1923	Bro-N	13	46	3	10	2	0	0	8	2	2	.217	.250	.261	36	-4	0	1	-1	1.000	-2	O-12	-0.7
Total	9	491	1531	189	442	47	21	2	185	115	112	.289	.343	.351	93	-12	28	23		.959	-29	O-330/1-89,2	-7.6

■ BRET BARBERIE
Barberie, Bret Edward b: 8/16/67, Long Beach, Cal. BB/TR, 5'11", 185 lbs. Deb: 6/16/91

YEAR	TM/L	G	AB	R	H	2B	3B	HR	RBI	BB	SO	AVG	OBP	SLG	PRO+	BR/A	SB	CS	SBR	FA	FR	G/POS	TPR
1991	Mon-N	57	136	16	48	12	2	2	18	20	22	.353	.443	.515	171	14	0	0	0	.931	-2	S-19,2-10,3/1	1.4
1992	Mon-N	111	285	26	66	11	0	1	24	47	62	.232	.356	.281	83	-4	9	5	-0	.932	5	3-63,2-26/S	0.2
1993	Fla-N	99	375	45	104	16	2	5	33	33	58	.277	.347	.371	87	-6	2	4	-2	.982	11	2-97	0.6
1994	Fla-N	107	372	40	112	20	2	5	31	23	65	.301	.356	.406	93	-3	2	0	1	.975	10	*2-106	1.0
Total	4	374	1168	127	330	59	6	13	106	123	207	.283	.364	.377	98	1	13	9	-2	.980	24	2-239/3-73,S1	3.2

■ JIM BARBIERI
Barbieri, James Patrick b: 9/15/41, Schenectady, N.Y. BL/TR, 5'7", 155 lbs. Deb: 7/5/66

YEAR	TM/L	G	AB	R	H	2B	3B	HR	RBI	BB	SO	AVG	OBP	SLG	PRO+	BR/A	SB	CS	SBR	FA	FR	G/POS	TPR
1966	*LA-N	39	82	9	23	5	0	0	3	9	7	.280	.352	.341	102	0	2	0	1	.939	0	O-20	0.1

■ GEORGE BARCLAY
Barclay, George Oliver "Deerfoot" b: 5/16/1876, Millville, Pa. d: 4/3/09, Philadelphia, Pa. TR, 5'10", 162 lbs. Deb: 4/17/02

YEAR	TM/L	G	AB	R	H	2B	3B	HR	RBI	BB	SO	AVG	OBP	SLG	PRO+	BR/A	SB	CS	SBR	FA	FR	G/POS	TPR
1902	StL-N	137	543	79	163	14	2	3	53	31		.300	.345	.350	119	12	30			.904	-7	*O-137	-0.5
1903	StL-N	108	419	37	104	10	8	0	42	15		.248	.278	.310	70	-18	12			.901	-6	*O-107	-3.1
1904	StL-N	103	375	41	75	7	4	1	28	12		.200	.237	.248	52	-22	14			.947	-6	*O-103	-3.6
	Bos-N	24	93	5	21	3	1	0	10	2		.226	.258	.280	68	-4	3			.935	-3	O-24	-0.9
	Yr	127	468	46	96	10	5	1	38	14		.205	.241	.254	55	-25	17			.945	-9	*O-127	-4.5
1905	Bos-N	29	108	5	19	1	0	0	7	2		.176	.205	.185	17	-11	2			.854	-5	O-28	-1.8
Total	4	401	1538	167	382	35	15	4	140	62		.248	.286	.298	79	-42	61			.911	-29	O-399	-9.9

YEAR	TM/L	G	AB	R	H	2B	3B	HR	RBI	BB	SO	AVG	OBP	SLG	PRO+	BR/A	SB	CS	SBR	FA	FR	G/POS	TPR
■ **JESSE BARFIELD**			Barfield, Jesse Lee		b: 10/29/59, Joliet, Ill.				BR/TR, 6'1", 205 lbs.		Deb: 9/3/81												
1981	Tor-A	25	95	7	22	3	2	2	9	4	19	.232	.270	.368	77	-3	4	3	-1	1.000	5	O-25	0.1
1982	Tor-A	139	394	54	97	13	2	18	58	42	79	.246	.323	.426	95	-3	1	4	-2	.963	-6	*O-137/D-1	-1.4
1983	Tor-A	128	388	58	98	13	3	27	68	22	110	.253	.300	.510	111	4	2	5	-2	.966	4	*O-120/D-5	0.3
1984	Tor-A	110	320	51	91	14	1	14	49	35	81	.284	.359	.466	122	9	8	2	1	.952	6	O-88/D-9	1.4
1985	*Tor-A	155	539	94	156	34	9	27	84	66	143	.289	.371	.536	141	30	22	8	2	.989	22	*O-154	4.8
1986	Tor-A★	158	589	107	170	35	2	**40**	108	69	146	.289	.371	.559	145	36	8	8	-2	.992	21	*O-157	**4.8**
1987	Tor-A	159	590	89	155	25	3	28	84	58	141	.263	.332	.458	104	3	3	5	-2	.992	16	*O-158	1.2
1988	Tor-A	137	468	62	114	21	5	18	56	41	108	.244	.306	.425	102	0	7	3	0	.988	13	*O-136/D-1	0.9
1989	Tor-A	21	80	8	16	4	0	5	11	5	28	.200	.256	.438	94	-1	0	2	-1	.979	3	O-21	0.0
	NY-A	129	441	71	106	19	1	18	56	82	122	.240	.362	.410	119	13	5	3	0	.972	9	*O-129	1.9
	Yr	150	521	79	122	23	1	23	67	87	150	.234	.347	.415	115	12	5	5	-2	.973	12	*O-150	1.9
1990	NY-A	153	476	69	117	21	2	25	78	82	150	.246	.362	.456	127	18	4	3	-1	.973	9	*O-151	2.3
1991	NY-A	84	284	37	64	12	0	17	48	36	80	.225	.313	.447	107	2	1	0	0	1.000	11	O-81	1.2
1992	NY-A	30	95	8	13	2	0	2	7	9	27	.137	.212	.221	21	-10	1	1	0	.966	0	O-30	-1.1
Total	12	1428	4759	715	1219	216	30	241	716	551	1234	.256	.338	.466	116	99	66	47	-8	.980	114	*O-1387/D-16	16.4
■ **AL BARKER**			Barker, Alfred L		b: 1/18/1839, Rockford, Ill.			d: 9/15/12, Rockford, Ill.			Deb: 6/1/1871												
1871	Rok-n	1	4	0	1	0	0	0	2	1	0	.250	.400	.250	97	0	0					/O-1	0.0
■ **RAY BARKER**			Barker, Raymond Herrell "Buddy"		b: 3/12/36, Martinsburg, W.Va.			BL/TR, 6', 192 lbs.		Deb: 9/13/60													
1960	Bal-A	5	6	0	0	0	0	0	0	0	3	.000	.000	.000	-99	-2	0	0	0	.000	-0	/O-1	-0.2
1965	Cle-A	11	6	0	0	0	0	0	0	2	2	.000	.250	.000	-22	-1	0	0	0	1.000	-0	/1-3	-0.1
	NY-A	98	205	21	52	11	0	7	31	20	46	.254	.329	.410	109	2	1	0	0	.991	6	1-61/3-3	0.7
	Yr	109	211	21	52	11	0	7	31	22	48	.246	.326	.398	105	1	1	0	0	.991	6	1-64/3-3	0.6
1966	NY-A	61	75	11	14	5	0	3	13	4	20	.187	.228	.373	72	-3	0	0	0	.987	5	1-47	0.1
1967	NY-A	17	26	2	2	0	0	0	0	3	5	.077	.172	.077	-25	-4	0	0	0	.961	1	1-13	-0.4
Total	4	192	318	34	68	16	0	10	44	29	76	.214	.286	.358	84	-7	1	0	0	.987	12	1-124/3-3,O	0.1
■ **RED BARKLEY**			Barkley, John Duncan		b: 9/19/13, Childress, Tex.			BR/TR, 5'11", 160 lbs.		Deb: 9/2/37													
1937	StL-A	31	101	9	27	6	0	0	14	14	17	.267	.357	.327	73	-4	1	0		.969	-4	2-31	-0.5
1939	Bos-N	12	11	1	0	0	0	0	0	1	2	.000	.083	.000	-82	-3	0			.842	4	/S-7,3-4	0.1
1943	Bro-N	20	51	6	16	3	0	0	7	4	7	.314	.364	.373	113	1	1			.894	-3	S-18	-0.1
Total	3	63	163	16	43	9	0	0	21	19	26	.264	.341	.319	75	-6	2	0		.882	-3	/2-31,S-25,3	-0.5
■ **SAM BARKLEY**			Barkley, Samuel E		b: 5/24/1858, Wheeling, W.Va.			d: 4/20/12, Wheeling, W.Va.		BR/TR, 5'11.5", 180 lbs.		Deb: 5/1/1884		M									
1884	Tol-a	104	435	71	133	**39**	9	1		22		.306	.342	.444	149	22				.930	25	*2-103/C-2	**4.4**
1885	*StL-a	106	418	67	112	18	10	3		25		.268	.312	.380	113	5				.921	15	*2-96,1-11	1.9
1886	Pit-a	122	478	77	127	31	8	1		58		.266	.345	.370	125	15	22			.936	-4	*2-112/O-8,1	1.3
1887	Pit-N	89	340	44	76	10	4	1	35	30	24	.224	.294	.285	66	-15	6			.979	-5	1-53,2-36	-2.0
1888	KC-a	116	482	67	104	21	6	4	51	26		.216	.262	.309	78	-14	15			.938	-7	*2-116/M	-1.6
1889	KC-a	45	176	36	50	6	2	0	23	15	20	.284	.340	.341	89	-3	8			.923	-12	2-41/1-4	-1.1
Total	6	582	2329	362	602	125	39	10	109	176	44	.258	.314	.359	105	10	51			.929	12	2-504/1-70,OC	2.9
■ **TOM BARLOW**			Barlow, Thomas H.		Deb: 5/2/1872																		
1872	Atl-n	37	170	34	56	2	0	0	10	3	2	.329	.341	.341	94	-4						*C-34/S-2	-0.5
1873	Atl-n	55	271	48	74	2	2	1	13	4	0	.273	.284	.306	82	-4						*C-55/2-1,S	-0.3
1874	Har-n	32	156	37	44	4	1	0		1		.282	.287	.321	89	-3						S-32	-0.3
1875	NH-n	1	5	1	1	0	0	0		0		.200	.200	.200	44	-0						/S-1	0.0
	Atl-n	1	4	0	0	0	0	0		0		.000	.000	.000	-99	-1						/2-1	-0.1
	Yr	2	9	1	1	0	0	0		0		.111	.111	.111	-26	-1						/S-1,2-1	-0.1
Total	4 n	126	606	120	175	8	3	1		8		.289	.298	.317	86	-12						/C-89,S-36,2	-1.2
■ **BRUCE BARMES**			Barmes, Bruce Raymond "Squeaky"		b: 10/23/29, Vincennes, Ind.			BL/TR, 5'8", 165 lbs.		Deb: 9/13/53													
1953	Was-A	5	5	1	1	0	0	0	0	0	0	.200	.200	.200	8	-1	0	0	0	1.000	0	/O-1	-0.1
■ **BABE BARNA**			Barna, Herbert Paul		b: 3/2/15, Clarksburg, W.Va.			d: 5/18/72, Charleston, W.Va.		BL/TR, 6'2", 210 lbs.		Deb: 9/16/37											
1937	Phi-A	14	36	10	14	2	0	2	9	2	6	.389	.421	.611	159	3	1	0	0	.800	-2	/O-9,1-1	0.1
1938	Phi-A	9	30	4	4	0	0	0	2	3	5	.133	.212	.133	-12	-5	0	0	0	.917	-1	/O-7	-0.6
1941	NY-N	10	42	5	9	3	0	1	5	2	6	.214	.250	.357	68	-2	0			1.000	1	O-10	-0.2
1942	NY-N	104	331	39	85	8	7	6	58	38	48	.257	.333	.378	107	3	3			.983	-5	O-89	-0.7
1943	NY-N	40	113	11	23	5	1	1	12	16	9	.204	.302	.292	72	-4	3			.984	-1	O-31	-0.7
	Bos-A	30	112	19	19	4	1	2	10	15	24	.170	.268	.277	58	-6	2	1	0	.940	-4	O-29	-1.3
Total	5	207	664	88	154	22	9	12	96	76	98	.232	.311	.346	88	-11	9	1		.969	-13	O-175/1-1	-3.4
■ **RED BARNES**			Barnes, Emile Deering		b: 12/25/03, Suggsville, Ala.			d: 7/3/59, Mobile, Ala.		BL/TR, 5'10.5", 158 lbs.		Deb: 9/29/27											
1927	Was-A	3	11	5	4	1	0	0	0	1	3	.364	.417	.455	127	0	0	0	0	1.000	0	/O-3	0.0
1928	Was-A	114	417	82	127	22	15	6	51	55	38	.305	.391	.472	127	17	7	3	0	.978	4	*O-104	1.3
1929	Was-A	72	130	16	26	5	2	1	15	13	12	.200	.273	.292	45	-11	1	0	0	.877	-6	O-30	-1.7
1930	Was-A	12	12	1	2	1	0	0	0	0	3	.167	.167	.250	4	-2	0	0	0	.000	0	H	-0.2
	Chi-A	85	266	48	66	12	7	1	31	26	20	.248	.317	.357	73	-11	4	2	0	.939	-0	O-72	-1.4
	Yr	97	278	49	68	13	7	1	31	26	23	.245	.311	.353	70	-13	4	2	0	.939	-0	O-72	-1.6
Total	4	286	836	152	225	41	24	8	97	95	76	.269	.347	.404	95	-6	12	5	1	.953	-2	O-209	-2.0
■ **EPPIE BARNES**			Barnes, Everett Duane		b: 12/1/1900, Ossining, N.Y.			d: 11/17/80, Mineola, N.Y.		BL/TL, 5'9", 175 lbs.		Deb: 9/25/23											
1923	Pit-N	2	2	0	1	0	0	0	0	0	1	.500	.500	.500	161	0	0	0	0	1.000	0	/1-1	0.0
1924	Pit-N	2	5	0	0	0	0	0	0	0	1	.000	.000	.000	-98	-1	0	0	0	1.000	0	/1-1	-0.1
Total	2	4	7	0	1	0	0	0	0	0	2	.143	.143	.143	-23	-1	0	0	0	1.000	1	/1-2	-0.1
■ **HONEY BARNES**			Barnes, John Francis		b: 1/29/1900, Fulton, N.Y.			d: 6/18/81, Lockport, N.Y.		BL/TR, 5'10", 175 lbs.		Deb: 4/20/26											
1926	NY-A	1	0	0	0	0	0	0	0	1	0	—	1.000	—	179	0	0	0	0	.000	0	/C-1	0.0
■ **LUTE BARNES**			Barnes, Luther Owens		b: 4/28/47, Forest City, Iowa			BR/TR, 5'10", 160 lbs.		Deb: 8/6/72													
1972	NY-N	24	72	5	17	2	2	0	6	6	4	.236	.295	.319	76	-2	0	1	-1	.959	1	2-14/S-6	-0.1
1973	NY-N	3	2	2	1	0	0	0	1	0	1	.500	.500	.500	181	0	0	0	0	.000	0	H	0.0
Total	2	27	74	7	18	2	2	0	7	6	5	.243	.300	.324	79	-2	0	1	-1	.959	1	2-14,S-6	-0.1
■ **ROSS BARNES**			Barnes, Roscoe Charles		b: 5/8/1850, Mount Morris, Ill.			d: 2/5/15, Chicago, Ill.		BR/TR, 5'8.5", 145 lbs.		Deb: 5/5/1871		U									
1871	Bos-n	31	157	**66**	63	10	9	0	34	13	1	.401	.447	.580	186	17	11					2-16,S-15/3	1.0
1872	Bos-n	45	230	81	**97**	**28**	2	1	44	9	4	**.422**	.444	**.574**	200	25						*2-45	**1.6**
1873	Bos-n	60	322	**125**	137	28	10	3	61	**18**	2	**.425**	**.456**	**.602**	193	34						*2-47,3-13	**2.2**
1874	Bos-n	51	259	72	89	12	4	0		8		.344	.363	.421	141	11						*2-52	0.6
1875	Bos-n	78	393	**114**	142	22	6	1		7		.361	**.373**	.455	178	29						*2-78	2.3
1876	Chi-N	66	322	**126**	138	21	14	1	59	**20**	8	**.429**	**.462**	**.590**	222	39				.910	5	*2-66/P-1	**3.7**
1877	Chi-N	22	92	16	25	1	0	0	5	7	4	.272	.323	.283	83	-2				.838	-8	2-22	-0.9

YEAR	TM/L	G	AB	R	H	2B	3B	HR	RBI	BB	SO	AVG	OBP	SLG	PRO+	BR/A	SB	CS	SBR	FA	FR	G/POS	TPR
1879	Cin-N	77	323	55	86	9	2	1	30	16	25	.266	.301	.316	109	4				.864	-1	*S-61,2-16	0.7
1881	Bos-N	69	295	42	80	14	1	0	17	16	16	.271	.309	.325	104	2				.854	-0	*S-63/2-7	0.6
Total	5 n	265	1361	458	528	100	31	5	139	55	7	.388	.412	.518	180	116						2-238/S-15,3	7.7
Total	4	234	1032	239	329	45	17	2	111	59	53	.319	.356	.401	143	43				.859	-5	S-124,2-111/P	4.1

■ SAM BARNES Barnes, Samuel Thomas b: 12/18/1899, Suggsville, Ala. d: 2/19/81, Montgomery, Ala. BL/TR, 5'8", 150 lbs. Deb: 9/14/21

YEAR	TM/L	G	AB	R	H	2B	3B	HR	RBI	BB	SO	AVG	OBP	SLG	PRO+	BR/A	SB	CS	SBR	FA	FR	G/POS	TPR
1921	Det-A	7	11	2	2	1	0	0	0	2	1	.182	.357	.273	63	-1	0	0	0	.944	2	/2-2	0.1

■ BILL BARNES Barnes, William H. b: Indianapolis, Ind. Deb: 9/27/1884

YEAR	TM/L	G	AB	R	H	2B	3B	HR	RBI	BB	SO	AVG	OBP	SLG	PRO+	BR/A	SB	CS	SBR	FA	FR	G/POS	TPR
1884	StP-U	8	30	2	6	1	0	0		0		.200	.200	.233	32	-4				.727	-2	/O-8	-0.5

■ SKEETER BARNES Barnes, William Henry b: 3/3/57, Cincinnati, Ohio BR/TR, 5'10", 180 lbs. Deb: 9/6/83

YEAR	TM/L	G	AB	R	H	2B	3B	HR	RBI	BB	SO	AVG	OBP	SLG	PRO+	BR/A	SB	CS	SBR	FA	FR	G/POS	TPR
1983	Cin-N	15	34	5	7	0	0	1	4	7	3	.206	.372	.294	84	-0	2	2	-1	1.000	-0	/1-7,3-7	-0.2
1984	Cin-N	32	42	5	5	0	0	1	3	4	6	.119	.196	.190	8	-5	0	0	0	1.000	0	3-11/O-3	-0.5
1985	Mon-N	19	26	0	4	1	0	0	0	0	2	.154	.154	.192	-4	-4	0	1	-1	1.000	1	/3-4,O-3,1	-0.3
1987	StL-N	4	4	1	1	0	0	1	3	0	0	.250	.250	1.000	208	1	0	0	0	.000	0	/3-1	0.1
1989	Cin-N	5	3	1	0	0	0	0	0	0	0	.000	.000	.000	-97	-1	0	0	-1	.000	0	H	-0.2
1991	Det-A	75	159	28	46	13	2	5	17	9	24	.289	.327	.491	121	4	10	7	-1	1.000	-1	O-33,3-17/12D	0.1
1992	Det-A	95	165	27	45	8	1	3	25	10	18	.273	.322	.388	97	-1	3	1	0	.919	2	3-39,1-17,O/2D	0.1
1993	Det-A	84	160	24	45	8	1	2	27	11	19	.281	.327	.381	90	-2	5	5	-2	.984	-0	1-27,O-18,3D2/S	-0.5
1994	Det-A	24	21	4	6	0	0	1	4	0	2	.286	.286	.429	81	-1	0	1	-1	1.000	-1	1-15/O-4,D	-0.2
Total	9	353	614	95	159	30	4	14	83	41	74	.259	.310	.389	90	-9	20	18	-5	.938	1	/3-92,O-76,1D2S	-1.6

■ ED BARNEY Barney, Edmund J. b: 1/23/1890, Amery, Wis. d: 10/4/67, Rice Lake, Wis. BL/TR, 5'10.5", 178 lbs. Deb: 7/22/15

YEAR	TM/L	G	AB	R	H	2B	3B	HR	RBI	BB	SO	AVG	OBP	SLG	PRO+	BR/A	SB	CS	SBR	FA	FR	G/POS	TPR
1915	NY-A	11	36	1	7	0	0	0	8	3	6	.194	.256	.194	35	-3	2	1	0	1.000	-0	O-10	-0.4
	Pit-N	32	99	16	27	1	2	0	5	11	12	.273	.363	.323	110	2	7	3	0	.972	2	O-26	0.3
1916	Pit-N	45	137	16	27	4	0	0	9	23	15	.197	.313	.226	66	-4	8			.964	5	O-40	-0.2
Total	2	88	272	33	61	5	2	0	22	37	33	.224	.324	.257	78	-5	17	4		.971	7	/O-76	-0.3

■ CLYDE BARNHART Barnhart, Clyde Lee "Pooch" b: 12/29/1895, Buck Valley, Pa. d: 1/21/80, Hagerstown, Md. BR/TR, 5'10", 155 lbs. Deb: 9/22/20 F

YEAR	TM/L	G	AB	R	H	2B	3B	HR	RBI	BB	SO	AVG	OBP	SLG	PRO+	BR/A	SB	CS	SBR	FA	FR	G/POS	TPR
1920	Pit-N	12	46	5	15	4	2	0	5	1	2	.326	.340	.500	135	2	1	0	0	.971	0	3-12	0.3
1921	Pit-N	124	449	66	116	15	13	3	62	32	36	.258	.312	.370	78	-15	3	3	-1	.956	-19	*3-118	-2.6
1922	Pit-N	75	209	30	69	7	5	1	38	25	7	.330	.402	.426	112	5	3	2	-0	.918	-12	3-30,O-26	-0.6
1923	Pit-N	114	327	60	106	25	13	9	72	47	21	.324	.409	.563	151	24	5	7	-3	.985	3	O-92	1.8
1924	Pit-N	102	344	49	95	6	11	3	51	30	17	.276	.338	.384	91	-4	8	4	0	.970	2	O-88	-0.8
1925	*Pit-N	142	539	85	175	32	11	4	114	59	25	.325	.391	.447	106	6	9	5	-0	.962	1	*O-138	-0.2
1926	Pit-N	76	203	26	39	3	0	0	10	23	13	.192	.278	.207	30	-19	1			.991	-4	O-61	-2.7
1927	*Pit-N	108	360	65	115	23	4	3	54	37	19	.319	.384	.431	110	6	2			.978	4	O-94	0.4
1928	Pit-N	61	196	18	58	6	2	4	30	11	9	.296	.338	.408	89	-3	3			.971	-2	O-48/3-1	-0.8
Total	9	814	2673	404	788	121	61	27	436	265	149	.295	.360	.416	100	1	35	21		.973	-27	O-547,3-161	-5.2

■ VIC BARNHART Barnhart, Victor Dee b: 9/1/22, Hagerstown, Md. BR/TR, 6', 188 lbs. Deb: 10/1/44 F

YEAR	TM/L	G	AB	R	H	2B	3B	HR	RBI	BB	SO	AVG	OBP	SLG	PRO+	BR/A	SB	CS	SBR	FA	FR	G/POS	TPR
1944	Pit-N	1	2	0	1	0	0	0	0	1	1	.500	.667	.500	222	0	0			.889	1	/S-1	0.2
1945	Pit-N	71	201	21	54	7	0	0	19	9	11	.269	.300	.303	65	-9	2			.928	8	S-60/3-4	0.2
1946	Pit-N	2	1	0	0	0	0	0	0	0	0	.000	.000	.000	-98	-0	0			.000	0	H	0.0
Total	3	74	204	21	55	7	0	0	19	10	12	.270	.304	.304	67	-9	2			.927	9	/S-61,3-4	0.4

■ BILLY BARNIE Barnie, William Harrison "Bald Billy" b: 1/26/1853, New York, N.Y. d: 7/15/1900, Hartford, Conn. 5'7", 157 lbs. Deb: 5/7/1874 MU

YEAR	TM/L	G	AB	R	H	2B	3B	HR	RBI	BB	SO	AVG	OBP	SLG	PRO+	BR/A	SB	CS	SBR	FA	FR	G/POS	TPR
1874	Har-n	45	188	21	34	3	2	0			0	.181	.181	.218	25	-16						C-23,O-21/S	-1.2
1875	Wes-n	10	36	3	4	1	0	0			0	.111	.111	.139	-13	-4						/C-5,O-5	-0.3
	Mut-n	9	35	1	5	1	0	0			0	.143	.143	.171	8	-3						/C-5,O-5	-0.3
	Yr	19	71	4	9	2	0	0			0	.127	.127	.155	-3	-7						C-10,O-10	-0.6
1883	Bal-a	17	55	7	11	0	0	0			2	.200	.228	.200	38	-4				.846	-2	C-13/O-6,SM	-0.4
1886	Bal-a	2	6	0	0	0	0	0			1	.000	.143	.000	-55	-1	0			.000	-1	/O-1,C-1	-0.2
Total	2 n	64	259	25	43	5	2	0			0	.166	.166	.201	18	-23	0					/C-33,O-31,S	-1.8
Total	2	19	61	7	11	0	0	0			3	.180	.219	.180	29	-5				.848	-3	/C-14,O-7,S	-0.6

■ DICK BARONE Barone, Richard Anthony b: 10/13/32, San Jose, Cal. BR/TR, 5'9", 165 lbs. Deb: 9/22/60

YEAR	TM/L	G	AB	R	H	2B	3B	HR	RBI	BB	SO	AVG	OBP	SLG	PRO+	BR/A	SB	CS	SBR	FA	FR	G/POS	TPR
1960	Pit-N	3	6	0	0	0	0	0	0	0	0	.000	.000	.000	-99	-0	0	0	0	.875	-0	/S-2	-0.2

■ SCOTTY BARR Barr, Hyder Edward b: 10/6/1886, Bristol, Tenn. d: 12/2/34, Ft.Worth, Tex. BR/TR, 6', 175 lbs. Deb: 8/22/08

YEAR	TM/L	G	AB	R	H	2B	3B	HR	RBI	BB	SO	AVG	OBP	SLG	PRO+	BR/A	SB	CS	SBR	FA	FR	G/POS	TPR
1908	Phi-A	19	56	4	8	2	0	0	1			.143	.200	.179	22	-5	0			.923	-7	2-11/3-4,1O	-1.4
1909	Phi-A	22	51	5	4	1	0	0	1		11	.078	.254	.098	12	-5	2			.947	-1	O-15/1-7	-0.7
Total	2	41	107	9	12	3	0	0	2		14	.112	.228	.140	17	-9	2			.947	-8	/O-17,2-11,13	-2.1

■ CUNO BARRAGAN Barragan, Facundo Anthony b: 6/20/32, Sacramento, Cal. BR/TR, 5'11", 180 lbs. Deb: 9/1/61

YEAR	TM/L	G	AB	R	H	2B	3B	HR	RBI	BB	SO	AVG	OBP	SLG	PRO+	BR/A	SB	CS	SBR	FA	FR	G/POS	TPR
1961	Chi-N	10	28	3	6	0	0	1	2	2	7	.214	.267	.321	54	-2	0	0	0	1.000	-1	C-10	-0.3
1962	Chi-N	58	134	11	27	6	1	0	12	21	28	.201	.310	.261	53	-8	0	2	-1	.971	-7	C-55	-1.5
1963	Chi-N	1	1	0	0	0	0	0	0	0	1	.000	.000	.000	-95	-0	0	0	0	1.000	0	/C-1	0.0
Total	3	69	163	14	33	6	1	1	14	23	36	.202	.301	.270	53	-11	0	2	-1	.975	-8	/C-66	-1.8

■ GERMAN BARRANCA Barranca, German (Costales) b: 10/19/56, Veracruz, Mex. BL/TR, 6', 160 lbs. Deb: 9/2/79

YEAR	TM/L	G	AB	R	H	2B	3B	HR	RBI	BB	SO	AVG	OBP	SLG	PRO+	BR/A	SB	CS	SBR	FA	FR	G/POS	TPR
1979	KC-A	5	5	3	3	1	0	0	0	0	0	.600	.600	.800	269	1	3	1	0	1.000	3	/2-1,3-1	0.4
1980	KC-A	7	0	3	0	0	0	0	0	0	0	—	—	—	—	0	0	0	0	.000	0	/R	0.0
1981	Cin-N	9	6	2	2	0	0	0	1	0	0	.333	.333	.333	88	-0	0	0	0	.000	0	/H	0.0
1982	Cin-N	46	51	11	13	1	3	0	2	2	9	.255	.283	.392	85	-1	2	0	1	.824	-1	/2-6	-0.2
Total	4	67	62	19	18	2	3	0	3	2	9	.290	.313	.419	101	-0	5	1	1	.893	2	/2-7,3-1	0.2

■ JIMMY BARRETT Barrett, James Erigena b: 3/28/1875, Athol, Mass. d: 10/24/21, Detroit, Mich. BL/TR, 5'9", 170 lbs. Deb: 9/13/1899

YEAR	TM/L	G	AB	R	H	2B	3B	HR	RBI	BB	SO	AVG	OBP	SLG	PRO+	BR/A	SB	CS	SBR	FA	FR	G/POS	TPR
1899	Cin-N	26	92	30	34	2	4	0	10	18		.370	.477	.478	160	9	4			.936	-2	O-26	0.4
1900	Cin-N	137	545	114	172	11	7	5	42	72		.316	.400	.389	121	19	44			.929	4	*O-137	1.2
1901	Det-A	135	542	110	159	16	9	4	65	76		.293	.385	.378	107	8	26			.940	15	*O-135	1.1
1902	Det-A	136	509	93	154	19	6	4	44	74		.303	.397	.387	116	14	24			.961	8	*O-136	1.2
1903	Det-A	136	517	96	163	13	10	2	31	**74**		.315	**.407**	.391	144	32	27			.955	7	*O-136	3.2
1904	Det-A	162	624	83	167	10	5	0	31	79		.268	.353	.300	111	12	15			.971	12	*O-162	1.5
1905	Det-A	20	67	2	17	1	0	0	3	6		.254	.324	.269	88	-1	0			1.000	-3	O-18	-0.5
1906	Cin-N	5	12	1	0	0	0	0	0	2		.000	.143	.000	-53	-2	0			1.000	0	/O-4	-0.3
1907	Bos-A	106	390	52	95	11	6	1	28	38		.244	.314	.310	100	1	3			.966	4	O-99	0.1
1908	Bos-A	3	8	0	1	0	0	0	1	1		.125	.222	.125	13	-1	0			1.000	-1	/O-2	-0.2
Total	10	866	3306	580	962	83	47	16	255	440		.291	.379	.359	117	91	143			.954	44	O-855	7.7

■ JOHNNY BARRETT Barrett, John Joseph "Jack" b: 12/18/15, Lowell, Mass. d: 8/17/74, Seabrook Beach, N.H. BL/TL, 5'10.5", 170 lbs. Deb: 4/14/42

YEAR	TM/L	G	AB	R	H	2B	3B	HR	RBI	BB	SO	AVG	OBP	SLG	PRO+	BR/A	SB	CS	SBR	FA	FR	G/POS	TPR
1942	Pit-N	111	332	56	82	11	6	0	26	48	42	.247	.347	.316	92	-1	10			.973	6	O-94	0.0
1943	Pit-N	130	290	41	67	12	3	1	32	32	23	.231	.316	.303	77	-8	14			.988	-1	O-99	-2.5
1944	Pit-N	149	568	99	153	24	**19**	7	83	86	56	.269	.366	.415	115	13	**28**			.972	-1	*O-147	0.4
1945	Pit-N	142	507	97	130	29	4	15	67	79	68	.256	.357	.418	111	8	25			.976	-2	*O-132	-0.1

YEAR	TM/L	G	AB	R	H	2B	3B	HR	RBI	BB	SO	AVG	OBP	SLG	PRO+	BR/A	SB	CS	SBR	FA	FR	G/POS	TPR
1946	Pit-N	32	71	7	12	3	0	0	6	6	11	.169	.253	.211	32	-6	1			.919	-3	O-21	-1.1
	Bos-N	24	43	3	10	3	0	0	6	12	1	.233	.400	.302	100	1	0			.962	-3	O-17	-0.3
	Yr	56	114	10	22	6	0	0	12	20	12	.193	.313	.246	59	-6	1			.937	-6	O-38	-1.4
Total	5	588	1811	303	454	82	32	23	220	265	201	.251	.349	.369	100	5	69			.974	-15	O-510	-3.6

■ **MARTY BARRETT**   Barrett, Martin F.   b: 11/1860, Port Henry, N.Y.   d: 1/29/10, Holyoke, Mass.   BR/TR, 5'9", 170 lbs.   Deb: 6/24/1884

YEAR	TM/L	G	AB	R	H	2B	3B	HR	RBI	BB	SO	AVG	OBP	SLG	PRO+	BR/A	SB	CS	SBR	FA	FR	G/POS	TPR
1884	Bos-N	3	6	0	0	0	0	0	0	0	4	.000	.000	.000	-99	-1				.900	-1	/C-3	-0.2
	Ind-a	5	13	1	1	1	0	0		0	1	.077	.143	.154	-3	-1				.808	-3	/C-4,O-1	-0.4
Total		8	19	1	1	1	0	0	0	1	4	.053	.100	.105	-34	-3				.833	-4	/C-7,O-1	-0.6

■ **MARTY BARRETT**   Barrett, Martin Glenn   b: 6/23/58, Arcadia, Cal.   BR/TR, 5'10", 176 lbs.   Deb: 9/6/82   F

YEAR	TM/L	G	AB	R	H	2B	3B	HR	RBI	BB	SO	AVG	OBP	SLG	PRO+	BR/A	SB	CS	SBR	FA	FR	G/POS	TPR
1982	Bos-A	8	18	0	1	0	0	0	0	0	1	.056	.056	.056	-66	-4	0	0	0	1.000	5	/2-7	0.1
1983	Bos-A	33	44	7	10	1	1	0	2	3	1	.227	.277	.295	54	-3	0	0	0	.984	4	2-23/D-5	0.2
1984	Bos-A	139	475	56	144	23	3	3	45	42	25	.303	.361	.383	101	2	5	3	-0	**.987**	0	*2-136	0.6
1985	Bos-A	156	534	59	142	26	0	5	56	56	50	.266	.338	.343	84	-11	7	5	-1	.987	15	*2-156	0.8
1986	*Bos-A	158	625	94	179	39	4	4	60	65	31	.286	.355	.381	100	1	15	7	0	.982	-3	*2-158	0.5
1987	Bos-A	137	559	72	164	23	0	3	43	51	38	.293	.354	.351	85	-10	15	2	3	**.988**	**32**	*2-137	3.0
1988	*Bos-A	150	612	83	173	28	1	1	65	40	35	.283	.334	.337	85	-12	7	3	0	.990	2	*2-150	-0.3
1989	Bos-A	86	336	31	86	18	0	1	27	32	12	.256	.324	.318	77	-10	4	1	1	.975	1	2-80/D-4	-0.6
1990	*Bos-A	62	159	15	36	4	0	0	13	15	4	.226	.297	.252	53	-10	4	0	1	.992	9	2-60/3-1,D	0.1
1991	SD-N	12	16	1	3	1	0	1	3	0	3	.188	.235	.438	83	-0	0	0	0	1.000	1	/2-2,3-2	0.0
Total	10	941	3378	418	938	163	9	18	314	304	209	.278	.340	.347	86	-57	57	21	5	.986	66	2-908/D-10,3	4.4

■ **BOB BARRETT**   Barrett, Robert Schley "Jumbo"   b: 1/27/1899, Atlanta, Ga.   d: 1/18/82, Atlanta, Ga.   BR/TR, 5'11", 175 lbs.   Deb: 4/30/23

YEAR	TM/L	G	AB	R	H	2B	3B	HR	RBI	BB	SO	AVG	OBP	SLG	PRO+	BR/A	SB	CS	SBR	FA	FR	G/POS	TPR
1923	Chi-N	3	3	0	1	0	0	0	0	0	0	.333	.333	.333	76	-0				.000	0	H	0.0
1924	Chi-N	54	133	12	32	2	3	5	21	7	29	.241	.279	.414	82	-4	1	0	0	.943	-1	2-25,1-10/3	-0.5
1925	Chi-N	14	32	1	10	1	0	0	7	1	4	.313	.333	.344	72	-1	1	2	-1	1.000	-3	/3-6,2-4	-0.5
	Bro-N	1	1	0	0	0	0	0	1	0	0	.000	.000	.000	-99	-0	0	0	0	.000	0	H	0.0
	Yr	15	33	1	10	1	0	0	8	1	4	.303	.324	.333	67	-2	1	2	-1	1.000	-3	/3-6,2-4	-0.5
1927	Bro-N	99	355	29	92	10	2	5	38	14	22	.259	.289	.341	68	-17	1			.920	-8	3-96	-2.0
1929	Bos-A	68	126	15	34	10	0	0	19	10	6	.270	.324	.349	75	-5	3	1	0	.938	5	3-34/1-4,2O	0.2
Total	5	239	650	57	169	23	5	10	86	32	61	.260	.296	.357	72	-27	6	3		.924	-6	3-144/2-31,1O	-2.8

■ **TOM BARRETT**   Barrett, Thomas Loren   b: 4/2/60, San Fernando, Cal.   BB/TR, 5'9", 157 lbs.   Deb: 7/2/88   F

YEAR	TM/L	G	AB	R	H	2B	3B	HR	RBI	BB	SO	AVG	OBP	SLG	PRO+	BR/A	SB	CS	SBR	FA	FR	G/POS	TPR
1988	Phi-N	36	54	5	11	1	0	0	3	7	8	.204	.306	.222	53	-3	0	0	0	.959	2	2-10	-0.1
1989	Phi-N	14	27	3	6	0	0	0	1	1	7	.222	.250	.222	36	-2	0	0	0	.978	4	/2-9	0.2
1992	Bos-A	4	3	1	0	0	0	0	0	2	0	.000	.400	.000	19	-0	0	0	0	1.000	1	/2-2	0.0
Total	3	54	84	9	17	1	0	0	4	10	15	.202	.295	.214	47	-5	0	0	0	.970	7	/2-21	0.1

■ **BILL BARRETT**   Barrett, William   b: Washington, D.C.   Deb: 7/8/1871

YEAR	TM/L	G	AB	R	H	2B	3B	HR	RBI	BB	SO	AVG	OBP	SLG	PRO+	BR/A	SB	CS	SBR	FA	FR	G/POS	TPR
1871	Kek-n	1	5	1	1	1	0	0	1	0	0	.200	.200	.400	66	-0	0					/C-1,3-1	0.0
1872	Oly-n	1	4	0	0	0	0	0	0	0	0	.000	.000	.000	-99	-1						/C-1	-0.1
	Atl-n	8	35	6	7	2	0	0	1	0	1	.200	.200	.257	34	-3						/O-7	-0.2
	Yr	9	39	6	7	2	0	0	1	0	1	.179	.179	.231	22	-4						/O-7,C-1	-0.3
1873	Bal-n	1	4	0	1	0	0	0	0	0	0	.250	.250	.250	48	-0						/S-1,O-1	-0.1
Total	3 n	11	48	7	9	3	0	0	2	0	1	.188	.188	.250	28	-5						/O-8,C-2,S3	-0.4

■ **BILL BARRETT**   Barrett, William Joseph "Whispering Bill"   b: 5/28/1900, Cambridge, Mass.   d: 1/26/51, Cambridge, Mass.   BR/TR, 6', 175 lbs.   Deb: 5/13/21

YEAR	TM/L	G	AB	R	H	2B	3B	HR	RBI	BB	SO	AVG	OBP	SLG	PRO+	BR/A	SB	CS	SBR	FA	FR	G/POS	TPR
1921	Phi-A	14	30	3	7	2	1	0	3	0	5	.233	.233	.367	51	-2	0	0	0	.925	2	/S-8,P-4,31	0.1
1923	Chi-A	44	162	17	44	7	2	2	23	9	24	.272	.310	.377	81	-5	12	3	2	.940	0	O-40/3-1	-0.7
1924	Chi-A	119	406	52	110	18	5	2	56	30	38	.271	.326	.355	78	-14	15	10	-2	.904	-15	S-77,O-28/3	-2.2
1925	Chi-A	81	245	44	89	23	3	3	40	24	27	.363	.420	.518	145	16	5	6	-2	.943	-7	2-41,O-27/S3	0.7
1926	Chi-A	111	368	46	113	31	4	6	61	25	26	.307	.353	.462	115	6	9	7	-2	.969	-6	*O-102/1-2	-0.7
1927	Chi-A	147	556	62	159	35	9	4	83	52	46	.286	.347	.403	96	-4	20	13	-2	.963	7	O-147	-0.8
1928	Chi-A	76	235	34	65	11	2	3	26	14	30	.277	.320	.379	84	-6	8	3	1	.988	-5	O-37,2-25	-1.1
1929	Chi-A	3	3	0	0	0	0	0	0	0	0	.000	.667	.000	87	-0	0	0	0	.000	0	H	0.0
	Bos-A	111	370	57	100	23	4	3	35	51	38	.270	.363	.378	93	-3	11	8	-2	.974	4	*O-109/3-1	-0.7
	Yr	114	371	57	100	23	4	3	35	53	38	.270	.365	.377	94	-2	11	8	-2	.974	4	*O-109/3-1	-0.7
1930	Bos-A	6	18	3	3	1	0	0	1	1	3	.167	.211	.222	10	-2	0	0	0	1.000	-1	/O-5	-0.4
	Was-A	6	4	0	0	0	0	0	0	1	0	.000	.200	.000	-44	-1	0	0	0	1.000	-1	/O-1	-0.1
	Yr	12	22	3	3	1	0	0	1	2	3	.136	.208	.182	-0	-3	0	0	0	1.000	-1	/O-6	-0.5
Total	9	718	2395	318	690	151	30	23	328	209	239	.288	.347	.405	97	-14	80	50	-6	.964	-21	O-496/S-89,23P1	-5.7

■ **JOSE BARRIOS**   Barrios, Jose Manuel   b: 6/26/57, New York, N.Y.   BR/TR, 6'4", 195 lbs.   Deb: 4/23/82

YEAR	TM/L	G	AB	R	H	2B	3B	HR	RBI	BB	SO	AVG	OBP	SLG	PRO+	BR/A	SB	CS	SBR	FA	FR	G/POS	TPR
1982	SF-N	10	19	2	3	0	0	0	0	1	4	.158	.200	.158	1	-2	0	0	0	1.000	-1	/1-7	-0.4

■ **RED BARRON**   Barron, David Irenus   b: 6/21/1900, Clarksville, Ga.   d: 10/4/82, Atlanta, Ga.   BR/TR, 5'11.5", 185 lbs.   Deb: 6/10/29

YEAR	TM/L	G	AB	R	H	2B	3B	HR	RBI	BB	SO	AVG	OBP	SLG	PRO+	BR/A	SB	CS	SBR	FA	FR	G/POS	TPR
1929	Bos-N	10	21	3	4	1	0	0	1	1	4	.190	.227	.238	16	-3	2			.929	1	/O-6	-0.2

■ **FRANK BARROWS**   Barrows, Franklin L.   b: 10/22/1846, Hudson, Ohio   d: 2/6/22, Fitchburg, Mass.   Deb: 5/20/1871

YEAR	TM/L	G	AB	R	H	2B	3B	HR	RBI	BB	SO	AVG	OBP	SLG	PRO+	BR/A	SB	CS	SBR	FA	FR	G/POS	TPR
1871	Bos-n	18	86	13	13	2	1	0	11	0	0	.151	.151	.198	-1	-11	1					O-17/2-1	-0.7

■ **CUKE BARROWS**   Barrows, Roland   b: 10/20/1883, Gray, Maine   d: 2/10/55, Gorham, Maine   BL/TR, 5'8", 158 lbs.   Deb: 9/18/09

YEAR	TM/L	G	AB	R	H	2B	3B	HR	RBI	BB	SO	AVG	OBP	SLG	PRO+	BR/A	SB	CS	SBR	FA	FR	G/POS	TPR
1909	Chi-A	5	20	1	3	0	0	0		2	0	.150	.190	.150	8	-2	0			.923	2	/O-5	-0.1
1910	Chi-A	6	20	0	4	0	0	0		1	3	.200	.304	.200	61	-1	0			.875	1	/O-6	-0.3
1911	Chi-A	13	46	5	9	2	0	0		4	7	.196	.315	.239	57	-2	2			1.000	-2	/O-13	-0.5
1912	Chi-A	8	13	0	3	0	0	0		2	2	.231	.333	.231	64	-0	1			1.000	-0	/O-3	-0.1
Total	4	32	99	6	19	2	0	0		9	12	.192	.292	.212	50	-6	3			.950	-2	/O-27	-1.0

■ **SHAD BARRY**   Barry, John C.   b: 10/27/1878, Newburgh, N.Y.   d: 11/27/36, Los Angeles, Cal.   BR/TR,   Deb: 5/30/1899

YEAR	TM/L	G	AB	R	H	2B	3B	HR	RBI	BB	SO	AVG	OBP	SLG	PRO+	BR/A	SB	CS	SBR	FA	FR	G/POS	TPR
1899	Was-N	78	247	31	71	7	5	1	33	12		.287	.328	.368	92	-3	11			.946	-16	O-23,1-22/S3/2	-1.7
1900	Bos-N	81	254	40	66	10	7	1	37	13		.260	.301	.366	74	-10	9			.956	-16	O-24,S-18,21/3	-2.4
1901	Bos-N	11	40	3	7	2	0	0	6	2		.175	.233	.225	30	-4	1			.926	-0	O-11	-0.5
	Phi-N	67	252	35	62	10	0	1	22	15		.246	.294	.298	70	-10	13			.903	-13	2-35,3-16,O/S	-2.1
	Yr	78	292	38	69	12	0	1	28	17		.236	.285	.288	64	-13	14			.903	-13	2-35,O-24,3/S	-2.6
1902	Phi-N	138	543	65	156	20	6	3	58	44		.287	.343	.363	118	11	14			.939	-5	*O-137/1-1	-0.3
1903	Phi-N	138	550	75	152	24	5	1	60	30		.276	.321	.344	92	-6	26			.970	-2	*O-107,1-30/3	-1.5
1904	Phi-N	35	122	15	25	2	0	0	3	11		.205	.281	.221	58	-6	2			.979	13	O-32/3-1	0.6
	Cin-N	73	263	29	69	7	2	1	26	17		.262	.310	.316	93	-2	12			.917	-3	O-30,1-18,3/S2	0.1
	Yr	108	385	44	94	9	2	1	29	28		.244	.300	.286	82	-8	14			.955	12	O-62,1-18,3/S2	0.1
1905	Chi-N	27	104	10	22	2	0	0	10	5		.212	.255	.231	43	-7	5			.982	1	1-26	-0.8
	Cin-N	125	494	90	160	11	12	1	56	33		.324	.372	.401	118	9	16			.982	-7	*1-124/O-2	-0.2
	Yr	152	598	100	182	13	12	1	66	38		.304	.352	.371	105	3	21			.982	-7	*1-150/O-2	-1.0
1906	Cin-N	73	279	38	80	10	2	1	33	26		.287	.354	.369	120	7	11			.993	1	1-43,O-30	0.5
	StL-N	62	237	26	59	9	1	0	12	15		.249	.299	.295	89	-3	6			.930	-7	O-35,1-21/3	-1.3

YEAR	TM/L	G	AB	R	H	2B	3B	HR	RBI	BB	SO	AVG	OBP	SLG	PRO+	BR/A	SB	CS	SBR	FA	FR	G/POS	TPR
	Yr	135	516	64	139	19	6	1	45	41		.269	.329	.335	107	4	17			.922	-6	O-65,1-64/3	-0.8
1907	StL-N	81	294	30	73	5	2	0	19	28		.248	.320	.279	91	-2	4			.963	-6	O-81	-1.4
1908	StL-N	74	268	24	61	8	1	0	11	19		.228	.286	.265	80	-6	9			.967	-1	O-69/S-2	-1.1
	NY-N	37	67	5	10	1	0	0	5	9		.149	.260	.194	43	-4	1			.971	-6	O-31	-1.3
	Yr	111	335	29	71	9	2	0	16	28		.212	.281	.251	71	-10	10			.968	-7	*O-100/S-2	-2.4
Total	10	1100	4014	516	1073	128	47	10	391	279		.267	.321	.330	94	-37	140			.955	-65	O-625,1-295/23S	-14.0

■ JACK BARRY
Barry, John Joseph b: 4/26/1887, Meriden, Conn. d: 4/23/61, Shrewsbury, Mass. BR/TR, 5'9", 158 lbs. Deb: 7/13/08 M

YEAR	TM/L	G	AB	R	H	2B	3B	HR	RBI	BB	SO	AVG	OBP	SLG	PRO+	BR/A	SB	CS	SBR	FA	FR	G/POS	TPR
1908	Phi-A	40	135	13	30	4	3	0	8	10		.222	.291	.296	85	-2	5			.966	-11	2-20,S-14/3	-1.5
1909	Phi-A	124	409	56	88	11	2	1	23	44		.215	.307	.259	77	-9	17			.927	-31	*S-124	-4.4
1910	*Phi-A	145	487	64	126	19	5	3	60	52		.259	.336	.337	112	8	14			.916	-22	*S-145	-1.0
1911	*Phi-A	127	442	73	117	18	7	1	63	38		.265	.333	.344	90	-6	30			**.944**	-7	*S-127	-0.4
1912	Phi-A	140	483	75	126	19	9	0	55	47		.261	.335	.337	96	-2	22			.925	-6	*S-139	0.3
1913	*Phi-A	134	455	62	125	20	6	3	85	44	32	.275	.349	.365	111	7	15			.953	-8	*S-134	1.2
1914	*Phi-A	140	467	57	113	12	0	0	42	53	34	.242	.324	.268	81	-9	22	13	-1	.947	5	*S-140	0.7
1915	Phi-A	54	194	16	43	6	2	0	15	15	9	.222	.284	.273	69	-8	6	5	-1	.952	-4	S-54	-1.0
	*Bos-A	78	248	30	65	13	2	0	26	24	11	.262	.342	.331	104	2	0			.962	-4	2-78	-0.2
	Yr	132	442	46	108	19	4	0	41	39	20	.244	.317	.305	89	-6	6	5	-1	.962	-9	2-78,S-54	-1.2
1916	Bos-A	94	330	28	67	6	1	0	20	17	24	.203	.277	.227	52	-19	8			.974	2	2-94	-1.6
1917	Bos-A	116	388	45	83	9	0	2	30	47	27	.214	.305	.253	71	-12	12			**.974**	-11	*2-116,M	-1.9
1919	Bos-A	31	108	13	26	5	1	0	2	5	5	.241	.293	.306	72	-4	2			.922	-7	2-31	-0.7
Total	11	1223	4146	532	1009	142	38	10	429	396	142	.243	.321	.303	88	-54	153	18		.935	-105	S-877,2-339/3	-10.8

■ RICH BARRY
Barry, Richard Donovan b: 9/12/40, Berkeley, Cal. BR/TR, 6'4", 205 lbs. Deb: 7/4/69

YEAR	TM/L	G	AB	R	H	2B	3B	HR	RBI	BB	SO	AVG	OBP	SLG	PRO+	BR/A	SB	CS	SBR	FA	FR	G/POS	TPR
1969	Phi-N	20	32	4	6	1	0	0	5	6		.188	.316	.219	54	-2	0	0	0	.938	-0	/O-9	-0.2

■ DICK BARTELL
Bartell, Richard William "Rowdy Richard" b: 11/22/07, Chicago, Ill. BR/TR, 5'9", 160 lbs. Deb: 10/2/27 C

YEAR	TM/L	G	AB	R	H	2B	3B	HR	RBI	BB	SO	AVG	OBP	SLG	PRO+	BR/A	SB	CS	SBR	FA	FR	G/POS	TPR
1927	Pit-N	1	2	0	0	0	0	0	2	0		.000	.500	.000	41	0	0			1.000	0	/S-1	0.0
1928	Pit-N	72	233	27	71	8	4	1	36	21	18	.305	.377	.386	96	-1	4			.974	2	2-39,S-27/3	0.5
1929	Pit-N	143	610	101	184	40	13	2	57	40	29	.302	.347	.420	87	-13	11			.953	4	S-74,2-70	0.3
1930	Pit-N	129	475	69	152	32	13	0	75	39	34	.320	.378	.467	102	2	8			.941	-8	*S-126	1.9
1931	Phi-N	135	554	88	160	43	7	0	34	27	38	.289	.325	.392	85	-12	6			.948	3	*S-133/2-3	0.5
1932	Phi-N	154	614	118	189	48	7	1	53	64	47	.308	.374	.414	101	2	8			.963	10	*S-154	2.5
1933	Phi-N★	152	587	78	159	25	5	1	37	56	46	.271	.340	.336	83	-12	6			.951	9	*S-152	0.8
1934	Phi-N	146	604	102	187	30	4	0	37	64	59	.310	.384	.373	91	-6	13			.954	14	*S-146	1.6
1935	NY-N	137	539	60	141	28	3	14	53	37	52	.262	.316	.406	94	-5	5			.954	10	*S-137	1.2
1936	*NY-N	145	510	71	152	31	3	8	42	40	36	.298	.355	.418	109	6	6			.956	**45**	*S-144	**5.7**
1937	*NY-N★	128	516	91	158	38	2	14	62	40	38	.306	.367	.469	124	17	5			.958	**38**	*S-128	6.1
1938	NY-N	127	481	67	126	26	1	9	49	55	60	.262	.347	.376	98	-0	4			.952	22	*S-127	3.2
1939	Chi-N	105	336	37	80	24	2	3	34	42	25	.238	.335	.348	82	-8	6			.943	-5	*S-101/3-1	-0.4
1940	*Det-A	139	528	76	123	24	3	7	53	76	53	.233	.335	.330	67	-26	12	2	2	.953	12	*S-139	0.0
1941	Det-A	5	12	0	2	1	0	0	1	2	2	.167	.333	.250	51	-1	0	1	-1	.920	1	/S-5	0.0
	NY-N	104	373	44	113	20	0	5	35	52	29	.303	.394	.397	121	12	6			.959	-10	3-84,S-21	0.5
1942	NY-N	90	316	53	77	10	3	5	24	44	34	.244	.351	.342	102	2	4			.965	1	3-52,S-31	0.6
1943	NY-N	99	337	48	91	14	0	5	28	47	27	.270	.371	.356	110	6	5			.980	18	3-54,S-33	2.9
1946	NY-N	5	2	0	0	0	0	0	0	0	0	.000	.000	.000	-99	-1	0			1.000	1	/3-4,2-2	0.0
Total	18	2016	7629	1130	2165	442	71	79	710	748	627	.284	.355	.391	96	-36	109	3		.953	178	*S-1679,3-196,2	27.9

■ TONY BARTIROME
Bartirome, Anthony Joseph b: 5/9/32, Pittsburgh, Pa. BL/TL, 5'10", 155 lbs. Deb: 4/19/52 C

YEAR	TM/L	G	AB	R	H	2B	3B	HR	RBI	BB	SO	AVG	OBP	SLG	PRO+	BR/A	SB	CS	SBR	FA	FR	G/POS	TPR
1952	Pit-N	124	355	32	78	10	3	0	16	26	37	.220	.273	.265	48	-25	3	3	-1	.989	2	*1-118	-2.8

■ BOYD BARTLEY
Bartley, Boyd Owen b: 2/11/20, Chicago, Ill. BR/TR, 5'8.5", 165 lbs. Deb: 5/30/43

YEAR	TM/L	G	AB	R	H	2B	3B	HR	RBI	BB	SO	AVG	OBP	SLG	PRO+	BR/A	SB	CS	SBR	FA	FR	G/POS	TPR
1943	Bro-N	9	21	0	1	0	0	0	1	1	3	.048	.091	.048	-59	-4	0			.897	2	/S-9	-0.2

■ IRV BARTLING
Bartling, Irving Henry b: 6/27/14, Bay City, Mich. d: 6/12/73, Westland, Mich. BR/TR, 6', 175 lbs. Deb: 9/8/38

YEAR	TM/L	G	AB	R	H	2B	3B	HR	RBI	BB	SO	AVG	OBP	SLG	PRO+	BR/A	SB	CS	SBR	FA	FR	G/POS	TPR
1938	Phi-A	14	46	5	8	1	1	0	5	3	7	.174	.224	.239	17	-6	0	0	0	.914	-3	S-13/3-1	-0.7

■ HARRY BARTON
Barton, Harry Lamb b: 1/20/1875, Chester, Pa. d: 1/25/55, Upland, Pa. BB/TR, 5'6.5", 155 lbs. Deb: 4/15/05

YEAR	TM/L	G	AB	R	H	2B	3B	HR	RBI	BB	SO	AVG	OBP	SLG	PRO+	BR/A	SB	CS	SBR	FA	FR	G/POS	TPR
1905	Phi-A	29	60	5	10	2	1	0	3	3		.167	.206	.233	39	-4	2			.954	-6	C-13/1-2,3O	-1.0

■ BOB BARTON
Barton, Robert Wilbur b: 7/30/41, Norwood, O. BR/TR, 6', 175 lbs. Deb: 9/17/65

YEAR	TM/L	G	AB	R	H	2B	3B	HR	RBI	BB	SO	AVG	OBP	SLG	PRO+	BR/A	SB	CS	SBR	FA	FR	G/POS	TPR
1965	SF-N	4	7	1	4	0	0	0	1	0	0	.571	.571	.571	217	1	0	0	0	1.000	1	/C-2	0.2
1966	SF-N	43	91	1	16	2	1	0	3	5	5	.176	.219	.220	22	-9	0	0	0	.994	7	C-39	-0.1
1967	SF-N	7	19	0	4	0	0	0	1	0	2	.211	.250	.211	34	-2	0	0	0	1.000	1	/C-7	-0.1
1968	SF-N	46	92	4	24	2	0	0	5	7	18	.261	.313	.283	80	-2	0	0	0	.995	12	C-45	1.3
1969	SF-N	49	106	5	18	2	0	0	1	9	19	.170	.241	.189	22	-11	0	0	0	.985	1	C-49	-0.9
1970	SD-N	61	188	15	41	6	0	4	16	15	37	.218	.279	.314	61	-11	1	1	-0	.995	7	C-59	-0.1
1971	SD-N	121	376	23	94	17	2	5	23	35	49	.250	.317	.346	94	-3	0	5	-3	.981	14	*C-119	1.2
1972	SD-N	29	88	1	17	1	0	0	9	2	19	.193	.211	.205	20	-9	2	0	1	.989	1	C-29	-0.7
1973	Cin-N	3	1	0	0	0	0	0	0	1	0	.000	.500	.000	52	0	0	0	0	1.000	1	/C-2	0.1
1974	SD-N	30	81	4	19	1	0	0	7	13	19	.235	.340	.247	69	-3	0	0	0	.981	10	C-29	0.8
Total	10	393	1049	54	237	31	3	9	66	87	168	.226	.288	.287	65	-49	3	6	-3	.987	53	C-380	1.7

■ VINCE BARTON
Barton, Vincent David b: 2/1/08, Edmonton, Alberta, Canada d: 9/13/73, Toronto, Ont., Can BL/TR, 6', 180 lbs. Deb: 7/17/31

YEAR	TM/L	G	AB	R	H	2B	3B	HR	RBI	BB	SO	AVG	OBP	SLG	PRO+	BR/A	SB	CS	SBR	FA	FR	G/POS	TPR
1931	Chi-N	66	239	45	57	10	1	13	50	21	40	.238	.323	.452	104	1	1			.964	-4	O-61	-0.7
1932	Chi-N	36	134	19	30	2	3	3	15	8	22	.224	.273	.351	67	-6	0			1.000	-2	O-34	-1.0
Total	2	102	373	64	87	12	4	16	65	29	62	.233	.306	.416	91	-6	1			.976	-6	/O-95	-1.7

■ DAVE BARTOSCH
Bartosch, David Robert b: 3/24/17, St.Louis, Mo. BR/TR, 6'1", 190 lbs. Deb: 4/28/45

YEAR	TM/L	G	AB	R	H	2B	3B	HR	RBI	BB	SO	AVG	OBP	SLG	PRO+	BR/A	SB	CS	SBR	FA	FR	G/POS	TPR
1945	StL-N	24	47	9	12	1	0	0	1	6	3	.255	.340	.277	71	-2	0			.964	1	O-11	-0.2

■ MONTY BASGALL
Basgall, Romanus b: 2/8/22, Pfeifer, Kan. BR/TR, 5'10.5", 175 lbs. Deb: 4/19/48 C

YEAR	TM/L	G	AB	R	H	2B	3B	HR	RBI	BB	SO	AVG	OBP	SLG	PRO+	BR/A	SB	CS	SBR	FA	FR	G/POS	TPR
1948	Pit-N	38	51	12	11	1	0	2	6	3	5	.216	.259	.353	63	-3	0			1.000	6	2-22	0.3
1949	Pit-N	107	308	25	67	9	1	2	26	31	32	.218	.294	.273	51	-21	1			.972	-7	2-98/3-3	-2.4
1951	Pit-N	55	153	15	32	5	2	0	9	12	14	.209	.271	.268	44	-12	0	0	0	.969	11	2-55	0.1
Total	3	200	512	52	110	15	3	4	41	46	51	.215	.282	.279	50	-36	1	0		.973	9	2-175/3-3	-2.0

■ AL BASHANG
Bashang, Albert C. b: 8/22/1888, Cincinnati, Ohio d: 6/23/67, Cincinnati, Ohio BB/TR, 5'8", 150 lbs. Deb: 7/30/12

YEAR	TM/L	G	AB	R	H	2B	3B	HR	RBI	BB	SO	AVG	OBP	SLG	PRO+	BR/A	SB	CS	SBR	FA	FR	G/POS	TPR
1912	Det-A	6	12	2	1	0	0	0	0	3		.083	.267	.083	2	-1	0			1.000	-1	/O-6	-0.3
1918	Bro-N	2	5	0	1	0	0	0	0	0		.200	.200	.200	22	-0	0			1.000	0	/O-1	0.0
Total	2	8	17	2	2	0	0	0	0	3		.118	.250	.118	8	-2	0			1.000	-1	/O-7	-0.3

■ WALT BASHORE
Bashore, Walter Franklin (b: Walter Franklin Beshore) b: 10/6/09, Harrisburg, Pa. d: 9/26/84, Sebring, Fla. BR/TR, 6', 170 lbs. Deb: 7/14/36

YEAR	TM/L	G	AB	R	H	2B	3B	HR	RBI	BB	SO	AVG	OBP	SLG	PRO+	BR/A	SB	CS	SBR	FA	FR	G/POS	TPR
1936	Phi-N	10	10	1	2	1	0	0	1	3		.200	.273	.200	26	-1				1.000	-3	/O-6,3-1	-0.4

YEAR	TM/L	G	AB	R	H	2B	3B	HR	RBI	BB	SO	AVG	OBP	SLG	PRO+	BR/A	SB	CS	SBR	FA	FR	G/POS	TPR

■ EDDIE BASINSKI   Basinski, Edwin Frank "Bazooka" or "Fiddler" b: 11/4/22, Buffalo, N.Y.   BR/TR, 6'1", 172 lbs.   Deb: 5/20/44

1944	Bro-N	39	105	13	27	4	1	0	9	6	10	.257	.310	.314	77	-3	1			.960	-2	2-37/S-3	-0.3
1945	Bro-N	108	336	30	88	9	4	0	33	11	33	.262	.293	.313	69	-15	0			.926	-10	*S-101/2-6	-1.7
1947	Pit-N	56	161	15	32	6	2	4	17	18	27	.199	.279	.335	61	-9	0			.972	-1	2-56	-0.8
Total	3	203	602	58	147	19	7	4	59	35	70	.244	.292	.319	68	-27	1			.925	-13	S-104/2-99	-2.8

■ JOHN BASS   Bass, John E. b: 1850, Baltimore, Md.   5'6", 150 lbs.   Deb: 5/4/1871

1871	Cle-n	22	89	18	27	1	10	3	18	3	4	.303	.326	.640	179	9	0					*3-22	0.5
1872	Atl-n	2	7	0	1	1	0	0	1	0	0	.143	.143	.286	24	-1						/O-1	0.0
1877	Har-N	1	4	1	1	0	0	0	0	0	0	.250	.250	.250	65	-0				.000	-1	/O-1	-0.1
Total	2 n	24	96	18	28	2	10	3	19	3	4	.292	.313	.615	166	8						/3-22,O-1	0.5

■ KEVIN BASS   Bass, Kevin Charles b: 5/12/59, Menlo Park, Cal.   BB/TR, 6', 183 lbs.   Deb: 4/9/82

1982	Mil-A	18	9	4	0	0	0	0	0	1	1	.000	.100	.000	-74	-2	0	0	0	1.000	-5	O-14/D-2	-0.8
	Hou-N	12	24	2	1	0	0	0	1	0	8	.042	.042	.042	-83	-6	0	0	0	.917	-1	/O-7	-0.8
1983	Hou-N	88	195	25	46	7	3	2	18	6	27	.236	.259	.333	67	-10	2	2	-1	.945	-6	O-52	-1.9
1984	Hou-N	121	331	33	86	17	5	2	29	6	57	.260	.279	.360	84	-9	5	5	-2	.975	-2	O-81	-1.5
1985	Hou-N	150	539	72	145	27	5	16	68	31	63	.269	.316	.427	109	4	19	8	1	.997	6	*O-141	0.8
1986	*Hou-N★	157	591	83	184	33	5	20	79	38	72	.311	.359	.486	134	26	22	13	-1	.984	4	*O-155	2.4
1987	Hou-N	157	592	83	168	31	5	19	85	53	77	.284	.347	.449	113	10	21	8	2	.987	10	*O-155	1.6
1988	Hou-N	157	541	57	138	27	2	14	72	42	65	.255	.316	.390	106	3	31	6	6	.979	-5	O-147	0.7
1989	Hou-N	87	313	42	94	19	4	5	44	29	44	.300	.362	.435	131	12	11	4	1	.985	9	O-84	2.1
1990	SF-N	61	214	25	54	9	1	7	32	14	26	.252	.304	.402	96	-2	2	2	-1	.968	-5	O-55	-0.9
1991	SF-N	124	361	43	84	10	4	10	40	36	56	.233	.309	.366	92	-4	7	4	-0	.977	-1	*O-101	-0.8
1992	SF-N	89	265	25	71	11	3	7	30	16	53	.268	.312	.411	109	2	7	7	-2	.983	-5	O-72	-0.7
	NY-N	46	137	15	37	12	2	2	9	7	17	.270	.306	.431	108	1	7	2	1	.987	1	O-39	0.2
	Yr	135	402	40	108	23	5	9	39	23	70	.269	.310	.418	109	3	14	9	-1	.985	-5	*O-111	-0.5
1993	Hou-N	111	229	31	65	18	0	3	37	26	31	.284	.359	.402	107	3	7	1	2	.989	-6	O-64	-0.3
1994	Hou-N	82	203	37	63	15	1	6	35	28	24	.310	.397	.483	131	10	2	3	-1	.977	-4	O-57	0.4
Total	13	1460	4544	577	1236	236	40	113	579	333	621	.272	.327	.416	108	39	143	65	4	.982	-5	*O-1224/D-2	0.5

■ RANDY BASS   Bass, Randy William b: 3/13/54, Lawton, Okla.   BL/TR, 6'1", 210 lbs.   Deb: 9/3/77

1977	Min-A	9	19	0	2	0	0	0	0	0	5	.105	.105	.105	-43	-4	0	0	0	.000	0	/D-6	-0.4
1978	KC-A	2	2	0	0	0	0	0	0	0	0	.000	.000	.000	-97	-1	0	0	0	.000	-0	H	-0.1
1979	Mon-N	2	1	0	0	0	0	0	0	0	0	.000	.000	.000	-99	-0	0	0	0	1.000	-0	/1-1	0.0
1980	SD-N	19	49	5	14	0	1	3	8	7	7	.286	.386	.510	157	4	0	0	0	.985	-1	1-15	0.2
1981	SD-N	69	176	13	37	4	1	4	20	20	28	.210	.294	.330	78	-5	0	1	-1	.993	2	1-50	-0.7
1982	SD-N	13	30	1	6	0	0	1	8	2	4	.200	.273	.300	63	-2	0	0	0	1.000	-1	/1-9	-0.3
	Tex-A	16	48	5	10	2	0	1	6	1	7	.208	.240	.313	53	-3	0	0	0	1.000	-0	/1-6,D-7	-0.4
Total	6	130	325	24	69	6	3	9	42	30	51	.212	.287	.326	76	-11	0	1	-1	.993	-0	/1-81,D-13	-1.7

■ DOC BASS   Bass, Williams Capers (also played one game in 1918 under name of Johnson) b: 12/4/1899, Macon, Ga. d: 1/12/70, Macon, Ga.   BL/TL, 5'10", 165 lbs.   Deb: 7/29/18

| 1918 | Bos-N | 2 | 1 | 1 | 1 | 0 | 0 | 0 | 1 | 0 | 0 | 1.000 | 1.000 | 1.000 | 533 | 0 | 1 | | | .000 | 0 | /H | 0.1 |

■ CHARLEY BASSETT   Bassett, Charles Edwin b: 2/9/1863, Central Falls, R.I. d: 5/28/42, Pawtucket, R.I.   BR/TR, 5'10", 150 lbs.   Deb: 7/22/1884

1884	Pro-N	27	79	10	11	2	1	0	6	4	15	.139	.181	.190	17	-7				.815	0	3-13/S-7,O2	-0.6
1885	Pro-N	82	285	21	41	8	2	0	16	19	60	.144	.197	.186	26	-22				.900	5	2-39,S-23,3/C	-1.4
1886	KC-N	90	342	41	89	19	8	2	32	36	43	.260	.331	.380	109	3	6			.886	8	S-82/3-8	1.0
1887	Ind-N	119	452	41	104	14	6	1	47	25	31	.230	.278	.294	61	-23	25			.931	16	*2-119	-0.3
1888	Ind-N	128	481	58	116	20	3	6	60	32	41	.241	.297	.308	91	-4	24			.922	-16	2-128	-1.5
1889	Ind-N	127	477	64	117	12	5	4	68	37	38	.245	.304	.317	72	-19	15			.937	11	2-127	-0.1
1890	NY-N	100	410	52	98	13	8	0	54	29	25	.239	.300	.310	78	-12	14			.952	12	2-100	0.5
1891	NY-N	130	524	60	136	19	8	4	68	36	29	.260	.312	.349	96	-3	16			.908	8	*3-121/2-9	1.0
1892	NY-N	35	130	9	27	2	3	0	16	6	10	.208	.254	.269	59	-7	0			.938	9	2-30/3-5	0.3
	Lou-N	79	313	36	67	5	5	2	35	15	19	.214	.250	.281	66	-14	16			.861	-9	3-73/2-6	-1.1
	Yr	114	443	45	94	7	8	2	51	21	29	.212	.251	.278	64	-20	16			.858	-3	3-78,2-36	-0.8
Total	9	917	3493	392	806	114	49	15	402	239	311	.231	.285	.304	76	-108	116			.932	53	2-559,3-240,S/OC	-2.2

■ JOHNNY BASSLER   Bassler, John Landis b: 6/3/1895, Mechanics Grove, Pa. d: 6/29/79, Santa Monica, Cal   BL/TR, 5'9", 170 lbs.   Deb: 7/11/13   C

1913	Cle-A	1	2	0	0	0	0	0	0	0	0	.000	.000	.000	-97	-0				.500	-1	/C-1	-0.2
1914	Cle-A	43	77	5	14	1	1	0	6	15	8	.182	.323	.221	61	-3	3	2	-0	.946	-1	C-25/3-1,O	-0.2
1921	Det-A	119	388	37	119	18	5	0	56	58	16	.307	.401	.379	101	3	2	1	0	.975	2	*C-114	1.1
1922	Det-A	121	372	41	120	14	0	0	41	62	12	.323	.422	.360	109	9	2	1	0	.980	-3	C-118	1.2
1923	Det-A	135	383	45	114	12	3	0	49	76	13	.298	.414	.345	103	6	2	1	-1	.988	12	*C-128	2.3
1924	Det-A	124	379	43	131	20	3	1	68	62	11	.346	.441	.422	125	18	2	1	0	.979	-4	*C-122	2.1
1925	Det-A	121	344	40	96	19	3	0	52	74	6	.279	.408	.352	96	2	1	1	-0	.983	-8	*C-118	0.0
1926	Det-A	66	174	20	53	8	1	0	22	45	6	.305	.447	.362	111	6	0	0	0	1.000	6	C-63	1.2
1927	Det-A	81	200	19	57	7	0	0	24	45	9	.285	.416	.320	92	0	1	2	1	.974	-2	C-67	0.0
Total	9	811	2319	250	704	99	16	1	318	437	81	.304	.416	.361	104	42	13	8		.980	-1	C-756/O-1,3	7.8

■ CHARLIE BASTIAN   Bastian, Charles J. b: 7/4/1860, Philadelphia, Pa. d: 1/18/32, Pennsauken, N.J.   BR/TR, 5'6.5", 145 lbs.   Deb: 8/18/1884

1884	Wil-U	17	60	6	12	1	3	2		3		.200	.238	.417	73	-3				.907	1	2-16/P-1,S	0.7
	KC-U	11	46	6	9	3	0	1		4		.196	.260	.326	67	-2				.950	-1	2-11	-0.2
	Yr	28	106	12	21	4	3	3		7		.198	.248	.377	70	-5				.923	10	2-27/P-1,S	0.5
1885	Phi-N	103	389	63	65	11	5	4	29	35	82	.167	.236	.252	59	-17				.890	6	*S-103	-0.8
1886	Phi-N	105	373	46	81	9	11	2	38	33	73	.217	.281	.316	81	-9	29			.945	-5	*2-87,S-10/3	-0.9
1887	Phi-N	60	221	33	47	11	1	1	21	19	29	.213	.284	.285	55	-14	11			.921	-13	2-39,S-18/3	-2.2
1888	Phi-N	80	275	30	53	4	1	1	17	27	41	.193	.282	.225	60	-12	12			.945	12	2-65,3-14/S	0.3
1889	Chi-N	46	155	19	21	0	0	0	10	25	46	.135	.256	.135	14	-18	1			.919	6	S-45/2-1	-0.9
1890	Chi-P	80	283	38	54	10	5	0	29	33	37	.191	.287	.261	45	-23	4			.880	-10	S-64,2-12/3	-2.3
1891	Cin-a	1	4	0	0	0	0	0	0	0	0	.000	.000	.000	-92	-1	0			1.000	1	/2-1	0.0
	Phi-N	1										—	—	—		0	0			1.000	0	/S-1	0.0
Total	8	504	1806	241	342	49	26	11	144	179	308	.189	.268	.264	56	-97	57			.892	7	S-243,2-232/3P	-6.3

■ EMIL BATCH   Batch, Emil "Heinie" or "Ace" b: 1/21/1880, Brooklyn, N.Y. d: 8/23/26, Brooklyn, N.Y.   BR/TR, 5'7", 170 lbs.   Deb: 9/13/04

1904	Bro-N	28	94	9	24	1	2	2	7	1		.255	.271	.372	100	-1				.880	-2	3-28	-0.2
1905	Bro-N	145	568	64	143	20	11	5	49	26		.252	.285	.352	96	-5	21			.887	-8	*3-145	-0.9
1906	Bro-N	59	203	23	52	7	6	0	11	15		.256	.311	.350	115	3	3			.964	-3	O-50/3-2	0.1
1907	Bro-N	116	388	38	96	10	3	0	31	23		.247	.291	.289	89	-6	7			.937	-3	*O-102/3-2,2S	-1.4
Total	4	348	1253	134	315	38	22	7	98	65		.251	.290	.334	98	-9	37			.886	-11	3-177,O-152/S2	-2.4

■ JOHN BATEMAN   Bateman, John Alvin b: 7/21/42, Killeen, Tex.   BR/TR, 6'3", 220 lbs.   Deb: 4/19/63

| 1963 | Hou-N | 128 | 404 | 23 | 85 | 8 | 6 | 10 | 59 | 13 | 103 | .210 | .251 | .334 | 71 | -16 | 0 | 0 | 0 | .971 | 2 | *C-115 | -1.1 |
| 1964 | Hou-N | 74 | 221 | 18 | 42 | 8 | 0 | 5 | 19 | 17 | 48 | .190 | .251 | .294 | 56 | -13 | 0 | 1 | -1 | .987 | 6 | C-72 | -0.5 |

YEAR	TM/L	G	AB	R	H	2B	3B	HR	RBI	BB	SO	AVG	OBP	SLG	PRO+	BR/A	SB	CS	SBR	FA	FR	G/POS	TPR
1965	Hou-N	45	142	15	28	3	1	7	14	12	37	.197	.260	.380	83	-4	0	1	-1	.985	0	C-39	-0.2
1966	Hou-N	131	433	39	121	24	3	17	70	20	74	.279	.319	.467	123	12	0	0	0	.981	1	*C-121	2.1
1967	Hou-N	76	252	16	48	9	0	2	17	17	53	.190	.247	.250	44	-18	0	0	0	.989	1	C-71	-1.4
1968	Hou-N	111	350	28	87	19	0	4	33	23	46	.249	.301	.337	93	-3	1	1	-0	.985	-2	*C-108	0.1
1969	Mon-N	74	235	16	49	4	0	8	19	12	44	.209	.250	.328	60	-13	0	2	-1	.985	-0	C-66	-1.2
1970	Mon-N	139	520	51	123	21	5	15	68	28	75	.237	.277	.383	75	-20	8	4	0	.983	-2	*C-137	-1.5
1971	Mon-N	139	492	34	119	17	3	10	56	19	87	.242	.278	.350	76	-17	1	0	0	.985	-9	*C-137	-2.2
1972	Mon-N	18	29	0	7	1	0	0	3	3	4	.241	.313	.276	67	-1	0	0	0	1.000	-2	/C-7	-0.3
	Phi-N	82	252	10	56	9	0	3	17	8	39	.222	.249	.294	52	-16	0	1	-1	.972	1	C-80	-1.4
	Yr	100	281	10	63	10	0	3	20	11	43	.224	.256	.292	54	-17	0	1	-1	.973	-1	C-87	-1.7
Total	10	1017	3330	250	765	123	18	81	375	172	610	.230	.273	.350	77	-111	10	10	-3	.982	-2	C-953	-7.6

■ CHARLIE BATES
Bates, Charles William b: 9/17/07, Philadelphia, Pa. d: 1/29/80, Topeka, Kan. BR/TR, 5'10", 165 lbs. Deb: 9/22/27

YEAR	TM/L	G	AB	R	H	2B	3B	HR	RBI	BB	SO	AVG	OBP	SLG	PRO+	BR/A	SB	CS	SBR	FA	FR	G/POS	TPR
1927	Phi-A	9	38	5	9	2	2	0	2	3	5	.237	.293	.395	73	-2	3	1	0	.857	-0	/O-9	-0.2

■ DEL BATES
Bates, Delbert Oakley b: 6/12/40, Seattle, Wash. BL/TR, 6'2", 195 lbs. Deb: 5/6/70

YEAR	TM/L	G	AB	R	H	2B	3B	HR	RBI	BB	SO	AVG	OBP	SLG	PRO+	BR/A	SB	CS	SBR	FA	FR	G/POS	TPR
1970	Phi-N	22	60	1	8	2	0	0	6	15	16	.133	.257	.167	16	-7	0	1	-1	.992	-4	C-20	-1.1

■ BUD BATES
Bates, Hubert Edgar b: 3/16/12, Los Angeles, Cal. d: 4/29/87, Long Beach, Cal. BR/TR, 6', 165 lbs. Deb: 9/16/39

YEAR	TM/L	G	AB	R	H	2B	3B	HR	RBI	BB	SO	AVG	OBP	SLG	PRO+	BR/A	SB	CS	SBR	FA	FR	G/POS	TPR
1939	Phi-N	15	58	8	15	2	0	1	2	2	8	.259	.283	.345	70	-3	1			.978	3	O-14	-0.1

■ JOHNNY BATES
Bates, John William b: 8/21/1882, Steubenville, Ohio d: 2/10/49, Steubenville, Ohio BL/TL, 5'7", 168 lbs. Deb: 4/12/06

YEAR	TM/L	G	AB	R	H	2B	3B	HR	RBI	BB	SO	AVG	OBP	SLG	PRO+	BR/A	SB	CS	SBR	FA	FR	G/POS	TPR
1906	Bos-N	140	504	52	127	21	5	6	54	36		.252	.315	.349	110	5	9			.958	-10	*O-140	-1.4
1907	Bos-N	126	447	52	116	18	12	2	49	39		.260	.329	.367	118	9	11			.979	-2	*O-120	0.2
1908	Bos-N	127	445	48	115	14	6	1	29	35		.258	.315	.324	106	3	25			.948	-4	*O-117	-0.6
1909	Bos-N	63	236	27	68	15	3	1	23	20		.288	.354	.390	125	7	15			.945	5	O-60	1.0
	Phi-N	77	266	43	78	11	1	1	15	28		.293	.365	.353	122	7	22			.959	-2	O-73	0.3
	Yr	140	502	70	146	26	4	2	38	48		.291	.360	.371	123	14	37			.952	3	O-133	1.3
1910	Phi-N	135	498	91	152	26	11	3	61	61	49	.305	.385	.420	130	20	31			.954	12	*O-131	2.6
1911	Cin-N	148	518	89	151	24	13	1	61	103	59	.292	.415	.394	131	28	33			.966	7	*O-147	2.5
1912	Cin-N	81	239	45	69	12	7	1	29	47	16	.289	.406	.410	127	11	10			.950	7	O-65	1.4
1913	Cin-N	131	407	63	113	13	7	6	51	67	30	.278	.387	.388	122	15	21			.946	4	*O-111	1.4
1914	Cin-N	58	155	29	39	7	5	2	15	28	17	.252	.380	.400	128	6	4			.913	-6	O-54	-0.2
	Chi-N	9	8	2	1	0	0	0	1	1	1	.125	.300	.125	28	-1	0			1.000	0	/O-3	-0.1
	Yr	67	163	31	40	7	5	2	16	29	18	.245	.376	.387	124	6	4			.917	-6	O-57	-0.3
	Bal-F	59	190	24	58	6	3	1	29	38	16	.305	.429	.384	108	5	6			.950	-1	O-59	0.1
Total	9	1154	3913	565	1087	167	73	25	417	503	190	.278	.367	.377	121	114	187			.955	9	*O-1080	7.2

■ RAY BATES
Bates, Raymond b: 2/8/1890, Paterson, N.J. d: 8/15/70, Tucson, Ariz. BR/TR, 6', 165 lbs. Deb: 5/31/13

YEAR	TM/L	G	AB	R	H	2B	3B	HR	RBI	BB	SO	AVG	OBP	SLG	PRO+	BR/A	SB	CS	SBR	FA	FR	G/POS	TPR
1913	Cle-A	27	30	4	5	0	2	0	4	3	9	.167	.265	.300	63	-1	3			.905	-0	3-12/O-2	-0.2
1917	Phi-A	127	485	47	115	20	7	2	66	21	39	.237	.277	.320	83	-12	12			.933	6	*3-124	-0.4
Total	2	154	515	51	120	20	9	2	70	24	48	.233	.277	.318	82	-13	15			.932	6	3-136/O-2	-0.6

■ BILLY BATES
Bates, William Derrick b: 12/7/63, Houston, Tex. BL/TR, 5'7", 155 lbs. Deb: 8/17/89

YEAR	TM/L	G	AB	R	H	2B	3B	HR	RBI	BB	SO	AVG	OBP	SLG	PRO+	BR/A	SB	CS	SBR	FA	FR	G/POS	TPR
1989	Mil-A	7	14	3	3	0	0	0	0	0	1	.214	.214	.214	21	-1	2	0	1	.938	4	/2-7	0.3
1990	Mil-A	14	29	6	3	1	0	0	2	4	7	.103	.212	.138	-0	-4	4	0	1	.962	3	2-14	0.0
	*Cin-N	8	5	2	0	0	0	0	0	0	2	.000	.000	.000	-96	-1	2	1	0	1.000	0	/2-1	-0.1
Total	2	29	48	11	6	1	0	0	2	4	10	.125	.192	.146	-4	-7	8	1	2	.953	7	/2-22	0.2

■ BILL BATHE
Bathe, William David b: 10/14/60, Downey, Cal. BR/TR, 6'2", 200 lbs. Deb: 4/12/86

YEAR	TM/L	G	AB	R	H	2B	3B	HR	RBI	BB	SO	AVG	OBP	SLG	PRO+	BR/A	SB	CS	SBR	FA	FR	G/POS	TPR
1986	Oak-A	39	103	9	19	3	0	5	11	2	20	.184	.208	.359	55	-7	0	0	0	.991	1	C-39	-0.4
1989	*SF-N	30	32	3	9	1	0	0	6	0	7	.281	.281	.313	72	-1	0	0	0	1.000	-1	/C-7	-0.2
1990	SF-N	52	48	3	11	0	1	3	12	7	12	.229	.327	.458	118	1	0	0	0	1.000	-1	/C-8	0.0
Total	3	121	183	15	39	4	1	8	29	9	39	.213	.254	.377	75	-7	0	0	0	.992	-1	/C-54	-0.6

■ RAFAEL BATISTA
Batista, Rafael (Sanchez) b: 10/20/47, San Pedro De Macoris, D.R. BL/TL, 6'1", 195 lbs. Deb: 6/17/73

YEAR	TM/L	G	AB	R	H	2B	3B	HR	RBI	BB	SO	AVG	OBP	SLG	PRO+	BR/A	SB	CS	SBR	FA	FR	G/POS	TPR
1973	Hou-N	12	15	2	4	0	0	0	2	1	6	.267	.313	.267	62	-1	0	0	0	1.000	-0	/1-8	-0.1
1975	Hou-N	10	10	0	3	1	0	0	0	0	4	.300	.300	.400	100	-0	0	0	0	.000	0	H	-0.0
Total	2	22	25	2	7	1	0	0	2	1	10	.280	.308	.320	76	-1	0	0	0	1.000	0	/1-8	-0.1

■ KEVIN BATISTE
Batiste, Kevin Wade b: 10/21/66, Galveston, Tex. BR/TR, 6'2", 175 lbs. Deb: 6/13/89

YEAR	TM/L	G	AB	R	H	2B	3B	HR	RBI	BB	SO	AVG	OBP	SLG	PRO+	BR/A	SB	CS	SBR	FA	FR	G/POS	TPR
1989	Tor-A	6	8	1	2	0	0	0	0	0	5	.250	.250	.250	42	-1	0	0	0	1.000	-1	/O-5	-0.1

■ KIM BATISTE
Batiste, Kimothy Emil b: 3/15/68, New Orleans, La. BR/TR, 6', 175 lbs. Deb: 9/8/91

YEAR	TM/L	G	AB	R	H	2B	3B	HR	RBI	BB	SO	AVG	OBP	SLG	PRO+	BR/A	SB	CS	SBR	FA	FR	G/POS	TPR
1991	Phi-N	10	27	2	6	0	0	0	1	1	8	.222	.250	.222	34	-2	0	1	-1	.970	1	/S-7	-0.1
1992	Phi-N	44	136	9	28	4	0	1	10	4	18	.206	.229	.257	37	-11	0	0	0	.922	-8	S-41	-1.9
1993	*Phi-N	79	156	14	44	7	1	5	29	3	29	.282	.300	.436	95	-2	0	1	-1	.956	13	3-58,S-24	1.2
1994	Phi-N	64	209	17	49	6	0	1	13	1	32	.234	.242	.278	35	-20	1	1	-0	.919	3	3-42,S-17	-1.7
Total	4	197	528	42	127	17	1	7	53	9	87	.241	.256	.316	54	-35	1	3	-2	.933	3	3-100/S-89	-2.5

■ BILL BATSCH
Batsch, William McKinley b: 5/18/1892, Mingo Junction, O. d: 12/31/63, Canton, Ohio BR/TR, 5'10.5", 168 lbs. Deb: 9/9/16

YEAR	TM/L	G	AB	R	H	2B	3B	HR	RBI	BB	SO	AVG	OBP	SLG	PRO+	BR/A	SB	CS	SBR	FA	FR	G/POS	TPR
1916	Pit-N	1	0	0	0	0	0	0	0	1	0	—	1.000	—	218	0	0			.000	0	H	0.0

■ LARRY BATTAM
Battam, Lawrence J. b: 5/1/1878, Brooklyn, N.Y. d: 1/27/38, Brooklyn, N.Y. 5'11". Deb: 9/28/1895

YEAR	TM/L	G	AB	R	H	2B	3B	HR	RBI	BB	SO	AVG	OBP	SLG	PRO+	BR/A	SB	CS	SBR	FA	FR	G/POS	TPR
1895	NY-N	2	4	0	1	0	0	0	0	2	1	.250	.500	.250	99	0	0			.667	-1	/3-2	0.0

■ GEORGE BATTEN
Batten, George Burnett b: 10/7/1891, Haddonfield, N.J. d: 8/4/72, New Port Richey, Fla. BR/TR, 5'11", 165 lbs. Deb: 9/28/12

YEAR	TM/L	G	AB	R	H	2B	3B	HR	RBI	BB	SO	AVG	OBP	SLG	PRO+	BR/A	SB	CS	SBR	FA	FR	G/POS	TPR
1912	NY-A	1	3	0	0	0	0	0	0	0	0	.000	.000	.000	-94	-1	0			1.000	-1	/2-1	-0.1

■ EARL BATTEY
Battey, Earl Jesse b: 1/5/35, Los Angeles, Cal. BR/TR, 6'1", 205 lbs. Deb: 9/10/55

YEAR	TM/L	G	AB	R	H	2B	3B	HR	RBI	BB	SO	AVG	OBP	SLG	PRO+	BR/A	SB	CS	SBR	FA	FR	G/POS	TPR
1955	Chi-A	5	7	1	2	0	0	0	0	1	1	.286	.444	.286	97	0	0	0	0	1.000	2	/C-5	0.2
1956	Chi-A	4	4	1	1	0	0	0	0	1	1	.250	.400	.250	74	0	0	0	0	.800	-1	/C-3	-0.1
1957	Chi-A	48	115	12	20	2	3	3	6	11	38	.174	.246	.322	54	-8	0	2	-1	.989	6	C-43	-0.2
1958	Chi-A	68	168	24	38	8	0	8	26	34	34	.226	.330	.417	106	1	1	0	0	.988	4	C-49	0.6
1959	Chi-A	26	64	9	14	1	2	2	7	8	12	.219	.306	.391	91	-1	0	0	0	.990	4	C-20	0.4
1960	Was-A	137	466	49	126	24	2	15	60	48	68	.270	.340	.427	110	6	4	5	-2	.982	5	*C-136	1.8
1961	Min-A	133	460	70	139	24	1	17	55	53	66	.302	.378	.470	118	12	3	3	-1	.993	7	*C-131	2.4
1962	Min-A★	148	522	58	146	20	3	11	57	57	48	.280	.351	.393	96	-2	0	0	0	.991	6	*C-147	1.0
1963	Min-A★	147	508	64	145	17	1	26	84	61	75	.285	.371	.476	133	23	0	0	0	.994	1	*C-146	3.1
1964	Min-A	131	405	33	110	17	1	12	52	51	49	.272	.354	.407	111	7	1	1	-0	.990	-5	*C-125	0.7
1965	*Min-A★	131	394	36	117	22	2	6	60	50	23	.297	.379	.409	119	11	0	0	0	.986	-8	*C-128	1.0
1966	Min-A★	115	364	30	93	12	1	4	34	43	30	.255	.339	.327	87	-5	4	1	1	.995	6	*C-113	0.9
1967	Min-A	48	109	6	18	3	0	1	14	12	8	.165	.254	.211	36	-8	1	1	-0	.987	-2	C-41	-1.0
Total	13	1141	3586	393	969	150	17	104	449	421	470	.270	.351	.409	106	37	13	12	-3	.990	23	*C-1087	10.8

YEAR	TM/L	G	AB	R	H	2B	3B	HR	RBI	BB	SO	AVG	OBP	SLG	PRO+	BR/A	SB	CS	SBR	FA	FR	G/POS	TPR

■ JOE BATTIN   Battin, Joseph V.   b: 11/11/1851, Philadelphia, Pa.   d: 12/10/37, Akron, Ohio   BR/TR,   Deb: 8/11/1871   MU

YEAR	TM/L	G	AB	R	H	2B	3B	HR	RBI	BB	SO	AVG	OBP	SLG	PRO+	BR/A	SB	CS	SBR	FA	FR	G/POS	TPR
1871	Cle-n	1	3	0	0	0	0	0		0	1	0	.000	.250	.000	-21	-0	0					/O-1	0.0
1873	Ath-n	1	5	4	3	0	0	0	2	1	0	.600	.667	.600	257	1						/O-1	0.1
1874	Ath-n	51	226	40	52	11	1	0			1	.230	.233	.288	60	-11						*2-40/O-7,S	-1.0
1875	StL-n	67	284	31	71	7	3	0			0	.250	.250	.296	97	0						*2-60/3-6	-0.1
1876	StL-N	64	283	34	85	11	4	0	46	6	6	.300	.315	.367	134	10				.867	14	*3-63/2-1	2.2
1877	StL-N	57	226	28	45	3	7	1	22	6	17	.199	.220	.288	62	-9				.823	-3	3-32,2-21/OP	-0.9
1882	Pit-a	34	133	13	28	5	1	1			3	.211	.228	.286	76	-3				.876	21	3-34	1.7
1883	Pit-a	98	388	42	83	9	6	1		11		.214	.236	.276	67	-13				.891	29	*3-98/P-2M	1.3
1884	Pit-a	43	158	10	28	1	2	0			3	.177	.198	.209	32	-12				.919	8	3-43,M	-0.3
	CP-U	18	69	8	13	2	0	0				.188	.188	.217	10	-8				.908	11	3-18,M	0.2
	Bal-U	17	59	3	6	1	0	0				.102	.102	.119	-37	-11				.813	2	3-17	-0.8
	Yr	35	128	11	19	3	0	0				.148	.148	.172	-13	-20				.868	13	3-35	-0.6
1890	Syr-a	29	119	15	25	2	1	0		8		.210	.260	.244	54	-7	8			.794	-4	3-29	-0.9
Total	4 n	120	518	75	126	18	4	0	2	3		.243	.248	.293	80	-10	0					2-100/O-9,3S	-1.0
Total	6	360	1435	153	313	34	21	3	68	37	23	.218	.238	.277	65	-53	8			.870	77	3-334/2-22,OP	2.5

■ JIM BATTLE   Battle, James Milton   b: 3/26/01, Bailey, Tex.   d: 9/30/65, Chico, Cal.   BR/TR, 6'1", 170 lbs.   Deb: 9/9/27

YEAR	TM/L	G	AB	R	H	2B	3B	HR	RBI	BB	SO	AVG	OBP	SLG	PRO+	BR/A	SB	CS	SBR	FA	FR	G/POS	TPR
1927	Chi-A	6	8	1	3	0	0	0	1	0	1	.375	.375	.625	160	1	0	0	0	1.000	-1	/3-4,S-2	0.0

■ MATT BATTS   Batts, Matthew Daniel   b: 10/16/21, San Antonio, Tex.   BR/TR, 5'11", 200 lbs.   Deb: 9/10/47

YEAR	TM/L	G	AB	R	H	2B	3B	HR	RBI	BB	SO	AVG	OBP	SLG	PRO+	BR/A	SB	CS	SBR	FA	FR	G/POS	TPR
1947	Bos-A	7	16	3	8	1	0	1	5	1	1	.500	.529	.750	236	3	0	0	0	1.000	-1	/C-6	0.2
1948	Bos-A	46	118	13	37	12	1	1	24	15	9	.314	.391	.441	115	3	0	0	0	.986	-1	C-41	0.4
1949	Bos-A	60	157	23	38	9	1	3	31	25	22	.242	.350	.369	84	-4	1	0	0	.977	2	C-50	0.1
1950	Bos-A	75	238	27	65	15	3	4	34	18	19	.273	.327	.412	80	-8	0	0	0	.994	5	C-73	-0.2
1951	Bos-A	11	29	1	4	1	0	0	2	1	2	.138	.167	.172	-8	-4	0	0	0	.975	-0	C-11	-0.4
	StL-A	79	248	26	75	17	1	5	31	21	21	.302	.357	.440	111	3	2	0	1	.960	-8	C-64	-0.2
	Yr	90	277	27	79	18	1	5	33	22	23	.285	.338	.412	98	-1	2	0	1	.962	-9	C-75	-0.6
1952	Det-A	56	173	11	41	4	1	3	13	14	22	.237	.298	.324	72	-7	1	0	0	.983	-5	C-55	-0.1
1953	Det-A	116	374	38	104	24	3	6	43	24	36	.278	.322	.406	97	-3	2	3	-1	.986	-14	*C-103	-1.3
1954	Det-A	12	21	1	6	1	0	0	5	2	4	.286	.348	.333	89	-0	0	0	0	.967	1	/C-8	0.1
	Chi-A	55	158	16	36	7	1	3	19	17	15	.228	.303	.342	74	-6	0	1	-1	.992	7	C-42	0.2
	Yr	67	179	17	42	8	1	3	24	19	19	.235	.308	.341	76	-6	0	1	-1	.989	8	C-50	0.3
1955	Cin-N	26	71	4	18	4	1	0	13	4	11	.254	.293	.338	63	-4	0	0	0	.986	-1	C-21	-0.4
1956	Cin-N	3	2	0	0	0	0	0	0	0	1	.000	.333	.000	-0	-0	0	0	0	.000	0	H	0.0
Total	10	546	1605	163	432	95	11	26	220	143	163	.269	.330	.391	89	-27	6	4	-1	.983	-10	C-474	-1.6

■ HANK BAUER   Bauer, Henry Albert   b: 7/31/22, E.St.Louis, Ill.   BR/TR, 6', 192 lbs.   Deb: 9/6/48   MC

YEAR	TM/L	G	AB	R	H	2B	3B	HR	RBI	BB	SO	AVG	OBP	SLG	PRO+	BR/A	SB	CS	SBR	FA	FR	G/POS	TPR
1948	NY-A	19	50	6	9	1	1	1	9	6	13	.180	.268	.300	51	-4	1	0		.964	-1	O-14	-0.5
1949	*NY-A	103	301	56	82	6	6	10	45	37	42	.272	.354	.432	107	2	2	2	-1	.977	-9	O-95	-1.1
1950	*NY-A	113	415	72	133	16	2	13	70	35	41	.320	.380	.463	118	11	2	3	-1	.987	-1	*O-110	0.4
1951	*NY-A	118	348	53	103	19	3	10	54	42	39	.296	.373	.454	128	13	5	2	0	.990	-5	*O-107	0.5
1952	*NY-A★	141	553	86	162	31	6	17	74	50	61	.293	.355	.463	134	23	6	7	-2	.984	3	*O-139	1.8
1953	*NY-A★	133	437	77	133	20	6	10	57	59	45	.304	.394	.446	131	20	2	3	-1	.992	0	*O-126	1.5
1954	NY-A★	114	377	73	111	16	5	12	54	40	42	.294	.362	.459	128	14	4	4	-1	.989	-6	*O-108	0.2
1955	*NY-A	139	492	97	137	20	5	20	53	56	65	.278	.362	.461	122	14	8	4	0	.981	4	*O-133/C-1	1.2
1956	*NY-U	147	539	96	130	18	7	26	84	59	72	.241	.318	.445	103	-1	4	2	0	.969	-8	*O-146	-1.6
1957	*NY-A	137	479	70	124	22	9	18	65	42	64	.259	.324	.455	112	6	7	2	1	.986	-7	*O-135	-0.8
1958	*NY-A	128	452	62	121	22	6	12	50	32	56	.268	.318	.423	106	2	3	2	-0	.980	-9	*O-123	-1.3
1959	NY-A	114	341	44	81	20	0	9	39	33	54	.238	.309	.375	90	-5	4	2	0	.972	-13	*O-111	-2.3
1960	KC-A	95	255	30	70	15	0	3	31	21	36	.275	.332	.369	89	-4	1	0	0	.978	-6	O-67	-1.3
1961	KC-A	43	106	11	28	3	1	3	18	9	8	.264	.322	.396	89	-2	1	0	0	.958	-7	*O-35,M	-1.1
Total	14	1544	5145	833	1424	229	57	164	703	521	638	.277	.347	.439	114	90	50	33	-5	.982	-65	*O-1449/C-1	-4.3

■ PADDY BAUMANN   Baumann, Charles John   b: 12/20/1885, Indianapolis, Ind.   d: 11/20/69, Indianapolis, Ind.   BR/TR, 5'9", 160 lbs.   Deb: 8/10/11

YEAR	TM/L	G	AB	R	H	2B	3B	HR	RBI	BB	SO	AVG	OBP	SLG	PRO+	BR/A	SB	CS	SBR	FA	FR	G/POS	TPR
1911	Det-A	26	94	8	24	2	4	0	11	6		.255	.307	.362	82	-3	1			.956	6	2-23/O-3	0.2
1912	Det-A	16	42	3	11	1	0	0	7	6		.262	.354	.286	86	-0	4			.786	-2	/3-6,2-5,O	-0.2
1913	Det-A	50	191	31	57	7	4	1	22	16	18	.298	.353	.393	120	4	4			.943	-7	2-49	-0.4
1914	Det-A	3	11	1	0	0	0	0	2	1		.000	.154	.000	-52	-2	0			1.000	4	/2-3	-0.4
1915	NY-A	76	219	30	64	13	1	2	28	28	32	.292	.380	.388	130	9	9	10	-3	.978	-2	2-43,3-19/O	0.5
1916	NY-A	79	237	35	68	5	3	1	25	19	16	.287	.352	.346	108	2	10			.958	-7	O-28,3-26/2	-0.6
1917	NY-A	49	110	10	24	2	1	0	8	4	9	.218	.246	.255	52	-7	2			.941	-12	2-18/O-7,3	-2.1
Total	7	299	904	118	248	30	13	4	101	81	76	.274	.340	.350	103	4	30	10		.953	-26	2-150/3-52,O	-3.0

■ JIM BAUMER   Baumer, James Sloan   b: 1/29/31, Tulsa, Okla.   BR/TR, 6'2", 185 lbs.   Deb: 9/14/49

YEAR	TM/L	G	AB	R	H	2B	3B	HR	RBI	BB	SO	AVG	OBP	SLG	PRO+	BR/A	SB	CS	SBR	FA	FR	G/POS	TPR
1949	Chi-A	8	10	2	4	1	1	0	2	2	1	.400	.571	.700	243	2	0	0	0	.938	1	/S-7	0.3
1961	Cin-N	10	24	0	3	0	0	0	0	0	9	.125	.125	.125	-33	-4	0	0	0	1.000	-0	/2-9	-0.4
Total	2	18	34	2	7	1	1	0	2	2	10	.206	.289	.294	55	-2	0	0	0	1.000	1	/2-9,S-7	-0.1

■ JOHN BAUMGARTNER   Baumgartner, John Edward   b: 5/29/31, Birmingham, Ala.   BR/TR, 6'1", 190 lbs.   Deb: 4/14/53

YEAR	TM/L	G	AB	R	H	2B	3B	HR	RBI	BB	SO	AVG	OBP	SLG	PRO+	BR/A	SB	CS	SBR	FA	FR	G/POS	TPR
1953	Det-A	7	27	3	5	0	0	0	2	0	5	.185	.185	.185	0	-4	0	0	0	.913	-1	/3-7	-0.5

■ FRANK BAUMHOLTZ   Baumholtz, Frank Conrad   b: 10/7/18, Midvale, Ohio   BL/TL, 5'10.5", 175 lbs.   Deb: 4/15/47

YEAR	TM/L	G	AB	R	H	2B	3B	HR	RBI	BB	SO	AVG	OBP	SLG	PRO+	BR/A	SB	CS	SBR	FA	FR	G/POS	TPR
1947	Cin-N	151	643	96	182	32	9	5	45	56	53	.283	.341	.384	93	-7	6			.977	-5	*O-150	-1.9
1948	Cin-N	128	415	57	123	19	5	4	30	27	32	.296	.344	.395	103	1	8			.987	3	*O-110	-0.2
1949	Cin-N	27	81	12	19	5	3	1	8	6	8	.235	.295	.407	86	-2	0			.964	2	O-20	-0.1
	Chi-N	58	164	15	37	4	2	1	15	9	21	.226	.270	.293	52	-11	2			.986	-4	O-43	-1.8
	Yr	85	245	27	56	9	5	2	23	15	29	.229	.279	.331	64	-13	2			.976	-3	O-63	-1.9
1951	Chi-N	146	560	62	159	28	10	2	50	49	36	.284	.346	.380	94	-5	5	4	-1	.975	-7	*O-140	-1.7
1952	Chi-N	103	409	59	133	17	4	4	35	27	27	.325	.371	.416	116	9	5	7	-3	.974	3	*O-101	0.5
1953	Chi-N	133	520	75	159	36	7	3	25	42	36	.306	.359	.419	100	0	3	3	-1	.980	-3	*O-130	-0.8
1954	Chi-N	90	303	38	90	12	6	4	28	20	15	.297	.343	.416	95	-2	1	3	-2	.988	-10	O-71	-1.6
1955	Chi-N	105	280	23	81	12	1	2	27	16	24	.289	.330	.379	88	-5	0	1	-1	.993	2	O-63	-0.6
1956	Phi-N	76	100	13	27	0	0	0	9	6	6	.270	.318	.270	61	-9	2			.962	-0	O-15	-0.8
1957	Phi-N	2	2	0	0	0	0	0	0	0	0	.000	.000	.000	-99	-1	0	0	0	.000	0	H	-0.1
Total	10	1019	3477	450	1010	165	51	25	272	258	258	.290	.342	.389	95	-27	30	20		.980	-20	O-843	-9.1

■ DANNY BAUTISTA   Bautista, Daniel (Alcantara)   b: 5/24/72, Santo Domingo, D.R.   BR/TR, 5'11", 170 lbs.   Deb: 9/15/93

YEAR	TM/L	G	AB	R	H	2B	3B	HR	RBI	BB	SO	AVG	OBP	SLG	PRO+	BR/A	SB	CS	SBR	FA	FR	G/POS	TPR
1993	Det-A	17	61	6	19	3	1	1	9	1	10	.311	.323	.410	96	-1	3	1	0	1.000	1	O-16/D-1	0.1
1994	Det-A	31	99	12	23	4	1	4	15	3	18	.232	.255	.414	69	-5	1	2	-1	1.000	-1	O-30/D-1	-0.7
Total	2	48	160	18	42	7	1	5	24	4	28	.262	.280	.412	79	-5	4	3	-1	1.000	-0	/O-46,D-2	-0.6

■ JIM BAXES   Baxes, Dimitrios Speros   b: 7/5/28, San Francisco, Cal   BR/TR, 6'1", 190 lbs.   Deb: 4/11/59   F

YEAR	TM/L	G	AB	R	H	2B	3B	HR	RBI	BB	SO	AVG	OBP	SLG	PRO+	BR/A	SB	CS	SBR	FA	FR	G/POS	TPR
1959	LA-N	11	33	4	10	1	0	2	5	4	7	.303	.395	.515	130	2	1	0	0	.952	7	3-10	0.8

YEAR	TM/L	G	AB	R	H	2B	3B	HR	RBI	BB	SO	AVG	OBP	SLG	PRO+	BR/A	SB	CS	SBR	FA	FR	G/POS	TPR
	Cle-A	77	247	35	59	11	0	15	34	21	47	.239	.299	.466	111	2	0	1	-1	.956	-13	2-48,3-22	-0.8
Total	1	88	280	39	69	12	0	17	39	25	54	.246	.310	.471	113	4	1	1	-0	.931	-7	/2-48,3-32	0.0

■ MIKE BAXES
Baxes, Michael b: 12/18/30, San Francisco, Cal BR/TR, 5'10", 175 lbs. Deb: 4/17/56 F

YEAR	TM/L	G	AB	R	H	2B	3B	HR	RBI	BB	SO	AVG	OBP	SLG	PRO+	BR/A	SB	CS	SBR	FA	FR	G/POS	TPR
1956	KC-A	73	106	9	24	3	1	1	5	18	15	.226	.339	.302	70	-4	0	1	-1	.944	4	S-62/2-1	0.2
1958	KC-A	73	231	31	49	10	1	0	8	21	24	.212	.286	.264	52	-15	1	6	-3	.969	-4	2-61/S-4	-1.9
Total	2	146	337	40	73	13	2	1	13	39	39	.217	.303	.276	58	-19	1	7	-4	.946	-0	/S-66,2-62	-1.7

■ JOHN BAXTER
Baxter, John Morris b: 7/27/1876, Chippewa Falls, Wis. d: 8/7/26, Portland, Ore. 6'3", Deb: 4/19/07

YEAR	TM/L	G	AB	R	H	2B	3B	HR	RBI	BB	SO	AVG	OBP	SLG	PRO+	BR/A	SB	CS	SBR	FA	FR	G/POS	TPR
1907	StL-N	6	21	1	4	0	0	0	0	0		.190	.190	.190	20	-2	0			.921	-1	/1-6	-0.3

■ HARRY BAY
Bay, Harry Elbert "Deerfoot" b: 1/17/1878, Pontiac, Ill. d: 3/20/52, Peoria, Ill. BL/TL, 5'8", 138 lbs. Deb: 7/23/01

YEAR	TM/L	G	AB	R	H	2B	3B	HR	RBI	BB	SO	AVG	OBP	SLG	PRO+	BR/A	SB	CS	SBR	FA	FR	G/POS	TPR
1901	Cin-N	41	157	25	33	1	2	1	3	13		.210	.275	.261	60	-8	4			.953	-1	O-40	-1.1
1902	Cin-N	6	16	3	6	0	0	0	1	2		.375	.474	.375	148	1	0			.778	0	/O-3	0.1
	Cle-A	108	455	71	132	10	5	0	23	36		.290	.343	.334	92	-4	22			.973	4	*O-107	-0.7
1903	Cle-A	140	579	94	169	15	12	1	35	29		.292	.329	.364	110	7	45			.950	-3	*O-140	-0.5
1904	Cle-A	132	506	69	122	12	9	3	36	43		.241	.307	.318	99	-0	38			.987	7	*O-132	-0.1
1905	Cle-A	144	552	90	166	18	10	0	22	36		.301	.349	.370	126	16	36			.970	1	*O-144	1.1
1906	Cle-A	68	280	47	77	8	3	0	14	26		.275	.337	.325	109	3	17			.979	-3	O-68	-0.3
1907	Cle-A	34	95	14	17	1	1	0	7	10		.179	.271	.211	53	-5	7			.968	0	O-31	-0.6
1908	Cle-A	2	0	0	0	0	0	0	0	0		—	—	—	—	—	0			.000	0	R	0.0
Total	8	675	2640	413	722	65	42	5	141	195		.273	.328	.336	103	11	169			.968	6	O-665	-2.1

■ DICK BAYLESS
Bayless, Harry Owen b: 9/6/1883, Joplin, Mo. d: 12/16/20, Santa Rita, N.Mex. BL/TR, 5'9", 178 lbs. Deb: 9/9/08

YEAR	TM/L	G	AB	R	H	2B	3B	HR	RBI	BB	SO	AVG	OBP	SLG	PRO+	BR/A	SB	CS	SBR	FA	FR	G/POS	TPR
1908	Cin-N	19	71	7	16	1	0	1	3	6		.225	.304	.282	90	-1	0			.946	3	O-19	0.1

■ DON BAYLOR
Baylor, Don Edward b: 6/28/49, Austin, Tex. BR/TR, 6'1", 195 lbs. Deb: 9/18/70 CM

YEAR	TM/L	G	AB	R	H	2B	3B	HR	RBI	BB	SO	AVG	OBP	SLG	PRO+	BR/A	SB	CS	SBR	FA	FR	G/POS	TPR
1970	Bal-A	8	17	4	4	0	0	0	4	2	3	.235	.316	.235	54	-1	1	1	-0	1.000	0	/O-6	-0.2
1971	Bal-A	1	2	0	0	0	0	0	1	2	1	.000	.600	.000	83	0	0	0	0	1.000	0	/O-1	0.1
1972	Bal-A	102	320	33	81	13	3	11	38	29	50	.253	.332	.416	118	7	24	2	6	.975	-9	O-84/1-9	0.1
1973	*Bal-A	118	405	64	116	20	4	11	51	35	48	.286	.362	.437	125	14	32	9	4	.981	-1	*O-110/1-6,D	1.2
1974	*Bal-A	137	489	66	133	22	4	10	59	43	56	.272	.343	.382	112	8	29	12	2	.978	-17	*O-129/1-8,D	-1.4
1975	Bal-A	145	524	79	148	21	6	25	76	53	64	.282	.363	.489	148	32	32	17	-1	.982	-2	*O-135/1-2,D	2.4
1976	Oak-A	157	595	85	147	25	1	15	68	58	72	.247	.334	.368	110	8	52	12	8	.981	-9	O-76,1-69,D	0.0
1977	Cal-A	154	561	87	141	27	0	25	75	62	76	.251	.339	.433	113	10	26	12	1	.966	-1	O-77,D-61,1	0.3
1978	Cal-A	158	591	103	151	26	0	34	99	56	71	.255	.338	.472	131	23	22	9	1	.974	-2	*D-102,O-39,1	1.7
1979	*Cal-A★	162	628	**120**	186	33	3	36	**139**	71	51	.296	.377	.530	147	41	22	12	-1	.976	2	O-97,D-65/1	3.4
1980	Cal-A	90	340	39	85	12	2	5	51	24	32	.250	.320	.341	83	-7	6	6	-2	.969	3	O-54,D-36	-1.0
1981	Cal-A	103	377	52	90	18	1	17	66	42	51	.239	.326	.427	116	7	3	3	-1	1.000	1	D-97/1-4,O	0.4
1982	*Cal-A	157	608	80	160	24	1	24	93	57	69	.263	.333	.424	106	5	10	4	1	1.000	0	*D-155	0.0
1983	NY-A	144	534	82	162	33	3	21	85	40	53	.303	.366	.494	139	28	17	7	1	1.000	0	*D-136/O-5,1	2.3
1984	NY-A	134	493	84	129	29	1	27	89	38	68	.262	.343	.489	132	21	1	1	-0	.889	-1	*D-127/O-5	1.6
1985	NY-A	142	477	70	110	24	1	23	91	52	90	.231	.336	.430	111	8	0	4	-2	1.000	0	*D-140	0.3
1986	*Bos-A	160	585	93	139	23	1	31	94	62	111	.238	.346	.439	112	10	3	5	-2	.986	-0	*D-143,1-13/O	0.4
1987	Bos-A	108	339	64	81	8	0	16	57	40	47	.239	.360	.404	100	1	5	2	0	.000	0	D-97	-0.1
	*Min-A	20	49	3	14	1	0	0	6	5	12	.286	.397	.306	87	-0	0	1	-1	.000	0	D-14	-0.1
	Yr	128	388	67	95	9	0	16	63	45	59	.245	.364	.392	98	1	5	3	-0	.000	0	*D-111	-0.2
1988	*Oak-A	92	264	28	58	7	0	7	34	34	44	.220	.335	.326	89	-3	0	1	-1	.000	0	D-80	-0.5
Total	19	2292	8198	1236	2135	366	28	338	1276	805	1069	.260	.346	.436	119	212	285	120	14	.977	-37	*D-1285,O-822,1	10.9

■ JACK BEACH
Beach, Stonewall Jackson b: 1862, Alexandria, Va. d: 7/23/1896, Alexandria, Va. Deb: 5/1/1884

YEAR	TM/L	G	AB	R	H	2B	3B	HR	RBI	BB	SO	AVG	OBP	SLG	PRO+	BR/A	SB	CS	SBR	FA	FR	G/POS	TPR
1884	Was-a	8	31	3	3	2	0	0		0		.097	.097	.161	-20	-4				.667	-1	/O-8	-0.5

■ JOHNNY BEALL
Beall, John Woolf b: 3/12/1882, Beltsville, Md. d: 6/14/26, Beltsville, Md. BL/TR, 6', 180 lbs. Deb: 4/17/13

YEAR	TM/L	G	AB	R	H	2B	3B	HR	RBI	BB	SO	AVG	OBP	SLG	PRO+	BR/A	SB	CS	SBR	FA	FR	G/POS	TPR
1913	Cle-A	6	6	0	1	0	0	0	1	0	2	.167	.167	.167	-2	-1	0			.000	0	H	-0.1
	Chi-A	17	60	10	16	0	1	2	3	0	0	.267	.279	.400	99	-1	1			.953	1	O-17	-0.1
	Yr	23	66	10	17	0	1	2	4	0	2	.258	.269	.379	89	-1	1			.953	1	O-17	-0.2
1915	Cin-N	10	34	3	8	1	0	0	3	5	10	.235	.350	.265	86	-0	0	1	-1	.960	1	O-10	0.0
1916	Cin-N	6	21	3	7	2	0	1	4	3	7	.333	.417	.571	207	3	1			1.000	1	/O-6	0.4
1918	StL-N	19	49	2	11	1	0	0	6	3	6	.224	.269	.245	59	-2	0			1.000	-1	O-18	-0.5
Total	4	58	170	18	43	4	1	3	17	11	25	.253	.306	.341	95	-1	2	1		.972	2	/O-51	-0.3

■ BOB BEALL
Beall, Robert Brooks b: 4/24/48, Portland, Ore. BB/TL, 5'11", 180 lbs. Deb: 5/12/75

YEAR	TM/L	G	AB	R	H	2B	3B	HR	RBI	BB	SO	AVG	OBP	SLG	PRO+	BR/A	SB	CS	SBR	FA	FR	G/POS	TPR
1975	Atl-N	20	31	2	7	1	0	0	1	6	9	.226	.351	.290	77	-1	0	0	0	.984	-0	/1-8	-0.1
1978	Atl-N	108	185	29	45	8	0	1	16	36	27	.243	.369	.303	81	-3	4	5	-2	.987	-1	1-40/O-8	-0.9
1979	Atl-N	17	15	1	2	2	0	0	1	3	4	.133	.278	.267	46	-1	0	0	0	1.000	0	/1-3	-0.1
1980	Pit-N	3	3	0	0	0	0	0	0	0	1	.000	.000	.000	-99	-1	0	0	0	.000	0	/H	-0.1
Total	4	148	234	32	54	12	0	1	18	45	41	.231	.357	.295	76	-6	4	5	-2	.987	-1	/1-51,O-8	-1.2

■ TOMMY BEALS
Beals, Thomas L. (a.k.a. W.Thomas In 1871-1873) b: 8/1850, New York d: 10/2/15, San Francisco, Cal. BR , 5'5", 144 lbs. Deb: 7/27/1871

YEAR	TM/L	G	AB	R	H	2B	3B	HR	RBI	BB	SO	AVG	OBP	SLG	PRO+	BR/A	SB	CS	SBR	FA	FR	G/POS	TPR
1871	Oly-n	10	36	6	7	0	0	0	1	2	0	.194	.237	.194	27	-3	2					/O-8,2-2	-0.2
1872	Oly-n	9	36	7	12	0	2	0	5	1	1	.333	.351	.444	151	2						/2-5,S-2,O	0.1
1873	Was-n	37	169	35	46	8	6	0	20	1	1	.272	.276	.391	97	-0						2-26,C-13/O	-0.2
1874	Bos-n	19	97	20	19	3	4	0		0		.196	.196	.309	55	-5						2-10/O-8	-0.4
1875	Bos-n	36	164	41	42	1	5	0		2		.256	.266	.323	99	-1						2-31,O-6	-0.1
1880	Chi-N	13	46	4	7	0	0	0	3	1	6	.152	.170	.152	10	-4				.889	-6	O-10/2-3	-1.0
Total	5 n	111	502	109	126	12	17	0	26	6	2	.251	.260	.343	87	-7						/2-74,O-25,CS	-0.8

■ CHARLIE BEAMON
Beamon, Charles Alfonzo Jr. b: 12/4/53, Oakland, Cal. BL/TL, 6'1", 183 lbs. Deb: 9/11/78 F

YEAR	TM/L	G	AB	R	H	2B	3B	HR	RBI	BB	SO	AVG	OBP	SLG	PRO+	BR/A	SB	CS	SBR	FA	FR	G/POS	TPR
1978	Sea-A	10	11	2	2	0	0	0	0	1	1	.182	.250	.182	23	-1	0	0	0	1.000	1	/1-2,D-6	0.0
1979	Sea-A	27	25	5	5	1	0	0	0	0	5	.200	.200	.240	18	-3	1	0	0	1.000	-0	/1-7,O-2	-0.3
1981	Tor-A	8	15	1	3	1	0	0	0	2	2	.200	.294	.267	59	-1	0	0	0	1.000	0	/D-4,1-1	-0.1
Total	3	45	51	8	10	2	0	0	0	3	8	.196	.241	.235	32	-5	1	0	0	1.000	1	/D-10,1-10,O	-0.4

■ JOE BEAN
Bean, Joseph William b: 3/18/1874, Boston, Mass. d: 2/15/61, Atlanta, Ga. BR/TR, 5'8", 138 lbs. Deb: 4/28/02

YEAR	TM/L	G	AB	R	H	2B	3B	HR	RBI	BB	SO	AVG	OBP	SLG	PRO+	BR/A	SB	CS	SBR	FA	FR	G/POS	TPR
1902	NY-N	48	176	13	39	2	1	0	5	5		.222	.247	.244	52	-10	9			.889	-9	S-48	-1.7

■ BILL BEAN
Bean, William Daro b: 5/11/64, Santa Ana, Cal. BL/TL, 6' ", 185 lbs. Deb: 4/25/87

YEAR	TM/L	G	AB	R	H	2B	3B	HR	RBI	BB	SO	AVG	OBP	SLG	PRO+	BR/A	SB	CS	SBR	FA	FR	G/POS	TPR
1987	Det-A	26	66	6	17	0	0	0	4	5	11	.258	.310	.288	63	-3	1	1	-0	1.000	0	O-24	-0.4
1988	Det-A	10	11	2	2	0	1	0	0	0	2	.182	.182	.364	51	-1	0	0	0	1.000	-1	/O-4,1-2,D	-0.2
1989	Det-A	9	11	0	0	0	0	0	0	0	2	.000	.214	.000	-36	-2	0	0	0	.833	1	/O-6,1-2	-0.5
	LA-N	51	71	7	14	4	0	0	4	1	9	.197	.250	.254	45	-5	0	2	-1	1.000	-9	O-44	-1.7
1993	SD-N	88	177	19	46	9	0	5	32	6	29	.260	.292	.395	81	-5	2	4	-2	.987	-7	O-54,1-12	-1.6
1994	SD-N	84	135	7	29	5	1	0	14	7	25	.215	.254	.267	36	-13	0	1	-1	1.000	-5	O-39,1-16	-1.9
Total	5	268	471	41	108	20	2	5	53	24	80	.229	.273	.312	57	-29	3	8	-4	.992	-25	O-171/1-32,D	-6.3

YEAR	TM/L	G	AB	R	H	2B	3B	HR	RBI	BB	SO	AVG	OBP	SLG	PRO+	BR/A	SB	CS	SBR	FA	FR	G/POS	TPR

■ BILLY BEANE   Beane, William Lamar   b: 3/29/62, Orlando, Fla.   BR/TR, 6'4", 195 lbs.   Deb: 9/13/84

YEAR	TM/L	G	AB	R	H	2B	3B	HR	RBI	BB	SO	AVG	OBP	SLG	PRO+	BR/A	SB	CS	SBR	FA	FR	G/POS	TPR
1984	NY-N	5	10	0	1	0	0	0	0	0	2	.100	.100	.100	-44	-2	0	1	-1	1.000	-2	/O-5	-0.4
1985	NY-N	8	8	0	2	1	0	0	1	0	3	.250	.250	.375	74	-0	0	0	0	1.000	-1	/O-2	-0.1
1986	Min-A	80	183	20	39	6	0	3	15	11	54	.213	.258	.295	49	-13	2	3	-1	1.000	-5	O-67/D-5	-2.0
1987	Min-A	12	15	1	4	2	0	0	1	0	6	.267	.267	.400	71	-1	0	0	0	1.000	-1	/O-7	-0.2
1988	Det-A	6	6	1	1	0	0	0	0	0	2	.167	.167	.167	-7	-1	0	0	0	1.000	-2	/O-6	-0.3
1989	Oak-A	37	79	8	19	5	0	0	11	0	13	.241	.241	.304	54	-5	3	1	0	1.000	-2	O-25/1-4,C3D	-0.7
Total	6	148	301	30	66	14	0	3	29	11	80	.219	.247	.296	48	-22	5	5	-2	1.000	-11	O-112/D-9,13C	-3.7

■ TED BEARD   Beard, Cramer Theodore   b: 1/7/21, Woodsboro, Md.   BL/TL, 5'8", 165 lbs.   Deb: 9/5/48

YEAR	TM/L	G	AB	R	H	2B	3B	HR	RBI	BB	SO	AVG	OBP	SLG	PRO+	BR/A	SB	CS	SBR	FA	FR	G/POS	TPR
1948	Pit-N	25	81	15	16	1	3	0	7	12	18	.198	.316	.284	62	-4	5			1.000	2	O-22	-0.4
1949	Pit-N	14	24	1	2	0	0	0	1	2	2	.083	.154	.083	-34	-5	0			.900	-3	O-10	-0.8
1950	Pit-N	61	177	32	41	6	2	4	12	27	45	.232	.333	.356	79	-5	3			.983	2	O-49	-0.5
1951	Pit-N	22	48	7	9	1	0	1	3	6	14	.188	.291	.271	51	-3	0	0	0	1.000	-2	O-15	-0.5
1952	Pit-N	15	44	5	8	2	1	0	3	7	9	.182	.294	.273	57	-2	2	0	1	1.000	-3	O-13	-0.2
1957	Chi-A	38	78	15	16	1	0	0	7	18	14	.205	.354	.218	59	-3	3	2	-0	.974	-1	O-28	-0.6
1958	Chi-A	19	22	5	2	0	0	1	2	6	5	.091	.286	.227	44	-2	3	0	1	1.000	-4	O-15	-0.5
Total	7	194	474	80	94	11	6	6	35	78	107	.198	.315	.285	61	-25	16	2		.987	-5	O-152	-3.5

■ OLLIE BEARD   Beard, Oliver Perry   b: 5/2/1862, Lexington, Ky.   d: 5/28/29, Cincinnati, Ohio   BR/TR, 5'11", 180 lbs.   Deb: 4/17/1889

YEAR	TM/L	G	AB	R	H	2B	3B	HR	RBI	BB	SO	AVG	OBP	SLG	PRO+	BR/A	SB	CS	SBR	FA	FR	G/POS	TPR
1889	Cin-a	141	558	96	159	13	14	1	77	35	39	.285	.328	.364	94	-6	36			.896	20	*S-141	1.8
1890	Cin-N	122	492	64	132	17	15	3	72	44	13	.268	.331	.382	108	4	30			.897	1	*S-113/3-9	1.0
1891	Lou-a	68	257	35	62	4	5	0	24	33	9	.241	.330	.296	80	-6	7			.879	7	3-61/S-7	0.3
Total	3	331	1307	195	353	34	34	4	173	112	61	.270	.330	.357	97	-8	73			.896	28	S-261/3-70	3.1

■ LEW BEASLEY   Beasley, Lewis Paige   b: 8/27/48, Sparta, Va.   BL/TR, 5'10", 172 lbs.   Deb: 5/21/77

YEAR	TM/L	G	AB	R	H	2B	3B	HR	RBI	BB	SO	AVG	OBP	SLG	PRO+	BR/A	SB	CS	SBR	FA	FR	G/POS	TPR
1977	Tex-A	25	32	5	7	1	0	0	3	2	2	.219	.265	.250	41	-3	1	1	-0	.833	-6	O-18/S-1,D	-0.9

■ DAVE BEATLE   Beatle, David   b: 1861, New York, N.Y.   6'2", 200 lbs.   Deb: 6/17/1884

YEAR	TM/L	G	AB	R	H	2B	3B	HR	RBI	BB	SO	AVG	OBP	SLG	PRO+	BR/A	SB	CS	SBR	FA	FR	G/POS	TPR
1884	Det-N	1	3	0	0	0	0	0	0	0	2	.000	.000	.000	-99	-1				.500	-1	/O-1,C-1	-0.1

■ DESMOND BEATTY   Beatty, Aloysius Desmond "Desperate"   b: 4/7/1893, Baltimore, Md.   d: 10/6/69, Norway, Maine   BR/TR, 5'8.5", 158 lbs.   Deb: 9/28/14

YEAR	TM/L	G	AB	R	H	2B	3B	HR	RBI	BB	SO	AVG	OBP	SLG	PRO+	BR/A	SB	CS	SBR	FA	FR	G/POS	TPR
1914	NY-N	2	3	0	0	0	0	0	1	0	0	.000	.000	.000	-99	-1	0			.400	-1	/S-1,3-1	-0.1

■ JIM BEAUCHAMP   Beauchamp, James Edward   b: 8/21/39, Vinita, Okla.   BR/TR, 6'2", 205 lbs.   Deb: 9/22/63   C

YEAR	TM/L	G	AB	R	H	2B	3B	HR	RBI	BB	SO	AVG	OBP	SLG	PRO+	BR/A	SB	CS	SBR	FA	FR	G/POS	TPR
1963	StL-N	4	3	0	0	0	0	0	0	0	2	.000	.000	.000	-91	-1	0	0	0	.000	0	H	-0.1
1964	Hou-N	23	55	6	9	2	0	2	4	5	16	.164	.246	.309	58	-3	0	0	0	.913	-1	O-15/1-2	-0.5
1965	Hou-N	24	53	5	10	1	0	0	4	5	11	.189	.259	.208	36	-4	0	2	-1	1.000	2	/O-9,1-3	-0.5
	Mil-N	4	3	0	0	0	0	0	0	1	1	.000	.250	.000	-23	-1	0	1	-1	1.000	0	/1-2	-0.1
	Yr	28	56	5	10	1	0	0	4	6	12	.179	.258	.196	32	-5	0	3	-2	1.000	1	/O-9,1-5	-0.6
1967	Atl-N	4	3	0	0	0	0	0	1	0	0	.000	.000	.000	-99	-1	0	0	0	.000	0	H	-0.1
1968	Cin-N	31	57	10	15	2	0	2	14	4	19	.263	.311	.404	107	-0	0	0	0	1.000	0	O-13/1-1	0.0
1969	Cin-N	43	60	8	15	1	0	1	8	5	13	.250	.308	.317	71	-2	0	0	0	1.000	0	/O-9,1-3	-0.5
1970	Hou-N	31	26	3	5	0	0	1	4	3	7	.192	.276	.308	59	-2	0	1	-1	1.000	-4	O-16	-0.7
	StL-N	44	58	8	15	2	0	1	6	8	11	.259	.348	.345	85	-1	2	0	1	1.000	1	O-10/1-5	-0.1
	Yr	75	84	11	20	2	0	2	10	11	18	.238	.326	.333	78	-3	2	1	0	1.000	-4	O-26/1-5	-0.8
1971	StL-N	77	162	24	38	8	3	2	16	9	26	.235	.279	.358	76	-5	3	1	0	.982	-3	1-44/O-1	-1.1
1972	NY-N	58	120	10	29	1	0	5	19	7	33	.242	.289	.375	90	-2	0	0	0	.979	-3	1-35/O-5	-0.8
1973	*NY-N	50	61	5	17	1	1	0	14	7	11	.279	.353	.328	91	-1	0	0	0	.969	-1	1-11	-0.2
Total	10	393	661	79	153	18	4	14	90	54	150	.231	.292	.334	76	-22	6	5	-1	.980	-11	1-106/O-78	-4.7

■ GINGER BEAUMONT   Beaumont, Clarence Howeth   b: 7/23/1876, Rochester, Wis.   d: 4/10/56, Burlington, Wis.   BL/TR, 5'8", 190 lbs.   Deb: 4/21/1899

YEAR	TM/L	G	AB	R	H	2B	3B	HR	RBI	BB	SO	AVG	OBP	SLG	PRO+	BR/A	SB	CS	SBR	FA	FR	G/POS	TPR
1899	Pit-N	111	437	90	154	15	8	3	38	41		.352	.416	.444	137	23	31			.924	6	*O-100/1-2	1.9
1900	*Pit-N	138	567	105	158	14	9	5	50	40		.279	.331	.362	90	-8	27			.944	-12	*O-138	-2.8
1901	Pit-N	133	558	120	185	14	5	8	72	44		.332	.382	.418	128	20	36			.943	-5	*O-133	0.5
1902	Pit-N	130	541	100	**193**	21	6	0	67	39		**.357**	.404	.418	148	31	33			.975	0	*O-130	2.3
1903	*Pit-N	141	613	**137**	**209**	30	6	7	68	44		.341	.390	.444	133	25	23			.948	-7	*O-141	0.9
1904	Pit-N	153	615	97	**185**	12	12	3	54	34		.301	.338	.374	117	11	28			.968	-4	*O-153	-0.3
1905	Pit-N	103	384	60	126	12	8	3	40	22		.328	.365	.424	131	14	21			.972	-0	O-97	0.9
1906	Pit-N	80	310	48	82	9	3	2	32	19		.265	.311	.332	96	-2	1			.945	-4	O-78	-1.2
1907	Bos-N	150	580	67	**187**	19	14	4	62	37		.322	.366	.424	148	30	25			.962	5	*O-149	3.2
1908	Bos-N	125	476	66	127	20	6	2	52	42		.267	.328	.347	117	9	13			.965	-1	*O-121	0.4
1909	Bos-N	123	407	35	107	11	4	0	60	35		.263	.321	.310	92	-4	12			.969	1	*O-111	-0.8
1910	*Chi-N	76	172	30	46	5	1	2	22	28	14	.267	.373	.343	110	3	4			.957	-4	O-56	-0.3
Total	12	1463	5660	955	1759	182	82	39	617	425	14	.311	.362	.393	122	151	254			.956	-26	*O-1407/1-2	4.7

■ E. P. BEAVENS   Beavens, E. P. (a.k.a. E. P. Bevens)   b: 1848, Troy, N.Y.   TR, 5'8", 138 lbs.   Deb: 5/9/1871

YEAR	TM/L	G	AB	R	H	2B	3B	HR	RBI	BB	SO	AVG	OBP	SLG	PRO+	BR/A	SB	CS	SBR	FA	FR	G/POS	TPR
1871	Tro-n	3	15	7	6	0	0	0	5	0	0	.400	.400	.400	129	1	2					/2-3	0.0
1872	Atl-n	10	45	6	10	2	0	0	3	1	0	.222	.239	.267	47	-4						/2-8,S-1,O	-0.3
Total	2 n	13	60	13	16	2	0	0	8	1	0	.267	.279	.300	66	-3						/2-11,O-1,S	-0.3

■ BUCK BECANNON   Becannon, James Melvin   b: 8/22/1859, New York, N.Y.   d: 11/5/23, New York, N.Y.   5'10", 165 lbs.   Deb: 10/15/1884

YEAR	TM/L	G	AB	R	H	2B	3B	HR	RBI	BB	SO	AVG	OBP	SLG	PRO+	BR/A	SB	CS	SBR	FA	FR	G/POS	TPR
1884	*NY-a	1	3	0	0	0	0	0	0	0		.000	.000	.000	-99	-1				1.000	0	/P-1	0.0
1885	NY-a	10	33	3	10	0	0	0		0	1	.303	.343	.303	114	1				.947	0	P-10	0.0
1887	NY-N	1	5	0	0	0	0	0		0	2	.000	.000	.000	-99	-1	0			.667	-0	/3-1	-0.2
Total	3	12	41	3	10	0	0	0	0	1	2	.244	.279	.244	69	-1	0			.952	0	/P-11,3-1	-0.2

■ GEORGE BECHTEL   Bechtel, George A.   b: 1848, Philadelphia, Pa.   5'11", 165 lbs.   Deb: 5/20/1871

YEAR	TM/L	G	AB	R	H	2B	3B	HR	RBI	BB	SO	AVG	OBP	SLG	PRO+	BR/A	SB	CS	SBR	FA	FR	G/POS	TPR
1871	Ath-n	20	94	24	33	9	1	1	21	2	2	.351	.365	.500	147	6	4					O-15/P-3,3	0.4
1872	Mut-n	51	246	60	74	11	2	0	39	6	3	.301	.317	.362	116	6						*O-51/1-1	0.7
1873	Phi-n	53	258	53	63	12	1	1	38	9	1	.244	.270	.310	68	-11						*O-52/P-3	-0.6
1874	Phi-n	32	151	29	44	5	4	1		2		.291	.301	.397	116	2						O-27/P-6	0.3
1875	Cen-n	14	62	12	17	5	0	0		0	1	.274	.274	.355	126	2						P-14	0.0
	Ath-n	35	164	33	46	5	2	0		1		.280	.285	.335	102	-1						O-30/P-4	0.0
	Yr	49	226	45	63	10	2	0		1	1	.279	.282	.341	108	1						O-30/P-18	0.0
1876	Lou-N	14	55	2	10	1	0	0	2	0	1	.182	.182	.200	23	-5				.882	-2	O-14	-0.6
	NY-N	2	10	2	3	0	0	0	0	0	0	.300	.300	.300	115	0				.429	-1	/O-2	-0.1
	Yr	16	65	4	13	1	0	0	2	0	1	.200	.200	.215	34	-5				.750	-3	O-16	-0.7
Total	5 n	205	975	211	277	47	10	3	98	20	6	.284	.298	.362	103	4						O-175/P-30,31	0.8

■ CLYDE BECK   Beck, Clyde Eugene "Jersey"   b: 1/6/1900, Bassett, Cal.   d: 7/15/88, Temple City, Cal.   BR/TR, 5'10", 176 lbs.   Deb: 5/19/26

YEAR	TM/L	G	AB	R	H	2B	3B	HR	RBI	BB	SO	AVG	OBP	SLG	PRO+	BR/A	SB	CS	SBR	FA	FR	G/POS	TPR
1926	Chi-N	30	101	10	16	0	4	7	15	34	-7	.198	.261	.350	34	-7	0			.993	1	2-30	0.5
1927	Chi-N	117	391	44	101	20	5	2	44	43	37	.258	.332	.350	83	-5	0			.969	22	2-99,3-17/S	1.7
1928	Chi-N	131	483	72	124	18	4	3	52	58	58	.257	.341	.329	77	-15	3			.958	-1	3-87,S-47/2	-0.6
1929	Chi-N	54	190	28	40	7	0	0	9	19	24	.211	.282	.247	32	-20	3			.978	5	3-33,S-14	-1.1

YEAR	TM/L	G	AB	R	H	2B	3B	HR	RBI	BB	SO	AVG	OBP	SLG	PRO+	BR/A	SB	CS	SBR	FA	FR	G/POS	TPR
1930	Chi-N	83	244	32	52	7	0	6	34	36	32	.213	.314	.316	53	-19	2			.953	0	S-57,2-24/3	-1.1
1931	Cin-N	53	136	17	21	4	2	0	19	21	14	.154	.272	.213	34	-12	1			.960	-2	3-38/S-6	-1.2
Total	6	468	1525	203	354	56	11	12	162	184	180	.232	.317	.307	63	-83	9			.959	36	3-177,2-154,S	-1.8

■ ERVE BECK
Beck, Ervin Thomas "Dutch"　b: 7/19/1878, Toledo, Ohio　d: 12/23/16, Toledo, Ohio　BR/TR, 5'10", 168 lbs.　Deb: 9/19/1899

YEAR	TM/L	G	AB	R	H	2B	3B	HR	RBI	BB	SO	AVG	OBP	SLG	PRO+	BR/A	SB	CS	SBR	FA	FR	G/POS	TPR
1899	Bro-N	8	24	2	4	2	0	0	2		0	.167	.167	.250	13	-3	0			.931	-2	/2-6,S-2	-0.4
1901	Cle-A	135	539	78	156	26	8	6	79	23		.289	.319	.401	103	1	7			.927	-11	*2-132	-0.4
1902	Cin-N	48	187	19	57	10	3	1	20	3		.305	.319	.406	113	2	2			.936	-5	2-32/1-6,O	-0.3
	Det-A	41	162	23	48	4	0	2	22	4		.296	.313	.358	84	-4	3			.971	1	1-36/O-5	-0.3
Total	3	232	912	122	265	42	11	9	123	30		.291	.315	.390	99	-4	12			.929	-16	2-170/1-42,OS	-1.4

■ FRANK BECK
Beck, Frank J. (b: Frank J. Hengstebeck)　b: 4/29/1860, Poughkeepsie, N.Y.　d: 2/8/41, Detroit, Mich.　TR, 5'9", 141 lbs.　Deb: 5/2/1884

YEAR	TM/L	G	AB	R	H	2B	3B	HR	RBI	BB	SO	AVG	OBP	SLG	PRO+	BR/A	SB	CS	SBR	FA	FR	G/POS	TPR
1884	Pit-a	3	12	1	4	1	0	0	0			.333	.333	.417	141	0				1.000	0	/P-3	0.0
	Bal-U	5	20	1	2	1	0	0	0			.100	.100	.150	-30	-4				.500	-1	/O-4,P-2	-0.4
Total	1	8	32	2	6	2	0	0	0			.188	.188	.250	24	-3				1.000	-1	/P-5,O-4	-0.4

■ FRED BECK
Beck, Frederick Thomas　b: 11/17/1886, Havana, Ill.　d: 3/12/62, Havana, Ill.　BL/TL, 6'1", 180 lbs.　Deb: 4/14/09

YEAR	TM/L	G	AB	R	H	2B	3B	HR	RBI	BB	SO	AVG	OBP	SLG	PRO+	BR/A	SB	CS	SBR	FA	FR	G/POS	TPR
1909	Bos-N	96	334	20	66	4	6	3	27	17		.198	.245	.272	58	-17	5			.966	4	O-57,1-33	-1.8
1910	Bos-N	154	571	52	157	32	9	10	64	19	55	.275	.307	.415	105	-0	8			.963	2	*O-134,1-19	-0.5
1911	Cin-N	41	87	7	16	1	2	2	20	1		.184	.193	.310	41	-7	2			1.000	-2	O-16/1-6	-1.0
	Phi-N	66	210	26	59	8	3	3	25	17	21	.281	.346	.390	105	1	3			.957	-5	O-61	-0.8
	Yr	107	297	33	75	9	5	5	45	18	34	.253	.304	.367	88	-6	5			.966	-7	O-77/1-6	-1.8
1914	Chi-F	157	555	51	155	23	4	11	77	44	66	.279	.341	.395	96	-6	9			.982	-13	*1-157	-2.3
1915	Chi-F	121	373	35	83	9	3	5	38	24	38	.223	.277	.303	58	-24	4			.992	-6	*1-117	-3.6
Total	5	635	2130	191	536	77	27	34	251	122	193	.252	.301	.361	85	-53	31			.984	-20	1-332,O-268	-10.0

■ ZINN BECK
Beck, Zinn Bertram　b: 9/30/1885, Steubenville, O.　d: 3/19/81, W.Palm Beach, Fla.　BR/TR, 5'10.5", 160 lbs.　Deb: 9/14/13

YEAR	TM/L	G	AB	R	H	2B	3B	HR	RBI	BB	SO	AVG	OBP	SLG	PRO+	BR/A	SB	CS	SBR	FA	FR	G/POS	TPR
1913	StL-N	10	30	4	5	1	0	0	2	4	10	.167	.265	.200	34	-2	1			.833	1	/S-5,3-5	-0.2
1914	StL-N	137	457	42	106	15	11	3	45	28	32	.232	.282	.333	84	-11	14			.935	10	*3-122,S-16	0.5
1915	StL-N	70	223	21	52	9	4	0	15	12	31	.233	.282	.309	79	-6	3	10	-5	.935	0	3-62/S-4,2	-0.9
1916	StL-N	62	184	8	41	7	1	0	10	14	21	.223	.281	.272	71	-6	3			.910	-6	3-52/1-1,2	-1.2
1918	NY-A	11	8	0	0	0	0	0	0	1	0	.000	.000	.000	-98	-2	0			1.000	0	/1-5,3-1	-0.2
Total	5	290	902	75	204	32	16	3	73	58	95	.226	.279	.307	76	-27	21	10		.932	5	3-242/S-25,12	-2.0

■ HEINIE BECKENDORF
Beckendorf, Henry Ward　b: 6/15/1884, New York, N.Y.　d: 9/15/49, Jackson Heights, N.Y.　BR/TR, 5'9", 174 lbs.　Deb: 4/16/09

YEAR	TM/L	G	AB	R	H	2B	3B	HR	RBI	BB	SO	AVG	OBP	SLG	PRO+	BR/A	SB	CS	SBR	FA	FR	G/POS	TPR
1909	Det-A	15	27	1	7	1	0	0	1	2		.259	.310	.296	88	-0	0			.957	-0	C-15	0.0
1910	Det-A	3	7	0	3	0	0	0	2	1		.429	.500	.429	179	1	0			.909	-1	/C-2	0.0
	Was-A	37	103	8	15	1	0	0	10	5		.146	.207	.155	14	-10	0			.991	0	C-36	-0.7
	Yr	40	110	8	18	1	0	0	12	6		.164	.227	.173	26	-9	0			.988	-0	C-38	-0.7
Total	2	55	137	9	25	2	0	0	13	8		.182	.243	.197	39	-10	0			.983	-1	/C-53	-0.7

■ BEALS BECKER
Becker, David Beals　b: 7/5/1886, ElDorado, Kan.　d: 8/16/43, Huntington Park, Cal.　BL/TL, 5'9", 170 lbs.　Deb: 4/19/08

YEAR	TM/L	G	AB	R	H	2B	3B	HR	RBI	BB	SO	AVG	OBP	SLG	PRO+	BR/A	SB	CS	SBR	FA	FR	G/POS	TPR
1908	Pit-N	20	65	4	10	0	1	0	0	2		.154	.191	.185	20	-6	2			1.000	-1	O-17	-0.8
	Bos-N	43	171	13	47	3	1	0	7	7		.275	.303	.304	96	-1	7			.941	-4	O-43	-0.8
	Yr	63	236	17	57	3	2	0	7	9		.242	.272	.271	74	-7	9			.958	-5	O-60	-1.6
1909	Bos-N	152	562	60	138	15	6	6	24	47		.246	.305	.326	91	-7	21			.932	-2	*O-152	-1.6
1910	NY-N	80	126	18	36	2	4	3	24	14	25	.286	.357	.437	131	5	11			.972	-3	O-45/1-1	0.1
1911	*NY-N	88	172	28	45	11	1	1	20	26	22	.262	.359	.355	97	-0	19			.975	-5	O-55	-0.7
1912	*NY-N	125	402	66	106	18	8	6	58	54	35	.264	.354	.393	101	1	30			.958	-1	*O-117	-0.5
1913	Cin-N	30	108	11	32	5	3	0	14	6	12	.296	.333	.398	109	1	0			.971	2	O-28	0.2
	Phi-N	88	306	53	99	19	10	9	44	22	30	.324	.369	.539	151	19	11			.983	-2	O-77/1-1	1.4
	Yr	118	414	64	131	24	13	9	58	28	42	.316	.360	.502	140	20	11			.980	0	*O-105/1-1	1.6
1914	Phi-N	138	514	76	167	25	5	9	66	37	59	.325	.370	.446	133	20	16			.947	-8	*O-126	2.4
1915	*Phi-N	112	338	38	83	16	4	11	35	26	48	.246	.301	.414	114	4	12	15	-5	.943	-8	O-98	-1.4
Total	8	876	2764	367	763	114	43	45	292	241	231	.276	.335	.397	112	35	129	15		.955	-13	O-758/1-2	-1.7

■ HEINZ BECKER
Becker, Heinz Reinhard "Dutch"　b: 8/26/15, Berlin, Germany　d: 11/11/91, Dallas, Tex.　BB/TR, 6'2", 200 lbs.　Deb: 4/21/43

YEAR	TM/L	G	AB	R	H	2B	3B	HR	RBI	BB	SO	AVG	OBP	SLG	PRO+	BR/A	SB	CS	SBR	FA	FR	G/POS	TPR
1943	Chi-N	24	69	5	10	0	0	0	2	9	6	.145	.244	.145	14	-7	0			.983	1	1-18	-0.8
1945	*Chi-N	67	133	25	38	8	2	2	27	17	16	.286	.375	.421	124	4	0			1.000	-2	1-28	0.1
1946	Chi-N	9	7	0	2	0	0	0	1	1		.286	.375	.286	91	-0	0			.000	0	H	0.0
	Cle-A	50	147	15	44	10	1	0	17	23	18	.299	.401	.381	127	6	1	0	0	.995	0	1-44	0.5
1947	Cle-A	2	2	0	0	0	0	0	0	1		.000	.000	.000	-99	-1	0	0	0	.000	0	H	-0.1
Total	4	152	358	45	94	18	3	2	47	50	42	.263	.359	.346	102	1	1	0		.994	0	/1-90	-0.3

■ JOE BECKER
Becker, Joseph Edward　b: 6/25/08, St.Louis, Mo.　BR/TR, 6'1", 180 lbs.　Deb: 5/10/36　C

YEAR	TM/L	G	AB	R	H	2B	3B	HR	RBI	BB	SO	AVG	OBP	SLG	PRO+	BR/A	SB	CS	SBR	FA	FR	G/POS	TPR
1936	Cle-A	22	50	5	9	3	1	1	11	5	4	.180	.255	.340	45	-5	0	0	0	.977	-4	C-15	-0.8
1937	Cle-A	18	33	3	11	2	1	0	2	3	4	.333	.405	.455	116	1	0	0	0	.949	-1	C-12	0.1
Total	2	40	83	8	20	5	2	1	13	8	8	.241	.315	.386	73	-4	0	0	0	.964	-5	/C-27	-0.7

■ MARTY BECKER
Becker, Martin Henry　b: 12/25/1893, Tiffin, Ohio　d: 9/25/57, Cincinnati, Ohio　BB/TL, 5'8.5", 155 lbs.　Deb: 9/8/15

YEAR	TM/L	G	AB	R	H	2B	3B	HR	RBI	BB	SO	AVG	OBP	SLG	PRO+	BR/A	SB	CS	SBR	FA	FR	G/POS	TPR
1915	NY-N	17	52	5	13	2	0	0	3	2	9	.250	.278	.288	76	-2	3			.917	0	O-16	-0.1

■ RICH BECKER
Becker, Richard Godhard　b: 2/1/72, Aurora, Ill.　BB/TR, 5'10", 180 lbs.　Deb: 9/10/93

YEAR	TM/L	G	AB	R	H	2B	3B	HR	RBI	BB	SO	AVG	OBP	SLG	PRO+	BR/A	SB	CS	SBR	FA	FR	G/POS	TPR
1993	Min-A	3	7	3	2	2	0	0	0	5	4	.286	.583	.571	211	2	1	1	-0	.875	-0	/O-3	0.1
1994	Min-A	28	98	12	26	3	0	1	8	13	25	.265	.351	.327	76	-3	6	1	1	.989	5	/O-26/D-1	0.3
Total	2	31	105	15	28	5	0	1	8	18	29	.267	.374	.343	87	-1	7	2	1	.980	5	/O-29,D-1	0.4

■ GLENN BECKERT
Beckert, Glenn Alfred　b: 10/12/40, Pittsburgh, Pa.　BR/TR, 6'1", 190 lbs.　Deb: 4/12/65

YEAR	TM/L	G	AB	R	H	2B	3B	HR	RBI	BB	SO	AVG	OBP	SLG	PRO+	BR/A	SB	CS	SBR	FA	FR	G/POS	TPR
1965	Chi-N	154	614	73	147	21	3	3	30	28	52	.239	.276	.298	60	-32	6	8	-3	.973	9	*2-153	-1.3
1966	Chi-N	153	656	73	188	23	7	1	59	26	36	.287	.318	.348	84	-14	10	4	1	.970	-20	*2-152/S-1	-2.4
1967	Chi-N	146	597	91	167	32	3	5	40	30	25	.280	.314	.369	91	-8	10	3	1	.968	4	*2-144	0.8
1968	Chi-N	155	643	98	189	28	4	4	37	31	20	.294	.328	.369	102	1	8	4	0	.977	4	*2-155	1.9
1969	Chi-N★	131	543	69	158	22	1	1	37	24	24	.291	.328	.341	78	-16	6	0	2	.965	6	*2-129	0.3
1970	Chi-N★	143	591	99	170	15	6	3	36	32	22	.288	.324	.349	72	-24	4	1	1	.970	10	*2-138/O-1	-0.2
1971	Chi-N★	131	530	80	181	18	5	2	42	24	24	.342	.370	.406	104	3	2	3	-0	.986	-3	*2-129	1.1
1972	Chi-N★	120	474	51	128	22	3	2	43	23	17	.270	.307	.344	76	-15	2	1	0	.976	11	*2-118	0.3
1973	Chi-N	114	372	38	95	13	0	0	29	30	15	.255	.314	.290	64	-17	0	2	-1	.984	-12	2-88	-2.7
1974	SD-N	64	172	11	44	9	0	0	7	11	8	.256	.301	.262	61	-9	0	0	0	.938	-17	2-36/3-1	-2.6
1975	SD-N	9	16	2	6	1	0	0	0	3	0	.375	.412	.438	145	1	0	0	0	1.000	-1	/3-4	0.0
Total	11	1320	5208	685	1473	196	31	22	360	260	243	.283	.319	.345	81	-129	49	25	-0	.973	-7	*2-1242/3-5,OS	-4.8

■ JAKE BECKLEY
Beckley, Jacob Peter "Eagle Eye"　b: 8/4/1867, Hannibal, Mo.　d: 6/25/18, Kansas City, Mo.　BL/TL, 5'10", 200 lbs.　Deb: 6/20/1888　H

YEAR	TM/L	G	AB	R	H	2B	3B	HR	RBI	BB	SO	AVG	OBP	SLG	PRO+	BR/A	SB	CS	SBR	FA	FR	G/POS	TPR
1888	Pit-N	71	283	35	97	15	3	0	27	7	22	.343	.363	.417	160	18	20			.979	-3	1-71	0.9
1889	Pit-N	123	522	91	157	24	10	9	97	29		.301	.345	.437	130	19	11			.982	2	*1-122/O-1	1.1
1890	Pit-P	121	516	109	167	38	22	9	120	42	32	.324	.381	.535	156	39	24			.976	-0	*1-121	2.5
1891	Pit-N	133	554	94	162	20	19	4	73	44	46	.292	.353	.419	128	18	13			.982	13	*1-133	2.1

YEAR	TM/L	G	AB	R	H	2B	3B	HR	RBI	BB	SO	AVG	OBP	SLG	PRO+	BR/A	SB	CS	SBR	FA	FR	G/POS	TPR
1892	Pit-N	151	614	102	145	21	19	10	96	31	44	.236	.288	.381	102	-2	30			.978	21	*1-151	1.0
1893	Pit-N	131	542	108	164	32	19	5	106	54	26	.303	.386	.459	127	20	15			.986	11	*1-131	2.2
1894	Pit-N	131	533	121	183	36	18	7	120	43	16	.343	.412	.518	124	21	21			.978	5	*1-131	2.0
1895	Pit-N	129	533	104	174	31	19	5	110	24	20	.328	.381	.487	130	22	20			.978	-1	*1-129	1.5
1896	Pit-N	59	217	44	55	7	5	3	32	22	28	.253	.349	.373	94	-1	8			.982	-1	1-56/O-3,2	-0.1
	NY-N	46	182	37	55	8	4	5	38	9	7	.302	.352	.473	120	4	11			.982	-1	1-45/O-2	0.3
	Yr	105	399	81	110	15	9	8	70	31	35	.276	.351	.419	106	3	19			.982	-2	*1-101/O-5,2	0.2
1897	NY-N	17	68	8	17	2	3	1	11	2		.250	.301	.412	90	-1	2			.973	2	1-17	0.1
	Cin-N	97	365	76	126	17	9	7	76	18		.345	.395	.499	127	12	23			.979	-3	*1-97	0.8
	Yr	114	433	84	143	19	12	8	87	20		.330	.380	.485	121	11	25			.978	-1	*1-114	0.9
1898	Cin-N	118	459	86	135	20	12	4	72	28		.294	.348	.416	111	4	6			.983	-1	*1-118	0.3
1899	Cin-N	134	513	87	171	27	16	3	99	40		.333	.393	.466	133	22	20			.986	5	*1-134	2.5
1900	Cin-N	141	558	98	190	26	10	2	94	40		.341	.389	.434	130	23	23			.980	6	*1-140	2.5
1901	Cin-N	140	580	78	178	36	13	3	79	28		.307	.346	.429	133	22	4			.977	-1	*1-140	1.6
1902	Cin-N	129	531	82	175	23	7	5	69	34		.330	.377	.427	135	20	15			.983	-3	*1-129/P-1	1.5
1903	Cin-N	120	459	85	150	29	10	2	81	42		.327	.384	.447	123	12	23			.976	4	*1-119	1.3
1904	StL-N	142	551	72	179	22	9	1	67	35		.325	.375	.403	147	30	17			.988	-12	*1-142	1.6
1905	StL-N	134	514	48	147	20	10	1	57	30		.286	.333	.370	113	7	12			.982	-8	*1-134	-0.5
1906	StL-N	87	320	29	79	16	6	0	44	13		.247	.283	.334	96	-3	3			.987	-4	1-85	-1.1
1907	StL-N	32	115	6	24	3	0	0	7	1		.209	.222	.235	45	-8	0			.988	-2	1-32	-1.2
Total	20	2386	9526	1600	2930	473	243	86	1575	616	270	.308	.361	.435	125	299	315			.981	19	*1-2377/O-6,P2	22.9

■ JULIO BECQUER   Becquer, Julio (Villegas)   b: 12/20/31, Havana, Cuba   BL/TL, 5'11.5", 178 lbs.   Deb: 9/13/55

YEAR	TM/L	G	AB	R	H	2B	3B	HR	RBI	BB	SO	AVG	OBP	SLG	PRO+	BR/A	SB	CS	SBR	FA	FR	G/POS	TPR
1955	Was-A	10	14	1	3	0	0	0	1	0	1	.214	.214	.214	16	-2	0	0	0	1.000	1	/1-2	-0.1
1957	Was-A	105	186	14	42	6	2	2	22	10	29	.226	.269	.312	59	-11	3	3	-1	1.000	-0	1-43	-1.4
1958	Was-A	86	164	10	39	3	0	0	12	8	21	.238	.273	.256	47	-12	1	2	-1	.994	6	1-42/O-1	-1.0
1959	Was-A	108	220	20	59	12	5	1	26	8	17	.268	.297	.382	85	-5	3	2	0	.990	2	1-53	-0.6
1960	Was-A	110	298	41	75	15	7	4	35	12	35	.252	.283	.389	81	-9	1	3	-2	.989	-3	1-77/P-1	-1.9
1961	LA-A	11	8	0	0	0	0	0	0	1	5	.000	.111	.000	-61	-2	0	0	0	1.000	-0	/1-5	-0.2
	Min-A	57	84	13	20	1	2	5	18	2	12	.238	.256	.476	86	-2	1	1	-1	1.000	-1	1-18/O-5,P	-0.4
	Yr	68	92	13	20	1	2	5	18	3	17	.217	.242	.435	72	-4	1	1	-1	1.000	-1	1-23/O-5,P	-0.6
1963	Min-A	1	0	1	0	0	0	0	0	0	0	—	—	—	—	-0	0			.000	0	H	0.0
Total	7	488	974	100	238	37	16	12	114	41	120	.244	.277	.352	70	-42	8	11	-4	.993	5	1-240/O-6,P	-5.6

■ HOWIE BEDELL   Bedell, Howard William   b: 9/29/35, Clearfield, Pa.   BL/TR, 6'1", 185 lbs.   Deb: 4/10/62   C

YEAR	TM/L	G	AB	R	H	2B	3B	HR	RBI	BB	SO	AVG	OBP	SLG	PRO+	BR/A	SB	CS	SBR	FA	FR	G/POS	TPR
1962	Mil-N	58	138	15	27	1	2	0	2	11	22	.196	.255	.232	33	-13	1	0	0	.955	-3	O-45	-1.8
1968	Phi-N	9	7	0	1	0	0	0	1	1	0	.143	.250	.143	20	-1	0	0	0	.000	0	H	-0.1
Total	2	67	145	15	28	1	2	0	3	12	22	.193	.255	.228	32	-14	1	0	0	.955	-3	/O-45	-1.9

■ GENE BEDFORD   Bedford, William Eugene   b: 12/2/1896, Dallas, Tex.   d: 10/6/77, San Antonio, Tex.   BB/TR, 5'8", 170 lbs.   Deb: 6/25/25

YEAR	TM/L	G	AB	R	H	2B	3B	HR	RBI	BB	SO	AVG	OBP	SLG	PRO+	BR/A	SB	CS	SBR	FA	FR	G/POS	TPR
1925	Cle-A	2	3	1	0	0	0	0	0	0	1	.000	.000	.000	-99	-1	0	0	0	1.000	-1	/2-2	-0.2

■ ED BEECHER   Beecher, Edward "Scrap Iron"   b: 5/1876, Indiana   Deb: 9/26/1897

YEAR	TM/L	G	AB	R	H	2B	3B	HR	RBI	BB	SO	AVG	OBP	SLG	PRO+	BR/A	SB	CS	SBR	FA	FR	G/POS	TPR
1897	StL-N	3	12	1	4	0	0	0	1	0		.333	.333	.333	78	-0	1			1.000	-0	/O-3	-0.1
1898	Cle-N	8	25	1	5	2	0	0	0	0		.200	.200	.280	38	-2	0			.846	-2	/O-8	-0.4
Total	2	11	37	2	9	2	0	0	1	0		.243	.243	.297	51	-3	1			.895	-2	/O-11	-0.5

■ ED BEECHER   Beecher, Edward H.   b: 7/2/1860, Guilford, Conn.   d: 9/12/35, Hartford, Conn.   BL/TL, 5'10", 185 lbs.   Deb: 6/28/1887

YEAR	TM/L	G	AB	R	H	2B	3B	HR	RBI	BB	SO	AVG	OBP	SLG	PRO+	BR/A	SB	CS	SBR	FA	FR	G/POS	TPR
1887	Pit-N	41	169	15	41	8	0	2	22	7	8	.243	.281	.325	72	-6	8			.915	5	O-41	-0.2
1889	Was-N	42	179	20	53	9	0	0	30	5	4	.296	.319	.346	91	-2	3			.861	-3	O-39/1-3	-0.4
1890	Buf-P	126	536	69	159	22	10	3	90	29	23	.297	.341	.392	104	3	14			.810	-5	*O-126/P-1	-0.5
1891	Was-a	58	235	35	57	11	3	2	28	27	9	.243	.333	.340	97	-1	17			.824	3	O-58	0.1
	Phi-a	16	71	9	15	2	4	0	7	3	4	.211	.243	.352	68	-4	7			1.000	-1	O-16	-0.4
	Yr	74	306	44	72	13	7	2	35	30	13	.235	.314	.343	91	-4	24			.845	2	O-74	-0.3
Total	4	283	1190	148	325	52	17	7	177	71	48	.273	.322	.363	94	-10	49			.843	1	O-280/1-3,P	-1.4

■ JODIE BEELER   Beeler, Joseph Sam   b: 11/26/21, Dallas, Tex.   BR/TR, 6', 170 lbs.   Deb: 9/21/44

YEAR	TM/L	G	AB	R	H	2B	3B	HR	RBI	BB	SO	AVG	OBP	SLG	PRO+	BR/A	SB	CS	SBR	FA	FR	G/POS	TPR
1944	Cin-N	3	3	0	0	0	0	0	0	0	2	.000	.000	.000	-99	-1				.000	-1	/2-1,3-1	-0.2

■ GENE BEGLEY   Begley, Eugene T.   b: 6/7/1861, Brooklyn, N.Y.   Deb: 9/11/1886

YEAR	TM/L	G	AB	R	H	2B	3B	HR	RBI	BB	SO	AVG	OBP	SLG	PRO+	BR/A	SB	CS	SBR	FA	FR	G/POS	TPR
1886	NY-N	5	16	1	2	0	0	0	1	1	3	.125	.176	.125	-7	-2	1			.864	-1	/C-3,O-2	-0.2

■ JIM BEGLEY   Begley, James Lawrence "Imp"   b: 9/19/02, San Francisco, Cal.   d: 2/20/57, San Francisco, Cal   BR/TR, 5'6", 145 lbs.   Deb: 5/28/24

YEAR	TM/L	G	AB	R	H	2B	3B	HR	RBI	BB	SO	AVG	OBP	SLG	PRO+	BR/A	SB	CS	SBR	FA	FR	G/POS	TPR
1924	Cin-N	2	5	1	1	0	0	0	2	0	.200		.429	.200	75	-0	0	0	0	.933	1	/2-2	0.1

■ STEVE BEHEL   Behel, Stephen Arnold Douglas   b: 11/6/1860, Earlville, Ill.   d: 2/15/45, Los Angeles, Cal.   Deb: 9/27/1884

YEAR	TM/L	G	AB	R	H	2B	3B	HR	RBI	BB	SO	AVG	OBP	SLG	PRO+	BR/A	SB	CS	SBR	FA	FR	G/POS	TPR
1884	Mil-U	9	33	5	8	1	0	0		3		.242	.306	.273	108	-1				1.000	-1	/O-9	-0.1
1886	NY-a	59	224	32	46	5	2	0		22		.205	.279	.246	68	-7	16			.858	-4	O-59	-1.1
Total	2	68	257	37	54	6	2	0		25		.210	.283	.249	71	-8	16			.865	-5	/O-68	-1.2

■ OLLIE BEJMA   Bejma, Alojzy Frank   b: 9/12/07, South Bend, Ind.   BR/TR, 5'10", 165 lbs.   Deb: 4/24/34

YEAR	TM/L	G	AB	R	H	2B	3B	HR	RBI	BB	SO	AVG	OBP	SLG	PRO+	BR/A	SB	CS	SBR	FA	FR	G/POS	TPR
1934	StL-A	95	262	39	71	16	3	2	29	40	36	.271	.376	.378	87	-4	3	2	-0	.952	-12	S-32,2-14,3/O	-1.3
1935	StL-A	64	198	18	38	8	2	2	26	27	21	.192	.289	.283	46	-16	1	0	0	.952	-4	2-47/S-8,3	-1.5
1936	StL-A	67	139	19	36	2	3	2	18	27	21	.259	.380	.360	81	-3	0	0	0	.963	2	2-32/3-7,S	-1.2
1939	Chi-A	90	307	52	77	9	3	8	44	36	27	.251	.331	.378	79	-10	1	3	-2	.981	-14	2-81/S-1,3	-2.0
Total	4	316	906	128	222	35	11	14	117	130	105	.245	.343	.354	75	-34	5	5	-2	.967	-42	2-174/S-42,3O	-6.0

■ MARK BELANGER   Belanger, Mark Henry   b: 6/8/44, Pittsfield, Mass.   BR/TR, 6'1", 170 lbs.   Deb: 8/7/65

YEAR	TM/L	G	AB	R	H	2B	3B	HR	RBI	BB	SO	AVG	OBP	SLG	PRO+	BR/A	SB	CS	SBR	FA	FR	G/POS	TPR
1965	Bal-A	11	3	1	1	0	0	0	0	0	0	.333	.333	.333	88	-0	0	1	-1	1.000	1	/S-4	0.0
1966	Bal-A	8	19	2	3	1	0	0	0	0	3	.158	.158	.211	5	-2	0	0	0	1.000	4	/S-6	0.2
1967	Bal-A	69	184	19	32	5	0	1	10	12	46	.174	.224	.217	31	-16	6	1	1	.952	7	S-38,2-26/3	-0.4
1968	Bal-A	145	472	40	98	13	0	2	21	40	114	.208	.275	.248	59	-22	10	1	2	.969	12	*S-145	0.8
1969	*Bal-A	150	530	76	152	17	4	2	50	53	54	.287	.354	.345	95	-2	14	6	1	.968	-10	*S-148	0.5
1970	*Bal-A	145	459	53	100	6	5	1	36	52	65	.218	.304	.259	58	-26	13	2	3	.970	8	*S-143	-0.1
1971	*Bal-A	150	500	67	133	19	4	0	35	73	69	.266	.367	.320	97	1	10	8	-2	.978	-0	*S-149	2.0
1972	Bal-A	113	285	36	53	9	1	2	16	18	53	.186	.239	.246	43	-20	6	3	0	.975	21	*S-105	1.4
1973	*Bal-A	154	470	60	106	15	1	0	27	49	54	.226	.305	.262	61	-23	13	6	0	.971	3	*S-154	0.0
1974	*Bal-A	155	493	54	111	14	4	5	36	51	69	.225	.300	.300	75	-15	17	7	1	**.984**	9	*S-155	1.6
1975	Bal-A	152	442	44	100	11	1	3	27	36	53	.226	.286	.276	63	-21	16	4	2	.978	**28**	*S-152	2.5
1976	Bal-A★	153	522	66	141	22	2	1	40	51	64	.270	.337	.326	101	1	27	17	-2	.982	16	*S-153	3.6
1977	Bal-A	144	402	39	83	13	4	2	30	43	68	.206	.288	.274	58	-23	15	8	-0	**.985**	21	*S-142	1.1
1978	Bal-A	135	348	39	74	13	0	0	16	40	58	.213	.305	.250	61	-17	6	6	-2	**.985**	34	*S-134	3.0
1979	*Bal-A	101	198	28	33	6	2	0	9	29	33	.167	.276	.217	36	-17	5	1	0	.990	3	S-98	-0.6
1980	Bal-A	113	268	37	61	8	1	0	12	26	25	.228	.261	.276	48	-19	5	1	0	.975	-1	*S-109	-1.1
1981	Bal-A	64	139	9	23	3	2	1	10	12	25	.165	.242	.237	39	-11	2	1	0	.973	5	S-63	-0.2

YEAR	TM/L	G	AB	R	H	2B	3B	HR	RBI	BB	SO	AVG	OBP	SLG	PRO+	BR/A	SB	CS	SBR	FA	FR	G/POS	TPR
1982	LA-N	54	50	6	12	1	0	0	4	5	10	.240	.309	.260	62	-2	1	0	0	.953	8	S-44/2-1	0.7
Total	18	2016	5784	676	1316	175	33	20	389	576	839	.228	.302	.280	68	-234	167	75	5	.977	167	*S-1942/2-27,3	15.0

■ WAYNE BELARDI
Belardi, Carroll Wayne b: 9/5/30, St.Helena, Cal. d: 10/21/93, Santa Cruz, Cal. BL/TL, 6'1", 185 lbs. Deb: 4/18/50

YEAR	TM/L	G	AB	R	H	2B	3B	HR	RBI	BB	SO	AVG	OBP	SLG	PRO+	BR/A	SB	CS	SBR	FA	FR	G/POS	TPR
1950	Bro-N	10	10	0	0	0	0	0	0	0	4	.000	.000	.000	-98	-3	0	0	0	1.000	-0	/1-1	-0.3
1951	Bro-N	3	3	1	1	0	1	0	0	0	2	.333	.333	1.000	240	1	0	0	0	.000	0	H	0.1
1953	*Bro-N	69	163	19	39	3	2	11	34	16	40	.239	.311	.485	101	-0	0	0	0	.984	-0	1-38	-0.2
1954	Bro-N	11	9	0	2	0	0	0	1	2	3	.222	.364	.222	55	-0	0	0	0	.000	0	H	0.0
	Det-A	88	250	27	58	7	1	11	24	33	34	.232	.333	.400	102	0	1	0	0	.988	2	1-79	-0.1
1955	Det-A	3	3	0	0	0	0	0	0	0	1	.000	.000	.000	-99	-1	0	0	0	.000	0	H	0.0
1956	Det-A	79	154	24	43	3	1	6	15	15	13	.279	.373	.429	111	3	0	0	0	.988	-1	1-31/O-2	0.0
Total	6	263	592	71	143	13	5	28	74	66	97	.242	.332	.422	100	-1	1	0		.987	0	1-149/O-2	-0.6

■ KEVIN BELCHER
Belcher, Kevin Donnell b: 8/8/67, Waco, Tex. BR/TR, 6', 170 lbs. Deb: 9/3/90

YEAR	TM/L	G	AB	R	H	2B	3B	HR	RBI	BB	SO	AVG	OBP	SLG	PRO+	BR/A	SB	CS	SBR	FA	FR	G/POS	TPR
1990	Tex-A	16	15	4	2	1	0	0		2	6	.133	.235	.200	23	-2	0	0	0	1.000	-2	/O-9	-0.3

■ IRA BELDEN
Belden, Ira Allison b: 4/16/1874, Cleveland, Ohio d: 7/15/16, Lakewood, Ohio BL/TR, 5'11", 175 lbs. Deb: 9/17/1897

YEAR	TM/L	G	AB	R	H	2B	3B	HR	RBI	BB	SO	AVG	OBP	SLG	PRO+	BR/A	SB	CS	SBR	FA	FR	G/POS	TPR
1897	Cle-N	8	30	5	8	0	2	0		4	2	.267	.333	.400	88	-1	0			1.000	2	/O-8	0.0

■ CHARLIE BELL
Bell, Charles C. b: 8/12/1868, Cincinnati, Ohio d: 2/7/37, Cincinnati, Ohio TR , Deb: 10/13/1889 F

YEAR	TM/L	G	AB	R	H	2B	3B	HR	RBI	BB	SO	AVG	OBP	SLG	PRO+	BR/A	SB	CS	SBR	FA	FR	G/POS	TPR
1889	KC-a	2	6	1	1	1	0	0		3	2	.167	.375	.333	97	0	0			.000	-0	/O-1,P-1	-0.1
1891	Lou-a	10	28	3	1	0	0	0		6	8	.036	.206	.036	-31	-5	0			.783	-2	P-10	0.0
	Cin-a	1	4	1	2	0	0	0		1	0	.500	.500	.500	171	0	0			1.000	0	/P-1	0.0
Yr		11	32	4	3	0	0	0		1	6	8	.094	.237	.094	-5	-4	0			.815	-1	P-11	0.0
Total	2	13	38	5	4	1	0	0		4	8	10	.105	.261	.132	13	-4	0		.844	-1	/P-12,O-1	-0.1

■ BUDDY BELL
Bell, David Gus b: 8/27/51, Pittsburgh, Pa. BR/TR, 6'2", 185 lbs. Deb: 4/15/72 FC

YEAR	TM/L	G	AB	R	H	2B	3B	HR	RBI	BB	SO	AVG	OBP	SLG	PRO+	BR/A	SB	CS	SBR	FA	FR	G/POS	TPR
1972	Cle-A	132	466	49	119	21	1	9	36	34	29	.255	.310	.363	96	-2	5	6	-2	.990	7	*O-123/3-6	-0.3
1973	Cle-A★	156	631	86	169	23	7	14	59	49	47	.268	.327	.393	100	-1	7	15	-7	.958	24	*3-154/O-2	1.6
1974	Cle-A	116	423	51	111	15	1	7	46	35	29	.262	.323	.352	95	-3	1	3	-2	.963	4	*3-115/D-1	-0.1
1975	Cle-A	153	553	66	150	20	4	10	59	51	72	.271	.334	.376	100	0	6	5	-1	.950	-3	3-153	-0.5
1976	Cle-A	159	604	75	170	26	2	7	60	44	49	.281	.332	.366	105	4	3	8	-4	.956	5	*3-158/1-2	0.4
1977	Cle-A	129	479	64	140	23	4	11	64	45	63	.292	.354	.426	115	10	1	8	-5	.960	13	*3-118,O-11	1.6
1978	Cle-A	142	556	71	157	27	8	6	62	39	43	.282	.329	.392	103	2	1	3	-2	.970	28	*3-139/D-1	2.7
1979	Tex-A	162	670	89	200	42	3	18	101	30	45	.299	.331	.451	110	7	5	4	-1	.969	12	*3-147,S-33	2.0
1980	Tex-A★	129	490	76	161	24	4	17	83	40	39	.329	.379	.498	143	28	3	1	0	.981	22	*3-120/S-3	4.7
1981	Tex-A★	97	360	44	106	16	1	10	64	42	30	.294	.373	.428	137	18	3	3	-1	.961	30	3-96/S-1	4.6
1982	Tex-A★	148	537	62	159	27	2	13	67	70	50	.296	.379	.426	127	22	5	4	-1	.976	34	*3-145/S-4	5.1
1983	Tex-A	156	618	75	171	35	3	14	66	50	48	.277	.335	.411	106	5	3	5	-2	.967	16	*3-154	1.6
1984	Tex-A★	148	553	88	174	36	5	11	83	63	54	.315	.388	.458	129	23	2	1	0	.958	21	*3-147	4.1
1985	Tex-A	84	313	33	74	13	3	4	32	33	21	.236	.311	.335	76	-10	3	2	-0	.942	13	3-83	0.2
	Cin-N	67	247	28	54	15	2	6	36	34	27	.219	.313	.368	86	-5	0	1	-1	.946	-9	3-67	-1.6
1986	Cin-N	155	568	89	158	29	3	20	75	73	49	.278	.365	.445	117	14	2	8	-4	.975	1	*3-151/2-1	0.9
1987	Cin-N	143	522	74	148	19	2	17	70	71	39	.284	.370	.425	105	6	4	1	1	.979	-17	*3-142	-1.3
1988	Cin-N	21	54	3	10	0	0	0	3	7	3	.185	.279	.185	34	-4	0	0	0	.968	0	3-13/1-2	-0.5
	Hou-N	74	269	24	68	10	1	7	37	19	29	.253	.302	.375	97	-2	1	1	0	.924	-11	3-66/1-7	-1.6
Yr		95	323	27	78	10	1	7	40	26	32	.241	.298	.344	86	-6	1	1	0	.931	-11	3-79/1-9	-2.1
1989	Tex-A	34	82	4	15	4	0	0	3	7	10	.183	.247	.232	35	-7	0	0	0	1.000	0	D-22/3-9,1	-0.7
Total	18	2405	8995	1151	2514	425	56	201	1106	836	776	.279	.343	.406	108	105	55	79	-31	.964	191	*3-2183,O-136/SD12	22.9

■ GUS BELL
Bell, David Russell b: 11/15/28, Louisville, Ky. BL/TR, 6'2", 196 lbs. Deb: 5/30/50 F

YEAR	TM/L	G	AB	R	H	2B	3B	HR	RBI	BB	SO	AVG	OBP	SLG	PRO+	BR/A	SB	CS	SBR	FA	FR	G/POS	TPR
1950	Pit-N	111	422	62	119	22	11	8	53	28	46	.282	.330	.443	99	-2	4			.977	6	*O-104	0.0
1951	Pit-N	149	600	80	167	27	12	16	89	42	41	.278	.330	.443	103	1	1	4	-2	.986	3	*O-145	-0.3
1952	Pit-N	131	468	53	117	21	5	16	59	36	72	.250	.306	.419	97	-4	1	4	-2	.972	-7	*O-123	-1.8
1953	Cin-N★	151	610	102	183	37	5	30	105	48	72	.300	.354	.525	124	20	0	2	-1	.977	14	*O-151	2.5
1954	Cin-N	153	619	104	185	38	7	17	101	48	58	.299	.353	.465	108	9	7	5	-0	.986	2	*O-153	0.1
1955	Cin-N	154	610	89	188	30	6	27	104	54	57	.308	.364	.510	122	18	4	4	-1	.987	-8	*O-154	0.2
1956	Cin-N★	150	603	82	176	31	4	29	84	50	66	.292	.349	.501	117	14	6	2	1	.986	-7	*O-149	-0.1
1957	Cin-N	121	510	65	149	20	3	13	61	30	54	.292	.335	.420	95	-4	1	1	-1	.988	0	*O-121	-1.2
1958	Cin-N	112	385	42	97	16	2	10	46	36	40	.252	.318	.382	80	-11	2	3	-1	.996	-2	*O-107	-2.0
1959	Cin-N	148	580	59	170	27	2	19	115	29	44	.293	.329	.445	101	-0	2	3	-1	.996	7	*O-145	-0.2
1960	Cin-N	143	515	65	135	19	5	12	62	29	40	.262	.303	.388	86	-11	4	3	-1	.988	0	*O-131	-1.8
1961	*Cin-N	103	235	27	60	10	1	3	33	18	21	.255	.308	.345	72	-9	1	1	-0	.991	6	*O-71	-1.9
1962	NY-N	30	101	8	15	2	0	1	6	10	7	.149	.225	.198	14	-12	0	1	-0	.979	4	O-26	-1.1
	Mil-N	79	214	28	61	11	3	5	24	12	17	.285	.323	.435	104	1	0	0	0	.987	-3	O-58	-0.6
Yr		109	315	36	76	13	3	6	30	22	24	.241	.287	.359	74	-12	0	1	-0	.984	0	O-84	-1.7
1963	Mil-N	3	3	0	1	0	0	0	0	0	0	.333	.333	.333	94	-0	0	0	0	.000	0	H	0.0
1964	Mil-N	3	3	0	0	0	0	0	0	0	1	.000	.000	.000	-99	-1	0	0	0	.000	0	H	-0.1
Total	15	1741	6478	865	1823	311	66	206	942	470	636	.281	.333	.445	102	7	30	31		.985	0	*O-1642	-8.3

■ DEREK BELL
Bell, Derek Nathaniel b: 12/11/68, Tampa, Fla. BR/TR, 6'2", 200 lbs. Deb: 6/28/91

YEAR	TM/L	G	AB	R	H	2B	3B	HR	RBI	BB	SO	AVG	OBP	SLG	PRO+	BR/A	SB	CS	SBR	FA	FR	G/POS	TPR
1991	Tor-A	18	28	5	4	0	0	0	1	6	5	.143	.314	.143	30	-2	3	2	-0	.889	-3	O-13	-0.6
1992	*Tor-A	61	161	23	39	6	3	2	15	15	34	.242	.326	.354	86	-3	7	2	1	1.000	-1	O-56/D-1	-0.4
1993	SD-N	150	542	73	142	19	1	21	72	23	122	.262	.307	.417	90	-9	26	5	5	.976	6	*O-125,3-19	0.6
1994	SD-N	108	434	54	135	20	0	14	54	29	88	.311	.356	.454	110	6	24	8	2	.962	-0	*O-108	0.6
Total	4	337	1165	155	320	45	4	37	142	73	249	.275	.328	.415	96	-8	60	17	8	.972	2	O-302/3-19,D	-0.4

■ FERN BELL
Bell, Fernando Jerome Lee (b: Fern Oran Bell) "Danny" b: 1/21/13, Ada, Okla. BR/TR, 6', 180 lbs. Deb: 4/17/39

YEAR	TM/L	G	AB	R	H	2B	3B	HR	RBI	BB	SO	AVG	OBP	SLG	PRO+	BR/A	SB	CS	SBR	FA	FR	G/POS	TPR
1939	Pit-N	83	262	44	75	5	8	2	34	42	18	.286	.385	.389	110	5	2			.975	0	O-67/3-1	0.3
1940	Pit-N	6	3	0	0	0	0	0	1	1	1	.000	.250	.000	-26	-0	0			.000	0	H	-0.1
Total	2	89	265	44	75	5	8	2	35	43	19	.283	.383	.385	109	5	2		.975	0	/O-67,3-1	0.2

■ FRANK BELL
Bell, Frank Gustav b: 1863, Cincinnati, Ohio d: 4/14/1891, Cincinnati, Ohio 6', Deb: 7/7/1885 F

YEAR	TM/L	G	AB	R	H	2B	3B	HR	RBI	BB	SO	AVG	OBP	SLG	PRO+	BR/A	SB	CS	SBR	FA	FR	G/POS	TPR
1885	Bro-a	10	29	5	5	0	1	0		0		.172	.200	.241	39	-2				.739	-2	/C-5,O-4,3	-0.3

■ JAY BELL
Bell, Jay Stuart b: 12/11/65, Eglin A.F.B., Fla. BR/TR, 6'1", 180 lbs. Deb: 9/29/86

YEAR	TM/L	G	AB	R	H	2B	3B	HR	RBI	BB	SO	AVG	OBP	SLG	PRO+	BR/A	SB	CS	SBR	FA	FR	G/POS	TPR
1986	Cle-A	5	14	3	5	2	0	1	4	2	3	.357	.438	.714	211	2	0	0	0	.778	-0	/2-2,D-2	0.2
1987	Cle-A	38	125	14	27	9	1	2	13	8	31	.216	.269	.352	62	-7	2	0	1	.947	3	S-38	-0.1
1988	Cle-A	73	211	23	46	5	1	2	21	21	53	.218	.292	.280	59	-11	4	2	0	.965	-13	S-72/D-1	-1.9
1989	Pit-N	78	271	33	70	13	3	2	27	19	47	.258	.309	.351	91	-3	5	3	-0	.968	-15	S-78	-1.3
1990	*Pit-N	159	583	93	148	28	7	7	52	65	109	.254	.332	.362	94	-4	10	6	-1	.970	15	*S-159	0.6
1991	*Pit-N	157	608	96	164	32	8	16	67	52	99	.270	.331	.428	114	1	10	6	-1	.968	8	*S-156	3.0
1992	*Pit-N	159	632	87	167	36	9	9	55	55	103	.264	.327	.383	102	1	7	5	-1	.973	17	*S-159	3.0
1993	Pit-N★	154	604	102	187	32	9	9	51	77	122	.310	.393	.437	122	22	16	10	-1	.986	26	*S-154	5.7

YEAR	TM/L	G	AB	R	H	2B	3B	HR	RBI	BB	SO	AVG	OBP	SLG	PRO+	BR/A	SB	CS	SBR	FA	FR	G/POS	TPR
1994	Pit-N	110	424	68	117	35	4	9	45	49	82	.276	.355	.441	106	4	2	0	1	.973	19	*S-110	3.2
Total	9	933	3472	519	931	192	39	57	335	348	649	.268	.339	.395	102	13	56	32	-2	.972	42	S-926/D-3,2	12.4

■ RUDY BELL
Bell, John (b: Rudolph Fred Baerwald) b: 1/1/1881, Wausau, Wis. d: 7/28/55, Albuquerque, N.Mex. BR/TR, 5'8.5", 158 lbs. Deb: 9/16/07

YEAR	TM/L	G	AB	R	H	2B	3B	HR	RBI	BB	SO	AVG	OBP	SLG	PRO+	BR/A	SB	CS	SBR	FA	FR	G/POS	TPR
1907	NY-A	17	52	4	11	2	1	0	3	3		.212	.268	.288	72	-2	4			.897	-1	O-17	-0.3

■ GEORGE BELL
Bell, Jorge Antonio (Mathey) b: 10/21/59, San Pedro De Macoris, D.R. BR/TR, 6'1", 190 lbs. Deb: 4/9/81 F

YEAR	TM/L	G	AB	R	H	2B	3B	HR	RBI	BB	SO	AVG	OBP	SLG	PRO+	BR/A	SB	CS	SBR	FA	FR	G/POS	TPR
1981	Tor-A	60	163	19	38	2	1	5	12	5	27	.233	.256	.350	69	-7	3	2	-0	.969	1	O-44/D-8	-0.8
1983	Tor-A	39	112	5	30	5	4	2	17	4	17	.268	.305	.438	96	-1	1	1	-0	.954	-2	O-34/D-2	-0.4
1984	Tor-A	159	606	85	177	39	4	26	87	24	86	.292	.328	.498	121	15	11	2	1	.971	-1	*O-147/3-3,D	1.1
1985	*Tor-A	157	607	87	167	28	6	28	95	43	90	.275	.331	.479	116	12	21	6	3	.968	8	*O-157/3-2	1.7
1986	Tor-A	159	641	101	198	38	6	31	108	41	62	.309	.352	.532	133	27	7	8	-3	.966	7	*O-147,D-11/3	2.5
1987	Tor-A★	156	610	111	188	32	4	47	134	39	75	.308	.357	.605	146	37	5	1	1	.960	-8	*O-148/2-1,3D	3.2
1988	Tor-A	156	614	78	165	27	5	24	97	34	66	.269	.308	.446	108	4	4	2	0	.946	-7	*O-149/D-7	-0.8
1989	*Tor-A	153	613	88	182	41	2	18	104	33	60	.297	.337	.458	124	18	4	3	-1	.963	-4	*O-134,D-19	0.9
1990	Tor-A★	142	562	67	149	25	0	21	86	32	80	.265	.308	.422	100	-1	3	2	-0	.979	4	*O-106,D-36	-0.2
1991	Chi-N★	149	558	63	159	27	0	25	86	32	62	.285	.328	.468	116	10	2	6	-3	.962	-5	*O-146	-0.1
1992	Chi-A	155	627	74	160	27	0	25	112	31	97	.255	.297	.418	99	-3	5	2	-0	.964	-2	*D-140,O-15	-1.0
1993	Chi-A	102	410	36	89	17	2	13	64	13	64	.217	.248	.363	64	-23	1	1	-0	.000	-0	*D-102	-2.7
Total	12	1587	6123	814	1702	308	34	265	1002	331	771	.278	.320	.469	113	88	67	36	-2	.964	-0	*O-1227,D-339/32	3.4

■ JUAN BELL
Bell, Juan (Mathey) b: 3/29/68, San Pedro De Macoris, D.R. BR/TR, 5'11", 172 lbs. Deb: 9/6/89 F

YEAR	TM/L	G	AB	R	H	2B	3B	HR	RBI	BB	SO	AVG	OBP	SLG	PRO+	BR/A	SB	CS	SBR	FA	FR	G/POS	TPR
1989	Bal-A	8	4	2	0	0	0	0	0	0	1	.000	.000	.000	-99	-1	1	0	0	1.000	2	/2-2,S-2,D	0.1
1990	Bal-A	5	2	1	0	0	0	0	0	0	1	.000	.000	.000	-99	-1	0	0	0	1.000	0	/S-1,D-1	0.0
1991	Bal-A	100	209	26	36	9	2	1	15	8	51	.172	.203	.249	25	-22	0	0	0	.973	-1	2-77,S-15/OD	-2.1
1992	Phi-N	46	147	12	30	3	1	1	8	18	29	.204	.295	.259	58	-8	5	0	2	.972	4	S-46	0.1
1993	Phi-N	24	65	5	13	6	1	0	7	5	12	.200	.268	.323	58	-4	0	1	-1	.909	3	S-22	-0.1
	Mil-A	91	286	42	67	6	2	5	29	36	64	.234	.322	.322	75	-10	6	6	-2	.983	2	2-47,S-40/OD	-0.5
1994	Mon-N	38	97	12	27	4	0	2	10	15	21	.278	.375	.381	96	-0	4	0	1	.991	-2	2-25/3-3,S	0.0
Total	6	312	810	100	173	28	6	9	69	82	179	.214	.288	.296	60	-45	16	7	1	.980	9	2-151,S-127/DO3	-2.5

■ KEVIN BELL
Bell, Kevin Robert b: 7/13/55, Los Angeles, Cal. BR/TR, 6', 195 lbs. Deb: 6/16/76

YEAR	TM/L	G	AB	R	H	2B	3B	HR	RBI	BB	SO	AVG	OBP	SLG	PRO+	BR/A	SB	CS	SBR	FA	FR	G/POS	TPR
1976	Chi-A	68	230	24	57	7	6	5	20	18	56	.248	.305	.396	104	0	2	1	-0	.970	3	3-67/D-1	0.3
1977	Chi-A	9	28	4	5	1	0	1	6	3	8	.179	.258	.321	57	-2	0	0	-0	.909	0	/S-5,3-4,O	-0.1
1978	Chi-A	54	68	9	13	0	0	2	5	5	19	.191	.257	.279	50	-5	1	0	-0	.946	11	3-52/D-1	0.7
1979	Chi-A	70	200	20	49	8	1	4	22	15	43	.245	.298	.355	75	-7	2	4	-2	.923	12	3-68/S-2	0.3
1980	Chi-A	92	191	16	34	5	2	1	11	29	37	.178	.286	.241	46	-14	0	0	-0	.925	7	3-83/S-3,D	-0.8
1982	Oak-A	4	9	1	3	1	0	0	0	0	2	.333	.333	.444	117	0	0	0	-0	.857	0	/3-3,D-1	0.0
Total	6	297	726	74	161	22	9	13	64	70	165	.222	.292	.331	73	-26	5	5	-2	.940	33	3-277/S-10,DO	0.4

■ LES BELL
Bell, Lester Rowland b: 12/14/01, Harrisburg, Pa. d: 12/26/85, Hershey, Pa. BR/TR, 5'11", 165 lbs. Deb: 9/18/23

YEAR	TM/L	G	AB	R	H	2B	3B	HR	RBI	BB	SO	AVG	OBP	SLG	PRO+	BR/A	SB	CS	SBR	FA	FR	G/POS	TPR
1923	StL-N	15	51	5	19	2	1	0	9	9	7	.373	.467	.451	146	4	1	0	0	.917	-1	S-15	0.4
1924	StL-N	17	57	5	14	3	2	1	5	3	7	.246	.295	.421	91	-1	0	0	0	.905	-4	S-17	-0.3
1925	StL-N	153	586	80	167	29	9	11	88	43	47	.285	.334	.422	89	-10	4	5	-2	.924	-1	*3-153/S-1	-0.2
1926	*StL-N	155	581	85	189	33	14	17	100	54	62	.325	.383	.518	135	27	9			.950	-22	*3-155	1.5
1927	StL-N	115	390	48	101	26	6	9	65	34	63	.259	.320	.426	95	-4	5			.904	-14	*3-100,S-10	-1.3
1928	Bos-N	153	591	58	164	36	7	10	91	40	45	.277	.323	.413	96	-6	1			.948	5	*3-153	0.8
1929	Bos-N	139	483	58	144	23	5	9	72	50	42	.298	.364	.422	98	-1	4			.953	-20	*3-127/2-1,S	-1.5
1930	Chi-N	74	248	35	69	15	4	5	47	24	27	.278	.342	.431	85	-6	1			.948	-0	3-70/1-2	-0.3
1931	Chi-N	75	252	30	71	17	1	4	32	19	22	.282	.332	.405	95	-2	0			.944	4	3-70	0.6
Total	9	896	3239	404	938	184	49	66	509	276	322	.290	.346	.438	102	1	25	5		.939	-53	3-828/S-44,12	-0.3

■ MIKE BELL
Bell, Michael Allen b: 4/22/68, Lewiston, N.J. BL/TL, 6'1", 175 lbs. Deb: 5/2/90

YEAR	TM/L	G	AB	R	H	2B	3B	HR	RBI	BB	SO	AVG	OBP	SLG	PRO+	BR/A	SB	CS	SBR	FA	FR	G/POS	TPR
1990	Atl-N	36	45	8	11	5	1	1	5	2	9	.244	.292	.467	99	-0	0	1	-1	.981	1	1-24	-0.1
1991	Atl-N	17	30	4	4	0	0	1	2	7		.133	.188	.233	17	-3	1	0	-0	.975	0	1-14	-0.4
Total	2	53	75	12	15	5	1	2	6	4	16	.200	.250	.373	67	-4	1	1	-0	.979	1	/1-38	-0.5

■ BEAU BELL
Bell, Roy Chester b: 8/20/07, Bellville, Tex. d: 9/14/77, College Station, Tex. BR/TR, 6'2", 185 lbs. Deb: 4/16/35

YEAR	TM/L	G	AB	R	H	2B	3B	HR	RBI	BB	SO	AVG	OBP	SLG	PRO+	BR/A	SB	CS	SBR	FA	FR	G/POS	TPR
1935	StL-A	76	220	20	55	8	2	3	17	16	16	.250	.304	.345	65	-12	1	1	-0	.918	-5	O-37,1-15/3	-1.9
1936	StL-A	155	616	100	212	40	12	11	123	60	55	.344	.403	.502	119	18	4	1	1	.974	-2	*O-142,1-17	0.8
1937	StL-A☆	156	642	82	218	51	8	14	117	53	54	.340	.391	.509	124	23	2	2	-1	.984	3	*O-131,1-26/3	1.6
1938	StL-A	147	526	91	138	35	3	13	84	71	46	.262	.350	.414	91	-8	1	3	-2	.979	4	*O-132/1-4	-0.9
1939	StL-A	11	32	4	7	0	1	0	5	4	3	.219	.324	.344	69	-1	0	0	-1	1.000	-0	/O-9	-0.2
	Det-A	54	134	14	32	4	2	0	24	24	16	.239	.358	.299	65	-7	0	1	-1	1.000	1	O-37	-0.7
	Yr	65	166	18	39	5	2	1	29	28	19	.235	.352	.307	66	-8	0	1	-1	1.000	1	O-46	-0.9
1940	Cle-A	120	444	55	124	22	2	4	58	34	41	.279	.332	.365	83	-11	0	2	-1	.971	-2	O-97,1-14	-1.9
1941	Cle-A	48	104	12	20	4	3	0	9	10	8	.192	.270	.288	50	-8	1	2	-1	1.000	-3	O-14,1-10	-1.3
Total	7	767	2718	378	806	165	32	46	437	272	239	.297	.362	.432	99	-6	11	12	-4	.976	-5	O-599/1-86,3	-4.5

■ TERRY BELL
Bell, Terence William b: 10/27/62, Dayton, Ohio BR/TR, 6', 195 lbs. Deb: 9/3/86

YEAR	TM/L	G	AB	R	H	2B	3B	HR	RBI	BB	SO	AVG	OBP	SLG	PRO+	BR/A	SB	CS	SBR	FA	FR	G/POS	TPR
1986	KC-A	8	3	0	0	0	0	0	0	2	1	.000	.400	.000	20	-0	0	0	0	1.000	-0	/C-8	0.0
1987	Atl-N	1	1	0	0	0	0	0	0	0	1	.000	.000	.000	-95	-0	0	0	0	.000	0	/H	0.0
Total	2	9	4	0	0	0	0	0	0	2	2	.000	.333	.000	-0	-0	0	0	0	1.000	-0	/C-8	0.0

■ ZEKE BELLA
Bella, John b: 8/23/30, Greenwich, Conn. BR/TL, 5'11", 185 lbs. Deb: 9/11/57

YEAR	TM/L	G	AB	R	H	2B	3B	HR	RBI	BB	SO	AVG	OBP	SLG	PRO+	BR/A	SB	CS	SBR	FA	FR	G/POS	TPR
1957	NY-A	5	10	0	1	0	0	0	0	1	2	.100	.182	.100	-21	-2	0	0	0	1.000	1	/O-4	-0.1
1959	KC-A	47	82	10	17	2	1	1	9	9	14	.207	.293	.293	60	-4	0	0	0	1.000	-3	O-25/1-1	-0.9
Total	2	52	92	10	18	2	1	1	9	10	16	.196	.282	.272	52	-6	0	0	0	1.000	-3	/O-29,1-1	-1.0

■ STEVE BELLAN
Bellan, Esteban Enrique b: 1850, Cuba d: 8/8/32, Havana, Cuba 5'6", 154 lbs. Deb: 5/9/1871

YEAR	TM/L	G	AB	R	H	2B	3B	HR	RBI	BB	SO	AVG	OBP	SLG	PRO+	BR/A	SB	CS	SBR	FA	FR	G/POS	TPR
1871	Tro-n	29	128	26	32	3	3	0	23	9	2	.250	.299	.320	77	-4	4					*3-28/S-1	-0.4
1872	Tro-n	23	118	22	30	4	1	0	16	0		.254	.254	.305	70	-4						/S-9,3-8,O	-0.3
1873	Mut-n	8	32	4	7	2	0	0	3	2	0	.219	.265	.281	61	-1						/3-7,2-3	-0.1
Total	3 n	60	278	52	69	9	4	0	42	11	2	.248	.277	.309	73	-9						/3-43,S-10,O2	-0.8

■ ALBERT BELLE
Belle, Albert Jojuan "Joey" b: 8/25/66, Shreveport, La. BR/TR, 6'1", 190 lbs. Deb: 7/15/89

YEAR	TM/L	G	AB	R	H	2B	3B	HR	RBI	BB	SO	AVG	OBP	SLG	PRO+	BR/A	SB	CS	SBR	FA	FR	G/POS	TPR
1989	Cle-A	62	218	22	49	8	4	7	37	12	55	.225	.272	.394	84	-5	2	2	-1	.979	1	O-44,D-17	-0.7
1990	Cle-A	9	23	1	4	0	0	1	3	1	6	.174	.208	.304	42	-2	0	0	0	.000	-0	/O-1,D-6	-0.2
1991	Cle-A	123	461	60	130	31	2	28	95	25	99	.282	.326	.540	134	19	3	1	0	.952	3	O-89,D-32	1.9
1992	Cle-A	153	585	81	152	23	1	34	112	52	128	.260	.324	.477	124	16	8	2	1	.969	-4	*D-100,O-52	1.0
1993	Cle-A★	159	594	93	172	36	3	38	129	76	96	.290	.378	.552	147	39	23	12	-0	.986	19	*O-150/D-9	5.2
1994	Cle-A★	106	412	90	147	35	2	36	101	58	71	.357	.442	.714	183	51	9	6	-1	.973	3	*O-104/D-2	4.6
Total	6	612	2293	347	654	133	12	144	477	224	455	.285	.355	.542	140	117	45	23	-0	.974	22	O-440,D-166	11.8

■ RAFAEL BELLIARD
Belliard, Rafael Leonidas (Matias) b: 10/24/61, Pueblo Nuevo, D.R. BR/TR, 5'6", 160 lbs. Deb: 9/6/82

YEAR	TM/L	G	AB	R	H	2B	3B	HR	RBI	BB	SO	AVG	OBP	SLG	PRO+	BR/A	SB	CS	SBR	FA	FR	G/POS	TPR
1982	Pit-N	9	2	3	1	0	0	0	0	0	0	.500	.500	.500	175	0	1	0	0	1.000	1	/S-4	0.2

YEAR	TM/L	G	AB	R	H	2B	3B	HR	RBI	BB	SO	AVG	OBP	SLG	PRO+	BR/A	SB	CS	SBR	FA	FR	G/POS	TPR
1983	Pit-N	4	1	1	0	0	0	0	0	0	1	.000	.000	.000	-98	-0	0	0	0	1.000	1	/S-3	0.1
1984	Pit-N	20	22	3	5	0	0	0	0	0	1	.227	.227	.227	28	-2	4	1	1	.889	1	S-12/2-1	0.0
1985	Pit-N	17	20	1	4	0	0	0	1	0	5	.200	.200	.200	12	-2	0	0	0	.947	6	S-12	0.4
1986	Pit-N	117	309	33	72	5	2	0	31	26	54	.233	.299	.262	55	-18	12	2	2	.970	13	S-96,2-23	0.5
1987	Pit-N	81	203	26	42	4	3	1	15	20	25	.207	.288	.271	49	-15	5	1	1	.979	6	S-71/2-7	-0.3
1988	Pit-N	122	286	28	61	0	4	0	11	26	47	.213	.288	.241	54	-16	7	1	2	**.977**	-12	*S-117/2-3	-2.0
1989	Pit-N	67	154	10	33	4	0	0	8	8	22	.214	.253	.240	43	-11	5	2	0	.978	7	S-40,2-20/3	-0.2
1990	Pit-N	47	54	10	11	3	0	0	6	5	13	.204	.283	.259	52	-3	1	2	-1	1.000	5	2-21,S-10/3	0.1
1991	*Atl-N	149	353	36	88	9	2	0	27	22	63	.249	.296	.286	61	-18	3	1	0	.967	26	*S-145	1.7
1992	*Atl-N	144	285	20	60	6	1	0	14	14	43	.211	.255	.239	38	-23	0	1	-1	.969	**27**	*S-139/2-1	1.0
1993	*Atl-N	91	79	6	18	5	0	0	6	4	13	.228	.291	.291	56	-5	0	0	0	1.000	20	S-58,2-24	1.6
1994	Atl-N	46	120	9	29	7	1	0	9	2	29	.242	.266	.317	51	-9	0	2	-1	.984	-5	S-26,2-18	-1.3
Total	13	914	1888	186	424	43	13	1	128	127	316	.225	.281	.263	51	-123	38	13	4	.972	96	S-733,2-118/3	1.8

■ JACK BELLMAN
Bellman, John Hutchins "Happy Jack" b: 3/4/1864, Taylorsville, Ky. d: 12/8/31, Louisville, Ky. Deb: 4/23/1889

YEAR	TM/L	G	AB	R	H	2B	3B	HR	RBI	BB	SO	AVG	OBP	SLG	PRO+	BR/A	SB	CS	SBR	FA	FR	G/POS	TPR
1889	StL-a	1	2	1	1	0	0	0	0	0	1	.500	.667	.500	207	0	0			1.000	-0	/C-1	0.0

■ ROB BELLOIR
Belloir, Robert Edward b: 7/13/48, Heidelberg, Ger. BR/TR, 5'10", 155 lbs. Deb: 8/2/75

YEAR	TM/L	G	AB	R	H	2B	3B	HR	RBI	BB	SO	AVG	OBP	SLG	PRO+	BR/A	SB	CS	SBR	FA	FR	G/POS	TPR
1975	Atl-N	43	105	11	23	2	1	0	9	7	8	.219	.268	.257	45	-8	0	0	0	.922	-2	S-38/2-1	-0.7
1976	Atl-N	30	60	5	12	2	0	0	4	5	7	.200	.262	.233	39	-5	0	0	0	.929	-1	S-12,3-10/2	-0.5
1977	Atl-N	6	1	2	0	0	0	0	0	0	0	.000	.000	.000	-89	-0	0	0	0	1.000	1	/S-3	0.1
1978	Atl-N	2	1	0	1	1	0	0	0	0	0	1.000	1.000	2.000	647	1	0	0	0	1.000	-0	/S-1,3-1	0.1
Total	4	81	167	18	36	5	1	0	13	12	15	.216	.268	.257	45	-12	0	0	0	.924	-3	/S-54,3-11,2	-1.0

■ ESTEBAN BELTRE
Beltre, Esteban (Valera) b: 12/26/67, Ingenio Quisqueya, D.R. BR/TR, 5'10", 155 lbs. Deb: 9/3/91

YEAR	TM/L	G	AB	R	H	2B	3B	HR	RBI	BB	SO	AVG	OBP	SLG	PRO+	BR/A	SB	CS	SBR	FA	FR	G/POS	TPR
1991	Chi-A	8	6	0	1	0	0	0	0	0	1	.167	.286	.167	29	-1	1	0	0	1.000	-1	/S-8	-0.1
1992	Chi-A	49	110	21	21	2	0	1	10	3	18	.191	.212	.236	26	-11	1	0	0	.924	-1	S-43/D-4	-0.9
1994	Tex-A	48	131	12	37	5	0	0	12	16	25	.282	.361	.321	83	-3	2	5	-2	.961	8	S-41/3-5,2	0.5
Total	3	105	247	33	59	7	0	1	22	20	44	.239	.296	.279	57	-14	4	5	-2	.945	7	/S-92,3-5,D2	-0.5

■ HARRY BEMIS
Bemis, Harry Parker b: 2/1/1874, Farmington, N.H. d: 5/23/47, Cleveland, Ohio BR/TR, 5'6.5", 155 lbs. Deb: 4/23/02

YEAR	TM/L	G	AB	R	H	2B	3B	HR	RBI	BB	SO	AVG	OBP	SLG	PRO+	BR/A	SB	CS	SBR	FA	FR	G/POS	TPR
1902	Cle-A	93	317	42	99	12	7	1	29	19		.312	.366	.404	118	8	3			.964	7	C-87/O-2,2	2.2
1903	Cle-A	92	314	31	82	20	3	1	41	8		.261	.295	.354	96	-2	5			**.988**	-7	C-74,1-10/2	-0.2
1904	Cle-A	97	336	35	76	11	6	0	25	8		.226	.259	.295	76	-10	6			.958	-3	C-79,1-13/2	-0.4
1905	Cle-A	70	226	27	66	13	3	0	28	13		.292	.344	.376	127	7	3			.972	-5	C-58/2-4,31	0.9
1906	Cle-A	93	297	28	82	13	5	2	30	12		.276	.311	.374	116	4	8			.963	-9	C-81	0.3
1907	Cle-A	65	172	12	43	7	0	0	19	7		.250	.283	.291	82	-4	5			.957	-7	C-51/1-2	-0.8
1908	Cle-A	91	277	23	62	9	1	0	33	7		.224	.253	.264	68	-10	14			.964	-6	C-76/1-2	-1.1
1909	Cle-A	42	123	4	23	2	0	0	13	0		.187	.194	.252	39	-9	2			.971	-0	C-36	-0.7
1910	Cle-A	61	167	12	36	5	1	1	16	5		.216	.238	.275	60	-8	3			.961	-4	C-46	-0.9
Total	9	704	2229	214	569	92	29	5	234	79		.255	.292	.329	92	-24	49			.966	-36	C-588/1-28,230	-0.7

■ FREDDIE BENAVIDES
Benavides, Alfredo b: 4/7/66, Laredo, Tex. BR/TR, 6'2", 180 lbs. Deb: 5/14/91

YEAR	TM/L	G	AB	R	H	2B	3B	HR	RBI	BB	SO	AVG	OBP	SLG	PRO+	BR/A	SB	CS	SBR	FA	FR	G/POS	TPR
1991	Cin-N	24	63	11	18	1	0	0	3	1	15	.286	.308	.302	69	-3	1	0	0	.974	3	S-20/2-3	0.2
1992	Cin-N	74	173	14	40	10	1	1	17	10	34	.231	.277	.318	66	-8	1	0	-1	1.000	4	2-37,S-34/3	-0.3
1993	Col-N	74	213	20	61	10	3	3	26	6	27	.286	.306	.404	76	-8	3	2	-0	.937	3	S-48,2-19/31	-0.7
1994	Mon-N	47	85	8	16	5	1	0	6	3	15	.188	.225	.271	28	-9	0	0	0	.976	-5	2-36/3-5,1S	-1.3
Total	4	219	534	53	135	26	5	4	52	20	91	.253	.284	.343	65	-27	4	3	-1	.948	-0	S-105/2-95,31	-2.1

■ JOHNNY BENCH
Bench, Johnny Lee b: 12/7/47, Oklahoma City, Okla. BR/TR, 6'1", 208 lbs. Deb: 8/28/67 H

YEAR	TM/L	G	AB	R	H	2B	3B	HR	RBI	BB	SO	AVG	OBP	SLG	PRO+	BR/A	SB	CS	SBR	FA	FR	G/POS	TPR
1967	Cin-N	26	86	7	14	3	1	1	6	5	19	.163	.209	.256	29	-8	0	1	-1	.995	5	C-26	-0.2
1968	Cin-N★	154	564	67	155	40	2	15	82	31	96	.275	.315	.433	115	9	1	5	-3	.991	7	*C-154	2.6
1969	Cin-N★	148	532	83	156	23	1	26	90	49	86	.293	.357	.487	128	19	6	6	-2	.992	-3	*C-147	2.3
1970	*Cin-N★	158	605	97	177	35	4	**45**	**148**	54	102	.293	.351	.587	146	35	5	2	0	.986	4	*C-139,O-24,1/3	4.5
1971	Cin-N★	149	562	80	134	19	2	27	61	49	83	.238	.300	.423	105	1	2	1	0	.988	-4	*C-141,1-12,O/3	0.3
1972	*Cin-N★	147	538	87	145	22	2	**40**	**125**	100	84	.270	.386	.541	171	51	6	6	-2	.992	-5	*C-129,O-17/13	5.1
1973	*Cin-N★	152	557	83	141	17	3	25	104	83	83	.253	.350	.429	121	16	4	1	1	.995	-3	*C-134,O-23/13	1.9
1974	Cin-N★	160	621	108	174	38	2	33	**129**	80	90	.280	.365	.507	144	35	5	4	-1	.993	-5	*C-137,3-36/1	3.6
1975	*Cin-N★	142	530	83	150	39	1	28	110	65	108	.283	.363	.519	140	27	11	0	3	.989	3	*C-121,O-19/1	3.9
1976	*Cin-N★	135	465	62	109	24	1	16	74	81	95	.234	.350	.394	108	7	13	2	3	**.997**	-3	*C-128/O-5,1	1.0
1977	Cin-N★	142	494	67	136	34	2	31	109	58	95	.275	.353	.540	133	22	2	4	-2	.987	-13	*C-135/O-8,13	1.1
1978	Cin-N†	120	393	52	102	17	1	23	73	50	83	.260	.345	.483	129	14	4	2	0	.989	-9	*C-107,1-11/O	0.8
1979	*Cin-N†	130	464	73	128	19	0	22	80	67	73	.276	.367	.459	123	16	4	2	0	.986	-7	*C-126/1-2	1.4
1980	Cin-N★	114	360	52	90	12	0	24	68	41	64	.250	.330	.483	124	11	4	2	0	.991	-17	*C-105	-0.3
1981	Cin-N	52	178	14	55	8	0	8	25	17	21	.309	.369	.489	139	9	0	2	-1	.983	-2	1-38/C-7	0.4
1982	Cin-N	119	399	44	103	16	0	13	38	37	58	.258	.321	.396	98	-2	1	2	-1	.917	-17	*3-107/1-8,C	-2.4
1983	Cin-N★	110	310	32	79	15	2	12	54	24	38	.255	.308	.432	100	-1	0	1	-1	.933	-12	3-42,1-32/CO	-1.7
Total	17	2158	7658	1091	2048	381	24	389	1376	891	1278	.267	.345	.476	127	261	68	43	-5	.990	-80	*C-1742,3-195,10	24.3

■ ART BENEDICT
Benedict, Arthur Melville b: 3/31/1862, Cornwall, Ill. d: 1/20/48, Denver, Colo. BR/TR, Deb: 5/14/1883

YEAR	TM/L	G	AB	R	H	2B	3B	HR	RBI	BB	SO	AVG	OBP	SLG	PRO+	BR/A	SB	CS	SBR	FA	FR	G/POS	TPR
1883	Phi-N	3	15	3	4	1	0	0	4	0	4	.267	.267	.333	89	-0				.571	-5	/2-3	-0.4

■ BRUCE BENEDICT
Benedict, Bruce Edwin b: 8/18/55, Birmingham, Ala. BR/TR, 6'1", 190 lbs. Deb: 8/18/78

YEAR	TM/L	G	AB	R	H	2B	3B	HR	RBI	BB	SO	AVG	OBP	SLG	PRO+	BR/A	SB	CS	SBR	FA	FR	G/POS	TPR
1978	Atl-N	22	52	3	13	2	0	0	1	6	6	.250	.328	.288	66	-2	0	0	0	.990	2	C-22	0.0
1979	Atl-N	76	204	14	46	11	0	0	15	33	18	.225	.333	.279	64	-9	1	3	-2	.984	4	C-76	-0.8
1980	Atl-N	120	359	18	91	14	1	2	34	28	36	.253	.309	.315	72	-13	3	3	-1	.988	3	*C-120	-0.7
1981	Atl-N★	90	295	26	78	12	1	5	35	33	21	.264	.344	.363	98	-0	1	1	-0	.986	6	C-90	1.0
1982	*Atl-N	118	386	34	95	11	1	3	44	37	40	.246	.317	.303	71	-14	4	4	-1	**.993**	2	*C-118	-0.9
1983	Atl-N★	134	423	43	126	13	1	2	43	61	24	.298	.388	.348	98	2	1	3	-2	.992	9	*C-134	1.5
1984	Atl-N	95	300	26	67	8	1	4	25	34	25	.223	.304	.297	65	-13	1	2	-1	.991	1	C-95	-1.0
1985	Atl-N	70	208	12	42	6	0	0	20	22	12	.202	.281	.231	42	-16	1	1	-0	.989	-2	C-70	-1.6
1986	Atl-N	64	160	11	36	10	1	0	13	15	10	.225	.299	.300	68	-7	1	1	-1	.993	-3	C-57	-0.8
1987	Atl-N	37	95	4	14	1	0	0	5	17	15	.147	.277	.189	25	-10	0	1	-1	.989	4	C-35	-0.5
1988	Atl-N	90	236	11	57	7	0	0	19	19	26	.242	.298	.271	61	-11	0	2	-1	.989	8	C-89	0.0
1989	Atl-N	66	160	12	31	3	0	1	6	23	18	.194	.299	.231	52	-9	0	0	0	.995	16	C-65	1.0
Total	12	982	2878	214	696	98	6	18	260	328	251	.242	.322	.299	71	-104	12	20	-8	.990	47	C-971	-2.8

■ JOE BENES
Benes, Joseph Anthony "Bananas" b: 1/8/01, Long Island City, N.Y. d: 3/7/75, Elmhurst, N.Y. BR/TR, 5'8.5", 158 lbs. Deb: 5/9/31

YEAR	TM/L	G	AB	R	H	2B	3B	HR	RBI	BB	SO	AVG	OBP	SLG	PRO+	BR/A	SB	CS	SBR	FA	FR	G/POS	TPR
1931	StL-N	10	12	1	2	0	0	0	0	2	1	.167	.333	.167	37	-1	0			1.000	1	/S-6,2-2,3	0.0

■ BENNY BENGOUGH
Bengough, Bernard Oliver b: 7/27/1898, Niagara Falls, N.Y. d: 12/22/68, Philadelphia, Pa. BR/TR, 5'7.5", 168 lbs. Deb: 5/18/23 C

YEAR	TM/L	G	AB	R	H	2B	3B	HR	RBI	BB	SO	AVG	OBP	SLG	PRO+	BR/A	SB	CS	SBR	FA	FR	G/POS	TPR
1923	NY-A	19	53	1	7	2	0	0	3	4	2	.132	.193	.170	-4	-8	0	0	0	.973	1	C-19	-0.7
1924	NY-A	11	16	4	5	1	1	0	3	2	0	.313	.389	.500	128	1	0	0	0	1.000	3	C-11	0.4
1925	NY-A	95	283	17	73	14	2	0	23	19	9	.258	.305	.322	60	-18	0	2	-1	**.993**	6	C-94	-0.8
1926	NY-A	36	84	9	32	2	0	0	14	7	4	.381	.435	.452	134	4	1	0	0	.973	8	C-35	1.4

YEAR	TM/L	G	AB	R	H	2B	3B	HR	RBI	BB	SO	AVG	OBP	SLG	PRO+	BR/A	SB	CS	SBR	FA	FR	G/POS	TPR
1927	*NY-A	31	85	6	21	3	3	0	10	4	4	.247	.281	.353	66	-5	0	3	-2	.986	12	C-30	0.6
1928	*NY-A	58	161	12	43	3	1	0	9	7	8	.267	.302	.298	60	-9	0	0	0	.992	6	C-58	0.1
1929	NY-A	23	62	5	12	2	1	0	7	0	2	.194	.194	.258	16	-8	0	0	0	.982	-5	C-23	-1.1
1930	NY-A	44	102	10	24	4	2	0	12	3	8	.235	.257	.314	46	-9	1	0	0	.990	9	C-44	0.3
1931	StL-A	40	140	6	35	4	1	0	12	4	4	.250	.271	.293	46	-11	0	3	-2	.986	-1	C-37	-1.1
1932	StL-A	54	139	13	35	7	1	0	15	12	4	.252	.311	.317	60	-8	1	1	-1	.989	6	C-47	0.0
Total	10	411	1125	83	287	46	12	0	108	62	45	.255	.295	.317	59	-70	2	9	-5	.988	45	C-398	-0.9

■ JUAN BENIQUEZ
Beniquez, Juan Jose (Torres)   b: 5/13/50, San Sebastian, P.R.   BR/TR, 5'11", 165 lbs.   Deb: 9/4/71

YEAR	TM/L	G	AB	R	H	2B	3B	HR	RBI	BB	SO	AVG	OBP	SLG	PRO+	BR/A	SB	CS	SBR	FA	FR	G/POS	TPR
1971	Bos-A	16	57	8	17	2	0	0	4	3	4	.298	.333	.333	83	-1	3	1	0	.895	-8	S-15	-0.7
1972	Bos-A	33	99	10	24	4	1	1	8	7	11	.242	.292	.333	81	-2	0	2	1	.900	5	S-27	0.7
1974	Bos-A	106	389	60	104	14	3	5	33	25	61	.267	.313	.357	86	-7	19	11	-1	.978	2	O-97/D-4	-1.1
1975	*Bos-A	78	254	43	74	14	4	2	17	25	26	.291	.359	.402	106	2	7	10	-4	.991	1	O-44,D-20,3	-0.3
1976	Tex-A	145	478	49	122	14	4	0	33	39	56	.255	.315	.301	79	-12	17	6	2	.986	20	*O-141/2-1	0.5
1977	Tex-A	123	424	56	114	19	6	10	50	43	43	.269	.338	.413	102	1	26	18	-3	.988	7	*O-123	0.0
1978	Tex-A	127	473	61	123	17	3	11	50	20	59	.260	.294	.378	88	-9	10	12	-4	.972	-0	*O-126	-2.0
1979	NY-A	62	142	19	36	4	1	4	17	9	17	.254	.307	.394	90	-2	3	3	-1	.981	-6	O-60/3-3	-1.0
1980	Sea-A	70	237	26	54	10	0	6	21	17	25	.228	.280	.346	70	-10	2	3	-1	.957	1	O-65/D-1	-1.3
1981	Cal-A	58	166	18	30	5	0	3	13	15	16	.181	.253	.265	49	-11	2	1	0	.959	-7	O-55/D-1	-2.0
1982	*Cal-A	112	196	25	52	11	2	3	24	15	21	.265	.321	.388	93	-2	3	0	1	.983	-27	*O-107	-2.9
1983	Cal-A	92	315	44	96	15	0	3	34	15	29	.305	.344	.381	100	0	4	2	0	.968	-8	O-84/D-6	-1.0
1984	Cal-A	110	354	60	119	17	0	8	39	18	43	.336	.373	.452	128	13	3	5	-2	.971	-12	O-98	-0.3
1985	Cal-A	132	411	54	125	13	5	8	42	34	46	.304	.364	.418	114	9	4	3	-1	1.000	-15	O-71,1-46,D/3S	-1.1
1986	Bal-A	113	343	48	103	15	0	6	36	40	49	.300	.378	.397	113	7	2	3	-1	.963	-6	O-54,3-25,D1	-0.3
1987	KC-A	57	174	14	41	7	0	3	26	11	26	.236	.285	.328	60	-10	0	0	0	1.000	-4	O-22,D-15/13	-1.5
	Tor-A	39	81	6	23	5	1	5	21	5	13	.284	.333	.556	127	3	0	0	0	.875	-2	D-15/O-7,1	0.0
	Yr	96	255	20	64	12	1	8	47	16	39	.251	.300	.400	82	-7	0	0	0	.976	-6	D-30,O-29/13	-1.5
1988	Tor-A	27	58	9	17	2	0	1	8	8	6	.293	.379	.379	112	1	0	0	0	.000	0	D-19/O-1	0.0
Total	17	1500	4651	610	1274	190	30	79	476	349	551	.274	.329	.379	95	-29	104	76	-14	.977	-60	*O-1155,D-111/13S2	-14.3

■ STAN BENJAMIN
Benjamin, Alfred Stanley   b: 5/20/14, Framingham, Mass.   BR/TR, 6'2", 194 lbs.   Deb: 9/16/39

YEAR	TM/L	G	AB	R	H	2B	3B	HR	RBI	BB	SO	AVG	OBP	SLG	PRO+	BR/A	SB	CS	SBR	FA	FR	G/POS	TPR
1939	Phi-N	12	50	4	7	2	1	0	2	1	6	.140	.157	.220	0	-7	1			.867	-0	/O-7,3-5	-0.8
1940	Phi-N	8	9	1	2	0	0	0	1	1	1	.222	.300	.222	48	-1	0			1.000	1	/O-2	0.0
1941	Phi-N	129	480	47	113	20	7	3	27	20	81	.235	.266	.325	68	-22	17			.980	-4	*O-110/1-8,23	-3.4
1942	Phi-N	78	210	24	47	8	3	2	8	10	27	.224	.262	.319	73	-8	5			.976	-3	O-45,1-15	-1.4
1945	Cle-A	14	21	1	7	2	0	0	3	0	0	.333	.333	.429	126	1	0	1	-1	1.000	2	/O-4	0.1
Total	5	241	770	77	176	32	11	5	41	32	115	.229	.260	.318	66	-37	23	1		.975	-5	O-168/1-23,32	-5.5

■ MIKE BENJAMIN
Benjamin, Michael Paul   b: 11/22/65, Euclid, Ohio   BR/TR, 6'3", 195 lbs.   Deb: 7/7/89

YEAR	TM/L	G	AB	R	H	2B	3B	HR	RBI	BB	SO	AVG	OBP	SLG	PRO+	BR/A	SB	CS	SBR	FA	FR	G/POS	TPR
1989	SF-N	14	6	6	1	0	0	0	0	1	1	.167	.167	.167	-5	-1	0	0	0	1.000	2	/S-8	0.1
1990	SF-N	22	56	7	12	3	1	2	3	3	10	.214	.254	.411	83	-2	1	0	0	.988	5	S-21	0.5
1991	SF-N	54	106	12	13	3	0	2	8	7	26	.123	.191	.208	13	-13	3	0	1	.984	16	S-51/3-1	0.7
1992	SF-N	40	75	4	13	2	1	1	3	4	15	.173	.215	.267	38	-6	1	0	0	.991	5	S-33/3-2	0.0
1993	SF-N	63	146	22	29	7	0	4	16	9	23	.199	.264	.329	59	-9	0	0	0	.991	20	2-23,S-23,3	1.2
1994	SF-N	38	62	9	16	5	1	1	9	5	16	.258	.343	.419	101	0	5	0	2	.968	9	S-18,2-10/3	1.1
Total	6	231	451	60	84	20	3	10	39	28	91	.186	.248	.310	54	-30	10	0	3	.984	56	S-154/2-33,3	3.6

■ IKE BENNERS
Benners, Isaac B.   b: 6/7/1856, Philadelphia, Pa.   d: 4/18/32, Philadelphia, Pa.   BL, 175 lbs.   Deb: 5/1/1884

YEAR	TM/L	G	AB	R	H	2B	3B	HR	RBI	BB	SO	AVG	OBP	SLG	PRO+	BR/A	SB	CS	SBR	FA	FR	G/POS	TPR
1884	Bro-a	49	189	25	38	11	5	1		7		.201	.237	.328	82	-4				.815	-5	O-49	-0.9
	Wil-U	6	22	0	1	0	0	0		1		.045	.087	.045	-61	-5				.750	0	/O-6	-0.5
Total	1	55	211	25	39	11	5	1		8		.185	.222	.299	64	-9				.806	-5	/O-55	-1.4

■ CHARLIE BENNETT
Bennett, Charles Wesley   b: 11/21/1854, New Castle, Pa.   d: 2/24/27, Detroit, Mich.   BR/TR, 5'11", 180 lbs.   Deb: 5/1/1878

YEAR	TM/L	G	AB	R	H	2B	3B	HR	RBI	BB	SO	AVG	OBP	SLG	PRO+	BR/A	SB	CS	SBR	FA	FR	G/POS	TPR
1878	Mil-N	49	184	16	45	9	0	1	12	10	26	.245	.284	.310	89	-2				.831	-13	C-35,O-20	-1.5
1880	Wor-N	51	193	20	44	9	3	0	18	10	30	.228	.266	.306	86	-3				.913	-0	C-46/O-6	-0.3
1881	Det-N	76	299	44	90	18	7	7	64	18	37	.301	.341	.478	149	16				.962	18	*C-70/3-5,O	3.3
1882	Det-N	84	342	43	103	16	10	5	51	20	33	.301	.340	.450	151	22				.945	7	*C-65,3-11/2S1	2.5
1883	Det-N	92	371	56	113	34	7	5	55	26	59	.305	.350	.474	155	25				.944	-3	*C-72,2-15,O	2.3
1884	Det-N	90	341	37	90	18	6	3	40	36	40	.264	.334	.378	132	14				.917	-5	*C-80/O-5,S321	1.4
1885	Det-N	91	349	49	94	24	13	5	60	47	37	.269	.356	.456	161	24				.919	-1	C-62/O-19,3	2.6
1886	Det-N	72	235	37	57	13	5	4	34	48	29	.243	.371	.391	128	10	4			.955	12	C-69/O-4,S	2.6
1887	*Det-N	46	160	26	39	6	5	3	20	30	22	.244	.363	.400	108	2	7			.951	2	C-45/O-1,1	0.7
1888	Det-N	74	258	32	68	12	4	5	29	31	40	.264	.347	.399	138	12	4			.966	7	C-73/1-1	2.5
1889	Bos-N	82	247	42	57	8	2	4	28	21	43	.231	.296	.328	70	-11	6			.955	12	C-82	0.6
1890	Bos-N	85	281	59	60	17	2	3	40	72	56	.214	.377	.320	96	1	6			.959	10	C-85	1.6
1891	Bos-N	75	256	35	55	9	3	5	39	42	61	.215	.332	.332	84	-6	3			.960	14	C-75	1.3
1892	*Bos-N	35	114	19	23	4	0	1	16	27	23	.202	.355	.263	80	-2	6			.948	1	C-35	0.2
1893	Bos-N	60	191	34	40	6	0	4	27	40	36	.209	.352	.304	69	-8	5			.953	-3	C-60	-0.6
Total	15	1062	3821	549	978	203	67	55	533	478	572	.256	.340	.387	118	90	42			.942	57	C-954/O-70,32S1	19.2

■ HERSCHEL BENNETT
Bennett, Herschel Emmett   b: 9/21/1896, Elwood, Mo.   d: 9/9/64, Springfield, Mo.   BL/TR, 5'9.5", 160 lbs.   Deb: 4/19/23

YEAR	TM/L	G	AB	R	H	2B	3B	HR	RBI	BB	SO	AVG	OBP	SLG	PRO+	BR/A	SB	CS	SBR	FA	FR	G/POS	TPR
1923	StL-A	5	4	0	0	0	0	0	0	1	1	.000	.200	.000	-42	-1	0	0	0	1.000	-0	/O-1	-0.1
1924	StL-A	41	94	16	31	4	3	1	11	3	6	.330	.364	.468	107	1	1	0	0	.966	-4	O-21	-0.4
1925	StL-A	93	298	46	83	11	6	2	37	18	16	.279	.324	.376	73	-13	4	10	-5	.916	-2	O-73	-2.2
1926	StL-A	80	225	33	60	14	2	1	26	22	21	.267	.337	.360	78	-7	2	1	0	.950	3	O-50	-0.8
1927	StL-A	93	256	40	68	12	2	3	30	14	21	.266	.311	.363	72	-11	6	2	1	.946	1	O-55	-1.2
Total	5	312	877	135	242	41	13	7	104	58	65	.276	.327	.376	77	-31	13	13	-4	.937	-1	O-200	-4.7

■ FRED BENNETT
Bennett, James Fred "Red"   b: 3/15/02, Atkins, Ark.   d: 5/12/57, Atkins, Ark.   BR/TR, 5'9", 185 lbs.   Deb: 4/13/28

YEAR	TM/L	G	AB	R	H	2B	3B	HR	RBI	BB	SO	AVG	OBP	SLG	PRO+	BR/A	SB	CS	SBR	FA	FR	G/POS	TPR
1928	StL-A	7	8	0	2	1	0	0	0	0	2	.250	.250	.375	60	0	0	0	0	1.000	0	/O-1	-0.1
1931	Pit-N	32	89	6	25	5	0	1	7	7	4	.281	.333	.371	90	-1	0			.951	-2	O-21	-0.5
Total	2	39	97	6	27	6	0	1	7	7	6	.278	.327	.371	87	-2	0	0		.953	-2	/O-22	-0.6

■ JOE BENNETT
Bennett, Joseph Rosenblum   b: 7/2/1900, New York, N.Y.   d: 7/11/87, Morro Bay, Cal.   BR/TR, 5'9", 168 lbs.   Deb: 7/5/23

YEAR	TM/L	G	AB	R	H	2B	3B	HR	RBI	BB	SO	AVG	OBP	SLG	PRO+	BR/A	SB	CS	SBR	FA	FR	G/POS	TPR
1923	Phi-N	1	0	0	0	0	0	0	0	0	0	—	—	—	—		0	0	0	1.000	0	/3-1	0.0

■ PUG BENNETT
Bennett, Justin Titus   b: 2/20/1874, Ponca, Neb.   d: 9/12/35, Kirkland, Wash.   BR/TR, 5'11", 165 lbs.   Deb: 4/12/06

YEAR	TM/L	G	AB	R	H	2B	3B	HR	RBI	BB	SO	AVG	OBP	SLG	PRO+	BR/A	SB	CS	SBR	FA	FR	G/POS	TPR
1906	StL-N	153	595	66	156	16	7	1	34	56		.262	.334	.318	108	6	20			.948	-7	*2-153	0.0
1907	StL-N	87	324	20	72	8	2	0	21	21		.222	.272	.259	69	-12	7			.939	-16	2-83/3-3	-3.4
Total	2	240	919	86	228	24	9	1	55	77		.248	.312	.297	94	-6	27			.945	-23	2-236/3-3	-3.4

■ VERN BENSON
Benson, Vernon Adair   b: 9/19/24, Granite Quarry, N.C.   BL/TR, 5'11", 180 lbs.   Deb: 7/31/43   MC

YEAR	TM/L	G	AB	R	H	2B	3B	HR	RBI	BB	SO	AVG	OBP	SLG	PRO+	BR/A	SB	CS	SBR	FA	FR	G/POS	TPR
1943	Phi-A	2	2	0	0	0	0	0	0	0	0	.000	.000	.000	-99	-0	0	0	0	.000	0	H	-0.1
1946	Phi-A	7	5	1	0	0	0	0	0	1	3	.000	.167	.000	-51	-1	0	0	0	1.000	-0	/O-2	-0.1
1951	StL-N	13	46	8	12	3	1	1	7	6	8	.261	.346	.435	108	0	0	0	0	.950	0	/3-9,O-4	0.1

YEAR	TM/L	G	AB	R	H	2B	3B	HR	RBI	BB	SO	AVG	OBP	SLG	PRO+	BR/A	SB	CS	SBR	FA	FR	G/POS	TPR
1952	StL-N	20	47	6	9	2	0	2	5	5	9	.191	.269	.362	73	-2	0	0	0	.889	-1	3-15	-0.3
1953	StL-N	13	4	2	0	0	0	0	0	1	2	.000	.200	.000	-42	-1	0	0	0	.000	0	H	-0.1
Total	5	55	104	17	21	5	1	3	12	13	22	.202	.291	.356	75	-4	0	0	0	.911	-0	/3-24,O-6	-0.5

■ JACK BENTLEY
Bentley, John Needles b: 3/8/1895, Sandy Spring, Md. d: 10/24/69, Olney, Md. BL/TL, 5'11.5", 200 lbs. Deb: 9/6/13

YEAR	TM/L	G	AB	R	H	2B	3B	HR	RBI	BB	SO	AVG	OBP	SLG	PRO+	BR/A	SB	CS	SBR	FA	FR	G/POS	TPR
1913	Was-A	3	3	0	0	0	0	0	0	0	0	.000	.000	.000	-98	-1	0			1.000	0	/P-3	0.0
1914	Was-A	30	40	7	11	2	0	0	4	0	5	.275	.275	.325	77	-1	0			.930	-1	P-30	0.0
1915	Was-A	4	2	0	0	0	0	0	0	0	1	.000	.000	.000	-98	-0	0			.750	-0	/P-4	0.0
1916	Was-A	2	0	0	0	0	0	0	0	0	0	—	—	—	—	0				1.000	0	/P-2	0.0
1923	*NY-N	52	89	9	38	6	2	1	14	3	4	.427	.446	.573	169	9	0	0	0	.977	-1	P-31	0.0
1924	*NY-N	46	98	12	26	5	1	0	6	3	13	.265	.287	.337	68	-5	0	0	0	.979	-1	P-28	0.0
1925	NY-N	64	99	10	30	5	2	3	18	9	11	.303	.361	.485	119	3	0	0	0	.930	-2	P-28/O-3,1	-0.1
1926	Phi-N	75	240	19	62	12	3	2	27	5	4	.258	.273	.358	66	-12	0			.993	-2	1-56/P-7	-1.6
	NY-N	3	4	0	1	0	0	0	0	0	0	.250	.250	.250	35	-0	0			.000	-0	/P-1	0.0
	Yr	78	244	19	63	12	3	2	27	5	4	.258	.273	.357	65	-13	0			.993	-2	1-56/P-8	-1.6
1927	NY-N	9	9	1	2	0	1	0	2	1	1	.222	.300	.556	125	0	0			.750	-0	/P-4,1-2	0.0
Total	9	287	584	58	170	30	8	7	71	21	39	.291	.316	.406	91	-8	0	0	0	.949	-6	P-138/1-59,O	-1.7

■ BUTCH BENTON
Benton, Alfred Lee b: 8/24/57, Tampa, Fla. BR/TR, 6'1", 190 lbs. Deb: 9/14/78

YEAR	TM/L	G	AB	R	H	2B	3B	HR	RBI	BB	SO	AVG	OBP	SLG	PRO+	BR/A	SB	CS	SBR	FA	FR	G/POS	TPR
1978	NY-N	4	4	1	2	0	0	0	2	0	0	.500	.600	.500	218	1	0	0	0	1.000	0	/C-1	0.1
1980	NY-N	12	21	0	1	0	0	0	0	2	4	.048	.167	.048	-39	-4	0	0	0	.935	-1	/C-8	-0.5
1982	Chi-N	4	7	0	1	0	0	0	1	0	1	.143	.143	.143	-19	-1	0	0	0	1.000	2	/C-4	0.1
1985	Cle-A	31	67	5	12	4	0	0	7	3	9	.179	.214	.239	24	-7	0	0	0	.957	-3	C-26	-0.9
Total	4	51	99	6	16	4	0	0	10	5	14	.162	.217	.202	16	-11	0	0	0	.959	-2	/C-39	-1.2

■ RABBIT BENTON
Benton, Stanley W. "Stan" b: 9/29/01, Cannel City, Ky. d: 6/7/84, Mesquite, Tex. BR/TR, 5'7", 150 lbs. Deb: 9/13/22

YEAR	TM/L	G	AB	R	H	2B	3B	HR	RBI	BB	SO	AVG	OBP	SLG	PRO+	BR/A	SB	CS	SBR	FA	FR	G/POS	TPR
1922	Phi-N	6	19	1	4	1	0	0	3	2	1	.211	.286	.263	39	-2	0			.889	0	/2-5	-0.1

■ TODD BENZINGER
Benzinger, Todd Eric b: 2/11/63, Dayton, Ky. BB/TR, 6'1", 185 lbs. Deb: 6/21/87

YEAR	TM/L	G	AB	R	H	2B	3B	HR	RBI	BB	SO	AVG	OBP	SLG	PRO+	BR/A	SB	CS	SBR	FA	FR	G/POS	TPR
1987	Bos-A	73	223	36	62	11	1	8	43	22	41	.278	.348	.444	105	2	5	4	-1	.987	8	O-61/1-2	0.7
1988	*Bos-A	120	405	47	103	28	1	13	70	22	80	.254	.294	.425	95	-4	2	3	-1	.991	-4	1-85,O-48/D	-1.6
1989	Cin-N	161	628	79	154	28	3	17	76	44	120	.245	.297	.381	89	-10	3	7	-3	.995	-13	*1-158	-4.2
1990	*Cin-N	118	376	35	95	14	2	5	46	19	69	.253	.296	.340	71	-15	3	4	-2	.992	-1	1-95,O-10	-2.6
1991	Cin-N	51	123	7	23	3	2	1	11	10	20	.187	.248	.268	43	-9	2	0	1	.986	-1	1-21,O-15	-1.2
	KC-A	78	293	29	86	15	3	2	40	17	46	.294	.339	.386	99	-0	2	6	-5	.996	-5	1-75/D-1	-1.3
1992	LA-N	121	293	24	70	16	2	4	31	15	54	.239	.276	.348	77	-10	2	4	-2	.989	0	O-51,1-42	-1.5
1993	SF-N	86	177	25	51	7	2	6	26	13	35	.288	.337	.452	112	3	0	0	0	1.000	-4	1-40/O-7,3	-0.4
1994	SF-N	107	328	32	87	13	2	9	31	17	84	.265	.305	.399	85	-8	2	1	0	.994	-4	1-99	-1.9
Total	8	915	2846	314	731	135	18	65	374	179	549	.257	.304	.385	88	-52	21	29	-11	.994	-24	1-617,O-192/D3	-14.0

■ JOHNNY BERARDINO
Berardino, John "Bernie" b: 5/1/17, Los Angeles, Cal. BR/TR, 6', 180 lbs. Deb: 4/22/39

YEAR	TM/L	G	AB	R	H	2B	3B	HR	RBI	BB	SO	AVG	OBP	SLG	PRO+	BR/A	SB	CS	SBR	FA	FR	G/POS	TPR
1939	StL-A	126	468	42	120	24	5	5	58	37	36	.256	.314	.361	71	-21	6	2	1	.958	4	*2-114/3-8,S	-1.0
1940	StL-A	142	523	71	135	31	4	16	85	32	46	.258	.301	.424	84	-14	6	8	-3	.939	13	*S-112,2-13/3	0.6
1941	StL-A	128	469	48	127	30	4	5	89	41	27	.271	.332	.384	86	-10	3	5	-2	.954	-14	*S-123/3-1	-1.6
1942	StL-A	29	74	11	21	6	0	1	10	4	2	.284	.329	.405	104	-1	3	1	0	.950	0	/S-6,3-6,12	0.1
1946	StL-A	144	582	70	154	29	5	5	68	34	58	.265	.306	.357	81	-16	2	4	-2	.972	-2	*2-143	-1.0
1947	StL-A	90	306	29	80	22	1	1	20	44	26	.261	.358	.350	95	-1	6	5	-1	.977	-9	2-86	-0.5
1948	Cle-A	66	147	19	28	5	1	2	10	27	16	.190	.328	.279	64	-7	0	1	-1	.988	4	2-20,1-18,S/3	-0.3
1949	Cle-A	50	116	11	23	6	1	0	13	14	14	.198	.295	.267	50	-8	0	1	-1	.935	-1	3-25/2-8,S	-1.0
1950	Cle-A	4	5	1	2	0	0	0	3	1	0	.400	.500	.400	137	0	0	0	0	1.000	1	/2-1,3-1	0.1
	Pit-N	40	131	12	27	3	1	1	12	19	11	.206	.307	.267	51	-9	0			.964	3	2-36/3-3	-0.5
1951	StL-A	39	119	13	27	7	1	0	13	17	18	.227	.324	.303	68	-5	1	1	-0	.917	-7	3-31/2-2,1O	-1.2
1952	Cle-A	35	32	5	3	0	0	0	2	10	8	.094	.310	.094	17	-3	0	1	-1	.960	2	/2-8,S-8,31	-0.2
	Pit-N	19	56	2	8	4	0	0	4	4	6	.143	.200	.214	14	-7	0	0	0	.960	6	2-18	0.1
Total	11	912	3028	334	755	167	23	36	387	284	268	.249	.316	.355	77	-101	27	29		.968	1	2-453,S-266/310	-6.4

■ LOU BERBERET
Berberet, Louis Joseph b: 11/20/29, Long Beach, Cal. BL/TR, 5'11", 212 lbs. Deb: 9/17/54

YEAR	TM/L	G	AB	R	H	2B	3B	HR	RBI	BB	SO	AVG	OBP	SLG	PRO+	BR/A	SB	CS	SBR	FA	FR	G/POS	TPR
1954	NY-A	5	5	1	2	0	0	0	3	1	1	.400	.500	.400	154	0	0	0	0	1.000	1	/C-3	0.2
1955	NY-A	5	5	1	2	0	0	0	2	1	0	.400	.500	.400	147	0	0	0	0	1.000	1	/C-1	0.1
1956	Was-A	95	207	25	54	6	3	4	27	46	33	.261	.402	.377	107	4	0	0	0	.997	-1	C-59	0.6
1957	Was-A	99	264	24	69	11	2	7	36	41	38	.261	.365	.398	110	4	0	1	-1	**1.000**	-3	C-77	0.4
1958	Was-A	5	6	0	1	0	0	0	0	1	0	.167	.500	.167	94	0	0	0	0	.917	1	/C-2	0.1
	Bos-A	57	167	11	35	5	3	2	18	31	32	.210	.337	.311	74	-5	0	2	-1	.984	-6	C-49	-0.9
	Yr	62	173	11	36	5	3	2	18	35	33	.208	.344	.306	76	-5	0	2	-1	.981	-5	C-51	-0.8
1959	Det-A	100	338	38	73	8	2	13	44	35	59	.216	.290	.367	75	-12	0	0	0	.989	-11	C-95	-1.8
1960	Det-A	85	232	18	45	4	0	5	23	41	31	.194	.318	.276	60	-12	2	1	0	.993	-0	C-81	-0.7
Total	7	448	1224	118	281	34	10	31	153	200	195	.230	.341	.350	86	-19	2	3	-1	.992	-17	C-367	-2.0

■ MOE BERG
Berg, Morris b: 3/2/02, New York, N.Y. d: 5/29/72, Belleville, N.J. BR/TR, 6'1", 185 lbs. Deb: 7/4/23 C

YEAR	TM/L	G	AB	R	H	2B	3B	HR	RBI	BB	SO	AVG	OBP	SLG	PRO+	BR/A	SB	CS	SBR	FA	FR	G/POS	TPR
1923	Bro-N	49	129	9	24	3	2	0	6	3	20	.186	.198	.240	16	-16	1	0	0	.906	-6	S-47/2-1	-1.8
1926	Chi-A	41	113	4	25	6	0	0	7	6	9	.221	.261	.274	41	-10	0	2	-1	.948	6	S-31/2-2,3	-0.3
1927	Chi-A	35	69	4	17	4	0	0	4	4	10	.246	.288	.304	55	-5	0	0	0	.952	-4	2-11,C-10/S3	-0.7
1928	Chi-A	76	224	25	55	16	0	0	29	14	25	.246	.302	.317	64	-12	2	1	0	.990	5	C-73	-0.1
1929	Chi-A	107	352	32	101	7	0	0	47	17	16	.287	.323	.307	64	-18	5	1	1	.982	-3	*C-106	-1.0
1930	Chi-A	20	61	4	7	3	0	0	7	1	5	.115	.129	.164	-27	-12	0	0	0	.986	-1	C-20	-1.0
1931	Cle-A	10	13	1	1	1	0	0	0	1	1	.077	.143	.154	-21	-2	0	0	0	.889	-1	/C-8	-0.2
1932	Was-A	75	195	16	46	8	1	1	26	24	8	.236	.266	.303	48	-15	1	1	-0	1.000	7	C-75	-0.5
1933	Was-A	40	65	8	12	3	0	2	9	4	5	.185	.232	.323	46	-5	0	0	0	1.000	5	C-35	-0.2
1934	Was-A	33	86	5	21	4	0	1	9	1	7	.244	.301	.291	55	-6	2	1	-1	.988	-4	C-31	-0.8
	Cle-A	29	97	4	25	3	1	0	6	1	7	.258	.265	.309	47	-8	0	0	0	.980	5	C-28	-0.1
	Yr	62	183	9	46	7	1	0	15	7	11	.251	.283	.301	51	-13	2	1	0	.983	1	C-59	-0.9
1935	Bos-A	38	98	13	28	5	2	0	12	5	3	.286	.320	.398	79	-3	0	0	0	.991	2	C-37	0.0
1936	Bos-A	39	125	9	30	4	1	0	19	2	6	.240	.264	.288	34	-13	0	0	0	.986	12	C-39	0.0
1937	Bos-A	47	141	13	36	3	1	0	20	5	4	.255	.281	.291	43	-12	0	0	0	.979	3	C-47	-0.7
1938	Bos-A	10	12	0	4	0	0	0	3	1	1	.333	.333	.333	64	-1	0	0	0	1.000	1	/C-7,1-1	0.0
1939	Bos-A	14	33	3	9	1	0	1	5	3	4	.273	.314	.394	70	-1	0	0	0	.965	4	C-13	0.3
Total	15	663	1813	150	441	71	6	6	206	78	117	.243	.278	.299	49	-140	11	5	0	.986	29	C-529/S-84,231	-7.1

■ AUGIE BERGAMO
Bergamo, August Samuel b: 2/14/17, Detroit, Mich. d: 8/19/74, Grosse Pointe, Mich. BL/TL, 5'9", 165 lbs. Deb: 4/25/44

YEAR	TM/L	G	AB	R	H	2B	3B	HR	RBI	BB	SO	AVG	OBP	SLG	PRO+	BR/A	SB	CS	SBR	FA	FR	G/POS	TPR
1944	*StL-N	80	192	35	55	6	3	2	19	35	23	.286	.399	.380	118	6	0			.988	-7	O-50/1-2	-0.4
1945	StL-N	94	304	51	96	17	2	3	44	43	21	.316	.401	.414	124	11	0			.969	-1	O-77/1-2	0.6
Total	2	174	496	86	151	23	5	5	63	78	44	.304	.400	.401	122	17	0			.975	-9	O-127/1-4	0.2

■ MARTY BERGEN
Bergen, Martin b: 10/25/1871, N.Brookfield, Mass. d: 1/19/1900, N.Brookfield, Mass. TR, 5'10", 170 lbs. Deb: 4/17/1896 F

YEAR	TM/L	G	AB	R	H	2B	3B	HR	RBI	BB	SO	AVG	OBP	SLG	PRO+	BR/A	SB	CS	SBR	FA	FR	G/POS	TPR
1896	Bos-N	65	245	39	66	6	4	4	37	11	22	.269	.309	.376	75	-10	6			.920	6	C-63/1-1	0.2

YEAR	TM/L	G	AB	R	H	2B	3B	HR	RBI	BB	SO	AVG	OBP	SLG	PRO+	BR/A	SB	CS	SBR	FA	FR	G/POS	TPR
1897	*Bos-N	87	327	47	81	11	3	2	45	18		.248	.295	.318	58	-21	5			.963	4	C-85/O-1	-0.6
1898	Bos-N	120	446	62	125	16	5	3	60	13		.280	.302	.359	85	-11	9			.962	2	*C-117/1-2	0.2
1899	Bos-N	72	260	32	67	11	3	1	34	10		.258	.290	.335	65	-14	4			.955	3	C-72	-0.5
Total	4	344	1278	180	339	44	15	10	176	52	22	.265	.299	.347	72	-56	24			.954	15	C-337/1-3,O	-0.7

■ BILL BERGEN
Bergen, William Aloysius b: 6/13/1878, N.Brookfield, Mass. d: 12/19/43, Worcester, Mass. BR/TR, 6', 184 lbs. Deb: 5/6/01 F

YEAR	TM/L	G	AB	R	H	2B	3B	HR	RBI	BB	SO	AVG	OBP	SLG	PRO+	BR/A	SB	CS	SBR	FA	FR	G/POS	TPR
1901	Cin-N	87	308	15	55	6	4	1	17	8		.179	.199	.234	27	-29	2			.970	-4	C-87	-2.4
1902	Cin-N	89	322	19	58	8	3	0	36	14		.180	.214	.224	32	-26	2			.959	17	C-89	0.0
1903	Cin-N	58	207	21	47	4	2	0	19	7		.227	.252	.266	43	-16	2			.980	2	C-58	-0.8
1904	Bro-N	96	329	17	60	4	2	0	12	9		.182	.204	.207	28	-28	3			.959	14	C-93/1-1	-0.4
1905	Bro-N	79	247	12	47	3	2	0	22	7		.190	.213	.219	31	-21	4			.954	12	C-76	-0.3
1906	Bro-N	103	353	9	56	3	3	0	19	7		.159	.175	.184	13	-37	2			.977	5	*C-103	-2.4
1907	Bro-N	51	138	2	22	3	0	0	14	1		.159	.165	.181	9	-15	1			.968	3	C-51	-1.0
1908	Bro-N	99	302	8	53	8	2	0	15	5		.175	.189	.215	30	-24	1			.989	16	C-99	0.0
1909	Bro-N	112	346	16	48	1	1	1	15	10		.139	.163	.156	-1	-41	1			.976	22	*C-112	-1.1
1910	Bro-N	89	249	11	40	2	1	0	14	6		.161	.180	.177	4	-31	0			.981	18	C-89	-0.5
1911	Bro-N	84	227	8	30	3	1	0	10	14	42	.132	.183	.154	-6	-32	2			.981	15	C-84	-1.0
Total	11	947	3028	138	516	45	21	2	193	88	81	.170	.194	.201	20	-301	23			.972	119	C-941/1-1	-9.9

■ CLARENCE BERGER
Berger, Clarence Edward b: 11/1/1894, E.Cleveland, Ohio d: 6/30/59, Washington, D.C. BL/TR, 6', 185 lbs. Deb: 9/23/14

YEAR	TM/L	G	AB	R	H	2B	3B	HR	RBI	BB	SO	AVG	OBP	SLG	PRO+	BR/A	SB	CS	SBR	FA	FR	G/POS	TPR
1914	Pit-N	6	13	2	1	0	0	0	0	1	4	.077	.143	.077	-36	-2	0			1.000	-2	/O-5	-0.5

■ JOHNNY BERGER
Berger, John Henne b: 8/27/01, Philadelphia, Pa. d: 5/7/79, Lake Charles, La. BR/TR, 5'9", 165 lbs. Deb: 4/20/22

YEAR	TM/L	G	AB	R	H	2B	3B	HR	RBI	BB	SO	AVG	OBP	SLG	PRO+	BR/A	SB	CS	SBR	FA	FR	G/POS	TPR
1922	Phi-A	2	1	0	1	0	0	0	0	0	0	1.000	1.000	1.000	412	0	1	0	0	1.000	1	/C-2	0.1
1927	Was-A	9	15	1	4	0	0	0	1	2	3	.267	.353	.267	63	-1	0	0	0	.926	0	/C-9	0.0
Total	2	11	16	1	5	0	0	0	1	2	3	.313	.389	.313	85	-0	1	0	0	.935	1	/C-11	0.1

■ TUN BERGER
Berger, John Henry b: 12/6/1867, Pittsburgh, Pa. d: 6/10/07, Pittsburgh, Pa. TR, 204 lbs. Deb: 5/9/1890

YEAR	TM/L	G	AB	R	H	2B	3B	HR	RBI	BB	SO	AVG	OBP	SLG	PRO+	BR/A	SB	CS	SBR	FA	FR	G/POS	TPR
1890	Pit-N	104	391	64	104	18	4	0	40	35	23	.266	.337	.332	108	5	11			.912	-7	O-41,S-33,C/23	0.1
1891	Pit-N	43	134	15	32	2	1	1	14	12	10	.239	.315	.291	79	-3	4			.920	-13	C-18,2-17/SO	-1.2
1892	Was-N	26	97	9	14	2	1	0	3	7	9	.144	.210	.186	20	-9	3			.872	-11	S-18/C-9	-1.8
Total	3	173	622	88	150	22	6	1	57	54	42	.241	.313	.301	87	-8	18			.837	-30	/S-57,C-48,O23	-2.9

■ JOE BERGER
Berger, Joseph August "Fats" b: 12/20/1886, St.Louis, Mo. d: 3/5/56, Rock Island, Ill. BR/TR, 5'10.5", 170 lbs. Deb: 4/11/13

YEAR	TM/L	G	AB	R	H	2B	3B	HR	RBI	BB	SO	AVG	OBP	SLG	PRO+	BR/A	SB	CS	SBR	FA	FR	G/POS	TPR
1913	Chi-A	79	223	27	48	6	2	2	20	36	28	.215	.330	.287	82	-4	5			.959	6	2-71/S-4,3	-0.2
1914	Chi-A	48	148	11	23	3	1	0	3	13	9	.155	.224	.189	25	-14	2	8	-4	.922	-2	S-28,2-12/3	-2.0
Total	2	127	371	38	71	9	3	2	23	49	37	.191	.289	.248	60	-18	7	8		.956	1	/2-83,S-32,3	-2.2

■ BOZE BERGER
Berger, Louis William b: 5/13/10, Baltimore, Md. d: 11/3/92, Bethesda, Md. BR/TR, 6'2", 180 lbs. Deb: 8/17/32

YEAR	TM/L	G	AB	R	H	2B	3B	HR	RBI	BB	SO	AVG	OBP	SLG	PRO+	BR/A	SB	CS	SBR	FA	FR	G/POS	TPR
1932	Cle-A	1	1	0	0	0	0	0	0	0	1	.000	.000	.000	-94	-0	0	0	0	1.000	1	/S-1	0.1
1935	Cle-A	124	461	62	119	27	5	5	43	34	97	.258	.310	.371	74	-19	7	5	-1	.964	13	*2-120/S-3,13	0.2
1936	Cle-A	28	52	1	9	2	0	0	3	1	14	.173	.189	.212	-1	-8	0	0	0	.959	4	/1-8,2-8,3S	-0.4
1937	Chi-A	52	130	19	31	5	0	5	13	15	24	.238	.322	.392	79	-5	1	1	-0	.931	-1	3-40/2-1,S	-0.4
1938	Chi-A	118	470	60	102	15	3	3	36	43	80	.217	.284	.281	41	-43	4	1	1	.946	-10	S-67,2-42/3	-4.1
1939	Bos-A	20	30	4	9	2	0	0	2	1	10	.300	.323	.367	73	-1	0	0	0	.947	3	S-10/3-5,2	0.0
Total	6	343	1144	146	270	51	8	13	97	94	226	.236	.296	.329	57	-77	12	7	-1	.954	9	2-173/S-84,31	-4.6

■ WALLY BERGER
Berger, Walter Antone b: 10/10/05, Chicago, Ill. d: 11/30/88, Redondo Beach, Cal BR/TR, 6'2", 198 lbs. Deb: 4/15/30

YEAR	TM/L	G	AB	R	H	2B	3B	HR	RBI	BB	SO	AVG	OBP	SLG	PRO+	BR/A	SB	CS	SBR	FA	FR	G/POS	TPR
1930	Bos-N	151	555	98	172	27	14	38	119	54	69	.310	.375	.614	139	31	3			.966	4	*O-145	2.2
1931	Bos-N	156	617	94	199	44	8	19	84	55	70	.323	.380	.512	143	36	13			.977	11	*O-156/1-1	3.5
1932	Bos-N	145	602	90	185	34	6	17	73	33	66	.307	.346	.468	121	16	5			.993	5	*O-134,1-11	1.2
1933	Bos-N★	137	528	84	165	37	8	27	106	41	77	.313	.365	.566	177	49	2			.977	4	*O-136	4.7
1934	Bos-N★	150	615	92	183	35	8	34	121	49	65	.298	.352	.546	148	38	2			.978	1	*O-150	3.1
1935	Bos-N★	150	589	91	174	39	4	34	130	50	80	.295	.355	.548	151	39	3			.965	9	*O-149	4.0
1936	Bos-N☆	138	534	88	154	23	3	25	91	53	84	.288	.361	.483	134	24	1			.966	7	*O-133	2.5
1937	Bos-N	30	113	14	31	9	1	5	22	11	33	.274	.344	.504	140	6	0			1.000	-2	O-28	0.3
	*NY-N	59	199	40	58	11	2	12	43	18	30	.291	.359	.548	141	11	3			.965	-2	O-52	0.7
	Yr	89	312	54	89	20	3	17	65	29	63	.285	.354	.532	141	16	3			.976	-4	O-80	1.0
1938	NY-N	16	32	5	6	0	0	0	4	2	4	.188	.235	.188	17	-4	0			1.000	1	/O-9	-0.3
	Cin-N	99	407	74	125	23	4	16	56	29	44	.307	.356	.501	137	19	2			.966	-3	O-98	1.3
	Yr	115	439	79	131	23	4	16	60	31	48	.298	.347	.478	128	15	2			.970	-2	*O-107	1.0
1939	*Cin-N	97	329	36	85	15	1	14	44	36	63	.258	.341	.438	107	3	1			.970	-8	O-95	-0.8
1940	Cin-N	2	2	0	0	0	0	0	0	0	1	.000	.000	.000	-99	-1	0			.000	0	H	-0.1
	Phi-N	20	41	3	13	0	1	0	4	2	7	.317	.378	.439	130	2	1			.947	-2	O-11/1-1	-0.1
	Yr	22	43	3	13	0	1	0	4	2	8	.302	.362	.419	119	1	1			.947	-2	O-11/1-1	-0.2
Total	11	1350	5163	809	1550	299	59	242	898	435	694	.300	.359	.522	140	269	36			.974	26	*O-1296/1-13	22.2

■ JOHN BERGH
Bergh, John Baptist b: 10/8/1857, Boston, Mass. d: 4/16/1883, Boston, Mass. Deb: 8/5/1876

YEAR	TM/L	G	AB	R	H	2B	3B	HR	RBI	BB	SO	AVG	OBP	SLG	PRO+	BR/A	SB	CS	SBR	FA	FR	G/POS	TPR
1876	Phi-N	1	4	0	0	0	0	0	0	0	2	.000	.000	.000	-99	-1				1.000	-0	/O-1,C-1	-0.1
1880	Bos-N	11	40	2	8	3	0	0	0	2	5	.200	.238	.275	76	-1				.844	-3	C-11	-0.4
Total	2	12	44	2	8	3	0	0	0	2		.182	.217	.250	59	-2				.841	-4	/C-12,O-1	-0.5

■ MARTY BERGHAMMER
Berghammer, Martin Andrew "Pepper" b: 6/18/1888, Elliott, Pa. d: 12/21/57, Pittsburgh, Pa. BL/TR, 5'9", 172 lbs. Deb: 9/8/11

YEAR	TM/L	G	AB	R	H	2B	3B	HR	RBI	BB	SO	AVG	OBP	SLG	PRO+	BR/A	SB	CS	SBR	FA	FR	G/POS	TPR
1911	Chi-A	2	5	0	0	0	0	0	0	0	0	.000	.167	.000	-54	-1	0			1.000	0	/2-2	-0.1
1913	Cin-N	74	188	25	41	4	1	1	13	10	29	.218	.269	.266	53	-11	16			.909	5	S-54,2-13	-0.3
1914	Cin-N	77	112	15	25	2	0	0	6	10	18	.223	.287	.241	56	-6	4			.906	7	S-33,2-13	0.3
1915	Pit-F	132	469	96	114	10	6	0	33	83	44	.243	.371	.290	79	-10	26			.943	-16	*S-132	-1.6
Total	4	285	774	136	180	16	7	1	52	103	91	.233	.335	.275	69	-28	46			.931	-5	S-219/2-28	-1.7

■ AL BERGMAN
Bergman, Alfred Henry "Dutch" b: 9/27/1890, Peru, Ind. d: 6/20/61, Fort Wayne, Ind. BR/TR, 5'7", 155 lbs. Deb: 8/29/16

YEAR	TM/L	G	AB	R	H	2B	3B	HR	RBI	BB	SO	AVG	OBP	SLG	PRO+	BR/A	SB	CS	SBR	FA	FR	G/POS	TPR
1916	Cle-A	8	14	2	3	0	0	0	1			.214	.313	.357	95	-0				.889	-2	/2-3	-0.2

■ DAVE BERGMAN
Bergman, David Bruce b: 6/6/53, Evanston, Ill. BL/TL, 6'1.5", 185 lbs. Deb: 8/26/75

YEAR	TM/L	G	AB	R	H	2B	3B	HR	RBI	BB	SO	AVG	OBP	SLG	PRO+	BR/A	SB	CS	SBR	FA	FR	G/POS	TPR
1975	NY-A	7	17	0	0	0	0	0	0	0	2	.000	.105	.000	-70	-4	0	0	0	.917	0	/O-6	-0.4
1977	NY-A	5	4	1	1	0	0	0	1	0	0	.250	.250	.250	37	-0	0	0	0	1.000	-1	/O-3,1-2	-0.1
1978	Hou-N	104	186	15	43	5	1	0	12	39	32	.231	.364	.269	86	-2	2	0	1	.993	-2	1-66,O-29	-0.6
1979	Hou-N	13	15	4	6	0	0	0	2	0	3	.400	.400	.600	179	1	0	0	0	1.000	-1	/1-4	0.1
1980	*Hou-N	90	78	12	20	6	1	0	3	10	10	.256	.341	.359	104	0	2	0	0	.995	2	1-59/O-5	0.2
1981	Hou-N	6	6	1	1	0	0	0	0	0	0	.167	.167	.667	134	0	0	0	0	1.000	0	/1-1	0.1
	SF-N	63	145	16	37	9	0	0	13	19	18	.255	.341	.379	106	1	2	0	1	.992	-1	1-33,O-15	0.1
	Yr	69	151	17	38	9	0	0	14	19	18	.252	.335	.391	108	2	2	0	1	.992	1	1-34,O-15	0.2
1982	SF-N	100	121	22	33	3	1	0	14	18	11	.273	.367	.413	118	3	3	0	0	.991	1	1-69/O-6	0.4
1983	SF-N	90	140	16	40	4	1	6	24	24	21	.286	.394	.457	140	4	3	0	0	.994	2	1-50/O-6	0.9
1984	*Det-A	120	271	42	74	8	5	7	44	33	40	.273	.358	.417	115	4	3	4	-2	.989	8	*1-114/O-2	0.8
1985	Det-A	69	140	8	25	2	0	3	7	14	15	.179	.253	.257	41	-11	0	0	0	.991	1	1-44/O-1,D	-1.2

YEAR	TM/L	G	AB	R	H	2B	3B	HR	RBI	BB	SO	AVG	OBP	SLG	PRO+	BR/A	SB	CS	SBR	FA	FR	G/POS	TPR
1986	Det-A	65	130	14	30	6	1	1	9	21	16	.231	.338	.315	79	-3	0	0	0	.986	2	1-41/O-2,D	-0.3
1987	*Det-A	91	172	25	47	7	3	6	22	30	23	.273	.384	.453	127	7	0	1	-1	.992	-1	1-65/O-7,D	0.3
1988	Det-A	116	289	37	85	14	0	5	35	38	34	.294	.376	.394	121	9	0	2	-1	.990	-0	1-64,D-30,O	0.3
1989	Det-A	137	385	38	103	13	1	7	37	44	44	.268	.346	.361	102	2	1	3	-2	.993	5	*1-123/O-1,D	-0.3
1990	Det-A	100	205	21	57	10	1	2	26	33	17	.278	.378	.366	108	4	3	2	-0	.995	-3	D-51,1-27/O	-0.3
1991	Det-A	86	194	23	46	10	1	7	29	35	40	.237	.354	.407	108	3	1	1	-0	.997	-1	1-49,D-13/O	-0.1
1992	Det-A	87	181	17	42	3	0	1	10	20	19	.232	.308	.265	62	-9	1	0	0	.986	-2	1-55,D-12/O	-1.4
Total	17	1349	2679	312	690	100	16	54	289	380	347	.258	.351	.367	102	17	19	14	-3	.992	10	1-866,D-133,O	-1.5

■ FRANK BERKELBACH
Berkelbach, Francis P. b: Philadelphia, Pa. 6', 182 lbs. Deb: 7/4/1884

YEAR	TM/L	G	AB	R	H	2B	3B	HR	RBI	BB	SO	AVG	OBP	SLG	PRO+	BR/A	SB	CS	SBR	FA	FR	G/POS	TPR
1884	Cin-a	6	25	3	6	0	1	0	0	0		.240	.296	.320	96	-0				.667	-2	/O-6	-0.2

■ NATE BERKENSTOCK
Berkenstock, Nathan b: 1831, Pennsylvania d: 2/23/1900, Philadelphia, Pa. Deb: 10/30/1871

YEAR	TM/L	G	AB	R	H	2B	3B	HR	RBI	BB	SO	AVG	OBP	SLG	PRO+	BR/A	SB	CS	SBR	FA	FR	G/POS	TPR
1871	Ath-n	1	4	0	0	0	0	0	0	0	3	.000	.000	.000	-99	-1	0					/O-1	-0.1

■ BOB BERMAN
Berman, Robert Leon b: 1/24/1899, New York, N.Y. d: 8/2/88, Bridgeport, Conn. BR/TR, 5'8", 147 lbs. Deb: 6/4/18

YEAR	TM/L	G	AB	R	H	2B	3B	HR	RBI	BB	SO	AVG	OBP	SLG	PRO+	BR/A	SB	CS	SBR	FA	FR	G/POS	TPR
1918	Was-A	2	0	0	0	0	0	0	0	0	0	—	—	—	—	-0	0			1.000	0	/C-1	0.0

■ CURT BERNARD
Bernard, Curtis Henry b: 2/18/1878, Parkersburg, W.Va. d: 4/10/55, Culver City, Cal. BL/TR, 5'10", 150 lbs. Deb: 9/17/00

YEAR	TM/L	G	AB	R	H	2B	3B	HR	RBI	BB	SO	AVG	OBP	SLG	PRO+	BR/A	SB	CS	SBR	FA	FR	G/POS	TPR
1900	NY-N	20	71	9	18	2	0	0	8	6		.254	.329	.282	73	-2	1			.929	-2	O-19/S-1	-0.6
1901	NY-N	23	76	11	17	0	2	0	6	7		.224	.289	.276	67	-3	2			.800	-1	O-15/2-4,S3	-0.5
Total	2	43	147	20	35	2	2	0	14	13		.238	.309	.279	70	-5	3			.857	-3	/O-34,2-4,S3	-1.1

■ TONY BERNAZARD
Bernazard, Antonio (Garcia) b: 8/24/56, Caguas, P.R. BB/TR, 5'9", 160 lbs. Deb: 7/13/79

YEAR	TM/L	G	AB	R	H	2B	3B	HR	RBI	BB	SO	AVG	OBP	SLG	PRO+	BR/A	SB	CS	SBR	FA	FR	G/POS	TPR
1979	Mon-N	22	40	11	12	2	0	1	8	15	12	.300	.500	.425	156	5	1	2	-1	.982	-1	2-14	0.3
1980	Mon-N	82	183	26	41	7	1	5	18	17	41	.224	.290	.355	79	-5	9	2	2	.976	2	2-39,S-22	0.2
1981	Chi-A	106	384	53	106	14	4	6	34	54	66	.276	.368	.380	118	11	4	4	-1	.987	-1	*2-104/S-1	1.6
1982	Chi-A	137	540	90	138	25	9	11	56	67	88	.256	.340	.396	101	2	11	0	3	.985	25	*2-137	3.7
1983	Chi-A	59	233	30	61	16	2	2	26	17	45	.262	.312	.373	85	-5	2	1	0	.976	-2	2-59	-0.4
	Sea-A	80	300	35	80	18	1	6	30	38	52	.267	.353	.393	101	1	21	8	2	.971	1	2-79	0.7
	Yr	139	533	65	141	34	3	8	56	55	97	.265	.336	.385	94	-4	23	9	2	.973	-1	*2-138	0.3
1984	Cle-A	140	439	44	97	15	4	2	38	43	70	.221	.293	.287	60	-23	20	13	-2	.971	-11	*2-136/D-1	-3.1
1985	Cle-A	153	500	73	137	26	3	11	59	69	72	.274	.363	.404	111	9	17	9	-0	.978	-29	*2-147/S-1	-1.5
1986	Cle-A	146	562	88	169	28	4	17	73	53	91	.301	.367	.456	125	19	17	8	0	.979	-1	*2-146	2.6
1987	Cle-A	79	293	39	70	12	1	11	30	25	49	.239	.301	.399	83	-8	7	4	-0	.983	-16	2-78	-1.9
	Oak-A	61	214	34	57	14	1	3	19	30	30	.266	.357	.383	103	2	4	4	-1	.953	-18	2-59/D-3	-1.5
	Yr	140	507	73	127	26	2	14	49	55	79	.250	.325	.393	91	-6	11	8	-2	.971	-34	*2-137/D-3	-3.4
1991	Det-A	6	12	0	2	0	0	0	1	4		.167	.167	.167	-7	-2	0			.900	1	/2-2,D-2	0.0
Total	10	1071	3700	523	970	177	30	75	391	428	606	.262	.341	.387	100	6	113	55	1	.978	-48	2-1000/S-24,D	0.7

■ JUAN BERNHARDT
Bernhardt, Juan Ramon (Coradin) b: 8/31/53, San Pedro De Macoris, D.R. BR/TR, 5'11", 160 lbs. Deb: 7/10/76

YEAR	TM/L	G	AB	R	H	2B	3B	HR	RBI	BB	SO	AVG	OBP	SLG	PRO+	BR/A	SB	CS	SBR	FA	FR	G/POS	TPR
1976	NY-A	10	21	1	4	1	0	0	1	0	4	.190	.190	.238	25	-2	0	0	0	.800	-1	/O-4,3-1,D	-0.3
1977	Sea-A	89	305	32	74	9	2	6	30	5	26	.243	.260	.354	66	-15	2	3	-1	.982	-1	D-54,3-21/1	-1.9
1978	Sea-A	54	165	13	38	9	0	2	12	9	10	.230	.274	.321	67	-7	1	1	-0	.989	-0	1-25,3-22/D	-1.0
1979	Sea-A	1	1	0	1	0	0	0	0	0	0	1.000	1.000	1.000	434	0	0	0	0	.000	0	/H	0.0
Total	4	154	492	46	117	19	2	9	43	14	40	.238	.263	.339	66	-24	3	4	-2	.965	-2	/D-58,3-44,1O	-3.2

■ CARLOS BERNIER
Bernier, Carlos (Rodriguez) b: 1/28/29, Juana Diaz, P.R. d: 4/6/89, Juana Diaz, P.R. BR/TR, 5'9", 180 lbs. Deb: 4/22/53

YEAR	TM/L	G	AB	R	H	2B	3B	HR	RBI	BB	SO	AVG	OBP	SLG	PRO+	BR/A	SB	CS	SBR	FA	FR	G/POS	TPR
1953	Pit-N	105	310	48	66	7	8	3	31	51	53	.213	.332	.316	70	-12	15	14	-4	.970	5	O-86	-1.4

■ JOHNNY BERO
Bero, John George b: 12/22/22, Gary, W.Va. d: 5/11/85, Gardena, Cal. BL/TR, 6', 170 lbs. Deb: 9/26/48

YEAR	TM/L	G	AB	R	H	2B	3B	HR	RBI	BB	SO	AVG	OBP	SLG	PRO+	BR/A	SB	CS	SBR	FA	FR	G/POS	TPR
1948	Det-A	4	9	2	0	0	0	0	0	1	1	.000	.100	.000	-70	-2	0			1.000	-1	/2-2	-0.3
1951	StL-A	61	160	24	34	5	0	5	17	26	30	.213	.323	.338	76	-5	1	1	-0	.954	-9	S-55/2-1	-1.1
Total	2	65	169	26	34	5	0	5	17	27	31	.201	.311	.320	69	-7	1	1	-0	1.000	-10	/S-55,2-3	-1.4

■ DALE BERRA
Berra, Dale Anthony b: 12/13/56, Ridgewood, N.J. BR/TR, 6', 190 lbs. Deb: 8/22/77 F

YEAR	TM/L	G	AB	R	H	2B	3B	HR	RBI	BB	SO	AVG	OBP	SLG	PRO+	BR/A	SB	CS	SBR	FA	FR	G/POS	TPR
1977	Pit-N	17	40	0	7	1	0	0	3	1	8	.175	.195	.200	6	-5	0	0	0	.973	3	3-14	-0.3
1978	Pit-N	56	135	16	28	2	0	6	14	13	20	.207	.287	.356	75	-5	3	1	0	.908	4	3-55/S-2	-0.4
1979	Pit-N	44	123	11	26	5	0	3	15	11	17	.211	.276	.325	61	-7	0	0	0	.940	1	S-22,3-22	-0.5
1980	Pit-N	93	245	21	54	8	2	6	31	16	52	.220	.271	.343	69	-11	2	0	0	.968	-2	3-48,S-45/2	-0.5
1981	Pit-N	81	232	21	56	12	0	2	27	17	34	.241	.302	.319	74	-8	11	1	3	.976	2	3-42,S-30,2	-0.1
1982	Pit-N	156	529	64	139	25	5	10	61	33	83	.263	.311	.386	91	-7	6	6	-2	.961	-2	*S-153/3-6	0.3
1983	Pit-N	161	537	51	135	25	1	10	52	61	84	.251	.328	.358	88	-8	8	5	-1	.963	16	*S-161	2.3
1984	Pit-N	136	450	31	100	16	0	9	52	34	78	.222	.278	.318	67	-20	1	3	-0	.955	-2	*S-135/3-1	-1.1
1985	NY-A	48	109	8	25	5	1	1	8	7	20	.229	.276	.321	64	-5	1	1	-0	.917	-3	3-41/S-6	-0.3
1986	NY-A	42	108	10	25	7	0	2	13	9	14	.231	.297	.352	77	-4	0	0	0	.972	-1	S-19,3-18/D	-0.3
1987	Hou-N	19	45	3	8	0	0	2	8	12	12	.178	.302	.244	49	-3	0	0	0	.963	-3	S-18/2-3	-0.5
Total	11	853	2553	236	603	109	9	49	278	210	422	.236	.297	.344	76	-83	32	17	-1	.959	21	S-591,3-247/2D	-1.3

■ YOGI BERRA
Berra, Lawrence Peter b: 5/12/25, St.Louis, Mo. BL/TR, 5'8", 194 lbs. Deb: 9/22/46 FMCH

YEAR	TM/L	G	AB	R	H	2B	3B	HR	RBI	BB	SO	AVG	OBP	SLG	PRO+	BR/A	SB	CS	SBR	FA	FR	G/POS	TPR
1946	NY-A	7	22	3	8	1	0	2	4	1	1	.364	.391	.682	193	2	0	0	0	1.000	2	/C-6	0.5
1947	*NY-A	83	293	41	82	15	3	11	54	13	12	.280	.310	.464	115	2	0	1	-1	.972	-6	C-51,O-24	-0.1
1948	NY-A☆	125	469	70	143	24	10	14	98	25	24	.305	.341	.488	120	10	3	3	-1	.979	-9	C-71,O-50	0.2
1949	*NY-A★	116	415	59	115	20	2	20	91	22	25	.277	.323	.480	111	2	2	1	0	.989	11	*C-109	1.9
1950	*NY-A★	151	597	116	192	30	6	28	124	55	12	.322	.383	.533	136	29	4	2	0	.985	-3	*C-148	3.4
1951	*NY-A★	141	547	92	161	19	4	27	88	44	20	.294	.350	.492	131	20	5	4	-1	.984	9	*C-141	3.3
1952	*NY-A★	142	534	97	146	17	1	30	98	66	24	.273	.358	.478	139	26	2	3	-1	.992	-5	*C-140	3.5
1953	*NY-A★	137	503	80	149	23	5	27	108	50	32	.296	.363	.523	142	27	0	3	-2	.986	3	*C-133	3.4
1954	*NY-A★	151	584	88	179	28	6	22	125	56	29	.307	.371	.488	139	29	0	1	-0	.990	-0	*C-149/3-1	3.6
1955	*NY-A★	147	541	84	147	20	3	27	108	60	20	.272	.352	.470	121	14	1	0	0	.984	-5	*C-145	1.9
1956	*NY-A★	140	521	93	155	29	2	30	105	65	29	.298	.381	.534	144	31	3	2	-1	.986	7	*C-135/O-1	4.2
1957	*NY-A★	134	482	74	121	14	2	24	82	57	24	.251	.331	.438	110	8	1	2	-1	.995	16	*C-121/O-6	2.6
1958	*NY-A★	122	433	60	115	17	3	22	90	35	35	.266	.323	.471	120	10	3	0	1	**1.000**	6	C-88,O-21/1	2.1
1959	*NY-A★	131	472	64	134	25	1	19	69	43	38	.284	.349	.462	125	15	1	2	-1	**.997**	7	*C-116/O-7	2.8
1960	*NY-A★	120	359	46	99	14	1	15	62	38	23	.276	.350	.446	120	10	2	1	0	.989	-10	C-63,O-36	0.2
1961	*NY-A★	119	395	62	107	11	0	22	61	35	28	.271	.333	.466	117	8	2	1	0	.988	3	O-87,C-15	0.7
1962	*NY-A	86	232	25	52	8	0	10	35	24	18	.224	.302	.388	87	-5	0	1	-1	.990	8	C-31,O-28	0.2
1963	*NY-A	64	147	20	43	6	0	8	28	15	17	.293	.362	.497	139	8	1	0	0	.988	8	C-35	1.8
1965	NY-N	4	9	1	2	0	0	0	0	0	0	.222	.222	.222	27	-1	0	0	0	.941	1	/C-2	0.0
Total	19	2120	7555	1175	2150	321	49	358	1430	704	414	.285	.350	.482	126	245	30	26	-7	.989	57	*C-1699,O-260/13	36.2

■ DENNIS BERRAN
Berran, Dennis Martin b: 10/8/1887, Merrimac, Mass. d: 4/28/43, Boston, Mass. BL/TL, Deb: 8/11/12

YEAR	TM/L	G	AB	R	H	2B	3B	HR	RBI	BB	SO	AVG	OBP	SLG	PRO+	BR/A	SB	CS	SBR	FA	FR	G/POS	TPR
1912	Chi-A	2	4	1	1	0	0	0	0	0		.250	.250	.250	44	-0	0			1.000	-1	/O-2	-0.1

■ RAY BERRES
Berres, Raymond Frederick b: 8/31/07, Kenosha, Wis. BR/TR, 5'9", 170 lbs. Deb: 4/24/34 C

YEAR	TM/L	G	AB	R	H	2B	3B	HR	RBI	BB	SO	AVG	OBP	SLG	PRO+	BR/A	SB	CS	SBR	FA	FR	G/POS	TPR
1934	Bro-N	39	79	7	17	4	0	0	3	1	16	.215	.225	.266	32	-8	0			.969	-2	C-37	-0.8

YEAR	TM/L	G	AB	R	H	2B	3B	HR	RBI	BB	SO	AVG	OBP	SLG	PRO+	BR/A	SB	CS	SBR	FA	FR	G/POS	TPR
1936	Bro-N	105	267	16	64	10	1	1	13	14	35	.240	.280	.296	55	-17	1			.988	23	*C-105	0.9
1937	Pit-N	2	6	0	1	0	0	0	0	0	0	.167	.167	.167	-9	-1	0			1.000	1	/C-2	0.0
1938	Pit-N	40	100	7	23	2	0	0	6	8	10	.230	.287	.250	48	-7	0			.993	4	C-40	-0.1
1939	Pit-N	81	231	22	53	6	1	0	16	11	25	.229	.267	.264	44	-18	1			.993	-2	C-80	-1.7
1940	Pit-N	21	32	2	6	0	0	0	2	1	1	.188	.212	.188	11	-4	0			.980	3	C-21	-0.1
	Bos-N	85	229	12	44	4	1	0	14	18	19	.192	.251	.218	32	-21	0			.981	1	C-85	-1.5
	Yr	106	261	14	50	4	1	0	16	19	20	.192	.246	.215	29	-25	0			.981	3	*C-106	-1.6
1941	Bos-N	120	279	21	56	10	0	1	19	17	20	.201	.247	.247	41	-22	2			**.995**	9	*C-120	-0.6
1942	NY-N	12	32	0	6	0	0	0	1	2	3	.188	.235	.188	24	-3	0			.973	-2	C-12	-0.4
1943	NY-N	20	28	1	4	1	0	0	0	1	2	.143	.172	.179	1	-4	0			.981	4	C-17	0.1
1944	NY-N	16	17	4	8	0	0	1	2	1	0	.471	.526	.647	230	3	0			1.000	0	C-12	0.4
1945	NY-N	20	30	4	5	0	0	0	2	3	1	.167	.219	.167	8	-4	0			1.000	1	C-20	-0.2
Total	11	561	1330	96	287	37	3	3	78	76	134	.216	.260	.255	43	-105	4			.989	40	C-551	-4.0

■ GERONIMO BERROA
Berroa, Geronimo Emiliano Letta (b: Geronimo Emiliano Letta (Berroa))   b: 3/18/65, Santo Domingo, D.R.   BR/TR, 6', 165 lbs.   Deb: 4/5/89

YEAR	TM/L	G	AB	R	H	2B	3B	HR	RBI	BB	SO	AVG	OBP	SLG	PRO+	BR/A	SB	CS	SBR	FA	FR	G/POS	TPR
1989	Atl-N	81	136	7	36	4	0	2	9	7	32	.265	.301	.338	80	-4	0	1	-1	.971	1	O-34	-0.4
1990	Atl-N	7	4	0	0	0	0	0	0	0	0	.000	.200	.000	-38	-1	0	0	0	1.000	-1	/O-3	-0.2
1992	Cin-N	13	15	2	4	1	0	0	0	2	1	.267	.389	.333	103	0	0	1	-1	1.000	0	/O-3	0.0
1993	Fla-N	14	34	3	4	1	0	0	0	2	9	.118	.167	.147	-14	-5	0	0	0	.833	-1	/O-9	-0.7
1994	Oak-A	96	340	55	104	18	2	13	65	41	62	.306	.385	.485	134	17	7	2	1	1.000	1	D-44,O-42/1	1.5
Total	5	211	529	67	148	24	2	15	74	53	103	.280	.350	.418	108	8	7	4	-0	.976	-0	/O-91,D-44,1	0.2

■ KEN BERRY
Berry, Allen Kent   b: 5/10/41, Kansas City, Mo.   BR/TR, 5'11", 180 lbs.   Deb: 9/9/62

YEAR	TM/L	G	AB	R	H	2B	3B	HR	RBI	BB	SO	AVG	OBP	SLG	PRO+	BR/A	SB	CS	SBR	FA	FR	G/POS	TPR
1962	Chi-A	3	6	2	2	0	0	0	0	0	0	.333	.333	.333	80	-0	0	0	0	1.000	1	/O-2	0.0
1963	Chi-A	4	5	2	1	0	0	0	0	0	1	.200	.333	.200	55	-0	0	0	0	.857	-0	/O-2,2,-1	0.0
1964	Chi-A	12	32	4	12	1	0	1	4	5	3	.375	.459	.500	171	3	0	1	-1	1.000	-3	O-12	0.0
1965	Chi-A	157	472	51	103	17	4	12	42	28	96	.218	.269	.347	79	-15	4	2	0	.980	3	*O-156	-1.9
1966	Chi-A	147	443	50	120	20	2	8	34	28	63	.271	.317	.379	106	2	7	10	-4	.991	-9	*O-141	-1.8
1967	Chi-A★	147	485	49	117	14	4	7	41	46	68	.241	.311	.330	93	-4	9	8	-2	.992	-15	*O-143	-3.1
1968	Chi-A	153	504	49	127	21	2	7	32	25	64	.252	.289	.343	90	-7	6	6	-2	.981	3	*O-151	-1.5
1969	Chi-A	130	297	25	69	12	2	4	18	24	50	.232	.296	.327	71	-12	1	2	-1	**1.000**	-5	O-120	-2.3
1970	Chi-A	141	463	45	128	12	2	7	50	43	61	.276	.346	.356	90	-5	6	4	-1	.988	5	*O-138	-0.6
1971	Cal-A	111	298	29	66	17	0	3	22	18	33	.221	.273	.309	69	-13	2	4	-0	.988	2	*O-101	-1.6
1972	Cal-A	119	409	41	118	15	3	5	39	35	47	.289	.348	.377	122	11	5	3	-0	**1.000**	14	*O-116	2.2
1973	Cal-A	136	415	48	118	11	2	3	36	26	50	.284	.328	.342	96	-3	1	6	-3	**.997**	3	*O-129	-0.8
1974	Mil-A	98	267	21	64	9	2	1	24	18	26	.240	.295	.300	72	-10	3	1	0	.995	-3	O-82,D-13	-1.7
1975	Cle-A	25	40	6	8	1	0	0	1	1	7	.200	.238	.225	31	-4	0	1	-1	.926	-2	O-18/D-5	-0.7
Total	14	1383	4136	422	1053	150	23	58	343	298	569	.255	.309	.344	90	-56	45	46	-14	.989	-5	*O-1311/D-18,2	-13.8

■ CHARLIE BERRY
Berry, Charles Francis   b: 10/18/02, Phillipsburg, N.J.   d: 9/6/72, Evanston, Ill.   BR/TR, 6', 185 lbs.   Deb: 6/15/25   FUC

YEAR	TM/L	G	AB	R	H	2B	3B	HR	RBI	BB	SO	AVG	OBP	SLG	PRO+	BR/A	SB	CS	SBR	FA	FR	G/POS	TPR
1925	Phi-A	10	14	1	3	1	0	0	3	0	2	.214	.214	.286	24	-2	0	0	0	.900	-1	/C-4	-0.2
1928	Bos-A	80	177	18	46	7	3	1	19	21	19	.260	.342	.350	84	-4	1	1	-0	.959	-9	C-63	-0.9
1929	Bos-A	77	207	19	50	11	4	1	21	15	29	.242	.302	.348	69	-10	2	4	-2	.983	-7	C-72	-0.3
1930	Bos-A	88	256	31	74	9	6	6	35	16	22	.289	.331	.441	98	-2	2	0	1	.988	7	C-85	1.2
1931	Bos-A	111	357	41	101	16	2	6	49	29	38	.283	.337	.389	96	-3	4	0	1	.985	-3	*C-102	0.2
1932	Bos-A	10	32	0	6	3	0	0	6	3	2	.188	.257	.281	40	-3	0	0	0	.944	-1	C-10	-0.3
	Chi-A	72	226	33	69	15	6	4	31	21	23	.305	.364	.478	124	7	3	0	1	.981	-2	C-70	1.0
	Yr	82	258	33	75	18	6	4	37	24	25	.291	.351	.453	114	4	3	0	1	.977	-2	C-80	0.7
1933	Chi-A	86	271	25	69	8	3	2	28	17	16	.255	.301	.388	70	-12	1	0	0	.987	-8	C-83	-1.5
1934	Phi-A	99	269	14	72	10	2	0	34	22	23	.268	.323	.320	69	-12	1	0	0	.987	0	C-99	-0.8
1935	Phi-A	62	190	14	48	7	3	3	29	10	20	.253	.290	.368	70	-9	0	0	0	.987	-1	C-56	-0.7
1936	Phi-A	13	17	0	1	1	0	0	1	6	2	.059	.304	.118	8	-2	0	0	0	.971	1	C-12	-0.1
1938	Phi-A	1	2	0	0	0	0	0	0	0	0	.000	.000	.000	-99	-2	0	0	0	1.000	0	/C-1	0.0
Total	11	709	2018	196	539	88	29	23	256	160	196	.267	.322	.374	83	-52	13	5	1	.982	-12	C-657	-2.4

■ CHARLIE BERRY
Berry, Charles Joseph   b: 9/6/1860, Elizabeth, N.J.   d: 1/22/40, Phillipsburg, N.J.   BR/TR, 5'11", 175 lbs.   Deb: 4/30/1884   F

YEAR	TM/L	G	AB	R	H	2B	3B	HR	RBI	BB	SO	AVG	OBP	SLG	PRO+	BR/A	SB	CS	SBR	FA	FR	G/POS	TPR
1884	Alt-U	7	25	2	6	0	0	0		0		.240	.240	.240	30	-2				.862	-6	/2-7	-0.8
	KC-U	29	118	15	29	6	1	1		1		.246	.252	.339	68	-5	3			.887	3	2-22/O-8,3	-0.2
	CP-U	7	27	4	3	2	0	0				.111	.111	.185	-21	-4				.833	1	/2-7	-0.3
	Yr	43	170	21	38	8	1	1		1		.224	.228	.300	46	-13	3			.871	-3	2-36/O-8,3	-1.3

■ CLAUDE BERRY
Berry, Claude Elzy "Admiral"   b: 2/14/1880, Losantville, Ind.   d: 2/1/74, Richmond, Ind.   BR/TR, 5'7", 165 lbs.   Deb: 4/22/04

YEAR	TM/L	G	AB	R	H	2B	3B	HR	RBI	BB	SO	AVG	OBP	SLG	PRO+	BR/A	SB	CS	SBR	FA	FR	G/POS	TPR
1904	Chi-A	3	1	1	0	0	0	0	0	1		.000	.500	.000	68	0	0			1.000	1	/C-3	0.1
1906	Phi-A	10	30	2	7	0	0	0	2	2		.233	.281	.233	60	-1	1			.938	6	C-10	0.5
1907	Phi-A	8	19	2	4	2	0	0	1	2		.211	.286	.316	90	-0	0			.944	-2	/C-8	-0.2
1914	Pit-F	124	411	35	98	18	9	2	36	26	50	.238	.284	.341	62	-25	6			.970	1	*C-122	-1.4
1915	Pit-F	100	292	32	56	11	1	1	26	29	42	.192	.269	.247	39	-25	7			.980	-0	C-99	-2.0
Total	5	245	753	72	165	31	10	3	65	60	92	.219	.279	.299	54	-52	14			.971	4	C-242	-3.0

■ NEIL BERRY
Berry, Cornelius John   b: 1/11/22, Kalamazoo, Mich.   BR/TR, 5'10", 170 lbs.   Deb: 4/20/48

YEAR	TM/L	G	AB	R	H	2B	3B	HR	RBI	BB	SO	AVG	OBP	SLG	PRO+	BR/A	SB	CS	SBR	FA	FR	G/POS	TPR
1948	Det-A	87	256	46	68	8	1	0	16	37	23	.266	.358	.305	75	-8	1	3	-2	.930	-4	S-41,2-26	-0.2
1949	Det-A	109	329	38	78	9	1	0	18	27	24	.237	.299	.271	51	-23	4	2	0	.970	-0	2-95/S-4	-1.9
1950	Det-A	39	40	9	10	1	0	0	7	6	11	.250	.348	.275	59	-2	1	1	0	.944	2	S-12/2-2,3	0.1
1951	Det-A	67	157	17	36	5	2	0	9	10	15	.229	.275	.287	52	-11	4	2	0	.944	8	S-38,2-10/3	0.0
1952	Det-A	73	189	22	43	4	3	0	13	22	19	.228	.311	.280	65	-9	1	3	-2	.965	4	S-66/3-2	-0.3
1953	StL-A	57	99	14	28	1	2	0	11	9	10	.283	.343	.333	82	-2	1	2	-1	.825	-1	3-18,2-15/S	-0.4
	Chi-A	5	8	1	1	0	0	0	0	1	1	.125	.222	.125	-4	-1	0	0	0	1.000	2	/2-3	0.1
	Yr	62	107	15	29	1	2	0	11	10	11	.271	.333	.318	75	-4	1	2	-1	.825	1	3-18,2-18/S	-0.3
1954	Bal-A	5	9	1	1	0	0	0	0	0	0	.111	.200	.111	-14	-1	0	0	0	1.000	0	/S-5	-0.1
Total	7	442	1087	148	265	28	9	0	74	113	105	.244	.317	.286	62	-58	11	12	-4	.949	19	S-172,2-151/3	-2.7

■ JOE BERRY
Berry, Joseph Howard Jr. "Nig"   b: 12/31/1894, Philadelphia, Pa.   d: 4/29/76, Philadelphia, Pa.   BB/TR, 5'10.5", 159 lbs.   Deb: 7/18/21   F

YEAR	TM/L	G	AB	R	H	2B	3B	HR	RBI	BB	SO	AVG	OBP	SLG	PRO+	BR/A	SB	CS	SBR	FA	FR	G/POS	TPR
1921	NY-N	9	6	0	2	0	1	0	2	1	1	.333	.429	.667	185	1	0	0	0	.875	0	/2-7	0.1
1922	NY-N	6	0	0	0	0	0	0	0	0	0	—	—	—	—		0	0	0	.000	0	R	0.0
Total	2	15	6	0	2	0	1	0	2	1	1	.333	.429	.667	185	1	0	0	0	.875	0	/2-7	0.1

■ JOE BERRY
Berry, Joseph Howard Sr. "Hodge"   b: 9/10/1872, Wheeling, W.Va.   d: 3/13/61, Allenwood, N.J.   BB/TR, 5'9", 172 lbs.   Deb: 9/4/02   F

YEAR	TM/L	G	AB	R	H	2B	3B	HR	RBI	BB	SO	AVG	OBP	SLG	PRO+	BR/A	SB	CS	SBR	FA	FR	G/POS	TPR
1902	Phi-N	1	4	0	1	0	0	0		1	1	.250	.400	.250	101	0	1			1.000	-1	/C-1	-0.1

■ SEAN BERRY
Berry, Sean Robert   b: 3/22/66, Santa Monica, Cal.   BR/TR, 5'11", 200 lbs.   Deb: 9/17/90

YEAR	TM/L	G	AB	R	H	2B	3B	HR	RBI	BB	SO	AVG	OBP	SLG	PRO+	BR/A	SB	CS	SBR	FA	FR	G/POS	TPR
1990	KC-A	8	23	2	5	1	1	0	4	2	5	.217	.280	.348	76	-1	0	0	0	.944	1	/3-8	0.0
1991	KC-A	31	60	5	8	3	0	0	1	5	23	.133	.212	.183	10	-7	0	0	0	.970	8	3-30	0.1
1992	Mon-N	24	57	5	19	1	0	1	4	4	11	.333	.345	.404	112	1	2	1	0	.879	-3	3-20	-0.2
1993	Mon-N	122	299	50	78	15	2	14	49	41	70	.261	.354	.465	112	5	12	2	2	.936	5	3-96	1.3

YEAR	TM/L	G	AB	R	H	2B	3B	HR	RBI	BB	SO	AVG	OBP	SLG	PRO+	BR/A	SB	CS	SBR	FA	FR	G/POS	TPR
1994	Mon-N	103	320	43	89	19	2	11	41	32	50	.278	.349	.453	105	2	14	0	4	.938	-2	*3-100	0.4
Total	5	288	759	105	199	39	5	26	99	81	159	.262	.338	.430	101	0	28	3	7	.938	8	3-254	1.6

■ TOM BERRY
Berry, Thomas Haney b: 12/31/1842, Chester, Pa. d: 6/6/15, Chester, Pa. 5'6", 140 lbs. Deb: 9/2/1871

YEAR	TM/L	G	AB	R	H	2B	3B	HR	RBI	BB	SO	AVG	OBP	SLG	PRO+	BR/A	SB	CS	SBR	FA	FR	G/POS	TPR
1871	Ath-n	1	4	0	1	0	0	0	0	0	0	.250	.250	.250	45	-0	0					/O-1	0.0

■ DAMON BERRYHILL
Berryhill, Damon Scott b: 12/3/63, South Laguna, Cal. BB/TR, 6' ", 210 lbs. Deb: 9/5/87

YEAR	TM/L	G	AB	R	H	2B	3B	HR	RBI	BB	SO	AVG	OBP	SLG	PRO+	BR/A	SB	CS	SBR	FA	FR	G/POS	TPR
1987	Chi-N	12	28	2	5	1	0	0	1	3	5	.179	.258	.214	26	-3	0	1	-1	.909	-4	C-11	-0.7
1988	Chi-N	95	309	19	80	19	1	7	38	17	56	.259	.298	.395	93	-3	1	0	0	.982	-3	C-90	0.0
1989	Chi-N	91	334	37	86	13	0	5	41	16	54	.257	.295	.341	76	-11	0	0	0	.992	-12	C-89	-1.8
1990	Chi-N	17	53	6	10	4	0	1	9	5	14	.189	.259	.321	54	-3	0	0	0	.978	-3	C-15	-0.5
1991	Chi-N	62	159	13	30	7	0	5	14	11	41	.189	.246	.327	57	-3	1	2	-1	.967	-6	C-48	-1.5
	Atl-N	1	1	0	0	0	0	0	0	0	1	.000	.000	.000	-94	-0	0	0	0	1.000	0	/C-1	0.0
	Yr	63	160	13	30	7	0	5	14	11	42	.188	.244	.325	56	-10	1	2	-1	.967	-6	C-49	-1.5
1992	*Atl-N	101	307	21	70	8	1	10	43	17	67	.228	.271	.384	79	-9	0	2	-1	.998	-8	C-84	-1.5
1993	*Atl-N	115	335	24	82	18	2	8	43	21	64	.245	.293	.382	78	-11	0	0	0	.990	9	*C-105	0.3
1994	Bos-A	82	255	30	67	17	2	6	34	19	59	.263	.314	.416	81	-8	0	1	-1	.995	-1	C-67/D-6	-0.5
Total	8	576	1781	152	430	95	6	42	223	109	361	.241	.287	.372	77	-58	3	6	-3	.988	-27	C-510/D-6	-6.2

■ HARRY BERTE
Berte, Harry Thomas b: 5/10/1872, Covington, Ky. d: 5/6/52, Los Angeles, Cal. TR, Deb: 9/17/03

YEAR	TM/L	G	AB	R	H	2B	3B	HR	RBI	BB	SO	AVG	OBP	SLG	PRO+	BR/A	SB	CS	SBR	FA	FR	G/POS	TPR
1903	StL-N	4	15	1	5	0	0	0		1	1	.333	.375	.333	106	0	0			.778	-4	/2-3,S-1	-0.4

■ DICK BERTELL
Bertell, Richard George b: 11/21/35, Oak Park, Ill. BR/TR, 6'0.5", 200 lbs. Deb: 9/22/60

YEAR	TM/L	G	AB	R	H	2B	3B	HR	RBI	BB	SO	AVG	OBP	SLG	PRO+	BR/A	SB	CS	SBR	FA	FR	G/POS	TPR
1960	Chi-N	5	15	0	2	0	0	0	2	3	1	.133	.278	.133	17	-2	0	0	0	1.000	-1	/C-5	-0.3
1961	Chi-N	92	267	20	73	7	1	2	33	15	33	.273	.312	.330	70	-11	0	0	0	.982	4	C-90	-0.4
1962	Chi-N	77	215	19	65	6	2	2	18	13	30	.302	.345	.377	90	-3	0	0	0	.986	-13	C-76	-1.4
1963	Chi-N	100	322	15	75	7	2	2	14	24	41	.233	.286	.286	62	-15	0	2	-1	.988	16	C-99	0.4
1964	Chi-N	112	353	29	84	11	3	4	35	33	67	.238	.307	.320	74	-12	2	1	0	.981	-5	*C-110	-1.2
1965	Chi-N	34	84	6	18	2	0	0	7	11	10	.214	.305	.238	54	-5	0	0	0	.981	3	C-34	-0.1
	SF-N	22	48	1	9	1	0	0	3	7	5	.188	.291	.208	42	-3	0	0	0	.992	3	C-22	-0.1
	Yr	56	132	7	27	3	0	0	10	18	15	.205	.300	.227	50	-8	0	0	0	.986	5	C-56	-0.2
1967	Chi-N	2	6	1	1	0	1	0		0	1	.167	.167	.500	80	-0	0	0	0	1.000	0	/C-2	0.0
Total	7	444	1310	91	327	34	9	10	112	106	188	.250	.307	.312	70	-51	2	4	-2	.985	7	C-438	-3.1

■ HARRY BERTHRONG
Berthrong, Henry W. b: 1/1/1844, Mumford, N.Y. d: 4/28/28, Chelsea, Mass. TR, 5'6.5", 140 lbs. Deb: 5/5/1871

YEAR	TM/L	G	AB	R	H	2B	3B	HR	RBI	BB	SO	AVG	OBP	SLG	PRO+	BR/A	SB	CS	SBR	FA	FR	G/POS	TPR
1871	Oly-n	17	73	17	17	1	1	0	8	4	2	.233	.273	.274	61	-3	3					O-12/2-4,3	-0.2

■ RENO BERTOIA
Bertoia, Reno Peter b: 1/8/35, St.Vito Udine, Italy BR/TR, 5'11.5", 185 lbs. Deb: 9/22/53

YEAR	TM/L	G	AB	R	H	2B	3B	HR	RBI	BB	SO	AVG	OBP	SLG	PRO+	BR/A	SB	CS	SBR	FA	FR	G/POS	TPR
1953	Det-A	1	1	0	0	0	0	0	0	0	1	.000	.000	.000	-99	-0	0	0	0	.500	-0	/2-1	-0.1
1954	Det-A	54	37	13	6	2	0	1	2	5	9	.162	.262	.297	54	-2	1	0	0	.969	17	2-15/3-8,S	1.5
1955	Det-A	38	68	13	14	2	1	1	10	5	11	.206	.260	.309	54	-5	0	0	0	.923	1	3-14/2-6,S	0.2
1956	Det-A	22	66	7	12	2	0	1	5	6	12	.182	.260	.258	37	-6	0	0	0	.982	10	2-18/3-2	0.5
1957	Det-A	97	295	28	81	16	2	4	28	19	43	.275	.327	.383	91	-4	2	3	-1	.953	-19	3-83/S-7,2	-2.3
1958	Det-A	86	240	28	56	6	0	6	27	20	35	.233	.298	.333	68	-10	5	2	0	.950	4	3-68/S-5,O	-0.5
1959	Was-A	90	308	33	73	10	0	8	29	29	48	.237	.305	.347	79	-9	2	5	-2	.971	-11	2-71/3-5,S	-1.7
1960	Was-A	121	460	44	122	17	7	4	45	26	58	.265	.316	.359	83	-11	3	5	-2	.961	-0	*3-112,2-21	-1.4
1961	Min-A	35	104	17	22	2	0	1	8	20	12	.212	.339	.260	59	-5	0	0	0	.900	-5	3-32	-1.1
	KC-A	39	120	12	29	2	0	3	13	9	15	.242	.296	.258	48	-9	3	1	0	.942	5	3-29/2-6	-0.3
	Det-A	24	46	6	10	1	0	1	4	3	8	.217	.265	.304	50	-3	2	0	1	.931	0	3-13/2-7,S	-0.2
	Yr	98	270	35	61	5	0	5	25	32	35	.226	.308	.267	53	-17	5	1	1	.923	-1	3-74,2-13/S	-1.6
1962	Det-A	5	0	3	0	0	0	0	0	0	0	—	—	—	—	0	0	0	0	1.000	0	/2-1,S-1,3	0.0
Total	10	612	1745	204	425	60	10	27	171	142	252	.244	.306	.336	73	-65	16	15	-4	.949	9	3-367,2-148/SO	-5.4

■ BOB BESCHER
Bescher, Robert Henry b: 2/25/1884, London, Ohio d: 11/29/42, London, Ohio BB/TL, 6'1", 200 lbs. Deb: 9/5/08

YEAR	TM/L	G	AB	R	H	2B	3B	HR	RBI	BB	SO	AVG	OBP	SLG	PRO+	BR/A	SB	CS	SBR	FA	FR	G/POS	TPR
1908	Cin-N	32	114	16	31	5	5	0	17	9		.272	.336	.404	140	5	10			1.000	4	O-32	0.8
1909	Cin-N	124	446	73	107	17	6	1	34	56		.240	.335	.312	102	3	**54**			.953	-0	*O-117	-0.3
1910	Cin-N	150	589	95	147	20	10	4	48	81	75	.250	.344	.338	104	4	**70**			.947	2	*O-150	-0.2
1911	Cin-N	153	599	106	165	32	10	1	45	102	78	.275	.385	.367	115	16	**80**			.954	-8	*O-153	0.0
1912	Cin-N	145	548	**120**	154	29	11	4	38	83	61	.281	.381	.396	116	15	**67**			.963	4	*O-143	1.1
1913	Cin-N	141	511	86	132	22	11	1	37	**94**	68	.258	.377	.350	109	10	38			.968	4	*O-138	0.8
1914	NY-N	135	512	82	138	23	4	6	35	45	48	.270	.336	.365	112	7	36			.960	9	*O-126	1.1
1915	StL-N	130	486	71	128	15	7	4	34	52	53	.263	.342	.348	109	6	27	19	-3	.971	-1	*O-129	-0.5
1916	StL-N	151	561	78	132	24	8	6	43	60	50	.235	.316	.339	102	2	39	12	5	.953	-0	*O-151	-0.1
1917	StL-N	42	110	10	17	1	1	1	8	20	13	.155	.290	.209	56	-5	3			.984	-3	O-32	-1.1
1918	Cle-A	25	60	12	20	2	1	0	6	11	5	.333	.487	.400	153	5	3			.969	-0	O-17	0.4
Total	11	1228	4536	749	1171	190	74	28	345	619	<u>451</u>	.258	.353	.351	109	68	427	<u>31</u>		.960	9	*O-1188	2.0

■ BESTICK
Bestick b: New York, N.Y. Deb: 6/10/1872

YEAR	TM/L	G	AB	R	H	2B	3B	HR	RBI	BB	SO	AVG	OBP	SLG	PRO+	BR/A	SB	CS	SBR	FA	FR	G/POS	TPR
1872	Eck-n	4	14	0	3	0	0	0	1		0	.214	.214	.214	38	-1						/C-4	-0.1

■ JIM BESWICK
Beswick, James William b: 2/12/58, Wilkinsburg, Pa. BB/TR, 6'1", 180 lbs. Deb: 8/9/78

YEAR	TM/L	G	AB	R	H	2B	3B	HR	RBI	BB	SO	AVG	OBP	SLG	PRO+	BR/A	SB	CS	SBR	FA	FR	G/POS	TPR
1978	SD-N	17	20	2	1	0	0	0	0	1	7	.050	.095	.050	-63	-4	0	0	0	1.000	-1	/O-6	-0.6

■ FRANK BETCHER
Betcher, Franklin Lyle (b: Franklin Lyle Bettger)
b: 2/15/1888, Philadelphia, Pa. d: 11/27/81, Wynnewood, Pa. BB/TR, 5'11", 173 lbs. Deb: 5/21/10

YEAR	TM/L	G	AB	R	H	2B	3B	HR	RBI	BB	SO	AVG	OBP	SLG	PRO+	BR/A	SB	CS	SBR	FA	FR	G/POS	TPR
1910	StL-N	35	89	7	18	2	0	0	6	7	14	.202	.276	.225	48	-6	1			.928	0	S-12/3-7,2O	-0.5

■ BILL BETHEA
Bethea, William Lamar "Spot" b: 1/1/42, Houston, Tex. BR/TR, 6', 175 lbs. Deb: 9/13/64

YEAR	TM/L	G	AB	R	H	2B	3B	HR	RBI	BB	SO	AVG	OBP	SLG	PRO+	BR/A	SB	CS	SBR	FA	FR	G/POS	TPR
1964	Min-A	10	30	4	5	1	0	0	2	4	4	.167	.265	.200	31	-3	0	0	0	1.000	-1	/2-7,S-3	-0.3

■ LARRY BETTENCOURT
Bettencourt, Lawrence Joseph b: 9/22/05, Newark, Cal. d: 9/15/78, New Orleans, La. BR/TR, 5'11", 195 lbs. Deb: 6/2/28

YEAR	TM/L	G	AB	R	H	2B	3B	HR	RBI	BB	SO	AVG	OBP	SLG	PRO+	BR/A	SB	CS	SBR	FA	FR	G/POS	TPR
1928	StL-A	67	159	30	45	9	4	4	24	22	19	.283	.377	.465	117	4	2	1	0	.946	-11	3-41/O-2,C	-0.4
1931	StL-A	74	206	27	53	9	2	3	26	31	35	.257	.357	.364	87	-3	4	3	-1	.963	-2	O-58	-0.9
1932	StL-A	27	30	4	4	1	0	1	3	7	6	.133	.297	.267	45	-2	1	0	0	1.000	-0	/O-4,3-2	-0.2
Total	3	168	395	61	102	19	6	8	53	60	60	.258	.360	.397	95	-2	7	4	-0	.966	-13	/O-64,3-43,C	-1.5

■ BRUNO BETZEL
Betzel, Christian Frederick Albert John Henry David
b: 12/6/1894, Chattanooga, Ohio d: 2/7/65, W.Hollywood, Fla. BR/TR, 5'9", 158 lbs. Deb: 9/3/14

YEAR	TM/L	G	AB	R	H	2B	3B	HR	RBI	BB	SO	AVG	OBP	SLG	PRO+	BR/A	SB	CS	SBR	FA	FR	G/POS	TPR
1914	StL-N	7	9	2	0	0	0	0	0	1	1	.000	.100	.000	-70	-2	0			1.000	2	/2-4,3-1	0.0
1915	StL-N	117	367	42	92	12	4	0	27	18	48	.251	.291	.305	80	-9	10	13	-5	.937	5	*3-105/2-3,S	-0.5
1916	StL-N	142	510	49	119	15	11	1	37	39	77	.233	.288	.312	85	-10	22	16	-3	.960	28	*2-113,3-33/O	2.3
1917	StL-N	106	328	24	71	4	3	1	17	20	47	.216	.266	.256	62	-15	9			.962	12	2-75,O-23/3	-0.1
1918	StL-N	76	230	18	51	6	7	0	13	12	16	.222	.260	.309	76	-7	8			.914	-3	3-34,O-21,2	-1.0
Total	5	448	1444	135	333	37	25	2	94	90	189	.231	.278	.295	76	-42	49	<u>29</u>		.956	46	2-205,3-177/OS	0.7

YEAR	TM/L	G	AB	R	H	2B	3B	HR	RBI	BB	SO	AVG	OBP	SLG	PRO+	BR/A	SB	CS	SBR	FA	FR	G/POS	TPR

■ KURT BEVACQUA

Bevacqua, Kurt Anthony   b: 1/23/47, Miami Beach, Fla.   BR/TR, 6'1", 185 lbs.   Deb: 6/22/71

YEAR	TM/L	G	AB	R	H	2B	3B	HR	RBI	BB	SO	AVG	OBP	SLG	PRO+	BR/A	SB	CS	SBR	FA	FR	G/POS	TPR
1971	Cle-A	55	137	9	28	3	1	3	13	4	28	.204	.227	.307	46	-10	0	0	0	.971	-9	2-36/O-5,3S	-1.8
1972	Cle-A	19	35	2	4	0	0	1	1	3	10	.114	.184	.200	14	-4	0	0	0	.900	-1	O-11/3-1	-0.6
1973	KC-A	99	276	39	71	8	3	2	40	25	42	.257	.321	.330	78	-8	2	3	-1	.935	-11	3-40,2-16,DO/1	-2.1
1974	Pit-N	18	35	1	4	1	0	0	0	2	10	.114	.162	.143	-15	-5	0	0	0	.955	-1	/3-8,O-1	-0.6
	KC-A	39	90	10	19	0	0	0	3	9	20	.211	.290	.211	43	-6	1	1	-0	.987	-4	1-14,3-13/2SD	-1.1
1975	Mil-A	104	258	30	59	14	0	2	24	26	45	.229	.302	.306	72	-9	3	4	-2	.948	1	3-60,2-32/S1D	-0.8
1976	Mil-A	12	7	3	1	0	0	0	0	0	0	.143	.143	.143	-17	-1	0	0	0	1.000	2	/2-2,D-3	0.1
1977	Tex-A	39	96	13	32	7	2	5	28	6	13	.333	.373	.604	159	7	0	1	-1	1.000	-7	O-14,3-11/12D	0.0
1978	Tex-A	90	248	21	55	12	0	6	30	18	31	.222	.274	.343	72	-10	1	2	-1	.877	-4	3-49,D-16,2/1	-1.6
1979	SD-N	114	297	23	75	12	4	1	34	38	25	.253	.337	.330	88	-4	2	5	-2	.954	-5	3-64,2-16/1O	-1.2
1980	SD-N	62	71	4	19	6	1	0	12	6	1	.268	.325	.380	102	0	1	1	-0	.929	-3	3-13/O-4,21	-0.4
	Pit-N	22	43	1	7	1	0	0	4	6	7	.163	.280	.186	32	-4	0	0	0	.958	0	/3-9,1-2	-0.4
	Yr	84	114	5	26	7	1	0	16	12	8	.228	.307	.307	75	-4	1	1	-0	.947	-3	3-22/O-4,12	-0.8
1981	Pit-N	29	27	2	7	1	0	1	4	4	6	.259	.355	.407	112	0	0	0	0	.941	1	/2-4,3-2	0.2
1982	SD-N	64	123	15	31	9	0	2	24	17	22	.252	.343	.325	93	-1	2	0	1	.989	-3	1-30/O-3,3	-0.4
1983	SD-N	74	156	17	38	7	0	2	24	18	33	.244	.322	.327	83	-3	0	3	-2	.995	-1	1-27,3-12,O	-0.8
1984	*SD-N	59	80	7	16	3	0	1	9	14	19	.200	.326	.275	71	-3	0	0	0	1.000	-4	1-20,3-10/O	-0.5
1985	SD-N	71	138	17	33	6	0	3	25	25	17	.239	.356	.348	99	1	0	0	0	.946	-2	3-33/1-9,O	-0.2
Total	15	970	2117	214	499	90	11	27	275	221	329	.236	.309	.327	78	-59	12	20	-8	.938	-46	3-329,2-133,1/ODS	-12.2

■ HAL BEVAN

Bevan, Joseph Harold   b: 11/15/30, New Orleans, La.   d: 10/5/68, New Orleans, La.   BR/TR, 6'2", 198 lbs.   Deb: 4/24/52

YEAR	TM/L	G	AB	R	H	2B	3B	HR	RBI	BB	SO	AVG	OBP	SLG	PRO+	BR/A	SB	CS	SBR	FA	FR	G/POS	TPR
1952	Bos-A	1	1	0	0	0	0	0	0	0	0	.000	.000	.000	-93	-0	0	0	0	.000	0	/3-1	0.0
	Phi-A	8	17	1	6	0	0	0	4	0	0	.353	.353	.353	91	-0	2	0	1	1.000	1	/3-6	0.1
	Yr	9	18	1	6	0	0	0	4	0	1	.333	.333	.333	81	-0	2	0	1	1.000	1	/3-7	0.1
1955	KC-A	3	3	0	0	0	0	0	0	0	0	.000	.000	.000	-99	-1	0	0	0	1.000	0	/3-1	-0.1
1961	Cin-N	3	3	1	1	0	0	1	1	0	2	.333	.333	1.333	311	1	0	0	0	.000	0	H	0.1
Total	3	15	24	2	7	0	0	1	5	0	3	.292	.292	.417	89	-0	2	0	1	1.000	1	/3-8	0.1

■ MONTE BEVILLE

Beville, Henry Monte   b: 2/24/1875, Dublin, Ind.   d: 1/24/55, Grand Rapids, Mich   BL/TR, 5'11", 180 lbs.   Deb: 4/24/03

YEAR	TM/L	G	AB	R	H	2B	3B	HR	RBI	BB	SO	AVG	OBP	SLG	PRO+	BR/A	SB	CS	SBR	FA	FR	G/POS	TPR
1903	NY-A	82	258	23	50	14	1	0	29	16		.194	.252	.256	49	-16	4			.960	-11	C-75/1-3	-2.0
1904	NY-A	9	22	2	6	2	0	0	2	2		.273	.333	.364	115	-2	0			.906	-2	/1-4,C-3	-0.1
	Det-A	54	174	14	36	5	1	0	13	8		.207	.250	.247	59	-8	2			.957	-3	C-30,1-24	-1.0
	Yr	63	196	16	42	7	1	0	15	10		.214	.260	.260	66	-8	2			.950	-5	C-33,1-28	-1.1
Total	2	145	454	39	92	21	2	0	44	26		.203	.255	.258	56	-23	6			.957	-16	C-108/1-31	-3.1

■ BUDDY BIANCALANA

Biancalana, Roland Americo   b: 2/2/60, Larkspur, Cal.   BB/TR, 5'11", 160 lbs.   Deb: 9/12/82

YEAR	TM/L	G	AB	R	H	2B	3B	HR	RBI	BB	SO	AVG	OBP	SLG	PRO+	BR/A	SB	CS	SBR	FA	FR	G/POS	TPR
1982	KC-A	3	2	0	1	0	1	0	0	1	0	.500	.667	1.500	474	1	0	0	0	1.000	3	/S-3	0.3
1983	KC-A	6	15	2	3	0	0	0	0	1	7	.200	.200	.200	10	-2	1	0	0	.914	4	/S-6	0.3
1984	*KC-A	66	134	18	26	6	1	2	9	6	44	.194	.229	.299	44	-10	1	2	-1	.946	6	S-33,2-29/D	-0.2
1985	*KC-A	81	138	21	26	5	1	1	6	17	34	.188	.277	.261	48	-10	1	4	-2	.961	11	S-74/2-4,D	0.3
1986	KC-A	100	190	24	46	4	4	2	8	15	50	.242	.298	.337	71	-8	5	1	1	.946	2	S-89,2-12	0.1
1987	KC-A	37	47	4	10	1	0	1	7	1	10	.213	.229	.298	37	-4	0	0	0	.886	4	S-22,2-12/D	0.1
	Hou-N	18	24	1	1	0	0	0	0	1	12	.042	.080	.042	-69	-6	0	0	0	.889	1	S-16/2-3	-0.6
Total	6	311	550	70	113	16	7	6	30	41	157	.205	.261	.293	50	-38	8	7	-2	.945	28	S-243/2-60,D	0.1

■ TOMMY BIANCO

Bianco, Thomas Anthony   b: 12/16/52, Rockville Centre, N.Y.   BB/TR, 5'11", 190 lbs.   Deb: 5/28/75

YEAR	TM/L	G	AB	R	H	2B	3B	HR	RBI	BB	SO	AVG	OBP	SLG	PRO+	BR/A	SB	CS	SBR	FA	FR	G/POS	TPR
1975	Mil-A	18	34	6	6	1	0	0	4	3	9	.176	.263	.206	34	-3	0	0	0	.941	-1	/3-7,1-5,D	-0.4

■ HANK BIASATTI

Biasatti, Henry Arcado   b: 1/14/22, Beano, Italy   BL/TL, 5'11", 175 lbs.   Deb: 4/23/49

YEAR	TM/L	G	AB	R	H	2B	3B	HR	RBI	BB	SO	AVG	OBP	SLG	PRO+	BR/A	SB	CS	SBR	FA	FR	G/POS	TPR
1949	Phi-A	21	24	6	2	2	0	0	2	8	5	.083	.313	.167	30	-2	0	0	0	.979	-1	/1-8	-0.3

■ DANTE BICHETTE

Bichette, Alphonse Dante   b: 11/18/63, W.Palm Beach, Fla.   BR/TR, 6'3", 215 lbs.   Deb: 9/5/88

YEAR	TM/L	G	AB	R	H	2B	3B	HR	RBI	BB	SO	AVG	OBP	SLG	PRO+	BR/A	SB	CS	SBR	FA	FR	G/POS	TPR
1988	Cal-A	21	46	1	12	2	0	0	8	0	7	.261	.261	.304	59	-3	0	0	0	.979	-2	O-21	-0.5
1989	Cal-A	48	138	13	29	7	0	3	15	6	24	.210	.243	.326	60	-8	3	0	1	.990	6	O-40/D-1	-0.2
1990	Cal-A	109	349	40	89	15	1	15	53	16	79	.255	.293	.433	103	-0	5	2	0	.965	-4	*O-105	-0.7
1991	Mil-A	134	445	53	106	18	3	15	59	22	107	.238	.276	.393	85	-11	14	8	-1	.976	11	*O-127/3-1	-0.4
1992	Mil-A	112	387	37	111	27	2	5	41	16	74	.287	.320	.406	104	1	18	7	1	.990	-2	*O-101/D-4	-0.1
1993	Col-N	141	538	93	167	43	5	21	89	28	99	.310	.353	.526	113	8	14	8	-1	.973	13	*O-137	1.7
1994	Col-N★	116	484	74	147	33	2	27	95	19	70	.304	.335	.548	107	3	21	8	2	.991	9	*O-116	0.6
Total	7	681	2387	311	661	145	13	86	360	107	460	.277	.313	.457	101	-10	75	33	3	.979	25	O-647/D-5,3	0.4

■ OSCAR BIELASKI

Bielaski, Oscar   b: 3/21/1847, Washington, D.C.   d: 11/8/11, Washington, D.C.   BR/TR, 5'10.5", 170 lbs.   Deb: 4/24/1872

YEAR	TM/L	G	AB	R	H	2B	3B	HR	RBI	BB	SO	AVG	OBP	SLG	PRO+	BR/A	SB	CS	SBR	FA	FR	G/POS	TPR
1872	Nat-n	10	46	13	9	0	0	0	2	0	0	.196	.196	.196	18	-5						O-10	-0.3
1873	Was-n	38	173	35	49	2	3	0	20	4	5	.283	.299	.329	88	-2						*O-38	-0.1
1874	Bal-n	44	191	24	47	1	0	0		2		.246	.254	.251	62	-8						O-42/1-1,2	-0.5
1875	Chi-n	51	196	21	49	2	0	0		2		.250	.258	.260	79	-4						*O-52	-0.3
1876	Chi-N	32	139	24	29	3	0	0	10	2	3	.209	.220	.230	45	-9				.763	-2	O-32	-1.0
Total	4 n	143	606	93	154	5	3	0	22	8	5	.254	.264	.272	71	-19						O-142/2-1,1	-1.2

■ LOU BIERBAUER

Bierbauer, Louis W.   b: 9/28/1865, Erie, Pa.   d: 1/31/26, Erie, Pa.   BL/TR, 5'8", 140 lbs.   Deb: 4/17/1886

YEAR	TM/L	G	AB	R	H	2B	3B	HR	RBI	BB	SO	AVG	OBP	SLG	PRO+	BR/A	SB	CS	SBR	FA	FR	G/POS	TPR
1886	Phi-a	137	522	56	118	17	5	2		21		.226	.256	.289	70	-19	19			.910	-3	*2-133/C-4,SP	-1.4
1887	Phi-a	126	530	74	144	19	7	1		13		.272	.289	.340	75	-19	40			.921	-8	*2-126/P-1	-2.0
1888	Phi-a	134	535	83	143	20	9	0	80	25		.267	.301	.338	105	2	34			.916	22	*2-121,3-13/P	2.7
1889	Phi-a	130	549	80	167	27	7	7	105	29	30	.304	.344	.417	118	11	17			.941	37	*2-130/C-1	4.5
1890	Bro-P	133	589	128	180	31	11	7	99	40	15	.306	.350	.431	102	-3	16			.931	25	*2-133	2.4
1891	Pit-N	121	500	60	103	13	6	1	47	28	19	.206	.252	.262	51	-32	12			.929	-2	*2-121	-2.5
1892	Pit-N	152	649	81	153	20	4	8	65	25	29	.236	.264	.331	79	-19	11			.950	32	*2-152	1.4
1893	Pit-N	128	528	84	150	19	11	4	94	36	12	.284	.335	.384	93	-7	11			**.959**	16	*2-128	0.9
1894	Pit-N	130	525	86	159	19	13	3	107	26	9	.303	.337	.406	79	-19	19			.938	9	*2-130	-0.3
1895	Pit-N	117	466	53	120	13	11	0	69	19	8	.258	.290	.333	64	-26	18			.946	14	*2-117	-0.5
1896	Pit-N	59	258	33	74	10	6	0	39	5	7	.287	.300	.372	80	-9	7			.966	12	2-59	0.6
1897	StL-N	12	46	1	10	0	0	0	1	0		.217	.217	.217	15	-6	2			.921	-2	2-12	-0.7
1898	StL-N	4	9	0	0	0	0	0	0	1		.000	.100	.000	-69	-2	0			.429	-1	/2-2,S-1,3	-0.3
Total	13	1383	5706	819	1521	208	95	33	706	268	129	.267	.301	.354	83	-148	206			.935	150	*2-1364/3-14,CPS	4.8

■ CHARLIE BIERMAN

Bierman, Charles S.   b: 1845, Hoboken, N.J.   d: 8/4/1879, Hoboken, N.J.   6', 180 lbs.   Deb: 6/21/1871

YEAR	TM/L	G	AB	R	H	2B	3B	HR	RBI	BB	SO	AVG	OBP	SLG	PRO+	BR/A	SB	CS	SBR	FA	FR	G/POS	TPR
1871	Kek-n	1	2	0	0	0	0	0	0	1	0	.000	.333	.000	6	-0	0					/1-1	0.0

■ CARSON BIGBEE

Bigbee, Carson Lee "Skeeter"   b: 3/31/1895, Waterloo, Ore.   d: 10/17/64, Portland, Ore.   BL/TR, 5'9", 157 lbs.   Deb: 8/25/16   F

YEAR	TM/L	G	AB	R	H	2B	3B	HR	RBI	BB	SO	AVG	OBP	SLG	PRO+	BR/A	SB	CS	SBR	FA	FR	G/POS	TPR
1916	Pit-N	43	164	17	41	3	6	0	3	7	14	.250	.285	.341	91	-2	8			.946	-5	2-23,O-19/3	-0.8
1917	Pit-N	133	469	46	112	11	6	0	21	37	16	.239	.301	.288	78	-11	19			.961	-3	*O-107,2-16/S	-2.2
1918	Pit-N	92	310	47	79	11	3	1	19	42	10	.255	.344	.319	99	1	19			.958	0	O-92	-0.4
1919	Pit-N	125	478	61	132	11	4	2	27	37	26	.276	.332	.328	95	-2	31			.971	18	*O-124	0.8
1920	Pit-N	137	550	78	154	19	15	4	32	45	28	.280	.341	.391	106	5	31	15	0	.971	6	*O-133	0.1

YEAR	TM/L	G	AB	R	H	2B	3B	HR	RBI	BB	SO	AVG	OBP	SLG	PRO+	BR/A	SB	CS	SBR	FA	FR	G/POS	TPR
1921	Pit-N	147	632	100	204	23	17	3	42	41	19	.323	.364	.427	106	6	21	20	-6	.977	16	*O-146	0.5
1922	Pit-N	150	614	113	215	29	15	5	99	56	13	.350	.405	.471	124	23	24	15	-2	.956	17	*O-150	2.6
1923	Pit-N	123	499	79	149	18	7	0	54	43	15	.299	.355	.363	88	-8	10	9	-2	.990	10	*O-122	-0.8
1924	Pit-N	89	282	42	74	4	1	0	15	26	12	.262	.331	.284	65	-13	15	7	0	.943	0	O-75	-1.7
1925	*Pit-N	66	126	31	30	7	0	0	8	7	8	.238	.278	.294	43	-11	2	2	-1	.942	-6	O-42	-1.8
1926	Pit-N	42	68	15	15	3	1	2	4	3	0	.221	.264	.382	69	-3	2			.966	-3	O-21	-0.7
Total	11	1147	4192	629	1205	139	75	17	324	344	161	.287	.345	.369	96	-16	182	68		.966	50	*O-1031/2-39,S3	-4.4

■ LYLE BIGBEE
Bigbee, Lyle Randolph "Al" b: 8/22/1893, Sweet Home, Ore. d: 8/5/42, Portland, Ore. BL/TR, 6', 180 lbs. Deb: 4/15/20 F

YEAR	TM/L	G	AB	R	H	2B	3B	HR	RBI	BB	SO	AVG	OBP	SLG	PRO+	BR/A	SB	CS	SBR	FA	FR	G/POS	TPR
1920	Phi-A	38	75	5	14	2	0	1	8	9	12	.187	.282	.253	42	-6	1	0	0	.857	-2	O-13,P-12	-0.7
1921	Pit-N	5	2	0	0	0	0	0	0	0	1	.000	.000	.000	-97	-1	0	0	0	1.000	0	/P-5	0.0
Total	2	43	77	5	14	2	0	1	8	9	13	.182	.276	.247	39	-7	1	0	0	1.000	-2	/P-17,O-13	-0.7

■ ELLIOT BIGELOW
Bigelow, Elliot Allardice "Babe" or "Gilly" b: 10/13/1897, Tarpon Springs, Fla. d: 8/10/33, Tampa, Fla. BL/TL, 5'11", 185 lbs. Deb: 4/18/29

YEAR	TM/L	G	AB	R	H	2B	3B	HR	RBI	BB	SO	AVG	OBP	SLG	PRO+	BR/A	SB	CS	SBR	FA	FR	G/POS	TPR
1929	Bos-A	100	211	23	60	16	0	1	26	23	18	.284	.357	.374	91	-2	1	4	-2	.944	-10	O-59	-1.7

■ CRAIG BIGGIO
Biggio, Craig Alan b: 12/14/65, Smithtown, N.Y. BR/TR, 5'11", 185 lbs. Deb: 6/26/88

YEAR	TM/L	G	AB	R	H	2B	3B	HR	RBI	BB	SO	AVG	OBP	SLG	PRO+	BR/A	SB	CS	SBR	FA	FR	G/POS	TPR
1988	Hou-N	50	123	14	26	6	1	3	5	7	29	.211	.254	.350	74	-5	6	1	1	.991	16	C-50	1.6
1989	Hou-N	134	443	64	114	21	2	13	60	49	64	.257	.339	.402	115	9	21	3	5	.990	-6	*C-125/O-5	1.5
1990	Hou-N	150	555	53	153	24	2	4	42	53	79	.276	.342	.348	93	-4	25	11	1	.985	-7	*C-113,O-50	-0.5
1991	Hou-N★	149	546	79	161	23	4	4	46	53	71	.295	.359	.374	113	10	19	6	2	.990	-14	*C-139/2-3,O	0.6
1992	Hou-N★	162	613	96	170	32	3	6	39	94	95	.277	.380	.369	118	18	38	15	2	.984	-21	*2-161	0.4
1993	Hou-N	155	610	98	175	41	5	21	64	77	93	.287	.376	.474	130	27	15	17	-6	.982	-2	*2-155	2.4
1994	Hou-N★	114	437	88	139	44	5	6	56	62	58	.318	.412	.483	135	25	39	4	9	.988	-5	*2-113	3.2
Total	7	914	3327	492	938	191	22	57	312	395	489	.282	.364	.404	116	81	163	57	15	.984	-39	2-432,C-427/O	9.2

■ PETE BIGLER
Bigler, Ivan Edward b: 12/13/1892, Bradford, Ohio d: 4/1/75, Coldwater, Mich. BR/TR, 5'9", 150 lbs. Deb: 5/6/17

YEAR	TM/L	G	AB	R	H	2B	3B	HR	RBI	BB	SO	AVG	OBP	SLG	PRO+	BR/A	SB	CS	SBR	FA	FR	G/POS	TPR
1917	StL-A	1	0	0	0	0	0	0	0	0	0	—	—	—			0	0		.000	0	/R	0.0

■ GEORGE BIGNELL
Bignell, George William b: 7/18/1858, Taunton, Mass. d: 1/16/25, Providence, R.I. 5'9", 160 lbs. Deb: 9/27/1884

YEAR	TM/L	G	AB	R	H	2B	3B	HR	RBI	BB	SO	AVG	OBP	SLG	PRO+	BR/A	SB	CS	SBR	FA	FR	G/POS	TPR
1884	Mil-U	4	9	4	2	0	0	0				.222	.300	.222	81	-0				.951	3	/C-4	0.3

■ LARRY BIITTNER
Biittner, Lawrence David b: 7/27/45, Pocahontas, Ia. BL/TL, 6'2", 205 lbs. Deb: 7/17/70

YEAR	TM/L	G	AB	R	H	2B	3B	HR	RBI	BB	SO	AVG	OBP	SLG	PRO+	BR/A	SB	CS	SBR	FA	FR	G/POS	TPR
1970	Was-A	2	2	0	0	0	0	0	0	0	0	.000	.000	.000	-99	-1	0	0	0	.000	0	H	-0.1
1971	Was-A	66	171	12	44	4	1	0	16	16	20	.257	.324	.292	80	-4	1	0	0	.940	-0	O-41/1-3	-0.7
1972	Tex-A	137	382	34	99	18	1	3	31	29	37	.259	.315	.335	98	-2	1	3	-2	.991	-1	1-65,O-65	-1.2
1973	Tex-A	83	258	19	65	8	2	1	12	20	21	.252	.308	.310	78	-8	1	0	0	.980	1	O-57,1-20/D	-1.0
1974	Mon-N	18	26	2	7	1	0	0	3	0	2	.269	.269	.308	58	-1	0	0	0	1.000	4	/O-4	-0.1
1975	Mon-N	121	346	34	109	13	5	3	28	34	33	.315	.376	.408	113	6	2	1	0	.972	6	O-93	0.3
1976	Mon-N	11	32	2	6	1	0	0	1	0	3	.188	.188	.219	14	-4	0	0	0	.947	1	/O-7	-0.3
	Chi-N	78	192	21	47	13	1	0	17	10	6	.245	.286	.323	66	-9	0	2	-1	.985	4	1-33,O-24	-0.9
	Yr	89	224	23	53	14	1	0	18	10	9	.237	.272	.308	59	-12	0	2	-1	.985	5	1-33,O-31	-1.2
1977	Chi-N	138	493	74	147	28	1	12	62	35	36	.298	.346	.432	97	-3	2	1	0	.987	6	1-80,O-52/P	-0.3
1978	Chi-N	120	343	32	88	15	1	4	50	23	37	.257	.305	.341	72	-13	0	1	0	.987	5	1-62,O-29	-1.3
1979	Chi-N	111	272	35	79	13	3	3	50	21	23	.290	.341	.393	91	-3	1	1	-0	.925	-6	O-44,1-32	-1.3
1980	Chi-N	127	273	21	68	12	2	1	34	18	33	.249	.300	.319	68	-12	1	3	-2	.996	1	1-41,O-38	-1.6
1981	Cin-N	42	61	1	13	4	0	0	4	4	4	.213	.262	.279	52	-4	0	0	0	1.000	-0	/1-8,O-3	-0.3
1982	Cin-N	97	184	18	57	9	2	2	24	17	16	.310	.374	.413	118	5	0	0	0	.978	-2	O-31,1-15	0.2
1983	Tex-A	66	116	5	32	5	1	0	18	9	16	.276	.328	.336	85	-2	0	0	0	.987	2	1-22/O-2,D	-0.1
Total	14	1217	3151	310	861	144	20	29	354	236	287	.273	.326	.359	87	-53	10	12	-4	.970	14	O-490,1-381/DP	-8.7

■ DANN BILARDELLO
Bilardello, Dann James b: 5/26/59, Santa Cruz, Cal. BR/TR, 6', 190 lbs. Deb: 4/11/83

YEAR	TM/L	G	AB	R	H	2B	3B	HR	RBI	BB	SO	AVG	OBP	SLG	PRO+	BR/A	SB	CS	SBR	FA	FR	G/POS	TPR
1983	Cin-N	109	298	27	71	18	0	9	38	15	49	.238	.277	.389	80	-9	2	1	0	.991	-1	*C-105	-0.7
1984	Cin-N	68	182	16	38	7	0	2	10	19	34	.209	.287	.280	57	-10	0	1	-1	.992	1	C-68	-0.7
1985	Cin-N	42	102	6	17	0	0	1	9	4	15	.167	.206	.196	12	-12	0	0	0	.986	8	C-42	-0.2
1986	Mon-N	79	191	12	37	5	0	4	17	14	34	.194	.249	.283	47	-14	1	0	0	.982	2	C-77	-0.9
1989	Pit-N	33	80	11	18	6	0	2	8	2	18	.225	.244	.375	77	-3	1	2	-1	.970	5	C-33	0.3
1990	Pit-N	19	37	1	2	0	0	0	3	0	6	.054	.146	.054	-44	-7	0	0	0	1.000	3	C-19	-0.4
1991	SD-N	15	26	4	7	2	1	0	5	3	4	.269	.345	.423	111	0	0	0	0	1.000	5	C-13	0.6
1992	SD-N	17	33	2	4	1	0	0	1	8	10	.121	.216	.152	6	-4	0	0	0	1.000	5	C-14	0.2
Total	8	382	949	79	194	39	1	18	91	65	170	.204	.258	.305	55	-59	4	4	-1	.988	28	C-371	-1.8

■ STEVE BILKO
Bilko, Stephen Thomas b: 11/13/28, Nanticoke, Pa. d: 3/7/78, Wilkes-Barre, Pa. BR/TR, 6'1", 230 lbs. Deb: 9/22/49

YEAR	TM/L	G	AB	R	H	2B	3B	HR	RBI	BB	SO	AVG	OBP	SLG	PRO+	BR/A	SB	CS	SBR	FA	FR	G/POS	TPR
1949	StL-N	6	17	3	5	2	0	0	2	5	6	.294	.455	.412	128	1	0			1.000	0	/1-5	0.1
1950	StL-N	10	33	1	6	1	0	0	2	4	10	.182	.270	.212	27	-3	0			.989	0	/1-9	-0.3
1951	StL-N	21	72	5	16	4	0	2	12	9	10	.222	.309	.361	79	-2	0	0	0	.984	-0	1-19	-0.3
1952	StL-N	20	72	7	19	6	1	1	6	4	15	.264	.303	.417	97	-1	0	0	0	.995	4	1-20	0.3
1953	StL-N	154	570	72	143	23	3	21	84	70	125	.251	.334	.412	93	-6	0	1	-1	.991	7	*1-154	-0.5
1954	StL-N	8	14	1	2	0	0	0	1	3	1	.143	.294	.143	18	-2	0	0	0	1.000	1	/1-6	0.0
	Chi-N	47	92	11	22	8	1	4	12	11	24	.239	.320	.478	104	1	0	0	0	1.000	8	1-22	0.5
	Yr	55	106	12	24	8	1	4	13	14	25	.226	.317	.434	92	-1	0	0	0	1.000	8	1-28	0.5
1958	Cin-N	31	87	12	23	4	2	4	17	10	20	.264	.340	.494	111	1	0	0	0	.995	-1	1-21	-0.1
	LA-N	47	101	13	21	1	2	7	18	8	37	.208	.266	.465	86	-3	0	0	0	.995	2	1-25	-0.2
	Yr	78	188	25	44	5	4	11	35	18	57	.234	.301	.479	98	-1	0	0	0	.995	0	1-46	-0.3
1960	Det-A	78	222	20	46	11	2	9	25	27	31	.207	.293	.396	82	-6	0	0	0	.991	0	1-62	-1.1
1961	LA-A	114	294	49	82	16	1	20	59	58	81	.279	.398	.544	134	14	1	1	-0	.989	1	1-86/O-3	1.0
1962	LA-A	64	164	26	47	9	1	8	38	25	35	.287	.387	.500	141	10	1	1	-0	.995	4	1-50	0.6
Total	10	600	1738	220	432	85	13	76	276	234	435	.249	.339	.444	103	5	2	4		.992	22	1-479/O-3	0.0

■ JOSH BILLINGS
Billings, John Augustus b: 11/30/1891, Grantville, Kan. d: 12/30/81, Santa Monica, Cal. BR/TR, 5'11", 165 lbs. Deb: 9/9/13

YEAR	TM/L	G	AB	R	H	2B	3B	HR	RBI	BB	SO	AVG	OBP	SLG	PRO+	BR/A	SB	CS	SBR	FA	FR	G/POS	TPR
1913	Cle-A	1	3	0	0	0	0	0	0	0	3	.000	.000	.000	-97	-1	0			.857	0	/C-1	-0.1
1914	Cle-A	11	8	2	2	1	0	0	0	1	1	.250	.333	.375	109	-1	0			.813	3	/C-3	0.3
1915	Cle-A	8	21	2	4	1	0	0	0	0	6	.190	.190	.238	28	-2	1			1.000	-1	/C-7,O-1	-0.3
1916	Cle-A	22	31	2	5	0	1	0	0	2	11	.161	.212	.161	42	-3	0			.981	3	C-12	-0.1
1917	Cle-A	66	129	8	23	3	2	0	9	8	21	.178	.243	.233	42	-9	2			.974	7	C-48	-0.4
1918	Cle-A	2	3	0	1	0	0	0	0	0	0	.333	.333	.333	92	-0	0			1.000	-0	/C-1	-0.0
1919	StL-A	38	76	9	15	1	0	3	12	5	12	.197	.218	.237	27	-7	0			.982	5	C-26/1-1	-0.1
1920	StL-A	66	155	19	43	5	2	0	11	11	10	.277	.353	.335	81	-4	0			.967	-5	C-40	-0.3
1921	StL-A	20	46	2	10	0	0	0	4	0	7	.217	.217	.217	11	-6	0			.982	2	C-12	-0.4
1922	StL-A	3	7	1	3	1	0	0	0	0	0	.429	.429	.571	153	1	0			1.000	0	/C-3	0.1
1923	StL-A	4	9	0	0	0	0	0	0	0	0	.000	.000	.000	-95	-2	0			.917	0	/C-4	-0.2
Total	11	243	488	44	106	12	5	0	29	23	73	.217	.268	.262	47	-35	5	0		.970	14	C-157/1-1,O	-1.6

YEAR	TM/L	G	AB	R	H	2B	3B	HR	RBI	BB	SO	AVG	OBP	SLG	PRO+	BR/A	SB	CS	SBR	FA	FR	G/POS	TPR
■ DICK BILLINGS			Billings, Richard Arlin		b: 12/4/42, Detroit, Mich.			BR/TR, 6'1", 195 lbs.		Deb: 9/11/68													
1968	Was-A	12	33	3	6	1	0	1	3	5	13	.182	.289	.303	82	-1	0	0	0	.929	0	/O-8,3-4	-0.1
1969	Was-A	27	37	3	5	0	0	0	0	6	8	.135	.256	.135	13	-4	0	1	-1	1.000	0	/O-6,3-1	-0.5
1970	Was-A	11	24	3	6	2	0	1	2	2	3	.250	.308	.458	114	0	0	0	0	1.000	0	/C-8	-0.1
1971	Was-A	116	349	32	86	14	0	6	48	21	54	.246	.299	.338	85	-8	2	5	-2	.992	-3	C-62,O-32/3	-1.3
1972	Tex-A	133	469	41	119	15	1	5	58	29	77	.254	.300	.322	89	-7	1	5	-3	.981	-5	C-92,O-41/31	-1.5
1973	Tex-A	81	280	17	50	11	0	3	32	20	43	.179	.238	.250	39	-23	1	1	-0	.975	-19	C-72/O-4,1D	-4.1
1974	Tex-A	16	31	2	7	1	0	0	0	4	6	.226	.314	.258	68	-1	2	0	1	1.000	1	C-13/O-1,D	0.1
	StL-N	1	5	0	1	0	0	0	0	0	1	.200	.200	.200	12	-1	0	0	0	1.000	0	/C-1	0.0
1975	StL-N	3	3	0	0	0	0	0	0	0	2	.000	.000	.000	-97	-1	0	0	0	.000	0	H	-0.1
Total	8	400	1231	101	280	44	1	16	142	87	207	.227	.283	.304	73	-45	6	12	-5	.984	-27	C-248/O-92,31D	-7.6
■ GEORGE BINKS			Binks, George Alvin "Bingo" (b: George Alvin Binkowski)			b: 7/11/16, Chicago, Ill.			BL/TL, 6', 175 lbs.		Deb: 9/23/44												
1944	Was-A	5	12	0	3	0	0	0	0	0	1	.250	.250	.250	45	-1	0	0	0	1.000	-1	/O-3	-0.2
1945	Was-A	145	550	62	153	32	6	6	81	34	52	.278	.324	.391	117	8	11	7	-1	.977	4	*O-128,1-20	0.4
1946	Was-A	65	134	13	26	3	0	0	12	6	16	.194	.229	.216	26	-13	1	0	0	1.000	-0	O-28	-1.5
1947	Phi-A	104	333	33	86	19	4	2	34	23	36	.258	.308	.357	83	-8	8	2	1	.965	1	O-75,1-13	-1.1
1948	Phi-A	17	41	2	4	1	0	0	2	2	2	.098	.140	.122	-30	-8	1	0	0	1.000	-2	O-14	-1.0
	StL-A	15	23	2	5	0	0	0	1	2	1	.217	.280	.217	32	-2	0	0	0	1.000	-1	/O-5,1-4	-0.4
	Yr	32	64	4	9	1	0	0	3	4	3	.141	.191	.156	-7	-10	1	0	0	1.000	-3	O-19/1-4	-1.4
Total	5	351	1093	112	277	55	10	8	130	67	108	.253	.299	.344	86	-24	21	9	1	.977	-0	O-253/1-37	-3.8
■ STEVE BIRAS			Biras, Stephen Alexander		b: 2/26/22, E.St.Louis, Ill.		d: 4/21/65, St.Louis, Mo.			BR/TR, 5'11", 185 lbs.		Deb: 9/15/44											
1944	Cle-A	2	2	0	2	0	0	0	2	0	0	1.000	1.000	1.000	491	1	0	0	0	.667	0	/2-1	0.1
■ JUD BIRCHALL			Birchall, Adoniram Judson		b: 1858, Germantown, Pa.		d: 12/22/1887, Philadelphia, Pa.			Deb: 5/2/1882													
1882	Phi-a	75	338	65	89	12	1	0			8	.263	.280	.305	87	-7				.860	0	*O-74/2-1	-0.6
1883	Phi-a	96	448	95	108	10	1	1			20	.241	.274	.275	71	-16				.809	6	*O-96	-1.0
1884	Phi-a	54	221	36	57	2	2	0			4	.258	.287	.285	82	-5				.838	3	O-52/3-2	-0.2
Total	3	225	1007	196	254	24	4	1			32	.252	.279	.287	79	-27				.832	9	O-222/3-2,2	-1.8
■ FRANK BIRD			Bird, Frank Zepherin "Dodo"		b: 3/10/1869, Spencer, Mass.		d: 5/20/58, Worcester, Mass.			BR/TR, 5'10", 195 lbs.		Deb: 4/16/1892											
1892	StL-N	17	50	9	10	3	1	1	6	6	11	.200	.286	.360	100	-0	2			.920	-4	C-17	-0.3
■ GEORGE BIRD			Bird, George Raymond		b: 6/23/1850, Stillman Valley, Ill.		d: 11/9/40, Rockford, Ill.			BR/TR, 5'9", 150 lbs.		Deb: 5/6/1871											
1871	Rok-n	25	106	19	28	2	5	0	13	3	2	.264	.284	.377	92	-1	1					*O-25	0.0
■ DAVE BIRDSALL			Birdsall, David Solomon		b: 7/16/1838, New York, N.Y.		d: 12/30/1896, Boston, Mass.			BR/TR, 5'9", 126 lbs.		Deb: 5/5/1871											
1871	Bos-n	29	152	51	46	3	3	0	24	4	4	.303	.321	.362	93	-2	6					*O-26/C-3	-0.1
1872	Bos-n	16	76	11	14	3	0	0	14	1	0	.184	.195	.224	27	-7						C-11/O-5	-0.6
1873	Bos-n	3	12	4	1	0	0	0	1	0	0	.083	.083	.083	-47	-2						/O-3	-0.2
Total	3 n	48	240	66	61	6	3	0	39	5	4	.254	.269	.304	65	-11						/O-34,C-14	-0.9
■ JOE BIRMINGHAM			Birmingham, Joseph Leo "Dode"		b: 8/6/1884, Elmira, N.Y.		d: 4/24/46, Tampico, Mexico			BR/TR, 5'10", 185 lbs.		Deb: 9/12/06	M										
1906	Cle-A	10	41	5	13	2	1	0	6	1		.317	.333	.415	136	1	2			1.000	-1	/O-9,3-1	0.3
1907	Cle-A	136	476	55	112	10	9	1	33	16		.235	.265	.300	79	-12	23			.949	12	*O-130/S-5	-0.5
1908	Cle-A	122	413	32	88	10	4	1	38	19		.213	.253	.257	65	-16	15			.957	6	*O-121/S-1	-1.7
1909	Cle-A	100	343	29	99	10	5	1	38	19		.289	.333	.356	113	5	12			.948	4	O-98	0.6
1910	Cle-A	104	367	41	84	11	2	0	35	23		.229	.284	.270	72	-12	18			.961	14	*O-103/3-1	-0.3
1911	Cle-A	125	447	55	136	18	5	2	51	15		.304	.334	.380	98	-3	16			.973	8	*O-102,3-16	0.0
1912	Cle-A	107	369	49	94	19	3	1	45	26		.255	.311	.331	81	-10	15			.952	5	O-96/1-9M	-1.0
1913	Cle-A	47	131	16	37	9	1	0	15	8	22	.282	.324	.366	99	-1	7			.974	-3	O-36,M	-0.5
1914	Cle-A	19	47	2	6	0	0	0	4	2	5	.128	.163	.128	-12	-6	0	1	-1	1.000	-2	O-14,M	-1.1
Total	9	770	2634	284	669	89	27	7	265	129	27	.254	.295	.316	85	-53	108	1		.958	46	O-709/3-18,1S	-4.2
■ JOHN BISCHOFF			Bischoff, John George "Smiley"		b: 10/28/1894, Granite City, Ill.		d: 12/28/81, Granite City, Ill.			BR/TR, 5'7", 165 lbs.		Deb: 4/18/25											
1925	Chi-A	7	11	1	1	0	0	0	0	1	5	.091	.167	.091	-35	-2	0	0	0	1.000	-0	/C-4	-0.2
	Bos-A	41	133	13	37	9	1	1	16	6	11	.278	.309	.383	75	-6	1	2	-1	.952	-3	C-40	-0.7
	Yr	48	144	14	38	9	1	1	16	7	16	.264	.298	.361	67	-8	1	2	-1	.955	-3	C-44	-0.9
1926	Bos-A	59	127	6	33	11	2	0	19	15	16	.260	.343	.378	91	-2	1	3	-2	.974	-1	/C-46	-0.2
Total	2	107	271	20	71	20	3	1	35	22	32	.262	.320	.369	78	-10	2	5	-2	.964	-4	/C-90	-1.1
■ FRANK BISHOP			Bishop, Frank H.		b: 9/21/1860, Belvidere, Ill.		d: 6/18/29, Chicago, Ill.			Deb: 5/27/1884													
1884	CP-U	4	16	1	3	1	0	0		0		.188	.188	.250	18	-2				.667	-2	/3-3,S-1	-0.3
■ MAX BISHOP			Bishop, Max Frederick "Tilly" or "Camera Eye"		b: 9/5/1899, Waynesboro, Pa.		d: 2/24/62, Waynesboro, Pa.			BL/TR, 5'8.5", 165 lbs.		Deb: 4/15/24										
1924	Phi-A	91	294	52	75	13	2	2	21	54	30	.255	.380	.333	84	-5	4	3	-1	.969	6	2-80	0.1
1925	Phi-A	105	368	66	103	18	4	4	27	87	37	.280	.420	.383	98	3	5	9	-4	.957	5	*2-104	0.5
1926	Phi-A	122	400	77	106	20	2	0	33	116	41	.265	.431	.325	94	4	4	5	-2	**.987**	0	*2-119	0.5
1927	Phi-A	117	372	80	103	15	1	0	22	105	28	.277	.442	.323	95	5	8	6	1	.967	3	*2-106	1.0
1928	Phi-A	126	472	104	149	27	5	6	50	97	36	.316	.435	.432	125	23	9	9	-3	**.978**	-11	*2-125	1.2
1929	*Phi-A	129	475	102	110	19	6	3	36	**128**	44	.232	.398	.316	83	-6	1	4	-2	.970	-26	*2-129	-2.7
1930	*Phi-A	130	441	117	111	27	6	10	38	128	60	.252	.426	.408	108	11	3	2	-0	.976	-6	*2-127	1.1
1931	*Phi-A	130	497	115	146	30	4	5	37	112	51	.294	.426	.400	111	14	3	1	0	.984	-0	*2-130	2.1
1932	Phi-A	114	409	89	104	24	3	5	37	110	43	.254	.412	.359	98	4	2	2	-1	**.988**	-9	*2-106	0.0
1933	Phi-A	117	391	80	115	27	1	4	42	106	46	.294	.446	.399	124	21	1	5	-3	.975	-13	*2-113	1.1
1934	Bos-A	97	253	65	66	13	1	1	22	82	22	.261	.445	.332	96	4	2	3	-0	.990	0	2-57,1-15	0.5
1935	Bos-A	60	122	19	28	3	1	1	14	28	14	.230	.377	.295	71	-4	2	1	-1	.978	-5	2-34,1-11/S	-0.8
Total	12	1338	4494	966	1216	236	35	41	379	1153	452	.271	.423	.366	102	72	43	50	-17	.976	-56	*2-1230/1-26,S	4.6
■ MIKE BISHOP			Bishop, Michael David		b: 11/5/58, Santa Maria, Cal.			Deb: 4/16/83															
1983	NY-N	3	8	2	1	0	0	0	3	4		.125	.364	.250	74	-0	0	0	0	.944	-0	/C-3	0.0
■ RIVINGTON BISLAND			Bisland, Rivington Martin		b: 2/17/1890, New York, N.Y.		d: 1/11/73, Salzburg, Austria			BR/TR, 5'9", 155 lbs.		Deb: 9/13/12										
1912	Pit-N	1	1	0	0	0	0	0	0	0	0	.000	.000	.000	-99	-0	0			.000	0	H	0.0
1913	StL-A	12	44	3	6	1	0	0	3	2	5	.136	.191	.136	-4	-6	0			.963	-5	S-12	-1.1
1914	Cle-A	18	57	9	6	0	1	0	4	6	2	.105	.190	.123	-5	-7	2	5	-2	.962	-5	/S-15/3-1	-1.0
Total	3	31	102	12	12	1	1	0	7	8	7	.118	.189	.127	-6	-13	2	5		.962	-5	/S-27,3-1	-2.1
■ DEL BISSONETTE			Bissonette, Delphia Louis		b: 9/6/1899, Winthrop, Me.		d: 6/9/72, Augusta, Maine			BL/TL, 5'11", 180 lbs.		Deb: 4/11/28	MC										
1928	Bro-N	155	587	90	188	30	13	25	106	70	75	.320	.396	.543	145	38	5			.987	-4	*1-155	2.0
1929	Bro-N	116	431	68	121	28	10	12	75	46	58	.281	.351	.476	105	2	2			.987	-9	*1-113	-1.7
1930	Bro-N	146	572	102	192	33	13	16	113	56	66	.336	.396	.523	121	20	4			.987	-9	*1-146	-0.3
1931	Bro-N	152	587	90	170	19	14	12	87	59	53	.290	.354	.431	111	9	7			.990	-7	*1-152	-1.2

YEAR	TM/L	G	AB	R	H	2B	3B	HR	RBI	BB	SO	AVG	OBP	SLG	PRO+	BR/A	SB	CS	SBR	FA	FR	G/POS	TPR
1933	Bro-N	35	114	9	28	7	0	1	10	2	17	.246	.259	.333	71	-5	2			.988	0	1-32	-0.8
Total	5	604	2291	359	699	117	50	66	391	233	269	.305	.371	.486	119	64	17			.988	-28	1-598	-2.0

■ RED BITTMAN
Bittman, Henry Peter b: 7/22/1862, Cincinnati, Ohio d: 11/8/29, Cincinnati, Ohio Deb: 10/10/1889

1889	KC-a	4	14	2	4	0	0	0	2	1	1	.286	.333	.286	73	-1	1			1.000	1	/2-4	0.1

■ GEORGE BJORKMAN
Bjorkman, George Anton b: 8/26/56, Ontario, Cal. BR/TR, 6'2", 190 lbs. Deb: 7/10/83

1983	Hou-N	29	75	8	17	4	0	2	14	16	29	.227	.370	.360	110	2	0	0	0	.993	-3	C-29	0.0

■ JOHN BLACK
Black, John Falcnor "Jack" (b: John Falcnor Haddow) b: 2/23/1890, Covington, Ky. d: 3/20/62, Rutherford, N.J. BR/TR, 6'1", 185 lbs. Deb: 6/20/11

1911	StL-A	54	186	13	28	4	0	0	7	10		.151	.202	.172	5	-24	4			.972	0	1-54	-2.4

■ BILL BLACK
Black, John William "Jigger" b: 8/12/1899, Philadelphia, Pa. d: 1/14/68, Philadelphia, Pa. BL/TR, 5'11", 168 lbs. Deb: 5/4/24

1924	Chi-A	6	5	0	1	0	0	0	0	0	0	.200	.200	.200	3	-1	0	0	0	.000	0	/2-1	-0.1

■ BOB BLACK
Black, Robert Benjamin b: 12/10/1862, Cincinnati, Ohio d: 3/21/33, Sioux City, Iowa Deb: 8/19/1884

1884	KC-U	38	146	25	36	14	2	1		10		.247	.295	.390	97	-1				.784	-1	O-19,P-16/2S	-0.3

■ ETHAN BLACKABY
Blackaby, Ethan Allen b: 7/24/40, Cincinnati, O. BL/TL, 5'11", 190 lbs. Deb: 9/6/62

1962	Mil-N	6	13	0	2	1	0	0	1	0	8	.154	.214	.231	20	-1	0	0	0	1.000	-1	/O-3	-0.2
1964	Mil-N	9	12	0	1	0	0	0	1	1	2	.083	.154	.083	-31	-2	0	0	0	.500	-2	/O-5	-0.4
Total	2	15	25	0	3	1	0	0	2	1	10	.120	.185	.160	-4	-4	0	0	0	.800	-2	/O-8	-0.6

■ EARL BLACKBURN
Blackburn, Earl Stuart b: 11/1/1892, Leesville, Ohio d: 8/3/66, Mansfield, Ohio BR/TR, 5'11", 180 lbs. Deb: 9/17/12

1912	Pit-N	1	0	0	0	0	0	0	0	0	0					0		0		1.000	0	/C-1	0.0
	Cin-N	1	0	0	0	0	0	0	0	1	0	—	1.000	—	191	0		0		1.000	0	/C-1	0.1
	Yr	2	0	0	0	0	0	0	0	1	0	—	1.000	—	190	0		0		1.000	0	/C-2	0.1
1913	Cin-N	17	27	1	7	0	0	0	3	2	5	.259	.310	.259	64	-1	2			.848	-1	C-12	-0.2
1915	Bos-N	3	6	0	1	0	0	0	0	2	1	.167	.375	.167	70	-0				1.000	-0	C-3	0.0
1916	Bos-N	47	110	12	30	4	4	0	7	9	21	.273	.328	.382	123	3	2			.972	-1	C-44	0.5
1917	Cin-N	2	2	0	0	0	0	0	0	0	0	.000	.000	.000	-93	-0				.000	0	H	-0.1
Total	5	71	145	13	38	4	4	0	10	14	27	.262	.327	.345	107	1	4			.954	-2	/C-61	0.3

■ LENA BLACKBURNE
Blackburne, Russell Aubrey "Slats"
b: 10/23/1886, Clifton Heights, Pa. d: 2/29/68, Riverside, N.J. BR/TR, 5'11", 160 lbs. Deb: 4/14/10 MC

1910	Chi-A	75	242	16	42	3	1	0	10	19		.174	.245	.194	39	-16	4			.911	19	S-74	0.6
1912	Chi-A	5	1	0	0	0	0	0	0	0		.000	.500	.000	48	0	1			.800	1	/S-4,3-1	0.1
1914	Chi-A	144	474	52	105	10	5	1	35	66	58	.222	.324	.270	80	-9	25	15	-1	.963	1	*2-143	-1.2
1915	Chi-A	96	283	33	61	5	1	0	25	35	34	.216	.304	.240	61	-13	13	11	-3	.949	-10	3-83/S-9	-2.3
1918	Cin-N	125	435	34	99	8	10	1	45	25	30	.228	.271	.299	75	-14	6			.938	10	*S-125	0.2
1919	Bos-N	31	80	5	21	3	0	0	4	6	7	.262	.322	.325	99	-0	3			.948	3	3-24/1-1,2S	0.5
	Phi-N	72	291	32	58	10	5	2	19	10	22	.199	.228	.289	51	-18	2			.933	6	3-72/1-1	-1.0
	Yr	103	371	37	79	13	5	2	23	16	29	.213	.249	.296	61	-18	5			.937	10	3-96/1-2,2S	-0.5
1927	Chi-A	1	1	1	1	0	0	0	1	0	0	1.000	1.000	1.000	431	0	0	0	0	.000	0	H	0.0
1929	Chi-A	1	0	0	0	0	0	0	0	0	0				—	0	0	0	0	.000	0	/P-1,M	0.0
Total	8	550	1807	173	387	39	23	4	139	162	151	.214	.284	.268	67	-69	54	26		.927	30	S-213,3-180,2/1P	-3.1

■ GEORGE BLACKERBY
Blackerby, George Franklin b: 11/10/03, Luther, Okla. d: 5/30/87, Wichita Falls, Tex. BR/TR, 6'1", 176 lbs. Deb: 8/10/28

1928	Chi-A	30	83	8	21	0	0	0	12	4	10	.253	.287	.253	44	-7	2	1	0	.953	-1	O-20	-0.9

■ FRED BLACKWELL
Blackwell, Fredrick William "Blacky" b: 9/7/1891, Bowling Green, Ky. d: 12/8/75, Morgantown, Ky. BL/TR, 5'11.5", 160 lbs. Deb: 9/25/17

1917	Pit-N	3	10	1	2	0	0	0	2	0	3	.200	.200	.200	22	-1	0			1.000	0	/C-3	-0.1
1918	Pit-N	8	13	1	2	0	0	0	4	3	4	.154	.313	.154	42	-1	0			.926	1	/C-8	0.0
1919	Pit-N	24	65	3	14	3	0	0	4	3	9	.215	.261	.262	55	-4	0			.964	-0	C-22	-0.2
Total	3	35	88	5	18	3	0	0	10	6	16	.205	.263	.239	50	-5	0			.961	0	C-33	-0.3

■ TIM BLACKWELL
Blackwell, Timothy P b: 8/19/52, San Diego, Cal. BB/TR, 5'11", 180 lbs. Deb: 7/3/74

1974	Bos-A	44	122	9	30	1	1	0	8	10	21	.246	.308	.270	63	-5	1	1	-0	.971	2	C-44	-0.2
1975	Bos-A	59	132	15	26	3	2	0	6	19	13	.197	.303	.270	53	-8	0	0	0	.984	8	C-57/D-2	0.2
1976	Phi-N	4	8	0	2	0	0	0	1	0	1	.250	.250	.250	41	-1	0	0	0	1.000	1	/C-4	0.0
1977	Phi-N	1	0	1	0	0	0	0	0	0	0	—	—	—	—	0	0	0	0	1.000	0	/C-1	0.0
	Mon-N	16	22	3	2	1	0	0	2	2	7	.091	.167	.136	-18	-4	0	0	0	.925	-1	C-14	-0.4
	Yr	17	22	4	2	1	0	0	2	2	7	.091	.167	.136	-18	-4	0	0	0	.929	-1	C-15	-0.4
1978	Chi-N	49	103	8	23	3	0	0	7	23	17	.223	.370	.252	68	-3	0	0	0	.987	7	C-49	0.5
1979	Chi-N	63	122	8	20	3	1	0	12	32	25	.164	.342	.205	48	-8	0	0	0	.975	1	C-63	-0.5
1980	Chi-N	103	320	24	87	16	4	5	30	41	62	.272	.355	.394	101	1	0	1	-1	.982	17	*C-103	2.2
1981	Chi-N	58	158	21	37	10	2	1	11	23	23	.234	.331	.342	87	-2	2	1	0	.993	2	C-56	0.1
1982	Mon-N	23	42	2	8	2	1	0	3	1	11	.190	.244	.286	47	-3	0	0	0	.985	2	C-18	-0.1
1983	Mon-N	6	15	0	3	1	0	0	2	1	3	.200	.250	.267	43	-1	0	0	0	.935	1	/C-5	-0.1
Total	10	426	1044	91	238	40	11	6	80	154	183	.228	.329	.305	73	-34	3	3	-1	.981	40	C-414/D-2	1.7

■ RAY BLADES
Blades, Francis Raymond b: 8/6/1896, Mt.Vernon, Ill. d: 5/18/79, Lincoln, Ill. BR/TR, 5'7.5", 163 lbs. Deb: 8/19/22 MC

1922	StL-N	37	130	27	39	2	4	3	21	25	21	.300	.428	.446	132	8	3	3	-1	.931	-1	O-29/S-4,3	0.4
1923	StL-N	98	317	48	78	21	5	5	44	37	46	.246	.342	.391	95	-2	4			.967	-6	O-83/3-4	-0.1
1924	StL-N	131	456	86	142	21	13	11	68	35	38	.311	.373	.487	131	19	7	9	-3	.956	-3	*O-109/2-7,3	0.7
1925	StL-N	122	462	112	158	37	8	12	57	59	47	.342	.423	.535	140	29	6	8	-3	.979	11	*O-114/3-1	2.7
1926	StL-N	107	416	81	127	17	12	8	43	62	57	.305	.409	.462	129	19	6			.980	4	*O-105	1.6
1927	StL-N	61	180	33	57	8	5	2	29	28	22	.317	.414	.450	127	8	3			.914	-13	O-50	-0.8
1928	*StL-N	51	85	9	20	7	1	1	19	20	26	.235	.393	.376	100	1	0			.972	-2	O-19	-0.2
1930	*StL-N	45	101	26	40	6	2	4	25	21	15	.396	.504	.614	163	12	1			.957	-3	O-32	0.6
1931	*StL-N	35	67	10	19	4	1	0	5	10	7	.284	.392	.388	106	1	1			.871	-4	O-20	-0.4
1932	StL-N	80	201	35	46	10	3	0	29	34	31	.229	.340	.333	80	-5	2			.975	-5	O-62/3-1	-1.3
Total	10	767	2415	467	726	133	51	50	340	331	310	.301	.395	.460	123	90	33	22		.963	-10	O-623/3-14,2S	3.2

■ RICK BLADT
Bladt, Richard Alan b: 12/9/46, Santa Cruz, Cal. BR/TR, 6'1", 160 lbs. Deb: 6/15/69

1969	Chi-N	10	13	1	2	0	0	0	0	1	5	.154	.154	.154	-12	-2	0	0	0	1.000	0	/O-7	-0.2
1975	NY-A	52	117	13	26	3	1	1	11	10	8	.222	.295	.291	68	-5	6	2	1	.973	-2	/O-51	-0.8
Total	2	62	130	14	28	3	1	1	11	11	13	.215	.282	.277	59	-7	6	2	1	.976	-2	/O-58	-1.0

■ RAE BLAEMIRE
Blaemire, Rae Bertrum b: 2/8/11, Gary, Ind. d: 12/23/75, Champaign, Ill. BR/TR, 6', 178 lbs. Deb: 9/13/41

1941	NY-N	2	5	0	2	0	0	0	0	0	0	.400	.400	.400	123	0	0			1.000	-0	/C-2	0.0

■ FOOTSIE BLAIR
Blair, Clarence Vick b: 7/13/1900, Enterprise, Okla. d: 7/1/82, Texarkana, Tex. BL/TR, 6'1", 180 lbs. Deb: 4/28/29

1929	*Chi-N	26	72	10	23	5	0	1	8	3	8	.319	.347	.431	91	-1	1			.897	1	/3-8,1-7,2	0.0
1930	Chi-N	134	578	97	158	24	12	6	59	20	58	.273	.306	.388	66	-33	9			.958	8	*2-115,3-13	-1.6

YEAR	TM/L	G	AB	R	H	2B	3B	HR	RBI	BB	SO	AVG	OBP	SLG	PRO+	BR/A	SB	CS	SBR	FA	FR	G/POS	TPR
1931	Chi-N	86	240	31	62	19	4	3	29	14	26	.258	.302	.408	88	-5	1			.956	-6	2-44,1-23/3	-0.9
Total	3	246	890	138	243	48	16	10	96	37	88	.273	.308	.397	73	-39	11			.958	4	2-161/1-30,3	-2.5

■ BUDDY BLAIR   Blair, Louis Nathan b: 9/10/10, Columbia, Miss.   BL/TR, 6', 186 lbs.   Deb: 4/14/42

YEAR	TM/L	G	AB	R	H	2B	3B	HR	RBI	BB	SO	AVG	OBP	SLG	PRO+	BR/A	SB	CS	SBR	FA	FR	G/POS	TPR
1942	Phi-A	137	484	48	135	26	8	5	66	30	30	.279	.325	.397	103	0	1	6	-3	.931	-7	*3-126	-0.8

■ PAUL BLAIR   Blair, Paul L D b: 2/1/44, Cushing, Okla.   BR/TR, 6', 171 lbs.   Deb: 9/9/64

YEAR	TM/L	G	AB	R	H	2B	3B	HR	RBI	BB	SO	AVG	OBP	SLG	PRO+	BR/A	SB	CS	SBR	FA	FR	G/POS	TPR
1964	Bal-A	8	1	0	0	0	0	0	0	0	1	.000	.000	.000	-99	-0	0	1	-1	1.000	-2	/O-6	-0.3
1965	Bal-A	119	364	49	85	19	2	5	25	32	52	.234	.303	.338	80	-9	8	5	-1	.992	3	*O-116	-1.3
1966	*Bal-A	133	303	35	84	20	2	6	33	15	36	.277	.311	.416	109	2	5	6	-2	.990	-11	*O-127	-1.5
1967	Bal-A	151	552	72	162	27	12	11	64	50	68	.293	.357	.446	137	25	4	8	-1	.985	21	*O-146	4.1
1968	Bal-A	141	421	48	89	22	1	7	38	37	60	.211	.278	.318	80	-10	4	2	0	.993	0	*O-132/3-1	-1.8
1969	*Bal-A★	150	625	102	178	32	5	26	76	40	72	.285	.330	.477	122	15	20	6	2	.988	25	*O-150	3.5
1970	*Bal-A	133	480	79	128	24	2	18	65	56	93	.267	.347	.438	114	9	24	11	1	.990	19	*O-128/3-1	2.3
1971	*Bal-A	141	516	75	135	24	8	10	44	32	94	.262	.306	.397	99	-3	14	11	-2	.991	2	*O-138	-1.0
1972	Bal-A	142	477	47	111	20	8	4	49	25	78	.233	.271	.358	84	-11	7	8	-3	.991	9	*O-139	-1.2
1973	*Bal-A★	146	500	73	140	25	3	10	64	43	72	.280	.337	.402	108	5	18	8	1	.990	7	*O-144/D-1	0.7
1974	*Bal-A	151	552	77	144	27	4	17	62	43	59	.261	.317	.417	113	7	27	9	3	.985	7	*O-151	1.2
1975	Bal-A	140	440	51	96	13	4	5	31	25	82	.218	.260	.300	62	-23	17	11	0	.991	-2	*O-138/1-1,D	-3.3
1976	Bal-A	145	375	29	74	16	0	3	16	22	49	.197	.246	.264	52	-23	15	6	1	.979	-8	*O-139/D-1	-3.6
1977	*NY-A	83	164	20	43	4	3	4	25	9	16	.262	.309	.396	91	-2	3	2	-0	.969	-13	O-79/D-1	-1.7
1978	*NY-A	75	125	10	22	5	0	2	13	9	17	.176	.231	.264	40	-10	1	1	-0	.989	-15	O-64/2-5,S3	-2.8
1979	NY-A	2	5	0	1	0	0	0	0	0	1	.200	.200	.200	8	-1	0	0		1.000	0	/O-2	0.0
	Cin-N	75	140	7	21	4	1	2	15	11	27	.150	.212	.236	22	-15	0	0		.992	-10	O-67	-2.8
1980	NY-A	12	2	2	0	0	0	0	0	0	0	.000	.000	.000	-99	-1	0	0		1.000	-4	O-12	-0.5
Total	17	1947	6042	776	1513	282	55	134	620	449	877	.250	.305	.382	96	-45	171	93	-5	.988	29	*O-1878/2-5,3SD1	-10.0

■ WALTER BLAIR   Blair, Walter Allen "Heavy" b: 10/13/1883, Landrus, Pa. d: 8/20/48, Lewisburg, Pa.   BR/TR, 6', 185 lbs.   Deb: 9/17/07 M

YEAR	TM/L	G	AB	R	H	2B	3B	HR	RBI	BB	SO	AVG	OBP	SLG	PRO+	BR/A	SB	CS	SBR	FA	FR	G/POS	TPR
1907	NY-A	7	22	1	4	0	0	0	1	2		.182	.250	.182	35	-2	0			.922	2	/C-7	0.1
1908	NY-A	76	211	9	40	5	1	1	13	11		.190	.237	.237	53	-11	4			.956	-14	C-60/O-9,1	-2.3
1909	NY-A	42	110	5	23	2	2	0	11	7		.209	.269	.264	68	-4	2			.964	-8	C-42	-1.0
1910	NY-A	6	22	2	5	0	1	0	2	0		.227	.227	.318	67	-1	0			.970	-2	/C-6	-0.3
1911	NY-A	85	222	18	43	9	2	0	26	16		.194	.257	.252	40	-18	2			.970	-1	C-84/1-1	-0.7
1914	Buf-F	128	378	22	92	11	2	0	33	32	64	.243	.304	.283	52	-27	6			.984	5	*C-128	-1.2
1915	Buf-F	98	290	23	65	15	3	2	20	18	32	.224	.274	.317	57	-19	4			**.981**	5	C-97,M	-0.7
Total	7	442	1255	80	272	42	11	3	106	86	96	.217	.272	.275	52	-81	18			.974	-9	C-424/O-9,1	-6.1

■ HARRY BLAKE   Blake, Harry Cooper b: 6/16/1874, Portsmouth, Ohio d: 10/14/19, Chicago, Ill.   BR/TR, 5'7", 165 lbs.   Deb: 7/7/1894

YEAR	TM/L	G	AB	R	H	2B	3B	HR	RBI	BB	SO	AVG	OBP	SLG	PRO+	BR/A	SB	CS	SBR	FA	FR	G/POS	TPR
1894	Cle-N	73	296	51	78	15	4	1	51	30	22	.264	.335	.351	63	-18	1			.932	2	O-73	-1.6
1895	*Cle-N	84	315	50	87	10	1	3	45	30	33	.276	.341	.343	72	-14	11			.898	-2	O-83	-1.8
1896	Cle-N	104	383	66	92	12	5	1	43	46	30	.240	.322	.305	62	-21	10			.944	5	*O-103/S-1	-2.4
1897	Cle-N	32	117	17	30	3	1	1	15	12		.256	.331	.325	70	-5	5			.989	4	O-32	-0.3
1898	Cle-N	136	474	65	116	18	7	0	58	69		.245	.342	.312	89	-5	12			.952	8	*O-136/1-2	-0.7
1899	StL-N	97	292	50	70	9	4	2	41	43		.240	.318	.318	80	-7	16			.979	-2	O-87/2-4,S1C	-1.3
Total	6	526	1877	299	473	67	22	8	253	230	85	.252	.336	.324	73	-71	55			.948	12	O-514/2-4,1SC	-8.1

■ LINC BLAKELY   Blakely, Lincoln Howard b: 2/12/12, Oakland, Cal. d: 9/28/76, Oakland, Cal.   BR/TR, 6', 180 lbs.   Deb: 4/29/34

YEAR	TM/L	G	AB	R	H	2B	3B	HR	RBI	BB	SO	AVG	OBP	SLG	PRO+	BR/A	SB	CS	SBR	FA	FR	G/POS	TPR
1934	Cin-N	34	102	11	23	1	1	0	10	5	14	.225	.269	.255	42	-8	1			.987	3	O-28	-0.6

■ BOB BLAKISTON   Blakiston, Robert J. (b: Robert J. Blackstone)
b: 10/2/1855, San Francisco, Cal. d: 12/25/18, San Francisco, Cal   5'8.5", 180 lbs.   Deb: 5/2/1882

YEAR	TM/L	G	AB	R	H	2B	3B	HR	RBI	BB	SO	AVG	OBP	SLG	PRO+	BR/A	SB	CS	SBR	FA	FR	G/POS	TPR
1882	Phi-a	72	281	40	64	4	1	0		9		.228	.252	.249	62	-12				.855	0	O-38,3-34/2	-1.1
1883	Phi-a	44	167	26	41	3	3	0		9		.246	.284	.299	82	-4				.857	-4	O-37/1-6,3	-0.7
1884	Phi-a	32	128	21	33	6	0	0		11		.258	.336	.305	104	1				.902	2	O-28/3-2,12S	0.2
	Ind-a	6	18	0	4	1	0	0		1		.222	.263	.278	79	-0				.884	-1	/1-5,O-1	-0.1
	Yr	38	146	21	37	7	0	0		12		.253	.324	.301	101	0				.902	1	O-29/1-6,32S	0.1
Total	3	154	594	87	142	14	4	0		30		.239	.280	.276	77	-16				.872	-2	O-104/3-41,12S	-1.7

■ JOHNNY BLANCHARD   Blanchard, John Edwin b: 2/26/33, Minneapolis, Minn.   BL/TR, 6'1", 198 lbs.   Deb: 9/25/55

YEAR	TM/L	G	AB	R	H	2B	3B	HR	RBI	BB	SO	AVG	OBP	SLG	PRO+	BR/A	SB	CS	SBR	FA	FR	G/POS	TPR
1955	NY-A	1	3	0	0	0	0	0	0	1	0	.000	.250	.000	-29	-1	0	0	0	1.000	0	/C-1	0.0
1959	NY-A	49	59	6	10	1	0	2	4	7	12	.169	.258	.288	51	-4	0	0	0	.963	-2	C-12/O-8,1	-0.6
1960	*NY-A	53	99	8	24	3	1	4	14	6	17	.242	.292	.414	94	-1	0	0	0	.988	10	C-28	0.9
1961	*NY-A	93	243	38	74	10	1	21	54	27	28	.305	.383	.613	170	23	0	0	0	.990	-8	C-48,O-15	2.3
1962	*NY-A	93	246	33	57	7	0	13	39	28	32	.232	.313	.419	98	-1	0	0	0	.987	-7	O-47,C-15/1	-1.1
1963	*NY-A	76	218	22	49	4	0	16	45	26	30	.225	.307	.463	114	3	0	0	0	.987	-9	O-64	-0.9
1964	*NY-A	77	161	18	41	8	0	7	28	24	24	.255	.351	.435	115	4	1	0	0	.984	-3	C-25,O-14/1	0.1
1965	NY-A	12	34	1	5	1	0	1	3	7	3	.147	.293	.265	60	-2	0	0	0	.961	-1	C-12	-0.2
	KC-A	52	120	10	24	2	0	2	11	9	16	.200	.256	.267	49	-8	0	0	0	1.000	-10	O-20,C-14	-2.0
	Yr	64	154	11	29	3	0	3	14	15	19	.188	.265	.266	52	-10	0	0	0	.971	-1	C-26,O-20	-2.2
	Mil-N	10	10	1	1	0	0	1	2	2	4	.100	.250	.400	79	-0	0	0	0	.000	-0	/O-1	-0.1
Total	8	516	1193	137	285	36	2	67	200	136	163	.239	.320	.441	109	13	2	0	1	.987	-25	O-169,C-155/1	-1.6

■ DAMASO BLANCO   Blanco, Damaso (Caripe) b: 12/11/41, Curiepe, Venez.   BR/TR, 5'10", 165 lbs.   Deb: 5/26/72

YEAR	TM/L	G	AB	R	H	2B	3B	HR	RBI	BB	SO	AVG	OBP	SLG	PRO+	BR/A	SB	CS	SBR	FA	FR	G/POS	TPR
1972	SF-N	39	20	5	7	1	0	0	2	4	3	.350	.458	.400	144	1	2	1	0	.889	6	3-19/S-8,2	0.8
1973	SF-N	28	12	4	0	0	0	0	0	1	2	.000	.077	.000	-74	-3	0	0	0	1.000	2	/3-7,S-5,2	-0.1
1974	SF-N	5	1	0	0	0	0	0	0	0	1	.000	.000	.000	-96	-0	1	0	0	.000	0	H	0.0
Total	3	72	33	9	7	1	0	0	2	5	6	.212	.316	.242	58	-2	3	1	0	.929	8	/3-26,S-13,2	0.7

■ OSSIE BLANCO   Blanco, Oswaldo Carlos (Diaz) b: 9/8/45, Caracas, Venez.   BR/TR, 6', 185 lbs.   Deb: 5/26/70

YEAR	TM/L	G	AB	R	H	2B	3B	HR	RBI	BB	SO	AVG	OBP	SLG	PRO+	BR/A	SB	CS	SBR	FA	FR	G/POS	TPR
1970	Chi-A	34	66	4	13	0	0	0	8	3	14	.197	.232	.197	19	-7	0	1	-1	.993	-1	1-22/O-1	-1.0
1974	Cle-A	18	36	1	7	0	0	0	2	7	4	.194	.326	.194	53	-2	0	3	-2	.992	-1	1-16/D-1	-0.6
Total	2	52	102	5	20	0	0	0	10	10	18	.196	.268	.196	31	-9	0	4	-2	.993	-2	/1-38,D-1,O	-1.6

■ COONIE BLANK   Blank, Frank Ignatz b: 10/18/1892, St.Louis, Mo. d: 12/8/61, St.Louis, Mo.   BR/TR, 5'11", 165 lbs.   Deb: 8/15/09

YEAR	TM/L	G	AB	R	H	2B	3B	HR	RBI	BB	SO	AVG	OBP	SLG	PRO+	BR/A	SB	CS	SBR	FA	FR	G/POS	TPR
1909	StL-N	1	2	0	0	0	0	0	0	0	0	.000	.000	.000	-99	-0	0			1.000	-0	/C-1	-0.1

■ CLIFF BLANKENSHIP   Blankenship, Clifford Douglas b: 4/10/1880, Columbus, Ga. d: 4/26/56, Oakland, Cal.   BR/TR, 5'10.5", 165 lbs.   Deb: 4/17/05

YEAR	TM/L	G	AB	R	H	2B	3B	HR	RBI	BB	SO	AVG	OBP	SLG	PRO+	BR/A	SB	CS	SBR	FA	FR	G/POS	TPR
1905	Cin-N	19	56	8	11	1	1	0	7	4		.196	.250	.250	44	-4	1			.960	-2	1-15	-0.7
1907	Was-A	37	102	4	23	2	0	0	6	3		.225	.248	.245	62	-5	3			.991	-0	C-22/1-9	-0.3
1909	Was-A	39	60	4	15	1	0	0	9	0		.250	.250	.267	66	-3	2			.907	-9	C-17/O-4	-1.2
Total	3	95	218	16	49	4	1	0	22	7		.225	.249	.252	58	-11	6			.964	-11	/C-39,1-24,O	-2.2

■ LANCE BLANKENSHIP   Blankenship, Lance Robert b: 12/6/63, Portland, Ore.   BR/TR, 6', 190 lbs.   Deb: 9/4/88

YEAR	TM/L	G	AB	R	H	2B	3B	HR	RBI	BB	SO	AVG	OBP	SLG	PRO+	BR/A	SB	CS	SBR	FA	FR	G/POS	TPR
1988	Oak-A	10	3	1	0	0	0	0	0	0	0	.000	.000	.000	-99	-1	0	0	0	/2-4,D-4			-0.1
1989	*Oak-A	58	125	22	29	5	1	1	4	8	31	.232	.278	.312	68	-5	5	1	1	1.000	3	O-25,2-24,D	-0.1
1990	*Oak-A	86	136	18	26	3	0	0	10	20	23	.191	.295	.213	46	-9	3	1	0	.947	-2	3-28,O-28,2/1D	-1.1

YEAR	TM/L	G	AB	R	H	2B	3B	HR	RBI	BB	SO	AVG	OBP	SLG	PRO+	BR/A	SB	CS	SBR	FA	FR	G/POS	TPR
1991	Oak-A	90	185	33	46	8	0	3	21	23	42	.249	.341	.341	95	-1	12	3	2	.983	8	2-45,O-28,3/D	0.9
1992	*Oak-A	123	349	59	84	24	1	3	34	82	57	.241	.394	.341	113	11	21	7	2	.992	-3	2-78,O-51/1D	1.1
1993	Oak-A	94	252	43	48	8	1	2	23	67	64	.190	.364	.254	74	-6	13	5	1	.994	4	O-66,2-19/1SD	-0.2
Total	6	461	1050	176	233	48	3	9	92	200	218	.222	.352	.299	86	-11	54	18	5	.987	10	O-198,2-190/3D1S	0.5

■ LARVELL BLANKS
Blanks, Larvell b: 1/28/50, Del Rio, Tex. BR/TR, 5'8", 167 lbs. Deb: 7/19/72

YEAR	TM/L	G	AB	R	H	2B	3B	HR	RBI	BB	SO	AVG	OBP	SLG	PRO+	BR/A	SB	CS	SBR	FA	FR	G/POS	TPR
1972	Atl-N	33	85	10	28	5	0	1	7	7	12	.329	.380	.424	117	2	0	0	0	1.000	6	2-18/S-4,3	1.0
1973	Atl-N	17	18	1	4	0	0	0	1	0	3	.222	.263	.222	33	-2	0	0	0	.000	-3	/3-3,2-2,S	-0.4
1974	Atl-N	3	8	0	2	0	0	0	1	0	0	.250	.250	.250	38	-1	0	0	0	.889	-0	/S-2	-0.1
1975	Atl-N	141	471	49	110	13	3	3	38	38	43	.234	.294	.293	61	-25	4	3	-1	.960	-12	*S-129,2-12	-2.5
1976	Cle-A	104	328	45	92	8	7	5	41	30	31	.280	.341	.393	116	6	1	2	-1	.977	-20	S-56,2-46/3D	-0.6
1977	Cle-A	105	322	43	92	10	4	6	38	19	37	.286	.327	.398	100	-1	3	0	1	.960	-25	S-66,3-18,2/D	-1.8
1978	Cle-A	70	193	19	49	10	0	2	20	10	16	.254	.291	.337	77	-6	0	0	0	.926	-10	S-43,2-17/3D	-1.0
1979	Tex-A	68	120	13	24	5	0	1	15	11	9	.200	.267	.267	45	-9	0	0	0	.972	-9	S-49,2-16	-1.4
1980	Atl-N	88	221	23	45	6	0	2	12	16	27	.204	.257	.258	43	-17	1	2	-1	.947	7	S-56,3-43/2	-0.8
Total	9	629	1766	203	446	57	14	20	172	132	178	.253	.306	.335	78	-51	9	7	-2	.957	-66	S-407,2-124/3D	-7.6

■ DON BLASINGAME
Blasingame, Don Lee b: 3/16/32, Corinth, Miss. BL/TR, 5'10", 165 lbs. Deb: 9/20/55

YEAR	TM/L	G	AB	R	H	2B	3B	HR	RBI	BB	SO	AVG	OBP	SLG	PRO+	BR/A	SB	CS	SBR	FA	FR	G/POS	TPR
1955	StL-N	5	16	4	6	1	0	0	6	0	0	.375	.545	.438	165	2	1	1	-0	.955	2	/2-3,S-2	0.4
1956	StL-N	150	587	94	153	22	7	0	27	72	52	.261	.344	.322	81	-14	8	8	-2	.986	22	2-98,S-49/3	1.8
1957	StL-N	154	650	108	176	25	7	8	58	71	49	.271	.343	.368	89	-8	21	9	1	.984	26	*2-154	3.1
1958	StL-N★	143	547	71	150	19	10	2	36	57	47	.274	.344	.356	83	-12	20	5	3	.964	-1	*2-137	-0.1
1959	StL-N	150	615	90	178	26	7	1	24	67	42	.289	.361	.359	87	-9	15	15	-5	.979	21	*2-150	1.8
1960	SF-N	136	523	72	123	12	8	2	31	49	53	.235	.302	.300	70	-21	14	2	3	.979	-13	*2-133	-1.9
1961	SF-N	3	1	1	0	0	0	0	0	2	1	.000	.667	.000	100	0	0	0	0	.000	-0	H	0.0
	*Cin-N	123	450	59	100	18	4	1	21	39	38	.222	.287	.287	52	-30	4	3	-1	.972	-19	*2-116	-3.8
	Yr	126	451	60	100	18	4	1	21	41	39	.222	.289	.286	53	-30	4	3	-1	.972	-19	*2-116	-3.8
1962	Cin-N	141	494	77	139	9	7	2	35	63	44	.281	.365	.340	88	-6	4	3	-1	.976	-10	*2-137	-0.2
1963	Cin-N	18	31	4	5	2	0	0	0	7	5	.161	.316	.226	57	-1	0	1	-1	.974	0	2-11/3-2	-0.1
	Was-A	69	254	29	65	10	2	2	12	24	18	.256	.320	.335	84	-5	3	2	-0	.991	1	2-64	0.2
1964	Was-A	143	506	56	135	17	2	1	34	40	44	.267	.321	.314	78	-14	8	5	-1	.977	-30	*2-135	-3.6
1965	Was-A	129	403	47	90	8	1	1	18	35	45	.223	.289	.290	66	-18	5	4	-1	.984	1	*2-110	-1.0
1966	Was-A	68	200	18	43	9	0	1	11	18	21	.215	.280	.275	61	-10	2	1	0	.984	-1	2-58/S-1	-0.8
	KC-A	12	19	1	3	0	0	0	1	2	3	.158	.238	.158	17	-2	0	1	-1	1.000	-0	/2-4	-0.3
	Yr	80	219	19	46	9	0	1	12	20	24	.210	.276	.265	57	-12	2	2	-1	.985	-2	2-62/S-1	-1.1
Total	12	1444	5296	731	1366	178	62	21	308	552	462	.258	.330	.327	78	-149	105	60	-4	.979	-3	*2-1310/S-52,3	-4.5

■ JOHNNY BLATNIK
Blatnik, John Louis b: 3/10/21, Bridgeport, Ohio BR/TR, 6', 195 lbs. Deb: 4/21/48

YEAR	TM/L	G	AB	R	H	2B	3B	HR	RBI	BB	SO	AVG	OBP	SLG	PRO+	BR/A	SB	CS	SBR	FA	FR	G/POS	TPR
1948	Phi-N	121	415	56	108	27	8	6	45	31	77	.260	.315	.407	96	-4	3			.946	-1	*O-105	-1.0
1949	Phi-N	6	8	3	1	0	0	0	0	4	1	.125	.417	.125	53	-0	0			1.000	-0	/O-2	-0.1
1950	Phi-N	4	4	0	1	0	0	0	0	2	3	.250	.500	.250	106	0	0			1.000	-0	/O-1	0.0
	StL-N	7	20	0	3	0	0	0	1	3	2	.150	.261	.150	11	-3	0			.875	-2	/O-7	-0.5
	Yr	11	24	0	4	0	0	0	1	5	5	.167	.310	.167	29	-2	0			.900	-2	/O-8	-0.5
Total	3	138	447	59	113	27	8	6	46	40	83	.253	.317	.389	91	-6	3			.945	-3	O-115	-1.6

■ BUDDY BLATTNER
Blattner, Robert Garnett b: 2/8/20, St.Louis, Mo. BR/TR, 6'0.5", 180 lbs. Deb: 4/18/42

YEAR	TM/L	G	AB	R	H	2B	3B	HR	RBI	BB	SO	AVG	OBP	SLG	PRO+	BR/A	SB	CS	SBR	FA	FR	G/POS	TPR
1942	StL-N	19	23	3	1	0	0	0	1	3	6	.043	.185	.043	-29	-4	0			.900	-0	S-13/2-3	-0.4
1946	NY-N	126	420	63	107	18	6	11	49	56	52	.255	.351	.405	113	8	12			.976	1	*2-114/1-1	1.7
1947	NY-N	55	153	28	40	9	2	0	13	21	19	.261	.351	.346	85	-3	4			.947	-3	2-34,3-11	-0.4
1948	NY-N	8	20	3	4	1	0	0	0	3	2	.200	.304	.250	51	-1	2			1.000	2	/2-7	0.1
1949	Phi-N	64	97	15	24	6	0	5	21	19	17	.247	.371	.464	126	4	0			.981	-10	2-15,3-12/S	-0.6
Total	5	272	713	112	176	34	8	16	84	102	96	.247	.347	.384	102	4	18			.971	-11	2-173/3-23,S1	0.4

■ JEFF BLAUSER
Blauser, Jeffrey Michael b: 11/8/65, Los Gatos, Cal. BR/TR, 6'1", 180 lbs. Deb: 7/5/87

YEAR	TM/L	G	AB	R	H	2B	3B	HR	RBI	BB	SO	AVG	OBP	SLG	PRO+	BR/A	SB	CS	SBR	FA	FR	G/POS	TPR
1987	Atl-N	51	165	11	40	6	3	2	15	18	34	.242	.328	.352	76	-5	7	3	0	.962	10	S-50	0.9
1988	Atl-N	18	67	7	16	3	1	2	7	2	11	.239	.271	.403	87	-1	0	1	-1	.967	3	/2-9,S-8	0.2
1989	Atl-N	142	456	63	123	24	2	12	46	38	101	.270	.327	.410	107	3	5	2	0	.929	-17	3-78,2-39,S/O	-1.0
1990	Atl-N	115	386	46	104	24	3	8	39	35	70	.269	.338	.409	99	-1	3	2	0	.961	-3	S-93,2-14/3O	-0.9
1991	*Atl-N	129	352	49	91	14	3	11	54	54	59	.259	.360	.409	109	5	5	6	-2	.948	-36	S-85,2-32,3	-2.9
1992	*Atl-N	123	343	61	90	19	3	14	46	46	82	.262	.356	.458	122	10	5	5	-2	.968	-47	*S-106,2-21/3	-3.5
1993	*Atl-N★	161	597	110	182	29	2	15	73	85	109	.305	.405	.436	124	24	16	6	1	.970	-23	*S-161	1.5
1994	Atl-N	96	380	56	98	21	4	6	45	38	64	.258	.333	.382	86	-8	1	3	-2	.970	8	S-96	0.1
Total	8	835	2746	403	744	140	21	70	325	316	530	.271	.354	.414	106	28	42	31	-6	.965	-109	S-629,2-115,3/O	-4.5

■ MARV BLAYLOCK
Blaylock, Marvin Edward b: 9/30/29, Ft.Smith, Ark. d: 10/23/93, Conway, Ark. BL/TL, 6'1.5", 175 lbs. Deb: 9/26/50

YEAR	TM/L	G	AB	R	H	2B	3B	HR	RBI	BB	SO	AVG	OBP	SLG	PRO+	BR/A	SB	CS	SBR	FA	FR	G/POS	TPR
1950	NY-N	1	1	0	0	0	0	0	0	0	0	.000	.000	.000	-99	-0	0			.000	0	H	0.0
1955	Phi-N	113	259	30	54	7	7	3	24	31	43	.208	.294	.324	66	-13	6	1	1	.991	3	1-77/O-6	-1.2
1956	Phi-N	136	460	61	117	14	8	10	50	50	86	.254	.330	.385	93	-4	5	1	1	.992	-5	*1-124/O-1	-1.7
1957	Phi-N	37	26	5	4	0	2	0	4	3	8	.154	.313	.385	89	-0	0	0	0	1.000	0	1-12/O-1	0.0
Total	4	287	746	96	175	21	15	15	78	84	137	.235	.317	.363	83	-18	11	2		.992	-2	1-213/O-8	-2.9

■ CURT BLEFARY
Blefary, Curtis Le Roy b: 7/5/43, Brooklyn, N.Y. BL/TR, 6'2", 195 lbs. Deb: 4/14/65

YEAR	TM/L	G	AB	R	H	2B	3B	HR	RBI	BB	SO	AVG	OBP	SLG	PRO+	BR/A	SB	CS	SBR	FA	FR	G/POS	TPR
1965	Bal-A	144	462	72	120	23	4	22	70	88	73	.260	.382	.470	138	25	4	2	0	.979	-9	*O-136	2.3
1966	*Bal-A	131	419	73	107	14	3	23	64	73	56	.255	.373	.468	142	25	1	4	-2	.976	-3	*O-109,1-20	1.5
1967	Bal-A	155	554	69	134	19	5	22	81	73	94	.242	.339	.413	122	16	4	4	-1	.968	13	*O-103,1-52	2.2
1968	Bal-A	137	451	50	90	8	1	15	39	65	66	.200	.306	.322	90	-4	6	3	0	.962	-9	O-92,C-40,1	-1.8
1969	Hou-N	155	542	66	137	26	7	12	67	77	79	.253	.350	.393	110	8	7		-2	.987	6	*1-152/O-1	0.0
1970	NY-A	99	269	34	57	6	0	9	37	43	37	.212	.327	.335	87	-4	1	2	-2	.972	-11	O-79/1-6	-2.1
1971	NY-A	21	36	4	7	1	0	1	2	5	7	.194	.256	.306	62	-2	0	0	0	.875	-1	/O-6,1-4	-0.4
	*Oak-A	50	101	15	22	2	0	5	12	15	15	.218	.325	.386	103	0	0	1	-1	.975	-5	C-14,O-14/32	-0.5
	Yr	71	137	19	29	3	0	6	14	18	20	.212	.308	.365	93	-1	0	1	-1	.958	-5	O-20,C-14/312	-0.9
1972	Oak-A	8	11	1	5	2	0	0	1	0	1	.455	.455	.636	234	2	0	0	0	.000	-0	/1-1,2-1,O	0.1
	SD-N	74	102	10	20	3	0	1	9	19	18	.196	.322	.314	88	-1	0	0	0	.982	-8	C-12/1-6,3O	-1.0
Total	8	974	2947	394	699	104	20	112	382	456	444	.237	.345	.400	115	65	24	24	-7	.972	-15	O-544,1-253/C32	0.3

■ IKE BLESSITT
Blessitt, Isaiah b: 9/30/49, Detroit, Mich. BR/TR, 5'11", 185 lbs. Deb: 9/7/72

YEAR	TM/L	G	AB	R	H	2B	3B	HR	RBI	BB	SO	AVG	OBP	SLG	PRO+	BR/A	SB	CS	SBR	FA	FR	G/POS	TPR
1972	Det-A	4	5	0	0	0	0	0	0	0	2	.000	.000	.000	-97	-1	0	0	0	1.000	-0	/O-1	-0.2

■ NED BLIGH
Bligh, Edwin Forrest b: 6/30/1864, Brooklyn, N.Y. d: 4/18/1892, Brooklyn, N.Y. BR/TR, 5'11", 172 lbs. Deb: 6/26/1886

YEAR	TM/L	G	AB	R	H	2B	3B	HR	RBI	BB	SO	AVG	OBP	SLG	PRO+	BR/A	SB	CS	SBR	FA	FR	G/POS	TPR
1886	Bal-a	3	9	0	0	0	0	0	0	0	1	.000	.000	.000	-69	-2	0			.833	-2	/C-3	-0.3
1888	Cin-a	3	5	0	0	0	0	0	0	0	0	.000	.000	.000	-95	-1	0			1.000	-1	/C-2,O-1	-0.2
1889	Col-a	28	93	6	13	1	1	0	5	4	14	.140	.200	.172	7	-11	2			.927	-3	C-28	-1.0
1890	Col-a	8	29	2	6	2	0	0			2	.207	.258	.276	62	-1	0			.933	2	C-8	0.1
	*Lou-a	24	73	9	15	0	0				9	.205	.293	.247	60	-3	1			.921	-0	C-24	-0.2

YEAR	TM/L	G	AB	R	H	2B	3B	HR	RBI	BB	SO	AVG	OBP	SLG	PRO+	BR/A	SB	CS	SBR	FA	FR	G/POS	TPR
	Yr	32	102	11	21	2	0	1		11		.206	.283	.255	61	-5	1			.925	1	C-32	-0.1
Total	4	66	209	17	34	3	1	1	5	16	14	.163	.232	.201	28	-19	3			.923	-5	/C-65,O-1	-1.6

■ ELMER BLISS
Bliss, Elmer Ward b: 3/9/1875, Penfield, Pa. d: 3/18/62, Bradford, Pa. BL/TR, 6', 180 lbs. Deb: 9/28/03

YEAR	TM/L	G	AB	R	H	2B	3B	HR	RBI	BB	SO	AVG	OBP	SLG	PRO+	BR/A	SB	CS	SBR	FA	FR	G/POS	TPR
1903	NY-A	1	3	0	0	0	0	0	0	0		.000	.000	.000	-94	-1	0			.000	-0	/P-1	0.0
1904	NY-A	1	1	0	0	0	0	0	0	0		.000	.000	.000	-96	-0	0			.000	-0	/O-1	-0.1
Total	2	2	4	0	0	0	0	0	0	0		.000	.000	.000	-94	-1	0			—	-1	/O-1,P-1	-0.1

■ FRANK BLISS
Bliss, Frank Eugene b: 12/10/1852, Chicago, Ill. d: 1/8/29, Nashville, Tenn. Deb: 6/20/1878

YEAR	TM/L	G	AB	R	H	2B	3B	HR	RBI	BB	SO	AVG	OBP	SLG	PRO+	BR/A	SB	CS	SBR	FA	FR	G/POS	TPR
1878	Mil-N	2	8	1	1	0	0	0	0	0	0	.125	.125	.125	-17	-1				1.000	-0	/3-1,C-1	-0.1

■ JACK BLISS
Bliss, John Joseph Albert b: 1/9/1882, Vancouver, Wash. d: 10/23/68, Temple City, Cal. BR/TR, 5'9", 185 lbs. Deb: 5/10/08

YEAR	TM/L	G	AB	R	H	2B	3B	HR	RBI	BB	SO	AVG	OBP	SLG	PRO+	BR/A	SB	CS	SBR	FA	FR	G/POS	TPR
1908	StL-N	44	136	9	29	4	0	1	5	8		.213	.267	.265	73	-4	3			.992	5	C-43	0.5
1909	StL-N	35	113	12	25	2	1	1	8	12		.221	.307	.283	89	-1	2			.951	1	C-32	0.3
1910	StL-N	16	33	2	2	0	0	0	3	4	8	.061	.162	.061	-36	-6	0			.980	-1	C-13	-0.7
1911	StL-N	97	258	36	59	6	4	1	27	42	25	.229	.341	.295	81	-5	5			.952	-9	C-84/S-1	-0.7
1912	StL-N	49	114	11	28	3	1	0	18	19	14	.246	.372	.289	84	-1	3			.973	-6	C-41	-0.3
Total	5	241	654	70	143	15	6	3	61	85	47	.219	.318	.274	76	-18	13			.966	-10	C-213/S-1	-0.9

■ BRUNO BLOCK
Block, James John (b: James John Blochowicz)
b: 3/13/1885, Wisconsin Rapids, Wis. d: 8/6/37, S.Milwaukee, Wis. BR/TR, 5'9", 185 lbs. Deb: 8/5/07

YEAR	TM/L	G	AB	R	H	2B	3B	HR	RBI	BB	SO	AVG	OBP	SLG	PRO+	BR/A	SB	CS	SBR	FA	FR	G/POS	TPR
1907	Was-A	24	57	3	8	2	1	0	2	2		.140	.169	.211	23	-5	0			.949	-6	C-21	-1.0
1910	Chi-A	55	152	12	32	1	1	0	9	13		.211	.273	.230	60	-7	3			.964	1	C-47	-0.2
1911	Chi-A	39	115	11	35	6	1	1	18	6		.304	.339	.400	109	1	0			.972	-3	C-38	0.2
1912	Chi-A	46	136	8	35	5	6	0	26	7		.257	.294	.382	96	-2	1			.980	2	C-46	0.4
1914	Chi-F	44	105	8	21	4	1	0	14	11	17	.200	.276	.257	41	-9	1			.966	-0	C-34	-0.7
Total	5	208	565	42	131	18	10	1	69	39	17	.232	.281	.304	72	-22	5			.969	-5	C-186	-1.3

■ CY BLOCK
Block, Seymour b: 5/4/19, Brooklyn, N.Y. BR/TR, 6', 180 lbs. Deb: 9/7/42

YEAR	TM/L	G	AB	R	H	2B	3B	HR	RBI	BB	SO	AVG	OBP	SLG	PRO+	BR/A	SB	CS	SBR	FA	FR	G/POS	TPR
1942	Chi-N	9	33	6	12	1	1	0	4	3	3	.364	.417	.455	161	3	2			.917	-2	/3-8,2-1	0.0
1945	*Chi-N	2	7	1	1	0	0	0	1	0	0	.143	.143	.143	-21	-1	0			1.000	1	/2-1,3-1	0.0
1946	Chi-N	6	13	2	3	0	0	0	0	4	0	.231	.412	.231	86	0	0			1.000	1	/3-4	0.1
Total	3	17	53	9	16	1	1	0	5	7	3	.302	.383	.358	118	2	2			.947	-0	/3-13,2-2	0.1

■ TERRY BLOCKER
Blocker, Terry Fennell b: 8/18/59, Columbia, S.C. BL/TL, 6'2", 195 lbs. Deb: 4/11/85

YEAR	TM/L	G	AB	R	H	2B	3B	HR	RBI	BB	SO	AVG	OBP	SLG	PRO+	BR/A	SB	CS	SBR	FA	FR	G/POS	TPR
1985	NY-N	18	15	1	1	0	0	0	1	2		.067	.125	.067	-46	-3	0	0	0	1.000	-1	/O-5	-0.4
1988	Atl-N	66	198	13	42	4	2	2	10	10	20	.212	.250	.283	50	-13	1	1	-0	.994	4	O-61	-1.2
1989	Atl-N	26	31	1	7	1	0	0	1	1	5	.226	.250	.258	44	-2	1	0	0	1.000	-2	/O-8,P-1	-0.4
Total	3	110	244	15	50	5	2	2	11	12	27	.205	.242	.266	44	-18	2	1	0	.994	1	/O-74,P-1	-2.0

■ WES BLOGG
Blogg, Wesley Collins b: 1855, Norfolk, Va. d: 3/10/1897, Baltimore, Md. Deb: 6/20/1883

YEAR	TM/L	G	AB	R	H	2B	3B	HR	RBI	BB	SO	AVG	OBP	SLG	PRO+	BR/A	SB	CS	SBR	FA	FR	G/POS	TPR
1883	Pit-a	9	34	0	5	0	0	0		0		.147	.147	.147	-5	-4				.881	-1	/C-6,O-3	-0.4

■ RON BLOMBERG
Blomberg, Ronald Mark "Boomer" b: 8/23/48, Atlanta, Ga. BL/TR, 6'1", 205 lbs. Deb: 9/10/69

YEAR	TM/L	G	AB	R	H	2B	3B	HR	RBI	BB	SO	AVG	OBP	SLG	PRO+	BR/A	SB	CS	SBR	FA	FR	G/POS	TPR
1969	NY-A	4	6	0	3	0	0	0		3		.500	.571	.500	210	1	0	0	0	1.000	-0	/O-2	0.1
1971	NY-A	64	199	30	64	6	2	7	31	14	23	.322	.366	.477	146	11	2	4	-2	.970	-5	O-57	0.2
1972	NY-A	107	299	36	80	22	1	14	49	38	26	.268	.356	.488	155	20	0	2	-1	.985	-8	1-95	0.4
1973	NY-A	100	301	45	99	13	1	12	57	34	25	.329	.397	.498	156	22	2	0	1	.980	-5	D-55,1-41	1.9
1974	NY-A	90	264	39	82	11	2	10	48	29	33	.311	.383	.481	151	18	2	1	0	1.000	0	D-58,O-19	1.6
1975	NY-A	34	106	18	27	8	2	4	17	13	10	.255	.336	.481	132	4	1	0	0	1.000	0	D-27/O-1	0.3
1976	NY-A	1	2	0	0	0	0	0	0	0	0	.000	.000	.000	-99	-0	0	0	0	.000	0	/D-1	-0.1
1978	Chi-A	61	156	16	36	7	0	5	22	11	17	.231	.281	.372	81	-4	0	0	0	.986	-1	D-36/1-7	-0.7
Total	8	461	1333	184	391	67	8	52	224	140	134	.293	.363	.473	142	71	6	7	-2	.983	-14	D-177,1-143/O	3.7

■ JOE BLONG
Blong, Joseph Myles b: 9/17/1853, St.Louis, Mo. d: 9/16/1892, St.Louis, Mo. BR/TR, Deb: 5/4/1875

YEAR	TM/L	G	AB	R	H	2B	3B	HR	RBI	BB	SO	AVG	OBP	SLG	PRO+	BR/A	SB	CS	SBR	FA	FR	G/POS	TPR
1875	RS-n	16	68	3	10	2	0	0				.147	.147	.176	13	-5						P-15/O-3	0.1
1876	StL-N	62	264	30	62	7	4	0	30	2	9	.235	.241	.292	81	-5				.895	1	*O-62/P-1	-0.4
1877	StL-N	58	218	17	47	8	3	0	13	4	22	.216	.230	.280	63	-9				.835	-3	*O-40,P-25	-0.8
Total	2	120	482	47	109	15	7	0	43	6	31	.226	.236	.286	72	-13				.867	-2	O-102/P-26	-1.2

■ JIMMY BLOODWORTH
Bloodworth, James Henry b: 7/26/17, Tallahassee, Fla. BR/TR, 5'11", 180 lbs. Deb: 9/14/37

YEAR	TM/L	G	AB	R	H	2B	3B	HR	RBI	BB	SO	AVG	OBP	SLG	PRO+	BR/A	SB	CS	SBR	FA	FR	G/POS	TPR
1937	Was-A	15	50	3	11	2	1	0	8	5	8	.220	.291	.300	51	-4	0	1	-1	.946	-1	2-14	-0.4
1939	Was-A	83	318	34	92	24	1	4	40	10	26	.289	.313	.409	90	-7	3	1	0	.972	14	2-73/O-5	1.1
1940	Was-A	119	469	47	115	17	8	11	70	16	71	.245	.272	.386	73	-21	3	1	0	.978	13	2-96,1-17/3	-0.3
1941	Was-A	142	506	59	124	24	3	7	66	41	58	.245	.303	.346	75	-20	1	1	-0	.971	**35**	*2-132/3-6,S	2.3
1942	Det-A	137	533	62	129	23	1	13	57	35	63	.242	.295	.362	78	-17	2	8	-4	.972	10	*2-134/S-2	-0.3
1943	Det-A	129	474	41	114	23	4	6	52	29	59	.241	.289	.344	79	-14	4	7	-3	.972	17	*2-129	0.8
1946	Det-A	76	249	25	61	8	1	5	36	12	26	.245	.285	.345	71	-10	3	3	-1	.974	-1	2-71	-0.7
1947	Pit-N	88	316	27	79	9	0	7	48	16	39	.250	.290	.345	66	-16	1			.979	-14	2-87	-2.4
1949	Cin-N	134	452	40	118	27	1	9	59	27	36	.261	.304	.385	83	-12	1			.981	-3	2-92,1-23/3	-1.2
1950	Cin-N	4	14	1	3	1	0	0	4	0	0	.214	.313	.286	58	-1	0			1.000	-3	/2-4	-0.4
	*Phi-N	54	96	6	22	2	0	4	13	6	12	.229	.275	.250	40	-8	0			1.000	-2	2-27/1-7,3	-0.9
	Yr	58	110	7	25	3	0	4	14	8	12	.227	.280	.255	42	-9	0			1.000	-5	2-31/1-7,3	-1.3
1951	Phi-N	21	42	2	6	0	0	1	3	9		.143	.200	.143	-6	-6	1	0		1.000	-1	/2-8,1-6	-0.7
Total	11	1002	3519	347	874	160	20	62	451	202	407	.248	.292	.358	74	-136	19	22		.975	64	2-867/1-53,30S	-3.1

■ BUD BLOOMFIELD
Bloomfield, Clyde Stalcup b: 1/5/36, Oklahoma City, Okla. BR/TR, 5'11.5", 175 lbs. Deb: 9/25/63

YEAR	TM/L	G	AB	R	H	2B	3B	HR	RBI	BB	SO	AVG	OBP	SLG	PRO+	BR/A	SB	CS	SBR	FA	FR	G/POS	TPR
1963	StL-N	1	0	0	0	0	0	0	0	0		—	—	—		0	0	0	0	.000	0	/3-1	0.0
1964	Min-A	7	7	1	1	0	0	0	0	0	0	.143	.143	.143	-20	-1	0	0	0	1.000	1	/2-3,S-2	0.0
Total	2	8	7	1	1	0	0	0	0	0	0	.143	.143	.143	-20	-1	0	0	0	1.000	1	/2-3,S-2,3	0.0

■ GREG BLOSSER
Blosser, Gregory Brent b: 6/26/71, Manatee, Fla. BL/TL, 6'3", 200 lbs. Deb: 9/5/93

YEAR	TM/L	G	AB	R	H	2B	3B	HR	RBI	BB	SO	AVG	OBP	SLG	PRO+	BR/A	SB	CS	SBR	FA	FR	G/POS	TPR
1993	Bos-A	17	28	1	2	1	0	0	1	2	7	.071	.133	.107	-33	-5	1	0	0	1.000	-1	/O-9,D-1	-0.6
1994	Bos-A	5	11	2	1	0	0	0	1	4	4	.091	.333	.091	16	-1	0	0	0	.727	-0	/O-3,D-1	-0.1
Total	2	22	39	3	3	1	0	0	2	6	11	.077	.200	.103	-16	-7	1	0	0	.870	-1	/O-12,D-2	-0.7

■ JACK BLOTT
Blott, John Leonard b: 8/24/02, Girard, Ohio d: 6/11/64, Ann Arbor, Mich. BR/TR, 6', 210 lbs. Deb: 7/30/24

YEAR	TM/L	G	AB	R	H	2B	3B	HR	RBI	BB	SO	AVG	OBP	SLG	PRO+	BR/A	SB	CS	SBR	FA	FR	G/POS	TPR
1924	Cin-N	2	1	0	0	0	0	0	0	0	0	.000	.000	.000	-99	-0	0	0	0	1.000	-0	/C-1	0.0

■ MIKE BLOWERS
Blowers, Michael Roy b: 4/24/65, Wurzburg, Germany BR/TR, 6'2", 190 lbs. Deb: 9/1/89

YEAR	TM/L	G	AB	R	H	2B	3B	HR	RBI	BB	SO	AVG	OBP	SLG	PRO+	BR/A	SB	CS	SBR	FA	FR	G/POS	TPR
1989	NY-A	13	38	2	10	0	0	0	3	3	13	.263	.317	.263	66	-2	0	0	0	.852	-3	3-13	-0.4
1990	NY-A	48	144	16	27	4	0	5	21	12	50	.188	.255	.319	59	-8	1	0	0	.899	-3	3-45/D-2	-1.6
1991	NY-A	15	35	3	7	1	0	1	1	4	13	.200	.282	.286	57	-2	0	0	0	.870	-3	3-14	-0.5
1992	Sea-A	31	73	7	14	3	0	1	2	6	20	.192	.253	.274	47	-5	0	0	0	.984	6	3-29/1-3	0.0
1993	Sea-A	127	379	55	106	23	3	15	57	44	98	.280	.358	.475	120	10	1	5	-3	.951	12	*3-117/O-2,C1D	2.0

YEAR	TM/L	G	AB	R	H	2B	3B	HR	RBI	BB	SO	AVG	OBP	SLG	PRO+	BR/A	SB	CS	SBR	FA	FR	G/POS	TPR
1994	Sea-A	85	270	37	78	13	0	9	49	25	60	.289	.351	.437	100	-0	2	2	-1	.939	10	3-48,1-20/OD	0.7
Total	6	319	939	120	242	43	3	31	133	94	244	.258	.328	.409	95	-7	4	7	-3	.937	13	3-266/1-24,DOC	0.2

■ BERT BLUE
Blue, Bird Wayne   b: 12/9/1877, Bettsville, Ohio   d: 9/2/29, Detroit, Mich.   BR/TR, 6'3", 200 lbs.   Deb: 6/15/08

YEAR	TM/L	G	AB	R	H	2B	3B	HR	RBI	BB	SO	AVG	OBP	SLG	PRO+	BR/A	SB	CS	SBR	FA	FR	G/POS	TPR
1908	StL-A	11	24	2	9	1	2	0	1	1	3	.375	.444	.583	232	3	0			.942	1	/C-8	0.5
	Phi-A	6	18	2	3	0	0	0	1	0		.167	.167	.167	8	-2	0			1.000	1	/C-6	0.0
	Yr	17	42	4	12	1	2	0	2	1	3	.286	.333	.405	136	2	0			.967	2	C-14	0.5

■ LU BLUE
Blue, Luzerne Atwell   b: 3/5/1897, Washington, D.C.   d: 7/28/58, Alexandria, Va.   BB/TL, 5'10", 165 lbs.   Deb: 4/14/21

YEAR	TM/L	G	AB	R	H	2B	3B	HR	RBI	BB	SO	AVG	OBP	SLG	PRO+	BR/A	SB	CS	SBR	FA	FR	G/POS	TPR
1921	Det-A	153	585	103	180	33	11	5	75	103	47	.308	.416	.427	117	19	13	17	-6	.990	-7	*1-152	0.2
1922	Det-A	145	584	131	175	31	9	6	45	82	48	.300	.392	.414	114	15	8	5	-1	.991	0	*1-144	0.8
1923	Det-A	129	504	100	143	27	7	1	46	96	40	.284	.402	.371	106	10	10	11	-4	.992	5	*1-129	0.3
1924	Det-A	108	395	81	123	26	7	2	53	64	26	.311	.413	.428	119	14	9	4	0	.986	3	*1-108	1.0
1925	Det-A	150	532	91	163	18	9	3	94	83	29	.306	.403	.391	104	7	19	5	3	.988	0	*1-148	0.1
1926	Det-A	128	429	92	123	24	14	1	52	90	18	.287	.413	.415	115	13	13	7	-0	.985	-5	*1-109/O-1	0.1
1927	Det-A	112	365	71	95	17	9	1	42	71	28	.260	.384	.364	94	-1	13	7	-0	.984	-2	*1-104	-0.9
1928	StL-A	154	549	116	154	32	11	14	80	105	43	.281	.400	.455	120	19	12	7	-0	.989	2	*1-154	0.7
1929	StL-A	151	573	111	168	40	10	6	61	126	32	.293	.422	.429	115	19	12	6	-0	.994	-3	*1-151	0.1
1930	StL-A	117	425	85	100	27	5	4	42	81	44	.235	.363	.351	79	-12	12	7	-1	.987	-3	*1-111	-2.1
1931	Chi-A	155	589	119	179	23	15	1	62	127	60	.304	.430	.399	126	31	13	3	2	.990	-3	*1-155	1.5
1932	Chi-A	112	373	51	93	21	2	0	43	64	21	.249	.364	.316	83	-7	17	6	2	.986	9	*1-105	-0.4
1933	Bro-N	1	1	0	0	0	0	0	0	0	0	.000	.000	.000	-99	-0	0			1.000	-0	/1-1	0.0
Total	13	1615	5904	1151	1696	319	109	44	695	1092	436	.287	.402	.401	109	126	151	85		.989	1	*1-1571/O-1	1.4

■ OSSIE BLUEGE
Bluege, Oswald Louis   b: 10/24/1900, Chicago, Ill.   d: 10/14/85, Edina, Minn.   BR/TR, 5'11", 162 lbs.   Deb: 4/24/22   FMC

YEAR	TM/L	G	AB	R	H	2B	3B	HR	RBI	BB	SO	AVG	OBP	SLG	PRO+	BR/A	SB	CS	SBR	FA	FR	G/POS	TPR
1922	Was-A	19	61	5	12	1	0	0	2	7	7	.197	.300	.213	37	-5	1	0		.925	-3	3-17/S-2	-0.7
1923	Was-A	109	379	48	93	15	7	2	42	48	53	.245	.343	.338	84	-8	5	3	-0	.936	4	*3-106/2-4	-1.1
1924	*Was-A	117	402	59	113	15	4	2	49	39	36	.281	.358	.353	86	-7	7	5	-1	.943	-12	*3-102,2-10/S	-1.1
1925	*Was-A	145	522	77	150	27	4	4	79	59	56	.287	.362	.377	89	-8	16	15	-4	.953	1	*3-144/S-4	-0.1
1926	Was-A	139	487	69	132	19	8	3	65	70	46	.271	.368	.361	93	-3	12	9	-2	.952	-19	*3-134/S-8	-1.5
1927	Was-A	146	503	71	138	21	10	1	66	57	47	.274	.354	.362	87	-9	15	5	2	.961	15	*3-146	1.4
1928	Was-A	146	518	78	154	33	4	2	75	46	27	.297	.364	.400	101	1	18	6	2	.960	12	*3-144/2-1	2.2
1929	Was-A	64	220	35	65	6	0	5	31	19	15	.295	.354	.391	91	-3	6	4	-1	.967	-3	3-35,2-14,S	0.2
1930	Was-A	134	476	64	138	27	7	3	69	51	40	.290	.368	.395	93	-4	15	8	-0	.964	-1	*3-134	0.3
1931	Was-A	152	570	82	155	25	7	3	98	56	39	.272	.336	.382	88	-10	16	10	-1	**.960**	-5	*3-152/S-1	-0.7
1932	Was-A	149	507	64	131	22	4	5	64	83	41	.258	.367	.347	87	-7	9	7	-2	.970	6	*3-149	0.8
1933	*Was-A	140	501	63	131	14	0	6	71	55	34	.261	.338	.325	77	-15	6	7	-2	.965	-8	*3-138	-1.6
1934	Was-A	99	285	39	70	9	4	0	11	23	15	.246	.306	.291	57	-18	2	1	0	.950	8	3-41,S-30/2O	-0.6
1935	Was-A★	100	320	44	84	13	4	2	34	37	21	.262	.341	.325	75	-11	2	2	-1	.967	1	S-58,3-25/2	-0.6
1936	Was-A	90	319	43	92	12	1	1	55	38	16	.288	.357	.342	83	-7	5	3	-0	.993	0	2-52,S-23,3	-0.1
1937	Was-A	42	127	12	36	4	2	1	13	13	9	.283	.355	.370	87	-2	1	1	-0	.952	3	S-28/1-2,3	0.1
1938	Was-A	58	184	25	48	12	1	0	21	21	11	.261	.340	.337	75	-7	3	1	0	.990	1	2-38,S-10/13	-0.3
1939	Was-A	18	59	5	9	0	0	0	3	7	2	.153	.242	.153	3	-9	1	0	0	.989	1	1-11/2-2,S3	-0.8
Total	18	1867	6440	883	1751	276	67	43	848	723	515	.272	.352	.356	85	-131	140	87	-10	.957	4	*3-1487,S-180,2/10	-2.7

■ OTTO BLUEGE
Bluege, Otto Adam "Squeaky"   b: 7/20/09, Chicago, Ill.   d: 6/28/77, Chicago, Ill.   BR/TR, 5'10", 154 lbs.   Deb: 4/12/32   F

YEAR	TM/L	G	AB	R	H	2B	3B	HR	RBI	BB	SO	AVG	OBP	SLG	PRO+	BR/A	SB	CS	SBR	FA	FR	G/POS	TPR
1932	Cin-N	1	0	1	0	0	0	0	0	0	0	—	—	—		0	0			.000	0	R	0.0
1933	Cin-N	108	291	17	62	6	2	0	18	26	29	.213	.278	.247	52	-18	0			.937	-9	S-95,2-10/3	-2.2
Total	2	109	291	18	62	6	2	0	18	26	29	.213	.278	.247	52	-18	0			.937	-9	/S-95,2-10,3	-2.2

■ RED BLUHM
Bluhm, Harvey Fred   b: 6/27/1894, Cleveland, Ohio   d: 5/7/52, Flint, Mich.   BR/TR, 5'11", 165 lbs.   Deb: 7/3/18

YEAR	TM/L	G	AB	R	H	2B	3B	HR	RBI	BB	SO	AVG	OBP	SLG	PRO+	BR/A	SB	CS	SBR	FA	FR	G/POS	TPR
1918	Bos-A	1	1	0	0	0	0	0	0	0	0	.000	.000	.000	-99	-0	0			.000	0	H	0.0

■ CHET BOAK
Boak, Chester Robert   b: 6/19/35, New Castle, Pa.   d: 11/28/83, Emporium, Pa.   BR/TR, 6', 180 lbs.   Deb: 9/18/60

YEAR	TM/L	G	AB	R	H	2B	3B	HR	RBI	BB	SO	AVG	OBP	SLG	PRO+	BR/A	SB	CS	SBR	FA	FR	G/POS	TPR
1960	KC-A	5	13	1	2	0	0	0	1	0	2	.154	.214	.154	1	-2	0	0		.957	1	/2-5	-0.1
1961	Was-A	5	7	0	0	0	0	0	0	1	1	.000	.125	.000	-64	-2	1	0		1.000	-1	/2-1	-0.2
Total	2	10	20	1	2	0	0	0	1	1	3	.100	.182	.100	-22	-3	1	0		.962	0	/2-6	-0.3

■ FREDERICK BOARDMAN
Boardman, Frederick   Deb: 8/29/1874

YEAR	TM/L	G	AB	R	H	2B	3B	HR	RBI	BB	SO	AVG	OBP	SLG	PRO+	BR/A	SB	CS	SBR	FA	FR	G/POS	TPR
1874	Bal-n	1	3	0	1	0	0	0		0	0	.333	.333	.333	114	0						/O-1	0.0

■ RANDY BOBB
Bobb, Mark Randall   b: 1/1/48, Los Angeles, Cal.   d: 6/13/82, Carnelian Bay, Cal   BR/TR, 6'1", 185 lbs.   Deb: 8/15/68

YEAR	TM/L	G	AB	R	H	2B	3B	HR	RBI	BB	SO	AVG	OBP	SLG	PRO+	BR/A	SB	CS	SBR	FA	FR	G/POS	TPR
1968	Chi-N	7	8	0	1	0	0	0	0	1	2	.125	.222	.125	6	-1	0	0	0	1.000	0	/C-7	-0.1
1969	Chi-N	3	2	0	0	0	0	0	0	0	1	.000	.000	.000	-89	-0	0	0	0	1.000	1	/C-2	0.0
Total	2	10	10	0	1	0	0	0	0	1	3	.100	.182	.100	-14	-1	0	0	0	1.000	1	/C-9	-0.1

■ JOHN BOCCABELLA
Boccabella, John Dominic   b: 6/29/41, San Francisco, Cal   BR/TR, 6'1", 200 lbs.   Deb: 9/2/63

YEAR	TM/L	G	AB	R	H	2B	3B	HR	RBI	BB	SO	AVG	OBP	SLG	PRO+	BR/A	SB	CS	SBR	FA	FR	G/POS	TPR
1963	Chi-N	24	74	7	14	4	1	1	5	6	21	.189	.250	.311	57	-4	0	1	-1	.996	-1	1-24	-0.7
1964	Chi-N	9	23	4	9	2	1	0	6	0	3	.391	.391	.565	159	2	0	0	0	1.000	-1	/1-5,O-2	0.1
1965	Chi-N	6	12	5	4	0	0	2	4	1	2	.333	.385	.833	227	2	0	0	0	1.000	-0	/1-2,O-1	0.2
1966	Chi-N	75	206	22	47	9	0	6	25	14	39	.228	.277	.359	74	-7	0	1	-1	.981	0	O-33,1-30/C	-1.0
1967	Chi-N	25	35	0	6	1	0	0	8	3	7	.171	.256	.257	45	-2	0	0	0	1.000	-1	/O-9,1-3,C	-0.4
1968	Chi-N	7	14	0	1	0	0	0	1	2	2	.071	.188	.071	-19	-2	0	0	0	1.000	-1	/C-4,O-1	-0.3
1969	Mon-N	40	86	4	9	2	0	1	6	6	30	.105	.172	.163	-6	-12	1	0	0	1.000	0	C-32	-1.1
1970	Mon-N	61	145	18	39	3	1	5	17	11	24	.269	.321	.407	94	-2	0	1	-1	.993	10	1-33,C-24/3	0.6
1971	Mon-N	74	177	15	39	11	0	3	15	14	26	.220	.281	.333	73	-6	0	1	-1	.979	-1	C-37,1-37/3	-1.0
1972	Mon-N	83	207	14	47	8	1	1	10	9	29	.227	.263	.290	56	-12	1	2	-1	.983	8	C-73/1-7,3	-0.4
1973	Mon-N	118	403	25	94	13	0	7	46	26	57	.233	.281	.318	63	-20	1	1	-0	.980	1	*C-117/1-1	-1.5
1974	SF-N	29	80	6	11	3	0	0	5	4	6	.138	.179	.175	-1	-11	0	0	0	.991	-2	C-26	-0.5
Total	12	551	1462	117	320	56	5	26	148	96	246	.219	.269	.317	62	-76	3	7	-4	.984	14	C-319,1-142/O3	-6.8

■ MILT BOCEK
Bocek, Milton Frank   b: 7/16/12, Chicago, Ill.   BR/TR, 6'1", 185 lbs.   Deb: 9/3/33

YEAR	TM/L	G	AB	R	H	2B	3B	HR	RBI	BB	SO	AVG	OBP	SLG	PRO+	BR/A	SB	CS	SBR	FA	FR	G/POS	TPR
1933	Chi-A	11	22	3	8	1	0	1	3	4	6	.364	.462	.545	173	2	0	0	0	1.000	-2	/O-6	0.0
1934	Chi-A	19	38	3	8	1	0	0	3	5	5	.211	.302	.237	39	-3	0	0	0	1.000	2	O-10	-0.1
Total	2	30	60	6	16	2	0	1	6	9	11	.267	.362	.350	86	-2	0	0	0	1.000	0	/O-16	-0.1

■ BRUCE BOCHTE
Bochte, Bruce Anton   b: 11/12/50, Pasadena, Cal.   BL/TL, 6'3", 200 lbs.   Deb: 7/19/74

YEAR	TM/L	G	AB	R	H	2B	3B	HR	RBI	BB	SO	AVG	OBP	SLG	PRO+	BR/A	SB	CS	SBR	FA	FR	G/POS	TPR
1974	Cal-A	57	196	24	53	4	5	2	26	18	23	.270	.335	.378	111	3	6	3	0	.985	-4	O-39,1-24	-0.4
1975	Cal-A	107	375	41	107	19	3	3	48	45	43	.285	.365	.376	118	10	3	4	-2	.987	-7	*1-105/D-1	-0.5
1976	Cal-A	146	466	53	120	17	1	2	49	64	53	.258	.350	.311	101	3	4	5	-2	.988	5	O-86,1-59/D	-0.9
1977	Cal-A	25	100	12	29	4	0	2	8	7	4	.290	.336	.390	110	2	0	0	0	1.000	2	O-24/D-1	0.1
	Cle-A	112	392	52	119	19	1	5	43	40	38	.304	.368	.395	112	7	3	1	-0	.966	5	O-76,1-36/D	0.8
	Yr	137	492	64	148	23	1	7	51	47	42	.301	.362	.394	110	7	3	1	-1	.974	7	*O-100,1-36/D	0.8
1978	Sea-A	140	486	58	128	25	3	11	51	60	47	.263	.346	.395	108	6	3	4	-2	.984	-4	O-91,D-43/1	-0.5
1979	Sea-A★	150	554	81	175	38	6	16	100	67	64	.316	.392	.493	134	28	2	2	-1	.991	5	*1-147	2.2

YEAR	TM/L	G	AB	R	H	2B	3B	HR	RBI	BB	SO	AVG	OBP	SLG	PRO+	BR/A	SB	CS	SBR	FA	FR	G/POS	TPR
1980	Sea-A	148	520	62	156	34	4	13	78	72	81	.300	.385	.456	128	22	2	3	-1	.996	6	*1-133,D-11	1.8
1981	Sea-A	99	335	39	87	16	4	6	30	47	53	.260	.354	.361	102	2	1	3	-2	.995	-5	1-82,O-14/D	-0.9
1982	Sea-A	144	509	58	151	21	0	12	70	67	71	.297	.382	.409	114	12	8	5	-1	.988	-5	O-99,1-34/D	0.1
1984	Oak-A	148	469	58	124	23	0	5	52	52	59	.264	.338	.345	96	-2	2	5	-2	.993	-13	*1-144/D-2	-2.6
1985	Oak-A	137	424	48	125	17	1	14	60	49	58	.295	.368	.439	129	17	3	1	0	.990	-9	*1-128	0.2
1986	Oak-A	125	407	57	104	13	1	6	43	65	68	.256	.358	.337	98	1	3	2	-0	.991	2	*1-115/D-1	-0.6
Total	12	1538	5233	643	1478	250	21	100	658	653	662	.282	.363	.396	114	109	43	41	-12	.992	-30	*1-1008,O-429/D	-1.3

■ BRUCE BOCHY
Bochy, Bruce Douglas b: 4/16/55, Landes De Bussac, France   BR/TR, 6'4", 210 lbs.   Deb: 7/19/78   C

YEAR	TM/L	G	AB	R	H	2B	3B	HR	RBI	BB	SO	AVG	OBP	SLG	PRO+	BR/A	SB	CS	SBR	FA	FR	G/POS	TPR
1978	Hou-N	54	154	8	41	8	0	3	15	11	35	.266	.315	.377	100	-1	0	0	0	.974	3	C-53	0.3
1979	Hou-N	56	129	11	28	4	0	1	6	13	25	.217	.294	.271	59	-7	0	0	0	.970	-1	C-55	-0.7
1980	*Hou-N	22	22	0	4	1	0	0	0	5	7	.182	.357	.227	72	-1	0	0	0	1.000	-2	C-10/1-1	-0.3
1982	NY-N	17	49	4	15	4	0	2	8	4	6	.306	.358	.510	141	3	0	0	0	.961	4	C-16/1-1	0.7
1983	SD-N	23	42	2	9	1	1	0	3	0	9	.214	.214	.286	39	-4	0	0	0	1.000	2	C-11	-0.2
1984	*SD-N	37	92	10	21	5	1	4	15	3	21	.228	.253	.435	90	-2	0	1	-1	.988	5	C-36	0.4
1985	SD-N	48	112	16	30	2	0	6	13	6	30	.268	.305	.446	109	1	0	0	0	.988	1	C-46	0.3
1986	SD-N	63	127	16	32	9	0	8	22	14	23	.252	.326	.512	130	5	1	0	0	.991	3	C-48	1.0
1987	SD-N	38	75	8	12	3	0	2	11	11	21	.160	.267	.280	47	-6	0	1	-1	.962	-4	C-23	-0.9
Total	9	358	802	75	192	37	2	26	93	67	177	.239	.300	.388	92	-12	1	2	-1	.979	9	C-298/1-2	0.6

■ EDDIE BOCKMAN
Bockman, Joseph Edward b: 7/26/20, Santa Ana, Cal.   BR/TR, 5'9", 175 lbs.   Deb: 9/11/46

YEAR	TM/L	G	AB	R	H	2B	3B	HR	RBI	BB	SO	AVG	OBP	SLG	PRO+	BR/A	SB	CS	SBR	FA	FR	G/POS	TPR
1946	NY-A	4	12	2	1	1	0	0	0	1	4	.083	.154	.167	-10	-2	0	0	0	.933	1	/3-4	0.0
1947	Cle-A	46	66	8	17	2	2	1	14	5	17	.258	.310	.394	97	-1	0	0	0	.946	9	3-12/2-4,SO	0.8
1948	Pit-N	70	176	23	42	7	1	4	23	17	35	.239	.309	.358	79	-5	2			.962	8	3-51/2-1	0.2
1949	Pit-N	79	220	21	49	6	1	6	19	23	31	.223	.296	.341	69	-10	3			.959	6	3-68/2-5	-0.5
Total	4	199	474	54	109	16	4	11	56	46	87	.230	.299	.350	74	-18	5	0		.958	24	3-135/2-10,OS	0.5

■ PING BODIE
Bodie, Frank Stephan (b: Francesco Stephano Pezzolo) b: 10/8/1887, San Francisco, Cal. d: 12/17/61, San Francisco, Cal   BR/TR, 5'8", 195 lbs.   Deb: 4/22/11

YEAR	TM/L	G	AB	R	H	2B	3B	HR	RBI	BB	SO	AVG	OBP	SLG	PRO+	BR/A	SB	CS	SBR	FA	FR	G/POS	TPR
1911	Chi-A	145	551	75	159	27	13	4	97	49		.289	.348	.407	114	9	14			.969	7	*O-128,2-16	0.9
1912	Chi-A	138	472	58	139	24	7	5	72	43		.294	.358	.407	123	13	12			.969	-12	*O-130	-0.6
1913	Chi-A	127	406	39	107	14	8	8	48	35	57	.264	.325	.397	112	4	5			.968	-5	*O-119	-0.6
1914	Chi-A	107	327	21	75	9	5	3	29	21	35	.229	.278	.315	79	-9	12	11	-3	.959	-2	O-95	-2.1
1917	Phi-A	148	557	51	162	28	11	7	74	53	40	.291	.356	.418	138	24	13			.963	5	*O-145/1-1	2.2
1918	NY-A	91	324	36	83	12	6	3	46	27	24	.256	.319	.358	102	-0	6			.971	4	O-90	-0.1
1919	NY-A	134	475	45	132	27	6	6	59	36	46	.278	.334	.406	107	3	15			.959	-8	*O-134	-1.5
1920	NY-A	129	471	63	139	26	12	7	79	40	30	.295	.350	.446	106	3	6	14	-7	.968	-10	*O-129	-2.2
1921	NY-A	31	87	5	15	2	2	0	12	8	8	.172	.242	.241	23	-10	0	1	-1	.944	-6	O-25	-1.8
Total	9	1050	3670	393	1011	169	72	43	516	312	240	.275	.335	.396	110	36	83	26		.965	-27	O-995/2-16,1	-5.8

■ TONY BOECKEL
Boeckel, Norman Doxie b: 8/25/1892, Los Angeles, Cal. d: 2/16/24, Torrey Pines, Cal.   BR/TR, 5'10.5", 175 lbs.   Deb: 7/23/17

YEAR	TM/L	G	AB	R	H	2B	3B	HR	RBI	BB	SO	AVG	OBP	SLG	PRO+	BR/A	SB	CS	SBR	FA	FR	G/POS	TPR
1917	Pit-N	64	219	16	58	11	1	0	23	8	31	.265	.297	.324	87	-4	6			.935	-4	3-62	-0.7
1919	Pit-N	45	152	18	38	9	2	0	16	18	20	.250	.333	.336	97	0	11			.930	-8	3-45	-0.7
	Bos-N	95	365	42	91	11	5	1	26	35	13	.249	.317	.315	94	-2	10			.960	-4	3-93	-0.2
	Yr	140	517	60	129	20	7	1	42	53	33	.250	.322	.321	95	-2	21			.951	-12	*3-138	-0.9
1920	Bos-N	153	582	70	156	28	5	3	62	38	50	.268	.314	.349	94	-5	18	15	-4	.936	-7	*3-149/S-3,2	-0.8
1921	Bos-N	153	592	93	185	20	13	10	84	52	41	.313	.370	.441	120	17	20	15	-3	.933	-12	*3-153	1.2
1922	Bos-N	119	402	61	116	19	6	6	47	35	32	.289	.349	.410	99	-1	14	8	-1	.952	-11	*3-106	-0.4
1923	Bos-N	148	568	72	169	32	4	7	79	51	31	.298	.357	.405	105	4	11	8	-2	.939	-10	*3-147/S-1	0.6
Total	6	777	2880	372	813	130	36	27	337	237	218	.282	.339	.381	102	10	90	46		.941	-55	3-755/S-4,2	-1.0

■ LEN BOEHMER
Boehmer, Leonard Joseph Stephen b: 6/28/41, Flinthill, Mo.   BR/TR, 6'1", 192 lbs.   Deb: 6/18/67

YEAR	TM/L	G	AB	R	H	2B	3B	HR	RBI	BB	SO	AVG	OBP	SLG	PRO+	BR/A	SB	CS	SBR	FA	FR	G/POS	TPR
1967	Cin-N	2	3	0	0	0	0	0	0	0	0	.000	.000	.000	-90	-1	0	0	0	1.000	-0	/2-1	-0.1
1969	NY-A	45	108	5	19	4	0	0	7	8	10	.176	.233	.213	26	-11	0	1	-1	.995	1	1-21/3-8,2S	-1.2
1971	NY-A	3	5	0	0	0	0	0	0	0	0	.000	.000	.000	-99	-1	0	0	0	1.000	-0	/3-1	-0.2
Total	3	50	116	5	19	4	0	0	7	8	10	.164	.218	.198	18	-13	0	1	-1	.933	2	/1-21,3-9,2S	-1.5

■ TIM BOGAR
Bogar, Timothy Paul b: 10/28/66, Indianapolis, Ind.   BR/TR, 6'2", 198 lbs.   Deb: 4/21/93

YEAR	TM/L	G	AB	R	H	2B	3B	HR	RBI	BB	SO	AVG	OBP	SLG	PRO+	BR/A	SB	CS	SBR	FA	FR	G/POS	TPR
1993	NY-N	78	205	19	50	13	0	3	25	14	29	.244	.302	.351	75	-7	0	1	-1	.972	15	S-66/3-7,2	1.1
1994	NY-N	50	52	5	8	0	0	2	5	4	11	.154	.214	.269	25	-6	1	0	0	.909	8	3-22,1-14/S20	0.2
Total	2	128	257	24	58	13	0	5	30	18	40	.226	.284	.335	65	-13	1	1	-0	.976	23	/S-73,3-29,120	1.3

■ TERRY BOGENER
Bogener, Terry Wayne b: 9/28/55, Hannibal, Mo.   BL/TL, 6', 193 lbs.   Deb: 6/14/82

YEAR	TM/L	G	AB	R	H	2B	3B	HR	RBI	BB	SO	AVG	OBP	SLG	PRO+	BR/A	SB	CS	SBR	FA	FR	G/POS	TPR
1982	Tex-A	24	60	6	13	2	1	1	4	8	4	.217	.288	.333	74	-2	2	0	1	1.000	-4	O-16/D-4	-0.5

■ WADE BOGGS
Boggs, Wade Anthony b: 6/15/58, Omaha, Neb.   BL/TR, 6'2", 197 lbs.   Deb: 4/10/82

YEAR	TM/L	G	AB	R	H	2B	3B	HR	RBI	BB	SO	AVG	OBP	SLG	PRO+	BR/A	SB	CS	SBR	FA	FR	G/POS	TPR
1982	Bos-A	104	338	51	118	14	1	5	44	35	21	.349	.410	.441	126	13	1	0	0	.994	18	1-49,3-44/OD	2.8
1983	Bos-A	153	582	100	210	44	7	5	74	92	36	**.361**	**.449**	.486	147	41	3	3	-1	.947	8	*3-153	4.5
1984	Bos-A	158	625	109	203	31	4	6	55	89	44	.325	.409	.416	123	23	3	2	-0	.959	21	*3-156/D-2	4.2
1985	Bos-A★	161	653	107	**240**	42	3	8	78	96	61	**.368**	**.452**	.478	149	49	2	1	0	.965	8	*3-161	5.3
1986	*Bos-A★	149	580	107	207	47	2	8	71	**105**	44	**.357**	**.455**	.486	156	51	0	4	-2	.953	-1	*3-149	4.3
1987	Bos-A	147	551	108	200	40	6	24	89	105	48	**.363**	**.461**	.588	173	63	1	3	-2	.965	3	*3-145/1-1,D	**5.8**
1988	*Bos-A★	155	584	**128**	214	**45**	6	5	58	**125**	34	.366	**.480**	.490	165	60	2	3	-1	.971	-5	*3-151/D-3	5.3
1989	Bos-A★	156	621	**113**	205	**51**	7	3	54	107	51	.330	**.434**	.449	141	39	2	6	-3	.958	-4	*3-152/D-3	3.3
1990	*Bos-A★	155	619	89	187	44	5	6	63	87	68	.302	.389	.418	120	19	0	3	-3	.946	-22	*3-152/D-3	-0.2
1991	Bos-A★	144	546	93	181	42	2	8	51	89	32	.332	.425	.460	138	32	1	2	-1	.952	-1	*3-140	3.2
1992	Bos-A★	143	514	62	133	22	4	7	50	74	31	.259	.356	.358	94	-2	1	3	-2	.952	-1	*3-117,D-21	-0.5
1993	NY-A★	143	560	83	169	26	1	2	59	74	49	.302	.383	.363	105	7	0	1	-1	**.970**	20	*3-134/D-8	2.6
1994	NY-A★	97	366	61	125	19	1	11	55	61	29	.342	.437	.489	148	29	2	1	0	.962	13	3-93/1-4	3.8
Total	13	1865	7139	1211	2392	467	49	98	801	1139	548	.335	.428	.455	138	425	18	29	-12	.960	58	*3-1747/1-54,DO	44.4

■ CHARLIE BOHN
Bohn, Charles b: 1857, Cleveland, Ohio d: 8/1/03, Cleveland, Ohio   BR/TR, 5'9", 165 lbs.   Deb: 6/20/1882

YEAR	TM/L	G	AB	R	H	2B	3B	HR	RBI	BB	SO	AVG	OBP	SLG	PRO+	BR/A	SB	CS	SBR	FA	FR	G/POS	TPR
1882	Lou-a	4	13	0	2	0	0	0				.154	.154	.154	4	-1				.667	1	/O-2,P-2	0.0

■ SAM BOHNE
Bohne, Samuel Arthur (b: Samuel Arthur Cohen) b: 10/22/1896, San Francisco, Cal d: 5/23/77, Palo Alto, Cal.   BR/TR, 5'8.5", 175 lbs.   Deb: 9/9/16

YEAR	TM/L	G	AB	R	H	2B	3B	HR	RBI	BB	SO	AVG	OBP	SLG	PRO+	BR/A	SB	CS	SBR	FA	FR	G/POS	TPR
1916	StL-N	14	38	3	9	0	0	0		4	6	.237	.310	.237	69	-1	3			.870	-4	S-14	-0.5
1921	Cin-N	153	613	98	175	28	16	3	44	54	38	.285	.347	.398	101	1	26	22	-5	.973	8	*2-102,3-53	1.0
1922	Cin-N	112	383	53	105	14	5	3	51	39	18	.274	.344	.360	83	-9	13	8	-1	.958	11	2-85,S-20	0.5
1923	Cin-N	139	539	77	136	18	10	3	48	37	37	.252	.316	.340	74	-20	16	19	-7	.975	5	2-96,3-35/S1	-1.6
1924	Cin-N	100	349	42	89	15	9	4	46	18	24	.255	.293	.384	81	-10	9	6	-1	.941	-9	2-48,S-40,3	-1.5
1925	Cin-N	73	214	24	55	9	1	2	24	14	14	.257	.303	.336	65	-12	6	4	-1	.933	-8	S-49,2-10/013	-1.4
1926	Cin-N	25	54	8	11	0	0	2	11	6	11	.204	.259	.278	46	-4	1			.931	-3	S-20	-0.5
	Bro-N	47	125	4	25	3	1	1	11	12	9	.200	.270	.280	49	-9	1			.965	11	2-31,3-15	0.3
	Yr	72	179	12	36	3	1	3	16	16	17	.201	.267	.279	48	-13	2			.965	8	2-31,S-20,3	-0.2
Total	7	663	2315	309	605	87	45	16	228	193	154	.261	.321	.359	81	-64	75	59		.966	11	2-372,S-152,3/01	-3.7

YEAR	TM/L	G	AB	R	H	2B	3B	HR	RBI	BB	SO	AVG	OBP	SLG	PRO+	BR/A	SB	CS	SBR	FA	FR	G/POS	TPR

■ BRUCE BOISCLAIR
Boisclair, Bruce Armand   b: 12/9/52, Putnam, Conn.   BL/TL, 6'2", 190 lbs.   Deb: 9/11/74

YEAR	TM/L	G	AB	R	H	2B	3B	HR	RBI	BB	SO	AVG	OBP	SLG	PRO+	BR/A	SB	CS	SBR	FA	FR	G/POS	TPR
1974	NY-N	7	12	0	3	1	0	0	1	1	4	.250	.308	.333	81	-0	0	0	0	.923	1	/O-5	0.1
1976	NY-N	110	286	42	82	13	3	2	13	28	55	.287	.350	.374	112	4	9	5	-0	.981	-6	O-87	-0.5
1977	NY-N	127	307	41	90	21	1	4	44	31	57	.293	.360	.407	110	5	6	4	-1	.959	-9	O-91/1-9	-0.8
1978	NY-N	107	214	24	48	7	1	4	15	23	43	.224	.300	.322	77	-7	3	3	-1	.983	-5	O-69/1-1	-1.6
1979	NY-N	59	98	7	18	5	1	0	4	3	24	.184	.216	.255	29	-10	0	2	-1	1.000	-2	O-24/1-1	-1.5
Total	5	410	917	114	241	47	6	10	77	86	183	.263	.327	.360	94	-8	18	14	-3	.975	-21	O-276/1-11	-4.3

■ BOB BOKEN
Boken, Robert Anthony   b: 2/23/08, Maryville, Ill.   d: 10/6/88, Las Vegas, Nev.   BR/TR, 6'2", 165 lbs.   Deb: 4/25/33

YEAR	TM/L	G	AB	R	H	2B	3B	HR	RBI	BB	SO	AVG	OBP	SLG	PRO+	BR/A	SB	CS	SBR	FA	FR	G/POS	TPR
1933	Was-A	55	133	19	37	5	2	3	26	9	16	.278	.324	.414	95	-1	0	0		.969	-2	2-31,3-19,S	-0.1
1934	Was-A	11	27	5	6	1	1	0	6	3	1	.222	.300	.333	66	-1	2	0	1	.864	1	/3-6,2-1	0.1
	Chi-A	81	297	30	70	9	1	3	40	15	32	.236	.275	.303	47	-24	2	1	0	.929	-10	2-57,S-22	-2.7
	Yr	92	324	35	76	10	2	3	46	18	33	.235	.277	.306	49	-25	4	1	1	.929	-9	2-58,S-22/3	-2.6
Total	2	147	457	54	113	15	4	6	72	27	49	.247	.291	.337	62	-26	4	1	1	.941	-11	/2-89,S-32,3	-2.7

■ BOLAND
Boland   Deb: 9/4/1875

YEAR	TM/L	G	AB	R	H	2B	3B	HR	RBI	BB	SO	AVG	OBP	SLG	PRO+	BR/A	SB	CS	SBR	FA	FR	G/POS	TPR
1875	Atl-n	1	4	0	0	0	0	0		0		.000	.000	.000	-99	-1						/O-1	-0.1

■ ED BOLAND
Boland, Edward John   b: 4/18/08, Long Island City, N.Y.   d: 2/5/93, Clearwater, Fla.   BL/TL, 5'10", 165 lbs.   Deb: 9/18/34

YEAR	TM/L	G	AB	R	H	2B	3B	HR	RBI	BB	SO	AVG	OBP	SLG	PRO+	BR/A	SB	CS	SBR	FA	FR	G/POS	TPR
1934	Phi-N	8	30	2	9	1	1	0	5	0	2	.300	.300	.400	76	-1	1			.778	-2	/O-7	-0.3
1935	Phi-N	30	47	5	10	0	0	0	4	4	6	.213	.277	.213	30	-5	1			.833	-3	O-10	-0.7
1944	Was-A	19	59	4	16	4	0	0	14	0	6	.271	.271	.339	77	-2	0	0	0	.889	-1	O-14	-0.4
Total	3	57	136	11	35	5	1	0	23	4	14	.257	.279	.309	59	-8	2	0		.852	-5	/O-31	-1.4

■ CHARLIE BOLD
Bold, Charles Dickens "Dutch"   b: 10/27/1894, Karlskrona, Sweden   d: 7/29/78, Chelsea, Mass.   BR/TR, 6'2", 185 lbs.   Deb: 8/24/14

YEAR	TM/L	G	AB	R	H	2B	3B	HR	RBI	BB	SO	AVG	OBP	SLG	PRO+	BR/A	SB	CS	SBR	FA	FR	G/POS	TPR
1914	StL-A	2	1	0	0	0	0	0		0	1	.000	.000	.000	-99	-0	0			.500	-0	/1-1	-0.1

■ CARL BOLES
Boles, Carl Theodore   b: 10/31/34, Center Point, Ark.   BR/TR, 5'11", 185 lbs.   Deb: 8/2/62

YEAR	TM/L	G	AB	R	H	2B	3B	HR	RBI	BB	SO	AVG	OBP	SLG	PRO+	BR/A	SB	CS	SBR	FA	FR	G/POS	TPR
1962	SF-N	19	24	4	9	0	0	0	1	0	6	.375	.375	.375	104	0	0	0	0	.833	-1	/O-7	-0.2

■ JOE BOLEY
Boley, John Peter (b: John Peter Bolinsky)   b: 7/19/1896, Mahanoy City, Pa.   d: 12/30/62, Mahanoy City, Pa.   BR/TR, 5'11", 170 lbs.   Deb: 4/12/27

YEAR	TM/L	G	AB	R	H	2B	3B	HR	RBI	BB	SO	AVG	OBP	SLG	PRO+	BR/A	SB	CS	SBR	FA	FR	G/POS	TPR
1927	Phi-A	118	370	49	115	18	8	1	52	26	14	.311	.361	.411	95	-3	8	5	-1	.951	-11	*S-114	-0.3
1928	Phi-A	132	425	49	112	20	3	0	49	32	11	.264	.317	.325	67	-20	5	1	0	.949	-17	*S-132	-2.1
1929	*Phi-A	91	303	36	76	17	6	2	47	24	16	.251	.310	.366	71	-14	1	0	0	.963	-10	S-88/3-1	-1.2
1930	*Phi-A	121	420	41	116	22	2	4	55	32	26	.276	.335	.367	74	-16	1	0	0	.970	-7	*S-120	-0.9
1931	*Phi-A	67	224	26	51	9	3	0	20	15	13	.228	.282	.295	49	-17	1	1	-0	.954	-13	S-62/2-1	-2.3
1932	Phi-A	10	34	2	7	2	0	0	4	1	4	.206	.229	.265	26	-4	0	1	-0	.897	-7	S-10	-1.0
	Cle-A	1	4	0	1	0	0	0	0	0	0	.250	.250	.250	28	-0	0	0	0	.000	0	/S-1	0.0
	Yr	11	38	2	8	2	0	0	4	1	4	.211	.231	.263	27	-4	0	1	-0	.897	-7	S-11	-1.0
Total	6	540	1780	203	478	88	22	7	227	130	84	.269	.323	.354	72	-74	15	8	-0	.957	-64	S-527/2-1,3	-7.8

■ JIM BOLGER
Bolger, James Cyril "Dutch"   b: 2/23/32, Cincinnati, Ohio   BR/TR, 6'2", 180 lbs.   Deb: 6/24/50

YEAR	TM/L	G	AB	R	H	2B	3B	HR	RBI	BB	SO	AVG	OBP	SLG	PRO+	BR/A	SB	CS	SBR	FA	FR	G/POS	TPR
1950	Cin-N	2	1	0	0	0	0	0	0	0	0	.000	.000	.000	-99	-0	0			.000	-1	/O-2	-0.1
1951	Cin-N	2	0	1	0	0	0	0	0	0	0	—	—	—	—	0	1	0	0	1.000	0	R	0.0
1954	Cin-N	5	3	1	1	0	0	0	0	0	1	.333	.333	.333	72	-0	0	0	0	.000	-1	/O-2	-0.1
1955	Chi-N	64	160	19	33	5	4	0	7	9	17	.206	.257	.287	45	-13	2	2	-0	.955	-3	O-51	-1.8
1957	Chi-N	112	273	28	75	4	1	5	29	10	36	.275	.308	.352	78	-9	0	1	-1	.987	2	O-63/3-3	-1.1
1958	Chi-N	84	120	15	27	4	1	1	11	9	20	.225	.285	.300	56	-8	0	1	-1	.940	-6	O-37	-1.5
1959	Cle-A	8	7	0	0	0	0	0	0	1	1	.000	.125	.000	-65	-2	0	0	0	.000	0	H	-0.2
	Phi-N	35	48	1	4	1	0	0	1	3	8	.083	.137	.104	-34	-9	0	0	-0	.938	-1	/O-9	-1.0
Total	7	312	612	65	140	14	6	6	48	32	83	.229	.274	.301	54	-40	3	4		.966	-9	O-164/3-3	-5.8

■ FRANK BOLICK
Bolick, Frank Charles   b: 6/28/66, Ashland, Pa.   BB/TR, 5'10", 180 lbs.   Deb: 4/5/93

YEAR	TM/L	G	AB	R	H	2B	3B	HR	RBI	BB	SO	AVG	OBP	SLG	PRO+	BR/A	SB	CS	SBR	FA	FR	G/POS	TPR
1993	Mon-N	95	213	25	45	13	0	4	24	23	37	.211	.300	.329	65	-10	1	0	0	.992	3	1-51,3-24	-1.1

■ FRANK BOLLING
Bolling, Frank Elmore   b: 11/16/31, Mobile, Ala.   BR/TR, 6'1", 175 lbs.   Deb: 4/13/54   F

YEAR	TM/L	G	AB	R	H	2B	3B	HR	RBI	BB	SO	AVG	OBP	SLG	PRO+	BR/A	SB	CS	SBR	FA	FR	G/POS	TPR
1954	Det-A	117	368	46	87	15	2	6	38	36	51	.236	.304	.337	77	-12	3	5	-2	.974	-29	*2-113	-3.8
1956	Det-A	102	366	53	103	21	7	7	45	42	51	.281	.359	.434	108	4	6	2	1	.978	-15	*2-102	-0.2
1957	Det-A	146	576	72	149	27	6	15	40	57	64	.259	.328	.405	96	-3	4	9	-4	.980	-3	*2-146	1.2
1958	Det-A	154	610	91	164	25	4	14	75	54	54	.269	.332	.392	92	-7	6	4	-1	.985	8	*2-154	1.2
1959	Det-A	127	459	56	122	18	3	13	55	45	37	.266	.341	.403	98	-1	4	1	1	.987	-1	*2-126	0.7
1960	Det-A	139	536	64	136	20	4	9	59	40	44	.254	.308	.356	77	-18	7	4	-0	.978	-5	*2-138	-0.9
1961	Mil-N★	148	585	86	153	16	4	15	56	57	62	.262	.330	.379	93	-6	7	3	0	.988	1	*2-148	1.1
1962	Mil-N★	122	406	45	110	17	4	9	43	35	45	.271	.335	.399	99	-1	2	2	-1	.989	-9	*2-119	0.1
1963	Mil-N	142	542	73	132	18	2	5	43	41	48	.244	.300	.312	77	-15	2	1	0	.981	-5	*2-141	-0.8
1964	Mil-N	120	352	35	70	11	1	5	34	21	44	.199	.248	.278	48	-24	1	1	-1	.985	-9	*2-117	-2.7
1965	Mil-N	148	535	55	141	26	3	7	50	24	41	.264	.295	.363	84	-12	0	4	-2	.976	-16	*2-147	-1.9
1966	Atl-N	75	227	16	48	7	0	1	18	10	14	.211	.248	.256	40	-18	1	1	-0	.983	-15	2-67	-3.2
Total	12	1540	5562	692	1415	221	40	106	556	462	558	.254	.315	.366	85	-114	40	38	-11	.982	-98	*2-1518	-10.2

■ JACK BOLLING
Bolling, John Edward   b: 2/20/17, Mobile, Ala.   BL/TL, 5'11", 168 lbs.   Deb: 6/10/39

YEAR	TM/L	G	AB	R	H	2B	3B	HR	RBI	BB	SO	AVG	OBP	SLG	PRO+	BR/A	SB	CS	SBR	FA	FR	G/POS	TPR
1939	Phi-N	69	211	27	61	11	0	3	13	11	10	.289	.324	.384	92	-3	6			.982	2	1-48	-0.6
1944	Bro-N	56	131	21	46	14	1	1	25	14	4	.351	.418	.496	159	10	0			.991	1	1-27	1.0
Total	2	125	342	48	107	25	1	4	38	25	14	.313	.361	.427	118	8	6			.985	3	/1-75	0.4

■ MILT BOLLING
Bolling, Milton Joseph   b: 8/9/30, Mississippi City, Miss.   BR/TR, 6'1", 180 lbs.   Deb: 9/10/52   F

YEAR	TM/L	G	AB	R	H	2B	3B	HR	RBI	BB	SO	AVG	OBP	SLG	PRO+	BR/A	SB	CS	SBR	FA	FR	G/POS	TPR
1952	Bos-A	11	36	4	8	1	0	1	3	3	5	.222	.282	.333	66	-2	0	1	-1	.984	6	S-11	0.4
1953	Bos-A	109	323	30	85	12	1	5	28	23	41	.263	.318	.353	77	-11	1	4	-2	.956	5	*S-109	-0.1
1954	Bos-A	113	370	42	92	20	3	6	36	47	55	.249	.340	.368	84	-8	2	4	-2	.946	15	*S-107/3-5	1.5
1955	Bos-A	6	5	0	1	0	0	0	0	0	0	.200	.200	.200	7	-1	0	0	0	.800	1	/S-2	-0.1
1956	Bos-A	45	118	19	25	2	3	3	8	18	20	.212	.321	.347	68	-6	0	1	-1	.947	-8	S-26,3-11/2	-1.2
1957	Bos-A	1	1	0	0	0	0	0	0	0	0	.000	.000	.000	-95	-0	0	0	0	.000	0	H	0.0
	Was-A	91	277	29	63	12	4	1	19	18	59	.227	.279	.321	64	-14	2	2	-1	.982	8	2-53,S-37/3	-0.1
	Yr	92	278	29	63	12	4	1	19	18	59	.227	.279	.320	64	-14	2	2	-1	.982	8	2-53,S-37/3	-0.1
1958	Det-A	24	31	3	6	2	0	0	2	6	7	.194	.306	.258	53	-2	0	0	0	.946	2	S-13/2-1,3	0.1
Total	7	400	1161	127	280	50	11	19	94	114	188	.241	.314	.345	74	-43	5	12	-6	.952	28	S-305/2-55,3	0.5

■ DON BOLLWEG
Bollweg, Donald Raymond   b: 2/12/21, Wheaton, Ill.   BL/TL, 6'1", 190 lbs.   Deb: 9/28/50

YEAR	TM/L	G	AB	R	H	2B	3B	HR	RBI	BB	SO	AVG	OBP	SLG	PRO+	BR/A	SB	CS	SBR	FA	FR	G/POS	TPR
1950	StL-N	4	11	1	2	1	0	0	1	1	1	.182	.250	.182	15	-1	0			1.000	-1	/1-4	-0.2
1951	StL-N	6	9	1	1	0	0	0	1	0	1	.111	.111	.222	-13	-1	0	0	0	.941	-1	/1-2	-0.2
1953	*NY-A	70	155	24	46	6	4	6	24	21	31	.297	.384	.503	143	9	1	0	0	.983	-4	1-43	0.4
1954	Phi-A	103	268	35	60	15	3	5	24	35	33	.224	.320	.358	85	-5	1	0	0	.978	1	1-71	-0.7
1955	KC-A	12	9	1	1	0	0	0	3	3	2	.111	.333	.111	23	-1	0	0	0	1.000	-0	/1-3	-0.1
Total	5	195	452	62	110	22	7	11	53	60	68	.243	.337	.396	100	0	2	0		.980	-3	1-123	-0.8

YEAR	TM/L	G	AB	R	H	2B	3B	HR	RBI	BB	SO	AVG	OBP	SLG	PRO+	BR/A	SB	CS	SBR	FA	FR	G/POS	TPR

■ CECIL BOLTON Bolton, Cecil Glenford "Glenn" b: 2/13/04, Booneville, Miss. d: 8/25/93, Jackson, Miss. BL/TR, 6'4", 195 lbs. Deb: 9/21/28

| 1928 | Cle-A | 4 | 13 | 1 | 2 | 0 | 2 | 0 | 0 | 2 | 2 | .154 | .267 | .462 | 87 | -0 | 0 | 0 | 0 | .955 | -1 | /1-4 | -0.2 |

■ CLIFF BOLTON Bolton, William Clifton b: 4/10/07, High Point, N.C. d: 4/21/79, Lexington, N.C. BL/TR, 5'9", 160 lbs. Deb: 4/20/31

1931	Was-A	23	43	3	11	1	1	0	6	1	5	.256	.273	.326	56	-3	0	0	0	.947	-6	C-13	-0.7
1933	*Was-A	33	39	4	16	1	1	0	6	6	3	.410	.500	.487	164	4	0	0	0	.889	-2	/C-9,O-1	0.3
1934	Was-A	42	148	12	40	9	1	1	17	11	9	.270	.321	.365	80	-5	2	0	1	.981	-5	C-39	-0.5
1935	Was-A	110	375	47	114	18	11	2	55	58	13	.304	.399	.427	117	11	0	1	-1	.971	-23	*C-106	-0.6
1936	Was-A	86	289	41	84	18	4	2	51	25	12	.291	.349	.401	90	-5	1	2	-1	.979	-3	C-83	-0.4
1937	Det-A	27	57	6	15	2	0	1	7	8	6	.263	.354	.351	76	-2	0	0	0	.982	0	C-13	-0.1
1941	Was-A	14	11	0	0	0	0	0	1	1	2	.000	.083	.000	-80	-3	0	0	0	1.000	0	/C-3	-0.3
Total	7	335	962	113	280	49	18	6	143	110	50	.291	.366	.398	98	-2	3	3	-1	.974	-36	C-266/O-1	-2.3

■ TOMMY BOND Bond, Thomas Henry b: 4/2/1856, Granard, Ireland d: 1/24/41, Boston, Mass. BR/TR, 5'7.5", 160 lbs. Deb: 5/5/1874 MU

1874	Atl-n	55	247	25	54	11	0	0		1		.219	.222	.263	61	-9						*P-55	0.0
1875	Har-n	71	289	32	78	12	3	0		0		.270	.270	.332	102	-1						P-40,O-29/12	0.3
1876	Har-N	45	182	18	50	8	0	0	21	0	4	.275	.275	.319	90	-3				.887	5	P-45	0.0
1877	Bos-N	61	259	32	59	4	3	0	30	1	15	.228	.231	.266	54	-14				.937	3	*P-58/O-3	-0.1
1878	Bos-N	59	236	22	50	4	1	0	23	0	4	.212	.212	.237	44	-15				.941	1	*P-59/O-2	-0.1
1879	Bos-N	65	257	35	62	3	1	0	21	6	8	.241	.259	.261	70	-8				.957	5	*P-64/O-5,1	-0.2
1880	Bos-N	76	282	27	62	4	1	0	24	8	14	.220	.241	.241	66	-9				.940	13	*P-63,O-26/31	0.0
1881	Bos-N	3	10	0	2	0	0	0	0	0	0	.200	.200	.200	27	-1				1.000	1	/P-3	0.0
1882	Wor-N	8	30	1	4	0	0	0	2	2	3	.133	.188	.133	5	-3				.714	-3	/O-8,P-2M	-0.5
1884	Bos-U	37	162	21	48	8	0	0		0	4	.296	.313	.346	80	-4				.863	1	P-23,O-17/3	-0.4
	Ind-a	7	23	0	3	1	1	0		0		.130	.130	.261	25	-2				.700	-2	/P-5,O-2	-0.1
Total	2 n	126	536	57	132	23	3	0		1		.246	.248	.300	84	-9						/P-95,O-29,21	0.3
Total	8	361	1441	156	340	32	7	0	121	21	53	.236	.247	.268	64	-59				.927	24	P-322/O-63,31	-1.4

■ WALT BOND Bond, Walter Franklin b: 10/19/37, Denmark, Tenn. d: 9/14/67, Houston, Tex. BL/TR, 6'7", 228 lbs. Deb: 4/19/60

1960	Cle-A	40	131	19	29	2	1	5	18	13	14	.221	.306	.366	84	-3	4	1	1	1.000	2	O-36	-0.2
1961	Cle-A	38	52	7	9	1	1	2	7	6	10	.173	.271	.346	65	-3	1	0	0	1.000	-1	O-12	-0.4
1962	Cle-A	12	50	10	19	3	0	6	17	4	9	.380	.426	.800	228	9	1	0	0	1.000	-0	O-12	0.8
1964	Hou-N	148	543	63	138	16	7	20	85	38	90	.254	.312	.420	110	6	2	2	-1	.989	-6	1-76,O-71	-0.9
1965	Hou-N	117	407	46	107	17	2	7	47	42	51	.263	.339	.366	106	3	2	1	0	.983	-5	1-74,O-38	-0.7
1967	Min-A	10	16	4	5	1	0	1	5	3	1	.313	.421	.563	174	2	0	0	0	.875	0	/O-3	0.2
Total	6	365	1199	149	307	40	11	41	179	106	175	.256	.325	.410	110	14	10	4	1	.974	-11	O-172,1-150	-1.2

■ BARRY BONDS Bonds, Barry Lamar b: 7/24/64, Riverside, Cal. BL/TL, 6'1", 185 lbs. Deb: 5/30/86 F

1986	Pit-N	113	413	72	92	26	3	16	48	65	102	.223	.331	.416	102	2	36	7	7	.983	15	*O-110	2.0
1987	Pit-N	150	551	99	144	34	9	25	59	54	88	.261	.331	.492	114	9	32	10	4	.986	20	*O-145	2.7
1988	Pit-N	144	538	97	152	30	5	24	58	72	82	.283	.369	.491	147	33	17	11	-2	.980	5	*O-136	3.4
1989	Pit-N	159	580	96	144	34	6	19	58	93	93	.248	.353	.426	126	21	32	10	4	.984	20	*O-156	4.2
1990	*Pit-N★	151	519	104	156	32	3	33	114	93	83	.301	.410	.565	172	53	52	13	8	.983	15	*O-150	7.2
1991	*Pit-N★	153	510	95	149	28	5	25	116	107	73	.292	.419	.514	163	47	43	13	5	.991	14	*O-150	6.4
1992	*Pit-N★	140	473	109	147	36	5	34	103	127	69	.311	.461	.624	207	73	39	8	7	.991	11	*O-139	9.2
1993	SF-N★	159	539	129	181	38	4	46	123	126	79	.336	.463	.677	207	87	29	12	2	.984	5	*O-157	8.8
1994	SF-N★	112	391	89	122	18	1	37	81	74	43	.312	.429	.647	182	49	29	9	3	.986	8	*O-112	5.5
Total	9	1281	4514	890	1287	276	41	259	760	811	712	.285	.397	.537	158	373	309	93	37	.985	113	*O-1255	49.4

■ BOBBY BONDS Bonds, Bobby Lee b: 3/15/46, Riverside, Cal. BR/TR, 6'1", 190 lbs. Deb: 6/25/68 FC

1968	SF-N	81	307	55	78	10	5	9	35	38	84	.254	.338	.407	123	9	16	7	1	.978	-3	O-80	0.3
1969	SF-N	158	622	120	161	25	6	32	90	81	187	.259	.353	.473	132	26	45	4	11	.978	-0	*O-155	2.9
1970	SF-N	157	663	134	200	36	10	26	78	77	189	.302	.376	.504	135	32	48	10	8	.969	7	*O-157	5.4
1971	*SF-N★	155	619	110	178	32	4	33	102	62	137	.288	.357	.512	146	35	26	8	3	.994	3	*O-154	3.5
1972	SF-N	153	626	118	162	29	5	26	80	60	137	.259	.329	.446	116	12	44	6	10	.978	11	*O-153	2.7
1973	SF-N	160	643	131	182	34	4	39	96	87	148	.283	.372	.530	141	35	43	17	3	.970	9	*O-158	4.1
1974	SF-N	150	567	97	145	22	8	21	71	95	134	.256	.366	.434	118	15	41	11	6	.966	7	*O-148	2.1
1975	NY-A★	145	529	93	143	26	3	32	85	89	137	.270	.378	.512	154	38	30	17	-1	.987	7	*O-129,D-12	3.8
1976	Cal-A	99	378	48	100	10	5	10	54	41	90	.265	.341	.386	120	10	30	15	0	.977	5	*O-98/D-1	1.1
1977	Cal-A	158	592	103	156	23	9	37	115	74	141	.264	.347	.520	138	30	41	18	2	.986	5	*O-140,D-18	3.0
1978	Chi-A	26	90	8	25	4	0	2	8	10	10	.278	.350	.389	107	1	6	2	1	.956	1	O-22/D-3	0.1
	Tex-A	130	475	85	126	15	4	29	82	69	110	.265	.361	.497	139	24	37	20	-1	.970	5	*O-111,D-18	2.3
	Yr	156	565	93	151	19	4	31	90	79	120	.267	.359	.480	133	25	43	22	-0	.968	5	*O-133,D-21	2.4
1979	Cle-A	146	538	93	148	24	1	25	85	74	135	.275	.371	.463	123	18	34	23	-4	.979	11	*O-116,D-29	1.9
1980	StL-N	86	231	37	47	5	3	5	24	33	74	.203	.308	.316	72	-8	15	5	2	.967	-5	O-70	-1.5
1981	Chi-N	45	163	26	35	7	1	6	19	24	44	.215	.323	.380	95	-1	5	6	-1	.982	-0	O-45	-0.5
Total	14	1849	7043	1258	1886	302	66	332	1024	914	1757	.268	.356	.471	129	277	461	169	37	.977	61	*O-1736/D-81	29.6

■ GEORGE BONE Bone, George Drummond b: 8/28/1876, New Haven, Conn. d: 5/26/18, West Haven, Conn. BB/TR, 5'7", 152 lbs. Deb: 9/18/01

| 1901 | Mil-A | 12 | 43 | 6 | 13 | 2 | 0 | 0 | 6 | 4 | | .302 | .362 | .349 | 103 | -2 | | | | .869 | -2 | S-12 | -0.1 |

■ NINO BONGIOVANNI Bongiovanni, Anthony Thomas b: 12/21/11, Pikes Peak, La. BL/TL, 5'10", 175 lbs. Deb: 4/23/38

1938	Cin-N	2	7	0	2	1	0	0	0	0	0	.286	.286	.429	97	-0	0			1.000	0	/O-2	0.0
1939	*Cin-N	66	159	17	41	6	0	0	16	9	8	.258	.298	.296	60	-9	0			.989	1	O-39	-0.9
Total	2	68	166	17	43	7	0	0	16	9	8	.259	.297	.301	61	-9	0			.990	1	/O-41	-0.9

■ JUAN BONILLA Bonilla, Juan Guillermo b: 2/12/55, Santurce, P.R. BR/TR, 5'9", 170 lbs. Deb: 4/9/81

1981	SD-N	99	369	30	107	13	2	1	25	25	23	.290	.338	.344	101	0	4	9	-4	.976	-11	2-97	-1.0
1982	SD-N	45	182	21	51	6	2	0	8	11	15	.280	.325	.335	90	-3	0	1	-1	.975	-8	2-45	-0.9
1983	SD-N	152	556	55	132	17	4	4	45	50	40	.237	.304	.304	71	-21	3	0	1	.986	-15	*2-149	-3.0
1985	NY-A	8	16	0	2	1	0	0	2	0	3	.125	.125	.188	-16	-3	0	0	0	.955	1	/2-7	-0.1
1986	Bal-A	102	284	33	69	10	1	1	18	25	21	.243	.311	.296	66	-12	0	0	0	.981	-9	2-70,3-33/D	-2.0
1987	NY-A	23	55	6	14	3	0	1	3	5	6	.255	.317	.364	81	-2	0	0	0	.965	1	2-22/3-1,D	0.0
Total	6	429	1462	145	375	50	9	7	101	116	108	.256	.315	.317	79	-40	7	10	-4	.980	-41	2-390/3-34,D	-7.0

■ BOBBY BONILLA Bonilla, Roberto Martin Antonio b: 2/23/63, Bronx, N.Y. BB/TR, 6'3", 230 lbs. Deb: 4/9/86

1986	Chi-A	75	234	27	63	10	2	2	26	33	49	.269	.362	.355	93	-1	4	1	1	.989	-1	O-43,1-30	-0.5
	Pit-N	63	192	28	46	6	2	1	17	29	39	.240	.342	.307	79	-5	4	4	-1	.974	-7	O-51/1-4,3	-1.6
1987	Pit-N	141	466	58	140	33	3	15	77	39	64	.300	.351	.481	119	12	3	5	-2	.932	-20	3-89,O-46/1	-1.2
1988	Pit-N★	159	584	87	160	32	7	24	100	85	82	.274	.370	.476	143	34	3	5	-2	.935	-1	*3-159	3.1
1989	Pit-N★	163	616	96	173	37	10	24	86	76	93	.281	.361	.490	146	36	8	5	-1	.929	6	*3-156/1-8,O	4.2
1990	*Pit-N★	160	625	112	175	39	7	32	120	45	103	.280	.329	.518	135	26	4	3	-1	.961	-2	*O-149,3-14/1	2.0
1991	*Pit-N★	157	577	102	174	44	6	18	100	90	67	.302	.398	.492	151	41	2	4	-2	.989	3	*O-104,3-67/1	4.1
1992	NY-N	128	438	62	109	23	0	19	70	66	73	.249	.349	.432	121	13	4	3	-1	.992	7	*O-121/1-6	1.8
1993	NY-N★	139	502	81	133	21	3	34	87	72	96	.265	.357	.522	133	23	3	3	-1	.969	-2	O-85,3-52/1	1.8

YEAR	TM/L	G	AB	R	H	2B	3B	HR	RBI	BB	SO	AVG	OBP	SLG	PRO+	BR/A	SB	CS	SBR	FA	FR	G/POS	TPR
1994	NY-N	108	403	60	117	24	1	20	67	55	101	.290	.376	.504	126	16	1	3	-2	.942	3	*3-107	1.7
Total	9	1293	4637	713	1290	269	41	189	750	590	767	.278	.361	.476	131	194	36	39	-13	.933	-15	3-648,O-600/1	15.4

■ LUTHER BONIN Bonin, Ernest Luther "Bonnie" b: 1/13/1888, Green Hill, Ind. d: 1/3/65, Sycamore, Ohio BL/TR, 5'9.5", 178 lbs. Deb: 4/13/13

YEAR	TM/L	G	AB	R	H	2B	3B	HR	RBI	BB	SO	AVG	OBP	SLG	PRO+	BR/A	SB	CS	SBR	FA	FR	G/POS	TPR
1913	StL-A	1	1	0	0	0	0	0	0	0	0	.000	.000	.000	-99	-0				.000	0	H	0.0
1914	Buf-F	20	76	6	14	4	1	0	4	7	11	.184	.253	.263	33	-8	3			.970	1	O-20	-0.9
Total	2	21	77	6	14	4	1	0	4	7	11	.182	.250	.260	32	-8	3			.970	1	/O-20	-0.9

■ BARRY BONNELL Bonnell, Robert Barry b: 10/27/53, Clermont County, O. BR/TR, 6'3", 200 lbs. Deb: 5/4/77

YEAR	TM/L	G	AB	R	H	2B	3B	HR	RBI	BB	SO	AVG	OBP	SLG	PRO+	BR/A	SB	CS	SBR	FA	FR	G/POS	TPR
1977	Atl-N	100	360	41	108	11	0	1	45	37	32	.300	.368	.339	81	-8	7	5	-1	.989	8	O-75,3-32	-0.4
1978	Atl-N	117	304	36	73	11	0	1	16	20	30	.240	.287	.306	59	-17	12	6	0	.984	-9	*O-105,3-15	-3.1
1979	Atl-N	127	375	47	97	20	3	12	45	26	55	.259	.312	.424	92	-5	8	7	-2	.983	-15	*O-124/3-1	-2.7
1980	Tor-A	130	463	55	124	22	4	13	56	37	59	.268	.325	.417	97	-2	3	4	-2	.973	6	*O-122/D-3	-0.3
1981	Tor-A	66	227	21	50	7	4	4	28	12	25	.220	.262	.339	68	-10	4	3	-1	.975	2	O-66	-1.1
1982	Tor-A	140	437	59	128	26	3	6	49	32	51	.293	.345	.407	97	-2	14	2	3	.979	-18	*O-125/3-9,D	-2.0
1983	Tor-A	121	377	49	120	21	3	10	54	33	52	.318	.373	.469	123	12	10	7	-1	.986	-13	*O-117/3-4,D	-0.5
1984	Sea-A	110	363	42	96	15	4	8	48	25	51	.264	.315	.394	96	-2	5	2	0	.994	-11	O-94,3-10/1D	-1.6
1985	Sea-A	48	111	9	27	8	0	1	10	6	19	.243	.282	.342	70	-5	1	2	-1	.976	-1	O-22/1-5,D	-0.7
1986	Sea-A	17	51	4	10	2	0	0	4	1	13	.196	.212	.235	21	-6	0	1	-1	.941	1	/O-9,1-8,D	-0.6
Total	10	976	3068	363	833	143	24	56	355	229	387	.272	.325	.389	89	-45	64	39	-4	.982	-51	O-859/3-71,D1	-13.0

■ FRANK BONNER Bonner, Frank J b: 8/20/1869, Lowell, Mass. d: 12/31/05, Kansas City, Mo. BR/TR, 5'7.5", 169 lbs. Deb: 4/26/1894

YEAR	TM/L	G	AB	R	H	2B	3B	HR	RBI	BB	SO	AVG	OBP	SLG	PRO+	BR/A	SB	CS	SBR	FA	FR	G/POS	TPR
1894	*Bal-N	33	118	27	38	10	2	0	24	17	5	.322	.412	.441	101	0	12			.904	-15	2-27/O-4,3S	-1.0
1895	Bal-N	11	42	9	14	1	1	0	7	5	1	.333	.404	.405	106	0	4			.742	-5	3-11	-0.4
	StL-N	15	59	3	8	0	1	1	8	1	8	.136	.164	.220	-1	-9	2			.656	-5	3-10/O-5,C	-1.2
	Yr	26	101	12	22	1	2	1	15	6	9	.218	.269	.297	46	-9	6			.698	-10	3-21/O-5,C	-1.6
1896	Bro-N	9	34	8	6	2	0	0	5	2	8	.176	.263	.235	34	-3	1			.915	-1	2-9	-0.3
1899	Was-N	85	347	41	95	20	4	2	44	18		.274	.313	.372	89	-7	6			.940	2	2-85	0.0
1902	Cle-A	34	132	14	37	6	0	0	14	5		.280	.312	.326	80	-4	1			.907	-10	2-34	-1.2
	Phi-A	11	44	2	8	0	0	0	3	0		.182	.200	.182	6	-6	0			.933	2	2-11	-0.3
	Yr	45	176	16	45	6	0	0	17	5		.256	.284	.290	61	-9	1			.915	-8	2-45	-1.5
1903	Bos-N	48	173	11	38	5	0	1	10	7		.220	.262	.266	53	-11	2			.957	-4	2-24,S-22	-1.2
Total	6	246	949	115	244	44	8	4	115	55	22	.257	.305	.333	73	-38	28			.931	-36	2-190/S-23,30C	-5.6

■ BOBBY BONNER Bonner, Robert Averill b: 8/12/56, Uvalde, Tex. BR/TR, 6', 185 lbs. Deb: 9/12/80

YEAR	TM/L	G	AB	R	H	2B	3B	HR	RBI	BB	SO	AVG	OBP	SLG	PRO+	BR/A	SB	CS	SBR	FA	FR	G/POS	TPR
1980	Bal-A	4	4	1	0	0	0	0	0	0	0	.000	.000	.000	-99	-1	0	0	0	.889	1	/S-3	0.0
1981	Bal-A	10	27	6	8	2	0	0	2	1	4	.296	.321	.370	99	-0	1	0	0	.976	1	/S-9	0.2
1982	Bal-A	41	77	8	13	3	1	0	5	3	12	.169	.200	.234	19	-9	0	0	0	.959	-5	S-38/2-3	-1.2
1983	Bal-A	6	0	0	0	0	0	0	0	0	0	—	—	—	0	-0	0	0	0	1.000	-0	/2-5,D-1	0.0
Total	4	61	108	15	21	5	1	0	8	4	16	.194	.223	.259	34	-10	1	0	0	.960	-4	/S-50,2-8,D	-1.0

■ ZEKE BONURA Bonura, Henry John b: 9/20/08, New Orleans, La. d: 3/9/87, New Orleans, La. BR/TR, 6', 210 lbs. Deb: 4/17/34

YEAR	TM/L	G	AB	R	H	2B	3B	HR	RBI	BB	SO	AVG	OBP	SLG	PRO+	BR/A	SB	CS	SBR	FA	FR	G/POS	TPR
1934	Chi-A	127	510	86	154	35	4	27	110	64	31	.302	.380	.545	132	22	0	2	-1	**.996**	5	*1-127	1.4
1935	Chi-A	138	550	107	162	34	4	21	92	57	28	.295	.364	.485	115	11	4	0		.994	2	*1-138	-0.1
1936	Chi-A	148	587	120	194	39	7	12	138	94	29	.330	.426	.482	119	21	4	2	0	**.996**	12	*1-146	1.6
1937	Chi-A	116	447	79	154	41	2	19	100	49	24	.345	.404	.573	146	30	5	1	1	.989	-2	*1-115	1.5
1938	Was-A	137	540	72	156	27	6	22	114	44	29	.289	.346	.472	111	6	2	2	-1	**.993**	3	*1-129	-0.6
1939	NY-N	123	455	72	146	26	6	11	85	46	22	.321	.388	.477	130	20	1			.992	-1	*1-122	1.2
1940	Was-A	79	311	41	85	16	3	3	45	40	13	.273	.358	.373	96	-1	2	0	1	.982	-4	1-79	-1.2
	Chi-N	49	182	20	48	14	0	4	20	10	4	.264	.302	.407	96	-2	1			.991	5	1-44	-0.1
Total	7	917	3582	600	1099	232	29	119	704	404	180	.307	.380	.487	121	106	19	7		.992	27	1-900	3.7

■ EVERETT BOOE Booe, Everett Little b: 9/28/1891, Mocksville, N.C. d: 5/21/69, Kenedy, Tex. BL/TR, 5'8.5", 165 lbs. Deb: 4/13/13

YEAR	TM/L	G	AB	R	H	2B	3B	HR	RBI	BB	SO	AVG	OBP	SLG	PRO+	BR/A	SB	CS	SBR	FA	FR	G/POS	TPR
1913	Pit-N	29	80	9	16	0	2	0		5	6	.200	.256	.250	47	-6	2			1.000	-1	O-22	-0.8
1914	Ind-F	20	31	5	7	1	0	0	6	7	6	.226	.368	.258	58	-2	4			.778	-2	/O-5,S-3	-0.3
	Buf-F	76	241	29	54	9	2	0	14	21	50	.224	.289	.278	46	-19	8			.959	-4	O-58/S-8,32	-2.6
	Yr	96	272	34	61	10	2	0	20	28	56	.224	.299	.276	48	-21	12			.944	-5	O-63,S-11/32	-2.9
Total	2	125	352	43	77	10	2	0	22	34	65	.219	.289	.270	48	-26	14			.959	-6	/O-85,S-11,32	-3.7

■ BUDDY BOOKER Booker, Richard Lee b: 5/28/42, Lynchburg, Va. BL/TR, 5'10", 170 lbs. Deb: 6/4/66

YEAR	TM/L	G	AB	R	H	2B	3B	HR	RBI	BB	SO	AVG	OBP	SLG	PRO+	BR/A	SB	CS	SBR	FA	FR	G/POS	TPR
1966	Cle-A	18	28	6	6	1	0	2	5	2	6	.214	.267	.464	105	0	0	0	0	.964	-5	C-12	-0.5
1968	Chi-A	5	5	0	0	0	0	0	0	0	2	.000	.167	.000	-46	-1	0	0	0	1.000	-1	/C-3	-0.2
Total	2	23	33	6	6	1	0	2	5	3	8	.182	.250	.394	83	-1	0	0	0	.967	-6	/C-15	-0.7

■ ROD BOOKER Booker, Roderick Stewart b: 9/4/58, Los Angeles, Cal. BL/TR, 6' ", 175 lbs. Deb: 4/29/87

YEAR	TM/L	G	AB	R	H	2B	3B	HR	RBI	BB	SO	AVG	OBP	SLG	PRO+	BR/A	SB	CS	SBR	FA	FR	G/POS	TPR
1987	StL-N	44	47	9	13	1	1	0	8	7	7	.277	.370	.340	88	-1	2	0	1	.960	3	2-18/3-4,S	0.4
1988	StL-N	18	35	6	12	3	0	0	3	4	3	.343	.410	.429	140	2	2	2	-1	.889	-3	3-13/2-1	-0.1
1989	StL-N	10	8	1	2	0	0	0	0	0	1	.250	.250	.250	42	-1	0	0	0	.867	2	/2-5,3-1	0.2
1990	Phi-N	73	131	19	29	5	2	0	10	15	26	.221	.301	.290	64	-6	3	1	0	.976	-6	S-27,2-23,3	-1.0
1991	Phi-N	28	53	3	12	1	0	0	7	1	7	.226	.241	.245	37	-4	0	0	0	1.000	3	S-20/3-3	-0.6
Total	5	173	274	38	68	10	3	0	28	27	44	.248	.316	.307	72	-10	7	3	0	.985	-5	/S-48,2-47,3	-1.1

■ AL BOOL Bool, Albert J. b: 8/24/1897, Lincoln, Neb. d: 9/27/81, Lincoln, Neb. BR/TR, 5'11", 180 lbs. Deb: 9/29/28

YEAR	TM/L	G	AB	R	H	2B	3B	HR	RBI	BB	SO	AVG	OBP	SLG	PRO+	BR/A	SB	CS	SBR	FA	FR	G/POS	TPR
1928	Was-A	2	7	0	1	0	0	0	1	0	0	.143	.143	.143	-25	-1	0	0	0	1.000	0	/C-2	-0.1
1930	Pit-N	78	216	30	56	12	4	7	46	25	29	.259	.336	.449	87	-5	0			.967	-1	C-65	0.0
1931	Bos-N	49	85	5	16	1	0	0	6	9	13	.188	.266	.200	28	-8	0			.989	-2	C-37	-0.9
Total	3	129	308	35	73	13	4	7	53	34	42	.237	.313	.373	71	-15	0	0		.973	-2	C-104	-1.0

■ BRET BOONE Boone, Bret Robert b: 4/6/69, ElCajon, Cal. BR/TR, 5'10", 180 lbs. Deb: 8/19/92 F

YEAR	TM/L	G	AB	R	H	2B	3B	HR	RBI	BB	SO	AVG	OBP	SLG	PRO+	BR/A	SB	CS	SBR	FA	FR	G/POS	TPR
1992	Sea-A	33	129	15	25	4	0	4	15	4	34	.194	.224	.318	50	-9	1	1	-0	.965	-0	2-32/3-6	-0.9
1993	Sea-A	76	271	31	68	12	2	12	38	17	52	.251	.305	.443	97	-2	2	3	-1	.991	-8	2-74/D-1	-1.0
1994	Cin-N	108	381	59	122	25	2	12	68	24	74	.320	.373	.491	124	13	3	4	-2	.978	-17	*2-106/3-2	-0.3
Total	3	217	781	105	215	41	4	28	121	45	160	.275	.325	.446	103	2	6	8	-3	.978	-26	2-212/3-8,D	-2.2

■ IKE BOONE Boone, Isaac Morgan b: 2/17/1897, Samantha, Ala. d: 8/1/58, Northport, Ala. BL/TR, 6', 195 lbs. Deb: 4/22/22 F

YEAR	TM/L	G	AB	R	H	2B	3B	HR	RBI	BB	SO	AVG	OBP	SLG	PRO+	BR/A	SB	CS	SBR	FA	FR	G/POS	TPR
1922	NY-N	2	2	0	1	0	0	0	0	0	1	.500	.500	.500	157	0	0			.000	0	H	0.0
1923	Bos-A	5	15	1	4	0	1	0	2	1	0	.267	.313	.400	86	-0	0	1	-1	.929	0	/O-4	-0.1
1924	Bos-A	128	487	72	164	31	4	13	98	54	32	.337	.404	.497	131	22	2	2	-1	.976	-7	*O-124	0.6
1925	Bos-A	133	476	79	157	34	5	9	68	60	19	.330	.406	.479	124	18	1	4	-2	.941	-7	*O-118	0.1
1927	Chi-A	29	53	10	12	4	0	1	11	3	4	.226	.268	.358	63	-3	0	0	0	1.000	-2	O-11	-0.6
1930	Bro-N	40	101	13	30	9	1	3	13	14	8	.297	.388	.495	111	2	0			.960	-2	O-27	-0.1
1931	Bro-N	6	5	0	1	0	0	0	0	1	0	.200	.333	.200	47	-0	0			1.000	-1	/O-8	-0.3
1932	Bro-N	13	21	2	3	1	0	0	2	5	1	.143	.308	.190	38	-2	0			1.000	-1	/O-8	-0.3
Total	8	356	1160	177	372	79	11	26	194	138	67	.321	.394	.475	121	37	3	7		.960	-18	O-292	-0.4

YEAR	TM/L	G	AB	R	H	2B	3B	HR	RBI	BB	SO	AVG	OBP	SLG	PRO+	BR/A	SB	CS	SBR	FA	FR	G/POS	TPR
■ LUKE BOONE			Boone, Lute Joseph "Danny"			b: 5/6/1890, Pittsburgh, Pa.				d: 7/29/82, Pittsburgh, Pa.			BR/TR, 5'9", 160 lbs.			Deb: 9/9/13							
1913	NY-A	6	12	3	4	0	0	0	1	3	1	.333	.467	.333	134	1	0			.857	-1	/S-4	0.0
1914	NY-A	106	370	34	82	8	2	0	21	31	41	.222	.285	.254	63	-17	10	18	-8	.960	23	2-90/3-9,O	-0.2
1915	NY-A	130	431	44	88	12	2	5	43	41	53	.204	.285	.276	68	-17	14	17	-6	.965	**21**	*2-115,S-11/3	0.0
1916	NY-A	46	124	14	23	4	0	1	8	8	10	.185	.252	.242	47	-8	7			.973	7	3-25,S-12/2	0.1
1918	Pit-N	27	91	7	18	3	0	0	3	8	6	.198	.263	.231	49	-5	1			.921	-0	S-26/2-1	-0.5
Total	5	315	1028	102	215	27	4	6	76	91	111	.209	.282	.261	63	-46	32	<u>35</u>		.964	50	2-214/S-53,3O	-0.6
■ RAY BOONE			Boone, Raymond Otis "Ike"			b: 7/27/23, San Diego, Cal.			BR/TR, 6'1", 188 lbs.			Deb: 9/3/48	F									
1948	*Cle-A	6	5	0	2	0	0	0	1	0	1	.400	.400	.600	168	0	0	0	0	.889	1	/S-4	0.2
1949	Cle-A	86	258	39	65	4	4	4	26	38	17	.252	.352	.345	87	-5	0	2	-1	.947	2	S-76	0.1
1950	Cle-A	109	365	53	110	14	6	7	58	56	27	.301	.397	.430	116	10	4	3	-1	.945	-9	*S-102	0.7
1951	Cle-A	151	544	65	127	14	1	12	51	48	36	.233	.302	.329	75	-21	5	3	-0	.957	-7	*S-151	-1.7
1952	Cle-A	103	316	57	83	8	2	7	45	53	33	.263	.372	.367	113	7	0	1	-1	.941	-10	S-96/3-2,2	0.3
1953	Cle-A	34	112	21	27	1	2	4	21	24	21	.241	.375	.393	110	2	1	2	-1	.952	-1	S-31	0.3
	Det-A	101	385	73	120	16	6	22	93	48	47	.312	.395	.556	156	30	2	1	0	.958	1	3-97/S-3	2.8
	Yr	135	497	94	147	17	8	26	114	72	68	.296	.390	.519	146	32	3	3	-1	.958	-0	3-97,S-34	3.1
1954	Det-A★	148	543	76	160	19	7	20	85	71	53	.295	.378	.466	133	24	4	2	0	.964	2	*3-148/S-1	2.3
1955	Det-A	135	500	61	142	22	7	20	**116**	50	49	.284	.350	.476	123	14	1	1	-0	.953	-5	*3-126	0.8
1956	Det-A★	131	481	77	148	14	6	25	81	77	46	.308	.406	.518	142	30	0	0	-0	.959	-7	*3-130	2.5
1957	Det-A	129	462	48	126	25	3	12	65	57	47	.273	.356	.418	108	6	1	1	-0	.990	-10	*1-117/3-4	-1.2
1958	Det-A	39	114	16	27	4	1	6	20	14	13	.237	.326	.447	103	0	0	2	-1	.988	-1	1-32	-0.4
	Chi-A	77	246	25	60	12	1	7	41	18	33	.244	.298	.386	89	-4	1	1	-0	.986	-2	1-63	-1.1
	Yr	116	360	41	87	16	2	13	61	32	46	.242	.307	.406	93	-4	1	3	-2	.986	-3	1-95	-1.5
1959	Chi-A	9	21	3	5	0	0	1	5	7	5	.238	.429	.381	126	1	1	0	-0	.955	0	/1-6	0.1
	KC-A	61	132	19	36	6	0	2	12	27	17	.273	.396	.364	108	3	1	0	-0	.983	1	1-38/3-3	0.2
	Yr	70	153	22	41	6	0	3	17	34	22	.268	.401	.366	111	4	2	0	-1	.980	1	1-44/3-3	0.3
	Mil-N	13	15	3	3	0	0	1	2	4	2	.200	.368	.400	114	0	0	0	-0	1.000	-0	/1-3	0.0
1960	Mil-N	7	12	3	3	1	0	0	4	5	1	.250	.471	.333	135	1	0	0	-0	1.000	-0	/1-4	0.0
	Bos-A	34	78	6	16	1	0	1	11	11	15	.205	.303	.256	51	-5	0	0	-0	.994	-0	1-22	-0.7
Total	13	1373	4589	645	1260	162	46	151	737	608	463	.275	.363	.429	115	95	21	19	-5	.958	-46	3-510,S-464,1/2	5.3
■ BOB BOONE			Boone, Robert Raymond			b: 11/19/47, San Diego, Cal.			BR/TR, 6'2", 202 lbs.			Deb: 9/10/72	FC									
1972	Phi-N	16	51	4	14	1	0	1	4	5	7	.275	.339	.353	95	-0	1	0	0	.936	-6	C-14	-0.6
1973	Phi-N	145	521	42	136	20	2	10	61	41	36	.261	.315	.365	86	-10	3	4	-2	.990	6	*C-145	0.0
1974	Phi-N	146	488	41	118	24	3	3	52	35	29	.242	.298	.322	70	-20	3	1	-0	.976	-7	*C-146	-2.0
1975	Phi-N	97	289	28	71	14	2	2	20	32	14	.246	.323	.329	78	-8	1	3	-2	.990	1	C-92/3-3	-0.6
1976	*Phi-N★	121	361	40	98	18	2	4	54	45	44	.271	.354	.366	101	2	2	5	-2	.993	-9	*C-108/1-4	-0.8
1977	*Phi-N	132	440	55	125	26	4	11	66	42	54	.284	.349	.436	105	3	5	5	-2	.989	3	*C-131/3-2	0.8
1978	*Phi-N★	132	435	48	123	18	4	12	62	46	37	.283	.353	.425	115	9	2	5	-2	**.991**	-9	*C-129/1-3,O	-0.3
1979	Phi-N★	119	398	38	114	21	3	9	58	49	33	.286	.367	.422	111	7	1	4	-2	.988	-12	*C-117/3-2	-0.3
1980	Phi-N	141	480	34	110	23	1	9	55	48	41	.229	.301	.338	74	-12	3	4	-2	.979	5	*C-138	-0.9
1981	Phi-N	76	227	19	48	7	0	4	24	22	16	.211	.281	.295	61	-12	2	2	-1	.985	-2	C-75	-1.3
1982	*Cal-A	143	472	42	121	17	0	7	58	39	34	.256	.313	.337	79	-14	0	2	-1	.989	7	*C-143	-0.2
1983	Cal-A★	142	468	46	120	18	0	9	52	24	42	.256	.293	.353	77	-15	4	3	-1	.980	4	*C-142	-0.5
1984	Cal-A	139	450	33	91	16	1	3	32	25	45	.202	.244	.262	40	-36	3	3	-1	.984	7	*C-137	-2.4
1985	Cal-A	150	460	37	114	17	0	5	55	37	35	.248	.308	.317	72	-17	1	1	-0	.987	5	*C-147	-0.6
1986	*Cal-A	144	442	48	98	12	2	7	49	43	30	.222	.291	.305	63	-22	1	0	-0	.988	12	*C-144	-0.1
1987	Cal-A	128	389	42	94	18	0	3	33	35	36	.242	.306	.311	66	-18	0	1	-1	.983	0	*C-127/D-1	-1.1
1988	Cal-A	122	352	38	104	17	0	5	39	29	26	.295	.352	.386	110	5	2	2	-1	.986	-6	*C-121	0.6
1989	KC-A	131	405	33	111	13	2	1	43	49	37	.274	.355	.323	93	-2	3	2	-0	.991	9	*C-129	0.9
1990	KC-A	40	117	11	28	3	0	0	9	17	12	.239	.336	.265	71	-4	1	1	-0	.985	2	C-40	0.0
Total	19	2264	7245	679	1838	303	26	105	826	663	608	.254	.318	.346	82	-170	38	50	-19	.986	6	*C-2225/1-7,3DO	-9.1
■ BOOTH		Booth		Deb: 5/1/1875																			
1875	NH-n	1	2	0	0	0	0	0		0		.000	.000	.000	-99	-0						/S-1	0.0
■ AMOS BOOTH			Booth, Amos Smith "Darling"			b: 9/14/1853, Cincinnati, O.			d: 7/1/21, Miamisburg, Ohio			BR/TR, 5'9", 159 lbs.			Deb: 4/25/1876							
1876	Cin-N	63	272	31	71	3	0	0	14	9	11	.261	.285	.272	101	2				.760	-18	3-24,C-24,S/OP	-1.3
1877	Cin-N	44	157	16	27	2	1	0	13	12	10	.172	.231	.197	41	-9				.853	-5	S-13,C-12,P2/3O	-0.9
1880	Cin-N	1	2	0	0	0	0	0	0	0	0	.000	.000	.000	-99	-0				.000	0	/3-1	0.0
1882	Bal-a	1	3	0	0	0	0	0	0	0	0	.000	.000	.000	-99	-1				1.000	0	/3-1	-0.1
	Lou-a	1	4	0	0	0	0	0	0	0	0	.000	.000	.000	-99	-1				1.000	-1	/2-1	-0.1
	Yr	2	7	0	0	0	0	0	0	0	0	.000	.000	.000	-99	-1				1.000	-1	/3-1,2-1	-0.2
Total	4	110	438	47	98	5	1	0	<u>27</u>	21	21	.224	.259	.240	73	-9				.746	-24	/C-36,S-35,3P2O	-2.4
■ EDDIE BOOTH			Booth, Edward H.			b: Brooklyn, N.Y.			Deb: 4/26/1872													
1872	Man-n	24	118	24	40	3	2	0	15	0	1	.339	.339	.398	134	5						2-20/O-4	0.2
	Atl-n	15	62	11	18	5	0	0	8	0	0	.290	.290	.371	87	-2						O-13/2-1	-0.2
	Yr	39	180	35	58	8	2	0	23	0	1	.322	.322	.389	114	2						2-21,O-17	0.0
1873	Res-n	18	72	11	21	2	1	0	4	0	2	.292	.292	.375	103	1						O-17/2-1	0.1
	Atl-n	16	69	8	14	3	1	0	7	3	0	.203	.236	.275	56	-3						O-16	-0.2
	Yr	34	141	19	35	5	2	0	11	3	2	.248	.264	.326	80	-2						O-33/2-1	-0.1
1874	Atl-n	44	187	24	47	2	4	1		3		.251	.263	.321	96	1						*O-44	0.1
1875	Mut-n	68	278	33	55	3	4	0		1		.198	.201	.237	48	-15						*O-62/2-6	-1.2
1876	NY-N	57	228	17	49	2	1	0	7	2	4	.215	.222	.232	59	-8				.764	-5	*O-53/2-5,P	-1.2
Total	4 n	185	786	111	195	18	13	1	<u>34</u>	7	<u>3</u>	.248	.255	.308	81	-14						O-156/2-28D	-1.2
■ FRENCHY BORDAGARAY			Bordagaray, Stanley George			b: 1/3/10, Coalinga, Cal.			BR/TR, 5'7.5", 175 lbs.			Deb: 4/17/34								
1934	Chi-A	29	87	12	28	3	1	0	3	3	9	.322	.344	.379	84	-2	1	2	-1	.938	-1	O-17	-0.4
1935	Bro-N	120	422	69	119	19	6	1	39	17	29	.282	.319	.363	85	-9	18			.980	1	*O-105	-1.2
1936	Bro-N	125	372	63	117	21	3	4	31	17	42	.315	.346	.419	104	2	12			.991	0	O-92,2-11/3	-0.1
1937	StL-N	96	300	43	88	11	4	1	37	15	25	.293	.331	.367	88	-5	11			.942	-9	3-50,O-28	-1.4
1938	StL-N	81	156	19	44	5	1	0	21	8	9	.282	.325	.327	76	-5	2			.959	0	O-29/3-4	-0.6
1939	*Cin-N	63	122	19	24	5	1	0	12	9	10	.197	.252	.254	36	-11	3			1.000	-6	O-43/2-2	-1.8
1941	*NY-A	36	73	10	19	1	2	0	4	6	8	.260	.325	.274	61	-4	1	0	0	.967	-3	O-19	-0.7
1942	Bro-N	48	58	11	14	2	0	0	5	3	3	.241	.279	.276	62	-3	2			1.000	-4	O-17	-0.7
1943	Bro-N	89	268	47	81	18	2	0	19	30	15	.302	.379	.384	120	8	6			.989	-15	O-53,3-25	-0.9
1944	Bro-N	130	501	85	141	26	4	6	51	36	22	.281	.331	.385	103	1	3			.945	-9	3-98,O-25	-2.0
1945	Bro-N	113	273	32	70	9	6	2	49	29	15	.256	.328	.355	91	-4	7			.886	-11	3-57,O-22	-1.4
Total	11	930	2632	410	745	120	28	14	270	173	166	.283	.331	.366	91	-32	66	<u>2</u>		.982	-66	O-450,3-240/2	-11.2
■ PAT BORDERS			Borders, Patrick Lance			b: 5/14/63, Columbus, Ohio			BR/TR, 6'2", 190 lbs.			Deb: 4/6/88								
1988	Tor-A	56	154	15	42	6	3	5	21	3	24	.273	.287	.448	102	-0	0	0	0	.973	2	C-43/2-1,3D	0.4

YEAR	TM/L	G	AB	R	H	2B	3B	HR	RBI	BB	SO	AVG	OBP	SLG	PRO+	BR/A	SB	CS	SBR	FA	FR	G/POS	TPR
1989	*Tor-A	94	241	22	62	11	1	3	29	11	45	.257	.292	.349	81	-6	2	1	0	.980	0	C-68,D-18	-0.4
1990	*Tor-A	125	346	36	99	24	2	15	49	18	57	.286	.321	.497	123	9	0	1	-1	.993	0	*C-115/D-1	1.5
1991	*Tor-A	105	291	22	71	17	0	5	36	11	45	.244	.274	.354	70	-13	0	0	0	.993	13	*C-102	0.5
1992	*Tor-A	138	480	47	116	26	2	13	53	33	75	.242	.293	.385	85	-11	1	1	-0	.991	5	*C-137	0.2
1993	*Tor-A	138	488	38	124	30	0	9	55	20	66	.254	.286	.371	75	-19	2	2	-1	.986	5	*C-138	-0.6
1994	Tor-A	85	295	24	73	13	1	3	26	15	50	.247	.284	.329	57	-19	1	1	-0	.988	7	C-85	-0.7
Total	7	741	2295	204	587	127	9	53	269	111	362	.256	.292	.388	83	-59	6	6	-2	.988	32	C-688/D-26,32	0.9

■ MIKE BORDICK
Bordick, Michael Todd b: 7/21/65, Marquette, Mich. BR/TR, 5'11", 170 lbs. Deb: 4/11/90

YEAR	TM/L	G	AB	R	H	2B	3B	HR	RBI	BB	SO	AVG	OBP	SLG	PRO+	BR/A	SB	CS	SBR	FA	FR	G/POS	TPR
1990	*Oak-A	25	14	0	1	0	0	0	0	1	4	.071	.133	.071	-43	-3	0	0	0	1.000	-0	3-10/S-9,2	-0.3
1991	Oak-A	90	235	21	56	5	1	0	21	14	37	.238	.290	.268	59	-13	3	4	-2	.972	-4	S-84/2-5,3	-1.2
1992	Oak-A	154	504	62	151	19	4	3	48	40	59	.300	.362	.371	111	8	12	.6	0	.987	8	2-95,S-70	2.3
1993	Oak-A	159	546	60	136	21	2	3	48	60	58	.249	.335	.311	80	-14	10	10	-3	.982	-16	*S-159/2-1	-2.0
1994	Oak-A	114	391	38	99	18	4	2	37	38	44	.253	.324	.335	77	-13	7	2	1	.974	-2	*S-112/2-4	-0.5
Total	5	542	1690	181	443	63	11	8	154	153	202	.262	.333	.322	84	-34	32	22	-4	.975	-13	S-434,2-112/3	-1.7

■ GLENN BORGMANN
Borgmann, Glenn Dennis b: 5/25/50, Paterson, N.J. BR/TR, 6'4", 210 lbs. Deb: 7/1/72

YEAR	TM/L	G	AB	R	H	2B	3B	HR	RBI	BB	SO	AVG	OBP	SLG	PRO+	BR/A	SB	CS	SBR	FA	FR	G/POS	TPR
1972	Min-A	56	175	11	41	4	0	3	14	25	25	.234	.330	.309	86	-2	0	0	0	.965	-1	C-56	-0.1
1973	Min-A	12	34	7	9	2	0	0	9	6	10	.265	.375	.324	95	0	0	0	0	1.000	-2	C-12	-0.2
1974	Min-A	128	345	33	87	8	1	3	45	39	44	.252	.330	.307	81	-7	2	1	0	**.997**	-1	*C-128	-0.4
1975	Min-A	125	352	34	73	15	2	2	33	47	59	.207	.304	.278	64	-16	0	1	-1	.989	-2	*C-125	-1.3
1976	Min-A	24	65	10	16	3	0	1	6	19	7	.246	.417	.338	119	3	1	1	-0	.976	2	C-24	0.5
1977	Min-A	17	43	12	11	1	0	2	7	11	9	.256	.407	.419	128	2	0	0	0	1.000	2	C-17	0.4
1978	Min-A	49	123	16	26	4	1	3	15	18	17	.211	.312	.333	80	-1	0	0	0	.990	5	C-46/D-1	0.3
1979	Min-A	31	70	4	14	3	0	0	8	12	11	.200	.317	.243	52	-4	1	0	0	.993	7	C-31	0.0
1980	Chi-A	32	87	10	19	2	0	2	14	14	9	.218	.327	.310	76	-3	0	0	0	1.000	2	C-32	0.0
Total	9	474	1294	137	296	42	4	16	151	191	191	.229	.329	.304	79	-30	4	3	-1	.989	10	C-471/D-1	-0.4

■ BOB BORKOWSKI
Borkowski, Robert Vilarian b: 1/27/26, Dayton, Ohio BR/TR, 6', 182 lbs. Deb: 4/22/50

YEAR	TM/L	G	AB	R	H	2B	3B	HR	RBI	BB	SO	AVG	OBP	SLG	PRO+	BR/A	SB	CS	SBR	FA	FR	G/POS	TPR
1950	Chi-N	85	256	27	70	7	4	4	29	16	30	.273	.319	.379	84	-6	1			.975	1	O-65/1-1	-0.8
1951	Chi-N	58	89	9	14	1	0	0	10	3	16	.157	.185	.169	-4	-13	0	0	0	.933	-4	O-25	-1.8
1952	Cin-N	126	377	42	95	11	4	4	24	26	53	.252	.300	.334	76	-13	1	3	-2	.991	-6	*O-103/1-5	-2.5
1953	Cin-N	94	249	32	67	11	1	7	29	21	41	.269	.328	.406	89	-4	0	1	-1	.982	-7	O-67/1-2	-1.3
1954	Cin-N	73	162	13	43	12	1	1	19	8	18	.265	.304	.370	73	-7	0	2	-1	1.000	4	O-36/1-3	-0.9
1955	Cin-N	25	18	1	3	1	0	0	1	1	2	.167	.211	.222	14	-2	0	0	0	1.000	-4	O-11/1-1	-0.6
	Bro-N	9	19	2	2	0	0	0	0	1	6	.105	.150	.105	-30	-4	0	0	0	1.000	-3	/O-9	-0.6
	Yr	34	37	3	5	1	0	0	1	2	8	.135	.179	.162	-8	-6	0	0	0	1.000	-6	O-20/1-1	-1.2
Total	6	470	1170	126	294	43	10	16	112	76	166	.251	.299	.346	71	-48	2	6		.982	-22	O-316/1-12	-8.5

■ RED BOROM
Borom, Edward Jones b: 10/30/15, Spartanburg, S.C. BL/TR, 5'11", 180 lbs. Deb: 4/23/44

YEAR	TM/L	G	AB	R	H	2B	3B	HR	RBI	BB	SO	AVG	OBP	SLG	PRO+	BR/A	SB	CS	SBR	FA	FR	G/POS	TPR
1944	Det-A	7	14	1	1	0	0	0	1	2	2	.071	.188	.071	-23	-2	0	0	0	.950	1	/2-4,S-1	-0.1
1945	*Det-A	55	130	19	35	4	0	0	9	7	8	.269	.307	.300	72	-5	4	2	0	.966	5	2-28/3-4,S	0.2
Total	2	62	144	20	36	4	0	0	10	9	10	.250	.294	.278	62	-7	4	2	0	.964	6	/2-32,3-4,S	0.1

■ STEVE BOROS
Boros, Stephen b: 9/3/36, Flint, Mich. BR/TR, 6', 185 lbs. Deb: 6/19/57 MC

YEAR	TM/L	G	AB	R	H	2B	3B	HR	RBI	BB	SO	AVG	OBP	SLG	PRO+	BR/A	SB	CS	SBR	FA	FR	G/POS	TPR
1957	Det-A	24	41	4	6	1	0	0	2	1	8	.146	.167	.171	-7	-6	0	0	0	.906	3	/3-9,S-5	-0.3
1958	Det-A	6	2	0	0	0	0	0	0	0	0	.000	.000	.000	-93	-1	0	0	0	1.000	-0	/2-1	0.0
1961	Det-A	116	396	51	107	18	2	5	62	68	42	.270	.388	.364	99	3	4	2	0	.953	-21	*3-116	-1.7
1962	Det-A	116	356	46	81	14	1	16	47	53	62	.228	.333	.407	95	-3	3	1	0	.931	-15	*3-105/2-6	-1.6
1963	Chi-N	41	90	9	19	5	1	3	7	12	19	.211	.304	.389	93	-1	0	2	-1	.975	-3	1-14,O-11	-0.6
1964	Cin-N	117	370	31	95	12	3	2	31	47	43	.257	.344	.322	86	-5	4	1	1	.961	4	*3-114	-0.3
1965	Cin-N	2	0	0	0	0	0	0	0	0	0	—	—	—	—	—	0	0	0	1.000	0	/3-2	0.0
Total	7	422	1255	141	308	50	7	26	149	181	174	.245	.346	.359	90	-13	11	6	-0	.948	-31	3-346/1-14,02S	-4.5

■ BABE BORTON
Borton, William Baker b: 8/14/1888, Marion, Ill. d: 7/29/54, Berkeley, Cal. BL/TL, 6', 178 lbs. Deb: 9/2/12

YEAR	TM/L	G	AB	R	H	2B	3B	HR	RBI	BB	SO	AVG	OBP	SLG	PRO+	BR/A	SB	CS	SBR	FA	FR	G/POS	TPR
1912	Chi-A	31	105	15	39	3	1	0	17	8		.371	.416	.419	143	6	1			.997	0	1-30	0.6
1913	Chi-A	28	80	9	22	5	0	0	13	23	5	.275	.442	.338	130	5	1			.991	-2	1-26	0.3
	NY-A	33	108	8	14	2	0	0	11	18	19	.130	.260	.148	20	-10	1			.978	4	1-33	-0.7
	Yr	61	188	17	36	7	0	0	24	41	24	.191	.342	.229	68	-5	2			.984	3	1-59	-0.4
1915	StL-F	159	549	**97**	157	20	14	3	83	**92**	64	.286	.395	.390	105	7	17			.993	-10	*1-159	-0.6
1916	StL-A	66	98	10	22	1	2	1	12	19	13	.224	.350	.306	102	1	1			.991	-1	1-22	-0.1
Total	4	317	940	139	254	31	17	4	136	160	101	.270	.381	.352	102	9	21			.991	-8	1-270	-0.5

■ DON BOSCH
Bosch, Donald John b: 7/15/42, San Francisco, Cal BB/TR, 5'10", 160 lbs. Deb: 9/19/66

YEAR	TM/L	G	AB	R	H	2B	3B	HR	RBI	BB	SO	AVG	OBP	SLG	PRO+	BR/A	SB	CS	SBR	FA	FR	G/POS	TPR
1966	Pit-N	3	2	0	0	0	0	0	0	0	0	.000	.000	.000	-99	-1	0	0	0	.000	-0	/O-1	-0.1
1967	NY-N	44	93	7	13	0	1	0	2	5	24	.140	.184	.161	-0	-12	3	1	0	1.000	-4	O-39	-1.9
1968	NY-N	50	111	14	19	1	0	3	7	9	33	.171	.233	.261	48	-7	0	2	-1	.974	2	O-33	-0.9
1969	Mon-N	49	112	13	20	5	0	1	4	8	20	.179	.233	.250	35	-10	1	0	0	.964	-3	O-32	-1.4
Total	4	146	318	34	52	6	1	4	13	22	77	.164	.218	.226	28	-29	4	3	-1	.979	-5	O-105	-4.3

■ RICK BOSETTI
Bosetti, Richard Alan b: 8/5/53, Redding, Cal. BR/TR, 5'11", 185 lbs. Deb: 9/9/76

YEAR	TM/L	G	AB	R	H	2B	3B	HR	RBI	BB	SO	AVG	OBP	SLG	PRO+	BR/A	SB	CS	SBR	FA	FR	G/POS	TPR
1976	Phi-N	13	18	6	5	1	0	0	0	1	3	.278	.316	.333	82	-0	3	0	1	1.000	-0	/O-6	0.0
1977	StL-N	41	69	12	16	0	0	0	3	6	11	.232	.303	.232	47	-5	4	4	-1	1.000	-4	O-35	-1.1
1978	Tor-A	136	568	61	147	25	5	5	42	30	65	.259	.300	.347	80	-16	6	10	-4	.986	25	*O-135	-0.1
1979	Tor-A	162	619	59	161	35	2	8	65	22	70	.260	.289	.362	73	-24	13	12	-3	.974	17	*O-162	-1.7
1980	Tor-A	53	188	24	40	7	1	4	18	15	29	.213	.278	.324	62	-10	4	6	-2	.985	-1	O-51	-1.6
1981	Tor-A	25	47	5	11	2	0	0	4	4	3	.234	.265	.277	53	-3	0	2	-1	1.000	-2	O-19/D-1	-0.7
	*Oak-A	9	19	4	2	0	0	0	1	3	3	.105	.227	.105	-2	-2	0	0	0	1.000	-0	/O-5,D-2	-0.3
	Yr	34	66	9	13	2	0	0	5	5	9	.197	.254	.227	38	-5	0	2	-1	1.000	-2	O-24/D-3	-1.0
1982	Oak-A	6	5	1	3	0	0	0	0	0	1	.200	.200	.200	11	-2	0	0	0	1.000	-1	/O-6	-0.1
Total	7	445	1543	172	385	70	8	17	133	79	188	.250	.290	.338	71	-62	30	34	-11	.982	37	O-419/D-3	-5.6

■ THAD BOSLEY
Bosley, Thaddis b: 9/17/56, Oceanside, Cal. BL/TL, 6'3", 175 lbs. Deb: 6/29/77

YEAR	TM/L	G	AB	R	H	2B	3B	HR	RBI	BB	SO	AVG	OBP	SLG	PRO+	BR/A	SB	CS	SBR	FA	FR	G/POS	TPR
1977	Cal-A	58	212	19	63	10	2	0	19	16	32	.297	.349	.363	98	-0	5	4	-1	.963	1	O-55	-0.3
1978	Chi-A	66	219	25	59	5	1	2	13	13	32	.269	.310	.329	79	-6	12	11	-3	.975	0	O-64	-1.2
1979	Chi-A	36	77	13	24	1	1	1	8	9	14	.312	.384	.390	109	1	4	1	1	.967	1	O-28	0.2
1980	Chi-A	70	147	12	33	2	0	2	14	10	27	.224	.274	.279	52	-10	3	2	-0	.958	-7	O-52	-1.8
1981	*Mil-A	42	105	11	24	2	0	0	3	6	13	.229	.270	.248	53	-6	1	0	1	.966	-6	O-37/D-1	-1.4
1982	Sea-A	22	46	3	8	1	0	0	2	4	6	.174	.240	.196	21	-5	3	1	0	1.000	-5	O-19	-1.1
1983	Chi-N	43	72	12	21	4	1	2	12	10	12	.292	.378	.458	125	1	1	1	-0	1.000	1	O-20	0.0
1984	*Chi-N	55	98	17	29	7	0	2	14	13	22	.296	.378	.418	113	2	5	1	1	.976	-4	O-33	-0.2
1985	Chi-N	108	180	25	59	6	3	7	27	20	29	.328	.395	.511	137	5	8	7	-0	.988	-7	O-55	0.0
1986	Chi-N	87	120	15	33	4	1	1	14	25	34	.275	.370	.350	92	-1	5	6	-1	.969	-10	O-41	-1.0
1987	KC-A	80	140	13	39	2	6	2	16	9	26	.279	.322	.357	78	-6	6	6	-0	.966	-6	O-28,D-13	-1.1
1988	KC-A	15	21	1	4	0	0	0	2	2	6	.190	.261	.190	28	-2	0	0	0	1.000	-2	/O-6,D-4	-0.4

YEAR	TM/L	G	AB	R	H	2B	3B	HR	RBI	BB	SO	AVG	OBP	SLG	PRO+	BR/A	SB	CS	SBR	FA	FR	G/POS	TPR
	Cal-A	35	75	9	21	5	0	0	7	6	12	.280	.333	.347	93	-1	1	1	-0	.965	-1	O-26/D-2	-0.2
	Yr	50	96	10	25	5	0	0	9	8	18	.260	.317	.313	78	-3	1	1	-0	.967	-3	O-32/D-6	-0.6
1989	Tex-A	37	40	5	9	2	0	1	9	3	11	.225	.279	.350	75	-1	2	0	1	1.000	0	/O-8,D-5	-0.1
1990	Tex-A	30	29	3	4	0	0	1	3	4	7	.138	.242	.241	36	-3	1	0	0	1.000	-3	/O-9,D-4	-0.5
Total	14	784	1581	183	430	50	12	20	158	143	275	.272	.333	.357	89	-24	47	24	-0	.972	-48	O-481/D-29	-8.9

■ HARLEY BOSS
Boss, Elmer Harley "Lefty" b: 11/19/08, Hodge, La. d: 5/15/64, Nashville, Tenn. BL/TL, 5'11.5", 185 lbs. Deb: 7/19/28

YEAR	TM/L	G	AB	R	H	2B	3B	HR	RBI	BB	SO	AVG	OBP	SLG	PRO+	BR/A	SB	CS	SBR	FA	FR	G/POS	TPR
1928	Was-A	12	12	1	3	0	0	0	2	3	1	.250	.400	.250	75	-0	0	0	0	.970	-1	/1-5	-0.1
1929	Was-A	28	66	9	18	2	1	0	6	2	6	.273	.294	.333	61	-4	0	0	0	.977	0	1-18	-0.5
1930	Was-A	3	3	0	0	0	0	0	0	0	0	.000	.000	.000	-99	-1	0	0	0	1.000	-0	/1-1	-0.1
1933	Cle-A	112	438	54	118	17	7	1	53	25	27	.269	.310	.347	71	-19	2	5	-2	.994	6	1-110	-2.5
Total	4	155	519	64	139	19	8	1	61	30	34	.268	.309	.341	69	-24	2	5	-2	.992	5	1-134	-3.2

■ HENRY BOSTICK
Bostick, Henry Landers (b: Henry Lipschitz) b: 1/12/1895, Boston, Mass. d: 9/16/68, Denver, Colo. BR/TR, Deb: 5/18/15

YEAR	TM/L	G	AB	R	H	2B	3B	HR	RBI	BB	SO	AVG	OBP	SLG	PRO+	BR/A	SB	CS	SBR	FA	FR	G/POS	TPR
1915	Phi-A	2	7	0	0	0	0	0	2	1		.000	.125	.000	-65	-1	0			1.000	-1	/3-2	-0.3

■ LYMAN BOSTOCK
Bostock, Lyman Wesley b: 11/22/50, Birmingham, Ala. d: 9/23/78, Gary, Ind. BL/TR, 6'1", 180 lbs. Deb: 4/8/75

YEAR	TM/L	G	AB	R	H	2B	3B	HR	RBI	BB	SO	AVG	OBP	SLG	PRO+	BR/A	SB	CS	SBR	FA	FR	G/POS	TPR
1975	Min-A	98	369	52	104	21	5	0	29	28	42	.282	.332	.366	95	-2	2	3	-1	.985	-3	O-92/D-1	-1.0
1976	Min-A	128	474	75	153	21	9	4	60	33	37	.323	.368	.430	130	17	12	6	0	.988	6	*O-124	1.9
1977	Min-A	153	593	104	199	36	12	14	90	51	59	.336	.394	.508	146	38	16	7	1	.989	4	*O-149	3.5
1978	Cal-A	147	568	74	168	24	4	5	71	59	36	.296	.364	.379	113	11	15	12	-3	.989	11	*O-146/D-1	1.3
Total	4	526	2004	305	624	102	30	23	250	171	174	.311	.368	.427	124	63	45	28	-3	.988	18	O-511/D-2	5.7

■ DARYL BOSTON
Boston, Daryl Lamont b: 1/4/63, Cincinnati, Ohio BL/TL, 6'3", 193 lbs. Deb: 5/13/84

YEAR	TM/L	G	AB	R	H	2B	3B	HR	RBI	BB	SO	AVG	OBP	SLG	PRO+	BR/A	SB	CS	SBR	FA	FR	G/POS	TPR
1984	Chi-A	35	83	8	14	3	1	0	3	4	20	.169	.207	.229	20	-9	6	0	2	.910	-6	O-34/D-1	-1.4
1985	Chi-A	95	232	20	53	13	1	3	15	14	44	.228	.272	.332	62	-12	8	6	-1	.989	-6	O-93/D-2	-2.1
1986	Chi-A	56	199	29	53	11	3	5	22	21	33	.266	.336	.427	103	1	9	5	-0	.969	5	O-53/D-1	0.3
1987	Chi-A	103	337	51	87	21	2	10	29	25	68	.258	.309	.421	89	-6	12	6	0	.991	-0	O-92/D-5	-0.8
1988	Chi-A	105	281	37	61	12	6	15	31	21	44	.217	.272	.434	95	-3	9	3	1	.951	-3	O-85/D-5	-0.7
1989	Chi-A	101	218	34	55	3	4	5	23	24	31	.252	.326	.372	99	-0	7	2	1	.971	-7	O-75/D-9	-0.8
1990	Chi-A	5	1	0	0	0	0	0	0	0	0	.000	.000	.000	-99	-0	1	0	0	.000	-0	/O-1,D-3	0.0
	NY-N	115	366	65	100	21	2	12	45	28	50	.273	.328	.440	110	4	18	7	1	.986	-5	*O-109	-0.2
1991	NY-N	137	255	40	70	16	4	4	21	30	42	.275	.351	.416	116	5	15	8	-0	.981	-17	*O-115	-1.4
1992	NY-N	130	289	37	72	14	2	11	35	38	60	.249	.342	.426	118	7	12	6	0	.993	-6	O-95	-1.5
1993	Col-N	124	291	46	76	15	5	14	40	26	57	.261	.326	.464	93	-4	1	6	-3	.985	-6	O-79	-1.5
1994	NY-A	52	77	11	14	2	0	4	14	6	20	.182	.250	.364	60	-5	0	1	-1	1.000	-4	O-16/D-9	-0.9
Total	11	1058	2629	378	655	131	22	83	278	237	469	.249	.313	.410	95	-23	98	50	-1	.977	-54	O-847/D-35	-9.5

■ KEN BOSWELL
Boswell, Kenneth George b: 2/23/46, Austin, Tex. BL/TR, 6', 172 lbs. Deb: 9/18/67

YEAR	TM/L	G	AB	R	H	2B	3B	HR	RBI	BB	SO	AVG	OBP	SLG	PRO+	BR/A	SB	CS	SBR	FA	FR	G/POS	TPR
1967	NY-N	11	40	2	9	3	0	1	4	1	5	.225	.244	.375	76	-1	0	0	0	.971	2	/2-6,3-4	0.1
1968	NY-N	75	284	37	74	7	2	4	11	16	27	.261	.302	.342	93	-3	7	2	1	.965	-1	2-69	0.1
1969	*NY-N	102	362	48	101	14	7	3	32	36	47	.279	.348	.381	102	1	7	3	0	.959	-15	2-96	-0.7
1970	NY-N	105	351	32	89	13	2	5	44	41	32	.254	.335	.345	82	-8	5	4	-1	.996	-15	*2-101	-1.6
1971	NY-N	116	392	46	107	20	1	5	40	36	31	.273	.337	.367	101	1	5	2	0	.973	-29	*2-109	-2.1
1972	NY-N	100	355	35	75	9	1	9	33	32	35	.211	.276	.318	70	-14	2	2	-1	.990	-31	2-94	-4.5
1973	*NY-N	76	110	12	25	2	1	2	14	12	11	.227	.303	.318	74	-4	0	0	0	.973	0	3-17/2-3	-0.4
1974	NY-N	96	222	19	48	6	1	2	15	18	19	.216	.278	.279	57	-13	0	1	-1	1.000	7	2-28,3-20/O	-0.6
1975	Hou-N	86	178	16	43	8	2	0	21	30	12	.242	.354	.309	92	-1	0	3	-2	.991	-10	2-31,3-23	-1.2
1976	Hou-N	91	126	12	33	8	1	0	18	8	8	.262	.306	.341	92	-2	1	0	0	.933	-5	3-16/2-3,O	-0.7
1977	Hou-N	72	97	7	21	1	0	1	10	12	8	.216	.290	.247	50	-7	0	0	0	1.000	-3	2-26/3-2	-0.9
Total	11	930	2517	266	625	91	19	31	244	240	239	.248	.316	.337	85	-51	27	17	-2	.979	-100	2-566/3-82,O	-12.5

■ JOHN BOTTARINI
Bottarini, John Charles b: 9/14/08, Crockett, Cal. d: 10/8/76, Jemez Springs, N.Mex. BR/TR, 6', 190 lbs. Deb: 4/22/37

YEAR	TM/L	G	AB	R	H	2B	3B	HR	RBI	BB	SO	AVG	OBP	SLG	PRO+	BR/A	SB	CS	SBR	FA	FR	G/POS	TPR
1937	Chi-N	26	40	3	11	3	0	1	7	5	10	.275	.370	.425	111	1	0			1.000	1	C-18/O-1	0.2

■ JIM BOTTOMLEY
Bottomley, James Leroy "Sunny Jim" b: 4/23/1900, Oglesby, Ill. d: 12/11/59, St.Louis, Mo. BL/TL, 6', 180 lbs. Deb: 8/18/22 MCH

YEAR	TM/L	G	AB	R	H	2B	3B	HR	RBI	BB	SO	AVG	OBP	SLG	PRO+	BR/A	SB	CS	SBR	FA	FR	G/POS	TPR
1922	StL-N	37	151	29	49	8	5	5	35	6	13	.325	.358	.543	136	7	3	1	0	.986	-3	1-34	0.3
1923	StL-N	134	523	79	194	34	14	8	94	45	44	.371	.425	.535	155	42	4	6	-2	.986	-12	*1-130	1.9
1924	StL-N	137	528	87	167	31	12	14	111	35	35	.316	.362	.500	131	21	5	4	-1	.982	-12	*1-133/2-1	0.0
1925	StL-N	153	619	92	227	44	12	21	128	47	36	.367	.413	.578	147	42	3	4	-2	.987	-4	*1-153	2.6
1926	*StL-N	154	603	98	180	40	14	19	120	58	52	.299	.364	.506	127	21	4			.989	-15	*1-154	-0.3
1927	StL-N	152	574	95	174	31	15	19	124	74	49	.303	.387	.509	134	28	8			.989	-11	*1-152	0.6
1928	*StL-N	149	576	123	187	42	20	31	136	71	54	.325	.402	.628	163	50	10			.987	-14	*1-148	2.2
1929	StL-N	146	560	108	176	31	12	29	137	70	54	.314	.391	.568	133	28	3			.991	-6	*1-145	0.7
1930	*StL-N	131	487	92	148	33	7	15	97	44	36	.304	.368	.493	102	1	5			.990	-14	*1-124	-2.2
1931	*StL-N	108	382	73	133	34	5	9	75	34	24	.348	.403	.534	144	23	3			.987	-3	1-93	1.1
1932	StL-N	91	311	45	92	16	3	11	48	25	32	.296	.350	.473	115	6	2			.986	-3	1-74	-0.2
1933	Cin-N	145	549	57	137	23	9	13	83	42	28	.250	.311	.395	102	1	3			.991	-9	*1-145	-2.3
1934	Cin-N	142	556	72	158	31	11	11	78	39	40	.284	.324	.439	105	2	1			.989	-4	*1-139	-1.3
1935	Cin-N	107	399	44	103	21	1	1	49	18	24	.258	.294	.323	68	-18	3			.992	-3	1-97	-3.1
1936	StL-A	140	544	72	162	39	11	12	95	44	55	.298	.354	.476	100	-2	0	0	0	.992	-10	*1-140	-2.2
1937	StL-A	65	109	11	26	7	0	1	12	18	15	.239	.346	.330	71	-5	1	0	0	.995	1	1-24,M	-0.5
Total	16	1991	7471	1177	2313	465	151	219	1422	664	591	.310	.369	.500	124	247	58	15		.988	-120	*1-1885/2-1	-2.7

■ ED BOUCHEE
Bouchee, Edward Francis b: 3/7/33, Livingston, Mont. BL/TL, 6'1", 205 lbs. Deb: 9/19/56

YEAR	TM/L	G	AB	R	H	2B	3B	HR	RBI	BB	SO	AVG	OBP	SLG	PRO+	BR/A	SB	CS	SBR	FA	FR	G/POS	TPR
1956	Phi-N	9	22	0	6	2	0	0	1	5	6	.273	.407	.364	112	1	0	0	0	1.000	-0	/1-6	0.0
1957	Phi-N	154	574	78	168	35	8	17	76	84	91	.293	.396	.470	136	32	1	0	0	.988	4	*1-154	2.7
1958	Phi-N	89	334	55	86	19	5	9	39	51	74	.257	.356	.425	107	4	1	0	0	.993	0	1-89	-0.1
1959	Phi-N	136	499	75	142	29	4	15	74	70	74	.285	.378	.449	117	14	0	4	-2	.986	-0	*1-134	0.2
1960	Phi-N	22	65	1	17	4	0	0	8	9	11	.262	.360	.323	89	-1	0	0	0	.994	1	1-22	-0.1
	Chi-N	98	299	33	71	11	1	5	44	45	51	.237	.341	.331	86	-5	2	0		.991	-0	1-80	-1.1
	Yr	120	364	34	88	15	1	5	52	54	62	.242	.344	.330	86	-5	2	0		.992	1	1-102	-1.2
1961	Chi-N	112	319	49	79	12	3	12	58	58	77	.248	.372	.417	108	5	1	4	-2	.983	1	*1-107	-0.4
1962	NY-N	50	87	7	14	2	0	3	10	18	17	.161	.305	.287	59	-5	0	0	0	.976	3	1-19	-0.2
Total	7	670	2199	298	583	114	21	61	290	340	401	.265	.370	.419	112	46	5	8	-3	.988	9	1-611	1.0

■ AL BOUCHER
Boucher, Alexander Francis "Bo" b: 11/13/1881, Franklin, Mass. d: 6/23/74, Torrance, Cal. BR/TR, 5'8.5", 156 lbs. Deb: 4/16/14

YEAR	TM/L	G	AB	R	H	2B	3B	HR	RBI	BB	SO	AVG	OBP	SLG	PRO+	BR/A	SB	CS	SBR	FA	FR	G/POS	TPR
1914	StL-F	147	516	62	119	26	4	2	49	52	88	.231	.304	.308	56	-34	13			.916	-4	*3-147	-3.4

■ MEDRIC BOUCHER
Boucher, Medric Charles Francis b: 3/12/1886, St.Louis, Mo. d: 3/12/74, Martinez, Cal. BR/TR, 5'10", 165 lbs. Deb: 6/3/14

YEAR	TM/L	G	AB	R	H	2B	3B	HR	RBI	BB	SO	AVG	OBP	SLG	PRO+	BR/A	SB	CS	SBR	FA	FR	G/POS	TPR
1914	Bal-F	16	16	2	5	1	1	0	2	1	1	.313	.353	.500	116	-0	0			.950	0	/C-7,1-1,O	0.1
	Pit-F	1	1	0	0	0	0	0	0	0	0	.000	.000	.000	-99	0	0			.000	0	H	0.0
	Yr	17	17	2	5	1	1	0	2	1	1	.294	.333	.471	104	-0	0			.950	0	/C-7,1-1,O	0.1

YEAR	TM/L	G	AB	R	H	2B	3B	HR	RBI	BB	SO	AVG	OBP	SLG	PRO+	BR/A	SB	CS	SBR	FA	FR	G/POS	TPR

■ LOU BOUDREAU Boudreau, Louis b: 7/17/17, Harvey, Ill. BR/TR, 5'11", 185 lbs. Deb: 9/9/38 MH

1938	Cle-A	1	1	0	0	0	0	0	0	0	0	.000	.500	.000	36	0	0	0	0	.000	0	/3-1	0.0
1939	Cle-A	53	225	42	58	15	4	0	19	28	24	.258	.340	.360	82	-6	2	1	0	.953	8	S-53	0.6
1940	Cle-A★	155	627	97	185	46	10	9	101	73	39	.295	.370	.443	113	13	6	3	0	**.968**	12	*S-155	3.5
1941	Cle-A★	148	579	95	149	45	8	10	56	85	57	.257	.355	.415	108	7	9	4	0	**.966**	13	*S-147	3.1
1942	Cle-A★	147	506	57	143	18	10	2	58	75	39	.283	.379	.370	118	15	7	16	-8	**.965**	-0	*S-146,M	1.6
1943	Cle-A☆	152	539	69	154	32	7	3	67	90	31	.286	.388	.388	135	27	4	7	-3	**.970**	28	*S-152/C-1M	6.7
1944	Cle-A☆	150	584	91	191	45	5	3	67	73	39	**.327**	.406	.437	146	37	11	3	2	**.978**	26	*S-149/C-1M	7.8
1945	Cle-A†	97	345	50	106	24	1	3	48	35	20	.307	.374	.409	133	14	0	4	-2	.983	1	S-97,M	2.2
1946	Cle-A	140	515	51	151	30	6	6	62	40	14	.293	.345	.410	118	11	6	7	-2	**.970**	16	*S-139,M	3.4
1947	Cle-A	150	538	79	165	45	3	4	67	67	10	.307	.388	.424	129	22	1	0	0	**.982**	17	*S-148,M	4.8
1948	*Cle-A★	152	560	116	199	34	6	18	106	98	9	.355	.453	.534	166	56	3	2	-0	**.975**	9	*S-151/C-1M	6.9
1949	Cle-A	134	475	53	135	20	3	4	60	70	10	.284	.381	.364	100	2	0	1	-1	.982	5	S-88,3-38/12M	1.1
1950	Cle-A	81	260	23	70	13	2	1	29	31	5	.269	.349	.346	81	-7	1	2	-1	.986	0	S-61/1-8,23M	-0.3
1951	Bos-A	82	273	37	73	18	1	5	47	30	12	.267	.353	.396	93	-3	1	0	0	.951	-1	S-52,3-15/1	-0.1
1952	Bos-A	4	2	1	0	0	0	0	2	0	0	.000	.000	.000	-93	-1	0	0	0	1.000	-0	/S-1,3-1M	-0.1
Total	15	1646	6029	861	1779	385	66	68	789	796	309	.295	.380	.415	121	187	51	50	-15	.973	134	*S-1539/3-57,12C	41.3

■ CHRIS BOURJOS Bourjos, Christopher b: 10/16/55, Chicago, Ill. BR/TR, 6', 185 lbs. Deb: 8/31/80

| 1980 | SF-N | 13 | 22 | 4 | 5 | 1 | 0 | 1 | 2 | 2 | 7 | .227 | .292 | .409 | 96 | -0 | 0 | 0 | 0 | 1.000 | -1 | /O-6 | -0.2 |

■ RAFAEL BOURNIGAL Bournigal, Rafael Antonio (Pelletier) b: 5/12/66, Azua, D.R. BR/TR, 5'11", 160 lbs. Deb: 9/1/92

1992	LA-N	10	20	1	3	1	0	0	0	1	2	.150	.227	.200	22	-2	0	0	0	.967	2	/S-9	0.1
1993	LA-N	8	18	0	9	1	0	0	3	0	2	.500	.500	.556	193	2	0	0	0	1.000	1	/2-4,S-4	0.3
1994	LA-N	40	116	2	26	3	1	0	11	9	5	.224	.291	.267	50	-8	0	0	0	.981	0	S-40	-0.6
Total	3	58	154	3	38	5	1	0	14	10	9	.247	.305	.292	62	-8	0	0	0	.980	3	/S-53,2-4	-0.2

■ PAT BOURQUE Bourque, Patrick Daniel b: 3/23/47, Worcester, Mass. BL/TL, 6', 210 lbs. Deb: 9/6/71

1971	Chi-N	14	37	3	7	0	1	1	3	3	9	.189	.250	.324	54	-2	0	0	0	.957	2	1-11	-0.1
1972	Chi-N	11	27	3	7	1	0	0	5	2	2	.259	.310	.296	66	-1	0	0	0	1.000	1	/1-7	-0.1
1973	Chi-N	57	139	11	29	6	0	7	20	16	21	.209	.299	.403	86	-3	1	1	-0	.986	5	1-38	0.0
	*Oak-A	23	42	8	8	4	1	2	9	15	10	.190	.404	.476	155	4	0	0	0	1.000	-1	D-15/1-5	0.3
1974	Oak-A	73	96	6	22	4	0	1	16	15	20	.229	.333	.302	90	-1	2	2	-1	.988	-1	1-39/D-8	-0.4
	Min-A	23	64	5	14	2	0	1	8	7	11	.219	.296	.297	68	-3	0	0	0	.987	3	1-21	-0.1
	Yr	96	160	11	36	6	0	2	24	22	31	.225	.319	.300	82	-3	2	2	-1	.988	2	1-60/D-8	-0.5
Total	4	201	405	36	87	17	2	12	61	58	73	.215	.316	.356	87	-6	1	3	-2	.985	11	1-121/D-23	-0.4

■ LARRY BOWA Bowa, Lawrence Robert b: 12/6/45, Sacramento, Cal. BB/TR, 5'10", 155 lbs. Deb: 4/7/70 MC

1970	Phi-N	145	547	50	137	17	6	0	34	21	48	.250	.278	.303	57	-34	24	13	-1	.979	-21	*S-143/2-1	-3.9
1971	Phi-N	159	650	74	162	18	5	0	25	36	61	.249	.294	.292	66	-28	28	11	2	**.987**	10	*S-157	0.5
1972	Phi-N	152	579	67	145	11	**13**	1	31	32	51	.250	.292	.320	72	-22	17	9	-0	**.987**	5	*S-150	0.4
1973	Phi-N	122	446	42	94	11	3	0	23	24	31	.211	.253	.249	38	-37	10	6	1	.979	-0	*S-122	-2.3
1974	Phi-N★	162	669	97	184	19	10	1	36	23	52	.275	.300	.338	75	-23	39	11	5	**.984**	-16	*S-162	-1.4
1975	Phi-N★	136	583	79	178	18	9	2	38	24	32	.305	.335	.377	94	-6	24	6	4	.962	-12	*S-135	0.1
1976	*Phi-N★	156	624	71	155	15	9	0	49	32	31	.248	.285	.301	65	-29	30	8	4	.975	-14	*S-156	-2.2
1977	*Phi-N★	154	624	93	175	19	3	4	41	32	32	.280	.316	.340	73	-24	32	3	8	.983	1	*S-154	0.3
1978	Phi-N★	156	654	78	192	31	5	3	43	24	40	.294	.320	.370	91	-9	27	5	5	**.986**	2	*S-156	1.9
1979	Phi-N★	147	539	74	130	17	11	0	31	61	32	.241	.319	.314	71	-20	20	9	1	**.991**	-12	*S-146	-1.6
1980	*Phi-N	147	540	57	144	16	4	2	39	24	28	.267	.302	.322	70	-21	21	6	3	.975	-13	*S-147	-1.6
1981	*Phi-N	103	360	34	102	14	3	0	31	26	17	.283	.332	.339	87	-6	16	7	1	.975	-10	*S-102	-0.5
1982	Chi-N	142	499	50	123	15	7	0	29	39	38	.246	.302	.305	68	-21	8	1	1	.973	-30	*S-140	-3.9
1983	Chi-N	147	499	73	133	20	5	2	43	35	30	.267	.315	.339	77	-15	7	3	0	**.984**	15	*S-145	1.5
1984	*Chi-N	133	391	33	87	14	2	0	17	28	24	.223	.274	.269	49	-26	10	4	1	.974	7	*S-132	-0.8
1985	Chi-N	72	195	13	48	6	4	0	13	11	20	.246	.286	.318	62	-10	5	1	1	.970	12	S-66	0.8
	NY-N	14	19	2	2	1	0	0	2	2	2	.105	.190	.158	-2	-3	0	0	0	.882	1	/S-9,2-4	-0.2
	Yr	86	214	15	50	7	4	0	15	13	22	.234	.278	.304	57	-12	5	1	1	.965	12	S-75/2-4	0.6
Total	16	2247	8418	987	2191	262	99	15	525	474	569	.260	.301	.320	71	-333	318	105	32	.980	-75	*S-2222/2-5	-12.9

■ BENNY BOWCOCK Bowcock, Benjamin James b: 10/28/1879, Fall River, Mass. d: 6/16/61, New Bedford, Mass BR/TR, 5'7", 150 lbs. Deb: 9/18/03

| 1903 | StL-A | 14 | 50 | 7 | 16 | 3 | 1 | 1 | 10 | 3 | | .320 | .358 | .480 | 154 | 3 | 1 | | | .885 | -7 | 2-14 | -0.3 |

■ TIM BOWDEN Bowden, David Timon b: 8/15/1891, McDonough, Ga. d: 10/25/49, Emory, Ga. BL/TR, 5'10", 175 lbs. Deb: 9/17/14

| 1914 | StL-A | 7 | 9 | 0 | 2 | 0 | 0 | 0 | 0 | 1 | 6 | .222 | .300 | .222 | 59 | -0 | 0 | | | 1.000 | -1 | /O-4 | -0.2 |

■ CHICK BOWEN Bowen, Emmons Joseph b: 7/26/1897, New Haven, Conn. d: 8/9/48, New Haven, Conn. BR/TR, 5'7", 165 lbs. Deb: 9/15/19

| 1919 | NY-N | 3 | 5 | 0 | 1 | 0 | 0 | 0 | 1 | 1 | 2 | .200 | .333 | .200 | 63 | -0 | 0 | | | 1.000 | -0 | /O-2 | -0.1 |

■ SAM BOWEN Bowen, Samuel Thomas b: 9/18/52, Brunswick, Ga. BR/TR, 5'9", 170 lbs. Deb: 8/25/77

1977	Bos-A	3	2	0	0	0	0	0	0	0	2	.000	.000	.000	-90	-1	0	0	0	1.000	-1	/O-3	-0.1
1978	Bos-A	6	7	3	1	0	0	1	1	1	2	.143	.250	.571	112	-1	0	0	0	1.000	-2	/O-4	-0.2
1980	Bos-A	7	13	0	2	0	0	0	0	2	3	.154	.267	.154	17	-1	1	0	0	1.000	1	/O-6	0.0
Total	3	16	22	3	3	0	0	1	1	3	7	.136	.240	.273	38	-2	1	0	0	1.000	-1	/O-13	-0.3

■ SAM BOWENS Bowens, Samuel Edward b: 3/23/39, Wilmington, N.C. BR/TR, 6'1.5", 195 lbs. Deb: 9/7/63

1963	Bal-A	15	48	8	16	3	1	1	9	4	5	.333	.385	.500	151	3	1	1	-0	.952	-1	O-13	0.1
1964	Bal-A	139	501	58	132	25	2	22	71	42	99	.263	.325	.453	114	9	4	3	-1	.981	-0	*O-135	0.2
1965	Bal-A	84	203	16	33	4	1	7	20	10	41	.163	.202	.296	39	-17	7	1	2	.982	-2	O-68	-2.1
1966	Bal-A	89	243	26	51	9	1	6	20	17	52	.210	.275	.329	74	-8	9	3	1	.960	-0	O-68	-1.1
1967	Bal-A	62	120	13	22	2	1	5	12	11	43	.183	.258	.342	76	-4	3	4	-2	.977	-2	O-32	-0.9
1968	Was-A	57	115	14	22	4	0	4	7	11	39	.191	.262	.330	81	-3	1	0	-0	.957	-1	O-27	-0.6
1969	Was-A	33	57	6	11	1	0	0	4	5	14	.193	.258	.211	34	-5	1	1	-0	.971	-5	O-30	-1.2
Total	7	479	1287	141	287	48	6	45	143	100	293	.223	.284	.375	87	-25	25	13	-0	.974	-12	O-373	-5.6

■ FRANK BOWERMAN Bowerman, Frank Eugene "Mike" b: 12/5/1868, Romeo, Mich. d: 11/30/48, Romeo, Mich. BR/TR, 6'2", 190 lbs. Deb: 8/24/1895 M

1895	Bal-N	1	1	0	0	0	0	0	0	0	0	.000	.000	.000	-97	-0	0			1.000	0	/C-1	0.0
1896	Bal-N	4	16	0	2	0	0	0	4	1	0	.125	.176	.125	-20	-3	0			.900	0	/C-3,1-1	-0.2
1897	*Bal-N	38	130	16	41	5	0	1	21	1		.315	.331	.377	86	-3	3			.948	3	C-36	0.3
1898	Bal-N	5	16	5	7	1	0	0	1	2		.438	.526	.500	191	2	1			.950	-0	/C-4	0.2
	Pit-N	69	241	17	66	6	3	0	29	7		.274	.297	.324	79	-7	4			.946	5	C-59/1-9	0.3
	Yr	74	257	22	73	7	3	0	30	9		.284	.313	.335	87	-5	5			.946	5	C-63/1-9	0.5
1899	Pit-N	109	424	49	110	16	10	3	53	11		.259	.286	.366	79	-15	10			.948	12	C-79,1-28	0.3
1900	NY-N	80	270	25	65	5	3	1	42	6		.241	.268	.293	57	-16	10			.929	14	C-75/S-2	0.4
1901	NY-N	59	191	20	38	5	3	0	14	7		.199	.235	.257	44	-14	3			.950	13	C-46/2-3,S31	0.4
1902	NY-N	107	367	38	93	14	2	0	26	13		.253	.279	.324	87	-7	12			.956	2	C-98/1-3	0.4
1903	NY-N	64	210	22	58	6	2	1	31	6		.276	.306	.338	80	-6	5			.977	0	C-55/1-4,O	0.0

YEAR	TM/L	G	AB	R	H	2B	3B	HR	RBI	BB	SO	AVG	OBP	SLG	PRO+	BR/A	SB	CS	SBR	FA	FR	G/POS	TPR
1904	NY-N	93	289	38	67	11	4	2	27	16		.232	.288	.318	84	-6	7			.976	-3	C-79/1-9,2P	-0.1
1905	NY-N	98	297	37	80	8	1	3	41	12		.269	.322	.333	93	-3	6			.982	-3	C-72,1-17/2	0.0
1906	NY-N	103	285	23	65	7	3	1	42	15		.228	.274	.284	72	-10	5			.984	3	C-67,1-20	-0.1
1907	NY-N	96	311	31	81	8	2	0	32	17		.260	.309	.299	88	-4	11			.990	-5	C-62,1-29	-0.5
1908	Bos-N	86	254	16	58	8	1	1	25	13		.228	.274	.280	78	-7	4			.971	-3	C-63,1-11	-0.5
1909	Bos-N	33	99	6	21	2	0	0	4	2		.212	.228	.232	41	-7	0			.928	1	C-27,M	-0.4
Total	15	1045	3401	343	852	102	38	13	392	129	0	.251	.287	.314	77	-105	81			.963	40	C-826,1-132/2S3PO	0.6

■ BILLY BOWERS
Bowers, Grover Bill   b: 3/25/23, Parkin, Ark.   BL/TR, 5'9.5", 176 lbs.   Deb: 4/24/49

YEAR	TM/L	G	AB	R	H	2B	3B	HR	RBI	BB	SO	AVG	OBP	SLG	PRO+	BR/A	SB	CS	SBR	FA	FR	G/POS	TPR
1949	Chi-A	26	78	5	15	2	1	0	6	4	5	.192	.232	.244	27	-9	1	1	-0	.980	0	O-20	-1.0

■ STEW BOWERS
Bowers, Stewart Cole "Doc"   b: 2/26/15, New Freedom, Pa.   BB/TR, 6', 170 lbs.   Deb: 8/5/35

YEAR	TM/L	G	AB	R	H	2B	3B	HR	RBI	BB	SO	AVG	OBP	SLG	PRO+	BR/A	SB	CS	SBR	FA	FR	G/POS	TPR
1935	Bos-A	11	5	1	1	0	0	0	0	1	2	.200	.333	.200	38	-0	0	0	0	.875	-0	P-10	0.0
1936	Bos-A	6	0	1	0	0	0	0	0	0	0	—	—	—	—	-0	0	0	0	.000	-0	/P-5	0.0
1937	Bos-A	1	0	1	0	0	0	0	0	0	0	—	—	—	—		0	0	0	.000	0	R	0.0
Total	3	18	5	3	1	0	0	0	0	1	2	.200	.333	.200	38	-0	0	0	0	.875	-0	/P-15	0.0

■ FRANK BOWES
Bowes, Frank M.   b: 1865, Bath, N.Y.   d: 1/21/1895, New York, N.Y.   TR , 5'9", 160 lbs.   Deb: 4/17/1890

YEAR	TM/L	G	AB	R	H	2B	3B	HR	RBI	BB	SO	AVG	OBP	SLG	PRO+	BR/A	SB	CS	SBR	FA	FR	G/POS	TPR
1890	Bro-a	61	232	28	51	5	2	0		7		.220	.246	.259	50	-15	11			.813	-9	C-25,O-19,3/1S	-2.0

■ JIM BOWIE
Bowie, James R.   b: 2/17/65, Tokyo, Japan   BL/TL, 6', 205 lbs.   Deb: 8/3/94

YEAR	TM/L	G	AB	R	H	2B	3B	HR	RBI	BB	SO	AVG	OBP	SLG	PRO+	BR/A	SB	CS	SBR	FA	FR	G/POS	TPR
1994	Oak-A	6	14	0	3	0	0	0	0	0	2	.214	.214	.214	12	-2	0	0	0	1.000	0	/1-6	-0.2

■ WELDON BOWLIN
Bowlin, Lois Weldon "Hoss"   b: 12/10/40, Paragould, Ark.   BR/TR, 5'9", 155 lbs.   Deb: 9/27/67

YEAR	TM/L	G	AB	R	H	2B	3B	HR	RBI	BB	SO	AVG	OBP	SLG	PRO+	BR/A	SB	CS	SBR	FA	FR	G/POS	TPR
1967	KC-A	2	5	0	1	0	0	0	0	0	0	.200	.200	.200	19	-1	0	0	0	1.000	0	/3-2	0.0

■ STEVE BOWLING
Bowling, Stephen Shaddon   b: 6/26/52, Tulsa, Okla.   BR/TR, 6', 185 lbs.   Deb: 9/7/76

YEAR	TM/L	G	AB	R	H	2B	3B	HR	RBI	BB	SO	AVG	OBP	SLG	PRO+	BR/A	SB	CS	SBR	FA	FR	G/POS	TPR
1976	Mil-A	14	42	4	7	2	0	0	2	2	5	.167	.205	.214	23	-4	0	0	0	.975	-0	O-13/D-1	-0.3
1977	Tor-A	89	194	19	40	8	1	1	13	37	42	.206	.333	.273	67	-8	2	3	-1	.987	-0	O-87	-1.2
Total	2	103	236	23	47	10	1	1	15	39	47	.199	.313	.263	60	-12	2	3	-1	.985	1	O-100/D-1	-1.5

■ ELMER BOWMAN
Bowman, Elmari Wilhelm "Big Bow"   b: 3/19/1897, Proctor, Vt.   d: 12/17/85, Los Angeles, Cal.   BR/TR, 6'0.5", 193 lbs.   Deb: 8/3/20

YEAR	TM/L	G	AB	R	H	2B	3B	HR	RBI	BB	SO	AVG	OBP	SLG	PRO+	BR/A	SB	CS	SBR	FA	FR	G/POS	TPR
1920	Was-A	2	1	1	0	0	0	0	0	0	0	.000	.500	.000	42	-0	0	0	0	.000	0	H	0.0

■ ERNIE BOWMAN
Bowman, Ernest Ferrell   b: 7/28/35, Johnson City, Tenn.   BR/TR, 5'10", 160 lbs.   Deb: 4/12/61

YEAR	TM/L	G	AB	R	H	2B	3B	HR	RBI	BB	SO	AVG	OBP	SLG	PRO+	BR/A	SB	CS	SBR	FA	FR	G/POS	TPR
1961	SF-N	38	38	10	8	0	2	0	2	1	8	.211	.231	.316	45	-3	2	0	1	.885	3	2-13,S-12/3	0.1
1962	*SF-N	46	42	9	8	1	0	1	4	1	10	.190	.227	.286	37	-4	0	1	-1	1.000	3	2-17,3-11,S	-0.1
1963	SF-N	81	125	10	23	3	0	0	4	0	15	.184	.184	.208	13	-14	1	2	-1	.952	3	S-40,2-26,3	-1.0
Total	3	165	205	29	39	4	2	1	10	2	33	.190	.202	.244	24	-21	3	3	-1	.950	9	/S-62,2-56,3	-1.0

■ JOE BOWMAN
Bowman, Joseph Emil   b: 6/17/10, Kansas City, Kan.   d: 11/22/90, Kansas City, Mo.   BL/TR, 6'2", 190 lbs.   Deb: 4/18/32

YEAR	TM/L	G	AB	R	H	2B	3B	HR	RBI	BB	SO	AVG	OBP	SLG	PRO+	BR/A	SB	CS	SBR	FA	FR	G/POS	TPR
1932	Phi-A	7	1	0	1	0	0	0	0	0	0	1.000	1.000	1.000	405		0	0	0	.875	1	/P-7	0.0
1934	NY-N	31	29	4	5	0	1	0	4	2	3	.172	.226	.241	26	-3	0			1.000	-0	P-30	0.0
1935	Phi-N	49	67	6	13	1	1	1	7	4	7	.194	.239	.284	36	-6	1			.947	-1	P-33/O-1	0.0
1936	Phi-N	44	77	9	15	1	0	0	6	6	14	.195	.253	.208	23	-8	0			.886	-2	P-40	0.0
1937	Pit-N	35	47	3	10	1	0	0	4	5	9	.213	.288	.234	43	-4	0			1.000	0	P-30	0.0
1938	Pit-N	18	21	5	7	0	1	0	1	1	3	.333	.364	.429	116	-0	0			.909	-1	P-17	0.0
1939	Pit-N	70	96	9	33	8	1	0	18	5	9	.344	.382	.448	124	3	0			1.000	0	P-37	0.0
1940	Pit-N	57	90	11	22	5	1	0	14	14	14	.244	.352	.356	96	-0	0			.981	0	P-32	0.0
1941	Pit-N	22	31	4	8	1	0	0	1	1	2	.258	.281	.290	61	-2	0			1.000	0	P-18	0.0
1944	Bos-A	59	100	7	20	5	2	0	16	5	19	.200	.238	.290	51	-7	1	0		.935	-2	P-26	0.0
1945	Bos-A	9	9	0	2	0	0	0	1	1	1	.222	.300	.222	51	-1	0	0		1.000	0	/P-3	0.0
	Cin-N	29	71	4	5	2	1	0	3	2	9	.070	.096	.127	-39	-13	1			.927	-2	P-25	0.0
Total	11	430	639	62	141	24	8	2	75	46	90	.221	.275	.293	55	-39	3	0		.958	-8	P-298/O-1	0.0

■ BOB BOWMAN
Bowman, Robert Leroy   b: 5/10/31, Laytonville, Cal.   BR/TR, 6'1", 195 lbs.   Deb: 4/16/55

YEAR	TM/L	G	AB	R	H	2B	3B	HR	RBI	BB	SO	AVG	OBP	SLG	PRO+	BR/A	SB	CS	SBR	FA	FR	G/POS	TPR
1955	Phi-N	3	3	0	0	0	0	0	0	0	0	.000	.000	.000	-99	-1	0	0	0	1.000	-0	/O-2→	-0.1
1956	Phi-N	6	16	2	3	0	1	1	2	0	6	.188	.188	.500	78	-1	0	0	0	.833	-1	/O-5	-0.2
1957	Phi-N	99	237	31	63	8	2	6	23	27	50	.266	.356	.392	104	2	0	0	0	.929	-2	O-81	-0.4
1958	Phi-N	91	184	31	53	11	2	8	24	16	30	.288	.345	.500	122	5	0	1	-1	.988	-6	O-57	-0.3
1959	Phi-N	57	79	7	10	0	0	2	5	5	23	.127	.179	.203	1	-11	0	0	0	1.000	-1	O-20/P-5	-1.2
Total	5	256	519	71	129	19	5	17	54	48	109	.249	.319	.403	93	-5	0	1	-1	.955	-10	O-165/P-5	-2.2

■ BILL BOWMAN
Bowman, William G.   b: 1869, Chicago, Ill.   d: 4/6/18, Arlington Heights, Ill.   5'11", 180 lbs.   Deb: 6/18/1891

YEAR	TM/L	G	AB	R	H	2B	3B	HR	RBI	BB	SO	AVG	OBP	SLG	PRO+	BR/A	SB	CS	SBR	FA	FR	G/POS	TPR
1891	Chi-N	15	45	2	4	1	0	0	5	5	9	.089	.196	.111	-10	-6	0			.915	-5	C-15	-0.9

■ RED BOWSER
Bowser, James Harvey   b: 9/20/1881, Freeport, Pa.   d: 5/22/43, Moundsville, W.Va.   Deb: 9/13/10

YEAR	TM/L	G	AB	R	H	2B	3B	HR	RBI	BB	SO	AVG	OBP	SLG	PRO+	BR/A	SB	CS	SBR	FA	FR	G/POS	TPR
1910	Chi-A	1	2	0	0	0	0	0	0	0		.000	.000	.000	-99	-0	0			.000	0	/O-1	-0.1

■ FRANK BOYD
Boyd, Frank Jay   b: 4/2/1868, West Middletown, Pa   d: 12/16/37, Oil City, Pa.   BR/TR,   Deb: 5/18/1893

YEAR	TM/L	G	AB	R	H	2B	3B	HR	RBI	BB	SO	AVG	OBP	SLG	PRO+	BR/A	SB	CS	SBR	FA	FR	G/POS	TPR
1893	Cle-N	2	5	3	1	1	0	0	3	1	0	.200	.333	.400	89	-0	0			1.000	-0	/C-2	0.0

■ JAKE BOYD
Boyd, Jacob Henry   b: 1/19/1874, Martinsburg, W.Va.   d: 8/12/32, Gettysburg, Pa.   TL , 160 lbs.   Deb: 9/20/1894

YEAR	TM/L	G	AB	R	H	2B	3B	HR	RBI	BB	SO	AVG	OBP	SLG	PRO+	BR/A	SB	CS	SBR	FA	FR	G/POS	TPR
1894	Was-N	6	21	1	3	0	1	1	1	1	4	.143	.182	.143	-22	-4	2			.833	1	/O-3,P-3	-0.2
1895	Was-N	51	157	29	42	5	1	1	16	20	28	.268	.375	.331	84	-3	2			.786	-14	O-21,P-14,2/S3	-1.4
1896	Was-N	4	13	1	1	0	0	0	1	1	1	.077	.200	.077	-25	-2	0			.909	0	/P-4	0.0
Total	3	61	191	31	46	5	1	1	18	22	33	.241	.344	.293	65	-9	4			.794	-12	/O-24,P-21,2S3	-1.6

■ BOB BOYD
Boyd, Robert Richard "The Rope"   b: 10/1/25, Potts Camp, Miss.   BL/TL, 5'10", 170 lbs.   Deb: 9/8/51

YEAR	TM/L	G	AB	R	H	2B	3B	HR	RBI	BB	SO	AVG	OBP	SLG	PRO+	BR/A	SB	CS	SBR	FA	FR	G/POS	TPR
1951	Chi-A	12	18	3	3	0	0	0	4	3	3	.167	.286	.278	54	-1	0	0	0	1.000	-1	/1-6	-0.2
1953	Chi-A	55	165	20	49	6	2	3	23	13	11	.297	.352	.412	103	0	1	4	-2	1.000	-2	1-29,O-16	-0.5
1954	Chi-A	29	56	10	10	3	0	0	5	4	3	.179	.233	.232	27	-6	2	0	1	.955	-1	O-13,1-12	-0.7
1956	Bal-A	70	225	28	70	8	3	2	11	30	14	.311	.395	.400	119	7	0	5	-3	.990	-7	1-60/O-8	-0.7
1957	Bal-A	141	485	73	154	16	8	4	34	55	31	.318	.389	.408	126	18	2	4	-2	.991	-3	*1-132/O-1	0.6
1958	Bal-A	125	401	58	124	21	5	7	36	25	24	.309	.353	.439	123	11	1	1	0	.994	-2	1-99	0.4
1959	Bal-A	128	415	42	110	20	2	3	41	29	14	.265	.315	.345	83	-10	3	1	0	.985	-9	*1-109	-2.6
1960	Bal-A	71	82	9	26	5	2	0	9	6	2	.317	.364	.427	114	2	0	0	0	1.000	0	1-17	0.1
1961	KC-A	26	48	7	11	0	0	0	9	1	2	.229	.245	.271	37	-4	0	2	-1	1.000	-1	/1-8	-0.7
	Mil-N	36	41	3	10	2	0	0	2	4	1	.244	.262	.244	38	-4	0	0	0	1.000	1	/1-3	-0.3
Total	9	693	1936	253	567	81	23	19	175	167	114	.293	.351	.388	105	14	9	17	-8	.991	-24	1-475/O-38	-4.6

■ BILL BOYD
Boyd, William J.   b: 12/22/1852, New York, N.Y.   d: 9/30/12, Jamaica, N.Y.   Deb: 4/22/1872   MU

YEAR	TM/L	G	AB	R	H	2B	3B	HR	RBI	BB	SO	AVG	OBP	SLG	PRO+	BR/A	SB	CS	SBR	FA	FR	G/POS	TPR
1872	Mut-n	35	164	26	44	6	1	1	32	6	7	.268	.294	.335	100	1						*3-33/S-1,O	-0.1
1873	Atl-n	50	228	31	63	10	5	1	30	2	2	.276	.283	.377	103	2						*O-43/3-8	0.2
1874	Har-n	26	116	22	41	9	4	0		2		.353	.364	.500	164	8						3-25,O-21	0.6

YEAR	TM/L	G	AB	R	H	2B	3B	HR	RBI	BB	SO	AVG	OBP	SLG	PRO+	BR/A	SB	CS	SBR	FA	FR	G/POS	TPR
1875	Atl-n	36	148	14	44	8	2	1			1	.297	.302	.399	161	10						2-15,O-11/3P1M	0.8
Total	4 n	147	656	93	192	33	12	3			11	.293	.304	.393	125	21						/O-76,3-75,21PS	1.5

■ CLETE BOYER   Boyer, Cletis Leroy b: 2/9/37, Cassville, Mo.   BR/TR, 6', 182 lbs.   Deb: 6/5/55 FC

YEAR	TM/L	G	AB	R	H	2B	3B	HR	RBI	BB	SO	AVG	OBP	SLG	PRO+	BR/A	SB	CS	SBR	FA	FR	G/POS	TPR
1955	KC-A	47	79	3	19	1	0	0	6	3	17	.241	.268	.253	40	-7	0	0	0	.963	6	S-12,3-11,2	0.0
1956	KC-A	67	129	15	28	3	1	1	4	11	24	.217	.284	.279	49	-10	1	1	-0	.971	18	2-51/3-7	1.0
1957	KC-A	10	0	0	0	0	0	0	0	0	0	—	—	—	—		0	0	0	.000	0	/2-1,3-1	0.0
1959	NY-A	47	114	4	20	2	0	0	3	6	23	.175	.217	.193	14	-13	1	0	0	.990	6	S-26,3-16	-0.6
1960	*NY-A	124	393	54	95	20	1	14	46	23	85	.242	.289	.405	90	-7	2	3	-1	.967	28	3-99,S-33	2.0
1961	*NY-A	148	504	61	113	19	5	11	55	63	83	.224	.313	.347	80	-14	1	3	-2	.967	30	*3-141,S-12/O	1.6
1962	*NY-A	158	566	85	154	24	1	18	68	51	106	.272	.335	.413	104	2	3	2	-0	.964	36	*3-157	4.0
1963	*NY-A	152	557	59	140	20	3	12	54	33	91	.251	.296	.363	84	-13	4	2	0	.954	22	*3-141/S-9,2	1.1
1964	*NY-A	147	510	43	111	10	5	8	52	36	93	.218	.271	.304	59	-29	6	1	1	.968	19	*3-123,S-21	-0.9
1965	NY-A	148	514	69	129	23	6	18	58	39	79	.251	.306	.424	106	3	4	1	1	.968	26	*3-147/S-2	2.7
1966	NY-A	144	500	59	120	22	4	14	57	46	48	.240	.307	.384	101	-0	6	0	2	.966	20	3-85,S-59	2.7
1967	Atl-N	154	572	63	140	18	3	26	96	39	81	.245	.295	.423	105	1	6	3	0	.970	5	*3-150/S-6	0.6
1968	Atl-N	71	273	19	62	7	2	4	17	16	32	.227	.275	.311	75	-8	2	0	1	.981	-0	3-69	-0.9
1969	*Atl-N	144	496	57	124	16	1	14	57	55	87	.250	.330	.371	96	-3	3	7	-3	.965	3	*3-141	-0.3
1970	Atl-N	134	475	44	117	14	1	16	62	41	71	.246	.308	.381	79	-15	2	5	-2	.954	12	*3-126/S-5	-0.6
1971	Atl-N	30	98	10	24	1	0	6	19	8	11	.245	.302	.439	101	-0	0	0	0	.961	3	3-25/S-1	0.2
Total	16	1725	5780	645	1396	200	33	162	654	470	931	.242	.301	.372	87	-112	41	28	-5	.965	233	*3-1439,S-186/2O	12.6

■ KEN BOYER   Boyer, Kenton Lloyd b: 5/20/31, Liberty, Mo.   d: 9/7/82, St.Louis, Mo.   BR/TR, 6'2", 200 lbs.   Deb: 4/12/55 FMC

YEAR	TM/L	G	AB	R	H	2B	3B	HR	RBI	BB	SO	AVG	OBP	SLG	PRO+	BR/A	SB	CS	SBR	FA	FR	G/POS	TPR
1955	StL-N	147	530	78	140	27	2	18	62	37	67	.264	.313	.425	94	-6	22	17	-4	.952	4	*3-139,S-18	-0.5
1956	StL-N★	150	595	91	182	30	2	26	98	38	65	.306	.349	.494	123	18	8	3	1	.961	9	*3-149	3.0
1957	StL-N	142	544	79	144	18	3	19	62	44	77	.265	.321	.414	94	-5	12	8	-1	.996	4	*O-105,3-41	-0.7
1958	StL-N	150	570	101	175	21	9	23	90	49	53	.307	.365	.496	121	16	11	6	-0	.962	23	*3-144/O-6,S	4.0
1959	StL-N	149	563	86	174	18	5	28	94	67	77	.309	.384	.508	127	22	12	6	0	.956	14	*3-143,S-12	3.6
1960	StL-N★	151	552	95	168	26	10	32	97	56	77	.304	.373	.562	139	29	8	7	-2	.959	13	*3-146	4.0
1961	StL-N	153	589	109	194	26	11	24	95	68	91	.329	.400	.533	132	27	6	3	0	.951	13	*3-153	4.1
1962	StL-N	160	611	92	178	27	3	24	98	75	104	.291	.370	.470	113	11	12	7	-1	.956	4	*3-160	1.6
1963	StL-N★	159	617	86	176	28	2	24	111	70	90	.285	.360	.454	121	18	1	0	0	.925	-13	*3-159	0.5
1964	*StL-N★	162	628	100	185	30	10	24	119	70	85	.295	.367	.489	128	23	3	5	-2	.951	3	*3-162	2.3
1965	StL-N	144	535	71	139	18	2	13	75	57	73	.260	.332	.374	90	-6	2	7	-4	.968	-11	*3-143	-2.6
1966	NY-N	136	496	62	132	28	2	14	61	30	64	.266	.308	.415	101	-0	4	3	-1	.951	11	*3-130/1-2	0.7
1967	NY-N	56	166	17	39	7	2	3	13	26	22	.235	.339	.355	100	1	2	1	0	.949	-2	3-44/1-8	-0.3
	Chi-A	57	180	17	47	5	1	4	21	7	25	.261	.289	.367	96	-2	0	2	-1	.957	1	3-33,1-18	-0.3
1968	Chi-A	10	24	0	3	0	0	0	0	1	6	.125	.160	.125	-13	-3	0	0	0	.900	-1	/3-5,1-1	-0.5
	LA-N	83	221	20	60	7	2	6	41	16	34	.271	.324	.403	127	6	2	2	-1	.922	-4	3-34,1-32	0.0
1969	LA-N	25	34	0	7	0	0	0	4	2	7	.206	.250	.265	48	-2	0	0	0	.971	-0	/1-4	-0.3
Total	15	2034	7455	1104	2143	318	68	282	1141	713	1017	.287	.351	.462	115	147	105	77	-15	.952	69	*3-1785,O-111/1S	18.6

■ DOE BOYLAND   Boyland, Dorian Scott b: 1/6/55, Chicago, Ill.   BL/TL, 6'4", 200 lbs.   Deb: 9/4/78

YEAR	TM/L	G	AB	R	H	2B	3B	HR	RBI	BB	SO	AVG	OBP	SLG	PRO+	BR/A	SB	CS	SBR	FA	FR	G/POS	TPR
1978	Pit-N	6	8	1	2	0	0	0	1	0	1	.250	.250	.250	38	-1	0	0	0	1.000	-0	/1-1	-0.1
1979	Pit-N	4	3	0	0	0	0	0	0	0	2	.000	.000	.000	-96	-1	0	0	0	.000	-0	/H	-0.1
1981	Pit-N	11	8	0	0	0	0	0	0	1	3	.000	.111	.000	-64	-2	0	0	0	.000	-0	/H	-0.2
Total	3	21	19	1	2	0	0	0	1	1	6	.105	.150	.105	-26	-3	0	0	0	1.000	-0	/1-1	-0.4

■ EDDIE BOYLE   Boyle, Edward J. b: 5/8/1874, Cincinnati, Ohio   d: 2/9/41, Cincinnati, Ohio   BR/TR, 6'3", 200 lbs.   Deb: 4/17/1896 F

YEAR	TM/L	G	AB	R	H	2B	3B	HR	RBI	BB	SO	AVG	OBP	SLG	PRO+	BR/A	SB	CS	SBR	FA	FR	G/POS	TPR
1896	Lou-N	3	9	0	0	0	0	0	0	2	2	.000	.182	.000	-52	-2	0			.938	1	/C-3	-0.1
	Pit-N	2	5	0	0	0	0	0	0	0	1	.000	.000	.000	-99	-1	0			.833	-0	/C-2	-0.1
	Yr	5	14	0	0	0	0	0	0	2	3	.000	.125	.000	-68	-3	0			.909	0	/C-5	-0.2

■ HENRY BOYLE   Boyle, Henry J. "Handsome Henry" b: 9/20/1860, Philadelphia, Pa.   d: 5/25/32, Philadelphia, Pa.   TR ,   Deb: 7/9/1884

YEAR	TM/L	G	AB	R	H	2B	3B	HR	RBI	BB	SO	AVG	OBP	SLG	PRO+	BR/A	SB	CS	SBR	FA	FR	G/POS	TPR
1884	StL-U	65	262	41	68	10	3	4		9		.260	.284	.366	73	-10				.885	5	O-43,P-19/3S21	-0.2
1885	StL-N	72	258	24	52	9	1	1	21	13	38	.202	.240	.256	64	-10				.907	-4	P-42,O-31/2	-0.7
1886	StL-N	30	108	8	27	2	1	2	13	5	19	.250	.283	.333	93	-1	0			.852	1	P-25/O-6	0.0
1887	Ind-N	41	141	17	27	9	1	2	13	6	18	.191	.250	.312	57	-8	2			.912	-5	P-38/O-4	-0.2
1888	Ind-N	37	125	13	18	2	0	1	6	6	31	.144	.189	.184	19	-11	1			.933	3	P-37/1-1	0.0
1889	Ind-N	46	155	17	38	10	0	1	17	9	23	.245	.291	.329	72	-6	1			.958	-5	P-46/3-1	0.0
Total	6	291	1049	120	230	42	7	10	70	51	129	.219	.258	.301	65	-47	7			.912	-5	P-207/O-84,321S	-1.1

■ JIM BOYLE   Boyle, James John b: 1/19/04, Cincinnati, Ohio   d: 12/24/58, Cincinnati, Ohio   BR/TR, 6', 180 lbs.   Deb: 6/20/26 F

YEAR	TM/L	G	AB	R	H	2B	3B	HR	RBI	BB	SO	AVG	OBP	SLG	PRO+	BR/A	SB	CS	SBR	FA	FR	G/POS	TPR
1926	NY-N	1	0	0	0	0	0	0	0	0	0	—	—	—	—		0		0	.000	0	/C-1	0.0

■ JACK BOYLE   Boyle, John Anthony "Honest Jack" b: 3/22/1866, Cincinnati, Ohio   d: 1/7/13, Cincinnati, Ohio   BR/TR, 6'4", 190 lbs.   Deb: 10/8/1886 F

YEAR	TM/L	G	AB	R	H	2B	3B	HR	RBI	BB	SO	AVG	OBP	SLG	PRO+	BR/A	SB	CS	SBR	FA	FR	G/POS	TPR
1886	Cin-a	1	5	0	1	0	0	0		0		.200	.200	.200	25	-0	0			.769	-0	/C-1	0.0
1887	*StL-a	88	350	48	66	3	1	2		20		.189	.237	.220	25	-37	7			.897	-11	C-86/O-2,13	-3.3
1888	*StL-a	71	257	33	62	8	1	1	23	13		.241	.286	.292	77	-8	11			.932	14	C-70/O-1	1.1
1889	StL-a	99	347	54	85	11	5	3	42	21	42	.245	.301	.331	71	-16	5			.947	5	C-80,3-12/O12	-0.3
1890	Chi-P	100	369	56	96	9	5	1	49	44	29	.260	.347	.320	76	-13	11			.940	-4	C-50,3-30,S/10	-0.9
1891	StL-a	123	439	78	123	18	8	5	79	47	36	.280	.365	.392	101	-3	19			.936	-14	C-91,S-26/3O21	-0.7
1892	NY-N	120	436	52	80	8	8	0	32	36	40	.183	.252	.239	49	-27	10			.922	14	C-79,1-40/OS	-0.8
1893	Phi-N	116	504	105	144	29	9	4	81	41	30	.286	.351	.403	100	-1	22			.988	6	*1-112/C-6,2	0.2
1894	Phi-N	114	495	98	149	21	10	4	88	45	26	.301	.363	.408	88	-10	21			.983	1	*1-114/3-1,2	-0.6
1895	Phi-N	133	565	90	143	17	4	0	67	35	23	.253	.302	.297	55	-38	13			.973	-6	*1-133	-3.4
1896	Phi-N	40	145	17	43	4	1	1	28	6	3	.297	.346	.359	87	-3	3			.920	-7	C-28,1-12	-0.5
1897	Phi-N	75	288	37	73	9	1	2	36	19		.253	.306	.313	65	-15	3			.962	-9	C-50,1-24	-1.5
1898	Phi-N	2	11	0	1	0	1	0	0	0		.091	.130	.182	-11	-3	0			.919	-0	/1-4,C-3	-0.3
Total	13	1086	4222	668	1067	137	54	23	528	328	233	.253	.315	.327	72	-174	125			.929	-10	C-544,1-455/3SO2	-11.0

■ JACK BOYLE   Boyle, John Bellew b: 7/9/1889, Morris, Ill.   d: 4/3/71, Ft.Lauderdale, Fla.   BL/TR, 5'11.5", 165 lbs.   Deb: 6/28/12

YEAR	TM/L	G	AB	R	H	2B	3B	HR	RBI	BB	SO	AVG	OBP	SLG	PRO+	BR/A	SB	CS	SBR	FA	FR	G/POS	TPR
1912	Phi-N	15	54	4	7	1	0	0	2	9	5	.280	.308	.320	67	-1	0			.905	5	/3-6,S-2	0.4

■ BUZZ BOYLE   Boyle, Ralph Francis b: 2/9/08, Cincinnati, Ohio   d: 11/12/78, Cincinnati, Ohio   BL/TL, 5'11.5", 170 lbs.   Deb: 9/11/29 F

YEAR	TM/L	G	AB	R	H	2B	3B	HR	RBI	BB	SO	AVG	OBP	SLG	PRO+	BR/A	SB	CS	SBR	FA	FR	G/POS	TPR
1929	Bos-N	17	57	8	15	2	1	1	2	6	11	.263	.333	.386	81	-2	2			1.000	-0	O-17	-0.3
1930	Bos-N	1	1	0	0	0	0	0	0	0	1	.000	.000	.000	-99	-0	0			.000	-1	/O-1	-0.1
1933	Bro-N	93	338	38	101	13	4	0	31	16	24	.299	.331	.361	102	0	7			.975	-6	O-90	-1.1
1934	Bro-N	128	472	88	144	26	10	7	48	51	44	.305	.376	.447	126	18	8			.970	11	*O-121	2.3
1935	Bro-N	127	475	51	129	17	9	4	44	43	45	.272	.332	.371	90	-6	7			.963	3	*O-124	-0.8
Total	5	366	1343	185	389	58	24	12	125	116	125	.290	.347	.395	105	10	24			.970	6	O-353	-0.0

■ GIBBY BRACK   Brack, Gilbert Herman b: 3/29/08, Chicago, Ill.   d: 1/20/60, Greenville, Tex.   BR/TR, 5'9", 170 lbs.   Deb: 4/23/37

YEAR	TM/L	G	AB	R	H	2B	3B	HR	RBI	BB	SO	AVG	OBP	SLG	PRO+	BR/A	SB	CS	SBR	FA	FR	G/POS	TPR
1937	Bro-N	112	372	60	102	27	9	5	38	44	93	.274	.351	.435	111	5	9			.969	1	*O-101	0.3
1938	Bro-N	40	56	10	12	2	1	1	6	4	14	.214	.267	.339	64	-3	1			1.000	2	O-13	-0.1

YEAR	TM/L	G	AB	R	H	2B	3B	HR	RBI	BB	SO	AVG	OBP	SLG	PRO+	BR/A	SB	CS	SBR	FA	FR	G/POS	TPR
	Phi-N	72	282	40	81	20	4	4	28	18	30	.287	.332	.429	111	3	2			.964	-2	O-68	-0.1
	Yr	112	338	50	93	22	5	5	34	22	44	.275	.321	.414	102	-0	3			.969	-0	O-81	-0.2
1939	Phi-N	91	270	40	78	21	4	6	41	26	49	.289	.351	.463	121	7	1			.959	-4	O-48,1-19	-0.1
Total	3	315	980	150	273	70	18	16	113	92	186	.279	.341	.436	111	13	13			.967	-4	O-230/1-19	0.0

■ BUDDY BRADFORD
Bradford, Charles William   b: 7/25/44, Mobile, Ala.   BR/TR, 5'11", 191 lbs.   Deb: 9/9/66

YEAR	TM/L	G	AB	R	H	2B	3B	HR	RBI	BB	SO	AVG	OBP	SLG	PRO+	BR/A	SB	CS	SBR	FA	FR	G/POS	TPR
1966	Chi-A	14	28	3	4	0	0	0	0	2	6	.143	.200	.143	0	-4	0	0	0	.833	-3	/O-9	-0.7
1967	Chi-A	24	20	6	2	1	0	0	1	1	7	.100	.143	.150	-14	-3	1	0	0	.900	-4	O-14	-0.8
1968	Chi-A	103	281	32	61	11	0	5	24	23	67	.217	.281	.310	78	-7	8	4	0	.965	-12	O-99	-2.7
1969	Chi-A	93	273	36	70	8	2	11	27	34	75	.256	.347	.421	109	3	5	2	0	.961	-13	O-88	-1.5
1970	Chi-A	32	91	8	17	3	0	2	8	10	30	.187	.267	.286	51	-6	1	2	-1	.979	-4	O-27	-1.3
	Cle-A	75	163	25	32	6	1	7	23	21	43	.196	.292	.374	79	-5	0	1	-1	.984	-4	O-64/3-1	-1.3
	Yr	107	254	33	49	9	1	9	31	31	73	.193	.283	.343	69	-11	1	3	-2	.982	-8	O-91/3-1	-2.6
1971	Cle-A	20	38	4	6	2	1	0	3	6	10	.158	.273	.263	48	-3	0	0	0	.930	-0	O-18	-0.4
	Cin-N	79	100	17	20	3	0	2	12	14	23	.200	.316	.290	74	-3	4	2	0	.986	-13	O-66	-1.9
1972	Chi-A	35	48	13	13	2	0	2	8	4	13	.271	.340	.438	127	2	3	2	-0	1.000	-5	O-28	-0.5
1973	Chi-A	53	168	24	40	3	1	8	15	17	43	.238	.316	.411	100	-0	4	5	2	.992	-4	O-51	0.0
1974	Chi-A	39	96	16	32	2	0	5	10	13	11	.333	.418	.510	162	8	1	2	-1	.980	-3	O-32/D-1	0.3
1975	Chi-A	25	58	8	9	3	1	2	15	8	22	.155	.290	.345	78	-2	3	2	-0	.966	-2	O-18/D-4	-0.4
	StL-N	50	81	12	22	1	0	4	15	12	24	.272	.366	.432	117	2	0	2	-1	.935	-1	O-25	-0.1
1976	Chi-A	55	160	20	35	5	2	4	14	19	37	.219	.309	.350	92	-1	6	0	2	.978	-3	O-48/D-3	-0.5
Total	11	697	1605	224	363	50	8	52	175	184	411	.226	.313	.364	91	-19	36	24	-4	.971	-64	O-587/D-8,3	-11.8

■ VIC BRADFORD
Bradford, Henry Victor   b: 3/5/15, Brownsville, Tenn.   BR/TR, 6'2", 190 lbs.   Deb: 5/1/43

YEAR	TM/L	G	AB	R	H	2B	3B	HR	RBI	BB	SO	AVG	OBP	SLG	PRO+	BR/A	SB	CS	SBR	FA	FR	G/POS	TPR
1943	NY-N	6	5	1	1	0	0	0	1	1	1	.200	.333	.200	55	-0				1.000	0	/O-1	0.0

■ AL BRADLEY
Bradley, Al   5'10", 185 lbs.   Deb: 5/21/1884

YEAR	TM/L	G	AB	R	H	2B	3B	HR	RBI	BB	SO	AVG	OBP	SLG	PRO+	BR/A	SB	CS	SBR	FA	FR	G/POS	TPR
1884	Was-U	1	3	0	0	0	0	0			2	.000	.400	.000	18	-0				1.000	0	/O-1	0.0

■ GEORGE BRADLEY
Bradley, George Washington "Grin"   b: 7/13/1852, Reading, Pa.   d: 10/2/31, Philadelphia, Pa.   BR/TR, 5'10.5", 175 lbs.   Deb: 5/4/1875

YEAR	TM/L	G	AB	R	H	2B	3B	HR	RBI	BB	SO	AVG	OBP	SLG	PRO+	BR/A	SB	CS	SBR	FA	FR	G/POS	TPR
1875	StL-n	60	254	28	62	8	3	0		1		.244	.247	.299	97	0						*P-60/3-1,O	0.5
1876	StL-N	64	265	29	66	7	6	0	28	3	12	.249	.257	.321	97	-0				.919	1	*P-64	0.0
1877	Chi-N	55	214	31	52	7	3	0	12	6	19	.243	.264	.304	70	-8				.950	-2	*P-50,3-16/1O	-0.3
1879	Tro-N	63	251	36	62	9	5	0	23	1	20	.247	.250	.323	93	-1				.867	7	P-54/3-5,10S	0.2
1880	Pro-N	82	309	32	70	7	6	0	23	5	38	.227	.239	.288	80	-6				.858	19	*3-57,P-28/O1	1.5
1881	Det-N	1	4	0	0	0	0	0	0	0	0	.000	.000	.000	-96	-1				.667	-1	/S-1	-0.2
	Cle-N	60	241	21	60	10	1	2	18	4	25	.249	.261	.324	88	-3				.865	-9	3-48/P-6,SO	-0.9
	Yr	61	245	21	60	10	1	2	18	4	25	.245	.257	.318	84	-4				.865	-10	3-48/S-7,PO	-1.1
1882	Cle-N	30	115	16	21	5	0	0	6	4	16	.183	.210	.226	41	-7				.897	3	P-18/O-9,1	-0.4
1883	Cle-N	4	16	0	5	0	1	0	1	0	1	.313	.313	.438	126	-0				.792	-0	/S-4	0.0
	Phi-a	76	312	47	73	8	5	1		8		.234	.253	.301	72	-11				.779	3	3-44,P-26,O/1	-0.3
1884	Cin-U	58	226	31	43	4	7	0		7		.190	.215	.270	29	-23				.912	-0	P-41,O-16/S1	-0.9
1886	Phi-a	13	48	1	4	0	1	0		1		.083	.102	.125	-29	-7	2			.849	1	S-13	-0.5
1888	Bal-a	1	3	0	0	0	0	0	0	0		.000	.000	.000	-99	-1	0			.600	-1	/S-1	-0.1
Total	10	507	2004	244	456	57	35	3	111	39	131	.228	.242	.295	70	-69	2			.896	22	P-287,3-170/OS1	-1.9

■ GEORGE BRADLEY
Bradley, George Washington   b: 4/1/14, Greenwood, Ark.   d: 10/19/82, Lawrenceburg, Tenn   BR/TR, 6'1.5", 185 lbs.   Deb: 4/28/46

YEAR	TM/L	G	AB	R	H	2B	3B	HR	RBI	BB	SO	AVG	OBP	SLG	PRO+	BR/A	SB	CS	SBR	FA	FR	G/POS	TPR
1946	StL-A	4	12	2	2	1	0	0	3	0	1	.167	.167	.250	15	-1	0	0	0	1.000	-1	/O-3	-0.2

■ HUGH BRADLEY
Bradley, Hugh Frederick "Corns"   b: 5/23/1885, Grafton, Mass.   d: 1/26/49, Worcester, Mass.   BR/TR, 5'10", 175 lbs.   Deb: 4/25/10

YEAR	TM/L	G	AB	R	H	2B	3B	HR	RBI	BB	SO	AVG	OBP	SLG	PRO+	BR/A	SB	CS	SBR	FA	FR	G/POS	TPR
1910	Bos-A	32	83	8	14	6	2	0	7	5		.169	.216	.289	57	-5	2			.995	-2	1-21/C-3,O	-0.7
1911	Bos-A	12	41	9	13	2	0	1	4	2		.317	.364	.439	125	1	1			.993	1	1-12	0.2
1912	Bos-A	40	137	16	26	11	1	1	19	15		.190	.275	.307	63	-7	3			.989	0	1-40	-0.8
1914	Pit-F	118	427	41	131	20	6	0	61	27	27	.307	.359	.382	93	-4	7			.990	-0	*1-118	-0.8
1915	Pit-F	26	66	3	18	4	1	0	6	4	5	.273	.314	.364	82	-2	2			.952	-3	O-15	-0.6
	Bro-F	37	126	7	31	3	2	0	18	4	9	.246	.269	.302	53	-9	6			.996	2	1-26/O-7,C	-0.8
	New-F	12	33	0	5	0	0	0	2	3	3	.152	.243	.152	7	-4	2			.986	-2	/1-8	-0.7
	Yr	75	225	10	54	7	3	0	26	10	17	.240	.278	.298	55	-15	10			.994	-2	1-34,O-22/C	-2.1
Total	5	277	913	84	238	46	12	2	117	59	44	.261	.314	.344	77	-30	23			.991	-3	1-225/O-23,C	-4.2

■ JACK BRADLEY
Bradley, John Thomas   b: 9/20/1893, Denver, Colo.   d: 3/18/69, Tulsa, Okla.   BR/TR, 5'11", 175 lbs.   Deb: 6/18/16

YEAR	TM/L	G	AB	R	H	2B	3B	HR	RBI	BB	SO	AVG	OBP	SLG	PRO+	BR/A	SB	CS	SBR	FA	FR	G/POS	TPR
1916	Cle-A	2	3	0	0	0	0	0	0	0	1	.000	.000	.000	-94	-1	0			1.000	-0	/C-1	-0.1

■ MARK BRADLEY
Bradley, Mark Allen   b: 12/3/56, Elizabethtown, Ky.   BR/TR, 6'1", 180 lbs.   Deb: 9/3/81

YEAR	TM/L	G	AB	R	H	2B	3B	HR	RBI	BB	SO	AVG	OBP	SLG	PRO+	BR/A	SB	CS	SBR	FA	FR	G/POS	TPR
1981	LA-N	9	6	2	1	1	0	0	0	1	1	.167	.167	.333	41	-1	0	0	0	1.000	-1	/O-6	-0.2
1982	LA-N	8	3	1	1	0	0	0	0	0	0	.333	.333	.333	89	-0	0	0	0	1.000	-1	/O-3	-0.1
1983	NY-N	73	104	10	21	4	0	3	5	11	35	.202	.278	.327	68	-5	4	2	0	1.000	-5	O-35	-1.1
Total	3	90	113	13	23	5	0	3	5	11	36	.204	.274	.327	67	-5	4	2	0	1.000	-7	/O-44	-1.4

■ PHIL BRADLEY
Bradley, Philip Poole   b: 3/11/59, Bloomington, Ind.   BR/TR, 6', 185 lbs.   Deb: 9/2/83

YEAR	TM/L	G	AB	R	H	2B	3B	HR	RBI	BB	SO	AVG	OBP	SLG	PRO+	BR/A	SB	CS	SBR	FA	FR	G/POS	TPR
1983	Sea-A	23	67	8	18	2	0	0	5	8	5	.269	.347	.299	77	-2	3	1	0	.974	-6	O-21/D-1	-0.8
1984	Sea-A	124	322	49	97	12	4	0	24	34	61	.301	.373	.363	106	4	21	8	2	.992	-11	*O-117/D-3	-0.8
1985	Sea-A★	159	641	100	192	33	8	26	88	55	129	.300	.366	.498	133	29	22	9	1	.986	6	*O-159	3.0
1986	Sea-A	143	526	88	163	27	4	12	50	77	134	.310	.406	.445	130	25	21	12	-1	.996	1	*O-140	2.1
1987	Sea-A	158	603	101	179	38	10	14	67	84	119	.297	.390	.463	119	18	40	10	6	.983	1	*O-158	1.9
1988	Phi-N	154	569	77	150	30	5	11	56	54	106	.264	.344	.392	109	7	11	9	-2	.990	9	*O-153	1.0
1989	Bal-A	144	545	83	151	23	10	11	55	70	103	.277	.367	.417	124	19	20	6	2	.990	-2	*O-140/D-2	1.5
1990	Bal-A	72	289	39	78	9	1	4	26	30	35	.270	.353	.340	100	1	10	4	1	.987	2	O-70/D-2	0.2
	Chi-A	45	133	20	30	5	1	0	5	20	26	.226	.344	.278	78	-3	7	3	0	.973	-4	O-38/D-7	-0.8
	Yr	117	422	59	108	14	2	4	31	50	61	.256	.350	.327	93	-2	17	7	1	.982	-3	*O-108/D-9	-0.6
Total	8	1022	3695	565	1058	179	43	78	376	432	718	.286	.371	.421	118	99	155	62	9	.988	-3	O-996/D-15	7.3

■ SCOTT BRADLEY
Bradley, Scott William   b: 3/22/60, Glen Ridge, N.J.   BL/TR, 5'11", 185 lbs.   Deb: 9/9/84

YEAR	TM/L	G	AB	R	H	2B	3B	HR	RBI	BB	SO	AVG	OBP	SLG	PRO+	BR/A	SB	CS	SBR	FA	FR	G/POS	TPR
1984	NY-A	9	21	3	6	1	0	0	2	1	1	.286	.318	.333	84	-0	0	0	0	1.000	-1	/O-5,C-3	-0.1
1985	NY-A	19	49	4	8	2	1	0	1	1	5	.163	.196	.245	20	-5	0	0	0	.923	-1	/C-3,D-9	-0.6
1986	Chi-A	9	21	3	6	0	0	0	1	1	5	.286	.375	.286	81	-0	0	2	-1	1.000	-0	/O-1,D-6	-0.2
	Sea-A	68	199	17	60	8	3	5	28	12	7	.302	.347	.447	113	3	1	0	0	.990	-13	C-59/D-3	-0.6
	Yr	77	220	20	66	8	3	5	29	13	7	.300	.350	.432	110	3	1	2	-1	.990	-14	C-59/D-9,O	-0.8
1987	Sea-A	102	342	34	95	15	1	5	43	15	18	.278	.314	.371	77	-11	0	1	-1	.983	-6	C-82/3-8,OD	-1.3
1988	Sea-A	103	335	45	86	17	1	4	33	17	16	.257	.297	.349	77	-11	1	1	0	.991	4	C-85/O-4,31	-0.1
1989	Sea-A	103	270	21	74	16	0	3	37	21	23	.274	.329	.367	93	-3	1	1	0	.993	3	C-70/1-2,OD	0.4
1990	Sea-A	101	233	11	52	9	1	0	28	15	19	.223	.270	.270	52	-15	1	1	0	.993	-5	C-63/3-5,1D	-1.2
1991	Sea-A	83	172	10	35	7	0	1	11	19	19	.203	.283	.244	47	-12	1	1	0	.993	-5	C-65/3-4,1D	-1.4
1992	Sea-A	2	1	0	0	0	0	0	0	1	1	.000	.500	.000	51	-0	0	0	0	1.000	1	/C-1	0.1

YEAR	TM/L	G	AB	R	H	2B	3B	HR	RBI	BB	SO	AVG	OBP	SLG	PRO+	BR/A	SB	CS	SBR	FA	FR	G/POS	TPR
	Cin-N	5	5	1	2	0	0	0	1	1	0	.400	.500	.400	154	0	0	0	0	1.000	-1	/C-2	0.0
Total	9	604	1648	149	424	75	6	18	184	104	110	.257	.306	.343	76	-54	3	6	-3	.990	-19	C-433/D-38,3O1	-5.0

■ BILL BRADLEY
Bradley, William Joseph b: 2/13/1878, Cleveland, Ohio d: 3/11/54, Cleveland, Ohio BR/TR, 6', 185 lbs. Deb: 8/26/1899 M

YEAR	TM/L	G	AB	R	H	2B	3B	HR	RBI	BB	SO	AVG	OBP	SLG	PRO+	BR/A	SB	CS	SBR	FA	FR	G/POS	TPR
1899	Chi-N	35	129	26	40	6	1	2	18	12		.310	.378	.419	122	4	4			.884	-3	3-30/S-5	0.1
1900	Chi-N	122	444	63	125	21	8	5	49	27		.282	.330	.399	104	1	14			.882	17	*3-106,1-15	1.7
1901	Cle-A	133	516	95	151	28	13	1	55	26		.293	.336	.403	109	5	15			.930	10	*3-133/P-1	1.5
1902	Cle-A	137	550	104	187	39	12	11	77	27		.340	.375	.515	151	35	11			.923	12	*3-137	4.4
1903	Cle-A	136	536	101	168	36	22	6	68	25		.313	.348	.496	154	33	21			.924	12	*3-136	4.7
1904	Cle-A	154	609	94	183	32	8	5	83	26		.300	.334	.404	134	22	23			.955	9	*3-154	3.9
1905	Cle-A	146	541	63	145	34	6	0	51	27		.268	.321	.353	112	7	22			.945	13	*3-146,M	2.8
1906	Cle-A	82	302	32	83	16	2	2	25	18		.275	.324	.361	116	5	13			.966	5	3-82	1.3
1907	Cle-A	139	498	48	111	20	1	0	34	35		.223	.286	.267	76	-13	20			.938	5	*3-139	-0.5
1908	Cle-A	148	548	70	133	24	7	1	46	29		.243	.297	.318	99	-1	18			.939	-31	*3-118,S-30	-3.1
1909	Cle-A	95	334	30	62	6	3	0	22	19		.186	.236	.222	43	-22	8			.957	-11	3-87/1-3,2	-3.4
1910	Cle-A	61	214	12	42	3	0	0	12	10		.196	.236	.210	39	-15	6			.956	-1	3-61	-1.6
1914	Bro-F	7	6	1	3	1	0	0	3	0	0	.500	.500	.667	202	1	0			.000	0	HM	0.1
1915	KC-F	66	203	15	38	9	1	0	9	9	18	.187	.225	.241	26	-22	6			.949	-6	3-61	-2.9
Total	14	1461	5430	754	1471	275	84	33	552	290	18	.271	.317	.371	107	40	181			.933	29	*3-1390/S-35,12P	9.0

■ DALLAS BRADSHAW
Bradshaw, Dallas Carl "Windy" b: 11/23/1895, Wolf Creek, Ill. d: 12/11/39, Herrin, Ill. BL/TR, 5'7", 145 lbs. Deb: 6/5/17

YEAR	TM/L	G	AB	R	H	2B	3B	HR	RBI	BB	SO	AVG	OBP	SLG	PRO+	BR/A	SB	CS	SBR	FA	FR	G/POS	TPR
1917	Phi-A	2	4	0	0	0	0	0	0	0	1	.000	.000	.000	-99	-1	0			1.000	1	/2-1	0.0

■ GEORGE BRADSHAW
Bradshaw, George Thomas b: 9/12/24, Salisbury, N.C. BR/TR, 6'2", 185 lbs. Deb: 8/10/52

YEAR	TM/L	G	AB	R	H	2B	3B	HR	RBI	BB	SO	AVG	OBP	SLG	PRO+	BR/A	SB	CS	SBR	FA	FR	G/POS	TPR
1952	Was-A	10	23	3	5	2	0	0	6	1	2	.217	.280	.304	65	-1	0	0	0	.917	-3	/C-9	-0.4

■ BRADY
Brady Deb: 9/25/1875

YEAR	TM/L	G	AB	R	H	2B	3B	HR	RBI	BB	SO	AVG	OBP	SLG	PRO+	BR/A	SB	CS	SBR	FA	FR	G/POS	TPR
1875	Chi-n	1	4	1	1	0	1	0		0		.250	.250	.750	230	1						/O-1	0.0

■ BRIAN BRADY
Brady, Brian Phelan b: 7/11/62, Elmhurst, N.Y. BL/TL, 5'11", 185 lbs. Deb: 4/16/89

YEAR	TM/L	G	AB	R	H	2B	3B	HR	RBI	BB	SO	AVG	OBP	SLG	PRO+	BR/A	SB	CS	SBR	FA	FR	G/POS	TPR
1989	Cal-A	2	2	0	1	1	0	0	1	0	1	.500	.500	1.000	319	1	0	0	0	.000	-0	/O-1	0.0

■ CLIFF BRADY
Brady, Clifford Francis b: 3/6/1897, St.Louis, Mo. d: 9/25/74, Belleville, Ill. BR/TR, 5'5.5", 140 lbs. Deb: 8/8/20

YEAR	TM/L	G	AB	R	H	2B	3B	HR	RBI	BB	SO	AVG	OBP	SLG	PRO+	BR/A	SB	CS	SBR	FA	FR	G/POS	TPR
1920	Bos-A	53	180	16	41	5	1	0	12	13	12	.228	.284	.267	48	-13	0	1	-1	.974	17	2-53	0.5

■ BOB BRADY
Brady, Robert Jay b: 11/8/22, Lewistown, Pa. BL/TR, 6'1", 175 lbs. Deb: 8/24/46

YEAR	TM/L	G	AB	R	H	2B	3B	HR	RBI	BB	SO	AVG	OBP	SLG	PRO+	BR/A	SB	CS	SBR	FA	FR	G/POS	TPR
1946	Bos-N	3	5	0	1	0	0	0	0	1	1	.200	.333	.200	52	-0	0			.857	0	/C-1	0.0
1947	Bos-N	1	1	0	0	0	0	0	0	0	0	.000	.000	.000	-99	-0	0			.000	0	H	0.0
Total	2	4	6	0	1	0	0	0	0	1	1	.167	.286	.167	29	-1	0			.857	0	/C-1	0.0

■ STEVE BRADY
Brady, Stephen A. b: 7/14/1851, Worcester, Mass. d: 11/1/17, Hartford, Conn. 5'9.5", 165 lbs. Deb: 7/23/1874

YEAR	TM/L	G	AB	R	H	2B	3B	HR	RBI	BB	SO	AVG	OBP	SLG	PRO+	BR/A	SB	CS	SBR	FA	FR	G/POS	TPR
1874	Har-n	27	115	19	38	5	2	0		3		.330	.347	.409	133	4						3-17/O-8	0.3
1875	Was-n	21	90	6	13	1	1	0		0		.144	.144	.178	11	-7						2-16/O-2,1	-0.7
	Har-n	1	4	0	0	0	0	0		0		.000	.000	.000	-95	-1						/O-1	-0.1
	Yr	22	94	6	13	1	1	0		0		.138	.138	.170	6	-8						2-16/O-3,1	-0.8
1883	NY-a	97	432	69	117	12	6	0		11		.271	.289	.326	94	-4				.961	3	*1-81,O-16	-0.8
1884	*NY-a	112	485	102	122	11	3	1		21		.252	.283	.293	90	-5				.918	1	*O-110/1-5,2	-0.5
1885	NY-a	108	434	60	128	14	5	3		25		.295	.342	.371	136	19				.879	-6	*O-105/1-4,23	0.9
1886	NY-a	124	466	56	112	8	5	0		35		.240	.298	.279	85	-7	16			.830	-5	*O-123/1-1	-1.3
Total	2 n	49	209	25	51	6	3	0		3		.244	.255	.301	82	-5	0					/3-17,2-16,O1	-0.5
Total	4	441	1817	287	479	45	19	4		92		.264	.302	.316	100	3	16			.875	-6	O-354/1-91,23	-1.7

■ BOBBY BRAGAN
Bragan, Robert Randall "Nig" b: 10/30/17, Birmingham, Ala. BR/TR, 5'10.5", 175 lbs. Deb: 4/16/40 MC

YEAR	TM/L	G	AB	R	H	2B	3B	HR	RBI	BB	SO	AVG	OBP	SLG	PRO+	BR/A	SB	CS	SBR	FA	FR	G/POS	TPR
1940	Phi-N	132	474	36	105	14	1	7	44	28	34	.222	.265	.300	58	-28	2			.936	1	*S-132/3-2	-1.7
1941	Phi-N	154	557	37	140	19	3	4	69	26	29	.251	.285	.318	72	-22	7			.944	-7	*S-154/2-2,3	-1.8
1942	Phi-N	109	335	17	73	12	2	2	15	20	21	.218	.264	.284	63	-16	0			.939	9	S-78,C-22/23	-0.1
1943	Bro-N	74	220	17	58	7	2	2	24	15	16	.264	.311	.341	88	-4	0			.973	6	C-57,3-12	0.5
1944	Bro-N	94	266	26	71	8	4	0	17	13	14	.267	.304	.327	79	-8	2			.954	-0	S-51,C-35/32	-0.3
1947	*Bro-N	25	36	3	7	2	0	0	3	7	3	.194	.326	.250	53	-2	1			1.000	0	C-21	0.2
1948	Bro-N	9	12	0	2	0	0	0	0	1	0	.167	.231	.167	9	-2	0			1.000	-0	/C-5	-0.2
Total	7	597	1900	136	456	62	12	15	172	110	117	.240	.282	.309	69	-82	12			.941	10	S-415,C-140/32	-3.4

■ DARREN BRAGG
Bragg, Darren William b: 9/7/69, Waterbury, Conn. BL/TR, 5'9", 180 lbs. Deb: 4/12/94

YEAR	TM/L	G	AB	R	H	2B	3B	HR	RBI	BB	SO	AVG	OBP	SLG	PRO+	BR/A	SB	CS	SBR	FA	FR	G/POS	TPR
1994	Sea-A	8	19	4	3	1	0	0	2	2	5	.158	.238	.211	17	-2	0	0	0	1.000	-1	/O-3,D-3	-0.3

■ GLENN BRAGGS
Braggs, Glenn Erick b: 10/17/62, San Bernardino, Cal BR/TR, 6'3", 210 lbs. Deb: 7/18/86

YEAR	TM/L	G	AB	R	H	2B	3B	HR	RBI	BB	SO	AVG	OBP	SLG	PRO+	BR/A	SB	CS	SBR	FA	FR	G/POS	TPR
1986	Mil-A	58	215	19	51	8	2	4	18	11	47	.237	.278	.349	67	-10	1	1	-0	.910	1	O-56/D-2	-1.1
1987	Mil-A	132	505	67	136	28	7	13	77	47	96	.269	.336	.430	98	-1	12	5	1	.972	14	*O-123/D-8	0.9
1988	Mil-A	72	272	30	71	14	0	10	42	14	60	.261	.309	.423	102	0	6	4	-1	.978	4	O-54,D-18	0.1
1989	Mil-A	144	514	77	127	12	3	15	66	42	111	.247	.309	.370	91	-6	17	5	2	.972	-0	*O-132,D-13	-0.8
1990	Mil-A	37	113	19	28	5	0	3	13	12	21	.248	.336	.372	98	-0	5	3	-0	.965	2	O-32/D-2	0.1
	*Cin-N	72	201	22	60	9	1	6	28	26	43	.299	.387	.443	122	7	3	4	-2	.968	6	O-60	1.0
1991	Cin-N	85	250	36	65	10	0	11	39	23	46	.260	.327	.432	108	2	11	3	2	.966	-2	O-74	0.0
1992	Cin-N	92	266	40	63	16	3	8	38	36	48	.237	.332	.410	106	2	3	1	0	.946	-9	O-79	-0.8
Total	7	692	2336	308	601	102	16	70	321	211	472	.257	.325	.405	98	-6	58	26	2	.963	16	O-610/D-43	-0.6

■ DAVE BRAIN
Brain, David Leonard b: 1/24/1879, Hereford, England d: 5/25/59, Los Angeles, Cal. BR/TR, 5'10", 170 lbs. Deb: 4/24/01

YEAR	TM/L	G	AB	R	H	2B	3B	HR	RBI	BB	SO	AVG	OBP	SLG	PRO+	BR/A	SB	CS	SBR	FA	FR	G/POS	TPR
1901	Chi-A	5	20	2	7	1	0	0	5	1		.350	.381	.400	120	1	0			.909	1	/2-5	0.1
1903	StL-N	119	464	44	107	8	15	1	60	25		.231	.270	.319	70	-20	21			.908	10	S-72,3-46	-0.6
1904	StL-N	127	488	57	130	24	12	7	72	17		.266	.291	.408	120	8	18			.927	3	S-59,3-30,O2/1	1.4
1905	StL-N	44	158	11	36	4	5	1	17	8		.228	.269	.335	82	-4	4			.910	-9	S-29/3-6,O	-1.3
	Pit-N	85	307	31	79	17	6	3	46	15		.257	.296	.381	99	-2	8			.923	6	3-78/S-4	0.7
	Yr	129	465	42	115	21	11	4	63	23		.247	.287	.366	93	-6	12			.929	-3	3-84,S-33/O	-0.6
1906	Bos-N	139	525	43	131	19	5	5	45	29		.250	.293	.333	98	-3	11			.917	26	*3-139	2.9
1907	Bos-N	133	509	60	142	24	9	**10**	56	29		.279	.324	.420	134	17	10			.916	25	*3-130/O-3	5.0
1908	Cin-N	16	55	4	6	0	0	0	1	8		.109	.222	.109	7	-5	0			.947	-1	O-16	-0.8
	NY-N	11	17	2	3	0	0	0	1	2		.176	.263	.176	39	-1	1			.867	-3	/2-3,O-3,3S	-0.4
	Yr	27	72	6	9	0	0	0	2	10		.125	.232	.125	14	-7	1			.947	-3	O-19/2-3,3S	-1.2
Total	7	679	2543	254	641	97	52	27	303	134		.252	.292	.363	101	-10	73			.913	58	3-431,S-165/O21	7.0

■ ASA BRAINARD
Brainard, Asa "Count" b: 1841, Albany, N.Y. d: 12/29/1888, Denver, Colo. TR, 5'8.5", 150 lbs. Deb: 5/5/1871

YEAR	TM/L	G	AB	R	H	2B	3B	HR	RBI	BB	SO	AVG	OBP	SLG	PRO+	BR/A	SB	CS	SBR	FA	FR	G/POS	TPR
1871	Oly-n	30	134	24	30	4	0	0	21	7	2	.224	.262	.254	52	-7	4					*P-30	0.0
1872	Oly-n	9	41	8	16	3	0	0	6	0	0	.390	.390	.463	170	3						/P-9	0.0
	Man-n	6	25	2	5	0	0	0	0	0	0	.200	.231	.200	36	-2						/2-4,P-2	-0.1
	Yr	15	66	10	21	3	0	0	6	0	0	.318	.328	.364	119	2						P-11/2-4	-0.1
1873	Bal-n	16	69	18	18	2	0	0	8	0	2	.261	.261	.290	62	-3						P-14/O-2,2	0.1

YEAR	TM/L	G	AB	R	H	2B	3B	HR	RBI	BB	SO	AVG	OBP	SLG	PRO+	BR/A	SB	CS	SBR	FA	FR	G/POS	TPR
1874	Bal-n	46	198	19	50	5	0	0			2	.253	.260	.278	72	-6						P-29,2-17/O	0.1
Total	4 n	107	467	71	119	14	0	0			10	.255	.270	.285	71	-14						/P-84,2-22,O	0.1

■ FRED BRAINERD
Brainerd, Frederick F.   b: 2/17/1892, Champaign, Ill.   d: 4/17/59, Galveston, Tex.   BR/TR, 6', 176 lbs.   Deb: 10/6/14

YEAR	TM/L	G	AB	R	H	2B	3B	HR	RBI	BB	SO	AVG	OBP	SLG	PRO+	BR/A	SB	CS	SBR	FA	FR	G/POS	TPR
1914	NY-N	2	5	1	1	0	0	0	0	1	0	.200	.333	.200	62	-0				.923	1	/2-2	0.1
1915	NY-N	91	249	31	50	7	5	1	21	21	44	.201	.266	.257	62	-11	6	7	-2	.988	7	1-43,3-15/S20	-0.8
1916	NY-N	2	7	0	0	0	0	0	0	0	0	.000	.000	.000	-99	-2				.625	-1	/3-2	-0.3
Total	3	95	261	32	51	7	5	1	21	22	44	.195	.261	.249	58	-13	6	7		.857	7	/1-43,3-17,S20	-1.0

■ ART BRAMHALL
Bramhall, Arthur Washington   b: 2/22/09, Oak Park, Ill.   d: 9/4/85, Madison, Wis.   BR/TR, 5'11", 170 lbs.   Deb: 4/18/35

YEAR	TM/L	G	AB	R	H	2B	3B	HR	RBI	BB	SO	AVG	OBP	SLG	PRO+	BR/A	SB	CS	SBR	FA	FR	G/POS	TPR
1935	Phi-N	2	1	0	0	0	0	0	0	0	0	.000	.000	.000	-91	-0	0			1.000	1	/S-1,3-1	0.0

■ AL BRANCATO
Brancato, Albert "Bronk"   b: 5/29/19, Philadelphia, Pa.   BR/TR, 5'9.5", 188 lbs.   Deb: 9/7/39

YEAR	TM/L	G	AB	R	H	2B	3B	HR	RBI	BB	SO	AVG	OBP	SLG	PRO+	BR/A	SB	CS	SBR	FA	FR	G/POS	TPR
1939	Phi-A	21	68	12	14	5	0	1	8	8	4	.206	.299	.324	60	-4	1	0	0	.939	-1	3-20/S-1	-0.5
1940	Phi-A	107	298	42	57	11	2	1	23	28	36	.191	.265	.252	36	-29	3	1	0	.949	5	S-80,3-25	-2.1
1941	Phi-A	144	530	60	124	20	9	2	49	59	49	.234	.311	.317	68	-24	1	5	-3	.915	-19	*S-139/3-7	-3.5
1945	Phi-A	10	34	3	4	1	0	0	0	1	3	.118	.143	.147	-16	-5	0	0	0	.959	-1	S-10	-0.6
Total	4	282	930	117	199	37	11	4	80	96	92	.214	.290	.290	54	-62	5	6	-2	.927	-21	S-230/3-52	-6.7

■ RON BRAND
Brand, Ronald George   b: 1/13/40, Los Angeles, Cal.   BR/TR, 5'8", 170 lbs.   Deb: 5/26/63

YEAR	TM/L	G	AB	R	H	2B	3B	HR	RBI	BB	SO	AVG	OBP	SLG	PRO+	BR/A	SB	CS	SBR	FA	FR	G/POS	TPR
1963	Pit-N	46	66	8	19	2	0	1	7	10	11	.288	.390	.364	118	2	0	1		.968	9	C-33/2-2,3	1.2
1965	Hou-N	117	391	27	92	6	3	2	37	19	34	.235	.281	.281	63	-19	10	5	0	.988	-7	*C-102/3-6,O	-2.3
1966	Hou-N	56	123	12	30	7	0	0	10	9	13	.244	.306	.260	64	-6	0	2	-1	.986	-5	C-25/2-9,O3	-1.1
1967	Hou-N	84	215	22	52	8	1	0	18	23	17	.242	.321	.288	78	-5	4	0	1	.998	-3	C-67/2-1,O	-0.4
1968	Hou-N	43	81	7	13	2	0	0	4	9	11	.160	.261	.185	36	-6	1	1	-0	1.000	1	C-29/3-1,O	-0.2
1969	Mon-N	103	287	19	74	12	0	0	20	30	19	.258	.330	.300	77	-8	2	3	1	.985	-8	C-84/O-2	-1.3
1970	Mon-N	72	126	10	30	2	3	0	9	9	16	.238	.289	.302	59	-7	2	1	0	.952	-7	S-19,3-12/CO2	-1.3
1971	Mon-N	47	56	3	12	0	0	0	1	3	5	.214	.254	.214	34	-5	1	1	0	.957	3	S-22/3-4,OC2	-0.1
Total	8	568	1345	108	322	34	7	3	106	112	126	.239	.305	.282	68	-55	20	13	-2	.988	-16	C-350/S-41,3O2	-5.5

■ JACKIE BRANDT
Brandt, John George   b: 4/28/34, Omaha, Neb.   BR/TR, 5'11", 170 lbs.   Deb: 4/21/56

YEAR	TM/L	G	AB	R	H	2B	3B	HR	RBI	BB	SO	AVG	OBP	SLG	PRO+	BR/A	SB	CS	SBR	FA	FR	G/POS	TPR
1956	StL-N	27	42	9	12	3	0	1	3	4	5	.286	.362	.429	111	1	0	1	-1	1.000	-3	O-26	-0.4
	NY-N	98	351	45	105	16	8	11	47	17	31	.299	.332	.484	116	7	3	4	-2	.989	-6	O-96	-0.5
	Yr	125	393	54	117	19	8	12	50	21	36	.298	.335	.478	116	8	3	5	-2	.990	-9	*O-122	-0.9
1958	SF-N	18	52	7	13	1	0	0	3	6	5	.250	.328	.269	62	-3	1	0	0	1.000	-0	O-14	-0.3
1959	SF-N	137	429	63	116	16	5	12	57	35	69	.270	.325	.415	98	-2	11	4	1	.984	-7	*O-116,3-18/12	-1.3
1960	Bal-A	145	511	73	130	24	6	15	65	47	69	.254	.321	.413	98	-2	5	3	-0	.983	-10	*O-142/3-2,1	-2.0
1961	Bal-A★	139	516	93	153	18	5	16	72	62	51	.297	.373	.444	122	16	10	2	0	.974	-16	*O-136/3-1	-0.6
1962	Bal-A	143	505	76	129	29	5	19	75	55	64	.255	.333	.446	115	9	9	3	1	.976	9	*O-138/3-2	1.1
1963	Bal-A	142	451	49	112	15	5	15	61	34	85	.248	.301	.404	99	-2	4	5	-2	.986	-7	*O-134/3-1	-1.8
1964	Bal-A	137	523	66	127	25	1	13	47	45	104	.243	.306	.369	87	-9	1	4	-2	.981	16	*O-134	-0.2
1965	Bal-A	96	243	35	59	17	0	8	24	21	40	.243	.303	.412	99	-1	1	2	-1	.961	-6	O-84	-1.1
1966	Phi-N	82	164	16	41	6	1	1	15	17	36	.250	.320	.317	78	-4	0	2	-1	.988	-12	O-71	-2.1
1967	Phi-N	16	19	1	2	1	0	0	1	0	6	.105	.105	.158	-25	-3	0	0	0	1.000	-1	/O-3	-0.4
	Hou-N	41	89	7	21	4	1	1	15	8	9	.236	.299	.337	85	-2	0	0	0	.991	-2	1-14/O-6,3	-0.6
	Yr	57	108	8	23	5	1	1	16	8	15	.213	.267	.306	65	-5	0	0	0	.991	-3	1-14/O-9,3	-1.0
Total	11	1221	3895	540	1020	175	37	112	485	351	574	.262	.325	.412	102	5	45	30	-4	.980	-46	*O-1100/3-25,12	-10.2

■ OTIS BRANNAN
Brannan, Otis Owen   b: 3/13/1899, Greenbrier, Ark.   d: 6/6/67, Little Rock, Ark.   BL/TR, 5'9", 160 lbs.   Deb: 4/11/28

YEAR	TM/L	G	AB	R	H	2B	3B	HR	RBI	BB	SO	AVG	OBP	SLG	PRO+	BR/A	SB	CS	SBR	FA	FR	G/POS	TPR
1928	StL-A	135	483	68	118	18	3	10	66	60	19	.244	.333	.356	79	-15	3	9	-5	.964	-8	*2-135	-2.3
1929	StL-A	23	51	4	15	1	0	1	8	4	4	.294	.345	.373	82	-1	0	0	0	.975	-1	2-19	-0.2
Total	2	158	534	72	133	19	3	11	74	64	23	.249	.334	.358	79	-15	3	9	-5	.966	-9	2-154	-2.5

■ MIKE BRANNOCK
Brannock, Michael J.   b: 1853, Guelph, Ont., Canada   5'8", 162 lbs.   Deb: 10/21/1871

YEAR	TM/L	G	AB	R	H	2B	3B	HR	RBI	BB	SO	AVG	OBP	SLG	PRO+	BR/A	SB	CS	SBR	FA	FR	G/POS	TPR
1871	Chi-n	3	14	2	1	0	0	0	0	0	0	.071	.071	.071	-53	-3	0					/3-3	-0.2
1875	Chi-n	2	9	2	1	0	0	0	0	0	0	.111	.111	.111	-23	-1						/3-2	-0.1
Total	2 n	5	23	4	2	0	0	0			0	.087	.087	.087	-43	-4						/3-5	-0.3

■ DUD BRANOM
Branom, Edgar Dudley   b: 11/30/1897, Sulphur Springs, Tex.   d: 2/4/80, Sun City, Ariz.   BL/TL, 6'1", 190 lbs.   Deb: 4/12/27

YEAR	TM/L	G	AB	R	H	2B	3B	HR	RBI	BB	SO	AVG	OBP	SLG	PRO+	BR/A	SB	CS	SBR	FA	FR	G/POS	TPR
1927	Phi-A	30	94	8	22	1	0	0	13	2	5	.234	.250	.245	27	-10	2	1	0	.973	-0	1-26	-1.1

■ KITTY BRANSFIELD
Bransfield, William Edward   b: 1/7/1875, Worcester, Mass.   d: 5/1/47, Worcester, Mass.   BR/TR, 5'11", 207 lbs.   Deb: 8/22/1898   U

YEAR	TM/L	G	AB	R	H	2B	3B	HR	RBI	BB	SO	AVG	OBP	SLG	PRO+	BR/A	SB	CS	SBR	FA	FR	G/POS	TPR
1898	Bos-N	5	9	2	2	0	1	0	1	0	0	.222	.222	.444	85	-0	0			.889	-1	/C-4,1-1	-0.1
1901	Pit-N	139	566	92	167	26	16	0	91	29		.295	.335	.398	109	5	23			.981	-10	*1-139	-0.7
1902	Pit-N	102	413	49	126	21	8	0	69	17		.305	.336	.395	121	8	23			.984	-6	*1-101	0.1
1903	*Pit-N	127	505	69	134	23	7	2	57	33		.265	.314	.350	87	-10	13			.981	6	*1-127	-0.6
1904	Pit-N	139	520	47	116	17	4	0	60	22		.223	.259	.290	68	-21	11			.981	-3	*1-139	-2.9
1905	Phi-N	151	580	55	150	23	9	3	76	27		.259	.294	.345	93	-7	27			.985	-1	*1-151	-1.3
1906	Phi-N	140	524	47	144	28	5	1	60	16		.275	.300	.353	104	-1	12			.980	-2	*1-139	-0.7
1907	Phi-N	94	348	25	81	15	2	0	38	14		.233	.262	.287	73	-12	8			.978	-3	1-92	-2.0
1908	Phi-N	144	527	53	160	25	7	3	71	23		.304	.335	.395	128	15	30			.986	-1	*1-143	1.3
1909	Phi-N	140	527	47	154	27	6	1	59	18		.292	.319	.372	113	8	17			**.989**	7	*1-138	1.3
1910	Phi-N	123	427	39	102	17	4	3	52	20	34	.239	.275	.319	71	-18	10			.982	-4	*1-110	-2.4
1911	Phi-N	23	43	4	11	1	1	0	3	0	5	.256	.256	.326	61	-2	1			.987	0	/1-8	-0.2
	Chi-N	3	10	0	4	2	0	0	2	0	2	.400	.500	.600	207	2	0			1.000	-0	/1-3	0.1
	Yr	26	53	4	15	3	1	0	3	2	7	.283	.309	.377	91	-0	1			.991	-0	1-11	-0.1
Total	12	1330	4999	529	1351	225	75	13	637	221	41	.270	.304	.353	97	-35	175			.983	-18	*1-1291/C-4	-8.1

■ JEFF BRANSON
Branson, Jeffery Glenn   b: 1/26/67, Waynesboro, Miss.   BL/TR, 6', 180 lbs.   Deb: 4/12/92

YEAR	TM/L	G	AB	R	H	2B	3B	HR	RBI	BB	SO	AVG	OBP	SLG	PRO+	BR/A	SB	CS	SBR	FA	FR	G/POS	TPR
1992	Cin-N	72	115	12	34	7	1	0	15	5	16	.296	.325	.374	95	-1	0	1	-1	.946	2	2-33/3-8,S	0.1
1993	Cin-N	125	381	40	92	15	1	3	22	19	73	.241	.278	.310	57	-23	4	1	1	.978	5	S-59,2-45,3/1	-1.3
1994	Cin-N	58	109	18	31	4	1	6	16	5	16	.284	.316	.505	110	1	0	0	0	.980	-4	2-19,3-18/S1	-0.2
Total	3	255	605	70	157	26	3	9	53	29	105	.260	.293	.357	74	-23	4	2	0	.966	3	/2-97,S-68,31	-1.4

■ MARSHALL BRANT
Brant, Marshall Lee   b: 9/17/55, Garberville, Cal.   BR/TR, 6'5", 185 lbs.   Deb: 10/1/80

YEAR	TM/L	G	AB	R	H	2B	3B	HR	RBI	BB	SO	AVG	OBP	SLG	PRO+	BR/A	SB	CS	SBR	FA	FR	G/POS	TPR
1980	NY-A	3	6	0	0	0	0	0	0	0	0	.000	.000	.000	-99	-2	0	0	0	1.000	0	/1-2,D-1	-0.1
1983	Oak-A	5	14	2	2	0	0	0	2	0	3	.143	.143	.143	-22	-2	0	0	0	.905	-1	/1-3,D-1	-0.4
Total	2	8	20	2	2	0	0	0	2	0	3	.100	.100	.100	-47	-4	0	0	0	.935	-1	/1-5,D-2	-0.5

■ MICKEY BRANTLEY
Brantley, Michael Charles   b: 6/17/61, Catskill, N.Y.   BR/TR, 5'10", 180 lbs.   Deb: 8/9/86

YEAR	TM/L	G	AB	R	H	2B	3B	HR	RBI	BB	SO	AVG	OBP	SLG	PRO+	BR/A	SB	CS	SBR	FA	FR	G/POS	TPR
1986	Sea-A	27	102	12	20	3	2	3	7	10	21	.196	.268	.353	67	-5	1	1	-0	.983	0	O-25	-0.6
1987	Sea-A	92	351	52	106	23	2	14	54	24	44	.302	.347	.499	115	7	13	4	2	.982	-6	O-82/D-8	-0.1
1988	Sea-A	149	577	76	152	25	4	15	56	26	64	.263	.298	.399	89	-10	18	7	1	.982	-5	*O-147/D-2	-1.8
1989	Sea-A	34	108	14	17	5	0	0	8	7	7	.157	.209	.204	16	-12	2	2	0	1.000	1	O-23/D-7	-1.2
Total	4	302	1138	154	295	56	8	32	125	67	136	.259	.302	.407	89	-20	34	14	2	.984	-9	O-277/D-17	-3.7

YEAR	TM/L	G	AB	R	H	2B	3B	HR	RBI	BB	SO	AVG	OBP	SLG	PRO+	BR/A	SB	CS	SBR	FA	FR	G/POS	TPR

■ ROY BRASHEAR
Brashear, Roy Parks b: 1/3/1874, Ashtabula, Ohio d: 4/20/51, Los Angeles, Cal. BR/TR, 5'11", 205 lbs. Deb: 4/25/02 F

YEAR	TM/L	G	AB	R	H	2B	3B	HR	RBI	BB	SO	AVG	OBP	SLG	PRO+	BR/A	SB	CS	SBR	FA	FR	G/POS	TPR
1902	StL-N	110	388	36	107	8	2	1	40	32		.276	.333	.314	104	2	9			.980	-9	1-67,2-21,O/S	-0.8
1903	Phi-N	20	75	9	17	3	0	0	4	6		.227	.284	.267	59	-4	2			.918	-4	2-18/1-2	-0.7
Total	2	130	463	45	124	11	2	1	44	38		.268	.325	.307	96	-2	11			.978	-13	/1-69,2-39,OS	-1.5

■ JOE BRATCHER
Bratcher, Joseph Warlick "Goobers" b: 7/22/1898, Grand Saline, Tex d: 10/13/77, Fort Worth, Tex. BL/TR, 5'8.5", 140 lbs. Deb: 8/26/24

YEAR	TM/L	G	AB	R	H	2B	3B	HR	RBI	BB	SO	AVG	OBP	SLG	PRO+	BR/A	SB	CS	SBR	FA	FR	G/POS	TPR
1924	StL-N	4	1	1	0	0	0	0	0	0	0	.000	.000	.000	-99	-0	0	0	0	.000	-1	/O-1	-0.1

■ FRED BRATSCHI
Bratschi, Frederick Oscar "Fritz" b: 1/16/1892, Alliance, Ohio d: 1/10/62, Massillon, Ohio BR/TR, 5'10", 170 lbs. Deb: 7/24/21

YEAR	TM/L	G	AB	R	H	2B	3B	HR	RBI	BB	SO	AVG	OBP	SLG	PRO+	BR/A	SB	CS	SBR	FA	FR	G/POS	TPR
1921	Chi-A	16	28	0	8	1	0	0	3	0	2	.286	.286	.321	55	-2	0	0	0	1.000	-0	/O-5	-0.1
1926	Bos-A	72	167	12	46	10	1	0	19	14	15	.275	.335	.347	81	-5	0	1	-1	.949	-7	O-37	-1.4
1927	Bos-A	1	1	0	0	0	0	0	0	0	0	.000	.000	.000	-99	-0	0	0	0	.000	0	H	0.0
Total	3	89	196	12	54	11	1	0	22	14	17	.276	.327	.342	76	-7	0	1	-1	.956	-6	/O-42	-1.5

■ STEVE BRAUN
Braun, Stephen Russell b: 5/8/48, Trenton, N.J. BL/TR, 5'10", 180 lbs. Deb: 4/6/71 C

YEAR	TM/L	G	AB	R	H	2B	3B	HR	RBI	BB	SO	AVG	OBP	SLG	PRO+	BR/A	SB	CS	SBR	FA	FR	G/POS	TPR
1971	Min-A	128	343	51	87	12	2	5	35	48	50	.254	.344	.344	95	-1	8	3	1	.933	-13	3-73,2-28,S/O	-1.1
1972	Min-A	121	402	40	116	21	4	2	50	45	38	.289	.363	.356	109	6	4	5	-2	.970	-12	3-74,2-20,S/O	-0.8
1973	Min-A	115	361	46	102	28	5	6	42	74	48	.283	.409	.438	133	19	4	3	-1	.941	-11	*3-102/O-6	0.7
1974	Min-A	129	453	53	127	12	1	8	40	56	51	.280	.362	.364	105	5	4	4	-1	.964	-6	*O-108,3-17	0.1
1975	Min-A	136	453	70	137	18	3	11	45	66	55	.302	.392	.428	129	19	0	2	-1	.971	-2	*O-106/1-9,32D	1.2
1976	Min-A	122	417	73	120	12	3	3	61	67	43	.288	.388	.353	114	11	12	4	1	.971	-3	D-71,O-32,3	0.6
1977	Sea-A	139	451	51	106	19	1	5	31	80	59	.235	.353	.315	84	-7	8	3	1	.975	5	*O-100,D-32/3	-0.6
1978	Sea-A	32	74	11	17	4	0	3	15	9	5	.230	.313	.405	101	0	1	0	0	1.000	-1	D-14/O-4	-0.1
	*KC-A	64	137	16	36	10	1	0	14	28	16	.263	.388	.350	106	3	3	2	0	.964	-5	O-33,3-11	-0.5
	Yr	96	211	27	53	14	1	3	29	37	21	.251	.363	.370	105	3	4	2	0	.967	-6	O-37,D-14,3	-0.6
1979	KC-A	58	116	15	31	2	0	4	10	22	11	.267	.384	.388	107	2	0	0	0	1.000	1	O-18,D-11/3	0.2
1980	KC-A	14	23	0	1	0	0	0	1	2	2	.043	.120	.043	-53	-5	0	0	0	1.000	-2	/O-5,D-1	-0.7
	Tor-A	37	55	4	15	2	0	1	9	8	5	.273	.365	.364	96	-0	0	0	0	1.000	0	D-13/3-1	0.0
	Yr	51	78	4	16	2	0	1	10	10	7	.205	.295	.269	54	-5	0	0	0	1.000	-2	D-14/O-5,3	-0.7
1981	StL-N	44	46	9	9	2	1	0	2	15	7	.196	.393	.283	92	-0	0	0	0	1.000	-1	O-12/3-1	0.0
1982	*StL-N	58	62	6	17	4	0	0	4	11	10	.274	.384	.339	103	0	0	0	0	1.000	-5	O-8,3-5	-0.4
1983	StL-N	78	92	8	25	2	1	3	7	21	7	.272	.407	.413	128	4	0	1	-1	1.000	-5	O-22/3-4	-0.2
1984	StL-N	86	98	6	27	6	1	0	16	17	17	.276	.383	.327	104	3	0	0	0	1.000	-5	O-19/3-1	-0.4
1985	*StL-N	64	67	7	16	4	0	1	6	10	9	.239	.346	.343	94	-0	0	0	0	1.000	-2	O-14	-0.3
Total	15	1425	3650	466	989	155	19	52	388	579	433	.271	.373	.367	108	59	45	27	-3	.973	-57	O-498,3-310,D/2S1	-2.2

■ ANGEL BRAVO
Bravo, Angel Alfonso (Urdaneta) b: 8/4/42, Maracaibo, Venez. BL/TL, 5'8", 150 lbs. Deb: 6/6/69

YEAR	TM/L	G	AB	R	H	2B	3B	HR	RBI	BB	SO	AVG	OBP	SLG	PRO+	BR/A	SB	CS	SBR	FA	FR	G/POS	TPR
1969	Chi-A	27	90	10	26	4	1	0	3	3	5	.289	.319	.411	98	-0	0	0	1	.978	-4	O-25	-0.6
1970	*Cin-N	65	65	10	18	1	1	0	3	9	13	.277	.365	.323	86	-1	0	1	-1	.947	-5	O-22	-0.7
1971	Cin-N	5	5	0	1	0	0	0	0	1	1	.200	.200	.200	14	-1	0	0	0	.000	0	H	-0.1
	SD-N	52	58	6	9	2	0	0	6	8	12	.155	.269	.190	34	-5	0	1	-1	.833	-3	O-9	-0.9
	Yr	57	63	6	10	2	0	0	6	8	13	.159	.264	.190	33	-5	0	1	-1	.833	-3	/O-9	-1.0
Total	3	149	218	26	54	7	3	1	12	20	31	.248	.317	.321	77	-7	2	2	-1	.957	-12	/O-56	-2.3

■ BUSTER BRAY
Bray, Clarence Wilbur b: 4/1/13, Birmingham, Ala. d: 9/4/82, Evansville, Ind. BL/TL, 6', 170 lbs. Deb: 4/18/41

YEAR	TM/L	G	AB	R	H	2B	3B	HR	RBI	BB	SO	AVG	OBP	SLG	PRO+	BR/A	SB	CS	SBR	FA	FR	G/POS	TPR
1941	Bos-N	4	11	2	1	1	0	0	1	1	2	.091	.167	.182	-2	-2	0			1.000	-0	/O-3	-0.2

■ FRANK BRAZILL
Brazill, Frank Leo b: 8/11/1899, Spangler, Pa. d: 11/3/76, Oakland, Cal. BL/TR, 5'11.5", 175 lbs. Deb: 4/13/21

YEAR	TM/L	G	AB	R	H	2B	3B	HR	RBI	BB	SO	AVG	OBP	SLG	PRO+	BR/A	SB	CS	SBR	FA	FR	G/POS	TPR
1921	Phi-A	66	177	17	48	3	1	0	19	23	21	.271	.361	.299	70	-7	2	4	-2	.984	-1	1-36/3-9	-1.0
1922	Phi-A	6	13	0	1	0	0	0	1	0	1	.077	.077	.077	-58	-3	0	0	0	.750	-2	/3-2	-0.5
Total	2	72	190	17	49	3	1	0	20	23	22	.258	.344	.284	62	-10	2	4	-2	.892	-3	/1-36,3-11	-1.5

■ SID BREAM
Bream, Sidney Eugene b: 8/3/60, Carlisle, Pa. BL/TL, 6'4", 220 lbs. Deb: 9/1/83

YEAR	TM/L	G	AB	R	H	2B	3B	HR	RBI	BB	SO	AVG	OBP	SLG	PRO+	BR/A	SB	CS	SBR	FA	FR	G/POS	TPR
1983	LA-N	15	11	0	2	0	0	0	2	2	2	.182	.308	.182	39	-1	0	0	0	1.000	-0	/1-4	-0.1
1984	LA-N	27	49	2	9	3	0	0	6	6	9	.184	.273	.245	47	-3	1	0	0	1.000	2	1-14	-0.2
1985	LA-N	24	53	4	7	0	0	3	6	7	10	.132	.233	.302	50	-4	0	0	0	.994	2	1-16	-0.3
	Pit-N	26	95	14	27	7	0	3	15	11	14	.284	.358	.453	127	3	0	2	-1	.992	2	1-25	0.2
	Yr	50	148	18	34	7	0	6	21	18	24	.230	.313	.399	100	-0	0	2	-1	.993	4	1-41	-0.1
1986	Pit-N	154	522	73	140	37	5	16	77	60	73	.268	.345	.450	115	10	13	7	-0	.989	23	*1-153/O-2	2.3
1987	Pit-N	149	516	64	142	25	3	13	65	49	69	.275	.338	.411	97	-3	9	8	-2	.988	11	*1-144	-0.4
1988	Pit-N	148	462	50	122	37	0	10	65	47	64	.264	.333	.409	114	4	9	9	-3	.995	21	*1-138	1.7
1989	Pit-N	19	36	3	8	3	0	0	4	12	10	.222	.417	.306	113	2	0	4	-2	.992	-0	1-13	-0.2
1990	*Pit-N	147	389	39	105	23	2	15	67	48	65	.270	.353	.455	125	13	8	4	-2	.993	10	*1-142	1.5
1991	*Atl-N	91	265	32	67	12	0	11	45	25	31	.253	.317	.423	100	0	0	3	-2	.996	0	1-85	-0.7
1992	*Atl-N	125	372	30	97	25	1	10	61	46	51	.261	.344	.414	107	4	6	0	-0	.989	-3	*1-120	-0.5
1993	*Atl-N	117	277	33	72	14	1	9	35	31	43	.260	.334	.415	98	-1	4	2	0	.996	5	1-90	-0.1
1994	Hou-N	46	61	7	21	5	0	0	7	9	9	.344	.429	.426	127	3	0	1	-1	.986	2	1-10	0.4
Total	12	1088	3108	351	819	191	12	90	455	353	450	.264	.340	.420	107	31	50	40	-9	.992	74	1-954/O-2	3.6

■ JIM BREAZEALE
Breazeale, James Leo b: 10/3/49, Houston, Tex. BL/TR, 6'2", 210 lbs. Deb: 9/13/69

YEAR	TM/L	G	AB	R	H	2B	3B	HR	RBI	BB	SO	AVG	OBP	SLG	PRO+	BR/A	SB	CS	SBR	FA	FR	G/POS	TPR
1969	Atl-N	2	1	1	0	0	0	0	2	0	0	.000	.667	.000	101	0	0	0	0	.833	-0	/1-1	0.0
1971	Atl-N	10	21	1	4	0	0	1	3	0	4	.190	.190	.333	43	-2	0	0	0	1.000	0	/1-4	-0.2
1972	Atl-N	52	85	10	21	3	0	5	17	6	12	.247	.297	.447	100	-0	0	1	-1	1.000	-2	1-16/3-1	-0.4
1978	Chi-A	25	72	8	15	3	0	3	13	8	10	.208	.287	.375	84	-2	0	0	0	.992	-3	1-19/D-4	-0.5
Total	4	89	179	20	40	5	0	9	33	16	25	.223	.287	.402	88	-3	0	1	-1	.993	-5	/1-40,D-4,3	-1.1

■ DANNY BREEDEN
Breeden, Danny Richard b: 6/27/42, Albany, Ga. BR/TR, 5'11.5", 185 lbs. Deb: 7/24/69 F

YEAR	TM/L	G	AB	R	H	2B	3B	HR	RBI	BB	SO	AVG	OBP	SLG	PRO+	BR/A	SB	CS	SBR	FA	FR	G/POS	TPR
1969	Cin-N	3	8	0	1	0	0	0	1	0	3	.125	.125	.125	-28	-1	0	0	0	.941	0	/C-3	-0.1
1971	Chi-N	25	65	3	10	1	0	0	4	9	18	.154	.267	.169	23	-6	0	0	0	.975	4	C-25	-0.2
Total	2	28	73	3	11	1	0	0	5	9	21	.151	.253	.164	18	-8	0	0	0	.972	5	/C-28	-0.3

■ HAL BREEDEN
Breeden, Harold Noel b: 6/28/44, Albany, Ga. BR/TL, 6'2", 200 lbs. Deb: 4/7/71 F

YEAR	TM/L	G	AB	R	H	2B	3B	HR	RBI	BB	SO	AVG	OBP	SLG	PRO+	BR/A	SB	CS	SBR	FA	FR	G/POS	TPR
1971	Chi-N	23	36	1	5	1	0	2	7	2	7	.139	.184	.250	19	-4	0	0	0	.982	1	/1-8	-0.3
1972	Mon-N	42	87	6	20	2	0	3	10	7	15	.230	.287	.356	80	-2	0	0	0	.994	-1	1-26/O-1	-0.6
1973	Mon-N	105	258	36	71	10	6	15	43	29	45	.275	.353	.535	138	12	0	1	-1	.991	3	1-66	1.1
1974	Mon-N	79	190	14	47	13	0	2	20	24	35	.247	.332	.347	85	-3	0	0	0	.987	1	1-56	-0.7
1975	Mon-N	24	37	4	5	2	0	0	1	7	5	.135	.273	.189	29	-3	0	0	0	.989	-0	1-12	-0.5
Total	5	273	608	61	148	28	6	21	76	69	107	.243	.323	.413	99	-1	0	2	-1	.990	4	1-168/O-1	-1.0

■ MARV BREEDING
Breeding, Marvin Eugene b: 3/8/34, Decatur, Ala. BR/TR, 6', 175 lbs. Deb: 4/19/60

YEAR	TM/L	G	AB	R	H	2B	3B	HR	RBI	BB	SO	AVG	OBP	SLG	PRO+	BR/A	SB	CS	SBR	FA	FR	G/POS	TPR
1960	Bal-A	152	551	69	147	25	2	3	43	35	80	.267	.314	.336	77	-18	10	4	1	.977	5	*2-152	0.2
1961	Bal-A	90	244	32	51	8	0	1	16	14	33	.209	.252	.254	37	-22	5	2	0	.970	7	2-80	-0.8
1962	Bal-A	95	240	27	59	10	1	2	18	6	41	.246	.273	.321	63	-13	2	2	-1	.977	21	2-73/S-1,3	1.3
1963	Was-A	58	197	20	54	11	1	4	14	7	21	.274	.299	.345	80	-5	1	1	-0	.914	-9	3-29,2-22/S	-1.3

YEAR	TM/L	G	AB	R	H	2B	3B	HR	RBI	BB	SO	AVG	OBP	SLG	PRO+	BR/A	SB	CS	SBR	FA	FR	G/POS	TPR
	LA-N	20	36	6	6	0	0	0	1	2	5	.167	.211	.167	11	-4	1	0	0	.972	-4	2-17/S-1,3	-0.8
Total	4	415	1268	154	317	50	5	7	92	66	180	.250	.289	.314	65	-63	19	9	0	.975	20	2-344/3-31,S	-1.4

■ HERB BREMER
Bremer, Herbert Frederick   b: 10/26/13, Chicago, Ill.   d: 11/28/79, Columbus, Ga.   BR/TR, 6', 195 lbs.   Deb: 9/16/37

YEAR	TM/L	G	AB	R	H	2B	3B	HR	RBI	BB	SO	AVG	OBP	SLG	PRO+	BR/A	SB	CS	SBR	FA	FR	G/POS	TPR
1937	StL-N	11	33	2	7	1	0	0	3	2	4	.212	.257	.242	36	-3	0			.979	-0	C-10	-0.3
1938	StL-N	50	151	14	33	5	1	2	14	9	36	.219	.262	.305	53	-10	1			.977	3	C-50	-0.5
1939	StL-N	9	9	0	1	0	0	0	1	0	2	.111	.111	.111	-38	-2	0			1.000	1	/C-8	-0.1
Total	3	70	193	16	41	6	1	2	18	11	42	.212	.255	.285	45	-15	1			.979	3	/C-68	-0.9

■ SAM BRENEGAN
Brenegan, Olaf Selmar   b: 9/1/1890, Galesville, Wis.   d: 4/20/56, Galesville, Wis.   BL/TR, 6'2", 185 lbs.   Deb: 4/24/14

YEAR	TM/L	G	AB	R	H	2B	3B	HR	RBI	BB	SO	AVG	OBP	SLG	PRO+	BR/A	SB	CS	SBR	FA	FR	G/POS	TPR
1914	Pit-N	1	0	0	0	0	0	0	0	0	0	—	—	—			0			.000	-0	/C-1	0.0

■ BOB BRENLY
Brenly, Robert Earl   b: 2/25/54, Coshocton, Ohio   BR/TR, 6'2", 210 lbs.   Deb: 8/14/81   C

YEAR	TM/L	G	AB	R	H	2B	3B	HR	RBI	BB	SO	AVG	OBP	SLG	PRO+	BR/A	SB	CS	SBR	FA	FR	G/POS	TPR
1981	SF-N	19	45	5	15	2	1	4	6	4	.333	.423	.489	161	4	0	1	-1	.964	-4	C-14/3-3,O	0.0
1982	SF-N	65	180	26	51	4	1	4	15	18	26	.283	.352	.383	106	2	6	2	1	.961	1	C-61/3-1	0.5
1983	SF-N	104	281	36	63	12	2	7	34	37	48	.224	.319	.356	89	-4	10	7	-1	.983	1	C-90,1-10/O	-0.1
1984	SF-N★	145	506	74	147	28	0	20	80	48	52	.291	.355	.464	133	21	6	9	-4	.986	-18	*C-127,1-22/O	0.5
1985	SF-N	133	440	41	97	16	1	19	56	57	62	.220	.313	.391	100	-0	1	4	-2	.984	-7	*C-110,3-17,1	-0.4
1986	SF-N	149	472	60	116	26	0	16	62	74	97	.246	.352	.403	113	9	10	6	-1	.995	-7	*C-101,3-45,1	0.6
1987	*SF-N	123	375	55	100	19	1	18	51	47	85	.267	.353	.467	121	11	10	7	-1	.988	9	*C-108/1-6,3	2.5
1988	SF-N	73	206	13	39	7	0	5	22	24	40	.189	.268	.296	64	-10	1	2	-1	.984	-4	C-69	-1.1
1989	Tor-A	48	88	9	15	3	1	1	6	10	17	.170	.255	.261	47	-6	1	0	0	.975	2	D-28,C-13/1	-0.5
	SF-N	12	22	2	4	2	0	0	3	1	7	.182	.217	.273	40	-2	0	0	0	1.000	0	C-12	-0.1
Total	9	871	2615	321	647	119	7	91	333	318	438	.247	.333	.403	107	25	45	38	-9	.984	-26	C-705/1-72,3DO	1.9

■ JIM BRENNAN
Brennan, James Augustus (b: John Gottlieb Dorn)   b: 1862, St.Louis, Mo.   d: 10/18/04, Philadelphia, Pa.   Deb: 4/20/1884

YEAR	TM/L	G	AB	R	H	2B	3B	HR	RBI	BB	SO	AVG	OBP	SLG	PRO+	BR/A	SB	CS	SBR	FA	FR	G/POS	TPR
1884	StL-U	56	231	38	50	6	1	0		12		.216	.255	.251	37	-20				.891	-2	C-33,O-16/3S	-1.8
1885	StL-N	3	10	0	1	0	0	0	1	1	1	.100	.182	.100	-7	-1				.750	-1	/O-2,3-1	-0.2
1888	KC-a	34	118	5	20	2	0	0	6	3		.169	.203	.186	24	-10	3			.884	-3	C-25/O-5,3	-1.0
1889	Phi-a	31	113	12	25	4	0	0	15	10	15	.221	.285	.257	55	-6	1			.818	-4	C-13/O-7,23	-0.8
1890	Cle-P	59	233	32	59	3	7	0	26	13	29	.253	.304	.326	74	-9	8			.845	-4	C-42,3-14/O	-0.7
Total	5	183	705	87	155	15	8	0	48	39	45	.220	.267	.264	49	-46	12			.869	-15	C-113/O-36,32S	-4.5

■ BILL BRENZEL
Brenzel, William Richard   b: 3/3/10, Oakland, Cal.   d: 6/12/79, Oakland, Cal.   BR/TR, 5'10", 173 lbs.   Deb: 4/13/32

YEAR	TM/L	G	AB	R	H	2B	3B	HR	RBI	BB	SO	AVG	OBP	SLG	PRO+	BR/A	SB	CS	SBR	FA	FR	G/POS	TPR
1932	Pit-N	9	24	0	1	1	0	0	2	0	4	.042	.042	.083	-69	-6	0			1.000	2	/C-9	-0.3
1934	Cle-A	15	51	4	11	3	0	0	3	2	1	.216	.245	.275	33	-5	0	0	0	1.000	1	C-15	-0.2
1935	Cle-A	52	142	12	31	5	1	0	14	6	10	.218	.250	.268	33	-14	2	2	-1	.975	-7	C-51	-1.8
Total	3	76	217	16	43	9	1	0	19	8	15	.198	.227	.249	23	-25	2	2		.985	-2	/C-75	-2.3

■ ROGER BRESNAHAN
Bresnahan, Roger Philip "The Duke Of Tralee"   b: 6/11/1879, Toledo, Ohio   d: 12/4/44, Toledo, Ohio   BR/TR, 5'9", 200 lbs.   Deb: 8/27/1897   MCH

YEAR	TM/L	G	AB	R	H	2B	3B	HR	RBI	BB	SO	AVG	OBP	SLG	PRO+	BR/A	SB	CS	SBR	FA	FR	G/POS	TPR
1897	Was-N	6	16	1	6	0	0	0	3	1	.375	.412	.375	109	-1	0			1.000	-1	/P-6,O-1	0.0
1900	Chi-N	2	2	0	0	0	0	0	0	0	.000	.000	.000	-99	-1	0			.000	-0	/C-1	-0.1
1901	Bal-A	86	295	40	79	9	9	1	32	23	.268	.323	.369	88	-5	10			.919	-19	C-69/O-8,3P2	-1.6
1902	Bal-A	65	235	30	64	8	6	4	34	21	.272	.337	.409	102	0	12			.880	-7	3-30,C-22,O	-0.5
	NY-N	51	178	16	51	9	3	1	22	16	.287	.352	.388	129	6	6			.946	0	O-27,C-16/1S3	0.7
1903	NY-N	113	406	87	142	30	8	4	55	61	.350	.443	.493	160	34	34			.965	0	O-84,1-13,C/3	2.8
1904	NY-N	109	402	81	114	22	7	5	33	58	.284	.381	.410	138	20	13			.954	0	O-93,1-10/S23	1.5
1905	*NY-N	104	331	58	100	18	3	0	46	50	.302	.411	.375	132	16	11			.970	-1	C-87/O-8	2.5
1906	NY-N	124	405	69	114	22	4	0	43	81	.281	**.419**	.356	139	25	25			.974	5	C-82,O-40	3.9
1907	NY-N	110	328	57	83	9	7	4	38	61	.253	.380	.360	128	13	15			.986	-7	C-95/1-6,O3	1.7
1908	NY-N	140	449	70	127	25	3	1	54	**83**	.283	.401	.359	146	23	14			.985	-18	*C-139	2.1
1909	StL-N	72	234	27	57	4	1	0	23	46	.244	.370	.269	105	5	11			.960	-6	C-59/2-9,3M	0.3
1910	StL-N	88	234	35	65	15	3	0	27	55	17	.278	.419	.368	135	14	13			.961	-9	C-77/O-2,PM	1.2
1911	StL-N	81	227	22	63	17	8	3	41	45	19	.278	.404	.463	146	15	4			.968	-2	C-77/2-2M	2.0
1912	StL-N	48	108	8	36	7	2	1	15	14	9	.333	.419	.463	145	7	4			.974	7	C-28,M	1.7
1913	Chi-N	69	162	20	37	5	2	1	21	21	11	.228	.324	.302	79	-4	7			.963	-5	C-58	-0.5
1914	Chi-N	101	248	42	69	10	4	0	24	49	20	.278	.401	.351	125	11	14			.978	-3	C-85,2-14/O	1.5
1915	Chi-N	77	221	19	45	8	1	1	19	29	23	.204	.296	.262	70	-7	19	3	**4**	.982	3	C-68,M	0.5
Total	17	1446	4481	682	1252	218	71	26	530	714	99	.279	.386	.377	126	172	212	3		.971	-63	C-974,O-281/312PS	19.7

■ RUBE BRESSLER
Bressler, Raymond Bloom   b: 10/23/1894, Coder, Pa.   d: 11/7/66, Cincinnati, Ohio   BR/TL, 6', 187 lbs.   Deb: 4/24/14

YEAR	TM/L	G	AB	R	H	2B	3B	HR	RBI	BB	SO	AVG	OBP	SLG	PRO+	BR/A	SB	CS	SBR	FA	FR	G/POS	TPR
1914	Phi-A	29	51	6	11	1	1	0	4	6	7	.216	.310	.275	79	-1	0			.941	-2	P-29	0.0
1915	Phi-A	33	55	9	8	0	1	1	4	9	13	.145	.277	.236	56	-3	0			.900	0	P-32	0.0
1916	Phi-A	4	5	1	1	0	1	0	1	0	0	.200	.200	.600	147	0	0			1.000	-0	/P-4	0.0
1917	Cin-N	3	5	0	1	0	0	0	0	0	2	.200	.200	.200	24	-0	0			1.000	-0	/P-2	0.0
1918	Cin-N	23	62	10	17	5	0	0	6	5	4	.274	.328	.355	110	1	0			.982	2	P-17/O-3	-0.1
1919	Cin-N	61	165	22	34	3	4	2	17	23	15	.206	.311	.309	89	-2	2			.965	1	O-48,P-13	-0.5
1920	Cin-N	21	30	4	8	1	0	0	3	1	4	.267	.290	.300	71	-1	1	0	0	1.000	-2	P-10/O-3,1	-0.2
1921	Cin-N	109	323	41	99	18	6	1	54	39	20	.307	.385	.409	115	8	5	5	-2	.953	-6	O-85/1-6	-0.6
1922	Cin-N	52	53	7	14	0	2	0	8	4	4	.264	.316	.340	70	-2	0	0	0	1.000	-2	/1-3,O-2	-0.4
1923	Cin-N	54	119	25	33	3	1	0	18	20	4	.277	.399	.319	93	0	3	1	0	.983	-3	1-22/O-6	-0.3
1924	Cin-N	115	383	41	133	14	13	4	49	22	20	.347	.389	.483	134	18	9	10	-3	.990	-3	1-50,O-49	1.3
1925	Cin-N	97	319	43	111	17	6	4	61	40	16	.348	.424	.476	133	17	9	5	-0	.982	-3	1-52,O-38	0.8
1926	Cin-N	86	297	58	106	15	9	1	51	37	20	.357	.433	.478	149	22	4			.970	-4	O-80/1-4	1.3
1927	Cin-N	124	467	43	136	14	8	3	77	32	22	.291	.338	.375	94	-4	4			.972	7	*O-120	-0.5
1928	Bro-N	145	501	78	148	29	13	4	70	80	33	.295	.398	.429	118	16	2			**.985**	-6	*O-137	0.1
1929	Bro-N	136	456	72	145	22	8	9	77	67	27	.318	.406	.461	117	14	4			.954	3	*O-122	0.8
1930	Bro-N	109	335	53	100	12	8	3	52	51	19	.299	.394	.409	96	-1	4			.995	6	O-90/1-7	0.0
1931	Bro-N	67	153	22	43	4	5	0	26	11	10	.281	.329	.373	89	-2	0			.982	-4	O-35/1-1	-0.9
1932	Phi-N	27	83	9	19	1	0	0	6	2	5	.229	.247	.325	47	-6	0			1.000	3	O-18	-0.4
	StL-N	10	19	0	3	0	0	0	2	0	1	.158	.158	.158	-14	-3	0			1.000	-0	/O-4	-0.3
	Yr	37	102	9	22	1	0	0	8	2	6	.216	.231	.294	37	-9	0			1.000	3	O-22	-0.7
Total	19	1305	3881	544	1170	164	87	32	586	449	246	.301	.378	.413	110	71	47	21		.971	-4	O-840,1-147,P	0.1

■ EDDIE BRESSOUD
Bressoud, Edward Francis   b: 5/2/32, Los Angeles, Cal.   BR/TR, 6'1", 175 lbs.   Deb: 6/14/56

YEAR	TM/L	G	AB	R	H	2B	3B	HR	RBI	BB	SO	AVG	OBP	SLG	PRO+	BR/A	SB	CS	SBR	FA	FR	G/POS	TPR
1956	NY-N	49	163	15	37	4	2	1	9	12	20	.227	.284	.276	52	-11	1	0	0	.950	-9	S-48	-1.7
1957	NY-N	49	127	11	34	2	2	5	10	4	19	.268	.301	.433	94	-1	0	1	-1	.940	1	S-33,3-12	0.2
1958	SF-N	66	137	19	36	5	3	0	8	14	22	.263	.331	.343	81	-1	1	0	0	.966	-2	2-57/3-6,S	-0.3
1959	SF-N	104	315	36	79	17	2	9	26	28	55	.251	.312	.403	91	-5	0	0	0	.974	-6	S-92/1-1,23	-0.4
1960	SF-N	116	386	37	87	19	6	9	43	35	72	.225	.293	.376	87	-8	1	2	-1	.960	6	*S-115	0.6
1961	SF-N	59	114	14	24	6	1	3	11	13	23	.211	.280	.342	66	-6	1	1	-0	.964	-9	*S-34/3-3,2	-1.3
1962	Bos-A	153	599	79	166	40	9	14	68	46	118	.277	.331	.444	103	3	2	1	-0	.965	25	*S-153	3.8
1963	Bos-A	140	497	61	129	23	6	20	60	52	93	.260	.332	.451	113	9	1	1	-0	.962	-9	*S-137	0.9
1964	Bos-A☆	158	566	86	166	41	3	15	55	72	99	.293	.374	.456	123	19	1	1	-0	.972	-14	*S-158	1.7

YEAR	TM/L	G	AB	R	H	2B	3B	HR	RBI	BB	SO	AVG	OBP	SLG	PRO+	BR/A	SB	CS	SBR	FA	FR	G/POS	TPR
1965	Bos-A	107	296	29	67	11	1	8	25	29	77	.226	.298	.351	79	-8	0	1	-1	.963	-5	S-86/3-2,O	-0.9
1966	NY-N	133	405	48	91	15	5	10	49	47	107	.225	.307	.360	87	-7	2	2	-1	.960	8	S-94,3-32/12	0.7
1967	*StL-N	52	67	8	9	1	1	1	9	18	.134	.237	.224	33	-6	0	0	0	.929	-4	S-48/3-1	-0.9
Total	12	1186	3672	443	925	184	40	94	365	359	723	.252	.321	.401	96	-26	9	13	-5	.963	-19	*S-1002/2-66,310	2.4

■ JIM BRETON

Breton, John Frederick b: 7/15/1891, Chicago, Ill. d: 5/30/73, Beloit, Wis. BR/TR, 5'10.5", 178 lbs. Deb: 8/25/13

YEAR	TM/L	G	AB	R	H	2B	3B	HR	RBI	BB	SO	AVG	OBP	SLG	PRO+	BR/A	SB	CS	SBR	FA	FR	G/POS	TPR
1913	Chi-A	12	30	1	5	1	1	0	2	1	5	.167	.194	.267	35	-3	0			.938	3	/S-7,3-3	0.0
1914	Chi-A	81	231	21	49	7	2	0	24	24	42	.212	.292	.260	67	-9	9	6	-1	.910	3	3-79	-0.5
1915	Chi-A	16	36	3	5	1	0	0	1	5	9	.139	.262	.167	27	-3	2	1	0	.882	-2	3-14/2-1,S	-0.5
Total	3	109	297	25	59	9	3	0	27	30	56	.199	.279	.249	59	-15	11	7		.906	4	/3-96,S-8,2	-1.0

■ GEORGE BRETT

Brett, George Howard b: 5/15/53, Glen Dale, W.Va. BL/TR, 6', 200 lbs. Deb: 8/2/73 F

YEAR	TM/L	G	AB	R	H	2B	3B	HR	RBI	BB	SO	AVG	OBP	SLG	PRO+	BR/A	SB	CS	SBR	FA	FR	G/POS	TPR
1973	KC-A	13	40	2	5	2	0	0	0	5	.125	.125	.175	-15	-6	0	0	0	.974	3	3-13	-0.3
1974	KC-A	133	457	49	129	21	5	2	47	21	38	.282	.314	.363	89	-7	8	5	-1	.948	-9	*3-132/S-1	-1.9
1975	KC-A	159	634	84	195	35	13	11	89	46	49	.308	.356	.456	125	19	13	10	-2	.949	-6	*3-159/S-1	1.1
1976	*KC-A★	159	645	94	215	34	14	7	67	49	36	.333	.381	.462	145	35	21	11	-0	.948	3	*3-157/S-4	4.0
1977	*KC-A★	139	564	105	176	32	13	22	88	55	24	.312	.375	.532	143	33	14	12	-3	.957	17	*3-135/S-1,D	4.4
1978	*KC-A★	128	510	79	150	45	8	9	62	39	35	.294	.345	.467	123	14	23	7	3	.961	5	*3-128/S-1	2.1
1979	*KC-A★	154	645	119	212	42	20	23	107	51	36	.329	.376	.563	147	40	17	10	-1	.944	14	*3-149/1-8	4.9
1980	*KC-A†	117	449	87	175	33	9	24	118	58	22	.390	.461	.664	203	64	15	6	1	.955	4	*3-112/1-1	6.4
1981	*KC-A★	89	347	42	109	27	7	6	43	27	23	.314	.365	.484	144	19	14	6	1	.946	-9	3-88	0.9
1982	KC-A★	144	552	101	166	32	9	21	82	71	51	.301	.381	.505	141	32	6	1	1	.959	-6	*3-134,O-12	2.3
1983	*KC-A★	123	464	90	144	38	2	25	93	57	39	.310	.387	.563	157	36	0	1	-1	.919	-25	*3-102,1-14,O/D	0.8
1984	*KC-A★	104	377	42	107	21	3	13	69	38	37	.284	.349	.459	121	10	0	2	-1	.949	-4	*3-101	0.4
1985	*KC-A★	155	550	108	184	38	5	30	112	103	49	.335	.442	.585	178	63	9	1	2	.967	12	*3-152/D-1	7.2
1986	KC-A†	124	441	70	128	28	4	16	73	80	45	.290	.404	.481	137	25	1	2	-1	.952	-2	*3-115/S-2,D	1.9
1987	KC-A	115	427	71	124	18	2	22	78	72	47	.290	.394	.496	131	21	6	3	0	.993	-5	1-83,D-21,3	0.8
1988	KC-A★	157	589	90	180	42	3	24	103	82	51	.306	.393	.509	149	40	14	3	2	.992	-9	*1-124,D-33/S	2.2
1989	KC-A	124	457	67	129	26	3	12	80	59	47	.282	.368	.431	125	16	14	4	2	.998	4	*1-104,D-17/O	1.3
1990	KC-A	142	544	82	179	45	7	14	87	56	63	.329	.392	.515	154	39	9	2	1	.993	-1	*1-102,D-32/O3	3.0
1991	KC-A	131	505	77	129	40	2	10	61	58	75	.255	.332	.402	102	1	2	0	1	.989	-1	*D-118,1-10	-0.5
1992	KC-A	152	592	55	169	35	5	7	61	35	69	.285	.332	.397	101	-0	8	6	-1	.987	0	*D-132,1-15/3	-0.7
1993	KC-A	145	560	69	149	31	3	19	75	39	67	.266	.317	.434	94	-6	7	5	-1	.000	0	*D-140	-1.3
Total	21	2707	10349	1583	3154	665	137	317	1595	1096	908	.305	.373	.487	135	488	201	97	-2	.951	-17	*3-1692,D-505,1/OS	39.0

■ TONY BREWER

Brewer, Anthony Bruce b: 11/25/57, Shreveport, La. BR/TR, 5'11", 190 lbs. Deb: 8/1/84 F

YEAR	TM/L	G	AB	R	H	2B	3B	HR	RBI	BB	SO	AVG	OBP	SLG	PRO+	BR/A	SB	CS	SBR	FA	FR	G/POS	TPR
1984	LA-N	24	37	3	4	1	0	1	4	3	9	.108	.195	.216	16	-4	1	0	0	1.000	-2	O-10	-0.6

■ MIKE BREWER

Brewer, Michael Quinn b: 10/24/59, Shreveport, La. BR/TR, 6'5", 190 lbs. Deb: 6/11/86 F

YEAR	TM/L	G	AB	R	H	2B	3B	HR	RBI	BB	SO	AVG	OBP	SLG	PRO+	BR/A	SB	CS	SBR	FA	FR	G/POS	TPR
1986	KC-A	12	18	0	3	1	0	0	2	6	.167	.250	.222	29	-2	0	1	-1	1.000	-2	/O-9,D-1	-0.4

■ ROD BREWER

Brewer, Rodney Lee b: 2/24/66, Eustis, Fla. BL/TL, 6'3", 210 lbs. Deb: 9/5/90

YEAR	TM/L	G	AB	R	H	2B	3B	HR	RBI	BB	SO	AVG	OBP	SLG	PRO+	BR/A	SB	CS	SBR	FA	FR	G/POS	TPR
1990	StL-N	14	25	4	6	1	0	0	2	0	4	.240	.240	.280	42	-2	0	0	0	.981	1	/1-9	-0.2
1991	StL-N	19	13	0	1	0	0	0	1	0	5	.077	.077	.077	-56	-3	0	0	0	1.000	-0	1-15/O-3	-0.3
1992	StL-N	29	103	11	31	6	0	0	10	8	12	.301	.357	.359	107	1	0	1	-1	1.000	1	1-27/O-4	-0.1
1993	StL-N	110	147	15	42	8	0	2	20	17	26	.286	.364	.381	102	1	1	0	-0	.960	-6	O-33,1-32/P	-0.6
Total	4	172	288	30	80	15	0	2	33	25	47	.278	.340	.351	92	-3	1	1	-0	.995	-4	/1-83,O-40,P	-1.2

■ CHARLIE BREWSTER

Brewster, Charles Lawrence b: 12/27/16, Marthaville, La. BR/TR, 5'8.5", 175 lbs. Deb: 5/2/43

YEAR	TM/L	G	AB	R	H	2B	3B	HR	RBI	BB	SO	AVG	OBP	SLG	PRO+	BR/A	SB	CS	SBR	FA	FR	G/POS	TPR
1943	Cin-N	7	8	0	1	0	0	0	0	0	1	.125	.125	.125	-28	-1	0			1.000	-0	/2-2	-0.1
	Phi-N	49	159	13	35	2	0	0	12	10	19	.220	.275	.233	49	-10	1			.901	-20	S-46	-3.0
	Yr	56	167	13	36	2	0	0	12	10	20	.216	.268	.228	45	-12	1			.901	-20	S-46/2-2	-3.1
1944	Chi-N	10	44	4	11	2	0	0	2	5	7	.250	.327	.295	76	-1	0	0	0	.903	0	S-10	0.0
1946	Cle-A	3	2	0	0	0	0	0	0	1	1	.000	.333	.000	-1	-0	0	0	0	1.000	0	/S-1	0.0
Total	3	69	213	17	47	4	0	0	14	16	28	.221	.281	.239	52	-13	1	0		.902	-20	/S-57,2-2	-3.1

■ FRITZ BRICKELL

Brickell, Fritz Darrell b: 3/19/35, Wichita, Kan. d: 10/15/65, Wichita, Kan. BR/TR, 5'5", 157 lbs. Deb: 4/30/58 F

YEAR	TM/L	G	AB	R	H	2B	3B	HR	RBI	BB	SO	AVG	OBP	SLG	PRO+	BR/A	SB	CS	SBR	FA	FR	G/POS	TPR
1958	NY-A	2	0	0	0	0	0	0	0	0						0	0	0	0	1.000	0	/2-2	0.0
1959	NY-A	18	39	4	10	1	0	1	4	1	10	.256	.275	.359	75	-1	0	0	0	.925	0	S-15/2-3	0.0
1961	LA-A	21	49	3	6	0	0	0	3	6	9	.122	.218	.122	-6	-7	0	0	0	.901	0	S-17	-0.6
Total	3	41	88	7	16	1	0	1	7	7	19	.182	.242	.227	26	-9	0	0	0	.911	0	/S-32,2-5	-0.6

■ FRED BRICKELL

Brickell, George Frederick b: 11/9/06, Saffordville, Kan. d: 4/8/61, Wichita, Kan. BL/TR, 5'7", 160 lbs. Deb: 8/19/26 F

YEAR	TM/L	G	AB	R	H	2B	3B	HR	RBI	BB	SO	AVG	OBP	SLG	PRO+	BR/A	SB	CS	SBR	FA	FR	G/POS	TPR
1926	Pit-N	24	55	11	19	3	1	0	4	3	6	.345	.400	.436	119	2				.920	-0	O-14	0.1
1927	*Pit-N	32	21	6	6	1	0	1	4	1	0	.286	.318	.476	103	-0				1.000	-1	/O-3	0.0
1928	Pit-N	81	202	34	65	4	4	3	41	20	18	.322	.383	.426	107	2	5			.958	0	O-50	0.1
1929	Pit-N	60	118	13	37	4	2	0	17	7	12	.314	.352	.381	80	-4	3			1.000	0	O-27	-0.5
1930	Pit-N	68	219	36	65	9	3	1	14	15	20	.297	.342	.379	74	-9	3			.951	-4	O-61	-1.5
	Phi-N	53	240	33	59	12	6	0	17	13	21	.246	.290	.346	49	-20	1			.963	5	O-53	-1.7
	Yr	121	459	69	124	21	9	1	31	28	41	.270	.315	.362	61	-29	4			.958	0	*O-114	-3.2
1931	Phi-N	130	514	77	130	14	5	1	31	42	39	.253	.316	.305	63	-26	5			.978	4	*O-122	-3.1
1932	Phi-N	45	66	9	22	6	1	0	2	4	5	.333	.389	.455	112	1	2			.935	-0	O-12	0.0
1933	Phi-N	8	13	2	4	1	1	0	1	1	0	.308	.357	.538	136	1	0			1.000	1	/O-4	0.1
Total	8	501	1448	221	407	54	23	6	131	106	121	.281	.335	.363	75	-53	19			.967	5	O-346	-6.5

■ GEORGE BRICKLEY

Brickley, George Vincent b: 7/19/1894, Everett, Mass. d: 2/23/47, Everett, Mass. BR/TR, 5'9", 180 lbs. Deb: 9/26/13

YEAR	TM/L	G	AB	R	H	2B	3B	HR	RBI	BB	SO	AVG	OBP	SLG	PRO+	BR/A	SB	CS	SBR	FA	FR	G/POS	TPR
1913	Phi-A	5	12	0	2	0	1	0	0	0	4	.167	.231	.333	66	-1	0			1.000	-1	/O-4	-0.2

■ JIM BRIDEWESER

Brideweser, James Ehrenfeld b: 2/13/27, Lancaster, Ohio d: 8/25/89, ElToro, Cal. BR/TR, 6', 165 lbs. Deb: 9/29/51

YEAR	TM/L	G	AB	R	H	2B	3B	HR	RBI	BB	SO	AVG	OBP	SLG	PRO+	BR/A	SB	CS	SBR	FA	FR	G/POS	TPR
1951	NY-A	2	8	1	3	0	0	0	0	0	1	.375	.375	.375	107	0	0	0	0	.818	-2	/S-2	0.0
1952	NY-A	42	38	12	10	0	0	0	2	3	5	.263	.317	.263	67	-2	0	0	0	.935	2	S-22/2-4,3	0.1
1953	NY-A	7	3	3	3	0	1	0	3	1	0	1.000	1.000	1.667	631	2	0	0	0	.833	0	/S-3	0.3
1954	Bal-A	73	204	18	54	7	2	0	12	15	27	.265	.318	.319	81	-6	1	1	-0	.944	-12	S-48,2-19	-1.4
1955	Chi-A	34	58	6	12	3	2	0	4	3	7	.207	.246	.328	52	-4	0	0	0	.949	6	S-26/3-3,2	0.3
1956	Chi-A	10	11	0	2	1	0	0	1	0	3	.182	.250	.273	37	-1	0	0	0	.938	0	S-10	-0.1
	Det-A	70	156	23	34	4	0	1	10	20	19	.218	.307	.244	47	-12	3	1	0	.987	14	S-32,2-31/3	0.6
	Yr	80	167	23	36	5	0	1	11	20	22	.216	.303	.246	46	-13	3	1	0	.979	14	S-42,2-31/3	0.5
1957	Bal-A	91	142	16	38	7	1	1	18	21	15	.268	.362	.352	102	1	2	0	1	.943	5	S-74/3-3,2	1.1
Total	7	329	620	79	156	22	6	1	50	63	77	.252	.323	.311	75	-21	6	2	1	.946	15	S-217/2-57,3	0.9

■ ROCKY BRIDGES

Bridges, Everett Lamar b: 8/7/27, Refugio, Tex. BR/TR, 5'8", 175 lbs. Deb: 4/17/51 C

YEAR	TM/L	G	AB	R	H	2B	3B	HR	RBI	BB	SO	AVG	OBP	SLG	PRO+	BR/A	SB	CS	SBR	FA	FR	G/POS	TPR
1951	Bro-N	63	134	13	34	7	0	1	15	10	10	.254	.306	.328	69	-6	0	0		.871	3	3-40,2-10/S	-0.2
1952	Bro-N	51	56	9	11	3	0	0	2	9	9	.196	.286	.250	49	-4	0	1	-1	.986	12	2-24,S-13/3	0.8
1953	Cin-N	122	432	52	98	13	2	1	21	37	42	.227	.288	.273	47	-33	5			.976	11	*2-115/S-6,3	-1.6
1954	Cin-N	53	52	4	12	1	0	0	2	7	7	.231	.322	.250	50	-4	1			1.000	11	S-20,2-19,3	0.7

YEAR	TM/L	G	AB	R	H	2B	3B	HR	RBI	BB	SO	AVG	OBP	SLG	PRO+	BR/A	SB	CS	SBR	FA	FR	G/POS	TPR
1955	Cin-N	95	168	20	48	4	0	1	18	15	19	.286	.344	.327	75	-6	1	1	-0	.965	7	3-59,S-26/2	0.1
1956	Cin-N	71	19	9	4	0	0	0	1	4	3	.211	.348	.211	52	-1	1	2	-1	.966	8	3-51/2-8,SO	0.6
1957	Cin-N	5	1	1	0	0	0	0	0	1	1	.000	.500	.000	46	0	0	0	0		-1	/2-2,S-1,3	-0.1
	Was-A	120	391	40	89	17	2	3	47	40	32	.228	.303	.304	67	-17	0	2	-1	.971	29	*S-108,2-14/3	2.2
1958	Was-A☆	116	377	38	99	14	3	5	28	27	32	.263	.317	.355	86	-7	0	3	-2	.976	3	*S-112/2-3,3	0.4
1959	Det-A	116	381	38	102	16	3	5	35	30	35	.268	.323	.349	80	-10	1	2	-1	.952	-6	*S-110/2-5	-0.7
1960	Det-A	10	5	0	1	0	0	0	0	0	0	.200	.200	.200	8	-1	0	0	0	1.000	3	/3-7,S-3	0.2
	Cle-A	10	27	1	9	0	0	0	3	1	2	.333	.357	.333	91	-0	0	0	0	1.000	3	/S-7,3-3	0.3
	Yr	20	32	1	10	0	0	0	3	1	2	.313	.333	.313	76	-1	0	0	0	1.000	6	3-10,S-10	0.5
	StL-N	3	0	0	0	0	0	0	0	0	0	—	—	—	—	0	0	0	0	1.000	0	/2-3	0.1
1961	LA-A	84	229	20	55	5	1	2	15	26	37	.240	.320	.297	59	-13	1	0	0	.988	10	2-58,S-25/3	0.4
Total	11	919	2272	245	562	80	11	16	187	205	229	.247	.312	.313	67	-102	10	15	-6	.968	95	S-447,2-270,3/O	3.2

■ AL BRIDWELL
Bridwell, Albert Henry b: 1/4/1884, Friendship, Ohio d: 1/23/69, Portsmouth, Ohio BL/TR, 5'9", 170 lbs. Deb: 4/16/05

YEAR	TM/L	G	AB	R	H	2B	3B	HR	RBI	BB	SO	AVG	OBP	SLG	PRO+	BR/A	SB	CS	SBR	FA	FR	G/POS	TPR
1905	Cin-N	82	254	17	64	3	1	0	17	19		.252	.309	.272	66	-11	8			.944	0	3-43,O-18/2S1	-1.0
1906	Bos-N	120	459	41	104	9	1	0	22	44		.227	.297	.251	73	-14	6			.930	17	*S-119/O-1	0.8
1907	Bos-N	140	509	49	111	8	2	0	26	61		.218	.309	.242	73	-13	17			**.942**	7	*S-140	-0.4
1908	NY-N	147	467	53	133	14	1	0	46	52		.285	.364	.319	113	9	20			.933	11	*S-147	2.6
1909	NY-N	145	476	59	140	11	5	0	55	67		.294	.386	.338	123	16	32			.940	5	*S-145	2.2
1910	NY-N	142	492	74	136	15	7	0	48	73	23	.276	.374	.335	107	7	14			.946	6	*S-141	2.0
1911	NY-N	76	263	28	71	10	1	0	31	33	10	.270	.358	.316	86	-4	8			.917	6	S-76	0.7
	Bos-N	51	182	29	53	5	0	0	10	33	8	.291	.403	.319	95	0	2			.950	-11	S-51	-0.7
	Yr	127	445	57	124	15	1	0	41	66	18	.279	.377	.317	90	-3	10			.929	-5	*S-127	0.0
1912	Bos-N	31	106	6	25	5	1	0	14	5	5	.236	.270	.302	55	-7	2			.936	-6	S-31	-1.0
1913	Chi-N	136	405	35	97	6	6	1	37	74	28	.240	.358	.291	86	-4	12			.948	2	*S-136	1.1
1914	StL-F	117	381	46	90	6	5	1	33	71	18	.236	.359	.286	65	-17	9			.944	-11	*S-103,2-11	-2.0
1915	StL-F	65	175	20	40	3	2	0	9	25	6	.229	.328	.269	58	-10	6			.952	1	2-42,3-15/1	-0.8
Total	11	1252	4169	457	1064	95	32	2	348	557	98	.255	.347	.295	87	-45	136			.939	23	*S-1094/2-60,3O1	3.5

■ BUNNY BRIEF
Brief, Anthony Vincent (b: Antonio Bordetzki) b: 7/3/1892, Remus, Mich. d: 2/10/63, Milwaukee, Wis. BR/TR, 6', 185 lbs. Deb: 9/22/12

YEAR	TM/L	G	AB	R	H	2B	3B	HR	RBI	BB	SO	AVG	OBP	SLG	PRO+	BR/A	SB	CS	SBR	FA	FR	G/POS	TPR
1912	StL-A	15	42	9	13	3	0	0	5	6		.310	.408	.381	131	2	2			.826	-1	/O-9,1-4	0.1
1913	StL-A	85	258	24	56	11	6	1	26	21	46	.217	.284	.318	78	-8	3			.986	-1	1-62/O-8	-1.1
1915	Chi-A	48	154	13	33	6	2	1	17	16	28	.214	.305	.318	84	-3	8	6	-1	.986	-2	1-46	-0.8
1917	Pit-N	36	115	15	25	5	1	2	11	15	21	.217	.318	.330	96	-0	4			.988	2	1-34	0.0
Total	4	184	569	61	127	25	9	5	59	58	95	.223	.306	.325	87	-9	17	6		.987	-2	1-146/O-17	-1.8

■ CHARLIE BRIGGS
Briggs, Charles R. b: 1861, Batavia, Ill. 5'7", 170 lbs. Deb: 5/2/1884

YEAR	TM/L	G	AB	R	H	2B	3B	HR	RBI	BB	SO	AVG	OBP	SLG	PRO+	BR/A	SB	CS	SBR	FA	FR	G/POS	TPR
1884	CP-U	49	182	29	31	8	2	1		11		.170	.218	.253	28	-18				.814	-5	O-37,2-12/S	-2.1

■ DAN BRIGGS
Briggs, Dan Lee b: 11/18/52, Scotia, Cal. BL/TL, 6', 180 lbs. Deb: 9/10/75

YEAR	TM/L	G	AB	R	H	2B	3B	HR	RBI	BB	SO	AVG	OBP	SLG	PRO+	BR/A	SB	CS	SBR	FA	FR	G/POS	TPR
1975	Cal-A	13	31	3	7	1	0	1	3	2	6	.226	.273	.355	82	-1	0	2	-1	.953	-1	/1-6,O-5,D	-0.4
1976	Cal-A	77	248	19	53	13	2	1	14	13	47	.214	.256	.294	65	-12	0	3	-2	.993	-0	1-44,O-40/D	-1.9
1977	Cal-A	59	74	6	12	2	0	1	4	8	14	.162	.244	.230	31	-7	0	0	0	.993	-0	1-45,O-13	-0.8
1978	Cle-A	15	49	4	8	1	0	1	4	4	9	.163	.226	.265	38	-4	0	0	0	1.000	2	O-15	-0.3
1979	SD-N	104	227	34	47	4	3	8	30	18	45	.207	.280	.357	77	-8	2	1	0	.986	-1	1-50,O-44	-1.2
1981	Mon-N	9	11	0	1	0	0	0	0	0	3	.091	.091	.091	-48	-2	0	1	-1	1.000	-1	/1-3,O-2	-0.4
1982	Chi-N	48	48	1	6	0	0	0	1	0	9	.125	.143	.125	-24	-8	0	0	0	.875	-2	O-10/1-4	-1.0
Total	7	325	688	67	134	20	6	12	53	45	133	.195	.251	.294	56	-42	2	7	-4	.989	-2	1-152,O-130/D	-6.0

■ GRANT BRIGGS
Briggs, Grant b: 3/16/1865, Pittsburgh, Pa. d: 5/31/28, Pittsburgh, Pa. 5'11", 170 lbs. Deb: 4/17/1890

YEAR	TM/L	G	AB	R	H	2B	3B	HR	RBI	BB	SO	AVG	OBP	SLG	PRO+	BR/A	SB	CS	SBR	FA	FR	G/POS	TPR
1890	Syr-a	86	316	44	57	6	5	0		16		.180	.222	.231	37	-25	7			.928	-4	C-46,O-33/3S	-2.3
1891	Lou-a	1	4	0	1	0	0	0	0	0		.250	.250	.250	44	-0	0			1.000	-0	/C-1	0.0
1892	StL-N	22	55	2	4	1	0	0		5	16	.073	.164	.091	-24	-8	2			.902	-11	C-15/O-8	-1.8
1895	Lou-N	1	3	0	0	0	0	0	0	0	1	.000	.000	.000	-99	-1	0			1.000	-1	/C-1	-0.2
Total	4	110	378	46	62	7	5	0	1	21	17	.164	.212	.209	27	-35	9			.925	-15	/C-63,O-41,3S	-4.3

■ JOHNNY BRIGGS
Briggs, John Edward b: 3/10/44, Paterson, N.J. BL/TL, 6'1", 195 lbs. Deb: 4/17/64

YEAR	TM/L	G	AB	R	H	2B	3B	HR	RBI	BB	SO	AVG	OBP	SLG	PRO+	BR/A	SB	CS	SBR	FA	FR	G/POS	TPR
1964	Phi-N	61	66	16	17	2	0	1	6	9	12	.258	.347	.333	94	-0	1	1	-0	.957	-2	O-19/1-1	-0.3
1965	Phi-N	93	229	47	54	9	4	4	23	42	44	.236	.354	.362	104	3	3	2	-0	.982	-3	O-66	-0.4
1966	Phi-N	81	255	43	72	13	5	10	23	41	55	.282	.382	.490	140	15	3	2	-0	.977	-4	O-69	0.7
1967	Phi-N	106	332	47	77	12	4	9	30	41	72	.232	.316	.373	96	-2	3	5	-2	.979	-2	O-94	-1.1
1968	Phi-N	110	338	36	86	13	1	7	31	58	72	.254	.365	.361	119	10	8	5	-1	.968	-3	O-65,1-36	0.1
1969	Phi-N	124	361	51	86	20	3	12	46	64	78	.238	.353	.410	116	9	9	6	-1	.971	-4	*O-108/1-2	0.2
1970	Phi-N	110	341	43	92	15	7	9	47	39	65	.270	.345	.434	110	5	5	4	-1	.980	6	O-95	0.5
1971	Phi-N	10	22	3	4	1	0	0	3	6	2	.182	.357	.227	69	-1	0	0	0	.846	1	/O-8	-0.2
	Mil-A	125	375	51	99	11	1	21	59	71	79	.264	.383	.467	141	22	9	2	-1	.958	1	O-65,1-60	1.5
1972	Mil-A	135	418	58	111	14	1	21	65	54	67	.266	.351	.455	141	21	1	2	-1	.980	-2	*O-106,1-28	1.3
1973	Mil-A	142	488	78	120	20	7	18	57	87	83	.246	.362	.426	124	17	15	9	-1	.968	7	*O-137/D-1	1.7
1974	Mil-A	154	554	72	140	30	8	17	73	71	102	.253	.338	.428	120	14	9	7	-2	.973	5	*O-149/D-2	1.2
1975	Mil-A	28	74	12	22	1	0	3	5	20	13	.297	.447	.432	149	6	0	2	-1	.962	3	O-21/D-1	0.6
	Min-A	87	264	44	61	9	2	7	39	60	41	.231	.373	.360	106	4	6	2	-0	.983	7	1-49,O-35/D	0.8
	Yr	115	338	56	83	10	2	10	44	80	54	.246	.390	.376	115	10	6	4	-1	.983	9	O-56,1-49/D	1.4
Total	12	1366	4117	601	1041	170	43	139	507	663	785	.253	.357	.416	121	123	64	49	-10	.973	12	*O-1037,1-176/D	6.6

■ HARRY BRIGHT
Bright, Harry James b: 9/22/29, Kansas City, Mo. BR/TR, 6', 190 lbs. Deb: 8/7/58

YEAR	TM/L	G	AB	R	H	2B	3B	HR	RBI	BB	SO	AVG	OBP	SLG	PRO+	BR/A	SB	CS	SBR	FA	FR	G/POS	TPR
1958	Pit-N	15	24	4	6	1	0	1	3	1	6	.250	.280	.417	84	-1	0	0	0	1.000	0	/3-7	0.0
1959	Pit-N	40	48	4	12	1	0	3	8	5	10	.250	.321	.458	105	-0	0	0	0	1.000	-2	/O-4,3-3,2	-0.2
1960	Pit-N	4	4	0	0	0	0	0	0	0	2	.000	.000	.000	-99	-1	0	0	0	.000	0	H	-0.1
1961	Was-A	72	183	20	44	6	0	4	21	19	23	.240	.312	.339	75	-7	0	2	-1	.928	7	3-40/C-8,2	0.0
1962	Was-A	113	392	55	107	15	4	17	67	26	51	.273	.321	.462	109	3	2	4	-0	.989	-1	1-99/C-3,3	-0.4
1963	Cin-N	1	1	0	0	0	0	0	0	0	1	.000	.000	.000	-97	-0	0	0	0	1.000	-0	/1-1	0.0
	*NY-A	60	157	15	37	7	0	7	23	13	31	.236	.298	.414	98	-1	0	0	0	.985	-5	1-35,3-12	-0.7
1964	NY-A	4	5	0	1	0	0	0	0	1	0	.200	.333	.200	52	-0	0	0	0	1.000	-0	/1-2	-0.1
1965	Chi-N	27	25	1	7	1	0	0	4	0	9	.280	.280	.320	67	-1	0	0	0	.000	0	H	-0.1
Total	8	336	839	99	214	31	4	32	126	65	133	.255	.311	.416	96	-7	2	5	-1	.988	-1	1-137/3-63,CO2	-1.6

■ GREG BRILEY
Briley, Gregory "Peewee" b: 5/24/65, Greenville, N.C. BL/TR, 5'9", 175 lbs. Deb: 6/27/88

YEAR	TM/L	G	AB	R	H	2B	3B	HR	RBI	BB	SO	AVG	OBP	SLG	PRO+	BR/A	SB	CS	SBR	FA	FR	G/POS	TPR
1988	Sea-A	13	36	6	9	2	0	1	4	5	6	.250	.341	.389	100	0	0	1	-1	.929	-2	O-11	-0.3
1989	Sea-A	115	394	52	105	22	4	13	52	39	82	.266	.340	.442	115	7	11	5	0	.958	-5	*O-105,2-10/D	-0.4
1990	Sea-A	125	337	40	83	18	2	5	29	37	48	.246	.323	.356	89	-5	16	4	2	.989	-4	*O-107/D-4	-0.9
1991	Sea-A	139	381	39	99	17	3	2	26	27	51	.260	.309	.336	78	-11	23	11	6	.980	-17	*O-125/2-1,3D	-3.0
1992	Sea-A	86	200	18	55	10	0	5	12	12	31	.275	.293	.400	92	-3	9	2	2	.967	-9	O-42,D-12/23	-1.1
1993	Fla-N	120	170	17	33	6	0	3	12	12	42	.194	.251	.282	40	-14	6	2	1	.986	-12	O-67	-2.7
Total	6	598	1518	172	384	75	9	29	135	124	260	.253	.313	.372	88	-26	65	25	4	.975	-48	O-457/D-20,23	-7.9

YEAR	TM/L	G	AB	R	H	2B	3B	HR	RBI	BB	SO	AVG	OBP	SLG	PRO+	BR/A	SB	CS	SBR	FA	FR	G/POS	TPR

■ BILL BRINKER
Brinker, William Hutchinson "Dode" b: 8/30/1883, Warrensburg, Mo. d: 2/5/65, Arcadia, Cal. BB/TR, 6'1", 190 lbs. Deb: 4/24/12

| 1912 | Phi-N | 9 | 18 | 1 | 4 | 1 | 0 | 0 | 2 | 2 | 3 | .222 | .300 | .278 | 55 | -1 | 0 | | | .778 | -1 | /3-2,O-2 | -0.2 |

■ CHUCK BRINKMAN
Brinkman, Charles Ernest b: 9/16/44, Cincinnati, O. BR/TR, 6'1", 185 lbs. Deb: 7/10/69 F

1969	Chi-A	14	15	2	1	0	0	0	0	1	5	.067	.125	.067	-43	-3	0	0	0	1.000	1	C-14	-0.2
1970	Chi-A	9	20	4	5	1	0	0	0	3	3	.250	.348	.300	77	-1	0	0	0	.974	1	/C-9	0.1
1971	Chi-A	15	20	0	4	0	0	0	1	3	5	.200	.304	.200	44	-1	0	0	0	1.000	2	C-14	0.1
1972	Chi-A	35	52	1	7	0	0	0	0	4	7	.135	.196	.135	-0	-6	0	0	0	.985	7	C-33	0.2
1973	Chi-A	63	139	13	26	6	0	1	10	11	37	.187	.252	.252	41	-11	0	0	0	.987	10	C-63	0.1
1974	Chi-A	8	14	1	2	0	0	0	0	1	3	.143	.200	.143	-0	-2	0	0	0	1.000	-1	/C-8	-0.3
	Pit-N	4	7	1	1	0	0	0	1	0	0	.143	.143	.143	-21	-1	0	0	0	1.000	-0	/C-4	-0.2
Total	6	148	267	22	46	7	0	1	12	23	60	.172	.241	.210	28	-25	0	0	0	.988	20	C-145	-0.2

■ ED BRINKMAN
Brinkman, Edwin Albert b: 12/8/41, Cincinnati, O. BR/TR, 6', 170 lbs. Deb: 9/6/61 FC

1961	Was-A	4	11	0	1	0	0	0	0	1	1	.091	.167	.091	-30	-2	0	0	0	.889	0	/3-3	-0.2
1962	Was-A	54	133	8	22	7	1	0	4	11	28	.165	.229	.233	25	-14	1	0	0	.942	2	S-38,3-10	-1.0
1963	Was-A	145	514	44	117	20	3	7	45	31	86	.228	.277	.319	67	-23	5	3	-0	.950	7	*S-143	-1.5
1964	Was-A	132	447	54	100	20	3	8	34	26	99	.224	.273	.336	68	-20	2	2	-1	.969	-3	*S-125	-1.5
1965	Was-A	154	444	35	82	13	2	5	35	38	82	.185	.252	.257	46	-32	1	2	-1	.964	4	*S-150	-2.1
1966	Was-A	158	582	42	133	18	9	7	48	29	105	.229	.265	.326	70	-24	7	9	-3	.965	12	*S-158	-0.1
1967	Was-A	109	320	21	60	9	2	1	18	24	58	.188	.253	.237	47	-21	1	3	-2	.979	14	*S-109	-0.5
1968	Was-A	77	193	12	36	3	0	0	6	19	31	.187	.259	.202	43	-13	0	0	0	.967	3	S-74/2-2,O	-0.5
1969	Was-A	151	576	71	153	18	5	2	43	50	42	.266	.330	.325	88	-9	2	2	-1	.976	15	*S-150	2.3
1970	Was-A	158	625	63	164	17	2	1	40	60	41	.262	.332	.301	79	-16	3	4	-3	.974	31	*S-157	3.2
1971	Det-A	159	527	40	120	18	2	1	37	44	54	.228	.296	.275	60	-27	1	4	-2	.980	12	*S-159	0.3
1972	*Det-A	156	516	42	105	19	1	6	49	38	51	.203	.262	.279	59	-26	0	0	0	.990	2	*S-156	-0.2
1973	Det-A★	162	515	55	122	16	4	7	40	34	79	.237	.285	.324	67	-23	0	1	-1	.968	-13	*S-162	-1.7
1974	Det-A	153	502	55	111	15	3	14	54	29	71	.221	.268	.347	73	-19	2	0	1	.972	13	*S-151/3-2	1.5
1975	StL-N	28	75	6	18	4	0	1	6	7	10	.240	.313	.333	77	-2	0	0	0	.948	0	S-24	0.0
	Tex-A	1	2	0	0	0	0	0	0	0	1	.000	.000	.000	-99	-1	0	0	0	1.000	-0	/3-1	-0.1
	NY-A	44	63	2	11	4	1	0	2	3	6	.175	.224	.270	40	-5	0	0	0	.933	-3	S-39/2-3,3	-0.6
	Yr	45	65	2	11	4	1	0	2	3	7	.169	.217	.262	36	-6	0	0	0	.933	-3	S-39/3-4,2	-0.7
Total	15	1845	6045	550	1355	201	38	60	461	444	845	.224	.282	.300	65	-276	30	35	-12	.970	94	*S-1795/3-19,2O	-1.4

■ LEON BRINKOPF
Brinkopf, Leon Clarence b: 10/20/26, Cape Girardeau, Mo BR/TR, 5'11.5", 185 lbs. Deb: 4/18/52

| 1952 | Chi-N | 9 | 22 | 1 | 4 | 0 | 0 | 0 | 2 | 4 | 5 | .182 | .308 | .182 | 38 | -2 | 0 | 0 | 0 | .955 | -2 | /S-6 | -0.4 |

■ FATTY BRIODY
Briody, Charles F. "Alderman" b: 8/13/1858, Lansingburg, N.Y. d: 6/22/03, Chicago, Ill. TR, 5'8.5", 190 lbs. Deb: 6/16/1880

1880	Tro-N	1	4	0	0	0	0	0	0	0	0	.000	.000	.000	-95	-1				.700	-1	/C-1	-0.2
1882	Cle-N	53	194	30	50	13	0	0	13	9	13	.258	.291	.325	100	0				.902	2	C-53	0.3
1883	Cle-N	40	145	23	34	5	1	0	10	3	13	.234	.250	.283	62	-6				.900	4	C-33/2-4,13	-0.1
1884	Cle-N	43	148	17	25	6	0	1	12	6	19	.169	.201	.230	34	-11				.922	10	C-42/O-1	0.2
	Cin-U	22	89	11	30	2	2	0	1		1	.337	.344	.404	95	-1				.943	17	C-22	1.5
1885	StL-N	62	215	14	42	9	0	1	17	12	23	.195	.238	.251	62	-8				.893	-9	C-60/O-1,32	-1.2
1886	KC-N	56	215	14	51	10	3	0	29	3	35	.237	.248	.312	65	-10	0			.919	2	C-54/O-2,1	-0.2
1887	Det-N	33	128	24	29	6	1	1	26	9	10	.227	.283	.313	63	-7	6			.907	6	C-33	0.2
1888	KC-a	13	48	1	10	1	0	0	8	1		.208	.224	.229	43	-3	0			.896	-4	C-13	-0.5
Total	8	323	1186	134	271	52	7	3	115	44	113	.228	.257	.292	67	-47	6			.910	25	C-311/2-5,O13	0.0

■ GEORGE BRISTOW
Bristow, George T. b: 5/1870, Paw Paw, Ill. TR , Deb: 4/15/1899

| 1899 | Cle-N | 3 | 8 | 0 | 1 | 1 | 0 | 0 | 1 | | | .125 | .222 | .250 | 32 | -1 | 0 | | | 1.000 | 0 | /O-3 | -0.1 |

■ BERNARDO BRITO
Brito, Bernardo b: 12/4/63, San Cristobal, D.R. BR/TR, 6'1", 190 lbs. Deb: 9/15/92

1992	Min-A	8	14	1	2	1	0	0	2	0	4	.143	.143	.214	-1	-1	0	1	-1	.750	-1	/O-3,D-1	-0.4
1993	Min-A	27	54	8	13	2	0	4	9	1	20	.241	.255	.500	97	-1	0	0	0	1.000	-1	O-10/D-7	-0.2
Total	2	35	68	9	15	3	0	4	11	1	24	.221	.232	.441	77	-3	0	1	-1	.941	-2	/O-13,D-8	-0.6

■ GUS BRITTAIN
Brittain, August Schuster b: 11/29/09, Wilmington, N.C. d: 2/16/74, Wilmington, N.C. BR/TR, 5'10", 192 lbs. Deb: 7/22/37

| 1937 | Cin-N | 3 | 6 | 0 | 1 | 0 | 0 | 0 | 0 | 0 | 3 | .167 | .167 | .167 | -10 | -1 | 0 | | | 1.000 | -0 | /C-1 | -0.1 |

■ GIL BRITTON
Britton, Stephen Gilbert b: 9/21/1891, Parsons, Kan. d: 6/20/83, Parsons, Kan. BR/TR, 5'10", 160 lbs. Deb: 9/20/13

| 1913 | Pit-N | 3 | 12 | 0 | 0 | 0 | 0 | 0 | 0 | 0 | 2 | .000 | .000 | .000 | -99 | -3 | 0 | | | .824 | -1 | /S-3 | -0.4 |

■ GREG BROCK
Brock, Gregory Allen b: 6/14/57, McMinnville, Ore. BL/TR, 6'3", 205 lbs. Deb: 9/1/82

1982	LA-N	18	17	1	2	1	0	0	1	1	5	.118	.167	.176	-4	-4	0	0	0	1.000	-0	/1-3	-0.3
1983	*LA-N	146	455	64	102	14	2	20	66	83	81	.224	.345	.396	105	5	5	1	1	.991	5	*1-140	0.3
1984	LA-N	88	271	33	61	6	0	14	34	39	37	.225	.323	.402	104	1	8	0	2	.995	7	1-83	0.7
1985	*LA-N	129	438	64	110	19	0	21	66	54	72	.251	.333	.438	118	10	4	2	0	.994	2	*1-122	0.4
1986	LA-N	115	325	33	76	19	0	16	52	37	60	.234	.312	.422	108	5	2	5	-2	.996	12	1-99	0.6
1987	Mil-A	141	532	81	159	29	3	13	85	57	63	.299	.363	.438	111	10	5	4	-1	.993	4	*1-141	0.2
1988	Mil-A	115	364	53	77	16	1	6	50	63	48	.212	.333	.310	81	-8	6	2	1	.993	9	*1-114/D-1	-0.7
1989	Mil-A	107	373	40	99	16	0	12	52	43	49	.265	.346	.405	112	5	6	1	1	.995	-5	*1-100/D-7	-0.5
1990	Mil-A	123	367	42	91	23	0	7	50	49	45	.248	.330	.368	96	-2	2	0	0	.995	-4	*1-115	-1.4
1991	Mil-A	31	60	9	17	4	0	1	9	9	9	.283	.419	.400	131	3	1	1	-0	1.000	-1	1-25	0.1
Total	10	1013	3202	420	794	141	6	110	462	434	469	.248	.340	.399	105	25	41	18	2	.994	29	1-942/D-8	-0.6

■ JOHN BROCK
Brock, John Roy b: 10/16/1896, Hamilton, Ill. d: 10/27/51, Clayton, Mo. BR/TR, 5'6.5", 165 lbs. Deb: 8/10/17

1917	StL-N	7	15	4	6	1	0	0	2	0	2	.400	.400	.467	170	1	2			.944	-1	/C-4	0.1
1918	StL-N	27	52	9	11	2	0	0	4	3	10	.212	.255	.250	56	-3	5			.951	-2	C-18/O-1	-0.4
Total	2	34	67	13	17	3	0	0	6	3	12	.254	.286	.299	81	-2	7			.949	-2	/C-22,O-1	-0.3

■ LOU BROCK
Brock, Louis Clark b: 6/18/39, ElDorado, Ark. BL/TL, 5'11.5", 170 lbs. Deb: 9/10/61 H

1961	Chi-N	4	11	1	1	0	0	0	0	0	3	.091	.167	.091	-29	-2	0	0	0	.750	-1	/O-3	-0.3
1962	Chi-N	123	434	73	114	24	7	9	35	35	96	.263	.322	.412	92	-5	16	7	1	.965	0	*O-106	-1.0
1963	Chi-N	148	547	79	141	19	11	9	37	31	122	.258	.302	.382	91	-7	24	12	0	.973	13	*O-140	-0.1
1964	Chi-N	52	215	30	54	9	2	2	14	13	40	.251	.300	.340	77	-7	10	3	1	.959	2	O-52	-0.6
	*StL-N	103	419	81	146	21	9	12	44	27	87	.348	.391	.527	143	23	33	15	1	.949	6	*O-102	2.6
	Yr	155	634	111	200	30	11	14	58	40	127	.315	.360	.464	121	17	43	18	2	.953	8	*O-154	2.0
1965	StL-N	155	631	107	182	35	8	16	69	45	116	.288	.345	.445	110	8	63	27	3	.959	8	*O-153	1.3
1966	StL-N	156	643	94	183	24	12	15	46	31	134	.285	.321	.429	106	4	74	18	11	.936	5	*O-154	1.2
1967	*StL-N★	159	689	113	206	32	12	21	76	24	109	.299	.328	.472	128	22	52	18	5	.956	7	*O-157	2.7
1968	*StL-N	159	660	92	184	46	14	6	51	46	124	.279	.329	.418	125	18	62	12	11	.952	6	*O-156	3.1
1969	StL-N	157	655	97	195	33	10	12	47	50	115	.298	.349	.434	118	14	53	14	8	.949	5	*O-157	1.8
1970	StL-N	155	664	114	202	29	5	13	57	60	99	.304	.363	.422	107	7	51	15	8	.962	-1	*O-152	0.8
1971	StL-N★	157	640	126	200	37	7	7	61	76	107	.313	.386	.425	125	23	64	19	8	.951	-1	*O-157	2.3

YEAR	TM/L	G	AB	R	H	2B	3B	HR	RBI	BB	SO	AVG	OBP	SLG	PRO+	BR/A	SB	CS	SBR	FA	FR	G/POS	TPR
1972	StL-N☆	153	621	81	193	26	8	3	42	47	93	.311	.360	.393	115	12	**63**	18	8	.952	-4	*O-149	1.1
1973	StL-N	160	650	110	193	29	8	7	63	71	88	.297	.366	.398	112	12	**70**	20	9	.963	1	*O-159	1.5
1974	StL-N★	153	635	105	194	25	7	3	48	61	88	.306	.368	.381	111	10	**118**	33	**16**	.967	2	*O-152	2.2
1975	StL-N★	136	528	78	163	27	6	3	47	38	64	.309	.359	.400	106	1	56	16	7	.966	1	*O-128	0.7
1976	StL-N	133	498	73	150	24	5	4	67	35	75	.301	.348	.394	109	6	56	19	5	.983	0	*O-123	0.7
1977	StL-N	141	489	69	133	22	6	2	46	30	74	.272	.317	.354	81	-13	35	24	-4	.954	-11	*O-130	-3.4
1978	StL-N	92	298	31	66	9	0	0	12	17	29	.221	.263	.252	45	-22	17	5	2	.975	-6	O-79	-3.1
1979	StL-N★	120	405	56	123	15	4	5	38	23	43	.304	.346	.398	101	1	21	12	-1	.958	-3	O-98	-0.8
Total	19	2616	10332	1610	3023	486	141	149	900	761	1730	.293	.344	.410	109	110	938	307	97	.959	32	*O-2507	12.7

■ MATT BRODERICK
Broderick, Matthew Thomas   b: 12/1/1877, Lattimer, Pa.   d: 2/26/40, Freeland, Pa.   BR/TR, 5'6.5", 135 lbs.   Deb: 5/1/03

YEAR	TM/L	G	AB	R	H	2B	3B	HR	RBI	BB	SO	AVG	OBP	SLG	PRO+	BR/A	SB	CS	SBR	FA	FR	G/POS	TPR
1903	Bro-N	2	2	0	0	0	0	0	0	0	0	.000	.000	.000	-99	-1	0			1.000	0	/2-1	0.0

■ STEVE BRODIE
Brodie, Walter Scott   b: 9/11/1868, Warrenton, Va.   d: 10/30/35, Baltimore, Md.   BL/TR, 5'11", 180 lbs.   Deb: 4/21/1890

YEAR	TM/L	G	AB	R	H	2B	3B	HR	RBI	BB	SO	AVG	OBP	SLG	PRO+	BR/A	SB	CS	SBR	FA	FR	G/POS	TPR
1890	Bos-N	132	514	77	152	19	9	0	67	66	20	.296	.387	.368	111	8	29			**.953**	3	*O-132	0.6
1891	Bos-N	133	523	84	136	13	6	2	78	63	39	.260	.351	.319	85	-11	25			.951	10	*O-133	-0.4
1892	StL-N	154	602	85	152	10	9	4	60	52	31	.252	.316	.319	97	-2	28			.943	8	*O-137,2-16/3	0.1
1893	StL-N	107	469	71	149	16	8	2	79	33	16	.318	.376	.399	106	4	41			.951	9	*O-107	0.6
	Bal-N	25	97	18	35	7	2	0	19	12	2	.361	.446	.474	142	6	8			.963	-3	O-25	0.2
	Yr	132	566	89	184	23	10	2	98	45	18	.325	.389	.412	112	10	49			.953	6	*O-132	0.8
1894	*Bal-N	129	573	134	210	25	11	3	113	18	8	.366	.399	.464	103	1	42			.950	-6	*O-129	-1.0
1895	*Bal-N	131	528	85	184	27	10	2	134	26	15	.348	.394	.449	114	10	35			.965	5	*O-131	0.4
1896	*Bal-N	132	516	98	153	19	11	2	87	36	17	.297	.363	.388	97	-2	25			.972	11	*O-132	-0.2
1897	Pit-N	100	370	47	108	7	12	2	53	25		.292	.348	.392	99	-1	11			**.983**	-0	*O-100	-0.7
1898	Pit-N	42	156	15	41	5	0	0	21	6		.263	.303	.295	73	-6	3			.958	3	O-42	-0.5
	Bal-N	23	98	12	30	3	2	0	19	5		.306	.346	.378	105	0	3			.923	3	O-23	0.1
	Yr	65	254	27	71	8	2	0	40	11		.280	.320	.327	86	-5	6			.946	6	O-65	-0.4
1899	Bal-N	137	531	82	164	26	1	3	87	31		.309	.373	.379	101	1	19			**.979**	1	*O-137	-0.8
1901	Bal-A	83	306	41	95	6	6	2	41	25		.310	.378	.389	108	4	9			.963	-3	O-83	-0.5
1902	NY-N	109	416	37	117	8	2	3	42	22		.281	.327	.332	104	2	11			.953	7	O-109	0.1
Total	12	1437	5699	886	1726	191	89	25	900	420	148	.303	.364	.381	102	15	289			.959	48	*O-1420/2-16,3	-2.0

■ RICO BROGNA
Brogna, Rico Joseph   b: 4/18/70, Turners Falls, Mass.   BL/TL, 6'2", 202 lbs.   Deb: 8/8/92

YEAR	TM/L	G	AB	R	H	2B	3B	HR	RBI	BB	SO	AVG	OBP	SLG	PRO+	BR/A	SB	CS	SBR	FA	FR	G/POS	TPR
1992	Det-A	9	26	3	5	1	0	1	3	3	5	.192	.276	.346	73	-1	0	0	0	.982	1	/1-8,D-2	-0.1
1994	NY-N	39	131	16	46	11	2	7	20	6	29	.351	.380	.626	155	10	1	0	0	.997	2	1-35	0.9
Total	2	48	157	19	51	12	2	8	23	9	34	.325	.361	.580	142	9	1	0	0	.995	2	/1-43,D-2	0.8

■ JACK BROHAMER
Brohamer, John Anthony   b: 2/26/50, Maywood, Cal.   BL/TR, 5'10", 165 lbs.   Deb: 4/18/72

YEAR	TM/L	G	AB	R	H	2B	3B	HR	RBI	BB	SO	AVG	OBP	SLG	PRO+	BR/A	SB	CS	SBR	FA	FR	G/POS	TPR
1972	Cle-A	136	527	49	123	13	2	5	35	27	46	.233	.272	.294	66	-22	3	2	-0	.977	6	*2-132/3-1	-1.1
1973	Cle-A	102	300	29	66	12	1	4	29	32	23	.220	.295	.307	69	-12	0	2	-1	.971	17	2-97	0.8
1974	Cle-A	101	315	33	85	11	1	2	30	26	22	.270	.331	.330	92	-3	2	1	0	.987	-4	2-99	-0.3
1975	Cle-A	69	217	15	53	5	0	6	16	14	14	.244	.290	.350	80	-6	2	2	-1	.976	4	2-66	-0.1
1976	Chi-A	119	354	33	89	12	2	7	40	44	28	.251	.339	.356	103	2	1	3	-2	.984	18	*2-117/3-1	2.7
1977	Chi-A	59	152	26	39	10	3	2	20	21	8	.257	.351	.401	105	1	0	0	0	.923	2	3-38,2-18/D	0.4
1978	Bos-A	81	244	34	57	14	1	1	25	25	13	.234	.305	.311	62	-11	1	3	-2	.974	-3	3-30,D-25,2	-1.6
1979	Bos-A	64	192	25	51	7	1	1	11	15	15	.266	.319	.328	71	-8	0	3	-2	.982	0	2-36,3-22	-0.7
1980	Bos-A	21	57	5	18	2	0	1	6	4	3	.316	.361	.404	104	0	0	0	0	.900	-1	3-13/2-4,D	-0.1
	Cle-A	53	142	13	32	5	1	1	15	14	6	.225	.295	.296	62	-7	0	1	-1	.979	-4	2-47/D-1	-0.9
	Yr	74	199	18	50	7	1	2	21	18	9	.251	.313	.327	74	-7	0	1	-1	.981	-5	2-51,3-13/D	-1.0
Total	9	805	2500	262	613	91	12	30	227	222	178	.245	.309	.327	79	-65	9	17	-8	.979	33	2-639,3-105/D	-0.8

■ HERMAN BRONKIE
Bronkie, Herman Charles "Dutch"   b: 3/31/1885, S.Manchester, Conn.   d: 5/27/68, Somers, Conn.   BR/TR, 5'9", 165 lbs.   Deb: 9/20/10

YEAR	TM/L	G	AB	R	H	2B	3B	HR	RBI	BB	SO	AVG	OBP	SLG	PRO+	BR/A	SB	CS	SBR	FA	FR	G/POS	TPR
1910	Cle-A	5	9	1	2	0	0	0	0	0	1	.222	.300	.222	63	-0	1			.625	-1	/3-3,S-1	-0.2
1911	Cle-A	2	6	0	1	0	0	0	0	0	0	.167	.167	.167	-7	-1	0			1.000	-1	/3-2	-0.2
1912	Cle-A	6	16	1	0	0	0	0	0	0	1	.000	.059	.000	-80	-4	0			.917	3	/3-6	-0.1
1914	Chi-N	1	1	1	1	1	0	0	0	0	0	1.000	1.000	2.000	786	1	0			.000	-0	/3-1	0.0
1918	StL-N	18	68	7	15	3	0	1	7	2	4	.221	.243	.309	70	-3	0			.984	-1	3-18	-0.4
1919	StL-A	67	196	23	50	8	4	0	14	23	23	.255	.336	.327	84	-4	2			.939	4	3-34,2-16/1	0.2
1922	StL-A	23	64	7	18	4	1	0	2	6	7	.281	.343	.375	84	-1	0	2	-1	.917	-0	3-18	-0.2
Total	7	122	360	40	87	14	5	1	24	33	34	.242	.307	.317	75	-12	3	2		.931	2	/3-82,2-16,1S	-0.9

■ TOM BROOKENS
Brookens, Thomas Dale   b: 8/10/53, Chambersburg, Pa.   BR/TR, 5'10", 170 lbs.   Deb: 7/10/79

YEAR	TM/L	G	AB	R	H	2B	3B	HR	RBI	BB	SO	AVG	OBP	SLG	PRO+	BR/A	SB	CS	SBR	FA	FR	G/POS	TPR
1979	Det-A	60	190	23	50	5	2	4	21	11	40	.263	.310	.374	81	-5	10	3	1	.945	11	3-42,2-19	0.7
1980	Det-A	151	509	64	140	25	9	10	66	32	71	.275	.319	.418	98	-2	13	11	-3	.931	4	*3-138/2-9,SD	-0.3
1981	Det-A	71	239	19	58	10	1	4	25	14	43	.243	.290	.343	79	-7	5	3	-0	.952	-4	3-71	-1.3
1982	Det-A	140	398	40	92	15	3	9	58	27	63	.231	.280	.352	72	-16	5	9	-4	.939	10	*3-113,2-26/SO	-1.1
1983	Det-A	138	332	50	71	13	3	6	32	29	46	.214	.281	.325	68	-15	10	4	1	.928	5	*3-103,S-30,2/D	-0.9
1984	*Det-A	113	224	32	55	11	4	5	26	19	33	.246	.307	.397	94	-2	6	6	-2	.969	20	3-68,S-28,2/D	1.8
1985	Det-A	156	485	54	115	34	6	7	47	27	78	.237	.277	.375	77	-16	14	5	4	.943	3	*3-151/S-8,2CD	-1.4
1986	Det-A	98	281	42	76	11	2	3	25	20	42	.270	.321	.356	84	-6	11	8	-2	.955	-2	3-35,2-31/SD/O	-0.5
1987	*Det-A	143	444	59	107	15	3	13	59	33	63	.241	.296	.376	80	-13	4	7	-0	.954	-2	*3-122/S-16,2	-1.1
1988	Det-A	136	441	62	107	23	5	5	38	44	74	.243	.316	.351	90	-6	4	4	-1	.952	-3	3-136/S-3,2	-1.1
1989	NY-A	66	168	14	38	6	0	4	14	11	27	.226	.274	.333	71	-7	1	3	-2	.926	-4	3-51/S-7,2OD	-1.2
1990	Cle-A	64	154	18	41	7	2	1	20	14	25	.266	.327	.357	92	-2	0	0	0	.923	4	3-35,2-21/S1D	0.3
Total	12	1336	3865	477	950	175	40	71	431	281	605	.246	.299	.367	83	-97	86	60	-10	.943	48	*3-1065,2-162,S/DO1O	-6.1

■ HARRY BROOKS
Brooks, Harry Frank   b: 11/30/1865, Philadelphia, Pa.   d: 12/5/45, Philadelphia, Pa.   Deb: 7/24/1886

YEAR	TM/L	G	AB	R	H	2B	3B	HR	RBI	BB	SO	AVG	OBP	SLG	PRO+	BR/A	SB	CS	SBR	FA	FR	G/POS	TPR
1886	NY-a	1	1	0	0	0	0	0		0		.000	.000	.000	-99	-0	0			.500	-1	/O-1,P-1	0.0

■ HUBIE BROOKS
Brooks, Hubert   b: 9/24/56, Los Angeles, Cal.   BR/TR, 6', 200 lbs.   Deb: 9/4/80

YEAR	TM/L	G	AB	R	H	2B	3B	HR	RBI	BB	SO	AVG	OBP	SLG	PRO+	BR/A	SB	CS	SBR	FA	FR	G/POS	TPR
1980	NY-N	24	81	8	25	2	1	1	10	5	9	.309	.364	.395	115	-1	1	1	-0	.966	-1	3-23	0.3
1981	NY-N	98	358	34	110	21	2	4	38	23	65	.307	.351	.411	117	7	9	5	-0	.924	-2	3-93/O-3,S	0.3
1982	NY-N	126	457	40	114	21	2	2	40	28	76	.249	.300	.317	73	-16	6	3	0	.931	-8	*3-126	-2.9
1983	NY-N	150	586	53	147	18	4	5	58	24	96	.251	.285	.321	68	-26	6	5	-1	.950	-3	*3-145/2-7	-2.7
1984	NY-N	153	561	61	159	23	2	16	73	48	79	.283	.342	.417	114	10	6	5	-1	.929	-18	*3-129,S-26	-2.0
1985	Mon-N	156	605	67	163	34	7	13	100	34	79	.269	.314	.413	108	4	6	4	-4	.958	-34	*S-155	-2.0
1986	Mon-N★	80	306	50	104	18	5	14	58	25	60	.340	.393	.569	164	25	4	2	0	.958	-14	S-80	2.0
1987	Mon-N	112	430	57	113	22	3	14	72	24	72	.263	.303	.426	88	-9	4	3	-1	.953	-26	*S-109	-2.7
1988	Mon-N	151	588	61	164	35	2	20	90	35	108	.279	.321	.447	113	8	7	3	0	.968	-2	*O-149	0.3
1989	Mon-N	148	542	56	145	30	1	14	70	39	108	.268	.321	.404	105	2	6	11	-5	.964	-2	*O-140	-0.8
1990	LA-N	153	568	74	151	28	1	20	91	33	108	.266	.313	.424	106	1	2	3	0	.972	-1	*O-100	0.0
1991	NY-N	103	357	48	85	11	1	16	50	44	62	.238	.327	.409	106	2	3	1	-1	.986	-0	D-70/1-6	-2.1
1992	Cal-A	82	306	28	66	13	0	8	36	12	46	.216	.248	.337	62	-16	3	3	-1	.986	-0	D-70/1-6	-2.1
1993	KC-A	75	168	14	48	12	0	1	24	11	27	.286	.333	.375	85	-4	2	1	-1	.966	-3	O-40/1-3,D	-0.8

YEAR	TM/L	G	AB	R	H	2B	3B	HR	RBI	BB	SO	AVG	OBP	SLG	PRO+	BR/A	SB	CS	SBR	FA	FR	G/POS	TPR
1994	KC-A	34	61	5	14	2	0	1	14	2	10	.230	.254	.311	41	-5	1	0	0	1.000	-0	D-19/1-4	-0.6
Total	15	1645	5974	656	1608	290	31	149	824	387	1005	.269	.318	.403	100	-14	64	56	-14	.966	-112	O-582,3-516,S/D12	-13.7

■ JERRY BROOKS
Brooks, Jerome Edward b: 3/23/67, Syracuse, N.Y. BR/TR, 6', 195 lbs. Deb: 9/6/93

YEAR	TM/L	G	AB	R	H	2B	3B	HR	RBI	BB	SO	AVG	OBP	SLG	PRO+	BR/A	SB	CS	SBR	FA	FR	G/POS	TPR
1993	LA-N	9	9	2	2	1	0	1	1	1	2	.222	.222	.667	135	0	0	0	0	.000	-1	/O-2	-0.1

■ MANDY BROOKS
Brooks, Jonathan Joseph (b: Jonathan Joseph Brozek)
b: 8/18/1897, Milwaukee, Wis. d: 6/17/62, Kirkwood, Mo. BR/TR, 5'9", 165 lbs. Deb: 5/30/25

YEAR	TM/L	G	AB	R	H	2B	3B	HR	RBI	BB	SO	AVG	OBP	SLG	PRO+	BR/A	SB	CS	SBR	FA	FR	G/POS	TPR
1925	Chi-N	90	349	55	98	25	7	14	72	19	28	.281	.322	.513	108	2	10	3	1	.977	5	O-89	0.2
1926	Chi-N	26	48	7	9	1	0	1	6	5	5	.188	.278	.271	48	-4	0			1.000	-2	O-18	-0.7
Total	2	116	397	62	107	26	7	15	78	24	33	.270	.316	.484	101	-2	10	3		.979	2	O-107	-0.5

■ BOBBY BROOKS
Brooks, Robert b: 11/1/45, Los Angeles, Cal. BR/TR, 5'8.5", 165 lbs. Deb: 9/1/69

YEAR	TM/L	G	AB	R	H	2B	3B	HR	RBI	BB	SO	AVG	OBP	SLG	PRO+	BR/A	SB	CS	SBR	FA	FR	G/POS	TPR
1969	Oak-A	29	79	13	19	5	0	3	10	20	24	.241	.400	.418	135	5	0	2	-1	1.000	0	O-21	0.3
1970	Oak-A	7	18	2	6	1	0	2	5	1	7	.333	.368	.722	201	2	0	1	-1	1.000	-1	/O-5	0.0
1972	Oak-A	15	39	4	7	0	0	0	5	8	8	.179	.319	.179	54	-2	0	1	-1	.930	2	O-11	-0.1
1973	Cal-A	4	7	0	1	0	0	0	0	0	3	.143	.143	.143	-21	-7	0	0	0	.000	-0	/O-1	-0.2
Total	4	55	143	19	33	6	0	5	20	29	42	.231	.364	.378	116	-4	0	4	-2	.964	1	O-38	0.0

■ SCOTT BROSIUS
Brosius, Scott David b: 8/15/66, Hillsboro, Ore. BR/TR, 6'1", 185 lbs. Deb: 8/7/91

YEAR	TM/L	G	AB	R	H	2B	3B	HR	RBI	BB	SO	AVG	OBP	SLG	PRO+	BR/A	SB	CS	SBR	FA	FR	G/POS	TPR
1991	Oak-A	36	68	9	16	5	0	2	4	3	11	.235	.268	.397	86	-2	3	1	0	1.000	-1	2-18,O-13/3D	-0.2
1992	Oak-A	38	87	13	19	2	0	4	13	3	13	.218	.261	.379	82	-3	3	0	1	1.000	-8	O-20,3-12/1SD	-1.1
1993	Oak-A	70	213	26	53	10	1	6	25	14	37	.249	.298	.390	89	-4	6	0	2	.991	-2	O-46,1-11,3/SD	-0.5
1994	Oak-A	96	324	31	77	14	1	14	49	24	57	.238	.294	.417	88	-7	2	6	-3	.946	-4	3-93/O-7,1	-1.4
Total	4	240	692	79	165	31	2	26	91	44	118	.238	.289	.402	87	-16	14	7	0	.953	-15	3-122/O-86,21SD	-3.2

■ SIG BROSKIE
Broskie, Sigmund Theodore "Chops" b: 3/23/11, Iselin, Pa. d: 5/17/75, Canton, Ohio BR/TR, 5'11.5", 200 lbs. Deb: 9/11/40

YEAR	TM/L	G	AB	R	H	2B	3B	HR	RBI	BB	SO	AVG	OBP	SLG	PRO+	BR/A	SB	CS	SBR	FA	FR	G/POS	TPR
1940	Bos-N	11	22	1	6	1	0	0	4	1	2	.273	.304	.318	76	-1	0			.935	0	C-11	0.0

■ TONY BROTTEM
Brottem, Anton Christian b: 4/30/1892, Halstad, Minn. d: 8/5/29, Chicago, Ill. BR/TR, 6'0.5", 176 lbs. Deb: 4/17/16

YEAR	TM/L	G	AB	R	H	2B	3B	HR	RBI	BB	SO	AVG	OBP	SLG	PRO+	BR/A	SB	CS	SBR	FA	FR	G/POS	TPR
1916	StL-N	26	33	3	6	1	0	0	4	3	10	.182	.250	.212	43	-2	1			.950	-1	C-15/O-2	-0.3
1918	StL-N	2	4	0	0	0	0	0	0	1	0	.000	.200	.000	-39	-1	0			1.000	1	/1-2	0.0
1921	Was-A	4	7	1	1	0	0	0	0	2	1	.143	.333	.143	26	-1	0	0	0	1.000	1	/C-4	0.1
	Pit-N	30	91	6	22	2	0	0	9	3	11	.242	.266	.264	40	-8	0	1	-1	.983	-2	C-29	-0.9
Total	3	62	135	10	29	3	0	0	13	9	22	.215	.264	.237	38	-11	1	1		.977	-1	/C-48,1-2,O	-1.1

■ CAL BROUGHTON
Broughton, Cecil Calvert b: 12/28/1860, Magnolia, Wis. d: 3/15/39, Evansville, Wis. BR/TR, Deb: 5/2/1883

YEAR	TM/L	G	AB	R	H	2B	3B	HR	RBI	BB	SO	AVG	OBP	SLG	PRO+	BR/A	SB	CS	SBR	FA	FR	G/POS	TPR
1883	Cle-N	4	10	2	2	0	0	0	1	2	2	.200	.333	.200	68	-0				.950	-0	/C-4	0.0
	Bal-a	9	32	1	6	0	0	0		1		.188	.212	.188	29	-2				.825	-2	/C-8,O-1	-0.3
1884	Mil-U	11	39	5	12	5	0	0		0		.308	.308	.436	184	2				.937	-1	/C-7,O-5	0.2
1885	StL-a	4	17	1	1	0	0	0		0		.059	.059	.059	-60	-3				.889	-1	/C-4	-0.4
	NY-a	11	41	1	6	1	0	0		0		.146	.167	.171	7	-4				.860	-2	C-11	-0.4
	Yr	15	58	2	7	1	0	0		0		.121	.136	.138	-14	-7				.867	-3	C-15	-0.8
1888	Det-N	1	4	0	0	0	0	0	0	0	0	.000	.000	.000	-99	-1	0			1.000	1	/C-1	0.0
Total	4	40	143	10	27	6	0	0	1	4	2	.189	.211	.231	39	-8	0			.887	-5	/C-35,O-6	-0.9

■ MARK BROUHARD
Brouhard, Mark Steven b: 5/22/56, Burbank, Cal. BR/TR, 6'1", 210 lbs. Deb: 4/12/80

YEAR	TM/L	G	AB	R	H	2B	3B	HR	RBI	BB	SO	AVG	OBP	SLG	PRO+	BR/A	SB	CS	SBR	FA	FR	G/POS	TPR
1980	Mil-A	45	125	17	29	6	0	5	16	7	24	.232	.278	.400	86	-3	1	0	0	.964	0	D-21,O-12,1	-0.4
1981	Mil-A	60	186	19	51	6	3	2	20	7	41	.274	.308	.371	100	-1	1	1	-0	.990	1	O-51/D-7	-0.1
1982	*Mil-A	40	108	16	29	4	1	4	10	9	17	.269	.336	.435	117	2	3	-2	.986	2	O-30/D-7	0.2
1983	Mil-A	56	185	25	51	10	1	7	23	9	39	.276	.316	.454	118	4	0	4	-3	.991	4	O-42,D-11	0.2
1984	Mil-A	66	197	20	47	7	0	6	22	16	36	.239	.302	.365	87	-4	0	3	-2	.983	-4	O-52/D-8	-0.3
1985	Mil-A	37	108	11	28	7	2	1	13	5	26	.259	.298	.389	87	-2	0	0	-0	.964	-3	O-29/D-1	-0.6
Total	6	304	909	108	235	40	7	25	104	53	183	.259	.307	.400	99	-3	2	11	-6	.983	7	O-216/D-55,1	-1.0

■ ART BROUTHERS
Brouthers, Arthur H. b: 11/25/1882, Montgomery, Ala. d: 9/28/59, Charleston, S.C. TR, 6'1", Deb: 4/14/06

YEAR	TM/L	G	AB	R	H	2B	3B	HR	RBI	BB	SO	AVG	OBP	SLG	PRO+	BR/A	SB	CS	SBR	FA	FR	G/POS	TPR
1906	Phi-A	37	144	18	30	5	1	0	14	5		.208	.240	.257	54	-8	4			.900	-4	3-35/2-1	-1.2

■ DAN BROUTHERS
Brouthers, Dennis Joseph "Big Dan" b: 5/8/1858, Sylvan Lake, N.Y. d: 8/2/32, E.Orange, N.J. BL/TL, 6'2", 207 lbs. Deb: 6/23/1879 H

YEAR	TM/L	G	AB	R	H	2B	3B	HR	RBI	BB	SO	AVG	OBP	SLG	PRO+	BR/A	SB	CS	SBR	FA	FR	G/POS	TPR
1879	Tro-N	39	168	17	46	12	1	4	17	1	18	.274	.278	.429	138	7				.926	-5	1-37/P-3	0.1
1880	Tro-N	3	12	0	2	0	0	0	1	1	0	.167	.231	.167	35	-1				.893	-1	/1-3	-0.2
1881	Buf-N	65	270	60	86	18	9	8	45	18	22	.319	.361	.541	182	25				.797	-5	O-35,1-30	1.5
1882	Buf-N	84	351	71	**129**	23	11	6	63	21	7	**.368**	.403	**.547**	198	37				**.974**	1	*1-84	2.6
1883	Buf-N	98	425	85	**159**	41	**17**	3	**97**	16	17	**.374**	.397	.572	186	42				.961	2	*1-97/3-1,P	2.9
1884	Buf-N	94	398	82	130	22	15	14	79	33	20	.327	.378	.563	186	38				.964	0	*1-93/3-1	2.4
1885	Buf-N	98	407	87	146	32	11	7	59	34	10	.359	.408	.543	199	43				.975	-2	*1-98	2.7
1886	Det-N	121	489	139	181	**40**	15	**11**	72	66	16	.370	.445	**.581**	204	62	21			.968	-8	*1-121	3.5
1887	*Det-N	123	500	**153**	169	**36**	20	12	101	71	9	.338	**.426**	.562	167	46	34			.969	-4	*1-123	2.4
1888	Det-N	129	522	**118**	160	**33**	11	9	66	68	13	.307	.399	.464	174	47	34			.971	-2	*1-129	3.2
1889	Bos-N	126	485	105	181	26	9	7	118	66	6	**.373**	.462	.507	161	42	22			.974	1	*1-126	2.9
1890	Bos-P	123	460	117	152	36	9	1	97	99	17	.330	**.466**	.454	137	29	28			.963	2	*1-123	1.9
1891	Bos-a	130	486	117	170	26	19	5	109	87	20	**.350**	**.471**	.512	184	59	31			.978	-7	*1-130	3.8
1892	Bro-N	152	588	121	**197**	30	20	5	**124**	84	30	**.335**	.432	.480	182	62	31			.982	12	*1-152	**6.1**
1893	Bro-N	77	282	57	95	21	11	2	59	52	10	.337	.450	.511	162	28	9			.986	3	1-77	2.4
1894	*Bal-N	123	525	137	182	39	23	9	128	67	9	.347	.425	.560	130	24	38			.976	-2	*1-123	1.8
1895	Bal-N	5	23	2	6	2	0	0	5	1	1	.261	.292	.348	63	-1	0			1.000	0	/1-5	-0.1
	Lou-N	24	97	13	30	10	1	2	15	11	2	.309	.380	.495	133	5	1			.953	-2	1-24	0.2
	Yr	29	120	15	36	12	1	2	20	12	3	.300	.364	.467	119	3	1			.960	-2	1-29	0.1
1896	Phi-N	57	218	42	75	13	3	1	41	44	11	.344	.462	.445	141	16	7			.983	-2	1-57	1.2
1904	NY-N	2	5	0	0	0	0	0	0	0		.000	.000	.000	-96	-1	0			1.000	-0	/1-1	-0.2
Total	19	1673	6711	1523	2296	460	205	106	1296	840	238	.342	.423	.519	170	609	256			.971	-18	*1-1633/O-35,P3	41.1

■ JOE BROVIA
Brovia, Joseph John "Ox" b: 2/18/22, Davenport, Cal. d: 8/15/94, Santa Cruz, Cal. BL/TR, 6'3", 195 lbs. Deb: 7/3/55

YEAR	TM/L	G	AB	R	H	2B	3B	HR	RBI	BB	SO	AVG	OBP	SLG	PRO+	BR/A	SB	CS	SBR	FA	FR	G/POS	TPR
1955	Cin-N	21	18	0	2	0	0	0	4	1	6	.111	.158	.111	-25	-3	0	0	0	.000	0	H	-0.3

■ FRANK BROWER
Brower, Frank Willard "Turkeyfoot" b: 3/26/1893, Gainesville, Va. d: 11/20/60, Baltimore, Md. BL/TR, 6'2", 180 lbs. Deb: 8/14/20

YEAR	TM/L	G	AB	R	H	2B	3B	HR	RBI	BB	SO	AVG	OBP	SLG	PRO+	BR/A	SB	CS	SBR	FA	FR	G/POS	TPR
1920	Was-A	36	119	21	37	7	2	1	13	9	11	.311	.374	.429	115	3	1	1	-0	.900	-0	O-20/1-9,3	0.1
1921	Was-A	83	203	31	53	12	3	1	35	18	7	.261	.330	.365	81	-6	1	1	-0	.917	3	O-46/1-4	-0.6
1922	Was-A	139	471	61	138	20	6	9	71	52	25	.293	.375	.418	112	9	8	6	-1	.978	-4	*O-121/1-7	-0.4
1923	Cle-A	126	397	77	113	25	8	16	66	62	32	.285	.392	.509	136	21	6	5	-1	.988	-1	*1-112/O-4	1.1
1924	Cle-A	66	107	16	30	10	1	3	20	27	9	.280	.434	.477	133	6	1	1	-0	.990	-1	1-26/P-4,O	0.3
Total	5	450	1297	206	371	74	20	30	205	168	84	.286	.379	.443	117	33	17	14	-3	.952	-4	O-194,1-158/P3	0.5

■ LOUIS BROWER
Brower, Louis Lester b: 7/1/1900, Cincinnati, Ohio d: 3/4/94, Tyler, Tex. BR/TR, 5'10", 155 lbs. Deb: 6/13/31

YEAR	TM/L	G	AB	R	H	2B	3B	HR	RBI	BB	SO	AVG	OBP	SLG	PRO+	BR/A	SB	CS	SBR	FA	FR	G/POS	TPR
1931	Det-A	21	62	3	10	1	0	0	6	8	5	.161	.278	.177	21	-7	1	0	0	.886	-7	S-20/2-2	-1.1

YEAR	TM/L	G	AB	R	H	2B	3B	HR	RBI	BB	SO	AVG	OBP	SLG	PRO+	BR/A	SB	CS	SBR	FA	FR	G/POS	TPR

■ **BOB BROWER**   Brower, Robert Richard   b: 1/10/60, Jamaica, N.Y.   BR/TR, 5'11", 185 lbs.   Deb: 9/3/86

1986	Tex-A	21	9	3	1	1	0	0	0	0	3	.111	.111	.222	-12	-1	1	2	-1	1.000	-5	O-17/D-1	-0.8
1987	Tex-A	127	303	63	79	10	3	14	46	36	66	.261	.339	.452	107	3	15	9	-1	.964	-13	*O-106/D-7	-1.3
1988	Tex-A	82	201	29	45	7	0	1	11	27	38	.224	.316	.274	65	-9	10	5	0	.972	-7	O-59,D-13	-1.8
1989	NY-A	26	69	9	16	3	0	2	3	6	11	.232	.293	.362	85	-2	3	1	0	.970	2	O-25/D-1	0.1
Total	4	256	582	104	141	21	3	17	60	69	118	.242	.323	.376	89	-9	29	17	-2	.968	-24	O-207/D-22	-3.8

■ **BROWN**   Brown   Deb: 7/29/1874

1874	Bal-n	2	9	0	0	0	0	0		0		.000	.000	.000	-99	-2						/S-1	-0.2

■ **CURTIS BROWN**   Brown, Curtis   b: 9/14/45, Sacramento, Cal.   BR/TR, 5'11", 180 lbs.   Deb: 5/27/73   F

1973	Mon-N	1	4	0	0	0	0	0	0	0	0	.000	.000	.000	-97	-1	0	0	0	1.000	0	/O-1	-0.1

■ **DARRELL BROWN**   Brown, Darrell Wayne   b: 10/29/55, Oklahoma City, Okla   BB/TR, 6', 184 lbs.   Deb: 4/11/81

1981	Det-A	16	4	4	1	0	0	0	0	1	1	.250	.250	.250	43	-0	1	0	0	1.000	-2	/O-6,D-4	-0.2
1982	Oak-A	8	18	2	6	0	1	0	3	1	2	.333	.368	.444	128	1	1	0	0	1.000	-1	/O-7,D-1	0.0
1983	Min-A	91	309	40	84	6	2	0	22	10	28	.272	.297	.304	64	-15	3	3	-1	.995	-4	O-81/D-3	-2.2
1984	Min-A	95	260	36	71	9	3	1	19	14	16	.273	.310	.342	77	-8	4	1	1	.993	4	O-55,D-13	-0.5
Total	4	210	591	82	162	15	6	1	44	25	47	.274	.305	.325	71	-23	9	4	0	.994	-3	O-149/D-21	-2.9

■ **DELOS BROWN**   Brown, Delos Hight   b: 10/4/1892, Anna, Ill.   d: 12/21/64, Carbondale, Ill.   BR/TR, 5'9", 160 lbs.   Deb: 6/12/14

1914	Chi-A	1	1	0	0	0	0	0	0	0	0	.000	.000	.000	-99	-0	0			.000	0	H	0.0

■ **DRUMMOND BROWN**   Brown, Drummond Nicol   b: 1/31/1885, Los Angeles, Cal.   d: 1/27/27, Parkville, Mo.   BR/TR, 6', 180 lbs.   Deb: 4/25/13

1913	Bos-N	15	34	3	11	0	1	0	2	2	9	.324	.361	.441	126	1	0			.960	-4	C-12	-0.2
1914	KC-F	31	58	4	11	3	0	0	5	7	6	.190	.277	.241	36	-6	1			.954	5	C-23/1-2	0.1
1915	KC-F	77	227	13	55	10	1	1	26	12	23	.242	.289	.308	62	-13	3			.961	-2	C-65/1-1	-1.1
Total	3	123	319	20	77	14	1	2	33	21	38	.241	.294	.310	64	-17	4			.960	-2	C-100/1-3	-1.2

■ **ED BROWN**   Brown, Edward P.   b: Chicago, Ill.   TR, 178 lbs.   Deb: 8/19/1882

1882	StL-a	17	60	4	11	0	0	0		4		.183	.234	.183	41	-4				.808	-2	O-15/2-2,P	-0.5
1884	Tol-a	42	153	13	27	3	0	0		2		.176	.187	.196	24	-13				.815	-8	3-40/O-2,CP	-1.9
Total	2	59	213	17	38	3	0	0		6		.178	.201	.192	29	-16				.815	-10	/3-40,O-17,P2C	-2.4

■ **EDDIE BROWN**   Brown, Edward William "Glass Arm Eddie"   b: 7/17/1891, Milligan, Neb.   d: 9/10/56, Vallejo, Cal.   BR/TR, 6'3", 190 lbs.   Deb: 9/26/20

1920	NY-N	3	8	1	1	1	0	0	0	0	3	.125	.125	.250	6	-1	0	0	0	1.000	0	/O-2	-0.1
1921	NY-N	70	128	16	36	6	2	0	12	4	11	.281	.324	.359	80	-4	1	0	0	.956	-3	O-30	-0.8
1924	Bro-N	114	455	56	140	30	4	5	78	26	15	.308	.345	.424	108	5	3	5	-2	.975	-2	*O-114	-0.3
1925	Bro-N	153	618	88	189	39	11	5	99	22	18	.306	.332	.429	95	-6	3	4	-2	.972	8	*O-153	-1.0
1926	Bos-N	153	612	71	**201**	31	8	2	84	23	20	.328	.355	.415	117	12	5			.965	8	*O-153	1.0
1927	Bos-N	155	558	64	171	35	6	2	75	28	20	.306	.340	.401	106	3	11			.980	3	*O-150/1-1	-0.4
1928	Bos-N	142	523	45	140	28	2	2	59	24	22	.268	.305	.340	72	-22	6			.960	-4	*O-129/1-1	-3.5
Total	7	790	2902	341	878	170	33	16	407	127	109	.303	.334	.400	99	-14	29	9		.970	13	O-731/1-2	-5.1

■ **RANDY BROWN**   Brown, Edwin Randolph   b: 8/29/44, Leesburg, Fla.   BL/TR, 5'7", 170 lbs.   Deb: 9/11/69

1969	Cal-A	13	25	3	4	1	0	0		6	1	.160	.323	.200	52	-1	0	0	0	1.000	-1	C-10/O-1	-0.2
1970	Cal-A	5	4	0	0	0	0	0		0	0	.000	.000	.000	-99	-1	0	0	0	1.000	-0	/C-5	-0.1
Total	2	18	29	3	4	1	0	0		6	1	.138	.286	.172	32	-2	0	0	0	1.000	-1	/C-15,O-1	-0.3

■ **FRED BROWN**   Brown, Fred Herbert   b: 4/12/1879, Ossipee, N.H.   d: 2/3/55, Somersworth, N.H.   BR/TR, 5'10.5", 190 lbs.   Deb: 5/4/01

1901	Bos-N	7	14	1	2	0	0	0	0	0		.143	.143	.143	-16	-2	0			.000	0	/O-5	-0.2
1902	Bos-N	2	6	1	2	1	0	0	0	0		.333	.333	.500	155	0	0			1.000	0	/O-2	0.0
Total	2	9	20	2	4	1	0	0	0	0		.200	.200	.250	30	-2	0			1.000	0	/O-7	-0.2

■ **IKE BROWN**   Brown, Isaac   b: 4/13/42, Memphis, Tenn.   BR/TR, 6'1", 205 lbs.   Deb: 6/17/69

1969	Det-A	70	170	24	39	4	3	5	12	26	43	.229	.338	.376	96	-1	2	3	-1	.962	-6	2-45,3-12/OS	-0.5
1970	Det-A	56	94	17	27	5	0	4	15	13	26	.287	.380	.468	132	4	0	0	0	.935	-3	2-23/O-4,3	0.3
1971	Det-A	59	110	20	28	1	0	8	19	19	25	.255	.364	.482	133	5	0	1	-1	1.000	-1	1-17/O-9,23S	0.2
1972	*Det-A	51	84	12	21	3	0	2	10	17	23	.250	.376	.357	115	2	1	2	-1	1.000	3	O-22,1-13/2S3	0.3
1973	Det-A	42	76	12	22	2	1	1	9	15	13	.289	.407	.382	115	2	0	1	-1	.983	-2	1-21,O-12/3D	-0.2
1974	Det-A	2	2	0	0	0	0	0	0	0	0	.000	.000	.000	-97	-0	0	0	0	1.000	0	/3-2	0.0
Total	6	280	536	85	137	15	4	20	65	90	130	.256	.366	.410	115	13	3	7	-3	.956	-9	/2-79,1-51,03SD	0.1

■ **JIM BROWN**   Brown, James Donaldson "Don" or "Moose"   b: 3/31/1897, Laurel, Md.   BR/TR, 6', 178 lbs.   Deb: 9/13/15

1915	StL-N	1	2	0	1	0	0	0	0	2	1	.500	.750	.500	281	1	0			1.000	-0	/O-1	0.1
1916	Phi-A	14	42	6	10	2	1	1	5	4	9	.238	.304	.405	119	1	0			.895	-1	O-12	-0.1
Total	2	15	44	6	11	2	1	1	5	6	10	.250	.340	.409	131	2	0			.900	-2	O-13	0.0

■ **JIMMY BROWN**   Brown, James Roberson   b: 4/25/10, Jamesville, N.C.   d: 12/29/77, Bath, N.C.   BB/TR, 5'8.5", 165 lbs.   Deb: 4/23/37   C

1937	StL-N	138	525	86	145	20	9	2	53	27	29	.276	.313	.360	81	-15	10			.964	-14	*2-112,S-25/3	-1.9
1938	StL-N	108	382	50	115	12	6	0	38	27	9	.301	.350	.364	91	-4	7			.968	1	2-49,S-30,3	0.2
1939	StL-N	147	645	88	192	31	8	3	51	32	18	.298	.335	.384	87	-12	4			.957	-5	*S-104,2-50	-0.5
1940	StL-N	107	454	56	127	17	4	0	30	24	15	.280	.317	.335	76	-15	9			.977	-22	2-48,3-41,S	-3.2
1941	StL-N	132	549	81	168	28	9	1	56	45	22	.306	.363	.406	109	7	2			.965	3	*3-123,2-11	1.3
1942	*StL-N★	145	606	75	155	28	4	1	71	52	11	.256	.315	.320	80	-15	4			.970	-12	2-82,3-66,S	-2.3
1943	StL-N	34	110	16	20	4	2	0	8	8	4	.182	.224	.255	37	-9	0			.978	2	2-19/3-9,S	-0.6
1946	Pit-N	79	241	23	58	6	0	0	12	18	5	.241	.293	.266	58	-13	3			.960	-2	S-30,2-21/3	-1.3
Total	8	890	3512	465	980	146	42	9	319	231	110	.279	.326	.352	84	-76	39			.968	-50	2-392,3-273,S	-8.3

■ **JIM BROWN**   Brown, James W. H.   b: 12/12/1860, Clinton Co., Pa.   d: 4/6/08, Williamsport, Pa.   Deb: 4/17/1884

1884	Alt-U	21	88	12	22	2	2	1			1	.250	.258	.352	63	-5				.615	-3	O-14,P-11	-0.6
	NY-N	1	3	0	0	0	0	0		0	0	.000	.000	.000	-98	-1				.333	-0	/P-1	0.0
	StP-U	6	16	5	5	4	0	0		0	1	.313	.353	.563	267	3				.706	-0	/P-6,1-1,O	0.0
1886	Phi-a	1	3	0	0	0	0	0		0		.000	.000	.000	-99	-1	0			1.000	-0	/P-1	0.0
Total	2	29	110	17	27	6	2	1		0	2	.245	.259	.364	73	-3	0			.741	-4	/P-19,O-15,1	-0.6

■ **JARVIS BROWN**   Brown, Jarvis Ardel   b: 3/26/67, Waukegan, Ill.   BR/TR, 5'7", 165 lbs.   Deb: 7/2/91

1991	*Min-A	38	37	10	8	0	0	0	0	2	8	.216	.256	.216	31	-3	7	1	2	.955	-11	O-32/D-4	-1.3
1992	Min-A	35	15	8	1	0	0	0	2	4	4	.067	.222	.067	-15	-4	2	2	-1	.952	-10	O-31/D-2	-1.4
1993	SD-N	47	133	21	31	9	2	0	8	15	26	.233	.338	.331	78	-4	3	3	-1	.982	2	O-43	-0.4
1994	Atl-N	17	15	3	2	1	0	1	1	0	2	.133	.133	.400	32	-2	0	0	0	1.000	-2	/O-9	-0.3
Total	4	137	200	42	42	10	2	1	9	19	40	.210	.301	.295	60	-11	12	6	0	.976	-21	O-115/D-6	-3.4

■ **JAKE BROWN**   Brown, Jerald Ray   b: 3/22/48, Sumrall, Miss.   d: 12/18/81, Houston, Tex.   BR/TR, 6'2", 200 lbs.   Deb: 5/17/75

1975	SF-N	41	43	6	9	1	0	0	4	5	13	.209	.292	.279	57	-2	2			.857	-3	O-14	-0.6

YEAR	TM/L	G	AB	R	H	2B	3B	HR	RBI	BB	SO	AVG	OBP	SLG	PRO+	BR/A	SB	CS	SBR	FA	FR	G/POS	TPR

■ CHRIS BROWN
Brown, John Christopher   b: 8/15/61, Jackson, Miss.   BR/TR, 6'2", 210 lbs.   Deb: 9/3/84

1984	SF-N	23	84	6	24	7	0	1	11	9	19	.286	.362	.405	119	2	2	1	0	.900	-2	3-23	0.0
1985	SF-N	131	432	50	117	20	3	16	61	38	78	.271	.345	.442	125	14	2	3	-1	.971	5	*3-120	1.7
1986	SF-N★	116	416	57	132	16	3	7	49	33	43	.317	.380	.421	127	16	13	9	-2	.933	-14	*3-111/S-2	-0.2
1987	SF-N	38	132	17	32	6	0	6	17	9	16	.242	.306	.424	95	-1	1	3	-2	.905	-2	3-37/S-1	-0.5
	SD-N	44	155	17	36	3	0	6	23	11	30	.232	.296	.368	77	-5	3	1	0	.942	-4	3-43	-0.9
	Yr	82	287	34	68	9	0	12	40	20	46	.237	.300	.394	86	-7	4	4	-1	.923	-6	3-80/S-1	-1.4
1988	SD-N	80	247	14	58	6	0	2	19	19	49	.235	.297	.283	69	-10	0	0	0	.949	5	3-72	-0.6
1989	Det-A	17	57	3	11	3	0	0	6	3	17	.193	.207	.246	28	-6	0	0	0	.909	-1	3-17	-0.7
Total	6	449	1523	164	410	61	6	38	184	120	252	.269	.335	.392	99	9	21	17	-4	.943	-13	3-423/S-3	-1.2

■ LINDSAY BROWN
Brown, John Lindsay "Red"   b: 7/22/11, Mason, Tex.   d: 1/1/67, San Antonio, Tex.   BR/TR, 5'10", 160 lbs.   Deb: 7/13/37

| 1937 | Bro-N | 48 | 115 | 16 | 31 | 3 | 1 | 0 | 6 | 3 | 17 | .270 | .288 | .313 | 62 | -6 | 1 | | | .937 | 6 | S-45 | 0.2 |

■ JOE BROWN
Brown, Joseph E.   b: 4/4/1859, Warren, Pa.   d: 6/28/1888, Warren, Pa.   5'10", 162 lbs.   Deb: 8/16/1884

1884	Chi-N	15	61	6	13	1	0	0	3	0	15	.213	.213	.230	36	-5				.750	-3	/O-9,P-7,1C	-0.5
1885	Bal-a	5	19	2	3	0	0	0	0	0		.158	.158	.158	-0	-2				1.000	0	/P-4,2-1	0.0
Total	2	20	80	8	16	1	0	0	3	0	15	.200	.200	.213	28	-7				.895	-3	/P-11,0-9,2C1	-0.5

■ LARRY BROWN
Brown, Larry Leslie   b: 3/1/40, Shinnston, W.Va.   BR/TR, 5'11", 165 lbs.   Deb: 7/6/63   F

1963	Cle-A	74	247	28	63	6	0	5	18	22	27	.255	.319	.340	85	-5	4	3	-1	.938	-8	S-46,2-27	-0.9
1964	Cle-A	115	335	33	77	12	1	12	40	24	55	.230	.285	.379	84	-8	1	2	-1	.981	11	*2-103/S-4	1.0
1965	Cle-A	124	438	52	111	22	2	8	40	38	62	.253	.316	.368	93	-4	5	7	-3	.977	3	S-95,2-26	0.5
1966	Cle-A	105	340	29	78	12	0	3	17	36	58	.229	.309	.291	73	-11	0	1	-1	.961	-4	S-90,2-10	-0.7
1967	Cle-A	152	485	38	110	16	2	7	37	53	62	.227	.311	.311	84	-9	4	4	-1	.967	1	*S-150	0.6
1968	Cle-A	154	495	43	116	18	0	6	35	48	46	.234	.302	.319	90	-6	1	1	-0	.966	-14	*S-154	0.6
1969	Cle-A	132	469	48	112	10	2	4	24	44	43	.239	.305	.294	66	-21	5	3	-0	.959	-17	*S-101,3-29/2	-2.8
1970	Cle-A	72	155	17	40	5	0	2	15	20	14	.258	.343	.316	79	-4	1	0	0	.950	-2	S-27,3-17,2	-0.2
1971	Cle-A	13	50	4	11	1	0	0	5	3	3	.220	.278	.240	44	-4	0	0	0	.980	-6	S-13	-0.9
	Oak-A	70	189	14	37	2	1	1	9	7	19	.196	.228	.233	31	-17	1	2	-1	.959	4	S-31,2-23,3	-1.1
	Yr	83	239	18	48	3	1	1	14	10	22	.201	.239	.234	35	-21	1	2	-1	.965	-2	S-44,2-23,3	-2.0
1972	Oak-A	47	142	11	26	2	0	4	13	8	18	.183	.252	.197	37	-11	0	0	0	.974	-8	2-46/3-1	-1.9
1973	*Bal-A	17	28	4	7	0	0	1	5	5	4	.250	.364	.357	104	0	0	0	0	.880	-2	3-15/2-1	-0.2
1974	Tex-A	54	76	10	15	2	0	0	5	9	13	.197	.282	.224	48	-5	0	0	0	.931	-3	3-47/2-8,S	0.3
Total	12	1129	3449	331	803	108	13	47	254	317	414	.233	.301	.313	76	-103	22	23	-7	.964	-34	S-712,2-265,3	-6.9

■ LEON BROWN
Brown, Leon   b: 11/16/49, Sacramento, Cal.   BR/TR, 6', 185 lbs.   Deb: 5/19/76   F

| 1976 | NY-N | 64 | 70 | 11 | 15 | 3 | 0 | 0 | 2 | 4 | 4 | .214 | .257 | .257 | 49 | -5 | 2 | 4 | -2 | 1.000 | -18 | O-43 | -2.7 |

■ LEW BROWN
Brown, Lewis J. "Blower"   b: 2/1/1858, Leominster, Mass.   d: 1/16/1889, Boston, Mass.   BR/TR, 5'10.5", 185 lbs.   Deb: 6/17/1876

1876	Bos-N	45	195	23	41	6	6	2	21	3	22	.210	.222	.333	82	-4				.856	-2	C-45/O-1	-0.4
1877	Bos-N	58	221	27	56	12	8	1	31	6	33	.253	.273	.394	104	0				.897	15	*C-55/1-4	1.6
1878	Pro-N	58	243	44	74	21	6	1	43	7	37	.305	.324	.453	153	13				.880	3	*C-45,1-15/OP	1.5
1879	Pro-N	53	229	23	59	13	4	2	38	4	24	.258	.270	.376	112	3				.847	-4	C-48/O-6	0.0
	Chi-N	6	21	2	6	1	0	0	3	1	4	.286	.318	.333	109	0				.974	0	/1-6	0.0
	Yr	59	250	25	65	14	4	2	41	5	28	.260	.275	.372	112	3				.847	-4	C-48/O-6,1	0.0
1881	Det-N	27	108	16	26	3	1	3	14	3	16	.241	.261	.370	93	-1				.959	-1	1-27	-0.4
	Pro-N	18	75	9	18	3	1	0	10	4	13	.240	.278	.307	85	-1				.833	-4	O-13/1-5	-0.5
	Yr	45	183	25	44	6	2	3	24	7	29	.240	.268	.344	90	-2				.960	-4	1-32,O-13	-0.9
1883	Bos-N	14	54	5	13	4	1	0	9	3	6	.241	.281	.352	89	-1				.943	-2	1-14	-0.3
	Lou-a	14	60	6	11	2	1	0		1		.183	.197	.250	46	-3				.891	-2	1-14/C-1	-0.6
1884	Bos-U	85	325	50	75	18	3	1		13		.231	.260	.314	56	-20				.914	13	C-54,1-33/OP	-0.5
Total	7	378	1531	205	379	83	31	10	169	45	155	.248	.269	.362	94	-13				.884	17	C-248,1-118/OP	0.4

■ MARTY BROWN
Brown, Marty Leo   b: 1/23/63, Lawton, Okla.   BR/TR, 6'1", 190 lbs.   Deb: 9/4/88

1988	Cin-N	10	16	0	3	1	0	0	2	1	2	.188	.235	.250	38	-1	0	1	-1	1.000	1	/3-8	-0.1
1989	Cin-N	16	30	2	5	1	0	0	4	4	9	.167	.265	.200	34	-3	0	0	0	.913	2	3-11	-0.1
1990	Bal-A	9	15	1	3	0	0	0	0	1	7	.200	.250	.200	28	-1	0	0	0	1.000	0	/2-3,3-2,D	-0.1
Total	3	35	61	3	11	2	0	0	6	6	18	.180	.254	.213	34	-5	0	1	-1	.943	3	/3-21,D-4,2	-0.3

■ MIKE BROWN
Brown, Michael Charles   b: 12/29/59, San Francisco, Cal.   BR/TR, 6'2", 195 lbs.   Deb: 7/21/83

1983	Cal-A	31	104	12	24	5	1	3	9	7	20	.231	.279	.385	81	-3	1	0	0	.949	-2	O-31	-0.5
1984	Cal-A	62	148	19	42	8	3	7	22	13	23	.284	.342	.520	136	7	0	2	-1	.968	-6	O-44/D-3	-0.1
1985	Cal-A	60	153	23	41	9	1	4	20	7	21	.268	.304	.418	96	-1	0	1	-1	1.000	-3	O-48/D-7	-0.5
	Pit-N	57	205	29	68	18	2	5	33	22	27	.332	.396	.512	154	15	2	2	-1	.938	-2	O-56	1.0
1986	Pit-N	87	243	18	53	7	0	4	26	27	32	.218	.296	.296	62	-12	2	4	-1	.973	-4	O-71	-2.1
1988	Cal-A	18	50	4	11	2	0	0	3	1	12	.220	.235	.260	40	-4	0	0	0	.946	-1	O-18	-0.5
Total	5	315	903	105	239	49	7	23	113	77	135	.265	.323	.411	102	2	5	8	-3	.964	-17	O-268/D-10	-2.7

■ OLIVER BROWN
Brown, Oliver S.   b: 1849, Brooklyn, N.Y.   d: 9/23/32, Brooklyn, N.Y.   Deb: 8/1/1872

1872	Atl-n	4	16	0	1	0	0	0	0	0	1	.063	.063	.063	-52	-3						/O-4	-0.2
1875	Atl-n	3	10	0	0	0	0	0	0	0	0	.000	.000	.000	-99	-2						/1-3	-0.2
Total	2 n	7	26	0	1	0	0	0	0		0	.038	.038	.038	-71	-5						/O-4,1-3	-0.4

■ OLLIE BROWN
Brown, Ollie Lee "Downtown"   b: 2/11/44, Tuscaloosa, Ala.   BR/TR, 6'3", 200 lbs.   Deb: 9/10/65   F

1965	SF-N	6	10	0	2	1	0	0	0	0	2	.200	.200	.300	38	-1	0	0	0	1.000	-1	/O-4	-0.2
1966	SF-N	115	348	32	81	7	1	7	33	33	66	.233	.303	.319	71	-13	2	5	-2	.978	-7	*O-114	-2.9
1967	SF-N	120	412	44	110	12	1	13	53	25	65	.267	.315	.396	104	1	0	2	-1	.985	-6	*O-115	-1.3
1968	SF-N	40	95	7	22	4	0	0	11	3	23	.232	.270	.274	64	-4	1	0	-0	1.000	0	O-35	-1.5
1969	SD-N	151	568	76	150	18	3	20	61	44	97	.264	.320	.412	108	4	1	0	0	.976	7	*O-148	0.2
1970	SD-N	139	534	79	156	34	1	23	89	34	78	.292	.335	.489	123	14	5	3	-0	.964	7	*O-137	1.3
1971	SD-N	145	484	36	132	16	0	9	55	52	74	.273	.347	.362	108	6	3	3	-2	.982	5	*O-134	0.3
1972	SD-N	23	70	3	12	2	0	0	3	5	9	.171	.227	.200	24	-7	0	0	0	1.000	1	O-17	-0.8
	Oak-A	20	54	5	13	1	0	1	4	5	14	.241	.317	.315	93	-0	1	1	-0	1.000	-2	O-16	-0.4
	Mil-A	66	179	21	50	8	0	3	25	17	24	.279	.345	.374	116	4	1	2	-1	.992	5	O-56/3-1	0.8
	Yr	86	233	26	63	9	0	4	29	23	38	.270	.339	.361	111	3	1	3	-2	.994	5	O-72/3-1	0.4
1973	Mil-A	97	296	28	83	16	1	7	32	33	53	.280	.356	.392	113	6	4	1	1	1.000	-1	D-82/O-4	0.3
1974	Hou-N	27	69	8	15	1	0	2	6	5	15	.217	.260	.362	76	-3	0	0	0	1.000	-1	O-20	-0.4
	Phi-N	43	99	11	24	2	0	3	13	6	20	.242	.286	.455	101	-1	0	0	0	.921	-5	O-33	-0.8
	Yr	70	168	19	39	3	0	5	19	10	35	.232	.275	.417	91	-3	0	0	0	.961	-6	O-53	-1.2
1975	Phi-N	84	145	19	36	6	0	6	26	15	29	.248	.369	.510	137	7	1	0	-0	1.000	-14	O-63	-0.9
1976	*Phi-N	92	209	30	53	10	1	5	30	33	33	.254	.355	.383	106	2	2	1	-0	.949	-6	O-75	-0.6
1977	*Phi-N	53	70	5	17	3	1	1	13	4	14	.243	.284	.357	68	-3	1	1	-0	1.000	-4	O-21	-0.8
Total	13	1221	3642	404	964	144	11	102	454	314	616	.265	.326	.394	103	11	30	27	-7	.977	-29	O-992/D-82,3	-7.7

YEAR	TM/L	G	AB	R	H	2B	3B	HR	RBI	BB	SO	AVG	OBP	SLG	PRO+	BR/A	SB	CS	SBR	FA	FR	G/POS	TPR

■ OSCAR BROWN Brown, Oscar Lee b: 2/8/46, Long Beach, Cal. BR/TR, 6', 175 lbs. Deb: 9/3/69 F

1969	Atl-N	7	4	2	1	0	0	0	0	0	1	.250	.250	.250	40	-0	0	0	0	1.000	-1	/O-3	-0.1
1970	Atl-N	28	47	6	18	2	1	1	7	7	7	.383	.473	.532	159	4	0	2	-1	.960	-5	O-25	-0.2
1971	Atl-N	27	43	4	9	4	0	0	5	3	8	.209	.261	.302	56	-3	0	0	0	1.000	-2	O-15	-0.5
1972	Atl-N	76	164	19	37	5	1	3	16	4	29	.226	.244	.323	55	-10	0	2	-1	.899	-4	O-59	-1.8
1973	Atl-N	22	58	3	12	3	0	0	0	3	10	.207	.246	.259	37	-5	0	0	0	1.000	2	O-13	-0.4
Total	5	160	316	34	77	14	2	4	28	17	55	.244	.284	.339	68	-13	0	4	-2	.939	-10	O-115	-3.0

■ DICK BROWN Brown, Richard Ernest b: 1/17/35, Shinnston, W.Va. d: 4/17/70, Baltimore, Md. BR/TR, 6'3", 190 lbs. Deb: 6/20/57 F

1957	Cle-A	34	114	10	30	4	0	4	22	4	23	.263	.288	.404	88	-2	1	1	-0	.986	1	C-33	0.0
1958	Cle-A	68	173	20	41	5	0	7	20	14	27	.237	.305	.387	91	-2	1	0	0	.987	6	C-62	0.6
1959	Cle-A	48	141	15	31	7	0	5	16	11	39	.220	.290	.376	85	-3	0	0	0	.996	3	C-48	0.2
1960	Chi-A	16	43	4	7	0	0	3	5	3	11	.163	.217	.372	57	-3	0	0	0	.986	3	C-14	0.1
1961	Det-A	93	308	32	82	12	2	16	45	22	57	.266	.315	.474	105	1	0	2	-1	.990	-1	C-91	0.4
1962	Det-A	134	431	40	104	12	0	12	40	21	66	.241	.280	.353	67	-21	0	1	-1	.994	3	*C-132	-1.4
1963	Bal-A	59	171	13	42	7	0	2	13	15	35	.246	.310	.322	80	-4	1	0	0	.986	6	C-58	0.4
1964	Bal-A	88	230	24	59	6	0	8	32	12	45	.257	.296	.387	89	-4	2	2	-1	.988	4	C-84	0.3
1965	Bal-A	96	255	17	59	9	1	5	30	17	53	.231	.282	.333	73	-9	2	1	-1	.983	10	C-92	0.4
Total	9	636	1866	175	455	62	3	62	223	119	356	.244	.293	.380	83	-49	7	6	-2	.989	35	C-614	1.0

■ BOBBY BROWN Brown, Robert William "Doc" b: 10/25/24, Seattle, Wash. BL/TR, 6'1", 180 lbs. Deb: 9/22/46

1946	NY-A	7	24	1	8	1	0	0	1	4	0	.333	.429	.375	124	1	0	0	0	1.000	-4	/S-5,3-2	-0.2
1947	*NY-A	69	150	21	45	6	1	1	18	21	9	.300	.390	.373	114	4	0	2	-1	.932	-11	3-27,S-11/O	-0.9
1948	NY-A	113	363	62	109	19	5	3	48	48	16	.300	.383	.405	111	6	0	1	-1	.946	-18	3-41,S-26,2/O	-1.0
1949	*NY-A	104	343	61	97	14	4	6	61	38	18	.283	.359	.399	101	-0	4	3	-1	.949	-4	3-86/O-3	-0.6
1950	*NY-A	95	277	33	74	4	2	4	37	39	18	.267	.360	.390	82	-7	3	1	0	.958	-4	3-82	-0.1
1951	*NY-A	103	313	44	84	15	2	6	51	47	18	.268	.369	.387	108	5	1	1	-0	.955	-5	3-90	-0.1
1952	NY-A	29	89	6	22	2	0	1	14	9	6	.247	.323	.303	80	-2	1	1	-0	.894	3	3-24	0.0
1954	NY-A	28	60	5	13	1	0	1	7	8	3	.217	.309	.283	65	-3	0	1	-1	1.000	-0	3-17	-0.4
Total	8	548	1619	233	452	62	14	22	237	214	88	.279	.367	.376	100	4	9	10	-3	.948	-43	3-369/S-42,2O	-4.2

■ BOBBY BROWN Brown, Rogers Lee b: 5/24/54, Norfolk, Va. BB/TR, 6'1", 205 lbs. Deb: 4/5/79

1979	Tor-A	4	10	1	0	0	0	0	0	2	1	.000	.167	.000	-50	-2	0	0	0	1.000	-0	/O-4	-0.2
	NY-A	30	68	7	17	3	1	0	3	2	17	.250	.271	.324	61	-4	2	1	0	.949	-3	O-27	-0.8
	Yr	34	78	8	17	3	1	0	3	4	18	.218	.256	.282	46	-6	2	1	0	.955	-3	O-31	-1.0
1980	*NY-A	137	412	65	107	12	5	14	47	29	82	.260	.308	.415	98	-2	27	8	3	.972	-1	*O-131/D-1	-0.4
1981	*NY-A	31	62	5	14	1	0	0	6	5	15	.226	.284	.242	53	-4	4	2	0	.949	-2	O-29/D-2	-0.6
1982	Sea-A	79	245	29	59	7	1	4	17	17	32	.241	.290	.327	67	-11	28	6	5	.968	3	O-68/D-3	-0.5
1983	SD-N	57	225	40	60	5	3	5	22	23	38	.267	.335	.382	102	0	27	9	3	.963	-1	O-54	0.0
1984	*SD-N	85	171	28	43	7	2	3	29	11	33	.251	.297	.368	86	-4	16	4	2	.971	-2	O-53	-0.5
1985	SD-N	79	84	8	13	3	0	0	6	5	20	.155	.202	.190	11	-10	6	4	-1	1.000	-7	O-28	-1.9
Total	7	502	1277	183	313	38	12	26	130	94	238	.245	.297	.355	80	-36	110	34	13	.968	-13	O-394/D-6	-4.9

■ SAM BROWN Brown, Samuel Wakefield b: 5/21/1878, Webster, Pa. d: 11/8/31, Mount Pleasant, Pa. BR/TR Deb: 4/21/06

1906	Bos-N	71	231	12	48	6	1	0	20	13		.208	.262	.242	59	-11	4			.970	-1	C-35,O-13,3/12	-1.0
1907	Bos-N	70	208	17	40	6	0	0	14	12		.192	.250	.221	48	-12	0			.970	7	C-63/1-2	0.0
Total	2	141	439	29	88	12	1	0	34	25		.200	.256	.232	54	-24	4			.970	6	/C-98,O-13,312	-1.0

■ TOMMY BROWN Brown, Thomas Michael "Buckshot" b: 12/6/27, Brooklyn, N.Y. BR/TR, 6'1", 170 lbs. Deb: 8/3/44

1944	Bro-N	46	146	17	24	4	0	0	8	8	17	.164	.208	.192	13	-17	0			.925	-9	S-46	-2.4
1945	Bro-N	57	196	13	48	3	4	2	19	6	16	.245	.267	.332	66	-10	3			.918	-4	S-55/O-1	-1.0
1947	Bro-N	15	34	3	8	1	0	0	2	1	6	.235	.257	.265	37	-3	0			1.000	2	/3-6,O-3,S	-0.1
1948	Bro-N	54	145	18	35	4	0	2	20	7	17	.241	.281	.310	58	-9	1			.936	-3	3-43/1-1	-1.0
1949	*Bro-N	41	89	14	27	2	0	3	18	6	8	.303	.347	.427	102	0	0			.931	-2	O-27	-0.3
1950	Bro-N	48	86	15	25	2	1	8	20	11	9	.291	.378	.616	153	6	0			.917	-0	O-16	0.6
1951	Bro-N	11	25	2	4	2	0	0	1	2	4	.160	.222	.240	24	-3	0	0	0	.909	-0	/O-5	-0.3
	Phi-N	78	196	24	43	2	1	10	32	15	21	.219	.278	.393	80	-6	1	2	-1	.966	-12	O-32,2-14,1/3	-2.0
	Yr	89	221	26	47	4	1	10	33	17	25	.213	.272	.376	73	-9	1	2	-1	.957	-11	O-37,2-14,1/3	-2.3
1952	Phi-N	18	25	2	4	1	0	1	2	4	3	.160	.276	.320	65	-1	0	0	0	1.000	-1	/1-3,O-3	-0.2
	Chi-N	61	200	24	64	11	0	3	24	12	24	.320	.358	.420	114	3	1	2	-1	.911	-19	S-39,2-10/1	-1.4
	Yr	79	225	26	68	12	0	4	26	16	27	.302	.349	.409	109	2	1	2	-1	.911	-20	S-39,2-10/1O	-1.6
1953	Chi-N	65	138	19	27	7	1	2	13	13	17	.196	.279	.304	51	-10	1	0	0	.903	-6	S-25/O-6	-1.4
Total	9	494	1280	151	309	39	7	31	159	85	142	.241	.292	.355	74	-48	7	4		.916	-52	S-166/O-93,321	-9.5

■ TOM BROWN Brown, Thomas Tarlton b: 9/21/1860, Liverpool, England d: 10/25/27, Washington, D.C. BL/TR, 5'10", 168 lbs. Deb: 7/6/1882 MU

1882	Bal-a	45	181	30	55	5	2	1		6		.304	.326	.370	146	9				.728	-0	O-45/P-2	0.8
1883	Col-a	97	420	69	115	12	7	5		20		.274	.307	.371	127	14				.805	-2	*O-96/P-3	1.1
1884	Col-a	107	451	93	123	9	11	5		24		.273	.315	.375	135	18				.847	-6	*O-107/P-4	1.0
1885	Pit-a	108	437	81	134	16	12	4		34		.307	.366	.426	152	26				.828	-3	*O-108/P-2	1.9
1886	Pit-a	115	460	106	131	11	11	1		56		.285	.365	.363	129	17	30			.837	6	*O-115/P-1	1.8
1887	Pit-N	47	192	30	47	3	4	0	6	11	40	.245	.289	.302	69	-8	12			.870	5	O-47	-0.3
	Ind-N	36	140	20	25	3	0	2	9	8	25	.179	.228	.243	32	-13	13			.813	-2	O-36	-1.3
	Yr	83	332	50	72	6	4	2	15	19	65	.217	.263	.277	53	-21	25			.851	3	O-83	-1.6
1888	Bos-N	107	420	62	104	10	7	9	49	30	68	.248	.299	.369	110	4	46			.896	-3	*O-107	-0.1
1889	Bos-N	90	362	93	84	10	5	2	24	59	56	.232	.341	.304	76	-11	63			.901	3	O-90	-0.9
1890	Bos-P	128	543	146	150	23	14	4	61	86	84	.276	.378	.392	99	-1	79			.911	4	*O-128	-0.1
1891	Bos-a	137	589	177	189	30	21	5	72	70	96	.321	.397	.469	150	37	**106**			.878	-10	*O-137	1.9
1892	Lou-N	153	660	105	150	16	8	2	45	47	94	.227	.284	.285	78	-17	78			.919	19	*O-153	-0.5
1893	Lou-N	122	529	104	127	15	7	5	54	56	63	.240	.319	.323	77	-17	**66**			.929	27	*O-122	0.3
1894	Lou-N	129	536	122	136	22	14	9	57	60	73	.254	.332	.397	81	-18	66			.912	3	*O-129	-1.8
1895	StL-N	83	350	72	76	11	4	1	31	48	44	.217	.315	.280	55	-23	34			.950	8	O-83	-1.7
	Was-N	34	134	25	32	8	3	2	16	18	16	.239	.329	.388	86	-3	8			.909	-7	O-34	-1.0
	Yr	117	484	97	108	19	7	3	47	66	60	.223	.319	.310	63	-26	42			.942	2	*O-117	-2.7
1896	Was-N	116	435	87	128	17	6	2	59	58	49	.294	.385	.375	101	3	28			.928	-5	*O-116	-1.0
1897	Was-N	116	469	91	137	17	2	5	45	52		.292	.364	.369	94	-3	25			.928	1	*O-115/M	-0.9
1898	Was-N	16	55	8	9	1	0	0	2	5		.164	.233	.182	19	-6	3			.925	0	O-15/M	-0.6
Total	17	1786	7363	1521	1952	239	138	64	530	748	708	.265	.337	.361	101	9	657			.890	38	*O-1783/P-12	-1.4

■ TOM BROWN Brown, Thomas William b: 12/12/40, Laureldale, Pa. BB/TL, 6'1", 190 lbs. Deb: 4/8/63

| 1963 | Was-A | 61 | 116 | 8 | 17 | 4 | 0 | 1 | 4 | 11 | 45 | .147 | .227 | .207 | 23 | -12 | 2 | 1 | 0 | 1.000 | -2 | O-16,1-14 | -1.6 |

■ WILLARD BROWN Brown, Willard "Big Bill" or "California" b: 1866, San Francisco, Cal. d: 12/20/1897, San Francisco, Cal BR/TR, 6'2", 190 lbs. Deb: 5/10/1887

| 1887 | NY-N | 49 | 170 | 17 | 37 | 3 | 2 | 0 | 25 | 10 | 15 | .218 | .273 | .259 | 51 | -11 | 10 | | | .914 | -0 | C-46/3-3,O | -0.6 |

YEAR	TM/L	G	AB	R	H	2B	3B	HR	RBI	BB	SO	AVG	OBP	SLG	PRO+	BR/A	SB	CS	SBR	FA	FR	G/POS	TPR
1888	*NY-N	20	59	4	16	1	0	0	6	1	8	.271	.283	.288	84	-1	1			.893	3	C-20	0.3
1889	*NY-N	40	139	16	36	10	0	1	29	9	9	.259	.318	.353	87	-3	6			.846	-5	C-37/O-3	-0.5
1890	NY-P	60	230	47	64	8	4	4	43	13	13	.278	.320	.400	84	-7	5			.900	-5	C-34,O-13/132	-0.8
1891	Phi-N	115	441	62	107	20	4	0	50	34	35	.243	.303	.306	75	-14	7			.989	5	*1-97,C-19/O	-1.2
1893	Bal-N	7	32	5	4	3	0	0	5	1	3	.125	.152	.219	-2	-5				.985	-0	/1-7	-0.5
	Lou-N	111	461	80	140	23	7	1	85	50	32	.304	.373	.390	112	9	9			.989	-2	*1-111/C-1	0.3
	Yr	118	493	85	144	26	7	1	90	51	35	.292	.360	.379	104	3	9			.988	-2	*1-118/C-1	-0.2
1894	Lou-N	13	48	5	10	2	0	0	9	5	7	.208	.283	.250	32	-5	1			.977	4	1-13	-0.1
	StL-N	3	9	0	1	0	0	0	0	0	2	.111	.111	.111	-46	-2	0			1.000	0	/1-3	-0.1
	Yr	16	57	5	11	2	0	0	9	5	9	.193	.258	.228	19	-8	1			.982	4	1-16	-0.2
Total	7	418	1589	236	415	70	17	6	252	123	124	.261	.319	.338	82	-40	39			.987	-0	1-240,C-157/O32	-3.2

■ WILLARD BROWN

Brown, Willard Jessie b: 6/26/15, Shreveport, La. BR/TR, 5'11.5", 200 lbs. Deb: 7/19/47

YEAR	TM/L	G	AB	R	H	2B	3B	HR	RBI	BB	SO	AVG	OBP	SLG	PRO+	BR/A	SB	CS	SBR	FA	FR	G/POS	TPR
1947	StL-A	21	67	4	12	3	0	1	6	0	7	.179	.179	.269	23	-7	2	2	-1	1.000	0	O-18	-0.9

■ GATES BROWN

Brown, William James b: 5/2/39, Crestline, O. BL/TR, 5'11", 220 lbs. Deb: 6/19/63 C

YEAR	TM/L	G	AB	R	H	2B	3B	HR	RBI	BB	SO	AVG	OBP	SLG	PRO+	BR/A	SB	CS	SBR	FA	FR	G/POS	TPR
1963	Det-A	55	82	16	22	3	1	2	14	8	13	.268	.341	.402	104	1	2	1	0	1.000	4	O-16	0.3
1964	Det-A	123	426	65	116	22	6	15	54	31	53	.272	.328	.458	114	7	11	4	1	.981	8	*O-106	1.1
1965	Det-A	96	227	33	58	14	2	10	43	17	33	.256	.328	.467	115	4	6	0	2	.973	2	O-56	0.6
1966	Det-A	88	169	27	45	5	1	7	27	16	19	.266	.344	.432	119	4	3	0	1	.980	-3	O-43	0.1
1967	Det-A	51	91	17	17	1	1	2	9	13	15	.187	.288	.286	68	-3	0	0	0	1.000	1	O-20	-0.6
1968	*Det-A	67	92	15	34	7	2	6	15	12	4	.370	.442	.685	231	14	0	0	0	1.000	-1	O-17/1-1	1.4
1969	Det-A	60	93	13	19	1	2	1	6	5	17	.204	.253	.290	49	-6	0	0	0	.906	1	O-14	-0.7
1970	Det-A	81	124	18	28	3	0	3	24	20	14	.226	.338	.323	82	-2	0	0	0	.950	-1	O-26	-0.5
1971	Det-A	82	195	37	66	2	3	11	29	21	17	.338	.408	.549	163	16	4	2	0	.986	-6	O-56	0.9
1972	*Det-A	103	252	33	58	5	0	10	31	26	28	.230	.307	.369	97	-1	3	0	1	.977	2	O-72	-0.1
1973	Det-A	125	377	48	89	11	1	12	50	52	41	.236	.330	.366	90	-5	1	1	-0	1.000	-1	*D-119/O-2	-0.9
1974	Det-A	73	99	7	24	2	0	4	17	10	15	.242	.312	.384	96	-0	0	0	0	.000	0	D-13	-0.1
1975	Det-A	47	35	1	6	2	0	1	3	9	6	.171	.356	.314	87	-0	0	0	0	.000	0	H	-0.1
Total	13	1051	2262	330	582	78	19	84	322	242	275	.257	.333	.420	109		27	8	4	.977	3	O-428,D-132/1	1.4

■ BILL BROWN

Brown, William Verna "Verna" b: 7/8/1893, Coleman, Tex. d: 5/13/65, Lubbock, Tex. BL/TL, 5'8", 185 lbs. Deb: 8/15/12

YEAR	TM/L	G	AB	R	H	2B	3B	HR	RBI	BB	SO	AVG	OBP	SLG	PRO+	BR/A	SB	CS	SBR	FA	FR	G/POS	TPR
1912	StL-A	9	20	0	4							.200	.200	.200	15	-2	0			.909	-2	/O-7	-0.4

■ BYRON BROWNE

Browne, Byron Ellis b: 12/27/42, St.Joseph, Mo. BR/TR, 6'2", 200 lbs. Deb: 9/9/65

YEAR	TM/L	G	AB	R	H	2B	3B	HR	RBI	BB	SO	AVG	OBP	SLG	PRO+	BR/A	SB	CS	SBR	FA	FR	G/POS	TPR
1965	Chi-N	4	6	0	0	0	0	0	0	0	2	.000	.000	.000	-98	-2	0	0	0	.667	-1	/O-4	-0.3
1966	Chi-N	120	419	46	102	15	7	16	51	40	143	.243	.317	.427	103	2	3	3	-1	.967	-4	*O-114	-0.9
1967	Chi-N	10	19	3	3	2	0	0	2	4	5	.158	.304	.263	61	-1	1	1	-0	1.000	-1	/O-8	-0.3
1968	Hou-N	10	13	0	3	0	0	0	1	4	6	.231	.412	.231	99	0	0	0	0	1.000	1	/O-2	0.2
1969	StL-N	22	53	9	12	0	1	1	7	11	14	.226	.359	.321	92	-0	0	0	0	1.000	3	O-16	0.2
1970	Phi-N	104	270	29	67	17	2	10	36	33	72	.248	.330	.437	107	2	1	2	-1	.975	-2	O-88	-0.5
1971	Phi-N	58	68	5	14	3	0	3	5	8	23	.206	.289	.382	89	-1	0	0	0	1.000	-8	O-30	-1.1
1972	Phi-N	21	21	2	4	0	0	0	0	1	8	.190	.227	.190	19	-2	0	0	0	1.000	-3	/O-9	-0.6
Total	8	349	869	94	205	37	10	30	102	101	273	.236	.319	.405	98	-2	5	6	-2	.973	-16	O-271	-3.3

■ EARL BROWNE

Browne, Earl James "Snitz" b: 3/5/11, Louisville, Ky. d: 1/12/93, Whittier, Cal. BL/TL, 6', 175 lbs. Deb: 9/12/35

YEAR	TM/L	G	AB	R	H	2B	3B	HR	RBI	BB	SO	AVG	OBP	SLG	PRO+	BR/A	SB	CS	SBR	FA	FR	G/POS	TPR
1935	Pit-N	9	32	6	8	2	0	0	6	2	8	.250	.294	.313	61	-2	0			1.000	0	/1-9	-0.3
1936	Pit-N	8	23	7	7	1	2	0	3	1	4	.304	.333	.522	124	1	0			1.000	0	/O-4,1-1	0.1
1937	Phi-N	105	332	42	97	19	3	6	52	21	41	.292	.342	.422	98	-1	4			.980	1	O-54,1-23	-0.5
1938	Phi-N	21	74	4	19	4	0	0	8	5	12	.257	.304	.311	71	-3	0			.978	-0	1-16/O-2	-0.5
Total	4	143	461	59	131	26	5	6	69	29	64	.284	.332	.401	93	-5	4			.983	1	/O-60,1-49	-1.2

■ GEORGE BROWNE

Browne, George Edward b: 1/12/1876, Richmond, Va. d: 12/9/20, Hyde Park, N.Y. BL/TR, 5'10.5", 160 lbs. Deb: 9/27/01

YEAR	TM/L	G	AB	R	H	2B	3B	HR	RBI	BB	SO	AVG	OBP	SLG	PRO+	BR/A	SB	CS	SBR	FA	FR	G/POS	TPR
1901	Phi-N	8	26	2	5	1	0	0	4	1		.192	.250	.231	39	-2	2			1.000	0	/O-8	-0.4
1902	Phi-N	70	281	41	73	7	1	0	26	16		.260	.304	.292	84	-5	11			.910	8	O-70	-0.3
	NY-N	53	216	30	69	9	5	0	14	9		.319	.355	.407	136	8	13			.895	-0	O-53	0.5
	Yr	123	497	71	142	16	6	0	40	25		.286	.326	.342	107	3	24			.904	7	*O-123	0.2
1903	NY-N	141	591	105	185	23	3	4	45	43		.313	.364	.372	106	4	27			.918	-4	*O-141	-0.8
1904	NY-N	150	596	99	169	16	5	4	39	39		.284	.332	.347	105	3	24			.925	-5	*O-149	-1.2
1905	*NY-N	127	536	95	157	16	14	4	43	20		.293	.321	.397	111	5	26			.915	-9	*O-127	-1.0
1906	NY-N	122	477	61	126	10	4	0	38	27		.264	.304	.302	87	-8	32			.934	-5	*O-121	-2.1
1907	NY-N	127	458	54	119	11	10	5	37	31		.260	.308	.360	106	2	15			.941	-9	*O-121	-1.4
1908	Bos-N	138	536	61	122	10	6	1	34	36		.228	.276	.274	77	-14	17			.950	4	*O-138	-1.9
1909	Chi-N	12	39	7	8	0	1	0	1	5		.205	.295	.256	70	-1	3			.944	-2	O-12	-0.4
	Was-A	103	393	40	107	15	5	1	16	17		.272	.308	.344	111	3	13			.935	-2	*O-101	-0.4
1910	Was-A	7	22	1	4	0	0	0	0	1		.182	.217	.182	26	-2	0			.667	-2	/O-5	-0.4
	Chi-A	30	112	17	27	4	1	0	4	12		.241	.315	.295	95	-0	5			.952	-3	O-29	-0.6
	Yr	37	134	18	31	4	1	0	4	13		.231	.299	.276	84	-2	5			.917	-5	O-34	-1.0
1911	Bro-N	8	12	1	4	0	0	0	0	2		.333	.385	.333	106	-0	2			1.000	-0	/O-2	0.0
1912	Phi-N	6	5	0	1	0	0	0	0	1		.200	.333	.200	45	-0	0			.000	0	H	0.0
Total	12	1102	4300	614	1176	119	55	18	303	259	1	.273	.318	.339	100	-8	190			.927	-32	*O-1077	-10.4

■ JERRY BROWNE

Browne, Jerome Austin b: 2/13/66, Christiansted, V.I. BB/TR, 5'10", 170 lbs. Deb: 9/6/86

YEAR	TM/L	G	AB	R	H	2B	3B	HR	RBI	BB	SO	AVG	OBP	SLG	PRO+	BR/A	SB	CS	SBR	FA	FR	G/POS	TPR
1986	Tex-A	12	24	6	10	2	0	0	3	1	4	.417	.440	.500	151	2	0	2	-1	.923	-1	/2-8	0.0
1987	Tex-A	132	454	63	123	16	6	1	38	61	50	.271	.360	.339	87	-7	27	17	-2	.980	-17	*2-130/D-1	-1.9
1988	Tex-A	73	214	26	49	9	2	1	17	25	32	.229	.310	.304	71	-8	7	5	-1	.958	-25	2-70/D-1	-3.2
1989	Cle-A	153	598	83	179	31	4	5	45	68	64	.299	.372	.390	113	12	14	6	1	.979	-48	*2-151/D-2	-3.1
1990	Cle-A	140	513	92	137	26	5	6	50	72	46	.267	.359	.372	105	6	12	7	-1	.985	-21	2-139	-1.3
1991	Cle-A	107	290	28	66	5	2	1	29	27	29	.228	.296	.259	57	-16	2	4	-2	.964	-10	2-47,O-17,3/D	-2.7
1992	*Oak-A	111	324	43	93	12	2	3	40	40	40	.287	.372	.364	113	7	2	4	-1	.965	-11	3-58,O-43,2/SD	-0.6
1993	Oak-A	76	260	27	65	13	0	2	19	22	17	.250	.309	.323	74	-9	4	0	1	.985	-4	O-56,3-13/21	-1.3
1994	Fla-N	101	329	42	97	12	4	3	30	52	23	.295	.394	.398	102	3	3	0	1	.931	-7	3-62,O-30,2	-0.3
Total	9	905	3006	410	819	131	25	22	271	368	305	.272	.354	.355	95	-11	72	44	-5	.977	-143	2-582,3-148,O/D1S	-14.4

■ PIDGE BROWNE

Browne, Prentice Almont b: 3/21/29, Peekskill, N.Y. BL/TL, 6'1", 190 lbs. Deb: 4/13/62

YEAR	TM/L	G	AB	R	H	2B	3B	HR	RBI	BB	SO	AVG	OBP	SLG	PRO+	BR/A	SB	CS	SBR	FA	FR	G/POS	TPR
1962	Hou-N	65	100	8	21	4	2	1	10	13	19	.210	.301	.320	72	-4	0	0	0	.983	1	1-26	-0.4

■ PETE BROWNING

Browning, Louis Rogers "The Gladiator" b: 6/17/1861, Louisville, Ky. d: 9/10/05, Louisville, Ky. BR/TR, 6', 180 lbs. Deb: 5/2/1882

YEAR	TM/L	G	AB	R	H	2B	3B	HR	RBI	BB	SO	AVG	OBP	SLG	PRO+	BR/A	SB	CS	SBR	FA	FR	G/POS	TPR
1882	Lou-a	69	288	67	109	17	3	5			26	.378	.430	.510	229	40				.890	12	2-42,S-18,3	4.7
1883	Lou-a	84	358	95	121	15	9	4			23	.338	.378	.464	183	34				.861	12	O-48,S-26,3/21	2.3
1884	Lou-a	103	447	101	150	33	8	4			13	.336	.357	.472	176	36				.806	-9	3-52,O-24,1/2P	2.1
1885	Lou-a	112	481	98	174	34	10	9			25	.362	.393	.530	190	47				.900	5	*O-112	4.3
1886	Lou-a	112	467	86	159	29	6	2			30	.340	.389	.441	151	25	26			.791	-10	*O-112	1.1
1887	Lou-a	134	547	137	220	35	16	4			55	.402	.464	.547	178	58	103			.868	-3	*O-134	4.2
1888	Lou-a	99	383	58	120	22	8	3	72		37	.313	.380	.436	164	28	36			.888	-1	*O-99	2.2

YEAR	TM/L	G	AB	R	H	2B	3B	HR	RBI	BB	SO	AVG	OBP	SLG	PRO+	BR/A	SB	CS	SBR	FA	FR	G/POS	TPR
1889	Lou-a	83	324	39	83	19	5	2	32	34	30	.256	.327	.364	98	-1	21			.882	-3	O-83	-0.5
1890	Cle-P	118	493	112	184	**40**	8	5	93	75	36	**.373**	.459	.517	**175**	**57**	35			.893	4	*O-118	**4.5**
1891	Pit-N	50	203	35	59	14	1	4	28	27	31	.291	.377	.429	138	10	4			.904	5	O-50	1.2
	Cin-N	55	216	29	74	10	3	0	33	24	23	.343	.413	.417	141	12	12			.924	-1	O-55	0.8
	Yr	105	419	64	133	24	4	4	61	51	54	.317	.395	.422	139	22	16			.913	5	*O-105	2.0
1892	Lou-N	21	77	10	19	4	0	0	4	12	7	.247	.348	.299	104	1	5			.911	-1	O-21	-0.1
	Cin-N	83	307	47	93	12	5	3	52	40	25	.303	.383	.404	140	16	8			.917	-2	O-82/1-2	0.9
	Yr	104	384	57	112	16	5	3	56	52	32	.292	.376	.383	133	17	13			.916	-3	*O-103/1-2	0.8
1893	Lou-N	57	220	38	78	11	3	1	37	44	15	.355	.466	.445	155	21	8			.881	-3	O-57	1.2
1894	StL-N	2	7	1	1	0	0	0	0	0	0	.143	.143	.143	-31	-1	0			1.000	-0	/O-2	-0.2
	Bro-N	1	2	1	2	0	0	0	2	0	0	1.000	1.000	1.000	413	1	0			1.000	-0	/O-1	0.1
	Yr	3	9	2	3	0	0	0	2	1	0	.333	.400	.333	80	-0	0			1.000	-1	/O-3	-0.1
Total	13	1183	4820	954	1646	295	85	46	353	466	167	.341	.403	.467	164	384	258			.883	-16	O-998/3-75,2S1P	28.8

■ **BILL BRUBAKER**   Brubaker, Wilbur Lee b: 11/7/10, Cleveland, Ohio d: 4/2/78, Laguna Hills, Cal. BR/TR, 6'2", 185 lbs. Deb: 9/8/32 F

YEAR	TM/L	G	AB	R	H	2B	3B	HR	RBI	BB	SO	AVG	OBP	SLG	PRO+	BR/A	SB	CS	SBR	FA	FR	G/POS	TPR
1932	Pit-N	7	24	3	10	3	0	0	4	3	4	.417	.481	.542	178	3	1			.909	-0	/3-7	0.3
1933	Pit-N	2	2	0	0	0	0	0	0	0	0	.000	.000	.000	-99	-1	0			1.000	0	/3-1	0.0
1934	Pit-N	3	6	0	2	1	0	0	1	1	0	.333	.429	.500	144	0	0			1.000	1	/3-3	0.1
1935	Pit-N	6	11	1	0	0	0	0	0	2	5	.000	.154	.000	-53	-2	0			.889	-0	/3-5	-0.3
1936	Pit-N	145	554	77	160	27	4	6	102	50	96	.289	.352	.384	96	-2	5			.940	-15	*3-145	-1.2
1937	Pit-N	120	413	57	105	20	4	6	48	47	51	.254	.335	.366	90	-5	2			.952	2	*3-115/S-3,1	0.0
1938	Pit-N	45	112	18	33	5	0	3	19	9	14	.295	.347	.420	109	1	2			.875	-1	3-18/1-9,SO	0.0
1939	Pit-N	100	345	41	80	23	1	7	43	29	51	.232	.297	.365	78	-11	3			.950	10	2-65,3-32/S	0.2
1940	Pit-N	38	78	8	15	3	1	0	7	8	16	.192	.267	.256	45	-6	0			.955	6	3-19/S-8,1	0.0
1943	Bos-N	13	19	3	8	3	0	0	1	2	2	.421	.476	.579	207	3	0			.778	-1	/3-5,1-3	0.2
Total	10	479	1564	208	413	85	10	22	225	151	239	.264	.333	.373	90	-20	13			.938	2	3-350/2-65,1SO	-0.7

■ **LOU BRUCE**   Bruce, Louis R. b: 1/16/1877, St.Regis, N.Y. d: 2/9/68, Ilion, N.Y. BL/TR, 5'5", 145 lbs. Deb: 6/22/04

YEAR	TM/L	G	AB	R	H	2B	3B	HR	RBI	BB	SO	AVG	OBP	SLG	PRO+	BR/A	SB	CS	SBR	FA	FR	G/POS	TPR
1904	Phi-A	30	101	9	27	3	0	0	8	5		.267	.302	.297	85	-2	2			.969	-2	O-25/P-2,23	-0.6

■ **EARLE BRUCKER**   Brucker, Earle Francis Jr. b: 8/29/25, Los Angeles, Cal. BL/TR, 6'2", 210 lbs. Deb: 10/2/48 F

YEAR	TM/L	G	AB	R	H	2B	3B	HR	RBI	BB	SO	AVG	OBP	SLG	PRO+	BR/A	SB	CS	SBR	FA	FR	G/POS	TPR
1948	Phi-A	2	6	0	1	1	0	0	0	1	1	.167	.286	.333	64	-0	0	0	0	1.000	-0	/C-2	-0.1

■ **EARLE BRUCKER**   Brucker, Earle Francis Sr. b: 5/6/01, Albany, N.Y. d: 5/8/81, San Diego, Cal. BR/TR, 5'11", 175 lbs. Deb: 4/19/37 FMC

YEAR	TM/L	G	AB	R	H	2B	3B	HR	RBI	BB	SO	AVG	OBP	SLG	PRO+	BR/A	SB	CS	SBR	FA	FR	G/POS	TPR
1937	Phi-A	102	317	40	82	16	5	6	37	48	30	.259	.356	.397	91	-4	1	2	-1	.971	-6	C-92	-0.6
1938	Phi-A	53	171	26	64	21	1	3	35	19	16	.374	.437	.561	152	14	1	1	-0	.986	-2	C-44/1-1	1.3
1939	Phi-A	62	172	18	50	15	1	3	31	24	16	.291	.381	.442	112	3	0	1	-1	1.000	-5	C-47	0.3
1940	Phi-A	23	46	3	9	1	1	0	2	6	3	.196	.288	.261	44	-4	0	0	0	.966	2	C-13	-0.1
1943	Phi-A	1	1	0	0	0	0	0	0	0	0	.000	.000	.000	-99	-0	0	0	0	.000	0	H	0.0
Total	5	241	707	87	205	53	8	12	105	97	65	.290	.376	.438	108	9	2	4	-2	.980	-11	C-196/1-1	0.6

■ **J. T. BRUETT**   Bruett, Joseph Timothy b: 10/8/67, Milwaukee, Wis. BL/TL, 5'11", 175 lbs. Deb: 6/3/92

YEAR	TM/L	G	AB	R	H	2B	3B	HR	RBI	BB	SO	AVG	OBP	SLG	PRO+	BR/A	SB	CS	SBR	FA	FR	G/POS	TPR
1992	Min-A	56	76	7	19	4	0	0	2	6	12	.250	.313	.303	71	-3	6	3	0	.979	-12	O-45/D-3	-1.6
1993	Min-A	17	20	2	5	2	0	0	1	1	4	.250	.318	.350	79	-1	0	0	0	.857	-4	O-13	-0.5
Total	2	73	96	9	24	6	0	0	3	7	16	.250	.314	.313	73	-3	6	3	0	.952	-16	/O-58,D-3	-2.1

■ **FRANK BRUGGY**   Bruggy, Frank Leo b: 5/4/1891, Elizabeth, N.J. d: 4/5/59, Elizabeth, N.J. BR/TR, 5'11", 195 lbs. Deb: 4/13/21

YEAR	TM/L	G	AB	R	H	2B	3B	HR	RBI	BB	SO	AVG	OBP	SLG	PRO+	BR/A	SB	CS	SBR	FA	FR	G/POS	TPR
1921	Phi-N	96	277	28	86	11	2	5	28	23	37	.310	.370	.419	100	1	6	2	1	.953	-9	C-86/1-2	-0.3
1922	Phi-A	53	111	10	31	7	0	0	9	6	11	.279	.322	.342	71	-5	1	2	-1	.925	-2	C-31	-0.6
1923	Phi-A	54	105	4	22	3	0	1	6	4	9	.210	.245	.267	34	-10	1	1	-0	.950	-1	C-34/1-5	-0.9
1924	Phi-A	50	113	9	30	6	0	0	8	8	15	.265	.314	.319	63	-6	4	0	1	.928	-8	C-44	-1.0
1925	Cin-N	6	14	2	3	0	0	0	1	2	0	.214	.313	.214	38	-1	0	0	0	.870	-2	/C-6	-0.1
Total	5	259	620	53	172	27	2	6	52	43	72	.277	.329	.356	76	-22	12	5	1	.941	-18	C-201/1-7	-2.9

■ **JACOB BRUMFIELD**   Brumfield, Jacob Donnell b: 5/27/65, Bogalusa, La. BR/TR, 6', 170 lbs. Deb: 4/6/92

YEAR	TM/L	G	AB	R	H	2B	3B	HR	RBI	BB	SO	AVG	OBP	SLG	PRO+	BR/A	SB	CS	SBR	FA	FR	G/POS	TPR
1992	Cin-N	24	30	6	4	2	0	0	2	2	4	.133	.212	.133	-0	-4	6	0	2	1.000	-2	O-16	-0.4
1993	Cin-N	103	272	40	73	17	3	6	23	21	47	.268	.323	.419	97	-2	20	8	1	.978	-5	O-96/2-4	-0.7
1994	Cin-N	68	122	36	38	10	2	4	11	15	18	.311	.387	.525	136	6	6	3	0	.987	-3	O-43	0.3
Total	3	195	424	82	115	27	5	10	36	38	69	.271	.334	.429	101	1	32	11	3	.982	-10	O-155/2-4	-0.8

■ **MIKE BRUMLEY**   Brumley, Anthony Michael b: 4/9/63, Oklahoma City, Okla. BB/TR, 5'10", 165 lbs. Deb: 6/16/87 F

YEAR	TM/L	G	AB	R	H	2B	3B	HR	RBI	BB	SO	AVG	OBP	SLG	PRO+	BR/A	SB	CS	SBR	FA	FR	G/POS	TPR
1987	Chi-N	39	104	8	21	2	2	1	9	10	30	.202	.278	.288	49	-8	7	1	2	.965	4	S-34/2-1	0.0
1989	Det-A	92	212	33	42	6	2	1	11	14	45	.198	.251	.255	44	-16	8	4	0	.980	-8	S-42,2-24,3/OD	-2.1
1990	Sea-A	62	147	19	33	5	4	0	7	10	22	.224	.274	.313	63	-7	2	0	1	.983	-1	S-47/2-6,3OD	-0.5
1991	Bos-A	63	118	16	25	5	0	0	5	10	22	.212	.273	.254	45	-9	2	0	1	.950	15	S-31,3-17/2OD	0.8
1992	Bos-A	2	1	0	0	0	0	0	0	0	0	.000	.000	.000	-94	-0	0	0	0	.000	0	/H	0.0
1993	Hou-N	8	10	1	3	0	0	0	2	1	3	.300	.364	.300	83	-0	0	1	-1	.000	-1	/3-1,S-1,O	-0.2
1994	Oak-A	11	25	0	6	0	0	0	2	1	8	.240	.269	.240	36	-2	0	0	0	.929	-3	/2-4,3-4,OS	-0.5
Total	7	277	617	77	130	17	8	2	36	46	130	.211	.268	.274	49	-42	19	6	2	.972	6	S-156/2-42,3OD	-2.5

■ **MIKE BRUMLEY**   Brumley, Tony Mike b: 7/10/38, Granite, Okla. BL/TR, 5'10", 195 lbs. Deb: 4/18/64 F

YEAR	TM/L	G	AB	R	H	2B	3B	HR	RBI	BB	SO	AVG	OBP	SLG	PRO+	BR/A	SB	CS	SBR	FA	FR	G/POS	TPR
1964	Was-A	136	426	36	104	19	2	2	35	40	54	.244	.310	.312	74	-14	1	1	-0	.991	-13	*C-132	-2.3
1965	Was-A	79	216	15	45	4	0	3	15	20	33	.208	.282	.269	58	-12	1	1	-0	.990	2	C-66	-0.8
1966	Was-A	9	18	1	2	1	0	0	0	0	2	.111	.111	.167	-22	-3	0	0	0	1.000	-1	/C-7	-0.4
Total	3	224	660	52	151	24	2	5	50	60	89	.229	.296	.294	67	-29	2	2	-1	.991	-12	C-205	-3.5

■ **GLENN BRUMMER**   Brummer, Glenn Edward b: 11/23/54, Olney, Ill. BR/TR, 6', 200 lbs. Deb: 5/25/81

YEAR	TM/L	G	AB	R	H	2B	3B	HR	RBI	BB	SO	AVG	OBP	SLG	PRO+	BR/A	SB	CS	SBR	FA	FR	G/POS	TPR
1981	StL-N	21	30	2	6	1	0	0	2	1	2	.200	.226	.233	30	-3	0	0	0	1.000	2	C-19	-0.1
1982	*StL-N	35	64	4	15	4	0	0	9	0	12	.234	.234	.297	47	-5	2	0	1	.970	3	C-32	0.0
1983	StL-N	45	87	7	24	7	0	0	9	10	11	.276	.351	.356	96	-0	1	3	-2	.978	0	C-41	0.0
1984	StL-N	28	58	3	12	0	0	1	3	3	7	.207	.246	.259	43	-4	0	0	0	.973	4	C-26	0.0
1985	Tex-A	49	108	7	30	4	0	1	5	11	22	.278	.355	.315	84	-2	1	5	-3	.989	-4	C-47/O-1,D	-0.7
Total	5	178	347	23	87	16	0	3	27	25	54	.251	.305	.305	70	-14	4	8	-4	.981	5	C-165/D-1,O	-0.8

■ **TOM BRUNANSKY**   Brunansky, Thomas Andrew b: 8/20/60, Covina, Cal. BR/TR, 6'4", 211 lbs. Deb: 4/9/81

YEAR	TM/L	G	AB	R	H	2B	3B	HR	RBI	BB	SO	AVG	OBP	SLG	PRO+	BR/A	SB	CS	SBR	FA	FR	G/POS	TPR
1981	Cal-A	11	33	7	5	0	0	3	6	8	10	.152	.317	.424	112	4	1	0	0	.938	3	O-11	0.3
1982	Min-A	127	463	77	126	30	1	20	46	71	101	.272	.378	.471	128	19	1	2	-1	.986	19	*O-127	2.7
1983	Min-A	151	542	70	123	24	5	28	82	61	95	.227	.310	.445	101	-0	2	5	-2	.985	18	*O-146/D-4	1.1
1984	Min-A	155	567	75	144	21	0	32	85	57	94	.254	.322	.460	109	5	4	5	-2	.984	5	*O-153/D-1	0.4
1985	Min-A★	157	567	71	137	28	4	27	90	71	86	.242	.326	.448	103	2	5	3	-0	.984	5	*O-155	0.2
1986	Min-A	157	593	69	152	28	1	23	75	53	98	.256	.318	.423	97	-3	12	4	1	.982	8	*O-152/D-2	0.1
1987	*Min-A	155	532	83	138	22	2	32	85	74	104	.259	.354	.489	116	12	11	11	-3	.990	-2	*O-138,D-17	0.2
1988	Min-A	14	49	5	9	1	0	1	6	7	11	.184	.286	.265	54	-3	1	0	0	.864	-2	O-13/D-1	-0.7
	StL-N	143	523	69	128	22	3	22	79	79	82	.245	.348	.428	121	15	16	6	1	**.996**	4	*O-143	1.7
1989	StL-N	158	556	67	133	29	3	20	85	59	107	.239	.314	.410	102	1	5	9	-4	.977	4	*O-155/1-1	-0.3

YEAR	TM/L	G	AB	R	H	2B	3B	HR	RBI	BB	SO	AVG	OBP	SLG	PRO+	BR/A	SB	CS	SBR	FA	FR	G/POS	TPR
1990	StL-N	19	57	5	9	3	0	1	2	12	10	.158	.314	.263	60	-3	0	0	0	.950	1	O-17	-0.2
	*Bos-A	129	461	61	123	24	5	15	71	54	105	.267	.347	.438	113	8	5	10	-5	.982	10	*O-121/D-7	1.0
1991	Bos-A	142	459	54	105	24	1	16	70	49	72	.229	.307	.390	87	-9	1	2	-1	.989	3	*O-137/D-1	-1.0
1992	Bos-A	138	458	47	122	31	3	15	74	66	96	.266	.359	.445	116	10	2	5	-2	.980	3	O-92,1-28,D	0.7
1993	Mil-A	80	224	20	41	7	3	6	29	25	59	.183	.265	.321	58	-14	3	4	-2	.987	1	O-71/D-6	-1.6
1994	Mil-A	16	28	2	6	2	0	0	0	1	9	.214	.241	.286	34	-3	0	0	0	1.000	-3	/O-6,1-2,D	-0.5
	Bos-A	48	177	22	42	10	1	10	34	23	48	.237	.325	.475	96	-2	0	2	-1	.989	-3	O-42/1-5,D	-0.6
	Yr	64	205	24	48	12	1	10	34	24	57	.234	.314	.449	89	-4	0	2	-1	.989	-5	O-48/1-7,D	-1.1
Total	14	1800	6289	804	1543	306	33	271	919	770	1187	.245	.331	.434	105	38	69	70	-21	.984	65	*O-1679/D-61,1	3.5

■ ARLO BRUNSBERG   Brunsberg, Arlo Adolph b: 8/15/40, Fertile, Minn.   BL/TR, 6', 195 lbs.   Deb: 9/23/66

| 1966 | Det-A | 2 | 3 | 1 | 1 | 1 | 0 | 0 | 0 | 0 | 0 | .333 | .500 | .667 | 227 | 1 | 0 | 0 | 0 | 1.000 | -1 | /C-2 | 0.0 |

■ BOB BRUSH   Brush, Robert b: 3/8/1875, Osage, Iowa   d: 4/2/44, San Bernardino, Cal.   Deb: 4/20/07

| 1907 | Bos-N | 2 | 2 | 0 | 0 | 0 | 0 | 0 | 0 | 0 | 0 | .000 | .000 | .000 | -99 | -0 | 0 | | | 1.000 | -0 | /1-1 | -0.1 |

■ BILL BRUTON   Bruton, William Haron b: 12/22/25, Panola, Ala.   BL/TR, 6'0.5", 169 lbs.   Deb: 4/13/53

1953	Mil-N	151	613	82	153	18	14	1	41	44	100	.250	.306	.330	70	-27	**26**	11	1	.979	8	*O-150	-2.3
1954	Mil-N	142	567	89	161	20	7	4	30	40	78	.284	.330	.365	88	-11	**34**	13	2	.981	1	*O-141	-1.3
1955	Mil-N	149	636	106	175	30	12	9	47	43	72	.275	.325	.403	97	-4	**25**	11	1	.968	15	*O-149	0.4
1956	Mil-N	147	525	73	143	23	**15**	8	56	26	63	.272	.308	.419	99	-3	8	6	-1	.969	3	*O-145	-0.9
1957	Mil-N	79	306	41	85	16	9	5	30	19	35	.278	.322	.438	110	3	11	4	1	.981	1	O-79	0.0
1958	*Mil-N	100	325	47	91	11	3	3	28	27	37	.280	.339	.360	93	-4	4	1	1	.977	-7	O-96	-1.4
1959	Mil-N	133	478	72	138	22	6	6	41	35	54	.289	.339	.397	104	1	13	5	1	.991	4	*O-133	0.0
1960	Mil-N	151	629	**112**	180	27	**13**	12	54	41	97	.286	.332	.428	115	10	22	13	-1	.986	4	*O-149	0.5
1961	Det-A	160	596	99	153	15	5	17	63	61	66	.257	.329	.384	87	-11	22	6	3	.988	12	*O-155	-0.5
1962	Det-A	147	561	90	156	27	5	16	74	55	67	.278	.348	.430	104	3	14	7	0	.983	19	*O-145	1.4
1963	Det-A	145	524	84	134	21	8	8	48	59	70	.256	.331	.372	93	-4	14	7	0	.991	10	*O-138	-0.1
1964	Det-A	106	296	42	82	11	5	5	33	32	54	.277	.348	.399	105	3	14	5	1	.987	-1	O-81	0.0
Total	12	1610	6056	937	1651	241	102	94	545	482	793	.273	.329	.393	96	-43	207	89	9	.981	68	*O-1561	-4.2

■ ED BRUYETTE   Bruyette, Edward T. b: 8/31/1874, Manawa, Wis.   d: 8/5/40, Peshastin, Wash.   BL/TR, 5'10", 170 lbs.   Deb: 8/6/01

| 1901 | Mil-A | 26 | 82 | 7 | 15 | 3 | 0 | 0 | 4 | 12 | | .183 | .295 | .220 | 46 | -5 | 1 | | | .778 | -6 | O-21/2-3,S3 | -1.2 |

■ BILLY BRYAN   Bryan, William Ronald b: 12/4/38, Morgan, Ga.   BL/TR, 6'4", 200 lbs.   Deb: 9/12/61

1961	KC-A	9	19	2	3	0	0	1	2	2	7	.158	.238	.316	46	-2	0	0	0	1.000	-2	/C-4	-0.3
1962	KC-A	25	74	5	11	2	1	2	7	5	32	.149	.203	.284	28	-8	0	0	0	.976	-3	C-22	-1.0
1963	KC-A	24	65	11	11	1	1	3	7	9	22	.169	.270	.354	69	-3	0	0	0	.981	5	C-24	0.3
1964	KC-A	93	220	19	53	9	2	13	36	16	69	.241	.292	.477	107	1	0	0	0	.991	-6	C-65	-0.6
1965	KC-A	108	325	36	82	11	5	14	51	29	87	.252	.317	.446	116	6	0	0	0	.984	-6	C-95	0.6
1966	KC-A	32	76	0	10	4	0	0	7	6	17	.132	.195	.184	10	-9	0	0	0	.965	-1	C-21/1-3	-1.0
	NY-A	27	69	5	15	2	0	4	5	5	19	.217	.270	.420	99	-0	0	0	0	.988	-0	C-14/1-3	0.0
	Yr	59	145	5	25	6	0	4	12	11	36	.172	.231	.297	52	-9	0	0	0	.975	-2	C-35/1-6	-1.0
1967	NY-A	16	12	1	2	0	0	0	2	5	3	.167	.412	.417	151	1	0	0	0	1.000	1	/C-1	0.2
1968	Was-A	40	108	5	22	3	0	3	8	14	27	.204	.301	.315	90	-1	0	1	-1	.983	-4	C-28	-0.4
Total	8	374	968	86	209	32	9	41	125	91	283	.216	.285	.395	91	-14	0	1	-1	.984	-18	C-274/1-6	-2.2

■ DEREK BRYANT   Bryant, Derek Roszell b: 10/9/51, Lexington, Ky.   BR/TR, 5'11", 185 lbs.   Deb: 4/24/79

| 1979 | Oak-A | 39 | 106 | 8 | 19 | 2 | 1 | 0 | 13 | 10 | 10 | .179 | .250 | .217 | 29 | -11 | 0 | 0 | 0 | 1.000 | -2 | O-33/D-2 | -1.3 |

■ DON BRYANT   Bryant, Donald Ray b: 7/13/41, Jasper, Fla.   BR/TR, 6'5", 200 lbs.   Deb: 7/17/66   C

1966	Chi-N	13	26	2	8	2	0	0	4	1	4	.308	.357	.385	105	0	1	0	0	.978	0	C-10	0.1
1969	Hou-N	31	59	2	11	1	0	1	6	4	13	.186	.250	.254	42	-5	0	0	0	.993	3	C-28	-0.1
1970	Hou-N	15	24	2	5	0	0	0	3	1	8	.208	.240	.208	22	-3	0	0	0	.957	-0	C-13	-0.3
Total	3	59	109	6	24	3	0	1	13	6	25	.220	.274	.275	53	-7	1	0	0	.983	3	/C-51	-0.3

■ G. BRYANT   Bryant, G.   Deb: 8/6/1885

| 1885 | Det-N | 1 | 4 | 0 | 0 | 0 | 0 | 0 | 0 | 0 | 2 | .000 | .000 | .000 | -99 | -1 | | | | 1.000 | -1 | /2-1 | -0.2 |

■ RALPH BRYANT   Bryant, Ralph Wendell b: 5/20/61, Fort Gaines, Ga.   BL/TR, 6'2", 200 lbs.   Deb: 9/8/85

1985	LA-N	6	6	0	2	0	0	0	1	0	2	.333	.333	.333	90	-0	0	0	0	.000	-1	/O-3	-0.1
1986	LA-N	27	75	15	19	4	2	6	13	5	25	.253	.309	.600	156	5	0	1	-1	.953	-1	O-26	0.3
1987	LA-N	46	69	7	17	2	1	2	10	10	24	.246	.350	.391	99	0	2	1	0	.917	-3	O-19	-0.4
Total	3	79	150	22	38	6	3	8	24	15	51	.253	.329	.493	125	5	2	2	-1	.940	-5	/O-48	-0.2

■ STEVE BRYE   Brye, Stephen Robert b: 2/4/49, Alameda, Cal.   BR/TR, 6', 190 lbs.   Deb: 9/3/70

1970	Min-A	9	11	1	2	1	0	0	2	2	4	.182	.308	.273	60	-1	0	0	0	1.000	-2	/O-6	-0.2
1971	Min-A	28	107	10	24	1	0	3	11	7	15	.224	.272	.318	65	-5	3	1	0	.966	1	O-28	-0.6
1972	Min-A	100	253	18	61	9	3	0	12	17	38	.241	.292	.300	73	-8	3	5	-2	.994	2	O-93	-1.0
1973	Min-A	92	278	39	73	9	5	6	33	35	46	.263	.345	.396	104	2	3	5	-2	.986	1	O-87/D-1	-0.3
1974	Min-A	135	488	52	138	32	1	2	41	22	59	.283	.320	.365	93	-5	1	3	-2	**.997**	3	*O-129	-1.1
1975	Min-A	86	246	41	62	13	1	9	34	21	37	.252	.316	.423	105	1	2	3	0	.983	-0	O-72/D-6	-0.4
1976	Min-A	87	258	33	68	11	0	2	23	13	31	.264	.299	.329	82	-6	1	2	-1	.987	-13	O-78/D-3	-2.5
1977	Mil-A	94	241	27	60	14	3	7	28	16	39	.249	.298	.419	93	-3	1	0	0	1.000	1	O-83/D-6	-0.6
1978	Pit-N	66	115	16	27	7	0	1	9	11	10	.235	.307	.322	73	-4	2	1	0	.983	-6	O-47	-1.2
Total	9	697	1997	237	515	97	13	30	193	144	276	.258	.311	.365	89	-29	16	14	-4	.991	-19	O-623/D-16	-7.9

■ HAL BUBSER   Bubser, Harold Fred b: 9/28/1895, Chicago, Ill.   d: 6/22/59, Melrose Park, Ill   BR/TR, 5'11", 170 lbs.   Deb: 4/15/22

| 1922 | Chi-A | 3 | 3 | 0 | 0 | 0 | 0 | 0 | 0 | 0 | 2 | .000 | .000 | .000 | -99 | -1 | 0 | 0 | 0 | .000 | 0 | H | -0.1 |

■ JOHNNY BUCHA   Bucha, John George b: 1/22/25, Allentown, Pa.   BR/TR, 5'11", 190 lbs.   Deb: 5/2/48

1948	StL-N	2	1	0	0	0	0	0	0	1	0	.000	.500	.000	43	-0	0			1.000	-0	/C-1	0.0
1950	StL-N	22	36	1	5	1	0	0	1	4	7	.139	.225	.167	5	-5	0			.959	0	C-17	-0.5
1953	Det-A	60	158	17	35	9	0	1	14	20	14	.222	.309	.297	65	-2	1	1	-0	.984	-4	C-56	-1.0
Total	3	84	195	18	40	10	0	1	15	25	21	.205	.295	.272	53	-12	1	1		.980	-4	/C-74	-1.5

■ JERRY BUCHEK   Buchek, Gerald Peter b: 5/9/42, St.Louis, Mo.   BR/TR, 5'11", 185 lbs.   Deb: 6/30/61

1961	StL-N	31	90	6	12	2	0	0	6	9	28	.133	.152	.156	-16	-15	0	0	0	.912	-6	S-31	-1.9
1963	StL-N	3	4	0	1	0	0	0	0	0	2	.250	.250	.250	41	-0	0	0	0	1.000	0	/S-1	0.0
1964	*StL-N	35	30	7	6	0	0	2	3	1	11	.200	.273	.333	64	-1	0	0	0	.929	3	S-20/2-9,3	0.6
1965	StL-N	55	166	17	41	8	3	3	21	13	46	.247	.302	.386	84	-4	0	0	0	.994	10	2-33,S-18/3	1.1
1966	StL-N	100	284	23	67	10	4	4	25	23	71	.236	.293	.342	75	-9	0	5	-3	.974	-13	2-49,S-48/3	-2.0
1967	NY-N	124	411	35	97	11	2	14	41	26	101	.236	.285	.375	89	-7	3	5	-2	.977	4	2-95,3-17/S	0.1
1968	NY-N	73	192	8	35	4	2	1	11	10	53	.182	.304	.219	36	-15	1	1	0	.935	-1	3-37,2-12/O	-1.8
Total	7	421	1177	96	259	35	11	22	108	75	312	.220	.271	.325	67	-51	5	11	-5	.978	2	2-198,S-127/3O	-3.9

YEAR	TM/L	G	AB	R	H	2B	3B	HR	RBI	BB	SO	AVG	OBP	SLG	PRO+	BR/A	SB	CS	SBR	FA	FR	G/POS	TPR

■ JIM BUCHER   Bucher, James Quinter   b: 3/11/11, Manassas, Va.   BL/TR, 5'11", 170 lbs.   Deb: 4/18/34

1934	Bro-N	47	84	12	19	5	2	0	8	4	7	.226	.261	.333	61	-5	1			.920	-1	2-20/3-6	-0.5
1935	Bro-N	123	473	72	143	22	1	7	58	10	33	.302	.317	.397	93	-6	4			.950	-11	2-41,3-39,O	-1.4
1936	Bro-N	110	370	49	93	12	8	2	41	29	27	.251	.306	.343	74	-14	5			.910	-3	3-39,2-32,O	-2.0
1937	Bro-N	125	380	44	96	11	2	4	37	20	18	.253	.295	.324	67	-18	5			.951	-14	2-49,3-43/O	-2.7
1938	StL-N	17	57	7	13	3	1	0	7	2	2	.228	.254	.316	53	-4	0			.955	-4	2-14/3-1	-0.7
1944	Bos-A	80	277	39	76	9	2	4	31	19	13	.274	.326	.365	98	-1	3	3	-1	.958	-9	3-44,2-21	-1.0
1945	Bos-A	52	151	19	34	4	3	0	11	7	13	.225	.264	.291	60	-8	1	3	-2	.940	-2	3-32/2-2	-1.1
Total	7	554	1792	242	474	66	19	17	193	91	113	.265	.302	.351	78	-55	19	6		.939	-48	3-204,2-179/O	-9.4

■ KEVIN BUCKLEY   Buckley, Kevin John   b: 1/16/59, Quincy, Mass.   BR/TR, 6'1", 200 lbs.   Deb: 9/4/84

| 1984 | Tex-A | 5 | 7 | 1 | 2 | 1 | 0 | 0 | 2 | 0 | 4 | .286 | .444 | .429 | 138 | 0 | 0 | 0 | 0 | .000 | 0 | /D-3 | 0.0 |

■ DICK BUCKLEY   Buckley, Richard D.   b: 9/21/1858, Troy, N.Y.   d: 12/12/29, Pittsburgh, Pa.   TR, 5'10", 195 lbs.   Deb: 4/20/1888

1888	Ind-N	71	260	28	71	9	3	5	22	6	24	.273	.289	.388	112	3	4			.898	-21	C-51,3-22/O1	-1.3
1889	Ind-N	68	260	35	67	11	0	8	41	15	32	.258	.301	.392	91	-5	5			.877	-21	C-55,3-12/O1	-1.8
1890	NY-N	70	266	39	68	11	0	2	26	23	35	.256	.324	.320	88	-4	3			.931	9	C-62/3-8	1.0
1891	NY-N	75	253	23	55	9	1	4	31	11	30	.217	.258	.308	67	-11	3			.958	19	C-74/3-1	1.2
1892	StL-N	121	410	43	93	17	4	5	52	22	34	.227	.275	.324	85	-9	7			.937	-5	*C-119/1-2	-0.5
1893	StL-N	9	23	2	4	1	0	0	1	0		.174	.174	.217	4	-3	0			.914	1	/C-9	-0.1
1894	StL-N	29	89	5	16	1	2	1	3	6	3	.180	.240	.270	23	-12	1			.936	2	C-27/1-1	-0.6
	Phi-N	43	160	18	47	7	3	1	26	6	13	.294	.327	.394	75	-7	0			.966	3	C-42/1-1	0.0
	Yr	72	249	23	63	8	5	2	29	12	16	.253	.295	.349	56	-19	1			.954	4	C-69/1-2	-0.6
1895	Phi-N	38	112	20	28	6	1	0	14	9	17	.250	.333	.321	69	-5	2			.919	6	C-38	0.3
Total	8	524	1833	213	449	72	14	26	216	98	188	.245	.291	.342	81	-53	25			.931	-7	C-477/3-43,1O	-1.8

■ BILL BUCKNER   Buckner, William Joseph   b: 12/14/49, Vallejo, Cal.   BL/TL, 6', 185 lbs.   Deb: 9/21/69

1969	LA-N	1	1	0	0	0	0	0	0	0	0	.000	.000	.000	-99	-0	0	0	0	.000	0	H	0.0
1970	LA-N	28	68	6	13	3	1	0	4	3	7	.191	.225	.265	32	-7	0	1	-1	1.000	1	O-20/1-1	-0.7
1971	LA-N	108	358	37	99	15	1	5	41	11	18	.277	.307	.366	96	-3	4	1	1	.994	-9	O-86,1-11	-0.6
1972	LA-N	105	383	47	122	14	3	5	37	17	13	.319	.349	.410	118	8	10	3	1	.992	-3	O-61,1-35	0.1
1973	LA-N	140	575	68	158	20	0	8	46	17	34	.275	.299	.351	83	-15	12	2	2	.998	-3	1-93,O-48	-2.6
1974	*LA-N	145	580	83	182	30	3	7	58	30	21	.314	.352	.412	118	12	31	13	2	.976	-3	*O-137/1-6	0.4
1975	LA-N	92	288	30	70	11	2	6	31	17	15	.243	.290	.358	82	-8	3	1	1	.986	2	O-72	-0.9
1976	LA-N	154	642	76	193	28	4	7	60	26	26	.301	.329	.389	105	2	28	9	3	.985	7	*O-153/1-1	0.6
1977	Chi-N	122	426	40	121	27	0	11	60	21	23	.284	.319	.425	88	-8	7	5	-1	.990	-0	1-99	-1.5
1978	Chi-N	117	446	47	144	26	1	5	74	18	17	.323	.349	.419	102	0	7	5	-1	.995	8	*1-105	0.1
1979	Chi-N	149	591	72	168	34	7	14	66	30	28	.284	.321	.437	96	-5	9	4	0	.995	18	*1-140	0.5
1980	Chi-N	145	578	69	187	41	3	10	68	30	18	**.324**	.357	.457	117	12	1	2	-1	.993	8	1-94,O-50	1.2
1981	Chi-N★	106	421	45	131	**35**	3	10	75	26	16	.311	.353	.480	129	14	5	2	0	.984	1	*1-105	1.0
1982	Chi-N	161	657	93	201	34	5	15	105	36	26	.306	.347	.441	116	13	15	5	2	.993	16	*1-161	2.2
1983	Chi-N	153	626	79	175	**38**	6	16	66	25	30	.280	.313	.436	101	-2	12	4	1	.992	21	*1-144,O-15	1.2
1984	Chi-N	21	43	3	9	0	0	0	2	1	1	.209	.244	.209	26	-4	0	0	0	1.000	2	/1-7,O-2	-0.3
	Bos-A	114	439	51	122	21	2	11	67	24	38	.278	.323	.410	97	-2	2	2	-1	.986	5	*1-113	-0.6
1985	Bos-A	162	673	89	201	46	3	16	110	30	36	.299	.330	.447	106	4	18	4	3	.992	25	*1-162	2.2
1986	*Bos-A	153	629	73	168	39	2	18	102	40	25	.267	.315	.421	98	-3	6	4	-1	.989	20	*1-138,D-15	0.6
1987	Bos-A	75	286	23	78	6	1	2	42	13	12	.273	.304	.322	65	-14	1	3	0	.991	3	1-74	-1.7
	Cal-A	57	183	16	56	12	1	3	32	9	7	.306	.339	.432	106	1	1	0	0	1.000	-0	1-39/1-5	0.0
	Yr	132	469	39	134	18	2	5	74	22	26	.286	.318	.365	80	-13	2	3	-1	.992	3	1-79,D-39	-1.7
1988	Cal-A	19	43	1	9	0	0	0	9	4	0	.209	.277	.209	39	-3	2	0	1	1.000	0	D-11/1-1	-0.3
	KC-A	89	242	18	62	14	0	3	34	13	19	.256	.294	.351	79	-7	3	1	0	.994	-0	D-42,1-21	-1.0
	Yr	108	285	19	71	14	0	-3	43	17	19	.249	.291	.330	73	-10	5	1	1	.994	-0	D-53,1-22	-1.3
1989	KC-A	79	176	7	38	4	1	0	16	6	11	.216	.242	.267	43	-13	1	0	0	.985	0	1-24,D-19	-1.6
1990	Bos-A	22	43	4	8	0	0	1	3	4	4	.186	.239	.256	37	-4	0	0	0	1.000	0	1-15	-0.5
Total	22	2517	9397	1077	2715	498	49	174	1208	450	453	.289	.324	.408	99	-31	183	73	11	.992	127	*1-1555,O-644,D	-2.2

■ MARK BUDASKA   Budaska, Mark David   b: 12/27/52, Sharon, Pa.   BB/TL, 6', 180 lbs.   Deb: 6/6/78

1978	Oak-A	4	4	0	1	1	0	0	0	1	2	.250	.400	.500	160	0	0	0	0	.500	-1	/O-2	-0.1
1981	Oak-A	9	32	3	5	1	0	0	2	4	10	.156	.250	.188	29	-3	0	1	-1	.000	0	/D-9	-0.4
Total	2	13	36	3	6	2	0	0	2	5	12	.167	.268	.222	44	-3	0	1	-1	.500	-1	/D-9,O-2	-0.5

■ BUDD   Budd   Deb: 9/10/1890

| 1890 | Cle-P | 1 | 4 | 0 | 0 | 0 | 0 | 0 | 0 | 0 | 3 | .000 | .000 | .000 | -99 | -1 | 0 | | | 1.000 | -0 | /O-1 | -0.1 |

■ DON BUDDIN   Buddin, Donald Thomas   b: 5/5/34, Turbeville, S.C.   BR/TR, 5'11", 178 lbs.   Deb: 4/17/56

1956	Bos-A	114	377	49	90	24	0	5	37	65	62	.239	.357	.342	76	-12	2	0	1	.953	14	*S-113	1.1
1958	Bos-A	136	497	74	118	25	2	12	43	82	106	.237	.350	.368	92	-4	0	4	-2	.958	15	*S-136	2.1
1959	Bos-A	151	485	75	117	24	1	10	53	92	99	.241	.368	.357	95	0	6	1	1	.949	-17	*S-150	-0.3
1960	Bos-A	124	428	62	105	21	5	6	36	62	59	.245	.342	.360	87	-7	4	2	0	.951	-5	*S-124	-0.2
1961	Bos-A	115	339	58	89	22	3	6	42	72	45	.263	.395	.398	110	5	2	1	0	.956	-1	*S-109	1.5
1962	Hou-N	40	80	10	13	4	1	2	10	17	17	.162	.316	.313	75	-3	0	0	0	.952	0	S-27/3-9	0.2
	Det-A	31	83	14	19	3	0	2	4	20	16	.229	.385	.265	76	-2	1	0	0	.978	-2	S-19/2-5,3	-0.2
Total	6	711	2289	342	551	123	12	41	225	410	404	.241	.360	.359	90	-19	15	8	-0	.954	7	S-678/3-11,2	4.2

■ STEVE BUECHELE   Buechele, Steven Bernard   b: 9/26/61, Lancaster, Cal.   BR/TR, 6'2", 190 lbs.   Deb: 7/19/85

1985	Tex-A	69	219	22	48	6	3	6	21	14	38	.219	.272	.356	70	-10	3	2	-0	.969	6	3-69/2-1	-0.4
1986	Tex-A	153	461	54	112	19	2	18	54	35	98	.243	.303	.413	90	-7	5	8	-3	.968	19	*3-137,2-33/O	0.6
1987	Tex-A	136	363	45	86	20	0	13	50	28	66	.237	.293	.399	81	-11	2	2	-1	.964	-1	*3-123,2-18/O	-0.9
1988	Tex-A	155	503	68	126	21	4	16	58	40	79	.250	.342	.404	105	4	2	4	-2	.962	4	*3-153/2-2	1.0
1989	Tex-A	155	486	60	114	22	2	16	59	36	107	.235	.294	.387	89	-3	1	3	-2	.969	15	*3-145,2-18/SD	0.7
1990	Tex-A	91	251	30	54	10	0	7	30	27	63	.215	.296	.339	77	-8	1	0	0	.966	6	3-88/2-4	-0.1
1991	Tex-A	121	416	58	111	17	2	18	66	39	69	.267	.337	.447	117	9	0	4	-2	**.991**	20	*3-111,2-13/S	2.7
	*Pit-N	31	114	16	28	5	1	4	19	10	26	.246	.317	.412	105	1	0	1	-1	.956	3	3-31	0.3
1992	Pit-N	80	285	27	71	14	1	8	43	34	61	.249	.333	.389	105	2	0	2	-1	.957	6	3-80	0.8
	Chi-N	65	239	25	66	9	1	1	21	18	44	.276	.340	.351	94	-2	1	1	-0	.960	-2	3-63/2-2	-0.5
	Yr	145	524	52	137	23	2	9	64	52	105	.261	.336	.372	100	1	1	3	-2	.958	4	*3-143/2-2	0.3
1993	Chi-N	133	460	53	125	27	2	15	65	48	87	.272	.347	.433	110	6	1	1	-0	**.975**	7	*3-129/1-6	0.7
1994	Chi-N	104	339	33	82	11	1	14	52	39	80	.242	.327	.404	92	-4	1	0	0	.974	-10	3-99/1-6,2	-1.3
Total	10	1293	4136	491	1023	181	21	136	538	393	820	.247	.319	.400	96	-27	17	28	-12	.969	75	*3-1228/2-92,1SOD	3.6

■ CHARLIE BUELOW   Buelow, Charles John   b: 1/12/1877, Dubuque, Iowa   d: 5/4/51, Dubuque, Iowa   BR/TR,   Deb: 6/1/01

| 1901 | NY-N | 22 | 72 | 3 | 8 | 4 | 0 | 0 | 4 | 2 | | .111 | .147 | .167 | -10 | -10 | 0 | | | .853 | 3 | 3-17/2-2 | -0.7 |

■ FRITZ BUELOW   Buelow, Frederick William Alexander   b: 2/13/1876, Berlin, Germany   d: 12/27/33, Detroit, Mich.   BR/TR, 5'10.5", 170 lbs.   Deb: 9/28/1899

| 1899 | StL-N | 7 | 15 | 4 | 7 | 0 | 2 | 0 | 2 | 2 | | .467 | .556 | .733 | 247 | 3 | 0 | | | 1.000 | -2 | /C-4,O-2 | 0.1 |

YEAR	TM/L	G	AB	R	H	2B	3B	HR	RBI	BB	SO	AVG	OBP	SLG	PRO+	BR/A	SB	CS	SBR	FA	FR	G/POS	TPR
1900	StL-N	6	17	2	4	0	0	0	3	0		.235	.235	.235	30	-2	2			.864	-1	/C-4,O-1	-0.2
1901	Det-A	70	231	28	52	5	5	2	29	11		.225	.269	.316	59	-13	2			.967	5	C-69	-0.2
1902	Det-A	66	224	23	50	5	2	2	29	9		.223	.256	.290	50	-15	3			.927	0	C-63/1-2	-0.8
1903	Det-A	63	192	24	41	3	6	1	13	6		.214	.249	.307	68	-8	4			.961	1	C-60/1-2	-0.1
1904	Det-A	42	136	6	15	1	1	0	5	8		.110	.160	.132	-7	-16	2			.975	1	C-42	-1.3
	Cle-A	42	119	11	21	4	1	0	5	11		.176	.252	.227	52	-6	2			.979	1	C-42	-0.1
	Yr	84	255	17	36	5	2	0	10	19		.141	.204	.176	21	-22	4			.977	1	C-84	-1.4
1905	Cle-A	75	239	11	41	4	1	1	18	6		.172	.198	.209	29	-19	7			.963	-7	C-60/O-8,13	-2.3
1906	Cle-A	34	86	7	14	2	0	0	7	9		.163	.250	.186	38	-6	0			.938	3	C-33/1-1	-0.1
1907	StL-N	26	75	9	11	1	0	0	1	7		.147	.220	.160	21	-6	0			.983	1	C-25	-0.4
Total	9	431	1334	125	256	25	18	6	112	69		.192	.238	.251	46	-89	20			.960	1	C-402/O-11,13	-5.4

■ ART BUES
Bues, Arthur Frederick   b: 3/3/1888, Milwaukee, Wis.   d: 11/7/54, Whitefish Bay, Wis.   BR/TR, 5'11", 184 lbs.   Deb: 4/17/13

YEAR	TM/L	G	AB	R	H	2B	3B	HR	RBI	BB	SO	AVG	OBP	SLG	PRO+	BR/A	SB	CS	SBR	FA	FR	G/POS	TPR
1913	Bos-N	2	1	0	0	0	0	0	0	0	1	.000	.000	.000	-98	-0	0			.000	0	/2-1,3-1	0.0
1914	Chi-N	14	45	3	10	1	1	0	4	5	6	.222	.300	.289	76	-1	1			.968	-2	3-12	-0.4
Total	2	16	46	3	10	1	1	0	4	5	7	.217	.294	.283	72	-2	1			.968	-2	/3-13,2-1	-0.4

■ CHARLIE BUFFINTON
Buffinton, Charles G.   b: 6/14/1861, Fall River, Mass.   d: 9/23/07, Fall River, Mass.   BR/TR, 6'1", 180 lbs.   Deb: 5/17/1882   M

YEAR	TM/L	G	AB	R	H	2B	3B	HR	RBI	BB	SO	AVG	OBP	SLG	PRO+	BR/A	SB	CS	SBR	FA	FR	G/POS	TPR
1882	Bos-N	15	50	5	13	1	0	0	4	2	3	.260	.288	.280	83	-1				.615	-1	/O-7,P-5,1	-0.2
1883	Bos-N	86	341	28	81	8	3	1	26	6	24	.238	.251	.287	62	-16				.756	-7	O-51,P-43/1	-1.4
1884	Bos-N	87	352	48	94	18	3	1	39	16	12	.267	.299	.344	102	1				.946	-1	P-67,O-13,1	-0.5
1885	Bos-N	82	338	26	81	12	3	1	33	3	26	.240	.246	.302	79	-8				.912	-0	P-51,O-18,1	-1.1
1886	Bos-N	44	176	27	51	4	1	1	30	6	12	.290	.313	.341	103	1	3			.968	-6	1-19,P-18/O	-0.7
1887	Phi-N	66	269	34	72	12	1	1	46	11		.268	.299	.331	71	-11	8			.931	2	P-40,O-22,1	-0.9
1888	Phi-N	46	160	14	29	4	1	0	12	7	5	.181	.216	.219	37	-11	1			.939	9	P-46/O-1	0.0
1889	Phi-N	47	154	16	32	2	0	0	21	9	5	.208	.256	.221	31	-15	1			.916	1	P-47/O-1	0.0
1890	Phi-P	42	150	24	41	3	2	1	24	9	3	.273	.340	.340	74	-6	1			.864	0	P-36/O-5,1M	-0.1
1891	Bos-a	58	181	16	34	2	1	1	16	19	15	.188	.269	.227	43	-13	1			.934	3	P-48,O-10/1	-0.5
1892	Bal-N	13	43	5	15	1	1	0	4	3	6	.349	.391	.419	141	2	1			.892	2	P-13	0.0
Total	11	586	2214	245	543	67	16	7	255	91	114	.245	.276	.299	72	-78	14			.916	2	P-414,O-137/1	-5.4

■ DAMON BUFORD
Buford, Damon Jackson   b: 6/12/70, Baltimore, Md.   BR/TR, 5'10", 170 lbs.   Deb: 5/4/93   F

YEAR	TM/L	G	AB	R	H	2B	3B	HR	RBI	BB	SO	AVG	OBP	SLG	PRO+	BR/A	SB	CS	SBR	FA	FR	G/POS	TPR
1993	Bal-A	53	79	18	18	5	0	2	9	9	19	.228	.315	.367	79	-2	2	2	-1	.984	-1	O-30,D-17	-0.5
1994	Bal-A	4	2	2	1	0	0	0	0	0	0	.500	.500	.500	149	0	0	0	0	.000	-0	/O-1	0.0
Total	2	57	81	20	19	5	0	2	9	9	20	.235	.319	.370	81	-2	2	2	-1	.984	-1	/O-31,D-17	-0.5

■ DON BUFORD
Buford, Donald Alvin   b: 2/2/37, Linden, Tex.   BB/TR, 5'8", 165 lbs.   Deb: 9/14/63   FC

YEAR	TM/L	G	AB	R	H	2B	3B	HR	RBI	BB	SO	AVG	OBP	SLG	PRO+	BR/A	SB	CS	SBR	FA	FR	G/POS	TPR
1963	Chi-A	12	42	9	12	1	2	0	5	5	7	.286	.362	.405	116	1	1	0	0	.955	-5	/3-9,2-2	-0.3
1964	Chi-A	135	442	62	116	14	6	4	30	46	62	.262	.339	.348	94	-3	12	7	-1	.968	-16	2-92,3-37	-1.3
1965	Chi-A	155	586	93	166	22	5	10	47	67	76	.283	.361	.389	120	17	17	7	1	.981	3	*2-139,3-41	3.3
1966	Chi-A	163	607	85	148	26	7	8	52	69	71	.244	.324	.349	100	1	51	22	2	.939	1	*3-133,2-37,O	0.4
1967	Chi-A	156	535	61	129	10	9	4	32	65	51	.241	.324	.316	93	-3	34	21	-2	.948	4	*3-121,2-51/O	0.0
1968	Bal-A	130	426	65	120	13	4	15	46	57	46	.282	.372	.437	144	24	27	12	1	1.000	6	O-65,2-58/3	2.0
1969	*Bal-A	144	554	99	161	31	3	11	64	96	62	.291	.400	.417	128	24	19	18	-5	.983	-4	*O-128,2-10/3	0.9
1970	*Bal-A	144	504	99	137	15	2	17	66	109	55	.272	.409	.411	125	23	16	8	0	.987	6	*O-130/2-3,3	2.3
1971	*Bal-A★	122	449	**99**	130	19	4	19	54	89	62	.290	.413	.477	153	35	15	7	0	.987	3	*O-115	3.5
1972	Bal-A	125	408	46	84	6	2	5	22	69	83	.206	.326	.267	76	-9	8	3	1	.989	-1	*O-105	-1.6
Total	10	1286	4553	718	1203	157	44	93	418	672	575	.264	.364	.379	115	109	200	105	-3	.988	-15	O-555,2-392,3	9.2

■ JAY BUHNER
Buhner, Jay Campbell   b: 8/13/64, Louisville, Ky.   BR/TR, 6'3", 205 lbs.   Deb: 9/11/87

YEAR	TM/L	G	AB	R	H	2B	3B	HR	RBI	BB	SO	AVG	OBP	SLG	PRO+	BR/A	SB	CS	SBR	FA	FR	G/POS	TPR
1987	NY-A	7	22	0	5	2	0	0	1	1	6	.227	.261	.318	53	-2	0	0	-0	1.000	0	/O-7	-0.2
1988	NY-A	25	69	8	13	0	0	3	13	3	25	.188	.253	.319	60	-4	0	0	-0	.964	1	O-22	-0.4
	Sea-A	60	192	28	43	13	1	10	25	25	68	.224	.323	.458	111	3	1	1	-0	.993	9	O-59	1.0
	Yr	85	261	36	56	13	1	13	38	28	93	.215	.305	.421	98	-1	1	1	-0	.985	10	O-81	0.6
1989	Sea-A	58	204	27	56	15	1	9	33	19	55	.275	.342	.490	128	7	1	4	-2	.966	1	O-57	0.4
1990	Sea-A	51	163	16	45	12	0	7	33	17	50	.276	.339	.479	131	7	2	2	-1	.966	-4	O-40,D-10	0.1
1991	Sea-A	137	406	64	99	14	4	27	77	53	117	.244	.340	.498	128	15	0	1	-1	.981	6	*O-131	1.7
1992	Sea-A	152	543	69	132	16	3	25	79	71	146	.243	.337	.422	111	8	0	6	-4	.994	11	*O-150	1.2
1993	Sea-A	158	563	91	153	28	3	27	98	100	144	.272	.383	.476	128	24	2	5	-2	.978	-2	*O-148,D-10	1.5
1994	Sea-A	101	358	74	100	23	4	21	68	66	63	.279	.394	.542	137	21	0	1	-1	.990	6	O-96/D-4	2.2
Total	8	749	2520	377	646	123	16	129	427	355	674	.256	.355	.471	122	78	6	20	-10	.983	27	O-710/D-24	7.5

■ HARRY BUKER
Buker, Henry L. "Happy"   b: 1859, Chicago, Ill.   d: 8/10/1899, Chicago, Ill.   Deb: 6/11/1884

YEAR	TM/L	G	AB	R	H	2B	3B	HR	RBI	BB	SO	AVG	OBP	SLG	PRO+	BR/A	SB	CS	SBR	FA	FR	G/POS	TPR
1884	Det-N	30	111	5	15	1	0	0	3	4	15	.135	.165	.144	-2	-12				.867	1	S-19,O-11	-1.0

■ GEORGE BULLARD
Bullard, George Donald "Curly"   b: 10/24/28, Lynn, Mass.   BR/TR, 5'9.5", 165 lbs.   Deb: 9/17/54

YEAR	TM/L	G	AB	R	H	2B	3B	HR	RBI	BB	SO	AVG	OBP	SLG	PRO+	BR/A	SB	CS	SBR	FA	FR	G/POS	TPR
1954	Det-A	4	1	0	0	0	0	0	0	0	0	.000	.000	.000	-99	-0	0	0	0	.800	1	/S-1	0.1

■ SIM BULLAS
Bullas, Simeon Edward   b: 4/10/1861, Cleveland, Ohio   d: 1/14/08, Cleveland, Ohio   5'7.5", 150 lbs.   Deb: 5/2/1884

YEAR	TM/L	G	AB	R	H	2B	3B	HR	RBI	BB	SO	AVG	OBP	SLG	PRO+	BR/A	SB	CS	SBR	FA	FR	G/POS	TPR
1884	Tol-a	13	45	4	4	0	1	0	1	2		.089	.109	.133	-21	-6				.909	-6	C-12/O-2	-1.0

■ SCOTT BULLETT
Bullett, Scott Douglas   b: 12/25/68, Martinsburg, W.Va.   BB/TL, 6'2", 200 lbs.   Deb: 9/3/91

YEAR	TM/L	G	AB	R	H	2B	3B	HR	RBI	BB	SO	AVG	OBP	SLG	PRO+	BR/A	SB	CS	SBR	FA	FR	G/POS	TPR
1991	Pit-N	11	4	0	0	0	0	0	0	0	3	.000	.200	.000	-40	-1	1	1	-0	1.000	-1	/O-3	-0.2
1993	Pit-N	23	55	2	11	0	2	0	4	3	15	.200	.241	.273	37	-5	3	2	-0	1.000	-2	O-19	-0.7
Total	2	34	59	2	11	0	2	0	4	3	18	.186	.238	.254	32	-6	4	3	-1	1.000	-3	/O-22	-0.9

■ BUD BULLING
Bulling, Terry Charles "Terry"   b: 12/15/52, Lynwood, Cal.   BR/TR, 6'1", 200 lbs.   Deb: 7/3/77

YEAR	TM/L	G	AB	R	H	2B	3B	HR	RBI	BB	SO	AVG	OBP	SLG	PRO+	BR/A	SB	CS	SBR	FA	FR	G/POS	TPR
1977	Min-A	15	32	2	5	1	0	0	5	5	5	.156	.270	.188	28	-3	0	0	0	.952	-0	C-10/D-3	-0.3
1981	Sea-A	62	154	15	38	3	0	2	15	21	20	.247	.341	.305	84	-2	0	0	0	.977	-3	C-62	-0.3
1982	Sea-A	56	154	17	34	7	0	1	8	19	16	.221	.306	.286	62	-8	2	1	0	.991	7	C-56	0.1
1983	Sea-A	5	5	0	0	0	0	0	0	0	0	.000	.000	.000	-96	-1	0	0	0	1.000	1	/C-5	0.0
Total	4	138	345	34	77	11	0	3	28	45	41	.223	.315	.281	66	-14	2	1	0	.983	6	C-133/D-3	-0.5

■ ERIC BULLOCK
Bullock, Eric Gerald   b: 2/16/60, Los Angeles, Cal.   BL/TL, 5'11", 185 lbs.   Deb: 8/26/85

YEAR	TM/L	G	AB	R	H	2B	3B	HR	RBI	BB	SO	AVG	OBP	SLG	PRO+	BR/A	SB	CS	SBR	FA	FR	G/POS	TPR
1985	Hou-N	18	25	2	7	2	0	0	2	0	3	.280	.308	.360	89	-0	0	1	-1	.750	-2	/O-7	-0.3
1986	Hou-N	6	21	0	1	0	0	0	1	0	3	.048	.048	.048	-76	-5	2	0	1	.875	-1	/O-6	-0.6
1988	Min-A	16	17	3	5	0	0	0	3	3	1	.294	.400	.294	95	-1	0	0	0	.875	-1	/O-4,D-2	-0.1
1989	Phi-N	6	4	1	0	0	0	0	0	0	0	.000	.000	.000	-99	-1	0	0	0	1.000	-1	/O-3	-0.2
1990	Mon-N	4	2	0	1	0	0	0	0	0	0	.500	.500	.500	183	-0	0	0	0	.000	0	/H	0.0
1991	Mon-N	73	72	6	16	4	0	1	6	9	13	.222	.309	.319	78	-2	6	1	1	1.000	-1	/O-9,1-3	-0.2
1992	Mon-N	8	5	0	0	0	0	0	0	0	0	.000	.000	.000	-99	-1	0	0	0	.000	0	/H	-0.2
Total	7	131	146	13	30	6	0	1	12	13	20	.205	.270	.267	52	-9	9	2	2	.892	-5	/O-29,1-3,D	-1.6

■ AL BUMBRY
Bumbry, Alonza Benjamin (b: Alonza Benjamin Bumbrey)   b: 4/21/47, Fredericksburg, Va.   BL/TR, 5'8", 175 lbs.   Deb: 9/5/72   C

YEAR	TM/L	G	AB	R	H	2B	3B	HR	RBI	BB	SO	AVG	OBP	SLG	PRO+	BR/A	SB	CS	SBR	FA	FR	G/POS	TPR
1972	Bal-A	9	11	5	4	0	0	0	0	0	0	.364	.364	.545	164	1	1	1	-0	1.000	0	/O-2	0.1
1973	*Bal-A	110	356	73	120	15	**11**	7	34	34	49	.337	.399	.500	153	25	23	10	1	.978	-10	O-86/D-7	1.2

YEAR	TM/L	G	AB	R	H	2B	3B	HR	RBI	BB	SO	AVG	OBP	SLG	PRO+	BR/A	SB	CS	SBR	FA	FR	G/POS	TPR
1974	*Bal-A	94	270	35	63	10	3	1	19	21	46	.233	.291	.304	74	-9	12	4	1	.953	-1	O-67/D-7	-1.2
1975	Bal-A	114	349	47	94	19	4	2	32	32	81	.269	.338	.364	105	2	16	3	3	1.000	-2	D-48,O-39/3	0.1
1976	Bal-A	133	450	71	113	15	7	9	36	43	76	.251	.318	.376	109	4	42	10	7	.989	-12	*O-116,D-10	-0.6
1977	Bal-A	133	518	74	164	31	3	4	41	45	88	.317	.373	.411	121	16	19	8	1	.991	-10	*O-130	0.1
1978	Bal-A	33	114	21	27	5	2	2	6	17	15	.237	.346	.368	108	2	5	3	-0	.985	-2	O-28	-0.2
1979	*Bal-A	148	569	80	162	29	1	7	49	43	74	.285	.338	.376	96	-3	37	12	4	.982	-3	*O-146	-0.8
1980	Bal-A★	160	645	118	205	29	9	9	53	78	75	.318	.394	.433	128	27	44	11	7	.990	15	*O-160	4.2
1981	Bal-A	101	392	61	107	18	2	1	27	51	51	.273	.360	.337	102	3	22	15	-2	.992	4	*O-100	0.1
1982	Bal-A	150	562	77	147	20	4	5	40	44	77	.262	.315	.338	80	-15	10	5	0	.986	8	*O-147/D-1	-1.1
1983	*Bal-A	124	378	63	104	14	4	3	31	31	33	.275	.330	.357	91	-4	12	5	1	.988	-11	*O-104,D-11	-1.8
1984	Bal-A	119	344	47	93	12	1	3	24	25	35	.270	.320	.337	84	-7	9	5	-0	.988	-6	O-99/D-9	-1.7
1985	SD-N	68	95	6	19	3	0	1	10	7	9	.200	.255	.263	46	-7	2	0	1	.939	-2	O-17	-0.9
Total	14	1496	5053	778	1422	220	52	54	402	471	709	.281	.345	.378	104	33	254	92	21	.986	-31	*O-1241/D-93,3	-2.5

■ JOSH BUNCE
Bunce, Joshua b: 5/10/1847, Brooklyn, N.Y. d: 4/28/12, Brooklyn, N.Y. Deb: 8/27/1877

YEAR	TM/L	G	AB	R	H	2B	3B	HR	RBI	BB	SO	AVG	OBP	SLG	PRO+	BR/A	SB	CS	SBR	FA	FR	G/POS	TPR
1877	Har-N	1	4	0	0	0	0	0	0	0	0	.000	.000	.000	-99	-1				1.000	-0	/O-1	-0.1

■ NELSON BURBRINK
Burbrink, Nelson Edward b: 12/28/21, Cincinnati, Ohio BR/TR, 5'10", 195 lbs. Deb: 6/5/55

YEAR	TM/L	G	AB	R	H	2B	3B	HR	RBI	BB	SO	AVG	OBP	SLG	PRO+	BR/A	SB	CS	SBR	FA	FR	G/POS	TPR
1955	StL-N	58	170	11	47	8	1	0	15	14	13	.276	.335	.335	79	-5	1	1	-0	.979	-1	C-55	-0.4

■ AL BURCH
Burch, Albert William b: 10/7/1883, Albany, N.Y. d: 10/5/26, Brooklyn, N.Y. BL/TR, 5'8.5", 160 lbs. Deb: 6/19/06

YEAR	TM/L	G	AB	R	H	2B	3B	HR	RBI	BB	SO	AVG	OBP	SLG	PRO+	BR/A	SB	CS	SBR	FA	FR	G/POS	TPR
1906	StL-N	91	335	40	89	5	1	0	11	37		.266	.339	.287	99	1	15			.934	1	O-91	-0.3
1907	StL-N	48	154	18	35	3	1	0	5	17		.227	.304	.260	79	-3	7			.922	0	O-48	-0.6
	Bro-N	40	120	12	35	2	2	0	12	11		.292	.351	.342	127	4	5			.890	2	O-36/2-1	0.5
	Yr	88	274	30	70	5	3	0	17	28		.255	.325	.296	100	0	12			.908	2	O-84/2-1	-0.1
1908	Bro-N	123	456	45	111	8	4	2	18	33		.243	.294	.292	91	-5	15			.971	13	*O-116	0.3
1909	Bro-N	152	601	80	163	20	6	1	30	51		.271	.329	.329	108	5	38			.955	6	*O-151/1-1	0.6
1910	Bro-N	103	352	41	83	8	3	1	20	22	30	.236	.281	.284	67	-16	13			.957	-1	O-70,1-13	-2.1
1911	Bro-N	54	167	18	38	2	3	0	7	15	22	.228	.291	.275	61	-9	3			.972	2	O-43/2-3	-0.9
Total	6	611	2185	254	554	48	20	4	103	186	<u>52</u>	.254	.312	.299	91	-23	96			.950	22	O-555/1-14,2	-2.5

■ ERNIE BURCH
Burch, Earnest W. b: 1856, Dekalb Co., Ill. BL, Deb: 8/15/1884

YEAR	TM/L	G	AB	R	H	2B	3B	HR	RBI	BB	SO	AVG	OBP	SLG	PRO+	BR/A	SB	CS	SBR	FA	FR	G/POS	TPR
1884	Cle-N	32	124	9	26	4	0	0	7	5	24	.210	.240	.242	50	-7				.899	4	O-32	-0.3
1886	Bro-a	113	456	78	119	22	6	2		39		.261	.321	.349	109	4	16			.884	-13	*O-113	-1.0
1887	Bro-a	49	188	47	55	4	4	2		29		.293	.395	.388	118	6	15			.899	1	O-49	0.4
Total	3	194	768	134	200	30	10	4	<u>7</u>	73	<u>24</u>	.260	.328	.341	102	3	31			.891	-8	O-194	-0.9

■ BOB BURDA
Burda, Edward Robert b: 7/16/38, St.Louis, Mo. BL/TL, 5'11", 180 lbs. Deb: 8/25/62

YEAR	TM/L	G	AB	R	H	2B	3B	HR	RBI	BB	SO	AVG	OBP	SLG	PRO+	BR/A	SB	CS	SBR	FA	FR	G/POS	TPR
1962	StL-N	7	14	0	1	0	0	0	0	3	1	.071	.235	.071	-12	-2	1	0	0	.917	-0	/O-6	-0.2
1965	SF-N	31	27	0	3	0	0	0	5	5	6	.111	.250	.111	6	-3	0	0	0	.969	-1	1-11/O-1	-0.4
1966	SF-N	37	43	3	7	3	0	0	2	2	5	.163	.200	.233	19	-5	0	0	0	1.000	-1	/1-7,O-4	-0.6
1969	SF-N	97	161	20	37	8	0	6	27	21	12	.230	.319	.391	100	-0	0	1	-1	.995	-1	1-45,O-19	-0.4
1970	SF-N	28	23	1	6	0	0	0	3	5	2	.261	.414	.261	86	-0	0	0	0	.933	-1	/1-8,O-1	-0.1
	Mil-A	78	222	19	55	9	0	4	20	16	17	.248	.307	.342	78	-7	1	0	0	.987	-7	O-64/1-7	-1.8
1971	StL-N	65	71	6	21	0	0	1	12	10	11	.296	.390	.338	104	1	0	0	0	1.000	0	1-13/O-1	0.0
1972	Bos-A	45	73	4	12	1	0	2	9	8	11	.164	.247	.260	48	-5	0	0	0	.992	-0	1-15/O-1	-0.7
Total	7	388	634	53	142	21	0	13	78	70	65	.224	.306	.319	74	-21	2	1	0	.992	-11	1-106/O-97	-4.2

■ JACK BURDOCK
Burdock, John Joseph "Black Jack" b: 4/1852, Brooklyn, N.Y. d: 11/27/31, Brooklyn, N.Y. BR/TR, 5'9.5", 158 lbs. Deb: 5/2/1872 MU

YEAR	TM/L	G	AB	R	H	2B	3B	HR	RBI	BB	SO	AVG	OBP	SLG	PRO+	BR/A	SB	CS	SBR	FA	FR	G/POS	TPR
1872	Atl-n	37	174	26	45	2	1	0	15	1	1	.259	.263	.282	58	-12						*S-33/C-2,2	-0.9
1873	Atl-n	55	245	56	62	9	2	2	33	7	4	.253	.274	.331	86	-2						*2-55/C-2	-0.4
1874	Mut-n	61	272	45	76	16	3	2		1		.279	.282	.382	106	1						*3-61	0.1
1875	Har-n	74	347	72	102	14	5	0		5		.294	.304	.363	123	7						*2-72/3-1	0.5
1876	Har-n	69	309	66	80	9	1	0	23	13	16	.259	.289	.294	87	-5				.895	1	*2-69/3-1	-0.4
1877	Har-N	58	277	35	72	6	0	0	9	2	16	.260	.265	.282	81	-5				**.903**	7	*2-55/3-3	0.3
1878	Bos-N	60	246	37	64	12	6	0	25	3	16	.260	.269	.358	97	-2				**.918**	21	*2-60	2.2
1879	Bos-N	84	359	64	86	10	3	0	36	9	28	.240	.258	.284	77	-9				.911	10	*2-84	0.6
1880	Bos-N	86	356	58	90	17	4	2	35	7	26	.253	.269	.340	108	3				**.923**	12	*2-86	1.9
1881	Bos-N	73	282	36	67	12	4	1	24	7	18	.238	.256	.319	84	-5				.911	-11	*2-72/S-1	-1.2
1882	Bos-N	83	319	36	76	6	7	0	27	9	24	.238	.259	.301	79	-7				**.932**	3	*2-83	-0.2
1883	Bos-N	96	400	80	132	27	8	5	88	14	35	.330	.353	.475	145	20				.921	-1	*2-96/M	1.8
1884	Bos-N	87	361	65	97	14	4	6	49	15	52	.269	.298	.380	112	5				**.922**	1	*2-87/3-1	0.7
1885	Bos-N	45	169	18	24	5	0	0	7	8	18	.142	.181	.172	15	-15				.917	-4	2-45	-1.7
1886	Bos-N	59	221	26	48	6	1	0	25	11	27	.217	.254	.253	57	-11	3			.904	-8	2-59	-1.5
1887	Bos-N	65	237	36	61	6	0	0	29	18	22	.257	.320	.283	69	-9	19			.882	-19	2-65	-2.3
1888	Bos-N	22	79	5	16	0	0	0	4	2	5	.203	.232	.203	39	-5	1			.903	0	2-22	-0.4
	Bro-a	70	246	15	30	1	2	1	8	8		.122	.166	.154	3	-26	9			.904	2	2-70	-2.4
1891	Bro-N	3	12	1	1	0	0	0	1	1	1	.083	.154	.083	-31	-2	0			1.000	-1	/2-3	-0.2
Total	4 n	227	1038	199	285	41	11	4	<u>48</u>	14	<u>5</u>	.275	.284	.347	97	-6	3					2-128/3-62,SC	-0.7
Total	14	960	3873	578	944	131	40	15	390	128	<u>305</u>	.244	.270	.310	83	-74	32			.912	13	2-956/3-5,S	-2.5

■ JOE BURG
Burg, Joseph Peter b: 6/4/1882, Chicago, Ill. d: 4/28/69, Joliet, Ill. BR/TR, 5'9", 150 lbs. Deb: 9/26/10

YEAR	TM/L	G	AB	R	H	2B	3B	HR	RBI	BB	SO	AVG	OBP	SLG	PRO+	BR/A	SB	CS	SBR	FA	FR	G/POS	TPR
1910	Bos-N	13	46	7	15	0	1	0	10	7	12	.326	.415	.370	124	2	5			.867	3	3-12/S-1	0.5

■ SMOKY BURGESS
Burgess, Forrest Harrill b: 2/6/27, Caroleen, N.C. d: 9/15/91, Asheville, N.C. BL/TR, 5'8", 187 lbs. Deb: 4/19/49

YEAR	TM/L	G	AB	R	H	2B	3B	HR	RBI	BB	SO	AVG	OBP	SLG	PRO+	BR/A	SB	CS	SBR	FA	FR	G/POS	TPR
1949	Chi-N	46	56	4	15	0	0	1	12	4	4	.268	.317	.321	73	-2	0			1.000	1	/C-8	-0.1
1951	Chi-N	94	219	21	55	4	2	4	20	21	12	.251	.317	.315	69	-9	2	0	1	.980	-3	C-64	-0.9
1952	Phi-N	110	371	49	110	27	2	6	56	49	21	.296	.380	.429	125	14	3	1	0	.978	-6	*C-104	1.4
1953	Phi-N	102	312	31	91	17	5	4	36	37	17	.292	.370	.417	105	3	3	2	0	**.993**	-8	C-95	-0.1
1954	Phi-N	108	345	41	127	27	5	4	46	42	11	.368	.437	.510	146	25	1	5	-3	.975	-8	C-91	1.8
1955	Phi-N	7	21	4	4	2	0	1	1	3	1	.190	.292	.429	90	-0	0	0	0	1.000	1	/C-6	0.0
	Cin-N★	116	421	67	129	15	3	20	77	47	35	.306	.377	.499	123	14	1	1	-0	.986	-9	*C-107	0.8
	Yr	123	442	71	133	17	3	21	78	50	36	.301	.373	.495	122	14	1	1	-0	.987	-9	*C-113	0.8
1956	Cin-N	90	229	28	63	10	0	12	39	26	18	.275	.349	.476	112	4	0	1	-1	1.000	-2	C-55	0.3
1957	Cin-N	90	205	29	58	14	1	14	39	24	16	.283	.358	.566	134	9	0	0	0	.988	-5	C-45	0.6
1958	Cin-N	99	251	28	71	12	1	6	31	22	20	.283	.343	.410	93	-2	0	0	0	.988	4	C-58	0.5
1959	Pit-N★	114	377	41	112	28	5	11	59	31	16	.297	.354	.485	122	11	0	0	0	.984	-17	*C-101	0.0
1960	*Pit-N★	110	337	33	99	15	2	7	39	35	13	.294	.360	.412	110	5	0	1	-1	**.994**	1	C-89	1.1
1961	Pit-N★	100	323	37	98	17	3	12	52	30	16	.303	.366	.486	123	11	1	0	0	**.991**	-14	C-92	0.2
1962	Pit-N	130	360	38	118	19	2	13	61	31	19	.328	.381	.500	134	17	0	1	-0	.988	-11	*C-101	0.9
1963	Pit-N	91	264	20	74	10	1	6	37	24	14	.280	.343	.394	111	4	0	1	-1	.990	-11	C-72	-0.6
1964	Pit-N☆	68	171	9	42	3	1	2	17	13	14	.246	.303	.310	73	-6	2	1	0	.992	-8	C-44	-1.2
	Chi-A	7	5	1	1	0	0	0	1	0	0	.200	.429	.800	239	1	0	0	0	1.000	0	H	0.1
1965	Chi-A	80	77	2	22	4	0	2	24	11	7	.286	.375	.416	132	BR/3	0	0	0	1.000	-0	/C-5	0.4
1966	Chi-A	79	67	0	21	5	0	0	15	11	8	.313	.418	.388	143	4	0	0	0	1.000	-0	/C-2	0.5

YEAR	TM/L	G	AB	R	H	2B	3B	HR	RBI	BB	SO	AVG	OBP	SLG	PRO+	BR/A	SB	CS	SBR	FA	FR	G/POS	TPR
1967	Chi-A	77	60	2	8	1	0	2	11	14	8	.133	.307	.250	69	-2	0	0	0	.000	0	H	-0.2
Total	18	1691	4471	485	1318	230	33	126	673	477	270	.295	.364	.446	116	104	13	14		.988	-96	*C-1139	5.5

■ **TOM BURGESS** Burgess, Thomas Roland "Tim" b: 9/1/27, London, Ont., Can. BL/TL, 6', 180 lbs. Deb: 4/17/54 C

YEAR	TM/L	G	AB	R	H	2B	3B	HR	RBI	BB	SO	AVG	OBP	SLG	PRO+	BR/A	SB	CS	SBR	FA	FR	G/POS	TPR
1954	StL-N	17	21	2	1	1	0	0	1	3	9	.048	.167	.095	-29	-4	0	0	0	.750	-1	/O-4	-0.6
1962	LA-A	87	143	17	28	7	1	2	13	36	20	.196	.358	.301	82	-2	2	0	1	.997	-3	1-35/O-2	-0.6
Total	2	104	164	19	29	8	1	2	14	39	29	.177	.335	.274	67	-6	2	0	1	.857	-4	/1-35,O-6	-1.2

■ **BILL BURGO** Burgo, William Ross b: 11/5/19, Johnstown, Pa. d: 10/19/88, Morgan City, La. BR/TR, 5'8", 185 lbs. Deb: 9/22/43

YEAR	TM/L	G	AB	R	H	2B	3B	HR	RBI	BB	SO	AVG	OBP	SLG	PRO+	BR/A	SB	CS	SBR	FA	FR	G/POS	TPR
1943	Phi-A	17	70	12	26	4	2	1	9	4	1	.371	.421	.529	178	7	0	2	-1	.979	2	O-17	0.7
1944	Phi-A	27	88	6	21	2	0	1	3	7	3	.239	.316	.295	76	-3	1	3	-2	.955	2	O-22	-0.3
Total	2	44	158	18	47	6	2	2	12	11	4	.297	.362	.399	121	4	1	5	-3	.965	4	/O-39	0.4

■ **BILL BURICH** Burich, William Max b: 5/29/18, Calumet, Mich. BR/TR, 6', 180 lbs. Deb: 4/15/42

YEAR	TM/L	G	AB	R	H	2B	3B	HR	RBI	BB	SO	AVG	OBP	SLG	PRO+	BR/A	SB	CS	SBR	FA	FR	G/POS	TPR
1942	Phi-N	25	80	3	23	1	0	0	7	6	13	.287	.337	.300	92	-1	2			.917	-5	S-19/3-3	-0.5
1946	Phi-N	2	1	1	0	0	0	0	0	0	0	.000	.000	.000	-99	-0	0			.000	0	/3-1	0.0
Total	2	27	81	4	23	1	0	0	7	6	13	.284	.333	.296	89	-1	2			1.000	-5	/S-19,3-4	-0.5

■ **MACK BURK** Burk, Mack Edwin b: 4/21/35, Nacogdoches, Tex. BR/TR, 6'4", 180 lbs. Deb: 5/25/56

YEAR	TM/L	G	AB	R	H	2B	3B	HR	RBI	BB	SO	AVG	OBP	SLG	PRO+	BR/A	SB	CS	SBR	FA	FR	G/POS	TPR
1956	Phi-N	15	1	3	1	0	0	0	0	0	0	1.000	1.000	1.000	449	0	0	0	0	1.000	0	/C-1	0.1
1958	Phi-N	1	1	0	0	0	0	0	0	0	0	.000	.000	.000	-99	-0	0	0	0	.000	0	H	0.0
Total	2	16	2	3	1	0	0	0	0	0	0	.500	.500	.500	171	0	0	0	0	1.000	0	/C-1	0.0

■ **CHRIS BURKAM** Burkam, Chauncey De Pew b: 10/13/1892, Benton Harbor, Mich. d: 5/9/64, Kalamazoo, Mich. BL/TR, 5'11", 175 lbs. Deb: 6/24/15

YEAR	TM/L	G	AB	R	H	2B	3B	HR	RBI	BB	SO	AVG	OBP	SLG	PRO+	BR/A	SB	CS	SBR	FA	FR	G/POS	TPR
1915	StL-A	1	1	0	0	0	0	0	0	0	1	.000	.000	.000	-99	-0	0			.000	0	H	0.0

■ **DAN BURKE** Burke, Daniel L. b: 10/25/1868, Abington, Mass. d: 3/20/33, Taunton, Mass. BR/TR, 5'10", 190 lbs. Deb: 4/18/1890

YEAR	TM/L	G	AB	R	H	2B	3B	HR	RBI	BB	SO	AVG	OBP	SLG	PRO+	BR/A	SB	CS	SBR	FA	FR	G/POS	TPR
1890	Roc-a	32	102	14	22	1	0	0	17			.216	.333	.225	70	-3	2			.944	-5	O-29/C-4,1	-0.7
	Syr-a	9	20	1	0	0	0	0			5	.000	.231	.000	-35	-3	0			.900	3	/C-9	0.0
	Yr	41	122	15	22	1	0	0			22	.180	.315	.189	53	-6	2			.944	-2	O-29,C-13/1	-0.7
1892	Bos-N	1	4	0	0	0	0	0	0	0		.000	.000	.000	-92	-1	0			.900	1	/C-1	0.0
Total	2	42	126	15	22	1	0	0	0	22	2	.175	.307	.183	48	-7	2			.892	-2	/O-29,C-14,1	-0.7

■ **EDDIE BURKE** Burke, Edward D. b: 10/6/1866, Northumberland, Pa. d: 11/26/07, Utica, N.Y. BL/TR, 5'6", 161 lbs. Deb: 4/19/1890

YEAR	TM/L	G	AB	R	H	2B	3B	HR	RBI	BB	SO	AVG	OBP	SLG	PRO+	BR/A	SB	CS	SBR	FA	FR	G/POS	TPR
1890	Phi-N	100	430	85	113	16	11	4	50	49	40	.263	.349	.379	109	5	38			.904	4	*O-96/2-4	0.5
	Pit-N	31	124	17	26	5	2	1	7	14	9	.210	.295	.306	85	-2	6			.911	1	O-31	-0.2
	Yr	131	554	102	139	21	13	5	57	63	49	.251	.337	.363	105	4	44			.906	4	*O-127/2-4	0.3
1891	Mil-a	35	144	31	34	9	0	2	21	12	19	.236	.337	.340	78	-6	7			.918	3	O-35	-0.4
1892	Cin-N	15	41	6	6	1	0	0	4	9	4	.146	.300	.171	44	-2	2			1.000	-3	O-14/3-1	-0.5
	NY-N	89	363	81	94	10	5	6	41	46	37	.259	.350	.364	118	9	42			.857	-3	2-59,O-30	0.5
	Yr	104	404	87	100	11	5	6	45	55	41	.248	.344	.344	110	6	44			.857	-6	2-59,O-44/3	0.0
1893	NY-N	135	537	122	150	23	10	9	80	51	32	.279	.369	.410	106	5	54			.912	2	*O-135	0.5
1894	*NY-N	136	566	121	172	23	11	4	77	37	35	.304	.357	.405	84	-15	34			.933	-4	*O-136	-2.2
1895	NY-N	39	167	38	43	6	2	1	12	7	9	.257	.299	.335	65	-9	14			.914	2	O-39	-0.8
	Cin-N	56	228	52	61	8	6	1	25	22	14	.268	.343	.368	80	-7	19			.899	2	O-56	-0.8
	Yr	95	395	90	104	14	8	2	37	29	23	.263	.325	.354	74	-16	33			.905	4	O-95	-1.6
1896	Cin-N	122	521	120	177	24	9	1	52	41	29	.340	.392	.426	108	6	53			.935	3	*O-122	-0.1
1897	Cin-N	95	387	71	103	10	7	1	41	29		.266	.327	.323	67	-19	52			.940	7	*O-95	-1.6
Total	8	853	3508	744	979	142	57	30	410	317	228	.279	.352	.378	93	-37	291			.921	14	O-789/2-63,3	-5.6

■ **FRANK BURKE** Burke, Frank Aloysius b: 2/16/1880, Carbon, Co., Pa. d: 9/17/46, Los Angeles, Cal. TR, Deb: 9/14/06

YEAR	TM/L	G	AB	R	H	2B	3B	HR	RBI	BB	SO	AVG	OBP	SLG	PRO+	BR/A	SB	CS	SBR	FA	FR	G/POS	TPR
1906	NY-N	8	9	2	3	1	1	0	1	1		.333	.400	.667	227	1	1			.667	-2	/O-4	0.0
1907	Bos-N	43	129	6	23	0	1	0	8	11		.178	.243	.194	37	-9	3			.955	-4	O-36	-1.6
Total	2	51	138	8	26	1	2	0	9	12		.188	.253	.225	50	-8	4			.942	-5	/O-40	-1.6

■ **GLENN BURKE** Burke, Glenn Lawrence b: 11/16/52, Oakland, Cal. BR/TR, 6', 195 lbs. Deb: 4/9/76

YEAR	TM/L	G	AB	R	H	2B	3B	HR	RBI	BB	SO	AVG	OBP	SLG	PRO+	BR/A	SB	CS	SBR	FA	FR	G/POS	TPR
1976	LA-N	25	46	9	11	2	0	0	5	3	8	.239	.300	.283	67	-2	3	2	-0	.971	-3	O-20	-0.7
1977	*LA-N	83	169	16	43	8	1	2	13	9	22	.254	.280	.320	61	-9	13	5	1	.971	-15	O-74	-2.6
1978	LA-N	16	19	2	4	0	0	0	2	0	4	.211	.211	.211	18	-2	1	0	0	1.000	-5	O-15	-0.7
	Oak-A	78	200	19	47	6	1	1	14	10	26	.235	.271	.290	61	-11	15	8	-0	.987	-4	O-67/1-1,D	-1.8
1979	Oak-A	23	89	4	19	2	1	0	4	0	10	.213	.247	.258	39	-8	3	1	0	1.000	1	O-23	-0.7
Total	4	225	523	50	124	18	2	2	38	22	70	.237	.271	.291	56	-32	35	16	1	.983	-26	O-199/D-2,1	-6.5

■ **JIMMY BURKE** Burke, James Timothy "Sunset Jimmy" b: 10/12/1874, St.Louis, Mo. d: 3/26/42, St.Louis, Mo. BR/TR, 5'7", 160 lbs. Deb: 10/6/1898 MC

YEAR	TM/L	G	AB	R	H	2B	3B	HR	RBI	BB	SO	AVG	OBP	SLG	PRO+	BR/A	SB	CS	SBR	FA	FR	G/POS	TPR
1898	Cle-N	13	38	1	4	1	0	0			1	.105	.150	.132	-19	-6	1			.853	-4	3-13	-1.0
1899	StL-N	2	6	1	2	0	0	0	0	1		.333	.429	.333	108	0	0			.923	1	/2-2	0.1
1901	Mil-A	64	233	24	48	8	0	0	26	17		.206	.266	.240	43	-17	6			.860	-7	3-64	-2.2
	Chi-A	42	148	20	39	5	0	0	21	12		.264	.327	.297	76	-4	11			.867	-1	S-31,3-11	-0.3
	Yr	106	381	44	87	13	0	0	47	29		.228	.290	.262	56	-22	17			.859	-9	3-75,S-31	-2.5
	Pit-N	14	51	4	10	0	0	0	4	4		.196	.268	.196	35	-4	0			.877	3	3-14	-0.1
1902	Pit-N	60	203	24	60	12	2	0	26	17		.296	.358	.374	122	5	9			.895	-5	2-27,O-18/3S	0.1
1903	StL-N	115	431	55	123	13	3	0	42	23		.285	.326	.329	90	-6	28			.911	6	3-93,2-15/O	0.2
1904	StL-N	118	406	37	92	10	3	0	37	15		.227	.271	.266	69	-15	17			.897	-7	*3-118	-2.0
1905	StL-N	122	431	34	97	9	5	1	30	21		.225	.276	.276	67	-18	15			.924	3	*3-122,M	-1.1
Total	7	550	1947	200	475	58	13	1	187	112		.244	.295	.289	73	-65	87			.899	-12	3-444/2-44,SO	-6.3

■ **JOHN BURKE** Burke, John Patrick b: 1/27/1877, Hazleton, Pa. d: 8/4/50, Jersey City, N.J. BR/TR, Deb: 6/27/02

YEAR	TM/L	G	AB	R	H	2B	3B	HR	RBI	BB	SO	AVG	OBP	SLG	PRO+	BR/A	SB	CS	SBR	FA	FR	G/POS	TPR
1902	NY-N	4	13	0	2	0	0	0	0	0		.154	.154	.154	-5	-2	0			1.000	-1	/P-2,O-4	-0.2

■ **JOE BURKE** Burke, Joseph A. b: Cincinnati, Ohio 5'7", 160 lbs. Deb: 9/26/1890

YEAR	TM/L	G	AB	R	H	2B	3B	HR	RBI	BB	SO	AVG	OBP	SLG	PRO+	BR/A	SB	CS	SBR	FA	FR	G/POS	TPR
1890	StL-a	2	6	3	4	0	0	0			1	.667	.750	.667	278	2	0			.750	-0	/3-2	0.1
1891	Cin-a	1	4	0	1	0	0	0	1	0	2	.250	.250	.250	40	-0	0			1.000	1	/2-1	0.1
Total	2	3	10	3	5	0	0	0	1	1	2	.500	.583	.500	192	1	0			.750	1	/3-2,2-1	0.2

■ **LEO BURKE** Burke, Leo Patrick b: 5/6/34, Hagerstown, Md. BR/TR, 5'10", 190 lbs. Deb: 9/7/58

YEAR	TM/L	G	AB	R	H	2B	3B	HR	RBI	BB	SO	AVG	OBP	SLG	PRO+	BR/A	SB	CS	SBR	FA	FR	G/POS	TPR
1958	Bal-A	7	11	4	5	1	0	1	4	1	2	.455	.500	.818	271	2	0	0	0	1.000	-2	/O-3,3-1	0.1
1959	Bal-A	5	10	2	2	0	0	0	0	0	0	.200	.273	.200	33	-1	0	0	0	1.000	-2	/2-2,3-2	-0.3
1961	LA-A	6	5	0	0	0	0	0	0	1	0	.000	.000	.000	-90	-1	0	0	0	.000	0	H	-0.1
1962	LA-A	19	64	8	17	1	0	4	14	5	11	.266	.329	.469	115	1	0	0	0	.958	-1	O-12/3-4,S	0.0
1963	StL-N	30	49	6	10	1	2	1	4	6	12	.204	.286	.347	68	-2	0	0	0	1.000	-3	O-11/3-5	0.0
	Chi-N	27	49	4	9	0	1	2	7	4	13	.184	.245	.306	55	-3	0	1	-1	.925	3	2-10/1-4	0.0
	Yr	57	98	10	19	1	3	3	12	8	25	.194	.255	.327	61	-5	0	1	-1	1.000	1	O-11,2-10/31	-0.5
1964	Chi-N	59	103	11	27	3	0	3	12	4	15	.262	.315	.340	81	0	0	0	0	1.000	0	O-18/2-5,31C	-0.5
1965	Chi-N	12	10	0	2	0	0	0	1	0	4	.200	.200	.200	13	-0	0	0	0	1.000	0	/C-2,O-1	0.0
Total	7	165	301	33	72	7	3	9	45	21	79	.239	.295	.365	81	-7	0	1	-1	.985	-6	/O-45,2-17,31CS	-1.4

YEAR	TM/L	G	AB	R	H	2B	3B	HR	RBI	BB	SO	AVG	OBP	SLG	PRO+	BR/A	SB	CS	SBR	FA	FR	G/POS	TPR

■ LES BURKE   Burke, Leslie Kingston "Buck"   b: 12/18/02, Lynn, Mass.   d: 5/6/75, Danvers, Mass.   BL/TR, 5'9", 168 lbs.   Deb: 5/2/23

1923	Det-A	7	10	2	1	0	0	0	2	0	1	.100	.100	.100	-48	-2	0	0	0	.500	-1	/3-2,2-1	-0.3
1924	Det-A	72	241	30	61	10	4	0	17	22	20	.253	.321	.328	69	-11	2	4	-2	.957	-6	2-58/S-6	-1.7
1925	Det-A	77	180	32	52	6	3	0	24	17	8	.289	.357	.356	82	-4	4	1	1	.962	2	2-52	-0.2
1926	Det-A	38	75	9	17	1	0	0	4	7	3	.227	.301	.240	42	-6	1	2	-1	.942	4	2-15/3-7,S	-0.2
Total	4	194	506	73	131	17	7	0	47	46	32	.259	.327	.320	67	-24	7	7	-2	.958	-1	2-126/3-9,S	-2.4

■ MIKE BURKE   Burke, Michael E.   b: Cincinnati, Ohio   d: 6/9/1889, Albany, N.Y.   BR/TR, 6', 190 lbs.   Deb: 5/1/1879

1879	Cin-N	28	117	13	26	3	0	0	8	2	5	.222	.235	.248	63	-4				.786	-8	S-19/O-5,3	-1.0

■ PAT BURKE   Burke, Patrick Edward   b: 5/13/01, St.Louis, Mo.   d: 7/7/65, St.Louis, Mo.   BR/TR, 5'10.5", 170 lbs.   Deb: 9/23/24

1924	StL-A	1	3	0	0	0	0	0	1	0	0	.000	.000	.000	-94	-1	0	0	0	.000	0	/3-1	-0.1

■ JESSE BURKETT   Burkett, Jesse Cail "Crab"   b: 12/4/1868, Wheeling, W.Va.   d: 5/27/53, Worcester, Mass.   BL/TL, 5'8", 155 lbs.   Deb: 4/22/1890   CH

1890	NY-N	101	401	67	124	23	13	4	60	33	52	.309	.366	.461	140	19	14			.824	3	O-90,P-21	1.3
1891	Cle-N	40	167	29	45	7	4	0	13	23	19	.269	.358	.359	105	1	1			.892	-3	O-40	-0.3
1892	*Cle-N	145	608	119	167	15	14	6	66	67	59	.275	.348	.375	114	9	36			.904	3	*O-145	0.5
1893	Cle-N	125	511	145	178	25	15	6	82	98	23	.348	.459	.491	144	35	39			.849	-8	*O-125	1.7
1894	*Cle-N	125	523	138	187	27	14	6	94	84	27	.358	.447	.509	125	23	28			.915	-4	*O-125/P-1	0.8
1895	*Cle-N	131	550	153	**225**	22	13	5	83	74	31	**.409**	.486	.524	152	45	41			.884	-3	*O-131	2.5
1896	*Cle-N	133	586	**160**	**240**	27	16	6	72	49	19	**.410**	.461	.541	155	46	34			.926	-2	*O-133	2.7
1897	Cle-N	127	517	129	198	28	7	2	60	76		.383	.468	.476	142	35	28			.949	-2	*O-127	2.0
1898	Cle-N	150	624	114	213	18	9	0	42	69		.341	.415	.399	135	32	19			.938	-8	*O-150	1.2
1899	StL-N	141	558	116	221	21	8	7	71	67		.396	.463	.500	160	48	25			.938	3	*O-140/2-1	3.1
1900	StL-N	141	559	88	203	11	15	7	68	62		.363	.429	.474	150	40	32			.934	4	*O-141	3.0
1901	StL-N	142	601	**142**	**226**	20	15	10	75	59		**.376**	**.440**	.509	**184**	**66**	27			.923	-1	*O-142	5.2
1902	StL-A	138	553	97	169	29	9	5	52	71		.306	.380	.418	126	22	23			.924	6	*O-137/P-1,S3	1.7
1903	StL-A	132	515	73	151	20	7	3	40	52		.293	.361	.377	125	17	17			.941	-5	*O-132	0.5
1904	StL-A	147	575	72	156	15	10	2	27	78		.271	.363	.343	132	24	12			.942	5	*O-147	2.3
1905	Bos-A	148	573	78	147	12	13	4	47	67		.257	.339	.344	115	11	13			.929	-1	*O-148	0.3
Total	16	2066	8421	1720	2850	320	182	75	952	1029	<u>230</u>	.338	.415	.446	140	474	389			.917	-18	*O-2053/P-23,3S2	28.5

■ ELLIS BURKS   Burks, Ellis Rena   b: 9/11/64, Vicksburg, Miss.   BR/TR, 6'2", 200 lbs.   Deb: 4/30/87

1987	Bos-A	133	558	94	152	30	2	20	59	41	98	.272	.324	.441	98	-3	27	6	5	.988	14	*O-132/D-1	1.1
1988	*Bos-A	144	540	93	159	37	5	18	92	62	89	.294	.370	.481	131	22	25	9	2	.977	12	*O-142/D-2	3.2
1989	Bos-A	97	399	73	121	19	6	12	61	36	52	.303	.368	.471	127	14	21	5	3	.977	7	O-95/D-1	2.2
1990	*Bos-A†	152	588	89	174	33	8	21	89	48	82	.296	.350	.486	126	19	9	11	-4	.994	-2	*O-143/D-6	1.3
1991	Bos-A	130	474	56	119	33	3	14	56	39	81	.251	.316	.422	97	-3	6	11	-5	.993	-3	*O-126/D-2	-1.3
1992	Bos-A	66	235	35	60	8	3	8	30	25	48	.255	.330	.417	101	0	5	2	0	.984	-7	O-63/D-1	-0.8
1993	*Chi-A	146	499	75	137	24	4	17	74	60	97	.275	.357	.441	116	11	6	9	-4	.982	0	*O-146	0.5
1994	Col-N	42	149	33	48	8	3	13	24	16	39	.322	.388	.678	147	9	3	1	0	.964	-2	O-39	0.7
Total	8	910	3442	548	970	192	34	123	485	327	586	.282	.348	.465	116	71	102	54	-2	.984	23	O-886/D-13	6.9

■ RICK BURLESON   Burleson, Richard Paul "Rooster"   b: 4/29/51, Lynwood, Cal.   BR/TR, 5'10", 165 lbs.   Deb: 5/4/74   C

1974	Bos-A	114	384	36	109	22	0	4	44	21	34	.284	.324	.372	93	-4	3	3	-1	.957	-5	S-88,2-31/3	0.2
1975	*Bos-A	158	580	66	146	25	1	6	62	45	44	.252	.309	.329	74	-20	8	5	-1	.963	-1	*S-158	-0.4
1976	Bos-A	152	540	75	157	27	1	7	42	60	37	.291	.367	.383	107	5	14	9	-1	.957	-7	*S-152	1.7
1977	Bos-A★	154	663	80	194	36	7	3	52	47	69	.293	.341	.382	87	-12	13	12	-3	.970	12	*S-154	1.4
1978	Bos-A†	145	626	75	155	32	5	5	49	40	71	.248	.297	.339	71	-25	8	8	-2	.981	19	*S-144	1.1
1979	Bos-A★	153	627	93	174	32	5	5	60	35	54	.278	.319	.368	80	-18	9	5	-0	.980	22	*S-153	2.1
1980	Bos-A	155	644	89	179	29	2	8	51	62	51	.278	.343	.366	90	-8	12	13	-4	.974	26	*S-155	3.1
1981	Cal-A★	109	430	53	126	17	1	5	33	42	38	.293	.360	.372	111	7	4	6	-2	.979	21	*S-109	3.8
1982	Cal-A	11	45	4	7	1	0	0	2	6	3	.156	.255	.178	21	-5	0	0	0	.986	7	S-11	0.4
1983	Cal-A	33	119	22	34	7	0	0	11	12	12	.286	.351	.345	93	-1	0	2	-1	.969	-0	S-31	0.1
1984	Cal-A	7	4	2	0	0	0	0	0	0	2	.000	.000	.000	-99	-1	0	0	0	.000	0	/H	-0.1
1986	*Cal-A	93	271	35	77	14	0	5	29	33	32	.284	.364	.391	107	3	1	3	-2	.984	-7	D-38,S-37/23	-0.3
1987	Bal-A	62	206	26	43	14	1	2	14	17	30	.209	.273	.316	59	-12	0	2	-1	.977	-1	2-55/D-7	-1.2
Total	13	1346	5139	656	1401	256	23	50	449	420	477	.273	.331	.361	87	-89	72	68	-19	.971	86	*S-1192/2-92,D3	11.9

■ HERCULES BURNETT   Burnett, Hercules H.   b: 8/13/1865, Louisville, Ky.   d: 10/4/36, Louisville, Ky.   BR, 177 lbs.   Deb: 6/26/1888

1888	Lou-a	1	4	1	0	0	0	0	1			.000	.200	.000	-34	-1	1			.667	-0	/O-1	-0.1
1895	Lou-N	5	17	6	7	0	1	2	3	2	2	.412	.474	.882	261	4	2			.769	-0	/O-4,1-1	0.3
Total	2	6	21	7	7	0	1	2	3	3	<u>2</u>	.333	.417	.714	211	3	3			.750	-0	/O-5,1-1	0.2

■ JOHNNY BURNETT   Burnett, John Henderson   b: 11/1/04, Bartow, Fla.   d: 8/13/59, Tampa, Fla.   BL/TR, 5'11", 175 lbs.   Deb: 5/7/27

1927	Cle-A	17	8	5	0	0	0	0	0	0	3	.000	.000	.000	-99	-2	1	0	0	.833	2	/2-2	0.0
1928	Cle-A	3	10	3	5	0	0	0	1	0	1	.500	.500	.500	162	1	0	0	0	.867	0	/S-2	0.1
1929	Cle-A	19	33	2	5	1	0	0	2	1	2	.152	.200	.182	-1	-5	0	0	0	.923	6	S-10/2-8	0.1
1930	Cle-A	54	170	28	53	13	0	0	20	17	8	.312	.378	.388	91	-5	2	2	-1	.973	-5	3-27,S-19	-0.3
1931	Cle-A	111	427	85	128	25	5	1	52	39	25	.300	.360	.389	92	-5	5	2	0	.938	-15	S-63,2-35,3/O	-1.0
1932	Cle-A	129	512	81	152	23	5	4	53	46	27	.297	.359	.385	87	-9	2	5	-2	.946	-22	*S-103,2-26	-2.2
1933	Cle-A	83	261	39	71	11	2	1	29	23	14	.272	.333	.341	76	-9	3	2	-0	.938	-5	S-41,2-17,3	-0.9
1934	Cle-A	72	208	28	61	11	2	3	30	18	11	.293	.352	.409	94	-2	1	1	-0	.981	-8	3-42/S-9,2O	-0.7
1935	StL-A	70	206	17	46	10	1	0	26	19	16	.223	.289	.282	46	-17	1	0	0	.939	-1	3-31,S-18,2	-1.8
Total	9	558	1835	288	521	94	15	9	213	163	107	.284	.345	.366	81	-50	15	12	-3	.935	-53	S-265,3-133,2/O	-6.7

■ JACK BURNETT   Burnett, John P.   b: 12/2/1889, Missouri   d: 9/8/29, Taft, Cal.   Deb: 7/2/07

1907	StL-N	59	206	18	49	8	4	0	12	15		.238	.296	.316	95	-2	5			.955	-4	O-59	-1.0

■ JEROMY BURNITZ   Burnitz, Jeromy Neal   b: 4/15/69, Westminster, Cal.   BL/TR, 6', 190 lbs.   Deb: 6/21/93

1993	NY-N	86	263	49	64	10	6	13	38	38	66	.243	.341	.475	117	6	3	6	-3	.977	2	O-79	0.4
1994	NY-N	45	143	26	34	4	0	3	15	23	45	.238	.347	.329	77	-4	1	1	-0	.970	-5	O-42	-1.0
Total	2	131	406	75	98	14	6	16	53	61	111	.241	.343	.424	103	2	4	7	-3	.975	-2	O-121	-0.6

■ C.B. BURNS   Burns, Charles Birmingham   b: 5/15/1879, Bay View, Md.   d: 6/6/68, Havre De Grace, Md   BR/TR, 6', 175 lbs.   Deb: 8/19/02

1902	Bal-A	1	1	0	1	0	0	0	0	0	0	1.000	1.000	1.000	436	0				.000	0	H	0.0

■ ED BURNS   Burns, Edward James   b: 10/31/1888, San Francisco, Cal.   d: 6/1/42, Monterey, Cal.   BR/TR, 5'6", 165 lbs.   Deb: 6/25/12

1912	StL-N	1	1	0	0	0	0	0	1	0	0	.000	.000	.000	-99	-0				.000	0	/C-1	0.0
1913	Phi-N	17	30	3	6	3	0	0	3	6	3	.200	.351	.300	83	-0	2			.980	-4	C-15	-0.4
1914	Phi-N	70	139	8	36	3	4	0	16	20	12	.259	.352	.338	99	-3	5			.947	-2	C-55	0.2
1915	*Phi-N	67	174	11	42	5	0	0	12	17	10	.241	.327	.270	81	-3	1			.981	-6	C-62	-0.5
1916	Phi-N	78	219	14	51	8	1	0	14	16	10	.233	.294	.279	74	-6	3			.981	-12	C-75/S-1,O	-1.5
1917	Phi-N	20	49	2	10	0	0	0	6	1	5	.204	.220	.224	35	-4	2			.971	-1	C-15	-0.5

YEAR	TM/L	G	AB	R	H	2B	3B	HR	RBI	BB	SO	AVG	OBP	SLG	PRO+	BR/A	SB	CS	SBR	FA	FR	G/POS	TPR
1918	Phi-N	68	184	10	38	1	1	0	9	20	9	.207	.288	.223	53	-10	1			.981	-4	C-68	-1.0
Total	7	321	796	48	183	21	6	0	65	83	59	.230	.308	.271	73	-23	14			.974	-29	C-291/O-1,S	-3.7

■ GEORGE BURNS   Burns, George Henry "Tioga George"   b: 1/31/1893, Niles, Ohio   d: 1/7/78, Kirkland, Wash.   BR/TR, 6'1.5", 180 lbs.   Deb: 4/14/14

YEAR	TM/L	G	AB	R	H	2B	3B	HR	RBI	BB	SO	AVG	OBP	SLG	PRO+	BR/A	SB	CS	SBR	FA	FR	G/POS	TPR
1914	Det-A	137	478	55	139	22	5	5	57	32	56	.291	.351	.389	119	10	23	13	-1	.982	-5	*1-137	0.1
1915	Det-A	105	392	49	99	18	3	5	50	22	51	.253	.301	.352	91	-6	9	3	1	.986	-4	*1-104	-1.2
1916	Det-A	135	479	60	137	22	6	4	73	22	30	.286	.327	.382	109	3	12			.985	-10	*1-124	-1.3
1917	Det-A	119	407	42	92	14	10	1	40	15	33	.226	.264	.317	77	-13	3			.990	-4	*1-104	-2.3
1918	Phi-A	130	505	61	178	22	9	6	70	23	25	.352	.390	.467	157	32	8			.983	6	*1-128/O-2	3.6
1919	Phi-A	126	470	63	139	29	9	8	57	19	18	.296	.339	.447	118	9	15			.980	2	1-86,O-34	0.7
1920	Phi-A	22	60	1	14	3	0	1	7	6	7	.233	.313	.333	71	-3	4	0	1	.958	1	O-13	-0.2
	*Cle-A	44	56	7	15	4	1	0	13	4	3	.268	.339	.375	86	-1	1	0	0	.979	1	1-12/O-1	0.0
	Yr	66	116	8	29	7	1	1	20	10	10	.250	.326	.353	78	-4	5	0	2	.958	1	O-14,1-12	-0.2
1921	Cle-A	84	244	52	88	21	4	0	49	13	19	.361	.398	.480	121	7	3	1	0	.990	2	1-73	0.7
1922	Bos-A	147	558	71	171	32	5	12	73	20	28	.306	.341	.446	104	1	8	2	1	.987	-1	*1-140	-0.4
1923	Bos-A	146	551	91	181	47	5	7	82	45	33	.328	.386	.470	124	18	9	7	-2	.990	-1	*1-146	0.8
1924	Cle-A	129	462	64	143	37	4	6	68	29	27	.310	.370	.437	106	3	14	5	1	.987	8	*1-127	0.5
1925	Cle-A	127	488	69	164	41	4	6	79	24	24	.336	.371	.473	112	7	16	11	-2	.989	-1	*1-126	-0.2
1926	Cle-A	151	603	97	216	64	3	4	114	28	33	.358	.394	.494	129	24	13	7	-0	.988	1	*1-151	1.5
1927	Cle-A	140	549	84	175	51	2	3	78	24	33	.319	.375	.435	109	7	13	11	-3	.990	3	*1-139	-0.2
1928	Cle-A	82	209	29	52	12	1	5	30	17	11	.249	.328	.388	85	-5	2	3	-1	.984	2	1-53	-0.8
	NY-A	4	4	1	2	0	0	0	0	0	0	.500	.500	.500	169	0	0	0	0	1.000	-0	/1-2	0.0
	Yr	86	213	30	54	12	1	5	30	17	12	.254	.326	.390	87	-4	2	3	-1	.985	2	1-55	-0.8
1929	NY-A	9	9	0	0	0	0	0	0	0	4	.000	.000	.000	-99	-3	0			.000	0	H	-0.3
	*Phi-A	29	49	5	13	5	0	1	11	2	3	.265	.294	.429	81	-2	1	0		1.000	-0	1-19	-0.2
	Yr	38	58	5	13	5	0	1	11	2	7	.224	.250	.362	55	-4	1	0		1.000	-0	1-19	-0.5
Total	16	1866	6573	901	2018	444	72	72	951	363	433	.307	.354	.429	112	91	154	63		.987	0	*1-1671/O-50	0.8

■ GEORGE BURNS   Burns, George Joseph   b: 11/24/1889, Utica, N.Y.   d: 8/15/66, Gloversville, N.Y.   BR/TR, 5'7", 160 lbs.   Deb: 10/3/11   C

YEAR	TM/L	G	AB	R	H	2B	3B	HR	RBI	BB	SO	AVG	OBP	SLG	PRO+	BR/A	SB	CS	SBR	FA	FR	G/POS	TPR
1911	NY-N	6	17	2	1	0	0	0	0	1	0	.059	.111	.059	-50	-3	0			1.000	-2	/O-6	-0.5
1912	NY-N	29	51	11	15	4	0	0	3	8	8	.294	.400	.373	109	1	7			1.000	-4	O-23	-0.4
1913	*NY-N	150	605	81	173	37	4	2	54	58	74	.286	.352	.370	106	5	40			.963	7	*O-150	0.5
1914	NY-N	154	561	100	170	35	10	3	60	89	53	.303	.403	.417	149	38	62			.950	8	*O-154	4.1
1915	NY-N	155	622	83	169	27	14	3	51	56	57	.272	.333	.373	121	15	27	20	-4	.960	-6	*O-155	-0.3
1916	NY-N	155	623	105	174	24	8	5	41	63	47	.279	.346	.368	126	19	37	26	-5	.962	3	*O-155	1.1
1917	*NY-N	152	597	103	180	25	13	5	45	75	55	.302	.380	.412	148	35	40			.974	5	*O-152	3.5
1918	NY-N	119	465	80	135	22	6	4	51	43	37	.290	.354	.389	129	16	40			.965	9	*O-119	2.0
1919	NY-N	139	534	86	162	30	9	2	46	82	37	.303	.396	.404	142	31	40			.990	1	*O-139	2.5
1920	NY-N	154	631	115	181	35	9	6	46	76	48	.287	.365	.399	121	19	22	22	-7	.983	1	*O-154	0.2
1921	*NY-N	149	605	111	181	28	9	4	61	80	24	.299	.386	.395	107	9	19	20	-6	.972	3	*O-149/3-1	-0.5
1922	Cin-N	156	631	104	180	20	10	1	53	78	38	.285	.366	.353	88	-9	30	23	-5	.976	6	*O-156	-1.8
1923	Cin-N	154	614	99	168	27	13	3	45	101	46	.274	.376	.375	101	4	12	14	-5	.960	-1	*O-154	-1.2
1924	Cin-N	93	336	43	86	19	2	2	33	29	21	.256	.315	.342	77	-11	3	6	-3	.963	1	O-90	-1.8
1925	Phi-N	88	349	65	102	29	1	1	22	33	20	.292	.353	.390	82	-9	4	8	-4	.990	0	O-88	-1.7
Total	15	1853	7241	1188	2077	362	108	41	611	872	565	.287	.366	.384	115	161	383	139		.970	32	*O-1844/3-1	5.7

■ JIM BURNS   Burns, James M.   b: Quincy, Ill.   5'7", 168 lbs.   Deb: 9/25/1888

YEAR	TM/L	G	AB	R	H	2B	3B	HR	RBI	BB	SO	AVG	OBP	SLG	PRO+	BR/A	SB	CS	SBR	FA	FR	G/POS	TPR
1888	KC-a	15	66	13	20	0	0	0		4	1	.303	.343	.303	101	-0	6			.853	2	O-15	0.1
1889	KC-a	134	579	103	176	23	11	5	97	20	68	.304	.335	.408	105	-0	56			.913	-7	*O-134/3-1	-0.9
1891	Was-a	20	82	15	26	6	0	0	10	6	10	.317	.378	.390	125	3	2			.771	-4	O-20/S-1	-0.1
Total	3	169	727	131	222	29	11	5	111	27	78	.305	.341	.396	107	3	64			.897	-9	O-169/S-1,3	-0.9

■ JACK BURNS   Burns, John Irving "Slug"   b: 8/31/07, Cambridge, Mass.   d: 4/18/75, Brighton, Mass.   BL/TL, 5'10.5", 175 lbs.   Deb: 9/17/30   C

YEAR	TM/L	G	AB	R	H	2B	3B	HR	RBI	BB	SO	AVG	OBP	SLG	PRO+	BR/A	SB	CS	SBR	FA	FR	G/POS	TPR
1930	StL-A	8	30	5	9	3	0	0	2	5	5	.300	.400	.400	100	0	0	0	0	1.000	1	/1-8	0.0
1931	StL-A	144	570	75	148	27	7	4	70	42	58	.260	.312	.353	72	-24	19	12	-2	.993	18	*1-143	-1.9
1932	StL-A	150	617	111	188	33	8	11	70	61	43	.305	.368	.438	102	2	17	11	-2	.992	4	*1-150	-0.7
1933	StL-A	144	556	89	160	43	4	7	71	56	51	.288	.353	.417	97	-3	11	11	-3	.992	3	*1-143	-1.6
1934	StL-A	154	612	86	157	28	8	13	70	62	47	.257	.327	.392	78	-22	9	3	1	.992	-0	*1-154	-3.2
1935	StL-A	143	549	77	157	28	5	5	67	68	49	.286	.366	.368	86	-10	4	3	-0	.992	-8	*1-141	-3.1
1936	StL-A	9	14	2	3	1	0	0	1	3	1	.214	.353	.286	58	-1	0	0	0	1.000	0	/1-2	-0.1
	Det-A	138	558	96	158	36	3	4	63	79	45	.283	.375	.380	87	-10	4	8	-4	.994	1	*1-138	-2.3
	Yr	147	572	98	161	37	3	4	64	82	46	.281	.374	.378	86	-11	4	8	-4	.994	1	*1-140	-2.4
Total	7	890	3506	541	980	199	31	44	417	376	299	.280	.351	.392	87	-67	63	47	-9	.992	19	1-879	-12.9

■ JACK BURNS   Burns, John Joseph   b: 5/13/1880, Avoca, Pa.   d: 6/24/57, Waterford, Conn.   BR/TR, 5'10", 160 lbs.   Deb: 9/11/03

YEAR	TM/L	G	AB	R	H	2B	3B	HR	RBI	BB	SO	AVG	OBP	SLG	PRO+	BR/A	SB	CS	SBR	FA	FR	G/POS	TPR
1903	Det-A	11	37	2	10	0	0	0	3		1	.270	.325	.270	82	-1	0			.981	1	2-11	0.0
1904	Det-A	4	16	3	2	0	0	0	1		1	.125	.176	.125	-4	-2	1			.952	-1	/2-4	-0.4
Total	2	15	53	5	12	0	0	0	4		2	.226	.281	.226	57	-3	1			.973	-1	/2-15	-0.4

■ JOE BURNS   Burns, Joseph Francis   b: 3/26/1889, Ipswich, Mass.   d: 7/12/87, Beverly, Ma.   BL/TL, 5'11", 170 lbs.   Deb: 6/19/10

YEAR	TM/L	G	AB	R	H	2B	3B	HR	RBI	BB	SO	AVG	OBP	SLG	PRO+	BR/A	SB	CS	SBR	FA	FR	G/POS	TPR
1910	Cin-N	1	1	0	1	0	0	0	0	0	0	1.000	1.000	1.000	506	0	1			.000	0	H	0.1
1913	Det-A	4	13	0	5	0	0	0	1	2	4	.385	.500	.385	162	1	0			1.000	-1	/O-4	0.1
Total	2	5	14	0	6	0	0	0	1	2	4	.429	.529	.429	184	2	1			1.000	-1	/O-4	0.2

■ JOE BURNS   Burns, Joseph Francis   b: 2/25/1900, Trenton, N.J.   d: 1/7/86, Trenton, N.J.   BR/TR, 6', 175 lbs.   Deb: 4/18/24

YEAR	TM/L	G	AB	R	H	2B	3B	HR	RBI	BB	SO	AVG	OBP	SLG	PRO+	BR/A	SB	CS	SBR	FA	FR	G/POS	TPR
1924	Chi-A	8	19	1	2	0	0	0	0	0	2	.105	.105	.105	-47	-4	0	0		.933	-2	/C-6	-0.6

■ JOE BURNS   Burns, Joseph James   b: 6/17/16, Bryn Mawr, Pa.   d: 6/24/74, Bryn Mawr, Pa.   BR/TR, 5'10.5", 175 lbs.   Deb: 4/24/43

YEAR	TM/L	G	AB	R	H	2B	3B	HR	RBI	BB	SO	AVG	OBP	SLG	PRO+	BR/A	SB	CS	SBR	FA	FR	G/POS	TPR
1943	Bos-N	52	135	12	28	3	0	1	5	8	25	.207	.262	.252	49	-9	2			.933	-1	3-34/O-4	-1.0
1944	Phi-A	28	75	5	18	2	0	1	8	4	8	.240	.278	.307	68	-3	0	1	-1	.919	-8	3-17/2-9	-1.2
1945	Phi-A	31	90	7	23	1	1	0	3	4	17	.256	.287	.289	68	-4	0	1	-1	1.000	-4	O-19/3-5,1	-1.0
Total	3	111	300	24	69	6	1	2	16	16	50	.230	.274	.277	60	-16	2	2		.920	-12	/3-56,O-23,21	-3.2

■ PAT BURNS   Burns, Patrick   Deb: 8/11/1884

YEAR	TM/L	G	AB	R	H	2B	3B	HR	RBI	BB	SO	AVG	OBP	SLG	PRO+	BR/A	SB	CS	SBR	FA	FR	G/POS	TPR
1884	Bal-a	6	25	3	5	2	1	0	3			.200	.286	.360	105	0				.953	-1	/1-6	-0.1
	Bal-U	1	4	0	2	0	0	0	0			.500	.500	.500	156	0				.917	-1	/1-1	0.0
Total	1	7	29	3	7	2	1	0	3			.241	.313	.379	113	0				.947	-1	/1-7	-0.1

■ DICK BURNS   Burns, Richard Simon   b: 12/26/1863, Holyoke, Mass.   d: 11/16/37, Holyoke, Mass.   BL/TL, 5'7", 140 lbs.   Deb: 5/3/1883

YEAR	TM/L	G	AB	R	H	2B	3B	HR	RBI	BB	SO	AVG	OBP	SLG	PRO+	BR/A	SB	CS	SBR	FA	FR	G/POS	TPR
1883	Det-N	37	140	11	26	7	1	0	5	2	22	.186	.197	.250	36	-10				.758	-6	O-24,P-17	-1.0
1884	Cin-U	79	350	84	107	17	12	4		5		.306	.315	.457	100	-2				.827	-3	O-44,P-40/S	-0.5
1885	StL-N	14	54	2	12	2	1	0	4	3	8	.222	.263	.296	86	-1				.682	-3	O-14,P-1	-0.5
Total	3	130	544	97	145	26	14	4	9	10	30	.267	.280	.388	85	-13				.785	-12	/O-82,P-58,S	-2.0

YEAR	TM/L	G	AB	R	H	2B	3B	HR	RBI	BB	SO	AVG	OBP	SLG	PRO+	BR/A	SB	CS	SBR	FA	FR	G/POS	TPR

■ TOM BURNS   Burns, Thomas Everett b: 3/30/1857, Honesdale, Pa. d: 3/19/02, Jersey City, N.J. BR/TR, 5'7", 152 lbs. Deb: 5/1/1880 MU

YEAR	TM/L	G	AB	R	H	2B	3B	HR	RBI	BB	SO	AVG	OBP	SLG	PRO+	BR/A	SB	CS	SBR	FA	FR	G/POS	TPR
1880	Chi-N	85	333	47	103	17	3	0	43	12	23	.309	.333	.378	133	10				.864	-24	*S-79/3-9,CP	-0.9
1881	Chi-N	84	342	41	95	20	3	4	42	14	22	.278	.306	.389	112	4				.870	-5	*S-80/3-3,2	0.4
1882	Chi-N	84	355	55	88	23	6	0	48	15	28	.248	.278	.346	95	-3				.911	0	2-43,S-41	0.0
1883	Chi-N	97	405	69	119	37	7	2	67	13	31	.294	.316	.435	118	7				.872	-1	*S-79,2-19/O	0.7
1884	Chi-N	83	343	54	84	14	2	7	44	13	50	.245	.272	.359	89	-6				.838	-2	*S-80/3-3	-0.6
1885	*Chi-N	111	445	82	121	23	9	7	71	16	48	.272	.297	.411	111	1				.844	-2	*S-111/2-1	0.1
1886	*Chi-N	112	445	64	123	18	10	3	65	14	40	.276	.298	.382	92	-8	15			.890	13	*3-112	0.7
1887	Chi-N	115	424	57	112	20	10	3	60	34	32	.264	.320	.380	83	-13	32			.872	21	*3-107/O-8	0.9
1888	Chi-N	134	483	60	115	12	6	3	70	26	49	.238	.281	.306	81	-11	34			.905	17	*3-134	0.8
1889	Chi-N	136	525	64	127	27	6	4	66	32	57	.242	.288	.350	71	-23	18			.880	3	*3-136	-1.3
1890	Chi-N	139	538	86	149	17	6	5	86	57	45	.277	.348	.359	102	1	44			.898	3	*3-139	0.7
1891	Chi-N	59	243	36	55	8	1	1	17	21	21	.226	.288	.280	66	-11	18			.892	-2	3-53/S-4,O	-0.9
1892	Pit-N	12	39	7	8	0	0	0	4	3	8	.205	.262	.205	41	-3	1			.690	-5	/3-8,O-3M	-0.7
Total	13	1251	4920	722	1299	236	69	39	683	270	454	.264	.303	.364	95	-53	162			.886	16	3-704,S-474/2OCP	-0.1

■ OYSTER BURNS   Burns, Thomas P. b: 9/6/1864, Philadelphia, Pa. d: 11/11/28, Brooklyn, N.Y. BR/TR, 5'8", 183 lbs. Deb: 8/18/1884

YEAR	TM/L	G	AB	R	H	2B	3B	HR	RBI	BB	SO	AVG	OBP	SLG	PRO+	BR/A	SB	CS	SBR	FA	FR	G/POS	TPR
1884	Wil-U	2	7	0	1	0	1	0		1		.143	.250	.429	79	-0				.778	-1	/S-2	0.0
	Bal-a	35	131	34	39	2	6	6		7		.298	.348	.542	179	11				.826	-5	O-24,2-10/P3	0.5
1885	Bal-a	78	321	47	74	11	6	5		16		.231	.280	.349	99	-0				.908	-0	O-45,P-15,S/321	-0.1
1887	Bal-a	140	551	122	188	33	19	9		63		.341	.414	.519	169	53	58			.841	-19	*S-98,3-42/P2	2.8
1888	Bal-a	79	325	54	97	18	9	4	42	24		.298	.349	.446	158	20	23			.855	-5	O-56,S-23/P32	1.3
	Bro-a	52	204	40	58	9	6	2	25	14		.284	.339	.417	142	9	21			.851	-13	S-36,O-14/2	-0.3
	Yr	131	529	94	155	27	15	6	67	38		.293	.345	.435	152	30	44			.847	-18	O-70,S-59/P23	1.0
1889	*Bro-a	131	504	105	153	19	13	5	100	68	26	.304	.391	.423	131	22	32			.920	-3	*O-113,S-19	1.0
1890	*Bro-N	119	472	102	134	22	12	13	128	51	42	.284	.359	.464	139	21	21			.941	-3	*O-116/3-3	1.3
1891	Bro-N	123	470	75	134	24	13	4	83	53	30	.285	.358	.417	126	15	21			.922	2	*O-113/S-6,3	1.2
1892	Bro-N	141	542	88	171	27	18	4	96	65	42	.315	.395	.454	163	42	33			.937	-13	*O-129/3-7,S	2.2
1893	Bro-N	109	415	68	112	22	8	7	60	36	16	.270	.334	.412	102	-0	14			.932	-1	*O-108/S-1	-0.5
1894	Bro-N	125	505	106	179	32	14	5	107	44	18	.354	.409	.503	128	23	30			.949	-4	*O-125	0.9
1895	Bro-N	20	76	7	14	0	1	0	7	8	2	.184	.271	.211	27	-8	0			.918	1	O-19	-0.7
	NY-N	33	114	21	35	5	3	1	25	14	6	.307	.388	.430	113	3	10			.870	-5	O-32/1-1	-0.3
	Yr	53	190	28	49	5	4	1	32	22	8	.258	.341	.342	80	-5	10			.893	-3	O-51/1-1	-1.0
Total	11	1187	4637	869	1389	224	129	65	673	464	182	.300	.368	.446	135	210	263			.920	-73	O-894,S-200/3P21	9.3

■ ALEX BURR   Burr, Alexander Thomson b: 11/1/1893, Chicago, Ill. d: 10/12/18, Cazaux, France BR/TR, 6'3.5", 190 lbs. Deb: 4/21/14

YEAR	TM/L	G	AB	R	H	2B	3B	HR	RBI	BB	SO	AVG	OBP	SLG	PRO+	BR/A	SB	CS	SBR	FA	FR	G/POS	TPR
1914	NY-A	1	0	0	0	0	0	0	0	0	0	—	—	—	—	0	0			.000	-1	/O-1	-0.1

■ BUSTER BURRELL   Burrell, Frank Andrew b: 12/22/1866, Weymouth, Mass. d: 5/8/62, Weymouth, Mass. BR/TR, 5'10", 165 lbs. Deb: 8/1/1891

YEAR	TM/L	G	AB	R	H	2B	3B	HR	RBI	BB	SO	AVG	OBP	SLG	PRO+	BR/A	SB	CS	SBR	FA	FR	G/POS	TPR
1891	NY-N	15	53	1	5	0	0	0	1	3	12	.094	.158	.094	-27	-8	2			.856	-5	C-15/O-1	-1.2
1895	Bro-N	12	28	7	4	0	0	1	5	4	3	.143	.250	.250	32	-3	0			.838	-2	C-12	-0.3
1896	Bro-N	62	206	19	62	11	3	0	23	15	13	.301	.348	.383	98	-1	1			.928	-9	C-60	-0.3
1897	Bro-N	33	103	15	25	2	0	2	18	10		.243	.310	.320	70	-4	1			.884	-4	C-27/1-4	-0.5
Total	4	122	390	42	96	13	3	3	47	32	28	.246	.305	.318	70	-16	4			.896	-19	C-114/1-4,O	-2.3

■ LARRY BURRIGHT   Burright, Larry Allen "Possum" b: 7/10/37, Roseville, Ill. BR/TR, 5'11", 170 lbs. Deb: 4/12/62

YEAR	TM/L	G	AB	R	H	2B	3B	HR	RBI	BB	SO	AVG	OBP	SLG	PRO+	BR/A	SB	CS	SBR	FA	FR	G/POS	TPR
1962	LA-N	115	249	35	51	6	5	4	30	21	67	.205	.267	.317	60	-15	4	3	-1	.962	14	*2-109/S-1	0.6
1963	NY-N	41	100	9	22	2	1	0	3	8	25	.220	.291	.260	59	-5	1	0	0	.946	12	S-19,2-15/3	1.0
1964	NY-N	3	0	0	0	0	0	0	0	0	0	.000	.000	.000	-99	-2	0	0	0	1.000	4	/2-3	0.3
Total	3	159	356	44	73	8	6	4	33	29	92	.205	.269	.295	56	-22	5	3	-0	.964	30	2-127/S-20,3	1.9

■ PAUL BURRIS   Burris, Paul Robert b: 7/21/23, Hickory, N.C. BR/TR, 6', 190 lbs. Deb: 10/2/48

YEAR	TM/L	G	AB	R	H	2B	3B	HR	RBI	BB	SO	AVG	OBP	SLG	PRO+	BR/A	SB	CS	SBR	FA	FR	G/POS	TPR
1948	Bos-N	2	4	0	2	0	0	0	0	0	0	.500	.500	.500	174	0				1.000	1	/C-2	0.1
1950	Bos-N	10	23	1	4	1	0	0	3	1	2	.174	.208	.217	13	-3	0			1.000	1	/C-8	-0.1
1952	Bos-N	55	168	14	37	4	0	2	21	7	19	.220	.256	.280	50	-12	0	0	0	1.000	-4	C-50	-1.4
1953	Mil-N	2	1	0	0	0	0	0	0	0	0	.000	.000	.000	-99	-0	0	0	0	1.000	-0	/C-2	0.0
Total	4	69	196	15	43	5	0	2	24	8	21	.219	.254	.276	47	-14	0			1.000	-2	/C-62	-1.4

■ HENRY BURROUGHS   Burroughs, Henry F. b: 1845, Detroit, Mich. 5'8", 147 lbs. Deb: 5/5/1871

YEAR	TM/L	G	AB	R	H	2B	3B	HR	RBI	BB	SO	AVG	OBP	SLG	PRO+	BR/A	SB	CS	SBR	FA	FR	G/POS	TPR
1871	Oly-n	12	63	11	15	2	3	1	14	1	1	.238	.250	.413	91	-0						/O-8,3-5	0.0
1872	Oly-n	2	7	1	1	1	0	0	0	1	0	.143	.250	.286	68	-0						/O-2	0.0
Total	2 n	14	70	12	16	3	3	1	14	2	1	.229	.250	.400	89	-1						/O-10,3-5	0.0

■ JEFF BURROUGHS   Burroughs, Jeffrey Alan b: 3/7/51, Long Beach, Cal. BR/TR, 6'1", 200 lbs. Deb: 7/20/70

YEAR	TM/L	G	AB	R	H	2B	3B	HR	RBI	BB	SO	AVG	OBP	SLG	PRO+	BR/A	SB	CS	SBR	FA	FR	G/POS	TPR
1970	Was-A	6	12	1	2	0	0	0	2	5	.167	.286	.167	29	-1	0	0	0	1.000	-0	/O-3	-0.1
1971	Was-A	59	181	20	42	9	0	5	25	22	55	.232	.319	.365	99	-1	1	0	0	.966	-5	O-50	-0.8
1972	Tex-A	22	65	4	12	1	0	1	3	5	22	.185	.243	.246	48	-4	0	2	-1	.935	-1	O-19/1-1	-0.8
1973	Tex-A	151	526	71	147	17	1	30	85	67	88	.279	.362	.487	143	29	0	0	0	.975	13	*O-148/1-3,D	3.5
1974	Tex-A★	152	554	84	167	33	2	25	118	91	104	.301	.405	.504	164	48	2	3	-1	.972	-8	*O-150/1-2,D	3.3
1975	Tex-A	152	585	81	132	20	0	29	94	79	155	.226	.319	.409	105	3	4	4	-1	.966	-8	*O-148/D-3	-1.3
1976	Tex-A	158	604	71	143	22	2	18	86	69	93	.237	.317	.369	98	-1	0	2	-1	.987	-2	*O-155/D-3	-1.0
1977	Atl-N	154	579	91	157	19	1	41	114	86	126	.271	.365	.520	120	16	4	1	1	.974	-4	*O-154	0.6
1978	Atl-N☆	153	488	72	147	30	6	23	77	117	92	.301	.436	.529	151	38	1	2	-1	.975	-0	*O-146	3.2
1979	Atl-N	116	397	49	89	14	1	11	47	73	75	.224	.349	.348	84	-7	2	2	-1	.963	-1	*O-110	-1.3
1980	Atl-N	99	278	35	73	14	0	13	51	35	57	.263	.349	.453	118	7	1	1	-0	.977	-4	O-73	-1.0
1981	Sea-A	89	319	32	81	13	1	10	41	41	64	.254	.339	.395	107	3	0	1	-1	.985	-9	O-87/D-1	-1.0
1982	Oak-A	113	285	42	79	13	2	16	48	45	61	.277	.376	.505	146	18	1	3	-2	.981	-5	D-48,O-34	0.9
1983	Oak-A	121	401	43	108	15	1	10	56	47	79	.269	.346	.387	108	5	0	2	-1	1.000	0	*D-114	-0.1
1984	Oak-A	58	71	5	15	1	0	2	8	18	23	.211	.371	.310	97	1	0	0	0	1.000	-2	D-23/O-4	-0.2
1985	*Tor-A	86	191	19	49	9	3	6	28	34	36	.257	.369	.429	115	5	0	1	-1	1.000	-0	D-75	0.3
Total	16	1689	5536	720	1443	230	20	240	882	831	1135	.261	.359	.439	120	159	16	22	-8	.974	-36	*O-1281,D-269/1	5.2

■ DICK BURRUS   Burrus, Maurice Lennon b: 1/29/1898, Hatteras, N.C. d: 2/2/72, Elizabeth City, N.C BL/TL, 5'11", 175 lbs. Deb: 6/23/19

YEAR	TM/L	G	AB	R	H	2B	3B	HR	RBI	BB	SO	AVG	OBP	SLG	PRO+	BR/A	SB	CS	SBR	FA	FR	G/POS	TPR
1919	Phi-A	70	194	17	50	3	4	0	8	9	25	.258	.294	.314	70	-8	2			.986	-4	1-38,O-10	-1.5
1920	Phi-A	71	135	11	25	8	0	0	10	5	7	.185	.225	.244	24	-15	0	3	-2	.989	-2	1-31/O-2	-1.9
1925	Bos-N	152	588	82	200	41	4	5	87	51	29	.340	.396	.449	126	24	8	9	-3	.990	1	*1-151	1.2
1926	Bos-N	131	486	59	131	21	1	3	61	37	16	.270	.324	.335	85	-11	4			.991	12	*1-128	-0.6
1927	Bos-N	72	220	22	70	8	0	0	32	17	10	.318	.370	.382	110	3	3			.972	-2	1-61	0.1
1928	Bos-N	64	137	15	37	6	3	3	13	19	8	.270	.367	.380	101	1	1			.977	-2	1-32	-0.4
Total	6	560	1760	206	513	87	12	11	211	138	95	.291	.347	.373	97	-6	18	12		.986	7	1-441/O-12	-3.1

■ FRANK BURT   Burt, Frank J. b: Camden, N.J. Deb: 5/2/1882

YEAR	TM/L	G	AB	R	H	2B	3B	HR	RBI	BB	SO	AVG	OBP	SLG	PRO+	BR/A	SB	CS	SBR	FA	FR	G/POS	TPR
1882	Bal-a	10	36	2	4	2	1	0		1		.111	.135	.222	20	-3				.815	-1	O-10	-0.3

YEAR	TM/L	G	AB	R	H	2B	3B	HR	RBI	BB	SO	AVG	OBP	SLG	PRO+	BR/A	SB	CS	SBR	FA	FR	G/POS	TPR

■ ELLIS BURTON
Burton, Ellis Narrington b: 8/12/36, Los Angeles, Cal. BB/TR, 5'11", 165 lbs. Deb: 9/18/58

YEAR	TM/L	G	AB	R	H	2B	3B	HR	RBI	BB	SO	AVG	OBP	SLG	PRO+	BR/A	SB	CS	SBR	FA	FR	G/POS	TPR
1958	StL-N	8	30	5	7	0	1	2	4	3	8	.233	.324	.500	110	0	0	1	-1	1.000	-0	/O-7	-0.1
1960	StL-N	29	28	5	6	1	0	0	2	4	14	.214	.313	.250	52	-2	0	2	-1	1.000	-7	O-23	-1.1
1963	Cle-N	26	31	6	6	3	0	1	1	4	4	.194	.286	.387	87	-1	0	0	0	1.000	-4	O-16	-0.5
	Chi-N	93	322	45	74	16	1	12	41	36	59	.230	.315	.398	98	-1	6	3	0	.975	-9	O-90	-1.5
1964	Chi-N	42	105	12	20	3	2	2	7	17	22	.190	.303	.314	71	-4	0	0	1	.981	-4	O-29	-0.9
1965	Chi-N	17	40	6	7	1	0	0	4	1	10	.175	.195	.200	11	-5	1	0	0	1.000	-0	O-12	-0.5
Total	5	215	556	79	120	24	4	17	59	65	117	.216	.304	.365	85	-11	11	6	-0	.981	-24	O-177	-4.6

■ JIM BUSBY
Busby, James Franklin b: 1/8/27, Kenedy, Tex. BR/TR, 6'1", 175 lbs. Deb: 4/23/50 C

YEAR	TM/L	G	AB	R	H	2B	3B	HR	RBI	BB	SO	AVG	OBP	SLG	PRO+	BR/A	SB	CS	SBR	FA	FR	G/POS	TPR
1950	Chi-A	18	48	5	10	0	0	0	4	1	5	.208	.224	.208	12	-6	0	2	-1	.964	-1	O-12	-0.8
1951	Chi-A★	143	477	59	135	15	2	5	68	40	46	.283	.344	.354	91	-6	26	11	1	.982	3	*O-139	-0.6
1952	Chi-A	16	39	5	5	0	0	0	0	2	7	.128	.171	.128	-16	-6	0	2	-1	1.000	-0	O-16	-0.9
	Was-A	129	512	58	125	24	4	2	47	22	48	.244	.281	.318	69	-23	5	6	-2	.993	14	*O-128	-1.8
	Yr	145	551	63	130	24	4	2	47	24	55	.236	.273	.305	62	-29	5	8	-3	.994	13	*O-144	-2.7
1953	Was-A	150	586	68	183	28	7	6	82	38	45	.312	.358	.415	111	8	13	6	0	.988	19	*O-150	2.1
1954	Was-A	155	628	83	187	22	7	7	80	43	56	.298	.346	.389	107	4	17	2	4	.988	12	*O-155	1.4
1955	Was-A	47	191	23	44	6	2	6	14	13	22	.230	.279	.377	79	-7	5	0	2	.993	2	O-47	-0.6
	Chi-A	99	337	38	82	13	4	1	27	25	37	.243	.296	.315	62	-18	7	3	0	.984	2	*O-99	-2.0
	Yr	146	528	61	126	19	6	7	41	38	59	.239	.290	.337	68	-25	12	3	2	.987	5	*O-146	-2.5
1956	Cle-A	135	494	72	116	17	3	12	50	43	47	.235	.301	.354	71	-22	8	3	1	.989	5	*O-133	-2.3
1957	Cle-A	30	74	9	14	2	1	2	4	1	8	.189	.200	.324	41	-6	0	1	-1	.978	-3	O-26	-1.2
	Bal-A	86	288	31	72	10	1	3	19	23	36	.250	.305	.323	77	-10	6	3	0	.984	10	O-85	-0.5
	Yr	116	362	40	86	12	2	5	23	24	44	.238	.285	.323	69	-16	6	4	-1	.983	6	*O-111	-1.7
1958	Bal-A	113	215	32	51	7	2	3	19	24	37	.237	.322	.330	84	-4	6	4	-1	.995	-9	*O-103/3-1	-1.7
1959	Bos-A	61	102	16	23	8	0	1	5	5	18	.225	.269	.333	61	-6	0	1	-1	.980	-6	O-34	-1.3
1960	Bos-A	1	0	0	0	0	0	0	0	0	0	—	—	—	—	0	0	0	0	.000	-0	/O-1	0.0
	Bal-A	79	159	25	41	7	1	0	12	20	14	.258	.341	.314	79	-4	2	3	-1	.985	-5	O-71	-1.3
	Yr	80	159	25	41	7	1	0	12	20	14	.258	.341	.314	79	-4	2	3	-1	.985	-6	O-72	-1.3
1961	Bal-A	75	89	15	23	3	1	0	6	8	10	.258	.320	.315	73	-3	2	0	1	.987	-16	O-71	-2.1
1962	Hou-N	15	11	2	2	0	0	0	1	2	3	.182	.308	.182	38	-1	0	1	-1	1.000	-4	O-10/C-1	-0.5
Total	13	1352	4250	541	1113	162	35	48	438	310	439	.262	.316	.350	82	-110	97	48	-0	.988	22	*O-1280/C-1,3	-14.0

■ PAUL BUSBY
Busby, Paul Miller "Red" b: 8/25/18, Waynesboro, Miss. BL/TR, 6'1", 175 lbs. Deb: 9/14/41

YEAR	TM/L	G	AB	R	H	2B	3B	HR	RBI	BB	SO	AVG	OBP	SLG	PRO+	BR/A	SB	CS	SBR	FA	FR	G/POS	TPR
1941	Phi-N	10	16	3	5	0	0	0	2	0	1	.313	.313	.313	79	-0	0			1.000	-1	/O-5	-0.1
1943	Phi-N	26	40	13	10	1	0	0	5	2	1	.250	.286	.275	65	-2	2			1.000	0	O-10	-0.2
Total	2	36	56	16	15	1	0	0	7	2	2	.268	.293	.286	69	-2	2			1.000	-1	/O-13	-0.3

■ ED BUSCH
Busch, Edgar John b: 11/16/17, Lebanon, Ill. d: 1/17/87, St.Clair Co., Ill. BR/TR, 5'10", 175 lbs. Deb: 9/30/43

YEAR	TM/L	G	AB	R	H	2B	3B	HR	RBI	BB	SO	AVG	OBP	SLG	PRO+	BR/A	SB	CS	SBR	FA	FR	G/POS	TPR
1943	Phi-A	4	17	2	5	0	0	0	1	2	.294	.368	.294		95	-0	0	1	-1	.941	-3	/S-4	-0.3
1944	Phi-A	140	484	41	131	11	3	0	40	29	17	.271	.313	.306	78	-14	5	3	-0	.940	-30	*S-111,2-27/3	-3.6
1945	Phi-A	126	416	37	104	10	3	0	35	32	9	.250	.305	.288	73	-14	2	3	-1	.952	1	*S-116/2-2,31	-0.6
Total	3	270	917	80	240	21	6	0	75	62	28	.262	.311	.298	76	-28	7	7	-2	.946	-32	S-231/2-29,31	-4.5

■ DONIE BUSH
Bush, Owen Joseph b: 10/8/1887, Indianapolis, Ind. d: 3/28/72, Indianapolis, Ind. BB/TR, 5'6", 140 lbs. Deb: 9/18/08 M

YEAR	TM/L	G	AB	R	H	2B	3B	HR	RBI	BB	SO	AVG	OBP	SLG	PRO+	BR/A	SB	CS	SBR	FA	FR	G/POS	TPR
1908	Det-A	20	68	13	20	1	1	0	4	7		.294	.360	.338	122	2	2			.938	-4	S-20	-0.2
1909	*Det-A	157	532	114	145	18	2	0	33	88		.273	.380	.314	114	13	53			.925	4	*S-157	2.3
1910	Det-A	142	496	90	130	13	4	3	34	78		.262	.365	.323	108	7	49			.940	9	*S-141/3-1	2.4
1911	Det-A	150	561	126	130	18	5	1	36	98		.232	.349	.287	74	-16	40			.925	17	*S-150	1.0
1912	Det-A	144	511	107	118	14	8	2	38	117		.231	.377	.301	98	5	35			.929	29	*S-144	4.6
1913	Det-A	153	597	98	150	19	10	1	40	80	32	.251	.344	.322	96	-1	44			.938	2	*S-153	1.6
1914	Det-A	157	596	97	150	18	4	0	32	112	54	.252	.373	.295	98	4	35	26	-5	.944	34	*S-157	5.0
1915	Det-A	155	561	99	128	12	8	1	44	118	44	.228	.364	.283	89	-2	35	27	-6	.937	9	*S-155	1.4
1916	Det-A	145	550	73	124	5	9	0	34	75	42	.225	.319	.267	74	-16	19			.954	-15	*S-144	-2.6
1917	Det-A	147	581	112	163	18	3	0	24	80	40	.281	.370	.322	111	11	34			.932	-18	*S-147	0.0
1918	Det-A	128	500	74	117	10	3	0	22	79	24	.234	.340	.266	86	-5	9			.931	-20	*S-128	-2.2
1919	Det-A	129	509	82	124	11	3	0	26	75	24	.244	.343	.289	80	-11	22			.943	-12	*S-129	-1.5
1920	Det-A	141	506	85	133	18	5	1	33	73	32	.263	.357	.324	83	-9	15	7	0	.938	-17	*S-140	-1.4
1921	Det-A	104	402	72	113	6	5	0	27	45	23	.281	.355	.321	74	-14	8	11	-4	.949	-5	S-81,2-23	-1.4
	Was-A	23	84	15	18	1	0	0	2	12	4	.214	.313	.226	41	-7	2	2	-1	.932	-4	S-21	-1.0
	Yr	127	486	87	131	7	5	0	29	57	27	.270	.347	.305	69	-21	10	13	-5	.946	-10	*S-102,2-23	-2.4
1922	Was-A	41	134	17	32	4	1	0	7	21	7	.239	.342	.284	68	-6	1	1	-0	.957	-2	3-37/2-1	-0.5
1923	Was-A	10	22	6	9	0	0	0	0	1	0	.409	.409	.409	122	1	1	1	-0	.813	-2	/3-5,2-2M	-0.1
Total	16	1946	7210	1280	1804	186	74	9	436	1158	346	.250	.356	.300	91	-42	404	75		.936	5	*S-1867/3-43,2	7.4

■ RANDY BUSH
Bush, Robert Randall b: 10/5/58, Dover, Del. BL/TL, 6'1", 186 lbs. Deb: 5/1/82

YEAR	TM/L	G	AB	R	H	2B	3B	HR	RBI	BB	SO	AVG	OBP	SLG	PRO+	BR/A	SB	CS	SBR	FA	FR	G/POS	TPR
1982	Min-A	55	119	13	29	6	1	4	13	8	28	.244	.308	.412	93	-1	0	0	0	1.000	-1	D-26/O-6	-0.4
1983	Min-A	124	373	43	93	24	3	11	56	34	51	.249	.324	.418	99	-1	0	1	-1	1.000	1	*D-103/1-3	-0.5
1984	Min-A	113	311	46	69	17	1	11	43	31	60	.222	.301	.389	85	-7	1	2	-1	1.000	-6	D-89/1-2	-1.0
1985	Min-A	97	234	26	56	13	3	10	35	24	30	.239	.323	.449	103	1	3	0	1	.969	-6	O-41,D-28/1	-0.6
1986	Min-A	130	357	50	96	19	7	7	45	39	63	.269	.346	.420	105	-3	5	2	0	.977	-7	*O-102/1-3,D	-0.7
1987	*Min-A	122	293	46	74	10	2	11	46	43	49	.253	.354	.413	99	0	10	3	1	.982	-8	O-75/1-9,D	-0.9
1988	Min-A	136	394	51	103	20	3	14	51	58	49	.261	.369	.434	120	12	8	6	-1	.979	-6	*O-109/1-6,D	0.2
1989	Min-A	141	391	60	103	17	4	14	54	48	73	.263	.348	.435	112	6	5	8	-3	.986	-9	*O-109,1-25/D	-1.0
1990	Min-A	73	181	17	44	8	0	6	18	21	27	.243	.341	.387	97	-0	0	3	-2	1.000	-6	O-32,D-29/1	-0.6
1991	*Min-A	93	165	21	50	10	1	6	23	24	25	.303	.401	.485	137	9	2	1	-1	1.000	-5	O-38,1-12,D	0.2
1992	Min-A	100	182	14	39	8	1	2	22	11	37	.214	.267	.302	57	-11	1	1	-0	1.000	-3	O-24,D-24/1	-1.6
1993	Min-A	35	45	1	7	2	0	1	3	7	13	.156	.269	.200	28	-4	0	0	0	1.000	-1	/1-4,O-1,D	-0.5
Total	12	1219	3045	388	763	154	26	96	409	348	505	.251	.337	.413	101	7	33	29	-8	.983	-48	O-537,D-341/1	-7.4

■ DOC BUSHONG
Bushong, Albert John b: 9/15/1856, Philadelphia, Pa. d: 8/19/08, Brooklyn, N.Y. BR/TR, 5'11", 165 lbs. Deb: 7/19/1875

YEAR	TM/L	G	AB	R	H	2B	3B	HR	RBI	BB	SO	AVG	OBP	SLG	PRO+	BR/A	SB	CS	SBR	FA	FR	G/POS	TPR
1875	Atl-n	1	5	0	3	0	1	0	0			.600	.600	1.000	509	2						/C-1	0.2
1876	Phi-N	5	21	4	1	0	0	0	1	0		.048	.048	.048	-69	-4				.769	-1	/C-5	-0.4
1880	Wor-N	41	146	13	25	3	0	0	19	1	16	.171	.177	.192	23	-12				.918	16	C-40/O-1,3	0.5
1881	Wor-N	76	275	35	64	7	4	0	21	21	23	.233	.287	.287	77	-7				.918	11	*C-76	0.6
1882	Wor-N	69	253	20	40	4	1	1	15	5	17	.158	.174	.194	18	-23				.897	-3	*C-69	-2.1
1883	Cle-N	63	215	15	37	5	0	0	9	7	19	.172	.198	.195	21	-20				.909	15	C-63	-0.1
1884	Cle-N	62	203	24	48	6	1	0	10	17	11	.236	.295	.276	78	-5				.886	0	C-62/O-1	0.1
1885	*StL-a	85	300	42	80	13	5	0		11		.267	.297	.343	97	-2				.932	14	*C-85/3-1	1.7
1886	*StL-a	107	386	56	86	8	0	1		31		.223	.281	.251	64	-16	12			.942	16	*C-106/1-1	1.0
1887	*StL-a	53	201	35	51	4	0	0		11		.254	.299	.274	55	-13	14			.927	7	C-52/O-2,3	-0.2
1888	Bro-a	69	253	23	53	1	0	0	16	5		.209	.231	.237	50	-14	9			.915	-7	C-69	-1.4
1889	*Bro-a	25	84	15	13	1	0	0	8	9	7	.155	.237	.167	16	-9	2			.894	-1	C-25	-0.7

YEAR	TM/L	G	AB	R	H	2B	3B	HR	RBI	BB	SO	AVG	OBP	SLG	PRO+	BR/A	SB	CS	SBR	FA	FR	G/POS	TPR
1890	*Bro-N	16	55	5	13	2	0	0	7	6	4	.236	.311	.273	70	-2	2			.913	-1	C-15/O-2	-0.2
Total	12	671	2392	287	511	58	12	2	106	124	97	.214	.254	.250	55	-127	39			.916	66	C-667/O-6,31	-1.2

■ JOE BUSKEY
Buskey, Joseph Henry "Jazzbow" b: 12/18/02, Cumberland, Md. d: 4/11/49, Cumberland, Md. BR/TR, 5'10", 175 lbs. Deb: 4/19/26

YEAR	TM/L	G	AB	R	H	2B	3B	HR	RBI	BB	SO	AVG	OBP	SLG	PRO+	BR/A	SB	CS	SBR	FA	FR	G/POS	TPR
1926	Phi-N	5	8	1	0	0	0	0	0	0	1	.000	.111	.000	-65	-2	0			.810	-0	/S-5	-0.2

■ MIKE BUSKEY
Buskey, Michael Thomas b: 1/13/49, San Francisco, Cal. BR/TR, 5'11", 160 lbs. Deb: 9/2/77

YEAR	TM/L	G	AB	R	H	2B	3B	HR	RBI	BB	SO	AVG	OBP	SLG	PRO+	BR/A	SB	CS	SBR	FA	FR	G/POS	TPR
1977	Phi-N	6	7	1	2	0	1	0	1	0	1	.286	.375	.571	143	0	0	0	0	.882	2	/S-6	0.2

■ RAY BUSSE
Busse, Raymond Edward b: 9/25/48, Daytona Beach, Fla. BR/TR, 6'4", 175 lbs. Deb: 7/24/71

YEAR	TM/L	G	AB	R	H	2B	3B	HR	RBI	BB	SO	AVG	OBP	SLG	PRO+	BR/A	SB	CS	SBR	FA	FR	G/POS	TPR
1971	Hou-N	10	34	2	5	3	0	0	4	2	9	.147	.194	.235	22	-4	0	0	0	.929	-2	/S-5,3-3	-0.6
1973	StL-N	24	70	6	10	4	2	2	5	5	21	.143	.200	.343	48	-5	0	1	-1	.898	-2	S-23	-0.6
	Hou-N	15	17	1	1	0	0	0	0	1	12	.059	.111	.059	-52	-3	0	0	0	1.000	-1	/S-5,3-3	-0.2
	Yr	39	87	7	11	4	2	2	5	6	33	.126	.183	.287	28	-9	0	1	-1	.906	-1	S-28/3-3	-0.8
1974	Hou-N	19	34	3	7	1	0	0	0	3	12	.206	.270	.235	44	-3	0	0	0	.864	-0	/3-8	-0.3
Total	3	68	155	12	23	8	2	2	9	11	54	.148	.205	.265	31	-15	0	1	-1	.908	-3	/S-33,3-14	-1.7

■ HANK BUTCHER
Butcher, Henry Joseph b: 7/12/1886, Chicago, Ill. d: 12/28/79, Hazel Crest, Ill. BR/TR, 5'10", 180 lbs. Deb: 7/8/11

YEAR	TM/L	G	AB	R	H	2B	3B	HR	RBI	BB	SO	AVG	OBP	SLG	PRO+	BR/A	SB	CS	SBR	FA	FR	G/POS	TPR
1911	Cle-A	38	133	21	32	7	3	1	11	11		.241	.303	.361	84	-3	9			.984	0	O-34	-0.5
1912	Cle-A	26	82	9	16	4	1	1	10	6		.195	.250	.305	57	-5	1			.920	1	O-21	-0.5
Total	2	64	215	30	48	11	4	2	21	17		.223	.283	.340	74	-8	10			.956	0	/O-55	-1.0

■ SAL BUTERA
Butera, Salvatore Philip b: 9/25/52, Richmond Hill, N.Y. BR/TR, 6', 190 lbs. Deb: 4/10/80

YEAR	TM/L	G	AB	R	H	2B	3B	HR	RBI	BB	SO	AVG	OBP	SLG	PRO+	BR/A	SB	CS	SBR	FA	FR	G/POS	TPR
1980	Min-A	34	85	4	23	1	0	0	2	3	6	.271	.303	.282	57	-5	0	0	0	.950	-1	C-32/D-2	-0.5
1981	Min-A	62	167	13	40	7	1	0	18	22	14	.240	.328	.293	75	-5	0	0	0	.970	5	C-59/1-1,D	0.2
1982	Min-A	54	126	9	32	2	0	0	8	17	12	.254	.347	.270	70	-4	0	0	0	.988	6	C-53	0.3
1983	Det-A	4	5	1	1	0	0	0	0	0	0	.200	.200	.200	11	-1	0	0	0	.929	1	/C-4	0.1
1984	Mon-N	3	3	0	0	0	0	0	0	1	0	.000	.250	.000	-26	-0	0	0	0	1.000	1	/C-2	0.0
1985	Mon-N	67	120	11	24	1	0	3	12	13	12	.200	.284	.283	63	-6	0	0	0	.984	0	C-66/P-1	-0.4
1986	Cin-N	56	113	14	27	6	1	2	16	21	10	.239	.363	.363	95	-0	0	0	0	.979	1	C-53/P-1	0.3
1987	Cin-N	5	11	1	2	0	0	1	2	1	6	.182	.250	.455	78	-0	0	0	0	.920	1	/C-5	0.1
	*Min-A	51	111	7	19	5	0	1	12	7	16	.171	.220	.243	22	-13	0	0	0	.983	1	C-51	-0.9
1988	Tor-A	23	60	3	14	2	1	1	6	1	9	.233	.246	.350	65	-3	0	0	0	.991	3	C-23	0.1
Total	9	359	801	63	182	24	3	8	76	86	85	.227	.304	.295	65	-37	0	0	0	.978	17	C-348/D-3,P1	-0.7

■ ED BUTKA
Butka, Edward Luke "Babe" b: 1/7/16, Canonsburg, Pa. BR/TR, 6'3", 193 lbs. Deb: 9/26/43

YEAR	TM/L	G	AB	R	H	2B	3B	HR	RBI	BB	SO	AVG	OBP	SLG	PRO+	BR/A	SB	CS	SBR	FA	FR	G/POS	TPR
1943	Was-A	3	9	0	3	1	0	0	1	0	3	.333	.333	.444	132	0	0	0	0	1.000	1	/1-3	0.1
1944	Was-A	15	41	1	8	1	0	0	1	2	11	.195	.233	.220	31	-4	0	0	0	.972	0	1-14	-0.5
Total	2	18	50	1	11	2	0	0	2	2	14	.220	.250	.260	48	-3	0	0	0	.977	1	/1-17	-0.4

■ ART BUTLER
Butler, Arthur Edward (b: Arthur Edward Bouthillier)
b: 12/19/1887, Fall River, Mass. d: 10/7/84, Fall River, Mass. BR/TR, 5'9", 160 lbs. Deb: 4/14/11

YEAR	TM/L	G	AB	R	H	2B	3B	HR	RBI	BB	SO	AVG	OBP	SLG	PRO+	BR/A	SB	CS	SBR	FA	FR	G/POS	TPR
1911	Bos-N	27	68	11	12	2	0	0	6	6		.176	.263	.206	30	-6	0			.930	-3	3-14/2-4,S	-1.0
1912	Pit-N	43	154	19	42	4	2	1	17	15	13	.273	.337	.344	88	-2	2			.960	-22	2-43	-2.6
1913	Pit-N	82	214	40	60	9	3	0	20	32	14	.280	.379	.350	114	5	9			.919	-12	2-28,S-26/3O	-0.5
1914	StL-N	86	274	29	55	12	3	1	24	39	23	.201	.311	.277	76	-7	14			.927	-19	S-83/O-1	-2.1
1915	StL-N	130	469	73	119	12	5	1	31	47	34	.254	.323	.307	91	-4	26	14	-1	.916	-34	*S-125/2-2	-3.2
1916	StL-N	86	110	9	23	5	0	0	7	12	9	.209	.256	.255	57	-6	3			.882	-6	O-15/2-8,S3	-1.4
Total	6	454	1289	181	311	44	13	3	101	146	102	.241	.323	.303	85	-20	54	14		.919	-96	S-236/2-85,O3	-10.8

■ BRETT BUTLER
Butler, Brett Morgan b: 6/15/57, Los Angeles, Cal. BL/TL, 5'10", 160 lbs. Deb: 8/20/81

YEAR	TM/L	G	AB	R	H	2B	3B	HR	RBI	BB	SO	AVG	OBP	SLG	PRO+	BR/A	SB	CS	SBR	FA	FR	G/POS	TPR
1981	Atl-N	40	126	17	32	2	3	0	4	19	17	.254	.352	.317	89	-1	9	1	2	.987	-2	O-37	-0.2
1982	*Atl-N	89	240	35	52	2	0	0	7	25	35	.217	.291	.225	44	-17	21	8	2	1.000	-10	O-77	-2.9
1983	Atl-N	151	549	84	154	21	**13**	5	37	54	56	.281	.347	.393	98	-1	39	23	-2	.987	6	*O-143	-0.2
1984	Cle-A	159	602	108	162	25	9	3	49	86	62	.269	.364	.355	98	2	52	22		.991	15	*O-156	1.4
1985	Cle-A	152	591	106	184	28	14	5	50	63	42	.311	.379	.431	122	19	47	20		**.998**	22	*O-150/D-1	3.7
1986	Cle-A	161	587	92	163	17	**14**	4	51	70	65	.278	.359	.375	102	3	32	15		.993	9	*O-159	0.7
1987	Cle-A	137	522	91	154	25	8	9	41	91	55	.295	.401	.425	119	18	33	16		.990	15	*O-136	2.7
1988	SF-N	157	568	**109**	163	27	9	6	43	97	64	.287	.395	.398	134	29	43	20	1	.988	6	*O-155	3.4
1989	*SF-N	154	594	100	168	22	4	4	36	59	69	.283	.351	.354	105	5	31	16	-0	.986	14	*O-152	1.6
1990	SF-N	160	622	108	**192**	20	9	3	44	90	62	.309	.401	.384	122	23	51	19	4	.986	7	*O-159	3.0
1991	LA-N★	161	615	**112**	182	13	5	2	38	**108**	79	.296	.402	.343	114	18	38	28	-5	**1.000**	12	*O-161	2.1
1992	LA-N	157	553	86	171	14	11	3	39	95	67	.309	.413	.391	131	28	41	21	-0	.995	2	*O-155	2.8
1993	LA-N	156	607	80	181	21	10	1	42	86	69	.298	.390	.371	111	14	39	19	0	**1.000**	3	*O-155	1.3
1994	LA-N	111	417	79	131	13	**9**	8	33	68	52	.314	.413	.446	132	22	27	8	3	.993	5	*O-111	2.7
Total	14	1945	7193	1207	2089	250	118	53	514	1011	794	.290	.381	.380	112	161	503	236		.992	105	*O-1906/D-1	22.1

■ FRANK BUTLER
Butler, Frank Dean "Stuffy" or "Goldbrick" b: 7/18/1860, Savannah, Ga. d: 7/10/45, Jacksonville, Fla BL/TL, Deb: 7/30/1895

YEAR	TM/L	G	AB	R	H	2B	3B	HR	RBI	BB	SO	AVG	OBP	SLG	PRO+	BR/A	SB	CS	SBR	FA	FR	G/POS	TPR
1895	NY-N	5	22	5	6	1	0	0	2	1	1	.273	.304	.318	62	-1	0			1.000	-1	/O-5	-0.2

■ KID BUTLER
Butler, Frank Edward b: 5/1861, Boston, Mass. d: 4/9/21, S.Boston, Mass. Deb: 5/20/1884

YEAR	TM/L	G	AB	R	H	2B	3B	HR	RBI	BB	SO	AVG	OBP	SLG	PRO+	BR/A	SB	CS	SBR	FA	FR	G/POS	TPR
1884	Bos-U	71	255	36	43	15	0	0		12		.169	.206	.227	18	-29				.810	-6	O-53,2-12/S3	-3.2

■ JOHN BUTLER
Butler, John Albert (a.k.a. Frederick King In 1901) b: 7/26/1879, Boston, Mass. d: 2/2/50, Boston, Mass. BR/TR, 5'7", 170 lbs. Deb: 9/28/01

YEAR	TM/L	G	AB	R	H	2B	3B	HR	RBI	BB	SO	AVG	OBP	SLG	PRO+	BR/A	SB	CS	SBR	FA	FR	G/POS	TPR
1901	Mil-A	1	3	0	0	0	0	0	0	0	1	.000	.250	.000	-28	-0	0			1.000	-1	/C-1	-0.1
1904	StL-N	12	37	0	6	1	0	0	1	4		.162	.262	.189	42	-2	0			.968	-2	C-12	-0.4
1906	Bro-N	1	0	0	0	0	0	0	0			—	—	—		0	0			1.000	0	/C-1	0.0
1907	Bro-N	30	79	6	10	1	0	0	2	9		.127	.216	.139	12	-8	0			.946	-5	C-28/O-1	-1.2
Total	4	44	119	6	16	2	0	0	3	14		.134	.231	.151	21	-11	0			.953	-8	/C-42,O-1	-1.7

■ JOHNNY BUTLER
Butler, John Stephen "Trolley Line" b: 3/20/1893, Fall River, Kan. d: 4/29/67, Seal Beach, Cal. BR/TR, 6', 175 lbs. Deb: 4/18/26 C

YEAR	TM/L	G	AB	R	H	2B	3B	HR	RBI	BB	SO	AVG	OBP	SLG	PRO+	BR/A	SB	CS	SBR	FA	FR	G/POS	TPR
1926	Bro-N	147	501	54	135	27	5	1	68	54	44	.269	.346	.349	89	-6	6			.949	-7	*S-102,3-42/2	0.0
1927	Bro-N	149	521	39	124	13	6	2	57	34	33	.238	.292	.298	58	-31	9			.959	-2	S-90,3-60	-2.0
1928	Chi-N	62	174	17	47	7	0	0	16	19	7	.270	.352	.310	75	-5	2			.950	10	3-59/S-2	0.7
1929	StL-N	17	55	5	9	1	1	0	5	4	5	.164	.220	.218	9	-8	0			.964	0	/3-9,S-8	-0.5
Total	4	375	1251	115	315	48	12	3	146	111	89	.252	.320	.317	70	-51	17			.954	2	S-202,3-170/2	-1.8

■ DICK BUTLER
Butler, Richard H. b: Brooklyn, N.Y. Deb: 6/16/1897

YEAR	TM/L	G	AB	R	H	2B	3B	HR	RBI	BB	SO	AVG	OBP	SLG	PRO+	BR/A	SB	CS	SBR	FA	FR	G/POS	TPR
1897	Lou-N	10	38	3	7	0	0	0	2	0		.184	.184	.184	-3	-6	1			.818	-2	C-10	-0.6
1899	Was-N	12	36	4	10	0	1	0	2	1		.278	.316	.333	79	-1	1			.892	-3	C-11	-0.3
Total	2	22	74	7	17	0	1	0	2	1		.230	.250	.257	37	-7	2			.852	-6	/C-21	-0.9

■ ROB BUTLER
Butler, Robert Frank John b: 4/10/70, E.York, Ont., Can. BL/TL, 5'11", 185 lbs. Deb: 6/12/93

YEAR	TM/L	G	AB	R	H	2B	3B	HR	RBI	BB	SO	AVG	OBP	SLG	PRO+	BR/A	SB	CS	SBR	FA	FR	G/POS	TPR
1993	*Tor-A	17	48	8	13	4	0	2	7	12		.271	.375	.354	97	-0	2	2	0	.970	-0	O-16	-0.1
1994	Tor-A	41	74	13	13	0	0	0	5	7	8	.176	.256	.203	20	-9	0	1	-1	.977	-5	O-31/D-1	-1.4
Total	2	58	122	21	26	4	0	2	7	14	20	.213	.304	.262	50	-9	2	3	-1	.974	-5	/O-47,D-1	-1.5

YEAR	TM/L	G	AB	R	H	2B	3B	HR	RBI	BB	SO	AVG	OBP	SLG	PRO+	BR/A	SB	CS	SBR	FA	FR	G/POS	TPR

■ BILL BUTLER Butler, William J. b: 1861, New Orleans, La. Deb: 6/29/1884

| 1884 | Ind-a | 9 | 31 | 7 | 7 | 3 | 2 | 0 | | | 1 | .226 | .250 | .452 | 128 | 1 | | | | .700 | -2 | /O-9 | -0.1 |

■ KID BUTLER Butler, Willis Everett b: 8/9/1887, Franklin, Pa. d: 2/22/64, Richmond, Cal. BR/TR, 5'11", 155 lbs. Deb: 4/30/07

| 1907 | StL-A | 20 | 59 | 4 | 13 | 2 | 0 | 0 | 6 | 2 | | .220 | .246 | .254 | 60 | -3 | 1 | | | .940 | -1 | 2-11/3-5,S | -0.4 |

■ FRANK BUTTERY Buttery, Frank b: 5/13/1851, Silvermine, Conn. d: 12/16/02, Silvermine, Conn. Deb: 4/26/1872

| 1872 | Man-n | 18 | 93 | 18 | 25 | 0 | 0 | 0 | 8 | 0 | 2 | .269 | .269 | .269 | 70 | -3 | | | | | | /P-6,3-6,O | -0.1 |

■ JOE BUZAS Buzas, Joseph John b: 10/2/19, Alpha, N.J. BR/TR, 6'1", 180 lbs. Deb: 4/17/45

| 1945 | NY-A | 30 | 65 | 8 | 17 | 0 | 0 | 0 | 6 | 2 | 5 | .262 | .284 | .323 | 73 | -2 | 2 | 0 | 1 | .898 | -3 | S-12 | -0.4 |

■ BURLEY BYERS Byers, Burley (b: Christopher A. Bayer) b: 12/19/1875, Louisville, Ky. d: 5/30/33, Louisville, Ky. 175 lbs. Deb: 6/17/1899

| 1899 | Lou-N | 1 | 3 | 0 | 0 | 0 | 0 | 0 | 0 | 0 | | .000 | .000 | .000 | -99 | -1 | 0 | | | .600 | -1 | /S-1 | -0.2 |

■ BILL BYERS Byers, James William b: 10/3/1877, Bridgeton, Ind. d: 9/8/48, Baltimore, Md. BR/TR, 5'7", Deb: 4/15/04

| 1904 | StL-N | 19 | 60 | 3 | 13 | 0 | 0 | 0 | 4 | 1 | | .217 | .230 | .217 | 40 | -4 | .0 | | | .971 | -1 | C-16/1-1 | -0.4 |

■ RANDY BYERS Byers, Randell Parker b: 10/2/64, Bridgeton, N.J. BL/TR, 6'2", 180 lbs. Deb: 9/7/87

1987	SD-N	10	16	1	5	1	0	0	1	1	5	.313	.353	.375	96	-0	1	0	0	1.000	0	/O-5	0.0
1988	SD-N	11	10	0	2	1	0	0	0	0	5	.200	.200	.300	42	-1	0	0	0	.000	-1	/O-2	-0.2
Total	2	21	26	1	7	2	0	0	1	1	10	.269	.296	.346	77	-1	1	0	0	1.000	-1	/O-7	-0.2

■ JIM BYRD Byrd, James Edward b: 10/3/68, WeWahitchka, Fla. BR/TR, 6'1", 185 lbs. Deb: 5/31/93

| 1993 | Bos-A | 2 | 0 | 0 | 0 | 0 | 0 | 0 | 0 | 0 | 0 | — | — | — | | | 0 | 0 | 0 | .000 | 0 | /R | 0.0 |

■ SAMMY BYRD Byrd, Samuel Dewey "Babe Ruth's Legs" b: 10/15/07, Bremen, Ga. d: 5/11/81, Mesa, Ariz. BR/TR, 5'10.5", 175 lbs. Deb: 5/11/29

1929	NY-A	62	170	32	53	12	0	5	28	28	18	.312	.409	.471	135	10	1	4	-2	.950	-0	O-54	0.4
1930	NY-A	92	218	46	62	12	6	3	31	30	18	.284	.371	.440	110	4	5	1	1	.992	-12	O-85	-1.0
1931	NY-A	115	248	51	67	18	2	3	32	29	26	.270	.349	.395	101	0	5	0	2	.974	-13	O-88	-1.4
1932	*NY-A	105	209	49	62	12	1	8	30	30	20	.297	.385	.478	129	9	1	2	-1	.964	-18	O-91	-1.2
1933	NY-A	85	107	26	30	6	1	2	11	15	12	.280	.369	.411	113	2	0	1	-1	.987	-16	O-71	-1.5
1934	NY-A	106	191	32	47	8	0	3	23	18	22	.246	.318	.335	73	-8	1	2	-1	.988	-13	*O-104	-2.3
1935	Cin-N	121	416	51	109	25	4	9	52	37	51	.262	.322	.406	97	-2	4			.970	3	*O-115	-0.4
1936	Cin-N	59	141	17	35	8	2	1	13	11	11	.248	.300	.348	80	-4	0			.989	-1	O-37	-0.6
Total	8	745	1700	304	465	101	10	38	220	198	178	.274	.350	.412	104	11	17	10		.975	-71	O-645	-8.0

■ BOBBY BYRNE Byrne, Robert Matthew b: 12/31/1884, St.Louis, Mo. d: 12/31/64, Wayne, Pa. BR/TR, 5'7.5", 145 lbs. Deb: 4/11/07

1907	StL-N	149	559	55	143	11	5	0	29	35		.256	.307	.293	91	-6	21			.920	22	*3-148/S-1	2.3
1908	StL-N	127	439	27	84	7	1	0	14	23		.191	.238	.212	46	-27	16			.925	9	3-122/S-4	-1.6
1909	StL-N	105	421	61	90	13	6	1	33	46		.214	.302	.280	86	-6	21			.922	17	3-105	1.6
	*Pit-N	46	168	31	43	6	2	0	7	32		.256	.387	.315	109	4	8			.987	6	3-46	1.2
	Yr	151	589	92	133	19	8	1	40	78		.226	.327	.290	93	-2	29			.939	23	3-151	2.8
1910	Pit-N	148	602	101	**178**	43	12	2	52	66	27	.296	.366	.417	121	15	36			.929	-7	3-148	1.3
1911	Pit-N	153	598	96	155	24	17	2	52	67	41	.259	.342	.366	95	-4	23			.930	-3	3-152	-0.5
1912	Pit-N	130	528	99	152	31	11	3	35	54	40	.288	.358	.405	110	7	20			.948	-23	3-130	-1.5
1913	Pit-N	113	448	54	121	22	0	1	47	29	28	.270	.322	.326	89	-7	10			.940	-9	3-110	-1.5
	Phi-N	19	58	9	13	1	0	1	4	5	3	.224	.308	.293	69	-2	2			.963	3	3-15	0.1
	Yr	132	506	63	134	23	0	2	51	34	31	.265	.320	.322	86	-9	12			.943	-7	*3-125	-1.4
1914	Phi-N	126	467	61	127	12	1	0	26	45	44	.272	.339	.302	85	-7	9			.934	-3	*2-101,3-22	-1.1
1915	*Phi-N	105	387	50	81	6	4	0	21	39	28	.209	.290	.245	62	-16	4	12	-6	.969	-7	*3-105	-2.8
1916	Phi-N	48	141	22	33	10	1	0	9	14	7	.234	.308	.319	89	-2	6			.933	3	3-40	0.3
1917	Phi-N	13	14	1	5	0	0	0	0	1	2	.357	.400	.357	128	0	0			1.000	-1	/3-4	-0.1
	Chi-A	1	1	0	0	0	0	0	0	0	0	.000	.000	.000	-98	-0	0			1.000	0	/2-1	0.0
Total	11	1283	4831	667	1225	186	60	10	329	456	220	.254	.324	.323	91	-51	176	12		.934	6	3-1147,2-102/S	-2.3

■ JIM BYRNES Byrnes, James Joseph b: 1/5/1880, San Francisco, Cal. d: 7/31/41, San Francisco, Cal BR/TR, 5'9", 150 lbs. Deb: 4/19/06

| 1906 | Phi-A | 10 | 23 | 2 | 4 | 0 | 1 | 0 | 0 | 0 | | .174 | .174 | .261 | 34 | -2 | 0 | | | .889 | -0 | /C-9 | -0.1 |

■ MILT BYRNES Byrnes, Milton John "Skippy" b: 11/15/16, St.Louis, Mo. d: 2/1/79, St.Louis, Mo. BL/TL, 5'10.5", 170 lbs. Deb: 4/21/43

1943	StL-A	129	429	58	120	28	7	4	50	53	49	.280	.362	.406	122	12	1	4	-2	.997	8	*O-114	1.3
1944	*StL-A	128	407	63	120	20	4	4	45	68	50	.295	.394	.393	119	12	1	7	-4	.976	-6	*O-122	-0.3
1945	StL-A	133	442	53	110	29	4	8	59	78	84	.249	.363	.387	112	8	1	3	-2	.988	5	*O-125/1-2	0.6
Total	3	390	1278	174	350	77	15	16	154	199	183	.274	.373	.395	117	33	3	14	-8	.987	8	O-361/1-2	1.6

■ PUTSY CABALLERO Caballero, Ralph Joseph b: 11/5/27, New Orleans, La. BR/TR, 5'10", 170 lbs. Deb: 9/14/44

1944	Phi-N	4	4	0	0	0	0	0	0	0	1	.000	.000	.000	-99	-1	0			.889	2	/3-2	0.1
1945	Phi-N	9	1	1	0	0	0	0	1	0	0	.000	.000	.000	-99	-0	0			.857	3	/3-5	0.1
1947	Phi-N	2	7	2	1	0	0	0	1	0	1	.143	.250	.143	7	-1	0			1.000	-0	/2-2,3-1	-0.1
1948	Phi-N	113	351	33	86	12	1	0	19	24	18	.245	.293	.285	58	-20	7			.962	6	3-79,2-23	-1.4
1949	Phi-N	29	68	8	19	3	0	0	3	0	2	.279	.279	.324	63	-4	0			.981	6	2-21/S-1	0.1
1950	*Phi-N	46	24	12	4	0	0	0	0	2	2	.167	.231	.167	7	-3	1			.950	6	/2-5,3-4,S	0.3
1951	Phi-N	84	161	15	30	3	2	1	11	12	7	.186	.243	.248	33	-15	1	2	-1	.985	9	2-54/3-3,S	-0.5
1952	Phi-N	35	42	10	10	3	0	0	6	2	3	.238	.273	.310	62	-2	1	0	0	.857	2	/S-8,2-7,3	0.1
Total	8	322	658	81	150	21	3	1	40	41	34	.228	.273	.274	49	-47	10	2		.968	31	2-112,3-101/S	-1.3

■ ENOS CABELL Cabell, Enos Milton b: 10/8/49, Fort Riley, Kan. BR/TR, 6'5", 185 lbs. Deb: 9/17/72

1972	Bal-A	3	5	0	0	0	0	0	1	0	0	.000	.000	.000	-97	-1	0	0	0	1.000	-0	/1-1	-0.2
1973	Bal-A	32	47	12	10	2	0	0	3	3	9	.213	.260	.319	63	-2	1	3	-2	.991	-1	1-23/3-1	-0.6
1974	*Bal-A	80	174	24	42	4	2	3	17	7	20	.241	.271	.339	77	-6	5	3	-0	.995	2	1-28,O-22,3/2D	-0.6
1975	Hou-N	117	348	43	92	17	6	2	43	18	53	.264	.306	.365	92	-5	12	3	2	.973	-0	O-67,1-25,3	-0.7
1976	Hou-N	144	586	85	160	13	7	2	43	29	79	.273	.310	.329	89	-10	35	8	6	.958	-9	*3-143/1-3	-1.5
1977	Hou-N	150	625	101	176	36	7	16	68	27	55	.282	.315	.438	109	4	42	22	-1	.948	-6	*3-144/1-8,S	-0.4
1978	Hou-N	162	660	92	195	31	8	7	71	22	80	.295	.323	.398	109	4	33	15	1	.958	-16	*3-153,1-14/S	-1.4
1979	Hou-N	155	603	60	164	30	5	6	67	21	68	.272	.300	.368	86	-14	37	18	0	.957	-23	*3-132,1-51	-4.1
1980	*Hou-N	152	604	69	167	23	8	2	55	26	84	.276	.307	.351	90	-10	21	13	-2	.927	-20	*3-150/1-1	-3.6
1981	SF-N	96	396	41	101	20	1	2	36	10	47	.255	.275	.326	71	-16	6	7	-2	.987	-1	1-69,3-22	-2.6
1982	Det-A	125	464	45	121	17	3	2	37	15	48	.261	.285	.323	67	-21	15	6	1	.992	-8	1-83,3-59/O	-3.3
1983	Det-A	121	392	62	122	23	5	6	46	16	41	.311	.340	.434	114	7	4	8	-4	.997	7	*1-106/3-4,SD	0.4
1984	Hou-N	127	436	52	135	17	3	8	44	21	47	.310	.343	.417	121	10	8	11	-4	.993	-1	*1-112	-0.1
1985	Hou-N	60	143	20	35	8	1	2	14	16	15	.245	.321	.357	92	-2	3	1	0	.994	-1	1-49	-0.5
	*LA-N	57	192	20	56	11	0	0	22	14	21	.292	.340	.349	96	-1	6	2	0	.920	-3	3-32,1-21/O	-0.4
	Yr	117	335	40	91	19	1	2	36	30	36	.272	.332	.352	94	-3	9	3	1	.993	-3	1-70,3-32/O	-0.9
1986	LA-N	107	277	27	71	11	0	2	29	14	26	.256	.297	.318	75	-10	10	4	1	.987	0	1-61,O-16/3	-1.4
Total	15	1688	5952	753	1647	263	56	60	596	259	691	.277	.309	.370	93	-74	238	124	-3	.944	-77	3-888,1-655,O/DS2	-21.0

YEAR	TM/L	G	AB	R	H	2B	3B	HR	RBI	BB	SO	AVG	OBP	SLG	PRO+	BR/A	SB	CS	SBR	FA	FR	G/POS	TPR

■ AL CABRERA
Cabrera, Alfredo A.　b: 1883, Canary Islands　d: Havana, Cuba　TR ,　Deb: 5/16/13

| 1913 | StL-N | 1 | 2 | 0 | 0 | 0 | 0 | 0 | 0 | 0 | 0 | .000 | .000 | .000 | -99 | -1 | 0 | | | .000 | 0 | /S-1 | -0.1 |

■ FRANCISCO CABRERA
Cabrera, Francisco (Paulino)　b: 10/10/66, Santo Domingo, D.R.　BR/TR, 6'4", 195 lbs.　Deb: 7/24/89

1989	Tor-A	3	12	1	2	1	0	0	1	0	3	.167	.231	.250	36	-1	0	0	0	.000	0	/D-3	-0.1
	Atl-N	4	14	0	3	0	0	0	0	0	3	.214	.214	.357	59	-1	0	0	0	1.000	-1	/1-2,C-1	-0.2
1990	Atl-N	63	137	14	38	5	1	7	25	5	21	.277	.303	.482	106	1	1	0	0	.990	-2	1-48/C-3	-0.3
1991	*Atl-N	44	95	7	23	6	0	4	23	6	20	.242	.287	.432	94	-1	1	1	-0	.987	-3	C-17,1-14	-0.4
1992	*Atl-N	12	10	2	3	0	0	2	3	1	1	.300	.364	.900	233	2	0	0	0	.000	0	/C-1	0.2
1993	*Atl-N	70	83	8	20	3	0	4	11	8	21	.241	.308	.422	92	-1	0	0	0	1.000	2	1-12/C-2	0.0
Total	5	196	351	32	89	17	1	17	62	21	69	.254	.296	.453	99	-2	2	1	0	.989	-3	/1-76,C-24,D	-0.8

■ CRAIG CACEK
Cacek, Craig Thomas　b: 9/10/54, Hollywood, Cal.　BR/TR, 6'1", 200 lbs.　Deb: 6/18/77

| 1977 | Hou-N | 7 | 20 | 0 | 1 | 0 | 0 | 0 | 1 | 1 | 3 | .050 | .095 | .050 | -66 | -5 | 0 | 0 | 0 | .981 | -1 | /1-6 | -0.6 |

■ CHARLIE CADY
Cady, Charles B.　b: 12/1865, Chicago, Ill.　d: 6/7/09, Kankakee, Ill.　5'11", 180 lbs.　Deb: 9/5/1883

1883	Cle-N	3	11	0	0	0	0	0	0	0	5	.000	.083	.000	-73	-2				1.000	-1	/O-2,P-1	-0.2
1884	CP-U	6	20	4	2	1	1	0		0	1	.100	.143	.250	5	-3				.909	-0	/P-4,O-2	-0.1
	KC-U	2	3	0	0	0	0	0		0	0	.000	.000	.000	-99	-1				.600	-2	/C-1,2-1	-0.2
	Yr	8	23	4	2	1	1	0		0	1	.087	.125	.217	-9	-4				.909	-2	/P-4,O-2,C2	-0.3
Total	2	11	34	4	2	1	1	0	0	2	5	.059	.111	.147	-28	-6				.917	-3	/P-5,O-4,2C	-0.5

■ HICK CADY
Cady, Forrest Leroy　b: 1/26/1886, Bishop Hill, Ill.　d: 3/3/46, Cedar Rapids, Iowa　BR/TR, 6'2", 179 lbs.　Deb: 4/26/12

1912	*Bos-A	47	135	19	35	13	2	0	9	10		.259	.324	.385	98	-1	0			.990	11	C-43/1-4	1.4
1913	Bos-A	40	96	10	24	5	2	0	6	5	14	.250	.294	.344	84	-2	1			.992	8	C-39	0.9
1914	Bos-A	61	159	14	41	6	1	0	8	12	22	.258	.310	.308	86	-3	2	1	0	.971	-3	C-58	-0.1
1915	*Bos-A	78	205	25	57	10	2	0	17	19	25	.278	.342	.346	109	2	0	2	-1	.980	-2	C-77	0.5
1916	*Bos-A	78	162	5	31	6	3	0	13	15	16	.191	.264	.265	59	-8	0			.967	-13	C-63/1-3	-2.0
1917	Bos-A	17	46	4	7	1	1	0	2	1	6	.152	.170	.217	18	-5	0			.959	1	C-14	-0.3
1919	Phi-N	34	98	6	21	6	0	1	19	4	8	.214	.252	.306	63	-5	1			.984	-7	C-29	-1.0
Total	7	355	901	83	216	47	11	1	74	66	91	.240	.297	.320	82	-21	4	3		.979	-4	C-323/1-7	-0.6

■ TOM CAFEGO
Cafego, Thomas　b: 8/21/11, Whipple, W.Va.　d: 10/29/61, Detroit, Mich.　BL/TR, 5'10", 160 lbs.　Deb: 9/3/37

| 1937 | StL-A | 4 | 4 | 1 | 0 | 0 | 0 | 0 | 0 | 0 | 1 | .000 | .000 | .000 | -99 | -1 | 0 | 0 | 0 | .500 | -1 | /O-1 | -0.2 |

■ JOE CAFFIE
Caffie, Joseph Clifford "Rabbit"　b: 2/14/31, Ramer, Ala.　BL/TR, 5'10.5", 180 lbs.　Deb: 9/13/56

1956	Cle-A	12	38	7	13	0	0	1	4	1	8	.342	.432	.342	104	1	3	2	-0	1.000	1	O-10	0.1
1957	Cle-A	32	89	14	24	2	1	3	10	4	11	.270	.301	.416	95	-1	0	1	-1	.976	-0	O-19	-0.3
Total	2	44	127	21	37	2	1	4	14	5	19	.291	.343	.394	99	-0	3	3	-1	.984	1	/O-29	-0.2

■ BEN CAFFYN
Caffyn, Benjamin Thomas　b: 2/10/1880, Peoria, Ill.　d: 11/22/42, Peoria, Ill.　BL/TL,　Deb: 8/21/06

| 1906 | Cle-A | 30 | 103 | 16 | 20 | 4 | 0 | 0 | 3 | 12 | | .194 | .291 | .233 | 65 | -4 | 2 | | | .909 | -4 | O-29 | -1.0 |

■ WAYNE CAGE
Cage, Wayne Levell　b: 11/23/51, Monroe, La.　BL/TL, 6'4", 205 lbs.　Deb: 4/22/78

1978	Cle-A	36	98	11	24	6	1	4	13	9	28	.245	.308	.449	112	1	1	2	-1	.988	1	D-20,1-11	0.0
1979	Cle-A	29	56	6	13	2	0	1	6	5	16	.232	.295	.321	66	-3	0	2	-1	1.000	1	/1-7,D-9	-0.3
Total	2	65	154	17	37	8	1	5	19	14	44	.240	.304	.403	94	-2	1	4	-2	.992	2	/D-29,1-18	-0.3

■ JOHN CAHILL
Cahill, John Patrick Francis "Patsy"　b: 4/30/1865, San Francisco, Cal　d: 10/31/01, Pleasanton, Cal.　BR/TR, 5'7.5", 168 lbs.　Deb: 5/31/1884

1884	Col-a	59	210	28	46	3	3	0		6		.219	.248	.262	72	-6				.843	-1	O-56/S-5,P	-0.6
1886	StL-N	125	463	43	92	17	6	1	32	9	79	.199	.214	.268	49	-28	16			.866	2	*O-124/P-2,S3	-2.7
1887	Ind-N	68	263	22	54	4	3	0	26	9	5	.205	.234	.243	34	-23	34			.826	-6	O-56/3-9,PS	-2.4
Total	3	252	936	93	192	24	12	1	58	24	84	.205	.227	.260	49	-57	50			.851	-5	O-236/3-10,PS	-5.7

■ TOM CAHILL
Cahill, Thomas H.　b: 10/1868, Fall River, Mass.　d: 12/25/1894, Scranton, Pa.　Deb: 4/9/1891

| 1891 | Lou-a | 120 | 433 | 70 | 111 | 18 | 7 | 3 | 47 | 41 | 51 | .256 | .329 | .351 | 96 | -3 | 39 | | | .931 | -3 | C-56,S-49,O/23 | 0.2 |

■ BOB CAIN
Cain, Robert Max "Sugar"　b: 10/16/24, Longford, Kan.　BL/TL, 6', 165 lbs.　Deb: 9/18/49

1949	Chi-A	6	3	0	0	0	0	0	0	0	1	.000	.000	.000	-99	-1	0	0	0	1.000	-0	/P-6	0.0
1950	Chi-A	35	61	7	12	2	0	0	2	3	15	.197	.234	.230	20	-7	0	0	0	.974	-0	P-34	0.0
1951	Chi-A	4	9	1	3	1	0	0	0	0	3	.333	.333	.444	111	-0	0	0	0	1.000	-0	/P-4	0.0
	Det-A	35	53	9	13	3	0	0	9	6	9	.245	.322	.302	69	-2	0	0	0	.972	0	P-35	0.0
	Yr	39	62	10	16	4	0	0	9	6	12	.258	.324	.323	75	-2	0	0	0	.975	-0	P-39	0.0
1952	StL-A	35	58	7	8	0	1	0	4	1	14	.138	.194	.172	2	-8	0	0	0	.966	-2	P-29	0.0
1953	StL-A	34	30	3	6	2	0	0	2	1	3	.200	.226	.267	32	-3	0	0	0	1.000	-2	P-32	0.0
1954	Chi-A	1	0	1	0	0	0	0	0	0	0	—	—	—	0	0	0	0	0	.000	0	R	0.0
Total	6	150	214	28	42	8	1	0	14	14	45	.196	.246	.243	31	-21	0	0	0	.975	-4	P-140	0.0

■ GEORGE CAITHAMER
Caithamer, George Theodore "Sidel"　b: 7/22/10, Chicago, Ill.　d: 6/1/54, Chicago, Ill.　BR/TR, 5'7.5", 160 lbs.　Deb: 9/17/34

| 1934 | Chi-A | 5 | 19 | 1 | 6 | 1 | 0 | 0 | 3 | 1 | | .316 | .350 | .368 | 83 | -0 | 0 | 0 | 0 | .958 | -1 | /C-5 | -0.1 |

■ IVAN CALDERON
Calderon, Ivan (Perez)　b: 3/19/62, Fajardo, P.R.　BR/TR, 6'1", 220 lbs.　Deb: 8/10/84

1984	Sea-A	11	24	2	5	1	0	1	2	5		.208	.269	.375	77	-1	1	0	0	1.000	-1	O-11	-0.1
1985	Sea-A	67	210	37	60	16	4	8	28	19	45	.286	.351	.514	132	9	4	2	0	.981	1	O-53/1-2,D	0.8
1986	Sea-A	37	131	13	31	5	0	2	13	6	33	.237	.275	.321	61	-7	3	1	0	.937	-1	O-32	-0.9
	Chi-A	13	33	3	10	2	1	0	2	3	6	.303	.361	.424	109	-0	0	0	0	.900	-0	O-5,D-6	-0.0
	Yr	50	164	16	41	7	1	2	15	9	39	.250	.293	.341	71	-7	3	1	0	.932	-1	O-37/D-6	-0.9
1987	Chi-A	144	542	93	159	38	2	28	83	60	109	.293	.365	.526	129	22	10	5	0	.984	5	*O-139/D-3	2.2
1988	Chi-A	73	264	40	56	14	0	14	35	34	66	.212	.302	.424	101	-0	4	4	-1	.954	2	O-67/D-3	-0.2
1989	Chi-A	157	622	83	178	34	9	14	87	43	94	.286	.335	.437	119	14	7	1	2	.978	0	*O-103,D-36,1	1.0
1990	Chi-A	158	607	85	166	44	2	14	74	51	79	.273	.331	.422	111	8	32	16	0	.975	4	*O-130,D-27/1	0.8
1991	Mon-N★	134	470	69	141	22	3	19	75	53	64	.300	.375	.481	141	26	31	16	-0	.974	5	*O-122/1-4	2.8
1992	Mon-N	48	170	19	45	14	2	3	24	14	22	.265	.324	.424	111	2	1	2	-1	.988	0	O-46	0.1
1993	Bos-A	73	213	25	47	8	2	1	19	21	28	.221	.294	.291	54	-14	4	2	0	1.000	-1	O-47,D-19	-1.6
	Chi-A	9	26	1	3	2	0	0	0	0	5	.115	.115	.192	-19	-4	0	0	0	.000	0	/D-6	-0.5
	Yr	82	239	26	50	10	2	1	22	21	33	.209	.276	.280	47	-18	4	2	0	.960	-1	O-47,D-19/H	-2.1
Total	10	924	3312	470	901	200	25	104	444	306	556	.272	.336	.442	113	55	97	49	-0	.976	15	O-755,D-103/1	4.4

■ SAM CALDERONE
Calderone, Samuel Francis　b: 2/6/26, Beverly, N.J.　BR/TR, 5'10.5", 185 lbs.　Deb: 4/19/50

1950	NY-N	34	67	9	20	1	0	1	12	12	5	.299	.319	.358	77	-2	0			.972	-4	C-33	-0.5
1953	NY-N	35	45	4	10	2	0	0	8	1	4	.222	.239	.267	31	-5	0	0	0	.966	-1	C-31	-0.4
1954	Mil-N	22	29	3	11	2	0	0	5	4	4	.379	.455	.448	146	2	0	0	0	1.000	3	C-16	0.5
Total	3	91	141	16	41	5	0	1	25	17	13	.291	.324	.348	76	-5	0	0	0	.978	-2	/C-80	-0.4

■ BRUCE CALDWELL
Caldwell, Bruce　b: 2/8/06, Ashton, R.I.　d: 2/15/59, West Haven, Conn.　BR/TR, 6', 195 lbs.　Deb: 6/30/28

| 1928 | Cle-A | 18 | 27 | 2 | 6 | 1 | 1 | 0 | 3 | 2 | 1 | .222 | .300 | .333 | 66 | -1 | 1 | 0 | 0 | 1.000 | -2 | O-10/1-1 | -0.3 |

YEAR	TM/L	G	AB	R	H	2B	3B	HR	RBI	BB	SO	AVG	OBP	SLG	PRO+	BR/A	SB	CS	SBR	FA	FR	G/POS	TPR
1932	Bro-N	7	11	2	1	0	0	0	2	2	2	.091	.231	.091	-10	-2	0			.875	-1	/1-6	-0.3
Total	2	25	38	4	7	1	1	0	5	4	4	.184	.279	.263	44	-3	1	0		.900	-3	/O-10,1-7	-0.6

■ RAY CALDWELL
Caldwell, Raymond Benjamin "Rube" or "Slim" b: 4/26/1888, Corydon, Pa. d: 8/17/67, Salamanca, N.Y. BL/TR, 6'2", 190 lbs. Deb: 9/9/10

YEAR	TM/L	G	AB	R	H	2B	3B	HR	RBI	BB	SO	AVG	OBP	SLG	PRO+	BR/A	SB	CS	SBR	FA	FR	G/POS	TPR
1910	NY-A	6	6	0	0	0	0	0	0	0	0	.000	.000	.000	-95	-1	0			1.000	-0	/P-6	0.0
1911	NY-A	59	147	14	40	4	1	0	17	11		.272	.323	.313	73	-5	5			.953	-2	P-41,O-11	-0.1
1912	NY-A	44	76	18	18	1	2	0	6	5		.237	.284	.303	64	-4	4			.938	1	P-30/O-1	0.0
1913	NY-A	59	97	10	28	3	2	0	11	3	15	.289	.310	.361	96	-1	3			1.000	-1	P-27/O-3	-0.1
1914	NY-A	59	113	9	22	4	0	0	10	7	24	.195	.248	.230	44	-8	2	1	0	.967	-4	P-31/1-6	-0.3
1915	NY-A	72	144	27	35	4	1	4	20	9	32	.243	.288	.368	96	-2	4	3	-1	.988	-3	P-36	0.0
1916	NY-A	45	93	6	19	2	0	0	4	2	17	.204	.221	.226	34	-8	1			.960	-1	P-21/O-2	0.0
1917	NY-A	63	124	12	32	6	1	2	12	16	16	.258	.343	.371	117	3	2			.973	-3	P-32/O-8	-0.2
1918	NY-A	65	151	14	44	10	0	1	18	13	23	.291	.352	.377	117	3	2			.977	-2	P-24,O-19	0.1
1919	Bos-A	33	48	5	13	1	1	0	4	0	9	.271	.271	.333	73	-2	0			.950	-2	P-18/O-2	-0.1
	Cle-A	6	23	4	8	4	0	0	2	0	4	.348	.348	.522	134	1	0			.900	-1	/P-6	0.0
	Yr	39	71	9	21	5	1	0	6	0	13	.296	.296	.394	97	-1	0			.933	-3	P-24/O-2	-0.1
1920	*Cle-A	41	89	17	19	3	0	0	7	10	13	.213	.300	.247	45	-7	0	2	-1	.917	-3	P-34	0.0
1921	Cle-A	38	53	2	11	4	0	1	3	2	5	.208	.236	.340	45	-5	0	0	0	.930	-0	P-37	0.0
Total	12	590	1164	138	289	46	8	8	114	78	158	.248	.297	.322	78	-36	23	6		.960	-20	P-343/O-46,1	-0.7

■ JACK CALHOUN
Calhoun, John Charles "Red" b: 12/14/1879, Pittsburgh, Pa. d: 2/27/47, Cincinnati, Ohio BR/TR, 6', 185 lbs. Deb: 6/27/02

YEAR	TM/L	G	AB	R	H	2B	3B	HR	RBI	BB	SO	AVG	OBP	SLG	PRO+	BR/A	SB	CS	SBR	FA	FR	G/POS	TPR
1902	StL-N	20	64	3	10	2	1	0	8	8		.156	.260	.219	50	-4	1			.972	-2	3-12/1-5,O	-0.6

■ BILL CALHOUN
Calhoun, William Davitte "Mary" b: 6/23/1890, Rockmart, Ga. d: 1/28/55, Sandersville, Ga. BL/TL, 6', 180 lbs. Deb: 4/24/13

YEAR	TM/L	G	AB	R	H	2B	3B	HR	RBI	BB	SO	AVG	OBP	SLG	PRO+	BR/A	SB	CS	SBR	FA	FR	G/POS	TPR
1913	Bos-N	6	13	0	1	0	0	0	0	0	3	.077	.077	.077	-55	-3	0			.970	-0	/1-3	-0.3

■ MARTY CALLAGHAN
Callaghan, Martin Francis b: 6/9/1900, Norwood, Mass. d: 6/23/75, Norfolk, Mass. BL/TL, 5'10", 157 lbs. Deb: 4/13/22

YEAR	TM/L	G	AB	R	H	2B	3B	HR	RBI	BB	SO	AVG	OBP	SLG	PRO+	BR/A	SB	CS	SBR	FA	FR	G/POS	TPR
1922	Chi-N	74	175	31	45	7	4	0	20	17	17	.257	.326	.343	71	-7	2	3	-1	.946	-9	O-53	-2.0
1923	Chi-N	61	129	18	29	1	3	0	14	8	18	.225	.275	.279	47	-10	2	5	-2	.969	-4	O-38	-1.7
1928	Cin-N	81	238	29	69	11	4	0	24	27	10	.290	.362	.370	93	-2	5			.980	-4	O-69	-1.0
1930	Cin-N	79	225	28	62	9	2	0	16	19	25	.276	.335	.333	66	-12	1			.986	3	O-54	-1.2
Total	4	295	767	106	205	28	13	0	74	71	70	.267	.332	.338	72	-31	10	8		.973	-14	O-214	-5.9

■ DAVE CALLAHAN
Callahan, David Joseph b: 7/20/1888, Ottawa, Ill. d: 10/28/69, Ottawa, Ill. BL/TR, 5'10", 165 lbs. Deb: 9/14/10

YEAR	TM/L	G	AB	R	H	2B	3B	HR	RBI	BB	SO	AVG	OBP	SLG	PRO+	BR/A	SB	CS	SBR	FA	FR	G/POS	TPR
1910	Cle-A	13	44	6	8	1	0	0	2	4		.182	.265	.205	47	-3	5			1.000	0	O-12	-0.3
1911	Cle-A	6	16	1	4	0	1	0	0	1		.250	.294	.375	85	-0	0			1.000	0	/O-4	0.0
Total	2	19	60	7	12	1	1	0	2	5		.200	.273	.250	58	-3	5			1.000	1	/O-16	-0.3

■ ED CALLAHAN
Callahan, Edward Joseph b: 12/11/1857, Boston, Mass. d: 2/5/47, New York, N.Y. Deb: 7/19/1884

YEAR	TM/L	G	AB	R	H	2B	3B	HR	RBI	BB	SO	AVG	OBP	SLG	PRO+	BR/A	SB	CS	SBR	FA	FR	G/POS	TPR
1884	StL-U	1	3	0	0	0	0	0		0		.000	.000	.000	-97	-1				1.000	0	/O-1	0.0
	KC-U	3	11	0	4	0	0	0		0		.364	.364	.364	113	0				.800	1	/S-3	0.1
	Bos-U	4	13	2	5	0	0	0		1		.385	.429	.385	125	1				.750	-1	/O-4	0.0
	Yr	8	27	2	9	0	0	0		1		.333	.357	.333	94	-0				.778	0	/O-5,S-3	0.1

■ NIXEY CALLAHAN
Callahan, James Joseph b: 3/18/1874, Fitchburg, Mass. d: 10/4/34, Boston, Mass. BR/TR, 5'10.5", 180 lbs. Deb: 5/12/1894 M

YEAR	TM/L	G	AB	R	H	2B	3B	HR	RBI	BB	SO	AVG	OBP	SLG	PRO+	BR/A	SB	CS	SBR	FA	FR	G/POS	TPR
1894	Phi-N	9	21	4	5	0	0	0	0	0	7	.238	.238	.238	16	-3	0			.923	1	/P-9	0.0
1897	Chi-N	94	360	60	105	18	6	3	47	10		.292	.320	.400	86	-9	12			.918	5	2-30,P-23,OS/3	-0.3
1898	Chi-N	43	164	27	43	7	5	0	22	4		.262	.280	.366	85	-4	3			.947	-2	P-31/O-9,S21	-0.4
1899	Chi-N	47	150	21	39	4	3	0	18	8		.260	.306	.327	76	-5	9			.904	3	P-35/O-9,S2	-0.3
1900	Chi-N	32	115	16	27	3	2	0	9	6		.235	.273	.296	59	-7	5			.975	6	P-32	0.0
1901	Chi-A	45	118	15	39	7	3	1	19	10		.331	.383	.466	138	6	10			.944	4	P-27/3-6,2	0.4
1902	Chi-A	70	218	27	51	7	2	0	13	6		.234	.261	.284	53	-14	4			.941	2	P-35,O-23/S	-1.0
1903	Chi-A	118	439	47	128	26	5	2	56	20		.292	.324	.387	118	9	24			.895	-6	*3-102/O-8,PM	0.3
1904	Chi-A	132	482	66	126	23	2	0	54	39		.261	.318	.317	105	4	29			.977	-17	*O-104,2-28M	-2.1
1905	Chi-A	96	345	50	94	18	6	1	43	29		.272	.336	.368	128	11	26			.956	-8	O-93	-0.1
1911	Chi-A	120	466	64	131	13	5	3	60	15		.281	.306	.350	86	-11	45			.963	-9	*O-114	-2.6
1912	Chi-A	111	408	45	111	9	7	1	52	12		.272	.298	.336	84	-10	19			.939	-16	*O-107,M	-3.1
1913	Chi-A	6	9	0	2	0	0	0	1	0	2	.222	.222	.222	30	-1	0			1.000	-0	/O-1,M	-0.1
Total	13	923	3295	442	901	135	46	11	394	159	9	.273	.311	.352	94	-34	186			.953	-36	O-489,P-195,3/2S1	-9.7

■ JIM CALLAHAN
Callahan, James Timothy "Red" (b: James Timothy Callaghan)
b: 1/12/1879, Allegheny Co., Pa. d: 3/9/68, Carnegie, Pa. BR/TR, 5'9", 145 lbs. Deb: 5/25/02

YEAR	TM/L	G	AB	R	H	2B	3B	HR	RBI	BB	SO	AVG	OBP	SLG	PRO+	BR/A	SB	CS	SBR	FA	FR	G/POS	TPR
1902	NY-N	1	4	0	0	0	0	0	0	0	1	.000	.200	.000	-38	-1	0			.000	-0	/O-1	-0.1

■ LEO CALLAHAN
Callahan, Leo David b: 8/9/1890, Jamaica Plain, Mass d: 5/2/82, Erie, Pa. BL/TL, 5'8", 142 lbs. Deb: 4/9/13

YEAR	TM/L	G	AB	R	H	2B	3B	HR	RBI	BB	SO	AVG	OBP	SLG	PRO+	BR/A	SB	CS	SBR	FA	FR	G/POS	TPR
1913	Bro-N	33	41	6	7	3	1	0	3	4	5	.171	.244	.293	52	-3	0			.857	-2	/O-8	-0.5
1919	Phi-N	81	235	26	54	14	4	1	9	29	19	.230	.317	.336	90	-2	5			.950	1	O-58	-0.6
Total	2	114	276	32	61	17	5	1	12	33	24	.221	.306	.330	84	-5	5			.941	-1	/O-66	-1.1

■ PAT CALLAHAN
Callahan, Patrick Henry b: 10/15/1866, Cleveland, Ohio d: 2/4/40, Louisville, Ky. Deb: 5/1/1884

YEAR	TM/L	G	AB	R	H	2B	3B	HR	RBI	BB	SO	AVG	OBP	SLG	PRO+	BR/A	SB	CS	SBR	FA	FR	G/POS	TPR
1884	Ind-a	61	258	38	67	8	5	2		8		.260	.282	.353	109	2				.812	-7	3-61	-0.4

■ WESLEY CALLAHAN
Callahan, Wesley Leroy b: 7/3/1888, Lyons, Ind. d: 9/13/53, Dayton, Ohio BR/TR, 5'7.5", 155 lbs. Deb: 9/7/13

YEAR	TM/L	G	AB	R	H	2B	3B	HR	RBI	BB	SO	AVG	OBP	SLG	PRO+	BR/A	SB	CS	SBR	FA	FR	G/POS	TPR
1913	StL-N	7	14	0	4	0	0	0	1	2	2	.286	.375	.286	91	-0	1			.920	1	/S-6	0.1

■ FRANK CALLAWAY
Callaway, Frank Burnett b: 2/26/1898, Knoxville, Tenn. d: 8/21/87, Knoxville, Tenn. BR/TR, 6', 170 lbs. Deb: 9/17/21

YEAR	TM/L	G	AB	R	H	2B	3B	HR	RBI	BB	SO	AVG	OBP	SLG	PRO+	BR/A	SB	CS	SBR	FA	FR	G/POS	TPR
1921	Phi-A	14	50	7	12	1	1	0	2	2	11	.240	.283	.300	49	-4	1	0	0	.878	-5	S-14	-0.7
1922	Phi-A	29	48	5	13	0	2	0	4	0	13	.271	.271	.354	60	-3	0	0	0	.880	1	2-11/3-5,S	-0.1
Total	2	43	98	12	25	1	3	0	8	2	24	.255	.277	.327	54	-7	1	0	0	.889	-4	/S-18,2-11,3	-0.8

■ JOHNNY CALLISON
Callison, John Wesley b: 3/12/39, Qualls, Okla. BL/TR, 5'10", 175 lbs. Deb: 9/9/58

YEAR	TM/L	G	AB	R	H	2B	3B	HR	RBI	BB	SO	AVG	OBP	SLG	PRO+	BR/A	SB	CS	SBR	FA	FR	G/POS	TPR
1958	Chi-A	18	64	10	19	4	2	1	12	6	14	.297	.357	.469	128	2	1	0	0	.976	3	O-18	0.4
1959	Chi-A	49	104	12	18	3	0	3	12	13	20	.173	.271	.288	54	-7	0	1	-1	.983	-3	O-41	-1.2
1960	Phi-N	99	288	36	75	11	5	9	30	45	70	.260	.360	.427	114	7	0	4	-2	.989	1	O-86	0.1
1961	Phi-N	138	455	74	121	20	11	9	47	69	76	.266	.366	.418	109	7	10	4	1	.967	5	*O-124	0.6
1962	Phi-N★	157	603	107	181	26	**10**	23	83	54	96	.300	.353	.491	131	25	10	3	1	.980	23	*O-152	3.9
1963	Phi-N	157	626	96	178	36	11	26	78	50	111	.284	.339	.502	140	31	8	3	1	.994	23	*O-157	4.8
1964	Phi-N★	162	654	101	179	30	10	31	104	36	95	.274	.318	.492	126	20	6	3	0	.988	19	*O-162	3.3
1965	Phi-N☆	160	619	93	162	25	**16**	32	101	57	117	.262	.330	.509	135	26	6	5	-1	.982	19	*O-159	3.8
1966	Phi-N	155	612	93	169	**40**	7	11	55	56	83	.276	.340	.418	109	8	8	8	-2	.990	8	*O-154	0.4
1967	Phi-N	149	556	62	145	30	5	14	64	55	63	.261	.331	.408	109	7	6	12	-5	.977	9	*O-147	0.5
1968	Phi-N	121	398	46	97	18	4	14	40	42	70	.244	.321	.415	119	9	4	3	-1	**1.000**	2	*O-109	0.6
1969	Phi-N	134	495	66	131	29	5	16	64	49	73	.265	.335	.440	119	11	5	2	1	.990	16	*O-129	2.0
1970	Chi-N	147	477	65	126	23	2	19	68	60	63	.264	.350	.440	98	-2	7	2	1	.973	-0	*O-144	-0.8
1971	Chi-N	103	290	27	61	12	2	8	38	36	55	.210	.302	.341	71	-11	2	1	0	.982	-3	O-89	-1.9
1972	NY-A	92	275	28	71	10	0	9	34	18	34	.258	.304	.393	110	2	3	0	1	.992	-3	O-74	-0.3

YEAR	TM/L	G	AB	R	H	2B	3B	HR	RBI	BB	SO	AVG	OBP	SLG	PRO+	BR/A	SB	CS	SBR	FA	FR	G/POS	TPR
1973	NY-A	45	136	10	24	4	0	1	10	4	24	.176	.200	.228	21	-14	1	1	-0	.960	-2	O-32,D-10	-1.9
Total	16	1886	6652	926	1757	321	89	226	840	650	1064	.264	.333	.441	114	121	74	51	-8	.984	113	*O-1777/D-10	14.1

■ JACK CALVO
Calvo, Jacinto (Gonzalez) (Born Jacinto Del Calvo) b: 6/11/1894, Havana, Cuba d: 6/15/65, Miami, Fla. BL/TL, 5'10", 156 lbs. Deb: 5/9/13

YEAR	TM/L	G	AB	R	H	2B	3B	HR	RBI	BB	SO	AVG	OBP	SLG	PRO+	BR/A	SB	CS	SBR	FA	FR	G/POS	TPR
1913	Was-A	17	33	5	8	0	0	1	2	1	4	.242	.265	.333	73	-1	0			.900	-2	O-13	-0.4
1920	Was-A	17	23	5	1	0	1	0	2	2	2	.043	.120	.130	-35	-5	0	0	0	1.000	-4	O-10	-0.9
Total	2	34	56	10	9	0	1	1	4	3	6	.161	.203	.250	27	-6	0	0		.938	-6	/O-23	-1.3

■ HANK CAMELLI
Camelli, Henry Richard b: 12/12/14, Gloucester, Mass. BR/TR, 5'11", 190 lbs. Deb: 10/3/43

YEAR	TM/L	G	AB	R	H	2B	3B	HR	RBI	BB	SO	AVG	OBP	SLG	PRO+	BR/A	SB	CS	SBR	FA	FR	G/POS	TPR
1943	Pit-N	1	3	1	0	0	0	0	1	0	1	.000	.250	.000	-24	-0	0			1.000	0	/C-1	0.0
1944	Pit-N	63	125	14	37	5	1	1	10	18	12	.296	.385	.376	110	-0	0			.959	4	C-61	0.8
1945	Pit-N	1	2	0	0	0	0	0	0	1	0	.000	.333	.000	-3	-0	0			1.000	-0	/C-1	0.0
1946	Pit-N	42	96	8	20	2	2	0	5	8	9	.208	.269	.271	52	-6	0			.971	4	C-39	-0.1
1947	Bos-N	52	150	10	29	8	1	1	11	18	18	.193	.280	.280	50	-11	0			.977	6	C-51	-0.2
Total	5	159	376	33	86	15	4	2	26	46	39	.229	.313	.306	70	-15	0			.970	14	C-153	0.5

■ JACK CAMERON
Cameron, John William "Happy Jack" b: 9/1884, Nova Scotia, Can. d: 8/17/51, Boston, Mass. Deb: 9/13/06

YEAR	TM/L	G	AB	R	H	2B	3B	HR	RBI	BB	SO	AVG	OBP	SLG	PRO+	BR/A	SB	CS	SBR	FA	FR	G/POS	TPR
1906	Bos-N	18	61	3	11	0	0	0	4	2		.180	.206	.180	21	-6	0			.852	-1	O-16/P-2	-0.8

■ DOLPH CAMILLI
Camilli, Adolph Louis b: 4/23/07, San Francisco, Cal BL/TL, 5'10", 185 lbs. Deb: 9/9/33 F

YEAR	TM/L	G	AB	R	H	2B	3B	HR	RBI	BB	SO	AVG	OBP	SLG	PRO+	BR/A	SB	CS	SBR	FA	FR	G/POS	TPR
1933	Chi-N	16	58	8	13	2	1	2	7	4	11	.224	.274	.397	90	-1	3			.994	2	1-16	-0.1
1934	Chi-N	32	120	17	33	8	0	4	19	5	25	.275	.315	.442	102	-0	1			.988	2	1-32	-0.1
	Phi-N	102	378	52	100	20	3	12	68	48	69	.265	.350	.429	95	-3	3			.985	-4	*1-102	-1.5
	Yr	134	498	69	133	28	3	16	87	53	94	.267	.342	.432	96	-3	4			.986	-2	*1-134	-1.6
1935	Phi-N	156	602	88	157	23	5	25	83	65	113	.261	.336	.440	97	-4	9			.987	-1	*1-156	-2.2
1936	Phi-N	151	530	106	167	29	13	28	102	116	84	.315	.441	.577	156	45	5			.988	-10	*1-150	2.0
1937	Phi-N	131	475	101	161	23	7	27	80	90	82	.339	**.446**	.587	165	45	6			**.994**	4	*1-131	3.4
1938	Bro-N	146	509	106	128	25	11	24	100	**119**	101	.251	.393	.485	137	29	6			.995	-1	*1-145	1.2
1939	Bro-N★	157	565	105	164	30	12	26	104	**110**	107	.290	.409	.524	144	38	1			.990	10	*1-157	3.0
1940	Bro-N	142	512	92	147	29	13	23	96	89	83	.287	.397	.529	144	32	9			.992	-4	*1-140	1.5
1941	*Bro-N†	149	529	92	151	29	6	**34**	**120**	104	115	.285	.407	.556	162	**45**	3			.989	3	*1-148	3.7
1942	Bro-N	150	524	89	132	23	7	26	109	97	85	.252	.372	.471	144	30	10			.992	-1	*1-150	2.2
1943	Bro-N	95	353	56	87	15	6	6	43	65	48	.246	.365	.374	113	8	2			.992	-1	1-95	0.2
1945	Bos-A	63	198	24	42	5	2	2	19	35	38	.212	.330	.288	78	-4	2	0	1	.991	2	1-54	-0.6
Total	12	1490	5353	936	1482	261	86	239	950	947	961	.277	.388	.492	134	260	60	0		.990	2	*1-1476	12.7

■ DOUG CAMILLI
Camilli, Douglas Joseph b: 9/22/36, Philadelphia, Pa. BR/TR, 5'11", 195 lbs. Deb: 9/25/60 FC

YEAR	TM/L	G	AB	R	H	2B	3B	HR	RBI	BB	SO	AVG	OBP	SLG	PRO+	BR/A	SB	CS	SBR	FA	FR	G/POS	TPR
1960	LA-N	6	24	4	8	2	0	1	3	1	4	.333	.385	.542	141	1	0	0	0	.980	0	/C-6	0.2
1961	LA-N	13	30	3	4	0	0	3	4	1	9	.133	.161	.433	47	-2	0	0	0	.986	2	C-12	0.0
1962	LA-N	45	88	16	25	5	2	4	22	12	21	.284	.370	.523	145	5	0	0	0	.983	-5	C-39	0.1
1963	LA-N	49	117	9	19	1	1	3	10	11	22	.162	.234	.265	47	-8	0	0	0	.977	4	C-47	0.1
1964	LA-N	50	123	1	22	3	0	0	10	8	19	.179	.229	.203	25	-12	0	0	0	.990	8	C-46	-0.2
1965	Was-A	75	193	13	37	6	1	3	18	16	34	.192	.257	.280	53	-12	0	0	0	.980	1	C-59	-0.9
1966	Was-A	44	107	5	22	4	0	2	8	3	19	.206	.234	.299	53	-7	0	0	0	.990	4	C-39	-0.1
1967	Was-A	30	82	5	15	1	0	2	5	4	16	.183	.221	.268	46	-6	0	0	0	.993	1	C-24	-0.5
1969	Was-A	1	3	0	1	0	0	0	0	0	2	.333	.333	.333	92	-0	0	0	0	1.000	-0	/C-1	0.0
Total	9	313	767	56	153	22	4	18	80	56	146	.199	.257	.309	61	-41	0	0	0	.984	19	C-273	-1.3

■ LOU CAMILLI
Camilli, Louis Steven b: 9/24/46, ElPaso, Tex. BB/TR, 5'10", 170 lbs. Deb: 8/9/69

YEAR	TM/L	G	AB	R	H	2B	3B	HR	RBI	BB	SO	AVG	OBP	SLG	PRO+	BR/A	SB	CS	SBR	FA	FR	G/POS	TPR
1969	Cle-A	13	14	0	0	0	0	0	0	3	3	.000	.000	.000	-97	-4	0	0	0	1.000	3	3-13	0.0
1970	Cle-A	16	15	0	0	0	0	0	0	2	2	.000	.118	.000	-62	-3	0	0	0	1.000	-1	/S-3,2-2,3	-0.4
1971	Cle-A	39	81	5	16	2	0	0	8	8	10	.198	.270	.222	37	-6	0	0	0	.938	1	S-23,2-16	-0.4
1972	Cle-A	39	41	2	6	2	0	0	3	3	8	.146	.205	.195	19	-4	0	0	0	1.000	-2	/S-8,2-2	-0.6
Total	4	107	151	7	22	4	0	0	3	13	23	.146	.213	.172	11	-18	0	0	0	.951	1	/S-34,2-20,3	-1.4

■ KEN CAMINITI
Caminiti, Kenneth Gene b: 4/21/63, Hanford, Cal. BB/TR, 6', 200 lbs. Deb: 7/16/87

YEAR	TM/L	G	AB	R	H	2B	3B	HR	RBI	BB	SO	AVG	OBP	SLG	PRO+	BR/A	SB	CS	SBR	FA	FR	G/POS	TPR
1987	Hou-N	63	203	10	50	7	1	3	23	12	44	.246	.288	.335	67	-10	0			.949	3	3-61	-0.7
1988	Hou-N	30	83	5	15	2	0	1	7	5	18	.181	.227	.241	36	-7	0	0	0	.948	0	3-28	-0.8
1989	Hou-N	161	585	71	149	31	3	10	72	51	93	.255	.318	.369	99	-1	4	1	0	.954	13	*3-160	1.4
1990	Hou-N	153	541	52	131	20	2	4	51	48	97	.242	.304	.309	71	-21	9	4	0	.945	-11	*3-149	-3.2
1991	Hou-N	152	574	65	145	30	3	13	80	46	85	.253	.314	.383	101	-1	4	5	-2	.948	3	*3-152	0.6
1992	Hou-N	135	506	68	149	31	2	13	62	44	68	.294	.352	.441	129	18	10	4	1	.966	-9	*3-129	1.0
1993	Hou-N	143	543	75	142	31	0	13	75	49	88	.262	.323	.390	93	-6	8	5	-1	.942	5	*3-143	-0.1
1994	Hou-N★	111	406	63	115	28	2	18	75	43	71	.283	.355	.495	121	12	4	3	-1	**.969**	2	*3-108	1.3
Total	8	948	3441	409	896	180	13	75	445	298	564	.260	.321	.386	98	-16	39	22	-2	.952	11	3-930	-0.5

■ HOWIE CAMP
Camp, Howard Lee "Red" b: 7/1/1893, Munford, Ala. d: 5/8/60, Eastaboga, Ala. BL/TR, 5'9", 169 lbs. Deb: 9/19/17

YEAR	TM/L	G	AB	R	H	2B	3B	HR	RBI	BB	SO	AVG	OBP	SLG	PRO+	BR/A	SB	CS	SBR	FA	FR	G/POS	TPR
1917	NY-A	5	21	3	6	1	0	0	1	0	2	.286	.318	.333	98	-0	0			.857	1	/O-5	0.0

■ LEW CAMP
Camp, Llewellyn Robert b: 2/22/1868, Columbus, Ohio d: 10/1/48, Omaha, Neb. BL/TR, 6', 175 lbs. Deb: 8/26/1892 F

YEAR	TM/L	G	AB	R	H	2B	3B	HR	RBI	BB	SO	AVG	OBP	SLG	PRO+	BR/A	SB	CS	SBR	FA	FR	G/POS	TPR
1892	StL-N	42	145	19	30	3	1	2	13	17	27	.207	.294	.283	79	-3	12			.780	-16	3-39/O-3	-1.7
1893	Chi-N	38	156	37	41	7	7	2	17	19	19	.263	.347	.436	109	1	30			.847	-10	3-16,O-11/2S	-0.7
1894	Chi-N	8	33	1	6	2	0	0	1	1	6	.182	.206	.242	7	-5	0			.830	-3	/2-8	-0.6
Total	3	88	334	57	77	12	8	4	31	37	52	.231	.311	.350	85	-7	42			.801	-28	/3-55,2-17,OS	-3.0

■ ROY CAMPANELLA
Campanella, Roy b: 11/19/21, Philadelphia, Pa. d: 6/26/93, Woodland Hills, Cal. BR/TR, 5'8", 200 lbs. Deb: 4/20/48 H

YEAR	TM/L	G	AB	R	H	2B	3B	HR	RBI	BB	SO	AVG	OBP	SLG	PRO+	BR/A	SB	CS	SBR	FA	FR	G/POS	TPR
1948	Bro-N	83	279	32	72	11	3	9	45	36	45	.258	.345	.416	102	1	3			.981	10	C-78	1.6
1949	*Bro-N★	130	436	65	125	22	2	22	82	67	36	.287	.385	.498	130	19	3			.985	5	*C-127	3.0
1950	Bro-N★	126	437	70	123	19	3	31	89	55	51	.281	.364	.551	134	21	1			.985	-4	*C-123	2.1
1951	Bro-N★	143	505	90	164	33	1	33	108	53	51	.325	.393	.590	158	40	1	2	-1	.986	9	*C-140	5.2
1952	*Bro-N★	128	468	73	126	18	1	22	97	57	59	.269	.352	.453	120	13	8	4	0	**.994**	-7	*C-122	1.3
1953	*Bro-N★	144	519	103	162	26	3	41	**142**	67	58	.312	.395	.611	154	40	4	2	0	.989	3	*C-140	4.7
1954	Bro-N★	111	397	43	82	14	3	19	51	42	49	.207	.286	.401	74	-17	1	4	-2	.989	3	*C-111	-1.6
1955	*Bro-N†	123	446	81	142	20	1	32	107	56	41	.318	.402	.583	153	34	2	3	-1	.992	1	*C-121	3.8
1956	*Bro-N★	124	388	39	85	6	1	20	73	66	61	.219	.334	.394	88	-6	1	0	0	.985	3	*C-121	0.3
1957	Bro-N	103	330	31	80	9	0	13	62	34	50	.242	.321	.388	81	-9	1	0	0	**.993**	16	*C-100	1.2
Total	10	1215	4205	627	1161	178	18	242	856	533	501	.276	.362	.500	123	136	25	15		.988	33	*C-1183	21.6

■ BERT CAMPANERIS
Campaneris, Dagoberto (Blanco) "Campy" (b: Dagoberto Campaneria (Blanco))
b: 3/9/42, Pueblo Nuevo, Cuba BR/TR, 5'10", 160 lbs. Deb: 7/23/64

YEAR	TM/L	G	AB	R	H	2B	3B	HR	RBI	BB	SO	AVG	OBP	SLG	PRO+	BR/A	SB	CS	SBR	FA	FR	G/POS	TPR
1964	KC-A	67	269	27	69	14	3	4	22	15	41	.257	.306	.375	86	-5	10	2	2	.981	-6	S-38,O-27/3	-0.9
1965	KC-A	144	578	67	156	23	**12**	6	42	41	75	.270	.328	.384	103	2	**51**	19	-4	.938	-14	*S-109,O-39/PC123	-0.3
1966	KC-A	142	573	82	153	29	10	5	42	25	72	.267	.303	.379	98	-3	**52**	16	10	.971	-17	*S-138	0.3
1967	KC-A	147	601	85	149	29	3	3	32	36	82	.248	.298	.331	89	-9	**55**	16	7	.954	-19	*S-145	-0.8
1968	Oak-A★	159	642	87	**177**	25	9	4	38	50	69	.276	.332	.361	116	11	**62**	22	5	.956	1	*S-155/O-3	3.8

YEAR	TM/L	G	AB	R	H	2B	3B	HR	RBI	BB	SO	AVG	OBP	SLG	PRO+	BR/A	SB	CS	SBR	FA	FR	G/POS	TPR
1969	Oak-A	135	547	71	142	15	2	2	25	30	62	.260	.303	.305	74	-20	62	8	**14**	.967	-5	*S-125	0.2
1970	Oak-A	147	603	97	168	28	4	22	64	36	73	.279	.323	.448	115	9	**42**	10	7	.973	-10	*S-143	2.4
1971	*Oak-A	134	569	80	143	18	4	5	47	29	64	.251	.290	.323	75	-20	34	7	6	.960	-5	*S-133	-0.1
1972	*Oak-A☆	149	625	85	150	25	2	8	32	32	88	.240	.279	.325	84	-15	**52**	14	7	.977	7	*S-148	2.3
1973	*Oak-A★	151	601	89	150	17	6	4	46	50	79	.250	.311	.318	82	-14	34	10	4	.969	-7	*S-149	0.2
1974	*Oak-A★	134	527	77	153	18	8	2	41	47	81	.290	.348	.366	113	9	34	15	1	.966	-9	*S-133/D-1	1.9
1975	*Oak-A★	137	509	69	135	15	3	4	46	50	71	.265	.339	.330	92	-4	24	12	0	.962	-31	*S-137	-2.1
1976	Oak-A	149	536	67	137	14	1	1	52	63	80	.256	.337	.291	89	-5	54	12	**9**	.969	-6	*S-149	1.6
1977	Tex-A★	150	552	77	140	19	7	5	46	47	86	.254	.317	.341	78	-16	27	20	-4	.968	18	*S-149	1.4
1978	Tex-A	98	269	30	50	5	3	1	17	20	36	.186	.247	.238	37	-22	22	4	4	.954	4	S-89/D-4	-0.4
1979	Tex-A	8	9	2	1	0	0	0	0	1	3	.111	.200	.111	-14	-1	1	0	0	.962	4	/S-8	0.3
	*Cal-A	85	239	27	56	4	4	0	15	19	32	.234	.296	.285	59	-13	12	4	1	.957	4	S-82	0.0
	Yr	93	248	29	57	4	4	0	15	20	35	.230	.293	.278	57	-15	13	4	2	.957	7	S-90	0.3
1980	Cal-A	77	210	32	53	8	1	2	18	14	33	.252	.302	.329	75	-7	10	5	0	.957	-5	S-64/2-1,D	-0.6
1981	Cal-A	55	82	11	21	2	1	1	10	5	10	.256	.299	.341	84	-2	5	2	0	.900	-2	3-45/S-3,2	-0.4
1983	NY-A	60	143	19	46	5	0	0	11	8	9	.322	.358	.357	101	5	6	7	-2	.964	-3	2-32,3-24	-0.4
Total	19	2328	8684	1181	2249	313	86	79	646	618	1142	.259	.313	.342	89	-127	649	199	75	.964	-102	*S-2097/3-76,02D1CP	8.4

■ AL CAMPANIS
Campanis, Alexander Sebastian (b: Alessandro Campani)   b: 11/2/16, Kos, Dodecanese Islands   BB/TR, 6′, 185 lbs.   Deb: 9/23/43   F

YEAR	TM/L	G	AB	R	H	2B	3B	HR	RBI	BB	SO	AVG	OBP	SLG	PRO+	BR/A	SB	CS	SBR	FA	FR	G/POS	TPR
1943	Bro-N	7	20	3	2	0	0	0	0	4	5	.100	.250	.100	3	-2	0			1.000	4	/2-7	0.2

■ JIM CAMPANIS
Campanis, James Alexander   b: 2/9/44, New York, N.Y.   BR/TR, 6′, 195 lbs.   Deb: 9/20/66   F

YEAR	TM/L	G	AB	R	H	2B	3B	HR	RBI	BB	SO	AVG	OBP	SLG	PRO+	BR/A	SB	CS	SBR	FA	FR	G/POS	TPR
1966	LA-N	1	1	0	0	0	0	0	0	0	0	.000	.000	.000	-99	-0	0	0	0	1.000	0	/C-1	0.0
1967	LA-N	41	62	3	10	1	0	2	9	1	14	.161	.268	.274	60	-3	0	0	0	.990	-0	C-23	-0.3
1968	LA-N	4	11	0	1	0	0	0	0	1	2	.091	.167	.091	-23	-2	0	0	0	.960	1	/C-4	0.0
1969	KC-A	30	83	4	13	5	0	0	5	5	19	.157	.205	.217	18	-9	0	0	0	.982	3	C-26	-0.5
1970	KC-A	31	54	6	7	0	0	2	2	4	14	.130	.203	.241	22	-6	0	0	0	.986	1	C-13/O-1	-0.5
1973	Pit-N	6	6	0	1	0	0	0	0	0	0	.167	.167	.167	-8	-1	0	0	0	.000	0	H	-0.1
Total	6	113	217	13	32	6	0	4	9	19	49	.147	.219	.230	27	-21	0	0	0	.983	5	/C-67,O-1	-1.4

■ COUNT CAMPAU
Campau, Charles Columbus   b: 10/17/1863, Detroit, Mich.   d: 4/3/38, New Orleans, La.   BL/TR, 5′11″, 160 lbs.   Deb: 7/7/1888   M

YEAR	TM/L	G	AB	R	H	2B	3B	HR	RBI	BB	SO	AVG	OBP	SLG	PRO+	BR/A	SB	CS	SBR	FA	FR	G/POS	TPR
1888	Det-N	70	251	28	51	5	3	1	18	19	36	.203	.259	.259	66	-9	27			.933	-4	O-70	-1.5
1890	StL-a	75	314	68	101	9	12	**9**		26		.322	.374	.513	141	12	36			.934	3	O-74/3-1,1M	1.1
1894	Was-N	2	7	1	1	0	0	0	1	1	4	.143	.250	.143	-3	-1	0			1.000	-0	/O-2	-0.1
Total	3	147	572	97	153	14	15	10	18	46	40	.267	.322	.397	109	1	63			.934	-1	O-146/1-1,3	-0.5

■ VIN CAMPBELL
Campbell, Arthur Vincent   b: 1/30/1888, St.Louis, Mo.   d: 11/16/69, Towson, Md.   BL/TR, 6′, 185 lbs.   Deb: 6/6/08

YEAR	TM/L	G	AB	R	H	2B	3B	HR	RBI	BB	SO	AVG	OBP	SLG	PRO+	BR/A	SB	CS	SBR	FA	FR	G/POS	TPR
1908	Chi-N	1	1	0	0	0	0	0	0	0	0	.000	.000	.000	-96	-0	0			.000	0	H	0.0
1910	Pit-N	97	282	42	92	9	5	4	21	26	23	.326	.391	.436	133	12	17			.895	-4	O-74	0.4
1911	Pit-N	42	93	12	29	3	1	0	10	8	7	.312	.366	.366	101	0	6			.923	-3	O-21	-0.3
1912	Bos-N	145	624	102	185	32	9	3	48	32	44	.296	.334	.391	96	-5	19			.938	5	*O-144	-1.2
1914	Ind-F	134	544	92	173	23	11	7	44	37	47	.318	.368	.439	98	-2	26			.925	-6	*O-132	-1.4
1915	New-F	127	525	78	163	18	10	1	44	29	35	.310	.352	.389	104	1	24			.947	-5	*O-126	-1.0
Total	6	546	2069	326	642	85	36	15	167	132	156	.310	.357	.408	104	6	92			.929	-17	O-497	-3.5

■ BRUCE CAMPBELL
Campbell, Bruce Douglas   b: 10/20/09, Chicago, Ill.   BL/TR, 6′1″, 185 lbs.   Deb: 9/12/30

YEAR	TM/L	G	AB	R	H	2B	3B	HR	RBI	BB	SO	AVG	OBP	SLG	PRO+	BR/A	SB	CS	SBR	FA	FR	G/POS	TPR
1930	Chi-A	5	10	4	5	1	1	0	5	1	2	.500	.545	.800	245	2	0	0	0	1.000	-0	/O-4	0.2
1931	Chi-A	4	17	4	7	2	0	2	5	0	4	.412	.444	.882	256	2	0	0	0	.900	-0	/O-4	0.3
1932	Chi-A	7	18	3	4	1	0	0	2	0	2	.222	.222	.278	31	-2	0	1	-1	1.000	-1	/O-4	-0.3
	StL-A	139	593	83	169	35	11	14	85	40	102	.285	.336	.452	97	-5	7	5	-1	.935	6	*O-139	-0.8
	Yr	146	611	86	173	36	11	14	87	40	104	.283	.333	.447	95	-6	7	6	-2	.935	5	*O-143	-1.1
1933	StL-A	148	567	87	157	38	8	16	106	69	77	.277	.357	.457	108	5	10	4	1	.950	-1	*O-144	-0.3
1934	StL-A	138	481	62	134	25	6	9	74	51	64	.279	.350	.412	88	-9	4	4	-1	.935	3	*O-123	-1.1
1935	Cle-A	80	308	56	100	26	3	7	54	31	33	.325	.390	.497	126	11	2	1	0	.992	-5	O-75	0.3
1936	Cle-A	76	172	35	64	15	2	6	30	19	17	.372	.440	.587	150	14	2	1	0	.960	-4	O-47	0.7
1937	Cle-A	134	448	82	135	42	11	4	61	67	49	.301	.392	.471	116	12	4	5	-2	.978	-2	*O-123	0.4
1938	Cle-A	133	511	90	148	27	12	12	72	53	57	.290	.360	.460	106	3	11	7	-1	.967	-0	*O-132	-0.1
1939	Cle-A	130	450	84	129	23	13	8	72	67	48	.287	.383	.449	116	12	7	6	-2	.942	-3	*O-115	0.3
1940	*Det-A	103	297	56	84	15	5	8	44	45	28	.283	.381	.448	104	2	7	4	-2	.959	-2	O-74	-0.7
1941	Det-A	141	512	72	141	28	10	15	93	68	67	.275	.364	.457	105	3	3	3	-1	.976	-8	*O-133	-1.3
1942	Was-A	122	378	41	105	17	5	5	63	37	34	.278	.344	.389	107	3	0	6	-4	.955	-1	O-87	-0.6
Total	13	1360	4762	759	1382	295	87	106	766	548	584	.290	.367	.455	108	55	53	50	-14	.956	-19	*O-1194	-3.0

■ SOUP CAMPBELL
Campbell, Clarence   b: 3/7/15, Sparta, Va.   BL/TR, 6′1″, 188 lbs.   Deb: 4/21/40

YEAR	TM/L	G	AB	R	H	2B	3B	HR	RBI	BB	SO	AVG	OBP	SLG	PRO+	BR/A	SB	CS	SBR	FA	FR	G/POS	TPR
1940	Cle-A	35	62	8	14	1	0	0	2	7	12	.226	.304	.242	45	-5	0	0	0	1.000	-2	O-16	-0.7
1941	Cle-A	104	328	36	82	10	4	3	35	31	21	.250	.317	.332	75	-12	1	9	-5	.981	2	O-78	-1.9
Total	2	139	390	44	96	11	4	3	37	38	33	.246	.315	.318	70	-17	1	9	-5	.984	0	/O-94	-2.6

■ DAVE CAMPBELL
Campbell, David Wilson   b: 1/14/42, Manistee, Mich.   BR/TR, 6′, 185 lbs.   Deb: 9/17/67

YEAR	TM/L	G	AB	R	H	2B	3B	HR	RBI	BB	SO	AVG	OBP	SLG	PRO+	BR/A	SB	CS	SBR	FA	FR	G/POS	TPR
1967	Det-A	2	2	0	0	0	0	0	0	0	1	.000	.000	.000	-97	-0	0	0	0	.500	-0	/1-1	-0.1
1968	Det-A	9	8	1	1	0	0	1	2	1	3	.125	.222	.500	111	0	0	0	0	1.000	0	/2-5	0.1
1969	Det-A	32	39	4	4	1	0	0	2	4	15	.103	.205	.128	-5	-5	0	1	-1	.967	-2	1-13/2-5,3	-0.8
1970	SD-N	154	581	71	127	28	2	12	40	40	115	.219	.270	.336	64	-32	18	6	2	.974	12	*2-153	-0.6
1971	SD-N	108	365	38	83	14	2	9	29	37	75	.227	.299	.334	85	-4	8	6	-1	.968	-2	2-69,3-40/S10	-0.6
1972	SD-N	33	100	6	24	5	0	0	3	11	12	.240	.315	.290	79	-3	0	4	-2	.988	4	3-31/2-1	-0.1
1973	SD-N	33	98	2	22	0	0	8	7	15	.224	.276	.255	52	-6	1	1	-0	.979	-1	2-27/1-3,3	-0.7
	StL-N	13	21	1	0	0	0	0	1	1	6	.000	.045	.000	-87	-6	0	0	0	.933	-3	/2-6	-0.8
	Hou-N	9	15	1	4	0	0	0	1	1	4	.267	.267	.400	83	-0	0	0	0	1.000	2	/3-5,1-2,O	0.1
	Yr	55	134	4	26	0	0	9	11	8	25	.194	.239	.231	33	-12	1	1	-0	.975	-2	2-33/3-7,1O	-1.4
1974	Hou-N	35	23	4	2	1	0	0	1	1	6	.087	.125	.130	-30	-4	1	0	0	.895	6	/2-9,1-6,3O	0.2
Total	8	428	1252	128	267	54	4	20	89	102	254	.213	.274	.311	64	-64	29	18	-2	.971	16	2-275/3-81,1OS	-3.3

■ JIM CAMPBELL
Campbell, James Robert   b: 6/24/37, Palo Alto, Cal.   BR/TR, 6′, 190 lbs.   Deb: 7/17/62

YEAR	TM/L	G	AB	R	H	2B	3B	HR	RBI	BB	SO	AVG	OBP	SLG	PRO+	BR/A	SB	CS	SBR	FA	FR	G/POS	TPR
1962	Hou-N	27	86	6	19	4	0	6	6	6	23	.221	.272	.372	77	-3	0	0	0	.970	6	C-25	0.4
1963	Hou-N	55	158	9	35	3	0	4	19	10	40	.222	.268	.316	72	-6	0	0	0	.979	-2	C-42	-0.7
Total	2	82	244	15	54	7	0	4	25	16	63	.221	.269	.336	74	-9	0	0	0	.975	4	/C-67	-0.3

■ JIM CAMPBELL
Campbell, James Robert   b: 1/10/43, Hartsville, S.C.   BL/TR, 6′, 205 lbs.   Deb: 4/11/70

YEAR	TM/L	G	AB	R	H	2B	3B	HR	RBI	BB	SO	AVG	OBP	SLG	PRO+	BR/A	SB	CS	SBR	FA	FR	G/POS	TPR
1970	StL-N	13	13	0	3	0	0	0	1	0	3	.231	.231	.231	24	-1	0	0	0	.000	0	H	-0.1

■ JOE CAMPBELL
Campbell, Joseph Earl   b: 3/10/44, Louisville, Ky.   BR/TR, 6′1″, 175 lbs.   Deb: 5/3/67

YEAR	TM/L	G	AB	R	H	2B	3B	HR	RBI	BB	SO	AVG	OBP	SLG	PRO+	BR/A	SB	CS	SBR	FA	FR	G/POS	TPR
1967	Chi-N	1	3	0	0	0	0	0	0	0	3	.000	.000	.000	-96	-1	0	0	0	.000	-0	/O-1	-0.1

■ MARC CAMPBELL
Campbell, Marc Thaddeus   b: 11/29/1884, Punxsutawney, Pa.   d: 2/13/46, New Bethlehem, Pa.   BL/TR, 5′10″, 155 lbs.   Deb: 9/30/07

YEAR	TM/L	G	AB	R	H	2B	3B	HR	RBI	BB	SO	AVG	OBP	SLG	PRO+	BR/A	SB	CS	SBR	FA	FR	G/POS	TPR
1907	Pit-N	2	4	0	1	0	0	0	1	1	1	.250	.400	.250	102	0	0			.889	0	/S-2	0.0

YEAR	TM/L	G	AB	R	H	2B	3B	HR	RBI	BB	SO	AVG	OBP	SLG	PRO+	BR/A	SB	CS	SBR	FA	FR	G/POS	TPR

■ MAT CAMPBELL
Campbell, Mathew   b: New Jersey   Deb: 4/28/1873   F

| 1873 | Res-n | 21 | 82 | 9 | 12 | 0 | 0 | 0 | 3 | 3 | 6 | .146 | .176 | .146 | -4 | -10 | | | | | | 1-18/S-3,O | -0.6 |

■ PAUL CAMPBELL
Campbell, Paul McLaughlin   b: 9/1/17, Paw Creek, N.C.   BL/TL, 5'10", 185 lbs.   Deb: 4/15/41

1941	Bos-A	1	0	0	0	0	0	0	0	0	0	—	—	—		0	0	0	0	.000	0	R	0.0
1942	Bos-A	26	15	4	1	0	0	0	0	1	5	.067	.125	.067	-44	-3	1	0	0	1.000	-2	/O-4	-0.5
1946	*Bos-A	28	26	3	3	1	0	0	0	2	7	.115	.179	.154	-6	-4	0	0	0	1.000	-0	/1-5	-0.4
1948	Det-A	59	83	15	22	1	1	1	11	1	10	.265	.274	.337	60	-5	0	0	0	.969	-3	1-27	-0.2
1949	Det-A	87	255	38	71	15	4	3	30	24	32	.278	.343	.404	97	-2	3	3	-1	.988	-3	1-74	-0.6
1950	Det-A	3	1	1	0	0	0	0	0	0	0	.000	.000	.000	-97	-0	0	0	0	.000	0	H	0.0
Total	6	204	380	61	97	17	5	4	41	28	54	.255	.308	.358	76	-14	4	3	-1	.984	-2	1-106/O-4	-1.7

■ RON CAMPBELL
Campbell, Ronald Thomas   b: 4/5/40, Chattanooga, Tenn.   BR/TR, 6'1", 180 lbs.   Deb: 9/1/64

1964	Chi-N	26	92	7	25	6	1	1	10	1	21	.272	.280	.391	83	-2	0	1	-1	.941	14	2-26	1.3
1965	Chi-N	2	0	0	0	0	0	0	0	0	0	.000	.000	.000	-98	-1	0	0	0	.000	0	H	-0.1
1966	Chi-N	24	60	4	13	1	0	0	4	6	5	.217	.288	.233	46	-4	1	1	-0	.980	4	S-11/3-7	0.0
Total	3	52	154	11	38	7	1	1	14	7	26	.247	.280	.325	67	-7	1	2	-1	.941	18	/2-26,S-11,3	1.2

■ SAM CAMPBELL
Campbell, Samuel   b: Philadelphia, Pa.   Deb: 10/11/1890

| 1890 | Phi-a | 2 | 5 | 0 | 0 | 0 | 0 | 0 | | 1 | | .000 | .167 | .000 | -52 | -1 | 0 | | | .833 | -2 | /2-2 | -0.3 |

■ GILLY CAMPBELL
Campbell, William Gilthorpe   b: 2/13/08, Kansas City, Kan.   d: 2/21/73, Los Angeles, Cal.   BL/TR, 5'7.5", 182 lbs.   Deb: 4/25/33

1933	Chi-N	46	89	11	25	3	1	1	10	7	4	.281	.347	.371	105	1	0			.949	-2	C-20	0.0
1935	Cin-N	88	218	26	56	7	0	3	30	42	7	.257	.379	.330	95	1	3			.986	5	C-66/1-5,O	0.3
1936	Cin-N	89	235	28	63	13	1	1	40	43	14	.268	.384	.345	104	3	2			.984	6	C-71/1-1	1.2
1937	Cin-N	18	40	3	11	2	0	0	2	5	1	.275	.356	.325	90	-0	0			.967	-1	C-17	0.0
1938	Bro-N	54	126	10	31	5	0	0	11	19	9	.246	.354	.286	76	-3	0			.958	-1	C-44	-0.1
Total	5	295	708	78	186	30	2	5	93	116	35	.263	.371	.332	96	1	5			.975	4	C-218/1-6,O	1.4

■ FRANK CAMPOS
Campos, Francisco Jose (Lopez)   b: 5/11/24, Havana, Cuba   BL/TL, 5'11", 180 lbs.   Deb: 9/11/51

1951	Was-A	8	26	4	11	3	1	0	3	0	1	.423	.423	.615	182	3	0	0	0	1.000	-2	/O-7	0.1
1952	Was-A	53	112	9	29	6	1	0	8	1	13	.259	.278	.330	71	-5	0	0	0	.978	-2	O-23	-0.8
1953	Was-A	10	9	0	1	0	0	0	2	1	0	.111	.200	.111	-14	-1	0	0	0	.000	0	H	-0.1
Total	3	71	147	13	41	9	2	0	13	2	14	.279	.298	.367	86	-4	0	0	0	.981	-4	/O-30	-0.8

■ SIL CAMPUSANO
Campusano, Silvestre (Diaz)   b: 12/31/65, Santo Domingo, D.R.   BR/TR, 6', 175 lbs.   Deb: 4/4/88

1988	Tor-A	73	142	14	31	10	2	2	12	9	33	.218	.284	.359	78	-4	0	0	0	.934	-10	O-69/D-2	-1.6
1990	Phi-N	66	85	10	18	1	1	2	9	6	16	.212	.272	.318	62	-5	1	0	0	.976	-13	O-47	-1.9
1991	Phi-N	15	35	2	4	0	0	1	2	1	10	.114	.139	.200	-6	-5	0	0	0	1.000	-1	O-15	-0.6
Total	3	154	262	26	53	11	3	5	23	16	59	.202	.261	.324	62	-14	1	0	0	.953	-24	O-131/D-2	-4.1

■ GEORGE CANALE
Canale, George Anthony   b: 8/11/65, Memphis, Tenn.   BL/TR, 6'1", 190 lbs.   Deb: 9/3/89

1989	Mil-A	13	26	5	5	1	0	1	3	2	3	.192	.250	.346	67	-1	0	1	-1	.989	-0	1-11	-0.3
1990	Mil-A	10	13	4	1	1	0	0	2	0	6	.077	.200	.154	0	-2	0	1	-1	1.000	1	/1-6,D-3	-0.2
1991	Mil-A	21	34	6	6	2	0	3	10	8	6	.176	.333	.500	130	1	0	0	0	.983	3	1-19	0.3
Total	3	44	73	15	12	4	0	4	13	12	15	.164	.282	.384	85	-2	0	2	-1	.988	3	/1-36,D-3	-0.2

■ WILLIE CANATE
Canate, Emisael William (Librada)   b: 12/11/71, Maracaibo, Venez.   BR/TR, 6', 170 lbs.   Deb: 4/16/93

| 1993 | *Tor-A | 38 | 47 | 12 | 10 | 0 | 0 | 1 | 3 | 6 | 15 | .213 | .315 | .277 | 60 | -2 | 1 | 1 | -0 | 1.000 | -4 | O-31/D-1 | -0.7 |

■ JIM CANAVAN
Canavan, James Edward   b: 11/26/1866, New Bedford, Mass.   d: 5/27/49, New Bedford, Mass.   BR/TR, 5'8", 160 lbs.   Deb: 4/8/1891

1891	Cin-a	101	426	74	97	13	14	7	66	27	44	.228	.282	.373	80	-16	21			.860	-11	*S-101	-1.8
	Mil-a	35	142	33	38	2	4	3	21	16	10	.268	.342	.401	94	-3	7			.864	-2	2-24,S-11	-0.3
	Yr	136	568	107	135	15	18	10	87	43	54	.238	.297	.380	84	-19	28			.860	-13	*S-112,2-24	-2.1
1892	Chi-N	118	439	48	73	10	11	0	32	48	48	.166	.248	.239	47	-28	33			.923	-2	*2-112/O-4,S	-2.7
1893	Cin-N	121	461	65	104	13	7	5	64	51	20	.226	.305	.317	64	-25	31			.931	-1	*O-117/2-5,3	-2.6
1894	Cin-N	101	356	77	97	16	9	13	70	62	25	.272	.380	.478	102	-0	13			.904	-2	*O-95/S-3,321	-0.7
1897	Bro-N	63	240	25	52	9	2	2	34	26		.217	.299	.304	63	-13	9			.909	-21	2-63	-2.7
Total	5	539	2064	322	461	63	48	30	287	230	147	.223	.304	.344	74	-86	114			.920	-40	O-216,2-205,S/31	-10.8

■ CASEY CANDAELE
Candaele, Casey Todd   b: 1/12/61, Lompoc, Cal.   BB/TR, 5'9", 165 lbs.   Deb: 6/5/86

1986	Mon-N	30	104	9	24	4	1	0	6	5	15	.231	.266	.288	53	-7	3	5	-2	.983	-2	2-24/3-4	-1.0
1987	Mon-N	138	449	62	122	23	4	1	23	38	28	.272	.331	.347	78	-14	7	10	-4	.985	-1	2-68,O-67,S/1	-1.7
1988	Mon-N	36	116	9	20	5	1	0	4	10	11	.172	.238	.233	34	-10	1	0	0	.988	1	2-35	-0.8
	Hou-N	21	31	2	5	3	0	1	1	1	6	.161	.188	.258	28	-3	0	1	-1	1.000	1	2-10/O-5,3	-0.3
	Yr	57	147	11	25	8	1	0	5	11	17	.170	.228	.238	33	-13	1	1	-1	.990	2	2-45/O-5,3	-1.1
1990	Hou-N	130	262	30	75	8	6	3	22	31	42	.286	.364	.397	112	5	7	5	-1	1.000	-14	O-58,2-49,S/3	-1.0
1991	Hou-N	151	461	44	121	20	7	4	50	40	49	.262	.321	.362	97	-2	9	3	1	.982	5	*2-109,O-26,3	0.6
1992	Hou-N	135	320	19	68	12	1	1	18	24	36	.213	.274	.266	56	-19	7	1	2	.968	-5	S-65,3-29,O/2	-2.0
1993	Hou-N	75	121	18	29	8	1	0	7	10	14	.240	.298	.331	70	-5	2	3	-1	1.000	-6	2-19,O-17,S/3	-1.2
Total	7	716	1864	193	464	83	20	10	131	159	201	.249	.310	.331	78	-54	36	28	-6	.986	-20	2-323,O-194,S/31	-7.4

■ JOHN CANGELOSI
Cangelosi, John Anthony   b: 3/10/63, Brooklyn, N.Y.   BB/TL, 5'8", 150 lbs.   Deb: 6/3/85

1985	Chi-A	5	2	2	0	0	0	0	0	0	0	.000	.333	.000	1	-0	0	0	0	1.000	-2	/O-3,D-2	-0.2
1986	Chi-A	137	438	65	103	16	3	2	32	71	61	.235	.351	.299	77	-12	50	17	5	.969	-5	*O-129/D-3	-1.6
1987	Pit-N	104	182	44	50	8	3	4	18	46	33	.275	.429	.418	125	9	21	6	3	.962	-4	O-47	0.7
1988	Pit-N	75	118	18	30	4	1	0	8	17	16	.254	.353	.305	92	-1	9	4	0	.963	-2	O-24/P-1	-0.3
1989	Pit-N	112	160	18	35	4	2	0	9	35	20	.219	.369	.269	88	-0	11	8	-2	.973	-6	O-46	-1.0
1990	Pit-N	58	76	13	15	2	0	0	1	11	12	.197	.307	.224	50	-5	7	2	1	1.000	-1	O-12	-0.5
1992	Tex-A	73	85	12	16	2	0	1	6	18	16	.188	.330	.247	66	-3	6	5	-1	.964	-13	O-65/D-6	-1.9
1994	NY-N	62	111	14	28	4	0	2	4	19	20	.252	.371	.288	75	-3	5	1	1	1.000	-6	O-50	-0.9
Total	8	626	1172	186	277	40	9	7	78	217	179	.236	.364	.304	85	-15	109	43	7	.972	-38	O-376/D-11,P	-5.7

■ RIP CANNELL
Cannell, Virgin Wirt   b: 1/23/1880, S.Bridgton, Maine   d: 8/26/48, Bridgton, Maine   BL/TR, 5'10.5", 180 lbs.   Deb: 4/14/04

1904	Bos-N	100	346	32	81	5	1	0	18	23		.234	.286	.254	70	-12	10			.897	-11	O-93	-3.0
1905	Bos-N	154	567	52	140	14	4	0	36	51		.247	.311	.286	80	-13	17			.935	-8	*O-154	-3.0
Total	2	254	913	84	221	19	5	0	54	74		.242	.302	.274	76	-25	27			.923	-19	O-247	-6.0

■ CHRIS CANNIZZARO
Cannizzaro, Christopher John   b: 5/3/38, Oakland, Cal.   BR/TR, 6', 190 lbs.   Deb: 4/17/60   C

1960	StL-N	7	9	0	2	0	0	0	1	1	3	.222	.300	.222	42	-1	0	0	0	1.000	1	/C-6	0.1
1961	StL-N	6	2	0	1	0	0	0	0	0	0	.500	.500	.500	151	0	0	0	0	.000	0	/C-5	0.1
1962	NY-N	59	133	9	32	2	1	0	9	19	26	.241	.340	.271	65	-6	1	1	-0	.973	2	C-56/O-1	-0.3
1963	NY-N	16	33	4	8	1	0	0	4	1	8	.242	.265	.273	54	-2	0	0	0	1.000	-1	C-15	-0.2
1964	NY-N	60	164	11	51	10	0	0	10	14	28	.311	.369	.372	112	3	0	5	-3	.988	2	C-53	0.4
1965	NY-N	114	251	17	46	8	1	1	7	28	60	.183	.270	.231	44	-18	0	2	-1	.977	12	*C-112	-0.3

YEAR	TM/L	G	AB	R	H	2B	3B	HR	RBI	BB	SO	AVG	OBP	SLG	PRO+	BR/A	SB	CS	SBR	FA	FR	G/POS	TPR
1968	Pit-N	25	58	5	14	2	2	1	7	9	13	.241	.343	.397	123	2	0	0	0	.976	-0	C-25	0.3
1969	SD-N☆	134	418	23	92	14	3	4	33	42	81	.220	.291	.297	68	-18	0	1	-1	.988	-14	*C-132	-2.7
1970	SD-N	111	341	27	95	13	3	5	42	48	49	.279	.369	.378	105	4	2	7	-4	.980	-16	*C-110	-1.0
1971	SD-N	21	63	2	12	1	0	1	8	11	10	.190	.320	.254	69	-2	0	0	0	.992	-2	C-19	-0.3
	Chi-N	71	197	18	42	8	1	5	23	28	24	.213	.314	.340	74	-7	0	0	0	.983	-11	C-70	-1.6
	Yr	92	260	20	54	9	1	6	31	39	34	.208	.316	.319	73	-9	0	0	0	.985	-12	C-89	-1.9
1972	LA-N	73	200	14	48	6	0	2	18	31	38	.240	.342	.300	86	-3	0	1	-1	.983	-8	C-72	-0.9
1973	LA-N	17	21	0	4	0	0	0	3	3	3	.190	.292	.190	38	-2	0	0	0	1.000	0	C-13	-0.2
1974	SD-N	26	60	2	11	1	0	0	4	6	11	.183	.258	.200	31	-6	0	0	0	.979	5	C-26	0.0
Total	13	740	1950	132	458	66	12	18	169	241	354	.235	.321	.309	77	-55	3	17	-9	.983	-28	C-714/O-1	-6.6

■ JOE CANNON
Cannon, Joseph Jerome   b: 7/13/53, Camp Lejeune, N.C.   BL/TR, 6'3", 193 lbs.   Deb: 9/22/77

YEAR	TM/L	G	AB	R	H	2B	3B	HR	RBI	BB	SO	AVG	OBP	SLG	PRO+	BR/A	SB	CS	SBR	FA	FR	G/POS	TPR
1977	Hou-N	9	17	3	2	2	0	0	1	0	5	.118	.118	.235	-9	-3	1	1	-0	1.000	1	/O-3	-0.3
1978	Hou-N	8	18	1	4	0	0	0	1	0	1	.222	.222	.222	26	-2	0	1	-1	.778	-1	/O-5	-0.4
1979	Tor-A	61	142	14	30	1	1	1	5	1	34	.211	.217	.254	26	-15	12	2	1	1.000	-4	O-50	-1.8
1980	Tor-A	70	50	16	4	0	0	0	4	0	14	.080	.098	.080	-48	-10	2	2	-1	.968	-10	O-33/D-1	-2.2
Total	4	148	227	34	40	3	1	1	11	1	54	.176	.183	.211	7	-29	15	6	1	.977	-15	/O-91,D-1	-4.7

■ JOSE CANSECO
Canseco, Jose (Capas)   b: 7/2/64, Havana, Cuba   BR/TR, 6'3", 240 lbs.   Deb: 9/2/85   F

YEAR	TM/L	G	AB	R	H	2B	3B	HR	RBI	BB	SO	AVG	OBP	SLG	PRO+	BR/A	SB	CS	SBR	FA	FR	G/POS	TPR
1985	Oak-A	29	96	16	29	3	0	5	13	4	31	.302	.330	.490	130	3	1	1	-0	.951	-0	O-26	0.2
1986	Oak-A☆	157	600	85	144	29	1	33	117	65	175	.240	.322	.457	118	13	15	7	0	.958	-3	*O-155/D-1	0.5
1987	Oak-A	159	630	81	162	35	3	31	113	50	157	.257	.314	.470	111	8	15	3	3	.975	11	*O-130,D-30	1.5
1988	*Oak-A★	158	610	120	187	34	0	42	124	78	128	.307	.394	.569	172	59	40	16	2	.978	8	*O-144,D-13	6.4
1989	*Oak-A†	65	227	40	61	9	1	17	57	23	69	.269	.341	.542	151	14	6	3	0	.976	4	O-56/D-5	1.6
1990	*Oak-A★	131	481	83	132	14	2	37	101	72	158	.274	.375	.543	160	38	19	10	-0	.995	-3	O-88/D-43	4.0
1991	Oak-A	154	572	115	152	32	1	44	122	78	152	.266	.363	.556	159	45	26	6	4	.965	-3	*O-131,D-24	4.2
1992	Oak-A†	97	366	66	90	11	0	22	72	48	104	.246	.338	.456	127	13	5	7	-3	.988	4	O-77,D-20	1.2
	Tex-A	22	73	8	17	4	0	4	15	15	24	.233	.385	.452	139	4	1	0	0	.970	1	O-13/D-8	0.5
	Yr	119	439	74	107	15	0	26	87	63	128	.244	.346	.456	129	17	6	7	-2	.929	5	O-90,D-28	1.7
1993	Tex-A	60	231	30	59	14	1	10	46	16	62	.255	.312	.455	107	1	6	6	-2	.970	1	O-49/P-1	0.0
1994	Tex-A	111	429	88	121	19	2	31	90	69	114	.282	.388	.552	149	32	15	8	-0	.000	0	*D-111	2.4
Total	10	1143	4315	732	1154	204	11	276	870	518	1174	.267	.353	.512	140	230	149	67	6	.973	27	O-869,D-255/P	22.5

■ OZZIE CANSECO
Canseco, Osvaldo (Capas)   b: 7/2/64, Havana, Cuba   BR/TR, 6'2", 220 lbs.   Deb: 7/18/90   F

YEAR	TM/L	G	AB	R	H	2B	3B	HR	RBI	BB	SO	AVG	OBP	SLG	PRO+	BR/A	SB	CS	SBR	FA	FR	G/POS	TPR
1990	Oak-A	9	19	1	2	1	0	0	1	1	10	.105	.150	.158	-14	-3	0	0	0	1.000	-0	/O-2,D-4	-0.3
1992	StL-N	9	29	7	8	5	0	0	3	7	4	.276	.417	.448	150	2	0	0	0	.889	-2	/O-8	0.0
1993	StL-N	6	17	0	3	0	0	0	0	1	3	.176	.222	.176	8	-2	0	0	0	.500	-2	/O-5	-0.5
Total	3	24	65	8	13	6	0	0	4	9	17	.200	.297	.292	67	-3	0	0	0	.857	-4	/O-15,D-4	-0.8

■ BART CANTZ
Cantz, Bartholomew L.   b: 1/29/1860, Philadelphia, Pa.   d: 2/12/43, Philadelphia, Pa.   Deb: 7/25/1888

YEAR	TM/L	G	AB	R	H	2B	3B	HR	RBI	BB	SO	AVG	OBP	SLG	PRO+	BR/A	SB	CS	SBR	FA	FR	G/POS	TPR
1888	Bal-a	37	126	7	21	2	1	0	9	2		.167	.180	.198	22	-11	0			.904	-9	C-33/O-4	-1.6
1889	Bal-a	20	69	6	12	2	0	0	8	4	14	.174	.219	.203	20	-7	2			.860	-7	C-18/O-2	-1.1
1890	Phi-a	5	22	1	1	0	0	0	0	0		.045	.045	.045	-75	-5	0			.893	-3	/C-5	-0.6
Total	3	62	217	14	34	4	1	0	17	6	14	.157	.179	.184	11	-23	2			.890	-19	/C-56,O-6	-3.3

■ NICK CAPRA
Capra, Nick Lee   b: 3/8/58, Denver, Colo.   BR/TR, 5'8", 165 lbs.   Deb: 9/6/82

YEAR	TM/L	G	AB	R	H	2B	3B	HR	RBI	BB	SO	AVG	OBP	SLG	PRO+	BR/A	SB	CS	SBR	FA	FR	G/POS	TPR
1982	Tex-A	13	15	2	4	0	0	1	1	3	4	.267	.421	.467	151	1	2	1	0	1.000	1	/O-9	0.2
1983	Tex-A	8	2	2	0	0	0	0	0	0	0	.000	.000	.000	-99	-1	0	0	0	1.000	-2	/O-4	-0.2
1985	Tex-A	8	8	1	1	0	0	0	0	0	0	.125	.125	.125	-31	-1	0	0	0	1.000	-1	/O-8	-0.3
1988	KC-A	14	29	3	4	1	0	0	0	2	3	.138	.194	.172	3	-4	1	0	0	1.000	-2	O-11/D-1	-0.6
1991	Tex-A	2	0	1	0	0	0	0	0	1	0	—	1.000	—	205	0	0	0	0	1.000	0	/O-2	-0.0
Total	5	45	54	9	9	1	0	1	1	6	7	.167	.262	.241	41	-4	3	1	0	1.000	-5	/O-34,D-1	-0.9

■ PAT CAPRI
Capri, Patrick Nicholas   b: 11/27/18, New York, N.Y.   d: 6/14/89, New York, N.Y.   BR/TR, 6'0.5", 170 lbs.   Deb: 7/16/44

YEAR	TM/L	G	AB	R	H	2B	3B	HR	RBI	BB	SO	AVG	OBP	SLG	PRO+	BR/A	SB	CS	SBR	FA	FR	G/POS	TPR
1944	Bos-N	7	1	1	0	0	0	0	0	0	1	.000	.000	.000	-96	-0	0			1.000	1	/2-1	0.1

■ RALPH CAPRON
Capron, Ralph Earl   b: 6/16/1889, Minneapolis, Minn   d: 9/19/80, Los Angeles, Cal.   BL/TR, 5'11.5", 165 lbs.   Deb: 4/25/12

YEAR	TM/L	G	AB	R	H	2B	3B	HR	RBI	BB	SO	AVG	OBP	SLG	PRO+	BR/A	SB	CS	SBR	FA	FR	G/POS	TPR
1912	Pit-N	1	0	0	0	0	0	0	0	0	0	—	—	—			0			.000	0	R	0.0
1913	Phi-N	2	1	1	0	0	0	0	0	0	0	.000	.000	.000	-96	-0	0			.000	-1	/O-1	-0.1
Total	2	3	1	1	0	0	0	0	0	0	0	.000	.000	.000	-96	-0	0			—	-1	/O-1	-0.1

■ RAMON CARABALLO
Caraballo, Ramon (Sanchez)   b: 5/23/69, Rio San Juan, D.R.   BB/TR, 5'7", 150 lbs.   Deb: 9/9/93

YEAR	TM/L	G	AB	R	H	2B	3B	HR	RBI	BB	SO	AVG	OBP	SLG	PRO+	BR/A	SB	CS	SBR	FA	FR	G/POS	TPR
1993	Atl-N	6	0	0	0	0	0	0	0	0	0	—	—	—			0			1.000	2	/2-5	0.2

■ JOHN CARBINE
Carbine, John C.   b: 10/12/1855, Syracuse, N.Y.   d: 9/11/15, Chicago, Ill.   6', 187 lbs.   Deb: 5/8/1875

YEAR	TM/L	G	AB	R	H	2B	3B	HR	RBI	BB	SO	AVG	OBP	SLG	PRO+	BR/A	SB	CS	SBR	FA	FR	G/POS	TPR
1875	Wes-n	10	36	0	3	0	0	0		0		.083	.083	.083	-40	-5						1-10	-0.4
1876	Lou-N	7	25	3	4	0	0	0	1	0	0	.160	.160	.160	6	-3				.878	-0	/1-6,O-1	-0.3

■ BERNIE CARBO
Carbo, Bernardo   b: 8/5/47, Detroit, Mich.   BL/TR, 6', 175 lbs.   Deb: 9/2/69

YEAR	TM/L	G	AB	R	H	2B	3B	HR	RBI	BB	SO	AVG	OBP	SLG	PRO+	BR/A	SB	CS	SBR	FA	FR	G/POS	TPR
1969	Cin-N	4	3	0	0	0	0	0	0	0	2	.000	.000	.000	-95	-1	0	0	0	.000	0	H	-0.1
1970	*Cin-N	125	365	54	113	19	3	21	63	94	77	.310	.456	.551	168	40	10	4	1	.979	0	*O-119	3.5
1971	Cin-N	106	310	33	68	20	1	5	20	54	56	.219	.339	.339	94	-1	2	1	-0	.982	0	O-90	-0.3
1972	Cin-N	19	21	2	3	0	0	0	0	6	3	.143	.357	.143	50	-1	0	0	0	1.000	0	/O-4	-0.1
	StL-N	99	302	42	78	13	1	7	34	57	56	.258	.385	.377	119	10	0	1	-1	.967	8	O-92/3-1	1.4
	Yr	118	323	44	81	13	1	7	34	63	59	.251	.383	.362	115	9	0	1	-1	.969	8	O-96/3-1	1.3
1973	StL-N	111	308	42	88	18	0	8	40	58	52	.286	.401	.422	128	14	2	0	1	.978	9	O-94	1.4
1974	Bos-A	117	338	40	84	20	6	12	61	58	90	.249	.365	.414	116	8	4	3	-1	.994	-1	O-87,D-15	0.3
1975	*Bos-A	107	319	64	82	21	3	15	50	83	69	.257	.412	.483	140	20	4	4	-2	.976	-1	O-85,D-13	1.4
1976	Bos-A	17	55	5	13	4	0	2	6	8	17	.236	.333	.418	106	0	1	0	0	1.000	0	D-15/O-1	0.0
	Mil-A	69	183	20	43	7	0	3	15	33	55	.235	.352	.322	100	1	1	2	-1	1.000	4	O-33,D-24	0.2
	Yr	86	238	25	56	11	0	5	21	41	72	.235	.348	.345	102	2	2	2	-1	1.000	3	D-39,O-34	0.2
1977	Bos-A	86	228	36	66	15	0	15	34	47	72	.289	.411	.522	136	12	1	2	-1	.951	2	O-67/D-7	1.1
1978	Bos-A	17	46	7	12	3	0	1	6	8	8	.261	.370	.391	103	1	1	1	-0	1.000	1	/O-9,D-8	0.1
	Cle-A	60	174	21	50	8	0	4	16	20	31	.287	.364	.402	117	4	0	1	0	1.000	-2	D-49/O-4	0.1
	Yr	77	220	28	62	11	0	5	22	28	39	.282	.365	.400	113	5	1	2	-0	1.000	-0	D-57,O-13	0.2
1979	StL-N	52	64	6	18	1	0	3	12	10	12	.281	.378	.438	121	2	1	0	0	1.000	-5	O-17	-0.3
1980	StL-N	14	11	0	2	0	0	0	0	1	0	.182	.250	.182	22	-1	0	0	0	.000	0	H	-0.2
	Pit-N	7	6	0	2	0	0	0	1	1	1	.333	.429	.333	114	0	0	0	0	.000	0	/H	0.0
	Yr	21	17	0	4	0	0	0	1	2	1	.235	.316	.235	55	-1	0	0	0	.000	0	/H	-0.2
Total	12	1010	2733	372	722	140	9	96	358	538	611	.264	.389	.427	125	109	26	18	-3	.978	12	O-702,D-131/3	8.5

■ JOSE CARDENAL
Cardenal, Jose Rosario Domec (b: Jose Rosario Domec (Cardenal))   b: 10/7/43, Matanzas, Cuba   BR/TR, 5'10", 150 lbs.   Deb: 4/14/63   C

YEAR	TM/L	G	AB	R	H	2B	3B	HR	RBI	BB	SO	AVG	OBP	SLG	PRO+	BR/A	SB	CS	SBR	FA	FR	G/POS	TPR
1963	SF-N	9	5	1	1	0	0	0	0	0	0	.200	.333	.200	58	-0	0	1	-1	.000	-1	/O-2	-0.2
1964	SF-N	20	15	3	0	0	0	0	0	2	3	.000	.118	.000	-62	-3	0	0	0	.909	-3	O-16	-0.6
1965	Cal-A	134	512	58	128	23	2	11	57	27	72	.250	.290	.367	87	-10	37	17	1	.964	10	*O-129/3-2,2	-0.5

YEAR	TM/L	G	AB	R	H	2B	3B	HR	RBI	BB	SO	AVG	OBP	SLG	PRO+	BR/A	SB	CS	SBR	FA	FR	G/POS	TPR
1966	Cal-A	154	561	67	155	15	3	16	48	34	69	.276	.322	.399	109	5	24	11	1	.992	12	*O-146	1.2
1967	Cal-A	108	381	40	90	13	5	6	27	15	63	.236	.269	.344	83	-9	10	5	0	.986	0	*O-101	-1.6
1968	Cle-A	157	583	78	150	21	7	7	44	39	74	.257	.306	.353	101	-0	40	18	1	.974	13	*O-153	0.6
1969	Cle-A	146	557	75	143	26	3	11	45	49	58	.257	.317	.373	89	-8	36	6	7	.982	11	*O-142/3-5	0.2
1970	StL-N	148	552	73	162	32	6	10	74	45	70	.293	.348	.428	104	3	26	9	2	.969	-0	*O-134	0.0
1971	StL-N	89	301	37	73	12	4	7	48	29	35	.243	.309	.379	90	-4	12	3	2	.969	7	O-83	0.1
	Mil-A	53	198	20	51	10	0	3	32	13	20	.258	.307	.354	88	-4	9	5	-0	.979	7	O-52	0.0
1972	Chi-N	143	533	96	155	24	6	17	70	55	58	.291	.358	.454	117	12	25	14	-1	.971	-9	*O-137	-0.5
1973	Chi-N	145	522	80	158	33	2	11	68	58	62	.303	.378	.437	116	13	19	7	2	.980	-3	*O-142	0.4
1974	Chi-N	143	542	75	159	35	3	13	72	56	67	.293	.361	.441	118	13	23	9	2	.965	8	*O-137	1.7
1975	Chi-N	154	574	85	182	30	6	9	68	77	50	.317	.402	.423	124	21	34	12	3	.976	12	*O-151	3.0
1976	Chi-N	136	521	64	156	25	2	8	47	32	39	.299	.341	.401	101	0	23	14	-2	.981	7	*O-128	0.0
1977	Chi-N	100	226	33	54	12	1	3	18	28	30	.239	.325	.341	71	-9	5	4	-1	.989	-6	O-62/2-1,S	-1.9
1978	*Phi-N	87	201	27	50	12	0	4	33	23	16	.249	.326	.368	93	-2	2	3	-1	.990	-9	1-50,O-13	-1.5
1979	Phi-N	29	48	4	10	3	0	0	9	8	8	.208	.321	.271	61	-2	1	0	0	1.000	-3	O-12/1-1	-0.6
	NY-N	11	37	8	11	4	0	2	4	6	3	.297	.409	.568	170	4	1	0	0	1.000	-1	/O-9,1-2	0.2
	Yr	40	85	12	21	7	0	2	13	14	11	.247	.360	.400	106	1	2	0	1	1.000	-4	O-21/1-3	-0.4
1980	NY-N	26	42	4	7	1	0	0	4	6	4	.167	.271	.190	32	-4	0	1	-1	1.000	0	/O-1,1-5	-0.5
	*KC-A	25	53	8	18	2	0	0	5	5	5	.340	.397	.377	112	1	1	0	0	.970	-3	O-23	-0.2
Total	18	2017	6964	936	1913	333	46	138	775	608	807	.275	.335	.395	102	16	329	139	15	.976	48	*O-1778/1-58,32S	-0.9

■ LEO CARDENAS
Cardenas, Leonardo Lazaro (Alfonso) "Chico"   b: 12/17/38, Matanzas, Cuba   BR/TR, 5'10", 163 lbs.   Deb: 7/25/60

YEAR	TM/L	G	AB	R	H	2B	3B	HR	RBI	BB	SO	AVG	OBP	SLG	PRO+	BR/A	SB	CS	SBR	FA	FR	G/POS	TPR
1960	Cin-N	48	142	13	33	2	4	1	24	6	32	.232	.264	.324	59	-8	0	0	0	.958	7	S-47	0.2
1961	*Cin-N	74	198	23	61	18	1	5	24	15	39	.308	.357	.485	119	5	1	0	0	.973	-5	S-63	0.5
1962	Cin-N	153	589	77	173	31	4	10	60	39	99	.294	.343	.411	98	-2	2	5	-2	.972	-7	*S-149	0.3
1963	Cin-N	158	565	42	133	22	4	7	48	23	101	.235	.270	.326	69	-23	3	5	-2	.972	-3	*S-157	-1.9
1964	Cin-N★	163	597	61	150	32	2	9	69	41	110	.251	.302	.357	82	-14	4	4	-1	.960	-10	*S-163	-1.5
1965	Cin-N★	156	557	65	160	25	11	11	57	60	100	.287	.358	.431	113	10	1	4	-2	.975	-1	*S-155	1.9
1966	Cin-N★	160	568	59	145	25	4	20	81	45	87	.255	.311	.419	93	-6	9	4	0	.980	-15	*S-160	-0.6
1967	Cin-N	108	379	30	97	14	3	2	21	34	77	.256	.320	.325	76	-11	4	5	-2	.971	-10	*S-108	-1.3
1968	Cin-N★	137	452	45	106	13	2	7	41	36	83	.235	.294	.319	79	-11	2	1	0	.955	-23	*S-136	-2.3
1969	*Min-A	160	578	67	162	24	4	10	70	66	96	.280	.358	.388	106	6	5	6	-2	.965	34	*S-160	5.6
1970	*Min-A	160	588	67	145	34	4	11	65	42	101	.247	.301	.374	84	-14	2	5	-2	.978	3	*S-160	0.6
1971	Min-A☆	153	554	59	146	25	4	18	75	51	69	.264	.327	.421	107	4	3	3	-1	.985	-0	*S-153	2.4
1972	Cal-A	150	551	25	123	11	2	6	42	35	73	.223	.272	.283	69	-22	1	2	-1	.970	3	*S-150	0.2
1973	Cle-A	72	195	9	42	4	0	0	12	13	42	.215	.264	.236	41	-15	1	4	-0	.964	-8	S-67/3-5	-1.9
1974	Tex-A	34	92	5	25	3	0	0	7	2	14	.272	.287	.304	72	-3	1	0	0	1.000	2	3-21,S-10/D	-0.1
1975	Tex-A	55	102	15	24	0	0	1	5	14	12	.235	.328	.284	75	-3	0	0	0	.956	11	3-43/S-5,2	0.8
Total	16	1941	6707	662	1725	285	49	118	689	522	1135	.257	.313	.367	88	-107	39	48	-17	.971	-22	*S-1843/3-69,D2	2.9

■ ROD CAREW
Carew, Rodney Cline   b: 10/1/45, Gatun, C.Z.   BL/TR, 6', 182 lbs.   Deb: 4/11/67   CH

YEAR	TM/L	G	AB	R	H	2B	3B	HR	RBI	BB	SO	AVG	OBP	SLG	PRO+	BR/A	SB	CS	SBR	FA	FR	G/POS	TPR
1967	Min-A★	137	514	66	150	22	7	8	51	37	91	.292	.342	.409	112	7	5	9	-4	.976	-10	*2-134	0.2
1968	Min-A★	127	461	46	126	27	2	1	42	26	71	.273	.314	.347	95	-3	12	4	1	.968	-14	*2-117/S-4	-1.0
1969	*Min-A★	123	458	79	152	30	4	8	56	37	72	.332	.386	.467	135	21	19	8	1	.970	-17	*2-118	1.5
1970	*Min-A†	51	191	27	70	12	3	4	28	11	28	.366	.407	.524	153	13	4	6	-2	.961	-11	2-45/1-1	0.3
1971	Min-A★	147	577	88	177	16	10	2	48	45	81	.307	.358	.380	106	7	6	7	-2	.976	-25	*2-142/3-2	-1.2
1972	Min-A★	142	535	61	170	21	6	0	51	43	60	.318	.371	.379	118	13	12	6	0	.978	1	*2-139	2.3
1973	Min-A★	149	580	98	203	30	11	6	62	62	55	.350	.415	.471	143	35	41	16	3	.984	7	*2-147	5.3
1974	Min-A★	153	599	86	218	30	5	3	55	74	49	.364	.435	.446	148	40	38	16	2	.960	9	*2-148	5.9
1975	Min-A★	143	535	89	192	24	4	14	80	64	40	.359	.428	.497	158	42	35	9	5	.973	-2	*2-123,1-14/D	5.6
1976	Min-A★	156	605	97	200	29	12	9	90	67	52	.331	.398	.463	147	37	49	22	2	.989	-2	*1-152/2-7	2.8
1977	Min-A★	155	616	128	239	38	16	14	100	69	55	.388	.452	.570	179	69	23	13	-1	.994	6	*1-151/2-4,D	6.3
1978	Min-A★	152	564	85	188	26	10	5	70	78	62	.333	.415	.441	138	32	27	7	4	.989	1	*1-148/2-4,O	2.8
1979	*Cal-A†	110	409	78	130	15	3	3	44	73	46	.318	.421	.391	125	19	18	8	1	.988	-7	*1-103/D-6	0.5
1980	Cal-A★	144	540	74	179	34	7	3	59	59	38	.331	.398	.437	132	25	23	15	-2	.994	-4	*1-103,D-32	1.1
1981	Cal-A★	93	364	57	111	17	1	2	21	45	45	.305	.381	.374	118	10	16	9	-1	.995	-1	1-90/D-2	0.4
1982	*Cal-A†	138	523	88	167	25	5	3	44	67	49	.319	.399	.403	121	18	10	17	-7	.992	1	*1-134	0.5
1983	Cal-A★	129	472	66	160	24	2	2	44	57	48	.339	.411	.411	128	21	6	7	-2	.994	-9	1-89,D-24/2	0.3
1984	Cal-A★	93	329	42	97	8	1	3	31	40	39	.295	.371	.353	102	3	4	3	-1	.981	-4	1-83/D-1	-0.7
1985	Cal-A	127	443	69	124	17	3	2	39	64	47	.280	.372	.345	99	2	5	5	-2	.994	-8	*1-116	-1.5
Total	19	2469	9315	1424	3053	445	112	92	1015	1018	1028	.328	.395	.429	131	408	353	187	-6	.991	-85	*1-1184,*2-1130/DS3O	31.4

■ ANDY CAREY
Carey, Andrew Arthur   b: 10/18/31, Oakland, Cal.   BR/TR, 6'1", 195 lbs.   Deb: 5/2/52

YEAR	TM/L	G	AB	R	H	2B	3B	HR	RBI	BB	SO	AVG	OBP	SLG	PRO+	BR/A	SB	CS	SBR	FA	FR	G/POS	TPR
1952	NY-A	16	40	6	6	0	0	0	1	3	10	.150	.209	.150	1	-5	0	0	0	.889	-1	3-14/S-1	-0.7
1953	NY-A	51	81	14	26	5	0	4	8	9	12	.321	.389	.531	152	6	2	1	0	.988	8	3-40/S-2,2	1.4
1954	NY-A	122	411	60	124	14	6	8	65	43	38	.302	.377	.423	123	13	5	5	-2	.967	17	*3-120	2.7
1955	*NY-A	135	510	73	131	19	11	7	47	44	51	.257	.317	.378	88	-10	3	3	-1	.954	14	*3-135	0.2
1956	*NY-A	132	422	54	100	18	2	7	50	45	45	.237	.313	.339	75	-16	9	6	-1	.947	-3	*3-131	-1.8
1957	*NY-A	85	247	30	63	6	5	6	33	15	42	.255	.311	.393	92	-3	2	4	-1	.977	3	3-81	0.1
1958	*NY-A	102	315	39	90	19	4	12	45	34	43	.286	.366	.486	137	16	1	2	-1	.961	10	3-99	2.6
1959	NY-A	41	101	11	26	1	0	3	9	7	17	.257	.306	.356	84	-2	1	1	-0	.916	2	3-34	-0.1
1960	NY-A	4	3	1	1	0	0	0	1	0	1	.333	.333	.333	86	-0	0	0	0	1.000	-1	/3-2,O-1	-0.1
	KC-A	102	343	30	80	14	4	12	53	26	52	.233	.289	.402	84	-9	1	2	0	.975	-0	3-91	-0.9
	Yr	106	346	31	81	14	4	12	54	26	53	.234	.290	.402	85	-9	1	2	0	.975	-1	3-93/O-1	-1.0
1961	KC-A	39	123	20	30	6	2	3	11	15	23	.244	.336	.398	94	-1	0	0	0	.944	-1	3-39	-0.2
	Chi-A	56	143	21	38	12	3	0	14	11	24	.266	.327	.392	93	-2	1	1	-1	.961	-5	3-54	-0.7
	Yr	95	266	41	68	18	5	3	25	26	47	.256	.331	.395	93	-3	1	1	-1	.953	-6	3-93	-0.9
1962	LA-N	53	111	12	26	5	1	2	13	16	23	.234	.336	.351	90	-1	0	0	0	.932	1	3-42	0.0
Total	11	938	2850	371	741	119	38	64	350	268	389	.260	.329	.396	97	-15	23	21	-6	.958	45	3-882/S-3,O2	2.5

■ SCOOPS CAREY
Carey, George C.   b: 12/4/1870, Pittsburgh, Pa.   d: 12/17/16, E.Liverpool, Ohio   BR/TR, 175 lbs.   Deb: 4/26/1895

YEAR	TM/L	G	AB	R	H	2B	3B	HR	RBI	BB	SO	AVG	OBP	SLG	PRO+	BR/A	SB	CS	SBR	FA	FR	G/POS	TPR
1895	*Bal-N	123	490	59	128	21	6	1	75	27	32	.261	.305	.335	63	-28	2			.987	-6	*1-123/O-1,S3	-2.6
1898	Lou-N	8	32	1	6	1	1	0	1	1		.188	.212	.281	42	-3	0			.961	0	/1-8	-0.2
1902	Was-A	120	452	46	142	35	11	0	60	20		.314	.350	.440	117	9	3			.989	4	*1-120	1.0
1903	Was-A	48	183	8	37	3	2	0	23	4		.202	.223	.240	38	-14	0			.977	-3	1-47	-1.8
Total	4	299	1157	114	313	60	20	1	159	52	32	.271	.308	.360	80	-35	5			.986	-5	1-298/3-1,SO	-3.6

■ MAX CAREY
Carey, Max George "Scoops" (b: Maximilian Carnarius)
b: 1/11/1890, Terre Haute, Ind.   d: 5/30/76, Miami, Fla.   BB/TR, 5'11.5", 170 lbs.   Deb: 10/3/10   MCH

YEAR	TM/L	G	AB	R	H	2B	3B	HR	RBI	BB	SO	AVG	OBP	SLG	PRO+	BR/A	SB	CS	SBR	FA	FR	G/POS	TPR
1910	Pit-N	2	6	2	3	0	1	0	2	3	0	.500	.625	.833	307	2	0			1.000	2	/O-2	0.3
1911	Pit-N	129	427	77	110	15	10	5	43	44	75	.258	.337	.375	95	-3	27			.975	7	*O-122	-0.3
1912	Pit-N	150	587	114	177	23	8	5	66	61	79	.302	.372	.394	114	11	45			.968	9	*O-150	1.0
1913	Pit-N	154	620	99	172	23	10	5	49	55	67	.277	.339	.371	107	6	61			.961	15	*O-154	1.4
1914	Pit-N	156	593	76	144	25	17	1	31	59	56	.243	.313	.347	101	-0	38			.966	11	*O-154	0.4

YEAR	TM/L	G	AB	R	H	2B	3B	HR	RBI	BB	SO	AVG	OBP	SLG	PRO+	BR/A	SB	CS	SBR	FA	FR	G/POS	TPR
1915	Pit-N	140	564	76	143	26	5	3	27	57	53	.254	.326	.333	101	2	**36**	17	1	.982	13	*O-139	1.0
1916	Pit-N	154	599	90	158	23	11	7	42	59	58	.264	.337	.374	117	13	**63**	19	8	.983	30	*O-154	4.7
1917	Pit-N	155	588	82	174	21	12	1	51	58	38	.296	.369	.378	125	19	**46**			.979	25	*O-153	3.9
1918	Pit-N	126	468	70	128	14	6	3	48	**62**	25	.274	.363	.348	113	10	**58**			.958	19	*O-126	2.3
1919	Pit-N	66	244	41	75	10	2	0	9	25	24	.307	.376	.365	119	6	18			.947	2	O-63	0.4
1920	Pit-N	130	485	74	140	18	4	1	35	59	31	.289	.369	.348	104	5	**52**	10	10	.967	1	*O-129	0.6
1921	Pit-N	140	521	85	161	34	4	7	56	70	30	.309	.395	.430	115	14	37	12	4	.957	16	*O-139	2.3
1922	Pit-N	155	629	140	207	28	12	10	70	**80**	26	.329	.408	.459	122	23	**51**	2	**14**	.969	20	*O-155	4.2
1923	Pit-N	153	610	120	188	32	**19**	6	63	73	28	.308	.388	.452	119	18	**51**	8	**11**	.962	20	*O-153	3.6
1924	Pit-N	149	599	113	178	30	9	8	55	58	17	.297	.366	.417	108	7	**49**	13	**7**	.965	9	*O-149	1.3
1925	*Pit-N	133	542	109	186	39	13	5	44	66	19	.343	.418	.491	123	20	**46**	11	**7**	.950	9	*O-130	2.6
1926	Pit-N	86	324	46	72	14	5	0	28	30	14	.222	.288	.296	55	-21	10			.943	4	O-82	-2.2
	Bro-N	27	100	18	26	3	1	0	7	8	5	.260	.315	.310	70	-4	0			.933	-1	O-27	-0.7
	Yr	113	424	64	98	17	6	0	35	38	19	.231	.294	.300	58	-25	10			.941	3	*O-109	-2.9
1927	Bro-N	144	538	70	143	30	10	1	54	64	18	.266	.345	.364	90	-7	32			.970	6	*O-141	-1.0
1928	Bro-N	108	296	41	73	11	0	2	19	47	24	.247	.354	.304	74	-9	18			.986	-12	O-95	-2.7
1929	Bro-N	19	23	2	7	0	0	0	1	3	2	.304	.407	.304	81	-0	0			1.000	-1	/O-4	-0.1
Total	20	2476	9363	1545	2665	419	159	70	800	1040	695	.285	.361	.386	107	109	738	92		.966	199	*O-2421	23.0

■ PAUL CAREY
Carey, Paul Stephan b: 1/8/68, Boston, Mass. BL/TR, 6'4", 215 lbs. Deb: 5/25/93

YEAR	TM/L	G	AB	R	H	2B	3B	HR	RBI	BB	SO	AVG	OBP	SLG	PRO+	BR/A	SB	CS	SBR	FA	FR	G/POS	TPR
1993	Bal-A	18	47	1	10	1	0	0	3	5	14	.213	.288	.234	41	-4	0	0	0	.970	-2	/1-9,D-5	-0.6

■ ROGER CAREY
Carey, Roger J. Deb: 7/9/1887

| 1887 | NY-N | 1 | 4 | 0 | 0 | 0 | 0 | 0 | 2 | 0 | 1 | .000 | .000 | .000 | -99 | -1 | 0 | | | .800 | 1 | /2-1 | 0.0 |

■ TOM CAREY
Carey, Thomas Francis Aloysius "Scoops" b: 10/11/06, Hoboken, N.J. d: 2/21/70, Rochester, N.Y. BR/TR, 5'8.5", 170 lbs. Deb: 7/19/35 C

1935	StL-A	76	296	29	86	18	4	0	42	13	11	.291	.320	.378	77	-11	0	2	-1	.961	-1	2-76	-0.6
1936	StL-A	134	488	58	133	27	6	1	57	27	25	.273	.315	.359	64	-28	2	1	0	.967	-1	*2-128/S-1	-1.8
1937	StL-A	130	487	54	134	24	1	1	40	21	26	.275	.306	.335	61	-29	1	2	-1	.983	2	2-87,S-44/3	-1.8
1939	Bos-A	54	161	17	39	6	2	0	20	3	9	.242	.265	.304	44	-14	0	0	0	1.000	6	2-35,S-10	-0.6
1940	Bos-A	43	62	4	20	4	0	0	7	2	1	.323	.344	.387	86	0	0	0	0	.953	5	S-20/2-4,3	0.4
1941	Bos-A	25	21	7	4	0	0	0	0	0	0	.190	.190	.190	1	-3	0	0	0	1.000	4	/2-9,S-8,3	0.1
1942	Bos-A	1	1	0	1	0	0	0	0	0	0	1.000	1.000	1.000	448	0	0	0	0	1.000	-0	/2-1	0.0
1946	Bos-A	3	5	0	1	0	0	0	0	0	0	.200	.200	.200	11	-1	0	0	0	.900	1	/2-3	0.1
Total	8	466	1521	169	418	79	13	2	167	66	73	.275	.308	.348	63	-87	3	5	-2	.973	17	2-343/S-83,3	-4.2

■ TOM CAREY
Carey, Thomas John (b: J. J. Norton) b: 1849, Brooklyn, N.Y. d: 2/13/1899, Los Angeles, Cal. BR/TR, 5'8", 145 lbs. Deb: 5/4/1871 M

1871	Kek-n	19	87	16	20	2	0	0	10	2	1	.230	.247	.253	43	-6	5					2-18/S-1	-0.5
1872	Bal-n	42	197	43	58	7	1	2	27	0	2	.294	.294	.371	99	-1						2-26/S-8,301	-0.2
1873	Bal-n	56	290	76	97	18	3	2	55	1	2	.334	.337	.438	127	9						*2-54/3-4,SM	0.3
1874	Mut-n	64	286	54	82	10	3	1		2		.287	.292	.353	101	-0						*S-51,2-13M	-0.2
1875	Har-n	86	382	63	101	6	2	0		2		.264	.268	.291	89	-6						*S-85	-0.7
1876	Har-N	68	289	51	78	7	0	0	26	3	4	.270	.277	.294	84	-6				.882	-1	*S-68	-0.7
1877	Har-N	60	274	38	70	3	2	1	20	0	9	.255	.255	.292	81	-5				.826	-6	*S-60	-0.9
1878	Pro-N	61	253	33	60	10	3	0	24	0	14	.237	.237	.300	76	-7				.874	1	*S-61	-0.2
1879	Cle-N	80	335	30	80	14	1	0	32	5	20	.239	.250	.287	77	-8				.864	-3	*S-80	-0.6
Total	5 n	267	1242	252	358	43	9	5	92	7	5	.288	.292	.349	99	-5						S-148,2-111/301	-1.3
Total	4	269	1151	152	288	34	6	1	102	8	47	.250	.255	.293	79	-26				.862	-9	S-269	-2.4

■ BOBBY CARGO
Cargo, Robert J. b: 10/1868, Pittsburgh, Pa. d: 4/27/04, Atlanta, Ga. BR/TR, Deb: 10/6/1892

| 1892 | Pit-N | 2 | 4 | 0 | 1 | 0 | 0 | 0 | 0 | 0 | 0 | .250 | .250 | .250 | 51 | -0 | 0 | | | .636 | 1 | /S-2 | 0.0 |

■ FRED CARISCH
Carisch, Frederick Behlmer b: 11/14/1881, Fountain City, Wis. d: 4/19/77, San Gabriel, Cal. BR/TR, 5'10.5", 174 lbs. Deb: 8/31/03 C

1903	Pit-N	5	18	4	6	4	0	1	5	0		.333	.333	.722	192	2	0			.969	1	/C-4	0.3
1904	Pit-N	37	125	9	31	3	1	0	8	9		.248	.299	.288	79	-3	3			.984	2	C-22,1-14	0.1
1905	Pit-N	32	107	7	22	0	3	0	8	2		.206	.227	.262	44	-8	1			.973	2	C-30	-0.3
1906	Pit-N	4	12	0	1	0	0	0	0	1		.083	.154	.083	-25	-2	1			.909	-0	/C-4	-0.2
1912	Cle-A	24	69	4	19	3	1	0	5	1		.275	.286	.348	78	-2	3			.952	6	C-23	0.6
1913	Cle-A	82	222	11	48	4	2	0	26	21	19	.216	.287	.252	56	-12	6			.971	13	C-79	0.8
1914	Cle-A	40	102	8	22	3	2	0	5	12	18	.216	.298	.284	72	-2	2	2	-1	.909	0	C-38	-0.1
1923	Det-A	2	0	0	0	0	0	0	0	0	0	—	—	—		0	0	0	0	1.000	-0	/C-2	0.0
Total	8	226	655	43	149	17	9	1	57	46	37	.227	.280	.285	66	-28	16	2		.968	24	C-202/1-14	1.2

■ FRED CARL
Carl, Frederick E. b: 11/1856, Germany d: 5/4/19, Washington, D.C. TL, 5'6", 158 lbs. Deb: 7/25/1889

| 1889 | Lou-a | 25 | 99 | 13 | 20 | 2 | 2 | 0 | 13 | 16 | 22 | .202 | .313 | .263 | 66 | -4 | 0 | | | .735 | 0 | O-18/2-6,3 | -0.3 |

■ LEW CARL
Carl, Lewis b: Baltimore, Md. Deb: 9/9/1874

| 1874 | Bal-n | 1 | 3 | 0 | 0 | 0 | 0 | 0 | | 0 | | .000 | .000 | .000 | -99 | -1 | | | | | | /C-1 | 0.0 |

■ JIM CARLETON
Carleton, James b: 1849, New York 5'8", 155 lbs. Deb: 5/4/1871

1871	Cle-n	29	127	31	32	8	1	0	18	8	3	.252	.296	.331	85	-2	2					*1-29	0.0
1872	Cle-n	7	38	8	12	3	0	0	4	1	0	.316	.333	.395	130	2						1-7	0.2
Total	2 n	36	165	39	44	11	1	0	22	9	3	.267	.305	.345	94	0						/1-36	0.2

■ JIM CARLIN
Carlin, James Arthur b: 2/23/18, Wylam, Ala. BR/TR, 5'11", 165 lbs. Deb: 7/26/41

| 1941 | Phi-N | 16 | 21 | 2 | 3 | 1 | 0 | 1 | 2 | 3 | 4 | .143 | .250 | .333 | 66 | -1 | 0 | | | 1.000 | -5 | /O-9,3-2 | -0.7 |

■ WALTER CARLISLE
Carlisle, Walter G. "Rosy" b: 7/6/1883, Yorkshire, England d: 5/27/45, Los Angeles, Cal. BB/TR, 5'9", 154 lbs. Deb: 5/8/08

| 1908 | Bos-A | 3 | 10 | 0 | 1 | 0 | 0 | 0 | 0 | 1 | | .100 | .182 | .100 | -8 | -1 | 1 | | | 1.000 | 1 | /O-3 | -0.1 |

■ SWEDE CARLSTROM
Carlstrom, Albin Oscar b: 10/26/1886, Elizabeth, N.J. d: 4/28/35, Elizabeth, N.J. BR/TR, 6', 167 lbs. Deb: 9/13/11

| 1911 | Bos-A | 2 | 6 | 0 | 1 | 0 | 0 | 0 | 0 | 0 | | .167 | .167 | .167 | -7 | -1 | 0 | | | 1.000 | 0 | /S-2 | 0.0 |

■ CLEO CARLYLE
Carlyle, Hiram Cleo b: 9/7/02, Fairburn, Ga. d: 11/12/67, Los Angeles, Cal. BL/TR, 6', 170 lbs. Deb: 5/16/27 F

| 1927 | Bos-A | 95 | 278 | 31 | 65 | 12 | 8 | 1 | 28 | 36 | 40 | .234 | .324 | .345 | 75 | -10 | 4 | 4 | -1 | .965 | -7 | O-83 | -2.2 |

■ ROY CARLYLE
Carlyle, Roy Edward "Dizzy" b: 12/10/1900, Buford, Ga. d: 11/22/56, Norcross, Ga. BL/TR, 6'2.5", 195 lbs. Deb: 4/16/25 F

1925	Was-A	1	1	0	0	0	0	0	0	0	1	.000	.000	.000	-99	-0	0			.000	0	H	0.0
	Bos-A	93	276	36	90	20	3	7	49	16	28	.326	.365	.496	117	6	1	1	-0	.909	-6	O-67	-0.4
	Yr	94	277	36	90	20	3	7	49	16	29	.325	.364	.495	116	5	1	1	-0	.909	-6	O-67	-0.4
1926	Bos-A	45	165	22	47	6	2	2	16	4	18	.285	.310	.382	82	-5	0	0	0	.904	-4	O-38	-1.1
	NY-A	35	52	3	20	5	1	0	11	4	9	.385	.439	.519	151	4	0	0	0	.941	-3	O-15	0.0
	Yr	80	217	25	67	11	3	2	27	8	27	.309	.342	.415	99	-1	0	0	0	.911	-7	O-53	-1.1
Total	2	174	494	61	157	31	6	9	76	24	56	.318	.354	.460	109	4	1	1	-0	.910	-12	O-120	-1.5

YEAR	TM/L	G	AB	R	H	2B	3B	HR	RBI	BB	SO	AVG	OBP	SLG	PRO+	BR/A	SB	CS	SBR	FA	FR	G/POS	TPR

■ GEORGE CARMAN   Carman, George Wartman   b: 3/29/1866, Philadelphia, Pa.   d: 6/16/29, Lancaster, Pa.   Deb: 9/4/1890

| 1890 | Phi-a | 28 | 97 | 9 | 17 | 2 | 0 | 0 | | 8 | | .175 | .245 | .196 | 31 | -8 | 5 | | | .767 | -9 | S-15,O-10/23 | -1.5 |

■ DUKE CARMEL   Carmel, Leon James   b: 4/23/37, New York, N.Y.   BL/TL, 6'3", 202 lbs.   Deb: 9/10/59

1959	StL-N	10	23	2	3	1	0	0	3	1	6	.130	.167	.174	-9	-4	0	1	-1	1.000	-3	O-10	-0.7
1960	StL-N	4	3	0	0	0	0	0	0	1	1	.000	.250	.000	-23	-0	1	1	-0	1.000	0	/1-2,O-1	-0.1
1963	StL-N	57	44	9	10	1	0	1	2	9	11	.227	.358	.318	88	-0	0	0	0	.974	-7	O-38/1-1	-0.8
	NY-N	47	149	11	35	5	3	3	18	16	37	.235	.309	.369	93	-1	2	2	-1	.980	-1	O-21,1-18	-0.5
	Yr	104	193	20	45	6	3	4	20	25	48	.233	.321	.358	90	-2	2	2	-1	.977	-7	O-59,1-19	-1.3
1965	NY-A	6	8	0	0	0	0	0	0	0	5	.000	.000	.000	-99	-2	0	0	0	1.000	0	/1-2	-0.2
Total	4	124	227	22	48	7	3	4	23	27	60	.211	.295	.322	73	-8	3	4	-2	.981	-10	/O-70,1-23	-2.3

■ EDDIE CARNETT   Carnett, Edwin Elliott "Lefty"   b: 10/21/16, Springfield, Mo.   BL/TL, 6', 185 lbs.   Deb: 4/19/41

1941	Bos-N	2	0	0	0	0	0	0	0	0	0	—	—	—	—	0	0			.000	0	/P-2	0.0
1944	Chi-A	126	457	51	126	18	8	1	60	26	35	.276	.322	.357	95	-4	5	2	0	.949	-8	O-88,1-25/P	-1.8
1945	Cle-A	30	73	5	16	7	0	0	7	2	9	.219	.250	.315	66	-4	0	1	-1	.971	-0	O-16/P-2	-0.6
Total	3	158	530	56	142	25	8	1	67	28	44	.268	.312	.351	91	-7	5	3		.952	-8	O-104/1-25,P	-2.4

■ JOHN CARNEY   Carney, John Joseph "Handsome Jack"   b: 11/10/1866, Salem, Mass.   d: 10/19/25, Litchfield, N.H.   BR/TR, 5'10.5", 175 lbs.   Deb: 4/24/1889

1889	Was-N	69	273	25	63	7	0	1	29	14	14	.231	.271	.267	54	-17	12			.957	-7	1-53,O-16	-2.4
1890	Buf-P	28	107	11	29	3	0	0	13	7	14	.271	.333	.299	76	-3	2			.972	-7	1-24/O-4	-0.5
	Cle-P	25	89	15	31	5	3	0	21	14	5	.348	.442	.472	157	8	6			.857	-3	O-19/1-6	0.3
	Yr	53	196	26	60	8	3	0	34	21	19	.306	.385	.378	113	5	8			.969	-6	1-30,O-23	-0.2
1891	Cin-a	99	367	47	102	10	8	5	43	35	18	.278	.346	.373	97	-4	15			.974	1	1-99	-0.7
	Mil-a	31	110	22	33	5	2	3	23	13	8	.300	.389	.464	120	1	5			.986	4	1-31	0.3
	Yr	130	477	69	135	15	10	6	66	48	26	.283	.356	.394	103	-2	20			.977	5	*1-130	-0.4
Total	3	252	946	120	258	30	13	7	129	83	59	.273	.338	.354	92	-14	40			.971	-8	1-213/O-39	-3.0

■ PAT CARNEY   Carney, Patrick Joseph "Doc"   b: 8/7/1876, Holyoke, Mass.   d: 1/9/53, Worcester, Mass.   BL/TL, 6', 200 lbs.   Deb: 9/20/01

1901	Bos-N	13	55	6	16	2	1	0	6	3		.291	.339	.364	95	-0	0			.933	-3	O-13	-0.4
1902	Bos-N	137	522	75	141	17	4	2	65	42		.270	.339	.330	105	4	27			.930	-9	*O-137/P-2	-1.4
1903	Bos-N	110	392	37	94	12	4	1	49	28		.240	.297	.298	73	-14	10			.953	-6	O-92,P-10/1	-2.3
1904	Bos-N	78	279	24	57	5	2	0	11	12		.204	.240	.237	49	-17	6			.953	-2	O-71/P-4,1	-2.4
Total	4	338	1248	142	308	36	11	3	131	85		.247	.304	.300	82	-27	43			.942	-20	O-313/P-16,1	-6.5

■ BILL CARNEY   Carney, William John   b: 3/25/1874, St.Paul, Minn.   d: 7/31/38, Hopkins, Minn.   BB/TR, 5'10",   Deb: 8/22/04

| 1904 | Chi-N | 2 | 7 | 0 | 0 | 0 | 0 | 0 | 0 | 1 | | .000 | .125 | .000 | -60 | -1 | 0 | | | 1.000 | 0 | /O-2 | -0.2 |

■ HICK CARPENTER   Carpenter, Warren William   b: 8/16/1855, Grafton, Mass.   d: 4/18/37, San Diego, Cal.   BR/TL, 5'11", 186 lbs.   Deb: 5/1/1879

1879	Syr-N	65	261	30	53	6	0	0	20	2	15	.203	.209	.226	49	-13				.948	-4	1-34,3-18,O/2	-1.7
1880	Cin-N	77	300	32	72	6	4	0	23	2	15	.240	.245	.287	80	-6				.853	-1	*3-67/1-9,S	-0.5
1881	Wor-N	83	347	40	75	12	2	2	31	3	19	.216	.223	.280	54	-19				.848	3	*3-83	-1.4
1882	Cin-a	80	351	78	**120**	15	5	1			10	.342	.360	.422	154	18				**.835**	-1	*3-80	1.7
1883	Cin-a	95	435	99	130	18	4	3			19	.299	.328	.379	120	8				.870	-6	*3-95	0.2
1884	Cin-a	108	474	80	121	16	2	4		6		.255	.271	.323	89	-7				.881	-9	*3-108/O-1	-1.4
1885	Cin-a	112	473	89	131	8	2	2		9		.277	.295	.349	101	-1				.860	-6	*3-112	-0.5
1886	Cin-a	111	458	67	101	8	5	2		18		.221	.262	.273	66	-19	8			.841	-6	*3-111	-2.0
1887	Cin-a	127	498	70	124	12	6	1		19		.249	.282	.303	62	-27	44			.846	-13	*3-127	-3.0
1888	Cin-a	136	551	68	147	14	5	3	67	5		.267	.280	.327	89	-9	59			.866	-12	*3-136	-1.7
1889	Cin-a	123	486	67	127	23	6	0	63	18	41	.261	.293	.333	76	-17	47			.835	-25	*3-121/1-2	-3.3
1892	StL-N	1	3	0	1	0	0	0	0	1	1	.333	.500	.333	161	0				.714	0	/3-1	0.0
Total	12	1118	4637	720	1202	142	47	18	204	112	91	.259	.281	.322	86	-92	158			.853	-80	*3-1059/1-45,O2S	-13.6

■ CHARLIE CARR   Carr, Charles Carbitt   b: 12/27/1876, Coatesville, Pa.   d: 11/25/32, Memphis, Tenn.   BR/TR, 6'2", 195 lbs.   Deb: 9/15/1898

1898	Was-N	20	73	6	14	2	0	0	4	2		.192	.213	.219	24	-7	2			.950	-2	1-20	-0.9
1901	Phi-A	2	8	0	1	0	0	0	0	0		.125	.125	.125	-29	-1	0			.926	0	/1-2	-0.1
1903	Det-A	135	548	59	154	23	11	2	79	10		.281	.296	.374	103	0	10			.982	12	*1-135	1.1
1904	Det-A	92	360	29	77	13	3	0	40	14		.214	.245	.267	64	-15	6			.983	16	1-92	-0.1
	Cle-A	32	120	9	27	5	1	0	7	4		.225	.250	.283	69	-4	0			.973	-0	1-32	-0.6
	Yr	124	480	38	104	18	4	0	47	18		.217	.246	.271	65	-20	6			.980	16	*1-124	-0.7
1905	Cle-A	89	306	29	72	12	4	1	31	13		.235	.266	.310	82	-7	12			.991	-2	1-87	-1.3
1906	Cin-N	22	94	9	18	2	3	0	10	2		.191	.216	.277	51	-6	0			.983	1	1-22	-0.6
1914	Ind-F	115	441	44	129	11	10	3	69	26	47	.293	.333	.383	77	-15	19			**.991**	-1	*1-115	-1.8
Total	7	507	1950	185	492	68	32	6	240	71	47	.252	.280	.329	78	-56	49			.984	26	1-505	-4.3

■ CHUCK CARR   Carr, Charles Lee Glenn   b: 8/10/67, San Bernardino, Cal.   BB/TR, 5'10", 155 lbs.   Deb: 4/28/90

1990	NY-N	4	2	0	0	0	0	0	0	0	2	.000	.000	.000	-99	-1	1	0	0	.000	-0	/O-1	-0.1
1991	NY-N	12	11	1	2	0	0	0	1	0	2	.182	.182	.182	3	-1	1	0	0	1.000	-2	/O-9	-0.3
1992	StL-N	22	64	8	14	3	0	0	3	9	6	.219	.315	.266	68	-2	10	2	2	1.000	-1	/O-19	-0.2
1993	Fla-N	142	551	75	147	19	2	4	41	49	74	.267	.329	.330	73	-20	**58**	22	4	.985	16	*O-139	-0.3
1994	Fla-N	106	433	61	114	19	2	2	30	22	71	.263	.307	.330	63	-23	32	8	5	.980	10	*O-104	-1.1
Total	5	286	1061	145	277	41	4	6	75	80	155	.261	.317	.324	68	-48	102	32	11	.984	22	O-272	-2.0

■ LEW CARR   Carr, Lewis Smith   b: 8/15/1872, Union Springs, N.Y.   d: 6/15/54, Moravia, N.Y.   BR/TR, 6'2", 200 lbs.   Deb: 7/4/01

| 1901 | Pit-N | 9 | 28 | 2 | 7 | 1 | 1 | 0 | 4 | 2 | | .250 | .344 | .357 | 100 | 0 | 0 | | | .886 | -5 | /S-9,3-1 | -0.4 |

■ CHICO CARRASQUEL   Carrasquel, Alfonso (Colon)   b: 1/23/28, Caracas, Venez.   BR/TR, 6', 170 lbs.   Deb: 4/18/50

1950	Chi-A	141	524	72	148	21	5	4	46	66	46	.282	.368	.365	91	-6	0	2	-1	.961	11	*S-141	1.4
1951	Chi-A★	147	538	41	142	22	4	5	58	46	39	.264	.325	.331	79	-16	14	4	2	**.975**	13	*S-147	0.9
1952	Chi-A	100	359	36	89	7	4	1	42	33	27	.248	.315	.298	71	-14	2	2	-1	.964	-16	S-99	-2.4
1953	Chi-A★	149	552	72	154	30	4	5	47	38	47	.279	.330	.359	83	-13	5	3	-0	**.976**	3	*S-149	0.1
1954	Chi-A★	155	620	106	158	28	3	12	62	85	67	.255	.349	.368	93	-4	7	6	-2	**.975**	11	*S-155	1.9
1955	Chi-A★	145	523	83	134	11	2	11	52	61	59	.256	.338	.348	83	-12	1	6	-0	.973	0	*S-144	0.0
1956	Cle-A	141	474	60	115	15	1	7	48	52	61	.243	.325	.323	70	-20	0	4	-2	.967	-25	S-141/3-1	-3.6
1957	Cle-A	125	392	37	108	14	1	8	57	41	53	.276	.356	.378	102	3	0	2	-2	.960	-5	*S-122	0.7
1958	Cle-A	49	156	14	40	6	0	2	21	14	12	.256	.318	.333	81	-4	0	0	0	.931	-19	S-32,3-14	-2.1
	KC-A	59	160	19	34	5	1	2	13	21	15	.213	.304	.294	64	-8	0	1	-0	.976	-6	3-32,S-22	-1.3
	Yr	108	316	33	74	11	1	4	34	35	27	.234	.311	.313	72	-12	0	1	-0	.947	-25	S-54,3-46	-3.4
1959	Bal-A	114	346	28	77	13	0	3	30	31	41	.223	.294	.295	64	-12	0	2	-1	.970	-14	S-89,2-22/31	-2.4
Total	10	1325	4644	568	1199	172	25	55	474	491	467	.258	.334	.342	82	-111	31	28	-8	.969	-47	*S-1241/3-49,21	-6.8

■ CAM CARREON   Carreon, Camilo   b: 8/6/37, Colton, Cal.   d: 9/2/87, Tucson, Ariz.   BR/TR, 6', 198 lbs.   Deb: 9/27/59   F

1959	Chi-A	1	1	0	0	0	0	0	0	0	0	.000	.000	.000	-99	-0	0	0	0	1.000	0	/C-1	0.0
1960	Chi-A	8	17	2	4	0	0	0	2	1	3	.235	.278	.235	41	-0	0	0	0	1.000	0	/C-7	-0.1
1961	Chi-A	78	229	32	62	5	1	4	27	29	24	.271	.332	.354	85	-5	0	1	-1	.995	9	C-71	0.7

YEAR	TM/L	G	AB	R	H	2B	3B	HR	RBI	BB	SO	AVG	OBP	SLG	PRO+	BR/A	SB	CS	SBR	FA	FR	G/POS	TPR
1962	Chi-A	106	313	31	80	19	1	4	37	33	37	.256	.329	.361	86	-6	1	1	-0	.995	8	C-93	0.5
1963	Chi-A	101	270	28	74	10	1	2	35	23	32	.274	.333	.341	91	-3	1	1	-0	.987	0	C-92	0.0
1964	Chi-A	37	95	12	26	5	0	0	4	7	13	.274	.330	.326	86	-2	0	0	0	.987	-4	C-34	-0.5
1965	Cle-A	19	52	6	12	2	1	1	7	9	6	.231	.344	.365	101	0	1	1	0	1.000	0	C-19	0.1
1966	Bal-A	4	9	2	2	2	0	0	2	3	2	.222	.417	.444	150	1	0	0	0	1.000	0	/C-3	0.1
Total	8	354	986	113	260	43	4	11	114	97	117	.264	.331	.349	87	-16	3	4	-2	.993	14	C-320	0.8

■ MARK CARREON
Carreon, Mark Steven b: 7/19/63, Chicago, Ill. BR/TL, 6', 194 lbs. Deb: 9/8/87 F

YEAR	TM/L	G	AB	R	H	2B	3B	HR	RBI	BB	SO	AVG	OBP	SLG	PRO+	BR/A	SB	CS	SBR	FA	FR	G/POS	TPR
1987	NY-N	9	12	0	3	0	0	0	1	1	1	.250	.308	.250	53	-1	0	1	-1	.800	-1	/O-5	-0.3
1988	NY-N	7	9	5	5	2	0	1	1	2	1	.556	.636	1.111	413	4	0	0	0	1.000	-1	/O-4	0.3
1989	NY-N	68	133	20	41	6	0	6	16	12	17	.308	.370	.489	151	8	2	3	-1	.983	-3	O-39	0.4
1990	NY-N	82	188	30	47	12	0	10	26	15	29	.250	.312	.473	113	3	1	0	0	1.000	-8	O-60	-0.7
1991	NY-N	106	254	18	66	6	0	4	21	12	26	.260	.299	.331	77	-8	2	1	0	.971	-12	O-77	-2.2
1992	Det-A	101	336	34	78	11	1	10	41	22	57	.232	.281	.360	78	-11	3	1	0	.979	2	O-83,D-13	-1.1
1993	SF-N	78	150	22	49	9	1	7	33	13	16	.327	.384	.540	149	10	1	0	0	.943	-7	O-41/1-3	0.3
1994	SF-N	51	100	8	27	4	0	3	20	7	20	.270	.330	.400	93	-1	0	0	0	.978	-5	O-33	-0.6
Total	8	502	1182	137	316	50	2	41	159	84	167	.267	.321	.417	104	4	9	6	-1	.976	-36	O-342/D-13,1	-3.9

■ BILL CARRIGAN
Carrigan, William Francis "Rough" b: 10/22/1883, Lewiston, Me. d: 7/8/69, Lewiston, Me. BR/TR, 5'9", 175 lbs. Deb: 7/7/06 M

YEAR	TM/L	G	AB	R	H	2B	3B	HR	RBI	BB	SO	AVG	OBP	SLG	PRO+	BR/A	SB	CS	SBR	FA	FR	G/POS	TPR
1906	Bos-A	37	109	5	23	0	0	0	10	5		.211	.252	.211	45	-7	3			.940	-2	C-35	-0.5
1908	Bos-A	57	149	13	35	5	2	0	14	3		.235	.255	.295	77	-4	1			.955	6	C-47/1-3	0.6
1909	Bos-A	94	280	25	83	13	2	1	36	17		.296	.341	.368	121	6	2			.972	1	C-77/1-8	1.6
1910	Bos-A	114	342	36	85	11	1	3	53	23		.249	.307	.313	92	-3	10			.962	-21	*C-110	-1.6
1911	Bos-A	72	232	29	67	6	1	1	30	26		.289	.373	.336	99	1	5			.972	1	C-62/1-6	0.6
1912	*Bos-A	87	266	34	70	7	1	0	24	38		.263	.359	.297	84	-4	7			.970	-12	C-87	-0.7
1913	Bos-A	87	256	17	62	15	5	0	28	27	26	.242	.319	.340	91	-3	6			.979	-8	C-82,M	-0.4
1914	Bos-A	82	178	18	45	5	1	1	22	40	18	.253	.395	.309	112	5	1	2	-1	.984	3	C-78,M	1.5
1915	*Bos-A	46	95	10	19	3	0	0	7	16	12	.200	.321	.232	68	-3	0			.975	8	C-44,M	0.8
1916	*Bos-A	33	63	7	17	2	1	0	11	11	3	.270	.378	.333	113	2	2			1.000	6	C-27,M	1.0
Total	10	709	1970	194	506	67	14	6	235	206	59	.257	.334	.314	94	-11	37	2		.971	-18	C-649/1-17	2.9

■ MATIAS CARRILLO
Carrillo, Matias (Garcia) b: 2/24/63, Los Mochis, Mexico BL/TL, 5'11", 190 lbs. Deb: 5/23/91

YEAR	TM/L	G	AB	R	H	2B	3B	HR	RBI	BB	SO	AVG	OBP	SLG	PRO+	BR/A	SB	CS	SBR	FA	FR	G/POS	TPR
1991	Mil-A	3	0	0	0	0	0	0	0	0	0	—	—	—	—	—	0	0	0	.000	-1	/O-3	-0.1
1993	Fla-N	24	55	4	14	6	0	0	3	1	7	.255	.281	.364	67	-3	0	0	0	1.000	-3	O-16	-0.6
1994	Fla-N	80	136	13	34	7	0	0	9	9	31	.250	.297	.301	53	-9	3	3	-1	.982	-7	O-49	-1.8
Total	3	107	191	17	48	13	0	0	12	10	38	.251	.292	.319	57	-12	3	3	-1	.987	-12	/O-68	-2.5

■ DIXIE CARROLL
Carroll, Dorsey Lee b: 5/9/1891, Paducah, Ky. d: 10/13/84, Jacksonville, Fla BL/TR, 5'11", 165 lbs. Deb: 9/12/19

YEAR	TM/L	G	AB	R	H	2B	3B	HR	RBI	BB	SO	AVG	OBP	SLG	PRO+	BR/A	SB	CS	SBR	FA	FR	G/POS	TPR
1919	Bos-N	15	49	10	13	3	1	0	7	1		.265	.379	.367	130	2	5			.921	2	O-13	0.3

■ CHICK CARROLL
Carroll, Edward b: 1868, Arkansas d: 7/13/08, Chicago, Ill. Deb: 4/17/1884

YEAR	TM/L	G	AB	R	H	2B	3B	HR	RBI	BB	SO	AVG	OBP	SLG	PRO+	BR/A	SB	CS	SBR	FA	FR	G/POS	TPR
1884	Was-U	4	16	1	4	0	0	0		0		.250	.250	.250	38	-1				.500	-1	/O-4	-0.2

■ FRED CARROLL
Carroll, Frederick Herbert b: 7/2/1864, Sacramento, Cal. d: 11/7/04, San Rafael, Cal. BR/TR, 5'11", 185 lbs. Deb: 5/1/1884

YEAR	TM/L	G	AB	R	H	2B	3B	HR	RBI	BB	SO	AVG	OBP	SLG	PRO+	BR/A	SB	CS	SBR	FA	FR	G/POS	TPR
1884	Col-a	69	252	46	70	13	5	6	13			.278	.326	.440	161	17				.944	16	C-54,O-15	3.3
1885	Pit-a	71	280	45	75	13	8	0	7			.268	.298	.371	112	3				.926	4	C-60,O-12	1.1
1886	Pit-a	122	486	92	140	28	11	5	52			.288	.362	.422	146	26	20			.921	11	C-70,O-27,1/S	3.6
1887	Pit-N	102	421	71	138	24	15	6	54	36	21	.328	.383	.499	152	30	23			.833	-12	O-46,C-40,1/S	1.7
1888	Pit-N	97	366	62	91	14	5	2	48	32	31	.249	.326	.331	119	10	18			.897	-11	C-54,O-38/13	0.2
1889	Pit-N	91	318	80	105	21	11	2	51	85	26	.330	.486	.484	190	48	19			.930	-13	C-43,O-41/13	3.2
1890	Pit-P	111	416	95	124	20	7	2	71	75	22	.298	.418	.394	128	23	35			.856	-17	C-56,O-49/1	0.7
1891	Pit-N	91	353	55	77	13	4	4	48	48	36	.218	.315	.312	85	-6	22			.915	6	O-91	-0.3
Total	8	754	2892	546	820	146	66	27	272	348	136	.284	.370	.408	137	151	137			.913	-16	C-377,O-319/13S	13.5

■ SCRAPPY CARROLL
Carroll, John E. b: 8/27/1860, Buffalo, N.Y. d: 11/14/42, Buffalo, N.Y. 5'7.5", Deb: 9/27/1884

YEAR	TM/L	G	AB	R	H	2B	3B	HR	RBI	BB	SO	AVG	OBP	SLG	PRO+	BR/A	SB	CS	SBR	FA	FR	G/POS	TPR
1884	StP-U	9	31	3	3	1	0	0				.097	.152	.129	-43	-7				.824	3	/O-8,3-2	-0.4
1885	Buf-N	13	40	1	3	0	0	0	1	2	8	.075	.119	.075	-35	-6				.917	1	O-13	-0.5
1887	Cle-a	57	216	30	43	5	1	0	15			.199	.264	.231	40	-17	19			.843	-5	O-54/3-3,2	-1.9
Total	3	79	287	34	49	6	1	0	1	19	8	.171	.232	.199	24	-30	19			.853	-2	/O-75,3-5,2	-2.8

■ PAT CARROLL
Carroll, Patrick b: 3/1853, Philadelphia, Pa. d: 2/14/16, Philadelphia, Pa. Deb: 5/10/1884

YEAR	TM/L	G	AB	R	H	2B	3B	HR	RBI	BB	SO	AVG	OBP	SLG	PRO+	BR/A	SB	CS	SBR	FA	FR	G/POS	TPR
1884	Alt-U	11	49	4	13	1	0	0	1			.265	.280	.286	53	-3				.920	-4	/C-8,O-3	-0.5
	Phi-U	5	19	1	3	1	0	0	0			.158	.158	.211	-1	-3				.839	3	/C-5	0.0
	Yr	16	68	5	16	2	0	0	1			.235	.246	.265	39	-6				.877	-1	C-13/O-3	-0.5

■ DOC CARROLL
Carroll, Ralph Arthur "Red" b: 12/28/1891, Worcester, Mass. d: 6/27/83, Worcester, Mass. BR/TR, 6', 170 lbs. Deb: 6/27/16

YEAR	TM/L	G	AB	R	H	2B	3B	HR	RBI	BB	SO	AVG	OBP	SLG	PRO+	BR/A	SB	CS	SBR	FA	FR	G/POS	TPR
1916	Phi-A	10	22	1	2	0	0	0	0	1	8	.091	.167	.091	-24	-3	0			.942	0	C-10	-0.3

■ CLIFF CARROLL
Carroll, Samuel Clifford b: 10/18/1859, Clay Grove, Iowa d: 6/12/23, Portland, Ore. BB/TR, 5'8", 163 lbs. Deb: 8/3/1882

YEAR	TM/L	G	AB	R	H	2B	3B	HR	RBI	BB	SO	AVG	OBP	SLG	PRO+	BR/A	SB	CS	SBR	FA	FR	G/POS	TPR
1882	Pro-N	10	41	4	5	0	0	0	2	0	4	.122	.122	.122	-21	-5				1.000	1	O-10	-0.4
1883	Pro-N	58	238	37	63	12	3	1	20	4	28	.265	.277	.353	87	-4				.902	5	O-58	0.0
1884	*Pro-N	113	452	90	118	16	4	3	54	29	39	.261	.306	.334	104	3				.904	2	*O-113	0.2
1885	Pro-N	104	426	62	99	12	3	1	40	29	29	.232	.281	.282	86	-6				.886	4	*O-104	-0.5
1886	Was-N	111	433	73	99	11	6	2	22	44	26	.229	.300	.296	87	-5	31			.862	1	*O-111	-0.8
1887	Was-N	103	420	79	104	17	4	4	37	17	30	.248	.291	.336	78	-12	40			.902	-1	*O-103	-1.1
1888	Pit-N	5	20	1	0	0	0	0	0	0	8	.000	.000	.000	-99	-5	2			.667	-1	/O-5	-0.6
1890	Chi-N	136	582	134	166	16	6	7	65	53	44	.285	.352	.369	106	4	34			.936	15	*O-136	1.2
1891	Chi-N	130	515	87	132	20	8	7	80	50	42	.256	.340	.367	106	4	31			.915	-5	*O-130	-0.4
1892	StL-N	101	407	82	111	14	8	4	49	47	22	.273	.363	.376	130	16	30			.901	4	*O-101	1.4
1893	Bos-N	120	438	80	98	7	5	2	54	88	28	.224	.360	.276	65	-21	29			.917	2	*O-120	-2.1
Total	11	991	3972	729	995	125	47	31	423	361	290	.251	.320	.329	93	-31	197			.905	25	O-991	-3.1

■ TOM CARROLL
Carroll, Thomas Edward b: 9/17/36, Jamaica, N.Y. BR/TR, 6'3", 186 lbs. Deb: 5/7/55

YEAR	TM/L	G	AB	R	H	2B	3B	HR	RBI	BB	SO	AVG	OBP	SLG	PRO+	BR/A	SB	CS	SBR	FA	FR	G/POS	TPR
1955	*NY-A	14	6	3	2	0	0	0	0	0	2	.333	.333	.333	81	-0	0	0	0	.875	2	/S-4	0.2
1956	NY-A	36	17	11	6	0	0	0	0	1	3	.353	.389	.353	100	0	1	0	0	.857	5	3-11/S-1	0.5
1959	KC-A	14	7	1	1	0	0	0	1	0	1	.143	.143	.143	-21	-1	0	0	0	1.000	4	/S-9,3-3	0.3
Total	3	64	30	15	9	0	0	0	1	1	6	.300	.323	.300	69	-1	1	0	0	.813	11	/3-14,S-14	1.0

■ KID CARSEY
Carsey, Wilfred b: 10/22/1870, New York, N.Y. d: 3/29/60, Miami, Fla. BL/TR, 5'7", 168 lbs. Deb: 4/8/1891

YEAR	TM/L	G	AB	R	H	2B	3B	HR	RBI	BB	SO	AVG	OBP	SLG	PRO+	BR/A	SB	CS	SBR	FA	FR	G/POS	TPR
1891	Was-a	61	187	25	28	5	2	0	15	19	38	.150	.236	.198	25	-18	2			.922	5	P-54/O-7,S	-0.2
1892	Phi-N	44	131	8	20	2	1	1	10	9	24	.153	.207	.206	25	-12	2			.888	2	P-43/O-2	-0.1
1893	Phi-N	39	145	12	27	1	1	0	10	5	14	.186	.229	.207	16	-18	2			.925	2	P-39	0.0
1894	Phi-N	35	125	30	34	2	2	0	18	16	11	.272	.359	.320	67	-6	3			.937	2	P-35	0.0
1895	Phi-N	44	141	24	41	2	0	0	20	15	12	.291	.363	.305	73	-5	2			.878	1	P-44	0.0
1896	Phi-N	27	81	13	18	2	0	0	7	11	12	.222	.315	.296	62	-4	1			.908	1	P-27	0.0
1897	Phi-N	4	13	1	3	0	0	0	1	0		.231	.231	.231	23	-1	0			1.000	-0	/P-4	0.0

YEAR	TM/L	G	AB	R	H	2B	3B	HR	RBI	BB	SO	AVG	OBP	SLG	PRO+	BR/A	SB	CS	SBR	FA	FR	G/POS	TPR
	StL-N	13	43	2	13	2	2	0	5	1		.302	.318	.442	101	-0	1			.917	1	P-12	0.0
	Yr	17	56	3	16	2	2	0	6	1		.286	.298	.393	83	-2	1			.930	1	P-16	0.0
1898	StL-N	38	105	8	21	0	1	1	10	10		.200	.270	.248	47	-7	3			.935	-6	P-20,2-10/O	-1.0
1899	Cle-N	11	36	5	10	0	0	0	4	3		.278	.333	.278	74	-1	0			.879	3	P-10/S-1	0.1
	Was-N	4	11	1	0	0	0	0	0	0		.000	.000	.000	-99	-3	0			.923	1	/P-4	0.0
	NY-N	5	18	2	6	1	0	0	1	2		.333	.400	.389	121	1	2			.667	-1	/3-3,S-2	0.0
	Yr	20	65	8	16	1	0	0	5	5		.246	.300	.262	57	-4	2			.891	3	P-14/S-3,3	0.1
1901	Bro-N	2	2	0	0	0	0	0	0	0		.000	.000	.000	-97	-0	0			1.000	0	/P-2	0.0
Total	10	327	1038	131	221	17	11	2	101	91	111	.213	.281	.256	47	-76	17			.911	7	P-294/O-17,2S3	-1.2

■ KIT CARSON
Carson, Walter Lloyd   b: 11/15/12, Colton, Cal.   d: 6/21/83, Long Beach, Cal.   BL/TL, 6′, 180 lbs.   Deb: 7/21/34

YEAR	TM/L	G	AB	R	H	2B	3B	HR	RBI	BB	SO	AVG	OBP	SLG	PRO+	BR/A	SB	CS	SBR	FA	FR	G/POS	TPR
1934	Cle-A	5	18	4	5	1	0	0	2	2	3	.278	.350	.500	115	0	0	1		1.000	-1	/O-4	-0.1
1935	Cle-A	16	22	1	5	0	1	0	2	6	.227	.292	.318	57	-1	0	1	-1	1.000	-0	/O-4	-0.2
Total	2	21	40	5	10	1	1	0	2	4	9	.250	.318	.400	83	-1	0	1	-1	1.000	-2	/O-8	-0.3

■ FRANK CARSWELL
Carswell, Frank Willis "Tex" or "Wheels"   b: 11/6/19, Palestine, Tex.   BR/TR, 6′, 195 lbs.   Deb: 4/17/53

YEAR	TM/L	G	AB	R	H	2B	3B	HR	RBI	BB	SO	AVG	OBP	SLG	PRO+	BR/A	SB	CS	SBR	FA	FR	G/POS	TPR
1953	Det-A	16	15	2	4	1	0	0	2	1	1	.267	.389	.267	81	-0	0	0		1.000	-1	/O-3	-0.1

■ GARY CARTER
Carter, Gary Edmund   b: 4/8/54, Culver City, Cal.   BR/TR, 6′2″, 215 lbs.   Deb: 9/16/74

YEAR	TM/L	G	AB	R	H	2B	3B	HR	RBI	BB	SO	AVG	OBP	SLG	PRO+	BR/A	SB	CS	SBR	FA	FR	G/POS	TPR
1974	Mon-N	9	27	5	11	0	1	1	6	1	2	.407	.429	.593	174	2	2	0	1	1.000	-1	/C-6,O-2	0.3
1975	Mon-N★	144	503	58	136	20	1	17	68	72	83	.270	.363	.416	111	8	5	2	0	.974	-16	O-92,C-66/3	-0.8
1976	Mon-N	91	311	31	68	8	1	6	38	30	43	.219	.289	.309	67	-13	0	2	-1	.994	3	C-60,O-36	-1.2
1977	Mon-N	154	522	86	148	29	2	31	84	58	103	.284	.361	.525	138	27	5	5	-2	.990	3	*C-146/O-1	3.3
1978	Mon-N	157	533	76	136	27	1	20	72	62	70	.255	.338	.422	113	9	10	6	-1	.989	10	*C-152/1-1	2.3
1979	Mon-N★	141	505	74	143	26	5	22	75	40	62	.283	.342	.485	124	15	3	2	-0	.989	13	*C-138	3.4
1980	Mon-N	154	549	76	145	25	5	29	101	58	78	.264	.336	.486	127	18	3	2	-0	.993	14	*C-149	3.9
1981	*Mon-N★	100	374	48	94	20	2	16	68	35	35	.251	.317	.444	113	5	1	5	-3	.993	2	*C-100/1-1	0.9
1982	Mon-N★	154	557	91	163	32	1	29	97	78	64	.293	.385	.510	146	35	2	5	-2	.991	14	*C-153	5.4
1983	Mon-N★	145	541	63	146	37	3	17	79	51	57	.270	.341	.444	116	11	1	1	-0	**.995**	10	*C-144/1-1	2.8
1984	Mon-N★	159	596	75	175	32	1	27	**106**	64	57	.294	.368	.487	145	34	2	2	-1	.993	-5	*C-143,1-25	3.5
1985	NY-N†	149	555	83	156	17	1	32	100	69	46	.281	.367	.488	141	30	1	1	-0	.992	5	*C-143/1-6,O	4.3
1986	*NY-N★	132	490	81	125	14	2	24	105	62	63	.255	.346	.439	118	12	1	0	0	.991	6	*C-122/1-9,O3	2.7
1987	NY-N★	139	523	55	123	18	2	20	83	42	73	.235	.293	.392	84	-14	0	0	0	.991	-0	*C-135/1-4,O	-0.5
1988	*NY-N★	130	455	39	110	16	2	11	46	34	52	.242	.304	.358	94	-4	0	2	-1	.990	-3	*C-119,1-10/3	-0.5
1989	NY-N	50	153	14	28	8	0	2	15	12	15	.183	.242	.275	50	-10	0	0	0	.980	-2	C-47/1-1	-1.0
1990	SF-N	92	244	24	62	10	0	9	27	25	31	.254	.326	.406	104	1	1	1	0	.992	-3	C-80/1-3	0.1
1991	LA-N	101	248	22	61	14	0	6	26	22	26	.246	.325	.375	98	-2	0	2	-1	.988	3	C-68,1-10	0.6
1992	Mon-N	95	285	24	62	18	1	5	29	33	37	.218	.303	.340	83	-6	0	4	-2	.989	1	C-85/1-5	-0.4
Total	19	2296	7971	1025	2092	371	31	324	1225	848	997	.262	.338	.439	116	159	39	42	-14	.991	54	*C-2056,O-137/13	29.6

■ HOWIE CARTER
Carter, John Howard   b: 10/13/04, New York, N.Y.   d: 7/24/91, New York, N.Y.   BR/TR, 5′10″, 154 lbs.   Deb: 6/21/26

YEAR	TM/L	G	AB	R	H	2B	3B	HR	RBI	BB	SO	AVG	OBP	SLG	PRO+	BR/A	SB	CS	SBR	FA	FR	G/POS	TPR
1926	Cin-N	5	1	0	0	0	0	0	0	0	0	.000	.000	.000	-99	-0	0			1.000	0	/2-3,S-1	0.0

■ JOE CARTER
Carter, Joseph Chris   b: 3/7/60, Oklahoma City, Okla.   BR/TR, 6′3″, 215 lbs.   Deb: 7/30/83

YEAR	TM/L	G	AB	R	H	2B	3B	HR	RBI	BB	SO	AVG	OBP	SLG	PRO+	BR/A	SB	CS	SBR	FA	FR	G/POS	TPR
1983	Chi-N	23	51	6	9	1	1	0	1	0	21	.176	.176	.235	13	-6	1	0	0	1.000	-2	O-16	-0.8
1984	Cle-A	66	244	32	67	6	1	13	41	11	48	.275	.309	.467	109	2	2	4	-2	.956	1	O-59/1-7	-0.1
1985	Cle-A	143	489	64	128	27	0	15	59	25	74	.262	.300	.409	93	-6	24	6	4	.983	-1	*O-135,1-11/23D	-0.8
1986	Cle-A	162	663	108	200	36	9	29	**121**	32	95	.302	.339	.514	130	25	29	7	5	.976	-6	*O-104,1-70	1.5
1987	Cle-A	149	588	83	155	27	2	32	106	27	105	.264	.306	.480	103	1	31	6	6	.983	-8	1-84,O-62/D	-0.9
1988	Cle-A	157	621	85	168	36	6	27	98	35	82	.271	.317	.478	116	11	27	5	5	.985	14	*O-156	2.5
1989	Cle-A	162	651	84	158	32	4	35	105	39	112	.243	.294	.465	109	4	13	5	1	.978	-1	*O-146,1-11/D	-0.1
1990	SD-N	162	634	79	147	27	1	24	115	48	93	.232	.293	.391	86	-14	22	6	3	.988	9	*O-150,1-14	-0.7
1991	*Tor-A★	162	638	89	174	42	3	33	108	49	112	.273	.334	.503	124	18	20	9	1	.974	-3	*O-151,D-11	1.8
1992	Tor-A★	158	622	97	164	30	7	34	119	36	109	.264	.315	.498	119	13	12	5	1	.971	6	*O-129,D-24/1	1.5
1993	*Tor-A★	155	603	92	153	33	5	33	121	47	113	.254	.317	.489	113	8	8	3	1	.974	-3	*O-151/D-3	0.6
1994	Tor-A★	111	435	70	118	25	2	27	103	33	64	.271	.326	.524	113	7	11	0	3	.991	0	*O-110/D-1	0.7
Total	12	1610	6239	889	1641	322	41	302	1097	382	1028	.263	.313	.473	110	63	200	56	26	.979	15	*O-1369,1-201/D32	5.2

■ BLACKIE CARTER
Carter, Otis Leonard   b: 9/30/02, Langley, S.C.   d: 9/10/76, Greenville, S.C.   BR/TR, 5′10″, 175 lbs.   Deb: 10/3/25

YEAR	TM/L	G	AB	R	H	2B	3B	HR	RBI	BB	SO	AVG	OBP	SLG	PRO+	BR/A	SB	CS	SBR	FA	FR	G/POS	TPR
1925	NY-N	1	4	0	0	0	0	0	0	1		.000	.000	.000	-99	-1	0	0		1.000	1	/O-1	-0.1
1926	NY-N	5	17	4	4	1	0	1	1	1	0	.235	.278	.471	100	-0	0	0		.917	-1	/O-4	0.0
Total	2	6	21	4	4	1	0	1	1	2		.190	.227	.381	61	-1	0	0		.929	1	/O-5	-0.1

■ STEVE CARTER
Carter, Steven Jerome   b: 12/3/64, Charlottesville, Va.   BL/TR, 6′4″, 201 lbs.   Deb: 4/16/89

YEAR	TM/L	G	AB	R	H	2B	3B	HR	RBI	BB	SO	AVG	OBP	SLG	PRO+	BR/A	SB	CS	SBR	FA	FR	G/POS	TPR
1989	Pit-N	9	16	2	2	1	0	1	3	2	5	.125	.222	.375	70	-1	0	0	0	1.000	-1	/O-5	-0.2
1990	Pit-N	5	5	0	1	0	0	0	0	0	1	.200	.200	.200	11	-1	0	0	0	1.000	-1	/O-3	-0.2
Total	2	14	21	2	3	1	0	1	3	2	6	.143	.217	.333	56	-1	0	0	0	1.000	-2	/O-8	-0.4

■ ED CARTWRIGHT
Cartwright, Edward Charles "Jumbo"   b: 10/6/1859, Johnstown, Pa.   d: 9/3/33, St.Petersburg, Fla   BR/TR, 5′10″, 220 lbs.   Deb: 7/10/1890

YEAR	TM/L	G	AB	R	H	2B	3B	HR	RBI	BB	SO	AVG	OBP	SLG	PRO+	BR/A	SB	CS	SBR	FA	FR	G/POS	TPR
1890	StL-a	75	300	70	90	12	4	8		29		.300	.367	.447	123	5	26			.976	-1	1-75	0.0
1894	Was-N	132	507	88	149	35	13	12	106	57	43	.294	.374	.485	109	6	31			.973	-2	*1-132	0.4
1895	Was-N	122	472	95	156	34	17	3	90	54	41	.331	.400	.494	131	22	50			.984	14	*1-122	3.1
1896	Was-N	133	499	76	138	15	10	1	62	54	24	.277	.350	.353	85	-10	28			.978	-3	*1-133	-0.7
1897	Was-N	33	124	19	29	4	0	0	15	8		.234	.286	.266	46	-10	9			.963	2	1-33	-0.6
Total	5	495	1902	348	562	100	44	24	273	202	128	.295	.368	.432	106	14	144			.977	13	1-495	2.2

■ RICO CARTY
Carty, Ricardo Adolfo Jacobo (b: Ricardo Adolfo Jacobo (Carty)   b: 9/1/39, San Pedro De Macoris, D.R.   BR/TR, 6′3″, 200 lbs.   Deb: 9/15/63

YEAR	TM/L	G	AB	R	H	2B	3B	HR	RBI	BB	SO	AVG	OBP	SLG	PRO+	BR/A	SB	CS	SBR	FA	FR	G/POS	TPR
1963	Mil-N	2	2	0	0	0	0	0	0	0	2	.000	.000	.000	-99	-1	0	0		.000	0	H	-0.1
1964	Mil-N	133	455	72	150	28	4	22	88	43	78	.330	.391	.554	162	37	1	2	-1	.978	1	*O-121	3.3
1965	Mil-N	83	271	37	84	18	1	10	35	17	44	.310	.357	.494	136	12	1	4	-2	.958	1	O-73	0.8
1966	Atl-N	151	521	73	170	25	2	15	76	60	74	.326	.396	.468	137	28	4	6	-2	.971	5	*O-126,C-17/13	2.7
1967	Atl-N	134	444	41	113	16	2	15	64	49	70	.255	.330	.401	110	6	4	3	-1	.959	-4	*O-112/1-9	0.3
1969	*Atl-N	104	304	47	104	15	0	16	58	32	28	.342	.405	.549	164	26	0	3	-2	.952	-3	O-79	1.8
1970	Atl-N★	136	478	84	175	23	3	25	101	77	46	**.366**	**.456**	.584	167	48	1	2	-1	.974	4	*O-133	4.2
1972	Atl-N	86	271	31	75	12	2	6	29	44	33	.277	.378	.402	111	5	0	2	-0	.979	-1	O-78	0.1
1973	Tex-A	86	306	24	71	12	0	3	33	36	39	.232	.315	.301	77	-5	0	1	-1	1.000	0	O-53,D-31	-1.3
	Chi-N	22	70	4	15	0	0	1	8	6	10	.214	.276	.257	45	-5	0	0	-0	.947	-0	O-19	-0.7
	Oak-A	7	8	1	2	1	0	1	2	1	2	.250	.400	.750	230	1	0	0	0	.000	0	/D-2	0.1
1974	Cle-A	33	91	6	33	6	0	1	14	8	12	.363	.396	.451	144	5	0	0	0	.985	-2	D-14/1-8	0.3
1975	Cle-A	118	383	57	118	19	1	18	64	45	31	.308	.384	.504	149	25	2	2	-1	.990	-1	D-72,1-26,O	2.0
1976	Cle-A	152	552	67	171	34	0	13	83	67	45	.310	.384	.442	143	31	1	4	-0	1.000	-2	*D-137,1-12/O	2.5
1977	Cle-A	127	461	50	129	23	1	15	80	56	51	.280	.358	.432	118	11	0	2	-1	.000	0	*D-123/1-2	0.8
1978	Tor-A	104	387	51	110	16	0	20	68	36	41	.284	.345	.481	127	13	1	1	-0	.000	0	*D-101	1.0
	Oak-A	41	141	19	39	5	1	11	31	21	16	.277	.370	.560	167	12	0	0	0	.000	0	D-41	1.1
	Yr	145	528	70	149	21	1	31	99	57	57	.282	.352	.502	138	25	1	1	-0	.000	0	*D-142	2.1

YEAR	TM/L	G	AB	R	H	2B	3B	HR	RBI	BB	SO	AVG	OBP	SLG	PRO+	BR/A	SB	CS	SBR	FA	FR	G/POS	TPR
1979	Tor-A	132	461	48	118	26	0	12	55	46	45	.256	.325	.390	91	-6	3	1	0	.000	0	*D-129	-1.0
Total	15	1651	5606	712	1677	278	17	204	890	642	663	.299	.372	.464	132	240	21	26	-9	.970	3	O-807,D-650/1C3	17.9

■ BOB CARUTHERS

Caruthers, Robert Lee "Parisian Bob" b: 1/5/1864, Memphis, Tenn. d: 8/5/11, Peoria, Ill. BL/TR, 5'7", 138 lbs. Deb: 9/7/1884 MU

YEAR	TM/L	G	AB	R	H	2B	3B	HR	RBI	BB	SO	AVG	OBP	SLG	PRO+	BR/A	SB	CS	SBR	FA	FR	G/POS	TPR
1884	StL-a	23	82	15	21	2	0	2			4	.256	.291	.354	105	0				.750	-6	O-16,P-13	-0.5
1885	*StL-a	60	222	37	50	10	2	1			20	.225	.289	.302	83	-4				.902	-6	P-53/O-7	-0.1
1886	*StL-a	87	317	91	106	21	14	4			64	.334	.448	.527	196	37	26			.897	-6	P-44,O-43/2	1.1
1887	*StL-a	98	364	102	130	23	11	8			66	.357	.463	.547	164	31	49			.903	9	O-54,P-39/1	1.5
1888	Bro-a	94	335	58	77	10	5	5	53	46		.230	.328	.334	113	6	23			.899	1	O-51,P-44	0.1
1889	*Bro-a	59	172	45	43	8	3	2	31	44	17	.250	.408	.366	121	7	9			.968	0	P-56/O-3,1	-0.1
1890	*Bro-N	71	238	46	63	7	4	1	29	47	18	.265	.397	.340	115	7	13			.860	-4	O-39,P-37	-0.4
1891	Bro-N	56	171	24	48	5	3	2	23	25	13	.281	.372	.380	120	5	4			.940	-3	P-38,O-17/2	-0.2
1892	StL-N	143	513	76	142	16	8	3	69	86	29	.277	.386	.357	131	24	24			.892	-11	*O-122,P-16/21M	0.6
1893	Chi-N	1	3	0	0	0	0	0	0	0	1	.000	.000	.000	-99	-1	0			1.000	-0	/O-1	-0.1
	Cin-N	13	48	14	14	2	0	1	8	16	1	.292	.477	.396	130	3	4			.857	-1	O-13	0.1
	Yr	14	51	14	14	2	0	1	8	16	2	.275	.456	.373	119	3	4			.862	-1	O-14	0.0
Total	10	705	2465	508	694	104	50	29	213	417	79	.282	.391	.400	135	116	152			.875	-22	O-366,P-340/12	2.0

■ PAUL CASANOVA

Casanova, Paulino (Ortiz) b: 12/21/41, Colon, Matanzas, Cuba BR/TR, 6'4", 200 lbs. Deb: 9/18/65

YEAR	TM/L	G	AB	R	H	2B	3B	HR	RBI	BB	SO	AVG	OBP	SLG	PRO+	BR/A	SB	CS	SBR	FA	FR	G/POS	TPR
1965	Was-A	5	13	2	4	1	0	1	1	1	3	.308	.357	.385	112	-0				.938	-2	/C-4	-0.2
1966	Was-A	122	429	45	109	16	5	13	44	14	78	.254	.279	.406	95	-4	1	2	-1	.981	-10	*C-119	-0.8
1967	Was-A☆	141	528	47	131	19	1	9	53	17	65	.248	.274	.339	84	-13	1	1	-0	.984	-5	*C-137	-1.1
1968	Was-A	96	322	19	63	6	0	4	25	7	52	.196	.213	.252	42	-23	0	1	-1	.989	-9	C-92	-3.2
1969	Was-A	124	379	26	82	9	2	4	37	18	52	.216	.257	.282	54	-25	0	0	0	.992	-6	*C-122	-2.6
1970	Was-A	104	328	25	75	17	3	6	30	10	47	.229	.254	.354	69	-15	0	0	0	.988	-1	*C-100	-1.2
1971	Was-A	94	311	19	63	9	1	5	26	14	52	.203	.239	.286	51	-21	0	3	-2	.985	-4	C-83	-2.7
1972	Atl-N	49	136	8	28	3	0	2	10	4	28	.206	.229	.272	38	-11	0	1	-1	.975	-6	C-43	-1.8
1973	Atl-N	82	236	18	51	7	0	7	18	11	36	.216	.254	.335	58	-14	0	2	-1	.977	6	C-78	-0.7
1974	Atl-N	42	104	5	21	0	0	0	8	5	17	.202	.239	.202	23	-11	0	0	0	.986	-1	C-33	-1.1
Total	10	859	2786	214	627	87	12	50	252	101	430	.225	.254	.319	64	-137	2	10	-5	.985	-38	C-811	-15.4

■ GEORGE CASE

Case, George Washington b: 11/11/15, Trenton, N.J. d: 1/23/89, Trenton, N.J. BR/TR, 6', 183 lbs. Deb: 9/8/37 C

YEAR	TM/L	G	AB	R	H	2B	3B	HR	RBI	BB	SO	AVG	OBP	SLG	PRO+	BR/A	SB	CS	SBR	FA	FR	G/POS	TPR
1937	Was-A	22	90	14	26	6	2	0	11	3	5	.289	.312	.400	82	-3	2	1	0	.945	-0	O-22	-0.4
1938	Was-A	107	433	69	132	27	3	2	40	39	28	.305	.362	.395	96	-3	11	6	-0	.964	-4	*O-101	-0.9
1939	Was-A☆	128	530	103	160	20	7	2	35	56	36	.302	.369	.377	98	-0	51	17	5	.955	3	*O-123	0.3
1940	Was-A	154	656	109	192	29	5	5	56	52	39	.293	.349	.375	94	-4	35	10	5	.970	1	*O-154	-0.8
1941	Was-A	153	649	95	176	32	8	2	53	51	37	.271	.325	.354	84	-16	33	9	5	.975	15	*O-151	-0.6
1942	Was-A	125	513	101	164	26	2	5	43	44	30	.320	.377	.407	122	15	44	6	10	.951	-2	*O-120	1.7
1943	Was-A★	141	613	102	180	36	5	1	52	41	27	.294	.341	.374	113	8	61	14	10	.985	1	*O-140	1.3
1944	Was-A†	119	464	63	116	14	2	2	32	49	22	.250	.326	.302	83	-9	49	18	4	.970	6	*O-114	-0.6
1945	Was-A†	123	504	72	148	19	5	1	31	49	27	.294	.360	.357	118	12	30	16	-1	.979	13	*O-123	1.8
1946	Cle-A	118	484	46	109	23	4	1	22	34	38	.225	.280	.295	65	-24	28	11	2	.983	-4	*O-118	-3.4
1947	Was-A	36	80	11	12	1	0	0	7	9	9	.150	.227	.162	10	-10	5	1	1	.963	0	O-21	-1.0
Total	11	1226	5016	785	1415	233	43	21	377	426	297	.282	.341	.358	95	-36	349	109	39	.970	30	*O-1187	-2.6

■ DENNIS CASEY

Casey, Dennis Patrick b: 3/30/1858, Binghamton, N.Y. d: 1/19/09, Binghamton, N.Y. BL/TR, 5'9", 164 lbs. Deb: 8/18/1884 F

YEAR	TM/L	G	AB	R	H	2B	3B	HR	RBI	BB	SO	AVG	OBP	SLG	PRO+	BR/A	SB	CS	SBR	FA	FR	G/POS	TPR
1884	Wil-U	2	8	1	2	1	0	0			0	.250	.250	.375	66	-0				1.000	-0	/O-2	0.0
	Bal-a	37	149	20	37	7	4	3			5	.248	.273	.409	115	-2				.898	-1	O-37	0.1
1885	Bal-a	63	264	50	76	10	5	3			21	.288	.347	.398	137	12				.821	-5	O-63	0.4
Total	2	102	421	71	115	18	9	6			26	.273	.320	.401	128	13				.847	-6	O-102	0.5

■ DOC CASEY

Casey, James Patrick b: 3/15/1870, Lawrence, Mass. d: 12/31/36, Detroit, Mich. BB/TR, 5'6", 157 lbs. Deb: 9/14/1898

YEAR	TM/L	G	AB	R	H	2B	3B	HR	RBI	BB	SO	AVG	OBP	SLG	PRO+	BR/A	SB	CS	SBR	FA	FR	G/POS	TPR
1898	Was-N	28	112	13	31	2	0	0	15	3		.277	.302	.295	71	-4	15			.893	-3	3-22/S-4,C	-0.6
1899	Was-N	9	34	3	4	2	0	0	2	2		.118	.167	.176	-6	-5	1			.853	-1	/3-9	-0.5
	Bro-N	134	525	75	141	14	8	1	43	25		.269	.313	.331	75	-19	27			.892	-19	*3-134	-3.3
	Yr	143	559	78	145	16	8	1	45	27		.259	.304	.322	70	-24	28			.889	-20	*3-143	-3.8
1900	Bro-N	1	3	0	1	0	0	0		1	0	.333	.500	.333	125	0	0			1.000	-0	/3-1	0.0
1901	Det-A	128	540	105	153	16	9	2	46	32		.283	.335	.357	88	-9	34			.887	5	*3-127	-0.2
1902	Det-A	132	520	69	142	18	7	3	55	44		.273	.338	.352	90	-7	22			.904	2	*3-132	-0.4
1903	Chi-N	112	435	56	126	21	1	0	40	19		.290	.324	.329	89	-7	11			.915	-19	*3-112	-2.4
1904	Chi-N	136	548	71	147	20	4	1	43	18		.268	.300	.325	93	-6	21			.911	-10	*3-134/C-2	-1.2
1905	Chi-N	144	526	66	122	21	10	1	56	41		.232	.295	.316	79	-14	22			.949	-9	*3-142/S-1	-1.9
1906	Bro-N	149	571	71	133	17	8	0	34	52		.233	.306	.291	93	-4	22			.919	-17	*3-149	-1.8
1907	Bro-N	141	527	55	122	19	3	0	19	34		.231	.282	.279	82	-12	16			.955	-6	*3-138	-1.6
Total	10	1114	4341	584	1122	137	52	9	354	270		.258	.310	.320	85	-86	191			.915	-77	*3-1100/C-5,S	-13.9

■ JOE CASEY

Casey, Joseph Felix b: 8/15/1887, Boston, Mass. d: 6/2/66, Melrose, Mass. BR/TR, 5'9", 180 lbs. Deb: 10/1/09

YEAR	TM/L	G	AB	R	H	2B	3B	HR	RBI	BB	SO	AVG	OBP	SLG	PRO+	BR/A	SB	CS	SBR	FA	FR	G/POS	TPR
1909	Det-A	3	5	1	0	0	0	0		0	1	.000	.167	.000	-45	-1	0			1.000	2	/C-3	0.1
1910	Det-A	23	62	3	12	3	0	0	2	2		.194	.231	.242	45	-4	1			.964	5	C-22	0.4
1911	Det-A	15	33	2	5	0	0	0	3	3		.152	.222	.152	5	-4	0			.956	-3	C-12/O-3	-0.6
1918	Was-A	9	17	3	4	0	0	0	2	2	2	.235	.316	.235	68	-1	0			1.000	2	/C-8	0.1
Total	4	50	117	9	21	3	0	0	7	8	2	.179	.238	.205	32	-10	1			.970	6	/C-45,O-3	0.1

■ BOB CASEY

Casey, Orrin Robinson b: 1/26/1859, Adolphustown, Ontario, Canada 5'11", 190 lbs. Deb: 7/17/1882

YEAR	TM/L	G	AB	R	H	2B	3B	HR	RBI	BB	SO	AVG	OBP	SLG	PRO+	BR/A	SB	CS	SBR	FA	FR	G/POS	TPR
1882	Det-N	9	39	5	9	2	1	1	7	0	15	.231	.231	.410	101	-0				.667	-5	/3-8,2-1	-0.4

■ DAVE CASH

Cash, David b: 6/11/48, Utica, N.Y. BR/TR, 5'11", 175 lbs. Deb: 9/13/69

YEAR	TM/L	G	AB	R	H	2B	3B	HR	RBI	BB	SO	AVG	OBP	SLG	PRO+	BR/A	SB	CS	SBR	FA	FR	G/POS	TPR
1969	Pit-N	18	61	8	17	3	1	0	4	9	9	.279	.371	.361	108	1	2	0	1	.990	5	2-17	0.8
1970	*Pit-N	64	210	30	66	7	6	1	28	17	25	.314	.368	.419	113	4	5	2	0	.974	2	2-55	1.4
1971	*Pit-N	123	478	79	138	17	4	2	34	46	33	.289	.351	.354	101	1	13	5	1	.987	6	*2-105,3-24/S	1.7
1972	*Pit-N	99	425	58	120	22	4	3	30	22	31	.282	.318	.374	98	-2	9	9	-3	.992	28	2-97	3.0
1973	Pit-N	116	436	59	118	21	2	2	31	38	36	.271	.329	.342	88	-7	2	5	-2	.979	5	2-92,3-17	0.2
1974	Phi-N★	162	687	89	206	26	11	2	58	46	33	.300	.352	.378	100	0	10	8	-1	.977	29	*2-162	4.0
1975	Phi-N★	162	699	111	213	40	3	4	57	56	34	.305	.360	.388	103	4	13	6	0	.981	6	*2-162	2.3
1976	*Phi-N★	160	666	92	189	14	12	1	56	54	13	.284	.339	.345	92	-6	10	12	-4	.988	-2	*2-158	-0.2
1977	Mon-N	153	650	91	188	42	7	0	43	52	33	.289	.344	.375	96	-4	21	12	-1	.986	-11	*2-153	-0.5
1978	Mon-N	159	658	66	166	26	3	3	43	37	29	.252	.292	.315	70	-27	12	6	0	.986	-30	*2-159	-4.9
1979	Mon-N	76	187	24	60	11	2	2	19	12	12	.321	.362	.422	114	4	7	4	0	.971	-6	2-47	-1.1
1980	SD-N	130	397	25	90	14	2	1	23	24	31	.227	.289	.280	63	-20	6	3	-3	.987	4	2-123	-1.1
Total	12	1422	5554	732	1571	243	56	21	426	424	309	.283	.336	.358	93	-51	120	74	-8	.982	43	*2-1330/3-41,S	6.7

■ NORM CASH

Cash, Norman Dalton b: 11/10/34, Justiceburg, Tex. d: 10/12/86, Beaver Island, Mich. BL/TL, 6', 190 lbs. Deb: 6/18/58

YEAR	TM/L	G	AB	R	H	2B	3B	HR	RBI	BB	SO	AVG	OBP	SLG	PRO+	BR/A	SB	CS	SBR	FA	FR	G/POS	TPR
1958	Chi-A	13	8	2	2	0	0	0	0	0	1	.250	.250	.250	39	-1	0			1.000	1	/O-4	-0.2
1959	*Chi-A	58	104	16	25	0	1	4	16	16	9	.240	.378	.375	109	2	1	1	-0	.984	-1	1-31	-0.1
1960	Det-A	121	353	64	101	16	3	18	63	65	58	.286	.406	.501	140	22	4	2	0	.991	-2	1-99/O-4	1.3

YEAR	TM/L	G	AB	R	H	2B	3B	HR	RBI	BB	SO	AVG	OBP	SLG	PRO+	BR/A	SB	CS	SBR	FA	FR	G/POS	TPR
1961	Det-A★	159	535	119	**193**	22	8	41	132	124	85	**.361**	**.488**	.662	198	82	11	5	0	.992	5	*1-157	7.1
1962	Det-A	148	507	94	123	16	2	39	89	104	82	.243	.385	.513	134	27	6	3	0	.992	7	*1-146/O-3	2.4
1963	Det-A	147	493	67	133	19	1	26	79	89	76	.270	.388	.471	135	26	2	3	-1	.994	2	*1-142	2.1
1964	Det-A	144	479	63	123	15	5	23	83	70	64	.257	.355	.453	121	15	2	1	0	**.997**	4	*1-137	1.3
1965	Det-A	142	467	79	124	23	1	30	82	77	62	.266	.374	.512	147	30	6	6	-2	.992	5	*1-139	2.8
1966	Det-A★	160	603	98	168	18	3	32	93	66	91	.279	.354	.478	133	26	2	1	0	.988	4	*1-158	2.0
1967	Det-A	152	488	64	118	16	5	22	72	81	100	.242	.354	.430	127	18	3	2	-0	**.995**	9	*1-146	2.0
1968	*Det-A	127	411	50	108	15	1	25	63	39	70	.263	.331	.487	141	19	1	1	-0	.992	9	*1-117	2.2
1969	Det-A	142	483	81	135	15	4	22	74	63	80	.280	.370	.464	126	17	2	1	0	.994	6	*1-134	1.3
1970	Det-A	130	370	58	96	18	2	15	53	72	58	.259	.387	.441	127	16	0	1	-1	.989	2	*1-114	0.8
1971	Det-A★	135	452	72	128	10	3	32	91	59	86	.283	.375	.531	148	28	1	0	0	.992	-0	*1-131	1.8
1972	*Det-A★	137	440	51	114	16	0	22	61	50	64	.259	.340	.445	128	15	0	2	-1	.993	-0	*1-134	0.3
1973	Det-A	121	363	51	95	19	0	19	40	47	73	.262	.359	.471	124	11	1	0	0	.991	2	*1-114/D-3	0.6
1974	Det-A	53	149	17	34	3	2	7	12	19	30	.228	.327	.416	109	2	1	1	-0	.985	-1	1-44	-0.2
Total	17	2089	6705	1046	1820	241	41	377	1103	1043	1091	.271	.377	.488	138	355	43	30	-5	.992	50	*1-1943/O-11,D	27.5

■ RON CASH   Cash, Ronald Forrest   b: 11/20/49, Atlanta, Ga.   BR/TR, 6′, 180 lbs.   Deb: 9/4/73

YEAR	TM/L	G	AB	R	H	2B	3B	HR	RBI	BB	SO	AVG	OBP	SLG	PRO+	BR/A	SB	CS	SBR	FA	FR	G/POS	TPR
1973	Det-A	14	39	8	16	1	1	0	6	5	5	.410	.477	.487	161	3	0	0	0	.900	-2	/O-7,3-6	0.1
1974	Det-A	20	62	6	14	2	0	0	5	0	11	.226	.226	.258	38	-5	0	1	-1	.979	-1	1-15/3-4	-0.8
Total	2	34	101	14	30	3	1	0	11	5	16	.297	.330	.347	89	-2	0	1	-1	.933	-3	/1-15,3-10,O	-0.7

■ ED CASKIN   Caskin, Edward James   b: 12/30/1851, Danvers, Mass.   d: 10/9/24, Danvers, Mass.   BR/TR, 5′9.5″, 165 lbs.   Deb: 5/1/1879

YEAR	TM/L	G	AB	R	H	2B	3B	HR	RBI	BB	SO	AVG	OBP	SLG	PRO+	BR/A	SB	CS	SBR	FA	FR	G/POS	TPR
1879	Tro-N	70	304	32	78	13	2	0	21	2	14	.257	.261	.313	95	-1				.902	6	S-42,C-22/2	0.8
1880	Tro-N	82	333	36	75	5	4	0	28	7	24	.225	.241	.264	68	-12				.885	7	*S-82/C-2	0.1
1881	Tro-N	63	234	33	53	7	1	0	21	13	29	.226	.267	.265	65	-9				.906	1	*S-63	-0.5
1883	NY-N	95	383	47	91	11	2	1	40	14	25	.238	.264	.285	68	-14				.855	-5	*S-81,2-13/C	-1.5
1884	NY-N	100	351	49	81	11	1	1	40	34	55	.231	.299	.276	80	-7				.883	-1	*S-96/C-6	-0.1
1885	StL-N	71	262	31	47	3	0	1	12	12	22	.179	.215	.191	34	-18				.884	-4	3-69/C-2,S	-1.9
1886	NY-N	1	4	1	2	0	0	0	1	0	1	.500	.500	.500	203	0	0			1.000	-1	/S-1	0.0
Total	7	482	1871	229	427	50	10	2	163	82	170	.228	.261	.269	70	-61				.883	9	S-366/3-69,C2	-3.1

■ HARRY CASSADY   Cassady, Harry Delbert (b: Harry Delbert Cassaday)   b: 7/20/1880, Bellflower, Ill.   d: 4/19/69, Fresno, Cal.   BL/TL, 5′8″, 145 lbs.   Deb: 8/8/04

YEAR	TM/L	G	AB	R	H	2B	3B	HR	RBI	BB	SO	AVG	OBP	SLG	PRO+	BR/A	SB	CS	SBR	FA	FR	G/POS	TPR
1904	Pit-N	12	44	8	9	0	0	0	3	2		.205	.239	.205	36	-3	2			.867	-1	O-12	-0.5
1905	Was-A	10	30	1	4	0	0	0	1	0		.133	.133	.133	-16	-4	0			1.000	0	/O-9	-0.4
Total	2	22	74	9	13	0	0	0	4	2		.176	.197	.176	17	-7	2			.933	-1	/O-21	-0.9

■ JOHN CASSIDY   Cassidy, John P.   b: 1857, Brooklyn, N.Y.   d: 7/2/1891, Brooklyn, N.Y.   BR/TL, 5′8″, 168 lbs.   Deb: 4/24/1875

YEAR	TM/L	G	AB	R	H	2B	3B	HR	RBI	BB	SO	AVG	OBP	SLG	PRO+	BR/A	SB	CS	SBR	FA	FR	G/POS	TPR
1875	Atl-n	41	165	14	29	3	2	1		1		.176	.181	.236	49	-7						P-30,O-10/1	0.0
	NH-n	6	22	3	3	1	0	0		0		.136	.136	.182	10	-2						/1-6	-0.2
	Yr	47	187	17	32	4	2	1		1		.171	.176	.230	45	-9						P-30,1-13,O	-0.2
1876	Har-N	12	47	6	13	2	0	0	8	1	0	.277	.292	.319	95	-0				1.000	-1	/O-8,1-4	0.0
1877	Har-N	60	251	43	95	10	5	0	27	3	3	.378	.386	.458	184	24				.722	-5	*O-58/P-2	1.4
1878	Chi-N	60	256	33	68	7	1	0	29	9	11	.266	.291	.301	89	-4				.810	8	*O-60/C-1	0.2
1879	Tro-N	9	37	4	7	1	0	0	1	2	4	.189	.231	.216	52	-2				.889	-2	/O-8,1-2	-0.4
1880	Tro-N	83	352	40	89	14	8	0	29	12	34	.253	.277	.338	102	0				.880	-2	*O-82/2-1	-0.4
1881	Tro-N	85	370	57	82	13	3	1	11	18	21	.222	.258	.281	66	-15				.872	-9	*O-84/S-1	-2.4
1882	Tro-N	29	121	14	21	3	1	0	9	3	16	.174	.194	.215	32	-9				.778	-9	O-16,3-13	-1.6
1883	Pro-N	89	366	46	87	16	5	0	42	9	38	.238	.256	.309	69	-14				.864	1	*O-88/2-1,1	-1.2
1884	Bro-a	106	433	57	109	11	6	2		19		.252	.286	.319	96	-2				.847	-8	*O-101/3-4,S	-1.1
1885	Bro-a	54	221	36	47	6	2	1		8		.213	.250	.271	64	-9				.852	-7	O-54	-1.6
Total	10	587	2454	336	618	83	31	4	<u>156</u>	84	<u>127</u>	.252	.278	.316	89	-30				.845	-31	O-559/3-17,1S2PC	-7.1

■ JOE CASSIDY   Cassidy, Joseph Phillip   b: 2/8/1883, Chester, Pa.   d: 3/25/06, Chester, Pa.   BR/TR,   Deb: 4/18/04

YEAR	TM/L	G	AB	R	H	2B	3B	HR	RBI	BB	SO	AVG	OBP	SLG	PRO+	BR/A	SB	CS	SBR	FA	FR	G/POS	TPR
1904	Was-A	152	581	63	140	12	**19**	1	33	15		.241	.265	.332	90	-9	17			.937	12	S-99,O-32,3	0.6
1905	Was-A	151	576	67	124	16	4	1	43	25		.215	.250	.262	65	-24	23			.934	**33**	*S-151	1.4
Total	2	303	1157	130	264	28	23	2	76	40		.228	.258	.297	78	-32	40			.935	46	S-250/O-32,3	2.0

■ PETE CASSIDY   Cassidy, Peter Francis   b: 4/8/1873, Wilmington, Del.   d: 7/9/29, Wilmington, Del.   BR/TR, 5′10″, 165 lbs.   Deb: 4/18/1896

YEAR	TM/L	G	AB	R	H	2B	3B	HR	RBI	BB	SO	AVG	OBP	SLG	PRO+	BR/A	SB	CS	SBR	FA	FR	G/POS	TPR
1896	Lou-N	49	184	16	39	1	1	0	12	7	7	.212	.256	.228	29	-19	5			.973	-7	1-38,S-11	-2.2
1899	Bro-N	6	20	2	3	1	0	0	4	1		.150	.261	.200	27	-2	1			1.000	-4	/3-3,S-2	-0.5
	Was-N	46	178	21	56	13	0	3	32	9		.315	.365	.438	121	5	5			.970	-2	1-37/3-6,S	0.3
	Yr	52	198	23	59	14	0	3	36	10		.298	.353	.414	111	3	6			.970	-5	1-37/3-9,S	-0.2
Total	2	101	382	39	98	15	1	3	48	17	<u>7</u>	.257	.307	.325	72	-16	11			.972	-13	/1-75,S-16,3	-2.4

■ JACK CASSINI   Cassini, Jack Dempsey "Gabby" or "Scat"   b: 10/26/19, Dearborn, Mich.   BR/TR, 5′10″, 175 lbs.   Deb: 4/19/49

YEAR	TM/L	G	AB	R	H	2B	3B	HR	RBI	BB	SO	AVG	OBP	SLG	PRO+	BR/A	SB	CS	SBR	FA	FR	G/POS	TPR
1949	Pit-N	8	0	3	0	0	0	0	0	0	0	—	—	—		0	0			.000	0	R	0.0

■ PEDRO CASTELLANO   Castellano, Pedro Orlando (Arrieta)   b: 3/11/70, Lara, Venez.   BR/TR, 6′1″, 175 lbs.   Deb: 5/30/93

YEAR	TM/L	G	AB	R	H	2B	3B	HR	RBI	BB	SO	AVG	OBP	SLG	PRO+	BR/A	SB	CS	SBR	FA	FR	G/POS	TPR
1993	Col-N	34	71	12	13	2	0	3	7	8	16	.183	.266	.338	52	-5	1	1	-0	.909	-1	3-13,1-10/S2	-0.7

■ JIM CASTIGLIA   Castiglia, James Vincent   b: 9/30/18, Passaic, N.J.   BL/TR, 5′11″, 200 lbs.   Deb: 4/14/42

YEAR	TM/L	G	AB	R	H	2B	3B	HR	RBI	BB	SO	AVG	OBP	SLG	PRO+	BR/A	SB	CS	SBR	FA	FR	G/POS	TPR
1942	Phi-A	16	18	2	7	0	0	0	2	1	3	.389	.421	.389	129	1	0	0	0	.875	-1	/C-3	0.0

■ PETE CASTIGLIONE   Castiglione, Peter Paul   b: 2/13/21, Greenwich, Conn.   BR/TR, 5′11″, 175 lbs.   Deb: 9/10/47

YEAR	TM/L	G	AB	R	H	2B	3B	HR	RBI	BB	SO	AVG	OBP	SLG	PRO+	BR/A	SB	CS	SBR	FA	FR	G/POS	TPR
1947	Pit-N	13	50	6	14	0	0	0	1	2	5	.280	.308	.280	55	-3	0			.970	1	S-13	-0.1
1948	Pit-N	4	2	0	0	0	0	0	0	0	0	.000	.000	.000	-98	-1	1			1.000	0	/S-1	0.0
1949	Pit-N	118	448	57	120	20	2	6	43	20	43	.268	.299	.362	74	-17	2			.957	4	3-98,S-17/O	-1.9
1950	Pit-N	94	263	29	67	10	3	3	22	23	23	.255	.317	.350	73	-10	1			.970	-17	3-35,S-29/21	-2.6
1951	Pit-N	132	482	62	126	19	4	7	42	34	28	.261	.311	.361	78	-15	2	2	-1	.957	4	3-99,S-28	-1.1
1952	Pit-N	67	214	27	57	9	1	4	18	17	8	.266	.323	.374	90	-3	3	3	-1	.951	4	3-57/1-1,O	-1.1
1953	Pit-N	45	159	14	33	2	1	4	21	5	14	.208	.236	.308	41	-14	1	1	-0	.978	4	3-43	-1.1
	StL-N	67	52	9	9	2	0	0	3	2	5	.173	.204	.212	9	-7	0	0	0	.967	8	3-51/2-9,S	0.1
	Yr	112	211	23	42	4	1	4	24	7	19	.199	.228	.284	33	-21	1	1	-0	.976	12	3-94/2-9,S	-1.0
1954	StL-N	5	0	1	0	0	0	0	0	0	0	—	—	—		0	0			1.000	0	/3-5	0.0
Total	8	545	1670	205	426	62	11	24	150	103	126	.255	.300	.349	71	-70	10	<u>6</u>		.960	4	3-388/S-91,210	-6.6

■ VINNY CASTILLA   Castilla, Vinicio (Soria)   b: 7/4/67, Oaxaca, Mexico   BR/TR, 6′1″, 175 lbs.   Deb: 9/1/91

YEAR	TM/L	G	AB	R	H	2B	3B	HR	RBI	BB	SO	AVG	OBP	SLG	PRO+	BR/A	SB	CS	SBR	FA	FR	G/POS	TPR
1991	Atl-N	12	5	1	1	0	0	0	0	0	2	.200	.200	.200	12	-1	0	0	0	1.000	1	S-12	0.1
1992	Atl-N	9	16	1	4	1	0	0	1	1	4	.250	.333	.313	79	-0	0	0	0	.875	0	/3-4,S-4	0.0
1993	Col-N	105	337	36	86	9	7	9	30	13	45	.255	.287	.404	71	-15	2	5	-2	.975	8	*S-104	-0.2
1994	Col-N	52	130	16	43	11	1	3	18	7	23	.331	.365	.500	105	1	2	1	0	.984	5	S-18,2-14/31	0.2
Total	4	178	488	54	134	21	8	12	49	21	74	.275	.309	.424	80	-15	4	6	-2	.977	10	S-138/2-14,31	0.1

■ TONY CASTILLO   Castillo, Anthony   b: 6/14/57, San Jose, Cal.   BR/TR, 6′4″, 190 lbs.   Deb: 9/22/78

YEAR	TM/L	G	AB	R	H	2B	3B	HR	RBI	BB	SO	AVG	OBP	SLG	PRO+	BR/A	SB	CS	SBR	FA	FR	G/POS	TPR
1978	SD-N	5	8	0	1	0	0	0	1	0	2	.125	.125	.125	-33	-1	0	0	0	.950	1	/C-5	0.0

YEAR	TM/L	G	AB	R	H	2B	3B	HR	RBI	BB	SO	AVG	OBP	SLG	PRO+	BR/A	SB	CS	SBR	FA	FR	G/POS	TPR

■ BRAULIO CASTILLO
Castillo, Braulio Robinson Medrano (b: Braulio Robinson Medrano (Castillo))
b: 5/13/68, Elias Pina, D.R. BR/TR, 6', 160 lbs. Deb: 8/18/91

YEAR	TM/L	G	AB	R	H	2B	3B	HR	RBI	BB	SO	AVG	OBP	SLG	PRO+	BR/A	SB	CS	SBR	FA	FR	G/POS	TPR
1991	Phi-N	28	52	3	9	3	0	0	2	1	15	.173	.189	.231	18	-6	1	1	-0	.977	-2	O-26	-0.9
1992	Phi-N	28	76	12	15	3	1	2	7	4	15	.197	.237	.342	62	-4	1	0	0	.956	-2	O-24	-0.6
Total	2	56	128	15	24	6	1	2	9	5	30	.188	.218	.297	44	-10	2	1	0	.966	-4	/O-50	-1.5

■ MANNY CASTILLO
Castillo, Esteban Manuel Antonio (Cabrera) b: 4/1/57, Santo Domingo, D.R. BB/TR, 5'9", 160 lbs. Deb: 9/1/80

YEAR	TM/L	G	AB	R	H	2B	3B	HR	RBI	BB	SO	AVG	OBP	SLG	PRO+	BR/A	SB	CS	SBR	FA	FR	G/POS	TPR
1980	KC-A	7	10	1	2	0	0	0	0	0	0	.200	.200	.200	10	-1	0	0	0	1.000	2	/3-3,2-1,D	0.0
1982	Sea-A	138	506	49	130	29	1	3	49	22	35	.257	.291	.350	70	-21	2	8	-4	.938	-24	*3-130/2-9	-5.3
1983	Sea-A	91	203	13	42	6	3	0	24	7	20	.207	.237	.266	37	-17	1	1	-0	.971	8	3-55,1-11/2PD	-1.1
Total	3	236	719	63	174	35	4	3	73	29	55	.242	.274	.314	59	-40	3	9	-5	.949	-15	3-188/2-15,1DP	-6.4

■ JUAN CASTILLO
Castillo, Juan (Bryas) b: 1/25/62, San Pedro De Macoris, D.R. BB/TR, 5'11", 162 lbs. Deb: 4/12/86

YEAR	TM/L	G	AB	R	H	2B	3B	HR	RBI	BB	SO	AVG	OBP	SLG	PRO+	BR/A	SB	CS	SBR	FA	FR	G/POS	TPR
1986	Mil-A	26	54	6	9	0	1	0	5	5	12	.167	.250	.204	24	-6	1	1	-0	1.000	5	2-17/S-4,3OD	-0.1
1987	Mil-A	116	321	44	72	11	4	3	28	33	76	.224	.303	.312	62	-17	15	7	0	.973	-6	2-97,S-13/3	-1.7
1988	Mil-A	54	90	10	20	0	0	0	2	3	14	.222	.247	.222	32	-8	2	0	1	.932	7	2-18,3-17,S/OD	0.0
1989	Mil-A	3	4	0	0	0	0	0	3	0	2	.000	.000	.000	-99	-1	0	0	0	1.000	1	/2-3	0.0
Total	4	199	469	60	101	11	5	3	38	41	104	.215	.284	.279	51	-32	18	8	1	.972	6	2-135/S-30,3DO	-1.8

■ MARTY CASTILLO
Castillo, Martin Horace b: 1/16/57, Long Beach, Cal. BR/TR, 6'1", 190 lbs. Deb: 8/19/81

YEAR	TM/L	G	AB	R	H	2B	3B	HR	RBI	BB	SO	AVG	OBP	SLG	PRO+	BR/A	SB	CS	SBR	FA	FR	G/POS	TPR
1981	Det-A	6	8	1	1	0	0	0	0	0	2	.125	.125	.125	-27	-1	0	0	0	1.000	2	/3-4,C-1,O	0.1
1982	Det-A	1	0	0	0	0	0	0	0	0	0	—	—	—	—	0	0	0	0	1.000	-0	/C-1	0.0
1983	Det-A	67	119	10	23	4	0	2	10	7	22	.193	.238	.277	42	-9	2	0	1	.990	4	3-58,C-10	-0.5
1984	*Det-A	70	141	16	33	5	2	4	17	10	33	.234	.285	.383	83	-3	1	0	0	.970	2	C-36,3-33/D	-0.5
1985	Det-A	57	84	4	10	2	0	2	5	2	19	.119	.140	.214	-5	-12	0	2	-1	.977	7	C-32,3-25	-0.5
Total	5	201	352	31	67	11	2	8	32	19	76	.190	.232	.301	46	-26	3	2	-0	.978	15	3-120/C-80,DO	-0.9

■ CARMEN CASTILLO
Castillo, Monte Carmelo b: 6/8/58, San Pedro De Macoris, D.R. BR/TR, 6'1", 190 lbs. Deb: 7/17/82

YEAR	TM/L	G	AB	R	H	2B	3B	HR	RBI	BB	SO	AVG	OBP	SLG	PRO+	BR/A	SB	CS	SBR	FA	FR	G/POS	TPR
1982	Cle-A	47	120	11	25	4	0	2	11	6	17	.208	.258	.292	51	-8	0	0	0	.978	-3	O-43/D-2	-1.2
1983	Cle-A	23	36	9	10	2	1	1	3	4	6	.278	.366	.472	124	1	1	1	-0	.929	-1	O-19/D-1	-0.5
1984	Cle-A	87	211	36	55	9	2	10	36	21	32	.261	.333	.464	116	4	1	3	-2	.933	-6	O-70/D-2	-0.5
1985	Cle-A	67	184	27	45	5	1	11	25	11	40	.245	.298	.462	105	3	0	1	0	.953	-2	O-51/D-9	-0.2
1986	Cle-A	85	205	34	57	9	0	8	32	9	48	.278	.312	.439	103	0	3	0	1	.939	-2	O-37,D-35	-0.3
1987	Cle-A	89	220	27	55	17	0	11	31	16	52	.250	.301	.477	101	-0	1	1	-0	1.000	-1	D-43,O-23	-0.3
1988	Cle-A	66	176	16	48	8	0	4	14	5	31	.273	.297	.386	87	-3	0	2	-1	.933	-6	O-45/D-9	-1.0
1989	Min-A	94	218	23	56	13	0	8	33	15	40	.257	.308	.454	105	1	1	2	-1	.976	-3	O-67/D-16	-0.5
1990	Min-A	64	137	11	30	4	0	0	12	3	23	.219	.241	.248	35	-12	0	1	-1	.923	-5	D-35,O-21	-1.9
1991	Min-A	9	12	0	2	0	0	0	0	1	2	.167	.231	.333	52	-1	0	0	0	1.000	-1	/O-4,D-2	-0.2
Total	10	631	1519	190	383	71	8	55	197	90	291	.252	.300	.418	93	-18	15	11	-2	.953	-30	O-380,D-154	-6.1

■ JOHN CASTINO
Castino, John Anthony b: 10/23/54, Evanston, Ill. BR/TR, 5'11", 175 lbs. Deb: 4/6/79

YEAR	TM/L	G	AB	R	H	2B	3B	HR	RBI	BB	SO	AVG	OBP	SLG	PRO+	BR/A	SB	CS	SBR	FA	FR	G/POS	TPR
1979	Min-A	148	393	49	112	13	8	5	52	27	72	.285	.333	.397	92	-5	5	2	0	.963	18	*3-143/S-5	1.3
1980	Min-A	150	546	67	165	17	7	13	64	29	67	.302	.337	.430	101	-0	7	5	-1	.961	28	*3-138,S-18	2.6
1981	Min-A	101	381	41	102	13	9	6	36	18	52	.268	.303	.396	94	-4	4	5	-2	.975	11	3-98/2-4	0.4
1982	Min-A	117	410	48	99	12	6	6	37	36	51	.241	.306	.344	76	-13	2	5	-2	.995	4	2-96,3-21/OD	-0.8
1983	Min-A	142	563	83	156	30	4	11	57	62	54	.277	.350	.403	103	3	4	2	0	.990	7	*2-132/3-8,D	1.6
1984	Min-A	8	27	5	12	1	0	0	3	5	2	.444	.531	.481	174	3	0	0	0	1.000	-1	/3-8	0.2
Total	6	666	2320	293	646	86	34	41	249	177	298	.278	.331	.398	95	-16	22	19	-5	.967	67	3-416,2-232/SOD	5.3

■ VINCE CASTINO
Castino, Vincent Charles b: 10/11/17, Willisville, Ill. d: 3/6/67, Sacramento, Cal. BR/TR, 5'9", 175 lbs. Deb: 6/24/43

YEAR	TM/L	G	AB	R	H	2B	3B	HR	RBI	BB	SO	AVG	OBP	SLG	PRO+	BR/A	SB	CS	SBR	FA	FR	G/POS	TPR
1943	Chi-A	33	101	14	23	1	0	2	16	12	11	.228	.310	.297	78	-3	0	0	0	.971	-9	C-30	-1.1
1944	Chi-A	29	78	8	18	5	0	0	3	10	13	.231	.326	.295	79	-2	0	1	-1	.990	1	C-26	0.0
1945	Chi-A	26	36	2	8	1	0	0	4	3	7	.222	.282	.250	56	-2	0	0	0	.951	-2	C-25	-0.4
Total	3	88	215	24	49	7	0	2	23	25	31	.228	.311	.288	75	-7	0	1	-1	.976	-11	/C-81	-1.5

■ DON CASTLE
Castle, Donald Hardy b: 2/1/50, Kokomo, Ind. BL/TL, 6'1", 205 lbs. Deb: 9/11/73

YEAR	TM/L	G	AB	R	H	2B	3B	HR	RBI	BB	SO	AVG	OBP	SLG	PRO+	BR/A	SB	CS	SBR	FA	FR	G/POS	TPR
1973	Tex-A	4	13	0	4	1	0	0	2	1	3	.308	.357	.385	114	0	0	0	0	.000	0	/D-3	0.0

■ JOHN CASTLE
Castle, John Francis b: 6/1/1883, Honey Brook, Pa. d: 4/13/29, Philadelphia, Pa. 5'10.5", Deb: 4/30/10

YEAR	TM/L	G	AB	R	H	2B	3B	HR	RBI	BB	SO	AVG	OBP	SLG	PRO+	BR/A	SB	CS	SBR	FA	FR	G/POS	TPR
1910	Phi-N	3	4	1	1	0	0	0	0	0		.250	.250	.250	44	-1	1			.000	-1	/O-2	-0.1

■ FOSTER CASTLEMAN
Castleman, Foster Ephraim b: 1/1/31, Nashville, Tenn. BR/TR, 6', 175 lbs. Deb: 8/4/54

YEAR	TM/L	G	AB	R	H	2B	3B	HR	RBI	BB	SO	AVG	OBP	SLG	PRO+	BR/A	SB	CS	SBR	FA	FR	G/POS	TPR
1954	NY-N	13	12	0	3	0	0	0	0	0	3	.250	.308	.250	47	-1	0	0	0	.000	0	/3-2	-0.1
1955	NY-N	15	28	3	6	1	0	2	4	2	4	.214	.267	.464	89	-1	0	0	0	1.000	-3	/2-6,3-1	-0.3
1956	NY-N	124	385	33	87	16	3	14	45	15	50	.226	.259	.392	72	-16	2	1	0	.947	7	*3-107/S-2,2	-0.9
1957	NY-N	18	37	7	6	2	0	1	2	2	8	.162	.205	.297	33	-4	0	0	0	.867	-2	/3-7,2-1,S	-0.6
1958	Bal-A	98	200	15	34	5	0	3	14	16	34	.170	.242	.240	35	-18	2	0	1	.964	-19	S-91/2-4,3O	-3.2
Total	5	268	662	58	136	24	3	20	65	35	99	.205	.252	.341	60	-39	4	1	1	.944	-17	3-121/S-94,2O	-5.1

■ LOUIS CASTRO
Castro, Louis Manuel "Jud" b: 1877, Colombia d: Venezuela BR/TR, 5'7", Deb: 4/23/02

YEAR	TM/L	G	AB	R	H	2B	3B	HR	RBI	BB	SO	AVG	OBP	SLG	PRO+	BR/A	SB	CS	SBR	FA	FR	G/POS	TPR
1902	Phi-A	42	143	18	35	8	1	1	15	4		.245	.265	.336	63	-8	2			.916	-16	2-36/O-3,S	-2.2

■ DANNY CATER
Cater, Danny Anderson b: 2/25/40, Austin, Tex. BR/TR, 5'11.5", 180 lbs. Deb: 4/14/64

YEAR	TM/L	G	AB	R	H	2B	3B	HR	RBI	BB	SO	AVG	OBP	SLG	PRO+	BR/A	SB	CS	SBR	FA	FR	G/POS	TPR
1964	Phi-N	60	152	13	45	9	1	1	13	7	15	.296	.327	.388	102	0	1	0	0	.981	-1	O-39/1-7,3	-0.2
1965	Chi-A	142	514	74	139	18	4	14	55	33	65	.270	.318	.403	110	5	3	3	-1	.978	-9	*O-127,3-11/1	-1.2
1966	Chi-A	21	60	3	11	1	1	0	4	0	10	.183	.197	.233	25	-6	3	1	0	.909	-3	O-18	-1.1
	KC-A	116	425	47	124	16	3	7	52	28	37	.292	.337	.393	113	6	1	4	-2	.994	-5	1-53,3-42,O	-0.6
	Yr	137	485	50	135	17	4	7	56	28	47	.278	.320	.373	102	1	4	5	-2	.994	-8	1-53,3-42,O	-1.7
1967	KC-A	142	529	55	143	17	4	46	34	60		.270	.319	.340	98	-2	4	5	-2	.916	-15	3-56,O-55,1	-2.6
1968	Oak-A	147	504	53	146	28	3	6	62	35	43	.290	.338	.393	127	15	8	7	-2	.995	-4	*1-121,O-20/2	0.0
1969	Oak-A	152	584	64	153	24	2	10	76	28	40	.262	.298	.361	87	-12	1	4	-2	.992	6	*1-132,O-20/2	-2.0
1970	NY-A	155	582	64	175	26	5	6	76	34	44	.301	.341	.393	108	3	4	2	0	.992	-4	*1-131,3-42/O	-1.0
1971	NY-A	121	428	39	118	16	5	4	50	19	25	.276	.310	.364	96	-4	0	3	-2	.995	8	1-78,3-52	-0.4
1972	Bos-A	92	317	32	75	17	1	8	39	15	33	.237	.275	.372	87	-4	0	0	0	.993	6	1-90	-0.9
1973	Bos-A	63	195	30	61	12	0	1	24	10	22	.313	.350	.390	102	3	0	0	0	.997	1	1-37,3-21/D	-0.1
1974	Bos-A	56	126	14	31	5	0	5	20	10	13	.246	.312	.405	99	-1	1	0	0	1.000	1	1-23,D-14	-0.1
1975	StL-N	22	35	3	8	2	0	0	2	1	9	.229	.250	.286	47	-3	0	0	0	.981	0	1-12	-0.3
Total	12	1289	4451	491	1229	191	29	66	519	254	406	.276	.318	.377	102	-1	26	30	-10	.994	-20	1-731,O-308,3/D2	-10.5

■ ELI CATES
Cates, Eli Eldo b: 1/26/1877, Greensfork, Ind. d: 5/29/64, Anderson, Ind. BR/TR, 5'9.5", 175 lbs. Deb: 4/20/08

YEAR	TM/L	G	AB	R	H	2B	3B	HR	RBI	BB	SO	AVG	OBP	SLG	PRO+	BR/A	SB	CS	SBR	FA	FR	G/POS	TPR
1908	Was-A	40	59	5	11	1	1	0	3	6		.186	.273	.237	72	-2	0			.907	-0	P-19/2-3	-0.1

■ TED CATHER
Cather, Theodore Physick b: 5/20/1889, Chester, Pa. d: 4/9/45, Elkton, Md. BR/TR, 5'10.5", 178 lbs. Deb: 9/23/12

YEAR	TM/L	G	AB	R	H	2B	3B	HR	RBI	BB	SO	AVG	OBP	SLG	PRO+	BR/A	SB	CS	SBR	FA	FR	G/POS	TPR
1912	StL-N	5	19	4	8	1	0	2	4	0	4	.421	.421	.579	176	2	1			.944	2	/O-5	0.3
1913	StL-N	67	183	16	39	8	4	0	12	9	24	.213	.250	.301	58	-11	7			.915	-7	O-57/P-1,1	-2.1
1914	StL-N	39	99	11	27	4	0	0	13	3	15	.273	.294	.343	90	-2	4			.981	0	O-28	-0.3

YEAR	TM/L	G	AB	R	H	2B	3B	HR	RBI	BB	SO	AVG	OBP	SLG	PRO+	BR/A	SB	CS	SBR	FA	FR	G/POS	TPR
	*Bos-N	50	145	19	43	11	2	0	27	7	28	.297	.338	.400	120	3	7			.953	-9	O-48	-0.8
	Yr	89	244	30	70	18	2	0	40	10	43	.287	.320	.377	108	1	11			.966	-9	O-76	-1.1
1915	Bos-N	40	102	10	21	3	1	2	18	15	19	.206	.319	.314	96	-0	2	4	-2	.902	-7	O-32	-1.2
Total	4	201	548	60	138	30	8	2	72	34	90	.252	.300	.347	91	-7	21	4		.938	-21	O-170/1-1,P	-4.1

■ HOWDY CATON
Caton, James Howard "Buster" b: 7/16/1896, Zanesville, Ohio d: 1/8/48, Zanesville, Ohio BR/TR, 5'6", 165 lbs. Deb: 9/17/17

YEAR	TM/L	G	AB	R	H	2B	3B	HR	RBI	BB	SO	AVG	OBP	SLG	PRO+	BR/A	SB	CS	SBR	FA	FR	G/POS	TPR
1917	Pit-N	14	57	6	12	1	2	0	4	6	7	.211	.286	.298	77	-2	0			.895	-2	S-14	-0.4
1918	Pit-N	80	303	37	71	5	7	0	31	32	16	.234	.312	.297	83	-5	12			.928	-7	S-79	-1.0
1919	Pit-N	39	102	13	18	1	2	0	5	12	10	.176	.263	.225	46	-6	2			.927	-11	S-17,3-14/O	-1.8
1920	Pit-N	98	352	29	83	11	5	0	27	33	19	.236	.305	.295	71	-13	4	9	-4	.929	-22	S-96	-3.4
Total	4	231	814	85	184	18	16	0	53	83	52	.226	.301	.287	72	-26	18	9		.926	-43	S-206/3-14,O	-6.6

■ TOM CATTERSON
Catterson, Thomas Henry b: 8/25/1884, Warwick, R.I. d: 2/5/20, Portland, Maine BL/TL, 5'10", 170 lbs. Deb: 9/19/08

YEAR	TM/L	G	AB	R	H	2B	3B	HR	RBI	BB	SO	AVG	OBP	SLG	PRO+	BR/A	SB	CS	SBR	FA	FR	G/POS	TPR
1908	Bro-N	19	68	5	13	1	1	1	2	5		.191	.257	.279	74	-2	0			.976	-2	O-18	-0.3
1909	Bro-N	9	18	0	4	0	0	0	1	3		.222	.333	.222	75	-0	0			.833	-2	/O-6	-0.3
Total	2	28	86	5	17	1	1	1	3	8		.198	.274	.267	75	-2	0			.957	-2	/O-24	-0.6

■ JAKE CAULFIELD
Caulfield, John Joseph b: 11/23/17, Los Angeles, Cal. d: 12/16/86, San Francisco, Cal BR/TR, 5'11", 170 lbs. Deb: 4/24/46

YEAR	TM/L	G	AB	R	H	2B	3B	HR	RBI	BB	SO	AVG	OBP	SLG	PRO+	BR/A	SB	CS	SBR	FA	FR	G/POS	TPR
1946	Phi-A	44	94	13	26	8	0	0	10	4	11	.277	.306	.362	87	-2	0	0	0	.929	-6	S-31/3-1	-0.7

■ WAYNE CAUSEY
Causey, James Wayne b: 12/26/36, Ruston, La. BL/TR, 5'10.5", 175 lbs. Deb: 6/5/55

YEAR	TM/L	G	AB	R	H	2B	3B	HR	RBI	BB	SO	AVG	OBP	SLG	PRO+	BR/A	SB	CS	SBR	FA	FR	G/POS	TPR
1955	Bal-A	68	175	14	34	2	1	1	9	17	25	.194	.269	.234	39	-15	0	1	-1	.912	-8	3-55/2-7,S	-2.4
1956	Bal-A	53	88	7	15	0	1	1	4	8	23	.170	.240	.227	26	-10	0	0	0	.980	2	3-30/2-7	-0.7
1957	Bal-A	14	10	2	2	0	0	0	1	5	2	.200	.500	.200	105	1	0	0	0	.960	3	/2-6,3-5	0.4
1961	KC-A	104	312	37	86	14	1	8	49	37	28	.276	.352	.404	100	0	0	0	0	.955	20	3-88,S-11/2	2.2
1962	KC-A	117	305	40	77	14	1	4	38	41	30	.252	.345	.344	82	-7	2	0	1	.953	2	S-51,3-26/2	0.1
1963	KC-A	139	554	72	155	32	4	3	44	56	54	.280	.346	.395	101	2	4	2	0	.978	5	*S-135/3-2	1.7
1964	KC-A	157	604	82	170	31	4	8	49	88	65	.281	.379	.386	110	12	0	1	-1	.967	-1	*S-131,2-17/3	2.2
1965	KC-A	144	513	48	134	17	8	3	34	61	48	.261	.342	.347	97	-1	1	3	-2	.972	-19	S-62,2-45,3	-1.5
1966	KC-A	28	79	1	18	0	0	0	5	7	6	.228	.291	.228	53	-5	1	0	0	.871	-9	3-15,S-10	-1.0
	Chi-A	78	164	23	40	8	2	0	13	24	13	.244	.340	.317	97	-0	2	0	1	.980	-16	2-60/S-1,3	-1.3
	Yr	106	243	24	58	8	2	0	18	31	19	.239	.325	.288	83	-5	3	0	1	.980	-21	2-60,3-16,S	-2.3
1967	Chi-A	124	292	21	66	10	3	1	28	32	35	.226	.305	.291	80	-7	2	5	-2	.978	-8	2-96/S-2	-1.4
1968	Chi-A	59	100	8	18	2	0	0	7	14	7	.180	.287	.200	49	-6	0	0	0	.971	-13	2-41	-2.0
	Cal-A	4	11	0	0	0	0	0	0	0	1	.000	.000	.000	-99	-3	0	0	0	1.000	1	/2-4	-0.2
	Yr	63	111	8	18	2	0	0	7	14	8	.162	.262	.180	36	-8	0	0	0	.975	-13	2-45	-2.2
	Atl-N	16	37	2	4	0	1	1	4	0	4	.108	.108	.243	3	-4	0	0	0	1.000	-4	/2-6,S-2,3	-1.0
Total	11	1105	3244	357	819	130	26	35	285	390	341	.252	.335	.341	89	-42	12	12	-4	.969	-42	S-406,2-307,3	-4.9

■ JOHN CAVANAUGH
Cavanaugh, John J. b: 6/5/1900, Scranton, Pa. d: 1/14/61, New Brunswick, N.J. BR/TR, 5'9", 158 lbs. Deb: 7/7/19

YEAR	TM/L	G	AB	R	H	2B	3B	HR	RBI	BB	SO	AVG	OBP	SLG	PRO+	BR/A	SB	CS	SBR	FA	FR	G/POS	TPR
1919	Phi-N	1	1	0	0	0	0	0	0	0	1	.000	.000	.000	-93	-0	0			.000	0	/3-1	0.0

■ PHIL CAVARRETTA
Cavarretta, Philip Joseph b: 7/19/16, Chicago, Ill. BL/TL, 5'11.5", 175 lbs. Deb: 9/16/34 MC

YEAR	TM/L	G	AB	R	H	2B	3B	HR	RBI	BB	SO	AVG	OBP	SLG	PRO+	BR/A	SB	CS	SBR	FA	FR	G/POS	TPR
1934	Chi-N	7	21	5	8	0	1	1	6	2	3	.381	.435	.619	182	2	1			1.000	1	/1-5	0.3
1935	*Chi-N	146	589	85	162	28	12	8	82	39	61	.275	.322	.404	93	-6	4			.986	2	*1-145	-2.0
1936	Chi-N	124	458	55	125	18	1	9	56	17	36	.273	.306	.376	81	-13	8			.987	-2	*1-115	-2.6
1937	Chi-N	106	329	43	94	18	7	5	56	32	35	.286	.349	.429	106	2	7			.972	-1	O-55,1-43	-0.5
1938	*Chi-N	92	268	29	64	11	4	1	28	14	27	.239	.287	.321	65	-13	4			.962	-7	O-52,1-28	-2.4
1939	Chi-N	22	55	4	15	3	1	0	4	4	3	.273	.322	.364	82	-1	2			.991	-1	1-13/O-1	-0.4
1940	Chi-N	65	193	34	54	11	4	2	22	31	18	.280	.388	.409	122	7	3			.991	-1	1-52	0.1
1941	Chi-N	107	346	46	99	18	4	6	40	53	28	.286	.384	.413	129	15	2			.992	-8	O-66,1-33	0.1
1942	Chi-N	136	482	59	130	28	4	3	54	71	42	.270	.365	.363	118	13	7			.989	6	O-70,1-61	1.2
1943	Chi-N	143	530	93	154	27	9	8	73	75	42	.291	.382	.421	134	24	3			.987	-11	*1-134/O-7	0.6
1944	Chi-N★	152	614	106	**197**	35	15	5	82	67	42	.321	.390	.451	137	31	4			.992	-7	*1-139,O-13	1.6
1945	*Chi-N†	132	498	94	177	34	10	6	97	81	34	**.355**	**.449**	.500	167	49	5			.993	-1	*1-120,O-11	3.8
1946	Chi-N★	139	510	89	150	28	10	8	78	88	54	.294	.401	.435	140	30	2			.967	-0	O-86,1-51	2.4
1947	Chi-N★	127	459	56	144	22	5	2	63	58	35	.314	.391	.397	114	11	2			.977	-0	*O-100,1-24	0.4
1948	Chi-N	111	334	41	93	16	4	3	40	35	29	.278	.349	.383	102	1	4			.998	1	1-41,O-40	-0.1
1949	Chi-N	105	360	46	106	22	4	8	49	45	31	.294	.374	.444	122	12	2			.993	9	1-70,O-25	1.8
1950	Chi-N	82	256	49	70	11	1	10	31	40	31	.273	.376	.441	115	6	1			.986	-1	1-67/O-13	0.4
1951	Chi-N	89	206	24	64	7	1	6	28	27	28	.311	.393	.442	122	7	0	0	0	.994	4	1-53,M	0.8
1952	Chi-N	41	63	7	15	1	1	1	8	9	3	.238	.333	.333	84	-1	0	0	0	.991	1	1-13,M	-0.1
1953	Chi-N	27	21	3	6	0	0	0	3	6	3	.286	.444	.429	126	1	0			.000	0	HM	0.1
1954	Chi-A	71	158	21	50	6	0	3	24	26	12	.316	.419	.411	124	7	4	0	1	.993	-4	1-44/O-9	0.2
1955	Chi-A	6	4	1	0	0	0	0	0	0	1	.000	.000	.000	-97	-1	0	0	0	1.000	-0	/1-3	-0.1
Total	22	2030	6754	990	1977	347	99	95	920	820	598	.293	.372	.416	118	182	65	0		.990	-21	*1-1254,O-538	5.6

■ IKE CAVENEY
Caveney, James Christopher b: 12/10/1894, San Francisco, Cal d: 7/6/49, San Francisco, Cal BR/TR, 5'9", 168 lbs. Deb: 4/12/22

YEAR	TM/L	G	AB	R	H	2B	3B	HR	RBI	BB	SO	AVG	OBP	SLG	PRO+	BR/A	SB	CS	SBR	FA	FR	G/POS	TPR
1922	Cin-N	118	394	41	94	12	9	3	54	29	33	.239	.301	.338	66	-21	6	6	-2	.934	-6	*S-118	-1.6
1923	Cin-N	138	488	58	135	21	9	4	63	26	41	.277	.315	.381	84	-12	5	4	-1	.942	0	*S-138	0.0
1924	Cin-N	95	337	36	92	19	1	4	32	14	21	.273	.310	.371	83	-9	2	3	-1	.924	3	S-90/2-5	0.3
1925	Cin-N	115	358	38	89	9	5	2	47	28	31	.249	.303	.318	60	-21	2	0	1	.941	9	*S-111	-0.1
Total	4	466	1577	173	410	61	24	13	196	97	126	.260	.307	.354	74	-63	15	13	-3	.936	6	S-457/2-5	-1.4

■ ANDUJAR CEDENO
Cedeno, Andujar (Donastorg) b: 8/21/69, LaRomana, D.R. BR/TR, 6'1", 170 lbs. Deb: 9/2/90 F

YEAR	TM/L	G	AB	R	H	2B	3B	HR	RBI	BB	SO	AVG	OBP	SLG	PRO+	BR/A	SB	CS	SBR	FA	FR	G/POS	TPR
1990	Hou-N	7	8	0	0	0	0	0	0	0	5	.000	.000	.000	-99	-2	0	0	0	.833	-0	/S-3	-0.3
1991	Hou-N	67	251	27	61	13	2	9	36	9	74	.243	.272	.418	97	-3	4	3	-1	.930	-14	S-66	-1.3
1992	Hou-N	71	220	15	38	13	2	2	13	14	71	.173	.232	.277	46	-16	2	0	1	.959	-2	S-70	-1.5
1993	Hou-N	149	505	69	143	24	4	11	56	48	97	.283	.349	.412	107	5	9	7	-2	.955	-26	*S-149/3-1	-1.1
1994	Hou-N	98	342	38	90	26	0	9	49	29	79	.263	.335	.418	92	-2	1	1	-0	.947	1	S-95	0.6
Total	5	392	1326	149	332	76	8	31	154	100	326	.250	.310	.390	92	-18	16	11	-2	.949	-41	S-383/3-1	-3.6

■ CESAR CEDENO
Cedeno, Cesar (Encarnacion) b: 2/25/51, Santo Domingo, D.R. BR/TR, 6'2", 195 lbs. Deb: 6/20/70

YEAR	TM/L	G	AB	R	H	2B	3B	HR	RBI	BB	SO	AVG	OBP	SLG	PRO+	BR/A	SB	CS	SBR	FA	FR	G/POS	TPR
1970	Hou-N	90	355	46	110	21	4	7	42	15	57	.310	.341	.451	115	6	17	4	3	.968	3	O-90	0.7
1971	Hou-N	161	611	85	161	**40**	6	10	81	25	102	.264	.296	.398	97	-5	20	9	1	.989	-2	*O-157/1-2	-1.5
1972	Hou-N★	139	559	103	179	**39**	8	22	82	56	62	.320	.387	.537	163	45	55	21	4	.981	11	*O-137	5.6
1973	Hou-N★	139	525	86	168	35	2	25	70	41	79	.320	.377	.537	151	34	56	15	6	.981	15	*O-136	5.3
1974	Hou-N★	160	610	95	164	29	5	26	102	64	103	.269	.342	.461	129	21	57	17	7	.993	21	*O-157	4.3
1975	Hou-N	131	500	93	144	31	3	13	63	62	52	.288	.374	.440	135	24	50	17	5	.982	4	*O-131	2.8
1976	Hou-N★	150	575	89	171	26	5	18	83	55	51	.297	.360	.454	143	30	58	15	8	.980	10	*O-146	4.4
1977	Hou-N	141	530	92	148	36	8	14	71	47	50	.279	.350	.457	126	18	61	14	10	**.997**	12	*O-137	3.4
1978	Hou-N	50	192	31	54	7	2	7	23	25	15	.281	.333	.453	127	6	23	2	6	.987	8	O-50	1.8
1979	Hou-N	132	470	57	123	27	4	6	54	64	52	.262	.354	.374	117	9	43	10	13	.981	-5	1-91,O-40	-0.7
1980	*Hou-N	137	499	71	154	32	8	10	73	66	72	.309	.390	.465	150	34	48	15	8	.977	8	*O-136	4.3
1981	*Hou-N	82	306	42	83	19	0	5	34	24	31	.271	.326	.382	106	2	12	7	-1	.991	-1	1-46,O-34	-0.4

YEAR	TM/L	G	AB	R	H	2B	3B	HR	RBI	BB	SO	AVG	OBP	SLG	PRO+	BR/A	SB	CS	SBR	FA	FR	G/POS	TPR
1982	Cin-N	138	492	52	142	35	1	8	57	41	41	.289	.348	.413	110	6	16	11	-2	.990	4	*O-131/1-1	0.5
1983	Cin-N	98	332	40	77	16	0	9	39	33	53	.232	.307	.361	82	-8	13	9	-2	.993	2	O-73,1-17	-1.2
1984	Cin-N	110	380	59	105	24	2	10	47	25	54	.276	.323	.429	105	2	19	3	4	.980	-2	O-77,1-44	-0.1
1985	Cin-N	83	220	24	53	12	0	3	30	19	35	.241	.310	.336	77	-7	9	5	-0	.990	-1	O-53,1-34	-1.0
	*StL-N	28	76	14	33	4	1	6	19	5	7	.434	.469	.750	238	13	5	1	1	.993	-4	1-23/O-2	1.0
	Yr	111	296	38	86	16	1	9	49	24	42	.291	.350	.443	116	6	14	6	1	.993	-4	1-57,O-55	0.0
1986	LA-N	37	78	5	18	2	1	0	6	7	13	.231	.294	.282	64	-4	1	1	-0	.944	-4	O-31	-0.9
Total	17	2006	7310	1084	2087	436	60	199	976	664	938	.285	.350	.443	124	221	550	179	58	.985	79	*O-1718,1-258	28.3

■ DOMINGO CEDENO

Cedeno, Domingo Antonio (Donastorg) b: 11/4/68, LaRomana, D.R. BB/TR, 6', 170 lbs. Deb: 5/19/93 F

YEAR	TM/L	G	AB	R	H	2B	3B	HR	RBI	BB	SO	AVG	OBP	SLG	PRO+	BR/A	SB	CS	SBR	FA	FR	G/POS	TPR
1993	Tor-A	15	46	5	8	0	0	0	7	1	10	.174	.191	.174	-1	-6	1	0	0	.973	-3	S-10/2-5	-0.8
1994	Tor-A	47	97	14	19	2	3	0	10	10	31	.196	.271	.278	42	-8	1	2	-1	.935	-3	2-28/S-8,3O	-1.1
Total	2	62	143	19	27	2	3	0	17	11	41	.189	.247	.245	29	-15	2	2	-1	.944	-6	/2-33,S-18,3O	-1.9

■ ORLANDO CEPEDA

Cepeda, Orlando Manuel (Penne) "Baby Bull" or "Cha Cha" b: 9/17/37, Ponce, P.R. BR/TR, 6'2", 210 lbs. Deb: 4/15/58 C

YEAR	TM/L	G	AB	R	H	2B	3B	HR	RBI	BB	SO	AVG	OBP	SLG	PRO+	BR/A	SB	CS	SBR	FA	FR	G/POS	TPR
1958	SF-N	148	603	88	188	38	4	25	96	29	84	.312	.346	.512	126	20	15	11	-2	.989	-3	*1-147	0.6
1959	SF-N★	151	605	92	192	35	4	27	105	33	100	.317	.358	.522	134	27	23	9	2	.984	-8	*1-122,O-44/3	1.2
1960	SF-N★	151	569	81	169	36	3	24	96	34	91	.297	.345	.497	135	25	15	6	1	.983	0	O-91,1-63	1.7
1961	SF-N★	152	585	105	182	28	4	46	142	39	91	.311	.363	.609	158	45	12	8	-1	.997	-3	1-81,O-80	3.0
1962	*SF-N★	162	625	105	191	26	1	35	114	37	97	.306	.350	.518	132	26	10	4	1	.991	-8	*1-160/O-2	0.8
1963	SF-N☆	156	579	100	183	33	4	34	97	37	70	.316	.367	.563	166	47	8	3	1	.985	-8	*1-150/O-3	3.4
1964	SF-N★	142	529	75	161	27	2	31	97	43	83	.304	.366	.539	148	33	9	4	0	.986	-4	*1-139/O-1	2.4
1965	SF-N	33	34	1	6	1	0	1	5	3	9	.176	.243	.294	49	-2	0	0	-0	1.000	-0	/1-4,O-2	-0.3
1966	SF-N	19	49	5	14	2	0	3	15	4	11	.286	.352	.510	132	2	0	1	-1	.778	-3	/O-8,1-6	-0.2
	StL-N	123	452	65	137	24	0	17	58	34	68	.303	.369	.469	130	19	9	8	-2	.989	-6	*1-120	0.2
	Yr	142	501	70	151	26	0	20	73	38	79	.301	.367	.473	130	21	9	9	-3	.990	-9	*1-126/O-8	0.0
1967	*StL-N★	151	563	91	183	37	0	25	111	62	75	.325	.403	.524	166	49	11	2	2	.993	-0	*1-151	4.4
1968	*StL-N	157	600	71	149	26	2	16	73	43	96	.248	.308	.378	107	4	8	5	-1	.988	-5	*1-154	-1.6
1969	*Atl-N	154	573	74	147	28	2	22	88	55	76	.257	.327	.428	109	6	12	5	1	.994	3	*1-153	-0.3
1970	Atl-N	148	567	87	173	33	0	34	111	47	75	.305	.368	.543	133	25	6	5	-1	.992	3	*1-148	1.3
1971	Atl-N	71	250	31	69	10	1	14	44	22	29	.276	.335	.492	124	7	3	6	-3	.992	2	1-63	0.1
1972	Atl-N	28	84	6	25	3	0	4	9	7	17	.298	.352	.476	122	2	0	0	-0	1.000	1	1-22	0.1
	Oak-A	3	3	0	0	0	0	0	0	0	2	.000	.000	.000	-99	-1	0	0	0	.000	0	H	-0.1
1973	Bos-A	142	550	51	159	25	0	20	86	50	81	.289	.350	.444	116	11	0	2	-2	.000	0	*D-142	0.6
1974	KC-A	33	107	3	23	5	0	1	18	9	16	.215	.282	.290	61	-5	1	0	-0	.000	0	D-26	-0.6
Total	17	2124	7927	1131	2351	417	27	379	1365	588	1169	.297	.353	.499	133	338	142	80	-5	.990	-39	*1-1683,O-231,D/3	16.7

■ ED CERMAK

Cermak, Edward Hugo b: 3/10/1882, Cleveland, Ohio d: 11/22/11, Cleveland, Ohio BR/TR, 5'11", 170 lbs. Deb: 9/9/01

YEAR	TM/L	G	AB	R	H	2B	3B	HR	RBI	BB	SO	AVG	OBP	SLG	PRO+	BR/A	SB	CS	SBR	FA	FR	G/POS	TPR
1901	Cle-A	1	4	0	0	0	0	0	0	0		.000	.000	.000	-99	-1	0			1.000	1	/O-1	0.0

■ RICK CERONE

Cerone, Richard Aldo b: 5/19/54, Newark, N.J. BR/TR, 5'11", 192 lbs. Deb: 8/17/75

YEAR	TM/L	G	AB	R	H	2B	3B	HR	RBI	BB	SO	AVG	OBP	SLG	PRO+	BR/A	SB	CS	SBR	FA	FR	G/POS	TPR
1975	Cle-A	7	12	1	3	1	0	0	0	1	0	.250	.308	.333	81	-0	0	0	0	1.000	-1	/C-7	-0.1
1976	Cle-A	7	16	1	2	0	0	0	1	0	2	.125	.125	.125	-27	-3	0	0	0	.963	0	/C-6,D-1	-0.2
1977	Tor-A	31	100	7	20	4	0	1	10	6	12	.200	.245	.270	40	-8	0	0	0	.994	-2	C-31	-0.9
1978	Tor-A	88	282	25	63	8	2	3	20	23	32	.223	.284	.298	63	-14	0	3	-2	.992	-0	C-84/D-2	-1.5
1979	Tor-A	136	469	47	112	27	4	7	61	37	40	.239	.296	.358	75	-17	1	4	-2	.980	-8	*C-136	-2.2
1980	*NY-A	147	519	70	144	30	4	14	85	32	56	.277	.327	.432	108	4	1	3	-2	.990	-6	*C-147	1.4
1981	*NY-A	71	234	23	57	13	2	2	21	12	24	.244	.280	.342	80	-7	0	2	-1	.992	-6	C-69	-1.2
1982	NY-A	89	300	29	68	10	0	5	28	19	27	.227	.275	.310	61	-16	0	2	-1	.989	-8	C-89	-2.2
1983	NY-A	80	246	18	54	7	0	2	22	15	29	.220	.267	.272	51	-17	0	0	0	.991	-6	C-78/3-1	-1.4
1984	NY-A	38	120	8	25	3	0	2	13	9	15	.208	.269	.283	55	-7	1	0	0	.996	3	C-38	-0.2
1985	Atl-N	96	282	15	61	9	0	3	25	29	25	.216	.292	.280	57	-16	0	3	-2	.986	-8	C-91	-2.2
1986	Mil-A	68	216	22	56	14	0	4	18	15	28	.259	.310	.380	84	-5	1	1	-0	.991	7	C-68	0.6
1987	NY-A	113	284	28	69	12	1	4	23	30	46	.243	.324	.335	76	-9	0	1	-0	.998	4	*C-111/P-2,1	0.1
1988	Bos-A	84	264	31	71	13	1	3	27	20	32	.269	.328	.360	89	-4	0	0	0	1.000	-5	C-83/D-1	-0.3
1989	Bos-A	102	296	28	72	16	1	4	48	34	29	.243	.325	.345	84	-6	0	0	0	.984	3	C-97/O-1,D	0.1
1990	NY-A	49	139	12	42	6	0	2	11	5	13	.302	.326	.388	99	-0	0	0	0	.995	-3	C-35/2-1,D	-0.2
1991	NY-N	90	227	18	62	13	0	2	16	30	24	.273	.360	.357	103	2	1	1	-0	.987	-2	C-81	0.4
1992	Mon-N	33	63	10	17	4	0	1	7	3	5	.270	.313	.381	97	-0	1	2	-1	1.000	1	C-28	0.0
Total	18	1329	4069	393	998	190	15	59	436	320	450	.245	.304	.343	78	-123	6	22	-11	.990	-19	*C-1279/D-11,1P203	-10.0

■ BOB CERV

Cerv, Robert Henry b: 5/5/26, Weston, Neb. BR/TR, 6', 202 lbs. Deb: 8/1/51

YEAR	TM/L	G	AB	R	H	2B	3B	HR	RBI	BB	SO	AVG	OBP	SLG	PRO+	BR/A	SB	CS	SBR	FA	FR	G/POS	TPR
1951	NY-A	12	28	4	6	1	0	0	2	4	6	.214	.313	.250	55	-2	0	0	0	.875	-1	/O-9	-0.3
1952	NY-A	36	87	11	21	3	2	1	8	9	22	.241	.313	.356	91	-1	0	1	-1	1.000	-2	O-27	-0.5
1953	NY-A	8	6	0	0	0	0	0	0	1	1	.000	.143	.000	-61	-1	0	0	0	.000	0	H	-0.1
1954	NY-A	56	100	14	26	6	0	5	13	11	17	.260	.333	.470	122	3	0	2	-1	.897	-5	O-24	-0.4
1955	*NY-A	55	85	17	29	4	3	2	22	7	16	.341	.411	.541	157	7	4	0	1	1.000	-4	O-20	0.4
1956	*NY-A	54	115	16	35	5	6	3	25	18	13	.304	.398	.530	148	8	0	1	-0	.984	-4	O-44	0.2
1957	KC-A	124	345	35	94	14	2	11	44	20	57	.272	.314	.420	97	-2	1	1	-0	.964	-7	O-89	-1.5
1958	KC-A★	141	515	93	157	20	7	38	104	50	82	.305	.372	.592	158	39	3	3	-1	.985	20	*O-136	5.1
1959	KC-A	125	463	61	132	22	4	20	87	35	87	.285	.339	.479	120	11	3	2	-0	.980	6	*O-119	1.1
1960	KC-A	23	78	14	20	1	1	6	12	10	17	.256	.341	.526	130	3	0	0	0	.977	-3	O-21	0.5
	*NY-A	87	216	32	54	11	1	8	28	30	36	.250	.349	.421	114	4	0	0	0	.982	4	O-51/1-3	0.5
	Yr	110	294	46	74	12	2	14	40	40	53	.252	.347	.449	119	7	0	0	0	.980	6	O-72/1-3	1.0
1961	LA-A	18	57	3	9	3	0	2	6	1	9	.158	.172	.316	25	-6	0	0	0	.944	-2	O-15	-1.0
	NY-A	57	118	17	32	5	1	6	20	12	17	.271	.344	.483	125	1	0	0	0	.983	1	O-30/1-3	0.4
	Yr	75	175	20	41	8	1	8	26	13	25	.234	.291	.429	91	-3	0	0	0	.974	-1	*O-45/1-3	-0.6
1962	NY-A	14	17	1	2	1	0	0	3	2	4	.118	.250	.176	18	-2	0	0	0	1.000	-0	/O-3	-0.3
	Hou-N	19	31	2	7	0	0	2	3	2	10	.226	.273	.419	89	-1	0	0	0	.833	-2	/O-6	-0.1
Total	12	829	2261	320	624	96	26	105	374	212	392	.276	.343	.481	122	63	12	10	-2	.976	8	O-594/1-6	4.0

■ RON CEY

Cey, Ronald Charles b: 2/15/48, Tacoma, Wash. BR/TR, 5'10", 185 lbs. Deb: 9/3/71

YEAR	TM/L	G	AB	R	H	2B	3B	HR	RBI	BB	SO	AVG	OBP	SLG	PRO+	BR/A	SB	CS	SBR	FA	FR	G/POS	TPR
1971	LA-N	2	2	0	0	0	0	0	0	0	0	.000	.000	.000	-99	-1	0	0	0	.000	0	H	-0.1
1972	LA-N	11	37	3	10	1	0	1	3	7	10	.270	.400	.378	125	2	0	0	0	.900	-2	3-11	-0.1
1973	LA-N	152	507	60	124	18	4	15	80	74	75	.245	.343	.385	106	5	1	1	-0	.961	16	*3-146	2.1
1974	*LA-N★	159	577	88	151	20	2	18	97	76	68	.262	.355	.397	115	12	1	1	-0	.959	17	*3-158	2.9
1975	LA-N★	158	566	72	160	29	2	25	101	74	74	.283	.376	.473	141	31	5	2	0	.960	-4	*3-158	2.8
1976	LA-N★	145	502	69	139	18	3	23	80	89	74	.277	.389	.462	140	31	0	4	-2	.965	11	*3-144	4.1
1977	*LA-N★	153	564	77	136	22	3	30	110	93	106	.241	.351	.450	114	11	3	4	-2	.964	17	*3-153	2.5
1978	LA-N★	159	555	84	150	32	0	23	84	96	96	.270	.384	.452	134	28	2	5	-2	.966	5	*3-158	2.9
1979	LA-N★	150	487	77	137	20	1	28	81	86	85	.281	.391	.499	143	31	3	3	-1	.977	-1	*3-150	2.9
1980	LA-N	157	551	81	140	25	0	28	77	69	92	.254	.342	.452	122	16	2	2	-0	.972	7	*3-157	2.1
1981	*LA-N	85	312	42	90	15	2	13	50	40	55	.288	.375	.474	145	18	0	3	-1	.941	7	3-84	2.4
1982	LA-N	150	556	62	141	23	1	24	79	57	99	.254	.327	.428	113	8	3	2	-0	.963	11	*3-149	1.6

YEAR	TM/L	G	AB	R	H	2B	3B	HR	RBI	BB	SO	AVG	OBP	SLG	PRO+	BR/A	SB	CS	SBR	FA	FR	G/POS	TPR
1983	Chi-N	159	581	73	160	33	1	24	90	62	85	.275	.350	.460	117	13	0	0	-0	.955	-21	*3-157	-1.0
1984	*Chi-N	146	505	71	121	27	0	25	97	61	108	.240	.329	.442	105	3	3	2	-0	**.967**	-20	*3-144	-2.0
1985	Chi-N	145	500	64	116	18	2	22	63	58	106	.232	.317	.408	91	-6	1	1	-0	.943	-7	*3-140	-1.7
1986	Chi-N	97	256	42	70	21	0	13	36	44	66	.273	.386	.508	134	12	0	0	0	.952	-6	3-77	0.5
1987	Oak-A	45	104	12	23	6	4	4	11	22	32	.221	.362	.394	108	2	0	0	0	.982	-1	D-30/1-7,3	0.0
Total	17	2073	7162	977	1868	328	21	316	1139	1012	1235	.261	.357	.445	121	216	24	29	-10	.961	30	*3-1989/D-30,1	21.9

■ ELIO CHACON
Chacon, Elio (Rodriguez)   b: 10/26/36, Caracas, Venez.   d: 4/24/92, Caracas, Venez.   BR/TR, 5'9", 160 lbs.   Deb: 4/20/60

YEAR	TM/L	G	AB	R	H	2B	3B	HR	RBI	BB	SO	AVG	OBP	SLG	PRO+	BR/A	SB	CS	SBR	FA	FR	G/POS	TPR
1960	Cin-N	49	116	14	21	1	0	0	7	14	23	.181	.275	.190	29	-11	7	1	2	.980	5	2-43/O-2	-0.1
1961	*Cin-N	61	132	26	35	4	2	2	5	21	22	.265	.374	.371	97	0	1	4	-2	.989	0	2-42/O-7	0.2
1962	NY-N	118	368	49	87	10	3	2	27	76	64	.236	.369	.296	80	-7	12	7	-1	.961	-3	*S-110/2-2,3	-0.1
Total	3	228	616	89	143	15	5	4	39	111	109	.232	.353	.292	74	-18	20	12	-1	.985	3	S-110/2-87,O3	0.0

■ CHET CHADBOURNE
Chadbourne, Chester James "Pop"   b: 10/28/1884, Parkman, Me.   d: 6/21/43, Los Angeles, Cal.   BL/TR, 5'9", 170 lbs.   Deb: 9/17/06

YEAR	TM/L	G	AB	R	H	2B	3B	HR	RBI	BB	SO	AVG	OBP	SLG	PRO+	BR/A	SB	CS	SBR	FA	FR	G/POS	TPR
1906	Bos-A	11	43	7	13	1	0	0	3	3		.302	.348	.326	111	1	1			.926	3	2-11/S-1	0.4
1907	Bos-A	10	38	0	11	0	0	0	1	7		.289	.400	.289	121	1	1			1.000	-0	O-10	0.1
1914	KC-F	147	581	92	161	22	8	1	37	69	49	.277	.359	.348	87	-10	42			.965	9	*O-146	-0.8
1915	KC-F	152	587	75	133	16	9	1	35	62	29	.227	.307	.290	63	-31	29			**.979**	1	*O-152	-4.1
1918	Bos-N	27	104	9	27	2	1	0	6	5	5	.260	.300	.298	86	-2	5			.925	-3	O-27	-0.7
Total	5	347	1353	183	345	41	18	2	82	146	<u>83</u>	.255	.333	.316	78	-41	78			.969	10	O-335/2-11,S	-5.1

■ DAVE CHALK
Chalk, David Lee   b: 8/30/50, Del Rio, Tex.   BR/TR, 5'10", 175 lbs.   Deb: 9/4/73

YEAR	TM/L	G	AB	R	H	2B	3B	HR	RBI	BB	SO	AVG	OBP	SLG	PRO+	BR/A	SB	CS	SBR	FA	FR	G/POS	TPR
1973	Cal-A	24	69	14	16	2	0	0	6	9	13	.232	.329	.261	74	-2	0	0	0	.962	2	S-22	0.2
1974	Cal-A★	133	465	44	117	9	3	5	31	30	57	.252	.307	.316	84	-10	10	10	-3	.938	-2	S-99,3-38	-0.2
1975	Cal-A☆	149	513	59	140	24	2	3	56	66	49	.273	.358	.345	107	7	6	9	-4	.976	6	*3-149	0.9
1976	Cal-A	142	438	39	95	14	1	0	33	49	62	.217	.310	.253	71	-14	0	0	0	.971	5	*S-102,3-49	0.1
1977	Cal-A	149	519	58	144	27	2	3	45	52	69	.277	.349	.355	96	-1	12	8	-1	.948	-1	*3-141/2-7,S	-0.6
1978	Cal-A	135	470	42	119	12	0	1	34	38	34	.253	.318	.285	74	-15	5	8	-3	.955	-20	S-97,2-29,3/D	-2.6
1979	Tex-A	9	8	0	2	0	0	0	0	0	0	.250	.250	.250	36	-1	0	0	0	1.000	-0	/S-3,2-1	-0.1
	Oak-A	66	212	15	47	6	0	2	13	29	14	.222	.318	.278	66	-9	2	1	0	.988	-17	2-37,S-16,3	-2.2
	Yr	75	220	15	49	6	0	2	13	29	14	.223	.316	.277	65	-10	2	1	0	.988	-17	2-38,S-19,3	-2.3
1980	*KC-A	69	167	19	42	10	1	1	20	18	27	.251	.332	.341	84	-3	1	1	-0	.964	-3	3-33,2-17/SD	-0.7
1981	KC-A	27	49	2	11	3	0	0	5	4	2	.224	.283	.286	65	-2	0	1	-1	.955	-2	3-14,2-10/S	-0.4
Total	9	903	2910	292	733	107	9	15	243	295	327	.252	.328	.310	85	-52	36	38	-12	.962	-34	3-462,S-345,2/D	-5.6

■ JOE CHAMBERLAIN
Chamberlain, Joseph Jeremiah   b: 5/10/10, San Francisco, Cal   d: 1/28/83, San Francisco, Cal.   BR/TR, 6'1", 175 lbs.   Deb: 4/17/34

YEAR	TM/L	G	AB	R	H	2B	3B	HR	RBI	BB	SO	AVG	OBP	SLG	PRO+	BR/A	SB	CS	SBR	FA	FR	G/POS	TPR
1934	Chi-A	43	141	13	34	5	1	2	17	6	38	.241	.272	.333	54	-10	1	1	-0	.896	-6	S-26,3-14/2	-1.4

■ WES CHAMBERLAIN
Chamberlain, Wesley Polk   b: 4/13/66, Chicago, Ill.   BR/TR, 6'2", 210 lbs.   Deb: 8/31/90

YEAR	TM/L	G	AB	R	H	2B	3B	HR	RBI	BB	SO	AVG	OBP	SLG	PRO+	BR/A	SB	CS	SBR	FA	FR	G/POS	TPR
1990	Phi-N	18	46	9	13	3	0	2	4	1	9	.283	.298	.478	110	0	4	0	1	.958	-1	O-10	0.1
1991	Phi-N	101	383	51	92	16	3	13	50	31	73	.240	.300	.399	96	-3	9	4	0	.985	5	O-98	0.0
1992	Phi-N	76	275	26	71	18	0	9	41	10	55	.258	.287	.422	99	-2	4	0	1	.971	-1	O-73	-0.3
1993	*Phi-N	96	284	34	80	20	2	12	45	17	51	.282	.325	.493	117	6	2	1	0	.993	5	O-76	0.9
1994	Phi-N	24	69	7	19	5	0	2	6	3	12	.275	.306	.435	91	-1	0	0	0	1.000	-1	O-18	-0.1
	Bos-A	51	164	13	42	9	1	4	20	12	38	.256	.307	.396	75	-6	0	2	-1	1.000	4	O-34,D-12	-0.5
Total	5	366	1221	140	317	71	6	42	166	74	238	.260	.304	.431	99	-6	19	7	2	.985	12	O-309/D-12	0.1

■ AL CHAMBERS
Chambers, Albert Eugene   b: 3/24/61, Harrisburg, Pa.   BL/TL, 6'4", 217 lbs.   Deb: 7/23/83

YEAR	TM/L	G	AB	R	H	2B	3B	HR	RBI	BB	SO	AVG	OBP	SLG	PRO+	BR/A	SB	CS	SBR	FA	FR	G/POS	TPR
1983	Sea-A	31	67	11	14	3	0	1	7	18	20	.209	.376	.299	85	-1	0	1	0	1.000	-1	D-22/O-3	-0.3
1984	Sea-A	22	49	4	11	1	0	1	4	3	12	.224	.269	.306	60	-3	2	1	0	.947	-2	O-13/D-1	-0.5
1985	Sea-A	4	4	0	0	0	0	0	0	0	2	.000	.000	.000	-99	-1	0	0	0	.000	0	/H	-0.1
Total	3	57	120	15	25	4	0	2	11	21	34	.208	.326	.292	71	-4	2	2	-1	.955	-3	/D-23,O-16	-0.9

■ CHRIS CHAMBLISS
Chambliss, Carroll Christopher   b: 12/26/48, Dayton, O.   BL/TR, 6'1", 215 lbs.   Deb: 5/28/71   C

YEAR	TM/L	G	AB	R	H	2B	3B	HR	RBI	BB	SO	AVG	OBP	SLG	PRO+	BR/A	SB	CS	SBR	FA	FR	G/POS	TPR
1971	Cle-A	111	415	49	114	20	4	9	48	40	83	.275	.341	.407	102	1	2	0	1	.992	-5	*1-108	-1.4
1972	Cle-A	121	466	51	136	27	2	6	44	26	63	.292	.329	.397	112	3	3	4	-2	.993	-6	*1-119	-1.3
1973	Cle-A	155	572	70	156	30	2	11	53	58	76	.273	.343	.390	104	3	4	8	-4	.991	7	*1-154	-0.6
1974	Cle-A	17	67	8	22	4	0	0	7	5	5	.328	.375	.388	121	2	0	1	0	.982	-2	1-17	-0.2
	NY-A	110	400	38	97	16	3	6	43	23	43	.243	.284	.343	82	-10	0	0	0	.992	7	*1-106	-1.1
	Yr	127	467	46	119	20	3	6	50	28	48	.255	.297	.349	87	-9	0	1	-1	.990	5	*1-123	-1.3
1975	NY-A	150	562	66	171	38	4	9	72	29	50	.304	.340	.434	121	13	0	1	-1	.991	3	*1-147	0.6
1976	*NY-A★	156	641	79	188	32	6	17	96	27	80	.293	.325	.441	124	16	1	0	0	.994	-2	*1-155/D-1	0.4
1977	*NY-A	157	600	90	172	32	6	17	90	45	73	.287	.338	.445	113	10	4	0	0	.989	-5	*1-157	-0.3
1978	*NY-A	162	625	81	171	26	3	12	90	41	60	.274	.323	.382	100	-1	2	1	0	**.997**	4	*1-155/D-7	-0.6
1979	NY-A	149	554	61	155	27	3	18	63	34	53	.280	.327	.437	106	4	3	2	-0	.995	-2	*1-134,D-16	-0.5
1980	Atl-N	158	602	83	170	37	2	18	72	49	73	.282	.340	.440	114	9	7	3	0	.993	-2	*1-158	-0.2
1981	Atl-N	107	404	44	110	25	2	8	51	44	41	.272	.345	.403	109	5	4	1	1	.997	7	*1-107	0.7
1982	*Atl-N	157	534	57	144	25	2	20	86	57	57	.270	.340	.436	111	8	7	3	0	.993	14	*1-151	1.5
1983	Atl-N	131	447	59	125	24	3	20	78	63	68	.280	.369	.481	124	15	2	7	-4	.996	0	*1-126	0.5
1984	Atl-N	135	389	47	100	14	0	9	44	58	54	.257	.355	.362	95	-1	1	2	-1	.993	2	*1-109	-0.7
1985	Atl-N	101	170	16	40	7	0	3	21	18	22	.235	.309	.329	74	-6	0	0	0	.997	0	1-39	-0.6
1986	Atl-N	97	122	13	38	8	0	2	14	15	24	.311	.387	.426	117	3	0	2	-1	.993	-2	1-20	-0.1
1988	NY-A	1	1	0	0	0	0	0	0	0	1	.000	.000	.000	-99	-0	0	0	0	.000	0	/H	0.0
Total	17	2175	7571	912	2109	392	42	185	972	632	926	.279	.336	.415	108	77	40	35	-9	.993	25	*1-1962/D-24	-3.9

■ MIKE CHAMPION
Champion, Robert Michael   b: 2/10/55, Montgomery, Ala.   BR/TR, 6', 185 lbs.   Deb: 9/14/76

YEAR	TM/L	G	AB	R	H	2B	3B	HR	RBI	BB	SO	AVG	OBP	SLG	PRO+	BR/A	SB	CS	SBR	FA	FR	G/POS	TPR
1976	SD-N	11	38	4	9	2	0	1	2	0	6	.237	.256	.368	82	-1	0	0	0	.940	-4	2-11	-0.5
1977	SD-N	150	507	35	116	14	6	1	43	27	85	.229	.271	.286	55	-34	3	3	-1	.974	-26	*2-149	-5.3
1978	SD-N	32	53	3	12	0	2	0	4	6	10	.226	.293	.302	72	-2	0	0	0	.932	2	2-20/3-4	0.1
Total	3	193	598	42	137	16	8	2	49	33	101	.229	.272	.293	58	-37	3	3	-1	.968	-28	2-180/3-4	-5.7

■ FRANK CHANCE
Chance, Frank Leroy "Husk" or "The Peerless Leader"   b: 9/9/1877, Fresno, Cal.   d: 9/15/24, Los Angeles, Cal.   BR/TR, 6', 190 lbs.   Deb: 4/29/1898   MH

YEAR	TM/L	G	AB	R	H	2B	3B	HR	RBI	BB	SO	AVG	OBP	SLG	PRO+	BR/A	SB	CS	SBR	FA	FR	G/POS	TPR
1898	Chi-N	53	147	32	41	4	3	1	14	7		.279	.338	.367	102	0	7			.950	-5	C-33,O-17/1	-0.4
1899	Chi-N	64	192	37	55	6	2	1	22	15		.286	.351	.354	96	-1	10			.950	-2	C-57/O-1,1	0.2
1900	Chi-N	56	149	26	44	9	3	0	13	15		.295	.413	.396	129	8	8			.932	-1	C-51/1-1	1.0
1901	Chi-N	69	241	38	67	12	4	0	36	29		.278	.376	.361	119	8	27			.932	-5	O-51,C-13/1	0.0
1902	Chi-N	75	240	39	69	9	4	1	31	35		.287	.396	.371	141	14	27			.969	-4	1-38,C-29/O	1.2
1903	Chi-N	125	441	83	144	24	10	2	81	78		.327	.439	.440	155	37	**67**			.972	-3	*1-121/C-2	3.0
1904	Chi-N	124	451	89	140	16	10	6	49	36		.310	.382	.430	150	27	42			.990	12	*1-123/C-1	3.7
1905	Chi-N	118	392	92	124	16	12	2	70	78		.316	**.450**	.434	157	34	38			.990	2	*1-115,M	3.3
1906	*Chi-N	136	474	**103**	151	24	10	3	71	70		.319	.419	.430	156	34	**57**			.989	4	*1-136,M	3.2
1907	*Chi-N	111	382	58	112	19	2	1	49	51		.293	.395	.361	129	15	35			**.992**	7	*1-109,M	2.2
1908	*Chi-N	129	452	65	123	27	4	2	55	37		.272	.338	.363	119	10	27			.989	4	*1-126,M	1.3
1909	Chi-N	93	324	53	88	16	4	0	46	30		.272	.341	.346	110	4	29			.994	-2	1-92,M	0.2

YEAR	TM/L	G	AB	R	H	2B	3B	HR	RBI	BB	SO	AVG	OBP	SLG	PRO+	BR/A	SB	CS	SBR	FA	FR	G/POS	TPR
1910	*Chi-N	88	295	54	88	12	8	0	36	37	15	.298	.395	.393	131	13	16			.996	-2	1-87,M	1.2
1911	Chi-N	31	88	23	21	6	3	1	17	25	13	.239	.432	.409	136	6	9			.990	-2	1-29,M	0.4
1912	Chi-N	2	5	2	1	0	0	0	0	3	0	.200	.500	.200	96	0	1			1.000	-0	/1-2,M	0.0
1913	NY-A	12	24	3	5	0	0	0	6	8	1	.208	.406	.208	81	0	1			1.000	1	/1-7,M	0.1
1914	NY-A	1	0	0	0	0	0	0	0	0	0	—	—	—	—	—	0			1.000	-0	/1-1,M	0.0
Total	17	1287	4297	797	1273	200	79	20	596	554	29	.296	.394	.394	135	208	401			.987	-1	1-997,C-186/O	20.6

■ BOB CHANCE

Chance, Robert b: 9/10/40, Statesboro, Ga. BL/TR, 6'2", 219 lbs. Deb: 9/4/63

YEAR	TM/L	G	AB	R	H	2B	3B	HR	RBI	BB	SO	AVG	OBP	SLG	PRO+	BR/A	SB	CS	SBR	FA	FR	G/POS	TPR
1963	Cle-A	16	52	5	15	4	0	2	7	1	10	.288	.302	.481	116	1	0	1	-1	.909	-2	O-14	-0.2
1964	Cle-A	120	390	45	109	16	1	14	75	40	101	.279	.351	.433	118	9	3	3	-1	.988	-12	1-81,O-31	-0.9
1965	Was-A	72	199	20	51	9	0	4	14	18	44	.256	.318	.362	94	-2	0	1	-1	.988	-2	1-48/O-3	-0.7
1966	Was-A	37	57	1	10	3	0	1	8	2	23	.175	.203	.281	38	-5	0	1	-1	.974	-2	1-13	-0.7
1967	Was-A	27	42	5	9	2	0	3	7	7	13	.214	.340	.476	144	2	0	0		1.000	-0	1-10	0.2
1969	Cal-A	5	7	0	1	0	0	0	0	4	4	.143	.143	.143	-21	-1	0	0		.909	-0	/1-1	-0.2
Total	6	277	747	76	195	34	1	24	112	68	195	.261	.326	.406	106	5	3	5	-2	.987	-18	1-153/O-48	-2.5

■ DARREL CHANEY

Chaney, Darrel Lee b: 3/9/48, Hammond, Ind. BB/TR, 6'1", 190 lbs. Deb: 4/11/69

YEAR	TM/L	G	AB	R	H	2B	3B	HR	RBI	BB	SO	AVG	OBP	SLG	PRO+	BR/A	SB	CS	SBR	FA	FR	G/POS	TPR
1969	Cin-N	93	209	21	40	5	2	0	15	24	75	.191	.278	.234	43	-16	1	0	0	.947	-12	S-91	-2.2
1970	*Cin-N	57	95	7	22	3	0	1	4	3	26	.232	.263	.295	49	-7	1	1	-0	.941	5	S-30,2-18/3	0.0
1971	Cin-N	10	24	2	3	0	0	0		1	3	.125	.160	.125	-19	-4	0	1	-1	1.000	-1	/S-7,2-1,3	-0.4
1972	*Cin-N	83	196	29	49	7	2	2	19	29	28	.250	.347	.337	101	1	1	3	-2	.963	-7	S-64,2-12,3	-0.1
1973	*Cin-N	105	227	27	41	7	1	0	14	26	50	.181	.268	.220	39	-19	4	3	-1	.964	12	S-75,2-14,3	0.1
1974	Cin-N	117	135	27	27	6	1	2	16	26	33	.200	.329	.304	79	-3	1	2	-1	.952	17	3-81,2-38,S	1.5
1975	*Cin-N	71	160	18	35	6	0	2	26	14	38	.219	.282	.294	59	-9	3	0	1	.961	1	S-34,2-23,3	1.2
1976	Atl-N	153	496	42	125	20	8	1	50	54	92	.252	.327	.331	82	-11	5	7	-3	.950	-0	*S-151/2-1,3	0.4
1977	Atl-N	74	209	20	42	7	2	3	15	17	44	.201	.261	.297	44	-17	0	0		.979	4	S-41,2-24	-0.7
1978	Atl-N	89	245	27	55	9	1	3	20	25	48	.224	.290	.306	62	-12	1	0		.976	-6	S-77/3-8,2	-1.0
1979	Atl-N	63	117	15	19	5	0	0	10	19	34	.162	.279	.205	32	-11	2	1		.945	-3	S-39/2-5,3C	-1.1
Total	11	915	2113	237	458	75	17	14	190	238	471	.217	.297	.288	61	-107	19	18	-5	.959	26	S-621,2-137,3/C	-2.3

■ LES CHANNELL

Channell, Lester Clark "Goat" or "Gint" b: 3/3/1886, Crestline, Ohio d: 5/8/54, Denver, Colo. BL/TL, 6', 180 lbs. Deb: 5/11/10

YEAR	TM/L	G	AB	R	H	2B	3B	HR	RBI	BB	SO	AVG	OBP	SLG	PRO+	BR/A	SB	CS	SBR	FA	FR	G/POS	TPR
1910	NY-A	6	19	3	6	1	0	0	3		2	.316	.381	.316	112	0	2			1.000	-1	/O-6	-0.1
1914	NY-A	1	1	0	1	1	0	0	0	0	0	1.000	1.000	2.000	803	1	0			.000	0	H	0.1
Total	2	7	20	3	7	1	0	0	3	2	0	.350	.409	.400	145	1	2			1.000	-1	/O-6	0.0

■ CHARLIE CHANT

Chant, Charles Joseph b: 8/7/51, Bell, Cal. BR/TR, 6', 190 lbs. Deb: 9/12/75

YEAR	TM/L	G	AB	R	H	2B	3B	HR	RBI	BB	SO	AVG	OBP	SLG	PRO+	BR/A	SB	CS	SBR	FA	FR	G/POS	TPR
1975	Oak-A	5	5	1	0	0	0	0	0	0	0	.000	.000	.000	-99	-1	0	0	0	1.000	-2	/O-5,D-1	-0.3
1976	StL-N	15	14	0	2	0	0	0	0	0	4	.143	.143	.143	-19	-2	0	0	0	1.000	-2	O-14	-0.5
Total	2	20	19	1	2	0	0	0	0	0	4	.105	.105	.105	-40	-3	0	0	0	1.000	-4	/O-19,D-1	-0.8

■ ED CHAPLIN

Chaplin, Bert Edgar (b: Bert Edgar Chapman) b: 9/25/1893, Pelzer, S.C. d: 8/15/78, Sanford, Fla. BL/TR, 5'7", 158 lbs. Deb: 9/4/20

YEAR	TM/L	G	AB	R	H	2B	3B	HR	RBI	BB	SO	AVG	OBP	SLG	PRO+	BR/A	SB	CS	SBR	FA	FR	G/POS	TPR
1920	Bos-A	4	5	2	1	1	0	0	1	4	1	.200	.556	.400	163	1	0	0		.900	-1	/C-2	0.1
1921	Bos-A	3	2	0	0	0	0	0	0	0	1	.000	.000	.000	-99	-1	0	0		1.000	0	/C-1	0.0
1922	Bos-A	28	69	8	13	1	1	0	6	9	9	.188	.282	.232	35	-6	2	1		.960	-3	C-21	-0.8
Total	3	35	76	10	14	2	1	0	7	13	11	.184	.303	.237	43	-6	2	1		.953	-3	/C-24	-0.7

■ CALVIN CHAPMAN

Chapman, Calvin Louis b: 12/20/10, Courtland, Miss. d: 4/1/83, Batesville, Miss. BL/TR, 5'9", 160 lbs. Deb: 9/10/35

YEAR	TM/L	G	AB	R	H	2B	3B	HR	RBI	BB	SO	AVG	OBP	SLG	PRO+	BR/A	SB	CS	SBR	FA	FR	G/POS	TPR
1935	Cin-N	15	53	6	18	1	0	0	3	4	5	.340	.386	.358	105	1	2			.949	-3	S-12/2-4	-0.1
1936	Cin-N	96	219	35	54	7	3	1	22	16	19	.247	.301	.320	72	-9	5			.961	-14	O-31,2-23/3	-2.2
Total	2	111	272	41	72	8	3	1	25	20	24	.265	.317	.327	78	-8	7			.968	-16	/O-31,2-27,S3	-2.3

■ GLENN CHAPMAN

Chapman, Glenn Justice "Pete" b: 1/21/06, Cambridge City, Ind. d: 11/5/88, Richmond, Ind. BR/TR, 5'11.5", 170 lbs. Deb: 4/18/34

YEAR	TM/L	G	AB	R	H	2B	3B	HR	RBI	BB	SO	AVG	OBP	SLG	PRO+	BR/A	SB	CS	SBR	FA	FR	G/POS	TPR
1934	Bro-N	67	93	19	26	5	1	1	10	7	19	.280	.330	.387	96	-1	1			1.000	-7	O-40,2-14	-0.8

■ HARRY CHAPMAN

Chapman, Harry E. b: 10/26/1887, Severance, Kan. d: 10/21/18, Nevada, Mo. BR/TR, 5'11", 160 lbs. Deb: 10/6/12

YEAR	TM/L	G	AB	R	H	2B	3B	HR	RBI	BB	SO	AVG	OBP	SLG	PRO+	BR/A	SB	CS	SBR	FA	FR	G/POS	TPR
1912	Chi-N	1	4	1	1	0	0	0		0	1	.250	.250	.750	169	0	1			1.000	1	/C-1	0.1
1913	Cin-N	2	2	0	1	0	0	0	0	0	0	.500	.500	.500	187	0	0			.000	0	H	0.0
1914	StL-F	64	181	16	38	2	1	0	14	13	27	.210	.270	.232	29	-19	2			.973	-4	C-51/1-1,2O	-1.9
1915	StL-F	62	186	19	37	6	3	1	29	22	24	.199	.284	.280	48	-14	4			.989	8	C-53	-0.1
1916	StL-A	18	31	2	3	0	0	0		2	5	.097	.152	.097	-27	-5	0			.981	2	C-14	-0.2
Total	5	147	404	38	80	8	5	1	44	37	57	.198	.269	.250	37	-37	7			.982	7	C-119/O-1,21	-2.1

■ JACK CHAPMAN

Chapman, John Curtis "Death To Flying Things" b: 5/8/1843, Brooklyn, N.Y. d: 6/10/16, Brooklyn, N.Y. TR, 5'11", 170 lbs. Deb: 5/5/1874 M

YEAR	TM/L	G	AB	R	H	2B	3B	HR	RBI	BB	SO	AVG	OBP	SLG	PRO+	BR/A	SB	CS	SBR	FA	FR	G/POS	TPR
1874	Atl-n	53	238	32	64	7	3	0		5		.269	.284	.324	105	3						*O-52/1-1	0.3
1875	StL-N	43	195	28	44	6	3	0		1		.226	.230	.287	85	-2						O-43	-0.1
1876	Lou-N	17	67	4	16	1	0	0	5	1	3	.239	.250	.254	58	-4				.750	-4	O-17/3-1M	-0.7
Total	2 n	96	433	60	108	13	6	0		6		.249	.260	.307	96	1						/O-95,1-1	0.2

■ JOHN CHAPMAN

Chapman, John Joseph b: 10/15/1899, Centralia, Pa. d: 11/3/53, Philadelphia, Pa. BR/TR, 5'10.5", 175 lbs. Deb: 6/28/24

YEAR	TM/L	G	AB	R	H	2B	3B	HR	RBI	BB	SO	AVG	OBP	SLG	PRO+	BR/A	SB	CS	SBR	FA	FR	G/POS	TPR
1924	Phi-A	19	71	7	20	4	1	0	7	4	8	.282	.329	.366	78	-2				.958	-10	S-19	-1.0

■ KELVIN CHAPMAN

Chapman, Kelvin Keith b: 6/2/56, Willits, Cal. BR/TR, 5'11", 173 lbs. Deb: 4/5/79

YEAR	TM/L	G	AB	R	H	2B	3B	HR	RBI	BB	SO	AVG	OBP	SLG	PRO+	BR/A	SB	CS	SBR	FA	FR	G/POS	TPR
1979	NY-N	35	80	7	12	1	2	0	4	5	15	.150	.200	.213	13	-10	0	0	0	.980	-4	2-23/3-1	-1.3
1984	NY-N	75	197	27	57	13	0	3	23	19	30	.289	.358	.401	115	4	8	7	-2	.979	1	2-57/3-3	0.5
1985	NY-N	62	144	16	25	3	0	0	7	9	15	.174	.232	.194	21	-15	5	4	-1	.970	-6	2-48/3-1	-2.2
Total	3	172	421	50	94	17	2	3	34	33	60	.223	.286	.295	64	-21	13	11	-3	.976	-9	2-127/3-5	-3.0

■ RAY CHAPMAN

Chapman, Raymond Johnson b: 1/15/1891, Beaver Dam, Ky. d: 8/17/20, New York, N.Y. BR/TR, 5'10", 170 lbs. Deb: 8/30/12

YEAR	TM/L	G	AB	R	H	2B	3B	HR	RBI	BB	SO	AVG	OBP	SLG	PRO+	BR/A	SB	CS	SBR	FA	FR	G/POS	TPR
1912	Cle-A	31	109	29	34	6	3	0	19	10		.312	.375	.422	124	3	10			.904	-10	S-31	-0.4
1913	Cle-A	141	508	78	131	19	7	3	39	46	51	.258	.322	.341	91	-6	29			.936	-9	*S-138/O-1	-0.2
1914	Cle-A	106	375	59	103	16	10	2	42	48	48	.275	.358	.387	119	9	24	9	2	.913	-15	S-72,2-33	0.2
1915	Cle-A	154	570	101	154	14	17	3	67	70	82	.270	.353	.370	114	10	36	15	2	.944	9	*S-154	3.5
1916	Cle-A	109	346	50	80	10	5	0	27	50	46	.231	.330	.289	81	-7	21	14	-2	.935	13	S-52,3-36,2	0.9
1917	Cle-A	156	563	98	170	28	13	2	36	61	65	.302	.370	.409	128	18	52			.938	24	*S-156	5.4
1918	Cle-A	128	446	84	119	19	8	1	32	84	46	.267	.390	.352	113	10	30			.936	6	*S-128/O-1	2.4
1919	Cle-A	115	433	75	130	23	10	3	53	31	38	.300	.351	.420	109	4	18			.944	-0	*S-115	1.2
1920	Cle-A	111	435	97	132	27	8	3	49	52	38	.303	.380	.423	109	6	13	9	-2	.959	12	*S-111	2.5
Total	9	1051	3785	671	1053	162	81	17	364	452	414	.278	.358	.377	110	48	233	47		.939	30	S-957/2-49,3O	15.5

■ SAM CHAPMAN

Chapman, Samuel Blake b: 4/11/16, Tiburon, Cal. BR/TR, 6'1", 190 lbs. Deb: 5/16/38

YEAR	TM/L	G	AB	R	H	2B	3B	HR	RBI	BB	SO	AVG	OBP	SLG	PRO+	BR/A	SB	CS	SBR	FA	FR	G/POS	TPR
1938	Phi-A	114	406	60	105	17	7	17	63	56	94	.259	.353	.461	105	2	3	4	-2	.952	-2	*O-110	-0.4
1939	Phi-A	140	498	74	134	24	6	15	64	51	62	.269	.338	.432	98	-3	11	4	1	.955	4	*O-117,1-19	-0.4
1940	Phi-A	134	508	88	140	26	3	23	75	46	96	.276	.337	.474	110	6	8		-6	.963	4	*O-129	0.0
1941	Phi-A	143	552	97	178	29	9	25	106	47	49	.322	.378	.543	115	8	6		-3	.967	14	*O-141	3.4
1945	Phi-A	9	30	3	6	2	0	0	1	2	4	.200	.250	.267	50	-2	1	0		1.000	-1	/O-8	-0.4
1946	Phi-A★	146	545	77	142	22	5	20	67	54	66	.261	.327	.429	111	-2	6	1	-2	.970	10	*O-145	0.8

YEAR	TM/L	G	AB	R	H	2B	3B	HR	RBI	BB	SO	AVG	OBP	SLG	PRO+	BR/A	SB	CS	SBR	FA	FR	G/POS	TPR
1947	Phi-A	149	551	84	139	18	5	14	83	65	70	.252	.331	.379	95	-4	3	4	-2	.987	12	*O-146	-0.2
1948	Phi-A	123	445	58	115	18	6	13	70	55	50	.258	.341	.413	100	-1	6	1	1	.982	7	*O-118	0.1
1949	Phi-A	154	589	89	164	24	4	24	108	80	68	.278	.367	.455	121	16	3	4	-2	.979	11	*O-154	1.7
1950	Phi-A	144	553	93	139	20	6	23	95	68	79	.251	.338	.434	98	-4	3	3	-1	.978	10	*O-144	0.0
1951	Phi-A	18	65	7	11	1	0	0	5	12	12	.169	.299	.185	32	-6	0	0	0	.957	-1	O-17	-0.7
	Cle-A	94	246	24	56	9	1	6	36	27	32	.228	.304	.346	80	-8	3	0	1	.985	-18	O-84/1-1	-2.7
	Yr	112	311	31	67	10	1	6	41	39	44	.215	.303	.312	69	-14	3	0	1	.978	-19	*O-101/1-1	-3.4
Total	11	1368	4988	754	1329	210	52	180	773	562	682	.266	.342	.438	107	34	41	38	-11	.972	53	*O-1309/1-20	1.3

■ BEN CHAPMAN
Chapman, William Benjamin b: 12/25/08, Nashville, Tenn. d: 7/7/93, Hoover, Ala. BR/TR, 6', 190 lbs. Deb: 4/15/30 MC

YEAR	TM/L	G	AB	R	H	2B	3B	HR	RBI	BB	SO	AVG	OBP	SLG	PRO+	BR/A	SB	CS	SBR	FA	FR	G/POS	TPR
1930	NY-A	138	513	74	162	31	10	10	81	43	58	.316	.371	.474	118	13	14	6	1	.912	-6	3-91,2-45	1.4
1931	NY-A	149	600	120	189	28	11	17	122	75	77	.315	.396	.483	138	33	61	23	5	.963	8	*O-137,2-11	3.5
1932	*NY-A	151	581	101	174	41	15	10	107	71	55	.299	.381	.473	126	23	38	18	1	.949	-3	*O-150	1.1
1933	NY-A★	147	565	112	176	36	4	9	98	72	45	.312	.393	.437	127	24	27	18	-3	.975	11	*O-147	2.3
1934	NY-A★	149	588	82	181	21	13	5	86	67	68	.308	.381	.413	113	12	26	16	-2	.967	8	*O-149	1.1
1935	NY-A★	140	553	118	160	38	8	8	74	61	39	.289	.361	.430	110	8	17	10	-1	.964	17	*O-138	1.7
1936	NY-A	36	139	19	37	14	3	1	21	15	20	.266	.338	.432	92	-2	1	2	-1	.965	2	O-36	-0.2
	Was-A★	97	401	91	133	36	7	4	60	69	18	.332	.431	.486	133	24	19	7	2	.959	4	O-97	2.2
	Yr	133	540	110	170	50	10	5	81	84	38	.315	.408	.472	123	21	20	9	1	.961	7	*O-133	2.0
1937	Was-A	35	130	23	34	7	1	0	12	26	7	.262	.385	.331	86	-2	8	0	2	.957	-1	O-32	-0.2
	Bos-A	113	423	76	130	23	11	7	57	57	35	.307	.391	.463	110	7	27	12	1	.985	9	*O-112/S-1	1.2
	Yr	148	553	99	164	30	12	7	69	83	42	.297	.389	.432	105	6	35	12	3	.978	7	*O-144/S-1	1.0
1938	Bos-A	127	480	92	163	40	8	6	80	65	33	.340	.418	.494	122	17	13	6	0	.966	4	*O-126/3-1	1.8
1939	Cle-A	149	545	101	158	31	9	6	82	87	30	.290	.390	.413	109	10	18	6	2	.971	-4	*O-146	0.3
1940	Cle-A	143	548	87	157	40	6	4	50	78	45	.286	.377	.403	105	7	13	7	-0	.964	2	*O-140	0.0
1941	Was-A	28	110	9	28	6	0	1	10	10	6	.255	.317	.336	76	-4	2	2	-1	.983	1	O-26	-0.5
	Chi-A	57	190	26	43	9	1	2	19	19	14	.226	.297	.316	63	-10	2	2	-1	.992	1	O-49	-1.3
	Yr	85	300	35	71	15	1	3	29	29	20	.237	.304	.323	68	-14	4	4	-1	.989	2	O-75	-1.8
1944	Bro-N	20	38	11	14	4	0	0	11	5	4	.368	.442	.474	161	3	1			.900	-2	P-11	0.0
1945	Bro-N	13	22	2	3	0	0	0	3	2	1	.136	.208	.136	-3	-3	0			.938	1	P-10	0.0
	Phi-N	24	51	4	16	2	0	0	4	2	1	.314	.340	.353	95	-0	0			.933	-3	O-10/3-4,PM	-0.4
	Yr	37	73	6	19	2	0	0	7	4	2	.260	.299	.288	65	-3	0			.941	-3	P-13,O-10/3	-0.4
1946	Phi-N	1	1	1	0	0	0	0	0	0	0	.000	.000	.000	-99	-0	0			.000	0	/P-1,M	0.0
Total	15	1717	6478	1144	1958	407	107	90	977	824	556	.302	.383	.440	115	159	287	135		.967	50	*O-1495/3-96,2PS	14.0

■ FRED CHAPMAN
Chapman, William Fred "Chappie" b: 7/17/16, Liberty, S.C. BR/TR, 6'1", 185 lbs. Deb: 9/15/39

YEAR	TM/L	G	AB	R	H	2B	3B	HR	RBI	BB	SO	AVG	OBP	SLG	PRO+	BR/A	SB	CS	SBR	FA	FR	G/POS	TPR
1939	Phi-A	15	49	5	14	1	1	0	1	1	3	.286	.300	.347	66	-3	1	0	0	.899	-4	S-15	-0.4
1940	Phi-A	26	69	6	11	1	0	0	4	6	10	.159	.227	.174	6	-10	1	1	-0	.862	-5	S-25	-1.3
1941	Phi-A	35	69	1	11	1	0	0	4	4	15	.159	.205	.174	1	-10	1	2	-1	.917	-2	S-28/3-2,2	-1.1
Total	3	76	187	12	36	3	1	0	9	11	28	.193	.237	.219	20	-22	3	3	-1	.889	-11	/S-68,3-2,2	-2.8

■ HARRY CHAPPAS
Chappas, Harry Perry b: 10/26/57, Mt.Ranier, Md. BB/TR, 5'3", 150 lbs. Deb: 9/7/78

YEAR	TM/L	G	AB	R	H	2B	3B	HR	RBI	BB	SO	AVG	OBP	SLG	PRO+	BR/A	SB	CS	SBR	FA	FR	G/POS	TPR
1978	Chi-A	20	75	11	20	1	0	0	6	6	11	.267	.329	.280	72	-3	1	2	-1	1.000	0	S-20	-0.1
1979	Chi-A	26	59	9	17	1	4	0	4	5	5	.288	.354	.356	92	-0	1	1	-0	.929	3	S-23	0.3
1980	Chi-A	26	50	6	8	2	0	0	2	4	10	.160	.236	.200	21	-5	0	2	-1	.981	-1	S-19/2-1,D	-0.6
Total	3	72	184	26	45	4	1	0	12	15	26	.245	.312	.283	65	-8	2	5	-2	.967	1	/S-62,D-2,2	-0.4

■ LARRY CHAPPELL
Chappell, La Verne Ashford b: 2/19/1890, McClusky, Ill. d: 11/8/18, San Francisco, Cal. BL/TR, 6', 186 lbs. Deb: 7/18/13

YEAR	TM/L	G	AB	R	H	2B	3B	HR	RBI	BB	SO	AVG	OBP	SLG	PRO+	BR/A	SB	CS	SBR	FA	FR	G/POS	TPR
1913	Chi-A	60	208	20	48	8	1	0	15	18	22	.231	.295	.279	69	-8	7			.952	-1	O-59	-1.3
1914	Chi-A	21	39	3	9	0	0	0	1	4	11	.231	.302	.231	61	-2	0			.929	-2	O-9	-0.4
1915	Chi-A	1	1	0	0	0	0	0	0	0	0	.000	.000	.000	-97	-0	0			.000	0	H	0.0
1916	Cle-A	3	2	0	0	0	0	0	0	1	0	.000	.333	.000	1	-0	0			.000	0	H	0.0
	Bos-N	20	53	4	12	1	1	0	9	2	8	.226	.268	.283	72	-2	1			.957	-2	O-14	-0.5
1917	Bos-N	4	2	0	0	0	0	0	1	0	1	.000	.000	.000	-99	-0	0			.000	-1	/O-1	-0.1
Total	5	109	305	27	69	9	2	0	26	25	42	.226	.289	.269	66	-13	9			.951	-5	/O-83	-2.3

■ JOE CHARBONEAU
Charboneau, Joseph b: 6/17/55, Belvidere, Ill. BR/TR, 6'2", 205 lbs. Deb: 4/11/80

YEAR	TM/L	G	AB	R	H	2B	3B	HR	RBI	BB	SO	AVG	OBP	SLG	PRO+	BR/A	SB	CS	SBR	FA	FR	G/POS	TPR
1980	Cle-A	131	453	76	131	17	2	23	87	49	70	.289	.362	.488	130	18	2	4	-2	.963	1	O-67,D-57	1.3
1981	Cle-A	48	138	14	29	7	1	4	18	7	22	.210	.248	.362	75	-5	1	0	0	.963	-2	O-27,D-14	-0.8
1982	Cle-A	22	56	7	12	2	1	2	9	5	7	.214	.290	.393	86	-1	0	0	0	.955	-3	O-18/D-1	-0.5
Total	3	201	647	97	172	26	4	29	114	61	99	.266	.333	.453	115	12	3	4	-2	.962	-4	O-112/D-72	-0.0

■ ED CHARLES
Charles, Edwin Douglas b: 4/29/33, Daytona Beach, Fla. BR/TR, 5'10", 170 lbs. Deb: 4/11/62

YEAR	TM/L	G	AB	R	H	2B	3B	HR	RBI	BB	SO	AVG	OBP	SLG	PRO+	BR/A	SB	CS	SBR	FA	FR	G/POS	TPR
1962	KC-A	147	535	81	154	24	7	17	74	54	70	.288	.358	.454	111	9	20	4	4	.964	4	*3-140/2-2	1.8
1963	KC-A	158	603	82	161	28	2	15	79	58	79	.267	.336	.395	99	-1	15	8	-0	.949	-4	*3-158	-0.9
1964	KC-A	150	557	69	134	25	2	16	63	64	92	.241	.323	.379	92	-6	12	7	-1	.954	-15	*3-147	-2.4
1965	KC-A	134	480	55	129	19	7	8	56	44	72	.269	.335	.387	106	4	13	4	2	.971	-1	*3-128/2-1,S	0.2
1966	KC-A	118	385	52	110	18	8	9	42	30	53	.286	.337	.444	122	12	12	5	1	.963	-6	*3-104/1-1,O	0.5
1967	KC-A	19	61	5	15	1	0	0	5	12	13	.246	.378	.262	95	1	0	0	0	.966	0	3-18	0.1
	NY-N	101	323	32	77	13	2	3	31	24	58	.238	.305	.319	80	-8	4	1	1	.944	9	3-89	0.0
1968	NY-N	117	369	41	102	11	1	15	53	28	57	.276	.331	.434	127	12	5	4	1	.954	1	*3-106/1-2	1.3
1969	*NY-N	61	169	21	35	8	1	3	18	18	31	.207	.287	.320	68	-7	4	2	0	.946	-0	3-52	-0.8
Total	8	1005	3482	438	917	147	30	86	421	332	525	.263	.332	.397	103	16	86	35	5	.957	-15	3-942/1-3,2OS	-0.2

■ CHAPPY CHARLES
Charles, Raymond (b: Charles Shuh Achenbach) b: 3/25/1881, Phillipsburg, N.J. d: 8/4/59, Bethlehem, Pa. BR/TR, 5'11", 175 lbs. Deb: 4/15/08

YEAR	TM/L	G	AB	R	H	2B	3B	HR	RBI	BB	SO	AVG	OBP	SLG	PRO+	BR/A	SB	CS	SBR	FA	FR	G/POS	TPR
1908	StL-N	121	454	39	93	14	3	1	17	19		.205	.238	.256	61	-21	15			.921	-12	2-65,S-31,3	-3.9
1909	StL-N	99	339	33	80	7	3	0	29	31		.236	.309	.274	87	-5	7			.918	-2	2-71,S-26/3	-0.8
	Cin-N	13	43	3	11	2	0	0	5	4		.256	.319	.302	94	-0	2			.932	-3	2-10/S-3	-0.4
	Yr	112	382	36	91	9	3	0	34	35		.238	.310	.277	87	-5	9			.920	-5	2-81,S-29/3	-1.2
1910	Cin-N	4	15	1	2	0	1	0	0	0	1	.133	.133	.267	17	-2	0			.818	-2	/S-4	-0.3
Total	3	237	851	76	186	23	7	1	51	54	1	.219	.270	.266	72	-28	24			.920	-18	2-146/S-64,3	-5.4

■ MIKE CHARTAK
Chartak, Michael George "Shotgun" b: 4/28/16, Brooklyn, N.Y. d: 7/25/67, Cedar Rapids, Ia. BL/TL, 6'2", 180 lbs. Deb: 9/13/40

YEAR	TM/L	G	AB	R	H	2B	3B	HR	RBI	BB	SO	AVG	OBP	SLG	PRO+	BR/A	SB	CS	SBR	FA	FR	G/POS	TPR
1940	NY-A	11	15	2	2	1	0	0	3	5	5	.133	.350	.200	49	-1	0	0	0	1.000	-1	/O-3	-0.2
1942	NY-A	5	5	0	0	0	0	0	0	0	0	.000	.000	.000	-99	-1	0	0	0	.000	0	H	-0.1
	Was-A	24	92	11	20	4	1	2	8	14	16	.217	.321	.337	86	-2	0	1	-1	.926	-0	O-24	-0.4
	StL-A	73	237	37	59	11	2	9	43	40	27	.249	.362	.426	119	7	3	3	-1	.974	7	O-64	1.0
	Yr	102	334	48	79	15	4	11	51	54	43	.237	.346	.395	107	4	3	4	-2	.962	7	O-88	0.5
1943	StL-A	108	344	38	88	16	2	10	37	39	55	.256	.333	.401	112	5	1	3	-2	.970	-4	O-77,1-18	-0.5
1944	*StL-A	35	72	8	17	2	1	0	7	6	9	.236	.304	.333	77	-2	0	0	0	1.000	0	1-12/O-7	-0.3
Total	4	256	765	96	186	34	7	21	98	104	112	.243	.337	.388	105	5	4	7	-3	.967	3	O-175/1-30	-0.5

■ HAL CHASE
Chase, Harold Homer "Prince Hal" b: 2/13/1883, Los Gatos, Cal. d: 5/18/47, Colusa, Cal. BR/TL, 6', 175 lbs. Deb: 4/14/05 M

YEAR	TM/L	G	AB	R	H	2B	3B	HR	RBI	BB	SO	AVG	OBP	SLG	PRO+	BR/A	SB	CS	SBR	FA	FR	G/POS	TPR
1905	NY-A	128	465	60	116	16	6	3	49	15		.249	.277	.329	83	-11	22			.976	-9	*1-124/S-2,2	-2.7

YEAR	TM/L	G	AB	R	H	2B	3B	HR	RBI	BB	SO	AVG	OBP	SLG	PRO+	BR/A	SB	CS	SBR	FA	FR	G/POS	TPR
1906	NY-A	151	597	84	193	23	10	0	76	13		.323	.341	.395	118	10	28			.980	-3	*1-150/2-1	0.3
1907	NY-A	125	498	72	143	23	3	2	68	19		.287	.315	.357	106	1	32			.973	1	*1-121/O-4	-0.2
1908	NY-A	106	405	50	104	11	3	1	36	15		.257	.285	.306	91	-5	27			.980	-4	1-98/2-3,O3P	-1.2
1909	NY-A	118	474	60	134	17	3	4	63	20		.283	.317	.357	112	5	25			.978	-2	*1-118/S-1	0.2
1910	NY-A	130	524	67	152	20	5	3	73	16		.290	.312	.365	106	1	40			.981	-4	*1-130,M	-0.4
1911	NY-A	133	527	82	166	32	7	3	62	21		.315	.342	.419	105	1	36			.974	-2	*1-124/O-7,2M	-0.2
1912	NY-A	131	522	61	143	21	9	4	58	17		.274	.299	.372	86	-12	33			.979	-2	*1-122/2-7	-1.6
1913	NY-A	39	146	15	31	2	4	0	9	11	13	.212	.268	.281	60	-8	5			.982	-5	1-29/2-5,O	-1.4
	Chi-A	102	384	49	110	11	10	2	39	16	41	.286	.320	.383	107	1	9			.976	1	*1-102	0.1
	Yr	141	530	64	141	13	14	2	48	27	54	.266	.305	.355	94	-7	14			.977	-4	*1-131/2-5,O	-1.3
1914	Chi-A	58	206	27	55	10	5	0	20	23	19	.267	.343	.364	114	4	9	4	0	.981	2	1-58	0.5
	Buf-F	75	291	43	101	19	9	3	48	6	31	.347	.365	.505	121	7	10			.980	-1	1-73	0.5
1915	Buf-F	145	567	85	165	31	10	17	89	20	50	.291	.316	.471	107	1	23			.983	0	*1-143/O-1	-0.3
1916	Cin-N	142	542	66	**184**	29	12	4	82	19	48	**.339**	.363	.459	155	32	22	11	0	.986	-7	1-98,O-25,2	2.3
1917	Cin-N	152	602	71	167	28	15	4	86	15	49	.277	.296	.394	115	7	21			.983	-3	*1-151	-0.1
1918	Cin-N	74	259	30	78	12	6	2	38	13	15	.301	.339	.417	133	9	5			.980	-2	1-67/O-2	0.5
1919	NY-N	110	408	58	116	17	7	4	45	17	40	.284	.318	.397	115	6	16			.984	-1	*1-107	0.1
Total	15	1919	7417	980	2158	322	124	57	941	276	306	.291	.319	.391	109	51	363	15		.980	-42	*1-1815/O-47,2SP3	-3.6

■ BUSTER CHATHAM
Chatham, Charles L b: 12/25/01, West, Tex. d: 12/15/75, Waco, Tex. BR/TR, 5'5", 150 lbs. Deb: 6/1/30

YEAR	TM/L	G	AB	R	H	2B	3B	HR	RBI	BB	SO	AVG	OBP	SLG	PRO+	BR/A	SB	CS	SBR	FA	FR	G/POS	TPR
1930	Bos-N	112	404	48	108	20	11	5	56	37	41	.267	.332	.408	80	-13	8			.920	-14	3-92,S-17	-1.8
1931	Bos-N	17	44	4	10	1	0	1	3	6	6	.227	.320	.318	75	-1	0			.762	-6	/S-6,3-6	-0.6
Total	2	129	448	52	118	21	11	6	59	43	47	.263	.331	.400	80	-15	8			.924	-20	/3-98,S-23	-2.4

■ JIM CHATTERTON
Chatterton, James M. b: 10/14/1864, Brooklyn, N.Y. d: 12/15/44, Tewksbury, Mass. Deb: 6/7/1884

YEAR	TM/L	G	AB	R	H	2B	3B	HR	RBI	BB	SO	AVG	OBP	SLG	PRO+	BR/A	SB	CS	SBR	FA	FR	G/POS	TPR
1884	KC-U	4	15	4	2	1	0	0			2	.133	.235	.200	22	-2				1.000	0	/O-2,1-2,P	-0.1

■ OSSIE CHAVARRIA
Chavarria, Osvaldo (Quijano) b: 8/5/40, Colon, Panama BR/TR, 5'11", 155 lbs. Deb: 4/14/66

YEAR	TM/L	G	AB	R	H	2B	3B	HR	RBI	BB	SO	AVG	OBP	SLG	PRO+	BR/A	SB	CS	SBR	FA	FR	G/POS	TPR
1966	KC-A	86	191	26	46	10	0	2	10	18	43	.241	.306	.325	84	-4	3	2	-0	.939	-5	O-26,S-23,2/13	-0.8
1967	KC-A	38	59	2	6	2	0	0	4	7	16	.102	.209	.136	4	-7	1	0	0	1.000	2	2-17/3-7,OS	-0.4
Total	2	124	250	28	52	12	0	2	14	25	59	.208	.283	.280	65	-11	4	2	0	.990	-2	/2-31,O-29,S31	-1.2

■ HARRY CHEEK
Cheek, Harry G. b: 1879, Sedalia, Mo. d: 6/25/56, Paramas, N.J. TR, Deb: 5/12/10

YEAR	TM/L	G	AB	R	H	2B	3B	HR	RBI	BB	SO	AVG	OBP	SLG	PRO+	BR/A	SB	CS	SBR	FA	FR	G/POS	TPR
1910	Phi-N	2	4	1	2	1	0	0	0	0		.500	.500	.750	255	1	0			1.000	-1	/C-2	0.0

■ PAUL CHERVINKO
Chervinko, Paul b: 7/28/10, Trauger, Pa. d: 6/3/76, Danville, Ill. BR/TR, 5'8", 185 lbs. Deb: 5/30/37

YEAR	TM/L	G	AB	R	H	2B	3B	HR	RBI	BB	SO	AVG	OBP	SLG	PRO+	BR/A	SB	CS	SBR	FA	FR	G/POS	TPR
1937	Bro-N	30	48	1	7	0	1	0	2	3	16	.146	.196	.188	5	-6	0			1.000	0	C-26	-0.5
1938	Bro-N	12	27	0	4	0	0	0	3	2	0	.148	.207	.148	-1	-4	0			.974	0	C-12	-0.3
Total	2	42	75	1	11	0	1	0	5	5	16	.147	.200	.173	3	-10	0			.990	1	/C-38	-0.8

■ CUPID CHILDS
Childs, Clarence Algernon b: 8/14/1867, Calvert Co., Md. d: 11/8/12, Baltimore, Md. BL/TR, 5'8", 185 lbs. Deb: 4/23/1888

YEAR	TM/L	G	AB	R	H	2B	3B	HR	RBI	BB	SO	AVG	OBP	SLG	PRO+	BR/A	SB	CS	SBR	FA	FR	G/POS	TPR
1888	Phi-N	2	4	0	0	0	0	0	0	0		.000	.000	.000	-95	-1	0			.857	0	/2-2	-0.1
1890	Syr-a	126	493	109	170	**33**	14	2		72		.345	.434	.481	189	**59**	56			.928	12	*2-125/S-1	**6.7**
1891	Cle-N	141	551	120	155	21	12	2	83	97	32	.281	.395	.374	119	17	39			.910	-12	*2-141	1.0
1892	*Cle-N	145	558	**136**	177	14	11	3	53	117	20	.317	**.443**	.398	149	40	26			.938	-6	*2-145	3.4
1893	Cle-N	124	485	145	158	19	10	3	65	120	12	.326	.463	.425	129	26	23			.926	10	*2-123	3.1
1894	Cle-N	118	479	143	169	21	12	4	52	107	11	.353	.475	.459	122	23	17			.916	-3	*2-118	1.9
1895	*Cle-N	119	462	96	133	15	3	4	90	74	24	.288	.394	.359	90	-5	20			.921	10	*2-119	0.9
1896	*Cle-N	132	498	106	177	24	9	1	106	100	18	.355	.467	.446	134	30	25			.942	42	*2-132	6.6
1897	Cle-N	114	444	105	150	15	9	1	61	74		.338	.435	.419	119	15	25			.944	17	*2-114	3.2
1898	Cle-N	110	413	90	119	9	4	1	31	69		.288	.395	.337	112	10	9			.931	9	*2-110	2.4
1899	StL-N	125	464	73	123	11	11	1	48	74		.265	.369	.343	93	-2	11			.934	-12	*2-125	-0.6
1900	Chi-N	137	531	67	128	14	5	0	44	57		.241	.323	.286	71	-19	15			.935	16	*2-137	0.3
1901	Chi-N	63	236	24	61	9	0	0	21	30		.258	.359	.297	95	0	3			.939	9	2-63	1.2
Total	13	1456	5618	1214	1720	205	100	20	654	991	117	.306	.416	.389	119	194	269			.930	92	*2-1454/S-1	30.0

■ PETE CHILDS
Childs, Peter Pierre b: 11/15/1871, Philadelphia, Pa. d: 2/15/22, Philadelphia, Pa. TR, Deb: 4/24/01

YEAR	TM/L	G	AB	R	H	2B	3B	HR	RBI	BB	SO	AVG	OBP	SLG	PRO+	BR/A	SB	CS	SBR	FA	FR	G/POS	TPR
1901	StL-N	29	79	12	21	1	0	0	8	14		.266	.389	.278	100	1	0			.907	-7	2-19/O-2,S	-0.4
	Chi-N	60	210	23	48	5	1	0	14	26		.229	.319	.262	72	-6	4			.959	13	2-60	0.9
	Yr	89	289	35	69	6	1	0	22	40		.239	.339	.266	80	-5	4			.947	6	2-79/O-2,S	0.5
1902	Phi-N	123	403	25	78	5	0	0	25	34		.194	.256	.206	43	-26	6			.945	-9	*2-123	-3.3
Total	2	212	692	60	147	11	1	0	47	74		.212	.292	.231	59	-31	10			.946	-3	2-202/O-2,S	-2.8

■ PEARCE CHILES
Chiles, Pearce Nuget "What's The Use" b: 5/28/1867, Deepwater, Mo. BR/TR, 5'11", 185 lbs. Deb: 4/18/1899

YEAR	TM/L	G	AB	R	H	2B	3B	HR	RBI	BB	SO	AVG	OBP	SLG	PRO+	BR/A	SB	CS	SBR	FA	FR	G/POS	TPR
1899	Phi-N	97	338	57	108	28	7	2	76	16		.320	.352	.462	127	10	6			.944	-15	O-46,1-25,2	-0.6
1900	Phi-N	33	111	13	24	6	2	1	23	6		.216	.256	.333	63	-6	4			.987	-3	1-16,2-12/O	-0.8
Total	2	130	449	70	132	34	9	3	99	22		.294	.328	.430	111	4	10			.947	-18	/O-49,1-41,2	-1.4

■ RICH CHILES
Chiles, Richard Francis b: 11/22/49, Sacramento, Cal. BL/TL, 5'11", 170 lbs. Deb: 9/20/71

YEAR	TM/L	G	AB	R	H	2B	3B	HR	RBI	BB	SO	AVG	OBP	SLG	PRO+	BR/A	SB	CS	SBR	FA	FR	G/POS	TPR
1971	Hou-N	67	119	12	27	5	1	2	15	6	20	.227	.270	.336	73	-5	0	1	-1	1.000	-3	O-27	-1.0
1972	Hou-N	9	11	0	3	1	0	0	2	1	1	.273	.333	.364	100	0	0	0	0	1.000	0	/O-2	0.0
1973	NY-N	8	25	2	3	2	0	0	1	0	2	.120	.120	.200	-13	-4	0	0	0	1.000	2	/O-8	-0.2
1976	Hou-N	5	4	1	2	1	0	0	0	0	0	.500	.500	.750	276	1	0	0	0	1.000	-0	/O-1	0.1
1977	Min-A	108	261	31	69	16	1	3	36	23	17	.264	.329	.368	91	-3	0	1	-1	.946	-2	D-61,O-22	-0.8
1978	Min-A	87	198	22	53	12	0	1	22	20	25	.268	.341	.343	91	-2	1	2	-1	.965	-2	O-61/D-8	-0.7
Total	6	284	618	68	157	37	2	6	76	50	65	.254	.315	.350	85	-13	1	4	-2	.972	-5	O-121/D-69	-2.6

■ DINO CHIOZZA
Chiozza, Dino Joseph "Dynamo" b: 6/30/12, Memphis, Tenn. d: 4/23/72, Memphis, Tenn. BL/TR, 6', 170 lbs. Deb: 7/14/35 F

YEAR	TM/L	G	AB	R	H	2B	3B	HR	RBI	BB	SO	AVG	OBP	SLG	PRO+	BR/A	SB	CS	SBR	FA	FR	G/POS	TPR
1935	Phi-N	2	0	1	0	0	0	0	0	0	0	—	—	—			0			1.000	-0	/S-2	0.0

■ LOU CHIOZZA
Chiozza, Louis Peo b: 5/17/10, Tallulah, La. d: 2/28/71, Memphis, Tenn. BL/TR, 6', 172 lbs. Deb: 4/17/34 F

YEAR	TM/L	G	AB	R	H	2B	3B	HR	RBI	BB	SO	AVG	OBP	SLG	PRO+	BR/A	SB	CS	SBR	FA	FR	G/POS	TPR
1934	Phi-N	134	484	66	147	28	5	0	44	34	35	.304	.357	.382	86	-9	9			.938	-24	2-85,3-26,O	-2.7
1935	Phi-N	124	472	71	134	26	6	3	47	33	44	.284	.333	.383	84	-11	5			.947	3	*2-120/3-2	0.1
1936	Phi-N	144	572	83	170	32	6	1	48	37	39	.297	.336	.379	87	-11	5			.972	1	O-90,2-33,3	-1.1
1937	*NY-N	117	439	49	102	11	2	4	29	20	30	.232	.266	.294	51	-30	6			.939	2	3-93,O-12,2	-2.6
1938	NY-N	57	179	15	42	7	2	3	17	12	7	.235	.283	.346	72	-7	5			.944	-8	2-34,O-16/3	-1.4
1939	NY-N	40	142	19	38	3	1	0	12	9	10	.268	.311	.366	81	-4	3			.915	-3	3-30/S-8	-0.6
Total	6	616	2288	303	633	107	22	14	197	145	165	.277	.324	.361	78	-72	45			.943	-30	2-274,3-178,O/S	-8.3

■ WALT CHIPPLE
Chipple, Walter John (b: Walter John Chlipala) b: 9/26/18, Utica, N.Y. d: 6/8/88, Tonawanda, N.Y. BR/TR, 6'0.5", 168 lbs. Deb: 4/17/45

YEAR	TM/L	G	AB	R	H	2B	3B	HR	RBI	BB	SO	AVG	OBP	SLG	PRO+	BR/A	SB	CS	SBR	FA	FR	G/POS	TPR
1945	Was-A	18	44	4	6	0	0	0	5	6		.136	.224	.136	6	-5	0	1	-1	.978	3	O-13	-0.4

■ TOM CHISM
Chism, Thomas Raymond b: 5/9/55, Chester, Pa. BL/TL, 6'1", 195 lbs. Deb: 9/13/79

YEAR	TM/L	G	AB	R	H	2B	3B	HR	RBI	BB	SO	AVG	OBP	SLG	PRO+	BR/A	SB	CS	SBR	FA	FR	G/POS	TPR
1979	Bal-A	6	3	0	0	0	0	0	0	0	0	.000	.000	.000	-99	-1	0	0	0	1.000	-0	/1-4	-0.1

YEAR	TM/L	G	AB	R	H	2B	3B	HR	RBI	BB	SO	AVG	OBP	SLG	PRO+	BR/A	SB	CS	SBR	FA	FR	G/POS	TPR

■ HARRY CHITI
Chiti, Harry b: 11/16/32, Kincaid, Ill. BR/TR, 6'3", 225 lbs. Deb: 9/27/50

1950	Chi-N	3	6	0	2	0	0	0	0	0	0	.333	.333	.333	77	-0	0			1.000	-1	/C-1	-0.1
1951	Chi-N	9	31	1	11	2	0	0	5	2	2	.355	.394	.419	117	1	0	0	0	.913	0	/C-8	0.1
1952	Chi-N	32	113	14	31	5	0	5	13	5	8	.274	.305	.451	106	0	0	1	-1	.984	-2	C-32	0.7
1955	Chi-N	113	338	24	78	6	1	11	41	25	68	.231	.286	.352	68	-16	0	0	0	.984	1	*C-113	-1.2
1956	Chi-N	72	203	17	43	6	4	4	18	19	35	.212	.283	.340	68	-10	0	0	0	.981	2	C-67	-0.5
1958	KC-A	103	295	32	79	11	3	9	44	18	48	.268	.316	.417	98	-1	3	2	-0	.987	3	C-83	0.6
1959	KC-A	55	162	20	44	11	1	5	25	17	26	.272	.344	.444	113	3	0	1	-1	.988	2	C-47	0.7
1960	KC-A	58	190	16	42	7	0	5	28	17	33	.221	.288	.337	68	-9	1	0	0	.983	-1	C-52	-0.6
	Det-A	37	104	9	17	0	0	2	5	10	12	.163	.237	.221	24	-11	0	3	-2	.984	-1	C-36	-1.0
	Yr	95	294	25	59	7	0	7	33	27	45	.201	.270	.296	52	-20	1	3	-2	.984	1	C-88	-1.6
1961	Det-A	5	12	0	1	0	0	0	0	0	1	.083	.154	.083	-34	-2	0	0	0	1.000	1	/C-5	-0.1
1962	NY-N	15	41	2	8	1	0	0	0	1	8	.195	.233	.220	22	-4	0	0	0	.971	-1	C-14	-0.5
Total	10	502	1495	135	356	49	9	41	179	115	242	.238	.296	.365	77	-50	4	7		.983	13	C-458	-1.9

■ FELIX CHOUINARD
Chouinard, Felix George b: 10/5/1887, Hines, Ill. d: 4/28/55, Hines, Ill. BR/TR, 5'7", 150 lbs. Deb: 9/11/10

1910	Chi-A	24	82	6	16	3	2	0	9	8		.195	.275	.280	77	-2	4			.962	4	O-23/2-1	0.1
1911	Chi-A	14	17	3	3	0	0	0	0	0		.176	.176	.176	-2	-2	0			.857	1	/2-4,O-4	-0.1
1914	Pit-F	9	30	2	9	1	0	1	3	0	4	.300	.300	.433	89	-1	1			.917	-0	/2-4,O-3,S	-0.1
	Bro-F	32	79	7	20	1	2	0	8	3	13	.253	.289	.316	57	-5	3			.929	-1	O-20	-0.7
	Bal-F	5	9	3	4	0	0	0	1	0	1	.444	.444	.444	127	0	0			1.000	-0	/O-2	0.0
	Yr	46	118	12	33	2	2	1	12	4	18	.280	.303	.356	71	-5	4			.941	-1	O-25/2-4,S	-0.8
1915	Bro-F	4	4	1	2	0	0	0	2	0	0	.500	.500	.500	169	0	0			1.000	-1	/O-2	0.0
Total	4	88	221	22	54	5	4	1	23	12	18	.244	.286	.317	69	-10	8			.948	4	O-54,2-9,S	-0.8

■ HARRY CHOZEN
Chozen, Harry b: 9/27/15, Winnebago, Minn. d: 9/16/94, Houston, Tex. BR/TR, 5'9.5", 190 lbs. Deb: 9/21/37

| 1937 | Cin-N | 1 | 4 | 0 | 1 | 0 | 0 | 0 | 0 | 0 | 0 | .250 | .250 | .250 | 38 | -0 | 0 | | | .833 | -0 | /C-1 | -0.1 |

■ NEIL CHRISLEY
Chrisley, Barbra O'Neil b: 12/16/31, Calhoun Falls, S.C BL/TR, 6'3", 187 lbs. Deb: 4/15/57

1957	Was-A	26	51	6	8	2	1	0	3	7	7	.157	.259	.235	36	-4	0	0	0	.810	-1	O-11	-0.6
1958	Was-A	105	233	19	50	7	4	5	26	16	18	.215	.265	.343	67	-11	1	3	-2	.992	1	O-69/3-1	-1.6
1959	Det-A	65	106	7	14	3	0	6	11	12	10	.132	.227	.330	48	-8	0	0	0	1.000	-2	O-21	-1.1
1960	Det-A	96	220	27	56	10	3	5	24	19	26	.255	.317	.395	89	-4	2	0	1	.981	2	O-47/1-2	-0.3
1961	Mil-N	10	9	1	2	0	0	0	0	1	1	.222	.300	.222	44	-1	0	0	0	.000	0	H	-0.1
Total	5	302	619	60	130	22	8	16	64	55	62	.210	.277	.349	69	-28	3	3	-1	.975	-0	O-148/1-2,3	-3.7

■ LLOYD CHRISTENBURY
Christenbury, Lloyd Reid "Lou" b: 10/19/1893, Mecklenburg Co., N.C. d: 12/13/44, Birmingham, Ala. BL/TR, 5'7", 165 lbs. Deb: 9/20/19

1919	Bos-N	7	31	5	9	1	0	0	4	2	2	.290	.333	.323	102	0	0			.941	1	/O-7	0.1
1920	Bos-N	65	106	17	22	2	2	0	14	13	12	.208	.300	.264	66	-4	0	1	-1	.895	-7	O-14/S-7,23	-1.2
1921	Bos-N	62	125	34	44	6	2	3	16	21	7	.352	.449	.504	161	12	3	4	-2	.914	-13	2-32/S-2,3	-0.1
1922	Bos-N	71	152	22	38	5	2	1	13	18	11	.250	.337	.329	76	-5	2	4	-2	.946	0	O-32/2-5,3	-0.8
Total	4	205	414	78	113	14	6	4	47	54	32	.273	.362	.365	101	3	5	9		.936	-18	/O-53,2-43,S3	-2.0

■ BRUCE CHRISTENSEN
Christensen, Bruce Ray b: 2/22/48, Madison, Wis. BL/TR, 5'11", 160 lbs. Deb: 7/17/71

| 1971 | Cal-A | 29 | 63 | 4 | 17 | 1 | 0 | 0 | 3 | 6 | 5 | .270 | .333 | .286 | 83 | -1 | 0 | 1 | -1 | .988 | 2 | S-24 | 0.3 |

■ JOHN CHRISTENSEN
Christensen, John Lawrence b: 9/5/60, Downey, Cal. BR/TR, 6'3", 205 lbs. Deb: 9/13/84

1984	NY-N	5	11	2	3	2	0	0	3	1	2	.273	.333	.455	121	0	0	1	-1	.500	-2	/O-5	-0.2
1985	NY-N	51	113	10	21	4	1	3	13	19	23	.186	.303	.319	76	-3	1	2	-1	.956	-6	O-38	-1.2
1987	Sea-A	53	132	19	32	6	1	2	12	12	28	.242	.306	.348	69	-6	2	0	1	1.000	-3	O-43/D-8	-0.8
1988	Min-A	23	38	5	10	4	0	0	5	3	5	.263	.349	.368	98	0	0	0	0	1.000	-3	O-17/D-1	-0.3
Total	4	132	294	36	66	16	2	5	33	35	58	.224	.311	.344	77	-9	3	3	-1	.977	-13	O-103/D-9	-2.5

■ CUCKOO CHRISTENSEN
Christensen, Walter Niels "Seacap" b: 10/24/1899, San Francisco, Cal d: 12/20/84, Menlo Park, Cal. BL/TL, 5'6.5", 156 lbs. Deb: 4/13/26

1926	Cin-N	114	329	41	115	15	7	0	41	40	18	.350	.426	.438	136	19	8			.978	-10	O-93	0.3
1927	Cin-N	57	185	25	47	6	0	0	16	20	16	.254	.330	.286	68	-8	4			.957	-3	O-50	-1.4
Total	2	171	514	66	162	21	7	0	57	60	34	.315	.392	.383	112	11	12			.970	-13	O-143	-1.1

■ BOB CHRISTIAN
Christian, Robert Charles b: 10/17/45, Chicago, Ill. d: 2/20/74, San Diego, Cal. BR/TR, 5'10", 180 lbs. Deb: 9/2/68

1968	Det-A	3	3	0	1	1	0	0	0	0	0	.333	.333	.667	191	0	0	0	0	1.000	-0	/1-1,O-1	0.0
1969	Chi-A	39	129	11	28	4	0	3	16	10	19	.217	.279	.318	63	-6	3	0	1	.958	-0	O-38	-0.8
1970	Chi-A	12	15	3	4	0	0	1	3	1	4	.267	.313	.467	108	0	0	0	0	1.000	-1	/O-4	-0.1
Total	3	54	147	14	33	5	0	4	19	11	23	.224	.283	.340	70	-6	3	0	1	.959	-1	/O-43,1-1	-0.9

■ MARK CHRISTMAN
Christman, Marquette Joseph b: 10/21/13, Maplewood, Mo. d: 10/9/76, St.Louis, Mo. BR/TR, 5'11", 180 lbs. Deb: 4/20/38

1938	Det-A	95	318	35	79	6	4	1	44	27	21	.248	.307	.302	50	-24	5	2	0	.983	-9	3-69,S-21	-1.2
1939	Det-A	6	16	0	4	2	0	0	0	0	2	.250	.250	.375	54	-1	0	0	0	.900	-1	/3-5	-0.2
	StL-A	79	222	27	48	6	3	0	20	20	10	.216	.281	.270	41	-20	2	1	0	.960	21	S-64/2-1	0.6
	Yr	85	238	27	52	8	3	0	20	20	12	.218	.279	.277	42	-21	2	1	0	.960	20	S-64/3-5,2	0.4
1943	StL-A	98	336	31	91	11	5	2	35	19	19	.271	.318	.351	94	-3	0	3	-2	.991	-3	3-37,S-24,12	-0.4
1944	*StL-A	148	547	56	148	25	1	6	83	47	37	.271	.332	.353	90	-7	5	2	0	.972	4	*3-145/1-3	-0.1
1945	StL-A	78	289	32	80	7	4	4	34	19	19	.277	.328	.370	98	-1	1	0	0	.973	-3	3-77	-0.2
1946	StL-A	128	458	40	118	22	2	1	41	22	29	.258	.295	.321	68	-20	0	2	-1	.975	9	3-77,S-47	-0.8
1947	Was-A	110	374	27	83	15	2	1	33	32	16	.222	.287	.281	60	-21	4	4	-1	.978	-10	*S-106/2-1	-2.7
1948	Was-A	120	409	38	106	17	2	1	40	25	19	.259	.303	.318	67	-20	0	3	-2	.969	-32	*S-102/3-9,2	-4.8
1949	Was-A	49	112	8	24	2	0	3	18	8	7	.214	.273	.313	56	-8	0	1	-0	.967	3	3-23/1-6,S2	-0.5
Total	9	911	3081	294	781	113	23	19	348	219	179	.253	.306	.324	71	-125	17	17	-5	.975	-0	3-442,S-368/12	-10.3

■ STEVE CHRISTMAS
Christmas, Stephen Randall b: 12/9/57, Orlando, Fla. BL/TR, 6', 190 lbs. Deb: 9/1/83

1983	Cin-N	9	17	0	1	0	0	0	1	3	3	.059	.111	.059	-50	-7	0	0	0	1.000	-0	/C-7	-0.4
1984	Chi-A	12	11	1	4	1	0	1	4	0	2	.364	.364	.727	185	1	0	0	0	1.000	-0	/C-1	0.1
1986	Chi-N	3	9	0	1	1	0	0	2	0	1	.111	.111	.222	-10	-1	0	0	0	1.000	-0	/C-1,1-1	-0.2
Total	3	24	37	1	6	2	0	1	7	1	6	.162	.184	.297	30	-4	0	0	0	1.000	-0	/C-9,1-1	-0.5

■ JOE CHRISTOPHER
Christopher, Joseph O'Neal b: 12/13/35, Frederiksted, V.I. BR/TR, 5'10", 176 lbs. Deb: 5/26/59

1959	Pit-N	15	12	6	0	0	0	0	0	1	4	.000	.077	.000	-78	-3	0	0	0	1.000	-3	/O-9	-0.6
1960	*Pit-N	50	56	21	13	2	0	1	3	5	8	.232	.295	.321	68	-2	1	0	0	1.000	-2	O-17	-0.5
1961	Pit-N	76	186	25	49	7	3	0	14	18	24	.263	.328	.333	76	-6	6	4	-1	.978	-2	O-55	-1.1
1962	NY-N	119	271	36	66	10	2	6	32	35	42	.244	.339	.362	87	-4	11	3	2	.972	-9	O-94	-0.9
1963	NY-N	64	149	19	33	5	1	1	8	13	21	.221	.297	.289	68	-6	1	3	-2	.983	-5	O-45	-1.5
1964	NY-N	154	543	78	163	26	8	16	76	48	92	.300	.363	.466	135	25	6	5	-1	.974	1	*O-145	1.8
1965	NY-N	148	437	38	109	18	3	5	40	35	82	.249	.314	.339	87	-7	4	4	-1	.989	-3	*O-112	-1.8

YEAR	TM/L	G	AB	R	H	2B	3B	HR	RBI	BB	SO	AVG	OBP	SLG	PRO+	BR/A	SB	CS	SBR	FA	FR	G/POS	TPR
1966	Bos-A	12	13	1	1	0	0	0	0	2	4	.077	.200	.077	-15	-2	0	0	0	1.000	-1	/O-2	-0.3
Total	8	638	1667	224	434	68	17	29	173	157	277	.260	.331	.374	96	-6	29	19	-3	.979	-24	O-479	-5.6

■ LOYD CHRISTOPHER
Christopher, Loyd Eugene b: 12/31/19, Richmond, Cal. d: 9/5/91, Richmond, Cal. BR/TR, 6'2", 190 lbs. Deb: 4/20/45 F

YEAR	TM/L	G	AB	R	H	2B	3B	HR	RBI	BB	SO	AVG	OBP	SLG	PRO+	BR/A	SB	CS	SBR	FA	FR	G/POS	TPR
1945	Bos-A	8	14	4	4	0	0	0	4	3	2	.286	.412	.286	101	0	0	0	0	1.000	-1	/O-3	-0.1
	Chi-N	1	0	0	0	0	0	0	0	0	0	—	—	—	—	0	0	0		.000	-0	/O-1	0.0
1947	Chi-A	7	23	1	5	0	1	0	0	2	4	.217	.280	.304	65	-1	0	1	-1	1.000	1	/O-7	-0.1
Total	2	16	37	5	9	0	1	0	4	5	6	.243	.333	.297	80	-1	0	1		1.000	0	/O-11	-0.2

■ HI CHURCH
Church, Hiram Lincoln b: 11/23/1863, Central Square, N.Y. d: 2/23/26, Jacksonville, Fla. Deb: 8/23/1890

YEAR	TM/L	G	AB	R	H	2B	3B	HR	RBI	BB	SO	AVG	OBP	SLG	PRO+	BR/A	SB	CS	SBR	FA	FR	G/POS	TPR
1890	Bro-a	3	9	1	1	0	0	0		0		.111	.111	.111	-36	-2	0			1.000	-1	/O-3	-0.3

■ JOHN CHURRY
Churry, John b: 11/26/1900, Johnstown, Pa. d: 2/8/70, Zanesville, Ohio BR/TR, 5'9", 172 lbs. Deb: 5/24/24

YEAR	TM/L	G	AB	R	H	2B	3B	HR	RBI	BB	SO	AVG	OBP	SLG	PRO+	BR/A	SB	CS	SBR	FA	FR	G/POS	TPR
1924	Chi-N	6	7	0	1	1	0	0		1	0	.143	.333	.286	67	-0	0	0	0	1.000	0	/C-3	0.0
1925	Chi-N	3	6	1	3	0	0	0		1	0	.500	.500	.500	154	-0	0	0	0	1.000	-0	/C-3	0.0
1926	Chi-N	2	4	0	0	0	0	0		1	2	.000	.200	.000	-42	-1	0			1.000	0	/C-1	-0.1
1927	Chi-N	1	1	0	1	0	0	0		1	0	1.000	1.000	1.000	436	-0	0			1.000	0	/C-1	0.1
Total	4	12	18	1	5	1	0	0		1	3	2	.278	.381	.333	89	-0	0	0	0	1.000	0	/C-8	0.0

■ LARRY CIAFFONE
Ciaffone, Lawrence Thomas "Symphony Larry" b: 8/17/24, Brooklyn, N.Y. d: 12/14/91, Brooklyn, N.Y. BR/TR, 5'9.5", 185 lbs. Deb: 4/17/51

YEAR	TM/L	G	AB	R	H	2B	3B	HR	RBI	BB	SO	AVG	OBP	SLG	PRO+	BR/A	SB	CS	SBR	FA	FR	G/POS	TPR
1951	StL-N	5	5	0	0	0	0	0		0	1	2	.000	.167	.000	-51	-0	0	0	0	1.000	-0	/O-1	-0.1

■ ARCHI CIANFROCCO
Cianfrocco, Angelo Dominic b: 10/6/66, Rome, N.Y. BR/TR, 6'5", 200 lbs. Deb: 4/8/92

YEAR	TM/L	G	AB	R	H	2B	3B	HR	RBI	BB	SO	AVG	OBP	SLG	PRO+	BR/A	SB	CS	SBR	FA	FR	G/POS	TPR
1992	Mon-N	86	232	25	56	5	2	6	30	11	66	.241	.279	.358	80	-7	3	0	1	.993	1	1-56,3-19/O	-0.8
1993	Mon-N	12	17	3	4	1	0	1	1	0	5	.235	.235	.471	80	-1	0	0	0	1.000	-0	1-11	-0.1
	SD-N	84	279	27	68	10	2	11	47	17	64	.244	.294	.412	85	-7	2	0	1	.932	-5	3-64,1-31	-1.3
	Yr	96	296	30	72	11	2	12	48	17	69	.243	.291	.416	85	-7	2	0	1	.932	-6	3-64,1-42	-1.4
1994	SD-N	59	146	9	32	8	0	4	13	3	39	.219	.255	.356	58	-9	2	0	1	.920	2	3-37,1-16/S	-0.7
Total	3	241	674	64	160	24	4	22	91	31	174	.237	.279	.383	77	-23	7	0	2	.919	-2	3-120,1-114/OS	-2.9

■ DARRYL CIAS
Cias, Darryl Richard b: 4/23/57, New York, N.Y. BR/TR, 5'11", 190 lbs. Deb: 4/27/83

YEAR	TM/L	G	AB	R	H	2B	3B	HR	RBI	BB	SO	AVG	OBP	SLG	PRO+	BR/A	SB	CS	SBR	FA	FR	G/POS	TPR
1983	Oak-A	19	18	1	6	1	0	0	1	2	4	.333	.400	.389	126	-0	1	1	0	.967	-0	C-19	0.1

■ JOE CICERO
Cicero, Joseph Francis "Dode" b: 11/18/10, Atlantic City, N.J. d: 3/30/83, Clearwater, Fla. BR/TR, 5'8", 167 lbs. Deb: 9/20/29

YEAR	TM/L	G	AB	R	H	2B	3B	HR	RBI	BB	SO	AVG	OBP	SLG	PRO+	BR/A	SB	CS	SBR	FA	FR	G/POS	TPR
1929	Bos-A	10	32	6	10	2	2	0	4	0	2	.313	.313	.500	108	0	0	0	0	1.000	-1	/O-7	-0.1
1930	Bos-A	18	30	5	5	1	2	0	4	1	5	.167	.194	.333	32	-3	0	0	0	.000	-0	/O-5,3-2	-0.5
1945	Phi-A	12	19	3	3	0	0	0	0	1	6	.158	.238	.158	16	-2	0	0	0	1.000	-2	/O-7	-0.5
Total	3	40	81	14	18	3	4	0	8	2	13	.222	.250	.358	60	-5	0	0	0	1.000	-4	/O-19,3-2	-1.1

■ TED CIESLAK
Cieslak, Thaddeus Walter b: 11/22/16, Milwaukee, Wis. BR/TR, 5'10", 175 lbs. Deb: 4/18/44

YEAR	TM/L	G	AB	R	H	2B	3B	HR	RBI	BB	SO	AVG	OBP	SLG	PRO+	BR/A	SB	CS	SBR	FA	FR	G/POS	TPR
1944	Phi-N	85	220	18	54	10	0	2	11	21	17	.245	.314	.318	81	-5	1			.877	-15	3-48/O-5	-2.1

■ AL CIHOCKI
Cihocki, Albert Joseph b: 5/7/24, Nanticoke, Pa. BR/TR, 5'11", 185 lbs. Deb: 4/17/45

YEAR	TM/L	G	AB	R	H	2B	3B	HR	RBI	BB	SO	AVG	OBP	SLG	PRO+	BR/A	SB	CS	SBR	FA	FR	G/POS	TPR
1945	Cle-A	92	283	21	60	9	3	0	24	11	48	.212	.241	.265	49	-19	2	1	0	.946	1	S-41,3-29,2	-1.5

■ ED CIHOCKI
Cihocki, Edward Joseph "Cy" b: 5/9/07, Wilmington, Del. d: 11/9/87, Newark, Del. BR/TR, 5'8", 163 lbs. Deb: 5/29/32

YEAR	TM/L	G	AB	R	H	2B	3B	HR	RBI	BB	SO	AVG	OBP	SLG	PRO+	BR/A	SB	CS	SBR	FA	FR	G/POS	TPR
1932	Phi-A	1	1	0	0	0	0	0	0	0	0	.000	.000	.000	-97	-0	0	0	0	.000	0	H	0.0
1933	Phi-A	33	97	6	14	2	3	0	9	7	16	.144	.202	.227	13	-12	0	0	0	.904	-2	S-28/2-1,3	-1.3
Total	2	34	98	6	14	2	3	0	9	7	16	.143	.200	.224	12	-13	0	0	0	.904	-2	/S-28,3-1,2	-1.3

■ GINO CIMOLI
Cimoli, Gino Nicholas b: 12/18/29, San Francisco, Cal. BR/TR, 6'2", 200 lbs. Deb: 4/19/56

YEAR	TM/L	G	AB	R	H	2B	3B	HR	RBI	BB	SO	AVG	OBP	SLG	PRO+	BR/A	SB	CS	SBR	FA	FR	G/POS	TPR
1956	*Bro-N	73	36	3	4	1	0	0	4	1	8	.111	.135	.139	-24	-6	1	0	0	.946	-18	O-62	-2.6
1957	Bro-N★	142	532	88	156	22	5	10	57	39	86	.293	.346	.410	93	-5	3	1	0	.979	-3	*O-138	-1.5
1958	LA-N	109	325	35	80	6	3	9	27	18	49	.246	.292	.366	71	-14	3	3	-1	.974	-8	*O-104	-2.8
1959	StL-N	143	519	61	145	40	7	8	72	37	83	.279	.330	.430	94	-5	7	0	2	.979	5	*O-141	-0.5
1960	*Pit-N	101	307	36	82	14	4	0	28	32	43	.267	.338	.339	85	-5	1	0	0	.964	-7	O-91	-1.7
1961	Pit-N	21	67	4	20	3	1	0	6	2	13	.299	.319	.373	83	-2	0	0	0	.971	-0	O-19	-0.3
	Mil-N	37	117	12	23	5	0	3	4	11	15	.197	.266	.316	57	-8	1	0	0	.985	-3	O-31	-1.2
	Yr	58	184	16	43	8	1	3	10	13	28	.234	.284	.337	67	-9	1	0	0	.980	-3	O-50	-1.5
1962	KC-A	152	550	67	151	20	**15**	10	71	40	89	.275	.326	.420	95	-5	2	1	0	.968	-9	*O-147	-2.2
1963	KC-A	145	529	56	139	19	11	4	48	39	72	.263	.316	.363	85	-10	3	1	0	.985	2	*O-136	-1.6
1964	KC-A	4	9	1	0	0	0	0	0	0	1	.000	.000	.000	-97	-2	0	0	0	1.000	0	/O-4	-0.3
	Bal-A	38	58	6	8	3	2	0	3	2	13	.138	.167	.259	16	-7	0	0	0	.893	-9	O-35	-1.7
	Yr	42	67	7	8	3	2	0	3	2	14	.119	.145	.224	1	-9	0	0	0	.912	-9	O-39	-2.0
1965	Cal-A	4	5	1	0	0	0	0	1	0	2	.000	.000	.000	-99	-1	0	0	0	1.000	0	/O-1	-0.1
Total	10	969	3054	370	808	133	48	44	321	221	474	.265	.317	.383	84	-70	21	6	3	.974	-50	O-909	-16.5

■ FRANK CIPRIANI
Cipriani, Frank Dominick b: 4/14/41, Buffalo, N.Y. BR/TR, 6', 180 lbs. Deb: 9/8/61

YEAR	TM/L	G	AB	R	H	2B	3B	HR	RBI	BB	SO	AVG	OBP	SLG	PRO+	BR/A	SB	CS	SBR	FA	FR	G/POS	TPR
1961	KC-A	13	36	2	9	0	0	0	2	2	4	.250	.289	.250	45	-3	0	0	0	1.000	-1	O-11	-0.4

■ JEFF CIRILLO
Cirillo, Jeffrey Howard b: 9/23/69, Pasadena, Cal. BR/TR, 6'2", 190 lbs. Deb: 5/11/94

YEAR	TM/L	G	AB	R	H	2B	3B	HR	RBI	BB	SO	AVG	OBP	SLG	PRO+	BR/A	SB	CS	SBR	FA	FR	G/POS	TPR
1994	Mil-A	39	126	17	30	9	0	3	12	11	16	.238	.309	.381	75	-5	0	1	-1	.965	-1	3-37/2-1	-0.6

■ GEORGE CISAR
Cisar, George Joseph b: 8/25/12, Chicago, Ill. BR/TR, 6', 175 lbs. Deb: 9/9/37

YEAR	TM/L	G	AB	R	H	2B	3B	HR	RBI	BB	SO	AVG	OBP	SLG	PRO+	BR/A	SB	CS	SBR	FA	FR	G/POS	TPR
1937	Bro-N	20	29	8	6	0	0	0	4	2	6	.207	.258	.207	27	-3	3			1.000	-3	O-13	-0.6

■ BILL CISSELL
Cissell, Chalmer William b: 1/3/04, Perryville, Mo. d: 3/15/49, Chicago, Ill. BR/TR, 5'11", 170 lbs. Deb: 4/11/28

YEAR	TM/L	G	AB	R	H	2B	3B	HR	RBI	BB	SO	AVG	OBP	SLG	PRO+	BR/A	SB	CS	SBR	FA	FR	G/POS	TPR
1928	Chi-A	125	443	66	115	22	3	1	60	29	41	.260	.307	.330	68	-21	18	6	2	.938	-2	*S-123	-0.6
1929	Chi-A	152	618	83	173	27	12	5	62	28	53	.280	.312	.387	80	-20	25	17	-3	.937	-3	*S-152	-0.7
1930	Chi-A	141	562	82	152	28	9	2	48	28	32	.270	.307	.363	72	-25	16	9	-1	.948	-11	*2-107,3-24,S	-2.6
1931	Chi-A	109	409	42	90	13	5	1	46	16	26	.220	.256	.284	44	-34	18	6	-1	.944	-10	S-83,2-23/3	-3.1
1932	Chi-A	12	43	7	11	1	1	1	5	1	0	.256	.273	.395	76	-2	0	0	0	.928	1	S-12	-0.1
	Cle-A	131	541	78	173	35	6	6	93	28	25	.320	.354	.440	98	-3	18	15	-4	.964	11	*2-129/S-6	1.1
	Yr	143	584	85	184	36	7	7	98	29	25	.315	.349	.437	97	-4	18	15	-4	.964	11	*2-129,S-18	1.0
1933	Cle-A	112	409	53	94	21	3	6	33	31	29	.230	.284	.340	62	-23	6	6	-2	.947	-7	2-62,S-46/3	-2.5
1934	Bos-A	102	416	71	111	13	4	4	44	28	23	.267	.315	.346	66	-22	11	4	1	.959	-4	2-96/S-7,3	-1.8
1937	Phi-A	34	117	15	31	7	0	1	14	17	10	.265	.358	.350	81	-3	0	0	0	.962	3	2-33	0.2
1938	NY-N	38	149	19	40	6	0	2	18	6	11	.268	.297	.349	76	-5	1			.977	3	2-33/3-6	0.6
Total	9	956	3707	516	990	173	43	29	423	212	250	.267	.308	.360	73	-158	113	63		.958	-14	2-483,S-439/3	-9.5

■ MOOSE CLABAUGH
Clabaugh, John William b: 11/13/01, Albany, Mo. d: 7/11/84, Tucson, Ariz. BL/TR, 6', 185 lbs. Deb: 8/30/26

YEAR	TM/L	G	AB	R	H	2B	3B	HR	RBI	BB	SO	AVG	OBP	SLG	PRO+	BR/A	SB	CS	SBR	FA	FR	G/POS	TPR
1926	Bro-N	11	14	2	1	0	0	0	1	0	1	.071	.133	.143	-26	-3	0			.600	-1	/O-2	-0.3

■ BOBBY CLACK
Clack, Robert S. "Gentlemanly Bob" (b: Robert S. Clark) b: 6/1850, England d: 10/22/33, Danvers, Mass. BR/TR, 5'9", 153 lbs. Deb: 5/13/1874

YEAR	TM/L	G	AB	R	H	2B	3B	HR	RBI	BB	SO	AVG	OBP	SLG	PRO+	BR/A	SB	CS	SBR	FA	FR	G/POS	TPR
1874	Atl-n	33	134	22	23	2	0	0		2		.172	.184	.187	21	-11						O-30/1-2	-0.8
1875	Atl-n	17	59	1	6	0	0	0		0		.102	.102	.102	-34	-7						O-17	-0.6

YEAR	TM/L	G	AB	R	H	2B	3B	HR	RBI	BB	SO	AVG	OBP	SLG	PRO+	BR/A	SB	CS	SBR	FA	FR	G/POS	TPR
1876	Cin-N	32	118	10	19	0	1	0	5	5	12	.161	.195	.178	29	-8				.736	0	O-17/2-8,13P	-0.7
Total	2 n	50	193	23	29	2	0	0		2		.150	.159	.161	5	-18						/O-47,1-2D	-1.4

■ DANNY CLAIRE
Claire, David Matthew   b: 11/17/1897, Ludington, Mich.   d: 1/7/56, Las Vegas, Nev.   BR/TR, 5'8", 164 lbs.   Deb: 9/17/20

YEAR	TM/L	G	AB	R	H	2B	3B	HR	RBI	BB	SO	AVG	OBP	SLG	PRO+	BR/A	SB	CS	SBR	FA	FR	G/POS	TPR
1920	Det-A	3	7	1	1	0	0	0	0	0	0	.143	.143	.143	-25	-1	0	0	0	.800	-0	/S-3	-0.2

■ AL CLANCY
Clancy, Albert Harrison   b: 8/14/1888, Santa Fe, N.Mex.   d: 10/17/51, Las Cruces, N.Mex.   BR/TR, 5'10.5", 175 lbs.   Deb: 6/20/11

YEAR	TM/L	G	AB	R	H	2B	3B	HR	RBI	BB	SO	AVG	OBP	SLG	PRO+	BR/A	SB	CS	SBR	FA	FR	G/POS	TPR
1911	StL-A	3	5	0	0	0	0	0	0	0	0	.000	.167	.000	-54	-1	0			.800	0	/3-2	-0.1

■ BUD CLANCY
Clancy, John William   b: 9/15/1900, Odell, Ill.   d: 9/26/68, Ottumwa, Iowa   BL/TL, 6', 170 lbs.   Deb: 8/29/24

YEAR	TM/L	G	AB	R	H	2B	3B	HR	RBI	BB	SO	AVG	OBP	SLG	PRO+	BR/A	SB	CS	SBR	FA	FR	G/POS	TPR
1924	Chi-A	13	35	5	9	1	0	0	6	3	2	.257	.316	.286	58	-2	3	2	-0	.947	-2	/1-8	-0.4
1925	Chi-A	4	3	0	0	0	0	0	0	1	0	.000	.250	.000	-34	-1	0	0	0	.000	0	H	-0.1
1926	Chi-A	12	38	3	13	2	2	0	7	1	1	.342	.375	.500	131	2	0	0	0	.991	0	1-10	0.1
1927	Chi-A	130	464	46	139	21	2	3	53	24	24	.300	.337	.373	86	-10	4	3	-1	.991	0	*1-123	-1.8
1928	Chi-A	130	487	64	132	19	11	2	37	42	25	.271	.331	.368	85	-11	6	9	-4	.991	5	*1-128	-2.1
1929	Chi-A	92	290	36	82	14	6	3	45	16	19	.283	.320	.403	86	-7	3	1	0	.991	2	1-74	-1.1
1930	Chi-A	68	234	28	57	8	3	3	27	12	18	.244	.286	.342	61	-14	3	1	0	.995	-3	1-60	-2.2
1932	Bro-N	53	196	14	60	4	2	0	16	6	13	.306	.327	.347	83	-5				.996	3	1-53	-0.6
1934	Phi-N	20	49	8	12	0	0	1	7	6	4	.245	.339	.306	65	-2				1.000	-1	1-10	-0.4
Total	9	522	1796	204	504	69	26	12	198	111	106	.281	.325	.368	81	-50	19	<u>16</u>		.992	4	1-466	-8.6

■ BILL CLANCY
Clancy, William Edward   b: 4/12/1879, Redfield, N.Y.   d: 2/10/48, Oriskany, N.Y.   BR/TR, 6'2", 180 lbs.   Deb: 4/14/05

YEAR	TM/L	G	AB	R	H	2B	3B	HR	RBI	BB	SO	AVG	OBP	SLG	PRO+	BR/A	SB	CS	SBR	FA	FR	G/POS	TPR
1905	Pit-N	56	227	23	52	11	3	2	34	4		.229	.246	.330	69	-10	3			.983	-4	1-52/O-4	-1.6

■ UKE CLANTON
Clanton, Eucal "Cat"   b: 2/19/1898, Powell, Mo.   d: 2/24/60, Antlers, Okla.   BL/TL, 5'8", 165 lbs.   Deb: 9/21/22

YEAR	TM/L	G	AB	R	H	2B	3B	HR	RBI	BB	SO	AVG	OBP	SLG	PRO+	BR/A	SB	CS	SBR	FA	FR	G/POS	TPR
1922	Cle-A	1	1	0	0	0	0	0	0	0	1	.000	.000	.000	-99	-0	0	0	0	.500	-0	/1-1	-0.1

■ AARON CLAPP
Clapp, Aaron Bronson   b: 7/1856, Ithaca, N.Y.   d: 1/13/14, Sayre, Pa.   TR, 5'8", 175 lbs.   Deb: 5/1/1879   F

YEAR	TM/L	G	AB	R	H	2B	3B	HR	RBI	BB	SO	AVG	OBP	SLG	PRO+	BR/A	SB	CS	SBR	FA	FR	G/POS	TPR
1879	Tro-N	36	146	24	39	9	3	0	18	6	10	.267	.296	.370	126	4				.935	-4	1-25,O-11	0.0

■ JOHN CLAPP
Clapp, John Edgar   b: 7/17/1851, Ithaca, N.Y.   d: 12/18/04, Ithaca, N.Y.   BR/TR, 5'7", 194 lbs.   Deb: 4/26/1872   FM

YEAR	TM/L	G	AB	R	H	2B	3B	HR	RBI	BB	SO	AVG	OBP	SLG	PRO+	BR/A	SB	CS	SBR	FA	FR	G/POS	TPR
1872	Man-n	19	97	30	32	8	0	1	12	1	0	.330	.337	.443	147	6						C-19,M	0.4
1873	Ath-n	45	204	36	62	11	2	1	28	2	2	.304	.311	.392	98	-2						*C-43/S-6,2O	-0.3
1874	Ath-n	39	165	46	48	8	4	3		1		.291	.295	.442	121	2						C-26,O-13/S	0.3
1875	Ath-n	60	291	65	77	7	8	0		8		.265	.284	.344	104	-1						C-60	0.1
1876	StL-N	64	298	60	91	4	2	0	29	8	2	.305	.324	.332	125	9				.874	9	*C-61/O-4,2	1.7
1877	StL-N	60	255	47	81	6	6	0	34	8	6	.318	.338	.388	135	11				.887	-6	*C-53,O-10/1	0.5
1878	Ind-N	63	263	42	80	10	2	0	29	13	8	.304	.337	.357	148	15				.890	-7	*O-44,1-12/CS2M	0.5
1879	Buf-N	70	292	47	77	12	5	1	36	11	11	.264	.290	.349	107	2				.906	-9	*C-63/O-7M	-0.5
1880	Cin-N	80	323	33	91	16	4	1	20	21	10	.282	.326	.365	135	12				.897	17	*C-73,O-10M	2.9
1881	Cle-N	68	261	47	66	12	2	0	25	**35**	6	.253	.341	.314	113	6				.890	-5	C-48,O-21M	0.3
1883	NY-N	20	73	6	13	0	0	0	5	5		.178	.231	.178	27	-6				.895	5	C-16/O-5M	0.0
Total	4 n	163	757	177	219	34	14	5	40	12	<u>2</u>	.289	.300	.391	111	5						C-148/O-14,S2	0.5
Total	7	425	1765	282	499	60	21	2	178	101	47	.283	.322	.344	122	48				.892	4	C-323,O-101/1S2	5.4

■ DENNY CLARE
Clare, Dennis J.   b: 1/1853, Brooklyn, N.Y.   d: 11/26/28, Brooklyn, N.Y.   Deb: 9/14/1872

YEAR	TM/L	G	AB	R	H	2B	3B	HR	RBI	BB	SO	AVG	OBP	SLG	PRO+	BR/A	SB	CS	SBR	FA	FR	G/POS	TPR
1872	Atl-n	2	7	1	1	0	0	0	0	0	0	.143	.143	.143	-10	-1						/2-2	-0.1

■ DOUG CLAREY
Clarey, Douglas William   b: 4/20/54, Los Angeles, Cal.   BR/TR, 6', 180 lbs.   Deb: 4/20/76

YEAR	TM/L	G	AB	R	H	2B	3B	HR	RBI	BB	SO	AVG	OBP	SLG	PRO+	BR/A	SB	CS	SBR	FA	FR	G/POS	TPR
1976	StL-N	9	4	2	1	0	0	1	2	0	1	.250	.250	1.000	240	1	0	0	0	1.000	0	/2-7	0.1

■ ALLIE CLARK
Clark, Alfred Aloysius   b: 6/16/23, S.Amboy, N.J.   BR/TR, 6', 185 lbs.   Deb: 8/5/47

YEAR	TM/L	G	AB	R	H	2B	3B	HR	RBI	BB	SO	AVG	OBP	SLG	PRO+	BR/A	SB	CS	SBR	FA	FR	G/POS	TPR
1947	*NY-A	24	67	9	25	5	0	1	14	5	2	.373	.417	.493	154	5	0	0	0	1.000	0	O-16	0.4
1948	*Cle-A	81	271	43	84	5	2	9	38	23	13	.310	.364	.443	117	6	0	2	-1	.982	-6	O-65/3-5,1	-0.5
1949	Cle-A	35	74	8	13	4	0	1	9	4	7	.176	.218	.270	29	-8	0	0	0	1.000	-4	O-17/1-1	-1.3
1950	Cle-A	59	163	19	35	6	1	6	21	11	10	.215	.264	.374	64	-10	0	1	-1	.987	-3	O-41	-1.4
1951	Cle-A	3	10	3	3	2	0	1	3	1	2	.300	.364	.800	221	1	0	0	0	1.000	-1	O-3	0.1
	Phi-A	56	161	20	40	10	1	4	22	15	7	.248	.320	.398	91	-2	2	0	1	.984	-1	O-32,3-10	-0.4
	Yr	59	171	23	43	12	1	5	25	16	9	.251	.323	.421	98	-1	2	0	1	.985	-1	O-35,3-10	-0.3
1952	Phi-A	71	186	23	51	12	0	7	29	10	19	.274	.315	.452	105	0	0	2	-1	.988	-3	O-48/1-2	-0.6
1953	Phi-A	20	74	6	15	4	0	3	13	3	4	.203	.234	.378	61	-5	0	0	0	1.000	0	O-19	-0.6
	Chi-A	9	15	0	1	0	0	0	0	0	6	.067	.067	.067	-62	-3	0	0	0	1.000	-0	/1-1,O-1	-0.4
	Yr	29	89	6	16	4	0	3	13	3	10	.180	.207	.326	40	-8	0	0	0	1.000	-1	O-20/1-1	-1.0
Total	7	358	1021	131	267	48	4	32	149	72	70	.262	.312	.410	92	-16	2	5	-2	.988	-19	O-242/3-15,1	-4.7

■ DAD CLARK
Clark, Alfred Robert "Fred"   b: 7/16/1873, San Francisco, Cal.   d: 7/26/56, Ogden, Utah   BL/TL, 5'11", 170 lbs.   Deb: 7/3/02

YEAR	TM/L	G	AB	R	H	2B	3B	HR	RBI	BB	SO	AVG	OBP	SLG	PRO+	BR/A	SB	CS	SBR	FA	FR	G/POS	TPR
1902	Chi-N	12	43	1	8	1	0	0	2	4		.186	.255	.209	45	-3	1			.938	-1	1-12	-0.5

■ EARL CLARK
Clark, Bailey Earl   b: 11/6/07, Washington, D.C.   d: 1/16/38, Washington, D.C.   BR/TR, 5'10", 160 lbs.   Deb: 8/17/27

YEAR	TM/L	G	AB	R	H	2B	3B	HR	RBI	BB	SO	AVG	OBP	SLG	PRO+	BR/A	SB	CS	SBR	FA	FR	G/POS	TPR
1927	Bos-N	13	44	6	12	1	0	0	3	2	4	.273	.304	.295	66	-2	0			1.000	-1	O-13	-0.3
1928	Bos-N	28	112	18	34	9	1	0	10	4	8	.304	.339	.402	98	-1	0			.987	-1	O-27	-0.3
1929	Bos-N	84	279	43	88	13	3	1	30	12	30	.315	.346	.394	86	-6	6			.978	4	O-74	-0.6
1930	Bos-N	82	233	29	69	11	3	3	28	7	22	.296	.320	.408	77	-9	3			.977	1	O-63	-1.1
1931	Bos-N	16	50	8	11	2	0	0	4	7	4	.220	.316	.260	58	-3	1			.970	-1	O-14	-0.3
1932	Bos-N	50	44	11	11	2	0	0	4	2	7	.250	.283	.295	58	-3	1			1.000	-2	O-16	-0.5
1933	Bos-N	7	23	3	8	1	0	0	1	2	1	.348	.400	.391	138	1	0			1.000	-1	/O-6	0.0
1934	StL-A	13	41	4	7	2	0	0	1	1	3	.171	.190	.220	5	-6	0			1.000	-1	/O-9	-0.5
Total	8	293	826	122	240	41	7	4	81	37	79	.291	.324	.372	78	-28	11	<u>0</u>		.981	2	O-222	-3.6

■ DANNY CLARK
Clark, Daniel Curran   b: 1/18/1894, Meridian, Miss.   d: 5/23/37, Meridian, Miss.   BL/TR, 5'9", 167 lbs.   Deb: 4/12/22

YEAR	TM/L	G	AB	R	H	2B	3B	HR	RBI	BB	SO	AVG	OBP	SLG	PRO+	BR/A	SB	CS	SBR	FA	FR	G/POS	TPR
1922	Det-A	83	185	31	54	11	3	2	26	15	11	.292	.345	.432	105	1	1	0		.945	-6	2-38/O-5,3	-0.4
1924	Bos-A	104	325	36	90	23	3	2	54	51	19	.277	.378	.385	97	-0	4	7	-3	.943	-6	3-94	-0.2
1927	StL-N	58	72	8	17	2	2	1	13	8	7	.236	.313	.319	67	-3	0			.929	1	/O-9	-0.3
Total	3	245	582	75	161	36	8	5	93	74	37	.277	.360	.392	96	-3	5	<u>7</u>		.943	-11	/3-95,2-38,O	-0.9

■ DAVE CLARK
Clark, David Earl   b: 9/3/62, Tupelo, Miss.   BL/TR, 6'2", 200 lbs.   Deb: 9/3/86

YEAR	TM/L	G	AB	R	H	2B	3B	HR	RBI	BB	SO	AVG	OBP	SLG	PRO+	BR/A	SB	CS	SBR	FA	FR	G/POS	TPR
1986	Cle-A	18	58	10	16	3	0	3	9	7	11	.276	.354	.448	119	2	1	0	0	1.000	1	O-10/D-7	0.2
1987	Cle-A	29	87	11	18	5	0	3	12	2	24	.207	.225	.368	53	-6	1	0	0	1.000	0	O-13,D-12	-0.6
1988	Cle-A	63	156	11	41	4	1	3	18	17	28	.263	.333	.359	92	-1	0	2	-1	.947	-8	D-27,O-23	-0.8
1989	Cle-A	102	253	21	60	12	0	8	29	30	63	.237	.318	.379	94	-2	0	1	-1	.964	-5	D-55,O-21	-1.0
1990	Chi-N	84	171	22	47	4	5	5	20	8	40	.275	.307	.409	89	-3	7	1	2	1.000	-2	O-39	-0.5
1991	KC-A	11	10	1	2	0	0	0	1	1	9	.200	.273	.200	33	-1	0	0	0	1.000	-1	/O-1,D-1	-0.1
1992	Pit-N	23	33	3	7	0	0	2	7	6	8	.212	.333	.394	106	0	0	0	0	1.000	0	/O-8	-0.1
1993	Pit-N	110	277	43	75	11	2	11	46	38	58	.271	.361	.444	114	6	1	1	0	.957	-11	O-91	-0.6
1994	Pit-N	86	223	37	66	11	4	10	46	22	48	.296	.359	.489	119	6	2	5	-1	.974	-5	O-57	0.6
Total	9	526	1268	159	332	48	6	45	188	131	281	.262	.331	.416	100	1	12	7	-1	.973	-20	O-263,D-102	-2.9

YEAR	TM/L	G	AB	R	H	2B	3B	HR	RBI	BB	SO	AVG	OBP	SLG	PRO+	BR/A	SB	CS	SBR	FA	FR	G/POS	TPR

■ GLEN CLARK Clark, Glen Ester b: 3/7/41, Austin, Tex. BB/TR, 6'1", 190 lbs. Deb: 6/3/67

| 1967 | Atl-N | 4 | 4 | 0 | 0 | 0 | 0 | 0 | 0 | 0 | 1 | .000 | .000 | .000 | -99 | -1 | 0 | 0 | 0 | .000 | 0 | H | -0.1 |

■ PEP CLARK Clark, Harry b: 3/20/1883, Union City, Ohio d: 6/8/65, Milwaukee, Wis. BR/TR, 5'7.5", 175 lbs. Deb: 9/11/03

| 1903 | Chi-A | 15 | 65 | 7 | 20 | 4 | 2 | 0 | 9 | 2 | | .308 | .338 | .431 | 135 | 3 | 5 | | | .877 | -0 | 3-15 | 0.2 |

■ JACK CLARK Clark, Jack Anthony b: 11/10/55, New Brighton, Pa. BR/TR, 6'2", 205 lbs. Deb: 9/12/75

1975	SF-N	8	17	3	4	0	0	0	2	1	2	.235	.278	.235	42	-1	1	0	0	1.000	-0	/O-3,3-2	-0.2
1976	SF-N	26	102	14	23	6	2	2	10	8	18	.225	.282	.382	85	-2	6	2	1	.987	1	O-26	-0.2
1977	SF-N	136	413	64	104	17	4	13	51	49	73	.252	.334	.407	98	-1	12	4	1	.975	7	*O-114	0.3
1978	SF-N★	156	592	90	181	46	8	25	98	50	72	.306	.363	.537	155	40	15	11	-2	.982	14	*O-152	4.7
1979	SF-N★	143	527	84	144	25	2	26	86	63	95	.273	.352	.476	133	22	11	8	-2	.982	5	*O-140/3-2	2.0
1980	SF-N	127	437	77	124	20	8	22	82	74	52	.284	.390	.517	155	33	2	5	-2	.967	1	*O-120	2.8
1981	SF-N	99	385	60	103	19	2	17	53	45	45	.268	.346	.460	129	14	1	1	-0	.981	12	O-98	2.4
1982	SF-N	157	563	90	154	30	3	27	103	90	91	.274	.375	.481	138	30	6	9	-4	.980	3	O-155	2.6
1983	SF-N	135	492	82	132	25	0	20	66	74	79	.268	.365	.441	126	18	5	3	-0	.967	14	*O-133/1-2	2.8
1984	SF-N	57	203	33	65	9	1	11	44	43	29	.320	.439	.537	179	23	1	1	-0	.990	1	O-54/1-4	2.2
1985	*StL-N★	126	442	71	124	26	3	22	87	83	88	.281	.397	.502	151	32	1	4	-2	.988	-11	*1-121,O-12	1.3
1986	StL-N	65	232	34	55	12	2	9	23	45	61	.237	.363	.422	117	6	1	1	-0	.995	-7	1-64	-0.5
1987	*StL-N★	131	419	93	120	23	1	35	106	**136**	139	.286	**.461**	**.597**	174	52	1	2	-1	.989	-8	*1-126/O-1	3.3
1988	NY-A	150	496	81	120	14	0	27	93	113	141	.242	.385	.433	130	24	3	2	-0	.951	-1	*D-112,O-19,1	1.9
1989	SD-N	142	455	76	110	19	1	26	94	**132**	145	.242	.413	.459	149	36	6	2	-1	.988	-1	*1-131,O-12	2.8
1990	SD-N	115	334	59	89	12	1	25	62	**104**	91	.266	.443	.533	166	36	4	3	-1	.994	-3	*1-110	2.5
1991	Bos-A	140	481	75	120	18	1	28	87	96	133	.249	.378	.466	126	19	0	2	-1	.000	0	*D-135	1.2
1992	Bos-A	81	257	32	54	11	0	5	33	56	87	.210	.356	.311	83	-4	1	1	-0	.992	-1	D-64,1-13	-0.8
Total	18	1994	6847	1118	1826	332	39	340	1180	1262	1441	.267	.383	.476	138	377	77	61	-14	.978	27	*O-1039,1-581,D/3	31.1

■ JIM CLARK Clark, James (b: James Petrosky) b: 9/21/27, Baggaley, Pa. BR/TR, 5'9", 150 lbs. Deb: 8/17/48

| 1948 | Was-A | 9 | 12 | 1 | 3 | 0 | 0 | 0 | 0 | 0 | 2 | .250 | .250 | .250 | 34 | -1 | 0 | 0 | 0 | 1.000 | -0 | /S-1,3-1 | -0.1 |

■ JIM CLARK Clark, James Edward b: 4/30/47, Kansas City, Kan. BR/TR, 6'1", 190 lbs. Deb: 7/16/71

| 1971 | Cle-A | 13 | 18 | 2 | 3 | 1 | 0 | 0 | 0 | 2 | 7 | .167 | .250 | .278 | 45 | -1 | 0 | 0 | 0 | 1.000 | 0 | /O-3,1-1 | -0.1 |

■ JIM CLARK Clark, James Francis b: 12/26/1887, Brooklyn, N.Y. d: 3/20/69, Beaumont, Tex. BR/TR, 5'11", 175 lbs. Deb: 9/2/11

1911	StL-N	14	18	2	3	0	1	0	3	3	4	.167	.286	.278	60	-1	2			1.000	-3	/O-8	-0.4
1912	StL-N	2	1	0	0	0	0	0	0	0	1	.000	.000	.000	-99	-0	0			.000	0	H	0.0
Total	2	16	19	2	3	0	1	0	3	3	5	.158	.273	.263	51	-1	2			1.000	-3	/O-8	-0.4

■ JERALD CLARK Clark, Jerald Dwayne b: 8/10/63, Crockett, Tex. BR/TR, 6'4", 189 lbs. Deb: 9/19/88 F

1988	SD-N	6	15	0	3	1	0	0	3	0	4	.200	.200	.267	33	-1	0	0	0	1.000	1	/O-4	0.0
1989	SD-N	17	41	5	8	2	0	1	7	3	9	.195	.250	.317	61	-2	0	1	-1	.947	-1	O-14	-0.4
1990	SD-N	53	101	12	27	4	1	5	11	5	24	.267	.302	.475	109	1	0	0	-0	1.000	-1	1-15,O-13	-0.1
1991	SD-N	118	369	26	84	16	0	10	47	31	90	.228	.290	.352	80	-10	2	1	0	.994	-3	O-96,1-16	-1.7
1992	SD-N	146	496	45	120	22	6	12	58	22	97	.242	.280	.383	85	-12	3	0	1	.990	12	*O-134,1-11	-0.1
1993	Col-N	140	478	65	135	26	6	13	67	20	60	.282	.325	.444	89	-9	9	6	-1	.966	2	O-96,1-37	-1.2
Total	6	480	1500	153	377	71	13	41	193	81	284	.251	.299	.398	86	-33	14	8	-1	.982	11	O-357/1-79	-3.5

■ CAP CLARK Clark, John Carrol b: 9/19/06, Snow Camp, N.C. d: 2/16/57, Fayetteville, N.C. BL/TR, 5'11", 180 lbs. Deb: 4/23/38

| 1938 | Phi-N | 52 | 74 | 11 | 19 | 1 | 1 | 0 | 4 | 9 | 10 | .257 | .337 | .297 | 78 | -2 | 0 | | | .936 | -3 | C-29 | -0.4 |

■ MEL CLARK Clark, Melvin Earl b: 7/7/26, Letart, W.Va. BR/TR, 6', 180 lbs. Deb: 9/11/51

1951	Phi-N	10	31	2	10	1	0	1	3	0	3	.323	.323	.452	108	0	0	1	-1	1.000	-1	/O-7	-0.1
1952	Phi-N	47	155	20	52	6	4	1	15	6	13	.335	.364	.445	125	5	2	1	-0	1.000	4	O-38/3-1	0.7
1953	Phi-N	60	198	31	59	10	4	0	19	11	17	.298	.338	.389	89	-3	1	0	0	.991	1	O-51	-0.3
1954	Phi-N	83	233	26	56	9	7	1	24	17	21	.240	.292	.352	67	-12	0	1	-1	.961	2	O-63	-1.2
1955	Phi-N	10	32	3	5	0	0	1	3	3	4	.156	.229	.250	27	-3	0	0	0	1.000	3	O-8	-0.1
1957	Det-A	5	7	0	0	0	0	0	1	0	3	.000	.000	.000	-97	-2	0	0	0	1.000	1	/O-2	-0.2
Total	6	215	656	82	182	29	15	3	63	37	61	.277	.318	.381	85	-15	3	3	-1	.983	10	O-169/3-1	-1.2

■ SPIDER CLARK Clark, Owen F. b: 9/16/1867, Brooklyn, N.Y. d: 2/8/1892, Brooklyn, N.Y. TR, 5'10", 150 lbs. Deb: 5/2/1889

1889	Was-N	38	145	19	37	7	2	3	22	6	18	.255	.285	.393	94	-2	8			.887	6	C-14,S-13/O32	0.5
1890	Buf-P	69	260	45	69	11	1	1	25	20	16	.265	.325	.327	81	-6	8			.938	-4	O-34,C-14,2/13SP	-0.8
Total	2	107	405	64	106	18	3	4	47	26	34	.262	.311	.351	86	-8	16			.952	2	/O-43,C-28,2S13PD	-0.3

■ PHIL CLARK Clark, Phillip Benjamin b: 5/6/68, Crockett, Tex. BR/TR, 6', 180 lbs. Deb: 5/27/92 F

1992	Det-A	23	54	3	22	4	1	5	6	9	.407	.467	.537	179	6	1	0	0	.931	-1	O-13/D-7	0.5
1993	SD-N	102	240	33	75	17	0	9	33	8	31	.313	.348	.496	121	6	2	0	1	.963	7	O-36,1-24,C/3	1.2
1994	SD-N	61	149	14	32	6	0	5	20	5	17	.215	.255	.356	57	-10	1	2	-1	.992	-2	1-24,O-17/C3	-1.4
Total	3	186	443	50	129	27	1	15	58	19	57	.291	.332	.454	106	2	4	2	0	.942	4	/O-66,1-48,CD3	0.3

■ BOBBY CLARK Clark, Robert Cale b: 6/13/55, Sacramento, Cal. BR/TR, 6', 190 lbs. Deb: 8/21/79

1979	*Cal-A	19	54	8	16	2	2	1	5	5	11	.296	.356	.463	123	1	1	1	-0	.978	2	O-19	0.3
1980	Cal-A	78	261	26	60	10	1	5	23	11	42	.230	.266	.333	65	-13	0	1	-1	.982	8	O-77	-0.9
1981	Cal-A	34	88	12	22	2	1	4	19	7	18	.250	.305	.432	110	1	0	0	0	1.000	0	O-34	0.0
1982	*Cal-A	102	90	11	19	1	0	2	8	0	29	.211	.211	.289	36	-8	1	0	0	1.000	-29	*O-102	-3.8
1983	Cal-A	76	212	17	49	9	1	5	21	9	45	.231	.262	.354	68	-10	0	0	0	1.000	-11	O-72/3-1,D	-2.2
1984	Mil-A	58	169	17	44	7	2	2	16	16	35	.260	.328	.361	94	-1	1	5	-3	.981	-10	O-56	-1.6
1985	Mil-A	29	93	6	21	3	0	0	8	7	19	.226	.280	.258	49	-6	1	1	-0	1.000	1	O-27	-0.7
Total	7	396	967	97	231	34	7	19	100	55	199	.239	.282	.347	74	-36	4	8	-4	.990	-39	O-387/D-2,3	-8.9

■ BOB CLARK Clark, Robert H. b: 3/18/1863, Covington, Ky. d: 8/21/19, Covington, Ky. BR/TR, 5'10", 175 lbs. Deb: 4/17/1886

1886	Bro-a	71	269	37	58	8	2	0	17			.216	.262	.260	63	-12	14			.864	-13	C-44,O-17,S	-1.7
1887	Bro-a	48	177	24	47	3	1	0	7			.266	.297	.294	64	-9	15			.871	-1	C-45/O-3	-0.5
1888	Bro-a	45	150	23	36	5	3	1	20	9		.240	.292	.333	100	-0	11			.884	-2	C-36/O-8,1	0.1
1889	*Bro-a	53	182	32	50	5	2	0	22	26	7	.275	.368	.324	98	0	18			.870	7	C-53	1.0
1890	*Bro-N	43	151	24	33	3	3	0	15	15	9	.219	.306	.278	70	-5	10			.836	-14	C-42/O-1	-1.4
1891	Cin-N	16	54	2	6	0	0	0	3	6	9	.111	.213	.111	-5	-7	3			.868	-5	C-16	-1.0
1893	Lou-N	12	28	3	3	0	0	0	3	5	5	.107	.242	.143	4	-4	0			.947	-2	C-10/O-1,S	-0.4
Total	7	288	1011	145	233	25	11	2	63	85	29	.230	.296	.280	71	-36	71			.867	-30	C-246/O-30,S1	-3.9

■ RON CLARK Clark, Ronald Bruce b: 1/14/43, Ft.Worth, Tex. BR/TR, 5'10", 175 lbs. Deb: 9/11/66 C

1966	Min-A	5	1	1	1	0	0	0	0	0	0	1.000	1.000	1.000	448	0	0	0	0	.000	0	/3-1	0.0
1967	Min-A	20	60	7	10	3	1	2	11	4	9	.167	.219	.350	61	-3	0	0	0	.891	-1	3-16	-0.5
1968	Min-A	104	227	14	42	5	1	6	13	16	44	.185	.245	.229	42	-16	3	2	-0	.932	-8	3-52,S-43,2	-2.2
1969	Min-A	5	8	0	1	0	0	0	0	0	0	.125	.125	.125	-29	-1	0	0	0	1.000	-1	/3-2	-0.2

YEAR	TM/L	G	AB	R	H	2B	3B	HR	RBI	BB	SO	AVG	OBP	SLG	PRO+	BR/A	SB	CS	SBR	FA	FR	G/POS	TPR
	Sea-A	57	163	9	32	5	0	0	12	13	29	.196	.260	.227	38	-13	1	0	0	.966	-9	S-38,3-15/21	-1.9
	Yr	62	171	9	33	5	0	0	12	13	29	.193	.254	.222	35	-15	1	0	0	.966	-10	S-38,3-17/21	-2.1
1971	Oak-A	2	1	0	0	0	0	0	0	1	0	.000	.500	.000	53	0	0	0	0	.000	0	H	0.0
1972	Oak-A	14	15	1	4	2	0	0	1	2	4	.267	.353	.400	130	1	0	0	0	1.000	0	2-11/3-3	0.1
	Mil-A	22	54	8	10	1	1	2	5	5	11	.185	.254	.352	81	-1	0	0	0	.963	5	2-11,3-10	0.5
	Yr	36	69	9	14	3	1	2	6	7	15	.203	.276	.362	92	-1	0	0	0	.974	6	2-22,3-13	0.6
1975	Phi-N	1	1	0	0	0	0	0	0	0	1	.000	.000	.000	-96	-0	0	0	0	.000	0	H	0.0
Total	7	230	530	40	100	16	3	5	43	41	98	.189	.251	.258	49	-34	4	2	0	.904	-13	/3-99,S-81,21	-4.2

■ ROY CLARK
Clark, Roy Elliott "Pepper" b: 5/11/1874, New Haven, Conn. d: 11/1/25, Bridgeport, Conn. BL/TR, 5'8", 170 lbs. Deb: 4/19/02

YEAR	TM/L	G	AB	R	H	2B	3B	HR	RBI	BB	SO	AVG	OBP	SLG	PRO+	BR/A	SB	CS	SBR	FA	FR	G/POS	TPR
1902	NY-N	21	76	4	11	1	0	0	3	1		.145	.156	.158	-3	-9	5			.962	-3	O-20	-1.4

■ WILL CLARK
Clark, William Nuschler b: 3/13/64, New Orleans, La. BL/TL, 6'2", 190 lbs. Deb: 4/8/86

YEAR	TM/L	G	AB	R	H	2B	3B	HR	RBI	BB	SO	AVG	OBP	SLG	PRO+	BR/A	SB	CS	SBR	FA	FR	G/POS	TPR
1986	SF-N	111	408	66	117	27	2	11	41	34	76	.287	.346	.444	122	11	4	7	-3	.989	-2	*1-102	0.0
1987	*SF-N	150	529	89	163	29	5	35	91	49	98	.308	.372	.580	155	40	5	17	-9	.991	2	*1-139	2.3
1988	SF-N★	162	575	102	162	31	6	29	**109**	**100**	129	.282	.392	.508	163	**49**	9	1	2	.993	-3	*1-158	3.8
1989	*SF-N★	159	588	**104**	196	38	9	23	111	74	103	.333	.412	.546	177	59	8	3	1	.994	0	*1-158	5.0
1990	SF-N★	154	600	91	177	25	5	19	95	62	97	.295	.364	.448	127	22	8	2	1	.992	1	*1-153	1.2
1991	SF-N★	148	565	84	170	32	7	29	116	51	91	.301	.361	**.536**	154	38	4	2	0	**.997**	3	*1-144	3.3
1992	SF-N★	144	513	69	154	40	1	16	73	73	82	.300	.392	.476	153	37	12	7	-1	.993	-0	*1-141	2.8
1993	SF-N	132	491	82	139	27	2	14	73	63	68	.283	.371	.432	118	14	2	2	-1	.988	-3	*1-129	0.0
1994	Tex-A★	110	389	73	128	24	2	13	80	71	59	.329	.436	.501	151	33	5	1	1	.990	-1	*1-107/D-1	2.4
Total	9	1270	4658	760	1406	273	39	189	789	577	803	.302	.383	.499	148	303	57	42	-8	.992	-0	*1-1231/D-1	20.8

■ WILLIE CLARK
Clark, William Otis "Wee Willie" b: 8/16/1872, Pittsburgh, Pa. d: 11/13/32, Pittsburgh, Pa. BL, Deb: 6/20/1895

YEAR	TM/L	G	AB	R	H	2B	3B	HR	RBI	BB	SO	AVG	OBP	SLG	PRO+	BR/A	SB	CS	SBR	FA	FR	G/POS	TPR
1895	NY-N	23	88	9	23	3	2	0	16	5	6	.261	.301	.341	67	-5	1			.974	1	1-23	-0.3
1896	NY-N	72	247	38	72	12	4	0	33	15	12	.291	.332	.372	94	-2	8			.975	-4	1-65	-0.5
1897	NY-N	116	431	63	122	17	12	1	75	37		.283	.352	.385	97	-2	18			.984	2	*1-107/O-7,3	0.1
1898	Pit-N	57	209	29	64	9	7	1	31	22		.306	.378	.431	134	9	0			.984	1	1-57	0.9
1899	Pit-N	80	298	49	85	13	10	0	44	35		.285	.379	.396	113	6	11			.989	1	1-78	0.7
Total	5	348	1273	188	366	54	35	2	199	114	18	.288	.359	.390	104	7	38			.983	0	1-330/O-7,3	0.9

■ BILL CLARK
Clark, William Winfield b: 4/11/1875, Circleville, Ohio d: 4/15/59, Los Angeles, Cal. BR/TR, 5'10", 175 lbs. Deb: 7/12/1897

YEAR	TM/L	G	AB	R	H	2B	3B	HR	RBI	BB	SO	AVG	OBP	SLG	PRO+	BR/A	SB	CS	SBR	FA	FR	G/POS	TPR
1897	Lou-N	4	16	2	3	0	0	0	3	0		.188	.235	.188	13	-2	1			.810	-1	/2-3,3-1	-0.3

■ ARTIE CLARKE
Clarke, Arthur Franklin b: 5/6/1865, Providence, R.I. d: 11/14/49, Brookline, Mass. BR/TR, 5'8", 155 lbs. Deb: 4/19/1890

YEAR	TM/L	G	AB	R	H	2B	3B	HR	RBI	BB	SO	AVG	OBP	SLG	PRO+	BR/A	SB	CS	SBR	FA	FR	G/POS	TPR
1890	NY-N	101	395	55	89	12	8	0	49	32	38	.225	.290	.296	71	-15	44			.908	-3	C-36,O-33,32/S	-1.3
1891	NY-N	48	174	17	33	2	2	0	21	15	16	.190	.254	.224	41	-13	5			.916	-12	C-42/3-5,O	-1.9
Total	2	149	569	72	122	14	10	0	70	47	54	.214	.279	.274	62	-28	49			.912	-15	/C-78,O-35,32S	-3.2

■ FRED CLARKE
Clarke, Fred Clifford "Cap" b: 10/3/1872, Winterset, Iowa d: 8/14/60, Winfield, Kan. BL/TR, 5'10.5", 165 lbs. Deb: 6/30/1894 FMCH

YEAR	TM/L	G	AB	R	H	2B	3B	HR	RBI	BB	SO	AVG	OBP	SLG	PRO+	BR/A	SB	CS	SBR	FA	FR	G/POS	TPR
1894	Lou-N	75	310	54	83	11	7	7	48	25	27	.268	.330	.416	85	-9	25			.885	4	O-75	-0.8
1895	Lou-N	132	550	96	191	21	5	4	82	34	24	.347	.396	.425	119	17	40			.881	11	*O-132	1.4
1896	Lou-N	131	517	96	168	15	18	9	79	43	34	.325	.392	.476	133	25	34			.908	-2	*O-131	1.2
1897	Lou-N	128	518	120	202	30	13	6	67	45		.390	.462	.533	**168**	**53**	57			.926	6	*O-127,M	4.2
1898	Lou-N	149	599	116	184	23	12	3	47	48		.307	.373	.401	124	19	40			.940	6	*O-149,M	1.3
1899	Lou-N	148	602	122	206	23	9	5	70	49		.342	.406	.435	131	27	49			.964	1	*O-144/S-3M	1.5
1900	Pit-N	106	399	84	110	15	12	3	32	51		.276	.368	.396	110	6	21			.944	3	*O-104,M	0.1
1901	Pit-N	129	527	118	171	24	15	6	60	51		.324	.395	.461	143	30	23			.970	2	*O-127/S-1,3M	2.1
1902	Pit-N	113	459	103	145	27	14	2	53	51		.316	.401	.449	157	32	29			.958	-1	*O-113,M	2.4
1903	*Pit-N	104	427	88	150	**32**	15	5	70	41		.351	.414	**.532**	164	34	21			.962	-8	*O-101/S-2M	1.9
1904	Pit-N	72	278	51	85	7	11	0	25	22		.306	.367	.410	136	12	11			.979	0	O-70,M	0.8
1905	Pit-N	141	525	95	157	18	15	2	51	55		.299	.368	.402	126	17	24			.976	4	*O-137,M	1.5
1906	Pit-N	118	417	69	129	14	**13**	1	39	40		.309	.371	.412	138	18	18			.974	0	*O-110,M	2.0
1907	Pit-N	148	501	97	145	18	13	2	59	59		.289	.383	.389	140	25	37			**.987**	6	*O-144,M	2.9
1908	Pit-N	151	551	83	146	18	15	2	53	65		.265	.349	.363	127	18	24			.973	10	*O-151,M	2.5
1909	*Pit-N	152	550	97	158	16	11	3	68	**80**		.287	.384	.373	124	18	31			**.987**	7	*O-152,M	2.1
1910	Pit-N	123	429	57	113	23	9	2	63	53	23	.263	.350	.373	105	2	12			.967	0	*O-118,M	0.0
1911	Pit-N	110	392	73	127	25	13	5	49	53	27	.324	.407	.492	146	24	10			.970	0	*O-101,M	1.9
1913	Pit-N	9	13	0	1	1	0	0	0	0	0	.077	.077	.154	-37	-2	0			1.000	-1	/O-2,M	-0.3
1914	Pit-N	2	2	0	0	0	0	0	0	0	0	.000	.000	.000	-99	-0	0			.000	0	HM	-0.1
1915	Pit-N	1	2	0	1	0	0	0	0	0	0	.500	.500	.500	206	0	0			.000	-1	/O-1,M	0.0
Total	21	2242	8568	1619	2672	361	220	67	1015	874	135	.312	.386	.429	132	366	506			.952	59	*O-2189/S-6,3	28.6

■ HARRY CLARKE
Clarke, Harry Corson b: 1861, d: 3/3/23, Long Beach, Cal. Deb: 8/28/1889

YEAR	TM/L	G	AB	R	H	2B	3B	HR	RBI	BB	SO	AVG	OBP	SLG	PRO+	BR/A	SB	CS	SBR	FA	FR	G/POS	TPR
1889	Was-N	1	3	0	0	0	0	0	0	0	1	.000	.000	.000	-99	-1	0			1.000	1	/O-1	0.0

■ HENRY CLARKE
Clarke, Henry Tefft b: 8/28/1875, Bellevue, Neb. d: 3/28/50, Colorado Springs, Colo. BR/TR, Deb: 6/26/1897

YEAR	TM/L	G	AB	R	H	2B	3B	HR	RBI	BB	SO	AVG	OBP	SLG	PRO+	BR/A	SB	CS	SBR	FA	FR	G/POS	TPR
1897	Cle-N	7	25	3	7	0	0	0	3	2		.280	.333	.280	60	-1	0			.714	-1	/P-5,O-2	-0.1
1898	Chi-N	2	4	0	1	0	0	0	0	1		.250	.400	.250	87	0	0			.000	-1	/O-1,P-1	-0.1
Total	2	9	29	3	8	0	0	0	3	3		.276	.344	.276	64	-1	0			.750	-2	/P-6,O-3	-0.2

■ HORACE CLARKE
Clarke, Horace Meredith b: 6/2/40, Frederiksted, St.Croix, V.I. BB/TR, 5'9", 178 lbs. Deb: 5/13/65

YEAR	TM/L	G	AB	R	H	2B	3B	HR	RBI	BB	SO	AVG	OBP	SLG	PRO+	BR/A	SB	CS	SBR	FA	FR	G/POS	TPR
1965	NY-A	51	108	13	28	1	0	1	9	6	6	.259	.298	.296	70	-4	2	1	0	.923	3	3-17/2-7,S	-0.2
1966	NY-A	96	312	37	83	10	4	6	28	27	24	.266	.326	.381	107	2	5	3	-0	.970	-19	S-63,2-16/3	-1.1
1967	NY-A	143	588	74	160	17	0	3	29	42	64	.272	.321	.316	92	-6	21	4	4	**.990**	15	*2-140	2.5
1968	NY-A	148	579	52	133	6	1	2	26	23	46	.230	.259	.254	58	-30	20	7	2	.984	**30**	*2-139	1.1
1969	NY-A	156	641	82	183	26	7	4	48	53	41	.285	.340	.367	101	1	33	13	2	.982	-4	*2-156	1.2
1970	NY-A	158	686	81	172	24	4	4	46	35	35	.251	.289	.309	68	-31	23	7	3	.979	-7	*2-157	-2.2
1971	NY-A	159	625	76	156	23	7	2	41	64	43	.250	.321	.318	87	-11	17	7	1	.981	-3	*2-156	0.1
1972	NY-A	147	547	65	132	20	2	3	37	56	44	.241	.316	.302	87	-8	18	6	2	.985	6	*2-143	1.0
1973	NY-A	148	590	60	155	21	0	2	35	47	48	.263	.319	.308	80	-15	11	10	-3	.979	8	*2-147	-0.1
1974	NY-A	24	47	3	11	1	0	0	4	4	5	.234	.294	.255	61	-2	1	0	0	1.000	-4	2-20/D-1	-0.7
	SD-N	42	90	5	17	1	0	0	4	8	6	.189	.255	.200	30	-8	0	0	0	.978	-4	2-21	-1.3
Total	10	1272	4813	548	1230	150	23	27	304	365	362	.256	.310	.313	82	-112	151	58	11	.983	19	*2-1102/S-64,3D	0.3

■ NIG CLARKE
Clarke, Jay Justin b: 12/15/1882, Amherstburg, Ont., Canada d: 6/15/49, River Rouge, Mich BL/TR, 5'8", 165 lbs. Deb: 4/26/05

YEAR	TM/L	G	AB	R	H	2B	3B	HR	RBI	BB	SO	AVG	OBP	SLG	PRO+	BR/A	SB	CS	SBR	FA	FR	G/POS	TPR
1905	Cle-A	5	9	2	1	1	0	0	1			.111	.200	.222	33	-1	0			1.000	0	/C-5	-0.2
	Det-A	3	7	1	3	0	0	1	0			.429	.500	.857	326	2	0			1.000	0	/C-2	0.3
	Cle-A	37	114	9	23	5	1	0	8	10		.202	.266	.263	67	-4	0			.961	-1	C-37	-0.2
	Yr	45	130	12	27	6	1	1	9	11		.208	.275	.292	79	-3	0			.965	-2	C-44	-0.1
1906	Cle-A	57	179	22	64	12	4	1	21	13		.358	.404	.486	181	16	3			.982	-0	C-54	2.2
1907	Cle-A	120	390	44	105	19	6	3	33	35		.269	.333	.333	124	10	3			.961	-11	*C-115	1.1
1908	Cle-A	97	290	34	70	8	6	1	27	30		.241	.315	.321	106	6	6			.969	-8	C-90	0.3
1909	Cle-A	55	164	15	45	4	2	0	14	9		.274	.316	.323	98	-1	1			.952	-3	C-44	0.1

YEAR	TM/L	G	AB	R	H	2B	3B	HR	RBI	BB	SO	AVG	OBP	SLG	PRO+	BR/A	SB	CS	SBR	FA	FR	G/POS	TPR
1910	Cle-A	21	58	4	9	2	0	0	2	8		.155	.258	.190	40	-4	0			.974	3	C-17	0.0
1911	StL-A	82	256	22	55	10	1	0	18	26		.215	.287	.262	56	-15	2			.926	-5	C-73/1-4	-1.3
1919	Phi-N	26	62	4	15	3	0	0	2	4	5	.242	.299	.290	72	-2	1			.969	0	C-22	0.0
1920	Pit-N	3	7	0	0	0	0	0	0	2	4	.000	.222	.000	-32	-1	0	0	0	1.000	1	/C-3	0.0
Total	9	506	1536	157	390	64	20	6	127	138	9	.254	.318	.333	102	3	16	0		.960	-25	C-462/1-4	2.3

■ JOSH CLARKE
Clarke, Joshua Baldwin "Pepper"   b: 3/8/1879, Winfield, Kan.   d: 7/2/62, Ventura, Cal.   BL/TR, 5'10", 180 lbs.   Deb: 6/15/1898   F

YEAR	TM/L	G	AB	R	H	2B	3B	HR	RBI	BB	SO	AVG	OBP	SLG	PRO+	BR/A	SB	CS	SBR	FA	FR	G/POS	TPR
1898	Lou-N	6	18	0	3	0	0	0		1		.167	.211	.167	9	-2	0			.917	-1	/O-5	-0.3
1905	StL-N	50	167	31	43	3	2	3	18	27		.257	.361	.353	117	4	8			.942	-8	O-26,2-16/S	-0.5
1908	Cle-A	131	492	70	119	8	4	1	21	76		.242	.348	.280	104	6	37			.963	-3	*O-131	-0.2
1909	Cle-A	4	12	1	0	0	0	0	0	2		.000	.143	.000	-52	-2	0			.600	-2	/O-4	-0.4
1911	Bos-N	32	120	16	28	7	3	1	4	29	22	.233	.387	.367	103	1	6			.938	4	O-30	0.3
Total	5	223	809	118	193	18	9	5	43	135	22	.239	.351	.302	102	8	51			.949	-9	O-196/2-16,S	-1.1

■ GREY CLARKE
Clarke, Richard Grey "Noisy"   b: 9/26/12, Fulton, Ala.   BR/TR, 5'9", 183 lbs.   Deb: 4/19/44

YEAR	TM/L	G	AB	R	H	2B	3B	HR	RBI	BB	SO	AVG	OBP	SLG	PRO+	BR/A	SB	CS	SBR	FA	FR	G/POS	TPR
1944	Chi-A	63	169	14	44	10	1	0	27	22	6	.260	.352	.331	97	0	0	4	-2	.941	1	3-45	-0.1

■ SUMPTER CLARKE
Clarke, Sumpter Mills   b: 10/18/1897, Savannah, Ga.   d: 3/16/62, Knoxville, Tenn.   BR/TR, 5'11", 170 lbs.   Deb: 9/27/20   F

YEAR	TM/L	G	AB	R	H	2B	3B	HR	RBI	BB	SO	AVG	OBP	SLG	PRO+	BR/A	SB	CS	SBR	FA	FR	G/POS	TPR
1920	Chi-N	1	3	0	1	0	0	0	0	0	1	.333	.333	.333	90	-0	0	0	0	1.000	-0	/3-1	0.0
1923	Cle-A	1	3	0	0	0	0	0	0	0	0	.000	.000	.000	-99	-1	0	0	0	1.000	-0	/O-1	-0.1
1924	Cle-A	35	104	17	24	6	1	0	11	6	12	.231	.273	.308	49	-8	0	0	0	1.000	-5	O-33	-1.5
Total	3	37	110	17	25	6	1	0	11	6	13	.227	.267	.300	46	-9	0	0	0	1.000	-6	O-34,3-1	-1.6

■ TOMMY CLARKE
Clarke, Thomas Aloysius   b: 5/9/1888, New York, N.Y.   d: 8/14/45, Corona, N.Y.   BR/TR, 5'11", 175 lbs.   Deb: 8/26/09

YEAR	TM/L	G	AB	R	H	2B	3B	HR	RBI	BB	SO	AVG	OBP	SLG	PRO+	BR/A	SB	CS	SBR	FA	FR	G/POS	TPR
1909	Cin-N	18	52	8	13	3	2	0	10	6		.250	.328	.385	122	1	3			.965	5	C-17	0.8
1910	Cin-N	64	151	19	42	6	5	1	20	19	17	.278	.370	.404	131	6	1			.971	-1	C-56	1.0
1911	Cin-N	86	203	20	49	6	7	1	25	25	22	.241	.328	.355	94	-2	4			.970	2	C-81/1-1	0.7
1912	Cin-N	72	146	19	41	7	2	0	22	28	14	.281	.400	.356	111	4	9			.983	5	C-63	1.3
1913	Cin-N	114	330	29	87	11	8	1	38	39	40	.264	.345	.355	100	1	2			.979	-13	*C-100	-0.3
1914	Cin-N	113	313	30	82	13	7	2	25	31	30	.262	.332	.367	105	3	6			.973	-4	*C-106	0.7
1915	Cin-N	96	226	23	65	7	2	0	21	33	22	.288	.381	.336	116	6	7	3	0	.981	-4	C-72	0.8
1916	Cin-N	78	177	10	42	10	1	0	17	24	20	.237	.328	.305	97	0	0			.965	-10	C-51	-0.7
1917	Cin-N	58	110	11	32	3	3	1	13	11	12	.291	.361	.400	139	5	2			.991	-5	C-29	0.2
1918	Cin-N	1	0	0	0	0	0	0				—	—	—		0	0			.000	0	/C-1	0.0
Total	10	700	1708	169	453	66	37	6	191	216	177	.265	.351	.358	109	24	42	3		.975	-26	C-576/1-1	4.5

■ BOILERYARD CLARKE
Clarke, William Jones   b: 10/18/1868, New York, N.Y.   d: 7/29/59, Princeton, N.J.   BR/TR, 5'11.5", 170 lbs.   Deb: 5/1/1893

YEAR	TM/L	G	AB	R	H	2B	3B	HR	RBI	BB	SO	AVG	OBP	SLG	PRO+	BR/A	SB	CS	SBR	FA	FR	G/POS	TPR
1893	Bal-N	49	183	23	32	1	3	1	24	19	14	.175	.274	.230	34	-18	2			.909	-3	C-38,1-11	-1.4
1894	Bal-N	28	100	18	24	8	0	1	19	16	14	.240	.361	.350	69	-5	2			.903	-3	C-23/1-5	-0.4
1895	*Bal-N	67	241	38	70	15	3	0	35	13	18	.290	.350	.378	85	-6	8			.938	6	C-60/1-6	0.5
1896	Bal-N	80	300	48	89	14	7	2	71	14	12	.297	.345	.410	97	-2	7			.948	-11	C-67,1-14	-0.5
1897	*Bal-N	64	241	32	65	7	1	1	38	9		.270	.320	.320	69	-11	5			.939	-15	C-59/1-4	-1.6
1898	Bal-N	82	285	26	69	5	2	0	27	4		.242	.289	.274	60	-15	3			.962	3	C-70,1-10	-0.4
1899	Bos-N	60	223	25	50	3	2	2	32	10		.224	.270	.283	47	-17	2			.940	-1	C-60	-1.2
1900	Bos-N	81	270	35	85	15	2	1	30	9		.315	.344	.359	84	-7	0			.928	7	C-67/1-8	0.6
1901	Was-A	110	422	58	118	15	5	3	54	23		.280	.335	.360	94	-3	7			.952	-9	*C-107/1-3	-0.1
1902	Was-A	87	291	31	78	15	0	6	40	23		.268	.330	.381	96	-2	1			**.972**	-3	C-87	0.4
1903	Was-A	126	465	35	111	14	6	2	38	15		.239	.273	.308	72	-16	12			.981	-11	1-88,C-37	-2.5
1904	Was-A	85	275	23	58	8	1	0	17	17		.211	.269	.247	65	-10	1			.977	0	C-52,1-29	-0.6
1905	NY-N	31	50	2	9	1	0	0	4	4		.180	.241	.240	42	-4	1			.973	-1	1-15,C-12	-0.4
Total	13	950	3346	394	858	110	32	20	429	176	58	.256	.310	.326	75	-115	54			.947	-39	C-739,1-193	-7.6

■ STU CLARKE
Clarke, William Stuart   b: 1/24/06, San Francisco, Cal   d: 8/26/85, Hayward, Cal.   BR/TR, 5'8.5", 160 lbs.   Deb: 7/17/29

YEAR	TM/L	G	AB	R	H	2B	3B	HR	RBI	BB	SO	AVG	OBP	SLG	PRO+	BR/A	SB	CS	SBR	FA	FR	G/POS	TPR
1929	Pit-N	57	178	20	47	5	7	2	21	19	21	.264	.338	.404	81	-5	3			.919	-3	S-41,3-15/2	-0.8
1930	Pit-N	4	9	2	4	0	1	0	2	1	0	.444	.500	.667	178	1	0			1.000	-1	/2-2	0.0
Total	2	61	187	22	51	5	8	2	23	20	21	.273	.346	.417	86	-4	3			1.000	-9	/S-41,3-15,2	-0.8

■ BUZZ CLARKSON
Clarkson, James Buster   b: 3/13/18, Hopkins, S.C.   d: 1/18/89, Jeannette, Pa.   BR/TR, 5'11", 210 lbs.   Deb: 4/30/52

YEAR	TM/L	G	AB	R	H	2B	3B	HR	RBI	BB	SO	AVG	OBP	SLG	PRO+	BR/A	SB	CS	SBR	FA	FR	G/POS	TPR
1952	Bos-N	14	25	3	5	0	0	0	1	3	3	.200	.286	.200	38	-2	0	0	0	.938	-2	/S-6,3-2	-0.4

■ ELLIS CLARY
Clary, Ellis "Cat"   b: 9/11/16, Valdosta, Ga.   BR/TR, 5'8", 160 lbs.   Deb: 6/7/42   C

YEAR	TM/L	G	AB	R	H	2B	3B	HR	RBI	BB	SO	AVG	OBP	SLG	PRO+	BR/A	SB	CS	SBR	FA	FR	G/POS	TPR
1942	Was-A	76	240	34	66	9	0	0	16	45	25	.275	.394	.313	101	3	2		1	.969	-17	2-69/3-2	-0.9
1943	Was-A	73	254	36	65	19	1	0	19	44	31	.256	.370	.339	112	6	8	4	0	.945	-8	3-68/S-1	-0.1
	StL-A	23	69	15	19	2	0	0	5	11	6	.275	.375	.304	98	0	1	2	-1	.972	-1	3-14/2-3	-0.1
	Yr	96	323	51	84	21	1	0	24	55	37	.260	.371	.331	109	6	9	6	-1	.949	-9	3-82/2-3,S	-0.2
1944	*StL-A	25	49	6	13	1	1	0	4	12	9	.265	.410	.327	106	1	0	0		1.000	-1	3-11/2-6	0.0
1945	StL-A	26	38	6	8	1	0	1	2	2	3	.211	.250	.316	61	-2	0	2	-1	.947	3	3-16/2-3	-0.1
Total	4	223	650	97	171	32	2	1	46	114	74	.263	.376	.323	103	8	12	8	-1	.953	-25	3-111/2-81,S	-1.1

■ DAIN CLAY
Clay, Dain Elmer "Sniffy" or "Ding-A-Ling"   b: 7/10/19, Hicksville, Ohio   BR/TR, 5'10.5", 160 lbs.   Deb: 6/12/43

YEAR	TM/L	G	AB	R	H	2B	3B	HR	RBI	BB	SO	AVG	OBP	SLG	PRO+	BR/A	SB	CS	SBR	FA	FR	G/POS	TPR
1943	Cin-N	49	93	19	25	2	4	0	9	8	14	.269	.333	.376	106	1	1			.936	-9	O-33	-1.0
1944	Cin-N	110	356	51	89	15	0	0	17	17	18	.250	.290	.292	67	-16	8			.993	-2	O-98	-2.3
1945	Cin-N	153	656	81	184	29	2	1	50	37	58	.280	.321	.335	84	-15	19			.989	6	*O-152	-1.7
1946	Cin-N	121	435	52	99	17	0	2	22	53	40	.228	.318	.280	73	-14	11			**.988**	7	*O-120	-1.3
Total	4	433	1540	203	397	63	6	3	98	115	130	.258	.314	.312	79	-44	39			.987	3	O-403	-6.3

■ BILL CLAY
Clay, Frederick C.   b: 11/23/1874, Baltimore, Md.   d: 10/12/17, York, Pa.   TR,   Deb: 8/8/02

YEAR	TM/L	G	AB	R	H	2B	3B	HR	RBI	BB	SO	AVG	OBP	SLG	PRO+	BR/A	SB	CS	SBR	FA	FR	G/POS	TPR
1902	Phi-N	3	8	1	2	0	0	0	1	0		.250	.250	.250	54	-0	0			.750	-1	/O-3	-0.2

■ ROYCE CLAYTON
Clayton, Royce Spencer   b: 1/2/70, Burbank, Cal.   BR/TR, 6', 175 lbs.   Deb: 9/20/91

YEAR	TM/L	G	AB	R	H	2B	3B	HR	RBI	BB	SO	AVG	OBP	SLG	PRO+	BR/A	SB	CS	SBR	FA	FR	G/POS	TPR
1991	SF-N	9	26	0	3	1	0	0	2	1	6	.115	.148	.154	-15	-4	0	0	0	.880	-6	/S-8	-1.0
1992	SF-N	98	321	31	72	7	4	4	24	26	63	.224	.280	.308	71	-13	8	4	0	.973	-9	S-94/3-1	-1.6
1993	SF-N	153	549	54	155	21	5	6	70	38	91	.282	.334	.372	91	-7	11	10	-3	.963	1	*S-153	0.3
1994	SF-N	108	385	38	91	14	5	3	30	30	74	.236	.297	.327	65	-20	23	3	5	.973	7	*S-108	0.3
Total	4	368	1281	123	321	43	15	13	126	95	234	.251	.306	.338	76	-43	42	17	2	.967	-8	S-363/3-1	-2.3

■ CHET CLEMENS
Clemens, Chester Spurgeon   b: 5/10/17, San Fernando, Cal.   BR/TR, 6', 175 lbs.   Deb: 9/13/39

YEAR	TM/L	G	AB	R	H	2B	3B	HR	RBI	BB	SO	AVG	OBP	SLG	PRO+	BR/A	SB	CS	SBR	FA	FR	G/POS	TPR
1939	Bos-N	9	23	2	5	0	0	0	1	3	1	.217	.250	.217	29	-2	1			.867	-1	/O-7	-0.4
1944	Bos-N	19	17	7	3	1	1	0	2	2	4	.176	.263	.353	69	-1	0			1.000	-2	/O-7	-0.3
Total	2	28	40	9	8	1	1	0	3	5	5	.200	.256	.275	46	-3	1			.905	-3	/O-14	-0.7

■ CLEM CLEMENS
Clemens, Clement Lambert "Count" (b: Clement Lambert Ulatowski)
b: 11/21/1886, Chicago, Ill.   d: 11/2/67, St.Petersburg, Fla.   BR/TR, 5'11", 176 lbs.   Deb: 5/15/14

YEAR	TM/L	G	AB	R	H	2B	3B	HR	RBI	BB	SO	AVG	OBP	SLG	PRO+	BR/A	SB	CS	SBR	FA	FR	G/POS	TPR
1914	Chi-F	13	27	4	4	0	0	0	2	3	0	.148	.233	.148	0	-4	0			.950	-1	/C-8	-0.5
1915	Chi-F	11	22	3	3	0	0	0	3	1	0	.136	.174	.182	-5	-3	0			1.000	-1	/C-9,2-2	-0.4

YEAR	TM/L	G	AB	R	H	2B	3B	HR	RBI	BB	SO	AVG	OBP	SLG	PRO+	BR/A	SB	CS	SBR	FA	FR	G/POS	TPR
1916	Chi-N	10	15	0	0	0	0	0	0	1	6	.000	.063	.000	-72	-3	0			.941	1	/C-9	-0.2
Total	3	34	64	7	7	1	0	0	5	5	6	.109	.174	.125	-18	-10	0			.962	-1	/C-26,2-2	-1.1

■ DOUG CLEMENS
Clemens, Douglas Horace b: 6/9/39, Leesport, Pa. BL/TR, 6', 180 lbs. Deb: 10/2/60

YEAR	TM/L	G	AB	R	H	2B	3B	HR	RBI	BB	SO	AVG	OBP	SLG	PRO+	BR/A	SB	CS	SBR	FA	FR	G/POS	TPR
1960	StL-N	1	0	0	0	0	0	0	0	0	0	—	—	—	—	0	0	0	0	1.000	0	/O-1	0.0
1961	StL-N	6	12	1	2	1	0	0	0	3	1	.167	.333	.250	53	-1	0	0	0	.667	-1	/O-3	-0.2
1962	StL-N	48	93	12	22	1	1	1	12	17	19	.237	.355	.301	71	-3	0	0	0	.974	-6	O-34	-1.1
1963	StL-N	5	6	1	1	0	0	1	2	1	2	.167	.286	.667	151	0	0	0	0	1.000	0	/O-3	0.1
1964	StL-N	33	78	8	16	4	3	1	9	6	16	.205	.271	.372	73	-3	0	0	0	.970	0	O-22	-0.4
	Chi-N	54	140	23	39	10	2	2	12	18	22	.279	.365	.421	116	3	0	0	0	.923	0	O-40	0.2
	Yr	87	218	31	55	14	5	3	21	24	38	.252	.332	.404	100	0	0	0	0	.937	1	O-62	-0.2
1965	Chi-N	128	340	36	75	11	0	4	26	38	53	.221	.303	.288	66	-15	5	8	-3	.981	-6	*O-105	-2.9
1966	Phi-N	79	121	10	31	1	0	1	15	16	25	.256	.353	.289	81	-2	1	0	0	1.000	-1	O-28/1-1	-0.4
1967	Phi-N	69	73	2	13	5	0	0	4	8	15	.178	.268	.247	48	-5	0	0	0	1.000	-3	O-10	-0.8
1968	Phi-N	29	57	6	12	1	1	2	8	7	13	.211	.297	.368	99	-0	0	0	0	1.000	-1	O-17	-0.2
Total	9	452	920	99	211	34	7	12	88	114	166	.229	.319	.321	78	-25	6	8	-3	.969	-16	O-263/1-1	-5.7

■ BOB CLEMENS
Clemens, Robert Baxter b: 8/9/1886, Mt.Hebron, Mo. d: 4/5/64, Marshall, Mo. BR/TR, 5'9", 163 lbs. Deb: 9/17/14

YEAR	TM/L	G	AB	R	H	2B	3B	HR	RBI	BB	SO	AVG	OBP	SLG	PRO+	BR/A	SB	CS	SBR	FA	FR	G/POS	TPR
1914	StL-A	7	13	1	3	0	1	0	3	2	1	.231	.375	.385	133	1	0	2	-1	.750	-1	/O-5	-0.2

■ WALLY CLEMENT
Clement, Wallace Oakes b: 7/21/1881, Auburn, Me. d: 11/1/53, Coral Gables, Fla. BL/TR, 5'11", 175 lbs. Deb: 8/17/08

YEAR	TM/L	G	AB	R	H	2B	3B	HR	RBI	BB	SO	AVG	OBP	SLG	PRO+	BR/A	SB	CS	SBR	FA	FR	G/POS	TPR
1908	Phi-N	16	36	0	8	3	0	0				.222	.222	.306	66	-2	2			1.000	4	/O-8	0.2
1909	Phi-N	3	3	0	0	0	0	0				.000	.000	.000	-99	-1	0			.000	0	H	-0.1
	Bro-N	92	340	35	88	8	4	0	17	18		.259	.296	.306	90	-5	11			.965	4	O-88	-0.5
	Yr	95	343	35	88	8	4	0	17	18		.257	.294	.303	88	-6	11			.965	4	O-88	-0.6
Total	2	111	379	35	96	11	4	0	18	18		.253	.287	.303	86	-7	13			.970	8	/O-96	-0.4

■ ROBERTO CLEMENTE
Clemente, Roberto (Walker) "Bob" b: 8/18/34, Carolina, P.R. d: 12/31/72, San Juan, P.R. BR/TR, 5'11", 175 lbs. Deb: 4/17/55 H

YEAR	TM/L	G	AB	R	H	2B	3B	HR	RBI	BB	SO	AVG	OBP	SLG	PRO+	BR/A	SB	CS	SBR	FA	FR	G/POS	TPR
1955	Pit-N	124	474	48	121	23	11	5	47	18	60	.255	.285	.382	76	-17	2	5	-2	.978	12	*O-118	-1.4
1956	Pit-N	147	543	66	169	30	7	7	60	13	58	.311	.332	.431	105	3	6	6	-2	.957	2	*O-139/2-2,3	-0.4
1957	Pit-N	111	451	42	114	17	7	4	30	23	45	.253	.289	.348	72	-18	0	4	-2	.979	13	*O-109	-1.4
1958	Pit-N	140	519	69	150	24	10	6	50	31	41	.289	.329	.408	96	-4	8	2	1	.982	25	*O-135	1.6
1959	Pit-N	105	432	60	128	17	7	4	50	15	51	.296	.329	.431	91	-6	2	3	-1	.948	9	*O-104	-0.3
1960	*Pit-N★	144	570	89	179	22	6	16	94	39	72	.314	.360	.458	121	16	4	5	-2	.971	3	*O-142	1.1
1961	Pit-N★	146	572	100	201	30	10	23	89	35	59	.351	.392	.559	148	38	4	1	1	.969	14	*O-144	4.4
1962	Pit-N★	144	538	95	168	28	9	10	74	35	73	.312	.355	.454	115	11	6	4	0	.973	13	*O-142	1.5
1963	Pit-N★	152	600	77	192	23	8	17	76	31	64	.320	.357	.470	135	26	12	2	2	.958	-3	*O-151	1.9
1964	Pit-N★	155	622	95	211	40	7	12	87	51	87	.339	.391	.484	145	37	5	2	0	.968	11	*O-154	4.2
1965	Pit-N★	152	589	91	194	21	14	10	65	43	78	.329	.380	.463	136	28	8	0	2	.968	9	*O-145	3.4
1966	Pit-N★	154	638	105	202	31	11	29	119	46	109	.317	.363	.536	146	38	7	5	-1	.965	15	*O-154	4.6
1967	Pit-N★	147	585	103	209	26	10	23	110	41	103	.357	.402	.554	170	52	9	1	2	.970	9	*O-145	5.8
1968	Pit-N	132	502	74	146	18	12	18	57	51	77	.291	.357	.482	152	31	2	3	-1	.984	12	*O-131	3.9
1969	Pit-N★	138	507	87	175	20	12	19	91	56	73	.345	.413	.544	170	47	4	1	1	.980	7	*O-135	4.9
1970	*Pit-N★	108	412	65	145	22	10	14	60	38	66	.352	.409	.556	159	34	3	0	1	.966	7	*O-104	3.5
1971	*Pit-N★	132	522	82	178	29	8	13	86	26	65	.341	.372	.502	146	29	1	2	-1	.993	10	*O-124	3.5
1972	*Pit-N†	102	378	68	118	19	7	10	60	29	49	.312	.361	.479	140	18	0	0	0	1.000	6	O-94	2.1
Total	18	2433	9454	1416	3000	440	166	240	1305	621	1230	.317	.362	.475	130	363	83	46	-3	.973	175	*O-2370/2-2,3	42.9

■ ED CLEMENTS
Clements, Edward b: Philadelphia, Pa. Deb: 6/24/1890

YEAR	TM/L	G	AB	R	H	2B	3B	HR	RBI	BB	SO	AVG	OBP	SLG	PRO+	BR/A	SB	CS	SBR	FA	FR	G/POS	TPR
1890	Pit-N	1	1	0	0	0	0	0	0	0	0	.000	.000	.000	-99	-0	0			.400	-0	/S-1	-0.1

■ JACK CLEMENTS
Clements, John J. b: 7/24/1864, Philadelphia, Pa. d: 5/23/41, Norristown, Pa. BL/TL, 5'8.5", 204 lbs. Deb: 4/22/1884 M

YEAR	TM/L	G	AB	R	H	2B	3B	HR	RBI	BB	SO	AVG	OBP	SLG	PRO+	BR/A	SB	CS	SBR	FA	FR	G/POS	TPR
1884	Phi-U	41	177	37	50	13	2	3		9		.282	.317	.429	109	2				.764	1	O-22,C-20/S	0.3
	Phi-N	9	30	3	7	0	0	0	0	4	8	.233	.324	.233	82	-0				.827	1	/C-9	0.1
1885	Phi-N	52	188	14	36	11	3	1	14	2	30	.191	.200	.298	61	-8				.891	-8	C-41,O-11	-1.2
1886	Phi-N	54	185	15	38	5	1	0	11	7	34	.205	.234	.243	45	-12	4			.930	12	C-47/O-7	0.4
1887	Phi-N	66	246	48	69	13	7	1	47	9	24	.280	.317	.402	93	-3	7			.940	9	C-59/3-4,S	0.9
1888	Phi-N	86	326	26	80	8	4	1	32	10	36	.245	.276	.304	81	-8	3			.927	-1	C-85/O-1	0.0
1889	Phi-N	78	310	51	88	17	1	4	35	29	21	.284	.347	.384	96	-3	3			.916	-7	C-78	-0.2
1890	Phi-N	97	381	64	120	23	8	7	74	45	30	.315	.392	.472	148	22	10			.944	3	C-91/1-5M	2.9
1891	Phi-N	107	423	58	131	29	4	4	75	43	19	.310	.380	.426	131	16	3			.927	-5	*C-107/1-2	1.9
1892	Phi-N	109	402	50	106	25	6	8	76	43	40	.264	.339	.415	128	13	7			.950	6	*C-109	2.4
1893	Phi-N	94	376	64	107	20	3	17	80	39	29	.285	.360	.488	125	11	3			.942	-12	*C-92/1-1	0.6
1894	Phi-N	45	159	26	55	6	5	3	36	24	7	.346	.455	.503	134	11	6			.946	-2	C-45	1.0
1895	Phi-N	88	322	64	127	27	2	13	75	22	7	.394	.446	.612	170	32	3			.969	-10	*C-88	2.4
1896	Phi-N	57	184	35	66	5	7	5	45	17	14	.359	.427	.543	157	15	2			.966	-4	C-53	1.4
1897	Phi-N	55	185	18	44	4	2	6	36	12		.238	.305	.378	82	-6	3			.962	-2	C-49	-0.2
1898	StL-N	99	335	39	86	19	5	3	41	21		.257	.314	.370	94	-4	1			.971	-6	C-86	-0.2
1899	Cle-N	4	12	1	3	0	0	0	0			.250	.308	.250	58	-1	0			.938	0	/C-4	0.0
1900	Bos-N	16	42	6	13	1	0	1	10	3		.310	.370	.405	101	-0	0			.948	1	C-10	0.0
Total	17	1157	4283	619	1226	226	60	77	687	339	299	.286	.347	.421	115	78	55			.937	-26	*C-1073/O-41,13S	12.7

■ VERNE CLEMONS
Clemons, Verne James "Stinger" or "Tubby" b: 9/8/1891, Clemons, Iowa d: 5/5/59, Bay Pines, Fla. BR/TR, 5'9.5", 190 lbs. Deb: 4/22/16

YEAR	TM/L	G	AB	R	H	2B	3B	HR	RBI	BB	SO	AVG	OBP	SLG	PRO+	BR/A	SB	CS	SBR	FA	FR	G/POS	TPR
1916	StL-A	4	7	0	1	1	0	0	0	0	1	.143	.143	.286	30	-1	0			.889	0	/C-2	0.0
1919	StL-N	88	239	14	63	13	2	2	22	26	13	.264	.336	.360	116	5	4			.982	2	C-75	1.5
1920	StL-N	112	338	17	95	10	6	1	36	30	12	.281	.340	.355	103	2	1	1	-0	.977	-6	*C-103	0.2
1921	StL-N	117	341	29	109	16	2	2	48	33	17	.320	.380	.396	108	5	0	0	0	.985	-4	*C-107	0.6
1922	StL-N	71	160	9	41	4	0	0	15	18	5	.256	.331	.281	62	-8	1	0	0	.996	3	C-63	-0.3
1923	StL-N	57	130	6	37	9	1	0	13	10	11	.285	.345	.369	90	-2	1			.981	5	C-41	0.5
1924	StL-N	25	56	3	18	3	0	0	6	2	3	.321	.345	.375	94	0	0	0	0	.983	-2	C-17	-0.1
Total	7	474	1271	78	364	56	11	5	140	119	62	.286	.348	.360	99	0	6	1		.983	-2	C-408	2.4

■ DONN CLENDENON
Clendenon, Donn Alvin b: 7/15/35, Neosho, Mo. BR/TR, 6'3.5", 210 lbs. Deb: 9/22/61

YEAR	TM/L	G	AB	R	H	2B	3B	HR	RBI	BB	SO	AVG	OBP	SLG	PRO+	BR/A	SB	CS	SBR	FA	FR	G/POS	TPR
1961	Pit-N	9	35	7	11	1	1	0	5	2	10	.314	.400	.400	113	1	0	0	0	1.000	1	/O-8	0.1
1962	Pit-N	80	222	39	67	8	5	7	28	26	58	.302	.378	.477	128	9	16	4	2	.990	-1	1-52,O-19	0.6
1963	Pit-N	154	563	65	155	28	7	15	57	39	136	.275	.328	.430	116	10	22	13	-1	.991	7	*1-151	1.0
1964	Pit-N	133	457	53	129	23	8	12	64	26	96	.282	.324	.446	115	8	12	8	-1	.989	-1	*1-119	0.1
1965	Pit-N	162	612	89	184	32	14	14	96	48	128	.301	.356	.467	129	23	9	9	-3	.984	2	*1-158/3-1	1.5
1966	Pit-N	155	571	80	171	22	10	28	98	52	142	.299	.360	.520	141	31	8	7	-2	.985	-1	*1-152	1.8
1967	Pit-N	131	478	46	119	15	2	13	56	34	107	.249	.300	.395	90	-7	4	4	-1	.988	-1	*1-123	-1.2
1968	Pit-N	158	584	63	150	20	6	17	87	47	163	.257	.313	.399	114	9	10	3	1	.990	10	*1-155	0.9
1969	Mon-N	38	129	14	31	6	1	4	14	6	32	.240	.274	.395	85	-3	1			.987	-4	1-24,O-11	-0.3
	*NY-N	72	202	31	51	5	0	12	37	19	62	.252	.323	.455	113	3	3	2	-0	.984	-4	1-58/O-1	-0.5
	Yr	110	331	45	82	11	1	16	51	25	94	.248	.304	.432	103	-0	3	4	-2	.985	-0	1-82,O-12	-0.8
1970	NY-N	121	396	65	114	18	3	22	97	39	91	.288	.353	.515	129	15	4	1	1	.991	-2	*1-100	0.5

YEAR	TM/L	G	AB	R	H	2B	3B	HR	RBI	BB	SO	AVG	OBP	SLG	PRO+	BR/A	SB	CS	SBR	FA	FR	G/POS	TPR
1971	NY-N	88	263	29	65	10	0	11	37	21	78	.247	.305	.411	103	0	1	2	-1	.985	-2	1-72	-0.9
1972	StL-N	61	136	13	26	4	0	4	9	17	37	.191	.281	.309	68	-6	1	2	-1	.986	3	1-36	-0.6
Total	12	1362	4648	594	1273	192	57	159	682	379	1140	.274	.331	.442	117	94	90	57	-7	.988	20	*1-1200/O-39,3	3.0

■ ELMER CLEVELAND
Cleveland, Elmer Ellsworth b: 9/15/1862, Washington, D.C. d: 10/8/13, Zimmerman, Pa. BR/TR, Deb: 8/29/1884

YEAR	TM/L	G	AB	R	H	2B	3B	HR	RBI	BB	SO	AVG	OBP	SLG	PRO+	BR/A	SB	CS	SBR	FA	FR	G/POS	TPR
1884	Cin-U	29	115	24	37	9	2	0		4		.322	.345	.435	102	-0				.843	2	3-29	0.2
1888	NY-N	9	34	6	8	0	2	2	5	3	1	.235	.297	.529	161	2	1			.667	-7	/3-9	-0.4
	Pit-N	30	108	10	24	2	1	2	11	5	23	.222	.270	.315	93	-1	3			.831	-9	3-30	-0.9
	Yr	39	142	16	32	2	3	4	16	8	24	.225	.276	.366	110	2	4			.806	-15	3-39	-1.3
1891	Col-a	12	41	12	7	0	0	0	4	12	9	.171	.370	.171	59	-1	4			.843	3	3-12	0.2
Total	3	80	298	52	76	11	5	4	20	24	33	.255	.317	.366	101	0	8			.830	-10	/3-80	-0.9

■ STAN CLIBURN
Cliburn, Stanley Gene b: 12/19/56, Jackson, Miss. BR/TR, 6', 195 lbs. Deb: 5/6/80 F

YEAR	TM/L	G	AB	R	H	2B	3B	HR	RBI	BB	SO	AVG	OBP	SLG	PRO+	BR/A	SB	CS	SBR	FA	FR	G/POS	TPR
1980	Cal-A	54	56	7	10	2	0	2	6	3	9	.179	.220	.321	48	-4	0	0	0	.971	5	C-54	0.2

■ HARLOND CLIFT
Clift, Harlond Benton "Darkie" b: 8/12/12, ElReno, Okla. d: 4/27/92, Yakima, Wash. BR/TR, 5'11", 180 lbs. Deb: 4/17/34

YEAR	TM/L	G	AB	R	H	2B	3B	HR	RBI	BB	SO	AVG	OBP	SLG	PRO+	BR/A	SB	CS	SBR	FA	FR	G/POS	TPR
1934	StL-A	147	572	104	149	30	10	14	56	84	100	.260	.357	.421	92	-7	7	2	1	.929	-16	*3-141	-1.6
1935	StL-A	137	475	101	140	26	4	11	69	83	39	.295	.406	.436	113	11	0	3	-2	.934	-6	*3-127/2-6	0.8
1936	StL-A	152	576	145	174	40	11	20	73	115	68	.302	.424	.514	127	27	12	4	1	.951	3	*3-152	3.2
1937	StL-A☆	155	571	103	175	36	7	29	118	98	80	.306	.413	.546	139	35	8	5	-1	.947	41	*3-155	7.2
1938	StL-A	149	534	119	155	25	7	34	118	118	67	.290	.423	.554	143	38	10	5	0	.962	14	*3-149	4.8
1939	StL-A	151	526	90	142	25	2	15	84	111	55	.270	.402	.411	106	9	4	3	-1	.953	12	*3-149	2.0
1940	StL-A	150	523	92	143	29	5	20	87	104	62	.273	.396	.463	119	18	9	8	-2	.959	4	*3-147	2.1
1941	StL-A	154	584	108	149	33	9	17	84	113	93	.255	.376	.430	109	9	6	4	-1	.959	1	*3-154	1.3
1942	StL-A	143	541	108	148	39	4	7	55	106	48	.274	.394	.399	122	20	6	4	-1	.941	-1	*3-141/S-1	2.0
1943	StL-A	105	379	43	88	11	3	3	25	54	37	.232	.329	.301	83	-7	5	4	-1	.950	19	*3-104	1.3
	Was-A	8	30	4	9	0	0	0	4	5	3	.300	.417	.300	115	1	0	0	0	.968	-1	/3-8	0.1
	Yr	113	409	47	97	11	3	3	29	59	40	.237	.336	.301	85	-6	5	4	-1	.951	18	*3-112	1.4
1944	Was-A	12	44	4	7	3	0	0	3	3	3	.159	.213	.227	27	-4	0	0	0	.842	-3	3-12	-0.7
1945	Was-A	119	375	49	79	12	0	8	53	74	58	.211	.349	.307	99	-5	3	2	1	.934	-4	*3-111	0.2
Total	12	1582	5730	1070	1558	309	62	178	829	1070	713	.272	.390	.441	115	152	69	43	-5	.948	63	*3-1550/2-6,S	22.7

■ FLEA CLIFTON
Clifton, Herman Earl b: 12/12/09, Cincinnati, Ohio BR/TR, 5'10", 160 lbs. Deb: 4/29/34

YEAR	TM/L	G	AB	R	H	2B	3B	HR	RBI	BB	SO	AVG	OBP	SLG	PRO+	BR/A	SB	CS	SBR	FA	FR	G/POS	TPR
1934	Det-A	16	16	3	1	0	0	0	1	1	2	.063	.118	.063	-52	-4	0	0	0	1.000	2	/3-4,2-1	-0.2
1935	*Det-A	43	110	15	28	5	0	0	9	5	13	.255	.293	.300	56	-7	2	1	0	.934	-1	3-21/2-5,S	-0.7
1936	Det-A	13	26	5	5	1	0	0	1	4	3	.192	.300	.231	33	-3	0	1	-1	.926	-0	/S-6,3-2,2	-0.3
1937	Det-A	15	43	4	5	1	0	0	2	7	10	.116	.240	.140	-2	-7	3	0	1	.958	-0	/3-7,S-4,2	-0.5
Total	4	87	195	27	39	7	0	0	13	17	28	.200	.268	.236	30	-20	5	2	0	.937	-0	/3-34,S-14,2	-1.7

■ MONK CLINE
Cline, John P. b: 3/3/1858, Louisville, Ky. d: 9/23/16, Louisville, Ky. BL/TL, 5'4", 150 lbs. Deb: 7/4/1882

YEAR	TM/L	G	AB	R	H	2B	3B	HR	RBI	BB	SO	AVG	OBP	SLG	PRO+	BR/A	SB	CS	SBR	FA	FR	G/POS	TPR
1882	Bal-a	44	172	18	38	6	2	0		3		.221	.234	.279	79	-3				.825	6	O-39/S-8,23	0.3
1884	Lou-a	94	396	91	115	16	7	2		27		.290	.342	.381	142	19				.875	6	*O-90/S-6	2.1
1885	Lou-a	2	9	0	2	1	0	0		0		.222	.222	.333	74	-0				1.000	-1	/O-1,3-1	-0.1
1888	KC-a	73	293	45	69	13	2	0	19	20		.235	.289	.294	82	-7	29			.883	5	O-70/2-3,3	-0.3
1891	Lou-a	21	76	13	23	3	1	0	12	19	3	.303	.442	.368	134	5	2			.906	-3	O-21	0.1
Total	5	234	946	167	247	39	12	2	31	69	3	.261	.315	.334	111	13	31			.867	14	O-221/S-14,23	2.1

■ TY CLINE
Cline, Tyrone Alexander b: 6/15/39, Hampton, S.C. BL/TL, 6'0.5", 170 lbs. Deb: 9/14/60

YEAR	TM/L	G	AB	R	H	2B	3B	HR	RBI	BB	SO	AVG	OBP	SLG	PRO+	BR/A	SB	CS	SBR	FA	FR	G/POS	TPR
1960	Cle-A	7	26	2	8	1	1	0	2	0	4	.308	.308	.423	99	-0	0	0	0	1.000	2	/O-6	0.1
1961	Cle-A	12	43	9	9	2	1	0	1	6	1	.209	.333	.302	73	-1	1	0	0	1.000	-2	O-12	-0.4
1962	Cle-A	118	375	53	93	15	5	2	28	28	50	.248	.309	.331	74	-14	5	4	-1	.992	3	*O-107	-1.8
1963	Mil-N	72	174	17	41	2	1	0	10	10	31	.236	.285	.259	58	-9	2	1	0	.992	-0	O-62	-1.3
1964	Mil-N	101	116	22	35	4	2	1	13	8	22	.302	.362	.397	113	2	0	1	-1	.982	-10	O-54/1-6	-1.0
1965	Mil-N	123	220	27	42	5	3	0	10	16	50	.191	.246	.241	37	-18	2	2	-1	.969	-6	O-86/1-5	-2.9
1966	Chi-N	7	17	3	6	0	0	0	2	0	2	.353	.353	.353	96	-0	1	0	0	1.000	-1	/O-5	-0.1
	Atl-N	42	71	12	18	5	0	0	6	3	11	.254	.303	.254	56	-4	1	0	0	1.000	-5	O-19/1-6	-1.0
	Yr	49	88	15	24	5	0	0	8	3	13	.273	.312	.273	63	-4	2	0	0	1.000	-6	O-24/1-6	-1.1
1967	Atl-N	10	8	0	0	0	0	0	0	0	3	.000	.111	.000	-66	-2	0	0	0	1.000	-0	/O-1	-0.2
	SF-N	64	122	18	33	5	5	0	4	9	13	.270	.326	.393	106	1	2	1	0	1.000	-6	O-37	-0.7
	Yr	74	130	18	33	5	5	0	4	9	16	.254	.312	.369	96	-1	2	1	0	1.000	-6	O-38	-0.9
1968	SF-N	116	291	37	65	6	3	1	28	11	26	.223	.254	.275	59	-15	4	1	-24	.971	-4	O-70,1-24	-2.8
1969	Mon-N	101	209	26	50	5	3	2	12	32	22	.239	.346	.321	87	-2	4	3	-1	.988	-0	O-41,1-17	-0.7
1970	Mon-N	2	2	0	1	0	0	0	0	0	0	.500	.500	.500	169	0	0	0	0	.000	0	H	0.0
	*Cin-N	48	63	13	17	7	1	0	8	12	11	.270	.387	.413	114	2	1	2	0	.966	-2	O-20/1-2	-0.2
	Yr	50	65	13	18	7	1	0	8	12	11	.277	.390	.415	115	2	1	2	0	.966	-2	O-20/1-2	-0.2
1971	Cin-N	69	97	12	19	1	0	1	1	18	16	.196	.333	.206	57	-5	2	2	-1	1.000	-5	O-28/1-2	-1.2
Total	12	892	1834	251	437	53	25	6	125	153	262	.238	.304	.304	72	-65	22	19	-5	.986	-38	O-548/1-62	-14.2

■ GENE CLINES
Clines, Eugene Anthony b: 10/6/46, San Pablo, Cal. BR/TR, 5'9", 170 lbs. Deb: 6/28/70 C

YEAR	TM/L	G	AB	R	H	2B	3B	HR	RBI	BB	SO	AVG	OBP	SLG	PRO+	BR/A	SB	CS	SBR	FA	FR	G/POS	TPR
1970	Pit-N	31	37	4	15	2	0	0	3	2	5	.405	.436	.459	143	2	2	1	0	1.000	-2	/O-7	0.0
1971	*Pit-N	97	273	52	84	12	4	1	24	22	36	.308	.366	.392	115	6	15	6	1	.981	2	O-74	0.6
1972	*Pit-N	107	311	52	104	15	6	0	17	16	47	.334	.371	.421	127	11	12	6	0	.958	-9	O-83	-0.1
1973	Pit-N	110	304	42	80	11	3	1	23	26	36	.263	.327	.329	84	-6	8	7	-2	.968	-2	O-77	-1.3
1974	*Pit-N	107	276	29	62	5	1	0	14	30	40	.225	.310	.250	60	-14	14	2	3	.989	2	O-78	-1.2
1975	NY-N	82	203	25	46	6	3	0	10	11	21	.227	.270	.286	57	-12	4	1	0	.982	-4	O-60	-2.0
1976	Tex-A	116	446	52	123	12	5	0	38	16	52	.276	.307	.316	81	-11	11	9	-2	.987	3	*O-103,D-10	-1.6
1977	Chi-N	101	239	27	70	12	2	3	41	25	25	.293	.362	.397	93	-2	1	2	-1	.986	-8	O-63	-1.3
1978	Chi-N	109	229	31	59	10	2	0	17	21	28	.258	.323	.319	71	-8	4	3	-1	.978	-7	O-66	-2.0
1979	Chi-N	10	10	0	2	0	0	0	0	0	1	.200	.200	.200	9	-1	0	0	0	.000	0	/H	-0.2
Total	10	870	2328	314	645	85	24	5	187	169	291	.277	.331	.341	88	-36	71	40	-3	.979	-24	O-611/D-10	-9.1

■ BILLY CLINGMAN
Clingman, William Frederick b: 11/21/1869, Cincinnati, Ohio d: 5/14/58, Cincinnati, Ohio BB/TR, 5'11", 150 lbs. Deb: 9/9/1890

YEAR	TM/L	G	AB	R	H	2B	3B	HR	RBI	BB	SO	AVG	OBP	SLG	PRO+	BR/A	SB	CS	SBR	FA	FR	G/POS	TPR
1890	Cin-N	7	27	2	7	1	0	0	5	1	0	.259	.286	.296	70	-1	0			.892	-1	/S-6,2-1	-0.1
1891	Cin-a	1	5	0	1	0	0	0	0	0	0	.200	.200	.400	65	-0	0			.667	-1	/2-1	-0.1
1895	Pit-N	106	382	69	99	16	4	0	45	41	43	.259	.334	.322	74	-14	19			.887	14	*3-106	0.1
1896	Lou-N	121	423	57	99	10	2	0	37	57	51	.234	.329	.281	64	-20	19			.925	24	*3-121	0.5
1897	Lou-N	113	395	59	90	14	7	2	47	37		.228	.292	.314	65	-20	14			.947	29	*3-113	1.0
1898	Lou-N	154	538	65	138	12	6	0	50	51		.257	.327	.301	81	-12	15			.914	15	3-79,S-74/O2	0.7
1899	Lou-N	109	366	67	96	15	4	2	44	46		.262	.349	.342	90	-4	13			.916	-4	*S-109	0.0
1900	Chi-N	47	159	15	33	6	0	0	11	17		.208	.292	.245	51	-10	6			.872	-12	S-47	-1.7
1901	Was-A	137	480	66	116	10	7	2	55	42		.242	.308	.304	71	-18	10			.932	18	*S-137	1.0
1903	Cle-A	21	64	10	18	1	0	0	7	11		.281	.387	.328	118	2	2			.932	-0	2-11/S-7,3	0.3
Total	10	816	2839	410	697	86	31	8	301	303	94	.246	.323	.306	74	-97	98			.919	81	3-422,S-380/2O	1.7

YEAR	TM/L	G	AB	R	H	2B	3B	HR	RBI	BB	SO	AVG	OBP	SLG	PRO+	BR/A	SB	CS	SBR	FA	FR	G/POS	TPR
■ JIM CLINTON					Clinton, James Lawrence "Big Jim"			b: 8/10/1850, New York, N.Y.				d: 9/3/21, Brooklyn, N.Y.			BR/TR, 5'8.5", 174 lbs.			Deb: 5/18/1872	MU			
1872	Eck-n	25	97	13	23	3	1	0	7	0	2	.237	.237	.289	72	-2						/3-8,-9/OS2CM	-0.2
1873	Res-n	9	38	5	9	1	0	0				.237	.237	.263	51	-2						/3-9	-0.2
1874	Atl-n	2	11	3	2	1	0	0	0			.182	.182	.273	48	-1						/2-1,O-1	0.0
1875	Atl-n	22	81	3	10	0	0	0				.123	.123	.123	-16	-9						P-17/O-5,12	-0.2
1876	Lou-N	16	65	8	22	2	0	0	0	0	0	.338	.338	.369	115	0				.783	1	O-14/1-1,P	0.0
1882	Wor-N	26	98	9	16	2	0	0	3	7	13	.163	.219	.184	30	-7				.734	-4	O-26	-1.0
1883	Bal-a	94	399	69	125	16	8	0		27		.313	.357	.393	137	16				.842	5	*O-92/2-2	1.8
1884	Bal-a	104	437	82	118	12	6	4		29		.270	.334	.352	119	9				.807	-1	*O-104/2-1	0.6
1885	Cin-a	105	408	48	97	5	5	0		15		.238	.277	.275	73	-12				.877	-0	*O-105	-1.4
1886	Bal-a	23	83	8	15	1	0	0		4		.181	.227	.193	33	-6	3			.894	-0	O-23	-0.6
Total	4 n	58	227	24	44	5	1	0	10	0	2	.194	.194	.225	38	-13	0					/3-18,P-17,O21SC	-0.6
Total	6	368	1490	224	393	38	19	4	3	82	13	.264	.311	.323	101	-0	3			.838	0	O-364/2-3,P1	-0.6
■ LOU CLINTON					Clinton, Luciean Louis			b: 10/13/37, Ponca City, Okla.				BR/TR, 6'1", 185 lbs.			Deb: 4/22/60							
1960	Bos-A	96	298	37	68	17	5	6	37	20	66	.228	.283	.379	75	-11	4	3	-1	.966	2	O-89	-1.4
1961	Bos-A	17	51	4	13	2	1	0	3	2	10	.255	.283	.333	63	-3	0	0	0	1.000	3	O-13	0.0
1962	Bos-A	114	398	63	117	24	10	18	75	34	79	.294	.351	.540	132	16	2	1	0	.979	1	*O-103	1.2
1963	Bos-A	148	560	71	130	23	7	22	77	49	118	.232	.295	.416	94	-6	0	0	0	.982	11	*O-146	-0.3
1964	Bos-A	37	120	15	31	4	3	3	6	9	33	.258	.310	.417	95	-1	1	0	0	1.000	5	O-35	0.3
	LA-A	91	306	30	76	18	0	9	38	31	40	.248	.320	.395	108	2	3	1	0	.985	3	O-86	0.2
	Yr	128	426	45	107	22	3	12	44	40	73	.251	.317	.401	104	1	4	0	1	.990	7	*O-121	0.5
1965	Cal-A	89	222	29	54	12	3	1	8	23	37	.243	.317	.338	88	-3	2	3	-1	.983	-2	O-73	-0.9
	KC-A	1	1	0	0	0	0	0	0	0	0	.000	.000	.000	-99	-0	0	0	0	.000	-0	/O-1	-0.1
	Cle-A	12	34	2	6	1	0	1	2	3	7	.176	.243	.294	51	-2	0	0	0	.941	-0	/O-9	-0.3
	Yr	102	257	31	60	13	3	2	10	26	44	.233	.306	.331	83	-6	2	3	-1	.977	-2	O-83	-1.3
1966	NY-A	80	159	18	35	10	2	5	21	16	27	.220	.291	.403	101	-0	0	0	0	.976	-6	O-63	-0.9
1967	NY-A	6	4	1	2	1	0	0	1	1	1	.500	.600	.750	308	1	0	0	0	.000	-0	/O-1	0.1
Total	8	691	2153	270	532	112	31	65	269	188	418	.247	.310	.418	99	-7	12	7	-1	.980	15	O-619	-2.1
■ ED CLOUGH					Clough, Edgar George "Big Ed" or "Spec"			b: 10/28/06, Wiconisco, Pa.				d: 1/30/44, Harrisburg, Pa.			BL/TL, 6', 188 lbs.			Deb: 8/28/24				
1924	StL-N	7	14	0	1	0	0	0	1	0	3	.071	.071	.071	-63	-3	0	0	0	1.000	0	/O-6	-0.3
1925	StL-N	3	4	0	1	0	0	0	0	0	0	.250	.250	.250	28	-0	0	0	0	1.000	0	/P-3	0.0
1926	StL-N	1	1	0	0	0	0	0	0	0	0	.000	.000	.000	-96	-0	0	0	0	.000	-0	/P-1	0.0
Total	3	11	19	0	2	0	0	0	1	0	3	.105	.105	.105	-44	0	0	0	0	1.000	0	/O-6,P-4	-0.3
■ OTIS CLYMER					Clymer, Otis Edgar			b: 1/27/1876, Pine Grove, Pa.				d: 2/27/26, St.Paul, Minn.			BB/TR, 5'11", 180 lbs.			Deb: 4/14/05				
1905	Pit-N	96	365	74	108	11	5	0	23	19		.296	.332	.353	102	0	23			.986	-2	O-89/1-1	-0.6
1906	Pit-N	11	45	7	11	0	1	0	1	3		.244	.292	.289	78	-1	1			.900	-1	O-11	-0.3
1907	Pit-N	22	66	8	15	2	0	0	4	5		.227	.311	.258	77	-1	4			.923	-3	O-15/1-1	-0.5
	Was-A	57	206	30	65	5	5	1	16	18		.316	.382	.403	163	15	18			.912	-4	O-51/1-1	1.0
1908	Was-A	110	368	32	93	11	4	1	35	20		.253	.291	.313	105	1	19			.933	-7	O-82,2-13/3	-1.1
1909	Was-A	45	138	11	27	5	2	0	6	17		.196	.284	.261	76	-4	7			.922	-4	O-41	-1.1
1913	Chi-N	30	105	12	24	5	1	0	7	14	18	.229	.319	.295	76	-3	9			.933	-2	O-26	-0.6
	Bos-N	14	37	4	12	3	1	0	6	3	3	.324	.375	.459	135	2	2			.880	-2	O-11	-0.1
	Yr	44	142	20	36	8	2	0	13	17	21	.254	.333	.338	91	-1	11			.918	-4	O-37	-0.7
Total	6	385	1330	182	355	42	19	2	98	99	21	.267	.322	.332	106	8	83			.939	-24	O-326/2-13,13	-3.3
■ BILL CLYMER					Clymer, William Johnston "Derby Day Bill"			b: 12/18/1873, Philadelphia, Pa.				d: 12/26/36, Philadelphia, Pa.			Deb: 6/26/1891	C			
1891	Phi-a	3	11	0	0	0	0	0	0	1	2	.000	.154	.000	-54	-2	1			.867	-2	/S-3	-0.3
■ PETE COACHMAN					Coachman, Bobby Dean			b: 11/11/61, Cottonwood, Ala.				BR/TR, 5'9", 175 lbs.			Deb: 8/18/90							
1990	Cal-A	16	45	3	14	3	0	0	5	1	7	.311	.354	.378	107	0	0	1	-1	.958	1	/3-9,2-2,D	0.1
■ GIL COAN					Coan, Gilbert Fitzgerald			b: 5/18/22, Monroe, N.C.				BL/TR, 6', 180 lbs.			Deb: 4/27/46							
1946	Was-A	59	134	17	28	3	2	3	9	7	37	.209	.269	.328	70	-6	2	2	-1	.969	-2	O-29	-1.0
1947	Was-A	11	42	5	21	3	2	0	3	5	6	.500	.553	.667	245	8	2	1	0	1.000	1	O-11	0.8
1948	Was-A	138	513	56	119	13	9	7	60	41	78	.232	.298	.333	70	-24	23	9	2	.970	12	*O-131	-1.7
1949	Was-A	111	358	36	78	7	8	3	25	29	58	.218	.278	.307	56	-24	9	6	-1	.975	2	O-97	-2.8
1950	Was-A	104	366	58	111	17	4	7	50	28	46	.303	.349	.429	106	2	10	5	0	.970	-3	O-98	-0.4
1951	Was-A	135	538	85	163	25	7	9	62	39	62	.303	.357	.426	113	9	8	5	-1	.965	22	*O-132	2.4
1952	Was-A	107	332	50	68	11	6	5	20	32	35	.205	.277	.319	68	-15	9	4	0	.984	1	O-86	-1.9
1953	Was-A	68	168	28	33	1	4	2	17	22	23	.196	.301	.286	60	-9	7	0	2	1.000	4	O-46	-0.5
1954	Bal-A	94	265	29	74	11	1	2	20	16	17	.279	.323	.351	91	-4	9	4	0	.968	-4	O-67	-1.0
1955	Bal-A	61	130	18	31	7	1	1	11	13	15	.238	.313	.331	79	-4	4	2	0	.983	-4	O-43	-1.0
	Chi-A	17	17	0	3	0	0	0	1	0	5	.176	.176	.176	-5	-2	0	0	0	1.000	-1	/O-3	-0.3
	Yr	78	147	18	34	7	1	1	12	13	20	.231	.298	.313	68	-7	4	2	0	.984	-5	O-46	-1.3
	NY-N	9	13	0	2	0	0	0	0	1	1	.154	.154	.154	-18	-2	0	0	0	1.000	0	/O-6	-0.5
1956	NY-N	4	1	0	0	0	0	0	0	0	0	.000	.000	.000	-99	-0	0	0	0	.000	0	H	0.0
Total	11	918	2877	384	731	98	44	39	278	232	384	.254	.316	.359	84	-73	83	38	2	.973	24	O-749	-7.9
■ JOE COBB					Cobb, Joseph Stanley (b: Joseph Stanley Serafin)			b: 1/24/1895, Hudson, Pa.				d: 12/24/47, Allentown, Pa.			BR/TR, 5'9", 170 lbs.			Deb: 4/25/18				
1918	Det-A	1	0	0	0	0	0	0	0	1	0	—	1.000	—	210	0	0			.000	0	H	0.0
■ TY COBB					Cobb, Tyrus Raymond "The Georgia Peach"			b: 12/18/1886, Narrows, Ga.				d: 7/17/61, Atlanta, Ga.			BL/TR, 6'1", 175 lbs.			Deb: 8/30/05	MH			
1905	Det-A	41	150	19	36	6	0	1	15	10		.240	.287	.300	86	-3	2			.958	2	O-41	-0.3
1906	Det-A	98	358	45	113	15	5	1	34	19		.316	.355	.394	130	12	23			.961	6	O-96	1.5
1907	*Det-A	150	605	97	**212**	28	14	5	**119**	24		**.350**	.380	**.468**	164	40	49			.961	11	*O-150	5.0
1908	*Det-A	150	581	88	**188**	**36**	**20**	4	**108**	34		.324	.367	**.475**	166	40	39			.944	4	*O-150	4.2
1909	*Det-A	156	573	**116**	**216**	33	10	**9**	**107**	48		**.377**	**.431**	**.517**	190	58	**76**			.946	3	*O-156	6.1
1910	Det-A	140	506	**106**	194	35	13	8	91	64		**.383**	**.456**	**.551**	202	60	65			.958	9	*O-137	6.7
1911	Det-A	146	591	**147**	**248**	**47**	**24**	8	**127**	44		**.420**	.467	**.621**	193	71	**83**			.957	11	*O-146	7.1
1912	Det-A	140	553	120	**226**	30	23	7	83	43		**.409**	.456	**.584**	203	72	61			.940	7	*O-140	6.4
1913	Det-A	122	428	70	167	18	16	4	67	58	31	**.390**	**.467**	.535	196	53	51			.947	3	*O-122	5.3
1914	Det-A	98	345	69	127	22	11	2	57	57	22	.368	.466	.513	188	41	35	17	0	.949	-10	O-96	2.8
1915	Det-A	156	563	**144**	**208**	31	13	3	99	118	43	**.369**	**.486**	.487	182	64	**96**	38	6	.951	-3	*O-156	6.2
1916	Det-A	145	542	**113**	201	31	10	5	68	78	39	.371	.452	.493	177	53	**68**	24	6	.953	-7	*O-143/1-1	5.5
1917	Det-A	152	588	107	**225**	**44**	**24**	6	102	61	34	**.383**	.444	**.570**	210	75	**55**			.973	13	*O-152	8.5
1918	Det-A	111	421	83	161	19	**14**	3	64	41	21	**.382**	.440	.515	196	48	34			.975	0	O-95,1-13/P23	4.8
1919	Det-A	124	497	92	**191**	36	13	1	70	38	22	**.384**	.429	.515	168	44	28			.973	-2	*O-123	3.5
1920	Det-A	112	428	86	143	28	8	2	63	58	28	.334	.416	.451	133	22	15	10	-2	.966	-7	*O-112	0.5
1921	Det-A	128	507	124	197	37	16	12	101	56	19	.389	.452	.596	167	52	22	15	-2	.970	13	*O-121,M	4.9
1922	Det-A	137	526	99	211	42	16	4	99	55	24	.401	.462	.565	172	57	9	13	-5	.980	4	*O-134,M	4.3
1923	Det-A	145	556	103	189	40	7	6	88	66	14	.340	.413	.469	135	29	9	10	-3	.969	5	*O-141,M	2.0

YEAR	TM/L	G	AB	R	H	2B	3B	HR	RBI	BB	SO	AVG	OBP	SLG	PRO+	BR/A	SB	CS	SBR	FA	FR	G/POS	TPR
1924	Det-A	155	625	115	211	38	10	4	78	85	18	.338	.418	.450	126	26	23	14	-2	**.986**	5	*O-155,M	1.8
1925	Det-A	121	415	97	157	31	12	12	102	65	12	.378	.468	.598	**171**	47	13	9	-2	.948	-2	*O-105/P-1M	3.3
1926	Det-A	79	233	48	79	18	5	4	62	26	2	.339	.408	.511	137	12	9	4	0	.950	-5	O-55,M	0.4
1927	Phi-A	134	490	104	175	32	7	5	93	67	12	.357	.440	.482	131	25	22	16	-3	.969	-5	*O-127	0.9
1928	Phi-A	95	353	54	114	27	4	1	40	34	16	.323	.389	.431	112	7	5	8	-3	.964	-1	O-85	-0.2
Total	24	3035	11434	2246	4189	724	295	117	1937	1249	**357**	.366	.433	.512	167	1004	892	178		.961	56	*O-2935/1-14,P32	91.1

■ DAVE COBLE
Coble, David Lamar b: 12/24/12, Monroe, N.C. d: 10/15/71, Orlando, Fla. BR/TR, 6'1", 183 lbs. Deb: 5/1/39

YEAR	TM/L	G	AB	R	H	2B	3B	HR	RBI	BB	SO	AVG	OBP	SLG	PRO+	BR/A	SB	CS	SBR	FA	FR	G/POS	TPR
1939	Phi-N	15	25	2	7	1	0	0	0	0	3	.280	.280	.320	63	-1	0			.938	-1	C-13	-0.2

■ GEORGE COCHRAN
Cochran, George Leslie b: 2/12/1889, Rusk, Tex. d: 5/21/60, Harbor City, Cal. TR, Deb: 7/29/18

YEAR	TM/L	G	AB	R	H	2B	3B	HR	RBI	BB	SO	AVG	OBP	SLG	PRO+	BR/A	SB	CS	SBR	FA	FR	G/POS	TPR
1918	Bos-A	24	60	7	7	0	0	0	3	10	6	.117	.264	.117	15	-6	3			.960	-4	3-22/S-1	-1.0

■ DAVE COCHRANE
Cochrane, David Carter b: 1/31/63, Riverside, Cal. BB/TR, 6'2", 180 lbs. Deb: 9/2/86

YEAR	TM/L	G	AB	R	H	2B	3B	HR	RBI	BB	SO	AVG	OBP	SLG	PRO+	BR/A	SB	CS	SBR	FA	FR	G/POS	TPR
1986	Chi-A	19	62	4	12	2	0	1	2	5	22	.194	.254	.274	42	-5	0	0	0	.872	-3	3-18/S-1	-0.8
1989	Sea-A	54	102	13	24	4	1	3	7	14	27	.235	.333	.382	98	-0	0	2	-1	.905	-13	S-30/1-9,32OC	-1.5
1990	Sea-A	15	20	0	3	0	0	0	0	0	8	.150	.150	.150	-16	-3	0	0	0	1.000	0	/S-5,1-3,3C	-0.3
1991	Sea-A	65	178	16	44	13	0	2	22	9	38	.247	.287	.354	76	-6	0	1	-1	.969	-14	O-26,C-19,3/1D	-2.1
1992	Sea-A	65	152	10	38	5	0	2	12	12	34	.250	.309	.322	77	-5	1	0	0	.879	-8	O-25,C-21,3/1SD2	-1.2
Total	5	218	514	43	121	24	1	8	43	40	129	.235	.294	.333	73	-19	1	3	-2	.925	-38	/O-54,3-53,CS12D	-5.9

■ MICKEY COCHRANE
Cochrane, Gordon Stanley b: 4/6/03, Bridgewater, Mass. d: 6/28/62, Lake Forest, Ill. BL/TR, 5'10.5", 180 lbs. Deb: 4/14/25 MCH

YEAR	TM/L	G	AB	R	H	2B	3B	HR	RBI	BB	SO	AVG	OBP	SLG	PRO+	BR/A	SB	CS	SBR	FA	FR	G/POS	TPR
1925	Phi-A	134	420	69	139	21	5	6	55	44	19	.331	.397	.448	107	5	7	4	-0	.984	-10	*C-133	0.1
1926	Phi-A	120	370	50	101	8	9	8	47	56	15	.273	.369	.408	97	-1	5	2	0	.975	12	*C-115	1.7
1927	Phi-A	126	432	80	146	20	6	12	80	50	7	.338	.409	.495	127	17	9	6	-1	.986	3	*C-123	2.6
1928	Phi-A	131	468	92	137	26	12	10	57	76	25	.293	.395	.464	122	16	7	7	-2	.966	2	*C-130	2.6
1929	*Phi-A	135	514	113	170	37	8	7	95	69	8	.331	.412	.475	123	19	7	6	-2	.983	8	*C-135	3.6
1930	*Phi-A	130	487	110	174	42	5	10	85	55	18	.357	.424	.526	133	25	5	0	2	**.993**	6	*C-130	4.0
1931	*Phi-A	122	459	87	160	31	6	17	89	56	21	.349	.423	.553	146	30	2	3	-1	.986	10	*C-117	4.3
1932	Phi-A	139	518	118	152	35	4	23	112	100	22	.293	.412	.510	132	27	0	1	-1	**.993**	10	*C-137/O-1	4.1
1933	Phi-A	130	429	104	138	30	4	15	60	106	22	.322	**.459**	.515	156	41	8	6	-1	.989	7	*C-128	3.7
1934	*Det-A★	129	437	74	140	32	1	2	76	78	26	.320	.428	.412	117	16	8	4	0	.988	-4	*C-124,M	1.6
1935	*Det-A☆	115	411	93	131	33	3	5	47	96	15	.319	.452	.450	139	30	5	1	-1	.989	-5	*C-110,M	2.7
1936	Det-A	44	126	24	34	8	2	2	17	46	15	.270	.465	.381	111	5	1	1	0	.983	-4	C-42,M	-0.1
1937	Det-A	27	98	27	30	10	1	2	12	25	4	.306	.452	.490	134	6	0	1	-1	1.000	-2	C-27,M	0.5
Total	13	1482	5169	1041	1652	333	64	119	832	857	217	.320	.419	.478	127	237	64	46	-8	.985	14	*C-1451/O-1	31.4

■ JIM COCKMAN
Cockman, James b: 4/26/1873, Guelph, Ont., Can. d: 9/28/47, Guelph, Ont., Can. BR/TR, 5'6", 145 lbs. Deb: 9/28/05

YEAR	TM/L	G	AB	R	H	2B	3B	HR	RBI	BB	SO	AVG	OBP	SLG	PRO+	BR/A	SB	CS	SBR	FA	FR	G/POS	TPR
1905	NY-A	13	38	5	4	0	0	0	2	4		.105	.190	.105	-5	-4	2			.875	-2	3-13	-0.7

■ JACK COFFEY
Coffey, John Francis b: 1/28/1887, New York, N.Y. d: 2/14/66, Bronx, N.Y. BR/TR, 5'11", 178 lbs. Deb: 6/23/09

YEAR	TM/L	G	AB	R	H	2B	3B	HR	RBI	BB	SO	AVG	OBP	SLG	PRO+	BR/A	SB	CS	SBR	FA	FR	G/POS	TPR
1909	Bos-N	73	257	21	48	4	4	0	20	11		.187	.229	.233	41	-18	2			.896	-12	S-73	-3.2
1918	Det-A	22	67	7	14	0	2	0	4	8	6	.209	.303	.269	75	-2	2			.957	0	2-22	-0.1
	Bos-A	15	44	5	7	1	0	1	2	3	2	.159	.213	.250	40	-3	2			.955	2	3-14/2-1	-0.1
	Yr	37	111	12	21	1	2	1	6	11	8	.189	.268	.261	62	-5	4			.959	2	2-23,3-14	-0.2
Total	2	110	368	33	69	5	6	1	26	22	8	.188	.241	.242	47	-23	6			.896	-9	/S-73,2-23,3	-3.4

■ FRANK COGGINS
Coggins, Franklin b: 5/22/44, Griffin, Ga. BB/TR, 6'2", 187 lbs. Deb: 9/10/67

YEAR	TM/L	G	AB	R	H	2B	3B	HR	RBI	BB	SO	AVG	OBP	SLG	PRO+	BR/A	SB	CS	SBR	FA	FR	G/POS	TPR
1967	Was-A	19	75	9	23	3	0	1	8	2	17	.307	.325	.387	114	1	1	0	0	.964	3	2-19	0.6
1968	Was-A	62	171	15	30	6	1	0	7	9	33	.175	.217	.222	34	-14	1	1	-0	.953	4	2-52	-0.9
1972	Chi-N	6	1	1	0	0	0	0	0	1	0	.000	.500	.000	48	0	0	0	0	.000	0	H	-0.0
Total	3	87	247	25	53	9	1	1	15	12	50	.215	.251	.271	59	-13	2	1	0	.957	7	/2-71	-0.3

■ RICH COGGINS
Coggins, Richard Allen b: 12/7/50, Indianapolis, Ind. BL/TL, 5'8", 170 lbs. Deb: 8/29/72

YEAR	TM/L	G	AB	R	H	2B	3B	HR	RBI	BB	SO	AVG	OBP	SLG	PRO+	BR/A	SB	CS	SBR	FA	FR	G/POS	TPR
1972	Bal-A	16	39	5	13	4	0	0	1	1	6	.333	.350	.436	129	1	0	2	-1	1.000	2	O-13	0.2
1973	*Bal-A	110	389	54	124	19	9	7	41	28	24	.319	.365	.468	134	16	17	9	-0	.987	-3	*O-101/D-1	0.9
1974	*Bal-A	113	411	53	100	13	3	4	32	29	31	.243	.301	.319	81	-10	26	6	-4	.984	-7	*O-105	-1.9
1975	Mon-N	13	37	1	10	2	1	0	4	1	7	.270	.289	.405	87	-1	0	0	0	1.000	-1	O-10	-0.3
	NY-A	51	107	7	24	1	0	1	6	7	16	.224	.272	.262	53	-7	3	3	-1	.970	-3	O-36/D-9	-1.2
1976	NY-A	7	4	1	1	0	0	0	1	0	1	.250	.250	.250	47	-0	1	0	0	1.000	0	/O-2	-0.0
	Chi-A	32	96	4	15	2	0	0	5	6	15	.156	.206	.177	13	-10	3	1	0	1.000	-4	O-26/D-1	-1.6
	Yr	39	100	5	16	2	0	0	6	6	16	.160	.208	.180	14	-11	4	1	1	1.000	-4	O-28/D-1	-1.6
Total	5	342	1083	125	287	42	13	12	90	72	100	.265	.314	.361	94	-11	50	21	-2	.986	-17	O-293/D-11	-3.9

■ ED COGSWELL
Cogswell, Edward b: 2/25/1854, England d: 7/27/1888, Fitchburg, Mass. BR/TR, 5'8", 150 lbs. Deb: 7/11/1879

YEAR	TM/L	G	AB	R	H	2B	3B	HR	RBI	BB	SO	AVG	OBP	SLG	PRO+	BR/A	SB	CS	SBR	FA	FR	G/POS	TPR
1879	Bos-N	49	236	51	76	8	1	1	18	8	5	.322	.344	.377	135	8				.967	1	1-49	0.7
1880	Tro-N	47	209	41	63	7	3	0	13	11	10	.301	.336	.364	130	6				.961	1	1-47	0.3
1882	Wor-N	13	51	10	7	1	0	0	1	6	6	.137	.228	.157	26	-4				.937	-1	1-13	-0.6
Total	3	109	496	102	146	16	4	1	32	25	21	.294	.328	.349	121	11				.960	1	1-109	0.4

■ ALTA COHEN
Cohen, Alta Albert "Schoolboy" b: 12/25/08, New York, N.Y. BL/TL, 5'10.5", 170 lbs. Deb: 4/15/31

YEAR	TM/L	G	AB	R	H	2B	3B	HR	RBI	BB	SO	AVG	OBP	SLG	PRO+	BR/A	SB	CS	SBR	FA	FR	G/POS	TPR
1931	Bro-N	1	3	1	2	0	0	0	0	0	0	.667	.667	.667	261	1	0			1.000	1	/O-1	0.2
1932	Bro-N	9	32	1	5	1	0	0	0	3	7	.156	.229	.188	14	-4	0			.850	1	/O-8	-0.4
1933	Phi-N	19	32	6	6	1	0	0	1	6	4	.188	.316	.219	49	-2	0			1.000	-0	/O-7	-0.2
Total	3	29	67	8	13	2	0	0	2	9	11	.194	.289	.224	42	-5	0			.925		/O-16	-0.4

■ ANDY COHEN
Cohen, Andrew Howard b: 10/25/04, Baltimore, Md. d: 10/29/88, El Paso, Tex. BR/TR, 5'8", 155 lbs. Deb: 6/6/26 FMC

YEAR	TM/L	G	AB	R	H	2B	3B	HR	RBI	BB	SO	AVG	OBP	SLG	PRO+	BR/A	SB	CS	SBR	FA	FR	G/POS	TPR
1926	NY-N	32	35	4	9	1	0	0	8	1	2	.257	.278	.314	60	-2	0			.792	-3	2-10,S-10/3	0.0
1928	NY-N	129	504	64	138	24	7	9	59	31	17	.274	.314	.403	87	-11	3			.969	3	*2-126/S-3,3	-0.4
1929	NY-N	101	347	40	102	12	2	5	47	11	15	.294	.319	.383	73	-15	3			.964	12	2-94/S-1,3	0.1
Total	3	262	886	108	249	36	10	14	114	43	34	.281	.317	.392	81	-28	6			.964	16	2-230/S-14,3	-0.3

■ JIMMIE COKER
Coker, Jimmie Goodwin b: 3/28/36, Holly Hill, S.C. d: 10/29/91, Throckmorton, Tex. BR/TR, 5'11", 195 lbs. Deb: 9/11/58

YEAR	TM/L	G	AB	R	H	2B	3B	HR	RBI	BB	SO	AVG	OBP	SLG	PRO+	BR/A	SB	CS	SBR	FA	FR	G/POS	TPR
1958	Phi-N	2	6	0	1	0	0	0	0	0	2	.167	.167	.167	-12	-1	0	0	0	1.000	0	/C-2	-0.1
1960	Phi-N	81	252	18	54	5	3	6	34	23	45	.214	.290	.329	69	-11	0	3	-2	.982	2	C-76	-0.6
1961	Phi-N	11	25	3	10	1	0	1	4	7	4	.400	.531	.560	193	4	0	0	0	.984	0	C-11	0.5
1962	Phi-N	5	3	0	0	0	0	0	1	1	2	.000	.250	.000	-27	-1	0	0	0	.000	0	H	-0.1
1963	SF-N	4	5	0	1	0	0	0	0	1	2	.200	.333	.200	58	-0	0	0	0	1.000	-1	/C-2	-0.1
1964	Cin-N	11	32	3	10	2	0	1	6	3	5	.313	.371	.469	130	1	0	0	0	1.000	2	C-11	0.4
1965	Cin-N	24	61	3	15	2	0	2	9	6	16	.246	.333	.377	93	-0	0	1	0	.993	5	C-19	0.4
1966	Cin-N	50	111	9	28	3	0	4	14	8	5	.252	.303	.387	83	-2	0	1	0	.979	4	C-39/O-2	0.3
1967	Cin-N	45	97	8	18	2	1	2	7	4	20	.186	.218	.289	39	-8	1	0	0	.983	0	C-34	-0.8
Total	9	233	592	44	137	15	4	16	70	56	99	.231	.301	.351	77	-18	1	5	-3	.983	13	C-194/O-2	0.1

■ ROCKY COLAVITO
Colavito, Rocco Domenico b: 8/10/33, New York, N.Y. BR/TR, 6'3", 190 lbs. Deb: 9/10/55 C

YEAR	TM/L	G	AB	R	H	2B	3B	HR	RBI	BB	SO	AVG	OBP	SLG	PRO+	BR/A	SB	CS	SBR	FA	FR	G/POS	TPR
1955	Cle-A	5	9	3	4	0	0	0	0	0	2	.444	.444	.667	189	1	0	0	0	1.000	2	/O-2	0.3

YEAR	TM/L	G	AB	R	H	2B	3B	HR	RBI	BB	SO	AVG	OBP	SLG	PRO+	BR/A	SB	CS	SBR	FA	FR	G/POS	TPR
1956	Cle-A	101	322	55	89	11	4	21	65	49	46	.276	.375	.531	134	15	0	1	-1	.968	-1	O-98	0.9
1957	Cle-A	134	461	66	116	26	0	25	84	71	80	.252	.353	.471	124	15	1	6	-3	.962	12	*O-130	1.7
1958	Cle-A	143	489	80	148	26	3	41	113	84	89	.303	.407	.620	183	56	0	2	-1	.981	2	*O-129,1-11/P	5.0
1959	Cle-A★	154	588	90	151	24	0	42	111	71	86	.257	.339	.512	135	26	3	3	-1	.985	12	*O-154	2.9
1960	Det-A	145	555	67	138	18	1	35	87	53	80	.249	.319	.474	108	4	3	6	-3	.976	7	*O-144	0.1
1961	Det-A	163	583	129	169	30	2	45	140	113	75	.290	.407	.580	156	48	1	2	-1	.975	10	*O-161	4.7
1962	Det-A★	161	601	90	164	30	2	37	112	96	68	.273	.375	.514	132	27	2	0	1	.992	18	*O-161	3.6
1963	Det-A	160	597	91	162	29	2	22	91	84	78	.271	.362	.437	119	16	0	0	0	.988	7	*O-159	1.6
1964	KC-A★	160	588	89	161	31	2	34	102	83	56	.274	.368	.507	136	30	3	1	0	.973	1	*O-159	2.6
1965	Cle-A★	162	592	92	170	25	2	26	**108**	**93**	63	.287	.387	.468	140	34	1	1	-0	**1.000**	4	*O-162	3.1
1966	Cle-A★	151	533	68	127	13	0	30	72	76	81	.238	.337	.432	119	14	2	1	0	.982	7	*O-146	1.5
1967	Cle-A	63	191	10	46	9	0	5	21	24	31	.241	.329	.366	104	1	2	2	-1	.962	-4	O-50	-0.6
	Chi-A	60	190	20	42	4	1	3	29	25	10	.221	.312	.300	85	-3	1	1	-0	.977	-7	O-58	-1.4
	Yr	123	381	30	88	13	1	8	50	49	41	.231	.320	.333	95	-2	3	3	-1	.970	-11	O-108	-2.0
1968	LA-N	40	113	8	23	3	0	3	11	15	18	.204	.297	.310	89	-1	0	1	-1	1.000	-1	O-33	-0.6
	NY-A	39	91	13	20	2	2	5	13	14	17	.220	.330	.451	139	4	0	0	0	.933	-4	O-28/P-1	-0.2
Total	14	1841	6503	971	1730	283	21	374	1159	951	880	.266	.362	.489	132	287	19	27	-11	.980	66	*O-1774/1-11,P	25.2

■ MIKE COLBERN
Colbern, Michael Malloy b: 4/19/55, Santa Monica, Cal. BR/TR, 6'3", 205 lbs. Deb: 7/18/78

YEAR	TM/L	G	AB	R	H	2B	3B	HR	RBI	BB	SO	AVG	OBP	SLG	PRO+	BR/A	SB	CS	SBR	FA	FR	G/POS	TPR
1978	Chi-A	48	141	11	38	5	1	2	20	1	36	.270	.285	.362	80	-4	0	1	-1	.969	0	C-47/D-1	-0.4
1979	Chi-A	32	83	5	20	5	1	0	8	4	25	.241	.276	.325	61	-5	0	0	0	.971	3	C-32	-0.1
Total	2	80	224	16	58	10	2	2	28	5	61	.259	.281	.348	73	-9	0	1	-1	.970	3	/C-79,D-1	-0.5

■ CRAIG COLBERT
Colbert, Craig Charles b: 2/13/65, Iowa City, Iowa BR/TR, 6', 190 lbs. Deb: 4/6/92

YEAR	TM/L	G	AB	R	H	2B	3B	HR	RBI	BB	SO	AVG	OBP	SLG	PRO+	BR/A	SB	CS	SBR	FA	FR	G/POS	TPR
1992	SF-N	49	126	10	29	5	2	1	16	9	22	.230	.281	.325	76	-4	1	0	0	.994	-7	C-35/3-9,2	-1.0
1993	SF-N	23	37	2	6	2	0	1	5	3	13	.162	.225	.297	40	-3	0	0	0	.982	2	C-10/2-2,3	-0.1
Total	2	72	163	12	35	7	2	2	21	12	35	.215	.269	.319	67	-8	1	0	0	.990	-5	/C-45,3-10,2	-1.1

■ NATE COLBERT
Colbert, Nathan b: 4/9/46, St.Louis, Mo. BR/TR, 6'2", 209 lbs. Deb: 4/14/66

YEAR	TM/L	G	AB	R	H	2B	3B	HR	RBI	BB	SO	AVG	OBP	SLG	PRO+	BR/A	SB	CS	SBR	FA	FR	G/POS	TPR
1966	Hou-N	19	7	3	0	0	0	0	0	0	4	.000	.000	.000	-99	-2	0	0	0	.000	0	H	-0.2
1968	Hou-N	20	53	5	8	1	0	0	4	1	23	.151	.167	.170	1	-6	1	1	-0	.952	-1	O-11/1-5	-1.0
1969	SD-N	139	483	64	123	20	9	24	66	45	123	.255	.322	.482	128	15	6	4	-1	.990	1	*1-134	0.5
1970	SD-N	156	572	84	148	17	6	38	86	56	150	.259	.329	.509	126	18	3	5	-2	.991	-8	*1-153/3-1	-0.6
1971	SD-N★	156	565	81	149	25	3	27	84	63	119	.264	.342	.462	135	24	5	2	0	.993	1	*1-153	1.1
1972	SD-N★	151	563	87	141	27	2	38	111	70	127	.250	.335	.508	147	32	15	6	1	.996	7	*1-150	2.8
1973	SD-N★	145	529	73	143	25	2	22	80	54	146	.270	.347	.450	130	20	9	8	-2	.992	3	*1-144	0.9
1974	SD-N	119	368	53	76	16	0	14	54	62	108	.207	.323	.364	96	-2	10	2	2	.988	4	1-79,O-48	0.2
1975	Det-A	45	156	16	23	4	2	4	18	17	52	.147	.231	.276	41	-13	0	2	-1	.982	-4	1-44/D-1	-2.1
	Mon-N	38	81	10	14	4	1	4	11	5	31	.173	.230	.395	68	-4	0	0	0	.988	-1	1-22	-0.6
1976	Mon-N	14	40	5	8	2	0	2	6	9	16	.200	.347	.400	107	1	3	1	0	1.000	0	/O-7,1-6	0.1
	Oak-A	2	5	0	0	0	0	0	0	1	3	.000	.167	.000	-50	-1	0	0	0	.000	0	/D-2	-0.1
Total	10	1004	3422	481	833	141	25	173	520	383	902	.243	.324	.451	120	81	52	31	-3	.991	5	1-890/O-66,D3	1.0

■ GREG COLBRUNN
Colbrunn, Gregory Joseph b: 7/26/69, Fontana, Cal. BR/TR, 6', 190 lbs. Deb: 7/9/92

YEAR	TM/L	G	AB	R	H	2B	3B	HR	RBI	BB	SO	AVG	OBP	SLG	PRO+	BR/A	SB	CS	SBR	FA	FR	G/POS	TPR
1992	Mon-N	52	168	12	45	8	0	2	18	6	34	.268	.301	.351	85	-4	3	2	-0	.992	-1	1-47	-0.9
1993	Mon-N	70	153	15	39	9	0	4	23	6	33	.255	.287	.392	76	-5	4	2	0	.995	1	1-61	-0.8
1994	Fla-N	47	155	17	47	10	0	6	31	9	27	.303	.349	.484	108	2	1	1	0	.988	-1	1-41	-0.2
Total	3	169	476	44	131	27	0	12	72	21	94	.275	.313	.408	90	-7	8	5	-1	.992	-1	1-149	-1.9

■ ALEX COLE
Cole, Alexander b: 8/17/65, Fayetteville, N.C. BL/TL, 6'2", 170 lbs. Deb: 7/27/90

YEAR	TM/L	G	AB	R	H	2B	3B	HR	RBI	BB	SO	AVG	OBP	SLG	PRO+	BR/A	SB	CS	SBR	FA	FR	G/POS	TPR
1990	Cle-A	63	227	43	68	5	4	0	13	28	38	.300	.379	.357	107	3	40	9	7	.961	2	O-59/D-1	1.0
1991	Cle-A	122	387	58	114	17	3	0	21	58	47	.295	.388	.354	106	6	27	17	-2	.970	1	*O-107/D-6	0.2
1992	Cle-A	41	97	11	20	1	0	0	5	10	21	.206	.287	.216	44	-7	9	2	2	.971	-4	O-24/D-4	-1.0
	*Pit-N	64	205	33	57	3	7	0	10	18	46	.278	.336	.361	99	-0	7	4	-0	.989	-1	O-53	-0.2
1993	Col-N	126	348	50	89	9	4	0	24	43	58	.256	.341	.305	64	-17	30	13	1	.982	2	O-93	-1.6
1994	Min-A	105	345	68	102	15	5	4	23	44	60	.296	.377	.403	101	2	29	8	4	.969	-0	*O-100/D-1	0.3
Total	5	521	1609	263	450	50	23	4	96	201	270	.280	.362	.347	91	-13	142	53	11	.973	-1	O-436/D-12	-1.3

■ DICK COLE
Cole, Richard Roy b: 5/6/26, Long Beach, Cal. BR/TR, 6'2", 175 lbs. Deb: 4/27/51 C

YEAR	TM/L	G	AB	R	H	2B	3B	HR	RBI	BB	SO	AVG	OBP	SLG	PRO+	BR/A	SB	CS	SBR	FA	FR	G/POS	TPR
1951	StL-N	15	36	4	7	1	0	0	3	6	5	.194	.310	.222	45	-3	0	0	0	.969	5	2-14	0.2
	Pit-N	42	106	9	25	4	0	1	11	15	9	.236	.331	.302	69	-4	0	1	-1	.981	-2	2-34/S-8	-0.5
	Yr	57	142	13	32	5	0	1	14	21	14	.225	.325	.282	63	-7	0	1	-1	.978	2	2-48/S-8	-0.3
1953	Pit-N	97	235	29	64	13	1	0	23	38	26	.272	.374	.336	87	-3	2	2	-1	.965	-3	S-77/2-7,1	-0.2
1954	Pit-N	138	486	40	131	22	5	1	40	41	48	.270	.326	.342	75	-17	0	0	0	.949	-11	S-66,3-55,2	-2.3
1955	Pit-N	77	239	16	54	8	3	0	21	18	22	.226	.286	.285	53	-16	1	0	0	.935	1	3-33,2-24,S	-1.3
1956	Pit-N	72	99	7	21	2	1	0	9	11	9	.212	.291	.253	49	-7	0	0	0	.947	-8	3-18,2-12/S	-1.4
1957	Mil-N	15	14	1	1	0	0	0	0	3	5	.071	.235	.071	-13	-2	0	0	0	.952	0	2-10/1-1,3	-0.2
Total	6	456	1215	106	303	50	10	2	107	132	124	.249	.324	.312	69	-52	2	3	-1	.961	-19	S-169,2-118,3/1	-5.7

■ STU COLE
Cole, Stewart Bryan b: 2/7/66, Charlotte, N.C. BR/TR, 6'1", 175 lbs. Deb: 9/5/91

YEAR	TM/L	G	AB	R	H	2B	3B	HR	RBI	BB	SO	AVG	OBP	SLG	PRO+	BR/A	SB	CS	SBR	FA	FR	G/POS	TPR
1991	KC-A	9	7	1	1	0	0	0	0	2	2	.143	.333	.143	37	-	-1	0	0	1.000	0	/2-5,S-1,D	0.0

■ WILLIS COLE
Cole, Willis Russell b: 1/6/1882, Milton Junction, Wis. d: 10/11/65, Madison, Wis. BR/TR, 5'8", 170 lbs. Deb: 8/22/09

YEAR	TM/L	G	AB	R	H	2B	3B	HR	RBI	BB	SO	AVG	OBP	SLG	PRO+	BR/A	SB	CS	SBR	FA	FR	G/POS	TPR
1909	Chi-A	46	165	17	39	7	3	0	16	16		.236	.308	.315	101	0	3			.889	-3	O-46	-0.6
1910	Chi-A	22	80	6	14	2	1	0	2	4		.175	.224	.225	42	-5	0			.974	1	O-22	-0.7
Total	2	68	245	23	53	9	4	0	18	20		.216	.281	.286	82	-5	3			.912	-3	/O-68	-1.3

■ CHOO CHOO COLEMAN
Coleman, Clarence b: 8/25/37, Orlando, Fla. BL/TR, 5'9", 165 lbs. Deb: 4/16/61

YEAR	TM/L	G	AB	R	H	2B	3B	HR	RBI	BB	SO	AVG	OBP	SLG	PRO+	BR/A	SB	CS	SBR	FA	FR	G/POS	TPR
1961	Phi-N	34	47	3	6	1	0	0	4	2	6	.128	.180	.149	-12	-8	0	0	0	.977	-1	C-14	-0.8
1962	NY-N	55	152	24	38	7	2	6	17	11	24	.250	.305	.441	96	-1	2	4	-2	.995	-9	C-44	-1.0
1963	NY-N	106	247	22	44	0	0	3	9	24	49	.178	.264	.215	39	-19	5	5	-2	.969	3	C-91/O-1	-1.6
1966	NY-N	6	16	2	3	0	0	0	0	0	6	.188	.188	.188	5	-2	0	0	0	.963	0	/C-5	-0.2
Total	4	201	462	51	91	8	2	9	30	37	85	.197	.267	.281	52	-30	7	9	-3	.977	-6	C-154/O-1	-3.6

■ CURT COLEMAN
Coleman, Curtis Hancock b: 2/18/1887, Salem, Ore. d: 7/1/80, Newport, Ore. BL/TR, 5'11", 180 lbs. Deb: 4/13/12

YEAR	TM/L	G	AB	R	H	2B	3B	HR	RBI	BB	SO	AVG	OBP	SLG	PRO+	BR/A	SB	CS	SBR	FA	FR	G/POS	TPR
1912	NY-A	12	37	8	9	4	0	0				.243	.364	.351	99	0	0			.865	0	3-10	0.0

■ DAVE COLEMAN
Coleman, David Lee b: 10/26/50, Dayton, Ohio BR/TR, 6'3", 195 lbs. Deb: 4/13/77

YEAR	TM/L	G	AB	R	H	2B	3B	HR	RBI	BB	SO	AVG	OBP	SLG	PRO+	BR/A	SB	CS	SBR	FA	FR	G/POS	TPR
1977	Bos-A	11	12	1	0	0	0	0	0	1	3	.000	.077	.000	-69	-3	0	0	0	1.000	-3	/O-9	-0.6

■ JERRY COLEMAN
Coleman, Gerald Francis b: 9/14/24, San Jose, Cal. BR/TR, 6', 170 lbs. Deb: 4/20/49 M

YEAR	TM/L	G	AB	R	H	2B	3B	HR	RBI	BB	SO	AVG	OBP	SLG	PRO+	BR/A	SB	CS	SBR	FA	FR	G/POS	TPR
1949	*NY-A	128	447	54	123	21	5	2	42	63	44	.275	.367	.358	92	-4	8	6	-1	**.981**	1	*2-122/S-4	0.2
1950	*NY-A★	153	522	69	150	19	6	6	69	67	38	.287	.372	.381	96	-2	3	2	-0	.977	-15	*2-152/S-6	-1.1
1951	*NY-A	121	362	48	90	11	2	3	43	31	36	.249	.315	.315	73	-14	6	1	1	.968	3	*2-102/S-18	-0.4
1952	NY-A	11	42	6	17	2	1	0	4	5	4	.405	.468	.500	180	5	0	1	-1	.971	3	2-11	0.7
1953	NY-A	8	10	1	2	0	0	0	0	0	2	.200	.200	.200	9	-1	0	0	0	1.000	2	/2-7,S-1	0.1

YEAR	TM/L	G	AB	R	H	2B	3B	HR	RBI	BB	SO	AVG	OBP	SLG	PRO+	BR/A	SB	CS	SBR	FA	FR	G/POS	TPR
1954	NY-A	107	300	39	65	7	1	3	21	26	29	.217	.279	.277	54	-19	3	0		.977	18	2-79,S-30/3	0.5
1955	*NY-A	43	96	12	22	5	0	0	8	11	11	.229	.321	.281	64	-5	0	2	-1	.966	-2	S-29,2-13/3	-0.5
1956	*NY-A	80	183	15	47	5	1	0	18	12	33	.257	.306	.295	61	-10	1	1	-1	.979	17	2-41,S-24,3	0.9
1957	*NY-A	72	157	23	42	7	2	2	12	20	21	.268	.354	.376	101	1	1	1	-0	.969	5	2-45,3-21/S	0.8
Total	9	723	2119	267	558	77	18	16	217	235	218	.263	.341	.339	83	-49	22	15	-2	.976	31	2-572,S-116/3	1.2

■ GORDY COLEMAN
Coleman, Gordon Calvin b: 7/5/34, Rockville, Md. d: 3/12/94, Cincinnati, Ohio BL/TR, 6'2", 218 lbs. Deb: 9/19/59

YEAR	TM/L	G	AB	R	H	2B	3B	HR	RBI	BB	SO	AVG	OBP	SLG	PRO+	BR/A	SB	CS	SBR	FA	FR	G/POS	TPR
1959	Cle-A	6	15	5	8	0	1	0	2	1	2	.533	.563	.667	245	3	0	0	0	.955	0	/1-3	0.3
1960	Cin-N	66	251	26	68	10	1	6	32	12	32	.271	.309	.390	89	-4	1	1	-0	.998	7	1-66	-0.3
1961	*Cin-N	150	520	63	149	27	4	26	87	45	67	.287	.346	.504	120	14	1	3	-2	.991	7	*1-150	0.7
1962	Cin-N	136	476	73	132	13	1	28	86	36	68	.277	.332	.485	113	7	2	3	-1	.989	-1	*1-128	-0.4
1963	Cin-N	123	365	38	90	20	2	14	59	29	51	.247	.306	.427	105	2	1	0	0	.987	1	*1-107	-0.1
1964	Cin-N	89	198	18	48	6	2	5	27	13	30	.242	.292	.369	82	-5	2	0	1	.990	4	1-49	-0.3
1965	Cin-N	108	325	39	98	19	0	14	57	24	38	.302	.351	.489	125	10	0	0	0	.991	-1	1-89	0.5
1966	Cin-N	91	227	20	57	7	0	5	37	16	45	.251	.300	.348	73	-8	2	1	0	.986	-1	1-65	-1.3
1967	Cin-N	4	7	0	0	0	0	0	0	1	0	.000	.125	.000	-55	-1	0	0	0	1.000	0	/1-2	-0.2
Total	9	773	2384	282	650	102	11	98	387	177	333	.273	.326	.448	106	18	9	8	-2	.990	16	1-659	-1.1

■ JOHN COLEMAN
Coleman, John Francis b: 3/6/1863, Saratoga Springs, N.Y. d: 5/31/22, Detroit, Mich. BL/TR, 5'9.5", 170 lbs. Deb: 5/1/1883

YEAR	TM/L	G	AB	R	H	2B	3B	HR	RBI	BB	SO	AVG	OBP	SLG	PRO+	BR/A	SB	CS	SBR	FA	FR	G/POS	TPR
1883	Phi-N	90	354	33	83	12	8	0	32	15	39	.234	.266	.314	83	-6				.886	10	P-65,O-31/2	0.5
1884	Phi-N	43	171	16	42	7	2	0	22	8	20	.246	.279	.310	89	-2				.844	2	O-27,P-21/1	-0.1
	Phi-a	28	107	16	22	2	3	2		5		.206	.241	.336	81	-3				.743	-1	O-24/P-3,1	-0.4
1885	Phi-a	96	398	71	119	15	11	3		25		.299	.345	.415	131	13				.844	-1	*O-93/P-8	0.8
1886	Phi-a	121	492	67	121	18	16	0		33		.246	.296	.348	100	-1	28			.862	1	*O-115/1-6,P2	-0.2
	Pit-a	11	43	3	15	2	1	0		2		.349	.378	.442	157	3	1			.786	-2	O-11	0.0
	Yr	132	535	70	136	20	17	0		35		.254	.302	.355	105	2	29			.858	-1	*O-126/1-6,P2	-0.2
1887	Pit-N	115	475	75	139	21	11	2	54	31	40	.293	.337	.396	110	7	25			.899	1	*O-115/1-2	0.4
1888	Pit-N	116	438	49	101	11	4	0	26	29	52	.231	.285	.274	85	-6	15			.928	2	O-91,1-25	-0.9
1889	Phi-a	6	19	1	1	0	0	0	1	1	3	.053	.100	.053	-57	-4	1			.929	0	/P-5,O-1	-0.1
1890	Pit-N	3	11	1	2	0	0	0	0	0	3	.182	.357	.182	66	-0	1			1.000	-1	/O-2,P-2	-0.1
Total	8	629	2508	332	645	88	56	7	135	152	154	.257	.302	.345	100	0	71			.873	11	O-510,P-107/12	-0.1

■ ED COLEMAN
Coleman, Parke Edward b: 12/1/01, Canby, Ore. d: 8/5/64, Oregon City, Ore. BL/TR, 6'2", 200 lbs. Deb: 4/15/32

YEAR	TM/L	G	AB	R	H	2B	3B	HR	RBI	BB	SO	AVG	OBP	SLG	PRO+	BR/A	SB	CS	SBR	FA	FR	G/POS	TPR
1932	Phi-A	26	73	13	25	7	1	1	13	1	6	.342	.351	.507	115	1	1	0	0	1.000	-1	O-16	0.1
1933	Phi-A	102	388	48	109	26	3	6	68	19	51	.281	.318	.410	91	-7	0	0	0	.948	-1	O-89	-1.2
1934	Phi-A	101	329	53	92	14	6	14	60	29	34	.280	.342	.486	116	6	0	1	-1	.980	-2	O-86	0.0
1935	Phi-A	10	13	0	1	0	0	0	0	0	3	.077	.077	.077	-61	-3	0	0	0	.000	-0	/O-1	-0.3
	StL-A	108	397	66	114	15	9	17	71	53	41	.287	.373	.499	118	10	0	2	-1	.974	-3	*O-102	0.2
	Yr	118	410	66	115	15	9	17	71	53	44	.280	.364	.485	113	7	0	2	-1	.974	-3	*O-103	-0.1
1936	StL-A	92	137	13	40	5	4	2	34	15	17	.292	.366	.431	93	-2	0	0	0	.939	-3	O-18	-0.4
Total	5	439	1337	193	381	67	23	40	246	117	152	.285	.345	.459	105	6	1	3	-2	.966	-8	O-312	-1.6

■ RAY COLEMAN
Coleman, Raymond Leroy b: 6/4/22, Dunsmuir, Cal. BL/TR, 5'11", 170 lbs. Deb: 4/22/47

YEAR	TM/L	G	AB	R	H	2B	3B	HR	RBI	BB	SO	AVG	OBP	SLG	PRO+	BR/A	SB	CS	SBR	FA	FR	G/POS	TPR
1947	StL-A	110	343	34	89	9	7	2	30	26	32	.259	.314	.344	81	-9	2	5	-2	.984	-2	O-93	-1.9
1948	StL-A	17	29	2	5	0	1	0	2	2	5	.172	.226	.241	24	-3	1	0	0	.889	-1	/O-5	-0.4
	Phi-A	68	210	32	51	6	6	0	21	31	17	.243	.340	.329	78	-6	4	3	-1	.978	2	O-53	-0.8
	Yr	85	239	34	56	6	7	0	23	33	22	.234	.327	.318	72	-10	5	3	-0	.972	1	O-58	-1.2
1950	StL-A	117	384	54	104	25	6	8	55	32	37	.271	.330	.430	90	-8	7	5	0	.985	3	O-98	-0.9
1951	StL-A	91	341	41	96	16	5	5	55	24	32	.282	.329	.402	94	-4	3	4	-1	.975	1	O-87	-0.7
	Chi-A	51	181	21	50	8	7	3	21	15	14	.276	.332	.448	112	2	2	3	-1	.980	-3	O-51	-0.4
	Yr	142	522	62	146	24	12	8	76	39	46	.280	.330	.418	100	-2	5	7	-3	.977	-2	*O-138	-1.1
1952	Chi-A	85	195	19	42	7	1	2	14	13	17	.215	.264	.292	54	-12	0	0	0	.978	-7	O-73	-2.2
	StL-A	20	46	5	9	3	0	0	1	5	4	.196	.288	.261	52	-3	0	0	0	1.000	-2	O-16	-0.6
	Yr	105	241	24	51	10	1	2	15	18	21	.212	.269	.286	54	-15	0	0	0	.982	-9	O-89	-2.8
Total	5	559	1729	208	446	74	33	20	199	148	158	.258	.318	.374	84	-43	19	20	-6	.980	-9	O-476	-7.9

■ BOB COLEMAN
Coleman, Robert Hunter b: 9/26/1890, Huntingburg, Ind. d: 7/16/59, Boston, Mass. BR/TR, 6'2", 190 lbs. Deb: 6/13/13 MC

YEAR	TM/L	G	AB	R	H	2B	3B	HR	RBI	BB	SO	AVG	OBP	SLG	PRO+	BR/A	SB	CS	SBR	FA	FR	G/POS	TPR
1913	Pit-N	24	50	5	9	2	0	0	9	7	8	.180	.281	.220	46	-3	0			.978	-4	C-24	-0.6
1914	Pit-N	73	150	11	40	4	1	1	14	15	32	.267	.333	.327	101	0	3			.977	2	C-72	0.7
1916	Cle-A	19	28	3	6	2	0	0	4	7	6	.214	.371	.286	92	0	0			.972	-3	C-12	-0.2
Total	3	116	228	19	55	8	1	1	27	29	46	.241	.327	.298	87	-3	3			.976	-5	C-108	-0.1

■ VINCE COLEMAN
Coleman, Vincent Maurice b: 9/22/61, Jacksonville, Fla. BB/TR, 6', 170 lbs. Deb: 4/18/85

YEAR	TM/L	G	AB	R	H	2B	3B	HR	RBI	BB	SO	AVG	OBP	SLG	PRO+	BR/A	SB	CS	SBR	FA	FR	G/POS	TPR
1985	*StL-N	151	636	107	170	20	10	1	40	50	115	.267	.321	.335	84	-13	**110**	25	**18**	.979	9	*O-150	0.9
1986	StL-N	154	600	94	139	13	8	0	29	60	98	.232	.304	.280	63	-30	**107**	14	**24**	.972	9	*O-149	-0.2
1987	*StL-N	151	623	121	180	14	10	3	43	70	126	.289	.364	.358	90	-6	**109**	22	**20**	.970	9	*O-150	1.7
1988	StL-N★	153	616	77	160	20	10	3	38	49	111	.260	.315	.339	87	-10	**81**	27	8	.971	5	*O-150	-0.2
1989	StL-N★	145	563	94	143	21	9	2	28	50	90	.254	.317	.334	84	-11	**65**	10	**14**	.962	-5	*O-142	-0.7
1990	StL-N	124	497	73	145	18	9	6	39	35	88	.292	.341	.400	103	2	**77**	17	**13**	.981	8	*O-120	2.0
1991	NY-N	72	278	45	71	7	5	1	17	39	47	.255	.347	.327	91	-2	37	14	3	.979	0	O-70	-0.1
1992	NY-N	71	229	37	63	11	1	2	21	27	41	.275	.357	.358	104	2	24	9	2	.991	-1	O-61	0.2
1993	NY-N	92	373	64	104	14	8	2	25	21	58	.279	.317	.375	86	-8	38	13	4	.982	0	O-90	-0.6
1994	KC-A	104	438	61	105	14	12	2	33	29	72	.240	.288	.340	57	-29	50	8	10	.962	0	O-99/D-5	-1.9
Total	10	1217	4853	773	1280	152	82	22	313	430	846	.264	.325	.342	83	-105	698	159	114	.974	34	*O-1181/D-5	1.1

■ CAD COLES
Coles, Cadwallader b: 1/17/1886, Rock Hill, S.C. d: 6/30/42, Miami, Fla. BL/TR, 6'0.5", 174 lbs. Deb: 4/16/14

YEAR	TM/L	G	AB	R	H	2B	3B	HR	RBI	BB	SO	AVG	OBP	SLG	PRO+	BR/A	SB	CS	SBR	FA	FR	G/POS	TPR
1914	KC-F	78	194	17	49	7	3	1	25	5	30	.253	.271	.335	59	-13	6			.889	-7	O-39/1-3	-2.3

■ CHUCK COLES
Coles, Charles Edward b: 6/27/31, Fredericktown, Pa BL/TL, 5'9", 180 lbs. Deb: 9/19/58

YEAR	TM/L	G	AB	R	H	2B	3B	HR	RBI	BB	SO	AVG	OBP	SLG	PRO+	BR/A	SB	CS	SBR	FA	FR	G/POS	TPR
1958	Cin-N	5	11	0	2	1	0	0	2	2	6	.182	.308	.273	52	-1	0	0	0	1.000	1	/O-4	0.0

■ DARNELL COLES
Coles, Darnell b: 6/2/62, San Bernardino, Cal BR/TR, 6'1", 185 lbs. Deb: 9/4/83

YEAR	TM/L	G	AB	R	H	2B	3B	HR	RBI	BB	SO	AVG	OBP	SLG	PRO+	BR/A	SB	CS	SBR	FA	FR	G/POS	TPR
1983	Sea-A	27	92	9	26	7	1	0	6	7	12	.283	.333	.391	95	-1	0	3	-2	.941	-3	3-26	-0.6
1984	Sea-A	48	143	15	23	3	1	0	6	17	26	.161	.259	.196	28	-14	2	1	0	.918	-3	3-42/O-3,D	-1.8
1985	Sea-A	27	59	8	14	4	0	1	5	9	17	.237	.348	.356	93	-0	0	1	-1	.918	1	S-15/3-7,OD	-0.3
1986	Det-A	142	521	67	142	30	2	20	86	45	84	.273	.337	.453	113	9	6	2	1	.938	-5	*3-133/S-2,OD	0.1
1987	Det-A	53	149	14	27	5	1	4	15	15	23	.181	.265	.309	54	-10	0	1	-1	.847	-5	3-36/1-9,OSD	-1.6
	Pit-N	40	119	20	27	8	0	6	24	19	20	.227	.338	.445	105	1	1	3	-2	1.000	-5	O-26,3-10/1	-0.7
1988	Pit-N	68	211	20	49	13	1	5	36	20	41	.232	.308	.374	96	-1	1	1	-0	.990	-3	O-55/1-1,3	-0.7
	Sea-A	55	195	32	57	10	1	10	34	17	26	.292	.361	.508	134	9	3	2	-0	.986	-5	O-47/1-1,D	0.4
1989	Sea-A	146	535	54	135	21	3	10	59	27	61	.252	.296	.359	81	-14	5	4	-1	.975	7	O-89,3-26,1D	-1.1
1990	Sea-A	37	107	9	23	5	1	2	16	4	17	.215	.250	.336	62	-6	0	0	0	.970	1	O-20/3-6,1D	-0.5
	Det-A	52	108	13	22	2	0	1	4	12	21	.204	.283	.250	50	-7	0	4	-2	1.000	-1	D-30,O-11/3	-1.2
	Yr	89	215	22	45	7	1	3	20	16	38	.209	.267	.293	56	-13	0	4	-2	.977	-0	O-31,D-31,3/1	-1.7
1991	SF-N	11	14	1	3	0	0	0	0	0	2	.214	.214	.214	22	-1	0	0	0	.000	-1	/O-3,1-1	-0.3

YEAR	TM/L	G	AB	R	H	2B	3B	HR	RBI	BB	SO	AVG	OBP	SLG	PRO+	BR/A	SB	CS	SBR	FA	FR	G/POS	TPR
1992	Cin-N	55	141	16	44	11	2	3	18	3	15	.312	.326	.482	123	4	1	0	0	1.000	1	3-23,1-20/O	0.4
1993	Tor-A	64	194	26	49	9	1	4	26	16	29	.253	.322	.371	85	-4	1	1	-0	.957	-9	O-44,3-16/1D	-1.4
1994	Tor-A	48	143	15	30	6	1	4	15	10	25	.210	.266	.350	57	-10	0	0	0	.980	-3	O-29,1-10/3D	-1.3
Total	12	873	2731	319	671	134	14	71	350	221	419	.246	.309	.383	89	-46	20	23	-8	.979	-34	O-344,3-341/D1S	-10.2

■ CHRIS COLETTA
Coletta, Christopher Michael   b: 8/2/44, Brooklyn, N.Y.   BL/TL, 5'11", 190 lbs.   Deb: 8/15/72

YEAR	TM/L	G	AB	R	H	2B	3B	HR	RBI	BB	SO	AVG	OBP	SLG	PRO+	BR/A	SB	CS	SBR	FA	FR	G/POS	TPR
1972	Cal-A	14	30	5	9	1	0	1	7	1	4	.300	.323	.433	131	1	0	0	0	1.000	-2	/O-7	-0.1

■ ED COLGAN
Colgan, William H.   b: 8/St.Louis, Ill.   d: 8/8/1895, Great Falls, Mont.   180 lbs.   Deb: 5/3/1884

YEAR	TM/L	G	AB	R	H	2B	3B	HR	RBI	BB	SO	AVG	OBP	SLG	PRO+	BR/A	SB	CS	SBR	FA	FR	G/POS	TPR
1884	Pit-a	48	161	10	25	4	1	0		3		.155	.171	.193	18	-14				.906	2	C-44/O-4	-0.8

■ COLLINS
Collins   Deb: 9/12/1892

YEAR	TM/L	G	AB	R	H	2B	3B	HR	RBI	BB	SO	AVG	OBP	SLG	PRO+	BR/A	SB	CS	SBR	FA	FR	G/POS	TPR
1892	StL-N	1	2	0	0	0	0	0	0	0	0	.000	.000	.000	-99	-0	0			1.000	0	/O-1	0.0

■ CHUB COLLINS
Collins, Charles Augustine   b: 10/12/1857, Dundas, Ont., Canad   d: 5/20/14, Dundas, Ont., Can.   BB, 5'11.5", 165 lbs.   Deb: 5/1/1884

YEAR	TM/L	G	AB	R	H	2B	3B	HR	RBI	BB	SO	AVG	OBP	SLG	PRO+	BR/A	SB	CS	SBR	FA	FR	G/POS	TPR
1884	Buf-N	45	169	24	30	6	0	0	20	14	36	.178	.240	.213	42	-11				.914	0	2-42/S-3	-0.9
	Ind-a	38	138	18	31	3	1	0		9		.225	.272	.261	77	-3				.886	-8	2-38	-1.0
1885	Det-N	14	55	8	10	0	2	0	6	0	11	.182	.182	.255	40	-4				.792	-8	S-14	-1.1
Total	2	97	362	50	71	9	3	0	26	23	47	.196	.244	.238	55	-18				.901	-16	/2-80,S-17	-3.0

■ WILSON COLLINS
Collins, Cyril Wilson   b: 5/7/1889, Pulaski, Tenn.   d: 2/28/41, Knoxville, Tenn.   BR/TR, 5'9.5", 165 lbs.   Deb: 5/12/13

YEAR	TM/L	G	AB	R	H	2B	3B	HR	RBI	BB	SO	AVG	OBP	SLG	PRO+	BR/A	SB	CS	SBR	FA	FR	G/POS	TPR
1913	Bos-N	16	3	3	1	0	0	0	0	0	1	.333	.333	.333	89	-0	0			1.000	-4	/O-9	-0.4
1914	Bos-N	27	35	5	9	0	0	0	1	2	8	.257	.297	.257	66	-1	0			.917	-4	O-19	-0.7
Total	2	43	38	8	10	0	0	0	1	2	9	.263	.300	.263	68	-1	0			.926	-8	/O-28	-1.1

■ DAN COLLINS
Collins, Daniel Thomas   b: 7/12/1854, St.Louis, Mo.   d: 9/21/1883, New Orleans, La.   Deb: 6/8/1874

YEAR	TM/L	G	AB	R	H	2B	3B	HR	RBI	BB	SO	AVG	OBP	SLG	PRO+	BR/A	SB	CS	SBR	FA	FR	G/POS	TPR
1874	Chi-n	3	12	1	1	0	0	0		0		.083	.083	.083	-46	-2						/P-2,O-2,S	-0.1
1876	Lou-N	7	28	3	4	1	0	0	9	0	2	.143	.143	.179	5	-3				.909	1	/O-7	-0.2

■ DAVE COLLINS
Collins, David S   b: 10/20/52, Rapid City, S.D.   BB/TL, 5'11", 175 lbs.   Deb: 6/7/75   C

YEAR	TM/L	G	AB	R	H	2B	3B	HR	RBI	BB	SO	AVG	OBP	SLG	PRO+	BR/A	SB	CS	SBR	FA	FR	G/POS	TPR
1975	Cal-A	93	319	41	85	13	4	3	29	36	55	.266	.343	.361	106	3	24	10	1	.988	4	O-75,D-12	0.5
1976	Cal-A	99	365	45	96	12	1	4	28	40	55	.263	.336	.334	103	2	32	19	-2	.994	3	O-71,D-22	-0.1
1977	Sea-A	120	402	46	96	9	3	5	28	33	66	.239	.301	.313	69	-17	25	10	2	.985	0	O-73,D-40	-1.9
1978	Cin-N	102	102	13	22	1	0	0	7	15	18	.216	.316	.225	54	-6	7	7	-2	.969	-4	O-24	-1.3
1979	*Cin-N	122	396	59	126	14	4	3	35	27	44	.318	.365	.402	108	5	16	9	-1	.976	-9	O-91,1-10	-0.9
1980	Cin-N	144	551	94	167	20	4	3	35	53	68	.303	.367	.370	106	6	79	21	11	.986	9	*O-141	1.6
1981	Cin-N	95	360	63	98	18	6	3	23	41	41	.272	.356	.381	107	4	26	10	2	.977	1	O-94	0.5
1982	NY-A	111	348	41	88	12	3	3	25	24	49	.253	.318	.330	80	-9	13	8	-1	.992	-5	O-60,1-52/D	-1.9
1983	Tor-A	118	402	55	109	12	4	1	34	43	67	.271	.345	.328	81	-9	31	7	5	.989	6	O-112/1-5,D	-0.2
1984	Tor-A	128	441	59	136	24	15	2	44	33	41	.308	.369	.444	119	12	60	14	10	.991	1	*O-108/1-6,D	1.9
1985	Oak-A	112	379	52	95	16	4	4	29	29	37	.251	.306	.346	84	-9	29	8	4	.978	6	O-91	-0.1
1986	Det-N	124	419	44	113	18	2	1	27	44	49	.270	.342	.329	84	-8	27	12	1	.995	9	O-94,D-24	-0.7
1987	Cin-N	57	85	19	25	5	0	0	5	11	12	.294	.388	.353	94	-0	9	0	3	1.000	-1	O-21	0.1
1988	Cin-N	99	174	12	41	6	2	0	14	11	27	.236	.289	.293	65	-8	7	2	1	.965	-4	O-35/1-3	-1.2
1989	Cin-N	78	106	12	25	4	0	0	7	10	17	.236	.302	.274	63	-5	3	1	0	1.000	6	O-16	-0.3
1990	StL-N	99	58	12	13	1	0	0	3	13	10	.224	.366	.241	70	-2	7	1	2	1.000	6	1-49,O-12	-0.6
Total	16	1701	4907	667	1335	187	52	32	373	467	660	.272	.340	.351	93	-40	395	139	35	.986	3	*O-1118,1-125,D	-4.6

■ EDDIE COLLINS
Collins, Edward Trowbridge Jr.   b: 11/23/16, Lansdowne, Pa.   BL/TR, 5'10", 175 lbs.   Deb: 7/4/39   F

YEAR	TM/L	G	AB	R	H	2B	3B	HR	RBI	BB	SO	AVG	OBP	SLG	PRO+	BR/A	SB	CS	SBR	FA	FR	G/POS	TPR
1939	Phi-A	32	21	6	5	1	0	0	0	0	3	.238	.238	.286	34	-2	1	0	0	1.000	-0	/O-6,2-1	-0.2
1941	Phi-A	80	219	29	53	6	3	0	12	20	24	.242	.305	.297	61	-12	2	1	0	.968	-0	O-50	-1.5
1942	Phi-A	20	34	6	8	2	0	0	4	4	2	.235	.316	.294	72	-1	1	0	0	.800	-4	O-9	-0.5
Total	3	132	274	41	66	9	3	0	16	24	29	.241	.302	.296	61	-15	4	1	1	.959	-4	/O-65,2-1	-2.2

■ EDDIE COLLINS
Collins, Edward Trowbridge Sr. "Cocky" (a.k.a. Edward T. Sullivan in 1906)
b: 5/2/1887, Millerton, N.Y.   d: 3/25/51, Boston, Mass.   BL/TR, 5'9", 175 lbs.   Deb: 9/17/06   FMCH

YEAR	TM/L	G	AB	R	H	2B	3B	HR	RBI	BB	SO	AVG	OBP	SLG	PRO+	BR/A	SB	CS	SBR	FA	FR	G/POS	TPR
1906	Phi-A	6	15	2	3	0	0	0	0	0		.200	.200	.200	25	-1	0			.900	-0	/S-3,2-1,3	-0.2
1907	Phi-A	14	20	0	5	0	0	0	2	0		.250	.250	.250	58	-1	0			.833	1	/S-6	0.0
1908	Phi-A	102	330	39	90	18	7	1	40	16		.273	.312	.379	116	5	8			.944	-12	2-47,S-28,O	-0.8
1909	Phi-A	153	572	104	198	30	10	3	56	62		.346	.416	.449	170	47	67			.967	8	*2-152/S-1	5.7
1910	*Phi-A	153	583	81	188	16	15	3	81	49		.322	.381	.417	151	34	81			.972	34	*2-153	7.0
1911	*Phi-A	132	493	92	180	22	13	3	73	62		.365	.451	.481	163	45	38			.967	3	*2-132	4.4
1912	Phi-A	153	543	137	189	25	11	0	64	101		.348	.450	.435	159	48	63			.955	15	*2-153	5.8
1913	*Phi-A	148	534	125	184	23	13	3	73	85	37	.345	.441	.453	165	48	55			.965	16	*2-148	6.4
1914	*Phi-A	152	526	122	181	23	14	2	85	97	31	.344	.452	.452	179	56	58	30	-1	.970	-0	*2-152	6.0
1915	Chi-A	155	521	118	173	22	10	4	77	119	27	.332	.460	.436	163	48	46	30	-4	.974	13	*2-155	6.1
1916	Chi-A	155	545	87	168	14	17	0	52	86	36	.308	.405	.396	139	29	40	21	-1	.976	-6	*2-155	3.0
1917	*Chi-A	156	564	91	163	18	12	0	67	89	16	.289	.389	.363	127	22	53			.969	-26	*2-156	0.5
1918	Chi-A	97	330	51	91	8	2	2	30	73	13	.276	.407	.330	121	13	22			.974	-1	2-96	3.1
1919	*Chi-A	140	518	87	165	19	7	4	80	68	27	.319	.400	.405	126	20	33			.974	3	*2-140	3.1
1920	Chi-A	153	602	117	224	38	13	3	76	69	19	.372	.438	.493	146	42	20	8	1	.976	10	*2-153	5.6
1921	Chi-A	139	526	79	177	20	10	2	58	66	11	.337	.412	.424	115	15	12	10	-2	.968	27	*2-136	4.0
1922	Chi-A	154	598	92	194	20	12	1	69	73	16	.324	.401	.403	110	12	20	12	-1	.976	-10	*2-154	0.5
1923	Chi-A	145	505	89	182	22	5	5	67	84	8	.360	.455	.453	141	36	48	29	-3	.975	-4	*2-142	2.9
1924	Chi-A	152	556	108	194	27	7	6	86	89	16	.349	.441	.455	136	34	42	17	2	.977	-7	*2-150,M	2.9
1925	Chi-A	118	425	80	147	26	3	3	80	87	8	.346	.461	.442	137	31	19	6	2	.970	-9	2-116,M	2.4
1926	Chi-A	106	375	66	129	32	4	1	62	62	8	.344	.441	.459	140	25	13	8	-1	.973	-6	2-101,M	2.0
1927	Phi-A	95	226	50	76	12	1	1	15	56	9	.336	.468	.412	123	12	6	2	1	.965	-7	2-56/S-1	0.6
1928	Phi-A	36	33	3	10	3	0	0	7	4	4	.303	.378	.394	100	0	0	0	0	.000	-2	/2-2,S-1	-0.1
1929	Phi-A	9	7	0	0	0	0	0	0	2	0	.000	.222	.000	-37	-1	0	0	0	.000	0	H	-0.1
1930	Phi-A	3	2	1	1	0	0	0	0	0	0	.500	.500	.500	148	0	0	0	0	.000	0	H	0.0
Total	25	2826	9949	1821	3312	438	186	47	1300	1499	286	.333	.424	.428	141	619	744	173		.970	41	*2-2650/S-40,O3	69.7

■ HUB COLLINS
Collins, Hubert B.   b: 4/15/1864, Louisville, Ky.   d: 5/21/1892, Brooklyn, N.Y.   BR/TR, 5'8", 160 lbs.   Deb: 9/4/1886

YEAR	TM/L	G	AB	R	H	2B	3B	HR	RBI	BB	SO	AVG	OBP	SLG	PRO+	BR/A	SB	CS	SBR	FA	FR	G/POS	TPR
1886	Lou-a	27	101	12	29	3	2	0		5		.287	.321	.356	106	0	7			.885	-2	O-24/3-2,S21	-0.2
1887	Lou-a	130	559	122	162	22	8	1		39		.290	.338	.363	94	-6	71			.887	-8	*O-109,2-10/1S3	-1.3
1888	Lou-a	116	485	117	149	26	11	2	50	41		.307	.366	.419	154	30	62			.890	13	O-82,2-19,S	3.7
	Bro-a	12	42	16	13	5	1	0	3	9		.310	.442	.476	195	5	9			.897	-3	2-12	0.3
	Yr	128	527	133	162	31	12	2	53	50		.307	.373	.423	158	35	71			.890	10	O-82,2-31,S	4.0
1889	*Bro-a	138	560	139	149	18	3	2	73	80	41	.266	.365	.320	95	-0	65			.929	-2	*2-138	0.4
1890	*Bro-N	129	510	148	142	32	7	3	69	85	47	.278	.385	.386	124	18	85			.945	5	*2-129	2.7
1891	Bro-N	107	435	82	120	16	5	3	31	59	63	.276	.365	.379	111	8	32			.910	-22	2-72,O-35	-1.1
1892	Bro-N	21	87	17	26	5	1	0	17	14	13	.299	.396	.379	140	5	4			.925	-2	O-21	0.2
Total	7	680	2779	653	790	127	38	11	243	332	164	.284	.366	.369	115	60	335			.928	-21	2-381,O-271/S13	4.7

YEAR	TM/L	G	AB	R	H	2B	3B	HR	RBI	BB	SO	AVG	OBP	SLG	PRO+	BR/A	SB	CS	SBR	FA	FR	G/POS	TPR

■ HUGH COLLINS   Collins, Hugh   150 lbs.   Deb: 8/1/1887

1887	NY-a	1	4	0	1	0	0	0	0	0	0	.250	.250	.250	41	-0	0			.000	-0	/C-1	-0.1

■ RIPPER COLLINS   Collins, James Anthony   b: 3/30/04, Altoona, Pa.   d: 4/15/70, New Haven, Conn.   BB/TL, 5'9", 165 lbs.   Deb: 4/18/31   C

1931	*StL-N	89	279	34	84	20	10	4	59	18	24	.301	.350	.487	118	6	1			.995	5	1-68/O-3	0.5
1932	StL-N	149	549	82	153	28	8	21	91	38	67	.279	.329	.474	110	6	4			.999	-5	1-81,O-60	-0.9
1933	StL-N	132	493	66	153	26	7	10	68	38	49	.310	.363	.452	125	16	7			.994	3	*1-123	0.7
1934	*StL-N	154	600	116	200	40	12	35	128	57	50	.333	.393	.615	155	45	2			.991	8	*1-154	3.8
1935	StL-N★	150	578	109	181	36	10	23	122	65	45	.313	.385	.529	138	30	0			.987	1	*1-150	1.4
1936	StL-N★	103	277	48	81	15	3	13	48	48	30	.292	.399	.509	143	18	1			.990	-2	1-61/O-9	0.9
1937	Chi-N★	115	456	77	125	16	5	16	71	32	46	.274	.329	.436	102	0	2			.991	1	*1-111	-1.2
1938	*Chi-N	143	490	78	131	22	8	13	61	54	48	.267	.344	.424	107	5	1			**.996**	10	*1-135	-0.1
1941	Pit-N	49	62	5	13	2	2	0	11	6	14	.210	.279	.306	65	-3	0			.947	-5	1-11/O-3	-0.4
Total	9	1084	3784	615	1121	205	65	135	659	356	373	.296	.360	.492	125	123	18			.992	19	1-894/O-75	4.7

■ JIMMY COLLINS   Collins, James Joseph   b: 1/16/1870, Buffalo, N.Y.   d: 3/6/43, Buffalo, N.Y.   BR/TR, 5'9", 178 lbs.   Deb: 4/19/1895   MH

1895	Bos-N	11	38	10	8	3	0	1	8	4	4	.211	.302	.368	67	-2	0			.714	-2	O-10	-0.4
	Lou-N	96	373	65	104	17	5	6	49	33	16	.279	.352	.399	100	0	12			.926	21	3-77,O-18/2S	1.7
	Yr	107	411	75	112	20	5	7	57	37	20	.273	.347	.397	96	-2	12			.926	19	3-77,O-28/2S	1.3
1896	Bos-N	84	304	48	90	10	9	1	46	30	12	.296	.374	.398	98	-1	10			.909	20	3-80/S-4	1.7
1897	*Bos-N	134	529	103	183	28	13	6	132	41		.346	.400	.482	125	17	14			.917	21	*3-134	3.5
1898	Bos-N	152	597	107	196	35	5	15	111	40		.328	.377	.479	138	26	12			.932	15	*3-152	3.8
1899	Bos-N	151	599	98	166	28	11	5	92	40		.277	.335	.386	89	-12	12			.943	21	*3-151	0.9
1900	Bos-N	142	586	104	178	25	6	6	95	34		.304	.352	.394	94	-7	23			.935	10	*3-141/S-1	0.4
1901	Bos-A	138	564	108	187	42	16	6	94	34		.332	.375	.495	142	30	19			.914	14	*3-138,M	4.0
1902	Bos-A	108	429	71	138	21	10	6	61	24		.322	.360	.459	123	12	18			**.954**	9	*3-107,M	2.0
1903	*Bos-A	130	540	88	160	33	17	5	72	24		.296	.329	.448	125	14	23			**.952**	12	*3-130,M	2.9
1904	Bos-A	156	631	85	171	33	13	3	67	27		.271	.306	.379	110	6	19			.945	7	*3-156,M	1.9
1905	Bos-A	131	508	66	140	26	5	4	65	37		.276	.330	.370	120	11	18			.923	6	*3-131,M	2.4
1906	Bos-A	37	142	17	39	8	4	1	16	4		.275	.295	.408	120	2	1			.911	3	3-32,M	0.6
1907	Bos-A	41	158	13	46	8	0	0	10	10		.291	.333	.342	116	3	4			.874	-7	3-41	-0.4
	Phi-A	100	365	38	100	22	0	0	35	24		.274	.332	.334	110	4	4			.904	-3	3-98	0.6
	Yr	141	523	51	146	30	0	0	45	34		.279	.333	.337	112	7	8			.895	-10	3-139	0.2
1908	Phi-A	115	433	34	94	14	3	0	30	20		.217	.258	.263	65	-17	5			.928	-7	*3-115	-2.2
Total	14	1726	6796	1055	2000	353	116	65	983	426	32	.294	.344	.409	112	86	194			.929	139	*3-1683/O-28,S2	23.4

■ ZIP COLLINS   Collins, John Edgar   b: 5/2/1892, Brooklyn, N.Y.   d: 12/19/83, Manassas, Va.   BL/TL, 5'11", 152 lbs.   Deb: 7/31/14

1914	Pit-N	49	182	14	44	2	0	0	15	8	10	.242	.277	.253	61	-9	3			.962	1	O-49	-1.2
1915	Pit-N	101	354	51	104	8	5	1	23	24	38	.294	.340	.353	112	5	6	7	-2	.942	5	O-89	0.4
	Bos-N	5	14	3	4	1	1	0	0	2	1	.286	.375	.500	171	1	1			1.000	1	/O-4	0.2
	Yr	106	368	54	108	9	6	1	23	26	39	.293	.342	.359	114	6	7	7	-2	.944	6	O-93	0.6
1916	Bos-N	93	268	39	56	1	6	1	18	18	42	.209	.261	.269	66	-11	4			.947	-6	O-93	-2.4
1917	Bos-N	9	27	3	4	0	1	0	2	0	4	.148	.148	.222	14	-3	0			1.000	1	/O-5	-0.3
1921	Phi-A	24	71	14	20	5	1	0	5	6	5	.282	.354	.380	87	-1	1	2	-1	.915	0	O-20	-0.3
Total	5	281	916	124	232	17	14	2	63	58	100	.253	.301	.309	85	-18	15	9		.946	1	O-245	-3.6

■ SHANO COLLINS   Collins, John Francis   b: 12/4/1885, Charlestown, Mass.   d: 9/10/55, Newton, Mass.   BR/TR, 6', 185 lbs.   Deb: 4/21/10   FM

1910	Chi-A	97	315	29	62	10	8	1	24	25		.197	.258	.289	74	-10	10			.949	4	O-66,1-28	-1.0
1911	Chi-A	106	370	48	97	16	12	4	48	20		.262	.309	.403	101	-2	14			.978	4	1-98/2-3,O	0.2
1912	Chi-A	153	579	75	168	34	10	2	81	29		.290	.330	.394	110	5	26			.969	3	*O-105,1-46	0.2
1913	Chi-A	148	535	53	128	26	9	1	47	32	60	.239	.286	.327	80	-15	22			.949	1	*O-147	-2.2
1914	Chi-A	154	598	61	164	34	9	3	65	27	49	.274	.312	.376	108	3	30	24	-5	.970	6	*O-154	-0.4
1915	Chi-A	153	576	73	148	24	17	2	85	28	50	.257	.298	.368	96	-6	38	19	0	.963	2	*O-104,1-47	-1.1
1916	Chi-A	143	527	74	128	28	12	0	42	59	51	.243	.323	.342	98	-1	16			.959	8	*O-137/1-4	-0.1
1917	*Chi-A	82	252	38	59	13	3	1	14	10	27	.234	.269	.321	78	-8	14			.992	-2	O-73	-1.4
1918	Chi-A	103	365	30	100	18	11	1	56	17	19	.274	.310	.392	111	2	7			.973	14	O-93/1-5	1.2
1919	*Chi-A	63	179	21	50	6	3	1	16	7	11	.279	.317	.363	90	-3	3			.957	1	O-46/1-8	-0.5
1920	Chi-A	133	495	70	150	21	10	1	63	23	24	.303	.339	.392	93	-6	12	9	-2	.988	-9	*1-116,O-13	-1.9
1921	Bos-A	141	542	63	155	29	12	4	69	18	38	.286	.314	.406	85	-15	15	8	-0	.966	4	*O-139/1-3	-2.0
1922	Bos-A	135	472	33	128	24	7	1	52	7	30	.271	.289	.358	68	-23	9	9	-3	.951	-7	*O-117/1-1	-4.2
1923	Bos-A	97	342	41	79	10	5	0	18	11	29	.231	.265	.289	46	-28	7	8	-3	.953	-2	O-89	-3.7
1924	Bos-A	89	240	37	70	17	5	0	28	18	17	.292	.349	.404	94	-3	4	6	-2	.957	-10	O-56,1-12	-1.8
1925	Bos-A	2	3	1	1	0	0	0	0	0	0	.333	.333	.333	70	-0	0			.000	-1	/O-1	-0.1
Total	16	1799	6390	747	1687	310	133	22	709	331	405	.264	.306	.364	90	-109	225	83		.962	16	*O-1343,1-368/2	-18.8

■ JOE COLLINS   Collins, Joseph Edward (b: Joseph Edward Kollonige)   b: 12/3/22, Scranton, Pa.   d: 8/30/89, Union, N.J.   BL/TL, 6', 185 lbs.   Deb: 9/25/48

1948	NY-A	5	5	0	1	1	0	0	2	0	1	.200	.200	.400	58	-0	0			.000	0	H	0.0
1949	NY-A	7	10	2	1	0	0	0	4	6	2	.100	.438	.100	46	-0	0	0	0	.920	-1	/1-5	-0.2
1950	*NY-A	108	205	47	48	8	3	8	28	31	34	.234	.335	.420	95	-2	5	0	2	.987	0	1-99/O-2	-0.2
1951	*NY-A	125	262	52	75	8	5	9	48	34	23	.286	.368	.458	127	10	9	7	-2	.987	4	*1-114,O-15	0.8
1952	*NY-A	122	428	69	120	16	8	18	59	55	47	.280	.364	.481	142	23	4	2	0	.990	-3	*1-119	1.7
1953	*NY-A	127	387	72	104	11	2	17	44	59	36	.269	.365	.439	121	11	2	6	-3	.989	1	*1-113/O-4	0.5
1954	NY-A	130	343	67	93	20	2	12	46	51	37	.271	.365	.446	126	12	2	2	-1	.992	1	*1-117	0.9
1955	*NY-A	105	278	40	65	9	1	13	45	44	32	.234	.343	.414	104	2	0	2	-1	.998	5	1-73,O-27	0.2
1956	*NY-A	100	262	38	59	5	3	7	43	34	33	.225	.316	.347	78	-9	3	1	0	.990	2	O-51,1-43	-1.0
1957	*NY-A	79	149	17	30	1	0	2	10	24	18	.201	.312	.248	56	-8	2	1	0	.987	-3	1-32/O-15	-1.4
Total	10	908	2329	404	596	79	24	86	329	338	263	.256	.351	.421	112	37	27	21	-5	.990	7	1-715/O-114	1.3

■ KEVIN COLLINS   Collins, Kevin Michael "Casey"   b: 8/4/46, Springfield, Mass.   BL/TR, 6'2", 190 lbs.   Deb: 9/1/65

1965	NY-N	11	23	3	4	1	0	0	0	0	9	.174	.208	.217	21	-2	0		-1	1.000	-1	/3-7,S-3	-0.5
1967	NY-N	4	10	1	1	0	0	0	0	0	3	.100	.100	.100	-43	-2	1	0	0	1.000	-0	/2-2	-0.2
1968	NY-N	58	154	12	31	5	2	1	13	7	37	.201	.236	.279	54	-9	0	1	-1	.955	-7	3-40/2-6,S	-1.8
1969	NY-N	16	40	1	6	3	0	1	2	3	10	.150	.209	.300	40	-3	0	0	0	.925	3	3-14	-0.1
	Mon-N	52	96	5	23	5	1	2	12	8	16	.240	.298	.375	87	-2	0	0	0	1.000	-7	2-20,3-16	-0.9
	Yr	68	136	6	29	8	1	3	14	11	26	.213	.272	.353	73	-5	0	0	0	.917	-4	3-30,2-20	-1.0
1970	Det-A	25	24	2	5	1	0	1	3	1	10	.208	.240	.375	67	-1	0	0	0	1.000	0	/1-1	-0.1
1971	Det-A	35	41	6	11	2	1	1	4	0	12	.268	.268	.439	94	-1	0	0	0	1.000	1	/3-4,O-2,2	0.0
Total	6	201	388	30	81	17	4	6	34	20	97	.209	.248	.320	62	-20	1	2	-1	.944	-11	/3-81,2-29,SO1	-3.6

■ ORTH COLLINS   Collins, Orth Stein "Buck"   b: 4/27/1880, Lafayette, Ind.   d: 12/13/49, Ft.Lauderdale, Fla   BL/TR, 6', 150 lbs.   Deb: 6/1/04

1904	NY-A	5	17	3	6	1	1	0	1	1		.353	.389	.529	180	1	0			1.000	2	/O-5	0.4
1909	Was-A	8	7	0	0	0	0	0	0	0		.000	.000	.000	-99	-2	0			1.000	-1	/O-2,P-1	-0.2
Total	2	13	24	3	6	1	1	0	1	1		.250	.280	.375	104	-0	0			1.000	1	/O-7,P-1	0.2

YEAR	TM/L	G	AB	R	H	2B	3B	HR	RBI	BB	SO	AVG	OBP	SLG	PRO+	BR/A	SB	CS	SBR	FA	FR	G/POS	TPR
■ RIP COLLINS		Collins, Robert Joseph b: 9/18/09, Pittsburgh, Pa. d: 4/19/69, Pittsburgh, Pa. BR/TR, 5'11", 176 lbs. Deb: 4/28/40																					
1940	Chi-N	47	120	11	25	3	0	1	14	14	18	.208	.296	.258	55	-7	4			.951	-3	C-42	-0.7
1944	NY-A	3	3	0	1	0	0	0	0	1	0	.333	.500	.333	136	0	0	0	0	1.000	0	/C-3	0.1
Total	2	50	123	11	26	3	0	1	14	15	18	.211	.302	.260	58	-7	4	0		.953	-2	/C-45	-0.6
■ PAT COLLINS		Collins, Tharon Leslie b: 9/13/1896, Sweet Sprgs., Mo. d: 5/20/60, Kansas City, Kan. BR/TR, 5'9", 178 lbs. Deb: 9/5/19																					
1919	StL-A	11	21	2	3	1	0	0	1	4	2	.143	.280	.190	32	-2	0			.929	-1	/C-5	-0.2
1920	StL-A	23	28	5	6	1	0	0	6	3	5	.214	.290	.250	43	-2	0			1.000	-2	/C-7	-0.4
1921	StL-A	58	111	9	27	3	0	1	10	16	17	.243	.339	.297	60	-6	1	0		.961	-1	C-31	-0.5
1922	StL-A	63	127	14	39	6	0	8	23	21	21	.307	.405	.543	140	8	0	1	-1	.980	6	C-28/1-5	1.4
1923	StL-A	85	181	9	32	8	0	3	30	15	45	.177	.240	.271	32	-18	0	0		.980	-1	C-47	-1.7
1924	StL-A	32	54	9	17	2	0	1	11	11	14	.315	.431	.407	110	1	0	1	-1	.969	-1	C-20	0.1
1926	*NY-A	102	290	41	83	11	3	7	35	73	57	.286	.433	.417	124	15	3	2	-0	.971	2	*C-100	2.2
1927	*NY-A	92	251	38	69	9	3	7	36	54	24	.275	.407	.418	118	9	0	1	-1	.976	-7	C-89	0.7
1928	*NY-A	70	136	18	30	5	0	6	14	35	16	.221	.380	.390	106	2	0	0	0	.977	-5	C-70	0.2
1929	Bos-N	7	5	1	0	0	0	0	2	3	1	.000	.375	.000	2	-1	0			1.000	1	/C-6	0.1
Total	10	543	1204	146	306	46	6	33	168	235	202	.254	.378	.385	98	5	4	5		.974	-7	C-403/1-5	1.9
■ BILL COLLINS		Collins, William J. b: 1863, Dublin, Ireland d: 6/8/1893, New York, N.Y. BR Deb: 10/5/1889																					
1889	Phi-a	1	4	0	1	0	0	0		1	0	.250	.400	.250	88	0	1			.800	-1	/C-1	0.0
1890	Phi-a	1	1	0	0	0	0	0		0		.000	.000	.000	-99	-0	0			.500	-0	/S-1	0.0
1891	Cle-N	2	3	0	0	0	0	0	0	0	0	.000	.000	.000	-96	-1	0			.000	-1	/O-1,C-1	0.0
Total	3	4	8	0	1	0	0	0	1	1	0	.125	.222	.125	1	-1	1			.867	0	/C-2,O-1,S	0.0
■ BILL COLLINS		Collins, William Shirley b: 3/27/1882, Chesterton, Ind. d: 6/26/61, San Bernardino, Cal. BB/TR, 6', 170 lbs. Deb: 4/14/10																					
1910	Bos-N	151	584	67	141	6	7	3	40	43	48	.241	.308	.291	72	-21	36			**.977**	13	*O-151	-1.7
1911	Bos-N	17	44	8	6	1	1	0	8	1	8	.136	.156	.250	0	-6	4			1.000	0	O-13/3-1	-0.6
	Chi-N	7	3	2	1	1	0	0	0	1	0	.333	.500	.667	225	1	0			1.000	-2	/O-4	-0.1
	Yr	24	47	10	7	2	1	0	8	2	8	.149	.184	.234	16	-6	4			1.000	-2	O-17/3-1	-0.7
1913	Bro-N	32	95	8	18	1	0	0	4	8	11	.189	.267	.200	33	-8	2			.921	-3	O-27	-1.3
1914	Buf-F	21	47	6	7	2	2	0	2	1	8	.149	.167	.277	13	-6	0			.864	-1	O-15	-0.8
Total	4	228	773	91	173	11	10	3	54	54	75	.224	.287	.276	60	-41	42			.966	7	O-210/3-1	-4.5
■ BILL COLLVER		Collver, William J. b: 3/21/1867, Clyde, Ohio d: 3/24/1888, Detroit, Mich. Deb: 7/4/1885																					
1885	Bos-N	1	4	0	0	0	0	0	0	0	1	.000	.000	.000	-99	-1				.000	-0	/O-1	-0.1
■ FRANK COLMAN		Colman, Frank Lloyd b: 3/2/18, London, Ont., Canada d: 2/19/83, London, Ont., Can. BL/TL, 5'11", 188 lbs. Deb: 9/12/42																					
1942	Pit-N	10	37	2	5	0	0	1	2	2	2	.135	.179	.216	15	-4	0			1.000	0	/O-8	-0.4
1943	Pit-N	32	59	9	16	2	2	0	4	8	7	.271	.358	.373	108	1	0			1.000	0	O-11	0.0
1944	Pit-N	99	226	30	61	9	5	6	53	25	27	.270	.345	.434	113	4	0			.964	-3	O-53/1-6	-0.2
1945	Pit-N	77	153	18	32	11	1	4	30	9	16	.209	.253	.373	70	-7	0			.993	-1	1-22,O-12	-1.0
1946	Pit-N	26	53	3	9	3	0	1	6	2	7	.170	.214	.283	39	-4	0			1.000	0	/O-8,1-2	-0.5
	NY-A	5	15	2	4	0	0	1	5	1	1	.267	.313	.467	114	0	0	0	0	1.000	-0	/O-5	0.0
1947	NY-A	22	28	2	3	0	0	2	6	2	6	.107	.167	.321	34	-3	0	0	0	1.000	-1	O-6	-0.4
Total	6	271	571	66	130	25	8	15	106	49	66	.228	.291	.378	85	-14	0	0		.980	-4	O-103/1-30	-2.5
■ CRIS COLON		Colon, Cristobal b: 1/3/69, LaGuaira, Venez. BB/TR, 6'2", 180 lbs. Deb: 9/18/92																					
1992	Tex-A	14	36	5	6	0	0	0	1	1	8	.167	.189	.167		-5	0	0	0	.946	3	S-14	-0.1
■ BOB COLUCCIO		Coluccio, Robert Pasquali b: 10/2/51, Centralia, Wash. BR/TR, 5'11", 183 lbs. Deb: 4/15/73																					
1973	Mil-A	124	438	65	98	21	8	15	58	54	92	.224	.313	.411	105	2	13	6	0	.992	10	*O-108,D-11	0.7
1974	Mil-A	138	394	42	88	13	4	6	31	43	61	.223	.305	.322	81	-9	15	9	-1	.989	0	*O-131/D-2	-1.5
1975	Mil-A	22	62	8	12	0	1	1	5	11	11	.194	.324	.274	70	-2	1	4	-2	1.000	1	O-22	-0.5
	Chi-A	61	161	22	33	4	2	4	13	13	34	.205	.269	.329	67	-7	4	0	1	.980	-5	O-59/D-1	-1.4
	Yr	83	223	30	45	4	3	5	18	24	45	.202	.285	.314	68	-9	5	4	-1	.987	-5	O-81/D-1	-1.9
1977	Chi-A	20	37	4	10	0	0	0	7	6	2	.270	.372	.270	79	-1	0	2	-1	1.000	-2	O-19	-0.5
1978	StL-N	5	3	0	0	0	0	0	0	1	2	.000	.250	.000	-25	-0	0	0	0	1.000	-1	/O-2	-0.1
Total	5	370	1095	141	241	38	15	26	114	128	202	.220	.306	.353	87	-18	33	21	-3	.990	2	O-341/D-14	-3.3
■ EARLE COMBS		Combs, Earle Bryan "The Kentucky Colonel" b: 5/14/1899, Pebworth, Ky. d: 7/21/76, Richmond, Ky. BL/TR, 6', 185 lbs. Deb: 4/16/24 CH																					
1924	NY-A	24	35	10	14	5	0	2	4	2	2	.400	.462	.543	159	3	0	1		1.000	-3	O-11	-0.1
1925	NY-A	150	593	117	203	36	13	3	61	65	43	.342	.411	.462	123	22	12	13	-4	.979	4	*O-150	1.1
1926	*NY-A	145	606	113	181	31	12	8	55	47	23	.299	.352	.429	105	2	8	6	-1	.970	1	*O-145	-0.8
1927	*NY-A	152	648	137	**231**	36	23	6	64	62	31	.356	.414	.511	143	41	15	6	1	.968	2	*O-152	3.2
1928	*NY-A	149	626	118	194	33	21	7	56	77	33	.310	.387	.463	127	25	10	8	-2	.980	8	*O-149	2.0
1929	NY-A	142	586	119	202	33	15	3	65	69	32	.345	.414	.468	135	32	11	7	-1	.966	-4	*O-141	1.7
1930	NY-A	137	532	129	183	30	22	7	82	74	26	.344	.424	.523	145	38	16	10	-1	.969	-2	*O-135	2.1
1931	NY-A	138	563	120	179	31	13	5	58	68	34	.318	.394	.446	128	24	11	3	2	.974	-0	*O-129	1.5
1932	*NY-A	144	591	143	190	32	10	9	65	81	16	.321	.405	.455	129	28	3	9	-5	.967	-7	*O-139	0.6
1933	NY-A	122	417	86	125	22	16	5	64	47	19	.300	.372	.465	128	16	6	4	-1	.975	-4	*O-104	0.6
1934	NY-A	63	251	47	80	13	5	2	25	40	9	.319	.412	.434	127	12	3	1	-1	.993	-2	O-62	0.7
1935	NY-A	89	298	47	84	7	4	3	35	36	10	.282	.359	.362	92	-3	1	3	-2	.993	-4	O-70	-1.0
Total	12	1455	5746	1186	1866	309	154	58	632	670	278	.325	.397	.462	127	241	96	71	-14	.974	-14	*O-1387	11.6
■ MERL COMBS		Combs, Merrill Russell b: 12/11/19, Los Angeles, Cal. d: 7/8/81, Riverside, Cal. BL/TR, 6', 172 lbs. Deb: 9/12/47 C																					
1947	Bos-A	17	68	8	15	1	0	1	6	9	9	.221	.329	.279	65	-3	0	0	0	1.000	4	3-17	0.1
1949	Bos-A	14	24	5	5	1	0	0	1	9	0	.208	.424	.250	75	-0	0	0	0	.923	-0	/3-9,S-1	-0.1
1950	Bos-A	1	0	0	0	0	0	0	0	0	0	—	1.000	—	158	0	0			.000	0	H	0.0
	Was-A	37	102	19	25	1	0	0	6	22	16	.245	.379	.255	68	-4	0	0	0	.966	-1	S-30	-0.2
	Yr	38	102	19	25	1	0	0	6	23	16	.245	.384	.255	69	-3	0	0	0	.966	-1	S-30	-0.2
1951	Cle-A	19	28	2	5	2	0	0	2	2	3	.179	.233	.250	32	-3	0	0	0	.960	5	S-16	0.2
1952	Cle-A	52	139	11	23	1	1	0	10	14	15	.165	.242	.209	28	-14	0	1	-1	.972	9	S-49/2-3	-0.3
Total	5	140	361	45	73	6	1	2	25	57	43	.202	.314	.241	52	-23	0	1		.968	17	/S-96,3-26,2	-0.3
■ WAYNE COMER		Comer, Harry Wayne b: 2/3/44, Shenandoah, Va. BR/TR, 5'10", 175 lbs. Deb: 9/17/67																					
1967	Det-A	4	3	0	1	0	0	0	0	0	0	.333	.333	.333	95	-0	0	0	0	.000	-0	/O-1	0.0
1968	*Det-A	48	48	8	6	0	1	1	3	2	7	.125	.160	.229	16	-5	0	0	0	1.000	-5	O-27/C-1	-1.2
1969	Sea-A	147	481	88	118	18	1	15	54	82	79	.245	.356	.380	108	7	18	7	1	.980	3	*O-139/C-1,3	0.4
1970	Mil-A	13	17	1	1	0	0	0	1	0	9	.059	.059	.059	-67	-4	0	0	0	1.000	0	/O-5	-0.5
	Was-A	77	129	21	30	4	0	0	8	22	16	.233	.349	.264	75	-3	4	1	0	.960	-10	O-58/3-1	-1.5
	Yr	90	146	22	31	4	0	0	9	22	19	.212	.320	.240	59	-7	4	1	0	.962	-11	O-63/3-1	-2.0
1972	Det-A	27	9	1	1	0	0	0	1	0	1	.111	.111	.111	-33	-1	0	1	-1	1.000	-5	O-17	-0.9
Total	5	316	687	119	157	22	2	16	67	106	106	.229	.333	.336	90	-7	22	9		.978	-18	O-247/3-2,C	-3.7

YEAR	TM/L	G	AB	R	H	2B	3B	HR	RBI	BB	SO	AVG	OBP	SLG	PRO+	BR/A	SB	CS	SBR	FA	FR	G/POS	TPR

■ CHARLIE COMISKEY
Comiskey, Charles Albert "Commy" or "The Old Roman" b: 8/15/1859, Chicago, Ill. d: 10/26/31, Eagle River, Wis. BR/TR, 6', 180 lbs. Deb: 5/2/1882 MH

YEAR	TM/L	G	AB	R	H	2B	3B	HR	RBI	BB	SO	AVG	OBP	SLG	PRO+	BR/A	SB	CS	SBR	FA	FR	G/POS	TPR
1882	StL-a	78	329	58	80	9	5	1			4	.243	.252	.310	85	-6				.967	-1	*1-77/P-2	-1.4
1883	StL-a	96	401	87	118	17	9	2			11	.294	.313	.397	120	7				.963	-2	*1-96/O-1M	-0.4
1884	StL-a	108	460	76	110	17	6	2			5	.239	.255	.315	82	-10				.969	-2	*1-108/2-1,PM	-1.9
1885	*StL-a	83	340	68	87	15	7	2			14	.256	.293	.359	101	-1				.969	1	*1-83,M	-0.9
1886	*StL-a	131	578	95	147	15	9	3			10	.254	.267	.327	82	-15	41			.975	4	*1-122/2-9,OM	-2.3
1887	*StL-a	125	538	139	180	22	5	4			27	.335	.374	.416	109	2	117			.976	3	*1-116/2-9,OM	-0.5
1888	*StL-a	137	576	102	157	22	5	6	83	12		.273	.292	.359	98	-6	72			.970	-6	*1-133/O-5,2M	-2.3
1889	StL-a	137	587	105	168	28	10	3	102	19	19	.286	.312	.383	86	-17	65			.970	-1	*1-134/O-3,2PM	-2.3
1890	Chi-P	88	377	53	92	11	3	0	59	14	17	.244	.277	.289	49	-29	34			.965	-2	1-88,M	-2.9
1891	StL-a	141	580	86	152	16	2	3	93	33	25	.262	.310	.312	68	-30	41			.980	3	*1-141/O-2M	-2.9
1892	Cin-N	141	551	61	125	14	6	3	71	32	16	.227	.274	.290	72	-20	30			.984	1	*1-141,M	-2.4
1893	Cin-N	64	259	38	57	12	1	0	26	11	2	.220	.257	.274	40	-23	9			.979	-6	1-64,M	-2.6
1894	Cin-N	61	220	26	58	8	0	0	33	5	5	.264	.289	.300	41	-22	10			.972	-4	1-60/O-1M	-2.9
Total	13	1390	5796	994	1531	206	68	29	467	197	84	.264	.293	.338	82	-168	419			.973	-8	*1-1363/2-25,OP	-24.8

■ JIM COMMAND
Command, James Dalton "Igor" b: 10/15/28, Grand Rapids, Mich. BL/TR, 6'2", 200 lbs. Deb: 6/20/54

YEAR	TM/L	G	AB	R	H	2B	3B	HR	RBI	BB	SO	AVG	OBP	SLG	PRO+	BR/A	SB	CS	SBR	FA	FR	G/POS	TPR
1954	Phi-N	9	18	1	4	1	0	1	6	2	4	.222	.300	.444	91	-0	0	0	0	.929	-0	/3-6	-0.1
1955	Phi-N	5	5	0	0	0	0	0	0	0	0	.000	.000	.000	-99	-1	0	0	0	.000	0	H	-0.1
Total	2	14	23	1	4	1	0	1	6	2	4	.174	.240	.348	52	-2	0	0	0	.929	-0	/3-6	-0.2

■ ADAM COMOROSKY
Comorosky, Adam Anthony b: 12/9/05, Swoyersville, Pa. d: 3/2/51, Swoyersville, Pa. BR/TR, 5'10", 167 lbs. Deb: 9/13/26

YEAR	TM/L	G	AB	R	H	2B	3B	HR	RBI	BB	SO	AVG	OBP	SLG	PRO+	BR/A	SB	CS	SBR	FA	FR	G/POS	TPR
1926	Pit-N	8	15	2	4	1	1	0	0	1	2	.267	.313	.467	102	-0	1			1.000	-1	/O-6	-0.2
1927	Pit-N	18	61	5	14	1	0	0	4	3	1	.230	.266	.246	35	-6	0			.978	-1	O-16	-0.5
1928	Pit-N	51	176	22	52	6	3	2	34	15	6	.295	.354	.398	92	-2	1			.968	-1	O-49	-0.5
1929	Pit-N	127	473	86	152	26	11	6	97	46	22	.321	.377	.461	104	3	19			.963	0	*O-121	-0.5
1930	Pit-N	152	597	112	187	47	**23**	12	119	51	33	.313	.371	.529	114	12	14			.969	1	*O-152	0.2
1931	Pit-N	99	350	37	85	12	1	1	48	34	28	.243	.310	.291	63	-17	11			.978	3	O-90	-2.1
1932	Pit-N	108	370	54	106	18	4	4	46	25	20	.286	.337	.389	96	-2	7			.981	7	O-92	0.0
1933	Pit-N	64	162	18	46	8	1	1	15	4	9	.284	.301	.364	89	-3	2			1.000	-1	O-30	-0.5
1934	Cin-N	127	446	46	115	12	6	0	40	34	23	.258	.315	.312	70	-18	1			.970	1	*O-122	-2.2
1935	Cin-N	59	137	22	34	3	1	2	14	7	14	.248	.290	.328	68	-6	1			.953	-2	O-40	-0.9
Total	10	813	2787	404	795	134	51	28	417	214	158	.285	.339	.400	91	-39	57			.972	9	O-718	-7.2

■ PETE COMPTON
Compton, Anna Sebastian "Bash" b: 9/28/1889, San Marcos, Tex. d: 2/3/78, Kansas City, Mo. BL/TL, 5'11", 170 lbs. Deb: 9/6/11

YEAR	TM/L	G	AB	R	H	2B	3B	HR	RBI	BB	SO	AVG	OBP	SLG	PRO+	BR/A	SB	CS	SBR	FA	FR	G/POS	TPR
1911	StL-A	28	107	9	29	4	0	0	5	8		.271	.322	.308	79	-3	2			.917	1	O-28	-0.3
1912	StL-A	103	268	26	75	6	4	2	30	22		.280	.339	.354	102	1	11			.925	1	O-72	-0.9
1913	StL-A	63	100	14	18	5	2	2	17	13	13	.180	.274	.330	79	-3	2			.862	-4	O-21	-0.9
1915	StL-F	2	8	0	2	0	0	0	0	0	0	.250	.250	.250	32	-1	0			1.000	-1	/O-2	-0.2
	Bos-N	35	116	10	28	7	1	1	12	8	11	.241	.290	.345	96	-1	4	1	1	.971	-0	O-31	-0.1
1916	Bos-N	34	98	13	20	2	0	0	8	7	7	.204	.264	.224	53	-5	5			.939	-2	O-30	-1.0
	Pit-N	5	16	1	1	0	0	0	0	2	5	.063	.211	.063	-14	-2	0			.917	0	/O-5	-0.3
	Yr	39	114	14	21	2	0	0	8	9	12	.184	.262	.202	43	-7	5			.936	-2	O-35	-1.3
1918	NY-N	21	60	5	13	0	1	0	5	5	4	.217	.277	.250	62	-3	2			.971	-1	O-19	-0.5
Total	6	291	773	78	186	24	8	5	80	65	40	.241	.303	.312	83	-17	26	1		.933	-6	O-208	-3.5

■ MIKE COMPTON
Compton, Michael Lynn b: 8/15/44, Stamford, Tex. BR/TR, 5'10", 180 lbs. Deb: 4/17/70

YEAR	TM/L	G	AB	R	H	2B	3B	HR	RBI	BB	SO	AVG	OBP	SLG	PRO+	BR/A	SB	CS	SBR	FA	FR	G/POS	TPR
1970	Phi-N	47	110	8	18	0	1	1	7	9	22	.164	.240	.209	22	-12	0	0	0	.986	8	C-40	-0.3

■ CLINT CONATSER
Conatser, Clinton Astor "Connie" b: 7/24/21, Los Angeles, Cal. BR/TR, 5'11", 182 lbs. Deb: 4/21/48

YEAR	TM/L	G	AB	R	H	2B	3B	HR	RBI	BB	SO	AVG	OBP	SLG	PRO+	BR/A	SB	CS	SBR	FA	FR	G/POS	TPR
1948	*Bos-N	90	224	30	62	9	3	3	23	32	27	.277	.370	.384	106	3	0			.974	-9	O-76	-0.9
1949	Bos-N	53	152	10	40	6	0	3	16	14	19	.263	.329	.362	89	-3	0			.951	0	O-44	-0.4
Total	2	143	376	40	102	15	3	6	39	46	46	.271	.352	.375	99	0	0			.965	-8	O-120	-1.3

■ DAVE CONCEPCION
Concepcion, David Ismael (Benitez) b: 6/17/48, Aragua, Venez. BR/TR, 6'1", 180 lbs. Deb: 4/6/70

YEAR	TM/L	G	AB	R	H	2B	3B	HR	RBI	BB	SO	AVG	OBP	SLG	PRO+	BR/A	SB	CS	SBR	FA	FR	G/POS	TPR
1970	*Cin-N	101	265	38	69	6	3	1	19	23	45	.260	.326	.317	73	-10	10	2	2	.945	-8	S-93/2-3	-0.6
1971	Cin-N	130	327	24	67	4	4	1	20	18	51	.205	.246	.251	42	-25	9	3	1	.974	-4	*S-112,2-10/3O	-1.7
1972	*Cin-N	119	378	40	79	13	2	3	29	32	65	.209	.274	.270	58	-21	13	6	0	.969	3	*S-114/3-9,2	-0.3
1973	Cin-N†	89	328	39	94	18	3	8	46	21	55	.287	.331	.433	116	6	22	5	4	.974	2	S-88/O-2	2.3
1974	Cin-N	160	594	70	167	25	1	14	82	44	79	.281	.337	.397	106	4	41	6	9	.963	9	*S-160/O-1	4.3
1975	*Cin-N★	140	507	62	139	23	1	5	49	39	51	.274	.328	.353	88	-9	33	6	6	.977	8	*S-130/3-6	2.1
1976	*Cin-N★	152	576	74	162	28	7	9	69	49	68	.281	.339	.401	107	5	21	10	0	.968	17	*S-150	4.1
1977	Cin-N★	156	572	59	155	26	3	8	64	46	77	.271	.325	.369	84	-13	29	7	5	**.986**	8	*S-156	1.7
1978	Cin-N	153	565	75	170	33	4	6	67	51	83	.301	.360	.405	113	10	23	10	1	.969	-5	*S-152	2.7
1979	*Cin-N†	149	590	91	166	25	3	16	84	64	73	.281	.352	.415	108	7	19	7	2	.967	13	*S-148	3.8
1980	Cin-N	156	622	72	162	31	8	5	77	37	107	.260	.303	.360	84	-14	12	2	2	.978	-13	*S-155/2-1	-0.7
1981	Cin-N★	106	421	57	129	28	0	5	67	37	61	.306	.364	.409	117	10	4	5	-2	.960	4	*S-106	2.4
1982	Cin-N★	147	572	48	164	25	4	5	53	46	63	.287	.339	.371	96	-2	13	6	-1	.977	13	*S-145/1-1,3	2.5
1983	Cin-N	143	528	54	123	22	0	1	47	56	81	.233	.307	.280	61	-26	13	9	-1	.979	-22	*S-139/3-6,1	-3.8
1984	Cin-N	154	531	46	130	26	1	4	58	52	72	.245	.312	.320	75	-17	22	6	3	.978	-35	*S-104,3-54/1	-4.3
1985	Cin-N	155	560	59	141	19	2	7	48	50	67	.252	.316	.330	77	-16	16	12	0	.962	-32	*S-151/3-5	-3.9
1986	Cin-N	90	311	42	81	13	2	3	30	26	43	.260	.318	.344	79	-9	13	2	3	.965	-2	S-60,1-12,23	-0.3
1987	Cin-N	104	279	32	89	15	0	1	33	28	24	.319	.381	.384	99	1	4	3	-1	.992	0	2-59,1-26,3/S	-0.2
1988	Cin-N	84	197	11	39	9	0	0	8	18	23	.198	.265	.244	45	-14	3	2	-0	.994	1	2-46,1-16,S/3P	-1.3
Total	19	2488	8723	993	2326	389	48	101	950	736	1186	.267	.325	.357	88	-133	321	109	31	.971	-44	*S-2178,2-130,3/1OP	9.2

■ ONIX CONCEPCION
Concepcion, Onix Cardona (Cardona) b: 10/5/57, Dorado, P.R. BR/TR, 5'6", 180 lbs. Deb: 8/30/80

YEAR	TM/L	G	AB	R	H	2B	3B	HR	RBI	BB	SO	AVG	OBP	SLG	PRO+	BR/A	SB	CS	SBR	FA	FR	G/POS	TPR
1980	*KC-A	12	15	1	2	0	0	0	2	0	1	.133	.133	.133	-26	-3	0	0	0	.833	1	/S-6	-0.2
1981	KC-A	2	0	0	0	0	0	0	0	0	0	—	—	—	—	0	0	0	0	.000	0	/S-1	0.0
1982	KC-A	74	205	17	48	9	1	0	15	5	18	.234	.256	.288	49	-14	2	1	0	.948	-2	S-46,2-24/D	-1.1
1983	KC-A	80	219	22	53	11	3	0	20	12	12	.242	.284	.320	66	-10	10	3	1	.913	1	3-31,2-28,S/D	-0.6
1984	*KC-A	90	287	36	81	9	2	1	23	14	33	.282	.322	.338	82	-7	9	6	-1	.972	0	S-85/2-6,3	0.4
1985	*KC-A	131	314	32	64	5	1	2	20	16	29	.204	.256	.245	38	-27	4	4	-1	.959	5	*S-128/2-2	-1.2
1987	Pit-N	1	1	0	1	0	0	0	0	0	0	1.000	1.000	1.000	429	0	0	0	0	.000	0	/H	0.0
Total	7	390	1041	108	249	34	7	3	80	47	93	.239	.279	.294	58	-60	25	14	-1	.960	8	S-287/2-60,3D	-2.7

■ RAMON CONDE
Conde, Ramon Luis (Roman) "Wito" b: 12/29/34, Juana Diaz, P.R. BR/TR, 5'8", 172 lbs. Deb: 7/17/62

YEAR	TM/L	G	AB	R	H	2B	3B	HR	RBI	BB	SO	AVG	OBP	SLG	PRO+	BR/A	SB	CS	SBR	FA	FR	G/POS	TPR
1962	Chi-A	14	16	0	0	0	0	0	1	3	3	.000	.158	.000	-54	-4	0	0	0	.889	-1	/3-7	-0.4

■ FRED CONE
Cone, Joseph Frederick b: 5/1848, Rockford, Ill. d: 4/13/09, Chicago, Ill. 5'9.5", 171 lbs. Deb: 5/5/1871

YEAR	TM/L	G	AB	R	H	2B	3B	HR	RBI	BB	SO	AVG	OBP	SLG	PRO+	BR/A	SB	CS	SBR	FA	FR	G/POS	TPR
1871	Bos-n	19	77	17	20	3	1	0	16	8	1	.260	.329	.325	86	-1	12					O-18	0.0

■ BUNK CONGALTON
Congalton, William Millar b: 1/24/1875, Guelph, Ont., Can. d: 8/16/37, Cleveland, Ohio BL/TL, 5'11", 190 lbs. Deb: 4/18/02

YEAR	TM/L	G	AB	R	H	2B	3B	HR	RBI	BB	SO	AVG	OBP	SLG	PRO+	BR/A	SB	CS	SBR	FA	FR	G/POS	TPR
1902	Chi-N	45	179	14	40	3	0	1	24	7		.223	.253	.257	59	-9	3			.987	0	O-45	-1.3

YEAR	TM/L	G	AB	R	H	2B	3B	HR	RBI	BB	SO	AVG	OBP	SLG	PRO+	BR/A	SB	CS	SBR	FA	FR	G/POS	TPR
1905	Cle-A	12	47	4	17	0	0	0	5	2		.362	.388	.362	136	2	3			.923	-1	O-12	0.0
1906	Cle-A	117	419	51	134	13	5	3	50	24		.320	.361	.396	139	18	12			.957	-9	*O-114	0.4
1907	Cle-A	9	22	2	4	0	0	0	2	4		.182	.308	.182	56	-1	0			1.000	0	/O-6	-0.1
	Bos-A	124	496	44	142	11	8	2	47	20		.286	.318	.353	115	7	13			.969	-2	*O-123	0.0
	Yr	133	518	46	146	11	8	2	49	24		.282	.317	.346	112	6	13			.971	-2	*O-129	-0.1
Total	4	307	1163	115	337	27	13	6	128	57		.290	.326	.351	115	17	31			.967	-12	O-300	-1.0

■ TONY CONIGLIARO
Conigliaro, Anthony Richard b: 1/7/45, Revere, Mass. d: 2/24/90, Salem, Mass. BR/TR, 6'3", 185 lbs. Deb: 4/16/64 F

YEAR	TM/L	G	AB	R	H	2B	3B	HR	RBI	BB	SO	AVG	OBP	SLG	PRO+	BR/A	SB	CS	SBR	FA	FR	G/POS	TPR
1964	Bos-A	111	404	69	117	21	2	24	52	35	78	.290	.354	.530	135	18	2	4	-2	.973	3	*O-106	1.5
1965	Bos-A	138	521	82	140	21	5	32	82	51	116	.269	.340	.512	131	20	4	2	0	.976	14	*O-137	2.8
1966	Bos-A	150	558	77	148	26	7	28	93	52	112	.265	.333	.487	120	13	0	2	-1	.973	-0	*O-146	0.6
1967	Bos-A★	95	349	59	100	11	5	20	67	27	58	.287	.346	.519	141	17	4	6	-2	.983	3	O-95	1.4
1969	Bos-A	141	506	57	129	21	3	20	82	48	111	.255	.324	.427	103	1	2	4	-2	.981	-8	*O-137	-1.7
1970	Bos-A	146	560	89	149	20	1	36	116	43	93	.266	.327	.498	116	10	4	2	0	.977	3	*O-146	0.6
1971	Cal-A	74	266	23	59	18	0	4	15	23	52	.222	.286	.335	81	-8	3	3	-1	.994	6	O-72	-0.6
1975	Bos-A	21	57	8	7	1	0	2	9	8	9	.123	.231	.246	32	-5	1	0	0	.000	0	D-15	-0.6
Total	8	876	3221	464	849	139	23	166	516	287	629	.264	.330	.476	118	67	20	23	-8	.979	21	O-839/D-15	4.0

■ BILLY CONIGLIARO
Conigliaro, William Michael b: 8/15/47, Revere, Mass. BR/TR, 6', 190 lbs. Deb: 4/11/69 F

YEAR	TM/L	G	AB	R	H	2B	3B	HR	RBI	BB	SO	AVG	OBP	SLG	PRO+	BR/A	SB	CS	SBR	FA	FR	G/POS	TPR
1969	Bos-A	32	80	14	23	6	2	4	7	9	23	.287	.367	.563	149	5	1	1	-0	.926	-7	O-24	-0.3
1970	Bos-A	114	398	59	108	16	3	18	58	35	73	.271	.341	.462	112	6	3	7	-3	.968	0	*O-108	-0.3
1971	Bos-A	101	351	42	92	26	1	11	33	25	68	.262	.311	.436	102	0	3	2	-0	.983	4	*O-100	-0.1
1972	Mil-A	52	191	22	44	6	2	7	16	8	54	.230	.261	.393	95	-2	1	0	0	.992	6	O-50	0.2
1973	*Oak-A	48	110	5	22	2	2	0	14	9	26	.200	.261	.255	48	-8	1	0	0	1.000	-2	O-40/2-1	-1.1
Total	5	347	1130	142	289	56	10	40	128	86	244	.256	.313	.429	103	1	9	10	-3	.980	2	O-322/2-1	-1.6

■ JEFF CONINE
Conine, Jeffrey Guy b: 6/27/66, Tacoma, Wash. BR/TR, 6'1", 205 lbs. Deb: 9/16/90

YEAR	TM/L	G	AB	R	H	2B	3B	HR	RBI	BB	SO	AVG	OBP	SLG	PRO+	BR/A	SB	CS	SBR	FA	FR	G/POS	TPR
1990	KC-A	9	20	3	5	2	0	0	2	2	5	.250	.318	.350	88	-0	0	0	0	.977	0	/1-9	-0.1
1992	KC-A	28	91	10	23	5	2	0	9	8	23	.253	.313	.352	84	-2	0	0	0	1.000	-2	O-23/1-4	-0.5
1993	Fla-N	162	595	75	174	24	3	12	79	52	135	.292	.354	.403	97	-2	2	2	-1	.992	7	*O-147,1-43	-0.5
1994	Fla-N☆	115	451	60	144	27	6	18	82	40	92	.319	.376	.525	125	16	1	2	-1	.974	5	O-97,1-46	1.5
Total	4	314	1157	148	346	58	11	30	172	102	255	.299	.359	.446	107	12	3	4	-2	.986	5	O-267,1-102	0.4

■ JOCKO CONLAN
Conlan, John Bertrand b: 12/6/1899, Chicago, Ill. d: 4/16/89, Scottsdale, Ariz. BL/TL, 5'7.5", 165 lbs. Deb: 7/6/34 UH

YEAR	TM/L	G	AB	R	H	2B	3B	HR	RBI	BB	SO	AVG	OBP	SLG	PRO+	BR/A	SB	CS	SBR	FA	FR	G/POS	TPR
1934	Chi-A	63	225	35	56	11	3	0	16	19	7	.249	.310	.324	62	-13	2	1	-1	.955	-3	O-54	-1.8
1935	Chi-A	65	140	20	40	7	1	0	15	14	6	.286	.355	.350	81	-4	3	3	-1	.961	-3	O-37	-0.8
Total	2	128	365	55	96	18	4	0	31	33	13	.263	.327	.334	69	-17	5	5	-2	.957	-6	/O-91	-2.6

■ JOCKO CONLON
Conlon, Arthur Joseph b: 12/10/1897, Woburn, Mass. d: 8/5/87, Falmouth, Mass. BR/TR, 5'7", 145 lbs. Deb: 4/17/23

YEAR	TM/L	G	AB	R	H	2B	3B	HR	RBI	BB	SO	AVG	OBP	SLG	PRO+	BR/A	SB	CS	SBR	FA	FR	G/POS	TPR
1923	Bos-N	59	147	23	32	3	0	0	17	11	11	.218	.299	.238	45	-11	0	3	-2	.955	1	2-36/S-6,3	-1.0

■ BERT CONN
Conn, Albert Thomas b: 9/22/1879, Philadelphia, Pa. d: 11/2/44, Philadelphia, Pa. TR , Deb: 9/16/1898

YEAR	TM/L	G	AB	R	H	2B	3B	HR	RBI	BB	SO	AVG	OBP	SLG	PRO+	BR/A	SB	CS	SBR	FA	FR	G/POS	TPR
1898	Phi-N	1	3	1	1	0	1	0	1	0		.333	.333	1.000	291	1	0			1.000	-0	/P-1	0.0
1900	Phi-N	6	9	4	3	1	0	0	1	0		.333	.333	.444	115	0	0			.667	-1	/P-4	0.0
1901	Phi-N	5	18	2	4	1	0	0	0	0		.222	.263	.278	56	-1	0			.880	-1	/2-5	-0.2
Total	3	12	30	7	8	2	1	0	2	0		.267	.290	.400	95	-0	0			.714	-2	/2-5,P-5	-0.2

■ FRITZIE CONNALLY
Connally, Fritzie Lee b: 5/19/58, Bryan, Tex. BR/TR, 6'3", 210 lbs. Deb: 9/9/83

YEAR	TM/L	G	AB	R	H	2B	3B	HR	RBI	BB	SO	AVG	OBP	SLG	PRO+	BR/A	SB	CS	SBR	FA	FR	G/POS	TPR
1983	Chi-N	8	10	1	1	0	0	0	0	0	5	.100	.100	.100	-42	-2	0	0	0	1.000	0	/3-3	-0.2
1985	Bal-A	50	112	16	26	4	0	3	15	19	21	.232	.348	.348	94	-0	0	0	0	.976	-3	3-46/1-2,D	-0.4
Total	2	58	122	16	27	4	0	3	15	19	26	.221	.331	.328	83	-2	0	0	0	.977	-3	/3-49,1-2,D	-0.6

■ BRUCE CONNATSER
Connatser, Broadus Milburn b: 9/19/02, Sevierville, Tenn. d: 1/27/71, Terre Haute, Ind. BR/TR, 5'11.5", 170 lbs. Deb: 9/15/31

YEAR	TM/L	G	AB	R	H	2B	3B	HR	RBI	BB	SO	AVG	OBP	SLG	PRO+	BR/A	SB	CS	SBR	FA	FR	G/POS	TPR
1931	Cle-A	12	49	5	14	3	0	0	4	2	3	.286	.327	.347	73	-2	0	0	0	1.000	1	1-12	-0.2
1932	Cle-A	23	60	8	14	3	1	0	4	4	8	.233	.281	.317	51	-4	1	0	0	1.000	0	1-14	-0.4
Total	2	35	109	13	28	6	1	0	8	6	11	.257	.302	.330	61	-6	1	0	0	1.000	2	/1-26	-0.6

■ FRANK CONNAUGHTON
Connaughton, Frank Henry b: 1/1/1869, Clinton, Mass. d: 12/1/42, Boston, Mass. BR/TR, 5'9", 165 lbs. Deb: 5/28/1894

YEAR	TM/L	G	AB	R	H	2B	3B	HR	RBI	BB	SO	AVG	OBP	SLG	PRO+	BR/A	SB	CS	SBR	FA	FR	G/POS	TPR
1894	Bos-N	46	171	42	59	9	2	2	33	16	2	.345	.407	.456	100	-0	3			.892	-3	S-33/C-7,O	-0.1
1896	NY-N	88	315	53	82	3	2	2	43	25	7	.260	.319	.302	66	-15	22			.892	3	S-54,O-30	-1.1
1906	Bos-N	12	44	3	9	0	0	0	1	3		.205	.271	.205	50	-2	1			.918	-3	S-11/2-1	-0.5
Total	3	146	530	98	150	12	4	4	77	44	15	.283	.344	.343	78	-18	26			.894	-3	/S-98,O-34,C2	-1.7

■ GENE CONNELL
Connell, Eugene Joseph b: 5/10/06, Hazleton, Pa. d: 8/31/37, Waverly, N.Y. BR/TR, 6'0.5", 180 lbs. Deb: 7/4/31 F

YEAR	TM/L	G	AB	R	H	2B	3B	HR	RBI	BB	SO	AVG	OBP	SLG	PRO+	BR/A	SB	CS	SBR	FA	FR	G/POS	TPR
1931	Phi-N	6	12	1	3	0	0	0	0	0	3	.250	.250	.250	32	-1	0			1.000	-1	/C-6	-0.1

■ JOE CONNELL
Connell, Joseph Bernard b: 1/16/02, Bethlehem, Pa. d: 9/21/77, Trexlertown, Pa. BL/TL, 5'8", 165 lbs. Deb: 6/15/26 F

YEAR	TM/L	G	AB	R	H	2B	3B	HR	RBI	BB	SO	AVG	OBP	SLG	PRO+	BR/A	SB	CS	SBR	FA	FR	G/POS	TPR
1926	NY-N	2	1	1	0	0	0	0	0	0	0	.000	.000	.000	-99	-0	0			.000	0	H	0.0

■ PETE CONNELL
Connell, Peter J. b: Brooklyn, N.Y. Deb: 9/3/1886

YEAR	TM/L	G	AB	R	H	2B	3B	HR	RBI	BB	SO	AVG	OBP	SLG	PRO+	BR/A	SB	CS	SBR	FA	FR	G/POS	TPR
1886	NY-a	1	5	0	0	0	0	0		0		.000	.000	.000	-99	-1	0			.667	-1	/3-1	-0.2

■ TERRY CONNELL
Connell, Terence G. b: 6/17/1855, Philadelphia, Pa. d: 3/25/24, Philadelphia, Pa. Deb: 6/20/1874

YEAR	TM/L	G	AB	R	H	2B	3B	HR	RBI	BB	SO	AVG	OBP	SLG	PRO+	BR/A	SB	CS	SBR	FA	FR	G/POS	TPR
1874	Chi-n	1	4	0	0	0	0	0		0		.000	.000	.000	-99	-1						/C-1	-0.1

■ TOM CONNELLY
Connelly, Thomas Martin b: 10/20/1897, Chicago, Ill. d: 2/18/41, Hines, Ill. BL/TR, 5'11.5", 165 lbs. Deb: 9/24/20

YEAR	TM/L	G	AB	R	H	2B	3B	HR	RBI	BB	SO	AVG	OBP	SLG	PRO+	BR/A	SB	CS	SBR	FA	FR	G/POS	TPR
1920	NY-A	1	1	0	0	0	0	0	0	0	0	.000	.000	.000	-97	-0	0	0	0	.000	0	H	0.0
1921	NY-A	4	5	0	1	0	0	0	0	1	0	.200	.333	.200	38	-0	0	0	0	1.000	0	/O-3	-0.1
Total	2	5	6	0	1	0	0	0	0	1	0	.167	.286	.167	18	-1	0	0	0	1.000	0	/O-3	-0.1

■ ED CONNOLLY
Connolly, Edward Joseph Sr. b: 7/17/08, Brooklyn, N.Y. d: 11/12/63, Pittsfield, Mass. BR/TR, 5'8.5", 180 lbs. Deb: 9/20/29 F

YEAR	TM/L	G	AB	R	H	2B	3B	HR	RBI	BB	SO	AVG	OBP	SLG	PRO+	BR/A	SB	CS	SBR	FA	FR	G/POS	TPR
1929	Bos-A	5	8	0	0	0	0	0	0	2		.000	.000	.000	-99	-2	0	0	0	.889	-1	/C-5	-0.3
1930	Bos-A	27	48	1	9	2	0	0	7	4		.188	.250	.229	23	-6	0	0	0	1.000	-1	C-26	-0.5
1931	Bos-A	42	93	3	7	1	0	0	3	5	18	.075	.131	.086	-44	-20	0	0	0	.981	-1	C-41	-1.8
1932	Bos-A	75	222	9	50	8	4	0	21	20	27	.225	.289	.297	54	-15	0	1	-1	.957	-1	C-75	-0.8
Total	4	149	371	13	66	11	4	0	31	29	50	.178	.239	.229	23	-43	0	1	-1	.966	-3	C-147	-3.4

■ RED CONNOLLY
Connolly, John M. b: 1863, New York, N.Y. d: 3/2/1896, New York, N.Y. Deb: 7/1/1886

YEAR	TM/L	G	AB	R	H	2B	3B	HR	RBI	BB	SO	AVG	OBP	SLG	PRO+	BR/A	SB	CS	SBR	FA	FR	G/POS	TPR
1886	StL-N	2	7	0	0	0	0	0		0	3	.000	.000	.000	-99	-1	0			.000	-1	/O-2	-0.2

■ JOE CONNOLLY
Connolly, Joseph Aloysius b: 2/12/1888, N.Smithfield, R.I. d: 9/1/43, Springfield, R.I. BL/TL, 5'7.5", 165 lbs. Deb: 4/10/13

YEAR	TM/L	G	AB	R	H	2B	3B	HR	RBI	BB	SO	AVG	OBP	SLG	PRO+	BR/A	SB	CS	SBR	FA	FR	G/POS	TPR
1913	Bos-N	126	427	79	120	18	11	5	57	66	47	.281	.379	.410	123	14	18			.954	-8	*O-124	0.1
1914	*Bos-N	120	399	64	122	28	10	9	65	49	36	.306	.393	.494	164	32	12			.974	-5	*O-118	2.3
1915	Bos-N	104	305	48	91	14	6	0	23	39	35	.298	.387	.397	144	18	13	13	-3	.971	-4	O-93	0.8
1916	Bos-N	62	110	11	25	5	2	0	12	14	13	.227	.320	.309	98	0	5			.980	-1	O-31	-0.2
Total	4	412	1241	202	358	65	31	14	157	168	131	.288	.380	.425	139	63	48	12		.967	-17	O-366	3.0

YEAR	TM/L	G	AB	R	H	2B	3B	HR	RBI	BB	SO	AVG	OBP	SLG	PRO+	BR/A	SB	CS	SBR	FA	FR	G/POS	TPR

■ JOE CONNOLLY
Connolly, Joseph George "Coaster Joe" b: 6/4/1896, San Francisco, Cal d: 3/30/60, San Francisco, Cal BR/TR, 6', 170 lbs. Deb: 10/1/21

YEAR	TM/L	G	AB	R	H	2B	3B	HR	RBI	BB	SO	AVG	OBP	SLG	PRO+	BR/A	SB	CS	SBR	FA	FR	G/POS	TPR
1921	NY-N	2	4	0	0	0	0	0	1	1		.000	.200	.000	-42	-1	0	0		1.000	-0	/O-1	-0.1
1922	Cle-A	12	45	6	11	2	1	0	6	5	8	.244	.320	.333	70	-2	1	0	0	.972	2	O-12	-0.1
1923	Cle-A	52	109	25	33	10	1	3	25	13	7	.303	.377	.495	129	4	1	2	-1	.957	-1	O-39	-0.8
1924	Bos-A	14	10	1	1	0	0	0	1	2	2	.100	.250	.100	-8	-2	0	0		1.000	-1	/O-3	-0.2
Total	4	80	168	32	45	12	2	3	32	21	18	.268	.349	.417	100	-0	2	2	-1	.966	-9	/O-55	-1.2

■ BUD CONNOLLY
Connolly, Mervin Thomas "Mike" b: 5/25/01, San Francisco, Cal d: 6/12/64, Berkeley, Cal. BR/TR, 5'8", 154 lbs. Deb: 5/3/25

YEAR	TM/L	G	AB	R	H	2B	3B	HR	RBI	BB	SO	AVG	OBP	SLG	PRO+	BR/A	SB	CS	SBR	FA	FR	G/POS	TPR
1925	Bos-A	43	107	12	28	7	1	0	21	23	9	.262	.392	.346	88	-1	0	3	-2	.950	-11	S-34/3-2	-0.9

■ TOM CONNOLLY
Connolly, Thomas Francis "Blackie" or "Ham" b: 12/30/1892, Boston, Mass. d: 5/14/66, Boston, Mass. BL/TR, 5'11", 175 lbs. Deb: 5/12/15

YEAR	TM/L	G	AB	R	H	2B	3B	HR	RBI	BB	SO	AVG	OBP	SLG	PRO+	BR/A	SB	CS	SBR	FA	FR	G/POS	TPR
1915	Was-A	50	141	14	26	3	2	0	7	14	19	.184	.268	.234	49	-9	5	4	-1	.970	-7	3-24,O-19/S	-1.7

■ NED CONNOR
Connor, Edward b: 1850, New York 5'9", 156 lbs. Deb: 5/18/1871

YEAR	TM/L	G	AB	R	H	2B	3B	HR	RBI	BB	SO	AVG	OBP	SLG	PRO+	BR/A	SB	CS	SBR	FA	FR	G/POS	TPR
1871	Tro-n	7	33	6	7	0	0	0	2	0	0	.212	.212	.212	22	-3	0					/1-4,O-2,2	-0.2

■ JIM CONNOR
Connor, James Matthew (b: James Matthew O'Connor) b: 5/11/1863, Port Jervis, N.Y. d: 9/3/50, Providence, R.I. BR/TR, Deb: 7/11/1892

YEAR	TM/L	G	AB	R	H	2B	3B	HR	RBI	BB	SO	AVG	OBP	SLG	PRO+	BR/A	SB	CS	SBR	FA	FR	G/POS	TPR
1892	Chi-N	9	34	0	2	0	0	0	0	1	7	.059	.111	.059	-48	-6	0			.917	-6	/2-9	-1.1
1897	Chi-N	77	285	40	83	10	5	3	38	24		.291	.349	.393	94	-3	10			.936	22	2-76	2.0
1898	Chi-N	138	505	51	114	9	9	0	67	42		.226	.289	.279	63	-24	11			.946	-3	*2-138	-1.7
1899	Chi-N	69	234	26	48	7	1	0	24	18		.205	.265	.244	41	-19	6			.942	4	2-44,3-25	-1.1
Total	4	293	1058	117	247	26	15	3	129	85	7	.233	.296	.295	64	-52	27			.942	18	2-267/3-25	-1.9

■ JOE CONNOR
Connor, Joseph Francis b: 12/8/1874, Waterbury, Conn. d: 11/8/57, Waterbury, Conn. BR/TR, 6'2", 185 lbs. Deb: 9/9/1895 F

YEAR	TM/L	G	AB	R	H	2B	3B	HR	RBI	BB	SO	AVG	OBP	SLG	PRO+	BR/A	SB	CS	SBR	FA	FR	G/POS	TPR
1895	StL-N	2	7	0	0	0	0	0	1	0	2	.000	.000	.000	-99	-2	0			1.000	1	/3-2	-0.1
1900	Bos-N	7	19	2	4	0	0	0	4	2		.211	.286	.211	34	-2	1			.971	2	/C-7	0.1
1901	Mil-A	38	102	10	28	3	1	1	9	6		.275	.321	.353	91	-1	4			.949	0	C-30/2-1,3O	0.1
	Cle-A	37	121	13	17	3	1	0	6	7		.140	.200	.182	7	-15	2			.942	-0	C-32/O-4,S	-1.2
	Yr	75	223	23	45	6	2	1	15	13		.202	.255	.260	45	-16	6			.946	-0	C-62/O-5,23S	-1.1
1905	NY-A	8	22	4	5	1	0	0	2	3		.227	.320	.273	79	-0	1			.978	2	/C-6,1-2	0.2
Total	4	92	271	29	54	7	2	1	22	18	2	.199	.257	.251	43	-21	8			.952	5	/C-75,O-5,31S2	-0.9

■ ROGER CONNOR
Connor, Roger b: 7/1/1857, Waterbury, Conn. d: 1/4/31, Waterbury, Conn. BL/TL, 6'3", 220 lbs. Deb: 5/1/1880 FMH

YEAR	TM/L	G	AB	R	H	2B	3B	HR	RBI	BB	SO	AVG	OBP	SLG	PRO+	BR/A	SB	CS	SBR	FA	FR	G/POS	TPR
1880	Tro-N	83	340	53	113	18	8	3	47	13	21	.332	.357	.459	166	22				.821	-10	*3-83	1.4
1881	Tro-N	85	367	55	107	17	6	2	31	15	20	.292	.319	.387	115	5				.950	2	*1-85	-0.1
1882	Tro-N	81	349	65	115	22	18	4	42	13	20	.330	.354	.530	188	34				.951	3	1-43,O-24,3	2.9
1883	NY-N	98	409	80	146	28	15	1	50	25	16	.357	.394	.506	173	36				.958	3	*1-98	2.4
1884	NY-N	116	477	98	151	28	4	4	82	38	32	.317	.367	.417	143	23				.860	3	2-67,O-37,3	2.4
1885	NY-N	110	455	102	169	23	15	1	65	51	8	.371	.435	.495	203	53				.975	3	*1-110	4.0
1886	NY-N	118	485	105	172	29	20	7	71	41	15	.355	.405	.540	183	48	17			.973	10	*1-118	3.9
1887	NY-N	127	471	113	134	26	22	17	104	75	50	.285	.392	.541	164	43	43			.993	5	*1-127	2.9
1888	*NY-N	134	481	98	140	15	17	14	71	73	44	.291	.389	.480	178	45	27			.982	1	*1-133/2-1	3.3
1889	*NY-N	131	496	117	157	32	17	13	130	93	46	.317	.426	.528	166	46	21			.977	-8	*1-131/3-1	2.5
1890	NY-P	123	484	133	169	24	15	14	103	88	32	.349	.450	.548	152	35	22			.985	11	*1-123	3.1
1891	NY-N	129	479	112	139	29	13	7	94	83	39	.290	.399	.449	153	35	27			.983	1	*1-129	2.7
1892	Phi-N	155	564	123	166	37	11	12	73	116	39	.294	.420	.463	167	51	22			.985	-6	*1-155	3.4
1893	NY-N	135	511	111	156	25	8	11	105	91	26	.305	.413	.450	129	23	24			.974	1	*1-135/3-1	1.7
1894	NY-N	22	82	10	24	7	0	1	14	8	0	.293	.356	.415	86	-2	2			.976	2	1-21/O-1	0.0
	StL-N	99	380	83	122	28	25	7	79	51	17	.321	.411	.582	137	21	17			.974	5	*1-99	2.0
	Yr	121	462	93	146	35	25	8	93	59	17	.316	.400	.552	128	19	19			.974	7	*1-120/O-1	2.0
1895	StL-N	103	398	78	131	29	9	8	77	63	10	.329	.423	.508	141	26	9			.986	4	*1-103	2.6
1896	StL-N	126	483	71	137	21	9	11	72	52	14	.284	.356	.433	112	7	10			.988	13	*1-126,M	1.8
1897	StL-N	22	83	13	19	3	1	1	12	13		.229	.337	.325	76	-3	3			.984	-0	1-22	-0.2
Total	18	1997	7794	1620	2467	441	233	138	1322	1002	449	.317	.397	.486	154	549	244			.978	42	*1-1758,3-111/2O	42.7

■ JERRY CONNORS
Connors, Jeremiah b: Cleveland, Ohio Deb: 7/11/1882

YEAR	TM/L	G	AB	R	H	2B	3B	HR	RBI	BB	SO	AVG	OBP	SLG	PRO+	BR/A	SB	CS	SBR	FA	FR	G/POS	TPR
1892	Phi-N	1	3	0	0	0	0	0	0	0	1	.000	.000	.000	-99	-1	0			.000	-0	/O-1	-0.1

■ JOE CONNORS
Connors, Joseph P. b: Paterson, N.J. Deb: 5/3/1884

YEAR	TM/L	G	AB	R	H	2B	3B	HR	RBI	BB	SO	AVG	OBP	SLG	PRO+	BR/A	SB	CS	SBR	FA	FR	G/POS	TPR
1884	Alt-U	3	11	0	1	0	0	0		0		.091	.091	.091	-50	-2				1.000	-0	/P-1,3-1,O	-0.2
	KC-U	3	11	2	1	0	0	0		1		.091	.167	.091	-32	-2				1.000	0	/O-2,P-2	0.0
	Yr	6	22	2	2	0	0	0		1		.091	.130	.091	-41	-4				.750	-0	/P-3,O-3,3	-0.2

■ CHUCK CONNORS
Connors, Kevin Joseph Aloysius b: 4/10/21, Brooklyn, N.Y. d: 11/10/92, Los Angeles, Cal. BL/TL, 6'5", 190 lbs. Deb: 5/1/49

YEAR	TM/L	G	AB	R	H	2B	3B	HR	RBI	BB	SO	AVG	OBP	SLG	PRO+	BR/A	SB	CS	SBR	FA	FR	G/POS	TPR
1949	Bro-N	1	1	0	0	0	0	0	0	0	0	.000	.000	.000	-96	-0	0			.000	0	H	0.0
1951	Chi-N	66	201	16	48	5	1	2	18	12	25	.239	.282	.303	56	-12	4	0	1	.984	-1	1-57	-1.5
Total	2	67	202	16	48	5	1	2	18	12	25	.238	.280	.302	56	-13	4	0		.984	-1	/1-57	-1.5

■ MERV CONNORS
Connors, Mervyn James b: 1/23/14, Berkeley, Cal. BR/TR, 6'2", 192 lbs. Deb: 9/4/37

YEAR	TM/L	G	AB	R	H	2B	3B	HR	RBI	BB	SO	AVG	OBP	SLG	PRO+	BR/A	SB	CS	SBR	FA	FR	G/POS	TPR
1937	Chi-A	28	103	12	24	4	1	2	12	14	19	.233	.325	.350	70	-5	2	1	0	.926	-3	3-28	-0.7
1938	Chi-A	24	62	14	22	4	0	6	13	9	17	.355	.437	.710	178	7	0	0	0	.979	0	1-16	0.5
Total	2	52	165	26	46	8	1	8	25	23	36	.279	.367	.485	111	2	2	1	0	.926	-3	/3-28,1-16	-0.2

■ BEN CONROY
Conroy, Bernard Patrick b: 3/14/1871, Philadelphia, Pa. d: 11/25/37, Philadelphia, Pa. 160 lbs. Deb: 4/21/1890

YEAR	TM/L	G	AB	R	H	2B	3B	HR	RBI	BB	SO	AVG	OBP	SLG	PRO+	BR/A	SB	CS	SBR	FA	FR	G/POS	TPR
1890	Phi-a	117	404	45	69	13	1	0		45		.171	.262	.208	40	-30	17			.893	-6	S-74,2-42/O	-2.6

■ WID CONROY
Conroy, William Edward b: 4/5/1877, Camden, N.J. d: 12/6/59, Mt.Holly, N.J. BR/TR, 5'9", 158 lbs. Deb: 4/25/01 C

YEAR	TM/L	G	AB	R	H	2B	3B	HR	RBI	BB	SO	AVG	OBP	SLG	PRO+	BR/A	SB	CS	SBR	FA	FR	G/POS	TPR
1901	Mil-A	131	503	74	129	20	6	5	64	36		.256	.316	.350	89	-7	21			.922	19	*S-118,3-12	1.9
1902	Pit-N	99	365	55	89	10	6	1	47	24		.244	.299	.312	86	-6	10			.925	8	S-95/O-3	0.8
1903	NY-N	126	503	74	137	23	12	1	45	32		.272	.322	.372	101	1	33			.919	3	*3-123/S-4	0.6
1904	NY-A	140	489	58	119	18	12	1	52	43		.243	.314	.335	100	1	30			.944	4	*3-110,S-27/O	1.0
1905	NY-A	101	385	55	105	19	11	2	25	32		.273	.329	.395	116	6	25			.928	7	3-48,O-25,S1/2	1.5
1906	NY-A	148	567	67	139	17	10	4	54	47		.245	.303	.332	89	-8	32			.968	-1	O-97,S-49/3	-1.4
1907	NY-A	140	530	58	124	12	11	3	51	30		.234	.279	.315	83	-11	41			.955	12	*O-100,S-38	-0.4
1908	NY-A	141	531	44	126	22	3	1	39	14		.237	.258	.296	79	-14	23			.939	13	*3-119,2-12,O	0.3
1909	Was-A	139	488	44	119	13	4	1	20	30		.244	.298	.293	91	-5	24			.938	-0	*3-120,2-13/OS	-0.2
1910	Was-A	103	351	36	89	11	3	1	27	30		.254	.314	.311	100	0	11			.961	3	3-46,O-46/2	0.1
1911	Was-A	106	349	40	81	11	4	2	28	20		.232	.282	.304	64	-17	12			.930	5	3-85,O-15/2	-1.1
Total	11	1374	5061	605	1257	176	82	22	452	345		.248	.301	.329	91	-62	262			.934	72	3-665,S-349,O/21	3.1

■ BILL CONROY
Conroy, William Frederick "Pep" b: 1/9/1899, Chicago, Ill. d: 1/23/70, Chicago, Ill. BR/TR, 5'8.5", 160 lbs. Deb: 4/18/23

YEAR	TM/L	G	AB	R	H	2B	3B	HR	RBI	BB	SO	AVG	OBP	SLG	PRO+	BR/A	SB	CS	SBR	FA	FR	G/POS	TPR
1923	Was-A	18	60	6	8	2	2	0	4	9		.133	.188	.233	11	-8	0	0	0	.926	-2	3-10/1-6,O	-0.9

■ BILL CONROY
Conroy, William Gordon b: 2/26/15, Bloomington, Ill. BR/TR, 6', 185 lbs. Deb: 9/21/35

YEAR	TM/L	G	AB	R	H	2B	3B	HR	RBI	BB	SO	AVG	OBP	SLG	PRO+	BR/A	SB	CS	SBR	FA	FR	G/POS	TPR
1935	Phi-A	1	4	0	1	1	0	0	0	0	0	.250	.400	.500	133	0	0	0	0	1.000	1	/C-1	0.1
1936	Phi-A	1	2	0	1	0	0	0	0	0	1	.500	.500	.500	151	0	0	0	0	1.000	-0	/C-1	0.0

YEAR	TM/L	G	AB	R	H	2B	3B	HR	RBI	BB	SO	AVG	OBP	SLG	PRO+	BR/A	SB	CS	SBR	FA	FR	G/POS	TPR
1937	Phi-A	26	60	4	12	1	1	0	3	7	9	.200	.284	.250	36	-6	1	0	0	1.000	-1	C-18/1-1	-0.6
1942	Bos-A	83	250	22	50	4	2	4	20	40	47	.200	.315	.280	66	-11	2	0	1	.971	1	C-83	-0.3
1943	Bos-A	39	89	13	16	5	0	1	6	18	19	.180	.336	.270	77	-2	0	0	0	.969	2	C-38	0.2
1944	Bos-A	19	47	6	10	2	0	0	4	11	9	.213	.362	.255	79	-1	0	0	0	.972	-0	C-19	0.0
Total	6	169	452	45	90	13	3	5	33	77	85	.199	.322	.274	66	-19	3	0	1	.974	1	C-160/1-1	-0.6

■ BILLY CONSOLO Consolo, William Angelo b: 8/18/34, Cleveland, Ohio BR/TR, 5'11", 180 lbs. Deb: 4/20/53 C

YEAR	TM/L	G	AB	R	H	2B	3B	HR	RBI	BB	SO	AVG	OBP	SLG	PRO+	BR/A	SB	CS	SBR	FA	FR	G/POS	TPR
1953	Bos-A	47	65	9	14	2	1	1	6	2	23	.215	.239	.323	48	-5	1	2	-1	.808	10	3-16,2-11	0.4
1954	Bos-A	91	242	23	55	7	1	1	11	33	69	.227	.325	.277	59	-13	2	1	0	.953	-3	S-50,3-18,2	-1.2
1955	Bos-A	8	18	4	4	0	0	0	0	5	4	.222	.391	.222	63	-1	0	0	0	.889	-3	/2-4	-0.3
1956	Bos-A	48	11	13	2	0	0	0	1	3	5	.182	.357	.182	41	-1	0	0	0	.920	8	2-25	0.7
1957	Bos-A	68	196	26	53	6	1	4	19	23	48	.270	.347	.372	91	-2	1	3	-2	.933	12	S-42,2-16/3	1.3
1958	Bos-A	46	72	13	9	2	1	0	5	6	14	.125	.192	.181	3	-10	0	0	0	.925	7	2-13,S-11/3	-0.1
1959	Bos-A	10	14	3	3	1	0	0	0	2	5	.214	.313	.286	63	-1	0	0	0	.818	-2	/S-2	-0.2
	Was-A	79	202	25	43	5	3	0	10	36	54	.213	.332	.267	67	-8	1	0	0	.952	10	S-75/2-4	0.8
	Yr	89	216	28	46	6	3	0	10	38	59	.213	.331	.269	66	-9	1	0	0	.948	9	S-77/2-4	0.6
1960	Was-A	100	174	23	36	4	2	3	15	25	29	.207	.310	.305	68	-8	1	1	-0	.938	-1	S-82,2-12/3	-0.5
1961	Min-A	11	5	1	0	0	0	0	0	0	1	.000	.000	.000	-95	-1	0	0	0	1.000	0	/2-3,S-3,3	-0.1
1962	Phi-N	13	5	3	2	0	0	0	0	1	1	.400	.400	.400	119	0	0	0	0	0.000	0	/3-1	0.0
	LA-A	28	20	4	2	0	0	0	0	3	11	.100	.217	.100	-12	-3	2	0	1	.917	3	3-20/S-4,2	0.0
	KC-A	54	154	11	37	4	2	0	16	23	33	.240	.339	.292	68	-6	1	3	-2	.950	-1	S-48	-0.5
	Yr	82	174	15	39	4	2	0	16	26	44	.224	.325	.270	61	-9	3	3	-1	.944	3	S-52,3-20/2	-0.5
Total	10	603	1178	158	260	31	11	9	83	161	297	.221	.316	.289	63	-57	9	10	-3	.945	41	S-317,2-101/3	0.3

■ CHARLIE CONWAY Conway, Charles Connell b: 4/28/1886, Youngstown, Ohio d: 9/12/68, Youngstown, Ohio BR/TR, Deb: 4/15/11

YEAR	TM/L	G	AB	R	H	2B	3B	HR	RBI	BB	SO	AVG	OBP	SLG	PRO+	BR/A	SB	CS	SBR	FA	FR	G/POS	TPR
1911	Was-A	2	3	0	1	0	1	0	0	0	0	.333	.333	1.000	272	1	0			.000	-1	/O-2	0.0

■ JACK CONWAY Conway, Jack Clements b: 7/30/19, Bryan, Tex. BR/TR, 5'11.5", 175 lbs. Deb: 9/9/41

YEAR	TM/L	G	AB	R	H	2B	3B	HR	RBI	BB	SO	AVG	OBP	SLG	PRO+	BR/A	SB	CS	SBR	FA	FR	G/POS	TPR
1941	Cle-A	2	2	0	1	0	0	0	0	0	0	.500	.500	.500	174	0	0	0	0	1.000	1	/S-2	0.1
1946	Cle-A	68	258	24	58	6	2	0	18	20	36	.225	.281	.264	56	-15	2	2	-1	.955	-7	2-50,S-14/3	-2.0
1947	Cle-A	34	50	3	9	2	0	0	5	3	8	.180	.226	.220	25	-5	0	0	0	.877	6	S-24/2-5,3	-0.5
1948	NY-N	24	49	8	12	2	1	1	3	5	10	.245	.315	.388	89	-1	0			.985	6	2-13/S-6,3	0.6
Total	4	128	359	35	80	10	3	1	27	28	54	.223	.279	.276	57	-21	2	2		.962	0	/2-68,S-46,3	-1.8

■ OWEN CONWAY Conway, Owen Sylvester b: 10/23/1890, New York, N.Y. d: 3/12/42, Philadelphia, Pa. TR, Deb: 6/21/15

YEAR	TM/L	G	AB	R	H	2B	3B	HR	RBI	BB	SO	AVG	OBP	SLG	PRO+	BR/A	SB	CS	SBR	FA	FR	G/POS	TPR
1915	Phi-A	4	15	2	1	0	0	0	0	0	3	.067	.067	.067	-62	-3	0			.750	1	/3-4	-0.2

■ PETE CONWAY Conway, Peter J. b: 10/30/1866, Burmont, Pa. d: 1/13/03, Clifton Heights, Pa. BR/TR, 5'10.5", 162 lbs. Deb: 8/10/1885 F

YEAR	TM/L	G	AB	R	H	2B	3B	HR	RBI	BB	SO	AVG	OBP	SLG	PRO+	BR/A	SB	CS	SBR	FA	FR	G/POS	TPR
1885	Buf-N	29	90	7	10	5	0	1	7	5	28	.111	.158	.200	15	-8				.889	-1	P-27/O-2,S1	-0.2
1886	KC-N	51	194	22	47	8	2	1	18	5	34	.242	.261	.320	71	-7	3			.857	-3	O-31,P-23	-0.4
	Det-N	12	43	10	8	1	0	2	3	1	8	.186	.205	.349	64	-2	0			.846	-1	P-11/O-1	0.0
	Yr	63	237	32	55	9	2	3	21	6	42	.232	.251	.325	70	-9	3			.826	-1	P-34,O-32	-0.4
1887	*Det-N	24	95	16	22	5	1	1	7	2	9	.232	.247	.337	59	-6	0			.979	2	P-17/O-8	-0.2
1888	Det-N	45	167	28	46	4	2	3	23	8	25	.275	.320	.377	122	4	1			.938	2	P-45/O-1	0.0
1889	Pit-N	3	10	2	1	0	0	1	2	1	3	.100	.182	.400	67	-1	0			.875	-0	/P-3,O-1	0.0
Total	5	164	599	85	134	23	5	9	60	22	107	.224	.255	.324	74	-20	5			.907	-1	P-126/O-44,1S	-0.8

■ RIP CONWAY Conway, Richard Daniel b: 4/18/1896, White Bear Lake, Minn. d: 12/3/71, St.Paul, Minn. BL/TR, 5'6", 160 lbs. Deb: 4/16/18

YEAR	TM/L	G	AB	R	H	2B	3B	HR	RBI	BB	SO	AVG	OBP	SLG	PRO+	BR/A	SB	CS	SBR	FA	FR	G/POS	TPR
1918	Bos-N	14	24	4	4	0	0	0	2	2	4	.167	.231	.167	23	-2	1			.810	-4	/2-5,3-1	-0.7

■ BILL CONWAY Conway, William F. b: 11/28/1861, Lowell, Mass. d: 12/28/43, Somerville, Mass. BR/TR, 5'8", 170 lbs. Deb: 7/28/1884 F

YEAR	TM/L	G	AB	R	H	2B	3B	HR	RBI	BB	SO	AVG	OBP	SLG	PRO+	BR/A	SB	CS	SBR	FA	FR	G/POS	TPR
1884	Phi-N	1	4	0	0	0	0	0	0	0	1	.000	.000	.000	-99	-1				1.000	0	/C-1	-0.1
1886	Bal-a	7	14	4	2	0	0	0	0	0	7	.143	.429	.143	84	0	0			.925	-3	/C-7	-0.2
Total	2	8	18	4	2	0	0	0	0	0	7	1	.111	.360	.111	52	-0	0		.936	-3	/C-8	-0.3

■ ED CONWELL Conwell, Edward James "Irish" b: 1/29/1890, Chicago, Ill. d: 5/1/26, Norwood Park, Ill. BR/TR, 5'11", 155 lbs. Deb: 9/22/11

YEAR	TM/L	G	AB	R	H	2B	3B	HR	RBI	BB	SO	AVG	OBP	SLG	PRO+	BR/A	SB	CS	SBR	FA	FR	G/POS	TPR
1911	StL-N	1	1	0	0	0	0	0	0	0	1	.000	.000	.000	-99	-0	0			.000	-0	/3-1	-0.1

■ HERB CONYERS Conyers, Herbert Leroy b: 1/8/21, Cowgill, Mo. d: 9/16/64, Cleveland, Ohio BL/TR, 6'5", 210 lbs. Deb: 4/18/50

YEAR	TM/L	G	AB	R	H	2B	3B	HR	RBI	BB	SO	AVG	OBP	SLG	PRO+	BR/A	SB	CS	SBR	FA	FR	G/POS	TPR
1950	Cle-A	7	9	2	3	0	0	1	1	1	2	.333	.400	.667	175	1	1	0	0	1.000	-0	/1-1	0.1

■ DALE COOGAN Coogan, Dale Roger b: 8/14/30, Los Angeles, Cal. d: 3/8/89, Mission Viejo, Cal. BL/TL, 6'1", 190 lbs. Deb: 4/22/50

YEAR	TM/L	G	AB	R	H	2B	3B	HR	RBI	BB	SO	AVG	OBP	SLG	PRO+	BR/A	SB	CS	SBR	FA	FR	G/POS	TPR
1950	Pit-N	53	129	19	31	6	1	1	13	17	24	.240	.338	.326	73	-5				.980	2	1-32	-0.3

■ DAN COOGAN Coogan, Daniel George b: 2/16/1875, Philadelphia, Pa. d: 10/28/42, Philadelphia, Pa. 128 lbs. Deb: 4/25/1895

YEAR	TM/L	G	AB	R	H	2B	3B	HR	RBI	BB	SO	AVG	OBP	SLG	PRO+	BR/A	SB	CS	SBR	FA	FR	G/POS	TPR
1895	Was-N	26	77	9	17	2	1	0	7	13	6	.221	.333	.273	58	-4	1			.746	-11	S-18/C-5,O3	-1.2

■ JIM COOK Cook, James Fitchie b: 11/10/1879, Dundee, Ill. d: 6/17/49, St.Louis, Mo. BR/TR, 5'9", 163 lbs. Deb: 7/2/03

YEAR	TM/L	G	AB	R	H	2B	3B	HR	RBI	BB	SO	AVG	OBP	SLG	PRO+	BR/A	SB	CS	SBR	FA	FR	G/POS	TPR
1903	Chi-N	8	26	3	4	1	0	0	2		2	.154	.241	.192	25	-3	1			1.000	-2	/O-5,2-2,1	-0.4

■ DOC COOK Cook, Luther Almus b: 6/24/1886, Whitt, Tex. d: 6/30/73, Lawrenceburg, Tenn. BL/TR, 6', 170 lbs. Deb: 8/7/13

YEAR	TM/L	G	AB	R	H	2B	3B	HR	RBI	BB	SO	AVG	OBP	SLG	PRO+	BR/A	SB	CS	SBR	FA	FR	G/POS	TPR
1913	NY-A	20	72	9	19	2	1	0	1	10	4	.264	.369	.319	101	1	1			.939	1	O-20	0.0
1914	NY-A	132	470	59	133	11	3	1	40	44	60	.283	.356	.326	105	4	26	32	-11	.949	-5	*O-127	-2.0
1915	NY-A	132	476	70	129	16	5	2	33	62	43	.271	.364	.338	111	8	29	18	-2	.959	-4	*O-131	0.0
1916	NY-A	4	10	0	1	0	0	0	1	0	2	.100	.100	.100	-39	-2	0			1.000	-1	/O-3	-0.3
Total	4	288	1028	138	282	29	9	3	75	116	109	.274	.359	.329	106	11	56	50		.953	-4	O-281	-2.3

■ PAUL COOK Cook, Paul b: 5/5/1863, Caledonia, N.Y. d: 5/25/05, Rochester, N.Y. BR/TR, Deb: 9/13/1884

YEAR	TM/L	G	AB	R	H	2B	3B	HR	RBI	BB	SO	AVG	OBP	SLG	PRO+	BR/A	SB	CS	SBR	FA	FR	G/POS	TPR
1884	Phi-N	3	12	0	1	0	0	0	0	0	2	.083	.083	.083	-50	-2				.818	-2	/C-3	-0.3
1886	Lou-a	66	262	28	54	5	2	0	10			.206	.235	.240	46	-17	6			.945	-9	1-43,C-21/O	-2.6
1887	Lou-a	61	223	34	55	4	2	0	11			.247	.294	.283	60	-12	15			.916	-10	C-55/1-6	-1.4
1888	Lou-a	57	185	20	34	2	0	0	13		5	.184	.222	.195	35	-13	9			.901	-14	C-53/O-4,S	-2.1
1889	Lou-a	81	286	34	65	10	1	0	15	15	48	.227	.287	.269	60	-15	11			.925	5	C-74/O-7,S1	-0.3
1890	Bro-P	58	218	32	55	3	3	0	31	14	18	.252	.303	.294	56	-14	7			.890	-4	C-36,1-21/O	-1.0
1891	Lou-a	45	153	21	35	3	1	0	23	11	17	.229	.285	.261	57	-9	4			.909	-9	C-35,1-10	-1.4
	StL-a	7	25	3	5	0	0	0	1	1	2	.200	.259	.200	28	-3	0			.921	3	/C-7	0.1
	Yr	52	178	24	40	3	1	0	24	12	19	.225	.281	.253	52	-11	4			.912	-5	C-42,1-10	-1.3
Total	7	378	1364	172	304	27	9	0	83	67	87	.223	.270	.256	52	-84	52			.906	-35	C-284/1-81,OS	-9.0

■ CLIFF COOK Cook, Raymond Clifford b: 8/20/36, Dallas, Tex. BR/TR, 6', 188 lbs. Deb: 9/9/59

YEAR	TM/L	G	AB	R	H	2B	3B	HR	RBI	BB	SO	AVG	OBP	SLG	PRO+	BR/A	SB	CS	SBR	FA	FR	G/POS	TPR
1959	Cin-N	9	21	3	8	0	0	1	5	2	8	.381	.435	.571	161	2	1	0	0	.909	1	/3-9	0.3
1960	Cin-N	54	149	9	31	7	0	3	13	8	51	.208	.248	.315	52	-10	0	0	0	.954	4	3-47/O-4	-0.7
1961	Cin-N	4	5	0	0	0	0	0	0	0	2	.000	.000	.000	-99	-1	0	0	0	1.000	0	/3-1	-0.1
1962	Cin-N	6	5	0	0	0	0	0	0	0	0	.000	.000	.000	-97	-1	0	0	0	1.000	0	/3-4	-0.2
	NY-N	40	112	12	26	6	1	2	9	4	34	.232	.277	.357	68	-5	1	0	0	.875	-8	3-16,O-10	-1.4
	Yr	46	117	12	26	6	1	2	9	4	36	.222	.266	.342	61	-7	1	0	0	.878	-8	3-20,O-10	-1.6

YEAR	TM/L	G	AB	R	H	2B	3B	HR	RBI	BB	SO	AVG	OBP	SLG	PRO+	BR/A	SB	CS	SBR	FA	FR	G/POS	TPR
1963	NY-N	50	106	9	15	2	1	2	8	12	37	.142	.229	.236	34	-9	0	1	-1	1.000	4	O-21/3-9,1	-0.7
Total	5	163	398	33	80	17	3	7	35	26	136	.201	.255	.312	54	-25	2	1	0	.937	0	/3-86,O-35,1	-2.8

■ DUSTY COOKE
Cooke, Allen Lindsey b: 6/23/07, Swepsonville, N.C. d: 11/21/87, Raleigh, N.C. BL/TR, 6'1", 205 lbs. Deb: 4/15/30 MC

YEAR	TM/L	G	AB	R	H	2B	3B	HR	RBI	BB	SO	AVG	OBP	SLG	PRO+	BR/A	SB	CS	SBR	FA	FR	G/POS	TPR
1930	NY-A	92	216	43	55	12	3	6	29	32	61	.255	.353	.421	100	0	4	6	-2	.978	-6	O-73	-1.1
1931	NY-A	27	39	10	13	1	0	1	6	8	11	.333	.447	.436	141	3	4	1	1	1.000	-1	O-11	0.2
1932	NY-A	3	0	1	0	0	0	0	0	0	1	—	1.000	—	191	0	0			.000	0	H	0.0
1933	Bos-A	119	454	86	133	35	10	5	54	67	71	.293	.386	.447	121	15	7	5	-1	.956	-18	*O-118	-0.9
1934	Bos-A	74	168	34	41	8	5	1	26	36	25	.244	.377	.369	87	-2	7	2	1	.976	-4	O-44	-0.7
1935	Bos-A	100	294	51	90	18	6	3	34	46	24	.306	.400	.439	109	5	6	8	-3	.972	-6	O-82	-0.6
1936	Bos-A	111	341	58	93	20	3	6	47	72	48	.273	.401	.402	93	-2	0			.972	2	O-91	-0.4
1938	Cin-N	82	233	41	64	15	1	2	33	28	36	.275	.355	.373	103	2	0			.963	3	O-51	0.3
Total	8	608	1745	324	489	109	28	24	229	290	276	.280	.384	.416	106	21	32	25		.969	-30	O-470	-3.2

■ FRED COOKE
Cooke, Frederick B. b: Paulding, Ohio Deb: 7/30/1897

YEAR	TM/L	G	AB	R	H	2B	3B	HR	RBI	BB	SO	AVG	OBP	SLG	PRO+	BR/A	SB	CS	SBR	FA	FR	G/POS	TPR
1897	Cle-N	5	17	2	5	2	0	0	3	3		.294	.400	.412	109	0	0			.857	1	/O-5	0.1

■ SCOTT COOLBAUGH
Coolbaugh, Scott Robert b: 6/13/66, Binghamton, N.Y. BR/TR, 5'11", 185 lbs. Deb: 9/2/89

YEAR	TM/L	G	AB	R	H	2B	3B	HR	RBI	BB	SO	AVG	OBP	SLG	PRO+	BR/A	SB	CS	SBR	FA	FR	G/POS	TPR
1989	Tex-A	25	51	7	14	1	0	2	7	4	12	.275	.327	.412	105	0	0	0	0	.958	5	3-23/D-2	0.5
1990	Tex-A	67	180	21	36	6	0	2	13	15	47	.200	.265	.267	49	-12	1	0		.941	7	3-66	-0.5
1991	SD-N	60	180	12	39	8	1	2	15	19	45	.217	.295	.306	67	-8	0	3	-2	.952	4	3-54	-0.6
1994	StL-N	15	21	4	4	0	0	2	6	1	4	.190	.227	.476	80	-1	0	0	0	1.000	0	/1-4,3-4	-0.1
Total	4	167	432	44	93	15	1	8	41	39	108	.215	.283	.310	65	-20	1	3	-2	.949	16	3-147/1-4,D	-0.7

■ DUFF COOLEY
Cooley, Duff Gordan "Dick" b: 3/14/1873, Dallas, Tex. d: 8/9/37, Dallas, Tex. BL/TR, 5'11", 158 lbs. Deb: 7/27/1893

YEAR	TM/L	G	AB	R	H	2B	3B	HR	RBI	BB	SO	AVG	OBP	SLG	PRO+	BR/A	SB	CS	SBR	FA	FR	G/POS	TPR
1893	StL-N	29	107	20	37	2	3	0	21	8	9	.346	.391	.421	115	2	8			.947	-9	O-15,C-10/S	-0.5
1894	StL-N	54	206	35	61	3	1	1	21	12	16	.296	.335	.335	62	-13	7			.833	-11	O-39,3-13/S1	-2.0
1895	StL-N	132	563	106	191	9	20	7	75	36	29	.339	.382	.464	119	15	27			.936	11	*O-124/3-5,SC	1.3
1896	StL-N	40	166	29	51	5	3	0	13	7	3	.307	.335	.373	90	-3	12			.959	-1	O-40	-0.6
	Phi-N	64	287	63	88	6	4	2	22	18	16	.307	.348	.376	92	-4	18			.901	-5	O-64	-1.1
	Yr	104	453	92	139	11	7	2	35	25	19	.307	.343	.375	91	-6	30			.923	-5	*O-104	-1.7
1897	Phi-N	133	566	124	186	14	13	4	40	51		.329	.386	.420	116	14	31			.960	7	*O-131/1-2	0.9
1898	Phi-N	149	629	123	196	24	12	4	55	48		.312	.364	.407	126	21	17			.943	4	*O-149	1.2
1899	Phi-N	94	406	75	112	15	8	1	31	29		.276	.330	.360	92	-5	15			.971	-5	1-79,O-14/2	-1.0
1900	Pit-N	66	249	30	50	8	1	0	22	14		.201	.243	.241	34	-23	9			.989	-5	1-66	-2.6
1901	Bos-N	63	240	27	62	13	3	0	27	14		.258	.302	.338	78	-7	5			.943	2	O-53,1-10	-0.9
1902	Bos-N	135	548	73	162	26	8	0	58	34		.296	.339	.372	118	11	27			.952	-6	*O-127/1-7	-0.4
1903	Bos-N	138	553	76	160	26	10	1	70	44		.289	.342	.378	109	6	27			.952	-5	*O-126,1-13	-0.7
1904	Bos-N	122	467	41	127	18	7	5	70	24		.272	.312	.373	115	7	14			.976	-7	*O-116/1-6	-0.8
1905	Det-A	97	377	25	93	11	9	1	32	26		.247	.297	.332	99	-1	7			.959	7	O-96	0.2
Total	13	1316	5364	847	1576	180	102	26	557	365	73	.294	.341	.380	104	20	224			.945	-22	*O-1094,1-184/3CS2	-7.0

■ CECIL COOMBS
Coombs, Cecil Lysander b: 3/18/1888, Moweaqua, Ill. d: 11/25/75, Fort Worth, Tex. BR/TR, 5'9", 160 lbs. Deb: 8/7/14

YEAR	TM/L	G	AB	R	H	2B	3B	HR	RBI	BB	SO	AVG	OBP	SLG	PRO+	BR/A	SB	CS	SBR	FA	FR	G/POS	TPR
1914	Chi-A	7	23	1	4	1	0	0	1	1	7	.174	.208	.217	28	-2	0	1	-1	1.000	1	/O-7	-0.2

■ JACK COOMBS
Coombs, John Wesley "Colby Jack" b: 11/18/1882, LeGrand, Iowa d: 4/15/57, Palestine, Tex. BB/TR, 6', 185 lbs. Deb: 7/5/06 MC

YEAR	TM/L	G	AB	R	H	2B	3B	HR	RBI	BB	SO	AVG	OBP	SLG	PRO+	BR/A	SB	CS	SBR	FA	FR	G/POS	TPR
1906	Phi-A	24	67	9	16	2	0	0	3	1		.239	.261	.269	64	-3	2			.968	0	P-23	0.0
1907	Phi-A	24	48	4	8	0	0	1	4	0		.167	.167	.229	25	-4	1			.979	0	P-23	0.0
1908	Phi-A	78	220	24	56	9	5	1	23	9		.255	.287	.355	101	-1	6			.990	6	O-47,P-26/1	0.4
1909	Phi-A	37	83	4	14	4	0	0	10	4		.169	.216	.217	36	-6	1			.973	0	P-30	0.0
1910	*Phi-A	46	132	20	29	3	0	0	9	7		.220	.270	.242	61	-6	3			.990	-5	P-45	0.0
1911	*Phi-A	52	141	31	45	6	1	2	23	8		.319	.356	.418	118	3	5			.913	-3	P-47	0.0
1912	Phi-A	56	110	10	28	2	0	0	13	14		.255	.344	.273	80	-2	1			1.000	-1	P-40	0.0
1913	Phi-A	2	3	1	1	1	0	0	0	0		.333	.333	.667	195	0				.500	0	/P-2	0.0
1914	Phi-A	5	11	0	3	1	0	0	2	1		.273	.333	.364	114	0	0	1	-1	1.000	-1	/P-2,O-2	-0.1
1915	Bro-N	29	75	8	21	1	1	0	5	2	17	.280	.304	.320	86	-1	0	1	-1	.980	-4	P-29	0.0
1916	*Bro-N	27	61	2	11	2	0	0	3	2	10	.180	.206	.213	28	-5	0			1.000	-6	P-27	0.0
1917	Bro-N	32	44	4	10	0	0	0	2	4	9	.227	.292	.273	72	-1	1			.971	-3	P-31	0.0
1918	Bro-N	46	113	6	19	3	2	0	3	7	5	.168	.223	.230	38	-7	1			.962	-7	P-27,O-13	-0.8
1920	Det-A	2	2	0	0	0	0	0	0	0		.000	.000	.000	-99	-1				1.000	0	/P-2	0.0
Total	14	460	1110	123	261	34	10	4	100	59	44	.235	.278	.295	74	-35	21	2		.966	-23	P-354/O-62,1	-0.5

■ WILLIAM COON
Coon, William K. b: 3/21/1855, Pennsylvania d: 8/30/15, Burlington, N.J. Deb: 9/4/1875

YEAR	TM/L	G	AB	R	H	2B	3B	HR	RBI	BB	SO	AVG	OBP	SLG	PRO+	BR/A	SB	CS	SBR	FA	FR	G/POS	TPR
1875	Ath-n	3	12	1	2	0	0	0		0		.167	.167	.167	14	-1						/C-4	-0.1
1876	Phi-N	54	220	30	50	5	1	0	22	2	4	.227	.234	.259	65	-8				.761	-15	O-29,C-18/32P	-2.0

■ JIMMY COONEY
Cooney, James Edward "Scoops" b: 8/24/1894, Cranston, R.I. d: 8/7/91, Warwick, R.I. BR/TR, 5'11", 160 lbs. Deb: 9/22/17 F

YEAR	TM/L	G	AB	R	H	2B	3B	HR	RBI	BB	SO	AVG	OBP	SLG	PRO+	BR/A	SB	CS	SBR	FA	FR	G/POS	TPR
1917	Bos-A	11	36	4	8	1	0	0	3	6	2	.222	.333	.250	79	-1	0			1.000	5	2-10/S-1	0.5
1919	NY-N	5	14	3	3	0	0	0	1	0	0	.214	.214	.214	29	-1	0			1.000	-1	/S-4,2-1	-0.2
1924	StL-N	110	383	44	113	20	8	1	57	20	20	.295	.330	.397	96	-3	12	10	-2	.969	1	S-99/3-7,2	0.6
1925	StL-N	54	187	27	51	11	2	0	18	4	5	.273	.292	.353	62	-11	1	3	-2	.976	-11	S-37,2-15/O	-1.8
1926	Chi-N	141	513	52	129	18	5	1	47	23	10	.251	.288	.312	61	-29	11			.972	19	*S-141	0.6
1927	Chi-N	33	132	16	32	2	0	0	6	8	7	.242	.286	.258	46	-10	1			.973	-2	S-33	-0.9
	Phi-N	76	259	33	70	12	1	0	15	13	9	.270	.305	.324	68	-12	4			.980	17	S-74	1.2
	Yr	109	391	49	102	14	1	0	21	21	16	.261	.299	.302	61	-22	5			.978	15	*S-107	0.3
1928	Bos-N	18	51	2	7	0	0	0	2	4	3	.137	.170	.137	-20	-9	1			.982	2	S-11/2-4	-0.6
Total	7	448	1575	181	413	64	16	2	150	76	58	.262	.298	.327	67	-75	30	13		.974	30	S-400/2-31,3O	-0.6

■ JIMMY COONEY
Cooney, James Joseph b: 7/9/1865, Cranston, R.I. d: 7/1/03, Cranston, R.I. BB/TR, 5'9", 155 lbs. Deb: 4/19/1890

YEAR	TM/L	G	AB	R	H	2B	3B	HR	RBI	BB	SO	AVG	OBP	SLG	PRO+	BR/A	SB	CS	SBR	FA	FR	G/POS	TPR
1890	Chi-N	135	574	114	156	19	10	4	52	73	23	.272	.360	.361	106	5	45			.936	1	*S-135/C-1	1.2
1891	Chi-N	118	465	84	114	15	3	3	42	48	17	.245	.318	.290	78	-12	21			.917	8	*S-118	0.3
1892	Chi-N	65	238	18	41	1	0	0	20	23	5	.172	.248	.176	29	-20	10			.912	-8	S-65	-2.3
	Was-N	6	25	5	4	0	1	0	4	4		.160	.276	.240	58	-1	1			.862	-3	/S-6	-0.4
	Yr	71	263	23	45	1	1	0	24	27		.171	.251	.183	31	-21	11			.908	-11	S-71	-2.7
Total	3	324	1302	221	315	35	14	4	118	148	48	.242	.324	.300	82	-29	77			.923	-2	S-324/C-1	-1.2

■ JOHNNY COONEY
Cooney, John Walter b: 3/18/01, Cranston, R.I. d: 7/8/86, Sarasota, Fla. BR/TL, 5'10", 165 lbs. Deb: 4/19/21 FMC

YEAR	TM/L	G	AB	R	H	2B	3B	HR	RBI	BB	SO	AVG	OBP	SLG	PRO+	BR/A	SB	CS	SBR	FA	FR	G/POS	TPR
1921	Bos-N	8	5	0	1	0	0	0	0	0	1	.200	.200	.200	7	0	0	0	0	1.000	0	/P-8	0.0
1922	Bos-N	4	8	0	0	0	0	0	0	0	0	.000	.000	.000	-99	-2	0	0	0	1.000	0	/P-4	0.0
1923	Bos-N	42	66	7	25	1	0	0	3	6	2	.379	.414	.394	119	2	0	1	-1	1.000	0	P-23,O-11/1	0.2
1924	Bos-N	55	130	10	33	2	1	0	4	9	5	.254	.302	.285	61	-7	0	4	-2	.962	-6	P-34,O-16/1	-0.4
1925	Bos-N	54	103	10	33	7	0	0	13	3	6	.320	.346	.388	90	-1	1	0	0	.949	0	P-31/1-3,O	-0.1
1926	Bos-N	64	126	17	38	3	2	0	18	13	7	.302	.367	.357	105	1	6			.996	5	P-19/O	0.3
1927	Bos-N	10	1	2	0	0	0	0	0	0	0	.000	.000	.000	-99	-0	0			.000	0	H	0.0
1928	Bos-N	33	41	2	7	0	0	0	2	4	3	.171	.244	.171	11	-5	0			1.000	2	P-24/1-3,O	-0.2

YEAR	TM/L	G	AB	R	H	2B	3B	HR	RBI	BB	SO	AVG	OBP	SLG	PRO+	BR/A	SB	CS	SBR	FA	FR	G/POS	TPR
1929	Bos-N	41	72	10	23	4	1	0	6	3	3	.319	.355	.403	91	-1	1			1.000	2	O-16,P-14	-0.1
1930	Bos-N	4	3	0	0	0	0	0	0	0	0	.000	.000	.000	-99	-1	0			1.000	1	/P-2	0.0
1935	Bro-N	10	29	3	9	0	1	0	1	3	2	.310	.375	.379	106	0	0			1.000	-1	O-10	-0.1
1936	Bro-N	130	507	71	143	17	5	0	30	24	15	.282	.315	.335	74	-18	3			.994	8	*O-130	-1.6
1937	Bro-N	120	430	61	126	18	5	0	37	22	10	.293	.327	.358	85	-9	5			.976	6	*O-111/1-2	-0.7
1938	Bos-N	120	432	45	117	25	5	0	17	22	12	.271	.308	.352	90	-8	2			.982	-10	*O-110,1-13	-2.2
1939	Bos-N	118	368	39	101	8	1	2	27	21	8	.274	.317	.318	77	-12	2			.992	-6	*O-116/1-2	-2.2
1940	Bos-N	108	365	40	116	14	3	0	21	25	9	.318	.363	.373	109	5	4			.992	-1	O-99/1-7	-0.1
1941	Bos-N	123	442	52	141	25	2	0	29	27	15	.319	.358	.385	114	8	3			.996	4	*O-111/1-4	0.5
1942	Bos-N	74	198	23	41	6	0	0	7	23	5	.207	.290	.237	56	-10	2			.984	-14	O-54,1-23	-3.1
1943	Bro-N	37	34	7	7	0	0	0	2	4	3	.206	.287	.206	44	-2	1			1.000	-0	/1-3,O-2	-0.3
1944	Bro-N	7	4	0	3	0	0	0	1	0	0	.750	.750	.750	329	1	0			1.000	-0	/O-2	0.1
	NY-A	10	8	1	1	0	0	0	1	1	0	.125	.222	.125	1	-1	0	0	0	1.000	-0	/O-2	-0.1
Total	20	1172	3372	408	965	130	26	2	219	208	107	.286	.329	.342	87	-63	30	5		.988	-6	O-794,P-159/1	-10.1

■ PHIL COONEY   Cooney, Philip Clarence (b: Philip Clarence Cohen) b: 9/14/1882, New York, N.Y. d: 10/6/57, New York, N.Y. BL/TR, 5'8", 155 lbs. Deb: 9/27/05

YEAR	TM/L	G	AB	R	H	2B	3B	HR	RBI	BB	SO	AVG	OBP	SLG	PRO+	BR/A	SB	CS	SBR	FA	FR	G/POS	TPR
1905	NY-A	1	3	0	0	0	0	0	0	0	0	.000	.000	.000	-90	-1	0			1.000	-0	/3-1	-0.1

■ BILL COONEY   Cooney, William A. "Cush" b: 4/7/1883, Boston, Mass. d: 11/6/28, Roxbury, Mass. TR , Deb: 9/22/09

YEAR	TM/L	G	AB	R	H	2B	3B	HR	RBI	BB	SO	AVG	OBP	SLG	PRO+	BR/A	SB	CS	SBR	FA	FR	G/POS	TPR
1909	Bos-N	5	10	0	3	0	0	0	0	0	0	.300	.300	.300	82	-0	0			.500	-0	/P-3,2-1,S	0.0
1910	Bos-N	8	12	2	3	0	0	0	1	2	0	.250	.357	.250	74	-0	0			.000	-1	/O-2	-0.1
Total	2	13	22	2	6	0	0	0	1	2	0	.273	.333	.273	78	-1	0			.500	-1	/P-3,O-2,S2	-0.1

■ CECIL COOPER   Cooper, Cecil Celester b: 12/20/49, Brenham, Tex. BL/TL, 6'2", 190 lbs. Deb: 9/8/71

YEAR	TM/L	G	AB	R	H	2B	3B	HR	RBI	BB	SO	AVG	OBP	SLG	PRO+	BR/A	SB	CS	SBR	FA	FR	G/POS	TPR
1971	Bos-A	14	42	9	13	4	1	0	3	5	4	.310	.396	.452	130	2	1	0	0	.988	-2	1-11	-0.1
1972	Bos-A	12	17	0	4	1	0	0	2	2	5	.235	.316	.294	78	-0	0	0	0	1.000	-1	/1-3	-0.1
1973	Bos-A	30	101	12	24	2	0	3	11	7	12	.238	.287	.347	73	-4	1	2	-1	.984	-0	1-29	-0.7
1974	Bos-A	121	414	55	114	24	1	8	43	32	74	.275	.329	.396	101	-0	2	5	-2	.983	-1	1-74,D-41	-1.0
1975	*Bos-A	106	305	49	95	17	6	14	44	19	33	.311	.358	.544	140	14	1	4	-2	.995	2	D-54,1-35	1.2
1976	Bos-A	123	451	66	127	22	6	15	78	16	62	.282	.308	.457	109	2	7	1	2	.994	-1	1-66,D-53	-0.3
1977	Mil-A	160	643	86	193	31	7	20	78	28	110	.300	.329	.463	113	10	13	8	-1	.992	5	*1-148,D-10	0.5
1978	Mil-A	107	407	60	127	23	2	13	54	32	72	.312	.362	.474	133	17	3	4	-2	.988	2	1-84,D-19	1.2
1979	Mil-A★	150	590	83	182	44	1	24	106	56	77	.308	.368	.537	134	27	15	3	3	.993	-8	*1-135,D-15	1.2
1980	Mil-A★	153	622	96	219	33	4	25	122	39	42	.352	.392	.539	157	47	17	6	2	.997	4	*1-142,D-11	4.3
1981	*Mil-A	106	416	70	133	35	1	12	60	28	30	.320	.367	.495	154	27	5	4	-1	.992	-0	*1-101/D-5	2.1
1982	*Mil-A★	155	654	104	205	38	3	32	121	32	53	.313	.345	.528	145	36	2	3	-1	.997	-1	*1-154/D-1	2.5
1983	Mil-A★	160	661	106	203	37	3	30	126	37	63	.307	.345	.508	142	34	2	1	0	.993	-10	*1-158/D-2	1.5
1984	Mil-A	148	603	63	166	28	3	11	67	27	59	.275	.309	.386	95	-6	8	2	1	.991	-1	*1-122,D-26	-1.0
1985	Mil-A★	154	631	82	185	39	8	16	99	30	77	.293	.327	.456	112	9	10	3	1	.986	-2	*1-123,D-30	0.0
1986	Mil-A	134	542	46	140	24	1	12	75	41	85	.258	.312	.373	83	-13	1	2	-1	.988	-4	1-90,D-44	-2.6
1987	Mil-A	63	250	25	62	13	0	6	36	17	51	.248	.296	.372	74	-10	1	1	-0	.000	-3	D-62	-1.1
Total	17	1896	7349	1012	2192	415	47	241	1125	448	911	.298	.340	.466	121	193	89	49	-3	.992	-13	*1-1475,D-373	7.6

■ CLAUDE COOPER   Cooper, Claude William b: 4/1/1892, Troupe, Tex. d: 1/21/74, Plainview, Tex. BL/TL, 5'9", 158 lbs. Deb: 4/14/13

YEAR	TM/L	G	AB	R	H	2B	3B	HR	RBI	BB	SO	AVG	OBP	SLG	PRO+	BR/A	SB	CS	SBR	FA	FR	G/POS	TPR
1913	*NY-N	27	30	11	9	4	0	0	4	4	6	.300	.382	.433	132	1	3			.895	-5	O-15	-0.4
1914	Bro-F	113	399	56	96	14	11	2	25	26	60	.241	.294	.346	66	-22	25			.926	-4	*O-101	-2.8
1915	Bro-F	153	527	75	155	26	12	2	63	77	78	.294	.388	.400	112	11	31			.958	18	*O-121,1-32	2.5
1916	Phi-N	56	104	9	20	2	0	0	11	7	15	.192	.250	.212	41	-7	1			.945	-3	O-29/1-1	-1.3
1917	Phi-N	24	29	5	3	1	0	0	1	5	4	.103	.235	.138	15	-3	0			.923	-4	O-12	-0.9
Total	5	373	1089	156	283	47	23	4	104	119	163	.260	.338	.356	87	-19	60			.943	5	O-278/1-33	-2.9

■ GARY COOPER   Cooper, Gary Clifton b: 8/13/64, Lynwood, Cal. BR/TR, 6'1", 200 lbs. Deb: 9/15/91

YEAR	TM/L	G	AB	R	H	2B	3B	HR	RBI	BB	SO	AVG	OBP	SLG	PRO+	BR/A	SB	CS	SBR	FA	FR	G/POS	TPR
1991	Hou-N	9	16	1	4	1	0	0	2	3	6	.250	.368	.313	99	0	0	0	0	.833	-2	/3-4	-0.2

■ GARY COOPER   Cooper, Gary Nathaniel b: 12/22/56, Savannah, Ga. BB/TR, 6'3", 175 lbs. Deb: 8/25/80

YEAR	TM/L	G	AB	R	H	2B	3B	HR	RBI	BB	SO	AVG	OBP	SLG	PRO+	BR/A	SB	CS	SBR	FA	FR	G/POS	TPR
1980	Atl-N	21	2	3	0	0	0	0	0	0	1	.000	.000	.000	-97	-1	2	1	0	1.000	-4	O-13	-0.4

■ PAT COOPER   Cooper, Orge Patterson b: 11/26/17, Albemarle, N.C. d: 3/15/93, Charlotte, N.C. BR/TR, 6'3", 180 lbs. Deb: 5/11/46

YEAR	TM/L	G	AB	R	H	2B	3B	HR	RBI	BB	SO	AVG	OBP	SLG	PRO+	BR/A	SB	CS	SBR	FA	FR	G/POS	TPR
1946	Phi-A	1	0	0	0	0	0	0	0	0	0	—	—	—	—	—	0	0	0	.000	-0	/P-1	0.0
1947	Phi-A	13	16	0	4	2	0	0	3	0	5	.250	.250	.375	71	-1	0	0	0	1.000	-0	/1-1	-0.1
Total	2	14	16	0	4	2	0	0	3	0	5	.250	.250	.375	71	-1	0	0	0	1.000	-0	/1-1,P-1	-0.1

■ SCOTT COOPER   Cooper, Scott Kendrick b: 10/13/67, St.Louis, Mo. BL/TR, 6'3", 200 lbs. Deb: 9/5/90

YEAR	TM/L	G	AB	R	H	2B	3B	HR	RBI	BB	SO	AVG	OBP	SLG	PRO+	BR/A	SB	CS	SBR	FA	FR	G/POS	TPR
1990	Bos-A	2	1	0	0	0	0	0	0	0	1	.000	.000	.000	-96	-0	0	0	0	.000	0	/H	0.0
1991	Bos-A	14	35	6	16	4	2	0	7	2	2	.457	.486	.686	210	5	0	0	0	.933	2	3-13	0.7
1992	Bos-A	123	337	34	93	21	0	5	33	37	33	.276	.348	.383	98	-1	1	1	-0	.990	8	1-62,3-47/2SD	0.4
1993	Bos-A★	156	526	67	147	29	3	9	63	58	81	.279	.357	.397	96	-2	5	2	0	.937	-17	*3-154/1-2,S	-1.8
1994	Bos-A★	104	369	49	104	16	4	13	53	30	65	.282	.338	.453	95	-3	0	3	-2	.944	8	*3-104	0.2
Total	5	399	1268	156	360	70	9	27	156	127	182	.284	.352	.417	99	-1	6	6	-2	.944	1	3-318/1-64,DS2	-0.5

■ WALKER COOPER   Cooper, William Walker "Walk" b: 1/8/15, Atherton, Mo. d: 4/11/91, Scottsdale, Ariz. BR/TR, 6'3", 210 lbs. Deb: 9/25/40 FC

YEAR	TM/L	G	AB	R	H	2B	3B	HR	RBI	BB	SO	AVG	OBP	SLG	PRO+	BR/A	SB	CS	SBR	FA	FR	G/POS	TPR
1940	StL-N	6	19	3	6	1	0	0	2	2	2	.316	.381	.368	102	0	1			1.000	0	/C-6	0.0
1941	StL-N	68	200	19	49	9	1	1	20	13	14	.245	.291	.315	66	-9	1			.966	4	C-63	-0.1
1942	*StL-N★	125	438	58	123	32	7	7	65	29	29	.281	.327	.434	113	5	4			.972	3	*C-115	1.8
1943	*StL-N★	122	449	52	143	30	4	9	81	19	19	.318	.349	.463	128	14	1			.975	-3	*C-112	2.0
1944	*StL-N★	112	397	56	126	25	5	13	72	20	19	.317	.352	.504	136	17	4			.980	4	C-97	2.7
1945	StL-N	4	18	3	7	0	0	0	1	0	1	.389	.389	.389	114	0				.966	1	/C-4	0.2
1946	NY-N★	87	280	29	75	10	1	8	46	17	12	.268	.310	.396	99	-2	0			.972	-12	C-73	-1.0
1947	NY-N★	140	515	79	157	24	8	35	122	24	43	.305	.339	.586	141	29	2			.979	-9	*C-132	2.4
1948	NY-N★	91	290	40	77	12	0	16	54	28	29	.266	.332	.472	115	5	1			.979	-13	C-79	-0.2
1949	NY-N	42	147	14	31	4	2	4	21	7	8	.211	.261	.347	62	-8	0			.982	-2	C-40	-0.8
	Cin-N☆	82	307	34	86	9	2	16	62	21	24	.280	.330	.479	113	4	0			.978	-3	C-77	0.6
	Yr	124	454	48	117	13	4	20	83	28	32	.258	.308	.436	97	-4	0			.979	-5	*C-117	-0.2
1950	Cin-N	15	47	3	9	3	0	0	4	0	5	.191	.191	.255	16	-6	0			.972	1	C-13	-0.4
	Bos-N☆	102	337	52	111	19	3	14	60	30	26	.329	.389	.528	148	23	1			.973	-5	*C-88	2.1
	Yr	117	384	55	120	22	3	14	64	30	31	.313	.367	.495	132	16	1			.973	-4	*C-101	1.7
1951	Bos-N	109	342	42	107	14	1	18	59	28	18	.313	.367	.518	145	20	1	1	-0	.981	-2	*C-90	2.2
1952	Bos-N	102	349	33	82	15	1	10	55	22	32	.235	.282	.361	80	-11	1	0	0	.983	-4	*C-89	-1.0
1953	Mil-N	53	137	12	30	6	0	3	16	12	15	.219	.287	.328	64	-8	1	0	0	.983	2	C-35	-1.0
1954	Pit-N	14	15	0	3	2	0	0	1	2	1	.200	.294	.333	64	-1	0	0	0	1.000	-0	/C-2	-0.1
	Chi-N	57	158	21	49	10	2	7	32	21	23	.310	.398	.532	138	9	0	0	0	.978	-2	C-48	0.9
	Yr	71	173	21	52	12	2	7	33	23	24	.301	.389	.514	132	8	0	0	0	.979	-2	C-50	0.8
1955	Chi-N	54	111	11	31	8	1	7	15	6	19	.279	.322	.559	128	4	0	0	0	.961	-11	C-31	-0.6
1956	StL-N	40	68	5	18	8	1	2	14	3	8	.265	.296	.456	98	-0				.984	-3	C-16	-0.3

YEAR	TM/L	G	AB	R	H	2B	3B	HR	RBI	BB	SO	AVG	OBP	SLG	PRO+	BR/A	SB	CS	SBR	FA	FR	G/POS	TPR
1957	StL-N	48	78	7	21	5	2	1	10	5	10	.269	.313	.474	106	0	0	0	0	.957	-2	C-13	-0.1
Total	18	1473	4702	573	1341	240	40	173	812	309	357	.285	.332	.464	116	82	18	1		.977	-63	*C-1223	9.3

■ JOEY CORA
Cora, Jose Manuel (Amaro)   b: 5/14/65, Caguas, P.R.   BB/TR, 5'8", 150 lbs.   Deb: 4/6/87

YEAR	TM/L	G	AB	R	H	2B	3B	HR	RBI	BB	SO	AVG	OBP	SLG	PRO+	BR/A	SB	CS	SBR	FA	FR	G/POS	TPR
1987	SD-N	77	241	23	57	7	2	0	13	28	26	.237	.319	.282	63	-12	15	11	-2	.975	-2	2-66/S-6	-1.3
1989	SD-N	12	19	5	6	1	0	0	1	1	0	.316	.350	.368	105	0	1	0	0	.960	2	/S-7,3-2,2	0.3
1990	SD-N	51	100	12	27	3	0	0	2	6	9	.270	.311	.300	68	-4	8	3	1	.833	-3	S-21,2-15/C	-0.6
1991	Chi-A	100	228	37	55	2	3	0	18	20	21	.241	.316	.276	67	-10	11	6	-0	.970	-9	2-80/S-5,D	-1.8
1992	Chi-A	68	122	27	30	7	1	0	9	22	13	.246	.378	.320	99	1	10	3	1	.984	5	2-28,D-18/S3	0.7
1993	*Chi-A	153	579	95	155	15	13	2	51	67	63	.268	.353	.349	91	-5	20	8	1	.974	-17	*2-151/3-3	-1.6
1994	Chi-A	90	312	55	86	13	4	2	30	38	32	.276	.358	.362	87	-5	8	4	0	.978	-13	2-84/D-1	-1.5
Total	7	551	1601	254	416	48	23	4	124	182	164	.260	.343	.326	82	-35	73	35	1	.973	-37	2-425/S-45,D3C	-5.8

■ GENE CORBETT
Corbett, Eugene Louis   b: 10/25/13, Winona, Minn.   BL/TR, 6'1.5", 190 lbs.   Deb: 9/19/36

YEAR	TM/L	G	AB	R	H	2B	3B	HR	RBI	BB	SO	AVG	OBP	SLG	PRO+	BR/A	SB	CS	SBR	FA	FR	G/POS	TPR
1936	Phi-N	6	21	1	3	0	0	0	2	2	3	.143	.217	.143	-1	-3	0			1.000	-1	/1-6	-0.4
1937	Phi-N	7	12	4	4	2	0	0	1	0	0	.333	.333	.500	114	0	0			.800	-1	/3-3,2-1	-0.1
1938	Phi-N	24	75	7	6	1	0	2	7	6	11	.080	.148	.173	-12	-12	0			.995	-1	1-22	-1.5
Total	3	37	108	12	13	3	0	2	10	8	14	.120	.181	.204	5	-15	0			.996	-2	/1-28,3-3,2	-2.0

■ CLAUDE CORBITT
Corbitt, Claude Elliott   b: 7/21/15, Sunbury, N.C.   d: 5/1/78, Cincinnati, Ohio   BR/TR, 5'10", 170 lbs.   Deb: 9/23/45

YEAR	TM/L	G	AB	R	H	2B	3B	HR	RBI	BB	SO	AVG	OBP	SLG	PRO+	BR/A	SB	CS	SBR	FA	FR	G/POS	TPR
1945	Bro-N	2	4	1	2	0	0	0	0	1	0	.500	.600	.500	209	1	0			1.000	0	/3-2	0.1
1946	Cin-N	82	274	25	68	10	1	1	16	23	13	.248	.306	.303	77	-9	3			.947	-13	S-77	-1.9
1948	Cin-N	87	258	24	66	11	0	0	18	14	16	.256	.297	.298	64	-13	4			.973	-8	2-52,3-16,S	-1.8
1949	Cin-N	44	94	10	17	1	0	0	3	9	1	.181	.252	.191	20	-10	1			.984	-6	S-18,2-17/3	-1.5
Total	4	215	630	60	153	22	1	1	37	47	30	.243	.297	.286	63	-31	8			.956	-26	S-106/2-69,3	-5.1

■ ART CORCORAN
Corcoran, Arthur Andrew "Bunny"   b: 11/23/1894, Roxbury, Mass.   d: 7/27/58, Chelsea, Mass.   TR,   Deb: 9/9/15

YEAR	TM/L	G	AB	R	H	2B	3B	HR	RBI	BB	SO	AVG	OBP	SLG	PRO+	BR/A	SB	CS	SBR	FA	FR	G/POS	TPR
1915	Phi-A	1	4	0	0	0	0	0	0	0	2	.000	.000	.000	-99	-1	0			1.000	-0	/3-1	-0.1

■ JOHN CORCORAN
Corcoran, John A.   b: 1873, Cincinnati, Ohio   d: 11/2/01, Cincinnati, Ohio   TL,   Deb: 9/17/1895

YEAR	TM/L	G	AB	R	H	2B	3B	HR	RBI	BB	SO	AVG	OBP	SLG	PRO+	BR/A	SB	CS	SBR	FA	FR	G/POS	TPR
1895	Pit-N	6	20	0	3	0	0	0	1	0	2	.150	.150	.150	-24	-4				.895	-1	/S-4,3-2	-0.4

■ JACK CORCORAN
Corcoran, John H.   b: 1860, Lowell, Mass.   Deb: 5/1/1884

YEAR	TM/L	G	AB	R	H	2B	3B	HR	RBI	BB	SO	AVG	OBP	SLG	PRO+	BR/A	SB	CS	SBR	FA	FR	G/POS	TPR
1884	Bro-a	52	185	17	39	4	3	0			8	.211	.251	.265	68	-6				.873	-9	C-38/O-9,2SP	-1.1

■ LARRY CORCORAN
Corcoran, Lawrence J.   b: 8/10/1859, Brooklyn, N.Y.   d: 10/14/1891, Newark, N.J.   BL/TB, 120 lbs.   Deb: 5/1/1880   F

YEAR	TM/L	G	AB	R	H	2B	3B	HR	RBI	BB	SO	AVG	OBP	SLG	PRO+	BR/A	SB	CS	SBR	FA	FR	G/POS	TPR
1880	Chi-N	72	286	41	66	11	1	0	25	10	33	.231	.257	.276	76	-7				.957	3	*P-63/O-8,S	-0.3
1881	Chi-N	47	189	25	42	8	0	0	9	5	22	.222	.242	.265	57	-9				.893	-1	P-45/S-2,O	0.0
1882	Chi-N	40	169	23	35	10	2	1	24	6	18	.207	.234	.308	69	-6				.919	1	P-39/3-1	0.0
1883	Chi-N	68	263	40	55	12	7	0	25	6	62	.209	.227	.308	57	-14				.906	-3	P-56,O-13/S2	-0.6
1884	Chi-N	64	251	43	61	3	4	1	19	10	33	.243	.272	.299	73	-9				.882	7	P-60/O-4,S	-0.1
1885	Chi-N	7	22	6	6	1	0	0	4	6	1	.273	.429	.318	126	1				.905	0	/P-7,S-1	0.0
	NY-N	3	14	3	5	0	0	0	2	0	1	.357	.357	.357	133	0				1.000	1	/P-3	0.0
	Yr	10	36	9	11	1	0	0	6	6	2	.306	.405	.333	128	1				.935	1	P-10/S-1	0.0
1886	NY-N	1	4	0	0	0	0	0	0	0	2	.000	.000	.000	-99	-1	0			.000	-1	/O-1	-0.2
	Was-N	21	81	9	15	2	1	0	3	7	14	.185	.250	.235	51	-4	3			.619	-3	O-11/S-9,P	-0.6
	Yr	22	85	9	15	2	1	0	3	7	16	.176	.239	.224	44	-5	3			.591	-3	O-12/S-9,P	-0.8
1887	Ind-N	3	10	2	2	0	0	0		2	1	.200	.333	.200	53	-1	2			1.000	-0	/O-2,P-2	0.0
Total	8	326	1289	192	287	47	15	2	111	52	187	.223	.253	.287	67	-50	5			.910	3	P-277/O-40,S23	-1.8

■ MICKEY CORCORAN
Corcoran, Michael Joseph   b: 8/26/1882, Buffalo, N.Y.   d: 12/9/50, Buffalo, N.Y.   BR/TR, 5'8", 165 lbs.   Deb: 9/15/10

YEAR	TM/L	G	AB	R	H	2B	3B	HR	RBI	BB	SO	AVG	OBP	SLG	PRO+	BR/A	SB	CS	SBR	FA	FR	G/POS	TPR
1910	Cin-N	14	46	3	10	3	0	0	7	5	9	.217	.308	.283	76	-1				.911	-1	2-14	-0.2

■ TOMMY CORCORAN
Corcoran, Thomas William "Corky"   b: 1/4/1869, New Haven, Conn.   d: 6/25/60, Plainfield, Conn.   BR/TR, 5'9", 164 lbs.   Deb: 4/19/1890   U

YEAR	TM/L	G	AB	R	H	2B	3B	HR	RBI	BB	SO	AVG	OBP	SLG	PRO+	BR/A	SB	CS	SBR	FA	FR	G/POS	TPR
1890	Pit-P	123	503	80	117	14	13	1	61	38	45	.233	.289	.318	68	-24	43			.884	4	*S-123	-1.0
1891	Phi-a	133	511	84	130	11	15	7	71	29	56	.254	.307	.376	93	-8	30			.911	12	*S-133	1.0
1892	Bro-N	151	613	77	145	11	6	1	74	34	51	.237	.281	.279	72	-21	39			.925	-2	*S-151	-1.5
1893	Bro-N	115	459	61	126	11	10	2	58	27	12	.275	.318	.355	82	-13	14			.907	14	*S-115	0.5
1894	Bro-N	129	576	123	173	21	20	5	92	25	17	.300	.329	.432	89	-13	33			.904	-4	*S-129	-0.8
1895	Bro-N	127	535	81	142	17	10	2	69	23	11	.265	.299	.346	72	-23	17			.924	18	*S-127	0.0
1896	Bro-N	132	532	63	154	15	7	3	73	15	13	.289	.310	.361	81	-16	16			.926	24	*S-132	1.0
1897	Cin-N	109	445	76	128	30	5	3	57	13		.288	.311	.398	81	-15	15			.913	6	S-63,2-47	-0.4
1898	Cin-N	153	619	80	155	28	15	2	87	26		.250	.283	.354	77	-22	19			.932	14	*S-153	-0.1
1899	Cin-N	137	537	91	149	11	8	0	81	28		.277	.316	.328	75	-19	32			.931	4	*S-123,2-14	-0.4
1900	Cin-N	127	523	64	128	21	9	1	54	22		.245	.278	.325	68	-24	27			.921	-5	*S-124/2-5	-1.8
1901	Cin-N	31	115	14	24	3	3	0	15	11		.209	.278	.287	68	-5	6			.919	4	S-30	0.2
1902	Cin-N	138	538	54	136	18	4	0	54	11		.253	.268	.301	69	-21	13			.926	-13	*S-137/2-1	-2.8
1903	Cin-N	115	459	61	113	19	7	2	73	12		.246	.267	.329	63	-25	12			.943	6	*S-115	-1.3
1904	Cin-N	150	578	55	133	17	9	2	74	19		.230	.257	.301	66	-25	19			.936	2	*S-150	-2.0
1905	Cin-N	151	605	70	150	21	11	2	85	23		.248	.277	.329	72	-23	28			.952	20	*S-151	0.0
1906	Cin-N	117	430	29	89	13	1	1	33	19		.207	.242	.249	51	-25	8			.941	8	*S-117	-1.6
1907	NY-N	62	226	21	60	9	2	0	24	7		.265	.288	.323	88	-4	9			.939	-5	2-62	-1.1
Total	18	2200	8804	1184	2252	289	155	34	1135	382	205	.256	.289	.335	74	-327	387			.924	106	*S-2073,2-129	-12.1

■ TIM CORCORAN
Corcoran, Timothy Michael   b: 3/19/53, Glendale, Cal.   BL/TL, 5'11", 175 lbs.   Deb: 5/18/77

YEAR	TM/L	G	AB	R	H	2B	3B	HR	RBI	BB	SO	AVG	OBP	SLG	PRO+	BR/A	SB	CS	SBR	FA	FR	G/POS	TPR
1977	Det-A	55	103	13	29	3	0	3	15	6	9	.282	.321	.398	90	-2	0	1	-1	1.000	-0	O-18/D-3	-0.3
1978	Det-A	116	324	37	86	13	1	1	27	24	27	.265	.326	.321	80	-8	3	2	-0	.985	-6	*O-109/D-1	-1.9
1979	Det-A	18	22	4	5	1	0	0	6	4	2	.227	.346	.273	67	-1	1	1	-0	1.000	-1	/O-9,1-5	-0.3
1980	Det-A	84	153	20	44	7	1	3	18	22	10	.288	.381	.405	113	3	0	2	-1	.985	-2	1-48,O-18/D	-0.2
1981	Min-A	22	51	4	9	0	0	0	4	6	7	.176	.263	.235	42	-4	0	0	0	1.000	1	1-16/D-3	-0.4
1983	Phi-N	3	0	0	0	0	0	0	0	0	0	—	—	—		—	0	0	0	1.000	-0	/1-3	0.0
1984	Phi-N	102	208	30	71	13	1	5	36	37	27	.341	.443	.486	158	18	0	1	-1	.997	-4	1-51,O-17	1.1
1985	Phi-N	103	182	11	39	6	1	0	22	29	20	.214	.322	.258	63	-8	0	2	-1	.993	-1	1-59/O-3	-1.3
1986	NY-N	6	7	1	0	0	0	0	0	2	0	.000	.222	.000	-34	-1	0	0	0	1.000	0	/1-1	-0.1
Total	9	509	1050	120	283	46	4	12	128	130	102	.270	.354	.355	96	-7	4	7	-3	.993	-15	1-183,O-174/D	-3.4

■ WIL CORDERO
Cordero, Wilfredo (Nieva)   b: 10/3/71, Mayaguez, P.R.   BR/TR, 6'2", 185 lbs.   Deb: 7/24/92

YEAR	TM/L	G	AB	R	H	2B	3B	HR	RBI	BB	SO	AVG	OBP	SLG	PRO+	BR/A	SB	CS	SBR	FA	FR	G/POS	TPR
1992	Mon-N	45	126	17	38	4	1	2	8	9	31	.302	.353	.397	113	2	0	0	0	.949	-6	S-35/2-9	-0.2
1993	Mon-N	138	475	56	118	32	2	10	58	34	60	.248	.308	.387	81	-13	12	3	2	.941	-16	*S-134/3-2	-1.7
1994	Mon-N★	110	415	65	122	30	3	15	63	41	62	.294	.366	.489	118	11	16	3	3	.952	-9	*S-109	1.3
Total	3	293	1016	138	278	66	6	27	129	84	153	.274	.338	.430	100	-0	28	6	5	.947	-30	S-278/2-9,3	-0.6

■ FRED COREY
Corey, Frederick Harrison   b: 1857, S.Kingston, R.I.   d: 11/27/12, Providence, R.I.   BR/TR,   Deb: 5/1/1878

YEAR	TM/L	G	AB	R	H	2B	3B	HR	RBI	BB	SO	AVG	OBP	SLG	PRO+	BR/A	SB	CS	SBR	FA	FR	G/POS	TPR
1878	Pro-N	7	21	3	3	0	0	0	1	0		.143	.143	.143	-6	-2				1.000	0	/P-5,2-2,1	-0.1
1880	Wor-N	41	138	11	24	8	1	0	6	4	27	.174	.197	.246	45	-8				.759	-11	O-29,P-25/S31	-1.3
1881	Wor-N	51	203	22	45	8	4	0	10	5	10	.222	.240	.300	65	-8				.827	2	O-25,P-23/S	-0.2

YEAR	TM/L	G	AB	R	H	2B	3B	HR	RBI	BB	SO	AVG	OBP	SLG	PRO+	BR/A	SB	CS	SBR	FA	FR	G/POS	TPR
1882	Wor-N	64	255	33	63	7	12	0	29	5	31	.247	.262	.369	97	-1				.847	-13	S-26,P-21,O/31	-1.2
1883	Phi-a	71	298	45	77	16	2	1		12		.258	.287	.336	92	-4				.799	-2	3-34,P-18,O/2SC	-0.6
1884	Phi-a	104	439	64	121	17	16	5		17		.276	.306	.421	127	11				**.887**	13	*3-104	2.2
1885	Phi-a	94	384	61	94	14	8	1		17		.245	.282	.331	88	-7				.872	8	*3-92/S-1,P	0.2
Total	7	432	1738	239	427	70	43	7	46	60	70	.246	.273	.348	93	-20				.863	-4	3-237/P-93,OS21CD	-1.0

■ MARK COREY
Corey, Mark Mundell   b: 11/3/55, Tucumcari, N.Mex.   BR/TR, 6'2", 200 lbs.   Deb: 9/1/79

YEAR	TM/L	G	AB	R	H	2B	3B	HR	RBI	BB	SO	AVG	OBP	SLG	PRO+	BR/A	SB	CS	SBR	FA	FR	G/POS	TPR
1979	Bal-A	13	13	1	2	0	0	0	1	0	4	.154	.154	.154	-17	-2	1	0	0	1.000	-3	O-11	-0.5
1980	Bal-A	36	36	7	10	2	0	1	2	5	7	.278	.366	.417	115	1	0	1	-1	1.000	-10	O-34	-1.0
1981	Bal-A	10	8	2	0	0	0	0	0	2	2	.000	.200	.000	-38	-1	0	0	0	1.000	-2	/O-9	-0.4
Total	3	59	57	10	12	2	0	1	3	7	13	.211	.297	.298	65	-3	1	1	-0	1.000	-15	O-54	-1.9

■ CHUCK CORGAN
Corgan, Charles Howard   b: 12/4/02, Wagoner, Okla.   d: 6/13/28, Wagoner, Okla.   BB/TR, 5'11", 180 lbs.   Deb: 9/19/25

YEAR	TM/L	G	AB	R	H	2B	3B	HR	RBI	BB	SO	AVG	OBP	SLG	PRO+	BR/A	SB	CS	SBR	FA	FR	G/POS	TPR
1925	Bro-N	14	47	4	8	1	1	0	0	3	9	.170	.220	.234	16	-6	0			.908	4	S-14	-0.1
1927	Bro-N	19	57	3	15	1	0	0	1	4	4	.263	.311	.281	59	-3	0			.969	-1	2-13/S-3	-0.3
Total	2	33	104	7	23	2	1	0	1	7	13	.221	.270	.260	40	-9	0	0		.900	3	/S-17,2-13	-0.4

■ ROY CORHAN
Corhan, Roy George "Irish"   b: 10/21/1887, Indianapolis, Ind.   d: 11/24/58, San Francisco, Cal   BR/TR, 5'9.5", 165 lbs.   Deb: 4/20/11

YEAR	TM/L	G	AB	R	H	2B	3B	HR	RBI	BB	SO	AVG	OBP	SLG	PRO+	BR/A	SB	CS	SBR	FA	FR	G/POS	TPR
1911	Chi-A	43	131	14	28	6	2	0	8	15		.214	.304	.290	68	-5	2			.924	11	S-43	0.8
1916	StL-N	92	295	30	62	6	3	0	18	20	31	.210	.265	.251	59	-14	15			.917	1	S-84	-0.9
Total	2	135	426	44	90	12	5	0	26	35	31	.211	.277	.263	62	-19	17			.920	12	S-127	-0.1

■ POP CORKHILL
Corkhill, John Stewart   b: 4/11/1858, Parkesburg, Pa.   d: 4/4/21, Pennsauken, N.J.   BL/TR, 5'10", 180 lbs.   Deb: 5/1/1883

YEAR	TM/L	G	AB	R	H	2B	3B	HR	RBI	BB	SO	AVG	OBP	SLG	PRO+	BR/A	SB	CS	SBR	FA	FR	G/POS	TPR
1883	Cin-a	88	375	53	81	10	8	2		3		.216	.222	.301	63	-16				**.930**	1	*O-85/S-2,21	-1.4
1884	Cin-a	110	452	85	124	13	11	4		6		.274	.290	.378	111	4				**.934**	10	*O-92,S-11/13P	1.0
1885	Cin-a	112	440	64	111	10	8	1		7		.252	.275	.318	85	-8				.938	17	*O-110/P-8,1	0.5
1886	Cin-a	129	540	81	143	9	7	5		23		.265	.302	.335	96	-4	24			.919	-0	*O-112,3-12/1SP	-0.6
1887	Cin-a	128	541	79	168	19	11	5		14		.311	.333	.414	105	1	30			**.952**	15	*O-128/P-5	1.1
1888	Cin-a	118	490	68	133	11	9	1	74	15		.271	.299	.337	98	-3	27			.958	7	*O-116/P-2,12	0.0
	Bro-a	19	71	17	27	4	3	1	19	4		.380	.429	.563	217	9	3			.980	2	O-19	0.9
	Yr	137	561	85	160	15	12	2	93	19		.285	.316	.365	113	5	30			.961	8	*O-135/P-2,12	0.9
1889	*Bro-a	138	537	91	134	21	9	8	78	42	24	.250	.308	.367	91	-8	22			**.949**	12	*O-138/S-1,1	0.1
1890	Bro-N	51	204	23	46	4	2	1	21	15	11	.225	.279	.279	62	-10	6			.977	4	O-48/1-6	-0.7
1891	Phi-a	83	349	50	73	7	7	0	31	26	15	.209	.268	.269	52	-23	12			.956	7	O-83	-1.7
	Cin-N	1	4	0	0	0	0	0	0	0	1	.000	.000	.000	-99	-1	0			1.000	1	/O-1	0.0
	Pit-N	41	145	16	33	1	1	3	20	7	10	.228	.268	.310	70	-6	7			.935	2	O-41	-0.5
	Yr	42	149	16	33	1	1	3	20	7	11	.221	.261	.302	65	-7	7			.939	3	O-42	-0.5
1892	Pit-N	68	256	23	47	1	4	0	25	12	19	.184	.229	.219	35	-20	6			.953	7	O-68	-1.5
Total	10	1086	4404	650	1120	110	80	31	268	174	80	.254	.288	.337	87	-86	137			.947	83	*O-1041/1-26,PS32	-2.8

■ PAT CORRALES
Corrales, Patrick   b: 3/20/41, Los Angeles, Cal.   BR/TR, 6', 195 lbs.   Deb: 8/2/64   MC

YEAR	TM/L	G	AB	R	H	2B	3B	HR	RBI	BB	SO	AVG	OBP	SLG	PRO+	BR/A	SB	CS	SBR	FA	FR	G/POS	TPR
1964	Phi-N	2	1	1	0	0	0	0	0	1	0	.000	.500	.000	55	0	0	0	0	.000	0	H	0.0
1965	Phi-N	63	174	16	39	8	1	2	15	25	24	.224	.325	.316	83	-3	0	0	0	.982	-3	C-62	-0.4
1966	StL-N	28	72	5	13	2	0	0	3	2	17	.181	.224	.208	21	-8	1	0	0	.975	9	C-27	0.3
1968	Cin-N	20	56	3	15	4	0	0	6	6	16	.268	.349	.339	101	0	0	0	0	.991	0	C-20	0.2
1969	Cin-N	29	72	10	19	5	0	1	5	8	17	.264	.346	.375	97	0	0	1	-1	.986	3	C-29	0.4
1970	*Cin-N	43	106	9	25	5	1	1	10	8	22	.236	.289	.330	65	-5	0	0	0	.983	4	C-42	-0.8
1971	Cin-N	40	94	6	17	2	0	0	6	6	17	.181	.230	.202	24	-9	0	0	0	.980	1	C-39	-0.8
1972	Cin-N	2	1	0	0	0	0	0	0	2	0	.000	.667	.000	110	0	0	0	0	1.000	1	/C-2	0.2
	SD-N	44	119	6	23	0	0	0	6	11	26	.193	.267	.193	35	-10	0	0	0	.993	4	C-43	-0.5
	Yr	46	120	6	23	0	0	0	6	13	26	.192	.276	.192	38	-10	0	0	0	.993	5	C-45	-0.3
1973	SD-N	29	72	7	15	2	1	0	3	6	10	.208	.278	.264	55	-4	0	0	0	.986	-1	C-28	-0.5
Total	9	300	767	63	166	28	3	4	54	75	167	.216	.292	.276	61	-39	1	1	-0	.984	18	C-292	-1.1

■ ROD CORREIA
Correia, Ronald Douglas   b: 9/13/67, Providence, R.I.   BR/TR, 5'11", 180 lbs.   Deb: 6/20/93

YEAR	TM/L	G	AB	R	H	2B	3B	HR	RBI	BB	SO	AVG	OBP	SLG	PRO+	BR/A	SB	CS	SBR	FA	FR	G/POS	TPR
1993	Cal-A	64	128	12	34	5	0	0	9	6	20	.266	.319	.305	66	-6	2	4	-2	.981	18	S-40,2-11/3D	1.2
1994	Cal-A	6	17	4	4	1	0	0	0	0	0	.235	.316	.294	57	-1	0	0	0	1.000	-2	/2-5,S-1	-0.2
Total	2	70	145	16	38	6	0	0	9	6	20	.262	.318	.303	65	-7	2	4	-2	.982	16	/S-41,2-16,D3	1.0

■ VIC CORRELL
Correll, Victor Crosby   b: 2/5/46, Washington, D.C.   BR/TR, 5'10", 185 lbs.   Deb: 10/4/72

YEAR	TM/L	G	AB	R	H	2B	3B	HR	RBI	BB	SO	AVG	OBP	SLG	PRO+	BR/A	SB	CS	SBR	FA	FR	G/POS	TPR
1972	Bos-A	1	4	1	2	0	0	0	1	0	1	.500	.500	.500	188	0	0	0	0	1.000	1	/C-1	0.1
1974	Atl-N	73	202	20	48	15	1	4	29	21	38	.238	.322	.381	92	-2	0	2	-1	.988	6	C-59	0.6
1975	Atl-N	103	325	37	70	12	1	11	39	42	66	.215	.307	.360	82	-8	0	2	-1	.973	-2	C-97	-0.8
1976	Atl-N	69	200	26	45	6	2	5	16	21	37	.225	.302	.350	80	-5	0	1	-1	.981	4	C-65	-0.1
1977	Atl-N	54	144	16	30	7	0	7	16	24	33	.208	.317	.403	82	-4	2	3	-1	.973	4	C-49	-0.2
1978	Cin-N	52	105	9	25	7	0	1	6	8	17	.238	.292	.333	74	-4	0	2	-1	.980	1	C-52	-0.3
1979	Cin-N	48	133	14	31	12	0	1	15	14	26	.233	.311	.346	78	-4	0	0	0	.992	7	C-47	0.4
1980	Cin-N	10	19	1	8	1	0	0	3	0	2	.421	.421	.474	149	1	0	0	0	.919	-0	C-10	0.1
Total	8	410	1132	124	259	60	4	29	125	128	220	.229	.312	.366	83	-26	2	8	-4	.979	18	C-380	-0.2

■ PHIL CORRIDAN
Corridan, Philip   Deb: 7/16/1884

YEAR	TM/L	G	AB	R	H	2B	3B	HR	RBI	BB	SO	AVG	OBP	SLG	PRO+	BR/A	SB	CS	SBR	FA	FR	G/POS	TPR
1884	CP-U	2	7	1	1	0	0	0		0		.143	.143	.143	-22	-1				.800	-1	/2-2,O-1	-0.2

■ JOHN CORRIDEN
Corriden, John Michael Jr.   b: 10/6/18, Logansport, Ind.   BB/TR, 5'6", 160 lbs.   Deb: 4/20/46   F

YEAR	TM/L	G	AB	R	H	2B	3B	HR	RBI	BB	SO	AVG	OBP	SLG	PRO+	BR/A	SB	CS	SBR	FA	FR	G/POS	TPR
1946	Bro-N	1	0	1	0	0	0	0	0	0	0	—	—	—	—	0	0			.000	0	R	0.0

■ RED CORRIDEN
Corriden, John Michael Sr.   b: 9/4/1887, Logansport, Ind.   d: 9/28/59, Indianapolis, Ind   BR/TR, 5'9", 165 lbs.   Deb: 9/8/10   FMC

YEAR	TM/L	G	AB	R	H	2B	3B	HR	RBI	BB	SO	AVG	OBP	SLG	PRO+	BR/A	SB	CS	SBR	FA	FR	G/POS	TPR
1910	StL-A	26	84	19	13	3	0	1	4	13		.155	.297	.226	68	-2	5			.902	4	S-14,3-12	0.3
1912	Det-A	38	138	22	28	6	0	0	5	15		.203	.286	.246	54	-8	4			.929	-1	3-25/2-7,S	-1.2
1913	Chi-N	46	97	13	17	3	0	2	9	10	14	.175	.252	.268	48	-7	4			.907	-1	S-37/2-2,3	-0.6
1914	Chi-N	107	318	42	73	9	5	3	29	35	33	.230	.323	.318	91	-3	13			.894	-33	S-91/3-8,2	-3.0
1915	Chi-N	6	3	1	0	0	0	0	0	2	1	.000	.571	.000	79	1	0			.667	-1	/3-1,O-1	0.0
Total	5	223	640	97	131	21	5	6	47	75	48	.205	.304	.281	74	-19	26			.896	-35	3-145/3-47,2O	-4.5

■ JESS CORTAZZO
Cortazzo, John Francis   b: 9/26/04, Wilmerding, Pa.   d: 3/4/63, Pittsburgh, Pa.   BR/TR, 5'3.5", 142 lbs.   Deb: 9/1/23

YEAR	TM/L	G	AB	R	H	2B	3B	HR	RBI	BB	SO	AVG	OBP	SLG	PRO+	BR/A	SB	CS	SBR	FA	FR	G/POS	TPR
1923	Chi-A	1	1	0	0	0	0	0	0	0	0	.000	.000	.000	-99	-0	0	0	0	.000	0	H	0.0

■ JOE COSCARART
Coscarart, Joseph Marvin   b: 11/18/09, Escondido, Cal.   d: 4/5/93, Sequim, Wash.   BR/TR, 6', 185 lbs.   Deb: 4/26/35   F

YEAR	TM/L	G	AB	R	H	2B	3B	HR	RBI	BB	SO	AVG	OBP	SLG	PRO+	BR/A	SB	CS	SBR	FA	FR	G/POS	TPR
1935	Bos-N	86	284	30	67	11	2	2	29	16	28	.236	.277	.299	59	-17	2			.962	-4	3-41,S-27,2	-1.7
1936	Bos-N	104	367	28	90	11	2	2	44	19	37	.245	.292	.302	64	-19	0			.935	2	3-97/S-6,2	-1.3
Total	2	190	651	58	157	22	4	3	73	35	65	.241	.285	.301	62	-35	2			.943	-3	3-138/S-33,2	-3.0

■ PETE COSCARART
Coscarart, Peter Joseph   b: 6/16/13, Escondido, Cal.   BR/TR, 5'11.5", 175 lbs.   Deb: 4/26/38   F

YEAR	TM/L	G	AB	R	H	2B	3B	HR	RBI	BB	SO	AVG	OBP	SLG	PRO+	BR/A	SB	CS	SBR	FA	FR	G/POS	TPR
1938	Bro-N	32	79	10	12	3	0	0	9	8	18	.152	.256	.190	24	-8	0			.955	1	2-27	-0.6
1939	Bro-N	115	419	59	116	22	2	4	43	46	56	.277	.354	.368	91	-4	10			.960	-8	*2-107/3-4,S	-0.6
1940	Bro-N★	143	506	55	120	24	4	9	58	53	59	.237	.311	.354	78	-15	5			.958	-32	*2-140	-3.8

YEAR	TM/L	G	AB	R	H	2B	3B	HR	RBI	BB	SO	AVG	OBP	SLG	PRO+	BR/A	SB	CS	SBR	FA	FR	G/POS	TPR
1941	*Bro-N	43	62	13	8	1	0	0	5	7	12	.129	.217	.145	3	-8	1			.948	5	2-19/S-1	-0.2
1942	Pit-N	133	487	57	111	12	4	3	29	38	56	.228	.288	.287	67	-20	2			.952	-18	*S-108,2-25	-3.3
1943	Pit-N	133	491	57	119	19	6	0	48	46	48	.242	.307	.305	75	-16	4			.961	-4	2-85,S-47/3	-1.3
1944	Pit-N	139	554	89	146	30	4	4	42	41	57	.264	.315	.354	85	-12	10			.967	-4	*2-136/S-4,O	-1.2
1945	Pit-N	123	392	59	95	17	2	4	38	55	55	.242	.341	.357	91	-4	4			.978	21	*2-122/S-1	2.4
1946	Pit-N	3	2	0	1	1	0	0	0	0	0	.500	.500	1.000	312	1	0			.000	0	/S-1	0.1
Total	9	864	2992	399	728	129	22	28	269	295	361	.243	.314	.329	78	-87	34			.963	-41	2-661,S-164/3O	-8.5

■ RAY COSEY
Cosey, Donald Ray b: 2/15/56, San Rafael, Cal. BL/TL, 5'10", 185 lbs. Deb: 4/14/80

YEAR	TM/L	G	AB	R	H	2B	3B	HR	RBI	BB	SO	AVG	OBP	SLG	PRO+	BR/A	SB	CS	SBR	FA	FR	G/POS	TPR
1980	Oak-A	9	9	0	1	0	0	0	0	0	0	.111	.111	.111	-42	-2	0	0	0	.000	0	/H	-0.2

■ DAN COSTELLO
Costello, Daniel Francis "Dashing Dan" b: 9/9/1891, Jessup, Pa. d: 3/26/36, Pittsburgh, Pa. BL/TR, 6'0.5", 185 lbs. Deb: 7/2/13

YEAR	TM/L	G	AB	R	H	2B	3B	HR	RBI	BB	SO	AVG	OBP	SLG	PRO+	BR/A	SB	CS	SBR	FA	FR	G/POS	TPR
1913	NY-A	2	2	1	1	0	0	0	0	0	0	.500	.500	.500	192	0	0			.000	0	H	0.0
1914	Pit-N	21	64	7	19	1	0	0	5	8	16	.297	.375	.313	110	1	2			.970	-1	O-20	-0.1
1915	Pit-N	71	125	16	27	4	1	0	11	7	23	.216	.258	.264	59	-6	7	1	2	.893	-5	O-22/1-1	-1.3
1916	Pit-N	60	159	11	38	1	3	0	8	6	23	.239	.267	.283	68	-6	3			.976	-2	O-41	-1.2
Total	4	154	350	35	85	6	4	0	24	21	62	.243	.286	.283	73	-11	12	1		.959	-9	/O-83,1-1	-2.6

■ TIM COSTO
Costo, Timothy Roger b: 2/16/69, Melrose Park, Ill. BR/TR, 6'5", 220 lbs. Deb: 9/18/92

YEAR	TM/L	G	AB	R	H	2B	3B	HR	RBI	BB	SO	AVG	OBP	SLG	PRO+	BR/A	SB	CS	SBR	FA	FR	G/POS	TPR
1992	Cin-N	12	36	3	8	2	0	0	2	5	6	.222	.317	.278	68	-1	0	0	0	1.000	0	1-12	-0.2
1993	Cin-N	31	98	13	22	5	0	3	12	4	17	.224	.255	.367	64	-5	0	0	0	.980	0	O-26/1-2,3	-0.6
Total	2	43	134	16	30	7	0	3	14	9	23	.224	.273	.343	66	-7	0	0	0	1.000	1	/O-26,1-14,3	-0.8

■ HENRY COTE
Cote, Henry Joseph b: 2/19/1864, Troy, N.Y. d: 4/28/40, Troy, N.Y. 5'9.5", 165 lbs. Deb: 9/16/1894

YEAR	TM/L	G	AB	R	H	2B	3B	HR	RBI	BB	SO	AVG	OBP	SLG	PRO+	BR/A	SB	CS	SBR	FA	FR	G/POS	TPR
1894	Lou-N	10	31	7	9	2	2	0	3	5	6	.290	.389	.484	117	1	2			.918	5	C-10	0.5
1895	Lou-N	10	33	10	10	0	0	0	5	3	3	.303	.361	.303	77	-1	2			.872	-3	C-10	-0.3
Total	2	20	64	17	19	2	2	0	8	8	9	.297	.375	.391	98	0	4			.900	2	/C-20	0.2

■ PETE COTE
Cote, Warren Peter b: 8/30/02, Cambridge, Mass. d: 10/17/87, Middleton, Mass. BR/TR, 5'6", 148 lbs. Deb: 6/18/26

YEAR	TM/L	G	AB	R	H	2B	3B	HR	RBI	BB	SO	AVG	OBP	SLG	PRO+	BR/A	SB	CS	SBR	FA	FR	G/POS	TPR
1926	NY-N	2	1	0	0	0	0	0	0	0	0	.000	.000	.000	-99	-0	0			.000	0	H	0.0

■ ED COTTER
Cotter, Edward Chrsitopher b: 7/4/04, Hartford, Conn. d: 6/14/59, Hartford, Conn. BR/TR, 6', 185 lbs. Deb: 6/12/26

YEAR	TM/L	G	AB	R	H	2B	3B	HR	RBI	BB	SO	AVG	OBP	SLG	PRO+	BR/A	SB	CS	SBR	FA	FR	G/POS	TPR
1926	Phi-N	17	26	3	8	0	0	1	0	1	4	.308	.333	.385	88	-0	1			.833	0	/3-8,S-5	0.0

■ HOOKS COTTER
Cotter, Harvey Louis b: 5/22/1900, Holden, Mo. d: 8/6/55, Los Angeles, Cal. BL/TL, 5'10", 160 lbs. Deb: 4/15/22

YEAR	TM/L	G	AB	R	H	2B	3B	HR	RBI	BB	SO	AVG	OBP	SLG	PRO+	BR/A	SB	CS	SBR	FA	FR	G/POS	TPR
1922	Chi-N	1	1	0	1	1	0	0	0	0	0	1.000	1.000	2.000	644	1	0	0	0	.000	0	H	0.1
1924	Chi-N	98	310	39	81	16	4	4	33	36	31	.261	.338	.377	91	-4	3	5	-2	.989	4	1-90	-0.7
Total	2	99	311	39	82	17	4	4	33	36	31	.264	.340	.383	92	-3	3	5	-2	.989	4	/1-90	-0.6

■ DICK COTTER
Cotter, Richard Raphael b: 10/12/1889, Manchester, N.H. d: 4/4/45, Brooklyn, N.Y. BR/TR, 5'11", 172 lbs. Deb: 8/17/11

YEAR	TM/L	G	AB	R	H	2B	3B	HR	RBI	BB	SO	AVG	OBP	SLG	PRO+	BR/A	SB	CS	SBR	FA	FR	G/POS	TPR
1911	Phi-N	20	46	2	13	0	0	0	5	5	7	.283	.353	.283	78	-1	1			.975	-2	C-17	-0.1
1912	Chi-N	26	54	6	15	0	2	0	10	6	13	.278	.361	.352	96	-0	1			.954	-3	C-24	-0.2
Total	2	46	100	8	28	0	2	0	15	11	20	.280	.357	.320	87	-1	2			.964	-5	/C-41	-0.3

■ TOM COTTER
Cotter, Thomas B. b: 9/30/1866, Waltham, Mass. d: 11/22/06, Brookline, Mass. BR/TR, 5'10.5", 149 lbs. Deb: 9/3/1891

YEAR	TM/L	G	AB	R	H	2B	3B	HR	RBI	BB	SO	AVG	OBP	SLG	PRO+	BR/A	SB	CS	SBR	FA	FR	G/POS	TPR
1891	Bos-a	6	12	1	3	0	0	0	4	1	2	.250	.308	.250	61	-1	0			.938	-1	/C-5,O-1	-0.1

■ CHUCK COTTIER
Cottier, Charles Keith b: 1/8/36, Delta, Colo. BR/TR, 5'10.5", 175 lbs. Deb: 4/17/59 MC

YEAR	TM/L	G	AB	R	H	2B	3B	HR	RBI	BB	SO	AVG	OBP	SLG	PRO+	BR/A	SB	CS	SBR	FA	FR	G/POS	TPR
1959	Mil-N	10	24	1	3	1	0	0	1	3	7	.125	.222	.167	6	-3	0	0	0	.976	1	2-10	-0.2
1960	Mil-N	95	229	29	52	8	0	3	19	14	21	.227	.278	.301	63	-12	1	0	0	.968	17	2-92	1.2
1961	Det-A	10	7	2	2	0	0	0	1	1	1	.286	.375	.286	77	-0	0	0	0	.889	2	/S-8,2-2	0.1
	Was-A	101	337	37	79	14	4	2	34	30	51	.234	.299	.318	66	-16	9	1	2	.982	15	*2-100	1.2
	Yr	111	344	39	81	14	4	2	35	31	52	.235	.301	.317	66	-17	9	1	2	.982	17	*2-102/S-8	1.3
1962	Was-A	136	443	50	107	14	6	6	40	44	57	.242	.313	.341	75	-15	14	8	-1	.981	21	*2-134	1.8
1963	Was-A	113	337	30	69	16	4	5	21	24	63	.205	.258	.320	61	-18	2	1	0	.963	11	2-85,S-24/3	0.1
1964	Was-A	73	137	16	23	6	2	3	10	19	33	.168	.269	.307	60	-7	2	0	1	.982	14	2-53/3-3,S	1.0
1965	Was-A	7	1	1	0	0	0	0	0	0	0	.000	.000	.000	-99	-0	0	0	0	.000	0	H	0.0
1968	Cal-A	33	67	2	13	4	1	0	1	2	15	.194	.217	.284	53	-4	0	0	0	.963	2	3-27/2-4	-0.3
1969	Cal-A	2	2	0	0	0	0	0	0	0	0	.000	.000	.000	-99	-1	0	0	0	1.000	-0	/2-2	-0.1
Total	9	580	1584	168	348	63	17	19	127	137	248	.220	.284	.317	65	-77	28	10	2	.976	81	2-482/S-34,3	4.8

■ HENRY COTTO
Cotto, Henry b: 1/5/61, New York, N.Y. BR/TR, 6'2", 178 lbs. Deb: 4/5/84

YEAR	TM/L	G	AB	R	H	2B	3B	HR	RBI	BB	SO	AVG	OBP	SLG	PRO+	BR/A	SB	CS	SBR	FA	FR	G/POS	TPR
1984	*Chi-N	105	146	24	40	5	0	6	8	10	23	.274	.325	.308	72	-5	9	3	1	.984	-12	O-88	-1.8
1985	NY-A	34	56	4	17	1	0	1	6	3	12	.304	.339	.375	98	-0	1	1	-0	.977	-7	O-30	-0.8
1986	NY-A	35	80	11	17	3	0	1	6	2	17	.213	.232	.287	41	-7	3	0	1	1.000	-2	O-29/D-1	-0.8
1987	NY-A	68	149	21	35	10	0	5	20	6	35	.235	.269	.403	76	-6	4	2	0	.989	-8	O-57	-1.4
1988	Sea-A	133	386	50	100	18	1	8	33	23	53	.259	.304	.373	85	-8	27	3	6	.992	-5	*O-120/D-2	-1.0
1989	Sea-A	100	295	44	78	11	2	9	33	12	44	.264	.300	.407	94	-3	10	4	1	.988	-7	O-90/D-2	-1.1
1990	Sea-A	127	355	40	92	14	3	4	33	22	52	.259	.310	.349	83	-8	21	3	5	.990	-9	*O-118/D-3	-1.5
1991	Sea-A	66	177	35	54	6	2	6	23	10	27	.305	.349	.463	123	5	16	3	3	.981	-5	O-56/D-6	0.2
1992	Sea-A	108	294	42	76	11	1	5	27	14	49	.259	.294	.354	80	-8	23	2	6	1.000	-10	O-92/D-3	-1.4
1993	Sea-A	54	105	10	20	1	0	2	7	2	22	.190	.213	.257	25	-11	5	4	-1	.983	-5	O-34,D-15	-1.6
	Fla-N	54	135	15	40	7	0	3	14	3	18	.296	.317	.415	89	-2	11	1	3	.977	-4	O-46	-0.4
Total	10	884	2178	296	569	87	9	44	210	107	352	.261	.301	.370	83	-54	130	26	23	.989	-70	O-760/D-32	-11.6

■ DENNIS COUGHLIN
Coughlin, Dennis F. Deb: 4/27/1872

YEAR	TM/L	G	AB	R	H	2B	3B	HR	RBI	BB	SO	AVG	OBP	SLG	PRO+	BR/A	SB	CS	SBR	FA	FR	G/POS	TPR
1872	Nat-n	8	38	5	12	0	0	0	6	0	0	.316	.316	.316	81	-2						/O-5,S-2,2	-0.1

■ ED COUGHLIN
Coughlin, Edward E. b: 8/5/1861, Hartford, Conn. d: 12/25/52, Hartford, Conn. Deb: 5/15/1884

YEAR	TM/L	G	AB	R	H	2B	3B	HR	RBI	BB	SO	AVG	OBP	SLG	PRO+	BR/A	SB	CS	SBR	FA	FR	G/POS	TPR
1884	Buf-N	1	4	0	1	0	0	0	1	0	2	.250	.250	.250	56	-0				.750	0	/O-1,P-1	0.0

■ BILL COUGHLIN
Coughlin, William Paul "Scranton Bill" b: 7/12/1878, Scranton, Pa. d: 5/7/43, Scranton, Pa. BR/TR, 5'9", 140 lbs. Deb: 8/9/1899

YEAR	TM/L	G	AB	R	H	2B	3B	HR	RBI	BB	SO	AVG	OBP	SLG	PRO+	BR/A	SB	CS	SBR	FA	FR	G/POS	TPR
1899	Was-N	6	24	2	3	0	1	0	3	1		.125	.160	.208	1	-3	1			.818	-1	/3-6	-0.4
1901	Was-A	137	506	75	139	17	13	6	68	25		.275	.317	.395	98	-3	16			.922	-6	*3-137	-0.1
1902	Was-A	123	469	84	141	27	4	6	71	26		.301	.348	.414	110	5	29			.926	12	3-66,S-31,2	1.9
1903	Was-A	125	473	56	116	18	3	1	31	9		.245	.267	.302	69	-18	30			.952	4	*3-119/S-4,2	-1.3
1904	Was-A	65	265	28	73	15	4	0	17	9		.275	.307	.362	113	3	10			.939	2	3-64	0.8
	Det-A	56	206	22	47	6	0	0	17	5		.228	.257	.257	65	-8	1			.929	-3	3-56	-1.1
	Yr	121	471	50	120	21	4	0	34	14		.255	.285	.316	92	-5	11			.935	-1	3-120	-0.3
1905	Det-A	137	489	48	123	20	6	0	44	34		.252	.309	.317	98	-1	16			.914	-10	*3-136	-0.6
1906	Det-A	147	498	54	117	15	5	2	60	36		.235	.293	.297	83	-10	31			.940	-11	*3-147	-1.7
1907	*Det-A	134	519	80	126	10	2	0	46	35		.243	.301	.270	79	-11	15			.930	-10	*3-133	-1.9
1908	*Det-A	119	405	32	87	5	1	0	23	23		.215	.269	.232	61	-17	10			.941	-16	*3-119	-3.3
Total	9	1049	3854	481	972	133	39	15	380	203		.252	.299	.319	86	-63	159			.931	-32	3-983/S-35,2	-7.7

YEAR	TM/L	G	AB	R	H	2B	3B	HR	RBI	BB	SO	AVG	OBP	SLG	PRO+	BR/A	SB	CS	SBR	FA	FR	G/POS	TPR
■ **MARLAN COUGHTRY**				Coughtry, James Marlan				b: 9/11/34, Hollywood, Cal.				BL/TR, 6'1", 170 lbs.		Deb: 9/2/60								
1960	Bos-A	15	19	3	3	0	0	0	0	5	8	.158	.333	.158	36	-1	0	0	0	.909	1	2-13/3-1	0.0
1962	LA-A	11	22	0	4	0	0	0	2	0	6	.182	.182	.182	-2	-3	0	0	0	.867	3	/3-5,2-2	0.0
	KC-A	6	11	1	2	0	0	0	1	4	3	.182	.400	.182	60	-0	0	0	0	.917	1	/3-3	0.1
	Cle-A	3	2	1	1	0	0	0	1	1	1	.500	.667	.500	226	1	0	0	0	.000	0	H	0.1
	Yr	20	35	2	7	0	0	0	4	5	10	.200	.300	.200	38	-3	0	0	0	.889	4	/3-8,2-2	0.2
Total	2	35	54	5	10	0	0	0	4	10	18	.185	.313	.185	37	-4	0	0	0	.915	6	/2-15,3-9	0.2
■ **BOB COULSON**				Coulson, Robert Jackson				b: 6/17/1887, Courtney, Pa.		d: 9/11/53, Washington, Pa.		BR/TR, 5'10.5", 175 lbs.		Deb: 8/4/08								
1908	Cin-N	8	18	3	6	1	1	0	1	3		.333	.429	.500	202	2	0			1.000	1	/O-6	0.3
1910	Bro-N	25	89	14	22	3	4	1	13	6	14	.247	.302	.404	109	0	9			.922	0	O-25	-0.5
1911	Bro-N	146	521	52	122	23	7	0	50	42	78	.234	.301	.305	73	-19	32			.968	1	*O-145	-2.6
1914	Pit-F	18	64	7	13	1	0	0	3	7	10	.203	.282	.219	31	-6	2			.931	-2	O-18	-1.0
Total	4	197	692	76	163	28	12	1	67	58	102	.236	.303	.315	76	-23	43			.960	0	O-194	-3.3
■ **CHIP COULTER**				Coulter, Thomas Lee				b: 6/5/45, Steubenville, O.		BB/TR, 5'10", 172 lbs.		Deb: 9/18/69									
1969	StL-N	6	19	3	6	1	1	0	4	2	6	.316	.381	.474	138	1	0	1	-1	.960	-0	/2-6	0.1
■ **CLINT COURTNEY**				Courtney, Clinton Dawson "Scrap Iron"				b: 3/16/27, Hall Summit, La.		d: 6/16/75, Rochester, N.Y.		BL/TR, 5'8", 180 lbs.		Deb: 9/29/51 C								
1951	NY-A	1	2	0	0	0	0	0	0	0	1	.000	.333	.000	-5	-0	0	0	0	.800	1	/C-1	0.0
1952	StL-A	119	413	38	118	24	3	5	50	39	26	.286	.349	.395	104	2	0	2	-1	.996	3	*C-113	0.9
1953	StL-A	106	355	28	89	12	2	4	19	25	20	.251	.302	.330	69	-16	0	1	-1	.980	-5	*C-103	-1.7
1954	Bal-A	122	397	25	107	18	3	4	37	30	7	.270	.326	.360	95	-4	2	1	0	.990	-3	*C-111	-0.2
1955	Chi-A	19	37	7	14	3	0	1	10	7	0	.378	.477	.541	168	4	0	0	0	1.000	-1	C-17	0.3
	Was-A	75	238	26	71	8	4	2	30	19	9	.298	.353	.391	105	1	0	0	0	.983	-14	C-67	-1.0
	Yr	94	275	33	85	11	4	3	40	26	9	.309	.371	.411	114	5	0	0	0	.985	-15	C-84	-0.7
1956	Was-A	101	283	31	85	20	3	5	44	20	10	.300	.365	.445	113	5	0	5	-3	.979	-15	C-76	-1.0
1957	Was-A	91	232	23	62	14	1	6	27	16	11	.267	.346	.414	108	3	0	0	0	.994	-1	C-59	0.4
1958	Was-A	134	450	46	113	18	0	8	62	48	23	.251	.335	.344	89	-6	1	5	-3	.991	-3	*C-128	-0.4
1959	Was-A	72	189	19	44	4	1	2	18	20	19	.233	.310	.296	68	-8	0	1	-1	.987	-13	C-53	-1.9
1960	Bal-A	83	154	14	35	3	0	1	12	30	14	.227	.380	.266	79	-2	0	1	-1	.975	4	C-58	0.4
1961	KC-A	1	1	0	0	0	0	0	0	0	0	.000	.000	.000	-98	-0	0	0	0	.000	0	H	0.0
	Bal-A	22	45	3	12	2	0	0	4	10	3	.267	.400	.311	96	0	0	0	0	1.000	1	C-16	0.2
	Yr	23	46	3	12	2	0	0	4	10	3	.261	.393	.304	92	0	0	0	0	1.000	1	C-16	0.2
Total	11	946	2796	260	750	126	17	38	313	264	143	.268	.341	.366	94	-21	3	16	-9	.987	-45	C-802	-4.0
■ **ERNIE COURTNEY**				Courtney, Edward Ernest				b: 1/20/1875, Des Moines, Iowa		d: 2/29/20, Buffalo, N.Y.		BL/TR, 5'10",		Deb: 4/17/02								
1902	Bos-N	48	165	23	36	3	0	0	17	13		.218	.291	.236	62	-7	3			.974	-1	O-39/S-3	-1.1
	Bal-A	1	4	3	2	0	1	0	1	1		.500	.600	1.000	324	1	0			1.000	0	/3-1	0.1
1903	NY-A	25	79	7	21	3	3	1	8	7		.266	.341	.418	119	2	1			.916	-2	S-19/2-4,1	0.1
	Det-A	23	74	7	17	0	0	0	6	5		.230	.305	.230	64	-3	1			.938	-4	3-13/S-9	-0.6
	Yr	48	153	14	38	3	3	1	14	12		.248	.324	.327	94	-1	2			.921	-6	S-28,3-13/21	-0.5
1905	Phi-N	155	601	77	165	14	7	2	77	47		.275	.334	.331	102	2	17			.923	-17	*3-155	-1.0
1906	Phi-N	116	398	53	94	12	2	0	42	45		.236	.315	.276	84	-6	6			.923	-11	3-96,1-13/OS	-1.6
1907	Phi-N	130	440	42	107	17	4	2	43	55		.243	.335	.314	105	4	6			.907	-8	3-75,1-48/O2S	-0.3
1908	Phi-N	60	160	14	29	3	0	0	6	15		.181	.260	.200	46	-9	1			.915	-7	3-22,1-13/2S	-1.8
Total	6	558	1921	226	471	52	17	5	200	188		.245	.321	.298	91	-15	35			.920	-49	3-362/1-75,OS2	-6.2
■ **DEE COUSINEAU**				Cousineau, Edward Thomas				b: 12/16/1898, Watertown, Mass.		d: 7/14/51, Watertown, Mass.		BR/TR, 6', 170 lbs.		Deb: 10/6/23								
1923	Bos-N	1	2	1	2	0	0	0	2	0	0	1.000	1.000	1.000	447	1	0	0	0	.000	0	/C-1	0.1
1924	Bos-N	3	2	0	0	0	0	0	0	0	0	.000	.000	.000	-99	-1	0	0	0	.500	-1	/C-3	-0.1
1925	Bos-N	1	0	0	0	0	0	0	0	0	0	—	—	—			0	0	0	.000	0	/C-1	0.0
Total	3	5	4	1	2	0	0	0	2	0	0	.500	.500	.500	174	0	0	0	0	.500	-1	/C-5	0.0
■ **JACK COVENEY**				Coveney, John Patrick				b: 6/10/1880, S.Natick, Mass.		d: 3/28/61, Wayland, Mass.		BR/TR, 5'9", 175 lbs.		Deb: 9/19/03								
1903	StL-N	4	14	0	2	0	0	0	0	0		.143	.143	.143	-19	-2	0			.923	1	/C-4	-0.1
■ **SAM COVINGTON**				Covington, Clarence Otto				b: 12/17/1892, Henryville, Tenn.		d: 1/4/63, Denison, Tex.		BL/TR, 6'1", 190 lbs.		Deb: 8/25/13 F								
1913	StL-A	20	60	3	9	0	1	0	4	4	6	.150	.203	.183	14	-7	3			.994	3	1-16	-0.4
1917	Bos-N	17	66	8	13	2	1	0	10	5	5	.197	.264	.273	69	-2	1			.994	0	1-17	-0.3
1918	Bos-N	3	3	0	1	0	0	0	0	0	0	.333	.333	.333	108	0	0			.000	0	H	0.0
Total	3	40	129	11	23	2	2	0	14	9	11	.178	.237	.233	43	-9	4			.994	3	/1-33	-0.7
■ **WES COVINGTON**				Covington, John Wesley				b: 3/27/32, Laurinburg, N.C.		BL/TR, 6'1", 205 lbs.		Deb: 4/19/56									
1956	Mil-N	75	138	17	39	4	0	2	16	16	20	.283	.361	.355	100	0	1	0	0	.979	-3	O-35	-0.4
1957	*Mil-N	96	328	51	93	4	8	21	65	29	44	.284	.345	.537	143	18	4	1	1	.981	0	O-89	1.4
1958	*Mil-N	90	294	43	97	12	1	24	74	20	35	.330	.382	.622	175	30	0	0	0	.953	-4	O-82	2.1
1959	Mil-N	103	373	38	104	17	3	7	45	26	41	.279	.331	.397	101	-0	0	1	-1	.962	-3	O-94	-0.8
1960	Mil-N	95	281	25	70	16	1	10	35	15	37	.249	.290	.420	99	-2	1	2	-1	.964	-5	O-72	-1.1
1961	Mil-N	9	21	3	4	1	0	0	0	2	4	.190	.261	.238	36	-2	0	0	0	1.000	0	I/O-5	-0.4
	Chi-A	22	59	5	17	0	0	4	15	4	5	.288	.333	.508	123	2	0	0	0	.900	-1	O-14	0.0
	KC-A	17	44	3	7	0	0	1	6	4	7	.159	.260	.227	31	-4	0	0	0	1.000	-2	O-12	-0.7
	Yr	39	103	8	24	1	0	5	21	8	12	.233	.301	.388	83	-3	0	0	0	.941	-3	O-26	-0.7
	Phi-N	57	165	23	50	9	0	7	26	15	17	.303	.361	.485	124	5	0	0	0	.950	-5	O-45	-0.2
1962	Phi-N	116	304	36	86	12	1	9	44	19	44	.283	.329	.418	102	0	0	0	0	.944	-7	O-88	-1.1
1963	Phi-N	119	353	46	107	24	1	17	64	38	50	.303	.354	.521	150	22	1	0	0	.937	-8	*O-99	1.1
1964	Phi-N	129	339	37	95	18	0	13	58	42	56	.280	.358	.448	127	13	0	0	0	.972	-5	O-64	0.4
1965	Phi-N	101	235	27	58	10	1	15	45	26	47	.247	.324	.489	128	8	0	0	0	.968	-2	O-64	0.4
1966	Chi-N	9	11	0	1	0	0	0	0	1	2	.091	.167	.091	-26	-2	0	0	0	1.000	0	/O-1	-0.2
	*LA-N	37	33	1	4	0	1	1	6	6	5	.121	.293	.273	63	-2	0	0	0	1.000	-0	/O-3	-0.2
	Yr	46	44	1	5	0	1	1	6	7	7	.114	.264	.227	41	-3	0	0	0	1.000	-0	/O-4	-0.4
Total	11	1075	2978	355	832	128	17	131	499	247	414	.279	.339	.466	123	86	7	4	-0	.961	-49	O-803	-0.1
■ **BILLY COWAN**				Cowan, Billy Rolland				b: 8/28/38, Calhoun City, Miss.		BR/TR, 6', 170 lbs.		Deb: 9/9/63									
1963	Chi-N	14	36	1	9	1	1	2	2	0	11	.250	.250	.417	84	-1	0	1	-1	.917	-2	O-10	-0.4
1964	Chi-N	139	497	52	120	16	4	19	50	18	128	.241	.269	.404	83	-12	12	3	2	.968	-8	*O-134	-2.1
1965	NY-N	82	156	16	28	8	2	3	9	4	45	.179	.205	.314	45	-12	3	2	-0	1.000	-8	O-61/2-2,S	-2.3
	Mil-N	19	27	4	5	1	0	0	0	0	9	.185	.185	.222	14	-3	0	0	0	1.000	-2	O-10	-0.5
	Yr	101	183	20	33	9	2	3	9	4	54	.180	.202	.301	41	-15	3	2	-0	1.000	-10	O-71/2-2,S	-2.8
1967	Phi-N	34	59	11	9	1	1	2	8	1	15	.153	.206	.305	44	-2	1	0	0	1.000	0	O-20/2-1,3	-0.9
1969	NY-A	32	48	5	8	0	0	1	3	3	9	.167	.216	.229	25	-5	0	0	0	1.000	-2	O-14	-0.7
	Cal-A	28	56	10	17	0	0	4	10	3	16	.304	.350	.536	152	3	0	0	0	1.000	0	O-13/1-6	0.3
	Yr	60	104	15	25	1	0	5	13	6	18	.240	.288	.394	93	-1	0	0	0	1.000	-2	O-27/1-6	-0.4
1970	Cal-A	68	134	20	37	9	1	5	25	11	29	.276	.336	.470	124	2	1	0	-1	.929	-6	O-27,1-14/3	-0.5
1971	Cal-A	74	174	12	48	8	0	4	20	7	41	.276	.304	.391	103	-0	1	1	-0	1.000	-2	O-40/1-5	-0.5

YEAR	TM/L	G	AB	R	H	2B	3B	HR	RBI	BB	SO	AVG	OBP	SLG	PRO+	BR/A	SB	CS	SBR	FA	FR	G/POS	TPR
1972	Cal-A	3	3	0	0	0	0	0	0	0	2	.000	.000	.000	-99	-1	0	0	0	.000	0	H	-0.1
Total	8	493	1190	131	281	44	8	40	125	50	297	.236	.269	.387	83	-31	17	8	0	.977	-28	O-329/1-25,32S	-7.7

■ AL COWENS   Cowens, Alfred Edward b: 10/25/51, Los Angeles, Cal. BR/TR, 6'2", 200 lbs. Deb: 4/6/74

YEAR	TM/L	G	AB	R	H	2B	3B	HR	RBI	BB	SO	AVG	OBP	SLG	PRO+	BR/A	SB	CS	SBR	FA	FR	G/POS	TPR
1974	KC-A	110	269	28	65	7	1	1	25	23	38	.242	.304	.286	67	-11	5	0	2	.988	-9	*O-102/3-2,D	-2.3
1975	KC-A	120	328	44	91	13	8	4	42	28	36	.277	.342	.402	107	3	12	7	-1	.978	-10	*O-113/D-2	-1.1
1976	*KC-A	152	581	71	154	23	6	3	59	26	50	.265	.300	.341	87	-11	23	16	-3	.986	5	*O-148/D-1	-1.5
1977	*KC-A	162	606	98	189	32	14	23	112	41	64	.312	.363	.525	138	30	16	12	-2	.982	3	*O-159/D-1	2.4
1978	*KC-A	132	485	63	133	24	8	5	63	31	54	.274	.326	.388	97	-2	14	6	1	.990	2	*O-127/3-5,D	-0.5
1979	KC-A	136	516	69	152	18	7	9	73	40	44	.295	.349	.409	102	1	10	8	-2	.986	-0	*O-134	-0.6
1980	Cal-A	34	119	11	27	5	0	1	17	12	21	.227	.303	.294	66	-5	1	2	-1	1.000	1	O-30/D-1	-0.7
	Det-A	108	403	58	113	15	3	5	42	37	40	.280	.342	.370	93	-3	5	6	-2	.986	2	*O-107/D-1	-0.8
	Yr	142	522	69	140	20	3	6	59	49	61	.268	.333	.352	87	-8	6	8	-3	.989	3	*O-137/D-2	-1.5
1981	Det-A	85	253	27	66	11	4	1	18	22	36	.261	.322	.348	90	-3	3	3	-1	.994	-6	O-83	-1.3
1982	Sea-A	146	560	72	151	39	8	20	78	46	81	.270	.326	.475	114	9	11	7	-1	.987	7	*O-145/D-1	1.1
1983	Sea-A	110	356	39	73	19	2	7	35	23	38	.205	.257	.329	58	-21	10	2	2	.985	2	O-70,D-34	-2.1
1984	Sea-A	139	524	60	145	34	2	15	78	24	83	.277	.315	.435	106	3	9	5	-0	.987	-2	*O-130/D-7	-0.4
1985	Sea-A	122	452	59	120	32	5	14	69	30	56	.265	.313	.451	105	2	5	5	-0	.967	2	*O-110/D-5	0.0
1986	Sea-A	28	82	5	15	4	0	0	6	3	16	.183	.212	.232	20	-9	1	0	0	.971	-0	O-19/D-1	-0.9
Total	13	1584	5534	704	1494	276	68	108	717	389	659	.270	.322	.403	98	-18	120	74	-8	.985	-5	*O-1477/D-60,3	-8.7

■ DICK COX   Cox, Elmer Joseph b: 9/30/1897, Pasadena, Cal. d: 6/1/66, Morro Bay, Cal. BR/TR, 5'7.5", 158 lbs. Deb: 4/16/25

YEAR	TM/L	G	AB	R	H	2B	3B	HR	RBI	BB	SO	AVG	OBP	SLG	PRO+	BR/A	SB	CS	SBR	FA	FR	G/POS	TPR
1925	Bro-N	122	434	68	143	23	10	7	64	37	29	.329	.382	.477	121	14	4	3	-1	.968	-4	*O-111	0.2
1926	Bro-N	124	398	53	118	17	4	1	45	46	20	.296	.375	.367	102	3	6			.964	-8	*O-117	-1.2
Total	2	246	832	121	261	40	14	8	109	83	49	.314	.379	.424	112	17	10	3		.966	-12	O-228	-1.0

■ FRANK COX   Cox, Francis Bernard "Runt" b: 8/29/1857, Waltham, Mass. d: 6/24/28, Hartford, Conn. 5'6", Deb: 8/13/1884

YEAR	TM/L	G	AB	R	H	2B	3B	HR	RBI	BB	SO	AVG	OBP	SLG	PRO+	BR/A	SB	CS	SBR	FA	FR	G/POS	TPR
1884	Det-N	27	102	6	13	3	1	0	4	2	36	.127	.144	.176	0	-11				.812	-4	S-27	-1.3

■ JIM COX   Cox, James Charles b: 5/28/50, Bloomington, Ill. BR/TR, 5'11", 175 lbs. Deb: 7/19/73

YEAR	TM/L	G	AB	R	H	2B	3B	HR	RBI	BB	SO	AVG	OBP	SLG	PRO+	BR/A	SB	CS	SBR	FA	FR	G/POS	TPR
1973	Mon-N	9	15	1	2	1	0	0	0	1	4	.133	.188	.200	7	-2	0	0	0	.950	-1	/2-7	-0.2
1974	Mon-N	77	236	29	52	9	1	2	26	23	36	.220	.292	.292	61	-12	2	3	-1	.968	15	2-72	0.4
1975	Mon-N	11	27	1	7	1	0	1	5	1	2	.259	.286	.407	87	-1	1	0	0	1.000	0	/2-8	0.0
1976	Mon-N	13	29	2	5	0	1	0	2	2	2	.172	.226	.241	31	-3	0	0	0	.958	1	2-11	-0.1
Total	4	110	307	33	66	11	3	3	33	27	44	.215	.281	.293	58	-17	3	3	-1	.969	16	/2-98	0.1

■ JEFF COX   Cox, Jeffrey Lindon b: 11/9/55, Los Angeles, Cal. BR/TR, 5'11", 170 lbs. Deb: 7/1/80

YEAR	TM/L	G	AB	R	H	2B	3B	HR	RBI	BB	SO	AVG	OBP	SLG	PRO+	BR/A	SB	CS	SBR	FA	FR	G/POS	TPR
1980	Oak-A	59	169	20	36	3	0	0	9	14	23	.213	.273	.231	43	-13	8	5	-1	.979	-16	2-58	-2.6
1981	Oak-A	2	0	0	0	0	0	0	0	0	0	—	—	—			0	0	0	1.000	0	/2-1	0.0
Total	2	61	169	20	36	3	0	0	9	14	23	.213	.273	.231	43	-13	8	5	-1	.979	-16	/2-59	-2.6

■ LARRY COX   Cox, Larry Eugene b: 9/11/47, Bluffton, Ohio d: 2/17/90, Bellefontaine, Ohio BR/TR, 5'11", 190 lbs. Deb: 4/18/73 C

YEAR	TM/L	G	AB	R	H	2B	3B	HR	RBI	BB	SO	AVG	OBP	SLG	PRO+	BR/A	SB	CS	SBR	FA	FR	G/POS	TPR
1973	Phi-N	1	0	0	0	0	0	0	0	0	0				0	0	0	0	0	1.000	-0	/C-1	0.0
1974	Phi-N	30	53	5	9	2	0	0	4	4	9	.170	.241	.208	25	-5	0	0	0	.990	0	/C-29	-0.4
1975	Phi-N	11	5	0	1	0	0	0	1	1	0	.200	.333	.200	49	-0	1	0	0	1.000	-0	/C-10	0.0
1977	Sea-A	35	93	6	23	6	0	2	6	10	12	.247	.320	.376	90	-1	1	1	-0	.970	-1	C-35	-0.2
1978	Chi-N	59	121	10	34	5	0	2	18	12	16	.281	.346	.372	90	-2	0	0	0	.967	2	C-58	0.1
1979	Sea-A	100	293	32	63	11	3	4	36	22	39	.215	.270	.314	56	-18	2	1	0	.981	-2	C-99	-1.7
1980	Sea-A	105	243	18	49	6	2	4	20	19	36	.202	.260	.292	50	-17	1	2	-1	**.993**	12	*C-104	-0.3
1981	Tex-A	5	13	0	3	1	0	0	0	0	0	.231	.231	.308	57	-1	0	0	0	1.000	3	/C-5	0.3
1982	Chi-N	2	4	1	0	0	0	0	0	2	1	.000	.333	.000	1	-0	0	0	0	1.000	1	/C-2	0.1
Total	9	348	825	72	182	31	5	12	85	70	117	.221	.282	.314	61	-45	5	4	-1	.983	15	C-343	-2.1

■ BOBBY COX   Cox, Robert Joseph b: 5/21/41, Tulsa, Okla. BR/TR, 5'11", 180 lbs. Deb: 4/14/68 MC

YEAR	TM/L	G	AB	R	H	2B	3B	HR	RBI	BB	SO	AVG	OBP	SLG	PRO+	BR/A	SB	CS	SBR	FA	FR	G/POS	TPR
1968	NY-A	135	437	33	100	15	1	7	41	41	85	.229	.302	.316	90	-5	3	2	-0	.957	-5	*3-132	-1.2
1969	NY-A	85	191	17	41	7	1	2	17	34	41	.215	.336	.293	80	-4	0	1	-1	.935	11	3-56/2-6	0.7
Total	2	220	628	50	141	22	2	9	58	75	126	.225	.313	.309	87	-9	3	3	-1	.950	6	3-188/2-6	-0.5

■ BILLY COX   Cox, William Richard b: 8/29/19, Newport, Pa. d: 3/30/78, Harrisburg, Pa. BR/TR, 5'10", 150 lbs. Deb: 9/20/41

YEAR	TM/L	G	AB	R	H	2B	3B	HR	RBI	BB	SO	AVG	OBP	SLG	PRO+	BR/A	SB	CS	SBR	FA	FR	G/POS	TPR
1941	Pit-N	10	37	4	10	3	1	0	2	3	2	.270	.325	.405	105	0	1			.943	2	S-10	0.3
1946	Pit-N	121	411	32	119	22	6	2	36	26	15	.290	.333	.387	101	-0	4			.935	-16	*S-114	-1.0
1947	Pit-N	132	529	75	145	30	7	15	54	29	28	.274	.313	.442	96	-5	5			.968	-13	*S-129	-1.1
1948	Bro-N	88	237	36	59	13	2	1	15	38	19	.249	.353	.359	90	-3	3			.958	-4	3-70/S-6,2	-0.7
1949	*Bro-N	100	390	48	91	18	2	8	40	30	18	.233	.290	.351	68	-18	5			.964	9	*3-100	-1.1
1950	Bro-N	119	451	62	116	17	2	8	44	35	24	.257	.311	.357	74	-17	6			**.957**	12	*3-107,2-13/S	-0.6
1951	*Bro-N	142	455	62	127	25	4	9	51	37	30	.279	.336	.411	98	-2	5	5	-2	.967	-8	*3-139/S-1	-1.3
1952	*Bro-N	116	455	56	118	12	3	6	34	25	32	.259	.301	.338	76	-15	10	12	-4	.970	-9	*3-100,S-10/2	-3.0
1953	*Bro-N	100	327	44	95	18	1	10	44	37	21	.291	.363	.443	106	3	2	2	-1	.974	-2	3-89/S-6,2	-0.1
1954	Bro-N	77	226	26	53	9	2	2	17	21	13	.235	.300	.319	59	-13	0	0	0	.961	2	3-58,2-11/S	-1.1
1955	Bal-A	53	194	25	41	7	2	3	14	17	16	.211	.275	.314	63	-11	1	2	-1	.969	-9	3-37,2-18/S	-2.1
Total	11	1058	3712	470	974	174	32	66	351	298	218	.262	.318	.380	85	-82	42	21		.965	-36	3-700,S-299/2	-11.8

■ TED COX   Cox, William Ted b: 1/24/55, Oklahoma City, Okla BR/TR, 6'3", 195 lbs. Deb: 9/18/77

YEAR	TM/L	G	AB	R	H	2B	3B	HR	RBI	BB	SO	AVG	OBP	SLG	PRO+	BR/A	SB	CS	SBR	FA	FR	G/POS	TPR
1977	Bos-A	13	58	11	21	3	1	1	6	3	6	.362	.393	.500	127	2	0	0	0	.000	0	D-13	0.2
1978	Cle-A	82	227	14	53	7	0	1	19	16	30	.233	.287	.278	60	-12	0	1	-1	.980	-5	O-38,3-20,D/1S	-2.0
1979	Cle-A	78	189	17	40	6	0	4	22	14	27	.212	.273	.307	56	-12	3	4	-2	.964	0	3-52,O-16/2	-1.3
1980	Sea-A	83	247	17	60	9	0	4	23	19	25	.243	.297	.304	64	-12	0	0	0	.945	-2	3-80	-1.5
1981	Tor-A	16	50	6	15	4	0	2	9	5	10	.300	.364	.500	138	1	0	1	-1	.897	-4	3-14/1-1,D	-0.3
Total	5	272	771	65	189	29	1	10	79	57	98	.245	.300	.324	71	-31	3	6	-3	.947	-11	3-166/O-54,D12S	-4.9

■ TOOTS COYNE   Coyne, Martin Albert b: 10/20/1894, St.Louis, Mo. d: 9/18/39, St.Louis, Mo. TR, Deb: 9/28/14

YEAR	TM/L	G	AB	R	H	2B	3B	HR	RBI	BB	SO	AVG	OBP	SLG	PRO+	BR/A	SB	CS	SBR	FA	FR	G/POS	TPR
1914	Phi-A	1	2	0	0	0	0	0	0	0	2	.000	.000	.000	-99	-0				1.000	-0	/3-1	-0.1

■ ESTEL CRABTREE   Crabtree, Estel Crayton "Crabby" b: 8/19/03, Crabtree, Ohio d: 1/4/67, Logan, Ohio BL/TR, 6', 168 lbs. Deb: 4/18/29 C

YEAR	TM/L	G	AB	R	H	2B	3B	HR	RBI	BB	SO	AVG	OBP	SLG	PRO+	BR/A	SB	CS	SBR	FA	FR	G/POS	TPR
1929	Cin-N	1	0	0	0	0	0	0	0	0	0	.000	.000	.000	-99	-0	0			.000	0	H	0.0
1931	Cin-N	117	443	70	119	12	12	4	37	23	33	.269	.309	.377	89	-8	0			.974	10	*O-101/3-4,1	-0.5
1932	Cin-N	108	402	38	110	14	9	2	35	23	26	.274	.316	.368	86	-8	2			.990	9	O-95	-0.5
1933	StL-N	23	34	6	9	3	0	0	3	2	3	.265	.306	.353	83	-1	0			.947	-0	/O-7	-0.1
1941	StL-N	77	167	27	57	6	3	5	28	26	24	.341	.439	.503	154	13	1			1.000	-8	O-50/3-1	0.3
1942	StL-N	10	9	1	3	0	0	2	1	3	1	.333	.400	.556	166	1	0			.000	0	H	0.1
1943	Cin-N	95	254	25	70	12	0	2	26	24	19	.276	.345	.354	101	1	5			.939	-5	O-65	-0.8
1944	Cin-N	58	98	7	28	6	1	0	11	13	3	.286	.369	.347	106	1	0			.976	1	O-19/1-2	-0.4
Total	8	489	1408	174	396	53	25	13	142	113	109	.281	.339	.382	100	-2	8			.976	1	O-337/3-5,1	-1.9

■ HARRY CRAFT   Craft, Harry Francis "Wildfire" b: 4/19/15, Ellisville, Miss. BR/TR, 6'1", 185 lbs. Deb: 9/19/37 MC

YEAR	TM/L	G	AB	R	H	2B	3B	HR	RBI	BB	SO	AVG	OBP	SLG	PRO+	BR/A	SB	CS	SBR	FA	FR	G/POS	TPR
1937	Cin-N	10	42	7	13	2	1	0	4	1	3	.310	.326	.405	102	-0				1.000	0	O-10	0.0

YEAR	TM/L	G	AB	R	H	2B	3B	HR	RBI	BB	SO	AVG	OBP	SLG	PRO+	BR/A	SB	CS	SBR	FA	FR	G/POS	TPR
1938	Cin-N	151	612	70	165	28	9	15	83	29	46	.270	.305	.418	100	-3	3			.983	16	*O-151	0.9
1939	*Cin-N	134	502	58	129	20	7	13	67	27	54	.257	.299	.402	86	-11	5			.981	3	*O-134	-1.3
1940	*Cin-N	115	422	47	103	18	5	6	48	17	46	.244	.277	.353	72	-17	2			.997	6	*O-109/1-2	-1.7
1941	Cin-N	119	413	48	103	15	2	10	59	33	43	.249	.308	.368	90	-7	4			.983	2	*O-115	-1.2
1942	Cin-N	37	113	7	20	2	1	0	6	3	11	.177	.205	.212	22	-11	0			.987	1	O-33	-1.3
Total	6	566	2104	237	533	85	25	44	267	110	203	.253	.294	.380	85	-49	14			.986	28	O-552/1-2	-4.6

■ ROD CRAIG   Craig, Rodney Paul   b: 1/12/58, Los Angeles, Cal.   BB/TR, 6'1", 195 lbs.   Deb: 9/11/79

YEAR	TM/L	G	AB	R	H	2B	3B	HR	RBI	BB	SO	AVG	OBP	SLG	PRO+	BR/A	SB	CS	SBR	FA	FR	G/POS	TPR
1979	Sea-A	16	52	9	20	8	1	0	6	1	5	.385	.396	.577	156	4	1	1	-0	.923	-2	O-15	0.1
1980	Sea-A	70	240	30	57	15	1	3	20	17	35	.237	.293	.346	74	-9	3	6	-3	.987	-2	O-63	-1.6
1982	Cle-A	49	65	7	15	2	0	0	1	4	6	.231	.275	.262	49	-5	3	1	0	.966	-4	O-22/D-4	-0.9
1986	Chi-A	10	10	3	2	0	0	0	0	2	2	.200	.333	.200	48	-1	0	0	0	.000	-1	/O-2	-0.1
Total	4	145	367	49	94	25	2	3	27	24	48	.256	.305	.360	80	-10	7	8	-3	.977	-9	O-102/D-4	-2.5

■ DOC CRAMER   Cramer, Roger Maxwell "Flit"   b: 7/22/05, Beach Haven, N.J.   d: 9/9/90, Manahawkin, N.J.   BL/TR, 6'2", 185 lbs.   Deb: 9/18/29   C

YEAR	TM/L	G	AB	R	H	2B	3B	HR	RBI	BB	SO	AVG	OBP	SLG	PRO+	BR/A	SB	CS	SBR	FA	FR	G/POS	TPR
1929	Phi-A	2	6	0	0	0	0	0	0	0	2	.000	.000	.000	-97	-2	0	0	0	1.000	1	/O-1	-0.1
1930	Phi-A	30	82	12	19	1	1	0	6	2	8	.232	.250	.268	30	-9	0	0	0	.927	-2	O-21/S-1	-1.1
1931	*Phi-A	65	223	37	58	8	2	2	20	11	15	.260	.301	.341	64	-12	2	1	0	.979	1	O-55	-1.4
1932	Phi-A	92	384	73	129	27	6	3	46	17	27	.336	.367	.461	109	4	3	1	0	.976	8	O-86	0.7
1933	Phi-A	152	661	109	195	27	8	8	75	36	24	.295	.331	.396	91	-10	5	4	-1	.971	5	*O-152	-1.4
1934	Phi-A	153	649	99	202	29	9	6	46	40	35	.311	.353	.411	100	-1	1	5	-3	.985	5	*O-152	-0.4
1935	Phi-A★	149	644	96	214	37	4	3	70	37	34	.332	.373	.416	105	4	6	7	-2	.975	4	*O-149	0.0
1936	Bos-A	154	643	99	188	31	7	0	41	49	20	.292	.347	.362	71	-29	4	6	-1	.975	16	*O-154	-1.9
1937	Bos-A☆	133	560	90	171	22	11	0	51	35	14	.305	.351	.384	82	-15	8	6	-1	.969	6	*O-133	-1.4
1938	Bos-A★	148	658	116	198	36	8	0	71	51	19	.301	.354	.380	80	-20	4	9	-4	.986	9	*O-148/P-1	-1.8
1939	Bos-A★	137	589	110	183	30	6	0	56	36	17	.311	.352	.382	85	-13	3	3	-1	.984	2	*O-135	-1.6
1940	Bos-A☆	150	661	94	200	27	12	1	51	36	29	.303	.340	.384	84	-16	3	5	-2	.969	-5	*O-149	-3.0
1941	Was-A	154	660	93	180	25	6	2	66	37	15	.273	.317	.338	77	-23	4	4	1	.984	-7	*O-152	-3.8
1942	Det-A	151	630	71	166	26	4	0	43	43	18	.263	.314	.317	72	-24	4	4	-1	.981	-0	*O-150	-3.4
1943	Det-A	140	606	79	182	18	4	1	43	31	13	.300	.335	.348	93	-6	6	5	-1	.989	1	*O-138	-1.4
1944	Det-A	143	578	69	169	20	9	2	42	37	21	.292	.337	.369	96	-3	6	5	-1	.980	-8	*O-141	-2.1
1945	*Det-A	141	541	62	149	22	8	6	58	36	21	.275	.324	.379	97	-3	2	9	-5	.991	-8	*O-140	-2.5
1946	Det-A	68	204	26	60	8	2	1	26	15	8	.294	.342	.368	93	-2	3	0	1	1.000	6	O-50	-1.0
1947	Det-A	73	157	21	42	7	2	2	30	20	5	.268	.350	.344	91	-2	0	4	-2	.965	-2	O-35	-0.8
1948	Det-A	4	4	1	0	0	0	0	1	3	0	.000	.429	.000	19	-0	0	0	0	1.000	-0	/O-1	-0.0
Total	20	2239	9140	1357	2705	396	109	37	842	572	345	.296	.340	.375	87	-180	62	73	-25	.979	19	*O-2142/P-1,S	-28.4

■ DICK CRAMER   Cramer, William B.   b: Brooklyn, N.Y.   d: 8/12/1885, Camden, N.J.   Deb: 5/12/1883

YEAR	TM/L	G	AB	R	H	2B	3B	HR	RBI	BB	SO	AVG	OBP	SLG	PRO+	BR/A	SB	CS	SBR	FA	FR	G/POS	TPR
1883	NY-N	2	6	0	0	0	0	0	0	1	5	.000	.143	.000	-52	-1				.000	-1	/O-2	-0.2

■ DEL CRANDALL   Crandall, Delmar Wesley   b: 3/5/30, Ontario, Cal.   BR/TR, 6'1", 195 lbs.   Deb: 6/17/49   MC

YEAR	TM/L	G	AB	R	H	2B	3B	HR	RBI	BB	SO	AVG	OBP	SLG	PRO+	BR/A	SB	CS	SBR	FA	FR	G/POS	TPR
1949	Bos-N	67	228	21	60	10	1	4	34	9	18	.263	.291	.368	80	-7	2			.982	7	C-63	0.3
1950	Bos-N	79	255	21	56	11	0	4	37	13	24	.220	.257	.310	52	-19	0			.967	3	C-75/1-1	-1.3
1953	Mil-N†	116	382	55	104	13	1	15	51	33	47	.272	.330	.429	102	0	2	1	0	.986	15	*C-108	1.9
1954	Mil-N☆	138	463	60	112	18	2	21	64	40	56	.242	.306	.425	94	-6	0	3	-2	.989	14	*C-136	1.2
1955	Mil-N★	133	440	61	104	15	2	26	62	40	56	.236	.303	.457	103	-0	2	1	0	.985	-2	*C-131	0.3
1956	Mil-N†	112	311	37	74	14	2	16	48	35	30	.238	.317	.450	110	3	1	2	-1	.996	3	*C-109	1.0
1957	*Mil-N	118	383	45	97	11	2	15	46	30	38	.253	.309	.410	98	-2	1	2	-1	.987	-8	*C-102/O-9,1	-0.8
1958	*Mil-N★	131	427	50	116	23	1	18	63	48	38	.272	.351	.457	122	12	4	1	1	.990	6	*C-124	2.6
1959	Mil-N★	150	518	65	133	19	2	21	72	46	49	.257	.321	.423	105	2	5	1	1	.994	6	*C-146	1.7
1960	Mil-N★	142	537	81	158	14	1	19	77	34	36	.294	.341	.430	118	12	4	6	-2	.988	-15	*C-141	0.3
1961	Mil-N	15	30	3	6	3	0	0	1	1	0	.200	.226	.300	40	-3	0	0	0	1.000	-2	C-5	-0.4
1962	Mil-N★	107	350	35	104	12	3	8	45	27	24	.297	.351	.417	108	4	3	4	-2	.994	-4	C-90/1-5	0.2
1963	Mil-N	86	259	18	52	4	0	3	28	18	22	.201	.253	.251	46	-18	1	4	-2	.991	5	C-75/1-7	-1.4
1964	SF-N	69	195	12	45	8	1	3	11	22	21	.231	.309	.328	78	-5	3	3	-2	.993	13	C-65	0.8
1965	Pit-N	60	140	11	30	2	0	2	10	14	10	.214	.290	.271	59	-7	1	0	0	.996	5	C-60	0.0
1966	Cle-N	50	108	10	25	2	0	4	8	14	9	.231	.320	.361	95	-1	0	0	0	.991	15	C-49	1.8
Total	16	1573	5026	585	1276	179	18	179	657	424	477	.254	.315	.404	97	-35	26	28		.989	61	*C-1479/1-14,O	8.2

■ DOC CRANDALL   Crandall, James Otis   b: 10/8/1887, Wadena, Ind.   d: 8/17/51, Bell, Cal.   BR/TR, 5'10.5", 180 lbs.   Deb: 4/24/08

YEAR	TM/L	G	AB	R	H	2B	3B	HR	RBI	BB	SO	AVG	OBP	SLG	PRO+	BR/A	SB	CS	SBR	FA	FR	G/POS	TPR
1908	NY-N	34	72	8	16	4	0	2	6	4		.222	.273	.361	97	-1	0			.985	-2	P-32/2-1	0.0
1909	NY-N	30	41	4	10	0	1	1	1	1		.244	.262	.366	93	-1	0			.941	2	P-30	0.0
1910	NY-N	45	73	10	25	2	4	1	13	5	7	.342	.385	.521	163	5	0			.984	-2	P-42/S-1	0.0
1911	*NY-N	61	113	12	27	1	4	2	21	8	16	.239	.295	.372	83	-3	2			.958	-0	P-41/S-6,2	-0.2
1912	*NY-N	50	80	9	25	6	2	0	19	6	7	.313	.360	.438	114	1	0			.957	0	P-37/2-2,1	0.0
1913	*NY-N	31	25	4	7	2	1	0	2	1	5	.280	.308	.440	111	0	0			1.000	1	P-24/2-2	0.0
	StL-N	2	2	0	0	0	0	0	0	0		.000	.000	.000	-99	-1	0			.000	0	H	-0.1
	*NY-N	15	22	3	8	2	1	0	2	2	3	.364	.417	.455	148	1	0			1.000	1	P-11	0.0
	Yr	48	49	7	15	4	1	0	4	3	10	.306	.346	.429	120	1	0			1.000	2	P-35/2-2	-0.1
1914	StL-F	118	278	40	86	16	5	2	41	58	32	.309	.424	.424	115	9	3			.926	-18	2-63,P-27/SO	-1.1
1915	StL-F	84	141	18	40	2	2	1	19	27	15	.284	.406	.348	97	1	4			.958	1	P-51	0.0
1916	StL-A	16	12	0	1	0	0	0	0	2	4	.083	.214	.083	-11	-2	0			.000	-0	/P-2	0.0
1918	Bos-N	14	28	1	8	0	0	0	2	4	3	.285	.375	.286	107	0	0			1.000	-0	P-5,O-3	0.0
Total	10	500	887	109	253	35	19	9	126	118	94	.285	.372	.398	109	13	9			.962	-18	P-302/2-71,SO1	-1.4

■ ED CRANE   Crane, Edward Nicholas "Cannon-Ball"   b: 5/27/1862, Boston, Mass.   d: 9/19/1896, Rochester, N.Y.   BR/TR, 5'10.5", 204 lbs.   Deb: 4/17/1884

YEAR	TM/L	G	AB	R	H	2B	3B	HR	RBI	BB	SO	AVG	OBP	SLG	PRO+	BR/A	SB	CS	SBR	FA	FR	G/POS	TPR
1884	Bos-U	101	428	83	122	23	6	12		14		.285	.308	.451	105	2				.826	-5	O-57,C-42/1P	-0.2
1885	Pro-N	1	2	0	0	0	0	0	0	1	1	.000	.333	.000	16	-0				.500	0	/O-1	0.0
	Buf-N	13	51	5	14	0	1	2	9	3	8	.275	.315	.431	135	2				.769	-3	O-13	-0.1
	Yr	14	53	5	14	0	1	2	9	4	9	.264	.316	.415	131	2				.750	-2	O-14	-0.1
1886	Was-N	80	292	20	50	11	3	0	20	13	54	.171	.207	.229	34	-22	8			.866	3	O-68,P-10/C	-1.7
1888	*NY-N	12	37	3	6	2	0	1	2	3	11	.162	.225	.297	66	-1	1			.867	1	P-12	0.0
1889	*NY-N	29	103	16	21	1	0	2	11	13	21	.204	.293	.272	58	-6	6			.762	-4	P-29/1-1	-0.1
1890	NY-P	43	146	27	46	5	4	0	16	10	26	.315	.363	.404	96	-2	5			.846	-3	P-43	0.0
1891	Cin-a	34	110	13	17	0	0	1	7	8	28	.155	.212	.182	12	-13	4			.822	-2	P-32/O-3	-0.1
	Cin-N	15	46	3	5	0	0	0	2	3	12	.109	.163	.109	-20	-7	3			.906	0	P-15	0.0
1892	NY-N	48	163	20	40	1	0	0	14	11	30	.245	.297	.264	71	-4	3			.821	-8	P-47/O-1	-0.1
1893	NY-N	12	26	8	12	1	0	0	3	7	0	.462	.576	.500	186	4	0			.889	-1	P-10/1-1,O	0.0
	Bro-N	3	5	1	2	0	0	0	1	0	0	.400	.400	.600	172	0	0			.500	-1	/P-2,O-1	0.0
	Yr	15	31	9	14	1	0	0	4	7	0	.452	.553	.516	186	5	0			.850	-2	P-12/1-1,O	0.0
Total	9	391	1409	199	335	45	15	18	84	86	191	.238	.283	.329	74	-49	29			.842	-15	P-204,O-145/C1	-2.2

■ FRED CRANE   Crane, Frederic William Hotchkiss   b: 11/4/1840, Old Saybrook, Conn.   d: 4/27/25, Brooklyn, N.Y.   Deb: 5/26/1873

YEAR	TM/L	G	AB	R	H	2B	3B	HR	RBI	BB	SO	AVG	OBP	SLG	PRO+	BR/A	SB	CS	SBR	FA	FR	G/POS	TPR
1873	Res-n	1	4	0	1	0	0	0	1	0	0	.250	.250	.250	52	-0						/2-1	0.0

YEAR	TM/L	G	AB	R	H	2B	3B	HR	RBI	BB	SO	AVG	OBP	SLG	PRO+	BR/A	SB	CS	SBR	FA	FR	G/POS	TPR
1875	Atl-n	21	80	7	17	1	0	0		0		.213	.213	.225	59	-3						1-20/O-1	-0.2
Total	2 n	22	84	7	18	1	0	0		0		.214	.214	.226	59	-3						/1-20,O-1,2	-0.2

■ SAM CRANE
Crane, Samuel Byren "Lucky" or "Red" b: 9/13/1894, Harrisburg, Pa. d: 11/12/55, Philadelphia, Pa. BR/TR, 5'11.5", 154 lbs. Deb: 10/2/14

YEAR	TM/L	G	AB	R	H	2B	3B	HR	RBI	BB	SO	AVG	OBP	SLG	PRO+	BR/A	SB	CS	SBR	FA	FR	G/POS	TPR
1914	Phi-A	2	6	0	0	0	0	0	0	2	3	.000	.250	.000	-25	-1	0			.929	1	/S-2	0.0
1915	Phi-A	8	23	3	2	2	0	0	1	0	4	.087	.087	.174	-23	-4	0			.900	2	/S-6,2-1	-0.1
1916	Phi-A	2	4	1	1	0	0	0	0	2	1	.250	.500	.250	132	0				1.000	-0	/S-2	0.0
1917	Was-A	32	95	6	17	2	0	0	4	4	14	.179	.212	.200	26	-9	0			.889	-4	S-32	-1.3
1920	Cin-N	54	144	20	31	4	0	0	9	7	9	.215	.261	.243	46	-10	5	4	-1	.945	-9	S-25,3-10/2O	-1.9
1921	Cin-N	73	215	20	50	10	2	0	16	14	14	.233	.292	.298	59	-13	2	5	-2	.953	-17	S-63/3-2,O	-2.6
1922	Bro-N	3	8	1	2	1	0	0	0	0	1	.250	.333	.375	83	-0	0	0	0	.875	2	/S-3	0.2
Total	7	174	495	51	103	19	2	0	30	29	46	.208	.262	.255	46	-35	7	9		.931	-25	S-133/3-12,2O	-5.7

■ SAM CRANE
Crane, Samuel Newhall b: 1/2/1854, Springfield, Mass. d: 6/26/25, New York, N.Y. BR/TR, Deb: 5/1/1880 M

YEAR	TM/L	G	AB	R	H	2B	3B	HR	RBI	BB	SO	AVG	OBP	SLG	PRO+	BR/A	SB	CS	SBR	FA	FR	G/POS	TPR
1880	Buf-N	10	31	4	4	0	0	0	2	1	8	.129	.156	.129	-2	-3				.866	-2	2-10/O-1M	-0.5
1883	NY-a	96	349	57	82	8	5	0		13		.235	.262	.287	73	-11				.859	-11	*2-96/O-1	-1.8
1884	Cin-U	80	309	56	72	9	3	1		11		.233	.259	.291	46	-24				.858	-9	*2-80,M	-2.8
1885	Det-N	68	245	23	47	4	6	1	20	13	45	.192	.233	.269	62	-10	8			.908	-5	2-68	-1.2
1886	Det-N	47	185	24	26	2	1	0	12	8	34	.141	.176	.189	11	-20				.903	1	2-38/S-8,O	-1.6
	StL-N	39	116	10	20	3	1	0	7	13	27	.172	.256	.216	48	-7	6			.897	-11	2-39	-1.4
	Yr	86	301	34	46	5	3	1	19	21	61	.153	.208	.199	25	-27	14			.900	-10	2-77/S-8,O	-3.0
1887	Was-N	7	30	6	9	1	1	0	1	1	6	.300	.323	.400	105	0	5			.865	-1	/S-7	0.0
1890	NY-N	2	6	0	0	0	0	0	0	0	1	.000	.000	.000	-99	-2	1			.778	-1	/1-1,O-1	-0.2
	Pit-N	22	82	3	16	3	0	0	3	0	5	.195	.205	.232	31	-7	5			.880	3	2-15/S-7,O	-0.2
	NY-N	2	6	0	0	0	0	0	0	0	1	.000	.000	.000	-99	-2	0			1.000	1	/2-2	-0.1
	Yr	26	94	3	16	3	0	0	3	0	7	.170	.179	.202	12	-11	6			.883	3	2-17/S-7,O1	-0.5
Total	7	373	1359	183	276	30	18	3	45	60	127	.203	.237	.258	49	-85	25			.878	-34	2-348/S-22,O1	-9.8

■ GAVVY CRAVATH
Cravath, Clifford Carlton "Cactus" b: 3/23/1881, Escondido, Cal. d: 5/23/63, Laguna Beach, Cal. BR/TR, 5'10.5", 186 lbs. Deb: 4/18/08 MC

YEAR	TM/L	G	AB	R	H	2B	3B	HR	RBI	BB	SO	AVG	OBP	SLG	PRO+	BR/A	SB	CS	SBR	FA	FR	G/POS	TPR
1908	Bos-A	94	277	43	71	10	11	1	34	38		.256	.354	.383	136	12	6			.925	-2	O-77/1-5	0.8
1909	Chi-A	19	50	7	9	0	0	1	8	19		.180	.406	.240	109	2	3			.944	-2	O-18	-0.1
	Was-A	4	6	0	0	0	0	0	1	1		.000	.143	.000	-57	-1	0			1.000	1	/O-1	-0.1
	Yr	23	56	7	9	0	0	1	9	20		.161	.382	.214	93	1	3			.947	-2	O-19	-0.2
1912	Phi-N	130	436	63	124	30	9	11	70	47	77	.284	.358	.470	118	9	15			.966	5	*O-113	0.8
1913	Phi-N	147	525	78	179	34	14	19	128	55	63	.341	.407	.568	169	46	10			.958	-4	*O-141	3.7
1914	Phi-N	149	499	76	149	27	8	19	100	83	72	.299	.402	.499	157	36	14			.930	3	*O-143	3.5
1915	*Phi-N	150	522	89	149	31	7	24	115	86	77	.285	.393	.510	170	46	11	9	-2	.946	9	*O-149	4.9
1916	Phi-N	137	448	70	127	21	8	11	70	64	89	.283	.379	.440	146	26	9			.966	-3	*O-130	1.8
1917	Phi-N	140	503	70	141	29	16	12	83	70	57	.280	.369	.473	151	31	6			.946	-3	*O-139	2.2
1918	Phi-N	121	426	43	99	27	5	8	54	54	46	.232	.320	.376	105	3	7			.931	-4	*O-118	-0.9
1919	Phi-N	83	214	34	73	18	5	12	45	35	21	.341	.438	.640	207	28	8			.914	-5	O-56,M	2.2
1920	Phi-N	46	45	2	13	5	0	1	11	9	12	.289	.407	.467	144	5	0	0	0	.667	-2	/O-5,M	0.1
Total	11	1220	3951	575	1134	232	83	119	719	561	514	.287	.380	.478	149	240	89	9		.944	-6	*O-1090/1-5	18.9

■ BILL CRAVER
Craver, William H. b: 6/1844, Troy, N.Y. d: 6/17/01, Troy, N.Y. BR/TR, 5'9", 160 lbs. Deb: 5/9/1871 M

YEAR	TM/L	G	AB	R	H	2B	3B	HR	RBI	BB	SO	AVG	OBP	SLG	PRO+	BR/A	SB	CS	SBR	FA	FR	G/POS	TPR
1871	Tro-n	27	118	26	38	1	0	0	26	3	0	.322	.339	.407	112	2	6					2-18/S-4,C1M	0.0
1872	Bal-n	35	180	55	50	5	3	0	24	5	2	.278	.297	.339	91	-3						C-25/O-5,32M	-0.1
1873	Bal-n	41	196	45	57	7	4	0	27	2	3	.291	.298	.367	95	-1						C-21,S-15/O1	-0.2
1874	Phi-n	55	267	68	94	13	11	0		4		.352	.362	.483	161	17						*2-53/C-3M	1.1
1875	Cen-n	14	65	8	18	5	2	0		0		.277	.277	.415	148	3						/S-9,3-4,1M	0.2
	Ath-n	54	260	71	83	11	11	2		4		.319	.330	.469	156	12						2-53/C-1	0.9
	Yr	68	325	79	101	16	13	2		4		.311	.319	.458	155	16						2-53/S-9,31C	1.1
1876	NY-N	56	246	24	55	4	0	0	22	2	7	.224	.230	.240	65	-8				.814	-21	2-42,C-11/S	-2.6
1877	Lou-N	57	238	33	63	5	2	0	29	5	11	.265	.280	.303	71	-10				.904	-1	*S-57	-0.8
Total	5 n	226	1086	273	340	49	32	2	77	18	5	.313	.324	.423	129	30						2-126/C-53,SO31	1.9
Total	2	113	484	57	118	9	2	0	51	7	18	.244	.255	.271	69	-18				.897	-22	/S-63,2-42,C	-3.4

■ PAT CRAWFORD
Crawford, Clifford Rankin b: 1/28/02, Society Hill, S.C. d: 1/25/94, Morehead City, N.C BL/TR, 5'11", 170 lbs. Deb: 4/18/29

YEAR	TM/L	G	AB	R	H	2B	3B	HR	RBI	BB	SO	AVG	OBP	SLG	PRO+	BR/A	SB	CS	SBR	FA	FR	G/POS	TPR
1929	NY-N	65	57	13	17	3	0	3	24	11	5	.298	.412	.509	127	3	1			1.000	-0	/1-7,3-1	0.2
1930	NY-N	25	76	11	21	3	2	1	17	7	2	.276	.345	.487	100	-0	0			.966	-4	2-18/1-1	-0.3
	Cin-N	76	224	24	65	7	1	3	26	23	10	.290	.359	.371	81	-6	2			.969	-8	2-54,1-13	-1.2
	Yr	101	300	35	86	10	3	6	43	30	12	.287	.355	.400	86	-7	2			.968	-12	2-72,1-14	-1.5
1933	StL-N	91	224	24	60	8	2	0	21	14	9	.268	.317	.321	78	-6	1			.986	3	1-29,2-15/3	-0.6
1934	*StL-N	61	70	3	19	2	0	0	16	5	3	.271	.320	.300	63	-4	0			.900	2	/3-9,2-4	-0.1
Total	4	318	651	75	182	23	5	9	104	60	29	.280	.344	.372	85	-13	4			.969	-8	/2-91,1-50,3	-2.0

■ FORREST CRAWFORD
Crawford, Forrest A. b: 5/10/1881, Rockdale, Tex. d: 3/29/08, Austin, Tex. BL/TR, Deb: 7/30/06

YEAR	TM/L	G	AB	R	H	2B	3B	HR	RBI	BB	SO	AVG	OBP	SLG	PRO+	BR/A	SB	CS	SBR	FA	FR	G/POS	TPR
1906	StL-N	45	145	8	30	3	1	0	11	7		.207	.248	.241	55	-8	1			.927	-10	S-39/3-6	-1.8
1907	StL-N	7	22	0	5	0	0	0	3	2		.227	.292	.227	65	-1	0			.912	-1	/S-7	-0.2
Total	2	52	167	8	35	3	1	0	14	9		.210	.254	.240	56	-9	1			.924	-11	/S-46,3-6	-2.0

■ GEORGE CRAWFORD
Crawford, George Deb: 10/8/1890

YEAR	TM/L	G	AB	R	H	2B	3B	HR	RBI	BB	SO	AVG	OBP	SLG	PRO+	BR/A	SB	CS	SBR	FA	FR	G/POS	TPR
1890	Phi-a	5	17	1	2	0	0	0		0		.118	.118	.118	-31	-3	1			1.000	1	/O-4,S-1	-0.2

■ GLENN CRAWFORD
Crawford, Glenn Martin "Shorty" b: 12/2/13, North Branch, Mich. d: 1/2/72, Saginaw, Mich. BL/TR, 5'9", 165 lbs. Deb: 4/22/45

YEAR	TM/L	G	AB	R	H	2B	3B	HR	RBI	BB	SO	AVG	OBP	SLG	PRO+	BR/A	SB	CS	SBR	FA	FR	G/POS	TPR
1945	StL-N	4	3	0	0	0	0	0	1	0		.000	.250	.000	-26	-0	0			.000	-1	/O-1	-0.1
	Phi-N	82	302	41	89	13	2	2	24	36	15	.295	.372	.371	110	5	5			.976	-2	O-38,S-34,2	0.5
	Yr	86	305	41	89	13	2	2	24	37	15	.292	.370	.367	108	5	5			.976	-2	O-39,S-34,2	0.4
1946	Phi-N	1	1	0	0	0	0	0	0	0		.000	.000	.000	-99	-0	0			.000	0	H	0.0
Total	2	87	306	41	89	13	2	2	24	37	15	.291	.369	.366	108	4	5			.976	-2	/O-39,S-34,2	0.4

■ KEN CRAWFORD
Crawford, Kenneth Daniel b: 10/31/1894, South Bend, Ind. d: 11/11/76, Pittsburg, Pa. BL/TR, 5'9", 145 lbs. Deb: 9/6/15

YEAR	TM/L	G	AB	R	H	2B	3B	HR	RBI	BB	SO	AVG	OBP	SLG	PRO+	BR/A	SB	CS	SBR	FA	FR	G/POS	TPR
1915	Bal-F	23	82	4	20	2	1	0	7	1	18	.244	.253	.293	44	-7	0			.978	-2	1-14/O-4	-1.0

■ JAKE CRAWFORD
Crawford, Rufus b: 3/20/28, Campbell, Mo. BR/TR, 6'1.5", 185 lbs. Deb: 9/7/52

YEAR	TM/L	G	AB	R	H	2B	3B	HR	RBI	BB	SO	AVG	OBP	SLG	PRO+	BR/A	SB	CS	SBR	FA	FR	G/POS	TPR
1952	StL-A	7	11	1	2	1	0	0	0	1	5	.182	.250	.273	44	-1	1	0	0	1.000	-0	/O-3	-0.1

■ SAM CRAWFORD
Crawford, Samuel Earl "Wahoo Sam" b: 4/18/1880, Wahoo, Neb. d: 6/15/68, Hollywood, Cal. BL/TL, 6', 190 lbs. Deb: 9/10/1899 H

YEAR	TM/L	G	AB	R	H	2B	3B	HR	RBI	BB	SO	AVG	OBP	SLG	PRO+	BR/A	SB	CS	SBR	FA	FR	G/POS	TPR
1899	Cin-N	31	127	25	39	3	7	1	20	2		.307	.318	.465	111	1	6			.970	2	O-31	0.1
1900	Cin-N	101	389	68	101	15	15	7	59	28		.260	.314	.429	107	1	14			.948	12	O-95	0.5
1901	Cin-N	131	515	91	170	20	16	16	104	37		.330	.378	.524	172	44	13			.923	3	*O-127	3.6
1902	Cin-N	140	555	92	185	18	22	3	78	47		.333	.386	.461	147	29	16			.932	4	*O-140	2.5
1903	Det-A	137	550	88	184	23	25	4	89	25		.335	.366	.489	159	37	18			.960	4	*O-137	3.3
1904	Det-A	150	562	49	143	22	16	2	73	44		.254	.309	.361	148	9	20			.973	4	*O-150	0.5
1905	Det-A	154	575	73	171	38	10	6	75	50		.297	.357	.430	148	30	22			.988	11	*O-103,1-51	3.8

YEAR	TM/L	G	AB	R	H	2B	3B	HR	RBI	BB	SO	AVG	OBP	SLG	PRO+	BR/A	SB	CS	SBR	FA	FR	G/POS	TPR
1906	Det-A	145	563	65	166	25	16	2	72	38		.295	.341	.407	130	18	24			.984	1	*O-116,1-32	1.4
1907	*Det-A	144	582	102	188	34	17	4	81	37		.323	.366	.460	157	35	18			.965	8	*O-144/1-2	4.0
1908	*Det-A	152	591	102	184	33	16	7	80	37		.311	.355	.457	157	34	15			.970	-8	*O-134,1-17	2.3
1909	*Det-A	156	589	83	185	35	14	6	97	47		.314	.366	.452	151	32	30			.965	-7	*O-139,1-18	2.3
1910	Det-A	154	588	83	170	26	19	5	120	37		.289	.332	.423	128	16	20			.963	-11	*O-153/1-1	-0.2
1911	Det-A	146	574	109	217	36	14	7	115	61		.378	.438	.526	160	46	37			.975	-12	*O-146	2.6
1912	Det-A	149	581	81	189	30	21	4	109	42		.325	.373	.470	145	31	41			.984	-17	*O-149	0.7
1913	Det-A	153	609	78	193	32	23	9	83	52	28	.317	.371	.489	154	37	13			.964	-10	*O-140,1-13	2.2
1914	Det-A	157	582	74	183	22	26	8	104	69	31	.314	.388	.483	157	39	25	16	-2	.977	-8	*O-157	2.4
1915	Det-A	156	612	81	183	31	19	4	112	66	29	.299	.367	.431	132	22	24	14	-1	.974	-14	*O-156	0.0
1916	Det-A	100	322	41	92	11	13	0	42	37	10	.286	.359	.401	124	9	10			.978	-10	O-79/1-2	-0.6
1917	Det-A	61	104	6	18	4	0	2	12	4	6	.173	.204	.269	44	-7	0			.988	-3	1-15/O-3	-1.2
Total	19	2517	9570	1391	2961	458	309	97	1525	760	104	.309	.362	.452	143	464	366	30		.965	-50	*O-2299,1-151	30.2

■ **WILLIE CRAWFORD**   Crawford, Willie Murphy   b: 9/7/46, Los Angeles, Cal.   BL/TL, 6'1", 205 lbs.   Deb: 9/16/64

YEAR	TM/L	G	AB	R	H	2B	3B	HR	RBI	BB	SO	AVG	OBP	SLG	PRO+	BR/A	SB	CS	SBR	FA	FR	G/POS	TPR
1964	LA-N	10	16	3	5	1	0	0	0	1	7	.313	.353	.375	113	0	1	1	-0	1.000	0	/O-4	0.0
1965	*LA-N	52	27	10	4	0	0	0	0	2	8	.148	.207	.148	2	-4	2	0	1	1.000	-2	/O-8	-0.5
1966	LA-N	6	0	1	0	0	0	0	0	0	0	—	—	—	—	0	0	0	0	.000	0	R	-
1967	LA-N	4	4	0	1	0	0	0	0	1	3	.250	.400	.250	98	0	0	0	0	.000	-1	/O-1	-0.1
1968	LA-N	61	175	25	44	12	1	4	14	20	64	.251	.335	.400	130	6	1	3	-2	.966	3	O-48	0.6
1969	LA-N	129	389	64	96	17	5	11	41	49	85	.247	.331	.401	112	6	4	5	-2	.973	-4	*O-113	-0.6
1970	LA-N	109	299	48	70	8	6	8	40	33	88	.234	.314	.381	89	-5	4	4	-1	.960	-1	O-94	-1.1
1971	LA-N	114	342	64	96	16	6	9	40	28	49	.281	.337	.442	126	11	5	2	0	.981	-7	O-97	0.0
1972	LA-N	96	243	28	61	7	3	8	27	35	55	.251	.350	.403	116	6	4	2	0	.983	-8	O-74	-0.5
1973	LA-N	145	457	75	135	26	2	14	66	78	91	.295	.399	.453	142	28	12	5	1	.978	1	*O-138	2.5
1974	*LA-N	139	468	73	138	23	4	11	61	64	88	.295	.380	.432	132	21	7	8	-3	.966	-7	*O-133	0.6
1975	LA-N	124	373	46	98	15	2	9	46	49	43	.263	.348	.386	108	4	5	5	-2	.990	-5	O-113	-0.6
1976	StL-N	120	392	49	119	17	5	9	50	37	53	.304	.365	.441	127	14	2	1	0	.982	-1	*O-107	0.9
1977	Hou-N	42	114	14	29	3	0	2	18	16	10	.254	.346	.333	91	-1	0	0	0	.959	-2	O-30	-0.4
	Oak-A	59	136	7	25	7	1	1	16	18	20	.184	.279	.272	52	-9	0	0	0	.978	2	O-22,D-18	-0.8
Total	14	1210	3435	507	921	152	35	86	419	431	664	.268	.351	.408	117	77	47	36	-8	.975	-30	O-982/D-18	-0.0

■ **GEORGE CREAMER**   Creamer, George W. (b: George W. Triebel)   b: 1855, Philadelphia, Pa.   d: 6/27/1886, Philadelphia, Pa.   BR/TR, 6'2",   Deb: 5/1/1878   M

YEAR	TM/L	G	AB	R	H	2B	3B	HR	RBI	BB	SO	AVG	OBP	SLG	PRO+	BR/A	SB	CS	SBR	FA	FR	G/POS	TPR
1878	Mil-N	50	193	30	41	7	3	0	15	5	15	.212	.232	.280	63	-8				.839	-5	2-28,O-17/3	-1.1
1879	Syr-N	15	60	3	13	2	0	0	3	1	2	.217	.230	.250	65	-2				.825	-10	2-10/S-3,O	-1.0
1880	Wor-N	85	306	40	61	6	3	0	27	4	21	.199	.210	.239	47	-17				.883	-7	*2-85	-1.9
1881	Wor-N	80	309	42	64	9	2	0	25	11	27	.207	.234	.249	49	-18				.904	-9	*2-80	-2.2
1882	Wor-N	81	286	27	65	16	6	1	29	14	24	.227	.263	.336	88	-4				.907	11	*2-81	0.8
1883	Pit-a	91	369	54	94	7	9	0		20		.255	.293	.322	103	2				.897	9	*2-91	1.0
1884	Pit-a	98	339	38	62	8	5	0		16		.183	.224	.236	49	-18				.937	16	*2-98,M	0.0
Total	7	500	1862	234	400	55	28	1	99	71	89	.215	.244	.276	67	-65				.901	6	2-473/O-19,3S	-4.4

■ **BIRDIE CREE**   Cree, William Franklin   b: 10/23/1882, Khedive, Pa.   d: 11/8/42, Sunbury, Pa.   BR/TR, 5'6", 150 lbs.   Deb: 9/17/08

YEAR	TM/L	G	AB	R	H	2B	3B	HR	RBI	BB	SO	AVG	OBP	SLG	PRO+	BR/A	SB	CS	SBR	FA	FR	G/POS	TPR
1908	NY-A	21	78	5	21	0	2	0	4	7		.269	.345	.321	115	2	1			1.000	1	O-21	0.2
1909	NY-A	104	343	48	90	6	3	2	27	30		.262	.338	.315	105	3	10			.949	-7	O-79/S-6,23	-0.7
1910	NY-A	134	467	58	134	19	16	4	73	40		.287	.353	.422	135	18	28			.955	-12	*O-134	-0.1
1911	NY-A	137	520	90	181	30	22	4	88	56		.348	.415	.513	149	33	48			.964	0	*O-132/S-4,2	2.6
1912	NY-A	50	190	25	63	11	6	0	22	20		.332	.409	.453	138	10	12			.948	5	O-50	1.2
1913	NY-A	145	534	51	145	25	6	1	63	50	51	.272	.338	.346	100	0	22			.988	-4	*O-144	-1.1
1914	NY-A	77	275	45	85	18	5	0	40	30	24	.309	.389	.411	141	14	4	9	-4	.976	7	O-76	1.5
1915	NY-A	74	196	23	42	8	2	0	15	36	22	.214	.353	.276	88	-1	7	8	-3	.945	-3	O-53	-1.0
Total	8	742	2603	345	761	117	62	11	332	269	97	.292	.368	.398	124	78	132	17		.965	-13	O-689/S-10,23	2.6

■ **CONNIE CREEDEN**   Creeden, Cornelius Stephen   b: 7/21/15, Danvers, Mass.   d: 11/30/69, Santa Ana, Cal.   BL/TL, 6'1", 200 lbs.   Deb: 4/28/43

YEAR	TM/L	G	AB	R	H	2B	3B	HR	RBI	BB	SO	AVG	OBP	SLG	PRO+	BR/A	SB	CS	SBR	FA	FR	G/POS	TPR
1943	Bos-N	5	4	0	1	0	0	0	1	1	0	.250	.400	.250	91	0	0			.000	0	H	0.0

■ **PAT CREEDEN**   Creeden, Patrick Francis "Whoops"   b: 5/23/06, Newburyport, Mass.   d: 4/20/92, Brockton, Mass.   BL/TR, 5'8", 175 lbs.   Deb: 4/14/31

YEAR	TM/L	G	AB	R	H	2B	3B	HR	RBI	BB	SO	AVG	OBP	SLG	PRO+	BR/A	SB	CS	SBR	FA	FR	G/POS	TPR
1931	Bos-A	5	8	0	0	0	0	0	0	1	3	.000	.111	.000	-73	-2	0			.846	0	/2-2	-0.2

■ **MARTY CREEGAN**   Creegan, Martin   b: San Francisco, Cal.   Deb: 4/17/1884

YEAR	TM/L	G	AB	R	H	2B	3B	HR	RBI	BB	SO	AVG	OBP	SLG	PRO+	BR/A	SB	CS	SBR	FA	FR	G/POS	TPR
1884	Was-U	9	33	4	5	0	0	0		1		.152	.176	.152	-10	-5				.667	-1	/O-6,C-3,31	-0.5

■ **GUS CREELY**   Creely, August L.   b: 6/6/1870, Florissant, Mo.   d: 4/22/34, St.Louis, Mo.   5'6", 150 lbs.   Deb: 10/9/1890

YEAR	TM/L	G	AB	R	H	2B	3B	HR	RBI	BB	SO	AVG	OBP	SLG	PRO+	BR/A	SB	CS	SBR	FA	FR	G/POS	TPR
1890	StL-a	4	15	0	0	0	0	0	0	0		.000	.000	.000	-88	-4	1			.769	-3	/S-4	-0.6

■ **PETE CREGAN**   Cregan, Peter James "Peekskill Pete"   b: 4/13/1875, Kingston, N.Y.   d: 5/18/45, New York, N.Y.   BR/TR, 5'7.5", 150 lbs.   Deb: 9/8/1899

YEAR	TM/L	G	AB	R	H	2B	3B	HR	RBI	BB	SO	AVG	OBP	SLG	PRO+	BR/A	SB	CS	SBR	FA	FR	G/POS	TPR
1899	NY-N	1	2	0	0	0	0	0	0	0		.000	.000	.000	-99	-1	0			1.000	-0	/O-1	-0.1
1903	Cin-N	6	19	0	2	0	0	0	0	0	1	.105	.190	.105	-13	-3	0			.769	-1	/O-6	-0.4
Total	2	7	21	0	2	0	0	0	0	0	1	.095	.174	.095	-21	-3	0			.786	-2	/O-7	-0.5

■ **BERNIE CREGER**   Creger, Bernard Odell   b: 3/21/27, Wytheville, Va.   BR/TR, 6', 175 lbs.   Deb: 4/29/47

YEAR	TM/L	G	AB	R	H	2B	3B	HR	RBI	BB	SO	AVG	OBP	SLG	PRO+	BR/A	SB	CS	SBR	FA	FR	G/POS	TPR
1947	StL-N	15	16	3	3	1	0	0	0	0	3	.188	.235	.250	28	-2	1			.828	-3	S-13	-0.5

■ **CREEPY CRESPI**   Crespi, Frank Angelo Joseph   b: 2/16/18, St.Louis, Mo.   d: 3/1/90, Florissant, Mo.   BR/TR, 5'8.5", 175 lbs.   Deb: 9/14/38

YEAR	TM/L	G	AB	R	H	2B	3B	HR	RBI	BB	SO	AVG	OBP	SLG	PRO+	BR/A	SB	CS	SBR	FA	FR	G/POS	TPR
1938	StL-N	7	19	2	5	2	0	0	1	2	7	.263	.333	.368	88	-0	0			.813	-2	/S-7	-0.2
1939	StL-N	15	29	3	5	1	0	0	6	3	6	.172	.250	.207	23	-3	0			.962	-0	/2-6,S-4	-0.3
1940	StL-N	3	11	2	3	1	0	0	0	1	2	.273	.333	.364	87	-0	1			1.000	-1	/3-2,S-1	-0.1
1941	StL-N	146	560	85	156	24	2	4	46	57	58	.279	.355	.350	93	-4	3			.962	0	*2-145	0.7
1942	*StL-N	93	292	33	71	4	0	0	35	27	29	.243	.309	.271	65	-12	4			.967	-5	2-83/S-5	-1.3
Total	5	264	911	125	240	32	4	4	88	90	102	.263	.336	.321	82	-20	8			.963	-7	2-234/S-17,3	-1.2

■ **LOU CRIGER**   Criger, Louis   b: 2/3/1872, Elkhart, Ind.   d: 5/14/34, Tucson, Ariz.   BR/TR, 5'10", 165 lbs.   Deb: 9/21/1896

YEAR	TM/L	G	AB	R	H	2B	3B	HR	RBI	BB	SO	AVG	OBP	SLG	PRO+	BR/A	SB	CS	SBR	FA	FR	G/POS	TPR
1896	Cle-N	2	5	0	0	0	0	0	0	1	0	.000	.167	.000	-51	-1	1			1.000	1	/C-1	0.0
1897	Cle-N	39	138	15	31	4	1	0	22	23		.225	.340	.268	58	-8	5			.937	-1	C-37/1-2	-0.4
1898	Cle-N	84	287	43	80	13	4	1	32	40		.279	.377	.362	113	7	2			.957	15	C-82	2.8
1899	StL-N	77	258	39	66	4	5	0	44	28		.256	.333	.333	81	-6	14			.949	2	C-75	0.1
1900	StL-N	80	288	31	78	8	6	2	38	4		.271	.286	.361	78	-10	5			.953	6	C-75/3-1	0.3
1901	Bos-A	76	268	26	62	6	3	0	24	11		.231	.270	.276	52	-17	7			.967	22	C-68/1-8	1.0
1902	Bos-A	83	266	32	68	16	5	0	28	27		.256	.324	.361	87	-5	7			.965	14	C-80/O-1	1.7
1903	*Bos-A	96	317	41	61	7	10	3	31	26		.192	.256	.306	65	-14	5			.979	23	C-96	2.0
1904	Bos-A	98	299	34	63	10	5	2	34	27		.211	.283	.298	79	-7	1			.981	19	C-95	2.5
1905	Bos-A	109	313	33	62	6	7	1	36	54		.198	.322	.272	88	-2	5			.972	6	*C-109	1.6
1906	Bos-A	7	17	0	3	1	0	0	1	1		.176	.222	.235	43	-1	1			.981	5	/C-6	0.4
1907	Bos-A	75	226	12	41	4	0	0	14	19		.181	.251	.199	44	-14	2			.978	0	C-75	-0.7
1908	Bos-A	84	237	12	45	4	2	0	25	13		.190	.232	.224	47	-14	1			.980	13	C-84	0.7

YEAR	TM/L	G	AB	R	H	2B	3B	HR	RBI	BB	SO	AVG	OBP	SLG	PRO+	BR/A	SB	CS	SBR	FA	FR	G/POS	TPR
1909	StL-A	74	212	15	36	1	1	0	9	25		.170	.261	.184	44	-13	2			.986	8	C-73	0.2
1910	NY-A	27	69	3	13	2	0	0	4	10		.188	.291	.217	56	-3	0			.993	-1	C-27	-0.3
1912	StL-A	1	2	1	0	0	0	0	0	0		.000	.000	.000	-99	-1	0			1.000	1	/C-1	0.0
Total	16	1012	3202	337	709	86	50	11	342	309	0	.221	.295	.290	72	-108	58			.971	131	C-984/1-10,O3	11.9

■ DAVE CRIPE
Cripe, David Gordon   b: 4/7/51, Ramona, Cal.   BR/TR, 6', 180 lbs.   Deb: 9/10/78

YEAR	TM/L	G	AB	R	H	2B	3B	HR	RBI	BB	SO	AVG	OBP	SLG	PRO+	BR/A	SB	CS	SBR	FA	FR	G/POS	TPR
1978	KC-A	7	13	1	2	0	0	0	1	0	2	.154	.154	.154	-13	-2	0	0	0	1.000	-2	/3-5	-0.4

■ DAVE CRISCIONE
Criscione, David Gerald   b: 9/2/51, Dunkirk, N.Y.   BR/TR, 5'8", 185 lbs.   Deb: 7/17/77

YEAR	TM/L	G	AB	R	H	2B	3B	HR	RBI	BB	SO	AVG	OBP	SLG	PRO+	BR/A	SB	CS	SBR	FA	FR	G/POS	TPR
1977	Bal-A	7	9	1	3	0	0	1	1	0	1	.333	.333	.667	176	1	0	0	0	1.000	-1	/C-7	0.0

■ TONY CRISCOLA
Criscola, Anthony Paul   b: 7/9/15, Walla Walla, Wash.   BL/TR, 5'11.5", 180 lbs.   Deb: 4/15/42

YEAR	TM/L	G	AB	R	H	2B	3B	HR	RBI	BB	SO	AVG	OBP	SLG	PRO+	BR/A	SB	CS	SBR	FA	FR	G/POS	TPR
1942	StL-A	91	158	17	47	9	2	1	13	8	13	.297	.331	.399	103	0	2	2	-1	.955	-14	O-52	-1.7
1943	StL-A	29	52	4	8	0	0	0	1	8	7	.154	.267	.154	24	-5	0	0	0	.960	-2	O-13	-0.8
1944	Cin-N	64	157	14	36	3	2	0	14	14	12	.229	.297	.274	64	-7	0			.977	2	O-35	-0.8
Total	3	184	367	35	91	12	4	1	28	30	32	.248	.307	.311	75	-12	2	2		.966	-15	O-100	-3.3

■ PAT CRISHAM
Crisham, Patrick J.   b: 6/4/1877, Amesbury, Mass.   d: 6/12/15, Syracuse, N.Y.   6', 168 lbs.   Deb: 5/5/1899

YEAR	TM/L	G	AB	R	H	2B	3B	HR	RBI	BB	SO	AVG	OBP	SLG	PRO+	BR/A	SB	CS	SBR	FA	FR	G/POS	TPR
1899	Bal-N	53	172	23	50	5	3	0	20	4		.291	.311	.355	78	-6	4			.979	-5	1-26,C-22	-0.8

■ JOE CRISP
Crisp, Joseph Shelby   b: 7/8/1889, Higginsville, Mo.   d: 2/5/39, Kansas City, Mo.   BR/TR, 6'4", 200 lbs.   Deb: 9/2/10

YEAR	TM/L	G	AB	R	H	2B	3B	HR	RBI	BB	SO	AVG	OBP	SLG	PRO+	BR/A	SB	CS	SBR	FA	FR	G/POS	TPR
1910	StL-A	1	1	0	0	0	0	0	0	0		.000	.000	.000	-99	-0	0			1.000	-0	/C-1	0.0
1911	StL-A	1	1	0	1	0	0	0	0	0		1.000	1.000	1.000	477	0	0			.000	0	/H	0.0
Total	2	2	2	0	1	0	0	0	0	0		.500	.500	.500	206	0	0			1.000	-0	/C-1	0.0

■ DODE CRISS
Criss, Dode   b: 3/12/1885, Sherman, Miss.   d: 9/8/55, Sherman, Miss.   BL/TR, 6'2", 200 lbs.   Deb: 4/20/08

YEAR	TM/L	G	AB	R	H	2B	3B	HR	RBI	BB	SO	AVG	OBP	SLG	PRO+	BR/A	SB	CS	SBR	FA	FR	G/POS	TPR
1908	StL-A	64	82	15	28	6	0	0	14	9		.341	.407	.415	166	6	1			.933	-1	O-11/P-9,1	0.5
1909	StL-A	35	48	2	14	6	1	0	7	0		.292	.306	.458	152	2	0			1.000	-1	P-11	0.0
1910	StL-A	70	91	11	21	4	2	1	11	11		.231	.320	.352	118	2	2			.983	-1	1-11/P-6	0.1
1911	StL-A	58	83	10	21	3	1	2	15	11		.253	.347	.386	109	1	0			.956	-2	1-14/P-4	-0.1
Total	4	227	304	38	84	19	4	3	47	31		.276	.349	.395	133	11	3			.964	-5	/P-30,1-26,O	0.5

■ CHES CRIST
Crist, Chester Arthur "Squak"   b: 2/10/1882, Cozaddale, Ohio   d: 1/7/57, Cincinnati, Ohio   BR/TR, 5'11", 165 lbs.   Deb: 5/18/06

YEAR	TM/L	G	AB	R	H	2B	3B	HR	RBI	BB	SO	AVG	OBP	SLG	PRO+	BR/A	SB	CS	SBR	FA	FR	G/POS	TPR
1906	Phi-N	6	11	1	0	0	0	0	0	0		.000	.083	.000	-74	-2	0			.800	-3	/C-6	-0.6

■ HUGHIE CRITZ
Critz, Hugh Melville   b: 9/17/1900, Starkville, Miss.   d: 1/10/80, Greenwood, Miss.   BR/TR, 5'8", 147 lbs.   Deb: 5/31/24

YEAR	TM/L	G	AB	R	H	2B	3B	HR	RBI	BB	SO	AVG	OBP	SLG	PRO+	BR/A	SB	CS	SBR	FA	FR	G/POS	TPR
1924	Cin-N	102	413	67	133	15	14	3	35	19	18	.322	.352	.448	115	7	19	11	-1	.956	2	2-96/S-1	1.0
1925	Cin-N	144	541	94	150	14	8	2	51	34	17	.277	.321	.344	72	-23	13	13	-4	.970	22	*2-144	-0.3
1926	Cin-N	155	607	96	164	24	14	3	79	39	25	.270	.316	.371	87	-12	7			.981	24	*2-155	1.6
1927	Cin-N	113	396	50	110	10	8	4	49	16	18	.278	.306	.374	84	-10	7			.969	-2	*2-113	-0.8
1928	Cin-N	153	641	95	190	21	11	5	52	37	24	.296	.335	.387	90	-11	18			.971	-17	*2-153	-2.3
1929	Cin-N	107	425	55	105	17	9	1	50	27	21	.247	.292	.336	58	-29	9			.974	4	*2-106/S-1	-1.9
1930	Cin-N	28	104	15	24	3	2	0	11	6	6	.231	.273	.298	40	-10	1			.987	-3	2-28	-1.1
	NY-N	124	558	93	148	17	11	4	50	24	26	.265	.296	.357	58	-39	7			.972	5	*2-124	-2.4
	Yr	152	662	108	172	20	13	4	61	30	32	.260	.292	.347	55	-49	8			.974	2	*2-152	-3.5
1931	NY-N	66	238	33	69	7	2	4	17	8	17	.290	.313	.387	89	-4	4			.984	0	2-54	0.0
1932	NY-N	151	659	90	182	32	7	2	50	34	27	.276	.313	.355	81	-18	3			.974	1	*2-151	-0.9
1933	*NY-N	133	558	68	137	18	5	2	33	23	24	.246	.279	.306	68	-23	4			.982	47	*2-133	3.2
1934	NY-N	137	571	77	138	17	1	6	40	19	24	.242	.269	.306	55	-37	3			.978	25	*2-137	-0.3
1935	NY-N	65	219	19	41	0	3	2	14	3	10	.187	.198	.242	18	-25	2			.966	3	2-59	-1.8
Total	12	1478	5930	832	1591	195	95	38	531	289	257	.268	.303	.352	74	-235	97	24		.974	111	*2-1453/S-2	-6.0

■ DAVEY CROCKETT
Crockett, Daniel Solomon   b: 10/5/1875, Roanoke, Va.   d: 2/23/61, Charlottesville, Va.   BL/TR, 6'1", 175 lbs.   Deb: 7/11/01

YEAR	TM/L	G	AB	R	H	2B	3B	HR	RBI	BB	SO	AVG	OBP	SLG	PRO+	BR/A	SB	CS	SBR	FA	FR	G/POS	TPR
1901	Det-A	28	102	10	29	2	2	0	14	6		.284	.336	.343	85	-2	1			.968	-0	1-27	-0.3

■ ART CROFT
Croft, Arthur F.   b: 1/23/1855, St.Louis, Mo.   d: 3/16/1884, St.Louis, Mo.   Deb: 5/4/1875

YEAR	TM/L	G	AB	R	H	2B	3B	HR	RBI	BB	SO	AVG	OBP	SLG	PRO+	BR/A	SB	CS	SBR	FA	FR	G/POS	TPR
1875	RS-n	19	75	5	15	3	0	0				.200	.200	.240	57	-3						O-18	-0.2
1877	StL-N	54	220	23	51	5	2	0	27	1	15	.232	.235	.273	63	-9				.971	-3	1-28,O-25/2	-1.1
1878	Ind-N	60	222	22	35	6	0	0	16	5	23	.158	.176	.185	22	-18				.963	-1	*1-51/O-9	-2.0
Total	2	114	442	45	86	11	2	0	43	6	38	.195	.205	.229	43	-26				.965	-4	/1-79,O-34,2	-3.1

■ HARRY CROFT
Croft, Henry T.   b: 8/1/1875, Chicago, Ill.   d: 12/11/33, Oak Park, Ill.   Deb: 5/19/1899

YEAR	TM/L	G	AB	R	H	2B	3B	HR	RBI	BB	SO	AVG	OBP	SLG	PRO+	BR/A	SB	CS	SBR	FA	FR	G/POS	TPR
1899	Lou-N	2	2	0	0	0	0	0	0	0		.000	.000	.000	-99	-1	0			.000	0	/H	0.0
	Phi-N	2	7	0	1	0	0	0	0	0	1	.143	.250	.143	9	-1	0			1.000	-1	/2-2	-0.1
	Yr	4	9	0	1	0	0	0	0	0	1	.111	.200	.111	-14	-1	0			1.000	-1	/2-2	-0.1
1901	Chi-N	3	12	1	4	0	0	0	0	0		.333	.333	.333	97	-0	0			1.000	2	/O-3	0.2
Total	2	7	21	1	5	0	0	0	0	4	1	.238	.273	.238	47	-1	0			1.000	2	/O-3,2-2	0.1

■ FRED CROLIUS
Crolius, Fred Joseph   b: 12/16/1876, Jersey City, N.J.   d: 8/25/60, Ormond Beach, Fla.   Deb: 4/19/01

YEAR	TM/L	G	AB	R	H	2B	3B	HR	RBI	BB	SO	AVG	OBP	SLG	PRO+	BR/A	SB	CS	SBR	FA	FR	G/POS	TPR
1901	Bos-N	49	200	22	48	4	1	1	13	9		.240	.306	.285	66	-9	6			.850	-8	O-49	-2.0
1902	Pit-N	9	38	4	10	2	1	0	7	0		.263	.263	.368	91	-1	0			1.000	-1	/O-9	-0.2
Total	2	58	238	26	58	6	2	1	20	9		.244	.300	.298	69	-9	6			.868	-8	O-58	-2.2

■ WARREN CROMARTIE
Cromartie, Warren Livingston   b: 9/29/53, Miami Beach, Fla.   BL/TL, 6', 192 lbs.   Deb: 9/6/74

YEAR	TM/L	G	AB	R	H	2B	3B	HR	RBI	BB	SO	AVG	OBP	SLG	PRO+	BR/A	SB	CS	SBR	FA	FR	G/POS	TPR
1974	Mon-N	8	17	2	3	0	0	0	0	3	3	.176	.300	.176	34	-1	1	0		1.000	-1	/O-6	-0.2
1976	Mon-N	33	81	8	17	1	0	0	2	1	5	.210	.220	.222	25	-4	1	2	-1	.943	-2	O-20	-1.2
1977	Mon-N	155	620	64	175	41	7	5	50	33	40	.282	.323	.395	94	-6	10	3	1	.976	12	*O-155	0.1
1978	Mon-N	159	607	77	180	32	6	10	56	33	60	.297	.340	.418	112	9	8	8	-2	.978	25	*O-158/1-4	2.5
1979	Mon-N	158	659	84	181	46	5	8	46	38	78	.275	.315	.396	94	-7	3	4	-2	.976	20	*O-158	0.5
1980	Mon-N	162	597	74	172	33	5	14	70	51	64	.288	.346	.430	115	12	8	8	-2	.991	-4	*1-158/O-2	-0.5
1981	*Mon-N	99	358	41	109	19	2	6	42	39	27	.304	.373	.419	123	11	2	3	-1	.992	7	1-62/O-38	0.5
1982	Mon-N	144	497	59	126	24	3	14	62	69	60	.254	.348	.398	106	5	3	0	1	.979	11	*O-136/1-9	1.4
1983	Mon-N	120	360	37	100	26	2	3	43	43	48	.278	.356	.386	116	4	8	3	1	.973	12	*O-101/1-1	1.5
1991	KC-A	69	131	13	41	7	2	1	20	15	18	.313	.384	.420	122	4	1	3	-2	.996	-4	1-29/O-6,D	-0.3
Total	10	1107	3927	459	1104	229	32	61	391	325	403	.281	.339	.402	105	22	50	37	-7	.977	68	O-780,1-263/D	4.3

■ TRIPP CROMER
Cromer, Roy Bunyan   b: 11/21/67, Lake City, S.C.   BR/TR, 6'2", 165 lbs.   Deb: 9/7/93

YEAR	TM/L	G	AB	R	H	2B	3B	HR	RBI	BB	SO	AVG	OBP	SLG	PRO+	BR/A	SB	CS	SBR	FA	FR	G/POS	TPR
1993	StL-N	10	23	1	2	0	0	0	1	0	6	.087	.125	.087	-43	-5	0	0	0	.912	1	/S-9	-0.3
1994	StL-N	2	0	0	0	0	0	0	0	0	0					0	0	0	0	.000	-1	/S-2	-0.1
Total	2	12	23	1	2	0	0	0	1	0	6	.087	.125	.087	-43	-5	0	0	0	.886	0	/S-11	-0.4

■ NED CROMPTON
Crompton, Edward   b: 2/12/1889, Liverpool, England   d: 9/28/50, Aspinwall, Pa.   BL/TL, 5'10.5", 175 lbs.   Deb: 9/13/09

YEAR	TM/L	G	AB	R	H	2B	3B	HR	RBI	BB	SO	AVG	OBP	SLG	PRO+	BR/A	SB	CS	SBR	FA	FR	G/POS	TPR
1909	StL-A	17	63	7	10	2	1	0	2	7		.159	.254	.222	54	-3	1			.909	1	O-17	-0.3
1910	Cin-N	1	2	0	0	0	0	0	0	0	2	.000	.000	.000	-99	-1	0			.000	-1	/O-1	-0.1
Total	2	18	65	7	10	2	1	0	2	7	2	.154	.247	.215	49	-4	1			.909	1	/O-18	-0.4

YEAR	TM/L	G	AB	R	H	2B	3B	HR	RBI	BB	SO	AVG	OBP	SLG	PRO+	BR/A	SB	CS	SBR	FA	FR	G/POS	TPR

■ HERB CROMPTON
Crompton, Herbert Bryan "Workhorse" b: 11/7/11, Taylor Ridge, Ill. d: 8/5/63, Moline, Ill. BR/TR, 6', 185 lbs. Deb: 4/26/37

YEAR	TM/L	G	AB	R	H	2B	3B	HR	RBI	BB	SO	AVG	OBP	SLG	PRO+	BR/A	SB	CS	SBR	FA	FR	G/POS	TPR
1937	Was-A	2	3	0	1	0	0	0	0	0	0	.333 .333 .333	72	-0	0	0	0	1.000	0	/C-2	0.0
1945	NY-A	36	99	6	19	3	0	0	12	2	7	.192 .208 .222	24	-10	0	0	0	.984	1	/C-33	-0.8
Total	2	38	102	6	20	3	0	0	12	2	7	.196 .212 .225	25	-10	0	0	0	.984	1	/C-35	-0.8

■ CHRIS CRON
Cron, Christopher John b: 3/31/64, Albuquerque, N.Mex. BR/TR, 6'2", 200 lbs. Deb: 8/15/91

YEAR	TM/L	G	AB	R	H	2B	3B	HR	RBI	BB	SO	AVG	OBP	SLG	PRO+	BR/A	SB	CS	SBR	FA	FR	G/POS	TPR
1991	Cal-A	6	15	0	2	0	0	0	0	2	5	.133 .235 .133	5	-2	0	0	0	1.000	2	/1-5,D-1	-0.1
1992	Chi-A	6	10	0	0	0	0	0	0	0	4	.000 .000 .000	-99	-3	0	0	0	.923	-1	/1-5,O-1	-0.3
Total	2	12	25	0	2	0	0	0	0	2	9	.080 .148 .080	-35	-5	0	0	0	.980	1	/1-10,O-1,D	-0.4

■ DAN CRONIN
Cronin, Daniel T. b: 4/1/1857, S.Boston, Mass. d: 11/30/1885, Boston, Mass. 5'8", 170 lbs. Deb: 7/9/1884

YEAR	TM/L	G	AB	R	H	2B	3B	HR	RBI	BB	SO	AVG	OBP	SLG	PRO+	BR/A	SB	CS	SBR	FA	FR	G/POS	TPR
1884	CP-U	1	4	1	1	0	0	0		0		.250 .250 .250	36	-0				.200	-2	/2-1	-0.2
	StL-U	1	5	0	0	0	0	0		0		.000 .000 .000	-97	-1				.000	-1	/O-1	-0.2
	Yr	2	9	1	1	0	0	0		0		.111 .111 .111	-39	-2				.000	-3	/2-1,O-1	-0.4

■ JIM CRONIN
Cronin, James John b: 8/7/05, Richmond, Cal. d: 6/10/83, Concord, Cal. BB/TR, 5'10.5", 150 lbs. Deb: 7/4/29

YEAR	TM/L	G	AB	R	H	2B	3B	HR	RBI	BB	SO	AVG	OBP	SLG	PRO+	BR/A	SB	CS	SBR	FA	FR	G/POS	TPR
1929	Phi-A	25	56	7	13	2	1	0	4	5	7	.232 .295 .304	52	-4	0	0	0	.966	5	2-10/S-9,3	0.2

■ JOE CRONIN
Cronin, Joseph Edward b: 10/12/06, San Francisco, Cal d: 9/7/84, Osterville, Mass. BR/TR, 5'11.5", 180 lbs. Deb: 4/29/26 MH

YEAR	TM/L	G	AB	R	H	2B	3B	HR	RBI	BB	SO	AVG	OBP	SLG	PRO+	BR/A	SB	CS	SBR	FA	FR	G/POS	TPR
1926	Pit-N	38	83	9	22	2	2	0	11	6	15	.265 .315 .337	72	-3	0			.977	6	2-27/S-7	0.3
1927	Pit-N	12	22	2	5	1	0	0	3	2	3	.227 .292 .273	48	-2	0			1.000	-4	/2-7,S-4,1	-0.5
1928	Was-A	63	227	23	55	10	4	0	25	22	27	.242 .309 .322	66	-11	4	0	1	.953	8	S-63	0.5
1929	Was-A	145	494	72	139	29	8	8	61	85	37	.281 .388 .421	107	8	5	9	-4	.923	6	*S-143/2-1	2.6
1930	Was-A	154	587	127	203	41	9	13	126	72	36	.346 .422 .513	135	33	17	10	-1	.960	26	*S-154	6.7
1931	Was-A	156	611	103	187	44	13	12	126	81	52	.306 .391 .480	127	25	10	9	-2	.950	13	*S-155	4.6
1932	Was-A	143	557	95	177	43	**18**	6	116	66	45	.318 .393 .492	129	25	7	5	-1	**.959**	6	*S-141	3.9
1933	*Was-A★	152	602	89	186	45	11	5	118	87	49	.309 .398 .445	124	23	5	4	-1	**.960**	10	*S-152,M	4.0
1934	Was-A★	127	504	68	143	30	9	7	101	53	28	.284 .353 .421	103	1	8	0	2	.951	18	*S-127,M	2.7
1935	Bos-A★	144	556	70	164	37	14	9	95	63	40	.295 .370 .460	106	5	3	3	-1	.949	-13	*S-139/1-2M	-0.2
1936	Bos-A	81	295	36	83	22	4	2	43	32	21	.281 .354 .403	82	-9	1	3	-2	.930	-2	S-60,3-21M	-0.7
1937	Bos-A★	148	570	102	175	40	4	18	110	84	73	.307 .402 .486	118	17	5	3	-0	.958	-13	*S-148,M	1.3
1938	Bos-A★	143	530	98	172	**51**	5	17	94	91	60	.325 .428 .536	134	29	7	5	-1	.954	7	*S-142,M	4.2
1939	Bos-A★	143	520	97	160	33	3	19	107	87	48	.308 .407 .492	124	20	6	6	-2	.959	6	*S-142,M	3.4
1940	Bos-A	149	548	104	156	35	6	24	111	83	65	.285 .380 .502	122	17	7	5	-1	.948	2	*S-146/3-2M	2.9
1941	Bos-A★	143	518	98	161	38	8	16	95	82	55	.311 .406 .508	137	29	1	4	-2	.958	-8	*S-119,3-22/OM	2.7
1942	Bos-A	45	79	7	24	3	0	4	24	15	21	.304 .415 .494	150	6	0	1	-1	.865	-1	3-11/1-5,SM	0.4
1943	Bos-A	59	77	8	24	4	0	5	29	11	4	.312 .398 .558	176	7	0	0	0	.968	1	3-10,M	0.8
1944	Bos-A	76	191	24	46	7	0	5	28	34	19	.241 .358 .356	106	3	1	4	-2	.981	-2	1-49,M	-0.4
1945	Bos-A	3	8	1	3	0	0	0	1	3	2	.375 .545 .375	165	1	0	0	0	1.000	1	/3-3,M	0.2
Total	20	2124	7579	1233	2285	515	118	170	1424	1059	700	.301 .390 .468	119	223	87	71		.951	68	*S-1843/3-69,120	39.4

■ BILL CRONIN
Cronin, William Patrick "Crungy" b: 12/26/02, W.Newton, Mass. d: 10/26/66, Newton, Mass. BR/TR, 5'9", 167 lbs. Deb: 7/4/28

YEAR	TM/L	G	AB	R	H	2B	3B	HR	RBI	BB	SO	AVG	OBP	SLG	PRO+	BR/A	SB	CS	SBR	FA	FR	G/POS	TPR
1928	Bos-N	3	2	1	0	0	0	0	0	1	0	.000 .333 .000	-6	-0	0			1.000	-0	/C-3	0.0
1929	Bos-N	6	9	0	1	0	0	0	0	0	0	.111 .111 .111	-47	-2	0			1.000	1	/C-6	-0.1
1930	Bos-N	66	178	19	45	9	1	0	17	4	8	.253 .277 .315	44	-16	0			.983	7	C-64	-0.4
1931	Bos-N	51	107	8	22	6	1	0	10	7	5	.206 .267 .280	49	-8	0			.941	1	C-50	-0.5
Total	4	126	296	28	68	15	2	0	27	12	13	.230 .269 .294	43	-26	0			.968	9	C-123	-1.0

■ TOM CROOKE
Crooke, Thomas Aloysius b: 7/26/1884, Washington, D.C. d: 4/5/29, Quantico, Va. BR/TR, 6', 180 lbs. Deb: 9/29/09

YEAR	TM/L	G	AB	R	H	2B	3B	HR	RBI	BB	SO	AVG	OBP	SLG	PRO+	BR/A	SB	CS	SBR	FA	FR	G/POS	TPR
1909	Was-A	3	7	2	2	1	0	0	2	2		.286 .444 .429	184	1	1			.969	-1	/1-3	0.0
1910	Was-A	8	21	1	4	1	0	0	1	1		.190 .227 .238	48	-1	0			1.000	-0	/1-5	-0.2
Total	2	11	28	3	6	2	0	0	3	3		.214 .290 .286	85	-0	1			.988	-1	/1-8	-0.2

■ JACK CROOKS
Crooks, John Charles b: 11/9/1865, St.Paul, Minn. d: 2/2/18, St.Louis, Mo. BR/TR, 5'10", 170 lbs. Deb: 9/26/1889 M

YEAR	TM/L	G	AB	R	H	2B	3B	HR	RBI	BB	SO	AVG	OBP	SLG	PRO+	BR/A	SB	CS	SBR	FA	FR	G/POS	TPR
1889	Col-a	12	43	13	14	2	3	0	7	10	4	.326 .463 .512	187	6	10			.987	5	2-12	0.9
1890	Col-a	135	485	86	107	5	4	1		96		.221 .357 .254	86	-1	57			.937	-4	*2-134/3-1,O	0.3
1891	Col-a	138	519	110	127	19	13	0	46	103	47	.245 .379 .331	110	13	50			**.957**	20	*2-138	3.3
1892	StL-N	128	445	82	95	7	4	7	38	**136**	52	.213 .400 .294	116	20	23			.929	-7	*2-101,3-25/OM	1.5
1893	StL-N	128	448	93	106	10	9	1	48	**121**	37	.237 .408 .306	91	2	31			.908	4	*3-123/S-4,C	0.7
1895	Was-N	117	409	80	114	19	8	6	57	68	39	.279 .392 .408	108	7	36			**.956**	12	*2-117	2.1
1896	Was-N	25	84	20	24	3	0	3	20	16	8	.286 .406 .429	120	3	2			.916	3	2-20/3-4	0.1
	Lou-N	39	122	19	29	5	1	2	15	20	8	.238 .354 .344	88	-2	8			.925	5	2-39	0.5
	Yr	64	206	39	53	8	1	5	35	36	16	.257 .376 .379	101	2	10			.922	2	2-59/3-4	0.6
1898	StL-N	72	225	33	52	4	2	1	20	40		.231 .359 .280	82	-3	3			.959	7	2-66/3-3,SO	0.5
Total	8	794	2780	536	668	74	44	21	251	610	195	.240 .385 .321	102	44	220			.946	39	2-627,3-156/SOC	10.1

■ ED CROSBY
Crosby, Edward Carlton b: 5/26/49, Long Beach, Cal. BL/TR, 6'2", 180 lbs. Deb: 7/12/70

YEAR	TM/L	G	AB	R	H	2B	3B	HR	RBI	BB	SO	AVG	OBP	SLG	PRO+	BR/A	SB	CS	SBR	FA	FR	G/POS	TPR
1970	StL-N	38	95	9	24	4	1	0	6	7	5	.253 .311 .316	67	-4	0	0	0	.954	-1	S-35/3-3,2	-0.2
1972	StL-N	101	276	27	60	9	1	0	19	18	27	.217 .270 .257	51	-18	1	1	0	.979	-6	S-43,2-38,3	-1.9
1973	StL-N	22	39	4	5	2	1	0	1	4	4	.128 .209 .231	22	-4	0	0	0	.938	-3	/S-7,2-5,3	-0.7
	*Cin-N	36	51	4	11	1	1	0	5	7	12	.216 .333 .275	74	-2	0	0	-1	.953	5	S-29/2-5	0.5
	Yr	58	90	8	16	3	2	0	6	11	16	.178 .282 .256	52	-6	0	1	-1	.950	2	S-36,2-10/3	-0.2
1974	Cle-A	37	86	11	18	3	0	0	6	6	12	.209 .261 .244	46	-6	0	1	-1	.926	-10	3-18,S-13/2	-1.6
1975	Cle-A	61	128	12	30	3	0	0	7	13	14	.234 .305 .258	60	-6	0	4	-2	.974	4	S-30,2-19,3	-0.7
1976	Cle-A	2	2	0	1	0	0	0	0	0	0	.500 .500 .500	195	0	0	0	0	1.000	1	/3-1,D-1	0.1
Total	6	297	677	67	149	22	4	0	44	55	74	.220 .284 .264	55	-40	1	7	-4	.964	-11	S-157/2-72,3D	-4.0

■ FRANKIE CROSETTI
Crosetti, Frank Peter Joseph "Crow" b: 10/4/10, San Francisco, Cal. BR/TR, 5'10", 165 lbs. Deb: 4/12/32 C

YEAR	TM/L	G	AB	R	H	2B	3B	HR	RBI	BB	SO	AVG	OBP	SLG	PRO+	BR/A	SB	CS	SBR	FA	FR	G/POS	TPR
1932	*NY-A	116	398	47	96	20	9	5	57	51	51	.241 .335 .374	88	-7	3	2	-0	.937	-5	S-84,3-33/2	-0.4
1933	NY-A	136	451	71	114	20	5	9	60	55	40	.253 .337 .379	95	-3	4	1	1	.936	-8	*S-133	-0.2
1934	NY-A	138	554	85	147	22	10	11	67	61	58	.265 .344 .401	98	-3	5	6	-2	.945	-10	*S-119,3-23/2	-0.6
1935	NY-A	87	305	49	78	17	6	8	50	41	27	.256 .351 .430	107	3	3	1	0	.963	-7	S-87	0.1
1936	*NY-A★	151	632	137	182	35	7	15	78	90	83	.288 .387 .437	107	8	18	7	1	.948	-8	*S-151	1.0
1937	*NY-A	149	611	127	143	29	5	11	49	86	105	.234 .340 .352	74	-24	13	7	-0	.948	-8	*S-147	-1.1
1938	*NY-A	157	631	113	166	35	4	9	55	106	97	.263 .382 .371	90	-7	**27**	12	1	.948	18	*S-157	2.2
1939	*NY-A☆	152	656	109	153	25	5	10	56	65	81	.233 .315 .332	67	-33	11	7	-1	**.968**	8	*S-152	-1.2
1940	NY-A	145	546	84	106	23	4	4	31	72	77	.194 .299 .273	52	-39	14	8	-1	.954	-14	*S-145	-4.0
1941	NY-A	50	148	13	33	4	2	1	22	18	14	.223 .320 .284	62	-8	0	2	-1	.944	10	S-32,3-13	0.3
1942	*NY-A	74	285	50	69	5	4	4	23	31	31	.242 .335 .337	91	-3	1	1	-0	.951	-3	3-62/S-8,2	-0.4
1943	*NY-A	95	348	36	81	8	1	2	20	36	43	.233 .317 .279	74	-10	4	4	-1	.946	3	S-90	-0.9
1944	NY-A	55	197	20	47	4	2	1	30	11	21	.239 .299 .355	84	-5	3	0	1	.960	-9	S-55	-0.9
1945	NY-A	130	441	57	105	12	6	4	48	59	65	.238 .341 .293	81	-8	0	3	-1	.946	-8	*S-126	-0.5
1946	NY-A	28	59	4	17	0	0	3	8	2	8	.288 .382 .339	101	1	0	3	-2	.940	7	S-24	0.7
1947	NY-A	3	1	0	0	0	0	0	0	0	0	.000 .000 .000	-99	-0	0	0	0	.000	0	/2-1,S-1	0.0

YEAR	TM/L	G	AB	R	H	2B	3B	HR	RBI	BB	SO	AVG	OBP	SLG	PRO+	BR/A	SB	CS	SBR	FA	FR	G/POS	TPR
1948	NY-A	17	14	4	4	0	1	0	0	2	0	.286	.375	.429	115	0	0	0	0	1.000	0	/2-6,S-5	0.1
Total	17	1683	6277	1006	1541	260	65	98	649	792	799	.245	.341	.354	84	-137	113	62	-3	.949	-24	*S-1516,3-131/2	-5.1

■ AMOS CROSS
Cross, Amos C.   b: 1861, Czechoslovakia   d: 7/16/1888, Cleveland, Ohio   Deb: 4/22/1885   F

YEAR	TM/L	G	AB	R	H	2B	3B	HR	RBI	BB	SO	AVG	OBP	SLG	PRO+	BR/A	SB	CS	SBR	FA	FR	G/POS	TPR
1885	Lou-a	35	130	11	37	2	1	0		0		.285	.290	.315	91	-2				.936	-1	C-35	0.0
1886	Lou-a	74	283	51	78	14	6	1	44			.276	.375	.378	129	10	13			.910	-16	C-51,1-20/SO	-0.3
1887	Lou-a	8	28	0	3	0	0	0		1		.107	.138	.107	-31	-5	0			.808	-4	/C-5,1-2,O	-0.8
Total	3	117	441	62	118	16	7	1	45			.268	.338	.342	108	4	13			.916	-22	/C-91,1-22,OS	-1.1

■ CLARENCE CROSS
Cross, Clarence (b: Clarence Crause)   b: 3/4/1856, St.Louis, Mo.   d: 6/23/31, Seattle, Wash.   Deb: 5/5/1884

YEAR	TM/L	G	AB	R	H	2B	3B	HR	RBI	BB	SO	AVG	OBP	SLG	PRO+	BR/A	SB	CS	SBR	FA	FR	G/POS	TPR
1884	Alt-U	2	7	1	4	1	0	0		2		.571	.667	.714	272	2				.500	-2	/3-2	0.0
	Phi-U	2	9	0	2	0	0	0		0		.222	.222	.222	23	-1				.545	-2	/S-2	-0.2
	KC-U	25	93	13	20	1	0	0		6		.215	.263	.226	39	-8				.836	3	S-24/3-1	-0.4
	Yr	29	109	14	26	2	0	0		8		.239	.291	.257	57	-6				.813	-1	S-26/3-3	-0.6
1887	NY-a	16	55	9	11	2	1	0		2		.200	.267	.273	53	-3	0			.833	-3	/S-13/3-4	-0.5
Total	2	45	164	23	37	4	1	0		10		.226	.282	.262	55	-10	0			.818	-4	/S-39,3-7	-1.1

■ FRANK CROSS
Cross, Frank Atwell "Mickey"   b: 1/20/1873, Cleveland, Ohio   d: 11/2/32, Geauga Lake, Ohio   TR   Deb: 5/20/01   F

YEAR	TM/L	G	AB	R	H	2B	3B	HR	RBI	BB	SO	AVG	OBP	SLG	PRO+	BR/A	SB	CS	SBR	FA	FR	G/POS	TPR
1901	Cle-A	1	5	0	3	0	0	0				.600	.600	.600	243	1				.000	-0	/O-1	0.0

■ JEFF CROSS
Cross, Joffre James   b: 8/28/18, Tulsa, Okla.   BR/TR, 5'11", 160 lbs.   Deb: 9/27/42

YEAR	TM/L	G	AB	R	H	2B	3B	HR	RBI	BB	SO	AVG	OBP	SLG	PRO+	BR/A	SB	CS	SBR	FA	FR	G/POS	TPR
1942	StL-N	1	4	0	1	0	0	0		0		.250	.250	.250	43	-0	0			1.000	-1	/S-1	-0.1
1946	StL-N	49	69	17	15	3	0	0	6	10	8	.217	.316	.261	62	-3	4			.970	6	S-17/2-8,3	0.3
1947	StL-N	51	49	4	5	1	0	0	3	10	6	.102	.254	.122	3	-7	0			.947	5	3-15,S-14/2	-0.1
1948	StL-N	2	0	0	0	0	0	0	0	0	0	—	—	—	—	0	0			.000	-0	R	0.0
	Chi-N	16	20	1	2	0	0	0	0	0	4	.100	.100	.100	-48	-4	0			.786	-4	/S-9,2-1	-0.8
	Yr	18	20	1	2	0	0	0	0	0	4	.100	.100	.100	-47	-4	0			.786	-4	/S-9,2-1	-0.8
Total	4	119	142	22	23	4	0	0	10	20	18	.162	.265	.190	26	-14	4			.932	7	/S-41,3-16,2	-0.7

■ LAVE CROSS
Cross, Lafayette Napoleon   b: 5/12/1866, Milwaukee, Wis.   d: 9/6/27, Toledo, Ohio   BR/TR, 5'8.5", 155 lbs.   Deb: 4/23/1887   FM

YEAR	TM/L	G	AB	R	H	2B	3B	HR	RBI	BB	SO	AVG	OBP	SLG	PRO+	BR/A	SB	CS	SBR	FA	FR	G/POS	TPR
1887	Lou-a	54	203	32	54	8	3	0		15		.266	.320	.335	81	-5	15			.916	-3	C-44,O-10	-0.3
1888	Lou-a	47	181	20	41	3	0	0	15	2		.227	.239	.243	56	-9	10			.929	1	C-37,O-12/S	-0.5
1889	Phi-a	55	199	22	44	8	2	0	23	14	9	.221	.272	.281	58	-11	11			.934	19	C-55	1.1
1890	Phi-P	63	245	42	73	7	8	3	47	12	6	.298	.343	.429	100	-2	5			.885	2	C-49,O-15	0.0
1891	Phi-a	110	402	66	121	20	14	5	52	38	23	.301	.366	.458	131	14	14			.971	-4	O-43,C-43,3/S2	1.2
1892	Phi-N	140	541	84	149	15	10	4	69	39	16	.275	.328	.362	109	5	18			.921	-2	3-65,C-39,O2/S	0.6
1893	Phi-N	96	415	81	124	17	6	4	78	26	7	.299	.342	.398	96	-4	18			.974	15	C-40,3-30,OS/1	1.3
1894	Phi-N	119	529	123	204	34	9	7	125	29	7	.386	.421	.524	130	25	21			.919	20	*3-100,C-16/S2	3.6
1895	Phi-N	125	535	95	145	26	9	2	101	35	8	.271	.319	.364	76	-21	21			**.940**	34	*3-125	1.2
1896	Phi-N	106	406	63	104	23	5	1	73	32	14	.256	.312	.345	74	-16	8			.937	13	3-61,S-37/20C	0.0
1897	Phi-N	88	344	37	89	17	5	3	51	10		.259	.282	.363	71	-16	10			.912	2	3-47,2-38/OS	-0.9
1898	StL-N	151	602	71	191	28	8	3	79	28		.317	.348	.405	113	7	14			**.945**	18	*3-149/S-2	2.5
1899	Cle-N	38	154	15	44	5	0	1	20	7		.286	.325	.338	88	-3	2			.955	4	3-38,M	0.1
	StL-N	103	403	61	122	14	5	4	64	17		.303	.333	.392	96	-4	11			.960	29	*3-103	2.4
	Yr	141	557	76	166	19	5	5	84	25		.298	.330	.377	94	-6	13			**.959**	33	*3-141	2.5
1900	StL-N	16	61	6	18	1	0	0	6	1		.295	.306	.311	71	-2	1			.962	1	3-16	-0.1
	*Bro-N	117	461	73	135	14	4	4	67	25		.293	.332	.375	90	-8	20			.943	3	*3-117	-0.4
	Yr	133	522	79	153	15	4	4	73	26		.293	.329	.368	88	-10	21			**.945**	4	*3-133	-0.5
1901	Phi-A	100	424	82	139	28	12	0	73	19		.328	.358	.465	121	10	23			.919	5	*3-100	1.5
1902	Phi-A	137	559	90	191	39	8	0	108	27		.342	.374	.440	120	14	25			.942	7	*3-137	2.1
1903	Phi-A	137	559	60	163	22	4	2	90	10		.292	.304	.356	93	-6	14			.950	-3	*3-136/1-1	-0.7
1904	Phi-A	155	607	73	176	31	10	0	71	13		.290	.310	.379	112	-8	10			.936	-10	*3-155	0.1
1905	*Phi-A	147	587	69	156	29	5	0	77	26		.266	.299	.332	98	-2	8			.928	-9	*3-147	-0.7
1906	Was-A	130	494	55	130	14	6	1	46	28		.263	.303	.322	100	-1	19			**.952**	-4	*3-130	0.0
1907	Was-A	41	161	13	32	8	0	0	10	10		.199	.246	.248	62	-7	3			.978	7	3-41	-0.1
Total	21	2275	9072	1333	2645	411	135	47	1345	464	90	.292	.328	.382	99	-34	301			.938	145	*3-1721,C-324,O/S21	14.5

■ MONTE CROSS
Cross, Montford Montgomery   b: 8/31/1869, Philadelphia, Pa.   d: 6/21/34, Philadelphia, Pa.   BR/TR, 5'8.5", 148 lbs.   Deb: 9/27/1892   U

YEAR	TM/L	G	AB	R	H	2B	3B	HR	RBI	BB	SO	AVG	OBP	SLG	PRO+	BR/A	SB	CS	SBR	FA	FR	G/POS	TPR
1892	Bal-N	15	50	5	8	0	0	0		4	10	.160	.222	.160	16	-5	2			.864	-3	S-15	-0.7
1894	Pit-N	13	43	14	19	1	5	2	13	5	4	.442	.520	.837	225	9	6			.924	2	S-13	0.8
1895	Pit-N	108	393	67	101	14	13	3	54	38	38	.257	.327	.382	87	-8	39			.883	-13	*S-107/2-1	-1.3
1896	StL-N	125	427	66	104	10	6	6	52	58	48	.244	.342	.337	83	-9	40			.892	-12	*S-125	-1.4
1897	StL-N	131	462	59	132	17	11	4	55	62		.286	.379	.396	107	6	38			.920	28	*S-131	3.2
1898	Phi-N	149	525	68	135	25	5	1	50	55		.257	.337	.330	95	-2	20			.907	15	*S-149	1.8
1899	Phi-N	154	557	85	143	25	6	3	65	56		.257	.335	.339	88	-8	26			.909	2	*S-154	0.5
1900	Phi-N	131	466	59	94	11	3	3	62	51		.202	.289	.258	52	-30	19			.928	-3	*S-131	-2.0
1901	Phi-N	139	483	49	95	14	1	1	44	52		.197	.281	.236	50	-30	24			.924	-16	*S-139	-3.4
1902	Phi-A	137	497	72	115	22	2	3	59	32		.231	.289	.302	61	-26	17			.927	11	*S-137	-0.7
1903	Phi-A	137	470	44	116	21	2	3	45	49		.247	.326	.319	90	-4	31			.940	8	*S-137/2-1	1.0
1904	Phi-A	153	503	33	95	23	4	1	38	46		.189	.266	.256	62	-20	19			.937	-16	*S-153	-3.6
1905	*Phi-A	79	252	28	67	17	0	0	24	19		.266	.332	.349	114	4	8			.929	-5	S-77/2-2	0.1
1906	Phi-A	134	445	32	89	23	3	1	40	50		.200	.291	.272	74	-12	22			.938	4	*S-134	-0.4
1907	Phi-A	77	248	37	51	9	5	0	18	39		.206	.316	.282	89	-2	17			.954	13	S-74	1.4
Total	15	1682	5821	718	1364	232	68	31	621	616	100	.234	.316	.314	80	-138	328			.920	15	*S-1676/2-4	-4.7

■ FRANK CROSSIN
Crossin, Frank Patrick   b: 6/15/1891, Avondale, Pa.   d: 12/6/65, Kingston, Pa.   BR/TR, 5'10", 160 lbs.   Deb: 9/24/12

YEAR	TM/L	G	AB	R	H	2B	3B	HR	RBI	BB	SO	AVG	OBP	SLG	PRO+	BR/A	SB	CS	SBR	FA	FR	G/POS	TPR
1912	StL-A	8	22	2	5	0	0	0	2	1		.227	.261	.227	41	-2	1			.920	-5	/C-8	-0.6
1913	StL-A	4	4	1	1	0	0	0	0	1		.250	.500	.250	124	0	0			.857	-1	/C-2	0.0
1914	StL-A	43	90	5	11	1	1	0	5	10	10	.122	.225	.156	15	-9	3			.934	-1	C-41	-0.7
Total	3	55	116	8	17	1	1	0	7	12	11	.147	.244	.172	25	-10	4			.930	-6	/C-51	-1.3

■ JOE CROTTY
Crotty, Joseph P.   b: 12/24/1860, Cincinnati, O.   d: 6/22/26, Minneapolis, Minn   BR/TR,   Deb: 5/4/1882

YEAR	TM/L	G	AB	R	H	2B	3B	HR	RBI	BB	SO	AVG	OBP	SLG	PRO+	BR/A	SB	CS	SBR	FA	FR	G/POS	TPR
1882	Lou-a	5	20	1	2	0	0	0		0		.100	.100	.100	-34	-3				.882	-0	/C-5	-0.3
	StL-a	8	28	2	4	1	0	0		3		.143	.226	.179	37	-2				.882	-1	C-7,O-1	-0.3
	Yr	13	48	3	6	1	0	0		3		.125	.176	.146	10	-4				.882	-2	C-12/O-1	-0.6
1884	Cin-U	21	84	11	22	4	2	1		1		.262	.271	.393	72	-4				.896	-7	C-21	-0.8
1885	Lou-a	39	129	14	20	2	0	0		3		.155	.193	.171	15	-12				.931	1	C-38/1-1	-0.7
1886	NY-a	14	47	6	8	0	1	0		4		.170	.250	.213	48	-3	3			.933	-3	C-14	-0.3
Total	4	87	308	34	56	7	3	1		11		.182	.220	.234	38	-23	3			.915	-10	/C-85,1-1,O	-2.4

■ JACK CROUCH
Crouch, Jack Albert "Roxy"   b: 6/12/03, Salisbury, N.C.   d: 8/25/72, Leesburg, Fla.   BR/TR, 5'9", 165 lbs.   Deb: 9/18/30

YEAR	TM/L	G	AB	R	H	2B	3B	HR	RBI	BB	SO	AVG	OBP	SLG	PRO+	BR/A	SB	CS	SBR	FA	FR	G/POS	TPR
1930	StL-A	6	14	1	2	1	0	0	1	2		.143	.200	.214	5	-2	0	0	0	1.000	1	/C-5	-0.1
1931	StL-A	8	12	0	0	0	0	0	0	3		.000	.000	.000	-97	-3	0	0	0	.895	1	/C-7	-0.3
1933	StL-A	19	30	1	5	0	0	0	1	2		.167	.219	.267	26	-3	0	0	0	1.000	-1	/C-9	-0.3

YEAR	TM/L	G	AB	R	H	2B	3B	HR	RBI	BB	SO	AVG	OBP	SLG	PRO+	BR/A	SB	CS	SBR	FA	FR	G/POS	TPR
	Cin-N	10	16	5	2	0	0	0	1	0	0	.125	.222	.125	1	-2	1			1.000	2	/C-6	0.0
Total	3	43	72	7	9	1	0	1	8	3	13	.125	.182	.181	-3	-11	1	0		.976	3	/C-27	-0.7

■ FRANK CROUCHER
Croucher, Frank Donald "Dingle" b: 7/23/14, San Antonio, Tex. d: 5/21/80, Houston, Tex. BR/TR, 5'11", 165 lbs. Deb: 4/18/39

YEAR	TM/L	G	AB	R	H	2B	3B	HR	RBI	BB	SO	AVG	OBP	SLG	PRO+	BR/A	SB	CS	SBR	FA	FR	G/POS	TPR
1939	Det-A	97	324	38	87	15	0	5	40	16	42	.269	.303	.361	64	-18	2	2	-1	.934	-8	S-93/2-3	-1.8
1940	*Det-A	37	57	3	6	0	0	0	2	4	5	.105	.164	.105	-26	-11	0	0	0	.936	-2	S-26/2-7,3	-1.1
1941	Det-A	136	489	51	124	21	4	2	39	33	72	.254	.305	.325	61	-28	2	0	1	.935	-3	*S-136	-2.0
1942	Was-A	26	65	2	18	1	1	0	5	3	9	.277	.309	.323	79	-2	0	0	0	.950	5	2-18	0.4
Total	4	296	935	94	235	37	5	7	86	56	128	.251	.296	.324	58	-59	4	2	0	.934	-8	S-255/2-28,3	-4.5

■ BUCK CROUSE
Crouse, Clyde Elsworth b: 1/6/1897, Anderson, Ind. d: 10/23/83, Muncie, Ind. BL/TR, 5'8", 158 lbs. Deb: 8/1/23

YEAR	TM/L	G	AB	R	H	2B	3B	HR	RBI	BB	SO	AVG	OBP	SLG	PRO+	BR/A	SB	CS	SBR	FA	FR	G/POS	TPR
1923	Chi-A	23	70	6	18	2	1	1	7	3	4	.257	.297	.357	73	-3	0	0		.955	-2	C-22	-0.4
1924	Chi-A	94	305	30	79	10	1	1	44	23	12	.259	.319	.308	64	-16	3	2	-0	.945	1	C-90	-0.9
1925	Chi-A	54	131	18	46	7	0	2	25	12	4	.351	.410	.450	125	5	1	2	-1	.952	-2	C-48	0.4
1926	Chi-A	49	135	10	32	4	1	0	17	14	7	.237	.309	.281	57	-8	0	0	0	.985	5	C-45	-0.3
1927	Chi-A	85	222	22	53	11	0	0	20	21	10	.239	.307	.288	57	-14	4	1	1	.972	7	C-81	-0.2
1928	Chi-A	78	218	17	55	5	2	2	20	19	14	.252	.315	.321	68	-10	3	4	-2	.959	-1	C-76	-0.7
1929	Chi-A	45	107	11	29	7	0	2	12	5	7	.271	.316	.393	82	-3	2	0	1	.979	6	C-40	0.6
1930	Chi-A	42	118	14	30	8	1	0	15	17	10	.254	.348	.339	78	-4	1	1	-0	.979	-5	C-38	0.6
Total	8	470	1306	128	342	54	6	8	160	114	68	.262	.326	.331	72	-53	14	10	-2	.964	18	C-440	-0.9

■ DON CROW
Crow, Donald Le Roy b: 8/18/58, Yakima, Wash. BR/TR, 6'4", 200 lbs. Deb: 7/25/82

YEAR	TM/L	G	AB	R	H	2B	3B	HR	RBI	BB	SO	AVG	OBP	SLG	PRO+	BR/A	SB	CS	SBR	FA	FR	G/POS	TPR
1982	LA-N	4	4	0	0	0	0	0	0	0	3	.000	.000	.000	-99	-1	0	0	0	1.000	1	/C-4	0.0

■ GEORGE CROWE
Crowe, George Daniel "Big George" b: 3/22/21, Whiteland, Ind. BL/TL, 6'2", 212 lbs. Deb: 4/16/52

YEAR	TM/L	G	AB	R	H	2B	3B	HR	RBI	BB	SO	AVG	OBP	SLG	PRO+	BR/A	SB	CS	SBR	FA	FR	G/POS	TPR
1952	Bos-N	73	217	25	56	13	1	4	20	18	25	.258	.329	.382	100	-0	0	1	-1	.985	2	1-55	-0.1
1953	Mil-N	47	42	6	12	2	0	2	6	2	7	.286	.333	.476	115	1	0	0	0	1.000	0	/1-9	0.1
1955	Mil-N	104	303	41	85	12	4	15	55	45	44	.281	.375	.495	135	16	1	0	0	.989	2	1-79	1.3
1956	Cin-N	77	144	22	36	2	1	10	23	11	28	.250	.312	.486	104	0	0	0	0	.988	2	1-32	0.1
1957	Cin-N	133	494	71	134	20	1	31	92	32	62	.271	.317	.504	108	4	1	1	-0	.989	-2	*1-120	-0.5
1958	Cin-N☆	111	345	31	95	12	5	7	61	41	51	.275	.352	.400	94	-2	1	0	0	.992	-3	1-93/2-1	-1.0
1959	StL-N	77	103	14	31	6	0	8	29	5	12	.301	.333	.592	132	4	0	0	0	1.000	0	1-14	0.6
1960	StL-N	73	72	5	17	3	0	4	13	5	16	.236	.286	.444	89	-1	0	0	0	1.000	0	/1-5	-0.1
1961	StL-N	7	7	0	1	0	0	0	0	0	2	.143	.143	.143	-22	-1	0	0	0	.000	0	H	-0.1
Total	9	702	1727	215	467	70	12	81	299	159	246	.270	.335	.466	109	20	3	2	0	.990	4	1-407/2-1	0.3

■ ED CROWLEY
Crowley, Edgar Jewel b: 8/20/06, Watkinsville, Ga. d: 4/14/70, Birmingham, Ala. BR/TR, 6'1", 180 lbs. Deb: 6/21/28

YEAR	TM/L	G	AB	R	H	2B	3B	HR	RBI	BB	SO	AVG	OBP	SLG	PRO+	BR/A	SB	CS	SBR	FA	FR	G/POS	TPR
1928	Was-A	2	1	0	0	0	0	0	0	0	0	.000	.000	.000	-99	-0	0	0	0	.000	-0	/3-2	-0.1

■ JOHN CROWLEY
Crowley, John A. b: 1/12/1862, Lawrence, Mass. d: 9/23/1896, Lawrence, Mass. 5'10", 164 lbs. Deb: 5/1/1884

YEAR	TM/L	G	AB	R	H	2B	3B	HR	RBI	BB	SO	AVG	OBP	SLG	PRO+	BR/A	SB	CS	SBR	FA	FR	G/POS	TPR
1884	Phi-N	48	168	26	41	7	3	0	19	15	21	.244	.306	.321	102	1				.832	-23	C-48	-1.6

■ TERRY CROWLEY
Crowley, Terrence Michael b: 2/16/47, Staten Island, N.Y. BL/TL, 6', 180 lbs. Deb: 9/4/69 C

YEAR	TM/L	G	AB	R	H	2B	3B	HR	RBI	BB	SO	AVG	OBP	SLG	PRO+	BR/A	SB	CS	SBR	FA	FR	G/POS	TPR
1969	Bal-A	7	18	2	6	0	0	0	3	1	4	.333	.368	.333	97	-0	0	0	0	1.000	0	/1-3,O-2	0.0
1970	*Bal-A	83	152	25	39	5	0	5	20	35	26	.257	.396	.388	116	5	2	0	1	.973	-5	O-27,1-23	-0.2
1971	Bal-A	18	23	2	4	0	0	0	1	3	4	.174	.269	.174	28	-2	0	0	0	1.000	0	/O-6,1-2	-0.5
1972	Bal-A	97	247	30	57	10	0	11	29	32	26	.231	.321	.405	112	4	0	0	0	.990	-7	O-68,1-15	-0.7
1973	*Bal-A	54	131	16	27	4	0	3	15	16	14	.206	.297	.305	71	-5	0	0	0	.867	-1	D-23,O-10/1	-0.7
1974	Cin-N	84	125	11	30	12	0	1	20	10	16	.240	.301	.360	86	-3	1	0	0	1.000	-2	O-22/1-7	-0.6
1975	*Cin-N	66	71	8	19	6	0	1	11	7	6	.268	.333	.394	100	-0	0	0	0	1.000	1	/1-4,O-4	0.1
1976	Atl-N	7	6	0	0	0	0	0	1	0	0	.000	.000	.000	-94	-2	0	0	0	.000	0	H	-0.2
	Bal-A	33	61	5	15	1	0	0	5	7	11	.246	.333	.262	81	-1	0	0	0	1.000	1	D-17/1-1	-0.1
1977	Bal-A	18	22	3	8	1	0	1	9	1	3	.364	.391	.545	162	2	0	0	0	1.000	-0	/1-1,D-2	0.2
1978	Bal-A	62	95	9	24	7	0	0	12	8	12	.253	.317	.274	72	-3	0	0	0	1.000	0	D-17/O-2,1	-0.4
1979	*Bal-A	61	63	8	20	5	1	1	8	14	13	.317	.449	.476	155	6	0	0	0	1.000	-0	D-15/1-2	0.5
1980	Bal-A	92	233	33	67	9	0	12	50	29	21	.288	.366	.476	130	10	0	0	0	1.000	-6	D-65/1-3	0.3
1981	Bal-A	68	134	12	33	6	0	4	25	29	12	.246	.380	.381	120	5	0	0	0	1.000	0	D-42/1-4	0.3
1982	Bal-A	65	93	8	22	0	0	3	17	21	9	.237	.377	.355	103	1	0	0	0	.988	0	D-14,1-10	0.1
1983	Mon-N	50	44	2	8	0	0	0	3	9	4	.182	.333	.182	47	-3	0	0	0	1.000	-1	/1-4	-0.4
Total	15	865	1518	174	379	62	1	42	229	222	181	.250	.348	.375	104	13				.980	-13	D-195,O-141/1	-1.7

■ BILL CROWLEY
Crowley, William Michael b: 4/8/1857, Philadelphia, Pa. d: 7/14/1891, Gloucester, N.J. BR/TR, 5'7.5", 159 lbs. Deb: 4/26/1875

YEAR	TM/L	G	AB	R	H	2B	3B	HR	RBI	BB	SO	AVG	OBP	SLG	PRO+	BR/A	SB	CS	SBR	FA	FR	G/POS	TPR
1875	Phi-n	9	37	4	3	0	0	0		1		.081	.105	.081	-33	-5						/O-4,3-3,12	-0.4
1877	Lou-N	61	238	30	67	9	3	1	23	4	13	.282	.293	.357	88	-6				.849	9	*O-58/S-2,C32	0.1
1879	Buf-N	60	261	41	75	9	5	0	30	6	14	.287	.303	.360	115	4				.809	-1	O-43,C-10/12	0.1
1880	Buf-N	85	354	57	95	16	4	0	20	19	23	.268	.306	.336	115	6				.824	1	*O-74,C-22	0.5
1881	Bos-N	72	279	33	71	12	0	0	31	14	15	.254	.290	.297	89	-3				.880	-1	*O-72	-0.5
1883	Phi-a	23	96	16	24	4	3	0		3		.250	.273	.354	93	-1				.810	-2	O-22/1-1	-0.3
	Cle-N	11	41	3	12	5	0	0	5	1	7	.293	.310	.415	119	1				.923	-3	O-11	-0.2
1884	Bos-N	108	407	50	110	14	6	6	61	33	74	.270	.325	.378	121	10				.870	-5	*O-108	0.3
1885	Buf-N	92	344	29	83	14	1	1	36	21	32	.241	.285	.297	85	-6				.874	-5	*O-92	-1.2
Total	7	512	2020	259	537	83	22	8	206	101	178	.266	.301	.341	103	5				.853	-6	O-480/C-34,12S3	-1.2

■ WALTON CRUISE
Cruise, Walton Edwin b: 5/6/1890, Childersburg, Ala. d: 1/9/75, Sylacauga, Ala. BL/TR, 6', 175 lbs. Deb: 4/14/14

YEAR	TM/L	G	AB	R	H	2B	3B	HR	RBI	BB	SO	AVG	OBP	SLG	PRO+	BR/A	SB	CS	SBR	FA	FR	G/POS	TPR
1914	StL-N	95	256	20	58	9	3	4	28	25	42	.227	.303	.332	90	-3	3			.976	-3	O-81	-1.0
1916	StL-N	3	3	0	2	0	0	0	0	1	0	.667	.750	.667	339	1	0			1.000	-0	/O-2	0.0
1917	StL-N	153	529	70	156	20	10	6	59	38	73	.295	.343	.399	131	18	16			.965	-14	O-152	-0.4
1918	StL-N	70	240	34	65	5	4	6	39	30	26	.271	.359	.400	136	11	2			.964	-7	O-65	0.0
1919	StL-N	9	21	0	2	1	0	0	0	1	2	.095	.136	.143	-17	-3	0			.833	-2	/O-5,1-2	-0.6
	Bos-N	73	241	23	52	7	0	1	21	17	29	.216	.267	.257	61	-11	8			.978	-5	O-66	-2.4
	Yr	82	262	23	54	8	0	1	21	18	35	.206	.257	.248	55	-14	8			.971	-7	O-71/1-2	-3.0
1920	Bos-N	91	288	40	80	7	5	1	21	31	26	.278	.352	.347	106	3	5	3	-0	.950	-7	O-82	-1.1
1921	Bos-N	108	344	47	119	16	7	8	55	48	24	.346	.429	.503	154	29	10	8	-2	.963	-6	*O-102/1-2	1.4
1922	Bos-N	104	352	51	98	15	10	4	46	44	20	.278	.360	.412	103	2	4	4	-1	.948	-0	*O-100/1-2	-0.6
1923	Bos-N	21	38	4	8	2	0	0	3	6	2	.211	.268	.263	42	-3	1	0	0	.952	-0	/O-9	-0.4
1924	Bos-N	9	9	4	4	1	0	1	3	0	2	.444	.444	.889	260	2	0	0	0	.000	0	H	0.2
Total	10	736	2321	293	644	83	39	30	272	238	250	.277	.348	.386	114	44	49	15		.962	-45	O-664/1-6	-4.9

■ GENE CRUMLING
Crumling, Eugene Leon b: 4/5/22, Wrightsville, Pa. BR/TR, 6', 180 lbs. Deb: 9/11/45

YEAR	TM/L	G	AB	R	H	2B	3B	HR	RBI	BB	SO	AVG	OBP	SLG	PRO+	BR/A	SB	CS	SBR	FA	FR	G/POS	TPR
1945	StL-N	6	12	0	1	0	0	0	0	0	1	.083	.083	.083	-52	-2	0			1.000	2	/C-6	-0.1

■ BUDDY CRUMP
Crump, Arthur Elliott b: 11/29/01, Norfolk, Va. d: 9/7/76, Raleigh, N.C. BL/TL, 5'10", 156 lbs. Deb: 9/28/24

YEAR	TM/L	G	AB	R	H	2B	3B	HR	RBI	BB	SO	AVG	OBP	SLG	PRO+	BR/A	SB	CS	SBR	FA	FR	G/POS	TPR
1924	NY-N	1	4	0	0	0	0	0	1	0	1	.000	.000	.000	-99	-1	0	0	0	.500	-1	/O-1	-0.2

■ PRESS CRUTHERS
Cruthers, Charles Preston b: 9/8/1890, Marshallton, Del. d: 12/27/76, Kenosha, Wis. BR/TR, 5'9", 152 lbs. Deb: 9/29/13

YEAR	TM/L	G	AB	R	H	2B	3B	HR	RBI	BB	SO	AVG	OBP	SLG	PRO+	BR/A	SB	CS	SBR	FA	FR	G/POS	TPR
1913	Phi-A	3	12	0	3	1	0	0	0	0	0	.250	.250	.333	72	-1	0			.923	-3	/2-3	-0.4

YEAR	TM/L	G	AB	R	H	2B	3B	HR	RBI	BB	SO	AVG	OBP	SLG	PRO+	BR/A	SB	CS	SBR	FA	FR	G/POS	TPR
1914	Phi-A	4	15	1	3	0	1	0	0	0	4	.200	.200	.333	63	-1	0	1	-1	1.000	2	/2-4	0.0
Total	2	7	27	1	6	1	1	0	0	0	4	.222	.222	.333	67	-1	0	1		.973	-1	/2-7	-0.4

■ TOMMY CRUZ
Cruz, Cirilo (Dilan) b: 2/15/51, Arroyo, P.R. BL/TL, 5'9", 165 lbs. Deb: 9/4/73 F

YEAR	TM/L	G	AB	R	H	2B	3B	HR	RBI	BB	SO	AVG	OBP	SLG	PRO+	BR/A	SB	CS	SBR	FA	FR	G/POS	TPR
1973	StL-N	3	0	1	0	0	0	0	0	0	0	—	—	—	—	0	0	0	0	.000	-0	/O-1	0.0
1977	Chi-A	4	2	1	0	0	0	0	0	0	0	.000	.000	.000	-99	-1	0	0	0	1.000	-1	/O-2	-0.1
Total	2	7	2	2	0	0	0	0	0	0	0	.000	.000	.000	-99	-1	0	0	0	1.000	-1	/O-3	-0.1

■ FAUSTO CRUZ
Cruz, Fausto (Santiago) b: 5/1/72, Monte Cristi, D.R. BR/TR, 5'10", 165 lbs. Deb: 4/10/94

YEAR	TM/L	G	AB	R	H	2B	3B	HR	RBI	BB	SO	AVG	OBP	SLG	PRO+	BR/A	SB	CS	SBR	FA	FR	G/POS	TPR
1994	Oak-A	17	28	2	3	0	0	0	0	4	6	.107	.219	.107	-14	-5	0	0	0	.960	3	S-10/3-4,2	-0.1

■ HECTOR CRUZ
Cruz, Hector Louis (Dilan) "Heity" b: 4/2/53, Arroyo, P.R. BR/TR, 5'11", 170 lbs. Deb: 8/11/73 F

YEAR	TM/L	G	AB	R	H	2B	3B	HR	RBI	BB	SO	AVG	OBP	SLG	PRO+	BR/A	SB	CS	SBR	FA	FR	G/POS	TPR
1973	StL-N	11	11	1	0	0	0	0	0	1	3	.000	.083	.000	-75	-3	0	0	0	1.000	-1	/O-5	-0.4
1975	StL-N	23	48	7	7	2	2	0	6	2	4	.146	.180	.271	23	-5	0	0	0	.800	-1	3-12/O-6	-0.7
1976	StL-N	151	526	54	120	17	1	13	71	42	119	.228	.288	.338	77	-17	1	0	0	.934	-21	*3-148	-4.2
1977	StL-N	118	339	50	80	19	2	6	42	46	56	.236	.329	.357	85	-6	4	3	-1	.964	-9	*O-106/3-2	-2.0
1978	Chi-N	30	76	8	18	5	0	2	9	3	6	.237	.286	.382	70	-3	0	0	0	1.000	0	O-14/3-7	-0.4
	SF-N	79	197	19	44	8	1	6	24	21	39	.223	.301	.365	89	-3	0	2	-1	.978	-5	O-53,3-14	-1.2
	Yr	109	273	27	62	13	1	8	33	24	45	.227	.292	.370	83	-7	0	2	-1	.983	-5	O-67,3-21	-1.6
1979	SF-N	16	25	1	3	0	0	0	1	3	7	.120	.214	.120	-7	-4	0	0	0	1.000	-2	/O-6,3-2	-0.6
	*Cin-N	74	182	24	44	10	2	4	27	31	39	.242	.352	.385	100	1	0	1	-1	.984	-7	O-69	-1.0
	Yr	90	207	26	47	10	2	4	28	34	46	.227	.336	.353	89	-3	0	1	-1	.985	-9	O-75/3-2	-1.6
1980	Cin-N	52	75	5	16	4	1	1	5	8	16	.213	.289	.333	73	-3	0	0	0	.955	-4	O-29	-0.8
1981	Chi-N	53	109	15	25	5	0	7	15	17	24	.229	.333	.468	120	3	2	2	-1	.925	-6	3-18,O-16	-0.4
1982	Chi-N	17	19	1	4	1	0	0	0	2	4	.211	.286	.263	53	-1	0	0	0	1.000	-0	/O-4	-0.3
Total	9	624	1607	186	361	71	9	39	200	176	317	.225	.303	.353	81	-42	7	8	-3	.975	-57	O-308,3-203	-12.0

■ HENRY CRUZ
Cruz, Henry (Acosta) b: 2/27/52, Christiansted, V.I. BL/TL, 6', 175 lbs. Deb: 4/18/75

YEAR	TM/L	G	AB	R	H	2B	3B	HR	RBI	BB	SO	AVG	OBP	SLG	PRO+	BR/A	SB	CS	SBR	FA	FR	G/POS	TPR
1975	LA-N	53	94	8	25	3	1	0	5	7	6	.266	.317	.319	80	-3	1	1	-0	.960	-11	O-41	-1.5
1976	LA-N	49	88	8	16	2	1	4	14	9	11	.182	.258	.364	76	-3	0	2	-1	.976	-3	O-23	-0.9
1977	Chi-A	16	21	3	6	0	0	2	5	1	3	.286	.318	.571	137	1	0	0	0	.833	-3	/O-9	-0.2
1978	Chi-A	53	77	13	17	2	1	2	10	8	11	.221	.302	.351	82	-2	0	1	-1	1.000	-5	O-40/D-1	-0.8
Total	4	171	280	32	64	7	3	8	34	25	31	.229	.294	.361	84	-7	1	4	-2	.974	-22	O-113/D-1	-3.4

■ JOSE CRUZ
Cruz, Jose (Dilan) b: 8/8/47, Arroyo, P.R. BL/TL, 6', 175 lbs. Deb: 9/19/70 F

YEAR	TM/L	G	AB	R	H	2B	3B	HR	RBI	BB	SO	AVG	OBP	SLG	PRO+	BR/A	SB	CS	SBR	FA	FR	G/POS	TPR
1970	StL-N	6	17	2	6	1	0	0	1	4	0	.353	.500	.412	144	2	0	0	0	1.000	2	/O-4	0.3
1971	StL-N	83	292	46	80	13	2	9	27	49	35	.274	.380	.425	123	10	6	3	0	.975	2	O-83	0.9
1972	StL-N	117	332	33	78	14	4	2	23	36	54	.235	.312	.319	81	-8	9	3	1	.979	4	*O-102	-0.8
1973	StL-N	132	406	51	92	22	5	10	57	51	66	.227	.314	.379	92	-5	10	4	1	.979	0	*O-118	-1.0
1974	StL-N	107	161	24	42	4	3	5	20	20	27	.261	.343	.416	112	3	4	2	0	.975	-6	O-53/1-1	-0.5
1975	Hou-N	120	315	44	81	15	2	9	49	52	44	.257	.364	.403	121	10	6	3	0	.980	4	O-94	1.1
1976	Hou-N	133	439	49	133	21	5	4	61	53	46	.303	.378	.401	133	19	28	11	2	.972	10	*O-125	2.7
1977	Hou-N	157	579	87	173	31	10	17	87	69	69	.299	.373	.475	138	30	44	23	-1	.973	4	*O-155	2.7
1978	Hou-N	153	565	79	178	34	9	10	83	57	57	.315	.380	.460	144	32	37	9	6	.975	3	*O-152/1-2	3.6
1979	Hou-N	157	558	73	161	33	7	9	72	72	66	.289	.370	.421	122	18	36	14	2	.959	9	*O-156	2.3
1980	*Hou-N☆	160	612	79	185	29	7	11	91	60	66	.302	.365	.426	130	24	36	11	4	.969	15	*O-158	3.9
1981	*Hou-N	107	409	53	109	16	5	13	55	35	49	.267	.324	.425	117	7	5	7	-3	.984	9	*O-105	1.1
1982	Hou-N	155	570	62	157	27	2	9	68	60	67	.275	.345	.377	110	8	21	11	-0	.964	14	*O-155	1.8
1983	Hou-N	160	594	85	**189**	28	8	14	92	65	86	.318	.386	.463	143	34	30	16	-1	.979	8	*O-160	3.9
1984	Hou-N	160	600	96	187	28	13	12	95	73	68	.312	.386	.462	148	38	22	8	2	.976	13	*O-160	4.9
1985	Hou-N★	141	544	69	163	34	4	9	79	43	74	.300	.351	.426	120	14	16	5	2	.971	10	*O-137	2.2
1986	*Hou-N	141	479	48	133	22	4	10	72	55	66	.278	.352	.403	111	7	3	4	-2	.984	6	*O-134	0.8
1987	Hou-N	126	365	47	88	17	4	11	38	36	65	.241	.309	.400	90	-6	4	1	1	.984	6	O-97	-0.3
1988	NY-A	38	80	9	16	4	0	0	4	9	15	.200	.273	.262	51	-5	0	1	-1	.889	-2	D-12/O-8	-0.8
Total	19	2353	7917	1036	2251	391	94	165	1077	898	1031	.284	.358	.420	122	232	317	136	14	.974	111	*O-2156/D-12,1	28.8

■ JULIO CRUZ
Cruz, Julio Luis b: 12/2/54, Brooklyn, N.Y. BB/TR, 5'9", 165 lbs. Deb: 7/4/77

YEAR	TM/L	G	AB	R	H	2B	3B	HR	RBI	BB	SO	AVG	OBP	SLG	PRO+	BR/A	SB	CS	SBR	FA	FR	G/POS	TPR
1977	Sea-A	60	199	25	51	3	1	1	7	24	29	.256	.336	.296	75	-6	15	6	1	.983	2	2-54/D-1	0.1
1978	Sea-A	147	550	77	129	14	1	1	25	69	66	.235	.321	.269	68	-21	59	10	**12**	**.987**	8	*2-141/S-5,D	0.9
1979	Sea-A	107	414	70	112	16	2	1	29	62	61	.271	.366	.326	87	-5	49	9	9	.979	17	*2-107	2.7
1980	Sea-A	119	422	66	88	9	3	2	16	59	49	.209	.307	.258	56	-24	45	7	9	.983	1	*2-115/D-3	-0.7
1981	Sea-A	94	352	57	90	12	3	2	24	39	40	.256	.335	.324	87	-5	43	8	**8**	.982	6	2-92/S-1	1.8
1982	Sea-A	154	549	83	133	22	5	8	49	57	71	.242	.317	.344	79	-15	46	13	6	.987	4	*2-151/S-2,3D	0.3
1983	Sea-A	61	181	24	46	10	1	2	12	20	22	.254	.335	.354	86	-3	33	6	6	.984	7	2-60/D-1	1.3
	*Chi-A	99	334	47	84	9	4	1	40	29	44	.251	.315	.311	71	-13	24	6	4	.983	10	2-97	0.5
	Yr	160	515	71	130	19	5	3	52	49	66	.252	.322	.326	76	-16	57	12	10	.983	17	2-157/D-1	1.8
1984	Chi-A	143	415	42	92	14	4	5	40	45	58	.222	.298	.311	66	-19	14	6	1	.976	22	*2-141	0.9
1985	Chi-A	91	234	28	46	2	3	0	15	32	40	.197	.290	.231	46	-17	8	5	-1	.982	13	2-87/D-2	-0.2
1986	Chi-A	81	209	38	45	2	0	0	19	42	28	.215	.347	.225	58	-11	7	2	1	.985	2	2-78/D-3	-0.5
Total	10	1156	3859	557	916	113	27	23	279	478	508	.237	.324	.299	71	-138	343	78	56	.983	93	*2-1123/D-13,S3	7.1

■ TODD CRUZ
Cruz, Todd Ruben b: 11/23/55, Highland Park, Mich BR/TR, 6', 175 lbs. Deb: 9/4/78

YEAR	TM/L	G	AB	R	H	2B	3B	HR	RBI	BB	SO	AVG	OBP	SLG	PRO+	BR/A	SB	CS	SBR	FA	FR	G/POS	TPR
1978	Phi-N	3	4	0	2	0	0	0	2	0	0	.500	.500	.500	178	0	0	1	-1	1.000	2	/S-2	0.1
1979	KC-A	55	118	9	24	7	0	2	15	3	19	.203	.230	.314	44	-9	0	1	-1	.974	4	S-48/3-9	-0.3
1980	Cal-A	18	40	5	11	3	0	1	5	5	8	.275	.356	.425	116	1	0	0	0	.860	-6	S-12/3-4,2O	-0.4
	Chi-A	90	293	23	68	11	1	2	18	9	54	.232	.260	.297	52	-19	2	1	0	.956	5	S-90	-0.4
	Yr	108	333	28	79	14	1	3	23	14	62	.237	.272	.312	60	-18	2	1	0	.948	-1	*S-102/3-4,2O	-0.8
1982	Sea-A	136	492	44	113	20	2	16	57	12	95	.230	.248	.376	67	-24	2	10	-5	.963	19	*S-136	0.3
1983	Sea-A	65	216	21	41	4	2	7	21	7	44	.190	.222	.324	46	-16	1	3	-2	.964	21	S-63	0.9
	*Bal-A	81	221	16	46	9	1	3	27	15	52	.208	.262	.299	55	-14	3	4	-2	.942	5	3-79/2-2	-1.2
	Yr	146	437	37	87	13	3	10	48	22	108	.199	.242	.311	51	-30	4	7	-3	.942	25	3-79,S-63/2	-0.3
1984	Bal-A	96	142	15	31	4	0	3	9	8	33	.218	.265	.310	60	-8	1	4	-2	.955	11	3-89/P-1,D	-0.7
Total	6	544	1526	133	336	58	6	34	154	59	317	.220	.253	.333	59	-89	9	24	-12	.960	60	S-351,3-181/2DPO	-0.9

■ MIKE CUBBAGE
Cubbage, Michael Lee b: 7/21/50, Charlottesville, Va. BL/TR, 6', 180 lbs. Deb: 4/7/74 MC

YEAR	TM/L	G	AB	R	H	2B	3B	HR	RBI	BB	SO	AVG	OBP	SLG	PRO+	BR/A	SB	CS	SBR	FA	FR	G/POS	TPR
1974	Tex-A	9	15	0	0	0	0	0	0	0	4	.000	.000	.000	-99	-4	0	0	0	1.000	2	/3-3,2-2	-0.2
1975	Tex-A	58	143	12	32	6	0	4	21	18	14	.224	.311	.350	87	-2	0	0	0	.962	2	2-37/3-3,D	0.1
1976	Tex-A	14	32	2	7	0	0	0	7	7	7	.219	.359	.219	70	-1	0	0	0	1.000	-0	/2-5,3-1,D	-0.1
	Min-A	104	342	40	89	19	5	3	42	42	37	.260	.346	.371	107	4	1	1	-0	.940	3	3-99/2-2,D	0.6
	Yr	118	374	42	96	19	5	3	49	49	44	.257	.347	.358	104	3	1	1	-0	.940	2	*3-100/D-8,2	0.5
1977	Min-A	129	417	60	110	16	5	9	55	37	49	.264	.324	.391	95	-3	1	4	-2	.923	1	*3-126/D-1	-0.8
1978	Min-A	125	394	40	111	12	7	7	57	40	44	.282	.349	.401	108	5	3	1	0	.971	3	*3-115/2-5	0.5
1979	Min-A	94	243	26	67	10	1	2	23	39	24	.276	.376	.350	94	-1	1	6	-5	.928	-12	3-63,D-21/12	-1.8
1980	Min-A	103	285	29	70	9	0	8	42	23	37	.246	.304	.361	76	-10	0	1	-1	.996	7	1-72,3-32/2D	-0.7

YEAR	TM/L	G	AB	R	H	2B	3B	HR	RBI	BB	SO	AVG	OBP	SLG	PRO+	BR/A	SB	CS	SBR	FA	FR	G/POS	TPR
1981	NY-N	67	80	9	17	2	2	1	4	9	15	.213	.292	.325	76	-3	0	0	0	.963	1	3-12	-0.2
Total	8	703	1951	218	503	74	20	34	251	215	233	.258	.333	.369	94	-14	6	15	-7	.952	12	3-454/1-73,2D	-1.6

■ AL CUCCINELLO
Cuccinello, Alfred Edward b: 11/26/14, Long Island City, N.Y. BR/TR, 5'10", 165 lbs. Deb: 5/17/35 F

YEAR	TM/L	G	AB	R	H	2B	3B	HR	RBI	BB	SO	AVG	OBP	SLG	PRO+	BR/A	SB	CS	SBR	FA	FR	G/POS	TPR
1935	NY-N	54	165	27	41	7	1	4	20	1	20	.248	.262	.376	70	-7	0			.951	6	2-48/3-2	0.1

■ TONY CUCCINELLO
Cuccinello, Anthony Francis "Cooch" or "Chick" b: 11/8/07, Long Island City, N.Y. BR/TR, 5'7", 160 lbs. Deb: 4/15/30 FC

YEAR	TM/L	G	AB	R	H	2B	3B	HR	RBI	BB	SO	AVG	OBP	SLG	PRO+	BR/A	SB	CS	SBR	FA	FR	G/POS	TPR
1930	Cin-N	125	443	64	138	22	5	10	78	47	44	.312	.380	.451	105	4	5			.920	-19	*3-109,2-15/S	-0.7
1931	Cin-N	154	575	67	181	39	11	2	93	54	28	.315	.374	.431	123	19	1			.969	5	*2-154	3.3
1932	Bro-N	154	597	76	168	32	6	12	77	46	47	.281	.337	.415	103	2	5			.973	19	*2-154	2.9
1933	Bro-N★	134	485	58	122	31	4	9	65	44	40	.252	.316	.388	105	2	4			.977	-19	*2-120,3-14	-0.9
1934	Bro-N	140	528	59	138	32	2	14	94	49	45	.261	.325	.409	100	-1	0			.974	12	*2-101,3-43	1.8
1935	Bro-N	102	360	49	105	20	3	8	53	40	35	.292	.366	.431	116	9	3			.977	6	2-64,3-36	1.9
1936	Bos-N	150	565	68	174	26	3	7	86	58	49	.308	.374	.402	116	14	1			.971	22	*2-150	4.5
1937	Bos-N	152	575	77	156	36	4	11	80	61	40	.271	.341	.405	112	9	2			.967	-10	*2-151	1.0
1938	Bos-N☆	147	555	62	147	25	2	9	76	52	32	.265	.331	.366	102	0	4			.974	-26	*2-147	-1.7
1939	Bos-N	81	310	42	95	17	1	2	40	26	26	.306	.360	.387	109	4	5			.970	-2	2-80	0.5
1940	Bos-N	34	126	14	34	9	0	0	19	8	9	.270	.319	.341	87	-2	1			.978	1	3-33	0.0
	NY-N	88	307	26	64	9	2	5	36	16	42	.208	.248	.300	50	-21	1			.987	5	2-47,3-37	-1.3
	Yr	122	433	40	98	18	2	5	55	24	51	.226	.269	.312	60	-24	2			.971	3	3-70,2-47	-1.3
1942	Bos-N	40	104	8	21	3	0	1	8	9	11	.202	.265	.260	55	-6	1			.907	-4	3-20,2-14	-1.0
1943	Bos-N	13	19	0	0	0	0	0	2	3	1	.000	.136	.000	-60	-4	0			.929	0	/3-4,2-2,S	-0.4
	Chi-A	34	103	5	28	5	0	2	11	13	13	.272	.353	.379	114	2	3	1	0	.965	-2	3-30	0.1
1944	Chi-A	38	130	5	34	3	0	0	17	8	16	.262	.304	.285	70	-5	0	0	0	.959	-2	3-30/2-6	-0.7
1945	Chi-A†	118	402	50	124	25	3	2	49	45	19	.308	.379	.400	130	16	6	2	1	.936	-5	*3-112	1.5
Total	15	1704	6184	730	1729	334	46	94	884	579	497	.280	.343	.394	105	41	42	3		.973	-18	*2-1205,3-468/S	10.8

■ JIM CUDWORTH
Cudworth, James Alaric "Cuddy" b: 8/22/1858, Fairhaven, Mass. d: 12/21/43, Middleboro, Mass. BR/TR, 6', 165 lbs. Deb: 7/27/1884

YEAR	TM/L	G	AB	R	H	2B	3B	HR	RBI	BB	SO	AVG	OBP	SLG	PRO+	BR/A	SB	CS	SBR	FA	FR	G/POS	TPR
1884	KC-U	32	116	7	17	3	1	0		2		.147	.161	.190	-6	-17				.963	2	1-19,O-12/P	-1.4

■ MANUEL CUETO
Cueto, Manuel "Potato" b: 2/8/1892, Guanajay, Cuba d: 6/29/42, Regla, Cuba BR/TR, 5'5", 157 lbs. Deb: 6/25/14

YEAR	TM/L	G	AB	R	H	2B	3B	HR	RBI	BB	SO	AVG	OBP	SLG	PRO+	BR/A	SB	CS	SBR	FA	FR	G/POS	TPR
1914	StL-F	19	43	2	4	0	0	0	2	5	0	.093	.188	.093	-25	-8	0			.941	-1	3-10/S-5,2	-0.9
1917	Cin-N	56	140	14	28	3	0	1	11	16	17	.200	.287	.243	66	-5	4			.963	-1	O-38/2-6,C	-0.9
1918	Cin-N	47	108	14	32	5	0	0	14	19	5	.296	.406	.361	137	6	4			.929	-14	O-19,2-10/SC	-0.8
1919	Cin-N	29	88	10	22	2	0	0	4	10	4	.250	.340	.273	88	-1	5			.982	4	O-25/3-1	0.1
Total	4	151	379	36	86	10	1	2	31	50	26	.227	.323	.266	79	-8	13			.964	-13	/O-82,2-18,SC3	-2.5

■ JOHN CUFF
Cuff, John J. b: 6/1864, Jersey City, N.J. Deb: 9/11/1884

YEAR	TM/L	G	AB	R	H	2B	3B	HR	RBI	BB	SO	AVG	OBP	SLG	PRO+	BR/A	SB	CS	SBR	FA	FR	G/POS	TPR
1884	Bal-U	3	11	1	1	1	0	0		1		.091	.167	.182	-5	-2				.920	0	/C-3	-0.1

■ LEON CULBERSON
Culberson, Delbert Leon "Lee" b: 8/6/19, Halls, Ga. d: 9/17/89, Rome, Ga. BR/TR, 5'11", 180 lbs. Deb: 5/16/43

YEAR	TM/L	G	AB	R	H	2B	3B	HR	RBI	BB	SO	AVG	OBP	SLG	PRO+	BR/A	SB	CS	SBR	FA	FR	G/POS	TPR
1943	Bos-A	81	312	36	85	16	6	3	34	31	35	.272	.338	.391	111	4	14	0	4	.978	6	O-79	1.0
1944	Bos-A	75	282	41	67	11	5	2	21	20	20	.238	.288	.333	78	-9	6	4	-1	.979	-3	O-72	-1.7
1945	Bos-A	97	331	26	91	21	6	6	45	20	37	.275	.316	.429	113	4	4	3	-1	.967	5	O-91	0.3
1946	*Bos-A	59	179	34	56	10	2	3	18	16	19	.313	.369	.430	116	4	3	2	-0	.967	-7	O-49/3-4	-0.5
1947	Bos-A	47	84	10	20	1	0	0	11	12	10	.238	.354	.250	65	-3	1	1	-0	.974	-4	O-25/3-4	-0.9
1948	Was-A	12	29	1	5	0	0	0	2	8	5	.172	.351	.172	43	-2	0	0	0	1.000	-3	O-11	-0.5
Total	6	371	1217	148	324	59	18	14	131	107	126	.266	.327	.379	100	-3	28	10	2	.974	-6	O-327/3-8	-2.3

■ JOHN CULLEN
Cullen, John J. b: Marysville, Cal. Deb: 8/18/1884

YEAR	TM/L	G	AB	R	H	2B	3B	HR	RBI	BB	SO	AVG	OBP	SLG	PRO+	BR/A	SB	CS	SBR	FA	FR	G/POS	TPR
1884	Wil-U	9	31	2	6	0	0	0		1		.194	.219	.194	13	-4				.750	-1	/O-6,S-3	-0.5

■ TIM CULLEN
Cullen, Timothy Leo b: 2/16/42, San Francisco, Cal. BR/TR, 6'1", 185 lbs. Deb: 8/8/66

YEAR	TM/L	G	AB	R	H	2B	3B	HR	RBI	BB	SO	AVG	OBP	SLG	PRO+	BR/A	SB	CS	SBR	FA	FR	G/POS	TPR
1966	Was-A	18	34	8	8	1	0	0	2		8	.235	.278	.265	57	-2	0	0	0	.889	1	/3-8,2-5	0.0
1967	Was-A	124	403	35	95	7	0	2	31	40	47	.236	.307	.269	74	-12	4	5	-2	.951	15	S-69,2-46,3/O	1.1
1968	Chi-A	72	155	16	31	7	0	2	13	15	23	.200	.275	.284	69	-6	0	0	0	.966	2	2-71	0.3
	Was-A	47	114	8	31	4	2	1	16	7	12	.272	.325	.368	113	2	0	1	-1	.968	-1	S-33,2-16/3	0.4
	Yr	119	269	24	62	11	2	3	29	22	35	.230	.296	.320	87	-4	0	1	-1	.965	1	2-87,S-33/3	0.7
1969	Was-A	119	249	22	52	7	0	1	15	14	27	.209	.257	.249	44	-19	1	1	-0	.981	12	*2-105/S-9,3	-0.1
1970	Was-A	123	262	22	56	10	2	1	18	31	38	.214	.304	.279	65	-12	3	2	-0	**.994**	27	*2-112/S-6	2.1
1971	Was-A	125	403	34	77	13	4	2	26	33	47	.191	.252	.258	47	-29	2	0	1	.997	21	2-78,S-62	0.5
1972	*Oak-A	72	142	10	37	8	1	0	15	5	17	.261	.286	.331	48	-3	0	1	-1	.952	-1	2-65/3-4,S	0.2
Total		700	1761	155	387	57	9	9	134	147	219	.220	.283	.278	65	-80	10	9	-2	.979	80	2-498,S-180/3O	4.1

■ ROY CULLENBINE
Cullenbine, Roy Joseph b: 10/18/13, Nashville, Tenn. d: 5/28/91, Mt.Clemens, Mich. BB/TR, 6'1", 190 lbs. Deb: 4/19/38

YEAR	TM/L	G	AB	R	H	2B	3B	HR	RBI	BB	SO	AVG	OBP	SLG	PRO+	BR/A	SB	CS	SBR	FA	FR	G/POS	TPR
1938	Det-A	25	67	12	19	1	3	0	9	12	9	.284	.392	.388	91	-1	2	0	1	1.000	-0	O-17	-0.1
1939	Det-A	75	179	31	43	9	2	6	23	34	29	.240	.362	.413	91	-2	0	1	-1	.902	-5	O-46/1-2	-0.9
1940	Bro-N	22	61	8	11	1	0	1	9	23	11	.180	.405	.246	78	-0	2			1.000	1	O-19	-0.1
	StL-A	86	257	41	59	11	2	7	31	50	34	.230	.359	.370	87	-4	0	1	-1	.975	-2	O-57/1-6	-1.0
1941	StL-A★	149	501	82	159	29	9	9	98	121	43	.317	.452	.465	138	35	6	4	-1	.964	1	*O-120,1-22	2.5
1942	StL-A	38	109	15	21	7	1	2	14	30	20	.193	.367	.330	95	0	0	1	-1	.930	-1	O-27/1-5	-0.1
	Was-A	64	241	30	69	19	0	2	35	44	18	.286	.396	.390	123	9	1	2	-0	.966	8	O-35,3-28	1.5
	*NY-A	21	77	16	28	7	0	2	17	18	2	.364	.484	.532	190	10	0	1	-1	.980	2	O-19/1-1	1.1
	Yr	123	427	61	118	33	1	6	66	92	40	.276	.405	.400	127	20	1	4	-2	.959	11	O-81,3-28/1	2.5
1943	Cle-A	138	488	66	141	24	4	8	56	96	58	.289	.407	.404	146	33	3	4	-2	.981	3	*O-121,1-13	2.9
1944	Cle-A☆	154	571	98	162	34	5	16	80	87	49	.284	.380	.445	141	31	4	4	-1	.967	-2	*O-151	2.1
1945	Cle-A	8	13	3	1	0	1	0	0	11	0	.077	.500	.154	97	1	0	0	0	1.000	-2	/O-4,3-3	-0.1
	*Det-A	146	523	80	145	27	5	18	93	102	36	.277	.398	.451	137	28	0	0	0	.980	13	*O-146	3.5
	Yr	154	536	83	146	28	5	18	93	**113**	36	.272	.402	.444	137	29	2	0	1	.980	11	*O-150/3-3	3.4
1946	Det-A	113	328	63	110	21	0	15	56	88	39	.335	.477	.537	172	37	3	0	1	.965	2	O-81,1-21	3.5
1947	Det-A	142	464	82	104	18	1	24	78	137	51	.224	.401	.422	125	21	3	2	-0	.989	16	*1-138	3.3
Total	10	1181	3879	627	1072	209	32	110	599	853	399	.276	.408	.432	132	199	26	20		.969	34	O-843,1-208/3	18.1

■ DICK CULLER
Culler, Richard Broadus b: 1/15/15, High Point, N.C. d: 6/16/64, Chapel Hill, N.C. BR/TR, 5'9.5", 155 lbs. Deb: 9/19/36

YEAR	TM/L	G	AB	R	H	2B	3B	HR	RBI	BB	SO	AVG	OBP	SLG	PRO+	BR/A	SB	CS	SBR	FA	FR	G/POS	TPR
1936	Phi-A	9	38	3	9	0	0	0	1	1	3	.237	.256	.237	23	-5	0	0	0	.946	-3	/2-7,S-2	-0.7
1943	Chi-A	53	148	9	32	5	1	0	11	16	11	.216	.297	.264	65	-6	4	5	-2	.950	11	3-26,2-19/S	0.4
1944	Bos-N	8	28	2	2	0	0	0	0	4	2	.071	.188	.071	-24	-5	0			.904	2	/S-8	-0.2
1945	Bos-N	136	527	87	138	12	1	2	30	50	35	.262	.328	.300	75	-17	7			.954	-8	*S-126/3-6	-1.5
1946	Bos-N	134	482	70	123	15	3	0	33	62	18	.255	.342	.299	82	-9	7			.948	-8	*S-132	-1.1
1947	Bos-N	77	214	20	53	2	0	0	19	19	15	.248	.309	.280	59	-12	1			.967	3	S-77	-0.6
1948	Chi-N	48	89	4	15	2	0	0	5	13	3	.169	.275	.191	29	-9	0			.968	16	S-43/2-2	0.9
1949	NY-N	7	1	0	0	0	0	0	0	1	0	.000	.500	.000	45	-0	0			.889	2	/S-7	0.2
Total	8	472	1527	195	372	39	6	2	99	166	87	.244	.320	.281	68	-62	19	5		.954	14	S-398/3-32,2	-2.6

YEAR	TM/L	G	AB	R	H	2B	3B	HR	RBI	BB	SO	AVG	OBP	SLG	PRO+	BR/A	SB	CS	SBR	FA	FR	G/POS	TPR

■ NICK CULLOP   Cullop, Henry Nicholas "Tomato Face" b: 10/16/1900, St.Louis, Mo. d: 12/8/78, Westerville, Ohio BR/TR, 6′, 200 lbs. Deb: 4/14/26

YEAR	TM/L	G	AB	R	H	2B	3B	HR	RBI	BB	SO	AVG	OBP	SLG	PRO+	BR/A	SB	CS	SBR	FA	FR	G/POS	TPR
1926	NY-A	2	2	0	1	0	0	0	0	0	1	.500	.500	.500	164	0	0	0	0	.000	0	H	0.0
1927	Was-A	15	23	2	5	2	0	0	1	1	6	.217	.250	.304	44	-2	0			1.000	-1	/O-5,1-1	-0.3
	Cle-A	32	68	9	16	2	3	1	8	9	19	.235	.333	.397	88	-1	0	4	-2	.982	3	O-20/P-1	-0.2
	Yr	47	91	11	21	4	3	1	9	10	25	.231	.314	.374	78	-3	0	4	-2	.984	2	O-25/1-1,P	-0.5
1929	Bro-N	13	41	7	8	2	2	1	5	8	7	.195	.327	.415	84	-1	0			1.000	-1	O-11/1-1	-0.2
1930	Cin-N	7	22	2	4	0	0	1	5	1	9	.182	.217	.318	29	-3	0			1.000	0	/O-5	-0.2
1931	Cin-N	104	334	29	88	23	7	8	48	21	86	.263	.309	.446	107	1	1			.968	0	O-83	-0.4
Total	5	173	490	49	122	29	12	11	67	40	128	.249	.308	.424	96	-6	1	4		.975	2	O-124/1-2,P	-1.3

■ WIL CULMER   Culmer, Wilfred Hillard b: 11/11/58, Nassau, Bahamas BR/TR, 6′4″, 210 lbs. Deb: 4/12/83

YEAR	TM/L	G	AB	R	H	2B	3B	HR	RBI	BB	SO	AVG	OBP	SLG	PRO+	BR/A	SB	CS	SBR	FA	FR	G/POS	TPR
1983	Cle-A	7	19	0	2	0	0	0	1	0	4	.105	.105	.105	-40	-4	0	1	-1	1.000	-1	/O-4,D-2	-0.6

■ BENNY CULP   Culp, Benjamin Baldy b: 1/19/14, Philadelphia, Pa. BR/TR, 5′9″, 175 lbs. Deb: 9/17/42 C

YEAR	TM/L	G	AB	R	H	2B	3B	HR	RBI	BB	SO	AVG	OBP	SLG	PRO+	BR/A	SB	CS	SBR	FA	FR	G/POS	TPR
1942	Phi-N	1	0	0	0	0	0	0	0	0	0	—	—	—		0	0			.500	-0	/C-1	0.0
1943	Phi-N	10	24	4	5	1	0	0	2	3	3	.208	.296	.250	61	-1	0			.958	-3	C-10	-0.3
1944	Phi-N	4	2	1	0	0	0	0	0	0	0	.000	.000	.000	-99	-1	0			1.000	0	/C-1	0.0
Total	3	15	26	5	5	1	0	0	2	3	3	.192	.276	.231	49	-2	0			.926	-3	/C-12	-0.3

■ JACK CUMMINGS   Cummings, John William b: 4/1/04, Pittsburgh, Pa. d: 10/5/62, W.Mifflin, Pa. BR/TR, 6′, 195 lbs. Deb: 9/11/26

YEAR	TM/L	G	AB	R	H	2B	3B	HR	RBI	BB	SO	AVG	OBP	SLG	PRO+	BR/A	SB	CS	SBR	FA	FR	G/POS	TPR
1926	NY-N	7	16	3	5	3	0	0	4	4	2	.313	.450	.500	157	2	0			.958	0	/C-6	0.2
1927	NY-N	43	80	8	29	6	1	2	14	5	10	.363	.407	.538	151	6	0			.974	-5	C-34	0.2
1928	NY-N	33	27	4	9	2	0	2	9	3	4	.333	.400	.630	165	2	0			.833	0	/C-4	0.2
1929	NY-N	3	3	0	1	0	0	0	0	0	0	.333	.333	.333	66	-0	0			1.000	0	/C-1	0.0
	Bos-N	3	6	0	1	0	0	0	1	0	2	.167	.167	.167	-18	-1	0			.667	-1	/C-3	-0.2
	Yr	6	9	0	2	0	0	0	1	0	2	.222	.222	.222	11	-1	0			.714	-1	/C-4	-0.2
Total	4	89	132	15	45	11	1	4	28	12	18	.341	.400	.530	145	8	0			.947	-6	/C-48	0.4

■ MIDRE CUMMINGS   Cummings, Midre Almeric b: 10/14/71, St.Croix, V.I. BB/TR, 6′1″, 190 lbs. Deb: 9/10/93

YEAR	TM/L	G	AB	R	H	2B	3B	HR	RBI	BB	SO	AVG	OBP	SLG	PRO+	BR/A	SB	CS	SBR	FA	FR	G/POS	TPR
1993	Pit-N	13	36	5	4	1	0	0	3	4	9	.111	.200	.139	-7	-5	0	0	0	1.000	-1	O-11	-0.7
1994	Pit-N	24	86	11	21	4	1	0	12	4	18	.244	.286	.326	59	-5	0	0	0	.962	0	O-24	-0.6
Total	2	37	122	16	25	5	1	0	15	8	27	.205	.260	.270	40	-11	0	0	0	.973	-1	/O-35	-1.3

■ GEORGE CUNNINGHAM   Cunningham, George Harold b: 7/13/1894, Sturgeon Lake, Minn. d: 3/10/72, Chattanooga, Tenn. BR/TR, 5′11″, 185 lbs. Deb: 4/14/16

YEAR	TM/L	G	AB	R	H	2B	3B	HR	RBI	BB	SO	AVG	OBP	SLG	PRO+	BR/A	SB	CS	SBR	FA	FR	G/POS	TPR
1916	Det-A	35	41	7	11	2	2	0	3	8	12	.268	.388	.415	136	2	0			.948	5	P-35	0.0
1917	Det-A	44	34	5	6	0	0	1	3	3	13	.176	.243	.265	55	-2	0			.922	0	P-44	0.0
1918	Det-A	56	112	11	25	4	1	0	2	16	34	.223	.320	.277	84	-2	2			.923	-6	P-27,O-20	-0.8
1919	Det-A	26	23	4	5	0	0	0	5	9	8	.217	.438	.217	89	1	0			.857	0	P-17	0.0
1921	Det-A	1	0	0	0	0	0	0	0	0	0	—	—	—		0	0	0	0	1.000	-0	/O-1	0.0
Total	5	162	210	27	47	6	3	1	13	36	67	.224	.337	.295	91	-1	2	0		.923	-4	P-123/O-21	-0.8

■ JOE CUNNINGHAM   Cunningham, Joseph Robert b: 8/27/31, Paterson, N.J. BL/TL, 6′1″, 190 lbs. Deb: 6/30/54 C

YEAR	TM/L	G	AB	R	H	2B	3B	HR	RBI	BB	SO	AVG	OBP	SLG	PRO+	BR/A	SB	CS	SBR	FA	FR	G/POS	TPR
1954	StL-N	85	310	40	88	11	3	11	50	43	40	.284	.375	.445	112	6	1	1	-0	.989	2	1-85	0.3
1956	StL-N	4	3	1	0	0	0	0	0	1	1	.000	.250	.000	-25	-1	0	0	0	1.000	-0	/1-1	-0.1
1957	StL-N	122	261	50	83	15	0	9	52	56	29	.318	.447	.479	146	20	3	3	-1	1.000	-3	1-57,O-46	1.2
1958	StL-N	131	337	61	105	20	3	12	57	82	23	.312	.450	.496	144	26	4	4	-1	.997	-6	1-67,O-66	1.3
1959	StL-N★	144	458	65	158	28	6	7	60	88	47	.345	.456	.478	140	31	2	6	-3	.972	-7	*O-121,1-35	1.4
1960	StL-N	139	492	68	138	28	3	6	39	59	59	.280	.364	.386	97	-0	1	7	-4	.950	-7	*O-116,1-15	-1.9
1961	StL-N	113	322	60	92	11	2	7	40	53	32	.286	.404	.398	104	4	1	0	0	.964	-9	O-86,1-10	-1.0
1962	Chi-A	149	526	91	155	32	7	8	70	101	59	.295	.415	.428	128	26	3	3	-1	.994	-6	*1-143/O-5	0.9
1963	Chi-A	67	210	32	60	12	1	1	31	33	23	.286	.393	.367	116	6	1	0	0	.989	-7	1-58	-0.3
1964	Chi-A	40	108	13	27	7	0	0	10	14	15	.250	.352	.315	90	-1	0	1	-1	.996	-1	1-33	-0.3
	Was-A	49	126	15	27	4	0	0	7	23	13	.214	.344	.246	68	-4	0	1	-1	.997	-4	1-41	-1.1
	Yr	89	234	28	54	11	0	0	17	37	28	.231	.348	.278	78	-5	0	2	-2	.997	-5	1-74	-1.4
1965	Was-A	95	201	29	46	9	1	3	20	46	27	.229	.375	.328	103	3	0	1	-1	.986	-4	1-59	-0.5
1966	Was-A	3	8	0	1	0	0	0	0	1	1	.125	.125	.125	-28	-1	0	0	0	1.000	1	/1-3	0.0
Total	12	1141	3362	525	980	177	26	64	436	599	369	.291	.406	.417	119	116	16	27	-11	.993	-51	1-607,O-440	-0.1

■ RAY CUNNINGHAM   Cunningham, Raymond Lee b: 1/17/08, Mesquite, Tex. BR/TR, 5′7.5″, 150 lbs. Deb: 9/16/31

YEAR	TM/L	G	AB	R	H	2B	3B	HR	RBI	BB	SO	AVG	OBP	SLG	PRO+	BR/A	SB	CS	SBR	FA	FR	G/POS	TPR
1931	StL-N	3	4	0	0	0	0	0	1	0	0	.000	.000	.000	-96	-1	0			1.000	1	/3-3	0.0
1932	StL-N	11	22	4	4	1	0	0	0	3	4	.182	.280	.227	37	-2	0			1.000	3	/3-8,2-2	0.1
Total	2	14	26	4	4	1	0	0	1	3	4	.154	.241	.192	18	-3	0			1.000	4	/3-11,2-2	0.1

■ BILL CUNNINGHAM   Cunningham, William Aloysius b: 7/30/1895, San Francisco, Cal. d: 9/26/53, Colusa, Cal. BR/TR, 5′8″, 155 lbs. Deb: 7/14/21 C

YEAR	TM/L	G	AB	R	H	2B	3B	HR	RBI	BB	SO	AVG	OBP	SLG	PRO+	BR/A	SB	CS	SBR	FA	FR	G/POS	TPR
1921	NY-N	40	76	10	21	2	1	1	12	3	3	.276	.313	.368	79	-2	0	1	-1	1.000	-4	O-20	-0.8
1922	*NY-N	85	229	37	75	15	2	2	33	7	9	.328	.350	.437	101	-0	4	5	-2	.988	-4	O-71/3-1	-0.9
1923	*NY-N	79	203	22	55	1	7	5	27	10	9	.271	.305	.389	83	-6	5	2	0	.992	-7	O-68/2-4	-1.5
1924	Bos-N	114	437	44	119	15	8	1	40	32	27	.272	.326	.350	85	-9	8	5	-1	.970	6	*O-109	-1.1
Total	4	318	945	113	270	39	12	9	112	52	48	.286	.326	.381	88	-17	17	13	-3	.982	-8	O-268/2-4,3	-4.3

■ BILL CUNNINGHAM   Cunningham, William John b: 6/9/1888, Schenectady, N.Y. d: 2/21/46, Schenectady, N.Y. BR/TR, 5′9″, 170 lbs. Deb: 9/12/10

YEAR	TM/L	G	AB	R	H	2B	3B	HR	RBI	BB	SO	AVG	OBP	SLG	PRO+	BR/A	SB	CS	SBR	FA	FR	G/POS	TPR
1910	Was-A	21	74	3	22	5	1	0	14	12		.297	.402	.392	156	5	4			.957	-5	2-21	0.0
1911	Was-A	94	331	34	63	10	5	3	37	19		.190	.239	.278	45	-26	10			.932	-13	2-93	-4.1
1912	Was-A	8	27	5	5	1	0	1	8	3		.185	.267	.333	71	-1	2			.962	-3	2-7,S-1	-0.4
Total	3	123	432	42	90	16	6	4	59	34		.208	.271	.301	64	-21	16			.938	-21	2-121/S-1	-4.5

■ DOC CURLEY   Curley, Walter James b: 3/12/1874, Upton, Mass. d: 9/23/20, Framingham, Mass. BR/TR, Deb: 9/12/1899

YEAR	TM/L	G	AB	R	H	2B	3B	HR	RBI	BB	SO	AVG	OBP	SLG	PRO+	BR/A	SB	CS	SBR	FA	FR	G/POS	TPR
1899	Chi-N	10	37	7	4	0	1	0	2	3		.108	.233	.162	9	-5	0			.907	-6	2-10	-0.9

■ PETE CURREN   Curren, Peter b: Baltimore, Md. Deb: 9/12/1876

YEAR	TM/L	G	AB	R	H	2B	3B	HR	RBI	BB	SO	AVG	OBP	SLG	PRO+	BR/A	SB	CS	SBR	FA	FR	G/POS	TPR
1876	Phi-N	3	12	5	4	1	0	0		2	0	.333	.333	.417	150	1				.588	-1	/C-2,O-1	0.0

■ PERRY CURRIN   Currin, Perry Gilmore b: 9/27/28, Washington, D.C. BL/TR, 6′, 175 lbs. Deb: 6/29/47

YEAR	TM/L	G	AB	R	H	2B	3B	HR	RBI	BB	SO	AVG	OBP	SLG	PRO+	BR/A	SB	CS	SBR	FA	FR	G/POS	TPR
1947	StL-A	3	2	0	0	0	0	0	0	1	0	.000	.333	.000	-3	-0	0	0	0	1.000	1	/S-1	0.1

■ TONY CURRY   Curry, George Anthony b: 12/22/38, Nassau, Bahamas BL/TL, 5′11″, 185 lbs. Deb: 4/12/60

YEAR	TM/L	G	AB	R	H	2B	3B	HR	RBI	BB	SO	AVG	OBP	SLG	PRO+	BR/A	SB	CS	SBR	FA	FR	G/POS	TPR
1960	Phi-N	95	245	26	64	14	2	6	34	16	53	.261	.309	.408	94	-2	0	2	-1	.925	-8	O-64	-1.4
1961	Phi-N	15	36	3	7	2	0	0	3	1	8	.194	.216	.250	24	-4	0			.833	-0	/O-8	-0.5
1966	Cle-A	19	16	4	2	0	0	0	3	3	8	.125	.263	.125	16	-2	0			.000	0	H	-0.2
Total	3	129	297	33	73	16	2	6	40	20	69	.246	.296	.374	82	-8	0	2	-1	.915	-8	/O-72	-2.1

■ JIM CURRY   Curry, James E. b: 3/10/1893, Camden, N.J. d: 8/2/38, Lakeland, N.J. BR/TR, 5′11″, 160 lbs. Deb: 10/2/09

YEAR	TM/L	G	AB	R	H	2B	3B	HR	RBI	BB	SO	AVG	OBP	SLG	PRO+	BR/A	SB	CS	SBR	FA	FR	G/POS	TPR
1909	Phi-A	1	4	1	1	0	0	0	0	0		.250	.250	.250	57	-0	0			1.000	-1	/2-1	-0.1
1911	NY-A	4	11	3	2	0	0	0	1	0		.182	.250	.182	20	-1	0			.773	-1	/2-4	-0.3
1918	Det-A	5	20	1	5	1	0	0	0	1		.250	.286	.300	80	-1	0			.952	-3	/2-5	-0.3
Total	3	10	35	5	8	1	0	0	1	1	0	.229	.270	.257						.867	-5	/2-10	-0.7

YEAR	TM/L	G	AB	R	H	2B	3B	HR	RBI	BB	SO	AVG	OBP	SLG	PRO+	BR/A	SB	CS	SBR	FA	FR	G/POS	TPR

■ **CHAD CURTIS**   Curtis, Chad David   b: 11/6/68, Marion, Ind.   BR/TR, 5'10", 175 lbs.   Deb: 4/8/92

YEAR	TM/L	G	AB	R	H	2B	3B	HR	RBI	BB	SO	AVG	OBP	SLG	PRO+	BR/A	SB	CS	SBR	FA	FR	G/POS	TPR
1992	Cal-A	139	441	59	114	16	2	10	46	51	71	.259	.343	.372	100	1	43	18	2	.978	-3	*O-135/D-1	-0.2
1993	Cal-A	152	583	94	166	25	3	6	59	70	89	.285	.365	.369	95	-2	48	24	0	.980	17	*O-151/2-3	1.1
1994	Cal-A	114	453	67	116	23	4	11	50	37	69	.256	.319	.397	81	-13	25	11	1	.988	15	*O-114	0.0
Total	3	405	1477	220	396	64	9	27	155	158	229	.268	.345	.378	92	-15	116	53	3	.982	29	O-400/2-3,D	0.9

■ **ERVIN CURTIS**   Curtis, Ervin Duane   b: 12/27/1861, Coldwater, Mich.   d: 2/14/45, N.Adams, Mass.   BL/TL, 5'8.5", 157 lbs.   Deb: 7/15/1891

YEAR	TM/L	G	AB	R	H	2B	3B	HR	RBI	BB	SO	AVG	OBP	SLG	PRO+	BR/A	SB	CS	SBR	FA	FR	G/POS	TPR
1891	Cin-N	27	108	11	29	3	1	1	13	9	19	.269	.331	.380	106	1	3			.862	-0	O-27	-0.1
	Was-a	29	103	17	26	3	2	0	12	13	16	.252	.347	.320	96	-0	2			.797	-1	O-29	-0.2
Total	1	56	211	28	55	6	5	1	25	22	35	.261	.339	.351	101	0	5			.829	-2	/O-56	-0.3

■ **GENE CURTIS**   Curtis, Eugene Holmes "Eude"   b: 5/5/1883, Bethany, W.Va.   d: 1/1/19, Steubenville, Ohio   BR/TR, 6'3", 220 lbs.   Deb: 9/21/03

YEAR	TM/L	G	AB	R	H	2B	3B	HR	RBI	BB	SO	AVG	OBP	SLG	PRO+	BR/A	SB	CS	SBR	FA	FR	G/POS	TPR
1903	Pit-N	5	19	2	8	1	0	0	3	1		.421	.450	.474	158	1	0			.833	-0	/O-5	0.1

■ **FRED CURTIS**   Curtis, Frederick Marion   b: 10/30/1880, Beaver Lake, Mich.   d: 4/5/39, Minneapolis, Minn.   BR/TR, 6'1",   Deb: 7/24/05

YEAR	TM/L	G	AB	R	H	2B	3B	HR	RBI	BB	SO	AVG	OBP	SLG	PRO+	BR/A	SB	CS	SBR	FA	FR	G/POS	TPR
1905	NY-A	2	9	0	2	1	0	0	2	1		.222	.300	.333	90	-0	1			1.000	-0	/1-2	0.0

■ **HARRY CURTIS**   Curtis, Harry Albert   b: 2/19/1883, Portland, Maine   d: 8/1/51, Evanston, Ill.   TR, 5'10.5", 170 lbs.   Deb: 8/28/07

YEAR	TM/L	G	AB	R	H	2B	3B	HR	RBI	BB	SO	AVG	OBP	SLG	PRO+	BR/A	SB	CS	SBR	FA	FR	G/POS	TPR
1907	NY-N	6	9	2	2	0	0	0	1	2		.222	.364	.222	81	-0	2			.909	0	/C-6	0.0

■ **GUY CURTRIGHT**   Curtright, Guy Paxton   b: 10/18/12, Holliday, Mo.   BR/TR, 5'11", 200 lbs.   Deb: 4/21/43

YEAR	TM/L	G	AB	R	H	2B	3B	HR	RBI	BB	SO	AVG	OBP	SLG	PRO+	BR/A	SB	CS	SBR	FA	FR	G/POS	TPR
1943	Chi-A	138	488	67	142	20	7	3	48	69	60	.291	.382	.379	123	16	13	12	-3	.972	-2	*O-128	0.5
1944	Chi-A	72	198	22	50	8	2	2	23	23	21	.253	.330	.343	94	-1	4	3	-1	.948	1	O-51	-0.3
1945	Chi-A	98	324	51	91	15	7	4	32	39	29	.281	.358	.407	125	10	3	4	-2	.986	1	O-84	0.6
1946	Chi-A	23	55	7	11	2	0	0	5	11	14	.200	.333	.236	63	-2	0	1	-1	1.000	1	O-15	-0.3
Total	4	331	1065	147	294	45	16	9	108	142	124	.276	.363	.374	115	23	20	20	-6	.973	2	O-278	0.5

■ **TONY CUSICK**   Cusick, Andrew Daniel "Andy"   b: 12/1857, Fall River, Mass.   d: 8/6/29, Chicago, Ill.   BR/TR, 5'9.5", 190 lbs.   Deb: 8/21/1884

YEAR	TM/L	G	AB	R	H	2B	3B	HR	RBI	BB	SO	AVG	OBP	SLG	PRO+	BR/A	SB	CS	SBR	FA	FR	G/POS	TPR
1884	Wil-U	11	34	0	5	0	0	0			1	.147	.171	.147	-12	-5				.871	-0	/C-6,S-3,023	-0.4
	Phi-N	9	29	2	4	0	0	0	1	0	3	.138	.138	.138	-14	-4				.930	4	/C-9	0.1
1885	Phi-N	39	141	12	25	1	0	0	5	1	24	.177	.183	.184	19	-12				.808	-3	C-38/O-1	-1.2
1886	Phi-N	29	104	10	23	5	1	0	4	3	14	.221	.243	.288	61	-5	1			.891	-6	C-25/O-3,1	-0.7
1887	Phi-N	7	24	3	7	1	0	0	5	3	1	.292	.393	.333	98	0				.643	-3	/C-4,1-3,2	-0.3
Total	4	95	332	27	64	7	1	0	15	8	42	.193	.214	.220	33	-26	1			.844	-8	/C-82,0-7,1S23	-2.5

■ **JACK CUSICK**   Cusick, John Peter   b: 6/12/28, Weehawken, N.J.   d: 11/17/89, Edgewood, N.J.   BR/TR, 6', 170 lbs.   Deb: 4/24/51

YEAR	TM/L	G	AB	R	H	2B	3B	HR	RBI	BB	SO	AVG	OBP	SLG	PRO+	BR/A	SB	CS	SBR	FA	FR	G/POS	TPR
1951	Chi-N	65	164	16	29	3	2	6	16	17	29	.177	.254	.256	37	-15	2	1	0	.953	-2	S-56	-1.3
1952	Bos-N	49	78	5	13	1	0	0	6	6	9	.167	.226	.179	14	-9	0	1	-1	.969	-2	S-28/3-3	-1.1
Total	2	114	242	21	42	4	2	6	22	23	38	.174	.245	.231	30	-24	2	2	-1	.958	-4	/S-84,3-3	-2.4

■ **NED CUTHBERT**   Cuthbert, Edgar Edward   b: 6/20/1845, Philadelphia, Pa.   d: 2/6/05, St.Louis, Mo.   BR/TR, 5'6", 140 lbs.   Deb: 5/20/1871   MU

YEAR	TM/L	G	AB	R	H	2B	3B	HR	RBI	BB	SO	AVG	OBP	SLG	PRO+	BR/A	SB	CS	SBR	FA	FR	G/POS	TPR
1871	Ath-n	28	150	47	37	7	5	3	30	10	2	.247	.294	.420	103	1	16					*O-27/C-1	0.1
1872	Ath-n	47	258	82	90	9	0	1	47	6	10	.349	.364	.395	133	10						*O-46	0.9
1873	Phi-n	51	278	78	77	5	3	2	32	2	4	.277	.282	.338	79	-8						*O-51	-0.3
1874	Chi-n	58	293	65	81	6	1	1		7		.276	.293	.314	93	-2						*O-55/C-3	-0.1
1875	StL-n	68	318	68	77	9	2	0		3		.242	.249	.283	92	-1						*O-67/C-2	0.0
1876	StL-N	63	283	46	70	10	1	0	25	7	4	.247	.266	.290	90	-2				.843	-8	*O-63	-1.0
1877	Cin-N	12	56	6	10	5	0	0	2	1	2	.179	.193	.268	49	-3				.830	4	O-12	0.1
1882	StL-a	60	233	28	52	16	5	0		17		.223	.276	.335	101	0				.896	-4	*O-60,M	-0.4
1883	StL-a	21	71	3	12	1	0	0		4		.169	.213	.183	27	-6				.794	-1	O-20/1-1	-0.6
1884	Bal-U	44	168	29	34	5	0	0		10		.202	.247	.232	28	-17				.750	-5	O-44	-2.1
Total	5 n	252	1297	340	362	36	11	7	109	28	16	.279	.294	.340	99	-1						O-246/C-6	0.6
Total	5	200	811	112	178	37	6	0	27	39	6	.219	.255	.280	69	-28				.833	-14	O-199/1-1	-4.0

■ **GEORGE CUTSHAW**   Cutshaw, George William "Clancy"   b: 7/27/1887, Wilmington, Ill.   d: 8/22/73, San Diego, Cal.   BR/TR, 5'9", 160 lbs.   Deb: 4/25/12

YEAR	TM/L	G	AB	R	H	2B	3B	HR	RBI	BB	SO	AVG	OBP	SLG	PRO+	BR/A	SB	CS	SBR	FA	FR	G/POS	TPR
1912	Bro-N	102	357	41	100	14	4	0	28	31	16	.280	.341	.342	91	-4	16			.958	2	2-91/3-5,S	0.2
1913	Bro-N	147	592	72	158	23	13	2	80	39	22	.267	.315	.385	97	-4	39			.957	18	*2-147	1.2
1914	Bro-N	153	583	69	150	22	12	2	78	30	32	.257	.297	.346	89	-10	34			.959	28	*2-153	1.8
1915	Bro-N	154	566	68	139	18	9	0	62	34	35	.246	.293	.309	81	-13	28	23	-5	**.971**	17	*2-154	0.0
1916	*Bro-N	154	581	58	151	21	4	2	63	25	32	.260	.292	.320	85	-11	27	20	-4	.958	8	*2-154	-0.2
1917	Bro-N	135	487	42	126	17	7	4	49	21	26	.259	.292	.347	93	-5	22			.963	-9	*2-134	-0.9
1918	Pit-N	126	463	56	132	16	10	5	68	22	18	.285	.326	.395	115	7	25			.964	-3	*2-126	1.4
1919	Pit-N	139	512	49	124	15	8	3	51	30	22	.242	.287	.320	79	-13	36			**.980**	-11	*2-139	-2.0
1920	Pit-N	131	488	56	123	16	0	0	47	23	10	.252	.287	.318	71	-18	17	14	-3	.968	1	*2-129	-1.8
1921	Pit-N	98	350	46	119	18	4	0	53	11	11	.340	.362	.414	102	1	14	5	1	.951	-15	2-84	-1.1
1922	Det-A	132	499	57	133	14	8	2	61	20	13	.267	.300	.339	68	-24	11	5	0	.972	9	*2-132	-1.1
1923	Det-A	45	143	15	32	1	2	0	13	9	5	.224	.279	.259	43	-12	2	1	0	.988	12	2-43/3-2	0.0
Total	12	1516	5621	629	1487	195	89	25	653	300	242	.265	.305	.344	86	-106	271	68		.965	61	*2-1486/3-7,S	-2.5

■ **KIKI CUYLER**   Cuyler, Hazen Shirley   b: 8/30/1899, Harrisville, Mich.   d: 2/11/50, Ann Arbor, Mich.   BR/TR, 5'10.5", 180 lbs.   Deb: 9/29/21   CH

YEAR	TM/L	G	AB	R	H	2B	3B	HR	RBI	BB	SO	AVG	OBP	SLG	PRO+	BR/A	SB	CS	SBR	FA	FR	G/POS	TPR
1921	Pit-N	1	3	0	0	0	0	0	0	0	1	.000	.000	.000	-97	-1	0	0	0	1.000	-0	/O-1	-0.1
1922	Pit-N	1	0	0	0	0	0	0	0	0	0	—	—	—	—	0	0	0	0	.000	0	R	0.0
1923	Pit-N	11	40	4	10	1	1	0	2	5	3	.250	.348	.325	77	-1	2	3	-1	.931	-1	O-11	-0.4
1924	Pit-N	117	466	94	165	27	16	9	85	30	62	.354	.402	.539	147	30	32	11	3	.943	5	*O-114	3.0
1925	*Pit-N	153	617	**144**	220	43	**26**	18	102	58	56	.357	.423	.598	148	44	41	13	5	.967	7	*O-153	4.1
1926	Pit-N	157	614	113	197	31	15	8	92	50	66	.321	.380	.459	119	16	**35**			.968	13	*O-157	1.8
1927	Pit-N	85	285	60	88	13	9	2	31	37	36	.309	.394	.435	114	7	20			.980	1	O-73	0.3
1928	Chi-N	133	499	92	142	25	9	17	79	51	61	.285	.359	.473	117	12	**37**			.982	0	*O-127	0.9
1929	*Chi-N	139	509	111	183	29	7	15	102	66	56	.360	.438	.532	139	33	**43**			.974	-0	*O-129	2.2
1930	Chi-N	156	642	155	228	50	17	13	134	72	49	.355	.428	.547	133	36	**37**			.980	12	*O-156	3.2
1931	Chi-N	154	613	100	202	37	12	9	88	72	54	.330	.404	.473	133	30	13			.970	-4	*O-153	1.6
1932	*Chi-N	110	446	58	130	19	9	10	77	29	43	.291	.340	.442	109	5	9			.969	-7	*O-109	-0.8
1933	Chi-N	70	262	37	83	15	4	5	35	28	16	.317	.376	.477	135	12	4			.978	-7	O-69	0.1
1934	Chi-N★	142	559	80	189	**42**	8	6	69	31	62	.338	.377	.474	129	22	15			.971	0	*O-142	1.6
1935	Chi-N	45	157	22	42	5	1	4	18	10	16	.268	.331	.389	92	-2	3			.981	-1	O-42	-0.4
	Cin-N	62	223	36	56	8	3	2	22	27	18	.251	.337	.341	85	-4	5			.985	-3	O-57	-0.8
	Yr	107	380	58	98	13	4	6	40	37	34	.258	.335	.361	88	-6	8			.983	-3	O-99	-1.2
1936	Cin-N	144	567	96	185	29	11	7	74	47	67	.326	.380	.453	132	25	16			.974	-4	*O-140	1.5
1937	Cin-N	117	406	48	110	12	4	0	32	36	50	.271	.333	.320	82	-9	10			.973	-8	*O-106	-2.1
1938	Bro-N	82	253	45	69	10	8	2	23	34	23	.273	.363	.399	107	3	6			.993	0	O-68	0.1
Total	18	1879	7161	1295	2299	394	157	128	1065	676	752	.321	.386	.474	125	258	328	27		.972	12	*O-1807	15.8

■ **MILT CUYLER**   Cuyler, Milton   b: 10/7/68, Macon, Ga.   BB/TR, 5'10", 175 lbs.   Deb: 9/6/90

YEAR	TM/L	G	AB	R	H	2B	3B	HR	RBI	BB	SO	AVG	OBP	SLG	PRO+	BR/A	SB	CS	SBR	FA	FR	G/POS	TPR
1990	Det-A	19	51	8	13	3	0	0	8	5	10	.255	.321	.353	88	-1	1	2	-1	.976	1	O-17	-0.2
1991	Det-A	154	475	77	122	15	7	3	33	52	92	.257	.336	.337	86	-8	41	10	6	.986	8	*O-151	0.3

YEAR TM/L	G	AB	R	H	2B	3B	HR	RBI	BB	SO	AVG	OBP	SLG	PRO+	BR/A	SB	CS	SBR	FA	FR	G/POS	TPR
1992 Det-A	89	291	39	70	11	1	3	28	10	62	.241	.275	.316	65	-14	8	5	-1	.983	-0	O-89	-1.7
1993 Det-A	82	249	46	53	11	7	0	19	19	53	.213	.277	.313	59	-15	13	2	3	.968	1	O-80	-1.2
1994 Det-A	48	116	20	28	3	1	1	11	13	21	.241	.323	.310	65	-6	5	3	-0	.975	-9	O-45	-1.4
Total 5	392	1182	190	286	43	17	7	99	99	238	.242	.308	.325	73	-43	68	22	7	.980	0	O-382	-4.2

■ AL CYPERT Cypert, Alfred Boyd "Cy" b: 8/8/1889, Little Rock, Ark. d: 1/9/73, Washington, D.C. BR/TR, 5'10.5", 150 lbs. Deb: 6/27/14

YEAR TM/L	G	AB	R	H	2B	3B	HR	RBI	BB	SO	AVG	OBP	SLG	PRO+	BR/A	SB	CS	SBR	FA	FR	G/POS	TPR
1914 Cle-A	1	1	0	0	0	0	0	0	0	1	.000	.000	.000	-96	-0	0			.000	0	/3-1	0.0

■ PAUL DADE Dade, Lonnie Paul b: 12/7/51, Seattle, Wash. BR/TR, 6', 195 lbs. Deb: 9/12/75

YEAR TM/L	G	AB	R	H	2B	3B	HR	RBI	BB	SO	AVG	OBP	SLG	PRO+	BR/A	SB	CS	SBR	FA	FR	G/POS	TPR
1975 Cal-A	11	30	5	6	4	0	0	1	6	7	.200	.333	.333	96	-0	0	0	0	1.000	1	/O-3,3-1,D	0.0
1976 Cal-A	13	9	2	1	0	0	0	1	3	3	.111	.333	.111	36	-1	0	0	0	.750	-2	/O-4,2-2,3D	0.0
1977 Cle-A	134	461	65	134	15	3	3	45	32	58	.291	.339	.356	93	-4	16	8	0	.989	-7	O-99,3-26/2D	-1.6
1978 Cle-A	93	307	37	78	12	1	3	20	34	45	.254	.332	.329	88	-4	12	9	-2	.962	2	O-81/D-9	-0.8
1979 Cle-A	44	170	22	48	4	1	3	18	12	22	.282	.330	.371	88	-3	12	6	0	.962	2	O-37/3-2,D	-0.2
SD-N	76	283	38	78	19	2	1	19	14	48	.276	.314	.367	91	-4	13	5	1	.949	6	3-70/O-4	0.1
1980 SD-N	68	53	17	10	0	0	0	3	12	10	.189	.338	.189	54	-3	4	5	-2	.846	1	3-21/O-8,2	-0.3
Total 6	439	1313	186	355	54	7	10	107	113	193	.270	.331	.345	89	-19	57	33	-3	.970	4	O-236,3-121/D2	-2.8

■ ANGELO DAGRES Dagres, Angelo George "Junior" b: 8/22/34, Newburyport, Mass. BL/TL, 5'11", 175 lbs. Deb: 9/11/55

YEAR TM/L	G	AB	R	H	2B	3B	HR	RBI	BB	SO	AVG	OBP	SLG	PRO+	BR/A	SB	CS	SBR	FA	FR	G/POS	TPR
1955 Bal-A	8	15	5	4	0	0	0	3	1	2	.267	.313	.267	61	-1	0	0	0	.818	-1	/O-5	-0.2

■ BILL DAHLEN Dahlen, William Frederick "Bad Bill" b: 1/5/1870, Nelliston, N.Y. d: 12/5/50, Brooklyn, N.Y. BR/TR, 5'9", 180 lbs. Deb: 4/22/1891 M

YEAR TM/L	G	AB	R	H	2B	3B	HR	RBI	BB	SO	AVG	OBP	SLG	PRO+	BR/A	SB	CS	SBR	FA	FR	G/POS	TPR
1891 Chi-N	135	549	114	143	18	13	9	76	67	60	.260	.348	.390	115	11	21			.887	9	3-84,O-37,S	2.0
1892 Chi-N	143	581	114	169	23	19	5	58	45	56	.291	.347	.422	131	19	60			.909	25	S-72,3-68/O2	4.6
1893 Chi-N	116	485	113	146	28	15	5	64	58	30	.301	.381	.452	123	15	31			.892	3	*S-88,O-17,2/3	1.8
1894 Chi-N	121	502	149	179	32	14	15	107	76	33	.357	.444	.566	135	28	42			.898	32	S-66,3-55	**4.8**
1895 Chi-N	129	516	106	131	19	10	7	62	61	51	.254	.344	.370	79	-18	38			.904	36	*S-129/O-1	1.9
1896 Chi-N	125	474	137	167	30	19	9	74	64	36	.352	.438	.553	154	37	51			.915	25	*S-125	5.5
1897 Chi-N	75	276	67	80	18	8	6	40	43		.290	.399	.478	126	11	15			.930	28	S-75	3.4
1898 Chi-N	142	521	96	151	35	8	1	79	58		.290	.385	.393	123	18	27			.921	26	*S-142	**4.6**
1899 Bro-N	121	428	87	121	22	7	4	76	67		.283	.398	.395	115	12	29			.941	17	*S-110,3-11	3.4
1900 *Bro-N	133	483	87	125	16	11	4	69	73		.259	.364	.344	90	-5	31			.938	20	*S-133	2.3
1901 Bro-N	131	511	69	136	17	9	4	82	30		.266	.313	.358	92	-6	23			.929	14	*S-129/2-2	1.8
1902 Bro-N	138	527	67	139	25	8	2	74	43		.264	.329	.353	110	6	20			.916	-6	*S-138	0.8
1903 Bro-N	138	474	71	124	17	9	1	64	82		.262	.373	.342	107	8	34			**.948**	18	*S-138	3.0
1904 NY-L	145	523	70	140	26	2	2	**80**	44		.268	.326	.337	100	0	47			.930	28	*S-145	3.3
1905 *NY-L	148	520	67	126	20	4	7	81	62		.242	.337	.337	99	1	37			.948	20	*S-147/O-1	2.4
1906 NY-L	143	471	63	113	18	3	1	49	76		.240	.337	.297	102	5	16			.938	0	*S-143	1.1
1907 NY-L	143	464	40	96	20	1	0	34	51		.207	.291	.254	69	-16	11			.941	7	*S-143	-0.5
1908 Bos-N	144	524	50	125	23	2	3	48	35		.239	.296	.307	94	-4	10			.952	**38**	*S-144	4.2
1909 Bos-N	69	197	22	46	6	1	2	16	29		.234	.332	.305	93	-1	4			.908	9	S-49/2-6,3	1.0
1910 Bro-N	3	2	0	0	0	0	0	0	0		.000	.000	.000	-99	-1	0			.000	0	HM	-0.1
1911 Bro-N	1	3	0	0	0	0	0	0	0	3	.000	.000	.000	-99	-1	0			1.000	2	/S-1,M	0.1
Total 21	2443	9031	1589	2457	413	163	84	1233	1064	269	.272	.358	.382	109	121	547			.927	348	*S-2132,3-223/O2	51.4

■ BABE DAHLGREN Dahlgren, Ellsworth Tenney b: 6/15/12, San Francisco, Cal. BR/TR, 6', 190 lbs. Deb: 4/16/35 C

YEAR TM/L	G	AB	R	H	2B	3B	HR	RBI	BB	SO	AVG	OBP	SLG	PRO+	BR/A	SB	CS	SBR	FA	FR	G/POS	TPR
1935 Bos-A	149	525	77	138	27	7	9	63	56	67	.263	.337	.392	83	-14	6	5	-1	.988	-7	*1-149	-3.7
1936 Bos-A	16	57	6	16	3	1	1	7	7	1	.281	.359	.421	87	-1	2	1	0	.980	-1	1-16	-0.3
1937 NY-A	1	1	0	0	0	0	0	0	0	0	.000	.000	.000	-99	-0	0	0	0	.000	0	H	0.0
1938 NY-A	27	43	8	8	1	0	0	1	1	7	.186	.205	.209	4	-6	0	0	0	.826	-1	/3-8,1-6	-0.7
1939 *NY-A	144	531	71	125	18	6	15	89	57	54	.235	.312	.377	76	-20	2	3	-1	.991	-7	*1-144	-4.1
1940 NY-A	155	568	51	150	24	4	12	73	46	54	.264	.325	.384	86	-12	1	1	-0	.990	-10	*1-155	-3.6
1941 Bos-N	44	166	20	39	8	1	7	30	16	13	.235	.306	.422	108	1	0			.993	2	1-39/3-5	0.1
Chi-N	99	359	50	101	20	1	16	59	43	39	.281	.360	.476	139	18	2			.991	-8	1-98	0.2
Yr	143	525	70	140	28	2	23	89	59	52	.267	.343	.459	129	19	2			.992	-6	*1-137/3-5	0.3
1942 Chi-N	17	56	4	12	1	0	0	6	6	5	.214	.267	.232	48	-4	0			.986	1	1-14	-0.4
StL-A	2	2	0	0	0	0	0	0	0	0	.000	.000	.000	-99	-1	0			.000	0	H	-0.1
Bro-N	17	19	2	1	0	0	0	0	4	5	.053	.217	.053	-19	-3	0			1.000	1	1-10	-0.1
1943 Phi-N★	136	508	55	146	19	2	5	56	50	39	.287	.354	.362	111	8	2			.988	-23	1-73,3-35,S/C	-1.8
1944 Pit-N	158	599	67	173	28	7	12	101	47	56	.289	.347	.419	110	7	2			.987	8	*1-158	0.7
1945 Pit-N	144	531	55	133	24	6	5	75	51	51	.250	.318	.354	84	-12	1			**.996**	1	*1-144	-2.1
1946 StL-A	28	80	2	14	1	0	0	9	8	13	.175	.250	.188	22	-8	0			.981	1	1-24	-0.9
Total 12	1137	4045	470	1056	174	37	82	569	390	401	.261	.329	.383	92	-49	18	11		.990	-44	*1-1030/3-48,SC	-16.9

■ JOHN DAILEY Dailey, John G. b: Brooklyn, N.Y. Deb: 7/12/1875

YEAR TM/L	G	AB	R	H	2B	3B	HR	RBI	BB	SO	AVG	OBP	SLG	PRO+	BR/A	SB	CS	SBR	FA	FR	G/POS	TPR
1875 Was-n	27	106	17	20	3	5	0		0		.189	.189	.311	72	-3						S-17/3-7,2	-0.3
Atl-n	2	8	3	1	0	0	0		0		.125	.125	.125	-15	-1						/1-1,O-1	-0.1
Yr	29	114	20	21	3	5	0		0		.184	.184	.298	67	-3						S-17/3-7,210	-0.4

■ VINCE DAILEY Dailey, Vincent Perry b: 12/25/1864, Osceola, Pa. d: 11/14/19, Hornell, N.Y. 6', 200 lbs. Deb: 4/21/1890

YEAR TM/L	G	AB	R	H	2B	3B	HR	RBI	BB	SO	AVG	OBP	SLG	PRO+	BR/A	SB	CS	SBR	FA	FR	G/POS	TPR
1890 Cle-N	64	246	41	71	5	7	0	32	33	23	.289	.373	.366	118	6	17			.859	1	O-64/P-2	0.4

■ CON DAILY Daily, Cornelius F. b: 9/11/1864, Blackstone, Mass. d: 6/14/28, Brooklyn, N.Y. BL, 6', 192 lbs. Deb: 6/9/1884 F

YEAR TM/L	G	AB	R	H	2B	3B	HR	RBI	BB	SO	AVG	OBP	SLG	PRO+	BR/A	SB	CS	SBR	FA	FR	G/POS	TPR
1884 Phi-U	2	8	0	0	0	0	0		0		.000	.000	.000	-99	-2				.857	-1	/C-2	-0.3
1885 Pro-N	60	223	20	58	6	1	0	19	12	20	.260	.298	.296	96	-1				.876	-1	C-48/1-7,O	0.2
1886 Bos-N	50	180	25	43	4	2	0	21	19	29	.239	.312	.283	85	-2	2			.911	-11	C-49/O-1	-0.7
1887 Bos-N	36	120	12	19	5	0	0	13	9	8	.158	.229	.200	20	-13	7			.889	-2	C-36	-1.0
1888 Ind-N	57	202	14	44	6	1	0	14	10	28	.218	.255	.257	62	-8	15			.893	-1	C-42/O-5,312	-0.6
1889 Ind-N	62	219	35	55	6	2	0	26	28	21	.251	.347	.297	79	-5	14			.887	-12	C-51/O-6,13	-1.1
1890 Bro-P	46	168	20	42	6	3	0	35	15	14	.250	.315	.321	66	-9	6			.879	-7	C-40/1-6,O	-1.0
1891 Bro-N	60	206	25	66	10	1	0	30	15	13	.320	.387	.379	121	6	7			.925	-0	C-55/O-3,S1	0.9
1892 Bro-N	80	278	38	65	10	1	0	28	38	21	.234	.328	.277	87	-3	18			.943	2	C-68,O-13	-0.3
1893 Bro-N	61	215	33	57	4	2	1	32	32	12	.265	.342	.316	79	-6	13			.935	-1	C-51/O-9	-0.2
1894 Bro-N	67	234	40	60	14	7	0	32	31	22	.256	.351	.376	81	-7	8			.930	-2	C-60/1-7	-0.3
1895 Bro-N	40	142	17	30	3	1	0	11	10	18	.211	.268	.282	46	-12	3			.956	-3	C-39/O-1	-0.9
1896 Chi-N	9	27	1	2	0	0	0	1	1	2	.074	.107	.074	-50	-6	1			.969	-2	/C-9	-0.6
Total 13	630	2222	280	541	74	22	2	262	208	208	.243	.314	.299	76	-68	94			.912	-43	C-550/O-45,13S2	-5.6

■ ED DAILY Daily, Edward M. b: 9/7/1862, Providence, R.I. d: 10/21/1891, Washington, D.C. BR/TR, 5'10.5", 174 lbs. Deb: 5/4/1885 F

YEAR TM/L	G	AB	R	H	2B	3B	HR	RBI	BB	SO	AVG	OBP	SLG	PRO+	BR/A	SB	CS	SBR	FA	FR	G/POS	TPR
1885 Phi-N	50	184	22	38	8	2	1	13	0	25	.207	.207	.288	60	-8				.891	-4	P-50	0.0
1886 Phi-N	79	309	40	70	19	7	5	34	7		.227	.244	.327	72	-11	23			.827	5	O-56,P-27	-0.5
1887 Phi-N	26	106	18	30	11	1	1	17	3	9	.283	.303	.434	97	-1	6			.659	-6	O-22/P-6	-0.7
Was-N	78	311	39	78	6	10	2	36	14	27	.251	.285	.354	81	-8	26			.855	-5	O-77/P-1	-1.3
Yr	104	417	57	108	17	11	3	53	17	36	.259	.290	.374	85	-9	34			.812	-11	O-99/P-7	-2.0
1888 Was-N	110	453	56	102	8	4	7	39	7	42	.225	.239	.307	77	-12	44			.912	4	*O-100/P-9,1	-1.1

YEAR	TM/L	G	AB	R	H	2B	3B	HR	RBI	BB	SO	AVG	OBP	SLG	PRO+	BR/A	SB	CS	SBR	FA	FR	G/POS	TPR
1889	Col-a	136	578	105	148	22	8	3	70	38	65	.256	.303	.337	87	-11	60			.854	-3	*O-136/P-2	-1.5
1890	Bro-a	91	394	68	94	15	7	1		24		.239	.284	.320	81	-11	49			.892	6	O-64,P-27	-0.5
	NY-N	4	15	1	2	1	0	0	1	0	4	.133	.133	.200	-3	-2	0			.500	0	/O-3,P-2	-0.1
	*Lou-a	23	80	24	20	0	2	0		13		.250	.355	.300	95	0	13			.925	1	P-12,O-11	-0.1
1891	Lou-a	22	64	10	16	2	0	0	8	8	6	.250	.342	.281	80	-1	4			.884	0	P-15/O-7	-0.4
	Was-a	21	79	13	18	2	0	0	6	11	10	.228	.322	.253	68	-3	8			.719	-4	O-21	-0.6
	Yr	43	143	23	34	4	0	0	14	19	16	.238	.331	.266	73	-4	12			.750	-3	O-28,P-15	-0.7
Total	7	640	2573	396	616	92	35	19	240	125	222	.239	.276	.325	80	-69	235			.857	-6	O-497,P-151/1	-6.5

■ **GEORGE DAISEY**   Daisey, George K. b: Altoona, Pa. 5'11", 190 lbs. Deb: 5/31/1884

YEAR	TM/L	G	AB	R	H	2B	3B	HR	RBI	BB	SO	AVG	OBP	SLG	PRO+	BR/A	SB	CS	SBR	FA	FR	G/POS	TPR
1884	Alt-U	1	4	0	0	0	0	0				.000	.000	.000	-99	-1				.000	-1	/O-1	-0.2

■ **PETE DALENA**   Dalena, Peter Martin b: 6/26/60, Fresno, Cal. BL/TR, 5'11", 200 lbs. Deb: 7/7/89

YEAR	TM/L	G	AB	R	H	2B	3B	HR	RBI	BB	SO	AVG	OBP	SLG	PRO+	BR/A	SB	CS	SBR	FA	FR	G/POS	TPR
1989	Cle-A	5	7	0	1	0	0	0	0	0	3	.143	.143	.286	18	-1	0	0	0	.000	0	/D-1	-0.1

■ **MARK DALESANDRO**   Dalesandro, Mark Anthony b: 5/14/68, Chicago, Ill. BR/TR, 6', 185 lbs. Deb: 6/6/94

YEAR	TM/L	G	AB	R	H	2B	3B	HR	RBI	BB	SO	AVG	OBP	SLG	PRO+	BR/A	SB	CS	SBR	FA	FR	G/POS	TPR
1994	Cal-A	19	25	5	5	1	0	1	2	2	4	.200	.259	.360	56	-2	0	0	0	1.000	-2	C-11/3-5,O	-0.4

■ **JOHN DALEY**   Daley, John Francis b: 5/25/1887, Pittsburgh, Pa. d: 8/31/88, Mansfield, Ohio BR/TR, 5'7.5", 155 lbs. Deb: 7/19/12

YEAR	TM/L	G	AB	R	H	2B	3B	HR	RBI	BB	SO	AVG	OBP	SLG	PRO+	BR/A	SB	CS	SBR	FA	FR	G/POS	TPR
1912	StL-A	18	52	7	9	0	0	1	3	9		.173	.317	.231	60	-2	4			.833	-4	S-17	-0.5

■ **JUD DALEY**   Daley, Judson Lawrence b: 3/14/1884, S.Coventry, Conn. d: 1/26/67, Gadsden, Ala. BL/TR, 5'8", 172 lbs. Deb: 9/19/11

YEAR	TM/L	G	AB	R	H	2B	3B	HR	RBI	BB	SO	AVG	OBP	SLG	PRO+	BR/A	SB	CS	SBR	FA	FR	G/POS	TPR
1911	Bro-N	19	65	8	15	2	1	0	7	2	8	.231	.286	.292	65	-3	2			.952	2	O-16	-0.3
1912	Bro-N	61	199	22	51	9	1	1	13	24	17	.256	.342	.327	87	-3	2			.947	2	O-55	-0.4
Total	2	80	264	30	66	11	2	1	20	26	25	.250	.329	.318	82	-6	4			.949	3	/O-71	-0.7

■ **PETE DALEY**   Daley, Peter Harvey b: 1/14/30, Grass Valley, Cal. BR/TR, 6', 195 lbs. Deb: 5/3/55

YEAR	TM/L	G	AB	R	H	2B	3B	HR	RBI	BB	SO	AVG	OBP	SLG	PRO+	BR/A	SB	CS	SBR	FA	FR	G/POS	TPR
1955	Bos-A	17	50	4	11	2	1	0	5	3	6	.220	.264	.300	47	-4	0	0	0	1.000	3	C-14	0.0
1956	Bos-A	59	187	22	50	11	3	5	29	18	30	.267	.338	.439	92	-3	1	0	0	.992	-10	C-57	-1.0
1957	Bos-A	78	191	17	43	10	0	3	25	16	31	.225	.288	.325	64	-10	0	0	0	**1.000**	-2	C-77	-1.0
1958	Bos-A	27	56	10	18	2	1	2	8	7	11	.321	.397	.500	136	3	0	0	0	.990	2	C-27	0.6
1959	Bos-A	65	169	9	38	7	0	1	11	13	31	.225	.280	.284	53	-11	1	1	-0	.996	3	C-58	-0.6
1960	KC-A	73	228	19	60	10	2	5	25	16	41	.263	.311	.390	88	-4	0	0	0	.990	-5	C-61/O-1	-0.5
1961	Was-A	72	203	12	39	7	1	2	17	14	37	.192	.244	.266	37	-18	0	1	-1	.988	7	C-72	-1.0
Total	7	391	1084	93	259	49	8	18	120	87	187	.239	.297	.349	71	-47	2	2	-1	.993	-2	C-366/O-1	-3.5

■ **TOM DALEY**   Daley, Thomas Francis "Pete" b: 11/13/1884, Dubois, Pa. d: 12/2/34, Los Angeles, Cal. BL/TR, 5'5", 168 lbs. Deb: 8/29/08

YEAR	TM/L	G	AB	R	H	2B	3B	HR	RBI	BB	SO	AVG	OBP	SLG	PRO+	BR/A	SB	CS	SBR	FA	FR	G/POS	TPR
1908	Cin-N	14	46	5	5	0	0	0	1	3		.109	.196	.109	-2	-5	1			1.000	-0	O-13	-0.7
1913	Phi-A	62	141	13	36	2	1	0	11	13	28	.255	.327	.284	81	-3	4			.963	-1	O-39	-0.6
1914	Phi-A	28	86	17	22	1	3	0	7	12	14	.256	.347	.337	110	1	4	7	-3	1.000	0	O-24	-0.1
	NY-A	69	191	36	48	6	4	0	9	38	13	.251	.378	.325	112	5	8	8	-2	.958	6	O-58	0.6
	Yr	97	277	53	70	7	7	0	16	50	27	.253	.369	.292	111	6	12	15	-5	.969	7	O-82	0.5
1915	NY-A	10	8	2	2	0	0	0	1	2	2	.250	.400	.250	95	0	1			1.000	-0	/O-2	0.0
Total	4	183	472	73	113	9	8	0	29	68	57	.239	.341	.292	92	-2	18	15		.970	6	O-136	-0.8

■ **DOM DALLESSANDRO**   Dallessandro, Nicholas Dominic "Dim Dom" b: 10/3/13, Reading, Pa. d: 4/29/88, Indianapolis, Ind. BL/TL, 5'6", 168 lbs. Deb: 4/24/37

YEAR	TM/L	G	AB	R	H	2B	3B	HR	RBI	BB	SO	AVG	OBP	SLG	PRO+	BR/A	SB	CS	SBR	FA	FR	G/POS	TPR
1937	Bos-A	68	147	18	34	7	1	0	11	27	16	.231	.351	.293	61	-8	2	1	0	.965	-5	O-35	-1.3
1940	Chi-N	107	287	33	77	19	6	1	36	34	13	.268	.348	.387	104	2	4			.969	-3	O-74	-0.4
1941	Chi-N	140	486	73	132	36	2	6	85	68	37	.272	.362	.391	116	12	3			.987	-2	*O-131	0.2
1942	Chi-N	96	264	30	69	12	4	4	43	36	18	.261	.350	.383	119	7	4			.986	-2	O-66	0.2
1943	Chi-N	87	176	13	39	8	3	1	31	40	14	.222	.369	.318	101	2	1			.967	-4	O-45	-0.4
1944	Chi-N	117	381	53	116	19	4	8	74	61	29	.304	.400	.438	137	21	1			.982	-2	*O-106	1.3
1946	Chi-N	65	89	14	20	2	2	1	9	23	12	.225	.384	.326	104	2	1			.971	-3	O-20	-0.2
1947	Chi-N	66	115	18	33	7	1	1	14	21	11	.287	.397	.391	115	3	0			1.000	-2	O-28	0.0
Total	8	746	1945	242	520	110	23	22	303	310	150	.267	.369	.381	112	40	16	1		.980	-22	O-505	-0.6

■ **ABNER DALRYMPLE**   Dalrymple, Abner Frank b: 9/9/1857, Warren, Ill. d: 1/25/39, Warren, Ill. BL/TR, 5'10.5", 175 lbs. Deb: 5/1/1878

YEAR	TM/L	G	AB	R	H	2B	3B	HR	RBI	BB	SO	AVG	OBP	SLG	PRO+	BR/A	SB	CS	SBR	FA	FR	G/POS	TPR
1878	Mil-N	61	271	52	96	10	4	0	15	6	29	**.354**	.368	.421	149	13				.832	7	*O-61	1.5
1879	Chi-N	71	333	47	97	25	1	0	23	4	29	.291	.300	.372	113	-6				.728	-13	*O-71	-1.2
1880	Chi-N	86	382	**91**	**126**	25	12	0	36	3	18	.330	.335	.458	157	20				.859	4	*O-86	2.1
1881	Chi-N	82	362	72	117	22	4	1	37	15	22	.323	.350	.414	133	13				.835	-7	*O-82	0.4
1882	Chi-N	84	397	96	117	25	11	1	36	14	18	.295	.319	.421	129	12				.877	0	*O-84	1.0
1883	Chi-N	80	363	78	108	24	4	2	37	11	29	.298	.318	.402	111	3				.826	-1	*O-80	0.2
1884	Chi-N	111	521	111	161	18	9	22	69	14	39	.309	.327	.505	146	23				.882	1	*O-111	2.0
1885	*Chi-N	113	492	109	135	27	12	**11**	61	46	42	.274	.336	.445	131	13				.879	-1	*O-113	0.9
1886	*Chi-N	82	331	62	77	7	12	3	26	33	44	.233	.302	.353	86	-8	16			.952	4	*O-82	-0.6
1887	Pit-N	92	358	45	76	18	5	2	31	45	43	.212	.311	.307	77	-9	29			.900	4	*O-92	-0.6
1888	Pit-N	57	227	19	50	9	2	0	14	6	28	.220	.247	.278	72	-7				.909	-2	O-57	-1.1
1891	Mil-a	32	135	31	42	7	5	1	22	7	18	.311	.345	.459	108	-1	6			.909	-1	O-32	-0.2
Total	12	951	4172	813	1202	217	81	43	407	204	359	.288	.323	.410	120	76	58			.863	-4	O-951	4.4

■ **CLAY DALRYMPLE**   Dalrymple, Clayton Errol b: 12/3/36, Chico, Cal. BL/TR, 6', 199 lbs. Deb: 4/24/60

YEAR	TM/L	G	AB	R	H	2B	3B	HR	RBI	BB	SO	AVG	OBP	SLG	PRO+	BR/A	SB	CS	SBR	FA	FR	G/POS	TPR
1960	Phi-N	82	158	11	43	6	2	4	21	15	21	.272	.347	.411	106	2	0	0	0	.966	-5	C-48	-0.1
1961	Phi-N	129	378	23	83	11	1	5	42	30	30	.220	.284	.294	54	-25	0	2	-1	.978	0	*C-122	-2.0
1962	Phi-N	123	370	40	102	13	3	11	54	70	32	.276	.396	.416	122	15	1	3	-2	.987	-12	*C-119	0.6
1963	Phi-N	142	452	40	114	15	3	10	40	45	55	.252	.327	.365	100	1	0	1	-1	.981	-1	*C-142	0.6
1964	Phi-N	127	382	36	91	16	3	6	46	39	40	.238	.309	.343	84	-8	0	1	-1	.991	3	*C-124	0.0
1965	Phi-N	103	301	14	64	5	5	4	23	34	37	.213	.293	.302	69	-12	0	1	-1	.993	18	*C-102	1.0
1966	Phi-N	114	331	30	81	13	3	4	39	60	57	.245	.365	.338	97	1	0	0	0	.993	-4	*C-110	0.4
1967	Phi-N	101	268	12	46	7	1	3	21	36	49	.172	.272	.239	47	-18	1	2	-1	.994	20	*C-97	0.7
1968	Phi-N	85	241	19	50	9	1	3	26	22	57	.207	.277	.290	70	-9	2	2	-1	.990	-3	C-80	-0.9
1969	*Bal-A	37	80	8	19	1	0	4	13	13	8	.237	.344	.387	103	1	0	0	0	1.000	7	C-30	0.3
1970	Bal-A	13	32	4	7	1	0	0	3	7	4	.219	.359	.344	94	-0	0	0	0	1.000	6	C-11	0.6
1971	Bal-A	23	49	6	10	1	0	1	6	16	13	.204	.409	.286	101	1	0	0	0	.971	2	C-18	0.4
Total	12	1079	3042	243	710	98	23	55	327	387	403	.233	.324	.335	85	-51	3	13	-7	.987	27	*C-1003	1.6

■ **BILL DALRYMPLE**   Dalrymple, William Dunn b: 2/7/1891, Baltimore, Md. d: 7/14/67, San Diego, Cal. TR , Deb: 7/6/15

YEAR	TM/L	G	AB	R	H	2B	3B	HR	RBI	BB	SO	AVG	OBP	SLG	PRO+	BR/A	SB	CS	SBR	FA	FR	G/POS	TPR
1915	StL-A	3	2	0	0	0	0	0	0	0	0	.000	.000	.000	-99	-0	0			1.000	0	/3-1	0.0

■ **JACK DALTON**   Dalton, Talbot Percy b: 7/3/1885, Henderson, Tenn. BR/TR, 5'10.5", 187 lbs. Deb: 6/20/10

YEAR	TM/L	G	AB	R	H	2B	3B	HR	RBI	BB	SO	AVG	OBP	SLG	PRO+	BR/A	SB	CS	SBR	FA	FR	G/POS	TPR
1910	Bro-N	77	273	33	62	9	4	1	21	26	30	.227	.304	.300	79	-7	5			.966	3	O-72	-0.9
1914	Bro-N	128	442	65	141	13	8	1	45	53	39	.319	.396	.391	131	19	19			.965	-3	*O-116	1.1
1915	Buf-F	132	437	68	128	17	3	2	46	50	38	.293	.368	.359	93	-3	28			.966	-5	*O-119	-1.5
1916	Det-A	8	11	1	2	0	0	0	0	0	5	.182	.182	.182	9	-1	0			1.000	-1	/O-4	-0.3
Total	4	345	1163	167	333	39	15	4	112	129	112	.286	.362	.356	103	7	52			.966	-7	O-311	-1.6

YEAR	TM/L	G	AB	R	H	2B	3B	HR	RBI	BB	SO	AVG	OBP	SLG	PRO+	BR/A	SB	CS	SBR	FA	FR	G/POS	TPR

■ BERT DALY Daly, Albert Joseph b: 4/8/1881, Bayonne, N.J. d: 9/3/52, Bayonne, N.J. BR/TR, 5'9", 170 lbs. Deb: 8/7/03

| 1903 | Phi-A | 10 | 21 | 2 | 4 | 0 | 2 | 0 | 4 | 1 | | .190 | .227 | .381 | 76 | -1 | 0 | | | .700 | -4 | /2-4,3-3,S | -0.5 |

■ SUN DALY Daly, James J. b: 1/6/1865, Rutland, Vt. d: 4/30/38, Albany, N.Y. Deb: 9/30/1892

| 1892 | Bal-N | 13 | 48 | 5 | 12 | 0 | 2 | 0 | 7 | 1 | 4 | .250 | .265 | .333 | 79 | -2 | 0 | | | .923 | 0 | O-13 | -0.2 |

■ JOE DALY Daly, Joseph John b: 9/21/1868, Conshohocken, Pa. d: 3/21/43, Philadelphia, Pa. TR, 5'8", 157 lbs. Deb: 9/19/1890 F

1890	Phi-a	21	75	8	21	4	1	0			3	.280	.308	.360	99	-1	1			.900	-6	O-14/C-9	-0.5
1891	Cle-N	1	3	0	0	0	0	0	0	0	2	.000	.000	.000	-96	-1	0			1.000	0	/O-1	-0.1
1892	Bos-N	1	0	0	0	0	0	0	0	0	0	—	—	—	—	0	0			1.000	1	/C-1	0.0
Total	3	23	78	8	21	4	1	0	0	3	2	.269	.296	.346	91	-1	1			.909	-6	/O-15,C-10	-0.6

■ TOM DALY Daly, Thomas Daniel b: 12/12/1891, St.John, N.B., Can. d: 11/7/46, Medford, Mass. BR/TR, 5'11.5", 171 lbs. Deb: 9/23/13 C

1913	Chi-A	1	3	0	0	0	0	0	0	0	0	.000	.000	.000	-99	-1	0			1.000	1	/C-1	0.0
1914	Chi-A	62	133	13	31	2	0	0	8	7	13	.233	.271	.248	57	-7	3	4	-2	.909	-10	O-23/3-5,C1	-2.2
1915	Chi-A	29	47	5	9	1	0	0	3	5	9	.191	.269	.213	43	-3	0			.958	-3	C-19/1-1	-0.5
1916	Cle-A	31	73	3	16	1	1	0	8	1	2	.219	.230	.260	45	-5	0			.982	-2	C-25/O-1	-0.6
1918	Chi-N	1	1	0	0	0	0	0	0	0	0	.000	.000	.000	-98	-0	0			.667	-2	/C-1	0.0
1919	Chi-N	25	50	4	11	0	1	0	1	2	5	.220	.250	.260	53	-3	0			.956	-2	C-18	-0.5
1920	Chi-N	44	90	12	28	6	0	0	13	2	6	.311	.333	.378	102	0	1	1	-0	.981	-3	C-29	-0.2
1921	Chi-N	51	143	12	34	7	1	0	22	8	8	.238	.278	.301	53	-10	1	2	-1	.973	4	C-47	-0.4
Total	8	244	540	49	129	17	3	0	55	25	43	.239	.274	.281	59	-29	5	7		.972	-15	C-144/O-24,31	-4.4

■ TOM DALY Daly, Thomas Peter "Tido" b: 2/7/1866, Philadelphia, Pa. d: 10/29/38, Brooklyn, N.Y. BB/TR, 5'7", 170 lbs. Deb: 4/30/1887 F

1887	Chi-N	74	256	45	53	10	4	2	17	22	25	.207	.270	.301	52	-19	29			**.935**	33	C-64/O-8,S21	1.7
1888	Chi-N	65	219	34	42	2	6	0	29	10	26	.192	.230	.256	51	-12	10			.939	20	C-62/O-4	1.3
1889	Was-N	71	250	39	75	13	5	1	40	38	28	.300	.384	.404	131	12	18			.917	3	C-57/1-8,20S	1.7
1890	*Bro-N	82	292	55	71	9	4	5	43	32	43	.243	.326	.353	97	-1	20			.953	7	C-69,1-12/O	1.0
1891	Bro-N	58	200	29	50	11	5	2	27	21	34	.250	.327	.385	108	2	7			.881	-6	C-26,1-15,S/O	-0.2
1892	Bro-N	124	446	76	114	15	6	4	51	64	61	.256	.355	.343	116	11	34			.897	-11	3-57,O-30,C2	0.3
1893	Bro-N	126	470	94	136	21	14	8	70	76	65	.289	.388	.445	127	19	32			.915	-18	2-82,3-45	0.3
1894	Bro-N	123	492	135	168	22	10	8	82	77	42	.341	.436	.476	129	28	51			.908	-19	*2-123	1.1
1895	Bro-N	120	455	89	128	17	8	2	68	52	52	.281	.359	.367	95	-2	28			.930	-19	*2-120	-1.1
1896	Bro-N	67	224	43	63	13	6	3	29	33	25	.281	.385	.433	122	8	19			.909	-2	2-66/C-1	0.9
1898	Bro-N	23	73	11	24	3	1	0	11	14		.329	.443	.397	142	5	6			.993	3	2-23	0.9
1899	Bro-N	141	498	95	156	24	9	5	88	69		.313	.409	.428	127	21	43			.929	16	*2-141	4.0
1900	*Bro-N	97	343	72	107	17	3	4	55	46		.312	.403	.414	118	10	27			.921	-8	2-93/1-3,O	0.6
1901	Bro-N	133	520	88	164	**38**	10	3	90	42		.315	.371	.444	132	21	31			.944	11	*2-133	3.6
1902	Chi-A	137	489	57	110	22	3	1	54	55		.225	.303	.288	68	-20	19			.957	-15	*2-137	-2.9
1903	Chi-A	43	150	20	31	11	0	0	19	20		.207	.304	.280	80	-3	6			.948	-13	2-43	-1.6
	Cin-N	80	307	42	90	14	9	1	38	16		.293	.342	.407	99	-2	5			.937	-10	2-79	-0.9
Total	16	1564	5684	1024	1582	262	103	49	811	687	401	.278	.361	.387	108	77	385			.931	-27	*2-1056,C-306,3/O1S	10.7

■ BILL DAM Dam, Elbridge Rust b: 4/4/1885, Cambridge, Mass. d: 6/22/30, Quincy, Mass. Deb: 8/23/09

| 1909 | Bos-N | 1 | 2 | 1 | 1 | 0 | 0 | 0 | 0 | 1 | | .500 | .667 | 1.000 | 398 | 1 | 0 | | | 1.000 | -0 | /O-1 | 0.1 |

■ JACK DAMASKA Damaska, Jack Lloyd b: 8/21/37, Beaver Falls, Pa. BR/TR, 5'11", 168 lbs. Deb: 7/3/63

| 1963 | StL-N | 5 | 5 | 1 | 1 | 0 | 0 | 0 | 1 | 0 | 4 | .200 | .200 | .200 | 14 | -1 | 0 | 0 | 0 | .000 | -0 | /2-1,O-1 | -0.1 |

■ HARRY DAMRAU Damrau, Harry Robert (Also Known As Arthur Lee Whitehorn) b: 9/11/1890, Newburgh, N.Y. d: 8/21/57, Staten Island, N.Y BR/TR, 5'10", 178 lbs. Deb: 9/17/15

| 1915 | Phi-A | 16 | 56 | 4 | 11 | 1 | 0 | 0 | 3 | 5 | 17 | .196 | .262 | .214 | 44 | -4 | 1 | 1 | -0 | .870 | -4 | 3-16 | -0.8 |

■ JAKE DANIEL Daniel, Handley Jacob b: 4/22/11, Roanoke, Ala. BL/TL, 5'11", 175 lbs. Deb: 7/24/37

| 1937 | Bro-N | 12 | 27 | 3 | 5 | 1 | 0 | 0 | 3 | 3 | 4 | .185 | .267 | .222 | 34 | -2 | 0 | | | 1.000 | -0 | /1-7 | -0.3 |

■ BERT DANIELS Daniels, Bernard Elmer b: 10/13/1882, Danville, Ill. d: 6/6/58, Cedar Grove, N.J. BR/TR, 5'9.5", 180 lbs. Deb: 6/25/10

1910	NY-A	95	356	68	90	13	8	1	17	41		.253	.356	.343	112	7	41			.957	3	O-85/3-6,1	0.6
1911	NY-A	131	462	74	132	16	9	2	31	48		.286	.375	.372	102	2	40			.941	1	*O-120	-0.3
1912	NY-A	135	496	72	136	25	11	2	41	51		.274	.363	.381	106	4	37			.945	-2	*O-131	0.3
1913	NY-A	94	320	52	69	13	5	0	22	44	36	.216	.343	.287	85	-4	27			.966	1	O-87	-0.7
1914	Cin-N	71	269	29	59	9	7	0	19	19	40	.219	.274	.305	70	-10	14			.974	0	O-71	-1.5
Total	5	526	1903	295	486	76	40	5	130	203	76	.255	.349	.345	98	-1	159			.953	10	O-494/3-6,1	-1.6

■ TONY DANIELS Daniels, Frederick Clinton b: 12/28/24, Gastonia, N.C. BR/TR, 5'9.5", 185 lbs. Deb: 6/12/45

| 1945 | Phi-N | 76 | 230 | 15 | 46 | 3 | 2 | 0 | 10 | 12 | 22 | .200 | .249 | .230 | 35 | -20 | 1 | | | .955 | 7 | 2-75/3-1 | -0.9 |

■ JACK DANIELS Daniels, Harold Jack "Sour Mash Jack" b: 12/21/27, Chester, Pa. BL/TL, 5'10", 165 lbs. Deb: 4/18/52

| 1952 | Bos-N | 106 | 219 | 31 | 41 | 5 | 1 | 2 | 14 | 28 | 30 | .187 | .288 | .247 | 51 | -14 | 3 | 3 | -1 | .977 | -9 | O-87 | -2.8 |

■ KAL DANIELS Daniels, Kalvoski b: 8/20/63, Vienna, Ga. BL/TR, 5'11", 195 lbs. Deb: 4/9/86

1986	Cin-N	74	181	34	58	10	4	6	23	22	30	.320	.400	.519	145	11	15	2	3	.967	-0	O-47	1.4
1987	Cin-N	108	368	73	123	24	1	26	64	60	62	.334	.429	.617	166	36	26	8	3	.968	3	O-94	3.8
1988	Cin-N	140	495	95	144	29	1	18	64	87	94	.291	**.400**	.463	141	30	27	6	5	.982	4	*O-137	3.6
1989	Cin-N	44	133	26	29	11	0	2	9	36	28	.218	.392	.346	109	3	6	4	-1	1.000	2	O-38	0.4
	LA-N	11	38	7	13	2	0	2	8	7	5	.342	.444	.553	187	5	3	0	-1	1.000	0	O-11	0.5
	Yr	55	171	33	42	13	0	4	17	43	33	.246	.403	.392	125	8	9	4	0	1.000	-0	O-49	0.9
1990	LA-N	130	450	81	133	23	1	27	94	68	104	.296	.392	.531	156	35	4	3	-1	.987	2	*O-127	3.4
1991	LA-N	137	461	54	115	15	1	17	73	63	116	.249	.341	.397	109	6	6	1	1	.979	1	*O-132	0.5
1992	LA-N	35	104	9	24	5	0	2	8	10	32	.231	.304	.337	83	-2	0	0	0	.964	-2	O-21/1-8	-0.6
	Chi-N	48	108	12	27	6	0	4	17	12	24	.250	.331	.417	108	1	0	2	-1	1.000	-2	O-28	-0.2
	Yr	83	212	21	51	11	0	6	25	22	54	.241	.318	.377	95	-1	0	2	-1	.984	-4	O-49/1-8	-0.8
Total	7	727	2338	391	666	125	8	104	360	365	493	.285	.385	.479	137	125	87	26	11	.980	8	O-635/1-8	12.8

■ LAW DANIELS Daniels, Lawrence Long b: 7/14/1862, Newton, Mass. d: 1/7/29, Waltham, Mass. BR/TR, 5'10", 170 lbs. Deb: 4/25/1887

1887	Bal-a	48	165	23	41	5	1	0		8		.248	.287	.291	65	-7	7			.845	-8	C-26,O-15/12S3	-1.1
1888	KC-a	61	218	32	45	2	0	2	28	14		.206	.264	.243	59	-10	20			.855	-2	O-30,C-29/3S	-1.0
Total	2	109	383	55	86	7	1	2	28	22		.225	.274	.264	62	-18	27			.859	-10	/C-55,O-45,13S2	-2.1

■ BUCK DANNER Danner, Henry Frederick b: 6/8/1891, Dedham, Mass. d: 9/21/49, Boston, Mass. BR/TR, 5'6", 135 lbs. Deb: 9/17/15

| 1915 | Phi-A | 3 | 12 | 1 | 3 | 0 | 0 | 0 | 0 | 0 | 1 | .250 | .250 | .250 | 51 | -1 | 1 | | | .750 | -3 | /S-3 | -0.3 |

■ HARRY DANNING Danning, Harry "Harry The Horse" b: 9/6/11, Los Angeles, Cal. BR/TR, 6'1", 190 lbs. Deb: 7/30/33 F

1933	NY-N	3	2	0	0	0	0	0	0	0	0	.000	.333	.000	2	-0	0			1.000	0	/C-1	0.0
1934	NY-N	53	97	8	32	7	0	1	7	1	9	.330	.337	.433	107	1	1			.989	-0	C-37	0.1
1935	NY-N	65	152	16	37	11	1	2	20	9	16	.243	.286	.368	76	-6	0			.978	3	C-44	-0.1

YEAR	TM/L	G	AB	R	H	2B	3B	HR	RBI	BB	SO	AVG	OBP	SLG	PRO+	BR/A	SB	CS	SBR	FA	FR	G/POS	TPR
1936	*NY-N	32	69	3	11	2	2	0	4	1	5	.159	.183	.246	15	-8	0			.988	2	C-24	-0.6
1937	*NY-N	93	292	30	84	12	4	8	51	18	20	.288	.331	.438	106	2	0			.982	-5	C-86	0.1
1938	NY-N☆	120	448	59	137	26	3	9	60	23	40	.306	.345	.438	113	7	1			.984	-8	*C-114	0.5
1939	NY-N☆	135	520	79	163	28	5	16	74	35	42	.313	.359	.479	122	15	4			.991	7	*C-132	2.9
1940	NY-N★	140	524	65	157	34	4	13	91	35	31	.300	.349	.454	119	12	3			.980	7	*C-131	2.9
1941	NY-N★	130	459	58	112	22	4	7	56	30	25	.244	.292	.355	80	-13	1			.993	7	*C-116/1-1	0.4
1942	NY-N	119	408	45	114	20	3	1	34	34	29	.279	.335	.350	100	-0	3			.979	-5	*C-116	0.5
Total	10	890	2971	363	847	162	26	57	397	187	217	.285	.330	.415	104	9	13			.985	8	C-801/1-1	6.7

■ IKE DANNING   Danning, Ike b: 1/20/05, Los Angeles, Cal. d: 3/30/83, Santa Monica, Cal BR/TR, 5'10", 160 lbs. Deb: 9/21/28 F

1928	StL-A	2	6	0	3	0	0	0	1	1	2	.500	.571	.500	178	1	0	0	0	.917	1	/C-2	0.1

■ FATS DANTONIO   Dantonio, John James b: 12/31/18, New Orleans, La. d: 5/28/93, New Orleans, La. BR/TR, 5'8", 165 lbs. Deb: 9/18/44

1944	Bro-N	3	7	0	1	0	0	0	0	0	1	.143	.143	.143	-20	-1	0			.846	2	/C-3	-0.1
1945	Bro-N	47	128	12	32	6	1	0	12	11	6	.250	.309	.313	74	-5	3			.929	-5	C-45	-0.8
Total	2	50	135	12	33	6	1	0	12	11	7	.244	.301	.304	69	-6	3			.923	-5	/C-48	-0.9

■ BABE DANZIG   Danzig, Harold P. b: 4/30/1887, Binghamton, N.Y. d: 7/14/31, San Francisco, Cal. BR/TR, 6'2", 205 lbs. Deb: 4/12/09

1909	Bos-A	6	13	0	2	0	0	0	0	0	2	.154	.313	.154	47	-1	0			.960	-1	/1-3	-0.2

■ CLIFF DAPPER   Dapper, Clifford Roland b: 1/2/20, Los Angeles, Cal. BR/TR, 6'2", 190 lbs. Deb: 4/19/42

1942	Bro-N	8	17	2	8	1	0	1	9	2	2	.471	.526	.706	255	3	0			1.000	-0	/C-8	0.4

■ CLIFF DARINGER   Daringer, Clifford Clarence "Shanty" b: 4/10/1885, Hayden, Ind. d: 12/26/71, Sacramento, Cal. BL/TR, 5'7.5", 155 lbs. Deb: 4/20/14 F

1914	KC-F	64	160	12	42	2	1	0	16	11	7	.262	.322	.287	61	-9	9			.944	6	S-24,3-19,2	-0.1

■ ROLLA DARINGER   Daringer, Rolla Harrison b: 11/15/1888, N.Vernon, Ind. d: 5/23/74, Seymour, Ind. BL/TR, 5'10", 155 lbs. Deb: 9/19/14 F

1914	StL-N	2	4	1	2	1	0	0	0	1	2	.500	.600	.750	304	1	0			.667	-1	/S-1	0.0
1915	StL-N	10	23	3	2	0	0	0	0	9	5	.087	.344	.087	33	-1	0	1	-1	.947	-3	S-10	-0.5
Total	2	12	27	4	4	1	0	0	0	10	7	.148	.378	.185	72	-0	0	1		.927	-4	/S-11	-0.5

■ ALVIN DARK   Dark, Alvin Ralph "Blackie" b: 1/7/22, Comanche, Okla. BR/TR, 5'11", 185 lbs. Deb: 7/14/46 MC

1946	Bos-N	15	13	0	3	0	0	1	0	1	3	.231	.231	.462	93	-0	0			.905	2	S-12/O-1	0.2
1948	*Bos-N	137	543	85	175	39	6	3	48	24	36	.322	.353	.433	114	9	4			.963	-12	*S-133	0.4
1949	Bos-N	130	529	74	146	23	5	3	53	31	43	.276	.317	.355	85	-13	5			.961	-4	*S-125/3-4	-0.7
1950	NY-N	154	587	79	164	36	5	16	67	39	60	.279	.331	.440	100	-1	9			.962	-15	*S-154	-0.4
1951	*NY-N★	156	646	114	196	41	7	14	69	42	39	.303	.352	.454	114	11	12	7	-1	.944	1	*S-156	2.3
1952	NY-N☆	151	589	92	177	29	3	14	73	47	39	.301	.357	.431	117	13	6	6	-2	.965	3	*S-150	2.6
1953	NY-N	155	647	126	194	41	6	23	88	28	34	.300	.335	.488	109	7	7	2	1	.967	8	*S-110,2-26,O/3P	2.4
1954	*NY-N★	154	644	98	189	26	6	20	70	27	40	.293	.327	.446	98	-3	5	3	-0	.956	4	*S-154	1.3
1955	NY-N	115	475	77	134	20	5	9	45	22	32	.282	.321	.394	88	-9	2	1	0	.962	-14	*S-115	-1.2
1956	NY-N	48	206	19	52	12	0	2	17	8	13	.252	.284	.340	67	-10	0	0	0	.961	-5	S-48	-1.1
	StL-N	100	413	54	118	14	7	4	37	21	33	.286	.323	.383	89	-7	3	1	0	.959	-2	S-99	0.0
	Yr	148	619	73	170	26	7	6	54	29	46	.275	.310	.368	82	-16	3	1	0	.960	-7	*S-147	-1.1
1957	StL-N	140	583	80	169	25	6	4	64	29	56	.290	.328	.381	88	-10	3	4	-2	.965	6	*S-139/3-1	0.8
1958	StL-N	18	64	7	19	0	0	1	5	2	6	.297	.318	.344	72	-2	0	0	0	.943	-3	/S-8,3-8	-0.5
	Chi-N	114	464	54	137	16	4	3	43	29	23	.295	.343	.366	89	-7	1	1	-0	.949	-3	*3-111	-0.9
	Yr	132	528	61	156	16	4	4	48	31	29	.295	.340	.364	87	-9	1	1	-0	.948	-6	3-119/S-8	-1.4
1959	Chi-N	136	477	60	126	22	9	6	45	55	50	.264	.344	.386	95	-3	1	1	-0	.948	-3	*3-131/1-4,S	-0.5
1960	Phi-N	55	198	29	48	5	1	3	14	19	14	.242	.315	.323	75	-6	1	1	0	.953	-8	3-53/1-1	-1.5
	Mil-N	50	141	16	42	6	2	1	18	7	13	.298	.336	.390	106	1	0	0	0	.960	-1	O-25,1-10/32	-0.2
	Yr	105	339	45	90	11	3	4	32	26	27	.265	.323	.351	88	-6	1	1	-0	.954	-8	3-57,O-25,1/2	-1.7
Total	14	1828	7219	1064	2089	358	72	126	757	430	534	.289	.334	.411	98	-30	59	27		.960	-43	*S-1404,3-320/021P	3.0

■ DELL DARLING   Darling, Conrad b: 12/21/1861, Erie, Pa. d: 11/20/04, Erie, Pa. BR/TR, 5'8", 170 lbs. Deb: 7/3/1883

1883	Buf-N	6	18	1	3	0	0	0		1	2	.167	.250	.167	29	-1				.875	-2	/C-6	-0.3
1887	Chi-N	38	141	28	45	7	4	3	20	22	18	.319	.411	.489	132	6	19			.786	2	O-20,C-20	0.8
1888	Chi-N	20	75	12	16	3	1	2	7	3	12	.213	.253	.360	87	-1	0			.932	3	C-20	0.3
1889	Chi-N	36	120	14	23	1	1	0	7	25	22	.192	.331	.217	52	-7	5			.960	4	C-36	0.0
1890	Chi-P	58	221	45	57	12	4	2	39	29	28	.258	.352	.376	91	-3	9			.957	-9	1-29,S-15/CO23	-1.0
1891	StL-a	17	53	9	7	1	3	0	9	10	11	.132	.270	.264	46	-4	0			.894	2	C-17/2-2,S	-0.1
Total	6	175	628	109	151	24	13	7	83	91	96	.240	.340	.354	87	-12	29			.923	-1	C-108/1-29,0S23	-0.3

■ JACK DARRAGH   Darragh, James S. b: 7/17/1866, Ebensburg, Pa. d: 8/12/39, Rochester, Pa. Deb: 5/13/1891

1891	Lou-a	1	2	0	1	0	0	0	0	0	0	.500	.500	.500	189	0	0			1.000	0	/1-1	0.0

■ BOBBY DARWIN   Darwin, Arthur Bobby Lee b: 2/16/43, Los Angeles, Cal. BR/TR, 6'2", 200 lbs. Deb: 9/30/62

1962	LA-A	1	1	0	0	0	0	0	0	0	1	.000	.000	.000	-99	-0	0	0	0	.000	-0	/P-1	0.0
1969	LA-N	6	0	1	0	0	0	0	0	0	0						0	0	0	.000	-0	/P-3	0.0
1971	LA-N	11	20	2	5	1	0	1	4	2	9	.250	.318	.450	123	0	0	0	0	1.000	0	/O-4	0.0
1972	Min-A	145	513	48	137	20	2	22	80	38	145	.267	.327	.442	122	13	2	3	-1	.980	-1	*O-142	0.5
1973	Min-A	145	560	69	141	20	2	18	90	46	137	.252	.312	.391	93	-6	5	2	0	.980	-2	*O-140/D-1	-1.0
1974	Min-A	152	575	67	152	13	7	25	94	37	127	.264	.304	.442	114	9	1	3	-2	.970	-2	*O-142	-0.1
1975	Min-A	48	169	26	37	6	0	5	18	18	44	.219	.309	.343	82	-4	2	0	1	.969	-4	O-27,D-19	-0.9
	Mil-A	55	186	19	46	6	2	8	23	11	54	.247	.300	.430	104	0	4	1	1	.978	1	O-43/D-9	0.0
	Yr	103	355	45	83	12	2	13	41	29	98	.234	.304	.389	94	-4	6	1	1	.975	-3	O-70,D-28	-0.9
1976	Mil-A	25	73	6	18	3	1	1	6	6	16	.247	.321	.356	100	0	0	0	0	.977	-1	O-21/D-1	-0.2
	Bos-A	43	106	9	19	5	2	3	13	2	35	.179	.216	.349	57	-6	1	0	0	.964	-2	O-17,D-16	-0.9
	Yr	68	179	15	37	8	3	4	18	8	51	.207	.260	.352	73	-7	1	0	0	.972	-3	O-38,D-17	-1.1
1977	Bos-A	4	9	1	2	1	0	0	0	0	4	.222	.222	.333	44	-1	0	0	0	.500	-0	/O-1,D-2	-0.1
	Chi-N	11	12	2	2	1	0	0	0	0	5	.167	.167	.250	9	-2	0	0	0	.000	-0	/O-1	-0.2
Total	9	646	2224	250	559	76	16	83	328	160	577	.251	.312	.412	103	4	15	9	-1	.976	-8	O-538/D-48,P	-2.9

■ DOUG DASCENZO   Dascenzo, Douglas Craig b: 6/30/64, Cleveland, Ohio BB/TL, 5'7", 150 lbs. Deb: 9/2/88

1988	Chi-N	26	75	9	16	3	0	0	4	9	4	.213	.298	.253	57	-4	6	1	1	1.000	2	O-20	-0.1
1989	Chi-N	47	139	20	23	3	1	0	12	13	13	.165	.237	.194	23	-14	6	3	0	1.000	-2	O-45	-1.8
1990	Chi-N	113	241	27	61	9	5	1	26	21	18	.253	.316	.344	76	-8	15	6	1	1.000	-18	*O-107/P-1	-2.7
1991	Chi-N	118	239	40	61	11	0	1	18	24	26	.255	.328	.314	78	-6	14	7	0	.985	-19	O-86/P-3	-2.8
1992	Chi-N	139	376	37	96	13	4	0	20	27	32	.255	.305	.311	73	-13	6	8	-3	.978	-17	*O-122	-3.8
1993	Tex-A	76	146	20	29	5	1	2	10	8	22	.199	.240	.288	43	-12	2	0	1	.990	-12	O-68/D-2	-2.4
Total	6	519	1216	153	286	42	10	5	90	102	115	.235	.296	.299	64	-57	49	25	-0	.990	-65	O-448/P-4,D	-13.6

■ WALLY DASHIELL   Dashiell, John Wallace b: 5/9/02, Jewett, Tex. d: 5/20/72, Pensacola, Fla. BR/TR, 5'9.5", 170 lbs. Deb: 4/20/24

1924	Chi-A	1	2	0	0	0	0	0	0	0	0	.000	.000	.000	-99	-1	0	0	0	.667	-1	/S-1	-0.1

YEAR	TM/L	G	AB	R	H	2B	3B	HR	RBI	BB	SO	AVG	OBP	SLG	PRO+	BR/A	SB	CS	SBR	FA	FR	G/POS	TPR

■ JEFF DATZ
Datz, Jeffrey William b: 11/28/59, Camden, N.J. BR/TR, 6'4", 220 lbs. Deb: 9/5/89

| 1989 | Det-A | 7 | 10 | 0 | 2 | 0 | 0 | 0 | 0 | 1 | 1 | .200 | .333 | .200 | 55 | -0 | 0 | 0 | 0 | 1.000 | 0 | /C-6,D-1 | 0.0 |

■ HARRY DAUBERT
Daubert, Harry "Jake" b: 6/19/1892, Columbus, Ohio d: 1/8/44, Detroit, Mich. BR/TR, 6', 160 lbs. Deb: 9/4/15

| 1915 | Pit-N | 1 | 1 | 0 | 0 | 0 | 0 | 0 | 0 | 0 | 1 | .000 | .000 | .000 | -99 | -0 | 0 | | | .000 | 0 | H | 0.0 |

■ JAKE DAUBERT
Daubert, Jacob Ellsworth b: 4/7/1884, Shamokin, Pa. d: 10/9/24, Cincinnati, Ohio BL/TL, 5'10.5", 160 lbs. Deb: 4/14/10

1910	Bro-N	144	552	67	146	15	15	8	50	47	53	.264	.328	.389	112	7	23			.989	-3	*1-144	0.4
1911	Bro-N	149	573	89	176	17	8	5	45	51	56	.307	.366	.391	117	12	32			.989	2	*1-149	1.4
1912	Bro-N	145	559	81	172	19	16	3	66	48	45	.308	.369	.415	119	14	29			.993	0	*1-143	1.2
1913	Bro-N	139	508	76	178	17	7	2	52	44	40	.350	.405	.423	133	23	25			.991	3	*1-139	2.5
1914	Bro-N	126	474	89	156	17	7	6	45	30	34	.329	.375	.432	137	20	25			.993	-6	*1-126	1.2
1915	Bro-N	150	544	62	164	21	8	2	47	57	48	.301	.369	.381	125	17	11	13	-5	.993	9	*1-150	2.0
1916	*Bro-N	127	478	75	151	16	7	3	33	38	39	.316	.371	.397	132	19	21	7	2	.993	4	*1-126	2.2
1917	Bro-N	125	468	59	122	4	4	2	30	51	30	.261	.341	.299	94	-1	11			.991	6	*1-125	0.1
1918	Bro-N	108	396	50	122	12	15	2	47	27	18	.308	.360	.429	141	18	10			.991	0	*1-105	1.6
1919	*Cin-N	140	537	79	148	10	12	2	44	35	23	.276	.322	.350	105	3	11			.989	-2	*1-140	-0.4
1920	Cin-N	142	553	97	168	28	13	4	48	47	29	.304	.362	.423	127	19	11	13	-5	.990	-9	*1-140	0.2
1921	Cin-N	136	516	69	158	18	12	2	64	24	16	.306	.341	.399	100	-1	12	6	0	.993	2	*1-136	-0.2
1922	Cin-N	156	610	114	205	15	22	12	66	56	21	.336	.395	.492	130	27	14	17	-6	.994	-0	*1-156	1.3
1923	Cin-N	125	500	63	146	27	10	2	54	40	20	.292	.349	.398	99	-1	11	12	-4	.993	6	*1-121	-0.5
1924	Cin-N	102	405	47	114	14	9	1	31	28	17	.281	.331	.368	88	-7	5	10	-2	.990	7	*1-102	-1.1
Total	15	2014	7673	1117	2326	250	165	56	722	623	489	.303	.360	.401	117	170	251	78		.991	19	*1-2002	11.9

■ RICH DAUER
Dauer, Richard Fremont b: 7/27/52, San Bernardino, Cal. BR/TR, 6', 180 lbs. Deb: 9/11/76 C

1976	Bal-A	11	39	0	4	0	0	0	3	1	3	.103	.146	.103	-28	-6	0	0	0	1.000	-3	2-10	-0.9
1977	Bal-A	96	304	38	74	15	1	5	25	20	28	.243	.294	.349	79	-9	1	0	0	.982	6	2-83/3-9,D	0.2
1978	Bal-A	133	459	57	121	23	0	6	46	26	22	.264	.303	.353	89	-8	0	4	-2	.998	3	2-87,3-52/D	-0.2
1979	*Bal-A	142	479	63	123	20	0	9	61	36	36	.257	.310	.355	82	-13	0	1	-1	.979	-5	*2-103,3-44	-1.2
1980	Bal-A	152	557	71	158	32	0	6	63	46	19	.284	.342	.352	91	-6	3	2	-0	.991	-4	*2-137,3-35	-0.2
1981	Bal-A	96	369	41	97	27	0	4	38	27	18	.263	.318	.369	98	-1	0	0	0	.989	-14	2-94/3-4	-1.0
1982	Bal-A	158	558	75	156	24	2	8	57	50	34	.280	.340	.373	96	-2	0	1	-1	.987	-36	*2-123,3-61	-3.5
1983	*Bal-A	140	459	49	108	19	0	5	41	44	29	.235	.309	.309	72	-17	1	1	-0	.988	-29	*2-131,3-17	-4.1
1984	Bal-A	127	397	29	101	26	0	2	24	24	23	.254	.297	.335	76	-13	1	3	-2	.980	-19	*2-123/3-3	-2.9
1985	Bal-A	85	208	25	42	7	0	2	14	20	7	.202	.275	.264	50	-14	0	1	-1	.990	5	2-73,3-17/1	-0.8
Total	10	1140	3829	448	984	193	3	43	372	297	219	.257	.313	.343	83	-89	6	13	-6	.987	-96	2-964,3-242/D1	-14.6

■ DOC DAUGHERTY
Daugherty, Harold Ray b: 10/12/27, Paris, Pa. BR/TR, 6', 180 lbs. Deb: 4/22/51

| 1951 | Det-A | 1 | 1 | 0 | 0 | 0 | 0 | 0 | 0 | 0 | 1 | .000 | .000 | .000 | -99 | -0 | 0 | 0 | 0 | .000 | 0 | H | 0.0 |

■ JACK DAUGHERTY
Daugherty, John Michael b: 7/3/60, Hialeah, Fla. BB/TL, 6'", 188 lbs. Deb: 9/1/87

1987	Mon-N	11	10	1	1	1	0	0	0	0	3	.100	.100	.200	-22	-2	0	0	0	1.000	0	/1-1	-0.2
1989	Tex-A	52	106	15	32	4	2	1	10	11	21	.302	.373	.406	117	3	2	1	0	1.000	1	1-23/O-5,D	0.2
1990	Tex-A	125	310	36	93	20	2	6	47	22	49	.300	.350	.435	118	7	0	0	0	.982	-3	O-42,1-30,D	-0.5
1991	Tex-A	58	144	8	28	3	2	1	11	16	23	.194	.275	.264	51	-10	1	0	0	.981	-4	O-37,1-11/D	-1.5
1992	Tex-A	59	127	13	26	9	0	0	9	16	21	.205	.299	.276	64	-6	2	1	0	.939	-4	O-26,D-13/1	-1.1
1993	Hou-N	4	3	0	1	0	0	0	0	0	0	.333	.333	.333	82	-0	0	0	0	.000	0	/1-1,O-1	0.0
	Cin-N	46	59	7	13	2	0	2	9	11	15	.220	.343	.356	87	-1	0	0	0	.917	-4	O-16/1-2	-0.5
	Yr	50	62	7	14	2	0	2	9	11	15	.226	.342	.355	87	-1	0	0	0	.923	-4	O-17/1-3	-0.5
Total	6	355	759	80	194	39	6	10	87	76	132	.256	.327	.362	92	-8	5	2	0	.969	-15	O-127/1-76,D	-3.0

■ BOB DAUGHTERS
Daughters, Robert Francis "Red" b: 8/5/14, Cincinnati, Ohio d: 8/22/88, Southbury, Conn. BR/TR, 6'2", 185 lbs. Deb: 4/24/37

| 1937 | Bos-A | 1 | 0 | 1 | 0 | 0 | 0 | 0 | 0 | 0 | 0 | — | — | — | | | 0 | 0 | 0 | .000 | 0 | R | 0.0 |

■ DARREN DAULTON
Daulton, Darren Arthur b: 1/3/62, Arkansas City, Kan. BL/TR, 6'2", 195 lbs. Deb: 9/25/83

1983	Phi-N	2	3	1	1	0	0	0	0	1	1	.333	.500	.333	137	0	0	0	0	1.000	-0	/C-2	0.0
1985	Phi-N	36	103	14	21	3	1	4	11	16	37	.204	.311	.369	87	-2	3	0	1	.994	-9	C-28	0.1
1986	Phi-N	49	138	18	31	4	0	8	21	38	41	.225	.395	.428	123	6	2	3	-1	.985	-4	C-48	0.3
1987	Phi-N	53	129	10	25	6	0	3	13	16	37	.194	.283	.310	55	-8	0	0	0	.991	1	C-40/1-1	-0.5
1988	Phi-N	58	144	13	30	6	0	1	12	17	26	.208	.292	.271	61	-7	2	1	0	.977	-4	C-44/1-1	-1.1
1989	Phi-N	131	368	29	74	12	2	8	44	52	58	.201	.303	.310	76	-11	2	4	-1	.984	-11	*C-126	-1.7
1990	Phi-N	143	459	62	123	30	1	12	57	72	72	.268	.370	.416	116	12	7	1	2	.989	-9	*C-139	1.4
1991	Phi-N	89	285	36	56	12	0	12	42	41	66	.196	.302	.365	88	-5	5	0	2	.985	-17	C-88	-1.6
1992	Phi-N★	145	485	80	131	32	5	27	109	88	103	.270	.389	.524	157	38	11	2	2	.987	-14	*C-141	3.6
1993	*Phi-N★	147	510	90	131	35	4	24	105	117	111	.257	.397	.482	136	30	5	0	2	.991	-8	*C-146	3.1
1994	Phi-N	69	257	43	77	17	1	15	56	33	43	.300	.381	.549	140	15	4	1	1	.994	6	C-68	2.4
Total	11	922	2881	396	700	157	14	114	470	491	595	.243	.356	.426	115	68	41	9	7	.988	-62	C-870/1-2	6.0

■ YO-YO DAVALILLO
Davalillo, Pompeyo Antonio (Romero) b: 6/30/31, Caracas, Venez. BR/TR, 5'3", 140 lbs. Deb: 8/1/53 F

| 1953 | Was-A | 19 | 58 | 10 | 17 | 1 | 0 | 0 | 2 | 1 | 7 | .293 | .305 | .310 | 68 | -3 | 1 | 0 | 0 | .935 | 2 | S-17 | 0.0 |

■ VIC DAVALILLO
Davalillo, Victor Jose (Romero) b: 7/31/36, Cabimas, Venez. BL/TL, 5'7", 155 lbs. Deb: 4/9/63 F

1963	Cle-A	90	370	44	108	18	5	7	36	16	41	.292	.323	.424	108	3	3	3	-1	.988	17	O-89	1.5
1964	Cle-A	150	577	64	156	26	2	6	51	34	77	.270	.312	.354	85	-12	21	11	-0	.986	16	*O-143	-0.3
1965	Cle-A★	142	505	67	152	19	1	5	40	35	50	.301	.346	.372	103	2	26	7	4	.988	15	*O-134	1.6
1966	Cle-A	121	344	42	86	6	4	3	19	24	37	.250	.299	.317	77	-10	8	6	-1	.986	0	*O-108	-1.6
1967	Cle-A	139	359	47	103	17	5	2	22	10	30	.287	.308	.379	101	-1	6	7	-2	.986	-8	*O-125	-1.7
1968	Cle-A	51	180	15	43	2	3	2	13	3	19	.239	.255	.317	74	-6	8	6	-1	.967	-2	O-49	-0.9
	Cal-A	93	339	34	101	15	4	1	18	15	34	.298	.328	.375	117	6	17	10	-1	.995	6	O-86	0.7
	Yr	144	519	49	144	17	7	3	31	18	53	.277	.303	.355	102	-1	25	16	-2	.987	8	*O-135	-0.2
1969	Cal-A	33	71	10	11	1	1	0	1	6	5	.155	.231	.197	22	-8	3	0	1	1.000	-2	O-22/1-3	-1.0
	StL-N	63	98	15	26	3	0	2	10	7	8	.265	.314	.357	87	-2	1	1	-0	1.000	-2	O-23/P-2	-0.5
1970	StL-N	111	183	29	57	14	3	1	33	13	19	.311	.357	.437	109	2	4	1	1	.972	-8	O-54	-0.7
1971	*Pit-N	99	295	48	84	14	6	1	33	11	31	.285	.315	.383	97	-2	10	2	2	.983	-2	O-61,1-16	-0.6
1972	Pit-N	117	368	59	117	19	2	4	28	26	44	.318	.368	.413	124	11	14	1	4	.979	-1	O-97/1-8	1.1
1973	Pit-N	59	83	9	15	1	0	1	3	2	7	.181	.200	.229	19	-9	0	2	-1	.977	-0	1-10,O-10	-1.2
	*Oak-A	38	64	5	12	1	0	0	4	3	4	.188	.224	.203	22	-7	0	0	0	.967	-2	O-19/1-8,D	-0.9
1974	Oak-A	17	23	0	4	0	0	0	4	2	2	.174	.240	.174	22	-2	0	0	0	1.000	-2	/O-6,D-4	-0.5
1977	*LA-N	24	48	3	15	2	0	0	4	0	6	.313	.313	.354	79	-1	0	0	0	1.000	-3	O-12	-0.5
1978	*LA-N	75	77	15	24	1	1	1	11	3	7	.312	.338	.390	103	0	2	1	0	1.000	-6	O-25/1-1	-0.7
1979	LA-N	29	27	2	7	1	0	0	2	2	0	.259	.310	.296	67	-1	2	1	0	1.000	-2	/O-3	-0.1
1980	LA-N	7	6	1	1	0	0	0	1	0	0	.167	.167	.167	-7	-1	0	0	0	1.000	-0	/1-1	-0.1
Total	16	1458	4017	509	1122	160	37	36	329	212	422	.279	.317	.364	94	-36	125	58	3	.986	19	*O-1066/1-47,DP	-6.4

YEAR TM/L	G	AB	R	H	2B	3B	HR	RBI	BB	SO	AVG	OBP	SLG	PRO+	BR/A	SB	CS	SBR	FA	FR	G/POS	TPR
■ **JERRY DaVANON** DaVanon, Frank Gerald b: 8/21/45, Oceanside, Cal. BR/TR, 5'11", 175 lbs. Deb: 4/11/69																						
1969 SD-N	24	59	4	8	1	0	0	3	3	12	.136	.177	.153	-7	-8	0	3	-2	.932	0	2-15/S-7	-0.9
StL-N	16	40	7	12	3	0	1	7	6	8	.300	.391	.450	135	2	0	0	0	.958	1	S-16	0.4
Yr	40	99	11	20	4	0	1	10	9	20	.202	.269	.273	53	-6	0	3	-2	.959	1	S-23,2-15	-0.5
1970 StL-N	11	18	2	2	1	0	0	0	2	5	.111	.200	.167	-1	-3	0	0	0	1.000	1	/3-5,2-3	0.0
1971 Bal-A	38	81	14	19	5	0	0	4	12	20	.235	.340	.296	82	-1	0	0	0	.970	3	2-20,S-11/31	-0.3
1973 Cal-A	41	49	6	12	3	0	0	2	3	9	.245	.288	.306	73	-2	1	2	-1	.927	5	S-14,2-12/3	0.4
1974 StL-N	30	40	4	6	1	0	0	4	4	5	.150	.261	.175	24	-4	0	1	-1	.840	-2	S-14/3-8,2O	-0.6
1975 Hou-N	32	97	15	27	4	2	1	10	16	7	.278	.386	.392	125	4	2	0	1	.944	2	S-21/2-9,3	1.0
1976 Hou-N	61	107	19	31	3	3	1	20	21	12	.290	.411	.402	144	7	0	2	-1	.980	3	2-17,S-17/3	1.2
1977 StL-N	9	8	2	0	0	0	0	0	1	2	.000	.111	.000	-68	-2	0	0	0	.923	1	/2-5	0.0
Total 8	262	499	73	117	21	5	3	50	68	80	.234	.332	.315	86	-7	3	8	-4	.936	11	S-100/2-88,301	1.2
■ **JIM DAVENPORT** Davenport, James Houston b: 8/17/33, Siluria, Ala. BR/TR, 5'11", 175 lbs. Deb: 4/15/58 MC																						
1958 SF-N	134	434	70	111	22	3	12	41	33	64	.256	.319	.403	92	-6	1	3	-2	.960	-4	*3-130/S-5	-1.0
1959 SF-N	123	469	65	121	16	3	6	38	28	65	.258	.303	.343	73	-18	0	1	-1	.978	-3	*3-121/S-1	-2.2
1960 SF-N	112	363	43	91	15	3	6	38	26	58	.251	.308	.358	87	-7	0	2	-1	.961	-1	*3-103/S-7	-0.9
1961 SF-N	137	436	64	121	28	4	12	65	45	65	.278	.348	.443	112	7	4	3	-1	.965	8	*3-132	1.6
1962 *SF-N★	144	485	83	144	25	5	14	58	45	76	.297	.359	.456	119	13	2	5	-2	.952	4	*3-141	1.6
1963 SF-N	147	460	40	116	19	3	4	36	32	87	.252	.301	.333	83	-10	3	1	0	.962	1	*3-127,2-22/S	-0.8
1964 SF-N	116	297	24	70	10	6	2	26	29	46	.236	.304	.330	77	-9	2	0	1	.979	-3	S-64,3-41,2	-0.7
1965 SF-N	106	271	29	68	14	3	4	31	21	47	.251	.307	.369	87	-5	0	0	0	.949	-21	3-39,S-37,2	-2.4
1966 SF-N	111	305	42	76	6	2	9	30	22	40	.249	.302	.370	83	-7	1	1	0	.961	-18	S-58,3-36,2/1	-2.2
1967 SF-N	124	295	42	81	10	3	5	30	39	50	.275	.367	.380	116	7	1	4	-2	1.000	5	3-64,S-28,2	0.9
1968 SF-N	113	272	27	61	1	1	1	17	26	32	.224	.292	.246	63	-12	0	3	-2	.960	-7	3-82,S-17/2	-2.2
1969 SF-N	112	303	20	73	10	1	2	42	29	37	.241	.307	.300	72	-11	0	1	-1	.967	1	*3-104/1-1,SO	-1.1
1970 SF-N	22	37	3	9	1	0	0	4	7	6	.243	.364	.270	73	-1	0	0	0	1.000	-3	3-10	-0.4
Total 13	1501	4427	552	1142	177	37	77	456	382	673	.258	.320	.367	90	-58	16	25	-10	.964	-43	*3-1130,S-219,2/10	-9.8
■ **ANDRE DAVID** David, Andre Anter b: 5/18/58, Hollywood, Cal. BL/TL, 6', 170 lbs. Deb: 6/29/84																						
1984 Min-A	33	48	5	12	2	0	1	5	7	11	.250	.357	.354	93	-0	0	0	0	1.000	-3	O-14/D-2	-0.4
1986 Min-A	5	5	0	1	0	0	0	0	0	2	.200	.333	.200	48	-0	0	0	0	.000	-0	/D-1	0.0
Total 2	38	53	5	13	2	0	1	5	7	13	.245	.355	.340	89	-0	0	0	0	1.000	-3	/O-14,D-3	-0.4
■ **CLAUDE DAVIDSON** Davidson, Claude Boucher "Davey" b: 10/13/1896, Boston, Mass. d: 4/18/56, Weymouth, Mass. BL/TR, 5'11", 155 lbs. Deb: 4/25/18																						
1918 Phi-A	31	81	4	15	1	0	0	4	5	9	.185	.233	.198	29	-7	0			.943	-7	2-15/O-8,3	-1.5
1919 Was-A	2	7	1	3	0	0	0	0	1	1	.429	.500	.429	163	1	0			1.000	-0	/3-2	0.1
Total 2	33	88	5	18	1	0	0	4	6	10	.205	.255	.216	41	-6	0			1.000	-7	/2-15,O-8,3	-1.4
■ **HOMER DAVIDSON** Davidson, Homer Hurd "Divvy" b: 10/14/1884, Cleveland, Ohio d: 7/26/48, Detroit, Mich. BR/TR, 5'10.5", 155 lbs. Deb: 4/25/08																						
1908 Cle-A	9	4	2	0	0	0	0	0	0		.000	.000	.000	-99	-1	1			1.000	2	/C-5,O-1	0.1
■ **MARK DAVIDSON** Davidson, John Mark b: 2/15/61, Knoxville, Tenn. BR/TR, 6'2", 190 lbs. Deb: 6/20/86																						
1986 Min-A	36	68	5	8	3	0	0	2	6	22	.118	.189	.162	-3	-10	2	3	-1	.980	-4	O-31/D-3	-1.5
1987 *Min-A	102	150	32	40	4	1	1	14	13	26	.267	.325	.327	71	-6	9	2	2	1.000	-14	O-86/D-9	-1.8
1988 Min-A	100	106	22	23	7	0	1	10	10	20	.217	.291	.311	67	-5	3	3	-1	.955	-16	O-91/3-1,D	-2.3
1989 Hou-N	33	65	7	13	2	1	1	5	7	14	.200	.278	.308	70	-3	1	0	0	1.000	-3	O-23	-0.6
1990 Hou-N	57	130	12	38	5	1	1	16	10	18	.292	.343	.369	99	-0	0	3	-2	.981	-2	O-51	-0.5
1991 Hou-N	85	142	10	27	6	0	2	15	12	28	.190	.263	.275	54	-9	0	0	0	1.000	-11	O-63	-2.2
Total 6	413	661	88	149	27	3	6	57	58	128	.225	.291	.303	64	-32	15	11	-2	.983	-49	O-345/D-15,3	-8.9
■ **BILL DAVIDSON** Davidson, William Simpson b: 5/10/1884, Lafayette, Ind. d: 5/23/54, Lincoln, Neb. BR/TR, 5'10", 170 lbs. Deb: 9/29/09																						
1909 Chi-N	2	7	2	1	0	0	0	1			.143	.250	.143	22	-1	1			1.000	-0	/O-2	-0.1
1910 Bro-N	136	509	48	121	13	7	0	34	24	54	.238	.277	.291	68	-22	27			.961	-7	*O-131	-3.8
1911 Bro-N	87	292	33	68	3	4	1	26	16	21	.233	.275	.281	58	-17	18			.956	-5	O-74	-2.6
Total 3	225	808	83	190	16	11	1	60	41	75	.235	.276	.286	64	-40	46			.959	-12	O-207	-6.5
■ **CHICK DAVIES** Davies, Lloyd Garrison b: 3/6/1892, Peabody, Mass. d: 9/5/73, Middletown, Conn. BL/TL, 5'8", 145 lbs. Deb: 7/11/14																						
1914 Phi-A	19	46	6	11	3	1	0	5	5	13	.239	.314	.348	103	0	1			.926	0	O-10/P-1	-0.1
1915 Phi-A	56	132	13	24	5	3	0	11	14	31	.182	.270	.265	62	-6	2	4	-2	.973	4	O-32/P-4	-0.6
1925 NY-N	4	6	1	0	0	0	0	0	0	1	.000	.000	.000	-99	-2	0	0	0	1.000	1	/P-2,O-1	-0.1
1926 NY-N	38	18	4	4	0	0	0	1	3	5	.222	.333	.222	53	-1	0			.938	1	P-38	-0.1
Total 4	117	202	24	39	8	4	0	17	22	50	.193	.279	.272	65	-9	3	4		.938	6	/P-45,O-43	-0.7
■ **LEFTY DAVIS** Davis, Alphonzo De Ford b: 2/4/1875, Nashville, Tenn. d: 2/4/19, Collins, N.Y. BL/TL, 5'10", 170 lbs. Deb: 4/18/01																						
1901 Bro-N	25	91	11	19	2	0	0	7	10		.209	.287	.231	50	-6	4			.822	-5	O-24/2-1	-1.2
Pit-N	87	335	87	105	8	11	2	33	56		.313	.415	.421	138	19	22			.975	7	O-86	1.9
Yr	112	426	98	124	10	11	2	40	66		.291	.389	.380	120	13	26			.942	2	*O-110/2-1	0.7
1902 Pit-N	59	232	52	65	7	3	0	20	35		.280	.377	.336	116	6	19			.945	-2	O-59	0.0
1903 NY-A	104	372	54	88	10	0	0	25	43		.237	.319	.263	72	-11	11			.906	-7	*O-102/S-1	-2.6
1907 Cin-N	73	266	28	61	5	5	1	25	23		.229	.293	.297	82	-5	9			.972	5	O-70	-0.4
Total 4	348	1296	232	338	32	19	3	110	167		.261	.348	.322	98	2	65			.939	-2	O-341/S-1,2	-2.3
■ **ALVIN DAVIS** Davis, Alvin Glenn b: 9/9/60, Riverside, Cal. BL/TR, 6'1", 195 lbs. Deb: 4/11/84																						
1984 Sea-A★	152	567	80	161	34	3	27	116	97	78	.284	.395	.497	147	39	5	4	-1	.992	-4	*1-147/D-7	2.5
1985 Sea-A	155	578	78	166	33	1	18	78	90	71	.287	.385	.441	125	22	1	2	-1	.992	-5	*1-154	0.7
1986 Sea-A	135	479	66	130	18	1	18	72	76	68	.271	.375	.426	116	13	0	3	-2	.986	1	*1-101,D-32	0.4
1987 Sea-A	157	580	86	171	37	2	29	100	72	84	.295	.375	.516	126	22	0	0	-0	.994	-7	*1-157	0.3
1988 Sea-A	140	478	67	141	24	1	18	69	95	53	.295	.416	.462	139	29	1	1	-0	.994	-6	*1-115,D-25	1.3
1989 Sea-A	142	498	84	152	30	1	21	95	101	49	.305	.428	.496	155	41	0	1	-1	.992	-3	*1-125,D-14	2.7
1990 Sea-A	140	494	63	140	21	0	17	68	85	68	.283	.383	.429	128	22	0	2	-1	.994	-1	D-87,1-52	1.3
1991 Sea-A	145	462	39	102	15	1	12	69	56	78	.221	.305	.335	77	-14	0	3	-2	1.000	-1	*D-126,1-14	-2.3
1992 Cal-A	40	104	5	26	8	0	0	16	13	9	.250	.333	.327	85	-2	0	0	0	.995	-1	1-22/D-9	-0.4
Total 9	1206	4240	568	1189	220	10	160	683	685	558	.280	.384	.450	127	172	7	16	-8	.992	-26	1-887,D-300	6.5
■ **BILL DAVIS** Davis, Arthur Willard b: 6/6/42, Graceville, Minn. BL/TL, 6'7", 215 lbs. Deb: 9/16/65																						
1965 Cle-A	10	10	0	3	1	0	0	0	0	1	.300	.300	.400	96	-0	0	0	0	.000	0	H	0.0
1966 Cle-A	23	38	2	6	1	0	1	4	6	9	.158	.273	.263	55	-2	0	0	0	.981	0	1-9	-0.3
1969 SD-N	31	57	1	10	1	0	1	1	8	18	.175	.288	.193	39	-4	0	0	0	.992	-1	1-14	-0.7
Total 3	64	105	3	19	3	0	2	5	14	28	.181	.283	.238	50	-7	0	0	0	.988	-1	/1-23	-1.0
■ **BROCK DAVIS** Davis, Bryshear Barnett b: 10/19/43, Oakland, Cal. BL/TL, 5'10", 168 lbs. Deb: 4/9/63																						
1963 Hou-N	34	55	7	11	2	0	1	2	4	10	.200	.254	.291	60	-3	0	0	0	.864	-2	O-14	-0.6
1964 Hou-N	1	3	0	0	0	0	0	0	0	1	.000	.000	.000	-24	-0	0	0	0	1.000	0	/O-1	0.0
1966 Hou-N	10	27	2	4	1	0	0	1	5	4	.148	.281	.185	35	-2	1	0	0	1.000	-0	/O-7	-0.3

YEAR	TM/L	G	AB	R	H	2B	3B	HR	RBI	BB	SO	AVG	OBP	SLG	PRO+	BR/A	SB	CS	SBR	FA	FR	G/POS	TPR
1970	Chi-N	6	3	0	0	0	0	0	0	0	1	.000	.000	.000	-89	-1	0	0	0	.000	-0	/O-1	-0.1
1971	Chi-N	106	301	22	77	7	5	0	28	35	34	.256	.337	.312	74	-9	0	6	-4	.982	4	O-93	-1.4
1972	Mil-A	85	154	17	49	2	0	0	12	12	23	.318	.367	.331	111	2	6	4	-1	.970	-5	O-43	-0.5
Total	6	242	543	48	141	12	5	1	43	57	73	.260	.332	.306	79	-13	7	10	-4	.973	-3	O-159	-2.9

■ CHILI DAVIS
Davis, Charles Theodore b: 1/17/60, Kingston, Jamaica BB/TR, 6'3", 195 lbs. Deb: 4/10/81

YEAR	TM/L	G	AB	R	H	2B	3B	HR	RBI	BB	SO	AVG	OBP	SLG	PRO+	BR/A	SB	CS	SBR	FA	FR	G/POS	TPR
1981	SF-N	8	15	1	2	0	0	0	0	1	2	.133	.188	.133	-8	-2	2	0	1	1.000	-1	/O-6	-0.3
1982	SF-N*	154	641	86	167	27	6	19	76	45	115	.261	.311	.410	100	-1	24	13	-1	.972	18	*O-153	1.2
1983	SF-N	137	486	54	113	21	2	11	59	55	108	.233	.311	.352	86	-10	10	12	-4	.976	13	*O-133	-0.5
1984	SF-N★	137	499	87	157	21	6	21	81	42	74	.315	.369	.507	149	31	12	8	-1	.971	8	*O-123	3.4
1985	SF-N	136	481	53	130	25	2	13	56	62	74	.270	.354	.412	119	13	15	7	0	.980	13	*O-126	2.2
1986	SF-N★	153	526	71	146	28	3	13	70	84	96	.278	.378	.416	125	20	16	13	-3	.972	-2	*O-148	1.1
1987	*SF-N	149	500	80	125	22	1	24	76	72	109	.250	.347	.442	113	9	16	9	-1	.975	-13	*O-135	-0.9
1988	Cal-A	158	600	81	161	29	3	21	93	56	118	.268	.331	.432	115	11	9	10	-3	.942	-4	*O-153/D-3	-0.1
1989	Cal-A	154	560	81	152	24	1	22	90	61	109	.271	.343	.436	120	14	3	0	1	.979	-4	*O-147/D-6	0.7
1990	Cal-A	113	412	58	109	17	1	12	58	61	89	.265	.359	.398	114	9	1	2	-1	.965	-3	D-60,O-52	0.3
1991	*Min-A	153	534	84	148	34	1	29	93	95	117	.277	.387	.507	139	30	5	6	-2	1.000	-0	*D-150/O-2	2.1
1992	Min-A	138	444	63	128	27	2	12	66	73	76	.288	.392	.439	128	19	4	5	-2	1.000	-1	*D-125/O-4,1	1.2
1993	Cal-A	153	573	74	139	32	0	27	112	71	135	.243	.327	.440	101	-0	4	1	1	.000	-0	*D-150/P-1	-0.6
1994	Cal-A★	108	392	72	122	18	1	26	84	69	84	.311	.416	.561	145	27	3	2	-0	1.000	-0	*D-106/O-2	2.1
Total	14	1851	6663	945	1799	325	29	250	1014	847	1306	.270	.353	.440	119	169	124	88	-16	.971	24	*O-1184,D-600/P1	11.9

■ DOUG DAVIS
Davis, Douglas Raymond b: 9/24/62, Bloomsburg, Pa. BR/TR, 6', 180 lbs. Deb: 7/8/88

YEAR	TM/L	G	AB	R	H	2B	3B	HR	RBI	BB	SO	AVG	OBP	SLG	PRO+	BR/A	SB	CS	SBR	FA	FR	G/POS	TPR
1988	Cal-A	6	12	1	0	0	0	0	0	0	3	.000	.077	.000	-79	-3	0	0	0	1.000	-3	/C-3,3-3	-0.6
1992	Tex-A	1	1	0	1	0	0	0	0	0	0	1.000	1.000	1.000	479	0	0	0	0	.000	0	/C-1	0.0
Total	2	7	13	1	1	0	0	0	0	0	3	.077	.143	.077	-38	-2	0	0	0	1.000	-3	/C-4,3-3	-0.6

■ ERIC DAVIS
Davis, Eric Keith b: 5/29/62, Los Angeles, Cal. BR/TR, 6'3", 175 lbs. Deb: 5/19/84

YEAR	TM/L	G	AB	R	H	2B	3B	HR	RBI	BB	SO	AVG	OBP	SLG	PRO+	BR/A	SB	CS	SBR	FA	FR	G/POS	TPR
1984	Cin-N	57	174	33	39	10	1	10	30	24	48	.224	.322	.466	114	3	10	2	2	.992	1	O-51	0.5
1985	Cin-N	56	122	26	30	3	3	8	18	7	39	.246	.287	.516	114	2	16	3	3	.987	-6	O-47	-0.3
1986	Cin-N	132	415	97	115	15	3	27	71	68	100	.277	.380	.523	140	23	80	11	17	.975	-9	*O-121	2.9
1987	Cin-N★	129	474	120	139	23	4	37	100	84	134	.293	.401	.593	152	36	50	6	11	.990	28	*O-128	6.9
1988	Cin-N	135	472	81	129	18	3	26	93	65	124	.273	.365	.489	138	23	35	3	9	.981	-0	*O-130	3.0
1989	Cin-N★	131	462	74	130	14	2	34	101	68	116	.281	.375	.541	154	32	21	7	2	.984	2	*O-125	3.4
1990	*Cin-N	127	453	84	118	26	2	24	86	60	100	.260	.350	.486	122	13	21	3	5	.993	7	*O-122	2.2
1991	Cin-N	89	285	39	67	10	0	11	33	48	92	.235	.355	.386	104	3	14	2	3	.985	6	O-81	1.1
1992	LA-N	76	267	21	61	8	1	5	32	36	71	.228	.327	.322	86	-4	19	1	5	.961	-5	O-74	-0.6
1993	LA-N	108	376	57	88	17	0	14	53	41	88	.234	.331	.391	92	-5	33	5	7	.991	9	O-103	0.9
	Det-A	23	75	14	19	1	1	6	15	14	18	.253	.371	.533	141	4	2	2	-1	.981	1	O-18/D-5	0.4
1994	Det-A	37	120	19	22	4	0	3	13	18	45	.183	.290	.292	51	-9	5	0	2	.989	-1	O-35	-0.8
Total	11	1100	3695	665	957	149	20	205	645	533	975	.259	.355	.477	125	122	306	45	65	.985	33	*O-1035/D-5	19.6

■ GEORGE DAVIS
Davis, George Stacey b: 8/23/1870, Cohoes, N.Y. d: 10/17/40, Philadelphia, Pa. BB/TR, 5'9", 180 lbs. Deb: 4/19/1890 M

YEAR	TM/L	G	AB	R	H	2B	3B	HR	RBI	BB	SO	AVG	OBP	SLG	PRO+	BR/A	SB	CS	SBR	FA	FR	G/POS	TPR
1890	Cle-N	136	526	98	139	22	9	6	73	53	34	.264	.336	.375	109	6	22			.946	12	*O-133/2-2,S	1.2
1891	Cle-N	136	570	115	165	35	12	3	89	53	29	.289	.354	.409	117	11	42			.931	14	*O-116,3-22/P	1.9
1892	*Cle-N	144	597	95	144	27	12	5	82	58	51	.241	.312	.352	97	-4	36			.914	-10	3-79,O-44,S/2	-1.1
1893	NY-N	133	549	112	195	22	27	11	119	42	20	.355	.410	.554	155	40	37			.884	0	*3-133/S-1	3.4
1894	*NY-N	122	477	120	168	26	19	8	91	66	10	.352	.435	.537	134	28	40			.908	-1	*3-122	2.0
1895	NY-N	110	430	108	146	36	9	5	101	55	12	.340	.417	.500	139	26	48			.881	15	3-80,1-14,2/OM	3.4
1896	NY-N	124	494	98	158	25	12	6	99	50	24	.320	.387	.455	125	18	48			.917	11	3-74,S-45/O1	2.7
1897	NY-N	130	519	112	183	31	10	10	**136**	41		.353	.407	.509	145	33	65			.926	22	*S-129	4.9
1898	NY-N	121	486	80	149	20	5	2	86	32		.307	.351	.381	113	7	26			.933	**35**	*S-121	4.4
1899	NY-N	108	416	68	140	21	5	1	57	37		.337	.393	.418	127	16	34			**.945**	46	*S-108	6.2
1900	NY-N	114	426	69	136	20	4	3	61	35		.319	.376	.406	121	13	29			**.944**	29	*S-114,M	4.6
1901	NY-N	130	491	69	148	26	7	7	65	40		.301	.356	.426	131	19	27			.939	23	*S-113,3-17M	4.9
1902	Chi-A	132	485	76	145	27	7	3	93	65		.299	.386	.402	124	19	31			**.951**	-2	*S-129/1-3	2.3
1903	NY-N	4	15	2	4	0	0	0	1	1		.267	.313	.267	63	-1	0			.870	-2	/S-4	-0.2
1904	Chi-A	152	563	75	142	27	15	1	69	43		.252	.311	.359	116	10	32			.937	17	*S-152	3.4
1905	Chi-A	151	550	74	153	29	1	1	55	60		.278	.353	.340	125	18	31			**.948**	16	*S-151	4.0
1906	*Chi-A	133	484	63	134	26	6	0	80	41		.277	.338	.355	120	12	27			.946	10	*S-129/2-1	2.8
1907	Chi-A	132	466	59	111	16	2	1	52	47		.238	.313	.288	95	-1	15			.949	9	*S-132	1.2
1908	Chi-A	128	419	41	91	14	1	0	26	41		.217	.298	.255	81	-7	22			.960	4	2-95,S-23/1	-0.4
1909	Chi-A	28	68	5	9	1	0	0	2	10		.132	.253	.147	28	-5	4			.986	1	1-17/2-2	-0.5
Total	20	2368	9031	1539	2660	451	163	73	1437	870	_180_	.295	.361	.405	121	255	616			.940	249	*S-1372,3-527,O2/1P	51.1

■ KIDDO DAVIS
Davis, George Willis b: 2/12/02, Bridgeport, Conn. d: 3/4/83, Bridgeport, Conn. BR/TR, 5'11", 178 lbs. Deb: 6/15/26

YEAR	TM/L	G	AB	R	H	2B	3B	HR	RBI	BB	SO	AVG	OBP	SLG	PRO+	BR/A	SB	CS	SBR	FA	FR	G/POS	TPR
1926	NY-A	1	0	0	0	0	0	0	0	0	0	—	—	—			0	0	0	.000	-0	/O-1	0.0
1932	Phi-N	137	576	100	178	39	6	5	57	44	56	.309	.359	.424	98	-2	16			.975	14	*O-133	0.4
1933	*NY-N	126	434	61	112	20	4	7	37	25	30	.258	.298	.371	92	-6	10			.988	-10	*O-120	-2.3
1934	StL-N	16	33	6	10	3	0	1	4	3	1	.303	.361	.485	117	1	1			.960	1	/O-9	0.1
	Phi-N	100	393	50	115	25	5	3	48	27	28	.293	.338	.405	86	-8	1			.991	17	*O-100	0.5
	Yr	116	426	56	125	28	5	4	52	30	29	.293	.340	.411	89	-7	2			.988	18	*O-109	0.6
1935	NY-N	47	91	16	24	7	1	2	6	10	4	.264	.343	.429	108	1	2			.977	-1	O-21	-0.1
1936	*NY-N	47	67	6	16	1	0	0	5	6	5	.239	.301	.254	51	-4	0			1.000	-1	O-22	-0.6
1937	NY-N	56	76	20	20	10	0	0	9	10	7	.263	.356	.395	103	0	1			.932	-10	O-37	-1.0
	Cin-N	40	136	19	35	6	0	1	5	16	6	.257	.340	.324	85	-2	1			.959	2	O-35	-0.2
	Yr	96	212	39	55	16	0	1	14	26	13	.259	.346	.349	90	-2	2			.951	-8	O-72	-1.2
1938	Cin-N	5	18	3	5	1	0	0	0	1	4	.278	.316	.333	81	-0	1			1.000	-1	/O-5	-0.1
Total	8	575	1824	281	515	112	16	19	171	142	141	.282	.336	.393	92	-20	32	_0_		.980	10	O-483	-3.3

■ GERRY DAVIS
Davis, Gerald Edward b: 12/25/58, Trenton, N.J. BR/TR, 6', 185 lbs. Deb: 9/20/83

YEAR	TM/L	G	AB	R	H	2B	3B	HR	RBI	BB	SO	AVG	OBP	SLG	PRO+	BR/A	SB	CS	SBR	FA	FR	G/POS	TPR
1983	SD-N	5	15	3	5	2	0	0	1	3	4	.333	.444	.467	158	1	1	0	0	1.000	-0	/O-5	0.2
1985	SD-N	44	58	10	17	3	1	0	2	5	7	.293	.349	.379	105	0	0	0	0	.952	-4	O-23	-0.4
Total	2	49	73	13	22	5	1	0	3	8	11	.301	.370	.397	117	2	1	0	0	.967	-3	/O-28	-0.2

■ GLENN DAVIS
Davis, Glenn Earle b: 3/28/61, Jacksonville, Fla. BR/TR, 6'3", 210 lbs. Deb: 9/2/84

YEAR	TM/L	G	AB	R	H	2B	3B	HR	RBI	BB	SO	AVG	OBP	SLG	PRO+	BR/A	SB	CS	SBR	FA	FR	G/POS	TPR
1984	Hou-N	18	61	6	13	5	0	2	8	4	12	.213	.262	.393	88	-1	0	0	0	.988	2	1-16	0.0
1985	Hou-N	100	350	51	95	11	0	20	64	27	68	.271	.336	.474	128	12	0	0	0	.985	-2	1-89/O-9	0.4
1986	*Hou-N★	158	574	91	152	32	3	31	101	64	72	.265	.348	.493	133	24	3	1	0	.992	3	*1-156	1.6
1987	Hou-N	151	578	70	145	35	2	27	93	47	84	.251	.313	.458	105	2	4	1	1	.991	3	*1-151	-0.6
1988	Hou-N	152	561	78	152	26	0	30	99	53	77	.271	.346	.478	140	27	4	3	-1	**.996**	0	*1-151	1.5
1989	Hou-N★	158	581	87	156	26	1	34	89	69	123	.269	.353	.492	144	32	4	2	0	.992	3	*1-156	2.4
1990	Hou-N	93	327	44	82	15	4	22	64	46	54	.251	.357	.523	143	19	8	5	3	.995	-3	1-91	1.0
1991	Bal-A	49	176	29	40	9	1	10	28	16	29	.227	.310	.460	115	3	4	0	1	.976	4	1-36,D-12	0.5

YEAR	TM/L	G	AB	R	H	2B	3B	HR	RBI	BB	SO	AVG	OBP	SLG	PRO+	BR/A	SB	CS	SBR	FA	FR	G/POS	TPR
1992	Bal-A	106	398	46	110	15	2	13	48	37	65	.276	.341	.422	110	5	1	0	0	1.000	-0	*D-103/1-2	0.1
1993	Bal-A	30	113	8	20	3	0	1	9	7	29	.177	.231	.230	24	-12	0	1	-1	.990	-2	1-22/D-7	-1.6
Total	10	1015	3719	510	965	177	13	190	603	370	613	.259	.335	.467	124	111	28	11	2	.991	6	1-870,D-122/O	5.3

■ **HARRY DAVIS**   Davis, Harry Albert "Stinky"   b: 5/7/08, Shreveport, La.   BL/TL, 5'10.5", 160 lbs.   Deb: 4/13/32

YEAR	TM/L	G	AB	R	H	2B	3B	HR	RBI	BB	SO	AVG	OBP	SLG	PRO+	BR/A	SB	CS	SBR	FA	FR	G/POS	TPR
1932	Det-A	141	590	92	159	32	13	4	74	60	53	.269	.339	.388	84	-14	12	7	-1	.989	-5	*1-141	-2.9
1933	Det-A	66	173	24	37	8	2	0	14	22	8	.214	.303	.283	55	-11	2	3	-1	.978	-5	1-44	-2.0
1937	StL-A	120	450	89	124	25	3	3	35	71	26	.276	.374	.364	86	-7	7	6	-2	.991	-4	*1-112/O-1	-2.4
Total	3	327	1213	205	320	65	18	7	123	153	87	.264	.347	.364	81	-32	21	16	-3	.988	-14	1-297/O-1	-7.3

■ **HARRY DAVIS**   Davis, Harry H (b: Harry Davis) "Jasper"   b: 7/19/1873, Philadelphia, Pa.   d: 8/11/47, Philadelphia, Pa.   BR/TR, 5'10", 180 lbs.   Deb: 9/21/1895   M

YEAR	TM/L	G	AB	R	H	2B	3B	HR	RBI	BB	SO	AVG	OBP	SLG	PRO+	BR/A	SB	CS	SBR	FA	FR	G/POS	TPR
1895	NY-N	7	24	1	7	0	1	0	6	2	0	.292	.346	.375	88	-0	1			.957	0	/1-7	0.0
1896	NY-N	64	233	43	64	11	10	2	50	31	20	.275	.372	.433	115	5	16			.883	-4	O-40,1-23	-0.1
	Pit-N	44	168	24	32	5	6	0	23	13	21	.190	.257	.292	46	-14	9			.966	0	1-35,O-10/S	-1.2
	Yr	108	401	67	96	16	16	2	73	44	41	.239	.325	.374	87	-8	25			.973	-4	1-58,O-50/S	-1.3
1897	Pit-N	111	429	70	131	10	28	2	63	26		.305	.359	.471	123	13	21			.965	-12	1-64,3-32,O/S	0.1
1898	Pit-N	58	222	31	65	9	13	1	24	12		.293	.332	.464	130	7	7			.980	-2	1-53/O-6	0.4
	Lou-N	37	138	18	30	5	2	1	16	7		.217	.255	.304	61	-7	6			.967	0	1-34/2-2,O	-0.7
	Was-N	1	3	0	0	0	0	0	0	0		.000	.000	.000	-99	-1	0			.875	-0	/1-1	-0.1
	Yr	96	363	49	95	14	15	2	40	19		.262	.300	.399	102	-1	13			.974	-2	1-88/O-7,2	-0.4
1899	Was-N	18	64	3	12	2	3	0	8	8		.188	.288	.313	65	-3	2			.988	-1	1-18	-0.4
1901	Phi-A	117	496	92	152	28	10	3	76	23		.306	.340	.452	113	6	21			.976	8	*1-117	1.2
1902	Phi-A	133	561	89	172	43	8	6	92	30		.307	.343	.444	112	7	28			.984	7	*1-128/O-5	1.1
1903	Phi-A	106	420	77	125	28	7	6	55	24		.298	.343	.440	128	13	24			.972	-1	*1-104/O-2	1.1
1904	Phi-A	102	404	54	125	21	11	10	62	23		.309	.350	.490	156	24	12			.983	-1	*1-102	2.3
1905	*Phi-A	150	607	93	173	47	6	8	83	41		.285	.334	.422	137	23	36			.985	1	*1-150	2.1
1906	Phi-A	145	551	94	161	42	7	12	96	49		.292	.355	.459	150	30	23			.975	-0	*1-145	2.8
1907	Phi-A	149	582	84	155	37	8	8	87	42		.266	.318	.399	125	15	20			.977	4	*1-149	1.6
1908	Phi-A	147	513	65	127	23	9	5	62	61		.248	.332	.357	116	10	20			.986	1	*1-147	0.9
1909	Phi-A	149	530	73	142	22	11	4	75	51		.268	.338	.374	122	13	20			.988	-5	*1-149	0.8
1910	*Phi-A	139	492	61	122	19	4	1	41	53		.248	.332	.309	102	3	17			.986	-4	*1-139	-0.2
1911	*Phi-A	57	183	27	36	9	1	1	22	24		.197	.297	.273	60	-9	2			.977	2	1-53	-0.8
1912	Cle-A	2	5	0	0	0	0	0	0	0		.000	.000	.000	-97	-1	0			.941	0	/1-2,M	-0.1
1913	Phi-A	7	17	2	6	2	0	0	4	0	4	.353	.389	.471	155	1	0			1.000	1	/1-6	0.2
1914	Phi-A	5	7	0	3	0	0	0	2	1	0	.429	.556	.429	204	1	0	2	-1	1.000	-0	/1-1	0.0
1915	Phi-A	5	3	0	1	0	0	0	4	0	0	.333	.333	.333	103	-0	0			.000	0	/1-1	0.0
1916	Phi-A	1	0	0	0	0	0	0	0	1	0	—	1.000	—	213	-0	0			.000	0	H	0.0
1917	Phi-A	1	1	0	0	0	0	0	0	0	0	.000	.000	.000	-99	-0	0			.000	0	H	0.0
Total	22	1755	6653	1001	1841	363	145	75	951	525	45	.277	.335	.409	119	136	285	2		.980	-6	*1-1628/O-78,32S	11.0

■ **TOMMY DAVIS**   Davis, Herman Thomas   b: 3/21/39, Brooklyn, N.Y.   BR/TR, 6'2", 205 lbs.   Deb: 9/22/59   C

YEAR	TM/L	G	AB	R	H	2B	3B	HR	RBI	BB	SO	AVG	OBP	SLG	PRO+	BR/A	SB	CS	SBR	FA	FR	G/POS	TPR
1959	LA-N	1	1	0	0	0	0	0	0	0	1	.000	.000	.000	-93	-0	0	0	0	.000	0	H	0.0
1960	LA-N	110	352	43	97	18	1	11	44	13	35	.276	.305	.426	92	-5	6	2	1	.975	-0	O-87/3-5	-0.9
1961	LA-N	132	460	60	128	13	2	15	58	32	53	.278	.328	.413	87	-9	10	4	1	.973	-12	O-86,3-59	-2.4
1962	LA-N★	163	665	120	230	27	9	27	153	33	65	.346	.379	.535	151	45	18	6	2	.961	1	*O-146,3-39	3.9
1963	*LA-N★	146	556	69	181	19	3	16	88	29	59	.326	.363	.457	144	30	15	10	-2	.969	-7	*O-129,3-40	1.6
1964	LA-N	152	592	70	163	20	5	14	86	29	68	.275	.314	.397	106	3	11	8	-2	.982	14	*O-148	0.8
1965	LA-N	17	60	3	15	1	1	0	9	2	4	.250	.274	.300	66	-3	2	1	0	1.000	0	O-16	-0.4
1966	*LA-N	100	313	27	98	11	1	3	27	16	36	.313	.347	.383	111	4	3	3	-1	.972	-2	O-79/3-2	-0.3
1967	NY-N	154	577	72	174	32	0	16	73	31	71	.302	.341	.440	125	17	9	3	1	.975	-3	*O-149/1-1	0.9
1968	Chi-A	132	456	30	122	5	3	8	50	16	48	.268	.292	.344	91	-6	4	2	0	.962	-4	*O-116/1-6	-1.9
1969	Sea-A	123	454	52	123	29	1	6	80	30	46	.271	.322	.379	97	-3	19	4	3	.967	-3	*O-112/1-1	-1.3
	Hou-N	24	79	2	19	3	0	1	9	8	9	.241	.318	.316	80	-2	1	1	0	1.000	0	O-21	-0.4
1970	Hou-N	50	213	24	60	12	2	3	30	7	25	.282	.305	.399	91	-4	8	3	1	.949	-1	O-53	-0.7
	Chi-N	11	42	4	11	2	0	2	8	1	1	.262	.279	.452	83	-1	0	0	0	.938	-1	O-10	-0.2
	Yr	68	255	28	71	14	2	5	38	8	26	.278	.300	.408	89	-5	8	3	1	.947	-2	O-63	-0.9
	Oak-A	66	200	17	58	9	1	1	27	8	18	.290	.321	.360	91	-2	3	2	4	.963	-7	O-45/1-8	-1.5
1971	*Oak-A	79	219	26	71	8	1	3	42	15	19	.324	.368	.411	123	6	7	1	2	.989	2	1-35,O-16/23	0.7
1972	Chi-N	15	26	3	7	1	0	0	6	2	3	.269	.321	.308	72	-1	0	1	-1	1.000	-0	/1-3,O-2	-0.2
	Bal-A	26	82	9	21	3	0	0	6	6	18	.256	.307	.293	77	-2	2	0	1	1.000	0	O-18/1-3	-0.3
1973	*Bal-A	137	552	53	169	20	3	7	89	30	56	.306	.343	.391	107	5	11	3	2	.971	-0	*D-127/1-4	0.2
1974	*Bal-A	158	626	67	181	20	1	11	84	34	49	.289	.329	.377	106	4	6	3	2	.000	0	*D-155	0.0
1975	Bal-A	116	460	43	130	14	1	6	57	23	52	.283	.317	.357	96	-4	2	0	1	.000	0	*D-111	-0.6
1976	Cal-A	72	219	16	58	5	0	3	26	15	18	.265	.315	.329	95	-2	0	1	-1	1.000	-0	D-54/1-1	-0.4
	KC-A	8	19	1	5	0	0	0	0	1	0	.263	.300	.263	65	-1	0	0	0	.000	0	/D-3	-0.1
	Yr	80	238	17	63	5	0	3	26	16	18	.265	.314	.324	92	-3	0	1	-1	1.000	-0	D-54/H-3,1	-0.5
Total	18	1999	7223	811	2121	272	35	153	1052	381	754	.294	.332	.405	109	68	136	59	5	.970	-27	*O-1233,D-450,3/12	-3.5

■ **IKE DAVIS**   Davis, Isaac Marion   b: 6/14/1895, Pueblo, Col.   d: 4/2/84, Tucson, Ariz.   BR/TR, 5'7", 140 lbs.   Deb: 4/23/19

YEAR	TM/L	G	AB	R	H	2B	3B	HR	RBI	BB	SO	AVG	OBP	SLG	PRO+	BR/A	SB	CS	SBR	FA	FR	G/POS	TPR
1919	Was-A	8	14	0	0	0	0	0	0	0	6	.000	.000	.000	-99	-4	0			.857	-2	/S-4	-0.6
1924	Chi-A	10	33	5	8	1	1	0	4	2	5	.242	.286	.333	61	-2	0			.940	1	S-10	0.0
1925	Chi-A	146	562	105	135	31	9	0	61	71	58	.240	.333	.327	72	-24	19	14	-3	.937	8	*S-144	-0.3
Total	3	164	609	110	143	32	10	0	65	73	69	.235	.324	.320	68	-29	19	14		.936	8	S-158	-0.9

■ **IRA DAVIS**   Davis, J. Ira "Slats"   b: 7/8/1870, Philadelphia, Pa.   d: 12/21/42, Brooklyn, N.Y.   162 lbs.   Deb: 4/22/1899

YEAR	TM/L	G	AB	R	H	2B	3B	HR	RBI	BB	SO	AVG	OBP	SLG	PRO+	BR/A	SB	CS	SBR	FA	FR	G/POS	TPR
1899	NY-N	6	17	3	4	1	1	0	2	0		.235	.235	.412	79	-1	1			.750	-0	/S-3,1-2	-0.1

■ **JACKE DAVIS**   Davis, Jacke Sylvesta   b: 3/5/36, Carthage, Tex.   BR/TR, 5'11", 160 lbs.   Deb: 4/19/62

YEAR	TM/L	G	AB	R	H	2B	3B	HR	RBI	BB	SO	AVG	OBP	SLG	PRO+	BR/A	SB	CS	SBR	FA	FR	G/POS	TPR
1962	Phi-N	48	75	9	16	0	1	1	6	4	20	.213	.253	.280	44	-6	1	0	0	.926	-6	O-26	-1.2

■ **JUMBO DAVIS**   Davis, James J.   b: 9/5/1861, New York, N.Y.   d: 2/14/21, St.Louis, Mo.   BL/TR, 5'11", 195 lbs.   Deb: 7/27/1884   U

YEAR	TM/L	G	AB	R	H	2B	3B	HR	RBI	BB	SO	AVG	OBP	SLG	PRO+	BR/A	SB	CS	SBR	FA	FR	G/POS	TPR
1884	KC-U	7	29	3	6	0	0	0		0		.207	.207	.207	15	-3				.633	-2	/3-7	-0.5
1886	Bal-a	60	216	23	42	5	2	1		11		.194	.240	.250	55	-11	12			.848	5	3-60	-0.4
1887	Bal-a	130	485	81	150	23	19	8		28		.309	.353	.485	141	25	49			.826	4	3-87,S-43	2.4
1888	KC-a	121	491	70	131	22	8	3	61	20		.267	.304	.363	106	1	42			.843	30	*3-113/S-8	3.0
1889	KC-a	62	241	40	64	4	3	0	30	17	35	.266	.319	.307	74	-9	25			.803	-0	3-62	-0.6
	StL-a	2	4	1	0	0	0	0	0	0		.000	.000	.000	-36	-1	0			1.000	-0	/S-1,O-1	-0.1
	Yr	64	245	41	64	4	3	0	30	18	36	.261	.317	.302	72	-9	25			.803	-1	3-62/S-1,O	-0.7
1890	StL-a	21	71	8	18	3	1	0		9		.254	.338	.324	83	-2	5			.731	-1	3-21	-0.2
	Bro-a	38	142	33	43	9	2	2	15			.303	.385	.437	147	8	10			.845	-5	3-38	0.4
	Yr	59	213	41	61	12	3	2		24		.286	.369	.399	123	6	15			.800	-6	3-59	0.2
1891	Was-a	12	44	7	14	3	2	0	9	7	5	.318	.412	.477	162	4	8			.820	-2	3-12	0.2
Total	7	453	1723	266	468	69	37	14	100	108	41	.272	.322	.379	107	12	151			.824	28	3-400/S-52,O	4.2

YEAR	TM/L	G	AB	R	H	2B	3B	HR	RBI	BB	SO	AVG	OBP	SLG	PRO+	BR/A	SB	CS	SBR	FA	FR	G/POS	TPR

■ JODY DAVIS
Davis, Jody Richard b: 11/12/56, Gainesville, Ga. BR/TR, 6'3", 210 lbs. Deb: 4/21/81

1981	Chi-N	56	180	14	46	5	1	4	21	21	28	.256	.337	.361	94	-1	0	1	-1	.972	-1	C-56	-0.1
1982	Chi-N	130	418	41	109	20	2	12	52	36	92	.261	.321	.404	99	-1	0	1	-1	.984	8	*C-129	1.1
1983	Chi-N	151	510	56	138	31	2	24	84	33	93	.271	.317	.480	113	7	0	2	-1	.984	-14	*C-150	-0.2
1984	*Chi-N★	150	523	55	134	25	2	19	94	47	99	.256	.319	.421	97	-3	5	6	-2	.984	4	*C-146	0.7
1985	Chi-N	142	482	47	112	30	0	17	58	48	83	.232	.302	.400	85	-10	1	0	0	.990	-1	*C-138	-0.4
1986	Chi-N★	148	528	61	132	27	2	21	74	41	110	.250	.304	.428	92	-7	0	1	-1	.992	4	*C-145/1-1	0.6
1987	Chi-N	125	428	57	106	12	2	19	51	52	91	.248	.332	.418	93	-4	1	2	-1	.989	-3	*C-123	0.1
1988	Chi-N	88	249	19	57	9	0	6	33	29	51	.229	.312	.337	83	-5	0	3	-2	.995	-4	C-74	-0.7
	Atl-N	2	8	2	2	0	0	1	3	0	1	.250	.250	.625	137	0	0	0	0	1.000	1	/C-2	0.1
	Yr	90	257	21	59	9	0	7	36	29	52	.230	.310	.346	84	-5	0	3	-2	.995	-4	C-76	-0.6
1989	Atl-N	78	231	12	39	5	0	4	19	23	61	.169	.247	.242	39	-18	0	0	0	.985	-9	C-72/1-2	-2.6
1990	Atl-N	12	28	0	2	0	0	0	1	3	3	.071	.161	.071	-32	-5	0	0	0	1.000	1	/1-6,C-4	-0.4
Total	10	1082	3585	364	877	164	11	127	490	333	712	.245	.310	.403	91	-48	7	16	-8	.987	-15	*C-1039/1-9	-1.8

■ JOHN DAVIS
Davis, John Humphrey "Red" b: 7/15/15, Laurel Run, Pa. BR/TR, 5'11", 172 lbs. Deb: 9/9/41

| 1941 | NY-N | 21 | 70 | 8 | 15 | 3 | 0 | 0 | 5 | 8 | 12 | .214 | .295 | .257 | 55 | -4 | 0 | | | .970 | 1 | 3-21 | -0.2 |

■ CRASH DAVIS
Davis, Lawrence Columbus b: 7/14/19, Canon, Ga. BR/TR, 6', 173 lbs. Deb: 6/15/40

1940	Phi-A	23	67	4	18	1	1	0	9	3	10	.269	.310	.313	63	-4	1	0	0	.963	4	2-19/S-1	0.1
1941	Phi-A	39	105	8	23	3	0	0	8	11	16	.219	.293	.248	45	-8	0	0	0	.952	2	2-20,1-12	-0.5
1942	Phi-A	86	272	31	61	8	1	2	26	21	30	.224	.282	.283	60	-15	1	0	0	.965	-6	2-57,S-26/1	-1.6
Total	3	148	444	43	102	12	2	2	43	35	56	.230	.289	.279	57	-26	2	0	1	.961	0	/2-96,S-27,1	-2.0

■ MARK DAVIS
Davis, Mark Anthony b: 11/25/64, San Diego, Cal. BR/TR, 6', 180 lbs. Deb: 7/2/91 F

| 1991 | Cal-A | 3 | 2 | 0 | 0 | 0 | 0 | 0 | 0 | 0 | 0 | .000 | .000 | .000 | -99 | -1 | 0 | 0 | 0 | .500 | -1 | /O-3 | -0.2 |

■ MIKE DAVIS
Davis, Michael Dwayne b: 6/11/59, San Diego, Cal. BL/TL, 6'3", 185 lbs. Deb: 4/10/80 F

1980	Oak-A	51	95	11	20	2	1	1	8	7	14	.211	.265	.284	54	-6	2	1	0	1.000	0	O-18/1-7,D	-0.6
1981	*Oak-A	17	20	0	1	1	0	0	0	2	4	.050	.136	.100	-33	-3	0	0	0	1.000	-0	/O-2,1-1,D	-0.4
1982	Oak-A	23	75	12	30	4	0	1	10	2	8	.400	.416	.493	155	5	3	2	-0	.946	-1	O-13/1-7	0.4
1983	Oak-A	128	443	61	122	24	4	8	62	27	74	.275	.324	.402	105	2	32	15	1	.974	9	*O-121/D-3	0.8
1984	Oak-A	134	382	47	88	18	3	9	46	31	66	.230	.290	.364	85	-9	14	9	-1	.961	-1	*O-127/D-4	-1.4
1985	Oak-A	154	547	92	157	34	1	24	82	50	99	.287	.349	.484	135	25	24	10	1	.979	-2	*O-151	2.3
1986	Oak-A	142	489	77	131	28	3	19	55	34	91	.268	.317	.454	115	8	27	4	6	.973	2	*O-139	1.1
1987	Oak-A	139	494	69	131	32	1	22	72	42	94	.265	.324	.468	114	8	19	7	2	.942	-7	*O-124,D-14	-0.1
1988	*LA-N	108	281	29	55	11	2	2	17	25	59	.196	.261	.270	55	-17	7	3	0	.961	-9	O-76	-3.0
1989	LA-N	67	173	21	43	7	1	5	19	16	28	.249	.312	.387	101	-0	6	5	-1	.987	-3	O-48	-0.6
Total	10	963	2999	419	778	161	16	91	371	236	537	.259	.316	.415	105	14	134	56	7	.968	-8	O-819/D-30,1	-1.5

■ ODIE DAVIS
Davis, Odie Ernest b: 8/13/55, San Antonio, Tex. BR/TR, 6'1", 178 lbs. Deb: 9/3/80

| 1980 | Tex-A | 17 | 8 | 0 | 1 | 0 | 0 | 0 | 0 | 0 | 2 | .125 | .125 | .125 | -32 | -1 | 0 | 0 | 0 | .880 | 5 | S-13/3-1 | 0.3 |

■ OTIS DAVIS
Davis, Otis Allen "Scat" b: 9/24/20, Charleston, Ark. BL/TL, 6', 160 lbs. Deb: 4/22/46

| 1946 | Bro-N | 1 | 0 | 1 | 0 | 0 | 0 | 0 | 0 | 0 | 0 | — | — | — | — | 0 | 0 | | | 1.000 | 0 | R | 0.0 |

■ DICK DAVIS
Davis, Richard Earl b: 9/25/53, Long Beach, Cal. BR/TR, 6'3", 195 lbs. Deb: 7/12/77

1977	Mil-A	22	51	7	14	2	0	0	6	1	8	.275	.288	.314	64	-3	0	0	0	1.000	-2	O-12/D-6	-0.5
1978	Mil-A	69	218	28	54	10	1	5	26	7	23	.248	.278	.372	81	-6	2	5	-2	1.000	-1	D-34,O-28	-1.2
1979	Mil-A	91	335	51	89	13	1	12	41	16	46	.266	.299	.418	91	-5	3	3	-1	.973	-0	D-53,O-35	-0.9
1980	Mil-A	106	365	50	99	26	2	4	30	11	43	.271	.298	.386	89	-7	5	3	-0	.971	-2	D-63,O-38	-1.3
1981	*Phi-N	45	96	12	32	6	1	2	19	8	13	.333	.390	.479	139	5	1	2	-1	.974	-4	O-32	-0.1
1982	Phi-N	28	68	5	19	3	1	2	7	2	9	.279	.300	.441	103	-0	1	0	0	1.000	0	O-16	0.0
	Tor-A	3	7	0	2	0	0	0	2	0	1	.286	.286	.286	53	-0	0	0	0	1.000	0	/O-1,D-1	-0.1
	Pit-N	39	77	7	14	2	1	2	10	5	9	.182	.232	.312	49	-5	1	0	0	.971	-4	O-28	-1.0
Total	6	403	1217	160	323	62	7	27	141	50	152	.265	.298	.394	89	-22	13	13	-4	.981	-14	O-190,D-157	-5.1

■ BRANDY DAVIS
Davis, Robert Brandon b: 9/10/28, Newark, Del. BR/TR, 6', 170 lbs. Deb: 4/15/52 C

1952	Pit-N	55	95	14	17	1	1	0	1	11	28	.179	.264	.211	32	-9	9	2	2	.932	-3	O-29	-1.1
1953	Pit-N	12	39	5	8	2	0	0	2	0	3	.205	.205	.256	20	-5	0	2	-1	.955	0	/O-9	-0.6
Total	2	67	134	19	25	3	1	0	3	11	31	.187	.248	.224	29	-13	9	4	0	.938	-3	/O-38	-1.7

■ BOB DAVIS
Davis, Robert John Eugene b: 3/1/52, Pryor, Okla. BR/TR, 6', 180 lbs. Deb: 4/6/73

1973	SD-N	5	11	1	1	0	0	0	0	0	5	.091	.091	.091	-54	-2	0	0	0	.941	2	/C-5	-0.1
1975	SD-N	43	128	6	30	3	2	0	7	11	31	.234	.307	.289	71	-5	0	0	0	.986	3	C-43	0.0
1976	SD-N	51	83	7	17	0	1	0	5	5	13	.205	.250	.229	40	-7	0	0	0	.965	-4	C-47	-0.2
1977	SD-N	48	94	9	17	2	0	1	10	5	24	.181	.238	.234	30	-10	0	0	0	.975	-1	C-46	-1.0
1978	SD-N	19	40	3	8	1	0	0	2	1	5	.200	.220	.225	26	-4	0	1	-1	.960	-2	C-16	-0.7
1979	Tor-A	32	89	6	11	2	0	1	8	6	15	.124	.188	.180	-0	-13	0	0	0	.984	-4	C-32	-1.3
1980	Tor-A	91	218	18	47	11	0	4	19	12	25	.216	.260	.321	56	-14	0	1	-1	.983	-2	C-89	-1.3
1981	Cal-A	1	2	0	0	0	0	0	0	0	0	.000	.000	.000	-99	-1	0	0	0	1.000	-0	/C-1	-0.1
Total	8	290	665	50	131	19	3	6	51	40	118	.197	.250	.262	42	-54	0	1	-1	.978	1	C-279	-4.7

■ RON DAVIS
Davis, Ronald Everette b: 10/21/41, Roanoke Rapids, N.C d: 9/5/92, Houston, Tex. BR/TR, 6', 180 lbs. Deb: 8/1/62

1962	Hou-N	6	14	1	3	0	0	0	1	1	7	.214	.267	.214	33	-1	1	0	0	1.000	-1	/O-5	-0.2
1966	Hou-N	48	194	21	48	10	1	2	19	13	26	.247	.308	.340	86	-4	2	2	-1	.982	6	O-48	-0.1
1967	Hou-N	94	285	31	73	19	1	7	38	17	48	.256	.303	.404	104	0	5	3	-0	.976	-0	O-80	-0.4
1968	Hou-N	52	217	22	46	10	1	1	12	13	48	.212	.269	.281	67	-9	0	4	-2	.971	6	O-52	-0.9
	*StL-N	33	79	11	14	4	2	0	5	5	17	.177	.226	.278	51	-5	1	0	0	.979	0	O-25	-0.6
	Yr	85	296	33	60	14	3	1	17	18	65	.203	.258	.280	63	-14	1	4	-2	.973	6	O-77	-1.5
1969	Pit-N	62	64	10	15	1	1	0	4	7	14	.234	.310	.281	68	-3	0	0	0	.933	-13	O-51	-1.8
Total	5	295	853	96	199	44	6	10	79	56	160	.233	.288	.334	82	-21	9	9	-3	.974	-2	O-261	-4.0

■ RUSS DAVIS
Davis, Russell Stuart b: 9/13/69, Birmingham, Ala. BR/TR, 6', 170 lbs. Deb: 7/6/94

| 1994 | NY-A | 4 | 14 | 0 | 2 | 0 | 0 | 0 | 1 | 0 | 4 | .143 | .143 | .143 | -28 | -3 | 0 | 0 | 0 | 1.000 | 0 | /3-4 | -0.3 |

■ STEVE DAVIS
Davis, Steven Michael b: 12/30/53, Oakland, Cal. BR/TR, 6'1", 200 lbs. Deb: 9/23/79

| 1979 | Chi-N | 3 | 4 | 0 | 0 | 0 | 0 | 0 | 0 | 0 | 0 | .000 | .000 | .000 | -91 | 0 | 0 | 0 | 0 | 1.000 | 0 | /2-2,3-1 | -0.1 |

■ TOD DAVIS
Davis, Thomas Oscar b: 7/24/24, Los Angeles, Cal. d: 12/31/78, W.Covina, Cal. BR/TR, 6'2", 190 lbs. Deb: 4/27/49

1949	Phi-A	31	75	7	20	0	1	1	6	9	16	.267	.345	.333	83	-2	0	0	0	.912	-1	S-14,3-12/2	-0.2
1951	Phi-A	11	15	0	1	0	0	0	0	1	3	.067	.125	.067	-46	-3	0	0	0	1.000	-0	2-2,3-1	-0.3
Total	2	42	90	7	21	0	1	1	6	10	19	.233	.310	.289	61	-5	0	0	0	.966	-1	/S-14,3-13,2	-0.5

■ TRENCH DAVIS
Davis, Trench Neal b: 9/12/60, Baltimore, Md. BL/TL, 6'3", 171 lbs. Deb: 6/4/85

| 1985 | Pit-N | 2 | 7 | 1 | 1 | 0 | 0 | 0 | 0 | 0 | 0 | .143 | .143 | .143 | -20 | -1 | 1 | 0 | 0 | .667 | -1 | /O-2 | -0.2 |

YEAR	TM/L	G	AB	R	H	2B	3B	HR	RBI	BB	SO	AVG	OBP	SLG	PRO+	BR/A	SB	CS	SBR	FA	FR	G/POS	TPR
1986	Pit-N	15	23	2	3	0	0	0	1	0	4	.130	.130	.130	-27	-4	0	0	0	.917	-0	/O-7	-0.5
1987	Atl-N	6	3	0	0	0	0	0	0	0	0	.000	.000	.000	-95	-1	0	0	0	.000	0	/H	-0.1
Total	3	23	33	3	4	0	0	0	1	0	5	.121	.121	.121	-32	-6	1	0	0	.867	-1	/O-9	-0.8

■ SPUD DAVIS
Davis, Virgil Lawrence b: 12/20/04, Birmingham, Ala. d: 8/14/84, Birmingham, Ala. BR/TR, 6'1", 197 lbs. Deb: 4/30/28 MC

YEAR	TM/L	G	AB	R	H	2B	3B	HR	RBI	BB	SO	AVG	OBP	SLG	PRO+	BR/A	SB	CS	SBR	FA	FR	G/POS	TPR
1928	StL-N	2	5	1	1	0	0	0	1	1	0	.200	.333	.200	42	-0	0			.750	-1	/C-2	-0.1
	Phi-N	67	163	16	46	2	0	3	18	15	11	.282	.343	.350	79	-5	0			.980	3	C-49	0.2
	Yr	69	168	17	47	2	0	3	19	16	11	.280	.342	.345	78	-5	0			.971	2	C-51	0.1
1929	Phi-N	98	263	31	90	18	0	7	48	19	17	.342	.391	.490	110	4	1			.961	-12	C-89	-0.1
1930	Phi-N	106	329	41	103	16	1	14	65	19	20	.313	.349	.495	94	-4	1			.986	-2	C-96	0.1
1931	Phi-N	120	393	30	128	32	1	4	51	36	28	.326	.382	.443	112	7	0			.994	1	*C-114	1.6
1932	Phi-N	125	402	44	135	23	5	14	70	40	39	.336	.390	.522	130	17	1			.987	-3	*C-120	2.0
1933	Phi-N	141	495	51	173	28	3	9	65	32	24	.349	.395	.473	130	19	2			.983	-11	*C-132	1.7
1934	*StL-N	107	347	45	104	22	4	9	65	34	27	.300	.366	.464	113	6	1			.988	1	C-94	1.2
1935	StL-N	102	315	28	100	24	2	1	60	33	30	.317	.386	.416	111	6	0			**.992**	-5	C-81/1-5	0.4
1936	StL-N	112	363	24	99	26	2	4	59	35	34	.273	.342	.388	97	-2	0			.985	-13	*C-103/3-2	-1.0
1937	Cin-N	76	209	19	56	10	1	3	33	23	15	.268	.341	.368	97	-1	0			.980	12	C-59	1.4
1938	Cin-N	12	36	3	6	1	0	0	1	5	6	.167	.286	.194	35	-3	0			.962	0	C-11	-0.2
	Phi-N	70	215	11	53	7	0	2	23	14	14	.247	.293	.307	67	-10	1			.980	-12	C-63	-1.9
	Yr	82	251	14	59	8	0	2	24	19	20	.235	.292	.291	62	-13	1			.977	-12	C-74	-2.1
1939	Phi-N	87	202	10	62	8	1	0	23	24	20	.307	.383	.356	103	2	0			**1.000**	-2	C-85	0.3
1940	Pit-N	99	285	23	93	14	1	5	39	35	20	.326	.404	.435	132	14	0			.967	-6	C-87	1.4
1941	Pit-N	57	107	3	27	4	1	0	6	11	11	.252	.322	.308	78	-3	0			1.000	-2	C-49	-0.2
1944	Pit-N	54	93	6	28	7	0	2	14	10	8	.301	.369	.441	122	3	0			.966	-1	C-35	0.3
1945	Pit-N	23	33	2	8	2	0	0	6	2	2	.242	.306	.303	67	-1	0			.968	-0	C-13	-0.1
Total	16	1458	4255	388	1312	244	22	77	647	386	326	.308	.369	.430	108	49	6			.984	-55	*C-1282/1-5,3	7.0

■ BUTCH DAVIS
Davis, Wallace McArthur b: 6/19/58, Martin Co., N.C. BR/TR, 6', 190 lbs. Deb: 8/23/83

YEAR	TM/L	G	AB	R	H	2B	3B	HR	RBI	BB	SO	AVG	OBP	SLG	PRO+	BR/A	SB	CS	SBR	FA	FR	G/POS	TPR
1983	KC-A	33	122	13	42	2	6	2	18	4	19	.344	.365	.508	137	6	4	3	-1	.977	2	O-33	0.6
1984	KC-A	41	116	11	17	3	0	2	12	10	19	.147	.214	.224	21	-12	4	3	-1	.959	-1	O-35/D-2	-1.5
1987	Pit-N	7	7	3	1	1	0	0	0	1	3	.143	.250	.286	41	-1	0	0	0	1.000	0	/O-1	0.0
1988	Bal-A	13	25	2	6	1	0	0	0	0	8	.240	.240	.280	46	-2	1	0	0	1.000	-0	O-10/D-1	-0.2
1989	Bal-A	5	6	1	1	1	0	0	0	0	1	.167	.167	.333	39	-1	0	0	0	1.000	-1	/O-3,D-1	-0.1
1991	LA-N	1	1	0	0	0	0	0	0	0	0	.000	.000	.000	-99	-0	0	0	0	.000	-0	/H	0.0
1993	Tex-A	62	159	24	39	10	4	3	20	5	28	.245	.273	.415	85	-4	3	1	0	.960	-2	O-44,D-11	-0.6
1994	Tex-A	4	17	2	4	3	0	0	0	0	3	.235	.235	.412	67	-1	1	0	0	1.000	1	/O-4	0.0
Total	8	166	453	56	110	21	10	7	50	20	83	.243	.276	.380	78	-15	13	7	-0	.969	-1	O-130/D-15	-1.8

■ WILLIE DAVIS
Davis, William Henry b: 4/15/40, Mineral Springs, Ark. BL/TL, 6'2.5", 181 lbs. Deb: 9/8/60

YEAR	TM/L	G	AB	R	H	2B	3B	HR	RBI	BB	SO	AVG	OBP	SLG	PRO+	BR/A	SB	CS	SBR	FA	FR	G/POS	TPR
1960	LA-N	22	88	12	28	6	1	2	10	4	12	.318	.348	.477	116	2	3	5	-2	.981	1	O-22	-0.1
1961	LA-N	128	339	56	86	19	6	12	45	27	46	.254	.318	.451	93	-4	12	5	1	.983	-3	*O-114	-1.1
1962	LA-N	157	600	103	171	18	**10**	21	85	42	72	.285	.338	.453	117	13	32	7	5	.963	13	*O-156	2.1
1963	*LA-N	156	515	60	126	19	8	9	60	25	61	.245	.284	.365	92	-8	25	11	1	.978	14	*O-153	0.0
1964	LA-N	157	613	91	180	23	7	12	77	22	59	.294	.319	.413	112	7	42	13	5	.983	25	*O-155	3.1
1965	*LA-N	142	558	52	133	24	3	10	57	14	81	.238	.266	.346	76	-20	25	9	2	.967	9	*O-141	-1.6
1966	*LA-N	153	624	74	177	31	6	11	61	15	68	.284	.305	.405	104	-0	21	10	0	.970	9	*O-152	0.3
1967	LA-N	143	569	65	146	27	9	6	41	29	65	.257	.296	.367	97	-5	20	6	2	.971	-4	*O-138	-0.7
1968	LA-N	160	643	86	161	24	10	7	31	31	88	.250	.286	.351	98	-5	36	10	5	.973	5	*O-158	-0.4
1969	LA-N	129	498	66	155	23	8	11	59	33	39	.311	.359	.456	136	22	24	10	1	.979	5	*O-125	2.2
1970	LA-N	146	593	92	181	23	**16**	8	93	29	54	.305	.339	.438	111	7	38	14	3	.992	15	*O-143	1.7
1971	LA-N★	158	641	84	198	33	10	10	74	23	47	.309	.333	.438	124	17	20	8	1	.981	12	*O-157	2.3
1972	LA-N	149	615	81	178	27	7	19	79	27	61	.289	.320	.441	117	11	20	3	4	.987	11	*O-146	2.0
1973	LA-N★	152	599	82	171	29	9	16	77	29	62	.285	.324	.444	116	10	17	5	2	.980	4	*O-146	0.9
1974	Mon-N	153	611	86	180	27	9	12	89	27	69	.295	.328	.427	104	2	25	7	3	.969	6	*O-151	0.4
1975	Tex-A	42	169	16	42	8	2	5	17	4	25	.249	.270	.408	90	-3	13	5	1	.990	-1	O-42	-0.5
	StL-N	98	350	41	102	19	6	6	50	14	27	.291	.326	.431	105	1	10	1	2	.970	-4	O-89	0.3
1976	SD-N	141	493	61	132	18	10	5	46	19	34	.268	.298	.375	98	-4	14	2	3	.992	8	*O-128	0.2
1979	*Cal-A	43	56	9	14	2	1	0	2	4	7	.250	.300	.321	70	-2	1	0	0	1.000	-1	/O-7,D-6	-0.3
Total	18	2429	9174	1217	2561	395	138	182	1053	418	977	.279	.314	.412	106	40	398	131	41	.978	137	*O-2323/D-6	10.8

■ ANDRE DAWSON
Dawson, Andre Fernando b: 7/10/54, Miami, Fla. BR/TR, 6'3", 195 lbs. Deb: 9/11/76

YEAR	TM/L	G	AB	R	H	2B	3B	HR	RBI	BB	SO	AVG	OBP	SLG	PRO+	BR/A	SB	CS	SBR	FA	FR	G/POS	TPR
1976	Mon-N	24	85	9	20	4	1	0	7	5	13	.235	.278	.306	63	-4	1	2	-1	.969	2	O-24	-0.4
1977	Mon-N	139	525	64	148	26	9	19	65	34	93	.282	.328	.474	116	9	21	7	2	.989	7	*O-136	1.3
1978	Mon-N	157	609	84	154	24	8	25	72	30	128	.253	.301	.442	106	2	28	11	2	.988	21	*O-153	1.9
1979	Mon-N	155	639	90	176	24	12	25	92	27	115	.275	.311	.468	111	6	35	10	5	.988	6	*O-153	1.0
1980	Mon-N	151	577	96	178	41	7	17	87	44	69	.308	.364	.492	137	27	34	9	5	.986	20	*O-147	4.8
1981	*Mon-N★	103	394	71	119	21	3	24	64	35	50	.302	.369	.553	157	28	26	4	5	.980	18	*O-103	5.0
1982	Mon-N★	148	608	107	183	37	7	23	83	34	96	.301	.346	.498	131	23	39	10	6	.982	21	*O-147	4.7
1983	Mon-N★	159	633	104	**189**	36	10	32	113	38	81	.299	.347	.539	143	33	25	11	1	.980	-1	*O-157	4.5
1984	Mon-N	138	533	73	132	23	6	17	86	41	80	.248	.304	.409	103	0	13	5	1	.975	16	*O-134	1.3
1985	Mon-N	139	529	65	135	27	2	23	91	29	92	.255	.299	.444	112	5	13	4	2	.973	-4	*O-131	-0.2
1986	Mon-N	130	496	65	141	32	2	20	78	37	79	.284	.341	.478	125	15	18	12	-2	.986	-0	*O-127	0.9
1987	Chi-N★	153	621	90	178	24	2	**49**	**137**	32	103	.287	.329	.568	127	21	11	3	2	.986	6	*O-152	2.3
1988	Chi-N★	157	591	78	179	31	8	24	79	37	73	.303	.348	.504	136	25	12	4	1	.989	1	*O-147	2.5
1989	*Chi-N★	118	416	62	105	18	6	21	77	35	62	.252	.312	.476	114	6	8	5	-1	.987	5	*O-112	0.8
1990	Chi-N★	147	529	72	164	28	5	27	100	42	65	.310	.363	.535	134	23	16	2	4	.981	-0	*O-139	2.4
1991	Chi-N★	149	563	69	153	21	4	31	104	22	80	.272	.302	.488	114	8	4	5	-2	.988	-1	*O-137	0.1
1992	Chi-N	143	542	60	150	27	2	22	90	30	70	.277	.319	.456	114	8	6	2	1	.992	-1	*O-139	0.5
1993	Bos-A	121	461	44	126	29	1	13	67	17	49	.273	.318	.425	92	-6	2	1	0	1.000	0	D-97,O-20	-1.0
1994	Bos-A	75	292	34	70	18	0	16	48	9	53	.240	.272	.466	80	-10	2	2	-1	.000	0	D-74	-1.3
Total	19	2506	9643	1337	2700	491	95	428	1540	578	1451	.280	.327	.484	120	219	314	109	29	.984	130	*O-2258,D-171	31.1

■ BOOTS DAY
Day, Charles Frederick b: 8/31/47, Ilion, N.Y. BL/TL, 5'9", 160 lbs. Deb: 6/15/69

YEAR	TM/L	G	AB	R	H	2B	3B	HR	RBI	BB	SO	AVG	OBP	SLG	PRO+	BR/A	SB	CS	SBR	FA	FR	G/POS	TPR
1969	StL-N	11	6	1	0	0	0	0	0	1	1	.000	.143	.000	-57	-1	0	0	0	.000	-0	/O-1	-0.2
1970	Chi-N	11	8	2	2	0	0	0	0	0	1	.250	.250	.250	31	-1	0	0	0	.875	-1	/O-7	-0.2
	Mon-N	41	108	14	29	4	0	0	5	6	18	.269	.307	.306	65	-5	3	2	-0	.987	1	O-35	-0.6
	Yr	52	116	16	31	4	0	0	5	6	21	.267	.303	.302	61	-6	3	2	-0	.976	-0	O-42	-0.8
1971	Mon-N	127	371	53	105	10	2	4	33	33	39	.283	.343	.353	97	-1	9	4	0	.982	4	*O-120	-0.2
1972	Mon-N	128	386	32	90	7	4	0	30	29	44	.233	.288	.272	59	-20	3	6	-3	.979	-5	*O-117	-3.5
1973	Mon-N	101	207	36	57	7	0	4	28	21	28	.275	.342	.367	93	-2	0	3	-2	1.000	-9	O-51	-1.5
1974	Mon-N	52	65	8	12	0	0	0	2	5	8	.185	.243	.185	20	-7	0	0	0	1.000	-0	O-16	-1.0
Total	6	471	1151	146	295	28	6	8	98	95	141	.256	.314	.312	75	-37	15	15	-5	.983	-13	O-347	-7.2

■ BRIAN DAYETT
Dayett, Brian Kelly b: 1/22/57, New London, Conn. BR/TR, 5'10", 180 lbs. Deb: 9/11/83

YEAR	TM/L	G	AB	R	H	2B	3B	HR	RBI	BB	SO	AVG	OBP	SLG	PRO+	BR/A	SB	CS	SBR	FA	FR	G/POS	TPR
1983	NY-A	11	29	3	6	0	1	0	5	2	4	.207	.258	.276	49	-2	0	0	0	1.000	1	/O-9	-0.1
1984	NY-A	64	127	14	31	8	0	4	23	9	14	.244	.299	.402	96	-1	0	0	0	.988	-9	O-62/D-1	-1.1
1985	Chi-N	22	26	1	6	0	0	1	4	0	6	.231	.259	.346	61	-1	0	0	0	1.000	-2	O-10	-0.4
1986	Chi-N	24	67	7	18	4	0	4	11	6	10	.269	.329	.507	118	1	0	1	-1	1.000	-4	O-24	-0.3
1987	Chi-N	97	177	20	49	14	1	5	25	20	37	.277	.350	.452	106	2	0	0	0	1.000	-13	O-78	-1.3
Total	5	218	426	45	110	26	2	14	68	37	71	.258	.320	.427	99	-2	0	1	-1	.995	-26	O-183/D-1	-3.2

■ CHARLIE DEAL
Deal, Charles Albert b: 10/30/1891, Wilkinsburg, Pa. d: 9/16/79, Covina, Cal. BR/TR, 6', 160 lbs. Deb: 7/19/12

YEAR	TM/L	G	AB	R	H	2B	3B	HR	RBI	BB	SO	AVG	OBP	SLG	PRO+	BR/A	SB	CS	SBR	FA	FR	G/POS	TPR
1912	Det-A	42	142	13	32	4	2	0	11	9		.225	.272	.282	60	-8	4			.942	10	3-41	0.3
1913	Det-A	16	50	3	11	0	2	0	3	1	7	.220	.235	.300	57	-3	2			.862	2	3-15	-0.1
	Bos-N	10	36	6	11	1	0	0	3	2	1	.306	.359	.333	96	-0	1			.935	-6	2-10	-0.7
1914	*Bos-N	79	257	17	54	13	2	0	23	20	23	.210	.270	.276	63	-12	4			.948	-5	3-74/S-1	-1.6
1915	StL-F	65	223	21	72	12	4	1	27	12	16	.323	.357	.426	104	1	10			.951	5	3-65	0.9
1916	StL-A	23	74	7	10	1	0	0	10	6	8	.135	.200	.149	5	-9	4			.970	-2	3-22/2-1	-1.1
	Chi-N	2	8	2	2	1	0	0	3	0	0	.250	.250	.375	82	-0	0			1.000	2	/3-2	0.2
1917	Chi-N	135	449	46	114	11	3	0	47	19	18	.254	.284	.292	71	-16	10			.957	0	*3-130	-0.7
1918	*Chi-N	119	414	43	99	9	3	2	34	21	13	.239	.279	.290	72	-14	11			.942	-2	*3-118	-1.6
1919	Chi-N	116	405	37	117	23	5	2	52	12	12	.289	.316	.385	110	3	11			.973	7	*3-116	1.7
1920	Chi-N	129	450	48	108	10	5	3	39	20	14	.240	.285	.304	68	-19	5	8	-3	.973	10	*3-128	-0.7
1921	Chi-N	115	422	52	122	19	8	3	66	13	9	.289	.310	.393	85	-10	3	5	-2	.973	14	*3-112	0.9
Total	10	851	2930	295	752	104	34	11	318	135	121	.257	.293	.327	78	-86	65	13		.958	41	3-823/2-11,S	-2.5

■ LINDSAY DEAL
Deal, Fred Lindsay b: 9/3/11, Lenoir, N.C. d: 4/18/79, Little Rock, Ark. BL/TR, 6', 175 lbs. Deb: 9/13/39

YEAR	TM/L	G	AB	R	H	2B	3B	HR	RBI	BB	SO	AVG	OBP	SLG	PRO+	BR/A	SB	CS	SBR	FA	FR	G/POS	TPR
1939	Bro-N	4	7	0	0	0	0	0	0	0	2	.000	.000	.000	-97	-2	0			1.000	0	/O-1	-0.2

■ SNAKE DEAL
Deal, John Wesley b: 1/21/1879, Lancaster, Pa. d: 5/9/44, Harrisburg, Pa. BR/TR, 6', 164 lbs. Deb: 7/9/06

YEAR	TM/L	G	AB	R	H	2B	3B	HR	RBI	BB	SO	AVG	OBP	SLG	PRO+	BR/A	SB	CS	SBR	FA	FR	G/POS	TPR
1906	Cin-N	65	231	13	48	4	3	0	21	6		.208	.228	.251	47	-15	15			.985	2	1-65	-1.6

■ PAT DEALY
Dealy, Patrick E. b: Burlington, Vt. d: 12/16/24, Buffalo, N.Y. BR/TR, 5'8", 145 lbs. Deb: 9/30/1884

YEAR	TM/L	G	AB	R	H	2B	3B	HR	RBI	BB	SO	AVG	OBP	SLG	PRO+	BR/A	SB	CS	SBR	FA	FR	G/POS	TPR
1884	StP-U	5	15	2	2	0	0	0			0	.133	.133	.133	-50	-4				.871	3	/C-4,O-1	-0.1
1885	Bos-N	35	130	18	29	4	1	1	9	2	14	.223	.235	.292	72	-4				.903	0	C-29/3-3,OS1	-0.1
1886	Bos-N	15	46	9	15	1	1	0	3	4	4	.326	.380	.391	140	2	5			.929	-2	C-14/O-1	0.2
1887	Was-N	58	212	33	55	8	2	1	18	8	8	.259	.293	.330	77	-7	36			.931	-7	C-28,S-23/O3	-0.9
1890	Syr-a	18	66	9	12	1	0	0			5	.182	.250	.197	36	-5	4			.900	-6	C-10/3-6,O	-0.9
Total	5	131	469	71	113	14	4	2	30	19	26	.241	.275	.301	74	-17	45			.914	-12	/C-85,S-25,3O1	-1.8

■ CHUBBY DEAN
Dean, Alfred Lovill b: 8/24/16, Mt.Airy, N.C. d: 12/21/70, Riverside, Cal. BL/TL, 5'11", 181 lbs. Deb: 4/14/36

YEAR	TM/L	G	AB	R	H	2B	3B	HR	RBI	BB	SO	AVG	OBP	SLG	PRO+	BR/A	SB	CS	SBR	FA	FR	G/POS	TPR
1936	Phi-A	111	342	41	98	21	3	1	48	24	24	.287	.337	.374	77	-13	3	2	-0	.989	-1	1-77	-1.9
1937	Phi-A	104	309	36	81	14	4	2	31	42	10	.262	.350	.353	79	-9	2	1	0	.991	-2	1-78/P-2	-1.9
1938	Phi-A	16	20	3	6	2	0	0	1	1	4	.300	.333	.400	85	-1	0	0	0	1.000	1	/P-6	0.0
1939	Phi-A	80	77	12	27	4	0	0	19	8	4	.351	.412	.403	111	2	0	0	0	.935	1	P-54	0.0
1940	Phi-A	67	90	4	26	2	0	0	6	16	9	.289	.396	.311	88	-1	0	0	0	.976	1	P-30/1-1	0.0
1941	Phi-A	27	37	0	9	0	0	0	9	4	3	.243	.317	.297	65	-2	0	0	0	1.000	0	P-18/1-1	0.0
	Cle-A	17	25	2	4	1	0	0	2	3	2	.160	.250	.200	21	-3	0	0	0	1.000	1	/P-8	0.0
	Yr	44	62	2	13	1	0	0	11	7	5	.210	.290	.258	48	-5	0	0	0	1.000	1	P-26/1-1	0.0
1942	Cle-A	70	101	4	27	1	0	0	7	11	7	.267	.339	.277	79	-2	0	0	0	.939	-3	P-27	0.0
1943	Cle-A	41	56	2	9	0	0	0	5	6	2	.196	.288	.196	45	-3	0	0	0	.929	-1	P-17	0.0
Total	8	533	1047	106	287	47	7	3	128	115	65	.274	.347	.341	79	-32	5	3	-0	.964	-5	P-162,1-157	-3.8

■ TOMMY DEAN
Dean, Tommy Douglas b: 8/30/45, Iuka, Miss. BR/TR, 6', 165 lbs. Deb: 9/17/67

YEAR	TM/L	G	AB	R	H	2B	3B	HR	RBI	BB	SO	AVG	OBP	SLG	PRO+	BR/A	SB	CS	SBR	FA	FR	G/POS	TPR
1967	LA-N	12	28	1	4	1	0	0	2	0	9	.143	.143	.179	-9	-4	0	0	0	.981	6	S-12	0.3
1969	SD-N	101	273	14	48	9	2	2	9	27	54	.176	.252	.245	42	-21	0	3	-2	.978	4	S-97/2-2	-1.1
1970	SD-N	61	158	18	35	5	1	2	13	11	29	.222	.272	.304	56	-10	2	0	1	.974	6	S-55	0.2
1971	SD-N	41	70	2	8	0	0	0	1	4	13	.114	.162	.114	-22	-11	1	0	0	.969	6	S-28,3-11/2	-0.3
Total	4	215	529	35	95	15	3	4	25	42	105	.180	.241	.242	36	-47	3	3	-1	.976	23	S-192/3-11,2	-0.9

■ HARRY DEANE
Deane, John Henry b: 5/6/1846, Trenton, N.J. d: 5/31/25, Indianapolis, Ind. 5'7", 150 lbs. Deb: 7/20/1871 M

YEAR	TM/L	G	AB	R	H	2B	3B	HR	RBI	BB	SO	AVG	OBP	SLG	PRO+	BR/A	SB	CS	SBR	FA	FR	G/POS	TPR
1871	Kek-n	6	22	3	4	0	1	0	2			.182	.250	.273	49	-1	0					/O-5,M	-0.1
1874	Bal-n	47	204	29	50	9	2	0			4	.245	.260	.309	81	-4						*O-45/2-2	-0.2
Total	2 n	53	226	32	54	9	3	0			6	.239	.259	.305	77	-6						/O-50,2-2	-0.3

■ BUDDY DEAR
Dear, Paul Stanford b: 12/1/05, Norfolk, Va. d: 8/29/89, Christiansburg, Va. BR/TR, 5'8", 143 lbs. Deb: 9/9/27

YEAR	TM/L	G	AB	R	H	2B	3B	HR	RBI	BB	SO	AVG	OBP	SLG	PRO+	BR/A	SB	CS	SBR	FA	FR	G/POS	TPR
1927	Was-A	2	1	1	0	0	0	0	0	0	0	.000	.000	.000	-99	-0				.000	0	/2-1	0.0

■ CHARLIE DeARMOND
DeArmond, Charles Hommer "Hummer" b: 2/13/1877, Okeana, Ohio d: 12/17/33, Morning Sun, Ohio BR/TR, 5'10", 165 lbs. Deb: 9/19/03

YEAR	TM/L	G	AB	R	H	2B	3B	HR	RBI	BB	SO	AVG	OBP	SLG	PRO+	BR/A	SB	CS	SBR	FA	FR	G/POS	TPR
1903	Cin-N	11	39	10	11	2	1	0	7	3		.282	.349	.385	98	-0	1			.878	-1	3-11	-0.1

■ JOHN DEASLEY
Deasley, John b: 1/1861, Philadelphia, Pa. d: 12/25/10, Philadelphia, Pa. Deb: 6/17/1884 F

YEAR	TM/L	G	AB	R	H	2B	3B	HR	RBI	BB	SO	AVG	OBP	SLG	PRO+	BR/A	SB	CS	SBR	FA	FR	G/POS	TPR
1884	Was-U	31	134	20	29	1	1	0			3	.216	.234	.239	30	-13				.836	0	S-31	-1.1
	KC-U	13	40	3	7	2	0	0			2	.175	.214	.225	22	-4				.833	-0	S-13	-0.4
	Yr	44	174	23	36	3	1	0			5	.207	.229	.236	28	-17				.835	0	S-44	-1.5

■ PAT DEASLEY
Deasley, Thomas H. b: 11/17/1857, Ireland d: 4/1/43, Philadelphia, Pa. BR/TR, 5'8.5", 154 lbs. Deb: 5/18/1881 F

YEAR	TM/L	G	AB	R	H	2B	3B	HR	RBI	BB	SO	AVG	OBP	SLG	PRO+	BR/A	SB	CS	SBR	FA	FR	G/POS	TPR
1881	Bos-N	43	147	13	35	5	2	0	8	5	10	.238	.263	.299	80	-3				.914	-4	C-28/O-7,S1	-0.6
1882	Bos-N	67	264	36	70	8	0	0	29	7	22	.265	.284	.295	86	-4				.958	2	*C-56,O-14/S	-0.1
1883	StL-a	58	206	27	53	2	1	0			6	.257	.278	.277	75	-6				.930	8	C-56/O-2	0.4
1884	StL-a	75	254	27	52	5	4	0			7	.205	.235	.256	58	-12				.919	14	*C-75/O-2,1	0.7
1885	NY-N	54	207	22	53	5	1	0	24	9	20	.256	.287	.290	88	-3				.935	8	C-54/O-2,S	0.9
1886	NY-N	41	143	18	38	6	1	0	17	4	12	.266	.286	.322	84	-3				.925	7	C-30/O-15	0.5
1887	NY-N	30	118	12	37	5	0	0	23	9	7	.314	.367	.356	107	2				.867	-13	C-24/3-7,S	-0.8
1888	Was-N	34	127	6	20	1	0	0	4	2	18	.157	.171	.165	8	-13	2			.922	8	C-31/O-1,S2	-0.2
Total	8	402	1466	161	358	37	9	0	105	49	89	.244	.271	.282	75	-42	7			.927	28	C-354/O-43,S312	0.8

■ HANK DeBERRY
DeBerry, John Herman b: 12/29/1894, Savannah, Tenn. d: 9/10/51, Savannah, Tenn. BR/TR, 5'11", 195 lbs. Deb: 9/12/16

YEAR	TM/L	G	AB	R	H	2B	3B	HR	RBI	BB	SO	AVG	OBP	SLG	PRO+	BR/A	SB	CS	SBR	FA	FR	G/POS	TPR
1916	Cle-A	15	33	7	9	4	0	0	4	6	9	.273	.385	.394	126	1	0			1.000	-3	C-14	-0.1
1917	Cle-A	25	33	3	9	2	0	0	1	2	7	.273	.333	.333	96	-0	0			.968	1	/C-9	0.1
1922	Bro-N	85	259	29	78	10	1	3	35	20	9	.301	.354	.382	91	-3	4	1	1	.971	8	C-81	-0.1
1923	Bro-N	78	235	21	67	11	6	1	48	20	12	.285	.346	.396	98	-1	2	1	0	.971	8	C-60	1.0
1924	Bro-N	77	218	20	53	10	3	2	26	20	21	.243	.307	.358	80	-6	0	1	-1	.993	23	C-63	1.9
1925	Bro-N	67	193	26	50	8	1	2	24	16	8	.259	.322	.342	72	-8	2	2	-1	.981	19	C-55	1.3
1926	Bro-N	48	115	6	33	11	0	0	15	8	5	.287	.338	.383	94	-1	0			.976	8	C-37	0.9
1927	Bro-N	68	201	15	47	3	2	1	21	17	8	.234	.294	.284	55	-13	0			.988	23	C-67	1.5
1928	Bro-N	82	258	19	65	8	2	0	23	18	15	.252	.301	.298	58	-16	3			.977	18	C-80	0.9
1929	Bro-N	68	210	13	55	11	1	0	25	17	15	.262	.317	.338	64	-8	1			.991	6	C-68	0.0

YEAR	TM/L	G	AB	R	H	2B	3B	HR	RBI	BB	SO	AVG	OBP	SLG	PRO+	BR/A	SB	CS	SBR	FA	FR	G/POS	TPR
1930	Bro-N	35	95	11	28	3	0	0	14	4	10	.295	.323	.326	58	-6	0			.978	12	C-35	0.7
Total	11	648	1850	170	494	81	16	11	234	148	119	.267	.323	.346	76	-65	13	5		.982	113	C-569	8.1

■ ADAM DEBUS   Debus, Adam Joseph   b: 10/7/1892, Chicago, Ill.   d: 5/13/77, Chicago, Ill.   BR/TR, 5'10.5", 150 lbs.   Deb: 7/14/17

| 1917 | Pit-N | 38 | 131 | 9 | 30 | 5 | 4 | 0 | 7 | 7 | 14 | .229 | .279 | .328 | 83 | -3 | 2 | | | .898 | -6 | S-21,3-18 | -0.9 |

■ DOUG DeCINCES   DeCinces, Douglas Vernon   b: 8/29/50, Burbank, Cal.   BR/TR, 6'2", 194 lbs.   Deb: 9/9/73

1973	Bal-A	10	18	2	2	0	0	0	3	1	5	.111	.158	.111	-23	-3	0	0	0	.895	3	/3-8,2-2,S	0.0
1974	Bal-A	1	1	0	0	0	0	0	0	1	0	.000	.500	.000	55	0	0	0	0	1.000	0	/3-1	0.0
1975	Bal-A	61	167	20	42	6	3	4	23	13	32	.251	.309	.395	105	0	0	1	-1	.947	3	3-34,S-13,2/1	0.4
1976	Bal-A	129	440	36	103	17	2	11	42	29	68	.234	.285	.357	93	-6	8	4	0	.941	-1	*3-109,2-17,1/SD	-0.8
1977	Bal-A	150	522	63	135	28	3	19	69	64	86	.259	.342	.433	117	12	8	8	-2	.958	10	*3-148/1-1,2D	1.8
1978	Bal-A	142	511	72	146	37	1	28	80	46	81	.286	.347	.526	152	32	7	7	-2	.975	10	*3-130,2-12	4.0
1979	*Bal-A	120	422	67	97	27	1	16	61	54	68	.230	.322	.412	100	-0	5	3	-0	.964	-3	*3-120	-0.4
1980	Bal-A	145	489	64	122	23	2	16	64	49	83	.249	.322	.403	98	-2	11	6	-0	.960	25	*3-142/1-1	2.0
1981	Bal-A	100	346	49	91	23	2	13	55	41	32	.263	.343	.454	128	12	0	3	-2	.942	9	*3-100/1-1,O	0.7
1982	*Cal-A	153	575	94	173	42	5	30	97	66	80	.301	.374	.548	149	38	7	5	-1	.961	21	*3-153/S-2	5.3
1983	Cal-A★	95	370	49	104	19	3	18	65	32	56	.281	.338	.495	127	13	2	0	1	.955	9	3-84,D-10	2.0
1984	Cal-A	146	547	77	147	23	3	20	82	53	79	.269	.333	.431	111	7	4	1	1	.964	-6	*3-140/D-5	-0.3
1985	Cal-A	120	427	50	104	22	1	20	78	47	71	.244	.321	.440	107	3	1	4	-2	.958	-10	*3-111/D-3	-1.0
1986	*Cal-A	140	512	69	131	20	3	26	96	52	74	.256	.327	.459	112	8	2	2	-1	.965	-8	*3-132/S-1,D	-0.3
1987	Cal-A	133	453	65	106	23	0	16	63	70	87	.234	.339	.391	96	-2	3	4	-2	.948	-3	*3-128/1-4,SD	-0.7
	StL-N	4	9	1	2	2	0	0	1	0	2	.222	.222	.444	70	-0	0	0	0	.833	1	/3-3	0.1
Total	15	1649	5809	778	1505	312	29	237	879	618	904	.259	.333	.445	116	113	58	48	-11	.958	49	*3-1543/2-43,D1SO	13.1

■ HARRY DECKER   Decker, Earle Harry   b: 9/3/1854, Lockport, Ill.   BR/TR, 5'11", 180 lbs.   Deb: 8/23/1884

1884	Ind-a	4	15	1	4	1	0	0			1	.267	.313	.333	114	0				.870	-3	/C-4	-0.3
	KC-U	23	75	8	10	2	0	0			5	.133	.188	.160	-5	-11				.813	2	O-16,C-11	-0.8
1886	Det-N	14	54	2	12	1	0	0	5	2	9	.222	.250	.241	48	-3	0			.871	4	C-14/O-1	0.2
	Was-N	7	23	0	5	1	1	0	2	1	5	.217	.250	.348	85	-0				.946	1	/C-4,3-2,S	0.1
	Yr	21	77	2	17	2	1	0	7	3	14	.221	.250	.273	59	-4	0			.886	5	C-18/3-2,OS	0.3
1889	Phi-N	11	30	4	3	0	0	0	2	2	5	.100	.156	.100	-25	-5	1			.857	-1	/2-7,C-3,O	-0.5
1890	Phi-N	5	19	5	7	1	0	0	2	4	1	.368	.478	.421	159	2	4			.938	-1	/1-2,O-2,C	0.0
	Pit-N	92	354	52	97	14	3	5	38	26	36	.274	.324	.373	116	6	8			.909	-26	C-70,1-16/O2S	-1.3
	Yr	97	373	57	104	15	3	5	40	30	37	.279	.333	.375	119	8	12			.909	-27	C-71,1-18/O2S	-1.3
Total	4	156	570	72	138	20	4	5	49	41	56	.242	.293	.318	84	-11	13			.903	-25	C-107/O-24,12S3	-2.6

■ FRANK DECKER   Decker, Frank   b: 2/26/1856, St.Louis, Mo.   d: 2/5/40, St.Louis, Mo.   BR/TR,   Deb: 6/25/1879

1879	Syr-N	3	10	0	1	0	0	0			3	.100	.100	.100	-38	-1				.714	-2	/C-2,O-1,1	-0.3
1882	StL-a	2	8	0	2	0	0	0			0	.250	.250	.250	66	-0				.813	-0	/2-2	0.0
Total	2	5	18	0	3	0	0	0	0	0	3	.167	.167	.167	12	-2				.813	-2	/2-2,C-2,1O	-0.3

■ GEORGE DECKER   Decker, George A "Gentleman George"   b: 6/1/1869, York, Pa.   d: 6/7/09, Patton, Cal.   BL/TL, 6'1", 180 lbs.   Deb: 7/11/1892

1892	Chi-N	78	291	32	66	6	7	1	28	20	49	.227	.277	.306	75	-10	9			.876	-12	O-62,2-16	-2.2
1893	Chi-N	81	328	57	89	9	8	2	48	24	22	.271	.325	.366	85	-8	22			.878	-9	O-33,1-27,2/S	-1.6
1894	Chi-N	91	384	74	120	17	6	8	92	24	17	.313	.361	.451	90	-8	23			.974	-8	1-48,O-29/32S	-1.4
1895	Chi-N	73	297	51	82	9	2	5	41	17	22	.276	.324	.374	75	-13	11			.910	-8	O-57,1-11/3S2	-2.0
1896	Chi-N	107	421	68	118	23	11	5	61	23	14	.280	.318	.423	91	-8	20			.928	-3	O-71,1-36	-1.4
1897	Chi-N	111	428	72	124	12	7	5	63	24		.290	.333	.386	86	-10	11			.925	-3	O-75,1-38/2	-1.5
1898	StL-N	76	286	26	74	10	0	1	45	20		.259	.314	.304	76	-9	4			.980	-7	1-75	-1.6
	Lou-N	42	148	27	44	4	3	0	19	9		.297	.342	.365	104	1	9			.993	-1	1-32/O-6	-0.1
	Yr	118	434	53	118	14	3	1	64	29		.272	.323	.325	85	-9	13			**.984**	-9	*1-107/O-6	-1.7
1899	Lou-N	38	135	13	36	8	0	1	18	12		.267	.336	.348	88	-2	3			.968	-3	1-38	-0.4
	Was-N	4	9	0	0	0	0	0	0	0		.000	.000	.000	-99	-2	0			.955	-1	/1-2,O-1	-0.3
	Yr	42	144	13	36	8	0	1	18	12		.250	.316	.326	77	-5	3			.967	-3	1-40/O-1	-0.7
Total	8	701	2727	420	753	98	49	25	415	173	124	.276	.324	.376	84	-70	112			.900	-54	O-334,1-307/23S	-12.5

■ STEVE DECKER   Decker, Steven Michael   b: 10/25/65, Rock Island, Ill.   BR/TR, 6'3", 205 lbs.   Deb: 9/18/90

1990	SF-N	15	54	5	16	2	0	3	8	1	10	.296	.309	.500	123	1	0	0	0	.989	2	C-15	0.4
1991	SF-N	79	233	11	48	7	1	5	24	16	44	.206	.266	.309	63	-12	0	1	-1	.984	-3	C-78	-1.2
1992	SF-N	15	43	3	7	1	0	0	1	6	7	.163	.280	.186	36	-3	0	0	0	1.000	2	C-15	0.0
1993	Fla-N	8	15	0	0	0	0	0	1	3	3	.000	.167	.000	-48	-3	0	0	0	.968	1	/C-5	-0.2
Total	4	117	345	19	71	10	1	8	34	26	64	.206	.269	.310	64	-17	0	1	-1	.986	2	C-113	-1.0

■ ARTIE DEDE   Dede, Arthur Richard   b: 7/12/1895, Brooklyn, N.Y.   d: 9/6/71, Keene, N.H.   BR/TR, 5'9", 155 lbs.   Deb: 10/4/16

| 1916 | Bro-N | 1 | 1 | 0 | 0 | 0 | 0 | 0 | 0 | 0 | 0 | .000 | .000 | .000 | -97 | -0 | 0 | | | 1.000 | -0 | /C-1 | -0.1 |

■ ROD DEDEAUX   Dedeaux, Raoul Martial   b: 2/17/15, New Orleans, La.   BR/TR, 5'11", 160 lbs.   Deb: 9/28/35

| 1935 | Bro-N | 2 | 4 | 0 | 1 | 0 | 0 | 0 | 0 | 1 | 0 | .250 | .250 | .250 | 36 | -0 | 0 | | | .857 | 0 | /S-2 | 0.0 |

■ JIM DEE   Dee, James D.   b: Buffalo, N.Y.   Deb: 7/30/1884

| 1884 | Pit-a | 12 | 40 | 0 | 5 | 0 | 0 | 0 | | 1 | | .125 | .146 | .125 | -10 | -5 | | | | .860 | 1 | S-12 | -0.3 |

■ SHORTY DEE   Dee, Maurice Leo   b: 10/4/1889, Halifax, N.S., Can.   d: 8/12/71, Jamaica Plain, Mass.   BR/TR, 5'6", 155 lbs.   Deb: 9/14/15

| 1915 | StL-A | 1 | 3 | 1 | 0 | 0 | 0 | 0 | 0 | 1 | 0 | .000 | .250 | .000 | -26 | -0 | 1 | 1 | -1 | .500 | -1 | /S-1 | -0.3 |

■ ROB DEER   Deer, Robert George   b: 9/29/60, Orange, Cal.   BR/TR, 6'3", 210 lbs.   Deb: 9/4/84

1984	SF-N	13	24	5	4	0	0	3	3	7	10	.167	.375	.542	160	2	1	1	-0	.905	0	/O-9	0.2
1985	SF-N	78	162	22	30	5	1	8	20	23	71	.185	.286	.377	88	-3	0	1	-1	.982	-4	O-37,1-10	-1.0
1986	Mil-A	134	466	75	108	17	3	33	86	72	179	.232	.338	.494	119	12	5	2	0	.974	8	*O-131/1-4	1.5
1987	Mil-A	134	474	71	113	15	2	28	80	86	186	.238	.361	.456	112	9	12	4	1	.974	8	*O-123,1-12/D	1.3
1988	Mil-A	135	492	71	124	24	0	23	85	51	153	.252	.331	.441	113	8	9	5	-0	.990	7	*O-133/D-1	1.1
1989	Mil-A	130	466	72	98	18	2	26	65	60	158	.210	.305	.425	105	4	4	8	-4	.972	5	*O-125/D-5	0.8
1990	Mil-A	134	440	57	92	15	1	27	69	64	147	.209	.315	.432	108	4	2	3	-1	.970	9	*O-117,1-21/D	0.8
1991	Det-A	134	448	64	80	14	2	25	64	89	175	.179	.315	.386	91	-5	1	3	-2	.970	11	*O-132/D-2	0.2
1992	Det-A	110	393	66	97	20	1	32	64	51	131	.247	.338	.547	143	21	4	2	0	.983	5	*O-106/D-2	2.4
1993	Det-A	90	323	48	70	11	0	14	39	38	121	.217	.305	.381	84	-8	3	2	-0	.975	5	O-86/D-4	-0.5
	Bos-A	38	143	18	28	6	1	7	16	20	49	.196	.303	.399	82	-4	2	0	1	.970	5	O-36/D-2	0.1
	Yr	128	466	66	98	17	1	21	55	58	169	.210	.304	.386	83	-12	5	2	0	.973	9	*O-122/D-6	-0.4
Total	10	1130	3831	569	844	145	13	226	591	561	1379	.220	.325	.442	108	38	43	31	-6	.976	58	*O-1035/1-47,D	6.1

■ CHARLIE DEES   Dees, Charles Henry   b: 6/24/35, Birmingham, Ala.   BL/TL, 6'1", 173 lbs.   Deb: 5/26/63

1963	LA-A	60	202	23	62	11	1	3	27	11	31	.307	.367	.416	126	7	3	3	-1	.986	-2	1-56	0.6
1964	LA-A	26	26	3	2	1	0	0	1	1	3	.077	.143	.115	-30	-5	1	2	-1	.981	0	1-12	-0.6
1965	Cal-A	12	32	1	5	0	0	0	1	1	8	.156	.182	.156	-3	-4	1	2	-1	.986	-1	/1-8	-0.7
Total	3	98	260	27	69	12	1	3	29	13	43	.265	.323	.354	95	-2	5	7	-3	.986	-3	/1-76	-1.1

YEAR	TM/L	G	AB	R	H	2B	3B	HR	RBI	BB	SO	AVG	OBP	SLG	PRO+	BR/A	SB	CS	SBR	FA	FR	G/POS	TPR

■ TONY DeFATE DeFate, Clyde Herbert b: 2/22/1895, Kansas City, Mo. d: 9/3/63, New Orleans, La. BR/TR, 5'8.5", 158 lbs. Deb: 4/18/17

1917	StL-N	14	14	0	2	0	0	0	1	4	5	.143	.333	.143	50	-1	0			1.000	-1	/3-5,2-1	-0.1
	Det-A	3	2	1	0	0	0	0	0	0	1	.000	.000	.000	-99	-0	0			1.000	-0	/2-1	-0.1
Total	1	17	16	1	2	0	0	0	1	4	6	.125	.300	.125	33	-1	0			1.000	-1	/3-5,2-2	-0.2

■ ARTURO DeFREITAS DeFreitas, Arturo Marcelino (Simon) b: 4/26/53, San Pedro De Macoris, D.R. BR/TR, 6'2", 195 lbs. Deb: 9/7/78

1978	Cin-N	9	19	1	4	1	0	1	2	1	4	.211	.250	.421	84	-1	0	0	0	1.000	0	/1-6	-0.1
1979	Cin-N	23	34	2	7	2	0	0	4	0	16	.206	.206	.265	27	-3	0	0	0	.974	-1	/1-6,O-1	-0.5
Total	2	32	53	3	11	3	0	1	6	1	20	.208	.222	.321	47	-4	0	0	0	.988	-1	/1-12,O-1	-0.6

■ RUBE DeGROFF DeGroff, Edward Arthur b: 9/2/1879, Hyde Park, N.Y. d: 12/17/55, Poughkeepsie, N.Y. BL, 5'11", Deb: 9/22/05

1905	StL-N	15	56	3	14	2	1	0	5	5		.250	.311	.321	91	-1	1			.909	-0	O-15	-0.1
1906	StL-N	1	4	1	0	0	0	0	0	0		.000	.000	.000	-99	-1	0			.000	-0	/O-1	-0.2
Total	2	16	60	4	14	2	1	0	5	5		.233	.292	.300	80	-2	1			.909	-0	/O-16	-0.3

■ HERMAN DEHLMAN Dehlman, Herman J. "Dutch" b: 1850, Catasauqua, Pa. d: 3/13/1885, Wilkes-Barre, Pa. Deb: 5/2/1872

1872	Atl-n	37	164	30	36	3	0	0	15	3	1	.220	.234	.238	39	-15						*1-35	-0.9
1873	Atl-n	54	221	50	52	5	2	0	17	9	7	.235	.265	.276	67	-7						*1-54	-0.2
1874	Atl-n	53	216	40	50	5	1	0		7		.231	.256	.264	74	-4						*1-53	-0.3
1875	StL-N	67	254	42	57	12	2	0		11		.224	.257	.287	97	1						*1-67	0.0
1876	StL-N	64	245	40	45	6	0	0	9	9	10	.184	.213	.208	43	-13				.958	0	*1-64	-1.3
1877	StL-N	32	119	24	22	4	0	0	11	7	21	.185	.230	.218	44	-7				.931	-3	1-31/O-1	-0.9
Total 4 n	211	855	162	195	25	5	0	32	30	8	.228	.254	.269	70	-25						1-209/D-0	-1.4
Total 2	96	364	64	67	10	0	0	20	16	31	.184	.218	.212	43	-20				.950	-3	/1-95,O-1	-2.2

■ JIM DEIDEL Deidel, James Lawrence b: 6/6/49, Denver, Col. BR/TR, 6'2", 195 lbs. Deb: 5/31/74

| 1974 | NY-A | 2 | 2 | 0 | 0 | 0 | 0 | 0 | 0 | 0 | 0 | .000 | .000 | .000 | -99 | -1 | 0 | 0 | 0 | 1.000 | 1 | /C-2 | 0.1 |

■ PEP DEININGER Deininger, Otto Charles b: 10/10/1877, Wasseralfingen, Germany d: 9/25/50, Boston, Mass. BL/TL, 5'8.5", 180 lbs. Deb: 4/26/02

1902	Bos-A	2	6	0	2	1	1	0	0	1		.333	.333	.833	210	1	0			1.000	-1	/P-2	0.0
1908	Phi-N	1	0	0	0	0	0	0	0	0		—	—	—	—	0	0			.000	-1	/O-1	-0.1
1909	Phi-N	55	169	22	44	9	0	0	16	11		.260	.309	.314	93	-2	5			.989	-2	O-45/2-1	-0.6
Total	3	58	175	22	46	10	1	0	16	11		.263	.310	.331	97	-1	5			.989	-3	/O-46,P-2,2	-0.7

■ PAT DEISEL Deisel, Edward b: 4/29/1876, Ripley, Ohio d: 4/17/48, Cincinnati, Ohio BR/TR, 5'5", 145 lbs. Deb: 8/21/02

1902	Bro-N	1	3	0	2	0	0	0	1	1		.667	.800	.667	351	1	0			1.000	0	/C-1	0.1
1903	Cin-N	2	0	0	0	0	0	0	0	1		—	1.000	—	174	1	0			.000	0	/C-1	0.0
Total	2	3	3	0	2	0	0	0	1	2		.667	.833	.667	352	2	0			1.000	0	/C-2	0.1

☒ BILL DEITRICK Deitrick, William Alexander b: 4/20/02, Hanover Co., Va. d: 5/6/46, Bethesda, Md. BR/TR, 5'10", 160 lbs. Deb: 9/19/27

1927	Phi-N	5	6	1	1	0	0	0	0	0	0	.167	.167	.167	-10	-1	0			.750	-1	/S-5	-0.2
1928	Phi-N	52	100	13	20	6	0	0	7	17	10	.200	.322	.260	52	-7	1			1.000	-2	O-21/S-8	-0.9
Total	2	57	106	14	21	6	0	0	7	17	10	.198	.315	.255	49	-8	1			.895	-3	/O-21,S-13	-1.1

■ MIKE DEJAN Dejan, Michael Dan b: 1/13/15, Cleveland, Ohio d: 2/2/53, W.Los Angeles, Cal. BL/TL, 6'1", 185 lbs. Deb: 7/13/40

| 1940 | Cin-N | 12 | 16 | 1 | 3 | 0 | 1 | 0 | 2 | 3 | 3 | .188 | .316 | .313 | 73 | -1 | 0 | | | 1.000 | -0 | /O-2 | -0.1 |

■ IVAN DeJESUS DeJesus, Ivan (Alvarez) b: 1/9/53, Santurce, P.R. BR/TR, 5'11", 175 lbs. Deb: 9/13/74

1974	LA-N	3	3	1	1	0	0	0	0	0	2	.333	.333	.333	91	-0	0	0	0	1.000	-1	/S-2	-0.1
1975	LA-N	63	87	10	16	2	1	0	2	11	15	.184	.276	.230	43	-7	1	2	-1	.974	7	S-63	0.3
1976	LA-N	22	41	4	7	2	1	0	2	4	9	.171	.244	.268	46	-3	0	1	-1	.950	5	S-13/3-7	0.3
1977	Chi-N	155	624	91	166	31	7	3	40	56	90	.266	.330	.353	75	-21	24	12	0	.962	36	*S-154	3.2
1978	Chi-N	160	619	104	172	24	7	3	35	74	78	.278	.357	.354	88	-8	41	12	5	.967	13	*S-160	3.1
1979	Chi-N	160	636	92	180	26	10	5	52	59	82	.283	.346	.379	89	-9	24	20	-5	.959	1	*S-160	0.5
1980	Chi-N	157	618	78	160	26	3	3	33	60	81	.259	.328	.325	77	-17	44	16	4	.969	8	*S-156	1.3
1981	Chi-N	106	403	49	78	8	4	0	13	46	61	.194	.276	.233	44	-29	21	9	1	.959	10	*S-106	-0.8
1982	Phi-N	161	536	53	128	21	3	3	59	54	70	.239	.311	.313	73	-18	14	4	2	.973	-3	*S-154/3-7	-1.0
1983	*Phi-N	158	497	60	126	15	7	4	45	53	77	.254	.325	.336	85	-10	11	4	1	.966	-14	*S-158	-0.8
1984	Phi-N	144	435	40	112	15	3	0	35	43	76	.257	.327	.306	77	-12	12	5	1	.951	-21	*S-141	-2.1
1985	*StL-N	59	72	11	16	5	0	0	7	4	16	.222	.263	.292	55	-4	2	2	-1	1.000	2	3-20,S-13	-0.2
1986	NY-A	7	4	1	0	0	0	0	0	0	1	.000	.000	.000	-40	-1	0	0	0	.900	1	/S-7	-0.1
1987	SF-N	9	10	0	2	0	0	0	1	0	2	.200	.200	.200	7	-1	0	1	-1	.840	2	/S-9	0.1
1988	Det-A	7	17	1	3	0	0	0	0	1	4	.176	.222	.176	14	-2	0	0	0	.893	1	/S-7	-0.1
Total	15	1371	4602	595	1167	175	48	21	324	466	664	.254	.324	.326	76	-142	194	88	5	.963	41	*S-1303/3-34	3.6

■ MARK DeJOHN DeJohn, Mark Stephen b: 9/18/53, Middletown, Conn. BB/TR, 5'11", 170 lbs. Deb: 4/28/82

| 1982 | Det-A | 24 | 21 | 1 | 4 | 2 | 0 | 0 | 1 | 4 | 4 | .190 | .320 | .286 | 68 | -1 | 1 | 0 | 0 | .978 | 6 | S-20/3-4,2 | 0.6 |

■ BILL DeKONING DeKoning, William Callahan b: 12/19/18, Brooklyn, N.Y. d: 7/26/79, Palm Harbor, Fla. BR/TR, 5'11", 185 lbs. Deb: 5/27/45

| 1945 | NY-N | 3 | 1 | 0 | 0 | 0 | 0 | 0 | 0 | 0 | 1 | .000 | .000 | .000 | -99 | -0 | 0 | | | 1.000 | -0 | /C-2 | 0.0 |

■ ED DELAHANTY Delahanty, Edward James "Big Ed" b: 10/30/1867, Cleveland, Ohio d: 7/2/03, Niagara Falls, Ont., Canada BR/TR, 6'1", 170 lbs. Deb: 5/22/1888 FH

1888	Phi-N	74	290	40	66	12	1	1	31	12	26	.228	.261	.293	73	-9	38			.872	-10	2-56,O-17	-1.7
1889	Phi-N	56	246	37	72	13	3	0	27	14	17	.293	.333	.370	89	-5	19			.956	-13	O-31,2-24/S	-1.5
1890	Cle-P	115	517	107	154	26	13	3	64	24	30	.298	.339	.416	110	6	25			.830	-7	S-76,2-20,O/31	0.3
1891	Phi-N	128	543	92	132	19	9	5	86	33	50	.243	.296	.339	83	-14	25			.909	1	*O-91,1-27/2	-1.5
1892	Phi-N	123	477	79	146	30	21	6	91	31	32	.306	.360	.495	158	30	29			.944	10	O-121/3-4	3.3
1893	Phi-N	132	595	145	219	35	18	19	146	47	20	.368	.423	.583	167	53	37			.948	31	*O-117,2-15/1	6.3
1894	Phi-N	114	489	147	199	39	18	4	131	60	16	.407	.478	.585	159	50	21			.925	17	*O-88,1-12/3S2	4.7
1895	Phi-N	116	480	149	194	49	10	11	106	86	31	.404	.500	.617	186	66	46			.944	-0	*O-103/S-9,23	4.7
1896	Phi-N	123	499	131	198	44	17	13	126	62	22	.397	.472	.631	192	67	37			.952	14	*O-99,1-22/2	6.0
1897	Phi-N	129	530	109	200	40	15	5	96	60		.377	.444	.538	162	49	26			.970	9	*O-129/1-1	4.0
1898	Phi-N	144	548	115	183	36	9	4	92	77		.334	.426	.454	159	46	58			.964	6	*O-144	3.7
1899	Phi-N	146	581	135	238	55	9	9	137	55		.410	.464	.582	193	73	30			.969	0	*O-143	5.6
1900	Phi-N	131	539	82	174	32	10	2	109	41		.323	.378	.430	124	17	16			.981	-3	*1-130	1.2
1901	Phi-N	139	542	106	192	38	16	8	108	65		.354	.427	.528	173	51	29			.949	-5	O-84,1-58	3.7
1902	Was-A	123	473	103	178	43	14	10	93	62		.376	.453	.590	186	56	16			.961	2	*O-111,1-13	4.7
1903	Was-A	42	156	22	52	11	1	1	21	12		.333	.388	.436	144	9	3			.962	2	O-40/1-1	0.8
Total	16	1835	7505	1599	2597	522	185	101	1464	741	244	.346	.412	.505	153	544	455			.951	55	*O-1344,1-271,2/S3	44.3

■ FRANK DELAHANTY Delahanty, Frank George "Pudgie" b: 1/29/1883, Cleveland, Ohio d: 7/22/66, Cleveland, Ohio BR/TR, 5'9", 160 lbs. Deb: 8/23/05 F

1905	NY-A	9	27	0	6	1	0	0	2	2	1	.222	.250	.259	55	-1	0			.932	-1	/1-5,O-3	-0.3
1906	NY-A	92	307	37	73	11	8	2	41	16		.238	.282	.345	87	-6	11			.954	3	O-86	-0.7
1907	Cle-A	15	52	3	9	0	1	0	4	4		.173	.232	.212	41	-3	2			.917	-0	O-15	-0.5
1908	NY-A	37	125	12	32	1	2	0	10	10		.256	.316	.296	98	-0	9			.957	-1	O-36	-0.3

YEAR	TM/L	G	AB	R	H	2B	3B	HR	RBI	BB	SO	AVG	OBP	SLG	PRO+	BR/A	SB	CS	SBR	FA	FR	G/POS	TPR
1914	Buf-F	79	274	29	55	4	7	2	27	23	19	.201	.265	.288	42	-24	21			.976	-6	O-78	-3.5
	Pit-F	41	159	25	38	4	4	1	7	11	11	.239	.297	.333	63	-9	7			.984	-3	O-36/2-4	-1.4
	Yr	120	433	54	93	8	11	3	34	34	30	.215	.277	.305	50	-33	28			.979	-8	*O-114/2-4	-4.9
1915	Pit-F	14	42	3	10	1	0	0	3	1	0	.238	.256	.262	39	-4	0			1.000	1	O-11	-0.4
Total	6	287	986	109	223	22	22	5	94	66	30	.226	.280	.308	66	-47	50			.964	-7	O-265/1-5,2	-7.1

■ JIM DELAHANTY
Delahanty, James Christopher   b: 6/20/1879, Cleveland, Ohio   d: 10/17/53, Cleveland, Ohio   BR/TR, 5'10.5", 170 lbs.   Deb: 4/19/01   F

YEAR	TM/L	G	AB	R	H	2B	3B	HR	RBI	BB	SO	AVG	OBP	SLG	PRO+	BR/A	SB	CS	SBR	FA	FR	G/POS	TPR
1901	Chi-N	17	63	4	12	2	0	0	4	3		.190	.239	.222	35	-5	5			.877	-1	3-17/2-1	-0.6
1902	NY-N	7	26	3	6	1	0	0	3	1		.231	.259	.269	64	-1	0			.917	-1	/O-7	-0.2
1904	Bos-N	142	499	56	142	27	8	3	60	27		.285	.333	.389	127	15	16			.888	1	*3-113,2-18/OP	1.9
1905	Bos-N	125	461	50	119	11	8	5	55	28		.258	.315	.349	100	-1	12			.962	-7	*O-124/P-1	-1.5
1906	Cin-N	115	379	63	106	21	4	1	39	45		.280	.371	.364	124	12	21			.903	-19	3-105/S-5,O	-0.4
1907	StL-A	33	95	8	21	3	0	0	6	5		.221	.275	.253	68	-3	6			.889	-1	3-21/O-4,2	-0.4
	Was-A	108	404	44	118	18	7	2	54	36		.292	.367	.386	152	24	18			.941	-13	2-68,3-27/O1	1.3
	Yr	141	499	52	139	21	7	2	60	41		.279	.350	.361	135	20	24			.942	-14	2-70,3-48,O/1	0.9
1908	Was-A	83	287	33	91	11	4	1	30	24		.317	.376	.394	164	20	16			.963	3	2-80	2.5
1909	Was-A	90	302	18	67	13	5	1	21	23		.222	.290	.308	93	-3	4			.956	-3	2-85	-0.8
	*Det-A	46	150	29	38	10	1	0	20	17		.253	.364	.333	115	4	9			.943	-7	2-46	-0.5
	Yr	136	452	47	105	23	6	1	41	40		.232	.316	.316	101	2	13			.951	-10	*2-131	-1.3
1910	Det-A	108	378	67	111	16	2	3	45	43		.294	.379	.370	126	13	15			.940	-15	*2-106	-0.5
1911	Det-A	144	542	83	184	30	14	3	94	56		.339	.411	.463	137	27	15			.978	-10	1-71,2-59,3	1.6
1912	Det-A	79	266	34	76	14	1	0	41	42		.286	.397	.346	117	9	9			.930	-5	2-44,O-33	0.1
1914	Bro-F	74	214	28	62	13	5	0	15	25	21	.290	.372	.397	100	0	4			.957	-19	2-55/1-5	-2.0
1915	Bro-F	17	25	0	6	1	0	0	2	3	3	.240	.345	.280	69	-1	1			.857	-1	/2-4	-0.2
Total	13	1186	4091	520	1159	191	59	19	489	378	24	.283	.357	.373	121	110	151			.946	-97	2-568,3-296,O/1SP	0.3

■ JOE DELAHANTY
Delahanty, Joseph Nicholas   b: 10/18/1875, Cleveland, Ohio   d: 1/9/36, Cleveland, Ohio   BR/TR, 5'9", 168 lbs.   Deb: 9/30/07   F

YEAR	TM/L	G	AB	R	H	2B	3B	HR	RBI	BB	SO	AVG	OBP	SLG	PRO+	BR/A	SB	CS	SBR	FA	FR	G/POS	TPR
1907	StL-N	7	22	3	7	1	1	0	4	1		.318	.318	.455	147	1	3			.933	-1	/O-7	0.0
1908	StL-N	140	499	37	127	14	11	1	44	32		.255	.309	.333	110	5	11			.977	-5	*O-138	-0.6
1909	StL-N	123	411	28	88	16	4	2	52	42		.214	.292	.287	85	-7	10			.985	-16	O-63,2-48	-3.0
Total	3	270	932	68	222	30	15	4	100	74		.238	.301	.315	100	-2	24			.978	-21	O-208/2-48	-3.6

■ TOM DELAHANTY
Delahanty, Thomas James   b: 3/9/1872, Cleveland, Ohio   d: 1/10/51, Sanford, Fla.   BL/TR, 5'8", 175 lbs.   Deb: 9/29/1894   F

YEAR	TM/L	G	AB	R	H	2B	3B	HR	RBI	BB	SO	AVG	OBP	SLG	PRO+	BR/A	SB	CS	SBR	FA	FR	G/POS	TPR
1894	Phi-N	1	4	0	1	0	0	0	0	0	1	.250	.250	.250	21	-1	0			.875	-2	/2-1	0.0
1896	Cle-N	16	56	11	13	4	0	0	4	8	4	.232	.338	.304	66	-3	4			.823	-1	3-16	-0.3
	Pit-N	1	3	1	1	0	0	0	0	0		.333	.333	.333	79	-0	0			.750	-0	/S-1	0.0
	Yr	17	59	12	14	4	0	0	4	8	4	.237	.338	.305	67	-3	4			.823	-2	3-16/S-1	-0.3
1897	Lou-N	1	4	1	1	1	0	0	2	0		.250	.250	.500	99	-0	0			.333	-2	/2-1	-0.2
Total	3	19	67	13	16	5	0	0	6	8	5	.239	.329	.313	66	-3	4			.727	-4	/3-16,2-2,S	-0.5

■ MIKE de la HOZ
de la Hoz, Miguel Angel (Piloto)   b: 10/2/38, Havana, Cuba   BR/TR, 5'11", 175 lbs.   Deb: 7/22/60

YEAR	TM/L	G	AB	R	H	2B	3B	HR	RBI	BB	SO	AVG	OBP	SLG	PRO+	BR/A	SB	CS	SBR	FA	FR	G/POS	TPR
1960	Cle-A	49	160	20	41	6	2	6	23	9	12	.256	.300	.431	98	-1	0	0	0	.950	-15	S-38/3-8	-1.3
1961	Cle-A	61	173	20	45	10	0	3	23	7	10	.260	.297	.370	79	-6	0	0	0	.969	3	2-17,S-17,3	0.0
1962	Cle-A	12	12	0	1	0	0	0	0	0	3	.083	.083	.083	-57	-3	0	0	0	1.000	-0	/2-2	-0.3
1963	Cle-A	67	150	15	40	10	0	5	25	9	29	.267	.313	.433	107	1	0	0	0	.962	4	2-34/3-6,SO	0.9
1964	Mil-N	78	189	25	55	7	1	4	12	14	22	.291	.346	.402	109	1	1	1	0	.968	-4	2-25,3-25/S	0.0
1965	Mil-N	81	176	15	45	9	2	2	11	8	21	.256	.296	.330	75	-6	0	1	0	.963	-10	S-41,3-22,2/1	-1.6
1966	Atl-N	71	110	11	24	3	0	2	7	5	18	.218	.252	.300	52	-7	0	1	-1	.950	-2	3-30/2-8,S	-1.1
1967	Atl-N	74	143	10	29	3	0	3	14	4	14	.203	.224	.287	46	-10	0	1	0	1.000	-4	2-23,3-22/S	-1.5
1969	Cin-N	1	1	0	0	0	0	0	0	0	0	.000	.000	.000	-95	-0	0	0	0	.000	0	H	0.0
Total	9	494	1114	116	280	42	5	25	115	56	130	.251	.292	.365	82	-29	2	3	-1	.936	-28	3-129,2-119,S/O1	-4.9

■ BILL DeLANCEY
DeLancey, William Pinkney   b: 11/28/11, Greensboro, N.C.   d: 11/28/46, Phoenix, Ariz.   BL/TR, 5'11.5", 185 lbs.   Deb: 9/11/32

YEAR	TM/L	G	AB	R	H	2B	3B	HR	RBI	BB	SO	AVG	OBP	SLG	PRO+	BR/A	SB	CS	SBR	FA	FR	G/POS	TPR
1932	StL-N	8	26	1	5	0	2	0	2	2	1	.192	.250	.346	57	-2	0			.930	1	/C-8	-0.1
1934	*StL-N	93	253	41	80	18	3	13	40	41	37	.316	.414	.565	150	18	1			.980	5	C-77	2.5
1935	StL-N	103	301	37	84	14	5	6	41	42	34	.279	.369	.419	107	4	0			.971	-2	C-83	0.6
1940	StL-N	15	18	0	4	0	0	0	2	0	2	.222	.222	.222	22	-2	0			.929	1	C-12	0.0
Total	4	219	598	79	173	32	10	19	85	85	74	.289	.380	.472	121	19	1			.972	4	C-180	3.0

■ BILL DELANEY
Delaney, William L.   b: 3/4/1863, Cincinnati, O.   d: 3/1/42, Canton, Ohio   BR/TR,   Deb: 8/21/1890

YEAR	TM/L	G	AB	R	H	2B	3B	HR	RBI	BB	SO	AVG	OBP	SLG	PRO+	BR/A	SB	CS	SBR	FA	FR	G/POS	TPR
1890	Cle-N	36	116	16	22	1	1	1	7	21	19	.190	.314	.241	64	-5	5			.926	-10	2-36	-1.1

■ JESUS de la ROSA
de la Rosa, Jesus (b: Jesus De Los Santos (De La Rosa))   b: 8/5/53, Santo Domingo, D.R   BR/TR, 6'1", 153 lbs.   Deb: 8/2/75

YEAR	TM/L	G	AB	R	H	2B	3B	HR	RBI	BB	SO	AVG	OBP	SLG	PRO+	BR/A	SB	CS	SBR	FA	FR	G/POS	TPR
1975	Hou-N	3	3	1	1	1	0	0	0	0	0	.333	.333	.667	186	0	0	0	0	.000	0	H	0.0

■ CARLOS DELGADO
Delgado, Carlos Juan (Hernandez)   b: 6/25/72, Mayaguez, P.R.   BL/TR, 6'3", 215 lbs.   Deb: 10/1/93

YEAR	TM/L	G	AB	R	H	2B	3B	HR	RBI	BB	SO	AVG	OBP	SLG	PRO+	BR/A	SB	CS	SBR	FA	FR	G/POS	TPR
1993	Tor-A	2	1	0	0	0	0	0	0	1	0	.000	.500	.000	47	0	0	0	0	1.000	0	/C-1,D-1	0.0
1994	Tor-A	43	130	17	28	2	0	9	24	25	46	.215	.354	.438	102	1	1	1	-0	.966	-4	O-41/C-1	-0.4
Total	2	45	131	17	28	2	0	9	24	26	46	.214	.356	.435	102	1	1	1	-0	1.000	-4	/O-41,C-2,D	-0.4

■ PUCHY DELGADO
Delgado, Luis Felipe (Robles)   b: 2/2/54, Hatillo, P.R.   BB/TL, 5'11", 170 lbs.   Deb: 9/6/77

YEAR	TM/L	G	AB	R	H	2B	3B	HR	RBI	BB	SO	AVG	OBP	SLG	PRO+	BR/A	SB	CS	SBR	FA	FR	G/POS	TPR
1977	Sea-A	13	22	4	4	0	0	0	2	1	8	.182	.217	.182	10	-3	0	0	0	1.000	-2	O-13	-0.5

■ BOBBY Del GRECO
Del Greco, Robert George   b: 4/7/33, Pittsburgh, Pa.   BR/TR, 5'11", 190 lbs.   Deb: 4/16/52

YEAR	TM/L	G	AB	R	H	2B	3B	HR	RBI	BB	SO	AVG	OBP	SLG	PRO+	BR/A	SB	CS	SBR	FA	FR	G/POS	TPR
1952	Pit-N	99	341	34	74	14	2	1	20	38	70	.217	.301	.279	60	-18	6	5	-1	.977	6	O-93	-1.8
1956	Pit-N	14	20	4	4	0	0	0	3	3	3	.200	.304	.500	114	0	0	0	0	1.000	-2	/O-7,3-3	-0.2
	StL-N	102	270	29	58	16	2	5	18	32	50	.215	.312	.344	76	-9	1	1	-0	.987	-9	O-99	-2.3
	Yr	116	290	33	62	16	2	7	21	35	53	.214	.311	.355	79	-8	1	1	-0	.987	-10	*O-106/3-3	-2.5
1957	Chi-N	20	40	2	8	2	0	0	3	10	17	.200	.360	.250	69	-1	0	0	0	.967	-2	O-16	-0.2
	NY-A	8	7	3	3	0	0	0	0	2	2	.429	.556	.429	175	1	1	0	0	1.000	-2	/O-6	-0.1
1958	NY-A	12	5	1	1	0	0	0	0	1	1	.200	.333	.200	52	-0	0	1	-1	1.000	-4	O-12	-0.5
1960	Phi-N	100	300	48	71	16	4	10	26	54	64	.237	.355	.417	110	5	5	3	-3	.970	12	O-89	1.0
1961	Phi-N	41	112	14	29	5	2	2	11	12	17	.259	.346	.357	88	-2	0	0	0	1.000	1	O-32/2-1,3	-0.2
	KC-A	74	239	34	55	14	1	5	21	30	31	.230	.319	.360	79	-7	1	0	0	.983	5	O-73	-0.5
1962	KC-A	132	338	61	86	21	1	9	38	49	62	.254	.370	.402	103	3	4	1	1	.984	0	*O-124	-0.2
1963	KC-A	121	306	40	65	7	1	8	29	40	52	.212	.313	.320	74	-10	1	1	0	.981	-6	*O-110/3-2	-2.3
1965	Phi-N	8	4	1	0	0	0	0	0	0	3	.000	.000	.000	-99	-1	0	0	0	.000	-1	/O-4	-0.2
Total	9	731	1982	271	454	95	11	42	169	271	372	.229	.331	.352	84	-38	16	15	-4	.981	-2	O-665/3-6,2	-7.6

■ JUAN DELIS
Delis, Juan Francisco   b: 2/27/28, Santiago, Cuba   BR/TR, 5'11", 170 lbs.   Deb: 4/16/55

YEAR	TM/L	G	AB	R	H	2B	3B	HR	RBI	BB	SO	AVG	OBP	SLG	PRO+	BR/A	SB	CS	SBR	FA	FR	G/POS	TPR
1955	Was-A	54	132	12	25	3	1	0	11	3	15	.189	.219	.227	21	-15	1	2	-1	.918	-2	3-24/O-8,2	-1.8

■ EDDIE DELKER
Delker, Edward Alberts   b: 4/17/07, DeAlto, Pa.   BR/TR, 5'10.5", 170 lbs.   Deb: 4/28/29

YEAR	TM/L	G	AB	R	H	2B	3B	HR	RBI	BB	SO	AVG	OBP	SLG	PRO+	BR/A	SB	CS	SBR	FA	FR	G/POS	TPR
1929	StL-N	22	40	5	6	1	0	0	3	2	12	.150	.227	.200	7	-6	0			.750	-2	/S-9,2-7,3	-0.7
1931	StL-N	1	2	0	1	1	0	0	2	0	0	.500	.500	1.000	283	-0	0			1.000	-0	/3-1	0.0
1932	StL-N	20	42	1	5	4	0	0	2	8	7	.119	.260	.214	28	-4	0			1.000	4	2-10/3-5,S	0.1

YEAR	TM/L	G	AB	R	H	2B	3B	HR	RBI	BB	SO	AVG	OBP	SLG	PRO+	BR/A	SB	CS	SBR	FA	FR	G/POS	TPR
	Phi-N	30	62	7	10	1	1	1	7	6	14	.161	.235	.258	29	-6	0			.925	-2	2-27	-0.7
	Yr	50	104	8	15	5	1	1	9	14	21	.144	.246	.240	29	-11	0			.946	3	2-37/3-5,S	-0.6
1933	Phi-N	25	41	6	7	3	1	0	1	0	12	.171	.171	.293	27	-4	0			.968	5	2-17/3-4	0.3
Total 4		98	187	19	29	9	3	1	15	16	45	.155	.229	.251	26	-20	0			.952	6	/2-61,3-13,S	-1.0

■ BERT DELMAS
Delmas, Albert Charles   b: 5/20/11, San Francisco, Cal   d: 12/4/79, Huntington Beach, Cal.   BL/TR, 5'11", 165 lbs.   Deb: 9/10/33

YEAR	TM/L	G	AB	R	H	2B	3B	HR	RBI	BB	SO	AVG	OBP	SLG	PRO+	BR/A	SB	CS	SBR	FA	FR	G/POS	TPR
1933	Bro-N	12	28	4	7	0	0	0	0	1	7	.250	.276	.250	53	-2	0			.912	-3	2-10	-0.5

■ LUIS de los SANTOS
de los Santos, Luis Manuel (Martinez)   b: 12/29/66, San Cristobal, D.R.   BR/TR, 6'5", 205 lbs.   Deb: 9/7/88

YEAR	TM/L	G	AB	R	H	2B	3B	HR	RBI	BB	SO	AVG	OBP	SLG	PRO+	BR/A	SB	CS	SBR	FA	FR	G/POS	TPR
1988	KC-A	11	22	1	2	1	1	0	1	4	4	.091	.231	.227	29	-2	0	0	0	1.000	-0	/1-5,D-3	-0.3
1989	KC-A	28	87	6	22	3	1	0	6	5	14	.253	.293	.310	71	-3	0	0	0	.986	0	1-27	-0.5
1991	Det-A	16	30	1	5	2	0	0	0	2	4	.167	.219	.233	25	-3	0	0	0	1.000	-0	/O-3,1-2,3D	-0.4
Total 3		55	139	8	29	6	2	0	7	11	22	.209	.267	.281	53	-9	0	0	0	.988	-1	/1-34,D-12,O3	-1.2

■ GARTON Del SAVIO
Del Savio, Garton Orville   b: 11/26/13, New York, N.Y.   BR/TR, 5'9.5", 165 lbs.   Deb: 4/24/43

YEAR	TM/L	G	AB	R	H	2B	3B	HR	RBI	BB	SO	AVG	OBP	SLG	PRO+	BR/A	SB	CS	SBR	FA	FR	G/POS	TPR
1943	Phi-N	4	11	0	1	0	0	0	0	1	0	.091	.167	.091	-26	-2	0			.857	0	/S-4	-0.1

■ JIM DELSING
Delsing, James Henry   b: 11/13/25, Rudolph, Wis.   BL/TR, 5'10", 175 lbs.   Deb: 4/21/48

YEAR	TM/L	G	AB	R	H	2B	3B	HR	RBI	BB	SO	AVG	OBP	SLG	PRO+	BR/A	SB	CS	SBR	FA	FR	G/POS	TPR
1948	Chi-A	20	63	5	12	0	0	0	5	5	12	.190	.261	.190	2	-7	0	0	0	1.000	-1	O-15	-0.9
1949	NY-A	9	20	5	7	1	0	1	3	1	2	.350	.381	.550	145	1	0	0	0	1.000	-2	/O-5	-0.1
1950	NY-A	12	10	2	4	0	0	0	2	2	0	.400	.500	.400	137	1	0	0	0	.000	0	H	0.1
	StL-A	69	209	25	55	5	2	0	15	20	23	.263	.328	.306	61	-12	1	4	-2	.994	2	O-53	-1.4
	Yr	81	219	27	59	5	2	0	17	22	23	.269	.336	.311	65	-11	1	4	-2	.994	2	O-53	-1.3
1951	StL-A	131	449	59	112	20	2	8	45	56	39	.249	.338	.356	85	-9	2	9	-5	.983	9	*O-124	-0.9
1952	StL-A	93	298	34	76	13	6	1	34	25	29	.255	.323	.349	85	-6	3	3	-1	.986	-1	O-85	-1.1
	Det-A	33	113	14	31	2	1	3	15	11	8	.274	.344	.389	103	0	1	0	0	.958	-0	O-32	-0.1
	Yr	126	411	48	107	15	7	4	49	36	37	.260	.329	.360	90	-6	4	3	-1	.979	-1	*O-117	-1.2
1953	Det-A	138	479	77	138	26	6	11	62	66	39	.288	.380	.436	121	15	1	3	-2	.992	-0	*O-133	0.7
1954	Det-A	122	371	39	92	24	2	6	38	49	38	.248	.337	.372	96	-2	4	4	-1	.996	-0	*O-108	-0.8
1955	Det-A	114	356	49	85	15	2	10	60	48	40	.239	.331	.376	92	-4	2	0	0	.995	-5	*O-101	-1.3
1956	Det-A	10	12	0	0	0	0	0	0	3	3	.000	.250	.000	-29	-2	0	0	0	1.000	-1	/O-3	-0.3
	Chi-A	55	41	11	5	3	0	0	2	10	13	.122	.294	.195	31	-4	1	0	0	.957	-8	O-29	-1.2
	Yr	65	53	11	5	3	0	0	2	13	16	.094	.284	.151	17	-6	1	0	0	.962	-8	O-32	-1.5
1960	KC-A	16	40	2	10	3	0	0	5	3	5	.250	.302	.325	69	-2	0	0	0	1.000	1	O-10	-0.1
Total 10		822	2461	322	627	112	21	40	286	299	251	.255	.340	.366	91	-31	15	23	-9	.989	-8	O-698	-7.4

■ JOE DeMAESTRI
DeMaestri, Joseph Paul "Oats"   b: 12/9/28, San Francisco, Cal.   BR/TR, 6', 174 lbs.   Deb: 4/19/51

YEAR	TM/L	G	AB	R	H	2B	3B	HR	RBI	BB	SO	AVG	OBP	SLG	PRO+	BR/A	SB	CS	SBR	FA	FR	G/POS	TPR
1951	Chi-A	56	74	8	15	0	2	1	3	5	11	.203	.253	.297	49	-6	0	4	-2	.959	6	S-27,2-11/3	-0.1
1952	StL-A	81	186	13	42	9	1	1	18	8	25	.226	.258	.301	54	-12	0	1	-1	.939	2	S-77/2-1,3	-0.7
1953	Phi-A	111	420	53	107	17	3	6	35	24	39	.255	.297	.352	72	-17	0	1	-1	.964	-16	*S-108	-2.7
1954	Phi-A	146	539	49	124	16	3	8	40	20	63	.230	.262	.315	57	-33	1	4	-2	.965	-6	*S-142/2-1,3	-3.0
1955	KC-A	123	457	42	114	14	1	6	37	20	47	.249	.285	.324	63	-25	3	5	-2	.964	-12	*S-122	-2.9
1956	KC-A	133	434	41	101	16	1	6	39	25	73	.233	.279	.316	57	-28	3	3	-1	.964	8	*S-132/2-2	-1.3
1957	KC-A☆	135	461	44	113	14	6	9	33	22	82	.245	.282	.360	73	-18	6	1	1	.980	-7	*S-134	-1.2
1958	KC-A	139	442	32	97	11	1	6	38	16	84	.219	.248	.290	47	-32	1	0	0	.980	11	*S-137	-1.0
1959	KC-A	118	352	31	86	16	5	6	34	28	65	.244	.307	.369	83	-8	1	0	0	.957	5	*S-115	0.6
1960	*NY-A	49	35	8	8	1	0	0	2	0	9	.229	.229	.257	33	-3	0	0	0	.952	7	2-19,S-17	0.4
1961	NY-A	30	41	1	6	0	0	0	2	0	13	.146	.146	.146	-23	-7	0	0	0	.981	7	S-18/2-5,3	0.1
Total 11		1121	3441	322	813	114	23	49	281	168	511	.236	.275	.325	62	-190	15	19	-7	.967	4	*S-1029/2-39,3	-11.8

■ FRANK DEMAREE
Demaree, Joseph Franklin (b: Joseph Franklin Dimaria)
b: 6/10/10, Winters, Cal.   d: 8/30/58, Los Angeles, Cal.   BR/TR, 5'11.5", 185 lbs.   Deb: 7/22/32

YEAR	TM/L	G	AB	R	H	2B	3B	HR	RBI	BB	SO	AVG	OBP	SLG	PRO+	BR/A	SB	CS	SBR	FA	FR	G/POS	TPR
1932	*Chi-N	23	56	4	14	3	0	0	6	2	7	.250	.288	.304	60	-3	0			1.000	-1	O-17	-0.5
1933	Chi-N	134	515	68	140	24	6	6	51	22	42	.272	.304	.377	94	-5	4			.965	0	*O-133	-1.2
1935	*Chi-N	107	385	60	125	19	4	2	66	26	23	.325	.369	.410	108	5	6			.973	-2	O-98	0.0
1936	Chi-N★	154	605	93	212	34	3	16	96	49	30	.350	.400	.496	137	31	4			.968	-2	*O-154	2.2
1937	Chi-N★	154	615	104	199	36	6	17	115	57	31	.324	.382	.485	129	24	6			.980	2	*O-154	2.0
1938	*Chi-N	129	476	63	130	15	7	8	62	45	34	.273	.341	.384	96	-2	8			.972	-8	*O-125	-1.4
1939	NY-N	150	560	68	170	27	2	11	79	66	40	.304	.381	.418	114	12	2			.986	-1	*O-150	0.6
1940	NY-N	121	460	68	139	18	6	7	61	45	39	.302	.364	.413	113	9	5			.980	-6	*O-119	-0.3
1941	NY-N	16	35	3	6	0	0	0	1	4	1	.171	.256	.171	22	-4	0			1.000	-0	O-10	-0.5
	Bos-N	48	113	20	26	5	2	2	15	12	5	.230	.304	.363	91	-2	2			1.000	-4	O-28	-0.7
	Yr	64	148	23	32	5	2	2	16	16	6	.216	.293	.318	74	-5	2			1.000	-5	O-38	-1.2
1942	Bos-N	64	187	18	42	5	0	3	24	17	10	.225	.289	.299	74	-6	2			1.000	4	O-49	-0.6
1943	*StL-N	39	86	5	25	2	0	0	9	8	4	.291	.351	.314	89	-1	1			1.000	-3	O-23	-0.6
1944	StL-A	51	51	4	13	2	2	0	6	6	3	.255	.333	.294	76	-1	0			.969	-3	O-16	-0.3
Total 12		1155	4144	578	1241	190	36	72	591	359	269	.299	.357	.415	110	57	33	0		.978	-22	*O-1076	-1.3

■ BILLY DeMARS
DeMars, William Lester "Kid"   b: 8/26/25, Brooklyn, N.Y.   BR/TR, 5'10", 160 lbs.   Deb: 5/18/48   C

YEAR	TM/L	G	AB	R	H	2B	3B	HR	RBI	BB	SO	AVG	OBP	SLG	PRO+	BR/A	SB	CS	SBR	FA	FR	G/POS	TPR
1948	Phi-A	18	29	3	5	0	1	0	3	5	3	.172	.294	.172	26	-3	0	0	0	.927	4	/S-9,2-1,3	0.1
1950	StL-A	61	178	25	44	5	1	0	13	22	13	.247	.330	.287	57	-11	0	1	-1	.933	-7	S-54/3-5	-1.4
1951	StL-A	1	4	1	1	0	0	0	0	1	0	.250	.400	.250	76	-0	0	0	0	1.000	-0	/S-1	0.0
Total 3		80	211	29	50	5	2	0	14	28	16	.237	.326	.270	53	-14	0	1	-1	.933	-4	/S-64,3-6,2	-1.3

■ JOHN DeMERIT
DeMerit, John Stephen "Thumper"   b: 1/8/36, West Bend, Wis.   BR/TR, 6'1.5", 195 lbs.   Deb: 6/18/57

YEAR	TM/L	G	AB	R	H	2B	3B	HR	RBI	BB	SO	AVG	OBP	SLG	PRO+	BR/A	SB	CS	SBR	FA	FR	G/POS	TPR
1957	*Mil-N	33	34	8	5	0	0	0	1	0	8	.147	.147	.147	-22	-6	0	0	0	1.000	-3	O-13	-0.9
1958	Mil-N	3	3	1	2	0	0	0	0	0	0	.667	.667	.667	278	1	0	0	0	1.000	-1	/O-2	0.0
1959	Mil-N	11	5	4	1	0	0	0	0	1	2	.200	.333	.200	51	-0	0	0	0	1.000	-0	/O-4	-0.1
1961	Mil-N	32	74	5	12	3	0	2	5	5	19	.162	.225	.284	36	-7	0	0	0	1.000	-8	/O-21	-0.8
1962	NY-N	14	16	3	3	0	0	1	1	2	4	.188	.278	.375	72	-1	0	0	0	1.000	-3	/O-9	-0.4
Total 5		93	132	21	23	3	0	3	7	8	33	.174	.227	.265	32	-13	0	0	0	1.000	-6	/O-49	-2.2

■ DON DEMETER
Demeter, Donald Lee   b: 6/25/35, Oklahoma City, Okla   BR/TR, 6'4", 190 lbs.   Deb: 9/18/56

YEAR	TM/L	G	AB	R	H	2B	3B	HR	RBI	BB	SO	AVG	OBP	SLG	PRO+	BR/A	SB	CS	SBR	FA	FR	G/POS	TPR
1956	Bro-N	3	3	1	1	0	0	1	1	0	1	.333	.333	1.333	297	1	0	0	0	1.000	-0	/O-1	0.0
1958	LA-N	43	106	11	20	2	0	5	8	5	32	.189	.225	.349	48	-8	2	3	-1	1.000	-4	O-39	-1.6
1959	*LA-N	139	371	55	95	11	1	18	70	16	87	.256	.298	.437	86	-8	5	6	-2	.983	-6	*O-124	-2.1
1960	LA-N	64	168	23	46	7	1	9	29	8	34	.274	.311	.488	108	0	1	6	-1	.989	-8	O-62	-1.0
1961	LA-N	15	29	3	5	0	0	1	2	3	6	.172	.250	.276	36	-3	0	0	0	.950	-1	O-14	-0.4
	Phi-N	106	382	54	98	18	4	20	68	19	74	.257	.300	.482	105	1	1	1	-3	.995	6	O-79,1-22	0.1
	Yr	121	411	57	103	18	4	21	70	22	80	.251	.297	.467	99	-2	1	1	-3	.990	5	O-93,1-22	-0.3
1962	Phi-N	153	550	85	169	24	3	29	107	41	93	.307	.366	.520	139	29	2	7	-4	.937	-13	*3-105,O-63/1	1.0
1963	Phi-N	154	515	63	133	20	2	22	83	19	93	.258	.308	.433	112	7	1	4	-2	1.000	-7	*O-119,3-43,1	-0.8
1964	Det-A	134	441	57	113	22	1	22	80	17	85	.256	.292	.460	104	0	4	1	1	1.000	-8	O-88,1-23	-0.6
1965	Det-A	122	389	50	108	16	4	16	58	23	65	.278	.328	.463	121	9	4	2	0	.988	-2	O-82,1-34	0.3
1966	Det-A	32	99	12	21	5	0	5	12	3	19	.212	.235	.414	81	-3	1	0	0	.985	5	O-27/1-4	0.1

YEAR	TM/L	G	AB	R	H	2B	3B	HR	RBI	BB	SO	AVG	OBP	SLG	PRO+	BR/A	SB	CS	SBR	FA	FR	G/POS	TPR
	Bos-A	73	226	31	66	13	1	9	29	5	42	.292	.310	.478	111	2	1	0	0	.982	-2	O-57/1-2	-0.1
	Yr	105	325	43	87	18	1	14	41	8	61	.268	.287	.458	102	-0	2	0	1	.984	3	O-84/1-6	0.0
1967	Bos-A	20	43	7	12	5	0	1	4	3	11	.279	.326	.465	122	1	0	0	0	1.000	-1	O-12/3-1	0.0
	Cle-A	51	121	15	25	4	0	5	12	6	16	.207	.256	.364	80	-3	0	0	0	.985	-2	O-35/3-1	-0.7
	Yr	71	164	22	37	9	0	6	16	9	27	.226	.274	.390	92	-2	0	0	0	.988	-3	O-47/3-2	-0.7
Total	11	1109	3443	467	912	147	17	163	563	180	658	.265	.309	.459	108	26	22	25	-8	.990	-37	O-802,3-150,1	-5.8

■ STEVE DEMETER
Demeter, Stephen b: 1/27/35, Homer City, Pa. BR/TR, 5'9.5", 185 lbs. Deb: 7/29/59 C

YEAR	TM/L	G	AB	R	H	2B	3B	HR	RBI	BB	SO	AVG	OBP	SLG	PRO+	BR/A	SB	CS	SBR	FA	FR	G/POS	TPR
1959	Det-A	11	18	1	2	1	0	0	0	0	1	.111	.111	.167	-24	-3	0	0	0	.909	1	/3-4	-0.2
1960	Cle-A	4	5	0	0	0	0	0	0	0	1	.000	.000	.000	-99	-1	0	0	0	1.000	0	/3-3	-0.1
Total	2	15	23	1	2	1	0	0	0	0	2	.087	.087	.130	-40	-4	0	0	0	.933	1	/3-7	-0.3

■ RAY DEMMITT
Demmitt, Charles Raymond b: 2/2/1884, Illiopolis, Ill. d: 2/19/56, Glen Ellyn, Ill. BL/TR, 5'8", 170 lbs. Deb: 4/12/09

YEAR	TM/L	G	AB	R	H	2B	3B	HR	RBI	BB	SO	AVG	OBP	SLG	PRO+	BR/A	SB	CS	SBR	FA	FR	G/POS	TPR
1909	NY-A	123	427	68	105	12	12	4	30	55		.246	.340	.358	120	11	16			.908	5	*O-109	1.3
1910	StL-A	10	23	4	4	1	0	0	2	3		.174	.296	.217	65	-1	0			1.000	1	/O-8	0.0
1914	Det-A	1	0	0	0	0	0	0	0	0	0	—	—	—	—		0			.000	0	R	0.0
	Chi-A	146	515	63	133	13	12	2	46	61	48	.258	.344	.342	108	6	12	20	-8	.953	-5	*O-142	-1.5
	Yr	147	515	63	133	13	12	2	46	61	48	.258	.344	.342	108	6	12	20	-8	.953	-5	*O-142	-1.5
1915	Chi-A	9	6	0	0	0	0	0	0	1	2	.000	.143	.000	-55	-1	0			1.000	-1	/O-3	-0.2
1917	StL-A	14	53	6	15	1	2	0	7	0	8	.283	.296	.377	109	0	1			1.000	-3	O-14	-0.4
1918	StL-A	116	405	45	114	23	5	1	66	38	35	.281	.346	.370	120	9	10			.951	7	*O-114	1.1
1919	StL-A	79	202	19	48	11	2	1	19	14	27	.238	.290	.327	71	-8	3			.868	-7	O-49	-2.0
Total	7	498	1631	205	419	61	33	8	165	172	120	.257	.334	.349	108	16	42	20		.934	-3	O-439	-1.7

■ GENE DeMONTREVILLE
DeMontreville, Eugene Napoleon b: 3/26/1874, St.Paul, Minn. d: 2/18/35, Memphis, Tenn. BR/TR, 5'8", 165 lbs. Deb: 8/20/1894 F

YEAR	TM/L	G	AB	R	H	2B	3B	HR	RBI	BB	SO	AVG	OBP	SLG	PRO+	BR/A	SB	CS	SBR	FA	FR	G/POS	TPR
1894	Pit-N	2	8	0	2	0	0	0	0	0	4	.250	.333	.250	43	-1	0			.889	-1	/S-2	-0.1
1895	Was-N	12	46	7	10	1	3	0	9	3	4	.217	.265	.370	63	-3	5			.929	4	S-12	0.1
1896	Was-N	133	533	94	183	24	5	8	77	29	27	.343	.381	.452	119	13	28			.890	16	*S-133	2.8
1897	Was-N	133	566	92	193	27	8	3	93	21		.341	.366	.433	111	7	30			.886	10	*S-99,2-33	1.8
1898	Bal-N	151	567	93	186	19	2	0	86	52		.328	.394	.369	117	14	49			.944	0	*2-123,S-28	2.2
1899	Chi-N	82	310	43	87	6	3	0	40	17		.281	.328	.319	80	-8	26			.902	9	S-82	0.7
	Bal-N	60	240	40	67	13	4	1	36	10		.279	.313	.379	85	-6	21			.961	9	2-60	0.5
	Yr	142	550	83	154	19	7	1	76	27		.280	.322	.345	82	-14	47			.902	18	S-82,2-60	1.2
1900	Bro-N	69	234	34	57	8	1	0	28	10		.244	.283	.286	54	-15	21			.952	0	2-48,S-12/301	-1.1
1901	Bos-N	140	577	83	173	14	4	5	72	17		.300	.321	.364	90	-9	25			.954	5	*2-120,3-20	0.1
1902	Bos-N	124	481	51	125	16	5	0	53	12		.260	.278	.314	82	-12	23			.940	-17	*2-112,S-10	-2.5
1903	Was-A	12	44	0	12	2	0	0	3	0		.273	.273	.318	75	-1	0			.931	-4	2-11/S-1	-0.6
1904	StL-A	4	9	0	1	0	0	0	0	2		.111	.273	.111	25	-1	0			1.000	-1	/2-3	-0.1
Total	11	922	3615	537	1096	130	35	17	497	174	35	.303	.340	.373	97	-21	228			.948	31	2-510,S-379/310	3.8

■ LEE DeMONTREVILLE
DeMontreville, Leon b: 9/23/1879, St.Paul, Minn. d: 3/22/62, Pelham Manor, N.Y. BR/TR, 5'7", 140 lbs. Deb: 7/10/03 F

YEAR	TM/L	G	AB	R	H	2B	3B	HR	RBI	BB	SO	AVG	OBP	SLG	PRO+	BR/A	SB	CS	SBR	FA	FR	G/POS	TPR
1903	StL-N	26	70	8	17	3	1	0	7	3		.243	.338	.314	89	-1	3			.901	-3	S-15/2-4,O	-0.3

■ RICK DEMPSEY
Dempsey, John Rikard b: 9/13/49, Fayetteville, Tenn. BR/TR, 6', 190 lbs. Deb: 9/23/69

YEAR	TM/L	G	AB	R	H	2B	3B	HR	RBI	BB	SO	AVG	OBP	SLG	PRO+	BR/A	SB	CS	SBR	FA	FR	G/POS	TPR
1969	Min-A	5	6	1	3	1	0	0	0	1	0	.500	.571	.667	240	1	0	0	0	.833	-1	/C-3	0.0
1970	Min-A	5	7	1	0	0	0	0	0	0	1	.000	.125	.000	-62	-2	0	0	0	.923	0	/C-3	-0.2
1971	Min-A	6	13	2	4	1	0	0	0	1	1	.308	.357	.385	107	0	0	0	0	.944	2	/C-6	0.2
1972	Min-A	25	40	0	8	1	0	0	0	6	8	.200	.304	.225	56	-2	0	0	0	.986	-1	C-23	-0.3
1973	NY-A	6	11	0	2	0	0	0	0	1	3	.182	.250	.182	24	-1	0	0	0	.818	-2	/C-5	-0.3
1974	NY-A	43	109	12	26	3	0	0	12	8	7	.239	.291	.321	78	-3	1	0	0	.978	4	C-31/O-2,D	0.2
1975	NY-A	71	145	18	38	8	0	1	11	21	15	.262	.355	.338	100	1	0	0	0	.977	3	C-19,D-18/O3	0.3
1976	NY-A	21	42	1	5	0	0	0	2	5	4	.119	.213	.119	-1	-5	0	0	0	1.000	1	/C-9,O-4	-0.3
	Bal-A	59	174	11	37	2	0	0	10	13	17	.213	.275	.224	50	-11	1	1	-0	.987	5	C-58/O-3	-0.5
	Yr	80	216	12	42	2	0	0	12	18	21	.194	.263	.204	40	-16	1	1	-0	.988	7	C-67/O-7	-0.8
1977	Bal-A	91	270	27	61	7	4	3	34	34	34	.226	.317	.315	78	-8	2	3	-1	.977	-2	C-91	-0.9
1978	Bal-A	136	441	41	114	25	0	6	32	48	54	.259	.331	.356	99	-0	7	3	0	.985	-5	*C-135	-0.1
1979	*Bal-A	124	368	48	88	23	0	6	41	38	37	.239	.310	.351	81	-10	0	1	-1	.990	19	*C-124	1.2
1980	Bal-A	119	362	51	95	26	3	9	40	36	45	.262	.334	.425	108	4	3	1	0	.987	9	*C-112/O-6,1D	1.7
1981	Bal-A	92	251	24	54	10	1	6	15	32	36	.215	.306	.335	85	-5	0	1	-1	.998	3	C-90/D-1	0.1
1982	Bal-A	125	344	35	88	15	1	5	36	46	37	.256	.344	.349	91	-3	0	3	-2	.991	0	*C-124/D-1	0.0
1983	*Bal-A	128	347	33	80	16	2	4	32	40	54	.231	.315	.323	78	-10	1	1	-0	.997	21	*C-128	1.5
1984	Bal-A	109	330	37	76	11	0	11	34	40	58	.230	.315	.364	89	-5	1	2	-1	.992	-4	*C-108	-0.5
1985	Bal-A	132	362	54	92	19	0	12	52	50	87	.254	.346	.406	108	5	0	1	-1	.987	-11	*C-131	0.0
1986	Bal-A	122	327	42	68	15	1	13	29	45	78	.208	.309	.379	87	-6	1	0	0	.990	5	*C-121	0.6
1987	Cle-A	60	141	16	25	10	0	1	9	23	29	.177	.297	.270	51	-10	0	0	0	.984	1	C-59	-0.5
1988	*LA-N	77	167	25	42	13	0	7	30	25	44	.251	.349	.455	133	7	1	0	0	.989	5	C-74	1.7
1989	LA-N	79	151	16	27	7	0	4	16	30	37	.179	.319	.305	80	-3	1	0	0	.984	3	C-62	0.3
1990	LA-N	62	128	13	25	5	0	2	15	23	29	.195	.318	.281	68	-5	1	0	0	.992	0	C-53	-0.2
1991	Mil-A	61	147	15	34	5	0	2	21	23	20	.231	.335	.347	91	-1	0	1	-1	.993	4	C-56/P-2,1	0.4
1992	Bal-A	8	9	2	1	0	0	0	0	2	1	.111	.273	.111	11	-1	0	0	0	1.000	-1	/C-8	-0.2
Total	24	1766	4692	525	1093	223	12	96	471	592	736	.233	.321	.347	88	-72	20	19	-5	.988	59	*C-1633/O-23,D1P3	4.2

■ TOD DENNEHEY
Dennehey, Thomas Francis b: 5/12/1899, Philadelphia, Pa. d: 8/8/77, Philadelphia, Pa. BL/TL, 5'10", 180 lbs. Deb: 4/21/23

YEAR	TM/L	G	AB	R	H	2B	3B	HR	RBI	BB	SO	AVG	OBP	SLG	PRO+	BR/A	SB	CS	SBR	FA	FR	G/POS	TPR
1923	Phi-N	9	24	4	7	2	0	0	2	1	3	.292	.320	.375	74	-1	0	0	0	1.000	-1	/O-9	-0.2

■ OTTO DENNING
Denning, Otto George "Dutch" b: 12/28/12, Hays, Kan. d: 5/25/92, Chicago, Ill. BR/TR, 6', 180 lbs. Deb: 4/15/42

YEAR	TM/L	G	AB	R	H	2B	3B	HR	RBI	BB	SO	AVG	OBP	SLG	PRO+	BR/A	SB	CS	SBR	FA	FR	G/POS	TPR
1942	Cle-A	92	214	15	45	14	0	1	19	18	14	.210	.275	.290	62	-11	0	0	0	.992	-2	C-78/O-2	-0.9
1943	Cle-A	37	129	8	31	6	0	0	13	5	1	.240	.269	.287	67	-6	3	1	0	.966	-3	1-34	-1.2
Total	2	129	343	23	76	20	0	1	32	23	15	.222	.272	.289	64	-17	3	1	0	.99	-6	/C-78,1-34,O	-2.1

■ JERRY DENNY
Denny, Jeremiah Dennis (b: Jeremiah Dennis Eldridge) b: 3/16/1859, New York, N.Y. d: 8/16/27, Houston, Tex. BR/TR, 5'11.5", 180 lbs. Deb: 5/2/1881

YEAR	TM/L	G	AB	R	H	2B	3B	HR	RBI	BB	SO	AVG	OBP	SLG	PRO+	BR/A	SB	CS	SBR	FA	FR	G/POS	TPR
1881	Pro-N	85	320	38	77	16	2	1	24	5	44	.241	.252	.313	78	-8				.840	6	*3-85	-0.1
1882	Pro-N	84	329	54	81	10	9	2	42	4	46	.246	.255	.350	92	-3				.861	13	*3-84	1.0
1883	Pro-N	98	393	73	108	26	8	8	55	9	48	.275	.291	.443	116	6				.876	10	*3-98	1.4
1884	*Pro-N	110	439	57	109	22	9	6	59	14	58	.248	.272	.380	105	2				.874	-2	*3-99/1-9,2C	0.0
1885	Pro-N	83	318	40	71	14	4	3	24	12	53	.223	.252	.321	88	-4				.869	-0	*3-83	-0.3
1886	StL-N	119	475	58	122	24	6	9	62	14	68	.257	.278	.389	108	4	16			.895	23	*3-117/S-3	2.6
1887	Ind-N	122	510	86	165	34	12	11	97	13	22	.324	.344	.502	137	23	29			.889	23	*3-116/S-4,O2	4.0
1888	Ind-N	126	524	92	137	27	7	12	63	9	79	.261	.277	.408	114	6	32			.894	25	*3-96,S-25/20P	3.2
1889	Ind-N	133	578	96	163	24	0	18	112	27	51	.282	.314	.417	101	-2				.913	12	*3-123/2-7,S	1.3
1890	NY-N	114	437	50	93	18	7	3	42	28	62	.213	.270	.307	68	-19	11			.889	5	*3-106/S-7,2	-0.9
1891	NY-N	4	16	0	4	1	0	0	1	0	3	.250	.250	.313	66	-1	2			.700	-3	/3-4	-0.3
	Cle-N	36	138	17	31	5	0	0	21	12	23	.225	.291	.261	59	-7	3			.884	-3	3-29/O-7	-0.8
	Phi-N	19	73	5	21	1	0	0	11	4	6	.288	.325	.329	88	-1	1			.977	-1	1-12/3-7	-0.2

YEAR	TM/L	G	AB	R	H	2B	3B	HR	RBI	BB	SO	AVG	OBP	SLG	PRO+	BR/A	SB	CS	SBR	FA	FR	G/POS	TPR
	Yr	59	227	22	56	7	1	0	33	16	32	.247	.299	.286	69	-9	6			.876	-8	3-40,1-12/O	-1.3
1893	Lou-N	44	175	22	43	5	4	1	22	9	15	.246	.283	.337	70	-8	4			.920	1	S-42/3-2	-0.5
1894	Lou-N	60	221	26	61	11	7	0	32	13	12	.276	.325	.389	77	-9	10			.874	3	3-60	-0.5
Total	13	1237	4946	714	1286	238	76	74	667	173	602	.260	.287	.384	99	-22	130			.882	109	*3-1109/S-86,120PC	9.9

■ DREW DENSON   Denson, Andrew b: 11/16/65, Cincinnati, Ohio BB/TR, 6'5", 210 lbs. Deb: 9/13/89

YEAR	TM/L	G	AB	R	H	2B	3B	HR	RBI	BB	SO	AVG	OBP	SLG	PRO+	BR/A	SB	CS	SBR	FA	FR	G/POS	TPR
1989	Atl-N	12	36	1	9	1	0	0	5	3	9	.250	.308	.278	67	-1	1	0	0	.988	2	1-12	0.0
1993	Chi-A	4	5	0	1	0	0	0	0	0	2	.200	.200	.200	8	-1	0	0	0	.800	-0	/1-3	-0.1
Total	2	16	41	1	10	1	0	0	5	3	11	.244	.295	.268	60	-2	1	0	0	.977	2	/1-15	-0.1

■ BUCKY DENT   Dent, Russell Earl (b: Russell Earl O'Dey) b: 11/25/51, Savannah, Ga. BR/TR, 5'11", 181 lbs. Deb: 6/1/73 MC

YEAR	TM/L	G	AB	R	H	2B	3B	HR	RBI	BB	SO	AVG	OBP	SLG	PRO+	BR/A	SB	CS	SBR	FA	FR	G/POS	TPR
1973	Chi-A	40	117	17	29	2	0	0	10	10	18	.248	.313	.265	62	-6	2	3	-1	.963	5	S-36/2-3,3	0.3
1974	Chi-A	154	496	55	136	15	3	5	45	28	48	.274	.317	.347	89	-7	3	4	-2	.972	9	*S-154	2.0
1975	Chi-A★	157	602	52	159	29	4	3	58	36	48	.264	.306	.341	81	-15	2	4	-2	**.981**	27	*S-157	2.7
1976	Chi-A	158	562	44	138	18	4	2	52	43	45	.246	.301	.302	77	-16	3	5	-2	.976	-6	*S-158	-0.5
1977	*NY-A	158	477	54	118	18	4	8	49	39	28	.247	.306	.352	80	-14	1	1	-0	.974	-11	*S-158	-0.8
1978	NY-A	123	379	40	92	11	1	5	40	23	24	.243	.289	.317	72	-14	3	1	0	.981	-8	*S-123	-0.7
1979	NY-A	141	431	47	99	14	2	2	32	37	30	.230	.292	.285	58	-25	0	0	0	.977	32	*S-141	2.2
1980	*NY-A★	141	489	57	128	26	2	5	52	48	37	.262	.330	.354	89	-7	0	3	-2	**.982**	13	*S-141	2.1
1981	NY-A★	73	227	22	54	11	0	7	27	19	17	.238	.302	.379	97	-1	0	1	-1	.970	-2	S-73	0.4
1982	NY-A	59	160	11	27	1	1	0	9	8	11	.169	.208	.188	50	-20	0	0	0	.962	17	S-58	0.2
	Tex-A	46	146	16	32	9	0	1	14	13	10	.219	.283	.301	64	-7	0	0	0	.980	-2	S-45	-0.5
	Yr	105	306	27	59	10	1	1	23	21	21	.193	.245	.242	35	-27	0	0	0	.970	15	*S-103	-0.3
1983	Tex-A	131	417	36	99	15	2	2	34	23	31	.237	.299	.297	60	-23	3	7	-3	**.979**	-8	*S-129/D-1	-2.2
1984	KC-A	11	9	2	3	0	0	0	1	1	2	.333	.400	.333	105	0	0	0	0	1.000	-1	/S-9,3-2	0.0
Total	12	1392	4512	451	1114	169	23	40	423	328	349	.247	.300	.321	74	-155	17	29	-12	.976	66	*S-1382/3-3,2D	5.2

■ SAM DENTE   Dente, Samuel Joseph "Blackie" b: 4/26/22, Harrison, N.J. BR/TR, 5'11", 175 lbs. Deb: 7/10/47

YEAR	TM/L	G	AB	R	H	2B	3B	HR	RBI	BB	SO	AVG	OBP	SLG	PRO+	BR/A	SB	CS	SBR	FA	FR	G/POS	TPR
1947	Bos-A	46	168	14	39	4	2	0	11	19	15	.232	.310	.280	60	-9	0	1	-1	.939	-3	3-46	-1.3
1948	StL-A	98	267	26	72	11	2	0	22	22	8	.270	.328	.326	72	-11	1	3	-2	.958	-8	S-76/3-6	-1.0
1949	Was-A	153	590	48	161	24	4	1	53	31	24	.273	.309	.332	71	-26	4	4	-1	.957	-9	*S-153	-2.6
1950	Was-A	155	603	56	144	20	5	2	59	39	19	.239	.286	.299	52	-45	1	1	0	.952	1	*S-128,2-29	-3.1
1951	Was-A	88	273	21	65	8	1	0	29	25	10	.238	.302	.275	58	-16	3	0	1	.962	3	S-65,2-10/3	-0.7
1952	Chi-A	62	145	12	32	4	1	0	11	5	8	.221	.257	.234	37	-12	0	0	0	.942	2	S-27,3-18/201	-0.9
1953	Chi-A	2	0	0	0	0	0	0	0	0	0	—	—	—	—	0	0	0	0	.000	0	/S-1	0.0
1954	*Cle-A	68	169	18	45	7	1	1	19	14	4	.266	.322	.337	79	-5	0	0	0	.971	-3	S-60/2-7	-0.4
1955	Cle-A	73	105	10	27	4	0	0	10	12	8	.257	.333	.295	68	-4	0	0	0	.976	7	S-53,3-13/2	0.5
Total	9	745	2320	205	585	78	16	4	214	167	96	.252	.303	.305	62	-128	9	9	-3	.958	-5	S-563/3-88,201	-9.5

■ MIKE DePANGHER   DePangher, Michael Anthony b: 9/11/1858, Marysville, Cal. d: 7/7/15, San Francisco, Cal BL, 5'8", 190 lbs. Deb: 8/8/1884

YEAR	TM/L	G	AB	R	H	2B	3B	HR	RBI	BB	SO	AVG	OBP	SLG	PRO+	BR/A	SB	CS	SBR	FA	FR	G/POS	TPR
1884	Phi-N	4	10	0	2	0	0	0	1	3		.200	.273	.200	54	-0				.920	1	/C-4	0.0

■ TONY DePHILLIPS   DePhillips, Anthony Andrew b: 9/20/12, New York, N.Y. d: 5/5/94, Port Jefferson, N.Y. BR/TR, 6'2", 185 lbs. Deb: 4/25/43

YEAR	TM/L	G	AB	R	H	2B	3B	HR	RBI	BB	SO	AVG	OBP	SLG	PRO+	BR/A	SB	CS	SBR	FA	FR	G/POS	TPR
1943	Cin-N	35	20	0	2	1	0	0	2	1	5	.100	.143	.150	-16	-3	0			.981	5	C-35	0.3

■ GENE DERBY   Derby, Eugene A. b: 2/1860, New Hampshire 5'7", 160 lbs. Deb: 9/3/1885

YEAR	TM/L	G	AB	R	H	2B	3B	HR	RBI	BB	SO	AVG	OBP	SLG	PRO+	BR/A	SB	CS	SBR	FA	FR	G/POS	TPR
1885	Bal-a	10	31	4	4	0	0	0	1			.129	.182	.129	-1	-3				.952	1	/C-9,O-1	-0.2

■ BOB DERNIER   Dernier, Robert Eugene b: 1/5/57, Kansas City, Mo. BR/TR, 6', 165 lbs. Deb: 9/7/80

YEAR	TM/L	G	AB	R	H	2B	3B	HR	RBI	BB	SO	AVG	OBP	SLG	PRO+	BR/A	SB	CS	SBR	FA	FR	G/POS	TPR
1980	Phi-N	10	7	5	4	0	0	0	1	1	0	.571	.625	.571	224	1	3	0	1	1.000	0	/O-3	0.3
1981	Phi-N	10	4	0	3	0	0	0	0	0	0	.750	.750	.750	313	1	2	1	0	1.000	-2	/O-5	-0.1
1982	Phi-N	122	370	56	92	10	2	4	21	36	69	.249	.317	.319	77	-11	42	12	5	.981	-0	*O-119	-0.9
1983	*Phi-N	122	221	41	51	10	0	1	15	18	21	.231	.289	.290	61	-11	35	7	6	.988	-11	*O-107	-1.9
1984	*Chi-N	143	536	94	149	26	5	3	32	63	60	.278	.356	.362	94	-3	45	17	3	.986	5	*O-140	0.1
1985	Chi-N	121	469	63	119	20	3	1	21	40	44	.254	.316	.316	70	-18	31	8	5	.972	9	*O-116	-0.9
1986	Chi-N	108	324	32	73	14	1	4	18	22	41	.225	.275	.312	57	-19	27	2	7	.987	1	*O-105	-1.4
1987	Chi-N	93	199	38	63	4	4	8	21	19	19	.317	.379	.497	125	7	16	7	1	.989	-12	O-71	-0.5
1988	Phi-N	68	166	19	48	3	1	0	10	9	19	.289	.330	.337	90	-2	13	6	0	.980	-4	O-54	-0.8
1989	Phi-N	107	187	26	32	5	0	1	13	14	28	.171	.229	.214	27	-18	4	3	-1	.970	-13	O-74	-3.5
Total	10	904	2483	374	634	92	16	23	152	222	301	.255	.318	.333	77	-73	218	63	28	.982	-26	O-794	-9.6

■ CLAUD DERRICK   Derrick, Claud Lester "Deek" b: 6/11/1886, Burton, Ga. d: 7/15/74, Clayton, Ga. BR/TR, 6', 175 lbs. Deb: 9/8/10

YEAR	TM/L	G	AB	R	H	2B	3B	HR	RBI	BB	SO	AVG	OBP	SLG	PRO+	BR/A	SB	CS	SBR	FA	FR	G/POS	TPR
1910	Phi-A	2	1	0	0	0	0	0	0	0		.000	.000	.000	-99	-0	0			.500	-0	/S-1	-0.1
1911	Phi-A	36	100	14	23	1	2	0	5	7		.230	.294	.280	61	-5	7			.960	1	2-21/S-6,13	-0.5
1912	Phi-A	21	58	7	14	0	1	0	7	5		.241	.313	.276	71	-2	1			.884	1	S-18	0.0
1913	NY-A	23	65	7	19	1	0	1	7	5	8	.292	.352	.354	106	1	2			.874	3	S-17/3-4,2	0.2
1914	Cin-N	3	6	2	2	1	0	0	1	0		.333	.333	.500	142	0	0			.889	0	/S-2	0.1
	Chi-N	28	96	5	21	3	1	0	13	5	13	.219	.257	.271	57	-5	2			.895	3	/S-28	-0.1
	Yr	31	102	7	23	4	1	0	14	5	13	.225	.262	.284	62	-5	3			.894	3	S-30	0.0
Total	5	113	326	35	79	6	4	1	33	22	21	.242	.298	.294	72	-12	13			.892	4	/S-72,2-22,31	-0.4

■ MIKE DERRICK   Derrick, James Michael b: 9/19/43, Columbia, S.C. BL/TR, 6', 190 lbs. Deb: 4/9/70

YEAR	TM/L	G	AB	R	H	2B	3B	HR	RBI	BB	SO	AVG	OBP	SLG	PRO+	BR/A	SB	CS	SBR	FA	FR	G/POS	TPR
1970	Bos-A	24	33	3	7	1	0	0	5	0	11	.212	.212	.242	23	-3	0	1	-1	1.000	0	/O-2,1-1	-0.4

■ RUSS DERRY   Derry, Alva Russell b: 10/7/16, Princeton, Mo. BL/TR, 6'1", 180 lbs. Deb: 7/4/44

YEAR	TM/L	G	AB	R	H	2B	3B	HR	RBI	BB	SO	AVG	OBP	SLG	PRO+	BR/A	SB	CS	SBR	FA	FR	G/POS	TPR
1944	NY-A	38	114	14	29	3	0	4	14	20	19	.254	.366	.386	111	2	1	0	0	.949	-1	O-28	0.0
1945	NY-A	78	253	37	57	6	2	13	45	34	49	.225	.312	.419	107	1	1	0	0	.978	0	O-68	-0.2
1946	Phi-A	69	184	17	38	8	5	0	14	27	54	.207	.311	.304	73	-6	0	0	0	.985	4	O-50	-0.5
1949	StL-N	2	2	0	0	0	0	0	0	0	2	.000	.000	.000	-96	-1	0			.000	0	H	-0.1
Total	4	187	553	68	124	17	7	17	73	78	124	.224	.322	.373	95	-4	2	0		.976	3	O-146	-0.8

■ JOE DeSA   DeSa, Joseph b: 7/27/59, Honolulu, Hawaii d: 12/20/86, San Juan, P.R. BL/TL, 5'11", 170 lbs. Deb: 9/6/80

YEAR	TM/L	G	AB	R	H	2B	3B	HR	RBI	BB	SO	AVG	OBP	SLG	PRO+	BR/A	SB	CS	SBR	FA	FR	G/POS	TPR
1980	StL-N	7	11	0	3	0	0	0	0	0	2	.273	.273	.273	51	-1	0	0	0	1.000	-0	/1-1,O-1	-0.1
1985	Chi-A	28	44	5	8	2	0	2	7	3	6	.182	.234	.364	58	-3	0	0	0	1.000	1	/1-9,O-1,D	-0.2
Total	2	35	55	5	11	2	0	2	7	3	8	.200	.241	.345	57	-3	0	0	0	1.000	1	/1-10,D-4,O	-0.3

■ GENE DESAUTELS   Desautels, Eugene Abraham "Red" b: 6/13/07, Worcester, Mass. BR/TR, 5'11", 170 lbs. Deb: 6/22/30

YEAR	TM/L	G	AB	R	H	2B	3B	HR	RBI	BB	SO	AVG	OBP	SLG	PRO+	BR/A	SB	CS	SBR	FA	FR	G/POS	TPR
1930	Det-A	42	126	13	24	4	2	0	9	7	9	.190	.239	.254	25	-15	2	0	1	.996	9	C-42	-0.3
1931	Det-A	3	11	1	1	0	0	0	0	0	1	.091	.091	.091	-50	-2	0	0	0	1.000	-1	/C-3	-0.2
1932	Det-A	28	72	8	17	2	0	0	2	13	11	.236	.360	.264	62	-4	0	0	0	.984	4	C-24	0.2
1933	Det-A	30	42	5	6	1	0	0	4	4	6	.143	.234	.167	8	-6	0	0	0	.976	2	C-30	-0.2
1937	Bos-A	96	305	33	89	24	3	0	35	25	29	.292	.325	.295	55	-20	1	2	1	**.993**	4	C-94	-1.2
1938	Bos-A	108	333	47	97	16	2	2	48	57	31	.291	.396	.369	89	-4	1	1	-0	.985	6	*C-108	0.6
1939	Bos-A	76	226	26	55	14	0	1	21	33	13	.243	.340	.305	64	-12	3			.994	10	C-73	0.2
1940	Bos-A	71	222	19	50	7	1	0	17	32	13	.225	.328	.266	54	-14	0	1	-1	.992	-3	C-70	-1.2
1941	Cle-A	66	189	20	38	5	1	1	17	14	12	.201	.260	.254	38	-17	1	0	0	.997	6	C-66	-0.6

YEAR	TM/L	G	AB	R	H	2B	3B	HR	RBI	BB	SO	AVG	OBP	SLG	PRO+	BR/A	SB	CS	SBR	FA	FR	G/POS	TPR
1942	Cle-A	62	162	14	40	5	0	0	9	12	13	.247	.303	.278	68	-7	1	0	0	.975	-8	C-61	-1.1
1943	Cle-A	68	185	14	38	6	1	0	19	11	16	.205	.250	.249	49	-12	2	0	1	.982	2	C-66	-0.7
1945	Cle-A	10	9	1	1	0	0	0	0	1	1	.111	.200	.111	-9	-1	0	0	0	1.000	0	C-10	-0.1
1946	Phi-A	52	130	10	28	3	1	0	13	12	16	.215	.282	.254	51	-8	1	1	-0	.989	2	C-52	-0.5
Total	13	712	2012	211	469	73	11	3	187	232	168	.233	.315	.285	57	-122	12	6	0	.989	31	C-699	-5.1

◼ DELINO DeSHIELDS
DeShields, Delino Lamont b: 1/15/69, Seaford, Del. BL/TR, 6'1", 170 lbs. Deb: 4/9/90

YEAR	TM/L	G	AB	R	H	2B	3B	HR	RBI	BB	SO	AVG	OBP	SLG	PRO+	BR/A	SB	CS	SBR	FA	FR	G/POS	TPR
1990	Mon-N	129	499	69	144	28	6	4	45	66	96	.289	.376	.393	116	13	42	22	-1	.981	-8	*2-128	0.7
1991	Mon-N	151	563	83	134	15	4	10	51	95	151	.238	.350	.332	94	-1	56	23	3	.962	-22	*2-148	-1.7
1992	Mon-N	135	530	82	155	19	8	7	56	54	108	.292	.361	.398	116	12	46	15	5	.976	-22	*2-134	-0.3
1993	Mon-N	123	481	75	142	17	7	2	29	72	64	.295	.390	.372	101	4	43	10	7	.983	-1	*2-123	1.3
1994	LA-N	89	320	51	80	11	3	2	33	54	53	.250	.358	.322	84	-6	27	7	4	.986	6	2-88,S-10	0.7
Total	5	627	2393	360	655	90	28	25	214	341	472	.274	.367	.366	103	22	214	77	18	.977	-47	2-621/S-10	0.7

◼ ORESTES DESTRADE
Destrade, Orestes (Cucuas) b: 5/8/62, Santiago, Cuba BB/TR, 6'4", 210 lbs. Deb: 9/11/87

YEAR	TM/L	G	AB	R	H	2B	3B	HR	RBI	BB	SO	AVG	OBP	SLG	PRO+	BR/A	SB	CS	SBR	FA	FR	G/POS	TPR
1987	NY-A	9	19	5	5	0	0	0	1	5	5	.263	.417	.263	87	-0	0	0	0	1.000	-0	/1-3,D-2	0.0
1988	Pit-N	36	47	2	7	1	0	1	3	5	17	.149	.231	.234	34	-4	0	0	0	1.000	-1	/1-8	-0.6
1993	Fla-N	153	569	61	145	20	3	20	87	58	130	.255	.327	.406	90	-8	0	2	-1	.987	-7	*1-152	-2.9
1994	Fla-N	39	130	12	27	4	0	5	15	19	32	.208	.318	.354	71	-5	1	0	0	.983	-3	1-37	-1.1
Total	4	237	765	80	184	25	3	26	106	87	184	.241	.322	.383	84	-18	1	2	-1	.987	-11	1-200/D-2	-4.6

◼ BOB DETHERAGE
Detherage, Robert Wayne b: 9/20/54, Springfield, Mo. BR/TR, 6', 180 lbs. Deb: 4/11/80

YEAR	TM/L	G	AB	R	H	2B	3B	HR	RBI	BB	SO	AVG	OBP	SLG	PRO+	BR/A	SB	CS	SBR	FA	FR	G/POS	TPR
1980	KC-A	20	26	2	8	2	0	1	7	1	4	.308	.333	.500	124	1	1	1	-0	1.000	-7	O-20	-0.7

◼ GEORGE DeTORE
DeTore, George Francis b: 11/11/06, Utica, N.Y. d: 2/7/91, Utica, N.Y. BR/TR, 5'8", 170 lbs. Deb: 9/14/30 C

YEAR	TM/L	G	AB	R	H	2B	3B	HR	RBI	BB	SO	AVG	OBP	SLG	PRO+	BR/A	SB	CS	SBR	FA	FR	G/POS	TPR
1930	Cle-A	3	12	1	2	1	0	0	2	0	2	.167	.167	.250	4	-2	0	0	0	.750	-2	/3-3	-0.3
1931	Cle-A	30	56	3	15	6	0	0	7	8	2	.268	.359	.375	88	-1	0	2	-1	.958	4	3-13,S-10/2	0.3
Total	2	33	68	3	17	7	0	0	9	8	4	.250	.329	.353	74	-3	0	2	-1	.929	2	/3-16,S-10,2	0.0

◼ DUCKY DETWEILER
Detweiler, Robert Sterling b: 2/15/19, Trumbauersville, Pa. BR/TR, 5'11", 178 lbs. Deb: 9/12/42

YEAR	TM/L	G	AB	R	H	2B	3B	HR	RBI	BB	SO	AVG	OBP	SLG	PRO+	BR/A	SB	CS	SBR	FA	FR	G/POS	TPR
1942	Bos-N	12	44	3	14	2	1	0	5	2	7	.318	.348	.409	123	1	0			.929	-4	3-12	-0.3
1946	Bos-N	1	1	0	0	0	0	0	0	0	0	.000	.000	.000	-99	-0	0			.000	0	H	0.0
Total	2	13	45	3	14	2	1	0	5	2	7	.311	.340	.400	118	1	0			.929	-4	/3-12	-0.3

◼ MIKE DEVEREAUX
Devereaux, Michael b: 4/10/63, Casper, Wyo. BR/TR, 6' ", 195 lbs. Deb: 9/2/87

YEAR	TM/L	G	AB	R	H	2B	3B	HR	RBI	BB	SO	AVG	OBP	SLG	PRO+	BR/A	SB	CS	SBR	FA	FR	G/POS	TPR
1987	LA-N	19	54	7	12	3	0	0	4	3	10	.222	.263	.278	45	-4	3	1	0	1.000	-2	O-18	-0.6
1988	LA-N	30	43	4	5	1	0	0	2	2	10	.116	.156	.140	-15	-6	0	1	-1	1.000	-5	O-26	-1.4
1989	Bal-A	122	391	55	104	14	3	8	46	36	60	.266	.331	.379	103	1	22	11	0	.983	-4	*O-112/D-5	-0.5
1990	Bal-A	108	367	48	88	18	1	12	49	28	48	.240	.294	.392	93	-5	13	12	-3	.983	6	*O-104/D-3	-0.5
1991	Bal-A	149	608	82	158	27	10	19	59	47	115	.260	.315	.431	109	5	16	9	-1	.993	12	*O-149	1.2
1992	Bal-A	156	653	76	180	29	11	24	107	44	94	.276	.325	.464	116	11	10	8	-2	.989	5	*O-155	1.2
1993	Bal-A	131	527	72	132	31	3	14	75	43	99	.250	.308	.400	85	-12	3	3	-1	.988	-0	*O-130	-1.3
1994	Bal-A	85	301	35	61	8	2	9	33	22	72	.203	.259	.332	48	-24	1	2	-1	.995	0	O-84	-2.5
Total	8	800	2944	379	740	131	30	86	375	225	508	.251	.307	.404	93	-34	68	47	-8	.989	14	O-778/D-8	-4.4

◼ JIM DEVINE
Devine, Walter James b: 10/5/1858, Brooklyn, N.Y. d: 1/11/05, Syracuse, N.Y. TL , Deb: 5/9/1883

YEAR	TM/L	G	AB	R	H	2B	3B	HR	RBI	BB	SO	AVG	OBP	SLG	PRO+	BR/A	SB	CS	SBR	FA	FR	G/POS	TPR
1883	Bal-a	2	9	4	2	0	0	0		0		.222	.222	.222	42	-1				.500	-1	/P-2,O-1	0.0
1886	NY-N	1	3	0	0	0	0	0	0	0	1	.000	.000	.000	-99	-1				.000	-0	/O-1	-0.1
Total	2	3	12	4	2	0	0	0	0	0	1	.167	.167	.167	6	-1				—	-1	/O-2,P-2	-0.1

◼ MICKEY DEVINE
Devine, William Patrick b: 5/9/1892, Albany, N.Y. d: 10/1/37, Albany, N.Y. BR/TR, 5'10", 165 lbs. Deb: 8/2/18

YEAR	TM/L	G	AB	R	H	2B	3B	HR	RBI	BB	SO	AVG	OBP	SLG	PRO+	BR/A	SB	CS	SBR	FA	FR	G/POS	TPR
1918	Phi-N	4	8	0	1	1	0	0	0	0	0	.125	.125	.250	13	-1				.909	0	/C-3	-0.1
1920	Bos-A	8	12	1	2	0	0	0	0	1	2	.167	.231	.167	7	-2	1	0	0	.955	1	/C-5	0.0
1925	NY-N	21	33	6	9	3	0	0	4	2	4	.273	.314	.364	76	-1	1	0	0	.933	2	C-11/3-1	0.1
Total	3	33	53	7	12	4	0	0	4	3	6	.226	.268	.302	51	-4	1	0		.936	2	/C-19,3-1	0.0

◼ BERNIE DeVIVEIROS
DeViveiros, Bernard John b: 4/19/01, Oakland, Cal. d: 7/5/94, Oakland, Cal. BR/TR, 5'7", 160 lbs. Deb: 9/13/24

YEAR	TM/L	G	AB	R	H	2B	3B	HR	RBI	BB	SO	AVG	OBP	SLG	PRO+	BR/A	SB	CS	SBR	FA	FR	G/POS	TPR
1924	Chi-A	1	1	0	0	0	0	0	0	0	0	.000	.000	.000	-99	-0	0	0	0	.333	-1	/S-1	-0.1
1927	Det-A	24	22	4	5	1	0	0	2	2	8	.227	.292	.273	46	-2	1	0	0	.913	0	S-14/3-1	-0.1
Total	2	25	23	4	5	1	0	0	2	2	8	.217	.280	.261	40	-2	1	0	0	.846	-1	/S-15,3-1	-0.2

◼ ART DEVLIN
Devlin, Arthur McArthur b: 10/16/1879, Washington, D.C. d: 9/18/48, Jersey City, N.J. BR/TR, 6', 175 lbs. Deb: 4/14/04 C

YEAR	TM/L	G	AB	R	H	2B	3B	HR	RBI	BB	SO	AVG	OBP	SLG	PRO+	BR/A	SB	CS	SBR	FA	FR	G/POS	TPR
1904	NY-N	130	474	81	133	16	8	1	66	62		.281	.371	.354	119	13	33			.907	7	*3-130	2.5
1905	*NY-N	153	525	74	129	14	4	5	61	66		.246	.344	.310	94	-1	**59**			.932	5	*3-153	1.0
1906	NY-N	148	498	76	149	23	8	2	65	74		.299	.396	.390	142	27	54			.944	**28**	*3-148	6.5
1907	NY-N	143	491	61	136	16	2	1	54	63		.277	.376	.324	116	12	38			.940	0	*3-140/S-3	1.9
1908	NY-N	157	534	59	135	18	4	2	45	62		.253	.346	.313	106	6	19			**.947**	13	*3-157	2.8
1909	NY-N	143	491	61	130	19	8	0	56	65		.265	.362	.336	115	11	26			.934	18	*3-143	3.7
1910	NY-N	147	493	71	128	17	5	2	67	62	32	.260	.353	.327	98	1	28			.933	5	*3-147	1.0
1911	NY-N	95	260	42	71	16	2	0	25	42	19	.273	.386	.350	103	3	9			.944	2	3-79/1-6,2S	0.6
1912	Bos-N	124	436	59	126	18	8	0	54	51	37	.289	.367	.367	99	1	11			.992	-1	1-69,S-26,3/O	0.1
1913	Bos-N	73	210	19	48	7	5	0	12	29	17	.229	.328	.310	81	-4	8			.973	9	3-69	0.5
Total	10	1313	4412	603	1185	164	57	10	505	576	105	.269	.364	.338	109	68	285			.938	86	*3-1192/1-75,S2O	20.6

◼ JIM DEVLIN
Devlin, James Alexander b: 1849, Philadelphia, Pa. d: 10/10/1883, Philadelphia, Pa. BR/TR, 5'11", 175 lbs. Deb: 4/21/1873

YEAR	TM/L	G	AB	R	H	2B	3B	HR	RBI	BB	SO	AVG	OBP	SLG	PRO+	BR/A	SB	CS	SBR	FA	FR	G/POS	TPR
1873	Phi-n	23	99	18	24	4	0	0	9	2	4	.242	.257	.364	78	-3						1-12/3-6,SO	-0.2
1874	Chi-n	45	203	26	59	5	1	0		2		.291	.298	.325	97	-1						1-22,O-16/3	0.0
1875	Chi-n	69	315	60	92	18	5	0		5		.292	.303	.381	134	10						1-43,P-28/O	0.8
1876	Lou-N	62	298	38	94	14	1	0	28	1	11	.315	.318	.369	109	-1				.941	2	*P-68/1-1	0.0
1877	Lou-N	61	268	38	72	6	3	1	27	7	27	.269	.287	.325	78	-9				.933	2	*P-61	0.0
Total	3 n	137	617	104	175	27	10	0	9	9	4	.284	.294	.360	111	6						/1-77,P-28,O3S	0.6
Total	2	129	566	76	166	20	4	1	55	8	38	.293	.303	.348	94	-10				.937	4	P-129/1-1	0.0

◼ JIM DEVLIN
Devlin, James Raymond b: 8/25/22, Plains, Pa. BL/TR, 5'11.5", 165 lbs. Deb: 4/27/44

YEAR	TM/L	G	AB	R	H	2B	3B	HR	RBI	BB	SO	AVG	OBP	SLG	PRO+	BR/A	SB	CS	SBR	FA	FR	G/POS	TPR
1944	Cle-A	1	1	0	0	0	0	0	0	0	0	.000	.000	.000	-99	-0	0	0	0	1.000	0	/C-1	0.0

◼ REX DeVOGT
DeVogt, Rex Eugene b: 1/4/1888, Clare, Mich. d: 11/9/35, Alma, Mich. BR/TR, 5'9", 170 lbs. Deb: 4/17/13

YEAR	TM/L	G	AB	R	H	2B	3B	HR	RBI	BB	SO	AVG	OBP	SLG	PRO+	BR/A	SB	CS	SBR	FA	FR	G/POS	TPR
1913	Bos-N	3	6	0	0	0	0	0	0	0	3	.000	.000	.000	-98	-2	0			.941	1	/C-3	0.0

◼ JOSH DEVORE
Devore, Joshua D. b: 11/13/1887, Murray City, Ohio d: 10/6/54, Chillicothe, Ohio BL/TL, 5'6", 160 lbs. Deb: 9/25/08

YEAR	TM/L	G	AB	R	H	2B	3B	HR	RBI	BB	SO	AVG	OBP	SLG	PRO+	BR/A	SB	CS	SBR	FA	FR	G/POS	TPR
1908	NY-N	5	6	1	1	0	0	0		2	1	.167	.286	.167	43	-0	1			1.000	-1	/O-2	-0.1
1909	NY-N	22	26	8	6	4	1	0		0	4	.143	.250	.179	33	-2	3			.824	-4	/O-12	-0.7
1910	NY-N	133	490	92	149	11	10	2	27	46	67	.304	.371	.380	119	12	43			.929	-12	*O-130	-0.6
1911	*NY-N	149	565	96	158	19	10	3	50	81	69	.280	.376	.365	104	6	61			.934	1	*O-149	-0.1
1912	*NY-N	106	327	66	90	14	6	2	37	51	43	.275	.381	.373	104	3	27			.918	-8	O-96	-0.9
1913	NY-N	16	21	4	4	0	1	0	1	3	4	.190	.320	.286	73	-1	6			1.000	-2	/O-8	-0.3

YEAR	TM/L	G	AB	R	H	2B	3B	HR	RBI	BB	SO	AVG	OBP	SLG	PRO+	BR/A	SB	CS	SBR	FA	FR	G/POS	TPR
	Cin-N	66	217	30	58	6	4	3	14	12	21	.267	.309	.373	95	-2	17			.920	-3	O-57	-0.8
	Phi-N	23	39	9	11	1	0	0	5	4	7	.282	.364	.308	89	-0	0			.889	-3	O-14	-0.4
	Yr	105	277	43	73	7	5	3	20	19	32	.264	.318	.357	92	-3	23			.919	-9	O-79	-1.5
1914	Phi-N	30	53	5	16	2	0	0	7	4	5	.302	.351	.340	99	-0	0			.947	2	/O-9	0.2
	*Bos-N	51	128	22	29	0	0	1	5	18	14	.227	.327	.281	82	-2	2			.915	-8	O-42	-1.3
	Yr	81	181	27	45	6	0	1	12	22	19	.249	.333	.298	87	-2	2			.923	-6	O-51	-1.1
Total	7	601	1874	331	520	58	31	11	149	222	230	.277	.361	.359	103	13	160			.925	-38	O-519	-5.0

■ AL DeVORMER
DeVormer, Albert E. b: 8/19/1891, Grand Rapids, Mich d: 8/29/66, Grand Rapids, Mich BR/TR, 6'0.5", 175 lbs. Deb: 8/4/18

YEAR	TM/L	G	AB	R	H	2B	3B	HR	RBI	BB	SO	AVG	OBP	SLG	PRO+	BR/A	SB	CS	SBR	FA	FR	G/POS	TPR
1918	Chi-A	8	19	2	5	2	0	0	0	0	4	.263	.263	.368	90	-0	1			1.000	-2	/C-6,O-1	-0.2
1921	*NY-A	22	49	6	17	4	0	0	7	2	4	.347	.373	.429	102	0	2	0	1	.950	-1	C-17	0.1
1922	NY-A	24	59	8	12	4	1	0	11	1	6	.203	.217	.305	34	-6	0	0	0	.968	-1	C-17/1-1	-0.6
1923	Bos-A	74	209	20	54	7	3	0	18	6	21	.258	.282	.321	58	-13	3	0	1	.979	0	C-55/1-2	-0.9
1927	NY-N	68	141	14	35	3	1	2	21	11	11	.248	.312	.326	71	-6	1			.953	-4	C-54/1-3	-0.8
Total	5	196	477	50	123	20	5	2	57	20	46	.258	.292	.333	65	-25	7	0		.967	-7	C-149/1-6,O	-2.4

■ WALT DEVOY
Devoy, Walter Joseph b: 3/14/1886, St.Louis, Mo. d: 12/17/53, St.Louis, Mo. 5'11", 165 lbs. Deb: 9/13/09

YEAR	TM/L	G	AB	R	H	2B	3B	HR	RBI	BB	SO	AVG	OBP	SLG	PRO+	BR/A	SB	CS	SBR	FA	FR	G/POS	TPR
1909	StL-A	19	69	7	17	3	1	0	8	3		.246	.278	.319	95	-1	4			.944	-2	O-16/1-3	-0.3

■ JEFF DeWILLIS
DeWillis, Jeffrey Allen b: 4/13/65, Houston, Tex. BR/TR, 6'2", 170 lbs. Deb: 4/19/87

YEAR	TM/L	G	AB	R	H	2B	3B	HR	RBI	BB	SO	AVG	OBP	SLG	PRO+	BR/A	SB	CS	SBR	FA	FR	G/POS	TPR
1987	Tor-A	13	25	2	3	1	0	1	2	2	12	.120	.185	.280	21	-3	0	0	0	.964	2	C-13	-0.1

■ CHARLIE DEXTER
Dexter, Charles Dana b: 6/15/1876, Evansville, Ind. d: 6/9/34, Cedar Rapids, Iowa BR/TR, 5'7", 155 lbs. Deb: 4/17/1896

YEAR	TM/L	G	AB	R	H	2B	3B	HR	RBI	BB	SO	AVG	OBP	SLG	PRO+	BR/A	SB	CS	SBR	FA	FR	G/POS	TPR
1896	Lou-N	107	402	65	112	18	7	3	37	17	34	.279	.318	.381	87	-9	21			.903	-3	C-55,O-47	-0.8
1897	Lou-N	76	257	43	72	12	5	2	46	21		.280	.342	.389	96	-2	12			.907	-5	O-32,C-23,3/S	-0.5
1898	Lou-N	112	421	76	132	13	5	1	66	26		.314	.363	.375	114	7	44			.958	-1	O-95/2-8,C	0.1
1899	Lou-N	80	295	47	76	7	1	1	33	21		.258	.318	.298	69	-12	21			.942	2	O-71/S-6	-1.3
1900	Chi-N	40	125	7	25	5	0	2	20	1		.200	.213	.288	39	-11	2			.943	8	C-22,O-13/2	-0.2
1901	Chi-N	116	460	46	123	9	5	1	66	16		.267	.302	.315	82	-11	22			.982	5	1-54,3-25,02/C	-0.9
1902	Chi-N	69	266	30	60	12	0	2	26	19		.226	.290	.293	82	-5	13			.853	-13	3-39,1-22,O	-2.0
	Bos-N	48	183	33	47	3	0	1	18	16		.257	.323	.290	88	-2	16			.901	-4	S-22,2-19/O3	-0.4
	Yr	117	449	63	107	15	0	3	44	35		.238	.303	.292	85	-7	29			.854	-16	3-40,1-22,S2O	-2.4
1903	Bos-N	123	457	82	102	15	1	3	34	61		.223	.323	.280	75	-12	32			.941	-10	*O-106/S-9,C	-2.7
Total	8	771	2866	429	749	94	24	16	346	198	34	.261	.318	.328	85	-57	183			.942	-22	O-402,C-116/312S	-8.7

■ ALEX DIAZ
Diaz, Alexis b: 10/5/68, Brooklyn, N.Y. BB/TR, 5'11", 175 lbs. Deb: 7/25/92

YEAR	TM/L	G	AB	R	H	2B	3B	HR	RBI	BB	SO	AVG	OBP	SLG	PRO+	BR/A	SB	CS	SBR	FA	FR	G/POS	TPR
1992	Mil-A	22	9	5	1	0	0	0	1	0	0	.111	.111	.111	-38	-2	3	2	-0	1.000	-4	O-11/D-2	-0.7
1993	Mil-A	32	69	9	22	2	0	0	1	0	12	.319	.319	.348	80	-2	5	3	-0	.979	-4	O-28/D-1	-0.6
1994	Mil-A	79	187	17	47	5	7	1	17	10	19	.251	.289	.369	67	-10	5	5	-2	.993	-9	O-73/2-2	-1.9
Total	3	133	265	31	70	7	7	1	19	10	31	.264	.291	.355	67	-13	13	10	-2	.990	-17	O-112/D-3,2	-3.2

■ BO DIAZ
Diaz, Baudilio Jose (Seijas) b: 3/23/53, Cua, Venezuela d: 11/23/90, Caracas, Venez. BR/TR, 5'11", 190 lbs. Deb: 9/6/77

YEAR	TM/L	G	AB	R	H	2B	3B	HR	RBI	BB	SO	AVG	OBP	SLG	PRO+	BR/A	SB	CS	SBR	FA	FR	G/POS	TPR
1977	Bos-A	2	1	0	0	0	0	0	0	0	1	.000	.000	.000	-90	-0	0	0	0	1.000	1	/C-2	0.0
1978	Cle-A	44	127	12	30	4	0	2	11	4	17	.236	.260	.315	61	-7	0	0	0	.971	-1	C-44	-0.7
1979	Cle-A	15	32	0	5	2	0	0	1	0	6	.156	.206	.219	15	-4	0	0	0	.958	4	C-15	0.0
1980	Cle-A	76	207	15	47	11	2	3	32	7	27	.227	.252	.343	61	-12	1	0	0	.989	3	C-75	-0.6
1981	Cle-A★	63	182	25	57	19	0	7	38	13	23	.313	.362	.533	157	13	2	2	-1	.975	-3	C-51/D-3	1.1
1982	Phi-N	144	525	69	151	29	1	18	85	36	87	.288	.337	.450	116	10	3	6	-3	.989	-9	*C-144	0.4
1983	*Phi-N	136	471	49	111	17	0	15	64	38	57	.236	.295	.367	84	-11	1	4	-2	.986	14	*C-134	0.7
1984	Phi-N	27	75	5	16	4	0	1	9	5	13	.213	.262	.307	58	-4	0	0	0	.992	-0	C-23	-0.4
1985	Phi-N	26	76	9	16	5	1	2	16	6	7	.211	.268	.382	78	-3	0	0	0	.972	2	C-24	0.1
	Cin-N	51	161	12	42	8	0	3	15	15	18	.261	.328	.366	89	-2	0	0	0	.988	9	C-51	0.9
	Yr	77	237	21	58	13	1	5	31	21	25	.245	.309	.371	86	-5	0	0	0	.983	11	C-75	1.0
1986	Cin-N	134	474	50	129	21	0	10	56	40	52	.272	.329	.380	91	-6	1	1	-0	.984	-6	*C-134	-0.4
1987	Cin-N★	140	496	49	134	28	1	15	82	19	73	.270	.304	.421	86	-11	1	0	-0	.992	-6	*C-137	-0.7
1988	Cin-N	92	315	26	69	9	0	10	35	7	41	.219	.238	.343	63	-16	0	2	-1	.990	-6	C-88	-1.5
1989	Cin-N	43	132	6	27	5	0	1	8	6	7	.205	.239	.265	43	-10	0	2	-1	.984	-0	C-43	-1.0
Total	13	993	3274	327	834	162	5	87	452	198	429	.255	.300	.387	87	-63	9	17	-8	.986	3	C-965/D-3	-2.1

■ CARLOS DIAZ
Diaz, Carlos Francisco b: 12/24/64, Elizabeth, N.J. BR/TR, 6'3", 195 lbs. Deb: 5/8/90

YEAR	TM/L	G	AB	R	H	2B	3B	HR	RBI	BB	SO	AVG	OBP	SLG	PRO+	BR/A	SB	CS	SBR	FA	FR	G/POS	TPR
1990	Tor-A	9	3	1	1	0	0	0	0	0	2	.333	.333	.333	85	-0	0	0	0	1.000	2	/C-9	0.2

■ EDGAR DIAZ
Diaz, Edgar (Serrano) b: 2/8/64, Santurce, P.R. BR/TR, 6', 155 lbs. Deb: 9/16/86

YEAR	TM/L	G	AB	R	H	2B	3B	HR	RBI	BB	SO	AVG	OBP	SLG	PRO+	BR/A	SB	CS	SBR	FA	FR	G/POS	TPR
1986	Mil-A	5	13	0	3	0	0	0	1		3	.231	.286	.231	41	-1	0	0	0	.875	-1	/S-5	-0.1
1990	Mil-A	86	218	27	59	2	2	0	14	21	32	.271	.338	.298	80	-5	3	2	-0	.950	-1	S-65,2-15/3D	-0.1
Total	2	91	231	27	62	2	2	0	14	22	35	.268	.335	.294	78	-6	3	2	-0	.946	-1	/S-70,2-15,3D	-0.2

■ MARIO DIAZ
Diaz, Mario Rafael (Torres) b: 1/10/62, Humacao, P.R. BR/TR, 5'10", 160 lbs. Deb: 9/12/87

YEAR	TM/L	G	AB	R	H	2B	3B	HR	RBI	BB	SO	AVG	OBP	SLG	PRO+	BR/A	SB	CS	SBR	FA	FR	G/POS	TPR
1987	Sea-A	11	23	4	7	0	0	0	3	0	4	.304	.304	.391	79	-1	0	0	0	.972	4	S-10	0.3
1988	Sea-A	28	24	6	22	5	0	0	9	3	5	.306	.333	.375	94	-1	0	0	0	.985	-4	S-21/2-4,13	-0.3
1989	Sea-A	52	74	9	10	0	0	1	7	7	7	.135	.210	.176	9	-9	0	0	0	.930	-9	S-37/2-14/3	-1.7
1990	NY-N	16	22	0	3	1	0	0	1	0	3	.136	.136	.182	-13	-3	0	0	0	.958	-2	S-10/2-1	-0.2
1991	Tex-A	96	182	24	48	7	0	1	22	15	18	.264	.320	.319	79	-5	0	1	-1	.962	-2	S-65,2-20/3D	-0.5
1992	Tex-A	19	31	2	7	1	0	0	1	1	2	.226	.250	.258	44	-2	0	1	-1	.975	1	S-16/2-3,3	-0.1
1993	Tex-A	71	205	24	56	10	1	2	24	8	13	.273	.304	.361	81	-6	0	0	0	.986	-6	S-57,3-12/1	-0.6
1994	Fla-N	32	77	10	25	4	2	0	11	6	6	.325	.381	.429	105	1	0	0	0	.964	-0	3-11/2-7,S	0.1
Total	8	325	686	79	178	28	4	4	78	40	58	.259	.302	.329	72	-26	1	2	-1	.971	-13	S-223/2-49,31D	-3.0

■ MIKE DIAZ
Diaz, Michael Anthony b: 4/15/60, San Francisco, Cal. BR/TR, 6'2", 195 lbs. Deb: 9/15/83

YEAR	TM/L	G	AB	R	H	2B	3B	HR	RBI	BB	SO	AVG	OBP	SLG	PRO+	BR/A	SB	CS	SBR	FA	FR	G/POS	TPR
1983	Chi-N	6	7	2	2	1	0	0	1	0	0	.286	.286	.429	91	-0	0	0	0	1.000	-0	/C-3	-0.1
1986	Pit-N	97	209	22	56	9	0	12	36	19	43	.268	.335	.483	120	4	5	0	1	.966	-0	O-38,1-20/3C	-0.3
1987	Pit-N	103	241	28	58	8	2	16	48	31	42	.241	.335	.490	114	4	0	0	0	.960	-6	O-37,1-32/C	-0.4
1988	Pit-N	47	74	6	17	3	0	0	5	16	13	.230	.367	.270	87	-0	0	0	0	1.000	-5	O-19/1-6,C	-0.6
	Chi-A	40	152	12	36	6	0	3	12	5	30	.237	.266	.336	67	-7	0	1	-1	.987	-2	1-39/D-1	-1.3
Total	4	293	683	70	169	27	2	31	102	71	128	.247	.324	.429	103	-3	1	2	-1	.988	-18	/1-97,O-94,C3D	-2.7

■ PAUL DICKEN
Dicken, Paul Franklin b: 10/2/43, DeLand, Fla. BR/TR, 6'5", 195 lbs. Deb: 6/7/64

YEAR	TM/L	G	AB	R	H	2B	3B	HR	RBI	BB	SO	AVG	OBP	SLG	PRO+	BR/A	SB	CS	SBR	FA	FR	G/POS	TPR
1964	Cle-A	11	11	0	0	0	0	0	0	0	5	.000	.000	.000	-99	-3	0	0	0	.000	0	H	-0.3
1966	Cle-A	2	2	0	0	0	0	0	0	0	1	.000	.000	.000	-99	-1	0	0	0	.000	0	H	-0.1
Total	2	13	13	0	0	0	0	0	0	0	6	.000	.000	.000	-99	-3	0	0	0		0	-0,-0	-0.4

■ BUTTERCUP DICKERSON
Dickerson, Lewis Pessano b: 10/11/1858, Tyaskin, Md. d: 7/23/20, Baltimore, Md. BL/TR, 5'6", 140 lbs. Deb: 7/15/1878

YEAR	TM/L	G	AB	R	H	2B	3B	HR	RBI	BB	SO	AVG	OBP	SLG	PRO+	BR/A	SB	CS	SBR	FA	FR	G/POS	TPR
1878	Cin-N	29	123	17	38	5	1	0	9	0	7	.309	.309	.366	134	4				.877	-1	O-29	0.1
1879	Cin-N	81	350	73	102	18	**14**	2	57	3	27	.291	.297	.440	147	17				.801	-4	*O-81	0.8
1880	Tro-N	30	119	15	23	2	0	0	10	2	3	.193	.207	.244	49	-6				.903	6	O-30/S-1	-0.1
	Wor-N	31	133	22	39	8	6	0	20	1	2	.293	.299	.444	136	4				.852	-2	O-31	0.1

YEAR	TM/L	G	AB	R	H	2B	3B	HR	RBI	BB	SO	AVG	OBP	SLG	PRO+	BR/A	SB	CS	SBR	FA	FR	G/POS	TPR
	Yr	61	252	37	62	10	8	0	30	3	5	.246	.255	.349	96	-2				.883	4	O-61/S-1	0.0
1881	Wor-N	80	367	48	116	18	6	1	31	8	8	.316	.331	.406	123	8				.892	10	*O-80	1.5
1883	Pit-a	85	354	62	88	15	1	0		18		.249	.285	.297	92	-2				.798	0	*O-78/S-8,2	-0.2
1884	StL-U	46	211	49	77	15	1	0		8		.365	.388	.445	122	6				.895	5	O-42/3-4	0.9
	Bal-a	13	56	9	12	2	1	0		4		.214	.290	.286	85	-1				.941	-2	O-12/3-1	-0.3
	Lou-a	8	28	6	4	0	2	1		3		.143	.226	.393	103	0				.813	-1	/O-8	0.0
	Yr	21	84	15	16	2	3	1		7		.190	.269	.321	91	-1				.879	-3	O-20/3-1	-0.3
1885	Buf-N	5	21	1	1	1	0	0	0	1	4	.048	.091	.095	-38	-3				1.000	1	/O-5	-0.3
Total	7	408	1762	302	500	84	34	4	<u>127</u>	48	<u>51</u>	.284	.304	.377	115	28				.854	12	O-396/S-9,32	2.5

■ GEORGE DICKEY
Dickey, George Willard "Skeets" b: 7/10/15, Kensett, Ark. d: 6/16/76, DeWitt, Ark. BB/TR, 6'2", 180 lbs. Deb: 9/21/35 F

YEAR	TM/L	G	AB	R	H	2B	3B	HR	RBI	BB	SO	AVG	OBP	SLG	PRO+	BR/A	SB	CS	SBR	FA	FR	G/POS	TPR
1935	Bos-A	5	11	1	0	0	0	0	1	1	3	.000	.083	.000	-72	-3	0	0	0	1.000	-1	/C-4	-0.4
1936	Bos-A	10	23	0	1	1	0	0	0	2	3	.043	.120	.087	-46	-5	0	0	0	.912	0	C-10	-0.4
1941	Chi-A	32	55	6	11	1	0	2	8	5	7	.200	.267	.327	57	-4	0	0	0	1.000	1	C-17	-0.2
1942	Chi-A	59	116	6	27	3	0	1	17	9	11	.233	.288	.284	63	-6	0	0	0	.918	-4	C-29	-0.8
1946	Chi-A	37	78	8	15	1	0	0	1	12	10	.192	.300	.205	45	-5	0	2	-1	1.000	2	C-30	-0.4
1947	Chi-A	83	211	15	47	6	0	1	27	34	25	.223	.331	.265	69	-8	4	2	0	.985	2	C-80	-0.1
Total	6	226	494	36	101	12	0	4	54	63	62	.204	.294	.253	53	-31	4	4	-1	.974	-0	C-170	-2.3

■ BILL DICKEY
Dickey, William Malcolm b: 6/6/07, Bastrop, La. d: 11/12/93, Little Rock, Ark. BL/TR, 6'1.5", 185 lbs. Deb: 8/15/28 FMCH

YEAR	TM/L	G	AB	R	H	2B	3B	HR	RBI	BB	SO	AVG	OBP	SLG	PRO+	BR/A	SB	CS	SBR	FA	FR	G/POS	TPR
1928	NY-A	10	15	1	3	1	1	0	2	0	2	.200	.200	.400	56	-1	0	0	0	1.000	-1	/C-6	-0.2
1929	NY-A	130	447	60	145	30	6	10	65	14	16	.324	.346	.485	120	10	4	3	-1	.979	1	*C-127	2.1
1930	NY-A	109	366	55	124	25	7	5	65	21	14	.339	.375	.486	122	11	7	1	2	.977	-12	*C-101	0.9
1931	NY-A	130	477	65	156	17	10	6	78	39	20	.327	.378	.442	122	15	2	1	2	**.996**	4	*C-125	2.5
1932	*NY-A	108	423	66	131	20	4	15	84	34	13	.310	.361	.482	123	13	2	4	-2	.987	-2	*C-108	1.4
1933	NY-A☆	130	478	58	152	24	8	14	97	47	14	.318	.381	.490	138	25	3	4	-2	.993	0	*C-127	2.9
1934	NY-A★	104	395	56	127	24	4	12	72	38	18	.322	.384	.494	134	19	0	3	-2	.986	-1	*C-104	1.9
1935	NY-A	120	448	54	125	26	6	14	81	35	11	.279	.339	.458	111	5	1	1	-0	**.995**	-2	*C-118	0.9
1936	*NY-A★	112	423	99	153	26	8	22	107	46	16	.362	.428	.617	161	39	0	2	-1	.976	0	*C-107	3.8
1937	*NY-A★	140	530	87	176	35	2	29	133	73	22	.332	.417	.570	145	37	3	2	0	.991	12	*C-137	5.1
1938	*NY-A★	132	454	84	142	27	4	27	115	75	22	.313	.412	.568	144	31	3	0	1	.987	4	*C-126	3.7
1939	*NY-A★	128	480	98	145	23	3	24	105	77	37	.302	.403	.512	135	26	5	0	2	**.989**	8	*C-126	3.9
1940	NY-A★	106	372	45	92	11	1	9	54	48	32	.247	.336	.355	83	-9	0	3	-2	.994	-1	*C-102	-0.3
1941	*NY-A★	109	348	35	99	15	5	7	71	45	17	.284	.371	.417	110	3	5	2	0	**.994**	1	*C-104	1.4
1942	*NY-A†	82	268	28	79	13	1	2	37	26	11	.295	.359	.373	108	3	2	2	-1	.976	3	C-80	1.2
1943	*NY-A☆	85	242	29	85	18	2	4	33	41	12	.351	.445	.492	173	24	2	0	0	.994	-1	C-71	2.9
1946	NY-A★	54	134	10	35	8	0	2	10	19	12	.261	.357	.366	101	1	0	1	-1	.987	10	C-39,M	1.3
Total	17	1789	6300	930	1969	343	72	202	1209	678	289	.313	.382	.486	128	252	36	29	-7	.988	24	*C-1708	35.4

■ JOHNNY DICKSHOT
Dickshot, John Oscar "Ugly" (b: John Oscar Dicksus) b: 1/24/10, Waukegan, Ill. BR/TR, 6', 195 lbs. Deb: 4/16/36

YEAR	TM/L	G	AB	R	H	2B	3B	HR	RBI	BB	SO	AVG	OBP	SLG	PRO+	BR/A	SB	CS	SBR	FA	FR	G/POS	TPR
1936	Pit-N	9	9	2	2	0	0	0	1	1	2	.222	.300	.222	42	-1	0			.000	-1	/O-1	-0.1
1937	Pit-N	82	264	42	67	8	4	3	33	26	36	.254	.323	.348	82	-6	0			.950	-3	O-64	-1.1
1938	Pit-N	29	35	3	8	0	0	0	4	8	5	.229	.372	.229	68	-1	3			1.000	-1	O-10	-0.3
1939	NY-N	10	34	3	8	0	0	0	5	5	3	.235	.333	.235	55	-2	0			1.000	-1	O-10	-0.3
1944	Chi-A	62	162	18	41	8	5	0	15	13	10	.253	.313	.364	94	-2	2	0	1	.974	-3	O-40	-0.6
1945	Chi-A	130	486	74	147	19	10	4	58	48	41	.302	.366	.407	128	17	18	3	**4**	.971	1	*O-124	1.5
Total	6	322	990	142	273	35	19	7	116	101	97	.276	.345	.371	104	5	23	<u>3</u>		.968	-7	O-249	-0.9

■ BOB DIDIER
Didier, Robert Daniel b: 2/16/49, Hattiesburg, Miss. BB/TR, 6', 190 lbs. Deb: 4/7/69 C

YEAR	TM/L	G	AB	R	H	2B	3B	HR	RBI	BB	SO	AVG	OBP	SLG	PRO+	BR/A	SB	CS	SBR	FA	FR	G/POS	TPR
1969	*Atl-N	114	352	30	90	16	1	0	32	34	39	.256	.321	.307	76	-10	1	3	-2	.994	-2	*C-114	-0.9
1970	Atl-N	57	168	9	25	2	1	0	7	12	11	.149	.210	.173	3	-23	1	0	0	.988	1	C-57	-1.9
1971	Atl-N	51	155	9	34	4	1	0	6	17	17	.219	.248	.258	41	-12	0	0	0	1.000	3	C-50	-0.8
1972	Atl-N	13	40	5	12	2	1	0	5	2	4	.300	.349	.400	103	2	0	0	0	1.000	2	C-11	0.2
1973	Det-A	7	22	3	10	1	0	0	1	3	0	.455	.520	.500	177	2	0	0	0	1.000	2	/C-7	0.5
1974	Bos-A	5	14	0	1	0	0	0	1	2	1	.071	.188	.071	-22	-2	0	0	0	.968	1	/C-5	-0.1
Total	6	247	751	56	172	25	4	0	51	59	72	.229	.287	.273	55	-45	2	3	-1	.994	6	C-244	-3.0

■ ERNIE DIEHL
Diehl, Ernest Guy b: 10/2/1877, Cincinnati, Ohio d: 11/6/58, Miami, Fla. BR/TR, 6'1", 190 lbs. Deb: 5/31/03

YEAR	TM/L	G	AB	R	H	2B	3B	HR	RBI	BB	SO	AVG	OBP	SLG	PRO+	BR/A	SB	CS	SBR	FA	FR	G/POS	TPR
1903	Pit-N	1	3	0	1	0	0	0	0			.333	.333	.333	87	-0	0			.000	-1	/O-1	-0.1
1904	Pit-N	12	37	6	6	0	0	0	4		6	.162	.311	.162	46	-2	3			1.000	1	/O-7,S-4	-0.1
1906	Bos-N	3	11	1	5	0	1	0	0			.455	.455	.636	247	2	0			1.000	0	/O-2,S-1	0.2
1909	Bos-N	1	4	1	2	1	0	0	0			.500	.500	.750	274	1	0			.800	1	/O-1	0.1
Total	4	17	55	8	14	1	1	0	4		6	.255	.349	.309	101	0	3			.944	1	/O-11,S-5	0.1

■ CHUCK DIERING
Diering, Charles Edward Allen b: 2/5/23, St.Louis, Mo. BR/TR, 5'10", 165 lbs. Deb: 4/15/47

YEAR	TM/L	G	AB	R	H	2B	3B	HR	RBI	BB	SO	AVG	OBP	SLG	PRO+	BR/A	SB	CS	SBR	FA	FR	G/POS	TPR
1947	StL-N	105	74	22	16	3	1	2	11	19	22	.216	.383	.365	95	0	3			1.000	-22	O-75	-2.3
1948	StL-N	7	7	2	0	0	0	0	0	2	2	.000	.222	.000	-33	-1	1			1.000	-1	/O-5	-0.2
1949	StL-N	131	369	60	97	21	8	3	38	35	49	.263	.328	.388	87	-7	1			.987	-2	*O-124	-1.4
1950	StL-N	89	204	34	51	12	0	3	18	35	38	.250	.360	.353	84	-4	1			.989	-1	O-81	-0.7
1951	StL-N	64	85	9	22	5	1	0	8	6	15	.259	.308	.341	74	-3	0	1	-1	1.000	-8	O-44	-1.3
1952	NY-N	41	23	2	4	1	0	0	2	4	3	.174	.296	.304	66	-1	0	2	-1	1.000	-10	O-36	-1.3
1954	Bal-A	128	418	35	108	14	1	2	29	56	57	.258	.351	.311	89	-5	3	7	-3	.983	13	*O-119	0.0
1955	Bal-A	137	371	38	95	16	2	3	31	57	45	.256	.355	.334	93	-3	5	8	-3	.976	3	*O-107,3-34,S	-0.6
1956	Bal-A	50	97	15	18	4	0	1	4	23	19	.186	.342	.258	65	-4	2	5	-2	1.000	-4	O-40/3-2	-1.2
Total	9	752	1648	217	411	76	14	14	141	237	250	.249	.346	.338	86	-27	16	<u>23</u>		.987	-31	O-631/3-36,S	-9.0

■ DICK DIETZ
Dietz, Richard Allen b: 9/18/41, Crawfordsville, Ind. BR/TR, 6'1", 195 lbs. Deb: 6/18/66

YEAR	TM/L	G	AB	R	H	2B	3B	HR	RBI	BB	SO	AVG	OBP	SLG	PRO+	BR/A	SB	CS	SBR	FA	FR	G/POS	TPR
1966	SF-N	13	23	1	1	0	0	0	0	0	9	.043	.083	.043	-62	-5	0	0	0	1.000	-1	/C-6	-0.6
1967	SF-N	56	120	10	27	3	0	4	19	25	44	.225	.363	.350	106	2	0	1	-1	.983	5	C-43	0.4
1968	SF-N	98	301	21	82	14	2	6	38	34	68	.272	.348	.392	122	9	1	1	-0	.976	-8	C-90	0.7
1969	SF-N	79	244	28	56	8	1	11	35	53	53	.230	.373	.406	120	8	0	0	0	.973	-5	C-73	0.7
1970	SF-N★	148	493	82	148	36	2	22	107	109	106	.300	.430	.515	154	42	0	1	-1	.984	-18	*C-139	3.0
1971	*SF-N	142	453	58	114	19	0	19	72	97	86	.252	.388	.419	131	22	1	3	-2	.982	-12	*C-135	1.5
1972	LA-N	27	56	4	9	1	0	1	6	14	11	.161	.329	.232	63	-2	0	2	-1	1.000	3	C-22	0.3
1973	Atl-N	83	139	22	41	8	1	3	24	49	25	.295	.479	.432	143	12	0	0	0	.989	1	1-36,C-20	1.1
Total	8	646	1829	226	478	89	6	66	301	381	402	.261	.392	.425	130	88	2	8	-5	.980	-39	C-528/1-36	7.1

■ ROY DIETZEL
Dietzel, Leroy Louis b: 1/9/31, Baltimore, Md. BR/TR, 6', 190 lbs. Deb: 9/2/54

YEAR	TM/L	G	AB	R	H	2B	3B	HR	RBI	BB	SO	AVG	OBP	SLG	PRO+	BR/A	SB	CS	SBR	FA	FR	G/POS	TPR
1954	Was-A	9	21	1	5	0	0	0	1	2	1	.238	.385	.238	78	-0	0	0	0	.960	-2	/2-7,3-2	-0.2

■ JAY DIFANI
Difani, Clarence Joseph b: 12/21/23, Crystal City, Mo. BR/TR, 6', 170 lbs. Deb: 4/23/48

YEAR	TM/L	G	AB	R	H	2B	3B	HR	RBI	BB	SO	AVG	OBP	SLG	PRO+	BR/A	SB	CS	SBR	FA	FR	G/POS	TPR
1948	Was-A	2	2	0	0	0	0	0	0	0	2	.000	.000	.000	-99	-1	0	0	0	.000	0	H	-0.1
1949	Was-A	2	1	0	1	0	0	0	0	0	0	1.000	1.000	2.000	699	1	0	0	0	1.000	0	/2-1	0.1
Total	2	4	3	0	1	0	0	0	0	0	2	.333	.333	.667	166	0	0	0	0	1.000	0	/2-1	0.0

YEAR	TM/L	G	AB	R	H	2B	3B	HR	RBI	BB	SO	AVG	OBP	SLG	PRO+	BR/A	SB	CS	SBR	FA	FR	G/POS	TPR
■ STEVE DIGNAN						Dignan, Stephen E.		b: 5/16/1859, Boston, Mass.			d: 7/11/1881, Boston, Mass.			Deb: 6/1/1880									
1880	Bos-N	8	34	4	11	1	0	0	4	0	3	.324	.324	.353	133	1				.684	0	/O-8	0.1
	Wor-N	3	10	1	3	0	1	0	2	0	1	.300	.300	.500	153	0				.750	-1	/O-3	0.0
	Yr	11	44	5	14	1	1	0	6	0	4	.318	.318	.386	137	2				.696	-1	O-11	0.1
■ DON DILLARD						Dillard, David Donald		b: 1/8/37, Greenville, S.C.		BL/TR, 6'1", 200 lbs.			Deb: 4/24/59									
1959	Cle-A	10	10	0	4	0	0	0	1	0	2	.400	.400	.400	125	0	0	0	0	.000	0	H	0.0
1960	Cle-A	6	7	0	1	0	0	0	0	1	3	.143	.250	.143	9	-1	0	0	0	.000	-0	/O-1	-0.1
1961	Cle-A	74	147	27	40	5	0	7	17	15	28	.272	.340	.449	112	2	0	0	0	1.000	-4	O-39	-0.3
1962	Cle-A	95	174	22	40	5	1	5	14	11	25	.230	.276	.356	71	-8	0	1	-1	.965	-10	O-50	-2.1
1963	Mil-N	67	119	9	28	6	4	1	12	5	21	.235	.272	.378	86	-2	0	2	-1	.951	-0	O-30	-0.5
1965	Mil-N	20	19	1	3	0	0	1	3	0	6	.158	.158	.316	30	-2	0	0	0	.000	-0	/O-1	-0.2
Total	6	272	476	59	116	16	5	14	47	32	85	.244	.293	.387	86	-10	0	3	-2	.976	-15	O-121	-3.2
■ PAT DILLARD						Dillard, Robert Lee		b: 6/12/1873, Chattanooga, Tenn.		d: 7/22/07, Denver, Colo.		BL/TR, 6', 180 lbs.		Deb: 4/21/00								
1900	StL-N	57	183	24	42	5	2	0	12	13		.230	.284	.279	56	-11	7			.942	-4	O-26,3-21/S	-1.5
■ STEVE DILLARD						Dillard, Stephen Bradley		b: 2/8/51, Memphis, Tenn.		BR/TR, 6'1", 180 lbs.			Deb: 9/28/75									
1975	Bos-A	1	5	2	2	0	0	0	0	0	0	.400	.400	.400	117	0	1	0	0	1.000	1	/2-1	0.1
1976	Bos-A	57	167	22	46	14	0	1	15	17	20	.275	.342	.377	99	-0	6	4	-1	.918	-4	3-18,2-17,S/D	-0.3
1977	Bos-A	66	141	22	34	7	0	1	13	7	13	.241	.277	.312	54	-9	4	3	-1	.967	8	2-45/S-9,D	0.1
1978	Det-A	56	130	21	29	5	2	0	7	4	12	.223	.257	.292	53	-8	1	2	-1	.958	17	2-41/D-4	1.0
1979	Chi-N	89	166	31	47	6	1	5	24	17	24	.283	.353	.422	101	0	1	0	0	.988	5	2-60/3-9	1.3
1980	Chi-N	100	244	31	55	8	1	4	27	20	54	.225	.287	.316	63	-12	2	2	-1	.908	2	3-51,2-38/S	-1.0
1981	Chi-N	53	119	18	26	7	1	2	11	8	20	.218	.268	.345	70	-5	0	0	0	.974	3	2-32/3-7,S	-0.1
1982	Chi-A	16	41	1	7	3	1	0	5	1	5	.171	.190	.293	30	-4	0	1	-1	.959	3	2-16	-0.1
Total	8	438	1013	148	246	50	6	13	102	76	147	.243	.297	.343	73	-38	15	12	-3	.973	37	2-250/3-85,SD	1.0
■ PICKLES DILLHOEFER						Dillhoefer, William Martin		b: 10/13/1894, Cleveland, Ohio		d: 2/23/22, St.Louis, Mo.		BR/TR, 5'7", 154 lbs.		Deb: 4/16/17								
1917	Chi-N	42	95	3	12	1	1	0	8	2	9	.126	.144	.158	-7	-12	1			.985	8	C-37	-0.2
1918	Phi-N	8	11	0	1	0	0	0	0	1	1	.091	.167	.091	-19	-2	2			.923	-1	/C-6	-0.2
1919	StL-N	45	108	11	23	3	2	0	12	8	6	.213	.267	.278	68	-4	5			.967	-5	C-39	-0.7
1920	StL-N	76	224	26	59	8	3	0	13	13	7	.263	.304	.326	84	-5	2	1	0	.953	-0	C-74	-0.1
1921	StL-N	76	162	19	39	4	4	0	15	11	7	.241	.289	.315	61	-9	2	1	0	.953	2	C-69	-0.5
Total	5	247	600	59	134	16	10	0	48	35	30	.223	.266	.283	58	-32	12	2		.961	4	C-225	-1.7
■ BOB DILLINGER						Dillinger, Robert Bernard "Duke"		b: 9/17/18, Glendale, Cal.		BR/TR, 5'11.5", 170 lbs.		Deb: 4/16/46									
1946	StL-A	83	225	33	63	6	3	0	11	19	30	.280	.341	.333	85	-4	8	1	2	.922	-3	3-54/S-1	-0.5
1947	StL-A	137	571	70	168	23	6	3	37	56	38	.294	.361	.371	102	2	**34**	13	2	.958	2	*3-137	0.8
1948	StL-A	153	644	110	**207**	34	10	2	44	65	34	.321	.385	.415	110	9	**28**	11	2	.955	-16	*3-153	-0.6
1949	StL-A★	137	544	80	176	22	13	1	51	51	40	.324	.385	.417	108	6	**20**	14	-2	.938	-25	*3-133	-2.4
1950	Phi-A	84	356	55	110	21	9	3	41	31	20	.309	.366	.444	109	4	5	3	-0	.957	-2	3-84	0.0
	Pit-N	58	222	23	64	8	2	1	9	13	22	.288	.328	.356	77	-7	4			.957	-2	3-51	-0.6
1951	Pit-N	12	43	3	10	3	0	0	0	1	0	.233	.250	.302	47	-3	2	0	1	.963	-2	3-10	-0.5
	Chi-A	89	299	39	90	6	4	0	20	15	17	.301	.337	.348	87	-6	5	5	-2	.930	-6	3-70	-1.4
Total	6	753	2904	401	888	123	47	10	213	251	201	.306	.363	.391	100	1	106	47		.948	-50	3-692/S-1	-5.2
■ POP DILLON						Dillon, Frank Edward		b: 10/17/1873, Normal, Ill.		d: 9/12/31, Pasadena, Cal.		BL/TR, 6'1", 185 lbs.		Deb: 9/8/1899								
1899	Pit-N	30	121	21	31	5	0	0	20	5		.256	.286	.298	60	-7	5			.988	1	1-30	-0.5
1900	Pit-N	5	18	3	2	1	0	0	1	0		.111	.111	.167	-24	-3	0			.981	1	/1-5	-0.2
1901	Det-A	74	281	40	81	14	6	1	42	15		.288	.324	.391	94	-3	14			.979	3	1-74	-0.2
1902	Det-A	66	243	21	50	6	3	0	22	16		.206	.255	.255	41	-19	2			.976	5	1-66	-1.5
	Bal-A	2	7	1	2	0	1	0	0	2		.286	.444	.571	173	1	0			.960	1	/1-2	0.1
	Yr	68	250	22	52	6	4	0	22	18		.208	.261	.264	45	-19	2			.975	6	1-68	-1.4
1904	Bro-N	135	511	60	132	18	6	0	31	40		.258	.313	.317	97	-2	13			.982	3	*1-134	-0.2
Total	5	312	1181	146	298	44	16	1	116	78		.252	.299	.319	79	-33	34			.980	14	1-311	-2.5
■ JOHN DILLON						Dillon, John		Deb: 5/8/1875 F															
1875	RS-n	1	1	0	0	0	0	0		0		.000	.000	.000	-99	-0						/S-1	0.0
■ PACKY DILLON						Dillon, Packard Andrew		b: St.Louis, Mo.		d: 1/8/1890, Guelph, Ont., Canada		Deb: 5/4/1875 F									
1875	RS-n	3	13	1	3	1	0	0		0		.231	.231	.308	93	-0						/C-3	0.0
■ MIGUEL DILONE						Dilone, Miguel Angel (Reyes)		b: 11/1/54, Santiago, D.R.		BB/TR, 6', 160 lbs.		Deb: 9/2/74									
1974	Pit-N	12	2	3	0	0	0	0	0	1	0	.000	.333	.000	-1	-0	2	0	1	1.000	-1	/O-2	0.0
1975	Pit-N	18	6	8	0	0	0	0	0	0	0	.000	.000	.000	-99	-2	2	2	-1	1.000	-0	/O-2	-0.3
1976	Pit-N	16	17	7	4	0	0	0	0	0	0	.235	.235	.235	34	-1	5	1	1	1.000	1	/O-3	-0.3
1977	Pit-N	29	44	5	6	0	0	0	2	3		.136	.174	.136	-15	-7	12	0	4	1.000	-3	O-17	-0.7
1978	Oak-A	135	258	34	59	8	0	1	14	23	30	.229	.294	.271	63	-12	50	23	1	.985	-7	O-99,D-11/3	-2.2
1979	Oak-A	30	91	15	17	1	2	1	6	6	7	.187	.237	.275	40	-8	6	5	-1	.959	-2	O-25	-1.2
	Chi-N	43	36	14	11	0	0	0	2	6	5	.306	.342	.306	71	-1	15	5	2	1.000	-5	O-22	-0.5
1980	Cle-A	132	528	82	180	30	9	0	40	28	45	.341	.376	.432	120	15	61	18	8	.973	-0	*O-118,D-11	1.6
1981	Cle-A	72	269	33	78	5	5	0	19	18	28	.290	.334	.346	98	-1	29	10	3	.971	6	O-56,D-11	0.6
1982	Cle-A	104	379	50	89	12	3	3	25	25	36	.235	.286	.306	63	-19	33	5	7	.964	-3	O-97/D-1	-1.8
1983	Cle-A	32	68	15	13	3	1	0	7	10	5	.191	.295	.265	53	-4	5	1	1	1.000	-0	O-19	-0.3
	Chi-A	4	3	1	0	0	0	0	0	0	0	.000	.000	.000	-96	-1	1	0	0	1.000	-1	/O-2,D-2	-0.1
	Yr	36	71	16	13	3	1	0	7	10	5	.183	.284	.254	47	-5	6	1	1	1.000	0	O-21/D-2	-0.4
	Pit-N	7	0	1	0	0	0	0	0	0	0	—	—	—	—	0	2	0	0	1.000	0	/R	0.0
1984	Mon-N	88	169	28	47	8	1	0	10	17	18	.278	.348	.367	106	1	27	2	7	.987	1	O-41	0.9
1985	Mon-N	51	84	10	16	0	0	0	6	6	11	.190	.244	.238	38	-7	7	3	0	.974	-2	O-22	-1.0
	SD-N	27	46	8	10	0	1	0	1	4	8	.217	.280	.261	53	-3	10	3	1	.917	-2	O-14	-0.4
	Yr	78	130	18	26	0	1	0	7	10	19	.200	.257	.246	43	-10	17	6	2	.952	-4	O-36	-1.4
Total	12	800	2000	314	530	67	25	6	129	142	197	.265	.316	.333	81	-51	267	78	33	.975	-16	O-539/D-36,3	-5.4
■ DOM DiMAGGIO						DiMaggio, Dominic Paul "The Little Professor"		b: 2/12/17, San Francisco, Cal.		BR/TR, 5'9", 168 lbs.		Deb: 4/16/40 F								
1940	Bos-A	108	418	81	126	32	6	8	46	41	46	.301	.367	.464	109	6	7	6	-2	.977	10	O-94	0.8
1941	Bos-A★	144	584	117	165	37	6	8	58	90	57	.283	.385	.408	107	8	13	6	0	.964	6	O-144	0.6
1942	Bos-A☆	151	622	110	178	36	8	14	48	70	52	.286	.364	.437	121	17	16	10	-1	.987	17	*O-151	2.5
1946	*Bos-A★	142	534	85	169	24	7	7	73	66	58	.316	.393	.427	122	17	10	6	-1	.985	7	*O-142	1.8
1947	Bos-A	136	513	75	145	21	5	8	71	74	62	.283	.376	.390	105	5	10	4	-1	.977	19	*O-134	1.7
1948	Bos-A	155	648	127	185	40	4	9	87	101	58	.285	.383	.401	104	5	10	2	-2	.973	6	*O-155	1.4
1949	Bos-A★	145	605	126	186	34	5	8	60	96	55	.307	.404	.420	110	11	9	7	-2	.977	14	*O-144	1.6
1950	Bos-A★	141	588	**131**	193	30	**11**	7	70	82	68	.328	.414	.452	111	11	**15**	4	2	.983	9	*O-140	1.5
1951	Bos-A★	146	639	**113**	189	34	4	12	72	73	53	.296	.370	.418	103	2	4	7	-3	.973	3	*O-146	-0.4
1952	Bos-A★	128	486	81	143	20	1	6	33	57	61	.294	.371	.377	100	2	6	8	-3	.975	-7	*O-123	-0.7

YEAR	TM/L	G	AB	R	H	2B	3B	HR	RBI	BB	SO	AVG	OBP	SLG	PRO+	BR/A	SB	CS	SBR	FA	FR	G/POS	TPR
1953	Bos-A	3	3	0	1	0	0	0	0	0	1	.333	.333	.333	76	-0	0	0	0	.000	0	H	0.0
Total	11	1399	5640	1046	1680	308	57	87	618	750	571	.298	.383	.419	109	84	100	62	-7	.978	101	*O-1373	10.8

■ JOE DiMAGGIO DiMaggio, Joseph Paul "Joltin' Joe" or "The Yankee Clipper" b: 11/25/14, Martinez, Cal. BR/TR, 6'2", 193 lbs. Deb: 5/3/36 FCH

YEAR	TM/L	G	AB	R	H	2B	3B	HR	RBI	BB	SO	AVG	OBP	SLG	PRO+	BR/A	SB	CS	SBR	FA	FR	G/POS	TPR
1936	*NY-A★	138	637	132	206	44	15	29	125	24	39	.323	.352	.576	130	23	4	0	1	.978	15	*O-138	3.0
1937	*NY-A★	151	621	151	215	35	15	46	167	64	37	.346	.412	.673	168	60	3	0	1	.962	11	*O-150	6.0
1938	*NY-A★	145	599	129	194	32	13	32	140	59	21	.324	.386	.581	140	33	6	1	1	.963	4	*O-145	3.0
1939	*NY-A★	120	462	108	176	32	6	30	126	52	20	.381	.448	.671	185	58	3	0	1	.986	8	*O-117	5.7
1940	NY-A★	132	508	93	179	28	9	31	133	61	30	.352	.425	.626	176	56	1	2	-1	.978	1	*O-130	4.5
1941	*NY-A★	139	541	122	193	43	11	30	125	76	13	.357	.440	.643	186	66	4	2	0	.978	10	*O-139	6.4
1942	*NY-A★	154	610	123	186	29	13	21	114	68	36	.305	.376	.498	148	37	4	2	0	.981	2	*O-154	3.1
1946	NY-A☆	132	503	81	146	20	8	25	95	59	24	.290	.367	.511	142	27	1	0	0	.982	4	*O-131	2.5
1947	*NY-A★	141	534	97	168	31	10	20	97	64	32	.315	.391	.522	154	38	3	0	1	.997	-13	*O-139	1.8
1948	*NY-A★	153	594	110	190	26	11	39	155	67	30	.320	.396	.598	164	50	1	1	-0	.972	4	*O-152	4.3
1949	*NY-A★	76	272	58	94	14	6	14	67	55	18	.346	.459	.596	178	32	0	1	-1	.985	-1	O-76	2.5
1950	*NY-A★	139	525	114	158	33	10	32	122	80	33	.301	.394	.585	152	39	0	0	0	.976	1	*O-137/1-1	3.1
1951	*NY-A☆	116	415	72	109	22	4	12	71	61	36	.263	.365	.422	117	10	0	0	0	.990	4	*O-113	1.0
Total	13	1736	6821	1390	2214	389	131	361	1537	790	369	.325	.398	.579	156	529	30	9	4	.978	51	*O-1721/1-1	46.9

■ VINCE DiMAGGIO DiMaggio, Vincent Paul b: 9/6/12, Martinez, Cal. d: 10/3/86, N.Hollywood, Cal. BR/TR, 5'11", 183 lbs. Deb: 4/19/37 F

YEAR	TM/L	G	AB	R	H	2B	3B	HR	RBI	BB	SO	AVG	OBP	SLG	PRO+	BR/A	SB	CS	SBR	FA	FR	G/POS	TPR
1937	Bos-N	132	493	56	126	18	4	13	69	39	111	.256	.311	.387	98	-4	8			.982	16	*O-130	0.7
1938	Bos-N	150	540	71	123	28	3	14	61	65	134	.228	.313	.369	96	-4	11			.973	13	*O-149/2-1	0.5
1939	Cin-N	8	14	1	1	1	0	0	2	2	10	.071	.188	.143	-10	-2	0			1.000	-0	/O-7	-0.2
1940	Cin-N	2	4	2	1	0	0	0	0	1	0	.250	.400	.250	82	-0	0			1.000	-0	/O-1	0.0
	Pit-N	110	356	59	103	26	6	19	54	37	83	.289	.364	.522	143	20	11			.979	-2	*O-108	1.3
	Yr	112	360	61	104	26	6	19	54	38	83	.289	.365	.519	142	20	11			.979	-2	*O-109	1.3
1941	Pit-N	151	528	73	141	27	5	21	100	68	100	.267	.354	.456	128	19	10			.976	7	*O-151	1.7
1942	Pit-N	143	496	57	118	22	3	15	75	52	87	.238	.311	.385	101	-1	10			.978	20	*O-138	1.3
1943	Pit-N★	157	580	64	144	41	2	15	88	70	126	.248	.329	.403	107	5	11			.985	15	*O-156/S-1	1.2
1944	Pit-N★	109	342	41	82	20	4	9	50	33	83	.240	.307	.401	94	-4	6			.984	-6	*O-101/3-1	-1.5
1945	Phi-N	127	452	64	116	25	3	19	84	43	91	.257	.321	.451	117	7	12			.994	10	*O-121	1.1
1946	Phi-N	6	19	1	4	1	0	0	1	0	7	.211	.211	.263	35	-2	0			1.000	-1	/O-6	-0.3
	NY-N	15	25	2	0	0	0	0	0	2	5	.000	.074	.000	-78	-6	0			.967	-1	O-13	-0.8
	Yr	21	44	3	4	1	0	0	1	2	12	.091	.130	.114	-31	-8	0			.975	-2	O-19	-1.1
Total	10	1110	3849	491	959	209	24	125	584	412	837	.249	.324	.413	108	29	79			.981	71	*O-1081/3-1,S2	5.0

■ MIKE DIMMEL Dimmel, Michael Wayne b: 10/16/54, Albert Lea, Minn. BR/TR, 6', 180 lbs. Deb: 9/2/77

YEAR	TM/L	G	AB	R	H	2B	3B	HR	RBI	BB	SO	AVG	OBP	SLG	PRO+	BR/A	SB	CS	SBR	FA	FR	G/POS	TPR
1977	Bal-A	25	5	8	0	0	0	0	0	0	1	.000	.000	.000	-99	-1	1	0	0	1.000	-6	O-23	-0.7
1978	Bal-A	8	0	2	0	0	0	0	0	0	0	—	—	—			0	1	-1	.667	-3	/O-7	-0.4
1979	StL-N	6	3	1	1	0	0	0	0	0	0	.333	.333	.333	82	-0	0	1	-1	1.000	-2	/O-5	-0.3
Total	3	39	8	11	1	0	0	0	0	0	1	.125	.125	.125	-33	-1	1	2	-1	.952	-11	/O-35	-1.4

■ KERRY DINEEN Dineen, Kerry Michael b: 7/1/52, Englewood, N.J. BL/TL, 5'11", 165 lbs. Deb: 6/14/75

YEAR	TM/L	G	AB	R	H	2B	3B	HR	RBI	BB	SO	AVG	OBP	SLG	PRO+	BR/A	SB	CS	SBR	FA	FR	G/POS	TPR
1975	NY-A	7	22	3	8	1	0	0	1	2	1	.364	.417	.409	138	1	0	0	0	1.000	-0	/O-7	0.1
1976	NY-A	4	7	0	2	0	0	0	1	1	2	.286	.375	.286	96	-0	1	1	-0	.900	-0	/O-4	-0.1
1978	Phi-N	5	8	0	2	1	0	0	0	1	0	.250	.333	.375	97	-0	0	0	0	1.000	-0	/O-1	0.0
Total	3	16	37	3	12	2	0	0	2	4	3	.324	.390	.378	121	1	1	1	-0	.967	-0	/O-12	0.0

■ VANCE DINGES Dinges, Vance George b: 5/29/15, Elizabeth, N.J. d: 10/4/90, Harrisonburg, Va. BL/TL, 6'2", 175 lbs. Deb: 4/17/45

YEAR	TM/L	G	AB	R	H	2B	3B	HR	RBI	BB	SO	AVG	OBP	SLG	PRO+	BR/A	SB	CS	SBR	FA	FR	G/POS	TPR
1945	Phi-N	109	397	46	114	15	4	1	36	35	17	.287	.346	.353	97	-1	5			.986	-1	O-65,1-42	-0.8
1946	Phi-N	50	104	7	32	5	1	1	10	9	12	.308	.363	.404	121	3	2			.985	-1	1-26/O-1	0.1
Total	2	159	501	53	146	20	5	2	46	44	29	.291	.350	.363	102	1	7			.986	-1	/1-68,O-66	-0.7

■ BOB DiPIETRO DiPietro, Robert Louis Paul b: 9/1/27, San Francisco, Cal BR/TR, 5'11", 185 lbs. Deb: 9/23/51

YEAR	TM/L	G	AB	R	H	2B	3B	HR	RBI	BB	SO	AVG	OBP	SLG	PRO+	BR/A	SB	CS	SBR	FA	FR	G/POS	TPR
1951	Bos-A	4	11	0	1	0	0	0	0	0	1	.091	.167	.091	-26	-2	0	0	0	.833	0	/O-3	-0.2

■ GARY DISARCINA Disarcina, Gary Thomas b: 11/19/67, Malden, Mass. BR/TR, 6'1", 170 lbs. Deb: 9/23/89

YEAR	TM/L	G	AB	R	H	2B	3B	HR	RBI	BB	SO	AVG	OBP	SLG	PRO+	BR/A	SB	CS	SBR	FA	FR	G/POS	TPR
1989	Cal-A	2	0	0	0							—	—	—			0	0	0	.000	0	/S-1	0.0
1990	Cal-A	18	57	8	8	1	1	0	0	3	10	.140	.183	.193	5	-7	1	0	0	.940	2	S-14/2-3	-0.4
1991	Cal-A	18	57	5	12	2	0	0	3	3	4	.211	.274	.246	45	-4	0	0	0	.915	-1	S-10/2-7,3	-0.4
1992	Cal-A	157	518	48	128	19	0	3	42	20	50	.247	.284	.301	64	-25	9	7	-2	.967	12	*S-157	-0.4
1993	Cal-A	126	416	44	99	20	1	3	45	15	38	.238	.275	.313	56	-26	5	7	-3	.975	-13	*S-126	-3.1
1994	Cal-A	112	389	53	101	14	2	3	33	18	28	.260	.296	.329	59	-24	3	7	-3	.983	8	*S-110	-1.0
Total	6	433	1437	158	348	56	4	9	123	59	130	.242	.280	.305	57	-87	18	21	-7	.972	6	S-418/2-10,3	-5.3

■ BENNY DISTEFANO Distefano, Benito James b: 1/23/62, Brooklyn, N.Y. BL/TL, 6'1", 195 lbs. Deb: 5/18/84

YEAR	TM/L	G	AB	R	H	2B	3B	HR	RBI	BB	SO	AVG	OBP	SLG	PRO+	BR/A	SB	CS	SBR	FA	FR	G/POS	TPR
1984	Pit-N	45	78	10	13	1	2	3	9	5	13	.167	.226	.346	59	-5	0	1	-1	.946	1	O-20,1-17	-0.5
1986	Pit-N	31	39	3	7	1	0	1	5	1	5	.179	.200	.282	31	-4	0	0	0	1.000	-1	/O-9,1-1	-0.5
1988	Pit-N	16	29	6	10	3	1	1	6	3	4	.345	.406	.621	194	3	0	0	0	1.000	-0	/1-5,O-2	0.3
1989	Pit-N	96	154	12	38	8	0	2	15	17	30	.247	.333	.338	96	-1	0	0	0	.981	-3	1-48/C-3,O	-0.6
1992	Hou-N	52	60	4	14	0	2	0	7	5	14	.233	.303	.300	75	-2	0	0	0	1.000	-0	O-12/1-6	-0.3
Total	5	240	360	35	82	13	5	7	42	31	66	.228	.298	.350	85	-7	1	1	0	.985	-3	/1-77,O-44,C	-1.6

■ DUTCH DISTEL Distel, George Adam b: 4/15/1896, Madison, Ind. d: 2/12/67, Madison, Ind. BR/TR, 5'9", 165 lbs. Deb: 6/21/18

YEAR	TM/L	G	AB	R	H	2B	3B	HR	RBI	BB	SO	AVG	OBP	SLG	PRO+	BR/A	SB	CS	SBR	FA	FR	G/POS	TPR
1918	StL-N	8	17	3	3	1	1	0	1	2	3	.176	.263	.353	90	-0	0			.900	-2	/2-5,S-2,O	-0.2

■ JACK DITTMER Dittmer, John Douglas b: 1/10/28, Elkader, Iowa BL/TR, 6'1", 175 lbs. Deb: 6/17/52

YEAR	TM/L	G	AB	R	H	2B	3B	HR	RBI	BB	SO	AVG	OBP	SLG	PRO+	BR/A	SB	CS	SBR	FA	FR	G/POS	TPR
1952	Bos-N	93	326	26	63	7	2	7	41	26	24	.193	.255	.291	53	-21	1	0	0	.982	6	2-90	-1.1
1953	Mil-N	138	504	54	134	22	1	9	63	18	35	.266	.293	.367	75	-20	1	0	0	.965	-29	*2-138	-4.0
1954	Mil-N	66	192	22	47	8	0	6	20	19	17	.245	.322	.380	88	-4	0	1	-1	.977	-2	2-55	-0.4
1955	Mil-N	38	72	4	9	1	1	1	4	4	15	.125	.171	.208	0	-11	0	0	0	.977	-2	2-28	-1.1
1956	Mil-N	44	102	8	25	6	0	1	6	8	8	.245	.300	.314	69	-4	0	0	0	.979	3	2-42	0.0
1957	Det-A	16	22	3	5	1	0	0	2	2	1	.227	.292	.273	54	-1	0	0	0	1.000	-1	/3-3,2-1	-0.2
Total	6	395	1218	117	283	43	4	24	136	77	102	.232	.281	.333	66	-61	2	1	0	.974	-26	2-354/3-3	-6.8

■ MOXIE DIVIS Divis, Edward George b: 1/16/1894, Cleveland, Ohio d: 12/19/55, Lakewood, Ohio Deb: 8/4/16

YEAR	TM/L	G	AB	R	H	2B	3B	HR	RBI	BB	SO	AVG	OBP	SLG	PRO+	BR/A	SB	CS	SBR	FA	FR	G/POS	TPR
1916	Phi-A	3	6	0	1	0	0	0	1	0	2	.167	.167	.167	0	-1	0			1.000	1	/O-1	0.0

■ LEO DIXON Dixon, Leo Moses b: 9/4/1894, Chicago, Ill. d: 4/11/84, Chicago, Ill. BR/TR, 5'11", 170 lbs. Deb: 4/14/25

YEAR	TM/L	G	AB	R	H	2B	3B	HR	RBI	BB	SO	AVG	OBP	SLG	PRO+	BR/A	SB	CS	SBR	FA	FR	G/POS	TPR
1925	StL-A	76	205	27	46	11	1	1	19	24	42	.224	.318	.302	55	-14	3	2	-0	.981	9	C-75	-0.2
1926	StL-A	33	89	7	17	3	1	0	8	11	14	.191	.294	.247	40	-8	1	4	-2	.977	4	C-33	-0.4
1927	StL-A	36	103	6	20	3	1	0	12	7	6	.194	.245	.243	26	-11	0	1	-1	.937	3	C-35	-0.6
1929	Cin-N	14	30	0	5	2	0	0	2	3	7	.167	.242	.233	19	-4	0	0	0	1.000	4	C-14	0.1
Total	4	159	427	40	88	19	3	1	41	45	69	.206	.291	.272	43	-37	4	7		.971	21	C-157	-1.1

YEAR	TM/L	G	AB	R	H	2B	3B	HR	RBI	BB	SO	AVG	OBP	SLG	PRO+	BR/A	SB	CS	SBR	FA	FR	G/POS	TPR

■ WALT DOANE   Doane, Walter Rudolph b: 3/12/1887, Bellevue, Idaho   d: 10/19/35, W.Brandywine, Pa.   BL/TR, 6′, 165 lbs.   Deb: 9/20/09

YEAR	TM/L	G	AB	R	H	2B	3B	HR	RBI	BB	SO	AVG	OBP	SLG	PRO+	BR/A	SB	CS	SBR	FA	FR	G/POS	TPR
1909	Cle-A	4	9	1	1	0	0	0	0	0	1	.111	.200	.111	-1	-1	0			.778	1	/O-2,P-1	0.0
1910	Cle-A	6	7	0	2	1	0	0	2	2	1	.286	.375	.429	150	0	0			.750	-1	/P-6	0.0
Total	2	10	16	1	3	1	0	0	2	2	2	.188	.278	.250	64	-1	0			.800	-0	/P-7,O-2	0.0

■ DAN DOBBEK   Dobbek, Daniel John b: 12/6/34, Ontonagon, Mich.   BL/TR, 6′, 195 lbs.   Deb: 9/9/59

YEAR	TM/L	G	AB	R	H	2B	3B	HR	RBI	BB	SO	AVG	OBP	SLG	PRO+	BR/A	SB	CS	SBR	FA	FR	G/POS	TPR
1959	Was-A	16	60	8	15	1	2	1	5	5	13	.250	.308	.383	89	-1	0	0	0	1.000	1	O-16	-0.1
1960	Was-A	110	248	32	54	8	2	10	30	35	41	.218	.317	.387	90	-4	4	3	-1	.973	-8	O-78	-1.5
1961	Min-A	72	125	12	21	3	1	4	14	13	18	.168	.257	.304	47	-10	1	2	-1	.985	-9	O-48	-2.1
Total	3	198	433	52	90	12	5	15	49	53	72	.208	.299	.363	77	-14	5	5	-2	.980	-16	O-142	-3.7

■ JOHN DOBBS   Dobbs, John Gordon b: 6/3/1876, Chattanooga, Tenn.   d: 9/9/34, Charlotte, N.C.   BL/TR, 5′9.5″, 170 lbs.   Deb: 4/20/01

YEAR	TM/L	G	AB	R	H	2B	3B	HR	RBI	BB	SO	AVG	OBP	SLG	PRO+	BR/A	SB	CS	SBR	FA	FR	G/POS	TPR
1901	Cin-N	109	435	71	119	17	4	2	27	36		.274	.338	.345	105	3	19			.948	-7	*O-100/3-8	-1.0
1902	Cin-N	63	256	39	76	7	3	1	16	19		.297	.348	.359	108	2	7			.963	8	O-63	0.6
	Chi-N	59	235	31	71	8	2	0	35	18		.302	.352	.353	121	6	3			.977	5	O-59	0.3
	Yr	122	491	70	147	15	5	1	51	37		.299	.350	.356	114	8	10			.970	8	*O-122	0.9
1903	Chi-N	16	61	8	14	1	1	0	4	7		.230	.329	.279	76	-2	0			1.000	1	O-16	-0.2
	Bro-N	111	414	61	98	15	7	2	59	48		.237	.323	.321	86	-6	23			.966	4	*O-110	-0.9
	Yr	127	475	69	112	16	8	2	63	55		.236	.324	.316	85	-8	23			.970	4	*O-126	-1.1
1904	Bro-N	101	363	36	90	16	2	0	30	28		.248	.304	.303	90	-4	11			.936	0	O-92/2-2,S	-1.0
1905	Bro-N	123	460	59	117	21	4	2	36	31		.254	.304	.330	96	-3	15			.938	-6	*O-123	-1.6
Total	5	582	2224	305	585	85	23	7	207	187		.263	.325	.331	98	-4	78			.954	-0	O-563/3-8,S2	-3.8

■ LARRY DOBY   Doby, Lawrence Eugene b: 12/13/24, Camden, S.C.   BL/TR, 6′1″, 182 lbs.   Deb: 7/5/47   MC

YEAR	TM/L	G	AB	R	H	2B	3B	HR	RBI	BB	SO	AVG	OBP	SLG	PRO+	BR/A	SB	CS	SBR	FA	FR	G/POS	TPR
1947	Cle-A	29	32	3	5	1	0	0	2	1	11	.156	.182	.188	3	-4	0	0	0	1.000	-1	/2-4,1-1,S	-0.5
1948	*Cle-A	121	439	83	132	23	9	14	66	54	77	.301	.384	.490	135	21	9	9	-3	.955	3	*O-114	1.5
1949	Cle-A★	147	547	106	153	25	3	24	85	91	90	.280	.389	.468	129	23	10	9	-2	.976	-7	*O-147	0.6
1950	Cle-A★	142	503	110	164	25	5	25	102	98	71	.326	.442	.545	156	46	8	6	-1	.987	-6	*O-140	3.1
1951	Cle-A★	134	447	84	132	27	5	20	69	101	81	.295	.428	.512	163	43	4	1	1	.977	-1	*O-132	3.6
1952	Cle-A★	140	519	**104**	143	26	8	**32**	104	90	111	.276	.383	**.541**	166	45	5	2	0	.986	11	*O-136	**5.1**
1953	Cle-A★	149	513	92	135	18	5	29	102	96	121	.263	.385	.487	138	29	3	2	-0	.984	-7	*O-146	1.6
1954	*Cle-A★	153	577	94	157	18	4	**32**	126	85	94	.272	.368	.484	130	23	3	1	0	.995	6	*O-153	2.4
1955	Cle-A☆	131	491	91	143	17	5	26	75	61	100	.291	.372	.505	129	19	2	1	1	.994	3	*O-129	1.7
1956	Chi-A	140	504	89	135	22	3	24	102	102	105	.268	.395	.466	125	20	0	1	-1	.987	6	*O-137	1.8
1957	Cle-A	119	416	57	120	27	2	14	79	56	79	.288	.376	.464	127	16	2	3	-1	.985	-4	*O-110	0.5
1958	Cle-A	89	247	41	70	10	1	13	45	26	49	.283	.352	.490	132	10	0	2	-1	1.000	1	O-68	0.7
1959	Det-A	18	55	5	12	3	1	0	4	8	9	.218	.317	.309	69	-2	0	0	0	.960	-1	O-16	-0.4
	Chi-A	21	58	1	14	1	1	0	9	2	13	.241	.267	.293	54	-4	1	0	0	.955	-1	O-12/1-2	-0.5
	Yr	39	113	6	26	4	2	0	13	10	22	.230	.293	.301	62	-6	1	0	0	.957	-1	O-28/1-2	-0.9
Total	13	1533	5348	960	1515	243	52	253	970	871	1011	.283	.387	.490	137	285	47	36	-8	.983	3	*O-1440/2-4,1S	21.2

■ ORAN DODD   Dodd, Oran A. b: 9/14/1889, Bagwell, Tex.   d: 3/31/29, Newport, Ark.   BR/TR, 5′8″, 150 lbs.   Deb: 7/26/12

YEAR	TM/L	G	AB	R	H	2B	3B	HR	RBI	BB	SO	AVG	OBP	SLG	PRO+	BR/A	SB	CS	SBR	FA	FR	G/POS	TPR
1912	Pit-N	5	9	0	0	0	0	0	1	1	3	.000	.100	.000	-73	-2	0			1.000	0	/3-4,2-1	-0.2

■ TOM DODD   Dodd, Thomas Marion b: 8/15/58, Portland, Ore.   BR/TR, 6′, 190 lbs.   Deb: 7/25/86

YEAR	TM/L	G	AB	R	H	2B	3B	HR	RBI	BB	SO	AVG	OBP	SLG	PRO+	BR/A	SB	CS	SBR	FA	FR	G/POS	TPR
1986	Bal-A	8	13	1	3	0	0	1	2	2	2	.231	.375	.462	128	1	0	0	0	.000	-0	/3-1,D-6	0.0

■ JOHN DODGE   Dodge, John Lewis b: 4/27/1889, Bolivar, Tenn.   d: 6/19/16, Mobile, Ala.   BR/TR, 5′11.5″, 165 lbs.   Deb: 8/29/12

YEAR	TM/L	G	AB	R	H	2B	3B	HR	RBI	BB	SO	AVG	OBP	SLG	PRO+	BR/A	SB	CS	SBR	FA	FR	G/POS	TPR
1912	Phi-N	30	92	3	11	1	0	0	3	4	11	.120	.156	.130	-20	-15	2			1.000	8	3-23/2-5,S	-0.8
1913	Phi-N	3	3	0	1	0	0	0	0	2	0	.333	.600	.333	164	1	0			1.000	-1	/S-3	0.0
	Cin-N	94	323	35	78	8	8	4	45	10	34	.241	.269	.353	77	-11	11			.908	-1	3-91	-0.9
	Yr	97	326	35	79	8	8	4	45	12	34	.242	.274	.353	78	-10	11			.908	-1	3-91/S-3	-0.9
Total	2	127	418	38	90	9	8	4	48	16	45	.215	.248	.304	55	-26	13			.926	8	3-114/2-5,S	-1.7

■ PAT DODSON   Dodson, Patrick Neal b: 10/11/59, Santa Monica, Cal.   BL/TL, 6′4″, 210 lbs.   Deb: 9/5/86

YEAR	TM/L	G	AB	R	H	2B	3B	HR	RBI	BB	SO	AVG	OBP	SLG	PRO+	BR/A	SB	CS	SBR	FA	FR	G/POS	TPR
1986	Bos-A	9	12	3	5	2	0	1	3	3	3	.417	.533	.833	264	3	0	0	0	1.000	-1	/1-7	0.2
1987	Bos-A	26	42	4	7	3	0	2	6	8	13	.167	.300	.381	77	-1	0	0	0	1.000	-1	1-21/D-1	-0.3
1988	Bos-A	17	45	5	8	3	1	1	1	6	17	.178	.275	.356	72	-2	0	0	0	1.000	1	1-17	-0.1
Total	3	52	99	12	20	8	1	4	10	17	33	.202	.319	.424	97	-0	0	0	0	1.000	0	/1-45,D-1	-0.2

■ BOBBY DOERR   Doerr, Robert Pershing b: 4/7/18, Los Angeles, Cal.   BR/TR, 5′11″, 175 lbs.   Deb: 4/20/37   CH

YEAR	TM/L	G	AB	R	H	2B	3B	HR	RBI	BB	SO	AVG	OBP	SLG	PRO+	BR/A	SB	CS	SBR	FA	FR	G/POS	TPR
1937	Bos-A	55	147	22	33	5	1	2	14	18	25	.224	.313	.313	56	-10	2	4	-2	.973	4	2-47	-0.5
1938	Bos-A	145	509	70	147	26	7	5	80	59	39	.289	.360	.397	86	-11	5	10	-5	.968	6	*2-145	-0.1
1939	Bos-A	127	525	75	167	28	2	12	73	38	32	.318	.365	.448	103	1	1	10	-6	.976	27	*2-126	2.7
1940	Bos-A	151	595	87	173	37	10	22	105	57	53	.291	.353	.497	113	10	10	5	0	.977	18	*2-151	3.6
1941	Bos-A★	132	500	74	141	28	4	16	93	43	43	.282	.339	.450	105	2	1	3	-2	.971	4	*2-132	0.3
1942	Bos-A☆	144	545	71	158	35	5	15	102	67	55	.290	.369	.455	127	19	4	4	-1	**.975**	11	*2-142	3.8
1943	Bos-A★	155	604	78	163	32	3	16	75	62	59	.270	.339	.412	117	12	8	4	-1	**.990**	15	*2-155	3.5
1944	Bos-A★	125	468	95	152	30	10	15	81	58	31	.325	.399	**.528**	166	39	5	2	0	.976	4	*2-125	5.2
1946	*Bos-A★	151	583	95	158	34	9	18	116	66	67	.271	.346	.453	115	11	5	6	-2	**.986**	27	*2-151	4.8
1947	Bos-A★	146	561	79	145	23	10	17	95	59	47	.258	.329	.426	101	-1	3	3	-1	.981	24	*2-146	3.3
1948	Bos-A★	140	527	94	150	23	6	27	111	83	49	.285	.386	.505	129	21	3	2	-0	.993	8	*2-138	3.6
1949	Bos-A	139	541	91	167	30	9	18	109	75	33	.309	.393	.497	126	19	2	2	-1	.980	**28**	*2-139	5.0
1950	Bos-A★	149	586	103	172	29	**11**	27	120	67	42	.294	.367	.519	114	9	3	4	-2	**.988**	9	*2-149	2.1
1951	Bos-A★	106	402	60	116	21	2	13	73	57	33	.289	.378	.448	112	7	2	1	0	.981	6	*2-106	1.7
Total	14	1865	7093	1094	2042	381	89	223	1247	809	608	.288	.362	.461	114	127	54	64	-22	.980	181	*2-1852	39.0

■ JOHN DOHERTY   Doherty, John Michael b: 8/22/51, Woburn, Mass.   BL/TL, 5′11″, 185 lbs.   Deb: 6/1/74

YEAR	TM/L	G	AB	R	H	2B	3B	HR	RBI	BB	SO	AVG	OBP	SLG	PRO+	BR/A	SB	CS	SBR	FA	FR	G/POS	TPR
1974	Cal-A	74	223	20	57	14	1	3	15	8	13	.256	.281	.368	91	-4	2	1	0	.991	-1	1-70/D-2	-0.9
1975	Cal-A	30	94	7	19	3	0	1	12	8	12	.202	.265	.266	54	-6	1	1	-0	.983	-1	1-26/D-1	-0.9
Total	2	104	317	27	76	17	1	4	27	16	25	.240	.276	.338	80	-10	3	2	-0	.989	-2	/1-96,D-3	-1.8

■ COZY DOLAN   Dolan, Albert J. (b: James Alberts) b: 12/23/1889, Chicago, Ill.   d: 12/10/58, Chicago, Ill.   BR/TR, 5′10″, 160 lbs.   Deb: 8/15/09   C

YEAR	TM/L	G	AB	R	H	2B	3B	HR	RBI	BB	SO	AVG	OBP	SLG	PRO+	BR/A	SB	CS	SBR	FA	FR	G/POS	TPR
1909	Cin-N	3	6	2	1	0	0	0	0	2		.167	.375	.167	69	-0	1			.750	-1	/3-3	-0.1
1911	NY-A	19	69	19	21	1	2	0	6	8		.304	.385	.377	106	1	12			.947	-1	3-19	0.0
1912	NY-A	18	60	15	12	1	3	0	11	5		.200	.273	.317	64	-3	5			.768	-5	3-17	-0.8
	Phi-N	11	50	8	14	2	2	0	7	1	10	.280	.294	.400	83	-1	3			.872	-6	3-11	-0.2
1913	Phi-N	55	126	15	33	4	0	0	8	1	21	.262	.273	.294	59	-7	9			.905	-7	O-12,S-10/231	-1.4
	Pit-N	35	133	22	27	5	2	0	9	15	14	.203	.289	.271	63	-6	14			.937	-3	3-35	-0.7
	Yr	90	259	37	60	9	2	0	17	16	35	.232	.282	.282	61	-13	23			.932	-9	3-39,O-12,S/21	-2.1
1914	StL-N	126	421	76	101	16	3	4	32	55	74	.240	.335	.321	96	-0	42			.955	-8	O-96,3-27	-1.2
1915	StL-N	111	322	53	90	14	9	2	38	34	37	.280	.356	.398	127	11	17	11	-2	.929	-11	O-98	-0.6
1922	NY-N	1															0	0	0	.000	0	R	0.0
Total	7	379	1187	210	299	43	21	6	111	121	<u>156</u>	.252	.328	.339	95	-6	102	<u>11</u>		.940	-34	O-206,3-116/S21	-5.0

YEAR	TM/L	G	AB	R	H	2B	3B	HR	RBI	BB	SO	AVG	OBP	SLG	PRO+	BR/A	SB	CS	SBR	FA	FR	G/POS	TPR

■ JOE DOLAN
Dolan, Joseph b: 2/24/1873, Baltimore, Md. d: 3/24/38, Omaha, Neb. TR, 5'10", 155 lbs. Deb: 8/11/1896

1896	Lou-N	44	165	14	35	2	1	3	18	9	12	.212	.253	.291	45	-14	6			.940	10	S-44	-0.2
1897	Lou-N	36	133	10	28	2	2	0	7	8		.211	.271	.256	41	-11	6			.849	-3	S-18,2-18	-1.2
1899	Phi-N	61	222	27	57	6	3	1	30	11		.257	.298	.324	73	-9	3			.915	-11	2-61	-1.5
1900	Phi-N	74	257	39	51	7	3	1	27	16		.198	.259	.261	44	-20	10			.931	3	3-31,2-29,S	-1.4
1901	Phi-N	10	37	0	3	0	0	0	2	2		.081	.128	.081	-38	-6	0			.973	-3	2-10	-0.9
	Phi-A	98	338	50	73	21	2	1	38	26		.216	.282	.299	58	-19	3			.881	16	S-61,3-35/2O	0.1
Total	5	323	1152	140	247	38	11	6	122	72	12	.214	.270	.282	51	-79	28			.902	11	S-135,2-119/3O	-5.1

■ BIDDY DOLAN
Dolan, Leon Mark b: 7/9/1881, Onalaska, Wis. d: 7/15/50, Indianapolis, Ind BR/TR, 6', Deb: 4/16/14

| 1914 | Ind-F | 32 | 103 | 13 | 23 | 4 | 2 | 1 | 15 | 12 | 13 | .223 | .316 | .330 | 61 | -6 | 5 | | | .979 | 1 | 1-31 | -0.6 |

■ COZY DOLAN
Dolan, Patrick Henry b: 12/3/1872, Cambridge, Mass. d: 3/29/07, Louisville, Ky. BL/TL, 5'10", 160 lbs. Deb: 4/26/1895

1895	Bos-N	26	83	12	20	4	1	0	7	6	7	.241	.300	.313	54	-6	3			.949	3	P-25/O-1	-0.1
1896	Bos-N	6	14	4	2	0	0	0	0	0	1	.143	.143	.143	-23	-3	0			.765	-0	/P-6	0.0
1900	Chi-N	13	48	5	13	1	0	0	2	2		.271	.300	.292	66	-2	2			.826	-2	O-13	-0.4
1901	Chi-N	43	171	29	45	1	2	0	16	7		.263	.296	.292	74	-6	3			.878	2	O-41	-0.7
	Bro-N	66	253	33	66	11	1	0	29	17		.261	.313	.312	79	-7	7			.967	-2	O-64	-1.3
	Yr	109	424	62	111	12	3	0	45	24		.262	.306	.304	77	-12	10			.931	0	*O-105	-2.0
1902	Bro-N	141	592	72	166	16	7	1	54	33		.280	.324	.336	103	1	24			.936	-9	*O-141	-1.8
1903	Chi-A	27	104	16	27	5	1	0	7	6		.260	.313	.327	96	-0	5			.971	2	1-19/O-4	0.1
	Cin-N	93	385	64	111	20	3	0	58	28		.288	.340	.356	88	-7	11			.937	-7	O-93	-1.9
1904	Cin-N	129	465	88	132	8	10	6	51	39		.284	.342	.383	113	6	19			.939	-4	*O-102,1-24	-0.4
1905	Cin-N	22	77	7	18	2	1	0	4	7		.234	.306	.286	69	-3	2			.965	-4	1-13/O-9	-0.8
	Bos-N	112	433	44	119	11	7	3	48	27		.275	.322	.353	103	1	21			.946	4	*O-111/P-2,1	0.0
	Yr	134	510	51	137	13	8	3	52	34		.269	.319	.343	97	-2	23			.931	0	*O-120,1-15/P	-0.8
1906	Bos-N	152	549	54	136	20	4	0	39	55		.248	.318	.299	95	-2	17			.928	-2	*O-144/2-7,P1	-1.2
Total	9	830	3174	428	855	99	37	10	315	227	8	.269	.322	.333	94	-27	114			.931	-18	O-723/1-59,P2	-8.5

■ TOM DOLAN
Dolan, Thomas J. b: 1/10/1859, New York, N.Y. d: 1/16/13, St.Louis, Mo. BR/TR, Deb: 9/30/1879

1879	Chi-N	1	4	0	0	0	0	0	0	0	2	.000	.000	.000	-94	-1				1.000	1	/C-1	0.0
1882	Buf-N	22	89	12	14	0	1	0	8	2	11	.157	.176	.180	14	-8				.941	-8	C-18/O-4,3	-1.5
1883	StL-a	81	295	32	63	9	2	1		9		.214	.237	.268	59	-14				.957	12	C-42,O-40/P	0.0
1884	StL-a	35	137	19	36	6	2	0		6		.263	.299	.336	103	0				.873	-6	C-34/O-2	-0.3
	StL-U	19	69	9	13	3	0	0		4		.188	.233	.232	26	-7				.897	11	C-14/3-3,O	0.4
1885	StL-N	3	9	1	2	0	0	0	0	2	1	.222	.364	.222	99	0				.810	-1	/C-3	0.0
1886	StL-N	15	44	8	11	3	0	0	1	7	9	.250	.353	.318	113	1	2			.928	6	C-15	0.8
	Bal-a	38	125	13	19	3	2	0		8		.152	.203	.208	30	-10	8			.918	-6	C-35/O-3	-1.1
1888	StL-a	11	36	1	7	1	0	0	1	1		.194	.216	.222	37	-3	1			.914	-0	C-11	-0.2
Total	7	225	808	95	165	25	7	1	10	39	23	.204	.242	.256	55	-42	11			.916	8	C-173/O-51,3P	-1.9

■ LESTER DOLE
Dole, Lester Carrington b: 7/8/1855, Meriden, Conn. d: 12/10/18, Concord, N.H. 5'11", Deb: 5/27/1875

| 1875 | NH-n | 1 | 4 | 1 | 2 | 0 | 0 | 0 | | 0 | | .500 | .500 | .500 | 283 | 1 | | | | | | /O-1 | 0.1 |

■ FRANK DOLJACK
Doljack, Frank Joseph "Dolie" b: 10/5/07, Cleveland, Ohio d: 1/23/48, Cleveland, Ohio BR/TR, 5'11", 175 lbs. Deb: 9/4/30

1930	Det-A	20	74	10	19	5	1	3	17	2	11	.257	.286	.473	87	-2	0	1	-1	.930	0	O-20	-0.3
1931	Det-A	63	187	20	52	13	3	4	20	15	17	.278	.335	.444	100	-1	3	2	-0	.925	3	O-54	-0.1
1932	Det-A	8	26	5	10	1	0	1	7	2	2	.385	.429	.538	143	2	1	0	0	1.000	-2	/O-6	0.0
1933	Det-A	42	147	18	42	5	4	0	22	14	13	.286	.348	.347	83	-3	2	6	-3	.941	2	O-37	-0.6
1934	*Det-A	56	120	15	28	7	1	1	19	13	15	.233	.313	.333	67	-6	2	1	0	.943	-3	O-30/1-3	-0.9
1943	Cle-A	3	7	0	0	0	0	0	0	1	2	.000	.125	.000	-66	-1	0	0	0	1.000	-0	/O-2	-0.2
Total	6	192	561	68	151	31	7	9	85	47	60	.269	.329	.398	87	-12	8	10	-4	.934	-0	O-149/1-3	-2.1

■ ART DOLL
Doll, Arthur James "Moose" b: 5/7/13, Chicago, Ill. d: 4/28/78, Calumet City, Ill. BR/TR, 6'1", 190 lbs. Deb: 9/21/35

1935	Bos-N	3	10	0	1	0	0	0	0	0	1	.100	.100	.100	-50	-2	0			.867	0	/C-3	-0.2
1936	Bos-N	1	2	0	0	0	0	0	0	0	2	.000	.000	.000	-99	-1	0			1.000	-0	/P-1	0.0
1938	Bos-N	3	1	0	1	0	0	0	0	0		1.000	1.000	1.000	501	1	0			1.000	0	/P-3	0.0
Total	3	7	13	0	2	0	0	0	0	0	3	.154	.154	.154	-18	-2	0			1.000	0	/P-4,C-3	-0.2

■ SHE DONAHUE
Donahue, Charles Michael b: 6/29/1877, Oswego, N.Y. d: 8/28/47, New York, N.Y. BR/TR, 5'9", Deb: 4/29/04

1904	StL-N	4	15	1	4	0	0	0	2	0		.267	.267	.267	68	-1	3			.846	-3	/2-3,S-1	-0.4
	Phi-N	58	200	21	43	4	0	0	14	3		.215	.227	.235	44	-13	7			.857	-17	S-29,3-24/12	-3.1
	Yr	62	215	22	47	4	0	0	16	3		.219	.229	.237	46	-14	10			.852	-20	S-30,3-24/21	-3.5

■ JIM DONAHUE
Donahue, James Augustus b: 1/8/1862, Lockport, Ill. d: 4/19/35, Lockport, Ill. BR/TR, 6', 175 lbs. Deb: 4/19/1886

1886	NY-a	49	186	14	37	0	0	0		10		.199	.251	.199	44	-11	1			.803	-2	O-32,C-19	-1.1
1887	NY-a	60	220	33	62	4	1	1		21		.282	.350	.323	92	-1	6			.890	-8	C-51/O-5,132	-0.3
1888	KC-a	88	337	29	79	11	3	1	28	21		.234	.281	.294	79	-9	12			.902	-11	C-67,O-18/32	-1.3
1889	KC-a	67	252	30	59	5	4	0	32	21	20	.234	.293	.286	61	-13	12			.887	-8	C-46,O-14,3	-1.5
1891	Col-a	77	280	27	61	4	3	0	35	31	18	.218	.298	.254	62	-13	2			.942	3	C-75/O-1,1	-0.3
Total	5	341	1275	133	298	24	11	2	95	104	38	.234	.295	.275	69	-48	33			.911	-25	C-258/O-70,312	-4.5

■ JIGGS DONAHUE
Donahue, John Augustus b: 7/13/1879, Springfield, Ohio d: 7/19/13, Columbus, Ohio BL/TL, 6'1", 178 lbs. Deb: 9/10/00 F

1900	Pit-N	3	10	1	2	0	1	0	3	0		.200	.200	.400	63	-1				.889	-1	/C-2,O-1	-0.2
1901	Pit-N	2	0	0	0	0	0	0	0	0		—	—	—			0			.000	-1	/C-1,O-1	-0.1
	Mil-A	37	107	10	34	5	4	0	16	10		.318	.387	.439	135	5	4			.933	-2	C-19,1-13	0.5
1902	StL-A	30	89	11	21	1	1	1	7	12		.236	.327	.303	76	-2	2			.956	-1	C-23/1-5	-0.1
1904	Chi-A	102	367	46	91	9	7	1	48	25		.248	.298	.319	99	-1	18			.979	7	*1-101	0.4
1905	Chi-A	149	533	71	153	22	4	1	76	44		.287	.346	.349	126	16	32			.988	8	*1-149	2.1
1906	*Chi-A	154	556	70	143	17	7	1	57	48		.257	.320	.318	103	2	36			.988	9	*1-154	0.7
1907	Chi-A	157	609	75	158	16	4	0	68	28		.259	.295	.299	93	-6	27			.994	21	*1-157	1.1
1908	Chi-A	93	304	22	62	6	1	0	22	25		.204	.271	.243	69	-10	14			.994	5	1-83	-0.8
1909	Chi-A	2	4	0	0	0	0	0	2	1		.000	.200	.000	-38	-1	0			1.000	-0	/1-2	-0.1
	Was-A	84	283	13	67	12	1	0	28	22		.237	.294	.286	87	-4	9			.984	-4	1-81	-1.0
	Yr	86	287	13	67	12	1	0	30	23		.233	.293	.282	86	-5	9			.984	-4	1-83	-1.1
Total	9	813	2862	319	731	90	31	4	327	215		.255	.311	.313	99	-27	143			.987	40	1-745/C-45,O	2.5

■ JOHN DONAHUE
Donahue, John Frederick "Jiggs" b: 4/19/1894, Roxbury, Mass. d: 10/3/49, Boston, Mass. BB/TR, 5'8", 170 lbs. Deb: 9/25/23

| 1923 | Bos-A | 10 | 36 | 5 | 10 | 4 | 0 | 0 | 1 | 4 | 5 | .278 | .350 | .389 | 94 | -0 | 0 | 1 | -1 | 1.000 | 3 | /O-9 | 0.2 |

■ PAT DONAHUE
Donahue, Patrick William b: 11/8/1884, Springfield, Ohio d: 1/31/66, Springfield, Ohio BR/TR, 6', 175 lbs. Deb: 5/29/08 F

1908	Bos-A	35	86	8	17	2	0	1	6	9		.198	.289	.256	75	-2	0			.959	2	C-32/1-3	0.1
1909	Bos-A	64	176	14	42	4	1	2	25	17		.239	.309	.307	93	-1	2			.982	-3	C-58	0.1
1910	Bos-A	2	4	0	0	0	0	0	0	0		.000	.000	.000	-98	-1	0			1.000	0	/C-1	-0.1
	Phi-A	14	34	2	5	0	0	0	4	3		.147	.237	.147	21	-3	1			1.000	3	C-13	0.2

YEAR	TM/L	G	AB	R	H	2B	3B	HR	RBI	BB	SO	AVG	OBP	SLG	PRO+	BR/A	SB	CS	SBR	FA	FR	G/POS	TPR
	Cle-A	2	6	0	1	0	0	0	0	0	0	.167	.167	.167	4	-1	0			1.000	-1	/C-2,1-1	-0.1
	Phi-A	1	1	0	0	0	0	0	0	0	0	.000	.000	.000	-99	-0	0			1.000	1	/C-1	
	Yr	19	45	2	6	0	0	0		4	3	.133	.204	.133	6	-5	1			1.000	3	C-17/1-1	0.0
Total	3	118	307	24	65	6	1	3	35	29		.212	.288	.267	75	-8	3			.978	1	C-107/1-4	0.2

■ TIM DONAHUE — Donahue, Timothy Cornelius "Bridget" b: 6/8/1870, Raynham, Mass. d: 6/12/02, Taunton, Mass. BL/TR, 5'11", 180 lbs. Deb: 7/28/1891

YEAR	TM/L	G	AB	R	H	2B	3B	HR	RBI	BB	SO	AVG	OBP	SLG	PRO+	BR/A	SB	CS	SBR	FA	FR	G/POS	TPR
1891	Bos-a	4	7	0	0	0	0	0	0	0	5	.000	.000	.000	-99	-2	0			.833	-1	/C-4	-0.3
1895	Chi-N	63	219	29	59	9	1	2	36	20	25	.269	.339	.347	73	-9	5			.915	-2	C-63	-0.4
1896	Chi-N	57	188	27	41	10	1	0	20	11	15	.218	.276	.282	45	-15	11			.937	5	C-57	-0.3
1897	Chi-N	58	188	28	45	7	3	0	21	9		.239	.281	.309	54	-13	3			.947	7	C-55/S-2,1	0.0
1898	Chi-N	122	396	52	87	12	3	0	39	49		.220	.318	.265	68	-15	17			.962	6	*C-122	0.3
1899	Chi-N	92	278	39	69	9	3	0	29	34		.248	.345	.302	80	-6	10			.951	4	C-91/1-1	0.4
1900	Chi-N	67	216	21	51	10	1	0	17	19		.236	.313	.292	70	-8	8			.928	-7	C-66/2-1	-0.9
1902	Was-A	3	8	0	2	0	0	0	1	0		.250	.250	.250	39	-1	0			1.000	0	/C-3	
Total	8	466	1500	196	354	57	12	3	163	142	45	.236	.314	.294	66	-70	54			.943	11	C-461/1-2,S2	-1.2

■ JOHN DONALDSON — Donaldson, John David b: 5/5/43, Charlotte, N.C. BL/TR, 5'11", 165 lbs. Deb: 8/26/66

YEAR	TM/L	G	AB	R	H	2B	3B	HR	RBI	BB	SO	AVG	OBP	SLG	PRO+	BR/A	SB	CS	SBR	FA	FR	G/POS	TPR
1966	KC-A	15	30	4	4	0	0	0	3	4		.133	.212	.133	2	-4	1	0	0	1.000	-2	/2-9	-0.6
1967	KC-A	105	377	27	104	16	5	0	28	37	39	.276	.344	.345	107	4	6	3	0	.982	-18	*2-101/S-1	-0.8
1968	Oak-A	127	363	37	80	9	2	2	27	45	44	.220	.310	.273	82	-7	5	5	-2	.971	-4	2-98/3-5,S	-0.8
1969	Oak-A	12	13	1	1	0	0	0	0	2	4	.077	.200	.077	-21	-2	0	0	0	.857	0	/2-1	-0.2
	Sea-A	95	338	22	79	8	3	1	19	36	36	.234	.307	.284	67	-14	6	1	1	.974	-1	2-90/3-2,S	-0.6
	Yr	107	351	23	80	8	3	1	19	38	40	.228	.303	.276	64	-16	6	1	1	.972	-0	2-91/3-2,S	-0.8
1970	Oak-A	41	89	4	22	2	1	1	11	9	6	.247	.316	.326	80	-2	1	0	0	.986	-3	2-21/S-6,3	-0.3
1974	Oak-A	10	15	1	2	0	0	0	0	0	0	.133	.133	.133	-25	-2	0	0	0	.962	1	/2-7,3-3	-0.2
Total	6	405	1225	96	292	35	11	4	86	132	133	.238	.314	.295	81	-28	19	9	0	.976	-26	2-327/3-11,S	-3.5

■ LEN DONDERO — Dondero, Leonard Peter "Mike" b: 9/12/03, Newark, Cal. BR/TR, 5'11", 178 lbs. Deb: 4/21/29

YEAR	TM/L	G	AB	R	H	2B	3B	HR	RBI	BB	SO	AVG	OBP	SLG	PRO+	BR/A	SB	CS	SBR	FA	FR	G/POS	TPR
1929	StL-A	19	31	2	6	0	0	1	8	0	4	.194	.194	.290	22	-4	0	0	0	.857	-3	3-10/2-5	-0.6

■ MIKE DONLIN — Donlin, Michael Joseph "Turkey Mike" b: 5/30/1878, Peoria, Ill. d: 9/24/33, Hollywood, Cal. BL/TL, 5'9", 170 lbs. Deb: 7/19/1899

YEAR	TM/L	G	AB	R	H	2B	3B	HR	RBI	BB	SO	AVG	OBP	SLG	PRO+	BR/A	SB	CS	SBR	FA	FR	G/POS	TPR
1899	StL-N	66	266	49	86	9	6	6	27	17		.323	.366	.470	126	8	20			.873		O-51,1-13/SP	-0.4
1900	StL-N	78	276	40	90	8	6	10	48	14		.326	.361	.507	139	13	14			.922	-4	O-47,1-21	0.5
1901	Bal-A	121	476	107	162	23	13	5	67	53		.340	.409	.475	138	25	33			.918	9	O-74,1-47	2.5
1902	Cin-N	34	143	30	41	5	4	0	9	9		.287	.333	.378	109	1	9			.877	-1	O-32/P-1,S	-0.2
1903	Cin-N	126	496	110	174	25	18	7	67	56		.351	.420	.516	150	30	26			.900	-2	*O-118/1-7	2.0
1904	Cin-N	60	236	42	84	11	7	1	38	18		.356	.406	.475	158	15	21			.872	-3	O-53/1-6	1.0
	NY-N	42	132	17	37	7	3	2	14	10		.280	.340	.424	130	4	1			.918	-7	O-37	-0.4
	Yr	102	368	59	121	18	10	3	52	28		.329	.382	.457	148	20	22			.886	-9	O-90/1-6	0.6
1905	*NY-N	150	606	**124**	216	31	16	7	80	56		.356	.413	.495	166	49	33			.934	-12	*O-150	3.1
1906	NY-N	37	121	15	38	5	1	1	14	11		.314	.371	.397	136	5	9			.929	-6	O-29/1-1	-0.3
1908	NY-N	155	593	71	198	26	13	6	106	23		.334	.364	.452	153	32	30			.977	0	*O-155	3.0
1911	NY-N	12	12	3	4	0	0	1	0	1		.333	.333	.583	150	1	2			1.000	-1	/O-3	-0.1
	Bos-N	56	222	33	70	16	1	2	34	22	17	.315	.377	.423	115	4	7			.912	-3	O-56	-0.2
	Yr	68	234	36	74	16	1	3	35	22	18	.316	.375	.432	117	5	9			.913	-4	O-59	-0.3
1912	Pit-N	77	244	27	77	9	8	2	35	20	16	.316	.370	.443	124	7	8			.982	-2	O-62	0.2
1914	NY-N	35	31	1	5	1	1	0	3	3	5	.161	.235	.355	77	-1	0			.000	0	H	-0.1
Total	12	1049	3854	669	1282	176	97	51	543	312	39	.333	.386	.468	142	193	213			.924	-37	O-867/1-95,PS	10.6

■ JIM DONNELLY — Donnelly, James B. b: 7/19/1865, New Haven, Conn. d: 3/5/15, Meriden, Conn. BR/TR, Deb: 7/11/1884

YEAR	TM/L	G	AB	R	H	2B	3B	HR	RBI	BB	SO	AVG	OBP	SLG	PRO+	BR/A	SB	CS	SBR	FA	FR	G/POS	TPR
1884	KC-U	6	23	2	3	1	0	0			1	.130	.167	.174	-8	-3				.536	-4	/3-5,C-1	-0.6
	Ind-a	40	134	22	34	2	2	0			5	.254	.301	.299	99	0				.850	-5	3-24/S-8,O2	-0.4
1885	Det-N	56	211	24	49	4	3	1	22	10	29	.232	.267	.294	81	-4				.850	-3	3-55/1-1	-0.6
1886	KC-N	113	438	51	88	11	3	0	38	36	57	.201	.262	.240	50	-26	16			.845	0	*3-113	-2.2
1887	Was-N	117	425	51	85	9	6	1	46	16	26	.200	.234	.256	38	-35	42			.867	16	*3-115/S-2	-1.4
1888	Was-N	122	428	43	86	9	4	0	23	20	16	.201	.242	.241	57	-20	44			.875	-5	*3-117/S-5	-2.2
1889	Was-N	4	13	1	2	0	0	0	0	0	8	.154	.267	.154	20	-1	1			.667	-2	/3-4	-0.2
1890	StL-a	11	42	11	14	0	0	0			8	.333	.451	.333	115	1	5			.795	-3	3-11	-0.1
1891	Col-a	17	54	6	13	0	0	0	9	13	5	.241	.388	.241	85	0	7			.855	3	3-17	0.3
1896	Bal-N	106	396	70	130	14	10	0	71	34	11	.328	.387	.414	110	6	38			.884	-2	*3-106	0.5
1897	Pit-N	44	161	22	31	4	0	0	14	16		.193	.270	.217	31	-16	14			.920	1	3-44	-1.2
	NY-N	23	85	19	16	3	0	0	11	9		.188	.266	.224	31	-8	6			.869	3	3-23	-1.2
	Yr	67	246	41	47	7	0	0	25	25		.191	.268	.220	31	-24	20			.905	-5	3-67	-2.4
1898	StL-N	1	1	0	1	0	0	0				1.000	1.000	1.000	463	0				.500	0	/3-1	0.0
Total	11	660	2411	324	552	57	28	2	234	170	144	.229	.284	.278	65	-107	173			.862	-8	3-635/S-15,021C	-9.3

■ JOHN DONNELLY — Donnelly, John b: Elizabeth, N.J. Deb: 4/14/1873 F

YEAR	TM/L	G	AB	R	H	2B	3B	HR	RBI	BB	SO	AVG	OBP	SLG	PRO+	BR/A	SB	CS	SBR	FA	FR	G/POS	TPR
1873	Was-n	30	137	15	35	3	0	0	17	1	0	.255	.261	.277	60	-6						S-13,2-12/O3	-0.5
1874	Phi-n	6	22	2	5	0	0	0		0		.227	.227	.227	44	-1						/S-2,O-2,2	-0.1
Total	2 n	36	159	17	40	3	0	0				.252	.256	.270	58	-8						/S-15,2-13,O3	-0.6

■ PETE DONNELLY — Donnelly, Peter J. b: 10/8/1849, Philadelphia, Pa. d: 10/1/1890, Jersey City, N.J. Deb: 5/13/1871 F

YEAR	TM/L	G	AB	R	H	2B	3B	HR	RBI	BB	SO	AVG	OBP	SLG	PRO+	BR/A	SB	CS	SBR	FA	FR	G/POS	TPR
1871	Kek-n	9	34	7	7	1	1	0	3	1	2	.206	.229	.294	48	-2	0					/O-9,3-1	-0.1

■ CHRIS DONNELS — Donnels, Chris Barton b: 4/21/66, Los Angeles, Cal. BL/TR, 6', 185 lbs. Deb: 5/7/91

YEAR	TM/L	G	AB	R	H	2B	3B	HR	RBI	BB	SO	AVG	OBP	SLG	PRO+	BR/A	SB	CS	SBR	FA	FR	G/POS	TPR
1991	NY-N	37	89	7	20	2	0	0	5	14	19	.225	.330	.247	65	-4	1	1	-0	1.000	3	1-15,3-11	-0.2
1992	NY-N	45	121	8	21	4	0	0	6	17	25	.174	.275	.207	39	-9	1	0	0	.941	4	3-29,2-12	-0.6
1993	Hou-N	88	179	18	46	14	2	2	24	19	33	.257	.328	.391	95	-1	2	0	1	.898	0	3-31,1-23/2	-0.6
1994	Hou-N	54	86	12	23	5	0	3	13	18		.267	.364	.430	108	1	1	0	0	1.000	1	3-14/1-4,2	0.2
Total	4	224	475	45	110	25	2	5	40	63	95	.232	.322	.324	78	-13	5	1	1	.936	7	/3-85,1-42,2	-0.8

■ JOE DONOHUE — Donahue, Joseph F. b: 1869, Syracuse, N.Y. Deb: 8/24/1891

YEAR	TM/L	G	AB	R	H	2B	3B	HR	RBI	BB	SO	AVG	OBP	SLG	PRO+	BR/A	SB	CS	SBR	FA	FR	G/POS	TPR
1891	Phi-N	6	22	2	7	1	0	0	2	1	3	.318	.375	.364	113	0	0			1.000	-0	/O-4,S-2	0.0

■ TOM DONOHUE — Donohue, Thomas James b: 11/15/52, Mineola, N.Y. BR/TR, 6', 185 lbs. Deb: 4/6/79

YEAR	TM/L	G	AB	R	H	2B	3B	HR	RBI	BB	SO	AVG	OBP	SLG	PRO+	BR/A	SB	CS	SBR	FA	FR	G/POS	TPR
1979	Cal-A	38	107	13	24	3	1	3	14	3	29	.224	.259	.355	66	-5	2	0	1	.981	-3	C-38	-0.7
1980	Cal-A	84	218	18	41	4	1	2	14	7	63	.188	.217	.243	26	-22	5	1	1	.986	-10	C-84	-2.9
Total	2	122	325	31	65	7	2	5	28	10	92	.200	.231	.280	40	-28	7	1	2	.985	-12	C-122	-3.6

■ FRED DONOVAN — Donovan, Frederick Maurice b: 7/4/1864, New Hampshire d: 3/7/16, Bloomington, Ill. BR/TR, Deb: 6/23/1895

YEAR	TM/L	G	AB	R	H	2B	3B	HR	RBI	BB	SO	AVG	OBP	SLG	PRO+	BR/A	SB	CS	SBR	FA	FR	G/POS	TPR
1895	Cle-N	3	12	1	1	0	0	0	1	1	2	.083	.154	.083	-36	-2	0			.938	-0	/C-3	-0.2

■ JERRY DONOVAN — Donovan, Jeremiah Francis b: 9/3/1876, Lock Haven, Pa. d: 6/27/38, St.Petersburg, Fla. BR/TR, Deb: 4/12/06 F

YEAR	TM/L	G	AB	R	H	2B	3B	HR	RBI	BB	SO	AVG	OBP	SLG	PRO+	BR/A	SB	CS	SBR	FA	FR	G/POS	TPR
1906	Phi-N	61	166	11	33	4	0	0	15	6		.199	.236	.223	43	-11	2			.955	-4	C-53/S-1,O	-1.2

YEAR	TM/L	G	AB	R	H	2B	3B	HR	RBI	BB	SO	AVG	OBP	SLG	PRO+	BR/A	SB	CS	SBR	FA	FR	G/POS	TPR

◼ MIKE DONOVAN   Donovan, Michael Berchman   b: 10/18/1881, Brooklyn, N.Y.   d: 2/3/38, New York, N.Y.   BR/TR, 5'8", 155 lbs.   Deb: 5/29/04

1904	Cle-A	2	2	0	0	0	0	0	0	0		.000	.000	.000	-99	-0	0			.000		/S-1	-0.1
1908	NY-A	5	19	2	5	1	0	0	2	0		.263	.263	.316	87	-0	0			1.000	1	/3-5	0.1
Total	2	7	21	2	5	1	0	0	2	0		.238	.238	.286	69	-1	0			1.000	1	/3-5,S-1	0.0

◼ PATSY DONOVAN   Donovan, Patrick Joseph   b: 3/16/1865, County Cork, Ireland   d: 12/25/53, Lawrence, Mass.   BL/TL, 5'11.5", 175 lbs.   Deb: 4/19/1890   M

1890	Bos-N	32	140	17	36	0	0	0	9	8	17	.257	.307	.257	60	-7	10			.891	-5	O-32	-1.2
	*Bro-N	28	105	17	23	5	1	0	8	5	5	.219	.268	.286	61	-5	3			1.000	2	O-28	-0.4
	Yr	60	245	34	59	5	1	0	17	13	22	.241	.290	.269	61	-13	13			.952	-3	O-60	-1.6
1891	Lou-a	105	439	73	141	10	3	2	53	30	18	.321	.375	.371	115	9	27			.912	5	*O-105	0.9
	Was-a	17	70	9	14	1	0	0	3	4	5	.200	.243	.214	33	-6	1			.857	-2	O-17	-0.8
	Yr	122	509	82	155	11	3	2	56	34	23	.305	.358	.350	104	3	28			.907	2	*O-122	0.1
1892	Was-N	40	163	29	39	3	3	0	12	11	13	.239	.295	.294	81	-4	16			.844	1	O-40	-0.4
	Pit-N	90	388	77	114	15	3	2	26	20	16	.294	.333	.363	110	4	40			.872	-3	O-90	-0.3
	Yr	130	551	106	153	18	6	2	38	31	29	.278	.322	.343	102	0	56			.862	-2	*O-130	-0.7
1893	Pit-N	113	499	114	158	5	8	2	56	42	8	.317	.373	.371	100	1	46			.937	-1	*O-112	-0.5
1894	Pit-N	132	576	145	174	21	10	4	76	33	12	.302	.345	.394	79	-21	41			.932	8	*O-132	-1.7
1895	Pit-N	125	519	114	160	17	6	1	58	47	19	.308	.370	.370	98	1	36			.961	-5	*O-125	-1.2
1896	Pit-N	131	573	113	183	20	5	3	59	35	18	.319	.370	.387	104	0	48			.954	7	*O-131	0.0
1897	Pit-N	120	479	82	154	16	7	0	57	25		.322	.360	.384	100	0	34			.949	1	*O-120,M	-0.7
1898	Pit-N	147	610	112	184	16	9	0	37	34		.302	.346	.357	104	2	41			.928	0	*O-147	-0.7
1899	Pit-N	121	531	82	156	11	7	1	55	17		.294	.322	.347	84	-13	26			.941	-12	*O-121,M	-3.1
1900	StL-N	126	503	78	159	11	1	0	61	38		.316	.368	.342	97	-5	**45**			.951	-5	*O-124	-1.3
1901	StL-N	130	531	92	161	23	5	1	73	27		.303	.344	.371	113	8	28			.979	4	*O-129,M	0.2
1902	StL-N	126	502	70	158	12	4	0	35	28		.315	.363	.355	127	16	34			.959	10	*O-126,M	1.9
1903	StL-N	105	410	63	134	15	3	0	39	25		.327	.370	.378	117	9	25			.952	-1	*O-105,M	0.2
1904	Was-A	125	436	30	100	6	0	0	19	24		.229	.271	.243	64	-17	17			.963	9	*O-122,M	-1.7
1906	Bro-N	7	21	1	5	0	0	0	0	0		.238	.238	.238	53	-1	0			1.000	-1	/O-6,M	-0.2
1907	Bro-N	1	1	0	0	0	0	0	0	0		.000	.000	.000	-99	-0	0			1.000	0	/O-1,M	0.0
Total	17	1821	7496	1318	2253	207	75	16	736	453	131	.301	.347	.355	98	-22	518			.941	13	*O-1813	-11.0

◼ TOM DONOVAN   Donovan, Thomas Joseph   b: 1/1/1873, West Troy, N.Y.   d: 3/25/33, Watervliet, N.Y.   BR/TR, 6'2", 168 lbs.   Deb: 9/10/01   F

1901	Cle-A	18	71	9	18	3	1	0	5	0		.254	.254	.324	62	-4	1			.862	-1	O-18/P-1	-0.5

◼ BILL DONOVAN   Donovan, William Edward "Wild Bill"   b: 10/13/1876, Lawrence, Mass.   d: 12/9/23, Forsyth, N.Y.   BR/TR, 5'11", 190 lbs.   Deb: 4/22/1898   MC

1898	Was-N	39	103	11	17	2	2	2	8	4		.165	.211	.282	41	-8	2			.933	1	O-20,P-17/S2	-0.5
1899	Bro-N	5	13	2	3	1	0	0	0	4		.231	.231	.308	46	-1	0			.857	-0	/P-5	0.0
1900	Bro-N	5	13	0	0	0	0	0	0	0		.000	.000	.000	-94	-3	0			1.000	1	/P-5	0.0
1901	Bro-N	46	135	16	23	3	0	2	13	8		.170	.217	.237	31	-12	1			.927	-1	P-45	0.0
1902	Bro-N	48	161	16	28	3	2	1	16	9		.174	.227	.236	42	-11	7			.948	-2	P-35/1-8,O2	-0.3
1903	Det-A	40	124	11	30	3	2	0	12	4		.242	.266	.298	71	-4	3			.938	-2	P-35/S-2,2O	0.1
1904	Det-A	46	140	12	38	2	1	1	6	3		.271	.287	.321	95	-1	2			.967	-3	P-34/1-8,O	-0.4
1905	Det-A	44	130	16	25	4	0	0	5	12		.192	.266	.223	55	-6	8			.933	-0	P-34/O-8,2	0.1
1906	Det-A	28	91	5	11	0	1	0	0	1		.121	.130	.143	-14	-12	6			.949	-1	P-25/2-3,O	-0.2
1907	*Det-A	37	109	20	29	7	2	0	19	6		.266	.304	.367	110	1	4			.945	-6	P-32	0.0
1908	*Det-A	30	82	5	13	1	0	0	2	10		.159	.250	.171	36	-5	2			.917	-6	P-29	0.0
1909	*Det-A	22	45	6	9	0	0	0	1	2		.200	.250	.200	41	-3	0			.974	-2	P-21	0.0
1910	Det-A	26	69	6	10	1	0	0	2	5		.145	.203	.159	13	-7	0			.955	-6	P-26	0.0
1911	Det-A	24	60	11	12	3	1	1	6	11		.200	.324	.333	79	-2	1			.935	-5	P-20	0.0
1912	Det-A	6	13	3	1	0	0	0	0	1		.077	.143	.077	-38	-2	0			1.000	-1	/P-3,1-2,O	-0.3
1915	NY-A	10	12	1	1	0	0	0	0	1	6	.083	.154	.083	-29	-2	0			1.000	-1	/P-9,M	0.0
1916	NY-A	1	0	0	0	0	0	0	0	0		—	—	—		0	0			.000	-0	/P-1,M	0.0
1918	Det-A	2	2	1	1	0	0	0	1	0		.500	.500	.500	210	0	0			1.000	-0	/P-2	0.0
Total	18	459	1302	142	251	30	11	7	93	77	6	.193	.241	.249	49	-80	36			.958	-30	P-378/O-37,12S	-1.5

◼ RED DOOIN   Dooin, Charles Sebastian   b: 6/12/1879, Cincinnati, Ohio   d: 5/14/52, Rochester, N.Y.   BR/TR, 5'9.5", 165 lbs.   Deb: 4/18/02   M

1902	Phi-N	94	333	20	77	7	3	0	35	10		.231	.262	.270	64	-14	8			.950	5	C-84/O-6	-0.1
1903	Phi-N	62	188	18	41	5	1	0	14	8		.218	.254	.255	47	-13	9			.940	-4	C-51/1-1,O	-1.2
1904	Phi-N	108	355	41	86	11	4	6	36	8		.242	.261	.346	90	-6	15			.938	8	C-96/1-4,O3	1.2
1905	Phi-N	113	380	45	95	13	5	0	36	10		.250	.269	.311	75	-13	12			.965	8	*C-107/3-1	0.6
1906	Phi-N	113	351	25	86	19	1	0	32	13		.245	.274	.305	80	-9	15			.948	-11	*C-107	-1.0
1907	Phi-N	101	313	18	66	4	0	0	14	15		.211	.252	.262	62	-14	10			.959	2	*C-94/2-1,O	-0.4
1908	Phi-N	133	435	28	108	17	4	0	41	17		.248	.283	.306	85	-8	20			.966	12	*C-132	1.8
1909	Phi-N	141	468	42	105	14	1	2	38	21		.224	.264	.271	65	-20	14			.958	4	*C-140	-0.3
1910	Phi-N	103	331	30	80	13	4	0	30	22	17	.242	.289	.305	71	-13	10			.956	-4	C-91/O-3M	-0.8
1911	Phi-N	74	247	18	81	15	1	1	16	14	12	.328	.366	.409	115	4	6			.967	5	C-74/M	1.6
1912	Phi-N	69	184	20	43	9	0	0	22	5	12	.234	.262	.283	46	-14	8			.958	0	C-58,M	-0.9
1913	Phi-N	55	129	6	33	4	1	0	13	9	14	.256	.273	.302	62	-7	1			.962	3	C-50,M	-0.1
1914	Phi-N	53	118	10	21	2	0	1	8	4	14	.178	.205	.220	25	-11	4			.967	-0	C-40/O-2M	-0.9
1915	Cin-N	10	31	2	10	0	0	0	2	0	5	.323	.364	.323	106	0	1			.915	-4	C-10	-0.3
	NY-N	46	124	9	27	2	2	0	9	3	15	.218	.236	.266	55	-7	0	2	-1	.964	1	C-46	-0.5
	Yr	56	155	11	37	2	2	0	11	3	20	.239	.262	.277	66	-7	1	2	-1	.956	-3	C-56	-0.8
1916	NY-N	15	17	1	2	0	0	0	1	0	3	.118	.118	.118	-29	-3	0			.972	0	C-15	-0.2
Total	15	1290	4004	333	961	139	31	10	344	155	87	.240	.272	.298	72	-148	133	2		.957	25	*C-1195/O-16,132	-1.5

◼ MICKEY DOOLAN   Doolan, Michael Joseph "Doc" (b: Michael Joseph Doolittle)   b: 5/7/1880, Ashland, Pa.   d: 11/1/51, Orlando, Fla.   BR/TR, 5'10.5", 170 lbs.   Deb: 4/14/05   C

1905	Phi-N	136	492	53	125	27	11	1	48	24		.254	.292	.360	97	-4	17			.935	-9	*S-135	-1.1
1906	Phi-N	154	535	41	123	19	7	1	55	27		.230	.270	.297	77	-16	16			.930	6	*S-154	-0.6
1907	Phi-N	145	509	33	104	19	5	0	47	25		.204	.243	.275	63	-23	18			.929	14	*S-145	-0.6
1908	Phi-N	129	445	29	104	25	4	2	49	17		.234	.267	.321	85	-9	5			.939	0	*S-129	-0.7
1909	Phi-N	147	493	39	108	12	10	1	35	37		.219	.276	.290	75	-15	10			.939	**24**	*S-147	1.3
1910	Phi-N	148	536	58	141	31	6	2	57	35	56	.263	.315	.354	92	-7	16			**.948**	21	*S-148	2.1
1911	Phi-N	146	512	51	122	23	6	1	49	44	65	.238	.301	.313	71	-21	14			.936	20	*S-145	0.9
1912	Phi-N	146	532	47	137	26	6	1	62	34	59	.258	.305	.335	70	-23	6			.950	8	*S-146	-0.2
1913	Phi-N	151	518	32	113	12	1	1	43	29	68	.218	.262	.270	50	-34	17			.941	17	*S-148/2-3	-0.3
1914	Bal-F	145	486	58	119	23	6	1	53	40	47	.245	.311	.323	63	-27	30			**.949**	29	*S-145	1.5
1915	Bal-F	119	404	41	75	13	7	1	21	24	39	.186	.238	.267	34	-39	10			.946	32	*S-119	0.3
	Chi-F	24	86	9	23	1	1	0	5	2	7	.267	.292	.302	63	-5	5			.914	1	S-24	-0.2
	Yr	143	490	50	98	14	8	1	26	26	46	.200	.248	.273	39	-44	15			.941	**33**	*S-143	0.1
1916	Chi-N	28	70	4	15	2	1	0	5	6	7	.214	.295	.271	67	-3	0			.918	-2	S-24	0.2
	NY-N	18	51	4	12	3	1	0	3	2	4	.235	.264	.392	106	2	1			.975	2	S-16/2-2	0.3
	Yr	46	121	8	27	5	2	0	8	10	11	.223	.282	.322	82	-3	1			.939	4	S-40/2-2	0.5

YEAR	TM/L	G	AB	R	H	2B	3B	HR	RBI	BB	SO	AVG	OBP	SLG	PRO+	BR/A	SB	CS	SBR	FA	FR	G/POS	TPR
1918	Bro-N	92	308	14	55	8	2	0	18	22	24	.179	.233	.218	38	-23	8			**.968**	10	2-91	-0.8
Total	13	1728	5977	513	1376	244	81	15	554	370	376	.230	.279	.306		69	-248	173		.940	178	*S-1625/2-96	2.1

■ HARRY DOOMS
Dooms, Henry E. "Jack" b: 1/30/1867, St.Louis, Mo. d: 12/14/1899, St.Louis, Mo. Deb: 8/7/1892

| 1892 | Lou-N | 1 | 4 | 0 | 0 | 0 | 0 | 0 | 1 | 3 | .000 | .200 | .000 | -42 | -1 | 0 | | .000 | -1 | /O-1 | -0.1 |

■ TOM DORAN
Doran, Thomas J. "Long Tom" b: 12/2/1880, Westchester Co., N.Y. d: 6/22/10, New York, N.Y. BL/TR, 5'11", 152 lbs. Deb: 4/19/04

1904	Bos-A	12	32	1	4	0	1	0	4		0	.125	.243	.188	35	-2	1		.898	-5	C-11	-0.7
1905	Bos-A	3	3	0	0	0	0	0	0	0		.000	.000	.000	-99	-1	0		1.000	-0	/C-1	
	Det-A	34	94	8	15	3	0	0	4	8		.160	.248	.191	40	-6	2		.962	-6	C-32	-1.0
	Yr	37	97	8	15	3	0	0	4	8		.155	.241	.186	35	-7	2		.963	-6	C-33	-1.0
1906	Bos-A	2	3	1	0	0	0	0	0			.000	.000	.000	-99	-1	0		1.000	-0	/C-2	-0.1
Total	3	51	132	10	19	3	1	0	4	12		.144	.236	.182	33	-10	3		.949	-11	/C-46	-1.8

■ BILL DORAN
Doran, William Donald b: 5/28/58, Cincinnati, Ohio BB/TR, 5'11", 175 lbs. Deb: 9/6/82

1982	Hou-N	26	97	11	27	3	0	0	6	4	11	.278	.307	.309	79	-3	5	0	2	.975	-3	2-26	-0.3
1983	Hou-N	154	535	70	145	12	7	8	39	86	67	.271	.372	.364	112	11	12	12	-4	.979	5	*2-153	2.0
1984	Hou-N	147	548	92	143	18	11	4	41	66	69	.261	.343	.356	104	4	21	12	-1	.986	6	*2-139,S-13	1.5
1985	Hou-N	148	578	84	166	31	6	14	59	71	69	.287	.365	.434	126	21	23	15	-2	.980	7	*2-147	3.2
1986	*Hou-N	145	550	92	152	29	3	6	37	81	57	.276	.371	.373	109	9	42	19	1	.974	-42	*2-144	-2.7
1987	Hou-N	162	625	82	177	23	3	16	79	82	64	.283	.369	.406	109	10	31	11	3	**.992**	-16	*2-162/S-3	0.4
1988	Hou-N	132	480	66	119	18	1	7	53	65	60	.248	.339	.333	97	-0	17	4	3	**.987**	-3	*2-130	0.5
1989	Hou-N	142	507	65	111	25	2	8	58	59	63	.219	.303	.323	82	-12	22	3	5	.980	-27	*2-138	-3.2
1990	Hou-N	109	344	49	99	21	2	6	32	71	53	.288	.412	.413	131	18	18	9	0	.989	-11	2-99	0.9
	Cin-N	17	59	10	22	8	0	1	5	8	5	.373	.448	.559	168	6	5	0	2	.985	1	2-12/3-4	0.9
	Yr	126	403	59	121	29	2	7	37	79	58	.300	.415	.434	137	24	23	9	2	.988	-10	*2-111/3-4	1.8
1991	Cin-N	111	361	51	101	12	2	6	35	46	39	.280	.361	.374	103	3	5	4	-1	.981	-14	2-88/O-6,1	-1.1
1992	Cin-N	132	387	48	91	16	2	8	47	64	40	.235	.344	.349	94	-1	7	4	-0	.988	-9	2-104,1-25	-1.0
1993	Mil-A	28	60	7	13	4	0	0	6	6	3	.217	.288	.283	55	-4	1	0		.964	-5	2-17/1-4	-0.9
Total	12	1453	5131	727	1366	220	39	84	497	709	600	.266	.356	.373	107	62	209	93	7	.983	-112	*2-1359/1-33,SO3	0.2

■ BILL DORAN
Doran, William James b: 6/14/1898, San Francisco, Cal. d: 3/9/78, Santa Monica, Cal. BL/TR, 5'11.5", 175 lbs. Deb: 6/23/22

| 1922 | Cle-A | 3 | 2 | 0 | 1 | 0 | 0 | 0 | 0 | 1 | 0 | .500 | .667 | .500 | 206 | 0 | 0 | 0 | 0 | .000 | 0 | /3-2 | 0.0 |

■ JERRY DORGAN
Dorgan, Jeremiah F. b: 1856, Meriden, Conn. d: 6/10/1891, New Haven, Conn. BL/TR, 165 lbs. Deb: 7/8/1880 F

1880	Wor-N	10	35	2	7	1	0	0		1	0	1	.200	.200	.229	41	-2			.750	-3	/O-9,C-1	-0.5
1882	Phi-a	44	181	25	51	9	1	0		4		.282	.297	.343	103	-1			.880	-1	C-25,O-22/3	-0.1
1884	Ind-a	34	141	22	42	6	1	0		2		.298	.317	.355	122	3			.793	-2	O-29/C-5	0.1
	Bro-a	4	13	2	4	0	0	0				.308	.308	.308	101	-0			.921	2	/C-4	0.2
	Yr	38	154	24	46	6	1	0		2		.299	.316	.351	120	3			.793	-0	O-29/C-9	0.3
1885	Det-N	39	161	23	46	6	2	0	24	8	10	.286	.303	.348	115	3			.857	-3	O-39	-0.2
Total	4	131	531	74	150	22	4	0	25	14	11	.282	.303	.339	107	3			.817	-7	/O-99,C-35,3	-0.5

■ MIKE DORGAN
Dorgan, Michael Cornelius b: 10/2/1853, Middletown, Conn. d: 4/26/09, Hartford, Conn. BR/TR, 5'9", 180 lbs. Deb: 5/8/1877 FM

1877	StL-N	60	266	45	82	9	7	0	23	9	13	.308	.331	.395	135	11			.824	-8	*O-50,C-12/3S2	0.1
1879	Syr-N	59	270	38	72	11	5	1	17	4	13	.267	.277	.356	120	6			.954	-5	1-21,O-16,3/SCP2	0.0
1880	Pro-N	79	321	45	79	10	1	0	31	10	18	.246	.269	.283	90	-3			.858	2	*O-77/3-2,PM	-0.3
1881	Wor-N	51	220	36	61	5	0	0	18	8	4	.277	.303	.300	85	-4			.953	1	1-26,O-23/SM	-0.6
	Det-N	8	34	5	8	1	0	0	5	1	0	.235	.257	.265	62	-1			1.000	-0	/O-5,3-2,1	-0.2
	Yr	59	254	41	69	6	0	0	23	9	4	.272	.297	.295	82	-5			.897	0	O-28,1-27/S3	-0.8
1883	NY-N	64	261	32	61	11	3	0	27	2	23	.234	.240	.299	63	-11			.847	-5	O-59/C-6,P	-1.5
1884	NY-N	83	341	61	94	11	6	1	48	13	27	.276	.302	.352	103	0			.851	1	O-64,P-14/C2	0.0
1885	NY-N	89	347	60	113	17	8	0	46	11	24	.326	.346	.421	149	18			.905	-2	*O-88/1-1	1.2
1886	NY-N	118	442	61	129	19	4	2	79	29	37	.292	.335	.367	112	6	9			.888	-8	*O-116/1-3	-0.4
1887	NY-N	71	283	41	73	10	0	1	34	15	20	.258	.302	.293	69	-11	22			.870	-1	O-69/1-2	-1.2
1890	Syr-a	33	139	19	30	8	0	0		16		.216	.301	.273	77	-3	8			.900	-2	O-33	-0.6
Total	10	715	2924	443	802	112	34	4	328	118	179	.274	.303	.340	102	8	39			.867	-30	O-600/1-54,CP3S2	-3.5

■ CHARLIE DORMAN
Dorman, Charles William "Slats" b: 4/23/1898, San Francisco, Cal d: 11/15/28, San Francisco, Cal BR/TR, 6'2", 185 lbs. Deb: 5/14/23

| 1923 | Chi-A | 1 | 2 | 0 | 1 | 0 | 0 | 0 | 0 | 0 | 0 | .500 | .500 | .500 | 166 | 0 | 0 | 0 | 0 | 1.000 | -0 | /C-1 | 0.0 |

■ RED DORMAN
Dorman, Dwight Dexter "Curlie" b: 10/3/05, Jacksonville, Ill. d: 12/7/74, Anaheim, Cal. BR/TR, 5'10.5", 180 lbs. Deb: 8/21/28

| 1928 | Cle-A | 25 | 77 | 12 | 28 | 6 | 0 | 0 | 11 | 9 | 6 | .364 | .430 | .442 | 128 | 4 | 1 | 0 | 0 | .915 | -3 | O-24 | 0.0 |

■ BRIAN DORSETT
Dorsett, Brian Richard b: 4/9/61, Terre Haute, Ind. BR/TR, 6'3", 215 lbs. Deb: 9/8/87

1987	Cle-A	5	11	2	3	0	0	1	3	0	3	.273	.333	.545	127	0	0	0	0	1.000	-2	/C-4	-0.1
1988	Cal-A	7	11	0	1	0	0	0	2	1	5	.091	.167	.091	-26	-2	0	0	0	1.000	1	/C-7	-0.1
1989	NY-A	8	22	3	8	1	0	0	4	1	3	.364	.391	.409	127	1	0	0	0	1.000	-0	/C-8	0.1
1990	NY-A	14	35	2	5	2	0	0	0	2	5	.143	.189	.200	9	-4	0	0	0	1.000	-1	/C-9,D-5	-0.5
1991	SD-N	11	12	0	1	0	0	0	1	0	3	.083	.083	.083	-51	-2	0	0	0	1.000	0	/1-2	-0.2
1993	Cin-N	25	63	7	16	4	0	2	12	3	14	.254	.288	.413	85	-2	0	0	0	1.000	2	C-18/1-3	0.1
1994	Cin-N	76	216	21	53	8	0	5	26	21	33	.245	.315	.352	74	-8	0	0	0	.991	-1	C-73/1-1	-0.5
Total	7	146	370	35	87	15	0	8	48	28	65	.235	.292	.341	68	-17	0	0	0	.994	-2	C-119/1-6,D	-1.2

■ JERRY DORSEY
Dorsey, Jeremiah b: 1885, Oakland, Cal. BL/TL, 5'11", 175 lbs. Deb: 9/23/11

| 1911 | Pit-N | 2 | 6 | 0 | 0 | 0 | 0 | 0 | 0 | 0 | 1 | .000 | .000 | .000 | -96 | -2 | | | 1.000 | 0 | /O-1 | -0.1 |

■ JERRY DORSEY
Dorsey, Michael Jeremiah b: 1854, Canada d: 11/3/38, Auburn, N.Y. Deb: 7/9/1884

| 1884 | Bal-U | 1 | 3 | 0 | 0 | 0 | 0 | 0 | 0 | | | .000 | .000 | .000 | -91 | -1 | | | .000 | -0 | /O-1,P-1 | -0.1 |

■ HERM DOSCHER
Doscher, John Henry Sr. b: 12/20/1852, New York, N.Y. d: 3/20/34, Buffalo, N.Y. BR/TR, 5'10", 182 lbs. Deb: 9/4/1872 FU

1872	Atl-n	6	25	4	9	1	0	0		5	0	1	.360	.360	.400	114	-0					/O-6	0.0
1873	Atl-n	1	6	1	1	0	0	0		1	0		.167	.167	.167	-2	-1					/O-1	0.0
1875	Was-n	22	81	5	15	2	0	0					.185	.185	.210	38	-5					3-19/S-2	-0.4
1879	Tro-N	47	191	16	42	8	0	0	18	2	10	.220	.228	.262	65	-7			.806	-4	3-47	-0.9
	Chi-N	3	11	1	2	0	0	0	1	0	3	.182	.182	.182	19	-1			.700	-1	/3-3	-0.2
	Yr	50	202	17	44	8	0	0	19	2	13	.218	.225	.257	62	-8			.800	-5	3-50	-1.1
1881	Cle-N	5	19	2	4	0	0	0	0	0		.211	.211	.211	35	-1			.895	-0	/3-5	-0.2
1882	Cle-N	25	104	7	25	2	0	0	10	0	11	.240	.240	.260	62	-4			.857	-2	/3-22/O-2,S	-0.5
Total	3 n	29	112	10	25	3	0	0		6	0	1	.223	.223	.250	57	-6					/3-19,O-7,S	-0.4
Total	3	80	325	26	73	10	0	0	29	2	26	.225	.229	.255	61	-13			.823	-7	/3-77,O-2,S	-1.8

■ DUTCH DOTTERER
Dotterer, Henry John b: 11/11/31, Syracuse, N.Y. BR/TR, 6', 209 lbs. Deb: 9/25/57

1957	Cin-N	4	12	0	1	0	0	0	2	1	2	.083	.154	.083	-32	-2	0	0	0	1.000	-1	/C-4	-0.3
1958	Cin-N	11	28	1	7	1	0	1	2	2	4	.250	.300	.393	77	-1	0	0	0	.981	4	/C-8	0.3
1959	Cin-N	52	161	21	43	7	0	2	17	16	23	.267	.333	.348	79	-4	0	0	0	.992	-0	C-51	-0.2

YEAR	TM/L	G	AB	R	H	2B	3B	HR	RBI	BB	SO	AVG	OBP	SLG	PRO+	BR/A	SB	CS	SBR	FA	FR	G/POS	TPR
1960	Cin-N	33	79	4	18	5	0	2	11	13	10	.228	.337	.367	91	-1	0	1	-1	.979	1	C-31	0.1
1961	Was-A	7	19	1	5	2	0	0	1	3	5	.263	.364	.368	98	0	0	0	0	1.000	2	/C-7	0.2
Total	5	107	299	27	74	15	0	5	33	35	44	.247	.326	.348	79	-8	0	1	-1	.988	7	C-101	0.1

■ CHARLIE DOUGHERTY
Dougherty, Charles William   b: 2/7/1862, Darlington, Wis.   d: 2/18/25, Milwaukee, Wis.   Deb: 4/17/1884

YEAR	TM/L	G	AB	R	H	2B	3B	HR	RBI	BB	SO	AVG	OBP	SLG	PRO+	BR/A	SB	CS	SBR	FA	FR	G/POS	TPR
1884	Alt-U	23	85	6	22	5	0	0		2		.259	.276	.318	60	-5				.854	0	2-16/O-8,S	-0.4

■ PATSY DOUGHERTY
Dougherty, Patrick Henry   b: 10/27/1876, Andover, N.Y.   d: 4/30/40, Bolivar, N.Y.   BL/TR, 6'2", 190 lbs.   Deb: 4/19/02

YEAR	TM/L	G	AB	R	H	2B	3B	HR	RBI	BB	SO	AVG	OBP	SLG	PRO+	BR/A	SB	CS	SBR	FA	FR	G/POS	TPR
1902	Bos-A	108	438	77	150	12	6	0	34	42		.342	.407	.397	120	14	20			.899	-9	*O-102/3-1	-0.2
1903	*Bos-A	139	590	**107**	**195**	19	12	4	59	33		.331	.372	.424	131	22	35			.952	4	*O-139	1.8
1904	Bos-A	49	195	33	53	5	4	0	4	25		.272	.355	.338	113	4	10			.925	0	O-49	0.1
	NY-A	106	452	80	128	13	10	6	22	19		.283	.316	.396	119	9	11			.925	-8	*O-106	-0.7
	Yr	155	647	**113**	181	18	14	6	26	44		.280	.329	.379	117	12	21			.925	-8	*O-155	-0.6
1905	NY-A	116	418	56	110	9	6	3	29	28		.263	.319	.335	96	-2	17			.898	-6	*O-108/3-1	-1.5
1906	NY-A	12	52	3	10	2	0	0	4	0		.192	.192	.231	29	-4	0			1.000	0	O-12	-0.3
	*Chi-A	75	253	30	59	9	4	1	27	19		.233	.295	.312	92	-2	11			.985	-2	O-74	-0.8
	Yr	87	305	33	69	11	4	1	31	19		.226	.278	.298	81	-7	11			.987	1	O-86	-1.1
1907	Chi-A	148	533	69	144	17	2	1	59	36		.270	.322	.315	107	4	33			.946	-7	*O-148	-0.9
1908	Chi-A	138	482	68	134	11	6	0	45	58		.278	.367	.326	128	18	**47**			.947	-15	*O-128	-0.3
1909	Chi-A	139	491	71	140	23	13	1	55	51		.285	.359	.391	143	24	36			.942	-16	*O-138	0.4
1910	Chi-A	127	443	45	110	8	6	1	43	41		.248	.318	.300	98	-1	22			.923	-13	*O-121	-2.2
1911	Chi-A	76	211	39	61	10	9	0	32	26		.289	.380	.422	128	8	19			.933	-6	O-56	0.0
Total	10	1233	4558	678	1294	138	78	17	413	378		.284	.346	.360	117	94	261			.935	-75	*O-1181/3-2	-4.6

■ JOHN DOUGLAS
Douglas, John Franklin   b: 9/14/17, Thayer, W.Va.   d: 2/11/84, Miami, Fla.   BL/TL, 6'2.5", 195 lbs.   Deb: 4/21/45

YEAR	TM/L	G	AB	R	H	2B	3B	HR	RBI	BB	SO	AVG	OBP	SLG	PRO+	BR/A	SB	CS	SBR	FA	FR	G/POS	TPR
1945	Bro-N	5	9	0	0	0	0	0	0	2	4	.000	.182	.000	-47	-2	0			.971	-1	/1-4	-0.3

■ ASTYANAX DOUGLASS
Douglass, Astyanax Saunders   b: 9/19/1899, Covington, Tex.   d: 1/26/75, ElPaso, Tex.   BL/TR, 6'1", 190 lbs.   Deb: 7/30/21

YEAR	TM/L	G	AB	R	H	2B	3B	HR	RBI	BB	SO	AVG	OBP	SLG	PRO+	BR/A	SB	CS	SBR	FA	FR	G/POS	TPR
1921	Cin-N	4	7	1	1	0	0	0	0	0	1	.143	.143	.143	-25	-1	0	0	0	1.000	0	/C-4	-0.1
1925	Cin-N	7	17	1	3	0	0	0	1	1	3	.176	.222	.176	3	-2	0	0	0	.889	-1	/C-7	-0.3
Total	2	11	24	2	4	0	0	0	1	1	4	.167	.200	.167	-4	-4	0	0	0	.926	-0	/C-11	-0.4

■ KLONDIKE DOUGLASS
Douglass, William Bingham   b: 5/10/1872, Boston, Pa.   d: 12/13/53, Bend, Ore.   BL/TR, 6', 200 lbs.   Deb: 4/23/1896

YEAR	TM/L	G	AB	R	H	2B	3B	HR	RBI	BB	SO	AVG	OBP	SLG	PRO+	BR/A	SB	CS	SBR	FA	FR	G/POS	TPR
1896	StL-N	81	296	42	78	8	6	4	28	35	15	.264	.351	.321	81	-7	18			.894	-3	O-74/C-6,S	-1.6
1897	StL-N	125	516	77	170	15	3	6	50	52		.329	.403	.405	116	14	12			.948	-17	C-61,O-43,1/3S	0.1
1898	Phi-N	146	582	105	150	26	4	2	48	55		.258	.333	.326	93	-4	18			.976	2	*1-146	-0.2
1899	Phi-N	77	275	26	70	6	6	0	27	10		.255	.296	.320	71	-11	7			.970	-5	C-66/3-4,1O	-1.0
1900	Phi-N	50	160	23	48	9	4	0	25	13		.300	.360	.406	112	3	7			.934	-3	C-47/3-2	0.3
1901	Phi-N	51	173	14	56	6	1	0	23	11		.324	.371	.370	113	3	10			.979	2	C-41/1-6,O	0.8
1902	Phi-N	109	408	37	95	12	3	0	37	23		.233	.274	.277	70	-15	6			.986	-7	1-69,C-29,O	-2.2
1903	Phi-N	105	377	43	96	5	4	1	36	28		.255	.308	.297	75	-12	6			.985	-1	1-97	-1.4
1904	Phi-N	3	10	1	3	0	0	0	1	0		.300	.364	.300	109	0	0			.970	-0	/1-3	0.0
Total	9	747	2797	368	766	85	29	10	275	227	15	.274	.337	.336	91	-28	84			.981	-37	1-342,C-250,O/3S	-5.2

■ TAYLOR DOUTHIT
Douthit, Taylor Lee   b: 4/22/01, Little Rock, Ark.   d: 5/28/86, Fremont, Cal.   BR/TR, 5'11.5", 175 lbs.   Deb: 9/14/23

YEAR	TM/L	G	AB	R	H	2B	3B	HR	RBI	BB	SO	AVG	OBP	SLG	PRO+	BR/A	SB	CS	SBR	FA	FR	G/POS	TPR
1923	StL-N	9	27	3	5	0	2	0	0	0	4	.185	.185	.333	35	-3	1	0	0	1.000	-0	/O-7	-0.3
1924	StL-N	53	173	24	48	13	1	0	13	16	19	.277	.349	.364	93	-1	4	3	-1	.976	2	O-50	-0.3
1925	StL-N	30	73	13	20	3	1	1	8	2	6	.274	.312	.384	75	-3	0	0	0	.981	-1	O-21	-0.4
1926	*StL-N	139	530	96	163	20	4	3	52	55	46	.308	.375	.377	99	1	23			.958	18	*O-138	0.9
1927	StL-N	130	488	81	128	29	6	5	50	52	45	.262	.336	.377	88	-8	6			.964	8	*O-125	-0.8
1928	*StL-N	154	648	111	191	35	3	3	43	84	36	.295	.384	.372	97	0	11			.984	24	*O-154	1.4
1929	StL-N	150	613	128	206	42	7	9	62	79	49	.336	.416	.471	118	20	8			.974	-5	*O-150	1.3
1930	*StL-N	154	664	109	201	41	10	7	93	60	38	.303	.364	.426	87	-13	4			.964	8	*O-154	-1.4
1931	StL-N	36	133	21	44	11	2	1	21	11	9	.331	.386	.466	123	4	1			.972	0	O-36	0.2
	Cin-N	95	374	42	98	9	1	0	24	42	24	.262	.340	.291	76	-11	4			.983	5	O-95	-1.3
	Yr	131	507	63	142	20	3	1	45	53	33	.280	.352	.337	89	-6	5			.980	5	*O-131	-1.1
1932	Cin-N	96	333	28	81	12	1	0	25	31	29	.243	.311	.285	64	-16	3			.985	1	O-88	-2.0
1933	Cin-N	1	0	1	0	0	0	0	0	0	0	—	—	—	—	0	0			.000	-0	R	0.0
	Chi-N	27	71	8	16	5	0	0	5	11	7	.225	.329	.296	80	-1	2			.930	-0	O-18	-0.3
	Yr	28	71	9	16	5	0	0	5	11	7	.225	.329	.296	80	-1	2			.930	-0	O-18	-0.3
Total	11	1074	4127	665	1201	220	38	29	396	443	312	.291	.364	.384	93	-31	67	3		.972	69	*O-1036	-3.0

■ CLARENCE DOW
Dow, Clarence G.   b: 10/11/1854, Charlestown, Mass.   d: 3/11/1893, West Somerville, Mass.   Deb: 9/22/1884

YEAR	TM/L	G	AB	R	H	2B	3B	HR	RBI	BB	SO	AVG	OBP	SLG	PRO+	BR/A	SB	CS	SBR	FA	FR	G/POS	TPR
1884	Bos-U	1	6	1	2	0	0	0		0		.333	.333	.333	83	-0				.333	-1	/O-1	-0.1

■ JOHN DOWD
Dowd, John Leo (b: John Leo O'Dowd)   b: 1/3/1891, Weymouth, Mass.   d: 1/31/81, Ft.Lauderdale, Fla   BR/TR, 5'8", 170 lbs.   Deb: 7/3/12

YEAR	TM/L	G	AB	R	H	2B	3B	HR	RBI	BB	SO	AVG	OBP	SLG	PRO+	BR/A	SB	CS	SBR	FA	FR	G/POS	TPR
1912	NY-A	10	31	1	6	1	0	0	0	6		.194	.342	.226	60	-1	0			.840	-3	S-10	-0.4

■ SNOOKS DOWD
Dowd, Raymond Bernard   b: 12/20/1897, Springfield, Mass.   d: 4/4/62, Northampton, Mass.   BR/TR, 5'8", 163 lbs.   Deb: 4/27/19

YEAR	TM/L	G	AB	R	H	2B	3B	HR	RBI	BB	SO	AVG	OBP	SLG	PRO+	BR/A	SB	CS	SBR	FA	FR	G/POS	TPR
1919	Det-A	1	0	0	0	0	0	0	0	0	0	—	—	—	—	0	0			.000	0	R	0.0
	Phi-A	13	18	4	3	0	0	0	6	0	5	.167	.167	.167	-6	-3	2			.800	1	/2-3,S-2,3O	-0.2
	Yr	14	18	4	3	0	0	0	6	0	5	.167	.167	.167	-6	-3	2			.800	1	/2-3,S-2,3O	-0.2
1926	Bro-N	2	8	0	0	0	0	0	0	0	0	.000	.000	.000	-99	-2	0			1.000	0	/2-2	-0.5
Total	2	16	26	4	3	0	0	0	6	0	5	.115	.115	.115	-36	-5	2			.875	-1	/2-5,S-2,O3	-0.7

■ TOMMY DOWD
Dowd, Thomas Jefferson "Buttermilk Tommy"   b: 4/20/1869, Holyoke, Mass.   d: 7/2/33, Holyoke, Mass.   BR/TR, 5'8", 173 lbs.   Deb: 4/8/1891   M

YEAR	TM/L	G	AB	R	H	2B	3B	HR	RBI	BB	SO	AVG	OBP	SLG	PRO+	BR/A	SB	CS	SBR	FA	FR	G/POS	TPR
1891	Bos-a	4	11	1	1	0	0	0	0	0	1	.091	.091	.091	-49	-2	0			.000	-2	/O-4	-0.3
	Was-a	112	464	66	120	9	10	1	44	19	44	.259	.291	.328	80	-14	39			.885	-17	*2-107/O-5	-2.3
	Yr	116	475	67	121	9	10	1	44	19	45	.255	.286	.322	77	-16	39			.885	-19	*2-107/O-9	-2.6
1892	Was-N	144	584	94	142	9	10	1	50	34	49	.243	.286	.298	79	-16	49			.891	-33	2-98,O-23,3/S	-4.4
1893	StL-N	132	581	114	164	18	7	1	54	49	23	.282	.340	.343	81	-16	59			.944	3	*O-132/2-1	-1.6
1894	StL-N	123	524	92	142	16	8	4	62	54	33	.271	.341	.355	68	-27	31			.930	-7	*O-117/2-7,3	-3.3
1895	StL-N	126	505	95	163	19	17	7	74	30	31	.323	.364	.469	116	10	30			.927	-7	*O-115,3-17/2	-0.5
1896	StL-N	126	521	93	138	17	11	5	46	42	19	.265	.322	.369	85	-12	40			.920	-13	2-78,O-48M	-2.1
1897	StL-N	35	145	25	38	9	1	0	9	6		.262	.291	.338	67	-7	11			.915	-7	O-30/2-5M	-1.4
	Phi-N	91	391	68	114	14	4	0	43	19		.292	.324	.348	79	-12	30			.919	-6	O-73,2-19	-1.9
	Yr	126	536	93	152	23	5	0	52	25		.284	.316	.345	76	-19	41			.918	-13	O-103,2-24	-3.3
1898	StL-N	139	586	70	143	17	7	0	32	30		.244	.287	.297	66	-27	16			.920	-17	*O-129,2-11	-5.0
1899	Cle-N	147	605	81	168	17	6	2	35	48		.278	.333	.336	90	-8	28			.954	-2	*O-147	-2.0
1901	Bos-A	122	594	104	159	18	7	3	52	38		.268	.315	.337	82	-14	15			.937	1	*O-137/1-2,3	-2.6
Total	10	1320	5511	903	1492	163	88	24	501	369	200	.271	.319	.345	82	-146	366			.933	-106	*O-960,2-328/3S1	-26.9

■ KEN DOWELL
Dowell, Kenneth Allen   b: 1/19/61, Sacramento, Cal.   BR/TR, 5'9", 160 lbs.   Deb: 6/24/87

YEAR	TM/L	G	AB	R	H	2B	3B	HR	RBI	BB	SO	AVG	OBP	SLG	PRO+	BR/A	SB	CS	SBR	FA	FR	G/POS	TPR
1987	Phi-N	15	39	4	5	1	0	0	1	2	5	.128	.171	.128	-19	-7	0	0	0	1.000	0	S-15	-0.5

YEAR	TM/L	G	AB	R	H	2B	3B	HR	RBI	BB	SO	AVG	OBP	SLG	PRO+	BR/A	SB	CS	SBR	FA	FR	G/POS	TPR
■ JOE DOWIE									Dowie, Joseph E. b: 7/1865, New Orleans, La. 5'8", 150 lbs. Deb: 7/10/1889														
1889	Bal-a	20	75	12	17	5	0	0	8	2	10	.227	.266	.293	58	-4	5			.947	0	O-20	-0.4
■ RED DOWNEY									Downey, Alexander Cummings b: 2/6/1889, Aurora, Ind. d: 7/10/49, Detroit, Mich. BL/TL, 5'11", 174 lbs. Deb: 9/15/09														
1909	Bro-N	19	78	7	20	1	0	0	8	2		.256	.275	.269	71	-3	4			1.000	-1	O-19	-0.6
■ TOM DOWNEY									Downey, Thomas Edward b: 1/1/1884, Lewiston, Me. d: 8/3/61, Passaic, N.J. BR/TR, 5'10", 178 lbs. Deb: 5/7/09														
1909	Cin-N	119	416	39	96	9	6	1	32	32		.231	.287	.288	79	-10	16			.909	-7	*S-119/C-1	-1.7
1910	Cin-N	111	378	43	102	9	3	2	32	34	28	.270	.335	.325	97	-1	12			.879	-7	S-68,3-41	-0.5
1911	Cin-N	111	360	50	94	16	7	0	36	44	38	.261	.345	.344	97	-1	10			.906	-12	S-93/2-6,310	-0.7
1912	Phi-N	54	171	27	50	6	3	1	23	21	20	.292	.380	.380	99	-0	3			.893	-3	3-46/S-3	-0.2
	Chi-N	13	22	4	4	0	2	0	4	1	5	.182	.217	.364	58	-1	0			.792	1	/S-5,3-3,2	0.0
	Yr	67	193	31	54	6	5	1	27	22	25	.280	.353	.378	95	-1	3			.892	-2	3-49/S-8,2	-0.2
1914	Buf-F	151	541	69	118	20	3	2	42	40	55	.218	.273	.277	42	-47	35			**.962**	13	*2-129,S-16/3	-3.6
1915	Buf-F	92	282	24	56	9	1	1	19	26	26	.199	.269	.248	38	-25	11			.930	2	2-48,3-35/S1	-2.3
Total	6	651	2170	256	520	69	25	7	188	198	172	.240	.306	.304	71	-86	87			.901	-12	S-306,2-184,3/10C	-9.0
■ BRIAN DOWNING									Downing, Brian Jay b: 10/9/50, Los Angeles, Cal. BR/TR, 5'10", 194 lbs. Deb: 5/31/73														
1973	Chi-A	34	73	5	13	1	0	2	4	10	17	.178	.277	.274	54	-4	0	0	0	1.000	0	O-13,C-11/3D	-0.4
1974	Chi-A	108	293	41	66	12	1	10	39	51	72	.225	.344	.375	104	3	0	1	-1	.994	-7	C-63,O-39/D	-0.3
1975	Chi-A	138	420	58	101	12	1	7	41	76	75	.240	.361	.324	93	-1	13	4	2	.990	2	*C-137/D-1	0.9
1976	Chi-A	104	317	38	81	14	0	3	30	40	55	.256	.341	.328	96	-1	7	3	0	.988	-12	C-93,D-11	-1.0
1977	Chi-A	69	169	28	48	4	2	4	25	34	21	.284	.410	.402	123	7	1	2	-1	.983	3	C-61/O-3,D	1.0
1978	Cal-A	133	412	42	105	15	0	7	46	52	47	.255	.347	.342	98	0	3	2	-0	.993	-7	*C-128/D-2	-0.3
1979	*Cal-A★	148	509	87	166	27	3	12	75	77	57	.326	.420	.462	142	34	3	3	-1	.985	-21	*C-129/D-18	1.5
1980	Cal-A	30	93	5	27	6	0	2	25	12	12	.290	.371	.419	119	3	0	2	-1	1.000	-4	C-16,D-13	-0.2
1981	Cal-A	93	317	47	79	14	0	9	41	46	35	.249	.351	.379	110	5	1	1	-0	.990	-9	O-56,C-37/D	-0.4
1982	*Cal-A	158	623	109	175	37	2	28	84	86	58	.281	.373	.482	132	29	2	1	0	**1.000**	2	*O-158	2.6
1983	Cal-A	113	403	68	99	15	1	19	53	62	59	.246	.353	.429	115	9	1	2	-1	.994	-0	O-84,D-26	0.5
1984	Cal-A	156	539	65	148	28	2	23	91	70	66	.275	.365	.462	128	21	0	4	-2	**1.000**	1	*O-131,D-21	1.6
1985	Cal-A	150	520	80	137	23	1	20	85	78	61	.263	.373	.427	119	16	5	3	-0	.992	2	*O-121,D-25	1.3
1986	*Cal-A	152	513	90	137	27	4	20	95	90	84	.267	.394	.452	131	26	4	4	-1	.989	1	*O-138,D-10	2.1
1987	Cal-A	155	567	110	154	29	3	29	77	**106**	85	.272	.401	.487	139	36	5	5	-2	1.000	-3	*D-118,O-34	2.6
1988	Cal-A	135	484	80	117	18	2	25	64	81	63	.242	.366	.442	129	21	3	4	-2	1.000	0	*D-132	1.6
1989	Cal-A	142	544	59	154	25	2	14	59	56	87	.283	.354	.414	114	18	0	2	-1	1.000	0	*D-141	0.9
1990	Cal-A	96	330	47	90	18	2	14	51	50	45	.273	.378	.467	138	18	0	0	0	.000	0	D-87	1.5
1991	Tex-A	123	407	76	113	17	2	17	49	58	70	.278	.378	.455	132	19	1	1	-0	.000	0	*D-109	1.4
1992	Tex-A	107	320	53	89	16	0	10	39	62	58	.278	.408	.428	139	20	1	0	0	.000	0	D-93	1.7
Total	20	2344	7853	1188	2099	360	28	275	1073	1197	1127	.267	.373	.425	122	276	50	44	-11	.995	-51	D-824,O-777,C/3	18.6
■ RED DOWNS									Downs, Jerome Willis b: 8/22/1883, Neola, Iowa d: 10/19/39, Council Bluffs, Ia BR/TR, 5'11", 155 lbs. Deb: 5/2/07														
1907	Det-A	105	374	28	82	13	5	1	42	13		.219	.249	.289	69	-14	3			.930	-25	2-80,O-20/S3	-4.6
1908	*Det-A	84	289	29	64	10	3	1	35	5		.221	.237	.287	67	-11	2			.925	1	2-82/3-1	-1.3
1912	Bro-N	9	32	2	8	3	0	0	3	1	5	.250	.273	.344	71	-1	3			.881	-1	/2-9	-0.3
	Chi-N	43	95	9	25	4	3	1	14	9	17	.263	.327	.400	99	-0	5			.907	2	2-16/S-9,3	0.2
	Yr	52	127	11	33	7	3	1	17	10	22	.260	.314	.386	92	-2	8			.896	0	2-25/S-9,3	-0.1
Total	3	241	790	68	179	30	11	3	94	28	22	.227	.256	.304	72	-27	13			.924	-24	2-187/O-20,S3	-6.0
■ TOM DOWSE									Dowse, Thomas Joseph b: 8/12/1866, Ireland d: 12/14/46, Riverside, Cal. BR/TR, 5'11", 175 lbs. Deb: 4/21/1890														
1890	Cle-N	40	159	20	33	2	1	0	9	12	22	.208	.267	.233	47	-11	3			.870	-3	O-26,1-10/CP	-1.3
1891	Col-a	55	201	24	45	7	0	0	22	13	22	.224	.278	.259	57	-11	2			.919	-6	C-51/O-5	-1.2
1892	Lou-N	41	145	10	21	2	0	0	7	2	15	.145	.173	.159	1	-17	1			.918	2	C-29,1-11/O2	-1.3
	Cin-N	1	4	0	0	0	0	0	0	0	0	.000	.000	.000	-99	-1	0			1.000	0	/C-1	-0.2
	Phi-N	16	54	3	10	0	0	0	6	2	4	.185	.228	.185	25	-5	1			.973	-1	C-15	-0.4
	Was-N	7	27	5	7	1	0	0	2	0	0	.259	.259	.296	70	-1	0			.800	0	/O-4,C-3	-0.1
	Yr	65	230	18	38	3	0	0	15	4	22	.165	.193	.178	13	-24	2			.931	0	C-48,1-11/O2	-2.0
Total	3	160	590	62	116	12	1	0	46	29	66	.197	.243	.220	38	-46	7			.921	-9	C-102/O-38,12P	-4.5
■ BRIAN DOYLE									Doyle, Brian Reed b: 1/26/55, Glasgow, Ky. BL/TR, 5'10", 160 lbs. Deb: 4/30/78 F														
1978	*NY-A	39	52	6	10	0	0	0	0	0	3	.192	.192	.192	9	-6	0	3	-2	.989	13	2-29/S-7,3	0.6
1979	NY-A	20	32	2	4	2	0	0	5	3	1	.125	.200	.188	5	-4	0	0	0	.944	1	2-13/3-6	-0.3
1980	NY-A	34	75	8	13	1	0	0	5	6	7	.173	.235	.227	27	-7	1	1	-0	.953	5	2-20,S-12/3	-0.1
1981	Oak-A	17	40	2	5	0	0	0	3	1	2	.125	.146	.125	-22	-6	0	1	-1	1.000	1	2-17	-0.5
Total	4	110	199	18	32	3	0	0	13	10	13	.161	.201	.191	10	-24	1	5	-3	.977	20	/2-79,S-19,3	-0.3
■ CONNY DOYLE									Doyle, Cornelius J. b: 9/26/1857, Holyoke, Mass. d: 10/6/38, W.Springfield, Mass 5'10", 185 lbs. Deb: 6/23/1883														
1883	Phi-N	16	68	3	15	3	2	0	3	0	15	.221	.221	.324	69	-2				.788	-1	O-16	-0.3
1884	Pit-a	15	58	8	17	3	2	0		2	0	.293	.317	.414	134	2				.818	-1	O-14/S-1	0.0
Total	2	31	126	11	32	6	4	0	3	2	15	.254	.266	.365	100	-0				.800	-3	/O-30,S-1	-0.3
■ DANNY DOYLE									Doyle, Howard James b: 1/24/17, McLoud, Okla. BB/TR, 6'1", 195 lbs. Deb: 9/14/43														
1943	Bos-A	13	43	2	9	1	0	0	6	7	9	.209	.320	.233	62	-2	0	1	-1	.964	-2	C-13	-0.4
■ JIM DOYLE									Doyle, James Francis b: 12/25/1881, Detroit, Mich. d: 2/1/12, Syracuse, N.Y. BR/TR, 5'10", 168 lbs. Deb: 5/4/10														
1910	Cin-N	7	13	1	2	2	0	0	1	0	2	.154	.154	.308	36	-1	0			.875	-1	/3-3,O-1	-0.3
1911	Chi-N	130	472	69	133	23	12	5	62	40	54	.282	.340	.413	110	5	19			.922	10	*3-127	1.6
Total	2	137	485	70	135	25	12	5	63	40	56	.278	.336	.410	108	4	19			.921	8	3-130/O-1	1.3
■ JEFF DOYLE									Doyle, Jeffrey Donald b: 10/2/56, Havre, Mont. BB/TR, 5'9", 160 lbs. Deb: 9/13/83														
1983	StL-N	13	37	4	11	2	1	0	3	3		.297	.316	.432	105	0	0	0	0	.966	1	2-12	0.2
■ JACK DOYLE									Doyle, John Joseph "Dirty Jack" b: 10/25/1869, Killorglin, Ireland d: 12/31/58, Holyoke, Mass. BR/TR, 5'9", 155 lbs. Deb: 8/27/1889 MU														
1889	Col-a	11	36	6	10	1	1	0	3	6	6	.278	.381	.361	118	1	9			.897	-3	/C-7,O-3,2	-0.1
1890	Col-a	77	298	47	80	17	7	2		13		.268	.299	.393	111	2	27			.887	-6	C-38,S-25/O23	0.1
1891	Cle-N	69	250	43	69	14	4	0	43	26	44	.276	.351	.364	104	1	24			.897	-3	C-29,O-21,3/S	0.1
1892	Cle-N	24	88	17	26	4	1	1	14	6	10	.295	.340	.398	118	2	5			.875	-1	O-12/C-9,1S	0.1
	NY-N	90	366	61	109	22	1	5	55	18	30	.298	.336	.404	126	10	42			.864	-13	2-31,C-26,O3/S	-0.5
	Yr	114	454	78	135	26	2	6	69	24	40	.297	.337	.403	124	11	47			.890	-18	C-35,2-31,O3/S1	-0.4
1893	NY-N	82	332	56	102	17	5	1	51	27	12	.321	.383	.415	112	5	40			.919	3	C-48,O-29/S31	0.9
1894	*NY-N	105	422	90	155	30	4	3	100	35	3	.367	.420	.498	121	15	42			.965	-7	*1-99/C-6	1.2
1895	NY-N	82	319	52	100	21	3	1	66	24	12	.313	.365	.408	102	1	35			.968	-2	1-58,2-13/3CM	0.1
1896	*Bal-N	118	487	116	165	29	4	1	101	42	15	.339	.400	.421	115	11	73			.974	-11	*1-118/2-1	0.2
1897	*Bal-N	105	460	91	163	29	4	2	87	29		.354	.394	.448	122	14	62			.979	5	*1-114	1.6
1898	Was-N	43	177	26	54	3	2	2	26	7		.305	.335	.373	103	-0	9			.963	-2	1-38/2-5M	-0.2
	NY-N	82	297	42	84	15	3	1	43	12		.283	.317	.364	98	-2	14			.860	0	O-38,1-24,S/3C	-0.3

YEAR	TM/L	G	AB	R	H	2B	3B	HR	RBI	BB	SO	AVG	OBP	SLG	PRO+	BR/A	SB	CS	SBR	FA	FR	G/POS	TPR
	Yr	125	474	68	138	17	5	3	69	19		.291	.324	.367	100	-2	23			.970	-2	1-62,O-38,S/23C	-0.5
1899	NY-N	118	448	55	134	15	7	3	76	33		.299	.353	.384	106	3	35			.976	6	*1-113/C-5	0.9
1900	NY-N	133	505	69	135	24	1	1	66	34		.267	.317	.325	81	-13	34			.971	6	*1-133	-0.7
1901	Chi-N	75	285	21	66	9	2	0	39	7		.232	.263	.277	59	-15	8			.973	7	1-75	-0.9
1902	NY-N	49	186	21	56	13	0	1	19	10		.301	.340	.387	125	5	12			.991	4	1-49	0.8
	Was-A	78	312	52	77	15	2	1	20	29		.247	.311	.317	74	-11	6			.929	-11	2-68/1-7,OC	-1.9
1903	Bro-N	139	524	84	164	27	6	0	91	54		.313	.383	.387	123	17	34			.981	2	*1-139	1.6
1904	Bro-N	8	22	2	5	1	0	0	2	6		.227	.414	.273	116	1	1			1.000	1	/1-8	0.2
	Phi-N	66	236	20	52	10	3	1	22	19		.220	.281	.301	83	-5	4			.977	4	1-65/2-1	-0.3
	Yr	74	258	22	57	11	3	1	24	25		.221	.295	.298	86	-4	5			.980	5	1-73/2-1	-0.1
1905	NY-A	1	3	0	0	0	0	0				.000	.000	.000	-90	-1	0			.833	-1	/1-1	-0.1
Total	17	1564	6039	971	1806	315	64	26	**924**	437	**132**	.299	.351	.385	106	42	516			.975	-20	*1-1043,C-176,O2/S3	2.8

■ **JOE DOYLE**   Doyle, Joseph K.   b: Cincinnati, Ohio   Deb: 4/20/1872

YEAR	TM/L	G	AB	R	H	2B	3B	HR	RBI	BB	SO	AVG	OBP	SLG	PRO+	BR/A	SB	CS	SBR	FA	FR	G/POS	TPR
1872	Nat-n	9	42	7	12	0	0	0	8	0	0	.286	.286	.286	66	-2						/S-6,2-1,3	-0.2

■ **LARRY DOYLE**   Doyle, Lawrence Joseph "Laughing Larry"   b: 7/31/1886, Caseyville, Ill.   d: 3/1/74, Saranac Lake, N.Y.   BL/TR, 5'10", 165 lbs.   Deb: 7/22/07

YEAR	TM/L	G	AB	R	H	2B	3B	HR	RBI	BB	SO	AVG	OBP	SLG	PRO+	BR/A	SB	CS	SBR	FA	FR	G/POS	TPR
1907	NY-N	69	227	16	59	3	0	0	16	20		.260	.320	.273	83	-4	3			.917	-22	2-69	-3.1
1908	NY-N	104	377	65	116	16	9	0	33	22		.308	.354	.398	134	13	17			.935	-10	*2-102	0.3
1909	NY-N	147	570	86	**172**	27	11	6	49	45		.302	.360	.419	140	25	31			.940	-18	*2-146	0.5
1910	NY-N	151	575	97	164	21	14	8	69	71	26	.285	.369	.412	128	20	39			.930	-17	*2-151	0.0
1911	*NY-N	143	526	102	163	25	**25**	13	77	71	39	.310	.397	.527	153	36	38			.944	-24	*2-141	0.8
1912	*NY-N	143	558	98	184	33	8	10	90	56	20	.330	.393	.471	132	24	36			.948	-8	*2-143	1.2
1913	*NY-N	132	482	67	135	25	6	5	73	59	29	.280	.364	.388	114	10	38			.955	-13	*2-130	-0.5
1914	NY-N	145	539	87	140	19	8	5	63	58	25	.260	.343	.353	111	8	17			.959	-19	*2-145	-1.3
1915	NY-N	150	591	86	**189**	**40**	10	4	70	32	28	**.320**	.358	.442	150	32	22	18	-4	.947	-7	*2-147	2.6
1916	NY-N	113	441	55	118	24	10	2	47	27	23	.268	.316	.381	120	9	17			.960	16	*2-113	3.1
	Chi-N	9	38	6	15	5	1	1	7	1	1	.395	.410	.658	203	4	2			.982	5	/2-9	1.0
	Yr	122	479	61	133	29	11	3	54	28	24	.278	.323	.403	127	14	19			.962	20	*2-122	4.1
1917	Chi-N	135	476	48	121	19	5	6	61	48	28	.254	.323	.353	99	-0	5			.952	-2	*2-128	0.4
1918	NY-N	75	257	38	67	7	4	3	36	37	10	.261	.354	.354	118	7	10			.969	-12	2-73	-0.1
1919	NY-N	113	381	61	110	14	10	7	52	31	17	.289	.350	.433	136	16	12			.956	2	*2-100	2.5
1920	NY-N	137	471	48	134	21	2	4	50	47	28	.285	.352	.363	107	5	11	9	-2	.967	-26	*2-133	-2.0
Total	14	1766	6509	960	1887	299	123	74	793	625	**274**	.290	.357	.408	126	206	298	**27**		.949	-155	*2-1728	5.4

■ **DENNY DOYLE**   Doyle, Robert Dennis   b: 1/17/44, Glasgow, Ky.   BL/TR, 5'9", 175 lbs.   Deb: 4/7/70   F

YEAR	TM/L	G	AB	R	H	2B	3B	HR	RBI	BB	SO	AVG	OBP	SLG	PRO+	BR/A	SB	CS	SBR	FA	FR	G/POS	TPR
1970	Phi-N	112	413	43	86	10	7	2	16	33	64	.208	.267	.281	48	-31	6	5	-1	.978	-16	*2-103	-4.1
1971	Phi-N	95	342	34	79	12	1	2	24	19	31	.231	.281	.298	64	-16	4	2	0	.967	4	2-91	-0.5
1972	Phi-N	123	442	33	110	14	2	1	26	31	33	.249	.298	.296	68	-18	6	7	-2	.982	-9	*2-119	-2.6
1973	Phi-N	116	370	45	101	9	3	3	26	31	32	.273	.329	.338	83	-8	1	3	-2	.974	9	*2-114	0.6
1974	Cal-A	147	511	47	133	19	2	1	34	25	49	.260	.296	.311	79	-14	6	7	-2	.983	16	*2-146/S-2	0.7
1975	Cal-A	8	15	0	1	0	0	0	0	1	1	.067	.125	.067	-48	-3	0	0	0	.926	2	/2-6,3-1	-0.1
	*Bos-A	89	310	50	96	21	2	4	36	14	11	.310	.342	.429	107	2	5	7	-3	.974	-31	2-84/3-6,S	-2.8
	Yr	97	325	50	97	21	2	4	36	15	12	.298	.331	.412	102	-0	5	7	-3	.970	-29	2-90/3-7,S	-2.9
1976	Bos-A	117	432	51	108	15	5	0	26	22	39	.250	.286	.308	66	-19	8	5	-1	.977	-25	*2-112	-4.0
1977	Bos-A	137	455	54	109	13	6	2	49	29	50	.240	.291	.308	57	-27	2	4	-2	.979	-10	*2-137	-3.0
Total	8	944	3290	357	823	113	28	16	237	205	310	.250	.296	.316	70	-135	38	40	-13	.977	-61	2-912/3-7,S	-15.8

■ **D. J. DOZIER**   Dozier, William Henry   b: 9/21/65, Norfolk, Va.   BR/TR, 6', 202 lbs.   Deb: 5/6/92

YEAR	TM/L	G	AB	R	H	2B	3B	HR	RBI	BB	SO	AVG	OBP	SLG	PRO+	BR/A	SB	CS	SBR	FA	FR	G/POS	TPR
1992	NY-N	25	47	4	9	2	0	0	2	4	19	.191	.269	.234	44	-3	4	0	1	.971	0	O-17	-0.2

■ **DRAKE**   Drake   Deb: 6/29/1884

YEAR	TM/L	G	AB	R	H	2B	3B	HR	RBI	BB	SO	AVG	OBP	SLG	PRO+	BR/A	SB	CS	SBR	FA	FR	G/POS	TPR
1884	Was-a	2	7	0	2	1	0	0		0		.286	.286	.429	147	0				.000	-1	/O-2	-0.1

■ **DELOS DRAKE**   Drake, Delos Daniel   b: 12/3/1886, Girard, Ohio   d: 10/3/65, Findlay, Ohio   BR/TL, 5'11.5", 170 lbs.   Deb: 4/30/11

YEAR	TM/L	G	AB	R	H	2B	3B	HR	RBI	BB	SO	AVG	OBP	SLG	PRO+	BR/A	SB	CS	SBR	FA	FR	G/POS	TPR
1911	Det-A	95	315	37	88	9	9	1	36	17		.279	.324	.375	90	-5	20			.942	-10	O-83/1-2	-1.9
1914	StL-F	138	514	51	129	18	8	3	42	31	57	.251	.295	.335	60	-31	17			.957	-1	*O-116,1-18	-4.0
1915	StL-F	102	343	32	91	23	4	1	41	23	27	.265	.313	.364	77	-12	6			.974	-5	O-97/1-1	-2.3
Total	3	335	1172	120	308	50	21	5	119	71	**84**	.263	.308	.354	73	-48	43			.959	-16	O-296/1-21	-8.2

■ **LARRY DRAKE**   Drake, Larry Francis   b: 5/4/21, McKinney, Tex.   d: 7/14/85, Houston, Tex.   BL/TR, 6'1.5", 195 lbs.   Deb: 7/20/45

YEAR	TM/L	G	AB	R	H	2B	3B	HR	RBI	BB	SO	AVG	OBP	SLG	PRO+	BR/A	SB	CS	SBR	FA	FR	G/POS	TPR
1945	Phi-A	1	2	0	0	0	0	0	0	0	2	.000	.000	.000	-99	-1	0	0	0	1.000	-0	/O-1	-0.1
1948	Was-A	4	7	0	2	0	0	0	1	1	3	.286	.375	.286	79	-0	0	0	0	1.000	-0	/O-2	-0.0
Total	2	5	9	0	2	0	0	0	1	1	5	.222	.300	.222	44	-1	0	0	0	1.000	-0	/O-3	-0.2

■ **SAMMY DRAKE**   Drake, Samuel Harrison   b: 10/7/34, Little Rock, Ark.   BB/TR, 5'11", 175 lbs.   Deb: 4/17/60   F

YEAR	TM/L	G	AB	R	H	2B	3B	HR	RBI	BB	SO	AVG	OBP	SLG	PRO+	BR/A	SB	CS	SBR	FA	FR	G/POS	TPR
1960	Chi-N	15	15	5	1	0	0	0	0	1	4	.067	.125	.067	-46	-3	0	0	0	1.000	-1	/3-6,2-2	-0.4
1961	Chi-N	13	5	1	0	0	0	0	0	1	1	.000	.167	.000	-50	-1	0	0	0	1.000	-0	/O-1	-0.1
1962	NY-N	25	52	2	10	0	0	0	7	6	12	.192	.276	.192	28	-5	0	0	0	.977	-2	2-10/3-6	-0.6
Total	3	53	72	8	11	0	0	0	7	8	17	.153	.237	.153	8	-9	0	0	0	.978	-3	2-12,3-12,O	-1.1

■ **SOLLY DRAKE**   Drake, Solomon Louis   b: 10/23/30, Little Rock, Ark.   BB/TR, 6', 170 lbs.   Deb: 4/17/56   F

YEAR	TM/L	G	AB	R	H	2B	3B	HR	RBI	BB	SO	AVG	OBP	SLG	PRO+	BR/A	SB	CS	SBR	FA	FR	G/POS	TPR
1956	Chi-N	65	215	29	55	9	1	2	15	23	35	.256	.331	.335	81	-5	9	5	-0	.993	2	O-53	-0.6
1959	LA-N	9	8	2	2	0	0	0	0	1	3	.250	.333	.250	54	-0	1	0	0	.667	-1	/O-4	-0.2
	Phi-N	67	62	10	9	1	0	0	3	8	15	.145	.243	.161	10	-8	5	5	-2	1.000	-0	O-37	-2.0
	Yr	76	70	12	11	1	0	0	3	9	18	.157	.253	.171	15	-8	6	5	-1	.974	-11	O-41	-2.2
Total	2	141	285	41	66	10	1	2	18	32	53	.232	.311	.295	64	-14	15	10	-2	.989	-9	O-94	-2.8

■ **JAKE DRAUBY**   Drauby, Jacob C.   b: 1865, Harrisburg, Pa.   5'10", 163 lbs.   Deb: 10/3/1892

YEAR	TM/L	G	AB	R	H	2B	3B	HR	RBI	BB	SO	AVG	OBP	SLG	PRO+	BR/A	SB	CS	SBR	FA	FR	G/POS	TPR
1892	Was-N	10	34	3	7	0	1	0	3	2	12	.206	.250	.265	57	-2	0			.763	-2	3-10	-0.3

■ **BILL DREESEN**   Dreesen, William Richard   b: 7/26/04, New York, N.Y.   d: 11/9/71, Mt.Vernon, N.Y.   BL/TR, 5'7.5", 160 lbs.   Deb: 5/1/31

YEAR	TM/L	G	AB	R	H	2B	3B	HR	RBI	BB	SO	AVG	OBP	SLG	PRO+	BR/A	SB	CS	SBR	FA	FR	G/POS	TPR
1931	Bos-N	48	180	38	40	10	4	1	10	23	23	.222	.310	.339	77	-6	1			.910	-8	3-47	-1.1

■ **BILL DRESCHER**   Drescher, William Clayton "Dutch"   b: 5/23/21, Congers, N.Y.   d: 5/15/68, Haverstraw, N.Y.   BL/TR, 6'2", 190 lbs.   Deb: 4/19/44

YEAR	TM/L	G	AB	R	H	2B	3B	HR	RBI	BB	SO	AVG	OBP	SLG	PRO+	BR/A	SB	CS	SBR	FA	FR	G/POS	TPR
1944	NY-A	4	7	0	1	0	0	0	0	0	0	.143	.143	.143	-18	-1	0	0	0	.875	0	/C-1	-0.1
1945	NY-A	48	126	10	34	3	1	0	15	8	5	.270	.313	.310	77	-4	2	0	-1	.991	-8	C-33	-1.2
1946	NY-A	5	6	0	2	1	0	0	1	0	0	.333	.333	.500	129	-0	0	0	0	1.000	0	/C-3	0.1
Total	3	57	139	10	37	4	1	0	16	8	5	.266	.306	.309	75	-5	2	0	-1	.985	-7	/C-37	-1.2

■ **CHUCK DRESSEN**   Dressen, Charles Walter   b: 9/20/1898, Decatur, Ill.   d: 8/10/66, Detroit, Mich.   BR/TR, 5'5.5", 146 lbs.   Deb: 4/17/25   MC

YEAR	TM/L	G	AB	R	H	2B	3B	HR	RBI	BB	SO	AVG	OBP	SLG	PRO+	BR/A	SB	CS	SBR	FA	FR	G/POS	TPR
1925	Cin-N	76	215	35	59	8	2	3	19	12	4	.274	.319	.372	78	-7	5	3	-0	.951	2	3-47/2-5,O	-0.3
1926	Cin-N	127	474	76	126	27	11	4	48	49	31	.266	.338	.395	99	-1	0			.966	17	*3-123/S-1,O	2.3
1927	Cin-N	144	548	78	160	36	10	2	55	71	32	.292	.376	.405	113	12	7			**.967**	8	*3-142/S-2	3.0
1928	Cin-N	135	498	72	145	26	3	1	59	43	22	.291	.355	.361	89	-7	10			.938	-2	*3-135	-0.2
1929	Cin-N	110	401	49	98	22	3	1	36	41	21	.244	.321	.322	63	-23	8			.932	-20	3-98/2-8	-3.6

YEAR	TM/L	G	AB	R	H	2B	3B	HR	RBI	BB	SO	AVG	OBP	SLG	PRO+	BR/A	SB	CS	SBR	FA	FR	G/POS	TPR
1930	Cin-N	33	19	0	4	0	0	0	1	1	3	.211	.250	.211	14	-3	0			1.000	3	3-10/2-3	0.0
1931	Cin-N	5	15	0	1	0	0	0	0	1	1	.067	.125	.067	-50	-3	0			.846	-0	/3-4	-0.3
1933	NY-N	16	45	3	10	4	0	0	3	1	4	.222	.239	.311	57	-3	0			.972	0	3-16	-0.2
Total	8	646	2215	313	603	123	29	11	221	219	118	.272	.343	.369	89	-35	30	3		.953	12	3-575/2-16,OS	0.7

■ LEE DRESSEN
Dressen, Lee August b: 7/23/1889, Ellinwood, Kan. d: 6/30/31, Diller, Neb. BL/TL, 6', 165 lbs. Deb: 4/21/14

YEAR	TM/L	G	AB	R	H	2B	3B	HR	RBI	BB	SO	AVG	OBP	SLG	PRO+	BR/A	SB	CS	SBR	FA	FR	G/POS	TPR
1914	StL-N	46	103	16	24	1	2	0	7	11	20	.233	.307	.272	73	-3	2			.982	-1	1-38	-0.6
1918	Det-A	31	107	10	19	1	2	0	3	21	10	.178	.323	.224	68	-3	2			.988	-3	1-30	-0.9
Total	2	77	210	26	43	3	3	0	10	32	30	.205	.316	.248	71	-6	4			.985	-5	/1-68	-1.5

■ CAMERON DREW
Drew, Cameron Steward b: 2/12/64, Boston, Mass. BL/TR, 6'5", 230 lbs. Deb: 9/9/88

YEAR	TM/L	G	AB	R	H	2B	3B	HR	RBI	BB	SO	AVG	OBP	SLG	PRO+	BR/A	SB	CS	SBR	FA	FR	G/POS	TPR
1988	Hou-N	7	16	1	3	0	1	0	1	0	1	.188	.188	.313	43	-1	0	0	0	1.000	0	/O-5	-0.1

■ DAVE DREW
Drew, David Deb: 5/14/1884

YEAR	TM/L	G	AB	R	H	2B	3B	HR	RBI	BB	SO	AVG	OBP	SLG	PRO+	BR/A	SB	CS	SBR	FA	FR	G/POS	TPR
1884	Phi-U	2	9	1	4	0	0	0		0		.444	.444	.444	154	1				.000	-0	/P-1,2-1,S	0.1
	Was-U	13	53	8	16	1	2	0		1		.302	.315	.396	95	-0				.806	1	/S-8,1-5,O	0.0
	Yr	15	62	9	20	1	2	0		1		.323	.333	.403	103	0				.813	1	/S-9,1-5,P20	0.1

■ FRANK DREWS
Drews, Frank John b: 5/25/16, Buffalo, N.Y. d: 4/22/72, Buffalo, N.Y. BR/TR, 5'10", 175 lbs. Deb: 8/13/44

YEAR	TM/L	G	AB	R	H	2B	3B	HR	RBI	BB	SO	AVG	OBP	SLG	PRO+	BR/A	SB	CS	SBR	FA	FR	G/POS	TPR
1944	Bos-N	46	141	14	29	9	1	0	10	25	14	.206	.329	.284	71	-5	0			.959	1	2-46	-0.2
1945	Bos-N	49	147	13	30	4	1	0	19	16	18	.204	.282	.245	47	-10	0			.976	5	2-48	-0.3
Total	2	95	288	27	59	13	2	0	29	41	32	.205	.306	.264	59	-15	0			.967	5	/2-94	-0.5

■ DAN DRIESSEN
Driessen, Daniel b: 7/29/51, Hilton Head Island, S.C. BL/TR, 5'11", 190 lbs. Deb: 6/9/73

YEAR	TM/L	G	AB	R	H	2B	3B	HR	RBI	BB	SO	AVG	OBP	SLG	PRO+	BR/A	SB	CS	SBR	FA	FR	G/POS	TPR
1973	*Cin-N	102	366	49	110	15	2	4	47	24	37	.301	.347	.385	108	4	8	3	1	.946	-10	3-87,1-35/O	-0.7
1974	Cin-N	150	470	63	132	23	6	7	56	48	62	.281	.349	.400	111	6	10	5	0	.915	-21	*3-126,1-47/O	-1.7
1975	*Cin-N	88	210	38	59	8	1	7	38	35	30	.281	.389	.429	124	8	10	3	1	.986	-5	1-41,O-29	0.1
1976	*Cin-N	98	219	32	54	11	1	7	44	43	32	.247	.370	.402	116	6	14	1	4	.997	-3	1-40,O-20	0.3
1977	Cin-N	151	536	75	161	31	4	17	91	64	85	.300	.378	.468	123	18	31	13	2	.994	-3	*1-148	0.8
1978	Cin-N	153	524	68	131	23	3	16	70	75	79	.250	.348	.397	108	7	28	9	3	**.996**	3	*1-151	0.4
1979	*Cin-N	150	515	72	129	24	3	18	75	62	77	.250	.334	.414	102	2	11	5	0	.993	3	*1-143	-1.0
1980	Cin-N	154	524	81	139	36	1	14	74	**93**	68	.265	.382	.418	123	20	19	6	3	.995	-4	*1-151	0.9
1981	Cin-N	82	233	35	55	14	0	7	33	40	31	.236	.353	.386	108	3	2	4	-2	.995	-5	1-74	-0.8
1982	Cin-N	149	516	64	139	25	1	17	57	82	62	.269	.372	.421	119	15	11	6	-0	**.998**	-7	*1-144	0.0
1983	Cin-N	122	386	57	107	17	1	12	57	75	51	.277	.395	.420	121	14	6	4	-1	**.996**	-2	*1-112	0.5
1984	Cin-N	81	218	27	61	13	0	7	28	37	25	.280	.384	.436	124	8	2	1	0	.991	-4	1-70	0.1
	Mon-N	51	169	20	43	11	0	9	32	17	15	.254	.323	.479	128	6	0	1	-1	.995	-2	1-45	0.1
	Yr	132	387	47	104	24	0	16	60	54	40	.269	.358	.455	126	14	2	2	-1	.992	-5	*1-115	0.2
1985	Mon-N	91	312	31	78	18	0	6	25	33	29	.250	.326	.365	99	-1	2	1	-1	.997	3	1-88	-0.4
	SF-N	54	181	22	42	8	0	3	22	17	22	.232	.302	.326	79	-5	0	1	0	.998	-2	1-49	-1.0
	Yr	145	493	53	120	26	0	9	47	50	51	.243	.317	.351	92	-6	2	2	-1	.997	1	*1-137	-1.4
1986	SF-N	15	16	2	3	2	0	0	0	4	4	.188	.350	.313	89	-0	0	0	0	1.000	1	/1-4	0.0
	Hou-N	17	24	5	7	1	0	1	3	5	2	.292	.414	.458	144	2	0	0	0	1.000	-0	1-12	0.1
	Yr	32	40	7	10	3	0	1	3	9	6	.250	.388	.400	122	2	0	0	0	1.000	0	1-16	0.1
1987	*StL-N	24	60	5	14	2	0	1	11	7	8	.233	.313	.317	66	-3	0	0	0	.993	-0	1-21	-0.4
Total	15	1732	5479	746	1464	282	23	153	763	761	719	.267	.359	.411	113	109	154	63	8	.995	-64	*1-1375,3-213/O	-2.7

■ LEW DRILL
Drill, Lewis L b: 5/9/1877, Browerville, Minn. d: 7/4/69, St.Paul, Minn. BR/TR, 5'6", 186 lbs. Deb: 4/23/02

YEAR	TM/L	G	AB	R	H	2B	3B	HR	RBI	BB	SO	AVG	OBP	SLG	PRO+	BR/A	SB	CS	SBR	FA	FR	G/POS	TPR
1902	Was-A	38	123	21	34	7	2	1	16	16		.276	.369	.390	110	2	0			.919	-11	C-28/2-4,O3	-0.6
	Bal-A	2	8	2	2	0	0	0	0	0		.250	.250	.250	37	-1	0			1.000	1	/C-1,1-1	0.0
	Was-A	33	98	12	24	3	2	0	13	10		.245	.327	.316	78	-3	5			.926	-4	C-25/O-4,2	-0.4
	Yr	73	229	35	60	10	4	1	29	26		.262	.347	.354	94	-1	5			.924	-15	C-54/O-8,231	-1.0
1903	Was-A	51	154	11	39	9	3	0	23	15		.253	.331	.351	103	1	4			.966	-4	C-47/1-3	0.2
1904	Was-A	46	142	17	38	7	2	1	11	21		.268	.385	.366	140	8	3			.934	-7	C-29,O-14	0.4
	Det-A	51	160	7	39	6	1	0	13	20		.244	.335	.294	103	1	2			.950	-7	C-49/1-2	0.0
	Yr	97	302	24	77	13	3	1	24	41		.255	.359	.328	121	10	5			.944	-14	C-78,O-14/1	0.4
1905	Det-A	72	211	17	55	9	0	0	24	32		.261	.366	.303	112	5	7			.970	-2	C-71	1.1
Total	4	293	896	87	231	41	10	2	100	114		.258	.353	.333	108	14	21			.953	-34	C-250/O-22,123	0.7

■ JIM DRISCOLL
Driscoll, James Bernard b: 5/14/44, Medford, Mass. BL/TR, 5'11", 175 lbs. Deb: 6/17/70

YEAR	TM/L	G	AB	R	H	2B	3B	HR	RBI	BB	SO	AVG	OBP	SLG	PRO+	BR/A	SB	CS	SBR	FA	FR	G/POS	TPR
1970	Oak-A	21	52	2	10	0	0	1	2	2	15	.192	.236	.250	35	-5	0	0	0	.967	-3	/2-7,S-7	-0.6
1972	Tex-A	15	18	0	0	0	0	0	2	2	3	.000	.100	.000	-72	-4	0	0	0	.900	1	/2-4,3-2	-0.3
Total	2	36	70	2	10	0	0	1	4	4	18	.143	.200	.186	9	-8	0	0	0	.950	-1	/2-11,S-7,3	-0.9

■ DENNY DRISCOLL
Driscoll, John F. b: 11/19/1855, Lowell, Mass. d: 7/11/1886, Lowell, Mass. BL/TL, 5'10.5", 160 lbs. Deb: 7/1/1880

YEAR	TM/L	G	AB	R	H	2B	3B	HR	RBI	BB	SO	AVG	OBP	SLG	PRO+	BR/A	SB	CS	SBR	FA	FR	G/POS	TPR
1880	Buf-N	18	65	1	10	1	0	0	4	1	7	.154	.167	.169	14	-6				.895	-2	O-14/P-6	-0.6
1882	Pit-a	23	80	12	11	2	0	1		3		.138	.169	.200	25	-6				.885	-4	P-23	0.0
1883	Pit-a	41	148	19	27	2	1	0		4		.182	.204	.209	35	-10				.890	4	P-41/O-4,3	-0.2
1884	Lou-a	13	48	5	9	1	0	0		2		.188	.220	.208	42	-3				.816	7	P-13/O-2	-0.1
1885	Buf-N	7	19	2	3	0	0	0	0	2	5	.158	.238	.158	29	-1				.719	-5	/2-7	-0.6
Total	5	102	360	39	60	6	1	1	4	12	12	.167	.194	.197	30	-26				.872	-5	/P-83,O-20,23	-1.5

■ PADDY DRISCOLL
Driscoll, John Leo b: 1/11/1895, Evanston, Ill. d: 6/28/68, Chicago, Ill. BR/TR, 5'8.5", 155 lbs. Deb: 6/12/17

YEAR	TM/L	G	AB	R	H	2B	3B	HR	RBI	BB	SO	AVG	OBP	SLG	PRO+	BR/A	SB	CS	SBR	FA	FR	G/POS	TPR
1917	Chi-N	13	28	2	3	1	0	0	3	2	6	.107	.167	.143	-4	-3	2			.882	2	/2-8,3-2,S	-0.1

■ MIKE DRISSEL
Drissel, Michael F. b: 12/19/1864, St.Louis, Mo. d: 2/26/13, St.Louis, Mo. BR/TR, 5'11", Deb: 9/5/1885

YEAR	TM/L	G	AB	R	H	2B	3B	HR	RBI	BB	SO	AVG	OBP	SLG	PRO+	BR/A	SB	CS	SBR	FA	FR	G/POS	TPR
1885	StL-a	6	20	0	1	0	0	0	0			.050	.050	.050	-65	-4				.971	-0	/C-6	-0.3

■ WALT DROPO
Dropo, Walter "Moose" b: 1/30/23, Moosup, Conn. BR/TR, 6'5", 220 lbs. Deb: 4/19/49

YEAR	TM/L	G	AB	R	H	2B	3B	HR	RBI	BB	SO	AVG	OBP	SLG	PRO+	BR/A	SB	CS	SBR	FA	FR	G/POS	TPR
1949	Bos-A	11	41	3	6	2	0	0	1	3	7	.146	.205	.195	6	-6	0	0	0	1.000	-1	1-11	-0.7
1950	Bos-A★	136	559	101	180	28	8	34	**144**	45	75	.322	.378	.583	130	21	0	0	0	.988	-4	*1-134	1.3
1951	Bos-A	99	360	37	86	14	0	11	57	38	52	.239	.312	.369	76	-13	0	0	0	.987	-1	1-93	-1.8
1952	Bos-A	37	132	13	35	7	1	6	27	11	22	.265	.331	.470	112	2	0	0	0	.994	-1	1-35	-0.1
	Det-A	115	459	56	128	17	3	23	70	26	63	.279	.320	.479	120	9	2	2	-1	.989	-1	*1-115	0.3
	Yr	152	591	69	163	24	4	29	97	37	85	.276	.323	.477	118	10	2	2	-1	.990	-2	*1-150	0.2
1953	Det-A	152	606	61	150	30	3	13	96	29	69	.248	.289	.371	78	-21	0	0	0	.990	12	*1-150	-1.5
1954	Det-A	107	320	27	90	14	2	4	44	24	41	.281	.331	.375	95	-3	0	1	-1	.996	-1	1-95	-0.7
1955	Chi-A	141	455	55	127	15	2	19	79	42	71	.280	.344	.448	109	4	0	1	-1	.995	-5	*1-140	-0.9
1956	Chi-A	125	361	42	96	13	1	8	52	37	51	.266	.339	.374	87	-7	1	0	0	**.993**	-3	*1-117	-1.6
1957	Chi-A	93	223	24	57	12	0	13	49	16	40	.256	.305	.439	101	-1	0	1	-1	.987	6	1-69	-0.3
1958	Chi-A	28	52	3	10	1	0	2	8	5	11	.192	.276	.327	67	-2	0	0	0	1.000	0	1-16	-0.3
	Cin-N	63	162	18	47	7	2	9	21	18	47	.290	.343	.488	111	2	0	1	-1	1.000	1	1-43	0.1
1959	Cin-N	26	39	4	4	1	0	2	8	1	7	.103	.205	.205	9	-5	0	0	0	1.000	1	1-23	-0.3
	Bal-A	62	151	17	42	9	0	6	21	12	20	.278	.331	.457	117	3	0	0	0	.990	-2	1-54/3-2	-0.1
1960	Bal-A	79	179	16	48	8	0	4	21	20	19	.268	.345	.380	97	-1	0	1	-1	.993	-1	1-67/3-1	-0.6

YEAR	TM/L	G	AB	R	H	2B	3B	HR	RBI	BB	SO	AVG	OBP	SLG	PRO+	BR/A	SB	CS	SBR	FA	FR	G/POS	TPR
1961	Bal-A	14	27	1	7	0	0	1	2	4	3	.259	.355	.370	97	-0	0	0	0	1.000	1	1-12	0.0
Total	13	1288	4124	478	1113	168	22	152	704	328	582	.270	.327	.432	100	-17	5	6	-2	.992	-1	*1-1174/3-3	-7.3

■ KEITH DRUMRIGHT   Drumright, Keith Alan   b: 10/21/54, Springfield, Mo.   BL/TR, 5′10″, 170 lbs.   Deb: 9/1/78

YEAR	TM/L	G	AB	R	H	2B	3B	HR	RBI	BB	SO	AVG	OBP	SLG	PRO+	BR/A	SB	CS	SBR	FA	FR	G/POS	TPR
1978	Hou-N	17	55	5	9	0	0	0	2	3	4	.164	.207	.164	5	-7	0	1	-1	.944	-1	2-17	-0.8
1981	*Oak-A	31	86	8	25	1	1	0	11	4	4	.291	.322	.326	91	-1	0	0	0	.989	-5	2-19/D-5	-0.6
Total	2	48	141	13	34	1	1	0	13	7	8	.241	.277	.262	58	-8	0	1	-1	.969	-6	/2-36,D-5	-1.4

■ JEAN DUBUC   Dubuc, Jean Joseph Octave Arthur "Chauncey"   b: 9/15/1888, St.Johnsbury, Vt.   d: 8/28/58, Fort Myers, Fla.   BR/TR, 5′10.5″, 185 lbs.   Deb: 6/25/08   C

YEAR	TM/L	G	AB	R	H	2B	3B	HR	RBI	BB	SO	AVG	OBP	SLG	PRO+	BR/A	SB	CS	SBR	FA	FR	G/POS	TPR
1908	Cin-N	15	29	2	4	2	0	0	0	0		.138	.138	.172	-1	-3	0			.943	1	P-15	0.0
1909	Cin-N	19	18	1	3	0	0	0	0	0	2	.167	.250	.167	30	-1	0			.844	0	P-19	0.0
1912	Det-A	40	108	16	29	6	2	1	9	3		.269	.295	.389	98	-1	0			.972	4	P-37/O-2	0.0
1913	Det-A	68	135	17	36	5	3	2	11	2	17	.267	.277	.393	97	-2	1			.953	6	P-36/O-3	-0.2
1914	Det-A	71	124	9	28	8	1	1	11	7	11	.226	.273	.331	79	-4	1			.942	3	P-36	0.0
1915	Det-A	60	112	7	23	2	1	0	14	8	15	.205	.258	.241	47	-7	0			.969	-1	P-39	0.0
1916	Det-A	52	78	3	20	0	2	0	7	7	12	.256	.318	.308	85	-1	0			.952	4	P-36	0.0
1918	*Bos-A	5	6	0	1	0	0	0	0	1	2	.167	.286	.167	37	-0	0			1.000	-0	/P-2	0.0
1919	NY-N	37	42	2	6	1	1	0	2	0	6	.143	.143	.214	7	-5	0			.964	2	P-36	0.0
Total	9	367	652	57	150	23	10	4	56	30	63	.230	.266	.314	72	-25	2			.952	22	P-256/O-5	-0.2

■ ROB DUCEY   Ducey, Robert Thomas   b: 5/24/65, Toronto, Ont., Can.   BL/TR, 6′2″, 175 lbs.   Deb: 5/1/87

YEAR	TM/L	G	AB	R	H	2B	3B	HR	RBI	BB	SO	AVG	OBP	SLG	PRO+	BR/A	SB	CS	SBR	FA	FR	G/POS	TPR
1987	Tor-A	34	48	12	9	1	0	1	6	8	10	.188	.304	.271	53	-3	2	0	1	1.000	-7	O-28/D-1	-0.9
1988	Tor-A	27	54	15	17	4	1	0	6	5	7	.315	.373	.426	123	2	1	0	0	1.000	-6	O-26/D-1	-0.4
1989	Tor-A	41	76	5	16	4	0	0	7	9	25	.211	.294	.263	59	-4	2	1	0	1.000	-4	O-35/D-1	-0.6
1990	Tor-A	19	53	7	16	5	0	0	7	7	15	.302	.393	.396	119	2	1	1	-0	1.000	-6	O-19	0.1
1991	*Tor-A	39	68	8	16	2	2	1	4	6	26	.235	.297	.368	80	-2	2	0	1	.892	-4	O-24/D-2	-0.5
1992	Tor-A	23	21	3	1	1	0	0	0	0	10	.048	.048	.095	-58	-4	0	1	-1	1.000	-3	O-13/D-4	-0.9
	Cal-A	31	59	4	14	3	0	0	2	5	12	.237	.297	.288	64	-3	2	3	-1	.944	-1	O-20/D-1	-0.5
	Yr	54	80	7	15	4	0	0	2	5	22	.188	.235	.237	32	-7	2	4	-2	.957	-4	O-33/D-5	-1.4
1993	Tex-A	27	85	15	24	6	3	2	9	10	17	.282	.358	.494	132	4	2	3	-1	1.000	-2	O-26	0.0
1994	Tex-A	11	29	1	5	1	0	0	1	2	1	.172	.226	.207	13	-4	0	0	0	.882	-2	O-10	-0.5
Total	8	252	493	70	118	27	6	4	42	52	123	.239	.313	.343	80	-13	12	9	-2	.975	-26	O-201/D-10	-4.2

■ JOHN DUDRA   Dudra, John Joseph   b: 5/27/16, Assumption, Ill.   d: 10/24/65, Pana, Ill.   BR/TR, 5′11.5″, 175 lbs.   Deb: 9/7/41

YEAR	TM/L	G	AB	R	H	2B	3B	HR	RBI	BB	SO	AVG	OBP	SLG	PRO+	BR/A	SB	CS	SBR	FA	FR	G/POS	TPR
1941	Bos-N	14	25	3	9	3	1	0	3	3	4	.360	.429	.560	185	3	0			.933	0	/2-5,3-5,1S	0.3

■ PAT DUFF   Duff, Patrick Henry   b: 5/6/1875, Providence, R.I.   d: 9/11/25, Providence, R.I.   TR,   Deb: 4/16/06

YEAR	TM/L	G	AB	R	H	2B	3B	HR	RBI	BB	SO	AVG	OBP	SLG	PRO+	BR/A	SB	CS	SBR	FA	FR	G/POS	TPR
1906	Was-A	1	1	0	0	0	0	0	0	0	0	.000	.000	.000	-99	-0	0			.000	0	H	0.0

■ CHARLIE DUFFEE   Duffee, Charles Edward "Home Run"   b: 1/27/1866, Mobile, Ala.   d: 12/24/1894, Mobile, Ala.   BR/TR,   Deb: 4/17/1889

YEAR	TM/L	G	AB	R	H	2B	3B	HR	RBI	BB	SO	AVG	OBP	SLG	PRO+	BR/A	SB	CS	SBR	FA	FR	G/POS	TPR
1889	StL-a	137	509	93	124	15	11	16	86	60	81	.244	.327	.411	97	-7	21			.936	18	*O-132/3-5,2	0.6
1890	StL-a	98	378	68	104	11	7	3		37		.275	.344	.365	96	-5	20			.951	10	O-66,3-33/S	0.3
1891	Col-a	137	552	86	166	28	4	10	90	42	36	.301	.353	.420	129	18	41			.927	11	*O-128/3-7,S	2.2
1892	Was-N	132	492	64	122	12	11	6	51	36	33	.248	.302	.354	101	-1	28			.913	19	*O-125/3-6,1	1.2
1893	Cin-N	4	12	3	2	1	0	0	0	5	0	.167	.412	.250	76	-0	0			.400	-2	/O-4	-0.2
Total	5	508	1943	314	518	67	33	35	227	180	150	.267	.332	.389	106	5	110			.927	56	O-455/3-51,1S2	4.1

■ ED DUFFY   Duffy, Edward Charles   b: 1844, Ireland   d: 6/21/1889, Brooklyn, N.Y.   TR, 5′7.5″, 152 lbs.   Deb: 5/8/1871

YEAR	TM/L	G	AB	R	H	2B	3B	HR	RBI	BB	SO	AVG	OBP	SLG	PRO+	BR/A	SB	CS	SBR	FA	FR	G/POS	TPR
1871	Chi-n	26	121	30	28	5	0	0	15	3	2	.231	.250	.273	45	-10	11					S-24/3-1	-0.7

■ FRANK DUFFY   Duffy, Frank Thomas   b: 10/14/46, Oakland, Cal.   BR/TR, 6′1″, 180 lbs.   Deb: 9/4/70

YEAR	TM/L	G	AB	R	H	2B	3B	HR	RBI	BB	SO	AVG	OBP	SLG	PRO+	BR/A	SB	CS	SBR	FA	FR	G/POS	TPR
1970	Cin-N	6	11	1	2	2	0	0	0	1	2	.182	.250	.364	62	-1	1	0	0	1.000	1	/S-5	0.1
1971	Cin-N	13	16	0	3	1	0	0	1	1	2	.188	.235	.250	38	-1	0	0	0	.944	5	S-10	0.4
	*SF-N	21	28	4	5	0	0	0	2	0	10	.179	.179	.179	4	-4	0	0	0	.968	4	/S-6,2-1,3	0.2
	Yr	34	44	4	8	1	0	0	3	1	12	.182	.200	.205	15	-5	0	0	0	.955	10	S-16/2-1,3	0.6
1972	Cle-A	130	385	23	92	16	4	3	27	31	54	.239	.297	.325	82	-8	6	2	1	.977	3	*S-126	1.2
1973	Cle-A	116	361	34	95	16	4	8	50	25	61	.263	.314	.396	97	-2	6	6	-2	.986	12	*S-115	2.3
1974	Cle-A	158	549	62	128	18	0	8	48	30	64	.233	.273	.310	68	-23	7	8	-3	.980	-8	*S-158	-1.5
1975	Cle-A	146	482	44	117	22	2	1	47	27	60	.243	.286	.303	66	-22	10	10	-3	.977	14	*S-145	0.4
1976	Cle-A	133	392	38	83	11	2	2	30	29	50	.212	.270	.265	58	-21	10	0	3	.983	11	*S-132	0.7
1977	Cle-A	122	334	30	67	13	2	4	31	21	47	.201	.248	.287	47	-25	8	3	1	.967	3	*S-121	-1.1
1978	Bos-A	64	104	12	27	5	0	0	4	6	11	.260	.306	.308	66	-5	1	1	-0	.960	6	3-22,S-21,2/D	0.4
1979	Bos-A	6	3	0	0	0	0	0	0	0	0	.000	.000	.000	-95	-1	0	0	0	1.000	-0	/2-3,1-1	0.0
Total	10	915	2665	248	619	104	14	26	240	171	342	.232	.281	.311	69	-112	49	30	-3	.977	53	S-839/3-23,2D1	3.1

■ HUGH DUFFY   Duffy, Hugh   b: 11/26/1866, Cranston, R.I.   d: 10/19/54, Boston, Mass.   BR/TR, 5′7″, 168 lbs.   Deb: 6/23/1888   MCH

YEAR	TM/L	G	AB	R	H	2B	3B	HR	RBI	BB	SO	AVG	OBP	SLG	PRO+	BR/A	SB	CS	SBR	FA	FR	G/POS	TPR
1888	Chi-N	71	298	60	84	10	4	7	41	9	32	.282	.305	.413	119	5	13			.910	5	O-67/S-3,3	0.8
1889	Chi-N	136	584	144	172	21	7	12	89	46	30	.295	.348	.416	108	4	52			.894	-15	*O-126,S-10	-1.3
1890	Chi-P	138	596	161	191	36	16	7	82	59	20	.320	.384	.470	122	16	78			.917	13	*O-137	2.0
1891	Bos-a	127	536	134	180	20	8	9	110	61	29	.336	.408	.453	149	34	85			.917	0	*O-124/3-3,S	2.6
1892	*Bos-N	147	612	125	184	28	12	5	81	60	37	.301	.364	.410	123	14	51			.942	-9	*O-146/3-2	-0.1
1893	Bos-N	131	560	147	203	23	7	6	118	50	13	.363	.416	.461	123	16	44			.953	-2	*O-131	0.6
1894	Bos-N	125	539	160	237	51	16	18	145	66	15	.440	.502	.694	172	61	48			.927	4	*O-124/S-2	4.3
1895	Bos-N	130	531	110	187	30	6	9	100	63	16	.352	.425	.482	124	18	42			.945	6	*O-130	1.1
1896	Bos-N	131	527	97	158	16	8	5	113	52	19	.300	.365	.389	93	-6	39			.957	0	*O-120/2-9,S	-1.3
1897	*Bos-N	134	550	130	187	25	10	11	129	52		.340	.403	.482	125	18	41			.975	-1	*O-129/2-6,S	0.7
1898	Bos-N	152	568	97	169	13	3	8	108	59		.298	.365	.373	106	4	29			.956	2	*O-152/3-1,1C	-0.4
1899	Bos-N	147	588	103	164	29	7	5	102	39		.279	.327	.378	85	-15	26			.970	-4	*O-147	-2.7
1900	Bos-N	55	181	27	55	5	4	2	31	16		.304	.360	.409	100	-1	11			.957	-1	O-49/2-1	-0.5
1901	Mil-A	79	285	40	86	15	9	2	45	16		.302	.341	.439	121	7	12			.967	-6	O-77,M	-0.4
1904	Phi-N	18	46	10	13	1	1	0	5	13		.283	.439	.348	150	3	4			.850	-3	O-14,M	0.1
1905	Phi-N	15	40	7	12	2	1	0	3	1		.300	.317	.400	117	1	0			.909	1	/O-8,M	0.0
1906	Phi-N	1	1	0	0	0	0	0	0	0		.000	.000	.000	-99	-0	0			.000	0	HM	0.0
Total	17	1737	7042	1552	2282	325	119	106	1302	662	211	.324	.384	.449	121	181	574			.943	-10	*O-1681/S-20,23C1	5.5

■ JOE DUGAN   Dugan, Joseph Anthony "Jumping Joe"   b: 5/12/1897, Mahanoy City, Pa.   d: 7/7/82, Norwood, Mass.   BR/TR, 5′11″, 160 lbs.   Deb: 7/5/17

YEAR	TM/L	G	AB	R	H	2B	3B	HR	RBI	BB	SO	AVG	OBP	SLG	PRO+	BR/A	SB	CS	SBR	FA	FR	G/POS	TPR
1917	Phi-A	43	134	9	26	8	0	0	16	3	16	.194	.229	.254	48	-9	0			.917	1	S-39/2-2	-0.7
1918	Phi-A	121	411	26	80	11	3	3	34	16	15	.195	.230	.258	47	-28	4			.930	17	S-86,2-34	-0.6
1919	Phi-A	104	387	25	105	17	2	1	30	11	30	.271	.300	.333	77	-13	9			.929	1	S-98/2-4,3	-0.6
1920	Phi-A	123	491	65	158	40	5	3	60	19	51	.322	.351	.442	108	4	5	8	-3	.948	-1	3-60,S-32,2	0.6
1921	Phi-A	119	461	54	136	22	6	10	58	24	39	.295	.342	.434	96	-4	5	1	1	.953	-25	*3-119	-1.9
1922	Bos-A	84	341	45	98	22	3	3	38	9	28	.287	.308	.396	83	-10	2	3	-1	.943	-9	3-64,S-21	-1.3
	*NY-A	60	252	44	72	9	1	3	25	13	21	.286	.331	.365	79	-8	1	0	0	.967	-10	3-60	-1.2
	Yr	144	593	89	170	31	4	6	63	22	49	.287	.318	.383	81	-17	3	3	-1	.954	-19	*3-124,S-21	-2.5
1923	*NY-A	146	644	111	182	30	7	7	67	25	41	.283	.311	.384	81	-20	4	2	0	.974	-12	*3-146	-1.8

YEAR	TM/L	G	AB	R	H	2B	3B	HR	RBI	BB	SO	AVG	OBP	SLG	PRO+	BR/A	SB	CS	SBR	FA	FR	G/POS	TPR
1924	NY-A	148	610	105	184	31	7	3	56	31	33	.302	.341	.390	88	-12	1	2	-1	.962	-15	*3-148/2-2	-1.5
1925	NY-A	102	404	50	118	19	4	0	31	19	20	.292	.330	.359	76	-15	2	4	-2	.970	7	3-96	-0.3
1926	*NY-A	123	434	39	125	19	5	1	64	25	16	.288	.328	.362	81	-13	2	4	-2	.955	-16	*3-122	-2.2
1927	*NY-A	112	387	44	104	24	3	2	43	27	37	.269	.321	.362	79	-12	1	4	-2	.938	-19	*3-111	-2.8
1928	*NY-N	94	312	33	86	15	0	6	34	16	15	.276	.317	.381	85	-7	1	0	0	.952	-18	3-91/2-1	-2.0
1929	Bos-N	60	125	14	38	10	0	0	15	8	8	.304	.364	.384	84	-3	0			.918	-9	3-24/S-5,2O	-1.0
1931	Det-A	8	17	1	4	0	0	0	0	0	3	.235	.235	.235	23	-2	0	0	0	.900	-1	/3-5	-0.2
Total	14	1447	5410	665	1516	277	46	42	571	250	419	.280	.317	.372	82	-152	37	28		.957	-108	*3-1048,S-281/20	-17.5

■ BILL DUGAN
Dugan, William H. b: 1864, New York, N.Y. d: 7/24/21, New York, N.Y. Deb: 8/5/1884 F

YEAR	TM/L	G	AB	R	H	2B	3B	HR	RBI	BB	SO	AVG	OBP	SLG	PRO+	BR/A	SB	CS	SBR	FA	FR	G/POS	TPR
1884	Ric-a	9	28	4	2	1	0	0		0		.071	.103	.107	-32	-4				.889	-3	/C-9	-0.5
	KC-U	3	6	0	0	0	0	0		0		.000	.000	.000	-99	-2				.400	-1	/O-3	-0.3
Total	1	12	34	4	2	1	0	0		0		.059	.086	.088	-47	-6				.889	-4	/C-9,O-3	-0.8

■ GUS DUGAS
Dugas, Augustin Joseph b: 3/24/07, St.Jean Dematha, Que., Canada BL/TL, 5'9", 165 lbs. Deb: 9/17/30

YEAR	TM/L	G	AB	R	H	2B	3B	HR	RBI	BB	SO	AVG	OBP	SLG	PRO+	BR/A	SB	CS	SBR	FA	FR	G/POS	TPR
1930	Pit-N	9	31	8	9	2	0	1	7	4		.290	.421	.355	90	-0	0			.864	-1	/O-9	-0.2
1932	Pit-N	55	97	13	23	3	3	3	12	7	11	.237	.288	.423	90	-2	0			.952	-3	O-20	-0.5
1933	Phi-N	37	71	4	12	3	0	0	9	1	9	.169	.181	.211	10	-8	0			.984	-0	1-11/O-1	-1.0
1934	Was-A	24	19	2	1	1	0	0	1	3	3	.053	.182	.105	-25	-4	0	0	0	1.000	-0	/O-2	-0.4
Total	4	125	218	27	45	9	3	3	23	18	27	.206	.267	.317	54	-14	0	0		.926	-4	O-32,1-11	-2.1

■ DAN DUGDALE
Dugdale, Daniel Edward b: 10/28/1864, Peoria, Ill. d: 3/9/34, Seattle, Wash. 5'8", 180 lbs. Deb: 5/20/1886

YEAR	TM/L	G	AB	R	H	2B	3B	HR	RBI	BB	SO	AVG	OBP	SLG	PRO+	BR/A	SB	CS	SBR	FA	FR	G/POS	TPR
1886	KC-N	12	40	0	7	0	0	0		2	13	.175	.214	.175	18	-4	1			.884	-2	/C-7,O-6	-0.5
1894	Was-N	38	134	19	32	4	2	0	16	13	14	.239	.306	.299	48	-11	7			.874	-5	C-33/3-3,O	-1.1
Total	2	50	174	23	39	4	2	0	18	15	27	.224	.286	.270	42	-15	8			.877	-7	/C-40,O-8,3	-1.6

■ OSCAR DUGEY
Dugey, Oscar Joseph "Jake" b: 10/25/1887, Palestine, Tex. d: 1/1/66, Dallas, Tex. BR/TR, 5'8", 160 lbs. Deb: 9/13/13 C

YEAR	TM/L	G	AB	R	H	2B	3B	HR	RBI	BB	SO	AVG	OBP	SLG	PRO+	BR/A	SB	CS	SBR	FA	FR	G/POS	TPR
1913	Bos-N	5	8	1	2	0	0	0		1	1	.250	.333	.250	67	-0	0			.500	-1	/3-2,2-1,S	-0.1
1914	Bos-N	58	109	17	21	2	0	1	10	10	15	.193	.267	.239	51	-6	10			.933	-2	O-16,2-16/3	-1.0
1915	*Phi-N	42	39	4	6	1	0	0	0	7	5	.154	.283	.179	41	-3	2	1	0	.941	3	2-14	0.0
1916	Phi-N	41	50	9	11	3	0	0	1	9	8	.220	.339	.280	88	-0	3			.967	3	2-12	0.3
1917	Phi-N	44	72	12	14	0	0	0	9	4	9	.194	.237	.278	55	-4	2			.871	0	2-15/O-4	-0.4
1920	Bos-N	5	0	2	0	0	0	0	0	0	0	—	—	—	—		0	0	0	.000	0	R	
Total	6	195	278	45	54	10	1	1	20	31	38	.194	.277	.248	58	-14	17	1		.915	3	/2-58,O-20,3S	-1.2

■ JIM DUGGAN
Duggan, James Elmer "Mer" b: 6/3/1884, Whiteland, Ind. d: 12/5/51, Indianapolis, Ind. BL/TL, 5'10", 165 lbs. Deb: 6/29/11

YEAR	TM/L	G	AB	R	H	2B	3B	HR	RBI	BB	SO	AVG	OBP	SLG	PRO+	BR/A	SB	CS	SBR	FA	FR	G/POS	TPR
1911	StL-A	1	4	1	0	0	0	0		1	1	.000	.200	.000	-44	-1	0			1.000	0	/1-1	-0.1

■ TOM DUNBAR
Dunbar, Thomas Jerome b: 11/24/59, Graniteville, S.C. BL/TL, 6'2", 192 lbs. Deb: 9/7/83

YEAR	TM/L	G	AB	R	H	2B	3B	HR	RBI	BB	SO	AVG	OBP	SLG	PRO+	BR/A	SB	CS	SBR	FA	FR	G/POS	TPR
1983	Tex-A	12	24	3	6	0	0	0	3	5	7	.250	.379	.250	79	-0	3	1	0	.875	-3	/O-9,D-1	-0.3
1984	Tex-A	34	97	9	25	2	0	2	10	6	16	.258	.301	.340	75	-3	1	0	0	.939	-3	O-20/D-6	-0.6
1985	Tex-A	45	104	7	21	4	0	1	5	12	9	.202	.291	.269	54	-6	0	3	-2	.933	-3	D-18,O-14	-1.2
Total	3	91	225	19	52	6	0	3	18	23	32	.231	.305	.298	66	-10	4	4	-1	.929	-9	/O-43,D-25	-2.1

■ DAVE DUNCAN
Duncan, David Edwin b: 9/26/45, Dallas, Tex. BR/TR, 6'2", 200 lbs. Deb: 5/6/64 C

YEAR	TM/L	G	AB	R	H	2B	3B	HR	RBI	BB	SO	AVG	OBP	SLG	PRO+	BR/A	SB	CS	SBR	FA	FR	G/POS	TPR
1964	KC-A	25	53	2	9	0	1	1	5	2	20	.170	.200	.264	27	-5	0	0		.981	3	C-22	-0.1
1967	KC-A	34	101	9	19	4	0	5	11	4	50	.188	.219	.376	75	-4	0		-1	.979	-6	C-32	-1.0
1968	Oak-A	82	246	15	47	4	0	7	28	25	68	.191	.268	.293	73	-8	1	1	-0	.987	0	C-79	-0.4
1969	Oak-A	58	127	11	16	3	0	3	22	19	41	.126	.240	.220	31	-12	0	0	0	.982	-12	C-56	-2.3
1970	Oak-A	86	232	21	60	7	0	10	29	22	38	.259	.323	.418	107	1	0	0	0	.978	3	C-73	0.8
1971	*Oak-A☆	103	363	39	92	13	1	15	40	28	77	.253	.309	.419	106	2	1	1	-0	.984	3	*C-102	0.9
1972	*Oak-A	121	403	39	88	13	0	19	59	34	68	.218	.287	.392	106	1	0	2	-1	.993	2	*C-113	0.7
1973	Cle-A	95	344	43	80	11	1	17	43	35	86	.233	.309	.419	101	-0	3	3	-1	.988	-1	C-86/D-9	0.2
1974	Cle-A	136	425	45	85	10	1	16	46	42	91	.200	.275	.341	77	-13	0	4	-2	.976	-8	*C-134/1-3,D	-1.9
1975	Bal-A	96	307	30	63	7	0	12	41	16	82	.205	.247	.345	70	-14	0	0	0	.982	-7	C-95	-1.7
1976	Bal-A	93	284	20	58	7	0	4	17	25	54	.204	.271	.271	63	-13	0	0	0	.985	-11	C-93	-2.3
Total	11	929	2885	274	617	79	4	109	341	252	677	.214	.280	.357	85	-65	5	13	-6	.984	-32	C-885/D-10,1	-7.1

■ JIM DUNCAN
Duncan, James William b: 7/1/1871, Saltsburg, Pa. d: 10/16/01, Foxburg, Pa. BR/TR, 5'8", 140 lbs. Deb: 7/18/1899

YEAR	TM/L	G	AB	R	H	2B	3B	HR	RBI	BB	SO	AVG	OBP	SLG	PRO+	BR/A	SB	CS	SBR	FA	FR	G/POS	TPR
1899	Was-N	15	47	5	11	2	0	0	5	4		.234	.294	.277	57	-3	1			.940	-1	C-14	-0.2
	Cle-N	31	105	9	24	2	3	2	9	4		.229	.257	.362	74	-4	0			.971	-4	1-17,C-14	-0.7
	Yr	46	152	14	35	4	3	2	14	8		.230	.269	.336	69	-7	1			.904	-5	C-28,1-17	-0.9

■ PAT DUNCAN
Duncan, Louis Baird b: 10/6/1893, Coalton, Ohio d: 7/17/60, Columbus, Ohio BR/TR, 5'9", 170 lbs. Deb: 7/16/15

YEAR	TM/L	G	AB	R	H	2B	3B	HR	RBI	BB	SO	AVG	OBP	SLG	PRO+	BR/A	SB	CS	SBR	FA	FR	G/POS	TPR
1915	Pit-N	3	5	0	1	0	0	0	0		1	.200	.200	.200	22	-0	0			1.000	-0	/O-1	-0.1
1919	*Cin-N	31	90	9	22	3	3	2	17	8	7	.244	.306	.411	118	2	2			.982	-1	O-27	-0.1
1920	Cin-N	154	576	75	170	16	11	2	83	42	42	.295	.350	.372	109	7	7	18	-5	.964	5	*O-154	-0.5
1921	Cin-N	145	532	57	164	27	10	2	60	44	33	.308	.367	.408	110	8	7	18	-9	.971	9	*O-145	-0.3
1922	Cin-N	151	607	94	199	44	12	8	94	40	31	.328	.370	.479	120	16	12	28	-13	.971	3	*O-151	-0.4
1923	Cin-N	147	566	92	185	26	8	7	83	30	27	.327	.363	.438	113	9	15	13	-3	.993	1	*O-146	-0.4
1924	Cin-N	96	319	34	86	21	6	2	37	20	23	.270	.313	.392	89	-6	1	7	-4	.927	-14	O-83	-2.9
Total	7	727	2695	361	827	137	50	23	374	184	164	.307	.355	.420	110	36	55	84		.970	1	O-707	-4.7

■ MARIANO DUNCAN
Duncan, Mariano (Nalasco) b: 3/13/63, San Pedro De Macoris, D.R. BR/TR, 6', 185 lbs. Deb: 4/9/85

YEAR	TM/L	G	AB	R	H	2B	3B	HR	RBI	BB	SO	AVG	OBP	SLG	PRO+	BR/A	SB	CS	SBR	FA	FR	G/POS	TPR
1985	*LA-N	142	562	74	137	24	6	6	39	38	113	.244	.295	.340	79	-16	38	8	7	.954	-8	*S-123,2-19	-0.6
1986	LA-N	109	407	47	93	7	0	8	30	30	78	.229	.285	.305	67	-19	48	13	7	.951	-2	*S-106	-0.4
1987	LA-N	76	261	31	56	8	1	6	18	17	62	.215	.268	.322	57	-17	11	1	3	.930	-1	S-67/2-7,O	-0.9
1989	LA-N	49	84	9	21	5	1	0	8	0	15	.250	.267	.333	72	-3	3	3	-1	.943	-0	S-16/2-8,O	-0.4
	Cin-N	45	174	23	43	10	1	3	13	8	36	.247	.292	.368	85	-4	6	2	1	.955	-7	S-44/2-5	-0.8
	Yr	94	258	32	64	15	2	3	21	8	51	.248	.284	.357	81	-7	9	5	-0	.952	-8	S-60,2-13/O	-1.2
1990	*Cin-N	125	435	67	133	22	11	10	55	24	67	.306	.348	.476	119	10	13	7	-0	.973	1	*2-115,S-12/O	1.4
1991	Cin-N	100	333	46	86	7	4	12	40	12	57	.258	.290	.411	92	-5	5	4	-1	.974	-6	2-62,S-32/O	-0.9
1992	Phi-N	142	574	71	153	40	3	8	50	17	108	.267	.294	.389	92	-8	23	5	3	.976	-23	O-65,2-52,S/3	-2.5
1993	*Phi-N	124	496	68	140	26	4	11	73	12	88	.282	.305	.417	92	-7	6	5	-1	.969	-28	2-65,S-59	-3.0
1994	Phi-N★	88	347	49	93	22	1	8	48	17	72	.268	.310	.406	86	-8	10	2	2	.972	-17	2-37,3-28,S/1	-2.0
Total	9	1000	3673	485	955	171	32	72	374	175	696	.260	.299	.383	87	-76	163	48	20	.950	-92	S-520,2-370/O31	-10.1

■ TAYLOR DUNCAN
Duncan, Taylor McDowell b: 5/12/53, Memphis, Tenn. BR/TR, 6', 170 lbs. Deb: 9/15/77

YEAR	TM/L	G	AB	R	H	2B	3B	HR	RBI	BB	SO	AVG	OBP	SLG	PRO+	BR/A	SB	CS	SBR	FA	FR	G/POS	TPR
1977	StL-N	8	12	2	4	0	0	1	2	2	1	.333	.429	.583	172	1	0	0	0	1.000	-2	/3-5	-0.1
1978	Oak-A	104	319	25	82	15	2	3	37	19	38	.257	.299	.335	82	-8	1	2	-1	.953	-21	3-84,2-11/SD	-3.2
Total	2	112	331	27	86	15	2	3	39	21	39	.260	.304	.344	86	-7	1	2	-1	.953	-23	/3-89,2-11,DS	-3.3

■ VERN DUNCAN
Duncan, Vernon Van Duke b: 1/6/1890, Clayton, N.C. d: 6/1/54, Daytona Beach, Fla BL/TR, 5'9", 155 lbs. Deb: 9/11/13

YEAR	TM/L	G	AB	R	H	2B	3B	HR	RBI	BB	SO	AVG	OBP	SLG	PRO+	BR/A	SB	CS	SBR	FA	FR	G/POS	TPR
1913	Phi-N	8	12	3	5	1	0	0	1	0		.417	.417	.500	155	1	0			1.000	-0	/O-3	0.1
1914	Bal-F	157	557	99	160	20	8	2	53	67	55	.287	.375	.363	89	-7	13			.914	-3	*O-148/3-8,2	-1.7

YEAR	TM/L	G	AB	R	H	2B	3B	HR	RBI	BB	SO	AVG	OBP	SLG	PRO+	BR/A	SB	CS	SBR	FA	FR	G/POS	TPR
1915	Bal-F	146	531	68	142	18	4	2	43	54	40	.267	.337	.328	76	-17	19			.965	-0	*O-124,3-21/2	-2.4
Total	3	311	1100	170	307	39	12	4	97	121	98	.279	.357	.347	83	-23	32			.939	-3	O-275/3-29,2	-4.0

■ GUS DUNDON
Dundon, Augustus Joseph b: 7/10/1874, Columbus, Ohio d: 9/1/40, Pittsburgh, Pa. BR/TR, 5'10", 165 lbs. Deb: 4/14/04

YEAR	TM/L	G	AB	R	H	2B	3B	HR	RBI	BB	SO	AVG	OBP	SLG	PRO+	BR/A	SB	CS	SBR	FA	FR	G/POS	TPR
1904	Chi-A	108	373	40	85	9	3	0	36	30		.228	.292	.268	81	-7	19			**.973**	-15	*2-103/3-3,S	-2.2
1905	Chi-A	106	364	30	70	7	3	0	22	23		.192	.248	.228	53	-19	14			.983	13	*2-100/S-6	-0.6
1906	Chi-A	33	96	7	13	1	0	0	4	11		.135	.224	.146	17	-9	4			.921	7	2-18,S-14	-0.1
Total	3	247	833	77	168	17	6	0	62	64		.202	.265	.236	61	-35	37			.972	5	2-221/S-22,3	-2.9

■ ED DUNDON
Dundon, Edward Joseph "Dummy" b: 7/10/1859, Columbus, Ohio d: 8/18/1893, Columbus, Ohio TR, Deb: 6/2/1883

YEAR	TM/L	G	AB	R	H	2B	3B	HR	RBI	BB	SO	AVG	OBP	SLG	PRO+	BR/A	SB	CS	SBR	FA	FR	G/POS	TPR
1883	Col-a	26	93	8	15	1	0	0		3		.161	.188	.172	18	-8				.804	0	P-20/O-9,2	-0.2
1884	Col-a	26	86	6	12	2	2	0		5		.140	.196	.209	35	-6				.966	3	O-16,P-11/1	-0.2
Total	2	52	179	14	27	3	2	0		8		.151	.191	.190	26	-14				.866	4	/P-31,O-25,12	-0.4

■ SAM DUNGAN
Dungan, Samuel Morrison b: 7/29/1866, Ferndale, Cal. d: 3/16/39, Santa Ana, Cal. BR, 5'11", 180 lbs. Deb: 4/12/1892

YEAR	TM/L	G	AB	R	H	2B	3B	HR	RBI	BB	SO	AVG	OBP	SLG	PRO+	BR/A	SB	CS	SBR	FA	FR	G/POS	TPR
1892	Chi-N	113	433	46	123	19	7	0	53	35	19	.284	.346	.360	112	6	15			.905	-6	*O-113	-0.5
1893	Chi-N	107	465	86	138	23	7	2	64	29	8	.297	.350	.389	98	-2	11			.920	4	*O-107	-0.3
1894	Chi-N	10	39	5	9	2	0	0	3	7	1	.231	.348	.282	51	-3	1			1.000	0	O-10	-0.3
	Lou-N	8	32	6	11	1	0	0	3	4	1	.344	.417	.375	99	0	2			.941	0	/O-8	0.0
	Yr	18	71	11	20	3	0	0	6	11	2	.282	.378	.324	71	-3	3			.971	1	O-18	-0.3
1900	Chi-N	6	15	1	4	0	0	0	1	1		.267	.313	.267	63	-1	0			.800	-1	/O-3	-0.2
1901	Was-A	138	559	70	179	26	12	1	73	40		.320	.368	.415	118	14	9			.947	-5	*O-104,1-35	0.1
Total	5	382	1543	214	464	71	26	3	197	116	29	.301	.356	.386	107	14	38			.924	-8	O-345/1-35	-1.2

■ LEE DUNHAM
Dunham, Leland Huffield b: 6/9/02, Atlanta, Ill. d: 5/11/61, Atlanta, Ill. BL/TL, 5'11", 185 lbs. Deb: 4/17/26

YEAR	TM/L	G	AB	R	H	2B	3B	HR	RBI	BB	SO	AVG	OBP	SLG	PRO+	BR/A	SB	CS	SBR	FA	FR	G/POS	TPR
1926	Phi-N	5	4	0	1	0	0	0	1	0	1	.250	.250	.250	33	-0	0			1.000	-0	/1-2	0.0

■ FRED DUNLAP
Dunlap, Frederick C. "Sure Shot" b: 5/21/1859, Philadelphia, Pa. d: 12/1/02, Philadelphia, Pa. BR/TR, 5'8", 165 lbs. Deb: 5/1/1880 M

YEAR	TM/L	G	AB	R	H	2B	3B	HR	RBI	BB	SO	AVG	OBP	SLG	PRO+	BR/A	SB	CS	SBR	FA	FR	G/POS	TPR
1880	Cle-N	85	373	61	103	**27**	9	4	30	7	32	.276	.289	.429	143	16				.911	8	*2-85	2.7
1881	Cle-N	80	351	60	114	25	4	3	24	18	24	.325	.358	.444	159	24				.909	6	*2-79/3-1	3.0
1882	Cle-N	84	364	68	102	19	4	0	28	23	26	.280	.323	.354	121	9				.900	18	*2-84,M	2.6
1883	Cle-N	93	396	81	129	34	2	4	37	22	21	.326	.361	.452	147	22				.911	8	*2-93/O-1	2.7
1884	StL-U	101	449	**160**	**185**	39	8	**13**		29		**.412**	**.448**	**.621**	181	49				**.926**	31	*2-100/O-1,PM	**6.9**
1885	StL-N	106	423	70	114	11	5	2	25	41	24	.270	.334	.333	124	13				**.934**	26	*2-106,M	4.0
1886	StL-N	71	285	53	76	15	2	3	32	28	30	.267	.332	.365	119	8	7			.931	7	2-71/O-1	2.4
	Det-N	51	196	32	56	8	3	4	37	16	21	.286	.340	.418	126	6	13			.918	3	2-51	1.0
	Yr	122	481	85	132	23	5	7	69	44	51	.274	.335	.387	122	14	20			.926	9	*2-122/O-1	3.4
1887	*Det-N	65	272	60	72	13	10	5	45	25	12	.265	.327	.441	108	2	15			.948	24	2-65/P-1	2.3
1888	Pit-N	82	321	41	84	12	4	1	36	16	30	.262	.303	.333	111	4	24			.940	12	2-82	1.9
1889	Pit-N	121	451	59	106	19	0	2	65	46	33	.235	.309	.290	75	-14	21			**.950**	-6	*2-121,M	-1.2
1890	Pit-N	17	64	9	11	1	1	0	3	7	6	.172	.264	.219	46	-4	2			.874	-3	2-17	-0.5
	NY-P	1	4	1	2	0	0	0	0	0	0	.500	.500	.500	154	0				1.000	-1	/2-1	-0.1
1891	Was-a	8	25	4	5	1	1	0	4	5	4	.200	.355	.320	98	0	3			.818	-3	2-8	-0.3
Total	12	965	3974	759	1159	224	53	41	366	283	263	.292	.340	.406	129	136	85			.924	137	2-963/O-3,P3	27.4

■ GRANT DUNLAP
Dunlap, Grant Lester "Snap" b: 12/20/23, Stockton, Cal. BR/TR, 6'2", 180 lbs. Deb: 4/21/53

YEAR	TM/L	G	AB	R	H	2B	3B	HR	RBI	BB	SO	AVG	OBP	SLG	PRO+	BR/A	SB	CS	SBR	FA	FR	G/POS	TPR
1953	StL-N	16	17	2	6	0	1	1	3	0	2	.353	.353	.647	154	1	0	0	0	.000	-0	/O-1	0.1

■ BILL DUNLAP
Dunlap, William James b: 5/1/09, Palmer, Mass. d: 11/29/80, Reading, Pa. BR/TR, 5'11", 170 lbs. Deb: 9/2/29

YEAR	TM/L	G	AB	R	H	2B	3B	HR	RBI	BB	SO	AVG	OBP	SLG	PRO+	BR/A	SB	CS	SBR	FA	FR	G/POS	TPR
1929	Bos-N	10	29	6	12	0	1	1	4	4	4	.414	.485	.586	171	3	0			.889	-1	/O-9	0.1
1930	Bos-N	16	29	3	2	1	0	0	0	0	6	.069	.069	.103	-61	-8	0			1.000	-1	/O-7	-0.8
Total	2	26	58	9	14	1	1	1	4	4	10	.241	.290	.345	57	-4	0			.939	-2	/O-16	-0.7

■ JACK DUNLEAVY
Dunleavy, John Francis b: 9/14/1879, Harrison, N.J. d: 4/11/44, S.Norwalk, Conn. TL, 5'6", 167 lbs. Deb: 5/30/03

YEAR	TM/L	G	AB	R	H	2B	3B	HR	RBI	BB	SO	AVG	OBP	SLG	PRO+	BR/A	SB	CS	SBR	FA	FR	G/POS	TPR
1903	StL-N	61	193	23	48	3	3	0	10	13		.249	.306	.295	74	-6	10			.972	6	O-38,P-14	-0.2
1904	StL-N	51	172	23	40	7	3	1	14	16		.233	.305	.326	99	-0	8			.987	1	O-44/P-7	-0.3
1905	StL-N	119	435	52	105	8	8	1	25	55		.241	.328	.303	91	-3	15			.962	2	*O-118/2-1	-0.7
Total	3	231	800	98	193	18	14	2	49	84		.241	.318	.306	89	-9	33			.969	9	O-200/P-21,2	-1.2

■ GEORGE DUNLOP
Dunlop, George Henry b: 7/19/1888, Meriden, Conn. d: 12/12/72, Meriden, Conn. BR/TR, 5'10", 170 lbs. Deb: 9/9/13

YEAR	TM/L	G	AB	R	H	2B	3B	HR	RBI	BB	SO	AVG	OBP	SLG	PRO+	BR/A	SB	CS	SBR	FA	FR	G/POS	TPR
1913	Cle-A	7	17	3	4	1	0	0	0	0	5	.235	.235	.294	53	-1	0			.923	1	/S-4,3-3	0.0
1914	Cle-A	1	3	0	0	0	0	0	0	1	1	.000	.250	.000	-23	-0	0			1.000	-1	/S-1	-0.2
Total	2	8	20	3	4	1	0	0	0	1	6	.200	.238	.250	42	-1	0			.929	0	/S-5,3-3	-0.2

■ JACK DUNN
Dunn, John Joseph b: 10/6/1872, Meadville, Pa. d: 10/22/28, Towson, Md. BR/TR, 5'9", Deb: 5/6/1897

YEAR	TM/L	G	AB	R	H	2B	3B	HR	RBI	BB	SO	AVG	OBP	SLG	PRO+	BR/A	SB	CS	SBR	FA	FR	G/POS	TPR
1897	Bro-N	36	131	20	29	4	0	0	17	4		.221	.244	.252	33	-13	2			.911	-1	P-25/2-4,O3S	-0.5
1898	Bro-N	51	167	21	41	0	1	0	19	7		.246	.280	.257	54	-10	3			.939	-1	P-41/O-4,S3	-0.2
1899	Bro-N	43	122	21	30	2	1	0	16	3		.246	.270	.279	49	-9	3			.963	3	P-41/S-1	0.0
1900	Bro-N	10	26	2	6	0	0	0	1	1		.231	.259	.231	34	-2	0			.960	1	P-10	0.0
	Phi-N	10	33	3	10	1	0	0	5	0		.303	.303	.333	76	-1	1			.920	-1	P-10	0.0
	Yr	20	59	5	16	1	0	0	6	1		.271	.283	.288	56	-4	1			.940	1	P-20	0.0
1901	Phi-N	2	1	1	1	0	0	0	0	0		1.000	1.000	1.000	471	1	0			1.000	-0	/P-2	0.0
	Bal-A	96	362	41	90	9	4	0	36	21		.249	.301	.296	63	-18	10			.872	-7	3-67,S-19/P2O	-2.0
1902	NY-N	100	342	26	72	11	1	0	14	20		.211	.256	.249	56	-18	13			.962	-10	O-43,S-36,3/P2	-2.9
1903	NY-N	78	257	35	62	15	1	0	37	15		.241	.291	.307	68	-11	12			.907	-7	S-27,3-25,2/O	-1.5
1904	NY-N	64	181	27	56	12	2	1	19	11		.309	.356	.414	132	6	11			.914	-8	3-28,S-10/2OP	-0.1
Total	8	490	1622	197	397	54	10	1	164	83		.245	.287	.292	66	-75	55			.890	-31	3-143,P-142/SO2	-7.2

■ JOE DUNN
Dunn, Joseph Edward b: 3/11/1885, Springfield, Ohio d: 3/19/44, Springfield, Ohio BR/TR, 5'9", 160 lbs. Deb: 9/12/08

YEAR	TM/L	G	AB	R	H	2B	3B	HR	RBI	BB	SO	AVG	OBP	SLG	PRO+	BR/A	SB	CS	SBR	FA	FR	G/POS	TPR
1908	Bro-N	20	64	3	11	3	0	0	5	6		.172	.172	.219	26	-6	0			.957	7	C-20	0.4
1909	Bro-N	10	25	1	4	1	0	0	2	0		.160	.192	.200	22	-2	0			.952	-2	/C-7	-0.4
Total	2	30	89	4	15	4	0	0	7	0		.169	.178	.213	25	-8	0			.956	6	/C-27	0.0

■ RON DUNN
Dunn, Ronald Ray b: 1/24/50, Oklahoma City, Okla BR/TR, 5'11", 180 lbs. Deb: 9/3/74

YEAR	TM/L	G	AB	R	H	2B	3B	HR	RBI	BB	SO	AVG	OBP	SLG	PRO+	BR/A	SB	CS	SBR	FA	FR	G/POS	TPR
1974	Chi-N	23	68	6	20	7	0	2	15	12	8	.294	.400	.485	141	4	0	0	0	.917	-7	2-21/3-6	-0.2
1975	Chi-N	32	44	2	7	3	0	1	6	6	17	.159	.260	.295	52	-3	0	0	0	.957	-1	3-11/O-2,2	-0.4
Total	2	55	112	8	27	10	0	3	21	18	25	.241	.346	.411	106	1	0	0	0	.918	-7	/2-22,3-17,O	-0.6

■ STEVE DUNN
Dunn, Stephen B. b: 12/21/1858, London, Ont., Can. d: 5/5/33, London, Ont., Can. 5'9.5", 173 lbs. Deb: 9/27/1884

YEAR	TM/L	G	AB	R	H	2B	3B	HR	RBI	BB	SO	AVG	OBP	SLG	PRO+	BR/A	SB	CS	SBR	FA	FR	G/POS	TPR
1884	StP-U	9	32	2	8	2	0	0		0		.250	.250	.313	96	-2				.972	1	/1-9,3-1	-0.1

■ STEVE DUNN
Dunn, Steven Robert b: 4/18/70, Champaign, Ill. BL/TL, 6'4", 225 lbs. Deb: 5/3/94

YEAR	TM/L	G	AB	R	H	2B	3B	HR	RBI	BB	SO	AVG	OBP	SLG	PRO+	BR/A	SB	CS	SBR	FA	FR	G/POS	TPR
1994	Min-A	14	35	2	8	5	0	0	4	1	12	.229	.250	.371	57	-2	0	0	0	.990	1	1-12	-0.2

■ SHAWON DUNSTON
Dunston, Shawon Donnell b: 3/21/63, Brooklyn, N.Y. BR/TR, 6'1", 175 lbs. Deb: 4/9/85

YEAR	TM/L	G	AB	R	H	2B	3B	HR	RBI	BB	SO	AVG	OBP	SLG	PRO+	BR/A	SB	CS	SBR	FA	FR	G/POS	TPR
1985	Chi-N	74	250	40	65	12	4	4	18	19	42	.260	.312	.388	85	-5	11	3	2	.958	13	S-73	1.7

YEAR	TM/L	G	AB	R	H	2B	3B	HR	RBI	BB	SO	AVG	OBP	SLG	PRO+	BR/A	SB	CS	SBR	FA	FR	G/POS	TPR
1986	Chi-N	150	581	66	145	37	3	17	68	21	114	.250	.279	.411	82	-16	13	11	-3	.961	20	*S-149	1.6
1987	Chi-N	95	346	40	85	18	3	5	22	10	68	.246	.269	.358	62	-19	12	3	2	.969	5	S-94	-0.5
1988	Chi-N☆	155	575	69	143	23	6	9	56	16	108	.249	.272	.357	76	-19	30	9	4	.973	6	*S-151	0.3
1989	*Chi-N	138	471	52	131	20	6	9	60	30	86	.278	.323	.403	99	-1	19	11	--1	.972	7	*S-138	1.6
1990	Chi-N★	146	545	73	143	22	8	17	66	15	87	.262	.286	.426	87	-12	25	5	5	.970	6	*S-144	1.0
1991	Chi-N	142	492	59	128	22	7	12	50	23	64	.260	.299	.407	92	-6	21	6	3	.968	-6	*S-142	0.1
1992	Chi-N	18	73	8	23	3	1	0	2	3	13	.315	.342	.384	103	0	2	3	-1	.986	-5	S-18	-0.5
1993	Chi-N	7	10	3	4	2	0	0	2	0	1	.400	.400	.600	166	1	0	0	0	1.000	-1	/S-2	0.0
1994	Chi-N	88	331	38	92	19	0	11	35	16	48	.278	.315	.435	95	-3	3	8	-4	.966	-7	S-84	-0.7
Total	10	1013	3674	448	959	178	38	84	379	153	631	.261	.294	.399	85	-82	136	59	5	.968	39	S-995	4.6

■ DAN DURAN

Duran, Daniel James b: 3/16/54, Palo Alto, Cal. BL/TL, 5'11", 190 lbs. Deb: 4/17/81

YEAR	TM/L	G	AB	R	H	2B	3B	HR	RBI	BB	SO	AVG	OBP	SLG	PRO+	BR/A	SB	CS	SBR	FA	FR	G/POS	TPR
1981	Tex-A	13	16	1	4	0	0	0	0	1	1	.250	.294	.250	61	-1	0	0	0	1.000	-1	/O-7,1-1	-0.2

■ KID DURBIN

Durbin, Blaine Alphonsus b: 9/10/1886, Lamar, Mo. d: 9/11/43, Kirkwood, Mo. BL/TL, 5'8", 155 lbs. Deb: 4/24/07

YEAR	TM/L	G	AB	R	H	2B	3B	HR	RBI	BB	SO	AVG	OBP	SLG	PRO+	BR/A	SB	CS	SBR	FA	FR	G/POS	TPR
1907	Chi-N	11	18	2	6	0	0	0		0	1	.333	.368	.333	113	-0	0			1.000	0	/P-5,O-5	0.0
1908	Chi-N	14	28	3	7	1	0	0		0	2	.250	.323	.286	91	-0	0			1.000	-3	O-14	-0.4
1909	Cin-N	6	5	1	1	0	0	0		0	1	.200	.333	.200	66	-0	0			.000	0	H	0.0
	Pit-N	1	0	0	0	0	0	0		0	0	—	—	—	—		0	0		.000	0	R	0.0
	Yr	7	5	1	1	0	0	0		0	1	.200	.333	.200	65	-0	0			.000	0	-0,-0	0.0
Total	3	32	51	6	14	1	0	0		0	4	.275	.339	.294	96	-0	0			1.000	-2	/O-19,P-5	-0.4

■ JOE DURHAM

Durham, Joseph Vann "Pop" b: 7/31/31, Newport News, Va. Deb: 9/10/54

YEAR	TM/L	G	AB	R	H	2B	3B	HR	RBI	BB	SO	AVG	OBP	SLG	PRO+	BR/A	SB	CS	SBR	FA	FR	G/POS	TPR
1954	Bal-A	10	40	4	9	0	0	1	3	4	7	.225	.295	.300	68	-2	0	0	0	.917	-1	O-10	-0.3
1957	Bal-A	77	157	19	29	2	0	4	17	16	42	.185	.260	.274	49	-11	1	1	-0	1.000	-11	O-59	-2.7
1959	StL-N	6	5	2	0	0	0	0	0	0	1	.000	.000	.000	-94	-1	0	0	0	1.000	0	/O-1	-0.1
Total	3	93	202	25	38	2	0	5	20	20	50	.188	.261	.272	49	-15	1	1	0	.979	-12	O-70	-3.1

■ LEON DURHAM

Durham, Leon b: 7/31/57, Cincinnati, Ohio BL/TL, 6'2", 210 lbs. Deb: 5/27/80

YEAR	TM/L	G	AB	R	H	2B	3B	HR	RBI	BB	SO	AVG	OBP	SLG	PRO+	BR/A	SB	CS	SBR	FA	FR	G/POS	TPR
1980	StL-N	96	303	42	82	15	4	8	42	18	55	.271	.314	.426	101	-0	8	5	-1	.987	7	O-78/1-8	0.3
1981	Chi-N	87	328	42	95	14	6	10	35	27	53	.290	.344	.460	121	8	25	11	1	.970	2	O-83/1-3	0.9
1982	Chi-N☆	148	539	84	168	33	7	22	90	66	77	.312	.389	.521	148	35	28	14	0	.963	-3	*O-143/1-1	2.9
1983	Chi-N★	100	337	58	87	18	8	12	55	66	83	.258	.384	.466	128	15	12	6	0	.966	-7	O-95/1-6	0.5
1984	*Chi-N	137	473	86	132	30	4	23	96	69	96	.279	.372	.505	132	20	16	8	0	.994	6	*1-130	2.0
1985	Chi-N	153	542	58	153	32	2	21	75	64	99	.282	.358	.465	116	11	7	6	-2	.995	3	*1-151	0.3
1986	Chi-N	141	484	66	127	18	7	20	65	67	98	.262	.353	.452	112	8	8	7	-2	.995	-7	*1-141	-1.0
1987	Chi-N	131	439	70	120	22	1	27	63	51	92	.273	.349	.513	120	12	2	2	-1	.990	-9	*1-123	-0.6
1988	Chi-N	24	73	10	16	6	1	3	6	9	20	.219	.305	.452	110	1	0	1	-1	.995	1	1-20	-0.1
	Cin-N	21	51	4	11	3	0	1	2	5	12	.216	.286	.333	74	-2	0	0	0	.993	-1	1-17	-0.4
	Yr	45	124	14	27	9	1	4	8	14	32	.218	.297	.403	95	-1	0	1	-1	.994	-0	1-37	-0.5
1989	StL-N	29	18	2	1	1	0	0	1	2	4	.056	.190	.111	-11	-3	0	1	-1	.961	1	1-18	-0.5
Total	10	1067	3587	522	992	192	40	147	530	444	679	.277	.358	.475	122	105	106	61	-5	.994	-8	1-618,O-399	4.5

■ BOBBY DURNBAUGH

Durnbaugh, Robert Eugene "Scroggy" b: 1/15/33, Dayton, Ohio BR/TR, 5'8", 170 lbs. Deb: 9/22/57

YEAR	TM/L	G	AB	R	H	2B	3B	HR	RBI	BB	SO	AVG	OBP	SLG	PRO+	BR/A	SB	CS	SBR	FA	FR	G/POS	TPR
1957	Cin-N	2	1	0	0	0	0	0	0	0	0	.000	.000	.000	-93	-0	0	0	0	.500	-0	/S-2	0.0

■ GEORGE DURNING

Durning, George Dewey b: 5/9/1898, Philadelphia, Pa. d: 4/18/86, Tampa, Fla. BR/TR, 5'11", 175 lbs. Deb: 9/12/25

YEAR	TM/L	G	AB	R	H	2B	3B	HR	RBI	BB	SO	AVG	OBP	SLG	PRO+	BR/A	SB	CS	SBR	FA	FR	G/POS	TPR
1925	Phi-N	5	14	3	5	0	0	1	2	1		.357	.438	.357	97	0	0	0	0	1.000	2	/O-4	0.2

■ LEO DUROCHER

Durocher, Leo Ernest "Lippy" b: 7/27/05, W.Springfield, Mass. d: 10/7/91, Palm Springs, Cal. BR/TR, 5'10", 160 lbs. Deb: 10/2/25 MCH

YEAR	TM/L	G	AB	R	H	2B	3B	HR	RBI	BB	SO	AVG	OBP	SLG	PRO+	BR/A	SB	CS	SBR	FA	FR	G/POS	TPR
1925	NY-A	2	1	1	0	0	0	0	0	0	0	.000	.000	.000	-99	-0	0	0	0	.000	0	H	0.0
1928	*NY-A	102	296	46	80	8	6	0	31	22	52	.270	.327	.338	77	-10	1	4	-2	.948	12	2-66,S-29	0.5
1929	NY-A	106	341	53	84	4	5	0	32	34	33	.246	.320	.287	62	-19	3	1	0	.958	26	S-93,2-12	1.7
1930	Cin-N	119	354	31	86	15	3	2	32	20	45	.243	.287	.328	51	-29	0			.959	10	*S-103,2-13	-0.7
1931	Cin-N	121	361	26	82	11	5	1	29	18	32	.227	.264	.294	53	-25	0			.965	-4	*S-120	-1.9
1932	Cin-N	143	457	43	99	22	5	1	33	36	40	.217	.275	.293	55	-29	3			.960	-14	*S-142	-3.1
1933	Cin-N	16	51	6	11	1	0	1	3	4	5	.216	.273	.294	63	-2	0			.953	6	S-16	0.4
	StL-N	123	395	45	102	18	4	2	41	26	32	.258	.306	.339	80	-10	3			.961	-1	*S-123	-0.3
	Yr	139	446	51	113	19	4	3	44	30	37	.253	.302	.334	78	-13	3			**.960**	5	*S-139	0.1
1934	*StL-N	146	500	62	130	26	5	3	70	33	40	.260	.308	.350	71	-20	2			.957	1	*S-146	-1.1
1935	StL-N	143	513	62	136	23	5	8	78	29	46	.265	.304	.376	79	-16	4			.963	9	*S-142	0.1
1936	StL-N★	136	510	57	146	22	3	1	58	29	47	.286	.327	.347	82	-13	3			**.971**	-11	*S-136	-1.5
1937	StL-N	135	477	46	97	11	3	1	47	38	36	.203	.262	.245	38	-41	6			.959	-11	*S-134	-4.3
1938	Bro-N★	141	479	41	105	18	5	1	56	47	30	.219	.293	.284	58	-27	3			**.966**	-5	*S-141	-2.1
1939	Bro-N	116	390	42	108	21	6	1	34	27	24	.277	.325	.369	83	-9	2			.957	-7	*S-113/3-1M	-0.7
1940	Bro-N☆	62	160	10	37	9	1	1	14	12	13	.231	.285	.319	62	-8	1			.959	1	S-53/2-4M	-0.4
1941	Bro-N	18	42	2	12	1	0	0	6	1	3	.286	.302	.310	70	-2	0			.917	-0	S-12/2-1M	-0.1
1943	Bro-N	6	18	1	4	0	0	0	1	1	2	.222	.263	.222	41	-1	0			1.000	2	/S-6,M	0.1
1945	Bro-N	2	5	0	1	0	0	0	2	0	0	.200	.200	.200	11	-1	0			1.000	1	/2-2,M	0.0
Total	17	1637	5350	575	1320	210	56	24	567	377	480	.247	.299	.320	66	-262	31		5	.961	16	*S-1509/2-98,3	-13.4

■ RED DURRETT

Durrett, Elmer Cable b: 2/3/21, Sherman, Tex. d: 1/17/92, Waxahachie, Tex. BL/TL, 5'10", 170 lbs. Deb: 9/14/44

YEAR	TM/L	G	AB	R	H	2B	3B	HR	RBI	BB	SO	AVG	OBP	SLG	PRO+	BR/A	SB	CS	SBR	FA	FR	G/POS	TPR
1944	Bro-N	11	32	3	5	1	0	1	1	7	10	.156	.308	.281	68	-1	0			.933	1	/O-9	0.0
1945	Bro-N	8	16	2	2	0	0	0	0	3	3	.125	.263	.125	10	-2	0			1.000	-1	/O-4	-0.3
Total	2	19	48	5	7	1	0	1	1	10	13	.146	.293	.229	48	-3	0			.947	1	/O-13	-0.3

■ CEDRIC DURST

Durst, Cedric Montgomery b: 8/23/1896, Austin, Tex. d: 2/16/71, San Diego, Cal. BL/TL, 5'11", 160 lbs. Deb: 5/30/22

YEAR	TM/L	G	AB	R	H	2B	3B	HR	RBI	BB	SO	AVG	OBP	SLG	PRO+	BR/A	SB	CS	SBR	FA	FR	G/POS	TPR
1922	StL-A	15	12	5	4	1	0	0	0	0	1	.333	.333	.417	91	-0	0	0	0	.857	-2	/O-6	-0.2
1923	StL-A	45	85	12	18	2	0	5	11	8	14	.212	.280	.412	76	-4	0	0	0	1.000	-2	O-10/1-8	-0.7
1926	StL-A	80	219	32	52	7	5	3	16	22	19	.237	.310	.356	70	-10	0	5	-3	.980	-2	O-57/1-4	-1.5
1927	*NY-A	65	129	18	32	4	3	0	25	6	7	.248	.281	.326	59	-8	0	3	-2	.980	-7	O-36/1-2	-1.8
1928	*NY-A	74	135	18	34	2	1	2	10	7	9	.252	.289	.326	63	-7	1	0	0	.983	-3	O-33/1-3	-1.1
1929	NY-A	92	202	32	52	3	3	4	31	15	25	.257	.309	.361	77	-8	3	2	-0	.987	-0	O-72/1-1	-1.1
1930	NY-A	8	19	0	3	1	0	0	5	0	1	.158	.158	.211	-8	-3	0	0	0	1.000	-0	/O-6	-0.3
	Bos-A	102	302	29	74	19	5	1	24	17	24	.245	.290	.351	64	-17	3	1	0	.968	-2	O-75	-2.2
	Yr	110	321	29	77	20	5	1	29	17	25	.240	.282	.343	60	-20	3	1	0	.970	-2	O-81	-2.5
Total	7	481	1103	146	269	39	17	15	122	75	100	.244	.294	.351	67	-57	7	11	-5	.979	-15	O-295/1-18	-8.9

■ ERV DUSAK

Dusak, Ervin Frank "Four Sack" b: 7/29/20, Chicago, Ill. BR/TR, 6'2", 185 lbs. Deb: 9/18/41

YEAR	TM/L	G	AB	R	H	2B	3B	HR	RBI	BB	SO	AVG	OBP	SLG	PRO+	BR/A	SB	CS	SBR	FA	FR	G/POS	TPR
1941	StL-N	6	14	1	2	0	0	0	0	1	4	.143	.250	.143	12	-1	1			1.000	1	/O-4	0.0
1942	StL-N	12	27	4	5	3	0	0	3	3	7	.185	.267	.296	60	-1	0			1.000	0	/O-8,3-1	-0.1
1946	*StL-N	100	275	38	66	9	1	9	42	33	63	.240	.321	.378	94	-2	7			.993	0	O-77,3-11/2	-0.2
1947	StL-N	111	328	56	93	7	8	6	28	50	34	.284	.380	.381	97	-0	1			.970	1	O-89/3-7	-0.3
1948	StL-N	114	311	60	65	3	2	6	19	49	55	.209	.317	.309	66	-14	3			.992	-5	O-68,2-29/3PS	-2.1
1949	StL-N	1	0	1	0	0	0	0	0	0	0	—	—	—	—	-0	0			.000	0	R	0.0

YEAR	TM/L	G	AB	R	H	2B	3B	HR	RBI	BB	SO	AVG	OBP	SLG	PRO+	BR/A	SB	CS	SBR	FA	FR	G/POS	TPR
1950	StL-N	23	12	0	1	1	0	0	0	0	3	.083	.083	.167	-34	-2	0			1.000	0	P-14/O-2	-0.1
1951	StL-N	5	2	1	1	0	0	1	1	0	1	.500	.500	2.000	537	1	0	0	0	1.000	0	/P-5	0.0
	Pit-N	21	39	6	12	3	0	1	7	3	11	.308	.357	.462	115	1	0	0	0	1.000	-6	O-12/P-3,23	-0.5
	Yr	26	41	7	13	3	0	2	8	3	12	.317	.364	.537	136	2	0	0	0	1.000	-6	O-12/P-8,23	-0.5
1952	Pit-N	20	27	1	6	0	0	1	3	2	8	.222	.276	.333	66	0	0	0	0	.818	-2	O-11	-0.3
Total	9	413	1035	168	251	32	6	24	106	142	188	.243	.334	.355	84	-21	12	0		.981	-6	O-271/2-33,3PS	-3.6

■ **AL DWIGHT**   Dwight, Albert Ward   b: 1/4/1856, New York, N.Y.   d: 2/20/03, San Francisco, Cal   Deb: 6/19/1884

1884	KC-U	12	43	8	10	2	0	0		2		.233	.267	.279	56	-3				.953	-1	C-10/O-1,2	-0.2

■ **JIM DWYER**   Dwyer, James Edward   b: 1/3/50, Evergreen Park, Ill.   BL/TL, 5'10", 175 lbs.   Deb: 6/10/73

1973	StL-N	28	57	7	11	1	1	0	1	1	5	.193	.207	.246	25	-6	0	0	0	1.000	-2	O-20	-0.9
1974	StL-N	74	86	13	24	1	0	2	11	11	16	.279	.367	.360	105	1	0	0	0	1.000	-3	O-25/1-3	-0.3
1975	StL-N	21	31	4	6	1	0	0	1	4	6	.194	.286	.226	42	-2	0	0	0	1.000	-1	/O-9	-0.3
	Mon-N	60	175	22	50	7	1	3	20	23	30	.286	.369	.389	106	2	4	1	1	.959	1	O-52	0.2
	Yr	81	206	26	56	8	1	3	21	27	36	.272	.356	.364	96	-0	4	1	1	.966	1	O-61	-0.1
1976	Mon-N	50	92	7	17	3	1	0	5	11	10	.185	.272	.239	44	-7	0	0	0	.970	-2	O-19	-1.0
	NY-N	11	13	2	2	0	0	0	0	2	1	.154	.267	.154	23	-1	0	0	0	1.000	-0	/O-2	-0.2
	Yr	61	105	9	19	3	1	0	5	13	11	.181	.271	.229	42	-8	0	0	0	.972	-2	O-21	-1.2
1977	StL-N	13	31	3	7	1	0	0	2	4	5	.226	.351	.258	68	-1	0	0	0	1.000	-0	O-12	-0.4
1978	StL-N	34	65	8	14	3	0	1	4	9	3	.215	.320	.308	77	-2	1	0	0	.952	-4	O-22	-0.7
	SF-N	73	173	22	39	9	2	5	22	28	29	.225	.333	.387	105	1	6	0	0	.987	1	O-36,1-29	0.2
	Yr	107	238	30	53	12	2	6	26	37	32	.223	.330	.366	97	-1	7	0	2	.979	-3	O-58,1-29	-0.5
1979	Bos-A	76	113	19	30	7	0	2	14	17	9	.265	.366	.381	96	-0	3	1	0	.981	-1	1-25,O-19	-0.2
1980	Bos-A	93	260	41	74	11	1	9	38	28	23	.285	.359	.438	111	4	3	2	-0	.975	-3	O-65,D-12/1	-0.1
1981	Bal-A	68	134	16	30	0	1	3	10	20	19	.224	.325	.306	83	-2	0	2	-1	.977	-11	O-59/1-3,D	-1.6
1982	Bal-A	71	148	28	45	4	3	6	15	27	24	.304	.411	.493	148	11	2	0	1	.976	-8	O-49/1-1,D	0.3
1983	*Bal-A	100	196	37	56	17	1	8	38	31	29	.286	.383	.505	145	13	1	1	-0	.966	-7	O-56,D-10/1	0.3
1984	Bal-A	76	161	22	41	9	1	2	21	23	24	.255	.348	.360	98	-0	0	2	-1	.966	-4	O-52/D-3	-0.6
1985	Bal-A	101	233	35	58	8	3	7	36	37	31	.249	.354	.399	109	4	0	3	-2	.993	-3	O-78/D-3	-0.3
1986	Bal-A	94	160	18	39	13	1	8	31	23	31	.244	.346	.488	126	6	0	2	-1	1.000	-0	O-24,D-24/1	0.3
1987	Bal-A	92	241	54	66	7	1	15	33	37	57	.274	.373	.498	132	11	4	1	1	1.000	-1	D-41,O-30	0.9
1988	Bal-A	35	53	3	12	0	0	0	3	12	11	.226	.369	.226	73	-1	0	0	0	1.000	-0	D-17/O-2	-0.2
	Min-A	20	41	6	12	1	0	2	15	13	8	.293	.473	.463	159	4	0	0	0	1.000	-0	D-13	0.4
	Yr	55	94	9	24	1	0	2	18	25	19	.255	.417	.330	113	3	0	0	0	1.000	-0	D-30/O-2	0.4
1989	Min-A	88	225	34	71	11	0	3	23	28	23	.316	.391	.404	117	6	2	0	1	1.000	-0	D-74/O-1	0.4
	Mon-N	13	10	1	3	1	0	0	2	1	1	.300	.364	.400	116	0	0	0	0	1.000	0	H	0.0
1990	Min-A	37	63	7	12	0	0	1	5	12	7	.190	.320	.238	55	-3	0	0	0	1.000	-0	D-23/O-2	-0.5
Total	18	1328	2761	409	719	115	17	77	349	402	402	.260	.357	.398	107	37	26	15	-1	.979	-50	O-634,D-222/1	-4.3

■ **JOHN DWYER**   Dwyer, John E.   Deb: 5/16/1882

1882	Cle-N	1	3	0	0	0	0	0	1	0	0	.000	.000	.000	-99	-1				.000	-1	/O-1,C-1	-0.2

■ **DOUBLE JOE DWYER**   Dwyer, Joseph Michael   b: 3/27/03, Orange, N.J.   d: 10/21/92, Glen Ridge, N.J.   BL/TL, 5'9", 186 lbs.   Deb: 4/20/37

1937	Cin-N	12	11	2	3	0	0	0	1	1	0	.273	.333	.273	70	-0	0			.000	0	H	0.0

■ **JERRY DYBZINSKI**   Dybzinski, Jerome Matthew   b: 7/7/55, Cleveland, Ohio   BR/TR, 6'2", 180 lbs.   Deb: 4/11/80

1980	Cle-A	114	248	32	57	11	1	1	23	13	35	.230	.274	.294	55	-15	4	1	1	.971	21	S-73,2-29/3D	1.3
1981	Cle-A	48	57	10	17	0	0	0	6	5	8	.298	.355	.298	91	-0	7	1	2	.970	8	S-34/2-3,3D	1.1
1982	Cle-A	80	212	19	49	6	2	0	22	21	25	.231	.309	.278	63	-10	3	5	-2	.957	17	S-77/3-3	1.1
1983	*Chi-A	127	256	30	59	10	1	1	32	18	29	.230	.286	.289	57	-15	11	4	1	.966	1	*S-118/3-9	-0.5
1984	Chi-A	94	132	17	31	5	1	1	10	13	12	.235	.313	.311	70	-5	7	2	1	.974	18	S-76,3-14/2D	1.8
1985	Pit-N	5	4	0	0	0	0	0	0	0	0	.000	.000	.000	-99	-1	0	0	0	.900	1	/S-5	0.0
Total	6	468	909	108	213	32	5	3	93	70	109	.234	.296	.290	61	-47	32	13	2	.966	67	S-383/3-33,2D	4.8

■ **JIM DYCK**   Dyck, James Robert   b: 2/3/22, Omaha, Neb.   BR/TR, 6'2", 205 lbs.   Deb: 9/27/51

1951	StL-A	4	15	1	1	0	0	0	0	1	1	.067	.125	.067	-46	-3	0	0	0	1.000	0	/3-4	-0.3
1952	StL-A	122	402	60	108	22	3	15	64	50	68	.269	.354	.450	119	10	0	4	-2	.962	9	3-74,O-48	1.4
1953	StL-A	112	334	38	71	15	1	9	27	38	40	.213	.299	.344	72	-14	3	2	-0	.981	-6	O-55,3-51	-2.3
1954	Cle-A	2	1	0	1	0	0	0	1	0	0	1.000	1.000	1.000	441	1	0	0	0	.000	0	H	0.1
1955	Bal-A	61	197	32	55	13	1	2	22	28	21	.279	.372	.386	112	4	1	0	0	.989	-0	O-45,3-17	0.2
1956	Bal-A	11	23	3	5	2	0	0	0	10	5	.217	.455	.304	112	1	0	0	0	.923	0	/O-9	0.1
	Cin-N	18	11	5	1	0	0	0	0	3	5	.091	.286	.091	7	-1	0	0	0	1.000	0	/1-1,3-1	-0.1
Total	6	330	983	139	242	52	5	26	114	131	140	.246	.339	.389	98	-2	4	6	-2	.982	3	O-157,3-147/1	-0.9

■ **BEN DYER**   Dyer, Benjamin Franklin   b: 2/13/1893, Chicago, Ill.   d: 8/7/59, Kenosha, Wis.   BR/TR, 5'10", 170 lbs.   Deb: 5/23/14

1914	NY-N	7	4	1	1	0	0	0	0	1	1	.250	.250	.250	50	-0	1			1.000	1	/S-6,2-1	0.1
1915	NY-N	7	19	4	4	0	1	0	0	4	3	.211	.375	.316	117	1	0			.889	-0	/3-6,S-1	0.1
1916	Det-A	4	14	4	4	1	0	0	1	1	1	.286	.333	.357	104	0	0			1.000	-2	/S-4	-0.2
1917	Det-A	30	67	6	14	5	0	0	0	2	17	.209	.232	.284	57	-4	3			.846	1	S-14/3-8	-0.1
1918	Det-A	13	18	1	5	0	0	0	2	0	6	.278	.278	.278	71	-1	0			1.000	-0	/P-2,1-2,O2	-0.1
1919	Det-A	44	85	11	21	4	0	0	15	8	19	.247	.312	.294	72	-3	0			.953	6	3-23,S-11/O	0.4
Total	6	105	207	27	49	10	1	0	18	15	47	.237	.291	.295	74	-7	4			.937	7	/3-37,S-36,O1P2	0.2

■ **DUFFY DYER**   Dyer, Don Robert   b: 8/15/45, Dayton, Ohio   BR/TR, 6', 195 lbs.   Deb: 9/21/68   C

1968	NY-N	1	3	0	1	0	0	0	0	1	1	.333	.500	.333	153	0	0	0	0	1.000	0	/C-1	0.1
1969	*NY-N	29	74	5	19	3	1	3	12	4	22	.257	.295	.446	103	-0	0	0	0	.991	-1	C-19	0.0
1970	NY-N	59	148	8	31	1	0	2	12	21	32	.209	.308	.257	53	-9	1	1	-0	.991	2	C-57	-0.6
1971	NY-N	59	169	13	39	7	1	2	18	14	45	.231	.293	.320	75	-6	1	0	0	.992	0	C-53	-0.4
1972	NY-N	94	325	33	75	17	3	8	36	28	71	.231	.302	.375	94	-3	0	1	-1	.993	18	C-91/O-1	1.9
1973	NY-N	70	189	9	35	6	1	1	9	13	40	.185	.245	.243	36	-16	0	1	-1	.994	-1	C-60	-1.7
1974	NY-N	63	142	14	30	1	1	0	10	18	15	.211	.304	.232	53	-8	0	0	0	.982	-4	C-45	-1.2
1975	*Pit-N	48	132	8	30	5	2	3	16	6	22	.227	.266	.364	74	-5	0	0	0	.990	6	C-36	0.2
1976	Pit-N	69	184	12	41	8	0	3	29	35	35	.223	.338	.315	85	-3	0	0	0	.994	7	C-58	0.6
1977	Pit-N	94	270	27	65	11	1	3	19	54	49	.241	.373	.322	86	-3	6	0	2	**.996**	5	C-93	0.6
1978	Pit-N	58	175	7	37	8	1	0	13	18	32	.211	.296	.269	56	-10	2	1	0	.991	6	C-55	-0.3
1979	Mon-N	28	74	4	18	6	0	1	9	8	17	.243	.325	.365	89	-1	0	0	0	.993	7	C-27	0.6
1980	Det-A	48	108	11	20	1	0	4	11	13	34	.185	.273	.306	57	-6	0	0	0	.986	3	C-37,D-10	-0.3
1981	Det-A	2	0	0	0	0	0	0	0	0	0	—	—	—	—		0	0	0	.000	0	/C-2	0.0
Total	14	722	1993	151	441	74	11	30	173	228	415	.221	.307	.315	73	-71	10	4	1	.992	46	C-634/D-10,O	-0.5

■ **EDDIE DYER**   Dyer, Edwin Hawley   b: 10/11/1900, Morgan City, La.   d: 4/20/64, Houston, Tex.   BL/TL, 5'11.5", 168 lbs.   Deb: 7/8/22   M

1922	StL-N	6	3	1	1	1	0	0	0	0	0	.333	.333	.667	159	0	0	0	0	1.000	0	/P-2	0.0
1923	StL-N	35	45	17	12	3	0	2	5	3	5	.267	.313	.467	105	0	1	0	0	1.000	-1	/O-8,P-4	-0.1
1924	StL-N	50	76	8	18	2	3	0	8	3	8	.237	.266	.342	63	-4	1	0	0	.909	1	P-29/O-1	-0.1

YEAR	TM/L	G	AB	R	H	2B	3B	HR	RBI	BB	SO	AVG	OBP	SLG	PRO+	BR/A	SB	CS	SBR	FA	FR	G/POS	TPR
1925	StL-N	31	31	4	3	1	0	0	0	3	1	.097	.176	.129	-20	-6	1	1	-0	.917	0	P-27	0.0
1926	StL-N	6	2	1	1	0	0	0	0	0	0	.500	.500	.500	164	0	0			1.000	0	/P-6	0.0
1927	StL-N	1	0	0	0	0	0	0	0	1	0	—	1.000	—	181	0	0			.000	0	/P-1	0.0
Total	6	129	157	31	35	7	3	2	13	10	14	.223	.269	.344	61	-9	3	1		.921	-0	/P-69,O-9	-0.2

■ JIMMY DYKES
Dykes, James Joseph b: 11/10/1896, Philadelphia, Pa. d: 6/15/76, Philadelphia, Pa. BR/TR, 5'9", 185 lbs. Deb: 5/6/18 MC

YEAR	TM/L	G	AB	R	H	2B	3B	HR	RBI	BB	SO	AVG	OBP	SLG	PRO+	BR/A	SB	CS	SBR	FA	FR	G/POS	TPR
1918	Phi-A	59	186	13	35	3	3	0	13	19	32	.188	.267	.237	51	-11	3			.940	10	2-56/3-1	0.3
1919	Phi-A	17	49	4	9	1	0	0	1	7	11	.184	.286	.204	38	-4	0			.945	6	2-16	0.3
1920	Phi-A	142	546	81	140	25	4	8	35	55	73	.256	.334	.361	83	-13	6	9	-4	.957	14	*2-108,3-34	0.6
1921	Phi-A	155	613	88	168	32	13	16	77	60	75	.274	.353	.447	102	1	6	5	-1	.954	25	*2-155	2.7
1922	Phi-A	145	501	66	138	23	7	12	68	55	98	.275	.359	.421	100	0	6	2	1	.945	-8	*3-141/2-5	0.4
1923	Phi-A	124	416	50	105	28	1	4	43	35	40	.252	.318	.353	76	-15	6	4	-1	.964	4	*2-102,S-20/3	-0.8
1924	Phi-A	110	410	68	128	26	6	3	50	38	60	.312	.372	.427	105	3	1	3	-2	.961	16	2-77,3-27/S	1.9
1925	Phi-A	122	465	93	150	32	11	5	55	46	49	.323	.393	.471	111	8	3	2	-0	.944	10	3-64,2-58/S	2.1
1926	Phi-A	124	429	54	123	32	5	1	44	49	34	.287	.370	.392	93	-3	6	2	1	.950	26	3-82,2-44/S	2.8
1927	Phi-A	121	417	61	135	33	6	3	60	44	23	.324	.394	.453	113	8	2	3	-1	.989	-3	1-82,3-25/SO2P	0.0
1928	Phi-A	85	242	39	67	11	0	5	30	27	21	.277	.361	.384	93	-2	2	1	0	.982	-2	2-32,S-22,3/10	0.0
1929	*Phi-A	119	401	76	131	34	6	13	79	51	25	.327	.412	.539	138	23	8	3	1	.928	-11	S-60,3-48,2	2.1
1930	*Phi-A	125	435	69	131	28	4	6	73	74	53	.301	.414	.425	109	9	3	3	-1	.960	-13	*3-123/O-1	0.2
1931	*Phi-A	101	355	48	97	28	2	3	46	49	47	.273	.371	.389	94	-2	1	2	-1	.974	-2	3-87,S-15	0.2
1932	Phi-A	153	558	71	148	29	5	7	90	77	65	.265	.358	.373	87	-10	3	1	2	.980	-5	*3-141,S-10/2	-0.2
1933	Chi-A★	151	554	49	144	22	6	1	68	69	37	.260	.354	.327	85	-9	3	7	-3	.953	-1	*3-151	-0.4
1934	Chi-A☆	127	456	52	122	17	4	7	82	64	29	.268	.363	.368	86	-8	1	1	-0	.944	-5	3-74,1-27,2M	-1.0
1935	Chi-A	117	403	45	116	24	2	4	61	59	28	.288	.381	.387	97	-0	4	3	-1	.953	-5	3-98,1-16/2M	-0.4
1936	Chi-A	127	435	62	116	16	3	7	60	61	36	.267	.362	.366	77	-15	1	3	-2	.951	-6	*3-125,M	-1.7
1937	Chi-A	30	85	10	26	5	0	1	23	9	7	.306	.372	.400	95	-1	0	0	0	.993	1	1-15,3-11M	-0.1
1938	Chi-A	26	89	9	27	4	2	2	13	10	8	.303	.374	.461	105	1	0	0	0	.941	1	2-23/S-1,3M	0.3
1939	Chi-A	2	1	0	0	0	0	0	0	0	0	.000	.000	.000	-97	-0	0	0	0	.667	0	/3-2,M	0.0
Total	22	2282	8046	1108	2256	453	90	108	1071	958	850	.280	.365	.399	96	-42	70	55		.952	57	*3-1257,2-722,1S/OP	9.3

■ LENNY DYKSTRA
Dykstra, Leonard Kyle b: 2/10/63, Santa Ana, Cal. BL/TL, 5'10", 167 lbs. Deb: 5/3/85

YEAR	TM/L	G	AB	R	H	2B	3B	HR	RBI	BB	SO	AVG	OBP	SLG	PRO+	BR/A	SB	CS	SBR	FA	FR	G/POS	TPR
1985	NY-N	83	236	40	60	9	3	1	19	30	24	.254	.341	.331	91	-2	15	2	3	.994	4	O-74	0.3
1986	*NY-N	147	431	77	127	27	7	8	45	58	55	.295	.378	.445	130	18	31	7	5	.990	4	*O-139	2.4
1987	NY-N	132	431	86	123	37	3	10	43	40	67	.285	.352	.455	118	10	27	7	4	.988	1	*O-118	1.1
1988	*NY-N	126	429	57	116	19	3	8	33	30	43	.270	.323	.385	107	3	30	8	4	.996	7	*O-112	1.2
1989	NY-N	56	159	27	43	12	1	3	13	23	15	.270	.370	.415	130	7	13	1	3	.984	2	O-51	1.2
	Phi-N	90	352	39	78	20	3	4	19	37	38	.222	.297	.330	79	-10	17	11	-2	.991	6	O-88	-0.7
	Yr	146	511	66	121	32	4	7	32	60	53	.237	.321	.356	95	-3	30	12	2	.988	9	*O-139	0.5
1990	Phi-N★	149	590	106	192	35	3	9	60	89	48	.325	.420	.441	137	35	33	5	7	.987	20	*O-149	5.8
1991	Phi-N	63	246	48	73	13	5	3	12	37	20	.297	.391	.427	131	11	24	4	5	.977	8	O-63	2.3
1992	Phi-N	85	345	53	104	18	0	6	39	40	32	.301	.379	.406	123	11	30	5	6	.989	13	O-85	3.0
1993	*Phi-N	161	637	143	194	44	6	19	66	129	64	.305	.423	.482	144	45	37	12	4	.979	17	*O-160	6.1
1994	Phi-N†	84	315	68	86	26	5	5	24	68	44	.273	.405	.435	120	12	15	4	2	.984	9	O-82	2.1
Total	10	1176	4171	744	1196	260	39	76	373	581	450	.287	.377	.422	122	142	272	66	42	.987	90	*O-1121	24.8

■ JOHN DYLER
Dyler, John F. b: 6/1852, Louisville, Ky. Deb: 7/22/1882 U

YEAR	TM/L	G	AB	R	H	2B	3B	HR	RBI	BB	SO	AVG	OBP	SLG	PRO+	BR/A	SB	CS	SBR	FA	FR	G/POS	TPR
1882	Lou-a	1	4	0	0	0	0	0		0		.000	.000	.000	-99	-1				.000	-0	/O-1	-0.1

■ DON EADDY
Eaddy, Donald Johnson b: 2/16/34, Grand Rapids, Mich BR/TR, 5'11", 165 lbs. Deb: 4/24/59

YEAR	TM/L	G	AB	R	H	2B	3B	HR	RBI	BB	SO	AVG	OBP	SLG	PRO+	BR/A	SB	CS	SBR	FA	FR	G/POS	TPR
1959	Chi-N	15	1	3	0	0	0	0	0	0	1	.000	.000	.000	-99	-0	0	0	0	.500	0	/3-1	0.0

■ TRUCK EAGAN
Eagan, Charles Eugene b: 8/10/1877, San Francisco, Cal d: 3/19/49, San Francisco, Cal BR/TR, 5'11", 190 lbs. Deb: 5/1/01

YEAR	TM/L	G	AB	R	H	2B	3B	HR	RBI	BB	SO	AVG	OBP	SLG	PRO+	BR/A	SB	CS	SBR	FA	FR	G/POS	TPR
1901	Pit-N	4	12	0	1	0	0	0	2	0		.083	.083	.083	-50	-2	1			.923	-1	/S-3	-0.3
	Cle-A	5	18	2	3	0	1	0	2	1		.167	.211	.278	36	-2	0			1.000	0	/2-5,3-1	-0.1
Total	2	9	30	2	4	0	1	0	4	1		.133	.161	.200	2	-4	1			1.000	-1	/2-5,S-3,3	-0.4

■ BILL EAGAN
Eagan, William "Bad Bill" b: 6/1/1869, Camden, N.J. d: 2/14/05, Denver, Colo. Deb: 4/8/1891

YEAR	TM/L	G	AB	R	H	2B	3B	HR	RBI	BB	SO	AVG	OBP	SLG	PRO+	BR/A	SB	CS	SBR	FA	FR	G/POS	TPR
1891	StL-a	83	302	49	65	11	4	4	43	44	54	.215	.321	.318	72	-14	21			.929	20	2-83	0.8
1893	Chi-N	6	19	3	5	0	0	0	2	5	5	.263	.417	.263	83	-0	4			.912	0	/2-6	0.0
1898	Pit-N	19	61	14	20	2	3	0	5	8		.328	.453	.459	165	6	1			.914	3	2-17	0.9
Total	3	108	382	66	90	13	7	4	50	57	59	.236	.348	.338	86	-8	26			.925	23	2-106	1.7

■ BILL EAGLE
Eagle, William Lycurgus b: 7/25/1877, Rockville, Md. d: 4/27/51, Churchton, Md. Deb: 8/20/1898

YEAR	TM/L	G	AB	R	H	2B	3B	HR	RBI	BB	SO	AVG	OBP	SLG	PRO+	BR/A	SB	CS	SBR	FA	FR	G/POS	TPR
1898	Was-N	4	13	0	4	1	0	0		0		.308	.308	.385	98	-0				.750	0	/O-4	0.0

■ CHARLIE EAKLE
Eakle, Charles Emory b: 9/27/1887, Maryland d: 6/15/59, Baltimore, Md. Deb: 8/20/15

YEAR	TM/L	G	AB	R	H	2B	3B	HR	RBI	BB	SO	AVG	OBP	SLG	PRO+	BR/A	SB	CS	SBR	FA	FR	G/POS	TPR
1915	Bal-F	2	7	0	2	1	0	0	0	0	0	.286	.286	.429	87	-0	1			.600	-2	/2-2	-0.3

■ HOWARD EARL
Earl, Howard J. "Slim Jim" b: 2/27/1869, Massachusetts d: 12/22/16, North Bay, N.Y. 6'2", 180 lbs. Deb: 4/19/1890

YEAR	TM/L	G	AB	R	H	2B	3B	HR	RBI	BB	SO	AVG	OBP	SLG	PRO+	BR/A	SB	CS	SBR	FA	FR	G/POS	TPR
1890	Chi-N	92	384	57	95	10	3	7	51	18	47	.247	.285	.344	80	-12	17			.861	-4	O-49,2-39/S1	-1.3
1891	Mil-a	31	129	21	32	5	2	1	17	5	13	.248	.281	.341	65	-8	3			.978	-1	O-30/1-2	-0.9
Total	2	123	513	78	127	15	5	8	68	23	60	.248	.284	.343	76	-20	20			.904	-5	/O-79,2-39,1S	-2.2

■ SCOTT EARL
Earl, William Scott b: 9/18/60, Seymour, Ind. BR/TR, 5'11", 165 lbs. Deb: 9/10/84

YEAR	TM/L	G	AB	R	H	2B	3B	HR	RBI	BB	SO	AVG	OBP	SLG	PRO+	BR/A	SB	CS	SBR	FA	FR	G/POS	TPR
1984	Det-A	14	35	3	4	0	1	0	1	0	9	.114	.114	.171	-22	-6	1	0	0	.959	1	2-14	-0.4

■ BILLY EARLE
Earle, William Moffat "The Little Globetrotter" b: 11/10/1867, Philadelphia, Pa. d: 5/30/46, Omaha, Neb. BR/TR, 5'10.5", 170 lbs. Deb: 4/27/1889

YEAR	TM/L	G	AB	R	H	2B	3B	HR	RBI	BB	SO	AVG	OBP	SLG	PRO+	BR/A	SB	CS	SBR	FA	FR	G/POS	TPR
1889	Cin-a	53	169	37	45	4	4	4	31	30	24	.266	.386	.444	132	7	26			.776	-2	O-26,C-23/1	0.5
1890	StL-a	22	73	16	17	3	1	0		7		.233	.317	.301	72	-3	6			.955	5	C-18/O-3,S32	0.3
1892	Pit-N	5	13	5	7	2	0	0	3	4	1	.538	.647	.692	304	4	2			.909	-1	/C-5	0.3
1893	Pit-N	27	95	21	24	4	4	2	15	7	6	.253	.304	.442	99	-1	1			.959	1	C-27	0.1
1894	Lou-N	21	65	10	23	1	0	0	7	9	3	.354	.432	.369	102	1	2			.954	3	C-18/1-1,230	0.4
	Bro-N	14	50	13	17	6	0	0	6	6	2	.340	.421	.460	121	2	4			.930	-2	C-12/2-1	0.1
	Yr	35	115	23	40	7	0	0	13	15	5	.348	.427	.409	110	3	6			.944	2	C-30/2-2,130	0.5
Total	5	142	465	102	133	20	12	6	62	63	36	.286	.378	.419	114	10	41			.929	5	C-103/O-30,123S	1.7

■ JAKE EARLY
Early, Jacob Willard b: 5/19/15, Kings Mountain, N.C. d: 5/31/85, Melbourne, Fla. BL/TR, 5'11", 168 lbs. Deb: 5/4/39

YEAR	TM/L	G	AB	R	H	2B	3B	HR	RBI	BB	SO	AVG	OBP	SLG	PRO+	BR/A	SB	CS	SBR	FA	FR	G/POS	TPR
1939	Was-A	32	84	8	22	7	2	0	14	5	14	.262	.303	.393	83	-3	0	0	0	.963	-1	C-24	-0.2
1940	Was-A	80	206	26	53	8	4	5	14	23	22	.257	.335	.408	98	-1	0	1	-1	.969	5	C-56	0.7
1941	Was-A	104	355	42	102	20	7	10	54	24	38	.287	.338	.468	117	6	0	1	-1	.965	-11	*C-100	0.3
1942	Was-A	104	353	31	72	14	2	3	46	37	37	.204	.280	.280	59	-19	0	0	0	.981	-2	C-98	-1.5
1943	Was-A★	126	423	37	109	23	3	5	60	53	43	.258	.346	.362	111	6	5	3	-0	.980	-8	*C-122	0.7
1946	Was-A	64	189	13	38	6	0	4	18	23	27	.201	.288	.296	67	-9	0	0	0	.960	-1	C-64	-0.3
1947	StL-A	87	214	25	48	9	3	3	19	54	34	.224	.381	.336	98	1	0	1	-1	.989	-3	C-85	0.3
1948	Was-A	97	246	22	54	7	2	1	28	36	33	.220	.322	.276	62	-13	2	1	0	.991	2	C-92	-0.5

YEAR	TM/L	G	AB	R	H	2B	3B	HR	RBI	BB	SO	AVG	OBP	SLG	PRO+	BR/A	SB	CS	SBR	FA	FR	G/POS	TPR
1949	Was-A	53	138	12	34	4	0	1	11	26	11	.246	.370	.297	79	-3	0	1	-1	.973	-4	C-53	-0.4
Total	9	747	2208	216	532	98	23	32	264	281	259	.241	.330	.350	89	-33	7	8	-3	.976	-19	C-694	-0.9

■ MIKE EASLER
Easler, Michael Anthony b: 11/29/50, Cleveland, Ohio BL/TR, 6'1", 196 lbs. Deb: 9/5/73 C

YEAR	TM/L	G	AB	R	H	2B	3B	HR	RBI	BB	SO	AVG	OBP	SLG	PRO+	BR/A	SB	CS	SBR	FA	FR	G/POS	TPR
1973	Hou-N	6	7	1	0	0	0	0	0	2	4	.000	.222	.000	-34	-1	0	0	0	.500	-1	/O-2	-0.2
1974	Hou-N	15	15	0	1	0	0	0	0	0	5	.067	.067	.067	-65	-3	0	0	0	.000	-0	H	-0.4
1975	Hou-N	5	5	0	0	0	0	0	0	0	1	.000	.000	.000	-99	-1	0	0	0	.000	-0	H	-0.2
1976	Cal-A	21	54	6	13	1	1	0	4	2	11	.241	.268	.296	69	-2	1	1	-0	.000	-0	D-16	-0.3
1977	Pit-N	10	18	3	8	1	2	1	5	0	1	.444	.444	.722	202	2	0	0	0	1.000	-0	/O-4	0.2
1979	*Pit-N	55	54	8	15	1	1	2	11	8	13	.278	.371	.444	116	1	0	1	-1	.000	-2	/O-4	-0.1
1980	Pit-N	132	393	66	133	27	3	21	74	43	65	.338	.404	.583	170	36	5	9	-4	.986	-8	*O-119	2.1
1981	Pit-N★	95	339	43	97	18	5	7	42	24	45	.286	.333	.431	112	5	4	7	-3	.980	7	O-90	0.6
1982	Pit-N	142	475	52	131	27	2	15	58	40	85	.276	.340	.436	112	7	1	1	-0	.973	1	O-138	0.4
1983	Pit-N	115	381	44	117	17	2	10	54	22	64	.307	.350	.441	115	7	4	2	0	.965	-3	*O-105	0.1
1984	Bos-A	156	601	87	188	31	5	27	91	58	134	.313	.377	.516	138	31	1	1	-0	.976	2	*D-126,1-29	2.7
1985	Bos-A	155	568	71	149	29	4	16	74	53	129	.262	.329	.412	97	-2	0	1	-1	.914	-2	*D-130,O-20	-0.8
1986	NY-A	146	490	64	148	26	2	14	78	49	87	.302	.365	.449	122	15	3	2	-0	.958	-0	*D-129,O-11	1.2
1987	Phi-N	33	110	7	31	4	0	1	10	6	20	.282	.319	.345	74	-4	0	1	-1	.981	2	O-30	-0.4
	NY-A	65	167	13	47	6	0	4	21	14	32	.281	.341	.389	94	-1	1	0	0	1.000	-1	D-32,O-15	-0.3
Total	14	1151	3677	465	1078	189	25	118	522	321	696	.293	.353	.454	118	88	20	26	-10	.974	-5	O-538,D-433/1	4.6

■ DAMION EASLEY
Easley, Jacinto Damion b: 11/11/69, New York, N.Y. BR/TR, 5'11", 155 lbs. Deb: 8/13/92

YEAR	TM/L	G	AB	R	H	2B	3B	HR	RBI	BB	SO	AVG	OBP	SLG	PRO+	BR/A	SB	CS	SBR	FA	FR	G/POS	TPR
1992	Cal-A	47	151	14	39	5	0	1	12	8	26	.258	.309	.311	74	-5	9	5	-0	.970	8	3-45/S-3	0.3
1993	Cal-A	73	230	33	72	13	2	2	22	28	35	.313	.395	.413	114	5	6	6	-2	.978	-11	2-54,3-14/D	-0.5
1994	Cal-A	88	316	41	68	16	1	6	30	29	48	.215	.289	.320	57	-20	4	5	-2	.953	-7	3-47,2-40	-2.6
Total	3	208	697	88	179	34	3	9	64	65	109	.257	.329	.353	79	-20	19	16	-4	.964	-9	3-106/2-94,SD	-2.8

■ CARL EAST
East, Carlton William b: 8/27/1894, Marietta, Ga. d: 1/15/53, Whitesburg, Ga. BL/TR, 6'2", 178 lbs. Deb: 8/24/15

YEAR	TM/L	G	AB	R	H	2B	3B	HR	RBI	BB	SO	AVG	OBP	SLG	PRO+	BR/A	SB	CS	SBR	FA	FR	G/POS	TPR
1915	StL-A	1	1	0	0	0	0	0	0	0	0	.000	.000	.000	-99	-1	0			.000	-0	/P-1	0.0
1924	Was-A	2	6	1	2	1	0	0	2	2	1	.333	.500	.500	163	1	0	0	0	.800	-0	/O-2	0.0
Total	2	3	7	1	2	1	0	0	2	2	1	.286	.444	.429	134	0	0	0		.800	-1	/O-2,P-1	0.0

■ HARRY EAST
East, Henry H. b: 4/1863, St.Louis, Mo. Deb: 6/17/1882

YEAR	TM/L	G	AB	R	H	2B	3B	HR	RBI	BB	SO	AVG	OBP	SLG	PRO+	BR/A	SB	CS	SBR	FA	FR	G/POS	TPR
1882	Bal-a	1	4	0	0	0	0	0		0	0	.000	.000	.000	-99	-1				.600	-0	/3-1	-0.1

■ LUKE EASTER
Easter, Luscious Luke b: 8/4/15, Jonestown, Miss. d: 3/29/79, Euclid, Ohio BR/TR, 6'4.5", 240 lbs. Deb: 8/11/49 C

YEAR	TM/L	G	AB	R	H	2B	3B	HR	RBI	BB	SO	AVG	OBP	SLG	PRO+	BR/A	SB	CS	SBR	FA	FR	G/POS	TPR
1949	Cle-A	21	45	6	10	3	0	0	2	8	6	.222	.340	.289	68	-2	0	1	-1	1.000	-4	O-12	-0.7
1950	Cle-A	141	540	96	151	20	4	28	107	70	95	.280	.373	.487	123	17	0	3	-2	.991	-3	*1-128,O-13	0.8
1951	Cle-A	128	486	65	131	12	5	27	103	37	71	.270	.333	.481	125	13	0	1	-1	.988	-7	*1-125	0.8
1952	Cle-A	127	437	63	115	10	3	31	97	44	84	.263	.337	.513	144	22	1	1	-0	.983	4	*1-118	2.2
1953	Cle-A	68	211	26	64	9	0	7	31	15	35	.303	.361	.445	120	5	0	2	-1	.981	-2	1-56	0.4
1954	Cle-A	6	6	0	1	0	0	0	0	0	2	.167	.167	.167	-8	-1	0	0	0	.000	-0	H	-0.1
Total	6	491	1725	256	472	54	12	93	340	174	293	.274	.350	.481	126	55	1	8	-5	.986	-12	1-427/O-25	2.2

■ HENRY EASTERDAY
Easterday, Henry P. b: 9/16/1864, Philadelphia, Pa. d: 3/30/1895, Philadelphia, Pa. BR/TR, 5'6", 145 lbs. Deb: 6/23/1884

YEAR	TM/L	G	AB	R	H	2B	3B	HR	RBI	BB	SO	AVG	OBP	SLG	PRO+	BR/A	SB	CS	SBR	FA	FR	G/POS	TPR
1884	Phi-U	28	115	12	28	5	0	0		5		.243	.275	.287	57	-7				.875	6	S-28	0.0
1888	KC-a	115	401	42	76	7	6	3	37	31		.190	.256	.259	61	-18	23			.888	26	*S-115	1.0
1889	Col-a	95	324	43	56	5	8	4	34	41	57	.173	.270	.275	58	-17	10			.890	12	S-89/2-5,3	0.0
1890	Col-a	58	197	25	31	5	1	1		23		.157	.249	.208	37	-15	5			.879	1	S-58	-0.5
	Phi-a	19	68	17	10	1	0	1		10		.147	.256	.206	37	-5	4			.860	-2	S-19	-0.5
	Lou-a	7	24	2	2	0	0	0		2		.083	.185	.083	-21	-4	1			.886	1	/S-6,3-1	-0.2
	Yr	84	289	44	43	6	1	2		35		.149	.245	.197	32	-24	10			.875	5	S-83/3-1	-1.2
Total	4	322	1129	141	203	23	15	9	71	112	57	.180	.259	.251	53	-66	43			.884	50	S-315/2-5,3	-0.2

■ PAUL EASTERLING
Easterling, Paul b: 9/28/05, Reidsville, Ga. d: 3/15/93, Reidsville, Ga. BR/TR, 5'11", 180 lbs. Deb: 4/11/28

YEAR	TM/L	G	AB	R	H	2B	3B	HR	RBI	BB	SO	AVG	OBP	SLG	PRO+	BR/A	SB	CS	SBR	FA	FR	G/POS	TPR
1928	Det-A	43	114	17	37	7	1	3	12	8	24	.325	.374	.482	122	3	2	1	0	.921	-2	O-34	-0.1
1930	Det-A	29	79	7	16	6	0	1	14	6	18	.203	.259	.316	44	-7	0	1	-1	1.000	-0	O-25	-1.0
1938	Phi-A	4	7	1	2	0	0	0	0	1	2	.286	.375	.286	70	-0	0	0	0	.750	-0	/O-1	0.0
Total	3	76	200	25	55	13	1	4	26	15	44	.275	.329	.410	88	-4	2	2	-1	.938	-4	/O-60	-1.1

■ TED EASTERLY
Easterly, Theodore Harrison b: 4/20/1885, Lincoln, Neb. d: 7/6/51, Clearlake Highlands, Cal. BL/TR, 5'8", 165 lbs. Deb: 4/17/09

YEAR	TM/L	G	AB	R	H	2B	3B	HR	RBI	BB	SO	AVG	OBP	SLG	PRO+	BR/A	SB	CS	SBR	FA	FR	G/POS	TPR
1909	Cle-A	98	287	32	75	14	10	1	27	13		.261	.293	.390	111	2	8			.965	0	C-76	1.0
1910	Cle-A	110	363	34	111	16	6	0	55	21		.306	.344	.383	126	10	10			.964	-12	C-65,O-32	0.7
1911	Cle-A	99	287	34	93	19	5	1	37	8		.324	.345	.436	116	4	6			.910	-12	O-54,C-22	-0.8
1912	Cle-A	65	186	17	55	4	0	2	21	7		.296	.328	.349	91	-3	3			.958	-4	C-41	-0.1
	Chi-A	30	55	5	20	2	0	0	14	2		.364	.386	.400	129	2	1			.964	-4	C-10/O-1	-0.1
	Yr	95	241	22	75	6	0	2	35	9		.311	.341	.361	100	-1	4			.959	-8	C-61/O-1	-0.3
1913	Chi-A	60	97	3	23	1	0	0	8	4	9	.237	.267	.247	51	-6	2			.976	-9	C-19	-0.2
1914	KC-F	134	436	58	146	20	12	1	67	31	25	.335	.384	.443	119	11	10			.969	-18	*C-128	0.4
1915	KC-F	110	309	32	84	12	5	3	32	21	15	.272	.320	.372	89	-6	2			.969	-8	C-88	0.5
Total	7	706	2020	215	607	88	38	8	261	107	49	.300	.338	.394	108	14	42			.965	-41	C-459/O-87	1.3

■ ROY EASTERWOOD
Easterwood, Roy Charles "Shag" b: 1/12/15, Waxahachie, Tex. d: 8/24/84, Graham, Tex. BR/TR, 6'0.5", 196 lbs. Deb: 4/21/44

YEAR	TM/L	G	AB	R	H	2B	3B	HR	RBI	BB	SO	AVG	OBP	SLG	PRO+	BR/A	SB	CS	SBR	FA	FR	G/POS	TPR
1944	Chi-N	17	33	1	7	2	0	1	2	1	11	.212	.235	.364	67	-2	0			1.000	-1	C-12	-0.2

■ JOHN EASTON
Easton, John David "Goose" b: 3/4/33, Trenton, N.J. BR/TR, 6'2", 185 lbs. Deb: 6/19/55

YEAR	TM/L	G	AB	R	H	2B	3B	HR	RBI	BB	SO	AVG	OBP	SLG	PRO+	BR/A	SB	CS	SBR	FA	FR	G/POS	TPR
1955	Phi-N	1	0	0	0	0	0	0	0	0	0	—	—	—	—	0	0	0	0	.000	0	R	0.0
1959	Phi-N	3	3	0	0	0	0	0	0	0	3	.000	.000	.000	-98	-1	0	0	0	.000	0	H	-0.1
Total	2	4	3	0	0	0	0	0	0	0	3	.000	.000	.000	-98	-1	0	0	0		0	-0,-0	-0.1

■ EDDIE EAYRS
Eayrs, Edwin b: 11/10/1890, Blackstone, Mass. d: 11/30/69, Warwick, R.I. BL/TL, 5'7", 160 lbs. Deb: 6/30/13

YEAR	TM/L	G	AB	R	H	2B	3B	HR	RBI	BB	SO	AVG	OBP	SLG	PRO+	BR/A	SB	CS	SBR	FA	FR	G/POS	TPR
1913	Pit-N	4	6	0	1	0	0	0	0	0	1	.167	.167	.167	-5	-1	0			.667	-0	/P-2	0.0
1920	Bos-N	87	244	31	80	5	2	1	24	30	18	.328	.410	.377	133	12	4	3	-1	.950	-4	O-63/P-7	0.1
1921	Bos-N	15	15	0	1	0	0	0	1	0	4	.067	.067	.067	-68	-4	0	0	0	.000	-0	/P-2	0.0
	Bro-N	8	6	1	1	0	0	0	1	2	1	.167	.375	.167	47	-0	0			.000	-1	/O-1	-0.1
	Yr	23	21	1	2	0	0	0	2	2	5	.095	.174	.095	-27	-4	0			.000	-1	/P-2,O-1	-0.1
Total	3	114	271	32	83	5	2	1	26	32	23	.306	.388	.351	116	7	4	3		.950	-5	/O-64,P-11	0.0

■ HI EBRIGHT
Ebright, Hiram C. "Buck" b: 6/12/1859, Lancaster Co., Pa d: 10/24/16, Milwaukee, Wis. BR/TR, Deb: 4/24/1889

YEAR	TM/L	G	AB	R	H	2B	3B	HR	RBI	BB	SO	AVG	OBP	SLG	PRO+	BR/A	SB	CS	SBR	FA	FR	G/POS	TPR
1889	Was-N	16	59	7	15	2	2	1	6	3	8	.254	.302	.407	103	-0	1			.875	4	/C-9,O-4,S	0.4

■ JOHNNY ECHOLS
Echols, John Gresham b: 1/9/17, Atlanta, Ga. d: 11/13/72, Atlanta, Ga. BR/TR, 5'10.5", 175 lbs. Deb: 5/24/39

YEAR	TM/L	G	AB	R	H	2B	3B	HR	RBI	BB	SO	AVG	OBP	SLG	PRO+	BR/A	SB	CS	SBR	FA	FR	G/POS	TPR
1939	StL-N	1	0	0	0	0	0	0	0	0	0	—	—	—	—	0				.000	0	R	0.0

■ OX ECKHARDT
Eckhardt, Oscar George b: 12/23/01, Yorktown, Tex. d: 4/22/51, Yorktown, Tex. BL/TR, 6'1", 185 lbs. Deb: 4/16/32

YEAR	TM/L	G	AB	R	H	2B	3B	HR	RBI	BB	SO	AVG	OBP	SLG	PRO+	BR/A	SB	CS	SBR	FA	FR	G/POS	TPR
1932	Bos-N	8	8	1	2	0	0	0	1	0	1	.250	.250	.250	36	-1	0			.000	0	H	-0.1

YEAR	TM/L	G	AB	R	H	2B	3B	HR	RBI	BB	SO	AVG	OBP	SLG	PRO+	BR/A	SB	CS	SBR	FA	FR	G/POS	TPR
1936	Bro-N	16	44	5	8	1	0	1	6	5	2	.182	.265	.273	45	-3	0			1.000	1	O-10	-0.3
Total	2	24	52	6	10	1	0	1	7	5	3	.192	.263	.269	43	-4	0			1.000	1	/O-10	-0.4

■ CHARLIE EDEN
Eden, Charles M.   b: 1/18/1855, Lexington, Ky.   d: 9/17/20, Cincinnati, Ohio   BL/TL, 168 lbs.   Deb: 8/17/1877

YEAR	TM/L	G	AB	R	H	2B	3B	HR	RBI	BB	SO	AVG	OBP	SLG	PRO+	BR/A	SB	CS	SBR	FA	FR	G/POS	TPR
1877	Chi-N	15	55	9	12	0	1	0	5	3	6	.218	.259	.255	56	-3				.679	-2	O-15	-0.5
1879	Cle-N	81	353	40	96	31	7	3	34	6	20	.272	.284	.425	131	12				.808	-4	*O-80/1-3,C	0.3
1884	Pit-a	32	122	12	33	7	4	1	7			.270	.341	.418	144	6				.759	-4	O-31/P-2	0.1
1885	Pit-a	98	405	57	103	18	6	0	17			.254	.298	.328	99	-0				.814	-16	*O-96/P-4,3	-1.6
Total	4	226	935	118	244	56	18	4	39	33	26	.261	.296	.372	114	14				.793	-25	O-222/P-6,13C	-1.7

■ MIKE EDEN
Eden, Edward Michael   b: 5/22/49, Fort Clayton, Canal Zone   BB/TR, 5'10", 170 lbs.   Deb: 8/2/76

YEAR	TM/L	G	AB	R	H	2B	3B	HR	RBI	BB	SO	AVG	OBP	SLG	PRO+	BR/A	SB	CS	SBR	FA	FR	G/POS	TPR
1976	Atl-N	5	8	0	0	0	0	0	1	0	0	.000	.000	.000	-94	-2	0	0	0	1.000	1	/2-2	-0.1
1978	Chi-A	10	17	1	2	0	0	0	0	4	0	.118	.286	.118	17	-2	0	0	0	.905	-0	/S-5,2-4	-0.1
Total	2	15	25	1	2	0	0	0	1	4	0	.080	.207	.080	-16	-4	0	0	0	1.000	0	/2-6,S-5	-0.2

■ STUMP EDINGTON
Edington, Jacob Frank   b: 7/4/1891, Roleen, Ind.   d: 11/11/69, Bastrop, La.   BL/TL, 5'8", 170 lbs.   Deb: 6/20/12

YEAR	TM/L	G	AB	R	H	2B	3B	HR	RBI	BB	SO	AVG	OBP	SLG	PRO+	BR/A	SB	CS	SBR	FA	FR	G/POS	TPR
1912	Pit-N	15	53	4	16	0	2	0	12	3	1	.302	.339	.377	97	-0				1.000	1	O-14	0.0

■ DAVE EDLER
Edler, David Delmar   b: 8/5/56, Sioux City, Iowa   BR/TR, 6', 185 lbs.   Deb: 9/4/80

YEAR	TM/L	G	AB	R	H	2B	3B	HR	RBI	BB	SO	AVG	OBP	SLG	PRO+	BR/A	SB	CS	SBR	FA	FR	G/POS	TPR
1980	Sea-A	28	89	11	20	1	0	3	9	8	16	.225	.290	.337	70	-4	2	3	-1	.965	4	3-28	-0.2
1981	Sea-A	29	78	7	11	0	0	1	5	11	13	.141	.256	.179	26	-7	3	3	-1	.884	3	3-26/S-1	-1.2
1982	Sea-A	40	104	14	29	2	2	2	18	11	13	.279	.348	.394	100	0	4	2	0	.922	3	3-31/O-2,D	0.2
1983	Sea-A	29	63	2	12	1	1	1	4	5	11	.190	.261	.286	49	-4	3	3	-1	.875	-2	3-13/1-5,OD	-0.7
Total	4	126	334	34	72	7	3	6	36	35	53	.216	.294	.308	66	-15	12	11	-3	.922	2	/3-98,D-8,10S	-1.9

■ JIM EDMONDS
Edmonds, James Patrick   b: 6/27/70, Fullerton, Cal.   BL/TL, 6'1", 190 lbs.   Deb: 9/9/93

YEAR	TM/L	G	AB	R	H	2B	3B	HR	RBI	BB	SO	AVG	OBP	SLG	PRO+	BR/A	SB	CS	SBR	FA	FR	G/POS	TPR
1993	Cal-A	18	61	5	15	4	1	0	4	2	16	.246	.270	.344	62	-3	0	2	-1	.980	5	O-17	0.0
1994	Cal-A	94	289	35	79	13	1	5	37	30	72	.273	.344	.377	83	-7	4	2	0	.981	0	O-77,1-22	-0.9
Total	2	112	350	40	94	17	2	5	41	32	88	.269	.332	.371	80	-10	4	4	-1	.981	5	/O-94,1-22	-0.9

■ BOB EDMONDSON
Edmondson, Robert E.   b: 4/30/1879, Paris, Ky.   d: 8/14/31, Lawrence, Kan.   BR/TR, 5'11", 185 lbs.   Deb: 9/15/06

YEAR	TM/L	G	AB	R	H	2B	3B	HR	RBI	BB	SO	AVG	OBP	SLG	PRO+	BR/A	SB	CS	SBR	FA	FR	G/POS	TPR
1906	Was-A	3	3	1	1	0	0	0	0	0		.333	.333	.333	114	0				1.000	-0	/P-2,O-1	0.0
1908	Was-A	26	80	5	15	4	1	0	2	7		.188	.261	.262	77	-2	0			.878	-2	O-24	-0.6
Total	2	29	83	6	16	4	1	0	2	7		.193	.264	.265	78	-2	0			.878	-2	/O-25,P-2	-0.6

■ EDDIE EDMONSON
Edmonson, Earl Edward   b: 11/20/1889, Hopewell, Pa.   d: 5/10/71, Leesburg, Fla.   BL/TR, 6', 175 lbs.   Deb: 10/4/13

YEAR	TM/L	G	AB	R	H	2B	3B	HR	RBI	BB	SO	AVG	OBP	SLG	PRO+	BR/A	SB	CS	SBR	FA	FR	G/POS	TPR
1913	Cle-A	2	5	0	0	0	0	0	0	0	0	.000	.000	.000	-97	-1	0			1.000	-1	/1-1,O-1	-0.2

■ BRUCE EDWARDS
Edwards, Charles Bruce "Bull"   b: 7/15/23, Quincy, Ill.   d: 4/25/75, Sacramento, Cal.   BR/TR, 5'7", 194 lbs.   Deb: 6/23/46

YEAR	TM/L	G	AB	R	H	2B	3B	HR	RBI	BB	SO	AVG	OBP	SLG	PRO+	BR/A	SB	CS	SBR	FA	FR	G/POS	TPR
1946	Bro-N	92	292	24	78	13	5	1	25	34	20	.267	.348	.356	99	0	1			.982	6	C-91	1.2
1947	*Bro-N★	130	471	53	139	15	8	9	80	49	55	.295	.364	.418	103	3	2			.983	5	*C-128	1.6
1948	Bro-N	96	286	36	79	17	2	8	54	26	28	.276	.341	.434	105	1	4			.984	-8	C-48,O-21,3/1	-0.5
1949	*Bro-N	64	148	24	31	3	0	8	25	25	15	.209	.324	.392	87	-3	0			.990	-3	C-41/O-4,3	-0.4
1950	Bro-N	50	142	16	26	4	1	8	16	13	22	.183	.256	.394	67	-8	1			.980	-4	C-38/1-2	-0.9
1951	Bro-N	17	36	6	9	2	0	1	8	1	3	.250	.270	.389	74	-1	0	0	0	1.000	0	/C-9	-0.1
	Chi-N☆	51	141	19	33	9	2	3	17	16	14	.234	.316	.390	87	-3	1	2	-1	.962	-3	C-28/1-9	-0.6
	Yr	68	177	25	42	11	2	4	25	17	17	.237	.308	.390	85	-4	1	2	-1	.971	-3	C-37/1-9	-0.7
1952	Chi-N	50	94	7	23	2	1	1	12	12	10	.245	.304	.340	77	-3	0	0	0	.989	-3	C-22/2-1	-0.5
1954	Chi-N	4	3	1	0	0	0	0	1	2	2	.000	.400	.000	15	-0	0	0	0	.000	0	H	0.0
1955	Was-A	30	57	5	10	2	0	0	3	16	6	.175	.356	.211	58	-3	0	1	-1	.980	7	C-22/3-5	0.4
1956	Cin-N	7	5	0	1	0	0	0	0	2	2	.200	.200	.200	8	-1	0	0	0	.000	-1	/C-2,2-1,3	-0.1
Total	10	591	1675	191	429	67	20	39	241	190	179	.256	.335	.390	93	-17	9	3		.982	-3	C-429/O-25,312	0.1

■ DAVE EDWARDS
Edwards, David Leonard   b: 2/24/54, Los Angeles, Cal.   BR/TR, 6', 177 lbs.   Deb: 9/11/78   F

YEAR	TM/L	G	AB	R	H	2B	3B	HR	RBI	BB	SO	AVG	OBP	SLG	PRO+	BR/A	SB	CS	SBR	FA	FR	G/POS	TPR
1978	Min-A	15	44	7	11	3	0	1	3	7	13	.250	.377	.386	113	1	1	1	-0	.950	1	O-15	0.1
1979	Min-A	96	229	42	57	8	0	8	35	24	45	.249	.323	.389	88	-4	6	3	0	.983	-4	O-86	-1.0
1980	Min-A	81	200	26	50	9	1	2	20	12	51	.250	.296	.335	68	-9	3	3	-1	.932	-6	O-72/D-3	-1.7
1981	SD-N	58	112	13	24	4	1	2	13	11	24	.214	.285	.321	77	-4	3	0	1	.970	-5	O-49	-1.0
1982	SD-N	71	55	7	10	2	0	1	2	1	14	.182	.196	.273	32	-5	0	0	0	.944	-14	O-45/1-1	-2.1
Total	5	321	640	95	152	26	2	14	73	55	147	.237	.302	.350	77	-21	12	6		.958	-28	O-267/D-3,1	-5.7

■ HANK EDWARDS
Edwards, Henry Albert   b: 1/29/19, Elmwood Place, O.   d: 6/22/88, Santa Ana, Cal.   BL/TL, 6', 190 lbs.   Deb: 9/10/41

YEAR	TM/L	G	AB	R	H	2B	3B	HR	RBI	BB	SO	AVG	OBP	SLG	PRO+	BR/A	SB	CS	SBR	FA	FR	G/POS	TPR
1941	Cle-A	16	68	10	15	1	1	1	6	2	4	.221	.243	.309	47	-5	0	0	0	.929	-1	O-16	-0.7
1942	Cle-A	13	48	6	12	2	1	0	7	5	8	.250	.321	.333	89	-1	2	1	0	.968	-1	O-12	-0.3
1943	Cle-A	92	297	38	82	18	6	3	28	30	34	.276	.343	.407	127	9	4	8	-4	.983	-5	O-74	-0.3
1946	Cle-A	124	458	62	138	33	16	10	54	43	48	.301	.361	.509	151	28	1	3	-2	.968	1	O-123	2.3
1947	Cle-A	108	393	54	102	12	3	15	59	31	55	.260	.315	.420	106	1	1	3	-2	.990	-7	*O-100	-1.3
1948	Cle-A	55	160	27	43	9	2	3	18	18	18	.269	.346	.406	102	0	1	1	-2	.987	-3	O-41	-0.5
1949	Cle-A	5	15	3	4	0	1	0	1	1	2	.267	.313	.467	107	-0	0	0	0	1.000	-1	/O-5	-0.1
	Chi-N	58	176	25	51	8	4	7	21	19	22	.290	.359	.500	131	7	0			.988	-4	O-51	0.1
1950	Chi-N	41	110	13	40	11	1	2	21	10	13	.364	.417	.536	150	8	0			.976	-3	O-29	0.4
1951	Bro-N	35	31	1	7	3	0	0	3	6	4	.226	.314	.323	70	-1	0			.000	0	H	-0.1
	Cin-N	41	127	14	40	9	1	3	20	13	17	.315	.379	.472	126	5	0	2	-1	.985	-3	O-34	-0.1
	Yr	76	158	15	47	12	1	3	23	19	21	.297	.366	.443	115	3	0	2	-1	.985	-3	O-34	-0.2
1952	Cin-N	74	184	24	52	7	6	4	28	19	22	.283	.350	.484	129	7	0	3	-2	.988	-4	O-51	-0.1
	Chi-A	8	18	2	6	0	0	1	0	2	1	.333	.333	.333	85	-0	0	0	0	1.000	1	/O-3	0.0
1953	StL-A	65	106	6	21	3	0	0	9	13	16	.198	.286	.226	39	-9	0	1	-1	1.000	-1	O-21	-1.1
Total	11	735	2191	285	613	116	41	51	276	208	264	.280	.343	.440	119	48	9	22		.981	-31	O-560	-1.8

■ DOC EDWARDS
Edwards, Howard Rodney   b: 12/10/36, Red Jacket, W.Va.   BR/TR, 6'2", 215 lbs.   Deb: 4/21/62   MC

YEAR	TM/L	G	AB	R	H	2B	3B	HR	RBI	BB	SO	AVG	OBP	SLG	PRO+	BR/A	SB	CS	SBR	FA	FR	G/POS	TPR
1962	Cle-A	53	143	13	39	6	0	3	6	9	14	.273	.325	.378	91	-2	0	0	0	.992	9	C-39	0.8
1963	Cle-A	10	31	6	8	2	0	0	2	6		.258	.303	.323	76	-1	0	0	0	.988	5	C-10	0.4
	KC-A	71	240	16	60	12	0	6	35	11	23	.250	.289	.375	80	-7	0	1	-1	.987	-6	C-63	-1.1
	Yr	81	271	22	68	14	0	6	35	13	29	.251	.290	.369	79	-8	0	1	-1	.987	-1	C-73	-0.7
1964	KC-A	97	294	25	66	10	0	5	28	13	40	.224	.265	.310	57	-17	0	1	-1	.986	-1	C-79/1-7	-1.4
1965	KC-A	6	20	1	3	0	0	0	0	1	2	.150	.190	.150	-2	-3	0	0	0	1.000	1	/C-6	-0.3
	NY-A	45	100	3	19	3	0	1	9	13	14	.190	.289	.250	55	-6	1	2	-1	.986	2	C-43	-0.3
	Yr	51	120	4	22	3	0	1	9	14	16	.183	.274	.233	46	-8	1	2	-1	.988	2	C-49	-0.6
1970	Phi-N	35	78	5	21	0	0	4	8	4	10	.269	.313	.269	59	-4	0	0	0	.970	6	C-34	0.3
Total	5	317	906	69	216	33	0	15	87	53	109	.238	.287	.325	68	-39	1	4	-2	.986	17	C-274/1-7	-1.6

■ JOHNNY EDWARDS
Edwards, John Alban   b: 6/10/38, Columbus, Ohio   BL/TR, 6'4", 220 lbs.   Deb: 6/27/61

YEAR	TM/L	G	AB	R	H	2B	3B	HR	RBI	BB	SO	AVG	OBP	SLG	PRO+	BR/A	SB	CS	SBR	FA	FR	G/POS	TPR
1961	*Cin-N	52	145	14	27	5	0	2	14	18	28	.186	.280	.262	45	-11	1	1	0	.982	-4	C-52	-1.2
1962	Cin-N	133	452	47	115	28	5	8	50	45	70	.254	.323	.392	88	-8	1	1	-0	.987	12	*C-130	0.9
1963	Cin-N★	148	495	46	128	19	4	11	67	45	93	.259	.325	.380	99	-0	1	5	-3	**.995**	13	*C-148	1.7
1964	Cin-N★	126	423	47	119	23	1	7	55	34	65	.281	.336	.390	100	0	1	2	-1	.992	23	*C-120	2.9

YEAR	TM/L	G	AB	R	H	2B	3B	HR	RBI	BB	SO	AVG	OBP	SLG	PRO+	BR/A	SB	CS	SBR	FA	FR	G/POS	TPR
1965	Cin-N☆	114	371	47	99	22	2	17	51	50	45	.267	.355	.474	123	12	0	0	0	.990	5	*C-110	2.3
1966	Cin-N	98	282	24	54	8	0	6	39	31	42	.191	.272	.284	50	-19	1	3	-2	.992	9	C-98	-0.6
1967	Cin-N	80	209	10	43	6	0	2	20	16	28	.206	.262	.263	46	-15	1	4	-2	.990	15	C-73	0.2
1968	*StL-N	85	230	14	55	9	1	3	29	16	20	.239	.291	.326	86	-4	1	1	-0	.992	2	C-54	0.1
1969	Hou-N	151	496	52	115	20	6	6	50	53	69	.232	.309	.333	81	-12	2	1	0	**.994**	5	*C-151	0.1
1970	Hou-N	140	458	46	101	16	4	7	49	51	63	.221	.300	.319	69	-21	1	0	0	**.995**	13	*C-139	-0.1
1971	Hou-N	106	317	18	74	13	4	1	23	26	38	.233	.292	.309	72	-12	1	1	-0	**.995**	8	*C-104	-0.1
1972	Hou-N	108	332	33	89	16	2	5	40	50	39	.268	.366	.373	113	7	2	4	-2	.988	-8	*C-105	0.1
1973	Hou-N	79	250	24	61	10	2	5	27	19	23	.244	.303	.360	83	-6	1	0	0	.989	-1	C-76	-0.4
1974	Hou-N	50	117	8	26	7	1	1	10	11	12	.222	.295	.325	76	-4	1	1	0	.989	5	C-32	0.2
Total	14	1470	4577	430	1106	202	32	81	524	465	635	.242	.314	.353	85	-92	15	23	-9	.992	97	*C-1392	6.1

■ MARSHALL EDWARDS
Edwards, Marshall Lynn b: 8/27/52, Fort Lewis, Wash. BL/TL, 5'9", 157 lbs. Deb: 4/11/81 F

YEAR	TM/L	G	AB	R	H	2B	3B	HR	RBI	BB	SO	AVG	OBP	SLG	PRO+	BR/A	SB	CS	SBR	FA	FR	G/POS	TPR
1981	*Mil-A	40	58	10	14	1	1	0	4	0	2	.241	.241	.293	56	-3	6	2	1	.979	-9	O-36/D-1	-1.3
1982	*Mil-A	69	178	24	44	4	1	2	14	4	8	.247	.264	.315	62	-10	10	4	1	.984	-2	O-54/D-6	-1.2
1983	Mil-A	51	74	14	22	1	1	0	5	1	9	.297	.307	.338	84	-2	5	5	-2	1.000	-3	O-35/D-4	-0.7
Total	3	160	310	48	80	6	3	2	23	5	19	.258	.270	.316	66	-15	21	11	-0	.987	-13	O-125/D-11	-3.2

■ MIKE EDWARDS
Edwards, Michael Lewis b: 8/27/52, Fort Lewis, Wash. BR/TR, 5'10", 154 lbs. Deb: 9/10/77 F

YEAR	TM/L	G	AB	R	H	2B	3B	HR	RBI	BB	SO	AVG	OBP	SLG	PRO+	BR/A	SB	CS	SBR	FA	FR	G/POS	TPR
1977	Pit-N	7	6	1	0	0	0	0	0	0	3	.000	.000	.000	-56	-1	0	2	-1	1.000	3	/2-4	0.1
1978	Oak-A	142	414	48	113	16	2	1	23	16	32	.273	.303	.329	82	-11	27	21	-5	.964	-28	*2-133/S-9,D	-3.5
1979	Oak-A	122	400	35	93	12	2	1	23	15	37	.233	.264	.280	49	-29	10	6	-1	.962	-14	*2-113/S-3	-3.5
1980	Oak-A	46	59	10	14	0	0	0	3	1	5	.237	.250	.237	37	-5	1	1	-0	.971	4	2-23/O-1,D	-0.1
Total	4	317	879	94	220	28	4	2	49	32	77	.250	.281	.298	63	-46	38	30	-7	.964	-34	2-273/S-12,DO	-7.0

■ RALPH EDWARDS
Edwards, Ralph Strunk b: 12/14/1882, Brewster, N.Y. d: 1/5/49, White Plains, N.Y. BR/TR, 5'9", 165 lbs. Deb: 9/17/15

YEAR	TM/L	G	AB	R	H	2B	3B	HR	RBI	BB	SO	AVG	OBP	SLG	PRO+	BR/A	SB	CS	SBR	FA	FR	G/POS	TPR
1915	Phi-A	2	5	0	0	0	0	0	0	0	3	.000	.000	.000	-99	-1	0			1.000	-1	/2-1	-0.3

■ ROBERT EENHOORN
Eenhoorn, Robert Franciscus b: 2/9/68, Rotterdam, Holland BR/TR, 6'3", 170 lbs. Deb: 4/27/94

YEAR	TM/L	G	AB	R	H	2B	3B	HR	RBI	BB	SO	AVG	OBP	SLG	PRO+	BR/A	SB	CS	SBR	FA	FR	G/POS	TPR
1994	NY-A	3	4	1	2	0	0	0	0	0	0	.500	.500	.750	232	1	0	0	0	1.000	-1	/S-3	0.0

■ BEN EGAN
Egan, Arthur Augustus b: 11/20/1883, Augusta, N.Y. d: 2/18/68, Sherrill, N.Y. BR/TR, 6', 195 lbs. Deb: 9/29/08 C

YEAR	TM/L	G	AB	R	H	2B	3B	HR	RBI	BB	SO	AVG	OBP	SLG	PRO+	BR/A	SB	CS	SBR	FA	FR	G/POS	TPR
1908	Phi-A	2	6	1	1	1	0	0		0	1	.167	.286	.333	95	-0	0			.933	0	/C-2	0.0
1912	Phi-A	49	138	9	24	3	4	0	13	6		.174	.208	.254	33	-13	3			.958	4	C-46	-0.5
1914	Cle-A	29	88	7	20	2	1	0	11	3	0	.227	.277	.273	63	-4	0	1	-1	.975	4	C-27	0.2
1915	Cle-A	42	120	4	13	3	0	0	6	8	14	.108	.164	.133	-11	-16	0			.970	8	C-40	-0.6
Total	4	122	352	21	58	9	5	0	30	18	34	.165	.212	.219	27	-33	3	1		.966	16	C-115	-0.9

■ JIM EGAN
Egan, James K. "Troy Terrier" b: 1858, Derby, Conn. d: 9/26/1884, New Haven, Conn. TL, Deb: 5/15/1882

YEAR	TM/L	G	AB	R	H	2B	3B	HR	RBI	BB	SO	AVG	OBP	SLG	PRO+	BR/A	SB	CS	SBR	FA	FR	G/POS	TPR
1882	Tro-N	30	115	15	23	3	2	0	10	1	21	.200	.207	.261	51	-6				.625	-8	O-18,P-12/C	-0.8

■ DICK EGAN
Egan, Richard Joseph b: 6/23/1884, Portland, Ore. d: 7/7/47, Oakland, Cal. BR/TR, 5'11", 162 lbs. Deb: 9/15/08

YEAR	TM/L	G	AB	R	H	2B	3B	HR	RBI	BB	SO	AVG	OBP	SLG	PRO+	BR/A	SB	CS	SBR	FA	FR	G/POS	TPR
1908	Cin-N	18	68	8	14	3	0	0	5	2		.206	.229	.279	64	-3	7			.891	-3	2-18	-0.7
1909	Cin-N	127	480	59	132	14	3	2	53	37		.275	.329	.329	105	3	39			.950	24	*2-116,S-10	2.7
1910	Cin-N	135	474	70	116	11	5	0	46	53	38	.245	.322	.289	82	-10	41			.961	-11	*2-131/S-3	-2.5
1911	Cin-N	153	558	80	139	11	5	1	56	59	50	.249	.322	.292	75	-18	37			.949	10	*2-152	-1.1
1912	Cin-N	149	507	69	125	14	5	0	52	56	26	.247	.324	.294	72	-19	24			**.973**	3	*2-149	-1.9
1913	Cin-N	60	195	15	55	7	3	0	22	15	13	.282	.333	.349	95	-1	6			.972	-5	2-37,S-17/3	-0.5
1914	Bro-N	106	337	30	76	10	3	1	21	22	25	.226	.273	.282	64	-15	8			.914	-9	S-83,3-10/O21	-1.9
1915	Bro-N	3	3	0	0	0	0	0	0	0	0	.000	.000	.000	-98	-1	0			.000	0	H	-0.1
	Bos-N	83	220	20	57	9	1	0	21	28	18	.259	.343	.305	102	2	3	4	-2	.974	-2	O-24,2-22,S/13	-0.2
	Yr	86	223	20	57	9	1	0	21	28	18	.256	.339	.305	100	1	3	4	-2	.974	-2	O-24,2-22,S/13	-0.3
1916	Bos-N	83	238	23	53	8	3	0	16	19	21	.223	.280	.282	76	-7	2			.949	-21	2-59,S-12/3	-3.0
Total	9	917	3080	374	767	87	29	4	292	291	191	.249	.315	.300	82	-69	167	4		.956	-14	2-686,S-135/O31	-9.2

■ TOM EGAN
Egan, Thomas Patrick b: 6/9/46, Los Angeles, Cal. BR/TR, 6'4", 218 lbs. Deb: 5/27/65

YEAR	TM/L	G	AB	R	H	2B	3B	HR	RBI	BB	SO	AVG	OBP	SLG	PRO+	BR/A	SB	CS	SBR	FA	FR	G/POS	TPR
1965	Cal-A	18	38	3	10	0	1	0	1	1	12	.263	.317	.316	82	-1	0	0	0	1.000	-0	C-16	0.0
1966	Cal-A	7	11	0	0	0	0	0	0	1	5	.000	.083	.000	-76	-2	0	0	0	1.000	2	/C-6	-0.1
1967	Cal-A	1	1	0	0	0	0	0	0	0	0	.000	.000	.000	-99	-0	0	0	0	1.000	0	/C-1	0.0
1968	Cal-A	16	43	2	5	1	0	1	4	2	15	.116	.156	.209	10	-5	0	0	0	1.000	2	C-14	-0.3
1969	Cal-A	46	120	7	17	5	0	1	16	17	41	.142	.254	.275	50	-8	0	1	-1	.985	6	C-46	0.0
1970	Cal-A	79	210	14	50	6	0	4	20	14	67	.238	.289	.324	71	-9	0	0	0	.988	-1	C-79	-0.7
1971	Chi-A	85	251	29	60	11	1	10	34	26	94	.239	.320	.410	102	1	1	0	0	.986	3	C-77/1-1	0.7
1972	Chi-A	50	141	8	27	3	0	2	9	4	48	.191	.224	.255	42	-10	0	0	0	.986	3	C-46	-0.6
1974	Cal-A	43	94	4	11	0	1	0	3	6	29	.117	.194	.117	-9	-13	1	0	0	.996	16	C-41	0.4
1975	Cal-A	28	70	7	16	3	1	0	3	5	14	.229	.280	.300	69	-3	0	0	0	.965	4	C-28	0.2
Total	10	373	979	74	196	25	3	22	91	80	336	.200	.267	.299	62	-51	2	1	0	.987	35	C-354/1-1	-0.4

■ ELMER EGGERT
Eggert, Elmer Albert "Mose" b: 1/29/02, Rochester, N.Y. d: 4/9/71, Rochester, N.Y. BR/TR, 5'9", 160 lbs. Deb: 4/27/27

YEAR	TM/L	G	AB	R	H	2B	3B	HR	RBI	BB	SO	AVG	OBP	SLG	PRO+	BR/A	SB	CS	SBR	FA	FR	G/POS	TPR
1927	Bos-A	5	3	0	0	0	0	0	0	1	1	.000	.250	.000	-31	-1	0	0	0	.000	0	/2-1	-0.1

■ DAVE EGGLER
Eggler, David Daniel b: 4/30/1851, Brooklyn, N.Y. d: 4/5/02, Buffalo, N.Y. BR/TR, 5'9", 165 lbs. Deb: 5/18/1871

YEAR	TM/L	G	AB	R	H	2B	3B	HR	RBI	BB	SO	AVG	OBP	SLG	PRO+	BR/A	SB	CS	SBR	FA	FR	G/POS	TPR
1871	Mut-n	33	147	37	47	7	3	0	18	4	3	.320	.338	.408	124	6	14					*O-33	0.5
1872	Mut-n	56	287	95	97	20	0	0	19	8	9	.338	.356	.408	144	16						*O-56	1.4
1873	Mut-n	53	268	82	90	16	5	0	34	5	2	.336	.348	.433	129	10						*O-53/3-1	0.8
1874	Phi-n	58	296	71	96	14	7	0		6		.324	.338	.419	135	10						*O-56/2-2	0.9
1875	Ath-n	66	293	66	89	15	7	0		2		.304	.308	.403	130	6						*O-66	0.6
1876	Phi-N	39	174	28	52	4	0	0	19	2	4	.299	.307	.322	111	2				.913	3	O-39	0.6
1877	Chi-N	33	136	20	36	3	0	0	20	1	5	.265	.270	.287	67	-6				.861	5	O-33	-0.4
1879	Buf-N	78	317	41	66	5	7	0	27	11	41	.208	.235	.268	64	-12				.919	-6	*O-78	-2.0
1883	Bal-a	53	202	15	38	2	0	0		1		.188	.192	.198	25	-17				.916	1	O-53	-1.5
	Buf-N	38	153	13	38	2	1	0	13	2	29	.248	.258	.275	61	-7				.845	-1	O-38	-0.8
1884	Buf-N	63	241	25	47	3	1	0	20	6	54	.195	.215	.216	35	-18				.887	1	O-63	-1.7
1885	Buf-N	6	24	0	2	0	0	0	0	2	4	.083	.154	.083	-21	-3				.938	1	/O-6	-0.3
Total	5 n	266	1291	351	419	72	22	0	71	25	14	.325	.337	.414	133	48						O-264/2-2,3	4.2
Total	6	310	1247	142	279	19	9	0	99	25	137	.224	.239	.253	56	-61				.894	3	O-310	-6.1

■ RED EHRET
Ehret, Philip Sydney b: 8/31/1868, Louisville, Ky. d: 7/28/40, Cincinnati, Ohio BR/TR, 6', 175 lbs. Deb: 7/7/1888

YEAR	TM/L	G	AB	R	H	2B	3B	HR	RBI	BB	SO	AVG	OBP	SLG	PRO+	BR/A	SB	CS	SBR	FA	FR	G/POS	TPR
1888	KC-a	17	63	4	12	0	0			1		.190	.203	.254	43	-4	1			.750	-4	O-10/P-7,21	-0.7
1889	Lou-a	67	258	27	65	6	6	1	31	4	23	.252	.263	.333	71	-11	4			.891	-1	P-45,O-22/S32	-0.7
1890	*Lou-a	43	146	11	31	2	1	0				.212	.218	.240	36	-12	1			.859	-3	P-43	0.0
1891	Lou-a	26	91	9	22	0	0	0	9	5	15	.242	.281	.286	63	-5	3			.871	4	P-26	0.0
1892	Pit-N	40	132	12	34	0	0	0	19	7	22	.258	.295	.273	72	-5	1			.855	-4	P-39	0.0
1893	Pit-N	40	136	16	24	8	1	0	11	10	18	.176	.233	.221	21	-16	1			.893	1	P-39	0.0
1894	Pit-N	46	135	6	23	4	1	0	11	8	22	.170	.217	.215	4	-21	0			.859	-1	P-46	0.0

YEAR	TM/L	G	AB	R	H	2B	3B	HR	RBI	BB	SO	AVG	OBP	SLG	PRO+	BR/A	SB	CS	SBR	FA	FR	G/POS	TPR
1895	StL-N	37	96	13	21	2	1	1	9	6	12	.219	.265	.292	44	-8	0			.848	0	P-37	0.0
1896	Cin-N	34	102	10	20	2	0	1	20	10	12	.196	.268	.245	33	-10	2			.923	1	P-34/1-1	0.0
1897	Cin-N	34	66	6	13	2	0	0	6	4		.197	.254	.227	26	-7	2			.957	-1	P-34	0.0
1898	Lou-N	13	40	3	9	3	1	0	4	1		.225	.262	.350	76	-1	0			.800	-1	P-12	0.0
Total	11	397	1265	117	274	32	11	4	130	57	124	.217	.252	.269	44	-101	15			.882	-12	P-362/O-32,123S	-1.4

■ HACK EIBEL

Eibel, Henry Hack b: 12/6/1893, Brooklyn, N.Y. d: 10/16/45, Macon, Ga. BL/TL, 5'11", 220 lbs. Deb: 6/13/12

YEAR	TM/L	G	AB	R	H	2B	3B	HR	RBI	BB	SO	AVG	OBP	SLG	PRO+	BR/A	SB	CS	SBR	FA	FR	G/POS	TPR
1912	Cle-A	1	3	0	0	0	0	0	0	0		.000	.000	.000	-97	-1	0			.000	-0	/O-1	-0.1
1920	Bos-A	29	43	4	8	2	0	0	6	3	6	.186	.239	.232	26	-5	1	1	-0	.800	-2	/O-5,P-3,1	-0.6
Total	2	30	46	4	8	2	0	0	6	3	6	.174	.224	.217	19	-5	1	1		.800	-2	/O-6,P-3,1	-0.7

■ IKE EICHRODT

Eichrodt, Frederick George b: 1/6/03, Chicago, Ill. d: 7/14/65, Indianapolis, Ind BR/TR, 5'11.5", 167 lbs. Deb: 9/7/25

YEAR	TM/L	G	AB	R	H	2B	3B	HR	RBI	BB	SO	AVG	OBP	SLG	PRO+	BR/A	SB	CS	SBR	FA	FR	G/POS	TPR
1925	Cle-A	15	52	4	12	3	0	0	4	2	7	.231	.259	.327	48	-4	0	0	0	.938	-3	O-13	-0.7
1926	Cle-A	37	80	14	25	7	1	0	7	2	11	.313	.329	.425	95	-1	1	0	0	.976	-4	O-27	-0.5
1927	Cle-A	85	267	24	59	19	2	0	25	16	25	.221	.265	.307	48	-21	2	3	-1	.979	1	O-81	-2.5
1931	Chi-A	34	117	9	25	5	1	0	15	1	8	.214	.220	.274	31	-12	0	0		1.000	-5	O-32	-1.8
Total	4	171	516	51	121	34	5	0	51	21	51	.234	.264	.320	52	-39	3	3	-1	.979	-9	O-153	-5.5

■ JIM EISENREICH

Eisenreich, James Michael b: 4/18/59, St.Cloud, Minn. BL/TL, 5'11", 195 lbs. Deb: 4/6/82

YEAR	TM/L	G	AB	R	H	2B	3B	HR	RBI	BB	SO	AVG	OBP	SLG	PRO+	BR/A	SB	CS	SBR	FA	FR	G/POS	TPR
1982	Min-A	34	99	10	30	6	0	2	9	11	13	.303	.378	.424	117	3	0	0	0	.973	-1	O-30	0.1
1983	Min-A	2	7	1	2	1	0	0	0	1	1	.286	.375	.429	116	0	0	0	0	1.000	1	/O-2	0.1
1984	Min-A	12	32	1	7	1	0	0	3	2	4	.219	.265	.250	41	-3	2	0	1	1.000	-0	/O-3,D-6	-0.3
1987	KC-A	44	105	10	25	8	2	4	21	7	13	.238	.286	.467	93	-2	1	1	-0	.000	0	D-26	-0.2
1988	KC-A	82	202	26	44	8	1	1	19	6	31	.218	.240	.282	45	-15	9	3	1	.965	-8	O-64,D-13	-2.4
1989	KC-A	134	475	64	139	33	7	9	59	37	44	.293	.344	.448	122	13	27	8	3	.989	-11	*O-123,D-10	0.2
1990	KC-A	142	496	61	139	29	7	5	51	42	51	.280	.338	.397	106	4	12	14	-5	**.996**	-9	*O-138/D-2	-1.4
1991	KC-A	135	375	47	113	22	3	2	47	20	35	.301	.338	.392	101	0	5	3	-0	.973	-17	*O-105,1-15/D	-2.0
1992	KC-A	113	353	31	95	13	3	2	28	24	36	.269	.316	.340	81	-9	11	6	-0	.995	-2	O-88/D-8	-1.3
1993	*Phi-N	153	362	51	115	17	4	7	54	26	36	.318	.363	.445	117	9	5	0	2	.996	-6	*O-137/1-1	0.2
1994	Phi-N	104	290	42	87	15	4	4	43	33	31	.300	.373	.421	108	4	6	2	1	.989	0	O-93	0.3
Total	11	955	2796	344	796	153	31	36	334	209	295	.285	.336	.400	102	5	78	37	1	.988	-55	O-783/D-66,1	-6.7

■ ELAND

Eland Deb: 4/14/1873

YEAR	TM/L	G	AB	R	H	2B	3B	HR	RBI	BB	SO	AVG	OBP	SLG	PRO+	BR/A	SB	CS	SBR	FA	FR	G/POS	TPR
1873	Mar-n	1	3	0	0	0	0	0	0	0	0	.000	.000	.000	-99	-1						/O-1	-0.1

■ KID ELBERFELD

Elberfeld, Norman Arthur "The Tabasco Kid" b: 4/13/1875, Pomeroy, Ohio d: 1/13/44, Chattanooga, Tenn. BR/TR, 5'7", 158 lbs. Deb: 5/30/1898 M

YEAR	TM/L	G	AB	R	H	2B	3B	HR	RBI	BB	SO	AVG	OBP	SLG	PRO+	BR/A	SB	CS	SBR	FA	FR	G/POS	TPR
1898	Phi-N	14	38	1	9	4	0	0	7	5		.237	.420	.342	124	2	0			.795	-5	3-14	-0.3
1899	Cin-N	41	138	23	36	4	2	0	22	15		.261	.378	.319	90	-1	5			.878	-4	S-24,3-18	-0.3
1901	Det-A	121	432	76	133	21	11	3	76	57		.308	.397	.428	123	15	23			.907	22	*S-121	4.2
1902	Det-A	130	488	70	127	17	6	1	64	55		.260	.348	.326	86	-7	19			.921	9	*S-130	0.9
1903	Det-A	35	132	29	45	5	3	0	19	11		.341	.412	.424	156	10	6			.932	6	S-34/3-1	1.7
	NY-A	90	349	49	100	18	5	0	45	22		.287	.346	.367	107	4	16			.914	7	S-90	1.5
	Yr	125	481	78	145	23	8	0	64	33		.301	.365	.383	120	13	22			.919	13	*S-124/3-1	3.2
1904	NY-A	122	445	55	117	13	5	2	46	37		.263	.337	.328	106	4	18			.933	15	*S-122	2.6
1905	NY-A	111	390	48	102	18	2	0	53	23		.262	.329	.318	95	-2	18			.908	-6	*S-108	-0.6
1906	NY-A	99	346	59	106	11	5	2	31	30		.306	.378	.384	126	11	19			.925	-4	S-98	1.1
1907	NY-A	120	447	61	121	17	6	0	51	36		.271	.343	.336	108	5	22			.930	11	*S-118	2.0
1908	NY-A	19	56	11	11	3	0	0	5	6		.196	.328	.250	87	-0	1			.916	-3	S-17,M	-0.3
1909	NY-A	106	379	47	90	9	5	0	26	28		.237	.314	.288	89	-4	23			.943	-2	S-61,3-44	-0.4
1910	Was-A	127	455	53	114	9	2	2	42	35		.251	.322	.292	97	-1	19			**.943**	-10	*3-113,2-10/S	-0.8
1911	Was-A	127	404	58	110	19	4	0	47	65		.272	.405	.339	110	11	24			.957	10	2-68,3-52	2.0
1914	Bro-N	30	62	7	14	1	0	0	1	2	4	.226	.304	.242	62	-3	0			.901	-4	S-18/2-1	-0.6
Total	14	1292	4561	647	1235	169	56	10	535	427	4	.271	.355	.339	105	44	213			.920	44	S-944,3-242/2	12.7

■ GEORGE ELDER

Elder, George Rezin b: 3/10/21, Lebanon, Ky. BL/TR, 5'11", 180 lbs. Deb: 7/22/49

YEAR	TM/L	G	AB	R	H	2B	3B	HR	RBI	BB	SO	AVG	OBP	SLG	PRO+	BR/A	SB	CS	SBR	FA	FR	G/POS	TPR
1949	StL-A	41	44	9	11	3	0	0	2	4	11	.250	.313	.318	64	-2	0	0	0	1.000	-1	O-10	-0.4

■ LEE ELIA

Elia, Lee Constantine b: 7/16/37, Philadelphia, Pa. BR/TR, 5'11", 175 lbs. Deb: 4/23/66 MC

YEAR	TM/L	G	AB	R	H	2B	3B	HR	RBI	BB	SO	AVG	OBP	SLG	PRO+	BR/A	SB	CS	SBR	FA	FR	G/POS	TPR
1966	Chi-A	80	195	16	40	5	2	3	22	15	39	.205	.269	.297	67	-9	0	1	-1	.954	4	S-75	0.0
1968	Chi-N	15	17	1	3	0	0	0	3	0	6	.176	.222	.176	20	-2	0	0	0	1.000	-1	/S-2,2-1,3	-0.3
Total	2	95	212	17	43	5	2	3	25	15	45	.203	.265	.288	63	-10	0	1	-1	.954	3	/S-77,3-1,2	-0.3

■ PETE ELKO

Elko, Peter "Piccolo Pete" b: 6/17/18, Wilkes-Barre, Pa. BR/TR, 5'11", 185 lbs. Deb: 9/17/43

YEAR	TM/L	G	AB	R	H	2B	3B	HR	RBI	BB	SO	AVG	OBP	SLG	PRO+	BR/A	SB	CS	SBR	FA	FR	G/POS	TPR
1943	Chi-N	9	30	1	4	0	0	0	0	4	5	.133	.235	.133	8	-3	0			.852	-2	/3-9	-0.6
1944	Chi-N	7	22	2	5	1	0	0	0	0	0	.227	.227	.273	40	-2	0			1.000	-0	/3-6	-0.2
Total	2	16	52	3	9	1	0	0	0	4	5	.173	.232	.192	22	-5	0			.902	-2	/3-15	-0.8

■ ROY ELLAM

Ellam, Roy "Whitey" or "Slippery" b: 2/8/1886, W.Conshohocken, Pa. d: 10/28/48, Conshohocken, Pa. BR/TR, 5'10.5", 203 lbs. Deb: 9/18/09

YEAR	TM/L	G	AB	R	H	2B	3B	HR	RBI	BB	SO	AVG	OBP	SLG	PRO+	BR/A	SB	CS	SBR	FA	FR	G/POS	TPR
1909	Cin-N	10	21	4	4	0	1	1	4	7		.190	.393	.429	156	2	1			.895	-1	/S-9	0.1
1918	Pit-N	26	77	9	10	1	1	0	2	17	17	.130	.302	.169	43	-4	2			.924	-8	S-26	-1.3
Total	2	36	98	13	14	1	2	1	6	24	17	.143	.323	.224	67	-3	3			.917	-10	/S-35	-1.2

■ FRANK ELLERBE

Ellerbe, Francis Rogers "Governor" b: 12/25/1895, Marion Co., S.C. d: 7/8/88, Latta, S.C. BR/TR, 5'10.5", 165 lbs. Deb: 8/28/19

YEAR	TM/L	G	AB	R	H	2B	3B	HR	RBI	BB	SO	AVG	OBP	SLG	PRO+	BR/A	SB	CS	SBR	FA	FR	G/POS	TPR
1919	Was-A	28	105	13	29	4	1	0	16	2	15	.276	.290	.333	75	-4	5			.945	-4	S-28	-0.7
1920	Was-A	101	336	38	98	14	2	0	36	19	23	.292	.331	.345	82	-9	5	4	-1	.934	-5	3-75,S-19/O	-1.0
1921	Was-A	10	10	1	2	0	0	0	1	0	2	.200	.200	.400	52	-1	0	0	0	.000	0	H	-0.1
	StL-A	105	430	65	124	20	12	2	49	22	42	.288	.327	.405	81	-14	1	6	-3	.953	2	*3-105	-0.7
	Yr	115	440	66	126	20	12	2	50	22	44	.286	.325	.405	81	-14	1	6	-3	.953	2	*3-105	-0.8
1922	StL-A	91	342	42	84	16	1	0	33	25	36	.246	.303	.319	60	-20	1	1	-0	.955	16	3-91	0.2
1923	StL-A	18	49	6	9	0	0	0	1	1	5	.184	.200	.184	1	-7	0	1	-0	.967	-3	3-14	-0.9
1924	StL-A	21	61	7	12	0	2	0	2	3		.197	.242	.246	19	-7	0	1	-1	.953	3	3-21	-0.4
	Cle-A	46	120	7	31	1	3	1	14	1	10	.258	.270	.342	56	-8	0	0		.975	5	3-39/2-2	-0.1
	Yr	67	181	14	43	4	3	1	16	3	13	.238	.254	.309	44	-16	0	1	-1	.967	8	3-60/2-2	-0.5
Total	6	420	1453	179	389	58	22	4	152	72	136	.268	.306	.346	68	-70	12	13		.952	14	3-345/S-47,2O	-3.7

■ JOE ELLICK

Ellick, Joseph J. b: 4/3/1854, Cincinnati, Ohio d: 4/21/23, Kansas City, Kan. 5'10", 162 lbs. Deb: 5/13/1875 MU

YEAR	TM/L	G	AB	R	H	2B	3B	HR	RBI	BB	SO	AVG	OBP	SLG	PRO+	BR/A	SB	CS	SBR	FA	FR	G/POS	TPR
1875	RS-n	7	27	1	6	1	0	0		0		.222	.222	.259	73	-1						/3-3,O-2,S	-0.1
1878	Mil-N	3	13	2	2	0	0	0		0	1	.154	.154	.154	1	-1				.769	-3	/C-2,3-1,P	-0.3
1880	Wor-N	5	18	1	1	0	0	0		1	2	.056	.105	.056	-40	-3				.882	0	/3-5	-0.2
1884	CP-U	92	394	71	93	11	0	0		16		.236	.266	.264	45	-29				.903	-2	O-57,S-33/2M	-2.9
	KC-U	2	8	0	0	0	0	0		0		.000	.000	.000	-99	-2				.778	-1	/2-1,O-1	-0.3
	Bal-U	7	27	2	4	0	0	0		2		.148	.207	.148	-2	-4				.714	-1	/S-6,O-1	-0.4
	Yr	101	429	73	97	11	0	0		18		.226	.257	.252	39	-35				.894	-3	O-59,S-39/2	-3.6
Total	3	109	460	76	100	11	0	0	1	19	3	.217	.248	.241	35	-40				.889	-6	/O-59,S-39,32CP	-4.1

YEAR	TM/L	G	AB	R	H	2B	3B	HR	RBI	BB	SO	AVG	OBP	SLG	PRO+	BR/A	SB	CS	SBR	FA	FR	G/POS	TPR

■ LARRY ELLIOT   Elliot, Lawrence Lee b: 3/5/38, San Diego, Cal. BL/TL, 6'2", 200 lbs. Deb: 4/19/62

YEAR	TM/L	G	AB	R	H	2B	3B	HR	RBI	BB	SO	AVG	OBP	SLG	PRO+	BR/A	SB	CS	SBR	FA	FR	G/POS	TPR
1962	Pit-N	8	10	2	3	0	0	1	2	0	1	.300	.300	.600	135	0	0	0	0	1.000	-1	/O-3	0.0
1963	Pit-N	4	4	0	0	0	0	0	0	0	3	.000	.000	.000	-99	-1	0	0	0	.000	0	H	-0.1
1964	NY-N	80	224	27	51	8	0	9	22	28	55	.228	.322	.384	100	0	1	2	-1	.985	-2	O-63	-0.5
1966	NY-N	65	199	24	49	14	2	5	32	17	46	.246	.306	.412	100	-0	0	1	-1	.912	0	O-54	-0.3
Total	4	157	437	53	103	22	2	15	56	45	105	.236	.311	.398	99	-1	1	3	-2	.956	-2	O-120	-0.9

■ ALLEN ELLIOTT   Elliott, Allen Clifford "Ace" b: 12/25/1897, St.Louis, Mo. d: 5/6/79, St.Louis, Mo. BL/TR, 6', 170 lbs. Deb: 6/14/23

YEAR	TM/L	G	AB	R	H	2B	3B	HR	RBI	BB	SO	AVG	OBP	SLG	PRO+	BR/A	SB	CS	SBR	FA	FR	G/POS	TPR
1923	Chi-N	53	168	21	42	8	2	2	29	2	12	.250	.267	.357	63	-9	3	3	-1	.992	-2	1-52	-1.4
1924	Chi-N	10	14	0	2	0	0	0	0	0	1	.143	.143	.143	-23	-2	0	0		1.000	-0	1-10	-0.3
Total	2	63	182	21	44	8	2	2	29	2	13	.242	.258	.341	57	-12	3	3	-1	.992	-2	/1-62	-1.7

■ CARTER ELLIOTT   Elliott, Carter Ward b: 11/29/1893, Atchison, Kan. d: 5/21/59, Palm Springs, Cal. BL/TR, 5'11", 165 lbs. Deb: 9/10/21

YEAR	TM/L	G	AB	R	H	2B	3B	HR	RBI	BB	SO	AVG	OBP	SLG	PRO+	BR/A	SB	CS	SBR	FA	FR	G/POS	TPR
1921	Chi-N	12	28	5	7	2	0	0	5	3		.250	.364	.321	83	-0	0	0		.964	4	S-10	0.4

■ GENE ELLIOTT   Elliott, Eugene Birminghouse b: 2/8/1889, Fayette Co., Pa. d: 1/5/76, Huntingdon, Pa. BL/TR, 5'7", 150 lbs. Deb: 4/13/11

YEAR	TM/L	G	AB	R	H	2B	3B	HR	RBI	BB	SO	AVG	OBP	SLG	PRO+	BR/A	SB	CS	SBR	FA	FR	G/POS	TPR
1911	NY-A	5	13	1	1	1	0	0	1	2		.077	.200	.154	-1	-2	0			.000	-1	/O-2,3-1	-0.3

■ ROWDY ELLIOTT   Elliott, Harold B. b: 7/8/1890, Kokomo, Ind. d: 2/12/34, San Francisco, Cal. BR/TR, 5'9", 160 lbs. Deb: 9/24/10

YEAR	TM/L	G	AB	R	H	2B	3B	HR	RBI	BB	SO	AVG	OBP	SLG	PRO+	BR/A	SB	CS	SBR	FA	FR	G/POS	TPR
1910	Bos-N	3	2	0	0	0	0	0	0	0	0	.000	.000	.000	-96	-0	0			1.000	-0	/C-1	-0.1
1916	Chi-N	23	55	5	14	3	0	0	3	3	5	.255	.293	.309	77	-2	1			.969	-1	C-18	-0.1
1917	Chi-N	85	223	18	56	8	5	0	28	11	11	.251	.292	.332	84	-4	4			.969	4	C-73	0.5
1918	Chi-N	5	10	0	0	0	0	0	0	2	1	.000	.167	.000	-47	-2	0			.952	0	/C-5	-0.1
1920	Bro-N	41	112	13	27	4	0	1	13	3	6	.241	.267	.304	62	-6	0	0	0	.964	5	C-39	0.1
Total	5	157	402	36	97	15	5	1	44	19	23	.241	.281	.311	73	-14	5	0		.967	7	C-136	0.3

■ HARRY ELLIOTT   Elliott, Harry Lewis b: 12/30/23, San Francisco, Cal BR/TR, 5'9", 175 lbs. Deb: 8/1/53

YEAR	TM/L	G	AB	R	H	2B	3B	HR	RBI	BB	SO	AVG	OBP	SLG	PRO+	BR/A	SB	CS	SBR	FA	FR	G/POS	TPR
1953	StL-N	24	59	6	15	6	1	1	6	3	8	.254	.302	.441	91	-1	0	0	0	1.000	1	O-17	-0.1
1955	StL-N	68	117	9	30	4	0	1	12	11	9	.256	.326	.316	71	-5	0	2	-1	.978	-2	O-28	-0.9
Total	2	92	176	15	45	10	1	2	18	14	17	.256	.318	.358	78	-6	0	2	-1	.988	-2	/O-45	-1.0

■ RANDY ELLIOTT   Elliott, Randy Lee b: 6/5/51, Oxnard, Cal. BR/TR, 6'2", 190 lbs. Deb: 9/10/72

YEAR	TM/L	G	AB	R	H	2B	3B	HR	RBI	BB	SO	AVG	OBP	SLG	PRO+	BR/A	SB	CS	SBR	FA	FR	G/POS	TPR
1972	SD-N	14	49	5	10	3	1	0	6	2	11	.204	.235	.306	57	-3	0	0	0	1.000	1	O-13	-0.3
1974	SD-N	13	33	5	7	1	0	1	2	7	9	.212	.350	.333	96	0	0	1	-1	1.000	1	O-11/1-1	-0.4
1977	SF-N	73	167	17	40	5	1	7	26	8	24	.240	.278	.407	82	-5	0	2	-1	.973	1	O-46	-0.7
1980	Oak-A	14	39	4	5	3	0	0	1	1	13	.128	.150	.205	-4	-6	0	0	0	.000	0	D-11	-0.6
Total	4	114	288	31	62	12	2	8	35	18	57	.215	.264	.354	69	-14	0	3	-2	.982	-1	/O-70,D-11,1	-2.0

■ BOB ELLIOTT   Elliott, Robert Irving "Mr. Team" b: 11/26/16, San Francisco, Cal. d: 5/4/66, San Diego, Cal. BR/TR, 6', 185 lbs. Deb: 9/2/39 MC

YEAR	TM/L	G	AB	R	H	2B	3B	HR	RBI	BB	SO	AVG	OBP	SLG	PRO+	BR/A	SB	CS	SBR	FA	FR	G/POS	TPR
1939	Pit-N	32	129	18	43	10	3	3	19	9	4	.333	.377	.527	143	7	0			.978	3	O-30	0.9
1940	Pit-N	148	551	88	161	34	11	5	64	45	28	.292	.348	.421	112	9	13			.978	2	*O-147	0.3
1941	Pit-N★	141	527	74	144	24	10	3	76	64	52	.273	.353	.374	105	5	6			.970	2	*O-139	-0.2
1942	Pit-N★	143	560	75	166	26	7	9	89	52	35	.296	.358	.416	123	16	2			.927	-2	*3-142/O-1	1.7
1943	Pit-N	156	581	82	183	30	12	7	101	56	24	.315	.376	.444	132	23	4			.949	-7	*3-151/2-2,S	2.0
1944	Pit-N★	143	538	85	160	28	16	10	108	75	42	.297	.383	.465	132	24	9			.944	-1	*3-140/S-1	2.5
1945	Pit-N†	144	541	80	157	36	6	8	108	64	38	.290	.366	.423	115	11	5			.928	8	3-81,O-61	1.8
1946	Pit-N	140	486	50	128	25	3	5	68	64	44	.263	.351	.358	99	1	6			.995	3	O-92,3-43	0.0
1947	Bos-N†	150	555	93	176	35	5	22	113	87	60	.317	.410	.517	148	40	3			.956	-2	*3-148	3.7
1948	*Bos-N★	151	540	99	153	24	5	23	100	131	57	.283	.423	.474	145	40	6			.945	-10	*3-150	2.8
1949	Bos-N	139	482	77	135	29	5	17	76	90	38	.280	.395	.467	138	28	0			.963	11	*3-130	3.5
1950	Bos-N	142	531	94	162	28	5	24	107	68	67	.305	.386	.512	143	33	2			.952	-17	*3-137	1.3
1951	Bos-N★	136	480	73	137	29	2	15	70	65	56	.285	.371	.448	128	19	2	0	1	.941	-8	*3-127	1.1
1952	NY-N	98	272	33	62	6	2	10	35	36	20	.228	.323	.375	92	-3	1	0	0	.978	-6	O-65,3-13	-1.1
1953	StL-A	48	160	19	40	7	1	5	29	30	18	.250	.368	.400	105	2	0	1	-1	.954	-2	3-45	-0.1
	Chi-A	67	208	24	54	11	1	4	32	31	21	.260	.358	.380	96	-0	1	1	-0	.963	-11	3-58/O-2	-1.3
	Yr	115	368	43	94	18	2	9	61	61	39	.255	.363	.389	100	1	1	2	-1	.959	-12	*3-103/O-2	-1.4
Total	15	1978	7141	1064	2061	382	94	170	1195	967	604	.289	.375	.440	124	252	60	2		.947	-37	*3-1365,O-537/S2	18.9

■ BEN ELLIS   Ellis, Benjamin Franklin b: 7/1870, New York, N.Y. 5'10", 165 lbs. Deb: 7/16/1896

YEAR	TM/L	G	AB	R	H	2B	3B	HR	RBI	BB	SO	AVG	OBP	SLG	PRO+	BR/A	SB	CS	SBR	FA	FR	G/POS	TPR
1896	Phi-N	4	16	0	1	0	0	0		3	6	.063	.211	.063	-26	-3	0			.800	-1	/S-2,3-2	-0.3

■ RUBE ELLIS   Ellis, George William b: 11/17/1885, Downey, Cal. d: 3/13/38, Rivera, Cal. BL/TL, 6', 170 lbs. Deb: 4/15/09

YEAR	TM/L	G	AB	R	H	2B	3B	HR	RBI	BB	SO	AVG	OBP	SLG	PRO+	BR/A	SB	CS	SBR	FA	FR	G/POS	TPR
1909	StL-N	149	575	76	154	10	9	3	46	54		.268	.334	.332	114	9	16			.955	13	*O-145	1.8
1910	StL-N	142	550	87	142	18	8	4	54	62	70	.258	.339	.342	102	2	25			.942	0	*O-141	-0.5
1911	StL-N	155	555	69	139	20	11	2	66	66	64	.250	.332	.337	90	-7	9			.938	1	*O-148	-1.5
1912	StL-N	109	305	47	82	18	2	4	33	34	36	.269	.342	.380	100	-0	6			.929	0	O-76	-0.4
Total	4	555	1985	279	517	66	30	13	199	216	170	.260	.336	.344	101	4	56			.943	14	O-510	-0.6

■ JOHN ELLIS   Ellis, John Charles b: 8/21/48, New London, Conn. BR/TR, 6'2.5", 225 lbs. Deb: 5/17/69

YEAR	TM/L	G	AB	R	H	2B	3B	HR	RBI	BB	SO	AVG	OBP	SLG	PRO+	BR/A	SB	CS	SBR	FA	FR	G/POS	TPR
1969	NY-A	22	62	2	18	4	0	1	8	1	11	.290	.313	.403	103	-0	0	2	-1	.978	1	C-15	0.0
1970	NY-A	78	226	24	56	12	1	7	29	18	47	.248	.309	.403	100	-1	0	1	-1	.992	1	1-53/3-5,C	-0.5
1971	NY-A	83	238	16	58	12	1	3	34	23	42	.244	.326	.340	95	-2	0	0	-1	.990	-3	1-65/C-2	-1.1
1972	NY-A	52	136	13	40	5	1	5	25	8	22	.294	.333	.456	138	6	0	0	0	.965	1	C-25/1-8	0.8
1973	Cle-A	127	437	59	118	12	2	14	68	46	57	.270	.344	.403	108	5	0	0	0	.980	-18	C-72,D-38,1	-1.2
1974	Cle-A	128	477	58	136	23	6	10	64	32	53	.285	.331	.421	116	9	1	2	-1	.992	-8	1-69,C-42,D	-0.4
1975	Cle-A	92	296	22	68	11	1	7	32	14	33	.230	.269	.345	72	-12	0	1	-1	.976	-8	C-84/1-2,D	-1.7
1976	Tex-A	11	31	4	13	0	0	0	1	1	0	.419	.419	.581	187	3	0	0	0	1.000	-1	/C-7,D-3	0.2
1977	Tex-A	49	119	7	28	7	0	4	15	8	26	.235	.283	.395	82	-3	0	0	0	1.000	-2	C-16,D-15/1	-0.6
1978	Tex-A	34	94	7	23	4	0	3	17	6	20	.245	.290	.383	88	-2	0	1	-1	.958	-2	C-22/D-7	-0.4
1979	Tex-A	111	316	33	90	16	1	12	61	15	55	.285	.321	.437	103	1	2	2	-1	.978	-1	D-62,1-30/C	-0.6
1980	Tex-A	73	182	12	43	9	1	1	23	14	23	.236	.294	.313	69	-8	3	0	1	.992	-2	1-39,D-20/C	-1.2
1981	Tex-A	23	58	2	8	3	0	1	7	5	10	.138	.219	.241	34	-5	0	1	-1	.993	-1	1-18/D-1	-0.8
Total	13	883	2672	259	699	116	13	69	391	190	403	.262	.315	.392	99	-10	6	10	-4	.989	-45	1-304,C-297,D/3	-7.5

■ ROB ELLIS   Ellis, Robert Walter b: 7/3/50, Grand Rapids, Mich. BR/TR, 5'11", 180 lbs. Deb: 6/18/71

YEAR	TM/L	G	AB	R	H	2B	3B	HR	RBI	BB	SO	AVG	OBP	SLG	PRO+	BR/A	SB	CS	SBR	FA	FR	G/POS	TPR
1971	Mil-A	36	111	9	22	4	0	0	6	12	24	.198	.282	.216	43	-8	0	2	-1	.923	-7	3-19,O-15	-1.9
1974	Mil-A	22	48	4	14	2	0	0	4	4	11	.292	.346	.333	97	-0	0	0	0	1.000	-1	O-11/3-1,D	-0.1
1975	Mil-A	6	7	3	2	0	0	0	0	0	0	.286	.286	.286	62	-0	0	0	0	1.000	-2	/O-5,D-1	-0.2
Total	3	64	166	16	38	4	0	0	10	16	35	.229	.301	.253	59	-8	0	2	-1	.976	-10	/O-31,3-20,D	-2.2

■ BABE ELLISON   Ellison, Herbert Spencer "Bert" b: 11/15/1895, Rutland, Ark. d: 8/11/55, San Francisco, Cal BR/TR, 5'11", 170 lbs. Deb: 9/18/16

YEAR	TM/L	G	AB	R	H	2B	3B	HR	RBI	BB	SO	AVG	OBP	SLG	PRO+	BR/A	SB	CS	SBR	FA	FR	G/POS	TPR
1916	Det-A	2	7	0	1	0	0	0	1	0	1	.143	.143	.143	-14	-1				1.000	-1	/3-2	-0.3
1917	Det-A	9	29	2	5	1	2	1	4	6	3	.172	.333	.448	139	1				.980	-2	/1-9	-0.1
1918	Det-A	7	23	1	6	1	0	0	3	0	1	.261	.346	.304	100	0	1			1.000	-0	/O-4,2-3	0.0
1919	Det-A	56	134	18	29	4	0	0	11	13	24	.216	.291	.246	53	-8	4			.966	-7	2-25,O-10/S	-1.5

YEAR	TM/L	G	AB	R	H	2B	3B	HR	RBI	BB	SO	AVG	OBP	SLG	PRO+	BR/A	SB	CS	SBR	FA	FR	G/POS	TPR
1920	Det-A	61	155	11	34	7	2	0	21	8	26	.219	.258	.290	46	-12	4	1	1	.997	2	1-38/O-4,3	-1.1
Total	5	135	348	32	75	13	4	1	39	30	55	.216	.282	.284	58	-20	9	1		.994	-9	/1-47,2-28,O3S	-3.0

■ VERDO ELMORE
Elmore, Verdo Wilson "Ellie" b: 12/10/1899, Gordo, Ala. d: 8/5/69, Birmingham, Ala. BL/TR, 5'11", 185 lbs. Deb: 9/11/24

YEAR	TM/L	G	AB	R	H	2B	3B	HR	RBI	BB	SO	AVG	OBP	SLG	PRO+	BR/A	SB	CS	SBR	FA	FR	G/POS	TPR
1924	StL-A	7	17	2	3	3	0	0	0	1	3	.176	.222	.353	44	-2	0	0	0	.000	-2	/O-3	-0.3

■ ROY ELSH
Elsh, Eugene Reybold b: 3/1/1892, Penns Grove, N.J. d: 11/12/78, Philadelphia, Pa. BR/TR, 5'9", 165 lbs. Deb: 4/19/23

YEAR	TM/L	G	AB	R	H	2B	3B	HR	RBI	BB	SO	AVG	OBP	SLG	PRO+	BR/A	SB	CS	SBR	FA	FR	G/POS	TPR
1923	Chi-A	81	209	28	52	7	2	0	24	16	23	.249	.305	.301	61	-12	16	8	0	.957	1	O-57	-1.4
1924	Chi-A	60	147	21	45	9	1	0	11	10	14	.306	.350	.381	91	-2	6	1	1	.953	-6	O-38/1-2	-0.8
1925	Chi-A	32	48	6	9	1	0	0	4	5	7	.188	.264	.208	22	-6	2	0	1	.964	-1	O-16/1-3	-0.6
Total	3	173	404	55	106	17	3	0	39	31	44	.262	.317	.319	67	-20	24	9	2	.957	-6	O-111/1-5	-2.8

■ KEVIN ELSTER
Elster, Kevin Daniel b: 8/3/64, San Pedro, Cal. BR/TR, 6'2", 180 lbs. Deb: 9/2/86

YEAR	TM/L	G	AB	R	H	2B	3B	HR	RBI	BB	SO	AVG	OBP	SLG	PRO+	BR/A	SB	CS	SBR	FA	FR	G/POS	TPR
1986	*NY-N	19	30	3	5	1	0	0	0	3	8	.167	.242	.200	24	-3	0	0	0	.962	4	S-19	0.2
1987	NY-N	5	10	1	4	2	0	0	1	0	1	.400	.400	.600	169	-1	0	0	0	.909	-0	/S-3	0.1
1988	*NY-N	149	406	41	87	11	1	9	37	35	47	.214	.282	.313	74	-14	2	0	1	.977	5	*S-148	0.2
1989	NY-N	151	458	52	106	25	2	10	55	34	77	.231	.287	.360	88	-8	4	3	-1	.976	7	*S-150	1.0
1990	NY-N	92	314	36	65	20	1	9	45	30	54	.207	.278	.363	75	-11	2	0	1	.960	15	S-92	1.1
1991	NY-N	115	348	33	84	16	2	6	36	40	53	.241	.321	.351	90	-4	2	0	1	.970	11	*S-107	1.3
1992	NY-N	6	18	0	4	0	0	0	0	0	2	.222	.222	.222	27	-2	0	0	0	1.000	-1	/S-5	-0.2
1994	NY-A	7	20	0	0	0	0	0	0	1	6	.000	.048	.000	-93	-6	0	0	0	1.000	5	/S-7	-0.1
Total	8	544	1604	166	355	75	6	34	174	143	248	.221	.288	.339	79	-48	10	6	-1	.972	47	S-531	3.6

■ BONES ELY
Ely, William Frederick b: 6/7/1863, N.Girard, Pa. d: 1/10/52, Berkeley, Cal. BR/TR, 6'1", 155 lbs. Deb: 6/19/1884

YEAR	TM/L	G	AB	R	H	2B	3B	HR	RBI	BB	SO	AVG	OBP	SLG	PRO+	BR/A	SB	CS	SBR	FA	FR	G/POS	TPR
1884	Buf-N	1	4	0	0	0	0	0	0	0	2	.000	.000	.000	-97	-1				.000	-1	/O-1,P-1	-0.1
1886	Lou-a	10	32	5	5	0	0	0			2	.156	.206	.156	13	-3	1			1.000	-0	/P-6,O-5	-0.2
1890	Syr-a	119	496	72	130	16	6	0			31	.262	.308	.319	95	-4	44			.915	19	O-78,S-36/123P	1.3
1891	Bro-N	31	111	9	17	0	1	0	11	7	9	.153	.203	.171	9	-13	4			.870	8	S-28/3-2,2	-0.3
1893	StL-N	44	178	25	45	1	6	0	16	17	13	.253	.318	.326	71	-8	2			.905	-3	S-44	-0.7
1894	StL-N	127	510	85	156	20	12	12	89	30	34	.306	.344	.463	93	-9	23			.901	1	*S-126/2-1,P	-0.1
1895	StL-N	117	467	68	121	16	2	1	46	19	17	.259	.288	.308	55	-32	28			.925	6	*S-117	-1.7
1896	Pit-N	128	537	85	153	15	9	3	77	33	33	.285	.326	.363	85	-12	18			.918	-2	*S-128	-0.8
1897	Pit-N	133	516	63	146	20	8	2	74	25		.283	.317	.364	83	-14	10			.927	3	*S-133	-0.7
1898	Pit-N	148	519	49	110	14	5	2	44	24		.212	.247	.270	49	-36	6			.943	8	*S-148	-2.0
1899	Pit-N	138	522	66	145	18	6	3	72	22		.278	.313	.352	83	-14	8			.928	3	*S-132/2-6	0.9
1900	*Pit-N	130	475	60	116	6	6	0	51	17		.244	.272	.282	53	-31	6			.935	13	*S-130	-0.8
1901	Pit-N	65	240	18	50	6	3	0	28	6		.208	.234	.258	41	-18	5			.916	-8	S-64/3-1	-2.1
	Phi-A	45	171	11	37	6	2	0	16	3		.216	.230	.275	38	-15	5			.913	1	S-45	-0.9
1902	Was-A	105	381	39	100	11	2	1	62	21		.262	.301	.310	69	-16	3			.923	-9	*S-105	-1.8
Total	14	1341	5159	655	1331	149	68	24	586	257	108	.258	.295	.327	70	-225	164			.923	39	*S-1236/O-84,2P31	-10.9

■ CHESTER EMERSON
Emerson, Chester Arthur "Chuck" b: 10/27/1889, Stow, Me. d: 7/2/71, Augusta, Me. BL/TR, 5'8", 165 lbs. Deb: 9/27/11

YEAR	TM/L	G	AB	R	H	2B	3B	HR	RBI	BB	SO	AVG	OBP	SLG	PRO+	BR/A	SB	CS	SBR	FA	FR	G/POS	TPR
1911	Phi-A	7	18	2	4	0	0	0	0	0	6	.222	.417	.222	82	0	1			1.000	1	/O-7	0.0
1912	Phi-A	1	1	0	0	0	0	0	0	0	0	.000	.000	.000	-99	-0	0			.000	0	H	0.0
Total	2	8	19	2	4	0	0	0	0	0	6	.211	.400	.211	74	-0	1			1.000	1	/O-7	0.0

■ CAL EMERY
Emery, Calvin Wayne b: 6/28/37, Centre Hall, Pa. BL/TL, 6'2", 205 lbs. Deb: 7/15/63 C

YEAR	TM/L	G	AB	R	H	2B	3B	HR	RBI	BB	SO	AVG	OBP	SLG	PRO+	BR/A	SB	CS	SBR	FA	FR	G/POS	TPR
1963	Phi-N	16	19	0	3	1	0	0	0	0	2	.158	.158	.211	5	-2	0	0	0	1.000	-0	/1-2	-0.3

■ SPOKE EMERY
Emery, Herrick Smith b: 12/10/1898, Bay City, Mich. d: 6/2/75, Cape Canaveral, Fla. BR/TR, 5'9", 165 lbs. Deb: 7/18/24

YEAR	TM/L	G	AB	R	H	2B	3B	HR	RBI	BB	SO	AVG	OBP	SLG	PRO+	BR/A	SB	CS	SBR	FA	FR	G/POS	TPR
1924	Phi-N	5	3	3	2	0	0	0	0	0	0	.667	.667	.667	230	1	0	1	-1	1.000	-0	/O-1	0.0

■ FRANK EMMER
Emmer, Frank William b: 2/17/1896, Crestline, Ohio d: 10/18/63, Homestead, Fla. BR/TR, 5'8", 150 lbs. Deb: 4/25/16

YEAR	TM/L	G	AB	R	H	2B	3B	HR	RBI	BB	SO	AVG	OBP	SLG	PRO+	BR/A	SB	CS	SBR	FA	FR	G/POS	TPR
1916	Cin-N	42	89	8	13	3	1	0	2	7	27	.146	.208	.202	27	-8	1			.899	5	S-29/O-2,23	-0.2
1926	Cin-N	80	224	22	44	7	6	0	18	13	30	.196	.244	.281	42	-19	1			.918	-7	S-79	-1.9
Total	2	122	313	30	57	10	7	0	20	20	57	.182	.234	.259	38	-26	2			.913	-3	S-108/O-2,32	-2.1

■ BOB EMMERICH
Emmerich, Robert George b: 8/1/1897, New York, N.Y. d: 11/22/48, Bridgeport, Conn. BR/TR, 5'3", 155 lbs. Deb: 9/22/23

YEAR	TM/L	G	AB	R	H	2B	3B	HR	RBI	BB	SO	AVG	OBP	SLG	PRO+	BR/A	SB	CS	SBR	FA	FR	G/POS	TPR
1923	Bos-N	13	24	3	2	0	0	0	0	2	3	.083	.154	.083	-37	-5	1	1		1.000	-1	/O-8	-0.6

■ BILL ENDICOTT
Endicott, William Franklin b: 9/4/18, Acorn, Mo. BL/TL, 5'11.5", 175 lbs. Deb: 4/21/46

YEAR	TM/L	G	AB	R	H	2B	3B	HR	RBI	BB	SO	AVG	OBP	SLG	PRO+	BR/A	SB	CS	SBR	FA	FR	G/POS	TPR
1946	StL-N	20	20	2	4	3	0	0	3	4	4	.200	.333	.350	90	-0	0			1.000	-0	/O-2	0.0

■ CLYDE ENGLE
Engle, Arthur Clyde "Hack" b: 3/19/1884, Dayton, Ohio d: 12/26/39, Boston, Mass. BR/TR, 5'10", 190 lbs. Deb: 4/12/09

YEAR	TM/L	G	AB	R	H	2B	3B	HR	RBI	BB	SO	AVG	OBP	SLG	PRO+	BR/A	SB	CS	SBR	FA	FR	G/POS	TPR
1909	NY-A	135	492	66	137	20	5	3	71	47		.278	.347	.358	122	13	18			.946	14	*O-134	2.4
1910	NY-A	5	13	0	3	0	0	0	0	2		.231	.333	.231	73	-0	1			.857	-0	/O-3	-0.1
	Bos-A	106	363	59	96	18	7	2	38	31		.264	.326	.369	115	5	12			.915	-4	3-51,2-27,O/S	0.7
	Yr	111	376	59	99	18	7	2	38	33		.263	.326	.364	113	5	13			.915	-0	3-51,2-27,O/S	0.6
1911	Bos-A	146	514	58	139	13	3	2	48	51		.270	.343	.319	86	-8	24			.975	-4	1-65,3-51,2O	-1.2
1912	*Bos-A	58	171	32	40	5	3	0	18	28		.234	.348	.298	81	-3	12			.977	-8	1-25,2-15,3/SO	-1.2
1913	Bos-A	143	498	75	144	17	12	2	50	53	41	.289	.363	.384	116	10	28			.987	-7	*1-133/O-2	0.1
1914	Bos-A	59	134	14	26	2	0	0	9	14	11	.194	.275	.209	46	-8	4	9	-4	.976	-4	1-29/2-5,3O	-2.0
	Buf-F	32	110	12	28	4	1	0	12	11	18	.255	.328	.309	64	-6	7			.889	-7	3-23/O-9	-0.3
1915	Buf-F	141	501	56	131	22	8	3	71	34	43	.261	.312	.355	77	-17	24			.969	-3	*O-100,2-21,3/1	-2.6
1916	Cle-A	11	26	1	4	0	0	0	1	0	6	.154	.154	.154	-7	-3	0			.810	-2	/3-7,1-2,O	-0.6
Total	8	836	2822	373	748	101	39	12	318	271	119	.265	.335	.341	95	-19	128	9		.959	-21	O-276,1-255,3/2S	-5.8

■ CHARLIE ENGLE
Engle, Charlie August "Cholly" b: 8/27/03, New York, N.Y. d: 10/12/83, San Antonio, Tex. BR/TR, 5'8", 145 lbs. Deb: 9/14/25

YEAR	TM/L	G	AB	R	H	2B	3B	HR	RBI	BB	SO	AVG	OBP	SLG	PRO+	BR/A	SB	CS	SBR	FA	FR	G/POS	TPR
1925	Phi-A	1	0	0	0	0	0	0	0	0	0	—	—	—		0	0	0	0	.000	0	/O-1	0.0
1926	Phi-A	19	19	7	2	0	0	0	0	10	6	.105	.433	.105	43	-1	0	0	0	.930	5	S-16	0.2
1930	Pit-N	67	216	34	57	10	1	0	15	22	20	.264	.335	.319	59	-14	1			.975	-1	3-24,S-23,2	-0.9
Total	3	87	235	41	59	10	1	0	15	32	26	.251	.346	.302	59	-15	1	0		.937	2	/S-40,3-24,2	-0.7

■ DAVE ENGLE
Engle, Ralph David b: 11/30/56, San Diego, Cal. BR/TR, 6'3", 216 lbs. Deb: 4/14/81

YEAR	TM/L	G	AB	R	H	2B	3B	HR	RBI	BB	SO	AVG	OBP	SLG	PRO+	BR/A	SB	CS	SBR	FA	FR	G/POS	TPR
1981	Min-A	82	248	29	64	14	4	5	32	13	37	.258	.298	.407	95	-2	0	1	-1	.980	-0	O-76/3-1,D	-0.6
1982	Min-A	58	186	20	42	7	2	4	16	10	22	.226	.269	.349	67	-9	0	0	0	.985	-0	O-34,D-20	-1.0
1983	Min-A	120	374	46	114	22	4	8	43	28	39	.305	.355	.449	115	8	2	1	0	.973	-19	C-73,D-29/O	-0.9
1984	Min-A☆	109	391	56	104	20	1	4	38	26	22	.266	.312	.353	80	-11	0	1	-1	.981	-7	C-86,D-22	-1.5
1985	Min-A	70	172	28	44	8	2	7	25	21	28	.256	.337	.448	106	1	2	2	-1	.984	-0	D-38,C-17/O	-0.8
1986	Det-A	35	86	6	22	7	0	0	4	7	13	.256	.312	.337	77	-3	0	0	0	1.000	-0	1-23/O-4,CD	-0.5
1987	Mon-N	59	84	7	19	4	0	1	14	6	11	.226	.278	.310	54	-6	1	0	0	1.000	0	O-11/C-6,13	-0.6
1988	Mon-N	34	37	8	8	3	0	0	1	5	5	.216	.310	.297	72	-1	0	0	0	1.000	-0	/C-9,O-4,3	-0.2
1989	Mil-A	27	65	9	14	3	0	0	15	2	15	.215	.261	.354	72	-3	0	0	0	.973	0	1-18/C-3,D	-0.4
Total	9	594	1643	201	431	88	13	31	181	120	190	.262	.314	.388	90	-25	5	5	-2	.979	-29	C-197,O-136,D/13	-5.7

YEAR	TM/L	G	AB	R	H	2B	3B	HR	RBI	BB	SO	AVG	OBP	SLG	PRO+	BR/A	SB	CS	SBR	FA	FR	G/POS	TPR

■ CHARLIE ENGLISH
English, Charles Dewie b: 4/8/10, Darlington, S.C. BR/TR, 5'9.5", 160 lbs. Deb: 7/23/32

YEAR	TM/L	G	AB	R	H	2B	3B	HR	RBI	BB	SO	AVG	OBP	SLG	PRO+	BR/A	SB	CS	SBR	FA	FR	G/POS	TPR
1932	Chi-A	24	63	7	20	3	1	1	8	3	7	.317	.348	.444	111	1	0	0	0	.821	-2	3-13/S-1	-0.1
1933	Chi-A	3	9	2	4	2	0	0	1	1	1	.444	.500	.667	216	2	0	0	0	.923	-1	/2-3	0.1
1936	NY-N	6	1	0	0	0	0	0	0	0	0	.000	.000	.000	-99	-0	0			.000	0	/2-1	0.0
1937	Cin-N	17	63	1	15	3	1	0	4	0	2	.238	.238	.317	52	-4	0			.958	2	3-15/2-2	-0.2
Total	4	50	136	10	39	8	2	1	13	4	10	.287	.307	.397	90	-2	0	0	0	.897	-2	/3-28,2-6,S	-0.2

■ WOODY ENGLISH
English, Elwood George b: 3/2/07, Fredonia, Ohio BR/TR, 5'10", 155 lbs. Deb: 4/26/27

YEAR	TM/L	G	AB	R	H	2B	3B	HR	RBI	BB	SO	AVG	OBP	SLG	PRO+	BR/A	SB	CS	SBR	FA	FR	G/POS	TPR
1927	Chi-N	87	334	46	97	14	4	1	28	16	26	.290	.325	.365	84	-8	1			.940	7	S-84/3-1	0.7
1928	Chi-N	116	475	68	142	22	4	2	34	30	28	.299	.343	.375	89	-8	4			.946	6	*S-114/3-2	1.1
1929	*Chi-N	144	608	131	168	29	3	1	52	68	50	.276	.352	.339	72	-25	13			.955	15	*S-144	0.8
1930	Chi-N	156	638	152	214	36	17	14	59	100	72	.335	.430	.511	125	30	3			.973	-13	*S-138,3-18	2.7
1931	Chi-N	156	634	117	202	38	8	2	53	68	80	.319	.391	.413	114	15	12			.965	1	*S-138,3-18	3.1
1932	*Chi-N	127	522	70	142	23	7	3	47	55	73	.272	.344	.360	90	-6	5			.957	-2	3-93,S-38	0.1
1933	Chi-N★	105	398	54	104	19	2	3	41	53	44	.261	.348	.342	98	1	5			**.973**	-15	*3-103/S-1	-0.8
1934	Chi-N	109	421	65	117	26	5	3	31	48	65	.278	.353	.385	99	1	6			.971	-10	S-56,3-46/2	-0.4
1935	Chi-N	34	84	11	17	2	0	2	8	20	4	.202	.368	.298	81	-1	1			.868	-5	3-16,S-12	-0.5
1936	Chi-N	64	182	33	45	9	0	0	20	40	28	.247	.394	.297	86	-1	1			.976	1	S-42,3-17/2	0.3
1937	Bro-N	129	378	45	90	16	2	1	42	65	55	.238	.350	.299	77	-10	4			.956	-17	*S-116,2-11	-1.9
1938	Bro-N	34	72	9	18	2	0	0	7	8	11	.250	.333	.278	68	-3	2			.958	1	3-21/2-3,S	0.0
Total	12	1261	4746	801	1356	236	52	32	422	571	536	.286	.366	.378	95	-14	57			.957	-31	S-826,3-400/2	5.0

■ GIL ENGLISH
English, Gilbert Raymond b: 7/2/09, Glenola, N.C. BR/TR, 5'11", 180 lbs. Deb: 9/20/31

YEAR	TM/L	G	AB	R	H	2B	3B	HR	RBI	BB	SO	AVG	OBP	SLG	PRO+	BR/A	SB	CS	SBR	FA	FR	G/POS	TPR
1931	NY-N	3	8	0	0	0	0	0	0	1	3	.000	.111	.000	-69	-2	0			1.000	-1	/3-3	-0.3
1932	NY-N	59	204	22	46	7	5	2	19	5	20	.225	.244	.338	56	-13	0			.931	4	3-39,S-23	-0.5
1936	Det-A	1	1	0	0	0	0	0	0	0	1	.000	.000	.000	-99	-0	0	0	0	1.000	0	/3-1	0.0
1937	Det-A	18	65	6	17	1	0	1	6	6	4	.262	.333	.323	65	-3	1	1	-0	.962	-8	2-12/3-6	-1.0
	Bos-N	79	269	25	78	5	2	2	37	23	27	.290	.348	.346	98	-1	3			.958	-7	3-71	-0.6
1938	Bos-N	53	165	17	41	6	0	2	21	15	16	.248	.315	.321	84	-4	1			.956	-4	3-43/O-3,2S	-0.7
1944	Bro-N	27	79	4	12	3	0	1	7	6	7	.152	.212	.228	24	-8	0			.918	-3	S-13,3-11/2	-1.1
Total	6	240	791	74	194	22	7	8	90	56	78	.245	.298	.321	72	-31	5	1		.950	-18	3-174/S-38,2O	-4.2

■ DEL ENNIS
Ennis, Delmer b: 6/8/25, Philadelphia, Pa. BR/TR, 6', 195 lbs. Deb: 4/28/46

YEAR	TM/L	G	AB	R	H	2B	3B	HR	RBI	BB	SO	AVG	OBP	SLG	PRO+	BR/A	SB	CS	SBR	FA	FR	G/POS	TPR
1946	Phi-N★	141	540	70	169	30	6	17	73	39	65	.313	.364	.485	144	28	5			.975	14	*O-138	3.7
1947	Phi-N	139	541	71	149	25	6	12	81	37	51	.275	.325	.410	98	-4	9			.979	9	*O-135	-0.1
1948	Phi-N	152	589	86	171	40	4	30	95	47	58	.290	.345	.525	135	25	2			.957	5	*O-151	2.2
1949	Phi-N	154	610	92	184	39	11	25	110	59	61	.302	.367	.525	140	32	2			.966	6	*O-154	3.0
1950	*Phi-N	153	595	92	185	34	8	31	**126**	56	59	.311	.372	.551	142	34	2			.970	-1	*O-149	2.5
1951	Phi-N★	144	532	76	142	20	5	15	73	68	42	.267	.352	.408	105	5	4	2	0	.969	-1	*O-135	-0.2
1952	Phi-N	151	592	90	171	30	10	20	107	47	65	.289	.341	.475	125	18	6	4	-1	.970	-1	*O-149	1.0
1953	Phi-N	152	578	79	165	22	3	29	125	57	63	.285	.355	.484	117	13	1	3	-2	.980	4	*O-150	0.9
1954	Phi-N	145	556	73	145	23	2	25	119	50	60	.261	.324	.444	98	-3	2	1	0	.957	3	*O-142/1-1	-0.6
1955	Phi-N★	146	564	82	167	24	7	29	120	46	46	.296	.351	.518	129	22	4	7	0	.987	6	*O-145	2.0
1956	Phi-N	153	630	80	164	23	3	26	95	33	62	.260	.300	.430	95	-6	7	3	0	.962	0	*O-153	-1.5
1957	StL-N	136	490	61	140	24	3	24	105	37	50	.286	.337	.494	117	11	1	3	-2	.943	-15	*O-127	-1.3
1958	StL-N	106	329	22	86	18	1	3	47	15	35	.261	.296	.350	67	-15	0	1	-1	.993	3	O-84	-1.7
1959	Cin-N	5	12	1	4	0	0	0	1	2	2	.333	.429	.333	103	0	0	0	0	1.000	0	/O-3	0.0
	Chi-A	26	96	10	21	6	0	2	7	4	10	.219	.250	.344	62	-5	0	0	0	.909	-3	O-25	-1.0
Total	14	1903	7254	985	2063	358	69	288	1284	597	719	.284	.341	.472	117	154	45	19		.969	28	*O-1840/1-1	8.9

■ RUSS ENNIS
Ennis, Russell Elwood "Hack" b: 3/10/1897, Superior, Wis. d: 1/21/49, Superior, Wis. BR/TR, 5'11.5", 160 lbs. Deb: 9/19/26

YEAR	TM/L	G	AB	R	H	2B	3B	HR	RBI	BB	SO	AVG	OBP	SLG	PRO+	BR/A	SB	CS	SBR	FA	FR	G/POS	TPR
1926	Was-A	1	0	0	0	0	0	0	0	0	0	—	—	—	—	0	0	0	0	.000	0	/C-1	0.0

■ GEORGE ENRIGHT
Enright, George Albert b: 5/9/54, New Britain, Conn. BR/TR, 5'11", 175 lbs. Deb: 8/8/76

YEAR	TM/L	G	AB	R	H	2B	3B	HR	RBI	BB	SO	AVG	OBP	SLG	PRO+	BR/A	SB	CS	SBR	FA	FR	G/POS	TPR
1976	Chi-A	2	1	0	0	0	0	0	0	0	0	.000	.000	.000	-99	-0	0	0	0	1.000	1	/C-2	0.0

■ MUTZ ENS
Ens, Anton b: 11/8/1884, St.Louis, Mo. d: 6/28/50, St.Louis, Mo. BL/TL, 6'1", 180 lbs. Deb: 9/2/12 F

YEAR	TM/L	G	AB	R	H	2B	3B	HR	RBI	BB	SO	AVG	OBP	SLG	PRO+	BR/A	SB	CS	SBR	FA	FR	G/POS	TPR
1912	Chi-A	3	6	0	0	0	0	0	0	0	0	.000	.000	.000	-99	-2	0			.857	-1	/1-3	-0.2

■ JEWEL ENS
Ens, Jewel Winklemeyer b: 8/24/1889, St.Louis, Mo. d: 1/17/50, Syracuse, N.Y. BR/TR, 5'10.5", 165 lbs. Deb: 4/29/22 FMC

YEAR	TM/L	G	AB	R	H	2B	3B	HR	RBI	BB	SO	AVG	OBP	SLG	PRO+	BR/A	SB	CS	SBR	FA	FR	G/POS	TPR
1922	Pit-N	47	142	18	42	7	3	0	17	7	9	.296	.338	.387	85	-3	3	0	1	.951	-16	2-29/3-3,1S	-1.6
1923	Pit-N	12	29	3	8	1	1	0	5	0	3	.276	.276	.379	70	-1	2	0	1	.975	-0	/1-4,3-3	-0.1
1924	Pit-N	5	10	2	3	0	0	0	0	0	3	.300	.300	.300	60	-1	0	0	0	1.000	0	/1-5	-0.1
1925	Pit-N	3	5	2	1	0	0	1	2	0	1	.200	.200	.800	133	0	0	0	0	1.000	-0	/1-3	0.0
Total	4	67	186	25	54	8	4	1	24	7	16	.290	.323	.392	83	-5	5	0	2	.990	-17	/2-29,1-14,3S	-1.8

■ CHARLIE ENWRIGHT
Enwright, Charles Massey b: 10/6/1887, Sacramento, Cal. d: 1/19/17, Sacramento, Cal. BL/TR, 5'10", Deb: 4/19/09

YEAR	TM/L	G	AB	R	H	2B	3B	HR	RBI	BB	SO	AVG	OBP	SLG	PRO+	BR/A	SB	CS	SBR	FA	FR	G/POS	TPR
1909	StL-N	3	7	1	1	0	0	0	1	2		.143	.333	.143	51	-0	0			.444	-3	/S-2	-0.4

■ JACK ENZENROTH
Enzenroth, Clarence Herman b: 11/4/1885, Mineral Point, Wis. d: 2/21/44, Detroit, Mich. BR/TR, 5'10", 164 lbs. Deb: 5/1/14

YEAR	TM/L	G	AB	R	H	2B	3B	HR	RBI	BB	SO	AVG	OBP	SLG	PRO+	BR/A	SB	CS	SBR	FA	FR	G/POS	TPR
1914	StL-A	3	6	0	1	0	0	0	2	3		.167	.444	.167	88	0	0	1	-1	.923	-1	/C-3	-0.2
	KC-F	26	67	7	12	4	1	0	5	5	19	.179	.236	.269	32	-7	0			.965	-2	C-24	-0.8
1915	KC-F	14	19	3	3	0	0	0	3	6	0	.158	.360	.158	43	-1	0			.973	2	/C-8	0.1
Total	2	43	92	10	16	4	1	0	8	13	22	.174	.283	.239	40	-8	0	1		.963	-1	/C-35	-0.9

■ JIM EPPARD
Eppard, James Gerhard b: 4/27/60, South Bend, Ind. BL/TL, 6'2", 180 lbs. Deb: 9/8/87

YEAR	TM/L	G	AB	R	H	2B	3B	HR	RBI	BB	SO	AVG	OBP	SLG	PRO+	BR/A	SB	CS	SBR	FA	FR	G/POS	TPR
1987	Cal-A	8	9	2	3	0	0	0	2	0	1	.333	.455	.333	118	0	0	0	0	1.000	-0	/O-1	0.0
1988	Cal-A	56	113	7	32	3	1	0	14	11	15	.283	.347	.327	92	-1	0	0	0	.971	-0	O-17,D-10/1	-0.2
1989	Cal-A	12	12	0	3	0	0	0	2	1	4	.250	.308	.250	60	-1	0	0	0	1.000	-0	/1-4	-0.1
1990	Tor-A	6	5	0	1	0	0	0	0	2	1	.200	.333	.200	52	-0	0	0	0	.000	0	/H	0.0
Total	4	82	139	9	39	3	1	0	16	14	21	.281	.351	.317	90	-1	0	0	0	.972	-0	/O-18,1-10,D	-0.3

■ AUBREY EPPS
Epps, Aubrey Lee "Yo-Yo" b: 3/3/12, Memphis, Tenn. d: 11/13/84, Ackerman, Miss. BR/TR, 5'10", 170 lbs. Deb: 9/29/35

YEAR	TM/L	G	AB	R	H	2B	3B	HR	RBI	BB	SO	AVG	OBP	SLG	PRO+	BR/A	SB	CS	SBR	FA	FR	G/POS	TPR
1935	Pit-N	1	4	1	3	0	0	0	3	0	0	.750	.750	1.250	414	2	0			.750	-0	/C-1	0.1

■ HAL EPPS
Epps, Harold Franklin b: 3/26/14, Athens, Ga. BL/TL, 6', 175 lbs. Deb: 9/9/38

YEAR	TM/L	G	AB	R	H	2B	3B	HR	RBI	BB	SO	AVG	OBP	SLG	PRO+	BR/A	SB	CS	SBR	FA	FR	G/POS	TPR
1938	StL-N	17	50	8	15	0	0	0	3	2	4	.300	.327	.360	84	-1	2			.963	-0	O-10	-0.2
1940	StL-N	11	15	6	3	0	0	0	1	0	3	.200	.200	.200	10	-2	0			.800	-1	/O-3	-0.3
1943	StL-A	8	35	2	10	4	0	0	4	0	4	.286	.342	.400	114	1	1	1	-0	1.000	-1	/O-8	-0.1
1944	StL-A	22	62	15	11	1	1	0	3	14	14	.177	.338	.226	59	-3	0	1	-1	.962	1	O-18	-0.3
	Phi-A	67	229	27	60	8	8	0	13	18	18	.262	.316	.367	96	-2	2	1	-1	.973	-3	O-60	-0.8
	Yr	89	291	42	71	9	9	0	16	32	32	.244	.321	.337	88	-4	2	2	-1	.970	-2	O-78	-1.1
Total	4	125	391	58	99	13	9	0	21	37	43	.253	.319	.340	86	-7	5	3		.968	-4	/O-99	-1.7

MIKE EPSTEIN
Epstein, Michael Peter "Superjew" b: 4/4/43, Bronx, N.Y. BL/TL, 6'3.5", 230 lbs. Deb: 9/16/66

YEAR	TM/L	G	AB	R	H	2B	3B	HR	RBI	BB	SO	AVG	OBP	SLG	PRO+	BR/A	SB	CS	SBR	FA	FR	G/POS	TPR
1966	Bal-A	6	11	1	2	0	1	0	3	1	3	.182	.250	.364	75	-0	0	0	0	1.000	0	/1-4	0.0
1967	Bal-A	9	13	0	2	0	0	0	0	3	5	.154	.313	.154	42	-1	0	0	0	1.000	-0	/1-3	-0.1
	Was-A	96	284	32	65	7	4	9	29	38	74	.229	.332	.377	114	5	1	4	-2	.987	-2	1-80	-0.3
	Yr	105	297	32	67	7	4	9	29	41	79	.226	.331	.367	110	5	1	4	-2	.988	-2	1-83	-0.4
1968	Was-A	123	385	40	90	8	2	13	33	48	91	.234	.339	.366	117	9	1	1	-0	.987	1	*1-110	0.3
1969	Was-A	131	403	73	112	18	1	30	85	85	99	.278	.416	.551	178	45	2	5	-2	.990	-1	*1-118	3.4
1970	Was-A	140	430	55	110	15	3	20	56	73	117	.256	.375	.444	131	20	2	3	-1	.992	-3	*1-122	0.5
1971	Was-A	24	85	6	21	1	1	1	9	12	31	.247	.366	.318	101	1	1	0	0	.992	-1	1-24	-0.2
	*Oak-A	104	329	43	77	13	0	18	51	62	71	.234	.368	.438	130	15	0	3	-2	.995	-2	1-96	0.3
	Yr	128	414	49	98	14	1	19	60	74	102	.237	.368	.413	124	15	1	3	-2	.994	-2	*1-120	0.1
1972	*Oak-A	138	455	63	123	18	2	26	70	68	68	.270	.378	.490	166	38	0	1	-1	.990	-2	*1-137	2.6
1973	Tex-A	27	85	9	16	3	0	1	6	14	19	.188	.324	.259	69	-3	0	0	0	.991	-1	1-25	-0.6
	Cal-A	91	312	30	67	8	2	8	32	34	54	.215	.302	.330	84	-7	0	0	0	.993	-0	1-86	-1.4
	Yr	118	397	39	83	11	2	9	38	48	73	.209	.307	.315	81	-10	0	0	0	.993	-1	*1-111	-2.0
1974	Cal-A	18	62	10	10	2	0	4	6		13	.161	.288	.387	98	-0	0	1	0	.993	1	1-18	-0.1
Total	9	907	2854	362	695	93	16	130	380	448	645	.244	.360	.424	130	121	7	17	-8	.991	-10	1-823	4.4

JOE ERAUTT
Erautt, Joseph Michael "Stubby" b: 9/1/21, Vibank, Sask., Can. d: 10/6/76, Portland, Ore. BR/TR, 5'9", 175 lbs. Deb: 5/9/50 F

YEAR	TM/L	G	AB	R	H	2B	3B	HR	RBI	BB	SO	AVG	OBP	SLG	PRO+	BR/A	SB	CS	SBR	FA	FR	G/POS	TPR
1950	Chi-A	16	18	0	4	0	0	0	1	1	3	.222	.263	.222	26	-2	0	0	0	1.000	1	/C-5	-0.1
1951	Chi-A	16	25	3	4	1	0	0	0	3	2	.160	.276	.200	31	-2	0	0	0	.977	3	/C-12	0.1
Total	2	32	43	3	8	1	0	0	1	4	5	.186	.271	.209	29	-4	0	0	0	.983	4	/C-17	0.0

HANK ERICKSON
Erickson, Henry Nels "Popeye" b: 11/11/07, Chicago, Ill. d: 12/13/64, Louisville, Ky. BR/TR, 6'1", 185 lbs. Deb: 4/17/35

YEAR	TM/L	G	AB	R	H	2B	3B	HR	RBI	BB	SO	AVG	OBP	SLG	PRO+	BR/A	SB	CS	SBR	FA	FR	G/POS	TPR
1935	Cin-N	37	88	9	23	3	2	1	4	6	4	.261	.323	.375	90	-1	0			.972	2	C-25	0.2

CAL ERMER
Ermer, Calvin Coolidge b: 11/10/23, Baltimore, Md. BR/TR, 6'0.5", 175 lbs. Deb: 9/26/47 MC

YEAR	TM/L	G	AB	R	H	2B	3B	HR	RBI	BB	SO	AVG	OBP	SLG	PRO+	BR/A	SB	CS	SBR	FA	FR	G/POS	TPR
1947	Was-A	1	3	0	0	0	0	0	0	0	0	.000	.000	.000	-99	-1	0	0	0	1.000	1	/2-1	0.0

FRANK ERNAGA
Ernaga, Frank John b: 8/22/30, Susanville, Cal. BR/TR, 6'1", 195 lbs. Deb: 5/24/57

YEAR	TM/L	G	AB	R	H	2B	3B	HR	RBI	BB	SO	AVG	OBP	SLG	PRO+	BR/A	SB	CS	SBR	FA	FR	G/POS	TPR
1957	Chi-N	20	35	9	11	3	2	2	7	9	14	.314	.455	.686	204	6	0	0	0	.950	-0	O-10	0.5
1958	Chi-N	9	8	0	1	0	0	0	0	2	2	.125	.125	.125	-34	-2	0	0	0	.000	0	H	-0.2
Total	2	29	43	9	12	3	2	2	7	9	16	.279	.404	.581	163	4	0	0	0	.950	-0	/O-10	0.3

TEX ERWIN
Erwin, Ross Emil b: 12/22/1885, Forney, Tex. d: 4/5/53, Rochester, N.Y. BL/TR, 6', 185 lbs. Deb: 8/26/07

YEAR	TM/L	G	AB	R	H	2B	3B	HR	RBI	BB	SO	AVG	OBP	SLG	PRO+	BR/A	SB	CS	SBR	FA	FR	G/POS	TPR
1907	Det-A	4	5	0	1	0	0	0	1	1	1	.200	.333	.200	68	-0	0			.909	0	/C-4	0.0
1910	Bro-N	81	202	15	38	3	1	1	10	24	12	.188	.278	.228	49	-13	3			.949	-1	C-68	-0.8
1911	Bro-N	91	218	30	59	13	2	7	34	31	23	.271	.367	.445	132	9	5			.971	-5	C-74	1.1
1912	Bro-N	59	133	14	28	3	0	2	14	18	16	.211	.305	.278	62	-7	1			.949	-2	C-41	-0.5
1913	Bro-N	20	31	6	8	1	0	0	3	4	5	.258	.343	.290	80	-1	0			.950	-3	C-13	-0.3
1914	Bro-N	9	11	0	5	0	0	0	1	2	1	.455	.538	.455	192	1	1			1.000	-1	/C-4	0.1
	Cin-N	12	35	5	11	3	0	1	7	2	3	.314	.351	.486	144	2	0			.962	1	C-12	0.3
	Yr	21	46	5	16	3	0	1	8	4	4	.348	.400	.478	157	3	1			.966	0	C-16	0.4
Total	6	276	635	70	150	23	3	11	70	82	60	.236	.326	.334	90	-8	10			.957	-11	C-216	-0.1

NICK ESASKY
Esasky, Nicholas Andrew b: 2/24/60, Hialeah, Fla. BR/TR, 6'3", 205 lbs. Deb: 6/19/83

YEAR	TM/L	G	AB	R	H	2B	3B	HR	RBI	BB	SO	AVG	OBP	SLG	PRO+	BR/A	SB	CS	SBR	FA	FR	G/POS	TPR
1983	Cin-N	85	302	41	80	10	5	12	46	27	99	.265	.331	.450	111	4	6	2	1	.935	-10	3-84	-0.7
1984	Cin-N	113	322	30	62	10	5	10	45	52	103	.193	.305	.348	79	-9	1	2	-1	.910	-8	3-82,1-25	-2.1
1985	Cin-N	125	413	61	108	21	0	21	66	41	102	.262	.334	.465	115	8	3	4	-2	.946	-8	3-62,O-54,1	-0.3
1986	Cin-N	102	330	35	76	17	2	12	41	47	97	.230	.328	.403	96	-2	0	2	-1	.991	-3	1-70,O-42/3	-1.1
1987	Cin-N	100	346	48	94	19	2	22	59	29	76	.272	.328	.529	117	7	0	0	0	.994	-11	1-93/3-1,O	-1.1
1988	Cin-N	122	391	40	95	17	2	15	62	48	104	.243	.332	.412	108	4	7	2	1	.994	-9	*1-116	-1.4
1989	Bos-A	154	564	79	156	26	5	30	108	66	117	.277	.355	.500	130	22	1	2	-1	.996	4	*1-153/O-1	1.3
1990	Atl-N	9	35	2	6	0	0	0	0	4	14	.171	.256	.171	19	-4	0	0	0	.944	-2	/1-9	-0.6
Total	8	810	2703	336	677	120	21	122	427	314	712	.250	.332	.446	109	31	18	14	-3	.993	-45	1-478,3-230/O	-6.0

NINO ESCALERA
Escalera, Saturnino Cuadrado b: 12/1/29, Santurce, P.R. BL/TR, 5'10", 165 lbs. Deb: 4/17/54

YEAR	TM/L	G	AB	R	H	2B	3B	HR	RBI	BB	SO	AVG	OBP	SLG	PRO+	BR/A	SB	CS	SBR	FA	FR	G/POS	TPR
1954	Cin-N	73	69	15	11	1	1	0	3	7	11	.159	.237	.203	15	-9	0			.962	0	O-14/1-8,S	-0.8

JIM ESCHEN
Eschen, James Godrich b: 8/21/1891, Brooklyn, N.Y. d: 9/27/60, Sloatsburg, N.Y. BR/TR, 5'10.5", 160 lbs. Deb: 7/10/15 F

YEAR	TM/L	G	AB	R	H	2B	3B	HR	RBI	BB	SO	AVG	OBP	SLG	PRO+	BR/A	SB	CS	SBR	FA	FR	G/POS	TPR
1915	Cle-A	15	42	11	10	1	0	0	2	5	9	.238	.319	.262	73	-1	0	1	-1	.968	1	O-10	-0.1

LARRY ESCHEN
Eschen, Lawrence Edward b: 9/22/20, Suffern, N.Y. BR/TR, 6', 180 lbs. Deb: 6/16/42 F

YEAR	TM/L	G	AB	R	H	2B	3B	HR	RBI	BB	SO	AVG	OBP	SLG	PRO+	BR/A	SB	CS	SBR	FA	FR	G/POS	TPR
1942	Phi-A	12	11	0	0	0	0	0	0	4	6	.000	.267	.000	-22	-2	0	0	0	.824	-1	/S-7,2-1	-0.3

ANGEL ESCOBAR
Escobar, Angel Rubenque (Rivas) b: 5/12/65, LaSabana, Venez. BB/TR, 6', 160 lbs. Deb: 5/17/88

YEAR	TM/L	G	AB	R	H	2B	3B	HR	RBI	BB	SO	AVG	OBP	SLG	PRO+	BR/A	SB	CS	SBR	FA	FR	G/POS	TPR
1988	SF-N	3	3	1	1	0	0	0	1	0	0	.333	.333	.333	96	-0	0	0	0	1.000	0	/S-1,3-1	0.0

JOSE ESCOBAR
Escobar, Jose Elias (Sanchez) b: 10/30/60, Las Flores, Venez. BR/TR, 5'10", 140 lbs. Deb: 4/13/91

YEAR	TM/L	G	AB	R	H	2B	3B	HR	RBI	BB	SO	AVG	OBP	SLG	PRO+	BR/A	SB	CS	SBR	FA	FR	G/POS	TPR
1991	Cle-A	10	15	0	3	0	0	0	0	1	3	.200	.250	.200	26	-1	0	0	0	1.000	2	/S-5,2-4,3	0.0

JIMMY ESMOND
Esmond, James Joseph b: 10/8/1889, Albany, N.Y. d: 6/26/48, Troy, N.Y. BR/TR, 5'11", 167 lbs. Deb: 4/20/11

YEAR	TM/L	G	AB	R	H	2B	3B	HR	RBI	BB	SO	AVG	OBP	SLG	PRO+	BR/A	SB	CS	SBR	FA	FR	G/POS	TPR
1911	Cin-N	73	198	27	54	4	6	1	11	17	30	.273	.330	.369	99	-1	7			.918	1	S-44,3-14/2	0.2
1912	Cin-N	82	231	24	45	5	3	1	40	20	31	.195	.259	.255	42	-19	11			.930	-7	S-74	-2.0
1914	Ind-F	151	542	74	160	23	15	2	49	40	48	.295	.344	.404	84	-13	25			.919	-7	*S-151	-0.8
1915	New-F	155	569	79	147	20	10	5	62	59	54	.258	.329	.355	88	-11	18			.939	6	*S-155	0.8
Total	4	461	1540	204	406	52	34	9	162	136	163	.264	.324	.359	82	-44	61			.929	-8	S-424/3-14,2	-1.8

JUAN ESPINO
Espino, Juan (Reyes) b: 3/16/56, Bonao, D.R. BR/TR, 6'1", 190 lbs. Deb: 6/25/82

YEAR	TM/L	G	AB	R	H	2B	3B	HR	RBI	BB	SO	AVG	OBP	SLG	PRO+	BR/A	SB	CS	SBR	FA	FR	G/POS	TPR
1982	NY-A	3	2	0	0	0	0	0	0	0	1	.000	.000	.000	-99	-1	0	0	0	1.000	0	/C-3	0.0
1983	NY-A	10	23	1	6	0	0	1	3	1	5	.261	.292	.391	89	-0	0	0	0	1.000	-0	C-10	0.0
1985	NY-A	9	11	0	4	0	0	0	0	0	0	.364	.364	.364	102	0	0	0	0	1.000	0	C-9	0.1
1986	NY-A	27	37	1	6	2	0	0	5	2	9	.162	.205	.216	15	-4	0	0	0	.987	3	C-27	-0.1
Total	4	49	73	2	16	2	0	1	8	3	15	.219	.250	.288	48	-5	0	0	0	.993	4	/C-49	0.0

ALVARO ESPINOZA
Espinoza, Alvaro Alberto b: 2/19/62, Valencia, Venez. BR/TR, 6', 170 lbs. Deb: 9/14/84

YEAR	TM/L	G	AB	R	H	2B	3B	HR	RBI	BB	SO	AVG	OBP	SLG	PRO+	BR/A	SB	CS	SBR	FA	FR	G/POS	TPR
1984	Min-A	1	0	0	0	0	0	0	0	0	0	—	—	—	-99	0	0	0	0	.000	0	/S-1	0.0
1985	Min-A	32	57	5	15	2	0	0	9	1	9	.263	.288	.298	58	-3	0	1	-1	.949	7	S-31	0.4
1986	Min-A	37	42	4	9	1	0	0	1	1	10	.214	.233	.238	28	-4	0	1	-1	.941	6	2-19,S-18	0.2
1988	NY-A	3	0	0	0	0	0	0	0	0	0	.000	.000	.000	-99	-1	0	0	0	1.000	0	/2-2,S-1	0.0
1989	NY-A	146	503	51	142	23	1	0	41	14	60	.282	.303	.332	80	-14	3	3	-1	.970	17	*S-146	1.3
1990	NY-A	150	438	31	98	12	2	2	20	16	54	.224	.259	.274	49	-30	1	2	-1	.977	21	*S-150	0.2
1991	NY-A	148	480	51	123	23	2	5	33	16	57	.256	.283	.344	72	-19	4	1	0	.969	20	*S-147/3-2,P	1.3
1993	Cle-A	129	263	34	73	15	0	4	27	9	36	.278	.301	.380	82	-7	2	2	-1	.937	1	3-99,S-35/2	-0.5
1994	Cle-A	90	231	27	55	13	0	1	19	6	33	.238	.261	.307	44	-19	1	3	-2	.915	24	3-37,S-36,2/1	0.6
Total	9	736	2017	203	515	89	5	12	150	62	259	.255	.281	.322	65	-98	11	13	-5	.971	97	S-565,3-138/21P	3.5

YEAR	TM/L	G	AB	R	H	2B	3B	HR	RBI	BB	SO	AVG	OBP	SLG	PRO+	BR/A	SB	CS	SBR	FA	FR	G/POS	TPR
■ SAMMY ESPOSITO					Esposito, Samuel		b: 12/15/31, Chicago, Ill.			BR/TR, 5'9", 165 lbs.				Deb: 9/28/52									
1952	Chi-A	1	4	0	1	0	0	0	0	0	2	.250	.250	.250	39	-0	0	1	-1	.500	-1	/S-1	-0.3
1955	Chi-A	3	4	3	0	0	0	0	0	1	0	.000	.200	.000	-41	-1	0	0	0	1.000	-1	/3-2	-0.2
1956	Chi-A	81	184	30	42	8	2	3	25	41	19	.228	.374	.342	89	-1	1	2	-1	.962	-4	3-61,S-19/2	0.2
1957	Chi-A	94	176	26	36	3	0	2	15	38	27	.205	.346	.256	66	-7	5	1	1	.960	16	3-53,S-22/2O	1.3
1958	Chi-A	98	81	16	20	3	0	0	3	12	6	.247	.358	.284	81	-2	1	1	-0	.979	11	3-63,S-22/2O	1.0
1959	*Chi-A	69	66	12	11	1	0	1	5	11	16	.167	.286	.227	43	-5	0	1	-1	.979	9	3-45,S-14/2	0.4
1960	Chi-A	57	77	14	14	5	0	1	11	10	20	.182	.276	.286	53	-5	0	0	0	.929	1	3-37,S-11/2	-0.4
1961	Chi-A	63	94	12	16	5	0	1	8	12	21	.170	.264	.255	40	-8	0	1	0	.976	12	3-28,S-20,2	0.5
1962	Chi-A	75	81	14	19	1	0	0	4	17	13	.235	.367	.247	69	-3	0	1	-1	.846	3	3-41,S-20/2	0.2
1963	Chi-A	1	0	0	0	0	0	0	0	0	0	—	—	—	—	—	0	0	0	.000	0	R	0.0
	KC-A	18	25	3	5	0	0	0	2	3	3	.200	.286	.240	47	-2	0	0	0	1.000	-2	/2-7,S-4,3	-0.3
	Yr	19	25	3	5	0	0	0	2	3	3	.200	.286	.240	47	-2	0	0	0	1.000	-2	/2-7,S-4,3	-0.3
Total	10	560	792	130	164	27	2	8	73	145	127	.207	.333	.277	66	-33	7	7	-2	.957	51	3-333,S-133/2O	2.4
■ CECIL ESPY					Espy, Cecil Edward		b: 1/20/63, San Diego, Cal.			BB/TR, 6'3", 195 lbs.				Deb: 9/2/83									
1983	LA-N	20	11	4	3	1	0	0	1	1	2	.273	.333	.364	94	-0	0	0	0	1.000	-5	O-15	-0.5
1987	Tex-A	14	8	1	0	0	0	0	0	1	3	.000	.111	.000	-67	-2	2	0	1	1.000	-1	/O-8	-0.2
1988	Tex-A	123	347	46	86	17	6	2	39	20	83	.248	.291	.349	76	-11	33	10	4	.972	-4	O-98,D-12/SC12	-1.4
1989	Tex-A	142	475	65	122	12	7	3	31	38	99	.257	.315	.331	81	-12	45	20	2	.990	-3	*O-133/D-3	-1.7
1990	Tex-A	52	71	10	9	0	0	0	1	10	20	.127	.235	.127	4	-9	11	5	0	1.000	-7	O-39/2-1,D	-1.7
1991	*Pit-N	43	82	7	20	4	0	1	11	5	17	.244	.287	.329	74	-3	4	0	1	.966	-3	O-35	-0.6
1992	*Pit-N	112	194	21	50	7	3	1	20	15	40	.258	.311	.340	85	-4	6	3	0	.955	-20	O-82	-2.7
1993	Cin-N	40	60	6	14	2	0	0	5	14	13	.233	.378	.267	76	-1	2	2	-1	.931	-1	O-18	-0.3
Total	8	546	1248	160	304	43	16	7	108	104	277	.244	.303	.321	74	-42	103	40	7	.977	-43	O-428/D-19,S2C1	-9.1
■ CHUCK ESSEGIAN					Essegian, Charles Abraham		b: 8/9/31, Boston, Mass.			BR/TR, 5'11", 202 lbs.				Deb: 4/15/58									
1958	Phi-N	39	114	15	28	5	2	5	16	12	34	.246	.317	.456	103	0	0	0	0	.952	1	O-30	-0.1
1959	StL-N	17	39	2	7	2	1	0	5	1	13	.179	.200	.282	25	-4	0	0	0	1.000	-1	/O-9	-0.6
	*LA-N	24	46	6	14	6	0	1	5	4	11	.304	.360	.500	118	1	0	0	0	1.000	-1	O-10	-0.1
	Yr	41	85	8	21	8	1	1	10	5	24	.247	.289	.400	76	-3	0	0	0	1.000	-2	O-19	-0.7
1960	LA-N	52	79	8	17	3	0	3	11	8	24	.215	.287	.367	73	-3	0	0	0	.968	0	O-18	-0.4
1961	Bal-A	1	1	0	0	0	0	0	0	0	0	.000	.000	.000	-99	-0	0	0	0	.000	0	H	0.0
	KC-A	4	6	1	2	1	0	0	1	1	2	.333	.429	.500	145	0	0	0	0	1.000	0	/O-1	0.1
	Cle-A	60	166	25	48	7	1	12	35	10	33	.289	.333	.560	138	8	0	0	0	.968	-2	O-49	0.4
	Yr	65	173	26	50	8	1	12	36	11	35	.289	.335	.555	137	8	0	0	0	.969	-1	O-50	0.5
1962	Cle-A	106	336	59	92	12	0	21	50	42	68	.274	.366	.497	134	16	0	0	0	.994	-4	O-90	0.7
1963	KC-A	101	231	23	52	9	0	5	27	19	48	.225	.287	.329	68	-10	0	0	0	.990	-0	O-53	-1.3
Total	6	404	1018	139	260	45	4	47	150	97	233	.255	.326	.446	106	8	0	0	0	.981	-7	O-260	-1.3
■ JIM ESSIAN					Essian, James Sarkis		b: 1/2/51, Detroit, Mich.			BR/TR, 6'2", 195 lbs.				Deb: 9/15/73 M									
1973	Phi-N	2	3	0	0	0	0	0	0	0	1	.000	.000	.000	-97	-1	0	0	0	.000	0	/C-1	-0.1
1974	Phi-N	17	20	1	2	0	0	0	0	2	1	.100	.182	.100	-19	-3	0	0	0	.976	1	C-15/1-1,3	-0.2
1975	Phi-N	2	1	1	1	0	0	0	1	1	0	1.000	1.000	1.000	439	1	0	0	0	1.000	0	/C-2	0.1
1976	Chi-A	78	199	20	49	7	0	2	21	23	28	.246	.327	.281	79	-4	2	1	0	.974	3	C-77/1-2,3	0.0
1977	Chi-A	114	322	50	88	18	2	10	44	52	35	.273	.376	.435	120	10	1	4	-2	.986	5	*C-111/3-2	1.6
1978	Oak-A	126	278	21	62	9	1	3	26	44	22	.223	.329	.295	81	-6	0	1	0	.981	14	*C-119/1-3,2D	1.1
1979	Oak-A	98	313	34	76	16	0	8	40	25	29	.243	.303	.371	85	-7	0	1	-1	.981	10	C-70,3-10/10D	0.4
1980	Oak-A	87	285	19	66	11	0	5	29	30	18	.232	.305	.323	78	-9	1	3	-2	.987	6	C-68,D-11/1	-0.3
1981	Chi-A	27	52	6	16	3	0	0	5	4	5	.308	.357	.365	111	1	0	1	-1	.990	5	C-25/3-2	0.6
1982	Sea-A	48	153	14	42	8	0	3	20	11	7	.275	.327	.386	92	-2	2	0	1	.994	6	C-48	0.7
1983	Cle-A	48	93	11	19	4	0	1	11	16	8	.204	.321	.312	72	-3	0	1	-1	.989	4	C-47/3-1	0.1
1984	Oak-A	63	136	17	32	9	0	2	10	23	17	.235	.350	.346	100	1	1	1	-0	.985	11	C-59/3-1,D	1.3
Total	12	710	1855	194	453	85	3	33	207	231	171	.244	.330	.347	90	-22	9	13	-5	.984	63	C-642/3-18,D102	5.3
■ BOBBY ESTALELLA					Estalella, Roberto (Ventoza)		b: 4/25/11, Cardenas, Cuba		d: 1/6/91, Hialeah, Fla.		BR/TR, 5'8", 180 lbs.			Deb: 9/7/35									
1935	Was-A	15	51	7	16	2	0	2	10	17	7	.314	.485	.471	153	5	1	0	0	.895	2	3-15	0.8
1936	Was-A	13	9	2	2	0	2	0	0	4	5	.222	.462	.667	186	1	0	0	0	.000	0	H	0.1
1939	Was-A	82	280	51	77	18	6	8	41	40	27	.275	.368	.468	121	8	2	3	-1	.964	-3	O-74	0.2
1941	StL-A	46	83	7	20	6	1	0	14	18	13	.241	.376	.337	87	-1	0	0	0	1.000	-4	O-17	-0.6
1942	Was-A	133	429	68	119	24	5	8	65	85	42	.277	.400	.431	130	21	5	2	0	.941	-14	3-78,O-36	0.7
1943	Phi-A	117	367	43	95	14	4	11	63	52	44	.259	.352	.409	123	11	1	3	-2	.975	-2	O-97	0.3
1944	Phi-A	140	506	54	151	17	9	7	60	59	60	.298	.374	.409	125	17	3	3	-1	.988	-2	*O-128/1-6	0.8
1945	Phi-A	126	451	45	135	25	6	8	52	74	46	.299	.399	.436	142	26	1	6	-3	.988	1	*O-124	1.8
1949	Phi-A	8	20	2	5	0	0	0	3	1	2	.250	.286	.250	44	-2	0	0	0	1.000	0	/O-6	-0.2
Total	9	680	2196	279	620	106	33	44	308	350	246	.282	.383	.421	127	88	13	17	-6	.982	-21	O-482/3-93,1	3.9
■ DUDE ESTERBROOK					Esterbrook, Thomas John		b: 6/20/1857, Staten Is., N.Y.		d: 4/30/01, Middletown, N.Y.		BR/TR, 5'11", 167 lbs.			Deb: 5/1/1880 M									
1880	Buf-N	64	253	20	61	12	1	0	35	0	15	.241	.241	.296	80	-6				.939	-3	1-47,O-15/2SC	-1.2
1882	Cle-N	45	179	13	44	4	3	0	19	5	12	.246	.266	.302	85	-3				.893	10	O-45/1-1	0.6
1883	NY-a	97	407	55	103	9	7	0		0	15	.253	.280	.310	86	-7				.871	-5	3-97	-1.2
1884	*NY-a	112	477	110	150	29	11	1		12		.314	.345	.428	154	28				.886	9	*3-112	3.4
1885	NY-N	88	359	48	92	14	5	0	44	4	28	.256	.264	.340	96	-2				.885	2	*3-84/O-4	0.0
1886	NY-N	123	473	62	125	20	6	3	43	8	43	.264	.277	.351	89	-8	13			.895	-3	*3-123	-0.7
1887	NY-a	26	101	11	17	1	0	0		6		.168	.222	.178	13	-11	8			.950	-7	/1-9,O-7,S2	-1.6
1888	Ind-N	64	246	21	54	8	0	0	17	2	20	.220	.232	.252	53	-13	11			.976	-3	1-61/3-3	-2.2
	Lou-a	23	93	9	21	6	0	0	7	3		.226	.265	.290	80	-2	5			.962	0	1-23	-0.4
1889	Lou-a	11	44	8	14	3	0	0	9	5	2	.318	.400	.386	127	2	6			.931	-1	/1-8,O-2,SM	0.1
1890	NY-N	45	197	29	57	14	1	0	29	10	8	.289	.333	.371	105	1	12			.984	5	1-45	-0.2
1891	Bro-N	3	8	1	3	0	0	0	0	1		.375	.444	.375	140	0	1			1.000	-1	/O-2,2-1	0.0
Total	11	701	2837	387	741	120	34	5	<u>203</u>	70	<u>129</u>	.261	.284	.334	94	-22	55			.884	-2	3-419,1-194/O2SC	-3.4
■ FRANK ESTRADA					Estrada, Francisco (Soto)		b: 2/12/48, Navojoa, Mexico			BR/TR, 5'8", 182 lbs.			Deb: 9/14/71									
1971	NY-N	1	2	0	1	0	0	0	0	0	0	.500	.500	.500	187	0	0	0	0	1.000	-1	/C-1	-0.1
■ ANDY ETCHEBARREN					Etchebarren, Andrew Auguste		b: 6/20/43, Whittier, Cal.			BR/TR, 6'1", 197 lbs.			Deb: 9/26/62 C									
1962	Bal-A	2	6	0	2	0	0	0	1	0	2	.333	.333	.333	85	-0	0	0	0	.875	-1	/C-2	-0.1
1965	Bal-A	5	6	1	1	0	0	0	4	0	2	.167	.167	.667	123	-0	0	0	0	1.000	3	/C-5	0.3
1966	*Bal-A☆	121	412	49	91	14	6	11	50	38	106	.221	.295	.364	89	-6	0	1	-1	.989	-4	*C-121	-0.3
1967	Bal-A☆	112	330	29	71	13	0	7	35	38	80	.215	.300	.318	83	-6	1	0	0	.989	6	*C-110	0.0
1968	Bal-A	74	189	20	44	11	2	5	20	19	46	.233	.313	.392	112	3	0	0	0	.998	9	C-70	1.7
1969	*Bal-A	73	217	29	54	9	1	8	26	28	42	.249	.353	.350	96	-0	2	1	-1	.990	-1	C-72	0.5
1970	*Bal-A	78	230	19	56	10	3	4	28	21	41	.243	.315	.348	82	-6	4	5	-1	.984	2	C-76	0.0
1971	*Bal-A	70	222	21	60	8	0	9	29	16	40	.270	.322	.428	112	3	1	4	-2	.986	2	C-70	0.5

YEAR	TM/L	G	AB	R	H	2B	3B	HR	RBI	BB	SO	AVG	OBP	SLG	PRO+	BR/A	SB	CS	SBR	FA	FR	G/POS	TPR
1972	Bal-A	71	188	11	38	6	1	2	21	17	43	.202	.279	.277	64	-8	0	2	-1	.992	7	C-70	0.0
1973	*Bal-A	54	152	16	39	9	1	2	23	12	21	.257	.319	.368	94	-1	1	1	-0	.991	2	C-51	0.2
1974	*Bal-A	62	180	13	40	8	0	2	15	6	26	.222	.251	.300	60	-10	1	0	0	.976	6	C-60	-0.1
1975	Bal-A	8	20	0	4	1	0	0	3	0	3	.200	.200	.250	28	-2	0	0	0	1.000	0	/C-7	-0.1
	Cal-A	31	100	10	28	0	1	3	17	14	19	.280	.368	.390	123	3	1	0	0	.981	-4	C-31	0.1
	Yr	39	120	10	32	1	1	3	20	14	22	.267	.343	.367	108	1	1	0	0	.983	-3	C-38	0.0
1976	Cal-A	103	247	15	56	9	1	0	21	24	37	.227	.305	.271	74	-7	0	2	-1	.980	6	*C-102	-0.1
1977	Cal-A	80	114	11	29	2	2	0	14	12	19	.254	.325	.307	77	-3	3	1	0	.987	1	C-80	-0.1
1978	Mil-A	4	5	1	2	1	0	0	2	1	2	.400	.500	.600	207	1	0	0	0	1.000	2	/C-4	0.3
Total	15	948	2618	245	615	101	17	49	309	246	529	.235	.308	.343	88	-41	13	14	-5	.987	32	C-931	2.8

■ BUCK ETCHISON

Etchison, Clarence Hampton   b: 1/27/15, Baltimore, Md.   d: 1/24/80, E.New Market, Md.   BL/TL, 6'1", 190 lbs.   Deb: 9/22/43

YEAR	TM/L	G	AB	R	H	2B	3B	HR	RBI	BB	SO	AVG	OBP	SLG	PRO+	BR/A	SB	CS	SBR	FA	FR	G/POS	TPR
1943	Bos-N	10	19	2	6	3	0	0	2	2	2	.316	.381	.474	148	1	0			.956	-1	/1-6	0.0
1944	Bos-N	109	308	30	66	16	0	8	33	33	50	.214	.292	.344	76	-10	1			.993	-1	1-85	-1.6
Total	2	119	327	32	72	19	0	8	35	35	52	.220	.298	.352	79	-9	1			.991	-2	/1-91	-1.6

■ BOBBY ETHERIDGE

Etheridge, Bobby Lamar "Luke"   b: 11/25/42, Greenville, Miss.   BR/TR, 5'9", 170 lbs.   Deb: 7/16/67

YEAR	TM/L	G	AB	R	H	2B	3B	HR	RBI	BB	SO	AVG	OBP	SLG	PRO+	BR/A	SB	CS	SBR	FA	FR	G/POS	TPR
1967	SF-N	40	115	13	26	7	2	1	15	7	12	.226	.299	.348	86	-2	0	0	0	.925	-1	3-37	-0.4
1969	SF-N	56	131	13	34	9	0	1	10	19	26	.260	.358	.351	101	1	0	0	0	.899	-2	3-39/S-1	-0.1
Total	2	96	246	26	60	16	2	2	25	26	38	.244	.331	.350	94	-1	0	0	0	.911	-4	/3-76,S-1	-0.5

■ NICK ETTEN

Etten, Nicholas Raymond Thomas   b: 9/19/13, Spring Grove, Ill.   d: 10/18/90, Hinsdale, Ill.   BL/TL, 6'2", 198 lbs.   Deb: 9/8/38

YEAR	TM/L	G	AB	R	H	2B	3B	HR	RBI	BB	SO	AVG	OBP	SLG	PRO+	BR/A	SB	CS	SBR	FA	FR	G/POS	TPR
1938	Phi-A	22	81	6	21	6	2	0	11	9	7	.259	.333	.383	81	-3	1	0	0	.987	-2	1-22	-0.6
1939	Phi-A	43	155	20	39	11	2	3	29	16	11	.252	.322	.406	87	-4	0	0	0	.990	-3	1-41	-1.0
1941	Phi-N	151	540	78	168	27	4	14	79	82	33	.311	.405	.454	147	36	9			.984	-3	*1-150	2.3
1942	Phi-N	139	459	37	121	21	3	8	41	67	26	.264	.357	.375	120	13	3			.985	-1	*1-135	0.6
1943	*NY-A	154	583	78	158	35	5	14	107	76	31	.271	.355	.420	126	19	3	7	-3	.989	-11	*1-154	-0.5
1944	NY-A	154	573	88	168	25	4	**22**	91	**97**	29	.293	.399	.466	142	34	4	2	0	.989	4	*1-154	3.0
1945	NY-A†	152	565	77	161	24	4	18	**111**	90	23	.285	.387	.437	133	25	2	3	-1	.989	-9	*1-152	0.5
1946	NY-A	108	323	37	75	14	1	9	49	38	35	.232	.315	.365	88	-5	0	1	-1	.991	-0	1-84	-1.2
1947	Phi-N	14	41	5	10	4	0	1	8	5	4	.244	.326	.415	99	-0	0		1	.990	1	1-11	0.1
Total	9	937	3320	426	921	167	25	89	526	480	199	.277	.371	.423	125	115	22	13		.988	-22	1-903	3.2

■ FRED EUNICK

Eunick, Fernandas Bowen   b: 4/22/1892, Baltimore, Md.   d: 12/9/59, Baltimore, Md.   BR/TR, 5'6", 148 lbs.   Deb: 8/29/17

YEAR	TM/L	G	AB	R	H	2B	3B	HR	RBI	BB	SO	AVG	OBP	SLG	PRO+	BR/A	SB	CS	SBR	FA	FR	G/POS	TPR
1917	Cle-A	1	2	0	0	0	0	0	0	0	0	.000	.000	.000	-93	-0	0			1.000	-0	/3-1	-0.1

■ TONY EUSEBIO

Eusebio, Raul Antonio Bare (b: Raul Antontio Bare (Eusebio))   b: 4/27/67, San Jose De Los Llamos, D.R.   BR/TR, 6'2", 180 lbs.   Deb: 8/8/91

YEAR	TM/L	G	AB	R	H	2B	3B	HR	RBI	BB	SO	AVG	OBP	SLG	PRO+	BR/A	SB	CS	SBR	FA	FR	G/POS	TPR
1991	Hou-N	10	19	4	2	1	0	0	0	6	8	.105	.320	.158	41	-1	0	0	0	.981	2	/C-9	0.1
1994	Hou-N	55	159	18	47	9	1	5	30	8	33	.296	.329	.459	105	1	0	1	-1	.993	-4	C-52	-0.1
Total	2	65	178	22	49	10	1	5	30	14	41	.275	.328	.427	99	-1	0	1	-1	.991	-2	/C-61	0.0

■ FRANK EUSTACE

Eustace, Frank John   b: 11/7/1873, New York, N.Y.   d: 10/20/32, Pottsville, Pa.   5'9", 160 lbs.   Deb: 4/17/1896

YEAR	TM/L	G	AB	R	H	2B	3B	HR	RBI	BB	SO	AVG	OBP	SLG	PRO+	BR/A	SB	CS	SBR	FA	FR	G/POS	TPR
1896	Lou-N	25	100	18	17	2	2	1	11	6	14	.170	.217	.260	26	-11	4			.841	-5	S-22/2-3	-1.3

■ EVANS

Evans   Deb: 6/1/1875

YEAR	TM/L	G	AB	R	H	2B	3B	HR	RBI	BB	SO	AVG	OBP	SLG	PRO+	BR/A	SB	CS	SBR	FA	FR	G/POS	TPR
1875	NH-n	1	4	1	2	1	0	0		0		.500	.500	.750	374	1						/O-1	0.1

■ AL EVANS

Evans, Alfred Hubert   b: 9/28/16, Kenly, N.C.   d: 4/6/79, Wilson, N.C.   BR/TR, 5'11", 190 lbs.   Deb: 9/13/39

YEAR	TM/L	G	AB	R	H	2B	3B	HR	RBI	BB	SO	AVG	OBP	SLG	PRO+	BR/A	SB	CS	SBR	FA	FR	G/POS	TPR
1939	Was-A	7	21	2	7	1	0	0	1	5	2	.333	.462	.333	115	1	0	0	0	.964	-1	/C-6	0.1
1940	Was-A	14	25	1	8	2	0	0	7	6	7	.320	.452	.400	131	2	1	0	0	1.000	-1	/C-9	0.2
1941	Was-A	53	159	16	44	8	4	1	19	9	18	.277	.315	.396	91	-3	0	3	-2	.969	2	C-51	0.1
1942	Was-A	74	223	22	51	4	1	0	10	25	36	.229	.309	.256	60	-11	3	0	1	.961	-3	C-67	-0.9
1944	Was-A	14	22	5	2	0	0	0	0	2	6	.091	.167	.091	-27	-4	0	0	0	.933	-1	/C-8	-0.5
1945	Was-A	51	150	19	39	11	2	2	19	17	22	.260	.339	.400	125	4	2	1	0	.973	-6	C-41	0.0
1946	Was-A	88	272	30	69	10	4	2	30	30	28	.254	.332	.342	94	-2	1	2	-1	.966	-12	C-81	-1.1
1947	Was-A	99	319	17	77	8	3	2	23	28	25	.241	.303	.304	71	-13	2	1	0	.989	-3	C-94	-0.9
1948	Was-A	93	228	19	59	6	3	2	28	34	28	.259	.367	.338	91	-2	1	1	-0	.983	-3	C-85	0.0
1949	Was-A	109	321	32	87	12	3	2	42	50	19	.271	.369	.346	92	-3	4	1	1	**.992**	-16	*C-107	-1.1
1950	Was-A	90	289	24	68	8	3	2	30	29	21	.235	.309	.304	61	-18	0	0	0	.987	-13	C-88	-2.6
1951	Bos-A	12	24	1	3	1	0	0	2	4	2	.125	.250	.167	13	-3	0	0	0	1.000	1	C-10	-0.2
Total	12	704	2053	188	514	70	23	13	211	243	206	.250	.332	.326	82	-50	14	9	-1	.979	-56	C-647	-6.9

■ BARRY EVANS

Evans, Barry Steven   b: 11/30/56, Atlanta, Ga.   BR/TR, 6'1", 180 lbs.   Deb: 9/4/78

YEAR	TM/L	G	AB	R	H	2B	3B	HR	RBI	BB	SO	AVG	OBP	SLG	PRO+	BR/A	SB	CS	SBR	FA	FR	G/POS	TPR
1978	SD-N	24	90	7	24	1	1	0	4	4	10	.267	.298	.300	73	-3	0	0	0	.947	1	3-24	-0.3
1979	SD-N	56	162	9	35	5	0	1	14	5	16	.216	.240	.265	40	-14	0	2	-1	.952	11	3-53/S-2,2	-0.4
1980	SD-N	73	125	11	29	3	2	1	14	17	21	.232	.324	.312	83	-3	1	1	-0	.983	-3	3-43,2-19/S1	-0.5
1981	SD-N	54	93	11	30	5	0	1	9	7	9	.323	.382	.376	125	3	2	2	-1	.969	-4	3-24,1-10/2S	-0.2
1982	NY-A	17	31	2	8	3	0	0	2	6	6	.258	.395	.355	109	1	0	0	0	1.000	1	/2-8,3-6,S	0.2
Total	5	224	501	40	126	17	3	2	41	41	62	.251	.309	.309	77	-16	3	5	-2	.960	7	3-150/2-34,S1	-1.2

■ DARRELL EVANS

Evans, Darrell Wayne   b: 5/26/47, Pasadena, Cal.   BL/TR, 6'2", 205 lbs.   Deb: 4/20/69   C

YEAR	TM/L	G	AB	R	H	2B	3B	HR	RBI	BB	SO	AVG	OBP	SLG	PRO+	BR/A	SB	CS	SBR	FA	FR	G/POS	TPR
1969	Atl-N	12	26	3	6	0	0	0	1	1	8	.231	.259	.231	38	-2	0	0	0	.917	-2	/3-6	-0.4
1970	Atl-N	12	44	4	14	1	1	0	9	7	5	.318	.423	.386	112	1	0	0	0	.941	-1	3-12	0.0
1971	Atl-N	89	260	42	63	11	1	12	38	39	54	.242	.343	.431	111	4	2	3	-1	.937	4	3-72/O-3	0.6
1972	Atl-N	125	418	67	106	12	0	19	71	90	58	.254	.391	.419	119	14	4	2	0	.941	9	*3-123	2.3
1973	Atl-N★	161	595	114	167	25	8	41	104	**124**	104	.281	.407	.556	153	45	6	3	0	.953	8	*3-146,1-20	5.2
1974	Atl-N	160	571	99	137	21	3	25	79	**126**	88	.240	.383	.419	119	18	4	2	0	.955	16	*3-160	3.4
1975	Atl-N	156	567	82	138	22	2	22	73	105	106	.243	.364	.406	109	9	12	3	2	.938	23	*3-156/1-3	3.5
1976	Atl-N	44	139	11	24	0	0	1	10	30	33	.173	.320	.194	45	-9	3	0	1	.994	0	1-36/3-7	-1.1
	SF-N	92	257	42	57	9	1	10	36	42	38	.222	.331	.381	99	0	6	1	1	.991	9	1-83/3-5	0.5
	Yr	136	396	53	81	9	1	11	46	72	71	.205	.327	.316	80	-9	9	1	2	.992	9	*1-119,3-12	-0.6
1977	SF-N	144	461	64	117	18	3	17	72	69	50	.254	.355	.416	106	5	9	6	-1	.937	-1	O-81,1-41,3	-0.2
1978	SF-N	159	547	82	133	24	2	20	78	105	64	.243	.365	.404	119	17	4	5	-2	.952	10	*3-155	2.4
1979	SF-N	160	562	68	142	23	2	17	70	91	80	.253	.359	.391	112	11	6	7	-2	.943	22	*3-159	3.0
1980	SF-N	154	556	69	147	23	0	20	78	83	65	.264	.362	.414	119	15	17	5	2	.946	17	*3-140,1-14	3.3
1981	SF-N	102	357	51	92	13	4	12	48	54	33	.258	.358	.417	122	11	2	3	-1	.953	7	3-87,1-12	1.5
1982	SF-N	141	465	64	119	20	4	16	61	77	64	.256	.364	.419	119	13	5	4	-1	.933	-2	3-84,1-49,S	0.7
1983	SF-N★	142	523	94	145	29	3	30	82	84	81	.277	.379	.516	151	36	6	6	-2	.993	1	*1-113,3-32/S	3.0
1984	*Det-A	131	401	60	93	11	1	16	63	77	70	.232	.356	.384	105	5	2	2	-2	.997	-5	D-62,1-47,3	-0.1
1985	Det-A	151	505	81	125	17	0	**40**	94	85	85	.248	.357	.519	137	26	0	4	-2	.984	11	*1-113,D-33/3	2.7
1986	Det-A	151	507	78	122	15	0	29	85	91	105	.241	.357	.442	116	13	3	2	-0	.998	11	*1-105,D-42/3	1.5
1987	*Det-A	150	499	90	128	20	0	34	99	100	84	.257	.383	.501	138	29	6	5	-1	.997	12	*1-105,D-44/3	2.9
1988	Det-A	144	437	48	91	9	0	22	64	84	89	.208	.337	.380	104	4	1	4	-2	.993	5	D-72,1-65	-0.1
1989	Atl-N	107	276	31	57	2	0	11	39	41	46	.207	.309	.355	87	-4	0	1	-1	.985	6	1-50,3-28	-0.3
Total	21	2687	8973	1344	2223	329	36	414	1354	1605	1410	.248	.364	.431	119	263	98	68	-11	.946	165	*3-1442,1-856,D/OS	34.6

YEAR	TM/L	G	AB	R	H	2B	3B	HR	RBI	BB	SO	AVG	OBP	SLG	PRO+	BR/A	SB	CS	SBR	FA	FR	G/POS	TPR

■ DWIGHT EVANS
Evans, Dwight Michael "Dewey" b: 11/3/51, Santa Monica, Cal. BR/TR, 6'2", 205 lbs. Deb: 9/16/72 C

YEAR	TM/L	G	AB	R	H	2B	3B	HR	RBI	BB	SO	AVG	OBP	SLG	PRO+	BR/A	SB	CS	SBR	FA	FR	G/POS	TPR
1972	Bos-A	18	57	2	15	3	1	1	6	7	13	.263	.344	.404	115	1	0	0	0	1.000	1	O-17	0.2
1973	Bos-A	119	282	46	63	13	1	10	32	40	52	.223	.322	.383	92	-3	5	0	2	.995	-6	*O-113/D-2	-1.1
1974	Bos-A	133	463	60	130	19	8	10	70	38	77	.281	.338	.421	110	5	4	4	-1	.990	11	*O-122/D-7	1.0
1975	*Bos-A	128	412	61	113	24	6	13	56	47	60	.274	.354	.456	118	9	3	4	-2	.987	18	*O-115/D-7	2.2
1976	Bos-A	146	501	61	121	34	5	17	62	57	92	.242	.326	.431	107	3	6	7	-2	**.994**	9	*O-145/D-1	0.5
1977	Bos-A	73	230	39	66	9	2	14	36	28	58	.287	.364	.526	125	7	4	2	0	.992	-2	O-63/D-6	0.3
1978	Bos-A★	147	497	75	123	24	2	24	63	65	119	.247	.337	.449	108	4	8	5	-1	.982	8	*O-142/D-4	0.6
1979	Bos-A	152	489	69	134	24	1	21	58	69	76	.274	.365	.456	114	10	6	9	-4	.988	10	*O-149	1.0
1980	Bos-A	148	463	72	123	37	5	18	60	64	98	.266	.361	.484	123	15	3	1	0	.982	2	*O-144/D-2	1.2
1981	Bos-A★	108	412	84	122	19	4	**22**	71	**85**	85	.296	.418	.522	160	34	3	2	-0	.993	14	*O-108	4.5
1982	Bos-A	162	609	122	178	37	7	32	98	112	125	.292	**.403**	.534	146	41	3	2	-0	.973	6	*O-161/D-1	4.2
1983	Bos-A	126	470	74	112	19	4	22	58	70	97	.238	.339	.436	104	3	3	3	1	.987	7	O-99,D-21	0.7
1984	Bos-A	162	630	**121**	186	37	8	32	104	96	115	.295	.392	.532	146	41	3	1	0	.994	2	*O-161/D-1	3.7
1985	Bos-A	159	617	110	162	29	1	29	78	**114**	105	.263	.382	.454	123	22	7	2	1	.990	3	*O-152/D-7	2.0
1986	*Bos-A	152	529	86	137	33	2	26	97	97	117	.259	.380	.476	131	25	3	3	-1	.983	5	*O-149/D-1	2.3
1987	Bos-A★	154	541	109	165	37	2	34	123	**106**	98	.305	.422	.569	155	46	4	6	-2	.982	-7	1-79,O-77/D	2.7
1988	*Bos-A	149	559	96	164	31	7	21	111	76	99	.293	.379	.442	135	27	5	1	1	.987	-6	O-85,1-64/D	1.4
1989	Bos-A	146	520	82	148	27	3	20	100	99	84	.285	.402	.463	135	27	3	3	-1	.981	2	O-77,D-69	2.5
1990	*Bos-A	123	445	66	111	18	3	13	63	67	73	.249	.353	.391	103	3	3	4	-2	.000	0	*D-122	-0.2
1991	Bal-A	101	270	35	73	9	1	6	38	54	54	.270	.396	.378	120	10	2	3	-1	.984	0	O-67,D-21	0.7
Total	20	2606	8996	1470	2446	483	73	385	1384	1391	1697	.272	.373	.470	126	331	78	59	-12	.987	76	*O-2146,D-282,1	30.4

■ JOE EVANS
Evans, Joseph Patton "Doc" b: 5/15/1895, Meridian, Miss. d: 8/9/53, Gulfport, Miss. BR/TR, 5'9", 160 lbs. Deb: 7/3/15

YEAR	TM/L	G	AB	R	H	2B	3B	HR	RBI	BB	SO	AVG	OBP	SLG	PRO+	BR/A	SB	CS	SBR	FA	FR	G/POS	TPR
1915	Cle-A	42	109	17	28	4	2	0	11	22	18	.257	.382	.330	111	2	6	1	1	.885	-0	3-30/2-2	0.5
1916	Cle-A	33	82	4	12	1	0	0	1	7	12	.146	.213	.159	11	-9	4			.915	4	3-28	-0.5
1917	Cle-A	132	385	36	73	4	5	2	33	42	44	.190	.271	.242	53	-22	12			.939	3	*3-127	-1.9
1918	Cle-A	79	243	38	64	6	7	1	22	30	29	.263	.344	.358	102	1	7			.932	4	3-74	0.7
1919	Cle-A	21	14	9	1	0	0	0	0	2	1	.071	.188	.071	-24	-2	1			.923	4	/S-6	0.1
1920	*Cle-A	56	172	32	60	9	4	0	23	15	3	.349	.404	.506	136	9	6	2	1	.966	-3	O-43/S-6	0.4
1921	Cle-A	57	153	36	51	11	0	0	21	19	5	.333	.410	.405	107	3	4	1	1	.933	-1	O-47	0.0
1922	Cle-A	75	145	35	39	6	2	0	22	8	4	.269	.307	.338	67	-7	11	2	2	.969	-7	O-49	-1.4
1923	Was-A	106	372	42	98	15	3	0	38	27	18	.263	.313	.320	70	-16	6	4	-1	.982	-4	O-72,3-21/1	-2.3
1924	StL-A	77	209	30	53	3	3	0	19	24	12	.254	.330	.297	59	-12	4	4	-1	.969	2	O-49	-1.5
1925	StL-A	55	159	27	50	12	0	0	20	16	6	.314	.377	.390	90	-2	6	2	1	1.000	1	O-47	-0.5
Total	11	733	2043	306	529	71	31	3	210	212	152	.259	.329	.328	79	-57	67	16		.971	0	O-307,3-280/S12	-6.4

■ STEVE EVANS
Evans, Louis Richard b: 2/17/1885, Cleveland, Ohio d: 12/28/43, Cleveland, Ohio BL/TL, 5'10", 175 lbs. Deb: 4/16/08

YEAR	TM/L	G	AB	R	H	2B	3B	HR	RBI	BB	SO	AVG	OBP	SLG	PRO+	BR/A	SB	CS	SBR	FA	FR	G/POS	TPR
1908	NY-N	2	2	0	1	0	0	0		0		.500	.500	.500	209	-0	0			.000	-1	/O-1	0.0
1909	StL-N	143	498	67	129	17	6	2	56	66		.259	.362	.329	122	16	14			.947	-4	*O-141/1-2	0.7
1910	StL-N	151	506	73	122	21	8	2	73	78	63	.241	.376	.326	109	11	10			.968	-6	*O-141,1-10	-0.2
1911	StL-N	154	547	74	161	24	13	5	71	46	52	.294	.369	.413	122	16	13			.972	-2	*O-150	0.6
1912	StL-N	135	491	59	139	23	9	6	72	36	51	.283	.353	.403	109	6	11			.942	-0	*O-134	-0.1
1913	StL-N	97	245	18	61	15	6	1	31	20	28	.249	.321	.371	99	-1	5			.983	-6	O-74/1-1	-1.0
1914	Bro-F	145	514	93	179	41	**15**	12	96	50	49	.348	.416	**.556**	152	38	18			.941	-5	*O-112,1-27	2.9
1915	Bro-F	63	216	44	64	14	4	3	30	35	22	.296	.411	.440	129	10	7			.960	-2	O-61/1-1	0.6
	Bal-F	88	340	50	107	20	6	1	37	28	34	.315	.379	.418	110	5	8			.925	-6	O-88/1-4	-0.5
	Yr	151	556	94	171	**34**	10	4	67	63	56	.308	.392	.424	117	15	15			.940	-8	*O-149/1-5	0.1
Total	8	978	3359	444	963	176	67	32	466	359	**299**	.287	.374	.407	121	101	86			.955	-31	O-902/1-45	3.0

■ JAKE EVANS
Evans, Uriah L. P. "Bloody Jake" b: 9/1856, Baltimore, Md. d: 1/16/07, Baltimore, Md. TR, 5'8", 154 lbs. Deb: 5/1/1879

YEAR	TM/L	G	AB	R	H	2B	3B	HR	RBI	BB	SO	AVG	OBP	SLG	PRO+	BR/A	SB	CS	SBR	FA	FR	G/POS	TPR
1879	Tro-N	72	280	30	65	9	5	0	17	5	18	.232	.246	.300	84	-4				.884	18	*O-72	0.9
1880	Tro-N	47	180	31	46	8	1	0	22	7	15	.256	.283	.311	96	-1				.906	0	O-47/P-1	-0.2
1881	Tro-N	83	315	35	76	11	5	0	28	14	30	.241	.274	.308	78	-8				.926	14	*O-83	0.4
1882	Wor-N	80	334	33	71	10	4	0	25	7	22	.213	.229	.266	57	-16				.910	20	*O-68,S-11/32P	-0.7
1883	Cle-N	90	332	36	79	13	2	0	31	8	38	.238	.256	.289	66	-13				.902	5	*O-86/S-3,32P	-0.7
1884	Cle-N	80	313	32	81	18	3	1	38	15	49	.259	.293	.345	97	-2				**.917**	8	*O-76/2-4,S	0.4
1885	Bal-a	20	77	18	17	1	1	0		7		.221	.318	.260	85	-1				.894	2	O-20	0.1
Total	7	472	1831	215	435	70	21	1	161	63	172	.238	.264	.300	78	-45				.907	67	O-452/S-16,23P	1.3

■ CARL EVERETT
Everett, Carl Edward b: 6/3/70, Tampa, Fla. BB/TR, 6', 190 lbs. Deb: 7/1/93

YEAR	TM/L	G	AB	R	H	2B	3B	HR	RBI	BB	SO	AVG	OBP	SLG	PRO+	BR/A	SB	CS	SBR	FA	FR	G/POS	TPR
1993	Fla-N	11	19	0	2	0	0	0	0	1	9	.105	.150	.105	-29	-3	1	0	0	.857	-3	/O-8	-0.6
1994	Fla-N	16	51	7	11	1	0	2	6	3	15	.216	.259	.353	55	-3	4	0	1	1.000	-0	O-16	-0.3
Total	2	27	70	7	13	1	0	2	6	4	24	.186	.230	.286	32	-7	5	0	2	.973	-3	/O-24	-0.9

■ BILL EVERITT
Everitt, William Lee "Wild Bill" b: 12/13/1868, Ft.Wayne, Ind. d: 1/19/38, Denver, Colo. BL/TR, 6'0.5", 185 lbs. Deb: 4/18/1895

YEAR	TM/L	G	AB	R	H	2B	3B	HR	RBI	BB	SO	AVG	OBP	SLG	PRO+	BR/A	SB	CS	SBR	FA	FR	G/POS	TPR
1895	Chi-N	133	550	129	197	16	10	3	88	33	42	.358	.399	.440	109	6	47			.854	-8	*3-130/2-3	0.0
1896	Chi-N	132	575	130	184	16	13	2	64	41	43	.320	.367	.403	99	-2	46			.882	-10	*3-97,O-35	-1.1
1897	Chi-N	92	379	63	119	14	7	5	39	36		.314	.373	.427	107	3	26			.864	-5	3-83/O-8	0.0
1898	Chi-N	149	596	102	190	15	6	0	69	53		.319	.377	.364	113	11	28			.974	-2	*1-149	0.8
1899	Chi-N	136	536	87	166	15	7	1	74	31		.310	.351	.366	99	-1	30			.971	8	*1-136	0.7
1900	Chi-N	23	91	10	24	4	0	0	17	3		.264	.287	.308	67	-4	2			.979	-1	1-23	-0.5
1901	Was-A	33	115	14	22	3	2	0	8	15		.191	.301	.252	55	-6	7			.967	-4	1-33	-1.0
Total	7	698	2842	535	902	85	43	11	341	212	85	.317	.368	.389	103	7	186			.973	-23	1-341,3-310/O2	-1.1

■ JOHNNY EVERS
Evers, John Joseph "Crab" or "Trojan" b: 7/21/1881, Troy, N.Y. d: 3/28/47, Albany, N.Y. BL/TR, 5'9", 125 lbs. Deb: 9/1/02 FMCH

YEAR	TM/L	G	AB	R	H	2B	3B	HR	RBI	BB	SO	AVG	OBP	SLG	PRO+	BR/A	SB	CS	SBR	FA	FR	G/POS	TPR
1902	Chi-N	26	90	7	20	0	0	0	2	3		.222	.263	.222	51	-5	1			.990	9	2-18/S-8	-0.5
1903	Chi-N	124	464	70	136	27	7	0	52	19		.293	.325	.381	104	1	25			.937	-14	2-110,S-11/3	-0.9
1904	Chi-N	152	532	49	141	14	7	0	47	28		.265	.307	.318	93	-5	26			.943	31	*2-152	3.2
1905	Chi-N	99	340	44	94	11	2	1	37	27		.276	.333	.329	94	-2	19			.937	3	2-99	0.1
1906	*Chi-N	154	533	65	136	11	5	1	51	36		.255	.305	.315	88	-8	49			.947	6	*2-153/3-1	-0.2
1907	*Chi-N	151	508	66	127	18	4	2	51	38		.250	.309	.313	89	-7	46			.964	**28**	*2-151	2.2
1908	*Chi-N	126	416	83	125	19	6	0	37	66		.300	.402	.375	143	23	36			.960	-0	*2-122/O-1	2.5
1909	Chi-N	127	463	88	122	19	6	1	24	73		.263	.369	.337	116	12	28			.942	3	*2-126	1.3
1910	Chi-N	125	433	87	114	11	7	0	28	108	18	.263	.413	.321	115	16	28			.950	-4	*2-125	1.0
1911	Chi-N	46	155	29	35	4	3	0	7	34	10	.226	.372	.290	86	-1				.975	-6	2-33,3-11	-0.8
1912	Chi-N	143	478	73	163	23	11	1	63	74	18	.341	**.431**	.441	139	29	16			.959	6	*2-143	3.1
1913	Chi-N	136	446	81	127	20	5	3	49	50	14	.285	.361	.372	109	6	11			.960	**30**	*2-136,M	3.5
1914	*Bos-N	139	491	81	137	20	3	1	40	87	26	.279	.390	.338	118	16	12			**.976**	5	*2-139	2.1
1915	Bos-N	83	278	38	73	4	5	0	22	50	16	.263	.375	.295	109	6	7	8	-3	.959	-1	2-82	0.4
1916	Bos-N	71	241	33	52	4	1	0	15	40	19	.216	.330	.241	80	-4	5			.951	-18	2-71	-2.2
1917	Bos-N	24	83	5	16	0	0	0	0	13	8	.193	.302	.193	56	-4	1			.950	-7	2-24	-1.1
	Phi-N	56	183	20	41	5	1	0	12	30	13	.224	.333	.279	85	-2	8			.983	-5	2-49/3-7	-0.5
	Yr	80	266	25	57	5	1	0	12	43	21	.214	.324	.252	77	-5	9			.973	-12	2-73/3-7	-1.6

YEAR	TM/L	G	AB	R	H	2B	3B	HR	RBI	BB	SO	AVG	OBP	SLG	PRO+	BR/A	SB	CS	SBR	FA	FR	G/POS	TPR
1922	Chi-A	1	3	0	0	0	0	0	1	2	0	.000	.400	.000	12	-0	0	0	0	1.000	-0	/2-1	0.0
1929	Bos-N	1	0	0	0	0	0	0	0	0	0	—	—	—			0	0		.000	-1	/2-1	-0.1
Total	18	1784	6137	919	1659	216	70	12	538	778	142	.270	.356	.334	106	71	324	8		.955	54	*2-1735/3-21,SO	13.1

■ JOE EVERS   Evers, Joseph Francis   b: 9/10/1891, Troy, N.Y.   d: 1/4/49, Albany, N.Y.   BR/TR, 5'9", 135 lbs.   Deb: 4/24/13   F

1913	NY-N	1	0	0	0	0	0	0	0	0	0	—	—	—			0	0		.000	0	R	0.0

■ TOM EVERS   Evers, Thomas Francis   b: 3/31/1852, Troy, N.Y.   d: 3/23/25, Washington, D.C.   TL ,   Deb: 5/25/1882

1882	Bal-a	1	4	0	0	0	0	0		0		.000	.000	.000	-99	-1				.500	-2	/2-1	-0.3
1884	Was-U	109	427	54	99	6	1	0		7		.232	.244	.251	36	-37				.869	11	*2-109	-2.1
Total	2	110	431	54	99	6	1	0		7		.230	.242	.248	35	-38				.866	9	2-110	-2.4

■ HOOT EVERS   Evers, Walter Arthur   b: 2/8/21, St.Louis, Mo.   d: 1/25/91, Houston, Tex.   BR/TR, 6'2", 185 lbs.   Deb: 9/16/41   C

1941	Det-A	1	4	0	0	0	0	0	0	0	2	.000	.000	.000	-91	-1	0	0	0	.000	-0	/O-1	-0.2
1946	Det-A	81	304	42	81	8	4	4	33	34	43	.266	.344	.359	91	-3	7	1	2	.975	0	O-76	-0.5
1947	Det-A	126	460	67	136	24	5	10	67	45	49	.296	.366	.435	119	11	8	7	-2	.978	8	*O-123	1.1
1948	Det-A★	139	538	81	169	33	6	10	103	51	31	.314	.378	.454	117	12	3	4	-2	.973	2	*O-138	0.5
1949	Det-A	132	432	68	131	21	6	7	72	70	38	.303	.403	.428	120	14	6	7	-2	.994	11	*O-123	1.6
1950	Det-A★	143	526	100	170	35	**11**	21	103	71	40	.323	.408	.551	139	30	5	9	-4	**.997**	8	*O-139	2.6
1951	Det-A	116	393	47	88	15	2	11	46	40	47	.224	.297	.356	76	-14	5	3	-0	.976	-4	*O-108	-2.3
1952	Det-A	1	1	0	1	0	0	0	0	0	0	1.000	1.000	1.000	454	0	0	0	0	.000	-0	H	0.0
	Bos-A	106	401	53	105	17	4	14	59	29	55	.262	.318	.429	99	-2	5	2	0	.974	-5	*O-105	-1.2
	Yr	107	402	53	106	17	4	14	59	29	55	.264	.320	.430	100	-2	5	2	0	.974	-5	*O-105	-1.2
1953	Bos-A	99	300	39	72	10	1	11	31	23	41	.240	.301	.390	81	-9	2	1	0	.988	-7	O-93	-1.9
1954	Bos-A	6	8	1	0	0	0	0	0	0	2	.000	.000	.000	-90	-2	0	0	0	1.000	-0	/O-1	-0.2
	NY-N	12	11	1	1	0	0	1	0	0	6	.091	.091	.364	12	-2	0	0	0	1.000	-1	/O-4	-0.3
	Det-A	30	60	5	11	4	0	0	5	5	8	.183	.258	.250	40	-5	1	0	0	1.000	-4	O-24	-0.9
1955	Bal-A	60	185	21	44	10	1	6	30	19	28	.238	.309	.400	96	-2	2	1	0	.991	-5	O-55	-0.8
	Cle-A	39	66	10	19	7	1	2	9	3	12	.288	.319	.515	117	-1	0	1	-1	1.000	-4	O-25	-0.4
	Yr	99	251	31	63	17	2	8	39	22	40	.251	.311	.430	101	-1	2	2	-1	.993	-8	O-80	-1.2
1956	Cle-A	3	0	0	0	0	0	0	0	1	0	—	—	1.000	180	-1	0	0	0	.000	-0	H	0.0
	Bal-A	48	112	20	27	3	0	1	4	24	18	.241	.375	.295	85	-1	1	0	0	.985	-3	O-36	-0.5
	Yr	51	112	21	27	3	0	1	4	25	18	.241	.380	.295	86	-1	1	0	0	.985	-4	O-36	-0.5
Total	12	1142	3801	556	1055	187	41	98	565	415	420	.278	.353	.426	106	27	45	36	-8	.983	-4	*O-1051	-3.4

■ GEORGE EWELL   Ewell, George   b: Philadelphia, Pa.   Deb: 6/26/1871

1871	Cle-n	1	3	0	0	0	0	0	0	0	0	.000	.000	.000	-99	-1	0					/O-1	0.0

■ JOHN EWING   Ewing, John "Long Jong"   b: 6/1/1863, Cincinnati, Ohio   d: 4/23/1895, Denver, Colo.   TR ,   Deb: 6/18/1883   F

1883	StL-a	1	5	0	0	0	0	0		0		.000	.000	.000	-95	-1				.333	-1	/O-1	-0.2
1884	Cin-U	1	4	0	0	0	0	0		0		.000	.000	.000	-93	-1				1.000	-0	/O-1	-0.1
	Was-U	1	5	1	1	0	1	0		0		.200	.200	.600	113	0				.500	0	/O-1	0.0
	Yr	2	9	1	1	0	1	0		0		.111	.111	.333	16	-1				.600	0	/O-2	-0.1
1888	Lou-a	21	79	6	16	1	1	0	5	1		.203	.213	.241	46	-5	7			.907	5	P-21	0.0
1889	Lou-a	41	134	12	23	2	0	0	6	9	30	.172	.234	.187	21	-14	5			.953	-0	P-40/1-1	0.0
1890	NY-P	35	114	18	24	2	1	2	17	5	35	.211	.244	.298	41	-11	2			.949	0	P-35	0.0
1891	NY-N	33	113	10	23	1	0	0	8	3	14	.204	.224	.212	28	-10	4			.917	5	P-33	0.0
Total	6	133	454	47	87	6	3	2	36	18	79	.192	.226	.231	31	-41	18			.935	2	P-129/O-3,1	-0.3

■ REUBEN EWING   Ewing, Reuben (b: Reuben Cohen)   b: 11/30/1899, Odessa, Russia   d: 10/5/70, W.Hartford, Conn.   BR/TR, 5'4½", 150 lbs.   Deb: 6/21/21

1921	StL-N	3	1	0	0	0	0	0	0	0	1	.000	.000	.000	-99	-0	0	0	0	1.000	0	/S-1	0.0

■ SAM EWING   Ewing, Samuel James   b: 4/9/49, Lewisburg, Tenn.   BL/TL, 6'3", 200 lbs.   Deb: 9/11/73

1973	Chi-A	11	20	1	3	1	0	0	2	2	6	.150	.227	.200	20	-2	0	0	0	1.000	1	/1-4	-0.2
1976	Chi-A	19	41	3	9	2	1	0	2	2	8	.220	.256	.317	67	-2	0	0	0	1.000	-0	D-12/1-1	-0.2
1977	Tor-A	97	244	24	70	8	2	4	34	19	42	.287	.338	.385	95	-1	1	1	-0	.957	-5	O-46,D-27/1	-0.9
1978	Tor-A	40	56	3	10	0	0	2	9	5	9	.179	.246	.286	48	-4	0	0	0	1.000	-1	/O-3,D-9	-0.5
Total	4	167	361	31	92	11	3	6	47	28	65	.255	.308	.352	81	-9	1	1	-0	.959	-5	/O-49,D-48,1	-1.8

■ BUCK EWING   Ewing, William   b: 10/17/1859, Hoagland, Ohio   d: 10/20/06, Cincinnati, Ohio   BR/TR, 5'10", 188 lbs.   Deb: 9/9/1880   FMH

1880	Tro-N	13	45	1	8	1	0	0	5	1	3	.178	.196	.200	33	-3				.864	-4	C-10/O-4	-0.7
1881	Tro-N	67	272	40	68	14	7	0	25	7	8	.250	.269	.353	89	-4				.915	25	C-44,S-22/O3	2.2
1882	Tro-N	74	328	67	89	16	11	2	29	10	15	.271	.293	.405	127	10				.887	14	3-44,C-25/201P	2.3
1883	NY-N	88	376	90	114	11	13	**10**	41	20	14	.303	.338	.481	147	21				.922	1	C-63,O-14,2/S3	2.3
1884	NY-N	94	382	90	106	15	**20**	3	41	28	22	.277	.327	.445	137	16				.933	4	*C-80,O-12/S3P	2.4
1885	NY-N	81	342	81	104	15	12	6	63	13	17	.304	.330	.471	159	21				.918	9	C-63,O-14/3S1P	3.2
1886	NY-N	73	275	59	85	11	7	4	31	16	17	.309	.347	.455	138	12	18			.921	3	C-50,O-23/1	1.7
1887	NY-N	77	318	83	97	17	13	6	44	30	33	.305	.370	.497	146	20	26			.863	-1	3-51,2-19/C	1.8
1888	*NY-N	103	415	83	127	18	15	6	58	24	28	.306	.348	.465	159	27	53			.947	5	C-78,3-21/SP	3.9
1889	*NY-N	99	407	91	133	23	13	4	87	37	32	.327	.383	.477	139	20	34			.937	16	*C-97/P-3,O	3.8
1890	NY-P	83	352	98	119	19	15	8	72	39	12	.338	.406	.545	140	17	36			**.949**	14	C-81/2-1,PM	3.0
1891	NY-N	14	49	8	17	2	1	0	8	5	5	.347	.407	.429	150	3	5			.881	-3	/2-8,C-6	0.1
1892	NY-N	105	393	58	122	10	15	8	76	38	26	.310	.371	.473	158	26	42			.974	5	1-73,C-30/2	3.0
1893	Cle-N	116	500	117	172	28	15	6	122	41	18	.344	.394	.496	128	17	47			.927	-1	*O-112/2-5,1C	0.8
1894	Cle-N	53	211	32	53	12	4	2	39	24	9	.251	.328	.374	66	-13	18			.912	-2	O-52/2-1	-1.4
1895	Cin-N	105	434	90	138	24	13	5	94	30	22	.318	.363	.468	109	3	34			.976	8	*1-105,M	1.1
1896	Cin-N	69	263	41	73	14	4	1	38	29	13	.278	.349	.373	85	-6	41			.980	5	1-69,M	-0.1
1897	Cin-N	1	1	0	0	0	0	0		1		.000	.500	.000	36	0	0			.800	-0	/1-1,M	0.0
Total	18	1315	5363	1129	1625	250	178	71	883	392	294	.303	.351	.456	130	186	354			.931	101	C-636,1-253,O3/2SP	29.4

■ ART EWOLDT   Ewoldt, Arthur Lee "Sheriff"   b: 1/8/1894, Paullina, Iowa   d: 12/8/77, Des Moines, Iowa   BR/TR, 5'10", 165 lbs.   Deb: 9/17/19

1919	Phi-A	9	32	2	7	1	0	0	2	1	5	.219	.242	.250	38	-3	0			1.000	0	/3-9	-0.2

■ HOMER EZZELL   Ezzell, Homer Estell   b: 2/28/1896, Victoria, Tex.   d: 8/3/76, San Antonio, Tex.   BR/TR, 5'10", 158 lbs.   Deb: 4/22/23

1923	StL-A	88	279	31	68	6	0	0	14	15	20	.244	.287	.265	44	-23	4	3	-1	.961	8	3-73/2-8	-0.9
1924	Bos-A	90	277	35	75	8	4	0	32	14	21	.271	.311	.329	65	-15	12	5	1	.984	9	3-64,S-21/C	0.1
1925	Bos-A	58	186	40	53	6	4	0	15	19	18	.285	.351	.360	81	-5	9	7	-2	.916	-7	3-47/2-9	-1.0
Total	3	236	742	106	196	20	8	0	61	48	59	.264	.312	.313	61	-43	25	15	-1	.957	10	3-184/S-21,2C	-1.8

■ JAY FAATZ   Faatz, Jayson S.   b: 10/24/1860, Weedsport, N.Y.   d: 4/10/23, Syracuse, N.Y.   BR/TR, 6'4"   Deb: 8/22/1884   M

1884	Pit-a	29	112	18	27	2	3	0		1		.241	.274	.313	89	-1				.963	-1	1-29	-0.5
1888	Cle-a	120	470	73	124	10	2	0	51	12		.264	.312	.294	97	-1	64			**.989**	2	*1-120	-0.9
1889	Cle-N	117	442	50	102	12	5	2	38	17	28	.231	.275	.294	60	-24	27			.981	6	*1-117	-2.3
1890	Buf-P	32	111	18	21	0	2	1	16	9	5	.189	.297	.252	52	-7	2			.982	-3	1-32,M	-0.9
Total	4	298	1135	159	274	24	12	3	105	39	33	.241	.293	.292	76	-33	93			.982	4	1-298	-4.6

YEAR	TM/L	G	AB	R	H	2B	3B	HR	RBI	BB	SO	AVG	OBP	SLG	PRO+	BR/A	SB	CS	SBR	FA	FR	G/POS	TPR

■ JORGE FABREGAS Fabregas, Jorge b: 3/13/70, Miami, Fla. BL/TR, 6'3", 205 lbs. Deb: 4/24/94

| 1994 | Cal-A | 43 | 127 | 12 | 36 | 3 | 0 | 0 | 16 | 7 | 18 | .283 | .321 | .307 | 61 | -7 | 2 | 1 | 0 | .987 | -2 | C-41 | -0.6 |

■ BUNNY FABRIQUE Fabrique, Albert La Verne b: 12/23/1887, Clinton, Mich. d: 1/10/60, Ann Arbor, Mich. BB/TR, 5'8.5", 150 lbs. Deb: 10/4/16

1916	Bro-N	2	2	0	0	0	0	0	0	0	1	.000	.000	.000	-97	-0	0			1.000	0	/S-2	0.0
1917	Bro-N	25	88	8	18	3	0	1	3	8	9	.205	.271	.273	65	-4	0			.874	-2	S-21	-0.5
Total	2	27	90	8	18	3	0	1	3	8	10	.200	.265	.267	62	-4	0			.878	-2	/S-23	-0.5

■ LENNY FAEDO Faedo, Leonardo Lago b: 5/13/60, Tampa, Fla. BR/TR, 6', 170 lbs. Deb: 9/6/80

1980	Min-A	5	8	1	2	1	0	0	0	0	0	.250	.250	.375	64	-0	0	0	0	.818	-1	/S-5	-0.1
1981	Min-A	12	41	3	8	0	1	0	6	1	5	.195	.214	.244	30	-4	0	0	0	.971	2	S-12	-0.1
1982	Min-A	90	255	16	62	8	0	3	22	16	22	.243	.290	.310	63	-13	1	0	0	.967	3	S-88/D-1	-0.2
1983	Min-A	51	173	16	48	7	0	1	18	4	19	.277	.294	.335	70	-7	0	0	0	.954	-15	S-51	-1.8
1984	Min-A	16	52	6	13	1	0	1	6	4	3	.250	.304	.327	71	-2	0	0	0	.968	-5	S-15/D-1	-0.6
Total	5	174	529	42	133	17	1	5	52	25	49	.251	.286	.316	64	-26	1	0	0	.961	-16	S-171/D-2	-2.8

■ FRED FAGIN Fagin, Frederick H. b: Cincinnati, Ohio Deb: 6/25/1895

| 1895 | StL-N | 1 | 3 | 0 | 1 | 0 | 0 | 0 | 2 | 0 | | .333 | .333 | .333 | 73 | -0 | 0 | | | .636 | 0 | /C-1 | 0.0 |

■ FRANK FAHEY Fahey, Francis Raymond b: 1/22/1896, Milford, Mass. d: 3/19/54, Boston, Mass. BB/TR, 6'1", 190 lbs. Deb: 4/25/18

| 1918 | Phi-A | 10 | 17 | 2 | 3 | 1 | 0 | 0 | 1 | 0 | 3 | .176 | .176 | .235 | 24 | -2 | | | | 1.000 | -2 | /O-5,P-3 | -0.4 |

■ HOWARD FAHEY Fahey, Howard Simpson "Cap" or "Kid" b: 6/24/1892, Medford, Mass. d: 10/24/71, Clearwater, Fla. BR/TR, 5'7.5", 145 lbs. Deb: 7/23/12

| 1912 | Phi-A | 5 | 8 | 0 | 0 | 0 | 0 | 0 | 0 | 0 | | .000 | .000 | .000 | -99 | -2 | 0 | | | 1.000 | -1 | /3-2,2-1,S | -0.3 |

■ BILL FAHEY Fahey, William Roger b: 6/14/50, Detroit, Mich. BL/TR, 6', 200 lbs. Deb: 9/26/71 C

1971	Was-A	2	8	0	0	0	0	0	0	0	0	.000	.000	.000	-99	-2	0	0	0	.909	-0	/C-2	-0.3
1972	Tex-A	39	119	8	20	2	0	1	10	12	23	.168	.250	.210	40	-9	4	0	1	.992	11	C-39	0.5
1974	Tex-A	6	16	1	4	0	0	0	0	0	1	.250	.250	.250	45	-1	0	0	0	1.000	-1	/C-6	-0.2
1975	Tex-A	21	37	3	11	1	1	0	3	1	10	.297	.316	.378	96	-0	0	0	0	.983	-1	C-21	-0.1
1976	Tex-A	38	80	12	20	2	0	1	9	11	6	.250	.348	.313	92	-0	1	0	0	.993	-1	C-38	0.2
1977	Tex-A	37	68	3	15	4	0	0	5	1	8	.221	.232	.279	38	-6	0	0	0	1.000	-1	C-34	-0.6
1979	SD-N	73	209	14	60	8	1	3	19	21	17	.287	.352	.378	106	2	1	1	-0	.994	-3	C-68	0.1
1980	SD-N	93	241	18	62	4	0	1	22	21	16	.257	.317	.286	74	-8	2	0	1	.977	-4	C-85	-1.0
1981	Det-A	27	67	5	17	2	0	1	9	2	4	.254	.275	.328	71	-3	0	1	-0	.981	3	C-27	0.1
1982	Det-A	28	67	7	10	2	0	0	4	0	5	.149	.149	.179	-10	-10	1	0	0	1.000	5	C-28	-0.4
1983	Det-A	19	22	4	6	1	0	0	2	5	3	.273	.407	.318	106	0	0	0	0	1.000	-1	C-18	0.1
Total	11	383	934	75	225	26	2	7	83	74	93	.241	.298	.296	69	-37	9	2	2	.989	11	C-366	-1.6

■ FERRIS FAIN Fain, Ferris Roy "Burrhead" b: 5/29/21, San Antonio, Tex. BL/TL, 5'11", 186 lbs. Deb: 4/15/47

1947	Phi-A	136	461	70	134	28	6	7	71	95	34	.291	.414	.423	130	23	4	5	-2	.985	1	*1-132	1.8
1948	Phi-A	145	520	81	146	27	6	7	88	113	37	.281	.412	.396	115	16	10	5	0	.989	9	*1-145	2.3
1949	Phi-A	150	525	81	138	21	5	3	78	136	51	.263	.415	.339	104	11	8	1	2	.984	4	*1-150	1.4
1950	Phi-A★	151	522	83	147	25	4	10	83	133	26	.282	.430	.402	116	20	5	5	-1	.987	8	*1-151	2.3
1951	Phi-A★	117	425	63	146	30	3	6	57	80	20	**.344**	.451	.471	146	32	0	3	-2	.990	13	*1-108,O-11	3.6
1952	Phi-A☆	145	538	82	176	**43**	3	2	59	105	26	**.327**	**.438**	.429	133	30	3	5	-2	.984	16	*1-144	3.9
1953	Chi-A★	128	446	73	114	18	2	6	52	108	28	.256	.405	.345	101	7	3	2	-0	.989	10	*1-127	1.0
1954	Chi-A†	65	235	30	71	10	1	5	51	40	14	.302	.406	.417	121	9	5	1	0	.987	-4	1-64	0.2
1955	Det-A	58	140	23	37	8	0	2	23	52	12	.264	.464	.364	128	10	2	1	0	.988	0	1-44	0.8
	Cle-A	56	118	9	30	3	0	0	8	42	13	.254	.453	.280	97	3	3	0	0	.992	3	1-51	0.5
	Yr	114	258	32	67	11	0	2	31	94	25	.260	.459	.326	113	13	5	1	1	.990	4	1-95	1.3
Total	9	1151	3930	595	1139	213	30	48	570	904	261	.290	.425	.396	120	160	46	28	-3	.987	59	*1-1116/O-11	17.8

■ GEORGE FAIR Fair, George T. b: 1/14/1856, Boston, Mass. d: 2/12/39, Roslindale, Mass. 5'7.5", 140 lbs. Deb: 7/29/1876

| 1876 | NY-N | 1 | 4 | 0 | 0 | 0 | 0 | 0 | 0 | 0 | 0 | .000 | .000 | .000 | -99 | -1 | | | | .750 | 0 | /2-1 | -0.1 |

■ JIM FAIREY Fairey, James Burke b: 9/22/44, Orangeburg, S.C. BL/TL, 5'10", 190 lbs. Deb: 4/14/68

1968	LA-N	99	156	17	31	3	3	1	10	9	32	.199	.242	.276	60	-8	1	1	-0	.944	-8	O-63	-2.1
1969	Mon-N	20	49	6	14	1	0	1	6	1	7	.286	.300	.367	86	-1	0	2	-1	.913	-1	O-13	-0.4
1970	Mon-N	92	211	35	51	9	3	3	25	14	38	.242	.295	.355	74	-8	3	3	-2	.978	-8	O-59	-2.0
1971	Mon-N	92	200	19	49	8	1	1	19	12	23	.245	.288	.310	69	-8	3	3	-1	.968	1	O-58	-1.2
1972	Mon-N	86	141	9	33	7	0	1	15	10	21	.234	.285	.305	66	-4	1	3	-2	.932	-7	O-37	-1.7
1973	LA-N	10	9	0	2	0	0	0	0	1	1	.222	.300	.222	49	-1	0	0	0	.000	0	H	-0.1
Total	6	399	766	86	180	28	7	7	75	47	122	.235	.281	.317	69	-32	6	12	-5	.957	-23	O-230	-7.5

■ RON FAIRLY Fairly, Ronald Ray b: 7/12/38, Macon, Ga. BL/TL, 5'10", 181 lbs. Deb: 9/9/58

1958	LA-N	15	53	6	15	1	0	2	8	6	7	.283	.356	.415	100	0	0	0	0	.971	-1	O-15	-0.2
1959	*LA-N	118	244	27	58	12	1	4	23	31	29	.238	.326	.344	73	-9	0	4	-2	.963	-10	O-88	-2.5
1960	LA-N	14	37	6	4	0	3	1	3	7	12	.108	.250	.351	59	-2	0	0	0	1.000	0	O-13	-0.4
1961	LA-N	111	245	42	79	15	2	10	48	48	22	.322	.435	.522	140	16	0	0	0	.989	-6	O-71,1-23	0.5
1962	LA-N	147	460	80	128	15	7	14	71	75	59	.278	.383	.433	126	19	1	1	-0	.989	-23	*1-120,O-48	-1.3
1963	*LA-N	152	490	62	133	21	0	12	77	58	69	.271	.350	.388	120	11	5	2	0	**.995**	-11	*1-119,O-45	-0.5
1964	LA-N	150	454	62	116	19	5	10	74	65	59	.256	.351	.385	116	11	4	0	1	.987	-1	*1-141	0.5
1965	*LA-N	158	555	73	152	28	1	9	70	76	72	.274	.364	.377	117	14	2	0	1	.982	-1	*O-148,1-13	0.8
1966	*LA-N	117	351	53	101	20	0	14	61	52	38	.288	.383	.464	146	23	3	2	-0	.974	-15	O-98,1-25	0.3
1967	LA-N	153	486	45	107	19	0	10	55	54	51	.220	.299	.321	85	-10	1	4	-2	.986	-4	O-97,1-68	-2.6
1968	LA-N	141	441	32	103	15	1	4	43	41	61	.234	.305	.299	89	-6	0	2	-1	.989	-1	*O-105,1-36	-1.7
1969	LA-N	30	64	3	14	3	2	0	9	9	6	.219	.315	.328	86	-1	0	0	0	.981	-1	1-12,O-10	-0.4
	Mon-N	70	253	35	73	13	4	12	39	28	28	.289	.359	.514	142	13	1	0	0	.991	1	1-52,O-21	1.0
	Yr	100	317	38	87	16	6	12	47	37	28	.274	.350	.476	132	13	1	0	0	.989	-0	1-64,O-31	0.6
1970	Mon-N	119	385	54	111	19	0	15	61	72	64	.288	.406	.455	130	19	10	2	1	.995	5	*1-118,O-4	1.6
1971	Mon-N	146	447	58	115	23	0	13	71	81	65	.257	.377	.396	119	14	1	3	-2	.992	5	*1-135,O-10	0.6
1972	Mon-N	140	446	51	124	13	1	17	49	46	33	.298	.349	.430	118	11	3	4	-2	.985	6	O-70,1-68	0.6
1973	Mon-N★	142	413	70	123	13	1	17	49	86	33	.298	.422	.458	139	26	2	2	-1	.974	-8	*O-121/1-5	1.2
1974	Mon-N	101	282	35	69	9	1	12	43	57	28	.245	.374	.411	113	6	2	1	0	.989	-1	1-67,O-20	0.2
1975	StL-N	107	229	32	69	13	2	7	37	45	22	.301	.422	.467	142	15	0	1	0	.980	-0	1-56,O-20	1.1
1976	StL-N	73	110	13	29	4	0	2	23	21	12	.264	.391	.300	97	1	0	0	0	.995	3	1-27	0.2
	Oak-A	15	46	9	11	1	0	3	10	9	12	.239	.364	.457	145	3	0	0	0	1.000	1	1-15	0.3
1977	Tor-A★	132	458	60	128	24	2	19	64	58	58	.279	.363	.465	122	14	0	4	-2	.986	3	D-58,1-40,O	1.0
1978	Cal-A	91	235	23	51	5	0	10	40	25	51	.217	.295	.366	88	-4	1	0	-0	.998	-2	1-78/D-5	-1.1
Total	21	2442	7184	931	1913	307	33	215	1044	1052	877	.266	.363	.408	117	186	35	33	-9	.991	-60	*1-1218,O-1037/D	-0.6

■ ANTON FALCH Falch, Anton C. b: 12/4/1860, Milwaukee, Wis. d: 3/31/36, Wauwatosa, Wis. 6'6", 220 lbs. Deb: 9/30/1884

| 1884 | Mil-U | 5 | 18 | 0 | 2 | 0 | 0 | 0 | 0 | 0 | | .111 | .111 | .111 | -73 | -5 | | | | .600 | -1 | /O-3,C-2 | -0.6 |

YEAR	TM/L	G	AB	R	H	2B	3B	HR	RBI	BB	SO	AVG	OBP	SLG	PRO+	BR/A	SB	CS	SBR	FA	FR	G/POS	TPR

■ BIBB FALK   Falk, Bibb August "Jockey"   b: 1/27/1899, Austin, Tex.   d: 6/8/89, Austin, Tex.   BL/TL, 6', 175 lbs.   Deb: 9/17/20   FMC

YEAR	TM/L	G	AB	R	H	2B	3B	HR	RBI	BB	SO	AVG	OBP	SLG	PRO+	BR/A	SB	CS	SBR	FA	FR	G/POS	TPR
1920	Chi-A	7	17	1	5	1	1	0	2	0	5	.294	.294	.471	100	-0	0	0	0	1.000	-1	/O-4	-0.1
1921	Chi-A	152	585	62	167	31	11	5	82	37	69	.285	.330	.402	87	-13	4	4	-1	.958	-14	*O-149	-3.7
1922	Chi-A	131	483	58	144	27	1	12	79	27	55	.298	.335	.433	99	-2	2	6	-3	.963	-9	*O-129	-2.3
1923	Chi-A	87	274	44	84	18	6	5	38	25	12	.307	.367	.471	121	7	5	5	-2	.951	-7	O-80	-0.5
1924	Chi-A	138	526	77	185	37	8	6	99	47	21	.352	.406	.487	134	26	6	6	-2	.970	10	*O-134	2.4
1925	Chi-A	154	602	80	181	35	9	4	99	51	25	.301	.357	.409	99	-2	4	5	-2	.959	-4	*O-153	-1.7
1926	Chi-A	155	566	86	195	43	4	8	108	66	22	.345	.415	.477	137	32	9	10	-3	.992	8	*O-155	2.4
1927	Chi-A	145	535	76	175	35	6	9	83	52	19	.327	.391	.465	125	19	5	7	-3	.978	18	*O-145	2.4
1928	Chi-A	98	286	42	83	18	4	1	37	25	16	.290	.347	.392	95	-2	5	1	1	.972	2	O-78	-0.4
1929	Cle-A	125	426	65	133	30	7	13	93	42	14	.312	.374	.507	120	12	4	4	-1	.943	-4	*O-120	-0.1
1930	Cle-A	82	191	34	62	12	1	4	36	23	8	.325	.397	.461	113	4	2	0	1	.967	1	O-42	0.3
1931	Cle-A	79	161	30	49	13	1	2	28	17	13	.304	.371	.435	105	1	1	1	-0	.949	-3	O-33	-0.4
Total	12	1353	4652	655	1463	300	59	69	784	412	279	.314	.372	.449	113	82	47	49	-15	.967	-4	*O-1222	-1.7

■ CHARLIE FALLON   Fallon, Charles Augustus   b: 3/7/1881, New York, N.Y.   d: 6/10/60, Kings Park, N.Y.   BR/TR, 5'6",   Deb: 6/30/05

YEAR	TM/L	G	AB	R	H	2B	3B	HR	RBI	BB	SO	AVG	OBP	SLG	PRO+	BR/A	SB	CS	SBR	FA	FR	G/POS	TPR
1905	NY-A	1	0	0	0	0	0	0	0	0	0	—	—	—	—	0	0	0		.000	0	R	0.0

■ GEORGE FALLON   Fallon, George Decatur "Flash"   b: 7/8/16, Jersey City, N.J.   BR/TR, 5'9", 155 lbs.   Deb: 9/27/37

YEAR	TM/L	G	AB	R	H	2B	3B	HR	RBI	BB	SO	AVG	OBP	SLG	PRO+	BR/A	SB	CS	SBR	FA	FR	G/POS	TPR
1937	Bro-N	4	8	0	2	1	0	0	1	0	0	.250	.333	.375	91	-0	0			.895	1	/2-4	0.1
1943	StL-N	36	78	6	18	1	0	0	5	2	9	.231	.259	.244	44	-6	0			.968	15	2-36	1.1
1944	*StL-N	69	141	16	28	6	0	1	9	16	11	.199	.282	.262	54	-8	1			.973	4	2-38,S-24/3	-0.2
1945	StL-N	24	55	4	13	2	1	0	7	6	6	.236	.311	.309	71	-2	1			.948	-2	S-20/2-4	-0.3
Total	4	133	282	26	61	10	1	1	21	25	26	.216	.285	.270	56	-16	2			.966	18	/2-82,S-44,3	0.7

■ PETE FALSEY   Falsey, Peter James   b: 4/24/1891, New Haven, Conn.   d: 5/23/76, Los Angeles, Cal.   BL/TL, 5'6.5", 132 lbs.   Deb: 7/16/14

YEAR	TM/L	G	AB	R	H	2B	3B	HR	RBI	BB	SO	AVG	OBP	SLG	PRO+	BR/A	SB	CS	SBR	FA	FR	G/POS	TPR
1914	Pit-N	3	1	0	0	0	0	0	0	0	1	.000	.000	.000	-99	-0	0			.000	0	H	0.0

■ RIKKERT FANEYTE   Faneyte, Rikkert   b: 5/31/69, Amsterdam, Holland   BR/TR, 6'1", 170 lbs.   Deb: 8/29/93

YEAR	TM/L	G	AB	R	H	2B	3B	HR	RBI	BB	SO	AVG	OBP	SLG	PRO+	BR/A	SB	CS	SBR	FA	FR	G/POS	TPR
1993	SF-N	7	15	2	2	0	0	0	0	2	4	.133	.235	.133	2	-3	0	0	0	1.000	-1	/O-6	-0.3
1994	SF-N	19	26	1	3	3	0	0	4	3	11	.115	.207	.231	14	-3	0	0	0	.900	-1	/O-6	-0.4
Total	2	26	41	3	5	3	0	0	4	5	15	.122	.217	.195	10	-5	0	0	0	.950	-2	/O-12	-0.7

■ JIM FANNING   Fanning, William James   b: 9/14/27, Chicago, Ill.   BR/TR, 5'11", 180 lbs.   Deb: 9/11/54   MC

YEAR	TM/L	G	AB	R	H	2B	3B	HR	RBI	BB	SO	AVG	OBP	SLG	PRO+	BR/A	SB	CS	SBR	FA	FR	G/POS	TPR
1954	Chi-N	11	38	2	7	0	0	0	1	1	7	.184	.205	.184	2	-5	0	0	0	1.000	-1	C-11	-0.6
1955	Chi-N	5	10	0	0	0	0	0	0	1	2	.000	.091	.000	-73	-3	0	0	0	1.000	3	/C-5	0.1
1956	Chi-N	1	4	0	1	0	0	0	0	0	0	.250	.250	.250	36	-0	0	0	0	.800	1	/C-1	0.0
1957	Chi-N	47	89	3	16	2	0	0	4	4	17	.180	.223	.202	16	-11	0	0	0	.981	2	C-35	-0.7
Total	4	64	141	5	24	2	0	0	5	6	26	.170	.209	.184	6	-19	0	0	0	.979	5	/C-52	-1.2

■ CARMEN FANZONE   Fanzone, Carmen Ronald   b: 8/30/43, Detroit, Mich.   BR/TR, 6', 200 lbs.   Deb: 7/21/70

YEAR	TM/L	G	AB	R	H	2B	3B	HR	RBI	BB	SO	AVG	OBP	SLG	PRO+	BR/A	SB	CS	SBR	FA	FR	G/POS	TPR
1970	Bos-A	10	15	0	3	1	0	0	3	0	3	.200	.333	.267	63	-1	0	0	0	.750	0	/3-5	-0.1
1971	Chi-N	12	43	5	8	2	0	2	5	2	7	.186	.222	.372	57	-3	0	0	0	1.000	0	/O-6,3-3,1	-0.3
1972	Chi-N	86	222	26	50	11	0	8	42	35	45	.225	.338	.383	95	-1	2	3	-1	.923	3	3-36,1-21,2/SO	0.0
1973	Chi-N	64	150	22	41	7	0	6	22	20	38	.273	.359	.440	112	3	1	2	-0	.922	-3	3-25,1-24/O	-0.3
1974	Chi-N	65	158	13	30	6	0	4	22	15	27	.190	.269	.304	57	-9	0	1	-1	.885	-1	3-35,2-10/1O	-1.2
Total	5	237	588	66	132	27	0	20	94	74	119	.224	.317	.372	86	-11	3	6	-3	.896	-1	3-104/1-54,20S	-1.9

■ PAUL FARIES   Faries, Paul Tyrrell   b: 2/20/65, Berkeley, Cal.   BR/TR, 5'10", 165 lbs.   Deb: 9/6/90

YEAR	TM/L	G	AB	R	H	2B	3B	HR	RBI	BB	SO	AVG	OBP	SLG	PRO+	BR/A	SB	CS	SBR	FA	FR	G/POS	TPR
1990	SD-N	14	37	4	7	1	0	0	2	4	7	.189	.286	.216	40	-3	0	1	-1	1.000	6	/2-7,S-4,3	0.3
1991	SD-N	57	130	13	23	3	1	0	7	14	21	.177	.262	.215	35	-11	3	1	0	.988	2	2-36,3-12/S	-0.2
1992	SD-N	10	11	3	5	1	0	0	1	1	2	.455	.500	.545	193	1	0	0	0	1.000	-2	/2-4,3-2,S	0.2
1993	SF-N	15	36	6	8	2	1	0	4	1	4	.222	.243	.333	54	-2	2	0	1	1.000	-1	/2-7,S-4,3	-0.3
Total	4	96	214	26	43	7	2	0	14	20	34	.201	.275	.252	47	-15	5	2	0	.992	11	/2-54,S-17,3	-0.2

■ MONTY FARISS   Fariss, Monty Ted   b: 10/13/67, Cordell, Okla.   BR/TR, 6'4", 180 lbs.   Deb: 9/6/91

YEAR	TM/L	G	AB	R	H	2B	3B	HR	RBI	BB	SO	AVG	OBP	SLG	PRO+	BR/A	SB	CS	SBR	FA	FR	G/POS	TPR
1991	Tex-A	19	31	6	8	1	0	1	6	7	11	.258	.395	.387	119	1	0	0	4	/O-8,2-4,D	0.5
1992	Tex-A	67	166	13	36	7	1	3	21	17	51	.217	.297	.325	77	-5	0	2	-1	1.000	-15	O-49,2-17/1D	-2.3
1993	Fla-N	18	29	3	5	2	1	0	2	5	13	.172	.294	.310	59	-2	0	0	0	1.000	-1	/O-8	-0.2
Total	3	104	226	22	49	10	2	4	29	29	75	.217	.311	.332	81	-6	0	2	-1	1.000	-12	/O-65,2-21,D1	-2.0

■ BOB FARLEY   Farley, Robert Jacob   b: 11/15/37, Watsontown, Pa.   BL/TL, 6'2", 200 lbs.   Deb: 4/15/61

YEAR	TM/L	G	AB	R	H	2B	3B	HR	RBI	BB	SO	AVG	OBP	SLG	PRO+	BR/A	SB	CS	SBR	FA	FR	G/POS	TPR
1961	SF-N	13	20	3	2	0	0	0	1	3	5	.100	.217	.100	-13	-3	0	0	0	1.000	-1	/O-3,1-1	-0.4
1962	Chi-A	35	53	7	10	1	1	1	4	13	13	.189	.348	.302	77	-1	0	1	-1	.989	-1	1-14	-0.4
	Det-A	36	50	9	8	2	0	1	4	14	10	.160	.344	.260	63	-2	0	0	0	.857	-4	O-11/1-6	-0.7
	Yr	71	103	16	18	3	1	2	8	27	23	.175	.346	.282	70	-3	0	1	-1	.974	-5	1-20,O-11	-1.1
Total	2	84	123	19	20	3	1	2	9	30	28	.163	.327	.252	58	-7	0	1	-1	.975	-6	/1-21,O-14	-1.5

■ TOM FARLEY   Farley, Thomas T.   b: Chicago, Ill.   Deb: 6/24/1884

YEAR	TM/L	G	AB	R	H	2B	3B	HR	RBI	BB	SO	AVG	OBP	SLG	PRO+	BR/A	SB	CS	SBR	FA	FR	G/POS	TPR
1884	Was-a	14	52	5	11	4	0	0		1		.212	.241	.288	81	-1				.867	1	O-14	0.0

■ ALEX FARMER   Farmer, Alexander Johnson   b: 5/9/1880, New York, N.Y.   d: 3/5/20, New York, N.Y.   BR/TR, 6', 175 lbs.   Deb: 9/1/08

YEAR	TM/L	G	AB	R	H	2B	3B	HR	RBI	BB	SO	AVG	OBP	SLG	PRO+	BR/A	SB	CS	SBR	FA	FR	G/POS	TPR
1908	Bro-N	12	30	1	5	1	0	0	2	1		.167	.194	.200	27	-3	0			.966	-0	C-11	-0.2

■ JACK FARMER   Farmer, Floyd Haskell   b: 7/14/1892, Granville, Tenn.   d: 5/21/70, Columbia, La.   BR/TR, 6', 180 lbs.   Deb: 7/8/16

YEAR	TM/L	G	AB	R	H	2B	3B	HR	RBI	BB	SO	AVG	OBP	SLG	PRO+	BR/A	SB	CS	SBR	FA	FR	G/POS	TPR
1916	Pit-N	55	166	10	45	6	4	0	14	7	24	.271	.309	.355	103	0	1			.929	-9	2-31,O-15/S3	-1.0
1918	Cle-A	7	9	1	2	0	0	0	1	0	3	.222	.300	.222	53	-0	2			.429	-2	/O-3	-0.3
Total	2	62	175	11	47	6	4	0	15	7	27	.269	.308	.349	100	-0	3			.829	-11	/2-31,O-18,S3	-1.3

■ BILL FARMER   Farmer, William   b: 12/27/1870,   BR/TR, 5'11.5",   Deb: 5/1/1888

YEAR	TM/L	G	AB	R	H	2B	3B	HR	RBI	BB	SO	AVG	OBP	SLG	PRO+	BR/A	SB	CS	SBR	FA	FR	G/POS	TPR
1888	Pit-N	2	4	0	0	0	0	0	0	0	1	.000	.000	.000	-99	-1	0			.667	0	/C-1,O-1	-0.1
	Phi-a	3	12	0	2	0	0	0	1	0		.167	.167	.167	7	-1	0			.960	0	/C-3	-0.1
Total	1	5	16	0	2	0	0	0	1	0	1	.125	.125	.125	-20	-2	0			.903	1	/C-4,O-1	-0.2

■ SID FARRAR   Farrar, Sidney Douglas   b: 8/10/1859, Paris Hill, Me.   d: 5/7/35, New York, N.Y.   TR, 5'10", 185 lbs.   Deb: 5/1/1883

YEAR	TM/L	G	AB	R	H	2B	3B	HR	RBI	BB	SO	AVG	OBP	SLG	PRO+	BR/A	SB	CS	SBR	FA	FR	G/POS	TPR
1883	Phi-N	99	377	41	88	19	8	0	29	4	37	.233	.241	.326	77	-9				.965	-0	*1-99	-1.7
1884	Phi-N	111	428	62	105	16	6	1	45	9	25	.245	.261	.318	85	-7				.966	5	*1-111	-1.4
1885	Phi-N	111	420	49	103	20	3	3	36	28	34	.245	.292	.329	103	2				.975	2	*1-111	-0.9
1886	Phi-N	118	439	55	109	19	7	5	50	16	47	.248	.275	.358	90	-6	10			.980	3	*1-118	-1.6
1887	Phi-N	116	443	83	125	20	9	4	72	42	29	.282	.358	.395	103	1	24			.977	3	*1-116	-0.7
1888	Phi-N	131	508	53	124	24	7	1	53	31	38	.244	.304	.325	96	-3	21			.979	3	*1-131	-1.2
1889	Phi-N	130	477	70	128	22	3	3	58	52	36	.268	.348	.342	86	-2	15			.978	-5	*1-130	-2.1
1890	Phi-P	127	481	84	122	17	11	1	69	51	23	.254	.331	.341	78	-16	9			.973	-2	*1-127	-2.0
Total	8	943	3573	497	904	157	53	18	412	233	269	.253	.305	.342	90	-48	92			.974	8	1-943	-11.6

YEAR	TM/L	G	AB	R	H	2B	3B	HR	RBI	BB	SO	AVG	OBP	SLG	PRO+	BR/A	SB	CS	SBR	FA	FR	G/POS	TPR
■ **DUKE FARRELL**					Farrell, Charles Andrew			b: 8/31/1866, Oakdale, Mass.			d: 2/15/25, Boston, Mass.		BB/TR, 6'1", 208 lbs.			Deb: 4/21/1888							
1888	Chi-N	64	241	34	56	6	3	1	19	4	41	.232	.245	.320	73	-8	8			.874	-12	C-33,O-31/1	-1.7
1889	Chi-N	101	407	66	101	19	3	7	75	41	21	.248	.318	.410	98	-3	13			.910	4	C-76,O-25	0.6
1890	Chi-P	117	451	79	131	21	12	2	84	42	28	.290	.352	.404	98	-3	8			.929	**27**	C-90,1-22,O	2.4
1891	Bos-a	122	473	108	143	19	13	**12**	**110**	59	48	.302	.384	.474	147	28	21			.918	19	3-66,C-37,O/1	**4.4**
1892	Pit-N	152	605	96	130	10	13	8	77	46	53	.215	.276	.314	78	-18	20			.879	-3	*3-133,O-20	-1.6
1893	Was-N	124	511	84	143	13	13	4	75	47	12	.280	.346	.380	95	-4	11			.923	14	C-81,3-41/1	1.4
1894	*NY-N	114	401	47	114	20	12	4	66	35	15	.284	.346	.424	86	-11	9			.926	29	*C-104/3-5,1	2.2
1895	NY-N	90	312	38	90	16	9	1	58	38	18	.288	.371	.407	103	2	11			.941	-4	C-62,3-24/1	1.0
1896	NY-N	58	191	23	54	7	3	1	37	19	7	.283	.351	.366	92	-2	2			.954	-7	C-34,S-13/3	-0.4
	Was-N	37	130	18	39	7	3	1	30	7	3	.300	.345	.423	102	-0	2			1.000	-1	C-18,3-14	0.1
	Yr	95	321	41	93	14	6	2	67	26	10	.290	.349	.389	96	-2	4			.970	-7	C-52,3-21,S	-0.3
1897	Was-N	78	261	41	84	9	6	0	53	17		.322	.366	.402	103	1	8			.945	9	C-63/1-1	1.5
1898	Was-N	99	338	47	106	12	6	1	53	34		.314	.383	.393	123	11	12			.929	-6	C-61,1-28	1.0
1899	Was-N	5	12	2	4	1	0	0	1	2		.333	.429	.417	134	1	1			1.000	-0	/C-4	0.1
	Bro-N	80	254	40	76	10	7	2	55	35		.299	.399	.417	121	9	6			.948	11	C-78	2.3
	Yr	85	266	42	80	11	7	2	56	37		.301	.400	.417	122	9	7			.949	10	C-82	2.4
1900	*Bro-N	76	273	33	75	11	5	0	39	11		.275	.310	.352	78	-9	3			.944	-4	C-74	-0.6
1901	Bro-N	80	284	38	84	10	6	1	31	7		.296	.320	.384	101	-1	7			.979	6	C-59,1-17	1.1
1902	Bro-N	74	264	14	64	5	2	0	24	12		.242	.281	.277	71	-9	6			.976	7	C-49,1-24	0.3
1903	*Bos-A	17	52	5	21	5	1	0	8	5		.404	.466	.538	190	6	1			.960	-0	C-17	0.8
1904	Bos-A	68	198	11	42	9	2	0	15	15		.212	.281	.278	73	-8	1			.958	-7	C-56	-0.7
1905	Bos-A	7	21	2	6	1	0	0	2	1		.286	.318	.333	105	0	0			1.000	2	/C-7	0.3
Total	18	1563	5679	826	1563	211	123	51	912	477	246	.275	.337	.383	99	-17	150			.938	91	*C-1003,3-290,O1/S	14.5
■ **DOC FARRELL**					Farrell, Edward Stephen			b: 12/26/01, Johnson City, N.Y.			d: 12/20/66, Livingston, N.J.		BR/TR, 5'8", 160 lbs.		Deb: 6/15/25								
1925	NY-N	27	56	6	12	1	0	0	4	4	6	.214	.267	.232	30	-6	0	1	-1	.900	2	S-13/3-7,2	-0.4
1926	NY-N	67	171	19	49	10	1	2	23	12	17	.287	.341	.392	98	-1	4			.950	-11	S-53/2-3	-0.7
1927	NY-N	42	142	13	55	10	1	3	34	12	11	.387	.442	.535	161	12	0			.919	-1	S-36/3-2	1.5
	Bos-N	110	424	44	124	13	2	1	58	14	21	.292	.315	.340	82	-12	4			.931	-4	S-57,2-40,3	-0.8
	Yr	152	566	57	179	23	3	4	92	26	32	.316	.348	.389	103	1	4			.926	-4	S-93,2-40,3	0.7
1928	Bos-N	134	483	36	104	14	2	3	43	26	26	.215	.263	.271	42	-42	3			.933	-17	*S-132/2-1	-4.3
1929	Bos-N	5	8	0	1	0	0	0	2	0	1	.125	.125	.125	-39	-2	0			.000	-1	/2-1,S-1	-0.2
	NY-N	63	178	18	38	6	0	0	16	9	17	.213	.251	.247	24	-21	2			.925	7	3-28,2-25/S	-1.1
	Yr	68	186	18	39	6	0	0	18	9	18	.210	.246	.242	22	-23	2			.925	7	3-28,2-26/S	-1.3
1930	StL-N	23	61	3	13	1	1	0	6	4	2	.213	.262	.262	26	-7	1			.944	2	S-15/2-6,1	-0.4
	Chi-N	46	113	21	33	6	0	1	16	9	5	.292	.344	.372	73	-5	0			.937	3	S-38/2-1	0.2
	Yr	69	174	24	46	7	1	1	22	13	7	.264	.316	.333	56	-12	1			.938	5	S-53/2-7,1	-0.2
1932	NY-A	26	63	4	11	1	0	0	4	2	8	.175	.212	.222	13	-8	0	0	0	.963	-4	2-16/S-5,13	-0.7
1933	NY-A	44	93	16	25	0	0	0	6	16	6	.269	.376	.269	78	-2	0	0	0	.947	-4	S-22,2-20	-0.4
1935	Bos-A	4	7	1	2	1	0	0	1	1	0	.286	.375	.429	101	0	0	0	0	.917	-1	/2-4	0.0
Total	9	591	1799	181	467	63	8	10	213	109	120	.260	.306	.320	66	-93	14	1		.934	-24	S-376,2-118/31	-7.3
■ **JACK FARRELL**					Farrell, John "Hartford Jack"			b: 1/2/1856, Hartford, Conn.			d: 11/15/16, Hartford, Conn.			Deb: 10/27/1874								
1874	Har-n	3	14	3	5	0	0	0		0		.357	.357	.357	122	0						/O-3	0.0
■ **JACK FARRELL**					Farrell, John A. "Moose"			b: 7/5/1857, Newark, N.J.			d: 2/10/14, Overbrook, N.J.		BR/TR, 5'9", 165 lbs.		Deb: 5/1/1879 M							
1879	Syr-N	54	241	40	73	6	2	1	21	3	13	.303	.311	.357	135	9				.870	-15	2-54	-0.2
	Pro-N	12	51	5	13	2	0	0	5	0	0	.255	.255	.294	82	-1				.915	7	2-12	0.6
	Yr	66	292	45	86	8	2	1	26	3	13	.295	.302	.346	125	8				.879	-7	2-66	0.4
1880	Pro-N	80	339	46	92	12	5	3	36	10	6	.271	.292	.363	125	9				.887	-8	*2-80	0.4
1881	Pro-N	84	345	69	82	16	5	5	36	29	23	.238	.297	.357	106	3				.881	-5	*2-82/O-3M	0.1
1882	Pro-N	84	366	67	93	21	6	2	31	16	23	.254	.285	.361	106	2				.875	-5	*2-84	-0.1
1883	Pro-N	95	420	92	128	24	11	3	61	15	21	.305	.329	.436	126	12				**.924**	25	*2-95	3.3
1884	*Pro-N	111	469	70	102	13	6	1	37	35	44	.217	.272	.277	75	-12				.922	-4	*2-109/3-3	-1.2
1885	Pro-N	68	257	27	53	7	1	1	19	10	25	.206	.236	.253	61	-11				.900	-15	2-68	-2.3
1886	Phi-N	17	60	7	11	0	1	0	3	3	11	.183	.222	.217	34	-5	1			.825	-3	2-17	-0.6
	Was-N	47	171	24	41	11	4	2	18	15	12	.240	.301	.386	114	3	12			.913	-13	2-47	-0.7
	Yr	64	231	31	52	11	5	2	21	18	23	.225	.281	.342	92	-2	13			.888	-15	2-64	-1.3
1887	Was-N	87	339	40	75	14	9	0	41	20	12	.221	.267	.316	64	-16	31			.876	-8	S-48,2-40	-1.9
1888	Bal-a	103	398	72	81	19	4	0	36	26		.204	.256	.307	82	-8	29			.902	11	S-54,2-52	0.6
1889	Bal-a	42	157	25	33	3	0	1	26	9	15	.210	.287	.248	52	-10	14			.891	-6	S-42	-1.1
Total	11	884	3613	584	877	148	55	23	370	197	205	.243	.283	.333	94	-24	87			.899	-38	2-740,S-144/3O	-3.1
■ **JACK FARRELL**					Farrell, John J.			b: 6/16/1892, Chicago, Ill.			d: 3/24/18, Chicago, Ill.		BB/TR, 5'8", 145 lbs.		Deb: 4/16/14							
1914	Chi-F	156	524	58	123	23	4	0	35	52	65	.235	.307	.294	60	-32	12			.954	0	*2-155/S-3	-3.4
1915	Chi-F	70	222	27	48	10	1	0	14	25	18	.216	.298	.270	56	-14	8			.941	-5	2-70/S-1	-1.9
Total	2	226	746	85	171	33	5	0	49	77	83	.229	.305	.287	59	-46	20			.950	-4	2-225/S-4	-5.3
■ **JOHN FARRELL**					Farrell, John Sebastian			b: 12/4/1876, Covington, Ky.			d: 5/13/21, Kansas City, Mo.		BR/TR, 5'10", 160 lbs.		Deb: 4/26/01							
1901	Was-A	135	555	100	151	32	11	3	63	52		.272	.336	.386	101	1	25			.915	17	2-72,O-62/3	1.4
1902	StL-N	138	565	68	141	13	5	0	25	43		.250	.308	.290	88	-7	9			.947	**34**	*2-118,S-21	3.3
1903	StL-N	130	519	83	141	25	8	1	32	48		.272	.336	.356	100	0	17			.927	**28**	*2-118,O-12	3.0
1904	StL-N	131	509	72	130	23	3	0	20	46		.255	.320	.312	100	1	16			.934	16	*2-130	2.1
1905	StL-N	7	24	6	4	0	1	0	1	4		.167	.286	.250	62	-1	1			.892	-3	/2-7	-0.4
Total	5	541	2172	329	567	93	28	4	141	193		.261	.324	.335	97	-6	68			.932	92	2-445/O-74,S3	9.4
■ **JOE FARRELL**					Farrell, Joseph F.			b: 1857, Brooklyn, N.Y.			d: 4/18/1893, Brooklyn, N.Y.		BR, 5'6", 160 lbs.		Deb: 5/1/1882							
1882	Det-N	69	283	34	70	12	2	1	24	4	20	.247	.258	.314	83	-6				.816	-11	3-42,2-18/S	-1.4
1883	Det-N	101	444	58	108	13	5	0	36	5	29	.243	.252	.295	69	-16				.845	13	*3-101	-0.3
1884	Det-N	110	461	59	104	10	5	3	41	14	66	.226	.248	.289	73	-14				.842	-7	*3-110/O-1	-1.8
1886	Bal-a	73	301	36	63	8	3	1		12		.209	.240	.266	60	-14	5			.870	-15	2-45,3-27/O	-2.4
Total	4	353	1489	187	345	43	15	5	101	35	115	.232	.249	.291	71	-49	5			.840	-21	3-280/2-63,SO	-5.9
■ **KERBY FARRELL**					Farrell, Major Kerby			b: 9/3/13, Leapwood, Tenn.			d: 12/17/75, Nashville, Tenn.		BL/TL, 5'11", 172 lbs.		Deb: 4/24/43 MC							
1943	Bos-N	85	280	11	75	14	6	0	21	16	15	.268	.307	.325	84	-6	1			.996	2	1-69/P-5	-0.9
1945	Chi-A	103	396	44	102	11	3	0	34	24	18	.258	.300	.301	76	-12	4	9	-4	.989	-0	1-97	-2.5
Total	2	188	676	55	177	25	4	0	55	40	33	.262	.303	.311	80	-19	5	9		.992	1	1-166/P-5	-3.4
■ **BILL FARRELL**					Farrell, William			Deb: 5/3/1882															
1882	Phi-a	2	7	2	2	1	0	0		1		.286	.375	.429	153	0				.000	-1	/O-2,C-1	-0.1
1883	Bal-a	2	7	0	0	0	0	0		1		.000	.125	.000	-55	-1				.750	-1	/S-2	-0.2
Total	2	4	14	2	2	1	0	0		2		.143	.250	.214	51	-1				.750	-2	/S-2,O-2,C	-0.3

YEAR	TM/L	G	AB	R	H	2B	3B	HR	RBI	BB	SO	AVG	OBP	SLG	PRO+	BR/A	SB	CS	SBR	FA	FR	G/POS	TPR
■ JOHN FARROW	Farrow, John Jacob b: 11/8/1853, Verplanck, N.Y. d: 12/31/14, Perth Amboy, N.J. BL/TR, Deb: 4/28/1873																						
1873	Res-n	12	48	2	8	1	0	0	3	0	3	.167	.167	.188	4	-5						/C-9,O-3,1S	-0.4
1874	Atl-n	27	121	16	26	3	0	0		1		.215	.221	.240	53	-5						C-15,2-12	-0.4
1884	Bro-a	16	58	7	11	2	0	0			3	.190	.230	.224	48	-3				.915	-1	C-16	-0.2
Total	2 n	39	169	18	34	4	0	0	3	1	3	.201	.206	.225	38	-11						/C-24,2-12,OS1	-0.8
■ BUCK FAUSETT	Fausett, Robert Shaw "Leaky" b: 4/8/08, Sheridan, Ark. d: 5/2/94, College Station, Tex. BL/TR, 5'10", 170 lbs. Deb: 4/18/44																						
1944	Cin-N	13	31	2	3	0	1	0	1	1	2	.097	.125	.161	-21	-5	0			1.000	3	/3-6,P-2	-0.1
■ JOE FAUTSCH	Fautsch, Joseph Roamon b: 2/28/1887, Minneapolis, Minn. d: 3/16/71, New Hope, Minn. BR/TR, 5'10", 162 lbs. Deb: 4/24/16																						
1916	Chi-A	1	0	0	0	0	0	0	0			.000	.000	.000	-99	-0				.000	0	H	0.0
■ ERNIE FAZIO	Fazio, Ernest Joseph b: 1/25/42, Oakland, Cal. BR/TR, 5'7", 165 lbs. Deb: 7/3/62																						
1962	Hou-N	12	12	3	1	0	0	0	1	2	5	.083	.214	.083	-18	-2	0	0	0	.783	-0	S-10	-0.1
1963	Hou-N	102	228	31	42	10	3	2	5	27	70	.184	.273	.281	64	-11	4	4	-1	.972	-11	2-84/S-1,3	-1.8
1966	KC-A	27	34	3	7	0	1	0	2	4	10	.206	.289	.265	62	-2	1	0	0	1.000	2	2-10/S-4	0.1
Total	3	141	274	37	50	10	4	2	8	33	85	.182	.273	.270	60	-14	5	4	-1	.974	-9	/2-94,S-15,3	-1.8
■ AL FEDEROFF	Federoff, Alfred "Whitey" b: 7/11/24, Bairdford, Pa. BR/TR, 5'10.5", 165 lbs. Deb: 9/27/51																						
1951	Det-A	2	4	0	0	0	0	0	0	0	0	.000	.000	.000	-99	-1	0	0	0	.889	0	/2-1	0.0
1952	Det-A	74	231	14	56	4	2	0	14	16	13	.242	.294	.277	59	-13	1	0	0	.976	0	2-70/S-7	-0.9
Total	2	76	235	14	56	4	2	0	14	16	13	.238	.290	.272	56	-14	1	0	0	.973	1	/2-71,S-7	-0.9
■ BILL FEHRING	Fehring, William Paul "Dutch" b: 5/31/12, Columbus, Ind. BB/TR, 6', 195 lbs. Deb: 6/25/34																						
1934	Chi-A	1	1	0	0	0	0	0	0	0	1	.000	.000	.000	-97	-0	0	0	0	1.000	0	/C-1	0.0
■ EDDIE FEINBERG	Feinberg, Edward Isadore "Itzzy" b: 9/29/17, Philadelphia, Pa. d: 4/20/86, Hollywood, Fla. BB/TR, 5'9", 165 lbs. Deb: 9/11/38																						
1938	Phi-N	10	20	0	3	0	0	0	0	0	1	.150	.150	.150	-18	-3	0			.957	3	/S-4,O-2	0.0
1939	Phi-N	6	18	2	4	1	0	0	0	2	0	.222	.300	.278	58	-1	0			.909	-4	/2-4,S-1	-0.5
Total	2	16	38	2	7	1	0	0	0	2	1	.184	.225	.211	20	-4	0			.957	-2	/S-5,2-4,O	-0.5
■ MIKE FELDER	Felder, Michael Otis b: 11/18/61, Vallejo, Cal. BB/TR, 5'8", 160 lbs. Deb: 9/11/85																						
1985	Mil-A	15	56	8	11	1	0	0		5	6	.196	.262	.214	33	-5	4	1	1	1.000	-0	O-14	-0.5
1986	Mil-A	44	155	24	37	2	4	1	13	13	16	.239	.298	.323	67	-7	16	2	4	1.000	2	O-42/D-1	-0.3
1987	Mil-A	108	289	48	77	5	7	2	31	28	23	.266	.331	.353	79	-8	34	8	5	.975	1	O-99/2-1,D	-0.4
1988	Mil-A	50	81	14	14	1	0	0	5	0	11	.173	.183	.185	3	-10	8	2	1	.976	-5	O-28,D-16/2	-1.5
1989	Mil-A	117	315	50	76	11	3	3	23	23	38	.241	.293	.324	74	-11	26	5	5	.985	-1	O-93,D-11,2	-0.9
1990	Mil-A	121	237	38	65	7	2	3	27	22	17	.274	.336	.359	95	-1	20	9	1	.972	-12	*O-109/2-1,3D	-1.5
1991	SF-N	132	348	53	92	10	6	0	18	30	51	.264	.325	.328	87	-6	21	6	3	.985	-11	*O-107/3-3,2	-1.6
1992	SF-N	145	322	44	92	13	4	3	23	21	29	.286	.333	.382	108	3	14	4	2	.994	-20	O-105/2-3	-1.9
1993	Sea-A	109	342	31	72	7	5	1	20	22	34	.211	.262	.269	43	-28	15	9	-1	.987	-3	O-95/3-2,D	-3.3
1994	Hou-N	58	117	10	28	2	2	0	13	4	12	.239	.264	.291	46	-9	3	0	1	.974	-6	O-32	-1.4
Total	10	899	2262	318	564	59	32	14	173	168	217	.249	.303	.322	73	-83	161	46	21	.984	-55	O-724/D-38,23	-13.3
■ MARV FELDERMAN	Felderman, Marvin Wilfred "Coonie" b: 12/20/15, Bellevue, Iowa BR/TR, 6'1", 187 lbs. Deb: 4/19/42																						
1942	Chi-N	3	6	0	1	0	0	0	0	0	4	.167	.286	.167	35	-0				1.000	1	/C-2	0.0
■ GUS FELIX	Felix, August Guenther b: 5/24/1895, Cincinnati, Ohio d: 5/12/60, Montgomery, Ala. BR/TR, 6', 180 lbs. Deb: 4/19/23																						
1923	Bos-N	139	506	64	138	17	2	6	44	51	65	.273	.348	.350	88	-8	8	13	-5	.950	0	*O-123/2-5,3	-2.0
1924	Bos-N	59	204	25	43	7	1	1	10	18	16	.211	.275	.270	48	-15	0	3	-2	.950	5	O-51	-1.5
1925	Bos-N	121	459	60	141	25	7	2	66	30	34	.307	.356	.405	103	2	5	5	-2	.972	10	*O-114	0.3
1926	Bro-N	134	432	64	121	21	7	3	53	51	32	.280	.360	.382	101	2	9			.956	-2	*O-125	-0.8
1927	Bro-N	130	445	43	118	21	8	0	57	39	47	.265	.327	.348	81	-12	6			.947	-3	*O-119	-2.2
Total	5	583	2046	256	561	91	25	12	230	189	194	.274	.341	.361	89	-31	28	21		.957	11	O-532/2-5,3	-6.2
■ JUNIOR FELIX	Felix, Junior Francisco (Sanchez) b: 10/3/67, Laguna Salada, D.R. BB/TR, 6', 170 lbs. Deb: 5/3/89																						
1989	*Tor-A	110	415	62	107	14	8	9	46	33	101	.258	.317	.395	101	0	18	12	-2	.966	3	*O-107/D-2	-0.1
1990	Tor-A	127	463	73	122	23	7	15	65	45	99	.263	.331	.441	112	7	13	8	-1	.966	2	*O-125/D-1	0.4
1991	Cal-A	66	230	32	65	10	2	2	26	11	55	.283	.324	.370	91	-3	7	5	-1	.977	-6	O-65	-1.1
1992	Cal-A	139	509	63	125	22	5	9	72	33	128	.246	.294	.361	82	-13	8	8	-2	.983	7	O-128/D-8	-1.2
1993	Fla-N	57	214	25	51	11	1	7	22	10	50	.238	.276	.397	73	-9	2	1	0	.940	-2	O-52	-1.2
1994	Det-A	86	301	54	92	25	1	13	49	26	76	.306	.356	.525	130	13	1	6	-3	.980	5	O-81/D-2	1.2
Total	6	585	2132	309	562	105	24	55	280	158	509	.264	.320	.413	100	-5	49	40	-9	.972	8	O-558/D-13	-2.0
■ JACK FELLER	Feller, Jack Leland b: 12/10/36, Adrian, Mich. BR/TR, 5'10.5", 185 lbs. Deb: 9/13/58																						
1958	Det-A	1	0	0	0	0	0	0	0	0	0	—	—	—		0	0	0	0	1.000	-0	/C-1	0.0
■ HAPPY FELSCH	Felsch, Oscar Emil b: 8/22/1891, Milwaukee, Wis. d: 8/17/64, Milwaukee, Wis. BR/TR, 5'11", 175 lbs. Deb: 4/14/15																						
1915	Chi-A	121	427	65	106	18	11	3	53	51	59	.248	.334	.363	105	2	16	18	-6	.959	-3	*O-118	-1.3
1916	Chi-A	146	546	73	164	24	12	7	70	31	67	.300	.341	.427	129	16	13			**.981**	7	*O-141	1.7
1917	*Chi-A	152	575	75	177	17	10	6	102	33	52	.308	.352	.403	128	17	26			.985	19	*O-152	3.0
1918	Chi-A	53	206	16	52	5	1	0	20	15	13	.252	.306	.325	90	-3	6			.957	-9	*O-53	-0.1
1919	*Chi-A	135	502	68	138	34	11	7	86	40	35	.275	.336	.428	113	7	19			.968	21	*O-135	2.1
1920	Chi-A	142	556	88	188	40	15	14	115	37	25	.338	.384	.540	143	31	8	13	-5	.981	18	*O-142	3.2
Total	6	749	2812	385	825	135	64	38	446	207	251	.293	.347	.427	123	70	88	31		.975	67	O-741	8.6
■ JOHN FELSKE	Felske, John Frederick b: 5/30/42, Chicago, Ill. BR/TR, 6'3", 195 lbs. Deb: 7/26/68 MC																						
1968	Chi-N	4	2	0	0	0	0	0	0	0	0	.000	.000	.000	-94	-0	0	0	0	.833	1	/C-3	0.0
1972	Mil-A	37	80	6	11	3	0	1	5	8	23	.138	.216	.213	28	-7	0	0	0	.972	-2	C-23/1-8	-1.0
1973	Mil-A	13	22	1	3	0	1	0	4	1	11	.136	.174	.227	12	-3	0	0	0	1.000	0	/C-7,1-6	-0.3
Total	3	54	104	7	14	3	1	1	9	9	35	.135	.204	.212	23	-10	0	0	0	.969	-1	/C-33,1-14	-1.3
■ FRANK FENNELLY	Fennelly, Francis John b: 2/18/1860, Fall River, Mass. d: 8/4/20, Fall River, Mass. BR/TR, 5'8", 168 lbs. Deb: 5/1/1884																						
1884	Was-a	62	257	52	75	17	7	2		20		.292	.343	.436	172	21				.863	13	S-60/2-4	3.1
	Cin-a	28	122	42	43	5	8	2		11		.352	.415	.574	209	14				.813	-6	S-28	0.8
	Yr	90	379	94	118	22	15	4		31		.311	.367	.480	186	37				.849	7	S-88/2-4	3.9
1885	Cin-a	112	454	82	124	14	17	10		38		.273	.348	.445	142	21				.873	-11	*S-112	1.0
1886	Cin-a	132	497	113	124	13	17	6		60		.249	.351	.380	125	15	32			.848	14	*S-132	2.6
1887	Cin-a	134	526	133	140	15	16	8		82		.266	.369	.401	112	10	74			.855	-9	*S-134	0.2
1888	Cin-a	120	448	64	88	8	7	2	56	63		.196	.297	.259	75	-12	43			.858	17	*S-112/2-4,O	0.7
	Phi-a	15	47	13	11	2	2	1	12	9		.234	.357	.426	151	3	5			.912	-1	S-15	0.2
	Yr	135	495	77	99	10	9	3	68	72		.200	.303	.275	82	-9	48			.863	16	*S-127/2-4,O	0.9
1889	Phi-a	138	513	79	132	20	5	1	64	65	78	.257	.344	.322	91	-4	15			.872	-20	*S-138	-1.4
1890	Bro-a	45	159	40	44	8	3	2		30		.247	.356	.360	115	0				.858	0	S-38/3-7	0.6
Total	7	786	3042	609	781	102	82	34	132	378	78	.257	.345	.378	118	72	175			.860	-4	S-769/2-8,3O	7.8

YEAR	TM/L	G	AB	R	H	2B	3B	HR	RBI	BB	SO	AVG	OBP	SLG	PRO+	BR/A	SB	CS	SBR	FA	FR	G/POS	TPR

■ BOBBY FENWICK

Fenwick, Robert Richard b: 12/10/46, Naha, Okinawa BR/TR, 5'9", 165 lbs. Deb: 4/26/72

YEAR	TM/L	G	AB	R	H	2B	3B	HR	RBI	BB	SO	AVG	OBP	SLG	PRO+	BR/A	SB	CS	SBR	FA	FR	G/POS	TPR
1972	Hou-N	36	50	7	9	3	0	0	4	3	13	.180	.226	.240	33	-4	0	1	-1	.945	3	2-17/S-4,3	-0.1
1973	StL-N	5	6	0	1	0	0	0	1	0	2	.167	.167	.167	-7	-1	0	0	0	.750	-1	/2-3	-0.2
Total	2	41	56	7	10	3	0	0	5	3	15	.179	.220	.232	29	-5	0	1	-1	.932	3	/2-20,S-4,3	-0.3

■ JOE FERGUSON

Ferguson, Joseph Vance b: 9/19/46, San Francisco, Cal. BR/TR, 6'2", 200 lbs. Deb: 9/12/70 C

YEAR	TM/L	G	AB	R	H	2B	3B	HR	RBI	BB	SO	AVG	OBP	SLG	PRO+	BR/A	SB	CS	SBR	FA	FR	G/POS	TPR
1970	LA-N	5	4	0	1	0	0	0	1	2	2	.250	.500	.250	112	0	0	0	0	1.000	0	/C-3	0.0
1971	LA-N	36	102	13	22	3	0	2	7	12	15	.216	.304	.304	77	-3	1	0	0	.983	-2	C-35	-0.4
1972	LA-N	8	24	2	7	3	0	1	5	2	4	.292	.346	.542	152	2	0	0	0	1.000	2	/C-7,O-2	0.3
1973	LA-N	136	487	84	128	26	0	25	88	87	81	.263	.376	.470	139	27	1	1	-0	.996	-0	*C-122,O-20	3.2
1974	*LA-N	111	349	54	88	14	1	16	57	75	73	.252	.384	.436	134	18	2	2	0	.988	-10	C-82,O-32	1.0
1975	LA-N	66	202	15	42	2	1	5	23	35	47	.208	.328	.302	79	-5	2	1	0	.994	-1	C-35,O-34	-0.6
1976	LA-N	54	185	24	41	7	0	6	18	25	41	.222	.318	.357	93	-2	2	0	1	.966	-1	O-39,C-17	-0.3
	StL-N	71	189	22	38	8	4	4	21	32	40	.201	.320	.349	89	-2	4	2	0	.978	3	C-48,O-14	0.2
	Yr	125	374	46	79	15	4	10	39	57	81	.211	.319	.353	91	-4	6	2	1	.975	2	/2-20,S-4,3	-0.1
1977	Hou-N	132	421	59	108	21	3	16	61	85	79	.257	.381	.435	130	20	6	2	1	.985	-10	*C-122/1-1	1.4
1978	Hou-N	51	150	20	31	5	0	7	22	37	30	.207	.367	.380	118	5	0	0	0	.994	-6	C-51	0.1
	*LA-N	67	198	20	47	11	0	7	28	34	41	.237	.352	.399	110	3	1	2	-1	.984	-10	C-62/O-3	-0.7
	Yr	118	348	40	78	16	0	14	50	71	71	.224	.359	.391	113	8	1	2	-1	.989	-16	*C-113/O-3	-0.6
1979	LA-N	122	363	54	95	14	0	20	69	70	68	.262	.384	.466	133	18	1	0	0	.981	-12	C-67,O-52	0.7
1980	LA-N	77	172	20	41	3	2	9	29	38	46	.238	.376	.436	128	8	2	2	-1	.982	-3	C-66/O-1	0.6
1981	LA-N	17	14	2	2	1	0	0	1	2	5	.143	.250	.214	34	-1	0	0	0	.000	-0	/O-1	-0.2
	Cal-A	12	30	5	7	1	0	1	5	9	8	.233	.410	.367	125	2	0	0	0	.976	0	/C-8,O-4	0.2
1982	Cal-A	36	84	10	19	2	0	3	8	12	19	.226	.323	.357	87	-1	0	0	0	.993	5	C-32/O-2	0.5
1983	Cal-A	12	27	3	2	0	0	0	2	5	8	.074	.219	.074	-15	-4	0	0	0	.968	-2	/C-9,O-3	-0.6
Total	14	1013	3001	407	719	121	11	122	445	562	607	.240	.361	.409	117	84	22	12	-1	.987	-47	C-766,O-207/1	5.4

■ BOB FERGUSON

Ferguson, Robert Vavasour b: 1/31/1845, Brooklyn, N.Y. d: 5/3/1894, Brooklyn, N.Y. BB/TR, 5'9.5", 149 lbs. Deb: 5/18/1871 MU

YEAR	TM/L	G	AB	R	H	2B	3B	HR	RBI	BB	SO	AVG	OBP	SLG	PRO+	BR/A	SB	CS	SBR	FA	FR	G/POS	TPR
1871	Mut-n	33	158	30	38	6	1	0	25	3	2	.241	.255	.291	62	-6	4					3-19,2-10/CPM	-0.5
1872	Atl-n	37	166	33	45	6	0	0	19	3	0	.271	.284	.307	70	-9						*3-35,M	-0.8
1873	Atl-n	51	228	36	59	5	5	0	24	4	9	.259	.272	.325	83	-3						*3-50/P-4M	-0.2
1874	Atl-n	56	246	34	63	5	1	0		1		.256	.259	.285	82	-3						*3-55/C-2,PM	-0.2
1875	Har-n	85	366	66	88	12	4	0				.240	.245	.295	82	-8						*3-84/P-1M	-0.6
1876	Har-N	69	310	48	82	8	5	0	32	2	11	.265	.269	.323	89	-5				.826	2	*3-69,M	-0.1
1877	Har-N	58	254	40	65	7	2	0	35	3	10	.256	.265	.299	86	-3				.841	17	*3-56/P-3M	1.4
1878	Chi-N	61	259	44	91	10	2	0	39	10	12	.351	.375	.405	147	12				.881	16	*S-57/2-4,CM	2.8
1879	Tro-N	30	123	18	31	5	0	0	4	4	3	.252	.276	.325	104	1				.808	2	3-24/2-6M	0.4
1880	Tro-N	82	332	55	87	9	0	0	22	24	24	.262	.312	.289	100	0				.904	-3	*2-82,M	0.1
1881	Tro-N	85	339	56	96	13	5	1	35	29	12	.283	.340	.360	114	6				.904	-10	*2-85,M	-0.1
1882	Tro-N	81	319	44	82	15	2	0	32	23	21	.257	.307	.317	106	3				.914	-13	*2-79/S-2M	-0.7
1883	Phi-N	86	329	39	85	9	2	0	27	18	21	.258	.297	.298	89	-3				.862	-3	*2-86/P-1M	-0.8
1884	Pit-a	10	41	2	6	0	0	0		0		.146	.146	.146	-4	-5				.714	-3	/O-6,1-3,3M	-0.8
Total	5 n	262	1164	199	293	34	11	0	68	13	11	.252	.260	.300	77	-29						3-243/2-10,PC	-2.4
Total	9	562	2306	346	625	76	20	1	226	113	114	.271	.305	.323	102	6				.895	0	2-342,3-150/SOP1C	2.2

■ FELIX FERMIN

Fermin, Felix Jose (Minaya) b: 10/9/63, Mao Valverde, D.R. BR/TR, 5'11", 179 lbs. Deb: 7/8/87

YEAR	TM/L	G	AB	R	H	2B	3B	HR	RBI	BB	SO	AVG	OBP	SLG	PRO+	BR/A	SB	CS	SBR	FA	FR	G/POS	TPR
1987	Pit-N	23	68	6	17	0	0	0	4	8	9	.250	.301	.250	48	-5	0	0	0	.980	1	S-23	-0.2
1988	Pit-N	43	87	9	24	0	2	0	2	8	10	.276	.357	.322	98	0	3	1	0	.955	-5	S-43	-0.3
1989	Cle-A	156	484	50	115	9	1	0	21	41	27	.238	.302	.260	59	-25	6	4	-1	.967	18	*S-153/2-2	0.4
1990	Cle-A	148	414	47	106	13	2	1	40	26	22	.256	.300	.304	70	-17	3	5	-1	.975	4	*S-147/2-1	-0.2
1991	Cle-A	129	424	30	111	13	2	0	31	26	27	.262	.309	.302	69	-17	5	4	-1	.980	1	*S-129	-0.7
1992	Cle-A	79	215	27	58	7	2	0	13	18	10	.270	.329	.321	84	-4	0	0	0	.971	-5	S-55,3-17/21	-0.6
1993	Cle-A	140	480	48	126	16	2	2	45	24	14	.262	.303	.317	67	-22	4	5	-2	.960	-29	*S-140	-4.1
1994	Sea-A	101	379	52	120	21	0	1	35	11	22	.317	.343	.380	84	-9	4	1	0	.974	-6	S-77,2-25	-0.9
Total	8	819	2551	269	677	79	11	4	191	158	141	.265	.313	.310	71	-99	25	21	-5	.970	-21	S-767/2-35,31	-6.6

■ ED FERNANDES

Fernandes, Edward Paul b: 3/11/18, Oakland, Cal. d: 11/27/68, Hayward, Cal. BB/TR, 5'9", 185 lbs. Deb: 6/9/40

YEAR	TM/L	G	AB	R	H	2B	3B	HR	RBI	BB	SO	AVG	OBP	SLG	PRO+	BR/A	SB	CS	SBR	FA	FR	G/POS	TPR
1940	Pit-N	28	33	1	4	1	0	0	2	7	6	.121	.275	.152	21	-3	0			.981	0	C-27	-0.2
1946	Chi-A	14	32	4	8	2	0	0	4	8	7	.250	.400	.313	105	1	0	0	0	.922	-1	C-12	0.0
Total	2	42	65	5	12	3	0	0	6	15	13	.185	.338	.231	61	-3	0	0	0	.952	-0	/C-39	-0.2

■ FRANK FERNANDEZ

Fernandez, Frank b: 4/16/43, Staten Island, N.Y. BR/TR, 6'1", 192 lbs. Deb: 9/12/67

YEAR	TM/L	G	AB	R	H	2B	3B	HR	RBI	BB	SO	AVG	OBP	SLG	PRO+	BR/A	SB	CS	SBR	FA	FR	G/POS	TPR
1967	NY-A	9	28	1	6	2	0	1	4	2	7	.214	.290	.393	104	0	1	1	-0	1.000	0	/C-7,O-2	0.0
1968	NY-A	51	135	15	23	6	1	7	30	35	50	.170	.341	.385	124	5	1	0	0	.989	6	C-45/O-4	1.5
1969	NY-A	89	229	34	51	6	1	12	29	65	68	.223	.401	.415	133	13	1	3	-2	.994	-8	C-65,O-14	0.8
1970	Oak-A	94	252	30	54	5	0	15	44	40	76	.214	.327	.413	106	2	1	0	0	.993	-1	C-76/O-1	0.5
1971	Oak-A	2	4	0	0	0	0	0	0	1	2	.000	.200	.000	-40	-1	0	0	0	1.000	0	/C-2	0.1
	Was-A	18	30	0	3	0	0	0	4	4	10	.100	.206	.100	-12	-4	0	0	0	1.000	-1	/O-6,C-1	-0.6
	Oak-A	2	5	1	1	1	0	0	1	0	1	.200	.200	.400	68	-0	0	0	0	1.000	-0	/C-1	-0.1
	Yr	22	39	1	4	1	0	0	5	5	13	.103	.205	.128	-4	-5	0	0	0	1.000	0	/O-6,C-4	-0.6
	Chi-N	17	41	11	7	1	0	4	4	17	15	.171	.414	.488	135	2	0	0	0	.980	0	C-16	0.3
1972	Chi-N	3	3	0	0	0	0	0	0	0	2	.000	.000	.000	-90	-1	0	0	0	1.000	-0	/C-1	-0.1
Total	6	285	727	92	145	21	2	39	116	164	231	.199	.351	.395	114	17	4	4	-1	.992	-2	C-214/O-27	2.4

■ NANNY FERNANDEZ

Fernandez, Froilan b: 10/25/18, Wilmington, Cal. BR/TR, 5'9", 170 lbs. Deb: 4/14/42

YEAR	TM/L	G	AB	R	H	2B	3B	HR	RBI	BB	SO	AVG	OBP	SLG	PRO+	BR/A	SB	CS	SBR	FA	FR	G/POS	TPR
1942	Bos-N	145	577	63	147	29	3	6	55	38	61	.255	.303	.347	92	-8	15			.914	6	3-98,O-44	-0.3
1946	Bos-N	115	372	37	95	15	2	2	42	30	44	.255	.313	.323	79	-10	1			.940	-2	3-81,S-18,O	-1.2
1947	Bos-N	83	209	16	43	4	0	2	21	22	20	.206	.281	.254	44	-17	2			.933	-13	S-62/O-8,3	-2.7
1950	Pit-N	65	198	23	51	11	0	6	27	19	17	.258	.326	.404	88	-4	2			.925	-3	3-52	-0.7
Total	4	408	1356	139	336	59	5	16	145	109	142	.248	.306	.334	80	-38	20			.925	-13	3-237/S-80,O	-4.9

■ CHICO FERNANDEZ

Fernandez, Humberto (Perez) b: 3/2/32, Havana, Cuba BR/TR, 6', 170 lbs. Deb: 7/14/56

YEAR	TM/L	G	AB	R	H	2B	3B	HR	RBI	BB	SO	AVG	OBP	SLG	PRO+	BR/A	SB	CS	SBR	FA	FR	G/POS	TPR
1956	Bro-N	34	66	11	15	2	0	1	9	3	10	.227	.261	.303	47	-5	2	3	-1	.978	7	S-25	-0.2
1957	Phi-N	149	500	42	131	14	4	5	51	31	64	.262	.306	.336	75	-18	18	5	2	.960	-25	*S-149	-2.7
1958	Phi-N	148	522	38	120	18	5	6	51	37	48	.230	.283	.318	60	-31	12	6	0	.975	-12	*S-148	-3.0
1959	Phi-N	45	123	15	26	5	1	0	3	10	11	.211	.271	.268	43	-10	2	1	0	.958	-3	S-40/2-2	-1.0
1960	Det-A	133	435	44	105	13	3	4	35	39	50	.241	.305	.313	66	-21	13	4	-2	.947	-4	*S-133	-1.4
1961	Det-A	133	435	41	108	15	4	3	40	36	45	.248	.306	.322	66	-21	8	5	-1	.958	-8	*S-121/3-8	-1.9
1962	Det-A	141	503	64	125	17	2	20	59	42	69	.249	.306	.410	88	-10	10	3	1	.960	-27	*S-138/3-2,1	-2.4
1963	Det-A	15	49	3	7	1	0	0	2	6	9	.143	.236	.163	14	-6	0	1	-1	.947	2	S-14	-0.6
	NY-N	58	145	12	29	6	0	1	9	9	30	.200	.247	.262	46	-10	3	0	1	.944	-16	S-45/3-5,2	-2.5
Total	8	856	2778	270	666	91	19	40	259	213	338	.240	.295	.329	67	-130	68	28	4	.960	-86	S-810/3-15,21	-15.0

YEAR	TM/L	G	AB	R	H	2B	3B	HR	RBI	BB	SO	AVG	OBP	SLG	PRO+	BR/A	SB	CS	SBR	FA	FR	G/POS	TPR

■ CHICO FERNANDEZ
Fernandez, Lorenzo Marto (Mosquera)　b: 4/23/39, Havana, Cuba　BR/TR, 5'10", 160 lbs.　Deb: 4/20/68

| 1968 | Bal-A | 24 | 18 | 0 | 2 | 0 | 0 | 0 | 0 | 1 | 2 | .111 | .158 | .111 | -17 | -3 | 0 | 0 | 0 | .923 | 3 | /S-7,2-4 | 0.0 |

■ TONY FERNANDEZ
Fernandez, Octavio Antonio (Castro) (b: Octavio Antonio Fernando (Castro))　b: 6/30/62, San Pedro De Macoris, D.R.　BB/TR, 6'2", 175 lbs.　Deb: 9/2/83

1983	Tor-A	15	34	5	9	1	1	0	2	2	2	.265	.324	.353	81	-1	0	1	-1	1.000	-3	S-13/D-1	-0.4
1984	Tor-A	88	233	29	63	5	3	3	19	17	15	.270	.320	.356	84	-5	5	7	-3	.974	3	S-73,3-10/D	0.1
1985	*Tor-A	161	564	71	163	31	10	2	51	43	41	.289	.342	.390	97	-2	13	6	0	.962	5	*S-160	1.9
1986	Tor-A★	163	687	91	213	33	9	10	65	27	52	.310	.340	.428	105	4	25	12	0	**.983**	3	*S-163	2.2
1987	Tor-A★	146	578	90	186	29	8	5	67	51	48	.322	.382	.426	112	11	32	12	2	.979	6	*S-146	3.0
1988	Tor-A	154	648	76	186	41	4	5	70	45	65	.287	.337	.386	101	1	15	5	2	.981	10	*S-154	2.5
1989	*Tor-A★	140	573	64	147	25	9	11	64	29	51	.257	.296	.389	93	-7	22	6	3	**.992**	18	*S-140	2.6
1990	Tor-A	161	635	84	175	27	**17**	4	66	71	70	.276	.352	.391	106	7	26	13	0	.989	9	*S-161	2.8
1991	SD-N	145	558	81	152	27	5	4	38	55	74	.272	.338	.360	93	-4	23	9	2	.972	3	*S-145	1.2
1992	SD-N★	155	622	84	171	32	4	4	37	56	62	.275	.339	.359	96	-2	20	20	-6	.983	-17	*S-154	-1.6
1993	NY-N	48	173	20	39	5	2	1	14	25	19	.225	.327	.295	69	-7	6	2	1	.975	7	S-48	0.4
	*Tor-A	94	353	45	108	18	9	4	50	31	26	.306	.362	.442	114	7	15	8	-0	.985	5	S-94	1.8
1994	Cin-N	104	366	50	102	18	6	8	50	44	40	.279	.364	.426	106	4	12	7	-1	.991	2	3-93/S-9,2	0.6
Total	12	1574	6024	790	1714	292	87	61	593	496	565	.285	.343	.392	100	6	214	108	-1	.980	50	*S-1460,3-103/2D	17.1

■ AL FERRARA
Ferrara, Alfred John "The Bull"　b: 12/22/39, Brooklyn, N.Y.　BR/TR, 6'1", 203 lbs.　Deb: 7/30/63

1963	LA-N	21	44	2	7	0	0	1	1	6	9	.159	.275	.227	50	-3	0	0	0	.950	1	O-11	-0.3
1965	LA-N	41	81	5	17	2	1	1	10	9	20	.210	.297	.296	72	-3	0	0	0	.927	-3	O-27	-0.8
1966	*LA-N	63	115	15	31	4	0	5	23	9	35	.270	.339	.435	123	3	0	0	0	.956	-3	O-32	-0.1
1967	LA-N	122	347	41	96	16	1	16	50	33	73	.277	.345	.467	142	17	0	1	-1	.978	-10	O-94	0.3
1968	LA-N	2	7	0	1	0	0	0	0	0	2	.143	.143	.143	-15	-1	0	0	0	.500	-1	/O-2	-0.2
1969	SD-N	138	366	39	95	22	1	14	56	45	69	.260	.352	.440	125	12	0	0	0	.958	-2	O-96	0.5
1970	SD-N	138	372	44	103	15	4	13	51	46	63	.277	.373	.444	123	13	0	0	0	.968	-8	O-96	0.0
1971	SD-N	17	17	0	2	1	0	0	2	5	5	.118	.318	.176	47	-1	0	0	0	1.000	-1	/O-2	-0.2
	Cin-N	32	33	2	6	0	0	1	5	3	10	.182	.270	.273	55	-2	0	0	0	1.000	-1	/O-5	-0.3
	Yr	49	50	2	8	1	0	1	7	8	15	.160	.288	.240	53	-3	0	0	0	1.000	-1	/O-7	-0.5
Total	8	574	1382	148	358	60	7	51	198	156	286	.259	.346	.423	120	36	0	1	-1	.962	-28	O-365	-1.1

■ MIKE FERRARO
Ferraro, Michael Dennis　b: 8/18/44, Kingston, N.Y.　BR/TR, 5'11", 175 lbs.　Deb: 9/6/66　MC

1966	NY-A	10	28	4	5	0	0	0	0	3	3	.179	.281	.179	37	-2	0	0	0	.926	1	3-10	-0.1
1968	NY-A	23	87	5	14	0	1	0	1	2	17	.161	.180	.184	11	-9	0	0	0	.975	4	3-22	-0.6
1969	Sea-A	5	4	0	0	0	0	0	0	1	0	.000	.200	.000	-41	-1	0	0	0	.000	0	H	-0.1
1972	Mil-A	124	381	19	97	18	1	2	29	17	41	.255	.286	.323	83	-9	0	5	-3	.950	-16	*3-115/S-1	-3.3
Total	4	162	500	28	116	18	2	2	30	23	61	.232	.267	.288	67	-21	0	5	-3	.953	-10	3-147/S-1	-4.1

■ RICK FERRELL
Ferrell, Richard Benjamin　b: 10/12/05, Durham, N.C.　BR/TR, 5'10", 160 lbs.　Deb: 4/19/29　FCH

1929	StL-A	64	144	21	33	8	1	0	20	32	10	.229	.373	.285	69	-5	1	2	-1	.962	0	C-45	-0.2
1930	StL-A	101	314	43	84	18	4	1	41	46	10	.268	.363	.360	81	-8	1	4	-2	.983	-9	*C-101	-1.0
1931	StL-A	117	386	47	118	30	4	3	57	56	12	.306	.394	.427	112	8	2	3	-1	.973	4	*C-108	1.7
1932	StL-A	126	438	67	138	30	5	2	65	66	18	.315	.406	.420	108	7	5	5	-2	.986	-2	*C-120	1.1
1933	StL-A	22	72	8	18	2	0	1	5	12	4	.250	.357	.319	76	-2	2	0	1	.991	3	C-21	0.2
	Bos-A★	118	421	50	125	19	4	3	72	58	19	.297	.385	.382	105	5	2	2	-1	.990	5	*C-116	1.6
	Yr	140	493	58	143	21	4	4	77	70	23	.290	.381	.373	100	3	4	2	0	.990	8	*C-137	1.8
1934	Bos-A☆	132	437	50	130	29	4	1	48	66	20	.297	.388	.389	95	-2	0	0	0	**.990**	3	*C-128	0.7
1935	Bos-A☆	133	458	54	138	34	4	3	61	65	15	.301	.388	.413	100	2	5	8	-3	.979	13	*C-131	1.7
1936	Bos-A★	121	410	59	128	27	5	8	55	65	17	.312	.406	.461	108	6	0	1	-1	.987	9	*C-121	1.7
1937	Bos-A	18	65	8	20	2	0	1	4	15	4	.308	.438	.385	105	1	0	0	0	.990	0	C-18	0.2
	Was-A☆	86	279	31	64	6	0	1	32	50	18	.229	.348	.262	59	-16	1	1	-0	.987	-6	C-84	-1.6
	Yr	104	344	39	84	8	0	2	36	65	22	.244	.366	.285	68	-14	1	1	-0	.988	-6	*C-102	-1.4
1938	Was-A☆	135	411	55	120	24	5	1	58	75	17	.292	.401	.382	104	6	1	0	-0	.981	-5	*C-131	0.7
1939	Was-A	87	274	32	77	13	1	0	31	41	12	.281	.377	.336	90	-2	1	1	-0	.976	-6	C-83	-0.4
1940	Was-A	103	326	35	89	18	2	0	28	47	15	.273	.365	.340	90	-3	1	1	-0	.980	-6	C-99	-0.2
1941	Was-A	21	66	8	18	5	0	0	13	15	4	.273	.407	.348	107	1	1	0	-0	.980	-1	C-21	0.2
	StL-A	100	321	30	81	14	3	2	23	52	22	.252	.357	.333	81	-8	2	1	0	.995	-5	C-98	-0.4
	Yr	121	387	38	99	19	3	2	36	67	26	.256	.366	.336	85	-6	3	1	0	.992	-6	*C-119	-0.2
1942	StL-A	99	273	20	61	6	1	0	26	33	13	.223	.307	.253	57	-15	0	0	-1	.986	9	C-95	1.4
1943	StL-A	74	209	12	50	7	0	0	20	34	14	.239	.348	.273	81	-3	0	0	0	.987	13	C-70	1.4
1944	Was-A☆	99	339	14	94	11	1	0	25	46	13	.277	.364	.316	99	2	2	1	0	.981	-3	C-96	1.2
1945	Was-A†	91	286	33	76	12	1	1	38	43	13	.266	.366	.325	110	5	2	4	-2	.990	-2	C-83	0.6
1947	Was-A	37	99	10	30	11	0	0	12	14	7	.303	.389	.414	127	4	0	0	0	.994	3	C-37	0.9
Total	18	1884	6028	687	1692	324	45	28	734	931	277	.281	.378	.363	95	-17	29	35	-12	.984	20	*C-1806	10.1

■ WES FERRELL
Ferrell, Wesley Cheek　b: 2/2/08, Greensboro, N.C.　d: 12/9/76, Sarasota, Fla.　BR/TR, 6'2", 195 lbs.　Deb: 9/9/27　F

1927	Cle-A	1	0	0	0	0	0	0	0	0	0	—	—	—	—	0	0	0	0	.000	-0	/P-1	0.0
1928	Cle-A	2	4	0	1	0	1	0	0	0	0	.250	.250	.750	152	0	0	0	0	1.000	0	/P-2	0.0
1929	Cle-A	47	93	12	22	5	3	1	12	6	28	.237	.283	.387	68	-5	1	0	0	.973	6	P-43	0.0
1930	Cle-A	53	118	19	35	8	3	0	14	12	15	.297	.362	.415	93	-1	0	0	0	.967	-3	P-43	0.0
1931	Cle-A	48	116	24	37	6	1	9	30	10	21	.319	.373	.621	149	7	0	0	0	.969	5	P-40	0.0
1932	Cle-A	55	128	14	31	5	2	2	18	6	21	.242	.276	.359	59	-8	0	0	0	.986	1	P-38	0.0
1933	Cle-A☆	61	140	26	38	7	0	7	26	20	22	.271	.363	.471	114	3	0	0	0	**1.000**	2	P-28,O-13	0.1
1934	Bos-A	34	78	12	22	4	0	4	17	7	15	.282	.341	.487	104	4	1	0	0	.969	-2	P-26	0.0
1935	Bos-A	75	150	25	52	5	1	7	32	21	16	.347	.427	.533	138	9	0	0	0	.977	2	P-41	0.0
1936	Bos-A	61	135	20	36	6	1	5	24	14	10	.267	.336	.437	84	-4	0	0	0	.962	-3	P-39	0.0
1937	Bos-A	18	33	7	12	1	0	1	9	7	3	.364	.475	.515	144	3	0	0	0	.964	2	P-12	0.0
	Was-A☆	53	106	7	27	5	0	0	16	9	18	.255	.313	.302	58	-7	0	0	0	.975	-1	P-25	0.0
	Yr	71	139	14	39	7	0	1	25	16	21	.281	.355	.353	81	-4	0	0	0	.971	1	P-37	0.0
1938	Was-A	26	49	6	11	2	0	1	6	15	7	.224	.406	.327	92	1	0	0	0	.976	1	P-23	0.0
	NY-A	5	12	1	2	1	0	0	1	1	4	.167	.231	.250	20	-2	0	0	0	.917	-0	/P-5	0.0
	Yr	31	61	7	13	3	0	1	7	16	11	.213	.377	.311	79	-1	0	0	0	.962	2	P-28	0.0
1939	NY-A	3	8	0	1	1	0	0	1	0	2	.125	.125	.250	-6	-1	0	0	0	1.000	1	/P-3	0.0
1940	Bro-N	2	2	0	0	0	0	0	0	0	2	.000	.000	.000	-94	-1	0	0	0	1.000	1	/P-1	0.0
1941	Bos-N	4	4	2	2	0	0	1	2	1	1	.500	.600	1.250	430	2	0	0	0	1.000	-0	/P-4	0.0
Total	15	548	1176	175	329	57	12	38	208	129	185	.280	.351	.446	99	-5	2	0		.975	7	P-374/O-13	0.1

■ SERGIO FERRER
Ferrer, Sergio (Marrero)　b: 1/29/51, Santurce, P.R.　BB/TR, 5'7", 145 lbs.　Deb: 4/5/74

1974	Min-A	24	57	12	16	0	2	0	8	6		.281	.379	.351	107	1	3	2	-0	.855	-12	S-20/2-1	-1.0
1975	Min-A	32	81	14	20	3	1	0	2	3	11	.247	.282	.309	66	-4	3	4	-2	.924	-1	S-18,2-10/D	-0.5
1978	NY-N	37	33	8	7	0	1	0	4	7		.212	.316	.273	68	-1	1	0	0	.971	10	S-29/2-3,3	1.0

YEAR	TM/L	G	AB	R	H	2B	3B	HR	RBI	BB	SO	AVG	OBP	SLG	PRO+	BR/A	SB	CS	SBR	FA	FR	G/POS	TPR
1979	NY-N	32	7	7	0	0	0	0	0	2	3	.000	.222	.000	-35	-1	0	2	-1	.833	6	3-12/S-5,2	0.3
Total	4	125	178	41	43	3	4	0	3	17	27	.242	.318	.303	76	-5	7	8	-3	.922	2	/S-72,2-18,3D	-0.2

■ HOBE FERRIS
Ferris, Albert Sayles   b: 12/7/1877, Providence, R.I.   d: 3/18/38, Detroit, Mich.   BR/TR, 5'8", 162 lbs.   Deb: 4/26/01

YEAR	TM/L	G	AB	R	H	2B	3B	HR	RBI	BB	SO	AVG	OBP	SLG	PRO+	BR/A	SB	CS	SBR	FA	FR	G/POS	TPR
1901	Bos-A	138	523	68	131	16	15	2	63	23		.250	.290	.350	78	-17	13			.930	9	*2-138/S-1	-0.2
1902	Bos-A	134	499	57	122	16	14	8	63	21		.244	.276	.381	79	-17	11			.952	27	*2-134	1.4
1903	*Bos-A	141	525	69	132	19	7	9	66	25		.251	.287	.366	90	-8	11			.950	15	*2-139/S-2	1.3
1904	Bos-A	156	563	50	120	23	10	3	63	23		.213	.245	.306	70	-20	7			.962	2	*2-156	-1.6
1905	Bos-A	142	523	51	115	24	16	6	59	23		.220	.253	.361	93	-7	11			.960	15	*2-142	1.0
1906	Bos-A	130	495	47	121	25	13	2	44	10		.244	.262	.360	94	-6	8			.960	9	*2-126/3-4	0.4
1907	Bos-A	150	561	41	135	25	2	4	60	10		.241	.254	.314	82	-14	11			.967	15	*2-150	-0.1
1908	StL-A	148	555	54	150	26	7	2	74	14		.270	.291	.353	108	3	6			**.952**	16	*3-148	2.7
1909	StL-A	148	556	36	120	18	5	4	58	12		.216	.232	.288	69	-23	11			.937	7	*3-114,2-34	-1.4
Total	9	1287	4800	473	1146	192	89	40	550	161		.239	.265	.341	84	-108	89			.954	113	*2-1019,3-266/S	3.5

■ WILLY FETZER
Fetzer, William McKinnon   b: 6/24/1884, Concord, N.C.   d: 5/3/59, Butner, N.C.   BL/TR, 5'10.5", 180 lbs.   Deb: 9/4/06

YEAR	TM/L	G	AB	R	H	2B	3B	HR	RBI	BB	SO	AVG	OBP	SLG	PRO+	BR/A	SB	CS	SBR	FA	FR	G/POS	TPR
1906	Phi-A	1	1	0	0	0	0	0	0	0	0	.000	.000	.000	-97	-0	0			.000	0	H	0.0

■ CHICK FEWSTER
Fewster, Wilson Lloyd   b: 11/10/1895, Baltimore, Md.   d: 4/16/45, Baltimore, Md.   BR/TR, 5'11", 160 lbs.   Deb: 9/19/17

YEAR	TM/L	G	AB	R	H	2B	3B	HR	RBI	BB	SO	AVG	OBP	SLG	PRO+	BR/A	SB	CS	SBR	FA	FR	G/POS	TPR
1917	NY-A	11	36	2	8	0	0	1	5	5		.222	.317	.222	64	-1	1			.919	2	2-11	0.1
1918	NY-A	5	2	1	1	0	0	0	0	0	0	.500	.500	.500	197	0	0			.000	0	/2-2	0.0
1919	NY-A	81	244	38	69	9	3	1	15	34	36	.283	.386	.357	108	5	8			.946	8	O-41,S-24/23	1.1
1920	NY-A	21	21	8	6	1	0	0	1	7	2	.286	.464	.333	110	1	0	1	-1	.840	1	/S-6,2-3	0.1
1921	*NY-A	66	207	44	58	19	1	1	19	28	43	.280	.382	.386	94	-1	4	4	-1	.974	-3	O-43,2-15	-0.7
1922	NY-A	44	132	20	32	4	1	1	9	16	23	.242	.324	.311	65	-7	2	4	-2	.975	1	O-38/2-2	-0.9
	Bos-A	23	83	8	24	4	1	0	9	6	10	.289	.344	.361	85	-2	8	3	1	.959	4	3-23	0.4
	Yr	67	215	28	56	8	2	1	18	22	33	.260	.332	.330	72	-8	10	7	-1	.975	5	O-38,3-23/2	-0.5
1923	Bos-A	90	284	32	67	10	1	0	15	39	35	.236	.334	.278	62	-14	7	14	-6	.938	-10	2-49,S-37/3	-2.6
1924	Cle-A	101	322	36	86	12	2	0	36	24	36	.267	.324	.317	65	-17	12	12	-4	.961	-22	2-94/3-5	-4.0
1925	Cle-A	93	294	39	73	16	1	1	38	36	25	.248	.330	.320	65	-15	6	9	-4	.939	-9	2-83,3-10/O	-2.5
1926	Bro-N	105	337	53	82	16	3	2	24	45	49	.243	.341	.326	82	-7	9			.953	-15	*2-103	-1.9
1927	Bro-N	4	1	1	0	0	0	0	0	0	0	.000	.000	.000	-99	-0	0			.000	0	H	0.0
Total	11	644	1963	282	506	91	12	6	167	240	264	.258	.346	.326	77	-59	57	47		.945	-43	2-366,O-123/S3	-10.9

■ NEIL FIALA
Fiala, Neil Stephen   b: 8/24/56, St.Louis, Mo.   BL/TR, 6'1", 185 lbs.   Deb: 9/3/81

YEAR	TM/L	G	AB	R	H	2B	3B	HR	RBI	BB	SO	AVG	OBP	SLG	PRO+	BR/A	SB	CS	SBR	FA	FR	G/POS	TPR
1981	StL-N	3	3	0	0	0	0	0	0	1	1	.000	.000	.000	-97	-1	0	0	0	.000	0	/H	-0.1
	Cin-N	2	2	1	1	0	0	0	1	0	1	.500	.500	.500	181	0	0	0	0	.000	0	/H	0.0
	Yr	5	5	1	1	0	0	0	1	1	2	.200	.200	.200	13	-1	0	0	0	.000	0	-0,-0	-0.1

■ JIM FIELD
Field, James C.   b: 4/24/1863, Philadelphia, Pa.   d: 5/13/53, Atlantic City, N.J   6'1", 170 lbs.   Deb: 6/2/1883

YEAR	TM/L	G	AB	R	H	2B	3B	HR	RBI	BB	SO	AVG	OBP	SLG	PRO+	BR/A	SB	CS	SBR	FA	FR	G/POS	TPR
1883	Col-a	76	295	31	75	10	6	1		7		.254	.272	.339	104	2				.938	-7	*1-76	-1.1
1884	Col-a	105	417	74	97	9	7	4		23		.233	.292	.317	107	5				.958	-4	*1-105	-1.0
1885	Pit-a	56	209	28	50	7	1	0		13		.239	.306	.306	95	-1				.965	0	1-56	-0.7
	Bal-a	38	144	16	30	3	2	0		13		.208	.278	.257	71	-4				.963	1	1-38	-0.7
	Yr	94	353	44	80	12	3	1		26		.227	.295	.286	85	-5				.964	1	1-94	-1.4
1890	Roc-a	52	188	30	38	7	5	4		21		.202	.309	.356	104	1	8			.964	-1	1-51/P-2	-0.5
1898	Was-N	5	21	1	2	0	0	0	0	0		.095	.095	.095	-46	-4	1			.979	-0	/1-5	-0.4
Total	5	332	1274	180	292	38	21	10	0	77		.229	.288	.316	96	-1	9			.956	-15	1-331/P-2	-4.4

■ SAM FIELD
Field, Samuel Jay   b: 10/12/1848, Philadelphia, Pa.   d: 10/28/04, Sinking Spring, Pa   BR/TR, 5'9.5", 182 lbs.   Deb: 5/19/1875

YEAR	TM/L	G	AB	R	H	2B	3B	HR	RBI	BB	SO	AVG	OBP	SLG	PRO+	BR/A	SB	CS	SBR	FA	FR	G/POS	TPR
1875	Cen-n	3	11	2	1	0	0	0		0		.091	.091	.091	-40	-1						/C-2,O-1	-0.1
	Was-n	5	17	0	5	0	0	0		0		.294	.294	.294	108	0						/C-4,O-1	0.0
	Yr	8	28	2	6	0	0	0		0		.214	.214	.214	51	-1						/C-6,O-2	-0.1
1876	Cin-N	4	14	2	0	0	0	0	0	1	3	.000	.067	.000	-89	-3				.667	-3	/C-3,2-2	-0.5

■ CECIL FIELDER
Fielder, Cecil Grant   b: 9/21/63, Los Angeles, Cal.   BR/TR, 6'3", 230 lbs.   Deb: 7/20/85

YEAR	TM/L	G	AB	R	H	2B	3B	HR	RBI	BB	SO	AVG	OBP	SLG	PRO+	BR/A	SB	CS	SBR	FA	FR	G/POS	TPR
1985	*Tor-A	30	74	6	23	4	0	4	16	6	16	.311	.363	.527	137	4	0	0	0	.979	1	1-25	0.3
1986	Tor-A	34	83	7	13	2	0	4	13	6	27	.157	.222	.325	46	-7	0	0	0	1.000	-1	D-22/1-7,3O	-0.8
1987	Tor-A	82	175	30	47	7	1	14	32	20	48	.269	.347	.560	132	8	0	1	-1	1.000	-1	D-55,1-16/3	0.4
1988	Tor-A	74	174	24	40	6	1	9	23	14	53	.230	.291	.431	99	-1	0	1	-1	.991	0	D-50,1-17/32	-0.3
1990	Det-A★	159	573	104	159	25	1	**51**	**132**	90	182	.277	.380	**.592**	167	50	0	0	0	.989	3	*1-143,D-15	4.2
1991	Det-A★	162	624	102	163	25	0	**44**	**133**	78	151	.261	.347	.513	133	27	0	0	0	.993	-3	*1-122,D-42	1.4
1992	Det-A	155	594	80	145	22	0	35	**124**	73	151	.244	.329	.458	118	13	0	0	0	.991	-4	*1-114,D-43	0.5
1993	Det-A★	154	573	80	153	23	0	30	117	90	125	.267	.370	.464	124	20	0	1	-1	.991	-2	*1-119,D-36	0.7
1994	Det-A	109	425	67	110	16	2	28	90	50	110	.259	.340	.504	114	8	0	0	0	.993	16	*1-102/D-7	1.4
Total	9	959	3295	500	853	130	5	219	680	427	863	.259	.348	.501	128	122	0	4	-2	.991	16	1-665,D-270/32O	7.8

■ BRUCE FIELDS
Fields, Bruce Alan   b: 10/6/60, Cleveland, Ohio   BL/TR, 6', 185 lbs.   Deb: 9/3/86

YEAR	TM/L	G	AB	R	H	2B	3B	HR	RBI	BB	SO	AVG	OBP	SLG	PRO+	BR/A	SB	CS	SBR	FA	FR	G/POS	TPR
1986	Det-A	16	43	4	12	0	0	1	6	1	6	.279	.295	.349	75	-2	1	1	-0	.962	-1	O-14/D-1	-0.3
1988	Sea-A	39	67	8	18	5	1	0	5	4	11	.269	.310	.388	90	-1	0	1	-1	1.000	-5	O-23/D-6	-0.7
1989	Sea-A	3	3	2	1	1	0	0	0	0	1	.333	.333	.667	170	0	0	0	0	.000	-0	/O-1	0.0
Total	3	58	113	14	31	7	1	1	11	5	18	.274	.305	.381	86	-2	1	2	-1	.980	-6	/O-38,D-7	-1.0

■ GEORGE FIELDS
Fields, George W.   b: 7/1853, Waterbury, Conn.   d: 9/22/33, Waterbury, Conn.   Deb: 5/2/1872

YEAR	TM/L	G	AB	R	H	2B	3B	HR	RBI	BB	SO	AVG	OBP	SLG	PRO+	BR/A	SB	CS	SBR	FA	FR	G/POS	TPR
1872	Man-n	18	83	14	22	2	2	0		0		.265	.265	.337	89	-1						3-10/O-6,S	-0.1

■ JOCKO FIELDS
Fields, John Joseph   b: 10/20/1864, Cork, Ireland   d: 10/14/50, Jersey City, N.J.   BR/TR, 5'10", 160 lbs.   Deb: 5/31/1887

YEAR	TM/L	G	AB	R	H	2B	3B	HR	RBI	BB	SO	AVG	OBP	SLG	PRO+	BR/A	SB	CS	SBR	FA	FR	G/POS	TPR
1887	Pit-N	43	164	26	44	9	2	0	17	7	13	.268	.306	.348	86	-3	7			.933	1	O-27,C-14/13P	-0.1
1888	Pit-N	45	169	22	33	7	1	2	15	8	19	.195	.232	.278	67	-6	9			.887	-5	O-29,C-14/3	-1.0
1889	Pit-N	75	289	41	90	22	5	2	43	29	30	.311	.376	.443	142	16	7			.860	-6	O-60,C-16	0.9
1890	Pit-P	126	526	101	149	18	20	9	86	57	52	.283	.357	.445	124	17	24			.879	-13	O-80,2-30,C/S	0.3
1891	Pit-N	23	75	10	18	3	0	0	5	10	13	.240	.337	.280	82	-1	1			.897	-3	C-15/S-8	-0.2
	Phi-N	8	30	4	7	2	1	0	5	4	2	.233	.324	.367	98	-0	0			.769	-4	/C-8	-0.3
	Yr	31	105	14	25	5	1	0	10	14	15	.238	.333	.305	87	-1	1			.857	-7	C-23/S-8	-0.5
1892	NY-N	21	66	8	18	4	2	0	5	9	10	.273	.368	.394	133	3	2			.917	-1	O-11,C-10	0.2
Total	6	341	1319	212	359	65	32	12	176	124	139	.272	.338	.397	114	26	50			.883	-31	O-207/C-92,2S31P	-0.2

■ BIEN FIGUEROA
Figueroa, Bienvenido   b: 2/7/64, Santo Domingo, D.R.   BR/TR, 5'10", 170 lbs.   Deb: 5/17/92

YEAR	TM/L	G	AB	R	H	2B	3B	HR	RBI	BB	SO	AVG	OBP	SLG	PRO+	BR/A	SB	CS	SBR	FA	FR	G/POS	TPR
1992	StL-N	12	11	1	2	1	0	0	1	0	2	.182	.250	.273	49	-1	0	0	0	.938	1	/S-9,2-3	0.0

■ JESUS FIGUEROA
Figueroa, Jesus Maria (Figueroa)   b: 2/20/57, Santo Domingo, D.R.   BL/TL, 5'10", 160 lbs.   Deb: 4/22/80

YEAR	TM/L	G	AB	R	H	2B	3B	HR	RBI	BB	SO	AVG	OBP	SLG	PRO+	BR/A	SB	CS	SBR	FA	FR	G/POS	TPR
1980	Chi-N	115	198	20	50	5	1	0	11	14	16	.253	.308	.293	64	-9	2	1	0	.979	-4	O-57	-1.5

■ SAM FILE
File, Lawrence Samuel   b: 5/18/22, Chester, Pa.   BR/TR, 5'11", 160 lbs.   Deb: 9/10/40

YEAR	TM/L	G	AB	R	H	2B	3B	HR	RBI	BB	SO	AVG	OBP	SLG	PRO+	BR/A	SB	CS	SBR	FA	FR	G/POS	TPR
1940	Phi-N	7	13	0	1	0	0	0	1	0	1	.077	.077	.077	-60	-3	0			.850	1	/S-6,3-1	-0.2

YEAR	TM/L	G	AB	R	H	2B	3B	HR	RBI	BB	SO	AVG	OBP	SLG	PRO+	BR/A	SB	CS	SBR	FA	FR	G/POS	TPR

■ STEVE FILIPOWICZ
Filipowicz, Stephen Charles "Flip" b: 6/28/21, Donora, Pa. d: 2/21/75, Wilkes-Barre, Pa. BR/TR, 5'8", 195 lbs. Deb: 9/3/44

YEAR	TM/L	G	AB	R	H	2B	3B	HR	RBI	BB	SO	AVG	OBP	SLG	PRO+	BR/A	SB	CS	SBR	FA	FR	G/POS	TPR
1944	NY-N	15	41	10	8	2	1	0	7	3	7	.195	.250	.293	52	-3	0			1.000	-1	O-10/C-1	-0.5
1945	NY-N	35	112	14	23	5	0	2	16	4	13	.205	.239	.304	50	-8	0			.935	-6	O-31	-1.6
1948	Cin-N	7	26	0	9	0	1	0	3	2	1	.346	.393	.423	125	1	0			1.000	-0	/O-7	0.0
Total	3	57	179	24	40	7	2	2	26	9	21	.223	.265	.318	61	-10	0			.961	-8	/O-48,C-1	-2.1

■ JACK FIMPLE
Fimple, John Joseph b: 2/10/59, Darby, Pa. BR/TR, 6'2", 185 lbs. Deb: 7/30/83

YEAR	TM/L	G	AB	R	H	2B	3B	HR	RBI	BB	SO	AVG	OBP	SLG	PRO+	BR/A	SB	CS	SBR	FA	FR	G/POS	TPR
1983	*LA-N	54	148	16	37	8	1	2	22	11	39	.250	.302	.358	83	-4	1	0	0	.989	12	C-54	1.1
1984	LA-N	12	26	2	5	1	0	0	3	1	6	.192	.222	.231	28	-3	0	0	0	.983	2	C-12	-0.1
1986	LA-N	13	13	2	1	0	0	0	2	6	6	.077	.368	.077	32	-1	0	0	0	1.000	1	/C-7,1-1,2	0.0
1987	Cal-A	13	10	1	2	0	0	0	1	1	2	.200	.273	.200	29	-1	0	0	0	.913	1	C-13	0.0
Total	4	92	197	21	45	9	1	2	28	19	53	.228	.296	.315	70	-8	1	0	0	.986	15	/C-86,2-1,1	1.0

■ JIM FINIGAN
Finigan, James Leroy b: 8/19/28, Quincy, Ill. d: 5/16/81, Quincy, Ill. BR/TR, 5'11", 175 lbs. Deb: 4/25/54

YEAR	TM/L	G	AB	R	H	2B	3B	HR	RBI	BB	SO	AVG	OBP	SLG	PRO+	BR/A	SB	CS	SBR	FA	FR	G/POS	TPR
1954	Phi-A☆	136	487	57	147	25	6	7	51	64	66	.302	.383	.421	120	14	2	8	-4	.948	2	*3-136	1.0
1955	KC-A★	150	545	72	139	30	7	9	68	61	49	.255	.333	.385	92	-7	1	3	-2	.975	-7	2-90,3-59	-0.9
1956	KC-A	91	250	29	54	7	2	2	21	30	28	.216	.302	.284	55	-16	3	1	0	.969	-1	2-52,3-32	-1.2
1957	Det-A	64	174	20	47	4	2	0	17	23	18	.270	.359	.316	84	-3	1	1	-0	.954	1	3-59/2-3	0.2
1958	SF-N	23	25	3	5	2	0	0	1	3	5	.200	.310	.280	59	-1	0	0	0	.917	-2	/2-8,3-4	-0.3
1959	Bal-A	48	119	14	30	6	0	1	10	9	10	.252	.305	.328	75	-4	1	0	0	.959	0	3-42/2-6,S	-0.3
Total	6	512	1600	195	422	74	17	19	168	190	176	.264	.344	.367	92	-17	8	13	-5	.948	-3	3-332,2-159/S	-1.5

■ BOB FINLEY
Finley, Robert Edward b: 11/25/15, Ennis, Tex. d: 1/2/86, W.Covina, Cal. BR/TR, 6'1", 200 lbs. Deb: 7/4/43

YEAR	TM/L	G	AB	R	H	2B	3B	HR	RBI	BB	SO	AVG	OBP	SLG	PRO+	BR/A	SB	CS	SBR	FA	FR	G/POS	TPR
1943	Phi-N	28	81	9	21	2	0	1	7	4	10	.259	.294	.321	81	-2	0			.962	3	C-24	0.2
1944	Phi-N	94	281	18	70	11	1	1	21	12	25	.249	.292	.306	71	-11	1			.967	-2	C-74	-0.9
Total	2	122	362	27	91	13	1	2	28	16	35	.251	.292	.309	73	-13	1			.966	1	/C-98	-0.7

■ STEVE FINLEY
Finley, Steven Allen b: 3/12/65, Paducah, Ky. BL/TL, 6'2", 175 lbs. Deb: 4/3/89

YEAR	TM/L	G	AB	R	H	2B	3B	HR	RBI	BB	SO	AVG	OBP	SLG	PRO+	BR/A	SB	CS	SBR	FA	FR	G/POS	TPR
1989	Bal-A	81	217	35	54	5	2	2	25	15	30	.249	.300	.318	77	-7	17	3	3	.986	-8	O-76/D-3	-1.4
1990	Bal-A	142	464	46	119	16	4	3	37	32	53	.256	.307	.328	80	-12	22	9	1	.977	-1	*O-133/D-2	-1.5
1991	Hou-N	159	596	84	170	28	10	8	54	42	65	.285	.334	.406	114	9	34	18	-1	.985	-6	*O-153	0.0
1992	Hou-N	162	607	84	177	29	13	5	55	58	63	.292	.356	.407	121	17	44	9	8	.993	10	*O-160	3.3
1993	Hou-N	142	545	69	145	15	13	8	44	28	65	.266	.306	.385	87	-12	19	6	2	.988	9	*O-140	-0.3
1994	Hou-N	94	373	64	103	16	5	11	33	28	52	.276	.330	.434	99	-1	13	7	-0	.982	5	O-92	0.1
Total	6	780	2802	382	768	109	47	37	248	203	328	.274	.326	.386	100	-6	149	52	14	.986	9	O-754/D-5	0.2

■ BILL FINLEY
Finley, William James b: 10/4/1863, New York, N.Y. d: 10/6/12, Asbury Park, N.J. 5'3", 170 lbs. Deb: 7/12/1886

YEAR	TM/L	G	AB	R	H	2B	3B	HR	RBI	BB	SO	AVG	OBP	SLG	PRO+	BR/A	SB	CS	SBR	FA	FR	G/POS	TPR
1886	NY-N	13	44	2	8	0	0	0	5	1	8	.182	.200	.182	17	-4	2			.800	-3	/O-8,C-8	-0.6

■ NEAL FINN
Finn, Cornelius Francis "Mickey" b: 1/24/04, Brooklyn, N.Y. d: 7/7/33, Allentown, Pa. BR/TR, 5'11", 168 lbs. Deb: 4/21/30

YEAR	TM/L	G	AB	R	H	2B	3B	HR	RBI	BB	SO	AVG	OBP	SLG	PRO+	BR/A	SB	CS	SBR	FA	FR	G/POS	TPR
1930	Bro-N	87	273	42	76	13	6	3	30	26	18	.278	.350	.359	73	-11	3			.948	-6	2-81	-1.2
1931	Bro-N	118	413	46	113	22	2	0	45	21	42	.274	.314	.337	75	-14	2			.975	0	*2-112	-0.7
1932	Bro-N	65	189	22	45	5	2	0	14	11	15	.238	.284	.286	55	-12	2			.933	4	3-50/2-2,S	-0.5
1933	Phi-N	51	169	15	40	4	1	0	13	10	14	.237	.287	.272	54	-10	2			.964	-1	2-51	-0.9
Total	4	321	1044	125	274	44	5	3	102	68	89	.262	.314	.323	67	-48	9			.964	-3	2-246/3-50,S	-3.3

■ HAL FINNEY
Finney, Harold Wilson b: 7/30/05, Lafayette, Ala. d: 12/20/91, Lafayette, Ala. BR/TR, 5'11", 170 lbs. Deb: 6/24/31 F

YEAR	TM/L	G	AB	R	H	2B	3B	HR	RBI	BB	SO	AVG	OBP	SLG	PRO+	BR/A	SB	CS	SBR	FA	FR	G/POS	TPR
1931	Pit-N	10	26	2	8	1	0	0	2	0	1	.308	.333	.346	84	-1	1			1.000	-0	/C-6	0.0
1932	Pit-N	31	33	14	7	3	0	0	4	3	4	.212	.297	.303	63	-2	0			.971	3	C-11	0.1
1933	Pit-N	56	133	17	31	4	1	1	18	3	19	.233	.250	.301	57	-8	0			.993	-2	C-47	-0.8
1934	Pit-N	5	0	3	0	0	0	0	0	0	0	—	1.000	—	188	0	0			.000	0	/C-1	0.0
1936	Pit-N	21	35	3	0	0	0	0	3	0	8	.000	.000	.000	-98	-10	0			.956	1	C-14	-0.8
Total	5	123	227	39	46	8	1	1	27	6	32	.203	.233	.260	37	-19	1			.983	1	/C-79	-1.5

■ LOU FINNEY
Finney, Louis Klopsche b: 8/13/10, Buffalo, Ala. d: 4/22/66, Lafayette, Ala. BL/TR, 6', 180 lbs. Deb: 9/12/31 F

YEAR	TM/L	G	AB	R	H	2B	3B	HR	RBI	BB	SO	AVG	OBP	SLG	PRO+	BR/A	SB	CS	SBR	FA	FR	G/POS	TPR
1931	Phi-A	9	24	7	9	0	1	0	3	6	1	.375	.516	.458	149	2	0	0	0	1.000	1	/O-8	0.3
1933	Phi-A	74	240	26	64	12	2	3	32	13	17	.267	.307	.371	78	-8	1	3	-2	.947	2	O-63	-1.0
1934	Phi-A	92	272	32	76	11	4	1	28	14	17	.279	.315	.360	77	-10	4	3	-1	.943	0	O-54,1-15	-1.3
1935	Phi-A	109	410	45	112	11	6	0	31	18	18	.273	.307	.329	65	-22	7	3	1	.943	-2	O-76,1-18	-2.6
1936	Phi-A	151	653	100	197	26	10	1	41	47	22	.302	.351	.377	81	-19	7	9	-3	.990	-4	1-78,O-73	-3.3
1937	Phi-A	92	379	53	95	14	9	1	20	20	16	.251	.288	.343	59	-25	2	5	-2	.989	-4	1-50,O-39/2	-3.6
1938	Phi-A	122	454	61	125	21	12	10	48	39	25	.275	.331	.441	94	-6	5	8	-3	.990	-3	1-64,O-46	-1.9
1939	Phi-A	9	22	1	3	0	0	0	1	2	0	.136	.208	.136	-10	-4	0	0	0	1.000	0	/O-4	-0.3
	Bos-A	95	249	43	81	18	3	1	46	24	11	.325	.385	.434	105	2	2	5	-2	.986	-6	1-32,O-24	-1.0
	Yr	104	271	44	84	18	3	1	47	26	11	.310	.370	.410	96	-1	2	5	-2	.986	-6	1-32,O-28	-1.3
1940	Bos-A★	130	534	73	171	31	15	5	73	33	13	.320	.360	.463	107	5	5	2	0	.975	2	O-69,1-51	-0.2
1941	Bos-A	127	497	83	143	24	10	4	53	38	17	.288	.340	.400	93	-6	2	5	-2	.945	-3	O-92,1-24	-1.8
1942	Bos-A	113	397	58	113	16	7	3	61	29	11	.285	.335	.383	98	-2	3	3	-1	.976	2	O-95/1-2	-0.6
1944	Bos-A	68	251	37	72	11	4	0	32	23	7	.287	.347	.347	100	0	1	0	0	.987	-5	1-59/O-2	-0.8
1945	Bos-A	2	2	0	0	0	0	0	0	0	0	.000	.000	.000	-98	-0	0	0	0	.000	0	H	-0.1
	StL-A	57	213	24	59	8	4	2	22	21	7	.277	.345	.380	105	1	0	0	0	.986	-2	O-36,1-22/3	-0.4
	Yr	59	215	24	59	8	4	2	22	21	7	.274	.342	.377	103	1	0	0	0	.986	-2	O-36,1-22/3	-0.5
1946	StL-A	16	30	0	9	0	0	0	3	2	4	.300	.344	.300	77	-1	0	0	0	.938	0	/O-7	-0.1
1947	Phi-N	4	4	0	0	0	0	0	0	0	0	.000	.000	.000	-99	-1	0			.000	0	H	-0.1
Total	15	1270	4631	643	1329	203	85	31	494	329	186	.287	.336	.388	88	-92	39	45		.961	-22	O-688,1-415/32	-18.8

■ MIKE FIORE
Fiore, Michael Gary Joseph b: 10/11/44, Brooklyn, N.Y. BL/TL, 6', 185 lbs. Deb: 9/21/68

YEAR	TM/L	G	AB	R	H	2B	3B	HR	RBI	BB	SO	AVG	OBP	SLG	PRO+	BR/A	SB	CS	SBR	FA	FR	G/POS	TPR
1968	Bal-A	6	17	2	1	0	0	0	0	4	4	.059	.273	.059	5	-2	0	0	0	.943	-0	/1-5,O-1	-0.3
1969	KC-A	107	339	53	93	14	1	12	35	84	63	.274	.421	.428	137	21	4	4	-1	.988	10	1-91,O-13	2.3
1970	KC-A	25	72	6	13	2	0	0	4	13	24	.181	.306	.208	44	-5	1	1	-0	.986	1	1-20	-0.7
	Bos-A	41	50	5	7	0	0	0	4	8	4	.140	.259	.140	12	-6	0	0	0	1.000	0	1-17/O-2	-0.7
	Yr	66	122	11	20	2	0	0	8	21	28	.164	.287	.180	30	-11	1	1	-0	.991	1	1-37/O-2	-1.4
1971	Bos-A	51	62	9	11	2	0	1	6	12	14	.177	.311	.258	58	-3	0	3	-2	1.000	-0	1-12	-0.6
1972	StL-N	17	10	1	1	0	0	0	1	2	3	.100	.250	.100	3	-2	0	0	0	1.000	-1	/1-6,O-1	-0.1
	SD-N	7	6	0	0	0	0	0	0	1	3	.000	.143	.000	-61	-1	0	0	0	.000	0	H	-0.1
	Yr	24	16	0	1	0	0	0	1	3	6	.063	.190	.063	-20	-2	0	0	0	1.000	-1	/1-6,O-1	-0.3
Total	5	254	556	75	126	18	1	13	50	124	115	.227	.370	.333	97	-3	5	8	-3	.988	9	1-151/O-17	-0.3

■ DAN FIROVA
Firova, Daniel Michael b: 10/16/56, Refugio, Tex. BR/TR, 6', 185 lbs. Deb: 9/1/81

YEAR	TM/L	G	AB	R	H	2B	3B	HR	RBI	BB	SO	AVG	OBP	SLG	PRO+	BR/A	SB	CS	SBR	FA	FR	G/POS	TPR
1981	Sea-A	13	2	0	0	0	0	0	0	0	0	.000	.000	.000	-96	-0	0	0	0	1.000	1	C-13	0.0
1982	Sea-A	3	5	0	0	0	0	0	0	0	0	.000	.000	.000	-97	-1	0	0	0	.900	-0	/C-3	-0.1
1988	Cle-A	1	0	0	0	0	0	0	0	0	0						0	0	0	1.000	0	/C-1	0.0
Total	3	17	7	0	0	0	0	0	0	0	0	.000	.000	.000	-97	-0	0	0	0	.944	1	/C-17	-0.1

YEAR	TM/L	G	AB	R	H	2B	3B	HR	RBI	BB	SO	AVG	OBP	SLG	PRO+	BR/A	SB	CS	SBR	FA	FR	G/POS	TPR

■ WILLIAM FISCHER Fischer, William Charles b: 3/2/1891, New York, N.Y. d: 9/4/45, Richmond, Va. BL/TR, 6′, 174 lbs. Deb: 6/11/13

1913	Bro-N	62	165	16	44	9	4	1	12	10	5	.267	.313	.388	97	-1	0			.974	-3	C-51	0.0
1914	Bro-N	43	105	12	27	1	2	0	8	8	12	.257	.310	.305	81	-2	1			.958	3	C-30	0.3
1915	Chi-F	105	292	30	96	15	4	4	50	24	19	.329	.384	.449	130	11	5			.972	-6	C-80	1.2
1916	Chi-N	65	179	15	35	9	2	1	14	11	8	.196	.246	.285	57	-9	2			.973	4	C-56	-0.2
	Pit-N	42	113	11	29	7	1	1	6	10	3	.257	.323	.363	109	1	1			.974	5	C-35	1.0
	Yr	107	292	26	64	16	3	2	20	21	11	.219	.276	.315	76	-8	3			.973	8	C-91	0.8
1917	Pit-N	95	245	25	70	9	2	3	25	27	19	.286	.359	.376	121	7	11			.961	-9	C-69/1-2	0.4
Total	5	412	1099	109	301	50	15	10	115	90	66	.274	.332	.374	104	7	20			.969	7	C-321/1-2	2.7

■ MIKE FISCHLIN Fischlin, Michael Thomas b: 9/13/55, Sacramento, Cal. BR/TR, 6′1″, 165 lbs. Deb: 9/3/77

1977	Hou-N	13	15	0	3	0	0	0	0	0	2	.200	.200	.200	8	-2	0	0	0	1.000	1	S-12	0.0
1978	Hou-N	44	86	3	10	1	0	0	0	4	9	.116	.165	.128	-19	-14	1	0	0	.928	-4	S-41	-1.6
1980	Hou-N	1	1	0	0	0	0	0	0	0	0	.000	.000	.000	-99	-0	0	0	0	1.000	-0	/S-1	0.0
1981	Cle-A	22	43	3	10	1	0	0	5	3	6	.233	.283	.256	57	-2	3	2	-0	.955	-0	S-19/2-1	0.0
1982	Cle-A	112	276	34	74	12	1	0	21	34	36	.268	.353	.319	86	-4	9	5	-0	.970	-7	*S-101/3-8,2C	-0.3
1983	Cle-A	95	225	31	47	5	2	2	23	26	32	.209	.296	.276	56	-13	9	2	2	.965	21	2-71,S-15/3D	1.3
1984	Cle-A	85	133	17	30	4	2	1	14	12	20	.226	.290	.308	64	-6	2	2	-1	.981	18	2-55,S-17,S	1.3
1985	Cle-A	73	60	12	12	4	1	0	2	5	7	.200	.262	.300	54	-4	0	1	-1	.990	27	2-31,S-22/13D	2.3
1986	NY-A	71	102	9	21	2	0	0	3	8	29	.206	.264	.225	35	-9	0	1	-1	.955	7	S-42,2-27	-0.1
1987	Atl-N	1	0	0	0	0	0	0	0	0	0	—	—	—	—	0	0	0	0	.000	-0	/R	0.0
Total	10	517	941	109	207	29	6	3	68	92	142	.220	.293	.273	57	-54	24	13	-1	.959	63	S-268,2-191/31DC	2.7

■ SAM FISHBURN Fishburn, Samuel E. b: 5/15/1893, Haverhill, Mass. d: 4/11/65, Bethlehem, Pa. BR/TR, 5′9″, 157 lbs. Deb: 9/30/19

| 1919 | StL-N | 9 | 6 | 0 | 2 | 1 | 0 | 0 | 2 | 0 | 0 | .333 | .333 | .500 | 158 | 0 | 0 | | | 1.000 | 0 | /1-1,2-1 | 0.1 |

■ JOHN FISHEL Fishel, John Alan b: 11/8/62, Fullerton, Cal. BR/TR, 5′11″, 185 lbs. Deb: 7/14/88

| 1988 | Hou-N | 19 | 26 | 1 | 6 | 0 | 0 | 1 | 2 | 3 | 6 | .231 | .310 | .346 | 92 | -0 | 0 | 0 | 0 | 1.000 | -2 | /O-6 | -0.3 |

■ FISHER Fisher Deb: 6/15/1889

| 1889 | Lou-a | 1 | 2 | 0 | 1 | 0 | 0 | 0 | 0 | 0 | 0 | .500 | .500 | .500 | 189 | 0 | 0 | | | .000 | -1 | /O-1 | 0.0 |

■ GUS FISHER Fisher, August Harris b: 10/21/1885, Pottsboro, Tex. d: 4/8/72, Portland, Ore. BL/TR, 5′10″, 175 lbs. Deb: 4/18/11

1911	Cle-A	70	203	20	53	6	3	0	12	7		.261	.302	.320	73	-8	6			.956	8	C-58/1-1	0.5
1912	NY-A	4	10	1	1	0	0	0	0	0		.100	.100	.100	-40	-2	0			1.000	1	/C-4	-0.1
Total	2	74	213	21	54	6	3	0	12	7		.254	.293	.310	68	-10	6			.958	8	/C-62,1-1	0.4

■ CHARLES FISHER Fisher, Charles J. b: Philadelphia, Pa. Deb: 6/7/1884

1884	KC-U	10	40	3	8	2	0	0		0		.200	.200	.250	25	-4				.711	-0	/3-9,S-1	-0.4
	CP-U	1	3	1	2	0	0	0		1		.667	.750	.667	290	1				.500	-1	/3-1	0.0
	Yr	11	43	4	10	2	0	0		1		.233	.250	.279	49	-3				.702	-2	3-10/S-1	-0.4

■ SHOWBOAT FISHER Fisher, George Aloys b: 1/16/1899, Wesley, Iowa d: 5/15/94, St.Cloud, Minn. BL/TR, 5′10″, 170 lbs. Deb: 4/24/23

1923	Was-A	13	23	4	6	2	0	0	2	4	3	.261	.370	.348	95	-0	0			.750	0	/O-5	0.0
1924	Was-A	15	41	7	9	1	0	0	6	6	6	.220	.319	.244	48	-3	2	0	1	.933	-2	O-11	-0.5
1930	*StL-N	92	254	49	95	18	6	8	61	25	21	.374	.432	.587	139	16	4			.962	-3	O-67	0.8
1932	StL-A	18	22	2	4	0	0	0	2	2	5	.182	.250	.182	13	-3	0	0	0	1.000	-1	/O-5	-0.4
Total	4	138	340	62	114	21	6	8	71	37	35	.335	.402	.503	119	10	6	0		.946	-6	/O-88	-0.1

■ GEORGE FISHER Fisher, George C. b: Wilmington, Del. BL, Deb: 7/17/1884

1884	Phi-U	10	36	7	8	2	0	0		3		.222	.282	.278	57	-2				.667	-2	/P-8,1-2	-0.2
	Cle-N	6	24	2	3	0	0	0	0	3		.125	.125	.125	-20	-3				.897	-3	/2-6,C-1	-0.6
	Wil-U	8	29	0	2	0	0	0		0		.069	.069	.069	-61	-6				.818	-1	/O-6,S-2	-0.7
1885	Buf-N	1	4	0	0	0	0	0		0		.000	.000	.000	-97	-1				1.000	0	/P-1	0.0
Total	2	25	93	9	13	2	0	0	0	3	3	.140	.167	.161	-7	-12				.710	-6	/P-9,0-6,2S1C	-1.5

■ HARRY FISHER Fisher, Harry Devereux b: 1/3/26, Newbury, Ont., Can. d: 9/20/81, Waterloo, Ont., Canada BL/TR, 6′, 180 lbs. Deb: 9/16/51

1951	Pit-N	3	3	0	0	0	0	0	0	0	0	.000	.000	.000	-97	-1	0	0	0	.000	0	H	-0.1
1952	Pit-N	15	15	0	5	1	0	0	1	0	3	.333	.333	.400	100	-0	0	0	0	1.000	-1	/P-8	0.0
Total	2	18	18	0	5	1	0	0	1	0	3	.278	.278	.333	66	-1	0	0	0	1.000	-1	/P-8	-0.1

■ RED FISHER Fisher, John Gus b: 6/22/1887, Pittsburg, Pa. d: 1/31/40, Louisville, Ky. BL/TR, Deb: 4/25/10

| 1910 | StL-A | 23 | 72 | 5 | 9 | 2 | 1 | 0 | 3 | 8 | | .125 | .222 | .181 | 28 | -6 | 5 | | | .935 | -1 | O-19 | -0.9 |

■ NEWT FISHER Fisher, Newton "Ike" b: 6/28/1871, Nashville, Tenn. d: 2/28/47, Norwood Park, Ill. BR/TR, 5′9.5″, 171 lbs. Deb: 5/17/1898 F

| 1898 | Phi-N | 9 | 26 | 0 | 3 | 1 | 0 | 0 | 0 | 0 | | .115 | .148 | .154 | -14 | -4 | 1 | | | .844 | -1 | /C-8,3-1 | -0.4 |

■ BOB FISHER Fisher, Robert Taylor b: 11/3/1886, Nashville, Tenn. d: 8/4/63, Jacksonville, Fla. BR/TR, 5′9.5″, 170 lbs. Deb: 6/3/12 F

1912	Bro-N	82	257	27	60	10	3	0	26	14	32	.233	.273	.296	58	-16	7			.917	-14	S-74/2-1,3	-2.4
1913	Bro-N	132	474	42	124	11	10	4	54	10	43	.262	.278	.352	77	-16	16			.923	-19	*S-131	-2.4
1914	Chi-N	15	50	5	15	2	2	0	5	3	4	.300	.340	.420	126	1	2			.943	-1	S-15	0.1
1915	Chi-N	147	568	70	163	22	5	5	53	30	51	.287	.326	.370	110	0	9	20	-9	.933	-20	*S-145	-1.4
1916	Cin-N	61	136	9	37	4	3	0	11	8	14	.272	.313	.346	104	0	7			.905	-12	S-29/2-6,O	-1.1
1918	StL-N	63	246	36	78	11	3	2	20	15	11	.317	.356	.411	138	10	7			.979	19	2-63	3.5
1919	StL-N	3	11	0	3	1	0	0	1	0	2	.273	.273	.364	96	-0	0			.900	0	/2-3	0.1
Total	7	503	1742	189	480	61	26	11	170	80	157	.276	.309	.359	96	-13	48	20		.925	-48	S-394/2-73,O3	-3.6

■ WILBUR FISHER Fisher, Wilbur McCullough b: 7/18/1894, Green Bottom, W.Va. d: 10/24/60, Welch, W.Va. BL/TR, 6′, 174 lbs. Deb: 6/13/16

| 1916 | Pit-N | 1 | 1 | 0 | 0 | 0 | 0 | 0 | 0 | 0 | 0 | .000 | .000 | .000 | -99 | -0 | 0 | | | .000 | 0 | H | 0.0 |

■ CHEROKEE FISHER Fisher, William Charles b: 12/1845, Philadelphia, Pa. d: 9/26/12, New York, N.Y. BR/TR, 5′9″, 164 lbs. Deb: 5/6/1871

1871	Rok-n	25	123	24	28	3	3	1	22	3	1	.228	.246	.325	65	-5	1					*P-24/S-1	0.2
1872	Bal-n	46	226	40	52	10	2	1	39	2	5	.230	.237	.305	63	-11						P-19,3-17,O	-0.4
1873	Ath-n	51	253	50	66	4	3	1	35	4	5	.261	.272	.312	67	-12						*O-45/P-13,21	-0.5
1874	Har-n	52	242	28	54	8	0	0		0		.223	.223	.256	50	-14						P-39,O-10/3S	0.2
1875	Phi-n	41	177	26	41	2	1	0		1		.232	.236	.254	67	-6						P-41/O-1	0.4
1876	Cin-N	35	129	12	32	1	0	0	4	0	8	.248	.248	.256	80	-2				.793	-5	P-28,O-11/S1	-0.3
1877	Chi-N	1	4	0	0	0	0	0	0	0		.000	.000	.000	-89	-1				.667	-0	/3-1	-0.1
1878	Pro-N	1	3	0	0	0	0	0	0	0		.000	.000	.000	-99	-1				1.000	0	/P-1	0.0
Total	5 n	215	1021	168	241	27	9	3	96	10	11	.236	.243	.289	62	-48						P-136/O-72,32S1	-0.1
Total	3	37	136	12	32	1	0	0	4	0	10	.235	.235	.243	68	-4				.803	-5	/P-29,O-11,31S	-0.4

■ CARLTON FISK Fisk, Carlton Ernest "Pudge" b: 12/26/47, Bellows Falls, Vt. BR/TR, 6′2″, 220 lbs. Deb: 9/18/69

1969	Bos-A	2	5	0	0	0	0	0	0	0	0	.000	.000	.000	-95	-1	0	0	0	/C-1			-0.3
1971	Bos-A	14	48	7	15	2	1	2	6	1	10	.313	.327	.521	128	-1	0	0	0	.975	-1	C-14	0.1
1972	Bos-A★	131	457	74	134	28	9	22	61	52	83	.293	.370	.538	159	33	5	2	0	.984	1	*C-131	4.4

YEAR	TM/L	G	AB	R	H	2B	3B	HR	RBI	BB	SO	AVG	OBP	SLG	PRO+	BR/A	SB	CS	SBR	FA	FR	G/POS	TPR
1973	Bos-A★	135	508	65	125	21	0	26	71	37	99	.246	.310	.441	103	0	7	2	1	.983	6	*C-131/D-3	1.3
1974	Bos-A†	52	187	36	56	12	1	11	26	24	23	.299	.385	.551	156	13	5	1	1	.980	2	C-50/D-2	1.9
1975	*Bos-A	79	263	47	87	14	4	10	52	27	32	.331	.397	.529	147	16	4	3	-1	.979	-4	C-71/D-6	1.4
1976	Bos-A★	134	487	76	124	17	5	17	58	56	71	.255	.339	.415	107	4	12	5	1	.984	10	*C-133/D-1	1.9
1977	Bos-A★	152	536	106	169	26	3	26	102	75	85	.315	.408	.521	135	27	7	6	-2	.987	0	*C-151	3.0
1978	Bos-A★	157	571	94	162	39	5	20	88	71	83	.284	.370	.475	123	17	7	2	1	.980	11	*C-154/O-1,D	3.4
1979	Bos-A	91	320	49	87	23	2	10	42	10	38	.272	.307	.450	96	-3	3	0	1	.982	-12	D-42,C-39/O	-1.3
1980	Bos-A★	131	478	73	138	25	3	18	62	36	62	.289	.355	.467	117	11	11	5	0	.983	-7	*C-115/O-5,13D	0.8
1981	Chi-A★	96	338	44	89	12	0	7	45	38	37	.263	.358	.361	110	6	3	2	-0	.990	-1	C-95/1-1,3O	0.7
1982	Chi-A★	135	476	66	127	17	3	14	65	46	60	.267	.339	.403	103	2	17	2	4	.994	-1	*C-133/1-2	1.0
1983	*Chi-A	138	488	85	141	26	4	26	86	46	88	.289	.357	.518	133	21	9	6	-1	.991	-2	*C-133/D-2	2.4
1984	Chi-A	102	359	54	83	20	1	21	43	26	60	.231	.292	.468	102	-1	6	0	2	.987	-17	C-90/D-5	-1.1
1985	Chi-A★	153	543	85	129	23	1	37	107	52	81	.238	.324	.488	114	9	17	9	-0	.989	-4	*C-130,D-28	1.1
1986	Chi-A	125	457	42	101	11	0	14	63	22	92	.221	.266	.337	61	-25	2	4	-2	.991	2	C-71,O-31/D	-2.1
1987	Chi-A	135	454	68	116	22	1	23	71	39	72	.256	.325	.460	103	1	1	4	-2	.990	2	*C-122/1-9,OD	0.8
1988	Chi-A	76	253	37	70	8	1	19	50	37	40	.277	.380	.542	155	19	0	0	0	.995	-5	C-74	2.0
1989	Chi-A	103	375	47	110	25	2	13	68	36	60	.293	.360	.475	137	18	1	0	0	**.993**	-15	C-90,D-13	0.8
1990	Chi-A	137	452	65	129	21	0	18	65	61	73	.285	.379	.451	134	22	7	2	1	.994	5	*C-116,D-14	3.5
1991	Chi-A★	134	460	42	111	25	0	18	74	32	86	.241	.301	.413	98	-3	1	2	-1	.993	-2	*C-106,D-13,1	-0.1
1992	Chi-A	62	188	12	43	4	1	3	21	23	38	.229	.316	.309	77	-5	3	0	1	.993	-6	C-54/D-2	-0.7
1993	Chi-A	25	53	2	10	0	0	1	4	2	11	.189	.232	.245	29	-5	0	1	-1	1.000	-4	C-25	-0.9
Total	24	2499	8756	1276	2356	421	47	376	1330	849	1386	.269	.343	.457	116	176	128	58	4	.988	-44	*C-2229,D-166/O13	24.0

■ WES FISLER
Fisler, Weston Dickson "Icicle" b: 7/5/1841, Camden, N.J. d: 12/25/22, Philadelphia, Pa. 5'6", 137 lbs. Deb: 5/20/1871

YEAR	TM/L	G	AB	R	H	2B	3B	HR	RBI	BB	SO	AVG	OBP	SLG	PRO+	BR/A	SB	CS	SBR	FA	FR	G/POS	TPR
1871	Ath-n	28	143	41	41	8	2	0	16	3	2	.279	.293	.361	88	-2	6					*1-26/2-2	-0.1
1872	Ath-n	47	243	50	84	14	3	0	48	4	4	.346	.356	.428	140	11						*2-46	0.6
1873	Ath-n	44	218	44	75	12	4	1	42	2	2	.344	.350	.450	124	5						*2-36,1-10	0.1
1874	Ath-n	37	179	26	59	12	1	0		0		.330	.330	.408	123	3						1-28/2-9	0.2
1875	Ath-n	58	267	55	74	14	3	0		4		.277	.288	.352	108	0						1-44/O-9,2	0.0
1876	Phi-N	59	278	42	80	15	1	1	30	2	4	.288	.293	.360	117	5				.911	1	O-24,2-21,1/S	0.4
Total	5 n	214	1054	218	333	60	13	3	106	13	8	.316	.324	.400	118	16						1-108/2-97,OD	0.8

■ CHARLIE FITZBERGER
Fitzberger, Charles Casper b: 2/13/04, Baltimore, Md. d: 1/25/65, Baltimore, Md. BL/TL, 6'1.5", 170 lbs. Deb: 9/11/28

YEAR	TM/L	G	AB	R	H	2B	3B	HR	RBI	BB	SO	AVG	OBP	SLG	PRO+	BR/A	SB	CS	SBR	FA	FR	G/POS	TPR
1928	Bos-N	7	7	0	2	0	0	0	0	0	3	.286	.286	.286	52	-0	0			.000	0	H	0.0

■ DENNIS FITZGERALD
Fitzgerald, Dennis S. b: 3/1865, England d: 10/16/36, New Haven, Conn. 5'10", 160 lbs. Deb: 4/17/1890

YEAR	TM/L	G	AB	R	H	2B	3B	HR	RBI	BB	SO	AVG	OBP	SLG	PRO+	BR/A	SB	CS	SBR	FA	FR	G/POS	TPR
1890	Phi-a	2	8	0	2	0	0	0		0		.250	.250	.250	48	-1	0			.667	-2	/S-2	-0.2

■ ED FITZ GERALD
Fitz Gerald, Edward Raymond b: 5/21/24, Santa Ynez, Cal. BR/TR, 6', 180 lbs. Deb: 4/19/48 C

YEAR	TM/L	G	AB	R	H	2B	3B	HR	RBI	BB	SO	AVG	OBP	SLG	PRO+	BR/A	SB	CS	SBR	FA	FR	G/POS	TPR
1948	Pit-N	102	262	31	70	9	3	1	35	32	37	.267	.349	.336	84	-5	3			.961	-2	C-96	-0.1
1949	Pit-N	75	160	16	42	7	0	2	18	8	27	.262	.302	.344	71	-7	1			.974	-5	C-56	-0.9
1950	Pit-N	6	15	1	1	1	0	0	0	0	3	.067	.067	.133	-47	-3	0			.950	-1	/C-5	-0.3
1951	Pit-N	55	97	8	22	6	0	0	13	7	10	.227	.286	.289	53	-6	1	1	-0	.965	-2	C-38	-0.8
1952	Pit-N	51	74	3	17	1	0	1	7	7	15	.233	.300	.288	62	-4	0	2	-1	1.000	-1	C-18/3-2	-0.6
1953	Pit-N	6	17	2	2	1	0	0	1	0	2	.118	.118	.176	-25	-3	0	0	0	1.000	-1	/C-5	-0.4
	Was-A	88	288	23	72	13	0	3	39	19	34	.250	.299	.326	70	-12	2	1	0	.989	-3	C-85	-1.1
1954	Was-A	115	360	33	104	13	5	4	40	33	22	.289	.352	.386	108	3	0	1	-1	.973	-17	*C-107	-0.9
1955	Was-A	74	236	28	56	3	1	4	19	25	23	.237	.318	.305	73	-9	0	1	-1	.982	-7	C-72	-1.4
1956	Was-A	64	148	15	45	8	0	2	12	20	16	.304	.387	.399	108	2	0	0	0	.974	-2	C-50	0.6
1957	Was-A	45	125	14	34	8	0	1	13	10	9	.272	.331	.360	90	-2	2	0	1	.963	-8	C-37	-0.8
1958	Was-A	58	114	7	30	3	0	0	11	8	15	.263	.311	.289	68	-5	0	0	0	.970	-6	C-21/1-5	-1.1
1959	Was-A	19	62	5	12	3	0	0	5	4	8	.194	.242	.242	34	-6	0	0	0	1.000	-1	C-16	-0.6
	Cle-A	49	129	12	35	1	1	1	4	12	14	.271	.343	.357	96	-1	0	0	0	.978	1	C-45	0.2
	Yr	68	191	17	47	9	1	1	9	16	22	.246	.311	.319	76	-6	0	0	0	.984	0	C-61	-0.4
Total	12	807	2086	199	542	82	10	19	217	185	235	.260	.324	.336	80	-56	9	6		.975	-48	C-651/1-5,3	-8.2

■ HOWIE FITZGERALD
Fitzgerald, Howard Chumney "Lefty" b: 5/16/02, Eagle Lake, Tex. d: 2/27/59, Matthews, Tex. BL/TL, 5'11.5", 163 lbs. Deb: 9/17/22

YEAR	TM/L	G	AB	R	H	2B	3B	HR	RBI	BB	SO	AVG	OBP	SLG	PRO+	BR/A	SB	CS	SBR	FA	FR	G/POS	TPR
1922	Chi-N	10	24	3	8	1	0	0	4	3	2	.333	.407	.375	101	0	1	0	0	.818	-2	/O-6	-0.1
1924	Chi-N	7	19	1	3	0	0	0	2	0	2	.158	.158	.158	-15	-3	0	0	0	1.000	-1	/O-5	-0.5
1926	Bos-A	31	97	11	25	2	0	0	8	5	7	.258	.294	.278	51	-7	1	4	-2	.882	-5	O-23	-1.5
Total	3	48	140	15	36	3	0	0	14	8	11	.257	.297	.279	52	-10	2	4	-2	.878	-8	/O-34	-2.1

■ MIKE FITZGERALD
Fitzgerald, Justin Howard b: 6/22/1890, San Mateo, Cal. d: 1/17/45, San Mateo, Cal. BL/TR, 5'8", 160 lbs. Deb: 6/20/11

YEAR	TM/L	G	AB	R	H	2B	3B	HR	RBI	BB	SO	AVG	OBP	SLG	PRO+	BR/A	SB	CS	SBR	FA	FR	G/POS	TPR
1911	NY-A	16	37	6	10	1	0	0	6	4		.270	.341	.297	74	-1	4			1.000	-0	/O-9	-0.3
1918	Phi-N	66	133	21	39	8	0	0	6	13	6	.293	.361	.353	110	2	3			.966	-14	O-59	-1.6
Total	2	82	170	27	49	9	0	0	12	17	6	.288	.356	.341	102	1	7			.971	-15	/O-68	-1.9

■ MATTY FITZGERALD
Fitzgerald, Matthew William b: 8/31/1880, Albany, N.Y. d: 9/22/49, Albany, N.Y. BR/TR, 6', 185 lbs. Deb: 9/15/06

YEAR	TM/L	G	AB	R	H	2B	3B	HR	RBI	BB	SO	AVG	OBP	SLG	PRO+	BR/A	SB	CS	SBR	FA	FR	G/POS	TPR
1906	NY-N	4	6	2	4	0	0	0	2	0		.667	.667	.667	309	1	1			1.000	-1	/C-3	0.1
1907	NY-N	7	15	1	2	1	0	0	1	0		.133	.133	.200	4	-2	0			.952	-1	/C-6	-0.3
Total	2	11	21	3	6	1	0	0	3	0		.286	.286	.333	91	-0	1			.967	-2	/C-9	-0.2

■ MIKE FITZGERALD
Fitzgerald, Michael Patrick b: 3/28/64, Savannah, Ga. BR/TR, 6'1", 196 lbs. Deb: 6/23/88

YEAR	TM/L	G	AB	R	H	2B	3B	HR	RBI	BB	SO	AVG	OBP	SLG	PRO+	BR/A	SB	CS	SBR	FA	FR	G/POS	TPR
1988	StL-N	13	46	4	9	1	0	0	1	0	9	.196	.213	.217	23	-5	0	0	0	.990	-2	1-12	-0.8

■ MIKE FITZGERALD
Fitzgerald, Michael Roy b: 7/13/60, Long Beach, Cal. BR/TR, 5'11", 190 lbs. Deb: 9/13/83

YEAR	TM/L	G	AB	R	H	2B	3B	HR	RBI	BB	SO	AVG	OBP	SLG	PRO+	BR/A	SB	CS	SBR	FA	FR	G/POS	TPR
1983	NY-N	8	20	1	2	0	0	0	2	3	6	.100	.217	.250	29	-2	0	0	0	.957	2	/C-8	0.1
1984	NY-N	112	360	20	87	15	1	2	33	24	71	.242	.291	.306	69	-15	1	0	0	**.995**	8	*C-107	-0.2
1985	Mon-N	108	295	25	61	7	1	5	34	38	55	.207	.301	.288	70	-12	5	3	0	.987	-6	*C-108	-1.3
1986	Mon-N	73	209	20	59	13	1	6	37	27	34	.282	.367	.440	123	7	3	2	0	.993	-7	C-71	0.4
1987	Mon-N	107	287	32	69	11	0	3	36	42	54	.240	.339	.310	71	-11	3	4	-2	.981	-1	*C-104/1-1,2	-0.7
1988	Mon-N	63	155	17	42	6	1	5	23	19	22	.271	.351	.419	115	3	2	2	-1	.979	4	C-47/O-4	1.0
1989	Mon-N	100	290	33	69	18	2	7	42	35	61	.238	.324	.386	101	0	3	4	-2	.984	-6	C-77/3-8,O	-0.3
1990	Mon-N	111	313	36	76	18	1	9	41	60	60	.243	.368	.393	114	8	8	1	2	.990	4	C-98/O-6	1.2
1991	Mon-N	71	198	17	40	5	2	4	28	22	35	.202	.282	.308	67	-9	4	2	1	.994	2	C-54/1-3,O	-0.4
1992	Cal-A	95	189	19	40	2	0	6	17	22	34	.212	.294	.317	78	-7	2	2	-1	.990	-15	C-74,O-11/312D	-2.0
Total	10	848	2316	220	545	95	9	48	293	292	432	.235	.323	.346	87	-37	31	20	-3	.988	-21	C-748/O-30,312D	-2.2

■ RAY FITZGERALD
Fitzgerald, Raymond Francis b: 12/5/04, Chicopee, Mass. d: 9/6/77, Westfield, Mass. BR/TR, 5'9", 168 lbs. Deb: 4/18/31

YEAR	TM/L	G	AB	R	H	2B	3B	HR	RBI	BB	SO	AVG	OBP	SLG	PRO+	BR/A	SB	CS	SBR	FA	FR	G/POS	TPR
1931	Cin-N	1	1	0	0	0	0	0		0		.000	.000	.000	-99	-0	0			.000	0	H	0.0

■ SHAUN FITZMAURICE
Fitzmaurice, Shaun Earle b: 8/25/42, Worcester, Mass. BR/TR, 6', 180 lbs. Deb: 9/9/66

YEAR	TM/L	G	AB	R	H	2B	3B	HR	RBI	BB	SO	AVG	OBP	SLG	PRO+	BR/A	SB	CS	SBR	FA	FR	G/POS	TPR
1966	NY-N	9	13	2	2	0	0	0	2		6	.154	.267	.154	21	-1	1	0	0	1.000	1	/O-5	-0.1

■ ED FITZPATRICK
Fitzpatrick, Edward Henry b: 12/9/1889, Lewistown, Pa. d: 10/23/65, Bethlehem, Pa. BR/TR, 5'8", 165 lbs. Deb: 4/17/15

YEAR	TM/L	G	AB	R	H	2B	3B	HR	RBI	BB	SO	AVG	OBP	SLG	PRO+	BR/A	SB	CS	SBR	FA	FR	G/POS	TPR
1915	Bos-N	105	303	54	67	19	3	0	44	43	36	.221	.344	.304	101	3	13	8	-1	.967	-5	2-71,O-29	-0.4

YEAR	TM/L	G	AB	R	H	2B	3B	HR	RBI	BB	SO	AVG	OBP	SLG	PRO+	BR/A	SB	CS	SBR	FA	FR	G/POS	TPR
1916	Bos-N	83	216	17	46	8	0	1	18	15	26	.213	.280	.264	70	-7	5			.950	-12	2-46,O-28	-2.2
1917	Bos-N	63	178	20	45	8	4	0	17	12	22	.253	.318	.343	109	2	4			.929	-13	2-22,O-19,3	-1.2
Total	3	251	697	91	158	35	7	1	59	70	84	.227	.319	.301	94	-3	22	8		.956	-30	2-139/O-76,3	-3.8

■ TOM FITZSIMMONS
Fitzsimmons, Thomas William b: 4/6/1890, Oakland, Cal. d: 12/20/71, Oakland, Cal. BR/TR, 6'1", 190 lbs. Deb: 6/12/19

YEAR	TM/L	G	AB	R	H	2B	3B	HR	RBI	BB	SO	AVG	OBP	SLG	PRO+	BR/A	SB	CS	SBR	FA	FR	G/POS	TPR
1919	Bro-N	4	4	1	0	0	0	0	0	1	2	.000	.200	.000	-36	-1	0			.500	-1	/3-4	-0.2

■ MAX FLACK
Flack, Max John b: 2/5/1890, Belleville, Ill. d: 7/31/75, Belleville, Ill. BL/TL, 5'7", 148 lbs. Deb: 4/16/14

YEAR	TM/L	G	AB	R	H	2B	3B	HR	RBI	BB	SO	AVG	OBP	SLG	PRO+	BR/A	SB	CS	SBR	FA	FR	G/POS	TPR
1914	Chi-F	134	502	66	124	15	3	2	39	51	48	.247	.324	.301	66	-25	37			.973	-1	*O-133	-3.3
1915	Chi-F	141	523	88	164	20	14	3	45	40	21	.314	.365	.423	117	11	37			.969	2	*O-138	0.6
1916	Chi-N	141	465	65	120	14	3	3	20	42	43	.258	.320	.320	87	-7	24	19	-4	.991	2	*O-136	-1.8
1917	Chi-N	131	447	65	111	18	7	0	21	51	34	.248	.325	.320	91	-4	17			.947	-3	*O-117	-1.5
1918	*Chi-N	123	478	74	123	17	10	4	41	56	19	.257	.343	.360	112	8	17			.978	3	*O-121	0.4
1919	Chi-N	116	469	71	138	20	4	6	35	34	13	.294	.346	.392	121	12	18			.986	-0	*O-116	0.4
1920	Chi-N	135	520	85	157	30	6	4	49	52	15	.302	.373	.406	121	16	13	19	-8	.967	-5	*O-132	-0.8
1921	Chi-N	133	572	80	172	31	4	6	37	32	15	.301	.342	.400	96	-4	17	11	-2	.989	4	*O-130	-1.1
1922	Chi-N	17	54	7	12	1	0	0	6	2	4	.222	.250	.241	27	-6	2	1	0	.933	-2	O-15	-0.9
	StL-N	66	267	46	78	12	1	2	21	31	11	.292	.368	.367	95	-1	3	5	-2	.968	-4	O-66	-1.2
	Yr	83	321	53	90	13	1	2	27	33	15	.280	.349	.346	83	-8	5	6	-2	.961	-6	O-81	-2.1
1923	StL-N	128	505	82	147	16	9	3	28	41	15	.291	.348	.376	93	-5	7	8	-3	.951	-6	*O-121	-2.0
1924	StL-N	67	209	31	55	11	3	2	21	21	5	.263	.330	.373	90	-3	5	3	-2	.971	1	O-52	-0.7
1925	StL-N	79	241	23	60	7	8	0	28	21	9	.249	.309	.344	65	-13	5	3	-0	.991	-2	O-59	-1.8
Total	12	1411	5252	783	1461	212	72	35	391	474	253	.278	.342	.366	97	-21	200	71		.972	-12	*O-1336	-13.7

■ WALLY FLAGER
Flager, Walter Leonard b: 11/3/21, Chicago Heights, Ill. d: 12/16/90, Keizer, Ore. BL/TR, 5'11", 160 lbs. Deb: 4/17/45

YEAR	TM/L	G	AB	R	H	2B	3B	HR	RBI	BB	SO	AVG	OBP	SLG	PRO+	BR/A	SB	CS	SBR	FA	FR	G/POS	TPR
1945	Cin-N	21	52	5	11	1	0	0	6	8	5	.212	.317	.231	55	-3	0			.933	-7	S-15	-0.9
	Phi-N	49	168	21	42	4	1	2	15	17	15	.250	.323	.321	82	-4	1			.946	1	S-48/2-1	0.1
	Yr	70	220	26	53	5	1	2	21	25	20	.241	.321	.300	75	-7	1			.943	-6	S-63/2-1	-0.8

■ IRA FLAGSTEAD
Flagstead, Ira James "Pete" b: 9/22/1893, Montague, Mich. d: 3/13/40, Olympia, Wash. BR/TR, 5'9", 165 lbs. Deb: 7/20/17

YEAR	TM/L	G	AB	R	H	2B	3B	HR	RBI	BB	SO	AVG	OBP	SLG	PRO+	BR/A	SB	CS	SBR	FA	FR	G/POS	TPR
1917	Det-A	4	4	0	0	0	0	0	0	1		.000	.000	.000	-99	-1	0			.000	-1	/O-2	-0.2
1919	Det-A	97	287	43	95	22	3	5	41	35	39	.331	.416	.481	155	22	6			.951	8	O-83	1.9
1920	Det-A	110	311	40	73	13	5	3	35	37	27	.235	.318	.338	76	-11	3	4	-2	.967	7	O-82	-1.2
1921	Det-A	85	259	40	79	16	2	0	31	21	21	.305	.371	.382	93	-2	8	4	0	.903	-5	S-55,O-12/23	-0.3
1922	Det-A	44	91	21	28	5	3	3	8	14	16	.308	.411	.527	148	7	0	1	-1	.967	-2	O-32	0.3
1923	Det-A	1	1	0	0	0	0	0	0	0	0	.000	.000	.000	-99	-0	0	0	0	.000	0	H	0.0
	Bos-A	109	382	55	119	23	4	8	53	37	26	.312	.380	.455	119	10	7	10	-4	.965	19	*O-102/S-1	1.7
	Yr	110	383	55	119	23	4	8	53	37	26	.311	.379	.454	118	10	7	10	-4	.965	19	*O-102/S-1	1.7
1924	Bos-A	149	560	106	172	35	7	5	43	77	41	.307	.401	.421	112	13	10	13	-5	.975	-2	*O-144	-0.3
1925	Bos-A	148	572	84	160	38	2	6	61	63	30	.280	.356	.385	88	-10	5	6	-2	.976	20	*O-144	-0.2
1926	Bos-A	98	415	65	124	31	7	3	31	36	22	.299	.363	.429	109	5	4	6	-2	.982	9	O-98	0.4
1927	Bos-A	131	466	63	133	26	8	4	69	57	25	.285	.374	.401	103	2	4	12	2	.986	11	*O-129	0.8
1928	Bos-A	140	510	84	148	41	4	1	39	60	23	.290	.366	.392	101	2	12	9	-2	.973	5	*O-135	-0.3
1929	Bos-A	14	36	9	11	2	0	0	3	5	1	.306	.390	.361	97	-0	3	3	-2	.955	-3	O-13	-0.5
	Was-A	18	39	5	7	1	0	0	9	4	5	.179	.256	.205	20	-5	1	0	0	.971	3	O-11	-0.2
	Yr	32	75	14	18	3	0	0	12	9	6	.240	.321	.280	57	-5	2	3	-1	.965	0	O-24	-0.7
	Pit-N	26	50	8	14	2	1	0	6	4	2	.280	.333	.360	70	-2	1			1.000	0	/O-9	-0.2
1930	Pit-N	44	156	21	39	7	4	2	21	17	9	.250	.324	.385	70	-8	1			.961	-3	O-40	-1.2
Total	13	1218	4139	644	1202	262	50	40	450	467	288	.290	.370	.407	103	23	71	58		.974	59	*O-1036/S-56,23	0.5

■ JOHN FLAHERTY
Flaherty, John Timothy b: 10/21/67, New York, N.Y. BR/TR, 6'1", 195 lbs. Deb: 4/12/92

YEAR	TM/L	G	AB	R	H	2B	3B	HR	RBI	BB	SO	AVG	OBP	SLG	PRO+	BR/A	SB	CS	SBR	FA	FR	G/POS	TPR
1992	Bos-A	35	66	3	13	2	0	0	2	3	7	.197	.232	.227	27	-6	0	0	0	.982	-3	C-34	-0.9
1993	Bos-A	13	25	3	3	2	0	0	2	2	6	.120	.214	.200	11	-3	0	0	0	1.000	-1	C-13	-0.4
1994	Det-A	34	40	2	6	1	0	0	4	1	11	.150	.171	.175	-11	-7	0	1	-1	1.000	6	C-33/D-1	-0.1
Total	3	82	131	8	22	5	0	0	8	6	24	.168	.210	.206	13	-16	0	1		.992	2	/C-80,D-1	-1.4

■ MARTIN FLAHERTY
Flaherty, Martin J. b: 9/24/1853, Worcester, Mass d: 6/10/20, Providence, R.I. BL/TL, Deb: 8/18/1881

YEAR	TM/L	G	AB	R	H	2B	3B	HR	RBI	BB	SO	AVG	OBP	SLG	PRO+	BR/A	SB	CS	SBR	FA	FR	G/POS	TPR
1881	Wor-N	1	2	0	0	0	0	0	0	0	2	.000	.000	.000	-95	-0					-1	/O-1	-0.2

■ PAT FLAHERTY
Flaherty, Patrick Henry b: 1/31/1876, St.Louis, Mo. d: 1/28/46, Chicago, Ill. 5'9", 166 lbs. Deb: 7/11/1894

YEAR	TM/L	G	AB	R	H	2B	3B	HR	RBI	BB	SO	AVG	OBP	SLG	PRO+	BR/A	SB	CS	SBR	FA	FR	G/POS	TPR
1894	Lou-N	38	145	15	43	5	3	0	15	9	6	.297	.342	.372	77	-5	2			.855	-5	3-38	-0.8

■ PATSY FLAHERTY
Flaherty, Patrick Joseph b: 6/29/1876, Mansfield, Pa. d: 1/23/68, Alexandria, La. BL/TL, 5'8", 165 lbs. Deb: 9/8/1899

YEAR	TM/L	G	AB	R	H	2B	3B	HR	RBI	BB	SO	AVG	OBP	SLG	PRO+	BR/A	SB	CS	SBR	FA	FR	G/POS	TPR
1899	Lou-N	7	24	3	5	1	1	0	6	3		.208	.296	.333	73	-1	0			.692	-1	/P-5,O-2	0.0
1900	Pit-N	4	9	0	1	0	0	0	0	0		.111	.200	.111	-13	-1	0			1.000	1	/P-4	0.0
1903	Chi-A	40	102	7	14	4	0	0	5	5		.137	.178	.176	7	-11	4			.914	3	P-40	0.0
1904	Chi-A	5	12	1	4	1	0	0	0	4		.333	.500	.417	199	2	0			.880	1	/P-5	0.0
	Pit-N	36	104	9	22	3	4	2	19	8		.212	.268	.375	95	-1	0			.965	5	P-29/O-2	0.0
1905	Pit-N	30	76	7	15	4	2	0	4	3		.197	.228	.303	56	-4	0			.894	2	P-27/O-2	-0.1
1907	Bos-N	41	115	9	22	5	2	0	11	2		.191	.212	.304	62	-6	1			.907	3	P-27/O-8	-0.1
1908	Bos-N	32	86	8	12	0	2	0	5	6		.140	.196	.186	22	-8	2			.961	-4	P-31	0.0
1910	Phi-N	2	2	0	1	0	0	0	0	0	0	.500	.500	.500	186	0	0			.000	-0	/P-1,O-1	0.0
1911	Bos-N	38	94	9	27	3	2	1	20	8	11	.287	.343	.426	106	1	2			.933	-4	O-19/P-4	-0.4
Total	9	235	624	53	123	19	13	6	70	40	11	.197	.247	.298	63	-30	9			.921	11	P-173/O-34	-0.6

■ AL FLAIR
Flair, Albert Dell "Broadway" b: 7/24/16, New Orleans, La. d: 7/25/88, New Orleans, La. BL/TL, 6'4", 195 lbs. Deb: 9/6/41

YEAR	TM/L	G	AB	R	H	2B	3B	HR	RBI	BB	SO	AVG	OBP	SLG	PRO+	BR/A	SB	CS	SBR	FA	FR	G/POS	TPR
1941	Bos-A	10	30	3	6	2	1	0	2	1	7	.200	.226	.333	45	-3	1	1	-0	1.000	-0	/1-8	-0.3

■ CHARLIE FLANAGAN
Flanagan, Charles James b: 12/31/1891, Oakland, Cal. d: 1/8/30, San Francisco, Cal. BR/TR, 6', 175 lbs. Deb: 7/9/13

YEAR	TM/L	G	AB	R	H	2B	3B	HR	RBI	BB	SO	AVG	OBP	SLG	PRO+	BR/A	SB	CS	SBR	FA	FR	G/POS	TPR
1913	StL-A	4	4	0	0	0	0	0	0	0		.000	.250	.000	-26	-0	0			.000	-0	/3-1,O-1	-0.1

■ ED FLANAGAN
Flanagan, Edward J. "Sleepy" b: 9/15/1861, Lowell, Mass. d: 11/10/26, Lowell, Mass. 6'1", 190 lbs. Deb: 4/16/1887

YEAR	TM/L	G	AB	R	H	2B	3B	HR	RBI	BB	SO	AVG	OBP	SLG	PRO+	BR/A	SB	CS	SBR	FA	FR	G/POS	TPR
1887	Phi-a	19	80	12	20	5	0	1		3		.250	.286	.350	77	-3	1			.948	-1	1-19	-0.5
1889	Lou-a	23	88	11	22	7	3	0	8	7	11	.250	.305	.398	101	-0	1			.953	-1	1-23	-0.2
Total	2	42	168	23	42	12	3	1	8	10	11	.250	.296	.375	89	-3	4			.951	-2	/1-42	-0.7

■ STEAMER FLANAGAN
Flanagan, James Paul b: 4/20/1881, Kingston, Pa. d: 4/21/47, Wilkes-Barre, Pa. BL/TL, 6'1", 185 lbs. Deb: 9/25/05

YEAR	TM/L	G	AB	R	H	2B	3B	HR	RBI	BB	SO	AVG	OBP	SLG	PRO+	BR/A	SB	CS	SBR	FA	FR	G/POS	TPR
1905	Pit-N	7	25	7	7	1	1	0	3	1		.280	.308	.400	108	0	3			1.000	1	/O-5	0.1

■ JOHN FLANNERY
Flannery, John Michael b: 1/25/57, Long Beach, Cal. BR/TR, 6'3", 173 lbs. Deb: 9/2/77

YEAR	TM/L	G	AB	R	H	2B	3B	HR	RBI	BB	SO	AVG	OBP	SLG	PRO+	BR/A	SB	CS	SBR	FA	FR	G/POS	TPR
1977	Chi-A	7	2	1	0	0	0	0	0	0	1	.000	.333	.000	0	-0	0	0	0	1.000	1	/S-4,3-1,D	0.1

■ TIM FLANNERY
Flannery, Timothy Earl b: 9/29/57, Tulsa, Okla. BL/TR, 5'11", 175 lbs. Deb: 9/3/79

YEAR	TM/L	G	AB	R	H	2B	3B	HR	RBI	BB	SO	AVG	OBP	SLG	PRO+	BR/A	SB	CS	SBR	FA	FR	G/POS	TPR
1979	SD-N	22	65	2	10	0	1	0	4	4	5	.154	.225	.185	14	-8	0	0		.991	2	2-21	-0.4
1980	SD-N	95	292	15	70	12	0	0	25	18	30	.240	.284	.281	62	-15	2	2	-1	.988	-4	2-53,3-41	-1.9
1981	SD-N	37	67	4	17	4	1	0	6	2	4	.254	.275	.343	80	-2	1	0		.967	-1	3-15/2-7	-0.3

YEAR	TM/L	G	AB	R	H	2B	3B	HR	RBI	BB	SO	AVG	OBP	SLG	PRO+	BR/A	SB	CS	SBR	FA	FR	G/POS	TPR
1982	SD-N	122	379	40	100	11	7	0	30	30	32	.264	.321	.330	87	-7	1	0	0	.974	-24	*2-104/3-5,S	-2.7
1983	SD-N	92	214	24	50	7	3	3	19	20	23	.234	.314	.336	83	-5	2	2	-1	.969	10	3-52,2-21/S	0.5
1984	*SD-N	86	128	24	35	3	3	2	10	12	17	.273	.350	.391	108	2	4	1	1	.944	-6	2-22,3-14,S	-0.2
1985	SD-N	126	384	50	108	14	3	1	40	58	39	.281	.388	.341	107	7	2	5	-2	.977	-19	*2-121/3-1	-1.1
1986	SD-N	134	368	48	103	11	2	3	28	54	61	.280	.379	.345	103	4	3	6	-3	.993	-7	*2-108,3-23/S	-0.2
1987	SD-N	106	276	23	63	5	1	0	20	42	30	.228	.334	.254	61	-14	2	4	-2	.986	3	2-84/3-8,S	-0.9
1988	SD-N	79	170	16	45	5	4	0	19	24	32	.265	.369	.341	107	3	3	2	-0	.972	-4	3-51/2-2,S	-0.2
1989	SD-N	73	130	9	30	5	0	0	8	13	20	.231	.301	.269	64	-6	2	0	1	.920	2	3-33/2-1	-0.4
Total	11	972	2473	255	631	77	25	9	209	277	293	.255	.338	.317	86	-41	22	22	-7	.982	-47	2-544,3-243/S	-7.8

■ ROY FLASKAMPER   Flaskamper, Raymond Harold "Flash" b: 10/31/01, St.Louis, Mo.   d: 2/3/78, San Antonio, Tex.   BB/TR, 5'7", 140 lbs.   Deb: 8/16/27

YEAR	TM/L	G	AB	R	H	2B	3B	HR	RBI	BB	SO	AVG	OBP	SLG	PRO+	BR/A	SB	CS	SBR	FA	FR	G/POS	TPR
1927	Chi-A	26	95	12	21	5	0	0	6	3	8	.221	.260	.274	40	-9	0	0	0	.962	0	S-25	-0.6

■ FRANK FLEET   Fleet, Frank H. b: 1848, New York, N.Y.   d: 6/13/1900, New York, N.Y.   Deb: 10/18/1871

YEAR	TM/L	G	AB	R	H	2B	3B	HR	RBI	BB	SO	AVG	OBP	SLG	PRO+	BR/A	SB	CS	SBR	FA	FR	G/POS	TPR
1871	Mut-n	1	6	1	2	0	0	0	1	0	0	.333	.333	.333	101	0	0					/P-1	0.0
1872	Eck-n	13	54	10	13	2	0	0	6	0	1	.241	.241	.278	70	-1						3-10/2-2,O	-0.1
1873	Res-n	22	90	11	23	2	0	0	10	1	2	.256	.264	.278	65	-3						/2-9,S-9,P31	-0.3
1874	Atl-n	22	95	18	22	1	0	0			2	.232	.247	.242	64	-3						C-12/2-7,O	-0.2
1875	StL-n	4	16	1	1	0	0	0			0	.063	.063	.063	-62	-2						/P-3	0.0
	Atl-n	26	112	13	25	1	0	0			1	.223	.230	.232	69	-3						2-11,C-10/SP	-0.2
	Yr	30	128	14	26	1	0	0			1	.203	.209	.211	52	-5						2-11,C-10/SP	-0.2
Total	5 n	88	373	54	86	6	0	0			4	.231	.239	.247	62	-12						/2-29,C-22,S3P01D	-0.8

■ ANGEL FLEITAS   Fleitas, Angel Felix Husta b: 11/10/14, Los Abreus, Cuba   BR/TR, 5'9", 160 lbs.   Deb: 7/5/48

YEAR	TM/L	G	AB	R	H	2B	3B	HR	RBI	BB	SO	AVG	OBP	SLG	PRO+	BR/A	SB	CS	SBR	FA	FR	G/POS	TPR
1948	Was-A	15	13	1	1	0	0	0	1	3	5	.077	.250	.077	-11	-2	0	2	-1	.952	3	/S-7	0.0

■ LES FLEMING   Fleming, Leslie Harvey "Moe" b: 8/7/15, Singleton, Tex.   d: 3/5/80, Cleveland, Tex.   BL/TL, 5'10", 185 lbs.   Deb: 4/22/39

YEAR	TM/L	G	AB	R	H	2B	3B	HR	RBI	BB	SO	AVG	OBP	SLG	PRO+	BR/A	SB	CS	SBR	FA	FR	G/POS	TPR
1939	Det-A	8	16	0	0	0	0	0	1	0	4	.000	.000	.000	-93	-5	0	0	0	1.000	-0	/O-3	-0.5
1941	Cle-A	2	8	0	2	1	0	0	2	0	0	.250	.250	.375	67	-0	0	0	0	1.000	-0	/1-2	-0.1
1942	Cle-A	156	548	71	160	27	4	14	82	106	57	.292	.412	.432	146	38	6	8	-3	.993	-9	*1-156	1.7
1945	Cle-A	42	140	18	46	10	2	3	22	11	5	.329	.382	.493	160	10	0	0	0	.938	-2	O-33/1-5	0.6
1946	Cle-A	99	306	40	85	17	5	8	42	50	42	.278	.383	.444	140	17	1	0	0	.984	3	1-80/O-1	1.6
1947	Cle-A	103	281	39	68	14	2	4	43	53	42	.242	.362	.349	101	2	0	0	0	.989	5	1-77	0.3
1949	Pit-N	24	31	0	8	0	2	0	7	6	2	.258	.395	.387	108	1	0			1.000	-1	/1-5	0.0
Total	7	434	1330	168	369	69	15	29	199	226	152	.277	.386	.417	131	63	7	8		.990	-6	1-325/O-37	3.6

■ TOM FLEMING   Fleming, Thomas Vincent "Sleuth" b: 11/20/1873, Philadelphia, Pa.   d: 12/26/57, Boston, Mass.   BL/TL, 5'11", 155 lbs.   Deb: 9/19/1899

YEAR	TM/L	G	AB	R	H	2B	3B	HR	RBI	BB	SO	AVG	OBP	SLG	PRO+	BR/A	SB	CS	SBR	FA	FR	G/POS	TPR
1899	NY-N	22	77	9	16	1	1	0	4	1		.208	.218	.247	28	-8	1			.909	-1	O-22	-0.9
1902	Phi-N	5	16	2	6	0	0	0	2	1		.375	.412	.375	143	1	0			1.000	1	/O-5	0.1
1904	Phi-N	3	6	0	0	0	0	0	0	0		.000	.000	.000	-99	-1	0			1.000	1	/O-1	-0.1
Total	3	30	99	11	22	1	1	0	6	2		.222	.238	.253	39	-8	1			.920	1	/O-28	-0.9

■ ART FLETCHER   Fletcher, Arthur b: 1/5/1885, Collinsville, Ill.   d: 2/6/50, Los Angeles, Cal.   BR/TR, 5'10.5", 170 lbs.   Deb: 4/15/09   MC

YEAR	TM/L	G	AB	R	H	2B	3B	HR	RBI	BB	SO	AVG	OBP	SLG	PRO+	BR/A	SB	CS	SBR	FA	FR	G/POS	TPR
1909	NY-N	33	98	7	21	0	1	0	6	1		.214	.238	.235	46	-6	0			.893	4	S-22/2-7,3	-0.2
1910	NY-N	51	125	12	28	2	1	0	13	4	9	.224	.248	.256	47	-9	9			.895	-5	S-22,2-11,3	-1.4
1911	*NY-N	112	326	73	104	17	8	1	37	30	27	.319	.400	.429	128	13	20			.926	4	S-74,3-21,2	2.2
1912	*NY-N	129	419	64	118	17	9	1	57	16	29	.282	.330	.372	89	-7	16			.927	16	*S-126/2-2,3	1.9
1913	*NY-N	136	538	76	160	20	9	4	71	24	35	.297	.345	.390	109	6	32			.932	-7	*S-136	1.1
1914	NY-N	135	514	62	147	26	8	2	79	22	37	.286	.332	.379	115	8	15			.922	6	*S-135	2.7
1915	NY-N	149	562	59	143	17	7	3	74	6	36	.254	.280	.326	88	-10	12	18	-7	.936	34	*S-149	3.1
1916	NY-N	133	500	53	143	23	8	3	66	13	36	.286	.323	.382	122	11	15			.940	20	*S-133	4.3
1917	*NY-N	151	557	70	145	24	5	4	56	23	28	.260	.312	.343	104	2	12			.956	27	*S-151	4.1
1918	NY-N	124	468	51	123	20	2	0	47	18	26	.263	.311	.314	93	-4	12			.959	22	*S-124	2.6
1919	NY-N	127	488	54	135	20	5	3	54	9	28	.277	.300	.357	98	-3	6			.944	24	*S-127	3.2
1920	NY-N	41	171	21	44	7	2	0	24	1	15	.257	.282	.322	74	-6	3	2	-0	.914	-2	S-41	-0.5
	Phi-N	102	379	36	112	25	7	4	38	15	28	.296	.329	.430	112	5	4	6	-2	.958	12	*S-102	2.4
	Yr	143	550	57	156	32	9	4	62	16	43	.284	.315	.396	100	-1	7	8	-3	.945	10	*S-143	1.9
1922	Phi-N	110	396	46	111	20	5	7	53	21	14	.280	.325	.409	80	-13	3	2	-0	.939	7	*S-106	0.4
Total	13	1533	5541	684	1534	238	77	32	675	203	348	.277	.319	.365	100	-14	159	28		.939	162	*S-1448/3-39,2	25.9

■ DARRIN FLETCHER   Fletcher, Darrin Glen b: 10/3/66, Elmhurst, Ill.   BL/TR, 6'2", 195 lbs.   Deb: 9/10/89   F

YEAR	TM/L	G	AB	R	H	2B	3B	HR	RBI	BB	SO	AVG	OBP	SLG	PRO+	BR/A	SB	CS	SBR	FA	FR	G/POS	TPR
1989	LA-N	5	8	1	4	0	0	1	2	0	1	.500	.556	.875	308	2	0	0	0	1.000	0	/C-5	0.2
1990	LA-N	2	1	0	0	0	0	0	0	0	1	.000	.000	.000	-99	-0	0	0	0	.000	0	/C-1	0.0
	Phi-N	9	22	3	3	1	0	0	1	1	5	.136	.174	.182	-2	-3	0	0	0	1.000	1	/C-6	-0.2
	Yr	11	23	3	3	1	0	0	1	1	6	.130	.167	.174	-6	-3	0	0	0	1.000	1	/C-7	-0.2
1991	Phi-N	46	136	5	31	8	0	1	12	5	15	.228	.255	.309	59	-8	0	1	-1	.992	3	C-45	-0.3
1992	Mon-N	83	222	13	54	10	2	2	26	14	28	.243	.294	.333	78	-7	0	2	-1	.995	-0	C-69	-0.5
1993	Mon-N	133	396	33	101	20	1	9	60	34	40	.255	.323	.379	84	-9	0	0	0	.988	-10	*C-127	-1.3
1994	Mon-N★	94	285	28	74	18	1	10	57	25	23	.260	.326	.435	94	-3	0	3	-2	.996	-8	C-81	-0.7
Total	6	372	1070	83	267	57	4	23	158	80	112	.250	.308	.375	82	-27	0	3	-2	.993	-15	C-334	-2.8

■ ELBIE FLETCHER   Fletcher, Elburt Preston b: 3/18/16, Milton, Mass.   d: 3/9/94, Milton, Mass.   BL/TL, 6', 180 lbs.   Deb: 9/16/34

YEAR	TM/L	G	AB	R	H	2B	3B	HR	RBI	BB	SO	AVG	OBP	SLG	PRO+	BR/A	SB	CS	SBR	FA	FR	G/POS	TPR
1934	Bos-N	8	4	4	2	0	0	0	0	0	2	.500	.500	.500	182	0	1			.875	-0	/1-1	0.0
1935	Bos-N	39	148	12	35	7	1	1	9	7	13	.236	.271	.318	63	-8	1			.997	2	1-39	-1.0
1937	Bos-N	148	539	56	133	22	4	1	38	56	64	.247	.321	.308	79	-16	3			.993	1	*1-148	-3.2
1938	Bos-N	147	529	71	144	24	7	6	48	60	40	.272	.351	.378	112	8	5			.990	10	*1-146	0.3
1939	Bos-N	35	106	14	26	2	0	0	6	19	5	.245	.365	.264	77	-2	1			.986	-5	1-31	-1.1
	Pit-N	102	370	49	112	23	4	12	71	48	28	.303	.386	.484	134	18	3			.993	-4	*1-101	0.4
	Yr	137	476	63	138	25	4	12	77	67	33	.290	.381	.435	122	16	4			.991	-9	*1-132	-0.7
1940	Pit-N	147	510	94	139	22	7	16	104	**119**	54	.273	**.418**	.437	137	33	5			.993	4	*1-147	2.3
1941	Pit-N	151	521	95	150	29	13	11	74	**118**	54	.288	**.421**	.457	148	39	5			.991	9	*1-151	3.7
1942	Pit-N	145	506	86	146	22	5	7	57	105	60	.289	**.417**	.393	134	28	0			.992	12	*1-144	3.2
1943	Pit-N★	154	544	91	154	24	5	9	70	95	49	.283	.395	.395	124	21	1			**.996**	3	*1-154	1.7
1946	Pit-N	148	532	72	136	25	8	4	66	111	37	.256	.384	.355	108	10	4			.995	1	*1-147	0.3
1947	Pit-N	69	157	22	38	9	1	1	22	29	24	.242	.364	.331	83	-3	2			.986	-0	1-50	-0.4
1949	Bos-N	122	413	57	108	19	3	11	51	84	65	.262	.396	.402	121	16	1			.991	0	*1-121	1.5
Total	12	1415	4879	723	1323	228	58	79	616	851	495	.271	.384	.390	118	145	32			.993	33	*1-1380	7.7

■ GEORGE FLETCHER   Fletcher, George Horace Ellis b: 4/21/1845,   Deb: 6/21/1872

YEAR	TM/L	G	AB	R	H	2B	3B	HR	RBI	BB	SO	AVG	OBP	SLG	PRO+	BR/A	SB	CS	SBR	FA	FR	G/POS	TPR
1872	Eck-n	2	8	1	3	0	0	0	1	0	0	.375	.375	.375	155	1						/O-2	0.0

■ FRANK FLETCHER   Fletcher, Oliver Frank b: 3/6/1891, Hildreth, Ill.   d: 10/7/74, St.Petersburg, Fla.   BR/TR, 5'10", 165 lbs.   Deb: 7/14/14

YEAR	TM/L	G	AB	R	H	2B	3B	HR	RBI	BB	SO	AVG	OBP	SLG	PRO+	BR/A	SB	CS	SBR	FA	FR	G/POS	TPR
1914	Phi-N	1	1	0	0	0	0	0	0	0	1	.000	.000	.000	-94	-0	0			.000	0	H	0.0

YEAR	TM/L	G	AB	R	H	2B	3B	HR	RBI	BB	SO	AVG	OBP	SLG	PRO+	BR/A	SB	CS	SBR	FA	FR	G/POS	TPR
■ SCOTT FLETCHER				Fletcher, Scott Brian b: 7/30/58, Fort Walton Beach, Fla. BR/TR, 5'11", 173 lbs. Deb: 4/25/81																			
1981	Chi-N	19	46	6	10	4	0	0	1	2	4	.217	.250	.304	54	-3	0	0	0	.972	6	2-13/S-4,3	0.4
1982	Chi-N	11	24	4	4	0	0	0	1	4	5	.167	.286	.167	29	-2	1	0	0	1.000	-0	S-11	-0.2
1983	*Chi-A	114	262	42	62	16	5	3	31	29	22	.237	.317	.370	85	-5	5	1	1	.965	18	*S-100,2-12/3D	2.2
1984	Chi-A	149	456	46	114	13	3	3	35	46	46	.250	.329	.311	75	-14	10	4	1	.973	0	*S-134,2-28/3	-0.1
1985	Chi-A	119	301	38	77	8	1	2	31	35	47	.256	.333	.309	74	-10	5	5	-2	.934	-3	3-55,S-44,2/D	-1.1
1986	Tex-A	147	530	82	159	34	5	3	50	47	59	.300	.361	.400	104	4	12	11	-3	.973	-6	*S-136,3-12,2/D	0.7
1987	Tex-A	156	588	82	169	28	4	5	63	61	66	.287	.359	.374	95	-3	13	12	-3	.966	5	*S-155	1.2
1988	Tex-A	140	515	59	142	19	4	0	47	62	34	.276	.367	.328	94	-1	8	5	-1	.983	1	*S-139	1.1
1989	Tex-A	83	314	47	75	14	1	0	22	38	41	.239	.325	.290	73	-10	1	0	0	.960	-18	S-81	-2.2
	Chi-A	59	232	30	63	11	1	1	21	26	19	.272	.347	.341	97	-0	1	1	-0	1.000	-3	2-53/S-8,D	-0.1
	Yr	142	546	77	138	25	2	1	43	64	60	.253	.334	.311	83	-10	2	1	-0	.957	-21	S-89,2-53/D	-2.3
1990	Chi-A	151	509	54	123	18	3	4	56	45	63	.242	.307	.312	75	-16	1	3	-2	.988	-6	*2-151	-2.2
1991	Chi-A	90	248	14	51	10	1	1	28	17	26	.206	.265	.266	48	-17	0	2	-1	.992	-6	2-86/3-4	-2.3
1992	Mil-A	123	386	53	106	18	3	3	51	30	33	.275	.338	.360	98	-1	17	10	-1	.992	10	*2-106,S-22/3	1.1
1993	Bos-A	121	480	81	137	31	5	5	45	37	35	.285	.343	.402	94	-4	16	3	3	.982	5	*2-116/S-2,3D	0.7
1994	Bos-A	63	185	31	42	9	1	3	11	16	14	.227	.296	.335	58	-12	8	1	2	.996	19	2-53/D-4	1.0
Total	14	1545	5076	669	1334	233	37	33	493	495	514	.263	.335	.343	85	-94	98	58	-5	.971	21	S-836,2-666/3D	0.2
■ ELMER FLICK				Flick, Elmer Harrison b: 1/11/1876, Bedford, Ohio d: 1/9/71, Bedford, Ohio BL/TR, 5'9", 168 lbs. Deb: 5/2/1898 H																			
1898	Phi-N	134	453	84	137	16	13	8	81	86		.302	.430	.448	158	40	23			.931	7	*O-133	3.5
1899	Phi-N	127	485	98	166	22	11	2	98	42		.342	.407	.445	139	27	31			.931	9	*O-125	2.4
1900	Phi-N	138	545	106	200	32	16	11	**110**	56		.367	.441	.545	173	55	35			.914	-3	*O-138	4.3
1901	Phi-N	138	540	112	180	32	17	8	88	52		.333	.399	.500	157	39	30			.962	15	*O-138	4.2
1902	Phi-A	11	37	15	11	2	1	0	3	6		.297	.435	.405	128	2	4			.947	-0	O-11	0.1
	Cle-A	110	424	70	126	19	11	2	61	47		.297	.371	.408	121	13	20			.929	-4	*O-110	0.1
	Yr	121	461	85	137	21	12	2	64	53		.297	.377	.408	121	15	24			.930	-4	*O-121	0.2
1903	Cle-A	140	523	81	155	23	16	2	51	51		.296	.368	.413	136	24	24			.955	1	*O-140	1.7
1904	Cle-A	150	579	97	177	31	17	6	56	51		.306	.371	.449	160	40	**38**			.955	10	*O-145/2-6	4.5
1905	Cle-A	132	500	72	154	29	**18**	4	64	53		**.308**	.383	**.462**	**165**	**37**	35			.938	-3	*O-131/2-1	3.3
1906	Cle-A	157	624	**98**	194	34	**22**	1	62	54		.311	.372	.441	156	40	**39**			.981	-11	*O-150/2-8	2.3
1907	Cle-A	147	549	78	166	15	**18**	3	58	64		.302	.386	.412	153	35	41			.956	1	*O-147	3.3
1908	Cle-A	9	35	4	8	1	1	0	2	3		.229	.289	.314	96	-0	0			1.000	4	/O-9	-0.1
1909	Cle-A	66	235	28	60	10	2	0	15	22		.255	.322	.315	97	-0	9			.958	-4	*O-61	-0.7
1910	Cle-A	24	68	5	18	2	1	0	7	10		.265	.359	.368	126	2	1			.955	-3	O-18	-0.2
Total	13	1483	5597	948	1752	268	164	48	756	597		.313	.389	.445	149	353	330			.947	23	*O-1456/2-15	28.7
■ LEW FLICK				Flick, Lewis Miller "Noisy" b: 2/18/15, Bristol, Tenn. d: 12/7/90, Weber City, Va. BL/TL, 5'9", 155 lbs. Deb: 9/28/43																			
1943	Phi-A	1	5	2	3	0	0	0	0	0	0	.600	.600	.600	253	1	0	0	0	1.000	0	/O-1	0.1
1944	Phi-A	19	35	1	4	0	0	0	2	1	2	.114	.139	.114	-28	-6	1	0	0	1.000	-1	/O-6	-0.7
Total	2	20	40	3	7	0	0	0	2	1	2	.175	.195	.175	6	-5	1	0	0	1.000	-1	/O-7	-0.6
■ DON FLINN				Flinn, Don Raphael b: 11/17/1892, Bluff Dale, Tex. d: 3/9/59, Waco, Tex. BR/TR, 6'1", 185 lbs. Deb: 9/2/17																			
1917	Pit-N	14	37	1	11	1	1	0	1	1	6	.297	.316	.378	109	0	1			1.000	0	O-12	0.0
■ SILVER FLINT				Flint, Frank Sylvester b: 8/3/1855, Philadelphia, Pa. d: 1/14/1892, Chicago, Ill. BR/TR, 6', 180 lbs. Deb: 5/4/1875 M																			
1875	RS-n	17	61	4	5	0	0	0			1	.082	.097	.082	-42	-8						C-15/3-1	-0.6
1878	Ind-N	63	254	23	57	7	0	0	18	2	15	.224	.230	.252	67	-8				.908	-1	*C-59/O-9	-0.8
1879	Chi-N	79	324	46	92	22	6	1	41	6	44	.284	.297	.398	120	6				.915	3	*C-78/O-1M	1.0
1880	Chi-N	74	284	30	46	10	4	0	17	5	32	.162	.176	.225	33	-20				**.934**	8	*C-67,O-13	-1.0
1881	Chi-N	80	306	46	95	18	0	1	34	6	39	.310	.324	.379	115	4				.938	-8	*C-80/O-8,1	-0.1
1882	Chi-N	81	331	48	83	18	8	4	44	2	50	.251	.255	.390	99	-1				.935	-3	*C-81,O-10	-0.1
1883	Chi-N	85	332	57	88	23	4	0	32	3	69	.265	.272	.358	85	-7				.877	-3	*C-83,O-23	-0.9
1884	Chi-N	73	279	35	57	5	2	9	45	7	57	.204	.224	.333	67	-12				.884	-2	C-73	-0.6
1885	*Chi-N	68	249	27	52	8	2	1	17	2	52	.209	.215	.269	49	-16				**.927**	-1	C-68/O-1	0.3
1886	*Chi-N	54	173	30	35	6	2	1	13	12	36	.202	.254	.277	53	-11	1			.893	15	C-54/1-3	0.8
1887	Chi-N	49	187	22	50	8	5	2	21	4	28	.267	.283	.422	83	-6				.909	3	C-47/1-2	0.1
1888	Chi-N	22	77	6	14	3	0	0	3	1	21	.182	.203	.221	33	-6	1			.926	-2	C-22	-0.6
1889	Chi-N	15	56	6	13	1	0	1	9	3	18	.232	.271	.304	58	-3	1			.903	-1	C-15	-0.3
Total	12	743	2852	376	682	129	34	21	294	53	461	.239	.253	.330	78	-80	1			.913	19	C-727/O-65,1	-2.2
■ CURT FLOOD				Flood, Curtis Charles b: 1/18/38, Houston, Tex. BR/TR, 5'9", 165 lbs. Deb: 9/9/56																			
1956	Cin-N	5	1	0	0	0	0	0	0	0	1	.000	.000	.000	-94	-0	0	0	0	.000	0	H	0.0
1957	Cin-N	3	3	2	1	0	0	1	1	0	0	.333	.333	1.333	299	1	0	0	0	.000	-1	/3-2,2-1	0.0
1958	StL-N	121	422	50	110	17	2	10	41	31	56	.261	.317	.382	81	-12	2	12	-7	.978	19	*O-120/3-1	-0.5
1959	StL-N	121	208	24	53	7	3	7	26	16	35	.255	.308	.418	86	-5	2	1	0	.967	-19	*O-106/2-1	-2.7
1960	StL-N	140	396	37	94	20	1	8	38	35	54	.237	.306	.354	73	-14	0	3	-2	**.993**	0	*O-134/3-1	-2.2
1961	StL-N	132	335	53	108	15	5	2	21	35	33	.322	.391	.415	104	3	6	2	1	.984	2	*O-119	0.1
1962	StL-N	151	635	99	188	30	5	12	70	42	57	.296	.349	.416	95	-4	8	6	-1	.990	16	*O-151	0.1
1963	StL-N	158	662	112	200	34	9	5	63	42	57	.302	.346	.403	105	5	17	12	-2	.988	20	*O-158	1.4
1964	*StL-N★	162	679	97	**211**	25	3	5	46	43	53	.311	.356	.378	98	-0	8	11	-4	.988	13	*O-162	0.1
1965	StL-N	156	617	90	191	30	3	11	83	51	50	.310	.368	.421	111	10	9	3	1	.986	11	*O-151	1.6
1966	StL-N★	160	626	64	167	21	5	10	78	26	50	.267	.300	.364	83	-15	14	7	0	**1.000**	10	*O-159	-1.2
1967	*StL-N	134	514	68	172	24	1	5	50	37	46	.335	.382	.414	129	20	2	2	-1	.988	11	*O-126	2.5
1968	*StL-N★	150	618	71	186	17	4	5	60	33	58	.301	.341	.366	114	10	11	6	-0	.983	18	*O-149	2.1
1969	StL-N	153	606	80	173	31	3	4	57	48	57	.285	.345	.366	99	-0	9	7	-2	.989	17	*O-152	0.7
1971	Was-A	13	35	4	7	0	0	0	2	5	2	.200	.300	.200	47	-2	0	1	-1	.941	-2	O-10	-0.6
Total	15	1759	6357	851	1861	271	44	85	636	444	609	.293	.344	.389	99	-4	88	73	-17	.987	114	*O-1697/3-4,2	1.4
■ TIM FLOOD				Flood, Timothy A. b: 3/13/1877, Montgomery City, Mo. d: 6/15/29, St. Louis, Mo. BR/TR, 5'9", 160 lbs. Deb: 9/24/1899																			
1899	StL-N	10	31	0	9	0	0	0	3	4		.290	.371	.290	81	-1	1			.878	-2	2-10	-0.2
1902	Bro-N	132	476	43	104	11	4	3	51	23		.218	.268	.277	68	-18	8			.942	-16	*2-132/O-1	-3.1
1903	Bro-N	89	309	27	77	15	2	0	32	15		.249	.291	.311	73	-11	14			.924	-9	2-84/S-2,O	-1.6
Total	3	231	816	70	190	26	6	3	86	42		.233	.280	.290	70	-30	23			.933	-26	2-226/S-2,O	-4.9
■ KEVIN FLORA				Flora, Kevin Scot b: 6/10/69, Fontana, Cal. BR/TR, 6', 180 lbs. Deb: 9/27/91																			
1991	Cal-A	3	8	1	1	0	0	0	0	1	5	.125	.222	.125	-1	-1	1	0	0	.846	-2	/2-3	-0.3
■ PAUL FLORENCE				Florence, Paul Robert "Pep" b: 4/22/1900, Chicago, Ill. d: 5/28/86, Gainesville, Fla. BB/TR, 6'1", 185 lbs. Deb: 5/22/26																			
1926	NY-N	76	188	19	43	4	3	2	14	23	12	.229	.322	.314	73	-7	2			.937	-9	C-76	-1.1
■ GIL FLORES				Flores, Gilberto (Garcia) b: 10/27/52, Ponce, P.R. BR/TR, 6', 185 lbs. Deb: 5/8/77																			
1977	Cal-A	104	342	41	95	19	4	1	26	23	39	.278	.325	.365	92	-4	12	10	-2	.978	-2	O-85/D-8	-1.2
1978	NY-N	11	29	8	8	0	1	0	1	3	5	.276	.344	.345	96	-0	1	0	0	.944	-1	/O-8	-0.1

YEAR	TM/L	G	AB	R	H	2B	3B	HR	RBI	BB	SO	AVG	OBP	SLG	PRO+	BR/A	SB	CS	SBR	FA	FR	G/POS	TPR
1979	NY-N	70	93	9	18	1	1	1	10	8	17	.194	.265	.258	45	-7	2	0	1	.976	-7	O-32	-1.5
Total	3	185	464	58	121	20	6	2	37	34	61	.261	.314	.343	82	-11	15	10	-2	.976	-10	O-125/D-8	-2.8

■ DICKIE FLOWERS
Flowers, Charles Richard b: 1850, Philadelphia, Pa. d: 10/5/1892, Philadelphia, Pa. Deb: 6/3/1871

YEAR	TM/L	G	AB	R	H	2B	3B	HR	RBI	BB	SO	AVG	OBP	SLG	PRO+	BR/A	SB	CS	SBR	FA	FR	G/POS	TPR
1871	Tro-n	21	105	39	33	5	4	0	18	4	0	.314	.339	.438	120	2	8						*S-20/P-1,2	0.2
1872	Ath-n	3	15	1	4	0	0	0	4	2	2	.267	.353	.267	93	0							/S-3	0.0
Total	2 n	24	120	40	37	5	4	0	22	6	2	.308	.341	.417	117	2							/S-23,2-1,P	0.2

■ JAKE FLOWERS
Flowers, D'Arcy Raymond b: 3/16/02, Cambridge, Md. d: 12/27/62, Clearwater, Fla. BR/TR, 5'11.5", 170 lbs. Deb: 9/7/23 C

YEAR	TM/L	G	AB	R	H	2B	3B	HR	RBI	BB	SO	AVG	OBP	SLG	PRO+	BR/A	SB	CS	SBR	FA	FR	G/POS	TPR
1923	StL-N	13	32	0	3	1	0	0	2	2	7	.094	.147	.125	-28	-6	1	2	-1	.971	-1	/S-7,2-2,3	-0.7
1926	*StL-N	40	74	13	20	1	0	3	9	5	9	.270	.325	.405	92	-1	1			.984	1	2-11/1-3,S	0.0
1927	Bro-N	67	231	26	54	5	5	2	20	21	25	.234	.300	.325	67	-11	3			.944	-8	S-65/2-1	-1.2
1928	Bro-N	103	339	51	93	11	6	2	44	47	30	.274	.366	.360	92	-3	10			.971	-6	2-94/S-6	-0.6
1929	Bro-N	46	130	16	26	6	0	1	16	22	6	.200	.316	.269	47	-10	9			.962	-5	2-39	-1.3
1930	Bro-N	89	253	37	81	18	3	2	50	21	18	.320	.372	.439	96	-1	5			.949	-8	2-65/O-1	-0.5
1931	Bro-N	22	31	3	7	0	0	0	1	7	4	.226	.368	.226	64	-1	1			1.000	1	/2-6,S-1	0.1
	*StL-N	45	137	19	34	11	1	2	19	9	6	.248	.295	.387	79	-4	7			.971	3	S-24,2-21/3	0.1
	Yr	67	168	22	41	11	1	2	20	16	10	.244	.310	.357	77	-5	8			.991	4	2-27,S-25/3	0.2
1932	StL-N	67	.247	35	63	11	1	2	18	31	18	.255	.341	.332	79	-6	7			.980	-0	3-54/S-7,2	-0.2
1933	Bro-N	78	210	28	49	11	2	2	22	24	15	.233	.312	.333	88	-3	13			.955	-11	S-36,2-19/3O	-1.1
1934	Cin-N	13	9	1	3	0	0	0	0	1	1	.333	.455	.333	117	0	1			1.000	0	H	0.0
Total	10	583	1693	229	433	75	18	16	201	190	139	.256	.333	.350	80	-47	58	2		.967	-34	2-260,S-147/310	-5.4

■ CLIFF FLOYD
Floyd, Cornelius Clifford b: 12/5/72, Chicago, Ill. BL/TL, 6'4", 220 lbs. Deb: 9/18/93

YEAR	TM/L	G	AB	R	H	2B	3B	HR	RBI	BB	SO	AVG	OBP	SLG	PRO+	BR/A	SB	CS	SBR	FA	FR	G/POS	TPR
1993	Mon-N	10	31	3	7	0	0	1	2	2	11	.226	.226	.323	43	-3	0	0	0	1.000	-0	1-10	-0.4
1994	Mon-N	100	334	43	94	19	4	4	41	24	63	.281	.335	.398	88	-6	10	3	1	.991	-3	1-77,O-26	-1.3
Total	2	110	365	46	101	19	4	5	43	24	72	.277	.327	.392	85	-8	10	3	1	.992	-3	/1-87,O-26	-1.7

■ BUBBA FLOYD
Floyd, Leslie Roe b: 6/23/17, Dallas, Tex. BR/TR, 5'11", 160 lbs. Deb: 6/16/44

YEAR	TM/L	G	AB	R	H	2B	3B	HR	RBI	BB	SO	AVG	OBP	SLG	PRO+	BR/A	SB	CS	SBR	FA	FR	G/POS	TPR
1944	Det-A	3	9	1	4	1	0	0	0	1	0	.444	.500	.556	191	1	0	0	0	1.000	-1	/S-3	0.0

■ BOBBY FLOYD
Floyd, Robert Nathan b: 10/20/43, Hawthorne, Cal. BR/TR, 6', 181 lbs. Deb: 9/18/68

YEAR	TM/L	G	AB	R	H	2B	3B	HR	RBI	BB	SO	AVG	OBP	SLG	PRO+	BR/A	SB	CS	SBR	FA	FR	G/POS	TPR
1968	Bal-A	5	9	0	1	1	0	0	1	0	3	.111	.111	.222	-4	-1	0	0	0	1.000	2	/S-4	0.1
1969	Bal-A	39	84	7	17	4	0	0	1	6	17	.202	.256	.250	41	-7	0	0	0	.984	11	2-15,S-15/3	0.7
1970	Bal-A	3	2	0	0	0	0	0	0	0	0	.000	.000	.000	-99	-1	0	0	0	1.000	-1	/S-2,2-1	-0.1
	KC-A	14	43	5	14	4	0	0	9	4	9	.326	.383	.419	121	1	0	1	-1	.880	1	/S-8,3-6	0.3
	Yr	17	45	5	14	4	0	0	9	4	11	.311	.367	.400	111	1	0	1	-1	.882	1	S-10/3-6,2	0.2
1971	KC-A	31	66	8	10	3	0	0	2	7	21	.152	.233	.197	23	-7	0	0	0	.970	5	S-15/2-8,3	0.0
1972	KC-A	61	134	9	24	3	0	0	5	5	29	.179	.209	.201	23	-13	1	0	0	.967	-2	3-30,S-29/2	-1.4
1973	KC-A	51	78	10	26	3	1	0	8	4	14	.333	.366	.397	107	1	1	1	-0	1.000	9	2-25,S-24	1.1
1974	KC-A	10	9	1	1	0	0	0	0	2	4	.111	.273	.111	13	-1	0	0	0	1.000	1	/2-5,3-2,S	0.2
Total	7	214	425	40	93	18	1	0	26	28	99	.219	.267	.266	52	-27	2	2	-1	.940	27	/S-98,2-56,3	0.9

■ JOHN FLUHRER
Fluhrer, John L. (a.k.a. Wm. G. Morris 1 Game In 1915)
b: 1/3/1894, Adrian, Mich. d: 7/17/46, Columbus, Ohio BR/TR, 5'9", 165 lbs. Deb: 9/5/15

YEAR	TM/L	G	AB	R	H	2B	3B	HR	RBI	BB	SO	AVG	OBP	SLG	PRO+	BR/A	SB	CS	SBR	FA	FR	G/POS	TPR
1915	Chi-N	6	6	0	2	0	0	0	0	1	0	.333	.429	.333	132	0	1			.500	-1	/O-2	0.0

■ ED FLYNN
Flynn, Edward J. b: 1/25/1864, Chicago, Ill. BL, 5'9", 165 lbs. Deb: 5/5/1887

YEAR	TM/L	G	AB	R	H	2B	3B	HR	RBI	BB	SO	AVG	OBP	SLG	PRO+	BR/A	SB	CS	SBR	FA	FR	G/POS	TPR
1887	Cle-a	7	27	0	5	1	0	0		1		.185	.214	.222	22	-3	3			.786	-0	/3-6,O-1	-0.2

■ GEORGE FLYNN
Flynn, George A. "Dibby" b: 5/24/1871, Chicago, Ill. d: 12/28/01, Chicago, Ill. Deb: 4/17/1896

YEAR	TM/L	G	AB	R	H	2B	3B	HR	RBI	BB	SO	AVG	OBP	SLG	PRO+	BR/A	SB	CS	SBR	FA	FR	G/POS	TPR
1896	Chi-N	29	106	15	27	1	2	0	11	9		.255	.336	.302	66	-5	12			.878	2	O-29	-0.4

■ JOCKO FLYNN
Flynn, John A. b: 6/30/1864, Lawrence, Mass. d: 12/30/07, Lawrence, Mass. TR, 5'6.5", 143 lbs. Deb: 5/1/1886

YEAR	TM/L	G	AB	R	H	2B	3B	HR	RBI	BB	SO	AVG	OBP	SLG	PRO+	BR/A	SB	CS	SBR	FA	FR	G/POS	TPR
1886	Chi-N	57	205	40	41	6	2	4	19	18	45	.200	.265	.307	64	-10	9			.916	-5	P-32,O-28	-1.0
1887	Chi-N	1	0	0	0	0	0	0	0	0	0	—	—	—		0				.000	-1	/O-1	-0.1
Total	2	58	205	40	41	6	2	4	19	18	45	.200	.265	.307	64	-10	9			.850	-6	/P-32,O-29	-1.1

■ JOHN FLYNN
Flynn, John Anthony b: 9/7/1883, Providence, R.I. d: 3/23/35, Providence, R.I. BR/TR, 6'0.5", 175 lbs. Deb: 4/22/10

YEAR	TM/L	G	AB	R	H	2B	3B	HR	RBI	BB	SO	AVG	OBP	SLG	PRO+	BR/A	SB	CS	SBR	FA	FR	G/POS	TPR
1910	Pit-N	96	332	32	91	10	2	6	52	30	47	.274	.336	.370	100	-1	6			.977	-3	1-93	-0.4
1911	Pit-N	33	59	5	12	0	1	0	3	9	8	.203	.309	.237	52	-4	0			1.000	0	1-13/O-1	-0.3
1912	Was-A	20	71	9	12	4	1	0	5	7		.169	.253	.254	45	-5	2			.974	-1	1-20	-0.4
Total	3	149	462	46	115	14	4	6	60	46	55	.249	.320	.335	85	-9	8			.978	-1	1-126/O-1	-1.1

■ JOE FLYNN
Flynn, Joseph b: Philadelphia, Pa. Deb: 4/18/1884

YEAR	TM/L	G	AB	R	H	2B	3B	HR	RBI	BB	SO	AVG	OBP	SLG	PRO+	BR/A	SB	CS	SBR	FA	FR	G/POS	TPR
1884	Phi-U	52	209	38	52	9	4	4		11		.249	.286	.388	88	-4				.778	-15	O-43,C-10/1S	-1.7
	Bos-U	9	31	4	7	2	0	0		2		.226	.273	.290	54	-2				.864	4	/C-7,O-4,1	0.2
	Yr	61	240	42	59	11	4	4		13		.246	.285	.375	83	-6				.764	-11	O-47,C-17/1S	-1.5

■ MIKE FLYNN
Flynn, Michael J. b: 3/15/1872, County Kildare, Ireland d: 6/16/41, Los Angeles, Cal. Deb: 8/31/1891

YEAR	TM/L	G	AB	R	H	2B	3B	HR	RBI	BB	SO	AVG	OBP	SLG	PRO+	BR/A	SB	CS	SBR	FA	FR	G/POS	TPR
1891	Bos-a	1	2	0	0	0	0	0	0	0	1	.000	.000	.000	-99	-1	0			1.000	1	/C-1	0.0

■ DOUG FLYNN
Flynn, Robert Douglas b: 4/18/51, Lexington, Ky. BR/TR, 5'11", 165 lbs. Deb: 4/9/75

YEAR	TM/L	G	AB	R	H	2B	3B	HR	RBI	BB	SO	AVG	OBP	SLG	PRO+	BR/A	SB	CS	SBR	FA	FR	G/POS	TPR
1975	Cin-N	89	127	17	34	7	0	1	20	11	13	.268	.326	.346	85	-3	3	0	1	.962	10	3-40,2-30,S	1.0
1976	*Cin-N	93	219	20	62	5	2	1	20	10	24	.283	.314	.338	83	-5	2	0	1	.988	-4	2-55,3-23,S	-0.4
1977	Cin-N	36	32	0	8	1	1	0	5	0	6	.250	.250	.344	56	-2	0	0	0	1.000	7	3-25/2-9,S	0.5
	NY-N	90	282	14	54	6	1	0	14	11	23	.191	.222	.220	20	-32	1	3	-2	.954	-13	S-65,2-29/3	-4.0
	Yr	126	314	14	62	7	2	0	19	11	29	.197	.225	.232	24	-34	1	3	-2	.956	-6	S-69,2-38,3	-3.5
1978	NY-N	156	532	37	126	12	8	0	36	30	50	.237	.279	.289	61	-28	3	5	-2	.986	2	*2-128,S-60	-1.7
1979	NY-N	157	555	35	135	19	5	4	61	17	46	.243	.266	.317	61	-32	0	3	-2	.983	1	*2-148,S-20	-2.3
1980	NY-N	128	443	46	113	9	8	0	24	22	20	.255	.290	.312	70	-18	2	2	-1	.991	3	*2-128/S-3	-0.9
1981	NY-N	105	325	24	72	12	4	1	20	11	19	.222	.247	.292	53	-21	1	2	-1	.987	12	*2-100/S-5	-0.3
1982	Tex-A	88	270	13	57	6	2	0	19	4	14	.211	.223	.248	31	-26	6	2	1	.989	1	2-55,S-35	-1.6
	Mon-N	58	193	13	47	6	2	0	20	4	23	.244	.259	.295	54	-12	0	2	-1	.983	5	2-58	-0.6
1983	Mon-N	143	452	44	107	18	4	0	26	19	28	.237	.268	.294	56	-27	2	1	0	.986	7	*2-107,S-37	-1.4
1984	Mon-N	124	366	23	89	12	1	0	17	12	41	.243	.267	.281	57	-22	0	1	0	.979	-8	2-88,S-34	-2.6
1985	Mon-N	9	6	0	1	0	0	0	0	0	0	.167	.167	.167	-7	-1	0	0	0	1.000	-1	/2-6,S-1	-0.2
	Det-A	32	51	2	13	2	1	0	2	0	3	.255	.255	.333	60	-3	0	0	0	.984	-3	2-20/S-8,3	0.6
Total	11	1308	3853	288	918	115	39	7	284	151	320	.238	.267	.294	57	-231	20	20	-6	.986	33	2-961,S-309/3	-13.9

■ CLIPPER FLYNN
Flynn, William b: 4/29/1849, Lansingburg, N.Y. d: 11/11/1881, Lansingburg, N.Y. TR, 5'7", 140 lbs. Deb: 5/9/1871

YEAR	TM/L	G	AB	R	H	2B	3B	HR	RBI	BB	SO	AVG	OBP	SLG	PRO+	BR/A	SB	CS	SBR	FA	FR	G/POS	TPR
1871	Tro-n	29	142	43	48	6	0	0	27	4	2	.338	.356	.394	114	2	3					1-19/O-9,3	0.2
1872	Oly-n	9	40	4	9	1	0	0	2	0	0	.225	.225	.250	48	-2						/1-9	-0.1
Total	2 n	38	182	47	57	7	1	0	29	4	2	.313	.328	.363	101	0						/1-28,O-9,3	0.1

JIM FOGARTY
Fogarty, James G.   b: 2/12/1864, San Francisco, Cal.   d: 5/20/1891, Philadelphia, Pa.   BR/TR, 5'10.5", 180 lbs.   Deb: 5/1/1884   FM

YEAR	TM/L	G	AB	R	H	2B	3B	HR	RBI	BB	SO	AVG	OBP	SLG	PRO+	BR/A	SB	CS	SBR	FA	FR	G/POS	TPR
1884	Phi-N	97	378	42	80	12	6	1	37	20	54	.212	.251	.283	71	-12				.915	3	*O-78,3-14/2SP	-0.9
1885	Phi-N	111	427	49	99	13	3	0	39	30	37	.232	.282	.276	83	-7				.941	25	*O-88,2-10/S3	1.5
1886	Phi-N	77	280	54	82	13	5	3	47	42	16	.293	.385	.407	140	15	30			.953	-3	O-60,2-13/S3P	0.9
1887	Phi-N	126	495	113	129	26	12	8	50	**82**	44	.261	.376	.410	112	9	102			.920	32	*O-123/S-2,32P	3.3
1888	Phi-N	121	454	72	107	14	6	1	35	53	66	.236	.325	.300	95	-1	58			.930	14	*O-117/3-5,S	1.0
1889	Phi-N	128	499	107	129	15	17	3	54	65	60	.259	.352	.375	95	-5	**99**			**.961**	19	*O-128/P-4	1.0
1890	Phi-P	91	347	71	83	17	6	4	58	59	50	.239	.364	.357	91	-4	36			.963	8	O-91/3-1M	0.1
Total	7	751	2880	508	709	110	55	20	320	351	327	.246	.335	.343	98	-4	325			.940	98	O-685/3-30,2SP	6.9

JOE FOGARTY
Fogarty, Joseph J.   b: San Francisco, Cal.   Deb: 9/18/1885   F

YEAR	TM/L	G	AB	R	H	2B	3B	HR	RBI	BB	SO	AVG	OBP	SLG	PRO+	BR/A	SB	CS	SBR	FA	FR	G/POS	TPR
1885	StL-N	2	8	1	1	0	0	0	0	0	1	.125	.125	.125	-20	-1				1.000	-0	/O-2	-0.1

LEE FOHL
Fohl, Leo Alexander   b: 11/28/1876, Lowell, Ohio   d: 10/30/65, Cleveland, Ohio   BL/TR, 5'10", 175 lbs.   Deb: 8/29/02   M

YEAR	TM/L	G	AB	R	H	2B	3B	HR	RBI	BB	SO	AVG	OBP	SLG	PRO+	BR/A	SB	CS	SBR	FA	FR	G/POS	TPR
1902	Pit-N	1	3	0	0	0	0	0	1		0	.000	.000	.000	-97	-1	0			.875	0	/C-1	0.0
1903	Cin-N	4	14	3	5	1	1	0	2		0	.357	.400	.571	158	1	0			.955	-0	/C-4	0.1
Total	2	5	17	3	5	1	1	0	3		0	.294	.333	.471	120	0	0			.933	0	/C-5	0.1

HANK FOILES
Foiles, Henry Lee   b: 6/10/29, Richmond, Va.   BR/TR, 6', 195 lbs.   Deb: 4/21/53

YEAR	TM/L	G	AB	R	H	2B	3B	HR	RBI	BB	SO	AVG	OBP	SLG	PRO+	BR/A	SB	CS	SBR	FA	FR	G/POS	TPR
1953	Cin-N	5	13	1	2	0	0	0	0	1	2	.154	.214	.154	-2	-2	0	0	0	.909	-1	/C-3	-0.2
	Cle-A	7	7	2	1	0	0	0	0	1	1	.143	.250	.143	9	-1	0	0	0	.933	1	/C-7	
1955	Cle-A	62	111	13	29	9	0	1	7	17	18	.261	.359	.369	93	-1	0	0	0	.988	14	C-41	1.4
1956	Cle-A	1	0	0	0	0	0	0	0	0	0	—	—	—	—	—	0	0	0	.000	0	/C-1	0.0
	Pit-N	79	222	24	47	10	2	7	25	17	56	.212	.268	.369	71	-10	0	1	-1	.988	-2	C-73	-1.0
1957	Pit-N★	109	281	32	76	10	4	9	36	37	53	.270	.355	.431	113	6	1	3	-2	.981	-6	*C-109	0.2
1958	Pit-N	104	264	31	54	10	2	8	30	45	53	.205	.323	.348	80	-7	0	1	-1	.990	8	*C-103	0.6
1959	Pit-N	53	80	10	18	3	0	3	4	7	16	.225	.287	.375	75	-3	0	0	0	1.000	9	C-51	0.7
1960	KC-A	6	7	1	4	0	0	0	1	3	2	.571	.700	.571	246	1	0	0	0	.900	-0	/C-2	0.2
	Cle-A	24	68	9	19	1	0	1	6	7	5	.279	.347	.338	89	-1	0	0	0	.982	0	C-22	0.1
	Det-A	26	56	5	14	3	0	0	3	1	8	.250	.263	.304	51	-4	1	0	0	1.000	4	C-22	0.2
	Yr	56	131	15	37	4	0	1	10	11	15	.282	.338	.336	83	-3	1	0	0	.987	5	C-46	0.5
1961	Bal-A	43	124	18	34	6	0	6	19	12	27	.274	.338	.468	117	3	0	2	-1	.995	3	C-38	0.6
1962	Cin-N	43	131	17	36	6	1	7	25	13	39	.275	.340	.496	118	3	0	1	0	.981	1	C-41	0.5
1963	Cin-N	1	3	0	0	0	0	0	0	0	0	.000	.250	.000	-21	-0	0	0	0	1.000	-0	/C-1	0.0
	LA-A	41	84	8	18	1	1	4	10	8	13	.214	.290	.393	95	-1	0	0	0	.974	5	C-30	0.3
1964	LA-A	4	4	0	1	0	0	0	0	0	2	.250	.250	.250	44	-0	0	0	0	.000	0	H	0.0
Total	11	608	1455	171	353	59	10	46	166	170	295	.243	.323	.392	92	-17	3	7	-3	.986	35	C-544	3.6

CURRY FOLEY
Foley, Charles Joseph   b: 1/14/1856, Milltown, Ireland   d: 10/20/1898, Boston, Mass.   TL, 5'10", 160 lbs.   Deb: 5/13/1879

YEAR	TM/L	G	AB	R	H	2B	3B	HR	RBI	BB	SO	AVG	OBP	SLG	PRO+	BR/A	SB	CS	SBR	FA	FR	G/POS	TPR
1879	Bos-N	35	146	16	46	3	1	0	17	3	4	.315	.329	.349	121	3				.857	-7	P-21,O-17/1	-0.4
1880	Bos-N	80	332	44	97	13	2	2	31	8	14	.292	.309	.361	130	10				.953	-3	P-36,O-35,1	1.0
1881	Buf-N	83	375	58	96	20	2	1	25	7	27	.256	.270	.328	88	-5				.795	-4	O-55,1-27,P	-1.2
1882	Buf-N	84	341	51	104	16	4	3	49	12	26	.305	.329	.402	131	11				.833	0	*O-84/P-1	1.0
1883	Buf-N	23	111	23	30	5	3	0	14	2	5	.270	.296	.369	98	-0				.885	-2	O-23/P-1	-0.2
Total	5	305	1305	192	373	57	12	6	128	34	83	.286	.304	.362	114	19				.819	-16	O-214/P-69,1	-0.8

MARV FOLEY
Foley, Marvis Edwin   b: 8/29/53, Stanford, Ky.   BL/TR, 6', 195 lbs.   Deb: 9/11/78   C

YEAR	TM/L	G	AB	R	H	2B	3B	HR	RBI	BB	SO	AVG	OBP	SLG	PRO+	BR/A	SB	CS	SBR	FA	FR	G/POS	TPR
1978	Chi-A	11	34	3	12	0	0	0	6	4	6	.353	.421	.353	119	1	0	1	-1	.938	-3	C-10	-0.2
1979	Chi-A	34	97	6	24	3	0	2	10	7	5	.247	.298	.340	72	-4	0	0	0	.993	-1	C-33	-0.4
1980	Chi-A	68	137	14	29	5	0	4	15	9	22	.212	.270	.336	65	-7	0	0	0	.991	2	C-64/1-3	-0.3
1982	Chi-A	27	36	1	4	0	0	0	1	6	4	.111	.238	.111	-0	-5	0	0	0	.980	1	C-15/3-2,1D	-0.3
1984	Tex-A	63	115	13	25	2	0	6	19	15	24	.217	.313	.391	91	-1	0	0	0	.988	1	C-36/1-1,3D	0.1
Total	5	203	419	37	94	10	0	12	51	41	61	.224	.298	.334	73	-16	0	1	-1	.986	0	C-158/D-5,13	-1.1

RAY FOLEY
Foley, Raymond Kirwin   b: 6/23/06, Naugatuck, Conn.   d: 3/22/80, Vero Beach, Fla.   BL/TR, 5'11", 173 lbs.   Deb: 7/4/28

YEAR	TM/L	G	AB	R	H	2B	3B	HR	RBI	BB	SO	AVG	OBP	SLG	PRO+	BR/A	SB	CS	SBR	FA	FR	G/POS	TPR
1928	NY-N	2	1	1	0	0	0	0	0	0	1	.000	.500	.000	41	0	0			.000	0	H	0.0

TOM FOLEY
Foley, Thomas J.   b: 8/16/1842, Cashel, Ireland   d: 11/3/26, Chicago, Ill.   5'9.5", 157 lbs.   Deb: 5/8/1871

YEAR	TM/L	G	AB	R	H	2B	3B	HR	RBI	BB	SO	AVG	OBP	SLG	PRO+	BR/A	SB	CS	SBR	FA	FR	G/POS	TPR
1871	Chi-n	18	84	18	22	3	1	0	13	3	2	.262	.287	.321	67	-5	1					O-14/C-3,3	-0.3

TOM FOLEY
Foley, Thomas Michael   b: 9/9/59, Columbus, Ga.   BL/TR, 6'1", 175 lbs.   Deb: 4/9/83

YEAR	TM/L	G	AB	R	H	2B	3B	HR	RBI	BB	SO	AVG	OBP	SLG	PRO+	BR/A	SB	CS	SBR	FA	FR	G/POS	TPR
1983	Cin-N	68	98	7	20	4	1	0	9	13	17	.204	.297	.265	55	-6	1	0	0	.983	9	S-37/2-5	0.6
1984	Cin-N	106	277	26	70	8	3	5	27	24	36	.253	.312	.357	84	-6	3	2	-0	.965	1	S-83,2-10/3	0.1
1985	Cin-N	43	92	7	18	5	1	0	6	6	16	.196	.245	.272	42	-7	1	0	0	.983	3	2-18,S-15/3	-0.3
	Phi-N	46	158	17	42	8	0	3	17	13	18	.266	.322	.373	91	-2	1	3	-2	.981	-5	S-45	-0.4
	Yr	89	250	24	60	13	1	3	23	19	34	.240	.294	.336	73	-9	2	3	-1	.978	-3	S-60,2-18/3	-0.7
1986	Phi-N	39	61	8	18	2	1	0	5	10	11	.295	.394	.361	106	1	2	0	1	.975	0	S-24/2-1,3	0.3
	Mon-N	64	202	18	52	13	2	1	18	20	26	.257	.324	.356	88	-3	8	3	1	.965	-5	S-29,2-25,3	-0.5
	Yr	103	263	26	70	15	3	1	23	30	37	.266	.341	.357	92	-2	10	3	1	.970	-5	S-53,2-26,3	-0.2
1987	Mon-N	106	280	35	82	18	3	5	28	11	28	.293	.322	.432	95	-3	6	10	-4	.963	2	S-49,2-39/3	-0.1
1988	Mon-N	127	377	33	100	21	3	5	43	30	49	.265	.321	.377	95	-2	2	7	-4	.972	3	2-89,S-32/3	0.3
1989	Mon-N	122	375	34	86	19	2	6	39	45	53	.229	.317	.347	88	-5	2	3	-1	.988	20	*2-108,3-16,S/P	1.8
1990	Mon-N	73	164	11	35	2	1	0	12	12	22	.213	.267	.238	42	-13	0	1	-1	.987	3	S-45,2-20/31	-0.9
1991	Mon-N	86	168	12	35	11	1	0	15	14	30	.208	.273	.286	58	-9	2	0	1	.967	-2	S-43,1-31/32	-1.0
1992	Mon-N	72	115	7	20	3	1	0	5	8	21	.174	.234	.217	29	-11	3	0	1	.967	6	S-33,2-13,1/30	-0.2
1993	Pit-N	86	194	18	49	11	1	3	22	11	26	.253	.293	.366	75	-7	2	0	1	.993	1	2-35,1-12/3S	-0.5
1994	Pit-N	59	123	13	29	7	0	3	15	13	18	.236	.309	.366	75	-5	0	0	0	.986	11	2-17,3-14/S1	0.7
Total	12	1097	2684	246	656	132	20	32	261	230	383	.244	.306	.344	79	-78	31	29	-8	.972	46	S-463,2-382/310P	-0.1

WILL FOLEY
Foley, William Brown   b: 11/15/1855, Chicago, Ill.   d: 11/12/16, Chicago, Ill.   BR/TR, 5'9.5", 150 lbs.   Deb: 8/23/1875

YEAR	TM/L	G	AB	R	H	2B	3B	HR	RBI	BB	SO	AVG	OBP	SLG	PRO+	BR/A	SB	CS	SBR	FA	FR	G/POS	TPR
1875	Chi-n	3	12	0	3	1	0	0	0	0		.250	.250	.333	99	-0						/3-3	0.0
1876	Cin-N	58	221	19	50	3	2	0	9	0	14	.226	.226	.258	71	-6				.804	2	3-46,C-20	-0.2
1877	Cin-N	56	216	23	41	5	1	0	18	4	13	.190	.205	.222	39	-14				.836	6	*3-56	-0.5
1878	Mil-N	56	229	33	62	8	5	0	22	7	14	.271	.292	.349	103	-0				.812	-9	*3-53/C-7	-0.6
1879	Cin-N	56	218	22	46	5	1	0	25	2	16	.211	.218	.243	55	-10				.820	3	3-29,O-25/2	-0.7
1881	Det-N	5	15	0	2	0	0	0	0	1	3	.133	.235	.133	18	-1				.769	-1	/3-5	-0.3
1884	CP-U	19	71	15	20	1	1	0	5			.282	.329	.324	79	-2				.804	5	3-19	-0.5
Total	6	250	970	112	221	22	10	0	75	20	60	.228	.243	.271	69	-33				.817	-2	3-208/C-27,O2	-2.8

TIM FOLI
Foli, Timothy John   b: 12/8/50, Culver City, Cal.   BR/TR, 6', 179 lbs.   Deb: 9/11/70   C

YEAR	TM/L	G	AB	R	H	2B	3B	HR	RBI	BB	SO	AVG	OBP	SLG	PRO+	BR/A	SB	CS	SBR	FA	FR	G/POS	TPR
1970	NY-N	5	11	0	4	1	0	0	1	0	2	.364	.364	.364	95	-0	0	0	0	1.000	2	/S-2,3-2	0.2
1971	NY-N	97	288	32	65	12	2	0	24	8	50	.226	.274	.281	58	-16	5	0	2	.964	14	2-58,3-36,S/O	0.4
1972	Mon-N	149	540	45	130	12	2	2	35	25	43	.241	.282	.281	59	-28	11	7	-1	.966	9	*S-148/2-1	0.1
1973	Mon-N	126	458	37	110	11	0	2	36	28	40	.240	.285	.277	55	-28	6	3	0	.960	8	*S-123/2-2,O	-0.3
1974	Mon-N	121	441	41	112	10	0	0	39	28	27	.254	.303	.290	63	-21	8	2	1	.971	19	*S-120/3-1	1.6

YEAR	TM/L	G	AB	R	H	2B	3B	HR	RBI	BB	SO	AVG	OBP	SLG	PRO+	BR/A	SB	CS	SBR	FA	FR	G/POS	TPR
1975	Mon-N	152	572	64	136	25	2	1	29	36	49	.238	.285	.294	58	-32	13	3	2	.973	6	*S-151/2-1	-0.9
1976	Mon-N	149	546	41	144	36	1	6	54	16	33	.264	.285	.366	80	-16	6	5	-1	.975	7	*S-146/3-1	0.8
1977	Mon-N	13	57	2	10	5	1	0	3	0	4	.175	.175	.298	25	-6	0	0	0	1.000	1	S-13	-0.4
	SF-N	104	368	30	84	17	3	4	27	11	16	.228	.251	.323	53	-25	2	4	-2	.974	2	*S-102/2-1,3O	-1.4
	Yr	117	425	32	94	22	4	4	30	11	20	.221	.241	.320	49	-31	2	4	-2	.977	3	*S-115/2-1,3O	-1.8
1978	NY-N	113	413	37	106	21	1	1	27	14	30	.257	.284	.320	71	-17	2	5	-2	.966	-15	*S-112	-2.1
1979	NY-N	3	7	0	0	0	0	0	0	0	0	.000	.000	.000	-99	-2	0	0	0	1.000	1	/S-3	-0.1
	*Pit-N	133	525	70	153	23	1	1	65	28	14	.291	.338	.345	83	-12	6	5	-1	.978	-1	*S-132	0.2
	Yr	136	532	70	153	23	1	1	65	28	14	.288	.334	.340	81	-13	6	5	-1	.978	0	*S-135	0.1
1980	Pit-N	127	495	61	131	22	0	3	38	19	23	.265	.300	.327	74	-17	11	7	-1	**.981**	-0	*S-125	-0.4
1981	Pit-N	86	316	32	78	12	2	0	20	17	10	.247	.287	.297	64	-15	7	7	-2	.965	-9	S-81	-2.0
1982	*Cal-A	150	480	46	121	14	2	3	56	14	22	.252	.276	.308	60	-26	2	4	-2	**.985**	8	*S-139/2-8,3	-0.7
1983	Cal-A	88	330	29	83	10	0	2	29	5	18	.252	.265	.300	56	-20	2	3	-1	.975	10	S-74,3-13	-0.4
1984	NY-A	61	163	8	41	11	0	0	16	2	16	.252	.265	.319	63	-8	0	0	0	.950	7	S-28,2-21,3/1	0.1
1985	Pit-N	19	37	1	7	0	0	0	2	4	2	.189	.268	.189	30	-3	0	0	0	.980	3	S-13	0.1
Total	16	1696	6047	576	1515	241	20	25	501	265	399	.251	.286	.309	64	-293	81	55	-9	.973	73	*S-1524/2-92,3O1	-5.2

■ DEE FONDY
Fondy, Dee Virgil b: 10/31/24, Slaton, Tex. BL/TL, 6'3", 196 lbs. Deb: 4/17/51

YEAR	TM/L	G	AB	R	H	2B	3B	HR	RBI	BB	SO	AVG	OBP	SLG	PRO+	BR/A	SB	CS	SBR	FA	FR	G/POS	TPR
1951	Chi-N	49	170	23	46	7	2	3	20	11	20	.271	.319	.388	88	-3	5	6	-2	.976	-3	1-44	-1.0
1952	Chi-N	145	554	69	166	21	9	10	67	28	60	.300	.334	.424	108	4	13	11	-3	.990	7	*1-143	-0.2
1953	Chi-N	150	595	79	184	24	11	18	78	44	106	.309	.358	.477	113	10	10	7	-1	.987	4	*1-149	0.6
1954	Chi-N	141	568	77	162	30	4	9	49	35	84	.285	.328	.400	87	-11	20	5	**3**	.993	7	*1-138	-0.8
1955	Chi-N	150	574	69	152	23	8	17	65	35	87	.265	.309	.422	92	-8	8	9	-3	.991	1	*1-147	-1.9
1956	Chi-N	137	543	52	146	22	9	9	46	20	74	.269	.295	.392	84	-13	9	7	-2	.985	-3	*1-133	-2.8
1957	Chi-N	11	51	3	16	3	1	0	2	0	9	.314	.314	.412	94	-1	1	2	-1	.991	-1	1-11	-0.3
	Pit-N	95	323	42	101	13	2	2	35	25	59	.313	.364	.384	104	2	11	5	0	.982	-3	1-73	-0.5
	Yr	106	374	45	117	16	3	2	37	25	68	.313	.357	.388	103	2	12	7	-1	.983	-4	1-84	-0.8
1958	Cin-N	89	124	23	27	1	1	1	11	5	27	.218	.248	.266	34	-12	7	1	2	.987	-1	1-36,O-22	-1.3
Total	8	967	3502	437	1000	144	47	69	373	203	526	.286	.326	.413	95	-30	84	53	-7	.988	3	1-874/O-22	-8.2

■ LEW FONSECA
Fonseca, Lewis Albert b: 1/21/1899, Oakland, Cal. d: 11/26/89, Ely, Iowa BR/TR, 5'10.5", 180 lbs. Deb: 4/13/21 M

YEAR	TM/L	G	AB	R	H	2B	3B	HR	RBI	BB	SO	AVG	OBP	SLG	PRO+	BR/A	SB	CS	SBR	FA	FR	G/POS	TPR
1921	Cin-N	82	297	38	82	10	3	1	41	8	13	.276	.304	.340	74	-12	2	3	-1	.961	-3	2-50,1-16,O	-1.6
1922	Cin-N	81	291	55	105	20	3	4	45	14	18	.361	.390	.491	128	12	7	8	-3	.970	8	2-71	1.8
1923	Cin-N	65	237	33	66	11	4	3	28	9	16	.278	.310	.397	87	-5	4	0	1	.957	8	2-45,1-14	0.4
1924	Cin-N	20	57	5	13	2	1	0	9	4	4	.228	.279	.298	55	-4	1	0	0	1.000	-2	2-10/1-6	-0.6
1925	Phi-N	126	467	78	149	30	5	7	60	21	42	.319	.352	.450	95	-4	6	2	1	.956	-8	2-69,1-55	-1.3
1927	Cle-A	112	428	60	133	20	7	2	40	12	17	.311	.333	.404	90	-8	12	4	1	.973	-6	2-96,1-13	-0.9
1928	Cle-A	75	263	38	86	19	4	3	36	13	17	.327	.361	.464	114	5	4	2	0	1.000	5	1-56,3-15/S2	0.5
1929	Cle-A	148	566	97	209	44	15	6	103	50	23	**.369**	.427	.532	140	34	19	11	-1	.995	6	*1-147	2.3
1930	Cle-A	40	129	20	36	9	2	0	17	7	7	.279	.316	.380	73	-6	1	0	0	.980	2	1-28/3-6	-0.5
1931	Cle-A	26	108	21	40	9	1	1	14	8	7	.370	.419	.500	133	5	3	2	-0	.993	0	1-26	0.0
	Chi-A	121	465	65	139	26	5	2	71	32	22	.299	.348	.389	99	-1	4	4	-1	.974	-17	O-95,2-21/13	-2.2
	Yr	147	573	86	179	35	6	3	85	40	29	.312	.361	.410	106	5	7	6	-2	.974	-16	O-95,1-28,2/3	-1.9
1932	Chi-A	18	37	0	5	1	0	0	6	1	7	.135	.158	.162	-18	-7	0	0	0	1.000	1	/O-8,P-1M	-0.6
1933	Chi-A	23	59	8	12	2	0	2	15	7	6	.203	.288	.339	68	-3	1	0	0	1.000	2	1-12,M	-0.1
Total	12	937	3404	518	1075	203	50	31	485	186	199	.316	.355	.432	103	8	64	36	-2	.994	-3	1-375,2-363,O/3SP	-2.5

■ BARRY FOOTE
Foote, Barry Clifton b: 2/16/52, Smithfield, N.C. BR/TR, 6'3", 210 lbs. Deb: 9/14/73 C

YEAR	TM/L	G	AB	R	H	2B	3B	HR	RBI	BB	SO	AVG	OBP	SLG	PRO+	BR/A	SB	CS	SBR	FA	FR	G/POS	TPR
1973	Mon-N	6	6	0	4	0	1	0	1	0	0	.667	.667	1.000	343	2	0	0	0	.000	0	H	0.2
1974	Mon-N	125	420	44	110	23	4	11	60	35	74	.262	.323	.414	100	-1	2	1	0	.984	9	*C-122	1.3
1975	Mon-N	118	387	25	75	16	1	7	30	17	48	.194	.230	.295	43	-31	0	1	-1	.985	11	*C-115	-1.7
1976	Mon-N	105	350	32	82	12	2	7	27	17	32	.234	.272	.340	70	-15	0	1	0	.989	7	C-96/3-2,1	-0.5
1977	Mon-N	15	49	4	12	3	1	2	8	4	10	.245	.302	.469	106	0	0	0	0	.988	0	C-13	0.1
	Phi-N	18	32	3	7	1	0	1	3	6	7	.219	.286	.344	65	-2	0	0	0	.980	-1	C-17	-0.2
	Yr	33	81	7	19	4	1	3	11	7	6	.235	.295	.420	88	-2	0	0	0	.985	-0	C-30	-0.1
1978	*Phi-N	39	57	4	9	0	0	1	4	1	11	.158	.172	.211	6	-7	0	0	0	1.000	2	C-31	-0.5
1979	Chi-N	132	429	47	109	26	0	16	56	34	49	.254	.316	.427	90	-6	5	2	0	.979	-3	*C-129	-0.4
1980	Chi-N	63	202	16	48	13	1	6	28	13	18	.238	.284	.401	83	-5	1	1	-0	.992	1	C-55	-0.3
1981	Chi-N	9	22	0	0	0	0	0	1	3	7	.000	.120	.000	-61	-5	0	0	0	1.000	-1	/C-8	-0.6
	*NY-A	40	125	12	26	4	0	6	10	8	21	.208	.256	.384	83	-3	0	0	0	.996	9	C-34/1-1,D	0.7
1982	NY-A	17	48	4	7	5	0	0	2	1	11	.146	.163	.250	12	-6	0	0	0	.973	-4	C-17	-0.9
Total	10	687	2127	191	489	103	10	57	230	136	287	.230	.279	.368	75	-78	10	6	-1	.985	31	C-637/D-4,13	-2.8

■ JIM FORAN
Foran, James H. b: 1848, New York 5'6.5", 159 lbs. Deb: 5/4/1871

YEAR	TM/L	G	AB	R	H	2B	3B	HR	RBI	BB	SO	AVG	OBP	SLG	PRO+	BR/A	SB	CS	SBR	FA	FR	G/POS	TPR
1871	Kek-n	19	89	21	31	1	3	1	18	2	1	.348	.363	.461	132	3	1					1-15/O-4	0.3

■ DAVY FORCE
Force, David W. "Wee Davy" or "Tom Thumb" b: 7/27/1849, New York, N.Y. d: 6/21/18, Englewood, N.J. BR/TR, 5'4", 130 lbs. Deb: 5/5/1871

YEAR	TM/L	G	AB	R	H	2B	3B	HR	RBI	BB	SO	AVG	OBP	SLG	PRO+	BR/A	SB	CS	SBR	FA	FR	G/POS	TPR
1871	Oly-n	32	162	45	45	9	4	0	29	4	0	.278	.295	.383	98	0	8					*S-31/3-1	0.0
1872	Tro-n	25	133	40	53	7	1	0	16	1	0	.398	.403	.466	164	9						3-16/S-9	0.5
	Bal-n	19	96	29	40	3	2	0	13	1	0	.417	.423	.490	172	7						3-18	0.5
	Yr	44	229	69	93	10	3	0	29	2	0	.406	.411	.476	168	17						3-34/S-9	1.0
1873	Bal-n	49	234	77	86	12	3	0	31	9	0	.368	.391	.444	146	14						3-34,S-17/P	0.8
1874	Chi-n	59	296	61	93	10	0	0	2			.314	.319	.348	111	3						3-38,S-20/PO	0.2
1875	Ath-n	77	384	78	120	21	6	0			8	.313	.327	.398	134	10						S-77	0.6
1876	Phi-N	60	284	48	66	6	0	0	17	5	3	.232	.246	.254	67	-9				.898	21	*S-60/3-2	1.0
	NY-N	1	3	0	0	0	0	0	0	0	0	.000	.000	.000	-99	-1				.833	0	/S-1	0.0
	Yr	61	287	48	66	6	0	0	17	5	3	.230	.243	.251	66	-10				.897	21	S-61/3-2	1.0
1877	StL-N	58	225	24	59	5	3	0	22	11	15	.262	.297	.311	97	-0				**.914**	6	*S-50/3-8	0.6
1879	Buf-N	79	316	36	66	5	2	0	8	13	37	.209	.240	.237	57	-14				**.929**	2	*S-78/3-1	-0.8
1880	Buf-N	81	290	22	49	10	0	0	17	10	35	.169	.197	.203	35	-19				.939	31	2-53,S-30	1.6
1881	Buf-N	75	278	21	50	9	1	0	15	11	29	.180	.211	.219	36	-20				.937	24	2-51,S-21/O3	0.7
1882	Buf-N	73	278	39	67	10	1	1	28	12	17	.241	.272	.295	81	-6				**.908**	7	*S-61,3-11/2	0.4
1883	Buf-N	96	378	40	82	11	3	0	35	12	39	.217	.241	.262	52	-22				.884	-6	*S-78,3-13/2	-2.3
1884	Buf-N	106	403	47	83	13	3	0	36	27	41	.206	.256	.253	59	-19				**.898**	-3	*S-105/2-1	-1.9
1885	Buf-N	71	253	20	57	6	1	0	15	13	19	.225	.263	.257	66	-9				.882	-4	2-42,S-24/3	-0.1
1886	Was-N	68	242	26	44	5	1	0	16	17	26	.182	.236	.211	39	-17	9			.909	17	S-56/2-8,3	0.1
Total	5 n	261	1305	330	437	62	16	0	89		25	.335	.347	.407	132	44	14					S-154,3-107/PO	2.6
Total	10	768	2950	323	623	80	15	1	209	131	261	.211	.245	.249	58	-136	9			.908	96	S-564,2-163/3O	-1.6

■ CURT FORD
Ford, Curtis Glenn b: 10/11/60, Jackson, Miss. BL/TR, 5'10", 150 lbs. Deb: 6/22/85

YEAR	TM/L	G	AB	R	H	2B	3B	HR	RBI	BB	SO	AVG	OBP	SLG	PRO+	BR/A	SB	CS	SBR	FA	FR	G/POS	TPR
1985	StL-N	11	12	2	6	2	0	0	3	4	1	.500	.625	.667	264	3	1	0	0	.750	-2	/O-4	0.2
1986	StL-N	85	214	30	53	15	2	2	29	23	29	.248	.321	.364	89	-3	13	5	1	.975	1	O-64	-0.3
1987	*StL-N	89	228	32	65	9	5	3	26	14	32	.285	.329	.408	92	-3	11	8	-2	.981	1	O-75	-0.5
1988	StL-N	91	128	11	25	6	0	1	18	8	26	.195	.243	.266	45	-9	6	1	1	.965	-4	O-40/1-7	-1.4

YEAR	TM/L	G	AB	R	H	2B	3B	HR	RBI	BB	SO	AVG	OBP	SLG	PRO+	BR/A	SB	CS	SBR	FA	FR	G/POS	TPR
1989	Phi-N	108	142	13	31	5	1	1	13	16	33	.218	.302	.289	70	-5	5	3	-0	1.000	-8	O-52/1-1,2	-1.6
1990	Phi-N	22	18	0	2	0	0	0	0	1	5	.111	.158	.111	-25	-3	0	0	0	1.000	-1	/O-3	-0.4
Total	6	406	742	88	182	37	8	7	89	66	126	.245	.309	.345	80	-20	36	17	1	.977	-12	O-238/1-8,2	-4.0

■ DAN FORD
Ford, Darnell Glenn   b: 5/19/52, Los Angeles, Cal.   BR/TR, 6'1", 185 lbs.   Deb: 4/12/75

YEAR	TM/L	G	AB	R	H	2B	3B	HR	RBI	BB	SO	AVG	OBP	SLG	PRO+	BR/A	SB	CS	SBR	FA	FR	G/POS	TPR
1975	Min-A	130	440	72	123	21	1	15	59	30	79	.280	.333	.434	113	6	6	7	-2	.988	-9	*O-120/D-3	-0.9
1976	Min-A	145	514	87	137	24	7	20	86	36	118	.267	.327	.457	124	14	17	6	2	.968	-5	*O-139/D-3	0.5
1977	Min-A	144	453	66	121	25	7	11	60	41	79	.267	.341	.426	109	6	6	4	-1	.964	-10	*O-137/D-3	-0.9
1978	Min-A	151	592	78	162	36	10	11	82	48	88	.274	.333	.424	109	7	7	7	-2	.977	-2	*O-149/D-1	-0.4
1979	*Cal-A	142	569	100	165	26	5	21	101	40	86	.290	.340	.464	118	13	8	5	-1	.977	7	*O-141	1.3
1980	Cal-A	65	226	22	63	11	0	7	26	19	45	.279	.340	.420	110	3	0	1	-1	.940	-2	O-45,D-15	-0.2
1981	Cal-A	97	375	53	104	14	1	15	48	23	71	.277	.328	.440	119	8	2	2	-1	.960	-2	O-97	0.2
1982	Bal-A	123	421	46	99	21	3	10	43	23	71	.235	.281	.371	78	-14	5	2	0	.975	4	O-119/D-1	-1.2
1983	*Bal-A	103	407	63	114	30	4	9	55	29	55	.280	.333	.440	113	6	9	2	2	.987	1	*O-103	0.5
1984	Bal-A	25	91	7	21	4	0	1	5	7	13	.231	.286	.308	66	-4	1	0	0	1.000	-0	O-15/D-8	-0.3
1985	Bal-A	28	75	4	14	2	0	1	1	7	17	.187	.256	.253	41	-6	0	1	-1	.000	0	D-28	-0.7
Total	11	1153	4163	598	1123	214	38	121	566	303	722	.270	.326	.427	108	39	61	37	-4	.974	-17	*O-1065/D-62	-2.1

■ ED FORD
Ford, Edward L.   b: 1862, Richmond, Va.   5'9.5", 160 lbs.   Deb: 10/9/1884

YEAR	TM/L	G	AB	R	H	2B	3B	HR	RBI	BB	SO	AVG	OBP	SLG	PRO+	BR/A	SB	CS	SBR	FA	FR	G/POS	TPR
1884	Ric-a	2	5	0	0	0	0	0	0			.000	.000	.000	-99	-1				.556	1	/S-1,1-1	0.0

■ HOD FORD
Ford, Horace Hills   b: 7/23/1897, New Haven, Conn.   d: 1/29/77, Winchester, Mass.   BR/TR, 5'10", 165 lbs.   Deb: 9/8/19

YEAR	TM/L	G	AB	R	H	2B	3B	HR	RBI	BB	SO	AVG	OBP	SLG	PRO+	BR/A	SB	CS	SBR	FA	FR	G/POS	TPR
1919	Bos-N	10	28	4	6	0	1	0	3	2	6	.214	.290	.286	77	-1	0			.946	3	/S-8,3-2	0.3
1920	Bos-N	88	257	16	62	12	5	1	30	18	25	.241	.296	.339	86	-5	3	3	-1	.972	15	2-59,S-18/1	1.3
1921	Bos-N	152	555	50	155	29	5	2	61	36	49	.279	.328	.360	87	-11	2	11	-6	.973	16	*2-119,S-33	0.5
1922	Bos-N	143	515	58	140	23	9	2	60	30	36	.272	.317	.363	78	-17	2	1	-0	.953	-4	*S-115,2-28	-0.8
1923	Bos-N	111	380	27	103	16	7	2	50	31	30	.271	.326	.366	86	-8	1	1	-0	.970	-9	2-95,S-19	-1.4
1924	Phi-N	145	530	58	144	27	5	3	53	27	40	.272	.308	.358	70	-23	1	9	-5	.970	12	*2-145	-1.5
1925	Bro-N	66	216	32	59	11	0	1	15	26	15	.273	.357	.338	81	-5	0	3	-2	.966	-0	S-66	-0.1
1926	Cin-N	57	197	14	55	6	1	0	18	14	12	.279	.336	.320	79	-5	1			.963	5	S-57	0.5
1927	Cin-N	115	409	45	112	16	2	1	46	33	34	.274	.331	.330	80	-11	1			.952	-8	*S-104,2-12	-0.8
1928	Cin-N	149	506	49	122	17	4	0	54	47	31	.241	.308	.291	58	-30	1			.972	12	*S-149	-0.1
1929	Cin-N	148	529	68	146	14	6	3	50	41	25	.276	.329	.342	70	-25	8			.953	8	*S-108,2-42	-0.1
1930	Cin-N	132	424	36	98	16	7	1	34	24	28	.231	.272	.309	42	-40	2			.974	2	S-74,2-66	-2.6
1931	Cin-N	84	175	18	40	8	1	0	13	13	13	.229	.286	.286	57	-11	0			.954	1	S-73/2-3,3	-0.5
1932	StL-N	1	2	0	0	0	0	0	0	0	0	.000	.000	.000	-97	-1	0			.750	1	/S-1	0.0
	Bos-N	40	95	9	26	5	2	0	6	6	9	.274	.324	.368	89	-1	0			.984	-3	2-20,S-16/3	-0.2
	Yr	41	97	9	26	5	2	0	6	6	9	.268	.317	.361	85	-2	0			.984	-3	2-20,S-17/3	-0.2
1933	Bos-N	5	15	0	1	0	0	0	1	3	1	.067	.222	.067	-16	-2	0			1.000	5	/S-5	0.0
Total	15	1446	4833	484	1269	200	55	16	494	351	354	.263	.316	.337	72	-198	21	28		.960	-6	S-846,2-589/31	-5.2

■ TED FORD
Ford, Theodore Henry   b: 2/7/47, Vineland, N.J.   BR/TR, 5'10", 180 lbs.   Deb: 4/7/70

YEAR	TM/L	G	AB	R	H	2B	3B	HR	RBI	BB	SO	AVG	OBP	SLG	PRO+	BR/A	SB	CS	SBR	FA	FR	G/POS	TPR
1970	Cle-A	26	46	5	8	1	0	1	1	3	13	.174	.224	.261	32	-4	0	0	0	1.000	1	O-12	-0.4
1971	Cle-A	74	196	15	38	6	0	2	14	9	34	.194	.229	.255	34	-17	2	2	-1	1.000	-1	O-55	-2.2
1972	Tex-A	129	429	43	101	19	1	14	50	37	80	.235	.301	.382	107	2	4	3	-1	.977	9	*O-119	0.6
1973	Cle-A	11	40	3	9	0	1	0	3	2	7	.225	.262	.275	50	-3	1	0	0	1.000	-4	O-10	-0.7
Total	4	240	711	66	156	26	2	17	68	51	134	.219	.275	.333	76	-22	7	5	-1	.985	6	O-196	-2.7

■ FRANK FOREMAN
Foreman, Francis Isaiah "Monkey"   b: 5/1/1863, Baltimore, Md.   d: 11/19/57, Baltimore, Md.   BL/TL, 6', 160 lbs.   Deb: 5/15/1884   F

YEAR	TM/L	G	AB	R	H	2B	3B	HR	RBI	BB	SO	AVG	OBP	SLG	PRO+	BR/A	SB	CS	SBR	FA	FR	G/POS	TPR
1884	CP-U	3	11	0	1	0	0	0	0			.091	.091	.091	-51	-2				.857	-1	/P-3,O-2	-0.1
	KC-U	1	3	0	0	0	0	0	0			.000	.000	.000	-99	-1				.900	1	/P-1	0.0
	Yr	4	14	0	1	0	0	0	0			.071	.071	.071	-63	-3				.882	0	/P-4,O-2	-0.1
1885	Bal-a	3	14	4	4	0	1	0	0			.286	.286	.429	125	0				.800	-1	/P-3,O-1	0.0
1889	Bal-a	54	181	18	26	2	1	1	11	12	35	.144	.201	.182	9	-22	7			.853	-3	P-51/O-3	-0.1
1890	Cin-N	25	75	13	10	1	3	1	7	10	13	.133	.253	.267	52	-5	0			.867	-3	P-25/O-1	0.0
1891	Cin-N	1	4	0	1	1	0	0	0	0	0	.250	.250	.500	116	0	0			.000	-0	/O-1	0.0
	Was-a	50	153	26	34	4	5	4	19	23	35	.222	.339	.392	114	3	6			.952	-0	P-43/O-8	0.0
1892	Was-N	11	28	5	13	2	2	1	3	3	3	.464	.516	.786	301	7	1			.632	-3	P-11	0.0
	Bal-N	7	23	2	4	1	1	0	1	3	3	.174	.269	.304	71	-1	0			.750	-0	/O-5,P-4	-0.1
	Yr	18	51	7	17	3	3	1	4	6	6	.333	.404	.569	195	6	1			.731	-3	P-15/O-5	-0.1
1893	NY-N	2	3	0	0	0	0	0	0	0	0	.000	.000	.000	-99	-1	0			1.000	-0	/P-2	0.0
1895	Cin-N	32	94	14	29	7	0	2	11	4	14	.309	.350	.447	100	-0	1			.882	-3	P-32	0.0
1896	Cin-N	27	74	9	18	2	0	0	8	4	7	.243	.282	.270	43	-6	2			.911	5	P-27	0.0
1901	Bos-A	1	4	0	0	0	0	0	0	0	0	.000	.000	.000	-99	-1	0			1.000	-0	/P-1	0.0
	Bal-A	24	80	12	26	2	2	0	10	3		.325	.349	.400	103	0	1			.887	-3	P-24	0.0
	Yr	25	84	12	26	2	2	0	10	3		.310	.333	.381	94	-1	1			.891	-3	P-25	0.0
1902	Bal-A	2	7	1	3	1	0	0	1	0		.429	.429	.571	168	1	0			.818	1	/P-2	0.0
Total	11	243	754	104	169	23	15	9	71	62	110	.224	.291	.330	73	-29	18			.881	-16	P-229/O-21	-0.3

■ TOM FORSTER
Forster, Thomas W.   b: 5/1/1859, New York, N.Y.   d: 7/17/46, New York, N.Y.   BR, 5'9", 153 lbs.   Deb: 8/4/1882

YEAR	TM/L	G	AB	R	H	2B	3B	HR	RBI	BB	SO	AVG	OBP	SLG	PRO+	BR/A	SB	CS	SBR	FA	FR	G/POS	TPR
1882	Det-N	21	76	5	7	0	0	0	2	5	12	.092	.148	.092	-21	-10				.830	-7	2-21	-1.5
1884	Pit-a	35	126	10	28	5	0	0		7		.222	.263	.262	71	-4				.897	6	S-28/3-6,2	0.2
1885	NY-a	57	213	28	47	7	2	0		17		.221	.281	.272	82	-3				.903	-12	2-52/O-5	-1.2
1886	NY-a	67	251	33	49	3	2	1		20		.195	.263	.235	59	-11	9			.891	-7	2-62/O-4,S	-1.4
Total	4	180	666	76	131	15	4	1	2	49	12	.197	.256	.236	59	-28	9			.885	-19	2-136/S-29,O3	-3.9

■ ED FORSYTHE
Forsythe, Edward James   b: 4/30/1887, Kingston, N.Y.   d: 6/22/56, Hoboken, N.J.   BR/TR, 5'10", 155 lbs.   Deb: 10/2/15

YEAR	TM/L	G	AB	R	H	2B	3B	HR	RBI	BB	SO	AVG	OBP	SLG	PRO+	BR/A	SB	CS	SBR	FA	FR	G/POS	TPR
1915	Bal-F	1	3	0	0	0	0	0	0	1	0	.000	.250	.000	-29	-1	0			.667	-0	/3-1	-0.1

■ GEORGE FOSS
Foss, George Dueward "Deeby"   b: 6/13/1897, Register, Ga.   d: 11/10/69, Brandon, Fla.   BR/TR, 5'10.5", 170 lbs.   Deb: 4/16/21

YEAR	TM/L	G	AB	R	H	2B	3B	HR	RBI	BB	SO	AVG	OBP	SLG	PRO+	BR/A	SB	CS	SBR	FA	FR	G/POS	TPR
1921	Was-A	4	7	0	0	0	0	0	0	0	1	.000	.000	.000	-99	-2	0	0	0	.750	0	/3-1	-0.2

■ RAY FOSSE
Fosse, Raymond Earl   b: 4/4/47, Marion, Ill.   BR/TR, 6'2", 215 lbs.   Deb: 9/8/67

YEAR	TM/L	G	AB	R	H	2B	3B	HR	RBI	BB	SO	AVG	OBP	SLG	PRO+	BR/A	SB	CS	SBR	FA	FR	G/POS	TPR
1967	Cle-A	7	16	0	1	0	0	0	0	0	5	.063	.063	.063	-62	-3	0	0	0	1.000	5	/C-7	0.2
1968	Cle-A	1	0	0	0	0	0	0	0	0	0	—	—	—			0			1.000	0	/C-1	0.0
1969	Cle-A	37	116	11	20	3	0	2	9	8	29	.172	.232	.250	34	-10	1	0	0	.977	3	C-37	-0.5
1970	Cle-A★	120	450	62	138	17	1	18	61	39	55	.307	.363	.469	122	13	1	5	-3	.989	6	*C-120	2.3
1971	Cle-A†	133	486	53	134	21	1	12	62	36	62	.276	.331	.397	97	-2	4	1	1	.988	6	*C-126/1-4	-0.1
1972	Cle-A	134	457	42	110	20	1	10	41	45	62	.241	.313	.354	95	-3	5	1	1	.985	6	*C-124/1-3	1.0
1973	*Oak-A	143	492	37	126	23	2	7	52	25	62	.256	.293	.354	86	-11	2	2	-1	.987	2	*C-141/D-2	-0.3
1974	Oak-A	69	204	20	40	8	3	4	23	11	31	.196	.244	.324	66	-4	1	1	-0	.973	-1	C-68/D-1	-0.9
1975	*Oak-A	82	136	14	19	3	2	0	12	8	19	.140	.193	.191	9	-16	0	1	-1	.981	6	C-82/1-1,2	-1.0
1976	Cle-A	90	276	26	83	9	1	2	30	20	20	.301	.348	.362	109	3	1	2	-1	.987	6	C-85/1-3,D	0.6
1977	Cle-A	78	238	25	63	9	1	3	27	24	26	.265	.294	.378	84	-6	5	5	-3	.983	9	C-77/1-1,D	0.2
	Sea-A	11	34	3	12	3	0	0	5	2	2	.353	.389	.441	127	1	0	1	-1	.968	-3	/C-8,D-2	-0.2

YEAR	TM/L	G	AB	R	H	2B	3B	HR	RBI	BB	SO	AVG	OBP	SLG	PRO+	BR/A	SB	CS	SBR	FA	FR	G/POS	TPR
	Yr	89	272	28	75	10	1	6	32	9	28	.276	.306	.386	90	-4	0	6	-4	.982	5	C-85/D-3,1	0.0
1979	Mil-A	19	52	6	12	3	1	0	2	2	6	.231	.286	.327	65	-3	0	0	0	1.000	-1	C-13/1-1,D	-0.3
Total	12	924	2957	299	758	117	13	61	324	203	363	.256	.308	.367	90	-46	15	19	-7	.985	28	C-889/1-13,D2	1.0

■ POP FOSTER

Foster, Clarence Francis   b: 4/8/1878, New Haven, Conn.   d: 4/16/44, Princeton, N.J.   BR/TR, 5'8.5"   Deb: 9/13/1898

YEAR	TM/L	G	AB	R	H	2B	3B	HR	RBI	BB	SO	AVG	OBP	SLG	PRO+	BR/A	SB	CS	SBR	FA	FR	G/POS	TPR
1898	NY-N	32	112	10	30	6	1	0	9	0		.268	.268	.339	76	-4	0			.967	-5	O-21,3-10/S	-1.0
1899	NY-N	84	301	48	89	9	7	3	57	20		.296	.348	.402	109	3	7			.949	-10	O-84/S-1,3	-1.2
1900	NY-N	31	84	19	22	3	1	0	11	11		.262	.347	.321	89	-1	0			1.000	-3	O-12/S-7,2	-0.3
1901	Was-A	103	392	65	109	16	9	6	54	41		.278	.352	.411	113	7	10			.925	-1	*O-102/S-2	-0.1
	Chi-A	12	35	4	10	2	2	1	6	4		.286	.359	.543	152	2	0			.909	-1	/O-9	0.0
	Yr	115	427	69	119	18	11	7	60	45		.279	.353	.422	116	9	10			.924	-2	*O-111/S-2	-0.1
Total	4	262	924	146	260	36	20	10	137	76		.281	.341	.396	107	8	17			.938	-19	O-228/S-12,32	-2.6

■ EDDIE FOSTER

Foster, Edward Cunningham "Kid"   b: 2/13/1887, Chicago, Ill.   d: 1/15/37, Washington, D.C.   BR/TR, 5'6.5", 145 lbs.   Deb: 4/14/10

YEAR	TM/L	G	AB	R	H	2B	3B	HR	RBI	BB	SO	AVG	OBP	SLG	PRO+	BR/A	SB	CS	SBR	FA	FR	G/POS	TPR
1910	NY-A	30	83	5	11	2	0	0	1	8		.133	.217	.157	16	-8	2			.909	-2	S-22	-1.1
1912	Was-A	154	618	98	176	34	9	2	70	53		.285	.345	.379	106	4	27			.920	12	*3-154	1.7
1913	Was-A	106	409	56	101	11	5	1	41	36	31	.247	.309	.306	78	-11	22			.901	4	*3-105	-0.6
1914	Was-A	157	616	82	174	16	10	2	50	60	47	.282	.348	.351	106	5	31	18	-2	.929	-18	*3-157	-1.0
1915	Was-A	154	618	75	170	25	10	0	52	48	30	.275	.329	.348	101	-1	20	6	2	.919	-5	3-79,2-75	0.1
1916	Was-A	158	606	75	153	18	9	1	44	68	26	.252	.332	.317	96	-2	23	16	-3	.929	-16	3-84,2-72	-1.7
1917	Was-A	143	554	66	130	16	8	0	43	46	23	.235	.293	.292	80	-14	11			.935	-6	3-86,2-57	-1.7
1918	Was-A	129	519	70	147	13	3	0	29	41	20	.283	.339	.320	101	-0	12			.936	2	*3-127/2-2	0.6
1919	Was-A	120	478	57	126	12	5	0	26	33	21	.264	.314	.310	76	-15	20			.946	7	*3-115	-0.3
1920	Bos-A	117	386	48	100	17	6	0	41	42	17	.259	.336	.334	82	-10	10	4	1	.957	15	3-88,2-21	1.0
1921	Bos-A	120	412	51	117	18	6	0	35	57	15	.284	.371	.357	89	-5	13	7	-0	.943	-14	3-94,2-22	-1.2
1922	Bos-A	48	109	11	23	3	0	0	3	9	10	.211	.277	.239	36	-10	1	1	-0	.886	-11	3-28/S-3	-1.9
	StL-A	37	144	29	44	4	0	0	12	20	8	.306	.394	.333	88	-1	3	1	0	.916	-2	3-37	0.0
	Yr	85	253	40	67	7	0	0	15	29	18	.265	.345	.292	67	-11	4	2	0	.905	-12	3-65/S-3	-1.9
1923	StL-A	27	100	9	18	2	0	0	4	7	7	.180	.241	.200	16	-12	0	0		.961	-8	2-20/3-7	-0.2
Total	13	1500	5652	732	1490	191	71	6	451	528	255	.264	.329	.326	89	-81	195	53		.930	-42	*3-1161,2-269/S	-8.1

■ ELMER FOSTER

Foster, Elmer Ellsworth   b: 8/15/1861, Minneapolis, Minn.   d: 7/22/46, Deephaven, Minn.   BR/TL,   Deb: 6/18/1884

YEAR	TM/L	G	AB	R	H	2B	3B	HR	RBI	BB	SO	AVG	OBP	SLG	PRO+	BR/A	SB	CS	SBR	FA	FR	G/POS	TPR
1884	Phi-a	4	11	4	2	0	0	0		3		.182	.357	.182	76	-0				.885	-2	/C-4,O-1	-0.2
	Phi-U	1	3	0	1	0	1	0		0		.333	.333	1.000	269	1				.625	-1	/C-1	0.0
1886	NY-a	35	125	16	23	0	7	0		7		.184	.239	.200	40	-8	3			.853	-2	2-21,O-14	-0.7
1888	NY-N	37	136	15	20	3	2	0	10	9	20	.147	.216	.199	33	-10	13			.852	-3	O-37/3-1	-1.3
1889	NY-N	2	4	2	0	0	0	0	0	3	1	.000	.429	.000	25	-0	2			1.000	-0	/O-2	0.0
1890	Chi-N	27	105	20	26	4	2	5	23	9	21	.248	.325	.467	125	2	18			.986	2	O-27	0.3
1891	Chi-N	4	16	3	3	0	0	1	1	1	2	.188	.235	.375	77	-1	1			.875	-0	/O-4	-0.1
Total	6	110	400	60	75	7	6	6	34	32	44	.188	.261	.280	67	-16	37			.883	-4	/O-85,2-21,C3	-2.0

■ GEORGE FOSTER

Foster, George Arthur   b: 12/1/48, Tuscaloosa, Ala.   BR/TR, 6'1", 185 lbs.   Deb: 9/10/69

YEAR	TM/L	G	AB	R	H	2B	3B	HR	RBI	BB	SO	AVG	OBP	SLG	PRO+	BR/A	SB	CS	SBR	FA	FR	G/POS	TPR
1969	SF-N	9	5	1	2	0	0	0	1	0	1	.400	.400	.400	127	0	0	0	0	1.000	-3	/O-8	-0.3
1970	SF-N	9	19	2	6	1	1	1	4	2	5	.316	.381	.632	168	2	0	0	0	1.000	-0	/O-7	0.1
1971	SF-N	36	105	11	28	5	0	3	8	6	27	.267	.304	.400	100	-0	0	1	-1	.980	-2	O-30	-0.4
	Cin-N	104	368	39	86	18	4	10	50	23	93	.234	.291	.386	94	-5	7	6	-2	.986	11	*O-102	-0.1
	Yr	140	473	50	114	23	4	13	58	29	120	.241	.295	.389	94	-5	7	7	-2	.985	9	*O-132	-0.5
1972	*Cin-N	59	145	15	29	4	1	2	12	5	44	.200	.232	.283	48	-10	2	1	0	.973	-5	O-47	-1.8
1973	Cin-N	17	39	6	11	3	0	4	9	4	7	.282	.349	.667	185	4	0	1	-1	1.000	-3	O-13	0.0
1974	Cin-N	106	276	31	73	18	0	7	41	30	52	.264	.345	.406	111	4	3	2	-0	.989	-16	O-98	-1.6
1975	*Cin-N	134	463	71	139	24	4	23	78	40	73	.300	.360	.518	139	22	2	1	0	.990	5	*O-125/1-1	2.3
1976	*Cin-N★	144	562	86	172	21	9	29	121	52	89	.306	.369	.530	149	34	17	3	3	.994	-2	*O-142/1-1	3.1
1977	Cin-N★	158	615	124	197	31	2	52	149	61	107	.320	.386	.631	165	54	6	4	-1	.992	16	*O-158	6.1
1978	Cin-N★	158	604	97	170	26	7	40	120	70	138	.281	.363	.546	151	39	4	4	-1	.971	7	*O-157	4.0
1979	*Cin-N	121	440	68	133	18	3	30	98	59	105	.302	.388	.561	155	33	0	2	-1	.982	4	*O-116	3.1
1980	Cin-N	144	528	79	144	21	5	25	93	75	99	.273	.364	.473	132	23	1	0	0	.997	10	*O-141	2.9
1981	Cin-N★	108	414	64	122	23	2	22	90	51	75	.295	.376	.519	150	26	4	0	1	.991	8	*O-108	3.4
1982	NY-N	151	550	64	136	23	2	13	70	50	123	.247	.312	.367	90	-8	1	1	-0	.974	-5	*O-138	0.0
1983	NY-N	157	601	74	145	19	2	28	90	38	111	.241	.291	.419	95	-6	1	1	-0	.988	10	*O-153	-0.1
1984	NY-N	146	553	67	149	22	1	24	86	30	122	.269	.314	.443	112	7	2	2	-1	.976	11	*O-141	1.3
1985	NY-N	129	452	57	119	24	1	21	77	46	87	.263	.334	.460	123	13	0	1	-1	.976	1	*O-123	0.9
1986	NY-N	72	233	28	53	6	1	13	38	21	53	.227	.291	.429	99	-1	1	1	-0	.962	-0	O-62	-0.4
	Chi-A	15	51	2	11	0	2	1	4	3	8	.216	.259	.353	63	-3	0	0	0	1.000	-1	O-11/D-3	-0.2
Total	18	1977	7023	986	1925	307	47	348	1239	666	1419	.274	.341	.480	127	227	51	31	-3	.984	65	*O-1880/D-3,1	22.3

■ LEO FOSTER

Foster, Leonard Norris   b: 2/2/51, Covington, Ky.   BR/TR, 5'11", 165 lbs.   Deb: 7/9/71

YEAR	TM/L	G	AB	R	H	2B	3B	HR	RBI	BB	SO	AVG	OBP	SLG	PRO+	BR/A	SB	CS	SBR	FA	FR	G/POS	TPR
1971	Atl-N	9	10	1	0	0	0	0	0	0	1	.000	.000	.000	-94	-2	0	0	0	.900	2	/S-3	-0.1
1973	Atl-N	3	6	1	1	1	0	0	0	0	0	.167	.167	.333	33	-1	0	0	0	1.000	-0	/S-1	-0.1
1974	Atl-N	72	112	16	22	2	0	1	5	9	22	.196	.256	.241	38	-9	1	2	-1	.977	-1	S-43,2-10/3O	-0.8
1976	NY-N	24	59	11	12	2	0	1	15	5	7	.203	.299	.288	71	-2	3	0	1	.920	1	/3-9,S-7,2	-0.1
1977	NY-N	36	75	6	17	3	0	0	6	5	14	.227	.284	.267	51	-5	3	1	0	.968	-4	2-20/S-8,3	-0.8
Total	5	144	262	35	52	8	0	2	26	22	44	.198	.263	.252	44	-20	7	3	0	.964	-3	/S-62,2-33,3O	-1.8

■ REDDY FOSTER

Foster, Oscar E.   b: 8/1864, Richmond, Va.   d: 12/19/08, Richmond, Va.   Deb: 6/3/1896

YEAR	TM/L	G	AB	R	H	2B	3B	HR	RBI	BB	SO	AVG	OBP	SLG	PRO+	BR/A	SB	CS	SBR	FA	FR	G/POS	TPR
1896	NY-N	1	1	0	0	0	0	0	0	0	0	.000	.000	.000	-99	-0	0			.000	0	H	0.0

■ ROY FOSTER

Foster, Roy   b: 7/29/45, Bixby, Okla.   BR/TR, 6', 185 lbs.   Deb: 4/7/70

YEAR	TM/L	G	AB	R	H	2B	3B	HR	RBI	BB	SO	AVG	OBP	SLG	PRO+	BR/A	SB	CS	SBR	FA	FR	G/POS	TPR
1970	Cle-A	139	477	66	128	26	0	23	60	54	75	.268	.357	.468	120	13	3	3	-1	.965	-3	*O-131	0.2
1971	Cle-A	125	396	51	97	21	1	18	45	35	48	.245	.316	.439	103	0	6	1	1	.968	-1	*O-107	-0.5
1972	Cle-A	73	143	19	32	4	0	4	13	21	23	.224	.331	.336	96	-0	0	2	-1	.966	-6	O-45	-1.1
Total	3	337	1016	136	257	51	1	45	118	110	146	.253	.338	.438	110	13	9	6	-1	.967	-11	O-283	-1.4

■ BOB FOTHERGILL

Fothergill, Robert Roy "Fats"   b: 8/16/1897, Massillon, Ohio   d: 3/20/38, Detroit, Mich.   BR/TR, 5'10.5", 230 lbs.   Deb: 4/18/22

YEAR	TM/L	G	AB	R	H	2B	3B	HR	RBI	BB	SO	AVG	OBP	SLG	PRO+	BR/A	SB	CS	SBR	FA	FR	G/POS	TPR
1922	Det-A	42	152	20	49	12	4	0	29	8	9	.322	.356	.454	113	2	1	5	-3	.945	-7	O-38	-0.9
1923	Det-A	101	241	34	76	18	2	1	49	12	19	.315	.358	.419	106	2	5	4	-1	.977	-8	O-68	-1.0
1924	Det-A	54	166	28	50	8	3	0	15	5	13	.301	.326	.386	84	-4	2	3	-1	.968	-4	O-45	-1.1
1925	Det-A	71	204	38	72	14	0	2	28	6	21	.353	.377	.451	111	3	3	2	-0	.977	-2	O-59	-0.2
1926	Det-A	110	387	63	142	31	7	3	73	33	23	.367	.421	.506	139	22	4	12	-6	.961	-1	*O-103	0.8
1927	Det-A	143	527	93	189	38	9	9	114	47	31	.359	.413	.516	138	29	9	15	-6	.961	-6	*O-137	0.0
1928	Det-A	111	347	49	110	28	10	3	63	24	19	.317	.366	.481	119	9	8	3	1	.959	-3	O-90	0.0
1929	Det-A	115	277	42	98	24	9	6	62	11	11	.354	.378	.570	140	15	3	1	0	.967	-0	O-59	0.8
1930	Det-A	55	143	14	37	9	3	2	14	6	10	.259	.289	.406	72	-7	1	0	0	.947	-5	O-38	-1.3
	Chi-A	52	135	10	40	9	0	0	24	4	8	.296	.326	.363	77	-5	0	0	0	.879	-3	O-31	-0.9
	Yr	107	278	24	77	18	3	2	38	10	18	.277	.307	.385	75	-11	1	1	-0	.913	-8	O-69	-2.2
1931	Chi-A	108	312	25	88	9	4	3	56	17	17	.282	.323	.365	86	-7	2	2	-1	.972	1	O-74	-1.1

YEAR	TM/L	G	AB	R	H	2B	3B	HR	RBI	BB	SO	AVG	OBP	SLG	PRO+	BR/A	SB	CS	SBR	FA	FR	G/POS	TPR
1932	Chi-A	116	346	36	102	24	1	7	50	27	10	.295	.348	.431	107	3	4	4	-1	.952	-11	O-86	-1.4
1933	Bos-A	28	32	1	11	1	0	0	5	2	4	.344	.382	.375	102	0	0	0	0	1.000	-1	/O-4	-0.1
Total	12	1106	3269	453	1064	225	52	36	582	202	177	.325	.368	.459	115	62	42	52	-19	.961	-53	O-832	-5.6

■ JACK FOURNIER
Fournier, John Frank   b: 9/29/1892, AuSable, Mich.   d: 9/5/73, Tacoma, Wash.   BL/TR, 6′, 195 lbs.   Deb: 4/13/12

YEAR	TM/L	G	AB	R	H	2B	3B	HR	RBI	BB	SO	AVG	OBP	SLG	PRO+	BR/A	SB	CS	SBR	FA	FR	G/POS	TPR
1912	Chi-A	35	73	6	14	5	2	0	2	4		.192	.262	.315	67	-3	1			.988	3	1-17	-0.1
1913	Chi-A	68	172	20	40	8	5	1	23	23	23	.233	.323	.355	99	-0	9			.990	4	1-29,O-23	0.3
1914	Chi-A	109	379	44	118	14	9	6	44	31	44	.311	.368	.443	146	20	10	13	-5	.978	5	1-97/O-6	1.9
1915	Chi-A	126	422	86	136	20	18	5	77	64	37	.322	.429	**.491**	170	38	21	16	-3	.986	3	1-65,O-57	3.5
1916	Chi-A	105	313	36	75	13	9	3	44	36	40	.240	.328	.367	108	3	19			.976	-3	1-85/O-1	-0.4
1917	Chi-A	1	1	0	0	0	0	0	0	0	1	.000	.000	.000	-98	-0	0			.000	0	H	0.0
1918	NY-A	27	100	9	35	6	1	0	12	7	7	.350	.393	.430	145	5	7			.976	-2	1-27	0.2
1920	StL-N	141	530	77	162	33	14	3	61	42	42	.306	.370	.438	136	25	26	20	-4	.983	1	*1-138	2.0
1921	StL-N	149	574	103	197	27	9	16	86	56	48	.343	.409	.505	144	37	20	22	-7	.987	-4	*1-149	2.1
1922	StL-N	128	404	64	119	23	9	10	61	40	21	.295	.368	.470	120	12	6	8	-3	.982	2	*1-109/P-1	0.6
1923	Bro-N	133	515	91	181	30	13	22	102	43	28	.351	.411	.588	165	47	11	4	1	.985	4	*1-133	**4.3**
1924	Bro-N	154	563	93	188	25	4	**27**	116	83	46	.334	.428	.536	162	52	7	5	-1	.985	7	*1-153	4.7
1925	Bro-N	145	545	99	191	21	16	22	130	**86**	39	.350	.446	.569	162	54	4	6	-2	.989	3	*1-145	4.2
1926	Bro-N	87	243	39	69	9	2	11	48	30	16	.284	.365	.473	126	9	0			.986	-2	1-64	0.3
1927	Bos-N	122	374	55	106	18	2	10	53	44	16	.283	.368	.422	121	11	4			.989	0	*1-102	0.6
Total	15	1530	5208	822	1631	252	113	136	859	587	408	.313	.392	.483	143	308	145	94		.984	20	*1-1313/O-87,P	24.0

■ BILL FOUSER
Fouser, William C.   b: 10/1855, Philadelphia, Pa.   d: 3/1/19, Philadelphia, Pa.   Deb: 4/22/1876

YEAR	TM/L	G	AB	R	H	2B	3B	HR	RBI	BB	SO	AVG	OBP	SLG	PRO+	BR/A	SB	CS	SBR	FA	FR	G/POS	TPR
1876	Phi-N	21	89	11	12	0	1	0	2	0	0	.135	.135	.157	-3	-9				.827	3	2-14/O-7,1	-0.5

■ DAVE FOUTZ
Foutz, David Luther "Scissors"   b: 9/7/1856, Carroll Co., Md.   d: 3/5/1897, Waverly, Ind.   BR/TR, 6′2″, 161 lbs.   Deb: 7/29/1884   FM

YEAR	TM/L	G	AB	R	H	2B	3B	HR	RBI	BB	SO	AVG	OBP	SLG	PRO+	BR/A	SB	CS	SBR	FA	FR	G/POS	TPR
1884	StL-a	33	119	17	27	4	0	0		8		.227	.276	.261	73	-3				.940	-3	P-25,O-14	-0.5
1885	*StL-a	65	238	42	59	6	4	0		11		.248	.281	.307	82	-5				.899	6	P-47,1-15/O	-0.4
1886	*StL-a	102	414	66	116	18	9	3		9		.280	.297	.389	109	1	17			.949	4	P-59,O-34,1	0.0
1887	*StL-a	102	423	79	151	26	13	4		23		.357	.393	.508	136	16	22			.899	-2	O-50,P-40,1	0.3
1888	Bro-a	140	563	91	156	20	13	3	99	28		.277	.314	.375	121	11	35			.895	3	O-78,1-42,P	0.3
1889	*Bro-a	138	553	118	152	19	8	6	113	64	23	.275	.351	.371	106	5	43			.979	-3	*1-134,P-12	-0.7
1890	*Bro-N	129	509	106	154	25	13	6	98	52	25	.303	.368	.432	133	20	42			.978	-1	*1-113,O-13/P	1.1
1891	Bro-N	130	521	87	134	26	8	2	73	40	25	.257	.313	.349	93	-6	48			.976	-3	*1-124/P-6,S	-1.3
1892	Bro-N	61	220	33	41	5	3	1	26	14	14	.186	.235	.242	48	-14	19			.850	-2	O-29,P-27/1	-1.3
1893	Bro-N	130	557	91	137	20	10	7	67	32	34	.246	.287	.355	74	-24	39			.913	-6	O-77,1-54/P-1	-2.9
1894	Bro-N	72	293	40	90	12	9	0	51	14	13	.307	.341	.410	86	-7	14			.976	-3	1-72/P-1M	-0.7
1895	Bro-N	31	115	14	34	4	1	0	21	4	2	.296	.319	.348	78	-4	1			.879	-5	O-20/1-8M	-0.8
1896	Bro-N	2	8	0	2	0	0	0	0	1	0	.250	.333	.375	92	-0	0			1.000	0	/O-1,1-1M	0.0
Total	13	1135	4533	784	1253	186	91	31	548	300	136	.276	.323	.378	102	-10	280			.977	-14	1-595,O-320,P/S	-6.9

■ FRANK FOUTZ
Foutz, Frank Hayes   b: 4/8/1877, Baltimore, Md.   d: 12/25/61, Lima, Ohio   BR/TR, 5′11″, 165 lbs.   Deb: 4/26/01   F

YEAR	TM/L	G	AB	R	H	2B	3B	HR	RBI	BB	SO	AVG	OBP	SLG	PRO+	BR/A	SB	CS	SBR	FA	FR	G/POS	TPR
1901	Bal-A	20	72	13	17	4	1	2	14	8		.236	.321	.403	96	-1	0			.959	-0	1-20	-0.1

■ BOOB FOWLER
Fowler, Joseph Chester "Gink"   b: 11/11/1900, Waco, Tex.   d: 10/8/88, Dallas, Tex.   BL/TR, 5′11.5″, 180 lbs.   Deb: 5/6/23

YEAR	TM/L	G	AB	R	H	2B	3B	HR	RBI	BB	SO	AVG	OBP	SLG	PRO+	BR/A	SB	CS	SBR	FA	FR	G/POS	TPR
1923	Cin-N	11	33	9	11	0	1	1	6	1	3	.333	.353	.485	121	1	1	0	0	.847	-1	S-10	0.1
1924	Cin-N	59	129	20	43	6	1	0	9	5	15	.333	.358	.395	103	1	2	2	-1	.936	-7	S-32/2-4,3	-0.4
1925	Cin-N	6	5	0	2	0	0	0	2	0	1	.400	.400	.600	155	0	0	0	0	.000	0	H	0.0
1926	Bos-A	2	8	1	1	0	0	0	1	0	0	.125	.125	.125	-36	-2	0	0	0	.800	0	/3-2	-0.1
Total	4	78	175	30	57	7	2	1	18	6	19	.326	.348	.406	102	0	3	2	0	.910	-8	/S-42,3-4,2	-0.4

■ CHARLIE FOX
Fox, Charles Francis "Irish"   b: 10/7/21, New York, N.Y.   BR/TR, 5′11″, 180 lbs.   Deb: 9/24/42   MC

YEAR	TM/L	G	AB	R	H	2B	3B	HR	RBI	BB	SO	AVG	OBP	SLG	PRO+	BR/A	SB	CS	SBR	FA	FR	G/POS	TPR
1942	NY-N	3	7	1	3	0	0	0	1	1	2	.429	.500	.429	172	1	0			1.000	-1	/C-3	0.0

■ ERIC FOX
Fox, Eric Hollis   b: 8/15/63, Lemoore, Cal.   BB/TL, 5′10″, 180 lbs.   Deb: 7/7/92

YEAR	TM/L	G	AB	R	H	2B	3B	HR	RBI	BB	SO	AVG	OBP	SLG	PRO+	BR/A	SB	CS	SBR	FA	FR	G/POS	TPR
1992	*Oak-A	51	143	24	34	5	2	3	13	13	29	.238	.301	.364	90	-2	3	4	-2	.990	-5	O-43/D-4	-1.0
1993	Oak-A	29	56	5	8	1	0	1	5	2	7	.143	.172	.214	3	-8	0	2	-1	1.000	-3	O-26/D-2	-1.2
1994	Oak-A	26	44	7	9	2	0	1	1	3	8	.205	.255	.318	51	-3	2	0	1	1.000	-4	O-24	-0.6
Total	3	106	243	36	51	8	2	5	19	18	44	.210	.264	.321	63	-13	5	6	-2	.994	-12	/O-93,D-6	-2.8

■ PETE FOX
Fox, Ervin   b: 3/8/09, Evansville, Ind.   d: 7/5/66, Detroit, Mich.   BR/TR, 5′11″, 165 lbs.   Deb: 4/12/33

YEAR	TM/L	G	AB	R	H	2B	3B	HR	RBI	BB	SO	AVG	OBP	SLG	PRO+	BR/A	SB	CS	SBR	FA	FR	G/POS	TPR
1933	Det-A	128	535	82	154	26	13	7	57	23	38	.288	.320	.424	94	-7	9	6	-1	.978	1	*O-124	-1.3
1934	*Det-A	128	516	101	147	31	2	2	45	49	53	.285	.351	.364	85	-11	25	10	2	.974	8	*O-121	-0.6
1935	Det-A	131	517	116	166	38	8	15	73	45	52	.321	.382	.513	134	24	14	4	2	.988	0	*O-125	2.0
1936	Det-A	73	220	46	67	12	1	4	26	34	23	.305	.405	.423	104	3	1	3	-2	.968	0	O-55	-0.1
1937	Det-A	148	628	116	208	39	8	12	82	41	43	.331	.372	.476	110	8	12	8	-1	.976	-3	*O-143	-0.1
1938	Det-A	155	634	91	186	35	10	7	96	31	39	.293	.328	.413	80	-21	16	7	1	**.994**	-2	*O-155	-2.5
1939	Det-A	141	519	69	153	24	6	7	66	35	41	.295	.342	.405	84	-13	23	12	-0	.970	9	*O-126	-0.9
1940	*Det-A	93	350	49	101	17	4	5	48	21	30	.289	.329	.403	81	-10	7	7	-2	.967	0	O-85	-1.6
1941	Bos-A	73	268	38	81	12	7	0	31	21	21	.302	.357	.399	98	-1	9	2	-1	.977	-1	O-62	-0.4
1942	Bos-A	77	256	42	67	15	5	3	42	20	28	.262	.323	.395	98	-1	2	4	0	.966	-9	O-71	-1.6
1943	Bos-A	127	489	54	141	24	4	2	44	34	40	.288	.337	.366	104	2	22	8	2	.961	3	*O-125	-0.6
1944	Bos-A☆	121	496	70	156	37	6	1	64	27	34	.315	.354	.419	122	13	10	5	0	.987	-1	*O-119	0.5
1945	Bos-A	66	208	21	51	4	1	0	20	11	18	.245	.296	.274	64	-9	2	2	-1	.989	-6	O-57	-2.1
Total	13	1461	5636	895	1678	314	75	65	694	392	471	.298	.347	.415	98	-25	158	81	-1	.977	-7	*O-1368	-9.3

■ PADDY FOX
Fox, George B.   b: 12/1/1868, Pottstown, Pa.   d: 5/8/14, Philadelphia, Pa.   Deb: 7/13/1891

YEAR	TM/L	G	AB	R	H	2B	3B	HR	RBI	BB	SO	AVG	OBP	SLG	PRO+	BR/A	SB	CS	SBR	FA	FR	G/POS	TPR
1891	Lou-a	6	19	1	2	0	1	0	2	2	3	.105	.261	.211	36	-2	0			.929	-2	/3-6	-0.3
1899	Pit-N	13	41	4	10	0	1	0	3	3		.244	.311	.366	86	-1	2			.971	0	/1-9,C-3	0.1
Total	2	19	60	5	12	0	2	0	5	5	3	.200	.294	.317	70	-2	2			.971	-1	/1-9,3-6,C	-0.2

■ NELLIE FOX
Fox, Jacob Nelson   b: 12/25/27, St.Thomas, Pa.   d: 12/1/75, Baltimore, Md.   BL/TR, 5′9″, 150 lbs.   Deb: 6/8/47   C

YEAR	TM/L	G	AB	R	H	2B	3B	HR	RBI	BB	SO	AVG	OBP	SLG	PRO+	BR/A	SB	CS	SBR	FA	FR	G/POS	TPR
1947	Phi-A	7	3	2	0	0	0	0	0	1	0	.000	.250	.000	-26	-0	0	0	0	1.000	0	/2-1	0.0
1948	Phi-A	3	13	0	2	0	0	0	0	0	0	.154	.214	.154	-1	-2	1	0	0	.950	-2	/2-3	-0.3
1949	Phi-A	88	247	42	63	6	2	0	21	32	9	.255	.354	.296	75	-8	2	2	-1	.982	-1	2-77	-0.6
1950	Chi-A	130	457	45	113	12	7	0	30	35	17	.247	.304	.304	58	-30	4	3	-1	.974	-0	*2-121	-2.4
1951	Chi-A	147	604	93	189	32	12	4	55	43	11	.313	.372	.425	118	15	9	12	-5	.981	-3	*2-147	1.4
1952	Chi-A☆	152	648	76	**192**	25	10	0	39	34	14	.296	.334	.366	94	-6	5	5	-2	**.985**	8	*2-151	0.8
1953	Chi-A★	154	624	92	178	31	8	3	72	49	18	.285	.344	.375	91	-7	4	5	-2	.983	3	*2-154	0.3
1954	Chi-A★	155	631	111	**201**	24	8	2	47	51	12	.319	.374	.391	106	6	16	9	-1	**.989**	-6	*2-155	1.1
1955	Chi-A★	154	636	100	198	28	7	6	59	38	15	.311	.366	.406	104	4	7	4	-0	.974	27	*2-154	3.9
1956	Chi-A★	154	649	109	192	20	10	4	52	44	14	.296	.350	.376	90	-9	8	4	0	**.986**	-3	*2-154	0.7
1957	Chi-A★	155	619	110	**196**	27	8	6	61	75	13	.317	.404	.415	124	24	5	6	-2	.986	21	*2-155	5.6
1958	Chi-A★	155	623	82	**187**	21	6	0	49	47	11	.300	.360	.353	99	1	5	6	-2	.985	2	*2-155	1.2
1959	*Chi-A★	156	624	84	191	34	6	2	70	71	13	.306	.383	.389	114	15	5	6	-2	**.988**	-3	*2-156	2.2

YEAR	TM/L	G	AB	R	H	2B	3B	HR	RBI	BB	SO	AVG	OBP	SLG	PRO+	BR/A	SB	CS	SBR	FA	FR	G/POS	TPR
1960	Chi-A★	150	605	85	175	24	10	2	59	50	13	.289	.353	.372	97	-1	2	4	-2	.985	12	*2-149	2.4
1961	Chi-A★	159	606	67	152	11	5	2	51	59	12	.251	.326	.295	69	-25	2	3	-1	.982	-6	*2-159	-1.5
1962	Chi-A	157	621	79	166	27	7	2	54	38	12	.267	.317	.343	78	-19	1	2	-1	.990	1	*2-154	-0.3
1963	Chi-A★	137	539	54	140	19	0	2	42	24	17	.260	.300	.306	72	-20	0	2	-1	.988	-8	*2-134	-1.8
1964	Hou-N	133	442	45	117	12	6	0	28	27	13	.265	.322	.319	86	-8	0	2	-1	.977	-6	*2-115	-0.6
1965	Hou-N	21	41	3	11	2	0	0	1	0	2	.268	.286	.317	75	-1	0	0	0	1.000	-0	/3-6,1-2,2	-0.2
Total	19	2367	9232	1279	2663	355	112	35	790	719	216	.288	.349	.363	94	-73	76	80	-25	.984	42	*2-2295/3-6,1	11.9

■ JACK FOX

Fox, John Paul b: 5/21/1885, Reading, Pa. d: 6/28/63, Reading, Pa. BR/TR, 5'10", 185 lbs. Deb: 6/2/08

YEAR	TM/L	G	AB	R	H	2B	3B	HR	RBI	BB	SO	AVG	OBP	SLG	PRO+	BR/A	SB	CS	SBR	FA	FR	G/POS	TPR
1908	Phi-A	9	30	2	6	0	0	0	0	0	0	.200	.200	.200	28	-2	2			.923	-1	/O-8	-0.4

■ BILL FOX

Fox, William Henry b: 1/15/1872, Sturbridge, Mass. d: 5/7/46, Minneapolis, Minn. BB/TR, 5'10", 160 lbs. Deb: 8/20/1897

YEAR	TM/L	G	AB	R	H	2B	3B	HR	RBI	BB	SO	AVG	OBP	SLG	PRO+	BR/A	SB	CS	SBR	FA	FR	G/POS	TPR
1897	Was-N	4	14	4	4	0	0	0	0	1		.286	.333	.286	64	-1	0			.700	0	/S-2,2-2	0.0
1901	Cin-N	43	159	9	28	2	1	0	7	4		.176	.201	.201	18	-17	9			.948	5	2-43	-0.9
Total	2	47	173	13	32	2	1	0	7	5		.185	.212	.208	22	-17	9			.944	6	/2-45,S-2	-0.9

■ JIMMIE FOXX

Foxx, James Emory "Beast" or "Double X" b: 10/22/07, Sudlersville, Md. d: 7/21/67, Miami, Fla. BR/TR, 6', 195 lbs. Deb: 5/1/25 CH

YEAR	TM/L	G	AB	R	H	2B	3B	HR	RBI	BB	SO	AVG	OBP	SLG	PRO+	BR/A	SB	CS	SBR	FA	FR	G/POS	TPR
1925	Phi-A	10	9	2	6	1	0	0	0	0	1	.667	.667	.778	249	2	0	0	0	.000	0	/C-1	0.2
1926	Phi-A	26	32	8	10	2	1	0	5	1	6	.313	.333	.438	94	-0	1	0	0	1.000	2	C-12/O-3	0.2
1927	Phi-A	61	130	23	42	6	5	3	20	14	11	.323	.393	.515	127	5	2	1	0	.975	2	1-32/C-5	0.1
1928	Phi-A	118	400	85	131	29	10	13	79	60	43	.327	.416	.548	147	28	3	8	-4	.940	-2	3-60,1-30,C	2.4
1929	*Phi-A	149	517	123	183	23	9	33	118	103	70	.354	.463	.625	171	58	9	7	-2	.995	-4	*1-142/3-8	3.6
1930	*Phi-A	153	562	127	188	33	13	37	156	93	66	.335	.429	.637	159	51	7	7	-2	.990	-2	*1-153	2.8
1931	*Phi-A	139	515	93	150	32	10	30	120	73	84	.291	.380	.567	138	26	4	3	-1	.993	-3	*1-112,3-26/O	1.3
1932	Phi-A	154	585	151	213	33	9	58	169	116	96	.364	.469	.749	203	90	3	7	-3	.994	-5	*1-141,3-13	6.5
1933	Phi-A☆	149	573	125	204	37	9	48	163	96	93	.356	.449	.703	199	81	2	2	-1	.990	6	*1-149/S-1	6.7
1934	Phi-A★	150	539	120	180	28	6	44	130	111	75	.334	.449	.653	188	72	11	2	2	.993	-3	*1-140/3-9	6.1
1935	Phi-A★	147	535	118	185	33	7	36	115	114	99	.346	.461	.636	182	68	6	4	-1	.997	6	*1-121,C-26/3	5.7
1936	Bos-A★	155	585	130	198	32	8	41	143	105	119	.338	.440	.631	153	48	13	4	2	.991	-1	*1-139,O-16/3	3.1
1937	Bos-A	150	569	111	162	24	6	36	127	99	96	.285	.392	.538	127	23	10	8	-2	.994	10	*1-150/C-1	1.3
1938	Bos-A★	149	565	139	197	33	9	50	175	119	76	.349	.462	.704	180	70	5	4	-1	.987	6	*1-149	5.2
1939	Bos-A☆	124	467	130	168	31	10	35	105	89	72	.360	.464	.694	185	61	4	3	-1	.992	7	*1-123/P-1	4.9
1940	Bos-A★	144	515	106	153	30	4	36	119	101	87	.297	.412	.581	148	38	4	7	-3	.990	-2	*1-95,C-42/3	2.6
1941	Bos-A★	135	487	87	146	27	8	19	105	93	103	.300	.412	.505	138	29	2	5	-2	.992	7	*1-124/3-5,O	2.3
1942	Bos-A	30	100	18	27	4	0	5	14	18	15	.270	.392	.460	134	5	0	0	0	.996	6	1-27	1.0
	Chi-N	70	205	25	42	8	0	3	19	22	55	.205	.282	.288	69	-8	1			.983	-4	1-52/C-1	-1.6
1944	Chi-N	15	20	0	1	1	0	0	2	5	12	.050	.136	.100	-33	-4	0			1.000	2	/3-2,C-1	-0.2
1945	Phi-N	89	224	30	60	11	1	7	38	23	39	.268	.336	.420	112	3	0			.988	-3	1-40,3-14/P	-0.2
Total	20	2317	8134	1751	2646	458	125	534	1922	1452	1311	.325	.428	.609	161	746	87	72		.992	30	*1-1919,3-141,C/OPS	54.0

■ JOE FOY

Foy, Joseph Anthony b: 2/21/43, New York, N.Y. d: 10/12/89, Bronx, N.Y. BR/TR, 6', 215 lbs. Deb: 4/13/66

YEAR	TM/L	G	AB	R	H	2B	3B	HR	RBI	BB	SO	AVG	OBP	SLG	PRO+	BR/A	SB	CS	SBR	FA	FR	G/POS	TPR
1966	Bos-A	151	554	97	145	23	8	15	63	91	80	.262	.368	.413	112	11	2	5	-2	.953	-1	*3-139,S-13	0.7
1967	*Bos-A	130	446	70	112	22	4	16	49	46	87	.251	.325	.426	111	6	8	6	-1	.921	-10	*3-118/O-1	-0.7
1968	Bos-A	150	515	65	116	18	2	10	60	84	91	.225	.338	.326	96	0	26	8	3	.935	-3	*3-147/O-3	0.6
1969	KC-A	145	519	72	136	19	2	11	71	74	75	.262	.360	.370	104	5	37	15	2	.964	-9	*3-113,1-16,O/S2	-0.3
1970	NY-N	99	322	39	76	12	0	6	37	68	58	.236	.376	.329	90	-1	22	13	-1	.937	-1	3-97	-0.4
1971	Was-A	41	128	12	30	8	0	0	11	27	14	.234	.368	.297	96	1	4	1	1	.960	4	3-37/2-3,S	0.5
Total	6	716	2484	355	615	102	16	58	291	390	405	.248	.354	.372	103	21	99	48	1	.943	-14	3-651/O-20,S12	0.4

■ JULIO FRANCO

Franco, Julio Cesar (b: Julio Cesar Robles (Franco)) b: 8/23/58, Hato Mayor, D.R. BR/TR, 6', 175 lbs. Deb: 4/23/82

YEAR	TM/L	G	AB	R	H	2B	3B	HR	RBI	BB	SO	AVG	OBP	SLG	PRO+	BR/A	SB	CS	SBR	FA	FR	G/POS	TPR
1982	Phi-N	16	29	3	8	1	0	0	3	2	4	.276	.323	.310	76	-1	0	2	-1	1.000	1	S-11/3-2	-0.2
1983	Cle-A	149	560	68	153	24	8	8	80	27	50	.273	.309	.387	87	-11	32	12	2	.961	-7	*S-149	-0.1
1984	Cle-A	160	658	82	188	22	5	3	79	43	68	.286	.335	.348	88	-10	19	10	-0	.955	-1	*S-159/D-1	0.5
1985	Cle-A	160	636	97	183	33	4	6	90	54	74	.288	.347	.381	100	1	13	9	-2	.949	-22	*S-151/2-8,D	-0.7
1986	Cle-A	149	599	80	183	30	5	10	74	32	66	.306	.341	.422	108	6	10	7	-1	.971	-5	*S-134,2-13/D	1.2
1987	Cle-A	128	495	86	158	24	3	8	52	57	56	.319	.393	.428	117	14	32	9	4	.963	-24	*S-111/2-9,D	0.4
1988	Cle-A	152	613	88	186	23	6	10	54	56	72	.303	.364	.409	113	11	25	11	1	.982	-10	*2-151/D-1	0.9
1989	Tex-A★	150	548	80	173	31	5	13	92	66	69	.316	.390	.462	137	28	21	3	5	.980	-6	*2-140,D-10	3.1
1990	Tex-A★	157	582	96	172	27	1	11	69	82	83	.296	.384	.402	120	18	31	10	3	.975	-2	*2-152/D-3	2.3
1991	Tex-A☆	146	589	108	201	27	3	15	78	65	78	.341	.409	.474	146	38	36	9	5	.979	-31	*2-146	1.6
1992	Tex-A	35	107	19	25	7	0	2	8	15	17	.234	.328	.355	95	-1	1	1	-0	.906	-6	D-15/2-9,O	-0.7
1993	Tex-A	144	532	85	154	31	3	14	84	62	95	.289	.365	.438	119	15	9	3	1	1.000	0	*D-140	1.0
1994	Chi-A	112	433	72	138	19	2	20	98	62	75	.319	.410	.510	137	25	8	1	1	.969	-1	D-99,1-14	2.0
Total	13	1658	6381	964	1922	299	45	120	861	623	807	.301	.366	.419	114	135	237	87	19	.960	-115	S-715,2-628,D/103	11.3

■ TITO FRANCONA

Francona, John Patsy b: 11/4/33, Aliquippa, Pa. BL/TL, 5'11", 190 lbs. Deb: 4/17/56 F

YEAR	TM/L	G	AB	R	H	2B	3B	HR	RBI	BB	SO	AVG	OBP	SLG	PRO+	BR/A	SB	CS	SBR	FA	FR	G/POS	TPR
1956	Bal-A	139	445	62	115	16	4	9	57	51	60	.258	.336	.373	94	-5	11	5	0	.977	-8	*O-122,1-21	-1.8
1957	Bal-A	97	279	35	65	8	3	7	38	29	48	.233	.312	.358	88	-5	7	3	0	.992	-10	O-73/1-4	-1.9
1958	Chi-A	41	128	10	33	3	2	1	10	14	24	.258	.331	.336	86	-2	2	3	-1	1.000	-4	O-35	-0.9
	Det-A	45	69	11	17	5	0	0	10	15	16	.246	.381	.319	86	-1	0	0	0	1.000	-3	O-18/1-1	-0.5
	Yr	86	197	21	50	8	2	1	20	29	40	.254	.350	.330	86	-3	2	3	-1	1.000	-7	O-53/1-1	-1.4
1959	Cle-A	122	399	68	145	17	2	20	79	35	42	.363	.419	.566	174	40	2	0	1	.972	-4	O-64,1-35	3.1
1960	Cle-A	147	544	84	159	36	4	17	79	67	67	.292	.375	.460	128	22	4	1	1	.989	5	*O-138,1-13	2.0
1961	Cle-A☆	155	592	87	178	30	8	16	85	56	52	.301	.365	.459	122	18	2	1	0	.987	4	*O-138,1-14	1.3
1962	Cle-A	158	621	82	169	28	5	14	70	47	74	.272	.330	.401	99	-2	3	2	-0	.986	2	*1-158	-1.1
1963	Cle-A	142	500	57	114	29	0	10	41	47	77	.228	.297	.346	80	-13	9	1	2	.986	-2	*O-122,1-11	-2.2
1964	Cle-A	111	270	35	67	13	2	8	24	44	46	.248	.362	.400	113	6	1	3	-2	.985	-12	O-69,1-17	-1.2
1965	StL-N	81	174	15	45	6	2	5	19	17	30	.259	.325	.402	95	-1	0	4	-1	.972	-9	O-34,1-13	-1.3
1966	StL-N	83	156	14	33	4	1	4	17	7	27	.212	.250	.327	59	-9	1	0	-0	.987	1	1-30/O-9	-1.0
1967	Phi-N	27	73	7	15	1	0	3	7	10	10	.205	.275	.219	43	-5	0	0	0	1.000	1	1-24/O-1	-0.6
	Atl-N	82	254	28	63	5	1	6	25	20	34	.248	.305	.346	87	-4	0	0	0	.991	-1	1-56/O-6	-0.9
	Yr	109	327	35	78	6	1	6	28	27	44	.239	.299	.318	77	-10	0	0	0	.993	1	1-80/O-7	-1.5
1968	Atl-N	122	346	32	99	13	1	2	47	51	45	.286	.378	.344	118	10	3	0	0	.978	-8	O-65,1-33	-0.3
1969	Atl-N	51	88	15	26	1	0	2	22	13	10	.295	.386	.375	114	0	1	0	0	.957	-0	O-15/1-7	-0.3
	Oak-A	32	85	12	29	6	1	3	20	12	11	.341	.423	.541	175	9	0	0	0	.988	-2	O-19/1-7	0.5
1970	Oak-A	32	33	2	8	0	0	0	6	6	6	.242	.375	.333	100	0	0	0	0	1.000	1	/1-6,O-1	0.1
	Mil-A	52	65	4	15	3	0	1	6	6	15	.231	.296	.277	58	-4	1	0	0	1.000	1	1-13	-0.3
	Yr	84	98	6	23	3	0	1	12	12	21	.235	.324	.296	73	-3	1	0	0	1.000	2	1-19/O-1	-0.2
Total	15	1719	5121	650	1395	224	34	125	656	544	694	.272	.346	.403	108	56	46	21	1	.984	-49	O-911,1-475	-7.0

■ TERRY FRANCONA

Francona, Terry Jon b: 4/22/59, Aberdeen, S.D. BL/TL, 6'1", 190 lbs. Deb: 8/19/81 F

YEAR	TM/L	G	AB	R	H	2B	3B	HR	RBI	BB	SO	AVG	OBP	SLG	PRO+	BR/A	SB	CS	SBR	FA	FR	G/POS	TPR
1981	*Mon-N	34	95	11	26	0	1	1	8	5	6	.274	.317	.326	82	-2	1	0	0	1.000	1	O-26/1-1	-0.2
1982	Mon-N	46	131	14	42	3	0	0	9	8	11	.321	.360	.344	96	-0	2	3	-1	.936	-6	O-33,1-16	-0.9
1983	Mon-N	120	230	21	59	11	1	3	22	6	20	.257	.275	.352	73	-9	0	2	-1	.978	-2	O-51,1-47	-1.5

YEAR	TM/L	G	AB	R	H	2B	3B	HR	RBI	BB	SO	AVG	OBP	SLG	PRO+	BR/A	SB	CS	SBR	FA	FR	G/POS	TPR
1984	Mon-N	58	214	18	74	19	2	1	18	5	12	.346	.364	.467	138	10	0	0	0	.994	6	1-50/O-6	1.3
1985	Mon-N	107	281	19	75	15	1	2	31	12	12	.267	.299	.349	86	-6	5	5	-2	.988	2	1-57,O-28/3	-0.9
1986	Chi-N	86	124	13	31	3	0	2	8	6	8	.250	.290	.323	64	-6	0	1	-1	1.000	-7	O-30,1-23	-1.6
1987	Cin-N	102	207	16	47	5	0	3	12	10	12	.227	.266	.295	46	-16	2	0	1	.995	3	1-57/O-8	-1.6
1988	Cle-A	62	212	24	66	8	0	1	12	5	18	.311	.327	.363	91	-3	0	0	0	.977		D-38/1-5,O	-0.4
1989	Mil-A	90	233	26	54	10	1	3	23	4	20	.232	.257	.322	63	-12	2	1	0	.989	-2	1-46,D-23,O/P	-1.8
1990	Mil-A	3	4	1	0	0	0	0	0	0	0	.000	.000	.000	-99	-1	0	0	0	1.000	-0	/1-2,D-1	-0.9
Total	10	708	1731	163	474	74	6	16	143	65	119	.274	.302	.351	81	-46	12	12	-4	.992	-4	1-304,O-203/DP3	-7.7

■ CHARLIE FRANK
Frank, Charles　b: 5/30/1870, Mobile, Ala.　d: 5/24/22, Memphis, Tenn.　5'10", 170 lbs.　Deb: 8/18/1893

YEAR	TM/L	G	AB	R	H	2B	3B	HR	RBI	BB	SO	AVG	OBP	SLG	PRO+	BR/A	SB	CS	SBR	FA	FR	G/POS	TPR
1893	StL-N	40	164	29	55	6	3	1	17	18	8	.335	.408	.427	122	5	8			.930	3	O-40	0.5
1894	StL-N	80	319	52	89	12	7	4	42	44	13	.279	.372	.398	86	-7	14			.869	-2	O-77/1-3,P	-1.1
Total	2	120	483	81	144	18	10	5	59	62	21	.298	.384	.408	97	-2	22			.889	1	O-117/1-3,P	-0.6

■ FRED FRANK
Frank, Frederick　b: 3/11/1874, Louisa, Ky.　d: 3/27/50, Ashland, Ky.　Deb: 9/27/1898

YEAR	TM/L	G	AB	R	H	2B	3B	HR	RBI	BB	SO	AVG	OBP	SLG	PRO+	BR/A	SB	CS	SBR	FA	FR	G/POS	TPR
1898	Cle-N	17	53	3	11	1	1	0	3		4	.208	.276	.264	56	-3	1			.915	3	O-17	-0.1

■ FRANKLIN
Franklin　Deb: 9/27/1884

YEAR	TM/L	G	AB	R	H	2B	3B	HR	RBI	BB	SO	AVG	OBP	SLG	PRO+	BR/A	SB	CS	SBR	FA	FR	G/POS	TPR
1884	Was-U	1	3	0	0	0	0	0		0		.000	.000	.000	-99	-1				1.000	0	/O-1	-0.1

■ MOE FRANKLIN
Franklin, Murray Asher　b: 4/1/14, Chicago, Ill.　d: 3/16/78, Harbor City, Cal.　BR/TR, 6', 175 lbs.　Deb: 8/12/41

YEAR	TM/L	G	AB	R	H	2B	3B	HR	RBI	BB	SO	AVG	OBP	SLG	PRO+	BR/A	SB	CS	SBR	FA	FR	G/POS	TPR
1941	Det-A	13	10	1	3	1	0	0	0	2	2	.300	.417	.400	106	0	0	0	0	.750	-1	/S-4,3-1	-0.1
1942	Det-A	48	154	24	40	7	0	2	16	7	5	.260	.301	.344	75	-5	0	0	0	.967	-6	S-32/2-7	-0.9
Total	2	61	164	25	43	8	0	2	16	9	7	.262	.309	.348	77	-5	0	0	0	.961	-7	/S-36,2-7,3	-1.0

■ HERMAN FRANKS
Franks, Herman Louis　b: 1/4/14, Price, Utah　BL/TR, 5'10.5", 187 lbs.　Deb: 4/27/39　MC

YEAR	TM/L	G	AB	R	H	2B	3B	HR	RBI	BB	SO	AVG	OBP	SLG	PRO+	BR/A	SB	CS	SBR	FA	FR	G/POS	TPR
1939	StL-N	17	17	1	1	0	0	0	3	3	3	.059	.200	.059	-26	-3	0			.973	3	C-13	0.0
1940	Bro-N	65	131	11	24	4	0	1	14	20	6	.183	.296	.237	46	-9	2			.990	9	C-43	0.2
1941	*Bro-N	57	139	10	28	7	0	1	11	14	13	.201	.275	.273	52	-9	0			.986	2	C-54/O-1	-0.3
1947	Phi-A	8	15	2	3	0	1	0	1	4	4	.200	.368	.333	94	0	0	0	0	1.000	-1	/C-4	-0.1
1948	Phi-A	40	98	10	22	7	1	1	14	16	11	.224	.345	.347	84	-2	0	0	0	.977	3	C-27	0.2
1949	NY-N	1	3	1	2	0	0	0	0	0	0	.667	.667	.667	259	1	0			1.000	0	/C-1	0.1
Total	6	188	403	35	80	18	2	3	43	57	37	.199	.302	.275	57	-22	2	0		.985	16	C-142/O-1	0.1

■ LOU FRAZIER
Frazier, Arthur Louis　b: 1/26/65, St.Louis, Mo.　BB/TR, 6'2", 175 lbs.　Deb: 4/8/93

YEAR	TM/L	G	AB	R	H	2B	3B	HR	RBI	BB	SO	AVG	OBP	SLG	PRO+	BR/A	SB	CS	SBR	FA	FR	G/POS	TPR
1993	Mon-N	112	189	27	54	7	1	1	16	16	24	.286	.341	.349	82	-4	17	2	4	.986	-8	O-60/1-8,2	-0.9
1994	Mon-N	76	140	25	38	3	1	0	14	18	23	.271	.358	.307	74	-5	20	4	4	1.000	-2	O-36/2-6,1	-0.3
Total	2	188	329	52	92	10	2	1	30	34	47	.280	.349	.331	79	-9	37	6	8	.992	-10	/O-96,1-9,2	-1.2

■ JOE FRAZIER
Frazier, Joseph Filmore　b: 10/6/22, Liberty, N.C.　BL/TR, 6', 180 lbs.　Deb: 8/31/47　M

YEAR	TM/L	G	AB	R	H	2B	3B	HR	RBI	BB	SO	AVG	OBP	SLG	PRO+	BR/A	SB	CS	SBR	FA	FR	G/POS	TPR
1947	Cle-A	9	14	1	1	1	0	0	0	1	1	.071	.133	.143	-24	-2	0	0	0	.857	-1	/O-5	-0.4
1954	StL-N	81	88	8	26	5	2	3	18	13	17	.295	.392	.500	129	4	0	0	0	.938	-1	O-11/1-1	0.3
1955	StL-N	58	70	12	14	1	0	4	9	6	12	.200	.273	.386	72	-3	0	0	0	1.000	-3	O-14	-0.6
1956	StL-N	14	19	1	4	2	0	1	4	3	3	.211	.318	.474	109	0	0	0	-1	.800	-1	/O-3	-0.1
	Cin-N	10	17	2	4	0	0	1	2	1	7	.235	.278	.412	77	-1	0	0	0	.000	-2	/O-4	-0.2
	Yr	24	36	3	8	2	0	2	6	4	10	.222	.300	.444	94	-0	0	1	-1	.800	-2	/O-7	-0.3
	Bal-A	45	74	7	19	6	0	1	12	11	6	.257	.360	.378	103	0	0	0	0	1.000	-0	O-19	0.0
Total	4	217	282	31	68	15	2	10	45	35	46	.241	.331	.415	97	-1	0	1	-1	.961	-7	/O-56,1-1	-1.0

■ JOHNNY FREDERICK
Frederick, John Henry　b: 1/26/02, Denver, Colo.　d: 6/18/77, Tigard, Ore.　BL/TL, 5'11", 165 lbs.　Deb: 4/18/29

YEAR	TM/L	G	AB	R	H	2B	3B	HR	RBI	BB	SO	AVG	OBP	SLG	PRO+	BR/A	SB	CS	SBR	FA	FR	G/POS	TPR
1929	Bro-N	148	628	127	206	**52**	6	24	75	39	34	.328	.372	.545	126	23	6			.975	8	*O-143	1.9
1930	Bro-N	142	616	120	206	44	11	17	76	46	34	.334	.383	.524	118	17	1			.990	12	*O-142	1.7
1931	Bro-N	146	611	81	165	34	8	17	71	31	46	.270	.312	.435	99	-3	2			.965	2	*O-145	-1.0
1932	Bro-N	118	384	54	115	28	2	16	56	25	35	.299	.349	.508	130	15	1			.976	-3	O-88	0.6
1933	Bro-N	147	556	65	171	22	7	7	64	36	14	.308	.355	.410	123	16	9			.971	-7	O-138	0.3
1934	Bro-N	104	307	51	91	20	1	4	35	33	13	.296	.370	.407	114	7	4			.957	-3	O-77/1-1	0.1
Total	6	805	3102	498	954	200	35	85	377	210	176	.308	.357	.477	118	75	23			.974	9	O-733/1-1	3.6

■ ED FREED
Freed, Edwin Charles　b: 8/22/19, Centre Valley, Pa.　BR/TR, 5'6", 165 lbs.　Deb: 9/11/42

YEAR	TM/L	G	AB	R	H	2B	3B	HR	RBI	BB	SO	AVG	OBP	SLG	PRO+	BR/A	SB	CS	SBR	FA	FR	G/POS	TPR
1942	Phi-N	13	33	3	10	3	1	0	1	4	3	.303	.378	.455	151	2	1			1.000	-1	O-11	0.0

■ ROGER FREED
Freed, Roger Vernon　b: 6/2/46, Los Angeles, Cal.　BR/TR, 6', 190 lbs.　Deb: 9/18/70

YEAR	TM/L	G	AB	R	H	2B	3B	HR	RBI	BB	SO	AVG	OBP	SLG	PRO+	BR/A	SB	CS	SBR	FA	FR	G/POS	TPR
1970	Bal-A	4	13	0	2	0	0	0	1	3	4	.154	.313	.154	32	-1	0	0	0	1.000	0	/1-3,O-1	-0.1
1971	Phi-N	118	348	23	77	12	1	6	37	44	86	.221	.314	.313	78	-9	0	3	-2	.989	-5	*O-106/C-1	-2.2
1972	Phi-N	73	129	10	29	4	0	6	18	23	39	.225	.346	.395	108	2	0	1	-1	.971	-2	O-46	-0.2
1974	Cin-N	6	6	1	2	0	0	1	3	1	1	.333	.429	.833	251	1	0	0	0	1.000	-0	/1-1	0.1
1976	Mon-N	8	15	0	3	1	0	0	1	0	3	.200	.200	.267	30	-1	0	0	0	1.000	-0	/1-3,O-1	-0.2
1977	StL-N	49	83	10	33	2	1	5	21	11	9	.398	.468	.627	194	11	0	0	0	1.000	-2	1-18/O-6	0.8
1978	StL-N	52	92	3	22	6	0	2	20	8	17	.239	.300	.370	87	-2	1	0	0	.992	-1	1-15/O-6	-0.4
1979	StL-N	34	31	2	8	2	0	2	8	5	7	.258	.361	.516	135	1	0	0	0	.889	0	/1-1	-0.1
Total	8	344	717	49	176	27	2	22	109	95	166	.245	.337	.381	101	2	1	4	-2	.982	-10	O-166/1-41,C	-2.0

■ BILL FREEHAN
Freehan, William Ashley　b: 11/29/41, Detroit, Mich.　BR/TR, 6'2", 205 lbs.　Deb: 9/26/61

YEAR	TM/L	G	AB	R	H	2B	3B	HR	RBI	BB	SO	AVG	OBP	SLG	PRO+	BR/A	SB	CS	SBR	FA	FR	G/POS	TPR
1961	Det-A	4	10	1	4	0	0	0	4	1	0	.400	.455	.400	127	0	0	0	0	1.000	1	/C-3	0.2
1963	Det-A	100	300	37	73	12	2	9	36	39	56	.243	.334	.387	98	-0	2	0	1	.995	-1	C-73,1-19	0.2
1964	Det-A☆	144	520	69	156	14	8	18	80	36	68	.300	.355	.462	123	16	5	1	1	.993	-2	*C-141/1-1	2.2
1965	Det-A★	130	431	45	101	15	0	10	43	39	63	.234	.308	.373	83	-9	4	2	0	.996	-1	*C-129	-0.4
1966	Det-A★	136	492	47	115	22	0	12	46	40	72	.234	.295	.352	83	-11	5	2	0	**.996**	1	*C-132/1-5	-0.2
1967	Det-A★	155	517	66	146	23	1	20	74	73	71	.282	.392	.447	143	31	1	2	-1	.992	-9	*C-147,1-11	3.2
1968	*Det-A★	155	540	73	142	24	2	25	84	65	64	.263	.367	.454	143	30	0	1	-1	.994	6	*C-138,1-21/O	4.8
1969	Det-A★	143	489	61	128	16	3	16	49	53	55	.262	.344	.405	104	3	1	2	-1	.992	4	*C-120,1-20	1.2
1970	Det-A★	117	395	44	95	17	3	16	52	52	48	.241	.335	.420	106	3	0	3	-2	**.997**	-16	*C-114	-0.8
1971	Det-A★	148	516	57	143	26	4	21	71	54	48	.277	.356	.465	126	17	2	7	-4	.996	-12	*C-144/O-1	0.8
1972	*Det-A★	111	374	51	98	18	2	10	56	48	51	.262	.355	.401	121	11	0	1	-1	.989	0	*C-105/1-1	1.6
1973	Det-A☆	110	380	33	89	10	1	6	29	40	30	.234	.325	.313	75	-11	0	0	0	**.995**	9	C-98/1-7,D	0.1
1974	Det-A	130	445	58	132	17	5	18	60	42	44	.297	.364	.479	136	20	2	0	0	.994	-8	1-65,C-63/D	1.1
1975	Det-A☆	120	427	42	105	17	3	14	47	32	56	.246	.308	.398	94	-4	2	0	0	.991	-8	*C-113/1-5	-0.7
1976	Det-A	71	237	22	64	10	1	5	27	12	27	.270	.308	.384	98	-1	0	0	0	.983	-2	C-61/1-2,D	-0.7
Total	15	1774	6073	706	1591	241	35	200	758	626	753	.262	.342	.412	111	94	24	21	-5	.993	-38	*C-1581,1-157/DO	13.2

■ JERRY FREEMAN
Freeman, Frank Ellsworth "Buck"　b: 12/26/1879, Placerville, Cal.　d: 9/30/52, Los Angeles, Cal.　BL/TR, 6'2", 220 lbs.　Deb: 4/14/08

YEAR	TM/L	G	AB	R	H	2B	3B	HR	RBI	BB	SO	AVG	OBP	SLG	PRO+	BR/A	SB	CS	SBR	FA	FR	G/POS	TPR
1908	Was-A	154	531	45	134	15	5	1	45	36		.252	.304	.305	107	3	6			.975	-13	*1-154	-1.4
1909	Was-A	19	48	2	8	0	1	0	3	4		.167	.245	.208	46	-3	3			.956	-2	1-14/O-1	-0.5
Total	2	173	579	47	142	15	6	1	48	40		.245	.299	.297	101	0	9			.974	-14	1-168/O-1	-1.9

YEAR	TM/L	G	AB	R	H	2B	3B	HR	RBI	BB	SO	AVG	OBP	SLG	PRO+	BR/A	SB	CS	SBR	FA	FR	G/POS	TPR

■ JOHN FREEMAN
Freeman, John Edward b: 1/24/01, Boston, Mass. d: 4/14/58, Washington, D.C. BR/TR, 5'8", 160 lbs. Deb: 6/17/27

YEAR	TM/L	G	AB	R	H	2B	3B	HR	RBI	BB	SO	AVG	OBP	SLG	PRO+	BR/A	SB	CS	SBR	FA	FR	G/POS	TPR
1927	Bos-A	4	2	0	0	0	0	0	0	0	0	.000	.000	.000	-99	-1	0	0	0	.000	-2	/O-3	-0.2

■ BUCK FREEMAN
Freeman, John Frank b: 10/30/1871, Catasauqua, Pa. d: 6/25/49, Wilkes-Barre, Pa. BL/TL, 5'9", 169 lbs. Deb: 6/27/1891

YEAR	TM/L	G	AB	R	H	2B	3B	HR	RBI	BB	SO	AVG	OBP	SLG	PRO+	BR/A	SB	CS	SBR	FA	FR	G/POS	TPR
1891	Was-a	5	18	1	4	1	0	0	1	2	2	.222	.300	.278	69	-1	0			.769	-0	/P-5	0.0
1898	Was-N	29	107	19	39	2	3	3	21	7		.364	.424	.523	171	10	2			.978	1	O-29	0.8
1899	Was-N	155	588	107	187	19	25	25	122	23		.318	.362	.563	154	38	21			.944	-12	*O-155/P-2	1.3
1900	Bos-N	117	418	58	126	19	13	6	65	25		.301	.355	.452	109	2	10			.950	-11	O-91,1-19	-1.4
1901	Bos-A	129	490	88	166	23	15	12	114	44		.339	.400	.520	157	37	17			.974	-5	*1-128/2-1,O	2.7
1902	Bos-A	138	564	75	174	38	19	11	121	32		.309	.352	.502	131	21	17			.944	-1	*O-138	1.1
1903	*Bos-A	141	567	74	163	39	20	13	104	30		.287	.328	.496	137	23	5			.933	-6	*O-141	0.9
1904	Bos-A	157	597	64	167	20	19	7	84	32		.280	.329	.412	126	17	7			.954	-6	*O-157	0.2
1905	Bos-A	130	455	59	109	20	8	3	49	46		.240	.316	.338	106	4	8			.972	-15	1-66,O-57/3	-1.7
1906	Bos-A	121	392	42	98	18	9	1	30	28		.250	.302	.349	104	1	5			.989	5	O-65,1-43/3	-0.2
1907	Bos-A	4	12	1	2	0	0	0	2	3		.167	.333	.417	140	1	0			1.000	0	/O-3	0.1
Total	11	1126	4208	588	1235	199	131	82	713	272	2	.293	.346	.462	131	152	92			.950	-53	O-837,1-256/P32	3.8

■ LA VEL FREEMAN
Freeman, La Vel Maurice b: 2/18/63, Oakland, Cal. BL/TL, 5'9", 170 lbs. Deb: 4/7/89

YEAR	TM/L	G	AB	R	H	2B	3B	HR	RBI	BB	SO	AVG	OBP	SLG	PRO+	BR/A	SB	CS	SBR	FA	FR	G/POS	TPR
1989	Mil-A	2	3	1	0	0	0	0	0	0	2	.000	.000	.000	-99	-1	0	0	0	.000	0	/D-2	-0.1

■ GENE FREESE
Freese, Eugene Lewis "Augie" b: 1/8/34, Wheeling, W.Va. BR/TR, 5'11", 175 lbs. Deb: 4/13/55 F

YEAR	TM/L	G	AB	R	H	2B	3B	HR	RBI	BB	SO	AVG	OBP	SLG	PRO+	BR/A	SB	CS	SBR	FA	FR	G/POS	TPR
1955	Pit-N	134	455	69	115	21	8	14	44	34	57	.253	.310	.426	94	-5	5	1	1	.943	-2	3-65,2-57	-0.2
1956	Pit-N	65	207	17	43	9	0	3	16	14	45	.208	.274	.295	54	-13	2	1	0	.963	-7	3-47,2-26	-1.9
1957	Pit-N	114	346	44	98	18	2	6	31	17	42	.283	.321	.399	95	-3	9	4	0	.924	-3	3-74,2-10,O	-0.4
1958	Pit-N	17	18	1	3	0	0	0	2	1	2	.167	.211	.333	42	-2	0	0	0	.800	1	/3-1	-0.1
	StL-N	62	191	28	49	11	1	6	16	10	32	.257	.294	.419	83	-5	1	1	-0	.924	-25	S-28,2-14/3	-2.7
	Yr	79	209	29	52	11	1	7	18	11	34	.249	.286	.411	80	-7	1	1	-0	.924	-24	S-28,2-14/3	-2.8
1959	Phi-N	132	400	60	107	14	5	23	70	43	61	.268	.346	.500	120	11	8	4	0	.916	-24	*3-109/2-6	-1.2
1960	Chi-A	127	455	60	124	32	6	17	79	29	65	.273	.318	.481	114	7	10	6	-1	.946	0	*3-122	0.5
1961	*Cin-N	152	575	78	159	27	2	26	87	27	78	.277	.309	.466	101	-1	8	2	1	.950	-17	*3-151/2-1	-1.6
1962	Cin-N	18	42	2	6	1	0	1	6	8		.143	.250	.167	14	-5	0	0	0	1.000	-2	3-10	-0.7
1963	Cin-N	66	217	20	53	9	1	6	26	17	42	.244	.305	.378	93	-2	4	2	0	.930	-6	3-62/O-1	-0.9
1964	Pit-N	99	289	33	65	13	2	9	40	19	45	.225	.273	.377	81	-8	1	2	-1	.920	-5	3-72	-1.6
1965	Pit-N	43	80	6	21	4	0	0	8	3	16	.262	.330	.313	82	-2	0	2	-0	.951	-1	3-19	-0.4
	Chi-A	17	32	2	9	0	1	1	4	5	9	.281	.378	.438	140	2	0	0	0	.824	-3	/3-8	-0.1
1966	Chi-A	48	106	8	22	2	0	3	10	8	20	.208	.270	.311	71	-4	2	1	0	.894	3	3-34	-0.2
	Hou-N	21	33	1	3	0	0	0	0	5	11	.091	.211	.091	-13	-5	1	0	0	.800	-0	/3-4,2-3,O	-0.5
Total	12	1115	3446	429	877	161	28	115	432	243	535	.254	.307	.418	94	-37	51	26	0	.934	-90	3-781,2-117/SO	-12.0

■ GEORGE FREESE
Freese, George Walter "Bud" b: 9/12/26, Wheeling, W.Va. BR/TR, 6', 190 lbs. Deb: 4/29/53 F

YEAR	TM/L	G	AB	R	H	2B	3B	HR	RBI	BB	SO	AVG	OBP	SLG	PRO+	BR/A	SB	CS	SBR	FA	FR	G/POS	TPR
1953	Det-A	1	1	0	0	0	0	0	0	0	0	.000	.000	.000	-99	0	0	0	0	.000	0	H	0.0
1955	Pit-N	51	179	17	46	8	2	3	22	17	18	.257	.328	.374	87	-3	1	1	0	.936	-8	3-50	-1.2
1961	Chi-A	9	7	0	2	0	0	0	1	1	4	.286	.375	.286	78	-0	0	0	0	.000	0	H	0.0
Total	3	61	187	17	48	8	2	3	23	18	22	.257	.329	.369	86	-4	1	1	0	.936	-8	/3-50	-1.2

■ JIM FREGOSI
Fregosi, James Louis b: 4/4/42, San Francisco, Cal. BR/TR, 6'1", 190 lbs. Deb: 9/14/61 M

YEAR	TM/L	G	AB	R	H	2B	3B	HR	RBI	BB	SO	AVG	OBP	SLG	PRO+	BR/A	SB	CS	SBR	FA	FR	G/POS	TPR
1961	LA-A	11	27	7	6	0	0	0	1	4		.222	.250	.222	25	-3	0	0	0	.944	-0	S-11	-0.2
1962	LA-A	58	175	15	51	3	4	3	23	18	27	.291	.358	.406	108	2	2	1	0	.943	4	S-52	1.1
1963	LA-A	154	592	83	170	29	12	9	50	36	104	.287	.328	.422	115	10	2	2	-1	.964	2	*S-151	2.3
1964	LA-A★	147	505	86	140	22	9	18	72	72	87	.277	.372	.463	145	31	8	3	1	.966	1	*S-137	4.4
1965	Cal-A	161	602	66	167	19	7	15	64	54	107	.277	.341	.407	114	11	13	5	1	.968	6	*S-160	3.0
1966	Cal-A★	162	611	78	154	32	7	13	67	67	89	.252	.328	.391	109	7	17	8	0	.959	15	*S-162/1-1	3.9
1967	Cal-A★	151	590	75	171	23	6	9	56	49	77	.290	.349	.395	124	17	9	6	-1	.965	-7	*S-151	2.6
1968	Cal-A★	159	614	77	150	21	13	9	49	60	101	.244	.317	.365	110	7	9	4	0	.962	-14	*S-159	1.1
1969	Cal-A★	161	580	78	151	22	6	12	47	93	86	.260	.364	.381	114	13	9	2	2	.972	-16	*S-160	1.7
1970	Cal-A★	158	601	95	167	33	5	22	82	69	92	.278	.355	.459	127	22	0	2	-1	.973	4	*S-150/1-6	4.2
1971	Cal-A	107	347	31	81	15	1	5	33	39	61	.233	.320	.326	90	-5	2	1	0	.938	-10	S-74,1-18/O	-0.7
1972	NY-N	101	340	31	79	15	4	5	32	38	71	.232	.311	.344	88	-5	0	0	0	.935	-7	3-85/S-6,1	-1.4
1973	NY-N	45	124	7	29	4	1	0	11	20	25	.234	.340	.282	75	-3	1	2	-1	.906	-6	S-17,3-17/1O	-0.9
	Tex-A	45	157	25	42	6	2	6	16	12	31	.268	.324	.446	120	3	0	1	-0	.937	-3	3-34,1-10/S	-0.7
1974	Tex-A	78	230	31	60	5	0	12	34	22	41	.261	.325	.439	121	6	0	1	0	1.000	-1	1-47,3-32	0.1
1975	Tex-A	77	191	25	50	5	0	7	33	20	39	.262	.335	.398	107	2	0	0	0	.985	2	1-54,D-13/3	0.1
1976	Tex-A	58	133	17	31	7	0	2	12	23	33	.233	.346	.331	97	-0	2	0	0	.995	-0	1-26,D-18/3	-0.1
1977	Tex-A	13	28	4	7	1	0	1	5	3	4	.250	.323	.393	93	-0	0	0	0	1.000	-1	/1-5,D-3	0.0
	Pit-N	36	56	10	16	1	1	3	16	13	10	.286	.420	.500	142	4	2	0	0	.981	-1	1-15/3-1	0.3
1978	Pit-N	20	20	3	4	1	0	0	1	6	8	.200	.385	.250	77	-0	0	0	0	.667	-1	/3-5,1-2,2	-0.2
Total	18	1902	6523	844	1726	264	78	151	706	715	1097	.265	.340	.398	114	118	76	40		.963	-40	*S-1396,1-190,3/DO2	20.6

■ VERN FREIBERGER
Freiberger, Vern Donald b: 12/19/23, Detroit, Mich. BR/TL, 6'1", 170 lbs. Deb: 9/6/41

YEAR	TM/L	G	AB	R	H	2B	3B	HR	RBI	BB	SO	AVG	OBP	SLG	PRO+	BR/A	SB	CS	SBR	FA	FR	G/POS	TPR
1941	Cle-A	2	8	0	1	0	0	0	1	0	2	.125	.125	.125	-35	-2	0	0	0	.947		/1-2	-0.1

■ HOWARD FREIGAU
Freigau, Howard Earl "Ty" b: 8/1/02, Dayton, Ohio d: 7/18/32, Chattanooga, Tenn BR/TR, 5'10.5", 160 lbs. Deb: 9/13/22

YEAR	TM/L	G	AB	R	H	2B	3B	HR	RBI	BB	SO	AVG	OBP	SLG	PRO+	BR/A	SB	CS	SBR	FA	FR	G/POS	TPR
1922	StL-N	3	1	0	0	0	0	0	0	0	0	.000	.000	.000	-99	-0	0	0	0	1.000		/S-2,3-1	0.1
1923	StL-N	113	358	30	94	18	1	1	35	25	36	.263	.314	.327	71	-15	5	4	-1	.929	3	S-87,2-16/130	-0.6
1924	StL-N	98	376	35	101	17	6	2	39	19	24	.269	.306	.362	80	-11	10	3	1	.958	3	3-98/S-2	0.0
1925	StL-N	9	26	2	4	0	0	0	0	2	1	.154	.214	.154	-4	-4	0	0	0	.936	1	/S-7,2-1	0.0
	Chi-N	117	476	77	146	22	10	8	71	30	31	.307	.349	.445	100	-1	10	6	-1	.913	-5	3-96,S-17/1	0.2
	Yr	126	502	79	150	22	10	8	71	32	32	.299	.342	.430	94	-5	10	6	-1	.913	-1	3-96,S-24/12	0.2
1926	Chi-N	140	508	51	137	27	7	3	51	43	42	.270	.327	.368	86	-10	6			.966	-3	*3-135/S-2,O	-0.4
1927	Chi-N	30	86	12	20	5	0	0	9	10		.233	.313	.291	62	-4	0			.883	1	3-30	-0.3
1928	Bro-N	17	34	6	7	2	0	0	3	1	3	.206	.229	.265	29	-4	0			.810	-4	3-10/S-1	-0.7
	Bos-N	52	109	11	28	8	1	1	17	9	14	.257	.319	.376	86	-3	1			.938	-10	S-14,2-11	-1.0
	Yr	69	143	17	35	10	1	1	20	10	17	.245	.299	.350	72	-6	1			.938	-13	S-15,2-11,3	-1.7
Total	7	579	1974	224	537	99	25	15	226	138	161	.272	.322	.370	82	-52	32	13		.940	-11	3-371,S-132/210	-2.7

■ CHARLIE FRENCH
French, Charles Calvin b: 10/12/1883, Indianapolis, Ind. d: 3/30/62, Indianapolis, Ind. BL/TR, 5'6", 140 lbs. Deb: 5/23/09

YEAR	TM/L	G	AB	R	H	2B	3B	HR	RBI	BB	SO	AVG	OBP	SLG	PRO+	BR/A	SB	CS	SBR	FA	FR	G/POS	TPR
1909	Bos-A	51	167	15	42	3	1	0	13	15		.251	.324	.281	90	-1	8			.921	-8	2-28,S-23	-1.1
1910	Bos-A	9	40	4	8	1	0	0	3	1		.200	.220	.225	38	-3	0			.889	1	/2-8	-0.3
	Chi-A	45	170	17	28	1	1	0	4	10		.165	.224	.182	29	-14	5			.930	-14	2-28,O-16	-3.4
	Yr	54	210	21	36	2	1	0	7	11		.171	.223	.190	31	-17	5			.919	-14	2-36,O-16	-3.7
Total	2	105	377	36	78	5	2	0	20	26		.207	.269	.231	58	-18	13			.920	-22	/2-64,S-23,O	-4.8

■ PAT FRENCH
French, Frank Alexander b: 9/22/1893, Dover, N.H. d: 7/13/69, Bath, Maine BR/TR, 6'1", 180 lbs. Deb: 7/2/17

YEAR	TM/L	G	AB	R	H	2B	3B	HR	RBI	BB	SO	AVG	OBP	SLG	PRO+	BR/A	SB	CS	SBR	FA	FR	G/POS	TPR
1917	Phi-A	3	2	0	0	0	0	0	0	0	0	.000	.000	.000	-99	-0	0			1.000	-0	/O-1	-0.1

YEAR	TM/L	G	AB	R	H	2B	3B	HR	RBI	BB	SO	AVG	OBP	SLG	PRO+	BR/A	SB	CS	SBR	FA	FR	G/POS	TPR

■ RAY FRENCH French, Raymond Edward b: 1/9/1895, Alameda, Cal. d: 4/3/78, Alameda, Cal. BR/TR, 5'9.5", 158 lbs. Deb: 9/17/20

1920	NY-A	2	2	2	0	0	0	0	1	0	1	.000	.000	.000	-97	-1	0	0	0	.500	-0	/S-1	-0.1
1923	Bro-N	43	73	14	16	2	1	0	7	4	7	.219	.269	.274	45	-6	0	0	0	.874	4	S-30	0.0
1924	Chi-A	37	112	13	20	4	0	0	11	10	13	.179	.246	.214	20	-14	3	1	0	.927	-3	S-28/2-3	-1.2
Total	3	82	187	29	36	6	1	0	19	14	21	.193	.252	.235	28	-20	3	1	0	.897	2	/S-59,2-3	-1.3

■ JIM FRENCH French, Richard James b: 8/13/41, Warren, Ohio BL/TR, 5'7", 182 lbs. Deb: 9/12/65

1965	Was-A	13	37	4	11	0	0	1	7	9	5	.297	.435	.378	135	2	1	0	0	.974	-0	C-13	0.3
1966	Was-A	10	24	0	5	1	0	0	3	4	5	.208	.321	.250	67	-1	0	1	-1	.979	-1	C-10	-0.2
1967	Was-A	6	16	0	1	0	0	0	1	3	4	.063	.211	.063	-16	-2	0	0	0	.968	-1	/C-6	-0.3
1968	Was-A	59	165	9	32	5	0	1	10	19	19	.194	.281	.242	62	-7	1	2	-1	.984	2	C-53	-0.3
1969	Was-A	63	158	14	29	6	3	2	13	41	15	.184	.352	.297	88	-1	1	0	0	.989	9	C-63	1.2
1970	Was-A	69	166	20	35	3	1	1	13	38	23	.211	.358	.259	76	-4	0	1	-1	.973	-6	C-62/O-1	-0.8
1971	Was-A	14	41	6	6	2	0	0	4	7	7	.146	.271	.195	36	-3	0	2	-1	.985	-1	C-14	-0.5
Total	7	234	607	53	119	17	4	5	51	121	78	.196	.331	.262	74	-16	3	6	-3	.982	2	C-221/O-1	-0.6

■ WALTER FRENCH French, Walter Edward "Piggy" or "Fitz" b: 7/12/1899, Moorestown, N.J. d: 5/13/84, Mountain Home, Ark BL/TR, 5'7.5", 155 lbs. Deb: 9/15/23

1923	Phi-A	16	39	7	9	3	0	0	2	5	7	.231	.318	.308	64	-2	0	1	-1	1.000	-1	O-10	-0.4
1925	Phi-A	67	100	20	37	9	0	0	14	1	9	.370	.376	.460	104	0	1	1	-0	.971	0	O-19	-0.1
1926	Phi-A	112	397	51	121	18	7	1	36	18	24	.305	.340	.393	86	-9	2	3	-1	.971	3	O-94	-1.4
1927	Phi-A	109	326	48	99	10	5	0	41	16	14	.304	.338	.365	78	-11	9	1	2	.956	0	O-99	-1.3
1928	Phi-A	48	74	9	19	4	0	0	7	2	5	.257	.286	.311	55	-5	1	1	-0	1.000	-1	O-19	-0.7
1929	*Phi-A	45	45	7	12	1	0	1	9	2	3	.267	.298	.356	65	-2	0	0	0	1.000	-3	O-10	-0.5
Total	6	397	981	142	297	45	12	2	109	44	62	.303	.336	.379	81	-29	13	7	-0	.968	-2	O-251	-4.4

■ BILL FRENCH French, William b: Baltimore, Md. Deb: 4/14/1873

1873	Mar-n	5	18	3	4	0	0	0	1	0	0	.222	.222	.222	41	-1						/1-2,O-2,P3	0.0

■ LONNY FREY Frey, Linus Reinhard "Junior" b: 8/23/10, St.Louis, Mo. BL/TR, 5'10", 160 lbs. Deb: 8/29/33

1933	Bro-N	34	135	25	43	5	3	0	12	13	13	.319	.378	.400	128	5	4			.896	-14	S-34	-0.7
1934	Bro-N	125	490	77	139	24	5	8	57	52	54	.284	.358	.402	109	7	11			.945	13	*S-109,3-13	2.6
1935	Bro-N	131	515	88	135	35	11	11	77	66	68	.262	.352	.437	113	10	6			.937	-4	*S-127/2-4	1.3
1936	Bro-N	148	524	63	146	29	4	4	60	71	56	.279	.369	.372	99	2	7			.918	-32	S-117,2-30/O	-2.1
1937	Chi-N	78	198	33	55	9	3	1	22	33	15	.278	.381	.369	100	1	6			.938	-19	S-30,2-13/3O	-1.4
1938	Cin-N	124	501	76	133	26	6	4	36	49	50	.265	.331	.365	94	-4	5			.964	-8	*2-121/S-3	-0.4
1939	*Cin-N★	125	484	95	141	27	9	11	55	72	46	.291	.387	.452	124	18	5			.976	15	*2-124	4.0
1940	*Cin-N★	150	563	102	150	23	6	8	54	80	48	.266	.361	.371	101	3	22			.977	18	*2-150	3.1
1941	Cin-N★	146	543	78	138	29	5	6	59	72	37	.254	.345	.359	98	-0	16			.970	-2	*2-145	0.8
1942	Cin-N	141	523	66	139	23	2	9	39	87	38	.266	.373	.344	111	11	9			.977	5	*2-140	2.6
1943	Cin-N★	144	586	78	154	20	8	2	43	76	56	.263	.347	.334	99	1	7			.985	12	*2-144	2.2
1946	Cin-N	111	333	46	82	10	3	3	24	63	31	.246	.368	.321	100	3	5			.963	-3	2-65,O-28	0.3
1947	Chi-N	24	43	4	9	0	0	0	3	4	6	.209	.277	.209	32	-4	0			1.000	-2	/2-9	-0.6
	*NY-A	24	28	10	5	2	0	0	2	10	1	.179	.410	.250	87	0	3	0	1	.923	3	/2-8	0.5
1948	NY-A	1	0	1	0	0	0	0	0	0	0	—	—	—	—	0	0			.000	0	R	0.0
	NY-N	29	51	6	13	1	0	1	6	4	6	.255	.309	.333	73	-2	0			.920	-2	2-13	-0.3
Total	14	1535	5517	848	1482	263	69	61	549	752	525	.269	.359	.374	104	50	105	0		.973	-18	2-966,S-420/O3	11.9

■ PEPE FRIAS Frias, Jesus Maria (Andujar) b: 7/14/48, San Pedro De Macoris, D.R. BR/TR, 5'10", 159 lbs. Deb: 4/6/73

1973	Mon-N	100	225	19	52	10	1	0	22	10	24	.231	.267	.284	51	-15	1	3	-2	.950	17	S-46,2-44/3O	0.6
1974	Mon-N	75	112	12	24	4	1	0	7	7	10	.214	.261	.268	45	-8	1	0	0	.962	17	S-30,3-27,2/O	1.1
1975	Mon-N	51	64	4	8	2	0	0	4	3	13	.125	.164	.156	-10	-10	0	1	-1	.938	14	S-29,3-11/2	0.5
1976	Mon-N	76	113	7	28	5	0	0	6	4	14	.248	.274	.292	58	-6	1	1	0	.957	14	2-35,S-35/3O	1.1
1977	Mon-N	53	70	10	18	1	0	0	5	0	10	.257	.257	.271	43	-6	1	0	0	.978	2	2-16,S-14/3	0.3
1978	Mon-N	73	15	5	4	2	1	0	3	0	3	.267	.267	.533	120	0	0	0	0	1.000	13	2-61/S-3	1.4
1979	Atl-N	140	475	41	123	18	4	1	44	20	36	.259	.292	.320	62	-25	3	2	-0	.954	0	*S-137	-1.0
1980	Tex-A	116	227	27	55	5	1	0	10	4	23	.242	.259	.273	47	-16	5	1	1	.947	-16	*S-106/3-7,2	-2.4
	LA-N	14	9	1	2	1	0	0	0	0	0	.222	.222	.333	54	-1	0	0	0	.933	2	S-11	0.2
1981	LA-N	25	36	6	9	1	0	0	3	1	3	.250	.289	.278	64	-2	0	0	-0	.906	-5	S-15/2-6,3	-0.6
Total	9	723	1346	132	323	49	8	1	108	49	136	.240	.269	.290	52	-88	12	8	-1	.951	63	S-426,2-186/3O	1.2

■ BERNIE FRIBERG Friberg, Bernard Albert (b: Gustaf Bernhard Friberg) b: 8/18/1899, Manchester, N.H. d: 12/8/58, Lynn, Mass. BR/TR, 5'11", 178 lbs. Deb: 8/20/19

1919	Chi-N	8	20	0	4	1	0	0	1	0	2	.200	.200	.250	35	-2	0			1.000	-1	/O-7	-0.3
1920	Chi-N	50	114	11	24	5	1	0	7	6	20	.211	.250	.272	49	-8	2	2	-1	.963	1	2-24,O-24	-0.8
1922	Chi-N	97	296	51	92	8	2	0	23	37	37	.311	.391	.351	91	-2	8	10	-4	.972	-2	O-74/1-6,32	-1.2
1923	Chi-N	146	547	91	174	27	11	12	88	45	49	.318	.372	.473	122	16	13	19	-8	.955	7	*3-146	2.8
1924	Chi-N	142	495	67	138	19	3	5	82	66	53	.279	.369	.360	95	-1	19	27	-11	.954	4	*3-142	0.4
1925	Chi-N	44	152	12	39	5	3	1	16	14	22	.257	.327	.349	72	-6	0	1	-1	.889	-5	3-26,O-12/1S	-1.1
	Phi-N	91	304	41	82	12	1	5	22	39	35	.270	.353	.365	77	-10	1	1	-0	.965	0	2-77,3-14/PC	-0.4
	Yr	135	456	53	121	17	4	6	38	53	57	.265	.344	.360	75	-16	1	2	-1	.965	-2	2-77,3-40,O/1SPC	-1.5
1926	Phi-N	144	478	38	128	21	3	1	51	57	77	.268	.346	.331	79	-13	2			.976	22	*2-144	1.3
1927	Phi-N	111	335	31	78	8	2	1	28	41	49	.233	.322	.278	61	-17	3			.959	25	*3-103/2-5	1.3
1928	Phi-N	52	94	11	19	3	0	1	7	12	16	.202	.292	.266	45	-7	0			.908	1	S-31/3-5,201	-0.4
1929	Phi-N	128	455	74	137	21	10	7	55	49	54	.301	.363	.437	93	-5	1			.923	-26	S-73,O-40/21	-2.2
1930	Phi-N	105	331	62	113	21	1	4	42	47	35	.341	.425	.447	104	4	1			.953	-4	2-44,O-35,S/3	0.1
1931	Phi-N	103	353	33	92	19	5	1	26	33	25	.261	.324	.351	75	-12	1			.955	6	2-64,3-25/1S	-0.1
1932	Phi-N	61	154	17	37	8	2	0	14	19	23	.240	.324	.318	66	-7	0			.957	-1	2-56	-0.6
1933	Bos-A	17	41	5	13	3	0	0	9	6	1	.317	.404	.390	112	1	0	0	0	.950	1	/2-6,3-5,S	0.3
Total	14	1299	4169	544	1170	181	44	38	471	471	498	.281	.356	.373	87	-69	51	60		.953	32	3-479,2-434,OS/1CP	-0.9

■ JIM FRIDLEY Fridley, James Riley "Big Jim" b: 9/6/24, Philippi, W.Va. BR/TR, 6'2", 205 lbs. Deb: 4/15/52

1952	Cle-A	62	175	23	44	2	0	4	16	14	40	.251	.311	.331	84	-4	3	3	-1	.978	-5	O-54	-1.3
1954	Bal-A	85	240	25	59	8	5	4	36	21	41	.246	.312	.371	93	-4	0	1	-0	.985	-1	O-67	-0.8
1958	Cin-N	5	9	2	2	2	0	0	1	0	2	.222	.222	.444	67	-0	0	0	0	1.000	-1	/O-2	-0.1
Total	3	152	424	50	105	12	5	8	53	35	83	.248	.310	.356	89	-8	3	4	-2	.982	-7	O-123	-2.2

■ PAT FRIEL Friel, Patrick Henry b: 6/11/1860, Lewisburg, W.Va. d: 1/15/24, Providence, R.I. BB, 5'11", 170 lbs. Deb: 7/13/1890 F

1890	Syr-a	62	261	51	65	8	2	3		17		.249	.302	.330	96	-2	34			.913	-6	O-62	-0.9
1891	Phi-a	2	8	2	2	1	0	0	0	0	0	.250	.250	.375	76	-0	0			1.000	-1	/O-2	-0.1
Total	2	64	269	53	67	9	2	3	0	17	0	.249	.301	.331	96	-2	34			.916	-7	/O-64	-1.0

■ BILL FRIEL Friel, William Edward b: 4/1/1876, Renovo, Pa. d: 12/24/59, St.Louis, Mo. BL/TR, 5'10", 165 lbs. Deb: 5/3/01 FU

1901	Mil-A	106	376	51	100	13	7	4	35	23		.266	.310	.370	92	-4	15			.866	-9	3-61,O-29/2S	-1.2
1902	StL-A	80	267	26	64	9	2	2	20	14		.240	.283	.311	65	-13	4			.921	-14	O-33,2-25,1/3SPC	-2.5

YEAR	TM/L	G	AB	R	H	2B	3B	HR	RBI	BB	SO	AVG	OBP	SLG	PRO+	BR/A	SB	CS	SBR	FA	FR	G/POS	TPR
1903	StL-A	97	351	46	80	11	8	0	25	23		.228	.279	.305	77	-10	4			.915	-11	2-63,3-24/O	-1.9
Total	3	283	994	123	244	33	17	6	80	60		.245	.292	.331	80	-27	23			.924	-33	/2-97,3-93,O1SCP	-5.6

■ FRANK FRIEND
Friend, Frank B. (b: Frederick Freund) b: 7/5/1875, Jeffersonville, Ind. d: 11/5/33, Jeffersonville, Ind. TR , 5'10", 180 lbs. Deb: 8/2/1896

YEAR	TM/L	G	AB	R	H	2B	3B	HR	RBI	BB	SO	AVG	OBP	SLG	PRO+	BR/A	SB	CS	SBR	FA	FR	G/POS	TPR
1896	Lou-N	2	5	1	1	0	0	0	0	1	1	.200	.333	.200	44	-0	0			1.000	-0	/C-2	0.0

■ OWEN FRIEND
Friend, Owen Lacey "Red" b: 3/21/27, Granite City, Ill. BR/TR, 6'1", 180 lbs. Deb: 10/2/49 C

YEAR	TM/L	G	AB	R	H	2B	3B	HR	RBI	BB	SO	AVG	OBP	SLG	PRO+	BR/A	SB	CS	SBR	FA	FR	G/POS	TPR
1949	StL-A	2	8	1	3	0	0	0	1	0	0	.375	.375	.375	95	-0	0	0	0	1.000	0	/2-2	0.1
1950	StL-A	119	372	48	88	15	2	8	50	40	68	.237	.312	.352	67	-19	2	1	0	.961	10	2-93,3-24/S	-0.5
1953	Det-A	31	96	10	17	4	0	3	10	6	9	.177	.233	.313	47	-8	0	1	-1	.947	4	2-26	-0.3
	Cle-A	34	68	7	16	2	0	2	13	5	16	.235	.288	.353	74	-3	0	0	0	1.000	6	2-19/S-8,3	0.4
	Yr	65	164	17	33	6	0	5	23	11	25	.201	.256	.329	58	-10	0	1	-1	.964	10	2-45/S-8,3	0.1
1955	Bos-A	14	42	3	11	0	0	0	2	4	11	.262	.326	.333	71	-2	0	0	0	.951	2	S-14/2-1	0.1
	Chi-N	6	10	0	1	0	0	0	0	0	3	.100	.100	.100	-47	-2	0	0	0	1.000	-1	/3-2,S-1	-0.3
1956	Chi-N	2	2	0	0	0	0	0	0	0	0	.000	.000	.000	-99	-1	0	0	0	.000	0	H	-0.1
Total	5	208	598	69	136	24	2	13	76	55	109	.227	.295	.339	63	-34	2	2	-1	.963	23	2-141/3-27,S	-0.6

■ BUCK FRIERSON
Frierson, Robert Lawrence b: 7/29/17, Chicota, Tex. BR/TR, 6'3", 195 lbs. Deb: 9/9/41

YEAR	TM/L	G	AB	R	H	2B	3B	HR	RBI	BB	SO	AVG	OBP	SLG	PRO+	BR/A	SB	CS	SBR	FA	FR	G/POS	TPR
1941	Cle-A	5	11	2	3	1	0	0	2	1		.273	.333	.364	89	-0	0	0		1.000	-1	/O-3	-0.1

■ PETE FRIES
Fries, Peter Martin b: 10/30/1857, Scranton, Pa. d: 7/30/37, Chicago, Ill. BL/TL, 5'8", 160 lbs. Deb: 8/10/1883

YEAR	TM/L	G	AB	R	H	2B	3B	HR	RBI	BB	SO	AVG	OBP	SLG	PRO+	BR/A	SB	CS	SBR	FA	FR	G/POS	TPR
1883	Col-a	3	10	1	3	1	0	0		1		.300	.364	.400	158	1				.857	0	/P-3	0.0
1884	Ind-a	1	3	0	1	1	0	0		1		.333	.500	.667	285	1				.333	0	/O-1	0.1
Total	2	4	13	1	4	2	0	0		2		.308	.400	.462	190	1				.857	0	/P-3,O-1	0.1

■ FRED FRINK
Frink, Fred Ferdinand b: 8/25/11, Macon, Ga. BR/TR, 6'1", 180 lbs. Deb: 7/1/34

YEAR	TM/L	G	AB	R	H	2B	3B	HR	RBI	BB	SO	AVG	OBP	SLG	PRO+	BR/A	SB	CS	SBR	FA	FR	G/POS	TPR
1934	Phi-N	2	0	0	0	0	0	0	0	0	0	—	—	—	—		0	0		.000	-1	/O-1	-0.1

■ CHARLIE FRISBEE
Frisbee, Charles Augustus "Bunt" b: 2/2/1874, Dows, Iowa d: 11/7/54, Alden, Iowa BB/TR, 5'9", 175 lbs. Deb: 6/22/1899

YEAR	TM/L	G	AB	R	H	2B	3B	HR	RBI	BB	SO	AVG	OBP	SLG	PRO+	BR/A	SB	CS	SBR	FA	FR	G/POS	TPR
1899	Bos-N	42	152	22	50	4	2	0	20	9		.329	.374	.382	98	-1	10			.875	-2	O-40	-0.5
1900	NY-N	4	13	2	2	1	0	0	3	2		.154	.267	.231	40	-1	0			.400	-2	/O-4	-0.3
Total	2	46	165	24	52	5	2	0	23	11		.315	.365	.370	94	-2	10			.849	-4	O-44	-0.8

■ FRANKIE FRISCH
Frisch, Frank Francis "The Fordham Flash" b: 9/9/1898, Bronx, N.Y. d: 3/12/73, Wilmington, Del. BB/TR, 5'11", 165 lbs. Deb: 6/14/19 MCH

YEAR	TM/L	G	AB	R	H	2B	3B	HR	RBI	BB	SO	AVG	OBP	SLG	PRO+	BR/A	SB	CS	SBR	FA	FR	G/POS	TPR
1919	NY-N	54	190	21	43	3	2	2	24	4	14	.226	.242	.295	62	-9	15			.972	4	2-29,3-20/S	-0.4
1920	NY-N	110	440	57	123	10	10	4	77	20	18	.280	.311	.375	97	-3	34	11	4	.967	9	*3-109/S-2	1.6
1921	*NY-N	153	618	121	211	31	17	8	100	42	28	.341	.384	.485	128	25	49	13	7	.936	4	3-93,2-61	4.3
1922	*NY-N	132	514	101	168	16	13	5	51	47	13	.327	.387	.438	111	9	31	17	-1	.975	13	2-85,3-53/S	2.5
1923	*NY-N	151	641	116	**223**	32	10	12	111	46	12	.348	.395	.485	133	30	29	12	2	**.973**	-8	*2-135,3-17	2.6
1924	*NY-N	145	603	**121**	198	33	15	7	69	56	24	.328	.387	.468	132	27	22	9	1	.972	25	*2-143,S-10/3	5.4
1925	NY-N	120	502	89	166	26	6	11	48	32	14	.331	.374	.472	119	14	21	12	-1	.931	5	3-46,2-42,S	2.4
1926	NY-N	135	545	75	171	29	4	5	44	33	16	.314	.353	.409	106	4	23			.975	11	*2-127/3-7	1.9
1927	StL-N	153	617	112	208	31	11	10	78	49	10	.337	.387	.472	125	21	**48**			**.979**	49	*2-153/S-1	**7.3**
1928	*StL-N	141	547	107	164	29	9	10	86	64	17	.300	.374	.441	110	9	29			**.976**	3	*2-139	1.5
1929	StL-N	138	527	93	176	40	12	5	74	53	12	.334	.397	.484	116	14	24			.970	-4	*2-121,3-13/S	1.4
1930	*StL-N	133	540	121	187	46	9	10	114	55	16	.346	.407	.520	118	16	15			.969	28	*2-123,3-10	4.4
1931	*StL-N	131	518	96	161	24	4	4	82	45	13	.311	.368	.396	101	2	**28**			.974	16	*2-129	2.6
1932	StL-N	115	486	59	142	26	2	3	60	25	13	.292	.327	.372	85	-10	18			.971	16	2-75,3-37/S	1.3
1933	StL-N★	147	585	74	177	32	6	4	66	48	13	.303	.358	.398	110	8	18			.982	-3	*2-132,S-15M	1.5
1934	*StL-N★	140	550	74	168	30	6	3	75	42	10	.305	.359	.398	96	-2	11			.977	5	*2-115,3-25M	1.0
1935	StL-N☆	103	354	52	104	16	2	1	55	33	16	.294	.356	.359	89	-5	2			.982	-7	2-88/3-5M	-0.5
1936	StL-N	93	303	40	83	10	0	1	26	36	10	.274	.353	.317	82	-6	2			.965	-13	2-60,3-22/SM	-1.4
1937	StL-N	17	32	3	7	2	0	0	4	1	0	.219	.242	.281	41	-3	0			1.000	-1	/2-5,M	-0.3
Total	19	2311	9112	1532	2880	466	138	105	1244	728	272	.316	.369	.432	110	142	419	74		.974	150	*2-1762,3-459/S	39.1

■ EMIL FRISK
Frisk, John Emil b: 10/15/1874, Kalkaska, Mich. d: 1/27/22, Seattle, Wash. BL/TR, 6'1", 190 lbs. Deb: 9/2/1899

YEAR	TM/L	G	AB	R	H	2B	3B	HR	RBI	BB	SO	AVG	OBP	SLG	PRO+	BR/A	SB	CS	SBR	FA	FR	G/POS	TPR
1899	Cin-N	9	25	5	7	1	0	0	2	2		.280	.357	.320	85	-0	0			.950	0	/P-9	0.0
1901	Det-A	20	48	10	15	3	0	1	7	3		.313	.346	.438	117	1	0			.851	2	P-11/O-2	0.0
1905	StL-A	124	429	58	112	11	6	3	36	42		.261	.342	.336	122	12	7			.923	-8	*O-115	-0.1
1907	StL-A	5	4	0	1	0	0	0	0	1		.250	.400	.250	108	0	0			.000	0	H	0.0
Total	4	158	506	73	135	15	6	4	45	48		.267	.346	.344	119	13	7			.918	-6	O-117/P-20	-0.1

■ HARRY FRITZ
Fritz, Harry Koch "Dutchman" b: 9/30/1890, Philadelphia, Pa. d: 11/4/74, Columbus, Ohio BR/TR, 5'8", 170 lbs. Deb: 9/29/13

YEAR	TM/L	G	AB	R	H	2B	3B	HR	RBI	BB	SO	AVG	OBP	SLG	PRO+	BR/A	SB	CS	SBR	FA	FR	G/POS	TPR
1913	Phi-A	5	13	1	0	0	0	0	0	2	4	.000	.188	.000	-45	-2	0			.846	1	/3-5	-0.4
1914	Chi-F	65	174	16	37	5	1	0	13	18	18	.213	.297	.253	46	-14	2			.912	-9	3-46/S-9,2	-2.2
1915	Chi-F	79	236	27	59	8	4	3	26	13	27	.250	.298	.356	79	-8	4			.964	-8	3-70/2-6,S	-1.5
Total	3	149	423	44	96	13	5	3	39	33	49	.227	.294	.303	62	-25	6			.941	-18	3-121/S-10,2	-4.1

■ LARRY FRITZ
Fritz, Lawrence Joseph b: 2/14/49, E.Chicago, Ind. BL/TL, 6'2", 225 lbs. Deb: 5/30/75

YEAR	TM/L	G	AB	R	H	2B	3B	HR	RBI	BB	SO	AVG	OBP	SLG	PRO+	BR/A	SB	CS	SBR	FA	FR	G/POS	TPR
1975	Phi-N	1	1	0	0	0	0	0	0	0	0	.000	.000	.000	-96	-0	0	0	0	.000	0	H	0.0

■ DOUG FROBEL
Frobel, Douglas Steven b: 6/6/59, Ottawa, Ont., Can. BL/TR, 6'4", 196 lbs. Deb: 9/5/82

YEAR	TM/L	G	AB	R	H	2B	3B	HR	RBI	BB	SO	AVG	OBP	SLG	PRO+	BR/A	SB	CS	SBR	FA	FR	G/POS	TPR
1982	Pit-N	16	34	5	7	2	0	2	3	1	11	.206	.229	.441	81	-1	1	1	-0	1.000	1	O-12	-0.3
1983	Pit-N	32	60	10	17	4	1	3	11	4	17	.283	.328	.533	132	2	1	1	-0	.964	-4	O-24	-0.2
1984	Pit-N	126	276	33	56	9	3	12	28	24	84	.203	.272	.388	83	-7	7	5	-1	.956	1	*O-112	-1.0
1985	Pit-N	53	109	14	22	5	0	0	7	19	24	.202	.320	.248	62	-5	4	3	-1	.941	-3	O-36	-1.0
	Mon-N	12	23	3	3	1	0	1	4	2	6	.130	.200	.304	42	-2	0	0	0	.923	-0	/O-6	-0.3
	Yr	65	132	17	25	6	0	1	11	21	30	.189	.301	.258	59	-7	4	3	-1	.938	-3	O-42	-1.3
1987	Cle-A	29	40	5	4	0	0	2	5	5	13	.100	.200	.250	18	-5	0	0	0	1.000	-3	O-12/D-5	-0.8
Total	5	268	542	70	109	21	4	20	58	55	155	.201	.277	.365	78	-18	13	10	-2	.957	-10	O-202/D-5	-3.6

■ BEN FROELICH
Froelich, William Palmer b: 11/12/1887, Pittsburgh, Pa. d: 9/1/16, Pittsburgh, Pa. BR/TR, Deb: 7/2/09

YEAR	TM/L	G	AB	R	H	2B	3B	HR	RBI	BB	SO	AVG	OBP	SLG	PRO+	BR/A	SB	CS	SBR	FA	FR	G/POS	TPR
1909	Phi-N	1	1	0	0	0	0	0	0	0		.000	.000	.000	-99	-0	0			.000	0	/C-1	0.0

■ JERRY FRY
Fry, Jerry Ray b: 2/29/56, Salinas, Cal. BR/TR, 6', 185 lbs. Deb: 9/4/78

YEAR	TM/L	G	AB	R	H	2B	3B	HR	RBI	BB	SO	AVG	OBP	SLG	PRO+	BR/A	SB	CS	SBR	FA	FR	G/POS	TPR
1978	Mon-N	4	9	0	0	0	0	0	0	1	5	.000	.100	.000	-71	-2	0	0	0	1.000	1	/C-4	-0.1

■ JEFF FRYE
Frye, Jeffrey Dustin b: 8/31/66, Oakland, Cal. BR/TR, 5'9", 180 lbs. Deb: 7/9/92

YEAR	TM/L	G	AB	R	H	2B	3B	HR	RBI	BB	SO	AVG	OBP	SLG	PRO+	BR/A	SB	CS	SBR	FA	FR	G/POS	TPR
1992	Tex-A	67	199	24	51	9	1	1	12	16	27	.256	.321	.327	85	-4	1	3	-2	.978	8	2-67	0.4
1994	Tex-A	57	205	37	67	20	3	0	18	29	23	.327	.413	.454	132	11	6	1	1	.983	-16	2-54/3-1,D	-0.2
Total	2	124	404	61	118	29	4	1	30	45	50	.292	.369	.391	110	7	7	4	-0	.980	-8	2-121/D-1,3	0.2

■ TRAVIS FRYMAN
Fryman, David Travis b: 3/25/69, Lexington, Ky. BR/TR, 6'1", 180 lbs. Deb: 7/7/90

YEAR	TM/L	G	AB	R	H	2B	3B	HR	RBI	BB	SO	AVG	OBP	SLG	PRO+	BR/A	SB	CS	SBR	FA	FR	G/POS	TPR
1990	Det-A	66	232	32	69	11	1	9	27	17	51	.297	.348	.470	126	7	3	3	-1	.915	5	3-48,S-17/D	1.3
1991	Det-A	149	557	65	144	36	3	21	91	40	149	.259	.312	.447	106	2	12	5	1	.946	-9	3-85,S-71	-0.1
1992	Det-A★	161	659	87	175	31	4	20	96	45	144	.266	.318	.416	104	1	8	4	0	.970	-4	*S-137,3-26	0.7

YEAR	TM/L	G	AB	R	H	2B	3B	HR	RBI	BB	SO	AVG	OBP	SLG	PRO+	BR/A	SB	CS	SBR	FA	FR	G/POS	TPR
1993	Det-A★	151	607	98	182	37	5	22	97	77	128	.300	.382	.486	133	28	9	4	0	.953	-5	S-81,3-69/D	2.9
1994	Det-A★	114	464	66	122	34	5	18	85	45	128	.263	.335	.474	106	3	2	2	-1	**.955**	-5	*3-114	-0.2
Total	5	641	2519	348	692	149	18	90	396	224	600	.275	.339	.455	114	43	34	18	-1	.952	-19	3-342,S-306/D	4.6

■ MIKE FUENTES
Fuentes, Michael Jay b: 7/11/58, Miami, Fla. BR/TR, 6'3", 190 lbs. Deb: 9/2/83

YEAR	TM/L	G	AB	R	H	2B	3B	HR	RBI	BB	SO	AVG	OBP	SLG	PRO+	BR/A	SB	CS	SBR	FA	FR	G/POS	TPR
1983	Mon-N	6	4	1	1	0	0	0	0	0	2	.250	.250	.250	39	-0	0	0	0	.000	0	/H	-0.1
1984	Mon-N	3	4	0	1	0	0	0	0	1	2	.250	.400	.250	90	-0	0	0	0	1.000	0	/O-1	0.0
Total	2	9	8	1	2	0	0	0	0	1	4	.250	.333	.250	67	-0	0	0	0	1.000	0	/O-1	-0.1

■ TITO FUENTES
Fuentes, Rigoberto (Peat) b: 1/4/44, Havana, Cuba BB/TR, 5'11", 175 lbs. Deb: 8/18/65

YEAR	TM/L	G	AB	R	H	2B	3B	HR	RBI	BB	SO	AVG	OBP	SLG	PRO+	BR/A	SB	CS	SBR	FA	FR	G/POS	TPR
1965	SF-N	26	72	12	15	1	0	1	5	1	14	.208	.269	.222	39	-6	0	1	-1	.919	-7	S-18/2-7,3	-1.3
1966	SF-N	133	541	63	141	21	3	9	40	9	57	.261	.277	.360	73	-20	6	3	0	.957	-14	S-76,2-60	-2.3
1967	SF-N	133	344	27	72	12	1	5	29	27	61	.209	.267	.294	61	-17	4	3	-1	.980	25	*2-130/S-5	1.4
1969	SF-N	67	183	28	54	4	3	1	14	15	25	.295	.352	.366	103	1	2	4	-2	.925	-6	3-36,S-30	-0.5
1970	SF-N	123	435	49	116	13	7	2	32	36	52	.267	.327	.343	81	-12	4	5	-2	.966	-2	2-78,S-36,3	-0.7
1971	*SF-N	152	630	63	172	28	6	4	52	18	46	.273	.300	.356	86	-13	12	2	2	.973	1	*2-152	0.3
1972	SF-N	152	572	64	151	33	6	7	53	39	56	.264	.314	.379	95	-5	16	5	2	.964	-21	*2-152	-1.6
1973	SF-N	160	656	78	182	25	5	6	63	45	62	.277	.331	.358	87	-11	12	6	0	**.993**	-5	*2-160/3-1	-0.7
1974	SF-N	108	390	33	97	15	2	0	22	22	32	.249	.294	.297	63	-19	7	3	0	.979	-4	2-103	-1.9
1975	SD-N	146	565	57	158	21	3	4	43	25	51	.280	.314	.349	89	-10	8	8	-2	.970	4	*2-142	-0.1
1976	SD-N	135	520	48	137	18	0	2	36	18	38	.263	.289	.310	76	-18	5	3	-0	.971	2	*2-127	-0.9
1977	Det-A	151	615	83	190	19	10	5	51	38	61	.309	.351	.397	98	-1	4	4	-1	.970	3	*2-151/D-1	1.1
1978	Oak-A	13	43	5	6	1	0	0	2	1	6	.140	.159	.163	-10	-6	0	0	0	.944	-12	2-13	-1.9
Total	13	1499	5566	610	1491	211	46	45	438	298	561	.268	.309	.347	82	-137	80	47	-4	.974	-37	2-1275,S-165/3D	-9.1

■ OLLIE FUHRMAN
Fuhrman, Alfred George b: 7/20/1896, Jordan, Minn. d: 1/11/69, Peoria, Ill. BB/TR, 5'11", 185 lbs. Deb: 4/13/22

YEAR	TM/L	G	AB	R	H	2B	3B	HR	RBI	BB	SO	AVG	OBP	SLG	PRO+	BR/A	SB	CS	SBR	FA	FR	G/POS	TPR
1922	Phi-A	6	6	1	2	0	0	0	0	0	0	.333	.333	.500	112	0	0	0	0	1.000	0	/C-4	0.0

■ DOT FULGHUM
Fulghum, James Lavoisier b: 7/4/1900, Valdosta, Ga. d: 11/11/67, Miami, Fla. BR/TR, 5'8.5", 165 lbs. Deb: 9/15/21

YEAR	TM/L	G	AB	R	H	2B	3B	HR	RBI	BB	SO	AVG	OBP	SLG	PRO+	BR/A	SB	CS	SBR	FA	FR	G/POS	TPR
1921	Phi-A	2	2	0	0	0	0	0	0	0	1	.000	.333	.000	-9	-0	0	0	0	.000	0	/S-1	0.0

■ NIG FULLER
Fuller, Charles F. b: 3/30/1879, Toledo, Ohio d: 11/12/47, Toledo, Ohio BR/TR, 5'11", 165 lbs. Deb: 7/1/02

YEAR	TM/L	G	AB	R	H	2B	3B	HR	RBI	BB	SO	AVG	OBP	SLG	PRO+	BR/A	SB	CS	SBR	FA	FR	G/POS	TPR
1902	Bro-N	3	9	0	0	0	0	0	1	0		.000	.000	.000	-99	-2	0			1.000	-1	/C-3	-0.3

■ FRANK FULLER
Fuller, Frank Edward "Rabbit" b: 1/1/1893, Detroit, Mich. d: 10/29/65, Warren, Mich. BB/TR, 5'7", 150 lbs. Deb: 4/14/15

YEAR	TM/L	G	AB	R	H	2B	3B	HR	RBI	BB	SO	AVG	OBP	SLG	PRO+	BR/A	SB	CS	SBR	FA	FR	G/POS	TPR
1915	Det-A	14	32	6	5	0	0	0	2	9	7	.156	.341	.156	47	-2	2	3	-1	.962	-6	/2-9,S-1	-0.9
1916	Det-A	20	10	2	1	0	0	0	1	1	4	.100	.182	.100	-15	-1	3			.846	3	/2-8,S-1	0.1
1923	Bos-A	6	21	3	5	0	0	0	0	1	1	.238	.273	.238	35	-2	1	1	-0	.952	2	/2-6	0.0
Total	3	40	63	11	11	0	0	0	3	11	12	.175	.297	.175	35	-5	6	4		.938	-1	/2-23,S-2	-0.8

■ HARRY FULLER
Fuller, Henry W. b: 12/5/1862, Cincinnati, Ohio d: 12/12/1895, Cincinnati, Ohio Deb: 4/8/1891 F

YEAR	TM/L	G	AB	R	H	2B	3B	HR	RBI	BB	SO	AVG	OBP	SLG	PRO+	BR/A	SB	CS	SBR	FA	FR	G/POS	TPR
1891	StL-a	1	2	0	0	0	0	0				.000	.000	.000	-87	-0	0			.000	-1	/3-1	-0.1

■ JIM FULLER
Fuller, James Hardy b: 11/28/50, Bethesda, Md. BR/TR, 6'3", 215 lbs. Deb: 9/10/73

YEAR	TM/L	G	AB	R	H	2B	3B	HR	RBI	BB	SO	AVG	OBP	SLG	PRO+	BR/A	SB	CS	SBR	FA	FR	G/POS	TPR
1973	Bal-A	9	26	2	3	0	0	2	4	1	17	.115	.148	.346	36	-2	0	0	0	1.000	1	/O-5,1-2,D	-0.1
1974	Bal-A	64	189	17	42	11	0	7	28	8	68	.222	.265	.392	90	-4	1	0	0	.960	-2	O-59/1-4,D	-0.8
1977	Hou-N	34	100	5	16	6	0	2	9	10	45	.160	.243	.280	44	-8	0	1	-1	.983	5	O-27/1-1	-0.5
Total	3	107	315	24	61	17	0	11	41	19	130	.194	.249	.352	70	-14	1	1	-0	.969	4	/O-91,1-7,D	-1.4

■ JOHN FULLER
Fuller, John Edward b: 1/29/50, Lynwood, Cal. BL/TL, 6'2", 180 lbs. Deb: 5/9/74

YEAR	TM/L	G	AB	R	H	2B	3B	HR	RBI	BB	SO	AVG	OBP	SLG	PRO+	BR/A	SB	CS	SBR	FA	FR	G/POS	TPR
1974	Atl-N	3	3	1	1	0	0	0	0	0	0	.333	.333	.333	83	0	0	0	0	1.000	-0	/O-1	0.0

■ VERN FULLER
Fuller, Vernon Gordon b: 3/1/44, Menomonie, Wis. BR/TR, 6'1", 170 lbs. Deb: 9/5/64

YEAR	TM/L	G	AB	R	H	2B	3B	HR	RBI	BB	SO	AVG	OBP	SLG	PRO+	BR/A	SB	CS	SBR	FA	FR	G/POS	TPR
1964	Cle-A	2	1	0	0	0	0	0	0	0	0	.000	.000	.000	-99	-0	0	0	0	.000	0	H	0.0
1966	Cle-A	16	47	7	11	2	1	2	2	7	6	.234	.357	.447	129	2	0	0	0	1.000	-4	2-16	-0.1
1967	Cle-A	73	206	18	46	10	0	7	21	19	55	.223	.301	.374	98	-1	2	3	-1	.986	0	2-64/S-2	0.2
1968	Cle-A	97	244	14	59	8	2	0	18	24	49	.242	.320	.291	87	-3	2	2	-1	.988	-12	2-73,3-23/S	-1.4
1969	Cle-A	108	254	25	60	11	1	4	22	20	53	.236	.297	.335	74	-9	2	1	0	.978	9	*2-102/3-7	0.6
1970	Cle-A	29	33	3	6	2	0	1	2	3	6	.182	.250	.333	57	-2	0	0	0	.919	3	2-16/3-4,1	0.1
Total	6	325	785	67	182	33	4	14	65	73	172	.232	.307	.338	87	-13	6	6	-2	.982	-4	2-271/3-34,S1	-0.6

■ SHORTY FULLER
Fuller, William Benjamin b: 10/10/1867, Cincinnati, Ohio d: 4/11/04, Cincinnati, Ohio BR/TR, 5'6", 157 lbs. Deb: 7/19/1888 F

YEAR	TM/L	G	AB	R	H	2B	3B	HR	RBI	BB	SO	AVG	OBP	SLG	PRO+	BR/A	SB	CS	SBR	FA	FR	G/POS	TPR
1888	Was-N	49	170	11	31	5	2	0	12	10	14	.182	.232	.253	52	-9	6			.845	-6	S-47/2-2	-1.3
1889	StL-a	140	517	91	117	18	6	0	51	52	56	.226	.303	.284	60	-31	38			**.913**	0	*S-140	-1.9
1890	StL-a	130	526	118	146	9	9	1			73	.278	.377	.335	96	-4	60			.870	1	*S-130	0.3
1891	StL-a	137	586	107	127	15	7	2	63	67	28	.217	.301	.276	57	-38	42			.856	-10	*S-103,2-39	-3.5
1892	NY-N	141	508	74	115	11	4	1	48	52	22	.226	.298	.270	73	-16	37			.888	1	*S-141	-0.8
1893	NY-N	130	474	78	112	14	6	0	51	60	21	.236	.325	.300	66	-23	26			.911	11	*S-130	-0.5
1894	*NY-N	93	368	81	104	14	4	2	46	52	16	.283	.374	.359	78	-12	32			.884	-4	*S-89/O-2,32	-0.9
1895	NY-N	126	458	82	103	11	3	0	32	64	34	.225	.320	.262	53	-30	15			.913	34	*S-126	0.8
1896	NY-N	18	72	10	12	0	0	0	7	14	5	.167	.310	.167	28	-7	4			.874	1	S-18	-0.5
Total	9	964	3679	652	867	97	43	6	310	444	196	.236	.323	.290	67	-168	260			.891	26	S-924/2-42,3O	-8.3

■ CHICK FULLIS
Fullis, Charles Philip b: 2/27/04, Girardville, Pa. d: 3/28/46, Ashland, Pa. BR/TR, 5'9", 170 lbs. Deb: 4/13/28

YEAR	TM/L	G	AB	R	H	2B	3B	HR	RBI	BB	SO	AVG	OBP	SLG	PRO+	BR/A	SB	CS	SBR	FA	FR	G/POS	TPR
1928	NY-N	11	1	5	0	0	0	0	0	1	1	.000	.500	.000	41	0	0			.000	0	H	0.0
1929	NY-N	86	274	67	79	11	1	7	29	30	26	.288	.365	.412	92	-3	7			.962	-12	O-78	-1.8
1930	NY-N	13	6	2	0	0	0	0	0	0	1	.000	.000	.000	-99	-2	1			.000	-1	/O-2	-0.3
1931	NY-N	89	302	61	99	15	2	3	28	23	13	.328	.383	.421	119	8	13			.988	-4	O-68/2-9	0.1
1932	NY-N	96	235	35	70	14	1	1	21	11	12	.298	.332	.396	97	-1	1			.990	-8	O-55/2-1	-1.2
1933	Phi-N	151	647	91	200	31	6	1	45	36	34	.309	.350	.380	96	-3	18			.977	8	*O-151/3-1	-0.3
1934	Phi-N	28	102	8	23	6	0	0	12	10	4	.225	.301	.284	51	-7	2			.956	-4	O-27	-1.2
	*StL-N	69	199	21	52	9	1	0	26	14	11	.261	.310	.317	64	-10	4			.969	-3	O-56	-1.4
	Yr	97	301	29	75	15	1	0	38	24	15	.249	.307	.306	59	-17	6			.966	-6	O-83	-2.6
1936	StL-N	47	89	15	25	6	1	0	6	7	5	.281	.333	.371	90	-1	0			1.000	-0	O-28	-0.5
Total	8	590	1855	305	548	92	14	12	167	132	113	.295	.347	.380	92	-19	46			.977	-23	O-463/2-10,3	-6.4

■ CHICK FULMER
Fulmer, Charles John b: 2/12/1851, Philadelphia, Pa. d: 2/15/40, Philadelphia, Pa. BR/TR, 6', 158 lbs. Deb: 8/23/1871 FU

YEAR	TM/L	G	AB	R	H	2B	3B	HR	RBI	BB	SO	AVG	OBP	SLG	PRO+	BR/A	SB	CS	SBR	FA	FR	G/POS	TPR
1871	Rok-n	16	63	11	17	1	3	0	3	5	1	.270	.324	.381	106	1	0					S-15/1-1	0.1
1872	Mut-n	36	167	28	51	2	1	1	12	2	3	.305	.314	.347	110	3						3-23,S-13	0.0
1873	Phi-n	49	236	42	66	11	3	1	37	2	3	.280	.286	.364	87	-5						*S-49/P-2,C1	-0.4
1874	Phi-n	57	259	49	72	5	3	0			1	.278	.281	.320	88	-4						S-31,3-26	-0.4
1875	Phi-n	69	293	50	65	5	1	0			0	.222	.222	.246	59	-12						*S-54,3-14	-1.2
1876	Lou-N	66	267	30	73	9	5	1	29	1	10	.273	.276	.356	93	-5				.861	-3	*S-66	-0.8
1879	Buf-N	70	306	30	82	11	6	0	28	5	34	.268	.280	.337	100	-0				.905	17	*2-76	2.0
1880	Buf-N	11	44	3	7	0	0	0	2	3	4	.159	.196	.159	21	-3				.882	-2	2-11	-0.5
1882	Cin-a	79	324	54	91	13	4	0		10		.281	.302	.346	112	3				**.897**	-13	*S-79	-0.6

YEAR	TM/L	G	AB	R	H	2B	3B	HR	RBI	BB	SO	AVG	OBP	SLG	PRO+	BR/A	SB	CS	SBR	FA	FR	G/POS	TPR
1883	Cin-a	92	362	52	92	13	5	5		12		.254	.278	.359	98	-2				.863	-2	*S-92	-0.1
1884	Cin-a	31	114	13	20	2	1	0		1		.175	.183	.211	27	-9				.786	-10	S-29/O-2,3	-1.8
	StL-a	1	5	0	0	0	0	0		0		.000	.000	.000	-97	-1				.778	-1	/2-1	-0.2
	Yr	32	119	13	20	2	1	0		1		.168	.175	.202	22	-10				.786	-11	S-29/O-2,32	-2.0
Total	5 n	227	1018	180	271	24	11	2	52	10	7	.266	.273	.317	85	-17						S-162/3-63,P1C	-1.9
Total	6	356	1422	180	365	48	20	6	58	31	48	.257	.273	.331	92	-18				.867	-13	S-266/2-88,O3	-2.0

■ CHRIS FULMER
Fulmer, Christopher b: 7/4/1858, Tamaqua, Pa. d: 11/9/31, Tamaqua, Pa. BR/TR, 5'8", 165 lbs. Deb: 8/4/1884

YEAR	TM/L	G	AB	R	H	2B	3B	HR	RBI	BB	SO	AVG	OBP	SLG	PRO+	BR/A	SB	CS	SBR	FA	FR	G/POS	TPR
1884	Was-U	48	181	39	50	9	0	0		11		.276	.318	.326	78	-5				.937	0	C-34,O-16/1	-0.2
1886	Bal-a	80	270	54	66	9	3	1		48		.244	.363	.311	115	8	29			.949	-4	C-68,O-12/P	0.9
1887	Bal-a	56	201	52	54	11	4	0		36		.269	.382	.363	115	6	35			.913	-11	C-48/O-8	0.0
1888	Bal-a	52	166	20	31	5	1	0	10	21		.187	.286	.229	67	-5	10			.903	-16	C-45/O-7	-1.6
1889	Bal-a	16	58	11	15	3	1	0	13	6	12	.259	.338	.345	93	-1	2			.938	-5	O-14/C-2	-0.5
Total	5	252	876	176	216	37	9	1	23	122	12	.247	.343	.313	97	3	76			.929	-36	C-197/O-57,1P	-1.4

■ WASHINGTON FULMER
Fulmer, Washington Fayette b: 6/15/1840, Philadelphia, Pa. d: 12/8/07, Philadelphia, Pa. Deb: 7/19/1875 F

YEAR	TM/L	G	AB	R	H	2B	3B	HR	RBI	BB	SO	AVG	OBP	SLG	PRO+	BR/A	SB	CS	SBR	FA	FR	G/POS	TPR
1875	Atl-n	1	4	1	2	0	0	0		0		.500	.500	.500	284	1						/3-1	0.1

■ DAVE FULTZ
Fultz, David Lewis b: 5/29/1875, Staunton, Va. d: 10/29/59, DeLand, Fla. BR/TR, 5'11", 170 lbs. Deb: 7/1/1898

YEAR	TM/L	G	AB	R	H	2B	3B	HR	RBI	BB	SO	AVG	OBP	SLG	PRO+	BR/A	SB	CS	SBR	FA	FR	G/POS	TPR
1898	Phi-N	19	55	7	10	2	2	0	5	6		.182	.262	.291	61	-3	1			.871	-2	O-14/2-3,S	-0.5
1899	Phi-N	2	5	0	2	0	0	0	0	0		.400	.400	.400	124	0	1			.750	-1	/2-1,S-1	0.0
	Bal-N	57	210	31	62	3	2	0	18	13		.295	.342	.328	80	-6	17			.940	-7	O-31,3-20/21	-1.3
	Yr	59	215	31	64	3	2	0	18	13		.298	.343	.330	81	-6	18			.940	-7	O-31,3-20/2S1	-1.3
1901	Phi-A	132	561	95	164	17	9	0	52	32		.292	.334	.355	87	-10	36			.935	-6	*O-106,2-18/S	-2.1
1902	Phi-A	129	506	109	153	20	5	1	49	62		.302	.381	.368	104	5	44			.961	-5	*O-114,2-16	-0.8
1903	NY-A	79	295	39	66	12	1	0	25	25		.224	.295	.271	67	-11	29			.933	-2	O-77/3-2	-1.9
1904	NY-A	97	339	39	93	17	4	2	32	24		.274	.324	.366	113	5	17			.976	3	O-90	0.2
1905	NY-A	129	422	49	98	13	3	0	42	39		.232	.308	.277	77	-10	44			.966	-6	*O-122	-2.5
Total	7	644	2393	369	648	84	26	3	223	201		.271	.332	.331	89	-31	189			.952	-26	O-554/2-40,3S1	-8.9

■ MARK FUNDERBURK
Funderburk, Mark Clifford b: 5/16/57, Charlotte, N.C. BR/TR, 6'4", 226 lbs. Deb: 9/4/81

YEAR	TM/L	G	AB	R	H	2B	3B	HR	RBI	BB	SO	AVG	OBP	SLG	PRO+	BR/A	SB	CS	SBR	FA	FR	G/POS	TPR
1981	Min-A	8	15	2	3	1	0	0	2	1		.200	.294	.267	59	-1	0	0	0	1.000	-1	/O-6,D-1	-0.2
1985	Min-A	23	70	7	22	7	1	2	13	5	12	.314	.360	.529	132	3	0	1	-1	1.000	-1	D-15/O-5,1	0.1
Total	2	31	85	9	25	8	1	2	15	7	13	.294	.348	.482	120	2	0	1	-1	1.000	-2	/D-16,O-11,1	-0.1

■ LIZ FUNK
Funk, Elias Calvin b: 10/28/04, LaCygne, Kan. d: 1/16/68, Norman, Okla. BL/TL, 5'8.5", 160 lbs. Deb: 4/26/29

YEAR	TM/L	G	AB	R	H	2B	3B	HR	RBI	BB	SO	AVG	OBP	SLG	PRO+	BR/A	SB	CS	SBR	FA	FR	G/POS	TPR
1929	NY-A	1	0	0	0	0	0	0	0	0	0	—	—	—			0	0	0	.000	0	R	0.0
1930	Det-A	140	527	74	145	26	11	4	65	29	39	.275	.319	.389	77	-19	12	6	0	.965	8	*O-129	-1.9
1932	Chi-A	122	440	59	114	21	5	2	40	43	19	.259	.325	.343	78	-14	17	15	-4	.979	7	*O-120	-1.7
1933	Chi-A	10	9	1	2	0	0	0	0	1	0	.222	.300	.222	42	-1	0	0	0	.000	-1	/O-2	-0.2
Total	4	273	976	134	261	47	16	6	105	73	58	.267	.322	.367	77	-34	29	21	-4	.972	14	O-251	-3.8

■ CARL FURILLO
Furillo, Carl Anthony "Skoonj" or "The Reading Rifle"
b: 3/8/22, Stony Creek Mills, Pa. d: 1/21/89, Stony Creek Mills, Pa. BR/TR, 6', 190 lbs. Deb: 4/16/46

YEAR	TM/L	G	AB	R	H	2B	3B	HR	RBI	BB	SO	AVG	OBP	SLG	PRO+	BR/A	SB	CS	SBR	FA	FR	G/POS	TPR
1946	Bro-N	117	335	29	95	18	6	3	35	31	20	.284	.346	.400	110	4	6			.984	9	*O-112	0.9
1947	*Bro-N	124	437	61	129	24	7	8	88	34	24	.295	.347	.437	103	1	7			.977	9	*O-121	-0.2
1948	Bro-N	108	364	55	108	20	4	4	44	43	32	.297	.374	.407	108	5	6			.983	9	*O-104	0.8
1949	*Bro-N	142	549	95	177	27	10	18	106	37	29	.322	.368	.506	127	19	4			.965	5	*O-142	1.7
1950	Bro-N	153	620	99	189	30	6	18	106	41	40	.305	.353	.460	110	8	8			.971	3	*O-153	0.4
1951	Bro-N	158	667	93	197	32	4	16	91	43	33	.295	.344	.427	104	3	8	7	-2	.986	16	*O-157	1.2
1952	*Bro-N☆	134	425	52	105	18	4	8	59	31	33	.247	.304	.351	80	-12	1	4	-2	.988	-1	*O-131	-2.0
1953	*Bro-N☆	132	479	82	165	38	6	21	92	34	32	.344	.393	.580	146	31	1	1	-0	.988	4	*O-131	2.9
1954	Bro-N	150	547	56	161	23	1	19	96	49	35	.294	.358	.444	104	3	2	4	-2	.972	4	*O-149	0.0
1955	*Bro-N	140	523	83	164	24	3	26	95	43	43	.314	.373	.520	130	22	4	5	-2	.981	-3	*O-140	1.1
1956	Bro-N	149	523	66	151	30	0	21	83	57	41	.289	.360	.467	111	9	1	1	-0	.984	-9	*O-146	-0.9
1957	Bro-N	119	395	61	121	17	4	12	66	29	33	.306	.361	.461	108	5	0	2	-1	.988	-5	*O-107	-0.8
1958	LA-N	122	411	54	119	19	3	18	83	35	28	.290	.348	.482	113	7	0	2	-1	.975	-8	*O-119	-0.8
1959	*LA-N	50	93	8	27	6	0	4	13	7	11	.290	.340	.333	75	-3	0	0		.920	-5	O-25	-0.9
1960	LA-N	8	10	1	2	0	1	0	1	0	2	.200	.200	.400	56	-1	0	0		1.000	-0	/O-2	-0.1
Total	15	1806	6378	895	1910	324	56	192	1058	514	436	.299	.356	.458	112	102	48	26		.979	22	*O-1739	3.3

■ EDDIE FUSSELBACK
Fusselback, Edward L. b: 7/17/1856, Philadelphia, Pa. d: 4/14/26, Philadelphia, Pa. 5'6", 156 lbs. Deb: 5/3/1882

YEAR	TM/L	G	AB	R	H	2B	3B	HR	RBI	BB	SO	AVG	OBP	SLG	PRO+	BR/A	SB	CS	SBR	FA	FR	G/POS	TPR
1882	StL-a	35	136	13	31	2	0	0		5		.228	.255	.243	66	-5				.853	0	C-19,O-15/P	-0.1
1884	Bal-U	68	303	60	86	16	3	1		3		.284	.291	.366	70	-14				.912	19	C-54/3-6,SO	0.9
1885	Phi-a	5	19	2	6	1	0	0		0		.316	.316	.368	109	0				.911	1	/C-5	0.1
1888	Lou-a	1	4	0	1	0	0	0	1	0		.250	.250	.250	62	-0	0			1.000	0	/O-1	0.0
Total	4	109	462	75	124	19	3	1	1	8		.268	.281	.329	71	-19	0			.901	22	/C-78,O-20,3SP	0.9

■ LES FUSSELMAN
Fusselman, Lester Leroy b: 3/7/21, Pryor, Okla. d: 5/21/70, Cleveland, Ohio BR/TR, 6'1", 195 lbs. Deb: 4/16/52

YEAR	TM/L	G	AB	R	H	2B	3B	HR	RBI	BB	SO	AVG	OBP	SLG	PRO+	BR/A	SB	CS	SBR	FA	FR	G/POS	TPR
1952	StL-N	32	63	5	10	3	0	1	3	0	9	.159	.159	.254	13	-8	0	0	0	.991	3	C-32	-0.4
1953	StL-N	11	8	1	2	1	0	0	0	0	0	.250	.250	.375	60	-0	0	0	0	1.000	2	C-11	0.1
Total	2	43	71	6	12	4	0	1	3	0	9	.169	.169	.268	18	-8	0	0	0	.992	5	/C-43	-0.3

■ GABE GABLER
Gabler, William Louis b: 8/4/30, St.Louis, Mo. BL/TR, 6'1", 190 lbs. Deb: 9/16/58

YEAR	TM/L	G	AB	R	H	2B	3B	HR	RBI	BB	SO	AVG	OBP	SLG	PRO+	BR/A	SB	CS	SBR	FA	FR	G/POS	TPR
1958	Chi-N	3	3	0	0	0	0	0	0	0	0	.000	.000	.000	-99	-1	0	0	0	.000	0	H	-0.1

■ LEN GABRIELSON
Gabrielson, Leonard Gary b: 2/14/40, Oakland, Cal. BL/TR, 6'4", 210 lbs. Deb: 9/9/60 F

YEAR	TM/L	G	AB	R	H	2B	3B	HR	RBI	BB	SO	AVG	OBP	SLG	PRO+	BR/A	SB	CS	SBR	FA	FR	G/POS	TPR
1960	Mil-N	4	3	1	0	0	0	0	0	0	0	.000	.250	.000	-27	-1	0	0	0	.000	-0	/O-1	-0.1
1963	Mil-N	46	120	14	26	5	0	3	15	8	23	.217	.266	.333	72	-4	1	1	-0	1.000	-3	O-22,1-16/3	-1.0
1964	Mil-N	24	38	0	7	2	0	0	1	1		.184	.205	.237	24	-4	1	0		1.000	-1	1-12/O-2	-0.5
	Chi-N	89	272	22	67	11	2	5	23	19	37	.246	.298	.357	80	-7	9	4	0	.984	-1	O-68/1-8	-1.2
	Yr	113	310	22	74	13	2	5	24	20	45	.239	.287	.342	74	-11	10	4	1	.984	-2	O-70,1-20	-1.7
1965	Chi-N	28	48	4	12	0	0	3	5	7	16	.250	.345	.438	116	1	0	2	-1	1.000	-3	O-14/1-1	-0.4
	SF-N	88	269	36	81	6	5	4	26	26	48	.301	.367	.405	114	6	4	0	1	.975	1	O-77/1-5	0.4
	Yr	116	317	40	93	6	5	7	31	33	64	.293	.364	.410	114	7	4	2	0	.977	-2	O-91/1-6	0.0
1966	SF-N	94	240	27	52	7	0	4	16	21	51	.217	.280	.296	58	-13	0	0	-1	.948	-9	O-67/1-6	-2.8
1967	Cal-A	11	12	2	1	0	0	0	2	2	4	.083	.214	.083	-9	-2	0	0		.000	-0	/O-1	-0.2
	LA-N	90	238	20	62	10	3	7	29	15	41	.261	.307	.416	114	3	3	1	0	.980	-4	O-68	-0.3
1968	LA-N	108	304	38	82	16	1	10	35	32	47	.270	.339	.428	140	14	1	1	-0	.976	-3	O-86	0.7
1969	LA-N	83	178	13	49	5	1	4	18	12	25	.270	.316	.326	86	-4	1	2	-1	.981	-7	O-47/1-2	-1.4
1970	LA-N	43	42	1	8	2	0	0	2	2	5	.190	.209	.238	20	-5	0	0	0	1.000	-0	/O-2,1-1	-0.5
Total	9	708	1764	178	446	64	12	37	176	145	315	.253	.311	.366	94	-15	20	12	-1	.977	-31	O-455/1-51,3	-7.3

■ LEN GABRIELSON
Gabrielson, Leonard Hilbourne b: 9/8/15, Oakland, Cal. BL/TL, 6'3", 210 lbs. Deb: 4/21/39 F

YEAR	TM/L	G	AB	R	H	2B	3B	HR	RBI	BB	SO	AVG	OBP	SLG	PRO+	BR/A	SB	CS	SBR	FA	FR	G/POS	TPR
1939	Phi-N	5	18	3	4	0	0	0	1	2	3	.222	.300	.222	43	-1	0			.977	2	/1-5	0.0

YEAR	TM/L	G	AB	R	H	2B	3B	HR	RBI	BB	SO	AVG	OBP	SLG	PRO+	BR/A	SB	CS	SBR	FA	FR	G/POS	TPR

◼ EDDIE GAEDEL
Gaedel, Edward Carl b: 6/8/25, Chicago, Ill. d: 6/18/61, Chicago, Ill. BR/TL, 3'7", 65 lbs. Deb: 8/19/51

1951	StL-A	1	0	0	0	0	0	0	0	1	0	—	1.000	—	182	0	0	0	0	.000	0	H	0.0

◼ GARY GAETTI
Gaetti, Gary Joseph b: 8/19/58, Centralia, Ill. BR/TR, 6', 184 lbs. Deb: 9/20/81

1981	Min-A	9	26	4	5	0	0	2	3	0	6	.192	.192	.423	68	-1	0	0	0	1.000	1	/3-8,D-1	0.0
1982	Min-A	145	508	59	117	25	4	25	84	37	107	.230	.286	.443	94	-6	0	4	-2	.963	-3	*3-142/S-2,D	-1.5
1983	Min-A	157	584	81	143	30	3	21	78	54	121	.245	.313	.414	95	-5	7	1	2	.967	13	*3-154/S-3,D	0.7
1984	Min-A	162	588	55	154	29	4	5	65	44	81	.262	.318	.350	81	-15	11	5	0	.960	15	*3-154/O-8,S	-0.1
1985	Min-A	160	560	71	138	31	0	20	63	37	89	.246	.301	.409	87	-11	13	5	1	.962	17	*3-156/O-4,1D	0.4
1986	Min-A	157	596	91	171	34	1	34	108	52	108	.287	.350	.518	129	23	14	15	-5	.956	19	*3-156/S-2,2O	3.3
1987	*Min-A	154	584	95	150	36	2	31	109	37	92	.257	.304	.485	101	-1	10	7	-1	.973	-4	*3-150/D-2	-0.8
1988	Min-A★	133	468	66	141	29	2	28	88	36	85	.301	.358	.551	146	27	7	4	-0	.977	-6	*3-115/S-2,D	2.1
1989	Min-A★	130	498	63	125	11	4	19	75	25	87	.251	.291	.404	88	-10	6	2	1	.973	11	*3-125/1-2,D	0.3
1990	Min-A	154	577	61	132	27	5	16	85	36	101	.229	.278	.376	76	-20	6	1	1	.959	14	*3-151/1-2,S	-0.4
1991	Cal-A	152	586	58	144	22	1	18	66	33	104	.246	.295	.379	85	-13	5	5	-2	.965	25	*3-152	1.1
1992	Cal-A	130	456	41	103	13	2	12	48	21	79	.226	.269	.342	70	-19	3	1	0	.927	13	3-67,1-44,D	-1.0
1993	Cal-A	20	50	3	9	2	0	4	5	12	.180	.255	.220	28	-5	1	0	0	.857	2	/3-7,1-6,D	-0.3
	KC-A	82	281	37	72	18	1	14	46	16	75	.256	.315	.477	103	0	0	3	-2	.974	5	3-72,1-18/D	0.3
	Yr	102	331	40	81	20	1	14	50	21	87	.245	.306	.438	92	-5	1	3	-2	.970	7	3-79,1-24/D	0.0
1994	KC-A	90	327	53	94	15	3	12	57	19	63	.287	.330	.462	94	-4	0	2	-1	.982	3	3-85/1-9	-0.2
Total	14	1835	6689	838	1698	322	32	257	979	452	1210	.254	.307	.427	95	-60	83	55	-8	.964	125	*3-1694/1-82,DOS2	3.9

◼ FABIAN GAFFKE
Gaffke, Fabian Sebastian b: 8/5/13, Milwaukee, Wis. d: 2/8/92, Milwaukee, Wis. BR/TR, 5'10", 185 lbs. Deb: 9/9/36

1936	Bos-A	15	55	5	7	2	0	1	3	4	5	.127	.200	.218	3	-9	0	0	0	1.000	-1	O-15	-1.0
1937	Bos-A	54	184	32	53	10	4	6	34	15	25	.288	.342	.484	102	-0	1	2	-1	.965	-4	O-50	-0.7
1938	Bos-A	15	10	2	1	0	0	0	1	3	2	.100	.308	.100	6	-1	0	0	0	.000	-1	/O-2,C-1	-0.2
1939	Bos-A	1	1	0	0	0	0	0	1	0	0	.000	.000	.000	-96	0	0	0	0	.000	0	H	0.0
1941	Cle-A	4	4	0	1	0	0	0	0	2	2	.250	.500	.250	109	0	0	0	0	1.000	0	/O-2	0.0
1942	Cle-A	40	67	4	11	2	0	0	3	6	13	.164	.243	.194	25	-7	1	0	0	1.000	-2	O-16	-0.9
Total	6	129	321	43	73	14	4	7	42	30	47	.227	.297	.361	67	-17	2	2	-1	.979	-9	/O-85,C-1	-2.8

◼ PHIL GAGLIANO
Gagliano, Philip Joseph b: 12/27/41, Memphis, Tenn. BR/TR, 6'1", 185 lbs. Deb: 4/16/63 F

1963	StL-N	10	5	1	2	0	0	0	1	1	1	.400	.500	.400	149	0	0	0	0	1.000	2	/2-3,3-1	0.2
1964	StL-N	40	58	5	15	4	0	1	9	3	10	.259	.295	.379	81	-1	0	1	-1	.918	1	2-12/O-2,13	0.0
1965	StL-N	122	363	46	87	14	2	6	53	40	45	.240	.317	.355	81	-9	2	1	0	.960	-12	2-57,O-25,3	-1.8
1966	StL-N	90	213	23	54	8	2	2	15	24	29	.254	.332	.338	86	-3	2	1	0	.982	-4	3-41/1-8,O2	-0.9
1967	*StL-N	73	217	20	48	7	0	2	21	19	26	.221	.287	.281	64	-10	0	0	0	.972	-13	2-27,3-25/1S	-2.4
1968	*StL-N	53	105	13	24	4	2	0	13	7	12	.229	.283	.305	77	-3	0	0	0	.982	4	2-17,3-10/O	-0.6
1969	StL-N	62	128	7	29	2	0	1	10	14	12	.227	.303	.266	60	-6	0	1	-1	.989	-2	2-20/1-9,3O	-0.8
1970	StL-N	18	32	0	6	0	0	0	2	1	3	.188	.212	.188	8	-4	0	1	-1	1.000	-1	/3-6,1-3,2	-0.6
	Chi-N	26	40	5	6	0	0	0	5	5	5	.150	.244	.150	7	-5	0	0	0	.882	-1	2-16/1-1,3	-0.4
	Yr	44	72	5	12	0	0	0	7	6	8	.167	.231	.167	8	-9	0	1	-1	.980	-0	2-18/3-7,1	-1.0
1971	Bos-A	47	68	11	22	5	0	0	13	11	5	.324	.418	.397	123	3	0	0	0	1.000	-5	O-11/2-7,3	-0.2
1972	Bos-A	52	82	9	21	4	1	0	10	10	13	.256	.337	.329	94	-1	0	1	0	.962	2	O-12/3-5,21	0.2
1973	*Cin-N	63	69	8	20	2	0	0	7	13	16	.290	.402	.319	108	2	0	0	0	.824	-1	/3-7,2-4,1O	0.2
1974	Cin-N	46	31	2	2	0	0	0	0	15	7	.065	.370	.065	27	-2	0	0	0	1.000	0	/2-2,1-1,3	-0.2
Total	12	702	1411	150	336	50	7	14	159	163	184	.238	.319	.313	77	-40	5	4	-1	.969	-34	2-172,3-130/O1S	-7.5

◼ RALPH GAGLIANO
Gagliano, Ralph Michael b: 10/8/46, Memphis, Tenn. BL/TR, 5'11", 170 lbs. Deb: 9/21/65 F

1965	Cle-A	1	0	0	0	0	0	0	0	0	0	—	—	—	—	0	0	0	0	.000	0	R	0.0

◼ GREG GAGNE
Gagne, Gregory Carpenter b: 11/12/61, Fall River, Mass. BR/TR, 5'11", 185 lbs. Deb: 6/5/83

1983	Min-A	10	27	3	3	1	0	0	3	0	6	.111	.111	.148	-28	-5	0	0	0	.923	-5	S-10	-1.0
1984	Min-A	2	1	0	0	0	0	0	0	0	0	.000	.000	.000	-96	-0	0	0	0	.000	0	/H	0.0
1985	Min-A	114	293	37	66	15	3	2	23	20	57	.225	.282	.317	60	-16	10	4	1	.968	4	*S-106/D-5	-0.3
1986	Min-A	156	472	63	118	22	6	12	54	30	108	.250	.303	.398	87	-9	12	10	-2	.959	-16	*S-155/2-4	-1.3
1987	*Min-A	137	437	68	116	28	7	10	40	25	84	.265	.311	.430	91	-7	6	6	-2	.970	17	*S-136/O-4,2D	1.8
1988	Min-A	149	461	70	109	20	6	14	48	27	110	.236	.289	.397	87	-9	15	7	0	.970	-15	*S-146/O-2,23	-1.3
1989	Min-A	149	460	69	125	29	7	9	48	17	80	.272	.301	.424	96	-4	11	4	1	.971	-4	*S-146/O-1	0.3
1990	Min-A	138	388	38	91	22	3	7	38	24	76	.235	.281	.361	73	-15	8	8	-2	.976	2	*S-135/O-1,D	-0.6
1991	*Min-A	139	408	52	108	23	3	8	42	26	72	.265	.314	.395	90	-6	11	9	-2	.984	4	*S-137/D-1	0.5
1992	Min-A	146	439	53	108	23	0	7	39	19	83	.246	.280	.346	72	-17	6	7	-2	.973	21	*S-141	1.1
1993	KC-A	159	540	66	151	32	3	10	57	33	93	.280	.321	.406	89	-10	10	12	-4	.986	6	*S-159	0.4
1994	KC-A	107	375	39	97	23	3	7	51	27	79	.259	.315	.392	75	-15	10	7	-7	.977	8	*S-106	-0.5
Total	12	1406	4301	557	1092	238	41	86	443	248	848	.254	.299	.388	82	-112	99	84	-21	.973	21	*S-1377/D-9,O23	-0.9

◼ ED GAGNIER
Gagnier, Edward J. b: 4/16/1883, Paris, France d: 9/13/46, Detroit, Mich. BR/TR, 5'9", 170 lbs. Deb: 4/14/14

1914	Bro-F	94	337	22	63	12	6	0	25	13	24	.187	.219	.234	18	-42	8			.933	-1	S-88/3-6	-3.7
1915	Bro-F	20	50	8	13	1	0	0	4	10	5	.260	.393	.280	82	-1	2			.930	2	S-13/2-6	0.3
	Buf-F	1	2	0	0	0	0	0	0	0	0	.000	.000	.000	-98	-1	0			.800	-2	/2-1	-0.1
	Yr	21	52	8	13	1	0	0	4	10	5	.250	.381	.269	76	-1	2			.930	2	S-13/2-7	0.2
Total	2	115	389	30	76	13	6	0	29	23	29	.195	.244	.239	26	-43	10			.933	2	S-101/2-7,3	-3.5

◼ CHICK GAGNON
Gagnon, Harold Dennis b: 9/27/1897, Millbury, Mass. d: 4/30/70, Wilmington, Del. BR/TR, 5'7.5", 158 lbs. Deb: 6/27/22

1922	Det-A	10	4	2	1	0	0	0	0	0	2	.250	.250	.250	32	-0	0	0	0	.000	-1	/S-1,3-1	-0.1
1924	Was-A	4	5	1	1	0	0	0	1	0	0	.200	.200	.200	3	-1	0	0	0	1.000	1	/S-2	0.0
Total	2	14	9	3	2	0	0	0	1	0	2	.222	.222	.222	16	-1	0	0	0	.000	0	/S-3,3-1	-0.1

◼ DEL GAINER
Gainer, Dellos Clinton "Sheriff" b: 11/10/1886, Montrose, W.Va. d: 1/29/47, Elkins, W.Va. BR/TR, 6', 180 lbs. Deb: 10/2/09

1909	Det-A	2	5	0	1	0	0	0	0	0		.200	.200	.200	25	-0	0			.929	-0	/1-2	-0.1
1911	Det-A	70	248	32	75	11	4	2	25	20		.302	.366	.403	109	3	10			.975	-4	1-69	-0.1
1912	Det-A	52	179	28	43	5	6	0	20	18		.240	.320	.335	90	-2	14			.986	-3	1-50/O-1	-0.6
1913	Det-A	105	363	47	97	16	8	2	25	30	45	.267	.333	.372	108	3	10			.988	-5	*1-103	-0.3
1914	Det-A	1	0	0	0	0	0	0	0	0	0	—	—	—		0	0			1.000	0	/1-1	0.0
	Bos-A	38	84	11	20	9	2	2	13	8	14	.238	.312	.464	133	3	2	2	-1	.981	-3	1-18,2-11/O	-0.1
	Yr	39	84	11	20	9	2	2	13	8	14	.238	.312	.464	133	3	2	2	-1	.982	-3	1-19,2-11/O	-0.1
1915	*Bos-A	82	200	30	59	5	8	1	29	21	31	.295	.371	.415	139	9	7	2	1	.988	9	1-56/O-6	1.0
1916	*Bos-A	56	142	14	36	6	0	3	18	10	24	.254	.303	.359	98	-1	5			.997	1	1-48/2-2	-0.1
1917	Bos-A	52	172	28	53	10	2	0	15	11	19	.308	.374	.424	145	9	1			.989	-1	1-50	0.7
1919	Bos-A	47	118	9	28	6	2	0	13	13	15	.237	.318	.322	85	-2	5			.978	-3	1-21,O-18	-0.7
1922	StL-N	43	97	19	26	7	4	2	23	14	6	.268	.360	.485	122	3	0	2	-0	.979	-1	1-26,O-10	-0.1
Total	10	548	1608	218	438	75	36	14	185	149	156	.272	.342	.390	113	24	54	6		.985	-19	1-444/O-36,2	-0.4

◼ JAY GAINER
Gainer, Johnathan Keith b: 10/8/66, Panama City, Fla. BL/TL, 6', 190 lbs. Deb: 5/14/93

1993	Col-N	23	41	4	7	0	0	3	6	4	12	.171	.244	.390	57	-3	1	1	-0	.982	-1	/1-7	-0.5

YEAR	TM/L	G	AB	R	H	2B	3B	HR	RBI	BB	SO	AVG	OBP	SLG	PRO+	BR/A	SB	CS	SBR	FA	FR	G/POS	TPR

■ JOE GAINES
Gaines, Arnesta Joe b: 11/22/36, Bryan, Tex. BR/TR, 6'1", 190 lbs. Deb: 6/29/60

YEAR	TM/L	G	AB	R	H	2B	3B	HR	RBI	BB	SO	AVG	OBP	SLG	PRO+	BR/A	SB	CS	SBR	FA	FR	G/POS	TPR
1960	Cin-N	11	15	2	3	0	0	0	1	0	1	.200	.200	.200	10	-2	0	0	0	1.000	-1	/O-3	-0.3
1961	Cin-N	5	3	2	0	0	0	0	0	2	1	.000	.400	.000	18	-0	0	0	0	.500	-1	/O-3	-0.2
1962	Cin-N	64	52	12	12	3	0	1	7	8	16	.231	.333	.346	80	-1	0	0	0	1.000	-3	O-13	-0.4
1963	Bal-A	66	126	24	36	4	1	6	20	20	39	.286	.384	.476	145	8	2	1	0	.945	-6	O-39	0.1
1964	Bal-A	16	26	2	4	0	0	1	2	3	7	.154	.241	.269	42	-2	0	0	0	.846	0	/O-5	-0.2
	Hou-N	89	307	37	78	9	7	7	34	27	69	.254	.318	.397	106	2	8	2	1	.957	-2	O-81	-0.3
1965	Hou-N	100	229	21	52	8	1	6	31	18	59	.227	.292	.349	86	-5	4	1	0	.913	-8	O-65	-1.5
1966	Hou-N	11	13	4	1	1	0	0	0	3	5	.077	.250	.154	17	-1	0	0	0	.500	-1	/O-3	-0.3
Total	7	362	771	104	186	25	9	21	95	81	197	.241	.317	.379	99	-2	14	4	2	.934	-21	O-212	-3.1

■ TY GAINEY
Gainey, Telmanch b: 12/25/60, Cheraw, S.C. BL/TR, 6'1", 190 lbs. Deb: 4/24/85

YEAR	TM/L	G	AB	R	H	2B	3B	HR	RBI	BB	SO	AVG	OBP	SLG	PRO+	BR/A	SB	CS	SBR	FA	FR	G/POS	TPR
1985	Hou-N	13	37	5	6	0	0	0	0	2	9	.162	.244	.162	16	-4	0	0	0	.913	-0	/O-9	-0.5
1986	Hou-N	26	50	6	15	3	1	1	6	6	19	.300	.375	.460	133	2	3	1	0	1.000	-3	O-19	-0.1
1987	Hou-N	18	24	1	3	0	0	0	1	2	9	.125	.192	.125	-14	-4	1	0	0	1.000	-0	/O-6	-0.4
Total	3	57	111	12	24	3	1	1	7	10	37	.216	.293	.288	62	-6	4	1	1	.968	-3	/O-34	-1.0

■ AUGIE GALAN
Galan, August John b: 5/25/12, Berkeley, Cal. d: 12/28/93, Fairfield, Cal. BB/TR, 6', 175 lbs. Deb: 4/29/34 C

YEAR	TM/L	G	AB	R	H	2B	3B	HR	RBI	BB	SO	AVG	OBP	SLG	PRO+	BR/A	SB	CS	SBR	FA	FR	G/POS	TPR
1934	Chi-N	66	192	31	50	6	2	5	22	16	15	.260	.317	.391	90	-3	4			.961	-9	2-43/3-3,S	-0.9
1935	*Chi-N	154	646	133	203	41	11	12	79	87	53	.314	.399	.467	131	31	22			.978	7	*O-154	3.1
1936	Chi-N★	145	575	74	152	26	4	8	81	67	50	.264	.344	.365	89	-8	16			.987	5	*O-145	-0.8
1937	Chi-N	147	611	104	154	24	10	18	78	79	48	.252	.339	.412	99	-1	23			.980	13	*O-140/2-8,S	0.7
1938	*Chi-N	110	395	52	113	16	9	6	69	49	17	.286	.368	.418	112	8	8			.987	2	*O-103	0.7
1939	Chi-N	148	549	104	167	36	8	6	91	75	26	.304	.392	.432	119	17	8			.970	-2	*O-145	0.9
1940	Chi-N	68	209	33	48	14	2	3	22	37	23	.230	.346	.359	96	-0	9			.984	0	O-54/2-2	-0.3
1941	Chi-N	65	120	18	25	3	0	1	13	22	10	.208	.331	.258	70	-4	0			.959	-5	O-31	-1.1
	*Bro-N	17	27	3	7	3	0	0	4	3	1	.259	.333	.370	94	-0	0			1.000	-0	/O-6	-0.1
	Yr	82	147	21	32	6	0	1	17	25	11	.218	.331	.279	74	-4	0			.967	-5	O-37	-1.2
1942	Bro-N	69	209	24	55	16	0	0	22	24	12	.263	.339	.340	97	-0	2			.990	-5	O-55/1-4,2	-0.8
1943	Bro-N★	139	495	83	142	26	3	9	67	103	39	.287	.412	.406	136	28	6			.981	16	*O-124,1-13	3.9
1944	Bro-N★	151	547	96	174	43	9	12	93	101	23	.318	.426	.495	162	49	4			.988	-2	*O-147/2-2	4.0
1945	Bro-N	152	576	114	177	36	7	9	92	114	27	.307	.423	.441	142	38	13			.988	-8	1-66,O-49,3	2.3
1946	Bro-N	99	274	53	85	22	5	3	38	68	21	.310	.451	.460	157	25	8			.935	-10	O-60,3-19,1	1.3
1947	Cin-N	124	392	60	123	18	2	6	61	94	19	.314	.449	.455	132	24	0			.988	-4	*O-118	1.4
1948	Cin-N	54	77	18	22	3	2	1	16	26	4	.286	.471	.455	157	8	0			.967	-2	O-18	0.5
1949	NY-N	22	17	0	1	1	0	0	2	5	3	.059	.273	.118	8	-2	0			1.000	-1	/1-3,O-1	-0.3
	Phi-N	12	26	4	8	2	0	0	9	2	2	.308	.486	.385	136	2	0	0	0	1.000	-1	/O-9	0.1
Total	16	1742	5937	1004	1706	336	74	100	830	979	393	.287	.390	.419	122	212	123	0		.981	-5	*O-1359/1-98,32S	14.6

■ ANDRES GALARRAGA
Galarraga, Andres Jose (b: Andres Jose Padovani (Galarraga)) b: 6/18/61, Caracas, Venez. BR/TR, 6'3", 235 lbs. Deb: 8/23/85

YEAR	TM/L	G	AB	R	H	2B	3B	HR	RBI	BB	SO	AVG	OBP	SLG	PRO+	BR/A	SB	CS	SBR	FA	FR	G/POS	TPR
1985	Mon-N	24	75	9	14	1	0	2	4	3	18	.187	.228	.280	44	-6	1	2	-1	.995	4	1-23	-0.5
1986	Mon-N	105	321	39	87	13	0	10	42	30	79	.271	.339	.405	105	2	6	5	-1	.995	-8	*1-102	-1.4
1987	Mon-N	147	551	72	168	40	3	13	90	41	127	.305	.364	.459	113	10	7	10	-4	.993	0	*1-146	-0.4
1988	Mon-N★	157	609	99	184	42	8	29	92	39	153	.302	.354	.540	147	34	13	4	2	.991	-4	*1-156	2.0
1989	Mon-N	152	572	76	147	30	1	23	85	48	158	.257	.329	.434	115	10	12	5	1	.992	-2	*1-147	-0.4
1990	Mon-N	155	579	65	148	29	0	20	87	40	169	.256	.308	.409	99	-2	10	1	2	.993	-5	*1-154	-1.7
1991	Mon-N	107	375	34	82	13	2	9	33	23	86	.219	.268	.336	70	-16	5	6	-2	.991	-2	*1-105	-2.4
1992	StL-N	95	325	38	79	14	2	10	39	11	69	.243	.285	.391	92	-5	5	4	-1	.991	-1	1-90	-1.3
1993	Col-N★	120	470	71	174	35	4	22	98	24	73	.370	.408	.602	143	27	2	4	-2	.990	7	*1-119	2.2
1994	Col-N	103	417	77	133	21	0	31	85	19	93	.319	.360	.592	123	12	8	3	1	.992	-5	*1-103	-0.1
Total	10	1165	4294	580	1216	238	20	169	655	278	1025	.283	.336	.466	115	66	69	44	-6	.992	-12	*1-1145	-4.0

■ MILT GALATZER
Galatzer, Milton b: 5/4/07, Chicago, Ill. d: 1/29/76, San Francisco, Cal BL/TL, 5'10", 168 lbs. Deb: 6/25/33

YEAR	TM/L	G	AB	R	H	2B	3B	HR	RBI	BB	SO	AVG	OBP	SLG	PRO+	BR/A	SB	CS	SBR	FA	FR	G/POS	TPR
1933	Cle-A	57	160	19	38	2	1	1	17	23	21	.237	.333	.281	61	-8	2	3	-1	.975	-0	O-40/1-5	-1.2
1934	Cle-A	49	196	29	53	10	2	0	15	21	21	.270	.344	.342	76	-7	3	4		.980	3	O-49	-0.6
1935	Cle-A	93	259	45	78	9	3	0	19	35	16	.301	.389	.359	93	-1	4	5	-2	.934	-8	O-81	-1.3
1936	Cle-A	49	97	12	23	4	1	0	6	13	8	.237	.333	.299	57	-6	1	2	-1	.964	-8	O-42/P-1,1	-1.4
1939	Cin-N	3	5	0	0	0	0	0	0	0	1	.000	.000	.000	-99	-1	0			1.000	-0	/1-2	-0.2
Total	5	251	717	105	192	25	7	1	57	92	46	.268	.354	.326	75	-24	10	12		.959	-14	O-212/1-8,P	-4.7

■ AL GALLAGHER
Gallagher, Alan Mitchell Edward George Patrick Henry b: 10/19/45, San Francisco, Cal. BR/TR, 6', 180 lbs. Deb: 4/7/70

YEAR	TM/L	G	AB	R	H	2B	3B	HR	RBI	BB	SO	AVG	OBP	SLG	PRO+	BR/A	SB	CS	SBR	FA	FR	G/POS	TPR
1970	SF-N	109	282	31	75	15	2	4	28	30	37	.266	.337	.376	92	-3	2	1	0	.971	4	3-91	-0.3
1971	*SF-N	136	429	47	119	18	5	5	57	40	57	.277	.342	.378	105	3	2	1	0	.951	-16	*3-128	-1.5
1972	SF-N	82	233	19	52	3	1	2	18	33	39	.223	.322	.270	69	-8	2	1	0	.974	-4	3-69	-1.4
1973	SF-N	5	9	1	2	0	0	0	1	0	0	.222	.300	.222	45	-1	0	0	0	.833	-1	/3-5	-0.2
	Cal-A	110	311	16	85	6	1	0	26	35	31	.273	.349	.299	91	-3	1	3	-2	.961	4	3-98/2-1,S	0.0
Total	4	442	1264	114	333	42	9	11	130	138	164	.263	.338	.337	91	-12	7	6	-2	.961	-15	3-391/S-1,2	-3.4

■ SHORTY GALLAGHER
Gallagher, Charles William b: 4/30/1872, Detroit, Mich. d: 6/23/24, Detroit, Mich. Deb: 8/13/01

YEAR	TM/L	G	AB	R	H	2B	3B	HR	RBI	BB	SO	AVG	OBP	SLG	PRO+	BR/A	SB	CS	SBR	FA	FR	G/POS	TPR
1901	Cle-A	2	4	0	0	0	0	0	0	0	0	.000	.000	.000	-99	-1	0			.667	-1	/O-2	-0.2

■ DAVE GALLAGHER
Gallagher, David Thomas b: 9/20/60, Trenton, N.J. BR/TR, 6', 180 lbs. Deb: 4/12/87

YEAR	TM/L	G	AB	R	H	2B	3B	HR	RBI	BB	SO	AVG	OBP	SLG	PRO+	BR/A	SB	CS	SBR	FA	FR	G/POS	TPR
1987	Cle-A	15	36	2	4	1	1	0	1	2	5	.111	.158	.194	-7	-6	2	0	1	.972	1	O-14	-0.4
1988	Chi-A	101	347	59	105	15	3	5	31	29	40	.303	.356	.406	113	6	5	4	-1	1.000	-1	O-95/D-2	0.1
1989	Chi-A	161	601	74	160	22	2	1	46	46	79	.266	.320	.314	82	-14	5	6	-2	.993	1	*O-160/D-1	-2.0
1990	Chi-A	45	75	5	21	3	1	0	5	3	9	.280	.316	.347	87	-1	0	1	-1	.981	-6	O-37/D-4	-0.9
	Bal-A	23	51	7	11	1	0	0	2	4	3	.216	.273	.235	45	-4	1	1	-0	.980	2	O-20/D-2	-0.2
	Yr	68	126	12	32	4	1	0	7	7	12	.254	.299	.302	70	-5	1	2	-1	.980	-4	O-57/D-6	-1.1
1991	Cal-A	90	270	32	79	17	0	1	30	24	43	.293	.355	.367	100	1	2	4	-2	1.000	1	O-87/D-2	-0.2
1992	NY-N	98	175	20	42	11	1	1	21	19	16	.240	.318	.331	85	-3	4	5	-2	.982	-8	O-76	-1.5
1993	NY-N	99	201	34	55	12	2	6	28	20	18	.274	.339	.443	109	2	1	1	0	1.000	-7	O-72/1-9	-0.6
1994	Atl-N	89	152	27	34	5	2	2	14	22	17	.224	.326	.296	64	-8	0	2	-1	.989	-9	O-77/1-1	-1.8
Total	8	721	1908	260	511	87	10	16	178	169	230	.268	.330	.349	89	-26	20	24	-8	.993	-26	O-638/D-11,1	-7.5

■ JIM GALLAGHER
Gallagher, James E. b: Findlay, Ohio d: 3/29/1894, Scranton, Pa. Deb: 9/4/1886

YEAR	TM/L	G	AB	R	H	2B	3B	HR	RBI	BB	SO	AVG	OBP	SLG	PRO+	BR/A	SB	CS	SBR	FA	FR	G/POS	TPR
1886	Was-N	1	5	1	1	0	0	0	0	0	2	.200	.200	.200	23	-0	0			.875	1	/S-1	0.0

■ JOHN GALLAGHER
Gallagher, John Carroll b: 2/18/1892, Pittsburgh, Pa. d: 3/30/52, Norfolk, Va. BR/TR, 5'10.5", 156 lbs. Deb: 8/20/15

YEAR	TM/L	G	AB	R	H	2B	3B	HR	RBI	BB	SO	AVG	OBP	SLG	PRO+	BR/A	SB	CS	SBR	FA	FR	G/POS	TPR
1915	Bal-F	40	126	11	25	4	0	0	4	5	22	.198	.229	.230	22	-14	1			.945	-2	2-37/S-5,3	-1.7

■ JACKIE GALLAGHER
Gallagher, John Laurence b: 1/28/02, Providence, R.I. d: 9/10/84, Gladwyne, Pa. BL/TR, 5'10", 175 lbs. Deb: 8/24/23

YEAR	TM/L	G	AB	R	H	2B	3B	HR	RBI	BB	SO	AVG	OBP	SLG	PRO+	BR/A	SB	CS	SBR	FA	FR	G/POS	TPR
1923	Cle-A	1	1	0	1	0	0	0	0	0	0	1.000	1.000	1.000	428	0	0	0	0	.000	-1	/O-1	0.0

■ JOE GALLAGHER
Gallagher, Joseph Emmett "Muscles" b: 3/7/14, Buffalo, N.Y. BR/TR, 6'2", 210 lbs. Deb: 4/20/39

YEAR	TM/L	G	AB	R	H	2B	3B	HR	RBI	BB	SO	AVG	OBP	SLG	PRO+	BR/A	SB	CS	SBR	FA	FR	G/POS	TPR
1939	NY-A	14	41	8	10	0	1	2	9	3	8	.244	.311	.439	91	-1	1	0	0	1.000	-1	O-12	-0.2

YEAR	TM/L	G	AB	R	H	2B	3B	HR	RBI	BB	SO	AVG	OBP	SLG	PRO+	BR/A	SB	CS	SBR	FA	FR	G/POS	TPR
	StL-A	71	266	41	75	17	2	9	40	17	42	.282	.327	.462	98	-2	0	1	-1	.944	2	O-67	-0.3
	Yr	85	307	49	85	17	3	11	49	20	50	.277	.325	.459	97	-3	1	1	-0	.950	1	O-79	-0.5
1940	StL-A	23	70	14	19	3	1	2	8	4	12	.271	.311	.429	88	-2	2	0	1	.966	1	O-15	-0.3
	Bro-N	57	110	10	29	6	1	3	16	2	14	.264	.283	.418	86	-3	1			.941	-2	O-20	-0.6
Total	2	165	487	73	133	26	5	16	73	26	76	.273	.314	.446	93	-7	4	1		.950	-3	O-114	-1.4

■ GIL GALLAGHER
Gallagher, Lawrence Kirby b: 9/5/1896, Washington, D.C. d: 1/6/57, Washington, D.C. BB/TR, 5'8", 155 lbs. Deb: 9/13/22

YEAR	TM/L	G	AB	R	H	2B	3B	HR	RBI	BB	SO	AVG	OBP	SLG	PRO+	BR/A	SB	CS	SBR	FA	FR	G/POS	TPR
1922	Bos-N	7	22	1	1	1	0	0	2	1	7	.045	.087	.091	-57	-5	0	0		.893	-2	/S-6	-0.6

■ BOB GALLAGHER
Gallagher, Robert Collins b: 7/7/48, Newton, Mass. BL/TL, 6'3", 185 lbs. Deb: 5/17/72 F

YEAR	TM/L	G	AB	R	H	2B	3B	HR	RBI	BB	SO	AVG	OBP	SLG	PRO+	BR/A	SB	CS	SBR	FA	FR	G/POS	TPR
1972	Bos-A	7	5	0	0	0	0	0	0	0	3	.000	.000	.000	-95		0	0	0	.000	0	H	-0.1
1973	Hou-N	71	148	16	39	3	1	2	10	3	27	.264	.278	.338	70	-6	0	1	-1	1.000	-2	O-42/1-1	-1.1
1974	Hou-N	102	87	13	15	2	0	0	3	12	23	.172	.280	.195	36	-7	1	0	0	.978	-21	O-62/1-4	-3.0
1975	NY-N	33	15	5	2	1	0	0	0	1	3	.133	.188	.200	8	-2	0	0	0	.900	-5	O-16	-0.7
Total	4	213	255	34	56	6	1	2	13	16	56	.220	.268	.275	52	-17	1	1	-0	.985	-27	O-120/1-5	-4.9

■ WILLIAM GALLAGHER
Gallagher, William Howard b: 2/4/1874, Boston, Mass. d: 3/11/50, Worcester, Mass. Deb: 8/19/1896

YEAR	TM/L	G	AB	R	H	2B	3B	HR	RBI	BB	SO	AVG	OBP	SLG	PRO+	BR/A	SB	CS	SBR	FA	FR	G/POS	TPR
1896	Phi-N	14	49	9	15	2	0	0	6	10	0	.306	.433	.347	108	1	0			.894	-4	S-14	-0.2

■ BILL GALLAGHER
Gallagher, William John b: Philadelphia, Pa. TL, Deb: 5/2/1883

YEAR	TM/L	G	AB	R	H	2B	3B	HR	RBI	BB	SO	AVG	OBP	SLG	PRO+	BR/A	SB	CS	SBR	FA	FR	G/POS	TPR
1883	Bal-a	16	61	9	10	3	1	0		3		.164	.203	.246	43	-4				.824	-2	/O-9,P-7,S	-0.3
	Phi-N	2	8	1	0	0	0	0			4	.000	.000	.000	-99	-2				1.000	-0	/O-2	-0.2
1884	Phi-U	3	11	1	1	0	0	0		0		.091	.091	.091	-54	-2				.800	0	/P-3	0.0
Total	2	21	80	11	11	3	1	0	0	3	4	.138	.169	.200	15	-8				.850	-2	/O-11,P-10,S	-0.5

■ STAN GALLE
Galle, Stanley Joseph (b: Stanley Joseph Galazewski) b: 2/7/19, Milwaukee, Wis. BR/TR, 5'7", 165 lbs. Deb: 4/14/42

YEAR	TM/L	G	AB	R	H	2B	3B	HR	RBI	BB	SO	AVG	OBP	SLG	PRO+	BR/A	SB	CS	SBR	FA	FR	G/POS	TPR
1942	Was-A	13	18	3	2	0	0	0	1		0	.111	.158	.111	-24	-3	0	0		.857	-1	/3-3	-0.4

■ MIKE GALLEGO
Gallego, Michael Anthony b: 10/31/60, Whittier, Cal. BR/TR, 5'8", 160 lbs. Deb: 4/11/85

YEAR	TM/L	G	AB	R	H	2B	3B	HR	RBI	BB	SO	AVG	OBP	SLG	PRO+	BR/A	SB	CS	SBR	FA	FR	G/POS	TPR
1985	Oak-A	76	77	13	16	5	1	1	9	12	14	.208	.322	.338	87	-1	1	1	-0	.991	12	2-42,S-21,3	1.2
1986	Oak-A	20	37	2	10	2	0	0	4	1	6	.270	.289	.324	72	-1	0	2	-1	.986	9	2-19/3-2,S	0.6
1987	Oak-A	72	124	18	31	6	0	2	14	12	21	.250	.321	.347	83	-3	0	1	-1	.968	17	2-31,3-24,S	1.4
1988	*Oak-A	129	277	38	58	8	0	2	20	34	53	.209	.298	.260	60	-14	2	3	-1	.993	4	2-83,S-42,3	-0.8
1989	*Oak-A	133	357	45	90	14	2	3	30	35	43	.252	.329	.328	89	-4	7	5	-1	.967	18	S-94,2-41/3D	2.0
1990	*Oak-A	140	389	36	80	13	2	3	34	35	50	.206	.278	.272	57	-22	5	5	-2	.990	14	2-83,S-38,3/OD	-0.6
1991	Oak-A	159	482	67	119	15	4	12	49	67	84	.247	.345	.369	103	4	6	9	-4	.989	-16	*2-135,S-55	-1.1
1992	NY-A	53	173	24	44	7	1	3	14	20	22	.254	.345	.358	98	0	0	1	-1	.990	1	2-40,S-14	0.3
1993	NY-A	119	403	63	114	20	1	10	54	50	65	.283	.368	.412	113	8	3	2	-0	.976	15	S-55,2-52,3/D	2.9
1994	NY-A	89	306	39	73	17	1	6	41	38	46	.239	.330	.359	83	-7	0	1	-1	.970	20	S-72,2-26	1.6
Total	10	990	2625	345	635	107	12	42	269	304	404	.242	.327	.340	87	-42	24	30	-11	.987	95	2-552,S-409,3/DO	7.5

■ JIM GALLIGAN
Galligan, James M. b: 1862, Easton, Pa. d: 7/17/01, New York, N.Y. 5'10", 160 lbs. Deb: 9/2/1889

YEAR	TM/L	G	AB	R	H	2B	3B	HR	RBI	BB	SO	AVG	OBP	SLG	PRO+	BR/A	SB	CS	SBR	FA	FR	G/POS	TPR
1889	Lou-a	31	120	6	20	0	2	0	7	6	17	.167	.213	.200	18	-13	1			.915	2	O-31	-1.0

■ CHICK GALLOWAY
Galloway, Clarence Edward b: 8/4/1896, Clinton, S.C. d: 11/7/69, Clinton, S.C. BR/TR, 5'8", 160 lbs. Deb: 9/9/19

YEAR	TM/L	G	AB	R	H	2B	3B	HR	RBI	BB	SO	AVG	OBP	SLG	PRO+	BR/A	SB	CS	SBR	FA	FR	G/POS	TPR
1919	Phi-A	17	63	2	9	0	0	0	4	1	8	.143	.156	.143	-16	-10	0			.969	1	S-17	-0.8
1920	Phi-A	98	298	28	60	9	3	0	18	22	32	.201	.259	.252	35	-28	2	2	-1	.928	4	S-84/2-4,3	-1.7
1921	Phi-A	131	465	42	123	28	5	3	47	29	43	.265	.310	.366	72	-21	12	7	-1	.922	-22	*S-110,3-20/2	-3.1
1922	Phi-A	155	571	83	185	26	9	6	69	39	39	.324	.368	.433	105	4	10	19	-8	.952	1	*S-155	1.3
1923	Phi-A	134	504	64	140	18	9	2	62	37	30	.278	.327	.361	80	-15	12	10	-2	.944	2	*S-134	-0.3
1924	Phi-A	129	464	41	128	16	4	2	48	23	25	.276	.311	.341	67	-23	11	12	-4	.952	2	*S-129	-1.0
1925	Phi-A	149	481	52	116	11	4	3	71	59	28	.241	.324	.299	55	-32	16	9	-1	.954	-3	*S-148	-1.9
1926	Phi-A	133	408	37	98	13	6	0	49	31	20	.240	.295	.301	53	-28	8	7	-2	.935	-13	*S-133	-3.0
1927	Phi-A	77	181	25	48	10	4	0	22	18	9	.265	.332	.365	76	-6	1	3	-2	.946	5	S-61/3-7	0.2
1928	Det-A	53	148	17	39	5	2	1	17	15	3	.264	.331	.345	77	-5	7	2	1	.914	-4	S-22,3-21/1O	-0.4
Total	10	1076	3583	391	946	136	46	17	407	274	225	.264	.317	.342	69	-165	79	71		.943	-28	S-993/3-51,201	-10.7

■ JIM GALLOWAY
Galloway, James Cato "Bad News" b: 9/16/1887, Iredell, Tex. d: 5/3/50, Fort Worth, Tex. BB/TR, 6'3", 187 lbs. Deb: 8/24/12

YEAR	TM/L	G	AB	R	H	2B	3B	HR	RBI	BB	SO	AVG	OBP	SLG	PRO+	BR/A	SB	CS	SBR	FA	FR	G/POS	TPR
1912	StL-N	21	54	4	10	0				4	5	8	.185	.254	.222	32	-5	2			.971	-6	2-16/S-1	-0.4

■ JIM GALVIN
Galvin, James Joseph b: 8/11/07, Somerville, Mass. d: 9/30/69, Marietta, Ga. BR/TR, 5'11.5", 180 lbs. Deb: 9/27/30

YEAR	TM/L	G	AB	R	H	2B	3B	HR	RBI	BB	SO	AVG	OBP	SLG	PRO+	BR/A	SB	CS	SBR	FA	FR	G/POS	TPR
1930	Bos-A	2	2	0	0	0	0	0	0	0	0	.000	.000	.000	-99	-1	0	0	0	.000	0	H	-0.1

■ JOHN GALVIN
Galvin, John S. b: Brooklyn, N.Y. d: 4/20/04, Brooklyn, N.Y. Deb: 5/7/1872

YEAR	TM/L	G	AB	R	H	2B	3B	HR	RBI	BB	SO	AVG	OBP	SLG	PRO+	BR/A	SB	CS	SBR	FA	FR	G/POS	TPR
1872	Atl-n	1	4	0	0	0	0	0	0	0	0	.000	.000	.000	-85	-1						/2-1	-0.1

■ JOHN GAMBLE
Gamble, John Robert b: 2/10/48, Reno, Nev. BR/TR, 5'10", 165 lbs. Deb: 9/7/72

YEAR	TM/L	G	AB	R	H	2B	3B	HR	RBI	BB	SO	AVG	OBP	SLG	PRO+	BR/A	SB	CS	SBR	FA	FR	G/POS	TPR
1972	Det-A	6	3	0	0	0	0	0	0	0	0	.000	.000	.000	-97	-1	0	0	0	1.000	1	/S-1	0.1
1973	Det-A	7	0	1	0	0	0	0	0	0	0	—	—	—		0	0	0	0	.000	0	R	0.0
Total	2	13	3	1	0	0	0	0	0	0	0	.000	.000	.000	-97	-1	0	0	0	1.000	1	/S-1	0.1

■ LEE GAMBLE
Gamble, Lee Jesse b: 6/28/10, Renovo, Pa. d: 10/5/94, Punxsutawney, Pa. BL/TR, 6'1", 170 lbs. Deb: 9/15/35

YEAR	TM/L	G	AB	R	H	2B	3B	HR	RBI	BB	SO	AVG	OBP	SLG	PRO+	BR/A	SB	CS	SBR	FA	FR	G/POS	TPR
1935	Cin-N	2	4	2	2	1	0	0	2	1	0	.500	.600	.750	269	1	1			1.000	-0	/O-2	0.1
1938	Cin-N	53	75	13	24	3	1	0	5	0	6	.320	.320	.387	96	-1	0			1.000	-0	/O-9	-0.1
1939	*Cin-N	72	221	24	59	7	2	0	14	9	14	.267	.296	.317	64	-11	5			.989	-3	O-56	-1.6
1940	Cin-N	38	42	12	6	1	0	0	3	1	1	.143	.143	.167	-15	-6	0			1.000	-0	O-10	-0.7
Total	4	165	342	51	91	12	3	0	21	10	21	.266	.287	.319	64	-17	6			.993	-4	/O-77	-2.3

■ OSCAR GAMBLE
Gamble, Oscar Charles b: 12/20/49, Ramer, Ala. BL/TR, 5'11", 165 lbs. Deb: 8/27/69

YEAR	TM/L	G	AB	R	H	2B	3B	HR	RBI	BB	SO	AVG	OBP	SLG	PRO+	BR/A	SB	CS	SBR	FA	FR	G/POS	TPR
1969	Chi-N	24	71	6	16	1	1	1	5	10	12	.225	.321	.310	69	-3	0	2	-1	.913	-2	O-24	-0.8
1970	Phi-N	88	275	31	72	12	4	1	19	27	37	.262	.330	.345	84	-6	5	4	-1	.956	1	O-74	-1.0
1971	Phi-N	92	280	24	62	11	1	6	23	21	35	.221	.278	.332	72	-11	5	2	-0	.970	-4	O-80	-1.9
1972	Phi-N	74	135	17	32	5	2	1	13	19	16	.237	.335	.326	86	-2	0	1	-1	1.000	1	O-35/1-1	-0.5
1973	Cle-A	113	390	56	104	11	3	20	44	34	37	.267	.330	.464	120	9	3	4	-2	.971	-1	D-70,O-37	0.3
1974	Cle-A	135	454	74	132	16	4	19	59	42	51	.291	.365	.469	140	23	5	6	-2	1.000	-1	*D-115,O-13	1.7
1975	Cle-A	121	348	60	91	16	3	15	45	53	39	.261	.362	.443	130	14	11	5	-0	.987	-0	O-82,D-29	1.2
1976	*NY-A	110	340	43	79	13	1	17	57	38	38	.232	.317	.426	117	7	5	3	-0	.981	-0	*O-104/D-1	0.3
1977	Chi-A	137	408	75	121	22	2	31	83	54	54	.297	.387	.588	162	35	1	2	-0	.987	-5	D-79,O-49	2.4
1978	SD-N	126	375	46	103	15	3	7	47	51	45	.275	.370	.387	121	12	1	2	-0	.979	-0	*O-107	0.7
1979	Tex-A	64	161	27	54	6	0	8	32	37	15	.335	.462	.522	167	17	2	1	0	1.000	1	O-37,D-21	1.6
	NY-A	36	113	21	44	4	1	11	32	13	13	.389	.452	.735	219	19	0	0	0	.943	0	O-27/D-6	1.7
	Yr	100	274	48	98	10	1	19	64	50	28	.358	.458	.609	188	36	2	1	0	.969	2	O-48,D-43	3.3
1980	*NY-A	78	194	40	54	10	2	14	50	37	28	.278	.381	.567	159	16	2	2	0	1.000	-6	O-49/D-20	0.8
1981	*NY-A	80	189	24	45	8	0	10	27	35	23	.238	.360	.439	131	8	0	2	-0	1.000	-0	O-43/D-33	0.3
1982	NY-A	108	316	49	86	21	2	18	57	58	47	.272	.392	.522	151	23	0	0	0	1.000	5	D-74,O-29	2.4
1983	NY-A	74	180	26	47	10	2	7	26	25	23	.261	.361	.456	128	7	0	0	0	.942	-0	O-32,D-21	0.5

YEAR	TM/L	G	AB	R	H	2B	3B	HR	RBI	BB	SO	AVG	OBP	SLG	PRO+	BR/A	SB	CS	SBR	FA	FR	G/POS	TPR
1984	NY-A	54	125	17	23	2	0	10	27	25	18	.184	.320	.440	112	2	1	0	0	1.000	-1	D-28,O-12	0.1
1985	Chi-A	70	148	20	30	5	0	4	20	34	22	.203	.355	.318	83	-2	0	0	0	.000	0	D-48	-0.3
Total	17	1584	4502	656	1195	188	31	200	666	610	546	.265	.358	.454	127	168	47	37	-8	.977	-15	O-818,D-561/1	9.5

■ DAFF GAMMONS
Gammons, John Ashley b: 3/17/1876, New Bedford, Mass. d: 9/24/63, E.Greenwich, R.I. BR/TR, 5'11", 170 lbs. Deb: 4/23/01

YEAR	TM/L	G	AB	R	H	2B	3B	HR	RBI	BB	SO	AVG	OBP	SLG	PRO+	BR/A	SB	CS	SBR	FA	FR	G/POS	TPR
1901	Bos-N	28	93	10	18	0	1	0	10	3		.194	.242	.215	30	-8	5			.880	-3	O-23/2-2,3	-1.2

■ CHICK GANDIL
Gandil, Arnold b: 1/19/1887, St.Paul, Minn. d: 12/13/70, Calistoga, Cal. BR/TR, 6'1.5", 190 lbs. Deb: 4/14/10

YEAR	TM/L	G	AB	R	H	2B	3B	HR	RBI	BB	SO	AVG	OBP	SLG	PRO+	BR/A	SB	CS	SBR	FA	FR	G/POS	TPR
1910	Chi-A	77	275	21	53	7	3	2	21	24		.193	.267	.262	69	-10	12			.989	7	1-74/O-2	-0.4
1912	Was-A	117	443	59	135	20	15	2	81	27		.305	.350	.431	122	11	21			.990	3	*1-117	1.1
1913	Was-A	148	550	61	175	25	8	1	72	36	33	.318	.363	.398	120	13	22			.990	8	*1-145	2.1
1914	Was-A	145	526	48	136	24	10	3	75	44	44	.259	.324	.359	101	-0	30	19	-2	.991	24	*1-145	2.0
1915	Was-A	136	485	53	141	20	15	2	64	29	33	.291	.340	.406	121	10	20	13	-2	.986	-1	*1-134	0.5
1916	Cle-A	146	533	51	138	26	9	0	72	36	48	.259	.312	.341	91	-7	13			.995	8	*1-145	-0.5
1917	*Chi-A	149	553	53	151	9	7	0	57	30	36	.273	.316	.315	91	-7	16			.995	-6	*1-149	-2.0
1918	Chi-A	114	439	49	119	18	4	0	55	27	19	.271	.319	.330	95	-4	9			.992	-3	*1-114	-1.2
1919	*Chi-A	115	441	54	128	24	7	1	60	20	20	.290	.325	.383	98	-2	10			.997	-4	*1-115	-1.1
Total	9	1147	4245	449	1176	173	78	11	557	273	233	.277	.327	.362	103	3	153	32		.992	36	*1-1138/O-2	0.5

■ BOB GANDY
Gandy, Robert Brinkley "String" b: 8/25/1893, Jacksonville, Fla. d: 6/19/45, Jacksonville, Fla BL/TR, 6'3", 180 lbs. Deb: 10/5/16

YEAR	TM/L	G	AB	R	H	2B	3B	HR	RBI	BB	SO	AVG	OBP	SLG	PRO+	BR/A	SB	CS	SBR	FA	FR	G/POS	TPR
1916	Phi-N	1	2	0	0	0	0	0	0	0	1	.000	.000	.000	-97	-0	0			1.000	0	/O-1	0.0

■ BOB GANLEY
Ganley, Robert Stephen b: 4/23/1875, Lowell, Mass. d: 10/9/45, Lowell, Mass. BL/TL, 5'7", 156 lbs. Deb: 9/1/05

YEAR	TM/L	G	AB	R	H	2B	3B	HR	RBI	BB	SO	AVG	OBP	SLG	PRO+	BR/A	SB	CS	SBR	FA	FR	G/POS	TPR
1905	Pit-N	32	127	12	40	1	2	0	7	8		.315	.356	.354	109	1	3			1.000	-2	O-32	-0.3
1906	Pit-N	137	511	63	132	7	6	0	31	41		.258	.316	.295	87	-8	19			.965	-2	*O-134	-1.8
1907	Was-A	154	605	73	167	10	5	1	35	54		.276	.337	.314	117	13	40			.940	9	*O-154	1.7
1908	Was-A	150	549	61	131	19	9	1	36	45		.239	.299	.311	107	4	30			.964	4	*O-150	0.2
1909	Was-A	19	63	5	16	3	0	0	5	1		.254	.266	.302	83	-2	4			1.000	-3	O-17	-0.6
	Phi-A	80	274	32	54	4	2	0	9	28		.197	.272	.226	56	-13	16			.980	8	O-77	-1.0
	Yr	99	337	37	70	7	2	0	14	29		.208	.270	.240	61	-15	20			.982	5	O-94	-1.6
Total	5	572	2129	246	540	44	24	2	123	177		.254	.313	.300	97	-4	112			.962	13	O-564	-1.8

■ BILL GANNON
Gannon, William G. b: 1876, New Haven, Conn. d: 4/26/27, Fort Worth, Tex. 5'9", 170 lbs. Deb: 9/9/01

YEAR	TM/L	G	AB	R	H	2B	3B	HR	RBI	BB	SO	AVG	OBP	SLG	PRO+	BR/A	SB	CS	SBR	FA	FR	G/POS	TPR
1901	Chi-N	15	61	2	9	0	0	0	0	1		.148	.161	.148	-11	-8	5			1.000	-1	O-15	-1.1

■ RON GANT
Gant, Ronald Edwin b: 3/2/65, Victoria, Tex. BR/TR, 6' ", 192 lbs. Deb: 9/6/87

YEAR	TM/L	G	AB	R	H	2B	3B	HR	RBI	BB	SO	AVG	OBP	SLG	PRO+	BR/A	SB	CS	SBR	FA	FR	G/POS	TPR
1987	Atl-N	21	83	9	22	4	0	2	9	1	11	.265	.274	.386	69	-4	4	2	0	.972	-0	2-20	-0.3
1988	Atl-N	146	563	85	146	28	8	19	60	46	118	.259	.319	.439	110	6	19	10	-0	.963	-1	*2-122,3-22	1.0
1989	Atl-N	75	260	26	46	8	3	9	25	20	63	.177	.238	.335	61	-14	9	6	-1	.887	4	3-53,O-14	-1.3
1990	Atl-N	152	575	107	174	34	3	32	84	50	86	.303	.359	.539	136	26	33	16	0	.978	7	*O-146	3.0
1991	*Atl-N	154	561	101	141	35	3	32	105	71	104	.251	.341	.496	125	18	34	15	1	.983	8	*O-148	2.4
1992	*Atl-N★	153	544	74	141	22	6	17	80	45	101	.259	.324	.415	102	1	32	10	4	.986	-4	*O-147	-0.2
1993	*Atl-N	157	606	113	166	27	4	36	117	67	117	.274	.348	.510	125	20	26	9	2	.962	-3	*O-155	1.6
Total	7	858	3192	515	836	158	27	147	480	300	600	.262	.329	.466	114	53	157	68	6	.978	8	O-610,2-142/3	6.2

■ JOE GANTENBEIN
Gantenbein, Joseph Stephen "Sep" b: 8/25/16, San Francisco, Cal BL/TR, 5'9", 168 lbs. Deb: 4/20/39

YEAR	TM/L	G	AB	R	H	2B	3B	HR	RBI	BB	SO	AVG	OBP	SLG	PRO+	BR/A	SB	CS	SBR	FA	FR	G/POS	TPR
1939	Phi-A	111	348	47	101	14	4	4	36	32	22	.290	.353	.388	91	-4	1	5	-3	.948	-34	2-76,3-14/S	-3.4
1940	Phi-A	75	197	21	47	6	2	4	23	11	21	.239	.282	.350	64	-11	1	0		.930	-8	3-45/1-6,SO	-1.7
Total	2	186	545	68	148	20	6	8	59	43	43	.272	.328	.374	82	-15	2	5	-2	.934	-42	/2-76,3-59,S10	-5.1

■ JIM GANTNER
Gantner, James Elmer b: 1/5/53, Fond Du Lac, Wis. BL/TR, 6', 180 lbs. Deb: 9/3/76

YEAR	TM/L	G	AB	R	H	2B	3B	HR	RBI	BB	SO	AVG	OBP	SLG	PRO+	BR/A	SB	CS	SBR	FA	FR	G/POS	TPR
1976	Mil-A	26	69	6	17	1	0	0	7	6	11	.246	.316	.261	71	-2	1	0	0	.982	-3	3-24/D-2	-0.6
1977	Mil-A	14	47	4	14	1	0	1	2	2	5	.298	.327	.383	93	-1	2	1	0	.902	1	3-14	0.1
1978	Mil-A	43	97	14	21	1	0	1	8	5	10	.216	.269	.258	49	-7	2	0	1	.980	5	2-21,3-15/1S	0.0
1979	Mil-A	70	208	29	59	10	3	2	22	16	17	.284	.341	.389	96	-1	3	5	-2	.952	3	3-42,2-22/SP	0.2
1980	Mil-A	132	415	47	117	21	3	4	40	30	29	.282	.332	.376	97	-2	11	10	-3	.938	-1	3-69,2-66/S	-0.2
1981	*Mil-A	107	352	35	94	14	1	2	33	19	23	.267	.328	.330	95	-2	3	6	-3	.984	16	*2-107	1.8
1982	*Mil-A	132	447	48	132	17	2	4	43	26	36	.295	.337	.369	100	-0	6	3	0	.982	9	*2-131	1.5
1983	Mil-A	161	603	85	170	23	8	11	74	38	46	.282	.331	.401	109	6	5	6	-2	.984	10	*2-158	2.1
1984	Mil-A	153	613	61	173	27	1	3	56	30	51	.282	.319	.344	87	-11	6	5	-1	.985	10	*2-153	0.3
1985	Mil-A	143	523	63	133	15	4	5	44	33	42	.254	.302	.327	73	-19	11	8	-2	.988	5	*2-124,3-24/S	-1.5
1986	Mil-A	139	497	58	136	25	1	7	38	26	50	.274	.318	.370	84	-11	13	7	-0	.985	-12	2-135/3-3,SD	-1.8
1987	Mil-A	81	265	37	72	14	0	4	30	19	22	.272	.332	.370	84	-6	6	2	1	.984	5	2-57,3-38/D	0.2
1988	Mil-A	155	539	67	149	28	2	0	47	34	50	.276	.323	.336	84	-11	20	8	1	.986	-8	*2-154/3-1	-1.2
1989	Mil-A	116	409	51	112	18	3	0	34	21	33	.274	.325	.333	86	-7	20	6	2	.987	9	*2-114/D-2	0.8
1990	Mil-A	88	323	36	85	8	5	0	25	29	19	.263	.328	.319	82	-7	18	3	4	.982	-7	2-80/3-9	-0.9
1991	Mil-A	140	526	63	149	27	4	2	47	27	34	.283	.322	.361	91	-7	4	6	-2	.976	4	3-90,2-59	-0.4
1992	Mil-A	101	256	22	63	12	1	1	18	12	17	.246	.280	.313	67	-12	6	2	1	.994	7	2-68,3-31/1D	-0.3
Total	17	1801	6189	726	1696	262	38	47	568	383	501	.274	.322	.351	88	-100	137	78	-6	.985	50	*2-1449,3-360/DS1P	0.1

■ CHARLIE GANZEL
Ganzel, Charles William b: 6/18/1862, Waterford, Wis. d: 4/7/14, Quincy, Mass. BR/TR, 6', 161 lbs. Deb: 9/27/1884 F

YEAR	TM/L	G	AB	R	H	2B	3B	HR	RBI	BB	SO	AVG	OBP	SLG	PRO+	BR/A	SB	CS	SBR	FA	FR	G/POS	TPR
1884	StP-U	7	23	2	5	0	0	0				.217	.217	.217	34	-3				.956	-2	/C-6,O-1	-0.4
1885	Phi-N	34	125	15	21	3	1	0	6	4	13	.168	.194	.208	31	-9				.888	0	C-33/O-1	-0.6
1886	Phi-N	1	3	0	0	0	0	0	0	0	0	.000	.000	.000	-99	-1	0			.600	-1	/C-1	-0.1
	Det-N	57	213	28	58	7	2	1	31	7	22	.272	.295	.338	90	-3	5			.911	3	C-45/O-7,1	0.4
	Yr	58	216	28	58	7	2	1	31	7	23	.269	.291	.333	87	-4	5			.903	3	C-46/O-7,1	0.3
1887	*Det-N	57	227	40	59	6	5	0	20	8	2	.260	.288	.330	69	-10	3			.913	9	C-51/O-4,13	0.3
1888	Det-N	95	386	45	96	13	5	1	46	14	15	.249	.277	.316	89	-5	12			.900	-1	2-49,C-28/3OS1	-0.1
1889	Bos-N	73	275	30	73	3	5	1	43	15	11	.265	.308	.324	72	-11	13			.927	5	C-39,O-26/1S3	-0.3
1890	Bos-N	38	163	21	44	7	3	0	24	5	6	.270	.300	.350	83	-5	1			.958	3	C-22,O-15/S2	0.1
1891	Bos-N	70	263	33	68	18	5	1	29	12	13	.259	.304	.376	87	-6	7			.956	4	C-59,O-13	0.2
1892	*Bos-N	54	198	25	53	9	3	0	25	18	12	.268	.332	.343	96	-2	7			.933	-5	C-51/O-2,1	-0.4
1893	Bos-N	73	281	50	75	10	2	1	48	22	9	.267	.325	.327	68	-14	5			.952	-2	C-40,O-23,1	-1.1
1894	Bos-N	70	266	51	74	7	3	1	56	19	6	.278	.326	.383	65	-17	1			.897	-5	C-59/1-7,OS2	-1.3
1895	Bos-N	80	277	38	73	2	5	1	52	24	6	.264	.325	.318	61	-17	1			.962	19	C-76/S-2,1	0.7
1896	Bos-N	47	179	28	47	2	0	1	18	9	5	.263	.305	.291	54	-12	2			.989	6	C-41/1-3,S	-0.1
1897	Bos-N	30	105	15	28	4	1	0	14	4		.267	.300	.362	70	-5	2			.942	2	C-27/1-2	0.0
Total	14	786	2984	421	774	91	45	10	412	161	121	.259	.301	.330	73	-120	60			.934	35	C-578,O-100/21S3	-2.7

■ BABE GANZEL
Ganzel, Foster Pirie b: 5/22/01, Malden, Mass. d: 2/6/78, Jacksonville, Fla. BR/TR, 5'10.5", 172 lbs. Deb: 9/19/27 F

YEAR	TM/L	G	AB	R	H	2B	3B	HR	RBI	BB	SO	AVG	OBP	SLG	PRO+	BR/A	SB	CS	SBR	FA	FR	G/POS	TPR
1927	Was-A	13	48	7	21	4	2	1	13	7	3	.438	.509	.667	206	8	0	0	0	.944	0	O-13	0.7
1928	Was-A	10	26	2	2	1	0	0	4	1	5	.077	.111	.115	-41	-5	0	0	0	1.000	-1	/O-7	-0.7
Total	2	23	74	9	23	5	2	1	17	8	8	.311	.378	.473	122	2	0	0	0	.957	-1	/O-20	0.0

YEAR	TM/L	G	AB	R	H	2B	3B	HR	RBI	BB	SO	AVG	OBP	SLG	PRO+	BR/A	SB	CS	SBR	FA	FR	G/POS	TPR

■ JOHN GANZEL   Ganzel, John Henry   b: 4/7/1874, Kalamazoo, Mich.   d: 1/14/59, Orlando, Fla.   BR/TR, 6′0.5″, 195 lbs.   Deb: 4/21/1898   FM

1898	Pit-N	15	45	5	6	0	0	0	2	4		.133	.220	.133	2	-6	0			.963	-1	1-12	-0.7
1900	Chi-N	78	284	29	78	14	4	4	32	10		.275	.316	.394	99	-2	5			.980	-4	1-78	-0.5
1901	NY-N	138	526	42	113	13	3	2	66	20		.215	.256	.262	52	-32	6			**.986**	2	*1-138	-3.2
1903	NY-A	129	476	62	132	25	7	3	71	30		.277	.336	.378	107	4	9			**.988**	7	*1-129	0.9
1904	NY-A	130	465	50	121	16	10	6	48	24		.260	.309	.376	111	5	13			.988	-2	*1-118/2-9,S	0.0
1907	Cin-N	145	531	61	135	20	**16**	2	64	29		.254	.297	.363	102	-1	9			.990	1	*1-143	-0.5
1908	Cin-N	112	388	32	97	16	10	1	53	19		.250	.289	.351	107	1	6			**.990**	-2	*1-108,M	-0.3
Total	7	747	2715	281	682	104	50	18	336	136		.251	.298	.346	93	-29	48			.987	0	1-726/2-9,S	-4.3

■ JOE GARAGIOLA   Garagiola, Joseph Henry   b: 2/12/26, St.Louis, Mo.   BL/TR, 6′, 190 lbs.   Deb: 5/26/46

1946	*StL-N	74	211	21	50	4	1	3	22	23	25	.237	.312	.308	73	-7	0			.990	-5	C-70	-0.9
1947	StL-N	77	183	20	47	10	2	5	25	40	14	.257	.398	.415	111	4	0			.987	1	C-74	0.9
1948	StL-N	24	56	9	6	1	0	2	7	12	9	.107	.275	.232	36	-5	0			.990	2	C-23	-0.2
1949	StL-N	81	241	25	63	14	0	3	26	31	19	.261	.348	.357	85	-4	0			.984	7	C-80	0.7
1950	StL-N	34	88	8	28	6	1	2	20	10	7	.318	.388	.477	120	3	0			1.000	-3	C-30	0.1
1951	StL-N	27	72	9	14	3	2	2	9	9	7	.194	.284	.375	75	-3	0	0	0	1.000	-3	C-23	-0.4
	Pit-N	72	212	24	54	8	2	9	35	32	20	.255	.358	.439	110	3	4	1	1	.986	-9	C-61	-0.2
	Yr	99	284	33	68	11	4	11	44	41	27	.239	.339	.423	101	1	4	1	1	**.989**	-11	C-84	-0.6
1952	Pit-N	118	344	35	94	15	4	8	54	50	24	.273	.369	.410	113	7	0	1	-1	.978	-3	*C-105	0.9
1953	Pit-N	27	73	9	17	5	0	2	14	10	11	.233	.341	.384	89	-1	1	0	0	.989	-4	C-22	-0.3
	Chi-N	74	228	21	62	9	4	1	21	21	23	.272	.336	.360	80	-6	0	0	0	.988	0	C-68	-0.3
	Yr	101	301	30	79	14	4	3	35	31	34	.262	.337	.365	82	-7	1	0	0	.988	-4	C-90	-0.6
1954	Chi-N	63	153	16	43	5	0	5	21	28	12	.281	.405	.412	112	4	0	0	0	.982	-8	C-55	-0.1
	NY-N	5	11	1	3	2	0	0	1	1	2	.273	.333	.455	102	0	0	0	0	1.000	0	/C-3	0.0
	Yr	68	164	17	46	7	0	5	22	29	14	.280	.401	.415	112	4	0	0	0	.983	-8	C-58	-0.1
Total	9	676	1872	198	481	82	16	42	255	267	173	.257	.355	.385	96	-5	5	2		.986	-23	C-614	0.2

■ MIKE GARBARK   Garbark, Nathaniel Michael (b: Nathaniel Michael Garbach)   b: 2/2/16, Houston, Tex.   BR/TR, 6′, 200 lbs.   Deb: 4/18/44   F

1944	NY-A	89	299	23	78	9	4	6	33	25	27	.261	.320	.328	82	-7	0	1	-1	.988	8	C-85	0.6
1945	NY-A	60	176	23	38	5	3	1	26	23	12	.216	.310	.295	73	-6	0	1	-1	.972	4	C-59	0.1
Total	2	149	475	46	116	14	7	2	59	48	39	.244	.316	.316	79	-12	0	2	-1	.982	12	C-144	0.7

■ BOB GARBARK   Garbark, Robert Michael (b: Robert Michael Garbach)   b: 11/13/09, Houston, Tex.   d: 8/15/90, Meadville, Pa.   BR/TR, 5′11″, 178 lbs.   Deb: 9/3/34   F

1934	Cle-A	5	11	1	0	0	0	0	0	1	3	.000	.083	.000	-76	-3	0	0	0	1.000	-2	/C-5	-0.4
1935	Cle-A	6	18	4	6	1	0	0	4	5	1	.333	.478	.389	124	1	0	0	0	1.000	2	/C-6	0.3
1937	Chi-N	1	1	0	0	0	0	0	0	0	0	.000	.000	.000	-96	0	0			.000	0	H	0.0
1938	Chi-N	23	54	2	14	0	0	0	5	1	0	.259	.273	.259	46	-4	0			1.000	1	C-20/1-1	-0.2
1939	Chi-N	24	21	1	3	0	0	0	0	0	3	.143	.143	.143	-23	-4	0			1.000	1	C-21	-0.3
1944	Phi-A	18	23	2	6	2	0	0	2	1	0	.261	.292	.348	83	-1	0	0	0	1.000	-0	C-15	-0.1
1945	Bos-A	68	199	21	52	6	0	0	17	18	10	.261	.329	.291	79	-5	0	1	-1	.993	-3	C-67	-0.5
Total	7	145	327	31	81	9	0	0	28	26	17	.248	.307	.275	64	-15	0	1		.996	-2	C-134/1-1	-1.2

■ BARBARO GARBEY   Garbey, Barbaro (Garbey)   b: 12/4/56, Santiago, Cuba   BR/TR, 5′10″, 170 lbs.   Deb: 4/3/84

1984	*Det-A	110	327	45	94	17	1	5	52	17	35	.287	.327	.391	98	-1	6	7	-2	.989	-5	1-65,3-20,DO/2	-1.3
1985	Det-A	86	237	27	61	9	1	6	29	15	37	.257	.310	.380	88	-4	3	2	-0	.991	-2	1-37,O-24,D/3	-0.9
1988	Tex-A	30	62	4	12	2	0	0	5	4	11	.194	.242	.226	31	-6	0	0	0	.900	-0	/O-8,1-7,3D	-0.6
Total	3	226	626	76	167	28	2	11	86	36	83	.267	.312	.371	88	-11	9	9	-2	.990	-8	1-109/D-45,032	-2.8

■ ALEX GARBOWSKI   Garbowski, Alexander   b: 6/25/25, Yonkers, N.Y.   BR/TR, 6′1″, 185 lbs.   Deb: 4/16/52

1952	Det-A	2	0	0	0	0	0	0	0	0	0	—	—	—	—		0	0	0	.000	0	R	0.0

■ KIKO GARCIA   Garcia, Alfonso Rafael   b: 10/14/53, Martinez, Cal.   BR/TR, 5′11″, 180 lbs.   Deb: 9/11/76

1976	Bal-A	11	32	2	7	1	1	1	4	0	4	.219	.219	.406	86	-1	2	1	0	1.000	1	S-11	0.1
1977	Bal-A	65	131	20	29	6	0	2	10	6	31	.221	.255	.313	58	-8	2	3	-1	.966	20	S-61/2-2	1.5
1978	Bal-A	79	186	17	49	6	4	0	13	7	43	.263	.290	.339	81	-5	7	1	2	.945	4	S-74/2-3	0.7
1979	*Bal-A	126	417	54	103	15	9	5	24	32	87	.247	.304	.362	82	-11	11	9	-2	.955	-18	*S-113,2-25/3O	-1.9
1980	Bal-A	111	311	27	62	8	0	1	27	24	57	.199	.257	.235	36	-27	4	4	0	.974	5	S-96,2-27/O	-1.6
1981	*Hou-N	48	136	9	37	6	1	0	15	10	16	.272	.327	.331	91	-2	2	2	-1	.950	3	S-28,3-13/2	0.4
1982	Hou-N	34	76	5	16	5	0	1	5	3	15	.211	.241	.316	59	-5	0	1	-1	.946	5	S-21/3-2,2	0.2
1983	Phi-N	84	118	22	34	7	1	2	9	9	20	.288	.344	.415	111	2	1	2	-1	.970	19	2-52,S-22,3	2.2
1984	Phi-N	57	60	6	14	2	0	0	5	4	11	.233	.281	.267	54	-4	0	0	0	.965	5	S-30,3-23/2	0.2
1985	Phi-N	4	3	0	0	0	0	0	0	0	1	.000	.000	.000	-97	-1	0	0	0	1.000	-1	/S-3,3-1	-0.2
Total	10	619	1470	162	351	56	16	12	112	95	285	.239	.287	.323	70	-61	34	22	-3	.961	39	S-459,2-120/3O	1.6

■ CARLOS GARCIA   Garcia, Carlos Jesus (Guerrero)   b: 10/15/67, Tachira, Venez.   BR/TR, 6′1″, 185 lbs.   Deb: 9/20/90

1990	Pit-N	4	4	1	2	0	0	0	0	0	2	.500	.500	.500	183	0	0	0	0	1.000	1	/S-3	0.1
1991	Pit-N	12	24	2	6	0	2	0	1	1	8	.250	.280	.417	95	-0	0	0	0	.947	2	/S-9,3-2,2	0.2
1992	*Pit-N	22	39	4	8	1	0	0	4	0	9	.205	.205	.231	23	-4	0	0	0	.977	2	2-14/S-8	-0.1
1993	Pit-N	141	546	77	147	25	5	12	47	31	67	.269	.319	.399	91	-8	18	11	-1	.983	-26	*2-140/S-3	-3.1
1994	Pit-N★	98	412	49	114	15	2	6	28	16	67	.277	.310	.367	76	-15	18	9	0	.978	8	2-98	-0.4
Total	5	277	1025	133	277	41	9	18	80	48	153	.270	.311	.380	83	-26	36	20	-1	.981	-13	2-253/S-23,3	-3.3

■ DAMASO GARCIA   Garcia, Damaso Domingo (Sanchez)   b: 2/7/55, Moca, D.R.   BR/TR, 6′, 170 lbs.   Deb: 6/24/78

1978	NY-A	18	41	5	8	0	0	0	1	2	6	.195	.233	.195	22	-4	0	0	0	.959	2	2-16/S-3	-0.2
1979	NY-A	11	38	3	10	1	0	0	4	0	2	.263	.263	.289	50	-3	2	0	1	.902	-5	S-10/3-1	-0.6
1980	Tor-A	140	543	50	151	30	7	4	46	12	55	.278	.297	.381	81	-15	13	13	-4	.980	16	*2-138/D-1	0.5
1981	Tor-A	64	250	24	63	8	1	1	13	9	32	.252	.278	.304	64	-12	13	3	2	.972	-15	2-62/D-1	-2.2
1982	Tor-A	147	597	89	185	32	3	5	42	21	44	.310	.339	.399	93	-6	54	20	1	.980	10	*2-141/D-4	1.6
1983	Tor-A	131	525	84	161	23	6	3	38	24	34	.307	.330	.390	94	-4	31	17	-1	.981	-16	*2-130	-1.5
1984	Tor-A★	152	633	79	180	32	5	5	46	16	46	.284	.312	.374	86	-13	46	12	7	.980	-14	*2-149/D-1	-1.5
1985	*Tor-A★	146	600	70	169	25	4	8	65	15	41	.282	.304	.377	83	-15	28	15	-1	.981	-34	*2-143	-4.5
1986	Tor-A	122	424	57	119	22	0	6	46	13	32	.281	.299	.373	83	-10	9	6	-1	.985	-7	*2-106,D-11/1	-1.4
1988	Atl-N	21	60	3	7	1	0	0	3	4	10	.117	.159	.183	-2	-8	1	0	0	.984	-4	2-13	-1.2
1989	Mon-N	80	203	26	55	9	1	3	18	15	20	.271	.321	.369	96	-1	5	4	-1	.972	6	2-62/3-1	0.6
Total	11	1032	3914	490	1108	183	27	36	323	130	322	.283	.311	.371	84	-91	203	90	7	.980	-62	2-960/D-18,S31	-10.4

■ DANNY GARCIA   Garcia, Daniel Raphael   b: 4/29/54, Brooklyn, N.Y.   BL/TL, 6′1″, 182 lbs.   Deb: 4/26/81

1981	KC-A	12	14	4	2	0	0	0	0	0	2	.143	.143	.143	-18	-2	0	0	0	1.000	-2	/O-6,1-2	-0.4

■ LEO GARCIA   Garcia, Leonardo Antonio (Peralt)   b: 11/6/62, Santiago, D.R.   BL/TL, 5′8″, 160 lbs.   Deb: 4/6/87

1987	Cin-N	31	30	8	6	0	0	1	2	4	8	.200	.294	.300	55	-2	3	1	0	1.000	0	O-14	-0.4
1988	Cin-N	23	28	2	4	1	0	0	0	4	5	.143	.250	.179	24	-3	0	1	-1	1.000	-1	/O-9	-0.5
Total	2	54	58	10	10	1	0	1	2	8	13	.172	.273	.241	41	-5	3	2	-0	1.000	-4	/O-23	-0.9

YEAR	TM/L	G	AB	R	H	2B	3B	HR	RBI	BB	SO	AVG	OBP	SLG	PRO+	BR/A	SB	CS	SBR	FA	FR	G/POS	TPR

■ PEDRO GARCIA
Garcia, Pedro Modesto (Delfi) b: 4/17/50, Guayama, P.R. BR/TR, 5'10", 175 lbs. Deb: 4/6/73

YEAR	TM/L	G	AB	R	H	2B	3B	HR	RBI	BB	SO	AVG	OBP	SLG	PRO+	BR/A	SB	CS	SBR	FA	FR	G/POS	TPR
1973	Mil-A	160	580	67	142	**32**	5	15	54	40	119	.245	.299	.395	96	-5	11	10	-3	.970	-12	*2-160	-1.0
1974	Mil-A	141	452	46	90	15	4	12	54	26	67	.199	.251	.330	66	-21	8	5	-1	.970	-11	*2-140	-2.7
1975	Mil-A	98	302	40	68	15	2	6	38	18	59	.225	.273	.348	74	-11	12	6	0	.985	19	2-94/D-1	1.3
1976	Mil-A	41	106	12	23	7	1	9	4	23	.217	.259	.330	73	-4	2	2	1	.971	-3	2-39	-0.6
	Det-A	77	227	21	45	10	2	3	20	9	40	.198	.242	.300	56	-13	2	3	-1	.958	-0	2-77	-1.1
	Yr	118	333	33	68	17	3	4	29	13	63	.204	.247	.309	61	-17	4	5	-2	.962	-3	*2-116	-1.7
1977	Tor-A	41	130	10	27	10	1	0	9	5	21	.208	.254	.300	50	-9	0	0	0	.971	-2	2-34/D-4	-0.9
Total	5	558	1797	196	395	89	15	37	184	102	329	.220	.270	.348	75	-63	35	26	-5	.971	-8	2-544/D-5	-5.0

■ CHICO GARCIA
Garcia, Vinicio Uzcanga b: 12/24/24, Veracruz, Mexico BR/TR, 5'8", 170 lbs. Deb: 4/24/54

YEAR	TM/L	G	AB	R	H	2B	3B	HR	RBI	BB	SO	AVG	OBP	SLG	PRO+	BR/A	SB	CS	SBR	FA	FR	G/POS	TPR
1954	Bal-A	39	62	6	7	0	2	0	5	8	3	.113	.214	.177	9	-8	0	0	0	.962	8	2-24	0.0

■ AL GARDELLA
Gardella, Alfred Stephan b: 1/11/18, New York, N.Y. BL/TL, 5'10", 172 lbs. Deb: 5/17/45 F

YEAR	TM/L	G	AB	R	H	2B	3B	HR	RBI	BB	SO	AVG	OBP	SLG	PRO+	BR/A	SB	CS	SBR	FA	FR	G/POS	TPR
1945	NY-N	16	26	2	2	0	0	0	1	4	3	.077	.226	.077	-14	-4	0			.961	-1	/1-9,O-1	-0.6

■ DANNY GARDELLA
Gardella, Daniel Lewis b: 2/26/20, New York, N.Y. BL/TL, 5'7.5", 160 lbs. Deb: 5/14/44 F

YEAR	TM/L	G	AB	R	H	2B	3B	HR	RBI	BB	SO	AVG	OBP	SLG	PRO+	BR/A	SB	CS	SBR	FA	FR	G/POS	TPR
1944	NY-N	47	112	20	28	2	2	6	14	11	13	.250	.323	.464	120	2	0			.912	2	O-25	0.3
1945	NY-N	121	430	54	117	10	1	18	71	46	55	.272	.349	.426	113	7	2			.954	-2	O-94,1-15	-0.1
1950	StL-N	1	1	0	0	0	0	0	0	0	0	.000	.000	.000	-95	-0	0			.000	0	H	
Total	3	169	543	74	145	12	3	24	85	57	68	.267	.343	.433	114	9	2			.943	0	O-119/1-15	0.2

■ RON GARDENHIRE
Gardenhire, Ronald Clyde b: 10/24/57, Butzbach, Germany BR/TR, 6', 175 lbs. Deb: 9/1/81 C

YEAR	TM/L	G	AB	R	H	2B	3B	HR	RBI	BB	SO	AVG	OBP	SLG	PRO+	BR/A	SB	CS	SBR	FA	FR	G/POS	TPR
1981	NY-N	27	48	2	13	1	0	3	5	9	.271	.340	.292	82	-1	2	2	-1	.969	4	S-18/2-6,3	0.4
1982	NY-N	141	384	29	92	17	1	3	33	23	55	.240	.283	.313	67	-17	5	6	-2	.956	15	*S-135/2-1,3	0.7
1983	NY-N	17	32	1	2	0	0	0	1	4	.063	.091	.063	-57	-7	0	0	0	1.000	5	S-15	-0.6
1984	NY-N	74	207	20	51	7	1	1	10	9	43	.246	.278	.304	64	-10	6	1	1	.947	-4	S-49,2-18/3	-0.9
1985	NY-N	26	39	5	7	2	1	0	2	8	11	.179	.319	.282	71	-1	0	0	0	.911	-1	S-13/2-5,3	-0.1
Total	5	285	710	57	165	27	3	4	49	46	122	.232	.279	.296	62	-36	13	9	-2	.955	15	S-230/2-30,3	-0.5

■ ALEX GARDNER
Gardner, Alexander b: 4/28/1861, Toronto, Ont., Can. d: 6/18/26, Danvers, Mass. Deb: 5/10/1884

YEAR	TM/L	G	AB	R	H	2B	3B	HR	RBI	BB	SO	AVG	OBP	SLG	PRO+	BR/A	SB	CS	SBR	FA	FR	G/POS	TPR
1884	Was-a	1	3	0	0	0	0	0	0			.000	.000	.000	-99	-1				.600	-1	/C-1	-0.1

■ ART GARDNER
Gardner, Arthur Junior b: 9/21/52, Madden, Miss. BL/TL, 5'11", 175 lbs. Deb: 9/2/75

YEAR	TM/L	G	AB	R	H	2B	3B	HR	RBI	BB	SO	AVG	OBP	SLG	PRO+	BR/A	SB	CS	SBR	FA	FR	G/POS	TPR
1975	Hou-N	13	31	3	6	0	0	0	2	1	8	.194	.242	.194	24	-3	1	0	0	1.000	-1	/O-8	-0.4
1977	Hou-N	66	65	7	10	0	0	0	3	3	15	.154	.203	.154	-3	-10	0	0	0	1.000	-4	O-26	-1.4
1978	SF-N	7	3	2	0	0	0	0	0	0	2	.000	.000	.000	-99	-1	0	1	0	1.000	0	H	-0.2
Total	3	86	99	12	16	0	0	0	5	4	25	.162	.210	.162	2	-14	1	1	-0	1.000	-4	/O-34	-2.0

■ EARLE GARDNER
Gardner, Earle McClurkin b: 1/24/1884, Sparta, Ill. d: 3/2/43, Sparta, Ill. BR/TR, 5'11", 160 lbs. Deb: 9/18/08

YEAR	TM/L	G	AB	R	H	2B	3B	HR	RBI	BB	SO	AVG	OBP	SLG	PRO+	BR/A	SB	CS	SBR	FA	FR	G/POS	TPR
1908	NY-A	20	75	7	16	2	0	0	4	1		.213	.234	.240	53	-4	0			.947	4	2-20	0.0
1909	NY-A	22	85	12	28	4	0	0	15	3		.329	.352	.376	129	3	4			.945	-8	2-22	-0.6
1910	NY-A	86	271	36	66	4	2	1	24	10		.244	.303	.284	79	-6	9			.936	6	2-70	-0.2
1911	NY-A	102	357	36	94	13	2	0	39	20		.263	.312	.311	69	-15	14			.959	-3	*2-101	-2.0
1912	NY-A	43	160	14	45	3	1	0	26	5		.281	.303	.313	72	-6	11			.922	-4	2-43	-1.1
Total	5	273	948	105	249	26	5	1	108	50		.263	.305	.304	76	-29	38			.944	-5	2-256	-3.9

■ GID GARDNER
Gardner, Frank Washington b: 6/9/1859, Attleboro, Mass. d: 8/1/14, Cambridge, Mass. 165 lbs. Deb: 8/23/1879

YEAR	TM/L	G	AB	R	H	2B	3B	HR	RBI	BB	SO	AVG	OBP	SLG	PRO+	BR/A	SB	CS	SBR	FA	FR	G/POS	TPR
1879	Tro-N	2	6	1	1	0	0	0		0	0	.167	.167	.167	11	-1				.429	-1	/P-2	0.0
1880	Cle-N	10	32	0	6	1	1	0	4	2	4	.188	.235	.281	76	-1				.850	-1	/P-9,O-1	0.0
1883	Bal-a	42	161	28	44	10	3	1		18		.273	.346	.391	133	6				.837	-1	O-35/2-4,3P	0.5
1884	Bal-a	41	173	32	37	6	8	2		14		.214	.280	.376	108	1				.860	4	O-40/1-2	0.4
	CP-U	38	149	22	38	10	2	0		10		.255	.302	.349	77	-5				.872	-1	O-29/3-8,P2	-0.6
	Bal-U	1	4	0	1	0	0	0		0		.250	.250	.250	33	-0				.714	-0	/S-1	0.0
	Yr	39	153	22	39	10	2	0		10		.255	.301	.346	76	-5				.872	-1	O-29/3-8,P2S	-0.6
1885	Bal-a	44	170	22	37	5	4	0		12		.218	.269	.294	79	-4				.891	3	2-39/O-5,1P	0.1
1887	Ind-N	18	63	8	11	1	0	1	8	12	11	.175	.307	.238	55	-3	7			1.000	-3	O-11/2-7	-0.6
1888	Was-N	1	3	0	1	0	0	0		1	1	.333	.500	.333	180	1	0			.750	0	/S-1	0.1
	Phi-N	1	3	0	2	0	0	0	1	0	0	.667	.667	.667	310	1	0			1.000	-1	/2-1	0.0
	Was-N	1	1	0	0	0	0	0		0	0	.000	.000	.000	-99	-0	0			1.000	-1	/2-1	-0.1
	Yr	3	7	0	3	0	0	0	1	1	1	.429	.500	.429	202	1	0			1.000	-1	*2-2,S-1	0.0
Total	7	199	765	113	178	33	18	4	13	69	16	.233	.298	.339	94	-5	7			.855	0	O-121/2-53,P31S	-0.2

■ JEFF GARDNER
Gardner, Jeffrey Scott b: 2/4/64, Newport Beach, Cal. BL/TL, 5'11", 165 lbs. Deb: 9/10/91

YEAR	TM/L	G	AB	R	H	2B	3B	HR	RBI	BB	SO	AVG	OBP	SLG	PRO+	BR/A	SB	CS	SBR	FA	FR	G/POS	TPR
1991	NY-N	13	37	3	6	0	0	0	1	4	6	.162	.244	.162	17	-4	0	0	0	.818	-2	/S-8,2-3	-0.6
1992	SD-N	15	19	0	2	0	0	0	0	1	4	.105	.150	.105	-26	-3	0	0	0	1.000	4	2-11	0.1
1993	SD-N	140	404	53	106	21	7	1	24	45	69	.262	.338	.356	85	-8	2	6	-3	.983	-8	*2-133/3-1,S	-1.6
1994	Mon-N	18	32	4	7	0	1	0	1	3	5	.219	.286	.281	48	-2	0	0	0	.714	-5	/3-9,2-4	-0.8
Total	4	186	492	60	121	21	8	1	26	53	88	.246	.321	.327	73	-18	2	6	-3	.984	-11	2-151/3-10,S	-2.9

■ RAY GARDNER
Gardner, Raymond Vincent b: 10/25/01, Frederick, Md. d: 5/3/68, Frederick, Md. BR/TR, 5'8", 145 lbs. Deb: 4/16/29

YEAR	TM/L	G	AB	R	H	2B	3B	HR	RBI	BB	SO	AVG	OBP	SLG	PRO+	BR/A	SB	CS	SBR	FA	FR	G/POS	TPR
1929	Cle-A	82	256	28	67	3	2	1	24	29	16	.262	.337	.301	63	-13	10	13	-5	.952	8	S-82	-0.1
1930	Cle-A	33	13	7	1	0	0	0	1	0	0	.077	.077	.077	-59	-3	0	1	0	.861	8	S-22/2-5,3	0.4
Total	2	115	269	35	68	3	2	1	25	29	16	.253	.326	.290	57	-16	10	14	-5	.945	16	S-104/2-5,3	0.3

■ BILLY GARDNER
Gardner, William Frederick "Shotgun" b: 7/19/27, Waterford, Conn. BR/TR, 6', 180 lbs. Deb: 4/22/54 MC

YEAR	TM/L	G	AB	R	H	2B	3B	HR	RBI	BB	SO	AVG	OBP	SLG	PRO+	BR/A	SB	CS	SBR	FA	FR	G/POS	TPR
1954	NY-N	62	108	10	23	5	0	1	7	6	19	.213	.261	.287	42	-9	0	1	-1	.987	10	3-30,2-13/S	0.0
1955	NY-N	59	187	26	38	10	1	3	17	13	19	.203	.262	.316	52	-13	0	0	0	.940	3	S-38,3-10/2	-0.2
1956	Bal-A	144	515	53	119	16	2	11	50	29	53	.231	.281	.334	67	-27	5	5	-2	.974	-12	*2-132,S-25/3	-2.9
1957	Bal-A	154	644	79	169	**36**	3	6	55	53	67	.262	.326	.356	92	-8	10	7	-1	**.987**	6	*2-148/S-9	0.9
1958	Bal-A	151	560	32	126	28	2	3	33	34	53	.225	.273	.298	60	-31	2	3	-1	.985	-22	*2-151,S-13	-4.6
1959	Bal-A	140	401	34	87	13	2	6	27	38	61	.217	.286	.304	64	-20	2	1	0	.976	**31**	*2-139/S-1,3	2.0
1960	Was-A	145	592	71	152	26	5	9	56	43	76	.257	.314	.363	83	-14	0	4	-2	.973	-2	*2-145,S-13	-0.5
1961	Min-A	45	154	13	36	9	0	1	11	10	14	.234	.280	.312	55	-10	0	0	0	.973	-4	2-41/3-2	-1.0
	*NY-A	41	99	11	21	5	1	0	2	6	18	.212	.278	.293	56	-6	0	0	0	.952	3	3-33/2-6	-0.3
	Yr	86	253	24	57	14	1	1	13	16	32	.225	.279	.304	56	-16	0	0	0	.975	-1	2-47,3-35	-1.3
1962	NY-A	4	1	1	0	0	0	0	0	0	1	.000	.000	.000	-99	-0	0	0	0	1.000	1	/2-1,3-1	0.0
	Bos-A	53	199	22	54	9	2	0	12	10	39	.271	.310	.337	72	-8	0	0	0	.963	-8	2-38/3-7,S	-1.2
	Yr	57	200	23	54	9	2	0	12	10	40	.270	.308	.335	72	-8	0	0	0	.963	-7	2-39/3-8,S	-1.2
1963	Bos-A	36	84	4	16	2	1	0	4	1	19	.190	.236	.238	32	-8	0	0	0	.989	7	2-21/3-2	0.1
Total	10	1034	3544	356	841	159	18	41	271	246	439	.237	.293	.327	70	-155	19	22	-8	.978	8	2-839,S-108/3	-8.5

■ LARRY GARDNER
Gardner, William Lawrence b: 5/13/1886, Enosburg Falls, Vt d: 3/11/76, St.George, Vt. BL/TR, 5'8", 165 lbs. Deb: 6/25/08

YEAR	TM/L	G	AB	R	H	2B	3B	HR	RBI	BB	SO	AVG	OBP	SLG	PRO+	BR/A	SB	CS	SBR	FA	FR	G/POS	TPR
1908	Bos-A	3	10	0	3	1	0	0	1	0		.300	.300	.400	124	0	0			.333	-3	/3-3	-0.3
1909	Bos-A	19	37	7	11	1	2	0	5	4		.297	.381	.432	153	2	1			.800	-4	/3-8,S-5	-0.1

YEAR	TM/L	G	AB	R	H	2B	3B	HR	RBI	BB	SO	AVG	OBP	SLG	PRO+	BR/A	SB	CS	SBR	FA	FR	G/POS	TPR
1910	Bos-A	113	413	55	117	12	10	2	36	41		.283	.354	.375	125	12	8			.944	-9	*2-113	0.1
1911	Bos-A	138	492	80	140	17	8	4	44	64		.285	.373	.376	110	8	27			.962	24	3-72,2-62	3.1
1912	*Bos-A	143	517	88	163	24	18	3	86	56		.315	.383	.449	131	20	25			.930	-1	*3-143	2.0
1913	Bos-A	131	473	64	133	17	10	0	63	47	34	.281	.347	.359	104	3	18			.943	-16	*3-130	-1.2
1914	Bos-A	155	553	50	143	23	19	3	68	35	39	.259	.303	.385	107	1	16	23	-9	.942	0	*3-153	-0.3
1915	*Bos-A	127	430	51	111	14	6	1	55	39	24	.258	.327	.326	98	-1	11	12	-4	.933	-7	*3-127	-0.7
1916	*Bos-A	148	493	47	152	19	7	2	62	48	27	.308	.372	.387	128	17	12			.953	-14	*3-147	0.8
1917	Bos-A	146	501	53	133	23	7	1	61	54	37	.265	.341	.345	110	7	16			.937	-7	*3-146	0.3
1918	Phi-A	127	463	50	132	22	6	1	52	43	22	.285	.346	.365	113	7	9			.964	10	*3-127	2.2
1919	Cle-A	139	524	67	157	29	7	2	79	39	29	.300	.352	.393	103	1	7			.946	-6	*3-139	0.1
1920	*Cle-A	154	597	72	185	31	11	3	118	53	25	.310	.367	.414	103	3	3	20	-11	.976	-2	*3-154	0.5
1921	Cle-A	153	586	101	187	32	14	3	120	65	16	.319	.391	.437	109	9	3	3	-1	.950	-1	*3-152	1.7
1922	Cle-A	137	470	74	134	31	3	2	68	49	21	.285	.355	.377	90	-6	9	8	-2	.951	-5	*3-128	-0.4
1923	Cle-A	52	79	4	20	5	1	0	12	12	7	.253	.352	.342	83	-2	0	1	-1	.962	3	3-19	0.1
1924	Cle-A	38	50	3	10	0	0	0	4	5	1	.200	.273	.200	23	-6	0	1	-1	.875	-4	/3-8,2-6	-0.9
Total	17	1923	6688	866	1931	301	129	27	934	654	282	.289	.355	.384	109	75	165	68		.948	-40	*3-1656,2-181/S	6.3

■ **ART GARIBALDI**   Garibaldi, Arthur Edward b: 8/20/07, San Francisco, Cal d: 10/19/67, Sacramento, Cal. BR/TR, 5'8", 165 lbs. Deb: 6/20/36

1936	StL-N	71	232	30	64	12	0	1	29	16	30	.276	.323	.341	79	-7	3			.925	-5	3-46,2-24	-0.9

■ **DEBS GARMS**   Garms, Debs C. "Tex" b: 6/26/08, Bangs, Tex. d: 12/16/84, Glen Rose, Tex. BL/TR, 5'8.5", 165 lbs. Deb: 8/10/32

1932	StL-A	34	134	20	38	7	1	1	8	17	7	.284	.364	.373	86	-2	4	3	-1	.953	-1	O-33	-0.5
1933	StL-A	78	189	35	60	10	2	4	24	30	21	.317	.416	.455	123	7	2	5	-2	.960	-2	O-47	0.0
1934	StL-A	91	232	25	68	14	4	0	31	27	19	.293	.372	.388	89	-4	0	0	0	.942	-3	O-56	-0.8
1935	StL-A	10	15	1	4	0	0	0	0	2	2	.267	.353	.267	59	-1	0	0	0	.800	-0	/O-2	-0.1
1937	Bos-N	125	478	60	124	15	8	2	37	37	33	.259	.317	.337	85	-11	2			.977	-8	O-81,3-36	-2.0
1938	Bos-N	117	428	62	135	19	1	0	47	34	22	.315	.371	.364	114	9	4			.985	-7	O-63,3-54/2	0.1
1939	Bos-N	132	513	68	153	24	9	2	37	39	20	.298	.350	.392	107	4	2			.964	-4	O-96,3-37	-0.3
1940	Pit-N	103	358	76	127	23	7	5	57	23	6	.355	.395	.500	147	22	3			.964	-1	3-64,O-19	2.2
1941	Pit-N	83	220	25	58	9	3	3	42	22	12	.264	.331	.373	98	-1	0			.911	-10	3-29,O-24	-1.2
1943	*StL-N	90	249	26	64	10	2	0	22	13	8	.257	.299	.313	74	-9	1			.980	-5	O-47,3-23/S	-1.7
1944	*StL-N	73	149	17	30	3	0	0	5	13	8	.201	.265	.221	37	-12	0			1.000	-8	O-23,3-21	-2.2
1945	StL-N	74	146	23	49	7	2	0	18	31	3	.336	.452	.411	137	9	0			.956	-10	3-32,O-10	0.0
Total	12	1010	3111	438	910	141	39	17	328	288	161	.293	.355	.379	103	13	18	8		.966	-58	O-501,3-296/S2	-6.5

■ **PHIL GARNER**   Garner, Philip Mason b: 4/30/49, Jefferson City, Tenn. BR/TR, 5'10", 177 lbs. Deb: 9/10/73 MC

1973	Oak-A	9	5	0	0	0	0	0	0	0	3	.000	.000	.000	-99	-1	0	0	0	1.000	1	/3-9	-0.1
1974	Oak-A	30	28	4	5	1	0	0	1	1	5	.179	.207	.214	23	-3	1	1	-0	.955	4	3-19/S-8,2D	0.1
1975	*Oak-A	160	488	46	120	21	5	6	54	30	65	.246	.296	.346	83	-12	4	6	-2	.968	-16	*2-160/S-1	-2.2
1976	Oak-A★	159	555	54	145	29	12	8	74	36	71	.261	.309	.400	111	5	35	13	3	.975	-14	*2-159	0.5
1977	Pit-N	153	585	99	152	35	10	17	77	55	65	.260	.326	.441	101	-0	32	9	4	.971	1	*3-107,2-50,S	0.7
1978	Pit-N	154	528	66	138	25	9	10	66	66	71	.261	.349	.400	104	4	27	14	-0	.976	10	2-81,3-81/S	1.9
1979	*Pit-N	150	549	76	161	32	8	11	59	54	74	.293	.361	.441	112	9	17	8	0	.981	6	2-83,3-78,S	2.2
1980	Pit-N★	151	548	62	142	27	6	5	58	46	53	.259	.319	.358	87	-9	32	7	5	.976	16	*2-151/S-1	2.3
1981	Pit-N★	56	181	22	46	6	2	1	20	21	21	.254	.332	.326	84	-3	4	6	-2	.968	-6	2-50	-1.0
	*Hou-N	31	113	13	27	3	1	0	6	15	11	.239	.328	.283	79	-3	6	2	1	.982	0	2-31	0.0
	Yr	87	294	35	73	9	3	1	26	36	32	.248	.330	.310	82	-6	10	8	-2	.973	-6	2-81	-1.0
1982	Hou-N	155	588	65	161	33	8	13	83	40	92	.274	.323	.423	116	10	24	13	-1	.980	1	*2-136,3-18	1.8
1983	Hou-N	154	567	76	135	24	2	14	79	63	84	.238	.320	.362	94	-5	18	12	-2	.945	4	*3-154	-0.5
1984	Hou-N	128	374	60	104	17	6	4	45	43	63	.278	.359	.388	118	10	3	2	-0	.979	23	3-82,2-35	3.3
1985	Hou-N	135	463	65	124	23	10	6	51	34	72	.268	.321	.400	103	1	4	4	-1	.932	-9	*3-123,2-15	-1.1
1986	*Hou-N	107	313	43	83	14	3	9	41	30	45	.265	.331	.415	108	3	12	6	0	.896	1	3-84/2-7	0.2
1987	Hou-N	43	112	15	25	5	0	3	15	8	20	.223	.275	.348	66	-6	1	0	0	.976	2	3-36/2-2	-0.4
	LA-N	70	126	14	24	4	0	2	8	20	24	.190	.301	.270	54	-8	5	1	1	.923	6	3-46,2-12/S	-0.1
	Yr	113	238	29	49	9	0	5	23	28	44	.206	.289	.307	60	-14	6	1	1	.947	8	3-82,2-14/S	-0.5
1988	SF-N	15	13	0	2	0	0	0	1	1	3	.154	.214	.154	8	-2	0	1	-1	.000	0	/3-2	-0.2
Total	16	1860	6136	780	1594	299	82	109	738	564	842	.260	.326	.389	100	-10	225	105	4	.974	30	2-975,3-839/SD	7.4

■ **RALPH GARR**   Garr, Ralph Allen "Road Runner" b: 12/12/45, Monroe, La. BL/TR, 5'11", 197 lbs. Deb: 9/3/68

1968	Atl-N	11	7	3	2	0	0	0	0	1	0	.286	.375	.286	100	0	1	0	0	.000	0	H	0.0
1969	Atl-N	22	27	6	6	1	0	0	2	2	4	.222	.276	.259	50	-2	1	1	-0	.857	-1	/O-7	-0.4
1970	Atl-N	37	96	18	27	3	0	0	8	5	12	.281	.317	.313	65	-5	5	2	0	1.000	0	O-21	-0.5
1971	Atl-N	154	639	101	219	24	6	9	44	30	68	.343	.374	.441	122	18	30	14	1	.968	16	*O-153	2.9
1972	Atl-N	134	554	87	180	22	0	12	53	25	41	.325	.361	.430	113	9	25	9	2	.962	-4	*O-131	0.1
1973	Atl-N	148	668	94	200	32	6	11	55	22	64	.299	.324	.415	96	-5	35	11	4	.968	1	*O-148	-0.7
1974	Atl-N★	143	606	87	214	24	17	11	54	28	52	.353	.384	.503	141	30	26	16	-2	.967	-19	*O-139	0.4
1975	Atl-N	151	625	74	174	26	11	6	31	44	50	.278	.329	.384	94	-6	14	9	-1	.966	6	*O-148	-0.7
1976	Chi-A	136	527	63	158	22	6	4	36	17	41	.300	.324	.387	107	3	14	5	1	.978	-6	*O-125/D-6	-0.8
1977	Chi-A	134	543	78	163	29	7	10	54	27	44	.300	.333	.435	108	5	12	7	-1	.987	3	*O-126/D-2	0.1
1978	Chi-A	118	443	67	122	18	9	3	29	24	41	.275	.314	.377	93	-5	7	5	-1	.959	1	*O-109/D-9	-1.0
1979	Chi-A	102	307	34	86	10	2	9	39	17	19	.280	.320	.414	96	-2	4	4	-2	.951	-8	O-67,D-17	-1.4
	Cal-A	6	24	0	3	0	0	0	0	0	3	.125	.125	.125	-33	-4	0	0	0	.000	0	/D-6	-0.5
	Yr	108	331	34	89	10	2	9	39	17	22	.269	.307	.393	87	-7	4	4	-2	.951	-8	O-67,D-17/H	-1.9
1980	Cal-A	21	42	5	8	1	0	0	3	4	6	.190	.261	.214	33	-4	0	0	0	.750	-0	/O-2,D-8	-0.4
Total	13	1317	5108	717	1562	212	64	75	408	246	445	.306	.340	.416	106	33	172	83	2	.968	-11	*O-1176/D-48	-2.9

■ **ADRIAN GARRETT**   Garrett, Henry Adrian "Pat" b: 1/3/43, Brooksville, Fla. BL/TR, 6'3", 185 lbs. Deb: 4/13/66 FC

1966	Atl-N	4	3	0	0	0	0	0	0	0	2	.000	.000	.000	-99	-1	0	0	0	.000	-0	/O-1	-0.1
1970	Chi-N	3	3	0	0	0	0	0	0	0	3	.000	.000	.000	-89	-1	0	0	0	.000	0	H	-0.1
1971	Oak-A	14	21	1	3	0	0	1	2	5	7	.143	.308	.286	70	-1	0	0	0	1.000	-0	/O-5	-0.1
1972	Oak-A	14	11	0	0	0	0	0	0	1	4	.000	.083	.000	-78	-2	0	0	0	1.000	-1	/O-2	-0.3
1973	Chi-N	36	54	7	12	0	0	3	8	4	18	.222	.276	.389	77	-2	1	0	0	1.000	-1	/O-7,C-6	-0.3
1974	Chi-N	10	8	0	0	0	0	0	0	1	1	.000	.111	.000	-64	-2	0	0	0	1.000	0	/C-3,1-1,O	-0.1
1975	Chi-N	16	21	2	2	0	0	1	6	1	9	.095	.136	.238	2	-3	0	0	0	1.000	1	/1-4	-0.2
	Cal-A	37	107	17	28	5	0	6	18	14	28	.262	.347	.477	141	5	3	0	0	1.000	-0	D-23,1-10/OC	0.5
1976	Cal-A	29	48	4	6	3	0	0	3	5	16	.125	.208	.188	17	-5	0	0	0	.974	-4	C-15/1-1,D	-0.9
Total	8	163	276	30	51	8	0	11	37	31	87	.185	.267	.333	71	-11	0	0	0	.959	-5	/D-27,C-25,O1	-1.6

■ **WAYNE GARRETT**   Garrett, Ronald Wayne b: 12/3/47, Brooksville, Fla. BL/TR, 5'11", 183 lbs. Deb: 4/12/69 F

1969	*NY-N	124	400	38	87	11	3	1	39	40	75	.218	.293	.268	57	-22	4	2	0	.951	-13	3-72,2-47/S	-3.4
1970	NY-N	114	366	74	93	17	4	12	45	81	60	.254	.392	.421	118	12	5	1	1	.944	-3	3-70,2-45/S	-0.3
1971	NY-N	56	202	20	43	12	0	1	14	28	31	.213	.312	.238	58	-10	1	3	-2	.967	-4	3-53/2-9	-1.7
1972	NY-N	111	298	41	69	13	2	1	29	70	58	.232	.378	.315	101	4	3	2	-0	.960	2	3-82,2-22	0.7
1973	*NY-N	140	504	76	129	20	3	16	58	72	74	.256	.350	.403	110	8	6	5	-1	.942	11	*3-130/S-9,2	1.9

YEAR	TM/L	G	AB	R	H	2B	3B	HR	RBI	BB	SO	AVG	OBP	SLG	PRO+	BR/A	SB	CS	SBR	FA	FR	G/POS	TPR
1974	NY-N	151	522	55	117	14	3	13	53	89	96	.224	.339	.337	91	-4	4	6	-2	.955	14	*3-144/S-9	0.7
1975	NY-N	107	274	49	73	8	3	6	34	50	45	.266	.382	.383	118	8	3	2	-0	.966	11	3-94/S-3,2	1.9
1976	NY-N	80	251	36	56	8	1	4	26	52	26	.223	.359	.311	97	1	7	5	-1	.948	3	3-64,2-10/S	0.4
	Mon-N	59	177	15	43	4	1	2	11	30	20	.243	.353	.311	86	-2	2	2	-1	.982	1	2-54/3-2	0.2
	Yr	139	428	51	99	12	2	6	37	82	46	.231	.356	.311	92	-1	9	7	-2	.949	4	3-66,2-64/S	0.6
1977	Mon-N	68	159	17	43	6	1	2	22	30	18	.270	.389	.358	105	3	2	2	-1	1.000	2	3-49/2-1	0.4
1978	Mon-N	49	69	6	12	0	0	1	2	8	10	.174	.260	.217	35	-6	0	0	0	.969	1	3-13	-0.6
	StL-N	33	63	11	21	4	0	1	10	11	16	.333	.432	.444	148	5	1	0	0	.927	-2	3-19	0.3
	Yr	82	132	17	33	4	0	2	12	19	26	.250	.344	.326	89	-1	1	0	0	.945	-2	3-32	-0.3
Total	10	1092	3285	438	786	107	22	61	340	561	529	.239	.352	.341	95	-4	38	30	-7	.956	7	3-792,2-195/S	0.5

■ GIL GARRIDO   Garrido, Gil Gonzalo b: 6/26/41, Panama City, Pan. BR/TR, 5'8", 160 lbs. Deb: 4/24/64

YEAR	TM/L	G	AB	R	H	2B	3B	HR	RBI	BB	SO	AVG	OBP	SLG	PRO+	BR/A	SB	CS	SBR	FA	FR	G/POS	TPR
1964	SF-N	14	25	1	2	0	0	0	1	2	7	.080	.148	.080	-33	-4	1	0	0	.969	-1	S-14	-0.5
1968	Atl-N	18	53	5	11	0	0	0	2	2	2	.208	.236	.208	34	-4	0	0	0	.987	3	S-17	0.1
1969	*Atl-N	82	227	18	50	5	1	0	10	16	11	.220	.272	.251	47	-16	0	0	0	.973	-11	S-81	-2.1
1970	Atl-N	101	367	38	97	5	4	1	19	15	16	.264	.293	.308	58	-22	0	2	-1	.975	-1	S-80,2-26	-1.3
1971	Atl-N	79	125	8	27	3	0	0	12	15	12	.216	.300	.240	51	-8	0	1	-0	.961	4	S-32,3-28,2	0.0
1972	Atl-N	40	75	11	20	1	0	0	7	11	6	.267	.368	.280	79	-1	1	1	-0	.989	1	2-21,S-10/3	0.0
Total	6	334	872	81	207	14	5	1	51	61	54	.237	.288	.268	53	-55	2	4	-2	.974	-4	S-234/2-65,3	-3.8

■ CECIL GARRIOTT   Garriott, Virgil Cecil b: 8/15/16, Harristown, Ill. d: 2/20/90, Lake Elsinore, Cal BL/TR, 5'8", 165 lbs. Deb: 9/4/46

YEAR	TM/L	G	AB	R	H	2B	3B	HR	RBI	BB	SO	AVG	OBP	SLG	PRO+	BR/A	SB	CS	SBR	FA	FR	G/POS	TPR
1946	Chi-N	6	5	1	0	0	0	0	0	0	2	.000	.167	.000	-52	-1	0	0	0	.000	0	H	-0.1

■ FORD GARRISON   Garrison, Robert Ford "Rocky" or "Snapper" b: 8/29/15, Greenville, S.C. BR/TR, 5'10.5", 180 lbs. Deb: 4/22/43 C

YEAR	TM/L	G	AB	R	H	2B	3B	HR	RBI	BB	SO	AVG	OBP	SLG	PRO+	BR/A	SB	CS	SBR	FA	FR	G/POS	TPR
1943	Bos-A	36	129	13	36	5	1	1	11	5	14	.279	.306	.357	92	-0	2	1	-0	.988	-0	O-32	-0.5
1944	Bos-A	13	49	5	12	3	0	0	2	6	4	.245	.327	.306	82	-1	0	0	0	.969	1	O-12	-0.1
	Phi-A	121	449	58	121	13	2	4	37	22	40	.269	.307	.334	84	-10	10	4	1	.987	6	*O-119	-1.0
	Yr	134	498	63	133	16	2	4	39	28	44	.267	.309	.331	84	-11	10	4	1	.985	7	*O-131	-1.1
1945	Phi-A	6	23	3	7	1	0	1	6	4	3	.304	.407	.478	157	2	1	0	0	1.000	1	/O-5	0.2
1946	Phi-A	9	37	1	4	0	0	0	0	0	6	.108	.108	.108	-40	-7	0	0	0	1.000	-2	/O-8	-1.0
Total	4	185	687	80	180	22	3	6	56	37	67	.262	.302	.329	81	-18	11	5	1	.986	5	O-176	-2.4

■ HANK GARRITY   Garrity, Francis Joseph b: 2/4/08, Boston, Mass. d: 9/1/62, Boston, Mass. BR/TR, 6'1", 185 lbs. Deb: 7/26/31

YEAR	TM/L	G	AB	R	H	2B	3B	HR	RBI	BB	SO	AVG	OBP	SLG	PRO+	BR/A	SB	CS	SBR	FA	FR	G/POS	TPR
1931	Chi-A	8	14	0	3	1	0	0	2	1	2	.214	.267	.286	48	-1	0	0	0	.941	0	/C-7	-0.1

■ STEVE GARVEY   Garvey, Steven Patrick b: 12/22/48, Tampa, Fla. BR/TR, 5'10", 192 lbs. Deb: 9/1/69

YEAR	TM/L	G	AB	R	H	2B	3B	HR	RBI	BB	SO	AVG	OBP	SLG	PRO+	BR/A	SB	CS	SBR	FA	FR	G/POS	TPR
1969	LA-N	3	3	0	1	0	0	0	0	0	1	.333	.333	.333	94	-0	0	0	0	.000	0	H	0.0
1970	LA-N	34	93	8	25	5	0	1	6	6	17	.269	.313	.355	82	-3	1	1	-0	.943	6	3-27/2-1	0.3
1971	LA-N	81	225	27	51	12	1	7	26	21	33	.227	.293	.382	95	-2	1	2	-1	.939	17	3-79	1.6
1972	LA-N	96	294	36	79	14	2	9	30	19	36	.269	.315	.422	110	3	4	2	0	.902	13	3-85/1-3	1.6
1973	LA-N	114	349	37	106	17	3	8	50	11	42	.304	.331	.438	116	6	0	2	-1	.993	-8	1-76,O-10	-1.0
1974	*LA-N★	156	642	95	200	32	3	21	111	31	66	.312	.346	.469	132	23	5	4	-1	.995	-13	*1-156	-0.2
1975	LA-N★	160	659	85	210	38	6	18	95	33	66	.319	.364	.476	135	27	11	2	2	**.995**	-10	*1-160	0.9
1976	LA-N★	162	631	85	200	37	4	13	80	50	69	.317	.368	.450	134	27	19	8	1	**.998**	-16	*1-162	0.1
1977	*LA-N★	162	646	91	192	25	3	33	115	38	90	.297	.337	.498	121	17	9	6	1	**.995**	-16	*1-160	-1.0
1978	*LA-N★	162	639	89	**202**	36	9	21	113	40	70	.316	.357	.499	138	29	10	5	0	.994	-9	*1-161	1.1
1979	LA-N★	162	648	92	204	32	1	28	110	37	59	.315	.354	.497	131	25	3	6	-3	.995	-2	*1-162	1.2
1980	LA-N★	163	658	78	**200**	27	1	26	106	36	67	.304	.343	.467	126	21	6	11	-5	.996	-3	*1-162	1.0
1981	*LA-N★	110	431	63	122	23	1	10	64	25	49	.283	.324	.411	111	5	3	5	-2	**.999**	-6	*1-110	-1.1
1982	LA-N	162	625	66	176	35	1	16	86	20	86	.282	.305	.418	103	-0	5	3	-0	.995	1	*1-158	-0.8
1983	SD-N	100	388	76	114	22	0	14	59	29	39	.294	.348	.459	126	12	4	1	1	.994	-11	*1-100	-0.4
1984	*SD-N★	161	617	72	175	27	2	8	86	24	64	.284	.312	.373	92	-8	1	2	-1	**1.000**	-4	*1-159	-2.4
1985	SD-N	162	654	80	184	34	6	17	81	35	67	.281	.321	.430	110	6	0	0	0	.997	-3	*1-162	-1.3
1986	SD-N	155	557	58	142	22	0	21	81	23	72	.255	.286	.408	91	-9	1	2	-1	.994	-18	*1-148	-4.0
1987	SD-N	27	76	5	16	2	0	1	9	1	10	.211	.231	.276	35	-7	0	0	0	1.000	0	1-20	-0.8
Total	19	2332	8835	1143	2599	440	43	272	1308	479	1003	.294	.333	.446	117	171	83	62	-12	.996	-78	*1-2059,3-191/O2	-5.2

■ ROD GASPAR   Gaspar, Rodney Earl b: 4/3/46, Long Beach, Cal. BB/TR, 5'11", 165 lbs. Deb: 4/8/69

YEAR	TM/L	G	AB	R	H	2B	3B	HR	RBI	BB	SO	AVG	OBP	SLG	PRO+	BR/A	SB	CS	SBR	FA	FR	G/POS	TPR
1969	*NY-N	118	215	26	49	6	1	1	14	25	19	.228	.314	.279	66	-9	7	3	0	.983	-7	O-91	-2.0
1970	NY-N	11	14	4	0	0	0	0	0	1	4	.000	.067	.000	-80	-4	1	0	0	1.000	-1	/O-8	-0.4
1971	SD-N	16	17	1	2	0	0	0	2	3	3	.118	.250	.118	8	-2	0	1	-1	1.000	-1	/O-2	-0.3
1974	SD-N	33	14	4	3	0	0	0	1	4	3	.214	.389	.214	75	-0	0	0	0	1.000	-2	/O-8,1-2	-0.3
Total	4	178	260	35	54	6	1	1	17	33	29	.208	.302	.250	55	-15	8	4	0	.986	-10	O-109/1-2	-3.0

■ TOM GASTALL   Gastall, Thomas Everett b: 6/13/32, Fall River, Mass. d: 9/20/56, Riviera Beach, Md. BR/TR, 6'2", 187 lbs. Deb: 6/21/55

YEAR	TM/L	G	AB	R	H	2B	3B	HR	RBI	BB	SO	AVG	OBP	SLG	PRO+	BR/A	SB	CS	SBR	FA	FR	G/POS	TPR
1955	Bal-A	20	27	4	4	1	0	0	0	3	5	.148	.233	.185	15	-3	0	0	0	.967	-1	C-15	-0.4
1956	Bal-A	32	56	3	11	2	0	0	4	3	8	.196	.250	.232	30	-6	0	0	0	1.000	0	/C-20	-0.4
Total	2	52	83	7	15	3	0	0	4	6	13	.181	.244	.217	25	-9	0	0	0	.990	0	/C-35	-0.8

■ ED GASTFIELD   Gastfield, Edward b: 8/1/1865, Chicago, Ill. d: 12/1/1899, Chicago, Ill. BR, 5'9.5", 155 lbs. Deb: 8/13/1884

YEAR	TM/L	G	AB	R	H	2B	3B	HR	RBI	BB	SO	AVG	OBP	SLG	PRO+	BR/A	SB	CS	SBR	FA	FR	G/POS	TPR
1884	Det-N	23	82	6	6	1	0	0	2	2	34	.073	.095	.085	-45	-13				.827	9	C-19/O-2,1	-0.3
1885	Det-N	1	3	0	0	0	0	0	0	0	2	.000	.000	.000	-99	-1				.714	-0	/C-1	-0.1
	Chi-N	1	3	0	0	0	0	0	0	0	1	.000	.000	.000	-87	-1				1.000	1	/C-1	0.1
	Yr	2	6	0	0	0	0	0	0	0	3	.000	.000	.000	-93	-1				.889	1	/C-2	0.0
Total	2	25	88	6	6	1	0	0	2	2	37	.068	.089	.080	-49	-14				.832	10	/C-21,1-2,O	-0.3

■ ALEX GASTON   Gaston, Alexander Nathaniel b: 3/12/1893, New York, N.Y. d: 2/8/79, Santa Monica, Cal. BR/TR, 5'9", 170 lbs. Deb: 9/26/20 F

YEAR	TM/L	G	AB	R	H	2B	3B	HR	RBI	BB	SO	AVG	OBP	SLG	PRO+	BR/A	SB	CS	SBR	FA	FR	G/POS	TPR
1920	NY-N	4	10	1	1	0	0	0	1	1	1	.100	.182	.100	-18	-1	0	0	0	.917	-1	/C-3	-0.3
1921	NY-N	20	22	1	5	1	1	0	3	1	9	.227	.261	.364	63	-1	0	0	0	.950	-0	C-11	-0.1
1922	NY-N	16	26	1	5	0	0	0	1	0	3	.192	.192	.192	-1	-4	1	0	0	1.000	0	C-13	-0.3
1923	NY-N	22	39	3	8	2	0	1	5	0	6	.205	.225	.333	46	-3	0	0	0	.957	0	C-21	-0.3
1926	Bos-A	98	301	37	67	5	3	0	21	21	28	.223	.282	.259	43	-25	3	0	1	.981	-10	C-98	-2.8
1929	Bos-A	55	116	14	26	5	2	2	9	6	8	.224	.262	.353	58	-8	1	0	0	.986	-1	C-49	-0.5
Total	6	215	514	58	112	13	6	3	40	29	56	.218	.266	.284	45	-43	5	0	2	.979	-13	C-195	-4.3

■ CITO GASTON   Gaston, Clarence Edwin b: 3/17/44, San Antonio, Tex. BR/TR, 6'4", 210 lbs. Deb: 9/14/67 MC

YEAR	TM/L	G	AB	R	H	2B	3B	HR	RBI	BB	SO	AVG	OBP	SLG	PRO+	BR/A	SB	CS	SBR	FA	FR	G/POS	TPR
1967	Atl-N	9	25	1	3	0	1	0	1	0	5	.120	.120	.200	-10	-4	0	0	0	.800	-1	/O-7	-0.5
1969	SD-N	129	391	20	90	11	7	2	28	24	117	.230	.276	.309	67	-18	4	4	-1	.959	6	*O-113	-2.1
1970	SD-N★	146	584	92	186	26	9	29	93	41	142	.318	.365	.543	146	34	4	1	1	.975	4	*O-142	3.1
1971	SD-N	141	518	57	118	13	4	17	61	24	121	.228	.265	.386	88	-11	1	0	0	.982	-0	*O-133	-1.9
1972	SD-N	111	379	30	102	14	0	7	44	22	76	.269	.313	.361	98	-2	0	2	-1	.977	1	O-94	-0.8
1973	SD-N	133	476	51	119	18	4	16	57	20	88	.250	.282	.405	96	-6	0	2	-1	.947	2	*O-119	-1.0
1974	SD-N	106	267	19	57	11	0	6	33	16	51	.213	.261	.322	65	-14	0	0	0	.992	3	O-63	-1.4
1975	Atl-N	64	141	17	34	3	0	4	15	17	33	.241	.323	.397	95	-1	1	0	0	.974	-1	O-35/1-1	-0.5
1976	Atl-N	69	134	15	39	4	0	4	25	13	21	.291	.354	.410	109	2	1	0	0	.977	-2	O-28/1-2	-0.1

YEAR	TM/L	G	AB	R	H	2B	3B	HR	RBI	BB	SO	AVG	OBP	SLG	PRO+	BR/A	SB	CS	SBR	FA	FR	G/POS	TPR
1977	Atl-N	56	85	6	23	4	0	3	21	5	19	.271	.311	.424	85	-2	1	0	0	1.000	-0	O-9,1-5	-0.2
1978	Atl-N	60	118	5	27	1	0	1	9	3	20	.229	.248	.263	38	-10	0	0	0	.957	-4	O-29/1-4	-1.5
	Pit-N	2	2	1	1	0	0	0	0	0	0	.500	.500	.500	172	0	0	0	0	.000	-0	/O-1	0.0
	Yr	62	120	6	28	1	0	1	9	3	20	.233	.252	.267	41	-9	0	0	0	.957	-4	O-30/1-4	-1.5
Total	11	1026	3120	314	799	106	30	91	387	185	693	.256	.300	.397	95	-32	13	7	-0	.970	6	O-773/1-12	-6.7

■ BRENT GATES
Gates, Brent Robert b: 3/14/70, Grand Rapids, Mich. BB/TR, 6'1", 180 lbs. Deb: 5/5/93

YEAR	TM/L	G	AB	R	H	2B	3B	HR	RBI	BB	SO	AVG	OBP	SLG	PRO+	BR/A	SB	CS	SBR	FA	FR	G/POS	TPR
1993	Oak-A	139	535	64	155	29	2	7	69	56	75	.290	.361	.391	109	7	7	3	0	.981	-2	*2-139	1.0
1994	Oak-A	64	233	29	66	11	1	2	24	21	32	.283	.356	.365	91	-3	3	0	1	.974	-17	2-63/1-1	-1.6
Total	2	203	768	93	221	40	3	9	93	77	107	.288	.356	.383	103	4	10	3	1	.979	-18	2-202/1-1	-0.6

■ JOE GATES
Gates, Joseph Daniel b: 10/3/54, Gary, Ind. BL/TR, 5'7", 175 lbs. Deb: 9/12/78

YEAR	TM/L	G	AB	R	H	2B	3B	HR	RBI	BB	SO	AVG	OBP	SLG	PRO+	BR/A	SB	CS	SBR	FA	FR	G/POS	TPR
1978	Chi-A	8	24	6	6	0	0	0	1	4	6	.250	.379	.250	80	-0	1	0	0	.972	-2	/2-8	-0.2
1979	Chi-A	16	16	5	1	0	1	0	1	2	3	.063	.167	.188	-5	-2	1	1	-0	.966	5	/2-8,3-1	0.2
Total	2	24	40	11	7	0	1	0	2	6	9	.175	.298	.225	46	-3	2	1	0	.969	2	/2-16,3-1	0.0

■ MIKE GATES
Gates, Michael Grant b: 9/20/56, Culver City, Cal. BL/TR, 6', 165 lbs. Deb: 5/6/81

YEAR	TM/L	G	AB	R	H	2B	3B	HR	RBI	BB	SO	AVG	OBP	SLG	PRO+	BR/A	SB	CS	SBR	FA	FR	G/POS	TPR
1981	Mon-N	1	2	1	1	0	1	0	1	0	1	.500	.500	1.500	445	1	0	0	0	1.000	-0	/2-1	0.0
1982	Mon-N	36	121	16	28	2	3	0	8	9	19	.231	.285	.298	62	-6	0	0	0	1.000	-9	2-36	-1.5
Total	2	37	123	17	29	2	4	0	9	9	20	.236	.288	.317	68	-5	0	0	0	1.000	-10	/2-37	-1.5

■ FRANK GATINS
Gatins, Frank Anthony b: 3/6/1871, Johnstown, Pa. d: 11/8/11, Johnstown, Pa. Deb: 9/21/1898

YEAR	TM/L	G	AB	R	H	2B	3B	HR	RBI	BB	SO	AVG	OBP	SLG	PRO+	BR/A	SB	CS	SBR	FA	FR	G/POS	TPR
1898	Was-N	17	58	6	13	2	0	0	5	3		.224	.274	.259	53	-4	2			.790	-8	S-17	-1.0
1901	Bro-N	50	197	21	45	7	2	1	21	5		.228	.255	.299	59	-11	6			.919	-9	3-46/S-5	-1.9
Total	2	67	255	27	58	9	2	1	26	8		.227	.259	.290	58	-14	8			.841	-17	/3-46,S-22	-2.9

■ JIM GAUDET
Gaudet, James Jennings b: 6/3/55, New Orleans, La. BR/TR, 6', 185 lbs. Deb: 9/10/78

YEAR	TM/L	G	AB	R	H	2B	3B	HR	RBI	BB	SO	AVG	OBP	SLG	PRO+	BR/A	SB	CS	SBR	FA	FR	G/POS	TPR
1978	KC-A	3	8	0	0	0	0	0	0	0	3	.000	.000	.000	-97	-2	0	0	0	.938	1	/C-3	-0.1
1979	KC-A	3	6	0	1	0	0	0	0	0	0	.167	.167	.167	-10	-1	0	0	0	1.000	1	/C-3	0.0
Total	2	6	14	0	1	0	0	0	0	0	3	.071	.071	.071	-59	-3	0	0	0	.966	2	/C-6	-0.1

■ MIKE GAULE
Gaule, Michael John b: 8/4/1869, Baltimore, Md. d: 1/24/18, Baltimore, Md. BL/TL, 6'2", Deb: 6/15/1889

YEAR	TM/L	G	AB	R	H	2B	3B	HR	RBI	BB	SO	AVG	OBP	SLG	PRO+	BR/A	SB	CS	SBR	FA	FR	G/POS	TPR
1889	Lou-a	1	2	0	0	0	0	0	0	0	0	.000	.000	.000	-99	-1	0			.000	-1	/O-1	-0.1

■ DOC GAUTREAU
Gautreau, Walter Paul "Punk" b: 7/26/01, Cambridge, Mass. d: 8/23/70, Salt Lake City, Ut BR/TR, 5'4", 129 lbs. Deb: 6/22/25

YEAR	TM/L	G	AB	R	H	2B	3B	HR	RBI	BB	SO	AVG	OBP	SLG	PRO+	BR/A	SB	CS	SBR	FA	FR	G/POS	TPR
1925	Phi-A	4	7	0	0	0	0	0	0	0	3	.000	.000	.000	-94	-2	0	0	0	.933	1	/2-4	-0.1
	Bos-N	68	279	45	73	13	3	0	23	35	13	.262	.346	.330	81	-7	11	7	-1	.976	-4	2-68	-1.0
1926	Bos-N	79	266	36	71	9	4	0	8	35	24	.267	.356	.331	94	-1	17			.942	-20	2-74	-1.9
1927	Bos-N	87	236	38	58	12	2	0	20	25	20	.246	.321	.314	76	-8	11			.965	-2	2-57	-0.8
1928	Bos-N	23	18	3	5	0	1	0	1	4	3	.278	.409	.389	116	1	1			.750	1	/2-4,S-1	0.0
Total	4	261	806	122	207	34	10	0	52	99	63	.257	.341	.324	83	-18	40	7		.960	-25	2-207/S-1	-3.8

■ SID GAUTREAUX
Gautreaux, Sidney Allen "Pudge" b: 5/4/12, Schriever, La. d: 4/19/80, Morgan City, La. BB/TR, 5'8", 190 lbs. Deb: 4/15/36

YEAR	TM/L	G	AB	R	H	2B	3B	HR	RBI	BB	SO	AVG	OBP	SLG	PRO+	BR/A	SB	CS	SBR	FA	FR	G/POS	TPR
1936	Bro-N	75	71	8	19	3	0	0	16	9	7	.268	.358	.310	80	-2	0			.963	-1	C-15	-0.2
1937	Bro-N	11	10	0	1	1	0	0	2	1	1	.100	.182	.200	4	-1	0			.000	0	H	-0.1
Total	2	86	81	8	20	4	0	0	18	10	8	.247	.337	.296	71	-3	0			.963	-1	/C-15	-0.3

■ GAVERN
Gavern Deb: 6/15/1874

YEAR	TM/L	G	AB	R	H	2B	3B	HR	RBI	BB	SO	AVG	OBP	SLG	PRO+	BR/A	SB	CS	SBR	FA	FR	G/POS	TPR
1874	Atl-n	1	4	1	0	0	0	0		0		.000	.000	.000	-99	-1						/2-1	-0.1

■ MIKE GAZELLA
Gazella, Michael b: 10/13/1896, Olyphant, Pa. d: 9/11/78, Odessa, Tex. BR/TR, 5'7.5", 165 lbs. Deb: 7/2/23

YEAR	TM/L	G	AB	R	H	2B	3B	HR	RBI	BB	SO	AVG	OBP	SLG	PRO+	BR/A	SB	CS	SBR	FA	FR	G/POS	TPR
1923	NY-A	8	13	2	1	0	0	0	1	2	3	.077	.200	.077	-25	-2	0	0	0	1.000	-1	/S-4,2-2,3	-0.3
1926	*NY-A	66	168	21	39	6	0	0	20	25	24	.232	.335	.268	60	-9	2	2	-1	.913	-4	3-45,S-11	-1.0
1927	NY-A	54	115	17	32	8	4	0	9	23	16	.278	.403	.417	117	4	4	1	1	.961	-6	3-44/S-6	-0.4
1928	NY-A	32	56	11	13	0	0	0	2	6	7	.232	.317	.232	48	-4	2	1	0	.969	-1	3-16/2-4,S	-0.4
Total	4	160	352	51	85	14	4	0	32	56	50	.241	.350	.304	73	-12	8	4	0	.940	-12	3-107/S-24,2	-1.7

■ DALE GEAR
Gear, Dale Dudley b: 2/2/1872, Lone Elm, Kan. d: 9/23/51, Topeka, Kan. BR/TR, 5'11", 165 lbs. Deb: 8/15/1896

YEAR	TM/L	G	AB	R	H	2B	3B	HR	RBI	BB	SO	AVG	OBP	SLG	PRO+	BR/A	SB	CS	SBR	FA	FR	G/POS	TPR
1896	Cle-N	4	15	5	6	1	1	0	3	1	1	.400	.438	.600	163	1	0			.857	-1	/P-3,1-1	0.0
1897	Cle-N	7	24	3	4	1	0	0	2	3		.167	.286	.208	30	-2	2			.750	0	/O-6	-0.2
1901	Was-A	58	199	17	47	9	2	0	20	4		.236	.251	.302	54	-13	2			.944	1	O-35,P-24	-1.0
Total	3	69	238	25	57	11	3	0	25	8	1	.239	.267	.311	59	-14	4			.900	0	/O-41,P-27,1	-1.2

■ GARY GEARHART
Gearhart, Lloyd William b: 8/10/23, New Lebanon, Ohio BR/TL, 5'11", 180 lbs. Deb: 4/18/47

YEAR	TM/L	G	AB	R	H	2B	3B	HR	RBI	BB	SO	AVG	OBP	SLG	PRO+	BR/A	SB	CS	SBR	FA	FR	G/POS	TPR
1947	NY-N	73	179	26	44	9	0	6	17	17	30	.246	.315	.397	87	-4	1			.961	-1	O-44	-0.7

■ HUCK GEARY
Geary, Eugene Francis Joseph b: 1/22/17, Buffalo, N.Y. d: 1/27/81, Cuba, N.Y. BL/TR, 5'10.5", 170 lbs. Deb: 7/17/42

YEAR	TM/L	G	AB	R	H	2B	3B	HR	RBI	BB	SO	AVG	OBP	SLG	PRO+	BR/A	SB	CS	SBR	FA	FR	G/POS	TPR
1942	Pit-N	9	22	3	5	0	0	0	2	2	3	.227	.292	.227	52	-1	0			.939	-1	/S-8	-0.1
1943	Pit-N	46	166	17	25	4	0	1	13	18	6	.151	.234	.193	23	-16	3			.956	-6	S-46	-2.0
Total	2	55	188	20	30	4	0	1	15	20	9	.160	.240	.197	26	-17	3			.954	-5	/S-54	-2.1

■ ELMER GEDEON
Gedeon, Elmer John b: 4/15/17, Cleveland, Ohio d: 4/20/44, St.Pol, France BR/TR, 6'4", 196 lbs. Deb: 9/18/39

YEAR	TM/L	G	AB	R	H	2B	3B	HR	RBI	BB	SO	AVG	OBP	SLG	PRO+	BR/A	SB	CS	SBR	FA	FR	G/POS	TPR
1939	Was-A	5	15	1	3	0	0	0	1	2	5	.200	.294	.200	31	-2	0	0	0	1.000	1	/O-5	-0.1

■ JOE GEDEON
Gedeon, Elmer Joseph b: 12/5/1893, Sacramento, Cal. d: 5/19/41, San Francisco, Cal BR/TR, 6', 167 lbs. Deb: 5/13/13

YEAR	TM/L	G	AB	R	H	2B	3B	HR	RBI	BB	SO	AVG	OBP	SLG	PRO+	BR/A	SB	CS	SBR	FA	FR	G/POS	TPR
1913	Was-A	29	71	3	13	1	3	0	6	1	6	.183	.205	.282	41	-6	3			.929	2	O-15/3-7,2SP	-0.4
1914	Was-A	4	2	0	0	0	0	0	0	1	0	.000	.333	.000	1	-0	0			.667	-1	/O-4	-0.1
1916	NY-A	122	435	50	92	14	4	0	27	40	61	.211	.282	.262	62	-20	14			.955	-10	*2-122	-2.9
1917	NY-A	33	117	15	28	7	0	0	8	7	13	.239	.288	.299	78	-3	4			.983	4	2-31	0.2
1918	StL-A	123	441	39	94	14	3	1	41	27	29	.213	.271	.265	64	-20	7			.977	16	*2-123	0.4
1919	StL-A	120	437	57	111	13	4	0	27	50	36	.254	.340	.302	79	-11	4			.975	-3	*2-118	-0.8
1920	StL-A	153	606	95	177	33	6	0	61	55	36	.292	.355	.366	89	-9	1	3	-2	.964	-26	*2-153	-3.1
Total	7	584	2109	259	515	82	20	1	171	180	181	.244	.311	.303	75	-69	33	3		.969	-18	2-549/O-19,3SP	-6.7

■ RICH GEDMAN
Gedman, Richard Leo b: 9/26/59, Worcester, Mass. BL/TR, 6', 215 lbs. Deb: 9/7/80

YEAR	TM/L	G	AB	R	H	2B	3B	HR	RBI	BB	SO	AVG	OBP	SLG	PRO+	BR/A	SB	CS	SBR	FA	FR	G/POS	TPR
1980	Bos-A	9	24	2	5	1	0	0	0	0	5	.208	.208	.208	14	-3	0	0	0	.867	-0	/C-2,D-4	-0.3
1981	Bos-A	62	205	22	59	15	0	5	26	9	31	.288	.321	.434	109	2	0	0	0	.990	-6	C-59	0.2
1982	Bos-A	92	289	30	72	17	2	4	26	10	37	.249	.279	.363	71	-12	0	1	-1	.977	-7	C-86	-1.7
1983	Bos-A	81	204	21	60	16	1	2	18	15	37	.294	.345	.412	100	0	0	0	0	.980	-3	C-68	-0.5
1984	Bos-A	133	449	54	121	26	4	24	72	29	72	.269	.315	.506	118	9	0	0	0	.977	-8	*C-125	0.7
1985	Bos-A★	144	498	66	147	30	5	18	80	57	69	.295	.363	.484	124	17	2	0	1	.983	4	*C-139	2.7
1986	*Bos-A★	135	462	49	119	29	0	16	65	37	61	.258	.318	.424	100	-1	1	0	0	.994	10	*C-134	1.8
1987	Bos-A	52	151	11	31	8	0	1	13	10	24	.205	.255	.278	40	-13	1	0	1	.976	-4	C-51	-1.3
1988	*Bos-A	95	299	33	69	14	0	9	39	18	49	.231	.281	.368	77	-10	0	0	0	.992	2	C-93/D-1	-0.1
1989	Bos-A	93	260	24	55	8	0	4	16	23	47	.212	.276	.292	57	-15	0	1	-1	.981	-0	/C-9	-1.2
1990	Bos-A	10	15	3	3	0	0	0	1	5	6	.200	.429	.200	78	0	0	0	0	.970	0	/C-9	0.0

YEAR	TM/L	G	AB	R	H	2B	3B	HR	RBI	BB	SO	AVG	OBP	SLG	PRO+	BR/A	SB	CS	SBR	FA	FR	G/POS	TPR
	Hou-N	40	104	4	21	7	0	1	10	15	24	.202	.303	.298	68	-4	0	0	0	1.000	6	C-39	0.4
1991	StL-N	46	94	7	10	1	0	3	8	4	15	.106	.143	.213	-1	-13	0	1	-1	.976	10	C-43	-0.2
1992	StL-N	41	105	5	23	4	0	1	8	11	22	.219	.293	.286	67	-5	0	0	0	.988	11	C-40	0.8
Total	13	1033	3159	331	795	176	12	88	382	236	509	.252	.307	.399	90	-48	3	4	-2	.984	20	C-979/D-5	1.9

■ COUNT GEDNEY
Gedney, Alfred W. b: 5/10/1849, Brooklyn, N.Y. d: 3/26/22, Hackensack, N.J. 5'9", 140 lbs. Deb: 4/27/1872

YEAR	TM/L	G	AB	R	H	2B	3B	HR	RBI	BB	SO	AVG	OBP	SLG	PRO+	BR/A	SB	CS	SBR	FA	FR	G/POS	TPR
1872	Tro-n	10	51	15	21	2	1	3	18	0	0	.412	.412	.667	223	7						/O-9	0.5
	Eck-n	18	72	4	11	1	0	0	5	0	1	.153	.153	.167	-2	-7						O-18	-0.5
	Yr	28	123	19	32	3	1	3	23	0	1	.260	.260	.374	102	1						O-27	0.0
1873	Mut-n	53	224	41	60	5	5	1	25	7	5	.268	.290	.348	88	-3						*O-53	-0.1
1874	Ath-n	54	222	49	60	6	1	1		7		.270	.293	.320	87	-4						*O-50/1-4	-0.3
1875	Mut-n	68	266	30	54	12	4	0		2		.203	.209	.278	63	-10						*O-66/P-2	-0.8
Total	4 n	203	835	139	206	26	11	5		16		.247	.261	.322	82							O-196/1-4,P	-1.2

■ BILLY GEER
Geer, William Henry Harrison (b: George Harrison Geer) b: 8/13/1849, Syracuse, N.Y. TR, 5'8", 160 lbs. Deb: 10/15/1874

YEAR	TM/L	G	AB	R	H	2B	3B	HR	RBI	BB	SO	AVG	OBP	SLG	PRO+	BR/A	SB	CS	SBR	FA	FR	G/POS	TPR
1874	Mut-n	2	8	0	2	0	0	0		0		.250	.250	.250	58	-0						/O-2	0.0
1875	NH-n	37	162	20	40	6	1	0		1		.247	.252	.296	102	1						O-17,2-13/S13	0.1
1878	Cin-N	61	237	31	52	13	2	0	20	10	18	.219	.251	.291	86	-3				.867	-4	*S-60/2-2	-0.4
1880	Wor-N	2	6	0	0	0	0	0	0	0	0	.000	.000	.000	-92	-1				1.000	-1	/O-1,S-1	-0.2
1884	Phi-U	9	36	7	9	2	1	0		4		.250	.325	.361	93	-0				.772	1	/S-9	0.1
	Bro-a	107	391	68	82	15	7	0		38		.210	.281	.284	84	-6				.870	17	*S-107/P-2,2	1.1
1885	Lou-a	14	51	2	6	2	0	0		2		.118	.167	.157	3	-6				.872	2	S-14	-0.3
Total	2 n	39	170	20	42	6	1	0		1		.247	.251	.294	99	1						/O-19,2-13,S31	0.1
Total	4	193	721	108	149	32	10	0	20	54	18	.207	.264	.279	78	-15				.864	15	S-191/2-4,PO	0.3

■ LOU GEHRIG
Gehrig, Henry Louis "The Iron Horse" b: 6/19/03, New York, N.Y. d: 6/2/41, Riverdale, N.Y. BL/TL, 6', 200 lbs. Deb: 6/15/23 H

YEAR	TM/L	G	AB	R	H	2B	3B	HR	RBI	BB	SO	AVG	OBP	SLG	PRO+	BR/A	SB	CS	SBR	FA	FR	G/POS	TPR
1923	NY-A	13	26	6	11	4	1	1	9	2	5	.423	.464	.769	217	4				.933	-1	/1-9	0.3
1924	NY-A	10	12	2	6	1	0	0	5	1	3	.500	.538	.583	190	2	0	0	0	1.000	-0	/1-2,O-1	0.1
1925	NY-A	126	437	73	129	23	10	20	68	46	49	.295	.365	.531	127	15	6	3	0	.989	-1	*1-114/O-6	-0.1
1926	*NY-A	155	572	135	179	47	20	16	112	105	73	.313	.420	.549	154	46	6	5	-1	.991	-8	*1-155	2.6
1927	*NY-A	155	584	149	218	52	18	47	175	109	84	.373	.474	.765	224	107	10	8	-2	.992	-6	*1-155	8.1
1928	*NY-A	154	562	139	210	47	13	27	142	95	69	.374	.467	.648	197	81	4	11	-5	.989	-8	*1-154	5.1
1929	NY-A	154	553	127	166	32	10	35	126	122	68	.300	.431	.584	170	61	4	4	-1	.994	-5	*1-154	3.7
1930	NY-A	154	581	143	220	42	17	41	174	101	63	.379	.473	.721	207	97	12	14	-5	.989	1	*1-153/O-1	6.9
1931	NY-A	155	619	163	211	31	15	46	184	117	56	.341	.446	.662	199	90	17	12	-2	.991	-10	*1-154/O-1	5.8
1932	*NY-A	156	596	138	208	42	9	34	151	108	38	.349	.451	.621	184	77	4	11	-5	.987	-6	*1-156	4.9
1933	NY-A★	152	593	138	198	41	12	32	139	92	42	.334	.424	.605	181	68	9	13	-5	.993	-3	*1-152	4.3
1934	NY-A★	154	579	128	210	40	6	49	165	109	31	.363	.465	.706	213	98	9	5	-0	.994	1	*1-153/S-1	7.8
1935	NY-A★	149	535	125	176	26	10	30	119	132	38	.329	.466	.583	180	70	8	7	-2	.990	0	*1-149	4.8
1936	*NY-A★	155	579	167	205	37	7	49	152	130	46	.354	.478	.696	193	89	3	4	-2	.994	1	*1-155	6.4
1937	*NY-A★	157	569	138	200	37	9	37	159	127	49	.351	.473	.643	177	72	4	3	-1	.989	-6	*1-157	4.3
1938	*NY-A★	157	576	115	170	32	6	29	114	107	75	.295	.410	.523	133	30	6	1	1	.991	-1	*1-157	1.2
1939	NY-A†	8	28	2	4	0	0	0	1	5	1	.143	.273	.143	9	-4	0	0	0	.971	-1	/1-8	-0.5
Total	17	2164	8001	1888	2721	534	163	493	1995	1508	790	.340	.447	.632	182	1005	102	101	-30	.991	-60	*1-2137/O-9,S	65.7

■ CHARLIE GEHRINGER
Gehringer, Charles Leonard "The Mechanical Man" b: 5/11/03, Fowlerville, Mich. d: 1/21/93, Bloomfield Hills, Mich. BL/TR, 5'11", 180 lbs. Deb: 9/22/24 CH

YEAR	TM/L	G	AB	R	H	2B	3B	HR	RBI	BB	SO	AVG	OBP	SLG	PRO+	BR/A	SB	CS	SBR	FA	FR	G/POS	TPR
1924	Det-A	5	13	2	6	0	0	0	1	0	2	.462	.462	.462	141	1	1	1	-0	.967	4	/2-5	0.4
1925	Det-A	8	18	3	3	0	0	0	0	0	2	.167	.250	.167	7	-3	0	1	-1	1.000	4	/2-6	0.0
1926	Det-A	123	459	62	127	19	17	1	48	30	42	.277	.322	.399	86	-11	9	7	-2	.973	-10	*2-112/3-6	-1.8
1927	Det-A	133	508	110	161	29	11	4	61	52	31	.317	.383	.441	112	9	17	8	0	.965	20	*2-121	3.1
1928	Det-A	154	603	108	193	29	16	6	74	69	22	.320	.395	.451	120	19	15	9	-1	.962	2	*2-154	2.3
1929	Det-A	155	634	131	215	45	19	13	106	64	19	.339	.405	.532	139	36	27	9	3	.975	-3	*2-154	3.9
1930	Det-A	154	610	144	201	47	15	16	98	69	17	.330	.404	.534	133	19	19	15	-3	.979	2	*2-154	3.4
1931	Det-A	101	383	67	119	24	5	4	53	29	15	.311	.359	.431	103	1	13	4	2	.979	-1	2-78/1-9	0.6
1932	Det-A	152	618	112	184	44	11	19	107	68	34	.298	.370	.497	118	15	9	8	-2	.967	-1	*2-152	1.8
1933	Det-A★	155	628	103	204	42	6	12	105	68	27	.325	.393	.468	125	23	5	4	-1	.981	7	*2-155	3.6
1934	*Det-A★	154	601	134	214	50	7	11	127	99	25	.356	.450	.517	149	47	11	8	-2	.981	7	*2-154	5.7
1935	*Det-A★	150	610	123	201	32	8	19	108	79	16	.330	.409	.502	139	36	11	4	1	.985	3	*2-149	4.7
1936	Det-A★	154	641	144	227	60	12	15	116	83	13	.354	.431	.555	141	43	4	1	1	.974	16	*2-154	6.1
1937	Det-A★	144	564	133	209	40	1	14	96	90	25	.371	.458	.520	143	41	11	4	1	.986	1	*2-142	5.2
1938	Det-A★	152	568	133	174	32	5	20	107	113	21	.306	.425	.486	121	21	14	1	4	.976	-1	*2-152	3.0
1939	Det-A	118	406	86	132	29	6	16	86	68	16	.325	.423	.544	135	22	4	3	-1	.977	1	*2-107	2.6
1940	*Det-A	139	515	108	161	33	3	10	81	101	17	.313	.428	.447	116	16	10	3	3	.972	-20	*2-138	0.8
1941	Det-A	127	436	65	96	19	4	3	46	95	26	.220	.363	.303	71	-16	1	2	-1	.982	-3	*2-116	-1.1
1942	Det-A	45	45	6	12	0	0	1	7	6	5	.267	.365	.333	90	-0	0	0	0	1.000	1	/2-3	0.1
Total	19	2323	8860	1774	2839	574	146	184	1427	1186	372	.320	.404	.480	123	332	181	89	1	.976	33	*2-2206/1-9,3	44.4

■ PHIL GEIER
Geier, Philip Louis "Little Phil" b: 11/3/1875, Washington, D.C. d: 9/25/67, Spokane, Wash. BL/TR, 5'7", 145 lbs. Deb: 8/17/1896

YEAR	TM/L	G	AB	R	H	2B	3B	HR	RBI	BB	SO	AVG	OBP	SLG	PRO+	BR/A	SB	CS	SBR	FA	FR	G/POS	TPR
1896	Phi-N	17	56	12	13	0	1	0	6	7		.232	.317	.268	56	-3	3			.813	-2	O-12/2-3,C	-0.5
1897	Phi-N	92	316	51	88	6	2	1	35	56		.278	.392	.320	91	-0	19			.932	-7	O-45,2-37/S3	-0.7
1900	Cin-N	30	113	18	29	1	4	0	10	7		.257	.306	.336	79	-3	3			.941	1	O-27/3-2	-0.4
1901	Phi-A	50	211	42	49	5	2	0	23	24		.232	.314	.275	61	-11	7			.934	-5	O-50/S-2,3	-1.7
	Mil-A	11	39	4	7	1	1	0	1	5		.179	.273	.256	50	-3	4			1.000	-1	/O-8,3-3	-0.4
	Yr	61	250	46	56	6	3	0	24	29		.224	.307	.272	60	-13	11			.941	-6	O-58/3-4,S	-2.1
1904	Bos-N	149	580	70	141	17	2	1	27	56		.243	.314	.284	88	-6	18			.933	-3	*O-137/3-7,2S	-1.8
Total	5	349	1315	197	327	30	12	2	102	154	7	.249	.332	.294	81	-27	54			.932	-16	O-279/2-45,3SC	-5.5

■ GARY GEIGER
Geiger, Gary Merle b: 4/4/37, Sand Ridge, Ill. BL/TR, 6', 168 lbs. Deb: 4/15/58

YEAR	TM/L	G	AB	R	H	2B	3B	HR	RBI	BB	SO	AVG	OBP	SLG	PRO+	BR/A	SB	CS	SBR	FA	FR	G/POS	TPR
1958	Cle-A	91	195	28	45	3	1	1	6	27	43	.231	.333	.272	70	-7	2	2	-1	.986		O-53/3-2,P	-0.6
1959	Bos-A	120	335	45	82	10	4	11	48	21	55	.245	.289	.397	83	-9	9	3	1	.989	-10	O-95	-2.3
1960	Bos-A	77	245	32	74	13	3	9	33	23	38	.302	.369	.490	126	9	2	2	-1	1.000	4	O-66	0.9
1961	Bos-A	140	499	82	116	21	6	18	64	87	91	.232	.351	.407	99	1	16	4	2	.988	10	*O-137	0.5
1962	Bos-A	131	466	67	116	18	4	16	54	67	66	.249	.346	.408	99	-0	18	11	-1	.987	4	*O-129	-0.1
1963	Bos-A	121	399	67	105	13	5	16	44	36	63	.263	.329	.441	110	5	9	4	0	.984	14	O-95/1-6	1.4
1964	Bos-A	5	13	3	5	1	0	1	2	0	2	.385	.467	.538	170	5	0	0		1.000		O-4	0.1
1965	Bos-A	24	45	5	9	3	0	1	2	3	10	.200	.379	.333	98	1	1	1	0	.970		O-16	0.1
1966	Atl-N	78	126	23	33	5	4	5	10	21	29	.262	.372	.444	124	5	0	1	-1	.982	-9	O-49	-0.6
1967	Atl-N	69	117	17	19	1		1	5	20	35	.162	.285	.214	45	-8	1	1	-0	.980	-6	O-38	-1.6
1969	Hou-N	93	125	19	28	4	1	0	16	24	34	.224	.353	.272	79	-2	0	1	-1	.968	-7	O-65	-1.2
1970	Hou-N	5	4	0	1	0	0	0	0	0	0	.250	.250	.250	36	-0	0	0		1.000	-1	/O-2	-0.1
Total	12	954	2569	388	633	91	29	77	283	341	466	.246	.339	.394	98	-6	62	29	1	.986	8	O-749/1-6,3P	-3.5

YEAR	TM/L	G	AB	R	H	2B	3B	HR	RBI	BB	SO	AVG	OBP	SLG	PRO+	BR/A	SB	CS	SBR	FA	FR	G/POS	TPR

■ BILL GEIS   Geis, William J. (b: William J. Geiss) b: 7/15/1858, Chicago, Ill. d: 9/18/24, Chicago, Ill. 5'10", 164 lbs. Deb: 5/1/1884 F

| 1884 | Det-N | 75 | 283 | 22 | 50 | 11 | 4 | 2 | 16 | 6 | 60 | .177 | .194 | .265 | 46 | -17 | | | | .862 | -7 | 2-73/O-1,1P | -2.0 |

■ EMIL GEISS   Geiss, Emil August b: 3/20/1867, Chicago, Ill. d: 10/4/11, Chicago, Ill. BR/TR, 5'11", 170 lbs. Deb: 5/18/1887 F

| 1887 | Chi-N | 3 | 12 | 0 | 1 | 0 | 0 | 0 | 0 | 0 | 7 | .083 | .083 | .083 | -47 | -2 | 0 | | | .571 | -1 | /2-1,1-1,P | -0.3 |

■ CHARLIE GELBERT   Gelbert, Charles Magnus b: 1/26/06, Scranton, Pa. d: 1/13/67, Easton, Pa. BR/TR, 5'11", 170 lbs. Deb: 4/16/29

1929	StL-N	146	512	60	134	29	8	3	65	51	46	.262	.329	.367	71	-23	8			.948	7	*S-146	0.1
1930	*StL-N	139	513	92	156	39	11	3	72	43	41	.304	.360	.441	89	-9	6			.947	9	*S-139	1.3
1931	*StL-N	131	447	61	129	29	5	1	62	54	31	.289	.365	.383	97	-0	7			.959	13	*S-130	2.5
1932	StL-N	122	455	60	122	28	9	1	45	39	30	.268	.330	.376	87	-8	8			.945	0	*S-122	0.3
1935	StL-N	62	168	24	49	7	2	2	21	17	18	.292	.357	.393	97	-0				.978	5	3-37,S-21/2	0.6
1936	StL-N	93	280	33	64	15	2	3	27	25	26	.229	.292	.329	67	-13	2			.965	8	3-60,S-28/2	-0.2
1937	Cin-N	43	114	12	22	4	0	1	13	15	12	.193	.287	.254	51	-8	1			.968	-2	S-37/2-9,3	-0.7
	Det-A	20	47	4	4	2	0	0	1	4	11	.085	.157	.128	-27	-9	0	0	0	.934	-0	S-16	-0.8
1939	Was-A	68	188	36	48	7	5	3	29	30	11	.255	.361	.394	100	-0	2	0	1	.970	-4	S-28,3-20/2	0.0
1940	Was-A	22	54	7	20	7	1	0	7	4	3	.370	.424	.537	157	5	0	0	0	.920	-5	S-12/P-2,2	0.0
	Bos-A	30	91	9	18	2	0	0	8	8	16	.198	.263	.220	25	-10	0	0	0	.926	5	3-29/S-1	-0.5
	Yr	52	145	16	38	9	1	0	15	12	19	.262	.323	.338	72	-6	0	0	0	.926	-1	3-29,S-13/P2	-0.5
Total	9	876	2869	398	766	169	43	17	350	290	245	.267	.336	.374	82	-76	34	0		.951	35	S-680,3-147/2P	2.6

■ FRANK GENINS   Genins, C. Frank "Frenchy" b: 11/2/1866, St.Louis, Mo. d: 9/30/22, St.Louis, Mo. TR, Deb: 7/5/1892

1892	Cin-N	35	110	12	20	4	0	0	7	12	12	.182	.262	.218	46	-7	7			.901	4	S-17,O-14/3	-0.2
	StL-N	15	51	5	10	1	0	0	4	1	11	.196	.212	.216	31	-4	3			.821	-8	S-14/O-1	-1.1
	Yr	50	161	17	30	5	0	0	11	13	23	.186	.247	.217	42	-11	10			.868	-3	S-31/O-15/3	-1.3
1895	Pit-N	73	252	43	63	8	0	2	24	22	14	.250	.315	.306	64	-13	19			.931	-8	O-29,3-16,2/S1	-1.8
1901	Cle-A	26	101	15	23	5	0	0	9	8		.228	.284	.277	58	-6	3			.940	1	O-26	-0.6
Total	3	149	514	75	116	18	0	2	44	43	37	.226	.288	.272	56	-30	32			.934	-10	/O-70,S-39,321	-3.7

■ GEORGE GENOVESE   Genovese, George Michael b: 2/22/22, Staten Island, N.Y BL/TR, 5'6.5", 160 lbs. Deb: 4/29/50

| 1950 | Was-A | 3 | 1 | 1 | 0 | 0 | 0 | 0 | 0 | 1 | 0 | .000 | .500 | .000 | 39 | 0 | 0 | 0 | 0 | .000 | 0 | H | 0.0 |

■ JIM GENTILE   Gentile, James Edward "Diamond Jim" b: 6/3/34, San Francisco, Cal. BL/TL, 6'4", 215 lbs. Deb: 9/10/57

1957	Bro-N	4	6	1	1	0	0	1	1	1	1	.167	.286	.667	133	0	0	0	0	1.000	-0	/1-2	0.0
1958	LA-N	12	30	0	4	1	0	0	4	4	6	.133	.235	.167	9	-4	0	0	0	.981	-1	/1-8	-0.6
1960	Bal-A★	138	384	67	112	17	0	21	98	68	72	.292	.407	.500	146	27	0	0	0	.993	-6	*1-124	1.2
1961	Bal-A★	148	486	96	147	25	2	46	141	96	106	.302	.428	.646	189	64	1	1	-0	.989	2	*1-144	5.3
1962	Bal-A★	152	545	80	137	21	1	33	87	77	100	.251	.351	.475	128	21	1	0	0	.988	6	*1-150	1.7
1963	Bal-A	145	496	65	123	16	1	24	72	76	101	.248	.355	.429	123	17	1	0	0	.995	7	*1-143	1.9
1964	KC-A	136	439	71	110	10	0	28	71	84	122	.251	.376	.465	128	19	0	0	0	.988	-0	*1-128	1.4
1965	KC-A	38	118	14	29	5	0	10	22	9	26	.246	.305	.542	138	5	0	1	0	.981	-1	1-35	0.2
	Hou-N	81	227	22	55	11	1	7	31	34	72	.242	.353	.392	118	6	0	0	0	.993	2	1-68	0.5
1966	Hou-N	49	144	16	35	6	1	7	18	21	39	.243	.355	.444	129	6	0	0	0	.989	2	1-43	0.6
	Cle-A	33	47	2	6	1	0	2	4	5	18	.128	.212	.277	39	-4	0	0	0	.944	-0	/1-9	-0.5
Total	9	936	2922	434	759	113	6	179	549	475	663	.260	.372	.486	137	157	3	1	0	.990	10	1-854	11.7

■ SAM GENTILE   Gentile, Samuel Christopher b: 10/12/16, Charlestown, Mass. BL/TR, 5'11", 180 lbs. Deb: 4/24/43

| 1943 | Bos-N | 8 | 4 | 1 | 1 | 1 | 0 | 0 | 1 | 0 | .250 | .400 | .500 | 162 | 0 | 0 | | | .000 | 0 | H | 0.0 |

■ HARVEY GENTRY   Gentry, Harvey William b: 5/27/26, Winston-Salem, N.C BL/TR, 6', 170 lbs. Deb: 4/14/54 F

| 1954 | NY-N | 5 | 4 | 0 | 1 | 0 | 0 | 0 | 1 | 1 | 0 | .250 | .400 | .250 | 73 | -0 | 0 | 0 | 0 | .000 | 0 | H | 0.0 |

■ ALEX GEORGE   George, Alex Thomas M. b: 9/27/38, Kansas City, Mo. BL/TR, 5'11.5", 170 lbs. Deb: 9/16/55

| 1955 | KC-A | 5 | 10 | 0 | 1 | 0 | 0 | 0 | 0 | 1 | 7 | .100 | .182 | .100 | -22 | -2 | 0 | 0 | 0 | .917 | -1 | /S-5 | -0.3 |

■ GREEK GEORGE   George, Charles Peter b: 12/25/12, Waycross, Ga. BR/TR, 6'2", 200 lbs. Deb: 6/30/35

1935	Cle-A	2	0	0	0	0	0	0	0	0	0	—	—	—	—		0	0	0	1.000	0	/C-1	0.0
1936	Cle-A	23	77	3	15	3	0	0	5	9	16	.195	.279	.234	28	-9	0	0	0	.994	16	C-22	0.7
1938	Bro-N	7	20	0	4	0	1	0	4	0	3	.200	.200	.300	35	-2	0	0	0	1.000	2	/C-7	0.0
1941	Chi-N	35	64	4	10	2	0	0	6	2	10	.156	.182	.188	4	-8	0			.973	2	C-18	-0.5
1945	Phi-A	51	138	8	24	4	1	0	11	7	29	.174	.265	.217	41	-10	0	0	0	.972	-6	C-46	-1.5
Total	5	118	299	15	53	9	2	0	24	28	59	.177	.248	.221	29	-29	0	0	0	.983	14	/C-94	-1.3

■ BILL GEORGE   George, William M. b: 1/27/1865, Bellaire, Ohio d: 8/23/16, Wheeling, W.Va. BR/TL, 5'8", 165 lbs. Deb: 5/11/1887

1887	NY-N	13	53	6	9	0	0	0	5	1	6	.170	.185	.170	-1	-7	2			.854	1	P-13/O-1	0.0
1888	*NY-N	9	39	7	9	1	0	1	6	0	2	.231	.231	.333	79	-1	1			1.000	-1	/O-6,P-4	-0.2
1889	NY-N	3	15	1	4	0	0	0	0	0	3	.267	.267	.267	49	-1	1			.875	-0	/O-3	-0.1
	Col-a	5	17	1	4	0	0	0	3	1	1	.235	.278	.235	49	-1	1			.667	-1	/O-4,P-2	-0.2
Total	3	30	124	15	26	1	0	1	14	2	12	.210	.222	.242	36	-10	5			.860	-1	/P-19,O-14	-0.5

■ BEN GERAGHTY   Geraghty, Benjamin Raymond b: 7/19/12, Jersey City, N.J. d: 6/18/63, Jacksonville, Fla BR/TR, 5'11", 175 lbs. Deb: 4/17/36

1936	Bro-N	51	129	11	25	4	0	0	9	8	16	.194	.241	.225	26	-13	4			.922	-7	S-31/2-9,3	-1.8
1943	Bos-N	8	1	2	0	0	0	0	0	0	0	.000	.000	.000	-99	-0	0			1.000	1	/2-1,S-1,3	0.1
1944	Bos-N	11	16	3	4	0	0	0	0	1	2	.250	.294	.250	52	-1	0			1.000	0	/2-4,3-3	-0.1
Total	3	70	146	16	29	4	0	0	9	9	18	.199	.245	.226	28	-15	4			.922	-6	/S-32,2-14,3	-1.8

■ CRAIG GERBER   Gerber, Craig Stuart b: 1/8/59, Chicago, Ill. BL/TR, 6', 175 lbs. Deb: 4/11/85

| 1985 | Cal-A | 65 | 91 | 8 | 24 | 1 | 2 | 0 | 6 | 2 | 3 | .264 | .280 | .319 | 64 | -5 | 0 | 3 | -2 | .970 | 19 | S-53/3-9,2D | 1.4 |

■ WALLY GERBER   Gerber, Walter "Spooks" b: 8/18/1891, Columbus, Ohio d: 6/19/51, Columbus, Ohio BR/TR, 5'10", 152 lbs. Deb: 9/23/14

1914	Pit-N	17	54	5	13	1	1	0	5	2	8	.241	.281	.296	75	-2				.921	1	S-17	0.0
1915	Pit-N	56	144	8	28	2	0	0	7	9	16	.194	.252	.208	40	-10	6	1	1	.930	2	3-23,S-21/2	-0.5
1917	StL-A	14	39	2	12	1	1	0	2	3	2	.308	.357	.385	131	1	1			.939	2	S-12/2-2	0.0
1918	StL-A	56	171	10	41	4	0	0	10	19	11	.240	.316	.263	77	-4	2			.922	-9	S-56	-1.2
1919	StL-A	140	462	43	105	14	6	1	37	49	36	.227	.308	.290	67	-20	1			.940	-8	*S-140	-2.1
1920	StL-A	154	584	70	163	26	2	2	60	58	32	.279	.346	.341	80	-16	4	13	-7	.939	7	*S-154	-0.2
1921	StL-A	114	436	55	121	12	9	2	48	34	19	.278	.337	.360	73	-18	4	7	-3	.943	-3	*S-113	-1.2
1922	StL-A	153	604	81	161	22	8	1	51	52	34	.267	.326	.334	70	-26	6	4	-1	.944	6	*S-153	-1.1
1923	StL-A	154	605	85	170	26	3	1	62	54	50	.281	.342	.339	75	-21	4	6	-2	.950	6	*S-154	-0.2
1924	StL-A	148	496	61	135	20	4	0	55	43	34	.272	.341	.329	69	-22	4	5	-2	.946	-7	*S-147	-1.4
1925	StL-A	72	246	29	67	13	1	0	19	26	15	.272	.344	.333	69	-11	1	2	-1	.949	-5	S-71	-0.6
1926	StL-A	131	411	37	111	8	0	0	42	40	29	.270	.339	.290	62	-21	0	2	-1	.944	-5	*S-129	-0.6
1927	StL-A	142	438	44	98	13	9	0	45	35	25	.224	.284	.295	49	-34	3	6	-3	.946	9	*S-141/3-1	-1.3
1928	StL-A	6	18	1	5	1	0	0	0	0	3	.278	.316	.333	69	-2	1			.783	-2	/S-6	-0.2
	Bos-A	104	300	21	64	6	1	0	28	32	31	.213	.289	.240	41	-25	6	1	1	.955	34	*S-103	1.9

YEAR	TM/L	G	AB	R	H	2B	3B	HR	RBI	BB	SO	AVG	OBP	SLG	PRO+	BR/A	SB	CS	SBR	FA	FR	G/POS	TPR
	Yr	110	318	22	69	7	1	0	28	33	34	.217	.291	.245	43	-26	6	1	1	.948	32	*S-109	1.7
1929	Bos-A	61	91	6	15	3	1	0	5	8	12	.165	.232	.220	17	-11	1	0	0	.937	14	S-30,2-22	0.5
Total	15	1522	5099	558	1309	172	46	7	476	465	357	.257	.323	.313	67	-241	43	47		.943	52	*S-1447/2-26,3	-7.6

■ BOB GEREN
Geren, Robert Peter b: 9/22/61, San Diego, Cal. BR/TR, 6'3", 205 lbs. Deb: 5/17/88

YEAR	TM/L	G	AB	R	H	2B	3B	HR	RBI	BB	SO	AVG	OBP	SLG	PRO+	BR/A	SB	CS	SBR	FA	FR	G/POS	TPR
1988	NY-A	10	10	0	1	0	0	0	0	0	3	.100	.250	.100	2	-1	0	0	0	1.000	1	C-10	0.0
1989	NY-A	65	205	26	59	5	1	9	27	14	44	.288	.330	.454	120	5	0	0	0	.991	0	C-60/D-2	0.9
1990	NY-A	110	277	21	59	7	0	8	31	13	73	.213	.261	.325	63	-14	0	0	0	.993	12	*C-107/D-1	0.3
1991	NY-A	64	128	7	28	3	0	2	12	9	31	.219	.270	.289	55	-8	0	1	-1	.989	9	C-63	0.2
1993	SD-N	58	145	8	31	6	0	3	6	13	28	.214	.278	.317	58	-9	0	0	0	.993	4	C-49/1-3	-0.2
Total	5	307	765	62	178	21	1	22	76	49	179	.233	.284	.349	74	-28	0	1	-1	.992	26	C-289/D-3,31	1.2

■ JOE GERHARDT
Gerhardt, John Joseph "Move Up Joe" b: 2/14/1855, Washington, D.C. d: 3/11/22, Middletown, N.Y. BR/TR, 6', 160 lbs. Deb: 9/1/1873 M

YEAR	TM/L	G	AB	R	H	2B	3B	HR	RBI	BB	SO	AVG	OBP	SLG	PRO+	BR/A	SB	CS	SBR	FA	FR	G/POS	TPR
1873	Was-n	13	56	6	12	2	1	0	6	0	5	.214	.214	.286	47	-3						S-13	-0.3
1874	Bal-n	14	61	10	20	1	1	0		0		.328	.328	.377	125	2						S-14	0.1
1875	Mut-n	58	251	29	53	8	3	0		0		.211	.211	.267	61	-10						3-44,2-12/S	-0.9
1876	Lou-N	65	292	33	76	10	3	2	18	3	5	.260	.268	.336	85	-8				.944	5	*1-54/2-5,S03	-0.3
1877	Lou-N	59	250	41	76	6	5	1	35	5	8	.304	.318	.380	101	-2				.888	20	*2-57/O-1,S1	1.7
1878	Cin-N	60	259	46	77	7	2	0	28	7	14	.297	.316	.340	127	8				.906	5	*2-60	1.6
1879	Cin-N	79	313	22	62	12	3	1	39	3	19	.198	.206	.265	57	-14				.908	7	2-55,3-16/1S	-0.3
1881	Det-N	80	297	35	72	13	6	0	36	7	31	.242	.260	.327	80	-7				.908	8	*2-79/3-1	0.3
1883	Lou-a	78	319	56	84	11	9	0		14		.263	.294	.354	116	7				.906	20	*2-78,M	2.4
1884	Lou-a	106	404	39	89	7	8	0		13		.220	.254	.277	76	-10				.920	27	*2-106	1.8
1885	NY-N	112	399	43	62	12	2	0	33	24	47	.155	.203	.195	30	-30				.911	11	*2-112	-1.4
1886	NY-N	123	426	44	81	11	7	0	40	22	63	.190	.230	.249	45	-28	8			.924	14	*2-123	-0.8
1887	NY-N	1	4	0	0	0	0	0	0	0	0	.000	.000	.000	-99	-1	0			1.000	0	/3-1	-0.1
	NY-a	85	307	40	68	13	2	0		24		.221	.280	.277	58	-17	15			.896	15	2-84/3-1	0.0
1890	Bro-a	99	369	34	75	10	4	2		30		.203	.270	.268	61	-18	9			.938	37	*2-99	2.1
	StL-a	37	125	15	32	0	0	1		9		.256	.321	.280	68	-6	5			.955	5	2-20,3-17M	0.1
	Yr	136	494	49	107	10	4	3		39		.217	.283	.271	63	-24	14			.940	42	*2-119,3-17	2.2
1891	Lou-a	2	6	0	0	0	0	0	0	1	0	.000	.143	.000	-59	-1	0			.833	-0	/2-2	-0.1
Total	3 n	85	368	45	85	11	5	0	6	0	5	.231	.231	.288	69	-12	0					/3-44,S-28,2	-1.1
Total	12	986	3770	448	854	112	51	7	229	162	187	.227	.261	.289	72	-127	37			.913	173	2-880/1-63,3SO	7.0

■ KEN GERHART
Gerhart, Harold Kenneth b: 5/19/61, Charleston, S.C. BR/TR, 6', 190 lbs. Deb: 9/14/86

YEAR	TM/L	G	AB	R	H	2B	3B	HR	RBI	BB	SO	AVG	OBP	SLG	PRO+	BR/A	SB	CS	SBR	FA	FR	G/POS	TPR
1986	Bal-A	20	69	4	16	2	0	1	7	4	18	.232	.274	.304	58	-4	0	1	-1	.971	-3	O-20	-0.8
1987	Bal-A	92	284	41	69	10	2	14	34	17	53	.243	.288	.440	92	-4	9	2	2	.973	-6	O-91	-1.1
1988	Bal-A	103	262	27	51	10	1	9	23	21	57	.195	.260	.344	69	-11	7	3	0	.975	-8	O-93/D-3	-2.1
Total	3	215	615	72	136	22	3	24	64	42	128	.221	.274	.384	79	-20	16	6	1	.974	-16	O-204/D-3	-4.0

■ GEORGE GERKEN
Gerken, George Herbert "Pickles" b: 7/28/03, Chicago, Ill. d: 10/23/77, Arcadia, Cal. BR/TR, 5'11.5", 175 lbs. Deb: 4/19/27

YEAR	TM/L	G	AB	R	H	2B	3B	HR	RBI	BB	SO	AVG	OBP	SLG	PRO+	BR/A	SB	CS	SBR	FA	FR	G/POS	TPR
1927	Cle-A	6	14	1	3	0	0	0	2	1	3	.214	.267	.214	26	-2	0	0	0	.917	-0	/O-5	-0.2
1928	Cle-A	38	115	16	26	7	2	0	9	12	22	.226	.305	.322	64	-6	3	3	-1	.940	-1	O-34	-1.0
Total	2	44	129	17	29	7	2	0	11	13	25	.225	.301	.310	60	-8	3	3	-1	.937	-1	/O-39	-1.2

■ JOHNNY GERLACH
Gerlach, John Glenn b: 5/11/17, Shullsburg, Wis. BR/TR, 5'9", 165 lbs. Deb: 9/3/38

YEAR	TM/L	G	AB	R	H	2B	3B	HR	RBI	BB	SO	AVG	OBP	SLG	PRO+	BR/A	SB	CS	SBR	FA	FR	G/POS	TPR
1938	Chi-A	9	25	2	7	0	0	0	1	4	2	.280	.379	.280	66	-1	0	0	0	.949	1	/S-8	0.0
1939	Chi-A	3	2	0	2	0	0	0	0	0	0	1.000	1.000	1.000	402	1	0	0	0	1.000	0	/3-1	0.1
Total	2	12	27	2	9	0	0	0	1	4	2	.333	.419	.333	89	-0	0	0	0	.949	1	/S-8,3-1	0.1

■ DICK GERNERT
Gernert, Richard Edward b: 9/28/28, Reading, Pa. BR/TR, 6'3", 210 lbs. Deb: 4/16/52 C

YEAR	TM/L	G	AB	R	H	2B	3B	HR	RBI	BB	SO	AVG	OBP	SLG	PRO+	BR/A	SB	CS	SBR	FA	FR	G/POS	TPR
1952	Bos-A	102	367	58	89	20	2	19	67	36	83	.243	.317	.463	107	2	4	1	1	.987	-1	1-99	-0.3
1953	Bos-A	139	494	73	125	15	1	21	71	88	82	.253	.371	.415	106	6	0	7	-4	.986	-3	*1-136	-0.6
1954	Bos-A	14	23	2	6	2	0	0	1	6	4	.261	.414	.348	99	0	0	0	0	1.000	1	/1-6	-0.1
1955	Bos-A	7	20	6	5	1	0	1	4	5	2	.250	.238	.300	40	-2	0	0	0	.974	-0	/1-5	-0.2
1956	Bos-A	106	306	53	89	11	0	16	68	56	57	.291	.404	.484	119	9	1	0	0	.985	1	O-50,1-37	0.5
1957	Bos-A	99	316	45	75	13	3	14	58	39	62	.237	.327	.430	99	-1	1	1	-0	.989	-2	1-71,O-16	-0.8
1958	Bos-A	122	431	59	102	19	1	20	69	59	78	.237	.331	.425	100	-0	1	2	-1	.991	8	*1-114	0.1
1959	Bos-A	117	298	41	78	14	1	11	42	52	49	.262	.371	.426	113	6	1	2	-1	.995	3	1-75,O-25	0.4
1960	Chi-N	52	96	8	24	3	0	5	16	10	19	.250	.321	.281	67	-2	1	0	0	.995	3	1-18/O-5	-0.2
	Det-A	21	50	6	15	4	0	1	5	4	5	.300	.352	.440	110	1	0	0	0	1.000	-2	1-13/O-6	-0.2
1961	Det-A	6	5	1	1	0	0	1	1	2	1	.200	.333	.800	187	1	0	0	0	.000	0	H	0.1
	*Cin-N	40	63	4	19	1	0	0	7	7	9	.302	.371	.317	84	-1	0	0	0	.993	3	1-21	0.1
1962	Hou-N	10	24	1	5	0	0	0	1	5	7	.208	.345	.208	57	-1	0	0	0	1.000	1	/1-9	-0.2
Total	11	835	2493	357	632	104	8	103	402	363	462	.254	.352	.426	104	15	10	11	-4	.990	9	1-604,O-102	-1.4

■ CESAR GERONIMO
Geronimo, Cesar Francisco (Zorrilla) b: 3/11/48, ElSeibo, D.R. BL/TL, 6'2", 170 lbs. Deb: 4/16/69

YEAR	TM/L	G	AB	R	H	2B	3B	HR	RBI	BB	SO	AVG	OBP	SLG	PRO+	BR/A	SB	CS	SBR	FA	FR	G/POS	TPR
1969	Hou-N	28	8	8	2	1	0	0	0	0	3	.250	.250	.375	74	-0	0	0	0	1.000	-3	/O-9	-0.3
1970	Hou-N	47	37	5	9	0	0	0	2	5	9	.243	.300	.243	49	-3	0	0	0	.920	-6	O-26	-0.9
1971	Hou-N	94	82	13	18	2	2	1	6	5	31	.220	.264	.329	69	-4	2	2	-1	.977	-16	O-64	-2.2
1972	*Cin-N	120	255	32	70	9	7	4	29	24	64	.275	.344	.412	121	7	2	7	-4	.982	-10	*O-106	-1.1
1973	*Cin-N	139	324	35	68	14	3	4	33	23	74	.210	.269	.309	63	-17	5	5	-2	.992	-6	*O-130	-3.0
1974	Cin-N	150	474	73	133	17	4	7	54	46	96	.281	.347	.395	109	5	9	5	0	.987	12	*O-145	1.1
1975	*Cin-N	148	501	69	129	25	5	6	53	48	97	.257	.327	.363	90	-7	13	5	1	.993	14	*O-148	0.2
1976	*Cin-N	149	486	59	149	24	11	2	49	56	95	.307	.385	.414	124	17	22	5	4	.985	4	*O-146	2.0
1977	Cin-N	149	492	54	131	22	4	10	52	35	89	.266	.321	.388	88	-9	10	4	1	.992	12	*O-147	-0.1
1978	Cin-N	122	296	28	67	15	5	0	27	43	67	.226	.330	.334	86	-5	8	3	1	.981	0	*O-115	-0.8
1979	*Cin-N	123	356	38	85	17	4	4	38	37	56	.239	.314	.343	79	-10	1	1	-0	.993	7	*O-118	-0.8
1980	Cin-N	103	145	16	37	5	0	2	9	14	24	.255	.321	.331	86	-3	2	1	0	1.000	-18	O-86	-2.5
1981	*KC-A	59	118	14	29	6	2	1	13	11	16	.246	.310	.331	85	-2	0	1	-1	.980	-6	O-57	-0.9
1982	KC-A	53	119	14	32	6	3	4	23	8	16	.269	.315	.471	112	2	2	0	1	1.000	-2	O-44/D-1	-0.2
1983	KC-A	38	87	2	18	4	0	2	4	2	13	.207	.242	.253	36	-8	0	0	-1	.986	-2	O-35	-1.1
Total	15	1522	3780	460	977	161	50	51	392	354	746	.258	.327	.368	93	-37	82	40	1	.988	-20	*O-1376/D-1	-10.4

■ LOU GERTENRICH
Gertenrich, Louis Wilhelm b: 5/4/1875, Chicago, Ill. d: 10/23/33, Chicago, Ill. BR/TR, 5'8", 175 lbs. Deb: 9/15/01

YEAR	TM/L	G	AB	R	H	2B	3B	HR	RBI	BB	SO	AVG	OBP	SLG	PRO+	BR/A	SB	CS	SBR	FA	FR	G/POS	TPR
1901	Mil-A	2	3	1	1	0	0	0	0	0	0	.333	.333	.333	90	-0	0			.000	-0	/O-1	0.0
1903	Pit-N	1	3	0	0	0	0	0	0	0	0	.000	.000	.000	-97	-1	0			1.000	-0	/O-1	-0.1
Total	2	3	6	1	1	0	0	0	0	0	0	.167	.167	.167	-6	-1	0			1.000	-0	/O-2	-0.1

■ DOC GESSLER
Gessler, Harry Homer "Brownie" b: 12/23/1880, Indiana, Pa. d: 12/26/24, Pittsburgh, Pa. BL/TR, 5'10", 180 lbs. Deb: 4/23/03 M

YEAR	TM/L	G	AB	R	H	2B	3B	HR	RBI	BB	SO	AVG	OBP	SLG	PRO+	BR/A	SB	CS	SBR	FA	FR	G/POS	TPR
1903	Det-A	29	105	9	25	5	4	0	12	3		.238	.273	.362	92	-1	1			.974	-0	O-28	-0.5
	Bro-N	49	154	20	38	8	3	0	18	17		.247	.366	.338	104	2	9			.984	-3	O-43	-0.3
1904	Bro-N	104	341	41	99	18	4	2	28	30		.290	.355	.384	131	13	13			.920	2	*1-88/1-1,2	1.0
1905	Bro-N	126	431	44	125	17	3	3	46	38		.290	.366	.369	129	17	26			.973	2	*1-107,O-12	1.5
1906	Bro-N	9	33	3	8	1	2	0	4	3		.242	.324	.394	134	1	3			.946	1	/1-9	0.2

YEAR	TM/L	G	AB	R	H	2B	3B	HR	RBI	BB	SO	AVG	OBP	SLG	PRO+	BR/A	SB	CS	SBR	FA	FR	G/POS	TPR
	*Chi-N	34	83	8	21	3	0	0	10	12		.253	.354	.289	95	0	4			1.000	-1	O-21/1-1	-0.2
	Yr	43	116	11	29	4	2	0	14	15		.250	.346	.319	104	1	7			1.000	-1	O-21,1-10	0.0
1908	Bos-A	128	435	55	134	13	14	3	63	51		.308	**.394**	.423	161	31	19			.950	-7	*O-126	2.1
1909	Bos-A	111	396	57	115	24	1	0	46	31		.290	.354	.356	122	10	16			.933	-1	*O-109	0.6
	Was-A	17	54	10	13	2	1	0	8	12		.241	.406	.315	134	3	4			1.000	-1	O-16/1-1	0.2
	Yr	128	450	67	128	26	2	0	54	43		.284	.361	.351	123	13	20			.940	-2	*O-125/1-1	0.8
1910	Was-A	145	487	58	126	17	11	2	50	62		.259	.361	.351	129	19	18			.953	-3	*O-144	1.0
1911	Was-A	128	450	65	127	19	5	4	78	74		.282	.406	.373	120	17	29			.943	-10	O-126/1-1	0.1
Total	8	880	2969	370	831	127	49	14	363	333		.280	.370	.370	128	112	142			.945	-23	O-713,1-120/2	5.7

■ CHARLIE GETTIG   Gettig, Charles Henry   b: 12/1870, Baltimore, Md.   d: 4/11/35, Baltimore, Md.   BR, 5'10", 172 lbs.   Deb: 8/5/1896

YEAR	TM/L	G	AB	R	H	2B	3B	HR	RBI	BB	SO	AVG	OBP	SLG	PRO+	BR/A	SB	CS	SBR	FA	FR	G/POS	TPR
1896	NY-N	6	9	3	3	1	0	0	0	0	0	.333	.333	.444	107	0	0			1.000	0	/P-4	0.0
1897	NY-N	22	75	8	15	6	0	0	12	6		.200	.277	.280	49	-6	3			.556	-8	/3-7,2-6,0SP	-1.2
1898	NY-N	64	196	30	49	6	2	0	26	15		.250	.310	.301	78	-6	5			.833	-10	O-21,P-17,2/S31C	-1.4
1899	NY-N	34	97	7	24	3	0	0	9	7		.247	.305	.278	63	-5	4			.833	-4	P-18/3-8,21O	-0.5
Total	4	126	377	48	91	16	2	0	47	28	0	.241	.302	.294	68	-16	12			.879	-22	/P-42,O-25,23S1CD	-3.1

■ TOM GETTINGER   Gettinger, Lewis Thomas Leyton (b: Lewis Thomas Leyton Gittinger)   b: 12/11/1868, Frederick, Md.   d: 7/26/43, Pensacola, Fla.   BL/TL, 5'10", 180 lbs.   Deb: 9/21/1889

YEAR	TM/L	G	AB	R	H	2B	3B	HR	RBI	BB	SO	AVG	OBP	SLG	PRO+	BR/A	SB	CS	SBR	FA	FR	G/POS	TPR
1889	StL-a	4	16	2	7	0	0	1	2	2		.438	.500	.625	194	2	0			.750	-1	/O-4	0.0
1890	StL-a	58	227	31	54	7	5	3	20			.238	.302	.352	81	-8	8			.886	-6	O-58	-1.4
1895	Lou-N	63	260	28	70	11	5	2	32	8	15	.269	.296	.373	77	-10	6			.910	-3	O-63/P-2	-1.5
Total	3	125	503	61	131	18	10	6	34	30	16	.260	.306	.372	82	-16	14			.897	-10	O-125/P-2	-2.9

■ JAKE GETTMAN   Gettman, Jacob John   b: 10/25/1876, Frank, Russia   d: 10/4/56, Denver, Colo.   BB/TL, 5'11", 185 lbs.   Deb: 8/20/1897

YEAR	TM/L	G	AB	R	H	2B	3B	HR	RBI	BB	SO	AVG	OBP	SLG	PRO+	BR/A	SB	CS	SBR	FA	FR	G/POS	TPR
1897	Was-N	36	143	28	45	7	3	3	29	7		.315	.359	.469	118	3	8			.981	-3	O-36	-0.2
1898	Was-N	142	567	75	157	16	5	5	47	29		.277	.319	.349	92	-7	32			.926	2	*O-139/1-3	-1.5
1899	Was-N	19	62	5	13	1	0	0	2	4		.210	.258	.226	33	-6	4			1.000	-1	O-16/1-2	-0.8
Total	3	197	772	108	215	24	8	8	78	40		.278	.322	.361	92	-10	44			.941	-2	O-191/1-5	-2.5

■ GUS GETZ   Getz, Gustave "Gee-Gee"   b: 8/3/1889, Pittsburgh, Pa.   d: 5/28/69, Keansburg, N.J.   BR/TR, 5'11", 165 lbs.   Deb: 8/15/09

YEAR	TM/L	G	AB	R	H	2B	3B	HR	RBI	BB	SO	AVG	OBP	SLG	PRO+	BR/A	SB	CS	SBR	FA	FR	G/POS	TPR
1909	Bos-N	40	148	6	33	2	0	0	9	1		.223	.228	.236	42	-10	2			.934	0	3-36/2-2,S	-1.0
1910	Bos-N	54	144	14	28	0	1	0	7	6	10	.194	.232	.208	27	-13	2			.915	3	3-22,2-13/OS	-1.1
1914	Bro-N	55	210	13	52	8	1	0	20	2	15	.248	.255	.295	62	-10	9			.949	12	3-55	0.4
1915	Bro-N	130	477	39	123	10	5	2	46	8	14	.258	.275	.312	76	-15	19	15	-3	.951	8	*3-128/S-2	-0.5
1916	*Bro-N	40	96	9	21	1	2	0	8	0	5	.219	.219	.271	49	-6	9			.913	-3	3-20/S-7,1	-0.9
1917	Cin-N	7	14	2	4	0	0	0	3	3	0	.286	.412	.286	121	1	0			.875	-3	/2-4,3-3	-0.2
1918	Cle-A	6	15	2	2	1	0	0	0	4	1	.133	.350	.200	60	-0	0			.941	-0	/3-5	-0.1
	Pit-N	7	10	0	2	0	0	0	0	0	0	.200	.200	.200	21	-1	0			.875	-4	/3-2	0.0
Total	7	339	1114	85	265	22	9	2	93	24	46	.238	.257	.279	60	-56	41	15		.942	18	3-271/2-19,SO1	-3.4

■ CHAPPIE GEYGAN   Geygan, James Edward   b: 6/3/03, Ironton, Ohio   d: 3/15/66, Columbus, Ohio   BR/TR, 5'11", 170 lbs.   Deb: 7/16/24

YEAR	TM/L	G	AB	R	H	2B	3B	HR	RBI	BB	SO	AVG	OBP	SLG	PRO+	BR/A	SB	CS	SBR	FA	FR	G/POS	TPR
1924	Bos-A	33	82	7	21	5	2	0	4	4	16	.256	.307	.366	73	-4	0	2	-1	.952	4	S-32	0.2
1925	Bos-A	3	11	0	2	0	0	0	0	0	2	.182	.182	.182	-8	-2	0	0	0	.813	-1	/S-3	-0.3
1926	Bos-A	4	10	0	3	0	0	0	0	1	1	.300	.364	.300	77	-0	0	0	0	.800	-1	/3-3	-0.1
Total	3	40	103	7	26	5	2	0	4	5	19	.252	.300	.340	65	-6	0	2	-1	.938	2	/S-35,3-3	-0.2

■ PATSY GHARRITY   Gharrity, Edward Patrick   b: 3/13/1892, Parnell, Iowa   d: 10/10/66, Beloit, Wis.   BR/TR, 5'10", 170 lbs.   Deb: 5/16/16   C

YEAR	TM/L	G	AB	R	H	2B	3B	HR	RBI	BB	SO	AVG	OBP	SLG	PRO+	BR/A	SB	CS	SBR	FA	FR	G/POS	TPR
1916	Was-A	39	92	8	21	5	1	0	9	8	18	.228	.297	.304	81	-2	2			1.000	-3	C-16,1-16	-0.5
1917	Was-A	76	176	15	50	5	0	0	18	14	18	.284	.337	.313	99	-0	7			.980	-1	1-46/C-5,O	-0.1
1918	Was-A	4	4	0	1	1	0	0	2	0	1	.250	.250	.500	129	0	0			.000	0	H	0.0
1919	Was-A	111	347	35	94	19	4	2	43	25	39	.271	.325	.366	95	-3	4			.969	-5	C-60,O-33/1	-0.5
1920	Was-A	131	428	51	105	18	3	3	44	37	52	.245	.307	.322	69	-20	6	5	-1	.965	-3	*C-121/1-7,O	-1.5
1921	Was-A	121	387	62	120	19	8	7	55	45	44	.310	.386	.455	120	12	4	3	-1	.977	-0	*C-115	1.6
1922	Was-A	96	273	40	70	16	6	5	45	36	30	.256	.351	.414	104	1	3	3	-1	.981	3	C-87	0.7
1923	Was-A	93	251	26	52	9	4	3	33	22	27	.207	.276	.311	57	-17	6	2	1	.986	1	C-35,1-33	-1.5
1929	Was-A	3	2	0	0	0	0	0	0	1	2	.000	.333	.000	-7	-0	0	0	0	.000	0	H	0.0
1930	Was-A	2	1	0	0	0	0	0	0	0	0	.000	.000	.000	-99	-0	0	0	0	1.000	-0	/1-1	0.0
Total	10	676	1961	237	513	92	26	20	249	188	231	.262	.331	.366	90	-29	32	13		.974	-7	C-439,1-110/O	-1.8

■ RAY GIANNELLI   Giannelli, Raymond John   b: 2/5/66, Brooklyn, N.Y.   BL/TR, 6', 195 lbs.   Deb: 5/4/91

YEAR	TM/L	G	AB	R	H	2B	3B	HR	RBI	BB	SO	AVG	OBP	SLG	PRO+	BR/A	SB	CS	SBR	FA	FR	G/POS	TPR
1991	Tor-A	9	24	2	4	1	0	0	0	5	9	.167	.310	.208	45	-2	1	0	0	.923	-2	/3-9	-0.3

■ JOE GIANNINI   Giannini, Joseph Francis   b: 9/8/1888, San Francisco, Cal   d: 9/26/42, San Francisco, Cal.   BL/TR, 5'8", 155 lbs.   Deb: 8/7/11

YEAR	TM/L	G	AB	R	H	2B	3B	HR	RBI	BB	SO	AVG	OBP	SLG	PRO+	BR/A	SB	CS	SBR	FA	FR	G/POS	TPR
1911	Bos-A	1	2	0	1	1	0	0	0	0	0	.500	.500	1.000	317	1	0			.500	-0	/S-1	0.0

■ JOHN GIBBONS   Gibbons, John Michael   b: 6/8/62, Great Falls, Mont.   BR/TR, 5'11", 187 lbs.   Deb: 4/11/84

YEAR	TM/L	G	AB	R	H	2B	3B	HR	RBI	BB	SO	AVG	OBP	SLG	PRO+	BR/A	SB	CS	SBR	FA	FR	G/POS	TPR
1984	NY-N	10	31	1	2	0	0	0	1	3	11	.065	.171	.065	-32	-5	0	0	0	.983	-1	/C-9	-0.6
1986	NY-N	8	19	4	9	4	0	1	3	1	3	.474	.545	.842	285	5	0	0	0	1.000	1	/C-8	0.6
Total	2	18	50	5	11	4	0	1	2	6	16	.220	.316	.360	90	-1	0	0	0	.990	-0	/C-17	0.0

■ JAKE GIBBS   Gibbs, Jerry Dean   b: 11/7/38, Grenada, Miss.   BL/TR, 6', 185 lbs.   Deb: 9/11/62

YEAR	TM/L	G	AB	R	H	2B	3B	HR	RBI	BB	SO	AVG	OBP	SLG	PRO+	BR/A	SB	CS	SBR	FA	FR	G/POS	TPR
1962	NY-A	2	2	0	0	0	0	0	0	0	0	—	—			0	0	0	0	.000	0	/3-1	0.0
1963	NY-A	4	8	1	2	0	0	0	0	0	1	.250	.250	.250	41	-1	0	0	0	1.000	-1	/C-1	-0.1
1964	NY-A	3	6	1	1	0	0	0	0	0	0	.167	.167	.167	-7	-1	0	0	0	1.000	0	/C-2	0.0
1965	NY-A	37	68	6	15	1	0	2	7	4	20	.221	.274	.324	70	-3	0	0	0	.991	2	C-21	0.0
1966	NY-A	62	182	19	47	3	0	3	20	19	16	.258	.328	.341	96	-1	5	2	0	.988	4	C-54	0.8
1967	NY-A	116	374	33	87	7	1	4	25	28	57	.233	.293	.289	75	-11	7	6	-2	.975	1	C-99	-0.8
1968	NY-A	124	423	31	90	12	3	3	29	27	68	.213	.270	.277	68	-17	9	8	-2	.991	-4	*C-121	-1.7
1969	NY-A	71	219	18	49	9	2	0	18	23	30	.224	.298	.283	65	-10	3	4	-2	.990	8	C-66	0.0
1970	NY-A	49	153	23	46	9	2	8	26	7	14	.301	.335	.542	146	8	2	0	1	.987	3	C-44	1.4
1971	NY-A	70	206	23	45	9	0	5	21	12	23	.218	.271	.335	76	-8	2	2	-1	.988	-5	C-51	-1.2
Total	10	538	1639	157	382	53	8	25	146	120	231	.233	.291	.321	81	-42	28	22	-5	.986	8	C-459/3-1	-1.6

■ CHARLIE GIBSON   Gibson, Charles Ellsworth "Gibby"   b: 11/17/1879, Sharon, Pa.   d: 11/22/54, Sharon, Pa.   BR/TR, 6', 160 lbs.   Deb: 9/23/05

YEAR	TM/L	G	AB	R	H	2B	3B	HR	RBI	BB	SO	AVG	OBP	SLG	PRO+	BR/A	SB	CS	SBR	FA	FR	G/POS	TPR
1905	StL-A	1	3	0	0	0	0	0	0	0	0	.000	.000	.000	-99	-1	0			1.000	-0	/C-1	-0.1

■ CHARLIE GIBSON   Gibson, Charles Griffin   b: 11/21/1899, LaGrange, Ga.   d: 12/18/90, LaGrange, Ga.   BR/TR, 5'8", 160 lbs.   Deb: 5/30/24

YEAR	TM/L	G	AB	R	H	2B	3B	HR	RBI	BB	SO	AVG	OBP	SLG	PRO+	BR/A	SB	CS	SBR	FA	FR	G/POS	TPR
1924	Phi-A	12	15	1	2	0	0	0	0	1	3	.133	.235	.133	-3	-2	0	0	0	.870	-4	C-12	-0.2

■ FRANK GIBSON   Gibson, Frank Gilbert   b: 9/27/1890, Omaha, Neb.   d: 4/27/61, Austin, Tex.   BB/TR, 6'0.5", 172 lbs.   Deb: 4/22/13

YEAR	TM/L	G	AB	R	H	2B	3B	HR	RBI	BB	SO	AVG	OBP	SLG	PRO+	BR/A	SB	CS	SBR	FA	FR	G/POS	TPR
1913	Det-A	23	57	8	8	1	0	0	2	3	9	.140	.197	.158	4	-7	2			.914	-6	C-19/O-2	-1.3
1921	Bos-N	63	125	14	33	5	4	2	13	3	17	.264	.292	.416	90	-2	0	0	0	.979	1	C-41	0.0
1922	Bos-N	66	164	15	49	7	2	3	20	10	27	.299	.339	.421	99	-1	4	1	1	.981	-1	C-29,1-20	-0.1
1923	Bos-N	41	50	13	15	1	0	0	5	7	7	.300	.386	.320	92	-0	0	2	-1	.923	-2	C-20	-0.2
1924	Bos-N	90	229	25	71	15	6	1	30	10	23	.310	.342	.441	113	3	1	1	-0	.972	2	C-46,1-10/3	0.7

YEAR	TM/L	G	AB	R	H	2B	3B	HR	RBI	BB	SO	AVG	OBP	SLG	PRO+	BR/A	SB	CS	SBR	FA	FR	G/POS	TPR
1925	Bos-N	104	316	36	88	23	5	2	50	15	28	.278	.313	.402	89	-7	3	3	-1	.968	-2	C-86/1-2	-0.5
1926	Bos-N	24	47	3	16	4	0	0	7	4	6	.340	.392	.426	132	2	0			1.000	2	C-13	0.4
1927	Bos-N	60	167	7	37	1	2	0	19	3	10	.222	.235	.251	33	-16	2			.965	-3	C-47	-1.7
Total	8	471	1155	121	317	57	19	8	146	55	127	.274	.310	.377	86	-28	12	7		.967	-10	C-301/1-32,3O	-2.7

■ GEORGE GIBSON
Gibson, George C. "Moon" b: 7/22/1880, London, Ont., Can. d: 1/25/67, London, Ont., Can. BR/TR, 5'11.5", 190 lbs. Deb: 7/2/05 MC

YEAR	TM/L	G	AB	R	H	2B	3B	HR	RBI	BB	SO	AVG	OBP	SLG	PRO+	BR/A	SB	CS	SBR	FA	FR	G/POS	TPR
1905	Pit-N	46	135	14	24	2	2	2	14	15		.178	.270	.267	59	-7	2			.966	3	C-44	0.0
1906	Pit-N	81	259	8	46	6	1	0	20	16		.178	.225	.208	34	-20	1			.971	-6	C-81	-2.0
1907	Pit-N	113	382	28	84	8	7	3	35	18		.220	.261	.301	75	-12	2			.972	-3	*C-109/1-1	-0.6
1908	Pit-N	143	486	37	111	19	4	2	45	19		.228	.260	.296	78	-14	4			.973	-14	*C-140	-1.7
1909	*Pit-N	150	510	42	135	25	9	2	52	44		.265	.326	.361	104	1	9			.983	2	*C-150	1.9
1910	Pit-N	143	482	53	125	22	6	3	44	47	31	.259	.333	.349	93	-4	7			.984	3	*C-143	1.3
1911	Pit-N	100	311	32	65	12	2	0	19	29	16	.209	.281	.260	50	-21	3			.979	0	C-98	-1.1
1912	Pit-N	95	300	23	72	14	3	2	35	20	16	.240	.290	.327	69	-13	0			.990	-1	C-94	-0.5
1913	Pit-N	48	118	6	33	4	2	0	12	10	8	.280	.341	.347	101	0	2			.986	-9	C-48	-0.5
1914	Pit-N	102	274	19	78	9	5	0	30	27	27	.285	.359	.354	117	7	4			.974	-9	*C-101	0.6
1915	Pit-N	120	351	28	88	15	6	1	30	31	25	.251	.313	.336	98	-1	5	2	0	.965	8	*C-118	1.8
1916	Pit-N	33	84	4	17	2	0	0	4	3	7	.202	.239	.274	57	-4	0			.989	7	C-29	0.5
1917	NY-N	35	82	1	14	3	0	0	5	7	2	.171	.236	.207	38	-6	1			.986	1	C-35	-0.4
1918	NY-N	4	2	0	1	0	0	0	0	0	0	.500	.500	1.000	360	1	0			1.000	1	/C-4	0.1
Total	14	1213	3776	295	893	142	49	15	345	286	132	.236	.295	.312	81	-94	40	2		.977	-18	*C-1194/1-1	-0.6

■ RUSS GIBSON
Gibson, John Russell b: 5/6/39, Fall River, Mass. BR/TR, 6'1", 195 lbs. Deb: 4/14/67

YEAR	TM/L	G	AB	R	H	2B	3B	HR	RBI	BB	SO	AVG	OBP	SLG	PRO+	BR/A	SB	CS	SBR	FA	FR	G/POS	TPR
1967	*Bos-A	49	138	8	28	7	0	1	15	12	31	.203	.267	.275	56	-7	0	0	0	1.000	-6	C-48	-1.2
1968	Bos-A	76	231	15	52	11	1	3	20	8	38	.225	.251	.320	49	-9	1	2	-1	.983	1	C-74/1-1	-0.6
1969	Bos-A	85	287	21	72	9	1	3	27	15	25	.251	.290	.321	67	-13	1	1	-0	.979	-6	C-83	-1.6
1970	SF-N	24	69	3	16	6	0	0	6	7	12	.232	.303	.319	67	-3	0	0	0	.971	2	C-23	0.0
1971	SF-N	25	57	2	11	1	1	1	7	2	13	.193	.220	.298	46	-4	0	0	0	.965	1	C-22	-0.4
1972	SF-N	5	12	0	2	0	1	0	3	0	4	.167	.167	.333	38	-1	0	0	0	1.000	-1	/C-5	-0.2
Total	6	264	794	49	181	34	4	8	78	44	123	.228	.269	.311	64	-38	2	3	-1	.983	-10	C-255/1-1	-4.0

■ KIRK GIBSON
Gibson, Kirk Harold b: 5/28/57, Pontiac, Mich. BL/TL, 6'3", 215 lbs. Deb: 9/8/79

YEAR	TM/L	G	AB	R	H	2B	3B	HR	RBI	BB	SO	AVG	OBP	SLG	PRO+	BR/A	SB	CS	SBR	FA	FR	G/POS	TPR
1979	Det-A	12	38	3	9	3	0	1	4	1	3	.237	.256	.395	70	-2	3	3	-1	1.000	-1	O-10	-0.4
1980	Det-A	51	175	23	46	2	1	9	16	10	45	.263	.306	.440	100	-1	4	7	-3	.992	-2	O-49/D-1	-0.7
1981	Det-A	83	290	41	95	11	3	9	40	18	64	.328	.371	.479	138	14	17	5	2	.973	-4	O-67/D-9	1.0
1982	Det-A	69	266	34	74	16	2	8	35	25	41	.278	.342	.444	113	5	9	7	-2	.994	3	O-64/D-4	0.5
1983	Det-A	128	401	60	91	12	9	15	51	53	96	.227	.323	.414	104	2	14	3	2	.975	-1	D-66,O-54	-0.1
1984	*Det-A	149	531	92	150	23	10	27	91	63	103	.282	.367	.516	142	30	29	9	3	.954	-9	*O-139/D-6	2.0
1985	Det-A	154	581	96	167	37	5	29	97	71	137	.287	.370	.518	141	33	30	4	7	.963	-7	*O-144/D-8	2.7
1986	Det-A	119	441	84	118	11	2	28	86	68	107	.268	.374	.492	134	22	34	6	7	.990	-9	*O-114/D-4	1.6
1987	*Det-A	128	487	95	135	25	3	24	79	71	117	.277	.375	.489	132	24	26	7	4	.974	5	*O-121/D-4	2.7
1988	*LA-N	150	542	106	157	28	1	25	76	73	120	.290	.381	.483	151	37	31	4	7	.964	8	*O-148	5.0
1989	LA-N	71	253	35	54	8	2	9	28	35	55	.213	.314	.368	96	-1	12	3	2	.980	1	O-70	-0.1
1990	LA-N	89	315	59	82	20	0	8	38	39	65	.260	.347	.400	108	4	26	2	7	.995	5	O-81	1.4
1991	KC-A	132	462	81	109	17	6	16	55	69	103	.236	.343	.403	105	4	18	4	3	.976	-2	O-94,D-30	0.2
1992	Pit-N	16	56	6	11	0	0	2	5	3	12	.196	.237	.304	53	-4	3	1	0	1.000	1	O-13	-0.3
1993	Det-A	116	403	62	105	18	6	13	62	44	87	.261	.339	.432	106	3	15	6	1	.987	-1	D-76,O-32	-0.1
1994	Det-A	98	330	71	91	17	2	23	72	42	69	.276	.363	.548	131	15	4	5	-2	.988	-2	D-56,O-38	0.8
Total	16	1565	5571	948	1494	248	52	246	835	685	1224	.268	.354	.464	124	185	275	76	37	.976	-17	*O-1238,D-264	16.2

■ WHITEY GIBSON
Gibson, Leighton P. b: 10/6/1868, Lancaster, Pa. d: 10/11/07, Talmage, Pa. TR , 5'9", 178 lbs. Deb: 5/2/1888

YEAR	TM/L	G	AB	R	H	2B	3B	HR	RBI	BB	SO	AVG	OBP	SLG	PRO+	BR/A	SB	CS	SBR	FA	FR	G/POS	TPR
1888	Phi-a	1	3	0	0	0	0	0	0	0		.000	.000	.000	-99	-1	0			1.000	1	/C-1	0.0

■ JOE GIEBEL
Giebel, Joseph Henry b: 11/30/1891, Washington, D.C. d: 3/17/81, Silver Spring, Md. BR/TR, 5'10.5", 175 lbs. Deb: 9/30/13

YEAR	TM/L	G	AB	R	H	2B	3B	HR	RBI	BB	SO	AVG	OBP	SLG	PRO+	BR/A	SB	CS	SBR	FA	FR	G/POS	TPR
1913	Phi-A	1	3	0	1	0	0	0	0	0	1	.333	.333	.333	97	-0	0			1.000	-0	/C-1	0.0

■ NORM GIGON
Gigon, Norman Phillip b: 5/12/38, Teaneck, N.J. BR/TR, 6', 195 lbs. Deb: 4/12/67

YEAR	TM/L	G	AB	R	H	2B	3B	HR	RBI	BB	SO	AVG	OBP	SLG	PRO+	BR/A	SB	CS	SBR	FA	FR	G/POS	TPR
1967	Chi-N	34	70	8	12	3	1	1	6	4	14	.171	.237	.286	47	-5	0	0	0	.982	-3	2-12/O-4,3	-0.8

■ BENJI GIL
Gil, Romar Benjamin (Aguilar) b: 10/6/72, Tijuana, Mex. BR/TR, 6'2", 180 lbs. Deb: 4/5/93

YEAR	TM/L	G	AB	R	H	2B	3B	HR	RBI	BB	SO	AVG	OBP	SLG	PRO+	BR/A	SB	CS	SBR	FA	FR	G/POS	TPR
1993	Tex-A	22	57	3	7	0	0	0	2	5	22	.123	.194	.123	-13	-9	1	2	-1	.954	8	S-22	0.0

■ GUS GIL
Gil, Tomas Gustavo (Guillen) b: 4/19/39, Caracas, Venez. BR/TR, 5'10", 180 lbs. Deb: 4/11/67

YEAR	TM/L	G	AB	R	H	2B	3B	HR	RBI	BB	SO	AVG	OBP	SLG	PRO+	BR/A	SB	CS	SBR	FA	FR	G/POS	TPR
1967	Cle-A	51	96	11	11	4	0	0	5	9	18	.115	.198	.156	6	-11	0	0	0	1.000	2	2-49/1-1	-0.8
1969	Sea-A	92	221	20	49	7	0	0	17	16	28	.222	.274	.253	49	-15	2	0	1	.942	1	3-38,2-18,S	-1.2
1970	Mil-A	64	119	12	22	4	0	1	12	21	12	.185	.307	.244	53	-7	2	0	1	.978	3	2-38,3-14	-0.1
1971	Mil-A	14	32	3	5	1	0	0	3	10	5	.156	.357	.188	59	-1	1	0	0	.977	-0	/2-8,3-6	0.0
Total	4	221	468	46	87	16	0	1	37	56	63	.186	.274	.226	43	-34	5	0	2	.987	7	2-113/3-58,S1	-2.1

■ ANDY GILBERT
Gilbert, Andrew b: 7/18/14, Bradenville, Pa. d: 8/29/92, Davis, Cal. BR/TR, 6', 203 lbs. Deb: 9/14/42 C

YEAR	TM/L	G	AB	R	H	2B	3B	HR	RBI	BB	SO	AVG	OBP	SLG	PRO+	BR/A	SB	CS	SBR	FA	FR	G/POS	TPR
1942	Bos-A	6	11	0	1	0	0	0	1	1	3	.091	.167	.091	-26	-2	0	0	0	1.000	-2	/O-5	-0.4
1946	Bos-A	2	1	1	0	0	0	0	0	0	0	.000	.000	.000	-95	-0	0	0	0	.000	-1	/O-1	-0.1
Total	2	8	12	1	1	0	0	0	1	1	3	.083	.154	.083	-31	-2	0	0	0	1.000	-2	/O-6	-0.5

■ CHARLIE GILBERT
Gilbert, Charles Mader b: 7/8/19, New Orleans, La. d: 8/13/83, New Orleans, La. BL/TL, 5'9", 165 lbs. Deb: 4/16/40 F

YEAR	TM/L	G	AB	R	H	2B	3B	HR	RBI	BB	SO	AVG	OBP	SLG	PRO+	BR/A	SB	CS	SBR	FA	FR	G/POS	TPR
1940	Bro-N	57	142	23	35	9	1	2	8	8	13	.246	.287	.366	74	-5	0			.960	-2	O-43	-0.8
1941	Chi-N	39	86	11	24	2	1	0	12	11	6	.279	.361	.326	98	0	1			1.000	-1	O-22	-0.2
1942	Chi-N	74	179	18	33	6	3	0	7	25	24	.184	.284	.251	60	-9	1			.981	0	O-47	-1.1
1943	Chi-N	8	20	1	3	0	0	0	1	3	1	.150	.261	.150	20	-2	1			1.000	-1	/O-6	-0.3
1946	Chi-N	15	13	2	1	0	0	0	1	1	4	.077	.143	.077	-38	-2	0			1.000	0	/O-2	-0.3
	Phi-N	88	260	34	63	5	2	1	17	25	18	.242	.314	.288	73	-9	3			1.000	6	O-69	-0.6
	Yr	103	273	36	64	5	2	1	18	26	22	.234	.305	.278	68	-11	3			1.000	6	O-71	-0.9
1947	Phi-N	83	152	20	36	5	2	2	10	13	14	.237	.301	.336	72	-6	1			.961	-0	O-37	-0.8
Total	6	364	852	109	195	27	9	5	55	86	82	.229	.302	.299	70	-33	7			.982	3	O-226	-4.1

■ BUDDY GILBERT
Gilbert, Drew Edward b: 7/26/35, Knoxville, Tenn. BL/TR, 6'3", 195 lbs. Deb: 9/9/59

YEAR	TM/L	G	AB	R	H	2B	3B	HR	RBI	BB	SO	AVG	OBP	SLG	PRO+	BR/A	SB	CS	SBR	FA	FR	G/POS	TPR
1959	Cin-N	7	20	4	3	0	0	2	2	3	4	.150	.261	.450	82	-1	0	0	0	1.000	1	/O-6	0.0

■ TOOKIE GILBERT
Gilbert, Harold Joseph b: 4/4/29, New Orleans, La. d: 6/23/67, New Orleans, La. BL/TR, 6'2.5", 185 lbs. Deb: 5/5/50 F

YEAR	TM/L	G	AB	R	H	2B	3B	HR	RBI	BB	SO	AVG	OBP	SLG	PRO+	BR/A	SB	CS	SBR	FA	FR	G/POS	TPR
1950	NY-N	113	322	40	71	12	2	4	32	43	36	.220	.314	.307	64	-16	3			.988	1	1-111	-1.7
1953	NY-N	70	160	12	27	3	0	3	16	22	21	.169	.269	.244	34	-15	1			.995	1	1-44	-1.5
Total	2	183	482	52	98	15	2	7	48	65	57	.203	.299	.286	54	-32	4	0		.991	2	1-155	-3.2

■ HARRY GILBERT
Gilbert, Harry H. b: 7/7/1868, Pottstown, Pa. d: 12/23/09, Pottstown, Pa. Deb: 6/23/1890 F

YEAR	TM/L	G	AB	R	H	2B	3B	HR	RBI	BB	SO	AVG	OBP	SLG	PRO+	BR/A	SB	CS	SBR	FA	FR	G/POS	TPR
1890	Pit-N	2	8	1	2	0	0	0	0	0	3	.250	.250	.250	52	-1	0			1.000	-1	/2-2	-0.1

YEAR	TM/L	G	AB	R	H	2B	3B	HR	RBI	BB	SO	AVG	OBP	SLG	PRO+	BR/A	SB	CS	SBR	FA	FR	G/POS	TPR

■ **JOHN GILBERT**   Gilbert, John G.   b: 1/8/1864, Pottstown, Pa.   d: 11/12/03, Pottstown, Pa.   Deb: 6/23/1890   F

1890	Pit-N	2	8	0	0	0	0	0	0	0	2	.000	.000	.000	-99	-2	0			1.000	-0	/S-2	-0.2

■ **JACK GILBERT**   Gilbert, John Robert "Jackrabbit"   b: 9/4/1875, Rhinecliff, N.Y.   d: 7/7/41, Albany, N.Y.   Deb: 9/11/1898

1898	Was-N	2	5	0	1	0	0	0	1	1		.200	.429	.200	82	0	1			.500	-0	/O-2	0.0
	NY-N	1	4	0	1	0	0	0	0	0		.250	.250	.250	45	-0	1			.500	-0	/O-1	-0.1
	Yr	3	9	0	2	0	0	0	1	1		.222	.364	.222	70	-0	2			.500	-1	/O-3	-0.1
1904	Pit-N	25	87	13	21	0	0	0	3	12		.241	.353	.241	82	-1	3			.857	-6	O-25	-0.9
Total	2	28	96	13	23	0	0	0	4	13		.240	.354	.240	81	-1	5			.821	-6	/O-28	-1.0

■ **LARRY GILBERT**   Gilbert, Lawrence William   b: 12/3/1891, New Orleans, La.   d: 2/17/65, New Orleans, La.   BL/TL, 5'9", 158 lbs.   Deb: 4/14/14   F

1914	*Bos-N	72	224	32	60	6	1	5	25	26	34	.268	.347	.371	114	4	3			.979	-0	O-60	0.1
1915	Bos-N	45	106	11	16	4	0	0	4	11	13	.151	.231	.189	29	-9	4	1	1	.941	-2	O-27	-1.3
Total	2	117	330	43	76	10	1	5	29	37	47	.230	.310	.312	88	-5	7	1		.969	-3	/O-87	-1.2

■ **MARK GILBERT**   Gilbert, Mark David   b: 8/22/56, Atlanta, Ga.   BB/TR, 6', 175 lbs.   Deb: 7/21/85

| 1985 | Chi-A | 7 | 22 | 3 | 6 | 1 | 0 | 0 | 3 | 4 | 5 | .273 | .385 | .318 | 92 | -0 | 0 | 0 | 0 | 1.000 | -1 | /O-7 | -0.1 |

■ **PETE GILBERT**   Gilbert, Peter   b: 9/6/1867, Baltic, Conn.   d: 1/1/12, Springfield, Mass.   TR , 5'8", 180 lbs.   Deb: 9/6/1890

1890	Bal-a	29	100	25	28	2	1	1			10	.280	.363	.350	105	1	12			.899	-3	3-29	-0.1
1891	Bal-a	139	513	81	118	15	7	3	72	37	77	.230	.317	.304	77	-16	31			.862	2	*3-139	-0.6
1892	Bal-N	4	15	0	3	0	0	0	1	0	3	.200	.250	.200	35	-1	1			.889	1	/3-4	0.0
1894	Bro-N	6	25	1	2	0	0	0	1	1	3	.080	.148	.080	-47	-6	2			.938	1	/2-3,3-3	-0.4
	Lou-N	28	108	13	33	3	1	0	14	5	4	.306	.353	.380	82	-3	2			.742	-6	3-28	-0.7
	Yr	34	133	14	35	3	1	0	15	6	7	.263	.315	.323	58	-9	4			.766	-4	3-31/2-3	-1.1
Total	4	206	761	120	184	20	9	5	87	54	87	.242	.321	.311	76	-25	48			.851	-4	3-203/2-3	-1.8

■ **WALLY GILBERT**   Gilbert, Walter John   b: 12/19/1900, Oscoda, Mich.   d: 9/7/58, Duluth, Minn.   BR/TR, 6', 180 lbs.   Deb: 8/18/28

1928	Bro-N	39	153	26	31	4	0	0	3	14	8	.203	.274	.229	33	-15	2			.965	-1	3-39	-1.3
1929	Bro-N	143	569	88	173	31	4	3	58	42	29	.304	.359	.388	87	-11	7			.956	7	*3-142	0.2
1930	Bro-N	150	623	92	183	34	5	3	67	47	33	.294	.345	.379	76	-24	7			.944	9	*3-150	-0.6
1931	Bro-N	145	552	60	147	25	6	0	46	39	38	.266	.322	.333	77	-17	3			.948	8	*3-145	0.0
1932	Cin-N	114	420	35	90	18	2	1	40	20	23	.214	.252	.274	43	-34	2			.929	-6	*3-111	-3.3
Total	5	591	2317	301	624	112	17	7	214	162	131	.269	.322	.341	71	-101	21			.947	17	3-587	-5.0

■ **BILLY GILBERT**   Gilbert, William Oliver   b: 6/21/1876, Tullytown, Pa.   d: 8/8/27, New York, N.Y.   BR/TR, 5'4", 153 lbs.   Deb: 4/25/01

1901	Mil-A	127	492	77	133	14	7	0	43	31		.270	.320	.327	84	-10	19			.936	-0	*2-127	-0.4
1902	Bal-A	129	445	74	109	12	3	2	38	45		.245	.327	.299	71	-16	38			.907	-5	*S-129	-1.3
1903	NY-N	128	413	62	104	9	0	1	40	41		.252	.348	.281	77	-10	37			.935	11	*2-128	0.5
1904	NY-N	146	478	57	121	13	3	1	54	46		.253	.340	.299	94	-1	33			.946	8	*2-146	1.1
1905	*NY-N	115	376	45	93	11	3	0	24	41		.247	.331	.293	84	-6	11			.947	25	*2-115	2.1
1906	NY-N	104	307	44	71	6	1	1	27	42		.231	.341	.267	88	-2	22			.940	23	2-98	2.3
1908	StL-N	89	276	12	59	7	0	0	10	20		.214	.274	.239	67	-10	6			.952	6	2-89	-0.5
1909	StL-N	12	29	4	5	0	0	0	1	4		.172	.333	.172	61	-1	1			.922	0	2-12	-0.1
Total	8	850	2816	375	695	72	17	5	237	270		.247	.328	.290	81	-57	167			.942	68	2-715,S-129	3.7

■ **ROD GILBREATH**   Gilbreath, Rodney Joe   b: 9/24/52, Laurel, Miss.   BR/TR, 6'2", 185 lbs.   Deb: 6/17/72

1972	Atl-N	18	38	2	9	1	0	0	1	2	10	.237	.293	.263	54	-2	1	1	-0	1.000	3	/2-7,3-4	0.0
1973	Atl-N	29	74	10	21	2	1	0	2	6	10	.284	.346	.338	84	-1	2	1	0	.960	-0	3-22	-0.2
1974	Atl-N	3	6	2	2	0	0	0	0	2	0	.333	.500	.333	131	0	0	0	0	1.000	0	/2-2	0.1
1975	Atl-N	90	202	24	49	3	1	2	16	24	26	.243	.326	.297	71	-7	5	5	-2	.980	2	2-52,3-10/S	-0.4
1976	Atl-N	116	383	57	96	11	8	1	32	42	36	.251	.331	.329	83	-8	7	7	-2	.975	7	*2-104/3-7,S	0.4
1977	Atl-N	128	407	47	99	15	2	8	43	45	79	.243	.322	.349	71	-16	3	9	-5	.978	3	*2-122/3-1	-1.0
1978	Atl-N	116	326	22	80	13	3	3	31	26	51	.245	.301	.331	69	-14	7	6	-2	.968	-3	3-62,2-39	-1.8
Total	7	500	1436	164	356	45	15	14	125	147	212	.248	.322	.329	74	-48	25	29	-10	.978	11	2-326,3-106/S	-2.9

■ **DON GILE**   Gile, Donald Loren "Bear"   b: 4/19/35, Modesto, Cal.   BR/TR, 6'6", 220 lbs.   Deb: 9/25/59

1959	Bos-A	3	10	1	2	1	0	0	1	0	2	.200	.273	.300	55	-1	0	0	0	1.000	-0	/C-3	-0.1
1960	Bos-A	29	51	6	9	1	1	1	4	1	13	.176	.192	.294	29	-5	0	0	0	1.000	-1	C-15,1-11	-0.7
1961	Bos-A	8	18	2	5	0	1	1	1	1	5	.278	.316	.444	98	-0	0	0	0	.958	-1	/1-6,C-1	-0.1
1962	Bos-A	18	41	3	2	0	0	1	3	3	15	.049	.133	.122	-30	-8	0	0	0	.990	-1	1-14	-0.9
Total	4	58	120	12	18	2	1	3	9	5	35	.150	.197	.258	21	-14	0	0	0	.982	-2	/1-31,C-19	-1.8

■ **BRIAN GILES**   Giles, Brian Jeffrey   b: 4/27/60, Manhattan, Kan.   BR/TR, 6'1", 165 lbs.   Deb: 9/12/81

1981	NY-N	9	7	0	0	0	0	0	0	0	3	.000	.000	.000	-99	-2	0	0	0	1.000	3	/2-2,S-2	0.2
1982	NY-N	45	138	14	29	5	0	3	10	12	29	.210	.273	.312	64	-7	6	1	1	.992	15	2-45/S-2	1.2
1983	NY-N	145	400	39	98	15	0	2	27	36	77	.245	.311	.298	70	-16	17	10	-1	.980	15	*2-140,S-12	0.4
1985	Mil-A	34	58	6	10	1	0	1	7	7	16	.172	.262	.241	39	-1	5	2	1	.963	8	S-20,2-13/D	0.4
1986	Chi-A	9	11	0	3	0	0	0	1	0	2	.273	.273	.273	48	-1	0	0	0	1.000	4	/2-7,S-1	0.3
1990	Sea-A	45	95	15	22	6	0	4	11	15	24	.232	.336	.421	109	1	2	1	0	.978	7	S-37/2-2,3D	1.1
Total	6	287	709	74	162	27	0	10	50	70	151	.228	.300	.309	70	-29	27	13	0	.985	52	2-209/S-74,D3	3.6

■ **GEORGE GILHAM**   Gilham, George Louis   b: 9/17/1899, Shamokin, Pa.   d: 4/25/37, Lansdowne, Pa.   BR/TR, 5'11", 164 lbs.   Deb: 9/24/20

1920	StL-N	1	3	0	0	0	0	0	0	0	1	.000	.000	.000	-99	-1	0	0	0	.750	-1	/C-1	-0.2
1921	StL-N	1	1	0	0	0	0	0	0	0	0	.000	.000	.000	-99	-0	0	0	0	.000	0	H	-0.0
Total	2	2	4	0	0	0	0	0	0	0	1	.000	.000	.000	-99	-1	0	0	0	.750	-1	/C-1	-0.2

■ **FRANK GILHOOLEY**   Gilhooley, Frank Patrick "Flash"   b: 6/10/1892, Toledo, Ohio   d: 7/11/59, Toledo, Ohio   BL/TR, 5'8", 155 lbs.   Deb: 9/18/11

1911	StL-N	1	0	0	0	0	0	0	0	0	0	—	—	—						.000	-0	/O-1	0.0
1912	StL-N	13	49	5	11	0	0	0	2	3	8	.224	.269	.224	37	-4	0			1.000	-2	O-11	-0.7
1913	NY-A	24	85	10	29	2	1	0	14	4	9	.341	.378	.388	124	3	2			.977	-1	O-24	0.1
1914	NY-A	1	3	0	2	0	0	0	1	0	0	.667	.750	.667	327	1	0			.000	-0	/O-1	0.1
1915	NY-A	1	4	0	0	0	0	0	0	0	1	.000	.000	.000	-99	-1	0			1.000	-0	/O-1	-0.1
1916	NY-A	58	223	40	62	5	3	1	10	37	17	.278	.383	.341	115	6	16			.971	3	O-57	0.6
1917	NY-A	54	165	14	40	6	1	0	8	30	13	.242	.362	.291	99	1	6			.933	-1	O-46	-0.3
1918	NY-A	112	427	59	118	13	5	1	23	53	24	.276	.358	.337	107	5	7			.961	1	*O-111	-0.1
1919	Bos-A	48	112	14	27	4	0	0	1	12	8	.241	.315	.277	71	-4	2			.922	-5	O-33	-1.2
Total	9	312	1068	142	289	30	10	2	58	140	80	.271	.357	.323	102	6	37			.957	-7	O-285	-1.6

■ **BERNARD GILKEY**   Gilkey, Otis Bernard   b: 9/24/66, St.Louis, Mo.   BR/TR, 6', 170 lbs.   Deb: 9/4/90

1990	StL-N	18	64	11	19	1	3	1	3	8	5	.297	.375	.484	134	3	6	1	1	.961	3	O-18	0.7
1991	StL-N	81	268	28	58	7	2	5	20	39	33	.216	.318	.313	78	-7	14	8	-1	.994	9	O-74	-0.1
1992	StL-N	131	384	56	116	19	4	7	43	39	52	.302	.368	.427	128	14	18	12	-2	.978	7	*O-111	1.9
1993	StL-N	137	557	99	170	40	5	16	70	56	66	.305	.373	.481	129	23	15	10	-2	.969	3	*O-134/1-3	2.1

YEAR	TM/L	G	AB	R	H	2B	3B	HR	RBI	BB	SO	AVG	OBP	SLG	PRO+	BR/A	SB	CS	SBR	FA	FR	G/POS	TPR
1994	StL-N	105	380	52	96	22	1	6	45	39	65	.253	.338	.363	86	-7	15	8	-0	.983	5	*O-102	-0.4
Total	5	472	1653	246	459	93	14	35	181	181	221	.278	.355	.414	111	26	68	39	-3	.979	27	O-439/1-3	4.2

■ BOB GILKS   Gilks, Robert James   b: 7/2/1864, Cincinnati, Ohio   d: 8/21/44, Brunswick, Ga.   BR/TR, 5'8", 178 lbs.   Deb: 8/25/1887

YEAR	TM/L	G	AB	R	H	2B	3B	HR	RBI	BB	SO	AVG	OBP	SLG	PRO+	BR/A	SB	CS	SBR	FA	FR	G/POS	TPR
1887	Cle-a	22	83	12	26	2	0	0			3	.313	.352	.337	96	-0	5			.881	2	P-13/1-6,O2	0.0
1888	Cle-a	119	484	59	111	14	4	1	63	7		.229	.245	.281	70	-17	16			.899	-1	O-87,3-28/SP2	-1.8
1889	Cle-N	53	210	17	50	5	2	0	18	7	20	.238	.273	.281	56	-13	6			1.000	0	O-29,S-13,1/2	-1.1
1890	Cle-N	130	544	65	116	10	3	0	41	32	38	.213	.265	.243	49	-35	17			.941	1	*O-123/P-4,S2	-3.3
1893	Bal-N	15	64	10	17	2	0	0	7	0	3	.266	.277	.297	52	-5	3			.969	3	O-15	-0.2
Total	5	339	1385	163	320	33	9	1	129	49	61	.231	.265	.270	60	-69	47			.937	5	O-257/3-28,PS12	-6.4

■ JIM GILL   Gill, James C.   b: St.Louis, Mo.   Deb: 6/27/1889

YEAR	TM/L	G	AB	R	H	2B	3B	HR	RBI	BB	SO	AVG	OBP	SLG	PRO+	BR/A	SB	CS	SBR	FA	FR	G/POS	TPR
1889	StL-a	2	8	2	2	1	0	0	1	1	2	.250	.333	.375	90	-0	1			1.000	-0	/O-1,2-1	-0.1

■ JOHNNY GILL   Gill, John Wesley "Patcheye"   b: 3/27/05, Nashville, Tenn.   d: 12/26/84, Nashville, Tenn.   BL/TR, 6'2", 190 lbs.   Deb: 8/28/27

YEAR	TM/L	G	AB	R	H	2B	3B	HR	RBI	BB	SO	AVG	OBP	SLG	PRO+	BR/A	SB	CS	SBR	FA	FR	G/POS	TPR
1927	Cle-A	21	60	8	13	3	0	1	4	7	13	.217	.319	.317	65	-3	1	1	-0	1.000	-2	O-17	-0.6
1928	Cle-A	2	2	0	0	0	0	0	0	0	0	.000	.000	.000	-99	-1	0	0	0	.000	0	H	-0.1
1931	Was-A	8	30	2	8	2	1	0	5	1	6	.267	.313	.400	86	-1	0	1	-1	1.000	3	/O-8	0.1
1934	Was-A	13	53	7	13	3	0	2	7	2	3	.245	.286	.415	82	-2	0	0	0	1.000	-1	O-13	-0.3
1935	Chi-N	3	3	2	1	1	0	0	1	0	1	.333	.333	.667	161	-0	0			.000	0	H	0.0
1936	Chi-N	71	174	20	44	8	0	7	28	13	19	.253	.309	.420	92	-2	0			.938	-3	O-41	-0.6
Total	6	118	322	39	79	17	1	10	45	23	43	.245	.306	.398	84	-8	1	2		.968	-2	/O-79	-1.5

■ WARREN GILL   Gill, Warren Darst "Doc"   b: 12/21/1878, Ladoga, Ind.   d: 11/26/52, Laguna Beach, Cal.   BR/TR, 6'1", 175 lbs.   Deb: 8/26/08

YEAR	TM/L	G	AB	R	H	2B	3B	HR	RBI	BB	SO	AVG	OBP	SLG	PRO+	BR/A	SB	CS	SBR	FA	FR	G/POS	TPR
1908	Pit-N	27	76	10	17	0	1	0	14	11		.224	.366	.250	97	1	3			1.000	-3	1-25	-0.2

■ SAM GILLEN   Gillen, Samuel (b: Samuel Gilleland)   b: 1/1871, Pittsburgh, Pa.   d: 5/13/05, Pittsburgh, Pa.   5'8",   Deb: 8/19/1893

YEAR	TM/L	G	AB	R	H	2B	3B	HR	RBI	BB	SO	AVG	OBP	SLG	PRO+	BR/A	SB	CS	SBR	FA	FR	G/POS	TPR
1893	Pit-N	3	6	0	0	0	0	0	0	0	1	.000	.000	.000	-99	-2				.750	-0	/S-3	-0.2
1897	Phi-N	75	270	32	70	10	3	0	27	35		.259	.353	.312	80	-6	2			.896	-29	S-69/3-6	-3.0
Total	2	78	276	32	70	10	3	0	27	35	1	.254	.346	.312	76	-8	2			.892	-30	/S-72,3-6	-3.2

■ TOM GILLEN   Gillen, Thomas J.   b: 5/18/1862, Philadelphia, Pa.   d: 1/26/1889, Philadelphia, Pa.   5'8", 160 lbs.   Deb: 4/18/1884

YEAR	TM/L	G	AB	R	H	2B	3B	HR	RBI	BB	SO	AVG	OBP	SLG	PRO+	BR/A	SB	CS	SBR	FA	FR	G/POS	TPR
1884	Phi-U	29	116	5	18	0	0	0			1	.155	.162	.172	-10	-17				.895	-4	C-27/O-3	-1.7
1886	Det-N	2	10	2	4	0	0	0	4	0	1	.400	.400	.400	140	0				.889	-2	/C-2	-0.1
Total	2	31	126	7	22	2	0	0	4	1	1	.175	.181	.190	2	-17				.895	-6	/C-29,O-3	-1.8

■ CARDEN GILLENWATER   Gillenwater, Carden Edison   b: 5/13/18, Riceville, Tenn.   BR/TR, 6'1", 178 lbs.   Deb: 9/22/40

YEAR	TM/L	G	AB	R	H	2B	3B	HR	RBI	BB	SO	AVG	OBP	SLG	PRO+	BR/A	SB	CS	SBR	FA	FR	G/POS	TPR
1940	StL-N	7	25	1	4	1	0	0	5	0	2	.160	.160	.200	-1	-3	0			1.000	-1	/O-7	-0.5
1943	Bro-N	8	17	1	3	0	0	0	2	2	3	.176	.263	.176	28	-2	0			1.000	-0	/O-4	-0.4
1945	Bos-N	144	517	74	149	20	2	7	72	73	70	.288	.379	.375	110	9	13			.979	24	*O-140	2.5
1946	Bos-N	99	224	30	51	10	1	1	14	39	27	.228	.342	.295	81	-4	3			.979	1	O-78	-0.6
1948	Was-A	77	221	23	54	10	4	3	21	39	36	.244	.358	.367	96	-1	4	2	0	.974	-1	O-67	-0.5
Total	5	335	1004	129	261	41	7	11	114	153	138	.260	.359	.348	96	-1	20	2		.979	23	O-296	0.7

■ JIM GILLESPIE   Gillespie, James Wheatfield   b: 9/1858, Canada   BL/TR,   Deb: 10/1/1890

YEAR	TM/L	G	AB	R	H	2B	3B	HR	RBI	BB	SO	AVG	OBP	SLG	PRO+	BR/A	SB	CS	SBR	FA	FR	G/POS	TPR
1890	Buf-P	1	3	0	0	0	0	0	0		2	.000	.000	.000	-99	-1	0			.250	-0	/O-1	-0.1

■ PAUL GILLESPIE   Gillespie, Paul Allen   b: 9/18/20, Sugar Valley, Ga.   d: 8/11/70, Anniston, Ala.   BL/TR, 6'3", 195 lbs.   Deb: 9/11/42

YEAR	TM/L	G	AB	R	H	2B	3B	HR	RBI	BB	SO	AVG	OBP	SLG	PRO+	BR/A	SB	CS	SBR	FA	FR	G/POS	TPR
1942	Chi-N	5	16	3	4	0	0	1	2	1	2	.250	.294	.625	172	1				1.000	-1	/C-4	0.0
1944	Chi-N	9	26	2	7	1	0	1	2	3	3	.269	.345	.423	116	1	0			.903	-1	/C-7	0.0
1945	*Chi-N	75	163	12	47	6	0	3	25	18	9	.288	.366	.380	110	3	2			.989	1	C-45/O-1	0.6
Total	3	89	205	17	58	7	0	6	31	22	14	.283	.358	.405	115	4	2			.978	-1	/C-56,O-1	0.6

■ PETE GILLESPIE   Gillespie, Peter Patrick   b: 11/30/1851, Carbondale, Pa.   d: 5/5/10, Carbondale, Pa.   BL/TR, 6'1.5", 178 lbs.   Deb: 5/1/1880

YEAR	TM/L	G	AB	R	H	2B	3B	HR	RBI	BB	SO	AVG	OBP	SLG	PRO+	BR/A	SB	CS	SBR	FA	FR	G/POS	TPR
1880	Tro-N	82	346	50	84	20	5	2	24	17	35	.243	.278	.347	105	1				.905	7	*O-82	0.5
1881	Tro-N	84	348	43	96	14	3	0	41	9	24	.276	.294	.333	92	-4				.933	4	*O-84	-0.1
1882	Tro-N	74	298	46	82	5	4	2	33	9	14	.275	.296	.333	108	3				.827	-6	*O-74	-0.2
1883	NY-N	98	411	64	129	23	12	1	62	9	27	.314	.329	.436	131	15				.897	7	*O-98	1.8
1884	NY-N	101	413	75	109	3	4	2	44	19	35	.264	.296	.315	90	-5				.893	-3	*O-101	-0.9
1885	NY-N	102	420	67	123	17	6	0	52	15	32	.293	.317	.362	121	9				**.942**	-4	*O-102	0.2
1886	NY-N	97	396	65	108	13	8	0	58	16	30	.273	.301	.346	95	-3	17			.901	-10	*O-97	-1.4
1887	NY-N	76	295	40	78	9	3	3	37	12	21	.264	.304	.346	84	-6	37			.946	2	O-76/3-1	-0.8
Total	8	714	2927	450	809	108	45	10	351	106	218	.276	.303	.354	104	11	54			.903	-8	O-714/3-1	-0.9

■ JIM GILLIAM   Gilliam, James William "Junior"   b: 10/17/28, Nashville, Tenn.   d: 10/8/78, Inglewood, Cal.   BB/TR, 5'10.5", 175 lbs.   Deb: 4/14/53   C

YEAR	TM/L	G	AB	R	H	2B	3B	HR	RBI	BB	SO	AVG	OBP	SLG	PRO+	BR/A	SB	CS	SBR	FA	FR	G/POS	TPR
1953	*Bro-N	151	605	125	168	31	**17**	6	63	100	38	.278	.383	.415	106	8	21	14	-2	.976	3	*2-149	1.7
1954	Bro-N	146	607	107	171	28	8	13	52	76	30	.282	.364	.418	100	1	8	7	-2	.977	-11	*2-143/O-4	-0.3
1955	*Bro-N	147	538	110	134	20	8	7	40	70	37	.249	.342	.355	83	-12	15	15	-5	.968	-9	2-99,O-46	-2.0
1956	*Bro-N☆	153	594	102	178	23	8	6	43	95	39	.300	.400	.396	107	10	21	9	1	.981	18	*2-102,O-56	3.4
1957	Bro-N	149	617	89	154	26	4	2	37	64	31	.250	.324	.314	66	-28	26	10	2	**.986**	3	*2-148/O-2	-1.2
1958	LA-N	147	555	81	145	25	5	2	43	78	22	.261	.352	.335	81	-13	18	11	-1	.987	8	O-75,3-44,2	-0.8
1959	*LA-N★	145	553	91	156	18	4	3	34	**96**	25	.282	.388	.345	91	-3	23	10	1	.958	2	*3-132/2-8,O	0.0
1960	LA-N	151	557	96	138	20	2	5	40	96	28	.248	.361	.318	82	-10	12	9	-2	.960	9	*3-130,2-30	0.0
1961	LA-N	144	439	74	107	26	3	4	32	79	34	.244	.359	.344	81	-10	8	4	0	.956	2	3-74,2-71,O	-0.2
1962	LA-N	160	588	83	159	24	1	4	43	93	35	.270	.372	.335	97	2	17	7	1	.981	-14	*2-113,3-90/O	0.0
1963	*LA-N	148	525	77	148	27	4	6	49	60	28	.282	.358	.383	122	15	19	5	3	.985	-8	*2-119,3-55	2.2
1964	LA-N	116	334	44	76	8	3	2	27	42	21	.228	.319	.287	78	-9	4	4	-1	.936	-20	3-86,2-25/O	-3.1
1965	*LA-N	111	372	50	104	19	4	4	39	53	31	.280	.375	.384	123	13	9	5	-0	.960	-13	3-80,O-22/2	-0.3
1966	*LA-N	88	235	30	51	9	0	1	16	34	17	.217	.316	.268	70	-9	2	1	0	.953	-12	3-70/1-2,2	-2.4
Total	14	1956	7119	1163	1889	304	71	65	558	1036	416	.265	.361	.355	92	-45	203	111	-6	.979	-43	*2-1046,3-761,O/1	-3.0

■ BARNEY GILLIGAN   Gilligan, Andrew Bernard   b: 1/3/1856, Cambridge, Mass.   d: 4/1/34, Lynn, Mass.   BR/TR, 5'6.5", 130 lbs.   Deb: 9/25/1875

YEAR	TM/L	G	AB	R	H	2B	3B	HR	RBI	BB	SO	AVG	OBP	SLG	PRO+	BR/A	SB	CS	SBR	FA	FR	G/POS	TPR
1875	Atl-n	2	8	2	2	0	0	0			0	.250	.250	.250	84	-0						/C-1,O-1	0.0
1879	Cle-N	52	205	20	35	6	2	0	11	0	13	.171	.171	.220	28	-15				.870	-9	C-27,O-23/S	-1.5
1880	Cle-N	30	99	9	17	4	3	1	13	6	12	.172	.219	.303	77	-2				.969	4	C-23/O-4,S	0.3
1881	Pro-N	46	183	19	40	7	0	2	20	9	24	.219	.255	.279	69	-6				.930	-1	C-36,S-10/O	-0.5
1882	Pro-N	56	201	32	45	7	6	0	26	4	26	.224	.239	.318	77	-5				.932	5	C-54/S-2	0.6
1883	Pro-N	74	263	34	52	13	3	0	24	26	32	.198	.270	.270	63	-11				.900	10	*C-74	0.3
1884	*Pro-N	82	294	47	72	13	1	1	38	35	41	.245	.325	.313	104	3				.928	17	*C-81/3-1,1	2.4
1885	Pro-N	71	252	23	54	7	3	0	12	23	33	.214	.280	.266	80	-4				.872	-3	C-65/S-5,O2	-0.1
1886	Was-N	81	273	23	52	9	2	0	17	39	35	.190	.292	.238	66	-9	6			.925	-9	C-71,O-14/S3	-0.9
1887	Was-N	28	90	7	18	2	0	1	6	5	18	.200	.242	.256	40	-7	2			.874	-7	C-26,S-3,O	-0.7
1888	Det-N	1	5	1	1	0	0	0			1	.200	.200	.200	28	-0				.875	-0	/C-1	0.0
Total	10	521	1865	215	386	68	23	3	167	147	235	.207	.265	.273	71	-58	8			.912	24	C-458/O-44,S321	-0.1

YEAR	TM/L	G	AB	R	H	2B	3B	HR	RBI	BB	SO	AVG	OBP	SLG	PRO+	BR/A	SB	CS	SBR	FA	FR	G/POS	TPR

■ GRANT GILLIS   Gillis, Grant b: 1/24/01, Grove Hill, Ala. d: 2/4/81, Thomasville, Ala. BR/TR, 5'10", 165 lbs. Deb: 9/19/27

1927	Was-A	10	36	8	8	3	1	0	2	2	0	.222	.263	.361	61	-2	0	0	0	1.000	-2	S-10	-0.3
1928	Was-A	24	87	13	22	5	1	0	10	4	5	.253	.309	.333	69	-4	0	1	-1	.910	-10	S-16/2-5,3	-1.3
1929	Bos-A	28	73	5	18	4	0	0	11	6	8	.247	.304	.301	58	-5	0	1	-1	.956	-4	2-25	-0.7
Total	3	62	196	26	48	12	2	0	23	12	13	.245	.299	.327	63	-11	0	2	-1	.948	-16	/2-30,S-26,3	-2.3

■ JIM GILMAN   Gilman, James Deb: 7/10/1893

| 1893 | Cle-N | 2 | 7 | 1 | 2 | 0 | 0 | 0 | 1 | 0 | 2 | .286 | .286 | .286 | 49 | -1 | 0 | | | .667 | -1 | /3-2 | -0.1 |

■ PIT GILMAN   Gilman, Pitkin Clark b: 3/14/1864, Laporte, Ohio d: 8/17/50, Elyria, Ohio BL/TL, 170 lbs. Deb: 9/18/1884

| 1884 | Cle-N | 2 | 10 | 0 | 1 | 0 | 0 | 0 | 0 | 0 | 1 | .100 | .100 | .100 | -36 | -2 | | | | 1.000 | 0 | /O-2 | -0.1 |

■ GROVER GILMORE   Gilmore, Ernest Grover b: 11/1/1888, Chicago, Ill. d: 11/25/19, Sioux City, Iowa BL/TL, 5'9.5", 170 lbs. Deb: 4/18/14

1914	KC-F	139	530	91	152	25	5	1	32	37	108	.287	.337	.358	84	-14	23			.973	3	*O-132	-1.7
1915	KC-F	119	411	53	117	22	15	1	47	26	50	.285	.347	.418	109	3	19			.979	7	O-119	0.5
Total	2	258	941	144	269	47	20	2	79	63	158	.286	.341	.385	94	-10	42			.976	10	O-251	-1.2

■ JIM GILMORE   Gilmore, James b: 5/1853, Baltimore, Md. d: 11/18/28, Baltimore, Md. Deb: 4/26/1875

| 1875 | Was-n | 3 | 12 | 2 | 3 | 0 | 0 | 0 | | 0 | | .250 | .250 | .250 | 76 | -0 | | | | | | /C-2,2-1,3 | 0.0 |

■ GILROY   Gilroy Deb: 9/7/1874

1874	Chi-n	8	39	4	8	1	0	0		0		.205	.205	.231	38	-3						/C-8	-0.2
1875	Ath-n	2	6	0	1	0	0	0		0		.167	.167	.167	14	-1						/C-1,O-1	0.0
Total	2 n	10	45	4	9	1	0	0		0		.200	.200	.222	35	-3						/C-9,O-1	-0.2

■ TINSLEY GINN   Ginn, Tinsley Rucker b: 9/26/1891, Royston, Ga. d: 8/30/31, Atlanta, Ga. BL/TR, 5'9", 180 lbs. Deb: 6/27/14

| 1914 | Cle-A | 2 | 1 | 0 | 0 | 0 | 0 | 0 | 0 | 0 | 0 | .000 | .000 | .000 | -96 | -0 | 0 | | | .000 | 0 | /O-2 | 0.0 |

■ JOE GINSBERG   Ginsberg, Myron Nathan b: 10/11/26, New York, N.Y. BL/TR, 5'11", 180 lbs. Deb: 9/15/48

1948	Det-A	11	36	7	13	0	0	0	1	3	1	.361	.410	.361	103	0	0	0	0	.943	-2	C-11	0.0
1950	Det-A	36	95	12	22	6	0	0	12	11	6	.232	.318	.295	56	-6	1	0	0	.981	-4	C-31	-0.8
1951	Det-A	102	304	44	79	10	2	8	37	43	21	.260	.355	.385	100	0	0	2	-1	.978	-1	C-95	0.2
1952	Det-A	113	307	29	68	13	2	6	36	51	21	.221	.338	.336	87	-4	1	1	-0	.984	-14	*C-101	-1.4
1953	Det-A	18	53	6	16	2	0	0	3	10	1	.302	.422	.340	109	1	0	0	0	.988	0	C-15	0.2
	Cle-A	46	109	10	31	4	0	0	10	14	4	.284	.371	.321	91	-1	0	0	0	.966	-5	C-39	-0.4
	Yr	64	162	16	47	6	0	0	13	24	5	.290	.388	.327	97	1	0	0	0	.974	-5	C-54	-0.2
1954	Cle-A	3	2	0	1	0	1	0	1	0	0	.500	.667	1.500	473	1	0	0	0	1.000	0	/C-1	0.1
1956	KC-A	71	195	15	48	8	1	1	12	23	17	.246	.326	.313	69	-8	1	1	-0	.989	-2	C-57	-0.9
	Bal-A	15	28	0	2	0	0	0	2	2	4	.071	.133	.071	-48	-6	0	0	0	1.000	-0	/C-8	-0.6
	Yr	86	223	15	50	8	1	1	14	25	21	.224	.302	.283	56	-14	1	1	-0	.990	-3	C-65	-1.5
1957	Bal-A	85	175	15	48	8	2	1	18	18	19	.274	.349	.360	100	0	0	2	1	.986	1	C-66	0.3
1958	Bal-A	61	109	4	23	1	0	3	16	13	14	.211	.306	.303	72	-4	0	0	0	.994	3	C-39	0.1
1959	Bal-A	65	166	14	30	2	0	1	14	21	13	.181	.273	.211	35	-14	1	0	0	.993	3	C-62	-0.9
1960	Bal-A	14	30	3	8	1	0	0	6	6	1	.267	.389	.300	90	-0	0	0	0	.940	4	C-14	0.1
	Chi-A	28	75	8	19	4	0	0	9	10	8	.253	.349	.307	80	-2	1	0	0	.993	4	C-25	0.4
	Yr	42	105	11	27	5	0	0	15	16	9	.257	.361	.305	83	-2	1	0	0	.976	5	C-39	0.5
1961	Chi-A	6	3	0	0	0	0	0	0	1	2	.000	.250	.000	-27	-1	0	0	0	1.000	0	/C-2	0.0
	Bos-A	19	24	1	6	0	0	0	5	0	2	.250	.250	.250	33	-2	0	0	0	1.000	-1	/C-6	-0.3
	Yr	25	27	1	6	0	0	0	5	1	4	.222	.250	.222	27	-3	0	0	0	1.000	-1	/C-8	-0.3
1962	NY-N	2	5	0	0	0	0	0	0	0	0	.000	.000	.000	-98	-1	0	0	0	1.000	1	/C-2	0.0
Total	13	695	1716	168	414	59	8	20	182	226	135	.241	.334	.320	79	-47	7	5	-1	.983	-17	C-574	-3.9

■ AL GIONFRIDDO   Gionfriddo, Albert Francis b: 3/8/22, Dysart, Pa. BL/TL, 5'6", 165 lbs. Deb: 9/23/44

1944	Pit-N	4	6	0	1	0	0	0	1	1	1	.167	.286	.167	28	-1	0			1.000	0	/O-1	-0.1
1945	Pit-N	122	409	74	116	18	9	2	42	60	22	.284	.377	.386	108	6	12			.964	-8	*O-106	-0.8
1946	Pit-N	64	102	11	26	2	2	0	10	14	5	.255	.345	.314	85	-2	1			.944	-5	O-33	-0.8
1947	Pit-N	1	1	0	0	0	0	0	0	0	0	.000	.000	.000	-97	-0	0			.000	0	H	-0.0
	*Bro-N	37	62	10	11	2	1	0	6	16	11	.177	.346	.242	57	-3	2			.938	-2	O-17	-0.6
	Yr	38	63	10	11	2	1	0	6	16	11	.175	.342	.238	54	-4	2			.938	-2	O-17	-0.6
Total	4	228	580	95	154	22	12	2	58	91	39	.266	.366	.355	97	0	15			.959	-15	O-157	-2.3

■ TOMMY GIORDANO   Giordano, Thomas Arthur "T-Bone" b: 10/9/25, Newark, N.J. BR/TR, 6', 175 lbs. Deb: 9/11/53

| 1953 | Phi-A | 11 | 40 | 6 | 7 | 2 | 0 | 2 | 5 | 5 | 6 | .175 | .267 | .375 | 69 | -2 | 0 | 1 | -1 | .984 | 1 | 2-11 | -0.1 |

■ JOE GIRARDI   Girardi, Joseph Elliott b: 10/14/64, Peoria, Ill. BR/TR, 5'11", 195 lbs. Deb: 4/4/89

1989	*Chi-N	59	157	15	39	10	1	1	14	11	26	.248	.306	.331	76	-5	2	1	0	.981	13	C-59	1.2
1990	Chi-N	133	419	36	113	24	2	1	38	17	50	.270	.303	.344	72	-16	8	3	1	.985	-9	*C-133	-1.7
1991	Chi-N	21	47	3	9	2	0	0	6	6	6	.191	.283	.234	45	-3	0	0	0	.972	4	C-21	0.1
1992	Chi-N	91	270	19	73	3	1	1	12	19	38	.270	.321	.300	75	-8	0	2	-1	.991	-4	C-86	-1.0
1993	Col-N	86	310	35	90	14	5	3	31	24	41	.290	.347	.397	85	-7	6	6	-2	.989	-7	C-84	-1.1
1994	Col-N	93	330	47	91	9	4	4	34	21	48	.276	.323	.364	67	-16	3	3	-1	.992	5	C-93	-0.7
Total	6	483	1533	155	415	62	12	10	135	98	209	.271	.319	.346	74	-55	19	15	-3	.987	2	C-476	-3.2

■ TONY GIULIANI   Giuliani, Angelo John b: 11/24/12, St.Paul, Minn. BR/TR, 5'11", 175 lbs. Deb: 4/18/36

1936	StL-A	71	198	17	43	3	0	0	13	11	13	.217	.258	.232	21	-25	0	0	0	.966	5	C-66	-1.5
1937	StL-A	19	53	6	16	1	0	0	3	3	3	.302	.339	.321	67	-3	0	0	0	.986	-0	C-19	-0.2
1938	Was-A	46	115	10	25	4	0	0	15	8	3	.217	.268	.252	33	-12	1	0	0	1.000	-1	C-46	-1.0
1939	Was-A	54	172	20	43	6	2	0	18	4	7	.250	.267	.308	50	-13	0	1	-1	.979	1	C-50	-0.9
1940	Bro-N	1	1	0	0	0	0	0	0	0	1	.000	.000	.000	-94	-0	0	0	0	1.000	-0	/C-1	0.0
1941	Bro-N	3	2	0	0	0	0	0	0	0	0	.000	.000	.000	-96	-1	0	0	0	1.000	1	/C-3	0.0
1943	Was-A	49	133	5	30	4	0	0	20	12	14	.226	.290	.271	67	-6	0	1	-1	.962	-1	C-49	-0.5
Total	7	243	674	58	157	18	3	0	69	38	41	.233	.274	.269	42	-59	1	2		.976	6	C-234	-4.1

■ JIM GLADD   Gladd, James Walter b: 10/2/22, Ft.Gibson, Okla. d: 11/8/77, Long Beach, Cal. BR/TR, 6'2", 190 lbs. Deb: 9/9/46

| 1946 | NY-N | 4 | 11 | 0 | 1 | 0 | 0 | 0 | 0 | 1 | 4 | .091 | .167 | .091 | -26 | -2 | 0 | | | 1.000 | 4 | /C-4 | 0.2 |

■ DAN GLADDEN   Gladden, Clinton Daniel b: 7/7/57, San Jose, Cal. BR/TR, 5'11", 180 lbs. Deb: 9/5/83

1983	SF-N	18	63	6	14	2	0	1	9	5	11	.222	.279	.302	63	-3	4	3	-1	1.000	0	O-18	-0.2
1984	SF-N	86	342	71	120	17	2	4	31	33	37	.351	.411	.447	146	22	31	16	-0	.988	9	O-85	2.9
1985	SF-N	142	502	64	122	15	8	7	41	40	78	.243	.308	.347	87	-9	32	15	1	.975	1	*O-124	-1.3
1986	SF-N	102	351	55	97	16	1	4	29	39	59	.276	.357	.362	104	3	27	10	2	.987	12	O-89	1.4
1987	*Min-A	121	438	69	109	21	2	8	38	38	72	.249	.313	.361	75	-15	25	9	2	.987	6	*O-111/D-4	-1.0
1988	Min-A	141	576	91	155	32	6	11	62	46	74	.269	.327	.403	100	-0	28	8	4	.991	16	*O-140/2-1,3P	1.6
1989	Min-A	121	461	69	136	23	3	6	46	23	53	.295	.335	.410	102	1	23	7	3	.966	5	*O-117/P-1,D	0.6
1990	Min-A	136	534	64	147	27	6	5	40	26	67	.275	.316	.376	87	-10	25	9	2	.980	12	*O-133/D-2	0.1

YEAR	TM/L	G	AB	R	H	2B	3B	HR	RBI	BB	SO	AVG	OBP	SLG	PRO+	BR/A	SB	CS	SBR	FA	FR	G/POS	TPR
1991	*Min-A	126	461	65	114	14	9	6	52	36	60	.247	.309	.356	80	-13	15	9	-1	.988	1	*O-126	-1.6
1992	Det-A	113	417	57	106	20	1	7	42	30	64	.254	.307	.357	85	-9	4	2	0	.987	0	*O-108/D-2	-1.1
1993	Det-A	91	356	52	95	16	2	13	56	21	50	.267	.313	.433	99	-2	8	5	-1	.986	8	O-86/D-5	0.4
Total	11	1197	4501	663	1215	203	40	74	446	337	625	.270	.327	.382	94	-36	222	93	11	.984	73	*O-1137/D-15,P32	1.8

■ BUCK GLADMAN
Gladman, John H.   b: 1864, Washington, D.C.   Deb: 7/7/1883

YEAR	TM/L	G	AB	R	H	2B	3B	HR	RBI	BB	SO	AVG	OBP	SLG	PRO+	BR/A	SB	CS	SBR	FA	FR	G/POS	TPR
1883	Phi-N	1	4	1	0	0	0	0	0	0	2	.000	.000	.000	-99	-1				1.000	-1	/3-1	-0.1
1884	Was-a	56	224	17	35	5	3	1			3	.156	.178	.219	33	-16				.796	-3	3-53/O-2,S	-1.7
1886	Was-N	44	152	17	21	5	3	1	15	12	30	.138	.201	.230	33	-12	5			.830	-6	3-44	-1.6
Total	3	101	380	35	56	10	6	2	15	15	32	.147	.186	.221	31	-28	5			.812	-10	/3-98,O-2,S	-3.4

■ ROLAND GLADU
Gladu, Roland Edouard   b: 5/10/13, Montreal, Que., Can   BL/TR, 5'8.5", 185 lbs.   Deb: 4/18/44

YEAR	TM/L	G	AB	R	H	2B	3B	HR	RBI	BB	SO	AVG	OBP	SLG	PRO+	BR/A	SB	CS	SBR	FA	FR	G/POS	TPR
1944	Bos-N	21	66	5	16	2	1	1	7	3	8	.242	.275	.348	72	-3	0			.891	-5	3-15/O-3	-0.8

■ JACK GLASSCOCK
Glasscock, John Wesley "Pebbly Jack"   b: 7/22/1859, Wheeling, W.Va.   d: 2/24/47, Wheeling, W.Va.   BR/TR, 5'8", 160 lbs.   Deb: 5/1/1879   M

YEAR	TM/L	G	AB	R	H	2B	3B	HR	RBI	BB	SO	AVG	OBP	SLG	PRO+	BR/A	SB	CS	SBR	FA	FR	G/POS	TPR
1879	Cle-N	80	325	31	68	9	3	0	29	6	24	.209	.224	.255	58	-14				.919	-6	*2-66,3-14	-1.4
1880	Cle-N	77	296	37	72	13	3	0	27	2	21	.243	.248	.307	89	-3				.891	7	*S-77	0.8
1881	Cle-N	85	335	49	86	9	5	0	33	15	8	.257	.289	.313	94	-2				**.911**	9	*S-79/2-6	1.2
1882	Cle-N	84	358	66	104	27	9	4	46	13	9	.291	.315	.450	147	18				.900	**24**	*S-83/3-1	**4.1**
1883	Cle-N	96	383	67	110	19	6	0	46	13	23	.287	.311	.368	107	3				**.922**	17	*S-93/2-3	1.9
1884	Cle-N	72	281	45	70	4	1	2	22	25	16	.249	.310	.302	91	-3				.893	27	S-69/2-3,P	2.2
	Cin-U	38	172	48	72	9	5	2		8		.419	.444	.564	160	14				.889	1	S-36/2-2	1.3
1885	StL-N	111	446	66	125	18	3	1	40	29	10	.280	.324	.341	123	12				**.917**	19	*S-110/2-1	3.1
1886	StL-N	121	486	96	158	29	7	3	40	38	13	.325	.374	.432	154	33	38			.906	14	*S-120/O-1	4.2
1887	Ind-N	122	483	91	142	18	7	0	40	41	8	.294	.361	.360	105	5	62			.906	**35**	*S-122/P-1	3.5
1888	Ind-N	113	442	63	119	17	3	1	45	14	17	.269	.302	.328	99	-1	48			**.901**	11	*S-110/2-3,P	1.3
1889	Ind-N	134	582	128	**205**	40	3	7	85	31	10	.352	.390	.467	136	26	57			**.915**	**36**	*S-132/2-2,PM	**5.9**
1890	NY-N	124	512	91	**172**	32	9	1	66	41	8	**.336**	.395	.439	143	27	54			.910	22	*S-124	4.9
1891	NY-N	97	369	46	89	12	6	0	55	36	11	.241	.317	.306	85	-6	29			.913	-2	*S-97	-0.3
1892	StL-N	139	566	83	151	27	5	3	72	44	19	.267	.327	.348	110	-0	26			.916	3	*S-139,M	1.7
1893	StL-N	48	195	32	56	8	1	1	26	25	3	.287	.382	.354	96	-0	20			.907	-7	S-48	-0.4
	Pit-N	66	293	49	100	7	11	1	74	17	4	.341	.385	.451	124	9	16			.934	12	S-66	2.0
	Yr	114	488	81	156	15	12	2	100	42	7	.320	.384	.412	113	9	36			.923	6	*S-114	1.6
1894	Pit-N	86	332	46	93	10	7	1	63	31	4	.280	.349	.361	72	-15	18			.933	7	S-85	-0.2
1895	Lou-N	18	74	9	25	3	1	1	6	3	1	.338	.387	.446	122	2	1			.900	2	S-13/1-5	0.4
	Was-N	25	100	20	23	2	0	0	10	7	3	.230	.300	.250	43	-8	3			.895	6	S-25	-0.1
	Yr	43	174	29	48	5	1	1	16	10	4	.276	.337	.333	76	-6	4			.897	8	S-38/1-5	0.3
Total	17	1736	7030	1163	2040	313	98	27	825	439	212	.290	.337	.374	112	105	372			.910	240	*S-1628/2-86,31PO	36.1

■ TOMMY GLAVIANO
Glaviano, Thomas Giatano "Rabbit"   b: 10/26/23, Sacramento, Cal.   BR/TR, 5'9", 175 lbs.   Deb: 4/19/49

YEAR	TM/L	G	AB	R	H	2B	3B	HR	RBI	BB	SO	AVG	OBP	SLG	PRO+	BR/A	SB	CS	SBR	FA	FR	G/POS	TPR
1949	StL-N	87	258	32	69	16	1	6	36	41	35	.267	.380	.407	106	4	0			.929	14	3-73/2-7	1.6
1950	StL-N	115	410	92	117	29	2	11	44	90	74	.285	.421	.446	122	17	6			.935	6	*3-106/2-5,S	2.1
1951	StL-N	54	104	20	19	4	0	1	4	26	18	.183	.356	.250	66	-4	3	0	1	.972	-3	O-17/2-9	-0.6
1952	StL-N	80	162	30	39	5	1	3	19	27	26	.241	.366	.340	97	0	0	0	0	.934	4	3-52/2-1	0.4
1953	Phi-N	53	74	17	15	1		2	5	24	20	.203	.410	.392	111	2	2	0	1	.892	-2	3-14,2-12/S	0.1
Total	5	389	1008	191	259	55	6	24	108	208	173	.257	.395	.395	108	20	11	0		.931	18	3-245/2-34,OS	3.6

■ HARRY GLEASON
Gleason, Harry Gilbert   b: 3/28/1875, Camden, N.J.   d: 10/21/61, Camden, N.J.   BR/TR, 5'6", 160 lbs.   Deb: 9/27/01   F

YEAR	TM/L	G	AB	R	H	2B	3B	HR	RBI	BB	SO	AVG	OBP	SLG	PRO+	BR/A	SB	CS	SBR	FA	FR	G/POS	TPR
1901	Bos-A	1	1	0	1	0	0	0	0			1.000	1.000	1.000	464	0	1			.667	1	/3-1	0.1
1902	Bos-A	71	240	30	54	5	5	2	25		10	.225	.265	.313	58	-14	6			.930	-0	3-35,O-23/2	-1.5
1903	Bos-A	6	13	3	2	1	0	0	2		0	.154	.154	.231	13	-1	0			.750	-1	/3-2	-0.9
1904	StL-A	46	155	10	33	7	1	0	6		4	.213	.247	.271	68	-6	1			.908	-3	S-20,3-20/2O	-0.9
1905	StL-A	150	535	45	116	11	5	1	57		34	.217	.269	.262	72	-17	23			.911	-15	*3-144/2-7	-2.9
Total	5	274	944	88	206	24	11	3	90		48	.218	.263	.276	67	-38	31			.914	-19	3-202/O-24,S2	-5.5

■ JACK GLEASON
Gleason, John Day   b: 7/14/1854, St.Louis, Mo.   d: 9/4/44, St.Louis, Mo.   BR/TR, 170 lbs.   Deb: 10/2/1877   F

YEAR	TM/L	G	AB	R	H	2B	3B	HR	RBI	BB	SO	AVG	OBP	SLG	PRO+	BR/A	SB	CS	SBR	FA	FR	G/POS	TPR
1877	StL-N	1	4	0	1	0	0	0	0	0		.250	.250	.250	61	-0				.000	-0	/O-1	-0.1
1882	StL-a	78	331	53	84	10	1	2	**27**			.254	.310	.308	105	2				.768	2	*3-73/O-6,2	0.5
1883	StL-a	9	34	2	8	0	0	0	4			.235	.316	.235	76	-1				.833	0	/O-9,3-1	0.0
	Lou-a	84	355	69	106	11	4	2	25			.299	.345	.369	140	17				.795	-33	*3-83/S-1	-1.5
	Yr	93	389	71	114	11	4	2	29			.293	.342	.357	134	16				.798	-33	3-84/O-9,S	-1.5
1884	StL-U	92	395	90	128	30	2	4	23			.324	.361	.441	113	7				.768	-6	*3-92	0.1
1885	StL-N	2	7	0	1	0	0	0	0		1	.143	.143	.143	-8	-1				.857	-0	/3-2	-0.1
1886	Phi-a	77	299	39	56	8	7	1	6			.187	.255	.271	64	-13	8			.797	-6	3-77	-1.4
Total	6	343	1425	253	384	59	14	9	0	95	2	.269	.320	.349	105	11	8			.781	-43	3-328/O-16,S2	-2.5

■ ROY GLEASON
Gleason, Roy William   b: 4/9/43, Melrose Park, Ill.   BB/TR, 6'5.5", 220 lbs.   Deb: 9/3/63

YEAR	TM/L	G	AB	R	H	2B	3B	HR	RBI	BB	SO	AVG	OBP	SLG	PRO+	BR/A	SB	CS	SBR	FA	FR	G/POS	TPR
1963	LA-N	8	1	3	1	1	0	0	0			1.000	1.000	2.000	795	1	0	0	0	.000	0	H	0.1

■ BILL GLEASON
Gleason, William G. "Will"   b: 11/12/1858, St.Louis, Mo.   d: 7/21/32, St.Louis, Mo.   BR/TR, 5'8", 170 lbs.   Deb: 5/2/1882   FU

YEAR	TM/L	G	AB	R	H	2B	3B	HR	RBI	BB	SO	AVG	OBP	SLG	PRO+	BR/A	SB	CS	SBR	FA	FR	G/POS	TPR
1882	StL-a	79	347	63	100	11	6	1	6			.288	.300	.363	118	5				.833	9	*S-79	1.7
1883	StL-a	98	425	81	122	21	9	2	15			.287	.311	.393	119	7				.871	-2	*S-98	0.7
1884	StL-a	110	472	97	127	21	7	1	28			.269	.326	.350	116	8				.867	-17	*S-110/3-1	-0.7
1885	*StL-a	112	472	79	119	9	5	3	29			.252	.316	.311	94	-3				.869	-42	*S-112	-3.9
1886	*StL-a	125	524	97	141	18	5	0	43			.269	.333	.323	101	-0	19			.853	-29	*S-125	-2.5
1887	*StL-a	135	598	135	172	19	1	0	41			.288	.342	.323	78	-21	23			.875	-10	*S-135	-2.4
1888	Phi-a	123	499	55	112	10	2	0	61	12		.224	.256	.253	63	-20	27			.858	-14	*S-121/3-1,1	-2.9
1889	Lou-a	16	58	6	14	2	0	0	5	4		.241	.302	.276	66	-2	1			.822	-3	S-16	-0.4
Total	8	798	3395	613	907	111	35	7	66	178	1	.267	.314	.327	96	-26	70			.860	-106	S-796/3-2,1	-10.4

■ KID GLEASON
Gleason, William J.   b: 10/26/1866, Camden, N.J.   d: 1/2/33, Philadelphia, Pa.   BB/TR, 5'7", 158 lbs.   Deb: 4/20/1888   FMC

YEAR	TM/L	G	AB	R	H	2B	3B	HR	RBI	BB	SO	AVG	OBP	SLG	PRO+	BR/A	SB	CS	SBR	FA	FR	G/POS	TPR
1888	Phi-N	24	83	4	17	2	0	0		5	16	.205	.233	.229	45	-5	3			.841	-3	P-24/O-1	0.0
1889	Phi-N	30	99	11	25	5	0	0		8	12	.253	.308	.303	65	-5	4			.862	-1	P-29/O-3,2	-0.1
1890	Phi-N	63	224	22	47	3	0	0	17	12	21	.210	.250	.223	37	-18	10			.937	-1	P-60/2-2	-0.1
1891	Phi-N	65	214	31	53	5	2	0	17	20	17	.248	.318	.290	75	-7	6			.896	-6	P-53/O-9,S	-0.4
1892	StL-N	66	233	35	50	4	2	3	25	34	23	.215	.315	.288	87	-3	7			.934	5	P-47,O-10/21	-0.2
1893	StL-N	59	199	25	51	6	4	0	20	19	8	.256	.327	.327	74	-8	2			.907	-0	P-48,O-11/S	-0.3
1894	StL-N	9	28	3	7	0	1	0	1	2	1	.250	.300	.321	50	-2	0			.885	1	/P-8,1-1	0.0
	*Bal-N	26	86	22	30	5	1	0	17	7	2	.349	.398	.430	95	-1	1			.900	2	P-21/1-1	0.0
	Yr	35	114	25	37	5	2	0	18	9	3	.325	.374	.404	85	-3	1			.894	-0	P-29/1-2	0.0
1895	*Bal-N	112	421	90	130	14	12	0	74	33	18	.309	.366	.399	95	-4	19			.899	-17	2-85,3-12/PO	-1.3
1896	NY-N	133	541	99	162	17	4	5	89	42	13	.299	.352	.372	93	-5	46			.938	5	*2-130/3-3,O	0.5
1897	NY-N	131	540	85	172	16	4	1	106	26		.319	.353	.369	93	-5	43			.930	1	*2-129/S-3	0.2
1898	NY-N	150	570	78	126	28	4	0	62	39		.221	.278	.253	54	-34	21			.938	21	*2-144/S-6	-0.3
1899	NY-N	146	576	72	152	14	4	0	59	24		.264	.293	.302	66	-28	29			.946	26	*2-146	0.5

YEAR	TM/L	G	AB	R	H	2B	3B	HR	RBI	BB	SO	AVG	OBP	SLG	PRO+	BR/A	SB	CS	SBR	FA	FR	G/POS	TPR
1900	NY-N	111	420	60	104	11	3	1	29	17		.248	.280	.295	62	-22	23			.931	14	*2-111/S-1	-0.3
1901	Det-A	135	547	82	150	16	12	3	75	41		.274	.327	.364	87	-10	32			.925	6	*2-135	0.1
1902	Det-A	118	441	42	109	11	4	1	38	25		.247	.292	.297	62	-22	17			.941	6	*2-118	-1.2
1903	Phi-N	106	412	65	117	19	6	1	49	23		.284	.326	.367	101	-1	12			.959	-4	*2-102/O-4	-0.1
1904	Phi-N	153	587	61	161	23	6	0	42	37		.274	.319	.334	106	3	17			.942	1	*2-152/3-1	0.9
1905	Phi-N	155	608	95	150	17	7	1	50	45		.247	.302	.303	83	-12	16			.947	-8	*2-155	-2.0
1906	Phi-N	135	494	47	112	17	2	0	34	36		.227	.281	.269	71	-17	17			.947	-29	*2-135	-5.1
1907	Phi-N	36	126	11	18	3	0	0	6	7		.143	.200	.167	15	-12	3			.979	-2	2-26/1-4,SO	-1.7
1908	Phi-N	2	1	0	0	0	0	0	0	0		.000	.000	.000	-97	-0	0			1.000	-0	/2-1,O-1	0.0
1912	Chi-A	1	2	0	1	0	0	0	0	0		.500	.500	.500	192	0	0			1.000	-0	/2-1	0.0
Total	22	1966	7452	1020	1944	216	80	15	823	500	131	.261	.311	.317	78	-216	328			.938	8	*2-1583,P-299/OS31	-10.9

■ BILLY GLEASON   Gleason, William Patrick b: 9/6/1894, Chicago, Ill. d: 1/9/57, Holyoke, Mass. BR/TR, 5'6.5", 157 lbs. Deb: 9/25/16

YEAR	TM/L	G	AB	R	H	2B	3B	HR	RBI	BB	SO	AVG	OBP	SLG	PRO+	BR/A	SB	CS	SBR	FA	FR	G/POS	TPR
1916	Pit-N	1	2	0	0	0	0	0	0	0	0	.000	.000	.000	-99	-0	0			1.000	-0	/2-1	-0.1
1917	Pit-N	13	42	3	7	1	0	0	0	5	5	.167	.255	.190	36	-3	1			.978	-5	2-13	-0.9
1921	StL-A	26	74	6	19	0	1	0	8	6	6	.257	.329	.284	54	-5	0	1	-1	.960	-5	2-25	-0.9
Total	3	40	118	9	26	1	1	0	8	11	11	.220	.298	.246	47	-8	1	1		.966	-10	/2-39	-1.9

■ JIM GLEESON   Gleason, James Joseph "Gee Gee" b: 3/5/12, Kansas City, Mo. BB/TR, 6'1", 191 lbs. Deb: 4/25/36 C

YEAR	TM/L	G	AB	R	H	2B	3B	HR	RBI	BB	SO	AVG	OBP	SLG	PRO+	BR/A	SB	CS	SBR	FA	FR	G/POS	TPR
1936	Cle-A	41	139	26	36	9	2	4	12	18	17	.259	.344	.439	91	-2	2	1	0	.958	-2	O-33	-0.5
1939	Chi-N	111	332	43	74	19	6	4	45	39	46	.223	.308	.352	76	-11	7			.957	-4	O-91	-1.9
1940	Chi-N	129	485	76	152	39	11	5	61	54	52	.313	.389	.470	139	26	4			.983	3	*O-123	2.2
1941	Cin-N	102	301	47	70	10	0	3	34	45	30	.233	.340	.296	80	-6	7			.981	-8	O-84	-2.0
1942	Cin-N	9	20	3	4	0	0	0	2	2	2	.200	.304	.200	49	-1	0			.889	-0	/O-5	-0.2
Total	5	392	1277	195	336	77	19	16	154	158	147	.263	.350	.391	101	5	20	1		.972	-11	O-336	-2.4

■ FRANK GLEICH   Gleich, Frank Elmer "Inch" b: 3/7/1894, Columbus, Ohio d: 3/27/49, Columbus, Ohio BL/TR, 5'11", 175 lbs. Deb: 9/17/19

YEAR	TM/L	G	AB	R	H	2B	3B	HR	RBI	BB	SO	AVG	OBP	SLG	PRO+	BR/A	SB	CS	SBR	FA	FR	G/POS	TPR
1919	NY-A	5	4	0	1	0	0	0	1	1	0	.250	.400	.250	84	-0	0			.000	-2	/O-4	-0.2
1920	NY-A	24	41	6	5	0	0	0	3	6	10	.122	.234	.122	-4	-6	0	0	0	.864	-4	O-15	-1.1
Total	2	29	45	6	6	0	0	0	4	7	10	.133	.250	.133	4	-6	0	0		.826	-7	/O-19	-1.3

■ BOB GLENALVIN   Glenalvin, Robert J. (b: Robert J. Dowling) b: 1/17/1867, Indianapolis, Ind. d: 3/24/44, Detroit, Mich. TR, 5'9", 160 lbs. Deb: 7/12/1890

YEAR	TM/L	G	AB	R	H	2B	3B	HR	RBI	BB	SO	AVG	OBP	SLG	PRO+	BR/A	SB	CS	SBR	FA	FR	G/POS	TPR
1890	Chi-N	66	250	43	67	10	3	4	26	19	31	.268	.337	.380	105	1	30			.928	-14	2-66	-0.9
1893	Chi-N	16	61	11	21	3	1	0	12	7	3	.344	.412	.426	125	2	7			.928	-5	2-16	-0.2
Total	2	82	311	54	88	13	4	4	38	26	34	.283	.352	.389	109	3	37			.928	-19	/2-82	-1.1

■ ED GLENN   Glenn, Edward C. "Mouse" b: 9/19/1860, Richmond, Va. d: 2/10/1892, Richmond, Va. BR/TR, 5'10", 160 lbs. Deb: 8/5/1884

YEAR	TM/L	G	AB	R	H	2B	3B	HR	RBI	BB	SO	AVG	OBP	SLG	PRO+	BR/A	SB	CS	SBR	FA	FR	G/POS	TPR
1884	Ric-a	43	175	26	43	2	4			5		.246	.271	.320	93	-1				.833	5	O-43	0.2
1886	Pit-a	71	277	32	53	6	5	0		17		.191	.241	.249	54	-15	19			.865	0	O-71	-1.4
1888	KC-a	3	8	0	0	0	0	0	0	0	0	.000	.200	.000	-32	-1	1			.857	-0	O-3	-0.1
	Bos-N	20	65	8	10	2	0		3	2	8	.154	.203	.215	33	-5	0			.957	2	O-19/3-1	-0.3
Total	3	137	525	66	106	8	11	1	3	24	8	.202	.245	.265	62	-22	20			.867	7	O-136/3-1	-1.6

■ ED GLENN   Glenn, Edward D. b: 10/1875, Ohio d: 12/6/11, Ludlow, Ky. BR/TR, Deb: 9/7/1898

YEAR	TM/L	G	AB	R	H	2B	3B	HR	RBI	BB	SO	AVG	OBP	SLG	PRO+	BR/A	SB	CS	SBR	FA	FR	G/POS	TPR
1898	Was-N	1	4	0	0	0	0	0	0	0	0	.000	.000	.000	-99	-1	0			1.000	-1	/S-1	-0.2
	NY-N	2	4	1	1	0	0	0	0	0	3	.250	.571	.250	142	-0	1			.750	-3	/S-2	-0.2
	Yr	3	8	1	1	0	0	0	0	0	3	.125	.364	.125	42	-0	1			.857	-3	/S-3	-0.4
1902	Chi-N	2	7	0	0	0	0	0	0	0	1	.000	.125	.000	-63	-1	0			1.000	-1	/S-1	-0.3
Total	2	5	15	1	1	0	0	0	0	0	4	.067	.263	.067	-2	-2	1			.923	-5	/S-5	-0.7

■ HARRY GLENN   Glenn, Harry Melville "Husky" b: 6/9/1890, Shelburn, Ind. d: 10/12/18, St.Paul, Minn. BR/TR, 6'1", 200 lbs. Deb: 4/14/15

YEAR	TM/L	G	AB	R	H	2B	3B	HR	RBI	BB	SO	AVG	OBP	SLG	PRO+	BR/A	SB	CS	SBR	FA	FR	G/POS	TPR
1915	StL-N	6	16	1	5	0	0	0	1	3	0	.313	.421	.313	123	1	0			.929	-1	/C-5	0.0

■ JOHN GLENN   Glenn, John b: 7/10/28, Moultrie, Ga. BR/TR, 6'3", 180 lbs. Deb: 6/16/60

YEAR	TM/L	G	AB	R	H	2B	3B	HR	RBI	BB	SO	AVG	OBP	SLG	PRO+	BR/A	SB	CS	SBR	FA	FR	G/POS	TPR
1960	StL-N	32	31	4	8	0	1	0	5	0	9	.258	.258	.323	53	-2	0	0	0	1.000	-7	O-28	-1.0

■ JOHN GLENN   Glenn, John W. b: 1849, Rochester, N.Y. d: 11/10/1888, Sandy Hill, N.Y. BR/TR, 5'8.5", 169 lbs. Deb: 5/13/1871

YEAR	TM/L	G	AB	R	H	2B	3B	HR	RBI	BB	SO	AVG	OBP	SLG	PRO+	BR/A	SB	CS	SBR	FA	FR	G/POS	TPR
1871	Oly-n	26	120	25	37	3	2	0	21	3	1	.308	.325	.367	104	1	1					*O-26	0.2
1872	Oly-n	9	40	5	6	2	0	0	3	1	0	.150	.171	.200	14	-4						/O-9	-0.3
	Nat-n	1	4	0	2	0	0	0	0	0	0	.500	.500	.500	179	0						/O-1	0.0
	Yr	10	44	5	8	2	0	0	3	1	0	.182	.200	.227	32	-3						O-10	-0.3
1873	Was-n	39	185	39	49	9	2	1	18	3	0	.265	.277	.351	86	-3						*1-39	-0.1
1874	Chi-n	55	235	33	66	8	0	0	6			.281	.299	.315	95	-1						1-38,O-17	-0.1
1875	Chi-n	69	303	46	75	9	0	0	5			.248	.260	.277	85	-4						O-44,1-26	-0.4
1876	Chi-N	66	276	55	84	9	2	0	32	12	6	.304	.333	.351	115	2				.881	-2	*O-56,1-15	0.0
1877	Chi-N	50	202	31	46	6	1	0	20	8	16	.228	.257	.267	58	-10				.948	0	O-36,1-14	-1.1
Total	5 n	199	887	148	235	31	4	1	42	18	1	.265	.280	.312	88	-11						1-103/O-97	-0.7
Total	2	116	478	86	130	15	3	0	52	20	22	.272	.301	.316	90	-8				.904	-2	/O-92,1-29	-1.1

■ JOE GLENN   Glenn, Joseph Charles "Gabby" (b: Joseph Charles Gurzensky) b: 11/19/08, Dickson City, Pa. d: 5/6/85, Tunkhannock, Pa. BR/TR, 5'11", 175 lbs. Deb: 9/15/32

YEAR	TM/L	G	AB	R	H	2B	3B	HR	RBI	BB	SO	AVG	OBP	SLG	PRO+	BR/A	SB	CS	SBR	FA	FR	G/POS	TPR
1932	NY-A	6	16	0	2	0	0	0	0	1	5	.125	.222	.125	-8	-3	0	0	0	1.000	-2	/C-5	-0.4
1933	NY-A	5	21	1	3	0	0	0	1	0	3	.143	.143	.143	-26	-4	0	0	0	1.000	-2	/C-5	-0.5
1935	NY-A	17	43	7	10	0	0	0	6	4	1	.233	.298	.326	65	-2	0	0	0	.984	0	C-16	-0.1
1936	NY-A	44	129	21	35	7	0	1	20	10	10	.271	.373	.349	82	-3	1	1	-0	.970	3	C-44	0.1
1937	NY-A	25	53	6	15	2	2	0	4	10	11	.283	.397	.396	100	0	0	0	0	.978	4	C-24	0.4
1938	NY-A	41	123	10	32	7	2	0	25	10	14	.260	.316	.350	67	-6	1	0	0	.974	0	C-40	-0.4
1939	StL-A	88	286	29	78	13	1	4	29	31	40	.273	.344	.367	80	-8	4	4	-1	.968	-13	C-82	-1.7
1940	Bos-A	22	47	3	6	1	0	0	3	4	4	.128	.212	.149	-5	-7	0	0	0	.961	-0	C-19	-0.6
Total	8	248	718	77	181	34	5	5	89	81	91	.252	.330	.334	69	-33	6	5	-1	.972	-10	C-235	-3.2

■ NORM GLOCKSON   Glockson, Norman Stanley b: 6/15/1894, Blue Island, Ill. d: 8/5/55, Maywood, Ill. BR/TR, 6'2", 200 lbs. Deb: 9/16/14

YEAR	TM/L	G	AB	R	H	2B	3B	HR	RBI	BB	SO	AVG	OBP	SLG	PRO+	BR/A	SB	CS	SBR	FA	FR	G/POS	TPR
1914	Cin-N	7	12	0	0	0	0	0	0	1	6	.000	.077	.000	-74	-3	0			.923	-1	/C-7	-0.3

■ AL GLOSSOP   Glossop, Alban b: 7/23/15, Christopher, Ill. d: 7/2/91, Walnut Creek, Cal. BB/TR, 6', 170 lbs. Deb: 9/23/39

YEAR	TM/L	G	AB	R	H	2B	3B	HR	RBI	BB	SO	AVG	OBP	SLG	PRO+	BR/A	SB	CS	SBR	FA	FR	G/POS	TPR
1939	NY-N	10	32	3	6	0	0	0	3	4	2	.188	.278	.281	50	-2				.980	0	2-10	-0.1
1940	NY-N	27	91	16	19	3	0	4	8	10	16	.209	.294	.374	82	-2	1			.952	0	2-24	0.0
	Bos-N	60	148	17	35	2	1	3	14	17	22	.236	.315	.324	81	-4	1			.938	7	2-18,3-18/S	0.4
	Yr	87	239	33	54	5	1	7	22	27	38	.226	.307	.343	82	-6	2			.947	7	2-42,3-18/S	0.4
1942	Phi-N	121	454	33	102	15	1	4	40	29	35	.225	.273	.289	68	-20	3			.961	7	*2-118/3-1	-0.6
1943	Bro-N	87	217	28	37	9	0	3	21	28	27	.171	.268	.253	51	-13				.927	-3	S-33,2-24,3/O	-1.9
1946	Chi-N	4	10	2	0	0	0	0	0	1	3	.000	.231	.000	-32	-2				1.000	-2	2-2,S-2	-0.3
Total	5	309	952	99	199	29	2	15	86	89	105	.209	.280	.291	66	-43	5			.954	6	2-196/S-36,3O	-2.5

■ BILL GLYNN   Glynn, William Vincent b: 7/30/25, Sussex, N.J. BL/TL, 6', 190 lbs. Deb: 9/16/49

YEAR	TM/L	G	AB	R	H	2B	3B	HR	RBI	BB	SO	AVG	OBP	SLG	PRO+	BR/A	SB	CS	SBR	FA	FR	G/POS	TPR
1949	Phi-N	8	10	0	2	0	0	0	1	0	3	.200	.200	.200	8	-1	0			1.000	0	/1-1	-0.1

YEAR	TM/L	G	AB	R	H	2B	3B	HR	RBI	BB	SO	AVG	OBP	SLG	PRO+	BR/A	SB	CS	SBR	FA	FR	G/POS	TPR
1952	Cle-A	44	92	15	25	5	0	2	7	5	16	.272	.309	.391	101	-0	1	0	0	.973	0	1-32	-0.1
1953	Cle-A	147	411	60	100	14	2	3	30	44	65	.243	.324	.309	74	-14	1	3	-2	**.993**	6	*1-135/O-2	-1.5
1954	*Cle-A	111	171	19	43	3	2	5	18	12	21	.251	.301	.380	84	-4	3	2	-0	.987	3	1-96/O-1	-0.4
Total	4	310	684	94	170	22	4	10	56	61	105	.249	.315	.336	79	-21	5	5		.989	9	1-264/O-3	-2.1

■ JOHN GOCHNAUER
Gochnauer, John Peter b: 9/12/1875, Altoona, Pa. d: 9/27/29, Altoona, Pa. BR/TR, 5'9", 160 lbs. Deb: 9/29/01

YEAR	TM/L	G	AB	R	H	2B	3B	HR	RBI	BB	SO	AVG	OBP	SLG	PRO+	BR/A	SB	CS	SBR	FA	FR	G/POS	TPR
1901	Bro-N	3	11	1	4	0	0	0	2	1		.364	.417	.364	124	0	1			1.000	-1	/S-3	0.0
1902	Cle-A	127	459	45	85	16	4	0	37	38		.185	.247	.237	36	-39	7			.933	-3	*S-127	-3.3
1903	Cle-A	134	438	48	81	16	4	0	48	48		.185	.265	.240	53	-24	10			.867	-22	*S-134	-4.3
Total	3	264	908	94	170	32	8	0	87	87		.187	.258	.240	45	-63	18			.901	-26	S-264	-7.6

■ JOHN GODAR
Godar, John Michael b: 10/25/1864, Cincinnati, Ohio d: 6/23/49, Park Ridge, Ill. BR/TR, 5'9", 170 lbs. Deb: 7/8/1892

YEAR	TM/L	G	AB	R	H	2B	3B	HR	RBI	BB	SO	AVG	OBP	SLG	PRO+	BR/A	SB	CS	SBR	FA	FR	G/POS	TPR
1892	Bal-N	5	14	2	3	0	0	0	1	2	1	.214	.353	.214	71	-0	1			1.000	-0	/O-5	-0.1

■ DANNY GODBY
Godby, Danny Ray b: 11/4/46, Logan, W.Va. BR/TR, 6', 185 lbs. Deb: 8/10/74

YEAR	TM/L	G	AB	R	H	2B	3B	HR	RBI	BB	SO	AVG	OBP	SLG	PRO+	BR/A	SB	CS	SBR	FA	FR	G/POS	TPR
1974	StL-N	13	13	2	2	1	0	0	1	3	4	.154	.313	.154	34	-1	0	0	0	1.000	1	/O-4	0.0

■ JOE GODDARD
Goddard, Joseph Harold b: 7/23/50, Beckley, W.Va. BR/TR, 5'11", 181 lbs. Deb: 7/31/72

YEAR	TM/L	G	AB	R	H	2B	3B	HR	RBI	BB	SO	AVG	OBP	SLG	PRO+	BR/A	SB	CS	SBR	FA	FR	G/POS	TPR
1972	SD-N	12	35	0	7	2	0	0	2	5	9	.200	.300	.257	64	-2	0	0	0	.973	-2	C-12	-0.4

■ JOHN GODWIN
Godwin, John Henry "Bunny" b: 3/10/1877, E.Liverpool, Ohio d: 5/5/56, E.Liverpool, Ohio BR/TR, 6', 190 lbs. Deb: 8/14/05

YEAR	TM/L	G	AB	R	H	2B	3B	HR	RBI	BB	SO	AVG	OBP	SLG	PRO+	BR/A	SB	CS	SBR	FA	FR	G/POS	TPR
1905	Bos-A	15	43	4	14	1	0	0	10	3		.326	.408	.349	139	2	3			.950	-1	/O-7,2-5	0.3
1906	Bos-A	66	193	11	36	2	1	0	15	6		.187	.215	.207	32	-15	6			.907	2	3-27,S-14,O/21	-1.4
Total	2	81	236	15	50	3	1	0	25	9		.212	.253	.233	53	-13	9			.935	1	/3-27,O-17,S21	-1.1

■ ED GOEBEL
Goebel, Edwin b: 9/1/1899, Brooklyn, N.Y. d: 8/12/59, Brooklyn, N.Y. BR/TR, 5'11", 170 lbs. Deb: 5/13/22

YEAR	TM/L	G	AB	R	H	2B	3B	HR	RBI	BB	SO	AVG	OBP	SLG	PRO+	BR/A	SB	CS	SBR	FA	FR	G/POS	TPR
1922	Was-A	37	59	13	16	1	0	1	3	8	16	.271	.358	.339	87	-1	1	1	-0	1.000	-1	O-16	-0.3

■ BILLY GOECKEL
Goeckel, William John b: 9/3/1871, Wilkes-Barre, Pa. d: 11/1/22, Philadelphia, Pa. BR/TL, Deb: 8/10/1899

YEAR	TM/L	G	AB	R	H	2B	3B	HR	RBI	BB	SO	AVG	OBP	SLG	PRO+	BR/A	SB	CS	SBR	FA	FR	G/POS	TPR
1899	Phi-N	37	141	17	37	3	1	0	16	1		.262	.283	.298	61	-8	6			.978	-3	1-36	-0.9

■ JERRY GOFF
Goff, Jerry Leroy b: 4/12/64, San Rafael, Cal. BL/TR, 6'3", 205 lbs. Deb: 5/15/90

YEAR	TM/L	G	AB	R	H	2B	3B	HR	RBI	BB	SO	AVG	OBP	SLG	PRO+	BR/A	SB	CS	SBR	FA	FR	G/POS	TPR
1990	Mon-N	52	119	14	27	1	0	3	7	21	36	.227	.343	.311	84	-2	0	2	-1	.963	-1	C-38/1-3,3	-0.2
1992	Mon-N	3	3	0	0	0	0	0	0	0	3	.000	.000	.000	-99	-1	0	0	0	.000	0	/H	-0.1
1993	Pit-N	14	37	5	11	2	0	2	6	8	9	.297	.422	.514	149	3	0	0	0	.984	-2	C-14	0.3
1994	Pit-N	8	25	0	2	0	0	0	1	0	11	.080	.080	.080	-58	-6	0	0	0	.950	-1	/C-7	-0.7
Total	4	77	184	19	40	3	0	5	14	29	59	.217	.324	.315	76	-5	0	2	-1	.966	-5	/C-59,3-3,1	-0.9

■ CHUCK GOGGIN
Goggin, Charles Francis b: 7/7/45, Pompano Beach, Fla. BB/TR, 5'11", 175 lbs. Deb: 9/8/72

YEAR	TM/L	G	AB	R	H	2B	3B	HR	RBI	BB	SO	AVG	OBP	SLG	PRO+	BR/A	SB	CS	SBR	FA	FR	G/POS	TPR
1972	Pit-N	5	7	0	2	0	0	0	0	1	1	.286	.375	.286	92	-0	0	0	0	1.000	0	/2-1	0.0
1973	Pit-N	1	1	1	1	0	0	0	0	0	0	1.000	1.000	1.000	468	0	0	0	0	1.000	-0	/C-1	0.0
	Atl-N	64	90	18	26	5	0	0	7	9	19	.289	.354	.344	88	-1	0	1	-1	.938	-10	2-19/O-6,SC	-1.1
	Yr	65	91	19	27	5	0	0	7	9	19	.297	.360	.352	91	-1	0	1	-1	.938	-10	2-19/O-6,SC	-1.1
1974	Bos-A	2	1	0	0	0	0	0	0	0	1	.000	.000	.000	-93	-0	0	0	0	.667	1	/2-2	0.0
Total	3	72	99	19	29	5	0	0	7	10	21	.293	.358	.343	90	-1	0	1	-1	.927	-9	/2-22,O-6,SC	-1.1

■ MIKE GOLDEN
Golden, Michael Henry b: 9/11/1851, Shirley, Mass. d: 1/11/29, Rockford, Ill. BR/TR, 5'8", 168 lbs. Deb: 5/5/1875

YEAR	TM/L	G	AB	R	H	2B	3B	HR	RBI	BB	SO	AVG	OBP	SLG	PRO+	BR/A	SB	CS	SBR	FA	FR	G/POS	TPR
1875	Wes-n	13	46	5	6	0	0	0				.130	.130	.130	-9	-5						P-13	0.0
	Chi-n	39	155	16	40	3	0	0			2	.258	.268	.277	88	-2						O-24,P-14/1	0.0
	Yr	52	201	21	46	3	0	0			2	.229	.236	.244	65	-7						P-27,O-24/1	0.0
1878	Mil-N	55	214	16	44	6	3	0	20	3	35	.206	.217	.262	53	-11				.831	-3	O-39,P-22/1	-1.2

■ JONAH GOLDMAN
Goldman, Jonah John b: 8/29/06, New York, N.Y. d: 8/17/80, Palm Beach, Fla. BR/TR, 5'7", 170 lbs. Deb: 9/22/28

YEAR	TM/L	G	AB	R	H	2B	3B	HR	RBI	BB	SO	AVG	OBP	SLG	PRO+	BR/A	SB	CS	SBR	FA	FR	G/POS	TPR
1928	Cle-A	7	21	1	5	1	0	0	2	3	0	.238	.333	.286	63	-1	0	0	0	.878	0	/S-7	0.0
1930	Cle-A	111	306	32	74	18	0	1	44	28	25	.242	.312	.310	56	-20	3	5	-2	.945	21	S-93,3-20	0.7
1931	Cle-A	30	62	0	8	1	0	0	3	4	6	.129	.182	.145	-12	-10	1	1	-0	.947	14	S-30	0.5
Total	3	148	389	33	87	20	0	1	49	35	31	.224	.293	.283	46	-31	4	6	-2	.941	35	S-130/3-20	1.2

■ GORDON GOLDSBERRY
Goldsberry, Gordon Frederick b: 8/30/27, Sacramento, Cal. BL/TL, 6', 170 lbs. Deb: 4/20/49

YEAR	TM/L	G	AB	R	H	2B	3B	HR	RBI	BB	SO	AVG	OBP	SLG	PRO+	BR/A	SB	CS	SBR	FA	FR	G/POS	TPR
1949	Chi-A	39	145	25	36	3	2	1	13	18	9	.248	.331	.317	74	-5	2	0	1	.990	-1	1-38	-0.6
1950	Chi-A	82	127	19	34	8	2	2	25	26	18	.268	.392	.409	108	2	0	2	-1	.989	3	1-40/O-3	0.4
1951	Chi-A	10	11	4	1	0	0	0	1	2	2	.091	.231	.091	-11	-2	0	0	0	1.000	1	/1-8	0.0
1952	StL-A	86	227	30	52	9	3	3	17	34	37	.229	.330	.335	83	-5	2	2	-1	.983	-3	1-72/O-2	-1.1
Total	4	217	510	78	123	20	7	6	56	80	66	.241	.344	.343	85	-10	4	4	-2	.987	1	1-158/O-5	-1.3

■ WALT GOLDSBY
Goldsby, Walton Hugh b: 12/31/1861, Louisiana d: 1/11/14, Dallas, Tex. BL, Deb: 5/28/1884

YEAR	TM/L	G	AB	R	H	2B	3B	HR	RBI	BB	SO	AVG	OBP	SLG	PRO+	BR/A	SB	CS	SBR	FA	FR	G/POS	TPR
1884	StL-a	5	20	2	4	0	0	0		0		.200	.200	.200	30	-2				.800	-1	/O-5	-0.2
	Was-a	6	24	4	9	0	0	0		1		.375	.400	.375	174	2				.909	1	/O-6	0.2
	Ric-a	11	40	4	9	1	0	0		1		.225	.262	.250	69	-1				.737	-1	O-11	-0.2
	Yr	22	84	10	22	1	0	0		2		.262	.287	.274	81	-1				.800	-1	/O-22	-0.2
1886	Was-N	6	18	0	4	1	0	0	1	2		.222	.300	.278	76	-0	0			.818	-1	/O-6	-0.1
1888	Bal-a	45	165	13	39	1	1	0	14	8		.236	.288	.255	76	-4	17			.903	-6	O-45	-1.0
Total	3	73	267	23	65	3	1	0	15	12	3	.243	.289	.262	80	-5	17			.858	-8	/O-73	-1.3

■ FRED GOLDSMITH
Goldsmith, Fred Ernest b: 5/15/1856, New Haven, Conn. d: 3/28/39, Berkley, Mich. BR/TR, 6'1", 195 lbs. Deb: 10/23/1875 U

YEAR	TM/L	G	AB	R	H	2B	3B	HR	RBI	BB	SO	AVG	OBP	SLG	PRO+	BR/A	SB	CS	SBR	FA	FR	G/POS	TPR
1875	NH-n	1	4	0	2	0	0	0		0		.500	.500	.500	283	1						/2-1	0.1
1879	Tro-N	9	38	6	9	1	0	0	3	0		.237	.256	.263	77	-1				.833	0	/P-8,O-2,1	-0.2
1880	Chi-N	35	142	24	37	4	2	0	15	2	15	.261	.271	.317	93	-1				.968	-1	P-26,O-10/1	-0.2
1881	Chi-N	42	158	24	38	3	4	0	16	6	17	.241	.268	.310	78	-4				.863	5	P-39/O-3	0.0
1882	Chi-N	45	183	23	42	11	1	0	19	4	29	.230	.246	.301	71	-6				.939	-2	P-45/1-1	0.0
1883	Chi-N	60	235	38	52	12	3	1	16	4		.221	.234	.311	60	-12				.865	1	P-46,O-16/1	-0.3
1884	Chi-N	22	81	11	11	2	0	2	6	7	26	.136	.205	.235	35	-6				.774	-3	P-21/O-2	0.0
	Bal-a	4	14	2	2	0	0	0		0		.143	.143	.143	30	-1				.889	1	/P-4,1-1	0.0
Total	6	217	851	128	191	33	10	3	74	26	125	.224	.247	.297	69	-31				.882	4	P-189/O-33,1	-0.5

■ WALLY GOLDSMITH
Goldsmith, Wallace b: 1849, Baltimore, Md. 5'7", 146 lbs. Deb: 5/4/1871

YEAR	TM/L	G	AB	R	H	2B	3B	HR	RBI	BB	SO	AVG	OBP	SLG	PRO+	BR/A	SB	CS	SBR	FA	FR	G/POS	TPR
1871	Kek-n	19	88	8	18	1	0	0	12	4	2	.205	.239	.216	31	-8	0					S-12/3-5,C2	-0.5
1872	Oly-n	9	40	4	10	0	0	0	5	0		.250	.250	.250	57	-2						/S-5,2-4	-0.1
1873	Mar-n	1	4	0	0	0	0	0	0	0		.000	.000	.000	-99	-1						/2-1	-0.1
1875	Wes-n	13	51	3	6	0	0	0		0	2	.118	.118	.118	-17	-6						3-13	-0.5
Total	4 n	42	183	15	34	1	0	0		4		.186	.203	.191	21	-16						/3-18,S-17,2C	-1.2

■ LONNIE GOLDSTEIN
Goldstein, Leslie Elmer b: 5/13/18, Austin, Tex. BL/TL, 6'2.5", 190 lbs. Deb: 9/11/43

YEAR	TM/L	G	AB	R	H	2B	3B	HR	RBI	BB	SO	AVG	OBP	SLG	PRO+	BR/A	SB	CS	SBR	FA	FR	G/POS	TPR
1943	Cin-N	5	5	1	1	0	0	0	2	1		.200	.429	.200	85	0	0			1.000	-0	/1-2	0.0
1946	Cin-N	6	5	1	0	0	0	0	0	1	1	.000	.167	.000	-53	-1	0			.000	0	H	-0.1
Total	2	11	10	2	1	0	0	0	2	3	2	.100	.308	.100	20	-1	0			1.000	-0	/1-2	-0.1

YEAR	TM/L	G	AB	R	H	2B	3B	HR	RBI	BB	SO	AVG	OBP	SLG	PRO+	BR/A	SB	CS	SBR	FA	FR	G/POS	TPR

■ PURNAL GOLDY　　Goldy, Purnal William b: 11/28/37, Camden, N.J.　BR/TR, 6'5", 200 lbs.　Deb: 4/12/62

1962	Det-A	20	70	8	16	1	1	3	12	0	12	.229	.239	.400	66	-4	0	0	0	.964	-0	O-15	-0.5
1963	Det-A	9	8	1	2	0	0	0	0	0	4	.250	.250	.250	39	-1	0	0	0	.000	0	H	-0.1
Total	2	29	78	9	18	1	1	3	12	0	16	.231	.241	.385	64	-4	0	0	0	.964	-0	/O-15	-0.6

■ STAN GOLETZ　　Goletz, Stanley "Stash" b: 5/21/18, Crescent, Ohio　BL/TL, 6'3", 200 lbs.　Deb: 9/9/41

1941	Chi-A	5	5	0	3	0	0	0	0	0	2	.600	.600	.600	221	1	0	0	0	.000	0	H	0.1

■ MIKE GOLIAT　　Goliat, Mike Mitchel b: 11/5/25, Yatesboro, Pa.　BR/TR, 6', 180 lbs.　Deb: 8/3/49

1949	Phi-N	55	189	24	40	6	3	3	19	20	32	.212	.290	.323	66	-9	0			.969	-2	2-50/1-5	-0.9
1950	*Phi-N	145	483	49	113	13	6	13	64	53	75	.234	.314	.366	80	-15	3			.972	-18	*2-145	-2.6
1951	Phi-N	41	138	14	31	2	1	4	15	9	18	.225	.277	.341	66	-7	0	1	-1	.968	-7	2-37/3-2	-1.3
	StL-A	5	11	0	2	0	0	0	1	0	1	.182	.182	.182	-1	-2	0	0	0	1.000	0	/2-2	-0.1
1952	StL-A	3	4	0	0	0	0	0	0	1	1	.000	.200	.000	-40	-1	0	0	0	1.000	1	/2-3	0.0
Total	4	249	825	87	186	21	10	20	99	83	127	.225	.300	.348	73	-33	3	1		.971	-26	2-237/1-5,3	-4.9

■ WALT GOLVIN　　Golvin, Walter George b: 2/1/1894, Hershey, Neb. d: 6/11/73, Gardena, Cal.　BL/TL, 6', 165 lbs.　Deb: 4/15/22

1922	Chi-N	2	2	0	0	0	0	0	1	0	0	.000	.000	.000	-98	-1	0	0	0	1.000	-0	/1-2	-0.1

■ CHRIS GOMEZ　　Gomez, Christopher Cory b: 6/16/71, Los Angeles, Cal.　BR/TR, 6'1", 183 lbs.　Deb: 7/19/93

1993	Det-A	46	128	11	32	7	1	0	11	9	17	.250	.304	.320	69	-6	2	2	-1	.963	11	S-29,2-17/D	0.6
1994	Det-A	84	296	32	76	19	0	8	53	33	64	.257	.337	.402	90	-4	5	3	-0	.981	-17	S-57,2-30	-1.5
Total	2	130	424	43	108	26	1	8	64	42	81	.255	.328	.377	84	-10	7	5	-1	.975	-6	/S-86,2-47,D	-0.9

■ CHILE GOMEZ　　Gomez, Jose Luis (Gonzalez) b: 5/23/09, Villa Union, Mex. d: 12/1/92, Nuevo Laredo, Mex.　BR/TR, 5'10", 165 lbs.　Deb: 7/27/35

1935	Phi-N	67	222	24	51	3	0	0	16	17	34	.230	.285	.243	39	-19	2			.948	12	S-36,2-32	-0.3
1936	Phi-N	108	332	24	77	4	1	0	28	14	32	.232	.265	.250	36	-30	0			.948	18	2-71,S-40	-0.5
1942	Was-A	25	73	8	14	2	0	0	6	9	7	.192	.280	.274	57	-4	1	0	0	.973	-1	2-23/3-1	-0.4
Total	3	200	627	56	142	9	3	0	50	40	73	.226	.274	.250	39	-53	3	0		.954	29	2-126/S-76,3	-1.2

■ LEO GOMEZ　　Gomez, Leonardo (Velez) b: 3/2/66, Canovanas, P.R.　BR/TR, 6', 180 lbs.　Deb: 9/17/90

1990	Bal-A	12	39	3	9	0	0	0	1	8	7	.231	.362	.231	71	-1	0	0	0	.886	-2	3-12	-0.3
1991	Bal-A	118	391	40	91	17	2	16	45	40	82	.233	.307	.409	100	-1	1	1	-0	.972	-13	*3-105,D-10/1	-1.4
1992	Bal-A	137	468	62	124	24	0	17	64	63	78	.265	.362	.425	117	11	2	3	-1	.951	-13	*3-137	-0.3
1993	Bal-A	71	244	30	48	7	0	10	25	32	60	.197	.297	.348	70	-11	0	1	-1	.951	6	3-70/D-1	-0.5
1994	Bal-A	84	285	46	78	20	0	15	56	41	55	.274	.371	.502	115	6	0	0	0	.975	-3	3-78/1-1,D	0.9
Total	5	422	1427	181	350	68	2	58	191	184	282	.245	.338	.418	103	5	3	5	-2	.958	-19	3-402/D-16,1	-1.6

■ LUIS GOMEZ　　Gomez, Luis (Sanchez) b: 8/19/51, Guadalajara, Mex.　BR/TR, 5'9", 150 lbs.　Deb: 4/28/74

1974	Min-A	82	168	18	35	1	0	0	3	12	16	.208	.261	.214	37	-13	2	3	-1	.960	20	S-74/2-2,D	1.2
1975	Min-A	89	72	7	10	0	0	0	5	4	12	.139	.184	.139	-7	-10	0	2	-1	.975	20	S-70/2-6,D	1.0
1976	Min-A	38	57	5	11	1	0	0	3	3	3	.193	.233	.211	30	-5	1	0	-0	.988	5	S-24/2-8,30D	0.4
1977	Min-A	32	65	6	16	4	2	0	11	4	9	.246	.290	.369	79	-2	0	2	-1	.983	4	2-19/S-7,30D	0.2
1978	Tor-A	153	413	39	92	7	3	0	32	34	41	.223	.282	.254	51	-26	2	10	-5	.976	-10	*S-153	-2.5
1979	Tor-A	59	163	11	39	7	0	0	11	6	17	.239	.266	.282	48	-12	1	0	0	1.000	9	S-22,2-20,S	-0.6
1980	Atl-N	121	278	18	53	6	0	0	24	17	27	.191	.240	.212	26	-27	0	4	-2	.968	12	*S-119	-0.8
1981	Atl-N	35	35	4	7	0	0	0	1	6	4	.200	.317	.200	48	-2	0	1	-1	.895	-3	S-21/3-9,2P	-0.5
Total	8	609	1251	108	263	26	5	0	90	86	129	.210	.262	.239	40	-98	6	22	-11	.970	53	S-483/2-58,3DOP	-1.6

■ PRESTON GOMEZ　　Gomez, Pedro (Martinez) b: 4/20/23, Preston, Cuba　BR/TR, 5'11", 170 lbs.　Deb: 5/5/44　MC

1944	Was-A	8	7	2	2	1	0	0	2	0	4	.286	.286	.429	107	0	0	0	0	1.000	-1	/2-2,S-2	-0.1

■ RANDY GOMEZ　　Gomez, Randell Scott b: 2/4/57, San Mateo, Cal.　BR/TR, 5'10", 185 lbs.　Deb: 8/21/84

1984	SF-N	14	30	0	5	1	0	0	0	8	3	.167	.342	.200	57	-1	0	0	0	.951	3	C-14	0.3

■ JESSE GONDER　　Gonder, Jesse Lemar b: 1/20/36, Monticello, Ark.　BL/TR, 5'10", 190 lbs.　Deb: 9/23/60

1960	NY-A	7	7	1	2	0	0	1	3	1	1	.286	.375	.714	199	1	0	0	0	1.000	1	/C-1	0.2
1961	NY-A	15	12	2	4	1	0	0	3	3	1	.333	.467	.417	146	1	0	0	0	.000	0	H	0.1
1962	Cin-N	4	4	0	0	0	0	0	0	0	3	.000	.000	.000	-97	-1	0	0	0	.000	0	H	-0.1
1963	Cin-N	31	32	5	10	2	0	3	5	1	12	.313	.333	.656	172	3	0	0	0	1.000	1	/C-7	0.4
	NY-N	42	126	12	38	4	0	3	15	6	25	.302	.333	.405	110	1	1	2	-1	.978	-14	C-31	-1.4
	Yr	73	158	17	48	6	0	6	20	7	37	.304	.333	.456	122	4	1	2	-1	.981	-13	C-38	-1.0
1964	NY-N	131	341	28	92	11	1	7	35	29	65	.270	.331	.370	99	-0	0	0		.979	-1	C-97	0.3
1965	NY-N	53	105	6	25	4	0	4	9	11	20	.238	.310	.390	100	-0	0	0		.992	-5	C-31	-0.4
	Mil-N	31	53	2	8	2	0	1	5	4	9	.151	.211	.245	28	-5	0	0		.989	5	C-13	0.0
	Yr	84	158	8	33	6	0	5	14	15	29	.209	.277	.342	75	-5	0	0		.991	-0	C-44	-0.4
1966	Pit-N	59	160	13	36	3	1	7	16	12	39	.225	.287	.387	85	-3	0	0		.978	-2	C-52	-0.2
1967	Pit-N	36	36	4	5	1	0	0	3	5	9	.139	.279	.167	30	-3	0	0		.971	-0	C-18	-0.3
Total	8	395	876	73	220	28	2	26	94	72	184	.251	.312	.377	94	-7	1	2	-1	.981	-15	C-250	-1.4

■ DAN GONZALES　　Gonzales, Daniel David b: 9/30/53, Whittier, Cal.　BL/TR, 6'1", 195 lbs.　Deb: 4/7/79

1979	Det-A	7	18	1	4	1	0	0	0	0	2	.222	.222	.278	33	-2	1	0	0	1.000	-1	/O-3	-0.2
1980	Det-A	2	7	1	1	0	0	0	2	0	1	.143	.143	.143	-21	-1	0	0	0	.750	0	/O-1,D-1	-0.1
Total	2	9	25	2	5	1	0	0	2	0	3	.200	.200	.240	18	-3	1	0	0	.857	-1	/O-4,D-1	-0.3

■ LARRY GONZALES　　Gonzales, Lawrence Christopher b: 3/28/67, West Covina, Cal.　BR/TR, 6'3", 200 lbs.　Deb: 6/13/93

1993	Cal-A	2	2	0	1	0	0	0	1	1	0	.500	.667	.500	212	0	0	0	0	1.000	-0	/C-2	0.0

■ RENE GONZALES　　Gonzales, Rene Adrian b: 9/3/60, Austin, Tex.　BR/TR, 6'3", 191 lbs.　Deb: 7/27/84

1984	Mon-N	29	30	5	7	1	0	0	2	2	5	.233	.303	.267	64	-1	0	0	0	.957	1	S-27	0.4
1986	Mon-N	11	26	1	3	0	0	0	0	2	2	.115	.179	.115	-17	-4	0	2	-1	1.000	2	/S-6,3-5	-0.4
1987	Bal-A	37	60	14	16	2	1	1	7	3	11	.267	.302	.383	82	-2	1	0	0	.963	6	3-29/2-6,S	0.4
1988	Bal-A	92	237	13	51	6	0	2	15	13	32	.215	.265	.266	50	-16	2	0	-0	.966	15	3-80,2-14/S1O	-0.1
1989	Bal-A	71	166	16	36	4	1	0	11	12	30	.217	.270	.259	51	-11	5	3	-0	.978	-4	2-54,3-17/S	-1.1
1990	Bal-A	67	103	13	22	4	1	1	12	12	14	.214	.296	.291	67	-4	1	2	-1	.994	9	2-43,3-16/SO	0.5
1991	*Tor-A	71	118	16	23	3	0	1	6	12	22	.195	.291	.246	48	-8	0	0	0	.973	10	S-36,3-26,2/1	0.4
1992	Cal-A	104	329	47	91	17	1	7	38	41	46	.277	.364	.398	113	6	7	4	-0	.954	5	3-53,2-42,1/S	1.2
1993	Cal-A	118	335	34	84	17	0	2	31	49	45	.251	.348	.319	78	-9	5	5	-2	.956	-0	3-79,1-31/S2P	-1.2
1994	Cle-A	22	23	6	8	1	1	1	5	5	3	.348	.464	.609	166	2	2	0	1	.952	3	3-13/1-4,S2	0.5
Total	10	622	1427	165	341	54	4	16	127	151	215	.239	.317	.316	75	-46	23	16	-3	.956	48	3-318,2-175/S1OP	0.2

■ ALEX GONZALEZ　　Gonzalez, Alexander Scott b: 4/8/73, Miami, Fla.　BR/TR, 6', 180 lbs.　Deb: 4/4/94

1994	Tor-A	15	53	7	8	3	1	0	4	4	17	.151	.224	.245	21	-6	3	0	1	.918	-5	S-15	-0.3

■ TONY GONZALEZ　　Gonzalez, Andres Antonio (Gonzalez) b: 8/28/36, Central Cunagua, Cuba　BL/TR, 5'9", 170 lbs.　Deb: 4/12/60

1960	Cin-N	39	99	10	21	5	1	3	14	4	27	.212	.250	.374	67	-5	1	0	0	.957	-4	O-31	-1.0

YEAR	TM/L	G	AB	R	H	2B	3B	HR	RBI	BB	SO	AVG	OBP	SLG	PRO+	BR/A	SB	CS	SBR	FA	FR	G/POS	TPR
	Phi-N	78	241	27	72	17	5	6	33	11	47	.299	.337	.485	122	6	2	2	-1	.981	-1	O-67	0.3
	Yr	117	340	37	93	22	6	9	47	15	74	.274	.312	.453	106	2	3	2	-0	.975	-4	O-98	-0.7
1961	Phi-N	126	426	58	118	16	8	12	58	49	66	.277	.360	.437	112	8	15	5	2	.984	-1	*O-118	0.2
1962	Phi-N	118	437	76	132	16	4	20	63	40	82	.302	.372	.494	134	21	17	8	0	**1.000**	6	*O-114	2.0
1963	Phi-N	155	555	78	170	36	12	4	66	53	68	.306	.375	.436	134	25	13	8	-1	.986	-6	*O-151	1.2
1964	Phi-N	131	421	55	117	25	3	4	40	44	74	.278	.355	.380	108	6	0	5	-3	**.996**	1	*O-119	-0.1
1965	Phi-N	108	370	48	109	19	1	13	41	31	52	.295	.354	.457	129	14	3	4	-2	.983	-6	*O-104	0.2
1966	Phi-N	132	384	53	110	20	6	6	40	26	60	.286	.337	.406	105	3	2	6	-3	.986	-1	*O-121	-0.5
1967	Phi-N	149	508	74	172	23	9	9	59	47	58	.339	.400	.472	147	32	10	9	-2	**.993**	5	*O-143	3.0
1968	Phi-N	121	416	45	110	13	4	3	38	40	42	.264	.339	.337	103	3	6	5	-1	.979	-4	*O-117	-1.0
1969	SD-N	53	182	17	41	4	0	2	8	19	24	.225	.309	.280	69	-7	1	0	0	.975	5	O-49	-0.6
	*Atl-N	89	320	51	94	15	2	10	50	27	22	.294	.358	.447	124	10	3	1	0	.989	2	O-82	0.8
	Yr	142	502	68	135	19	2	12	58	46	46	.269	.340	.386	104	3	4	1	1	.983	6	*O-131	0.2
1970	Atl-N	123	430	57	114	18	2	7	55	46	45	.265	.347	.365	86	-8	3	5	-2	.987	-3	O-119	-1.8
	Cal-A	26	92	9	28	2	0	1	12	2	11	.304	.326	.359	92	-1	3	2	-0	.960	-1	O-24	-0.4
1971	Cal-A	111	314	32	77	9	2	3	38	28	28	.245	.313	.315	84	-7	0	1	-1	.987	-6	O-88	-1.9
Total	12	1559	5195	690	1485	238	57	103	615	467	706	.286	.353	.413	114	100	79	61	-13	.987	-12	*O-1447	0.4

■ DENNY GONZALEZ

Gonzalez, Denio Mariano (Manzueta)　b: 7/22/63, Sabana Grande Boya, D.R.　BR/TR, 5'11", 185 lbs.　Deb: 8/6/84

YEAR	TM/L	G	AB	R	H	2B	3B	HR	RBI	BB	SO	AVG	OBP	SLG	PRO+	BR/A	SB	CS	SBR	FA	FR	G/POS	TPR
1984	Pit-N	26	82	9	15	3	1	0	4	7	21	.183	.247	.244	38	-7	1	1	-0	1.000	1	3-11,S-10/O	-0.5
1985	Pit-N	35	124	11	28	4	0	4	12	13	27	.226	.299	.355	83	-3	2	4	-2	.894	-4	3-21,O-13/2	-1.0
1987	Pit-N	5	7	1	0	0	0	0	0	1	2	.000	.125	.000	-63	-2	0	0	0	1.000	-1	/S-1	-0.2
1988	Pit-N	24	32	5	6	1	0	0	1	6	10	.188	.316	.219	57	-2	0	0	0	1.000		S-14/2-4,3	-0.1
1989	Cle-A	8	17	3	5	1	0	0	1	0	4	.294	.333	.353	92	-0	0	0	0	1.000	-4	/3-1,D-6	-0.1
Total	5	98	262	29	54	9	1	4	18	27	64	.206	.283	.294	62	-13	3	5	-2	.925	-4	/3-35,S-25,O2D	-1.9

■ EUSEBIO GONZALEZ

Gonzalez, Eusebio Miguel (Lopez) "Papo"　b: 7/13/1892, Havana, Cuba　d: 2/14/76, Havana, Cuba　BR/TR, 5'10", 165 lbs.　Deb: 7/26/18

YEAR	TM/L	G	AB	R	H	2B	3B	HR	RBI	BB	SO	AVG	OBP	SLG	PRO+	BR/A	SB	CS	SBR	FA	FR	G/POS	TPR
1918	Bos-A	3	5	2	2	0	1	0	0	1	1	.400	.571	.800	319	1	0			1.000	-1	/S-2,3-1	0.1

■ FERNANDO GONZALEZ

Gonzalez, Jose Fernando (Quinones)　b: 6/19/50, Arecibo, P.R.　BR/TR, 5'10", 170 lbs.　Deb: 9/15/72

YEAR	TM/L	G	AB	R	H	2B	3B	HR	RBI	BB	SO	AVG	OBP	SLG	PRO+	BR/A	SB	CS	SBR	FA	FR	G/POS	TPR
1972	Pit-N	3	2	0	0	0	0	0	0	0	2	.000	.000	.000	-99	-1	0	0	0	.500	0	/3-1	-0.1
1973	Pit-N	37	49	5	11	0	1	1	5	1	11	.224	.255	.327	62	-3	0	0	0	.923	-1	/3-5	-0.4
1974	KC-A	9	21	1	3	1	0	0	2	0	4	.143	.143	.190	-5	-3	1	0	0	1.000	-0	/3-8,D-1	-0.3
	NY-A	51	121	11	26	5	1	1	7	7	7	.215	.258	.298	61	-6	0	0	0	.982	-0	2-42/3-7,S	-0.2
	Yr	60	142	12	29	6	1	1	9	7	11	.204	.242	.282	51	-9	1	0	0	.982	-0	2-42,3-15/SD	-0.5
1977	Pit-N	80	181	17	50	10	0	4	27	13	21	.276	.325	.398	90	-3	3	3	-1	.972	-8	3-37,O-16/2S	-1.2
1978	Pit-N	9	21	2	4	1	0	0	0	1	3	.190	.227	.238	29	-2	0	0	0	.923	-4	/2-4,3-3	-0.2
	SD-N	101	320	27	80	10	2	2	29	18	32	.250	.290	.313	74	-12	4	4	-1	.982	-0	2-94	-0.7
	Yr	110	341	29	84	11	2	2	29	19	35	.246	.286	.308	71	-14	4	4	-1	.981	-4	2-98/3-3	-1.4
1979	SD-N	114	323	22	70	13	3	9	34	18	34	.217	.258	.359	71	-15	0	0	0	.976	-14	*2-103/3-3	-2.3
Total	6	404	1038	85	244	40	7	17	104	58	114	.235	.276	.336	71	-44	8	7	-2	.979	-24	2-249/3-64,OSD	-5.9

■ JOSE GONZALEZ

Gonzalez, Jose Rafael (Gutierrez)　b: 11/23/64, Puerto Plata, D.R.　BR/TR, 6'2", 196 lbs.　Deb: 9/2/85

YEAR	TM/L	G	AB	R	H	2B	3B	HR	RBI	BB	SO	AVG	OBP	SLG	PRO+	BR/A	SB	CS	SBR	FA	FR	G/POS	TPR
1985	LA-N	23	11	6	3	2	0	0	1	0	3	.273	.333	.455	122	0	1	1	-0	1.000	-6	O-18	-0.6
1986	LA-N	57	93	15	20	5	1	2	6	7	29	.215	.270	.355	76	-3	4	3	-1	.924	-10	O-57	-1.6
1987	LA-N	19	16	2	3	2	0	0	1	1	2	.188	.235	.313	45	-1	5	0	2	1.000	-1	O-16	-0.1
1988	*LA-N	37	24	7	2	1	0	0	0	3	10	.083	.154	.125	-20	-4	3	0	1	.938	-8	O-24	-1.2
1989	LA-N	95	261	31	70	11	2	2	18	23	53	.268	.327	.360	98	-1	9	3	1	.968	-0	O-87	-0.2
1990	LA-N	106	99	15	23	5	3	2	8	6	27	.232	.283	.404	89	-2	3	1	0	1.000	-22	O-81	-2.5
1991	LA-N	42	28	3	0	0	0	0	0	2	9	.000	.067	.000	-82	-7	0	0	0	1.000	-7	O-27	-1.4
	Pit-N	16	20	2	2	0	0	1	3	0	6	.100	.100	.250	-5	-3	0	0	0	1.000	-1	O-14	-0.5
	Yr	58	48	5	2	0	0	1	3	2	15	.042	.080	.104	-50	-10	0	0	0	1.000	-8	O-41	-1.9
	Cle-A	33	69	10	11	2	1	1	4	11	27	.159	.284	.261	51	-4	8	0	2	.981	-3	O-32	-0.6
1992	Cal-A	33	55	4	10	2	0	0	2	7	20	.182	.274	.218	39	-4	0	1	-1	1.000	-4	O-22/D-1	-0.9
Total	8	461	676	95	144	30	7	9	42	60	186	.213	.279	.318	69	-29	33	9	5	.972	-62	O-378/D-1	-9.6

■ JUAN GONZALEZ

Gonzalez, Juan Alberto (Vazquez)　b: 10/20/69, Arecibo, P.R.　BR/TR, 6'3", 175 lbs.　Deb: 9/1/89

YEAR	TM/L	G	AB	R	H	2B	3B	HR	RBI	BB	SO	AVG	OBP	SLG	PRO+	BR/A	SB	CS	SBR	FA	FR	G/POS	TPR
1989	Tex-A	24	60	6	9	3	0	1	7	6	17	.150	.227	.250	34	-5	0	0	0	.964	-2	O-24	-0.7
1990	Tex-A	25	90	11	26	7	1	4	12	2	18	.289	.304	.522	131	3	0	1	-1	1.000	-1	O-16/D-9	0.1
1991	Tex-A	142	545	78	144	34	1	27	102	42	118	.264	.323	.479	121	13	4	4	-1	.981	-19	*O-136/D-4	-1.1
1992	Tex-A	155	584	77	152	24	2	**43**	109	35	143	.260	.308	.529	135	23	0	1	-1	.975	5	*O-148/D-4	2.4
1993	Tex-A★	140	536	105	166	33	1	**46**	118	37	99	.310	.369	**.632**	170	49	4	1	1	.985	4	*O-129,D-10	4.9
1994	Tex-A	107	422	57	116	18	4	19	85	30	66	.275	.330	.472	112	6	6	4	-1	.991	7	*O-107	1.0
Total	6	593	2237	334	613	119	9	140	433	152	461	.274	.329	.523	133	89	14	11	-2	.982	-6	O-560/D-27	6.6

■ JULIO GONZALEZ

Gonzalez, Julio Cesar (Hernandez)　b: 12/25/52, Caguas, P.R.　BR/TR, 5'11", 165 lbs.　Deb: 4/8/77

YEAR	TM/L	G	AB	R	H	2B	3B	HR	RBI	BB	SO	AVG	OBP	SLG	PRO+	BR/A	SB	CS	SBR	FA	FR	G/POS	TPR
1977	Hou-N	110	383	34	94	18	3	1	27	19	45	.245	.288	.316	68	-18	3	3	-1	.921	-26	S-63,2-45	-3.6
1978	Hou-N	78	223	24	52	3	1	1	16	8	31	.233	.263	.269	53	-15	6	1	1	.983	-20	2-54,S-17/3	-3.1
1979	Hou-N	68	181	16	45	5	2	0	10	5	14	.249	.280	.298	62	-10	2	1	0	.987	-1	2-32,S-21/3	-0.5
1980	Hou-N	40	52	5	6	1	0	0	1	1	8	.115	.132	.135	-28	-9	1	0	0	1.000	3	S-16,3-11/2	-0.5
1981	StL-N	20	22	2	7	1	0	0	3	1	3	.318	.348	.500	135	1	0	0	0	1.000	1	/S-5,2-4,3	0.2
1982	StL-N	42	87	9	21	3	2	1	7	1	24	.241	.258	.356	70	-4	1	1	-0	.907	-1	3-21/2-9,S	-0.6
1983	Det-A	12	21	0	3	1	0	0	2	1	7	.143	.182	.190	3	-3	0	0	0	.889	3	/S-6,2-5,3	0.1
Total	7	370	969	90	228	32	8	4	66	36	132	.235	.269	.297	59	-58	13	6	0	.976	-39	2-151,S-129/3	-8.0

■ LUIS GONZALEZ

Gonzalez, Luis Emilio　b: 9/3/67, Tampa, Fla.　BL/TR, 6'2", 180 lbs.　Deb: 9/4/90

YEAR	TM/L	G	AB	R	H	2B	3B	HR	RBI	BB	SO	AVG	OBP	SLG	PRO+	BR/A	SB	CS	SBR	FA	FR	G/POS	TPR
1990	Hou-N	12	21	1	4	2	0	0	0	2	5	.190	.261	.286	52	-1	0	0	0	1.000	2	/3-4,1-2	0.1
1991	Hou-N	137	473	51	120	28	9	13	69	40	101	.254	.322	.433	117	9	10	7	-1	.984	13	*O-133	1.9
1992	Hou-N	122	387	40	94	19	3	10	55	24	52	.243	.291	.385	94	-5	7	7	-2	.993	15	*O-111	0.7
1993	Hou-N	154	540	82	162	34	3	15	72	47	83	.300	.367	.457	124	18	20	9	1	.978	20	*O-149	3.5
1994	Hou-N	112	392	57	107	29	4	8	67	49	57	.273	.358	.429	106	4	15	13	-3	.991	12	*O-111	1.0
Total	5	537	1813	231	487	112	19	46	263	162	298	.269	.336	.427	111	25	52	36	-6	.985	62	O-504/3-4,1	7.2

■ MIKE GONZALEZ

Gonzalez, Miguel Angel (Cordero)　b: 9/24/1890, Havana, Cuba　d: 2/19/77, Havana, Cuba　BR/TR, 6'1", 200 lbs.　Deb: 9/28/12　MC

YEAR	TM/L	G	AB	R	H	2B	3B	HR	RBI	BB	SO	AVG	OBP	SLG	PRO+	BR/A	SB	CS	SBR	FA	FR	G/POS	TPR
1912	Bos-N	1	2	0	0	0	0	0	0	1	1	.000	.333	.000	-5	-0	0			.875	1	/C-1	0.1
1914	Cin-N	95	176	19	41	6	0	0	10	13	16	.233	.293	.267	65	-7	2			.954	10	C-83	0.8
1915	StL-N	51	97	12	22	2	2	0	10	8	14	.227	.306	.289	80	-2	4	2	0	.992	4	C-32/1-8	0.3
1916	StL-N	118	331	33	79	15	4	0	29	28	18	.239	.304	.308	89	-4	5			.981	7	C-93,1-13	1.0
1917	StL-N	106	290	28	76	8	1	2	28	22	24	.262	.316	.307	94	-2	12			.977	0	C-68,1-18/O	0.3
1918	StL-N	117	349	33	88	13	4	3	20	39	30	.252	.327	.338	107	3	14			.978	-1	*C-100/O-5,1	1.1
1919	NY-N	58	158	18	30	6	0	0	8	20	9	.190	.293	.228	58	-7	3			.962	-3	C-52/1-4	-0.7
1920	NY-N	11	13	1	3	0	0	0	0	0	0	.231	.375	.231	77	-0	0			1.000	-1	/C-8	0.0
1921	NY-N	13	24	3	9	0	0	0	3	3	2	.375	.400	.417	116	1	0			.981	-0	/1-6,C-2	0.0
1924	StL-N	120	402	34	119	27	1	0	53	24	22	.296	.337	.391	96	-2	3	5	-3	.986	-7	*C-119	-0.4
1925	StL-N	22	71	9	22	3	0	0	4	6	2	.310	.380	.352	86	-1	1	2	-1	.982	4	C-22	0.3

YEAR	TM/L	G	AB	R	H	2B	3B	HR	RBI	BB	SO	AVG	OBP	SLG	PRO+	BR/A	SB	CS	SBR	FA	FR	G/POS	TPR
	Chi-N	70	197	26	52	13	1	3	18	13	15	.264	.316	.386	77	-7	2	1	0	.989	1	C-50/1-9	-0.4
	Yr	92	268	35	74	16	1	3	22	19	17	.276	.333	.377	80	-8	3	3	-1	.987	5	C-72/1-9	-0.1
1926	Chi-N	80	253	24	63	13	3	1	23	13	17	.249	.288	.336	67	-12	3			**.989**	6	C-78	-0.1
1927	Chi-N	39	108	15	26	4	1	1	15	10	8	.241	.311	.324	70	-5	1			.994	9	C-36	0.6
1928	Chi-N	49	158	12	43	9	2	1	21	12	7	.272	.324	.373	83	-4	2			.983	8	C-45	0.8
1929	*Chi-N	60	167	15	40	3	0	0	18	18	14	.240	.317	.257	44	-14	1			.992	6	C-60	-0.3
1931	StL-N	15	19	1	2	0	0	0	3	0	3	.105	.105	.105	-42	-4	0			1.000	-0	C-12	-0.4
1932	StL-N	17	14	0	2	0	0	0	3	0	2	.143	.143	.143	-22	-2	0			1.000	2	/C-7	-0.1
Total	17	1042	2829	283	717	123	19	13	263	231	198	.253	.314	.324	81	-71	52	10		.980	45	C-868/1-60,O	2.9

■ ORLANDO GONZALEZ
Gonzalez, Orlando Eugene b: 11/15/51, Havana, Cuba BL/TL, 6'2", 180 lbs. Deb: 6/7/76

YEAR	TM/L	G	AB	R	H	2B	3B	HR	RBI	BB	SO	AVG	OBP	SLG	PRO+	BR/A	SB	CS	SBR	FA	FR	G/POS	TPR
1976	Cle-A	28	68	5	17	2	0	0	4	5	7	.250	.301	.279	72	-2	1	2	-1	.992	-2	1-15/O-7,D	-0.7
1978	*Phi-N	26	26	1	5	0	0	0	0	1	1	.192	.222	.192	17	-3	0	0	0	1.000	0	O-11/1-3	-0.6
1980	Oak-A	25	70	10	17	0	0	0	1	9	8	.243	.329	.243	64	-3	0	2	-1	.990	1	1-11/O-2,D	-0.4
Total	3	79	164	16	39	2	0	0	5	15	16	.238	.302	.250	59	-8	1	4	-2	.991	-3	/1-29,O-20,D	-1.7

■ PEDRO GONZALEZ
Gonzalez, Pedro (Olivares) b: 12/12/37, San Pedro De Macoris, D.R. BR/TR, 6', 176 lbs. Deb: 4/11/63

YEAR	TM/L	G	AB	R	H	2B	3B	HR	RBI	BB	SO	AVG	OBP	SLG	PRO+	BR/A	SB	CS	SBR	FA	FR	G/POS	TPR
1963	NY-A	14	26	3	5	1	0	0	1	0	5	.192	.192	.231	18	-3	0	1	-1	.963	-1	/2-7	-0.4
1964	*NY-A	80	112	18	31	8	1	0	5	7	22	.277	.331	.366	92	-1	3	4	-2	.992	1	1-31,O-20/32	-0.2
1965	NY-A	7	5	0	2	1	0	0	0	0	2	.400	.400	.600	181	0	0	0	0	.000	0	H	0.1
	Cle-A	116	400	38	101	14	3	5	39	18	57	.253	.290	.340	78	-12	7	4	-0	.980	8	*2-112/O-3,3	0.6
	Yr	123	405	38	103	15	3	5	39	18	59	.254	.291	.343	79	-12	7	4	-0	.980	8	*2-112/O-3,3	0.7
1966	Cle-A	110	352	21	82	9	2	2	17	15	54	.233	.268	.287	60	-18	8	5	-1	.984	11	*2-104/3-1,O	-0.1
1967	Cle-A	80	189	19	43	6	0	1	8	12	36	.228	.277	.275	63	-9	4	6	-2	.971	-5	2-64/1-4,3S	-1.4
Total	5	407	1084	99	264	39	6	8	70	52	176	.244	.283	.313	70	-43	22	20	-5	.980	14	2-293/1-35,O3S	-1.4

■ CHARLIE GOOCH
Gooch, Charles Furman b: 6/5/02, Smyrna, Tenn. d: 5/30/82, Lanham, Md. BR/TR, 5'9", 170 lbs. Deb: 4/18/29

YEAR	TM/L	G	AB	R	H	2B	3B	HR	RBI	BB	SO	AVG	OBP	SLG	PRO+	BR/A	SB	CS	SBR	FA	FR	G/POS	TPR
1929	Was-A	39	57	6	16	2	1	0	5	7	8	.281	.359	.351	83	-1	0	1	-1	.970	-2	/1-7,3-7,S	-0.3

■ JOHNNY GOOCH
Gooch, John Beverley b: 11/9/1897, Smyrna, Tenn. d: 5/15/75, Nashville, Tenn. BB/TR, 5'11", 175 lbs. Deb: 9/9/21 C

YEAR	TM/L	G	AB	R	H	2B	3B	HR	RBI	BB	SO	AVG	OBP	SLG	PRO+	BR/A	SB	CS	SBR	FA	FR	G/POS	TPR
1921	Pit-N	13	38	2	9	0	0	0	3	3	3	.237	.293	.237	41	-3	1	0	0	.985	3	C-13	0.1
1922	Pit-N	105	353	45	116	15	3	1	42	39	15	.329	.403	.397	106	5	1	1	-0	.970	-2	*C-103	0.8
1923	Pit-N	66	202	16	56	10	2	1	20	17	13	.277	.336	.361	82	-5	2	1	0	.975	5	C-66	0.3
1924	Pit-N	70	224	26	65	6	5	0	25	16	12	.290	.343	.362	88	-4	1	3	-2	.988	-6	C-69	-0.7
1925	*Pit-N	79	215	24	64	8	4	0	30	20	16	.298	.357	.372	81	-6	1			.968	-5	C-76	-0.6
1926	Pit-N	86	218	19	59	15	1	1	42	20	14	.271	.340	.362	85	-4	1			.980	-5	C-80	-0.5
1927	*Pit-N	101	291	22	75	17	2	2	48	19	21	.258	.305	.351	70	-12	1			.974	-5	C-91	-0.4
1928	Pit-N	31	80	7	19	2	1	0	5	3	6	.237	.265	.287	43	-7	0			.957	4	C-31	-0.1
	Bro-N	42	101	9	32	1	2	0	12	7	9	.317	.361	.366	92	-1	0			.969	-2	C-38	0.0
	Yr	73	181	16	51	3	3	0	17	10	15	.282	.319	.331	70	-8	0			.964	2	C-69	-0.1
1929	Bro-N	1	1	0	0	0	0	0	0	0	0	.000	.000	.000	-99	-0	0			.000	0	H	0.0
	Cin-N	92	287	22	86	13	5	0	34	24	10	.300	.356	.380	86	-6	4			.975	5	C-86	0.6
	Yr	93	288	22	86	13	5	0	34	24	10	.299	.355	.378	86	-6	4			.975	5	C-86	0.6
1930	Cin-N	82	276	29	67	10	3	2	30	27	15	.243	.315	.322	57	-19	0			.955	-5	C-79	-1.5
1933	Bos-A	37	77	6	14	1	1	0	2	11	7	.182	.284	.221	36	-7	0	0	0	.991	4	C-26	-0.1
Total	11	805	2363	227	662	98	29	7	293	206	141	.280	.342	.355	79	-69	11	5		.973	-1	C-758	-2.1

■ LEE GOOCH
Gooch, Lee Currin b: 2/23/1890, Oxford, N.C. d: 5/18/66, Raleigh, N.C. BR/TR, 6', 190 lbs. Deb: 8/17/15

YEAR	TM/L	G	AB	R	H	2B	3B	HR	RBI	BB	SO	AVG	OBP	SLG	PRO+	BR/A	SB	CS	SBR	FA	FR	G/POS	TPR
1915	Cle-A	2	2	0	1	0	0	0	0	0	0	.500	.500	.500	196	0	0			.000	0	H	0.0
1917	Phi-A	17	59	4	17	2	0	1	8	4	10	.288	.333	.373	117	1	0			.893	-2	O-16	-0.2
Total	2	19	61	4	18	2	0	1	8	4	10	.295	.338	.377	120	1	0			.893	-2	/O-16	-0.2

■ GENE GOOD
Good, Eugene J. b: 12/13/1882, Roxbury, Mass. d: 8/6/47, Boston, Mass. BL/TL, 5'6", 130 lbs. Deb: 4/12/06

YEAR	TM/L	G	AB	R	H	2B	3B	HR	RBI	BB	SO	AVG	OBP	SLG	PRO+	BR/A	SB	CS	SBR	FA	FR	G/POS	TPR
1906	Bos-N	34	119	4	18	0	0	0	0	13		.151	.246	.151	25	-10	2			.873	-2	O-34	-1.6

■ WILBUR GOOD
Good, Wilbur David "Lefty" b: 9/28/1885, Punxsutawney, Pa. d: 12/30/63, Brooksville, Fla. BL/TL, 5'6", 165 lbs. Deb: 8/18/05

YEAR	TM/L	G	AB	R	H	2B	3B	HR	RBI	BB	SO	AVG	OBP	SLG	PRO+	BR/A	SB	CS	SBR	FA	FR	G/POS	TPR
1905	NY-A	5	8	2	3	0	0	0	0	0	0	.375	.375	.375	124	0	0			.889	0	/P-5	0.0
1908	Cle-A	46	154	23	43	1	3	1	14	13		.279	.351	.344	126	5	7			.845	-8	O-42	-0.6
1909	Cle-A	94	318	33	68	6	5	0	17	28		.214	.296	.264	74	-9	13			.953	5	O-80	-1.1
1910	Bos-N	23	86	15	29	5	4	0	11	6	13	.337	.394	.488	150	5	5			.969	5	O-23	0.9
1911	Bos-N	43	165	21	44	9	3	0	15	12	22	.267	.316	.358	82	-5	5			.945	8	O-43	0.1
	Chi-N	58	145	27	39	5	4	2	21	11	17	.269	.329	.400	103	0	10			.928	-5	O-40	-0.7
	Yr	101	310	48	83	14	7	2	36	23	39	.268	.322	.377	92	-4	13			.938	3	O-83	-0.6
1912	Chi-N	39	35	7	5	0	0	0	1	3	7	.143	.211	.143	-2	-5	3			1.000	-3	O-10	-0.8
1913	Chi-N	49	91	11	23	3	2	1	12	11	16	.253	.340	.363	100	0	5			.974	-3	O-26	-0.4
1914	Chi-N	154	580	70	158	24	7	2	43	53	74	.272	.341	.348	105	4	31			.930	-4	*O-154	-0.4
1915	Chi-N	128	498	66	126	18	9	2	27	34	65	.253	.307	.337	95	-4	19	17	-5	.936	-2	*O-125	-1.8
1916	Phi-N	75	136	25	34	4	3	1	15	8	13	.250	.306	.346	96	-1	7			.983	-5	O-46	-0.8
1918	Chi-A	35	148	24	37	9	4	0	11	6	13	.250	.315	.365	104	0	1			.982	4	O-35	0.3
Total	11	749	2364	324	609	84	44	9	187	190	243	.258	.322	.342	98	-7	104	17		.942	-8	O-624/P-5	-5.3

■ BILL GOODENOUGH
Goodenough, William B. b: 1863, St.Louis, Mo. d: 5/24/05, St.Louis, Mo. 6'1", 170 lbs. Deb: 8/31/1893

YEAR	TM/L	G	AB	R	H	2B	3B	HR	RBI	BB	SO	AVG	OBP	SLG	PRO+	BR/A	SB	CS	SBR	FA	FR	G/POS	TPR
1893	StL-N	10	31	4	5	1	0	0	2	3	4	.161	.297	.194	31	-3	2			.880	-1	O-10	-0.4

■ MIKE GOODFELLOW
Goodfellow, Michael J. b: 10/3/1866, Port Jervis, N.Y. d: 2/12/20, Newark, N.J. BR/TR, 6', 180 lbs. Deb: 6/13/1887

YEAR	TM/L	G	AB	R	H	2B	3B	HR	RBI	BB	SO	AVG	OBP	SLG	PRO+	BR/A	SB	CS	SBR	FA	FR	G/POS	TPR
1887	StL-a	1	4	0	0	0	0	0		0		.000	.000	.000	-90	-1	0			.800	-0	/C-1	-0.1
1888	Cle-a	68	269	24	66	7	0	0	29	11		.245	.283	.271	80	-6	7			.863	-3	O-62/C-4,1S	-1.0
Total	2	69	273	24	66	7	0	0	29	11		.242	.279	.267	77	-7	7			.909	-3	/O-62,C-5,1S	-1.1

■ IVAL GOODMAN
Goodman, Ival Richard "Goodie" b: 7/23/08, Northview, Mo. d: 11/25/84, Cincinnati, Ohio BL/TR, 5'11", 170 lbs. Deb: 4/16/35

YEAR	TM/L	G	AB	R	H	2B	3B	HR	RBI	BB	SO	AVG	OBP	SLG	PRO+	BR/A	SB	CS	SBR	FA	FR	G/POS	TPR
1935	Cin-N	148	592	86	159	23	**18**	12	72	35	50	.269	.314	.429	101	-1	14			.960	8	*O-146	0.1
1936	Cin-N	136	489	81	139	15	**14**	17	71	38	53	.284	.347	.476	128	17	6			.972	3	*O-120	1.4
1937	Cin-N	147	549	86	150	25	12	12	55	55	58	.273	.347	.428	115	11	10			.974	6	*O-141	1.1
1938	Cin-N★	145	568	103	166	27	10	30	92	53	51	.292	.368	.533	149	36	3			.988	5	*O-142	3.7
1939	*Cin-N★	124	470	85	152	37	16	7	84	54	32	.323	.401	.515	144	29	2			.981	7	*O-123	3.1
1940	*Cin-N	136	519	78	134	20	6	12	63	60	54	.258	.335	.389	98	-1	9			.970	-5	*O-135	-1.4
1941	Cin-N	42	149	14	40	5	2	1	12	16	15	.268	.343	.349	95	-1	1			.966	1	O-40	-0.3
1942	Cin-N	87	226	21	55	18	1	0	15	24	32	.243	.319	.332	91	-3	0			.991	1	O-57	-0.5
1943	Chi-N	80	225	31	72	10	5	3	45	24	20	.320	.390	.449	144	13	4			.968	-7	O-61	0.4
1944	Chi-N	62	141	24	37	8	1	1	16	23	15	.262	.377	.355	107	2	0			1.000	-6	O-35	-0.5
Total	10	1107	3928	609	1104	188	85	95	525	382	380	.281	.352	.445	120	104	49			.975	12	O-1000	7.1

■ JAKE GOODMAN
Goodman, Jacob b: 9/14/1853, Lancaster, Pa. d: 3/9/1890, Reading, Pa. 6'1.5", Deb: 5/2/1878

YEAR	TM/L	G	AB	R	H	2B	3B	HR	RBI	BB	SO	AVG	OBP	SLG	PRO+	BR/A	SB	CS	SBR	FA	FR	G/POS	TPR
1878	Mil-N	60	252	28	62	4	3	1	27	7	33	.246	.266	.298	80	-6				.944	-4	*1-60	-1.1

YEAR	TM/L	G	AB	R	H	2B	3B	HR	RBI	BB	SO	AVG	OBP	SLG	PRO+	BR/A	SB	CS	SBR	FA	FR	G/POS	TPR
1882	Pit-a	10	41	5	13	2	2	0		2		.317	.349	.463	180	3				.962	1	1-10	0.3
Total	2	70	293	33	75	6	5	1	27	9	33	.256	.278	.321	92	-3				.946	-3	/1-70	-0.8

■ BILLY GOODMAN
Goodman, William Dale b: 3/22/26, Concord, N.C. d: 10/1/84, Sarasota, Fla. BL/TR, 5'11", 165 lbs. Deb: 4/19/47 C

YEAR	TM/L	G	AB	R	H	2B	3B	HR	RBI	BB	SO	AVG	OBP	SLG	PRO+	BR/A	SB	CS	SBR	FA	FR	G/POS	TPR
1947	Bos-A	12	11	1	2	0	0	0	1	1	2	.182	.250	.182	20	-1	0	0	0	1.000	0	/O-1	-0.1
1948	Bos-A	127	445	65	138	27	2	1	66	74	44	.310	.414	.387	108	9	5	3	-0	.993	-4	*1-117/2-2,3	0.4
1949	Bos-A★	122	443	54	132	23	3	0	56	58	21	.298	.382	.363	91	-4	2	0	1	.992	-1	*1-117	-0.6
1950	Bos-A	110	424	91	150	25	3	4	68	52	25	.354	.427	.455	115	11	2	4	-2	.991	-2	0-45,3-27,1/2S	0.4
1951	Bos-A	141	546	92	162	34	4	0	50	79	37	.297	.380	.374	97	-0	7	4	-0	.995	-2	1-62,2-44,O/3	-0.1
1952	Bos-A	138	513	79	157	27	4	4	56	44	23	.306	.370	.394	104	4	8	2	1	.975	20	*2-103,1-23/3O	3.0
1953	Bos-A★	128	514	73	161	33	5	2	41	57	11	.313	.384	.409	108	7	1	4	-2	.974	-11	*2-112,1-20	0.0
1954	Bos-A	127	489	71	148	25	4	1	36	51	15	.303	.371	.376	95	-3	3	3	-1	.979	1	2-72,1-27,O3	0.0
1955	Bos-A	149	599	100	176	31	2	0	52	99	44	.294	.391	.352	94	-1	5	5	-2	.969	-18	*2-143/1-5,O	-0.9
1956	Bos-A	105	399	61	117	22	8	2	38	40	22	.293	.358	.404	90	-6	0	3	-2	.966	-11	2-95	-1.0
1957	Bos-A	18	16	1	1	1	0	0	0	2	1	.063	.167	.125	-18	-3	0	0	0	.000	0	H	-0.3
	Bal-A	73	263	36	81	10	3	3	33	21	18	.308	.366	.403	117	6	0	2	-1	.961	-10	3-54/O-9,12S	-0.4
	Yr	91	279	37	82	11	3	3	33	23	19	.294	.354	.387	106	3	0	2	-1	.961	-10	3-54/O-9,12S	-0.7
1958	Chi-A	116	425	41	127	15	5	0	40	37	21	.299	.358	.358	100	1	1	0	0	.954	-18	*3-111/1-3,2S	-1.7
1959	*Chi-A	104	268	21	67	14	1	1	28	19	20	.250	.304	.321	73	-10	3	0	0	.950	-2	3-74/2-3	-1.1
1960	Chi-A	30	77	5	18	4	0	0	6	12	8	.234	.337	.286	71	-3	0	0	0	.982	3	3-20/2-7	0.1
1961	Chi-A	41	51	4	13	4	0	1	10	7	6	.255	.345	.392	98	-0	0	0	0	.944	0	/3-7,1-2,2	0.0
1962	Hou-N	82	161	12	41	4	1	0	10	12	11	.255	.306	.292	66	-8	0	0	0	.972	-9	2-31,3-17/1	-1.5
Total	16	1623	5644	807	1691	299	44	19	591	669	329	.300	.377	.378	98	-1	37	30	-7	.972	-63	2-624,1-406,3O/S	-4.1

■ ED GOODSON
Goodson, James Edward b: 1/25/48, Pulaski, Va. BL/TR, 6'3", 185 lbs. Deb: 9/5/70

YEAR	TM/L	G	AB	R	H	2B	3B	HR	RBI	BB	SO	AVG	OBP	SLG	PRO+	BR/A	SB	CS	SBR	FA	FR	G/POS	TPR
1970	SF-N	7	11	1	3	0	0	0	0	0	2	.273	.273	.273	47	-1	0	0	0	.941	0	/1-2	-0.1
1971	SF-N	20	42	4	8	1	0	0	1	2	4	.190	.227	.214	26	-4	0	0	0	1.000	1	1-14	-0.5
1972	SF-N	58	150	15	42	1	1	6	30	8	12	.280	.321	.420	107	4	0	0	0	.991	2	1-42	0.0
1973	SF-N	102	384	37	116	20	1	12	53	15	44	.302	.332	.453	111	4	0	1	-1	.911	-14	3-93	-1.1
1974	SF-N	98	298	25	81	15	0	6	48	18	22	.272	.320	.383	91	-4	1	0	0	.997	-4	1-73/3-8	-1.2
1975	SF-N	39	121	10	25	7	0	1	8	7	14	.207	.250	.289	47	-9	0	1	-1	.993	1	1-16,3-13	-0.9
	Atl-N	47	76	5	16	2	0	1	8	2	8	.211	.231	.276	39	-6	0	0	0	.990	0	1-13/3-1	-0.7
	Yr	86	197	15	41	9	0	2	16	9	22	.208	.243	.284	44	-15	0	1	-1	.992	2	1-29,3-14	-1.6
1976	LA-N	83	118	13	27	4	0	3	17	5	17	.229	.278	.339	76	-4	0	0	0	.833	-4	3-16/1-3,O2	-0.9
1977	*LA-N	61	66	3	11	1	0	1	5	3	10	.167	.203	.227	15	-8	0	1	-1	1.000	1	1-13/3-4	-0.8
Total	8	515	1266	108	329	51	2	30	170	63	135	.260	.298	.374	84	-31	1	3	-2	.994	-16	1-176,3-135/O2	-6.2

■ PEP GOODWIN
Goodwin, Claire Vernon b: 12/19/1891, Pocatello, Idaho d: 2/15/72, Oakland, Cal. BL/TR, 5'10.5", 160 lbs. Deb: 4/16/14

YEAR	TM/L	G	AB	R	H	2B	3B	HR	RBI	BB	SO	AVG	OBP	SLG	PRO+	BR/A	SB	CS	SBR	FA	FR	G/POS	TPR
1914	KC-F	112	374	38	88	15	6	1	32	27	23	.235	.290	.316	59	-24	4			.907	-13	S-67,3-40/1	-3.1
1915	KC-F	81	229	22	54	5	1	0	16	15	23	.236	.291	.266	52	-16	6			.906	-8	S-42,2-23	-2.2
Total	2	193	603	60	142	20	7	1	48	42	46	.235	.291	.297	57	-39	10			.907	-20	S-109/3-40,21	-5.3

■ DANNY GOODWIN
Goodwin, Danny Kay b: 9/2/53, St.Louis, Mo. BL/TR, 6'1", 195 lbs. Deb: 9/3/75

YEAR	TM/L	G	AB	R	H	2B	3B	HR	RBI	BB	SO	AVG	OBP	SLG	PRO+	BR/A	SB	CS	SBR	FA	FR	G/POS	TPR
1975	Cal-A	4	10	0	1	0	0	0	0	0	5	.100	.100	.100	-47	-2	0	0	0	.000	0	/D-3	-0.2
1977	Cal-A	35	91	5	19	6	1	1	8	5	19	.209	.250	.330	59	-5	0	0	0	.000	0	D-23	-0.6
1978	Cal-A	24	58	9	16	5	0	2	10	10	13	.276	.382	.466	143	4	0	0	0	.000	0	D-15	0.3
1979	Min-A	58	159	22	46	8	5	5	27	11	23	.289	.335	.497	117	3	0	0	0	1.000	0	D-51/1-8	0.1
1980	Min-A	55	115	12	23	5	0	1	11	17	32	.200	.303	.270	54	-7	0	0	0	1.000	0	D-38,1-13	-0.8
1981	Min-A	59	151	18	34	6	1	2	17	16	32	.225	.299	.318	73	-5	3	1	0	.992	-2	1-40/O-1,D	-1.0
1982	Oak-A	17	52	6	11	2	1	2	8	2	13	.212	.241	.404	77	-2	0	0	0	.000	0	D-15	-0.3
Total	7	252	636	72	150	32	8	13	81	61	137	.236	.303	.373	84	-15	3	1	0	.994	-2	D-150/1-61,O	-2.5

■ TOM GOODWIN
Goodwin, Thomas Jones b: 7/27/68, Fresno, Cal. BL/TR, 6'1", 165 lbs. Deb: 9/1/91

YEAR	TM/L	G	AB	R	H	2B	3B	HR	RBI	BB	SO	AVG	OBP	SLG	PRO+	BR/A	SB	CS	SBR	FA	FR	G/POS	TPR
1991	LA-N	16	7	3	1	0	0	0	0	0	0	.143	.143	.143	-20	-1	1	1	-0	1.000	-1	/O-5	-0.2
1992	LA-N	57	73	15	17	1	1	0	3	6	10	.233	.291	.274	62	-4	7	3	0	1.000	-9	O-45	-1.4
1993	LA-N	30	17	6	5	1	0	0	1	1	4	.294	.333	.353	89	-0	1	2	-1	1.000	-4	O-12	-0.5
1994	KC-A	2	2	0	0	0	0	0	0	0	1	.000	.000	.000	-93	-1	0	0	0	1.000	-0	/O-1	-0.1
Total	4	105	99	24	23	2	1	0	4	7	15	.232	.283	.273	57	-6	9	6	-1	1.000	-14	/O-63	-2.2

■ RAY GOOLSBY
Goolsby, Raymond Daniel "Ox" b: 9/5/19, Florala, Ala. BR/TR, 6'1", 185 lbs. Deb: 4/18/46

YEAR	TM/L	G	AB	R	H	2B	3B	HR	RBI	BB	SO	AVG	OBP	SLG	PRO+	BR/A	SB	CS	SBR	FA	FR	G/POS	TPR
1946	Was-A	3	4	0	0	0	0	0	0	1	1	.000	.200	.000	-43	-1	0	0	0	1.000	-0	/O-1	-0.1

■ GREG GOOSSEN
Goossen, Gregory Bryant b: 12/14/45, Los Angeles, Cal. BR/TR, 6'1.5", 210 lbs. Deb: 9/3/65

YEAR	TM/L	G	AB	R	H	2B	3B	HR	RBI	BB	SO	AVG	OBP	SLG	PRO+	BR/A	SB	CS	SBR	FA	FR	G/POS	TPR
1965	NY-N	11	31	2	9	0	0	1	2	1	5	.290	.313	.387	99	-0	0	0	0	.979	-1	/C-8	-0.1
1966	NY-N	13	32	1	6	2	0	1	5	1	11	.188	.235	.344	60	-2	0	0	0	1.000	4	C-11	-0.6
1967	NY-N	37	69	2	11	1	0	0	4	4	26	.159	.216	.174	13	-8	0	0	0	.973	-1	C-23	-0.9
1968	NY-N	38	106	4	22	7	0	0	6	10	21	.208	.288	.274	69	-4	0	0	0	.992	2	1-31/C-1	-0.5
1969	Sea-A	52	139	19	43	8	1	10	24	14	29	.309	.385	.597	174	13	1	1	-0	.993	2	1-31/O-2	1.3
1970	Mil-A	21	47	3	12	3	0	3	10	12	12	.255	.407	.383	118	2	0	0	0	.990	-1	1-15	-0.1
	Was-A	21	36	2	8	3	0	0	1	2	8	.222	.263	.306	59	-2	0	0	0	1.000	-1	/O-5,1-2	-0.3
	Yr	42	83	5	20	6	0	3	11	14	20	.241	.351	.349	96	-0	0	0	0	.992	-2	1-17/O-5	-0.4
Total	6	193	460	33	111	24	1	13	44	42	112	.241	.317	.383	90	-0	1	1	-0	.992	-5	/1-79,C-43,O	-1.2

■ GLEN GORBOUS
Gorbous, Glen Edward b: 7/8/30, Drumheller, Alberta, Canada d: 6/12/90, Calgary, Alberta, Canada BL/TR, 6'2", 175 lbs. Deb: 4/11/55

YEAR	TM/L	G	AB	R	H	2B	3B	HR	RBI	BB	SO	AVG	OBP	SLG	PRO+	BR/A	SB	CS	SBR	FA	FR	G/POS	TPR
1955	Cin-N	8	18	2	6	3	0	0	4	3	1	.333	.429	.500	137	1	0	0	0	.857	0	/O-5	0.1
	Phi-N	91	224	25	53	9	1	4	23	21	17	.237	.302	.339	71	-9	0	3	-2	.984	6	O-57	-0.7
	Yr	99	242	27	59	12	1	4	27	24	18	.244	.312	.351	77	-8	0	3	-2	.971	6	O-62	-0.6
1956	Phi-N	15	33	1	6	0	0	0	1	0	1	.182	.182	.182	-2	-5	0	0	0	1.000	-2	/O-8	-0.7
1957	Phi-N	3	2	1	1	1	0	0	1	1	0	.500	.667	1.000	351	1	0	0	0	.000	0	H	0.1
Total	3	117	277	29	66	13	1	4	29	25	19	.238	.301	.336	70	-12	0	3	-2	.973	4	O-70	-1.2

■ JOE GORDON
Gordon, Joseph Lowell "Flash" b: 2/18/15, Los Angeles, Cal. d: 4/14/78, Sacramento, Cal. BR/TR, 5'10", 180 lbs. Deb: 4/18/38 MC

YEAR	TM/L	G	AB	R	H	2B	3B	HR	RBI	BB	SO	AVG	OBP	SLG	PRO+	BR/A	SB	CS	SBR	FA	FR	G/POS	TPR
1938	*NY-A	127	458	83	117	24	7	25	97	56	72	.255	.340	.502	109	3	11	3	2	.960	24	*2-126	3.2
1939	*NY-A★	151	567	92	161	32	5	28	111	75	57	.284	.370	.506	124	19	11	10	-3	.967	6	*2-151	2.8
1940	NY-A★	155	616	112	173	32	10	30	103	52	57	.281	.340	.511	122	17	18	8	1	.975	14	*2-155	3.9
1941	NY-A★	156	588	104	162	26	7	24	87	72	80	.276	.358	.466	118	14	10	9	-2	.958	4	*2-131,1-30	2.5
1942	*NY-A★	147	538	88	173	29	4	18	103	79	95	.322	.409	.491	156	41	12	6	0	.966	4	*2-147	5.4
1943	*NY-A☆	152	543	82	135	28	5	17	69	98	75	.249	.365	.413	126	20	4	7	-3	.969	26	*2-152	5.4
1946	NY-A	112	376	35	79	15	0	11	47	49	72	.210	.308	.338	79	-10	2	4	-2	.974	22	*2-108	1.7
1947	Cle-A★	155	562	89	153	27	6	29	93	62	49	.272	.346	.496	136	24	7	3	0	.978	-4	*2-155	3.1
1948	*Cle-A★	144	550	96	154	21	4	32	124	77	81	.280	.371	.507	136	26	5	4	0	.971	-7	*2-144/S-2	2.7
1949	Cle-A★	148	541	74	136	18	3	20	84	83	33	.251	.355	.407	103	2	5	6	-2	.980	-18	*2-145	-1.1
1950	Cle-A	119	368	59	87	12	1	19	57	56	44	.236	.340	.429	99	-2	4	1	1	.969	-18	*2-105	-1.4
Total	11	1566	5707	914	1530	264	52	253	975	759	702	.268	.357	.466	121	153	89	60	-9	.970	54	*2-1519/1-30,S	28.2

YEAR	TM/L	G	AB	R	H	2B	3B	HR	RBI	BB	SO	AVG	OBP	SLG	PRO+	BR/A	SB	CS	SBR	FA	FR	G/POS	TPR

■ KEITH GORDON Gordon, Keith Bradley b: 1/22/69, Bethesda, Md. BR/TR, 6'1", 205 lbs. Deb: 7/9/93

| 1993 | Cin-N | 3 | 6 | 0 | 1 | 0 | 0 | 0 | 0 | 0 | 2 | .167 | .167 | .167 | -10 | -1 | 0 | 0 | 0 | 1.000 | -0 | /O-2 | -0.1 |

■ MIKE GORDON Gordon, Michael William b: 9/11/53, Leominster, Mass. BB/TR, 6'3", 215 lbs. Deb: 4/7/77

1977	Chi-N	8	23	0	1	0	0	0	2	2	8	.043	.120	.043	-49	-5	0	0	0	.970	-3	/C-8	-0.8
1978	Chi-N	4	5	0	1	0	0	0	0	3	2	.200	.556	.200	106	0	0	0	0	1.000	-0	/C-4	0.0
Total	2	12	28	0	2	0	0	0	2	5	10	.071	.235	.071	-11	-4	0	0	0	.979	-3	/C-12	-0.8

■ SID GORDON Gordon, Sidney b: 8/13/17, Brooklyn, N.Y. d: 6/17/75, New York, N.Y. BR/TR, 5'10", 185 lbs. Deb: 9/11/41

1941	NY-N	9	31	4	8	1	1	0	4	6	1	.258	.378	.355	105	0	0			1.000	-1	/O-9	-0.1
1942	NY-N	6	19	4	6	0	1	0	2	3	2	.316	.409	.421	142	1	0			.913	1	/3-6	0.3
1943	NY-N	131	474	50	119	9	11	9	63	43	32	.251	.315	.373	98	-2	2			.941	3	3-53,1-41,O/2	-0.2
1946	NY-N	135	450	64	132	15	4	5	45	60	27	.293	.380	.378	115	11	1			.995	1	*O-101,3-30	0.8
1947	NY-N	130	437	57	119	19	8	13	57	50	21	.272	.347	.442	107	4	2			.971	1	*O-124/3-2	-0.2
1948	NY-N☆	142	521	100	156	26	4	30	107	74	39	.299	.390	.537	148	34	8			.948	-5	*3-115,O-23	2.7
1949	NY-N★	141	489	87	139	26	2	26	90	95	37	.284	.404	.505	142	32	1			.958	-23	*3-123,O-15/1	0.6
1950	Bos-N	134	481	78	146	33	4	27	103	78	31	.304	.403	.557	160	42	2			.990	6	*O-123,3-10	4.1
1951	Bos-N	150	550	96	158	28	1	29	109	80	32	.287	.383	.500	146	35	2	0	1	.984	-4	*O-122,3-34	2.7
1952	Bos-N	144	522	69	151	22	2	25	75	77	49	.289	.384	.483	144	32	0	4	-2	.996	2	*O-142/3-2	2.6
1953	Mil-N	140	464	67	127	22	4	19	75	71	40	.274	.372	.461	123	17	1	1	-0	.977	-1	*O-137	1.0
1954	Pit-N	131	363	38	111	12	0	12	49	67	24	.306	.414	.438	124	16	0	0	0	.977	-6	O-73,3-40	0.6
1955	Pit-N	16	47	2	8	1	0	0	1	2	6	.170	.204	.191	6	-6	0	0	0	1.000	2	/3-8,O-4	-0.5
	NY-N	66	144	19	35	6	1	7	25	25	15	.243	.355	.444	110	2	0	0	0	1.000	6	3-31,O-17	0.7
	Yr	82	191	21	43	7	1	7	26	27	21	.225	.321	.382	86	-4	0	0	0	1.000	7	3-39,O-21	0.2
Total	13	1475	4992	735	1415	220	43	202	805	731	356	.283	.377	.466	130	218	19	5		.985	-19	O-918,3-454/12	15.1

■ GEORGE GORE Gore, George F. "Piano Legs" b: 5/3/1857, Saccarappa, Me. d: 9/16/33, Utica, N.Y. BL/TR, 5'11", 195 lbs. Deb: 5/1/1879 M

1879	Chi-N	63	266	43	70	17	4	0	32	8	30	.263	.285	.357	104	0				.872	-2	O-54/1-9	-0.4
1880	Chi-N	77	322	70	116	23	2	2	47	21	10	.360	.399	.463	180	26				.879	6	*O-74/1-7	2.8
1881	Chi-N	73	309	86	92	18	9	1	44	27	23	.298	.354	.424	137	13				.874	2	*O-72/3-1,1	1.2
1882	Chi-N	84	367	99	117	15	7	3	51	29	19	.319	.369	.422	146	19				.842	6	*O-84	2.1
1883	Chi-N	92	392	105	131	30	9	2	52	27	13	.334	.377	.472	148	21				.867	11	*O-92	2.7
1884	Chi-N	103	422	104	134	18	4	5	34	61	26	.318	.404	.415	146	23				.868	2	*O-103	2.0
1885	*Chi-N	109	441	115	138	21	13	5	57	68	25	.313	.405	.454	144	25				.884	-3	*O-109	1.8
1886	*Chi-N	118	444	150	135	20	12	6	63	102	19	.304	.434	.444	145	25	23			.876	-3	*O-118	1.7
1887	NY-N	111	459	95	133	16	5	1	49	42	18	.290	.358	.353	103	4	39			.889	1	*O-111	0.3
1888	*NY-N	64	254	37	56	4	4	2	17	30	31	.220	.308	.291	93	-1	11			.836	-9	O-64	-1.1
1889	*NY-N	120	488	132	149	21	7	7	54	84	28	.305	.416	.420	134	20	28			.864	-8	*O-120	1.3
1890	NY-P	93	399	132	127	26	8	10	55	77	23	.318	.432	.499	136	20	28			.877	-12	O-93	0.4
1891	NY-N	130	528	103	150	22	7	2	48	74	34	.284	.379	.364	122	18	19			.909	-6	*O-130	0.7
1892	NY-N	53	193	47	49	11	2	0	11	49	16	.254	.412	.332	128	10	20			.932	1	O-53	0.9
	StL-N	20	73	9	15	0	1	0	4	18	6	.205	.363	.233	85	0	2			.844	-2	O-20,M	-0.2
	Yr	73	266	56	64	11	3	0	15	67	22	.241	.399	.305	116	10	22			.908	-0	O-73	0.7
Total	14	1310	5357	1327	1612	262	94	46	618	717	332	.301	.386	.411	134	231	170			.876	-14	*O-1297/1-17,3	16.2

■ BOB GORINSKI Gorinski, Robert John b: 1/7/52, Latrobe, Pa. BR/TR, 6'3", 215 lbs. Deb: 4/10/77

| 1977 | Min-A | 54 | 118 | 14 | 23 | 4 | 1 | 3 | 22 | 5 | 29 | .195 | .228 | .322 | 49 | -9 | 1 | 0 | 0 | .936 | -7 | O-37/D-9 | -1.6 |

■ HERB GORMAN Gorman, Herbert Allen b: 12/18/24, San Francisco, Cal. d: 4/5/53, San Diego, Cal. BL/TL, 5'11", 180 lbs. Deb: 4/19/52

| 1952 | StL-N | 1 | 1 | 0 | 0 | 0 | 0 | 0 | 0 | 0 | 0 | .000 | .000 | .000 | -99 | -0 | 0 | 0 | 0 | .000 | 0 | H | 0.0 |

■ HOWIE GORMAN Gorman, Howard Paul "Lefty" b: 5/14/13, Pittsburgh, Pa. d: 4/29/84, Harrisburg, Pa. BL/TL, 6'2", 160 lbs. Deb: 8/7/37

1937	Phi-N	13	19	3	4	1	0	0	1	1	1	.211	.250	.263	37	-2	1			.500	-3	/O-7	-0.5
1938	Phi-N	1	1	0	0	0	0	0	0	0	0	.000	.000	.000	-99	-0	0			.000	0	H	0.0
Total	2	14	20	3	4	1	0	0	1	1	1	.200	.238	.250	30	-2	1			.500	-3	/O-7	-0.5

■ JACK GORMAN Gorman, John F. "Stooping Jack" b: 1859, St.Louis, Mo. d: 9/9/1889, St.Louis, Mo. Deb: 7/1/1883

1883	StL-a	1	4	0	0	0	0	0		0		.000	.000	.000	-95	-1				.667	0	/O-1	0.0
1884	KC-U	33	137	25	38	5	2	0		4		.277	.298	.343	85	-3				.954	-2	1-24/O-5,3	-0.7
	Pit-a	8	27	3	4	0	1	0		1		.148	.179	.222	30	-2				.750	-2	/P-3,O-3,3	-0.3
Total	2	42	168	28	42	5	3	0		5		.250	.272	.315	71	-6				.944	-4	/1-24,O-9,3P	-1.0

■ JOHNNY GORYL Goryl, John Albert b: 10/21/33, Cumberland, R.I. BR/TR, 5'10", 175 lbs. Deb: 9/20/57 MC

1957	Chi-N	9	38	7	8	2	0	1	5	9	.211	.318	.263	59	-2	0	1	-1	.952	-1	/3-9	-0.4
1958	Chi-N	83	219	27	53	9	3	4	14	27	34	.242	.331	.365	85	-4	0	1	-1	.931	11	3-44,2-35	0.8
1959	Chi-N	25	48	1	9	3	1	1	6	5	3	.188	.264	.354	63	-3	1	1	-0	.973	-0	2-11/3-4	-0.2
1962	Min-A	37	26	6	5	0	1	2	2	2	6	.192	.250	.500	93	-0	0	0	0	.923	-0	/2-4,S-1	-0.1
1963	Min-A	64	150	29	43	5	3	9	24	15	29	.287	.355	.540	144	9	0	0	0	.958	-9	2-34,3-11/S	0.3
1964	Min-A	58	114	9	16	0	2	0	1	10	25	.140	.216	.175	10	-14	1	0	0	.975	2	2-28,3-13	-1.0
Total	6	276	595	79	134	19	10	16	48	64	106	.225	.306	.371	83	-15	2	3	-1	.960	2	2-112/3-81,S	-0.6

■ JIM GOSGER Gosger, James Charles b: 11/6/42, Port Huron, Mich. BL/TL, 5'11", 185 lbs. Deb: 5/4/63

1963	Bos-A	19	16	3	1	0	0	0	0	3	5	.063	.211	.063	-19	-3	0	0	0	.818	-0	/O-4	-0.3
1965	Bos-A	81	324	45	83	15	4	9	35	29	61	.256	.321	.410	100	-0	3	1	0	.975	9	O-81	0.6
1966	Bos-A	40	126	16	32	4	0	5	17	15	20	.254	.333	.405	101	0	0	1	-1	.985	-1	O-32	-0.3
	KC-A	88	272	34	61	14	1	5	27	37	53	.224	.322	.338	93	-2	5	3	-0	.994	1	O-77	-0.5
	Yr	128	398	50	93	18	1	10	44	52	73	.234	.325	.359	96	-1	5	4	-1	.991	0	*O-109	-0.8
1967	KC-A	134	356	31	86	14	5	4	36	53	69	.242	.340	.351	108	5	5	7	-3	.981	-1	*O-113	-0.4
1968	Oak-A	88	150	7	27	1	1	0	11	17	21	.180	.263	.200	44	-10	4	0	1	1.000	-2	O-64	-1.5
1969	Sea-A	39	55	4	6	2	1	1	6	11	.109	.197	.236	21	-2	5	2	0	1.000	-1	O-26	-1.1
	NY-N	10	15	0	2	2	0	0	1	1	6	.133	.188	.267	25	-2	0	0	0	1.000	-1	/O-5	-0.3
1970	Mon-N	91	274	38	72	11	2	5	37	35	35	.263	.348	.372	93	-2	5	3	-0	1.000	-3	O-71,1-19	-0.9
1971	Mon-N	51	102	7	16	2	2	0	8	9	17	.157	.232	.216	27	-10	1	1	-0	.952	-2	O-23/1-6	-1.4
1973	NY-N	38	92	9	22	5	2	0	10	9	16	.239	.307	.261	60	-5	0	1	-1	1.000	-7	O-35	-1.4
1974	NY-N	26	33	3	3	0	0	3	2	6	.091	.167	.091	-27	-6	0	0	0	1.000	-7	O-24	-1.4
Total	10	705	1815	197	411	67	16	30	177	217	316	.226	.311	.331	83	-39	25	18	-3	.985	-17	O-555/1-25	-8.9

■ GOOSE GOSLIN Goslin, Leon Allen b: 10/16/1900, Salem, N.J. d: 5/15/71, Bridgeton, N.J. BL/TR, 5'11.5", 185 lbs. Deb: 9/16/21 H

1921	Was-A	14	50	8	13	1	1	1	6	6	5	.260	.351	.380	91	-1	0			1.000	0	O-14	-0.2
1922	Was-A	101	358	44	116	19	7	3	53	25	26	.324	.373	.441	117	8	4	4	-1	.932	-3	O-93	-0.2
1923	Was-A	150	600	86	180	29	18	9	99	40	53	.300	.347	.453	115	10	7	2	1	.957	7	*O-149	0.8
1924	*Was-A	154	579	100	199	30	17	12	129	68	29	.344	.421	.516	145	39	15	14	-4	.960	5	*O-154	2.9
1925	*Was-A	150	601	116	201	34	20	18	113	53	50	.334	.394	.547	140	33	27	8	3	.971	14	*O-150	3.7
1926	Was-A	147	568	105	201	26	15	17	108	63	38	.354	.425	.542	155	45	8	8	-2	.964	19	*O-147	4.9
1927	Was-A	148	581	96	194	37	15	13	120	50	28	.334	.392	.516	136	29	21	6	3	.955	2	*O-148	2.3

YEAR	TM/L	G	AB	R	H	2B	3B	HR	RBI	BB	SO	AVG	OBP	SLG	PRO+	BR/A	SB	CS	SBR	FA	FR	G/POS	TPR
1928	Was-A	135	456	80	173	36	10	17	102	48	19	.379	.442	.614	176	50	16	3	3	.962	3	*O-125	4.5
1929	Was-A	145	553	82	159	28	7	18	91	66	33	.288	.366	.461	111	8	10	3	1	.968	-4	*O-142	-0.4
1930	Was-A	47	188	34	51	11	5	7	38	19	19	.271	.344	.495	110	2	3	2	-0	.937	-5	O-47	-0.6
	StL-A	101	396	81	129	25	7	30	100	48	35	.326	.400	.652	156	32	14	9	-1	.973	12	*O-101	3.2
	Yr	148	584	115	180	36	12	37	138	67	54	.308	.382	.601	142	34	17	11	-2	.964	7	*O-148	2.6
1931	StL-A	151	591	114	194	42	10	24	105	80	41	.328	.412	.555	147	40	9	6	-1	.960	5	*O-151	3.1
1932	StL-A	150	572	88	171	28	9	17	104	92	35	.299	.384	.469	117	16	12	9	-2	.951	8	*O-149/3-1	1.2
1933	*Was-A	132	549	97	163	35	10	10	64	42	32	.297	.348	.452	112	7	5	2	0	.965	8	*O-128	0.8
1934	*Det-A	151	614	106	187	38	7	13	100	65	38	.305	.373	.453	112	10	5	4	-1	.953	2	*O-149	0.5
1935	*Det-A	147	590	88	172	34	6	9	109	56	31	.292	.355	.415	102	1	5	4	-1	.965	0	*O-144	-0.5
1936	Det-A★	147	572	122	180	33	8	24	125	85	50	.315	.403	.526	127	24	14	4	2	.955	-5	*O-144	1.4
1937	Det-A	79	181	30	43	11	1	4	35	35	18	.238	.367	.376	86	-3	0	1	-1	.954	-2	O-40/1-1	-0.7
1938	Was-A	38	57	6	9	3	0	2	8	8	5	.158	.262	.316	47	-5	0	0	0	1.000	-1	O-13	-0.6
Total	18	2287	8656	1483	2735	500	173	248	1609	949	585	.316	.387	.500	128	347	175	89	-1	.960	63	*O-2188/1-1,3	26.1

■ HOWIE GOSS   Goss, Howard Wayne b: 11/1/34, Wewoka, Okla. BR/TR, 6'4", 204 lbs. Deb: 4/10/62

YEAR	TM/L	G	AB	R	H	2B	3B	HR	RBI	BB	SO	AVG	OBP	SLG	PRO+	BR/A	SB	CS	SBR	FA	FR	G/POS	TPR
1962	Pit-N	89	111	19	27	6	0	2	10	9	36	.243	.306	.351	76	-4	5	2	0	.985	-12	O-66	-1.7
1963	Hou-N	133	411	37	86	18	2	9	44	31	128	.209	.265	.328	74	-15	4	6	-2	.993	7	*O-123	-1.8
Total	2	222	522	56	113	24	2	11	54	40	164	.216	.274	.333	75	-19	9	8	-2	.991	-5	O-189	-3.5

■ DICK GOSSETT   Gossett, John Star b: 8/21/1891, Dennison, Ohio d: 10/6/62, Massillon, Ohio BR/TR, 5'11", 185 lbs. Deb: 4/30/13

YEAR	TM/L	G	AB	R	H	2B	3B	HR	RBI	BB	SO	AVG	OBP	SLG	PRO+	BR/A	SB	CS	SBR	FA	FR	G/POS	TPR
1913	NY-A	39	105	9	17	2	0	0	9	10	22	.162	.254	.181	28	-9	1			.972	-5	C-38	-1.2
1914	NY-A	10	21	3	3	0	0	0	1	5	5	.143	.333	.143	44	-1	0			.977	-1	C-10	-0.2
Total	2	49	126	12	20	2	0	0	10	15	27	.159	.269	.175	31	-10	1			.973	-6	/C-48	-1.4

■ JULIO GOTAY   Gotay, Julio Enrique (Sanchez) b: 6/9/39, Fajardo, P.R. BR/TR, 6', 180 lbs. Deb: 8/6/60

YEAR	TM/L	G	AB	R	H	2B	3B	HR	RBI	BB	SO	AVG	OBP	SLG	PRO+	BR/A	SB	CS	SBR	FA	FR	G/POS	TPR
1960	StL-N	3	8	1	3	0	0	0	0	0	2	.375	.375	.375	98	-0	1	0	0	.750	-2	/S-2,3-1	-0.1
1961	StL-N	10	45	5	11	4	0	0	5	3	5	.244	.292	.333	59	-3	0	0	0	.804	-4	S-10	-0.6
1962	StL-N	127	369	47	94	12	1	2	27	27	47	.255	.316	.309	62	-19	7	3	0	.956	5	*S-120/2-8,O3	-0.4
1963	Pit-N	4	2	0	1	0	0	0	0	0	0	.500	.500	.500	188	0	0	0	0	.667	0	/2-1	0.0
1964	Pit-N	3	2	1	1	0	0	0	0	1	0	.500	.667	.500	235	1	0	0	0	.000	0	H	0.1
1965	Cal-A	40	77	6	19	4	0	1	3	4	9	.247	.284	.338	78	-2	0	0	0	.961	3	2-23/3-9,S	0.2
1966	Hou-N	4	5	0	0	0	0	0	0	0	0	.000	.000	.000	-99	-1	0	0	0	1.000	0	/3-1	-0.1
1967	Hou-N	77	234	30	66	10	2	2	15	15	30	.282	.331	.368	103	1	1	1	0	.971	-4	2-30,S-20/3	0.1
1968	Hou-N	75	165	9	41	3	0	1	11	4	21	.248	.271	.285	68	-7	1	2	-1	.982	10	2-48/3-1	0.6
1969	Hou-N	46	81	7	21	5	0	0	9	7	13	.259	.318	.321	81	-2	2	1	0	.987	6	2-16/3-1	0.5
Total	10	389	988	106	257	38	3	6	70	61	127	.260	.309	.323	75	-32	12	7	-1	.944	15	S-153,2-126/3O	0.3

■ CHARLIE GOULD   Gould, Charles Harvey b: 8/21/1847, Cincinnati, Ohio d: 4/10/17, Flushing, N.Y. BR/TR, 6', 172 lbs. Deb: 5/5/1871 M

YEAR	TM/L	G	AB	R	H	2B	3B	HR	RBI	BB	SO	AVG	OBP	SLG	PRO+	BR/A	SB	CS	SBR	FA	FR	G/POS	TPR
1871	Bos-n	31	151	38	43	9	2	2	32	3	1	.285	.299	.411	98	-1	6					*1-30/O-1	0.0
1872	Bos-n	45	214	39	57	7	8	0	33	2	3	.266	.273	.374	92	-3						*1-44/O-2	-0.1
1874	Bal-n	33	142	20	31	6	0	0		3		.218	.234	.261	58	-6						1-32/C-1	-0.5
1875	NH-n	27	109	9	29	2	1	0		1		.266	.274	.303	113	2						1-26/O-1M	0.2
1876	Cin-N	61	258	27	65	7	0	0	11	6	11	.252	.269	.279	97	1				.939	1	*1-61/P-2M	0.0
1877	Cin-N	24	91	5	25	2	1	0	13	5	5	.275	.313	.319	112	2				.922	-1	1-24/O-1	0.1
Total	4 n	136	616	106	160	24	11	2	65	9	4	.260	.270	.344	89	-9						1-132/O-4,C	-0.4
Total	2	85	349	32	90	9	1	0	24	11	16	.258	.281	.289	101	2				.934	0	/1-85,P-2,O	0.1

■ NICK GOULISH   Goulish, Nicholas Edward b: 11/13/17, Punxsutawney, Pa. d: 5/15/84, Youngstown, Ohio BL/TL, 6'1", 179 lbs. Deb: 4/19/44

YEAR	TM/L	G	AB	R	H	2B	3B	HR	RBI	BB	SO	AVG	OBP	SLG	PRO+	BR/A	SB	CS	SBR	FA	FR	G/POS	TPR
1944	Phi-N	1	1	0	0	0	0	0	0	0	0	.000	.000	.000	-99	-0	0			.000	0	H	0.0
1945	Phi-N	13	11	4	3	0	0	0	2	1	3	.273	.333	.273	72	-0	0			1.000	-1	/O-2	-0.1
Total	2	14	12	4	3	0	0	0	2	1	3	.250	.308	.250	58	-1	0			1.000	-1	/O-2	-0.1

■ CLAUDE GOUZZIE   Gouzzie, Claude b: 1873, France d: 9/21/07, Denver, Colo. BR/TR, 5'9", 170 lbs. Deb: 7/22/03

YEAR	TM/L	G	AB	R	H	2B	3B	HR	RBI	BB	SO	AVG	OBP	SLG	PRO+	BR/A	SB	CS	SBR	FA	FR	G/POS	TPR
1903	StL-A	1	1	0	0	0	0	0	0	0	0	.000	.000	.000	-99	-0	0			1.000	0	/2-1	0.0

■ HANK GOWDY   Gowdy, Henry Morgan b: 8/24/1889, Columbus, Ohio d: 8/1/66, Columbus, Ohio BR/TR, 6'2", 182 lbs. Deb: 9/13/10 MC

YEAR	TM/L	G	AB	R	H	2B	3B	HR	RBI	BB	SO	AVG	OBP	SLG	PRO+	BR/A	SB	CS	SBR	FA	FR	G/POS	TPR
1910	NY-N	7	14	1	3	1	0	0	2	3	3	.214	.313	.286	75	-0	1			.943	0	/1-5	0.0
1911	NY-N	4	4	1	1	0	0	0	0	2	0	.250	.500	.500	175	1	0			1.000	0	/1-2	0.0
	Bos-N	29	97	9	28	4	2	0	16	4	19	.289	.324	.371	87	-2	2			.966	-1	1-26/C-1	-0.3
	Yr	33	101	10	29	5	2	0	16	6	19	.287	.333	.376	92	-1	2			.969	-1	1-28/C-1	-0.3
1912	Bos-N	44	96	16	26	6	1	3	10	16	13	.271	.386	.448	126	4	3			.926	-2	C-22/1-7	0.3
1913	Bos-N	3	5	0	3	1	0	0	2	3	2	.600	.750	.800	336	2	0			1.000	-1	/C-2	0.1
1914	*Bos-N	128	366	42	89	17	6	3	46	48	40	.243	.337	.347	104	3	14			.968	-5	*C-115/1-9	0.7
1915	Bos-N	118	316	49	78	15	3	2	30	41	34	.247	.339	.332	108	4	10	4	1	.974	0	*C-114	1.5
1916	Bos-N	118	349	32	88	14	1	1	34	24	33	.252	.311	.307	94	-2	8			.980	3	*C-116	1.1
1917	Bos-N	49	154	12	33	7	0	0	14	15	13	.214	.288	.260	73	-5	2			.969	-1	C-49	-0.2
1919	Bos-N	78	219	18	61	8	1	1	22	19	16	.279	.339	.338	108	2	5			.977	5	C-74/1-1	1.4
1920	Bos-N	80	214	14	52	11	2	0	18	20	15	.243	.314	.313	84	-4	6	1		.980	11	C-74	1.3
1921	Bos-N	64	164	17	49	9	2	2	17	16	11	.299	.368	.402	110	3	2	1		.981	-1	C-53	0.4
1922	Bos-N	92	221	23	70	11	3	1	27	24	13	.317	.391	.389	107	3	2	1	0	.971	3	C-72/1-1	0.7
1923	Bos-N	23	48	5	6	1	1	0	5	15	5	.125	.354	.188	48	-3	1	1	-0	.982	-2	C-15	-0.4
	*NY-N	53	122	13	40	6	3	1	18	21	9	.328	.427	.451	133	7	2	0	1	.986	-7	C-43	0.2
	Yr	76	170	18	46	7	4	1	23	36	14	.271	.404	.376	109	4	3	1	0	.985	-10	C-58	-0.2
1924	*NY-N	87	191	25	62	9	4	2	37	26	11	.325	.411	.445	133	10	1	0	0	.982	5	C-78	1.9
1925	NY-N	47	114	14	37	4	3	2	19	12	7	.325	.389	.491	128	5	0	0	0	1.000	2	C-41	0.8
1929	Bos-N	10	16	1	7	0	0	0	2	3	1	.438	.438	.438	122	1	0			1.000	-0	/C-9	0.0
1930	Bos-N	16	25	0	5	1	0	0	2	3	1	.200	.310	.240	37	-3	0			.972	1	C-15	-0.1
Total	17	1050	2735	270	738	124	27	21	322	311	247	.270	.351	.358	105	25	59	7		.975	5	C-893/1-51	9.4

■ BILLY GRABARKEWITZ   Grabarkewitz, Billy Cordell b: 1/18/46, Lockhart, Tex. BR/TR, 5'10", 170 lbs. Deb: 4/22/69

YEAR	TM/L	G	AB	R	H	2B	3B	HR	RBI	BB	SO	AVG	OBP	SLG	PRO+	BR/A	SB	CS	SBR	FA	FR	G/POS	TPR
1969	LA-N	34	65	4	6	1	1	0	5	4	19	.092	.145	.138	-22	-11	1	0	0	.954	-2	S-18/3-6,2	-1.2
1970	LA-N★	156	529	92	153	20	8	17	84	95	149	.289	.403	.454	135	30	19	9	0	.959	-1	3-97,S-50,2	3.4
1971	LA-N	44	71	9	16	5	0	0	6	19	16	.225	.389	.296	102	1	1	0	0	1.000	6	2-13,3-10/S	0.6
1972	LA-N	53	144	17	24	4	0	4	16	18	53	.167	.268	.278	57	-8	3	0	1	.902	-4	3-24,2-19/S	-1.1
1973	Cal-A	61	129	27	21	6	1	3	9	28	27	.163	.316	.295	79	-3	2	2	-1	.965	-6	2-18,3-12/SOD	-0.9
	Phi-N	25	66	12	19	2	0	2	7	12	18	.288	.397	.409	121	2	1	0	0	.960	0	2-20/3-3,O	0.4
1974	Phi-N	34	30	7	4	0	0	1	2	5	10	.133	.257	.233	36	-3	1	0	0	1.000	-1	/O-5,3-1	-0.3
	Chi-N	53	125	21	31	3	2	1	12	21	28	.248	.361	.328	90	-1	1	2	-1	.954	2	2-45/S-7,3	0.2
	Yr	87	155	28	35	3	2	2	14	26	38	.226	.341	.310	80	-3	4	3	-1	.954	2	2-45/3-7,SO	-0.1
1975	Oak-A	6	2	0	0	0	0	0	0	0	1	.000	.000	.000	-99	-0	0	0	0	.833	-0	/2-4,D-1	0.0
Total	7	466	1161	189	274	41	12	28	141	202	321	.236	.354	.364	101	8	33	17	-0	.952	-8	3-159,2-142/SOD	1.1

■ ROD GRABER   Graber, Rodney Blaine b: 6/20/30, Massillon, Ohio BL/TL, 5'11", 175 lbs. Deb: 9/9/58

YEAR	TM/L	G	AB	R	H	2B	3B	HR	RBI	BB	SO	AVG	OBP	SLG	PRO+	BR/A	SB	CS	SBR	FA	FR	G/POS	TPR
1958	Cle-A	4	8	0	1	0	0	0	0	1	2	.125	.222	.125	-2	-1	0	0	0	1.000	-0	/O-2	-0.1

YEAR	TM/L	G	AB	R	H	2B	3B	HR	RBI	BB	SO	AVG	OBP	SLG	PRO+	BR/A	SB	CS	SBR	FA	FR	G/POS	TPR

■ JOHNNY GRABOWSKI
Grabowski, John Patrick "Nig" b: 1/7/1900, Ware, Mass. d: 5/23/46, Albany, N.Y. BR/TR, 5'10", 185 lbs. Deb: 7/11/24

1924	Chi-A	20	56	10	14	3	0	0	3	2	4	.250	.276	.304	51	-4	0	0	0	.972	1	C-19	-0.2
1925	Chi-A	21	46	5	14	4	1	0	10	2	4	.304	.333	.435	99	-0	0	1	-1	.983	0	C-21	0.0
1926	Chi-A	48	122	6	32	1	1	0	11	4	15	.262	.286	.311	58	-8	0	1	-1	.973	-2	C-38/1-1	-0.8
1927	*NY-A	70	195	29	54	2	4	0	25	20	15	.277	.350	.328	79	-5	0	0	0	.984	0	C-68	-0.1
1928	NY-A	75	202	21	48	7	1	1	21	10	21	.238	.274	.297	51	-15	0	0	0	.987	2	C-75	-0.7
1929	NY-A	22	59	4	12	1	0	0	2	3	6	.203	.242	.220	21	-7	1	0	0	.943	-0	C-22	-0.5
1931	Det-A	40	136	9	32	7	1	1	14	6	19	.235	.268	.324	53	-10	0	0	0	.984	2	C-39	-0.5
Total	7	296	816	84	206	25	8	3	86	47	84	.252	.295	.314	60	-49	1	2	-1	.979	4	C-282/1-1	-2.8

■ JOE GRACE
Grace, Joseph Laverne b: 1/5/14, Gorham, Ill. d: 9/18/69, Murphysboro, Ill. BL/TR, 6'1", 180 lbs. Deb: 9/24/38

1938	StL-A	12	47	7	16	1	0	0	4	2	3	.340	.367	.362	83	-1	0	1	-1	.933	-2	O-12	-0.4
1939	StL-A	74	207	35	63	11	2	3	22	19	24	.304	.363	.420	98	-1	3	2	-0	.968	-4	O-53	-0.6
1940	StL-A	80	229	45	59	14	2	5	25	26	23	.258	.336	.402	88	-4	2	2	-1	.958	-5	O-51,C-12	-1.1
1941	StL-A	115	362	53	112	17	4	6	60	57	31	.309	.410	.428	118	12	1	3	-2	.983	-2	O-88/C-9	0.3
1946	StL-A	48	161	21	37	7	2	1	13	16	20	.230	.307	.317	71	-6	1	3	-2	.967	1	O-43	-0.9
	Was-A	77	321	39	97	17	4	2	31	24	19	.302	.358	.399	118	7	1	4	-2	.959	4	O-74	0.5
	Yr	125	482	60	134	24	6	3	44	40	39	.278	.341	.371	101	0	2	7	-4	.962	5	*O-117	-0.4
1947	Was-A	78	234	25	58	9	4	3	17	35	15	.248	.348	.359	99	0	1	2	-1	.976	2	O-67	-0.2
Total	6	484	1561	225	442	76	18	20	172	179	135	.283	.362	.393	102	7	9	17	-8	.969	-6	O-388/C-21	-2.4

■ MARK GRACE
Grace, Mark Eugene b: 6/28/64, Winston-Salem, N.C BL/TL, 6'2", 190 lbs. Deb: 5/2/88

1988	Chi-N	134	486	65	144	23	4	7	57	60	43	.296	.374	.403	118	13	3	3	-1	.987	-4	*1-133	-0.3
1989	*Chi-N	142	510	74	160	28	3	13	79	80	42	.314	.407	.457	136	27	14	7	0	.996	19	*1-142	3.0
1990	Chi-N	157	589	72	182	32	1	9	82	59	54	.309	.377	.413	109	9	15	6	1	.992	27	*1-153	2.5
1991	Chi-N	160	619	87	169	28	5	8	58	70	53	.273	.350	.373	99	0	3	4	-2	.995	20	*1-160	0.9
1992	Chi-N	158	603	72	185	37	5	9	79	72	36	.307	.384	.430	127	23	6	1	1	.998	9	*1-157	2.4
1993	Chi-N★	155	594	86	193	39	4	14	98	71	32	.325	.398	.475	135	31	8	4	0	.997	1	*1-154	1.8
1994	Chi-N	106	403	55	120	23	3	6	44	48	41	.298	.373	.414	108	6	0	1	-1	.993	1	*1-103	-0.3
Total	7	1012	3804	511	1153	210	25	66	497	460	301	.303	.380	.424	119	108	49	26	-1	.994	67	*1-1002	10.0

■ MIKE GRACE
Grace, Michael Lee b: 6/14/56, Pontiac, Mich. BR/TR, 6', 175 lbs. Deb: 4/18/78

1978	Cin-N	5	3	0	0	0	0	0	0	0	2	.000	.000	.000	-99	-1	0	0	0	1.000	1	/3-2	0.0

■ EARL GRACE
Grace, Robert Earl b: 2/24/07, Barlow, Ky. d: 12/22/80, Phoenix, Ariz. BL/TR, 6', 175 lbs. Deb: 4/23/29

1929	Chi-N	27	80	7	20	1	0	2	17	9	7	.250	.333	.338	67	-4	0			1.000	3	C-27	0.1
1931	Chi-N	7	9	2	1	0	0	0	1	4	1	.111	.385	.111	39	-1	0			1.000	-0	/C-2	0.0
	Pit-N	47	150	8	42	6	1	1	20	13	5	.280	.337	.353	87	-3	0			.974	-1	C-45	0.0
	Yr	54	159	10	43	6	1	1	21	17	6	.270	.341	.340	84	-3	0			.976	-1	C-47	0.0
1932	Pit-N	115	390	41	107	17	5	8	55	14	23	.274	.305	.405	91	-6	0			.998	-7	*C-114	-0.6
1933	Pit-N	93	291	22	84	13	1	3	44	26	23	.289	.349	.371	106	3	0			.980	1	C-88	0.0
1934	Pit-N	95	289	27	78	17	1	4	24	20	19	.270	.317	.377	83	-7	0			.982	-9	C-83/1-1	-1.2
1935	Pit-N	77	224	19	59	8	1	3	29	32	17	.263	.355	.348	87	-3	1			.990	3	C-69	0.3
1936	Phi-N	86	221	24	55	11	0	4	32	34	20	.249	.352	.353	82	-5	0			.976	-4	C-65	-0.6
1937	Phi-N	80	223	19	47	10	1	6	29	33	15	.211	.313	.345	73	-8	0			.990	-2	C-64	-0.8
Total	8	627	1877	169	493	83	10	31	251	185	130	.263	.331	.367	86	-34	1			.987	-17	C-557/1-1	-1.9

■ JOHN GRADY
Grady, John J. b: 6/18/1860, Lowell, Mass. d: 7/15/1893, Lowell, Mass. 5'7", 150 lbs. Deb: 5/10/1884

1884	Alt-U	9	36	5	11	3	0	0		2		.306	.342	.389	97	-0				.909	-1	/1-8,O-1	-0.2

■ MIKE GRADY
Grady, Michael William b: 12/23/1869, Kennett Square, Pa d: 12/3/43, Kennett Square, Pa. BR/TR, 5'11", 190 lbs. Deb: 4/24/1894

1894	Phi-N	60	190	45	69	13	8	0	40	14	13	.363	.427	.516	130	10	3			.878	-12	C-44,1-11/O	0.1
1895	Phi-N	46	123	21	40	3	1	1	23	14	8	.325	.407	.390	106	2	5			.926	-11	C-38/O-5,31	-0.5
1896	Phi-N	71	242	49	77	20	7	1	44	16	19	.318	.382	.471	126	9	10			.942	-7	C-61/3-7	0.7
1897	Phi-N	4	13	1	2	0	0	0	0	1		.154	.214	.154	-2	-2	0			1.000	1	/C-3	-0.1
	StL-N	83	322	48	90	11	3	7	45	26		.280	.352	.398	100	-0	7			.974	-1	1-83/O-1	-0.1
	Yr	87	335	49	92	11	3	7	45	27		.275	.347	.388	96	-2	7			.974	-0	1-83/C-3,O	-0.2
1898	NY-N	93	287	64	85	19	5	3	49	38		.296	.399	.429	142	17	20			.944	-4	C-57,O-30/1S	1.5
1899	NY-N	86	311	47	104	18	8	2	54	29		.334	.403	.463	142	18	20			.939	-13	C-43,3-35/O1	0.8
1900	NY-N	83	251	36	55	8	4	0	27	34		.219	.331	.283	74	-7	9			.932	-14	C-41,1-12,S/302	-1.6
1901	Was-A	94	347	57	99	17	10	9	56	27		.285	.351	.470	128	12	14			.975	6	1-59,C-30/O	1.8
1904	StL-N	101	323	44	101	15	11	5	43	31		.313	.376	.474	169	26	6			.955	-19	C-77,1-11/23	1.6
1905	StL-N	100	311	41	89	20	7	4	41	33		.286	.360	.434	141	15	15			.956	-11	C-71,1-20	1.2
1906	StL-N	97	280	33	70	11	3	3	27	48		.250	.369	.343	127	11	5			.983	-11	C-60,1-38	0.5
Total	11	918	3000	486	881	155	67	35	449	311	40	.294	.374	.425	127	110	114			.946	-95	C-525,1-246/3OS2	5.9

■ FRED GRAFF
Graff, Frederick Gottleib b: 8/25/1889, Canton, Ohio d: 10/4/79, Chattanooga, Tenn. BR/TR, 5'10.5", 164 lbs. Deb: 5/14/13

1913	StL-A	4	5	1	2	1	0	0	2	3	3	.400	.625	.600	266	1	0			1.000	-1	/3-4	0.1

■ LOUIS GRAFF
Graff, Louis George "Chappie" b: 7/25/1866, Philadelphia, Pa. d: 4/16/55, Bryn Mawr, Pa. TR, Deb: 6/23/1890

1890	Syr-a	1	5	0	2	1	0	0	0			.400	.400	.600	217	1	0			.333	-2	/C-1	-0.1

■ MILT GRAFF
Graff, Milton Edward b: 12/30/30, Jefferson Center, Pa. BL/TR, 5'7.5", 158 lbs. Deb: 4/16/57 C

1957	KC-A	56	155	16	28	4	3	0	10	15	10	.181	.262	.245	39	-13	2	5	-2	.988	1	2-53	-1.1
1958	KC-A	5	1	0	0	0	0	0	0	0	0	.000	.000	.000	-98	-0	0	0	0	1.000	0	/2-1	0.0
Total	2	61	156	16	28	4	3	0	10	15	10	.179	.260	.244	38	-13	2	5	-2	.988	2	/2-54	-1.1

■ MOONLIGHT GRAHAM
Graham, Archibald Wright b: 11/9/1876, Fayetteville, N.C. d: 8/25/65, Chisolm, Minn. BL/TR, 5'10.5", 170 lbs. Deb: 6/29/05

1905	NY-N	1	0	0	0	0	0	0	0	0	0	—	—	—			0	0	0	.000	-0	/O-1	0.0

■ SKINNY GRAHAM
Graham, Arthur William b: 8/12/09, Somerville, Mass. d: 7/10/67, Cambridge, Mass. BL/TR, 5'7", 162 lbs. Deb: 9/14/34

1934	Bos-A	13	47	7	11	2	1	0	3	6	13	.234	.321	.319	61	-3	2	2	-1	1.000	-1	O-13	-0.5
1935	Bos-A	8	10	1	3	0	0	0	1	1	3	.300	.364	.300	69	-0	1	0	0	1.000	-1	O-2	-0.1
Total	2	21	57	8	14	2	1	0	4	7	16	.246	.328	.316	62	-3	3	2	-1	1.000	-2	/O-15	-0.6

■ BARNEY GRAHAM
Graham, Barney b: Philadelphia, Pa. d: 12/31/1896, Mobile, Ala. Deb: 9/4/1889

1889	Phi-a	4	18	0	3	0	0	0	0	0	0	.167	.167	.167	-5	-2	0			.933	1	/3-4	-0.1

■ BERNIE GRAHAM
Graham, Bernard W. b: 1860, Beloit, Wis. d: 10/30/1886, Mobile, Ala. BL, Deb: 7/11/1884

1884	CP-U	1	5	2	1	0	0	0		0		.200	.200	.200	9	-1				1.000	-0	/O-1	-0.1
	Bal-U	41	167	21	45	11	0	0		2		.269	.278	.335	60	-10				.814	1	O-40/1-1	-0.8
	Yr	42	172	23	46	11	0	0		2		.267	.276	.331	58	-10				.816	1	O-41/1-1	-0.9

■ BERT GRAHAM
Graham, Bert "B.G." b: 4/3/1886, Tilton, Ill. d: 6/19/71, Cottonwood, Ariz. BB/TR, 5'11.5", 187 lbs. Deb: 9/9/10

1910	StL-A	8	26	1	3	2	1	0	5	1		.115	.148	.269	32	-2	0			.964	1	/1-5,2-2	-0.1

YEAR	TM/L	G	AB	R	H	2B	3B	HR	RBI	BB	SO	AVG	OBP	SLG	PRO+	BR/A	SB	CS	SBR	FA	FR	G/POS	TPR

■ **CHARLIE GRAHAM**   Graham, Charles Henry b: 4/25/1878, Santa Clara, Cal. d: 8/29/48, San Francisco, Cal BR/TR, 5'11", 180 lbs. Deb: 4/16/06

YEAR	TM/L	G	AB	R	H	2B	3B	HR	RBI	BB	SO	AVG	OBP	SLG	PRO+	BR/A	SB	CS	SBR	FA	FR	G/POS	TPR
1906	Bos-A	30	90	10	21	1	0	1	12	10		.233	.330	.278	91	-0	1			.963	7	C-27	1.0

■ **DAN GRAHAM**   Graham, Daniel Jay b: 7/19/54, Ray, Ariz. BL/TR, 6'1", 205 lbs. Deb: 6/8/79

YEAR	TM/L	G	AB	R	H	2B	3B	HR	RBI	BB	SO	AVG	OBP	SLG	PRO+	BR/A	SB	CS	SBR	FA	FR	G/POS	TPR
1979	Min-A	2	4	0	0	0	0	0	0	0	0	.000	.000	.000	-96	-1	0	0	0	.000	0	/H	-0.1
1980	Bal-A	86	266	32	74	7	1	15	54	14	40	.278	.314	.481	116	4	0	0	0	.981	0	C-73/3-9,OD	0.7
1981	Bal-A	55	142	7	25	3	0	2	11	13	32	.176	.245	.239	40	-11	0	0	0	.975	-4	C-40/3-4,D	-1.5
Total	3	143	412	39	99	10	1	17	65	27	72	.240	.287	.393	88	-7	0	0	0	.979	-4	C-113/3-13,DO	-0.9

■ **TINY GRAHAM**   Graham, Dawson Francis b: 9/9/1892, Nashville, Tenn. d: 12/29/62, Nashville, Tenn. BR/TR, 6'2", 185 lbs. Deb: 8/30/14

YEAR	TM/L	G	AB	R	H	2B	3B	HR	RBI	BB	SO	AVG	OBP	SLG	PRO+	BR/A	SB	CS	SBR	FA	FR	G/POS	TPR
1914	Cin-N	25	61	5	14	1	0	0	3	3	10	.230	.266	.246	51	-4	1			.961	-2	1-25	-0.6

■ **PEACHES GRAHAM**   Graham, George Frederick b: 3/23/1877, Aledo, Ill. d: 7/25/39, Long Beach, Cal. BR/TR, 5'9", 180 lbs. Deb: 9/14/02 F

YEAR	TM/L	G	AB	R	H	2B	3B	HR	RBI	BB	SO	AVG	OBP	SLG	PRO+	BR/A	SB	CS	SBR	FA	FR	G/POS	TPR
1902	Cle-A	2	6	0	2	0	0	0		1	1	.333	.429	.333	118	0	0			1.000	0	/2-1	0.0
1903	Chi-N	1	2	0	0	0	0	0		0	0	.000	.000	.000	-99	-1	0			1.000	0	/P-1	0.0
1908	Bos-N	75	215	22	59	5	0	0	22	23		.274	.361	.298	112	4	4			.955	-3	C-62/2-5	0.8
1909	Bos-N	92	267	27	64	6	3	0	17	24		.240	.302	.285	79	-7	7			.948	-4	C-76/O-6,S3	-0.4
1910	Bos-N	110	291	31	82	13	2	0	21	33	15	.282	.359	.340	100	0	5			.966	-8	C-87/3-2,1O	0.1
1911	Bos-N	33	88	7	24	6	1	0	12	14	5	.273	.373	.364	98	-1	2			.912	-5	C-26	-0.3
	Chi-N	36	71	6	17	3	0	0	8	11	8	.239	.365	.282	82	-1	2			.972	-5	C-28	-0.4
	Yr	69	159	13	41	9	1	0	20	25	13	.258	.369	.327	92	-1	4			.937	-10	C-54	-0.7
1912	Phi-N	24	59	6	17	1	0	0	4	8	5	.288	.373	.356	94	-0	1			.944	-2	C-19	0.0
Total	7	373	999	99	265	34	6	1	85	114	33	.265	.347	.314	95	-3	21			.953	-25	C-298/O-7,231SP	-0.2

■ **JACK GRAHAM**   Graham, John Bernard b: 12/24/16, Minneapolis, Minn. BL/TL, 6'2", 200 lbs. Deb: 4/16/46 F

YEAR	TM/L	G	AB	R	H	2B	3B	HR	RBI	BB	SO	AVG	OBP	SLG	PRO+	BR/A	SB	CS	SBR	FA	FR	G/POS	TPR
1946	Bro-N	2	5	0	1	0	0	0	0	0	0	.200	.200	.200	14	-1	0			1.000	0	/1-2	-0.1
	NY-N	100	270	34	59	6	4	14	47	23	37	.219	.282	.426	99	-2	1			.949	-1	O-62/1-7	-0.7
	Yr	102	275	34	60	6	4	14	47	23	37	.218	.281	.422	97	-3	1			.949	-1	O-62/1-9	-0.8
1949	StL-A	137	500	71	119	22	1	24	79	61	62	.238	.326	.430	95	-7	0	1	-1	.984	-6	*1-136	-1.4
Total	2	239	775	105	179	28	5	38	126	84	99	.231	.310	.427	96	-9	1	1		.985	-7	1-145/O-62	-2.2

■ **LEE GRAHAM**   Graham, Lee Willard b: 9/22/59, Summerfield, Fla. BL/TL, 5'10", 170 lbs. Deb: 9/3/83

YEAR	TM/L	G	AB	R	H	2B	3B	HR	RBI	BB	SO	AVG	OBP	SLG	PRO+	BR/A	SB	CS	SBR	FA	FR	G/POS	TPR
1983	Bos-A	5	6	2	0	0	0	0	1	0	0	.000	.000	.000	-93	-2	0	1	-1	1.000	1	/O-3	-0.2

■ **ROY GRAHAM**   Graham, Roy Vincent b: 2/22/1895, San Francisco, Cal d: 4/26/33, Manila, Phillipines BR/TR, 5'10.5", 175 lbs. Deb: 5/28/22

YEAR	TM/L	G	AB	R	H	2B	3B	HR	RBI	BB	SO	AVG	OBP	SLG	PRO+	BR/A	SB	CS	SBR	FA	FR	G/POS	TPR
1922	Chi-A	5	3	0	0	0	0	0	0	0	0	.000	.400	.000	12	-0	0	0	0	1.000	-0	/C-3	0.0
1923	Chi-A	36	82	3	16	2	0	0	6	9	6	.195	.290	.220	36	-7	0	0	0	.949	-7	C-33	-1.3
Total	2	41	85	3	16	2	0	0	6	9	6	.188	.296	.212	35	-8	0	0	0	.950	-7	/C-36	-1.3

■ **WAYNE GRAHAM**   Graham, Wayne Leon b: 4/6/37, Yoakum, Tex. BR/TR, 6', 200 lbs. Deb: 4/10/63

YEAR	TM/L	G	AB	R	H	2B	3B	HR	RBI	BB	SO	AVG	OBP	SLG	PRO+	BR/A	SB	CS	SBR	FA	FR	G/POS	TPR
1963	Phi-N	10	22	1	4	0	0	0	3		1	.182	.280	.182	36	-2	0	0	0	.857	-1	/O-6	-0.3
1964	NY-N	20	33	1	3	1	0	0	0		5	.091	.091	.121	-42	-6	0	0	0	1.000	-2	3-11	-0.9
Total	2	30	55	2	7	1	0	0	3		6	.127	.172	.145	-9	-8	0	0	0	1.000	-3	/3-11,O-6	-1.2

■ **ALEX GRAMMAS**   Grammas, Alexander Peter b: 4/3/26, Birmingham, Ala. BR/TR, 6', 178 lbs. Deb: 4/13/54 MC

YEAR	TM/L	G	AB	R	H	2B	3B	HR	RBI	BB	SO	AVG	OBP	SLG	PRO+	BR/A	SB	CS	SBR	FA	FR	G/POS	TPR
1954	StL-N	142	401	57	106	17	4	2	29	40	29	.264	.339	.342	77	-13	6	1	1	.966	30	*S-142/3-1	2.8
1955	StL-N	128	366	32	88	19	2	3	25	33	36	.240	.308	.328	69	-16	4	1	1	.968	7	*S-126	0.1
1956	StL-N	6	12	1	3	0	0	0	1	1	1	.250	.308	.250	52	-1	0	0	0	1.000	0	/S-5	-0.1
	Cin-N	77	140	17	34	11	0	0	16	16	18	.243	.325	.321	70	-6	0	1	-1	.968	4	3-58,S-12/2	-0.2
	Yr	83	152	18	37	11	0	0	17	17	19	.243	.324	.316	69	-6	0	1	-1	.968	4	3-58,S-17/2	-0.3
1957	Cin-N	73	99	14	30	4	0	0	8	10	6	.303	.367	.343	86	-2	1	3	-2	.966	2	S-42,2-20/3	0.1
1958	Cin-N	105	216	25	47	8	0	0	12	34	24	.218	.329	.255	54	-13	2	2	-1	.993	-2	S-61,3-38,2	-1.3
1959	StL-N	131	368	43	99	14	2	3	30	38	26	.269	.339	.342	77	-11	3	3	-1	.964	12	*S-130	1.0
1960	StL-N	102	196	20	48	4	1	0	17	12	15	.245	.292	.337	66	-9	0	1	-1	.972	20	S-46,2-38,3	1.4
1961	StL-N	89	170	23	36	10	1	0	21	19	21	.212	.295	.282	49	-12	0	1	-1	.960	17	S-65,2-18/3	0.8
1962	StL-N	21	18	0	2	0	0	0	1	1	6	.111	.158	.111	-24	-3	0	0	0	.933	1	S-16/2-2	-0.1
	Chi-N	23	60	3	14	3	0	0	3	2	7	.233	.270	.283	47	-4	1	1	-0	1.000	1	S-13/2-3,3	-0.2
	Yr	44	78	3	16	3	0	0	3	3	13	.205	.244	.244	29	-8	1	1	-0	.978	3	S-29/2-5,3	-0.3
1963	Chi-N	16	27	1	5	0	0	0	0		3	.185	.185	.185	7	-3	0	0	0	.955	-3	S-13	-0.7
Total	10	913	2073	236	512	90	10	12	163	206	192	.247	.320	.317	67	-93	17	14	-3	.968	88	S-671,3-123,2	3.6

■ **JACK GRANEY**   Graney, John Gladstone b: 6/10/1886, St.Thomas, Ont., Can. d: 4/20/78, Louisiana, Mo. BL/TL, 5'9", 180 lbs. Deb: 4/30/08

YEAR	TM/L	G	AB	R	H	2B	3B	HR	RBI	BB	SO	AVG	OBP	SLG	PRO+	BR/A	SB	CS	SBR	FA	FR	G/POS	TPR
1908	Cle-A	2	0	0	0	0	0	0	0	0		—	—	—		0	0			.000	-0	/P-2	0.0
1910	Cle-A	116	454	62	107	13	9	1	31	37		.236	.293	.311	88	-7	18			.949	1	*O-114	-1.3
1911	Cle-A	146	527	84	142	25	5	1	45	66		.269	.363	.342	96	-1	21			.927	2	*O-142	-0.7
1912	Cle-A	78	264	44	64	13	2	0	20	50		.242	.367	.307	90	-1	9			.958	4	O-75	-0.1
1913	Cle-A	148	517	56	138	18	12	3	68	48	55	.267	.335	.366	102	1	27			.970	2	*O-148	-0.4
1914	Cle-A	130	460	63	122	17	10	1	39	67	46	.265	.362	.352	111	8	20	18	-5	.935	5	*O-127	0.3
1915	Cle-A	116	404	42	105	20	7	1	56	59	29	.260	.355	.351	110	6	12	15	-5	.972	5	*O-115	0.1
1916	Cle-A	155	589	106	142	41	14	5	54	102	72	.241	.355	.384	115	12	10			.959	3	*O-154	0.7
1917	Cle-A	146	535	87	122	29	7	3	35	94	49	.228	.348	.325	98	1	16			.959	-7	*O-145	-1.6
1918	Cle-A	70	177	27	42	7	4	0	19	28	13	.237	.351	.322	94	-0	3			.975	-6	O-45	-1.0
1919	Cle-A	128	461	79	108	22	8	1	30	105	39	.234	.380	.323	93	0	7			.961	6	*O-125	-0.3
1920	*Cle-A	62	152	31	45	11	1	0	13	27	21	.296	.412	.382	108	3	4	2	0	.941	-6	O-47	-0.6
1921	Cle-A	68	107	19	32	3	0	2	18	20	9	.299	.414	.383	103	2	1	1	-0	.933	-9	O-32	-0.9
1922	Cle-A	37	58	6	9	0	0	0	5	9	6	.155	.279	.155	16	-7	0	0	0	.862	-1	O-13	-0.9
Total	14	1402	4705	706	1178	219	79	18	420	712	345	.250	.354	.342	100	16	148	36		.953	-3	*O-1282/P-2	-6.7

■ **EDDIE GRANT**   Grant, Edward Leslie "Harvard Eddie" b: 5/21/1883, Franklin, Mass. d: 10/5/18, Argonne Forest, France BL/TR, 5'11.5", 168 lbs. Deb: 8/4/05

YEAR	TM/L	G	AB	R	H	2B	3B	HR	RBI	BB	SO	AVG	OBP	SLG	PRO+	BR/A	SB	CS	SBR	FA	FR	G/POS	TPR
1905	Cle-A	2	8	1	3	0	1	0		0	0	.375	.375	.375	136	0	0			.833	-2	/2-2	-0.2
1907	Phi-N	74	268	26	65	4	3	0	19	10		.243	.272	.280	74	-9	10			.916	-2	3-74	-1.0
1908	Phi-N	147	598	69	146	13	8	0	32	35		.244	.289	.293	83	-12	27			.930	3	*3-134,S-13	-0.5
1909	Phi-N	154	631	75	170	18	4	1	37	35		.269	.311	.315	94	-6	28			.957	3	*3-154	0.3
1910	Phi-N	152	579	70	155	15	5	1	67	39	54	.268	.315	.316	81	-14	25			.935	-10	*3-152	-2.2
1911	Cin-N	136	458	49	102	12	7	1	53	51	47	.223	.301	.286	67	-20	28			.953	-7	*3-122,S-11	-2.5
1912	Cin-N	96	255	37	61	6	1	2	20	18	27	.239	.292	.294	62	-13	11			.948	0	S-56,3-15	-0.9
1913	Cin-N	27	94	12	20	1	0	0	9	11	10	.213	.295	.223	49	-6	7			.929	-4	3-26	-1.0
	*NY-N	27	20	8	4	1	0	0	1	2	2	.200	.273	.250	49	-1	1			1.000	6	/3-5,2-3,S	0.5
	Yr	54	114	20	24	2	0	0	10	13	12	.211	.291	.228	49	-7	8			.940	2	3-31/2-3,S	-0.5
1914	NY-N	88	282	34	78	7	1	0	29	23	21	.277	.333	.309	94	-2	11			.948	-7	3-52,S-21,2	-0.6
1915	NY-N	87	192	18	40	2	1	0	10	9	20	.208	.248	.229	47	-12	5	6	-2	.970	-5	3-35/2-9,1S	-2.0
Total	10	990	3385	399	844	79	30	5	277	233	181	.249	.300	.295	78	-95	153	6		.942	-26	3-769,S-103/21	-10.1

■ **JIMMY GRANT**   Grant, James Charles b: 10/6/18, Racine, Wis. d: 7/8/70, Rochester, Minn. BL/TR, 5'8", 166 lbs. Deb: 9/8/42

YEAR	TM/L	G	AB	R	H	2B	3B	HR	RBI	BB	SO	AVG	OBP	SLG	PRO+	BR/A	SB	CS	SBR	FA	FR	G/POS	TPR
1942	Chi-A	12	36	0	6	1	1	0	1	5	6	.167	.268	.250	47	-3	0	0	0	.944	1	3-10	-0.2

YEAR	TM/L	G	AB	R	H	2B	3B	HR	RBI	BB	SO	AVG	OBP	SLG	PRO+	BR/A	SB	CS	SBR	FA	FR	G/POS	TPR
1943	Chi-A	58	197	23	51	9	2	4	22	18	34	.259	.321	.386	106	1	4	3	-1	.893	1	3-51	0.2
	Cle-A	15	22	3	3	2	0	0	1	4	7	.136	.269	.227	49	-1	0	0	0	.941	2	/3-5	0.0
	Yr	73	219	26	54	11	2	4	23	22	41	.247	.315	.370	101	-0	4	3	-1	.897	3	3-56	0.2
1944	Cle-A	61	99	12	27	4	3	1	12	11	20	.273	.357	.404	122	3	1	0	0	.926	-4	2-20/3-4	0.1
Total	3	146	354	38	87	16	6	5	36	38	67	.246	.322	.367	101	-0	5	3	-0	.907	-0	3-70,2-20	0.1

■ TOM GRANT   Grant, Thomas Raymond b: 5/28/57, Worcester, Mass.   BL/TR, 6'2", 190 lbs.   Deb: 6/17/83

YEAR	TM/L	G	AB	R	H	2B	3B	HR	RBI	BB	SO	AVG	OBP	SLG	PRO+	BR/A	SB	CS	SBR	FA	FR	G/POS	TPR
1983	Chi-N	16	20	2	3	1	0	0	2	3	4	.150	.261	.200	28	-2	0	0	0	1.000	-2	O-10	-0.4

■ GEORGE GRANTHAM   Grantham, George Farley "Boots" b: 5/20/1900, Galena, Kan.   d: 3/16/54, Kingman, Ariz.   BL/TR, 5'10", 170 lbs.   Deb: 9/20/22

YEAR	TM/L	G	AB	R	H	2B	3B	HR	RBI	BB	SO	AVG	OBP	SLG	PRO+	BR/A	SB	CS	SBR	FA	FR	G/POS	TPR
1922	Chi-N	7	23	3	4	1	1	0	3	1	3	.174	.208	.304	30	-2	2	0	1	1.000	-3	/3-5	-0.4
1923	Chi-N	152	570	81	160	36	8	8	70	71	92	.281	.360	.414	104	4	43	28	-4	.942	1	*2-150	0.3
1924	Chi-N	127	469	85	148	19	6	12	60	55	63	.316	.390	.458	125	18	21	21	-6	.941	1	*2-118/3-6	1.4
1925	*Pit-N	114	359	74	117	24	6	8	52	50	29	.326	.413	.493	122	13	14	4	2	.989	-4	*1-102	0.5
1926	Pit-N	141	449	66	143	27	13	8	70	60	42	.318	.400	.490	131	21	6			.990	-2	*1-132	1.0
1927	*Pit-N	151	531	96	162	33	11	8	66	74	39	.305	.396	.454	119	16	9			.953	-24	*2-124,1-29	-0.6
1928	Pit-N	124	440	93	142	24	9	10	85	59	37	.323	.408	.486	128	19	9			.986	1	*1-119/2-1,3	1.0
1929	Pit-N	110	349	85	107	23	10	12	90	93	38	.307	.454	.533	140	26	10			.967	-5	2-76,O-19,1	2.1
1930	Pit-N	146	552	120	179	34	14	18	99	81	66	.324	.413	.534	126	25	5			.958	-13	*2-141/1-4	1.6
1931	Pit-N	127	465	91	142	26	6	10	46	71	50	.305	.400	.452	130	22	5			.985	-22	1-78,2-51	-0.4
1932	Cin-N	126	493	81	144	29	6	8	39	56	40	.292	.364	.412	112	9	4			.959	-29	*2-115,1-10	-1.5
1933	Cin-N	87	260	32	53	14	3	4	28	38	21	.204	.310	.327	83	-5	4			.948	-11	2-72,1-12	-1.4
1934	NY-N	32	29	5	7	2	0	1	4	8	6	.241	.405	.414	123	1	0			1.000	0	/1-4,3-2	0.1
Total	13	1444	4989	912	1508	292	93	105	712	717	526	.302	.392	.461	121	166	132	53		.949	-109	2-848,1-502/O3	3.7

■ MICKEY GRASSO   Grasso, Newton Michael b: 5/10/20, Newark, N.J.   d: 10/15/75, Miami, Fla.   BR/TR, 6', 195 lbs.   Deb: 9/18/46

YEAR	TM/L	G	AB	R	H	2B	3B	HR	RBI	BB	SO	AVG	OBP	SLG	PRO+	BR/A	SB	CS	SBR	FA	FR	G/POS	TPR
1946	NY-N	7	22	1	3	0	0	0	1	0	3	.136	.136	.136	-22	-4	0	0	0	.967	0	/C-7	-0.3
1950	Was-A	75	195	25	56	4	1	1	22	25	31	.287	.374	.333	86	-3	1	1	-0	.942	6	C-69	0.5
1951	Was-A	52	175	16	36	3	0	1	14	14	17	.206	.268	.240	39	-15	0	0	0	.967	-2	C-49	-1.5
1952	Was-A	115	361	22	78	9	0	0	27	29	36	.216	.276	.241	46	-26	1	0	0	.970	6	*C-114	-1.5
1953	Was-A	61	196	13	41	7	0	2	22	9	20	.209	.251	.276	43	-16	0	0	0	.984	1	C-59	-1.3
1954	*Cle-A	4	6	1	2	0	0	1	1	1	1	.333	.500	.833	256	1	0	0	0	.833	-1	/C-4	0.1
1955	NY-N	8	2	0	0	0	0	0	0	3	0	.000	.600	.000	77	0	0	0	0	.900	-0	/C-8	-0.0
Total	7	322	957	78	216	23	1	5	87	81	108	.226	.291	.268	53	-62	2	1		.964	9	C-310	-4.0

■ LEW GRAULICH   Graulich, Lewis b: Camden, N.J.   Deb: 9/17/1891

YEAR	TM/L	G	AB	R	H	2B	3B	HR	RBI	BB	SO	AVG	OBP	SLG	PRO+	BR/A	SB	CS	SBR	FA	FR	G/POS	TPR
1891	Phi-N	7	26	2	8	0	0	0	3	1	2	.308	.333	.308	85	-1	0			.640	-3	/C-4,1-3	-0.3

■ FRANK GRAVES   Graves, Frank M. b: 11/2/1860, Cincinnati, Ohio   6', 163 lbs.   Deb: 5/10/1886

YEAR	TM/L	G	AB	R	H	2B	3B	HR	RBI	BB	SO	AVG	OBP	SLG	PRO+	BR/A	SB	CS	SBR	FA	FR	G/POS	TPR
1886	StL-N	43	138	7	21	2	0	0	9	7	48	.152	.193	.167	11	-14	11			.885	4	C-41/O-3,P	-0.5

■ JOE GRAVES   Graves, Joseph Ebenezer b: 2/26/06, Marblehead, Mass.   d: 12/22/80, Salem, Mass.   BR/TR, 5'10", 160 lbs.   Deb: 9/26/26   F

YEAR	TM/L	G	AB	R	H	2B	3B	HR	RBI	BB	SO	AVG	OBP	SLG	PRO+	BR/A	SB	CS	SBR	FA	FR	G/POS	TPR
1926	Chi-N	2	5	0	0	0	0	0	0	1	.000	.000	.000	-99	-1	0			.250	-1	/3-2	-0.3

■ SID GRAVES   Graves, Samuel Sidney "Whitey" b: 11/30/01, Marblehead, Mass.   d: 12/26/83, Biddeford, Maine   BR/TR, 6', 170 lbs.   Deb: 7/23/27   F

YEAR	TM/L	G	AB	R	H	2B	3B	HR	RBI	BB	SO	AVG	OBP	SLG	PRO+	BR/A	SB	CS	SBR	FA	FR	G/POS	TPR
1927	Bos-N	7	20	5	5	1	1	0	2	0	1	.250	.250	.400	78	-1	1			.857	1	/O-5	-0.1

■ GARY GRAY   Gray, Gary George b: 9/21/52, New Orleans, La.   BR/TR, 6', 203 lbs.   Deb: 6/23/77

YEAR	TM/L	G	AB	R	H	2B	3B	HR	RBI	BB	SO	AVG	OBP	SLG	PRO+	BR/A	SB	CS	SBR	FA	FR	G/POS	TPR
1977	Tex-A	1	2	0	0	0	0	0	0	0	1	.000	.000	.000	-99	-1	0	0	0	.000	-0	/O-1	-0.1
1978	Tex-A	17	50	4	12	1	0	2	6	1	12	.240	.255	.380	76	-2	1	0	0	.000	0	D-11	-0.2
1979	Tex-A	16	42	4	10	0	0	1	2	8	7	.238	.273	.238	40	-3	1	1	-0	.000	0	D-13	-0.4
1980	Cle-A	28	54	4	8	1	0	2	4	3	13	.148	.193	.278	27	-6	0	0	0	1.000	-2	/1-6,O-6,D	-0.8
1981	Sea-A	69	208	27	51	7	1	13	31	4	44	.245	.259	.476	104	-0	2	0	1	.993	-2	1-34,D-15/O	-0.5
1982	Sea-A	80	269	26	69	14	2	9	29	24	59	.257	.322	.401	95	-2	1	1	-0	.984	-3	1-60,D-14	-0.8
Total	6	211	625	65	150	23	3	24	71	34	137	.240	.281	.402	86	-14	5	2	0	.988	-7	1-100/D-62,O	-2.8

■ REDDY GRAY   Gray, James D.   TR,   Deb: 6/17/1890

YEAR	TM/L	G	AB	R	H	2B	3B	HR	RBI	BB	SO	AVG	OBP	SLG	PRO+	BR/A	SB	CS	SBR	FA	FR	G/POS	TPR
1890	Pit-P	2	9	3	2	0	0	1	3	0	2	.222	.222	.556	114	0	0			.813	-1	/2-2	-0.1
	Pit-N	1	3	0	0	0	0	0	0	0	1	.000	.000	.000	-99	-1	0			.571	-1	/S-1	-0.1
1893	Pit-N	2	9	0	4	1	0	0	2	0	1	.444	.444	.556	168	1	0			.800	-3	/S-2	-0.2
Total	2	5	21	3	6	1	0	1	5	0	4	.286	.286	.476	111	0				.667	-4	/S-3,2-2	-0.4

■ JIM GRAY   Gray, James W. b: 8/7/1862, Pittsburgh, Pa.   d: 1/31/38, Allegheny, Pa.   TR,   Deb: 10/9/1884

YEAR	TM/L	G	AB	R	H	2B	3B	HR	RBI	BB	SO	AVG	OBP	SLG	PRO+	BR/A	SB	CS	SBR	FA	FR	G/POS	TPR
1884	Pit-a	1	2	0	1	0	0	0	0		0	.500	.500	.500	224	0				.500	1	/3-1	0.0

■ LORENZO GRAY   Gray, Lorenzo b: 3/4/58, Mound Bayou, Miss.   BR/TR, 6'1", 180 lbs.   Deb: 7/8/82

YEAR	TM/L	G	AB	R	H	2B	3B	HR	RBI	BB	SO	AVG	OBP	SLG	PRO+	BR/A	SB	CS	SBR	FA	FR	G/POS	TPR
1982	Chi-A	17	28	4	8	1	0	0	2	4	5	.286	.333	.321	81	-1	1	0	0	.864	-3	3-16	-0.4
1983	Chi-A	41	78	18	14	3	0	1	8	6	16	.179	.256	.256	40	-6	1	0	0	.940	2	3-31/D-7	-0.4
Total	2	58	106	22	22	4	0	1	4	10	20	.208	.276	.274	50	-7	2	0	1	.921	-1	/3-47,D-7	-0.8

■ MILT GRAY   Gray, Milton Marshall b: 2/21/14, Louisville, Ky.   d: 6/30/69, Quincy, Fla.   BR/TR, 6'1", 170 lbs.   Deb: 5/27/37

YEAR	TM/L	G	AB	R	H	2B	3B	HR	RBI	BB	SO	AVG	OBP	SLG	PRO+	BR/A	SB	CS	SBR	FA	FR	G/POS	TPR
1937	Was-A	2	6	0	0	0	0	0	0	0	1	.000	.000	.000	-99	-2	0	0	0	1.000	0	/C-2	-0.1

■ PETE GRAY   Gray, Peter J. (b: Peter Wyshner) b: 3/6/15, Nanticoke, Pa.   BL/TL, 6'1", 169 lbs.   Deb: 4/17/45

YEAR	TM/L	G	AB	R	H	2B	3B	HR	RBI	BB	SO	AVG	OBP	SLG	PRO+	BR/A	SB	CS	SBR	FA	FR	G/POS	TPR
1945	StL-A	77	234	26	51	6	2	0	13	13	11	.218	.259	.261	49	-15	5	6	-2	.959	1	O-61	-2.1

■ DICK GRAY   Gray, Richard Benjamin b: 7/11/31, Jefferson, Pa.   BR/TR, 5'11", 165 lbs.   Deb: 4/15/58

YEAR	TM/L	G	AB	R	H	2B	3B	HR	RBI	BB	SO	AVG	OBP	SLG	PRO+	BR/A	SB	CS	SBR	FA	FR	G/POS	TPR
1958	LA-N	58	197	25	49	5	6	9	30	19	30	.249	.327	.472	105	1	1	1	-0	.929	14	3-55	1.5
1959	LA-N	21	52	8	8	1	0	2	4	6	12	.154	.241	.288	38	-5	0	0	0	1.000	-0	3-11	-0.5
	StL-N	36	51	9	16	1	0	1	6	6	8	.314	.386	.392	101	0	3	0	1	.958	-9	S-13/3-6,2O	-0.7
	Yr	57	103	17	24	2	0	3	10	12	20	.233	.313	.340	69	-4	3	0	1	.935	-9	3-17,S-13/2O	-1.2
1960	StL-N	9	5	1	0	0	0	0	1	2	2	.000	.286	.000	-13	-1	0	0	0	1.000	1	/2-4,3-1	0.1
Total	3	124	305	43	73	7	6	12	41	33	52	.239	.322	.420	91	-4	4	1	1	.930	6	/3-73,S-13,2O	0.4

■ STAN GRAY   Gray, Stanley Oscar "Dolly" b: 12/10/1888, Ladonia, Tex.   d: 10/11/64, Snyder, Tex.   BR/TR, 6'0.5", 184 lbs.   Deb: 9/17/12

YEAR	TM/L	G	AB	R	H	2B	3B	HR	RBI	BB	SO	AVG	OBP	SLG	PRO+	BR/A	SB	CS	SBR	FA	FR	G/POS	TPR
1912	Pit-N	6	20	4	5	0	0	0	2	0	3	.250	.250	.350	64	-1	0			1.000	-1	/1-4	-0.2

■ CRAIG GREBECK   Grebeck, Craig Allen b: 12/29/64, Johnstown, Pa.   BR/TR, 5'8", 160 lbs.   Deb: 4/13/90

YEAR	TM/L	G	AB	R	H	2B	3B	HR	RBI	BB	SO	AVG	OBP	SLG	PRO+	BR/A	SB	CS	SBR	FA	FR	G/POS	TPR
1990	Chi-A	59	119	7	20	3	1	1	9	8	24	.168	.233	.235	32	-11	0	0	0	.987	8	3-35,S-16/2D	-0.2
1991	Chi-A	107	224	37	63	16	3	6	31	38	40	.281	.388	.460	137	12	1	3	-2	.933	-1	3-49,2-36,S	1.2
1992	Chi-A	88	287	24	77	21	2	3	35	30	34	.268	.344	.387	106	2	0	3	-2	.980	-4	S-85/3-7,O	0.2
1993	*Chi-A	72	190	25	43	5	0	1	12	26	26	.226	.319	.268	61	-10	1	0	1	.983	14	S-46,2-16,3	-0.1
1994	Chi-A	35	97	17	30	5	0	0	5	12	5	.309	.391	.361	96	0	0	2	-1	.982	-3	2-14,S-14/3	-0.1
Total	5	361	917	110	233	50	6	11	92	114	129	.254	.341	.358	94	-6	2	8	-4	.975	14	S-187,3-112/2OD	1.8

■ DAVID GREEN   Green, David Alejandro (Casaya) b: 12/4/60, Managua, Nicaragua   BR/TR, 6'3", 170 lbs.   Deb: 9/4/81

YEAR	TM/L	G	AB	R	H	2B	3B	HR	RBI	BB	SO	AVG	OBP	SLG	PRO+	BR/A	SB	CS	SBR	FA	FR	G/POS	TPR
1981	StL-N	21	34	6	5	1	0	0	2	6	5	.147	.275	.176	29	-3	0	1	-1	.970	-3	O-18	-0.8

YEAR	TM/L	G	AB	R	H	2B	3B	HR	RBI	BB	SO	AVG	OBP	SLG	PRO+	BR/A	SB	CS	SBR	FA	FR	G/POS	TPR
1982	*StL-N	76	166	21	47	7	1	2	23	8	29	.283	.320	.373	92	-2	11	3	2	.991	-8	O-68	-1.0
1983	StL-N	146	422	52	120	14	10	8	69	26	76	.284	.327	.422	106	2	34	16	1	.970	-8	*O-136	-0.8
1984	StL-N	126	452	49	121	14	4	15	65	20	105	.268	.300	.416	102	-1	17	9	-0	.991	-5	*1-117,O-14	-1.4
1985	SF-N	106	294	36	73	10	2	5	20	22	58	.248	.303	.347	85	-6	6	5	-1	.987	-3	1-78,O-12	-1.6
1987	StL-N	14	30	4	8	2	1	1	1	2	5	.267	.313	.500	109	0	0	1	-1	.882	-1	O-10/1-3	-0.2
Total	6	489	1398	168	374	48	18	31	180	84	278	.268	.311	.394	97	-9	68	35	-1	.972	-27	O-258,1-198	-5.8

■ DANNY GREEN
Green, Edward b: 11/6/1876, Burlington, N.J. d: 11/9/14, Camden, N.J. BL/TR, Deb: 8/17/1898

YEAR	TM/L	G	AB	R	H	2B	3B	HR	RBI	BB	SO	AVG	OBP	SLG	PRO+	BR/A	SB	CS	SBR	FA	FR	G/POS	TPR
1898	Chi-N	47	188	26	59	4	3	4	27	7		.314	.342	.431	121	4	12			.970	5	O-47	0.5
1899	Chi-N	117	475	90	140	12	11	6	56	35		.295	.352	.404	110	6	18			.947	1	*O-115	-0.1
1900	Chi-N	103	389	63	116	21	5	5	49	17		.298	.339	.416	112	5	28			.938	0	*O-102	-0.2
1901	Chi-N	133	537	82	168	16	12	6	61	40		.313	.364	.421	132	21	31			.932	8	*O-133	1.9
1902	Chi-A	129	481	77	150	16	11	0	62	53		.312	.388	.391	122	17	35			.942	-3	*O-129	0.5
1903	Chi-A	135	499	75	154	26	7	6	62	47		.309	.375	.425	146	29	29			.933	2	*O-133	2.3
1904	Chi-A	147	536	83	142	16	10	2	62	63		.265	.352	.343	125	18	28			.964	1	*O-146	1.2
1905	Chi-A	112	379	56	92	13	6	0	44	53		.243	.345	.309	112	8	11			.914	-11	*O-107	-0.9
Total	8	923	3484	552	1021	124	65	29	423	315		.293	.359	.391	124	108	192			.941	3	O-912	5.2

■ PUMPSIE GREEN
Green, Elijah Jerry b: 10/27/33, Oakland, Cal. BB/TR, 6′, 175 lbs. Deb: 7/21/59

YEAR	TM/L	G	AB	R	H	2B	3B	HR	RBI	BB	SO	AVG	OBP	SLG	PRO+	BR/A	SB	CS	SBR	FA	FR	G/POS	TPR
1959	Bos-A	50	172	30	40	6	3	1	10	29	22	.233	.350	.320	81	-3	4	2	0	.972	4	2-45/S-1	0.4
1960	Bos-A	133	260	36	63	10	3	3	21	44	47	.242	.354	.338	85	-4	3	4	-2	.982	-13	2-69,S-41	-1.3
1961	Bos-A	88	219	33	57	12	3	6	27	42	32	.260	.379	.425	112	5	4	2	0	.940	-5	S-57/2-7	0.5
1962	Bos-A	56	91	12	21	2	1	2	11	11	18	.231	.314	.341	74	-3	1	0	0	.953	-9	2-18/S-5	-1.1
1963	NY-N	17	54	8	15	1	2	1	5	12	13	.278	.409	.426	139	3	0	2	-1	.857	-1	3-16	0.1
Total	5	344	796	119	196	31	12	13	74	138	132	.246	.360	.364	94	-3	12	10	-2	.975	-24	2-139,S-104/3	-1.4

■ GARY GREEN
Green, Gary Allan b: 1/14/62, Pittsburgh, Pa. BR/TR, 6′3″, 175 lbs. Deb: 9/14/86 F

YEAR	TM/L	G	AB	R	H	2B	3B	HR	RBI	BB	SO	AVG	OBP	SLG	PRO+	BR/A	SB	CS	SBR	FA	FR	G/POS	TPR
1986	SD-N	13	33	2	7	1	0	0	2	1	11	.212	.235	.242	33	-3	0	0	0	1.000	5	S-13	0.3
1989	SD-N	15	27	4	7	3	0	0	0	1	1	.259	.286	.370	86	-1	0	1	-1	.921	4	S-11/3-1	0.3
1990	Tex-A	62	88	10	19	3	0	0	8	6	18	.216	.266	.250	45	-6	1	1	-0	.972	21	S-58	1.6
1991	Tex-A	8	20	0	3	1	0	0	1	1	6	.150	.190	.200	8	-2	0	0	0	.968	1	/S-8	-0.2
1992	Cin-N	8	12	3	4	1	0	0	0	0	2	.333	.333	.417	108	0	0	0	0	1.000	-1	/S-6,3-1	-0.1
Total	5	106	180	19	40	9	0	0	11	9	38	.222	.259	.272	49	-12	1	2	-1	.970	29	/S-96,3-2	1.9

■ GENE GREEN
Green, Gene Leroy b: 6/26/33, Los Angeles, Cal. d: 5/23/81, St.Louis, Mo. BR/TR, 6′2″, 205 lbs. Deb: 9/10/57

YEAR	TM/L	G	AB	R	H	2B	3B	HR	RBI	BB	SO	AVG	OBP	SLG	PRO+	BR/A	SB	CS	SBR	FA	FR	G/POS	TPR
1957	StL-N	6	15	0	3	1	0	0	2	0	3	.200	.200	.267	23	-2	0	0	0	1.000	-1	/O-3	-0.3
1958	StL-N	137	442	47	124	18	3	13	55	37	48	.281	.338	.423	96	-3	2	1	0	.956	9	O-75,C-48	0.5
1959	StL-N	30	74	8	14	6	0	1	3	5	18	.189	.241	.311	43	-6	0	0	0	.944	4	O-19,C-11	-0.3
1960	Bal-A	1	4	0	1	0	0	0	0	0	0	.250	.250	.250	36	-0	0	0	0	1.000	0	/O-1	0.0
1961	Was-A	110	364	52	102	16	3	18	62	35	65	.280	.345	.489	122	10	0	2	-1	.986	-22	C-79,O-21	-0.9
1962	Cle-A	66	143	16	40	4	1	11	28	8	21	.280	.318	.552	133	6	0	0	0	.964	-2	O-33/1-2	0.2
1963	Cle-A	43	78	4	16	3	0	2	7	4	22	.205	.262	.321	63	-4	0	0	0	1.000	-6	/O-18	-0.8
	Cin-N	15	31	3	7	1	0	1	3	0	8	.226	.250	.355	70	-1	0	0	0	.932	-2	/C-8	-0.1
Total	7	408	1151	130	307	49	7	46	160	89	185	.267	.322	.441	101	-0	2	3	-1	.963	-16	O-170,C-146/1	-1.9

■ JIM GREEN
Green, James R. b: Cleveland, Ohio Deb: 7/19/1884

YEAR	TM/L	G	AB	R	H	2B	3B	HR	RBI	BB	SO	AVG	OBP	SLG	PRO+	BR/A	SB	CS	SBR	FA	FR	G/POS	TPR
1884	Was-U	10	36	4	5	1	0	0				.139	.139	.167	-18	-6				.818	-0	/3-9,O-1	-0.5

■ JOE GREEN
Green, Joseph Henry (a.k.a. Joseph Henry Greene) b: 9/17/1897, Philadelphia, Pa. d: 2/4/72, Bryn Mawr, Pa. BR/TR, 6′2″, 170 lbs. Deb: 7/2/24

YEAR	TM/L	G	AB	R	H	2B	3B	HR	RBI	BB	SO	AVG	OBP	SLG	PRO+	BR/A	SB	CS	SBR	FA	FR	G/POS	TPR
1924	Phi-A	1	1	0	0	0	0	0	0	0	0	.000	.000	.000	-99	-0	0	0	0	.000	0	H	0.0

■ LENNY GREEN
Green, Leonard Charles b: 1/6/33, Detroit, Mich. BL/TL, 5′11″, 170 lbs. Deb: 8/25/57

YEAR	TM/L	G	AB	R	H	2B	3B	HR	RBI	BB	SO	AVG	OBP	SLG	PRO+	BR/A	SB	CS	SBR	FA	FR	G/POS	TPR
1957	Bal-A	19	33	2	6	1	1	1	5	1	4	.182	.206	.364	56	-2	0	1	-1	.950	-4	O-15	-0.8
1958	Bal-A	69	91	10	21	4	0	0	4	9	10	.231	.300	.275	63	-5	0	2	-1	.965	-11	O-53	-1.8
1959	Bal-A	27	24	3	7	0	0	1	2	1	3	.292	.346	.417	111	0	0	0	0	1.000	0	O-23	-0.7
	Was-A	88	190	29	46	6	1	2	15	20	15	.242	.314	.316	74	-7	9	5	-0	.979	-4	O-58	-1.4
	Yr	115	214	32	53	6	1	3	17	21	18	.248	.318	.327	78	-6	9	5	-0	.981	-11	O-81	-2.1
1960	Was-A	127	330	62	97	16	7	5	33	43	25	.294	.385	.430	121	11	21	8	2	.991	-6	*O-100	0.3
1961	Min-A	156	600	92	171	28	7	9	50	81	50	.285	.376	.400	102	4	17	11	-2	.978	-15	*O-153	-2.2
1962	Min-A	158	619	97	168	33	3	14	63	88	36	.271	.369	.402	104	6	8	4	0	.995	-17	*O-156	-2.1
1963	Min-A	145	280	41	67	10	1	4	27	31	21	.239	.317	.325	80	-7	11	5	0	.988	-25	*O-119	-3.8
1964	Min-A	26	15	3	0	0	0	0	0	4	6	.000	.211	.000	-35	-3	0	1	-1	1.000	-2	/O-7	-0.6
	LA-A	39	92	13	23	2	0	2	4	10	8	.250	.330	.337	96	-1	2	0	1	.977	-1	O-23	-0.2
	Bal-A	14	21	0	4	0	0	0	1	7	3	.190	.393	.190	69	-0	1	0	0	1.000	-1	/O-8	0.1
	Yr	79	128	16	27	2	0	2	5	21	17	.211	.327	.273	72	-4	3	1	-0	.985	-2	O-38	-0.7
1965	Bos-A	119	373	69	103	24	6	7	24	48	43	.276	.363	.429	117	9	8	2	1	.980	2	O-95	0.8
1966	Bos-A	85	133	18	32	6	1	1	12	15	19	.241	.327	.308	76	-4	0	1	-1	.978	-1	O-27	-0.7
1967	Det-A	58	151	22	42	8	1	1	13	9	17	.278	.319	.364	99	-0	1	1	-0	.983	-4	O-44	-0.7
1968	Det-A	6	4	0	1	0	0	0	0	1	0	.250	.400	.250	97	0	0	0	0	.000	-1	/O-2	-0.1
Total	12	1136	2956	461	788	138	27	47	253	368	260	.267	.353	.379	99	2	78	41	-1	.984	-95	O-883	-13.9

■ DICK GREEN
Green, Richard Larry b: 4/21/41, Sioux City, Iowa BR/TR, 5′10″, 180 lbs. Deb: 9/9/63

YEAR	TM/L	G	AB	R	H	2B	3B	HR	RBI	BB	SO	AVG	OBP	SLG	PRO+	BR/A	SB	CS	SBR	FA	FR	G/POS	TPR
1963	KC-A	13	37	5	10	2	1	1	4	2	10	.270	.325	.405	98	-0	0	0	0	.941	2	/S-6,2-4	0.3
1964	KC-A	130	435	48	115	14	5	11	37	27	87	.264	.312	.395	92	-5	3	3	-1	.990	17	*2-120	2.1
1965	KC-A	133	474	64	110	15	1	15	55	50	110	.232	.309	.363	92	-5	0	2	-1	.980	-7	*2-126	-0.2
1966	KC-A	140	507	58	127	24	3	9	62	27	101	.250	.298	.363	92	-6	6	1	0	.979	-1	*2-137/3-2	0.4
1967	KC-A	122	349	26	69	12	4	5	37	30	68	.198	.261	.298	67	-15	6	3	0	.946	-2	3-59,2-50/1S	-1.6
1968	Oak-A	76	202	19	47	6	0	6	18	21	41	.233	.308	.351	104	1	3	1	0	.974	13	2-61/C-1,3	1.9
1969	Oak-A	136	483	61	133	25	6	12	64	53	94	.275	.357	.427	123	15	2	3	-1	.986	10	*2-131	3.0
1970	Oak-A	135	384	34	73	7	0	4	29	38	73	.190	.268	.240	43	-30	0	2	0	.978	-3	*2-127/3-5,C	-2.0
1971	*Oak-A	144	475	58	116	14	1	12	49	51	83	.244	.321	.354	93	-4	1	1	-0	.986	8	*2-143/S-1	1.6
1972	*Oak-A	26	42	1	12	1	0	3	3	3	5	.286	.348	.357	116	1	0	1	0	.964	2	2-26	0.3
1973	*Oak-A	133	332	33	87	17	0	3	42	21	63	.262	.310	.340	88	-6	0	2	-0	.988	-9	*2-133/S-1,3	-0.9
1974	*Oak-A	100	287	20	61	8	2	2	22	22	50	.213	.269	.275	61	-15	2	3	-1	.983	-5	*2-100	-1.8
Total	12	1288	4007	427	960	145	23	80	422	345	785	.240	.305	.347	87	-70	26	20	-4	.983	28	2-1158/3-68,SC1	3.6

■ SHAWN GREEN
Green, Shawn David b: 11/10/72, Des Plaines, Ill. BL/TL, 6′4″, 190 lbs. Deb: 9/28/93

YEAR	TM/L	G	AB	R	H	2B	3B	HR	RBI	BB	SO	AVG	OBP	SLG	PRO+	BR/A	SB	CS	SBR	FA	FR	G/POS	TPR
1993	Tor-A	3	6	0	0	0	0	0	0	1		.000	.000	.000	-99	-2	0	0	0	1.000	-1	/O-2,D-1	-0.2
1994	Tor-A	14	33	1	3	1	0	0	1	1	8	.091	.118	.121	-38	-7	1	0	0	1.000	-2	O-14	-0.8
Total	2	17	39	1	3	1	0	0	1	1	9	.077	.100	.103	-47	-8	1	0	0	1.000	-3	/O-16,D-1	-1.0

■ HANK GREENBERG
Greenberg, Henry Benjamin "Hammerin' Hank" b: 1/1/11, New York, N.Y. d: 9/4/86, Beverly Hills, Cal BR/TR, 6′3.5″, 210 lbs. Deb: 9/14/30 H

YEAR	TM/L	G	AB	R	H	2B	3B	HR	RBI	BB	SO	AVG	OBP	SLG	PRO+	BR/A	SB	CS	SBR	FA	FR	G/POS	TPR
1930	Det-A	1	1	0	0	0	0	0	0	0	0	.000	.000	.000	-98	-0	0	0	0	.000	0	H	0.0
1933	Det-A	117	449	59	135	33	3	12	87	46	78	.301	.367	.468	118	11	6	2	0	.988	1	*1-117	0.1
1934	*Det-A	153	593	118	201	63	7	26	139	63	93	.339	.404	.600	156	46	9	5	-0	.990	1	*1-153	3.2

YEAR	TM/L	G	AB	R	H	2B	3B	HR	RBI	BB	SO	AVG	OBP	SLG	PRO+	BR/A	SB	CS	SBR	FA	FR	G/POS	TPR
1935	*Det-A	152	619	121	203	46	16	36	170	87	91	.328	.411	.628	171	63	4	3	-1	.992	6	*1-152	4.7
1936	Det-A	12	46	10	16	6	2	1	16	9	6	.348	.455	.630	165	5	1	0	0	.992	1	1-12	0.4
1937	Det-A☆	154	594	137	200	49	14	40	183	102	101	.337	.436	.668	171	64	8	3	1	.992	5	*1-154	4.7
1938	Det-A†	155	556	144	175	23	4	58	146	119	92	.315	.438	.683	167	57	7	5	-1	.991	7	*1-155	4.0
1939	Det-A★	138	500	112	156	42	7	33	112	91	95	.312	.420	.622	152	38	8	3	1	.993	-1	*1-136	2.1
1940	*Det-A★	148	573	129	195	50	8	41	150	93	75	.340	.433	.670	166	55	6	3	0	.954	1	*O-148	4.4
1941	Det-A	19	67	12	18	5	1	2	12	16	12	.269	.410	.463	118	2	1	0	0	.914	-3	O-19	-0.2
1945	*Det-A†	78	270	47	84	20	2	13	60	42	40	.311	.404	.544	164	22	3	1	0	1.000	-6	O-72	1.3
1946	Det-A	142	523	91	145	29	5	44	127	80	88	.277	.373	.604	160	40	5	1	1	.989	2	*1-140	3.5
1947	Pit-N	125	402	71	100	13	2	25	74	104	71	.249	.408	.478	131	21	0			.992	2	*1-119	1.8
Total	13	1394	5193	1051	1628	379	71	331	1276	852	844	.313	.412	.605	157	422	58	26		.991	15	*1-1138,O-239	30.0

■ AL GREENE

Greene, Altar Alphonse b: 11/9/54, Detroit, Mich. BL/TR, 5'11", 190 lbs. Deb: 7/23/79

YEAR	TM/L	G	AB	R	H	2B	3B	HR	RBI	BB	SO	AVG	OBP	SLG	PRO+	BR/A	SB	CS	SBR	FA	FR	G/POS	TPR
1979	Det-A	29	59	9	8	1	0	3	6	10	15	.136	.261	.305	50	-4	0	1	-1	1.000	0	D-15/O-6	-0.5

■ JUNE GREENE

Greene, Julius Foust b: 6/25/1899, Ramseur, N.C. d: 3/19/74, Glendora, Cal. BL/TR, 6'2.5", 185 lbs. Deb: 4/20/28

YEAR	TM/L	G	AB	R	H	2B	3B	HR	RBI	BB	SO	AVG	OBP	SLG	PRO+	BR/A	SB	CS	SBR	FA	FR	G/POS	TPR
1928	Phi-N	11	6	0	3	0	0	0	0	3	1	.500	.667	.500	202	1	0			1.000	0	/P-1	0.0
1929	Phi-N	21	19	1	4	1	0	0	0	2	4	.211	.286	.263	35	-2	0			1.000	0	/P-5	0.0
Total	2	32	25	1	7	1	0	0	0	5	5	.280	.400	.320	79	-1	0			1.000	1	/P-6	0.0

■ PADDY GREENE

Greene, Patrick Joseph "Patsy" (a.k.a. Patrick Foley In 1902) b: 3/20/1875, Providence, R.I. d: 10/20/34, Providence, R.I. BR/TR, 5'8", 150 lbs. Deb: 9/10/02

YEAR	TM/L	G	AB	R	H	2B	3B	HR	RBI	BB	SO	AVG	OBP	SLG	PRO+	BR/A	SB	CS	SBR	FA	FR	G/POS	TPR
1902	Phi-N	19	65	6	11	1	0	0		1	2	.169	.206	.185	21	-6	2			.912	0	3-19	-0.6
1903	NY-A	4	13	1	4	1	0	0		0		.308	.308	.385	100	-0	0			1.000	1	/3-2,S-1	0.1
	Det-A	1	3	0	0	0	0	0		0		.000	.000	.000	-99	-1	0			.750	-0	/3-1	-0.1
	Yr	5	16	1	4	1	0	0		0		.250	.250	.313	65	-1	0			.933	1	/3-3,S-1	0.0
Total	2	24	81	7	15	2	0	0		1	2	.185	.214	.210	30	-7	2			.916	1	/3-22,S-1	-0.6

■ WILLIE GREENE

Greene, Willie Louis b: 9/23/71, Milledgeville, Ga. BL/TR, 5'11", 180 lbs. Deb: 9/1/92

YEAR	TM/L	G	AB	R	H	2B	3B	HR	RBI	BB	SO	AVG	OBP	SLG	PRO+	BR/A	SB	CS	SBR	FA	FR	G/POS	TPR
1992	Cin-N	29	93	10	25	5	2	2	13	10	23	.269	.340	.430	114	2	0	2	-1	.948	-1	3-25	0.0
1993	Cin-N	15	50	7	8	1	1	2	5	2	19	.160	.192	.340	39	-5	0	0	0	.978	4	S-10/3-5	0.0
1994	Cin-N	16	37	5	8	2	0	0	3	6	14	.216	.327	.270	58	-2	0	0	0	.958	0	3-13/O-1	-0.2
Total	3	60	180	22	41	8	3	4	21	18	56	.228	.298	.372	81	-5	0	2	-1	.957	3	/3-43,S-10,O	0.0

■ JIM GREENGRASS

Greengrass, James Raymond b: 10/24/27, Addison, N.Y. BR/TR, 6'1", 200 lbs. Deb: 9/9/52

YEAR	TM/L	G	AB	R	H	2B	3B	HR	RBI	BB	SO	AVG	OBP	SLG	PRO+	BR/A	SB	CS	SBR	FA	FR	G/POS	TPR
1952	Cin-N	18	68	10	21	2	1	5	24	7	12	.309	.373	.588	163	5	0	0	0	.965	2	O-17	0.6
1953	Cin-N	154	606	86	173	22	7	20	100	47	83	.285	.340	.444	102	1	6	4	-1	.983	8	*O-153	0.2
1954	Cin-N	139	542	79	152	27	4	27	95	41	81	.280	.331	.494	109	5	0	3	-2	.968	5	O-137	0.2
1955	Cin-N	13	39	1	4	2	0	0	1	9	9	.103	.271	.154	16	-5	0	0	0	1.000	2	O-11	-0.3
	Phi-N	94	323	43	88	20	2	12	37	33	43	.272	.342	.458	112	5	0	2	-1	.988	2	O-83/3-2	0.2
	Yr	107	362	44	92	22	2	12	38	42	52	.254	.333	.425	100	0	0	2	-1	.990	4	O-94/3-2	-0.1
1956	Phi-N	86	215	24	44	9	2	5	25	28	43	.205	.296	.335	71	-9	0	0	0	.991	-2	O-62	-1.4
Total	5	504	1793	243	482	82	16	69	282	165	271	.269	.332	.448	102	2	6	9	-4	.980	17	O-463/3-2	-0.5

■ MIKE GREENWELL

Greenwell, Michael Lewis b: 7/18/63, Louisville, Ky. BL/TR, 6', 200 lbs. Deb: 9/5/85

YEAR	TM/L	G	AB	R	H	2B	3B	HR	RBI	BB	SO	AVG	OBP	SLG	PRO+	BR/A	SB	CS	SBR	FA	FR	G/POS	TPR
1985	Bos-A	17	31	7	10	1	0	4	8	3	4	.323	.382	.742	191	4	1	0	0	1.000	-5	O-17	-0.1
1986	*Bos-A	31	35	4	11	2	0	0	4	5	7	.314	.400	.371	111	1	0	0	0	1.000	-1	O-15/D-3	-0.1
1987	Bos-A	125	412	71	135	31	6	19	89	35	40	.328	.389	.570	146	27	5	4	-1	.971	1	O-91,D-15/C	2.3
1988	*Bos-A★	158	590	86	192	39	8	22	119	87	38	.325	.420	.531	158	48	16	8	0	.981	7	*O-147,D-11	4.9
1989	Bos-A★	145	578	87	178	36	0	14	95	56	44	.308	.372	.443	121	17	13	5	1	.967	-4	*O-139/D-5	1.0
1990	*Bos-A	159	610	71	181	30	6	14	73	65	43	.297	.368	.434	118	15	8	7	-2	.977	4	*O-159	1.4
1991	Bos-A	147	544	76	163	26	6	9	83	43	35	.300	.354	.419	108	6	15	5	2	.989	6	*O-143/D-1	1.0
1992	Bos-A	49	180	16	42	2	0	2	18	18	19	.233	.310	.278	62	-9	2	3	-1	1.000	1	O-41/D-6	-1.1
1993	Bos-A	146	540	77	170	38	6	13	72	54	46	.315	.381	.480	122	17	5	4	-1	.993	3	*O-134/D-10	1.5
1994	Bos-A	95	327	60	88	25	1	11	45	38	26	.269	.352	.453	99	-1	2	2	-1	.993	2	O-84/D-6	-0.1
Total	10	1072	3847	555	1170	230	33	108	606	404	302	.304	.375	.465	123	124	67	38	-3	.983	14	O-970/D-57,C	10.7

■ BILL GREENWOOD

Greenwood, William F. b: 1857, Philadelphia, Pa. d: 5/2/02, Philadelphia, Pa. BB/TL, 5'7.5", 180 lbs. Deb: 9/16/1882

YEAR	TM/L	G	AB	R	H	2B	3B	HR	RBI	BB	SO	AVG	OBP	SLG	PRO+	BR/A	SB	CS	SBR	FA	FR	G/POS	TPR
1882	Phi-a	7	30	8	9	1	0	0	1			.300	.323	.333	109	-0				.909	-1	/O-7,2-2	-0.1
1884	Bro-a	92	385	52	83	8	3	3		10		.216	.237	.275	66	-14				.900	-8	*2-92/S-1	-1.8
1887	Bal-a	118	495	114	130	16	6	0		54		.263	.336	.319	88	-5	71			.928	7	*2-117/O-1	0.4
1888	Bal-a	115	409	69	78	13	1	0	29	30		.191	.246	.227	57	-19	46			.913	-22	2-86,S-28/O	-3.5
1889	Col-a	118	414	62	93	7	10	3	49	58	71	.225	.327	.312	86	-5	37			.914	-3	*2-118	-0.2
1890	Roc-a	124	437	76	97	11	6	2		48		.222	.310	.288	83	-8	40			.921	2	*2-123/S-1	0.1
Total	6	574	2170	381	490	56	26	8	78	201	71	.226	.298	.287	78	-51	194			.916	-26	2-538/S-30,O	-5.1

■ BRIAN GREER

Greer, Brian Keith b: 5/14/59, Lynwood, Cal. BR/TR, 6'3", 210 lbs. Deb: 9/13/77

YEAR	TM/L	G	AB	R	H	2B	3B	HR	RBI	BB	SO	AVG	OBP	SLG	PRO+	BR/A	SB	CS	SBR	FA	FR	G/POS	TPR
1977	SD-N	1	1	0	0	0	0	0	0	0	1	.000	.000	.000	-99	-0	0	0	0	.000	0	H	0.0
1979	SD-N	4	3	0	0	0	0	0	0	0	1	.000	.000	.000	-99	-1	0	0	0	1.000	-1	/O-4	-0.2
Total	2	5	4	0	0	0	0	0	0	0	2	.000	.000	.000	-99	-1	0	0	0	1.000	-1	/O-4	-0.2

■ ED GREER

Greer, Edward C. b: 1865, Philadelphia, Pa. d: 2/4/1890, Philadelphia, Pa. BR Deb: 6/24/1885

YEAR	TM/L	G	AB	R	H	2B	3B	HR	RBI	BB	SO	AVG	OBP	SLG	PRO+	BR/A	SB	CS	SBR	FA	FR	G/POS	TPR
1885	Bal-a	56	211	32	42	7	0	0	8			.199	.235	.232	49	-12				.908	-0	O-47,C-12	-1.2
1886	Bal-a	11	38	2	5	1	0	0	2			.132	.175	.158	5	-4	4			.875	-2	/O-9,C-2	-0.5
	Phi-a	71	264	33	51	5	3	1	12			.193	.223	.246	46	-17	12			.921	6	O-70/C-1	-1.1
	Yr	82	302	35	56	6	3	1	10			.185	.217	.235	41	-21	16			.919	4	O-79/C-3	-1.6
1887	Phi-a	3	11	1	2	0	0	0	0			.182	.182	.182	2	-1	2			.857	0	/O-3	-0.1
	Bro-a	91	327	49	83	13	2	2	25			.254	.318	.324	78	-9	33			.921	6	O-76,C-16	-0.5
	Yr	94	338	50	85	13	2	2	25			.251	.314	.320	76	-11	35			.918	6	O-79,C-16	-0.6
Total	3	232	851	117	183	26	5	3	43			.215	.261	.268	58	-44	51			.916	6	O-205/C-31	-3.4

■ RUSTY GREER

Greer, Thurman Clyde b: 1/21/69, Fort Rucker, Ala. BL/TL, 6', 190 lbs. Deb: 5/16/94

YEAR	TM/L	G	AB	R	H	2B	3B	HR	RBI	BB	SO	AVG	OBP	SLG	PRO+	BR/A	SB	CS	SBR	FA	FR	G/POS	TPR
1994	Tex-A	80	277	36	87	16	1	10	46	46	46	.314	.415	.487	141	19	0	0	0	.976	-7	O-73/1-9	0.9

■ TOMMY GREGG

Gregg, William Thomas b: 7/29/63, Boone, N.C. BL/TL, 6'1", 190 lbs. Deb: 9/14/87

YEAR	TM/L	G	AB	R	H	2B	3B	HR	RBI	BB	SO	AVG	OBP	SLG	PRO+	BR/A	SB	CS	SBR	FA	FR	G/POS	TPR
1987	Pit-N	10	8	3	2	1	0	0	0	0	0	.250	.250	.375	62	-0	0	0	0	1.000	-2	/O-4	-0.2
1988	Pit-N	14	15	4	3	1	0	1	3	1	4	.200	.250	.467	103	-0	0	1	-1	1.000	-2	/O-6	-0.3
	Atl-N	11	29	1	10	3	0	0	4	2	2	.345	.387	.448	132	1	0	0	0	1.000	2	/O-7	0.3
	Yr	25	44	5	13	4	0	1	7	3	6	.295	.340	.455	125	1	0	1	-1	1.000	0	O-13	-0.1
1989	Atl-N	102	276	24	67	8	0	6	23	18	45	.243	.289	.337	76	-9	3	4	-2	.967	-10	O-48,1-37	-2.5
1990	Atl-N	124	239	18	63	13	1	5	32	20	39	.264	.320	.389	90	-3	4	3	-1	.987	-2	1-50,O-20	-0.9
1991	*Atl-N	72	107	13	20	8	1	1	4	12	24	.187	.275	.308	60	-6	2	2	-1	1.000	0	O-14,1-13	-0.9
1992	Atl-N	18	19	1	5	0	0	0	1	1	7	.263	.300	.421	96	-0	0	0	0	1.000	-1	/O-9	-0.1
1993	Cin-N	10	12	1	2	0	0	0	1	0	0	.167	.167	.167	-10	-2	0	0	0	1.000	-1	/O-4	-0.3
Total	7	361	705	65	172	34	2	14	68	54	123	.244	.300	.357	80	-19	10	10	-3	.979	-17	O-112,1-100	-4.9

YEAR	TM/L	G	AB	R	H	2B	3B	HR	RBI	BB	SO	AVG	OBP	SLG	PRO+	BR/A	SB	CS	SBR	FA	FR	G/POS	TPR

■ **ED GREMMINGER** Gremminger, Lorenzo Edward "Battleship" b: 3/30/1874, Canton, Ohio d: 5/26/42, Canton, Ohio BR/TR, 6'1", 200 lbs. Deb: 4/21/1895

1895	Cle-N	20	78	10	21	1	0	0	15	5	13	.269	.313	.282	51	-6	0			.873	-1	3-20	-0.5
1902	Bos-N	140	522	55	134	20	12	1	65	39		.257	.314	.347	103	1	7			**.951**	3	*3-140	0.6
1903	Bos-N	140	511	57	135	24	9	5	56	31		.264	.313	.376	100	-2	12			.935	16	*3-140	1.5
1904	Det-A	83	309	18	66	13	3	1	28	14		.214	.257	.285	73	-10	3			.950	-16	3-83	-2.6
Total	4	383	1420	140	356	58	24	7	164	89	13	.251	.301	.340	92	-16	22			.940	2	3-383	-1.0

■ **BUDDY GREMP** Gremp, Lewis Edward b: 8/5/19, Denver, Col. BR/TR, 6'1", 175 lbs. Deb: 9/13/40

1940	Bos-N	4	9	0	2	0	0	0	2	0	0	.222	.222	.222	24	-1	0			1.000	-0	/1-3	-0.1
1941	Bos-N	37	75	7	18	3	0	0	10	5	3	.240	.287	.280	63	-4	0			.977	-3	1-21/2-6,C	-0.8
1942	Bos-N	72	207	12	45	11	0	3	19	13	21	.217	.267	.314	71	-8	1			.991	1	1-62/3-1	-1.1
Total	3	113	291	19	65	14	0	3	31	18	24	.223	.271	.302	67	-13	1			.988	-3	/1-86,2-6,C3	-2.0

■ **REDDY GREY** Grey, Romer Carl (b: Romer Carl Gray) b: 4/8/1875, Zanesville, Ohio d: 11/9/34, Altadena, Cal. BL/TL, 5'11", 175 lbs. Deb: 5/28/03

| 1903 | Pit-N | 1 | 3 | 1 | 1 | 0 | 0 | 0 | 1 | 1 | | .333 | .500 | .333 | 135 | 0 | 0 | | | 1.000 | -0 | /O-1 | 0.0 |

■ **BILL GREY** Grey, William Tobin b: 4/15/1871, Philadelphia, Pa. d: 12/8/32, Philadelphia, Pa. 5'11", 175 lbs. Deb: 5/14/1890

1890	Phi-N	34	128	20	31	8	4	0	21	6	3	.242	.287	.367	88	-3	5			1.000	-11	O-10/3-8,2C1	-1.1
1891	Phi-N	23	75	11	18	0	0	0	7	3	10	.240	.346	.240	55	-4	3			.804	-6	C-11,O-10/S3	-0.8
1895	Cin-N	52	181	24	55	17	4	1	29	15	8	.304	.364	.459	107	1	4			.906	-4	3-27,2-16/SCO	-0.1
1896	Cin-N	46	121	15	25	2	1	0	17	19	11	.207	.314	.240	44	-10	6			.927	1	2-12,C-11/SO13	-0.6
1898	Pit-N	137	528	56	121	17	5	0	67	28		.229	.283	.280	63	-26	5			.879	-20	*3-137	-4.2
Total	5	292	1033	126	250	44	14	1	141	71	32	.242	.303	.315	72	-41	23			.879	-40	3-174/2-36,COS1	-6.8

■ **BOBBY GRICH** Grich, Robert Anthony b: 1/15/49, Muskegon, Mich. BR/TR, 6'2", 190 lbs. Deb: 6/29/70

1970	Bal-A	30	95	11	20	1	3	0	8	9	21	.211	.279	.284	55	-6	1	1	-0	.915	2	S-20/2-9,3	-0.1
1971	Bal-A	7	30	7	9	0	0	1	6	5	8	.300	.400	.400	128	1	1	0	0	1.000	3	/S-5,2-2	0.5
1972	Bal-A★	133	460	66	128	21	3	12	50	53	96	.278	.362	.415	127	16	13	6	0	.950	-25	S-81,2-45,1/3	0.4
1973	*Bal-A	162	581	82	146	29	7	12	50	107	91	.251	.374	.387	116	16	17	9	-0	**.995**	21	*2-162	4.7
1974	*Bal-A★	160	582	92	153	29	6	19	82	90	117	.263	.380	.431	137	31	17	11	-2	.979	9	*2-160	4.8
1975	Bal-A	150	524	81	136	26	4	13	57	107	88	.260	.393	.399	133	28	14	10	-2	.977	24	*2-150	5.8
1976	Bal-A★	144	518	93	138	31	4	13	54	86	99	.266	.374	.417	140	28	14	6	1	.985	-1	*2-140/3-2,D	3.9
1977	Cal-A	52	181	24	44	6	0	7	23	37	40	.243	.374	.392	114	5	6	6	-2	.983	-3	S-52	0.6
1978	Cal-A	144	487	68	122	16	2	6	42	75	83	.251	.359	.329	98	2	4	3	-1	.983	0	*2-144	1.2
1979	*Cal-A★	153	534	78	157	30	5	30	101	59	84	.294	.366	.537	145	33	1	0	0	.984	2	*2-153	4.3
1980	Cal-A★	150	498	60	135	22	2	14	62	80	71	.271	.381	.408	119	16	3	7	-3	.989	3	*2-146/1-3	2.5
1981	Cal-A	100	352	56	107	14	2	**22**	61	40	71	.304	.381	**.543**	164	28	2	4	-0	.983	11	*2-100	4.5
1982	*Cal-A★	145	506	74	132	28	5	19	65	82	109	.261	.372	.449	124	19	3	3	-1	.986	11	*2-142/D-1	3.6
1983	Cal-A	120	387	65	113	17	0	16	62	76	62	.292	.417	.460	142	26	2	4	-2	.969	16	*2-118/S-1	4.5
1984	Cal-A	116	363	60	93	15	1	18	58	57	70	.256	.360	.452	124	13	2	5	-2	.982	3	2-91,1-25,3	1.5
1985	Cal-A	144	479	74	116	17	3	13	53	81	77	.242	.355	.372	100	2	3	5	-2	**.997**	15	*2-116,1-16,3/D	1.8
1986	*Cal-A	98	313	42	84	18	0	9	30	39	54	.268	.355	.412	109	5	1	3	-2	.980	-10	2-87,1-11/3	-0.4
Total	17	2008	6890	1033	1833	320	47	224	864	1087	1278	.266	.373	.424	125	264	104	83	-19	.984	80	*2-1765,S-159/13D	44.1

■ **TIM GRIESENBECK** Griesenbeck, Carlos Phillipe Timothy b: 12/10/1897, San Antonio, Tex. d: 3/25/53, San Antonio, Tex. BR/TR, 5'10.5", 190 lbs. Deb: 9/11/20

| 1920 | StL-N | 5 | 3 | 1 | 1 | 0 | 0 | 0 | 0 | 0 | 0 | .333 | .333 | .333 | 95 | -0 | 0 | 0 | 0 | 1.000 | 0 | /C-3 | 0.0 |

■ **TOM GRIEVE** Grieve, Thomas Alan b: 3/4/48, Pittsfield, Mass. BR/TR, 6'2", 190 lbs. Deb: 7/5/70

1970	Was-A	47	116	12	23	5	1	3	10	14	38	.198	.290	.336	76	-4	0	0	0	.939	-7	O-39	-1.3
1972	Tex-A	64	142	12	29	2	1	3	11	11	39	.204	.271	.296	72	-5	1	3	-2	.985	-4	O-49	-1.4
1973	Tex-A	66	123	22	38	6	0	7	21	7	25	.309	.351	.528	151	8	1	0	0	1.000	-12	O-59/D-1	-0.6
1974	Tex-A	84	259	30	66	10	4	9	32	20	48	.255	.313	.429	114	4	0	0	0	1.000	4	D-40,O-38/1	0.3
1975	Tex-A	118	369	46	102	17	1	14	61	22	74	.276	.317	.442	113	5	0	2	-1	.990	-7	O-63,D-45	-0.6
1976	Tex-A	149	546	57	139	23	3	20	81	35	119	.255	.304	.418	108	3	4	1	1	.983	2	D-96,O-52	0.1
1977	Tex-A	79	236	24	53	9	0	7	30	13	57	.225	.274	.352	68	-11	1	0	0	.976	-6	O-60,D-13	-1.9
1978	NY-N	54	101	5	21	3	0	2	9	9	23	.208	.273	.297	61	-5	0	1	-1	.979	1	O-26/1-2	-0.7
1979	StL-N	9	15	1	3	1	0	0	0	4	1	.200	.368	.267	76	-0	0	0	0	.875	-1	/O-5	-0.1
Total	9	670	1907	209	474	76	10	65	254	135	424	.249	.303	.401	100	-6	7	7	-2	.982	-31	O-391,D-195/1	-6.2

■ **KEN GRIFFEY** Griffey, George Kenneth Jr. "Junior" b: 11/21/69, Donora, Pa. BL/TL, 6'3", 195 lbs. Deb: 4/3/89 F

1989	Sea-A	127	455	61	120	23	0	16	61	44	83	.264	.331	.420	107	4	16	7	1	.969	5	*O-127	0.6
1990	Sea-A★	155	597	91	179	28	7	22	80	63	81	.300	.369	.481	134	27	16	11	-2	.980	1	*O-151/D-2	2.2
1991	Sea-A★	154	548	76	179	42	1	22	100	71	82	.327	.405	.527	156	42	18	6	2	.989	9	*O-152/D-1	4.9
1992	Sea-A★	142	565	83	174	39	4	27	103	44	67	.308	.363	.535	148	34	10	5	0	.997	6	*O-137/D-3	3.7
1993	Sea-A★	156	582	113	180	38	3	45	109	96	91	.309	.412	.617	170	58	17	9	-0	.991	2	*O-139,D-19/1	5.3
1994	Sea-A★	111	433	94	140	24	4	**40**	90	56	73	.323	.403	.674	168	43	11	3	2	.983	5	*O-103/D-9	4.2
Total	6	845	3180	518	972	194	19	172	543	374	477	.306	.382	.541	148	207	88	41	2	.985	27	O-809/D-34,1	20.9

■ **KEN GRIFFEY** Griffey, George Kenneth Sr. b: 4/10/50, Donora, Pa. BL/TL, 6', 200 lbs. Deb: 8/25/73 FC

1973	*Cin-N	25	86	19	33	5	1	3	14	6	10	.384	.424	.570	182	9	4	2	0	1.000	-3	O-21	0.5
1974	Cin-N	88	227	24	57	9	5	2	19	27	43	.251	.333	.361	96	-1	9	4	0	1.000	-1	O-70	-0.4
1975	*Cin-N	132	463	95	141	15	9	4	46	67	67	.305	.394	.402	119	14	16	7	1	.967	-5	*O-119	0.5
1976	*Cin-N★	148	562	111	189	28	9	6	74	62	65	.336	.403	.450	139	30	34	11	4	.979	-1	*O-144	2.8
1977	Cin-N☆	154	585	117	186	35	8	12	57	69	84	.318	.390	.467	126	23	17	8	0	.990	9	*O-147	2.7
1978	Cin-N	158	614	90	177	33	8	10	63	54	70	.288	.346	.417	112	9	23	5	4	.969	4	*O-154	1.2
1979	Cin-N	95	380	62	120	27	4	8	32	36	39	.316	.376	.471	129	15	12	5	1	.984	-3	O-93	0.9
1980	Cin-N★	146	544	89	160	28	10	13	85	62	72	.294	.367	.454	128	21	23	1	6	.978	-0	*O-138	2.2
1981	Cin-N	101	396	65	123	21	6	2	34	39	42	.311	.374	.409	120	11	12	4	1	.989	10	*O-99	2.0
1982	NY-A	127	484	70	134	23	2	12	54	39	58	.277	.331	.407	103	2	10	4	1	.983	7	*O-125	0.6
1983	NY-A	118	458	60	140	21	3	11	46	34	45	.306	.356	.437	121	13	6	1	1	.992	-2	*1-101/O-14,D	0.6
1984	NY-A	120	399	44	109	20	1	7	56	29	32	.273	.324	.381	98	-1	2	2	-0	.974	-0	O-82,1-27/D	-0.6
1985	NY-A	127	438	68	120	28	4	10	69	41	51	.274	.336	.425	109	5	7	7	-2	.970	5	*O-110/1-1,D	0.4
1986	NY-A	59	198	33	60	7	0	9	26	15	24	.303	.355	.475	125	7	2	2	-1	.971	1	O-51/D-2	0.5
	Atl-N	80	292	36	90	15	3	12	32	20	43	.308	.353	.503	126	10	12	7	1	.986	1	O-77/1-1	0.8
1987	Atl-N	122	399	65	114	24	1	14	64	46	47	.286	.361	.456	109	6	4	7	-3	.995	1	O-107/1-3	0.4
1988	Atl-N	69	193	21	48	8	0	2	19	17	26	.249	.310	.306	74	-6	4	4	-1	.969	-4	O-42,1-11	-1.5
	Cin-N	25	50	5	14	1	0	2	4	2	5	.280	.308	.420	103	0	0	0	0	.986	-0	1-10	-0.1
	Yr	94	243	26	62	9	0	4	23	19	31	.255	.309	.339	80	-6	1	3	-2	.969	-4	O-42,1-21	-1.6
1989	Cin-N	106	236	26	62	8	3	8	30	29	42	.263	.346	.424	115	1	4	1	0	.987	-8	O-58/1-9	-0.5
1990	Cin-N	46	63	6	13	2	0	1	9	5	11	.206	.242	.286	43	-5	2	1	0	.979	0	/1-9,O-6	-0.5
	Sea-A	21	77	13	29	2	0	3	18	10	3	.377	.448	.519	168	7	0	0	0	.963	-2	O-20	0.5
1991	Sea-A	30	85	10	24	1	0	2	7	9	14	.282	.347	.400	117	1	0	0	0	1.000	0	O-26/D-1	-0.2
Total	19	2097	7229	1129	2143	364	77	152	859	719	898	.296	.361	.431	118	175	200	83	10	.981	4	*O-1703,1-172/D	12.4

YEAR	TM/L	G	AB	R	H	2B	3B	HR	RBI	BB	SO	AVG	OBP	SLG	PRO+	BR/A	SB	CS	SBR	FA	FR	G/POS	TPR

■ ALFREDO GRIFFIN
Griffin, Alfredo Claudino (b: Alfredo Claudino Baptist (Griffin))   b: 10/6/57, Santo Domingo, D.R.   BB/TR, 5'11", 165 lbs.   Deb: 9/4/76

1976	Cle-A	12	4	0	1	0	0	0	0	0	2	.250	.250	.250	47	-0	0	1	-1	.750	0	/S-6,D-4	0.0
1977	Cle-A	14	41	5	6	1	0	0	3	3	5	.146	.205	.171	4	-5	2	2	-1	.940	-1	S-13/D-1	-0.6
1978	Cle-A	5	4	1	2	1	0	0	0	2	1	.500	.667	.750	301	1	0	0	0	.917	3	/S-2	0.4
1979	Tor-A	153	624	81	179	22	10	2	31	40	59	.287	.335	.364	87	-11	21	16	-3	.956	6	*S-153	0.9
1980	Tor-A	155	653	63	166	26	**15**	2	41	24	58	.254	.285	.349	70	-28	18	23	-8	.955	2	*S-155	-1.7
1981	Tor-A	101	388	30	81	19	6	0	21	17	38	.209	.244	.289	50	-25	8	12	-5	.937	-19	S-97/3-4,2	-4.2
1982	Tor-A	162	539	57	130	20	8	1	48	22	48	.241	.271	.314	55	-34	10	8	-2	.968	6	*S-162	-1.4
1983	Tor-A	162	528	62	132	22	9	4	47	27	44	.250	.290	.348	71	-22	8	11	-4	.965	-4	*S-157/2-5,D	-1.5
1984	Tor-A★	140	419	53	101	8	2	4	30	4	33	.241	.250	.298	49	-29	11	3	2	.962	-5	*S-115,2-21/D	-2.2
1985	Oak-A	162	614	75	166	18	7	2	64	20	50	.270	.293	.332	77	-21	24	9	2	.960	-15	*S-162	-1.8
1986	Oak-A	162	594	74	169	23	6	4	51	35	52	.285	.326	.364	95	-5	33	16	0	.966	-11	*S-162	-0.1
1987	Oak-A	144	494	69	130	23	5	3	60	28	41	.263	.308	.348	79	-15	26	13	0	.963	0	*S-137/2-1	-0.3
1988	*LA-N	95	316	39	63	8	3	1	27	24	39	.199	.260	.253	49	-21	7	5	-1	.965	2	S-93	-1.3
1989	LA-N	136	506	49	125	27	2	0	29	29	57	.247	.288	.308	72	-19	10	7	-1	.975	-8	*S-131	-1.9
1990	LA-N	141	461	38	97	11	3	1	35	29	65	.210	.260	.254	43	-36	6	3	0	.959	10	*S-139	-1.6
1991	LA-N	109	350	27	85	6	2	0	27	22	49	.243	.290	.271	60	-18	5	4	-1	.961	19	*S-109	0.8
1992	*Tor-A	63	150	21	35	7	0	0	10	9	19	.233	.277	.280	54	-9	3	1	0	.981	-1	S-48,2-16	-0.7
1993	*Tor-A	46	95	15	20	3	0	0	3	3	13	.211	.235	.242	28	-10	0	0	0	.960	4	S-20,2-11/3	-0.4
Total	18	1962	6780	759	1688	245	78	24	527	338	664	.249	.287	.319	67	-306	192	134	-23	.961	-10	*S-1861/2-55,D3	-17.6

■ DOUG GRIFFIN
Griffin, Douglas Lee   b: 6/4/47, South Gate, Cal.   BR/TR, 6', 170 lbs.   Deb: 9/11/70

1970	Cal-A	18	55	2	7	1	0	0	4	6	5	.127	.213	.145	1	-7	0	0	0	.964	1	2-11/3-8	-0.6
1971	Bos-A	125	483	51	118	23	2	3	27	31	45	.244	.293	.319	68	-20	11	5	0	.986	7	*2-124	-0.3
1972	Bos-A	129	470	43	122	12	1	2	35	45	48	.260	.327	.302	83	-8	9	2	2	.978	2	*2-129	0.3
1973	Bos-A	113	396	43	101	14	5	1	33	21	42	.255	.298	.323	71	-16	7	5	-1	.990	-14	*2-113	-2.5
1974	Bos-A	93	312	35	83	12	4	0	33	28	21	.266	.330	.330	85	-6	2	8	-4	.979	-13	2-91/S-1	-2.0
1975	*Bos-A	100	287	21	69	6	0	1	29	18	29	.240	.290	.272	55	-17	2	2	-1	.967	-10	2-99/S-1	-2.4
1976	Bos-A	49	127	14	24	2	0	0	4	9	14	.189	.248	.205	30	-11	2	1	0	.989	-1	2-44/D-2	-1.1
1977	Bos-A	5	6	0	0	0	0	0	0	0	0	.000	.000	.000	-90	-2	0	0	0	1.000	0	/2-3	-0.1
Total	8	632	2136	209	524	70	12	7	165	158	204	.245	.301	.299	68	-87	33	23	-4	.981	-28	2-614/3-8,DS	-8.7

■ PUG GRIFFIN
Griffin, Francis Arthur   b: 4/24/1896, Lincoln, Neb.   d: 10/12/51, Colorado Springs, Colo.   BR/TR, 5'11.5", 187 lbs.   Deb: 7/27/17

1917	Phi-A	18	25	4	5	1	0	1	3	1	9	.200	.231	.360	81	-1	1			1.000	1	/1-3	0.0
1920	NY-N	5	4	0	1	0	0	0	0	1	2	.250	.400	.250	90	-0	0	0	0	1.000	-0	/O-2	-0.1
Total	2	23	29	4	6	1	0	1	3	2	11	.207	.258	.345	83	-1	1	0		1.000	-0	/1-3,O-2	-0.1

■ IVY GRIFFIN
Griffin, Ivy Moore   b: 11/16/1896, Thomasville, Ala.   d: 8/25/57, Gainesville, Fla.   BL/TR, 5'11", 180 lbs.   Deb: 9/9/19

1919	Phi-A	17	68	5	20	2	2	0	6	3	10	.294	.333	.382	99	-0	0			.989	4	1-17	0.3
1920	Phi-A	129	467	46	111	15	1	0	20	17	49	.238	.281	.274	47	-36	3	3	-1	.990	5	*1-127/2-2	-3.4
1921	Phi-A	39	103	14	33	4	2	0	13	5	6	.320	.369	.398	95	-1	1	2	-1	.973	-2	1-27	-0.4
Total	3	185	638	65	164	21	5	0	39	25	65	.257	.301	.306	60	-36	4	5		.988	7	1-171/2-2	-3.5

■ MIKE GRIFFIN
Griffin, Michael Joseph   b: 3/20/1865, Utica, N.Y.   d: 4/10/08, Utica, N.Y.   BL/TR, 5'7", 160 lbs.   Deb: 4/16/1887   M

1887	Bal-a	136	532	142	160	32	13	3		55		.301	.375	.427	131	24	94			.924	-12	*O-136	0.8
1888	Bal-a	137	542	103	139	21	11	0	46	55		.256	.331	.336	117	12	46			.938	7	*O-137	1.4
1889	Bal-a	137	531	**152**	148	21	14	4	48	91	29	.279	.387	.394	120	17	39			.910	-10	*O-109,S-25/2	0.4
1890	Phi-P	115	489	127	140	29	6	6	54	64	19	.286	.377	.407	107	5	30			**.954**	18	*O-115	1.5
1891	Bro-N	134	521	106	139	**36**	9	3	65	57	31	.267	.340	.388	113	8	65			**.960**	26	*O-134	2.6
1892	Bro-N	129	452	103	125	17	11	3	66	68	36	.277	.376	.383	135	21	49			**.986**	13	*O-127/S-2	2.7
1893	Bro-N	95	362	85	103	21	7	6	59	59	23	.285	.396	.431	125	15	30			.965	9	*O-93/2-2	1.6
1894	Bro-N	107	402	122	144	28	4	5	75	78	14	.358	.467	.485	140	33	39			.969	7	*O-106	2.4
1895	Bro-N	131	519	140	173	38	7	4	65	93	29	.333	.444	.457	144	41	27			**.969**	14	*O-131/S-1	3.6
1896	Bro-N	122	493	101	152	27	9	5	51	48	25	.308	.380	.424	118	14	23			.961	3	*O-122	0.6
1897	Bro-N	134	534	136	169	25	11	2	56	81		.316	.416	.416	127	26	16			.956	5	*O-134	1.8
1898	Bro-N	134	537	88	161	18	6	2	40	60		.300	.379	.367	114	12	15			**.974**	10	*O-134,M	1.1
Total	12	1511	5914	1405	1753	313	108	42	625	809	206	.296	.388	.407	124	228	473			.956	88	*O-1478/S-28,2	20.5

■ THOMAS GRIFFIN
Griffin, Thomas William   b: 1/1857, Titusville, Pa.   d: 4/17/33, Rockford, Ill.   Deb: 9/27/1884

| 1884 | Mil-U | 11 | 41 | 5 | 9 | 2 | 0 | 0 | | 3 | | .220 | .273 | .268 | 88 | -2 | | | | .918 | -2 | 1-11 | -0.4 |

■ SANDY GRIFFIN
Griffin, Tobias Charles   b: 7/19/1858, Fayetteville, N.Y.   d: 6/5/26, Fayetteville, N.Y.   BR/TR, 5'10", 160 lbs.   Deb: 5/26/1884   M

1884	NY-N	16	62	7	11	2	0	0	6	1	19	.177	.190	.210	25	-5				.842	-3	O-16	-0.8
1890	Roc-a	107	407	85	125	28	4	5		50		.307	.388	.432	153	28	21			.856	-19	*O-107/2-1	0.5
1891	Was-a	20	69	15	19	4	2	0	10	10	3	.275	.398	.391	132	4	2			.939	-3	O-20,M	0.0
1893	StL-N	23	92	9	18	1	1	0	9	16	2	.196	.315	.228	45	-7	2			.906	-2	O-23	-0.8
Total	4	166	630	116	173	35	7	5	25	77	24	.275	.361	.376	120	19	25			.873	-27	O-166/2-1	-1.1

■ BERT GRIFFITH
Griffith, Bartholomew Joseph "Buck"   b: 3/30/1896, St.Louis, Mo.   d: 5/5/73, Bishop, Cal.   BR/TR, 5'11", 185 lbs.   Deb: 4/13/22

1922	Bro-N	106	325	45	100	22	8	2	35	5	11	.308	.322	.443	96	-3	5	7	-3	.981	-7	O-77/1-6	-1.2
1923	Bro-N	79	248	23	73	8	4	2	37	13	16	.294	.332	.383	91	-4	1	2	-1	.949	-8	O-62	-1.5
1924	Was-A	6	8	1	1	0	0	0	0	0	1	.125	.125	.125	-37	-2	0	0	0	1.000	0	/O-2	-0.1
Total	3	191	581	69	174	30	12	4	72	18	28	.299	.324	.413	92	-8	6	9	-4	.968	-9	O-141/1-6	-2.8

■ CLARK GRIFFITH
Griffith, Clark Calvin "The Old Fox"   b: 11/20/1869, Clear Creek, Mo.   d: 10/27/55, Washington, D.C.   BR/TR, 5'6.5", 156 lbs.   Deb: 4/11/1891   MH

1891	StL-a	27	77	11	12	1	0	1		8	15	.156	.253	.208	28	-8	2			.930	0	P-27	0.0
	Bos-a	10	23	6	4	1	1	0	3	6	5	.174	.367	.435	131	1	1			.778	-1	/P-7,O-3	0.0
	Yr	37	100	17	16	2	1	2	11	14	20	.160	.282	.250	50	-7	3			.909	-1	P-34/O-3	0.0
1893	Chi-N	4	11	1	2	0	0	0	2	0	1	.182	.182	.182	-3	-2	0			1.000	1	/P-4	0.0
1894	Chi-N	46	142	27	33	5	4	0	15	23	9	.232	.339	.324	58	-10	6			.942	-3	P-36/O-7,S	-0.4
1895	Chi-N	43	144	20	46	3	0	1	27	16	9	.319	.391	.361	89	-2	2			.923	1	P-42/O-1	0.0
1896	Chi-N	38	135	22	36	5	2	1	16	9	7	.267	.313	.356	73	-8	3			.917	1	P-36	0.0
1897	Chi-N	46	162	27	38	8	4	0	21	18		.235	.311	.333	67	-8	2			.947	2	P-41/O-2,S31	-0.1
1898	Chi-N	38	122	15	20	2	0	0	15	13		.164	.244	.230	36	-10	1			.952	1	P-38	0.0
1899	Chi-N	39	120	15	31	5	0	0	14	14		.258	.304	.300	80	-3	2			.933	1	P-38/S-1	-0.1
1900	Chi-N	30	95	16	24	4	1	0	7	8		.253	.311	.347	84	-2	1			.917	-1	P-30	0.0
1901	Chi-A	35	89	21	27	3	1	2	14	23		.303	.446	.427	147	7	0			.946	0	P-35,M	0.0
1902	Chi-A	35	92	11	20	3	0	0	8	7		.217	.273	.250	48	-6	0			**1.000**	-2	P-28/O-3M	-0.1
1903	NY-A	25	69	5	11	0	0	1	7	11		.159	.284	.261	60	-3	1			.983	-3	P-25,M	0.0
1904	NY-A	16	42	2	6	2	0	0	1	4		.143	.217	.190	28	-3	0			.946	-1	P-16,M	0.0
1905	NY-A	26	32	2	7	1	0	0	5	3		.219	.286	.313	80	-1	0			.960	-3	P-25/O-1M	0.0
1906	NY-A	17	18	0	2	0	0	0		1		.111	.238	.111	9	-2	0			1.000	1	P-17,M	0.0
1907	NY-A	5	2	0	0	0	0	0		0		.000	.000	.000	-93	-0	0			.800	1	/P-4,M	0.0

YEAR	TM/L	G	AB	R	H	2B	3B	HR	RBI	BB	SO	AVG	OBP	SLG	PRO+	BR/A	SB	CS	SBR	FA	FR	G/POS	TPR
1909	Cin-N	1	2	0	0	0	0	0	0	0	0	.000	.000	.000	-99	-0	0			1.000	1	/P-1,M	0.0
1910	Cin-N	1	0	1	0	0	0	0	0	0	0	—	—	—		0	0			.000	0	RM	0.0
1912	Was-A	1	1	0	0	0	0	0	0	0	0	.000	.000	.000	-99	-0	0			.000	1	/P-1,2-1M	0.0
1913	Was-A	1	1	0	1	1	0	0	1	0	0	1.000	1.000	2.000	758	1	0			.000	-0	/P-1,O-1M	0.0
1914	Was-A	1	1	0	1	1	0	0	1	0	0	1.000	1.000	2.000	769	1	0	1	-1	.000	-0	/P-1,M	0.0
Total	21	485	1380	202	321	49	17	8	166	166	46	.233	.318	.310	69	-57	22	1		.942	1	P-453/O-18,S213	-0.7

■ DERRELL GRIFFITH
Griffith, Robert Derrell   b: 12/12/43, Anadarko, Okla.   BL/TR, 6', 168 lbs.   Deb: 9/26/63

YEAR	TM/L	G	AB	R	H	2B	3B	HR	RBI	BB	SO	AVG	OBP	SLG	PRO+	BR/A	SB	CS	SBR	FA	FR	G/POS	TPR
1963	LA-N	1	2	0	0	0	0	0	0	0	0	.000	.000	.000	-99	-1	0	0	0	.000	0	/2-1	-0.1
1964	LA-N	78	238	27	69	16	2	4	23	5	21	.290	.307	.424	112	2	5	1	1	.769	-12	3-35,O-29	-1.1
1965	LA-N	22	41	3	7	0	0	1	2	0	9	.171	.171	.244	16	-5	0	0	0	1.000	-0	O-11	-0.5
1966	LA-N	23	15	3	1	0	0	0	2	2	3	.067	.176	.067	-32	-3	0	0	0	1.000	-2	/O-7	-0.5
Total	4	124	296	33	77	16	2	5	27	7	33	.260	.280	.378	90	-5	5	1	1	.970	-14	/O-47,3-35,2	-2.2

■ TOMMY GRIFFITH
Griffith, Thomas Herman   b: 10/26/1889, Prospect, Ohio   d: 4/13/67, Cincinnati, Ohio   BL/TR, 5'10", 175 lbs.   Deb: 8/28/13

YEAR	TM/L	G	AB	R	H	2B	3B	HR	RBI	BB	SO	AVG	OBP	SLG	PRO+	BR/A	SB	CS	SBR	FA	FR	G/POS	TPR
1913	Bos-N	37	127	16	32	4	1	1	12	9	8	.252	.301	.323	77	-4	1			.886	1	O-35	-0.4
1914	Bos-N	16	48	3	5	0	0	0	1	2	6	.104	.140	.104	-27	-7	0			.931	3	O-14	-0.6
1915	Cin-N	160	583	59	179	31	16	4	85	41	34	.307	.355	.436	136	24	6	24	-13	.952	-13	*O-160	-1.0
1916	Cin-N	155	595	50	158	28	7	2	61	36	37	.266	.310	.346	104	2	16			.967	6	*O-155	0.0
1917	Cin-N	115	363	45	98	18	7	1	45	19	23	.270	.308	.366	111	4	5			.974	6	*O-100	0.5
1918	Cin-N	118	427	47	113	10	4	2	48	39	30	.265	.326	.321	99	0	10			.969	2	*O-118	-0.5
1919	Bro-N	125	484	65	136	18	4	6	57	23	32	.281	.315	.372	104	1	8			.954	-1	*O-125	-0.9
1920	*Bro-N	93	334	41	87	9	4	2	30	15	18	.260	.292	.329	76	-11	3	3	-1	.972	-1	O-92	-3.1
1921	Bro-N	129	455	66	142	21	6	12	71	36	13	.312	.364	.464	113	8	3	3	-1	.972	7	*O-124	0.5
1922	Bro-N	99	329	44	104	17	8	4	49	23	10	.316	.361	.453	110	4	7	1	2	.952	4	O-82	0.4
1923	Bro-N	131	481	70	141	21	9	8	66	50	19	.293	.361	.424	109	7	8	2	1	.927	-7	*O-127	-0.7
1924	Bro-N	140	482	43	121	19	5	3	67	34	19	.251	.300	.330	71	-20	5	5	-3	.965	-11	*O-139	-4.3
1925	Bro-N	7	4	2	0	0	0	0	0	3	2	.000	.429	.000	20	-0	1	0	0	1.000	-1	/O-2	-0.1
	Chi-N	76	235	38	67	12	1	7	27	21	11	.285	.346	.434	97	-1	2	4	-2	.937	-4	O-60	-1.0
	Yr	83	239	40	67	12	1	7	27	24	13	.280	.348	.427	96	-2	3	4	-2	.938	-4	O-62	-1.1
Total	13	1401	4947	589	1383	208	72	52	619	351	262	.280	.328	.382	102	6	70	42		.956	-19	*O-1333	-11.2

■ ART GRIGGS
Griggs, Arthur Carle   b: 12/10/1883, Topeka, Kan.   d: 12/19/38, Los Angeles, Cal.   BR/TR, 5'11", 185 lbs.   Deb: 5/2/09

YEAR	TM/L	G	AB	R	H	2B	3B	HR	RBI	BB	SO	AVG	OBP	SLG	PRO+	BR/A	SB	CS	SBR	FA	FR	G/POS	TPR
1909	StL-A	108	364	38	102	17	5	0	43	24		.280	.330	.354	125	9	11			.982	-6	1-49,O-41/2S	0.1
1910	StL-A	123	416	28	98	22	5	2	30	25		.236	.281	.327	96	-4	11			.878	-1	O-49,2-41,1/S3	-0.8
1911	Cle-A	27	68	7	17	3	2	1	7	5		.250	.301	.397	93	-1	1			.949	-2	2-11/O-4,31	-0.3
1912	Cle-A	89	273	29	83	16	7	0	39	33		.304	.381	.414	123	9	10			.986	1	1-71	0.8
1914	Bro-F	40	112	10	32	6	1	1	15	5	11	.286	.328	.384	85	-3	1			.980	-3	1-27/O-1	-0.7
1915	Bro-F	27	38	4	11	1	0	1	2	3	7	.289	.372	.395	106	0	0			1.000	1	/1-5,O-1	0.1
1918	Det-A	28	99	11	36	8	0	0	16	10	5	.364	.422	.444	168	8	2			.986	-3	1-25	0.5
Total	7	442	1370	127	379	73	20	5	152	105	23	.277	.332	.370	114	19	36			.983	-13	1-195/O-96,23S	-0.3

■ DENVER GRIGSBY
Grigsby, Denver Clarence   b: 3/25/01, Jackson, Ky.   d: 11/10/73, Sapulpa, Okla.   BL/TR, 5'9", 155 lbs.   Deb: 9/1/23

YEAR	TM/L	G	AB	R	H	2B	3B	HR	RBI	BB	SO	AVG	OBP	SLG	PRO+	BR/A	SB	CS	SBR	FA	FR	G/POS	TPR
1923	Chi-N	24	72	8	21	5	2	0	5	7	5	.292	.363	.417	105	1	1	3	-2	1.000	-2	O-22	-0.4
1924	Chi-N	124	411	58	123	18	2	3	48	31	47	.299	.357	.375	95	-2	10	19	-8	.974	3	*O-121	-1.5
1925	Chi-N	51	137	20	35	5	0	0	20	19	12	.255	.346	.292	64	-7	1	1	-0	.966	-1	O-39	-1.0
Total	3	199	620	86	179	28	4	3	73	57	64	.289	.355	.361	89	-8	12	23	-10	.975	0	O-182	-2.9

■ JOHN GRIM
Grim, John Helm   b: 8/9/1867, Lebanon, Ky.   d: 7/28/61, Indianapolis, Ind   BR/TR, 6'2", 175 lbs.   Deb: 9/29/1888

YEAR	TM/L	G	AB	R	H	2B	3B	HR	RBI	BB	SO	AVG	OBP	SLG	PRO+	BR/A	SB	CS	SBR	FA	FR	G/POS	TPR
1888	Phi-N	2	7	0	1	0	0	0	0	0	0	.143	.143	.143	-8	-1	0			.000	-1	/O-1,2-1	-0.1
1890	Roc-a	50	192	30	51	6	9	2		0	7	.266	.299	.422	121	3	14			.851	-7	S-21,C-15/3201P	0.0
1891	Mil-a	29	119	14	28	5	1	1	14	2	5	.235	.248	.319	52	-9	1			.926	3	C-16,3-10/2	-0.3
1892	Lou-N	97	370	40	90	16	4	1	36	13	24	.243	.280	.316	87	-7	18			.940	-10	C-69,1-11,2/OS3	-1.1
1893	Lou-N	99	415	68	111	19	8	3	54	12	10	.267	.303	.373	86	-10	15			.952	-4	*C-92/1-3,20S	-0.6
1894	Lou-N	108	410	60	122	27	7	7	70	16	15	.298	.339	.449	95	-5	14			.931	11	C-77,2-24/13	1.0
1895	Bro-N	93	329	54	92	17	5	0	44	13	9	.280	.321	.362	83	-9	9			.947	-0	*C-91/O-1,1	-0.3
1896	Bro-N	81	281	32	75	13	1	2	35	12	14	.267	.311	.342	76	-10	4			.939	-1	C-77/1-5	-0.8
1897	Bro-N	80	290	26	72	10	1	0	25	1		.248	.259	.290	47	-23	3			.947	5	C-77	-0.8
1898	Bro-N	52	178	17	50	5	1	0	11	8		.281	.323	.320	85	-4	1			.950	-4	C-52	-0.3
1899	Bro-N	15	47	3	13	1	0	0	7	1		.277	.320	.298	68	-2	1			.966	1	C-12	-0.1
Total	11	706	2638	350	705	119	37	16	296	85	77	.267	.302	.359	82	-76	82			.943	-7	C-578/2-44,1S30P	-2.4

■ ED GRIMES
Grimes, Edward Adelbert   b: 9/8/05, Chicago, Ill.   d: 10/5/74, Chicago, Ill.   BR/TR, 5'10", 165 lbs.   Deb: 4/19/31

YEAR	TM/L	G	AB	R	H	2B	3B	HR	RBI	BB	SO	AVG	OBP	SLG	PRO+	BR/A	SB	CS	SBR	FA	FR	G/POS	TPR
1931	StL-A	43	57	9	15	1	2	0	5	9	3	.263	.364	.351	86	-1	1	0	0	.892	-2	3-22/2-4,S	-0.2
1932	StL-A	31	68	7	16	0	1	0	13	6	12	.235	.297	.265	44	-6	0	1	-1	.891	2	3-18/2-2,S	-0.3
Total	2	74	125	16	31	1	3	0	18	15	15	.248	.329	.304	63	-6	1	1	-0	.891	-0	/3-40,2-6,S	-0.5

■ ROY GRIMES
Grimes, Austin Roy "Bummer"   b: 9/11/1893, Bergholz, Ohio   d: 9/13/54, Gilford Lake, O.   BR/TR, 6'1", 176 lbs.   Deb: 7/31/20   F

YEAR	TM/L	G	AB	R	H	2B	3B	HR	RBI	BB	SO	AVG	OBP	SLG	PRO+	BR/A	SB	CS	SBR	FA	FR	G/POS	TPR
1920	NY-N	26	57	5	9	1	0	0	3	3	8	.158	.200	.175	8	-7	1	1	-0	.948	-1	2-21	-0.9

■ OSCAR GRIMES
Grimes, Oscar Ray Jr.   b: 4/13/15, Minerva, Ohio   d: 5/19/93, Westlake, Ohio   BR/TR, 5'11", 178 lbs.   Deb: 9/28/38   F

YEAR	TM/L	G	AB	R	H	2B	3B	HR	RBI	BB	SO	AVG	OBP	SLG	PRO+	BR/A	SB	CS	SBR	FA	FR	G/POS	TPR
1938	Cle-A	4	10	2	2	0	1	0	2	2	0	.200	.333	.400	85	-0	0	0	0	1.000	-1	/2-2,1-1	-0.1
1939	Cle-A	119	364	51	98	20	5	4	56	56	61	.269	.368	.385	96	-1	8	3	1	.968	-11	2-48,1-43,S/3	-1.0
1940	Cle-A	11	13	3	0	0	0	0	0	0	5	.000	.000	.000	-99	-4	0	0	0	.958	2	/1-4,3-1	-0.2
1941	Cle-A	77	244	28	58	9	3	4	24	39	47	.238	.346	.348	88	-4	4	0	1	.995	-5	1-62,2-13/3	-1.1
1942	Cle-A	51	84	10	15	2	0	2	13	17	.179	.289	.202	42	-6	3	2	-0	.944	-3	2-24/3-8,1S	-0.9
1943	NY-A	9	20	4	3	0	0	0	1	3	7	.150	.261	.150	21	-2	0	0	0	1.000	-1	/S-3,1-1	-0.3
1944	NY-A	116	387	44	108	17	8	5	46	59	65	.279	.377	.403	119	11	6	0	2	.945	-10	3-97,S-20	0.5
1945	NY-A†	142	480	64	127	19	7	4	45	97	73	.265	.395	.358	114	13	7	6	-2	.937	3	*3-141/1-1	1.9
1946	NY-A	14	39	1	8	1	0	0	4	1	7	.205	.225	.231	27	-4	0	1	-0	.895	1	/S-7,2-5	-0.4
	Phi-A	59	191	28	50	5	0	1	20	27	29	.262	.356	.304	86	-2	2	0	1	.958	-12	2-43/3-6,S	-1.1
	Yr	73	230	29	58	6	0	1	24	28	36	.252	.336	.291	76	-6	2	1	0	.957	-12	2-48,S-11/3	-1.5
Total	9	602	1832	235	469	73	24	18	200	297	303	.256	.363	.352	98	1	30	12	2	.940	-39	3-257,2-135,1/S	-2.7

■ RAY GRIMES
Grimes, Oscar Ray Sr.   b: 9/11/1893, Bergholz, Ohio   d: 5/25/53, Minerva, Ohio   BR/TR, 5'11", 168 lbs.   Deb: 9/24/20   F

YEAR	TM/L	G	AB	R	H	2B	3B	HR	RBI	BB	SO	AVG	OBP	SLG	PRO+	BR/A	SB	CS	SBR	FA	FR	G/POS	TPR
1920	Bos-A	1	4	1	1	0	0	0	1	0	1	.250	.400	.250	78	-0	0	0	0	1.000	-0	/1-1	0.0
1921	Chi-N	147	530	91	170	38	6	6	79	70	55	.321	.406	.449	126	22	5	8	-3	.993	-5	*1-147	1.1
1922	Chi-N	138	509	99	180	45	12	14	99	75	33	.354	.442	.572	157	45	7	7	-2	.987	-2	*1-138	3.3
1923	Chi-N	64	216	32	71	7	2	2	36	24	17	.329	.401	.407	114	5	5	0	2	.991	-1	1-62	0.3
1924	Chi-N	51	177	33	53	6	5	2	34	28	15	.299	.401	.475	132	9	4	2	0	.982	-7	1-50	-0.1
1926	Phi-N	32	101	13	30	5	0	3	14	7	12	.297	.343	.347	82	-2	0			.981	0	1-28	-0.4
Total	6	433	1537	269	505	101	25	27	263	204	133	.329	.413	.480	132	79	21	17		.989	-14	1-426	4.2

■ CHARLIE GRIMM
Grimm, Charles John "Jolly Cholly"   b: 8/28/1898, St.Louis, Mo.   d: 11/15/83, Scottsdale, Ariz.   BL/TL, 5'11.5", 173 lbs.   Deb: 7/30/16   MC

YEAR	TM/L	G	AB	R	H	2B	3B	HR	RBI	BB	SO	AVG	OBP	SLG	PRO+	BR/A	SB	CS	SBR	FA	FR	G/POS	TPR
1916	Phi-A	12	22	0	2	0	0	0	0	2	4	.091	.167	.091	-24	-3	0			.875	-2	/O-7	-0.6

YEAR	TM/L	G	AB	R	H	2B	3B	HR	RBI	BB	SO	AVG	OBP	SLG	PRO+	BR/A	SB	CS	SBR	FA	FR	G/POS	TPR
1918	StL-N	50	141	11	31	7	0	0	12	6	15	.220	.262	.270	64	-6	2			.971	-3	1-42/O-2,3	-1.2
1919	Pit-N	14	44	6	14	1	3	0	6	2	4	.318	.348	.477	141	2	1			.968	-3	1-13	-0.1
1920	Pit-N	148	533	38	121	13	7	2	54	30	40	.227	.273	.289	60	-28	7	8	-3	**.995**	4	*1-148	-3.2
1921	Pit-N	151	562	62	154	21	17	7	71	31	38	.274	.314	.409	88	-11	6	8	-3	.994	-6	*1-150	-2.4
1922	Pit-N	154	593	64	173	28	13	0	76	43	15	.292	.343	.383	86	-12	6	10	-4	.994	-3	*1-154	-2.5
1923	Pit-N	152	563	78	194	29	13	7	99	41	43	.345	.389	.480	125	20	6	9	-4	**.995**	2	*1-152	1.0
1924	Pit-N	151	542	53	156	25	12	2	63	37	22	.288	.336	.389	92	-6	3	6	-3	**.995**	-3	*1-151	-2.1
1925	Chi-N	141	519	73	159	29	5	10	76	38	25	.306	.354	.439	100	-1	4	3	-1	.989	0	*1-139	-0.8
1926	Chi-N	147	524	58	145	30	6	8	82	49	25	.277	.342	.403	99	-1	3			.988	-6	*1-147	-1.6
1927	Chi-N	147	543	68	169	29	6	2	74	45	21	.311	.367	.398	105	4	3			.990	3	*1-147	-0.3
1928	Chi-N	147	547	67	161	25	5	5	62	39	20	.294	.342	.386	91	-7	7			.993	-2	*1-147	-2.2
1929	*Chi-N	120	463	66	138	28	3	10	91	42	25	.298	.358	.436	95	-4	3			.992	0	*1-120	-1.4
1930	Chi-N	114	429	58	124	27	2	6	66	41	26	.289	.359	.403	83	-11	1			**.995**	1	*1-113	-1.9
1931	Chi-N	146	531	65	176	33	11	4	66	53	29	.331	.393	.458	126	20	1			**.993**	2	*1-144	0.8
1932	*Chi-N	149	570	66	175	42	2	7	80	35	22	.307	.349	.425	108	6	2			.993	10	*1-149,M	0.5
1933	Chi-N	107	384	38	95	15	2	3	37	23	15	.247	.290	.320	74	-13	1			**.996**	9	*1-104,M	-1.4
1934	Chi-N	75	267	24	79	8	1	5	47	16	12	.296	.338	.390	96	-2	1			.995	1	1-74,M	-0.6
1935	Chi-N	2	8	0	0	0	0	0	0	0	1	.000	.000	.000	-99	-2	0			1.000	-0	/1-2,M	-0.3
1936	Chi-N	39	132	13	33	4	0	1	16	5	8	.250	.277	.303	55	-8	0			1.000	5	1-35,M	-0.6
Total	20	2166	7917	908	2299	394	108	79	1078	578	410	.290	.341	.397	95	-63	57	44		.993	10	*1-2131/O-9,3	-20.9

■ MYRON GRIMSHAW

Grimshaw, Myron Frederick b: 11/30/1875, St.Johnsville, N.Y d: 12/11/36, Canajoharie, N.Y. BB/TR, 6'1", 173 lbs. Deb: 4/25/05

YEAR	TM/L	G	AB	R	H	2B	3B	HR	RBI	BB	SO	AVG	OBP	SLG	PRO+	BR/A	SB	CS	SBR	FA	FR	G/POS	TPR
1905	Bos-A	85	285	39	68	8	2	4	35	21		.239	.293	.323	94	-2	4			.980	-5	1-74	-1.0
1906	Bos-A	110	428	46	124	16	12	0	48	23		.290	.332	.383	124	11	5			.987	-1	*1-110	0.7
1907	Bos-A	64	181	19	37	7	2	0	33	16		.204	.273	.265	72	-5	6			.966	-7	O-23,1-15/S	-1.5
Total	3	259	894	104	229	31	16	4	116	60		.256	.307	.340	104	3	15			.984	-13	1-199/O-23,S	-1.8

■ MARQUIS GRISSOM

Grissom, Marquis Deon b: 4/17/67, Atlanta, Ga. BR/TR, 5'11", 190 lbs. Deb: 8/22/89

YEAR	TM/L	G	AB	R	H	2B	3B	HR	RBI	BB	SO	AVG	OBP	SLG	PRO+	BR/A	SB	CS	SBR	FA	FR	G/POS	TPR
1989	Mon-N	26	74	16	19	2	0	1	2	12	21	.257	.360	.324	96	0	1	0	0	.943	-4	O-23	-0.5
1990	Mon-N	98	288	42	74	14	2	3	29	27	40	.257	.321	.351	88	-5	22	2	5	.988	-4	O-87	-0.5
1991	Mon-N	148	558	73	149	23	9	6	39	34	89	.267	.310	.373	93	-6	**76**	17	**13**	.984	20	*O-138	2.4
1992	Mon-N	159	653	99	180	39	6	14	66	42	81	.276	.324	.418	110	7	**78**	13	**16**	.983	7	*O-157	2.8
1993	Mon-N★	157	630	104	188	27	2	19	95	52	76	.298	.351	.438	106	6	53	10	**10**	.984	11	*O-157	2.3
1994	Mon-N★	110	475	96	137	25	4	11	45	41	66	.288	.346	.427	98	-1	36	6	7	.985	16	*O-109	2.0
Total	6	698	2678	430	747	130	23	54	276	208	373	.279	.333	.405	101	0	266	48	51	.983	46	O-671	8.5

■ DICK GROAT

Groat, Richard Morrow b: 11/4/30, Wilkinsburg, Pa. BR/TR, 5'11.5", 180 lbs. Deb: 6/19/52

YEAR	TM/L	G	AB	R	H	2B	3B	HR	RBI	BB	SO	AVG	OBP	SLG	PRO+	BR/A	SB	CS	SBR	FA	FR	G/POS	TPR
1952	Pit-N	95	384	38	109	6	1	1	29	19	27	.284	.319	.313	74	-13	2	4	-2	.952	1	S-94	-0.7
1955	Pit-N	151	521	45	139	28	2	4	51	38	26	.267	.318	.351	78	-16	0	2	-1	.961	15	*S-149	1.1
1956	Pit-N	142	520	40	142	19	3	0	37	35	25	.273	.319	.321	74	-18	0	3	-2	.954	0	*S-141/3-2	-0.8
1957	Pit-N	125	501	58	158	30	5	7	54	27	26	.315	.354	.437	114	10	0	1	-1	.968	-1	*S-123/3-2	2.0
1958	Pit-N	151	584	67	175	36	9	3	66	23	32	.300	.331	.408	97	-4	2	2	-1	.975	3	*S-149	1.2
1959	Pit-N★	147	593	74	163	22	7	5	51	32	35	.275	.314	.361	89	-17	2	1	-1	.964	3	*S-145	-0.3
1960	*Pit-N★	138	573	85	186	26	4	2	50	39	35	**.325**	.372	.394	109	8	0	2	-2	.966	11	*S-136	2.9
1961	Pit-N★	148	596	71	164	25	6	6	55	40	44	.275	.322	.367	82	-15	0	4	-2	.957	9	*S-144/3-1	0.4
1962	Pit-N★	161	678	76	199	34	3	2	61	31	61	.294	.327	.361	85	-15	2	1	0	.956	14	*S-161	1.4
1963	StL-N★	158	631	85	201	**43**	11	6	73	56	58	.319	.380	.450	124	22	3	1	0	.964	-13	*S-158	2.2
1964	*StL-N★	161	636	70	186	35	4	5	70	44	42	.292	.338	.371	92	-6	2	3	-1	.949	-12	*S-160	-0.9
1965	StL-N	153	587	55	149	26	5	0	52	56	50	.254	.320	.315	73	-20	1	1	-0	.962	-8	*S-148/3-2	-2.0
1966	Phi-N	155	584	58	152	21	4	5	53	40	38	.260	.313	.320	77	-18	1	0	0	.974	11	*S-139,3-20/1	0.6
1967	Phi-N	10	26	3	3	0	0	0	1	4	4	.115	.233	.115	3	-3	0	0	0	.947	2	/S-6	-0.3
	SF-N	34	70	4	12	1	1	0	4	6	7	.171	.237	.214	30	-6	0	0	0	.912	-8	S-24/2-1	-1.4
	Yr	44	96	7	15	1	1	0	5	10	11	.156	.236	.188	23	-9	0	0	0	.925	-5	S-30/2-1	-1.4
Total	14	1929	7484	829	2138	352	67	39	707	490	512	.286	.332	.366	89	-112	14	27	-12	.961	28	*S-1877/3-27,21	5.7

■ HEINIE GROH

Groh, Henry Knight b: 9/18/1889, Rochester, N.Y. d: 8/22/68, Cincinnati, Ohio BR/TR, 5'8", 158 lbs. Deb: 4/12/12 FM

YEAR	TM/L	G	AB	R	H	2B	3B	HR	RBI	BB	SO	AVG	OBP	SLG	PRO+	BR/A	SB	CS	SBR	FA	FR	G/POS	TPR
1912	NY-N	27	48	8	13	2	1	0	3	8	7	.271	.375	.354	97	0	6			.887	3	2-12/S-7,3	0.3
1913	NY-N	4	2	0	0	0	0	0	0	0	1	.000	.000	.000	-99	-1	0			1.000	-0	/3-2,S-1	0.0
	Cin-N	117	397	51	112	19	5	3	48	38	36	.282	.351	.378	109	5	24			.963	10	*2-113/S-4	1.3
	Yr	121	399	51	112	19	5	3	48	38	37	.281	.349	.376	107	4	24			.963	10	*2-113/S-5,3	1.3
1914	Cin-N	139	455	59	131	18	4	2	32	64	34	.288	.391	.358	120	15	24			.936	-7	*2-134/S-2	0.7
1915	Cin-N	160	587	72	170	32	9	3	50	50	33	.290	.354	.390	123	17	12	17	-7	.969	11	*3-131,2-29	2.9
1916	Cin-N	149	553	85	149	24	14	2	28	**84**	34	.269	.370	.374	132	24	13			.957	19	*3-110,2-33/S	**5.4**
1917	Cin-N	156	599	91	**182**	39	11	1	53	71	30	.304	**.385**	.411	150	38	15			**.966**	8	*3-154/2-2	5.3
1918	Cin-N	126	493	**86**	158	**28**	3	1	37	54	24	.320	**.395**	.396	144	**28**	11			.969	2	*3-126,M	**3.6**
1919	*Cin-N	122	448	79	139	17	11	5	63	56	26	.310	.392	.431	151	29	21			.971	-2	*3-121	3.5
1920	Cin-N	145	550	86	164	28	12	0	49	60	29	.298	.375	.393	122	18	16	19	-7	.969	-6	*3-144/S-1	1.3
1921	Cin-N	97	357	54	118	19	6	0	48	36	17	.331	.398	.417	122	13	22	14	-2	.950	1	3-97	1.8
1922	*NY-N	115	426	63	113	21	3	3	51	53	29	.265	.353	.350	81	-10	5	6	-2	**.965**	4	*3-110	-0.3
1923	*NY-N	123	465	91	135	22	5	4	48	60	23	.290	.379	.385	103	3	3	4	-2	**.975**	4	*3-118	1.6
1924	*NY-N	145	559	82	157	32	3	2	46	52	29	.281	.354	.360	94	-3	8	6	-1	**.983**	3	*3-145	1.0
1925	NY-N	25	65	7	15	4	0	0	4	6	3	.231	.296	.292	53	-5	0	0	0	.909	-5	3-16/2-2	-0.9
1926	NY-N	12	35	2	8	2	0	0	3	2	1	.229	.270	.286	50	-2	0			.950	-1	/3-7	-0.3
1927	*Pit-N	14	35	2	10	1	0	0	3	2	2	.286	.324	.314	67	-2	0			.958	-1	3-12	-0.3
Total	16	1676	6074	918	1774	308	87	26	566	696	345	.292	.373	.384	119	167	180	66		.967	39	*3-1299,2-325/S	27.0

■ LEW GROH

Groh, Lewis Carl "Silver" b: 10/16/1883, Rochester, N.Y. d: 10/20/60, Rochester, N.Y. BR/TR, Deb: 8/2/19 F

YEAR	TM/L	G	AB	R	H	2B	3B	HR	RBI	BB	SO	AVG	OBP	SLG	PRO+	BR/A	SB	CS	SBR	FA	FR	G/POS	TPR
1919	Phi-A	2	4	0	0	0	0	0	0	0	2	.000	.000	.000	-99	-1	0			1.000	-0	/3-1	-0.1

■ HOWDIE GROSKLOSS

Groskloss, Howard Hoffman b: 4/9/07, Pittsburgh, Pa. BR/TR, 5'9", 176 lbs. Deb: 6/23/30

YEAR	TM/L	G	AB	R	H	2B	3B	HR	RBI	BB	SO	AVG	OBP	SLG	PRO+	BR/A	SB	CS	SBR	FA	FR	G/POS	TPR
1930	Pit-N	2	3	0	1	0	0	0	1	0	0	.333	.333	.333	62	-0	1			.000	-1	/S-1	-0.1
1931	Pit-N	53	161	13	45	7	2	0	20	11	16	.280	.326	.348	82	-4	1			.981	-1	2-39/S-3	-0.3
1932	Pit-N	17	20	1	2	0	0	0	0	0	3	.100	.100	.100	-47	-4	0			.800	1	/S-1	-0.5
Total	3	72	184	14	48	7	2	0	21	11	19	.261	.303	.321	68	-8	1			.700	-3	/2-39,S-5	-0.9

■ EMIL GROSS

Gross, Emil Michael b: 3/3/1858, Chicago, Ill. d: 8/24/21, Eagle River, Wis. BR/TR, 6', 190 lbs. Deb: 8/13/1879

YEAR	TM/L	G	AB	R	H	2B	3B	HR	RBI	BB	SO	AVG	OBP	SLG	PRO+	BR/A	SB	CS	SBR	FA	FR	G/POS	TPR
1879	Pro-N	30	132	31	46	9	5	0	24	4	8	.348	.368	.492	183	12				.897	-5	C-30	0.7
1880	Pro-N	87	347	43	90	18	3	1	34	16	15	.259	.292	.337	116	6				.866	-14	*C-87	-0.6
1881	Pro-N	51	182	15	50	9	4	1	24	13	11	.275	.323	.385	124	5				.893	-4	C-50/O-1	0.3
1883	Phi-N	57	231	39	71	25	7	1	25	12	16	.307	.342	.489	163	18				.789	-24	C-55/O-2	-0.3
1884	CP-U	23	95	13	34	6	2	4	6			.358	.396	.589	165	8				.860	-3	C-15/O-9	0.6
Total	5	248	987	141	291	67	21	7	107	51	52	.295	.329	.427	143	49				.859	-50	C-237/O-12	0.7

■ TURKEY GROSS

Gross, Ewell b: 2/21/1896, Mesquite, Tex. d: 1/11/36, Dallas, Tex. BR/TR, 6', 165 lbs. Deb: 4/14/25

YEAR	TM/L	G	AB	R	H	2B	3B	HR	RBI	BB	SO	AVG	OBP	SLG	PRO+	BR/A	SB	CS	SBR	FA	FR	G/POS	TPR
1925	Bos-A	9	32	2	3	0	1	0	2	2	2	.094	.171	.156	-16	-6	0	0	0	.976	-1	/S-9	-0.5

YEAR	TM/L	G	AB	R	H	2B	3B	HR	RBI	BB	SO	AVG	OBP	SLG	PRO+	BR/A	SB	CS	SBR	FA	FR	G/POS	TPR

■ GREG GROSS   Gross, Gregory Eugene   b: 8/1/52, York, Pa.   BL/TL, 5'11", 175 lbs.   Deb: 9/5/73

1973	Hou-N	14	39	5	9	2	1	0	1	4	4	.231	.302	.333	76	-1	2	1	0	1.000	1	/O-9	-0.1
1974	Hou-N	156	589	78	185	21	8	0	36	76	39	.314	.393	.377	121	20	12	20	-8	.994	-9	*O-151	-0.5
1975	Hou-N	132	483	67	142	14	10	0	41	63	37	.294	.375	.364	114	11	2	2	-1	.958	5	*O-121	1.0
1976	Hou-N	128	426	52	122	12	3	0	27	64	39	.286	.380	.329	112	10	2	6	-3	.978	3	*O-115	0.5
1977	Chi-N	115	239	43	77	10	4	5	32	33	19	.322	.404	.460	118	7	0	1	-1	.991	-8	O-71	-0.4
1978	Chi-N	124	347	34	92	12	7	1	39	33	19	.265	.329	.349	80	-9	3	1	0	.979	-14	*O-111	-2.8
1979	Phi-N	111	174	21	58	6	3	0	15	29	5	.333	.429	.402	124	7	5	2	0	.978	-12	O-73	-0.6
1980	*Phi-N	127	154	19	37	7	2	0	12	24	7	.240	.346	.312	80	-3	1	1	-0	.973	-22	O-91/1-1	-2.9
1981	*Phi-N	83	102	14	23	6	1	0	7	15	5	.225	.325	.304	76	-3	2	2	-1	.982	-7	O-55	-1.2
1982	Phi-N	119	134	14	40	4	0	0	10	19	8	.299	.386	.328	99	1	4	3	-1	.983	-18	O-71	-1.9
1983	*Phi-N	136	245	25	74	12	3	0	29	34	16	.302	.389	.376	114	6	3	5	-2	.991	-28	*O-110/1-1	-2.7
1984	Phi-N	112	202	19	65	9	1	0	16	24	11	.322	.396	.376	116	5	1	0	0	.986	-4	O-48,1-28	0.0
1985	Phi-N	93	169	21	44	5	2	0	14	32	9	.260	.378	.314	93	-0	1	0	0	1.000	-7	O-52/1-8	-0.8
1986	Phi-N	87	101	11	25	5	0	0	8	21	11	.248	.382	.297	87	-1	0	0	0	1.000	-3	O-27/1-5,P	-0.4
1987	Phi-N	114	133	14	38	4	1	1	12	25	12	.286	.403	.353	99	1	0	0	0	1.000	-12	O-50,1-11	-1.2
1988	Phi-N	98	133	10	27	1	0	0	5	16	3	.203	.293	.211	46	-9	0	0	0	1.000	-11	O-37,1-14	-2.3
1989	Hou-N	60	75	2	15	0	0	0	5	4	0	.200	.310	.200	51	-4	0	0	0	.929	-3	O-12/1-6,P	-0.8
Total	17	1809	3745	449	1073	130	46	7	308	523	250	.287	.375	.351	103	38	39	44	-15	.982	-148	*O-1204/1-74,P	-17.1

■ WAYNE GROSS   Gross, Wayne Dale   b: 1/14/52, Riverside, Cal.   BL/TR, 6'2", 210 lbs.   Deb: 8/21/76

1976	Oak-A	10	18	0	4	0	0	0	1	2	1	.222	.300	.222	57	-1	0	0	0	.966	-1	/1-3,O-2,D	-0.2
1977	Oak-A☆	146	485	66	113	21	1	22	63	86	84	.233	.354	.416	111	9	5	4	-1	.932	-23	*3-145/1-1	-1.7
1978	Oak-A	118	285	18	57	10	2	7	23	40	63	.200	.309	.323	82	-6	0	2	-1	.917	-8	*3-106/1-15	-1.7
1979	Oak-A	138	442	54	99	19	1	14	50	72	62	.224	.334	.367	94	-3	4	3	-1	.943	-10	*3-120,1-18/O	-1.5
1980	Oak-A	113	366	45	103	20	3	14	61	44	39	.281	.360	.467	134	17	5	3	-0	.948	-28	3-99,1-10/D	-1.3
1981	*Oak-A	82	243	29	50	7	1	10	31	34	28	.206	.308	.366	98	-0	2	1	-0	.946	-9	3-73/1-2,D	-1.2
1982	Oak-A	129	386	43	97	14	0	9	41	53	50	.251	.345	.358	98	-0	3	1	-0	.970	-7	*3-108,1-16/D	-1.0
1983	Oak-A	137	339	34	79	18	0	12	44	36	52	.233	.312	.392	98	-1	3	5	-2	.996	-5	1-74,3-67/PD	-1.2
1984	Bal-A	127	342	53	74	9	1	22	64	68	69	.216	.348	.442	119	10	1	2	-1	.937	-5	*3-117/1-3,D	0.3
1985	Bal-A	103	217	31	51	8	0	11	18	46	48	.235	.369	.424	120	7	1	1	-0	.933	-3	3-67,D-10/1	0.5
1986	Oak-A	3	2	0	0	0	0	0	0	1	0	.000	.333	.000	0	-0	0	0	0	.000	-0	/3-1	-0.1
Total	11	1106	3125	373	727	126	9	121	396	482	496	.233	.339	.395	106	31	24	22	-6	.941	-96	3-903,1-151/DOP	-9.1

■ GEORGE GROSSART   Grossart, George Albert   b: 4/11/1880, Meadville, Pa.   d: 4/18/02, Pittsburg, Pa.   Deb: 6/7/01

1901	Bos-N	7	26	4	3	0	0	0		1		.115	.115	.115	-30	-4	0			1.000	0	/O-7	-0.5

■ JERRY GROTE   Grote, Gerald Wayne   b: 10/6/42, San Antonio, Tex.   BR/TR, 5'10", 190 lbs.   Deb: 9/21/63

1963	Hou-N	3	5	0	1	0	0	0	1	1	3	.200	.333	.200	61	-0	0	0	0	1.000	-1	/C-3	-0.1
1964	Hou-N	100	298	26	54	9	3	3	24	20	75	.181	.242	.262	44	-22	0	2	-1	.985	2	C-98	-1.8
1966	NY-N	120	317	26	75	12	3	3	31	40	81	.237	.328	.315	82	-7	4	3	-1	.981	5	*C-115/3-2	-0.1
1967	NY-N	120	344	25	67	8	0	4	23	14	65	.195	.228	.253	38	-28	2	2	-1	.990	2	*C-119	-2.3
1968	NY-N★	124	404	29	114	18	0	3	31	44	81	.282	.357	.349	112	7	1	5	-3	.994	7	*C-115	2.3
1969	*NY-N	113	365	38	92	12	3	6	40	32	59	.252	.314	.351	84	-8	2	1	0	.991	19	*C-112	1.8
1970	NY-N	126	415	38	106	14	2	3	34	36	39	.255	.316	.308	68	-18	2	1	0	.991	10	*C-125	-0.2
1971	NY-N	125	403	35	109	25	0	2	35	40	47	.270	.339	.347	96	-1	1	4	-2	.990	5	*C-122	0.7
1972	NY-N	64	205	15	43	5	1	3	21	26	27	.210	.308	.288	72	-7	1	0	0	.998	5	C-59/3-3,O	-0.1
1973	*NY-N	84	285	17	73	10	2	1	32	13	23	.256	.291	.316	69	-12	0	0	0	.995	9	C-81/3-2	0.0
1974	NY-N★	97	319	25	82	8	1	5	36	33	33	.257	.331	.335	88	-5	0	1	-1	.988	-3	C-94	-0.5
1975	NY-N	119	386	28	114	14	5	2	39	38	23	.295	.360	.373	109	5	0	1	-1	**.995**	6	*C-111	1.6
1976	NY-N	101	323	30	88	14	2	4	28	38	19	.272	.351	.365	110	5	1	2	-1	.993	12	C-95/O-2	1.9
1977	NY-N	42	115	8	31	3	1	0	7	9	12	.270	.333	.313	78	-3	0	0	0	1.000	-2	C-28,3-11	-0.5
	*LA-N	18	27	3	7	0	0	0	4	2	5	.259	.310	.259	55	-2	0	1	-1	1.000	4	C-16/3-2	0.2
	Yr	60	142	11	38	3	1	0	11	11	17	.268	.329	.303	73	-5	0	1	-1	1.000	2	C-44,3-13	-0.3
1978	*LA-N	41	70	5	19	5	0	0	9	10	5	.271	.363	.343	98	0	0	0	0	.985	8	C-32/3-7	0.7
1981	KC-A	22	56	4	17	3	1	0	9	3	2	.304	.350	.446	129	2	1	0	0	1.000	4	C-22	0.7
	LA-N	2	2	0	0	0	0	0	0	0	0	.000	.000	.000	-99	-1	0	0	0	1.000	0	/C-1	0.0
Total	16	1421	4339	352	1092	160	22	39	404	399	600	.252	.318	.326	83	-95	15	23	-9	.991	85	*C-1348/3-27,O	4.5

■ JEFF GROTEWOLD   Grotewold, Jeffrey Scott   b: 12/8/65, Madera, Cal.   BL/TR, 6', 215 lbs.   Deb: 4/12/92

1992	Phi-N	72	65	7	13	2	0	3	9	16	9	.200	.307	.369	91	-1	0	0	0	1.000	-1	/C-2,O-2,1	-0.2

■ JOHNNY GROTH   Groth, John Thomas   b: 7/23/26, Chicago, Ill.   BR/TR, 6', 182 lbs.   Deb: 9/5/46

1946	Det-A	4	9	1	0	0	0	0	0	0	3	.000	.000	.000	-94	-2	0	0	0	1.000	-1	/O-4	-0.4
1947	Det-A	2	4	1	1	0	0	0	0	2	1	.250	.500	.250	109	0	0	0	0	1.000	1	/O-1	0.1
1948	Det-A	6	17	3	8	3	0	1	5	1	1	.471	.500	.824	242	3	0	0	0	.900	0	/O-4	0.3
1949	Det-A	103	348	60	102	19	5	11	73	65	27	.293	.407	.471	132	17	3	7	-3	.966	1	O-99	0.9
1950	Det-A	157	566	95	173	30	8	12	85	95	27	.306	.407	.451	116	16	1	5	-3	.985	-12	*O-157	-0.6
1951	Det-A	118	428	41	128	29	1	3	49	31	32	.299	.349	.393	100	-1	1	1	-0	**.993**	-1	*O-112	-0.5
1952	Det-A	141	524	56	149	22	2	4	51	51	39	.284	.348	.357	96	-3	2	10	-5	.986	0	*O-139	-1.4
1953	StL-A	141	557	65	141	27	4	10	57	42	53	.253	.308	.370	81	-16	5	6	-2	.991	17	*O-141	-0.7
1954	Chi-A	125	422	41	116	20	0	7	60	42	37	.275	.343	.372	93	-4	3	9	-5	.988	1	*O-125	-1.5
1955	Chi-A	32	77	13	26	7	0	2	11	6	13	.338	.386	.506	135	3	1	0	0	1.000	-0	O-26	0.2
	Was-A	63	183	22	40	4	5	2	17	18	18	.219	.289	.328	69	-9	2	0	1	.984	-1	O-48	-1.1
	Yr	95	260	35	66	11	5	4	28	24	31	.254	.317	.381	89	-5	3	0	1	.989	-1	O-74	-0.9
1956	KC-A	95	244	22	63	13	3	5	37	30	31	.258	.339	.398	94	-2	1	2	-1	1.000	-7	O-84	-1.4
1957	KC-A	55	59	10	15	0	0	0	2	7	6	.254	.333	.254	62	-3	0	0	0	.974	-13	O-50	-1.7
	Det-A	38	103	11	30	10	0	0	16	6	7	.291	.336	.388	95	-1	0	0	0	1.000	-3	O-36	-0.5
	Yr	93	162	21	45	10	0	0	18	13	13	.278	.335	.340	83	-4	0	0	0	.991	-16	O-86	-2.2
1958	Det-A	88	146	24	41	5	2	1	11	13	19	.281	.340	.384	92	-1	1	2	-1	.990	-11	O-80	-1.6
1959	Det-A	55	102	12	24	7	1	1	10	7	14	.235	.284	.353	70	-4	0	0	0	.983	-6	O-41	-0.8
1960	Det-A	25	19	3	7	1	0	0	4	2	1	.368	.455	.421	135	1	0	1	-1	1.000	-3	/O-8	-0.2
Total	15	1248	3808	480	1064	197	31	60	486	419	329	.279	.353	.395	99	-5	19	42	-20	.987	-40	*O-1155	-11.3

■ ROY GROVER   Grover, Roy Arthur   b: 1/17/1892, Snohomish, Wash.   d: 2/7/78, Milwaukie, Ore.   BR/TR, 5'8", 150 lbs.   Deb: 9/13/16

1916	Phi-A	20	77	8	21	1	2	0	7	6	10	.273	.325	.338	104	1	5			.952	-7	2-20	-0.7
1917	Phi-A	141	482	45	108	15	7	0	34	43	53	.224	.292	.284	77	-14	12			.960	5	*2-139	-0.2
1919	Phi-A	22	56	8	13	1	0	0	2	5	6	.232	.295	.250	53	-3	0			.915	-6	2-12/3-3	-0.9
	Was-A	24	75	6	14	0	0	0	7	6	10	.187	.256	.187	25	-7	2			.947	-4	2-24	-1.1
	Yr	46	131	14	27	1	0	0	9	11	16	.206	.273	.214	37	-11	2			.936	-10	2-36/3-3	-2.0
Total	3	207	690	67	156	17	9	0	50	60	79	.226	.292	.277	72	-24	19			.956	-12	2-195/3-3	-2.9

■ HARVEY GRUBB   Grubb, Harvey Harrison   b: 9/18/1890, Lexington, N.C.   d: 1/25/70, Corpus Christi, Tex.   BR/TR, 6', 165 lbs.   Deb: 9/27/12

1912	Cle-A	1	0	0	0	0	0	0	0	0		—	1.000	—	187	0	0			1.000	-0	/O-1	0.0

YEAR	TM/L	G	AB	R	H	2B	3B	HR	RBI	BB	SO	AVG	OBP	SLG	PRO+	BR/A	SB	CS	SBR	FA	FR	G/POS	TPR

■ JOHNNY GRUBB Grubb, John Maywood b: 8/4/48, Richmond, Va. BL/TR, 6'3", 188 lbs. Deb: 9/10/72

YEAR	TM/L	G	AB	R	H	2B	3B	HR	RBI	BB	SO	AVG	OBP	SLG	PRO+	BR/A	SB	CS	SBR	FA	FR	G/POS	TPR
1972	SD-N	7	21	4	7	1	1	0	1	1	3	.333	.364	.476	147	1	0	1	-1	1.000	0	/O-6	0.1
1973	SD-N	113	389	52	121	22	3	8	37	37	50	.311	.374	.445	137	19	9	3	1	.988	7	*O-102/3-2	2.2
1974	SD-N★	140	444	53	127	20	4	8	42	46	47	.286	.358	.403	118	10	4	0	1	.976	12	*O-122/3-2	1.9
1975	SD-N	144	553	72	149	36	2	4	38	59	59	.269	.345	.363	103	2	2	7	-4	.991	-4	*O-139	-1.1
1976	SD-N	109	384	54	109	22	1	5	27	65	53	.284	.393	.385	132	19	1	2	-1	.974	-9	O-98/1-9,3	0.4
1977	Cle-A	34	93	8	28	3	3	2	14	19	18	.301	.425	.462	146	7	0	3	-2	1.000	-0	O-28/D-4	0.4
1978	Cle-A	113	378	54	100	16	6	14	61	59	60	.265	.367	.450	130	16	5	1	1	.973	5	*O-110	1.8
	Tex-A	21	33	8	13	3	0	1	6	11	5	.394	.545	.576	215	6	1	1	-0	1.000	-1	O-13/D-3	0.5
	Yr	134	411	62	113	19	6	15	67	70	65	.275	.383	.460	137	22	6	2	1	.974	5	*O-123/D-3	2.3
1979	Tex-A	102	289	42	79	14	0	10	37	34	44	.273	.352	.426	110	4	2	4	-2	.986	-8	O-82	-0.8
1980	Tex-A	110	274	40	76	12	1	9	32	42	35	.277	.377	.427	124	10	2	3	-1	.952	-7	O-77/D-8	0.0
1981	Tex-A	67	199	26	46	9	1	3	26	23	25	.231	.317	.332	92	-2	0	3	-2	.990	-4	O-58	-1.0
1982	Tex-A	103	308	35	86	13	3	3	26	39	37	.279	.371	.370	110	6	0	3	-2	.965	-6	O-77,D-18	-0.4
1983	Det-A	57	134	20	34	5	2	4	22	28	17	.254	.390	.410	124	6	0	0	0	1.000	-3	O-26,D-18	0.1
1984	*Det-A	86	176	25	47	5	0	8	17	36	36	.267	.397	.432	130	9	1	0	0	1.000	-6	O-36,D-33	0.2
1985	Det-A	78	155	19	38	7	1	5	25	24	25	.245	.350	.400	106	2	0	1	-1	.1.000	-3	D-33,O-18	-0.2
1986	Det-A	81	210	32	70	13	1	13	51	28	28	.333	.417	.590	171	21	0	1	-1	1.000	-2	D-52,O-19	1.6
1987	*Det-A	59	114	9	23	6	0	2	13	15	16	.202	.295	.307	63	-6	0	0	0	1.000	-4	O-31,D-16/3	-1.0
Total	16	1424	4154	553	1153	207	29	99	475	566	558	.278	.369	.413	121	130	27	33	-12	.981	-31	*O-1042,D-185/13	4.7

■ FRANK GRUBE Grube, Franklin Thomas "Hans" b: 1/7/05, Easton, Pa. d: 7/2/45, New York, N.Y. BR/TR, 5'9", 190 lbs. Deb: 5/12/31

YEAR	TM/L	G	AB	R	H	2B	3B	HR	RBI	BB	SO	AVG	OBP	SLG	PRO+	BR/A	SB	CS	SBR	FA	FR	G/POS	TPR
1931	Chi-A	88	265	29	58	13	1	2	24	22	22	.219	.284	.294	55	-18	2	2	1	.977	-10	C-81	-2.2
1932	Chi-A	93	277	36	78	16	2	0	31	33	13	.282	.362	.354	92	-2	6	1	1	.957	-2	C-92	0.2
1933	Chi-A	85	256	23	59	13	0	0	23	38	20	.230	.334	.281	67	-11	1	1	-0	.984	-7	C-83	-1.3
1934	StL-A	65	170	22	49	10	0	0	11	24	11	.288	.379	.347	82	-4	2	1	0	.963	-6	C-55	-0.2
1935	StL-A	3	6	3	2	1	0	0	0	0	1	.333	.333	.500	108	0	0	0	0	1.000	0	/C-3	0.0
	Chi-A	9	19	1	7	2	0	0	6	3	2	.368	.455	.474	137	1	0	0	0	.944	3	/C-9	0.4
	Yr	12	25	4	9	3	0	0	6	3	3	.360	.429	.480	131	1	0	0	0	.955	3	C-12	0.4
1936	Chi-A	33	93	6	15	2	1	0	11	9	15	.161	.235	.204	9	-14	1	0	0	.991	2	C-32	-0.9
1941	StL-A	18	39	1	6	2	0	0	1	2	4	.154	.195	.205	6	-5	0	0	0	.951	3	C-18	-0.2
Total	7	394	1125	121	274	59	5	1	107	131	88	.244	.326	.308	67	-52	12	5	1	.970	-13	C-373	-4.2

■ KELLY GRUBER Gruber, Kelly Wayne b: 2/26/62, Houston, Tex. BR/TR, 6', 185 lbs. Deb: 4/20/84

YEAR	TM/L	G	AB	R	H	2B	3B	HR	RBI	BB	SO	AVG	OBP	SLG	PRO+	BR/A	SB	CS	SBR	FA	FR	G/POS	TPR
1984	Tor-A	15	16	1	1	0	0	1	2	0	5	.063	.063	.250	-18	-3	0	0	0	.933	1	3-12/O-2,S	-0.1
1985	Tor-A	5	13	0	3	0	0	0	1	0	3	.231	.231	.231	26	-1	0	0	0	1.000	-1	/3-5,2-1	-0.2
1986	Tor-A	87	143	20	28	4	1	5	15	5	27	.196	.223	.343	50	-10	2	5	-2	.940	7	3-42,2-14,D/OS	-0.6
1987	Tor-A	138	341	50	80	14	3	12	36	17	70	.235	.285	.399	77	-12	12	2	2	.948	3	*3-119,S-21/20D	-0.2
1988	Tor-A	158	569	75	158	33	5	16	81	38	92	.278	.331	.438	113	9	23	5	4	.971	25	*3-156/2-7,OSD	3.7
1989	*Tor-A☆	135	545	83	158	24	4	18	73	30	60	.290	.330	.448	120	12	10	5	0	.945	19	*3-119,O-16/SD	3.2
1990	Tor-A★	150	592	92	162	36	6	31	118	48	94	.274	.336	.512	132	23	14	2	3	.955	-3	*3-145/O-6,D	2.3
1991	*Tor-A	113	429	58	108	18	2	20	65	31	70	.252	.311	.443	102	0	12	7	-1	.962	4	*3-111/D-2	0.4
1992	*Tor-A	120	446	42	102	16	3	11	43	26	72	.229	.277	.352	72	-18	7	7	-2	.949	-4	*3-120	-2.4
1993	Cal-A	18	65	10	18	3	0	3	9	2	11	.277	.309	.462	101	-0	0	0	0	.938	6	3-17/O-1,D	0.6
Total	10	939	3159	431	818	148	24	117	443	197	504	.259	.310	.432	102	-1	80	33	4	.955	64	3-846/O-38,2SD	6.7

■ SIG GRYSKA Gryska, Sigmund Stanley b: 11/4/15, Chicago, Ill. BR/TR, 5'11.5", 173 lbs. Deb: 9/28/38

YEAR	TM/L	G	AB	R	H	2B	3B	HR	RBI	BB	SO	AVG	OBP	SLG	PRO+	BR/A	SB	CS	SBR	FA	FR	G/POS	TPR
1938	StL-A	7	21	3	10	2	1	0	4	3	3	.476	.542	.667	202	3	0	0	0	.912	1	/S-7	0.4
1939	StL-A	18	49	4	13	2	0	0	8	6	10	.265	.345	.306	66	-2	3	1	0	.873	-4	S-14	-0.5
Total	2	25	70	7	23	4	1	0	12	9	13	.329	.405	.414	107	1	3	1	0	.887	-4	/S-21	-0.1

◧ MARV GUDAT Gudat, Marvin John b: 8/27/05, Goliad, Tex. d: 3/1/54, Los Angeles, Cal. BL/TL, 5'11", 162 lbs. Deb: 5/21/29

YEAR	TM/L	G	AB	R	H	2B	3B	HR	RBI	BB	SO	AVG	OBP	SLG	PRO+	BR/A	SB	CS	SBR	FA	FR	G/POS	TPR
1929	Cin-N	9	10	0	2	0	0	0	0	0	0	.200	.200	.200	-1	-2	0			.800	-1	/P-7	0.0
1932	*Chi-N	60	94	15	24	4	1	0	15	16	10	.255	.369	.351	96	0	0			.933	-6	O-14/1-8,P	-0.7
Total	2	69	104	15	26	4	1	1	15	16	10	.250	.355	.337	87	-1	0			.800	-6	/O-14,1-8,P	-0.7

■ MIKE GUERRA Guerra, Fermin (Romero) b: 10/11/12, Havana, Cuba d: 10/9/92, Miami Beach, Fla. BR/TR, 5'9", 162 lbs. Deb: 9/19/37

YEAR	TM/L	G	AB	R	H	2B	3B	HR	RBI	BB	SO	AVG	OBP	SLG	PRO+	BR/A	SB	CS	SBR	FA	FR	G/POS	TPR
1937	Was-A	1	3	0	0	0	0	0	0	0	2	.000	.000	.000	-99	-1	0	0	0	.750	-1	/C-1	-0.1
1944	Was-A	75	210	29	59	7	2	1	29	13	14	.281	.323	.348	96	-2	8	2	1	.960	-5	C-58/O-1	-0.2
1945	Was-A	56	138	11	29	1	1	0	15	10	12	.210	.268	.254	57	-8	4	1	1	.990	5	C-38	0.0
1946	Was-A	41	83	3	21	2	1	0	4	5	6	.253	.295	.301	71	-3	1	0	0	.938	-2	C-27	-0.4
1947	Phi-A	72	209	20	45	2	2	0	18	10	15	.215	.251	.244	37	-18	1	2	-1	.964	1	C-62	-1.3
1948	Phi-A	53	142	18	30	4	2	1	23	18	13	.211	.300	.289	57	-9	2	3	-1	.973	-0	C-47	-0.7
1949	Phi-A	98	298	41	79	14	3	1	31	37	26	.265	.346	.349	87	-6	3	0	1	.982	-5	C-95	-0.2
1950	Phi-A	87	252	25	71	10	4	2	26	16	12	.282	.325	.377	81	-8	1	0	0	.990	-6	C-78	-1.0
1951	Bos-A	10	32	1	5	0	0	0	2	6	5	.156	.289	.156	21	-3	1	0	0	1.000	-1	C-10	-0.3
	Was-A	72	214	20	43	2	1	1	20	16	18	.201	.257	.234	34	-20	4	4	-1	.977	-11	C-66	-2.9
	Yr	82	246	21	48	2	1	1	22	22	23	.195	.261	.224	32	-23	5	4	-1	.982	-11	C-76	-3.2
Total	9	565	1581	168	382	42	14	9	168	131	123	.242	.300	.303	65	-77	25	12	0	.975	-20	C-482/O-1	-7.1

■ JUAN GUERRERO Guerrero, Juan Antonio b: 2/1/67, Los Llanos, D.R. BR/TR, 5'11", 160 lbs. Deb: 4/9/92

YEAR	TM/L	G	AB	R	H	2B	3B	HR	RBI	BB	SO	AVG	OBP	SLG	PRO+	BR/A	SB	CS	SBR	FA	FR	G/POS	TPR
1992	Hou-N	79	125	8	25	4	2	1	14	10	32	.200	.265	.288	59	-7	1	0	0	.980	-7	S-19,3-12/O2	-1.4

■ MARIO GUERRERO Guerrero, Mario Miguel (Abud) b: 9/28/49, Santo Domingo, D.R. BR/TR, 5'10", 155 lbs. Deb: 4/8/73

YEAR	TM/L	G	AB	R	H	2B	3B	HR	RBI	BB	SO	AVG	OBP	SLG	PRO+	BR/A	SB	CS	SBR	FA	FR	G/POS	TPR
1973	Bos-A	66	219	19	51	5	2	0	11	10	21	.233	.273	.274	51	-14	2	2	-1	.974	1	S-46,2-24	-0.8
1974	Bos-A	93	284	18	70	6	2	0	23	13	22	.246	.284	.282	59	-15	3	1	0	.969	-0	S-93	-0.4
1975	StL-N	64	184	17	44	9	0	1	11	10	7	.239	.286	.288	57	-11	0	0	0	.955	6	S-64	0.1
1976	Cal-A	83	268	24	76	12	0	1	18	7	12	.284	.309	.340	96	-2	0	0	0	.973	-12	2-41,S-41/D	-0.9
1977	Cal-A	86	244	17	69	8	2	1	28	4	16	.283	.294	.344	76	-8	0	0	0	.985	-2	S-31,D-19,2	-0.7
1978	Oak-A	143	505	27	139	18	4	3	38	15	35	.275	.304	.345	87	-10	0	5	-3	.958	-40	*S-142	-3.7
1979	Oak-A	46	166	12	38	5	0	0	18	6	7	.229	.256	.259	42	-14	0	1	-1	.952	-4	S-43	-1.3
1980	Oak-A	116	381	32	91	16	2	1	23	19	32	.239	.277	.307	64	-19	3	3	-1	.962	-42	*S-116	-5.0
Total	8	697	2251	166	578	79	12	7	170	84	152	.257	.288	.312	69	-93	8	12	-5	.961	-94	S-576/2-77,D	-12.7

■ PEDRO GUERRERO Guerrero, Pedro b: 6/29/56, San Pedro De Macoris, D.R. BR/TR, 6', 195 lbs. Deb: 9/22/78

YEAR	TM/L	G	AB	R	H	2B	3B	HR	RBI	BB	SO	AVG	OBP	SLG	PRO+	BR/A	SB	CS	SBR	FA	FR	G/POS	TPR
1978	LA-N	5	8	3	5	0	1	0	1	0	0	.625	.625	.875	316	2	0	0	0	1.000	0	/1-4	0.2
1979	LA-N	25	62	7	15	2	0	2	9	1	14	.242	.254	.371	69	-3	2	0	1	1.000	-0	O-12/1-8,3	-0.6
1980	LA-N	75	183	27	59	9	1	7	31	12	31	.322	.364	.497	141	9	2	1	0	.987	-3	O-40,2-12/31	0.6
1981	*LA-N★	98	347	46	104	17	2	12	48	34	57	.300	.366	.464	139	17	5	9	-4	.974	3	O-75,3-21/1	1.4
1982	LA-N	150	575	87	175	27	5	32	100	65	89	.304	.380	.536	157	43	22	5	4	.934	9	O-137,3-24	4.6
1983	*LA-N★	160	584	87	174	28	6	32	103	72	110	.298	.377	.531	150	38	23	7	3	.934	6	*3-157/1-2	4.6
1984	LA-N	144	535	85	162	29	4	16	72	49	105	.303	.362	.462	132	22	9	8	-2	.917	-8	3-76,O-58,1	0.8
1985	*LA-N†	137	487	99	156	22	2	33	87	83	68	.320	**.425**	**.577**	**183**	**56**	12	4	1	.974	8	O-81,3-44,1	6.3
1986	LA-N	31	61	7	15	3	0	5	10	2	19	.246	.281	.541	131	2	0	0	0	1.000	-2	O-10/1-4	-0.1

YEAR	TM/L	G	AB	R	H	2B	3B	HR	RBI	BB	SO	AVG	OBP	SLG	PRO+	BR/A	SB	CS	SBR	FA	FR	G/POS	TPR
1987	LA-N★	152	545	89	184	25	2	27	89	74	85	.338	.421	.539	156	46	9	7	-2	.971	1	*O-109,1-40	3.8
1988	LA-N	59	215	24	64	7	1	5	35	25	33	.298	.379	.409	130	9	2	1	0	.895	-13	3-45,1-15/O	-0.6
	StL-N	44	149	16	40	7	1	5	30	21	26	.268	.366	.430	126	6	2	0	1	1.000	-2	1-37/O-7	0.1
	Yr	103	364	40	104	14	2	10	65	46	59	.286	.373	.418	128	15	4	1	1	.998	-15	1-52,3-45/O	-0.5
1989	StL-N★	162	570	60	177	42	1	17	117	79	84	.311	.398	.477	145	35	2	0	1	.990	-14	*1-160	0.9
1990	StL-N	136	498	42	140	31	1	13	80	44	70	.281	.341	.426	109	6	1	1	-0	.989	-10	*1-132	-1.5
1991	StL-N	115	427	41	116	12	1	8	70	37	46	.272	.331	.361	94	-3	4	2	0	.985	-8	*1-112	-1.9
1992	StL-N	43	146	10	32	6	1	1	16	11	25	.219	.274	.295	63	-7	2	2	-1	.988	-7	1-28,O-10	-1.9
Total	15	1536	5392	730	1618	267	29	215	898	609	862	.300	.374	.480	138	277	97	47	1	.988	-49	1-573,O-541,3/2	16.7

■ OZZIE GUILLEN

Guillen, Oswaldo Jose (Barrios)   b: 1/20/64, Ocualre Del Tuy, Venezuela   BL/TR, 5'11", 150 lbs.   Deb: 4/9/85

YEAR	TM/L	G	AB	R	H	2B	3B	HR	RBI	BB	SO	AVG	OBP	SLG	PRO+	BR/A	SB	CS	SBR	FA	FR	G/POS	TPR
1985	Chi-A	150	491	71	134	21	9	1	33	12	36	.273	.292	.358	74	-18	7	4	-0	**.980**	12	*S-150	0.6
1986	Chi-A	159	547	58	137	19	4	2	47	12	52	.250	.286	.311	55	-34	8	4	0	.970	14	*S-157/D-1	-0.5
1987	Chi-A	149	560	64	156	22	7	2	51	22	52	.279	.307	.354	73	-22	25	8	3	.975	13	*S-149	0.6
1988	Chi-A†	156	566	58	148	16	7	0	39	25	40	.261	.295	.314	71	-22	25	13	-0	.977	**43**	*S-156	3.3
1989	Chi-A	155	597	63	151	20	8	1	54	15	48	.253	.271	.318	67	-27	36	17	1	.973	14	*S-155	0.0
1990	Chi-A★	160	516	61	144	21	4	1	58	26	37	.279	.315	.341	85	-11	13	17	-6	.977	3	*S-159	-0.1
1991	Chi-A★	154	524	52	143	20	3	3	49	11	38	.273	.288	.340	75	-19	21	15	-3	.970	-3	*S-149	-1.4
1992	Chi-A	12	40	5	8	4	0	0	7	1	5	.200	.220	.300	45	-3	1	0	0	1.000	1	S-12	-0.1
1993	*Chi-A	134	457	44	128	23	4	4	50	10	41	.280	.296	.374	80	-14	5	4	-1	.972	-12	*S-133	-1.6
1994	Chi-A	100	365	46	105	9	5	1	39	14	35	.288	.314	.348	71	-16	5	4	-1	.959	-23	S-99	-3.0
Total	10	1329	4663	522	1254	175	51	15	427	148	384	.269	.292	.338	72	-185	146	86	-8	.974	62	*S-1319/D-1	-2.2

■ BOBBY GUINDON

Guindon, Robert Joseph   b: 9/4/43, Brookline, Mass.   BL/TL, 6'2", 185 lbs.   Deb: 9/19/64

YEAR	TM/L	G	AB	R	H	2B	3B	HR	RBI	BB	SO	AVG	OBP	SLG	PRO+	BR/A	SB	CS	SBR	FA	FR	G/POS	TPR
1964	Bos-A	5	8	0	1	1	0	0	1	1	4	.125	.222	.250	30	-0	0	0	0	1.000	-0	/1-1,O-1	-0.1

■ BEN GUINEY

Guiney, Benjamin Franklin   b: 11/16/1858, Detroit, Mich.   d: 12/5/30, Detroit, Mich.   BB/TR, 6', 170 lbs.   Deb: 9/4/1883

YEAR	TM/L	G	AB	R	H	2B	3B	HR	RBI	BB	SO	AVG	OBP	SLG	PRO+	BR/A	SB	CS	SBR	FA	FR	G/POS	TPR
1883	Det-N	1	5	1	1	0	0	0	0	0	1	.200	.200	.200	23	-0				.000	-1	/O-1	-0.1
1884	Det-N	2	7	0	0	0	0	0	0	0	3	.000	.000	.000	-99	-2				.750	-2	/C-2	-0.3
Total	2	3	12	1	1	0	0	0	0	0	4	.083	.083	.083	-51	-2				.750	-2	/C-2,O-1	-0.4

■ BEN GUINTINI

Guintini, Benjamin John   b: 1/13/20, Los Banos, Cal.   BR/TR, 6'1.5", 190 lbs.   Deb: 4/21/46

YEAR	TM/L	G	AB	R	H	2B	3B	HR	RBI	BB	SO	AVG	OBP	SLG	PRO+	BR/A	SB	CS	SBR	FA	FR	G/POS	TPR
1946	Pit-N	2	3	0	0	0	0	0	0	0	0	.000	.000	.000	-98	-1	0			1.000	-0	/O-1	-0.1
1950	Phi-A	3	4	0	0	0	0	0	0	0	0	.000	.000	.000	-99	-1	0	0	0	1.000	-0	/O-1	-0.1
Total	2	5	7	0	0	0	0	0	0	0	0	.000	.000	.000	-99	-2	0	0	0	1.000	-0	/O-2	-0.2

■ LOU GUISTO

Guisto, Louis Joseph   b: 1/16/1895, Napa, Cal.   d: 10/15/89, Napa, Cal.   BR/TR, 5'11", 193 lbs.   Deb: 9/10/16

YEAR	TM/L	G	AB	R	H	2B	3B	HR	RBI	BB	SO	AVG	OBP	SLG	PRO+	BR/A	SB	CS	SBR	FA	FR	G/POS	TPR
1916	Cle-A	6	19	2	3	0	0	0	2	4	3	.158	.304	.158	37	-1	1			1.000	0	/1-6	-0.2
1917	Cle-A	73	200	9	37	4	2	0	29	25	18	.185	.282	.225	51	-11	3			.989	-1	1-59	-1.6
1921	Cle-A	2	2	0	1	0	0	0	1	0	1	.500	.500	.500	153	0	0	0	0	1.000	0	/1-1	0.0
1922	Cle-A	35	84	7	21	10	1	0	9	2	7	.250	.276	.393	72	-4	0	0	0	.995	1	1-24	-0.4
1923	Cle-A	40	144	17	26	5	0	0	18	15	15	.181	.262	.215	27	-15	1	1	-0	.988	1	1-40	-1.6
Total	5	156	449	35	88	19	3	0	59	46	44	.196	.277	.252	47	-31	5	1		.990	1	1-130	-3.8

■ BRAD GULDEN

Gulden, Bradley Lee   b: 6/10/56, New Ulm, Minn.   BL/TR, 5'11", 180 lbs.   Deb: 9/22/78

YEAR	TM/L	G	AB	R	H	2B	3B	HR	RBI	BB	SO	AVG	OBP	SLG	PRO+	BR/A	SB	CS	SBR	FA	FR	G/POS	TPR
1978	LA-N	3	4	0	0	0	0	0	0	0	2	.000	.000	.000	-99	-1	0	0	0	1.000	1	/C-3	0.0
1979	NY-A	40	92	10	15	4	0	0	6	9	16	.163	.238	.207	21	-10	0	1	-1	.995	11	C-40	0.2
1980	NY-A	2	3	1	1	0	0	0	2	0	0	.333	.333	1.333	340	1	0	0	0	1.000	-1	/C-2	0.0
1981	Sea-A	8	16	0	3	2	0	0	1	0	2	.188	.188	.313	40	-1	0	0	0	1.000	1	/C-6	0.1
1982	Mon-N	5	6	1	0	0	0	0	0	1	1	.000	.143	.000	-56	-1	0	0	0	1.000	1	/C-2	0.0
1984	Cin-N	107	292	31	66	8	2	4	33	33	35	.226	.309	.308	71	-11	2	2	-1	.975	-4	*C-100	-1.2
1986	SF-N	17	22	2	2	0	0	1	2	5	5	.091	.167	.091	-28	-4	0	0	0	1.000	0	C-10	-0.5
Total	7	182	435	45	87	14	2	5	43	45	61	.200	.278	.276	53	-27	2	3		.982	9	C-163	-1.4

■ TOM GULLEY

Gulley, Thomas Jefferson   b: 12/25/1899, Garner, N.C.   d: 11/24/66, St.Charles, Ark.   BL/TR, 5'11", 178 lbs.   Deb: 8/24/23

YEAR	TM/L	G	AB	R	H	2B	3B	HR	RBI	BB	SO	AVG	OBP	SLG	PRO+	BR/A	SB	CS	SBR	FA	FR	G/POS	TPR
1923	Cle-A	2	3	1	1	0	0	0	0	0	0	.333	.333	.667	159	0	0	0	0	1.000	-0	/O-1	0.0
1924	Cle-A	8	20	4	3	0	1	0	1	3	2	.150	.261	.250	32	-2	0	0	0	.933	0	/O-5	-0.2
1926	Chi-A	16	35	5	8	3	1	0	8	5	2	.229	.325	.371	84	-1	0	0	0	1.000	-2	O-12	-0.3
Total	3	26	58	10	12	4	2	0	9	8	4	.207	.303	.345	69	-3	0	0	0	.971	-2	/O-18	-0.5

■ TED GULLIC

Gullic, Theodore Jasper   b: 1/2/07, Koshkonong, Mo.   BR/TR, 6'2", 175 lbs.   Deb: 4/15/30

YEAR	TM/L	G	AB	R	H	2B	3B	HR	RBI	BB	SO	AVG	OBP	SLG	PRO+	BR/A	SB	CS	SBR	FA	FR	G/POS	TPR
1930	StL-A	92	308	39	77	7	5	4	44	27	43	.250	.310	.344	64	-17	4	0	1	.967	3	O-82/1-3	-1.8
1933	StL-A	104	304	34	74	18	3	5	35	15	38	.243	.281	.372	67	-15	3	1	0	.988	10	O-36,3-33,1	-0.6
Total	2	196	612	73	151	25	8	9	79	42	81	.247	.296	.358	65	-33	7	1	2	.975	12	O-118/3-33,1	-2.4

■ GLENN GULLIVER

Gulliver, Glenn James   b: 10/15/54, Detroit, Mich.   BL/TR, 5'11", 175 lbs.   Deb: 7/17/82

YEAR	TM/L	G	AB	R	H	2B	3B	HR	RBI	BB	SO	AVG	OBP	SLG	PRO+	BR/A	SB	CS	SBR	FA	FR	G/POS	TPR
1982	Bal-A	50	145	24	29	7	0	1	5	37	18	.200	.363	.269	77	-3	0	0	0	.970	-4	3-50	-0.8
1983	Bal-A	23	47	5	10	3	0	0	2	9	5	.213	.339	.277	73	-1	0	1	-1	1.000	0	3-21	-0.2
Total	2	73	192	29	39	10	0	1	7	46	23	.203	.357	.271	76	-4	0	1	-1	.978	-4	/3-71	-1.0

■ FRED GUNKLE

Gunkle, Frederick W.   b: Dubuque, Iowa   Deb: 5/17/1879

YEAR	TM/L	G	AB	R	H	2B	3B	HR	RBI	BB	SO	AVG	OBP	SLG	PRO+	BR/A	SB	CS	SBR	FA	FR	G/POS	TPR
1879	Cle-N	1	3	1	0	0	0	0	0	0	1	.000	.000	.000	-99	-1				1.000	-2	/O-1,C-1	-0.3

■ HY GUNNING

Gunning, Hyland   b: 8/6/1888, Maplewood, N.J.   d: 3/28/75, Togus, Me.   BL/TR, 6'1.5", 189 lbs.   Deb: 8/8/11

YEAR	TM/L	G	AB	R	H	2B	3B	HR	RBI	BB	SO	AVG	OBP	SLG	PRO+	BR/A	SB	CS	SBR	FA	FR	G/POS	TPR
1911	Bos-A	4	9	0	1	0	0	0	2	2		.111	.273	.111	9	-1	0			1.000	-1	/1-4	-0.2

■ TOM GUNNING

Gunning, Thomas Francis   b: 3/4/1862, Newmarket, N.H.   d: 3/17/31, Fall River, Mass.   BR/TR, 5'10", 160 lbs.   Deb: 7/26/1884   U

YEAR	TM/L	G	AB	R	H	2B	3B	HR	RBI	BB	SO	AVG	OBP	SLG	PRO+	BR/A	SB	CS	SBR	FA	FR	G/POS	TPR
1884	Bos-N	12	45	4	5	1	1	0	1	1	12	.111	.130	.178	-4	-5				.914	-5	C-12	-0.9
1885	Bos-N	48	174	17	32	3	0	0	15	5	29	.184	.207	.201	34	-12				.877	-7	C-48	-1.5
1886	Bos-N	27	98	15	22	2	1	0	7	3	19	.224	.248	.265	58	-5	3			.892	-5	C-27	-0.6
1887	Phi-N	28	104	22	27	6	1	1	16	5	6	.260	.306	.365	81	-3	18			.895	6	C-28	0.5
1888	Phi-a	23	92	18	18	0	0	0	5	2		.196	.237	.196	40	-6	14			.894	-1	C-23	-0.5
1889	Phi-a	8	24	3	6	0	1	1	2	0	4	.250	.250	.458	101	-0	3			.838	-2	/C-8	-0.1
Total	6	146	537	79	110	12	4	2	46	16	70	.205	.235	.253	50	-32	38			.887	-15	C-146	-3.1

■ JOE GUNSON

Gunson, Joseph Brook   b: 3/23/1863, Philadelphia, Pa.   d: 11/15/42, Philadelphia, Pa.   BR/TR, 5'6", 160 lbs.   Deb: 6/14/1884

YEAR	TM/L	G	AB	R	H	2B	3B	HR	RBI	BB	SO	AVG	OBP	SLG	PRO+	BR/A	SB	CS	SBR	FA	FR	G/POS	TPR
1884	Was-U	45	166	15	23	2	0	0		3		.139	.154	.151	-18	-27				.915	10	C-33,O-18	-1.3
1889	KC-a	34	122	15	24	3	1	0	12	3	17	.197	.228	.238	31	-11	2			.862	-6	C-32/O-1,3	-1.3
1892	Bal-N	89	314	35	67	10	5	0	32	16	17	.213	.267	.277	63	-15	2			.921	-1	C-67,O-20/12	-1.1
1893	StL-N	40	151	20	41	5	0	0	15	6	6	.272	.321	.305	66	-7	0			.927	3	C-35/O-5	-0.1
	Cle-N	21	73	11	19	1	0	0	9	6		.260	.316	.274	54	-5	0			.942	2	C-20	-0.1
	Yr	61	224	31	60	6	0	0	24	12	6	.268	.320	.295	62	-12	0			.932	5	C-55/O-5	-0.2
Total	4	229	826	96	174	21	6	0	68	34	40	.211	.254	.251	42	-65	4			.912	8	C-187/O-44,123	-3.9

■ ERNIE GUST

Gust, Ernest Herman Frank "Red"   b: 1/24/1888, Bay City, Mich.   d: 10/26/45, Maupin, Ore.   BR/TR, 6', 170 lbs.   Deb: 8/17/11

YEAR	TM/L	G	AB	R	H	2B	3B	HR	RBI	BB	SO	AVG	OBP	SLG	PRO+	BR/A	SB	CS	SBR	FA	FR	G/POS	TPR
1911	StL-A	3	12	0	0	0	0	0	0	0	0	.000	.000	.000	-99	-3	0			.974	-0	/1-3	-0.4

YEAR	TM/L	G	AB	R	H	2B	3B	HR	RBI	BB	SO	AVG	OBP	SLG	PRO+	BR/A	SB	CS	SBR	FA	FR	G/POS	TPR

■ FRANKIE GUSTINE
Gustine, Frank William   b: 2/20/20, Hoopeston, Ill.   d: 4/1/91, Davenport, Iowa   BR/TR, 6′, 180 lbs.   Deb: 9/13/39   C

1939	Pit-N	22	70	5	13	3	0	0	3	9	4	.186	.278	.229	38	-6	0			.896	4	3-22	-0.2
1940	Pit-N	133	524	59	147	32	7	1	55	35	39	.281	.328	.374	94	-5	7			.941	-8	*2-130	-0.4
1941	Pit-N	121	463	46	125	24	7	1	46	28	38	.270	.313	.359	89	-8	5			.954	-1	*2-104,3-15	-0.1
1942	Pit-N	115	388	34	89	11	4	2	35	29	27	.229	.286	.294	68	-16	5			.954	-10	*2-108/S-2,3C	-2.1
1943	Pit-N	112	414	40	120	21	3	0	43	32	36	.290	.341	.355	98	-1	12			.938	-5	S-68,2-40/1	0.1
1944	Pit-N	127	405	42	93	18	3	2	42	33	41	.230	.288	.304	64	-19	8			.938	-27	*S-116,2-11/3	-3.9
1945	Pit-N	128	478	67	134	27	5	2	66	37	33	.280	.335	.370	92	-5	8			.930	-19	*S-104,2-29/C	-1.5
1946	Pit-N★	131	495	60	128	23	6	8	52	40	52	.259	.318	.378	95	-5	2			.967	8	*2-113,S-13/3	1.2
1947	Pit-N★	156	616	102	183	30	6	9	67	63	65	.297	.364	.409	102	2	5			.944	15	*3-156	1.8
1948	Pit-N★	131	449	68	120	19	2	9	42	42	62	.267	.333	.379	90	-6	5			.947	9	*3-118	0.2
1949	Chi-N	76	261	29	59	13	4	4	27	18	22	.226	.279	.352	70	-12	3			.931	1	3-55,2-16	-1.1
1950	StL-A	9	19	1	3	1	0	0	2	3	8	.158	.273	.211	24	-2	0	1	-1	.857	-0	/3-6	-0.3
Total	12	1261	4582	553	1214	222	47	38	480	369	427	.265	.322	.359	87	-82	60	1		.955	-33	2-551,3-382,S/C1	-6.3

■ BUCKY GUTH
Guth, Charles Henry   b: 8/18/47, Baltimore, Md.   BR/TR, 6′1″, 180 lbs.   Deb: 9/12/72

1972	Min-A	3	3	1	0	0	0	0	0	0	0	.000	.000	.000	-95	-1	0	0	0	1.000	1	/S-1	0.0

▨ CESAR GUTIERREZ
Gutierrez, Cesar Dario "Coca"   b: 1/26/43, Coro, Venez.   BR/TR, 5′9″, 155 lbs.   Deb: 4/16/67

1967	SF-N	18	21	4	3	0	0	0	0	1	4	.143	.217	.143	5	-3	1	0	0	.946	3	S-15/2-1	0.1
1969	SF-N	15	23	4	5	1	0	0	0	6	2	.217	.379	.261	84	-0	1	0	0	.882	-0	/3-7,S-4	0.0
	Det-A	17	49	5	12	1	0	0	0	5	3	.245	.315	.265	61	-2	1	2	-1	.946	1	S-16	0.0
1970	Det-A	135	415	40	101	11	6	0	22	18	39	.243	.276	.299	58	-24	4	3	-1	.957	-18	*S-135	-2.9
1971	Det-A	38	37	8	7	0	0	0	4	0	3	.189	.189	.189	13	-4	0	0	0	.971	5	S-14/3-5,2	0.2
Total	4	223	545	61	128	13	6	0	26	30	51	.235	.279	.281	55	-33	7	5	-1	.955	-9	S-184/3-12,2	-2.6

■ JACKIE GUTIERREZ
Gutierrez, Joaquin Fernando   b: 6/27/60, Cartagena, Colombia   BR/TR, 5′11″, 175 lbs.   Deb: 9/6/83

1983	Bos-A	5	10	2	3	0	0	0	0	1	1	.300	.364	.300	79	-0	0	1	-1	.938	-0	/S-4	-0.1
1984	Bos-A	151	449	55	118	12	3	2	29	15	49	.263	.287	.316	64	-22	12	5	1	.949	-33	*S-150	-4.2
1985	Bos-A	103	275	33	60	5	2	2	21	12	37	.218	.251	.273	42	-22	10	2	2	.943	5	S-99	-0.7
1986	Bal-A	61	145	8	27	3	0	0	4	3	27	.186	.208	.207	14	-17	3	1	0	.990	7	2-53/3-6,D	-0.8
1987	Bal-A	3	1	0	0	0	0	0	0	0	0	.000	.000	.000	-99	-0	0	0	0	.000	0	/2-1,3-1	0.0
1988	Phi-N	33	77	8	19	4	0	0	9	2	9	.247	.266	.299	61	-4	0	0	0	.919	-2	S-22,3-13	-0.6
Total	6	356	957	106	227	24	5	4	63	33	123	.237	.263	.285	50	-66	25	9		.945	-23	S-275/2-54,3D	-6.4

■ RICKY GUTIERREZ
Gutierrez, Ricardo   b: 5/23/70, Miami, Fla.   BR/TR, 6′1″, 175 lbs.   Deb: 4/13/93

1993	SD-N	133	438	76	110	10	5	5	26	50	97	.251	.335	.331	78	-13	4	3	-1	.971	-14	*S-117/2-6,O3	-1.8
1994	SD-N	90	275	27	66	11	2	1	28	32	54	.240	.324	.305	66	-13	2	6	-3	.925	-8	S-78/2-7	-1.8
Total	2	223	713	103	176	21	7	6	54	82	151	.247	.330	.321	73	-26	6	9	-4	.954	-22	S-195/2-13,O3	-3.6

■ DON GUTTERIDGE
Gutteridge, Donald Joseph   b: 6/19/12, Pittsburg, Kan.   BR/TR, 5′10.5″, 165 lbs.   Deb: 9/7/36   MC

1936	StL-N	23	91	13	29	3	4	3	16	1	14	.319	.326	.538	130	3	3			.967	0	3-23	0.4
1937	StL-N	119	447	66	121	26	10	7	61	25	66	.271	.311	.421	95	-4	12			.978	2	*3-105/S-8	0.0
1938	StL-N	142	552	61	141	21	15	9	64	29	49	.255	.293	.397	83	-14	14			.945	0	3-73,S-68	-0.8
1939	StL-N	148	524	71	141	27	4	7	54	27	70	.269	.309	.376	78	-17	5			.934	-18	*3-143/S-2	-3.4
1940	StL-N	69	108	19	29	5	0	3	14	5	15	.269	.301	.398	86	-2	3			.877	-2	3-39	-0.3
1942	StL-A	147	616	90	157	27	11	1	50	59	54	.255	.320	.339	84	-13	16	13	-3	.973	3	*2-145/3-2	-0.5
1943	StL-A	132	538	77	147	35	6	1	36	50	46	.273	.335	.366	103	2	10	9	-2	.958	-31	*2-132	-2.6
1944	*StL-A	148	603	89	148	27	11	1	36	51	63	.245	.304	.342	80	-17	20	8	1	.957	-8	*2-146	-1.6
1945	StL-A	143	543	72	129	24	3	2	49	43	46	.238	.295	.304	70	-21	9	6	-1	.970	-20	*2-128,O-14	-3.7
1946	*Bos-A	22	47	8	11	3	0	1	6	2	7	.234	.265	.362	70	-2	0	0	0	1.000	-1	/2-9,3-8	-0.3
1947	Bos-A	54	131	20	22	2	0	2	5	17	13	.168	.264	.229	35	-11	3	1	0	.938	-1	2-20,3-19	-1.2
1948	Pit-N	4	2	0	0	0	0	0	0	0	1	.000	.000	.000	-98	-1	0			.000	0	H	-0.1
Total	12	1151	4202	586	1075	200	64	39	391	309	444	.256	.308	.362	84	-98	95	37		.964	-76	2-580,3-412/SO	-14.1

■ DOUG GWOSDZ
Gwosdz, Douglas Wayne   b: 6/20/60, Houston, Tex.   BR/TR, 5′11″, 185 lbs.   Deb: 8/17/81

1981	SD-N	16	24	1	4	2	0	0	3	3	6	.167	.259	.250	48	-2	0	0	0	1.000	2	C-13	0.1
1982	SD-N	7	17	1	3	0	0	0	0	2	7	.176	.263	.176	27	-2	0	0	0	1.000	2	/C-7	0.0
1983	SD-N	39	55	7	6	1	0	1	4	7	19	.109	.210	.182	10	-7	0	0	0	.971	2	C-32	-0.5
1984	SD-N	7	8	0	2	0	0	0	1	2	5	.250	.400	.250	86	-0	0	0	0	.963	2	/C-6	0.2
Total	4	69	104	9	15	3	0	1	8	14	37	.144	.246	.202	27	-10	0	0	0	.981	8	/C-58	-0.2

■ TONY GWYNN
Gwynn, Anthony Keith   b: 5/9/60, Los Angeles, Cal.   BL/TL, 5′11″, 200 lbs.   Deb: 7/19/82   F

1982	SD-N	54	190	33	55	12	2	1	17	14	16	.289	.338	.389	109	2	8	3	1	.991	-6	O-52	-0.5
1983	SD-N	86	304	34	94	12	2	1	37	23	21	.309	.358	.372	106	3	7	4	-0	.994	6	O-81	0.6
1984	*SD-N★	158	606	88	213	21	10	5	71	59	23	.351	.411	.444	140	34	33	18	-1	.989	16	*O-156	4.5
1985	SD-N	154	622	90	197	29	5	6	46	45	33	.317	.365	.408	118	15	14	11	-2	.989	17	*O-152	2.5
1986	SD-N★	160	642	107	211	33	7	14	59	52	35	.329	.382	.467	136	31	37	9	6	.989	20	*O-160	5.2
1987	SD-N★	157	589	119	218	36	13	7	54	82	35	.370	.450	.511	160	54	56	12	10	.981	16	*O-156	6.6
1988	SD-N★	133	521	64	163	22	5	7	70	51	40	.313	.374	.415	128	20	26	11	1	.982	3	*O-133	2.1
1989	SD-N★	158	604	82	203	27	7	4	62	56	30	.336	.393	.424	133	27	40	16	2	.984	11	*O-157	3.9
1990	SD-N★	141	573	79	177	29	10	4	72	44	23	.309	.359	.415	112	9	17	8	0	.985	15	*O-141	2.2
1991	SD-N★	134	530	69	168	27	11	4	62	34	19	.317	.355	.432	118	12	8	8	-2	.990	11	*O-134	1.8
1992	SD-N★	128	520	77	165	27	3	6	41	46	16	.317	.373	.415	121	15	3	6	-3	.982	12	*O-127	2.3
1993	SD-N★	122	489	70	175	41	3	7	59	36	19	.358	.403	.497	137	26	14	1	4	.981	4	*O-121	3.0
1994	SD-N★	110	419	79	165	35	1	12	64	48	19	.394	.458	.568	167	43	5	0	2	.985	2	*O-106	4.3
Total	13	1695	6609	991	2204	351	79	78	714	590	329	.333	.389	.446	131	290	268	107	12	.986	121	*O-1676	38.5

■ CHRIS GWYNN
Gwynn, Christopher Karlton   b: 10/13/64, Los Angeles, Cal.   BL/TL, 6′ ″, 200 lbs.   Deb: 8/14/87   F

1987	LA-N	17	32	2	7	1	0	0	2	1	7	.219	.242	.250	32	-3	0	0	0	1.000	-1	O-10	-0.5
1988	LA-N	12	11	1	2	0	0	0	0	1	2	.182	.250	.182	27	-1	0	0	0	.000	-2	/O-4	-0.3
1989	LA-N	32	68	8	16	4	1	0	7	2	9	.235	.257	.324	66	-3	1	0	0	1.000	-2	O-19	-0.6
1990	LA-N	101	141	19	40	2	1	5	22	7	28	.284	.318	.418	104	0	1	0	0	1.000	-9	O-44	-1.1
1991	LA-N	94	139	18	35	5	1	5	22	10	23	.252	.307	.410	102	-0	1	0	0	1.000	-9	O-41	-1.0
1992	KC-A	34	84	10	24	3	1	1	7	3	10	.286	.310	.405	96	-1	0	0	0	1.000	-5	O-19/D-2	-0.3
1993	KC-A	103	287	36	86	14	4	1	25	24	34	.300	.356	.387	94	-2	0	1	-1	.994	0	O-83/1-1,D	-0.4
1994	LA-N	58	71	9	19	0	0	3	13	7	7	.268	.333	.394	94	-1	0	2	-1	1.000	-4	O-20	-0.6
Total	8	451	833	103	229	29	9	15	98	55	120	.275	.321	.385	92	-11	2	4	-2	.997	-29	O-240/D-7,1	-4.8

■ DICK GYSELMAN
Gyselman, Richard Renald   b: 4/6/08, San Francisco, Cal.   d: 9/20/90, Seattle, Wash.   BR/TR, 6′2″, 170 lbs.   Deb: 4/20/33

1933	Bos-N	58	155	10	37	6	2	0	12	7	21	.239	.272	.303	70	-7	0			.926	6	3-42/2-5,S	0.2
1934	Bos-N	24	36	7	6	1	1	0	4	2	11	.167	.211	.250	25	-4	0			.739	-2	3-15/2-2	-0.5
Total	2	82	191	17	43	7	3	0	16	9	32	.225	.260	.293	61	-11	0			.901	4	/3-57,2-7,S	-0.3

YEAR	TM/L	G	AB	R	H	2B	3B	HR	RBI	BB	SO	AVG	OBP	SLG	PRO+	BR/A	SB	CS	SBR	FA	FR	G/POS	TPR

■ BERT HAAS
Haas, Berthold John b: 2/8/14, Naperville, Ill. BR/TR, 5'11", 180 lbs. Deb: 9/9/37

1937	Bro-N	16	25	2	10	3	0	0	2	1	1	.400	.423	.520	152	2	0			1.000	-1	/O-4,1-3	0.1
1938	Bro-N	1	0	0	0	0	0	0	0	0	0	—	—	—	—		0	0		.000	0	H	0.0
1942	Cin-N	154	585	59	140	21	6	6	54	59	54	.239	.310	.326	86	-10	6			.925	-10	*3-146/1-6,O	-2.0
1943	Cin-N	101	332	39	87	17	6	4	44	22	26	.262	.308	.386	101	-1	6			.993	9	1-44,3-23,O	0.5
1946	Cin-N	140	535	57	141	24	7	3	50	33	42	.264	.310	.351	91	-8	22			.994	0	*1-140/3-6	-1.7
1947	Cin-N★	135	482	58	138	17	7	3	67	42	27	.286	.346	.369	91	-6	9			.956	-4	O-69,1-53	-1.6
1948	Phi-N	95	333	35	94	9	2	4	34	36	25	.282	.354	.357	95	-2	8			.892	-8	3-54,1-35	-1.1
1949	Phi-N	2	1	0	0	0	0	0	0	1	1	.000	.500	.000	47	0	0			.000	0	H	0.0
	NY-N	54	104	12	27	2	3	1	10	5	8	.260	.294	.365	76	-4	0			.983	-1	1-23,3-11	-0.5
	Yr	56	105	12	27	2	3	1	10	6	9	.257	.297	.362	76	-4	0			.983	-1	1-23,3-11	-0.5
1951	Chi-A	23	43	1	7	0	1	1	2	5	4	.163	.250	.279	44	-4	0	0	0	1.000	-1	/1-7,O-4,3	0.0
Total	9	721	2440	263	644	93	32	22	263	204	188	.264	.323	.355	91	-33	51	0		.991	-17	1-311,3-241/O	-6.8

■ BRUNO HAAS
Haas, Bruno Philip "Boon" b: 5/5/1891, Worcester, Mass. d: 6/5/52, Sarasota, Fla. BB/TL, 5'10", 180 lbs. Deb: 6/23/15

| 1915 | Phi-A | 12 | 18 | 1 | 1 | 0 | 0 | 0 | 0 | 1 | 7 | .056 | .105 | .056 | -54 | -3 | 0 | | | .875 | 1 | /P-6,O-3 | -0.2 |

■ EDDIE HAAS
Haas, George Edwin b: 5/26/35, Paducah, Ky. BL/TR, 5'11", 178 lbs. Deb: 9/8/57 MC

1957	Chi-N	14	24	1	5	1	0	0	4	1	5	.208	.240	.250	32	-2	0	0	0	1.000	-1	/O-4	-0.3
1958	Mil-N	9	14	2	5	0	0	0	1	2	1	.357	.438	.357	124	1	0	0	0	1.000	-0	/O-3	0.0
1960	Mil-N	32	32	4	7	2	0	1	5	5	14	.219	.324	.375	98	-0	0	0	0	1.000	-0	/O-2	-0.1
Total	3	55	70	7	17	3	0	1	10	8	20	.243	.321	.329	80	-2	0	0	0	1.000	-2	/O-9	-0.4

■ MULE HAAS
Haas, George William b: 10/15/03, Montclair, N.J. d: 6/30/74, New Orleans, La. BL/TR, 6'1", 175 lbs. Deb: 8/15/25 C

1925	Pit-N	4	3	1	0	0	0	0	0	0	1	.000	.000	.000	-94	-1	0	0	0	1.000	-1	/O-2	-0.2
1928	Phi-A	91	332	41	93	21	4	6	39	23	20	.280	.331	.422	94	-4	2	3	-1	.974	-3	O-82	-1.3
1929	*Phi-A	139	578	115	181	41	9	16	82	34	38	.313	.356	.498	113	9	0	4	-2	.982	2	*O-139	-0.1
1930	*Phi-A	132	532	91	159	33	7	2	68	43	33	.299	.352	.398	86	-11	2	2	-1	.976	12	*O-131	-0.8
1931	*Phi-A	102	440	82	142	29	7	8	56	30	29	.323	.366	.475	113	7	0	0	0	.989	4	*O-102	0.3
1932	Phi-A	143	558	91	170	28	5	6	65	62	49	.305	.376	.405	99	0	1	0	0	.987	7	*O-137	-0.2
1933	Chi-A	146	585	97	168	33	4	1	51	65	41	.287	.360	.362	96	-2	0	5	-3	.983	-5	*O-146	-1.6
1934	Chi-A	106	351	54	94	16	3	2	22	47	22	.268	.354	.348	79	-10	1	0		.991	-2	O-89	-1.5
1935	Chi-A	92	327	44	95	22	1	2	40	37	11	.291	.363	.382	90	-4	4	1	1	.989	-1	O-84	-0.7
1936	Chi-A	119	408	75	116	26	2	0	46	64	29	.284	.383	.358	81	-10	1	0	0	.989	-6	O-96/1-7	-1.9
1937	Chi-A	54	111	8	23	3	3	0	15	16	10	.207	.313	.288	52	-8	1	0		.975	0	1-32/O-2	-1.0
1938	Phi-A	40	78	7	16	2	0	0	12	12	10	.205	.311	.231	39	-7	0	0	0	1.000	-2	O-12/1-6	-1.0
Total	12	1168	4303	706	1257	254	45	43	496	433	299	.292	.359	.402	93	-41	12	16	-6	.984	5	*O-1022/1-45	-10.0

■ EMIL HABERER
Haberer, Emil Karl b: 2/2/1878, Cincinnati, Ohio d: 10/19/51, Louisville, Ky. BR/TR, 6'1", 204 lbs. Deb: 7/9/01

1901	Cin-N	6	18	2	3	0	1	0	1	3		.167	.286	.278	68	-1	0			.545	-2	/3-3,1-2	-0.2
1903	Cin-N	5	13	1	1	0	0	0	0	2		.077	.200	.077	-18	-2	0			.933	-2	/C-4	-0.4
1909	Cin-N	5	16	1	3	1	0	0	2	0		.188	.188	.250	36	-1	0			.895	-2	/C-4	-0.3
Total	3	16	47	4	7	1	1	0	3	5		.149	.231	.213	31	-4	0			.912	-6	/C-8,3-3,1	-0.9

■ IRV HACH
Hach, Irvin William "Major" b: 6/6/1873, Louisville, Ky. d: 8/13/36, Louisville, Ky. BR/TR, Deb: 7/1/1897

| 1897 | Lou-N | 16 | 51 | 5 | 11 | 2 | 0 | 0 | 3 | 5 | | .216 | .322 | .255 | 55 | -3 | 1 | | | .889 | -2 | /2-9,3-7 | -0.3 |

■ STAN HACK
Hack, Stanley Camfield "Smiling Stan" b: 12/6/09, Sacramento, Cal d: 12/15/79, Dixon, Ill. BL/TR, 6', 170 lbs. Deb: 4/12/32 MC

1932	*Chi-N	72	178	32	42	5	6	2	19	17	16	.236	.306	.365	80	-5	5			.913	-5	3-51	-0.7
1933	Chi-N	20	60	10	21	3	1	1	2	8	3	.350	.451	.483	167	6	4			.983	6	3-17	1.3
1934	Chi-N	111	402	54	116	16	6	1	21	45	42	.289	.363	.366	98	0	11			.949	0	*3-109	0.5
1935	*Chi-N	124	427	75	133	23	9	4	64	65	17	.311	.406	.436	125	18	14			.942	11	*3-111/1-7	3.1
1936	Chi-N	149	561	102	167	27	4	6	78	89	39	.298	.396	.392	110	12	17			.950	-12	*3-140,1-11	0.4
1937	Chi-N	154	582	106	173	27	6	2	63	83	42	.297	.388	.375	104	6	16			.968	-9	*3-150/1-4	0.1
1938	*Chi-N★	152	609	109	195	34	11	4	67	94	39	.320	.411	.432	128	28	**16**			.954	7	*3-152	3.6
1939	Chi-N★	156	641	112	191	28	6	8	56	65	35	.298	.364	.398	103	4	**17**			.956	-7	*3-156	-0.1
1940	Chi-N	149	603	101	**191**	38	6	8	40	75	24	.317	.395	.439	132	29	21			.954	14	*3-148/1-1	4.5
1941	Chi-N★	151	586	111	**186**	23	5	7	45	99	40	.317	.417	.427	143	38	10			.954	-16	*3-150/1-1	2.6
1942	Chi-N	140	553	91	166	36	4	6	39	94	40	.300	.402	.409	143	34	9			**.965**	-10	*3-139	2.7
1943	Chi-N★	144	533	78	154	24	4	3	35	82	27	.289	.384	.366	119	16	5			.960	-7	*3-136	1.1
1944	Chi-N	98	383	65	108	16	1	3	32	53	11	.282	.369	.352	104	5	4			.939	2	3-75,1-18	0.6
1945	*Chi-N†	150	597	110	193	29	7	2	43	99	30	.323	.420	.405	133	32	12			**.975**	18	*3-146/1-5	5.2
1946	Chi-N	92	323	55	92	13	4	0	26	83	32	.285	.431	.350	125	17	3			.968	-3	3-90	1.6
1947	Chi-N	76	240	28	65	11	2	0	12	41	19	.271	.377	.333	94	-0	6			.962	7	3-66	0.7
Total	16	1938	7278	1239	2193	363	81	57	642	1092	466	.301	.394	.397	120	238	165			.957	-4	*3-1836/1-47	27.2

■ RICH HACKER
Hacker, Richard Warren b: 10/6/47, Belleville, Ill. BB/TR, 6', 160 lbs. Deb: 7/2/71 C

| 1971 | Mon-N | 16 | 33 | 2 | 4 | 1 | 0 | 0 | 3 | 2 | 12 | .121 | .194 | .152 | -1 | -4 | 0 | 0 | 0 | .984 | 5 | S-16 | 0.2 |

■ JIM HACKETT
Hackett, James Joseph "Sunny Jim" b: 10/1/1877, Jacksonville, Ill. d: 3/28/61, Douglas, Mich. BR/TR, 6'2", 185 lbs. Deb: 9/14/02

1902	StL-N	6	21	2	6	1	0	0	4	2		.286	.348	.333	115	0	1			.833	-1	/P-4,O-2	0.0
1903	StL-N	99	351	24	80	13	8	0	36	19		.228	.272	.311	68	-16	2			.972	-6	1-89/P-7	-2.2
Total	2	105	372	26	86	14	8	0	40	21		.231	.276	.312	70	-15	3			.893	-7	/1-89,P-11,O	-2.2

■ MERT HACKETT
Hackett, Mortimer Martin b: 11/11/1859, Cambridge, Mass. d: 2/22/38, Cambridge, Mass. BR/TR, 5'10.5", 175 lbs. Deb: 5/2/1883 F

1883	Bos-N	46	179	20	42	8	6	2	24	1	48	.235	.239	.380	82	-4				.909	-6	C-44/O-4	-0.7
1884	Bos-N	72	268	28	55	13	2	1	20	2	66	.205	.211	.280	53	-14				.928	12	C-71/3-1	0.3
1885	Bos-N	34	115	9	21	7	1	0	4	2	28	.183	.197	.261	49	-6				.901	5	C-34	0.2
1886	KC-N	62	230	18	50	8	3	3	25	4	59	.217	.231	.317	61	-11				.926	-17	C-53,O-13	-2.1
1887	Ind-N	42	147	12	35	6	3	2	10	7	24	.238	.282	.361	80	-4	4			.938	-9	C-40/O-2,1	-0.8
Total	5	256	939	87	203	42	15	8	83	16	225	.216	.231	.318	65	-40	5			.921	-15	C-242/O-19,13	-3.1

■ WALTER HACKETT
Hackett, Walter Henry b: 8/15/1857, Cambridge, Mass. d: 10/2/20, Cambridge, Mass. Deb: 4/17/1884 F

1884	Bos-U	103	415	71	101	19	0	1		7		.243	.256	.296	50	-28				**.855**	12	*S-103	-1.3
1885	Bos-N	35	125	8	23	3	0	0	9	3	22	.184	.203	.208	34	-9				.893	-12	2-20,S-15	-1.9
Total	2	138	540	79	124	22	0	1	9	10	22	.230	.244	.276	47	-37				.852	1	S-118/2-20	-3.2

■ KENT HADLEY
Hadley, Kent William b: 12/17/34, Pocatello, Idaho BL/TL, 6'3", 190 lbs. Deb: 9/14/58

1958	KC-A	3	11	1	2	0	0	0	0	0	6	.182	.182	.182	1	0	0	0	0	1.000	-1	/1-2	-0.2
1959	KC-A	113	288	40	73	11	1	10	39	24	74	.253	.313	.403	93	-3	1	2	-1	.989	-2	1-95	-1.1
1960	NY-A	55	64	8	13	2	0	4	11	6	19	.203	.271	.422	90	-0	0	0	0	.991	-0	1-24	-0.2
Total	3	171	363	49	88	13	1	14	50	30	97	.242	.302	.399	90	-6	1	2	-1	.989	-2	1-121	-1.5

■ BILL HAEFFNER
Haeffner, William Bernhard b: 7/8/1894, Philadelphia, Pa. d: 1/27/82, Springfield, Pa. BR/TR, 5'9", 165 lbs. Deb: 6/29/15

| 1915 | Phi-A | 3 | 4 | 0 | 1 | 0 | 0 | 0 | 0 | 0 | 1 | .250 | .250 | .250 | 51 | -0 | | | | 1.000 | -1 | /C-3 | -0.2 |

YEAR	TM/L	G	AB	R	H	2B	3B	HR	RBI	BB	SO	AVG	OBP	SLG	PRO+	BR/A	SB	CS	SBR	FA	FR	G/POS	TPR
1920	Pit-N	54	175	8	34	4	1	0	14	8	14	.194	.230	.229	31	-15	1	1	-0	.972	-3	C-52	-1.7
1928	NY-N	2	1	0	0	0	0	0	0	0	0	.000	.000	.000	-99	-0	0			.750	0	/C-2	0.0
Total	3	59	180	8	35	4	1	0	14	8	15	.194	.229	.228	30	-16	1	1		.968	-5	/C-57	-1.9

■ CHICK HAFEY

Hafey, Charles James b: 2/12/03, Berkeley, Cal. d: 7/2/73, Calistoga, Cal. BR/TR, 6', 185 lbs. Deb: 8/28/24 H

YEAR	TM/L	G	AB	R	H	2B	3B	HR	RBI	BB	SO	AVG	OBP	SLG	PRO+	BR/A	SB	CS	SBR	FA	FR	G/POS	TPR
1924	StL-N	24	91	10	23	5	2	2	22	4	8	.253	.292	.418	90	-2	1	0	0	.927	-1	O-24	-0.4
1925	StL-N	93	358	36	108	25	2	5	57	10	29	.302	.321	.425	87	-8	3	7	-3	.955	-1	O-88	-1.7
1926	*StL-N	78	225	30	61	19	2	4	38	11	36	.271	.311	.427	93	-3	2			.974	-6	O-64	-1.2
1927	StL-N	103	346	62	114	26	5	18	63	36	41	.329	.401	**.590**	157	27	12			.980	5	O-94	2.6
1928	*StL-N	138	520	101	175	46	6	27	111	40	53	.337	.386	.604	152	37	8			.965	3	*O-133	2.9
1929	StL-N	134	517	101	175	47	9	29	125	45	42	.338	.394	.632	148	36	7			.966	3	*O-130	2.7
1930	*StL-N	120	446	108	150	39	12	26	107	46	51	.336	.407	.652	146	31	12			.976	-3	*O-116	1.8
1931	*StL-N	122	450	94	157	35	8	16	95	39	43	**.349**	**.404**	.569	153	33	11			.983	-4	*O-118	2.0
1932	Cin-N	83	253	34	87	19	3	2	36	22	20	.344	.403	.466	137	14	4			.965	-3	O-65	0.7
1933	Cin-N★	144	568	77	172	34	6	7	62	40	44	.303	.351	.421	121	15	3			.987	8	*O-144	1.6
1934	Cin-N	140	535	75	157	29	6	18	67	52	63	.293	.359	.471	123	17	4			.967	4	*O-140	1.5
1935	Cin-N	15	59	10	20	6	1	1	9	4	5	.339	.400	.525	151	4	1			.912	-3	O-15	0.1
1937	Cin-N	89	257	39	67	11	5	9	41	23	42	.261	.324	.447	113	4	2			.971	-2	O-64	-0.1
Total	13	1283	4625	777	1466	341	67	164	833	372	477	.317	.372	.526	133	205	70	7		.971	1	*O-1195	12.5

■ BUD HAFEY

Hafey, Daniel Albert b: 8/6/12, Berkeley, Cal. d: 7/27/86, Sacramento, Cal. BR/TR, 6', 185 lbs. Deb: 4/21/35 F

YEAR	TM/L	G	AB	R	H	2B	3B	HR	RBI	BB	SO	AVG	OBP	SLG	PRO+	BR/A	SB	CS	SBR	FA	FR	G/POS	TPR
1935	Chi-A	2	0	1	0	0	0	0	0	0	0	—	—	—		0	0	0	0	.000	0	R	0.0
	Pit-N	58	184	29	42	11	2	6	16	16	48	.228	.290	.408	83	-5	0			.970	4	O-47	-0.3
1936	Pit-N	39	118	19	25	6	1	4	13	10	27	.212	.273	.381	73	-5	0			.932	0	O-29	-0.6
1939	Cin-N	6	13	1	2	1	0	0	1	1	4	.154	.214	.231	19	-1	1			1.000	-0	/O-4	-0.2
	Phi-N	18	51	3	9	1	0	0	3	3	12	.176	.222	.196	14	-6	1			1.000	1	O-13/P-2	-0.6
	Yr	24	64	4	11	2	0	0	4	4	16	.172	.221	.203	15	-8	2			1.000	1	O-17/P-2	-0.8
Total	3	123	366	53	78	19	3	10	33	30	91	.213	.273	.363	68	-18	2	0		.963	4	/O-93,P-2	-1.7

■ TOM HAFEY

Hafey, Thomas Francis "Heave-O" or "The Arm" b: 7/12/13, Berkeley, Cal. BR/TR, 6'1", 180 lbs. Deb: 7/21/39 F

YEAR	TM/L	G	AB	R	H	2B	3B	HR	RBI	BB	SO	AVG	OBP	SLG	PRO+	BR/A	SB	CS	SBR	FA	FR	G/POS	TPR
1939	NY-N	70	256	37	62	10	1	6	26	10	44	.242	.271	.359	67	-13	1			.960	-0	3-70	-1.2
1944	StL-A	8	14	1	5	2	0	0	2	1	4	.357	.400	.500	148	1	0	0	0	1.000	-0	/O-4,1-1	0.1
Total	2	78	270	38	67	12	1	6	28	11	48	.248	.278	.367	72	-12	1	0		.960	-0	/3-70,O-4,1	-1.1

■ JOE HAGUE

Hague, Joe Clarence b: 4/25/44, Huntington, W.Va. BL/TL, 6', 198 lbs. Deb: 9/19/68

YEAR	TM/L	G	AB	R	H	2B	3B	HR	RBI	BB	SO	AVG	OBP	SLG	PRO+	BR/A	SB	CS	SBR	FA	FR	G/POS	TPR
1968	StL-N	7	17	2	4	0	0	1	1	2	2	.235	.316	.412	119	0	0	0	0	.800	-1	/O-3,1-2	-0.1
1969	StL-N	40	100	8	17	2	1	2	8	12	23	.170	.259	.270	48	-7	0	2	-1	.939	-0	O-17/1-9	-1.1
1970	StL-N	139	451	58	122	16	4	14	68	63	87	.271	.361	.417	106	4	2	1	0	.994	-4	1-82,O-52	-0.9
1971	StL-N	129	380	46	86	9	3	16	54	58	69	.226	.332	.392	100	1	0	3	-2	.996	-3	1-91,O-36	-1.3
1972	StL-N	27	76	8	18	5	1	3	11	17	18	.237	.376	.447	135	4	0	1	-1	1.000	-1	1-22/O-3	0.1
	*Cin-N	69	138	17	34	7	1	4	20	20	18	.246	.342	.399	116	3	1	1	0	1.000	-2	1-22,O-19	-0.1
	Yr	96	214	25	52	12	2	7	31	37	36	.243	.355	.416	124	7	1	2	-1	1.000	-2	1-44,O-22	0.0
1973	Cin-N	19	33	2	5	2	0	0	1	5	5	.152	.263	.212	35	-3	1	0	0	1.000	-1	/O-5,1-4	-0.3
Total	6	430	1195	141	286	41	10	40	163	177	222	.239	.339	.391	101	3	4	8	-4	.996	-11	1-232,O-135	-3.8

■ BILL HAGUE

Hague, William L. (b: William L. Haug) b: 1852, Philadelphia, Pa. BR/TR, 5'9", 164 lbs. Deb: 5/4/1875

YEAR	TM/L	G	AB	R	H	2B	3B	HR	RBI	BB	SO	AVG	OBP	SLG	PRO+	BR/A	SB	CS	SBR	FA	FR	G/POS	TPR
1875	StL-n	62	260	24	56	2	0		2			.215	.221	.223	60	-9						*3-61/1-1	-0.8
1876	Lou-N	67	294	31	78	8	0	1	22	2	10	.265	.270	.303	77	-10				.754	-26	*3-67/S-1	-3.1
1877	Lou-N	59	263	38	70	7	1	1	24	7	18	.266	.285	.312	75	-10				.843	-19	*3-59	-2.5
1878	Pro-N	62	250	21	51	3	0	0	25	5	34	.204	.220	.216	44	-15				**.925**	19	*3-62	0.7
1879	Pro-N	51	209	20	47	3	1	0	21	3	19	.225	.236	.249	61	-8				.822	5	3-51	-0.3
Total	4	239	1016	110	246	21	2	2	92	17	81	.242	.255	.273	66	-43				.843	-22	3-239/S-1	-5.2

■ DON HAHN

Hahn, Donald Antone b: 11/16/48, San Francisco, Cal. BR/TR, 6'1", 185 lbs. Deb: 4/8/69

YEAR	TM/L	G	AB	R	H	2B	3B	HR	RBI	BB	SO	AVG	OBP	SLG	PRO+	BR/A	SB	CS	SBR	FA	FR	G/POS	TPR
1969	Mon-N	4	9	0	1	0	0	0	2	0	5	.111	.111	.111	-37	-2	0	0	0	1.000	-0	/O-3	-0.2
1970	Mon-N	82	149	22	38	8	0	0	8	27	27	.255	.376	.309	86	-2	4	2	0	.986	-7	O-61	-1.0
1971	NY-N	98	178	16	42	5	1	1	11	21	32	.236	.320	.292	76	-5	2	3	-1	.973	-6	O-80	-1.5
1972	NY-N	17	37	0	6	0	0	0	1	4	12	.162	.244	.162	18	-4	0	0	0	1.000	-2	O-10	-0.7
1973	*NY-N	93	262	22	60	10	0	2	21	22	43	.229	.289	.290	62	-13	2	1	0	.989	-3	O-87	-2.1
1974	NY-N	110	323	34	81	14	1	4	28	37	34	.251	.330	.337	88	-5	2	0	1	.987	-1	*O-106	-1.0
1975	Phi-N	9	5	0	0	0	0	0	0	0	2	.000	.000	.000	-96	-1	0	0	0	1.000	-2	/O-7	-0.3
	StL-N	7	8	3	1	0	0	0	0	1	1	.125	.222	.125	-2	-1	0	0	0	1.000	-1	/O-4	-0.2
	SD-N	34	26	7	6	1	2	0	3	10	2	.231	.444	.423	151	3	1	0	0	1.000	-0	O-26	-0.5
	Yr	50	39	10	7	1	2	0	3	11	5	.179	.360	.308	89	-0	1	0	0	1.000	-10	O-37	-1.0
Total	7	454	997	104	235	38	4	7	74	122	158	.236	.321	.303	75	-30	11	6	-0	.985	-29	O-384	-7.5

■ DICK HAHN

Hahn, Richard Frederick b: 7/24/16, Canton, Ohio d: 11/5/92, Orlando, Fla. BR/TR, 5'11", 176 lbs. Deb: 9/7/40

YEAR	TM/L	G	AB	R	H	2B	3B	HR	RBI	BB	SO	AVG	OBP	SLG	PRO+	BR/A	SB	CS	SBR	FA	FR	G/POS	TPR
1940	Was-A	1	3	0	0	0	0	0	0	0	0	.000	.000	.000	-99	-1	0	0	0	1.000	0	/C-1	-0.1

■ ED HAHN

Hahn, William Edgar b: 8/27/1875, Nevada, Ohio d: 11/29/41, Des Moines, Iowa BL/TR, 160 lbs. Deb: 8/31/05

YEAR	TM/L	G	AB	R	H	2B	3B	HR	RBI	BB	SO	AVG	OBP	SLG	PRO+	BR/A	SB	CS	SBR	FA	FR	G/POS	TPR
1905	NY-A	43	160	32	51	5	0	0	11	25		.319	.426	.350	132	7	1			.957	2	O-43	0.8
1906	NY-A	11	22	2	2	1	0	0	1	3		.091	.259	.136	23	-2	2			1.000	-1	/O-7	-0.3
	*Chi-A	130	484	80	110	7	5	0	27	69		.227	.335	.262	90	-2	19			.949	-6	*O-130	-1.5
	Yr	141	506	82	112	8	5	0	28	72		.221	.331	.257	86	-4	21			.952	-6	*O-137	-1.8
1907	Chi-A	156	592	87	151	9	7	0	45	84		.255	.359	.294	112	14	17			**.990**	-5	*O-156	0.3
1908	Chi-A	122	447	58	112	12	8	0	21	39		.251	.329	.313	111	7	11			.965	-11	*O-118	-1.1
1909	Chi-A	76	287	30	52	6	0	1	16	31		.181	.268	.213	54	-14	9			.990	-7	O-76	-2.8
1910	Chi-A	15	53	2	6	2	0	0	1	7		.113	.217	.151	16	-5	0			.933	-3	O-15	-1.0
Total	6	553	2045	291	484	42	20	1	122	258		.237	.335	.278	97	5	59			.970	-30	O-545	-5.6

■ ED HAIGH

Haigh, Edward E. b: 2/7/1867, Philadelphia, Pa. d: 2/13/53, Atlantic City, N.J Deb: 8/14/1892

YEAR	TM/L	G	AB	R	H	2B	3B	HR	RBI	BB	SO	AVG	OBP	SLG	PRO+	BR/A	SB	CS	SBR	FA	FR	G/POS	TPR
1892	StL-N	1	4	0	1	0	0	0	0	0	2	.250	.250	.250	54	-0				1.000	1	/O-1	0.0

■ HINKEY HAINES

Haines, Henry Luther b: 12/23/1898, Red Lion, Pa. d: 1/9/79, Sharon Hill, Pa. BR/TR, 5'10", 170 lbs. Deb: 4/20/23

YEAR	TM/L	G	AB	R	H	2B	3B	HR	RBI	BB	SO	AVG	OBP	SLG	PRO+	BR/A	SB	CS	SBR	FA	FR	G/POS	TPR
1923	*NY-A	28	25	9	4	2	0	0	3	4	5	.160	.276	.240	36	-2	3	1	0	1.000	-3	O-14	-0.5

■ JERRY HAIRSTON

Hairston, Jerry Wayne b: 2/16/52, Birmingham, Ala. BB/TR, 5'10", 180 lbs. Deb: 7/26/73 F

YEAR	TM/L	G	AB	R	H	2B	3B	HR	RBI	BB	SO	AVG	OBP	SLG	PRO+	BR/A	SB	CS	SBR	FA	FR	G/POS	TPR
1973	Chi-A	60	210	25	57	11	1	0	23	33	30	.271	.373	.333	97	1	0	0	0	.944	2	O-33,1-19/D	-0.1
1974	Chi-A	45	109	8	25	7	0	0	8	13	18	.229	.311	.294	73	-4	0	2	-1	.926	-4	O-22,D-10	-1.0
1975	Chi-A	69	219	26	62	8	0	0	23	46	23	.283	.410	.320	107	5	1	0	0	.951	1	O-59/D-8	0.4
1976	Chi-A	44	119	20	27	2	2	0	10	24	19	.227	.357	.277	87	-1	1	1	0	.973	-3	O-40	-0.6
1977	Chi-A	13	26	3	8	2	0	0	4	5	7	.308	.419	.385	121	1	0	0	0	1.000	-2	O-11	-0.1
	Pit-N	51	52	5	10	2	0	0	6	6	10	.192	.276	.346	64	-3	0	0	0	.923	-4	O-14/2-1	-0.7
1981	Chi-A	9	25	5	7	1	0	1	5	2	4	.280	.357	.440	131	0	0	0	0	.933	-1	/O-7	0.0
1982	Chi-A	85	90	11	21	5	0	5	18	19	15	.233	.303	.456	105	0	0	0	0	1.000	-8	O-36/D-2	-0.8

YEAR	TM/L	G	AB	R	H	2B	3B	HR	RBI	BB	SO	AVG	OBP	SLG	PRO+	BR/A	SB	CS	SBR	FA	FR	G/POS	TPR
1983	*Chi-A	101	126	17	37	9	1	5	22	23	16	.294	.403	.500	141	8	0	1	-1	.968	-9	O-32/D-4	-0.2
1984	Chi-A	115	227	41	59	13	2	5	19	41	29	.260	.375	.401	110	4	2	1	0	.967	-5	O-37,D-20	-0.2
1985	Chi-A	95	140	9	34	8	0	2	20	29	18	.243	.380	.343	96	1	0	0	0	1.000	-1	D-29/O-5	-0.1
1986	Chi-A	101	225	32	61	15	0	5	26	26	26	.271	.349	.404	101	1	0	0	0	1.000	-3	D-29,1-19,O	-0.4
1987	Chi-A	66	126	14	29	8	0	5	20	25	25	.230	.362	.413	102	1	0	0	0	1.000	-0	O-13,D-13/1	0.0
1988	Chi-A	2	2	0	0	0	0	0	0	0	0	.000	.000	.000	-99	-1	0	0	0	.000	0	/H	-0.1
1989	Chi-A	3	3	0	1	0	0	0	0	0	0	.333	.333	.333	91	-0	0	0	0	.000	0	/D-2	0.0
Total	14	859	1699	216	438	91	6	30	205	282	240	.258	.366	.371	103	15	4	5	-2	.963	-35	O-320,D-125/12	-3.9

■ JOHNNY HAIRSTON
Hairston, John Louis b: 8/27/44, Birmingham, Ala. BR/TR, 6'2", 200 lbs. Deb: 9/6/69 F

YEAR	TM/L	G	AB	R	H	2B	3B	HR	RBI	BB	SO	AVG	OBP	SLG	PRO+	BR/A	SB	CS	SBR	FA	FR	G/POS	TPR
1969	Chi-N	3	4	0	1	0	0	0	0	0	2	.250	.250	.250	36	-0	0	0	0	1.000	-1	/C-1,O-1	-0.1

■ SAMMY HAIRSTON
Hairston, Samuel Harding b: 1/20/20, Crawford, Miss. BR/TR, 5'10.5", 187 lbs. Deb: 7/21/51 FC

YEAR	TM/L	G	AB	R	H	2B	3B	HR	RBI	BB	SO	AVG	OBP	SLG	PRO+	BR/A	SB	CS	SBR	FA	FR	G/POS	TPR
1951	Chi-A	4	5	1	2	1	0	0	1	2	0	.400	.571	.600	222	1	0	0	0	1.000	-1	/C-2	0.0

■ CHET HAJDUK
Hajduk, Chester b: 7/21/18, Chicago, Ill. BR/TR, 6', 195 lbs. Deb: 4/16/41

YEAR	TM/L	G	AB	R	H	2B	3B	HR	RBI	BB	SO	AVG	OBP	SLG	PRO+	BR/A	SB	CS	SBR	FA	FR	G/POS	TPR
1941	Chi-A	1	1	0	0	0	0	0	0	0	0	.000	.000	.000	-99	-0	0	0	0	.000	0	H	0.0

■ GEORGE HALAS
Halas, George Stanley b: 2/2/1895, Chicago, Ill. d: 10/31/83, Chicago, Ill. BB/TR, 6', 164 lbs. Deb: 5/6/19

YEAR	TM/L	G	AB	R	H	2B	3B	HR	RBI	BB	SO	AVG	OBP	SLG	PRO+	BR/A	SB	CS	SBR	FA	FR	G/POS	TPR
1919	NY-A	12	22	0	2	0	0	0	0	0	8	.091	.091	.091	-49	-4	0			1.000	-1	/O-6	-0.6

■ JOHN HALDEMAN
Haldeman, John Avery b: 12/2/1855, Peewee Valley, Ky. d: 9/17/1899, Louisville, Ky. BL/TR, 5'10", 175 lbs. Deb: 7/3/1877

YEAR	TM/L	G	AB	R	H	2B	3B	HR	RBI	BB	SO	AVG	OBP	SLG	PRO+	BR/A	SB	CS	SBR	FA	FR	G/POS	TPR
1877	Lou-N	1	4	0	0	0	0	0	0	0	0	.000	.000	.000	-85	-1				.571	-1	/2-1	-0.2

■ ODELL HALE
Hale, Arvel Odell "Bad News" b: 8/10/08, Hosston, La. d: 6/9/80, ElDorado, Ark. BR/TR, 5'10", 175 lbs. Deb: 8/1/31

YEAR	TM/L	G	AB	R	H	2B	3B	HR	RBI	BB	SO	AVG	OBP	SLG	PRO+	BR/A	SB	CS	SBR	FA	FR	G/POS	TPR
1931	Cle-A	25	92	14	26	2	4	1	5	8	8	.283	.340	.424	94	-1	2	0	1	.918	-4	3-15,2-10/S	-0.3
1933	Cle-A	98	351	49	97	19	8	10	64	30	37	.276	.333	.462	104	0	2	3	-1	.954	3	2-73,3-21	0.8
1934	Cle-A	143	563	82	170	44	6	13	101	48	50	.302	.357	.471	110	7	8	12	-5	.956	**26**	*2-137/3-5	3.3
1935	Cle-A	150	589	80	179	37	11	16	101	52	55	.304	.361	.486	115	11	15	13	-3	.938	7	*3-149/2-1	1.9
1936	Cle-A	153	620	126	196	50	13	14	87	64	43	.316	.380	.506	116	14	8	5	-1	.946	17	*3-148/2-3	3.1
1937	Cle-A	154	561	74	150	32	4	6	82	56	41	.267	.335	.371	77	-20	9	6	-1	.964	26	3-90,2-64	1.1
1938	Cle-A	130	496	69	138	32	2	4	69	44	39	.278	.338	.399	86	-12	8	1	2	.963	-13	*2-127	-1.4
1939	Cle-A	108	253	36	79	16	2	4	48	25	18	.312	.374	.439	111	4	4	5	-2	.966	-16	2-73/3-2	-0.9
1940	Cle-A	48	50	3	11	3	1	0	6	5	7	.220	.291	.320	60	-3	0			.700	-1	/3-3	-0.4
1941	Bos-A	12	24	5	5	2	0	1	3	4		.208	.296	.417	85	-1	0			.857	-3	/3-6,2-1	-0.4
	NY-N	41	102	13	20	3	0	0	9	18	13	.196	.317	.225	53	-6	1			.964	1	2-29	-0.3
Total	10	1062	3701	551	1071	240	51	73	573	353	315	.289	.352	.441	100	-6	57	45		.959	42	2-518,3-439/S	6.5

■ GEORGE HALE
Hale, George Wagner "Ducky" b: 8/3/1894, Dexter, Kan. d: 11/1/45, Wichita, Kan. BR/TR, 5'10", 160 lbs. Deb: 8/24/14

YEAR	TM/L	G	AB	R	H	2B	3B	HR	RBI	BB	SO	AVG	OBP	SLG	PRO+	BR/A	SB	CS	SBR	FA	FR	G/POS	TPR
1914	StL-A	6	11	1	2	0	0	0	0	0	3	.182	.182	.182	10	-1	0			.895	-0	/C-6	-0.1
1916	StL-A	4	1	0	0	0	0	0	0	1	0	.000	.500	.000	54	-0	0			1.000	0	/C-3	0.0
1917	StL-A	38	61	4	12	2	1	0	8	10	12	.197	.310	.262	78	-1	0			.927	3	C-28	0.3
1918	StL-A	12	30	0	4	1	0	0	1	1	5	.133	.161	.167	-1	-4	0			.981	2	C-11	-0.1
Total	4	60	103	5	18	3	1	0	9	11	21	.175	.261	.223	49	-6	0			.940	5	/C-48	0.1

■ JOHN HALE
Hale, John Steven b: 8/5/53, Fresno, Cal. BL/TR, 6'2", 195 lbs. Deb: 9/8/74

YEAR	TM/L	G	AB	R	H	2B	3B	HR	RBI	BB	SO	AVG	OBP	SLG	PRO+	BR/A	SB	CS	SBR	FA	FR	G/POS	TPR
1974	LA-N	4	4	2	4	1	0	0	2	0	0	1.000	1.000	1.250	549	2	0			.000	-1	/O-3	0.1
1975	LA-N	71	204	20	43	7	0	6	22	26	51	.211	.306	.333	81	-5	1	2	-1	.977	-7	O-68	-1.7
1976	LA-N	44	91	4	14	2	1	0	8	16	14	.154	.294	.198	42	-6	4	1	1	.983	-4	O-37	-1.2
1977	LA-N	79	108	10	26	4	1	2	11	15	28	.241	.333	.352	84	-2	2	1	0	.986	-16	O-73	-2.0
1978	Sea-A	107	211	24	36	8	0	4	22	34	64	.171	.286	.265	56	-12	3	4	-2	.988	-13	O-98/D-3	-3.0
1979	Sea-A	54	63	6	14	3	0	2	7	12	26	.222	.347	.365	91	-1	0	0	0	1.000	-11	O-42	-1.2
Total	6	359	681	66	137	25	2	14	72	103	183	.201	.310	.305	72	-24	10	8	-2	.985	-52	O-321/D-3	-9.0

■ BOB HALE
Hale, Robert Houston b: 11/7/33, Sarasota, Fla. BL/TL, 5'10", 195 lbs. Deb: 7/4/55

YEAR	TM/L	G	AB	R	H	2B	3B	HR	RBI	BB	SO	AVG	OBP	SLG	PRO+	BR/A	SB	CS	SBR	FA	FR	G/POS	TPR
1955	Bal-A	67	182	13	65	7	1	0	29	5	19	.357	.378	.407	119	4	0	2	-1	.974	2	1-44	0.3
1956	Bal-A	85	207	18	49	10	1	1	24	11	10	.237	.279	.309	60	-13	0	2	-1	.975	-0	1-51	-1.7
1957	Bal-A	42	44	2	11	0	0	0	7	2	12	.250	.283	.250	50	-3	0	0	0	1.000	-0	/1-5	-0.4
1958	Bal-A	19	20	2	7	3	0	0	3	2	1	.350	.409	.450	144	1	0	0	0	1.000	1	/1-2	0.2
1959	Bal-A	40	54	2	10	3	0	0	7	2	6	.185	.214	.241	25	-6	0	0	0	1.000	-1	/1-8	-0.7
1960	Cle-A	70	70	0	21	7	0	0	12	3	6	.300	.329	.400	99	-0	0	0	0	.944	0	/1-5	0.0
1961	Cle-A	42	36	0	6	0	0	0	6	1	7	.167	.211	.167	2	-5	0	0	0	.000	0	H	-0.5
	NY-A	11	13	2	2	0	0	1	1	0	0	.154	.154	.385	41	-1	0	0	0	1.000	-0	/1-5	-0.1
	Yr	53	49	2	8	0	0	1	7	1	7	.163	.196	.224	12	-6	0	0	0	1.000	-0	/1-5	-0.6
Total	7	376	626	41	171	29	2	2	89	26	51	.273	.305	.335	76	-22	0	4	-2	.977	2	1-120	-2.9

■ SAMMY HALE
Hale, Samuel Douglas b: 9/10/1896, Glen Rose, Tex. d: 9/6/74, Wheeler, Tex. BR/TR, 5'8.5", 160 lbs. Deb: 4/20/20

YEAR	TM/L	G	AB	R	H	2B	3B	HR	RBI	BB	SO	AVG	OBP	SLG	PRO+	BR/A	SB	CS	SBR	FA	FR	G/POS	TPR
1920	Det-A	76	116	13	34	3	3	1	14	5	15	.293	.322	.397	92	-2	2	0	1	.886	-3	3-16/O-4,2	-0.3
1921	Det-A	9	2	2	0	0	0	0	0	0	1	.000	.000	.000	-99	-1	0	1	-1	.000	0	H	-0.1
1923	Phi-A	115	434	68	125	22	8	3	51	17	31	.288	.327	.396	89	-9	8	3	1	.916	-19	*3-107	-1.7
1924	Phi-A	80	261	41	83	14	2	2	17	17	19	.318	.367	.410	99	-1	3	2	-0	.948	-8	3-55/O-5,S	-0.4
1925	Phi-A	110	391	62	135	30	11	8	63	17	27	.345	.376	.540	122	11	7	4	-0	.919	-3	3-96/2-1	1.2
1926	Phi-A	111	327	49	92	22	9	4	43	13	36	.281	.311	.440	89	-7	1	4	-2	.947	-2	3-77/O-1	-0.6
1927	Phi-A	131	501	77	157	24	8	5	81	32	32	.313	.358	.423	97	-3	11	3	2	.961	7	*3-128	0.5
1928	Phi-A	88	314	38	97	20	4	4	58	9	21	.309	.334	.468	106	1	7			.932	12	3-79	1.7
1929	Phi-A	101	379	51	105	14	3	1	40	12	18	.277	.303	.338	62	-21	6	2	1	.956	-7	3-99/2-1	-2.3
1930	StL-A	62	190	21	52	8	1	2	25	8	18	.274	.303	.358	65	-10	1	1	-0	.947	-3	3-47	-1.0
Total	10	883	2915	422	880	157	54	30	392	130	218	.302	.336	.424	89	-42	41	20		.939	-33	3-704/O-10,2S	-3.0

■ CHIP HALE
Hale, Walter William b: 12/2/64, San Jose, Cal. BL/TR, 5'11", 180 lbs. Deb: 8/27/89

YEAR	TM/L	G	AB	R	H	2B	3B	HR	RBI	BB	SO	AVG	OBP	SLG	PRO+	BR/A	SB	CS	SBR	FA	FR	G/POS	TPR
1989	Min-A	28	67	6	14	3	0	0	4	1	6	.209	.221	.254	31	-6	0	0	0	.980	-3	2-16/3-9,D	-0.9
1990	Min-A	1	2	0	0	0	0	0	2	0	1	.000	.000	.000	-94	-1	0	0	0	1.000	1	/2-1	0.1
1993	Min-A	69	186	25	62	6	1	3	27	18	17	.333	.410	.425	124	7	2	1	0	.952	-3	2-21,3-19,D/1S	0.4
1994	Min-A	67	118	13	31	9	0	1	11	16	14	.263	.356	.364	86	-2	0	1	-1	.964	5	3-21,D-10/120	0.1
Total	4	165	373	44	107	18	1	4	44	35	38	.287	.359	.373	95	-1	2	2	-1	.970	-0	/3-49,2-43,D1OS	-0.3

■ FRED HALEY
Haley, Fred b: Wheeling, W.Va. TR , Deb: 6/22/1880

YEAR	TM/L	G	AB	R	H	2B	3B	HR	RBI	BB	SO	AVG	OBP	SLG	PRO+	BR/A	SB	CS	SBR	FA	FR	G/POS	TPR
1880	Tro-N	2	7	0	0	0	0	0	0	1	2	.000	.125	.000	-51	-1				.750	-2	/C-2	-0.3

■ RAY HALEY
Haley, Raymond Timothy "Pat" b: 1/23/1891, Danbury, Iowa d: 10/8/73, Bradenton, Fla. BR/TR, 5'11", 180 lbs. Deb: 4/21/15

YEAR	TM/L	G	AB	R	H	2B	3B	HR	RBI	BB	SO	AVG	OBP	SLG	PRO+	BR/A	SB	CS	SBR	FA	FR	G/POS	TPR
1915	Bos-A	5	7	2	1	0	0	0	1	0	1	.143	.250	.286	62	-0	0			1.000	0	/C-4	0.0
1916	Bos-A	1	1	0	0	0	0	0	0	0	1	.000	.000	.000	-99	-0	0			.000	0	H	0.0
	Phi-A	34	108	6	25	5	0	0	8	8	18	.231	.278	.278	70	-4	2			.982	6	C-33	0.5
	Yr	35	109	8	25	5	0	0	8	8	19	.229	.276	.275	69	-4	2			.982	6	C-33	0.5
1917	Phi-A	41	98	7	27	2	1	0	11	4	12	.276	.311	.316	93	-1	2			.947	-6	C-34	-0.6
Total	3	81	214	17	53	8	1	0	15	11	32	.248	.291	.294	80	-6	2			.970	1	/C-71	-0.1

YEAR	TM/L	G	AB	R	H	2B	3B	HR	RBI	BB	SO	AVG	OBP	SLG	PRO+	BR/A	SB	CS	SBR	FA	FR	G/POS	TPR

■ ALBERT HALL Hall, Albert b: 3/7/58, Birmingham, Ala. BB/TR, 5'11", 155 lbs. Deb: 9/12/81

1981	Atl-N	6	2	1	0	0	0	0	0	1	1	.000	.333	.000	1	-0	0	0	0	.000	-1	/O-2	-0.1
1982	Atl-N	5	0	1	0	0	0	0	0	0	0	—	—	—	—	0	0	0	0	.000	0	/R	0.0
1983	Atl-N	10	8	2	0	0	0	0	0	2	2	.000	.200	.000	-37	-1	1	1	-0	.750	-2	/O-4	-0.4
1984	Atl-N	87	142	25	37	6	1	1	9	10	18	.261	.309	.338	76	-4	6	4	-1	.932	-10	O-66	-1.7
1985	Atl-N	54	47	5	7	0	1	0	3	9	12	.149	.286	.191	34	-4	1	1	-0	.900	-4	O-13	-0.8
1986	Atl-N	16	50	6	12	2	0	0	1	5	6	.240	.309	.280	60	-3	8	3	1	.900	0	O-14	-0.3
1987	Atl-N	92	292	54	83	20	4	3	24	38	36	.284	.370	.411	102	2	33	10	4	.981	3	O-69	0.6
1988	Atl-N	85	231	27	57	7	1	1	15	21	35	.247	.315	.299	73	-7	15	10	-2	.973	2	O-63	-1.0
1989	Pit-N	20	33	4	6	2	1	0	1	3	5	.182	.250	.303	59	-2	3	0	1	.909	-3	O-12	-0.5
Total	9	375	805	125	202	37	8	5	53	89	115	.251	.329	.335	80	-20	67	29	3	.958	-15	O-243	-4.2

■ AL HALL Hall, Archibald W. b: Worcester, Mass. d: 2/10/1885, Warren, Pa. Deb: 5/1/1879

1879	Tro-N	67	306	30	79	7	3	0	14	3	13	.258	.265	.301	92	-2				.842	5	*O-67	-0.1
1880	Cle-N	3	8	1	1	0	0	0	0	0	0	.125	.125	.125	-15	-1				1.000	-1	/O-3	-0.2
Total	2	70	314	31	80	7	3	0	14	3	13	.255	.262	.296	90	-3				.843	4	/O-70	-0.3

■ CHARLIE HALL Hall, Charles Walter "Doc" b: 8/24/1863, Toulon, Ill. d: 6/24/21, Tacoma, Wash. Deb: 5/3/1887

| 1887 | NY-a | 3 | 12 | 1 | 1 | 0 | 0 | 0 | | 0 | 2 | .083 | .214 | .083 | -16 | -2 | 1 | | | 1.000 | 0 | /O-3 | -0.1 |

■ GEORGE HALL Hall, George William b: 3/29/1849, Stepney, England d: 6/11/23, Ridgewood, N.J. BL, 5'7", 142 lbs. Deb: 5/5/1871

1871	Oly-n	32	136	31	40	3	3	2	17	8	0	.294	.333	.404	117	4	2					*O-32	0.3
1872	Bal-n	53	252	69	82	14	8	1	40	3	1	.325	.333	.456	135	8						*O-53/1-1	0.8
1873	Bal-n	35	168	44	58	8	4	1	30	2	0	.345	.353	.458	137	8						O-35	0.6
1874	Bos-n	47	222	58	64	11	7	1		2		.288	.295	.414	117	3						*O-47	0.3
1875	Ath-n	77	360	71	107	12	13	5		8	1	.297	.299	.444	138	10						*O-77	0.9
1876	Phi-N	60	268	51	98	7	13	5	45	8	4	.366	.384	.545	208	30				.801	-2	*O-60	2.4
1877	Lou-N	61	269	53	87	15	6	0	26	12	19	.323	.352	.439	125	5				.900	-6	*O-61	-0.3
Total	5 n	244	1138	273	351	48	35	10	87	16	1	.308	.318	.438	130	33						O-244/1-1	2.9
Total		121	537	104	185	22	21	5	71	20	23	.345	.368	.492	162	35				.837	-7	O-121	2.1

■ IRV HALL Hall, Irvin Gladstone b: 10/7/18, Alberton, Md. BR/TR, 5'10.5", 160 lbs. Deb: 4/20/43

1943	Phi-A	151	544	37	139	15	4	0	54	22	42	.256	.292	.298	73	-19	10	7	-1	.948	-11	*S-148/2-1,3	-2.2
1944	Phi-A	143	559	60	150	20	8	0	45	31	46	.268	.309	.333	85	-12	2	5	-2	.980	-5	2-97,S-40/1	-1.2
1945	Phi-A	151	616	62	161	17	5	0	50	35	42	.261	.307	.305	78	-17	3	10	-5	.978	26	*2-151	1.4
1946	Phi-A	63	185	19	46	6	2	0	19	9	18	.249	.287	.303	65	-9	1	1	-0	.973	-4	2-40/S-7	-1.1
Total	4	508	1904	178	496	58	19	0	168	97	148	.261	.302	.311	77	-58	16	23	-9	.977	6	2-289,S-195/13	-3.1

■ JIM HALL Hall, James d: 1/30/1886, Brooklyn, N.Y. Deb: 5/20/1872

1872	Atl-n	13	56	9	16	1	1	0	6	1	0	.286	.298	.339	82	-2						2-12/O-1	-0.2
1874	Atl-n	2	9	0	1	0	0	0		0		.111	.111	.111	-33	-1						/2-2	-0.1
1875	Wes-n	1	3	0	1	0	1	0		0		.333	.333	1.000	325	1						/O-1	0.1
Total	3 n	16	68	9	18	1	2	0		1		.265	.275	.338	79	-3						/2-14,O-2	-0.2

■ JIMMIE HALL Hall, Jimmie Randolph b: 3/17/38, Mt.Holly, N.C. BL/TR, 6', 175 lbs. Deb: 4/9/63

1963	Min-A	156	497	88	129	21	5	33	80	63	101	.260	.343	.521	136	23	3	3	-1	.982	-10	*O-143	0.5
1964	Min-A★	149	510	61	144	20	3	25	75	44	112	.282	.341	.480	125	16	5	2	0	.985	13	*O-137	2.4
1965	*Min-A★	148	522	81	149	25	4	20	86	51	79	.285	.350	.464	124	16	14	7	0	.976	-2	*O-141	0.8
1966	Min-A	120	356	52	85	7	4	20	47	33	66	.239	.303	.449	106	2	1	2	-1	.978	-1	*O-103	-0.4
1967	Cal-A	129	401	54	100	8	3	16	55	42	65	.249	.321	.404	117	8	4	1	1	.990	-2	*O-120	0.1
1968	Cal-A	46	126	15	27	3	0	1	8	16	19	.214	.303	.262	75	-3	1	0	0	.981	-4	O-39	-1.0
	Cle-A	53	111	4	22	4	0	1	8	10	19	.198	.264	.261	61	-5	1	0	0	.983	2	O-29	-0.5
	Yr	99	237	19	49	7	0	2	16	26	38	.207	.285	.262	68	-9	2	0	1	.982	-1	O-68	-1.5
1969	Cle-A	4	10	1	0	0	0	0	0	2	3	.000	.167	.000	-48	-2	1	0	0	1.000	-0	/O-3	-0.2
	NY-A	80	212	21	50	8	5	3	26	19	34	.236	.299	.363	88	-4	8	3	1	.963	-5	O-50/1-7	-1.2
	Yr	84	222	22	50	8	5	3	26	21	37	.225	.292	.347	81	-6	9	3	1	.966	-5	O-53/1-7	-1.4
	Chi-N	11	24	1	5	1	0	1	1	1	5	.208	.240	.250	33	-2	0	0	0	1.000	-1	/O-5	-0.4
1970	Chi-N	28	32	2	3	1	0	0	1	4	12	.094	.194	.125	-11	-5	0	0	0	1.000	-2	/O-8	-0.7
	Atl-N	39	47	7	10	2	0	2	4	2	14	.213	.245	.383	62	-3	0	0	0	1.000	-6	O-28	-0.9
	Yr	67	79	9	13	3	0	2	5	6	26	.165	.224	.278	31	-8	0	0	0	1.000	-7	O-36	-1.6
Total	8	963	2848	387	724	100	24	121	391	287	529	.254	.323	.434	112	40	38	18	1	.982	-17	O-806/1-7	-1.5

■ MEL HALL Hall, Melvin b: 9/16/60, Lyons, N.Y. BL/TL, 6'1", 205 lbs. Deb: 9/3/81

1981	Chi-N	10	11	1	1	0	0	1	2	1	4	.091	.167	.364	45	-1	0	0	0	.000	-2	/O-3	-0.3
1982	Chi-N	24	80	6	21	3	2	0	4	5	17	.262	.322	.350	86	-1	0	1	-1	.939	1	O-22	-0.2
1983	Chi-N	112	410	60	116	23	5	17	56	42	101	.283	.354	.488	125	13	6	6	-2	.988	0	*O-112	0.8
1984	Chi-N	48	150	25	42	11	3	4	22	12	23	.280	.333	.473	114	2	2	1	0	.961	-2	O-46	-0.1
	Cle-A	83	257	43	66	13	1	7	30	35	55	.257	.350	.397	104	2	1	1	-0	.993	-3	O-69/D-9	0.0
1985	Cle-A	23	66	7	21	6	0	0	12	8	12	.318	.392	.409	121	2	0	1	-1	1.000	-3	O-15/D-5	-0.2
1986	Cle-A	140	442	68	131	29	2	18	77	33	65	.296	.348	.493	128	16	6	2	1	.972	-7	*O-126/D-7	0.6
1987	Cle-A	142	485	57	136	21	1	18	76	20	68	.280	.310	.439	95	-5	5	4	-1	.989	6	*O-122,D-14	-0.4
1988	Cle-A	150	515	69	144	32	4	6	71	28	50	.280	.317	.392	95	-4	7	3	0	.967	-3	*O-141/D-6	-1.1
1989	NY-A	113	361	54	94	9	0	17	58	21	37	.260	.301	.404	104	1	0	0	0	.993	6	O-75,D-34	-0.4
1990	NY-A	113	360	41	93	23	2	12	46	6	46	.258	.274	.433	95	-5	0	0	0	.973	-6	D-54,O-50	-1.3
1991	NY-A	141	492	67	140	23	2	19	80	26	40	.285	.324	.455	113	7	0	1	-1	.987	-0	*O-120,D-10	0.3
1992	NY-A	152	583	67	163	36	3	15	81	29	53	.280	.315	.429	107	3	4	2	0	.990	6	*O-136,D-11	0.6
Total	12	1251	4212	564	1168	229	25	134	615	266	571	.277	.323	.439	107	31	31	22	-4	.981	-12	*O-1037,D-150	-1.7

■ JOE HALL Hall, Joseph Geroy b: 3/6/66, Paducah, Ky. BR/TR, 6', 180 lbs. Deb: 4/5/94

| 1994 | Chi-A | 17 | 28 | 6 | 11 | 3 | 0 | 1 | 5 | 2 | 4 | .393 | .452 | .607 | 171 | 3 | 0 | 0 | 0 | .917 | -2 | /O-9,D-2 | 0.1 |

■ DICK HALL Hall, Richard Wallace b: 9/27/30, St.Louis, Mo. BR/TR, 6'6", 200 lbs. Deb: 4/15/52

1952	Pit-N	26	80	6	11	1	0	0	2	2	17	.138	.159	.150	-14	-12	0	1	-1	.972	0	O-14/3-5	-1.4
1953	Pit-N	7	24	2	4	0	0	0	1	1	3	.167	.200	.167	-3	-4	1	1	-0	.978	11	/2-7	0.6
1954	Pit-N	112	310	38	74	8	4	2	27	33	46	.239	.312	.310	64	-16	3	0	1	.956	-2	*O-102	-2.1
1955	Pit-N	21	40	3	7	1	0	1	3	6	5	.175	.283	.275	50	-3	0	0	0	1.000	-1	P-15/O-3	-0.2
1956	Pit-N	33	29	5	10	0	0	0	1	5	7	.345	.441	.345	118	1	0	0	0	1.000	-1	P-19/1-1	0.3
1957	Pit-N	10	1	0	0	0	0	0	0	0	1	.000	.000	.000	-99	-0	0	0	0	.000	-0	/P-8	0.0
1959	Pit-N	2	0	0	0	0	0	0	0	0	0	.000	.000	.000	-99	-1	0	0	0	1.000	-0	/P-2	0.0
1960	KC-A	32	56	6	6	0	0	0	4	4	15	.107	.167	.107	-24	-10	1	0	0	.925	-1	P-29	0.0
1961	Bal-A	30	36	4	5	0	0	0	3	3	13	.139	.205	.139	-6	-5	0	0	0	.970	-1	P-29	0.0
1962	Bal-A	44	24	3	4	1	0	0	3	0	1	.167	.286	.208	38	-2	0	0	0	1.000	-0	P-43	0.0
1963	Bal-A	48	28	7	13	1	0	1	5	3	3	.464	.464	.607	205	4	0	0	0	1.000	-0	P-47	0.3
1964	Bal-A	45	16	1	2	1	0	0	3	1	3	.125	.176	.125	-14	-2	0	0	0	1.000	-1	P-45	0.0
1965	Bal-A	49	15	1	5	2	0	0	0	1	4	.333	.412	.467	146	1	0	0	0	.923	-1	P-48	0.0

YEAR	TM/L	G	AB	R	H	2B	3B	HR	RBI	BB	SO	AVG	OBP	SLG	PRO+	BR/A	SB	CS	SBR	FA	FR	G/POS	TPR
1966	Bal-A	32	12	0	2	0	0	0	2	0	5	.167	.231	.167	17	-1	0	0	0	1.000	-0	P-32	0.0
1967	Phi-N	48	14	1	1	0	0	0	0	0	5	.071	.071	.071	-58	-3	0	0	0	1.000	1	P-48	0.0
1968	Phi-N	32	3	0	1	0	0	0	0	0	1	.333	.333	.333	101	-0	0	0	0	1.000	-0	P-32	0.0
1969	*Bal-A	39	7	1	2	0	0	0	2	1	0	.286	.375	.286	86	-0	1	0	0	1.000	-1	P-39	0.0
1970	*Bal-A	32	12	2	1	0	0	0	1	0	3	.083	.083	.083	-53	-2	0	0	0	1.000	-1	P-32	0.0
1971	*Bal-A	27	5	0	2	1	0	0	0	0	0	.400	.400	.600	182	-0	0	0	0	.800	-1	P-27	0.0
Total	19	669	714	79	150	15	4	4	56	61	147	.210	.274	.259	44	-56	6	2	1	.976	2	P-495,O-119/231	-3.1

■ BOB HALL
Hall, Robert Prill b: 12/20/1878, Baltimore, Md. d: 12/1/50, Wellesley, Mass. TR, 5'10", 158 lbs. Deb: 4/18/04

YEAR	TM/L	G	AB	R	H	2B	3B	HR	RBI	BB	SO	AVG	OBP	SLG	PRO+	BR/A	SB	CS	SBR	FA	FR	G/POS	TPR
1904	Phi-N	46	163	11	26	4	0	0	17	14		.160	.226	.184	28	-13	5			.843	-10	3-20,S-15,1	-2.5
1905	NY-N	1	3	1	1	0	0	0	0	0		.333	.333	.333	97	-0	0			.000	-0	/O-1	0.0
	Bro-N	56	203	21	48	4	1	2	15	11		.236	.279	.296	77	-6	8			.939	6	O-42/2-7,1	-0.3
	Yr	57	206	22	49	4	1	2	15	11		.238	.280	.296	77	-6	8			.939	5	O-43/2-7,1	-0.3
Total	2	103	369	33	75	8	1	2	32	25		.203	.256	.247	55	-20	13			.968	-5	/O-43,3-20,S12	-2.8

■ RUSS HALL
Hall, Robert Russell b: 9/29/1871, Shelbyville, Ky. d: 7/1/37, Los Angeles, Cal. TL, 5'10", 170 lbs. Deb: 4/15/1898

YEAR	TM/L	G	AB	R	H	2B	3B	HR	RBI	BB	SO	AVG	OBP	SLG	PRO+	BR/A	SB	CS	SBR	FA	FR	G/POS	TPR
1898	StL-N	39	143	13	35	2	1	0	10	7		.245	.285	.273	59	-8	1			.835	-14	S-35/3-3,O	-2.0
1901	Cle-A	1	4	2	2	0	0	0	0	0		.500	.500	.500	185	0	0			.500	-1	/S-1	-0.1
Total	2	40	147	15	37	2	1	0	10	7		.252	.290	.279	62	-7	1			.824	-16	/S-36,3-3,O	-2.1

■ BILL HALL
Hall, William Lemuel b: 7/30/28, Moultrie, Ga. d: 1/1/86, Moultrie, Ga. BL/TR, 5'11", 165 lbs. Deb: 4/18/54

YEAR	TM/L	G	AB	R	H	2B	3B	HR	RBI	BB	SO	AVG	OBP	SLG	PRO+	BR/A	SB	CS	SBR	FA	FR	G/POS	TPR
1954	Pit-N	5	7	0	0	0	0	0	0	0	0	.000	.000	.000	-99	-2	0	0	0	1.000	-0	/C-1	-0.2
1956	Pit-N	1	3	0	0	0	0	0	0	0	1	.000	.000	.000	-99	-1	0	0	0	1.000	1	/C-1	0.0
1958	Pit-N	51	116	15	33	6	0	1	15	15	13	.284	.366	.362	96	-0	0	0	0	.982	7	C-51	0.9
Total	3	57	126	15	33	6	0	1	15	15	14	.262	.340	.333	81	-3	0	0	0	.983	8	/C-53	0.7

■ TOM HALLER
Haller, Thomas Frank b: 6/23/37, Lockport, Ill. BL/TR, 6'4", 195 lbs. Deb: 4/11/61 C

YEAR	TM/L	G	AB	R	H	2B	3B	HR	RBI	BB	SO	AVG	OBP	SLG	PRO+	BR/A	SB	CS	SBR	FA	FR	G/POS	TPR
1961	SF-N	30	62	5	9	1	0	2	8	9	23	.145	.264	.258	41	-5	0	1	-1	1.000	2	C-25	-0.3
1962	*SF-N	99	272	53	71	13	1	18	55	51	59	.261	.385	.515	142	17	1	4	-2	.992	-2	C-91	1.6
1963	SF-N	98	298	32	76	8	1	14	44	34	45	.255	.335	.430	120	8	4	6	-2	.994	-4	C-85/O-7	0.4
1964	SF-N	117	388	43	98	14	3	16	48	55	51	.253	.348	.428	115	9	4	2	0	.989	-1	*C-113/O-3	1.3
1965	SF-N	134	422	40	106	4	3	16	49	47	67	.251	.338	.389	101	1	0	0	0	.987	-5	*C-133	0.4
1966	SF-N☆	142	471	74	113	19	2	27	67	53	74	.240	.325	.461	112	7	1	3	-2	.991	-7	*C-136/1-4	0.8
1967	SF-N★	141	455	54	114	23	5	14	49	62	61	.251	.345	.415	118	12	0	4	-2	.997	-1	*C-136/O-1	1.7
1968	LA-N★	144	474	37	135	27	5	4	53	46	76	.285	.351	.388	132	18	1	4	-2	.994	3	*C-139	3.2
1969	LA-N	134	445	46	117	18	3	6	39	48	58	.263	.337	.357	102	1	0	3	-2	.992	-9	*C-132	-0.3
1970	LA-N	112	325	47	93	16	6	10	47	32	35	.286	.354	.465	123	10	3	0	1	.993	-8	*C-106	0.7
1971	LA-N	84	202	23	54	5	0	5	32	25	30	.267	.354	.366	111	3	0	2	-1	.978	4	C-67	0.9
1972	*Det-A	59	121	7	25	5	2	2	13	15	14	.207	.294	.331	83	-2	0	1	-1	1.000	8	C-36	0.7
Total	12	1294	3935	461	1011	153	31	134	504	477	593	.257	.342	.414	114	78	14	30	-14	.992	-4	*C-1199/O-11,1	11.1

■ NEWT HALLIDAY
Halliday, Newton Reese b: 6/18/1896, Chicago, Ill. d: 4/6/18, Great Lakes, Ill. BR/TR, 6'1", 175 lbs. Deb: 8/19/16

YEAR	TM/L	G	AB	R	H	2B	3B	HR	RBI	BB	SO	AVG	OBP	SLG	PRO+	BR/A	SB	CS	SBR	FA	FR	G/POS	TPR
1916	Pit-N	1	1	0	0	0	0	0	0	0	1	.000	.000	.000	-99	-0	0			1.000	0	/1-1	0.0

■ JOCKO HALLIGAN
Halligan, William E. b: 12/8/1868, Avon, N.Y. d: 2/13/45, Buffalo, N.Y. BL, 5'9", 166 lbs. Deb: 5/13/1890

YEAR	TM/L	G	AB	R	H	2B	3B	HR	RBI	BB	SO	AVG	OBP	SLG	PRO+	BR/A	SB	CS	SBR	FA	FR	G/POS	TPR
1890	Buf-P	57	211	28	53	9	2	3	33	20	19	.251	.319	.355	87	-4	7			.824	-5	O-43,C-16	-0.8
1891	Cin-N	61	247	43	77	13	6	3	44	24	25	.312	.375	.449	139	12	5			.856	-3	O-61	0.6
1892	Cin-N	26	101	14	29	4	0	2	12	12	9	.287	.363	.386	128	4	3			.875	-1	O-26	0.2
	Bal-N	46	178	38	47	4	7	2	43	30	24	.264	.376	.399	131	7	8			.861	-7	O-22,1-19/C	-0.2
	Yr	72	279	52	76	8	7	4	55	42	33	.272	.372	.394	130	11	11			.869	-8	O-48,1-19/C	0.0
Total	3	190	737	123	206	30	15	10	132	86	77	.280	.358	.402	120	19	23			.848	-16	O-152/C-21,1	-0.2

■ ED HALLINAN
Hallinan, Edward S. b: 8/23/1888, San Francisco, Cal. d: 8/24/40, San Francisco, Cal. BR/TR, 5'9", 168 lbs. Deb: 5/13/11

YEAR	TM/L	G	AB	R	H	2B	3B	HR	RBI	BB	SO	AVG	OBP	SLG	PRO+	BR/A	SB	CS	SBR	FA	FR	G/POS	TPR
1911	StL-A	52	169	13	35	3	1	0	14	14		.207	.268	.237	43	-13	4			.902	-6	S-34,2-15/3	-1.7
1912	StL-A	29	86	11	19	2	0	0	1	5		.221	.272	.244	50	-6	3			.866	-7	S-26	-1.1
Total	2	81	255	24	54	5	1	0	15	19		.212	.269	.239	45	-19	7			.887	-12	/S-60,2-15,3	-2.8

■ JIMMY HALLINAN
Hallinan, James H. b: 5/27/1849, Ireland d: 10/28/1879, Chicago, Ill. BL/TL, 5'9", 172 lbs. Deb: 7/26/1871

YEAR	TM/L	G	AB	R	H	2B	3B	HR	RBI	BB	SO	AVG	OBP	SLG	PRO+	BR/A	SB	CS	SBR	FA	FR	G/POS	TPR
1871	Kek-n	5	25	7	5	0	0	0	2	2	0	.200	.259	.200	34	-2	1					/S-5	-0.1
1875	Wes-n	13	51	12	14	1	1	0		0		.275	.275	.333	104	-0						S-13	
	Mut-n	44	202	29	58	7	3	3		1		.287	.291	.396	128	5						S-43/3-1	0.3
	Yr	57	253	41	72	8	4	3		1		.285	.287	.383	123	5						S-56/3-1	0.3
1876	NY-N	54	240	45	67	7	6	2	36	2	4	.279	.285	.383	139	10				.764	-15	*S-50/2-4,O	-0.5
1877	Cin-N	16	73	18	27	1	1	0	7	1	1	.370	.378	.411	167	6				.854	-6	2-16	0.0
	Chi-N	19	89	17	25	4	1	0	11	4	2	.281	.312	.348	96	-1				.800	-2	O-19	-0.3
	Yr	35	162	35	52	5	2	0	18	5	3	.321	.341	.377	124	4				.800	-8	O-19,2-16	-0.3
1878	Chi-N	16	67	14	19	3	0	2	5	6	6	.284	.333	.328	111	1				.789	-4	O-11/2-5	-0.3
	Ind-N	3	12	0	3	2	0	1	0	2	2	.250	.250	.417	134	0				.667	-1	/O-3	0.0
	Yr	19	79	14	22	5	0	3	5	8	8	.278	.321	.342	114	1				.760	-5	O-14/2-5	-0.3
Total	2 n	62	278	48	77	8	4	3	2	3		.277	.285	.367	114	3						/S-61,3-1	0.2
Total	3	108	481	94	141	17	8	2	57	12	15	.293	.310	.374	129	16				.783	-28	/S-50,O-35,2	-1.1

■ BILL HALLMAN
Hallman, William Harry b: 3/15/1876, Philadelphia, Pa. d: 4/23/50, Philadelphia, Pa. BL/TL, Deb: 4/25/01

YEAR	TM/L	G	AB	R	H	2B	3B	HR	RBI	BB	SO	AVG	OBP	SLG	PRO+	BR/A	SB	CS	SBR	FA	FR	G/POS	TPR
1901	Mil-A	139	549	70	135	27	6	2	47	41		.246	.301	.328	78	-16	12			.905	-2	*O-139	-2.7
1903	Chi-A	63	207	29	43	7	4	0	18	31		.208	.320	.280	85	-2	11			.953	2	O-57	-0.4
1906	Pit-N	23	89	12	24	3	1	1	6	15		.270	.375	.360	124	3	3			.935	-1	O-23	0.2
1907	Pit-N	94	302	39	67	6	2	0	15	33		.222	.305	.255	74	-8	21			.966	-6	O-84	-1.9
Total	4	319	1147	150	269	43	13	3	86	120		.235	.311	.303	82	-24	47			.933	-7	O-303	-4.8

■ BILL HALLMAN
Hallman, William Wilson b: 3/31/1867, Pittsburgh, Pa. d: 9/11/20, Philadelphia, Pa. BR/TR, 5'8", 160 lbs. Deb: 4/23/1888 M

YEAR	TM/L	G	AB	R	H	2B	3B	HR	RBI	BB	SO	AVG	OBP	SLG	PRO+	BR/A	SB	CS	SBR	FA	FR	G/POS	TPR
1888	Phi-N	18	63	5	13	4	1	0	6	1	12	.206	.219	.302	61	-3	1			.898	-7	C-10/2-4,OS3	-0.9
1889	Phi-N	119	462	67	117	21	8	2	60	36	54	.253	.313	.346	77	-16	20			.895	7	*S-106,2-13/C	-0.2
1890	Phi-P	84	356	59	95	16	7	1	37	33	24	.267	.338	.360	84	-9	6			.885	-8	O-34,C-26,23/S	-1.1
1891	Phi-a	141	587	112	166	21	13	6	69	38	56	.283	.332	.394	104	-0	18			.930	-5	*2-141	0.1
1892	Phi-N	138	586	106	171	27	10	2	84	32	52	.292	.335	.382	117	10	19			.936	-24	*2-138	-1.0
1893	Phi-N	132	596	119	183	28	7	5	76	51	27	.307	.367	.403	105	3	22			.950	-15	*2-120,1-12	-0.7
1894	Phi-N	119	505	107	156	19	7	0	66	36	15	.309	.360	.374	79	-16	36			.930	-19	*2-119	-2.3
1895	Phi-N	124	539	94	169	26	5	1	91	34	20	.314	.359	.386	92	-7	16			.943	6	*2-122/S-3	0.4
1896	Phi-N	120	469	82	150	21	3	2	83	45	23	.320	.382	.390	105	5	16			.945	3	*2-120/P-1	1.2
1897	Phi-N	31	126	16	33	3	0	0	15	8		.262	.326	.286	64	-6	1			.958	-10	2-31	-1.2
	StL-N	79	298	31	66	6	2	0	26	24		.221	.288	.255	45	-23	12			.939	3	2-77/1-3M	-1.4
	Yr	110	424	47	99	9	2	0	41	32		.233	.302	.264	51	-29	13			.944	-7	2-108/1-3	-2.6
1898	Bro-N	134	509	57	124	10	7	2	63	29		.244	.291	.303	70	-20	9			.944	-3	*2-124,3-10	-1.4
1901	Cle-A	5	19	2	4	0	0	0	8	2		.211	.286	.211	41	-1	0			.815	-3	/S-5	-0.4
	Phi-N	123	445	46	82	13	5	0	38	26		.184	.236	.236	36	-36	13			.971	-5	2-90,3-33	-3.7

YEAR	TM/L	G	AB	R	H	2B	3B	HR	RBI	BB	SO	AVG	OBP	SLG	PRO+	BR/A	SB	CS	SBR	FA	FR	G/POS	TPR
1902	Phi-N	73	254	14	63	8	4	0	35	14		.248	.287	.311	84	-5	9			.932	-6	3-72	-1.1
1903	Phi-N	63	198	20	42	11	2	0	17	16		.212	.271	.288	61	-10	2			.932	-3	2-22,3-19/10S	-1.2
Total	14	1503	6012	937	1634	234	81	21	769	425	283	.272	.325	.348	84	-136	200			.940	-88	*2-1135,3-145,S/OC1P	-14.9

■ JIM HALPIN   Halpin, James Nathaniel   b: 10/4/1863, England   d: 1/4/1893, Boston, Mass.   Deb: 6/15/1882

YEAR	TM/L	G	AB	R	H	2B	3B	HR	RBI	BB	SO	AVG	OBP	SLG	PRO+	BR/A	SB	CS	SBR	FA	FR	G/POS	TPR
1882	Wor-N	2	8	0	0	0	0	0	0	0	2	.000	.000	.000	-98	-2				.625	-1	/3-2	-0.3
1884	Was-U	46	168	24	31	3	0	0		0	2	.185	.194	.202	8	-21				.809	-7	S-39/3-7	-2.5
1885	Det-N	15	54	3	7	2	0	0	1	1	12	.130	.145	.167	1	-6				.846	1	S-15	-0.5
Total	3	63	230	27	38	5	0	0	1	3	14	.165	.176	.187	3	-28				.821	-8	/S-54,3-9	-3.3

■ AL HALT   Halt, Alva William   b: 11/23/1890, Sandusky, Ohio   d: 1/22/73, Sandusky, Ohio   BR/TR, 6', 180 lbs.   Deb: 5/29/14

YEAR	TM/L	G	AB	R	H	2B	3B	HR	RBI	BB	SO	AVG	OBP	SLG	PRO+	BR/A	SB	CS	SBR	FA	FR	G/POS	TPR
1914	Bro-F	80	261	26	61	6	2	3	25	13	39	.234	.270	.307	49	-20	11			.890	-11	S-71/2-3,O	-2.7
1915	Bro-F	151	524	41	131	22	7	3	64	39	79	.250	.307	.336	72	-21	20			.930	3	*3-111,S-40	-1.2
1918	Cle-A	26	69	9	12	2	0	0	1	9	12	.174	.269	.203	39	-5	4			.971	-1	3-14/2-4,S1	-0.6
Total	3	257	854	76	204	30	9	6	90	61	130	.239	.293	.316	63	-47	35			.933	-9	3-125,S-115/210	-4.5

■ RALPH HAM   Ham, Ralph A.   b: 3/1849, Troy, N.Y.   d: 2/13/05, Troy, N.Y.   5'8", 158 lbs.   Deb: 5/6/1871

YEAR	TM/L	G	AB	R	H	2B	3B	HR	RBI	BB	SO	AVG	OBP	SLG	PRO+	BR/A	SB	CS	SBR	FA	FR	G/POS	TPR
1871	Rok-n	25	113	25	28	4	0	0	12	1	7	.248	.254	.283	57	-6	6					O-18/2-5,S	-0.3
1872	Man-n	1	5	0	2	0	0	0	1	0	0	.400	.400	.400	156	0						/S-1	0.0
Total	2 n	26	118	25	30	4	0	0	13	1	7	.254	.261	.288	61	-5						/O-18,2-5,S	-0.3

■ CHARLIE HAMBURG   Hamburg, Charles M. (b: Charles M. Hambrick)   b: 11/22/1863, Louisville, Ky.   d: 5/18/31, Union, N.J.   6', 175 lbs.   Deb: 4/18/1890

YEAR	TM/L	G	AB	R	H	2B	3B	HR	RBI	BB	SO	AVG	OBP	SLG	PRO+	BR/A	SB	CS	SBR	FA	FR	G/POS	TPR
1890	*Lou-a	133	485	93	132	22	2	3	69			.272	.370	.344	113	11	46			.946	-2	*O-133	0.4

■ JIM HAMBY   Hamby, James Sanford "Cracker"   b: 7/29/1897, Wilkesboro, N.C.   d: 10/21/91, Springfield, Ill.   BR/TR, 6', 170 lbs.   Deb: 9/20/26

YEAR	TM/L	G	AB	R	H	2B	3B	HR	RBI	BB	SO	AVG	OBP	SLG	PRO+	BR/A	SB	CS	SBR	FA	FR	G/POS	TPR
1926	NY-N	1	3	0	0	0	0	0	0	0	0	.000	.000	.000	-99	-1	0			.600	-1	/C-1	-0.2
1927	NY-N	21	52	6	10	0	1	0	5	7	7	.192	.288	.231	40	-4	1			.904	-0	C-19	-0.3
Total	2	22	55	6	10	0	1	0	5	7	7	.182	.274	.218	33	-5	1			.885	-1	/C-20	-0.5

■ BOB HAMELIN   Hamelin, Robert James   b: 11/29/67, Elizabeth, N.J.   BL/TL, 6', 235 lbs.   Deb: 9/12/93

YEAR	TM/L	G	AB	R	H	2B	3B	HR	RBI	BB	SO	AVG	OBP	SLG	PRO+	BR/A	SB	CS	SBR	FA	FR	G/POS	TPR
1993	KC-A	16	49	2	11	3	0	2	5	6	15	.224	.309	.408	86	-1	0	0	0	.986	-0	1-15	-0.2
1994	KC-A	101	312	64	88	25	1	24	65	56	62	.282	.393	.599	140	18	4	3	-1	.992	1	D-70,1-24	1.2
Total	2	117	361	66	99	28	1	26	70	62	77	.274	.382	.573	133	17	4	3	-1	.990	1	/D-70,1-39	1.0

■ DARRYL HAMILTON   Hamilton, Darryl Quinn   b: 12/3/64, Baton Rouge, La.   BL/TR, 6'1", 180 lbs.   Deb: 6/3/88

YEAR	TM/L	G	AB	R	H	2B	3B	HR	RBI	BB	SO	AVG	OBP	SLG	PRO+	BR/A	SB	CS	SBR	FA	FR	G/POS	TPR
1988	Mil-A	44	103	14	19	4	0	1	11	12	9	.184	.276	.252	49	-7	7	3	0	1.000	-1	O-37/D-3	-0.8
1990	Mil-A	89	156	27	46	5	0	1	18	9	12	.295	.333	.346	91	-2	10	3	1	.992	-6	O-72/D-9	-0.8
1991	Mil-A	122	405	64	126	15	6	1	57	33	38	.311	.363	.385	110	6	16	6	1	.996	-10	*O-117	-0.5
1992	Mil-A	128	470	67	140	19	7	5	62	45	42	.298	.360	.400	115	10	41	14	4	1.000	1	*O-124	1.2
1993	Mil-A	135	520	74	161	21	1	9	48	45	62	.310	.368	.406	109	8	21	13	-2	.992	6	*O-129/D-1	0.9
1994	Mil-A	36	141	23	37	10	1	1	13	11	15	.262	.333	.369	79	-4	3	0	1	1.000	-4	O-32/D-4	-0.7
Total	6	554	1795	269	529	74	15	18	209	159	180	.295	.354	.383	103	10	98	39	6	.996	-14	O-511/D-17	-0.7

■ JEFF HAMILTON   Hamilton, Jeffrey Robert   b: 3/19/64, Flint, Mich.   BR/TR, 6'3", 207 lbs.   Deb: 6/28/86

YEAR	TM/L	G	AB	R	H	2B	3B	HR	RBI	BB	SO	AVG	OBP	SLG	PRO+	BR/A	SB	CS	SBR	FA	FR	G/POS	TPR
1986	LA-N	71	147	22	33	5	0	5	19	2	43	.224	.235	.361	66	-8	0	0	0	.968	11	3-66/S-2	0.3
1987	LA-N	35	83	5	18	3	0	1	9	7	22	.217	.286	.253	45	-6	0	1	-1	.935	9	3-31/S-1	0.2
1988	*LA-N	111	309	34	73	14	2	6	33	10	51	.236	.269	.353	80	-9	0	2	-1	.941	-0	*3-105/S-2,1	-1.2
1989	LA-N	151	548	45	134	35	1	12	56	20	71	.245	.275	.378	86	-12	0	0	0	.951	5	*3-147/P-1,2S	-1.8
1990	LA-N	7	24	1	3	0	0	0	1	0	3	.125	.125	.125	-32	-4	0	0	0	1.000	1	/3-7	-0.4
1991	LA-N	41	94	4	21	4	0	1	14	4	21	.223	.255	.298	56	-6	0	0	0	.928	3	3-33/S-1	-0.6
Total	6	416	1205	111	282	61	3	24	124	43	211	.234	.265	.349	74	-45	0	3	-2	.948	15	3-389/S-7,2P1	-3.5

■ TOM HAMILTON   Hamilton, Thomas Ball "Ham"   b: 9/29/25, Altoona, Kan.   d: 11/29/73, Tyler, Tex.   BL/TR, 6'4", 213 lbs.   Deb: 9/4/52

YEAR	TM/L	G	AB	R	H	2B	3B	HR	RBI	BB	SO	AVG	OBP	SLG	PRO+	BR/A	SB	CS	SBR	FA	FR	G/POS	TPR
1952	Phi-A	9	10	1	2	1	0	0	1	1	1	.200	.273	.300	56	-1	0	0	0	1.000	-0	/1-5	-0.1
1953	Phi-A	58	56	8	11	2	0	0	5	7	11	.196	.286	.232	40	-5	0	0	0	1.000	-1	/1-7,O-2	-0.6
Total	2	67	66	9	13	3	0	0	6	8	12	.197	.284	.242	42	-5	0	0	0	1.000	-1	/1-12,O-2	-0.7

■ BILLY HAMILTON   Hamilton, William Robert "Sliding Billy"   b: 2/16/1866, Newark, N.J.   d: 12/16/40, Worcester, Mass.   BL/TR, 5'6", 165 lbs.   Deb: 7/31/1888   H

YEAR	TM/L	G	AB	R	H	2B	3B	HR	RBI	BB	SO	AVG	OBP	SLG	PRO+	BR/A	SB	CS	SBR	FA	FR	G/POS	TPR
1888	KC-a	35	129	21	34	4	4	0	11	4		.264	.307	.357	106	0	19			.961	-2	O-35	-0.3
1889	KC-a	137	534	144	161	17	12	3	77	87	41	.301	.413	.395	123	19	111			.857	-7	*O-137	0.7
1890	Phi-N	123	496	133	161	13	9	2	49	83	37	.325	.430	.399	139	29	102			.882	4	*O-123	2.5
1891	Phi-N	133	527	**141**	**179**	23	7	2	60	**102**	28	**.340**	**.453**	.421	151	41	111			.907	5	*O-133	3.7
1892	Phi-N	139	554	132	183	21	7	3	53	81	29	.330	.423	.410	153	39	57			.919	14	*O-139	4.3
1893	Phi-N	82	355	110	135	22	7	5	44	63	7	.380	**.490**	.524	170	40	43			.937	4	O-82	3.3
1894	Phi-N	129	544	**192**	220	25	15	4	87	**126**	17	.404	**.523**	.528	158	65	98			.964	1	*O-129	4.6
1895	Phi-N	123	517	**166**	201	22	6	7	74	**96**	30	.389	.490	.495	154	49	97			.913	-1	*O-123	3.1
1896	Bos-N	131	523	152	191	24	9	3	52	**110**	29	.365	**.477**	.463	140	36	83			.934	-11	*O-131	1.2
1897	*Bos-N	127	507	**152**	174	17	5	3	61	**105**		.343	.461	.414	124	24	66			.962	-3	*O-126	1.0
1898	Bos-N	110	417	110	154	16	5	3	50	87		.369	**.480**	.453	**159**	38	54			.904	-15	*O-110	1.4
1899	Bos-N	84	297	63	92	7	1	1	33	72		.310	.446	.350	109	9	19			.952	1	O-81	-0.1
1900	Bos-N	136	520	103	173	20	5	1	47	107		.333	.449	.396	119	18	32			.947	2	*O-136	0.9
1901	Bos-N	102	348	71	100	11	2	3	38	64		.287	.404	.356	111	8	20			.945	1	O-99	0.1
Total	14	1591	6268	1690	2158	242	94	40	736	1187	218	.344	.455	.432	139	414	912			.926	-5	*O-1584	26.4

■ KEN HAMLIN   Hamlin, Kenneth Lee   b: 5/18/35, Detroit, Mich.   BR/TR, 5'10", 170 lbs.   Deb: 6/17/57

YEAR	TM/L	G	AB	R	H	2B	3B	HR	RBI	BB	SO	AVG	OBP	SLG	PRO+	BR/A	SB	CS	SBR	FA	FR	G/POS	TPR
1957	Pit-N	2	1	0	0	0	0	0	0	0	0	.000	.000	.000	-99	-0	0	0	0	1.000	0	/S-1	0.0
1959	Pit-N	3	8	1	1	0	0	0	0	2	1	.125	.300	.125	19	-1	0	0	0	1.000	-1	/S-3	-0.2
1960	KC-A	140	428	51	96	10	2	2	24	44	48	.224	.298	.271	55	-26	1	1	-0	.955	-41	*S-139	-5.9
1961	LA-A	42	91	4	19	3	0	1	5	11	9	.209	.301	.275	49	-6	0	1	-1	.963	13	S-39	0.8
1962	Was-A	98	292	29	74	12	0	3	22	22	22	.253	.306	.325	70	-12	7	7	-2	.963	-11	S-87/2-2	-1.9
1965	Was-A	117	362	45	99	21	1	4	22	33	45	.273	.336	.370	102	1	8	2	1	.976	-29	*S-47/3	-2.0
1966	Was-A	66	158	13	34	7	1	1	16	13	21	.215	.275	.291	63	-7	1	0	0	.963	6	2-50/3-1	0.2
Total	7	468	1340	143	323	53	4	11	89	125	146	.241	.307	.311	71	-52	17	11	-2	.959	-63	S-316,2-129/3	-9.0

■ STEVE HAMMOND   Hammond, Steven Benjamin   b: 5/9/57, Atlanta, Ga.   BL/TR, 6'2", 190 lbs.   Deb: 6/28/82   F

YEAR	TM/L	G	AB	R	H	2B	3B	HR	RBI	BB	SO	AVG	OBP	SLG	PRO+	BR/A	SB	CS	SBR	FA	FR	G/POS	TPR
1982	KC-A	46	126	14	29	5	1	1	11	4	18	.230	.254	.310	54	-8	0	1	-1	1.000	3	O-37/D-1	-0.7

■ JACK HAMMOND   Hammond, Walter Charles "Wobby"   b: 2/26/1891, Amsterdam, N.Y.   d: 3/4/42, Kenosha, Wis.   BR/TR, 5'11", 170 lbs.   Deb: 4/15/15

YEAR	TM/L	G	AB	R	H	2B	3B	HR	RBI	BB	SO	AVG	OBP	SLG	PRO+	BR/A	SB	CS	SBR	FA	FR	G/POS	TPR
1915	Cle-A	35	84	9	18	2	1	0	4	7	19	.214	.224	.262	44	-6	0	1	-1	.957	-8	2-19	-1.6
1922	Cle-A	1	4	1	1	0	0	0	0	0	0	.250	.250	.250	30	-1	0	0	0	.333	-2	/2-1	-0.2
	Pit-N	9	11	3	3	0	0	0	0	1	0	.273	.333	.273	57	-1	0	0	0	1.000	2	/2-4	0.1
Total	2	45	99	13	22	2	1	0	4	2	19	.222	.238	.263	45	-7	0	1	-1	.943	-8	/2-24	-1.7

■ JEFFREY HAMMONDS   Hammonds, Jeffrey Bryan   b: 3/5/71, Plainfield, N.J.   BR/TR, 6', 195 lbs.   Deb: 6/25/93

YEAR	TM/L	G	AB	R	H	2B	3B	HR	RBI	BB	SO	AVG	OBP	SLG	PRO+	BR/A	SB	CS	SBR	FA	FR	G/POS	TPR
1993	Bal-A	33	105	10	32	8	0	3	19	2	16	.305	.318	.467	104	0	4	0	1	.961	1	O-23/D-8	0.1

YEAR	TM/L	G	AB	R	H	2B	3B	HR	RBI	BB	SO	AVG	OBP	SLG	PRO+	BR/A	SB	CS	SBR	FA	FR	G/POS	TPR
1994	Bal-A	68	250	45	74	18	2	8	31	17	39	.296	.346	.480	103	1	5	0	2	.962	4	O-66	0.4
Total	2	101	355	55	106	26	2	11	50	19	55	.299	.338	.476	103	1	9	0	3	.962	5	/O-89,D-8	0.5

■ GRANNY HAMNER
Hamner, Granville Wilbur   b: 4/26/27, Richmond, Va.   d: 9/12/93, Philadelphia, Pa.   BR/TR, 5'10", 163 lbs.   Deb: 9/14/44   F

YEAR	TM/L	G	AB	R	H	2B	3B	HR	RBI	BB	SO	AVG	OBP	SLG	PRO+	BR/A	SB	CS	SBR	FA	FR	G/POS	TPR
1944	Phi-N	21	77	6	19	1	0	0	5	3	7	.247	.275	.260	53	-5	0			.933	6	S-21	0.3
1945	Phi-N	14	41	3	7	2	0	0	6	1	3	.171	.190	.220	14	-5	0			.861	3	S-13	-0.1
1946	Phi-N	2	7	0	1	0	0	0	0	0	3	.143	.143	.143	-19	-1	0			.857	-1	/S-2	-0.2
1947	Phi-N	2	7	1	2	0	0	0	0	0	0	.286	.375	.286	81	-0	0			1.000	0	/S-2	0.0
1948	Phi-N	129	446	42	116	21	5	3	48	22	39	.260	.298	.350	76	-16	2			.967	-8	2-87,S-37/3	-1.7
1949	Phi-N	154	662	83	174	32	5	6	53	25	47	.263	.296	.353	74	-27	6			.961	-9	*S-154	-1.6
1950	*Phi-N	157	637	78	172	27	5	11	82	39	35	.270	.314	.380	83	-17	2			.944	-5	*S-157	-0.9
1951	Phi-N	150	589	61	150	23	7	9	72	29	32	.255	.290	.363	76	-22	10	5	0	.958	-2	*S-150	-1.3
1952	Phi-N★	151	596	74	164	30	5	17	87	27	51	.275	.307	.428	103	-0	7	3	0	.951	-4	*S-151	0.7
1953	Phi-N★	154	609	90	168	30	8	21	92	32	28	.276	.313	.455	98	-4	2	1	0	.970	-8	2-93,S-71	-0.3
1954	Phi-N★	152	596	83	178	39	11	13	89	53	44	.299	.356	.466	112	10	1	2	-1	.978	-23	*2-152/S-1	-0.3
1955	Phi-N	104	405	57	104	12	4	5	43	41	30	.257	.327	.343	79	-11	0	1	-1	.960	-36	2-82,S-32	-3.9
1956	Phi-N	122	401	42	90	24	3	4	42	30	42	.224	.278	.329	64	-21	2	0	1	.937	-13	*S-110,2-11/P	-2.4
1957	Phi-N	133	502	59	114	19	5	10	62	34	42	.227	.276	.345	68	-24	3	1	0	.963	-39	*2-125/S-5,P	-5.5
1958	Phi-N	35	133	18	40	7	3	2	18	8	16	.301	.340	.444	107	1	0	0	0	.984	-3	3-22,2-11/S	-0.1
1959	Phi-N	21	64	10	19	4	0	2	6	5	5	.297	.348	.453	109	1	0	1	-1	.947	-7	S-15/3-1	-0.6
	Cle-A	27	67	4	11	1	1	1	3	1	8	.164	.176	.254	17	-8	0	0	0	.960	-2	S-10/2-7,3	-0.9
1962	KC-A	3	0	0	0	0	0	0	0	0	0	—	—	—		0	0	0	0	1.000	0	/P-3	0.0
Total	17	1531	5839	711	1529	272	62	104	708	351	432	.262	.304	.383	84	-149	35	14		.946	-139	S-934,2-568/3P	-18.8

■ GARVIN HAMNER
Hamner, Wesley Garvin   b: 3/18/24, Richmond, Va.   BR/TR, 5'11", 172 lbs.   Deb: 4/17/45   F

YEAR	TM/L	G	AB	R	H	2B	3B	HR	RBI	BB	SO	AVG	OBP	SLG	PRO+	BR/A	SB	CS	SBR	FA	FR	G/POS	TPR
1945	Phi-N	32	101	12	20	3	0	0	5	7	9	.198	.250	.228	34	-9	2			.962	-4	2-21/S-9,3	-1.1

■ IKE HAMPTON
Hampton, Isaac Bernard   b: 8/22/51, Camden, S.C.   BB/TR, 6'1", 185 lbs.   Deb: 9/12/74

YEAR	TM/L	G	AB	R	H	2B	3B	HR	RBI	BB	SO	AVG	OBP	SLG	PRO+	BR/A	SB	CS	SBR	FA	FR	G/POS	TPR
1974	NY-N	4	4	0	0	0	0	0	1	0	1	.000	.000	.000	-99	-1	0	0	0	1.000	-0	/C-1	-0.1
1975	Cal-A	31	66	8	10	3	0	0	4	7	19	.152	.243	.197	28	-6	0	0	0	.947	-5	C-28/S-2,3	-1.0
1976	Cal-A	3	2	0	0	0	0	0	0	0	0	.000	.000	.000	-99	-1	0	0	0	1.000	1	/C-2,S-1	0.0
1977	Cal-A	52	44	5	13	1	0	3	9	2	10	.295	.340	.523	137	2	0	0	0	.968	1	C-47/D-2	0.3
1978	Cal-A	19	14	2	3	0	1	0	4	2	7	.214	.313	.571	149	2	1	0	0	.905	1	C-13/1-1,D	0.2
1979	Cal-A	4	5	0	2	0	0	0	0	0	1	.400	.400	.400	121	0	0	0	0	1.000	1	/1-2	0.1
Total	6	113	135	15	28	4	1	4	18	11	38	.207	.277	.341	75	-5	1	0	0	.953	-2	/C-91,D-6,1S3	-0.5

■ BERT HAMRIC
Hamric, Odbert Herman   b: 3/1/28, Clarksburg, W.Va.   d: 8/8/84, Springboro, Ohio   BL/TR, 6', 165 lbs.   Deb: 4/24/55

YEAR	TM/L	G	AB	R	H	2B	3B	HR	RBI	BB	SO	AVG	OBP	SLG	PRO+	BR/A	SB	CS	SBR	FA	FR	G/POS	TPR
1955	Bro-N	2	1	0	0	0	0	0	0	0	0	.000	.000	.000	-97	-1	0	0	0	.000	0	H	0.0
1958	Bal-A	8	8	0	1	0	0	0	0	0	6	.125	.125	.125	-33	-1	0	0	0	.000	0	H	-0.2
Total	2	10	9	0	1	0	0	0	0	0	7	.111	.111	.111	-41	-2	0	0	0		0	-0,-0	-0.2

■ RAY HAMRICK
Hamrick, Raymond Bernard   b: 8/1/21, Nashville, Tenn.   BR/TR, 5'11.5", 160 lbs.   Deb: 8/14/43

YEAR	TM/L	G	AB	R	H	2B	3B	HR	RBI	BB	SO	AVG	OBP	SLG	PRO+	BR/A	SB	CS	SBR	FA	FR	G/POS	TPR
1943	Phi-N	44	160	12	32	3	1	0	9	8	28	.200	.238	.231	37	-13	0			.960	-11	2-31,S-12	-2.4
1944	Phi-N	74	292	22	60	10	1	1	23	23	34	.205	.268	.257	50	-19	1			.948	20	S-74	0.7
Total	2	118	452	34	92	13	2	1	32	31	62	.204	.258	.248	46	-33	1			.946	9	/S-86,2-31	-1.7

■ BUDDY HANCKEN
Hancken, Morris Medlock   b: 8/30/14, Birmingham, Ala.   BR/TR, 6'1", 175 lbs.   Deb: 5/14/40   C

YEAR	TM/L	G	AB	R	H	2B	3B	HR	RBI	BB	SO	AVG	OBP	SLG	PRO+	BR/A	SB	CS	SBR	FA	FR	G/POS	TPR
1940	Phi-A	1	0	0	0	0	0	0	0	0	0	—	—	—		0	0			1.000	-0	/C-1	0.0

■ FRED HANCOCK
Hancock, Fred James   b: 3/28/20, Allenport, Pa.   d: 3/12/86, Clearwater, Fla.   BR/TR, 5'8", 170 lbs.   Deb: 4/26/49

YEAR	TM/L	G	AB	R	H	2B	3B	HR	RBI	BB	SO	AVG	OBP	SLG	PRO+	BR/A	SB	CS	SBR	FA	FR	G/POS	TPR
1949	Chi-A	39	52	7	7	2	1	0	9	8	9	.135	.262	.212	27	-6	0	1	-1	.978	-3	S-27/3-3,O	-0.9

■ GARRY HANCOCK
Hancock, Ronald Garry   b: 1/23/54, Tampa, Fla.   BL/TL, 6', 175 lbs.   Deb: 7/16/78

YEAR	TM/L	G	AB	R	H	2B	3B	HR	RBI	BB	SO	AVG	OBP	SLG	PRO+	BR/A	SB	CS	SBR	FA	FR	G/POS	TPR
1978	Bos-A	38	80	10	18	3	0	0	4	1	12	.225	.235	.262	36	-7	0	0	0	1.000	-0	O-19,D-13	-0.8
1980	Bos-A	46	115	9	33	6	0	4	19	3	11	.287	.305	.443	97	-1	0	3	-2	.963	-2	O-27,D-12	-0.6
1981	Bos-A	26	45	4	7	3	0	0	3	2	4	.156	.191	.222	18	-5	0	0	0	1.000	-0	/O-8,D-4	-0.5
1982	Bos-A	11	14	0	0	0	0	0	0	1	1	.000	.067	.000	-75	-3	0	0	0	1.000	-2	/O-7	-0.6
1983	Oak-A	101	256	29	70	7	3	8	30	5	13	.273	.290	.418	94	-2	2	0	1	.981	-9	O-67,1-27/D	-1.3
1984	Oak-A	51	60	2	13	2	0	0	8	0	1	.217	.217	.250	31	-6	0	0	0	1.000	-5	O-18/1-4,PD	-1.1
Total	6	273	570	57	141	21	3	12	64	12	42	.247	.264	.358	71	-23	2	3	-1	.982	-19	O-146/D-43,1P	-4.9

■ MIKE HANDIBOE
Handiboe, Aloysius James "Coalyard Mike"   b: 7/21/1887, Washington, D.C.   d: 1/31/53, Savannah, Ga.   BL/TL, 5'10", 155 lbs.   Deb: 9/8/11

YEAR	TM/L	G	AB	R	H	2B	3B	HR	RBI	BB	SO	AVG	OBP	SLG	PRO+	BR/A	SB	CS	SBR	FA	FR	G/POS	TPR
1911	NY-A	5	15	0	1	0	0	0		0	2	.067	.176	.067	-29	-3	0			1.000	-0	/O-4	-0.3

■ GENE HANDLEY
Handley, Eugene Louis   b: 11/25/14, Kennett, Mo.   BR/TR, 5'10.5", 165 lbs.   Deb: 4/16/46   F

YEAR	TM/L	G	AB	R	H	2B	3B	HR	RBI	BB	SO	AVG	OBP	SLG	PRO+	BR/A	SB	CS	SBR	FA	FR	G/POS	TPR
1946	Phi-A	89	251	31	63	8	5	0	21	22	25	.251	.311	.323	78	-8	8	3	1	.947	-17	2-68/3-4,S	-2.1
1947	Phi-A	36	90	10	23	2	1	0	8	10	2	.256	.330	.300	74	-3	1	0	0	.973	-5	2-17,3-10/S	-0.7
Total	2	125	341	41	86	10	6	0	29	32	27	.252	.316	.317	77	-10	9	3	1	.952	-23	/2-85,3-14,S	-2.8

■ LEE HANDLEY
Handley, Lee Elmer "Jeep"   b: 7/31/13, Clarion, Iowa   d: 4/8/70, Pittsburgh, Pa.   BR/TR, 5'7", 160 lbs.   Deb: 4/15/36   F

YEAR	TM/L	G	AB	R	H	2B	3B	HR	RBI	BB	SO	AVG	OBP	SLG	PRO+	BR/A	SB	CS	SBR	FA	FR	G/POS	TPR
1936	Cin-N	24	78	10	24	1	0	2	8	7	16	.308	.365	.397	112	1	3			.926	-0	2-16/3-7	0.2
1937	Pit-N	127	480	59	120	21	12	3	37	37	40	.250	.305	.363	81	-14	3			.950	-14	*2-126/3-1	-1.9
1938	Pit-N	139	570	91	153	25	8	6	51	53	31	.268	.332	.372	93	-6	7			.948	9	*3-136	0.5
1939	Pit-N	101	376	43	107	14	5	1	42	32	20	.285	.341	.356	89	-6	17			.936	-10	*3-100	-1.5
1940	Pit-N	98	302	50	85	7	4	1	19	27	16	.281	.340	.341	89	-4	4			.925	1	3-80/2-2	-0.2
1941	Pit-N	124	459	59	132	18	4	0	33	35	22	.288	.338	.344	93	-4	16			.947	-1	*3-114	-0.2
1944	Pit-N	40	86	7	19	2	0	0	5	5	3	.221	.247	.244	37	-7	1			.947	2	2-19,3-11/S	-0.4
1945	Pit-N	98	312	39	93	16	2	1	32	20	16	.298	.340	.372	94	-3	7			.947	15	3-79	1.4
1946	Pit-N	116	416	43	99	8	7	1	28	29	20	.238	.289	.298	65	-19	4			.958	13	*3-102/2-3	-0.5
1947	Phi-N	101	277	14	70	10	3	0	42	24	18	.253	.312	.310	68	-12	1			.975	2	3-83/2-3,S	-1.0
Total	10	968	3356	418	902	122	45	15	297	267	204	.269	.323	.345	84	-73	68			.949	16	3-713,2-169/S	-3.6

■ HARRY HANEBRINK
Hanebrink, Harry Aloysius   b: 11/12/27, St.Louis, Mo.   BL/TR, 6', 165 lbs.   Deb: 5/3/53

YEAR	TM/L	G	AB	R	H	2B	3B	HR	RBI	BB	SO	AVG	OBP	SLG	PRO+	BR/A	SB	CS	SBR	FA	FR	G/POS	TPR
1953	Mil-N	51	80	8	19	1	1	1	8	6	8	.237	.291	.313	61	-5	1	0	0	.979	8	2-21/3-1	0.0
1957	Mil-N	6	7	0	2	0	0	0	0	1	0	.286	.375	.286	87	-0	0	0	0	1.000	1	/3-2	0.1
1958	*Mil-N	63	133	14	25	3	0	4	10	13	9	.188	.270	.301	56	-9	0	1	-0	.982	-0	O-33/3-7	-1.1
1959	Phi-N	57	97	10	25	3	1	1	7	2	12	.258	.273	.340	61	-5	0	0	0	.889	-6	2-15/3-9,O	-1.1
Total	4	177	317	32	71	7	2	6	25	22	31	.224	.279	.315	60	-19	1	1	-0	.959	-2	/2-36,O-34,3	-2.1

■ FRED HANEY
Haney, Fred Girard "Pudge"   b: 4/25/1898, Albuquerque, N.Mex   d: 11/9/77, Beverly Hills, Cal.   BR/TR, 5'6", 170 lbs.   Deb: 4/18/22   MC

YEAR	TM/L	G	AB	R	H	2B	3B	HR	RBI	BB	SO	AVG	OBP	SLG	PRO+	BR/A	SB	CS	SBR	FA	FR	G/POS	TPR
1922	Det-A	81	213	41	75	7	4	0	25	32	14	.352	.438	.423	129	11	3	8	-4	.937	2	3-53,1-11/S	1.2
1923	Det-A	142	503	85	142	13	4	4	67	64	23	.282	.347	.348	85	-10	13	5	4	.955	-2	2-69,3-55,S	-0.5
1924	Det-A	86	256	54	79	11	1	1	30	39	13	.309	.400	.371	101	2	7	4	-0	.933	4	3-59/S-4,2	1.0
1925	Det-A	114	398	84	111	13	0	3	40	66	29	.279	.384	.332	84	-7	11	5	3	.953	-2	3-106	0.2
1926	Bos-A	138	462	47	102	15	4	0	52	74	28	.221	.330	.284	63	-23	13	6	6	.957	6	*3-137	-0.8
1927	Bos-A	47	116	23	32	4	1	3	12	25	14	.276	.404	.405	113	3	4	1	1	.936	-2	3-34/O-1	0.3

YEAR	TM/L	G	AB	R	H	2B	3B	HR	RBI	BB	SO	AVG	OBP	SLG	PRO+	BR/A	SB	CS	SBR	FA	FR	G/POS	TPR
	Chi-N	4	3	0	0	0	0	0	0	0	0	.000	.000	.000	-99	-1	0			.000	0	H	-0.1
1929	StL-N	10	26	4	3	1	1	0	2	1	2	.115	.179	.231	1	-4	0			.958	3	/3-6	-0.1
Total	7	622	1977	338	544	66	21	8	228	282	123	.275	.368	.342	87	-29	51	25		.949	9	3-450/2-72,S10	1.2

■ TODD HANEY
Haney, Todd Michael b: 7/30/65, Waco, Tex. BR/TR, 5'9", 165 lbs. Deb: 9/9/92

YEAR	TM/L	G	AB	R	H	2B	3B	HR	RBI	BB	SO	AVG	OBP	SLG	PRO+	BR/A	SB	CS	SBR	FA	FR	G/POS	TPR
1992	Mon-N	7	10	0	3	1	0	0	1	0	0	.300	.300	.400	97	-0	0	0	0	1.000	-0	/2-5	-0.1
1994	Chi-N	17	37	6	6	0	0	1	2	3	3	.162	.244	.243	28	-4	2	1	0	.979	-0	2-11/3-3	-0.4
Total	2	24	47	6	9	1	0	1	3	3	3	.191	.255	.277	42	-4	2	1	0	.982	-1	/2-16,3-3	-0.5

■ LARRY HANEY
Haney, Wallace Larry b: 11/19/42, Charlottesville, Va BR/TR, 6'2", 195 lbs. Deb: 7/27/66 FC

YEAR	TM/L	G	AB	R	H	2B	3B	HR	RBI	BB	SO	AVG	OBP	SLG	PRO+	BR/A	SB	CS	SBR	FA	FR	G/POS	TPR
1966	Bal-A	20	56	3	9	1	0	1	3	1	15	.161	.190	.232	21	-6	0	0	0	.985	3	C-20	-0.2
1967	Bal-A	58	164	13	44	11	0	3	20	6	28	.268	.294	.390	101	-0	1	0	0	.991	2	C-57	0.5
1968	Bal-A	38	89	5	21	3	1	1	5	0	19	.236	.236	.326	69	-4	0	0	0	.994	4	C-32	0.2
1969	Sea-A	22	59	3	15	3	0	2	7	6	12	.254	.323	.407	105	0	1	1	-0	.956	-2	C-20	-0.1
	Oak-A	53	86	8	13	4	0	2	12	7	19	.151	.223	.267	38	-7	0	0	0	.994	-0	C-53	-0.7
	Yr	75	145	11	28	7	0	4	19	13	31	.193	.264	.324	66	-7	1	1	-0	.979	-2	C-73	-0.8
1970	Oak-A	2	2	2	0	0	0	0	0	2	1	.000	.500	.000	51	0	0	0	0	1.000	-0	/C-1	0.0
1972	Oak-A	5	4	0	0	0	0	0	0	0	1	.000	.000	.000	-99	-1	0	0	0	.800	-1	/C-4,2-1	-0.3
1973	Oak-A	2	2	0	1	0	0	0	0	0	0	.500	.500	.500	192	-0	0	0	0	1.000	-0	/C-2	0.0
	StL-N	2	1	0	0	0	0	0	0	0	0	.000	.000	.000	-99	-0	0	0	0	1.000	-0	/C-2	0.0
1974	*Oak-A	76	121	12	20	4	0	2	3	3	18	.165	.185	.248	25	-12	1	0	0	.992	10	C-73/3-3,1	0.0
1975	Oak-A	47	26	3	5	0	0	1	2	1	4	.192	.222	.308	50	-2	0	0	0	1.000	7	C-43/3-4	0.6
1976	Oak-A	88	177	12	40	5	0	0	10	13	26	.226	.283	.237	56	-10	0	1	-1	.974	9	C-87	0.1
1977	Mil-A	63	127	7	29	2	0	0	10	5	30	.228	.258	.244	38	-11	0	0	0	.985	8	C-63	-0.2
1978	Mil-A	4	5	0	1	0	0	0	1	0	1	.200	.200	.200	13	-1	0	0	0	1.000	-0	/C-4	-0.1
Total	12	480	919	68	198	30	1	12	73	44	175	.215	.254	.289	57	-53	3	2	-0	.985	40	C-461/3-7,12	-0.2

■ CHARLIE HANFORD
Hanford, Charles Joseph b: 6/3/1881, Tunstall, England d: 7/19/63, Trenton, N.J. BR/TR, 5'6.5", 145 lbs. Deb: 4/13/14

YEAR	TM/L	G	AB	R	H	2B	3B	HR	RBI	BB	SO	AVG	OBP	SLG	PRO+	BR/A	SB	CS	SBR	FA	FR	G/POS	TPR
1914	Buf-F	155	597	83	174	28	13	12	90	32	81	.291	.332	.442	97	-5	37			.973	10	*O-155	-0.2
1915	Chi-F	77	179	27	43	4	5	0	22	12	28	.240	.295	.318	68	-9	10			.971	-4	O-43	-1.6
Total	2	232	776	110	217	32	18	12	112	44	109	.280	.323	.414	91	-14	47			.972	6	O-198	-1.8

■ JAY HANKINS
Hankins, Jay Nelson b: 11/7/35, St.Louis Co., Mo. BL/TR, 5'7", 170 lbs. Deb: 4/15/61

YEAR	TM/L	G	AB	R	H	2B	3B	HR	RBI	BB	SO	AVG	OBP	SLG	PRO+	BR/A	SB	CS	SBR	FA	FR	G/POS	TPR
1961	KC-A	76	173	23	32	0	3	3	16	8	17	.185	.225	.272	32	-17	2	0	0	.970	-10	O-65	-2.9
1963	KC-A	10	34	2	6	0	1	1	4	0	3	.176	.176	.324	35	-3	0	1	-1	.952	1	/O-9	-0.4
Total	2	86	207	25	38	0	4	4	10	8	20	.184	.218	.280	32	-20	2	1	0	.967	-10	/O-74	-3.3

■ FRANK HANKINSON
Hankinson, Frank Edward b: 4/29/1856, New York, N.Y. d: 4/5/11, Palisades Park, N.J BR/TR, 5'11", 168 lbs. Deb: 5/1/1878

YEAR	TM/L	G	AB	R	H	2B	3B	HR	RBI	BB	SO	AVG	OBP	SLG	PRO+	BR/A	SB	CS	SBR	FA	FR	G/POS	TPR
1878	Chi-N	58	240	38	64	8	3	1	27	5	36	.267	.282	.338	96	-2				.875	8	*3-57/P-1	0.8
1879	Chi-N	44	171	14	31	4	0	0	8	2	14	.181	.191	.205	29	-13				.933	6	P-26,O-14/3	-0.4
1880	Cle-N	69	263	32	55	7	4	1	19	1	23	.209	.212	.278	66	-9				.844	-12	*3-56,O-12/P	-2.0
1881	Tro-N	85	321	34	62	15	1	1	19	10	41	.193	.218	.249	44	-21				.907	7	*3-84/S-1	-1.1
1883	NY-N	94	337	40	74	13	6	2	30	19	38	.220	.261	.312	74	-10				.870	-4	*3-93/O-1	-1.3
1884	NY-N	105	389	44	90	16	7	2	43	23	59	.231	.274	.324	85	-7				.871	-1	*3-105/O-1	-0.6
1885	NY-a	94	362	43	81	12	2	2		12		.224	.251	.285	75	-10				**.906**	18	*3-94/P-1	0.9
1886	NY-a	136	522	66	126	14	5	2		49		.241	.306	.299	94	-2	10			.873	25	*3-136	2.3
1887	NY-a	127	512	79	137	29	11	1		38		.268	.318	.373	97	-3	19			.864	3	*3-127	0.6
1888	KC-a	37	155	20	27	4	1	0	20	11		.174	.229	.232	45	-10	2			.947	-5	2-13/S-9,O31	-1.3
Total	10	849	3272	410	747	122	39	13	166	170	211	.228	.267	.301	77	-85	31			.875	50	3-764/O-35,P2S1	-2.1

■ NED HANLON
Hanlon, Edward Hugh b: 8/22/1857, Montville, Conn. d: 4/14/37, Baltimore, Md. BL/TR, 5'9.5", 170 lbs. Deb: 5/1/1880 M

YEAR	TM/L	G	AB	R	H	2B	3B	HR	RBI	BB	SO	AVG	OBP	SLG	PRO+	BR/A	SB	CS	SBR	FA	FR	G/POS	TPR
1880	Cle-N	73	280	30	69	10	3	0	32	11	30	.246	.275	.304	98	-0				.804	-3	*O-69/S-4	-0.5
1881	Det-N	76	305	63	85	14	8	2	28	22	11	.279	.327	.397	122	7				.897	-5	*O-74/S-2	0.1
1882	Det-N	82	347	68	80	18	6	5	38	26	25	.231	.284	.360	105	3				.887	14	*O-82/2-1	1.4
1883	Det-N	100	413	65	100	13	2	1	40	34	44	.242	.300	.291	84	-6				.884	2	*O-90,2-11	-0.4
1884	Det-N	114	450	86	119	18	6	1	39	40	52	.264	.324	.364	124	14				.874	13	*O-114	2.2
1885	Det-N	105	424	93	128	18	8	1	29	47	18	.302	.372	.389	146	23				.863	4	*O-105	2.2
1886	Det-N	126	494	105	116	6	6	4	60	57	39	.235	.314	.296	84	-8	50			.929	-4	*O-126/2-1	-1.4
1887	*Det-N	118	471	79	129	13	7	4	69	30	24	.274	.320	.357	85	-10	69			.904	3	*O-118	-0.8
1888	Det-N	109	459	64	122	8	8	5	39	15	32	.266	.295	.346	104	1	38			.919	-6	*O-109	-0.7
1889	Pit-N	116	461	81	110	14	10	2	37	58	25	.239	.326	.325	91	-4	53			.919	-3	*O-116,M	-0.8
1890	Pit-P	118	472	106	131	16	6	1	44	80	24	.278	.389	.343	105	9	65			.911	-2	*O-118,M	0.3
1891	Pit-N	119	455	87	121	12	8	0	60	48	30	.266	.341	.327	97	-0	54			.881	0	*O-119/S-1M	-0.3
1892	Bal-N	11	43	3	7	1	1	0	2	3	3	.163	.217	.233	35	-3	0			.786	-0	O-11,M	-0.4
Total	13	1267	5074	930	1317	159	79	30	517	471	357	.260	.325	.340	102	25	329			.891	14	*O-1251/2-13,S	0.9

■ BILL HANLON
Hanlon, William Joseph "Big Bill" b: 6/24/1876, Los Angeles, Cal. d: 11/23/05, Los Angeles, Cal. 6', Deb: 4/16/03

YEAR	TM/L	G	AB	R	H	2B	3B	HR	RBI	BB	SO	AVG	OBP	SLG	PRO+	BR/A	SB	CS	SBR	FA	FR	G/POS	TPR
1903	Chi-N	8	21	4	2	0	0	0	2	6		.095	.296	.095	14	-2	1			.980	-0	/1-8	-0.2

■ JOHN HANNA
Hanna, John b: 11/3/1863, Philadelphia, Pa. d: 11/7/30, Philadelphia, Pa. Deb: 5/23/1884

YEAR	TM/L	G	AB	R	H	2B	3B	HR	RBI	BB	SO	AVG	OBP	SLG	PRO+	BR/A	SB	CS	SBR	FA	FR	G/POS	TPR
1884	Was-a	23	76	8	5	0	0	0		6		.066	.134	.066	-37	-11				.874	0	C-18/O-6	-0.9
	Ric-a	22	67	6	13	2	1	0		0		.194	.206	.254	50	-4				.924	4	C-21/S-1	0.2
	Yr	45	143	14	18	2	1	0		6		.126	.167	.154	6	-14				.900	4	C-39/O-6,S	-0.7

■ TRUCK HANNAH
Hannah, James Harrison b: 6/5/1889, Larimore, N.D. d: 4/27/82, Fountain Valley, Cal. BR/TR, 6'1", 190 lbs. Deb: 4/15/18

YEAR	TM/L	G	AB	R	H	2B	3B	HR	RBI	BB	SO	AVG	OBP	SLG	PRO+	BR/A	SB	CS	SBR	FA	FR	G/POS	TPR
1918	NY-A	90	250	24	55	6	0	2	21	51	25	.220	.361	.268	88	-1	5			.974	3	C-88	1.0
1919	NY-A	75	227	14	54	8	3	1	20	22	19	.238	.313	.313	76	-7	0			**.984**	-9	C-73/1-1	-1.0
1920	NY-A	79	259	24	64	11	1	2	25	24	35	.247	.313	.320	66	-13	2	0	1	.961	-6	C-78	-1.2
Total	3	244	736	62	173	25	4	5	66	97	79	.235	.331	.300	76	-21	7	0		.973	-11	C-239/1-1	-1.2

■ JACK HANNIFIN
Hannifin, John Joseph b: 2/25/1883, Holyoke, Mass. d: 10/27/45, Northampton, Mass. BR/TR, 5'11", 167 lbs. Deb: 4/19/06

YEAR	TM/L	G	AB	R	H	2B	3B	HR	RBI	BB	SO	AVG	OBP	SLG	PRO+	BR/A	SB	CS	SBR	FA	FR	G/POS	TPR
1906	Phi-A	1	1	0	1	0	0	0	0	0		1.000	1.000	1.000	511	0	0			.000	0	H	0.0
	NY-N	10	30	4	6	0	1	0	3	2		.200	.250	.267	60	-1	1			.903	-1	/S-6,3-3,2	-0.2
1907	NY-N	56	149	16	34	7	3	1	15	15		.228	.303	.336	97	-1	6			.996	-4	1-29,3-10/SO	-0.5
1908	NY-N	1	2	0	0	0	0	0	0	0		.000	.000	.000	-95	-0	0			.000	-0	/O-1	-0.1
	Bos-N	90	257	30	53	6	2	0	22	28		.206	.284	.268	78	-6	7			.930	5	3-35,2-22,S/O	-0.1
	Yr	91	259	30	53	6	2	0	22	28		.205	.282	.266	77	-6	7			.930	5	3-35,2-22,S/O	-0.1
Total	3	158	439	50	94	13	6	2	40	45		.214	.289	.292	84	-8	14			.937	0	/3-48,S-30,120	-0.8

■ PAT HANNIFIN
Hannifin, Patrick James b: 1868, Nova Scotia, Canada d: 11/5/08, Springfield, Mass. TL, Deb: 4/29/1897

YEAR	TM/L	G	AB	R	H	2B	3B	HR	RBI	BB	SO	AVG	OBP	SLG	PRO+	BR/A	SB	CS	SBR	FA	FR	G/POS	TPR
1897	Bro-N	10	20	4	5	0	0	0	2	1		.250	.375	.250	71	-1	4			.867	2	/O-3,2-2	0.1

■ DAVE HANSEN
Hansen, David Andrew b: 11/24/68, Long Beach, Cal. BL/TR, 6', 180 lbs. Deb: 9/16/90

YEAR	TM/L	G	AB	R	H	2B	3B	HR	RBI	BB	SO	AVG	OBP	SLG	PRO+	BR/A	SB	CS	SBR	FA	FR	G/POS	TPR
1990	LA-N	5	7	0	1	0	0	0	0	0	1	.143	.143	.143	-22	-0	0	0	0	.500	-1	/3-2	-0.2
1991	LA-N	53	56	3	15	4	0	1	5	2	12	.268	.293	.393	93	-1	0	0	0	1.000	2	3-21/S-1	0.1
1992	LA-N	132	341	30	73	11	0	6	22	34	49	.214	.287	.299	67	-15	0	2	-1	**.968**	7	*3-108	-1.0

YEAR	TM/L	G	AB	R	H	2B	3B	HR	RBI	BB	SO	AVG	OBP	SLG	PRO+	BR/A	SB	CS	SBR	FA	FR	G/POS	TPR
1993	LA-N	84	105	13	38	3	0	4	30	21	13	.362	.468	.505	170	12	0	1	-1	.927	-1	3-18	1.0
1994	LA-N	40	44	3	15	3	0	0	5	5	5	.341	.408	.409	121	2	0	0	0	.857	-1	/3-7	0.0
Total	5	314	553	49	142	21	0	11	63	62	82	.257	.333	.354	94	-3	1	3	-2	.960	6	3-156/S-1	-0.1

■ DOUG HANSEN
Hansen, Douglas William b: 12/16/28, Los Angeles, Cal. BR/TR, 6', 180 lbs. Deb: 9/4/51

YEAR	TM/L	G	AB	R	H	2B	3B	HR	RBI	BB	SO	AVG	OBP	SLG	PRO+	BR/A	SB	CS	SBR	FA	FR	G/POS	TPR
1951	Cle-A	3	0	2	0	0	0	0	0	0	0	—	—	—	—	0	0	0	0	.000	0	R	0.0

■ BOB HANSEN
Hansen, Robert Joseph b: 5/26/48, Boston, Mass. BL/TL, 6', 195 lbs. Deb: 5/10/74

YEAR	TM/L	G	AB	R	H	2B	3B	HR	RBI	BB	SO	AVG	OBP	SLG	PRO+	BR/A	SB	CS	SBR	FA	FR	G/POS	TPR
1974	Mil-A	58	88	8	26	4	1	2	9	3	16	.295	.319	.432	115	1	2	1	0	1.000	-0	D-18/1-3	0.1
1976	Mil-A	24	61	4	10	1	0	0	4	6	8	.164	.239	.180	24	-6	0	0	0	.000	-0	D-14/1-1	-0.7
Total	2	82	149	12	36	5	1	2	13	9	24	.242	.285	.329	78	-4	2	1	0	1.000	-0	/D-32,1-4	-0.6

■ RON HANSEN
Hansen, Ronald Lavern b: 4/5/38, Oxford, Neb. BR/TR, 6'3", 200 lbs. Deb: 4/15/58 C

YEAR	TM/L	G	AB	R	H	2B	3B	HR	RBI	BB	SO	AVG	OBP	SLG	PRO+	BR/A	SB	CS	SBR	FA	FR	G/POS	TPR
1958	Bal-A	12	19	1	0	0	0	0	0	0	7	.000	.050	.000	-90	-5	0	0	0	.943	-0	S-12	-0.5
1959	Bal-A	2	4	0	0	0	0	0	0	1	1	.000	.200	.000	-41	-1	0	0	0	.889	1	/S-2	0.0
1960	Bal-A★	153	530	72	135	22	5	22	86	69	94	.255	.343	.440	111	8	3	3	-1	.964	9	*S-153	2.5
1961	Bal-A	155	533	51	132	13	2	12	51	66	96	.248	.332	.347	85	-11	3	-2	.959	12	*S-149/2-7	1.3
1962	Bal-A	71	196	12	34	7	0	3	17	30	36	.173	.289	.255	51	-13	0	1	-1	.965	4	S-64	-0.5
1963	Chi-A	144	482	55	109	17	2	13	67	78	74	.226	.334	.351	94	-2	1	1	-0	.983	27	*S-144	3.6
1964	Chi-A	158	575	85	150	25	4	20	68	73	73	.261	.350	.419	116	13	1	0	0	.975	16	*S-158	4.3
1965	Chi-A	162	587	61	138	23	4	11	66	60	73	.235	.308	.344	91	-8	1	1	0	.969	17	*S-161/2-1	2.1
1966	Chi-A	23	74	3	13	1	0	0	4	15	10	.176	.322	.189	55	-4	0	1	-1	.946	3	S-23	0.0
1967	Chi-A	157	498	35	116	20	8	8	51	64	51	.233	.320	.321	94	-3	0	3	-2	.964	2	*S-157	1.4
1968	Was-A	86	275	28	51	12	0	8	28	35	49	.185	.282	.316	84	-5	0	0	0	.963	6	S-81/3-5	0.5
	Chi-A	40	87	7	20	3	0	1	4	11	12	.230	.316	.299	86	-1	0	0	0	.959	6	3-29/S-7,2	0.6
	Yr	126	362	35	71	15	0	9	32	46	61	.196	.290	.312	84	-7	0	0	0	.963	7	S-88,3-34/2	1.1
1969	Chi-A	85	185	15	48	6	1	2	22	18	25	.259	.328	.335	82	-4	2	0	1	.967	-1	2-26,1-21/S3	-0.4
1970	NY-A	59	91	13	27	4	0	4	14	19	9	.297	.423	.473	155	8	0	0	-1	.983	-3	S-15,3-11/2	0.6
1971	NY-A	61	145	6	30	3	0	2	20	9	27	.207	.253	.269	51	-10	0	0	0	.918	-3	3-30/2-9,S	-1.3
1972	KC-A	16	30	2	4	0	0	0	2	3	6	.133	.212	.133	4	-3	0	0	0	.944	3	/S-6,3-4,2	0.0
Total	15	1384	4311	446	1007	156	17	106	501	551	643	.234	.323	.351	92	-42	9	14	-6	.968	90	*S-1143/3-86,21	14.2

■ DON HANSKI
Hanski, Donald Thomas (b: Donald Thomas Hanyzewski) b: 2/27/16, LaPorte, Ind. d: 9/2/57, Worth, Ill. BL/TL, 5'11", 180 lbs. Deb: 5/6/43

YEAR	TM/L	G	AB	R	H	2B	3B	HR	RBI	BB	SO	AVG	OBP	SLG	PRO+	BR/A	SB	CS	SBR	FA	FR	G/POS	TPR
1943	Chi-A	9	21	1	5	1	0	0	2	0	5	.238	.238	.286	53	-1	0	1	-1	.952	-0	/1-5,P-1	-0.3
1944	Chi-A	2	1	0	0	0	0	0	0	0	0	.000	.000	.000	-99	-0	0	0	0	.000	-0	/P-2	0.0
Total	2	11	22	1	5	1	0	0	2	0	5	.227	.227	.273	46	-2	0	1	-1	—	-1	/1-5,P-3	-0.3

■ HARRY HANSON
Hanson, Harry Francis b: 1/17/1896, Elgin, Ill. d: 10/5/66, Savannah, Ga. BR/TR, 5'11", Deb: 7/14/13

YEAR	TM/L	G	AB	R	H	2B	3B	HR	RBI	BB	SO	AVG	OBP	SLG	PRO+	BR/A	SB	CS	SBR	FA	FR	G/POS	TPR
1913	NY-A	1	2	0	0	0	0	0	0	0	0	.000	.000	.000	-99	-0	0			1.000	-0	/C-1	-0.1

■ JOHN HAPPENNY
Happenny, John Clifford "Cliff" b: 5/18/01, Waltham, Mass. d: 12/29/88, Coral Springs, Fla BR/TR, 5'11", 165 lbs. Deb: 7/2/23

YEAR	TM/L	G	AB	R	H	2B	3B	HR	RBI	BB	SO	AVG	OBP	SLG	PRO+	BR/A	SB	CS	SBR	FA	FR	G/POS	TPR
1923	Chi-A	32	86	7	19	5	0	0	10	3	13	.221	.256	.279	41	-8	0	0	0	.947	0	2-19/S-9,3	-0.6

■ BILL HARBIDGE
Harbidge, William Arthur "Yaller Bill" b: 3/29/1855, Philadelphia, Pa. d: 3/17/24, Philadelphia, Pa. BL/TL, 162 lbs. Deb: 5/15/1875

YEAR	TM/L	G	AB	R	H	2B	3B	HR	RBI	BB	SO	AVG	OBP	SLG	PRO+	BR/A	SB	CS	SBR	FA	FR	G/POS	TPR
1875	Har-n	53	205	32	50	3	3	0		12		.244	.286	.288	94	-1						C-25,O-13,2/1	0.0
1876	Har-N	30	106	11	23	2	1	0	2	3	6	.217	.239	.255	59	-5				.799	4	C-24/O-6,1	-0.3
1877	Har-N	41	167	18	37	5	2	0	8	3	6	.222	.235	.275	68	-6				.881	-4	C-32/O-5,23	-0.8
1878	Chi-N	54	240	32	71	12	0	0	37	6	13	.296	.313	.346	109	2				.878	-8	*C-53/O-8	-0.6
1879	Chi-N	4	18	2	2	0	0	0	1	0	5	.111	.111	.111	-25	-2				.571	-1	/O-4	-0.3
1880	Tro-N	9	27	3	10	0	1	0		0	3	.370	.370	.444	166	2				.887	0	/C-9,O-1	0.2
1882	Tro-N	32	123	11	23	1	1	0	13	10	17	.187	.248	.211	52	-6				.836	-4	O-23/1-6,C	-0.9
1883	Phi-N	73	280	32	62	12	3	0	21	24	20	.221	.283	.286	81	-5				.796	-11	O-44,S-11/2C3	-1.4
1884	Cin-U	82	341	59	95	12	5	2		25		.279	.328	.361	81	-10				.906	5	*O-80/S-3,1	-0.6
Total	8	325	1302	168	323	44	13	2	88	71	66	.248	.287	.306	80	-30				.849	-21	O-171,C-128/S213	-4.7

■ SCOTT HARDESTY
Hardesty, Scott Durbin b: 1/26/1870, Bellville, Ohio d: 10/29/44, Fostoria, Ohio Deb: 8/17/1899

YEAR	TM/L	G	AB	R	H	2B	3B	HR	RBI	BB	SO	AVG	OBP	SLG	PRO+	BR/A	SB	CS	SBR	FA	FR	G/POS	TPR
1899	NY-N	22	72	4	16	0	0	0	4	1		.222	.243	.222	29	-7				.895	2	S-20/1-2	-0.3

■ PAT HARDGROVE
Hardgrove, William Henry b: 5/10/1895, Palmyra, Kan. d: 1/26/73, Jackson, Miss. BR/TR, 5'10", 158 lbs. Deb: 6/8/18

YEAR	TM/L	G	AB	R	H	2B	3B	HR	RBI	BB	SO	AVG	OBP	SLG	PRO+	BR/A	SB	CS	SBR	FA	FR	G/POS	TPR
1918	Chi-A	2	2	0	0	0	0	0	0	0	0	.000	.000	.000	-99	-0	0			.000	0	H	-0.1

■ LOU HARDIE
Hardie, Louis W. b: 8/24/1864, New York, N.Y. d: 3/5/29, Oakland, Cal. 5'11", 180 lbs. Deb: 5/22/1884

YEAR	TM/L	G	AB	R	H	2B	3B	HR	RBI	BB	SO	AVG	OBP	SLG	PRO+	BR/A	SB	CS	SBR	FA	FR	G/POS	TPR
1884	Phi-N	3	8	0	3	2	0	0	0	0	2	.375	.375	.625	219	1				.857	-3	/C-3	-0.1
1886	Chi-N	16	51	4	9	0	0	0	3	4	10	.176	.236	.176	24	-5	1			.964	-0	C-13/O-2,3	-0.4
1890	Bos-N	47	185	17	42	8	0	3	17	18	36	.227	.296	.319	73	-7	3			.886	-0	C-25,O-15/3S1	-0.5
1891	Bal-a	15	56	7	13	0	3	0	1	8	8	.232	.328	.339	90	-1	3			1.000	1	O-15	0.0
Total	4	81	300	28	67	10	3	3	21	30	56	.223	.294	.307	71	-12	8			.910	-2	/C-41,O-32,31S	-1.0

■ BUD HARDIN
Hardin, William Edgar b: 6/14/22, Shelby, N.C. BR/TR, 5'10", 165 lbs. Deb: 4/15/52

YEAR	TM/L	G	AB	R	H	2B	3B	HR	RBI	BB	SO	AVG	OBP	SLG	PRO+	BR/A	SB	CS	SBR	FA	FR	G/POS	TPR
1952	Chi-N	3	7	1	1	0	0	0	0	0	0	.143	.143	.143	-20	-1	0	0	0	1.000	-0	/S-2,2-1	-0.1

■ LOU HARDING
Harding, Louis Edward "Jumbo" b: 1865, San Francisco, Cal. 5'9.5", 213 lbs. Deb: 10/5/1886

YEAR	TM/L	G	AB	R	H	2B	3B	HR	RBI	BB	SO	AVG	OBP	SLG	PRO+	BR/A	SB	CS	SBR	FA	FR	G/POS	TPR
1886	StL-a	1	3	0	1	1	0	0		0		.333	.333	.667	201	0	0			.889	1	/C-1	0.1

■ CARROLL HARDY
Hardy, Carroll William b: 5/18/33, Sturgis, S.Dak. BR/TR, 6', 185 lbs. Deb: 4/15/58

YEAR	TM/L	G	AB	R	H	2B	3B	HR	RBI	BB	SO	AVG	OBP	SLG	PRO+	BR/A	SB	CS	SBR	FA	FR	G/POS	TPR
1958	Cle-A	27	49	10	10	3	0	1	6	6	14	.204	.304	.327	75	-2	1	2	-1	1.000	1	O-17	-0.3
1959	Cle-A	32	53	12	11	3	0	2	3	3	7	.208	.250	.226	33	-5	1	1	-0	1.000	1	O-15	-0.5
1960	Cle-A	29	18	7	2	1	0	0	1	2	2	.111	.200	.167	0	-3	0	0	0	1.000	-4	O-17	-0.7
	Bos-A	73	145	26	34	5	2	2	15	17	40	.234	.315	.338	74	-5	3	2	-0	.968	-6	O-59	-1.4
	Yr	102	163	33	36	6	2	2	16	19	42	.221	.302	.319	67	-7	3	2	-0	.973	-11	O-76	-2.1
1961	Bos-A	85	281	46	74	20	2	3	36	26	53	.263	.330	.381	87	-5	4	2	0	.961	-1	O-76	-1.0
1962	Bos-A	115	362	52	78	13	5	8	36	54	68	.215	.321	.345	77	-11	3	7	-3	.991	-1	*O-105	-1.9
1963	Hou-N	15	44	5	10	0	0	3	3	7	7	.227	.277	.295	69	-2	1	0	0	.947	1	O-10	-0.1
1964	Hou-N	46	157	13	29	1	1	2	12	8	30	.185	.234	.242	36	-13	0	0	0	.990	5	O-41	-1.2
1967	Min-A	11	8	1	3	0	0	1	2	1	2	.375	.444	.750	229	1	0	0	0	.000	-1	/O-4	0.0
Total	8	433	1117	172	251	47	10	17	113	120	222	.225	.304	.330	72	-45	13	14	-5	.981	-5	O-344	-7.1

■ JACK HARDY
Hardy, John Doolittle b: 6/23/1877, Cleveland, Ohio d: 10/20/21, Cleveland, Ohio BR/TR, 6', 185 lbs. Deb: 8/29/03

YEAR	TM/L	G	AB	R	H	2B	3B	HR	RBI	BB	SO	AVG	OBP	SLG	PRO+	BR/A	SB	CS	SBR	FA	FR	G/POS	TPR
1903	Cle-A	5	19	1	3	1	0	0		1		.158	.200	.211	24	-2	1			1.000	-1	/O-5	-0.3
1907	Chi-N	4	4	0	1	0	0	0	0	0		.250	.250	.250	53	-0	0			.909	0	/C-1	0.0
1909	Was-A	10	24	3	4	0	0	0	4	1		.167	.200	.167	17	-2	0			.974	-2	/C-9,2-1	-0.4
1910	Was-A	7	8	1	2	0	0	0	1	0		.250	.250	.250	59	-0	0			.933	1	/C-4,O-1	0.0
Total	4	23	55	5	10	1	0	0	5	2		.182	.211	.200	28	-5	1			.953	-2	/C-14,O-6,2	-0.7

■ SHAWN HARE
Hare, Shawn Robert b: 3/26/67, St.Louis, Mo. BL/TL, 6'2", 190 lbs. Deb: 9/6/91

YEAR	TM/L	G	AB	R	H	2B	3B	HR	RBI	BB	SO	AVG	OBP	SLG	PRO+	BR/A	SB	CS	SBR	FA	FR	G/POS	TPR
1991	Det-A	9	19	0	1	1	0	0	0	2	2	.053	.143	.105	-30	-3	0	0	0	1.000	0	/O-6,D-2	-0.4

YEAR	TM/L	G	AB	R	H	2B	3B	HR	RBI	BB	SO	AVG	OBP	SLG	PRO+	BR/A	SB	CS	SBR	FA	FR	G/POS	TPR
1992	Det-A	15	26	0	3	1	0	0	5	2	1	.115	.179	.154	-6	-4	0	0	0	1.000	-2	/O-9,1-4	-0.6
1994	NY-N	22	40	7	9	1	1	0	2	4	11	.225	.295	.300	55	-3	0	0	0	1.000	-0	O-14	-0.3
Total	3	46	85	7	13	3	1	0	7	8	16	.153	.226	.212	19	-10	0	0	0	1.000	-2	/O-29,1-4,D	-1.3

■ GARY HARGIS
Hargis, Gary Lynn   b: 11/2/56, Minneapolis, Minn.   BR/TR, 5'11", 165 lbs.   Deb: 9/29/79

YEAR	TM/L	G	AB	R	H	2B	3B	HR	RBI	BB	SO	AVG	OBP	SLG	PRO+	BR/A	SB	CS	SBR	FA	FR	G/POS	TPR
1979	Pit-N	1	0	0	0	0	0	0	0	0	0	—	—	—	—		0	0	0	.000	0	/R	0.0

■ BUBBLES HARGRAVE
Hargrave, Eugene Franklin   b: 7/15/1892, New Haven, Ind.   d: 2/23/69, Cincinnati, Ohio   BR/TR, 5'10.5", 174 lbs.   Deb: 9/18/13   F

YEAR	TM/L	G	AB	R	H	2B	3B	HR	RBI	BB	SO	AVG	OBP	SLG	PRO+	BR/A	SB	CS	SBR	FA	FR	G/POS	TPR
1913	Chi-N	3	3	0	1	0	0	0	1	0	0	.333	.333	.333	90	-0	0			1.000	0	/C-2	0.0
1914	Chi-N	23	36	3	8	2	0	0	2	0	4	.222	.222	.278	48	-2	2			.930	-4	C-16	-0.6
1915	Chi-N	15	19	2	3	0	1	0	2	1	5	.158	.200	.263	40	-1	0			1.000	-1	C-9	-0.2
1921	Cin-N	93	263	28	76	17	8	1	38	12	15	.289	.327	.426	102	0	4	2	0	.973	-7	C-73	-0.3
1922	Cin-N	98	320	49	101	22	10	7	57	26	18	.316	.371	.512	128	12	7	4	-0	.982	-9	C-87	0.7
1923	Cin-N	118	378	54	126	23	9	10	78	44	22	.333	.419	.521	150	28	4	5	-2	.988	3	*C-109	3.3
1924	Cin-N	98	312	42	94	19	10	3	33	30	20	.301	.370	.455	122	10	2	2	-1	.983	-1	C-91	1.4
1925	Cin-N	87	273	28	82	13	6	2	33	25	23	.300	.361	.414	100	4	4	3	-1	.979	-6	C-84	-0.2
1926	Cin-N	105	326	42	115	22	8	6	62	25	17	**.353**	.406	.525	153	24	2			.988	-12	C-93	1.8
1927	Cin-N	102	305	36	94	18	3	0	35	31	18	.308	.376	.387	108	4	0			**.988**	-10	C-92	0.1
1928	Cin-N	65	190	19	56	12	3	0	23	13	14	.295	.353	.389	95	-1	4			.991	2	C-57	0.5
1930	NY-A	45	108	11	30	7	0	0	12	10	9	.278	.339	.343	77	-4	0			.992	-5	C-34	-0.6
Total	12	852	2533	314	786	155	58	29	376	217	165	.310	.372	.452	119	70	29	16		.983	-50	C-747	5.9

■ PINKY HARGRAVE
Hargrave, William McKinley   b: 1/31/1896, New Haven, Ind.   d: 10/3/42, Ft.Wayne, Ind.   BB/TR, 5'8.5", 180 lbs.   Deb: 5/18/23   F

YEAR	TM/L	G	AB	R	H	2B	3B	HR	RBI	BB	SO	AVG	OBP	SLG	PRO+	BR/A	SB	CS	SBR	FA	FR	G/POS	TPR
1923	Was-A	33	59	4	17	2	0	1	8	2	6	.288	.311	.322	70	-3	0	0	0	.917	-4	/3-8,C-5,O	-0.6
1924	Was-A	24	33	3	5	1	1	0	5	1	4	.152	.176	.242	8	-5	0	0	0	1.000	-1	/C-8	-0.5
1925	Was-A	5	6	0	3	0	0	0	0	1	2	.500	.571	.500	177	1	0	0	0	1.000	1	/C-1	0.2
	StL-A	67	225	34	64	15	2	8	43	13	13	.284	.326	.476	97	-3	2	0	1	.981	-6	C-62	-0.5
	Yr	72	231	34	67	15	2	8	43	14	15	.290	.333	.476	99	-2	2	0	1	.981	-5	C-63	-0.3
1926	StL-A	92	235	20	66	16	3	7	37	10	38	.281	.319	.464	98	-2	2	0	1	.977	-2	C-58	0.0
1928	Det-A	121	320	38	88	13	5	10	63	32	28	.275	.343	.441	103	1	4	1	1	.977	-14	C-88	-0.5
1929	Det-A	76	185	26	61	12	0	3	26	20	24	.330	.401	.443	117	5	2	2	-1	.973	-4	C-48	0.7
1930	Det-A	55	137	18	39	8	0	5	18	20	12	.285	.380	.453	108	2	2	0	1	.984	-4	C-40	0.2
	Was-A	10	31	3	6	2	1	0	7	3	1	.194	.265	.484	85	-1	0	0	0	1.000	-1	/C-9	0.1
	Yr	65	168	21	45	10	2	6	25	23	13	.268	.359	.458	104	1	2	0	1	.987	-5	C-49	0.3
1931	Was-A	40	80	6	26	8	0	1	19	9	12	.325	.393	.463	124	3	1	0	0	.978	-2	C-25	0.2
1932	Bos-N	82	217	20	57	14	3	4	33	24	18	.263	.336	.410	103	1	1			.968	-4	C-73	0.1
1933	Bos-N	45	73	5	13	0	0	0	5	2	6	.178	.241	.178	23	-7	1			.957	1	C-25	-0.6
Total	10	650	1601	177	445	91	16	39	265	140	165	.278	.339	.428	98	-8	17	3		.976	-35	C-442/3-8,O	-1.2

■ CHARLIE HARGREAVES
Hargreaves, Charles Russell   b: 12/14/1896, Trenton, N.J.   d: 5/9/79, Neptune, N.J.   BR/TR, 6', 170 lbs.   Deb: 7/15/23

YEAR	TM/L	G	AB	R	H	2B	3B	HR	RBI	BB	SO	AVG	OBP	SLG	PRO+	BR/A	SB	CS	SBR	FA	FR	G/POS	TPR
1923	Bro-N	20	57	5	16	0	0	0	4	1	2	.281	.293	.281	54	-4	0			.921	-4	C-15	-0.7
1924	Bro-N	15	27	4	11	2	0	0	5	1	1	.407	.429	.481	148	2	0	1	-1	1.000	-1	/C-9	0.0
1925	Bro-N	45	83	9	23	3	1	0	13	6	1	.277	.326	.337	72	-3	1	1	-0	.986	2	C-18/1-2	-0.1
1926	Bro-N	85	208	14	52	13	2	2	23	19	10	.250	.316	.361	83	-5	1			.986	4	C-70	0.2
1927	Bro-N	46	133	9	38	3	1	0	11	14	7	.286	.362	.323	85	-2	1			.985	-1	C-44	0.0
1928	Bro-N	20	61	3	12	2	0	0	5	6	6	.197	.269	.230	32	-6	1			.979	2	C-20	-0.3
	Pit-N	79	260	15	74	8	2	1	32	12	9	.285	.319	.342	70	-11	1			.962	-5	C-77	-1.0
	Yr	99	321	18	86	10	2	1	37	18	15	.268	.309	.321	63	-17	2			.966	-3	C-97	-1.3
1929	Pit-N	102	328	33	88	12	5	1	44	16	12	.268	.306	.345	60	-21	1			.981	2	*C-101	-0.9
1930	Pit-N	11	31	4	7	1	0	0	2	2	1	.226	.273	.258	29	-4	0			1.000	6	C-11	0.3
Total	8	423	1188	96	321	44	11	4	139	77	49	.270	.318	.336	69	-55	6	2		.977	4	C-365/1-2	-2.5

■ MIKE HARGROVE
Hargrove, Dudley Michael   b: 10/26/49, Perryton, Tex.   BL/TL, 6', 195 lbs.   Deb: 4/7/74   MC

YEAR	TM/L	G	AB	R	H	2B	3B	HR	RBI	BB	SO	AVG	OBP	SLG	PRO+	BR/A	SB	CS	SBR	FA	FR	G/POS	TPR
1974	Tex-A	131	415	57	134	18	6	4	66	49	42	.323	.400	.424	141	23	0	0	0	.987	9	1-91,D-32/O	2.7
1975	Tex-A★	145	519	82	157	22	2	11	62	79	66	.303	.399	.416	132	25	4	3	-1	.964	3	O-96,1-48,D	2.1
1976	Tex-A	151	541	80	155	30	1	7	58	**97**	64	.287	.401	.384	128	24	2	3	-1	.984	1	*1-141/D-5	1.5
1977	Tex-A	153	525	98	160	28	4	18	69	103	59	.305	.424	.476	143	37	2	5	-2	.993	-0	*1-152	2.5
1978	Tex-A	146	494	63	124	24	1	7	40	**107**	47	.251	.391	.346	109	12	2	5	-2	.987	7	*1-140/D-4	0.8
1979	SD-N	52	125	15	24	5	0	0	8	25	15	.192	.327	.232	59	-6	0	2	-1	.986	-2	1-37	-1.2
	Cle-A	100	338	60	110	21	4	10	56	63	40	.325	.438	.500	152	28	2	3	-1	.993	-0	O-65,1-28/D	2.2
1980	Cle-A	160	589	86	179	22	2	11	85	111	36	.304	.421	.404	127	28	4	2	0	.993	-5	*1-160	1.3
1981	Cle-A	94	322	43	102	21	0	2	49	60	16	.317	**.432**	.401	143	22	5	4	-1	.989	6	1-88/D-4	2.3
1982	Cle-A	160	591	67	160	26	1	4	65	101	58	.271	.380	.338	100	5	2	4	-4	.996	11	*1-153/D-5	0.7
1983	Cle-A	134	469	57	134	21	4	3	57	78	40	.286	.393	.367	107	8	0	6	-4	.994	12	*1-131/D-1	0.9
1984	Cle-A	133	352	44	94	14	2	2	44	53	38	.267	.363	.335	93	-1	0	2	-1	.991	-0	*1-124	-0.3
1985	Cle-A	107	284	31	81	14	1	1	27	39	29	.285	.372	.352	100	2	1	0	0	.991	5	1-85	0.2
Total	12	1666	5564	783	1614	266	28	80	686	965	550	.290	.400	.391	121	205	24	37	-15	.991	52	*1-1378,O-167/D	15.7

■ TIM HARKNESS
Harkness, Thomas William   b: 12/23/37, Lachine, Que., Can.   BL/TL, 6'2", 182 lbs.   Deb: 9/12/61

YEAR	TM/L	G	AB	R	H	2B	3B	HR	RBI	BB	SO	AVG	OBP	SLG	PRO+	BR/A	SB	CS	SBR	FA	FR	G/POS	TPR
1961	LA-N	5	8	4	4	2	0	0	3		1	.500	.636	.750	245	2	1	0	0	1.000	-0	/1-2	0.2
1962	LA-N	92	62	9	16	2	0	2	7	10	20	.258	.370	.387	110	0	1	1	0	1.000	1	1-59	0.2
1963	NY-N	123	375	35	79	12	3	10	41	36	79	.211	.292	.339	80	-10	4	3	-1	.986	16	*1-106	0.2
1964	NY-N	39	117	11	33	2	1	2	13	9	18	.282	.339	.368	101	0	1	1	-0	.993	3	1-32	0.2
Total	4	259	562	59	132	18	4	14	64	56	118	.235	.316	.358	90	-6	7	4	-0	.989	21	1-199	0.8

■ DICK HARLEY
Harley, Richard Joseph   b: 9/25/1872, Philadelphia, Pa.   d: 4/3/52, Philadelphia, Pa.   BL/TR, 5'10.5", 165 lbs.   Deb: 6/2/1897

YEAR	TM/L	G	AB	R	H	2B	3B	HR	RBI	BB	SO	AVG	OBP	SLG	PRO+	BR/A	SB	CS	SBR	FA	FR	G/POS	TPR
1897	StL-N	89	330	43	96	6	4	3	35	36		.291	.379	.361	98	1	23			.899	-0	*O-89	-0.4
1898	StL-N	142	549	74	135	6	5	0	42	34		.246	.316	.275	68	-22	13			.926	9	*O-141	-2.2
1899	Cle-N	142	567	70	142	15	7	1	50	40		.250	.315	.307	76	-18	15			.924	5	*O-142	-2.2
1900	Cin-N	5	21	2	9	1	0	0	5	1		.429	.455	.476	161	2	4			1.000	-0	/O-5	0.0
1901	Cin-N	133	535	69	146	13	2	4	27	31		.273	.323	.327	95	-3	37			.898	-5	*O-133	-1.7
1902	Det-A	125	491	59	138	9	8	2	44	36		.281	.345	.344	90	-6	20			.930	-2	*O-125	-1.5
1903	Chi-N	104	386	72	89	9	1	0	33	45		.231	.328	.259	70	-13	27			.923	-4	*O-103	-1.5
Total	7	740	2879	389	755	59	27	10	236	223		.262	.332	.312	83	-58	139			.918	10	O-738	-9.5

■ LARRY HARLOW
Harlow, Larry Duane   b: 11/13/51, Colorado Springs, Colo.   BL/TL, 6'2", 185 lbs.   Deb: 9/20/75

YEAR	TM/L	G	AB	R	H	2B	3B	HR	RBI	BB	SO	AVG	OBP	SLG	PRO+	BR/A	SB	CS	SBR	FA	FR	G/POS	TPR
1975	Bal-A	4	3	1	1	0	0	0	0	0	0	.333	.333	.333	90	-0	0	0	0	1.000	-2	/O-4	-0.2
1977	Bal-A	46	48	4	10	0	1	0	0	5	8	.208	.283	.250	50	-3	6	1	1	.887	-12	O-38	-1.4
1978	Bal-A	147	460	67	112	25	1	8	26	55	72	.243	.326	.354	97	-2	14	11	-2	.979	-5	*O-138/P-1	-1.5
1979	Bal-A	38	41	5	11	1	0	0	1	7	4	.268	.375	.293	86	-0	1	3	-2	.970	-10	O-31	-1.2
	*Cal-A	62	159	22	37	8	2	0	14	25	34	.233	.344	.308	80	-4	1	3	-2	.975	-2	O-58	-0.9
	Yr	100	200	27	48	9	2	0	15	32	38	.240	.350	.305	81	-4	2	6	-3	.974	-12	O-89	-2.1
1980	Cal-A	109	301	47	83	13	4	4	27	48	61	.276	.377	.385	112	7	6	9	-1	.976	12	O-94/1-D	1.5
1981	Cal-A	43	82	13	17	1	0	0	4	16	25	.207	.337	.220	63	-3	1	5	-0	.981	-8	O-39	-0.9
Total	6	449	1094	159	271	48	8	12	72	156	205	.248	.344	.339	94	-5	26	21	-5	.971	-26	O-402/D-1,1P	-5.0

YEAR	TM/L	G	AB	R	H	2B	3B	HR	RBI	BB	SO	AVG	OBP	SLG	PRO+	BR/A	SB	CS	SBR	FA	FR	G/POS	TPR

■ BILL HARMAN
Harman, William Bell b: 1/2/19, Bridgewater, Va. BR/TR, 6'4", 200 lbs. Deb: 6/17/41

| 1941 | Phi-N | 15 | 14 | 1 | 1 | 0 | 0 | 0 | 0 | 0 | 3 | .071 | .071 | .071 | -62 | -3 | 0 | | | 1.000 | -1 | /P-5,C-5 | -0.2 |

■ CHUCK HARMON
Harmon, Charles Byron b: 4/23/24, Washington, Ind. BR/TR, 6'2", 175 lbs. Deb: 4/17/54

1954	Cin-N	94	286	39	68	7	3	2	25	17	27	.238	.283	.304	52	-20	7	3	0	.961	4	3-67/1-3	-1.7
1955	Cin-N	96	198	31	50	6	3	5	28	26	24	.253	.348	.389	90	-2	9	9	-3	.935	4	3-39,O-32/1	-0.3
1956	Cin-N	13	4	2	0	0	0	0	0	0	0	.000	.000	.000	-94	-1	1	0	0	1.000	-2	/O-6,1-2	-0.3
	StL-N	20	15	2	0	0	0	0	0	2	2	.000	.118	.000	-65	-4	0	0	0	1.000	-4	O-11/1-2,3	-0.8
	Yr	33	19	4	0	0	0	0	0	2	2	.000	.095	.000	-70	-5	1	0	0	1.000	-6	O-17/1-4,3	-1.1
1957	StL-N	9	3	2	1	0	1	0	1	0	0	.333	.333	1.000	236	1	1	0	0	1.000	-3	/O-8	-0.2
	Phi-N	57	86	14	22	2	1	0	5	1	4	.256	.264	.302	53	-6	7	2	1	1.000	-2	O-25/3-5,1	-0.7
	Yr	66	89	16	23	2	2	0	6	1	4	.258	.267	.326	60	-5	8	2	1	1.000	-5	O-33/3-5,1	-0.9
Total	4	289	592	90	141	15	8	7	59	46	57	.238	.298	.326	62	-33	25	14	-1	.952	-3	3-112/O-82,1	-4.0

■ TERRY HARMON
Harmon, Terry Walter b: 4/12/44, Toledo, Ohio BR/TR, 6'2", 180 lbs. Deb: 7/23/67

1967	Phi-N	2	0	0	0	0	0	0	0	—	—	—	—	—	—	0	0	0	0	.000	0	R	0.0
1969	Phi-N	87	201	25	48	8	1	0	16	22	31	.239	.323	.289	74	-6	1	2	-1	.968	8	S-38,2-19/3	0.7
1970	Phi-N	71	129	16	32	2	4	0	7	12	22	.248	.317	.326	75	-5	6	3	0	.989	-3	S-35,2-14/3	-0.4
1971	Phi-N	79	221	27	45	4	2	0	12	20	45	.204	.282	.240	49	-14	3	3	0	.986	8	2-58/S-9,31	-0.1
1972	Phi-N	73	218	35	62	8	2	2	13	29	23	.284	.373	.367	108	4	3	2	-0	.996	-1	2-50,S-15/3	0.6
1973	Phi-N	72	148	17	31	3	0	0	8	13	14	.209	.278	.230	41	-11	1	0	0	.988	2	2-43,S-19/3	-0.7
1974	Phi-N	27	15	5	2	0	0	0	0	3	3	.133	.278	.133	17	-2	0	0	0	1.000	3	/S-7,2-5	-0.2
1975	Phi-N	48	72	14	13	1	2	0	5	9	13	.181	.280	.250	46	-5	0	0	0	.989	1	S-25/2-7,3	-0.2
1976	*Phi-N	42	61	12	18	4	1	0	6	3	10	.295	.328	.393	101	-0	3	0	1	.960	3	S-19,2-13/3	0.6
1977	Phi-N	46	60	13	11	1	0	0	5	6	11	.183	.269	.300	50	-4	0	2	-1	.982	8	2-28,S-16/3	0.4
Total	10	547	1125	164	262	31	12	4	72	117	175	.233	.312	.292	69	-44	17	11	-2	.989	29	2-237,S-183/31	1.0

■ BRIAN HARPER
Harper, Brian David b: 10/16/59, Los Angeles, Cal. BR/TR, 6'2", 195 lbs. Deb: 9/29/79

1979	Cal-A	1	2	0	0	0	0	0	0	0	1	.000	.000	.000	-99	-1	0	0	0	.000	0	/H	-0.1
1981	Cal-A	4	11	1	3	0	0	0	1	0	0	.273	.273	.273	58	-1	1	0	0	.833	-0	/O-2,D-1	0.0
1982	Pit-N	20	29	4	8	1	0	2	4	1	4	.276	.300	.517	121	1	0	0	0	1.000	-1	/O-8	-0.1
1983	Pit-N	61	131	16	29	4	1	7	20	2	15	.221	.239	.427	79	-4	0	0	0	1.000	-5	O-35/1-1	-1.1
1984	Pit-N	46	112	4	29	4	0	2	11	5	11	.259	.303	.348	82	-3	0	0	0	.981	-2	O-37/C-2	-0.6
1985	*StL-N	43	52	5	13	4	0	0	8	2	3	.250	.278	.327	69	-2	0	0	0	1.000	-4	O-13/3-6,C1	-0.7
1986	Det-A	19	36	2	5	1	0	0	3	3	3	.139	.205	.167	3	-5	0	0	0	.929	-2	O-11/C-2,1D	-0.7
1987	Oak-A	11	17	1	4	1	0	0	3	0	4	.235	.235	.294	42	-1	0	0	0	.000	-0	/O-1,D-7	-0.2
1988	Min-A	60	166	15	49	11	1	3	20	10	12	.295	.346	.428	112	3	0	3	-2	.991	-7	C-48/3-2,D	-0.3
1989	Min-A	126	385	43	125	24	0	8	57	13	16	.325	.356	.449	118	8	2	4	-2	.978	-14	*C-101,D-19/O13	-0.3
1990	Min-A	134	479	61	141	42	3	6	54	19	27	.294	.331	.432	105	2	3	2	-0	.985	2	*C-120,D-11/31	1.1
1991	*Min-A	123	441	54	137	28	1	10	69	14	22	.311	.341	.447	111	5	1	2	-1	.988	-6	*C-119/1-1,OD	0.5
1992	Min-A	140	502	58	154	25	0	9	73	26	22	.307	.350	.410	109	5	0	1	-1	.984	-7	*C-133/D-2	0.6
1993	Min-A	147	530	52	161	26	1	12	73	29	29	.304	.350	.425	107	5	1	3	-2	.988	-13	*C-134/D-7	-0.2
1994	Mil-A	64	251	23	73	15	0	4	32	9	18	.291	.323	.398	83	-7	0	2	-1	.981	1	D-36,C-25/O	-0.6
Total	15	999	3144	339	931	186	7	63	428	133	187	.296	.334	.420	103	5	8	17	-8	.985	-58	C-686,O-114/D31	-2.7

■ GEORGE HARPER
Harper, George Washington b: 6/24/1892, Arlington, Ky. d: 8/18/78, Magnolia, Ark. BL/TR, 5'8", 167 lbs. Deb: 4/15/16

1916	Det-A	44	56	4	9	1	0	0	3	5	8	.161	.230	.179	22	-5	0			.938	-4	O-14	-1.0
1917	Det-A	47	117	6	24	3	0	0	12	11	15	.205	.290	.231	59	-5	2			.980	-3	O-31	-1.1
1918	Det-A	69	227	19	55	5	2	0	16	18	14	.242	.301	.282	79	-6	3			.956	-1	O-64	-1.2
1922	Cin-N	128	430	67	146	22	8	2	68	35	22	.340	.397	.442	118	13	11	10	-3	.955	1	*O-109	0.3
1923	Cin-N	61	125	14	32	4	2	3	16	11	9	.256	.316	.392	88	-3	0	2	-1	.967	-2	O-29	-0.7
1924	Cin-N	28	74	7	20	3	0	0	3	13	5	.270	.393	.311	92	0	1	3	-2	.964	1	O-22	-0.2
	Phi-N	109	411	68	121	26	6	16	55	38	23	.294	.361	.504	115	8	10	11	-4	.991	3	*O-109	0.0
	Yr	137	485	75	141	29	6	16	58	51	28	.291	.366	.474	113	8	11	14	-5	.986	4	*O-131	-0.2
1925	Phi-N	132	495	86	173	35	7	18	97	28	32	.349	.391	.558	128	19	10	8	-2	.971	6	*O-126	1.5
1926	Phi-N	56	194	32	61	6	5	7	38	16	7	.314	.367	.505	126	6	6			.942	-6	O-55	-0.3
1927	NY-N	145	483	85	160	19	6	16	87	84	27	.331	.435	.495	149	37	7			.975	-2	*O-142	2.7
1928	NY-N	19	57	11	13	1	0	2	7	10	4	.228	.353	.351	84	-1	1			.957	2	O-18	0.0
	*StL-N	99	272	41	83	8	2	17	58	51	15	.305	.418	.537	145	19	2			.988	1	O-84	1.4
	Yr	118	329	52	96	9	2	19	65	61	19	.292	.407	.505	135	18	3			.982	3	*O-102	1.4
1929	Bos-N	136	457	65	133	25	5	10	68	69	21	.291	.389	.433	108	7	5			.972	-1	*O-130	-0.3
Total	11	1073	3398	505	1030	158	43	91	528	389	208	.303	.380	.455	118	90	58	34		.970	-5	O-933	1.1

■ TERRY HARPER
Harper, Terry Joe b: 8/19/55, Douglasville, Ga. BR/TR, 6'4", 195 lbs. Deb: 9/12/80

1980	Atl-N	21	54	3	10	2	1	0	3	6	5	.185	.279	.259	49	-4	2	1	0	.968	-2	O-18	-0.6
1981	Atl-N	40	73	9	19	1	0	2	8	11	17	.260	.357	.356	100	0	5	1	1	.976	-2	O-27	-0.1
1982	*Atl-N	48	150	16	43	3	0	2	16	14	28	.287	.352	.347	92	-1	7	4	-0	.987	-0	O-41	-0.3
1983	Atl-N	80	201	19	53	13	1	3	26	20	43	.264	.333	.383	91	-2	6	5	-1	.952	-1	O-60	-0.7
1984	Atl-N	40	102	4	16	3	1	0	8	4	21	.157	.196	.206	12	-12	4	1	1	1.000	4	O-29	-0.9
1985	Atl-N	138	492	58	130	15	2	17	72	44	76	.264	.328	.407	98	-1	9	9	-3	.978	1	*O-131	-0.7
1986	Atl-N	106	265	26	68	12	0	8	30	29	39	.257	.332	.392	94	-1	3	4	-1	.970	-11	O-83	-1.9
1987	Det-A	31	64	4	13	3	0	3	10	9	8	.203	.301	.391	85	-1	1	0	0	.952	-2	O-15,O-14	-0.3
	Pit-N	36	66	8	19	3	0	1	7	7	11	.288	.356	.379	94	-0	0	1	-1	1.000	-3	O-20	-0.4
Total	8	540	1467	147	371	55	5	36	180	144	248	.253	.323	.371	88	-24	37	28	-6	.976	-16	O-423/D-15	-5.9

■ TOMMY HARPER
Harper, Tommy b: 10/14/40, Oak Grove, La. BR/TR, 5'10", 168 lbs. Deb: 4/9/62 C

1962	Cin-N	6	23	1	4	0	0	0	1	0	6	.174	.240	.174	13	-3	1	0	0	.929	-1	/3-6	-0.4
1963	Cin-N	129	408	67	106	12	3	10	37	44	72	.260	.336	.377	102	2	12	1	3	.983	6	*O-118/3-1	0.5
1964	Cin-N	102	317	42	77	5	2	4	22	39	56	.243	.328	.309	78	-8	24	3	5	.994	5	O-92/3-2	-0.2
1965	Cin-N	159	646	**126**	166	28	3	18	64	78	127	.257	.342	.393	99	1	35	6	7	.983	7	*O-159/3-2,2	0.8
1966	Cin-N	149	553	85	154	22	5	5	31	57	85	.278	.349	.363	91	-6	29	10	3	.996	-13	*O-147	-2.4
1967	Cin-N	103	365	55	82	17	3	7	22	43	51	.225	.306	.345	77	-10	23	8	2	.995	7	*O-100	-0.7
1968	Cle-A	130	235	26	51	15	2	6	26	26	61	.217	.298	.374	104	0	11	7	-1	.984	-16	*O-115/2-2	-2.3
1969	Sea-A	148	537	78	126	10	2	9	41	95	90	.235	.351	.311	88	-5	**73**	18	11	.959	-15	2-59,3-59,O	-0.6
1970	Mil-A★	154	604	104	179	35	4	31	82	77	107	.296	.380	.522	145	37	38	16	2	.943	-3	*3-128,2-22,O	3.6
1971	Mil-A	152	585	79	151	26	3	14	52	65	92	.258	.333	.385	104	3	25	3	6	.975	-19	O-90,3-70/2	-1.6
1972	Bos-A	144	556	92	141	29	2	14	49	67	104	.254	.343	.388	111	9	25	7	3	.985	1	*O-144	0.8
1973	Bos-A	147	566	92	159	23	3	17	71	61	93	.281	.352	.422	111	8	**54**	14	8	.985	-6	*O-143/D-1	1.2
1974	Bos-A	118	443	66	105	15	3	5	24	46	65	.237	.313	.318	75	-13	28	12	1	.982	-3	O-61,D-51	-1.9
1975	Cal-A	89	285	40	68	10	1	3	31	38	51	.239	.332	.312	89	-3	19	8	1	.992	-2	D-57,1-19/O	-0.7
	*Oak-A	34	69	11	22	4	0	2	7	5	9	.319	.373	.464	139	3	7	0	0	.963	-3	1-16/O-9,3D	0.1
	Yr	123	354	51	90	14	1	5	38	43	60	.254	.340	.342	99	0	26	8	1	.986	-5	D-60,1-35,O/3	-0.6
1976	Bal-A	46	77	8	18	5	0	1	7	10	16	.234	.322	.338	99	0	4	3	-1	1.000	-1	D-27/1-1,O	-0.2
Total	15	1810	6269	972	1609	256	36	146	567	753	1080	.257	.340	.379	100	15	408	116	53	.986	-47	*O-1227,3-270,D/21	-4.0

YEAR	TM/L	G	AB	R	H	2B	3B	HR	RBI	BB	SO	AVG	OBP	SLG	PRO+	BR/A	SB	CS	SBR	FA	FR	G/POS	TPR

■ TOBY HARRAH
Harrah, Colbert Dale   b: 10/26/48, Sissonville, W.Va.   BR/TR, 6', 180 lbs.   Deb: 9/5/69   MC

YEAR	TM/L	G	AB	R	H	2B	3B	HR	RBI	BB	SO	AVG	OBP	SLG	PRO+	BR/A	SB	CS	SBR	FA	FR	G/POS	TPR
1969	Was-A	8	1	4	0	0	0	0	0	0	0	.000	.000	.000	-99	-0	0	0	0	.000	0	/S-1	0.0
1971	Was-A	127	383	45	88	11	3	2	22	40	48	.230	.303	.290	73	-14	10	9	-2	.955	-7	*S-116/3-7	-1.0
1972	Tex-A†	116	374	47	97	14	3	1	31	34	31	.259	.321	.321	95	-2	16	7	1	.960	-9	*S-106	0.5
1973	Tex-A	118	461	64	120	16	1	10	50	46	49	.260	.330	.364	100	-0	10	3	1	.951	-13	S-76,3-52	-0.2
1974	Tex-A	161	573	79	149	23	2	21	74	50	65	.260	.322	.417	114	9	15	14	-4	.963	-2	*S-158/3-3	2.5
1975	Tex-A☆	151	522	81	153	24	1	20	93	98	71	.293	.406	.458	145	34	23	9	2	.963	14	*S-118,3-28,2	**6.2**
1976	Tex-A★	155	584	64	152	21	1	15	67	91	59	.260	.363	.377	114	13	8	5	-1	.955	-0	*S-146/3-5,D	3.2
1977	Tex-A	159	539	90	142	25	5	27	87	**109**	73	.263	.397	.479	136	31	27	5	5	.963	-24	*3-159/S-1	1.0
1978	Tex-A	139	450	56	103	17	3	12	59	83	66	.229	.351	.360	100	3	31	8	5	.965	-8	3-91,S-49	0.4
1979	Cle-A	149	527	99	147	25	1	20	77	89	60	.279	.391	.444	124	21	20	9	1	.940	-48	*3-127,S-33/D	-2.5
1980	Cle-A	160	561	100	150	22	4	11	72	98	60	.267	.383	.380	109	11	17	2	4	.971	2	*3-156/S-2,D	1.5
1981	Cle-A	103	361	64	105	12	4	5	44	57	44	.291	.389	.388	126	15	12	1	3	.949	-12	*3-101/S-3,D	0.4
1982	Cle-A☆	162	602	100	183	29	4	25	78	84	52	.304	.400	.490	144	39	17	3	3	.971	-19	*3-159/2-3,S	1.9
1983	Cle-A	138	526	81	140	23	1	9	53	75	49	.266	.365	.365	98	1	16	10	-1	**.971**	-11	*3-137/2-1,D	-1.3
1984	NY-A	88	253	40	55	9	4	1	26	42	28	.217	.333	.296	79	-6	3	0	1	.968	3	3-74/2-4,OD	-0.3
1985	Tex-A	126	396	65	107	18	1	9	44	113	60	.270	.437	.389	127	22	11	4	1	.989	-14	*2-122/S-2,D	1.4
1986	Tex-A	95	289	36	63	18	2	7	41	44	53	.218	.325	.367	86	-5	2	5	-2	.982	-20	2-93	-2.4
Total	17	2155	7402	1115	1954	307	40	195	918	1153	868	.264	.368	.395	114	171	238	94	15	.963	-166	*3-1099,S-813,2/DO	11.3

■ JOHN HARRELL
Harrell, John Robert   b: 11/27/47, Long Beach, Cal.   BR/TR, 6'2", 190 lbs.   Deb: 10/1/69

YEAR	TM/L	G	AB	R	H	2B	3B	HR	RBI	BB	SO	AVG	OBP	SLG	PRO+	BR/A	SB	CS	SBR	FA	FR	G/POS	TPR
1969	SF-N	2	6	0	3	0	0	0	2	2	1	.500	.625	.500	223	1	0	0	0	1.000	-0	/C-2	0.1

■ BILLY HARRELL
Harrell, William   b: 7/18/28, Norristown, Pa.   BR/TR, 6'1.5", 180 lbs.   Deb: 9/2/55

YEAR	TM/L	G	AB	R	H	2B	3B	HR	RBI	BB	SO	AVG	OBP	SLG	PRO+	BR/A	SB	CS	SBR	FA	FR	G/POS	TPR
1955	Cle-A	13	19	2	8	0	0	0	1	3	3	.421	.500	.421	144	1	1	0	0	.926	-0	S-11	0.2
1957	Cle-A	22	57	6	15	1	1	1	5	4	7	.263	.311	.368	86	-1	3	1	0	.893	-4	S-14/3-6,2	-0.4
1958	Cle-A	101	229	36	50	4	0	7	19	15	36	.218	.272	.328	66	-11	12	2	2	.986	-7	3-46,S-45/2O	-1.2
1961	Bos-A	37	37	10	6	2	0	0	1	1	8	.162	.184	.216	6	-5	1	0	0	1.000	7	3-10/S-7,1	0.2
Total	4	173	342	54	79	7	1	8	26	23	54	.231	.283	.327	68	-16	17	3	3	.933	-5	/S-77,3-62,210	-1.2

■ BUD HARRELSON
Harrelson, Derrel McKinley   b: 6/6/44, Niles, Cal.   BB/TR, 5'11", 160 lbs.   Deb: 9/2/65   MC

YEAR	TM/L	G	AB	R	H	2B	3B	HR	RBI	BB	SO	AVG	OBP	SLG	PRO+	BR/A	SB	CS	SBR	FA	FR	G/POS	TPR
1965	NY-N	19	37	3	4	1	1	0	0	2	11	.108	.154	.189	-4	-5	0	0	0	.955	4	S-18	-0.1
1966	NY-N	33	99	20	22	2	4	0	4	13	23	.222	.313	.323	79	-3	7	3	0	.993	5	S-29	0.5
1967	NY-N	151	540	59	137	16	4	1	28	48	64	.254	.319	.304	80	-13	12	13	-4	.958	7	*S-149	0.4
1968	NY-N	111	402	38	88	7	3	0	14	29	68	.219	.273	.251	58	-20	4	5	-2	.972	-5	*S-106	-1.8
1969	*NY-N	123	395	42	98	11	6	0	24	54	54	.248	.341	.306	81	-8	1	3	-2	.969	-5	*S-119	-0.2
1970	NY-N★	157	564	72	137	18	8	1	42	95	74	.243	.355	.309	79	-13	23	4	5	.971	-28	*S-156	-1.8
1971	NY-N★	142	547	55	138	16	6	0	32	53	59	.252	.321	.303	79	-14	28	7	4	.978	15	*S-140	2.0
1972	NY-N	115	418	54	90	10	4	1	24	58	57	.215	.314	.266	68	-16	12	4	1	.970	-12	*S-115	-1.0
1973	*NY-N	106	356	35	92	12	3	0	20	48	49	.258	.348	.309	85	-6	5	1	1	.979	-3	*S-103	0.6
1974	NY-N	106	331	48	75	10	0	1	13	71	39	.227	.366	.266	80	-5	9	4	0	.968	16	S-97	2.4
1975	NY-N	34	73	5	16	2	0	0	3	12	13	.219	.329	.247	65	-3	0	0	0	.941	1	S-34	0.0
1976	NY-N	118	359	34	84	12	4	1	26	63	56	.234	.351	.298	91	-2	9	3	1	.962	-5	*S-117	0.8
1977	NY-N	107	269	25	48	6	2	1	12	27	28	.178	.256	.227	32	-26	5	4	-1	.984	-2	S-98	-2.0
1978	Phi-N	71	103	16	22	1	0	0	9	18	21	.214	.331	.223	57	-5	5	2	0	.972	15	2-43,S-15	1.3
1979	Phi-N	53	71	7	20	6	0	0	7	13	14	.282	.400	.366	107	1	3	3	-1	.990	6	2-25,S-17/3O	0.8
1980	Tex-A	87	180	26	49	6	0	1	9	29	23	.272	.373	.322	95	0	4	4	-1	.952	11	S-87/2-2	1.7
Total	16	1533	4744	539	1120	136	45	7	267	633	653	.236	.329	.288	75	-136	127	60	2	.969	16	*S-1400/2-70,3O	3.6

■ KEN HARRELSON
Harrelson, Kenneth Smith "Hawk"   b: 9/4/41, Woodruff, S.C.   BR/TR, 6'2", 190 lbs.   Deb: 6/9/63

YEAR	TM/L	G	AB	R	H	2B	3B	HR	RBI	BB	SO	AVG	OBP	SLG	PRO+	BR/A	SB	CS	SBR	FA	FR	G/POS	TPR
1963	KC-A	79	226	16	52	10	1	6	23	23	58	.230	.301	.363	81	-6	1	1	-0	.980	-5	1-34,O-28	-1.5
1964	KC-A	49	139	15	27	5	0	7	12	13	34	.194	.263	.381	74	-5	0	1	-1	.977	3	O-24,1-15	-0.4
1965	KC-A	150	483	61	115	17	3	23	66	66	112	.238	.331	.429	116	10	9	7	-2	.992	-4	*1-125/O-4	-0.2
1966	KC-A	63	210	24	47	5	0	5	22	27	59	.224	.312	.319	85	-4	9	2	2	.985	2	1-58/O-3	-0.4
	Was-A	71	250	25	62	8	1	7	28	26	53	.248	.321	.372	100	-0	4	1	1	.991	-4	1-70	-0.9
	Yr	134	460	49	109	13	1	12	50	53	112	.237	.317	.348	93	-4	13	3	2	.989	-2	*1-128/O-3	-1.3
1967	Was-A	26	79	10	16	0	0	3	10	7	15	.203	.267	.316	75	-3	1	0	0	.996	0	1-23	-0.4
	KC-A	61	174	23	53	11	0	6	30	17	17	.305	.366	.471	151	11	8	2	1	.992	-1	1-45	0.9
	*Bos-A	23	80	9	16	4	1	3	14	5	12	.200	.247	.387	79	-2	1	1	-0	.929	-3	O-23/1-1	-0.8
	Yr	110	333	42	85	15	1	12	54	29	44	.255	.315	.414	115	5	10	3	1	.993	-4	1-69,O-23	-0.3
1968	Bos-A★	150	535	79	147	17	4	35	**109**	69	90	.275	.360	.518	153	34	2	6	-3	**1.000**	8	*O-132,1-19	3.5
1969	Bos-A	10	46	6	10	1	0	3	8	4	6	.217	.280	.435	92	-1	0	1	-1	.991	2	1-10	-0.1
	Cle-A	149	519	83	115	13	4	27	84	95	96	.222	.344	.418	109	7	17	8	0	.985	-0	*O-144,1-16	0.3
	Yr	159	565	89	125	14	4	30	92	99	102	.221	.339	.419	107	6	17	9	-0	.985	6	*O-144,1-26	0.2
1970	Cle-A	17	39	3	11	0	1	1	6	4	7	.282	.378	.385	106	0	0	0	0	1.000	1	1-13	0.0
1971	Cle-A	52	161	20	32	2	0	5	14	24	21	.199	.303	.304	66	-7	1	0	0	.988	-1	1-40/O-7	-1.3
Total	9	900	2941	374	703	94	14	131	421	382	577	.239	.328	.414	109	35	53	30	-2	.990	2	1-469,O-365	-1.3

■ ANDY HARRINGTON
Harrington, Andrew Matthew   b: 2/12/03, Mountain View, Cal   d: 1/26/79, Boise, Idaho   BR/TR, 5'11", 170 lbs.   Deb: 4/18/25

YEAR	TM/L	G	AB	R	H	2B	3B	HR	RBI	BB	SO	AVG	OBP	SLG	PRO+	BR/A	SB	CS	SBR	FA	FR	G/POS	TPR
1925	Det-A	1	1	0	0	0	0	0	0	0	0	.000	.000	.000	-99	-0	0	0	0	.000	0	H	0.0

■ MICKEY HARRINGTON
Harrington, Charles Michael   b: 10/8/34, Hattiesburg, Miss.   BR/TR, 6'4", 205 lbs.   Deb: 7/10/63

YEAR	TM/L	G	AB	R	H	2B	3B	HR	RBI	BB	SO	AVG	OBP	SLG	PRO+	BR/A	SB	CS	SBR	FA	FR	G/POS	TPR
1963	Phi-N	1	0	0	0	0	0	0	0	0	0	—	—	—	—	0	0	0	0	.000	0	R	0.0

■ JERRY HARRINGTON
Harrington, Jeremiah Peter   b: 8/12/1869, Keokuk, Iowa   d: 4/16/13, Keokuk, Iowa   BR/TR, 5'11", 220 lbs.   Deb: 4/30/1890

YEAR	TM/L	G	AB	R	H	2B	3B	HR	RBI	BB	SO	AVG	OBP	SLG	PRO+	BR/A	SB	CS	SBR	FA	FR	G/POS	TPR
1890	Cin-N	65	236	25	58	7	1	1	23	15	29	.246	.299	.297	74	-8	4			.957	5	C-65	0.3
1891	Cin-N	92	333	25	76	10	5	2	41	19	34	.228	.272	.306	68	-15	4			.908	-3	C-92/3-1	-0.8
1892	Cin-N	22	61	6	13	1	0	0	3	6	1	.213	.284	.230	56	-3	0			.989	2	C-22/1-1	-0.1
1893	Lou-N	10	36	4	4	1	0	0	6	3	9	.111	.179	.139	-16	-6	0			.853	-4	C-10	-0.8
Total	4	189	666	60	151	19	6	3	73	43	73	.227	.278	.287	64	-32	8			.932	-1	C-189/1-1,3	-1.4

■ JOE HARRINGTON
Harrington, Joseph C.   b: 12/21/1869, Fall River, Mass.   d: 9/13/33, Fall River, Mass.   BR/TR, 5'8.5", 162 lbs.   Deb: 9/10/1895

YEAR	TM/L	G	AB	R	H	2B	3B	HR	RBI	BB	SO	AVG	OBP	SLG	PRO+	BR/A	SB	CS	SBR	FA	FR	G/POS	TPR
1895	Bos-N	18	65	21	18	0	2	3	13	7	5	.277	.356	.431	95	-1	3			.912	0	2-18	0.0
1896	Bos-N	54	198	25	39	5	3	1	25	19	17	.197	.271	.268	40	-18	2			.816	-10	3-49/S-4,2	-2.3
Total	2	72	263	46	57	5	5	3	38	26	22	.217	.292	.308	54	-19	5			.901	-10	/3-49,2-19,S	-2.3

■ CANDY HARRIS
Harris, Alonzo   b: 9/17/47, Selma, Ala.   BB/TR, 6', 160 lbs.   Deb: 4/13/67

YEAR	TM/L	G	AB	R	H	2B	3B	HR	RBI	BB	SO	AVG	OBP	SLG	PRO+	BR/A	SB	CS	SBR	FA	FR	G/POS	TPR
1967	Hou-N	6	1	0	0	0	0	0	0	0	0	.000	.000	.000	-99	-0	0	0	0	.000	0	H	0.0

■ SPENCER HARRIS
Harris, Anthony Spencer   b: 8/12/1900, Duluth, Minn.   d: 7/3/82, Minneapolis, Minn.   BL/TL, 5'9", 145 lbs.   Deb: 4/14/25

YEAR	TM/L	G	AB	R	H	2B	3B	HR	RBI	BB	SO	AVG	OBP	SLG	PRO+	BR/A	SB	CS	SBR	FA	FR	G/POS	TPR
1925	Chi-A	56	92	12	26	2	0	1	13	14	13	.283	.383	.337	89	-1	3	3	-2	.957	-5	O-27	-0.8
1926	Chi-A	80	222	36	56	11	3	2	27	20	15	.252	.317	.356	78	-8	8	3	1	.949	-6	O-63	-1.6
1929	Was-A	6	14	1	3	1	0	0	1	4	3	.214	.214	.286	27	-2	1	0	0	1.000	-1	/O-4	-0.2
1930	Phi-A	22	49	4	9	1	0	0	5	5	2	.184	.259	.204	29	-6	0	0	0	.958	0	O-13	-0.6
Total	4	164	377	53	94	15	3	3	46	39	33	.249	.323	.329	70	-16	10	6	-1	.954	-11	O-107	-3.2

YEAR	TM/L	G	AB	R	H	2B	3B	HR	RBI	BB	SO	AVG	OBP	SLG	PRO+	BR/A	SB	CS	SBR	FA	FR	G/POS	TPR
■ GAIL HARRIS			Harris, Boyd Gail		b: 10/15/31, Abingdon, Va.			BL/TL, 6′, 195 lbs.			Deb: 6/3/55											
1955	NY-N	79	263	27	61	9	0	12	36	20	46	.232	.291	.403	82	-8	0	0	0	.982	0	1-75	-1.1
1956	NY-N	12	38	2	5	0	1	1	1	3	10	.132	.233	.263	33	-4	0	0	0	.975	0	1-11	-0.4
1957	NY-N	90	225	28	54	7	3	9	31	16	28	.240	.308	.418	93	-3	1	0	0	.985	-2	1-61	-0.8
1958	Det-A	134	451	63	123	18	8	20	83	36	60	.273	.332	.481	113	7	1	2	-1	.986	3	*1-122	0.1
1959	Det-A	114	349	39	77	4	3	9	39	29	49	.221	.292	.327	66	-16	0	1	-1	.992	5	1-93	-2.1
1960	Det-A	8	5	0	0	0	0	0	0	2	1	.000	.286	.000	-15	-1	0	0	0	1.000	0	/1-5	-0.1
Total	6	437	1331	159	320	38	15	51	190	106	194	.240	.306	.406	88	-25	2	3	-1	.986	4	1-367	-4.4
■ CHARLIE HARRIS			Harris, Charles Jenkins		b: 10/21/1877, Macon, Ga.			d: 3/14/63, Gainesville, Fla.			BR/TR, 5′8″, 200 lbs.			Deb: 5/25/1899								
1899	Bal-N	30	68	16	19	3	0	0	1	3		.279	.319	.324	73	-3	4			.872	-5	3-21/O-3,2S	-0.7
■ DAVE HARRIS			Harris, David Stanley "Sheriff"		b: 7/14/1900, Summerfield, N.C.			d: 9/18/73, Atlanta, Ga.			BR/TR, 5′11″, 170 lbs.			Deb: 4/14/25								
1925	Bos-N	92	340	49	90	8	7	5	36	27	44	.265	.321	.374	84	-9	6	4	-1	.962	8	O-90	-0.7
1928	Bos-N	7	17	2	2	1	0	0	0	2	6	.118	.211	.176	2	-2	0			.833	-1	/O-6	-0.4
1930	Chi-A	33	86	16	21	2	1	5	13	7	22	.244	.309	.465	96	-1	0	0	0	1.000	-0	O-23/2-1	-0.3
	Was-A	73	205	40	65	19	8	4	44	28	35	.317	.399	.546	137	11	6	3	0	.983	1	O-59	0.8
	Yr	106	291	56	86	21	9	9	57	35	57	.296	.373	.522	125	11	6	3	0	.988	1	O-82/2-1	0.5
1931	Was-A	77	231	49	72	14	8	5	50	49	35	.312	.434	.506	146	17	7	6	-2	.950	-2	O-60	0.9
1932	Was-A	81	156	26	51	7	4	6	29	19	34	.327	.400	.538	143	10	4	4	-1	.932	-2	O-34	0.4
1933	*Was-A	82	177	33	46	9	2	5	38	25	26	.260	.358	.418	106	2	3	1	0	.964	-7	O-45/1-6,3	-0.7
1934	Was-A	97	235	28	59	14	3	2	37	39	40	.251	.358	.362	89	-3	2	3	-1	.973	-4	O-64/3-5	-0.9
Total	7	542	1447	243	406	74	33	32	247	196	245	.281	.368	.444	112	25	28	21		.963	-8	O-381/3-7,12	-0.9
■ DONALD HARRIS			Harris, Donald		b: 11/12/67, Waco, Tex.			BR/TR, 6′1″, 185 lbs.			Deb: 9/4/91											
1991	Tex-A	18	8	4	3	0	0	1	2	1	3	.375	.444	.750	228	1	1	0	0	1.000	-5	O-12/D-3	-0.3
1992	Tex-A	24	33	3	6	1	0	0	1	0	15	.182	.182	.212	10	-4	1	0	0	.974	-4	O-24	-0.8
1993	Tex-A	40	76	10	15	2	0	1	8	5	18	.197	.256	.263	41	-6	0	1	-1	.943	-7	O-38/D-3	-1.5
Total	3	82	117	17	24	3	0	2	11	6	36	.205	.250	.282	46	-9	2	1	0	.959	-16	/O-74,D-6	-2.6
▣ FRANK HARRIS			Harris, Frank W.		b: 11/2/1858, Pittsburgh, Pa.			d: 11/26/39, E.Moline, Ill.			BR/TR,			Deb: 4/17/1884								
1884	Alt-U	24	95	10	25	2	1	0		3		.263	.286	.305	60	-5				.941	-1	1-17/O-7	-0.7
■ BILLY HARRIS			Harris, James William		b: 11/24/43, Hamlet, N.C.			BL/TR, 6′, 175 lbs.			Deb: 6/16/68											
1968	Cle-A	38	94	10	20	5	1	0	3	8	22	.213	.275	.287	71	-3	2	0	1	.970	-1	2-27,3-10/S	-0.3
1969	KC-A	5	7	1	2	1	0	0	0	0	1	.286	.286	.429	97	-0	0	0	0	1.000	-0	/2-1	0.0
Total	2	43	101	11	22	6	1	0	3	8	23	.218	.275	.297	73	-3	2	0	1	.971	-1	/2-28,3-10,S	-0.3
■ JOHN HARRIS			Harris, John Thomas		b: 9/13/54, Portland, Ore.			BL/TL, 6′3″, 205 lbs.			Deb: 9/26/79											
1979	Cal-A	1	2	0	0	0	0	0	0	0	0	.000	.000	.000	-99	-1	0	0	0	1.000	-0	/1-1	-0.1
1980	Cal-A	19	41	8	12	5	0	2	7	7	4	.293	.396	.561	163	4	0	1	-1	1.000	-0	1-10/O-3	0.2
1981	Cal-A	36	77	5	19	3	0	3	9	3	11	.247	.275	.403	93	-1	0	0	0	.976	-4	1-11,O-10/D	-0.6
Total	3	56	120	13	31	8	0	5	16	10	15	.258	.315	.450	115	2	0	1	-1	.987	-4	/1-22,O-13,D	-0.5
■ JOE HARRIS			Harris, Joseph "Moon"		b: 5/20/1891, Coulters, Pa.			d: 12/10/59, Renton, Pa.			BR/TR, 5′9″, 170 lbs.			Deb: 6/9/14								
1914	NY-A	2	1	0	0	0	0	0	0	3	1	.000	.800	.000	143	1	0			1.000	-1	/1-1,O-1	0.0
1917	Cle-A	112	369	40	112	22	4	0	65	55	32	.304	.398	.385	129	15	11			.985	10	1-95/O-5,3	2.3
1919	Cle-A	62	184	30	69	16	1	1	46	33	21	.375	.472	.489	160	17	2			.988	2	1-46/S-4	1.8
1922	Bos-A	119	408	53	129	30	9	6	54	30	15	.316	.364	.478	119	10	2	6	-3	.953	7	O-83,1-21	0.7
1923	Bos-A	142	483	82	162	28	11	13	76	52	27	.335	.406	.520	142	28	7	3	0	.968	-2	*O-132/1-9	1.8
1924	Bos-A	133	491	82	148	36	9	9	77	81	29	.301	.406	.430	115	14	6	1	1	.993	6	*1-128/O-3	1.2
1925	Bos-A	8	19	4	3	0	1	1	2	5	5	.158	.333	.421	90	-0	0	0	0	1.000	-1	/1-6	-0.1
	*Was-A	100	300	60	97	21	9	12	59	51	28	.323	.430	.573	156	26	6	3	0	.989	-0	1-58,O-41	1.9
	Yr	108	319	64	100	21	10	13	61	56	33	.313	.424	.564	152	26	6	3	0	.990	-1	1-64,O-41	1.8
1926	Was-A	92	257	43	79	13	9	5	55	37	9	.307	.405	.486	135	14	2	3	-1	.994	-3	1-36,O-35	0.5
1927	*Pit-N	129	411	57	134	27	9	5	73	48	19	.326	.402	.472	125	15	0			.990	2	*1-116/O-3	0.9
1928	Pit-N	16	23	2	9	2	1	0	2	4	2	.391	.500	.565	171	3	0			1.000	1	/1-6	0.3
	Bro-N	55	89	8	21	6	1	1	8	14	4	.236	.340	.360	84	-2	0			.958	-2	O-16	-0.4
	Yr	71	112	10	30	8	2	1	10	18	6	.268	.374	.402	103	1	0			.958	-0	O-16/1-6	-0.1
Total	10	970	3035	461	963	201	64	47	517	413	188	.317	.404	.472	131	140	36	16		.989	20	1-522,O-319/S3	10.9
■ LENNY HARRIS			Harris, Leonard Anthony		b: 10/28/64, Miami, Fla.			BL/TR, 5′10″, 195 lbs.			Deb: 9/7/88								
1988	Cin-N	16	43	7	16	1	0	0	8	5	4	.372	.438	.395	135	2	4	1	1	1.000	1	3-10/2-6	0.4
1989	Cin-N	61	188	17	42	4	0	2	11	9	20	.223	.263	.277	52	-12	10	6	-1	.980	1	2-32,S-17,3	-1.0
	LA-N	54	147	19	37	6	1	1	15	11	13	.252	.308	.327	83	-3	4	3	-1	1.000	-7	O-21,2-14/3S	-1.1
	Yr	115	335	36	79	10	1	3	26	20	33	.236	.283	.299	66	-15	14	9	-1	.975	-5	2-46,3-24,OS	-2.1
1990	LA-N	137	431	61	131	16	4	2	29	29	31	.304	.349	.374	102	1	15	10	-2	.959	-8	3-94,2-44/OS	-0.7
1991	LA-N	145	429	59	123	16	1	3	38	37	32	.287	.350	.350	100	1	12	3	2	.943	-1	*3-113,2-27,S/O	0.3
1992	LA-N	135	347	28	94	11	0	0	30	24	24	.271	.320	.303	78	-9	19	7	2	.963	17	2-81,3-33,OS	1.1
1993	LA-N	107	160	20	38	6	1	2	11	15	15	.237	.303	.325	72	-6	3	1	0	.987	2	2-35,3-17/SO	-0.3
1994	Cin-N	66	100	13	31	3	1	0	14	5	13	.310	.343	.360	84	-2	7	2	1	.846	-0	3-15/1-4,O2	-0.2
Total	7	721	1845	224	512	63	8	10	156	135	152	.278	.330	.337	88	-29	74	33	2	.941	5	3-306,2-241/SO1	-1.5
■ NED HARRIS			Harris, Robert Ned		b: 7/9/16, Ames, Iowa			d: 12/18/76, W.Palm Beach, Fla.			BL/TL, 5′11″, 175 lbs.			Deb: 4/20/41								
1941	Det-A	26	61	11	13	3	1	1	4	6	13	.213	.284	.344	59	-4	1	0	0	1.000	-2	O-12	-0.6
1942	Det-A	121	398	53	108	16	10	9	45	49	35	.271	.351	.430	110	5	5	4	-1	.944	-10	*O-104	-1.1
1943	Det-A	114	354	43	90	14	3	6	32	47	29	.254	.343	.362	99	-0	6	8	-3	.961	-3	O-96	-1.2
1946	Det-A	1	1	0	0	0	0	0	0	0	0	.000	.000	.000	-94	-0	0	0	0	.000	0	H	0.0
Total	4	262	814	107	211	33	14	16	81	102	77	.259	.342	.393	101	1	12	12	-4	.955	-15	O-212	-2.9
■ BUCKY HARRIS			Harris, Stanley Raymond		b: 11/8/1896, Port Jervis, N.Y.			d: 11/8/77, Bethesda, Md.			BR/TR, 5′9.5″, 156 lbs.			Deb: 8/28/19 MH								
1919	Was-A	8	28	0	6	2	0	0	4	1	3	.214	.267	.286	56	-2	0			.925	2	/2-8	0.1
1920	Was-A	136	506	76	152	26	6	1	68	41	36	.300	.377	.381	104	5	16	17	-5	.958	-19	*2-134	-0.6
1921	Was-A	154	584	82	169	22	8	0	54	54	39	.289	.367	.354	89	-7	29	9	3	.959	12	*2-154	1.1
1922	Was-A	154	602	95	162	24	8	2	40	52	38	.269	.341	.346	84	-14	25	11	1	.970	**26**	*2-154	1.7
1923	Was-A	145	532	60	150	21	13	2	70	50	29	.282	.358	.382	100	1	23	16	-3	.961	20	*2-144/S-1	1.8
1924	*Was-A	143	544	88	146	28	9	1	58	56	41	.268	.344	.358	84	-13	20	10	0	.968	-13	*2-143,M	-2.3
1925	*Was-A	144	551	91	158	30	3	1	66	64	21	.287	.370	.358	87	-9	14	12	-3	.970	3	*2-144,M	-0.6
1926	Was-A	141	537	94	152	39	9	1	63	58	41	.283	.363	.395	100	0	16	11	-2	.963	-11	*2-141,M	-0.8
1927	Was-A	128	475	98	127	20	3	1	55	66	33	.267	.363	.328	81	-11	18	3	4	**.972**	-3	*2-128,M	-0.1
1928	Was-A	99	358	34	73	11	5	0	28	27	26	.204	.264	.263	39	-32	5	2	0	.970	11	2-96/3-1,OM	-1.8
1929	Det-A	7	11	3	1	0	0	0	1	0	1	.091	.231	.091	-14	-2	1	0	0	.900	0	/2-4,S-1M	-0.1
1931	Det-A	8	8	1	1	1	0	0	1	3	2	.125	.222	.250	21	-1	0	0	0	1.000	0	/2-3,M	-0.1
Total	12	1263	4736	722	1297	224	64	9	506	472	310	.274	.352	.354	86	-85	167	91		.965	43	*2-1253/S-2,O3	-1.7

YEAR	TM/L	G	AB	R	H	2B	3B	HR	RBI	BB	SO	AVG	OBP	SLG	PRO+	BR/A	SB	CS	SBR	FA	FR	G/POS	TPR

■ VIC HARRIS   Harris, Victor Lanier   b: 3/27/50, Los Angeles, Cal.   BB/TR, 6', 170 lbs.   Deb: 7/21/72

1972	Tex-A	61	186	8	26	5	1	0	10	12	39	.140	.192	.177	11	-21	7	3	0	.960	0	2-58/S-1	-2.0
1973	Tex-A	152	555	71	138	14	7	8	44	55	81	.249	.319	.342	90	-7	13	12	-3	.977	2	*O-113,3-25,2	-1.4
1974	Chi-N	62	200	18	39	6	3	0	11	29	26	.195	.297	.255	53	-12	9	3	1	.943	-17	2-56	-2.7
1975	Chi-N	51	56	6	10	0	0	0	5	6	7	.179	.258	.179	22	-6	0	0	0	.900	-2	O-11/3-7,2	-0.8
1976	StL-N	97	259	21	59	12	3	1	19	16	55	.228	.275	.309	65	-12	1	2	-1	.945	-8	2-37,O-35,3/S	-2.1
1977	SF-N	69	165	28	43	12	0	2	14	19	36	.261	.337	.370	90	-2	2	1	0	.973	-10	2-27,S-11/3O	-0.9
1978	SF-N	53	100	8	15	4	0	1	11	11	24	.150	.234	.220	29	-10	0	0	0	.934	-7	S-22,2-10/O	-1.5
1980	Mil-A	34	89	8	19	4	1	1	7	12	13	.213	.307	.315	73	-3	4	1	1	.967	-2	O-31/3-2,2	-0.6
Total	8	579	1610	168	349	57	15	13	121	160	281	.217	.289	.295	65	-73	36	22	-2	.954	-43	2-212,O-199/3S	-12.0

■ CHUCK HARRISON   Harrison, Charles William   b: 4/25/41, Abilene, Tex.   BR/TR, 5'10", 190 lbs.   Deb: 9/15/65

1965	Hou-N	15	45	2	9	4	0	1	9	8	9	.200	.321	.356	97	-0	0	0	0	.983	0	1-12	-0.1
1966	Hou-N	119	434	52	111	23	2	9	52	37	69	.256	.317	.380	100	-1	2	0	1	.992	4	*1-114	-0.5
1967	Hou-N	70	177	13	43	7	3	2	26	13	30	.243	.295	.350	87	-3	0	0	0	.987	-0	1-59	-0.7
1969	KC-A	75	213	18	47	5	1	3	18	16	20	.221	.278	.296	60	-11	1	2	-1	.993	-0	1-55	-1.6
1971	KC-A	49	143	9	31	4	0	2	21	11	19	.217	.273	.287	59	-8	0	0	0	.992	0	1-39	-1.2
Total	5	328	1012	94	241	43	6	17	126	85	147	.238	.299	.343	83	-24	3	2	-0	.991	5	1-279	-4.1

■ BEN HARRISON   Harrison, Leo J.   BR ,   Deb: 9/27/01

1901	Was-A	1	2	0	0	0	0	0	0	1	0	.000	.333	.000	-2	-0	0			.000	-0	/O-1	-0.1

■ TOM HARRISON   Harrison, Thomas James   b: 1/18/45, Trail, B.C., Canada   BR/TR, 6'3", 200 lbs.   Deb: 5/7/65

1965	KC-A	2	0	0	0	0	0	0	0	0	0	—	—	—			0	0	0	.000	-0	/P-1	0.0

■ RIT HARRISON   Harrison, Washington Ritter   b: 9/16/1849, Waterbury, Conn.   d: 11/7/1888, Bridgeport, Conn.   Deb: 5/20/1875

1875	NH-n	1	4	0	2	1	0	0		0		.500	.500	.750	374	1				.000	-0	/C-1	0.1

■ SAM HARSHANY   Harshany, Samuel   b: 5/1/10, Madison, Ill.   BR/TR, 6', 180 lbs.   Deb: 9/28/37

1937	StL-A	5	11	0	1	1	0	0	0	3	0	.091	.286	.182	20	-1	0	0	0	.905	1	/C-4	-0.1
1938	StL-A	11	24	2	7	0	0	0	0	3	2	.292	.370	.292	68	-1	0	0	0	.975	-0	C-10	-0.1
1939	StL-A	42	145	15	35	2	0	0	15	9	8	.241	.290	.255	40	-13	0	1	-1	.994	-2	C-36	-1.2
1940	StL-A	3	1	0	0	0	0	0	0	1	0	.000	.500	.000	41	-0	0	0	0	.000	-0	/C-2	0.0
Total	4	61	181	17	43	3	0	0	15	16	10	.238	.303	.254	43	-15	0	1	-1	.983	-2	/C-52	-1.4

■ JACK HARSHMAN   Harshman, John Elvin   b: 7/12/27, San Diego, Cal.   BL/TL, 6'2", 185 lbs.   Deb: 9/16/48

1948	NY-N	5	8	0	2	0	0	0	1	1	3	.250	.333	.250	60	-0	0			1.000	0	/1-3	0.0
1950	NY-N	9	32	3	4	0	0	2	4	3	6	.125	.200	.313	32	-3	0			.989	0	/1-9	-0.3
1952	NY-N	3	2	0	0	0	0	0	0	0	0	.000	.000	.000	-99	-1	0	0	0	1.000	0	/P-2	0.0
1954	Chi-A	36	56	6	8	1	0	2	5	12	21	.143	.294	.268	53	-4	0	0	0	.967	-1	P-35/1-1	0.0
1955	Chi-A	32	60	6	11	1	0	2	8	9	17	.183	.290	.300	57	-4	0	0	0	.970	-0	P-32	0.0
1956	Chi-A	36	71	8	12	1	0	6	19	11	21	.169	.280	.437	86	-2	0	0	0	.886	-2	P-34	0.0
1957	Chi-A	30	45	5	10	1	0	2	5	10	17	.222	.364	.378	102	0	0	0	0	.947	-3	P-30	0.0
1958	Bal-A	47	82	11	16	1	0	6	14	17	22	.195	.333	.427	114	2	0	0	0	.980	-0	P-34/O-1	0.0
1959	Bal-A	15	10	3	2	0	0	1	1	2	2	.200	.333	.500	128	0	0	0	0	1.000	1	P-14	0.0
	Bos-A	9	7	1	1	0	0	0	2	2	2	.143	.333	.143	34	-1	0	0	0	1.000	-1	/P-8	0.0
	Cle-A	21	34	3	7	1	0	0	5	5	4	.206	.308	.235	53	-2	0	0	0	1.000	0	P-13	0.0
	Yr	45	51	7	10	1	0	1	8	9	8	.196	.317	.275	65	-2	0	0	0	1.000	0	P-35	0.0
1960	Cle-A	15	17	0	3	1	0	0	1	0	4	.176	.176	.235	11	-2	0	0	0	1.000	-1	P-15	0.0
Total	10	258	424	46	76	7	0	21	65	72	119	.179	.298	.344	74	-16	0	0	0	.962	-5	P-217/1-13,O	-0.3

■ BURT HART   Hart, James Burton   b: 6/28/1870, Brown Co., Minn.   d: 1/29/21, Sacramento, Cal.   BB , 6'3", 200 lbs.   Deb: 6/6/01

1901	Bal-A	58	206	33	64	3	5	0	23	20		.311	.383	.374	106	2	7			.976	-8	1-58	-0.6

■ HUB HART   Hart, James Henry   b: 2/2/1878, Everett, Mass.   d: 10/10/60, Fort Wayne, Ind.   BL/TR, 5'11", 170 lbs.   Deb: 7/16/05

1905	Chi-A	11	20	3	2	0	0	0	4	3		.100	.217	.100	2	-2	0			1.000	-2	/C-7	-0.4
1906	Chi-A	17	37	1	6	0	0	0	0	2		.162	.205	.162	16	-4	0			.935	-4	C-15	-0.7
1907	Chi-A	29	70	6	19	1	0	0	7	5		.271	.329	.286	100	-0	1			.956	-5	C-25	-0.3
Total	3	57	127	10	27	1	0	0	11	10		.213	.275	.220	29	-5	1			.957	-11	/C-47	-1.4

■ MIKE HART   Hart, James Michael   b: 12/20/51, Kalamazoo, Mich.   BB/TR, 6'3", 185 lbs.   Deb: 6/12/80

1980	Tex-A	5	4	1	1	0	0	0	1	0	1	.250	.400	.250	85	-0	0	0	0	1.000	-1	/O-2	-0.1

■ JIM RAY HART   Hart, James Ray   b: 10/30/41, Hookerton, N.C.   BR/TR, 5'11", 185 lbs.   Deb: 7/7/63

1963	SF-N	7	20	1	4	1	0	0	2	3	6	.200	.360	.250	80	-0	0	0	0	1.000	0	/3-7	0.0
1964	SF-N	153	566	71	162	15	6	31	81	47	94	.286	.345	.498	132	23	5	2	0	.937	4	*3-149/O-6	2.7
1965	SF-N	160	591	91	177	30	6	23	96	47	75	.299	.353	.487	130	23	6	4	-1	.919	-13	*3-144,O-15	0.6
1966	SF-N★	156	578	88	165	23	4	33	93	48	75	.285	.344	.510	130	22	2	5	-2	.941	-5	*3-139,O-17	1.2
1967	SF-N	158	578	98	167	26	7	29	99	77	100	.289	.376	.509	153	40	1	1	0	.937	-15	3-89,O-72	2.2
1968	SF-N	136	480	67	124	14	3	23	78	46	74	.258	.327	.444	130	17	3	1	0	.925	-12	3-72,O-65	0.2
1969	SF-N	95	236	27	60	9	0	3	26	28	49	.254	.346	.331	92	-2	0	0	0	.943	-7	O-68/3-3	-1.2
1970	SF-N	76	255	30	72	12	1	8	37	30	29	.282	.365	.431	114	3	0	1	0	.908	-17	3-56,O-18	-1.3
1971	*SF-N	31	39	5	10	0	0	2	5	6	8	.256	.356	.410	118	1	0	1	-1	.833	-1	/3-3,O-3	-0.1
1972	SF-N	24	79	10	24	5	0	5	8	6	10	.304	.360	.557	155	5	0	1	-1	.886	-9	3-20	-0.5
1973	SF-N	3	3	0	0	0	0	0	1	3	1	.000	.500	.000	48	-0	0	0	0	.600	-3	/3-1	0.0
	NY-A	114	339	29	86	13	2	13	52	36	45	.254	.325	.419	112	5	0	2	-1	.000	0	*D-106	0.1
1974	NY-A	10	19	1	1	0	0	0	0	3	7	.053	.182	.053	-31	-3	0	0	0	.000	0	/D-4	-0.3
Total	12	1125	3783	518	1052	148	29	170	578	380	573	.278	.348	.467	128	136	17	17	-5	.929	-73	3-683,O-264,D	3.6

■ MIKE HART   Hart, Michael Lawrence   b: 2/17/58, Milwaukee, Wis.   BL/TL, 5'11", 185 lbs.   Deb: 5/8/84

1984	Min-A	13	29	0	5	0	0	0	5	1	2	.172	.200	.172	4	-1	0	1	-1	1.000	1	O-11	-0.4
1987	Bal-A	34	76	7	12	2	0	4	12	6	19	.158	.220	.342	47	-6	1	4	-2	1.000	-2	O-32	-1.0
Total	2	47	105	7	17	2	0	4	17	7	21	.162	.214	.295	35	-10	1	5	-3	1.000	-1	/O-43	-1.4

■ TOM HART   Hart, Thomas Henry "Bushy"   b: 6/15/1869, Canaan, N.Y.   d: 9/17/39, Gardner, Mass.   5'7", 160 lbs.   Deb: 4/15/1891

1891	Was-a	8	24	1	3	0	0	0	2	1		.125	.192	.125	-9	-3	1			1.000	1	/C-5,O-3	-0.2

■ BILL HART   Hart, William Woodrow   b: 3/4/13, Wiconisco, Pa.   d: 7/29/68, Lykens, Pa.   BR/TR, 6', 175 lbs.   Deb: 9/18/43

1943	Bro-N	8	19	0	3	0	0	0	1	1	2	.158	.200	.158	4	-2	0			1.000	4	/3-6,S-1	0.2
1944	Bro-N	29	90	8	16	4	2	0	4	9	7	.178	.253	.267	47	-6	1			.941	-8	S-25/3-2	-1.3
1945	Bro-N	58	161	27	37	6	2	3	27	14	21	.230	.291	.348	78	-5	7			.913	-3	3-39/S-8	-0.6
Total	3	95	270	35	56	10	4	3	32	24	30	.207	.272	.307	63	-14	8			.924	-6	/3-47,S-34	-1.7

■ CHUCK HARTENSTEIN   Hartenstein, Charles Oscar "Twiggy"   b: 5/26/42, Seguin, Tex.   BR/TR, 5'11", 165 lbs.   Deb: 9/11/65   C

1965	Chi-N	1	0	0	0	0	0	0	0	0	0	—	—	—		0	0	0	0	.000	0	R	0.0
1966	Chi-N	5	0	0	0	0	0	0	0	0	0	—	—	—		0	0	0	0	1.000	0	/P-5	0.0

YEAR	TM/L	G	AB	R	H	2B	3B	HR	RBI	BB	SO	AVG	OBP	SLG	PRO+	BR/A	SB	CS	SBR	FA	FR	G/POS	TPR
1967	Chi-N	45	16	0	1	0	0	0	1	0	9	.063	.063	.063	-61	-3	0	0	0	.950	-0	P-45	0.0
1968	Chi-N	28	2	0	0	0	0	0	0	0	0	.000	.000	.000	-94	-0	0	0	0	.818	-0	P-28	0.0
1969	Pit-N	56	14	0	1	0	0	0	0	1	8	.071	.133	.071	-42	-3	0	0	0	1.000	1	P-56	0.0
1970	Pit-N	17	1	1	0	0	0	0	0	0	0	.000	.000	.000	-99	-0	0	0	0	.900	1	P-17	0.0
	StL-N	6	2	0	0	0	0	0	0	1	2	.000	.333	.000	-3	-0	0	0	0	1.000	0	/P-6	0.0
	Yr	23	3	1	0	0	0	0	0	1	2	.000	.250	.000	-27	-1	0	0	0	.923	1	P-23	0.0
	Bos-A	17	2	0	0	0	0	0	0	1	2	.000	.333	.000	-0	-0	0	0	0	1.000	-1	P-17	0.0
1977	Tor-A	13	0	0	0	0	0	0	0	0	0	—	—	—			0	0	0	1.000	-0	P-13	0.0
Total	7	188	37	1	2	0	0	0	1	3	21	.054	.125	.054	-47	-7	0	0	0	.952	2	P-187	0.0

■ BRUCE HARTFORD
Hartford, Bruce Daniel b: 5/14/1892, Chicago, Ill. d: 5/25/75, Los Angeles, Cal. BR/TR, 6'0.5", 190 lbs. Deb: 6/3/14

YEAR	TM/L	G	AB	R	H	2B	3B	HR	RBI	BB	SO	AVG	OBP	SLG	PRO+	BR/A	SB	CS	SBR	FA	FR	G/POS	TPR
1914	Cle-A	8	22	5	4	1	0	0	4	9		.182	.308	.227	59	-1	0			.913	-3	/S-8	-0.4

■ CHRIS HARTJE
Hartje, Christian Henry b: 3/25/15, San Francisco, Cal d: 6/26/46, Seattle, Wash. BR/TR, 5'10.5", 165 lbs. Deb: 9/9/39

YEAR	TM/L	G	AB	R	H	2B	3B	HR	RBI	BB	SO	AVG	OBP	SLG	PRO+	BR/A	SB	CS	SBR	FA	FR	G/POS	TPR
1939	Bro-N	9	16	2	5	1	0	0	5	1	0	.313	.353	.375	92	-0	0			.909	-2	/C-8	-0.2

■ GROVER HARTLEY
Hartley, Grover Allen "Slick" b: 7/2/1888, Osgood, Ind. d: 10/19/64, Daytona Beach, Fla BR/TR, 5'11", 175 lbs. Deb: 5/13/11 C

YEAR	TM/L	G	AB	R	H	2B	3B	HR	RBI	BB	SO	AVG	OBP	SLG	PRO+	BR/A	SB	CS	SBR	FA	FR	G/POS	TPR
1911	NY-N	11	18	1	4	2	0	0	1	1	1	.222	.263	.333	64	-1	1			.962	3	C-10	0.2
1912	NY-N	25	34	3	8	2	1	0	7	0	4	.235	.257	.353	64	-2	2			.960	2	C-25	0.1
1913	NY-N	23	19	4	6	0	0	0	0	1	2	.316	.350	.316	90	-0	4			.978	2	C-21/1-1	0.2
1914	StL-F	86	212	24	61	13	2	1	25	12	26	.288	.329	.382	80	-7	4			.956	-9	C-32,2-13/130	-1.4
1915	StL-F	120	394	47	108	21	6	1	50	42	21	.274	.356	.365	89	-5	10			.972	-7	*C-113/1-1	-0.3
1916	StL-A	89	222	19	50	8	0	0	12	30	24	.225	.325	.261	80	-4	4			.968	1	C-75	0.1
1917	StL-A	19	13	2	3	0	0	0	0	2	1	.231	.333	.231	75	-0	0			.875	1	/C-4,S-1,3	0.1
1924	NY-N	4	7	1	2	1	0	0	1	1	0	.286	.375	.429	118	0	1	0	0	1.000	-0	/C-3	0.1
1925	NY-N	46	95	9	30	1	1	0	8	8	3	.316	.373	.347	89	-1	2	0	1	.974	4	C-37/1-8	0.5
1926	NY-N	13	21	0	1	0	0	0	0	5	0	.048	.231	.048	-22	-4	0			1.000	0	C-13	-0.3
1927	Bos-A	103	244	23	67	11	0	1	31	22	14	.275	.337	.332	76	-8	1	0	0	.967	-13	C-86	-1.5
1929	Cle-A	24	33	2	9	0	1	0	8	2	1	.273	.314	.333	64	-2	0	0	0	1.000	-3	C-13	-0.4
1930	Cle-A	1	4	0	3	0	0	0	1	0	0	.750	.750	.750	271	0	0	0	0	.750	-0	/C-1	0.1
1934	StL-A	5	3	0	1	1	0	0	0	1	0	.333	.500	.667	183	0	0	0	0	1.000	0	/C-2	0.1
Total	14	569	1319	135	353	60	11	3	144	127	97	.268	.339	.337	81	-33	29	0		.968	-19	C-435/1-19,23OS	-2.4

■ CHICK HARTLEY
Hartley, Walter Scott b: 8/22/1880, Philadelphia, Pa. d: 7/18/48, Philadelphia, Pa. BR/TR, 5'8", 180 lbs. Deb: 6/4/02

YEAR	TM/L	G	AB	R	H	2B	3B	HR	RBI	BB	SO	AVG	OBP	SLG	PRO+	BR/A	SB	CS	SBR	FA	FR	G/POS	TPR
1902	NY-N	1	4	0	0	0	0	0	0	0		.000	.000	.000	-99	-1	0			1.000	-0	/O-1	-0.1

■ FRED HARTMAN
Hartman, Frederick Orrin "Dutch" b: 4/25/1868, Allegheny, Pa. d: 11/11/38, McKeesport, Pa. BR/TR, 5'8", 170 lbs. Deb: 7/26/1894

YEAR	TM/L	G	AB	R	H	2B	3B	HR	RBI	BB	SO	AVG	OBP	SLG	PRO+	BR/A	SB	CS	SBR	FA	FR	G/POS	TPR
1894	Pit-N	49	182	41	58	4	7	2	20	16	11	.319	.389	.451	103	1	12			.876	-4	3-49	-0.2
1897	StL-N	124	516	67	158	21	8	2	67	26		.306	.350	.390	97	-3	18			.867	-4	*3-124	-0.3
1898	NY-N	123	475	57	129	16	11	2	88	25		.272	.313	.364	97	-3	11			.882	9	*3-123	0.6
1899	NY-N	50	174	25	41	3	5	1	16	12		.236	.318	.328	80	-5	2			.886	-4	3-50	-0.7
1901	Chi-A	120	473	77	146	23	13	3	89	25		.309	.355	.431	120	12	31			.894	-6	*3-119	0.7
1902	StL-A	114	416	30	90	10	3	0	52	14		.216	.251	.255	58	-21	14			.908	-3	*3-105/S-4,1	-2.5
Total	6	580	2236	297	622	77	47	10	332	118	11	.278	.326	.368	95	-19	88			.886	-12	3-570/S-4,1	-2.4

■ J C HARTMAN
Hartman, J C b: 4/15/34, Cottonton, Ala. BR/TR, 6', 175 lbs. Deb: 7/21/62

YEAR	TM/L	G	AB	R	H	2B	3B	HR	RBI	BB	SO	AVG	OBP	SLG	PRO+	BR/A	SB	CS	SBR	FA	FR	G/POS	TPR
1962	Hou-N	51	148	11	33	5	0	0	5	4	16	.223	.248	.257	39	-13	1	1	-0	.972	7	S-48	-0.3
1963	Hou-N	39	90	2	11	1	0	0	3	2	13	.122	.151	.133	-19	-14	1	0	0	.950	0	S-32	-1.3
Total	2	90	238	13	44	6	0	0	8	6	29	.185	.211	.210	18	-27	2	1	0	.964	7	/S-80	-1.6

■ GABBY HARTNETT
Hartnett, Charles Leo b: 12/20/1900, Woonsocket, R.I. d: 12/20/72, Park Ridge, Ill. BR/TR, 6'1", 195 lbs. Deb: 4/12/22 MCH

YEAR	TM/L	G	AB	R	H	2B	3B	HR	RBI	BB	SO	AVG	OBP	SLG	PRO+	BR/A	SB	CS	SBR	FA	FR	G/POS	TPR
1922	Chi-N	31	72	4	14	1	1	0	4	6	8	.194	.256	.236	27	-8	1	0	0	.982	6	C-27	-0.1
1923	Chi-N	85	231	28	62	12	2	8	39	25	22	.268	.347	.442	107	2	4	0	1	.994	9	C-39,1-31	0.7
1924	Chi-N	111	354	56	106	17	7	16	67	39	37	.299	.377	.523	137	18	10	2	2	.963	-4	*C-105	2.3
1925	Chi-N	117	398	61	115	28	3	24	67	36	77	.289	.351	.555	126	13	1	5	-3	.958	10	*C-110	2.5
1926	Chi-N	93	284	35	78	25	3	8	41	32	37	.275	.352	.468	118	7	0			.978	5	C-88	1.7
1927	Chi-N	127	449	56	132	32	5	10	80	44	42	.294	.361	.454	117	10	2			.973	4	*C-126	2.3
1928	Chi-N	120	388	61	117	26	9	14	57	65	32	.302	.404	.523	143	25	3			.989	9	*C-118	4.2
1929	*Chi-N	25	22	2	6	2	1	1	9	5	5	.273	.407	.591	144	2	1			1.000	-0	/C-1	0.1
1930	Chi-N	141	508	84	172	31	3	37	122	55	62	.339	.404	.630	144	35	0			.989	3	*C-136	4.4
1931	Chi-N	116	380	53	107	32	1	8	70	52	48	.282	.370	.434	113	8	3			.981	2	*C-105	1.7
1932	*Chi-N	121	406	52	110	25	3	12	52	51	59	.271	.354	.436	112	7	0			.982	6	*C-117/1-1	2.0
1933	Chi-N★	140	490	55	135	21	4	16	88	37	51	.276	.326	.433	115	9	1			.989	7	*C-140	2.6
1934	Chi-N★	130	438	58	131	21	1	22	90	37	46	.299	.358	.502	130	18	0			.996	14	*C-129	3.5
1935	*Chi-N★	116	413	67	142	32	6	13	91	41	46	.344	.404	.545	152	30	1			.984	15	*C-110	4.8
1936	Chi-N★	121	424	49	130	25	6	7	64	30	36	.307	.341	.443	113	7	0			.991	9	*C-114	2.1
1937	Chi-N★	110	356	47	126	21	6	12	82	43	19	.354	.424	.548	156	28	0			.996	1	*C-103	3.3
1938	*Chi-N☆	88	299	40	82	19	1	10	59	48	17	.274	.380	.445	123	10	1			.995	-4	C-83,M	1.1
1939	Chi-N	97	306	36	85	18	2	12	59	37	32	.278	.358	.464	118	7	0			.992	-8	C-86,M	0.4
1940	Chi-N	37	64	3	17	3	0	1	12	8	7	.266	.347	.359	97	-0	0			.951	1	C-22/1-1M	0.3
1941	NY-N	64	150	20	45	5	0	5	26	12	14	.300	.356	.433	119	4	0			.994	-3	C-34	0.3
Total	20	1990	6432	867	1912	396	64	236	1179	703	697	.297	.370	.489	126	232	28	7		.984	74	*C-1793/1-33	40.1

■ PAT HARTNETT
Hartnett, Patrick J. "Happy" b: 10/20/1863, Boston, Mass. d: 4/10/35, Boston, Mass. 6'1", 175 lbs. Deb: 4/18/1890

YEAR	TM/L	G	AB	R	H	2B	3B	HR	RBI	BB	SO	AVG	OBP	SLG	PRO+	BR/A	SB	CS	SBR	FA	FR	G/POS	TPR
1890	StL-a	14	53	6	10	2	1	0	6			.189	.283	.264	54	-3	1			.954	-1	1-14	-0.4

■ GREG HARTS
Harts, Gregory Rudolph b: 4/21/50, Atlanta, Ga. BL/TL, 6', 168 lbs. Deb: 9/15/73

YEAR	TM/L	G	AB	R	H	2B	3B	HR	RBI	BB	SO	AVG	OBP	SLG	PRO+	BR/A	SB	CS	SBR	FA	FR	G/POS	TPR
1973	NY-N	3	2	0	1	0	0	0	0	0	0	.500	.500	.500	181	0	0	0	0	.000	0	H	0.0

■ TOPSY HARTSEL
Hartsel, Tully Frederick b: 6/26/1874, Polk, Ohio d: 10/14/44, Toledo, Ohio BL/TL, 5'5", 155 lbs. Deb: 9/14/1898

YEAR	TM/L	G	AB	R	H	2B	3B	HR	RBI	BB	SO	AVG	OBP	SLG	PRO+	BR/A	SB	CS	SBR	FA	FR	G/POS	TPR
1898	Lou-N	22	71	11	23	0	0	0	9	11		.324	.422	.324	116	2	2			.931	-2	O-21	-0.1
1899	Lou-N	30	75	8	18	1	1	0	7	11		.240	.345	.320	83	-1	1			.927	-2	O-22	-0.4
1900	Cin-N	18	64	10	21	2	1	2	5	8		.328	.403	.484	148	4	7			.957	-5	O-18	-0.2
1901	Chi-N	140	558	111	187	25	16	7	54	74		.335	.414	.475	164	47	41			.951	-1	*O-140	3.5
1902	Phi-A	137	545	109	154	20	12	5	58	87		.283	.383	.391	110	10	47			.955	-1	*O-137	0.0
1903	Phi-A	98	373	65	116	19	14	5	26	49		.311	.391	.477	152	25	13			.968	-6	*O-96	1.3
1904	Phi-A	147	534	79	135	17	12	2	25	75		.253	.347	.341	112	10	19			.959	-4	*O-147	-0.3
1905	*Phi-A	150	538	88	148	22	8	0	28	121		.275	.409	.346	138	31	37			.939	-7	*O-149	1.8
1906	Phi-A	144	533	96	136	21	9	1	30	88		.255	.363	.334	115	13	31			.969	-0	*O-144	0.7
1907	Phi-A	143	507	93	142	23	6	3	29	106		.280	.405	.367	143	31	20			.967	-11	*O-143	1.5
1908	Phi-A	129	460	73	112	16	6	4	29	93		.243	.371	.330	120	14	15			.960	-5	*O-129	0.5
1909	Phi-A	83	267	30	72	4	4	1	18	48		.270	.381	.326	121	9	3			.966	-4	O-74	0.3
1910	*Phi-A	90	285	45	63	10	3	0	22	58		.221	.353	.277	99	3	11			.945	-6	O-83	-0.8
1911	Phi-A	25	38	8	9	2	0	0	1	8		.237	.396	.289	94	1	0			.941	1	/O-9	0.1
Total	14	1356	4848	826	1336	182	92	31	341	837		.276	.384	.370	128	199	247			.956	-53	*O-1312	7.9

YEAR	TM/L	G	AB	R	H	2B	3B	HR	RBI	BB	SO	AVG	OBP	SLG	PRO+	BR/A	SB	CS	SBR	FA	FR	G/POS	TPR

■ ROY HARTSFIELD
Hartsfield, Roy Thomas "Spec" b: 10/25/25, Chattahoochee, Ga. BR/TR, 5'9", 165 lbs. Deb: 4/28/50 MC

1950	Bos-N	107	419	62	116	15	2	7	24	27	61	.277	.322	.372	88	-8	7			.949	-24	2-96	-2.8
1951	Bos-N	120	450	63	122	11	2	6	31	41	73	.271	.333	.344	89	-7	7	2	1	.969	-5	*2-114	-0.5
1952	Bos-N	38	107	13	28	4	3	0	4	5	12	.262	.295	.355	82	-3	0			.950	-6	2-29	-0.7
Total	3	265	976	138	266	30	7	13	59	73	146	.273	.324	.358	88	-18	14	2		.959	-34	2-239	-4.0

■ CLINT HARTUNG
Hartung, Clinton Clarence "Floppy" or "The Hondo Hurricane" b: 8/10/22, Hondo, Tex. BR/TR, 6'4", 215 lbs. Deb: 4/15/47

1947	NY-N	34	94	13	29	4	3	4	13	3	21	.309	.330	.543	127	3	0			1.000	-2	P-23/O-7	-0.1
1948	NY-N	43	56	5	10	1	1	0	3	7	24	.179	.270	.232	37	-5	0			1.000	-0	P-36	0.0
1949	NY-N	38	63	7	12	0	0	4	7	4	21	.190	.239	.381	64	-4	0			.957	2	P-33	0.0
1950	NY-N	32	43	7	13	2	1	3	10	1	13	.302	.318	.605	136	2	0			.939	3	P-20/O-2,1	0.0
1951	*NY-N	21	44	4	9	1	0	0	2	1	9	.205	.222	.227	21	-5	0	0	0	1.000	-1	O-12	-0.8
1952	NY-N	28	78	6	17	2	1	3	8	9	24	.218	.299	.385	88	-1	0			.932	-1	O-24	-0.3
Total	6	196	378	42	90	10	6	14	43	25	112	.238	.285	.407	84	-10	0	0		.972	-2	P-112/O-45,1	-1.2

■ ROY HARTZELL
Hartzell, Roy Allen b: 7/6/1881, Golden, Colo. d: 11/6/61, Golden, Colo. BL/TR, 5'8.5", 155 lbs. Deb: 4/17/06

1906	StL-A	113	404	43	86	7	0	0	24	19		.213	.266	.230	58	-19	21			.889	-2	*3-103/S-6,2	-2.0
1907	StL-A	60	220	20	52	3	5	0	13	11		.236	.285	.295	85	-4	7			.911	-3	3-38,2-12/SO	-0.3
1908	StL-A	115	422	41	112	5	6	2	32	19		.265	.302	.320	101	-0	24			.943	-6	O-82,S-18/32	-1.0
1909	StL-A	152	595	64	161	12	5	0	32	29		.271	.312	.308	103	1	14			.940	4	O-85,S-65/2	0.3
1910	StL-A	151	542	52	118	13	5	2	30	49		.218	.290	.271	81	-12	18			.929	1	3-89,S-38,O	-0.9
1911	NY-A	144	527	67	156	17	11	3	91	63		.296	.375	.387	106	5	22			.936	-12	*3-124,S-12/O	-0.5
1912	NY-A	125	416	50	113	10	11	1	38	64		.272	.370	.356	102	2	20			.906	-0	3-56,O-56,S/2	0.1
1913	NY-A	141	490	60	127	18	1	0	38	67	40	.259	.353	.300	91	-3	26			.942	-0	2-81,O-31,3/S	-0.5
1914	NY-A	137	481	55	112	15	9	1	32	68	38	.233	.335	.308	94	-2	22	25	-8	.973	0	*O-128/2-5	-1.8
1915	NY-A	119	387	39	97	11	2	3	60	57	37	.251	.351	.313	99	1	7	19	-9	.963	-3	*O-107/2-5,3	-1.7
1916	NY-A	33	64	12	12	1	0	0	7	3	8	.188	.297	.203	49	-4	1			1.000	-6	O-28	-1.2
Total	11	1290	4548	503	1146	112	55	12	397	455	118	.252	.327	.309	93	-33	182	44		.959	-26	O-550,3-440,S2	-9.5

■ LUTHER HARVEL
Harvel, Luther Raymond "Red" b: 9/30/05, Cambria, Ill. d: 4/10/86, Kansas City, Mo. BR/TR, 5'11", 180 lbs. Deb: 7/31/28

| 1928 | Cle-A | 40 | 136 | 12 | 30 | 6 | 1 | 0 | 12 | 4 | 17 | .221 | .264 | .279 | 42 | -11 | 1 | 1 | -0 | .948 | 2 | O-39 | -1.5 |

■ ERWIN HARVEY
Harvey, Ervin King "Zaza" b: 1/5/1879, Saratoga, Cal. d: 6/3/54, Santa Monica, Cal. BL/TL, 6', 190 lbs. Deb: 5/3/00

1900	Chi-N	2	3	0	0	0	0	0	0	0		.000	.000	.000	-99	-1	0			1.000	-0	/P-1	0.0
1901	Chi-A	17	40	11	10	3	1	0	3	2		.250	.302	.375	89	-1	1			.930	3	P-16	0.0
	Cle-A	45	170	21	60	5	5	1	24	9		.353	.392	.459	141	9	15			.890	2	O-45	0.7
	Yr	62	210	32	70	8	6	1	27	11		.333	.375	.443	131	9	16			.890	3	O-45,P-16	0.7
1902	Cle-A	12	46	5	16	2	0	0	5	3		.348	.388	.391	121	1	1			1.000	-0	O-12	0.1
Total	3	76	259	37	86	10	6	1	32	14		.332	.373	.429	127	9	17			.907	4	/O-57,P-17	0.8

■ ZIGGY HASBROOK
Hasbrook, Robert Lyndon "Ziggy" b: 11/21/1893, Grundy Center, Ia. d: 2/9/76, Garland, Tex. BR/TR, 6'1", 180 lbs. Deb: 9/6/16

1916	Chi-A	9	8	1	1	0	0	0	0	1	2	.125	.222	.125	4	-1	0			1.000	1	/1-7	0.0
1917	Chi-A	2	1	1	0	0	0	0	0	0	0	.000	.000	.000	-98	-0	0			1.000	1	/2-1	0.0
Total	2	11	9	2	1	0	0	0	0	1	2	.111	.200	.111	-6	-1	0			1.000	1	/1-7,2-1	0.0

■ BILL HASELMAN
Haselman, William Joseph b: 5/25/66, Long Branch, N.J. BR/TR, 6'3", 205 lbs. Deb: 9/3/90

1990	Tex-A	7	13	0	2	0	0	0	3	1	5	.154	.214	.154	5	-2	0	0	0	1.000	0	/C-1,D-3	-0.1
1992	Sea-A	8	19	1	5	0	0	0	0	0	7	.263	.263	.263	48	-1	0	0	0	1.000	-2	/C-5,O-2	-0.3
1993	Sea-A	58	137	21	35	8	0	5	16	12	19	.255	.320	.423	97	-1	2	1	0	.992	-2	C-49/O-2,D	-0.1
1994	Sea-A	38	83	11	16	7	1	1	8	3	11	.193	.230	.337	43	-7	1	0	0	.982	-1	C-33/O-2,D	-0.6
Total	4	111	252	33	58	15	1	6	27	16	42	.230	.281	.369	71	-11	3	1	0	.989	-5	/C-88,D-10,O	-1.1

■ DON HASENMAYER
Hasenmayer, Donald Irvin b: 4/4/27, Roslyn, Pa. BR/TR, 5'10.5", 180 lbs. Deb: 5/2/45

1945	Phi-N	5	18	1	2	0	0	0	1	2	1	.111	.200	.111	-13	-3	0			.920	3	/2-4,3-1	0.0
1946	Phi-N	6	12	0	1	1	0	0	0	0	1	.083	.083	.167	-31	-2	0			1.000	2	/3-3	0.0
Total	2	11	30	1	3	1	0	0	1	2	2	.100	.156	.133	-19	-5	0			1.000	5	/3-4,2-4	0.0

■ MICKEY HASLIN
Haslin, Michael Joseph b: 10/31/10, Wilkes-Barre, Pa. BR/TR, 5'8", 165 lbs. Deb: 9/7/33

1933	Phi-N	26	89	3	21	2	0	0	9	3	5	.236	.261	.258	43	-6	1			.956	-4	2-26	-1.0
1934	Phi-N	72	166	28	44	8	2	1	11	16	13	.265	.330	.355	74	-6	1			.941	-3	3-26,2-21/S	-0.7
1935	Phi-N	110	407	53	108	17	3	3	52	19	25	.265	.300	.344	66	-20	5			.931	-3	S-87,3-11/2	-1.7
1936	Phi-N	16	64	6	22	1	1	0	6	3	5	.344	.373	.391	96	-0	0			.938	5	2-12/3-5	-0.4
	Bos-N	36	104	14	29	1	2	2	11	5	9	.279	.312	.385	93	-1	0			.892	-5	3-17/2-7	-0.5
	Yr	52	168	20	51	2	3	2	17	8	14	.304	.335	.387	95	-1	0			.854	-10	3-22,2-19	-0.9
1937	NY-N	27	42	8	8	1	0	0	5	9	3	.190	.333	.214	51	-2	1			.920	6	/S-9,2-4,3	0.4
1938	NY-N	31	102	13	33	3	0	3	15	4	4	.324	.361	.441	119	2	0			.902	-3	3-15,2-13	0.1
Total	6	318	974	125	265	33	8	9	109	59	64	.272	.316	.350	74	-34	8			.927	-15	S-100/2-92,3	-3.8

■ PETE HASNEY
Hasney, Peter James b: 5/26/1865, England d: 5/24/08, Philadelphia, Pa. Deb: 9/13/1890

| 1890 | Phi-a | 2 | 7 | 1 | 1 | 0 | 0 | 0 | | 1 | | .143 | .250 | .143 | 16 | -1 | 0 | | | .000 | -1 | /O-2 | -0.2 |

■ BILL HASSAMAER
Hassamaer, William Louis "Roaring Bill" b: 7/26/1864, St.Louis, Mo. d: 5/29/10, St.Louis, Mo. 6', 180 lbs. Deb: 4/19/1894

1894	Was-N	118	494	106	159	33	17	4	90	41	20	.322	.375	.482	109	6	16			.916	5	O-68,3-31,2/S	0.5
1895	Was-N	85	358	42	100	18	4	1	60	26	13	.279	.328	.360	78	-12	8			.964	-7	O-75/1-9,S3	-2.0
	Lou-N	23	96	7	20	2	2	0	14	3	4	.208	.232	.271	31	-10	0			.980	3	1-21/2-1,S	-0.5
	Yr	108	454	49	120	20	6	1	74	29	17	.264	.308	.341	69	-22	8			.964	-4	O-75,1-30/S32	-2.5
1896	Lou-N	30	106	8	26	5	0	2	14	14	7	.245	.333	.349	83	-2	1			.976	6	1-29	0.4
Total	3	256	1054	163	305	58	23	7	178	84	44	.289	.342	.408	90	-19	25			.938	7	O-143/1-59,32S	-1.6

■ BUDDY HASSETT
Hassett, John Aloysius b: 9/5/11, New York, N.Y. BL/TL, 5'11", 180 lbs. Deb: 4/14/36

1936	Bro-N	156	635	79	197	29	11	3	82	35	17	.310	.350	.405	102	1	5			.983	5	*1-156	-0.9
1937	Bro-N	137	556	71	169	31	6	1	53	20	19	.304	.334	.387	94	-5	13			.984	9	*1-131/O-7	-1.2
1938	Bro-N	115	335	49	98	11	6	0	40	32	19	.293	.356	.361	95	-1	3			.945	-2	O-71/1-8	-0.7
1939	Bos-N	147	590	72	182	15	3	2	60	29	14	.308	.342	.354	94	-6	13			.985	9	*1-123,O-23	-1.1
1940	Bos-N	124	458	59	107	19	4	0	27	25	16	.234	.273	.293	59	-26	4			.979	7	1-98,O-13	-2.9
1941	Bos-N	118	405	59	120	9	4	1	33	36	15	.296	.354	.346	102	1	10			.991	7	1-99	0.1
1942	*NY-A	132	538	80	153	16	4	5	48	32	16	.284	.325	.364	95	-5	5	5	-2	.991	11	*1-132	-0.3
Total	7	929	3517	469	1026	130	40	12	343	209	116	.292	.333	.362	92	-40	53	5		.985	45	1-747,O-114	-7.0

■ RON HASSEY
Hassey, Ronald William b: 2/27/53, Tucson, Ariz. BL/TR, 6'2", 200 lbs. Deb: 4/23/78 C

1978	Cle-A	25	74	5	15	0	0	2	9	5	7	.203	.262	.284	54	-5	2	0	1	.993	5	C-24	0.2
1979	Cle-A	75	223	20	64	14	0	4	32	19	19	.287	.343	.404	100	0	1	0	0	.992	6	C-68/1-2	0.9
1980	Cle-A	130	390	43	124	18	4	8	65	49	51	.318	.395	.446	130	17	0	2	-1	.993	-7	*C-113/1-3,D	1.3
1981	Cle-A	61	190	8	44	4	0	5	25	16	11	.232	.301	.268	66	-8	0	0	-1	.991	8	C-56/1-5,D	0.2
1982	Cle-A	113	323	33	81	18	0	5	34	53	32	.251	.358	.353	97	0	3	2	-0	.993	8	*C-105/1-2,D	1.2

YEAR	TM/L	G	AB	R	H	2B	3B	HR	RBI	BB	SO	AVG	OBP	SLG	PRO+	BR/A	SB	CS	SBR	FA	FR	G/POS	TPR
1983	Cle-A	117	341	48	92	21	0	6	42	38	35	.270	.346	.384	97	-1	2	2	-1	.995	-3	*C-113/D-1	0.0
1984	Cle-A	48	149	11	38	5	1	0	19	15	26	.255	.323	.302	73	-5	1	0	0	1.000	-1	C-44/1-1,D	-0.4
	Chi-N	19	33	5	11	0	0	2	5	4	6	.333	.405	.515	144	2	0	1	-1	1.000	-0	/C-6,1-4	0.1
1985	NY-A	92	267	31	79	16	1	13	42	28	21	.296	.369	.509	141	15	0	0	0	.984	-2	C-69/1-2,D	1.6
1986	NY-A	64	191	23	57	14	0	6	29	24	16	.298	.382	.466	131	9	1	1	0	.985	-13	C-51/D-3	-0.2
	Chi-A	49	150	22	53	11	1	3	20	22	11	.353	.439	.500	150	11	0	0	0	1.000	1	D-34,C-11	1.2
	Yr	113	341	45	110	25	1	9	49	46	27	.323	.408	.481	140	20	1	1	0	.988	-12	C-62,D-37	1.0
1987	Chi-A	49	145	15	31	9	0	3	12	17	11	.214	.305	.338	69	-6	0	0	0	.994	-1	C-24,D-18	-0.4
1988	*Oak-A	107	323	32	83	15	0	7	45	30	42	.257	.328	.368	98	-1	2	0	1	.994	-1	C-91/D-9	0.4
1989	*Oak-A	97	268	29	61	12	0	5	23	24	45	.228	.294	.328	78	-8	1	0	0	.991	7	C-78/1-1,D	0.3
1990	*Oak-A	94	254	18	54	7	0	5	22	27	29	.213	.291	.299	68	-11	0	0	0	.997	3	C-59,D-15/1	-0.5
1991	Mon-N	52	119	5	27	8	0	1	14	13	16	.227	.303	.319	76	-4	1	1	0	.989	-4	C-34	-0.7
Total	14	1192	3440	348	914	172	7	71	438	385	378	.266	.343	.382	100	7	14	10	-2	.993	9	C-946/D-95,1	5.2

■ JOE HASSLER
Hassler, Joseph Frederick b: 4/7/05, Ft.Smith, Ark. d: 9/4/71, Duncan, Okla. BR/TR, 6', 165 lbs. Deb: 5/26/28

YEAR	TM/L	G	AB	R	H	2B	3B	HR	RBI	BB	SO	AVG	OBP	SLG	PRO+	BR/A	SB	CS	SBR	FA	FR	G/POS	TPR
1928	Phi-A	28	34	5	9	2	0	0	3	2	4	.265	.306	.324	64	-2	0	1	-1	.879	1	S-28	0.0
1929	Phi-A	4	4	1	0	0	0	0	0	0	2	.000	.000	.000	-97	-1	0	0	0	.600	-0	/S-2	-0.1
1930	StL-A	5	8	3	2	0	0	0	1	0	1	.250	.250	.250	26	-1	0	0	0	1.000	1	/S-3	0.1
Total	3	37	46	9	11	2	0	0	4	2	7	.239	.271	.283	43	-4	0	1	-1	.875	2	/S-33	0.0

■ GENE HASSON
Hasson, Charles Eugene b: 7/20/15, Connellsville, Pa BL/TL, 6', 197 lbs. Deb: 9/9/37

YEAR	TM/L	G	AB	R	H	2B	3B	HR	RBI	BB	SO	AVG	OBP	SLG	PRO+	BR/A	SB	CS	SBR	FA	FR	G/POS	TPR
1937	Phi-A	28	98	12	30	6	3	3	14	13	14	.306	.387	.520	129	4	0	0	0	1.000	-2	1-28	-0.1
1938	Phi-A	19	69	10	19	6	2	1	12	12	7	.275	.385	.464	114	2	0	0	0	.958	-4	1-19	-0.4
Total	2	47	167	22	49	12	5	4	26	25	21	.293	.385	.497	123	6	0	0	0	.985	-6	/1-47	-0.5

■ SCOTT HASTINGS
Hastings, Winfield Scott b: 8/10/1847, Hillsboro, Ohio d: 8/14/07, Sawtelle, Cal. BR/TR, 5'8", 161 lbs. Deb: 5/6/1871 M

YEAR	TM/L	G	AB	R	H	2B	3B	HR	RBI	BB	SO	AVG	OBP	SLG	PRO+	BR/A	SB	CS	SBR	FA	FR	G/POS	TPR
1871	Rok-n	25	118	27	30	6	4	0	20	2	4	.254	.267	.373	85	-7	11					*C-23/2-2,OM	-0.2
1872	Cle-n	22	117	34	45	6	0	0	16	3	2	.385	.400	.436	166	10						C-11/O-7,2M	0.7
	Bal-n	13	61	16	19	3	1	0	4	1	2	.311	.323	.393	114	1						/C-9,2-2	0.0
	Yr	35	178	50	64	9	1	0	20	4	4	.360	.374	.421	147	10						C-20/O-7,2	0.7
1873	Bal-n	30	146	41	41	5	0	0	12	4	1	.281	.300	.315	82	-3						C-19,O-11/2	-0.2
1874	Har-n	52	248	60	80	13	1	0	4			.323	.333	.383	121	5						C-31,O-20/2	0.5
1875	Chi-n	65	284	43	73	9	0	0			9	.257	.280	.289	96	-1						C-39,O-25/2	0.1
1876	Lou-N	67	283	36	73	6	1	0	21	5	11	.258	.271	.286	73	-11				.872	-7	*O-65/C-5	-1.7
1877	Cin-N	20	71	7	10	1	0	0	3	3	6	.141	.176	.155	6	-7				.791	-9	C-20/O-1	-1.4
Total	5 n	207	974	221	288	42	6	0	52	23	9	.296	.312	.351	108	9						C-132/O-64,2	0.9
Total	2	87	354	43	83	7	1	0	24	8	17	.234	.251	.260	61	-18				.872	-17	/O-66,C-25	-3.1

■ MICKEY HATCHER
Hatcher, Michael Vaughn b: 3/15/55, Cleveland, Ohio BR/TR, 6'2", 200 lbs. Deb: 8/3/79 C

YEAR	TM/L	G	AB	R	H	2B	3B	HR	RBI	BB	SO	AVG	OBP	SLG	PRO+	BR/A	SB	CS	SBR	FA	FR	G/POS	TPR
1979	LA-N	33	93	9	25	4	1	1	5	7	12	.269	.327	.366	90	-1	1	3	-2	.974	-1	O-19,3-17	-0.5
1980	LA-N	57	84	4	19	2	0	1	5	2	12	.226	.244	.286	48	-6	0	2	-1	1.000	-5	O-25,3-18	-1.4
1981	Min-A	99	377	36	96	23	2	3	37	15	29	.255	.287	.350	77	-11	3	1	0	.992	4	O-91/1-7,3D	-1.2
1982	Min-A	84	277	23	69	13	2	3	26	8	27	.249	.280	.343	65	-13	0	2	-1	.988	0	O-47,D-29/3	-1.7
1983	Min-A	106	375	50	119	15	3	9	47	14	19	.317	.344	.445	111	5	2	0	1	.979	6	O-56,D-39/13	0.8
1984	Min-A	152	576	61	174	35	5	5	69	37	34	.302	.346	.406	103	2	0	1	-1	.974	13	*O-100,D-37,1/3	1.0
1985	Min-A	116	444	46	125	28	0	5	49	16	23	.282	.310	.365	79	-13	0	0	0	.991	8	O-97,D-11/1	-0.9
1986	Min-A	115	317	40	88	13	3	3	32	19	26	.278	.318	.366	84	-7	2	1	0	.971	-3	O-46,D-28,1/3	-1.3
1987	LA-N	101	287	27	81	19	1	7	42	20	19	.282	.331	.429	102	0	2	3	-1	.929	1	3-49,1-37/O	-0.4
1988	*LA-N	88	191	22	56	8	0	1	25	7	7	.293	.325	.351	97	-1	0	0	0	1.000	-2	O-29,1-25/3	-0.6
1989	LA-N	94	224	18	66	9	2	1	25	11	22	.295	.336	.379	106	1	1	2	-1	.961	-3	O-48,3-16/1P	-0.4
1990	LA-N	85	132	12	28	3	1	0	13	6	22	.212	.252	.250	40	-11	0	0	0	1.000	-4	1-25,3-10,O	-1.7
Total	12	1130	3377	348	946	172	20	38	375	164	246	.280	.316	.377	89	-55	11	15	-6	.983	13	O-575,1-149,D3/P	-8.3

■ BILLY HATCHER
Hatcher, William Augustus b: 10/4/60, Williams, Ariz. BR/TR, 5'9", 175 lbs. Deb: 9/10/84

YEAR	TM/L	G	AB	R	H	2B	3B	HR	RBI	BB	SO	AVG	OBP	SLG	PRO+	BR/A	SB	CS	SBR	FA	FR	G/POS	TPR
1984	Chi-N	8	9	1	1	0	0	0	0	1	0	.111	.200	.111	-10	-1	2	0	1	1.000	-0	/O-4	-0.1
1985	Chi-N	53	163	24	40	12	1	2	10	8	12	.245	.293	.368	75	-6	2	4	-2	.988	-3	O-44	-1.2
1986	*Hou-N	127	419	55	108	15	4	6	36	22	52	.258	.303	.356	83	-10	38	14	3	.983	-5	*O-121	-1.7
1987	Hou-N	141	564	96	167	28	3	11	63	42	70	.296	.354	.415	107	6	53	9	11	.986	10	*O-140	2.2
1988	Hou-N	145	530	79	142	25	4	7	52	37	56	.268	.325	.370	103	2	32	13	2	.983	2	*O-142	0.1
1989	Hou-N	108	395	49	90	15	3	3	44	30	53	.228	.284	.304	71	-15	22	6	3	.991	2	*O-104	-1.4
	Pit-N	27	86	10	21	4	0	1	7	2	9	.244	.253	.326	67	-4	2	1	0	1.000	-4	O-20	-0.9
	Yr	135	481	59	111	19	3	4	51	32	62	.231	.279	.308	70	-19	24	7	3	.992	-2	*O-124	-2.3
1990	*Cin-N	139	504	68	139	28	5	5	25	33	42	.276	.328	.381	91	-6	30	10	3	**.997**	8	*O-131	0.1
1991	Cin-N	138	442	45	116	25	3	4	41	26	55	.262	.314	.360	86	-9	11	9	-2	.981	-2	*O-121	-1.6
1992	Cin-N	43	94	10	27	3	0	2	10	5	11	.287	.323	.383	97	-1	2	2	-1	.967	-3	O-23	-0.5
	Bos-A	75	315	37	75	16	2	1	23	17	41	.238	.284	.311	62	-16	4	6	-2	.968	-1	O-75	-2.2
1993	Bos-A	136	508	71	146	24	3	9	57	28	46	.287	.328	.400	92	-6	14	7	0	.993	-4	*O-130/2-2	-1.3
1994	Bos-A	44	164	24	40	9	1	1	18	11	14	.244	.295	.329	57	-11	4	5	-2	.968	1	O-43/D-1	-1.1
	Phi-N	43	134	15	33	5	1	2	13	6	14	.246	.279	.343	62	-8	4	1	1	1.000	-3	O-40	-1.1
Total	11	1227	4327	584	1145	209	30	54	399	266	475	.265	.315	.364	86	-85	218	87	13	.986	-2	*O-1138/2-2,D	-10.7

■ FRED HATFIELD
Hatfield, Fred James b: 3/18/25, Lanett, Ala. BL/TR, 6'1", 171 lbs. Deb: 8/31/50 C

YEAR	TM/L	G	AB	R	H	2B	3B	HR	RBI	BB	SO	AVG	OBP	SLG	PRO+	BR/A	SB	CS	SBR	FA	FR	G/POS	TPR
1950	Bos-A	10	12	3	3	0	0	0	2	3	1	.250	.400	.250	63	-1	0	0	0	1.000	3	/3-3	0.2
1951	Bos-A	80	163	23	28	4	2	1	14	22	27	.172	.274	.258	40	-14	1	0	0	.959	21	3-49	0.6
1952	Bos-A	19	25	6	8	1	1	1	3	4	2	.320	.433	.560	162	2	0	3	-2	1.000	4	3-17	0.4
	Det-A	112	441	42	104	12	2	2	25	35	52	.236	.301	.286	63	-21	2	2	-1	.968	14	*3-107/S-9	-1.0
	Yr	131	466	48	112	13	3	3	28	39	54	.240	.309	.300	69	-19	2	5	-2	**.971**	18	*3-124/S-9	-0.6
1953	Det-A	109	311	41	79	11	1	3	19	40	34	.254	.341	.325	81	-7	3	5	-2	.978	9	3-54,2-28/S	0.0
1954	Det-A	81	218	31	64	12	0	2	25	24	24	.294	.386	.376	112	5	4	2	0	.972	-7	2-54,3-15	0.0
1955	Det-A	122	413	51	96	15	3	8	33	61	49	.232	.338	.341	85	-6	3	2	0	.975	-6	2-92,3-16,S	-0.6
1956	Det-A	8	12	2	3	0	0	0	2	2	1	.250	.400	.250	75	-0	0	0	0	1.000	-1	/2-4	-0.1
	Chi-A	106	321	46	84	9	1	7	33	37	36	.262	.352	.361	88	-5	1	0	0	.961	5	*3-100/S-3	0.1
	Yr	114	333	48	87	9	1	7	35	39	37	.261	.354	.357	87	-5	1	0	0	.961	4	*3-100/2-4,S	0.0
1957	Chi-A	69	114	14	23	3	0	0	8	15	20	.202	.321	.228	52	-7	1	0	0	.951	2	3-44	-0.4
1958	Cle-A	3	8	0	1	0	0	0	1	1	1	.125	.222	.125	-2	-1	0	0	0	1.000	1	/3-2	0.0
	Cin-N	3	1	0	0	0	0	0	0	0	0	.000	.000	.000	-95	-0	0	0	0	1.000	0	/2-1,3-1	0.0
Total	9	722	2039	259	493	67	10	25	165	248	247	.242	.334	.321	78	-57	15	14	-4	.962	43	3-408,2-179/S	-0.8

■ GIL HATFIELD
Hatfield, Gilbert "Colonel" b: 1/27/1855, Hoboken, N.J. d: 5/27/21, Hoboken, N.J. TR, 5'9.5", 168 lbs. Deb: 9/24/1885 F

YEAR	TM/L	G	AB	R	H	2B	3B	HR	RBI	BB	SO	AVG	OBP	SLG	PRO+	BR/A	SB	CS	SBR	FA	FR	G/POS	TPR
1885	Buf-N	11	30	1	4	0	1	0	0	0	11	.133	.133	.200	6	-3				.913	-0	/3-8,2-3	-0.3
1887	NY-N	2	7	2	3	1	0	0	0	0	1	.429	.429	.571	184	2				1.000	0	/3-2	0.1
1888	*NY-N	28	105	7	19	1	0	0	9	2	6	.181	.211	.190	29	-8	8			.813	-1	3-14,S-13/O2	-0.9
1889	NY-N	32	125	21	23	2	0	1	12	9	15	.184	.250	.224	33	-11	9			.858	1	S-24/P-6,3	-0.6
1890	NY-P	71	287	32	80	13	6	2	37	17	19	.279	.328	.387	83	-9	12			.842	-19	3-42,S-27/PO	-2.0

YEAR	TM/L	G	AB	R	H	2B	3B	HR	RBI	BB	SO	AVG	OBP	SLG	PRO+	BR/A	SB	CS	SBR	FA	FR	G/POS	TPR
1891	Was-a	134	500	83	128	11	8	1	48	50	39	.256	.335	.316	90	-5	43			.869	9	*S-105,3-27/PO	1.0
1893	Bro-N	34	120	24	35	3	3	2	19	17	5	.292	.388	.417	119	4	9			.875	-7	3-34	-0.2
1895	Lou-N	5	16	3	3	0	0	0	1	1	1	.188	.278	.188	23	-2	0			.889	-1	/3-3,S-2	-0.2
Total	8	317	1190	173	295	31	18	6	129	96	109	.248	.315	.319	79	-34	81			.850	-17	S-171,3-132/PO2	-3.1

■ JOHN HATFIELD   Hatfield, John Van Buskirk b: 7/20/1847, New Jersey d: 2/20/09, Long Island City, N.Y. 5'10", 165 lbs. Deb: 5/18/1871 FM

YEAR	TM/L	G	AB	R	H	2B	3B	HR	RBI	BB	SO	AVG	OBP	SLG	PRO+	BR/A	SB	CS	SBR	FA	FR	G/POS	TPR
1871	Mut-n	33	168	41	43	3	2	0	22	4	0	.256	.273	.298	70	-5	10					*O-24/2-7,3	-0.3
1872	Mut-n	56	287	75	91	12	2	1	45	9	5	.317	.338	.383	130	12						*2-56,M	0.5
1873	Mut-n	52	255	54	78	6	7	2	45	3	2	.306	.314	.408	111	4						*3-45,2-11/OM	0.1
1874	Mut-n	63	289	46	68	12	2	0	8			.235	.256	.291	71	-10						*O-59/3-4,P1	-0.6
1875	Mut-n	2	9	2	3	1	0	0	0			.333	.333	.444	158	0						/O-2	0.0
1876	NY-N	1	4	0	1	0	0	0	1	0	0	.250	.250	.250	77	-0				.833	-0	/2-1	0.0
Total	5 n	206	1008	218	283	34	13	2	112	24	7	.281	.297	.349	98	2						/O-86,2-74,3P1	-0.3

■ GRADY HATTON   Hatton, Grady Edgebert b: 10/7/22, Beaumont, Tex. BL/TR, 5'9", 175 lbs. Deb: 4/16/46 MC

YEAR	TM/L	G	AB	R	H	2B	3B	HR	RBI	BB	SO	AVG	OBP	SLG	PRO+	BR/A	SB	CS	SBR	FA	FR	G/POS	TPR
1946	Cin-N	116	436	56	118	18	3	14	69	66	53	.271	.369	.422	129	17	6			.941	-19	*3-116/O-2	-0.1
1947	Cin-N	146	524	91	147	24	8	16	77	81	50	.281	.377	.448	119	15	7			.938	-8	*3-136	0.7
1948	Cin-N	133	458	58	110	17	2	9	44	72	50	.240	.343	.345	90	-5	7			.932	4	*3-123/2-3,SO	-0.2
1949	Cin-N	137	537	71	141	38	5	11	69	62	48	.263	.342	.413	101	0	4			**.975**	-1	*3-136	-0.3
1950	Cin-N	130	438	67	114	17	1	11	54	70	39	.260	.366	.379	96	-1	6			.954	-3	*3-126/2-1,S	-0.5
1951	Cin-N	96	331	41	84	9	3	4	37	33	32	.254	.321	.335	76	-11	4	2	0	.972	0	3-87/O-2	-0.9
1952	Cin-N☆	128	433	48	92	14	2	9	57	66	60	.212	.319	.312	76	-13	5	4	-1	**.990**	-17	*2-120	-2.6
1953	Cin-N	83	159	22	37	3	1	7	22	29	24	.233	.351	.396	94	-1	0	1	-1	.991	-11	2-35,1-10/3	-1.1
1954	Cin-N	1	1	0	0	0	0	0	0	0	0	.000	.000	.000	-97	-0	0	0	0	.000	0	H	0.0
	Chi-A	13	30	3	5	1	0	0	3	5	3	.167	.286	.200	34	-3	1	0	0	1.000	-1	3-10/1-3	-0.4
	Bos-A	99	302	40	85	12	3	5	33	58	25	.281	.401	.391	106	4	1	1	-0	.966	6	3-93/1-1,S	0.9
	Yr	112	332	43	90	13	3	5	36	63	28	.271	.390	.373	100	2	2	1	0	**.969**	5	*3-103/1-4,S	0.5
1955	Bos-A	126	380	48	93	11	4	4	49	76	28	.245	.371	.326	81	-8	0	1	-1	.976	-2	3-111/2-1	-1.1
1956	Bos-A	5	5	0	2	0	0	0	0	0	0	.400	.400	.400	100	0	0	0	0	.000	-0	H	0.0
	StL-N	44	73	10	18	1	2	0	7	13	7	.247	.360	.315	84	-1	1	0	0	.951	-4	2-13/3-1	-0.4
	Bal-A	27	61	4	9	1	0	1	3	13	6	.148	.297	.213	40	-5	0	0	0	1.000	-5	2-15,3-12	-0.9
1960	Chi-N	28	38	3	13	0	0	0	7	2	5	.342	.390	.342	104	0	0	0	0	.931	-2	/2-8	-0.1
Total	12	1312	4206	562	1068	166	33	91	533	646	430	.254	.355	.374	96	-10	42	9		.956	-60	3-956,2-196/10S	-7.0

■ ARTHUR HAUGER   Hauger, John Arthur b: 11/18/1893, Delhi, Ohio d: 8/2/44, Redwood City, Cal BL/TR, 5'11", 168 lbs. Deb: 7/17/12

YEAR	TM/L	G	AB	R	H	2B	3B	HR	RBI	BB	SO	AVG	OBP	SLG	PRO+	BR/A	SB	CS	SBR	FA	FR	G/POS	TPR
1912	Cle-A	15	18	0	1	0	0	0	0		1	.056	.105	.056	-52	-4	0			1.000	-2	/O-5	-0.5

■ ARNOLD HAUSER   Hauser, Arnold George "Peewee" or "Stub" b: 9/25/1888, Chicago, Ill. d: 5/22/66, Aurora, Ill. BR/TR, 5'6", 145 lbs. Deb: 4/21/10

YEAR	TM/L	G	AB	R	H	2B	3B	HR	RBI	BB	SO	AVG	OBP	SLG	PRO+	BR/A	SB	CS	SBR	FA	FR	G/POS	TPR
1910	StL-N	119	375	37	77	7	2	2	36	49	39	.205	.312	.251	67	-14	15			.931	-8	*S-117/3-1	-1.9
1911	StL-N	136	515	61	124	11	8	3	46	26	67	.241	.286	.311	69	-23	24			.918	-15	*S-134/3-2	-2.9
1912	StL-N	133	479	73	124	14	7	1	42	39	69	.259	.319	.324	78	-15	26			.934	10	*S-132	0.6
1913	StL-N	22	45	3	13	0	3	0	9	2	2	.289	.347	.422	121	1	1			.848	-3	/S-8,2-4	-0.2
1915	Chi-F	23	54	6	11	1	0	0	4	5	7	.204	.283	.222	38	-5	2			.851	-3	S-16/3-6	-0.7
Total	5	433	1468	180	349	33	20	6	137	121	184	.238	.305	.300	72	-55	68			.924	-19	S-407/3-9,2	-5.1

■ JOE HAUSER   Hauser, Joseph John "Unser Choe" b: 1/12/1899, Milwaukee, Wis. BL/TL, 5'10.5", 175 lbs. Deb: 4/18/22

YEAR	TM/L	G	AB	R	H	2B	3B	HR	RBI	BB	SO	AVG	OBP	SLG	PRO+	BR/A	SB	CS	SBR	FA	FR	G/POS	TPR
1922	Phi-A	111	368	61	119	21	5	9	43	30	37	.323	.378	.481	119	10	1	5	-3	.986	-3	1-94	0.0
1923	Phi-A	146	537	93	165	21	9	17	94	69	52	.307	.398	.475	127	22	6	6	-2	.990	-3	*1-146	0.9
1924	Phi-A	149	562	97	162	31	8	27	115	56	52	.288	.358	.516	123	15	7	5	-1	.993	-3	*1-146	0.2
1926	Phi-A	91	229	31	44	10	0	8	36	39	35	.192	.312	.341	66	-12	1	1	-0	.996	0	1-65	-1.5
1928	Phi-A	95	300	61	78	19	5	16	59	52	45	.260	.369	.517	127	11	4	2	0	.986	-6	1-88	-0.2
1929	Cle-A	37	48	8	12	1	1	3	9	4	8	.250	.321	.500	104	0	0	0	0	.986	1	/1-8	0.0
Total	6	629	2044	351	580	103	28	80	356	250	229	.284	.368	.479	117	46	19	19	-6	.990	-14	1-547	-0.6

■ GEORGE HAUSMANN   Hausmann, George John b: 2/11/16, St.Louis, Mo. BR/TR, 5'5", 145 lbs. Deb: 4/18/44

YEAR	TM/L	G	AB	R	H	2B	3B	HR	RBI	BB	SO	AVG	OBP	SLG	PRO+	BR/A	SB	CS	SBR	FA	FR	G/POS	TPR
1944	NY-N	131	466	70	124	20	4	1	30	40	25	.266	.324	.333	85	-9	3			.960	-7	*2-122	-0.9
1945	NY-N	154	623	98	174	15	8	2	45	73	46	.279	.356	.339	92	-5	5			.968	5	*2-154	1.0
1949	NY-N	16	47	5	6	0	1	0	3	7	6	.128	.241	.170	12	-6	0			.984	-0	2-13	-0.6
Total	3	301	1136	173	304	35	13	3	78	120	77	.268	.338	.329	86	-19	10			.965	-3	2-289	-0.5

■ CHARLIE HAUTZ   Hautz, Charles A. b: 2/5/1852, St.Louis, Mo. d: 1/24/29, St.Louis, Mo. BR, 5'7", 150 lbs. Deb: 5/4/1875

YEAR	TM/L	G	AB	R	H	2B	3B	HR	RBI	BB	SO	AVG	OBP	SLG	PRO+	BR/A	SB	CS	SBR	FA	FR	G/POS	TPR
1875	RS-n	19	83	5	25	2	0	0			1	.301	.310	.325	133	3						1-18	0.2
1884	Pit-a	7	24	0	5	0	0	0		0		.208	.296	.208	66	-1				.980	0	/1-5,O-2	-0.1

■ ROY HAWES   Hawes, Roy Lee b: 7/5/26, Shiloh, Ill. BL/TL, 6'2", 190 lbs. Deb: 9/23/51

YEAR	TM/L	G	AB	R	H	2B	3B	HR	RBI	BB	SO	AVG	OBP	SLG	PRO+	BR/A	SB	CS	SBR	FA	FR	G/POS	TPR
1951	Was-A	3	6	0	1	0	0	0	0	1	1	.167	.167	.167	-10	-1	0	0	0	1.000	-0	/1-1	-0.1

■ BILL HAWES   Hawes, William Hildreth b: 11/17/1853, Nashua, N.H. d: 6/16/40, Lowell, Mass. BR/TR, 5'10", 155 lbs. Deb: 5/1/1879

YEAR	TM/L	G	AB	R	H	2B	3B	HR	RBI	BB	SO	AVG	OBP	SLG	PRO+	BR/A	SB	CS	SBR	FA	FR	G/POS	TPR
1879	Bos-N	38	155	19	31	3	3	0	9	2	13	.200	.210	.258	52	-8				.828	-3	O-34/C-5	-1.2
1884	Cin-U	79	349	80	97	7	4	4		5		.278	.288	.355	68	-16				.827	-7	O-58,1-21	-2.4
Total	2	117	504	99	128	10	7	4	9	7	13	.254	.264	.325	64	-24				.827	-10	/O-92,1-21,C	-3.6

■ THORNY HAWKES   Hawkes, Thorndike Proctor b: 10/15/1852, Danvers, Mass. d: 2/3/29, Danvers, Mass. BR/TR, 5'8", 135 lbs. Deb: 5/1/1879

YEAR	TM/L	G	AB	R	H	2B	3B	HR	RBI	BB	SO	AVG	OBP	SLG	PRO+	BR/A	SB	CS	SBR	FA	FR	G/POS	TPR
1879	Tro-N	64	250	24	52	6	1	0	20	4	14	.208	.220	.240	55	-11				.896	16	*2-64	0.8
1884	Was-a	38	151	16	42	4	2	0		4		.278	.297	.331	118	3				.917	3	2-38/O-2	0.6
Total	2	102	401	40	94	10	3	0	20	8	14	.234	.249	.274	79	-8				.903	19	2-102/O-2	1.4

■ CHICKEN HAWKS   Hawks, Nelson Louis b: 2/3/1896, San Francisco, Cal. d: 5/26/73, San Rafael, Cal. BL/TL, 5'11", 167 lbs. Deb: 4/14/21

YEAR	TM/L	G	AB	R	H	2B	3B	HR	RBI	BB	SO	AVG	OBP	SLG	PRO+	BR/A	SB	CS	SBR	FA	FR	G/POS	TPR
1921	NY-A	41	73	16	21	2	3	2	15	5	12	.288	.333	.479	103	-0	0	1	-1	.970	-2	O-15	-0.3
1925	Phi-N	105	320	52	103	15	5	5	45	32	33	.322	.387	.447	103	2	3	6	-3	.986	-0	1-90	-0.5
Total	2	146	393	68	124	17	8	7	60	37	45	.316	.377	.453	103	2	3	7	-3	.986	-2	/1-90,O-15	-0.8

■ HOWIE HAWORTH   Haworth, Homer Howard "Cully" b: 8/27/1893, Newberg, Ore. d: 1/28/53, Troutdale, Ore. BL/TR, 5'10.5", 165 lbs. Deb: 8/14/15

YEAR	TM/L	G	AB	R	H	2B	3B	HR	RBI	BB	SO	AVG	OBP	SLG	PRO+	BR/A	SB	CS	SBR	FA	FR	G/POS	TPR
1915	Cle-A	7	7	0	1	0	0	0	1		2	.143	.333	.143	42	-0	0			.917	-1	/C-5	-0.1

■ JACK HAYDEN   Hayden, John Francis b: 10/21/1880, Bryn Mawr, Pa. d: 8/3/42, Haverford, Pa. BL/TL, 5'9", Deb: 4/26/01

YEAR	TM/L	G	AB	R	H	2B	3B	HR	RBI	BB	SO	AVG	OBP	SLG	PRO+	BR/A	SB	CS	SBR	FA	FR	G/POS	TPR
1901	Phi-A	51	211	35	56	6	4	0	17	18		.265	.323	.332	78	-6	4			.841	-4	O-50	-1.2
1906	Bos-A	85	322	22	80	6	4	1	14	17		.248	.292	.301	86	-5	6			.973	-1	O-85	-1.2
1908	Chi-N	11	45	3	9	2	0	0	2	1		.200	.217	.244	45	-3	1			1.000	-1	O-11	-0.5
Total	3	147	578	60	145	14	8	1	33	36		.251	.298	.308	80	-14	11			.929	-5	O-146	-2.9

■ CHARLIE HAYES   Hayes, Charles Dewayne b: 5/29/65, Hattiesburg, Miss. BR/TR, 6', 190 lbs. Deb: 9/11/88

YEAR	TM/L	G	AB	R	H	2B	3B	HR	RBI	BB	SO	AVG	OBP	SLG	PRO+	BR/A	SB	CS	SBR	FA	FR	G/POS	TPR
1988	SF-N	7	11	0	1	0	0	0	0	0	3	.091	.091	.091	-50	-2	0	0	0	1.000	-1	/O-4,3-3	-0.3
1989	SF-N	3	5	0	1	0	0	0	0	0	1	.200	.200	.200	15	-1	0	0	0	1.000	-0	/3-3	-0.1
	Phi-N	84	299	26	77	15	1	8	43	11	49	.258	.284	.395	92	-4	3	1	0	.910	10	3-82	0.7
	Yr	87	304	26	78	15	1	8	43	11	50	.257	.283	.391	91	-5	3	1	0	.911	10	3-85	0.6

YEAR	TM/L	G	AB	R	H	2B	3B	HR	RBI	BB	SO	AVG	OBP	SLG	PRO+	BR/A	SB	CS	SBR	FA	FR	G/POS	TPR
1990	Phi-N	152	561	56	145	20	0	10	57	28	91	.258	.296	.348	77	-19	4	4	-1	.957	24	*3-146/1-4,2	0.5
1991	Phi-N	142	460	34	106	23	1	12	53	16	75	.230	.258	.363	74	-18	3	3	-1	.958	7	*3-138/S-2	-1.1
1992	NY-A	142	509	52	131	19	2	18	66	28	100	.257	.300	.409	98	-4	3	5	-2	.963	-11	*3-139/1-4	-1.8
1993	Col-N	157	573	89	175	45	2	25	98	43	82	.305	.362	.522	114	9	11	6	-0	.954	4	*3-154/S-1	1.3
1994	Col-N	113	423	46	122	23	4	10	50	36	71	.288	.348	.433	88	-8	3	6	-3	.944	1	*3-110	-0.9
Total	7	800	2841	303	758	145	10	83	367	162	472	.267	.310	.413	91	-46	27	25	-7	.951	33	3-775/1-8,OS2	-1.7

■ FRANKIE HAYES
Hayes, Frank Witman "Blimp" b: 10/13/14, Jamesburg, N.J. d: 6/22/55, Point Pleasant, N.J. BR/TR, 6', 185 lbs. Deb: 9/21/33

YEAR	TM/L	G	AB	R	H	2B	3B	HR	RBI	BB	SO	AVG	OBP	SLG	PRO+	BR/A	SB	CS	SBR	FA	FR	G/POS	TPR
1933	Phi-A	3	5	0	0	0	0	0	0	0	2	.000	.000	.000	-99	-1	0	0	0	.889	0	/C-3	-0.1
1934	Phi-A	92	248	24	56	10	0	6	30	20	44	.226	.286	.339	63	-15	2	1	-0	.955	-11	C-89	-2.1
1936	Phi-A	144	505	59	137	25	2	10	67	46	58	.271	.335	.388	79	-17	3	5	-2	.972	-22	*C-143	-3.1
1937	Phi-A	60	188	24	49	11	1	10	38	29	34	.261	.359	.489	114	3	0	0	0	.971	-4	C-56	0.2
1938	Phi-A	99	316	56	92	19	3	11	55	54	51	.291	.396	.475	120	11	2	3	-1	.975	-16	C-90	-0.2
1939	Phi-A☆	124	431	66	122	28	5	20	83	40	55	.283	.348	.510	119	10	4	1	1	.978	-12	*C-114	0.5
1940	Phi-A★	136	465	73	143	23	4	16	70	61	59	.308	.389	.477	126	19	9	3	1	.971	-13	*C-134/1-2	1.5
1941	Phi-A★	126	439	66	123	27	4	12	63	62	56	.280	.369	.442	117	11	2	0	1	.983	-11	*C-123	1.0
1942	Phi-A	21	63	8	15	4	0	0	5	9	8	.238	.333	.302	80	-1	1	1	-0	1.000	1	C-20	-0.5
	StL-A	56	159	14	40	6	0	2	17	28	39	.252	.364	.327	94	-0	1	0	-0	.971	-8	C-51	-0.4
	Yr	77	222	22	55	10	0	2	22	37	47	.248	.355	.320	90	-2	1	1	-0	.979	-12	C-71	-0.9
1943	StL-A	88	250	16	47	7	0	5	30	37	36	.188	.295	.276	66	-10	1	0	0	.983	-9	C-76/1-1	-1.5
1944	Phi-A★	155	581	62	144	18	6	13	78	57	59	.248	.315	.367	96	-2	2	1	-0	.982	3	*C-155/1-1	0.9
1945	Phi-A	32	110	12	25	2	1	5	14	18	14	.227	.336	.345	98	0	1	0	-0	.994	2	C-32	0.4
	Cle-A†	119	385	39	91	15	6	6	43	53	52	.236	.335	.353	104	2	1	1	-0	.988	2	*C-119	1.2
	Yr	151	495	51	116	17	7	9	57	71	66	.234	.335	.352	103	3	2	1	0	.989	3	*C-151	1.6
1946	Cle-A★	51	156	11	40	12	0	3	18	21	26	.256	.345	.391	112	3	1	3	-2	.981	-1	C-50	0.3
	Chi-A	53	179	15	38	6	0	2	16	29	33	.212	.322	.279	72	-6	1	1	-0	.979	-3	C-52	-0.7
	Yr	104	335	26	78	18	0	5	34	50	59	.233	.332	.331	90	-4	2	4	-2	.980	-4	*C-102	-0.4
1947	Bos-A	5	13	0	2	0	0	0	1	0	1	.154	.154	.154	-13	-2	0	0	0	.917	1	/C-4	0.0
Total	14	1364	4493	545	1164	213	32	119	628	564	627	.259	.343	.400	100	1	30	20	-3	.977	-106	*C-1311/1-4	-2.6

■ JACKIE HAYES
Hayes, John J. b: 6/27/1861, Brooklyn, N.Y. TR, Deb: 5/2/1882

YEAR	TM/L	G	AB	R	H	2B	3B	HR	RBI	BB	SO	AVG	OBP	SLG	PRO+	BR/A	SB	CS	SBR	FA	FR	G/POS	TPR
1882	Wor-N	78	326	27	88	22	4	4	54	6	26	.270	.283	.399	113	4				.855	-10	*O-58,C-15/3S	-0.5
1883	Pit-a	85	351	41	92	23	5	3		15		.262	.292	.382	121	8				.911	-18	C-62,O-18/S12	-0.5
1884	Pit-a	33	124	11	28	6	1	0		4		.226	.256	.290	77	-3				.912	-1	C-24/1-5,O2	-0.2
	Bro-a	16	51	4	12	3	0	0		3		.235	.278	.294	86	-1				.946	6	C-14/O-2	0.6
	Yr	49	175	15	40	9	1	0		7		.229	.262	.291	79	-4				.925	6	C-38/1-5,O2	0.4
1885	Bro-a	42	137	10	18	3	0	0		5		.131	.179	.153	6	-14				.900	-2	C-42	-1.2
1886	Was-N	26	89	8	17	3	0	3	9	4	23	.191	.226	.326	70	-3	0			.926	-4	C-14,O-12/2	-0.6
1887	Bal-a	8	28	2	4	3	0	0		0		.143	.143	.250	9	-3	0			.250	-4	/O-4,3-3,C	-0.6
1890	Bro-P	12	42	3	8	0	0	0	5	2	4	.190	.227	.190	11	-5	0			.867	-3	/O-6,S-3,C2	-0.7
Total	7	300	1148	106	267	63	10	10	68	39	53	.233	.260	.331	87	-18				.906	-36	C-174,O-103/1S32	-3.7

■ MIKE HAYES
Hayes, Michael b: 1853, Cleveland, Ohio 5'7.5", 170 lbs. Deb: 9/9/1876

YEAR	TM/L	G	AB	R	H	2B	3B	HR	RBI	BB	SO	AVG	OBP	SLG	PRO+	BR/A	SB	CS	SBR	FA	FR	G/POS	TPR
1876	NY-N	5	21	1	3	0	2	0	2	0	0	.143	.143	.333	63	-1				.882	0	/O-5	-0.1

■ JACKIE HAYES
Hayes, Minter Carney b: 7/19/06, Clanton, Ala. d: 2/9/83, Birmingham, Ala. BR/TR, 5'10.5", 165 lbs. Deb: 8/5/27

YEAR	TM/L	G	AB	R	H	2B	3B	HR	RBI	BB	SO	AVG	OBP	SLG	PRO+	BR/A	SB	CS	SBR	FA	FR	G/POS	TPR
1927	Was-A	10	29	2	7	0	0	0	2	1	2	.241	.267	.241	33	-3	0	0	0	.969	-1	/S-8,3-1	-0.3
1928	Was-A	60	210	30	54	7	3	0	22	5	10	.257	.274	.319	56	-14	3	0	1	.974	8	2-41,S-15/3	-0.2
1929	Was-A	123	424	52	117	20	3	2	57	24	29	.276	.316	.351	71	-18	4	5	-2	.945	3	3-63,2-57/S	-1.1
1930	Was-A	51	166	25	47	7	2	1	20	7	8	.283	.312	.367	71	-7	2	3	-1	.981	8	2-29/3-9,1	0.1
1931	Was-A	38	108	11	24	2	1	0	8	6	4	.222	.263	.259	38	-10	2	4	-0	.962	-4	2-19/3-8,S	-1.1
1932	Chi-A	117	475	53	122	20	5	2	54	30	28	.257	.302	.333	69	-23	7	4	-0	.967	1	2-97,S-10,3	-1.5
1933	Chi-A	138	535	65	138	23	5	2	47	55	36	.258	.331	.331	79	-16	2	3	-1	.981	10	*2-138	0.1
1934	Chi-A	62	226	19	58	9	1	1	31	23	20	.257	.325	.319	65	-12	3	2	-0	.980	-9	2-61	-1.6
1935	Chi-A	89	329	45	88	14	0	4	45	29	15	.267	.327	.347	72	-13	5	6		.966	-6	2-85	-1.2
1936	Chi-A	108	417	53	130	34	3	6	84	35	25	.312	.366	.444	96	-4	4	2	0	.979	17	2-89,S-13/3	1.8
1937	Chi-A	143	573	63	131	27	4	2	79	41	37	.229	.282	.300	47	-47	1	6	-3	.984	21	*2-143	-1.9
1938	Chi-A	62	238	40	78	21	2	1	20	24	6	.328	.389	.445	106	2	3	2	-0	.976	-3	2-61	0.2
1939	Chi-A	72	269	34	67	12	3	0	23	27	10	.249	.320	.316	62	-15	0	3	-2	.974	5	2-69	-0.8
1940	Chi-A	18	41	2	8	0	1	0	1	2	11	.195	.233	.244	23	-5	0	0	-0	.981	-0	2-15	-0.4
Total	14	1091	4040	494	1069	196	33	20	493	309	241	.265	.318	.344	70	-184	34	31	-8	.976	52	2-904/3-95,S1	-7.9

■ VON HAYES
Hayes, Von Francis b: 8/31/58, Stockton, Cal. BL/TR, 6'5", 185 lbs. Deb: 4/14/81

YEAR	TM/L	G	AB	R	H	2B	3B	HR	RBI	BB	SO	AVG	OBP	SLG	PRO+	BR/A	SB	CS	SBR	FA	FR	G/POS	TPR
1981	Cle-A	43	109	21	28	8	2	1	14	14	10	.257	.352	.394	116	3	8	1	2	.939	1	D-21,O-13/3	0.4
1982	Cle-A	150	527	65	132	25	3	14	82	42	63	.250	.311	.389	91	-7	32	13	2	.981	6	*O-139/3-5,1	-0.3
1983	*Phi-N	124	351	45	93	9	5	6	32	36	55	.265	.338	.370	97	-1	20	12	-1	.972	-19	*O-103	-2.5
1984	Phi-N	152	561	85	164	27	6	16	67	59	84	.292	.360	.447	124	17	48	13	7	.988	-8	*O-148	1.3
1985	Phi-N	152	570	76	150	30	4	13	70	61	99	.263	.334	.398	101	1	21	8	2	.984	-6	*O-146	-0.8
1986	Phi-N	158	610	107	186	46	2	19	98	74	77	.305	.381	.480	131	27	24	12	6	.990	2	*1-134,O-31	1.9
1987	Phi-N	158	556	84	154	36	5	21	84	121	77	.277	.406	.473	128	26	16	7	1	.990	-13	*1-144,O-32	0.3
1988	Phi-N	104	367	43	100	28	2	6	45	49	59	.272	.360	.409	118	9	20	9	1	.990	-1	1-85,O-16/3	0.3
1989	Phi-N★	154	540	93	140	27	2	26	78	101	103	.259	.380	.461	139	30	28	7	3	.980	3	*O-128,1-30,3	3.4
1990	Phi-N	129	467	70	122	14	3	17	73	87	81	.261	.382	.413	119	15	16	7	1	.979	5	*O-127	1.8
1991	Phi-N	77	284	43	64	15	1	0	21	31	42	.225	.308	.285	69	-11	9	2	2	.990	11	O-72	-0.6
1992	Cal-A	94	307	35	69	17	1	4	29	37	54	.225	.308	.326	77	-9	11	6	-0	.983	-1	O-85/1-4,D	-1.3
Total	12	1495	5249	767	1402	282	36	143	696	712	804	.267	.357	.416	113	101	253	97	18	.983	-20	*O-1040,1-401/D3	4.3

■ BILL HAYES
Hayes, William Ernest b: 10/24/57, Cheverly, Md. BR/TR, 6', 195 lbs. Deb: 9/30/80

YEAR	TM/L	G	AB	R	H	2B	3B	HR	RBI	BB	SO	AVG	OBP	SLG	PRO+	BR/A	SB	CS	SBR	FA	FR	G/POS	TPR
1980	Chi-N	4	9	0	2	1	0	0	1	0	3	.222	.222	.333	49	-1	0	0	0	1.000	-0	/C-3	-0.1
1981	Chi-N	1	0	0	0	0	0	0	0	0	0	—	—	—	—	0	0	0	0	.000	0	/C-1	0.0
Total	2	5	9	0	2	1	0	0	1	0	3	.222	.222	.333	49	-1	0	0	0	1.000	-0	/C-4	-0.1

■ RED HAYWORTH
Hayworth, Myron Claude b: 5/14/15, High Point, N.C. BR/TR, 6'1.5", 200 lbs. Deb: 4/21/44 F

YEAR	TM/L	G	AB	R	H	2B	3B	HR	RBI	BB	SO	AVG	OBP	SLG	PRO+	BR/A	SB	CS	SBR	FA	FR	G/POS	TPR
1944	*StL-A	90	270	20	60	11	1	1	25	10	13	.222	.253	.281	50	-18	0	0	0	.967	1	C-87	-1.4
1945	StL-A	56	160	7	31	4	0	0	17	7	6	.194	.228	.219	28	-15	0	2	-1	.992	4	C-55	-1.0
Total	2	146	430	27	91	15	1	1	42	17	19	.212	.243	.258	42	-33	0	2	-1	.976	4	C-142	-2.4

■ RAY HAYWORTH
Hayworth, Raymond Hall b: 1/29/04, High Point, N.C. BR/TR, 6', 180 lbs. Deb: 6/27/26 FC

YEAR	TM/L	G	AB	R	H	2B	3B	HR	RBI	BB	SO	AVG	OBP	SLG	PRO+	BR/A	SB	CS	SBR	FA	FR	G/POS	TPR
1926	Det-A	12	11	1	3	0	0	0	5	1	1	.273	.333	.273	59	-1	0	0	0	1.000	-1	/C-8	-0.1
1929	Det-A	14	43	5	11	0	0	0	4	3	8	.256	.304	.256	45	-3	0	0	0	.951	0	C-14	-0.2
1930	Det-A	77	227	24	63	15	4	0	22	10	9	.278	.336	.379	79	-7	0	2	0	.977	-13	C-76	-1.3
1931	Det-A	88	273	28	70	10	3	0	25	19	27	.256	.307	.315	62	-15	0	1	0	.973	4	C-88	-0.6
1932	Det-A	109	338	41	99	20	2	2	44	31	22	.293	.354	.382	87	-6	1	1	0	.991	3	*C-106	0.2
1933	Det-A	134	425	37	104	14	3	1	45	35	28	.245	.302	.299	59	-25	0	1	0	.994	-8	*C-133	-1.5
1934	*Det-A	54	167	20	49	5	2	0	27	16	22	.293	.355	.347	82	-4	0	2	-1	.984	7	C-54	0.3

YEAR	TM/L	G	AB	R	H	2B	3B	HR	RBI	BB	SO	AVG	OBP	SLG	PRO+	BR/A	SB	CS	SBR	FA	FR	G/POS	TPR
1935	Det-A	51	175	22	54	14	2	0	22	9	14	.309	.342	.411	98	-1	0	0	0	.996	11	C-48	1.1
1936	Det-A	81	250	31	60	10	0	1	30	39	18	.240	.347	.292	59	-15	0	0	0	.988	-4	C-81	-1.4
1937	Det-A	30	78	9	21	2	0	1	8	14	15	.269	.394	.333	83	-1	0	0	0	.992	6	C-28	0.5
1938	Det-A	8	19	1	4	0	0	0	5	3	4	.211	.318	.211	33	-2	1	0	0	.971	2	/C-7	0.1
	Bro-N	5	4	0	0	0	0	0	0	1	1	.000	.200	.000	-40	-1				1.000	0	/C-3	-0.1
1939	Bro-N	21	26	0	4	2	0	0	1	4	7	.154	.267	.231	34	-2	0			1.000	1	C-18	-0.1
	NY-N	5	13	1	3	0	0	0	0	1	1	.231	.231	.231	24	-1	0			1.000	1	/C-5	0.0
	Yr	26	39	1	7	2	0	0	1	4	8	.179	.256	.231	31	-4	0			1.000	2	C-23	-0.1
1942	StL-A	1	1	0	1	0	0	0	0	0	0	1.000	1.000	1.000	456	0	0	0	0	.000	0	H	0.0
1944	Bro-N	7	10	0	0	0	0	0	0	2	1	.000	.167	.000	-51	-2	0			1.000	2	/C-6	0.0
1945	Bro-N	2	2	0	0	0	0	0	0	1	0	.000	.333	.000	-3	-0	0			1.000	2	/C-2	0.0
Total	15	699	2062	220	546	92	16	5	238	198	188	.265	.331	.332	71	-87	2	6		.987	20	C-677	-3.1

■ DRUNGO HAZEWOOD   Hazewood, Drungo La Rue b: 9/2/59, Mobile, Ala. BR/TR, 6'3", 210 lbs. Deb: 9/19/80

YEAR	TM/L	G	AB	R	H	2B	3B	HR	RBI	BB	SO	AVG	OBP	SLG	PRO+	BR/A	SB	CS	SBR	FA	FR	G/POS	TPR
1980	Bal-A	6	5	1	0	0	0	0	0	0	4	.000	.000	.000	-99	-1	0	0	0	1.000	-1	/O-3	-0.2

■ BOB HAZLE   Hazle, Robert Sidney "Hurricane" b: 12/9/30, Laurens, S.C. d: 4/25/92, Columbia, S.C. BL/TR, 6', 190 lbs. Deb: 9/8/55

YEAR	TM/L	G	AB	R	H	2B	3B	HR	RBI	BB	SO	AVG	OBP	SLG	PRO+	BR/A	SB	CS	SBR	FA	FR	G/POS	TPR
1955	Cin-N	6	13	0	3	0	0	0	0	0	3	.231	.231	.231	22	-1	0	0	0	1.000	2	/O-3	0.0
1957	*Mil-N	41	134	26	54	12	0	7	27	18	15	.403	.477	.649	214	22	1	3	-2	.906	-5	O-40	1.3
1958	Mil-N	20	56	6	10	0	0	0	5	9	4	.179	.303	.179	34	-5	0	0	0	1.000	-1	O-20	-0.7
	Det-A	43	58	5	14	2	0	2	5	5	13	.241	.302	.379	80	-2	0	0	0	1.000	-2	O-12	-0.4
Total	3	110	261	37	81	14	0	9	37	32	35	.310	.390	.467	135	14	1	3	-2	.951	-7	/O-75	0.2

■ DOC HAZLETON   Hazleton, Willard Carpenter b: 8/28/1876, Strafford, Vt. d: 3/17/41, Burlington, Vt. Deb: 4/17/02

YEAR	TM/L	G	AB	R	H	2B	3B	HR	RBI	BB	SO	AVG	OBP	SLG	PRO+	BR/A	SB	CS	SBR	FA	FR	G/POS	TPR
1902	StL-N	7	23	0	3	0	0	0	0	2		.130	.231	.130	12	-2	0			.973	0	/1-7	-0.3

■ FRAN HEALY   Healy, Francis Xavier b: 9/6/46, Holyoke, Mass. BR/TR, 6'5", 220 lbs. Deb: 9/3/69

YEAR	TM/L	G	AB	R	H	2B	3B	HR	RBI	BB	SO	AVG	OBP	SLG	PRO+	BR/A	SB	CS	SBR	FA	FR	G/POS	TPR
1969	KC-A	6	10	0	4	1	0	0	0	0	5	.400	.400	.500	149	1	0	0	0	1.000	0	/C-5	0.1
1971	SF-N	47	93	10	26	3	0	2	11	15	24	.280	.380	.376	117	3	1	0	0	.966	2	C-22	0.2
1972	SF-N	45	99	12	15	4	0	1	8	13	24	.152	.257	.222	37	-8	0	1	-1	.995	7	C-43	-0.1
1973	KC-A	95	279	25	77	15	2	6	34	31	56	.276	.348	.409	104	2	3	4	-2	.979	-3	C-92/D-1	0.1
1974	KC-A	139	445	59	112	24	2	9	53	62	73	.252	.344	.351	101	2	16	8	0	.977	-7	*C-138	0.1
1975	KC-A	56	188	16	48	5	2	3	18	14	19	.255	.307	.335	79	-5	4	3	-1	.982	-7	C-51/D-4	-1.1
1976	KC-A	8	24	2	3	0	0	0	1	4	10	.125	.250	.125	12	-3	2	0	1	1.000	0	/C-6,D-1	-0.2
	NY-A	46	120	10	32	3	0	0	9	9	17	.267	.318	.292	80	-3	3	1	0	.983	3	C-31/D-9	0.1
	Yr	54	144	12	35	3	0	0	10	13	27	.243	.306	.264	68	-5	5	1	1	.987	3	C-37,D-10	-0.1
1977	NY-A	27	67	10	15	5	0	0	7	6	13	.224	.288	.299	61	-4	1	0	0	.971	-0	C-26	-0.3
1978	NY-A	1	1	0	0	0	0	0	0	0	1	.000	.000	.000	-99	-0	0	0	0	.000	0	/C-1	0.0
Total	9	470	1326	144	332	60	6	20	141	154	242	.250	.329	.350	90	-16	30	17	-1	.980	-8	C-415/D-15	-1.1

■ FRANCIS HEALY   Healy, Francis Xavier Paul b: 6/29/10, Holyoke, Mass. BR/TR, 5'9.5", 175 lbs. Deb: 4/29/30

YEAR	TM/L	G	AB	R	H	2B	3B	HR	RBI	BB	SO	AVG	OBP	SLG	PRO+	BR/A	SB	CS	SBR	FA	FR	G/POS	TPR
1930	NY-N	7	2	2	0	0	0	0	0	0	0	.000	.000	.000	-99	-1	0			.000	0	/C-4	-0.1
1931	NY-N	6	7	1	1	0	0	0	0	0	0	.143	.143	.143	-24	-1	0			1.000	0	/C-4	0.0
1932	NY-N	14	32	5	8	2	0	0	4	2	8	.250	.294	.313	65	-2	0			.960	2	C-11	0.1
1934	StL-N	15	13	1	4	1	0	0	1	0	2	.308	.308	.385	79	-0	0			1.000	1	/C-2,3-1,O	0.0
Total	4	42	54	9	13	3	0	0	5	2	10	.241	.268	.296	51	-4	0			.969	3	/C-18,O-1,3	-0.1

■ THOMAS HEALY   Healy, Thomas Fitzgerald b: 10/30/1895, Altoona, Pa. d: 1/15/74, Cleveland, Ohio BR/TR, 6', 172 lbs. Deb: 7/13/15

YEAR	TM/L	G	AB	R	H	2B	3B	HR	RBI	BB	SO	AVG	OBP	SLG	PRO+	BR/A	SB	CS	SBR	FA	FR	G/POS	TPR
1915	Phi-A	23	77	11	17	1	0	0	5	6	4	.221	.310	.234	65	-3	0	4	-2	.933	5	3-17/S-1	0.1
1916	Phi-A	6	23	4	6	1	1	0	2	1	2	.261	.320	.391	119	0	1			.947	-1	/3-6	0.0
Total	2	29	100	15	23	2	1	0	7	7	6	.230	.313	.270	77	-3	1	4		.936	4	/3-23,S-1	0.1

■ CHARLIE HEARD   Heard, Charles b: 1/30/1872, Philadelphia, Pa. d: 2/20/45, Philadelphia, Pa. BR/TR, 6'2", 190 lbs. Deb: 7/14/1890

YEAR	TM/L	G	AB	R	H	2B	3B	HR	RBI	BB	SO	AVG	OBP	SLG	PRO+	BR/A	SB	CS	SBR	FA	FR	G/POS	TPR
1890	Pit-N	12	43	2	8	2	0	0	0	1	15	.186	.205	.233	31	-4	0			.600	-3	/O-6,P-6	-0.4

■ ED HEARN   Hearn, Edmund b: 9/17/1888, Ventura, Cal. d: 9/8/52, Sawtelle, Cal. BR/TR, 5'9", 160 lbs. Deb: 6/9/10

YEAR	TM/L	G	AB	R	H	2B	3B	HR	RBI	BB	SO	AVG	OBP	SLG	PRO+	BR/A	SB	CS	SBR	FA	FR	G/POS	TPR
1910	Bos-A	2	2	0	0	0	0	0	0	0	0	.000	.000	.000	-98	-0	0			1.000	2	/S-2	0.1

■ ED HEARN   Hearn, Edward John b: 8/23/60, Stuart, Fla. BR/TR, 6'3", 215 lbs. Deb: 5/17/86

YEAR	TM/L	G	AB	R	H	2B	3B	HR	RBI	BB	SO	AVG	OBP	SLG	PRO+	BR/A	SB	CS	SBR	FA	FR	G/POS	TPR
1986	NY-N	49	136	16	36	5	0	4	10	12	19	.265	.324	.390	99	-0	0	1	-1	.987	-6	C-45	-0.5
1987	KC-A	6	17	2	5	2	0	0	3	4	2	.294	.429	.412	121	1	0	0	0	1.000	-2	/C-5	-0.1
1988	KC-A	7	18	1	4	2	0	0	1	0	1	.222	.222	.333	53	-1	0	0	0	1.000	-0	/C-4,D-2	-0.1
Total	3	62	171	19	45	9	0	4	14	16	22	.263	.326	.386	97	-1	0	1	-1	.989	-8	/C-54,D-2	-0.7

■ HUGHIE HEARNE   Hearne, Hugh Joseph b: 4/18/1873, Troy, N.Y. d: 9/22/32, Troy, N.Y. BR/TR, 5'8", 182 lbs. Deb: 8/29/01

YEAR	TM/L	G	AB	R	H	2B	3B	HR	RBI	BB	SO	AVG	OBP	SLG	PRO+	BR/A	SB	CS	SBR	FA	FR	G/POS	TPR
1901	Bro-N	2	5	1	2	0	0	0	3	0		.400	.400	.400	129	0	0			1.000	0	/C-2	0.0
1902	Bro-N	66	231	22	65	10	0	0	28	16		.281	.336	.325	103	1	3			.966	-10	C-65	-0.2
1903	Bro-N	26	57	8	16	3	2	0	4	3		.281	.328	.404	111	1	2			.960	3	C-17/1-2	0.5
Total	3	94	293	31	83	13	2	0	35	19		.283	.335	.341	105	2	5			.965	-7	/C-84,1-2	0.3

■ JEFF HEARRON   Hearron, Jeffrey Vernon b: 11/19/61, Long Beach, Cal. BR/TR, 6'1", 195 lbs. Deb: 8/25/85

YEAR	TM/L	G	AB	R	H	2B	3B	HR	RBI	BB	SO	AVG	OBP	SLG	PRO+	BR/A	SB	CS	SBR	FA	FR	G/POS	TPR
1985	*Tor-A	4	7	0	1	0	0	0	0	0	2	.143	.143	.143	-21	-1	0	0	0	1.000	2	/C-4	0.0
1986	Tor-A	12	23	2	5	1	0	0	4	3	7	.217	.308	.261	55	-1	0	0	0	.980	1	C-12	0.0
Total	2	16	30	2	6	1	0	0	4	3	9	.200	.273	.233	39	-2	0	0	0	.985	2	/C-16	0.0

■ JEFF HEATH   Heath, John Geoffrey b: 4/1/15, Ft.William, Ont., Canada d: 12/9/75, Seattle, Wash. BL/TR, 5'11.5", 200 lbs. Deb: 9/13/36

YEAR	TM/L	G	AB	R	H	2B	3B	HR	RBI	BB	SO	AVG	OBP	SLG	PRO+	BR/A	SB	CS	SBR	FA	FR	G/POS	TPR
1936	Cle-A	12	41	6	14	3	3	1	8	3	4	.341	.386	.634	147	3	1	0	0	1.000	0	O-12	0.0
1937	Cle-A	20	61	8	14	1	4	0	8	0	9	.230	.230	.377	50	-5	0	1	-1	1.000	-1	O-14	-0.6
1938	Cle-A	126	502	104	172	31	**18**	21	112	33	55	.343	.383	.602	146	32	3	1	0	.974	1	*O-122	2.6
1939	Cle-A	121	431	64	126	31	7	14	69	41	64	.292	.354	.494	119	10	8	4	0	.964	6	O-108	1.1
1940	Cle-A	100	356	55	78	16	3	14	50	40	62	.219	.298	.399	81	-11	5	3	-0	.971	-2	O-90	-1.4
1941	Cle-A★	151	585	89	199	32	**20**	24	123	50	69	.340	.396	.586	165	51	18	12	-2	.949	-4	*O-151	3.4
1942	Cle-A	147	568	82	158	37	13	10	76	62	66	.278	.350	.442	130	20	9	9	-3	.980	-2	*O-146	1.2
1943	Cle-A★	118	424	58	116	22	6	18	79	63	58	.274	.369	.481	157	30	5	8	-3	.968	-4	*O-111	1.8
1944	Cle-A†	60	151	20	50	5	2	5	33	18	12	.331	.402	.490	160	12	0	1	0	.952	-1	O-37	0.9
1945	Cle-A	102	370	60	113	16	7	15	61	56	39	.305	.398	.508	169	33	3	1	0	.973	-4	*O-101	2.5
1946	Was-A	48	166	23	47	12	3	4	27	36	36	.283	.411	.464	153	13	0	4	-2	.969	-2	O-47	0.6
	StL-A	86	316	46	87	20	4	12	57	37	37	.275	.353	.478	124	10	0	2	-1	.962	-6	O-83	-0.2
	Yr	134	482	69	134	32	7	16	84	73	73	.278	.374	.473	134	22	0	6	-4	.965	-9	*O-130	0.4
1947	StL-A	141	491	81	123	20	7	27	85	88	87	.251	.366	.485	133	21	2	1	0	.987	-3	*O-140	1.1
1948	Bos-N	115	364	64	116	26	5	20	76	51	46	.319	.404	.582	167	33	2			**.991**	-2	*O-106	2.6
1949	Bos-N	36	111	17	34	7	0	9	23	15	26	.306	.389	.613	174	11	0			.983	-2	O-31	0.8
Total	14	1383	4937	777	1447	279	102	194	887	593	670	.293	.370	.509	140	262	56	47		.972	-20	*O-1299	16.4

■ KELLY HEATH   Heath, Kelly Mark b: 9/4/57, Plattsburgh, N.Y. BR/TR, 5'7", 155 lbs. Deb: 4/20/82

YEAR	TM/L	G	AB	R	H	2B	3B	HR	RBI	BB	SO	AVG	OBP	SLG	PRO+	BR/A	SB	CS	SBR	FA	FR	G/POS	TPR
1982	KC-A	1	1	0	0	0	0	0	0	0	0	.000	.000	.000	-99	-0	0	0	0	1.000	1	/2-1	0.1

YEAR	TM/L	G	AB	R	H	2B	3B	HR	RBI	BB	SO	AVG	OBP	SLG	PRO+	BR/A	SB	CS	SBR	FA	FR	G/POS	TPR

■ MIKE HEATH
Heath, Michael Thomas b: 2/5/55, Tampa, Fla. BR/TR, 5'11", 190 lbs. Deb: 6/3/78

YEAR	TM/L	G	AB	R	H	2B	3B	HR	RBI	BB	SO	AVG	OBP	SLG	PRO+	BR/A	SB	CS	SBR	FA	FR	G/POS	TPR
1978	*NY-A	33	92	6	21	3	1	0	8	4	9	.228	.268	.283	56	-5	0	0	0	.970	3	C-33	-0.2
1979	Oak-A	74	258	19	66	8	0	3	27	17	18	.256	.309	.322	75	-9	1	0	0	.978	-1	O-46,C-22/3D	-1.1
1980	Oak-A	92	305	27	74	10	2	1	33	16	28	.243	.280	.298	63	-16	3	3	-1	.986	8	C-47,D-31/O	-0.8
1981	*Oak-A	84	301	26	71	7	1	8	30	13	36	.236	.270	.346	80	-9	3	3	-1	.978	4	C-78/O-6	-0.3
1982	Oak-A	101	318	43	77	18	4	3	39	27	36	.242	.301	.352	82	-8	8	3	1	.973	-8	C-90,O-10/3	-1.2
1983	Oak-A	96	345	45	97	17	0	6	33	18	59	.281	.319	.383	98	-2	3	4	-2	.973	-10	C-80,O-24/3D	-1.1
1984	Oak-A	140	475	49	118	21	5	13	64	26	72	.248	.289	.396	94	-6	7	4	-0	.986	-19	*C-108,O-45/3S	-2.1
1985	Oak-A	138	436	71	109	18	6	13	55	41	63	.250	.316	.408	104	2	7	7	-2	.981	-13	*C-112,O-35,3	-0.9
1986	StL-N	65	190	19	39	8	1	4	25	23	36	.205	.294	.321	70	-8	2	3	-1	.967	-7	C-63/O-2	-1.2
	Det-A	30	98	11	26	3	0	4	11	4	17	.265	.294	.418	92	-1	4	1	1	.987	-2	C-29/3-1	-0.1
1987	*Det-A	93	270	34	76	16	0	8	33	21	42	.281	.340	.430	107	3	1	5	-3	.989	2	C-67,O-24/13S2	0.5
1988	Det-A	86	219	24	54	7	2	5	18	18	32	.247	.307	.365	91	-3	1	0	0	.984	-1	C-75/O-9	0.1
1989	Det-A	122	396	38	104	16	2	10	43	24	71	.263	.311	.389	98	-2	7	1	2	.986	0	*C-117/3-4,OD	0.6
1990	Det-A	122	370	46	100	18	2	7	38	19	71	.270	.313	.386	94	-4	7	6	-2	.980	-2	*C-117/O-3,SD	-0.9
1991	Atl-N	49	139	4	29	3	1	1	12	7	26	.209	.252	.266	43	-10	0	0	0	.991	-0	C-45	-0.9
Total	14	1325	4212	462	1061	173	27	86	469	278	616	.252	.302	.367	87	-79	54	40	-8	.981	-46	*C-1083,O-215/D31S2	-8.7

■ MICKEY HEATH
Heath, Minor Wilson b: 10/30/03, Toledo, Ohio d: 7/30/86, Dallas, Tex. BL/TL, 6', 175 lbs. Deb: 4/18/31

YEAR	TM/L	G	AB	R	H	2B	3B	HR	RBI	BB	SO	AVG	OBP	SLG	PRO+	BR/A	SB	CS	SBR	FA	FR	G/POS	TPR
1931	Cin-N	7	26	2	7	0	0	0	3	2	5	.269	.321	.269	64	-1	0			1.000	-0	/1-7	-0.2
1932	Cin-N	39	134	14	27	1	3	0	15	20	23	.201	.310	.254	55	-8	0			.991	2	1-39	-0.9
Total	2	46	160	16	34	1	3	0	18	22	28	.213	.311	.256	57	-9	0			.992	2	/1-46	-1.1

■ TOMMY HEATH
Heath, Thomas George b: 8/18/13, Akron, Col. d: 2/26/67, Los Gatos, Cal. BR/TR, 5'10", 185 lbs. Deb: 4/23/35

YEAR	TM/L	G	AB	R	H	2B	3B	HR	RBI	BB	SO	AVG	OBP	SLG	PRO+	BR/A	SB	CS	SBR	FA	FR	G/POS	TPR
1935	StL-A	47	93	10	22	3	0	0	9	20	13	.237	.372	.269	65	-4	0	0	0	.982	-2	C-37	-0.4
1937	StL-A	17	43	4	10	0	2	1	3	10	3	.233	.377	.395	94	-0	0	0	0	1.000	-0	C-14	0.0
1938	StL-A	70	194	22	44	13	0	2	22	35	24	.227	.345	.325	69	-9	0	1	-1	.986	7	C-65	0.0
Total	3	134	330	36	76	16	2	3	34	65	40	.230	.357	.318	71	-13	0	1	-1	.987	5	C-116	-0.4

■ BILL HEATH
Heath, William Chris b: 3/10/39, Yuba City, Cal. BL/TR, 5'8", 175 lbs. Deb: 10/3/65

YEAR	TM/L	G	AB	R	H	2B	3B	HR	RBI	BB	SO	AVG	OBP	SLG	PRO+	BR/A	SB	CS	SBR	FA	FR	G/POS	TPR
1965	Chi-A	1	1	0	0	0	0	0	0	0	0	.000	.000	.000	-99	-0	0	0	0	.000	0	H	0.0
1966	Hou-N	55	123	12	37	6	0	0	8	9	11	.301	.353	.350	103	1	1	0	0	.995	-1	C-37	0.2
1967	Hou-N	9	11	0	1	0	0	0	0	4	3	.091	.333	.091	28	-1	0	0	0	1.000	1	/C-5	0.0
	Det-A	20	32	0	4	0	0	0	4	1	4	.125	.152	.125	-17	-5	0	0	0	1.000	1	/C-7	-0.3
1969	Chi-N	27	32	1	5	0	1	0	1	12	4	.156	.386	.219	65	-1	0	0	0	.979	0	/C-9	-0.1
Total	4	112	199	13	47	6	1	0	13	26	22	.236	.327	.276	73	-6	1	0	0	.993	-1	/C-58	-0.2

■ CLIFF HEATHCOTE
Heathcote, Clifton Earl b: 1/24/1898, Glen Rock, Pa. d: 1/19/39, York, Pa. BL/TL, 5'10.5", 160 lbs. Deb: 6/4/18

YEAR	TM/L	G	AB	R	H	2B	3B	HR	RBI	BB	SO	AVG	OBP	SLG	PRO+	BR/A	SB	CS	SBR	FA	FR	G/POS	TPR
1918	StL-N	88	348	37	90	12	3	4	32	20	40	.259	.301	.345	100	-1	12			.934	-4	O-87	-1.1
1919	StL-N	114	401	53	112	13	4	1	29	20	41	.279	.315	.339	103	1	27			.967	-3	*O-101/1-2	-1.0
1920	StL-N	133	489	55	139	18	8	3	56	25	31	.284	.320	.372	102	0	21	14	-2	.964	10	*O-129	-0.1
1921	StL-N	62	156	18	38	6	2	0	9	10	9	.244	.293	.308	61	-9	7	5	-1	.926	-8	O-51	-2.1
1922	StL-N	34	98	11	24	5	2	0	14	9	4	.245	.315	.337	71	-4	0	2	-1	.950	2	O-32	-0.5
	Chi-N	76	243	37	68	8	7	1	34	18	15	.280	.330	.383	82	-7	5	2	0	.986	-2	O-60	-1.2
	Yr	110	341	48	92	13	9	1	48	27	19	.270	.325	.370	79	-11	5	4	-1	.971	0	O-92	-1.7
1923	Chi-N	117	393	48	98	14	3	1	27	25	22	.249	.298	.308	60	-23	32	17	-1	.980	4	*O-112	-2.5
1924	Chi-N	113	392	66	121	19	7	0	30	28	28	.309	.366	.393	100	0	26	24	-7	.979	-2	*O-111	-1.6
1925	Chi-N	109	380	57	100	14	5	5	39	39	26	.263	.343	.366	80	-11	15	11	-2	.970	14	O-99	-0.5
1926	Chi-N	139	510	98	141	33	3	10	53	58	30	.276	.353	.412	104	3	18			.985	13	*O-133	0.7
1927	Chi-N	83	228	28	67	12	4	2	25	20	16	.294	.359	.408	105	2	6			.987	6	O-57	0.7
1928	Chi-N	67	137	26	39	8	0	3	18	17	12	.285	.364	.409	103	1	6			.973	-2	O-39	-0.4
1929	*Chi-N	82	224	45	70	17	0	2	31	25	17	.313	.384	.415	98	-0	9			.985	3	O-52	-0.1
1930	Chi-N	70	150	30	39	10	1	9	18	19	15	.260	.343	.520	104	0	4			.986	-2	O-35	-0.3
1931	Cin-N	90	252	34	65	15	6	0	28	32	16	.258	.342	.365	96	-1	3			.989	12	O-59	0.7
1932	Cin-N	8	3	3	0	0	0	0	0	0	0	.000	.000	.000	-99	-1	0			.000	0	H	-0.1
	Phi-N	30	39	7	11	2	0	1	5	3	3	.282	.333	.410	88	-1	0			.962	-0	/1-7	-0.1
	Yr	38	42	10	11	2	0	1	5	3	3	.262	.311	.381	78	-1	0			.962	-0	/1-7	-0.2
Total	15	1415	4443	653	1222	206	55	42	448	367	325	.275	.333	.375	92	-51	191	75		.971	43	*O-1157/1-9	-9.5

■ RICHIE HEBNER
Hebner, Richard Joseph b: 11/26/47, Boston, Mass. BL/TR, 6'1", 197 lbs. Deb: 9/23/68 C

YEAR	TM/L	G	AB	R	H	2B	3B	HR	RBI	BB	SO	AVG	OBP	SLG	PRO+	BR/A	SB	CS	SBR	FA	FR	G/POS	TPR
1968	Pit-N	2	1	0	0	0	0	0	0	0	0	.000	.000	.000	-99	-0	0	0	0	.000	0	H	0.0
1969	Pit-N	129	459	72	138	23	4	8	47	53	53	.301	.383	.420	127	18	4	1	1	.944	3	*3-124/1-1	2.3
1970	*Pit-N	120	420	60	122	24	8	11	46	42	48	.290	.365	.464	123	13	2	3	-1	.940	1	*3-117	1.2
1971	*Pit-N	112	388	50	105	17	8	17	67	32	68	.271	.331	.487	130	14	2	2	-1	.949	-8	*3-108	0.4
1972	*Pit-N	124	427	63	128	24	4	19	72	52	54	.300	.384	.508	155	31	0	0	0	.969	-15	*3-121	1.5
1973	Pit-N	144	509	73	138	28	1	25	74	56	60	.271	.348	.477	130	19	0	1	-1	.939	-14	*3-139	0.4
1974	*Pit-N	146	550	97	160	21	6	18	68	60	53	.291	.367	.449	132	23	0	3	-2	.937	-6	*3-141	1.5
1975	*Pit-N	128	472	65	116	16	4	15	57	43	48	.246	.322	.392	98	-2	0	1	-1	.946	-15	*3-126	-1.9
1976	Pit-N	132	434	60	108	21	3	8	51	47	39	.249	.328	.366	96	-2	1	3	-2	.953	-10	*3-126	-1.5
1977	*Phi-N	118	397	67	113	17	4	18	62	61	46	.285	.384	.484	125	15	7	8	-3	.991	2	*1-103,3-13/2	0.9
1978	*Phi-N	137	435	61	123	22	3	17	71	53	58	.283	.362	.464	131	19	4	7	-3	.994	-7	*1-117,3-19/2	0.8
1979	NY-N	136	473	54	127	25	2	10	79	59	59	.268	.359	.393	109	7	3	1	0	.940	-7	*3-134/1-6	-0.1
1980	Det-A	104	341	48	99	10	7	12	82	38	45	.290	.365	.466	123	11	0	3	-2	.998	-5	1-61,3-32/D	0.0
1981	Det-A	78	226	19	51	8	2	5	28	27	28	.226	.314	.345	87	-4	1	2	-1	.995	-3	1-61,D-11	-1.2
1982	Det-A	68	179	25	49	6	0	8	18	25	21	.274	.363	.441	119	5	1	1	-0	.990	-2	1-40,D-20	0.4
	Pit-N	25	70	6	21	2	0	2	12	5	3	.300	.347	.414	109	1	4	0	1	.964	-2	O-21/1-4,3	-0.1
1983	Pit-N	78	162	23	43	4	1	5	26	17	28	.265	.339	.395	100	0	8	3	1	.967	-6	3-40/1-7,O	-0.6
1984	*Chi-N	44	81	12	27	3	0	2	8	10	15	.333	.407	.444	127	3	1	0	0	.963	-2	3-14/1-3,O	0.2
1985	Chi-N	83	120	10	26	2	0	3	22	7	15	.217	.266	.308	54	-7	0	1	-1	.991	-0	1-12/3-7,O	-0.9
Total	18	1908	6144	865	1694	273	57	203	890	687	741	.276	.356	.438	120	164	38	40	-13	.946	-85	*3-1262,1-415/DO2	3.3

■ MIKE HECHINGER
Hechinger, Michael Vincent b: 2/14/1890, Chicago, Ill. d: 8/13/67, Chicago, Ill. BR/TR, 6', 175 lbs. Deb: 9/27/12

YEAR	TM/L	G	AB	R	H	2B	3B	HR	RBI	BB	SO	AVG	OBP	SLG	PRO+	BR/A	SB	CS	SBR	FA	FR	G/POS	TPR
1912	Chi-N	2	3	0	0	0	0	0	0	2	0	.000	.400	.000	14	-0	0			1.000	0	/C-2	0.0
1913	Chi-N	2	2	0	0	0	0	0	0	0	0	.000	.000	.000	-99	-1	0			.000	0	H	-0.1
	Bro-N	9	11	1	2	1	0	0	0	0	2	.182	.182	.273	28	-1	0			1.000	-1	/C-4	-0.2
	Yr	11	13	1	2	1	0	0	0	0	2	.154	.154	.231	9	-2	0			1.000	-1	/C-4	-0.3
Total	2	13	16	1	2	1	0	0	0	2	2	.125	.222	.188	16	-2	0			1.000	-1	/C-6	-0.3

■ GUY HECKER
Hecker, Guy Jackson b: 4/3/1856, Youngsville, Pa. d: 12/3/38, Wooster, Ohio BR/TR, 6', 190 lbs. Deb: 5/2/1882 MU

YEAR	TM/L	G	AB	R	H	2B	3B	HR	RBI	BB	SO	AVG	OBP	SLG	PRO+	BR/A	SB	CS	SBR	FA	FR	G/POS	TPR
1882	Lou-a	78	340	62	94	14	4	3		5		.276	.287	.368	126	9				.958	5	*1-66,P-13/O	0.2
1883	Lou-a	79	322	56	88	6	7	1		11		.273	.297	.339	112	5				.936	3	P-51,O-23,1	0.0
1884	Lou-a	78	316	53	94	14	8	4		10		.297	.323	.430	151	17				.951	6	*P-75/O-5	0.0
1885	Lou-a	70	297	48	81	9	3	2		5		.273	.287	.337	97	-2				.927	3	P-53,1-17/O	-0.4
1886	Lou-a	84	343	76	117	14	5	4		32		.341	.402	.446	157	21	25			.875	-6	P-49,1-22,O	0.0

YEAR	TM/L	G	AB	R	H	2B	3B	HR	RBI	BB	SO	AVG	OBP	SLG	PRO+	BR/A	SB	CS	SBR	FA	FR	G/POS	TPR
1887	Lou-a	91	370	89	118	21	6	4		31		.319	.381	.441	126	13	48			.954	-4	1-43,P-34,O	-0.4
1888	Lou-a	56	211	32	48	9	2	0	29	11		.227	.285	.289	86	-3	20			.936	-4	1-30,P-26/O	-0.9
1889	Lou-a	81	327	42	93	17	5	1	36	18	27	.284	.333	.376	104	1	17			.969	-0	1-65,P-19/O	-0.4
1890	Pit-N	86	340	43	77	13	9	0	38	19	17	.226	.285	.318	86	-7	13			.962	1	1-69,P-14/OM	-0.7
Total	9	703	2866	501	810	117	47	19	103	142	44	.283	.324	.376	118	55	123			.935	4	P-334,1-322/O	-2.6

■ DANNY HEEP
Heep, Daniel William b: 7/3/57, San Antonio, Tex. BL/TL, 5'11", 185 lbs. Deb: 8/31/79

YEAR	TM/L	G	AB	R	H	2B	3B	HR	RBI	BB	SO	AVG	OBP	SLG	PRO+	BR/A	SB	CS	SBR	FA	FR	G/POS	TPR
1979	Hou-N	14	14	0	2	0	0	0	2	1	4	.143	.200	.143	-5	-2	0	0	0	1.000	1	/O-2	-0.1
1980	*Hou-N	33	87	6	24	8	0	0	6	8	9	.276	.344	.368	107	1	0	0	0	.990	-2	1-22	-0.2
1981	Hou-N	33	96	6	24	3	0	0	11	10	11	.250	.321	.281	76	-3	0	0	0	.990	-3	1-22/O-1	-0.8
1982	Hou-N	85	198	16	47	14	1	4	22	21	31	.237	.314	.379	100	-0	0	2	-1	1.000	-3	O-39,1-16	-0.7
1983	NY-N	115	253	30	64	12	0	8	21	29	40	.253	.332	.395	102	1	3	3	-1	1.000	-5	O-61,1-14	-0.7
1984	NY-N	99	199	36	46	9	2	1	12	27	22	.231	.326	.312	81	-4	3	1	0	.967	1	O-48,1-10	-0.5
1985	NY-N	95	271	26	76	17	0	7	42	27	27	.280	.348	.421	117	6	2	2	-1	.977	-5	O-78/1-4	-0.2
1986	*NY-N	86	195	24	55	8	2	5	33	30	31	.282	.381	.421	124	7	1	4	-2	.988	-2	O-56	0.1
1987	LA-N	60	98	7	16	4	0	0	9	8	10	.163	.226	.204	16	-12	1	0	0	.962	-1	O-22/1-6	-1.4
1988	*LA-N	95	149	14	36	2	0	0	11	22	13	.242	.343	.255	76	-3	2	0	1	1.000	-2	O-32,1-12/P	-0.7
1989	Bos-A	113	320	36	96	17	0	5	49	29	26	.300	.360	.400	107	3	0	1	-1	.989	-12	O-75,1-19/D	-1.2
1990	*Bos-A	41	69	3	12	1	1	0	8	7	14	.174	.260	.217	33	-6	0	0	0	1.000	-0	O-14/1-5,PD	-0.7
1991	Atl-N	12	12	4	5	1	0	0	3	1	4	.417	.462	.500	161	1	0	0	0	1.000	-0	/1-1,O-1	0.0
Total	13	883	1961	208	503	96	6	30	229	220	242	.257	.334	.357	95	-12	12	14	-5	.986	-34	O-429,1-131/DP	-7.1

■ BERT HEFFERNAN
Heffernan, Bertram Alexander b: 3/3/65, Centereach, N.Y. BL/TR, 5'10", 185 lbs. Deb: 5/13/92

YEAR	TM/L	G	AB	R	H	2B	3B	HR	RBI	BB	SO	AVG	OBP	SLG	PRO+	BR/A	SB	CS	SBR	FA	FR	G/POS	TPR
1992	Sea-A	8	11	0	1	1	0	0	1	0	1	.091	.091	.182	-25	-2	0	0	0	1.000	1	/C-5,D-1	-0.1

■ DON HEFFNER
Heffner, Donald Henry "Jeep" b: 2/8/11, Rouzerville, Pa. d: 8/1/89, Pasadena, Cal. BR/TR, 5'10", 155 lbs. Deb: 4/17/34 MC

YEAR	TM/L	G	AB	R	H	2B	3B	HR	RBI	BB	SO	AVG	OBP	SLG	PRO+	BR/A	SB	CS	SBR	FA	FR	G/POS	TPR
1934	NY-A	72	241	29	63	8	3	0	25	25	18	.261	.331	.320	73	-9	1	1	-0	.971	-8	2-68	-1.3
1935	NY-A	10	36	3	11	3	1	0	8	4	1	.306	.375	.444	118	1	0	0	0	.980	-1	2-10	0.1
1936	NY-A	19	48	7	11	2	1	0	6	6	5	.229	.315	.313	57	-3	0	0	0	.971	4	/3-8,2-5,S	0.1
1937	NY-A	60	201	23	50	6	5	0	21	19	19	.249	.314	.328	62	-12	1	4	-2	.980	-8	2-38,S-13/310	-1.7
1938	StL-A	141	473	47	116	23	3	2	69	65	53	.245	.341	.319	67	-23	1	1	-0	.971	-9	*2-141	-2.2
1939	StL-A	110	375	45	100	10	2	1	35	48	39	.267	.350	.312	69	-16	1	7	-4	.944	-4	S-73,2-32	-1.5
1940	StL-A	126	487	52	115	23	2	3	53	39	37	.236	.295	.310	56	-32	5	5	-2	**.977**	**19**	*2-125	-0.5
1941	StL-A	110	399	48	93	14	2	0	17	38	27	.233	.303	.278	53	-27	5	6	-2	.974	3	*2-105	-1.9
1942	StL-A	19	36	2	6	2	0	0	3	1	4	.167	.189	.222	15	-4	0	0	0	.906	1	/2-6,1-4	-0.2
1943	StL-A	18	33	2	4	1	0	0	2	2	2	.121	.171	.152	-5	-4	0	0	0	.974	-0	2-13/1-1	-0.5
	Phi-A	52	178	17	37	6	0	0	8	18	12	.208	.284	.242	55	-10	3	2	-0	.978	-10	2-47/1-1	-1.9
	Yr	70	211	19	41	7	0	0	10	20	14	.194	.267	.227	45	-14	3	2	-0	.978	-10	2-60/1-2	-2.4
1944	Det-A	6	19	0	4	1	0	0	1	0	0	.211	.375	.263	80	-0	0	0	0	.962	-1	/2-5	-0.1
Total	11	743	2526	275	610	99	19	6	248	270	218	.241	.317	.303	61	-140	18	26	-10	.973	-13	2-595/S-89,310	-11.6

■ JIM HEGAN
Hegan, James Edward b: 8/3/20, Lynn, Mass. d: 6/17/84, Swampscott, Mass. BR/TR, 6'2", 195 lbs. Deb: 9/9/41 FC

YEAR	TM/L	G	AB	R	H	2B	3B	HR	RBI	BB	SO	AVG	OBP	SLG	PRO+	BR/A	SB	CS	SBR	FA	FR	G/POS	TPR
1941	Cle-A	16	47	4	15	2	0	1	5	4	7	.319	.373	.426	116	1	0	0	0	.973	-0	C-16	0.2
1942	Cle-A	68	170	10	33	5	1	0	11	11	31	.194	.243	.224	34	-15	1	3	-2	.977	8	C-66	-0.5
1946	Cle-A	88	271	29	64	11	5	0	17	17	44	.236	.284	.314	71	-11	1	4	-2	.991	9	C-87	0.0
1947	Cle-A☆	135	378	38	94	14	5	4	42	41	49	.249	.324	.344	88	-6	3	1	0	.989	7	*C-133	0.9
1948	*Cle-A	144	472	60	117	21	6	14	61	48	74	.248	.317	.407	94	-7	6	3	0	.990	21	*C-142	2.3
1949	Cle-A☆	152	468	54	105	19	5	8	55	49	89	.224	.298	.338	69	-23	1	0	0	.990	10	*C-152	-0.3
1950	Cle-A★	131	415	53	91	16	5	14	58	42	52	.219	.291	.383	74	-19	1	0	0	.993	24	*C-129	1.0
1951	Cle-A★	133	416	60	99	17	5	6	43	38	72	.238	.302	.346	79	-13	0	3	-2	.991	11	*C-129	0.1
1952	Cle-A☆	112	333	39	75	17	2	4	41	29	47	.225	.287	.324	75	-13	0	2	-1	.987	7	*C-107	-0.2
1953	Cle-A	112	299	37	65	10	1	9	37	25	41	.217	.280	.348	71	-13	1	2	-1	.976	3	*C-106	-0.7
1954	*Cle-A	139	423	56	99	12	7	11	40	34	48	.234	.291	.374	80	-13	0	1	-1	**.994**	13	*C-137	0.5
1955	Cle-A	116	304	30	67	5	2	9	40	34	33	.220	.299	.339	69	-14	0	1	-1	**.997**	7	*C-111	-0.4
1956	Cle-A	122	315	42	70	15	2	6	34	49	54	.222	.327	.340	75	-11	0	0	0	.985	16	*C-118	0.8
1957	Cle-A	58	148	14	32	7	0	4	15	16	23	.216	.293	.345	74	-5	0	1	-1	1.000	5	C-58	-0.2
1958	Det-A	45	130	14	25	6	0	1	7	10	32	.192	.250	.262	38	-11	0	0	0	.996	1	C-45	-0.8
	Phi-N	25	59	5	13	6	0	0	5	8	16	.220	.270	.322	57	-4	0	0	0	.991	4	C-25	0.1
1959	Phi-N	25	51	1	10	1	0	0	8	3	10	.196	.241	.216	22	-6	0	1	-1	.990	1	C-25	-0.5
	SF-N	21	30	0	4	1	0	0	0	1	10	.133	.161	.167	-13	-5	0	1	-1	.975	5	C-21	0.0
	Yr	46	81	1	14	2	0	0	8	4	20	.173	.212	.198	10	-10	0	1	-1	.983	5	C-46	-0.5
1960	Chi-N	24	43	4	9	2	1	0	5	1	10	.209	.244	.372	67	-2	0	0	0	.977	2	C-22	0.1
Total	17	1666	4772	550	1087	187	46	92	525	456	742	.228	.296	.344	74	-191	15	24	-10	.990	149	*C-1629	2.4

■ MIKE HEGAN
Hegan, James Michael b: 7/21/42, Cleveland, Ohio BL/TL, 6'1", 190 lbs. Deb: 9/13/64 F

YEAR	TM/L	G	AB	R	H	2B	3B	HR	RBI	BB	SO	AVG	OBP	SLG	PRO+	BR/A	SB	CS	SBR	FA	FR	G/POS	TPR
1964	*NY-A	5	5	0	0	0	0	0	0	1	2	.000	.167	.000	-48	-1	0	0	0	1.000	1	/1-2	0.0
1966	NY-A	13	39	7	8	0	1	0	2	7	11	.205	.326	.256	73	-1	1	1	-0	.991	-0	1-13	-0.3
1967	NY-A	68	118	12	16	4	1	1	3	20	40	.136	.266	.212	44	-8	7	1	2	1.000	1	1-54,O-10	-0.8
1969	Sea-A†	95	267	54	78	9	6	8	37	62	61	.292	.427	.461	151	21	6	5	-1	.955	2	O-64,1-19	1.8
1970	Mil-A	148	476	70	116	21	2	11	52	67	116	.244	.338	.366	93	-3	9	7	-2	.994	11	*1-139/O-8	-0.6
1971	Mil-A	46	122	19	27	4	1	4	11	26	19	.221	.358	.369	107	2	1	1	0	1.000	-1	1-45	0.3
	*Oak-A	65	55	5	13	3	0	0	3	5	13	.236	.300	.291	69	-2	1	0	0	1.000	-2	1-47/O-2	-0.1
	Yr	111	177	24	40	7	1	4	14	31	32	.226	.341	.345	96	-0	2	1	0	1.000	6	1-92/O-2	0.2
1972	*Oak-A	98	79	13	26	3	1	1	5	7	20	.329	.384	.430	150	5	1	0	0	1.000	1	1-64/O-3	0.6
1973	Oak-A	75	71	8	13	2	0	1	5	5	17	.183	.237	.254	40	-6	0	0	0	.988	-3	1-56/O-3,D	-1.0
	NY-A	37	131	12	36	3	2	6	14	7	34	.275	.312	.466	121	3	0	0	0	.992	2	1-37	0.2
	Yr	112	202	20	49	5	2	7	19	12	51	.243	.285	.391	93	-3	0	0	0	.991	-1	1-93/O-3,D	-0.8
1974	NY-A	18	53	3	12	2	0	2	9	5	9	.226	.317	.377	102	1		1	-0	1.000	-0	1-17	-0.1
	Mil-A	89	190	21	45	7	1	7	32	33	34	.237	.350	.395	114	4	0	4	-2	.991	-2	D-37,1-17,O	-0.2
	Yr	107	243	24	57	9	1	9	41	38	43	.235	.343	.391	112	4	1	5	-3	.996	-2	D-37,1-34,O	-0.3
1975	Mil-A	93	203	19	51	11	0	5	22	31	42	.251	.350	.379	106	2	1	0	0	.984	-4	O-42,1-27/D	-0.4
1976	Mil-A	80	218	30	54	4	3	5	31	25	54	.248	.328	.362	104	1	0	0	0	1.000	-3	D-40,O-20,1	-0.4
1977	Mil-A	35	53	8	9	0	2	0	3	10	17	.170	.313	.283	64	-2	0	0	0	1.000	-3	/O-8,1-6,D	-0.6
Total	12	965	2080	281	504	73	18	53	229	311	489	.242	.343	.371	103	15	28	14	-4	.995	11	1-553,O-177/D	-1.6

■ BOB HEGMAN
Hegman, Robert Hilmer b: 2/26/58, Springfield, Minn. BR/TR, 6'1", 180 lbs. Deb: 8/8/85

YEAR	TM/L	G	AB	R	H	2B	3B	HR	RBI	BB	SO	AVG	OBP	SLG	PRO+	BR/A	SB	CS	SBR	FA	FR	G/POS	TPR
1985	KC-A	1	0	0	0	0	0	0	0	0	0	—	—	—			0	0	0	.000	0	/2-1	0.0

■ JACK HEIDEMANN
Heidemann, Jack Seale b: 7/11/49, Brenham, Tex. BR/TR, 6', 178 lbs. Deb: 5/2/69

YEAR	TM/L	G	AB	R	H	2B	3B	HR	RBI	BB	SO	AVG	OBP	SLG	PRO+	BR/A	SB	CS	SBR	FA	FR	G/POS	TPR
1969	Cle-A	3	3	0	0	0	0	0	0	0	0	.000	.250	.000	-24	-1	0	0	0	1.000	1	/S-3	0.0
1970	Cle-A	133	445	44	94	14	2	6	37	34	88	.211	.270	.292	52	-29	2	4	-2	.961	-2	*S-132	-1.9
1971	Cle-A	81	240	16	50	7	0	0	9	12	46	.208	.252	.237	36	-20	1	3	-2	.977	-9	S-81	-2.4
1972	Cle-A	10	20	0	3	0	0	0	0	2	3	.150	.261	.150	24	-2	0	0	0	.964	-1	S-10	-0.3
1974	Cle-A	12	11	2	1	0	0	0	0	0	2	.091	.091	.091	-48	-2	0	0	0	1.000	-1	/3-6,S-4,12	-0.3

YEAR	TM/L	G	AB	R	H	2B	3B	HR	RBI	BB	SO	AVG	OBP	SLG	PRO+	BR/A	SB	CS	SBR	FA	FR	G/POS	TPR
	StL-N	47	70	8	19	1	0	0	3	5	10	.271	.320	.286	71	-3	0	0	0	.967	-10	S-45/3-1	-1.0
1975	NY-N	61	145	12	31	4	2	1	16	17	28	.214	.296	.290	66	-7	1	0	0	.951	-12	S-44/3-4,2	-1.6
1976	NY-N	5	12	0	1	0	0	0	0	0	0	.083	.083	.083	-56	-2	0	0	0	1.000	0	/S-3,2-1	-0.2
	Mil-A	69	146	11	32	1	0	2	10	7	24	.219	.255	.267	54	-9	1	3	-2	.962	-7	3-40,2-24/D	-1.7
1977	Mil-A	5	1	1	0	0	0	0	0	1	0	.000	.500	.000	50	0	0	0	0	1.000	1	/2-1,D-3	0.1
Total	8	426	1093	94	231	27	4	9	75	78	203	.211	.268	.268	49	-73	5	10	-5	.965	-42	S-322/3-51,2D1	-9.3

■ EMMETT HEIDRICK
Heidrick, John Emmett "Snags" b: 7/9/1876, Queenstown, Pa. d: 1/20/16, Clarion, Pa. BL/TR, 6', 185 lbs. Deb: 9/14/1898

YEAR	TM/L	G	AB	R	H	2B	3B	HR	RBI	BB	SO	AVG	OBP	SLG	PRO+	BR/A	SB	CS	SBR	FA	FR	G/POS	TPR
1898	Cle-N	19	76	10	23	2	2	0	8	3		.303	.329	.382	105	0	3			.850	-1	O-19	-0.2
1899	StL-N	146	591	109	194	21	14	2	82	34		.328	.368	.421	114	9	55			.925	4	*O-145	0.2
1900	StL-N	85	339	51	102	6	8	2	45	18		.301	.338	.383	100	-1	22			.959	15	O-83	0.7
1901	StL-N	118	502	94	170	24	12	6	67	21		.339	.366	.470	149	29	32			.945	1	*O-118	2.0
1902	StL-A	110	447	75	129	19	10	3	56	34		.289	.339	.396	105	2	17			.940	2	*O-109/P-1,S3	-0.2
1903	StL-A	120	461	55	129	20	15	1	42	19		.280	.310	.395	113	6	19			.954	2	*O-119/C-1	0.1
1904	StL-A	133	538	66	147	14	10	1	36	16		.273	.294	.342	107	3	35			.963	11	*O-130	0.7
1908	StL-A	26	93	8	20	2	2	1	6	1		.215	.223	.312	73	-3	3			.957	-1	O-25	-0.6
Total	8	757	3047	468	914	108	73	16	342	146		.300	.333	.399	114	45	186			.946	33	O-748/C-1,3SP	2.7

■ FRANK HEIFER
Heifer, Franklin "Heck" b: 1/18/1854, Reading, Pa. d: 8/29/1893, Reading, Pa. 5'10.5", 175 lbs. Deb: 6/4/1875

YEAR	TM/L	G	AB	R	H	2B	3B	HR	RBI	BB	SO	AVG	OBP	SLG	PRO+	BR/A	SB	CS	SBR	FA	FR	G/POS	TPR
1875	Bos-n	11	51	11	14	1	0	3	0			.275	.275	.392	123	1						/1-7,O-6,P	0.1

■ CHINK HEILEMAN
Heileman, John George b: 8/10/1872, Cincinnati, Ohio d: 7/19/40, Cincinnati, Ohio BR/TR, 5'8", 155 lbs. Deb: 7/8/01

YEAR	TM/L	G	AB	R	H	2B	3B	HR	RBI	BB	SO	AVG	OBP	SLG	PRO+	BR/A	SB	CS	SBR	FA	FR	G/POS	TPR
1901	Cin-N	5	15	1	2	1	0	0	1	0		.133	.133	.200	-4	-2	0			.667	-1	/3-4,2-1	-0.3

■ HARRY HEILMANN
Heilmann, Harry Edwin "Slug" b: 8/3/1894, San Francisco, Cal. d: 7/9/51, Southfield, Mich. BR/TR, 6'1", 195 lbs. Deb: 5/16/14 CH

YEAR	TM/L	G	AB	R	H	2B	3B	HR	RBI	BB	SO	AVG	OBP	SLG	PRO+	BR/A	SB	CS	SBR	FA	FR	G/POS	TPR
1914	Det-A	69	182	25	41	8	1	2	18	22	29	.225	.316	.313	86	-3	1	8	-5	.870	-6	O-31,1-16/2	-1.6
1916	Det-A	136	451	57	127	30	11	2	73	42	40	.282	.349	.410	124	12	9			.952	-10	O-77,1-30/2	-0.2
1917	Det-A	150	556	57	156	22	11	5	86	41	54	.281	.333	.387	120	11	11			.960	-2	*O-123,1-27	0.2
1918	Det-A	79	286	34	79	10	6	5	39	35	10	.276	.359	.406	136	12	13			.957	-4	O-40,1-37/2	0.5
1919	Det-A	140	537	74	172	30	15	8	93	37	41	.320	.366	.477	139	25	7			.979	-10	*1-140	1.1
1920	Det-A	145	543	66	168	28	5	9	89	39	32	.309	.358	.429	111	7	3	7	-3	.985	-1	*1-122,O-22	-0.1
1921	Det-A	149	602	114	237	43	14	19	139	53	37	.394	.444	.606	167	60	2	6	-3	.962	-11	*O-147/1-3	3.2
1922	Det-A	118	455	92	162	27	10	21	92	58	28	.356	.432	.598	172	47	8	4	0	.948	-10	*O-115/1-5	2.7
1923	Det-A	144	524	121	211	44	11	18	115	74	40	.403	.481	.632	195	74	9	7	-2	.960	2	*O-130,1-12	6.2
1924	Det-A	153	570	107	197	45	16	10	114	78	41	.346	.428	.533	149	42	13	5	1	.970	-9	*O-147/1-4	3.9
1925	Det-A	150	573	97	225	40	11	13	134	67	27	.393	.457	.569	161	55	6	6	-2	.970	-3	*O-148	3.7
1926	Det-A	141	502	90	184	41	8	9	103	67	19	.367	.445	.534	152	40	6	7	-2	.972	-2	*O-134	2.6
1927	Det-A	141	505	106	201	50	9	14	120	72	16	.398	.475	.616	179	60	11	5	0	.966	-8	*O-135	4.2
1928	Det-A	151	558	83	183	38	10	14	107	57	45	.328	.390	.507	132	25	7	3	0	.971	1	*O-125,1-25	1.6
1929	Det-A	125	453	86	156	41	7	15	120	50	39	.344	.412	.565	148	32	5	6	-2	.966	-6	*O-114/1-2	1.6
1930	Cin-N	142	459	79	153	43	6	19	91	64	50	.333	.416	.577	144	33	2			.955	12	*O-106,1-19	3.1
1932	Cin-N	15	31	3	8	2	0	0	6	0	2	.258	.258	.323	57	-2	0			.981	-0	/1-6	-0.3
Total	17	2148	7787	1291	2660	542	151	183	1539	856	550	.342	.410	.520	148	532	113	64		.962	-48	*O-1594,1-448/2	32.4

■ VAL HEIM
Heim, Val Raymond b: 11/4/20, Plymouth, Wis. BL/TR, 5'11", 170 lbs. Deb: 8/31/42

YEAR	TM/L	G	AB	R	H	2B	3B	HR	RBI	BB	SO	AVG	OBP	SLG	PRO+	BR/A	SB	CS	SBR	FA	FR	G/POS	TPR
1942	Chi-A	13	45	6	9	1	1	0	7	5	3	.200	.294	.267	60	-2	1	0	0	.958	-1	O-12	-0.4

■ BUD HEINE
Heine, William Henry b: 9/22/1900, Elmira, N.Y. d: 9/2/76, Ft.Lauderdale, Fla BL/TR, 5'8", 145 lbs. Deb: 10/1/21

YEAR	TM/L	G	AB	R	H	2B	3B	HR	RBI	BB	SO	AVG	OBP	SLG	PRO+	BR/A	SB	CS	SBR	FA	FR	G/POS	TPR
1921	NY-N	1	2	0	0	0	0	0	0	0	0	.000	.000	.000	-99	-1	0	0	0	1.000	-0	/2-1	-0.1

■ TOM HEINTZELMAN
Heintzelman, Thomas Kenneth b: 11/3/46, St.Charles, Mo. BR/TR, 6'1", 180 lbs. Deb: 8/12/73 F

YEAR	TM/L	G	AB	R	H	2B	3B	HR	RBI	BB	SO	AVG	OBP	SLG	PRO+	BR/A	SB	CS	SBR	FA	FR	G/POS	TPR
1973	StL-N	23	29	5	9	0	0	0	3	3	3	.310	.375	.310	92	-0	0	0	0	1.000	1	/2-6	0.1
1974	StL-N	38	74	10	17	4	0	1	6	9	14	.230	.313	.324	79	-2	0	0	0	.978	0	2-28/3-2,S	-0.1
1977	SF-N	2	2	0	0	0	0	0	0	0	0	.000	.000	.000	-99	-1	0	0	0	.000	0	H	-0.1
1978	SF-N	27	35	2	8	1	0	2	6	2	5	.229	.270	.429	96	-0	0	0	0	1.000	2	/2-5,3-3,1	0.2
Total	4	90	140	17	34	5	0	3	12	14	22	.243	.312	.343	84	-3	0	0	0	.984	4	/2-39,3-5,1S	0.1

■ JACK HEINZMAN
Heinzman, John Peter b: 9/27/1863, New Albany, Ind. d: 11/10/14, Louisville, Ky. BR/TR, Deb: 10/2/1886

YEAR	TM/L	G	AB	R	H	2B	3B	HR	RBI	BB	SO	AVG	OBP	SLG	PRO+	BR/A	SB	CS	SBR	FA	FR	G/POS	TPR
1886	Lou-a	1	5	1	0	0	0	0	0			.000	.000	.000	-95	-1				1.000	-0	/1-1	-0.1

■ BOB HEISE
Heise, Robert Lowell b: 5/12/47, San Antonio, Tex. BR/TR, 6', 175 lbs. Deb: 9/12/67

YEAR	TM/L	G	AB	R	H	2B	3B	HR	RBI	BB	SO	AVG	OBP	SLG	PRO+	BR/A	SB	CS	SBR	FA	FR	G/POS	TPR
1967	NY-N	16	62	7	20	4	0	0	3	3	1	.323	.354	.387	114	1	0	1	-1	.973	2	2-12/S-3,3	0.3
1968	NY-N	6	23	3	5	0	0	0	1	1	1	.217	.250	.217	41	-2	0	0	0	.929	-5	/S-6,2-1	-0.8
1969	NY-N	4	10	1	3	1	0	0	0	3	2	.300	.462	.400	140	1	0	0	0	1.000	-3	/S-3	-0.2
1970	SF-N	67	154	15	36	5	1	1	22	5	13	.234	.258	.299	49	-11	0	0	0	.915	-1	S-33,2-28/3	-0.9
1971	SF-N	13	11	2	0	0	0	0	0	0	1	.000	.000	.000	-99	-3	0	0	0	.833	0	/S-3,3-2,2	-0.3
	Mil-A	68	189	10	48	7	0	0	7	7	15	.254	.281	.291	63	-9	1	1	0	.961	3	S-51,3-11/2O	0.3
1972	Mil-A	95	271	23	72	10	1	0	12	12	14	.266	.302	.310	84	-6	1	1	0	.990	-3	2-49,3-24/S	-0.7
1973	Mil-A	49	98	8	20	2	0	0	4	4	4	.204	.235	.224	31	-9	1	0	0	.956	-1	S-29/3-9,12D	-0.7
1974	StL-N	3	7	1	1	0	0	0	0	0	0	.143	.143	.143	-20	-1	0	0	0	1.000	2	/2-3	0.1
	Cal-A	29	75	7	20	0	0	0	6	5	10	.267	.313	.360	99	-0	0	1	0	1.000	2	2-17/3-6,S	0.2
1975	Bos-A	63	126	12	27	3	0	0	21	4	6	.214	.250	.238	35	-11	0	0	0	.940	11	3-45,2-14/S1	0.1
1976	Bos-A	32	56	5	15	2	0	0	5	1	2	.268	.293	.304	67	-2	0	1	0	.968	2	3-22/S-9,2	0.0
1977	KC-A	54	62	11	16	2	1	0	5	2	8	.258	.292	.323	67	-3	0	1	-1	1.000	10	2-21,S-21,3/1	0.8
Total	11	499	1144	104	283	43	3	1	86	47	77	.247	.281	.293	63	-55	3	7	-3	.945	23	S-174,2-154,3/1DO	-1.8

■ AL HEIST
Heist, Alfred Michael b: 10/5/27, Brooklyn, N.Y. BR/TR, 6'2", 185 lbs. Deb: 7/17/60 C

YEAR	TM/L	G	AB	R	H	2B	3B	HR	RBI	BB	SO	AVG	OBP	SLG	PRO+	BR/A	SB	CS	SBR	FA	FR	G/POS	TPR
1960	Chi-N	41	102	11	28	5	0	6	10	12		.275	.339	.412	106	1	3	1	0	.985	-2	O-33	-0.2
1961	Chi-N	109	321	48	82	14	3	7	37	39	51	.255	.338	.383	90	-4	3	3	-1	.978	0	O-99	-1.0
1962	Hou-N	27	72	4	16	1	0	3	3	9	21	.222	.263	.236	38	-6	0	0	0	.974	-3	O-23	-1.0
Total	3	177	495	63	126	20	3	16	46	52	72	.255	.328	.368	86	-10	6	4	-1	.979	-4	O-155	-2.2

■ HEINIE HEITMULLER
Heitmuller, William Frederick b: 5/25/1883, San Francisco, Cal d: 10/8/12, Los Angeles, Cal. BR/TR, 6'2", 215 lbs. Deb: 4/26/09

YEAR	TM/L	G	AB	R	H	2B	3B	HR	RBI	BB	SO	AVG	OBP	SLG	PRO+	BR/A	SB	CS	SBR	FA	FR	G/POS	TPR
1909	Phi-A	64	210	36	60	9	8	0	15	18		.286	.351	.405	136	8	7			.927	-2	O-61	0.5
1910	Phi-A	31	111	11	27	2	2	0	7	7		.243	.288	.297	84	-2	6			.981	-0	O-28	-0.4
Total	2	95	321	47	87	11	10	0	22	25		.271	.330	.368	118	6	13			.943	-2	/O-89	0.1

■ WOODIE HELD
Held, Woodson George b: 3/25/32, Sacramento, Cal. BR/TR, 5'11", 180 lbs. Deb: 9/5/54

YEAR	TM/L	G	AB	R	H	2B	3B	HR	RBI	BB	SO	AVG	OBP	SLG	PRO+	BR/A	SB	CS	SBR	FA	FR	G/POS	TPR
1954	NY-A	4	3	2	0	0	0	0	0	2	1	.000	.400	.000	17	-0	0	0	0	1.000	-1	/S-4,3-1	-0.1
1957	NY-A	1	1	0	0	0	0	0	0	0	0	.000	.000	.000	-99	-0	0	0	0	.000	0	H	0.0
	KC-A	92	326	48	78	14	3	20	50	37	81	.239	.322	.485	116	6	4	0	1	.996	17	O-92	1.8
	Yr	93	327	48	78	14	3	20	50	37	81	.239	.322	.483	115	5	4	0	1	.996	17	O-92	1.8
1958	KC-A	47	131	13	28	4	1	6	16	10	28	.214	.280	.321	64	-7	0	1	-1	1.000	-3	O-41/3-4,S	-1.3
	Cle-A	67	144	12	28	4	1	3	17	15	36	.194	.288	.299	63	-7	1	2	-1	.966	-0	O-43,S-14/3	-0.9
	Yr	114	275	25	56	6	1	7	33	25	64	.204	.284	.309	64	-14	1	3	-2	.982	-4	O-84,S-15/3	-2.2
1959	Cle-A	143	525	82	132	19	3	29	71	46	118	.251	.314	.465	115	8	1	2	-1	.962	-9	*S-103,3-40/O2	0.7

YEAR	TM/L	G	AB	R	H	2B	3B	HR	RBI	BB	SO	AVG	OBP	SLG	PRO+	BR/A	SB	CS	SBR	FA	FR	G/POS	TPR
1960	Cle-A	109	376	45	97	15	1	21	67	44	73	.258	.344	.471	122	11	0	1	-1	.967	9	*S-109	2.7
1961	Cle-A	146	509	67	136	23	5	23	78	69	111	.267	.358	.468	122	16	0	0	0	.960	-14	*S-144	1.4
1962	Cle-A	139	466	55	116	12	2	19	58	73	107	.249	.364	.406	110	8	5	1	1	.956	-14	*S-133/3-5,O	0.7
1963	Cle-A	133	416	61	103	19	4	17	61	61	96	.248	.355	.435	121	13	2	2	-1	.982	-3	2-96,O-35/S3	1.7
1964	Cle-A	118	364	50	86	13	0	18	49	43	88	.236	.329	.420	107	4	1	0	0	.966	0	2-52,O-41,3	0.6
1965	Was-A	122	332	46	82	16	2	16	54	49	74	.247	.349	.452	128	12	0	0	0	.963	-19	*O-106/3-5,2S	-1.1
1966	Bal-A	56	82	6	17	3	1	1	7	12	30	.207	.309	.305	78	-2	0	0	0	1.000	-4	O-10/2-5,S3	-0.6
1967	Bal-A	26	41	4	6	3	0	1	6	6	12	.146	.286	.293	72	-1	0	0	0	.974	1	/2-9,3-5,O	0.0
	Cal-A	58	141	15	31	3	0	4	17	18	41	.220	.317	.326	94	-1	0	2	-1	.979	-4	3-19,O-17,S/2	-0.7
	Yr	84	182	19	37	6	0	5	23	24	53	.203	.310	.319	88	-2	0	2	-1	.962	-3	3-24,O-19,S2	-0.7
1968	Cal-A	33	45	4	5	1	0	0	0	5	15	.111	.231	.133	13	-5	0	0	0	1.000	-3	/2-5,S-5,3O	-0.9
	Chi-A	40	54	5	9	1	0	0	2	5	14	.167	.250	.185	33	-4	0	0	0	1.000	-6	O-33/3-5,2	-1.2
	Yr	73	99	9	14	2	0	0	2	10	29	.141	.241	.162	24	-9	0	0	0	1.000	-9	O-36,3-10/2S	-2.1
1969	Chi-A	56	63	9	9	2	0	0	6	13	19	.143	.299	.317	69	-3	0	0	0	1.000	-3	O-18/S-3,32	-0.6
Total	14	1390	4019	524	963	150	22	179	559	508	944	.240	.333	.421	109	48	14	11	-2	.960	-56	S-539,O-448,23	2.2

■ HANK HELF

Helf, Henry Hartz b: 8/26/13, Austin, Tex. d: 10/27/84, Austin, Tex. BR/TR, 6'1", 196 lbs. Deb: 5/5/38

YEAR	TM/L	G	AB	R	H	2B	3B	HR	RBI	BB	SO	AVG	OBP	SLG	PRO+	BR/A	SB	CS	SBR	FA	FR	G/POS	TPR
1938	Cle-A	6	13	1	1	0	0	0	1	1	1	.077	.143	.077	-44	-3	0	0	0	.947	0	/C-5	-0.2
1940	Cle-A	1	1	0	0	0	0	0	0	0	0	.000	.000	.000	-99	-0	0	0	0	1.000	-0	/C-1	0.0
1946	StL-A	71	182	17	35	11	0	6	21	9	40	.192	.234	.352	59	-11	0	1	-1	.965	12	C-69	0.4
Total	3	78	196	18	36	11	0	6	22	10	41	.184	.227	.332	51	-14	0	1	-1	.964	12	/C-75	0.2

■ ERIC HELFAND

Helfand, Eric James b: 3/25/69, Erie, Pa. BL/TR, 6', 195 lbs. Deb: 9/4/93

YEAR	TM/L	G	AB	R	H	2B	3B	HR	RBI	BB	SO	AVG	OBP	SLG	PRO+	BR/A	SB	CS	SBR	FA	FR	G/POS	TPR
1993	Oak-A	8	13	1	3	0	0	0	1	0	1	.231	.231	.231	26	-1	0	0	0	1.000	4	/C-5	0.2
1994	Oak-A	7	6	1	1	0	0	0	1	0	1	.167	.167	.167	-15	-1	0	0	0	1.000	1	/C-6	0.0
Total	2	15	19	2	4	0	0	0	2	0	2	.211	.211	.211	13	-2	0	0	0	1.000	5	/C-11	0.2

■ TY HELFRICH

Helfrich, Emory Wilbur b: 10/9/1890, Pleasantville, N.J. d: 3/18/55, Pleasantville, N.J BR/TR, 5'10", 178 lbs. Deb: 6/30/15

YEAR	TM/L	G	AB	R	H	2B	3B	HR	RBI	BB	SO	AVG	OBP	SLG	PRO+	BR/A	SB	CS	SBR	FA	FR	G/POS	TPR
1915	Bro-F	43	104	12	25	6	0	0	5	15	21	.240	.336	.298	71	-4	2			.912	-4	2-34/O-1	-0.8

■ HELLINGS

Hellings b: Philadelphia, Pa. Deb: 7/19/1875

YEAR	TM/L	G	AB	R	H	2B	3B	HR	RBI	BB	SO	AVG	OBP	SLG	PRO+	BR/A	SB	CS	SBR	FA	FR	G/POS	TPR
1875	Atl-n	1	4	0	1	0	0	0		0		.250	.250	.250	84	-0						/2-1	0.0

■ TONY HELLMAN

Hellman, Anthony J. b: 1861, Cincinnati, Ohio d: 3/29/1898, Cincinnati, Ohio Deb: 10/10/1886

YEAR	TM/L	G	AB	R	H	2B	3B	HR	RBI	BB	SO	AVG	OBP	SLG	PRO+	BR/A	SB	CS	SBR	FA	FR	G/POS	TPR
1886	Bal-a	1	3	0	0	0	0	0		0		.000	.000	.000	-99	-1	0			1.000	1	/C-1	0.0

■ TOMMY HELMS

Helms, Tommy Vann b: 5/5/41, Charlotte, N.C. BR/TR, 5'10", 175 lbs. Deb: 9/23/64 MC

YEAR	TM/L	G	AB	R	H	2B	3B	HR	RBI	BB	SO	AVG	OBP	SLG	PRO+	BR/A	SB	CS	SBR	FA	FR	G/POS	TPR
1964	Cin-N	2	1	0	0	0	0	0	0	0	1	.000	.000	.000	-97	-0	0	0	0	.000	0	H	0.0
1965	Cin-N	21	42	4	16	2	2	0	6	3	7	.381	.435	.524	158	3	1	0	0	.973	-2	/S-8,3-2,2	0.3
1966	Cin-N	138	542	72	154	23	1	9	49	24	31	.284	.317	.380	85	-11	3	4	-2	.961	-13	*3-113,2-20	-2.8
1967	Cin-N★	137	497	40	136	27	4	2	35	24	41	.274	.307	.356	80	-13	5	10	-5	.978	-9	2-88,S-46	-1.8
1968	Cin-N★	127	507	35	146	28	2	2	47	12	27	.288	.307	.363	94	-4	5	6	-2	.979	8	*2-127/S-2,3	1.1
1969	Cin-N	126	480	38	129	18	1	1	40	18	33	.269	.297	.317	68	-20	4	6	-2	.975	-4	*2-125/S-4	-1.6
1970	*Cin-N	150	575	42	136	21	1	1	45	21	33	.237	.263	.282	46	-44	2	2	-1	.983	1	*2-148,S-12	-3.2
1971	Cin-N	150	547	40	141	26	1	3	52	26	33	.258	.293	.325	76	-18	3	4	-2	.990	14	*2-149	0.8
1972	Hou-N	139	518	45	134	20	5	5	60	24	27	.259	.297	.346	84	-12	4	3	-1	.979	27	*2-139	2.3
1973	Hou-N	146	543	44	156	28	2	4	61	32	21	.287	.327	.368	93	-6	1	1	-0	.988	-1	*2-145	0.1
1974	Hou-N	137	452	32	126	21	1	5	50	23	27	.279	.315	.363	93	-6	5	4	-1	.985	-11	*2-133	-1.2
1975	Hou-N	64	135	7	28	2	0	0	14	10	8	.207	.267	.222	40	-11	0	0	0	.988	-0	2-42/3-3,S	-1.0
1976	Pit-N	62	87	10	24	5	1	1	13	10	5	.276	.357	.391	111	1	0	0	0	.921	2	3-22,2-11/S	0.4
1977	Pit-N	15	12	0	0	0	0	0	0	0	3	.000	.000	.000	-97	-3	0	0	0	.000	0	H	-0.4
	Bos-N	21	59	5	16	2	0	1	5	4	4	.271	.328	.356	77	-2	0	0	0	1.000	-2	*2-13/3-2,2	-0.4
Total	14	1435	4997	414	1342	223	21	34	477	231	301	.269	.303	.342	79	-145	33	40	-14	.983	11	*2-1129,3-143/SD	-7.4

■ HEINIE HELTZEL

Heltzel, William Wade b: 12/21/13, York, Pa. BR/TR, 5'10", 150 lbs. Deb: 7/27/43

YEAR	TM/L	G	AB	R	H	2B	3B	HR	RBI	BB	SO	AVG	OBP	SLG	PRO+	BR/A	SB	CS	SBR	FA	FR	G/POS	TPR
1943	Bos-N	29	86	6	13	3	0	0	5	7	13	.151	.215	.186	17	-9	0			.880	-3	3-29	-1.3
1944	Phi-N	11	22	1	4	1	0	0	0	2	3	.182	.280	.227	45	-2	0			.919	-2	S-10	-0.3
Total	2	40	108	7	17	4	0	0	5	9	16	.157	.229	.194	23	-11	0			.880	-5	/3-29,S-10	-1.6

■ ED HEMINGWAY

Hemingway, Edson Marshall b: 5/8/1893, Sheridan, Mich. d: 7/5/69, Grand Rapids, Mich BB/TR, 5'11.5", 165 lbs. Deb: 9/17/14

YEAR	TM/L	G	AB	R	H	2B	3B	HR	RBI	BB	SO	AVG	OBP	SLG	PRO+	BR/A	SB	CS	SBR	FA	FR	G/POS	TPR
1914	StL-A	3	5	0	0	0	0	0	0	1	1	.000	.167	.000	-51	-1	1			1.000	0	/3-3	-0.1
1917	NY-N	7	25	3	8	1	1	0	1	2	1	.320	.370	.440	153	2	2			.958	1	3-7	0.3
1918	Phi-N	33	108	7	23	4	1	0	12	7	9	.213	.267	.269	59	-5	4			.955	2	2-25/3-3,1	-0.2
Total	3	43	138	10	31	5	2	0	13	10	11	.225	.282	.290	71	-5	7			.952	3	/2-25,3-13,1	0.0

■ SCOTT HEMOND

Hemond, Scott Mathew b: 11/18/65, Taunton, Mass. BR/TR, 6', 205 lbs. Deb: 9/9/89

YEAR	TM/L	G	AB	R	H	2B	3B	HR	RBI	BB	SO	AVG	OBP	SLG	PRO+	BR/A	SB	CS	SBR	FA	FR	G/POS	TPR
1989	Oak-A	4	0	2	0	0	0	0	0	0	0	—	—	—	—	0	0	0	0	.000	0	R	0.0
1990	Oak-A	7	13	0	2	0	0	0	1	0	5	.154	.154	.154	-14	-2	0	0	0	1.000	-1	/3-7,2-1	-0.3
1991	Oak-A	23	23	4	5	0	0	0	0	1	7	.217	.250	.217	32	-2	1	2	-1	.947	5	/C-8,2-7,3SD	0.2
1992	Oak-A	17	27	7	6	1	0	0	1	3	7	.222	.300	.259	61	-1	1	0	0	1.000	-0	/C-8,S-3,30D	-0.1
	Chi-A	8	13	1	3	1	0	0	1	1	6	.231	.286	.308	67	-1	0	0	0	1.000	-0	/O-2,C-1,3D	-0.1
	Yr	25	40	8	9	2	0	0	2	4	13	.225	.295	.275	63	-2	1	0	0	1.000	-1	/C-9,D-5,OS3	-0.2
1993	Oak-A	91	215	31	55	16	0	6	26	32	55	.256	.355	.414	113	4	14	5	1	.991	5	C-75/O-6,12D	1.3
1994	Oak-A	91	198	23	44	11	0	3	20	16	51	.222	.280	.323	60	-12	7	6	-2	1.000	7	C-39,2-25,3/10D	-0.5
Total	6	241	489	68	115	29	0	9	49	53	131	.235	.311	.350	81	-14	23	13	-1	.993	15	C-131/2-34,3DO1S	0.5

■ DUCKY HEMP

Hemp, William H. b: 12/27/1867, St.Louis, Mo. d: 3/6/23, St.Louis, Mo. Deb: 10/6/1887

YEAR	TM/L	G	AB	R	H	2B	3B	HR	RBI	BB	SO	AVG	OBP	SLG	PRO+	BR/A	SB	CS	SBR	FA	FR	G/POS	TPR
1887	Lou-a	1	3	1	1	1	0	0		1		.333	.500	.667	219	1	0			.000	-1	/O-1	0.0
1890	Pit-N	21	81	9	19	2	0	0	4	8	12	.235	.311	.284	83	-1	3			.867	0	O-21	-0.2
	Syr-a	9	33	1	5	1	0	0		0		.152	.176	.182	6	-4	1			.947	2	/O-9	-0.2
Total	2	31	117	11	25	2	2	0	4	9	12	.214	.281	.265	67	-5	2			.877	2	/O-31	-0.4

■ CHARLIE HEMPHILL

Hemphill, Charles Judson "Eagle Eye" b: 4/20/1876, Greenville, Mich. d: 6/22/53, Detroit, Mich. BL/TL, 5'9", 160 lbs. Deb: 6/27/1899 F

YEAR	TM/L	G	AB	R	H	2B	3B	HR	RBI	BB	SO	AVG	OBP	SLG	PRO+	BR/A	SB	CS	SBR	FA	FR	G/POS	TPR
1899	StL-N	11	37	4	9	0	0	0	3	6		.243	.364	.324	87	-0	0			.750	-2	O-10	-0.3
	Cle-N	55	202	23	56	3	5	2	23	6		.277	.301	.371	91	-4	3			.859	-8	O-54	-1.4
	Yr	66	239	27	65	3	5	3	26	12		.272	.312	.364	90	-4	3			.837	-10	O-64	-1.7
1901	Bos-A	136	545	71	142	10	10	3	62	39		.261	.312	.332	80	-14	11			.925	-4	*O-136	-2.6
1902	Cle-A	25	94	14	25	2	0	1	5	5		.266	.303	.287	67	-4	4			.860	-1	O-19	-0.6
	StL-A	103	416	67	132	14	11	6	58	44		.317	.383	.447	131	18	23			.952	-3	*O-101/2-2	0.8
	Yr	128	510	81	157	16	11	6	69	49		.308	.369	.418	120	14	27			.935	-3	*O-120/2-2	0.2
1903	StL-A	105	383	36	94	6	3	3	29	23		.245	.292	.300	80	-9	16			.961	2	*O-104	-1.3
1904	StL-A	114	438	47	112	13	2	2	45	35		.256	.311	.308	102	1	23			.926	-2	*O-108/2-1	-0.8
1906	StL-A	154	585	90	169	19	12	4	62	43		.289	.338	.383	131	20	33			.961	1	*O-154	1.4
1907	StL-A	153	603	66	156	20	9	0	38	51		.259	.319	.322	105	3	14			.957	-2	*O-153	-0.5
1908	NY-A	142	505	62	150	12	9	0	44	59		.297	.374	.356	136	22	42			.937	-2	*O-142	1.7

YEAR	TM/L	G	AB	R	H	2B	3B	HR	RBI	BB	SO	AVG	OBP	SLG	PRO+	BR/A	SB	CS	SBR	FA	FR	G/POS	TPR
1909	NY-A	73	181	23	44	5	1	0	10	32		.243	.357	.282	101	2	10			.976	-1	O-45	-0.1
1910	NY-A	102	351	45	84	9	4	0	21	55		.239	.350	.288	95	0	19			.971	-2	O-94	-0.7
1911	NY-A	69	201	32	57	4	2	1	15	37		.284	.397	.338	99	2	9			.952	-7	O-55	-0.8
Total	11	1242	4541	580	1230	117	68	22	421	435		.271	.337	.341	106	37	207			.944	-29	*O-1175/2-3	-5.2

■ FRANK HEMPHILL   Hemphill, Frank Vernon b: 5/13/1878, Greenville, Mich.   d: 11/16/50, Chicago, Ill.   BR/TR, 5'11", 165 lbs.   Deb: 4/17/06 F

YEAR	TM/L	G	AB	R	H	2B	3B	HR	RBI	BB	SO	AVG	OBP	SLG	PRO+	BR/A	SB	CS	SBR	FA	FR	G/POS	TPR
1906	Chi-A	13	40	0	3	0	0	0	2	9		.075	.275	.075	11	-3	1			.970	-1	O-13	-0.3
1909	Was-A	1	3	0	0	0	0	0	0	0		.000	.000	.000	-99	-1	0			1.000	0	/O-1	-0.1
Total	2	14	43	0	3	0	0	0	2	9		.070	.259	.070	5	-4	1			.971	1	/O-14	-0.4

■ ROLLIE HEMSLEY   Hemsley, Ralston Burdett b: 6/24/07, Syracuse, Ohio   d: 7/31/72, Washington, D.C.   BR/TR, 5'10", 170 lbs.   Deb: 4/13/28 C

YEAR	TM/L	G	AB	R	H	2B	3B	HR	RBI	BB	SO	AVG	OBP	SLG	PRO+	BR/A	SB	CS	SBR	FA	FR	G/POS	TPR
1928	Pit-N	50	133	14	36	2	3	0	18	4	10	.271	.292	.331	60	-8	1			.962	1	C-49	-0.4
1929	Pit-N	88	235	31	68	13	7	0	37	11	22	.289	.321	.404	77	-9	1			.954	8	C-80	0.4
1930	Pit-N	104	324	45	82	19	6	2	45	22	21	.253	.301	.367	60	-21	3			.979	3	C-98	-0.9
1931	Pit-N	10	35	3	6	3	0	0	1	3	3	.171	.237	.257	33	-3	0			1.000	1	/C-9	-0.2
	Chi-N	66	204	28	63	17	4	3	31	17	30	.309	.362	.475	121	6	4			.975	5	C-53	1.5
	Yr	76	239	31	69	20	4	3	32	20	33	.289	.344	.444	109	3	4			.978	6	C-62	1.3
1932	*Chi-N	60	151	27	36	10	3	4	20	10	16	.238	.286	.424	89	-3	2			.974	2	C-47/O-1	0.1
1933	Cin-N	49	116	9	22	8	0	0	7	6	8	.190	.230	.259	40	-9	0			.970	5	C-41	-0.3
	StL-A	32	95	7	23	2	1	1	15	11	12	.242	.321	.316	65	-5	0	0	0	.965	-3	C-27	-0.5
1934	StL-A	123	431	47	133	31	7	2	52	29	37	.309	.355	.427	93	-5	6	2	1	.973	23	*C-114/O-6	2.2
1935	StL-A★	144	504	57	146	32	7	0	48	44	41	.290	.349	.381	85	-11	3	2	-0	.979	10	*C-141	0.5
1936	StL-A☆	116	377	43	99	24	2	2	39	46	30	.263	.343	.353	70	-18	2	3	-1	.969	-11	*C-114	-2.1
1937	StL-A	100	334	30	74	12	3	2	28	25	29	.222	.276	.302	45	-29	0	0	0	.969	-5	C-94/1-2	-2.6
1938	Cle-A☆	66	203	27	60	11	3	2	28	23	14	.296	.367	.409	96	-1	1	0	-0	.980	15	C-58	1.4
1939	Cle-A☆	107	395	58	104	17	4	2	36	26	26	.263	.309	.342	69	-19	2	4	-2	.984	6	*C-106	-0.8
1940	Cle-A★	119	416	46	111	20	5	4	42	22	25	.267	.304	.368	75	-16	1	3	-2	**.994**	9	*C-117	0.0
1941	Cle-A	98	288	29	69	10	5	2	24	18	19	.240	.284	.330	65	-15	0			.982	-2	C-96	-0.9
1942	Cin-N	36	115	7	13	1	2	0	7	4	11	.113	.143	.157	-12	-16	0			.982	11	C-34	-0.3
	NY-A	31	85	12	25	3	1	0	15	5	9	.294	.333	.353	95	-1	1	0	0	.991	1	C-29	0.3
1943	NY-A	62	180	12	43	6	3	2	24	13	9	.239	.290	.339	83	-4	0	1	-1	.981	2	C-52	0.0
1944	NY-A★	81	284	23	76	12	5	2	26	9	13	.268	.290	.366	84	-7	0	2	-1	.983	-2	C-76	-0.6
1946	Phi-N	49	139	7	31	4	1	0	11	9	10	.223	.270	.266	54	-0	0			.977	11	C-45	0.4
1947	Phi-N	2	3	0	1	0	0	0	1	0	0	.333	.333	.333	80	-0	0			1.000	-0	/C-2	0.0
Total	19	1593	5047	562	1321	257	72	31	555	357	395	.262	.311	.360	74	-205	29	18		.978	90	*C-1482/O-7,1	-2.8

■ SOLLY HEMUS   Hemus, Solomon Joseph b: 4/17/23, Phoenix, Ariz.   BL/TR, 5'9", 175 lbs.   Deb: 4/27/49 MC

YEAR	TM/L	G	AB	R	H	2B	3B	HR	RBI	BB	SO	AVG	OBP	SLG	PRO+	BR/A	SB	CS	SBR	FA	FR	G/POS	TPR
1949	StL-N	20	33	8	11	1	0	0	2	7	3	.333	.450	.364	115	1	0			.981	2	2-16	0.3
1950	StL-N	11	15	1	2	1	0	0	0	2	4	.133	.235	.200	15	-2	0			1.000	1	/3-5	-0.1
1951	StL-N	120	420	68	118	18	9	2	32	75	31	.281	.395	.381	109	9	7	7	-2	.965	13	*S-105,2-12	2.8
1952	StL-N	151	570	**105**	153	28	8	15	52	96	55	.268	.392	.425	126	24	1	5	-3	.960	4	*S-148/3-2	3.8
1953	StL-N	154	585	110	163	32	11	14	61	86	40	.279	.382	.443	114	15	2	1	0	.964	7	*S-150/2-3	3.1
1954	StL-N	124	214	43	65	15	3	2	27	55	27	.304	.456	.430	131	14	5	1	1	.944	-20	S-66,3-27,2	-0.1
1955	StL-N	96	206	36	50	10	2	5	21	27	22	.243	.336	.383	91	-3	1	1	-0	.956	-4	3-43,2-10/S	-0.6
1956	StL-N	8	5	1	1	0	0	0	2	1	1	.200	.429	.200	77	-0	0	0	0	.000	0	H	0.0
	Phi-N	78	187	24	54	10	4	5	24	28	21	.289	.401	.465	134	10	1	1	-0	.974	-25	2-49/3-1	-1.1
	Yr	86	192	25	55	10	4	5	26	29	22	.286	.402	.458	133	10	1	1	-0	.974	-25	2-49/3-1	-1.1
1957	Phi-N	70	108	8	20	6	1	0	5	20	8	.185	.323	.259	61	-5	1	1	-0	.980	-3	2-24	-0.8
1958	Phi-N	105	334	53	95	14	3	8	36	51	34	.284	.392	.416	116	10	3	1	0	.969	-14	2-85/3-1	0.2
1959	StL-N	24	17	2	4	2	0	0	1	8	2	.235	.500	.353	124	1	0	0	0	1.000	1	/2-1,3-1M	0.2
Total	11	961	2694	459	736	137	41	51	263	456	248	.273	.390	.411	115	75	21	18		.962	-38	S-471,2-212/3	7.7

■ DAVE HENDERSON   Henderson, David Lee b: 7/21/58, Merced, Cal.   BR/TR, 6'2", 220 lbs.   Deb: 4/9/81

YEAR	TM/L	G	AB	R	H	2B	3B	HR	RBI	BB	SO	AVG	OBP	SLG	PRO+	BR/A	SB	CS	SBR	FA	FR	G/POS	TPR
1981	Sea-A	59	126	17	21	3	0	6	13	16	24	.167	.266	.333	69	-5	2	1	0	1.000	-7	O-58	-1.5
1982	Sea-A	104	324	47	82	17	1	14	48	36	67	.253	.328	.441	106	2	2	5	-2	.985	7	*O-101	0.5
1983	Sea-A	137	484	50	130	24	5	17	55	28	93	.269	.310	.444	101	-1	9	3	1	.982	12	*O-133/D-3	0.8
1984	Sea-A	112	350	42	98	23	0	14	43	19	56	.280	.321	.466	116	6	5	5	-2	.988	8	*O-97,D-10	1.0
1985	Sea-A	139	502	70	121	28	2	14	68	48	104	.241	.311	.388	90	-7	6	1	1	.986	-4	*O-138	-1.5
1986	Sea-A	103	337	51	93	19	4	14	44	37	95	.276	.351	.481	123	10	1	3	-2	.979	5	O-80,D-22	1.0
	*Bos-A	36	51	8	10	3	0	1	3	2	15	.196	.226	.314	45	-4	1	0	0	.981	-5	O-32	-0.9
	Yr	139	388	59	103	22	4	15	47	39	110	.265	.336	.459	113	6	2	3	-1	.980	0	*O-112,D-22	0.1
1987	Bos-A	75	184	30	43	10	0	8	25	22	48	.234	.316	.418	90	-3	1	1	-0	.958	-5	O-64/D-1	-1.0
	SF-N	15	21	2	5	2	0	0	1	8	5	.238	.448	.333	117	1	2	0	1	1.000	-1	/O-9	0.0
1988	*Oak-A	146	507	100	154	38	1	24	94	47	92	.304	.367	.525	152	34	2	4	-2	.982	5	*O-143	3.3
1989	*Oak-A	152	579	77	145	24	3	15	80	54	131	.250	.318	.380	99	-1	8	5	-1	.977	5	*O-149/D-2	-0.1
1990	*Oak-A	127	450	65	122	28	0	20	63	40	105	.271	.332	.467	126	14	3	1	0	.988	9	*O-116/D-6	2.1
1991	Oak-A★	150	572	86	158	33	0	25	85	58	113	.276	.347	.465	130	22	6	6	-2	.997	1	*O-140/2-1,D	2.7
1992	Oak-A	20	63	1	9	1	0	0	2	2	16	.143	.169	.159	-8	-9	0	0	0	.950	-3	O-12/D-4	-1.2
1993	Oak-A	107	382	37	84	19	0	20	53	32	113	.220	.280	.427	93	-6	0	3	-1	.991	9	O-76,D-28	-0.2
1994	KC-A	56	198	27	49	14	1	5	31	16	28	.247	.307	.404	75	-8	2	0	1	.962	-0	O-40,D-16	-0.8
Total	14	1538	5130	710	1324	286	17	197	708	465	1105	.258	.322	.436	108	46	50	38	-8	.984	44	*O-1388/D-99,2	4.2

■ KEN HENDERSON   Henderson, Kenneth Joseph b: 6/15/46, Carroll, Iowa   BB/TR, 6'2", 180 lbs.   Deb: 4/23/65

YEAR	TM/L	G	AB	R	H	2B	3B	HR	RBI	BB	SO	AVG	OBP	SLG	PRO+	BR/A	SB	CS	SBR	FA	FR	G/POS	TPR
1965	SF-N	63	73	10	14	1	1	0	7	9	19	.192	.280	.233	45	-5	1	1	-0	.980	-9	O-48	-1.6
1966	SF-N	11	29	4	9	1	1	1	3	2	3	.310	.375	.517	141	2	0	0	0	.917	-3	O-10	-0.2
1967	SF-N	65	179	15	34	3	0	4	14	19	52	.190	.275	.274	58	-9	0	1	-1	.947	-5	O-52	-1.9
1968	SF-N	3	3	1	1	0	0	0	0	2	1	.333	.600	.333	186	1	0	0	0	1.000	0	/O-2	0.0
1969	SF-N	113	374	42	84	14	4	6	44	42	64	.225	.311	.332	82	-9	6	4	-1	.969	-3	*O-111/3-3	-2.0
1970	SF-N	148	554	104	163	35	3	17	88	87	78	.294	.395	.460	130	26	20	3	4	.966	2	*O-146	2.4
1971	*SF-N	141	504	80	133	26	6	15	65	84	76	.264	.372	.429	128	21	18	3	4	.966	-1	*O-138/1-1	1.7
1972	SF-N	130	439	60	113	21	2	18	51	38	66	.257	.319	.437	112	5	14	7	0	.974	9	*O-123	0.9
1973	Chi-A	73	262	32	68	13	0	6	32	27	49	.260	.331	.378	96	-1	3	4	-2	.972	-1	O-44,D-26	-0.7
1974	Chi-A	162	602	76	176	35	5	20	95	66	112	.292	.364	.467	134	26	12	9	0	.987	9	*O-162	2.8
1975	Chi-A	140	513	65	129	20	3	9	53	74	65	.251	.350	.355	98	-1	5	3	0	.990	-13	*O-137/D-1	-1.6
1976	Atl-N	133	435	52	114	19	0	13	61	62	68	.262	.355	.395	106	5	5	7	-3	.987	-12	*O-122	-1.6
1977	Tex-A	75	244	23	63	14	0	5	23	18	37	.258	.317	.377	87	-4	2	1	0	.983	-6	O-65/D-3	-1.3
1978	NY-N	7	22	2	5	2	0	1	4	4	4	.227	.346	.455	127	1	0	1	0	1.000	0	/O-7	0.0
	Cin-N	64	144	10	24	6	1	3	19	23	32	.167	.285	.285	59	-8	0	0	0	1.000	-2	O-38	-1.2
	Yr	71	166	12	29	8	1	4	23	27	36	.175	.290	.307	67	-7	0	1	-1	1.000	-2	O-45	-1.2
1979	Cin-N	10	13	1	3	1	0	0	2	0	2	.231	.231	.308	45	-1	0	0	0	1.000	-0	/O-2	-0.2
	Chi-N	62	81	11	19	2	0	2	8	15	16	.235	.361	.333	83	-1	0	0	0	.950	-6	O-23	-0.8
	Yr	72	94	12	22	3	0	2	10	15	18	.234	.345	.330	79	-2	0	0	0	.955	-6	O-25	-1.0
1980	Chi-N	44	82	7	16	3	0	2	9	17	19	.195	.333	.305	74	-2	0	0	0	.944	-1	O-22	-0.4
Total	16	1444	4553	595	1168	216	26	122	576	589	763	.257	.346	.396	106	45	86	42	1	.977	-19	*O-1252/D-30,31	-3.3

YEAR	TM/L	G	AB	R	H	2B	3B	HR	RBI	BB	SO	AVG	OBP	SLG	PRO+	BR/A	SB	CS	SBR	FA	FR	G/POS	TPR
■ RICKEY HENDERSON							Henderson, Rickey Henley b: 12/25/58, Chicago, Ill. BR/TL, 5'10", 195 lbs. Deb: 6/24/79															
1979	Oak-A	89	351	49	96	13	3	1	26	34	39	.274	.341	.336	88	-5	33	11	3	.973	3	O-88	-0.3
1980	Oak-A★	158	591	111	179	22	4	9	53	117	54	.303	.422	.399	136	37	**100**	26	14	.984	23	*O-157/D-1	6.6
1981	*Oak-A	108	423	**89**	**135**	18	7	6	35	64	68	.319	.411	.437	152	31	**56**	22	4	.979	20	*O-107	5.2
1982	Oak-A★	149	536	119	143	24	4	10	51	**116**	94	.267	.399	.382	121	22	**130**	42	14	.977	9	*O-144/D-4	4.0
1983	Oak-A★	145	513	105	150	25	7	9	48	**103**	80	.292	.415	.421	139	33	**108**	19	21	.992	9	*O-142/D-1	5.7
1984	Oak-A★	142	502	113	147	27	4	16	58	86	81	.293	.401	.458	147	35	**66**	18	9	.969	8	*O-140	4.7
1985	NY-A★	143	547	**146**	172	28	5	24	72	99	65	.314	.422	.516	159	48	**80**	10	18	.980	16	*O-141/D-1	7.4
1986	NY-A★	153	608	**130**	160	31	5	28	74	89	81	.263	.359	.469	125	21	**87**	18	15	.986	12	*O-146/D-5	4.2
1987	NY-A★	95	358	78	104	17	3	17	37	80	52	.291	.423	.497	144	27	41	8	8	.980	7	O-69,D-24	3.5
1988	NY-A★	140	554	118	169	30	2	6	50	82	54	.305	.397	.399	125	22	**93**	13	20	.965	10	*O-136/D-3	4.7
1989	NY-A	65	235	41	58	13	1	3	22	56	29	.247	.394	.349	112	7	25	8	3	.993	4	O-65	1.2
	*Oak-A	85	306	72	90	13	2	9	35	70	39	.294	.429	.438	150	25	52	6	12	.985	7	O-82/D-3	4.1
	Yr	150	541	**113**	148	26	3	12	57	**126**	68	.274	.413	.399	133	31	77	14	15	.988	11	*O-147/D-3	5.3
1990	*Oak-A★	136	489	**119**	159	33	3	28	61	97	60	.325	**.441**	.577	**190**	63	65	10	14	.983	10	*O-118,D-15	8.2
1991	Oak-A★	134	470	105	126	17	1	18	57	98	73	.268	.402	.423	136	28	**58**	18	7	.970	10	*O-119,D-10	4.1
1992	*Oak-A★	117	396	77	112	18	3	15	46	95	56	.283	.429	.457	156	36	48	11	8	.984	6	*O-108/D-6	4.7
1993	Oak-A	90	318	77	104	19	1	17	47	85	46	.327	.472	.553	186	44	31	6	6	.974	9	O-74,D-16	5.3
	*Tor-A	44	163	37	35	3	1	4	12	35	19	.215	.360	.319	84	-2	22	2	5	.975	-2	O-44	0.0
	Yr	134	481	114	139	22	2	21	59	120	65	.289	.435	.474	150	41	53	8	11	.974	7	*O-118,D-16	5.3
1994	Oak-A	87	296	66	77	13	0	6	20	72	45	.260	.413	.365	112	10	22	7	2	.977	4	O-71,D-13	1.3
Total	16	2080	7656	1652	2216	364	56	226	804	1478	1035	.289	.408	.440	139	480	1117	255	182	.979	164	*O-1951,D-102	74.6
■ STEVE HENDERSON							Henderson, Stephen Curtis b: 11/18/52, Houston, Tex. BR/TR, 6'2", 190 lbs. Deb: 6/16/77 C															
1977	NY-N	99	350	67	104	16	6	12	65	43	79	.297	.376	.480	134	17	6	3	0	.980	6	O-97	1.9
1978	NY-N	157	587	83	156	30	9	10	65	60	109	.266	.336	.399	108	6	13	7	-0	.968	16	*O-155	1.6
1979	NY-N	98	350	42	107	16	8	5	39	38	58	.306	.380	.440	128	14	13	5	1	.990	9	O-94	2.1
1980	NY-N	143	513	75	149	17	8	8	58	62	90	.290	.370	.402	119	14	23	12	-0	.981	13	*O-136	2.3
1981	Chi-N	82	287	32	84	9	5	5	35	42	61	.293	.387	.411	121	9	5	7	-3	.951	1	O-77	0.5
1982	Chi-N	92	257	23	60	12	4	2	29	22	64	.233	.294	.335	73	-9	6	5	-1	.956	0	O-70	-1.2
1983	Sea-A	121	436	50	128	32	3	10	54	44	82	.294	.358	.450	116	10	10	14	-5	.970	1	*O-112/D-6	0.2
1984	Sea-A	109	325	42	85	12	3	10	35	38	62	.262	.341	.409	108	4	2	4	-2	.936	-2	O-53,D-51	-0.3
1985	Oak-A	85	193	25	58	8	3	3	31	18	34	.301	.360	.420	122	6	0	0	0	.953	-7	O-58/D-1	-0.2
1986	Oak-A	11	26	2	2	1	0	0	3	0	5	.077	.077	.115	-52	-5	0	0	0	.800	-2	/O-7,D-1	-0.7
1987	Oak-A	46	114	14	33	7	0	3	9	12	19	.289	.357	.430	115	3	0	0	0	.943	-7	O-31/D-9	-0.5
1988	Hou-N	42	46	4	10	2	0	0	5	7	14	.217	.321	.261	72	-1	1	1	-0	1.000	0	/O-8,1-1	-0.2
Total	12	1085	3484	459	976	162	49	68	428	386	677	.280	.354	.413	113	66	79	58	-11	.968	29	O-898/D-68,1	5.5
■ GEORGE HENDRICK							Hendrick, George Andrew b: 10/18/49, Los Angeles, Cal. BR/TR, 6'3", 195 lbs. Deb: 6/4/71															
1971	Oak-A	42	114	8	27	4	1	0	8	3	20	.237	.256	.289	55	-7	0	1	-1	.981	-7	O-36	-1.8
1972	*Oak-A	58	121	10	22	1	1	4	15	3	22	.182	.208	.306	54	-7	3	2	-0	1.000	-7	O-41	-1.8
1973	Cle-A	113	440	64	118	18	0	21	61	25	71	.268	.310	.452	111	4	7	6	-2	.988	-3	*O-110	-0.6
1974	Cle-A★	139	495	65	138	23	1	19	67	33	73	.279	.325	.444	121	11	6	4	-1	.989	-3	*O-133/D-1	0.8
1975	Cle-A★	145	561	82	145	21	2	24	86	40	78	.258	.308	.431	107	3	6	7	-2	.983	1	*O-143	-0.5
1976	Cle-A	149	551	72	146	20	3	25	81	51	82	.265	.327	.448	127	17	4	4	-1	.987	3	*O-146/D-3	1.3
1977	SD-N	152	541	75	168	25	2	23	81	61	74	.311	.382	.492	148	35	11	6	-0	.983	8	*O-142	3.8
1978	SD-N	36	111	9	27	4	0	3	8	12	16	.243	.317	.360	96	-1	1	1	-0	.986	-0	O-33	-0.3
	StL-N	102	382	55	110	27	1	17	67	28	44	.288	.340	.497	133	15	1	0	0	.996	6	*O-101	1.8
	Yr	138	493	64	137	31	1	20	75	40	60	.278	.335	.467	126	15	2	1	0	.994	6	*O-134	1.5
1979	StL-N	140	493	67	148	27	1	16	75	49	62	.300	.363	.456	121	14	2	3	-1	.993	6	*O-138	1.4
1980	StL-N★	150	572	73	173	33	2	25	109	32	67	.302	.344	.498	128	20	6	1	-1	.994	-6	*O-149	0.9
1981	StL-N	101	394	67	112	19	1	8	61	41	44	.284	.358	.485	134	17	4	2	0	.983	-4	*O-101	1.0
1982	*StL-N	136	515	65	145	20	5	19	104	37	80	.282	.331	.450	115	9	3	2	-0	.980	-2	*O-134	0.3
1983	StL-N☆	144	529	73	168	33	3	18	97	51	76	.318	.380	.493	140	28	3	4	-2	.992	1	1-92,O-51	2.1
1984	StL-N	120	441	57	122	28	1	9	69	32	75	.277	.327	.406	108	3	0	2	-1	.990	-1	*O-116/1-1	-0.2
1985	Pit-N	69	256	23	59	15	0	2	25	18	42	.230	.281	.313	66	-12	1	0	0	.971	3	O-65	-1.1
	Cal-A	16	41	5	5	1	0	2	6	4	8	.122	.200	.293	33	-4	0	0	0	1.000	-1	O-12/D-1	-0.5
1986	*Cal-A	102	283	45	77	13	1	14	47	26	41	.272	.335	.473	119	7	1	1	-0	.968	-6	O-93/1-7,D	-0.2
1987	Cal-A	65	162	14	39	10	0	5	25	14	18	.241	.301	.395	85	-4	0	0	0	.967	-8	O-45/1-9,D	-1.3
1988	Cal-A	69	127	12	31	1	0	3	19	7	20	.244	.289	.323	73	-5	0	0	-1	.933	-1	O-24,1-12/D	-0.8
Total	18	2048	7129	941	1980	343	27	267	1111	567	1013	.278	.333	.446	117	144	59	47	-11	.985	-17	*O-1813,1-121/D	4.3
■ HARVEY HENDRICK							Hendrick, Harvey "Gink" b: 11/9/1897, Mason, Tenn. d: 10/29/41, Covington, Tenn. BL/TR, 6'2", 190 lbs. Deb: 4/20/23															
1923	*NY-A	37	66	9	18	3	1	3	12	2	8	.273	.294	.485	101	-1	3	0	1	.947	-2	O-13	-0.2
1924	NY-A	40	76	7	20	0	0	1	11	2	7	.263	.291	.303	53	-5	1	0	0	.975	0	O-17	-0.6
1925	Cle-A	25	28	2	8	1	2	0	9	3	5	.286	.355	.464	106	0	0	0	0	1.000	0	/1-3	0.0
1927	Bro-N	128	458	55	142	18	11	4	50	24	40	.310	.350	.424	106	3	29			.969	-16	O-64,1-53/2	-2.0
1928	Bro-N	126	425	83	135	15	10	11	59	54	34	.318	.397	.478	129	19	16			.913	3	3-91,O-17	2.5
1929	Bro-N	110	384	69	136	26	6	14	82	31	20	.354	.404	.562	139	22	14			.975	-0	O-42,1-39/3S	1.5
1930	Bro-N	68	167	29	43	10	1	5	28	20	19	.257	.344	.419	84	-4	2			.947	-3	O-42/1-7	-0.9
1931	Bro-N	1	1	0	0	0	0	0	0	0	0	.000	.000	.000	-99	-0	0			.000	0	H	0.0
	Cin-N	137	530	74	167	32	9	1	75	53	40	.315	.379	.411	121	16	3			.987	-5	*1-137	-0.2
	Yr	138	531	74	167	32	9	1	75	53	40	.315	.379	.414	120	16	3			.987	-5	1-137	-0.2
1932	StL-N	28	72	8	18	2	0	1	5	5	9	.250	.299	.319	64	-4	0			.862	-3	3-12/O-5	-0.6
	Cin-N	94	398	56	120	30	4	0	40	23	29	.302	.341	.422	107	4	3			.986	-4	1-94	-0.8
	Yr	122	470	64	138	32	4	1	45	28	38	.294	.335	.406	100	-2	3			.986	-7	1-94,3-12/O	-1.4
1933	Chi-N	69	189	30	55	13	4	2	23	13	17	.291	.346	.455	128	6	0			.983	-1	1-38/O-8,3	0.2
1934	Phi-N	59	116	12	34	8	0	0	19	9	15	.293	.344	.362	79	-3	0			.962	-3	O-12/1-7,3	-0.7
Total	11	922	2910	434	896	157	46	48	413	239	243	.308	.364	.443	113	53	75	<u>0</u>		.986	-32	1-378,O-220,3/S2	-1.8
■ ELLIE HENDRICKS							Hendricks, Elrod Jerome b: 12/22/40, Charlotte Amalie, V.I. BL/TR, 6'1", 175 lbs. Deb: 4/13/68 C															
1968	Bal-A	79	163	19	37	8	1	7	23	19	51	.202	.281	.417	96	-1	0	0	0	.991	-5	C-53	-0.3
1969	Bal-A	105	295	36	72	9	0	12	38	39	44	.244	.336	.383	100	0	0	1	-1	**.998**	8	C-87/1-4	1.0
1970	*Bal-A	106	322	32	78	9	0	12	41	33	44	.242	.320	.382	92	-4	1	0	0	.986	-5	C-95	-0.7
1971	*Bal-A	101	316	33	79	14	1	9	42	39	38	.250	.336	.386	105	2	0	0	0	.985	-8	C-90/1-3	-0.2
1972	Bal-A	33	84	6	13	4	0	2	4	12	19	.155	.260	.202	38	-6	0	1	-1	.986	2	C-28	-0.5
	Chi-N	17	43	7	5	1	0	2	6	13	8	.116	.321	.279	65	-2	0	1	-1	.978	1	C-16	-0.1
1973	Bal-A	41	101	9	18	5	1	3	15	10	22	.178	.259	.337	67	-5	0	0	0	.994	4	C-38/D-1	0.1
1974	*Bal-A	66	159	18	33	8	2	4	8	17	25	.208	.288	.340	83	-4	0	0	0	1.000	4	C-54/1-1,D	-0.7
1975	Bal-A	85	223	32	48	8	0	5	38	34	40	.215	.322	.377	103	1	0	0	0	**.995**	-1	C-83	0.3
1976	Bal-A	28	79	2	11	4	0	1	4	7	13	.139	.209	.190	19	-8	0	0	0	.971	-5	C-27	-1.4
	*NY-A	26	53	6	12	0	0	3	6	3	10	.226	.268	.415	99	-0	0	0	0	1.000	1	C-18	0.1
	Yr	54	132	8	23	4	0	4	9	10	23	.174	.232	.280	52	-8	0	0	0	.982	-4	C-45	-1.3

YEAR	TM/L	G	AB	R	H	2B	3B	HR	RBI	BB	SO	AVG	OBP	SLG	PRO+	BR/A	SB	CS	SBR	FA	FR	G/POS	TPR
1977	NY-A	10	11	1	3	1	0	1	5	0	2	.273	.273	.636	140	0	0	0	0	1.000	0	/C-6	0.1
1978	Bal-A	13	18	4	6	1	0	1	1	3	3	.333	.429	.556	186	2	0	0	0	.955	0	/C-6,P-1,D	0.2
1979	Bal-A	1	1	0	0	0	0	0	0	0	0	.000	.000	.000	-99	-0	0	0	0	.500	-1	/C-1	-0.1
Total	12	711	1888	205	415	66	7	62	230	229	319	.220	.308	.361	90	-24	1	5	-3	.990	-17	C-602/1-8,DP	-2.2

■ JACK HENDRICKS
Hendricks, John Charles b: 4/9/1875, Joliet, Ill. d: 5/13/43, Chicago, Ill. BL/TL, 5'11.5", 160 lbs. Deb: 6/12/02 M

YEAR	TM/L	G	AB	R	H	2B	3B	HR	RBI	BB	SO	AVG	OBP	SLG	PRO+	BR/A	SB	CS	SBR	FA	FR	G/POS	TPR
1902	NY-N	8	26	1	6	2	0	0		0	2	.231	.286	.308	84	-1	2			.929	0	/O-7	-0.1
	Chi-N	2	7	0	4	0	1	0		0	0	.571	.571	.857	350	2	0			1.000	0	/O-2	0.2
	Yr	10	33	1	10	2	1	0		0	2	.303	.343	.424	138	1	2			.950	1	/O-9	0.1
1903	Was-A	32	112	10	20	1	3	0		4	13	.179	.264	.241	51	-6	3			.891	-4	O-32	-1.3
Total	2	42	145	11	30	3	4	0		4	15	.207	.281	.283	70	-5	5			.909	-3	O-41	-1.2

■ TIM HENDRYX
Hendryx, Timothy Green b: 1/31/1891, LeRoy, Ill. d: 8/14/57, Corpus Christi, Tex. BR/TR, 5'9", 170 lbs. Deb: 9/4/11

YEAR	TM/L	G	AB	R	H	2B	3B	HR	RBI	BB	SO	AVG	OBP	SLG	PRO+	BR/A	SB	CS	SBR	FA	FR	G/POS	TPR
1911	Cle-A	4	7	0	2	0	0	0	0	0	0	.286	.286	.286	59	-0	1			1.000	-1	/3-3	-0.1
1912	Cle-A	23	70	9	17	2	4	1	14	8		.243	.329	.429	113	1	3			1.000	-2	O-22	-0.2
1915	NY-A	13	40	4	8	2	0	0	1	4	2	.200	.289	.250	61	-2	3	3	-2	.968	1	O-12	-0.4
1916	NY-A	15	62	10	18	7	1	0	5	8	6	.290	.380	.435	142	3	4			1.000	-2	O-15	0.1
1917	NY-A	125	393	43	98	14	7	5	44	62	45	.249	.359	.359	118	10	6			.955	5	*O-107	1.0
1918	StL-A	88	219	22	61	14	3	0	33	37	35	.279	.388	.370	133	10	5			.982	-9	O-65	-0.2
1920	Bos-A	99	363	54	119	21	5	0	73	42	27	.328	.400	.413	121	12	7	9	-3	.964	-10	O-98	-0.7
1921	Bos-A	49	137	10	33	8	2	0	22	24	13	.241	.362	.328	79	-3	1	1	-0	.958	-4	O-41	-1.0
Total	8	416	1291	152	356	68	22	6	192	185	128	.276	.372	.376	115	31	26	13		.966	-22	O-360/3-3	-1.5

■ DAVE HENGEL
Hengel, David Lee b: 12/18/61, Oakland, Cal. BR/TR, 6', 185 lbs. Deb: 9/3/86

YEAR	TM/L	G	AB	R	H	2B	3B	HR	RBI	BB	SO	AVG	OBP	SLG	PRO+	BR/A	SB	CS	SBR	FA	FR	G/POS	TPR
1986	Sea-A	21	63	3	12	1	0	1	6	1	13	.190	.215	.254	27	-6	0	0	0	1.000	-1	D-11/O-8	-0.7
1987	Sea-A	10	19	2	6	0	0	1	4	0	4	.316	.316	.474	100	-0	0	0	0	.875	-2	/O-7,D-1	-0.2
1988	Sea-A	26	60	3	10	1	0	2	7	1	15	.167	.180	.283	27	-6	0	0	0	.952	-1	O-12,D-12	-0.8
1989	Cle-A	12	25	2	3	1	0	0	1	2	4	.120	.185	.160	-2	-3	0	0	0	1.000	-1	/O-9,D-3	-0.4
Total	4	69	167	10	31	3	0	4	18	4	36	.186	.209	.275	31	-16	0	0	0	.962	-5	/O-36,D-27	-2.1

■ MOXIE HENGLE
Hengle, Emery J. b: 10/7/1857, Chicago, Ill. d: 12/11/24, River Forest, Ill. BR, 5'8", 144 lbs. Deb: 4/20/1884

YEAR	TM/L	G	AB	R	H	2B	3B	HR	RBI	BB	SO	AVG	OBP	SLG	PRO+	BR/A	SB	CS	SBR	FA	FR	G/POS	TPR
1884	CP-U	19	74	9	15	2	1	0			3	.203	.234	.257	33	-7				.840	-7	2-19	-1.2
	StP-U	9	33	2	5	1	1	0			3	.152	.152	.242	10	-6				.923	1	/2-9	-0.4
	Yr	28	107	11	20	3	2	0			3	.187	.209	.252	29	-11				.870	-6	2-28	-1.6
1885	Buf-N	7	26	2	4	0	0	0		1	2	.154	.185	.154	10	-3				.864	-3	/2-5,O-3	-0.5
Total	2	35	133	13	24	3	2	0		1	2	.180	.204	.233	25	-15				.869	-9	/2-33,O-3	-2.1

■ GAIL HENLEY
Henley, Gail Curtice b: 10/15/28, Wichita, Kan. BL/TR, 5'9", 180 lbs. Deb: 4/13/54

YEAR	TM/L	G	AB	R	H	2B	3B	HR	RBI	BB	SO	AVG	OBP	SLG	PRO+	BR/A	SB	CS	SBR	FA	FR	G/POS	TPR
1954	Pit-N	14	30	7	9	1	0	1	4	4	4	.300	.382	.433	114	-0	1	0	0	1.000	-0	/O-9	0.0

■ BUTCH HENLINE
Henline, Walter John b: 12/20/1894, Ft.Wayne, Ind. d: 10/9/57, Sarasota, Fla. BR/TR, 5'10", 175 lbs. Deb: 4/13/21 U

YEAR	TM/L	G	AB	R	H	2B	3B	HR	RBI	BB	SO	AVG	OBP	SLG	PRO+	BR/A	SB	CS	SBR	FA	FR	G/POS	TPR
1921	NY-N	1	1	0	0	0	0	0	0	0	1	.000	.000	.000	-99	-0	0	0	0	.000	0	H	0.0
	Phi-N	33	111	8	34	2	0	0	8	2	6	.306	.319	.324	65	-5	1	0	0	.987	9	C-32	0.5
	Yr	34	112	8	34	2	0	0	8	2	7	.304	.316	.321	64	-6	1	0	0	.987	9	C-32	0.5
1922	Phi-N	125	430	57	136	20	4	14	64	36	33	.316	.380	.479	110	6	2	2	-1	.983	2	*C-119	1.2
1923	Phi-N	111	330	45	107	14	3	7	46	37	33	.324	.407	.448	112	7	7	5	-1	.978	-16	C-96/O-1	-0.5
1924	Phi-N	115	289	41	82	18	4	5	35	27	15	.284	.361	.426	98	-1	1	2	-1	.973	-1	C-83/O-2	0.2
1925	Phi-N	93	263	43	80	12	5	8	48	24	16	.304	.380	.479	108	3	3	1	0	.956	-2	C-68/O-1	0.5
1926	Phi-N	99	283	32	80	14	1	2	30	21	18	.283	.339	.360	84	-6	1			.970	-10	C-77/1-4,O	-1.1
1927	Bro-N	67	177	12	47	10	3	1	18	17	10	.266	.337	.373	90	-3				.947	-3	C-60	0.2
1928	Bro-N	55	132	12	28	3	1	2	8	17	8	.212	.302	.295	58	-8	2			.976	-4	C-45	-0.8
1929	Bro-N	27	62	5	15	2	0	1	7	9	9	.242	.338	.323	66	-3				.967	1	C-21	-0.1
1930	Chi-A	3	8	1	1	0	0	0	0	2	3	.125	.125	.125	-38	-2	0	0		1.000	0	/C-3	-0.1
1931	Chi-A	11	15	2	1	1	0	0	2	2	4	.067	.176	.133	-19	-3	0	0	0	.889	0	/C-4	-0.2
Total	11	740	2101	258	611	96	21	40	268	192	156	.291	.361	.414	96	-15	18	10		.971	-20	C-608/O-6,1	-0.2

■ LES HENNESSEY
Hennessey, Lester Baker b: 12/12/1893, Lynn, Mass. d: 11/20/76, New York, N.Y. BR/TR, 6', 190 lbs. Deb: 6/4/13

YEAR	TM/L	G	AB	R	H	2B	3B	HR	RBI	BB	SO	AVG	OBP	SLG	PRO+	BR/A	SB	CS	SBR	FA	FR	G/POS	TPR
1913	Det-A	14	22	2	3	0	0	0		3	6	.136	.240	.136	11	-2	2			.880	-2	2-10	-0.5

■ FRITZ HENRICH
Henrich, Frank Wilde b: 5/8/1899, Cincinnati, Ohio d: 5/1/59, Philadelphia, Pa. BL/TL, 5'10", 160 lbs. Deb: 4/21/24

YEAR	TM/L	G	AB	R	H	2B	3B	HR	RBI	BB	SO	AVG	OBP	SLG	PRO+	BR/A	SB	CS	SBR	FA	FR	G/POS	TPR
1924	Phi-N	36	90	4	19	4	0	0	4	2	12	.211	.228	.256	26	-9	0	0	0	.978	-9	O-32	-2.0

■ BOBBY HENRICH
Henrich, Robert Edward b: 12/24/38, Lawrence, Kan. BR/TR, 6'1", 185 lbs. Deb: 5/3/57

YEAR	TM/L	G	AB	R	H	2B	3B	HR	RBI	BB	SO	AVG	OBP	SLG	PRO+	BR/A	SB	CS	SBR	FA	FR	G/POS	TPR
1957	Cin-N	29	10	8	2	0	0	0	1	1	4	.200	.273	.200	28	-1	0	0	0	.875	0	/S-7,O-6,32	-0.1
1958	Cin-N	5	3	2	0	0	0	0	0	0	2	.000	.000	.000	-95	-1	0	0	0	1.000	1	/S-2	0.0
1959	Cin-N	14	3	3	0	0	0	0	0	0	1	.000	.000	.000	-97	-1	0	0	0	1.000	0	/S-5,3-1	-0.1
Total	3	48	16	13	2	0	0	0	1	1	7	.125	.176	.125	-17	-3	0	0	0	.929	1	/S-14,O-6,32	-0.2

■ TOMMY HENRICH
Henrich, Thomas David "The Clutch" or "Old Reliable" b: 2/20/13, Massillon, Ohio BL/TL, 6', 180 lbs. Deb: 5/11/37 C

YEAR	TM/L	G	AB	R	H	2B	3B	HR	RBI	BB	SO	AVG	OBP	SLG	PRO+	BR/A	SB	CS	SBR	FA	FR	G/POS	TPR
1937	NY-A	67	206	39	66	14	5	8	42	35	17	.320	.419	.553	142	14	4	0	1	.970	-4	O-59	0.8
1938	*NY-A	131	471	109	127	24	7	22	91	92	32	.270	.391	.490	120	15	6	2	1	.984	-1	*O-130	1.0
1939	NY-A	99	347	64	96	18	4	9	57	51	23	.277	.371	.429	106	3	7	0	2	.991	0	O-88/1-1	0.4
1940	NY-A	90	293	57	90	28	5	10	53	48	30	.307	.408	.539	149	22	1	2	-1	.969	-1	O-76/1-2	1.5
1941	*NY-A	144	538	106	149	27	5	31	85	81	40	.277	.377	.519	137	27	3	1	0	.980	-1	*O-139	1.8
1942	NY-A★	127	483	77	129	30	5	13	67	58	42	.267	.352	.431	122	13	4	4	-1	.987	-1	*O-119/1-7	0.4
1946	NY-A	150	565	92	142	25	4	19	83	87	63	.251	.358	.411	113	11	5	2	0	.992	2	*O-111,1-41	0.6
1947	*NY-A	142	550	109	158	35	13	16	98	71	54	.287	.372	.485	139	27	3	2	-0	.983	6	*O-132/1-6	2.7
1948	NY-A★	146	588	138	181	42	14	25	100	76	42	.308	.391	.554	151	40	2	3	-1	.978	-0	*O-102,1-46	3.1
1949	*NY-A☆	115	411	90	118	20	3	24	85	86	34	.287	.416	.526	148	30	2	3	-1	.958	-4	O-61,1-52	2.1
1950	NY-A★	73	151	20	41	6	8	6	34	27	6	.272	.382	.536	137	8	0	1	-1	.987	-5	1-34	0.1
Total	11	1284	4603	901	1297	269	73	183	795	712	383	.282	.382	.491	132	211	37	19	-0	.981	-7	*O-1017,1-189	14.5

■ OLAF HENRIKSEN
Henriksen, Olaf "Swede" b: 4/26/1888, Kirkerup, Denmark d: 10/17/62, Norwood, Mass. BL/TL, 5'7.5", 158 lbs. Deb: 8/11/11

YEAR	TM/L	G	AB	R	H	2B	3B	HR	RBI	BB	SO	AVG	OBP	SLG	PRO+	BR/A	SB	CS	SBR	FA	FR	G/POS	TPR
1911	Bos-A	27	93	17	34	2	1	0	8	14		.366	.449	.409	141	6	4			.953	-0	O-25	0.4
1912	*Bos-A	44	56	20	18	3	1	0	8	14		.321	.457	.411	142	4				.909	-2	O-11	0.1
1913	Bos-A	31	40	8	15	1	0	0	2	7	5	.375	.468	.400	151	3	3			1.000	-1	/O-7	0.2
1914	Bos-A	63	95	16	25	1	1	0	13	22	12	.263	.407	.337	124	4	5	4	-1	.947	-5	O-29	-0.3
1915	*Bos-A	73	92	9	18	1	0	0	13	18	7	.196	.333	.261	80	-1	1	5	-3	.967	-4	O-25	-0.9
1916	*Bos-A	68	99	13	20	0	1	0	11	19	15	.202	.331	.263	78	-2	2			1.000	-4	O-31	-0.1
1917	Bos-A	15	12	1	1	0	0	0	1	3	4	.083	.267	.083	7	-1	0			.000	0	H	-0.1
Total	7	321	487	84	131	12	7	1	48	97	43	.269	.392	.329	112	13	15	9		.966	-17	O-128	-1.4

■ SNAKE HENRY
Henry, Frederick Marshall b: 7/19/1895, Waynesville, N.C. d: 10/12/87, Wendell, N.C. BL/TL, 6', 170 lbs. Deb: 9/15/22

YEAR	TM/L	G	AB	R	H	2B	3B	HR	RBI	BB	SO	AVG	OBP	SLG	PRO+	BR/A	SB	CS	SBR	FA	FR	G/POS	TPR
1922	Bos-N	18	66	5	13	4	1	0	5	2	8	.197	.221	.288	32	-7	2	2	-1	.995	1	1-18	-0.7
1923	Bos-N	11	9	1	1	0	0	0	2	1	1	.111	.200	.111	-17	-2	0			.000	0	H	-0.1
Total	2	29	75	6	14	4	1	0	7	3	9	.187	.218	.267	26	-8	2	2	-1	.995	0	/1-18	-0.8

YEAR	TM/L	G	AB	R	H	2B	3B	HR	RBI	BB	SO	AVG	OBP	SLG	PRO+	BR/A	SB	CS	SBR	FA	FR	G/POS	TPR

■ **GEORGE HENRY**   Henry, George Washington   b: 8/10/1863, Philadelphia, Pa.   d: 12/30/34, Lynn, Mass.   BR/TR, 5'9", 180 lbs.   Deb: 4/27/1893

1893	Cin-N	21	83	11	23	3	0	0	13	11	12	.277	.375	.313	82	-2		2		.965	5	O-21	0.1

■ **JOHN HENRY**   Henry, John Michael   b: 9/2/1863, Springfield, Mass.   d: 6/11/39, Hartford, Conn.   TL ,   Deb: 8/13/1884

1884	Cle-N	9	26	2	4	0	0	0	0	0	12	.154	.154	.154	-3	-3				1.000	0	/P-5,O-4	-0.1
1885	Bal-a	10	34	4	9	3	0	0		0	1	.265	.286	.353	102	0				.931	2	/P-9,O-1	0.0
1886	Was-N	4	14	3	5	0	0	0	0	0	3	.357	.357	.357	125	0	0			.833	-0	/P-4	0.0
1890	NY-N	37	144	19	35	6	0	0	16	7	12	.243	.283	.285	65	-7	12			.870	-3	O-37	-0.9
Total	4	60	218	28	53	9	0	0	16	8	27	.243	.273	.284	66	-9	12			.867	-1	/O-42,P-18	-1.0

■ **JOHN HENRY**   Henry, John Park "Bull"   b: 12/26/1889, Amherst, Mass.   d: 11/24/41, Fort Huachuca, Ariz.   BR/TR, 6', 180 lbs.   Deb: 7/8/10

1910	Was-A	29	87	2	13	1	1	0	5	2		.149	.169	.184	11	-9	2			.989	2	C-18,1-10	-0.7
1911	Was-A	85	261	24	53	5	0	0	21	25		.203	.273	.222	39	-21	8			.969	9	C-51,1-30	-0.7
1912	Was-A	66	191	23	37	4	1	0	9	31		.194	.309	.225	53	-11	10			.977	8	C-65	0.4
1913	Was-A	96	273	26	61	8	4	1	26	30	43	.223	.309	.293	75	-8	5			.982	3	C-96	0.3
1914	Was-A	92	261	22	44	7	4	0	20	37	47	.169	.274	.226	49	-16	7	3	0	.980	6	C-92	-0.2
1915	Was-A	95	277	20	61	9	2	1	22	36	28	.220	.323	.278	78	-6	10	2	2	.972	4	C-94	0.7
1916	Was-A	117	305	28	76	12	3	0	46	49	40	.249	.364	.308	103	4	12			.981	-4	*C-116	0.8
1917	Was-A	65	163	10	31	6	0	0	18	24	16	.190	.302	.227	62	-6	1			.988	1	C-59	-0.1
1918	Bos-N	43	102	6	21	2	0	0	4	10	15	.206	.283	.225	58	-5	0			.964	3	C-38	-0.1
Total	9	688	1920	161	397	54	15	2	171	244	189	.207	.303	.254	65	-79	55	5		.978	31	C-629/1-40	0.4

■ **RON HENRY**   Henry, Ronald Baxter   b: 8/7/36, Chester, Pa.   BR/TR, 6'1", 180 lbs.   Deb: 4/15/61

1961	Min-A	20	28	1	4	0	0	0	3	2	7	.143	.200	.143	-6	-4	0	0	0	1.000	-1	/C-5,1-1	-0.5
1964	Min-A	22	41	4	5	1	1	2	5	2	17	.122	.163	.341	36	-4	0	0	0	.984	-0	C-13	-0.4
Total	2	42	69	5	9	1	1	2	8	4	24	.130	.178	.261	18	-8	0	0	0	.988	-1	/C-18,1-1	-0.9

■ **BABE HERMAN**   Herman, Floyd Caves   b: 6/26/03, Buffalo, N.Y.   d: 11/27/87, Glendale, Cal.   BL/TL, 6'4", 190 lbs.   Deb: 4/14/26   C

1926	Bro-N	137	496	64	158	35	11	11	81	44	53	.319	.375	.500	136	24	8			.986	0	*1-101,O-35	1.5
1927	Bro-N	130	412	65	112	26	9	14	73	39	41	.272	.336	.481	116	8	4			.980	9	*1-105/O-1	0.1
1928	Bro-N	134	486	64	165	37	6	12	91	38	36	.340	.390	.514	136	25	1			.937	-7	*O-127	1.0
1929	Bro-N	146	569	105	217	42	13	21	113	55	45	.381	.436	.612	160	52	21			.941	-17	*O-141/1-2	2.3
1930	Bro-N	153	614	143	241	48	11	35	130	66	56	.393	.455	.678	171	71	18			.978	-20	*O-153	3.4
1931	Bro-N	151	610	93	191	43	16	18	97	50	65	.313	.365	.525	137	30	17			.960	-1	*O-150	1.9
1932	Cin-N	148	577	87	188	38	**19**	16	87	60	45	.326	.389	.541	152	42	7			.969	16	*O-146	4.7
1933	Chi-N	137	508	77	147	36	12	16	93	50	57	.289	.353	.502	142	27	6			.957	-5	*O-131	1.5
1934	Chi-N	125	467	65	142	34	5	14	84	35	71	.304	.353	.488	125	15	1			.971	-10	*O-113/1-7	0.0
1935	Pit-N	26	81	8	19	8	1	0	7	3	10	.235	.271	.358	65	-4	0			.958	0	O-15/1-3	-0.8
	Cin-N	92	349	44	117	23	5	10	58	35	25	.335	.396	.516	147	23	4			.976	-1	O-76,1-14	1.7
	Yr	118	430	52	136	31	6	10	65	38	35	.316	.373	.486	131	19	5			.974	-4	O-91,1-17	0.9
1936	Cin-N	119	380	59	106	25	2	13	71	39	36	.279	.348	.458	123	11	4			.967	-7	O-92/1-4	0.1
1937	Det-A	17	20	2	6	3	0	0	3	1	6	.300	.364	.450	102	0	2	0	1	1.000	-0	/O-2	0.0
1945	Bro-N	37	34	6	9	1	0	1	9	5	7	.265	.359	.382	107	0	0			.000	-1	/O-3	-0.1
Total	13	1552	5603	882	1818	399	110	181	997	520	553	.324	.383	.532	141	323	94	0		.961	-55	*O-1185,1-236	17.3

■ **BILLY HERMAN**   Herman, William Jennings Bryan   b: 7/7/09, New Albany, Ind.   d: 9/5/92, W.Palm Beach, Fla.   BR/TR, 5'11", 180 lbs.   Deb: 8/29/31   MCH

1931	Chi-N	25	98	14	32	7	0	0	16	13	6	.327	.405	.398	115	3	2			.939	3	2-25	0.7
1932	*Chi-N	154	656	102	206	42	7	1	51	40	33	.314	.358	.404	105	6	14			.961	17	*2-154	3.0
1933	Chi-N	153	619	82	173	35	2	0	44	45	34	.279	.332	.342	93	-5	5			.956	29	*2-153	3.5
1934	Chi-N★	113	456	79	138	21	6	3	42	34	31	.303	.355	.395	102	2	6			.975	16	*2-111	2.3
1935	*Chi-N★	154	666	113	**227**	**57**	6	7	83	42	29	.341	.383	.476	128	26	6			.964	19	*2-154	5.4
1936	Chi-N★	153	632	101	211	57	7	5	93	59	30	.334	.392	.470	128	25	5			.975	15	*2-153	5.0
1937	Chi-N★	138	564	106	189	35	11	8	65	56	22	.335	.396	.479	131	25	2			.954	19	*2-137	5.2
1938	*Chi-N★	152	624	86	173	34	7	1	56	59	31	.277	.342	.359	90	-7	3			.981	25	*2-151	2.6
1939	Chi-N★	156	623	111	191	34	**18**	7	70	66	31	.307	.378	.453	120	18	9			.967	-3	*2-156	2.3
1940	Chi-N★	135	558	77	163	24	4	5	57	47	30	.292	.347	.376	101	1	1			.974	19	*2-135	2.9
1941	Chi-N	11	36	4	7	0	1	0	9	5	7	.194	.356	.250	75	-1	0			.898	1	2-11	-0.5
	*Bro-N★	133	536	77	156	30	4	3	41	58	38	.291	.361	.379	104	4	1			.970	-27	*2-133	-1.4
	Yr	144	572	81	163	30	5	3	41	67	43	.285	.361	.371	103	3	1			.964	-32	*2-144	-1.9
1942	Bro-N	155	571	76	146	34	2	2	65	72	52	.256	.339	.333	95	-2	6			.973	-11	*2-153/1-3	-0.4
1943	Bro-N★	153	585	76	193	41	2	2	100	66	25	.330	.398	.417	135	28	4			.971	-17	*2-117,3-37	1.9
1946	Bro-N	47	184	24	53	8	4	0	28	26	10	.288	.376	.375	112	4	2			.945	-2	3-29,2-16	0.4
	Bos-N	75	252	32	77	23	1	3	22	43	13	.306	.409	.440	139	14	1			.956	-16	2-44,1-22/3	0.0
	Yr	122	436	56	130	31	5	3	50	69	23	.298	.395	.413	128	18	3			.968	-18	2-60,3-34,1	0.4
1947	Pit-N	15	47	3	10	4	0	0	6	2	7	.213	.245	.298	42	-4	0			1.000	0	2-10/1-2M	-1.2
Total	15	1922	7707	1163	2345	486	82	47	839	737	428	.304	.367	.407	112	138	67			.967	71	*2-1813/3-71,1	31.7

■ **AL HERMANN**   Hermann, Albert Bartel   b: 3/28/1899, Milltown, N.J.   d: 8/20/80, Lewes, Del.   BR/TR, 6', 180 lbs.   Deb: 7/17/23

1923	Bos-N	31	93	2	22	4	0	0	11	0	7	.237	.237	.280	37	-9	3	2		.957	-6	2-15/3-5,1	-1.4
1924	Bos-N	1	1	0	0	0	0	0	0	0	1	.000	.000	.000	-99	-0	0	0	0	.000	0	H	0.0
Total	2	32	94	2	22	4	0	0	11	0	8	.234	.234	.277	36	-9	3	2	-0	.957	-6	/2-15,3-5,1	-1.4

■ **GENE HERMANSKI**   Hermanski, Eugene Victor   b: 5/11/20, Pittsfield, Mass.   BL/TR, 5'11.5", 185 lbs.   Deb: 8/15/43

1943	Bro-N	18	60	6	18	2	1	0	12	11	7	.300	.417	.367	127	3	1			.976	3	O-17	0.5
1946	Bro-N	64	110	15	22	8	0	1	8	17	10	.200	.313	.255	61	-5	2			.938	-7	O-34	-1.4
1947	*Bro-N	79	189	36	52	7	1	7	39	28	7	.275	.377	.434	111	3	5			.982	-7	O-66	-0.6
1948	Bro-N	133	400	63	116	22	7	15	60	64	46	.290	.391	.493	133	19	15			.971	-4	*O-119	1.7
1949	*Bro-N	87	224	48	67	12	3	8	42	47	21	.299	.431	.487	140	15	12			.980	-4	O-77	0.8
1950	Bro-N	94	289	36	86	17	5	7	34	36	26	.298	.381	.450	115	7	2			.989	3	O-78	0.7
1951	Bro-N	31	80	8	20	4	0	1	5	10	12	.250	.333	.338	79	-2	0	2	-1	.977	1	O-19	-0.3
	Chi-N	75	231	28	65	12	1	3	20	35	30	.281	.385	.381	105	3	3	0	1	.966	5	O-63	0.6
	Yr	106	311	36	85	16	1	4	25	45	42	.273	.372	.370	98	1	3	2	-0	.969	6	O-82	0.3
1952	Chi-N	99	275	28	70	6	0	4	34	29	32	.255	.330	.320	80	-7	2	0	1	.981	2	O-76	-0.7
1953	Chi-N	18	40	1	6	1	0	0	1	4	7	.150	.227	.175	7	-5	1	0	0	1.000	-2	O-13	-0.7
	Pit-N	41	62	7	11	0	0	1	4	8	14	.177	.282	.226	35	-6	0	0	0	1.000	-0	O-13	-0.6
	Yr	59	102	8	17	1	0	1	5	12	21	.167	.261	.206	24	-11	1	0	0	1.000	-2	O-26	-1.3
Total	9	739	1960	276	533	85	18	46	259	289	212	.272	.372	.404	107	25	43	2		.977	-1	O-575	-0.0

■ **REMY HERMOSO**   Hermoso, Angel Remigio   b: 10/1/46, Carabobo, Venezuela   BR/TR, 5'8", 155 lbs.   Deb: 9/14/67

1967	Atl-N	11	26	3	8	0	0	0	2	4		.308	.357	.308	93	-0	1	0	0	.952	1	/S-9,2-2	0.2
1969	Mon-N	28	74	6	12	0	3	0	5	10		.162	.225	.162	10	-9	3	1	0	.968	4	2-18/S-6	-0.3
1970	Mon-N	4	1	1	0	0	0	0	0	0	0	.000	.000	.000	-99	-0	0	0	0	1.000	0	/2-1,3-1	0.0
1974	Cle-A	48	122	15	27	3	1	0	5	7	7	.221	.264	.262	52	-8	2	2	-1	.967	7	2-45	0.1
Total	4	91	223	25	47	3	1	0	8	14	21	.211	.261	.233	42	-17	6	3	0	.968	12	/2-66,S-15,3	-0.0

YEAR	TM/L	G	AB	R	H	2B	3B	HR	RBI	BB	SO	AVG	OBP	SLG	PRO+	BR/A	SB	CS	SBR	FA	FR	G/POS	TPR

■ CARLOS HERNANDEZ   Hernandez, Carlos Alberto (Almeida) b: 5/24/67, San Felix, Venez.   BR/TR, 5'11", 185 lbs. Deb: 4/20/90

1990	LA-N	10	20	2	4	1	0	0	1	0	2	.200	.200	.250	24	-2	0	0	0	1.000	1	C-10	-0.1
1991	LA-N	15	14	1	3	1	0	0	1	0	5	.214	.267	.286	57	-1	1	0	0	.966	1	C-13/3-1	0.0
1992	LA-N	69	173	11	45	4	0	3	17	11	21	.260	.319	.335	87	-3	0	1	-1	.979	2	C-63	0.2
1993	LA-N	50	99	6	25	5	0	2	7	2	11	.253	.267	.364	71	-4	0	0	0	.966	7	C-43	0.4
1994	LA-N	32	64	6	14	2	0	2	6	1	14	.219	.231	.344	50	-5	0	0	0	1.000	5	C-27	0.1
Total	5	176	370	26	91	13	0	7	32	14	53	.246	.283	.338	72	-15	1	1	-0	.979	16	C-156/3-1	0.6

■ CESAR HERNANDEZ   Hernandez, Cesar Dario (Perez) b: 9/28/66, Yamasa, D.R.   BR/TR, 6', 160 lbs. Deb: 7/19/92

1992	Cin-N	34	51	6	14	4	0	0	4	0	10	.275	.275	.353	74	-2	3	1	0	.952	-2	O-18	-0.4
1993	Cin-N	27	24	3	2	0	0	0	1	1	8	.083	.120	.083	-44	-5	1	2	-1	.970	-2	O-23	-0.8
Total	2	61	75	9	16	4	0	0	5	1	18	.213	.224	.267	35	-7	4	3	-1	.963	-5	/O-41	-1.2

■ ENZO HERNANDEZ   Hernandez, Enzo Octavio b: 2/12/49, Valle De Guanape, Venez.   BR/TR, 5'8", 155 lbs. Deb: 4/17/71

1971	SD-N	143	549	58	122	9	3	0	12	54	34	.222	.295	.250	60	-28	21	5	3	.955	-11	*S-143	-1.9
1972	SD-N	114	329	33	64	11	2	1	15	22	25	.195	.245	.249	44	-25	24	3	5	.963	5	*S-107/O-3	-0.1
1973	SD-N	70	247	26	55	2	1	0	9	17	14	.223	.273	.239	47	-18	15	4	2	.977	-1	S-67	-0.9
1974	SD-N	147	512	55	119	19	2	0	34	38	36	.232	.285	.277	60	-27	37	10	5	.966	-8	*S-145	-1.2
1975	SD-N	116	344	37	75	12	2	0	19	26	25	.218	.277	.265	54	-22	20	4	4	.965	8	*S-111	0.0
1976	SD-N	113	340	31	87	13	3	1	24	32	16	.256	.320	.321	89	-5	12	7	-1	.964	4	*S-101	1.1
1977	SD-N	7	3	1	0	0	0	0	0	0	0	.000	.000	.000	-99	-1	0	0	0	1.000	0	/S-7	0.1
1978	LA-N	4	3	0	0	0	0	0	0	0	1	.000	.000	.000	-99	-1	0	0	0	.000	0	/S-2	-0.1
Total	8	714	2327	241	522	66	13	2	113	189	151	.224	.284	.266	59	-127	129	33	19	.964	-1	S-683/O-3	-3.0

■ JACKIE HERNANDEZ   Hernandez, Jacinto (Zulueta) b: 9/11/40, Central Tinguaro, Cuba   BR/TR, 6', 175 lbs. Deb: 9/14/65

1965	Cal-A	6	6	2	2	1	0	0	1	0	1	.333	.333	.500	137	0	1	0	0	1.000	-0	/S-2,3-1	0.0
1966	Cal-A	58	23	19	1	0	0	0	2	1	4	.043	.083	.043	-64	-5	1	1	-0	.857	13	3-11/2-8,SO	0.9
1967	Min-A	29	28	1	4	0	0	0	3	0	6	.143	.143	.143	-14	-4	0	0	0	.974	6	S-15,3-13	0.3
1968	Min-A	83	199	13	35	3	0	2	17	9	52	.176	.219	.221	32	-16	5	4	0	.927	9	S-79/1-1	-0.1
1969	KC-A	145	504	54	112	14	2	4	40	38	111	.222	.279	.282	57	-29	17	7	1	.954	-15	*S-144	-3.0
1970	KC-A	83	238	14	55	4	1	2	10	15	50	.231	.282	.282	56	-14	1	3	-2	.951	-5	S-77	-1.4
1971	*Pit-N	88	233	30	48	7	3	3	26	17	45	.206	.260	.300	59	-13	5	2	-1	.950	12	S-75/3-9	0.6
1972	Pit-N	72	176	12	33	7	1	1	14	9	43	.188	.227	.256	38	-15	4	3	-0	.929	17	S-68/3-4	0.9
1973	Pit-N	54	73	8	18	1	2	0	8	4	12	.247	.286	.315	68	-3	0	0	0	.940	17	S-49	1.6
Total	9	618	1480	153	308	37	9	12	121	93	324	.208	.258	.270	49	-99	25	15	-1	.945	53	S-517/3-38,201	-0.2

■ JOSE HERNANDEZ   Hernandez, Jose Antonio (Figueroa) b: 7/14/69, Rio Piedras, P.R.   BR/TR, 6'1", 180 lbs. Deb: 8/9/91

1991	Tex-A	45	98	8	18	2	1	0	4	3	31	.184	.208	.224	20	-11	0	1	-1	.975	9	S-44/3-1	0.0
1992	Cle-A	3	4	0	0	0	0	0	0	0	2	.000	.000	.000	-99	-1	0	0	0	.857	-0	/S-3	-0.1
1994	Chi-N	56	132	18	32	2	3	1	9	8	29	.242	.294	.326	62	-7	2	2	-1	.938	0	3-28,S-21/2O	-0.6
Total	3	104	234	26	50	4	4	1	13	11	62	.214	.252	.278	42	-19	2	3	-1	.972	9	/S-68,3-29,2O	-0.7

■ KEITH HERNANDEZ   Hernandez, Keith b: 10/20/53, San Francisco, Cal.   BL/TL, 6', 195 lbs. Deb: 8/30/74

1974	StL-N	14	34	3	10	1	2	0	2	7	8	.294	.415	.441	141	2	0	0	0	.973	-2	/1-9	0.0
1975	StL-N	64	188	20	47	8	2	3	20	17	26	.250	.312	.362	84	-4	0	1	-1	.996	3	1-56	-0.5
1976	StL-N	129	374	54	108	21	5	7	46	49	53	.289	.376	.428	126	14	4	2	0	.990	16	*1-110	2.4
1977	StL-N	161	560	90	163	41	4	15	91	79	88	.291	.380	.459	126	22	7	7	-2	.992	5	*1-158	1.5
1978	StL-N	159	542	90	138	32	4	11	64	82	68	.255	.355	.389	109	8	13	5	1	.994	9	*1-158	0.3
1979	StL-N★	161	610	**116**	210	**48**	11	11	105	80	78	**.344**	**.421**	.513	152	46	11	6	-0	.995	19	*1-160	5.6
1980	StL-N★	159	595	**111**	191	39	8	16	99	86	73	.321	**.410**	.494	147	40	14	8	-1	.995	5	*1-157	3.6
1981	StL-N	103	376	65	115	27	4	8	48	61	45	.306	.405	.463	142	23	12	5	1	.997	4	1-98/O-3	2.5
1982	*StL-N	160	579	79	173	33	6	7	94	100	67	.299	.404	.413	128	26	19	11	-1	.994	6	*1-158/O-4	2.4
1983	StL-N	55	218	34	62	15	4	3	26	24	30	.284	.355	.431	117	5	1	1	-0	.991	5	1-54	0.5
	NY-N	95	320	43	98	8	3	9	37	64	42	.306	.425	.434	140	21	8	4	0	.993	11	1-90	2.7
	Yr	150	538	77	160	23	7	12	63	88	72	.297	.398	.433	131	26	9	5	-0	.992	14	*1-144	3.2
1984	NY-N★	154	550	83	171	31	0	15	94	97	89	.311	.415	.449	145	37	2	3	-1	.994	18	*1-153	4.6
1985	NY-N	158	593	87	183	34	4	10	91	77	59	.309	.384	.430	132	28	3	3	-1	**.997**	16	*1-157	3.4
1986	*NY-N★	149	551	94	171	34	1	13	83	**94**	69	.310	.414	.446	141	35	2	1	0	**.996**	18	*1-149	4.4
1987	NY-N★	154	587	87	170	28	2	18	89	81	104	.290	.379	.436	122	20	0	2	-1	.993	18	*1-154	2.5
1988	*NY-N	95	348	43	96	16	0	11	55	31	57	.276	.337	.417	121	9	2	1	0	.998	8	1-93	1.0
1989	NY-N	75	215	18	50	8	0	4	19	27	39	.233	.324	.326	90	-2	0	3	-2	.991	-2	1-58	-1.1
1990	Cle-A	43	130	7	26	2	0	1	8	14	17	.200	.283	.238	47	-9	0	0	0	.994	-2	1-42	-1.4
Total	17	2088	7370	1124	2182	426	60	162	1071	1070	1012	.296	.388	.436	129	320	98	63	-8	.994	148	*1-2014/O-7	34.4

■ LEO HERNANDEZ   Hernandez, Leonardo Jesus b: 11/6/59, Santa Lucia, Venez.   BR/TR, 5'11", 170 lbs. Deb: 9/19/82

1982	Bal-A	2	2	0	0	0	0	0	0	0	2	.000	.000	.000	-99	-1	0	0	0	.000	0	/H	-0.1
1983	Bal-A	64	203	21	50	6	1	6	26	12	19	.246	.288	.374	82	-5	1	0	0	.922	-12	3-64	-1.8
1985	Bal-A	12	21	0	1	0	0	0	0	0	4	.048	.048	.048	-76	-5	0	0	0	1.000	-1	/1-1,O-1,D	-0.6
1986	NY-A	7	22	2	5	2	0	1	4	1	8	.227	.261	.455	91	-0	0	0	0	1.000	-1	/3-7,2-1	-0.1
Total	4	85	248	23	56	8	1	7	30	13	33	.226	.264	.351	69	-11	1	0	0	.927	-13	/3-71,D-8,201	-2.6

■ PEDRO HERNANDEZ   Hernandez, Pedro Julio (b: Pedro Julio Montas (Hernandez)) b: 4/4/59, LaRomana, D.R.   BR/TR, 6'1", 160 lbs. Deb: 9/8/79

1979	Tor-A	3	0	1	0	0	0	0	0	0	0	—	—	—	—	0	0	0	0	.000	0	/R	0.0
1982	Tor-A	8	9	1	0	0	0	0	0	0	3	.000	.000	.000	-92	-2	0	0	0	.000	-1	/3-2,O-1,D	-0.3
Total	2	11	9	2	0	0	0	0	0	0	3	.000	.000	.000	-92	-2	0	0	0	—	-1	/D-3,3-2,O	-0.3

■ TOBY HERNANDEZ   Hernandez, Rafael Tobias (Alvarado) b: 11/30/58, Calabozo, Venez.   BR/TR, 6'1", 160 lbs. Deb: 6/22/84

| 1984 | Tor-A | 3 | 2 | 1 | 1 | 0 | 0 | 0 | 0 | 0 | 0 | .500 | .500 | .500 | 171 | 0 | 0 | 0 | 0 | 1.000 | -1 | /C-3 | 0.0 |

■ RUDY HERNANDEZ   Hernandez, Rodolfo (Acosta) b: 10/18/51, Empalme, Mexico   BR/TR, 5'9", 150 lbs. Deb: 9/6/72

| 1972 | Chi-A | 8 | 21 | 0 | 4 | 0 | 0 | 0 | 1 | 0 | 3 | .190 | .190 | .190 | 13 | -2 | 0 | 0 | 0 | 1.000 | 1 | /S-6 | -0.1 |

■ CHICO HERNANDEZ   Hernandez, Salvador Jose (Ramos) b: 1/3/16, Havana, Cuba d: 1/3/86, Havana, Cuba   BR/TR, 6', 195 lbs. Deb: 4/16/42

1942	Chi-N	47	118	6	27	5	0	0	7	11	13	.229	.295	.271	69	-5	0			.975	-2	C-43	-0.4
1943	Chi-N	43	126	10	34	4	0	0	9	9	9	.270	.324	.302	82	-3	0			.981	-3	C-41	-0.3
Total	2	90	244	16	61	9	0	0	16	20	22	.250	.309	.287	76	-7	0			.978	-5	/C-84	-0.7

■ LARRY HERNDON   Herndon, Larry Darnell b: 11/3/53, Sunflower, Miss.   BR/TR, 6'3", 195 lbs. Deb: 9/4/74 C

1974	StL-N	12	1	3	1	0	0	0	0	0	0	1.000	1.000	1.000	465	0	0	0	0	1.000	-0	/O-1	0.0
1976	SF-N	115	337	42	97	11	3	2	23	23	45	.288	.337	.356	94	-2	12	10	-2	.967	-6	*O-110	-1.5
1977	SF-N	49	109	13	26	4	3	1	5	5	20	.239	.278	.358	69	-5	4	2	0	.957	-3	O-44	-0.9
1978	SF-N	151	471	52	122	15	9	1	32	35	71	.259	.312	.335	84	-11	13	8	-1	.974	4	*O-149	-1.4
1979	SF-N	132	354	35	91	14	5	7	36	29	70	.257	.315	.384	96	-3	8	6	-1	.963	-15	*O-122	-2.3
1980	SF-N	139	493	54	127	17	11	8	49	19	91	.258	.287	.385	88	-10	8	6	-2	.959	-4	*O-122	-2.3
1981	SF-N	96	364	48	105	15	8	5	41	20	55	.288	.327	.415	111	4	15	6	1	.977	5	O-93	0.8

YEAR	TM/L	G	AB	R	H	2B	3B	HR	RBI	BB	SO	AVG	OBP	SLG	PRO+	BR/A	SB	CS	SBR	FA	FR	G/POS	TPR
1982	Det-A	157	614	92	179	21	13	23	88	38	92	.292	.334	.480	120	15	12	9	-2	.983	6	*O-155/D-3	1.5
1983	Det-A	153	603	88	182	28	9	20	92	46	95	.302	.354	.478	130	23	9	3	1	.951	1	*O-133,D-19	2.0
1984	*Det-A	125	407	52	114	18	5	7	43	32	63	.280	.336	.400	103	2	6	2	1	.986	-5	*O-117/D-4	-0.5
1985	Det-A	137	442	45	108	12	7	12	37	33	79	.244	.298	.385	86	-9	2	1	0	.976	5	*O-136	-0.8
1986	Det-A	106	283	33	70	13	1	8	37	27	40	.247	.315	.385	90	-4	2	1	0	.988	-1	O-83,D-18	-0.8
1987	*Det-A	89	225	32	73	13	2	9	47	23	35	.324	.387	.520	144	14	1	0	0	.989	-4	O-57,D-23	0.8
1988	Det-A	76	174	16	39	5	0	4	20	23	37	.224	.318	.322	83	-4	0	1	0	1.000	-6	D-53,O-15	-0.8
Total	14	1537	4877	605	1334	186	76	107	550	353	793	.274	.325	.409	103	11	92	57	-7	.972	-19	*O-1337,D-120	-6.2

■ TOM HERNON
Hernon, Thomas H.   b: 11/4/1866, E.Bridgewater, Mass   d: 2/4/02, New Bedford, Mass.   BR/TR,   Deb: 9/13/1897

YEAR	TM/L	G	AB	R	H	2B	3B	HR	RBI	BB	SO	AVG	OBP	SLG	PRO+	BR/A	SB	CS	SBR	FA	FR	G/POS	TPR
1897	Chi-N	4	16	2	1	0	0	0	2	0		.063	.063	.063	-65	-4	1			1.000	0	/O-4	-0.4

■ ED HERR
Herr, Edward Joseph   b: 5/18/1862, St.Louis, Mo.   d: 7/18/43, St.Louis, Mo.   BR/TR, 5'9.5", 179 lbs.   Deb: 4/16/1887

YEAR	TM/L	G	AB	R	H	2B	3B	HR	RBI	BB	SO	AVG	OBP	SLG	PRO+	BR/A	SB	CS	SBR	FA	FR	G/POS	TPR
1887	Cle-a	11	44	6	12	2	0	0		6		.273	.360	.318	93	-0	2			.729	-3	3-11	-0.2
1888	*StL-a	43	172	21	46	7	1	3	43	11		.267	.323	.372	110	1	9			.872	-9	S-28,O-11/3	-0.7
1890	StL-a	12	41	5	9	2	1	0		5		.220	.347	.317	84	-1	2			.793	-7	/2-7,O-4,3	-0.7
Total	3	66	257	32	67	11	2	3	43	22		.261	.333	.354	102	-0	13			.762	-18	/S-28,3-16,O2	-1.6

■ TOM HERR
Herr, Thomas Mitchell   b: 4/4/56, Lancaster, Pa.   BB/TR, 6', 185 lbs.   Deb: 8/13/79

YEAR	TM/L	G	AB	R	H	2B	3B	HR	RBI	BB	SO	AVG	OBP	SLG	PRO+	BR/A	SB	CS	SBR	FA	FR	G/POS	TPR
1979	StL-N	14	10	4	2	0	0	0	1	2	2	.200	.333	.200	49	-1	1	0	0	1.000	6	/2-6	0.5
1980	StL-N	76	222	29	55	12	5	0	15	16	21	.248	.301	.347	78	-7	9	2	2	.984	2	2-58,S-14	0.1
1981	StL-N	103	411	50	110	14	9	0	46	39	30	.268	.333	.345	90	-5	23	7	3	**.992**	4	*2-103	0.9
1982	*StL-N	135	493	83	131	19	4	0	36	57	56	.266	.344	.320	86	-7	25	12	0	.987	2	*2-128	0.3
1983	StL-N	89	313	43	101	14	4	2	31	43	27	.323	.406	.412	127	13	6	8	-3	.986	-19	2-86	-0.4
1984	StL-N	145	558	67	154	23	2	4	49	49	56	.276	.337	.346	94	-3	13	7	-0	.992	-1	*2-144	0.1
1985	*StL-N★	159	596	97	180	38	3	8	110	80	55	.302	.386	.416	126	23	31	3	8	.985	-31	*2-158	0.6
1986	StL-N	152	559	48	141	30	4	2	61	73	75	.252	.344	.331	88	-7	22	8	2	.988	-22	*2-152	-2.2
1987	*StL-N	141	510	73	134	29	0	2	83	68	62	.263	.353	.331	81	-12	19	4	3	.989	-17	*2-137	-1.9
1988	StL-N	15	50	4	13	0	0	1	3	11	4	.260	.393	.320	106	1	3	0	1	.984	-6	2-15	-0.4
	Min-A	86	304	42	80	16	0	1	21	40	47	.263	.349	.326	88	-4	10	3	1	.988	-8	2-73/S-2,D	-0.8
1989	Phi-N	151	561	65	161	25	6	2	37	54	63	.287	.353	.364	105	5	10	7	-1	.990	2	*2-144	1.1
1990	Phi-N	119	447	39	118	21	3	4	50	36	47	.264	.322	.351	85	-9	7	1	2	.991	-3	*2-114	-0.8
	NY-N	27	100	9	25	5	0	1	10	14	11	.250	.342	.330	86	-2	0	0	0	.979	-5	2-26	-0.6
	Yr	146	547	48	143	26	3	5	60	50	58	.261	.326	.347	85	-10	7	1	2	.989	-8	*2-140	-1.4
1991	NY-N	70	155	17	30	7	0	1	14	32	21	.194	.332	.258	68	-5	7	2	1	1.000	7	2-57/O-1	0.3
	SF-N	32	60	6	15	1	1	0	7	13	7	.250	.384	.300	98	1	2	0	1	1.000	-6	2-15/3-3	-0.2
	Yr	102	215	23	45	8	1	1	21	45	28	.209	.346	.270	77	-5	9	2	2	1.000	1	2-72/3-3,O	-0.2
Total	13	1514	5349	676	1450	254	41	28	574	627	584	.271	.350	.350	95	-18	188	64	18	.989	-94	*2-1416/S-16,3DO	-3.7

■ JOSE HERRERA
Herrera, Jose Concepcion (Ontiveros) "Loco"   b: 4/8/42, San Lorenzo, Venez.   BR/TR, 5'8", 165 lbs.   Deb: 6/3/67

YEAR	TM/L	G	AB	R	H	2B	3B	HR	RBI	BB	SO	AVG	OBP	SLG	PRO+	BR/A	SB	CS	SBR	FA	FR	G/POS	TPR
1967	Hou-N	5	4	0	1	0	0	0	1	0	1	.250	.250	.250	45	-0	0	0	0	.000	0	H	0.0
1968	Hou-N	27	100	9	24	5	0	0	7	4	12	.240	.269	.290	69	-4	0	2	-1	.958	-2	O-17/2-7	-0.9
1969	Mon-N	47	126	7	36	5	0	2	12	3	14	.286	.302	.373	88	-2	1	2	-1	.980	-2	O-31/2-2,3	-0.7
1970	Mon-N	1	1	0	0	0	0	0	0	0	1	.000	.000	.000	-99	-0	0	0	0	.000	0	H	0.0
Total	4	80	231	16	61	10	0	2	20	7	28	.264	.286	.333	79	-7	1	4	-2	.973	-4	/O-48,2-9,3	-1.6

■ PANCHO HERRERA
Herrera, Juan Francisco (Willavicencio)   b: 6/16/34, Santiago, Cuba   BR/TR, 6'3", 220 lbs.   Deb: 4/15/58

YEAR	TM/L	G	AB	R	H	2B	3B	HR	RBI	BB	SO	AVG	OBP	SLG	PRO+	BR/A	SB	CS	SBR	FA	FR	G/POS	TPR
1958	Phi-N	29	63	5	17	3	0	1	6	7	15	.270	.352	.365	92	-1	1	2	-1	.980	2	3-16,1-11	0.0
1960	Phi-N	145	512	61	144	26	6	17	71	51	136	.281	.352	.455	119	13	2	3	-1	.988	10	*1-134,2-17	1.4
1961	Phi-N	126	400	56	103	17	2	13	51	55	120	.257	.353	.408	102	2	5	1	1	.993	6	*1-115	0.0
Total	3	300	975	122	264	46	8	31	128	113	271	.271	.352	.430	110	15	8	6	-1	.990	18	1-260/2-17,3	1.4

■ MIKE HERRERA
Herrera, Ramon   b: 12/19/1897, Havana, Cuba   d: 2/3/78, Havana, Cuba   BR/TR, 5'6", 147 lbs.   Deb: 9/22/25

YEAR	TM/L	G	AB	R	H	2B	3B	HR	RBI	BB	SO	AVG	OBP	SLG	PRO+	BR/A	SB	CS	SBR	FA	FR	G/POS	TPR
1925	Bos-A	10	39	2	15	0	0	0	8	2	2	.385	.415	.385	104	0	1	0	0	.958	3	2-10	0.4
1926	Bos-A	74	237	20	61	14	1	0	19	15	13	.257	.304	.325	66	-12	0	5	-3	.962	5	2-48,3-16/S	-0.8
Total	2	84	276	22	76	14	1	0	27	17	15	.275	.320	.333	72	-12	1	5	-3	.961	8	/2-58,3-16,S	-0.4

■ LEFTY HERRING
Herring, Silas Clarke   b: 3/4/1880, Philadelphia, Pa.   d: 2/11/65, Massapequa, N.Y.   BL/TL, 5'11", 160 lbs.   Deb: 5/16/1899

YEAR	TM/L	G	AB	R	H	2B	3B	HR	RBI	BB	SO	AVG	OBP	SLG	PRO+	BR/A	SB	CS	SBR	FA	FR	G/POS	TPR
1899	Was-N	2	1	1	1	0	0	0		1		1.000	1.000	1.000	454	1	0			1.000	0	/P-2	0.0
1904	Was-A	15	46	3	8	1	0	0	2	7		.174	.283	.196	54	-2	0			.991	1	1-10/O-5	-0.2
Total	2	17	47	4	9	1	0	0	2	8		.191	.309	.213	67	-1	0			.991	1	/1-10,O-5,P	-0.2

■ ED HERRMANN
Herrmann, Edward Martin   b: 8/27/46, San Diego, Cal.   BL/TR, 6'1", 210 lbs.   Deb: 9/1/67   F

YEAR	TM/L	G	AB	R	H	2B	3B	HR	RBI	BB	SO	AVG	OBP	SLG	PRO+	BR/A	SB	CS	SBR	FA	FR	G/POS	TPR
1967	Chi-A	2	3	1	2	1	0	0	1	0	0	.667	.750	1.000	429	1	0	0	0	1.000	1	/C-2	0.3
1969	Chi-A	102	290	31	67	8	0	8	31	30	35	.231	.307	.341	81	-7	0	2	-1	.983	-8	C-92	-0.7
1970	Chi-A	96	297	42	84	9	0	19	52	31	41	.283	.356	.505	130	12	0	1	-1	.988	5	C-88	2.0
1971	Chi-A	101	294	32	63	6	0	11	35	44	48	.214	.321	.347	86	-5	2	0	1	.995	9	C-97	0.9
1972	Chi-A	116	354	23	88	9	0	10	40	43	37	.249	.337	.359	105	3	0	0	0	.989	0	*C-112	0.9
1973	Chi-A	119	379	42	85	17	1	10	39	31	55	.224	.295	.354	79	-11	2	4	-2	.984	5	*C-114/D-2	-0.3
1974	Chi-A†	107	367	32	95	13	1	10	39	16	49	.259	.290	.381	90	-6	0	0	0	.987	3	*C-107	0.2
1975	NY-A	80	200	16	51	9	2	6	30	16	23	.255	.310	.410	105	2	0	0	0	.979	7	D-35,C-24	0.8
1976	Cal-A	29	46	5	8	3	0	2	8	7	8	.174	.283	.370	96	-0	0	0	0	.954	-6	C-27	-0.6
	Hou-N	79	265	14	54	8	0	3	25	22	40	.204	.275	.268	60	-14	0	0	0	.987	0	C-79	-1.3
1977	Hou-N	56	158	7	46	7	0	1	17	15	18	.291	.356	.354	100	0	1	1	-0	.990	9	C-49	1.0
1978	Hou-N	16	36	1	4	1	0	0	3	0	3	.111	.179	.139	-11	-5	0	0	0	1.000	-1	C-14	-0.6
	Mon-N	19	40	1	7	1	0	0	3	4	7	.175	.195	.200	11	-5	0	0	0	.977	-1	C-12	-0.6
	Yr	35	76	2	11	2	0	0	6	4	7	.145	.188	.171	1	-10	0	0	0	.991	-2	C-26	-1.2
Total	11	922	2729	247	654	92	4	80	320	260	361	.240	.312	.364	91	-37	6	8	-3	.987	29	C-817/D-37	2.0

■ RICK HERRSCHER
Herrscher, Richard Franklin   b: 11/3/36, St.Louis, Mo.   BR/TR, 6'2.5", 187 lbs.   Deb: 8/1/62

YEAR	TM/L	G	AB	R	H	2B	3B	HR	RBI	BB	SO	AVG	OBP	SLG	PRO+	BR/A	SB	CS	SBR	FA	FR	G/POS	TPR
1962	NY-N	35	50	5	11	3	0	1	6	5	11	.220	.291	.340	68	-2	0	0	0	1.000	2	1-10/3-6,OS	0.0

■ JOHN HERRNSTEIN
Herrnstein, John Ellett   b: 3/31/38, Hampton, Va.   BL/TL, 6'3", 215 lbs.   Deb: 9/15/62

YEAR	TM/L	G	AB	R	H	2B	3B	HR	RBI	BB	SO	AVG	OBP	SLG	PRO+	BR/A	SB	CS	SBR	FA	FR	G/POS	TPR
1962	Phi-N	6	5	0	1	0	0	0	1	1	3	.200	.333	.200	48	-0	0	0	0	.000	-0	/O-1	-0.1
1963	Phi-N	15	12	1	2	0	0	1	1	1	5	.167	.231	.417	83	-0	0	0	0	1.000	-1	/O-2,1-1	-0.1
1964	Phi-N	125	303	38	71	12	4	6	25	22	67	.234	.291	.360	83	-7	1	4	-0	.977	-20	O-69,1-68	-3.4
1965	Phi-N	63	85	8	17	2	0	1	5	2	18	.200	.227	.259	37	-7	0	0	0	.984	-3	1-18,O-14	-1.1
1966	Phi-N	4	10	0	1	0	0	0	1	0	3	.100	.100	.100	-44	-2	0	0	0	1.000	-0	/O-2	-0.2
	Chi-N	9	17	3	3	0	0	0	0	3	8	.176	.300	.176	36	-1	0	0	0	.975	-1	/1-4,O-1	-0.3
	Atl-N	17	18	2	4	0	0	0	1	0	7	.222	.222	.222	24	-2	0	0	0	1.000	-1	/O-5	-0.3
	Yr	30	45	5	8	0	0	0	2	3	22	.178	.229	.178	15	-5	0	0	0	1.000	-2	/O-8,1-4	-0.8
Total	5	239	450	52	99	14	4	8	34	29	115	.220	.272	.342	67	-20	1	4	-0	.983	-26	/O-94,1-91	-5.5

■ EARL HERSH
Hersh, Earl Walter   b: 5/21/32, Ebbvale, Md.   BL/TL, 6', 205 lbs.   Deb: 9/4/56

YEAR	TM/L	G	AB	R	H	2B	3B	HR	RBI	BB	SO	AVG	OBP	SLG	PRO+	BR/A	SB	CS	SBR	FA	FR	G/POS	TPR
1956	Mil-N	7	13	0	3	3	0	0	0	0	5	.231	.231	.462	85	-0	0	0	0	.000	-1	/O-2	-0.2

YEAR	TM/L	G	AB	R	H	2B	3B	HR	RBI	BB	SO	AVG	OBP	SLG	PRO+	BR/A	SB	CS	SBR	FA	FR	G/POS	TPR

■ MIKE HERSHBERGER
Hershberger, Norman Michael b: 10/9/39, Massillon, Ohio BR/TR, 5'10", 175 lbs. Deb: 9/5/61

YEAR	TM/L	G	AB	R	H	2B	3B	HR	RBI	BB	SO	AVG	OBP	SLG	PRO+	BR/A	SB	CS	SBR	FA	FR	G/POS	TPR
1961	Chi-A	15	55	9	17	3	0	0	5	2	2	.309	.333	.364	88	-1	1	1	-0	1.000	2	O-13	-0.1
1962	Chi-A	148	427	54	112	14	2	4	46	37	36	.262	.325	.333	78	-13	10	6	-1	.984	-7	*O-135	-2.7
1963	Chi-A	135	476	64	133	26	2	3	45	39	39	.279	.339	.361	98	-1	9	3	1	.976	-5	*O-119	-1.2
1964	Chi-A	141	452	55	104	15	3	2	31	48	47	.230	.310	.290	70	-18	8	6	-1	.984	-8	*O-134	-3.4
1965	KC-A	150	494	43	114	15	5	5	48	37	42	.231	.291	.312	72	-18	7	3	0	.988	4	*O-144	-2.1
1966	KC-A	146	538	55	136	27	7	2	57	47	37	.253	.316	.340	92	-6	13	5	1	.977	12	*O-143	0.1
1967	KC-A	142	480	55	122	25	1	1	49	38	40	.254	.318	.317	91	-5	10	3	1	.982	7	*O-130	-0.3
1968	Oak-A	99	246	23	67	9	2	5	32	21	22	.272	.332	.386	123	6	8	3	1	.978	-7	O-90	-0.4
1969	Oak-A	51	129	11	26	2	0	1	10	10	15	.202	.259	.240	42	-10	1	2	-1	.980	-5	O-35	-1.9
1970	Mil-A	49	98	7	23	5	0	1	6	10	8	.235	.306	.316	71	-4	1	2	-1	.946	-6	O-35	-1.2
1971	Chi-A	74	177	22	46	9	0	2	15	30	23	.260	.379	.345	103	2	6	2	1	.960	-8	O-59	-0.9
Total	11	1150	3572	398	900	150	22	26	344	319	311	.252	.319	.328	85	-66	74	36	1	.980	-21	*O-1037	-14.1

■ WILLARD HERSHBERGER
Hershberger, Willard McKee "Bill" b: 5/28/10, Lemoncove, Cal. d: 8/3/40, Boston, Mass. BR/TR, 5'10.5", 167 lbs. Deb: 4/19/38

YEAR	TM/L	G	AB	R	H	2B	3B	HR	RBI	BB	SO	AVG	OBP	SLG	PRO+	BR/A	SB	CS	SBR	FA	FR	G/POS	TPR
1938	Cin-N	49	105	12	29	3	1	0	12	5	6	.276	.315	.324	78	-3	1			.960	-2	C-39/2-1	-0.2
1939	*Cin-N	63	174	23	60	9	2	0	32	9	4	.345	.384	.420	115	4	1			.987	-2	C-60	0.5
1940	Cin-N	48	123	6	38	4	2	0	26	6	6	.309	.351	.374	99	-0	0			.985	-2	C-37	0.0
Total	3	160	402	41	127	16	5	0	70	20	16	.316	.356	.381	101	1	2			.980	-5	C-136/2-1	0.3

■ NEAL HERTWECK
Hertweck, Neal Charles b: 11/22/31, St.Louis, Mo. BL/TL, 6'1.5", 175 lbs. Deb: 9/27/52

YEAR	TM/L	G	AB	R	H	2B	3B	HR	RBI	BB	SO	AVG	OBP	SLG	PRO+	BR/A	SB	CS	SBR	FA	FR	G/POS	TPR
1952	StL-N	2	6	0	0	0	0	0	0	1	1	.000	.143	.000	-57	-1	0	0	0	1.000	-0	/1-2	-0.2

■ STEVE HERTZ
Hertz, Stephen Allan b: 2/26/45, Fairfield, Ohio BR/TR, 6'1", 195 lbs. Deb: 4/21/64

YEAR	TM/L	G	AB	R	H	2B	3B	HR	RBI	BB	SO	AVG	OBP	SLG	PRO+	BR/A	SB	CS	SBR	FA	FR	G/POS	TPR
1964	Hou-N	5	4	2	0	0	0	0	0	0	3	.000	.000	.000	-99	-1	0	0	0	1.000	0	/3-2	-0.1

■ BUCK HERZOG
Herzog, Charles Lincoln b: 7/9/1885, Baltimore, Md. d: 9/4/53, Baltimore, Md. BR/TR, 5'11", 160 lbs. Deb: 4/17/08 M

YEAR	TM/L	G	AB	R	H	2B	3B	HR	RBI	BB	SO	AVG	OBP	SLG	PRO+	BR/A	SB	CS	SBR	FA	FR	G/POS	TPR
1908	NY-N	64	160	38	48	6	2	0	11	36		.300	.448	.363	152	13	16			.921	1	2-42,S-12/3O	1.6
1909	NY-N	42	130	16	24	2	0	0	8	13		.185	.264	.200	43	-8	2			.914	-2	O-29/2-6,3S	-1.3
1910	Bos-N	106	380	51	95	20	3	3	32	30	34	.250	.329	.342	92	-4	13			.915	4	*3-105	0.3
1911	Bos-N	79	294	53	91	19	5	5	41	33	33	.310	.398	.459	129	11	26			.934	8	S-74/3-4	2.4
	*NY-N	69	247	37	66	14	4	1	26	14	19	.267	.325	.368	91	-4	22			.926	10	3-65/2-3,S	0.7
	Yr	148	541	90	157	33	9	6	67	47	40	.290	.365	.418	112	8	48			.935	18	S-75,3-69/2	3.1
1912	*NY-N	140	482	72	127	20	9	2	47	57	39	.263	.350	.355	90	-6	37			.942	19	*3-140	1.4
1913	*NY-N	96	290	46	83	15	3	3	31	22	12	.286	.349	.390	110	3	23			.947	1	3-84/2-2	0.6
1914	Cin-N	138	498	54	140	14	8	1	40	42	27	.281	.348	.347	104	3	46			.939	31	*S-137/1-2M	4.8
1915	Cin-N	155	579	61	153	14	10	1	42	34	21	.264	.314	.328	93	-5	35	16	1	.945	31	*S-153/1-2M	4.8
1916	Cin-N	79	281	30	75	14	2	1	24	21	12	.267	.329	.342	109	0	15	12	-3	.931	-2	S-65,3-12/OM	0.5
	NY-N	77	280	40	73	10	4	0	25	22	24	.261	.326	.325	106	2	19	16	-4	.978	14	2-44,3-27/S	2.1
	Yr	156	561	70	148	24	6	1	49	43	36	.264	.327	.333	107	5	34	28	-7	.926	12	S-74,2-44,3/O	2.6
1917	*NY-N	114	417	69	98	10	8	2	31	31	36	.235	.308	.312	93	-3	12			.948	-9	*2-113	-0.6
1918	Bos-N	118	473	57	108	12	6	0	26	29	28	.228	.280	.279	74	-15	10			.961	4	2-99,1-12/S	-0.6
1919	Bos-N	73	275	27	77	8	5	1	25	13	11	.280	.327	.356	110	3	16			.953	-14	2-70/1-1	-0.9
	Chi-N	52	193	15	53	4	4	0	17	10	7	.275	.336	.337	102	1	12			.987	-11	2-52	-0.8
	Yr	125	468	42	130	12	9	1	42	23	18	.278	.331	.348	106	4	28			.967	-25	*2-122/1-1	-1.7
1920	Chi-N	91	305	39	59	9	2	0	19	20	21	.193	.261	.236	43	-22	8	9	-3	.938	-6	2-59,3-28/1	-3.0
Total	13	1493	5284	705	1370	191	75	20	445	427	<u>307</u>	.259	.329	.335	96	-27	312	<u>53</u>		.954	77	2-490,3-473,S/O1	11.4

■ WHITEY HERZOG
Herzog, Dorrel Norman Elvert b: 11/9/31, New Athens, Ill. BL/TL, 5'11", 182 lbs. Deb: 4/17/56 MC

YEAR	TM/L	G	AB	R	H	2B	3B	HR	RBI	BB	SO	AVG	OBP	SLG	PRO+	BR/A	SB	CS	SBR	FA	FR	G/POS	TPR
1956	Was-A	117	421	49	103	13	7	4	35	35	74	.245	.303	.337	69	-20	8	5	-1	.980	1	*O-103/1-5	-2.4
1957	Was-A	36	78	7	13	3	0	0	4	13	12	.167	.301	.205	41	-6	1	2	-1	.981	-3	O-28	-1.2
1958	Was-A	8	5	0	0	0	0	0	0	1	5	.000	.167	.000	-51	-1	0	0	0	1.000	-2	/O-7	-0.3
	KC-A	88	96	11	23	1	2	0	9	16	21	.240	.348	.292	77	-2	0	3	-2	.968	-10	O-37,1-22	-1.6
	Yr	96	101	11	23	1	2	0	9	17	26	.228	.339	.277	71	-3	0	3	-2	.972	-12	O-44,1-22	-1.9
1959	KC-A	38	123	25	36	7	1	1	9	34	23	.293	.446	.390	129	7	1	0	0	.963	2	O-34/1-1	0.8
1960	KC-A	83	252	43	67	10	2	8	38	40	32	.266	.366	.417	111	4	0	1	-1	.985	1	O-69/1-2	0.1
1961	Bal-A	113	323	39	94	11	6	5	35	50	41	.291	.388	.409	117	9	1	4	-2	1.000	-11	O-98	-0.8
1962	Bal-A	99	263	34	70	8	1	7	35	41	36	.266	.371	.403	116	7	2	3	-1	.978	0	O-70	-0.5
1963	Det-A	52	53	5	8	2	1	0	7	11	17	.151	.308	.226	51	-3	0	0	0	.976	-2	/1-7,O-4	-0.5
Total	8	634	1614	213	414	60	20	25	172	241	261	.257	.356	.365	96	-4	13	18	-7	.982	-23	O-450/1-37	-5.7

■ OTTO HESS
Hess, Otto C. b: 10/10/1878, Bern, Switzerland d: 2/25/26, Tucson, Ariz. BL/TL, 6'1", 170 lbs. Deb: 8/3/02

YEAR	TM/L	G	AB	R	H	2B	3B	HR	RBI	BB	SO	AVG	OBP	SLG	PRO+	BR/A	SB	CS	SBR	FA	FR	G/POS	TPR
1902	Cle-A	7	14	2	1	0	0	0	1		2	.071	.188	.071	-27	-2	0			.870	1	/P-7	0.0
1904	Cle-A	34	100	4	12	2	1	0	5	3		.120	.146	.160	-3	-12	0			.951	-4	P-21,O-12	-0.5
1905	Cle-A	54	173	15	44	8	1	2	13	7		.254	.291	.347	101	-0	2			.950	3	O-28,P-26	0.1
1906	Cle-A	53	154	13	31	5	2	0	11	2		.201	.212	.260	48	-10	1			.949	-3	P-43/O-5	-0.2
1907	Cle-A	19	30	4	4	0	0	0	0	1		.133	.278	.133	30	-2	1			.941	-1	P-17/O-2	-0.1
1908	Cle-A	9	14	0	0	0	0	0	0	1		.000	.067	.000	-78	-3	0			1.000	-0	/P-4,O-4	-0.4
1912	Bos-N	33	94	10	23	4	4	0	10	0	26	.245	.245	.372	66	-5	0			.951	-4	P-33	0.0
1913	Bos-N	35	83	9	26	0	1	2	11	7	15	.313	.367	.410	119	2	0			.945	1	P-29	0.0
1914	Bos-N	31	47	5	11	1	0	1	6	1	11	.234	.250	.319	69	-2	0			.947	-4	P-14/1-5	-0.1
1915	Bos-N	5	5	1	2	1	0	0	1	0	2	.400	.400	.600	210	1	0			.800	-0	/P-4,1-1	0.0
Total	10	280	714	63	154	21	9	5	58	27	<u>54</u>	.216	.248	.291	64	-33	4			.941	-3	P-198/O-51,1	-1.2

■ TOM HESS
Hess, Thomas (b: Thomas Heslin) b: 8/15/1875, Brooklyn, N.Y. d: 12/15/45, Albany, N.Y. Deb: 6/6/1892

YEAR	TM/L	G	AB	R	H	2B	3B	HR	RBI	BB	SO	AVG	OBP	SLG	PRO+	BR/A	SB	CS	SBR	FA	FR	G/POS	TPR
1892	Bal-N	1	2	0	0	0	0	0	0	0	0	.000	.000	.000	-97	-0	0			.000	0	/C-1	0.0

■ GUS HETLING
Hetling, August Julius b: 11/21/1885, St.Louis, Mo. d: 10/13/62, Wichita, Kan. BR/TR, 5'10", 165 lbs. Deb: 10/6/06

YEAR	TM/L	G	AB	R	H	2B	3B	HR	RBI	BB	SO	AVG	OBP	SLG	PRO+	BR/A	SB	CS	SBR	FA	FR	G/POS	TPR
1906	Det-A	2	7	0	1	0	0	0	0		0	.143	.143	.143	-10	-1	0			1.000	-0	/3-2	-0.1

■ GEORGE HEUBEL
Heubel, George A. b: 1849, Paterson, N.J. d: 1/22/1896, Philadelphia, Pa. 5'11.5", 178 lbs. Deb: 5/20/1871 U

YEAR	TM/L	G	AB	R	H	2B	3B	HR	RBI	BB	SO	AVG	OBP	SLG	PRO+	BR/A	SB	CS	SBR	FA	FR	G/POS	TPR
1871	Ath-n	17	75	18	23	4	2	0	13	2	0	.307	.325	.413	111	1	1					O-16/1-1	0.1
1872	Oly-n	5	23	2	3	1	0	0	1	0	0	.130	.130	.174	-8	-3						/O-5	-0.2
1876	NY-N	1	4	0	0	0	0	0	0	0	0	.000	.000	.000	-99	-1				.750	-0	/1-1	-0.1
Total	2 n	22	98	20	26	5	2	0	<u>14</u>	2		.265	.280	.357	86	-2						/O-21,1-1	-0.1

■ JOHNNIE HEVING
Heving, John Aloysius b: 4/29/1896, Covington, Ky. d: 12/24/68, Salisbury, N.C. BR/TR, 6', 175 lbs. Deb: 9/24/20 F

YEAR	TM/L	G	AB	R	H	2B	3B	HR	RBI	BB	SO	AVG	OBP	SLG	PRO+	BR/A	SB	CS	SBR	FA	FR	G/POS	TPR
1920	StL-A	1	1	0	0	0	0	0	0	0	0	.000	.000	.000	-97	-0	0	0	0	.000	0	H	0.0
1924	Bos-A	45	109	15	31	5	1	0	11	10	7	.284	.345	.349	79	-3	0	0	0	.969	4	C-29	0.2
1925	Bos-A	45	119	14	20	7	0	0	6	12	7	.168	.244	.227	20	-15	0	1	-1	.958	3	C-34	-1.0
1928	Bos-A	82	158	11	41	7	2	0	11	11	10	.259	.308	.329	69	-7	1	1	-0	.967	-4	C-62	-0.7
1929	Bos-A	76	188	26	60	4	3	0	23	8	7	.319	.354	.372	88	-3	1	2	-1	.988	5	C-55	0.6
1930	Bos-A	75	220	15	61	5	3	0	17	11	14	.277	.312	.327	65	-12	2	0		.987	-4	C-71	-0.9
1931	*Phi-A	42	113	8	27	3	2	1	12	6	8	.239	.277	.327	55	-8	0	0	0	.993	2	C-40	-0.3

YEAR	TM/L	G	AB	R	H	2B	3B	HR	RBI	BB	SO	AVG	OBP	SLG	PRO+	BR/A	SB	CS	SBR	FA	FR	G/POS	TPR
1932	Phi-A	33	77	14	21	6	1	0	10	7	6	.273	.333	.377	81	-2	0	0	0	1.000	-1	C-28	-0.2
Total	8	399	985	103	261	37	12	1	90	65	59	.265	.312	.330	66	-50	4	4	-1	.981	4	C-319	-2.3

■ MIKE HEYDON
Heydon, Michael Edward "Ed"   b: 7/15/1874, Missouri   d: 10/13/13, Indianapolis, Ind.   BL/TR, 6',   Deb: 10/12/1898

YEAR	TM/L	G	AB	R	H	2B	3B	HR	RBI	BB	SO	AVG	OBP	SLG	PRO+	BR/A	SB	CS	SBR	FA	FR	G/POS	TPR
1898	Bal-N	3	9	2	1	0	0	0	1	2		.111	.333	.111	28	-1	0			.917	-1	/C-3	-0.1
1899	Was-N	3	3	0	0	0	0	0	0	2		.000	.000	.000	14	-0	0			.833	-1	/C-2	0.0
1901	StL-N	16	43	2	9	1	1	1	6	5		.209	.292	.349	90	-1	2			.941	-3	C-13/O-1	-0.2
1904	Chi-A	4	10	0	1	1	0	0	1	1		.100	.250	.200	45	-1	0			1.000	1	/C-4	0.1
1905	Was-A	77	245	20	47	7	4	1	26	21		.192	.261	.265	70	-8	5			.955	11	C-77	1.2
1906	Was-A	49	145	14	23	7	1	0	10	14		.159	.237	.221	46	-9	2			.937	-2	C-49	-0.7
1907	Was-A	62	164	14	30	3	0	0	9	25		.183	.302	.201	66	-5	3			.961	-8	C-57	-0.9
Total	7	214	619	52	111	19	6	2	53	70		.179	.271	.239	64	-24	12			.952	-0	C-205/O-1	-0.6

■ JACK HIATT
Hiatt, Jack E   b: 7/27/42, Bakersfield, Cal.   BR/TR, 6'2", 190 lbs.   Deb: 9/7/64   C

YEAR	TM/L	G	AB	R	H	2B	3B	HR	RBI	BB	SO	AVG	OBP	SLG	PRO+	BR/A	SB	CS	SBR	FA	FR	G/POS	TPR
1964	LA-A	9	16	2	6	0	0	0	2	2	3	.375	.444	.375	145	1	0	0	0	.889	-1	/C-3,1-2	0.0
1965	SF-N	40	67	5	19	4	0	1	7	12	14	.284	.392	.388	118	2	0	0	0	.987	-2	C-21/1-7	0.0
1966	SF-N	18	23	2	7	2	0	0	1	4	5	.304	.407	.391	120	1	0	0	0	.982	1	/1-7	0.2
1967	SF-N	73	153	24	42	6	0	6	26	27	37	.275	.387	.431	136	8	0	0	0	.990	-3	1-36/C-3,O	0.4
1968	SF-N	90	224	14	52	10	2	4	34	41	61	.232	.353	.348	111	5	0	0	0	.994	-1	C-58,1-10	0.8
1969	SF-N	69	194	18	38	4	0	7	34	48	58	.196	.355	.325	93	0	0	0	0	.992	0	C-60/1-3	0.3
1970	Mon-N	17	43	4	14	2	0	0	7	14	14	.326	.491	.372	135	3	0	0	0	.961	-4	C-12/1-2	0.1
	Chi-N	66	178	19	43	12	1	2	22	31	48	.242	.354	.354	81	-5	0	0	0	.990	5	C-63/1-2	0.3
	Yr	83	221	23	57	14	1	2	29	45	62	.258	.383	.357	91	-1	0	0	0	.986	2	C-75/1-4	0.4
1971	Hou-N	69	174	16	48	8	1	1	16	35	39	.276	.403	.351	118	6	0	1	-1	.991	-1	C-65/1-1	0.7
1972	Hou-N	10	25	2	5	3	0	0	0	5	5	.200	.333	.320	88	-0	0	0	0	1.000	-3	C-10	-0.3
	Cal-A	22	45	4	13	0	1	1	5	5	11	.289	.360	.400	133	2	0	0	0	1.000	-8	C-17	-0.7
Total	9	483	1142	110	287	51	5	22	154	224	295	.251	.350	.363	109	24	0	1	-1	.990	-16	C-312/1-70,O	1.8

■ PHIL HIATT
Hiatt, Philip Farrell   b: 5/1/69, Pensacola, Fla.   BR/TR, 6'3", 200 lbs.   Deb: 4/7/93

YEAR	TM/L	G	AB	R	H	2B	3B	HR	RBI	BB	SO	AVG	OBP	SLG	PRO+	BR/A	SB	CS	SBR	FA	FR	G/POS	TPR
1993	KC-A	81	238	30	52	12	1	7	36	16	82	.218	.287	.366	70	-11	6	3	0	.909	-1	3-70/D-9	-1.1

■ JIM HIBBS
Hibbs, James Kerr   b: 9/10/44, Klamath Falls, Ore.   BR/TR, 6', 190 lbs.   Deb: 4/12/67

YEAR	TM/L	G	AB	R	H	2B	3B	HR	RBI	BB	SO	AVG	OBP	SLG	PRO+	BR/A	SB	CS	SBR	FA	FR	G/POS	TPR
1967	Cal-A	3	3	0	0	0	0	0	0	0	2	.000	.000	.000	-99	-1	0	0	0	.000	0	H	-0.1

■ EDDIE HICKEY
Hickey, Edward A.   b: 8/18/1872, Cleveland, Ohio   d: 3/25/41, Tacoma, Wash.   Deb: 9/3/01

YEAR	TM/L	G	AB	R	H	2B	3B	HR	RBI	BB	SO	AVG	OBP	SLG	PRO+	BR/A	SB	CS	SBR	FA	FR	G/POS	TPR
1901	Chi-N	10	37	4	6	0	0	0	3	2		.162	.225	.162	14	-4				.743	-2	3-10	-0.6

■ MIKE HICKEY
Hickey, Michael Francis   b: 12/25/1871, Chicopee, Mass.   d: 6/11/18, Springfield, Mass   BR/TR, 5'10.5", 150 lbs.   Deb: 9/14/1899

YEAR	TM/L	G	AB	R	H	2B	3B	HR	RBI	BB	SO	AVG	OBP	SLG	PRO+	BR/A	SB	CS	SBR	FA	FR	G/POS	TPR
1899	Bos-N	1	3	0	1	0	0	0	0	0		.333	.333	.333	76	-0	0			.889	1	/2-1	0.1

■ CHARLIE HICKMAN
Hickman, Charles Taylor "Cheerful Charlie" or "Piano Legs"
b: 3/4/1876, Taylortown, Dunkard Township, Pa.   d: 4/19/34, Morgantown, W.Va.   BR/TR, 5'11.5", 215 lbs.   Deb: 9/8/1897

YEAR	TM/L	G	AB	R	H	2B	3B	HR	RBI	BB	SO	AVG	OBP	SLG	PRO+	BR/A	SB	CS	SBR	FA	FR	G/POS	TPR
1897	*Bos-N	2	3	1	2	0	0	0	2	0		.667	.667	1.667	475	1	0			1.000	0	/P-2	0.0
1898	Bos-N	19	58	4	15	2	0	0	7	1		.259	.283	.293	62	-3	0			1.000	-1	/O-7,1-6,P	-0.3
1899	Bos-N	19	63	15	25	2	7	0	15	2		.397	.433	.651	178	6	1			.941	-2	P-11/O-7,1	0.1
1900	NY-N	127	473	65	148	19	17	9	91	17		.313	.359	.482	137	21	10			.842	-4	*3-120/O-7	1.6
1901	NY-N	112	406	44	113	20	6	4	62	15		.278	.315	.387	107	2	5			.904	-7	O-50,S-23,3/P21	-0.6
1902	Bos-A	28	108	13	32	5	2	3	16	3		.296	.339	.463	118	2	1			.939	1	O-27	0.1
	Cle-A	102	426	61	161	31	11	8	94	12		.378	.399	.559	170	37	8			.966	-7	1-98/2-3,P	2.7
	Yr	130	534	74	**193**	36	13	11	110	15		.361	.387	.539	159	39	9			.966	-6	1-98,O-27/2P	2.8
1903	Cle-A	131	522	64	154	31	11	12	97	17		.295	.325	.466	137	21	14			.972	-7	*1-125/2-7	1.3
1904	Cle-A	86	337	34	97	22	10	4	45	13		.288	.318	.448	142	14	9			.943	-0	2-45,1-40/O	1.6
	Det-A	42	144	18	35	6	6	2	22	11		.243	.297	.410	126	4	3			.970	-2	1-39	0.1
	Yr	128	481	52	132	28	16	6	67	24		.274	.312	.437	137	18	12			.969	-3	1-79,2-45/O	1.7
1905	Det-A	59	213	21	47	12	3	2	20	12		.221	.278	.333	93	-2	3			.940	-2	O-47,1-12	-0.2
	Was-A	88	360	48	112	25	9	2	46	9		.311	.332	.447	152	19	3			.922	7	2-85/1-3	2.8
	Yr	147	573	69	159	37	12	4	66	21		.277	.311	.405	129	16	6			.922	9	2-85,O-47,1	2.6
1906	Was-A	120	451	53	128	25	5	9	57	14		.284	.311	.421	135	15	9			.955	-7	O-95,1-18/32	1.0
1907	Was-A	60	198	20	55	9	4	1	23	14		.278	.338	.379	139	8	4			.965	-4	1-30,O-18/2P	0.3
	Chi-A	21	23	1	6	2	0	0	1	4		.261	.370	.348	134	1	0			.667	-1	/O-3	0.0
	Yr	81	221	21	61	11	4	1	24	18		.276	.342	.376	138	9	4			.965	-5	1-30,O-21/2P	0.3
1908	Cle-A	65	197	16	46	6	1	2	16	9		.234	.271	.305	86	-3	2			.907	-0	O-28,1-20/2	-0.6
Total	12	1081	3982	478	1176	217	92	59	614	153		.295	.331	.440	134	145	72			.968	-26	1-394,O-290,23/PS	9.9

■ JIM HICKMAN
Hickman, David James   b: 5/19/1894, Johnson City, Tenn   d: 12/30/58, Brooklyn, N.Y.   BR/TR, 5'7.5", 170 lbs.   Deb: 9/17/15

YEAR	TM/L	G	AB	R	H	2B	3B	HR	RBI	BB	SO	AVG	OBP	SLG	PRO+	BR/A	SB	CS	SBR	FA	FR	G/POS	TPR
1915	Bal-F	20	81	7	17	4	1	1	7	4	14	.210	.256	.321	52	-6	3			.963	4	O-20	-0.3
1916	Bro-N	9	5	3	1	0	0	0	0	2	0	.200	.429	.200	94	0	1			1.000	-1	/O-3	-0.1
1917	Bro-N	114	370	46	81	15	4	6	36	17	66	.219	.253	.330	76	-12	14			.942	7	*O-101	-1.0
1918	Bro-N	53	167	14	39	4	1	6	16	8	31	.234	.281	.359	95	-2	5			.914	-4	O-46	-0.8
1919	Bro-N	57	104	14	20	3	1	0	11	6	17	.192	.236	.240	43	-7	2			.962	-4	O-29	-1.4
Total	5	253	727	84	158	26	13	13	70	37	128	.217	.259	.322	73	-26	27			.941	4	O-199	-3.6

■ JIM HICKMAN
Hickman, James Lucius   b: 5/10/37, Henning, Tenn.   BR/TR, 6'4", 205 lbs.   Deb: 4/14/62

YEAR	TM/L	G	AB	R	H	2B	3B	HR	RBI	BB	SO	AVG	OBP	SLG	PRO+	BR/A	SB	CS	SBR	FA	FR	G/POS	TPR
1962	NY-N	140	392	54	96	18	2	13	46	47	96	.245	.320	.401	94	-4	4	4	-1	.971	1	*O-124	-1.0
1963	NY-N	146	494	53	113	21	6	17	51	44	120	.229	.293	.399	96	-3	0	5	-3	.963	-0	O-82,3-59	-1.2
1964	NY-N	139	409	48	105	14	1	11	57	36	90	.257	.320	.377	98	-1	0	1	-1	.976	-9	*O-113/3-1	-1.6
1965	NY-N	141	369	32	87	18	0	15	40	27	76	.236	.291	.407	98	-2	3	1	0	.965	-8	O-91,1-30,3	-1.6
1966	NY-N	58	160	15	38	7	0	4	16	13	34	.237	.294	.356	83	-4	2	1	0	.986	1	O-45,1-17	-0.9
1967	LA-N	65	98	7	16	6	1	0	10	14	28	.163	.268	.245	52	-6	1	1	0	1.000	-3	O-37/1-2,3P	-1.1
1968	Chi-N	75	188	22	42	6	3	5	23	18	38	.223	.295	.367	91	-2	1	1	0	.975	-4	O-66	-1.1
1969	Chi-N	134	338	38	80	11	2	21	54	47	74	.237	.330	.467	107	2	2	1	0	.981	-14	*O-125	-1.8
1970	Chi-N★	149	514	102	162	33	4	32	115	93	99	.315	.421	.582	148	35	0	1	-1	.974	8	O-79,1-74	3.0
1971	Chi-N	117	383	50	98	13	2	19	60	50	61	.256	.346	.449	108	4	0	1	-1	.982	-4	O-69,1-44	-0.9
1972	Chi-N	115	368	65	100	15	2	17	64	52	64	.272	.365	.462	121	10	3	1	0	.992	-4	1-77,O-27	1.1
1973	Chi-N	92	201	27	49	1	2	3	20	42	42	.244	.374	.313	86	-2	1	1	0	.988	-2	1-51,O-13	-0.6
1974	StL-N	50	60	5	16	2	0	1	9	8	10	.267	.353	.367	102	0	0	0	0	.986	1	1-14/3-1	0.1
Total	13	1421	3974	518	1002	163	25	159	560	491	832	.252	.337	.426	106	28	17	19	-6	.976	-29	O-871,1-309/3P	-7.6

■ BUDDY HICKS
Hicks, Clarence Walter   b: 2/15/27, Belvedere, Cal.   BB/TR, 5'10", 170 lbs.   Deb: 4/17/56

YEAR	TM/L	G	AB	R	H	2B	3B	HR	RBI	BB	SO	AVG	OBP	SLG	PRO+	BR/A	SB	CS	SBR	FA	FR	G/POS	TPR
1956	Det-A	26	47	5	10	2	0	0	5	3	2	.213	.260	.255	36	-4	0	1	-1	1.000	-1	S-16/2-6,3	-0.5

■ JIM HICKS
Hicks, James Edward   b: 5/18/40, East Chicago, Ind.   BR/TR, 6'3", 205 lbs.   Deb: 10/2/64

YEAR	TM/L	G	AB	R	H	2B	3B	HR	RBI	BB	SO	AVG	OBP	SLG	PRO+	BR/A	SB	CS	SBR	FA	FR	G/POS	TPR
1964	Chi-A	2	0	0	0	0	0	0	0	0	0	—	—	—			0	0	0	.000	0	R	0.0
1965	Chi-A	13	19	2	5	1	0	1	2	0	9	.263	.263	.474	112	0	0	0	0	.750	-2	/O-5	-0.2
1966	Chi-A	18	26	3	5	0	1	0	1	1	5	.192	.222	.269	43	-2	0	0	0	1.000	-1	O-10/1-2	-0.4

YEAR	TM/L	G	AB	R	H	2B	3B	HR	RBI	BB	SO	AVG	OBP	SLG	PRO+	BR/A	SB	CS	SBR	FA	FR	G/POS	TPR
1969	StL-N	19	44	5	8	0	2	1	3	4	14	.182	.250	.341	64	-2	0	0	0	1.000	1	O-15	-0.2
	Cal-A	37	48	6	4	0	0	3	8	13	18	.083	.279	.271	57	-3	0	1	-1	1.000	-3	O-10/1-8	-0.8
1970	Cal-A	4	4	0	1	0	0	0	0	2	2	.250	.250	.250	40	-3	0	0	0	.000	0	H	0.0
Total	5	93	141	16	23	1	3	5	14	18	48	.163	.258	.319	64	-7	0	1	-1	.981	-6	/O-40,1-10	-1.6

■ NAT HICKS
Hicks, Nathaniel Woodhull b: 4/19/1845, Hempstead, N.Y. d: 4/21/07, Hoboken, N.J. BR/TR, 6'1", 186 lbs. Deb: 4/22/1872 M

YEAR	TM/L	G	AB	R	H	2B	3B	HR	RBI	BB	SO	AVG	OBP	SLG	PRO+	BR/A	SB	CS	SBR	FA	FR	G/POS	TPR
1872	Mut-n	56	266	55	81	12	2	0	35	5	3	.305	.317	.365	117	7						*C-55/O-2	0.4
1873	Mut-n	28	121	12	29	2	2	1	14	7	0	.240	.281	.314	75	-3						C-28	-0.2
1874	Phi-n	58	264	50	74	8	2	0			5	.280	.294	.326	94	-2						*C-56/O-2	-0.1
1875	Mut-n	62	269	32	67	11	2	0			2	.249	.255	.305	88	-4						*C-59/O-3M	-0.2
1876	NY-N	45	188	20	44	4	1	0	15	3	4	.234	.246	.266	81	-3				.741	-6	C-45	-0.6
1877	Cin-N	8	32	3	6	0	0	0	3	1	2	.188	.212	.188	30	-2				.868	0	/C-8	-0.2
Total	4 n	204	920	149	251	33	8	1	49	19	3	.273	.288	.329	96	-3						C-198/O-7	-0.1
Total	2	53	220	23	50	4	1	0	18	4	6	.227	.241	.255	73	-5				.757	-5	/C-53	-0.8

■ JOE HICKS
Hicks, William Joseph b: 4/7/33, Ivy, Va. BL/TR, 6', 180 lbs. Deb: 9/18/59

YEAR	TM/L	G	AB	R	H	2B	3B	HR	RBI	BB	SO	AVG	OBP	SLG	PRO+	BR/A	SB	CS	SBR	FA	FR	G/POS	TPR
1959	Chi-A	6	7	0	3	0	0	0	0	0	0	.429	.500	.429	160	1	0	1	-1	1.000	-0	/O-4	
1960	Chi-A	36	47	3	9	1	0	0	2	6	3	.191	.296	.213	40	-4	0	1	-1	1.000	-4	O-14	-0.9
1961	Was-A	12	29	2	5	0	0	1	0		4	.172	.172	.276	18	-3	0	1	-1	1.000	1	/O-7	-0.4
1962	Was-A	102	174	20	39	4	2	6	14	15	34	.224	.286	.374	76	-6	3	1	0	.962	-3	O-42	-1.1
1963	NY-N	56	159	16	36	6	1	5	22	7	31	.226	.272	.371	82	-4	0	1	0	.966	-2	O-41	-1.0
Total	5	212	416	41	92	11	3	12	39	29	73	.221	.278	.349	72	-17	3	6	-3	.970	-8	O-108	-3.4

■ MAHLON HIGBEE
Higbee, Mahlon Jesse b: 8/16/01, Louisville, Ky. d: 4/7/68, Depauw, Ind. BR/TR, 5'11", 165 lbs. Deb: 9/27/22

YEAR	TM/L	G	AB	R	H	2B	3B	HR	RBI	BB	SO	AVG	OBP	SLG	PRO+	BR/A	SB	CS	SBR	FA	FR	G/POS	TPR
1922	NY-N	3	10	2	4	0	0	1	5	0	2	.400	.400	.700	177	1	0	0	0	1.000	-1	/O-3	0.0

■ HIGBY
Higby Deb: 9/18/1872

YEAR	TM/L	G	AB	R	H	2B	3B	HR	RBI	BB	SO	AVG	OBP	SLG	PRO+	BR/A	SB	CS	SBR	FA	FR	G/POS	TPR
1872	Atl-n	1	4	0	0	0	0	0	0	0	0	.000	.000	.000	-85	-1						/O-1	-0.1

■ BILL HIGDON
Higdon, William Travis b: 4/27/24, Camp Hill, Ala. d: 8/30/86, Pascagoula, Miss. BL/TR, 6'1", 193 lbs. Deb: 9/10/49

YEAR	TM/L	G	AB	R	H	2B	3B	HR	RBI	BB	SO	AVG	OBP	SLG	PRO+	BR/A	SB	CS	SBR	FA	FR	G/POS	TPR
1949	Chi-A	11	23	3	7	3	0	0	1	6	3	.304	.448	.435	139	2	1	0	0	1.000	-1	/O-6	0.1

■ KEVIN HIGGINS
Higgins, Kevin Wayne b: 1/22/67, San Gabriel, Cal. BL/TR, 5'11", 170 lbs. Deb: 5/29/93

YEAR	TM/L	G	AB	R	H	2B	3B	HR	RBI	BB	SO	AVG	OBP	SLG	PRO+	BR/A	SB	CS	SBR	FA	FR	G/POS	TPR
1993	SD-N	71	181	17	40	4	1	0	13	16	17	.221	.295	.254	48	-13	0	1	-1	.983	-2	C-59/3-4,102	-1.3

■ MARK HIGGINS
Higgins, Mark Douglas b: 7/9/63, Miami, Fla. BR/TR, 6'2", 210 lbs. Deb: 9/7/89

YEAR	TM/L	G	AB	R	H	2B	3B	HR	RBI	BB	SO	AVG	OBP	SLG	PRO+	BR/A	SB	CS	SBR	FA	FR	G/POS	TPR
1989	Cle-A	6	10	1	1	0	0	0	0	1	6	.100	.182	.100	-18	-2	0	0	0	1.000	1	/1-5	-0.1

■ PINKY HIGGINS
Higgins, Michael Franklin "Mike" b: 5/27/09, Red Oak, Tex. d: 3/21/69, Dallas, Tex. BR/TR, 6'1", 185 lbs. Deb: 6/25/30 M

YEAR	TM/L	G	AB	R	H	2B	3B	HR	RBI	BB	SO	AVG	OBP	SLG	PRO+	BR/A	SB	CS	SBR	FA	FR	G/POS	TPR
1930	Phi-A	14	24	1	6	2	0	0	4	5		.250	.357	.333	73	-1	0	0	0	1.000	-2	/3-5,2-2,S	-0.3
1933	Phi-A	152	567	85	178	34	12	13	99	61	53	.314	.383	.485	127	22	2	7	-4	.947	-6	*3-152	2.0
1934	Phi-A☆	144	543	89	179	37	6	16	90	56	70	.330	.392	.508	136	28	9	2	-2	.914	-19	*3-144	1.5
1935	Phi-A	133	524	69	155	32	4	23	94	42	62	.296	.350	.504	120	12	6	2	1	.947	-14	*3-131	0.4
1936	Phi-A★	146	550	89	159	32	2	12	80	67	61	.289	.366	.420	96	-4	7	4	-0	.941	-14	*3-145	-1.2
1937	Bos-A	153	570	88	172	33	5	9	106	76	51	.302	.385	.425	100	1	2	6	-3	.935	-17	*3-152	-1.3
1938	Bos-A	139	524	77	159	29	5	5	106	71	55	.303	.388	.406	95	-3	10	9	-2	.914	-10	*3-138	-1.2
1939	Det-A	132	489	57	135	23	2	8	76	56	41	.276	.353	.380	81	-14	7	4	-0	.914	-11	*3-130	-2.1
1940	*Det-A	131	480	70	130	24	3	13	76	61	31	.271	.357	.415	91	-7	4	2	-0	.928	-11	*3-129	-1.4
1941	Det-A	147	540	79	161	28	5	11	73	67	45	.298	.378	.422	101	1	5	4	-1	.946	1	*3-145	0.5
1942	Det-A	143	499	65	133	34	2	11	79	72	21	.267	.362	.409	108	6	3	7	-3	.926	-14	*3-137	-0.9
1943	Det-A	138	523	62	145	20	1	10	84	57	31	.277	.349	.377	104	3	2	5	-2	.940	-7	*3-138	-0.5
1944	Det-A★	148	543	79	161	32	4	7	76	81	34	.297	.392	.409	122	18	4	4	-1	.954	-7	*3-146	1.2
1946	Det-A	18	60	2	13	3	1	0	8	5	6	.217	.277	.300	58	-3	0	1	-1	.949	-2	3-17	-0.6
	*Bos-A	64	200	18	55	11	1	2	28	24	24	.275	.356	.370	97	-3	0	2	-1	.947	0	3-59	0.0
	Yr	82	260	20	68	14	2	2	36	29	30	.262	.338	.354	88	-4	0	3	-2	.947	-2	3-76	-0.6
Total	14	1802	6636	930	1941	374	51	140	1075	800	590	.292	.370	.428	106	60	61	59	-17	.935	-131	*3-1768/2-2,S	-3.9

■ BOB HIGGINS
Higgins, Robert Stone b: 9/23/1886, Fayetteville, Tenn. d: 5/25/41, Chattanooga, Tenn. BR/TR, 5'8", 176 lbs. Deb: 9/13/09

YEAR	TM/L	G	AB	R	H	2B	3B	HR	RBI	BB	SO	AVG	OBP	SLG	PRO+	BR/A	SB	CS	SBR	FA	FR	G/POS	TPR
1909	Cle-A	8	23	0	2	0	0	0	0	0	0	.087	.087	.087	-43	-4	0			1.000	3	/C-8	0.0
1911	Bro-N	4	10	1	3	0	0	0	0	1	0	.300	.364	.300	90	-0	1			.933	0	/C-2,3-1	0.0
1912	Bro-N	1	2	0	0	0	0	0	0	0	1	.000	.000	.000	-99	-1	0			.750	-0	/C-1	-0.1
Total	3	13	35	1	5	0	0	0	2	1	1	.143	.167	.143	-6	-4	1			.970	3	/C-11,3-1	-0.1

■ BILL HIGGINS
Higgins, William Edward b: 9/8/1861, Wilmington, Del. d: 4/25/19, Wilmington, Del. TR, 5'9", 155 lbs. Deb: 8/9/1888

YEAR	TM/L	G	AB	R	H	2B	3B	HR	RBI	BB	SO	AVG	OBP	SLG	PRO+	BR/A	SB	CS	SBR	FA	FR	G/POS	TPR
1888	Bos-N	14	54	5	10	1	0	0	4	1	3	.185	.200	.204	28	-4	1			.906	5	2-14	0.2
1890	StL-a	67	258	39	65	6	2	0	24			.252	.316	.291	69	-12	7			.951	13	2-67	0.5
	Syr-a	1	4	1	1	1	0	0	0			.250	.250	.500	135	0	0			1.000	1	/2-1	0.1
	Yr	68	262	40	66	7	2	0	24			.252	.315	.294	70	-12	7			.952	14	2-68	0.6
Total	2	82	316	45	76	8	2	0	4	25	3	.241	.296	.278	64	-16	8			.943	20	/2-82	0.8

■ ANDY HIGH
High, Andrew Aird "Handy Andy" b: 11/21/1897, Ava, Ill. d: 2/22/81, Toledo, Ohio BL/TR, 5'6", 155 lbs. Deb: 4/12/22 FC

YEAR	TM/L	G	AB	R	H	2B	3B	HR	RBI	BB	SO	AVG	OBP	SLG	PRO+	BR/A	SB	CS	SBR	FA	FR	G/POS	TPR
1922	Bro-N	153	579	82	164	27	10	6	65	59	26	.283	.354	.396	94	-5	3	12	-6	.958	-5	*3-130,S-22/2	-0.4
1923	Bro-N	123	426	51	115	23	9	3	37	47	13	.270	.344	.387	95	-3	4	1	1	.969	-9	3-80,S-45/2	0.0
1924	Bro-N	144	582	98	191	26	13	6	61	57	16	.328	.390	.448	128	24	3	6	-3	.964	-9	*2-133,S-17/3	1.4
1925	Bro-N	44	115	11	23	4	1	0	6	14	5	.200	.287	.252	40	-10	0	1	-1	.938	-5	2-11,3-11/S	-1.4
	Bos-N	60	219	31	63	11	1	4	28	24	2	.288	.361	.402	104	1	3	5	-2	.979	-9	3-60/2-1	-0.6
	Yr	104	334	42	86	15	2	4	34	38	7	.257	.335	.350	80	-10	3	6	-3			3-71,2-12/S	-2.0
1926	Bos-N	130	476	55	141	17	10	2	66	39	9	.296	.351	.387	108	5	4			.963	-14	3-81,2-49	0.5
1927	Bos-N	113	384	59	116	15	9	4	46	26	11	.302	.350	.419	114	6	4			.962	-6	3-89/2-8,S	-0.9
1928	*StL-N	111	368	58	105	14	3	7	37	37	10	.285	.355	.389	93	-3	2			.935	-19	3-73,2-19	-1.8
1929	StL-N	146	603	95	178	32	4	10	63	38	18	.295	.340	.411	84	-15	7			.967	-19	*3-123,2-22	-2.6
1930	*StL-N	72	215	34	60	12	2	2	29	23	6	.279	.349	.381	74	-9	0			.990	-7	3-48/2-3	-1.1
1931	*StL-N	63	120	20	35	6	1	0	19	24	4	.267	.389	.328	91	-0	0			1.000	-5	3-23,2-19	-0.3
1932	Cin-N	84	191	16	36	4	2	0	12	23	6	.188	.282	.230	39	-16	1			.950	-10	3-46,2-12	-2.3
1933	Cin-N	24	43	4	9	2	0	1	6	5	1	.209	.292	.326	77	-1	0			.966	1	3-11/2-2	0.0
1934	Phi-N	47	68	4	14	2	0	0	7	9	3	.206	.299	.235	40	-6	1			.906	-2	3-14/2-2	-0.7
Total	13	1314	4400	618	1250	195	65	44	482	425	130	.284	.350	.388	94	-33	33	25		.956	-125	3-790,2-287/S	-10.2

■ CHARLIE HIGH
High, Charles Edwin b: 12/1/1898, Ava, Ill. d: 9/11/60, Oak Grove, Ore. BL/TR, 5'9", 170 lbs. Deb: 9/5/19 F

YEAR	TM/L	G	AB	R	H	2B	3B	HR	RBI	BB	SO	AVG	OBP	SLG	PRO+	BR/A	SB	CS	SBR	FA	FR	G/POS	TPR
1919	Phi-A	11	29	2	2	0	0	0	1	3	4	.069	.152	.069	-28	-5	2			.944	-0	/O-9	-0.6
1920	Phi-A	17	65	7	20	2	1	1	6	3	6	.308	.375	.415	108	1	0	2	-1	.882	-0	O-17	-0.2
Total	2	28	94	9	22	2	1	1	7	6	10	.234	.314	.309	68	-4	2	2		.904	-1	/O-26	-0.8

■ HUGH HIGH
High, Hugh Jenken "Bunny" b: 10/24/1887, Pottstown, Pa. d: 11/16/62, St.Louis, Mo. BL/TL, 5'7.5", 155 lbs. Deb: 4/11/13 F

YEAR	TM/L	G	AB	R	H	2B	3B	HR	RBI	BB	SO	AVG	OBP	SLG	PRO+	BR/A	SB	CS	SBR	FA	FR	G/POS	TPR
1913	Det-A	87	183	18	42	6	1	0	16	28	24	.230	.335	.273	80	-4	6			.982	1	O-52	-0.5
1914	Det-A	84	184	25	49	5	3	0	17	26	21	.266	.363	.326	104	2	7	6	-2	.959	-7	O-53	-1.0

YEAR	TM/L	G	AB	R	H	2B	3B	HR	RBI	BB	SO	AVG	OBP	SLG	PRO+	BR/A	SB	CS	SBR	FA	FR	G/POS	TPR
1915	NY-A	119	427	51	110	19	7	1	43	62	47	.258	.356	.342	109	6	22	13	-1	**.981**	-1	*O-117	-0.2
1916	NY-A	116	377	44	99	13	4	1	28	47	44	.263	.349	.326	101	1	13			.950	-1	*O-110	-0.6
1917	NY-A	103	365	37	86	11	6	1	19	48	31	.236	.329	.307	93	-2	8			.986	0	*O-100	-0.8
1918	NY-A	7	10	1	0	0	0	0	0	1	1	.000	.091	.000	-71	-2	0			1.000	0	/O-4	-0.2
Total	6	516	1546	176	386	54	21	3	123	212	168	.250	.345	.318	98	2	56	<u>19</u>		.972	-8	O-436	-3.3

■ DICK HIGHAM
Higham, Richard b: 1852, England d: 3/18/05, Chicago, Ill. BL/TR, 5'8.5", 171 lbs. Deb: 6/1/1871 MU

YEAR	TM/L	G	AB	R	H	2B	3B	HR	RBI	BB	SO	AVG	OBP	SLG	PRO+	BR/A	SB	CS	SBR	FA	FR	G/POS	TPR
1871	Mut-n	21	94	21	34	3	1	0	9	2	0	.362	.375	.415	139	6	3					2-11/O-8,C3	0.3
1872	Bal-n	50	244	72	85	9	2	2	40	2	3	.348	.354	.426	133	8						C-21,O-18/21	0.4
1873	Mut-n	49	245	57	77	6	7	0	34	2	1	.314	.320	.396	110	3						O-19,2-18,C	0.1
1874	Mut-n	65	331	58	87	13	4	1		4		.263	.272	.335	89	-5						*C-41,O-23/2M	-0.3
1875	Chi-n	42	204	44	49	3	3	0		0		.240	.240	.284	80	-4						C-23,2-15/O	-0.3
	Mut-n	15	64	12	25	5	0	0		0		.391	.391	.469	186	5						/C-7,2-4,O1	0.4
	Yr	57	268	56	74	8	3	0		0		.276	.276	.328	106	1						C-30,2-19/O1	0.1
1876	Har-N	67	312	59	102	**21**	2	0	35	2	7	.327	.331	.407	134	9				.869	-2	*O-59,C-13/S2	0.6
1878	Pro-N	62	281	**60**	90	**22**	1	1	29	5	16	.320	.332	.416	145	13				.811	3	*O-62/C-1	1.2
1880	Tro-N	1	5	1	1	0	0	0	0	0	0	.200	.200	.200	34	-0				.000	-2	/O-1,C-1	-0.3
Total	5 n	242	1182	264	357	39	17	3	83	10	4	.302	.308	.371	111	13						C-110/O-75,213	0.6
Total	3	130	598	120	193	43	3	1	64	7	23	.323	.331	.410	138	22				.834	-2	O-122/C-15,2S	1.5

■ JOHN HILAND
Hiland, John William b: 9/1860, Baltic, R.I. d: 4/10/01, Philadelphia, Pa. BL/TL, 5'8.5", 165 lbs. Deb: 8/20/1885

YEAR	TM/L	G	AB	R	H	2B	3B	HR	RBI	BB	SO	AVG	OBP	SLG	PRO+	BR/A	SB	CS	SBR	FA	FR	G/POS	TPR
1885	Phi-N	3	9	0	0	0	0	0	0	0	4	.000	.000	.000	-99	-2				.833	-2	/2-3	-0.4

■ GEORGE HILDEBRAND
Hildebrand, George Albert b: 9/6/1878, San Francisco, Cal. d: 5/30/60, Reseda, Cal. BR/TR, 5'8", 170 lbs. Deb: 4/17/02 U

YEAR	TM/L	G	AB	R	H	2B	3B	HR	RBI	BB	SO	AVG	OBP	SLG	PRO+	BR/A	SB	CS	SBR	FA	FR	G/POS	TPR
1902	Bro-N	11	41	3	9	1	0	0	5	3		.220	.289	.244	64	-2	0			1.000	2	O-11	0.0

■ PALMER HILDEBRAND
Hildebrand, Palmer Marion "Pete" b: 12/23/1884, Shauck, Ohio d: 1/25/60, N.Canton, Ohio BR/TR, 5'10", 170 lbs. Deb: 5/14/13

YEAR	TM/L	G	AB	R	H	2B	3B	HR	RBI	BB	SO	AVG	OBP	SLG	PRO+	BR/A	SB	CS	SBR	FA	FR	G/POS	TPR
1913	StL-N	26	55	3	9	2	0	0	1	1	10	.164	.207	.200	17	-6	1			.968	0	C-22/O-1	-0.5

■ R. E. HILDEBRAND
Hildebrand, R. E. Deb: 8/29/02

YEAR	TM/L	G	AB	R	H	2B	3B	HR	RBI	BB	SO	AVG	OBP	SLG	PRO+	BR/A	SB	CS	SBR	FA	FR	G/POS	TPR
1902	Chi-N	1	4	1	0	0	0	0	0	0	1	.000	.200	.000	-39	-1	0			1.000	-0	/O-1	-0.1

■ BELDEN HILL
Hill, Belden L. b: 8/24/1864, Kewanee, Ill. d: 10/22/34, Cedar Rapids, Iowa BR/TR, 6', Deb: 8/27/1890

YEAR	TM/L	G	AB	R	H	2B	3B	HR	RBI	BB	SO	AVG	OBP	SLG	PRO+	BR/A	SB	CS	SBR	FA	FR	G/POS	TPR
1890	Bal-a	9	30	3	5	2	0	0	3			.167	.306	.233	56	-2	6			.857	1	/3-9	0.0

■ DONNIE HILL
Hill, Donald Earl b: 11/12/60, Pomona, Cal. BB/TR, 5'10", 160 lbs. Deb: 7/25/83

YEAR	TM/L	G	AB	R	H	2B	3B	HR	RBI	BB	SO	AVG	OBP	SLG	PRO+	BR/A	SB	CS	SBR	FA	FR	G/POS	TPR
1983	Oak-A	53	158	20	42	7	0	2	15	4	21	.266	.284	.348	77	-5	1	1	-0	.961	0	S-53	-0.1
1984	Oak-A	73	174	21	40	6	0	2	16	5	12	.230	.251	.299	55	-11	4	1	-0	.949	-12	S-66/2-4,3D	-1.8
1985	Oak-A	123	393	45	112	13	2	3	48	23	33	.285	.325	.351	92	-5	9	4	0	.973	-41	*2-122	-4.1
1986	Oak-A	108	339	37	96	16	2	4	29	23	38	.283	.329	.378	99	-1	5	2	0	.984	-12	2-68,3-33/SD	-1.1
1987	Chi-A	111	410	57	98	14	6	9	46	30	35	.239	.293	.368	72	-17	1	0		.987	-29	2-84,3-32/D	-4.1
1988	Chi-A	83	221	17	48	6	1	2	20	26	32	.217	.300	.281	64	-10	3	1	0	.975	-11	2-59,3-12/D	-1.9
1990	Cal-A	103	352	36	93	18	2	3	32	29	27	.264	.322	.352	90	-5	1	2	-1	.990	3	2-60,S-24,3/1PD	0.0
1991	Cal-A	77	209	36	50	8	1	1	20	30	21	.239	.335	.301	77	-5	1	0		.971	-3	2-39,S-29/1	-0.5
1992	Min-A	25	51	7	15	3	0	0	2	5	6	.294	.368	.353	100	0	0	0		.944	1	S-10/2-7,3O	-0.2
Total	9	756	2307	276	594	91	14	26	228	175	225	.257	.311	.343	81	-59	22	11	0	.980	-107	2-443,S-184,3/D1OP	-13.8

■ GLENALLEN HILL
Hill, Glenallen b: 3/22/65, Santa Cruz, Cal. BR/TR, 6'3", 210 lbs. Deb: 9/1/89

YEAR	TM/L	G	AB	R	H	2B	3B	HR	RBI	BB	SO	AVG	OBP	SLG	PRO+	BR/A	SB	CS	SBR	FA	FR	G/POS	TPR
1989	Tor-A	19	52	4	15	0	0	1	7	3	12	.288	.327	.346	92	-1	2	1	0	.964	-2	O-16/D-3	-0.3
1990	Tor-A	84	260	47	60	11	3	12	32	18	62	.231	.281	.435	95	-3	8	3	1	.983	0	O-60,D-20	-0.4
1991	Tor-A	35	99	14	25	5	2	3	11	7	24	.253	.302	.434	97	-1	2	2	-1	.967	-1	D-16,O-13	-0.2
	Cle-A	37	122	15	32	3	0	5	14	16	30	.262	.348	.410	108	1	4	2	0	.978	-1	O-33/D-1	0.0
	Yr	72	221	29	57	8	2	8	25	23	54	.258	.328	.421	103	1	6	4	-1	.975	-0	O-46,D-17	-0.2
1992	Cle-A	102	369	38	89	16	1	18	49	20	73	.241	.288	.436	102	-1	9	6	-1	.956	2	O-59,D-34	-0.2
1993	Cle-N	66	174	19	39	7	2	5	25	11	50	.224	.274	.374	73	-7	7	3	0	.940	-4	O-39,D-18	-1.2
	Chi-N	31	87	14	30	7	0	10	22	6	21	.345	.387	.770	204	12	1	0		.957	1	O-21	1.3
1994	Chi-N	89	269	48	80	12	1	10	38	29	57	.297	.366	.461	117	7	19	6	2	.987	-6	O-78	0.1
Total	6	463	1432	199	370	61	9	64	198	110	329	.258	.314	.448	106	-9	52	23		.970	-9	O-319/D-92	-0.9

■ HERMAN HILL
Hill, Herman Alexander b: 10/12/45, Tuskegee, Ala. d: 12/14/70, Valencia, Venez. BL/TR, 6'2", 190 lbs. Deb: 9/2/69

YEAR	TM/L	G	AB	R	H	2B	3B	HR	RBI	BB	SO	AVG	OBP	SLG	PRO+	BR/A	SB	CS	SBR	FA	FR	G/POS	TPR
1969	Min-A	16	2	4	0	0	0	0	0	1		.000	.000	.000	-98	-1	1	2	-1	.000	-1	/O-2	-0.2
1970	Min-A	27	22	8	2	0	0	0	0	0	6	.091	.091	.091	-49	-4	0	0	0	1.000	-2	O-14	-0.7
Total	2	43	24	12	2	0	0	0	0	0	7	.083	.083	.083	-53	-5	1	2	-1	1.000	-3	/O-16	-0.9

■ HUGH HILL
Hill, Hugh Ellis b: 7/21/1879, Ringgold, Ga. d: 9/6/58, Cincinnati, Ohio BL/TR, 5'11.5", 168 lbs. Deb: 5/1/03 F

YEAR	TM/L	G	AB	R	H	2B	3B	HR	RBI	BB	SO	AVG	OBP	SLG	PRO+	BR/A	SB	CS	SBR	FA	FR	G/POS	TPR
1903	Cle-A	1	1	0	0	0	0	0	0	0		.000	.000	.000	-99	-0	0			.000	0	H	0.0
1904	StL-N	23	93	13	21	2	1	3	4	2		.226	.242	.366	91	-2	3			1.000	0	O-23	-0.3
Total	2	24	94	13	21	2	1	3	4	2		.223	.240	.362	89	-2	3			1.000	0	/O-23	-0.3

■ HUNTER HILL
Hill, Hunter Benjamin b: 6/21/1879, Austin, Tex. d: 2/22/59, Austin, Tex. BR/TR, Deb: 7/1/03

YEAR	TM/L	G	AB	R	H	2B	3B	HR	RBI	BB	SO	AVG	OBP	SLG	PRO+	BR/A	SB	CS	SBR	FA	FR	G/POS	TPR
1903	StL-A	86	317	30	77	11	3	0	25	8		.243	.264	.297	70	-12	2			.923	-1	3-86	-1.2
1904	StL-A	58	219	19	47	3	0	0	14	6		.215	.246	.228	54	-12	4			.826	-16	3-56/O-1	-3.0
	Was-A	77	290	18	57	6	1	0	17	11		.197	.228	.224	44	-18	10			.895	-6	3-71/O-5	-2.6
	Yr	135	509	37	104	9	1	0	31	17		.204	.236	.226	48	-30	14			.864	-23	*3-127/O-6	-5.6
1905	Was-A	104	374	37	78	12	1	1	24	32		.209	.278	.254	72	-11	10			.908	-1	*3-103	-0.9
Total	3	325	1200	104	259	32	5	1	80	57		.216	.257	.253	62	-53	26			.895	-24	3-316/O-6	-7.7

■ JESSE HILL
Hill, Jesse Terrill b: 1/20/07, Yates, Mo. d: 8/31/93, Pasadena, Cal. BR/TR, 5'9", 165 lbs. Deb: 4/17/35

YEAR	TM/L	G	AB	R	H	2B	3B	HR	RBI	BB	SO	AVG	OBP	SLG	PRO+	BR/A	SB	CS	SBR	FA	FR	G/POS	TPR
1935	NY-A	107	392	69	115	20	3	4	33	42	32	.293	.362	.390	100	0	14	4	2	.951	2	O-94	0.1
1936	Was-A	85	233	50	71	19	5	0	34	29	23	.305	.384	.429	106	3	11	0	3	.967	-8	O-60	-0.3
1937	Was-A	33	92	24	20	2	1	1	4	13	16	.217	.314	.293	57	-6	2	1	0	.986	2	O-21	-0.4
	Phi-A	70	242	32	71	12	3	1	37	31	20	.293	.374	.380	92	-2	16	3	3	.954	-5	O-68	-0.6
	Yr	103	334	56	91	14	4	2	41	44	36	.272	.357	.356	82	-8	18	4	3	.964	-3	O-89	-1.0
Total	3	295	959	175	277	53	12	6	108	115	91	.289	.366	.388	95	-4	43	8	8	.959	-9	O-243	-1.2

■ MARC HILL
Hill, Marc Kevin b: 2/18/52, Elsberry, Mo. BR/TR, 6'3", 210 lbs. Deb: 9/28/73 C

YEAR	TM/L	G	AB	R	H	2B	3B	HR	RBI	BB	SO	AVG	OBP	SLG	PRO+	BR/A	SB	CS	SBR	FA	FR	G/POS	TPR
1973	StL-N	1	3	0	0	0	0	0	0	0	1	.000	.000	.000	-99	-1	0	0	0	1.000	0	/C-1	-0.1
1974	StL-N	10	21	2	5	1	0	0	2	4	5	.238	.360	.286	83	-0	0	0	0	1.000	3	/C-9	0.3
1975	SF-N	72	182	14	39	4	0	5	23	25	27	.214	.309	.319	71	-7	0	0	0	.994	1	C-60/3-1	-0.4
1976	SF-N	54	131	11	24	5	0	3	15	10	19	.183	.246	.290	50	-9	0	1	-1	.995	1	C-49/1-1	-0.8
1977	SF-N	108	320	28	80	10	0	9	50	34	34	.250	.322	.366	84	-7	0	1	-1	.989	-3	*C-102	-0.7
1978	SF-N	117	358	20	87	15	1	3	36	45	39	.243	.329	.316	84	-7	1	2	-0	.986	0	*C-116/1-2	-0.5
1979	SF-N	63	169	20	35	3	0	3	15	26	25	.207	.313	.278	67	-7	0	1	-1	.991	-6	C-58/1-1	-1.2
1980	SF-N	17	41	1	7	2	0	0	1	0	7	.171	.190	.220	14	-5	0	0	0	.972	0	C-14	-0.3
	Sea-A	29	70	8	16	2	1	3	8	5	10	.229	.260	.371	70	-3	0	1	-0	.991	-0	C-29	-0.3
1981	Chi-A	16	6	0	0	0	0	0	0	0	1	.000	.000	.000	-99	-2	0	0	0	1.000	0	C-14/1-1,3	-0.1

YEAR	TM/L	G	AB	R	H	2B	3B	HR	RBI	BB	SO	AVG	OBP	SLG	PRO+	BR/A	SB	CS	SBR	FA	FR	G/POS	TPR
1982	Chi-A	53	88	9	23	2	0	3	13	6	13	.261	.316	.386	92	-1	0	0	0	.993	6	C-49/1-1,3	0.5
1983	Chi-A	58	133	11	30	6	0	1	11	9	24	.226	.275	.293	54	-8	0	1	-1	.991	5	C-55/1-1,D	-0.2
1984	Chi-A	77	193	15	45	10	1	5	20	9	26	.233	.275	.373	74	-7	0	1	-1	.991	4	C-72/1-2	-0.1
1985	Chi-A	40	75	5	10	2	0	0	4	12	9	.133	.253	.160	16	-9	0	0	0	.985	9	C-37/3-1	0.1
1986	Chi-A	22	19	2	3	0	0	0	0	1	3	.158	.238	.158	10	-2	0	0	0	1.000	7	C-22	0.5
Total	14	737	1809	146	404	62	3	34	198	185	243	.223	.298	.317	69	-74	1	7	-4	.990	30	C-687/1-9,3D	-3.3

■ OLIVER HILL
Hill, Oliver Clinton b: 10/16/12, Powder Springs, Ga d: 9/20/70, Decatur, Ga. BL/TR, 5'11", 178 lbs. Deb: 4/19/39

YEAR	TM/L	G	AB	R	H	2B	3B	HR	RBI	BB	SO	AVG	OBP	SLG	PRO+	BR/A	SB	CS	SBR	FA	FR	G/POS	TPR
1939	Bos-N	2	2	1	1	1	0	0	0	0	0	.500	.500	1.000	317	1	0			.000	0	H	0.1

■ HOMER HILLEBRAND
Hillebrand, Homer Hiller Henry "Doc" b: 10/10/1879, Freeport, Ill. d: 1/20/74, Elsinore, Cal. BR/TL, 5'8", 165 lbs. Deb: 4/24/05

YEAR	TM/L	G	AB	R	H	2B	3B	HR	RBI	BB	SO	AVG	OBP	SLG	PRO+	BR/A	SB	CS	SBR	FA	FR	G/POS	TPR
1905	Pit-N	39	110	9	26	3	2	0	7	6		.236	.282	.300	72	-4	1			.978	-3	1-16,P-10/OC	-0.6
1906	Pit-N	7	21	1	5	1	0	0	3	1		.238	.273	.286	71	-1	0			1.000	1	/P-7	0.0
1908	Pit-N	1	0	0	0	0	0	0	0	0		—	—	—	—	0	0			.000	0	/P-1	0.0
Total	3	47	131	10	31	4	2	0	10	7		.237	.281	.298	71	-5	1			1.000	-1	/P-18,1-16,OC	-0.6

■ CHUCK HILLER
Hiller, Charles Joseph b: 10/1/34, Johnsburg, Ill. BL/TR, 5'11", 170 lbs. Deb: 4/11/61 C

YEAR	TM/L	G	AB	R	H	2B	3B	HR	RBI	BB	SO	AVG	OBP	SLG	PRO+	BR/A	SB	CS	SBR	FA	FR	G/POS	TPR
1961	SF-N	70	240	38	57	12	1	2	12	32	30	.237	.330	.321	76	-7	4	4	-1	.973	-14	2-67	-1.6
1962	*SF-N	161	602	94	166	22	2	3	48	54	45	.276	.344	.334	84	-12	5	4	-1	.964	-18	*2-161	-1.4
1963	SF-N	111	417	44	93	10	2	6	33	20	23	.223	.262	.300	62	-21	3	2	-1	.963	-15	*2-109	-2.9
1964	SF-N	80	205	21	37	8	1	1	17	17	23	.180	.247	.244	38	-17	1	1	-0	.977	2	2-60/3-1	-1.2
1965	SF-N	7	7	1	1	0	0	1	1	0	1	.143	.143	.571	88	-0	0	0	0	1.000	-1	/2-2	-0.1
	NY-N	100	286	24	68	11	1	5	21	14	24	.238	.276	.336	74	-10	1	1	-0	.959	-12	2-80/O-4,3	-1.8
	Yr	107	293	25	69	11	1	6	22	14	25	.235	.273	.341	74	-11	1	1	-0	.959	-13	2-82/O-4,3	-1.9
1966	NY-N	108	254	25	71	8	2	2	14	15	22	.280	.332	.350	92	-2	0	0	0	.981	11	2-45,3-14/O	1.1
1967	NY-N	25	54	0	5	3	0	0	3	2	11	.093	.125	.148	-22	-9	0	0	0	.968	2	2-14	-0.6
	Phi-N	31	43	4	13	1	0	0	2	2	4	.302	.333	.326	88	-1	0	2	-1	.947	-3	/2-6	-0.4
	Yr	56	97	4	18	4	0	0	5	4	15	.186	.218	.227	27	-9	0	2	-1	.963	-0	2-20	-1.0
1968	Pit-N	11	13	2	5	1	0	0	1	0	1	.385	.385	.462	155	1	0	0	0	.857	-0	/2-2	0.1
Total	8	704	2121	253	516	76	9	20	152	157	187	.243	.301	.316	72	-78	14	14	-4	.967	-49	2-546/3-17,O	-8.8

■ HOB HILLER
Hiller, Harvey Max b: 5/12/1893, E.Mauch Chunk, Pa. d: 12/27/56, Leighton, Pa. BR/TR, 5'8", 162 lbs. Deb: 4/22/20

YEAR	TM/L	G	AB	R	H	2B	3B	HR	RBI	BB	SO	AVG	OBP	SLG	PRO+	BR/A	SB	CS	SBR	FA	FR	G/POS	TPR
1920	Bos-A	17	29	4	5	1	1	0	2	2	5	.172	.226	.276	34	-3	0	3	-2	.905	1	/3-6,S-5,2O	-0.4
1921	Bos-A	1	1	0	0	0	0	0	0	0	0	.000	.000	.000	-99	-0	0	0		.000	0	H	0.0
Total	2	18	30	4	5	1	1	0	2	2	5	.167	.219	.267	29	-3	0	3	-2	.905	1	/3-6,S-5,2O	-0.4

■ ED HILLEY
Hilley, Edward Garfield "Whitey" b: 6/17/1879, Cleveland, Ohio d: 11/14/56, Cleveland, Ohio BR/TR, 5'10.5", 170 lbs. Deb: 9/29/03

YEAR	TM/L	G	AB	R	H	2B	3B	HR	RBI	BB	SO	AVG	OBP	SLG	PRO+	BR/A	SB	CS	SBR	FA	FR	G/POS	TPR
1903	Phi-A	1	3	1	1	0	0	0	0	1		.333	.500	.333	147	0	0			.800	-0	/3-1	0.0

■ MACK HILLIS
Hillis, Malcolm David b: 7/23/01, Cambridge, Mass. d: 6/16/61, Cambridge, Mass. BR/TR, 5'10", 165 lbs. Deb: 9/13/24

YEAR	TM/L	G	AB	R	H	2B	3B	HR	RBI	BB	SO	AVG	OBP	SLG	PRO+	BR/A	SB	CS	SBR	FA	FR	G/POS	TPR
1924	NY-A	1	1	1	0	0	0	0	0	0	0	.000	.000	.000	-99	-0	0	0	0	.000	0	/2-1	0.0
1928	Pit-N	11	36	6	9	2	3	1	7	0	6	.250	.250	.556	101	-0	1			.973	-1	/2-8,3-1	-0.1
Total	2	12	37	7	9	2	3	1	7	0	6	.243	.243	.541	96	-1	1	0		.973	-1	/2-9,3-1	-0.1

■ PAT HILLY
Hilly, William Edward (b: William Edward Hilgerink) b: 2/24/1887, Fostoria, Ohio d: 7/25/53, Eureka, Mo. BR/TR, 5'11", 180 lbs. Deb: 5/7/14

YEAR	TM/L	G	AB	R	H	2B	3B	HR	RBI	BB	SO	AVG	OBP	SLG	PRO+	BR/A	SB	CS	SBR	FA	FR	G/POS	TPR
1914	Phi-N	8	10	2	3	0	0	0	1	1	5	.300	.364	.300		0	0			1.000	-1	/O-4	-0.1

■ CHARLIE HILSEY
Hilsey, Charles T. b: 3/23/1864, Philadelphia, Pa. d: 10/31/18, Philadelphia, Pa. 5'7", 180 lbs. Deb: 9/27/1883

YEAR	TM/L	G	AB	R	H	2B	3B	HR	RBI	BB	SO	AVG	OBP	SLG	PRO+	BR/A	SB	CS	SBR	FA	FR	G/POS	TPR
1883	Phi-N	3	10	0	1	0	0	0		0	4	.100	.100	.100	-43	-2				.714	-0	/P-3	0.0
1884	Phi-a	6	24	5	5	1	1	0		0		.208	.208	.333	70	-1				.250	-0	/O-3,P-3	-0.1
Total	2	9	34	5	6	1	1	0	1	0	4	.176	.176	.265	38	-3				.824	-1	/P-6,O-3	-0.1

■ DAVE HILTON
Hilton, John David b: 9/15/50, Uvalde, Tex. BR/TR, 5'11", 191 lbs. Deb: 9/10/72 C

YEAR	TM/L	G	AB	R	H	2B	3B	HR	RBI	BB	SO	AVG	OBP	SLG	PRO+	BR/A	SB	CS	SBR	FA	FR	G/POS	TPR
1972	SD-N	13	47	2	10	2	1	0	5	3	6	.213	.260	.298	63	-2	1	0	0	.939	-3	3-13	-0.5
1973	SD-N	70	234	21	46	9	0	5	16	19	35	.197	.260	.299	59	-14	2	1	0	.970	-4	3-47,2-23	-1.8
1974	SD-N	74	217	17	52	8	2	1	12	13	28	.240	.283	.309	68	-10	3	5	-2	.948	-5	3-55,2-15	-1.8
1975	SD-N	4	8	0	0	0	0	0	0	0	0	.000	.000	.000	-99	-2	0	0	0	.900	1	/3-4	-0.1
Total	4	161	506	40	108	19	3	6	33	35	69	.213	.266	.298	61	-28	6	6	-2	.954	-11	3-119/2-38	-4.2

■ JACK HIMES
Himes, John Herb b: 9/22/1878, Bryan, Ohio d: 12/16/49, Joliet, Ill. BL/TR, 6'2", 180 lbs. Deb: 9/18/05

YEAR	TM/L	G	AB	R	H	2B	3B	HR	RBI	BB	SO	AVG	OBP	SLG	PRO+	BR/A	SB	CS	SBR	FA	FR	G/POS	TPR
1905	StL-N	12	41	3	6	0	0	0	1	1		.146	.167	.146	-7	-5	0			1.000	-1	O-11	-0.7
1906	StL-N	40	155	10	42	5	2	0	14	7		.271	.307	.329	102	-0	4			.977	5	O-40	0.3
Total	2	52	196	13	48	5	2	0	14	8		.245	.278	.291	79	-5	4			.981	4	/O-51	-0.4

■ HARRY HINCHMAN
Hinchman, Harry Sibley b: 8/4/1878, Philadelphia, Pa. d: 1/19/33, Toledo, Ohio BB/TR, 5'11", 165 lbs. Deb: 7/29/07 F

YEAR	TM/L	G	AB	R	H	2B	3B	HR	RBI	BB	SO	AVG	OBP	SLG	PRO+	BR/A	SB	CS	SBR	FA	FR	G/POS	TPR
1907	Cle-A	15	51	3	11	3	1	0	9	5		.216	.286	.314	90	-1	2			.904	4	2-15	0.3

■ BILL HINCHMAN
Hinchman, William White b: 4/4/1883, Philadelphia, Pa. d: 2/20/63, Columbus, Ohio BR/TR, 5'11", 190 lbs. Deb: 9/24/05 FC

YEAR	TM/L	G	AB	R	H	2B	3B	HR	RBI	BB	SO	AVG	OBP	SLG	PRO+	BR/A	SB	CS	SBR	FA	FR	G/POS	TPR
1905	Cin-N	17	51	10	13	4	1	0	10	13		.255	.415	.373	122	2	4			.905	-3	O-12/3-4,1	-0.1
1906	Cin-N	18	54	7	11	1	1	0	1	8		.204	.306	.259	73	-1	2			.963	1	O-16	-0.2
1907	Cle-A	152	514	62	117	19	9	1	50	47		.228	.311	.305	96	-1	15			.958	-5	*O-148/1-4,2	-1.3
1908	Cle-A	137	464	55	107	23	8	6	59	38		.231	.301	.353	112	6	9			.975	-6	O-75,S-51/1	-0.3
1909	Cle-A	139	457	57	118	20	13	2	53	41		.258	.331	.372	117	9	22			.918	1	*O-131/S-6	0.6
1915	Pit-N	156	577	72	177	33	14	5	77	48	75	.307	.368	.438	146	31	17	17	-5	.969	-4	*O-156	2.4
1916	Pit-N	152	555	64	175	18	**16**	4	76	54	61	.315	.378	.427	146	30	10			.962	-4	*O-124,1-31	2.2
1917	Pit-N	69	244	27	46	5	5	2	29	33	27	.189	.288	.275	70	-8	5			.945	-1	O-48,1-20	-1.4
1918	Pit-N	50	111	10	26	5	2	0	13	15	8	.234	.336	.315	96	-0	1			1.000	-4	O-40/1-3	-0.6
1920	Pit-N	18	16	0	3	0	0	0	1	1	3	.188	.278	.188	34	-1	0	0	0	.000	0	H	-0.1
Total	10	908	3043	364	793	128	69	20	369	298	_174_	.261	.336	.368	118	66	85	_17_		.954	-17	O-750/1-63,S32	1.2

■ HUNKEY HINES
Hines, Henry Fred b: 9/29/1867, Elgin, Ill. d: 1/2/28, Rockford, Ill. BR/TR, 5'7", 165 lbs. Deb: 5/16/1895

YEAR	TM/L	G	AB	R	H	2B	3B	HR	RBI	BB	SO	AVG	OBP	SLG	PRO+	BR/A	SB	CS	SBR	FA	FR	G/POS	TPR
1895	Bro-N	2	8	3	2	0	0	0	1	2	0	.250	.400	.250	76	-0	0			1.000	0	/O-2	0.0

■ MIKE HINES
Hines, Michael P. b: 9/1862, Ireland d: 3/14/10, New Bedford, Mass. BR/TL, 5'10", 176 lbs. Deb: 5/1/1883

YEAR	TM/L	G	AB	R	H	2B	3B	HR	RBI	BB	SO	AVG	OBP	SLG	PRO+	BR/A	SB	CS	SBR	FA	FR	G/POS	TPR
1883	Bos-N	63	231	38	52	13	1	0	16	7	36	.225	.248	.290	61	-11				.887	8	C-59/O-7	0.1
1884	Bos-N	35	132	16	23	3	0	0	3	3	24	.174	.193	.197	23	-11				.919	6	C-35	-0.2
1885	Bos-N	14	56	11	13	4	0	0	4	4	5	.232	.283	.304	93	-3				.857	-3	O-14	-0.4
	Bro-a	3	13	1	1	0	1	0		0		.077	.077	.231	-6	-2				1.000	-1	/C-3	-0.2
	Pro-N	1	3	0	0	0	0	0		0	2	.000	.000	.000	-99	-1				.636	-1	/C-1	-0.1
1888	Bos-N	4	16	3	2	0	1	0	2	2	0	.125	.222	.250	49	-1	0			1.000	-1	/O-3,C-1	-0.1
Total	4	120	451	69	91	20	3	0	_25_	16	_67_	.202	.229	.259	51	-25	0			.896	9	/C-99,O-24	-0.9

■ PAUL HINES
Hines, Paul A. b: 3/1/1852, Washington, D.C. d: 7/10/35, Hyattsville, Md. BR/TR, 5'9.5", 173 lbs. Deb: 4/20/1872

YEAR	TM/L	G	AB	R	H	2B	3B	HR	RBI	BB	SO	AVG	OBP	SLG	PRO+	BR/A	SB	CS	SBR	FA	FR	G/POS	TPR
1872	Nat-n	11	50	10	12	1	0	0		1		.240	.240	.300	56	-3						1-10/3-1	-0.2
1873	Was-n	39	181	33	60	11	2	2	26	1	1	.331	.335	.448	132	7						*O-36/2-2,C	0.5
1874	Chi-n	59	270	47	81	12	1	0		4		.300	.310	.352	109	3						*O-46,2-12/S	0.2

YEAR	TM/L	G	AB	R	H	2B	3B	HR	RBI	BB	SO	AVG	OBP	SLG	PRO+	BR/A	SB	CS	SBR	FA	FR	G/POS	TPR
1875	Chi-n	69	308	45	97	13	4	0		1		.315	.317	.383	140	11						O-41,2-28	1.0
1876	Chi-N	64	305	62	101	**21**	3	2	59	1	3	.331	.333	.439	139	10				**.923**	5	*O-64/2-1	1.2
1877	Chi-N	60	261	44	73	11	7	0	23	1	8	.280	.282	.375	94	-3				.806	-10	*O-49,2-11	-1.3
1878	Pro-N	62	257	42	92	13	4	**4**	**50**	2	10	.358	.363	**.486**	178	20				.849	3	*O-61/S-1	1.8
1879	Pro-N	85	409	81	**146**	25	10	2	52	8	16	.357	.369	.482	181	**34**				.867	7	*O-85	3.3
1880	Pro-N	85	374	64	115	20	2	3	35	13	17	.307	.331	.396	150	19				**.927**	8	*O-75/2-6,1	2.4
1881	Pro-N	80	361	65	103	**27**	5	2	31	13	12	.285	.310	.404	125	10				.897	-1	*O-78/2-4,1	0.7
1882	Pro-N	84	379	73	117	28	5	4	34	10	14	.309	.326	.467	151	21				.861	1	*O-82/1-2	1.9
1883	Pro-N	97	442	94	132	32	4	4	45	18	23	.299	.326	.416	120	10				.905	7	*O-89/1-9	1.3
1884	*Pro-N	114	490	94	148	**36**	10	3	41	44	28	.302	.360	.435	152	30				.895	2	*O-108/1-7,P	2.6
1885	Pro-N	98	411	63	111	20	4	1	35	19	18	.270	.302	.345	114	6				.865	4	*O-92/1-4,S32	0.7
1886	Was-N	121	487	80	152	30	8	9	56	35	21	.312	.358	.462	157	33	21			.899	3	*O-92,3-15,1/S2	3.0
1887	Was-N	123	478	83	147	32	5	10	72	48	24	.308	.380	.458	139	27	46			.886	-14	*O-109/1-7,2S	0.9
1888	Ind-N	133	513	84	144	26	3	4	58	41	45	.281	.343	.366	124	15	31			.912	-7	*O-125/1-6,S	0.4
1889	Ind-N	121	486	77	148	27	1	6	72	49	22	.305	.374	.401	114	10	34			.964	4	*1-109,O-12	0.5
1890	Pit-N	31	121	11	22	1	0	0	9	11	7	.182	.256	.190	34	-10	6			.973	2	1-17,O-14	-0.8
	Bos-N	69	273	41	72	12	3	2	48	32	20	.264	.350	.352	97	-2	9			.881	-12	O-69/1-1	-1.4
	Yr	100	394	52	94	13	3	2	57	43	27	.239	.321	.302	80	-9	15			.871	-10	O-83,1-18	-2.2
1891	Was-a	54	206	25	58	7	5	0	31	21	16	.282	.376	.364	117	6	6			.856	-3	O-47/1-8	0.0
Total	4 n	178	809	135	250	37	8	2	30	6	1	.309	.314	.382	121	18	0					O-123/2-42,1SC3	1.5
Total	16	1481	6253	1083	1881	368	84	56	751	366	304	.301	.343	.413	133	236	153			.887	-3	*O-1251,1-185/23SP	17.2

■ GORDIE HINKLE
Hinkle, Daniel Gordon   b: 4/3/05, Toronto, Ohio   d: 3/19/72, Houston, Tex.   BR/TR, 6', 185 lbs.   Deb: 4/19/34

YEAR	TM/L	G	AB	R	H	2B	3B	HR	RBI	BB	SO	AVG	OBP	SLG	PRO+	BR/A	SB	CS	SBR	FA	FR	G/POS	TPR
1934	Bos-A	27	75	7	13	6	1	0	9	7	23	.173	.244	.280	33	-8	0	0	0	.992	4	C-26	-0.2

■ GEORGE HINSHAW
Hinshaw, George Addison   b: 10/23/59, Los Angeles, Cal.   BR/TR, 6', 185 lbs.   Deb: 9/19/82

YEAR	TM/L	G	AB	R	H	2B	3B	HR	RBI	BB	SO	AVG	OBP	SLG	PRO+	BR/A	SB	CS	SBR	FA	FR	G/POS	TPR
1982	SD-N	6	15	1	4	0	0	0	1	3	5	.267	.389	.267	91	0	0	0	0	1.000	0	/O-6	0.0
1983	SD-N	7	16	1	7	1	0	0	4	0	4	.438	.438	.500	165	1	1	0	0	1.000	-0	/3-5	0.1
Total	2	13	31	2	11	1	0	0	5	3	9	.355	.412	.387	129	1	1	0	0	1.000	0	/O-6,3-5	0.1

■ PAUL HINSON
Hinson, James Paul   b: 5/9/04, Vanleer, Tenn.   d: 9/23/60, Muskogee, Okla.   BR/TR, 5'10", 150 lbs.   Deb: 4/19/28

YEAR	TM/L	G	AB	R	H	2B	3B	HR	RBI	BB	SO	AVG	OBP	SLG	PRO+	BR/A	SB	CS	SBR	FA	FR	G/POS	TPR
1928	Bos-A	3	0	1	0	0	0	0	0	0	0	—	—	—		0	0	0	0	.000	0	R	0.0

■ CHUCK HINTON
Hinton, Charles Edward   b: 5/3/34, Rocky Mount, N.C.   BR/TR, 6'1", 197 lbs.   Deb: 5/14/61

YEAR	TM/L	G	AB	R	H	2B	3B	HR	RBI	BB	SO	AVG	OBP	SLG	PRO+	BR/A	SB	CS	SBR	FA	FR	G/POS	TPR
1961	Was-A	106	339	51	88	13	5	6	34	40	81	.260	.339	.381	93	-3	22	5	4	.963	4	O-92	-0.4
1962	Was-A	151	542	73	168	25	6	17	75	47	66	.310	.365	.472	124	18	28	10	2	.988	-10	*O-136,2-12/S	0.4
1963	Was-A	150	566	80	152	20	12	15	55	64	79	.269	.344	.426	115	11	25	9	2	.989	-1	*O-125,3-19/1S	0.6
1964	Was-A★	138	514	71	141	25	7	11	53	57	77	.274	.348	.414	112	8	17	6	2	.985	10	*O-131/3-2	1.4
1965	Cle-A	133	431	59	110	17	6	18	54	53	66	.255	.338	.444	120	11	17	3	3	.966	-9	O-72,1-40,2/3	0.3
1966	Cle-A	123	348	46	89	9	3	12	50	35	66	.256	.326	.402	108	3	10	6	-1	.973	-8	*O-104/1-6,2	-0.1
1967	Cle-A	147	498	55	122	19	3	10	37	43	100	.245	.306	.355	94	-4	6	8	-3	.976	-13	*O-136/2-5	-2.8
1968	Cal-A	116	267	28	52	10	3	7	23	24	61	.195	.261	.333	82	-6	3	1	0	.987	-6	1-48,O-37,3/2	-1.8
1969	Cle-A	94	121	18	31	3	2	3	19	8	22	.256	.308	.388	91	-2	2	0	1	.941	-10	O-40,3-14	-1.2
1970	Cle-A	107	195	24	62	7	0	9	29	25	34	.318	.395	.477	133	9	0	2	-1	.994	-6	1-40,O-35/C23	-0.1
1971	Cle-A	88	147	13	33	7	0	5	14	20	34	.224	.317	.374	87	-2	0	0	0	1.000	-7	1-20,O-20/C	-1.2
Total	11	1353	3968	518	1048	152	47	113	443	416	685	.264	.335	.412	108	44	130	50	9	.979	-59	O-928,1-160/23CS	-5.8

■ JOHN HINTON
Hinton, John Robert "Red"   b: 6/20/1876, Pittsburgh, Pa.   d: 7/19/20, Braddock, Pa.   BR/TR, 6', 200 lbs.   Deb: 6/3/01

YEAR	TM/L	G	AB	R	H	2B	3B	HR	RBI	BB	SO	AVG	OBP	SLG	PRO+	BR/A	SB	CS	SBR	FA	FR	G/POS	TPR
1901	Bos-N	4	13	0	1	0	0	0	0		2	.077	.200	.077	-17	-2	0			.750	-2	/3-4	-0.4

■ TOMMY HINZO
Hinzo, Thomas Lee   b: 6/18/64, San Diego, Cal.   BB/TR, 5'10", 170 lbs.   Deb: 7/16/87

YEAR	TM/L	G	AB	R	H	2B	3B	HR	RBI	BB	SO	AVG	OBP	SLG	PRO+	BR/A	SB	CS	SBR	FA	FR	G/POS	TPR
1987	Cle-A	67	257	31	68	9	3	3	21	10	47	.265	.297	.358	72	-10	9	4	0	.973	-4	2-67	-1.0
1989	Cle-A	18	19	4	0	0	0	0	0	2	6	.000	.105	.000	-67	-4	1	2	-1	.867	0	/2-6,S-1,D	-0.4
Total	2	85	274	35	68	9	3	3	21	12	53	.248	.285	.336	64	-14	10	6	-1	.968	-4	/2-73,D-1,S	-1.4

■ GENE HISER
Hiser, Gene Taylor   b: 12/11/48, Baltimore, Md.   BL/TL, 5'11", 175 lbs.   Deb: 8/20/71

YEAR	TM/L	G	AB	R	H	2B	3B	HR	RBI	BB	SO	AVG	OBP	SLG	PRO+	BR/A	SB	CS	SBR	FA	FR	G/POS	TPR
1971	Chi-N	17	29	4	6	0	0	0		4	8	.207	.303	.207	41	-2	1	0	0	1.000	-0	/O-9	-0.2
1972	Chi-N	32	46	2	9	0	0	0	4	6	8	.196	.288	.196	36	-4	1	0	0	1.000	-0	O-15	-0.4
1973	Chi-N	100	109	15	19	3	0	1	6	11	17	.174	.256	.229	33	-10	4	5	-2	.980	-18	O-64	-3.2
1974	Chi-N	12	17	2	4	1	0	0	3	0	3	.235	.235	.294	46	-1	0	0	0	1.000	-2	/O-8	-0.3
1975	Chi-N	45	62	11	15	3	0	0	6	11	7	.242	.356	.290	77	-1	0	1	-1	1.000	-3	O-18/1-1	-0.5
Total	5	206	263	34	53	7	0	1	18	32	43	.202	.291	.240	46	-18	6	6	-2	.992	-22	O-114/1-1	-4.6

■ LARRY HISLE
Hisle, Larry Eugene   b: 5/5/47, Portsmouth, Ohio   BR/TR, 6'2", 195 lbs.   Deb: 4/10/68   C

YEAR	TM/L	G	AB	R	H	2B	3B	HR	RBI	BB	SO	AVG	OBP	SLG	PRO+	BR/A	SB	CS	SBR	FA	FR	G/POS	TPR
1968	Phi-N	7	11	1	4	1	0	0		1	4	.364	.417	.455	161	1	0	0	0	1.000	-1	/O-6	0.0
1969	Phi-N	145	482	75	128	23	5	20	56	48	152	.266	.338	.459	125	14	18	8	1	.977	11	*O-140	1.9
1970	Phi-N	126	405	52	83	22	4	10	44	53	139	.205	.302	.353	77	-14	5	5	-2	.978	5	*O-121	-1.6
1971	Phi-N	36	76	7	15	0	0	3		6	22	.197	.256	.237	40	-6	1	0	0	.962	-0	O-27	-0.7
1973	Min-A	143	545	88	148	25	6	15	64	64	128	.272	.352	.422	113	10	11	4	1	.975	4	*O-143	1.0
1974	Min-A	143	510	68	146	20	7	19	79	48	112	.286	.357	.465	130	19	12	6	1	.979	-8	*O-137	0.5
1975	Min-A	80	255	37	80	9	2	11	51	27	39	.314	.382	.494	143	14	17	3	0	.976	-7	O-58,D-14	0.8
1976	Min-A	155	581	81	158	19	5	14	96	34	92	.272	.340	.394	111	8	31	18	-2	.984	14	*O-154	1.5
1977	Min-A★	141	546	95	165	36	3	28	**119**	56	106	.302	.373	.533	146	34	21	10	0	.974	4	*O-134/D-6	2.9
1978	Mil-A★	142	520	96	151	24	0	34	115	67	90	.290	.377	.533	153	36	10	6	-1	.978	-2	O-87,D-51	2.9
1979	Mil-A	26	96	18	27	7	0	3	14	11	19	.281	.355	.448	115	2	1	0	0	1.000	-0	D-15,O-10	0.2
1980	Mil-A	17	60	16	17	0	0	6	16	14	7	.283	.427	.583	180	7	1	1	-0	.000	0	D-17	0.6
1981	Mil-A	27	87	11	20	4	0	4	11	6	17	.230	.295	.414	108	1	0	0	0	.000	0	D-24	0.0
1982	Mil-A	9	31	7	4	0	0	2	5	5	13	.129	.250	.323	60	-2	0	0	0	.000	-0	/D-8	-0.2
Total	14	1197	4205	652	1146	193	32	166	674	462	941	.273	.350	.452	123	125	128	61	-6	.978	19	*O-1017,D-135	9.8

■ JIM HITCHCOCK
Hitchcock, James Franklin   b: 6/28/11, Inverness, Ala.   d: 6/23/59, Montgomery, Ala.   BR/TR, 5'11", 175 lbs.   Deb: 8/24/38   F

YEAR	TM/L	G	AB	R	H	2B	3B	HR	RBI	BB	SO	AVG	OBP	SLG	PRO+	BR/A	SB	CS	SBR	FA	FR	G/POS	TPR
1938	Bos-N	28	76	2	13	0	0	0	7	2	11	.171	.192	.171	1	-10	1			.881	-2	S-24/3-2	-1.1

■ BILLY HITCHCOCK
Hitchcock, William Clyde   b: 7/31/16, Inverness, Ala.   BR/TR, 6'1.5", 185 lbs.   Deb: 4/14/42   FMC

YEAR	TM/L	G	AB	R	H	2B	3B	HR	RBI	BB	SO	AVG	OBP	SLG	PRO+	BR/A	SB	CS	SBR	FA	FR	G/POS	TPR
1942	Det-A	85	280	27	59	8	1	0	29	26	21	.211	.280	.246	45	-20	2	2	-1	.944	-3	S-80/3-1	-2.0
1946	Det-A	3	3	0	0	0	0	0	0	1	0	.000	.250	.000	-25	-0	0	0	0	1.000	0	/2-1	0.0
	Was-A	98	354	27	75	8	3	0	25	26	52	.212	.268	.251	48	-25	2	4	-2	.966	-4	S-53,3-46	-2.8
	Yr	101	357	27	75	8	3	0	25	27	52	.210	.268	.249	48	-25	2	4	-2	.966	-3	S-53,3-46/2	-2.8
1947	StL-A	80	275	25	61	2	2	1	28	21	34	.222	.277	.255	47	-19	3	0	1	.977	11	2-46,3-17/S1	-0.4
1948	Bos-A	49	124	15	37	3	1	0	20	7	9	.298	.341	.379	87	-3	0	0	0	.951	6	2-15,3-15	0.4
1949	Bos-A	55	147	22	30	6	1	0	9	7	11	.204	.291	.259	43	-12	2	3	-1	.993	-8	1-29/2-8	-2.1
1950	Phi-A	115	399	35	109	25	5	1	54	45	32	.273	.347	.361	83	-10	3	1	0	.967	-3	2-107/S-1	-0.7
1951	Phi-A	77	222	27	68	10	4	1	36	21	23	.306	.371	.401	107	2	1	1	-0	.929	7	3-45,2-23/1	1.0
1952	Phi-A	119	407	45	100	8	3	4	56	39	45	.246	.318	.292	66	-18	1	1	-0	.942	-1	*3-104,1-13	-2.2

YEAR	TM/L	G	AB	R	H	2B	3B	HR	RBI	BB	SO	AVG	OBP	SLG	PRO+	BR/A	SB	CS	SBR	FA	FR	G/POS	TPR
1953	Det-A	22	38	8	8	0	0	0	0	3	3	.211	.268	.211	31	-4	0	0	0	.929	0	3-12/2-1,S	-0.4
Total	9	703	2249	231	547	67	22	5	257	206	230	.243	.310	.299	65	-109	15	11	-2	.938	7	3-240,2-201,S/1	-9.2

■ MYRIL HOAG
Hoag, Myril Oliver b: 3/9/08, Davis, Cal. d: 7/28/71, High Springs, Fla BR/TR, 5'11", 180 lbs. Deb: 4/15/31

YEAR	TM/L	G	AB	R	H	2B	3B	HR	RBI	BB	SO	AVG	OBP	SLG	PRO+	BR/A	SB	CS	SBR	FA	FR	G/POS	TPR
1931	NY-A	44	28	6	4	2	0	0	3	1	8	.143	.172	.214	1	-4	0	0	0	1.000	-7	O-23/3-1	-1.0
1932	*NY-A	46	54	18	20	5	0	1	7	7	13	.370	.443	.519	156	5	1	1	-0	.962	-10	O-35/1-1	-0.6
1934	NY-A	97	251	45	67	8	2	3	34	21	21	.267	.324	.351	79	-8	1	3	-2	.974	-9	O-86	-2.0
1935	NY-A	48	110	13	28	4	1	1	13	12	19	.255	.328	.336	76	-4	4	2	0	.986	-2	O-37/3-1	-0.6
1936	NY-A	45	156	23	47	9	4	3	34	7	16	.301	.343	.468	102	-0	3	1	0	.955	-4	O-39	-0.5
1937	*NY-A	106	362	48	109	19	8	3	46	33	33	.301	.364	.423	97	-2	4	7	-3	.955	-6	O-99	-1.3
1938	*NY-A	85	267	28	74	14	3	0	48	25	31	.277	.344	.352	75	-10	4	3	-1	.965	-4	O-70	-1.6
1939	StL-A★	129	482	58	142	23	4	10	75	24	35	.295	.329	.421	89	-10	9	5	-0	.971	-8	*O-117/P-1	-2.0
1940	StL-A	76	191	20	50	11	0	3	26	13	30	.262	.309	.366	73	-8	2	0	1	.971	-6	O-46	-1.5
1941	StL-A	1	1	0	0	0	0	0	0	0	0	.000	.000	.000	-97	-0	0	0	0	.000	0	H	0.0
	Chi-A	106	380	30	97	13	3	1	44	27	29	.255	.306	.313	65	-19	6	10	-4	.957	-6	O-99	-3.4
	Yr	107	381	30	97	13	3	1	44	27	29	.255	.306	.312	65	-20	6	10	-4	.957	-6	O-99	-3.4
1942	Chi-A	113	412	47	99	18	2	2	37	36	21	.240	.301	.308	73	-15	17	8	0	.972	-4	*O-112	-2.6
1944	Chi-A	17	48	5	11	1	0	0	4	10	1	.229	.362	.250	77	-1	1	3	-2	.969	-1	O-14	-0.4
	Cle-A	67	277	33	79	9	3	1	27	25	23	.285	.347	.350	103	1	6	4	-1	.947	-1	O-66	-0.4
	Yr	84	325	38	90	10	3	1	31	35	24	.277	.349	.335	99	0	7	7	-2	.950	-2	O-80	-0.8
1945	Cle-A	40	128	10	27	5	3	0	3	11	18	.211	.279	.297	70	-5	1	2	-1	.987	0	O-33/P-2	-0.8
Total	13	1020	3147	384	854	141	33	28	401	252	298	.271	.328	.364	83	-80	59	49	-12	.965	-67	O-876/P-3,31	-18.7

■ DON HOAK
Hoak, Donald Albert "Tiger" b: 2/5/28, Roulette, Pa. d: 10/9/69, Pittsburgh, Pa. BR/TR, 6', 175 lbs. Deb: 4/18/54 C

YEAR	TM/L	G	AB	R	H	2B	3B	HR	RBI	BB	SO	AVG	OBP	SLG	PRO+	BR/A	SB	CS	SBR	FA	FR	G/POS	TPR
1954	Bro-N	88	261	41	64	9	5	7	26	25	39	.245	.321	.398	83	-7	8	3	1	.950	4	3-75	-0.3
1955	*Bro-N	94	279	50	67	13	3	5	19	46	50	.240	.350	.362	87	-4	9	5	-0	.960	17	3-78	1.2
1956	Chi-N	121	424	51	91	18	4	5	37	41	46	.215	.285	.311	61	-23	8	3	1	.949	-18	*3-110	-4.1
1957	Cin-N★	149	529	78	155	**39**	2	19	89	74	54	.293	.384	.482	122	18	8	15	-7	**.971**	-0	*3-149/2-1	1.4
1958	Cin-N	114	417	51	109	30	0	6	50	43	36	.261	.333	.376	83	-10	6	8	-3	.964	4	*3-112/S-1	-0.8
1959	Pit-N	155	564	60	166	29	3	6	65	71	75	.294	.377	.399	108	9	9	2	2	.961	9	*3-155	2.0
1960	*Pit-N	155	553	97	156	24	9	16	79	74	74	.282	.368	.445	120	17	3	2	0	.948	6	*3-155	2.0
1961	Pit-N	145	503	72	150	27	7	12	61	73	53	.298	.390	.451	122	18	4	2	0	.953	-3	*3-143	1.6
1962	Pit-N	121	411	63	99	14	8	5	48	49	49	.241	.323	.350	81	-11	4	2	0	**.969**	-3	*3-116	-1.2
1963	Phi-N	115	377	35	87	11	3	6	24	27	52	.231	.284	.324	75	-12	5	5	-2	.958	6	*3-106	-0.8
1964	Phi-N	6	4	0	0	0	0	0	0	0	2	.000	.000	.000	-99	-1	0	0	0	.000	0	H	-0.1
Total	11	1263	4322	598	1144	214	44	89	498	523	530	.265	.347	.396	98	-6	64	47	-9	.959	20	*3-1199/S-1,2	0.9

■ BILL HOBBS
Hobbs, William Lee "Smokey" b: 5/7/1893, Grants Lick, Ky. d: 1/5/45, Hamilton, Ohio BR/TR, 5'9.5", 155 lbs. Deb: 8/9/13

YEAR	TM/L	G	AB	R	H	2B	3B	HR	RBI	BB	SO	AVG	OBP	SLG	PRO+	BR/A	SB	CS	SBR	FA	FR	G/POS	TPR
1913	Cin-N	4	4	0	0	0	0	0	0	0	3	.000	.000	.000	-99	-1	0			1.000	6	/2-1,3-1	0.0
1916	Cin-N	6	11	1	2	1	0	0	1	2	0	.182	.308	.273	81	-0	1			.947	6	/S-6	0.6
Total	2	10	15	1	2	1	0	0	1	2	3	.133	.235	.200	32	-1	1			.947	6	/S-6,3-1,2	0.6

■ DICK HOBLITZEL
Hoblitzel, Richard Carleton "Doc" (b: Richard Carleton Hoblitzell) b: 10/26/1888, Waverly, W.Va. d: 11/14/62, Parkersburg, W.Va. BL/TL, 6', 172 lbs. Deb: 9/5/08

YEAR	TM/L	G	AB	R	H	2B	3B	HR	RBI	BB	SO	AVG	OBP	SLG	PRO+	BR/A	SB	CS	SBR	FA	FR	G/POS	TPR
1908	Cin-N	32	114	8	29	3	2	0	8	7		.254	.309	.316	102	0	2			.985	2	1-32	0.1
1909	Cin-N	142	517	59	159	23	11	4	67	44		.308	.364	.418	144	25	17			.982	-3	*1-142	2.3
1910	Cin-N	155	611	85	170	24	13	4	70	47	32	.278	.332	.380	112	7	28			.984	-8	*1-148/2-7	-0.1
1911	Cin-N	158	622	81	180	19	13	11	91	42	44	.289	.342	.415	116	10	32			.990	2	*1-158	1.2
1912	Cin-N	148	558	73	164	32	12	2	85	48	28	.294	.352	.405	110	7	23			.985	2	*1-147	0.6
1913	Cin-N	137	502	59	143	23	7	3	62	35	26	.285	.334	.376	103	1	18			.988	-5	*1-134	-0.6
1914	Cin-N	78	248	31	52	8	7	0	26	26	26	.210	.287	.298	72	-9	7			.988	-4	1-75	-1.6
	Bos-A	69	229	31	73	10	3	0	33	19	21	.319	.386	.389	133	9	12	12	-4	.979	-5	1-68	-0.1
1915	*Bos-A	124	399	54	113	15	12	2	61	38	26	.283	.351	.396	128	13	9	14	-6	.987	-1	*1-117	0.3
1916	*Bos-A	130	417	57	108	17	1	0	39	47	28	.259	.338	.305	93	-3	10			.989	-1	*1-126	-0.9
1917	Bos-A	120	420	49	108	19	7	1	47	46	22	.257	.336	.343	108	4	12			.990	-8	*1-118	-0.9
1918	Bos-A	25	69	4	11	1	0	0	1	9	7	.159	.266	.174	33	-5	3			.996	1	1-19	-0.6
Total	11	1318	4706	591	1310	194	88	27	593	407	256	.278	.341	.374	111	61	173	26		.987	-29	*1-1284/2-7	-0.3

■ BUTCH HOBSON
Hobson, Clell Lavern b: 8/17/51, Tuscaloosa, Ala. BR/TR, 6'1", 193 lbs. Deb: 9/7/75 M

YEAR	TM/L	G	AB	R	H	2B	3B	HR	RBI	BB	SO	AVG	OBP	SLG	PRO+	BR/A	SB	CS	SBR	FA	FR	G/POS	TPR
1975	Bos-A	2	4	0	1	0	0	0	0	0	0	.250	.250	.250	38	-0	0	0	0	1.000	1	/3-1	0.0
1976	Bos-A	76	269	34	63	7	5	8	34	15	62	.234	.275	.387	82	-7	0	1	-1	.936	-7	3-76	-1.7
1977	Bos-A	159	593	77	157	33	5	30	112	27	162	.265	.301	.489	100	-3	5	4	-1	.946	-28	*3-159	-3.4
1978	Bos-A	147	512	65	128	26	2	17	80	50	122	.250	.317	.408	92	-6	1	0	-0	.899	-14	*3-133,D-14	-2.3
1979	Bos-A	146	528	74	138	26	5	28	93	30	92	.261	.301	.496	105	1	3	2	-0	.935	-21	*3-142/2-1	-2.1
1980	Bos-A	93	324	35	74	6	0	11	39	25	69	.228	.284	.349	69	-14	1	1	-0	.910	-9	3-57,D-36	-2.6
1981	Cal-A	85	268	27	63	7	4	4	36	35	60	.235	.326	.336	91	-2	1	1	-0	.929	-11	3-83/D-2	-1.7
1982	NY-A	30	58	2	10	2	0	0	3	1	14	.172	.186	.207	8	-7	0	0	0	.951	1	D-15,1-11	-0.9
Total	8	738	2556	314	634	107	23	98	397	183	569	.248	.300	.423	91	-40	11	9	-2	.926	-90	3-651/D-67,12	-14.7

■ ED HOCK
Hock, Edward Francis b: 3/27/1899, Franklin Furnace, Ohio d: 11/21/63, Portsmouth, Ohio BL/TL, 5'10.5", 165 lbs. Deb: 7/8/20

YEAR	TM/L	G	AB	R	H	2B	3B	HR	RBI	BB	SO	AVG	OBP	SLG	PRO+	BR/A	SB	CS	SBR	FA	FR	G/POS	TPR
1920	StL-N	1	0	0	0	0	0	0	0	0	0	—	—	—			0	0	0	.000	-1	/O-1	-0.1
1923	Cin-N	2	0	0	0	0	0	0	0	0	0	—	—	—			0	0	0	.000	0	R	0.0
1924	Cin-N	16	10	7	1	0	0	0	0	0	2	.100	.182	.100	-23	-2	0	0	0	1.000	-0	/O-2	-0.2
Total	3	19	10	7	1	0	0	0	0	0	2	.100	.182	.100	-23	-2	0	0	0	1.000	-0	/O-3	-0.3

■ ORIS HOCKETT
Hockett, Oris Leon "Brown" b: 9/29/09, Amboy, Ind. d: 3/23/69, Torrance, Cal. BL/TR, 5'9", 182 lbs. Deb: 9/4/38

YEAR	TM/L	G	AB	R	H	2B	3B	HR	RBI	BB	SO	AVG	OBP	SLG	PRO+	BR/A	SB	CS	SBR	FA	FR	G/POS	TPR
1938	Bro-N	21	70	8	23	5	1	1	8	4	9	.329	.365	.471	126	2	0			.893	-4	O-17	-0.2
1939	Bro-N	9	13	3	3	0	0	0	1	1	1	.231	.286	.231	39	-1	0			1.000	1	/O-1	-0.1
1941	Cle-A	2	6	0	2	0	0	0	1	2	0	.333	.500	.333	131	0	0	0	0	1.000	-1	/O-2	0.0
1942	Cle-A	148	601	85	150	22	7	7	48	45	45	.250	.305	.344	88	-12	12	12	-4	.980	-2	*O-145	-2.6
1943	Cle-A	141	601	70	166	33	4	2	51	45	45	.276	.331	.354	107	4	13	18	-7	.960	1	*O-139	-1.0
1944	Cle-A☆	124	457	47	132	29	5	1	50	35	27	.289	.339	.381	110	5	8	9	-3	.986	-4	*O-110	-0.8
1945	Chi-A	106	417	46	122	23	4	2	55	27	30	.293	.340	.381	112	5	10	9	-2	.982	1	*O-106	-0.1
Total	7	551	2165	259	598	112	21	13	214	159	157	.276	.329	.365	103	3	43	48		.974	-6	O-520	-4.8

■ DENNIS HOCKING
Hocking, Dennis Lee b: 4/2/70, Torrance, Cal. BB/TR, 5'10", 180 lbs. Deb: 9/10/93

YEAR	TM/L	G	AB	R	H	2B	3B	HR	RBI	BB	SO	AVG	OBP	SLG	PRO+	BR/A	SB	CS	SBR	FA	FR	G/POS	TPR
1993	Min-A	15	36	7	5	1	0	0	0	6	8	.139	.262	.167	18	-4	1	0	0	.971	-2	S-12/2-1	-0.5
1994	Min-A	11	31	3	10	3	0	0	2	0	4	.323	.323	.419	89	-1	2	0	1	1.000	1	S-10	0.1
Total	2	26	67	10	15	4	0	0	2	6	12	.224	.288	.284	51	-5	3	0	1	.986	-2	/S-22,2-1	-0.4

■ JOHNNY HODAPP
Hodapp, Urban John b: 9/26/05, Cincinnati, Ohio d: 6/14/80, Cincinnati, Ohio BR/TR, 6', 185 lbs. Deb: 8/19/25

YEAR	TM/L	G	AB	R	H	2B	3B	HR	RBI	BB	SO	AVG	OBP	SLG	PRO+	BR/A	SB	CS	SBR	FA	FR	G/POS	TPR
1925	Cle-A	37	130	12	31	5	1	0	14	11	7	.238	.298	.292	50	-10	2	3	-1	.960	3	3-37	-0.5
1926	Cle-A	3	5	0	1	0	0	0	0	0	0	.200	.200	.200	4	-1	0	0	0	.750	-1	/3-3	-0.1
1927	Cle-A	79	240	25	73	15	8	5	40	14	23	.304	.343	.454	105	2	2	3	-1	.935	1	3-67/1-4	0.3
1928	Cle-A	116	449	51	145	31	6	2	73	20	20	.323	.352	.432	104	2	2	1	0	.944	-2	*3-101,1-13	0.4

YEAR	TM/L	G	AB	R	H	2B	3B	HR	RBI	BB	SO	AVG	OBP	SLG	PRO+	BR/A	SB	CS	SBR	FA	FR	G/POS	TPR
1929	Cle-A	90	294	30	96	12	7	4	51	15	14	.327	.361	.456	105	2	3	3	-1	.977	5	2-72	0.8
1930	Cle-A	154	635	111	**225**	51	8	9	121	32	29	.354	.386	.502	119	17	6	5	-1	.970	12	*2-154	3.2
1931	Cle-A	122	468	71	138	19	4	2	56	27	23	.295	.336	.365	80	-14	1	5	-3	.969	16	*2-121	0.7
1932	Cle-A	7	16	2	2	1	0	0	0	0	2	.125	.125	.188	-19	-3	0	0	0	1.000	-2	/2-7	-0.4
	Chi-A	68	176	21	40	8	0	3	20	11	3	.227	.273	.324	58	-12	1	0	0	.967	-5	O-31/2-5,3	-1.7
	Yr	75	192	23	42	9	0	3	20	11	5	.219	.261	.313	51	-15	1	0	0	.967	-7	O-31,2-12/3	-2.1
1933	Bos-A	115	413	55	129	27	5	3	54	33	14	.312	.365	.424	109	5	1	1	-0	.960	3	*2-101,1-10	1.2
Total	9	791	2826	378	880	169	34	28	429	163	136	.311	.350	.425	98	-13	18	20	-7	.967	30	2-460,3-212/O1	3.9

■ MEL HODERLEIN
Hoderlein, Melvin Anthony   b: 6/24/23, Mt.Carmel, Ohio   BB/TR, 5'10", 185 lbs.   Deb: 8/16/51

YEAR	TM/L	G	AB	R	H	2B	3B	HR	RBI	BB	SO	AVG	OBP	SLG	PRO+	BR/A	SB	CS	SBR	FA	FR	G/POS	TPR
1951	Bos-A	9	14	1	5	1	1	0	1	6	2	.357	.550	.571	185	2	0	1	-1	1.000	1	/2-3,3-3	0.2
1952	Was-A	72	208	16	56	8	2	0	17	18	22	.269	.333	.327	87	-3	2	0	1	.978	-2	2-58	-0.2
1953	Was-A	23	47	5	9	0	0	0	5	6	9	.191	.283	.191	31	-4	0	0	0	.953	-3	2-11/S-2	-0.7
1954	Was-A	14	25	0	4	1	0	0	1	1	4	.160	.192	.200	8	-3	0	0	0	.939	1	/S-6,2-5	-0.1
Total	4	118	294	22	74	10	3	0	24	31	37	.252	.327	.306	78	-9	2	1	-0	.973	-3	/2-77,S-8,3	-0.8

■ CHARLIE HODES
Hodes, Charles   b: 1848, New York, N.Y.   d: 2/14/1875, Brooklyn, N.Y.   TR, 5'11.5", 175 lbs.   Deb: 5/8/1871

YEAR	TM/L	G	AB	R	H	2B	3B	HR	RBI	BB	SO	AVG	OBP	SLG	PRO+	BR/A	SB	CS	SBR	FA	FR	G/POS	TPR
1871	Chi-n	28	130	32	36	4	1	2	25	7	0	.277	.314	.369	86	-4	3					C-18/3-7,OS	-0.3
1872	Tro-n	13	65	17	15	5	0	0	12	1	0	.231	.242	.308	67	-3						/S-5,O-4,C3	-0.2
1874	Atl-n	22	82	8	13	2	1	0		0		.159	.159	.207	17	-7						O-19/2-2	-0.5
Total	3 n	63	277	57	64	11	2	2		8	8	.231	.253	.307	66	-13						/O-25,C-21,3S2	-1.0

■ BERT HODGE
Hodge, Edward Burton   b: 5/25/17, Knoxville, Tenn.   BL/TR, 5'11", 170 lbs.   Deb: 4/14/42

YEAR	TM/L	G	AB	R	H	2B	3B	HR	RBI	BB	SO	AVG	OBP	SLG	PRO+	BR/A	SB	CS	SBR	FA	FR	G/POS	TPR
1942	Phi-N	8	11	0	2	0	0	0	0	1	1	.182	.250	.182	29	-1	0			1.000	-1	/3-2	-0.2

■ GOMER HODGE
Hodge, Harold Morris   b: 4/3/44, Rutherfordton, N.C.   BB/TR, 6'2", 185 lbs.   Deb: 4/6/71

YEAR	TM/L	G	AB	R	H	2B	3B	HR	RBI	BB	SO	AVG	OBP	SLG	PRO+	BR/A	SB	CS	SBR	FA	FR	G/POS	TPR
1971	Cle-A	80	83	3	17	3	0	1	9	4	19	.205	.258	.277	47	-6	0	0	0	1.000	-2	/1-3,3-3,2	-0.8

■ GIL HODGES
Hodges, Gilbert Raymond (b: Gilbert Ray Hodge)   b: 4/4/24, Princeton, Ind.   d: 4/2/72, West Palm Beach, Fla   BR/TR, 6'1.5", 200 lbs.   Deb: 10/3/43   M

YEAR	TM/L	G	AB	R	H	2B	3B	HR	RBI	BB	SO	AVG	OBP	SLG	PRO+	BR/A	SB	CS	SBR	FA	FR	G/POS	TPR
1943	Bro-N	1	2	0	0	0	0	0	0	1	2	.000	.333	.000	0	-0	1			.600	0	/3-1	0.0
1947	*Bro-N	28	77	9	12	3	1	1	7	14	19	.156	.286	.260	44	-6	0			.958	-2	C-24	-0.7
1948	Bro-N	134	481	48	120	18	5	11	70	43	61	.249	.341	.376	82	-13	7			.986	-1	1-96,C-38	-1.2
1949	*Bro-N★	156	596	94	170	23	4	23	115	66	64	.285	.360	.453	112	10	10			**.995**	-4	*1-156	0.5
1950	Bro-N☆	153	561	98	159	26	2	32	113	73	73	.283	.367	.508	125	20	6			**.994**	1	*1-153	1.6
1951	*Bro-N★	158	582	118	156	25	3	40	103	93	99	.268	.374	.527	137	30	9	7	-2	.992	4	*1-158	2.9
1952	*Bro-N☆	153	508	87	129	27	1	32	102	107	90	.254	.386	.500	142	31	2	4	-2	.992	5	*1-153	3.0
1953	*Bro-N★	141	520	101	157	22	7	31	122	75	84	.302	.393	.550	139	31	1	4	-2	.993	8	*1-127,O-24	2.9
1954	Bro-N★	154	579	106	176	23	5	42	130	74	84	.304	.384	.579	142	35	3	3	-1	.995	9	*1-154	3.4
1955	*Bro-N	150	546	75	158	24	5	27	102	80	91	.289	.383	.500	128	23	2	1	0	.991	1	*1-139,O-16	1.6
1956	*Bro-N	153	550	86	146	29	4	32	87	76	91	.265	.355	.507	119	15	3	3	-1	.992	4	*1-138,O-30/C	0.6
1957	Bro-N★	150	579	94	173	28	7	27	98	63	91	.299	.370	.511	122	18	5	3	1	.990	2	*1-150/3-2,2	1.0
1958	LA-N	141	475	68	123	15	1	22	64	52	87	.259	.332	.434	98	-2	8	2	1	.992	1	*1-122,3-15/OC	-0.7
1959	*LA-N	124	413	57	114	19	2	25	80	58	92	.276	.369	.513	123	14	3	2	-0	**.992**	0	*1-113/3-4	0.6
1960	LA-N	101	197	22	39	8	1	8	30	26	37	.198	.295	.371	76	-7	0	1	-1	.995	0	1-92,3-10	-1.0
1961	LA-N	109	215	25	52	4	0	8	31	24	43	.242	.318	.372	76	-7	3	1	0	.998	0	*1-100	-1.1
1962	NY-N	54	127	15	32	1	0	9	17	15	27	.252	.331	.472	111	2	0	0	0	.986	3	1-47	0.3
1963	NY-N	11	22	2	5	0	0	0	3	3	2	.227	.320	.227	60	-1	0	0	0	1.000	2	1-10	0.0
Total	18	2071	7030	1105	1921	295	48	370	1274	943	1137	.273	.361	.487	119	191	63	31		.992	34	*1-1908/O-79,C32	13.7

■ RON HODGES
Hodges, Ronald Wray   b: 6/22/49, Rocky Mount, Va.   BL/TR, 6'1", 185 lbs.   Deb: 6/13/73

YEAR	TM/L	G	AB	R	H	2B	3B	HR	RBI	BB	SO	AVG	OBP	SLG	PRO+	BR/A	SB	CS	SBR	FA	FR	G/POS	TPR
1973	*NY-N	45	127	5	33	2	1	1	18	11	19	.260	.319	.299	73	-4	0	1	-1	.992	2	C-40	-0.1
1974	NY-N	59	136	16	30	4	0	4	14	19	11	.221	.316	.338	84	-3	0	0	0	.953	-2	C-44	-0.3
1975	NY-N	9	34	3	7	1	0	2	4	1	4	.206	.229	.412	79	-1	0	0	0	1.000	0	/C-9	-0.1
1976	NY-N	56	155	21	35	6	0	4	24	27	16	.226	.341	.342	100	1	2	0	1	.976	-9	C-52	-0.7
1977	NY-N	66	117	6	31	4	0	1	5	9	17	.265	.317	.325	76	-4	0	2	-1	.992	-1	C-27	-0.5
1978	NY-N	47	102	4	26	4	1	0	7	10	11	.255	.327	.314	83	-2	1	2	-1	.982	6	C-30	0.4
1979	NY-N	59	86	4	14	4	0	0	5	19	16	.163	.314	.209	47	-6	0	0	0	.980	1	C-22	-0.4
1980	NY-N	36	42	4	10	2	0	0	5	10	13	.238	.385	.286	92	0	1	1	-0	.982	1	/C-9	0.4
1981	NY-N	35	43	5	13	2	0	1	6	5	8	.302	.375	.419	127	2	1	0	0	1.000	-1	/C-7	0.1
1982	NY-N	80	228	26	56	12	1	5	27	41	40	.246	.361	.373	106	3	4	3	-1	.980	-4	C-74	0.5
1983	NY-N	110	250	20	65	12	0	0	21	49	42	.260	.385	.308	95	1	0	3	-2	.971	-10	C-96	-0.7
1984	NY-N	64	106	5	22	3	0	1	11	23	18	.208	.354	.264	77	-2	1	1	-0	.979	-1	C-35	-0.2
Total	12	666	1426	119	342	56	2	19	147	224	217	.240	.345	.322	88	-16	10	13	-5	.978	-9	C-445	-1.6

■ RALPH HODGIN
Hodgin, Elmer Ralph   b: 2/10/16, Greensboro, N.C.   BL/TR, 5'10", 170 lbs.   Deb: 4/19/39

YEAR	TM/L	G	AB	R	H	2B	3B	HR	RBI	BB	SO	AVG	OBP	SLG	PRO+	BR/A	SB	CS	SBR	FA	FR	G/POS	TPR
1939	Bos-N	32	48	4	10	1	0	0	4	3	4	.208	.255	.229	33	-5	0			1.000	-1	/O-9	-0.6
1943	Chi-A	117	407	52	128	22	8	1	50	20	24	.314	.356	.415	125	12	3	5	-2	.945	-7	3-56,O-42	1.5
1944	Chi-A	121	465	56	137	25	7	1	51	21	14	.295	.333	.385	106	2	3	1	0	.942	12	3-82,O-33	1.5
1946	Chi-A	87	258	32	65	10	1	0	25	19	6	.252	.308	.298	73	-9	0	1	0	.983	-2	O-57	-1.6
1947	Chi-A	59	180	26	53	10	3	1	24	14	4	.294	.352	.400	113	3	1	0	0	.990	-1	O-41	0.2
1948	Chi-A	114	331	28	88	11	5	1	34	21	11	.266	.310	.338	75	-13	0	3	-2	.970	5	O-79	-1.4
Total	6	530	1689	198	481	79	24	4	188	97	63	.285	.330	.367	98	-10	7	10		.985	7	O-261,3-138	-1.7

■ PAUL HODGSON
Hodgson, Paul Joseph Denis   b: 4/14/60, Montreal, Que., Can.   BR/TR, 6'2", 190 lbs.   Deb: 8/31/80

YEAR	TM/L	G	AB	R	H	2B	3B	HR	RBI	BB	SO	AVG	OBP	SLG	PRO+	BR/A	SB	CS	SBR	FA	FR	G/POS	TPR
1980	Tor-A	20	41	5	9	0	1	1	5	3	12	.220	.273	.341	64	-2	0	1	-1	1.000	-0	O-11/D-3	-0.3

■ ART HOELSKOETTER
Hoelskoetter, Arthur "Holley" or "Hoss" (a.k.a. Arthur H. Hostetter)
   b: 9/30/1882, St.Louis, Mo.   d: 8/3/54, St.Louis, Mo.   BR/TR, 6'2",   Deb: 9/10/05

YEAR	TM/L	G	AB	R	H	2B	3B	HR	RBI	BB	SO	AVG	OBP	SLG	PRO+	BR/A	SB	CS	SBR	FA	FR	G/POS	TPR
1905	StL-N	24	83	7	20	2	1	0	5	3		.241	.267	.289	68	-3	1			.972	1	3-20/2-3,P	-0.2
1906	StL-N	94	317	21	71	6	3	0	14	4		.224	.238	.262	58	-17	2			.943	-6	3-53,S-16,PO/2	-2.1
1907	StL-N	119	397	21	98	6	3	2	28	27		.247	.298	.292	88	-6	5			.927	10	2-73,1-27/COP3	0.4
1908	StL-N	62	155	10	36	7	1	0	6	6		.232	.265	.290	81	-4	1			.948	-2	C-41/3-2,12	-0.1
Total	4	299	952	59	225	21	8	2	53	40		.236	.271	.282	75	-30	9			.924	3	/2-78,3-77,C1OSP	-1.9

■ JACK HOEY
Hoey, John Bernard   b: 11/10/1881, Watertown, Mass.   d: 11/14/47, Waterbury, Conn.   BL/TL, 5'9", 185 lbs.   Deb: 6/27/06

YEAR	TM/L	G	AB	R	H	2B	3B	HR	RBI	BB	SO	AVG	OBP	SLG	PRO+	BR/A	SB	CS	SBR	FA	FR	G/POS	TPR
1906	Bos-A	94	361	27	88	8	4	0	24	14		.244	.274	.288	76	-10	10			.915	-8	O-94	-2.5
1907	Bos-A	39	96	7	21	2	1	0	8	1		.219	.227	.260	56	-5	2			.857	-5	O-21	-1.3
1908	Bos-A	13	43	5	7	0	0	0	3	0		.163	.163	.163	6	-4	1			1.000	0	O-11	-0.6
Total	3	146	500	39	116	10	5	0	35	15		.232	.256	.272	66	-20	13			.913	-13	O-126	-4.4

■ STEW HOFFERTH
Hofferth, Stewart Edward   b: 1/27/13, Logansport, Ind.   BR/TR, 6'2", 195 lbs.   Deb: 4/19/44

YEAR	TM/L	G	AB	R	H	2B	3B	HR	RBI	BB	SO	AVG	OBP	SLG	PRO+	BR/A	SB	CS	SBR	FA	FR	G/POS	TPR
1944	Bos-N	66	180	14	36	8	1	0	26	11	5	.200	.246	.261	41	-14	0			.984	0	C-47	-1.2
1945	Bos-N	50	170	13	40	2	0	3	15	14	11	.235	.297	.300	66	-8	1			.980	6	C-45	0.1
1946	Bos-N	20	58	3	12	1	0	0	10	3	6	.207	.246	.259	43	-4	0			1.000	-1	C-15	-0.5
Total	3	136	408	30	88	11	1	4	51	28	22	.216	.268	.277	52	-26	1			.985	6	C-107	-1.6

YEAR	TM/L	G	AB	R	H	2B	3B	HR	RBI	BB	SO	AVG	OBP	SLG	PRO+	BR/A	SB	CS	SBR	FA	FR	G/POS	TPR
■ **DUTCH HOFFMAN**				Hoffman, Clarence Casper "Red"				b: 1/28/04, Freeburg, Ill.			d: 12/6/62, Belleville, Ill.			BR/TR, 6', 175 lbs.		Deb: 4/23/29							
1929	Chi-A	107	337	27	87	16	5	3	37	24	28	.258	.307	.362	73	-14	6	3	0	.984	-1	O-88	-2.0
■ **DANNY HOFFMAN**				Hoffman, Daniel John		b: 3/2/1880, Canaan, Conn.			d: 3/14/22, Manchester, Conn.			BL/TL, 5'9", 175 lbs.			Deb: 4/20/03								
1903	Phi-A	74	248	29	61	5	7	2	22	6		.246	.267	.347	79	-7	7			.950	0	O-62/P-1	-1.0
1904	Phi-A	53	204	31	61	7	5	3	24	5		.299	.329	.426	131	6	9			.936	0	O-51	0.4
1905	*Phi-A	120	459	66	120	10	10	1	35	33		.261	.312	.333	103	1	**46**			.942	-2	*O-118	-0.7
1906	Phi-A	7	22	4	5	0	0	0	0	3		.227	.320	.227	70	-1	1			1.000	1	/O-7	0.0
	NY-A	100	320	34	82	10	6	0	23	27		.256	.318	.325	92	-3	32			.938	-9	O-98	-1.8
	Yr	107	342	38	87	10	6	0	23	30		.254	.318	.319	91	-4	33			.943	-8	*O-105	-1.8
1907	NY-A	136	517	81	131	10	3	5	46	42		.253	.325	.313	96	-2	30			.953	8	*O-135	0.1
1908	StL-A	99	363	41	91	9	7	1	25	23		.251	.304	.322	103	1	17			.962	11	O-99	0.9
1909	StL-A	110	387	44	104	6	7	2	26	41		.269	.349	.336	125	12	24			.968	2	*O-110	1.1
1910	StL-A	106	380	20	90	11	5	0	27	34		.237	.306	.292	93	-3	16			.960	1	*O-106	-0.8
1911	StL-A	24	81	11	17	3	2	0	7	12		.210	.326	.296	77	-2	3			.908	3	O-23	0.0
Total	9	829	2981	361	762	71	52	14	235	226		.256	.316	.328	101	4	185			.951	15	O-809/P-1	-1.8
■ **TEX HOFFMAN**			Hoffman, Edward Adolph		b: 11/30/1893, San Antonio, Tex.			d: 5/19/47, New Orleans, La.			BL/TR, 5'9", 195 lbs.			Deb: 7/11/15									
1915	Cle-A	9	13	1	2	0	0	0	2	1	5	.154	.214	.154	10	-1	0			.750	-2	/3-3	-0.3
■ **GLENN HOFFMAN**				Hoffman, Glenn Edward		b: 7/7/58, Orange, Cal.			BR/TR, 6'2", 190 lbs.		Deb: 4/12/80		F									
1980	Bos-A	114	312	37	89	15	4	4	42	19	41	.285	.330	.397	94	-3	2	4	-2	.946	-0	*3-110/S-5,2	-0.6
1981	Bos-A	78	242	28	56	10	0	1	20	12	25	.231	.271	.285	57	-13	0	1	-1	.960	5	S-78/3-1	-0.1
1982	Bos-A	150	469	53	98	23	2	7	49	30	69	.209	.264	.311	54	-30	0	4	-2	.972	13	*S-150	-0.6
1983	Bos-A	143	473	56	123	24	1	4	41	30	76	.260	.307	.340	73	-18	1	1	0	.962	-6	*S-143	-1.0
1984	Bos-A	64	74	8	14	4	0	0	4	5	10	.189	.241	.243	33	-7	0	1	-1	.957	5	S-56/3-4,2	0.0
1985	Bos-A	96	279	40	77	17	2	6	34	25	40	.276	.346	.416	103	1	2	2	-1	.975	-1	S-93/2-3,3	0.8
1986	Bos-A	12	23	1	5	2	0	0	1	2	3	.217	.280	.304	59	-1	0	0	0	.923	-2	S-11/3-1	-0.3
1987	Bos-A	21	55	5	11	3	0	0	6	3	9	.200	.267	.255	38	-5	0	0	0	.984	1	S-16/3-3,2	-0.1
	LA-N	40	132	10	29	5	0	0	10	7	23	.220	.270	.258	42	-11	0	1	-1	.966	1	S-40	-0.7
1989	Cal-A	48	104	9	22	3	0	1	3	3	13	.212	.241	.269	44	-8	0	2	-1	.982	3	S-23,3-18/21D	-0.2
Total	9	766	2163	247	524	106	9	23	210	136	309	.242	.293	.331	68	-94	5	16	-8	.966	21	S-615,3-140/2D1	-3.1
■ **IZZY HOFFMAN**			Hoffman, Harry C.		b: 1/5/1875, Bridgeport, N.J.			d: 11/13/42, Philadelphia, Pa.			BL/TL, 5'9", 160 lbs.			Deb: 4/14/04									
1904	Was-A	10	30	1	3	1	0	0	1	2		.100	.156	.133	-8	-4	0			1.000	1	/O-9	-0.4
1907	Bos-N	19	86	17	24	3	1	0	3	6		.279	.326	.337	108	1	2			.897	-2	O-19	-0.2
Total	2	29	116	18	27	4	1	0	4	8		.233	.282	.284	79	-3	2			.939	-1	/O-28	-0.6
■ **JOHN HOFFMAN**			Hoffman, John Edward "Pork Chop"		b: 10/31/43, Aberdeen, S.D.			BL/TR, 6', 190 lbs.		Deb: 7/30/64												
1964	Hou-N	6	15	1	1	0	0	0	0	1	7	.067	.125	.067	-47	-3	0	0	0	1.000	-2	/C-5	-0.5
1965	Hou-N	2	6	1	2	0	0	0	1	0	3	.333	.333	.333	95	-0	0	0	0	1.000	-1	/C-2	-0.1
Total	2	8	21	2	3	0	0	0	1	1	10	.143	.182	.143	-8	-3	0	0	0	1.000	-2	/C-7	-0.6
■ **LARRY HOFFMAN**			Hoffman, Lawrence Charles		b: 7/18/1878, Chicago, Ill.			d: 12/29/48, Chicago, Ill.			BR/TR,		Deb: 7/9/01										
1901	Chi-N	6	22	2	7	1	0	0	6	0		.318	.348	.364	111	0	1			.800	-2	/3-5,2-1	-0.1
■ **HICKEY HOFFMAN**				Hoffman, Otto Charles		b: 10/27/1856, Cleveland, Ohio			d: 10/27/15, Peoria, Ill.			Deb: 5/10/1879											
1879	Cle-N	2	6	0	0	0	0	0	0	0	3	.000	.000	.000	-99	-1				.857	0	/C-2,O-1	-0.1
■ **RAY HOFFMAN**			Hoffman, Raymond Lamont		b: 6/14/17, Detroit, Mich.			BL/TR, 6'0.5", 175 lbs.		Deb: 8/30/42													
1942	Was-A	7	19	2	1	0	0	0	2	1	1	.053	.100	.053	-57	-4	0	0	0	.815	2	/3-6	-0.2
■ **JESSE HOFFMEISTER**				Hoffmeister, Jesse H.		b: Toledo, Ohio			Deb: 7/24/1897														
1897	Pit-N	48	188	33	58	6	9	3	36	8		.309	.337	.484	120	4	6			.792	-12	3-48	-0.6
■ **SOLLY HOFMAN**				Hofman, Arthur Frederick "Circus Solly"		b: 10/29/1882, St.Louis, Mo.			d: 3/10/56, St.Louis, Mo.			BR/TR, 6', 160 lbs.		Deb: 7/28/03								
1903	Pit-N	3	2	1	0	0	0	0	0	0		.000	.000	.000	-97	-1	0			.000	-1	/O-2	-0.1
1904	Chi-N	7	26	7	7	0	0	1	4	1		.269	.296	.385	110	-0	2			1.000	0	/O-6,S-1	0.0
1905	Chi-N	86	287	43	68	14	4	1	38	20		.237	.289	.324	79	-8	15			.955	4	2-59/1-9,S3O	-0.4
1906	*Chi-N	64	195	30	50	2	3	2	20	20		.256	.326	.328	98	-0	13			.976	-1	O-23,3-21/S23	-0.3
1907	Chi-N	134	470	67	126	11	3	1	36	41		.268	.328	.311	94	-3	29			.938	2	O-69,S-42,1/32	-0.4
1908	*Chi-N	120	411	55	100	15	5	2	42	33		.243	.309	.319	96	-2	15			.955	5	O-50,1-37,2/3	0.2
1909	Chi-N	153	527	60	150	21	4	2	58	53		.285	.351	.351	115	10	20			.965	5	*O-153	1.0
1910	*Chi-N	136	477	83	155	24	16	3	86	65	34	.325	.406	.461	154	33	29			.975	5	*O-110,1-24/3	3.4
1911	Chi-N	143	512	66	129	17	2	2	70	66	40	.252	.341	.305	81	-11	30			.968	-6	*O-107,1-36	-2.4
1912	Chi-N	36	125	28	34	11	0	0	18	22	13	.272	.385	.360	105	2	5			.987	4	O-27/1-9	0.4
	Pit-N	17	53	7	15	4	1	0	2	5	6	.283	.345	.396	104	1	0			1.000	2	O-15	0.2
	Yr	53	178	35	49	15	1	0	20	27	19	.275	.374	.371	105	2	5			.991	6	O-42/1-9	0.6
1913	Pit-N	28	83	11	19	5	2	0	7	8	6	.229	.297	.337	84	-2	3			.964	-1	O-24	-0.4
1914	Bro-F	147	515	65	148	25	12	5	83	54	41	.287	.357	.412	100	-1	34			.951	5	*2-108,1-22,O/S	0.2
1915	Buf-F	109	346	29	81	10	6	0	27	30	28	.234	.295	.298	58	-21	12			.961	1	O-82,1-11/32S	-2.6
1916	NY-A	6	27	0	8	1	1	0	2	1	1	.296	.321	.407	116	0	1			1.000	2	/O-6	0.2
	Chi-N	5	16	2	5	2	1	0	2	2	2	.313	.389	.563	172	1	0			1.000	0	/O-4	0.2
Total	14	1194	4072	554	1095	162	60	19	495	421	171	.269	.340	.352	99	-1	208			.967	26	O-702,2-198,1/S3	-0.8
■ **BOBBY HOFMAN**				Hofman, Robert George		b: 10/5/25, St.Louis, Mo.			d: 4/5/94, Chesterfield, Mo.			BR/TR, 5'11", 175 lbs.		Deb: 4/19/49		C						
1949	NY-N	19	48	4	10	0	0	0	3	5	6	.208	.296	.208	38	-4	0			.939	-0	2-16	-0.4
1952	NY-N	32	63	11	18	2	2	4	8	8	10	.286	.375	.476	134	3	0	0	0	.964	3	2-21/3-2,1	0.7
1953	NY-N	74	169	21	45	7	2	12	34	12	23	.266	.315	.544	117	3	1	1	-0	.918	2	3-23,2-17	0.5
1954	NY-N	71	125	12	28	5	0	8	30	17	15	.224	.322	.456	99	-1	0	0	0	.994	-4	1-21,2-10/3	-0.5
1955	NY-N	96	207	32	55	7	2	10	28	22	31	.266	.339	.464	110	3	0	2	-1	1.000	-5	1-24,C-19,2/3	-0.4
1956	NY-N	47	56	1	10	1	0	2	6	2	8	.179	.270	.196	28	-6	0	0	0	1.000	1	/C-7,3-7,12	-0.4
1957	NY-N	2	2	0	0	0	0	0	0	0	1	.000	.000	.000	-99	-1	0	0	0	.000	0	H	-0.1
Total	7	341	670	81	166	22	6	32	101	70	94	.248	.323	.442	100	-2	1	3		.969	-3	/2-85,1-49,3C	-0.6
■ **FRED HOFMANN**				Hofmann, Fred "Bootnose"		b: 6/10/1894, St.Louis, Mo.			d: 11/19/64, St.Helena, Cal.			BR/TR, 5'11.5", 175 lbs.		Deb: 9/26/19		C						
1919	NY-A	1	1	0	0	0	0	0	0	0		.000	.000	.000	-99	-0	0			1.000	0	/C-1	0.0
1920	NY-A	15	24	3	7	0	0	0	1	1	2	.292	.346	.292	68	-1	0			.905	-4	C-14	-0.4
1921	NY-A	23	62	7	11	1	1	0	5	5	13	.177	.250	.274	33	-6	0			.952	-0	C-18/1-1	-0.6
1922	NY-A	37	91	13	27	5	3	2	10	9	12	.297	.360	.484	116	2	0			.962	-4	C-29	-0.1
1923	*NY-A	72	238	24	69	10	4	3	26	18	27	.290	.350	.403	96	-2	2	1	0	.979	-3	C-70	-0.2
1924	NY-A	62	166	17	29	6	1	1	11	12	15	.175	.239	.241	24	-19	2	1	-0	.991	2	C-54	-1.4
1925	NY-A	3	2	0	0	0	0	0	0	0		.000	.000	.000	-99	-1	0	0	0	1.000	0	/C-1	0.0
1927	Bos-A	87	217	20	59	19	1	0	24	21	26	.272	.342	.369	86	-4	0	0	1	.943	-2	C-81	-0.1

YEAR	TM/L	G	AB	R	H	2B	3B	HR	RBI	BB	SO	AVG	OBP	SLG	PRO+	BR/A	SB	CS	SBR	FA	FR	G/POS	TPR
1928	Bos-A	78	199	14	45	8	1	0	16	11	25	.226	.270	.276	45	-16	0	1	-1	.982	4	C-71	-0.7
Total	9	378	1000	98	247	49	11	7	93	77	120	.247	.308	.339	68	-48	6	3		.969	-7	C-339/1-1	-3.5

■ HARRY HOGAN
Hogan, Harry S. b: 11/1/1875, Syracuse, N.Y. d: 1/24/34, Syracuse, N.Y. Deb: 8/13/01

YEAR	TM/L	G	AB	R	H	2B	3B	HR	RBI	BB	SO	AVG	OBP	SLG	PRO+	BR/A	SB	CS	SBR	FA	FR	G/POS	TPR
1901	Cle-A	1	4	0	0	0	0	0	0	0	0	.000	.000	.000	-99	-1	0			.000	-0	/O-1	-0.1

■ SHANTY HOGAN
Hogan, James Francis b: 3/21/06, Somerville, Mass. d: 4/7/67, Boston, Mass. BR/TR, 6'1", 240 lbs. Deb: 6/23/25

YEAR	TM/L	G	AB	R	H	2B	3B	HR	RBI	BB	SO	AVG	OBP	SLG	PRO+	BR/A	SB	CS	SBR	FA	FR	G/POS	TPR
1925	Bos-N	9	21	2	6	1	1	0	3	1	3	.286	.318	.429	97	-0	0	0	0	1.000	-1	/O-5	-0.1
1926	Bos-N	4	14	1	4	1	1	0	5	0	0	.286	.286	.500	119	0	0			.852	1	/C-4	0.1
1927	Bos-N	71	229	24	66	17	1	3	32	9	23	.288	.324	.410	104	-0	2			.985	2	C-61	0.6
1928	NY-N	131	411	48	137	25	2	10	71	42	25	.333	.406	.477	129	19	0			.978	-10	*C-124	1.9
1929	NY-N	102	317	19	95	13	0	5	45	25	22	.300	.362	.388	86	-6	1			.979	-4	C-93	-0.2
1930	NY-N	122	389	60	132	26	2	13	75	21	24	.339	.378	.517	116	9	2			.982	-3	C-96	1.3
1931	NY-N	123	396	42	119	17	1	12	65	29	29	.301	.354	.439	115	8	1			.996	-0	*C-113	1.5
1932	NY-N	140	502	36	144	18	2	8	77	26	22	.287	.323	.378	90	-7	0			.983	-8	*C-136	-0.7
1933	Bos-N	96	328	15	83	7	0	3	30	13	9	.253	.288	.302	75	-12	0			.997	-1	C-95	-0.7
1934	Bos-N	92	279	20	73	5	2	4	34	16	13	.262	.316	.337	81	-8	0			.986	-2	C-90	-0.6
1935	Bos-N	59	163	9	49	8	0	2	25	21	8	.301	.394	.387	120	6	0			.990	-4	C-56	0.4
1936	Was-A	19	65	8	21	4	0	1	7	11	2	.323	.421	.431	117	2	0	1	-1	.989	0	C-19	0.4
1937	Was-A	21	66	4	10	4	0	0	5	6	8	.152	.222	.212	10	-9	0	1	-1	.979	2	C-21	-0.7
Total	13	989	3180	288	939	146	12	61	474	220	188	.295	.348	.406	101	1	6	2		.985	-26	C-908/O-5	3.2

■ KENNY HOGAN
Hogan, Kenneth Sylvester b: 10/9/02, Cleveland, Ohio d: 1/2/80, Cleveland, Ohio BL/TR, 5'9", 145 lbs. Deb: 10/2/21

YEAR	TM/L	G	AB	R	H	2B	3B	HR	RBI	BB	SO	AVG	OBP	SLG	PRO+	BR/A	SB	CS	SBR	FA	FR	G/POS	TPR
1921	Cin-N	1	2	0	0	0	0	0	0	0	1	.000	.000	.000	-99	-1	0	0	0	.000	-1	/O-1	-0.1
1923	Cle-A	1	0	0	0	0	0	0	0	0	0	—	—	—		0	0	0	0	.000	0	R	0.0
1924	Cle-A	2	1	0	0	0	0	0	0	0	0	.000	.000	.000	-99	-0	0	0	0	.000	0	H	-0.1
Total	3	4	3	0	0	0	0	0	0	0	1	.000	.000	.000	-99	-1	0	0	0	—	-1	/O-1	-0.1

■ MARTY HOGAN
Hogan, Martin F. b: 10/15/1869, Wensbury, England d: 8/15/23, Youngstown, Ohio BR, 5'8", 145 lbs. Deb: 8/6/1894

YEAR	TM/L	G	AB	R	H	2B	3B	HR	RBI	BB	SO	AVG	OBP	SLG	PRO+	BR/A	SB	CS	SBR	FA	FR	G/POS	TPR
1894	Cin-N	6	23	4	3	0	0	0	3	1	4	.130	.167	.130	-27	-5	2			.846	-0	/O-6	-0.4
	StL-N	29	100	11	28	3	4	0	13	3	13	.280	.308	.390	67	-6	2			.887	-1	O-29	-0.7
	Yr	35	123	15	31	3	4	0	16	4	17	.252	.281	.341	49	-11	9			.879	-2	O-35	-1.1
1895	StL-N	5	18	2	3	1	0	0	2	3	0	.167	.286	.222	32	-2	2			.833	1	/O-5	-0.1
Total	2	40	141	17	34	4	4	0	18	7	17	.241	.282	.326	47	-12	11			.869	-1	/O-40	-1.2

■ EDDIE HOGAN
Hogan, Robert Edward b: 4/1860, St.Louis, Mo. BR, 5'7", 153 lbs. Deb: 7/5/1882

YEAR	TM/L	G	AB	R	H	2B	3B	HR	RBI	BB	SO	AVG	OBP	SLG	PRO+	BR/A	SB	CS	SBR	FA	FR	G/POS	TPR
1882	StL-a	1	3	1	1	0	0	0				.333	.333	.333	121	0				.333	-1	/P-1	0.0
1884	Mil-U	11	37	6	3	1	0	0		7		.081	.227	.108	-11	-7				.806	7	O-11	0.0
1887	NY-a	32	120	22	24	6	1	0		30		.200	.373	.267	84	-0	12			.750	-7	O-29/S-4,3	-0.6
1888	Cle-a	78	269	60	61	16	6	0	24	50		.227	.368	.331	128	12	30			.896	-5	O-78	0.5
Total	4	122	429	89	89	23	7	0	24	87		.207	.357	.294	106	5	42			.844	-6	O-118/S-4,3P	-0.1

■ WILLIE HOGAN
Hogan, William Henry "Happy" b: 9/14/1884, N.San Juan, Cal. d: 9/28/74, San Jose, Cal. BR/TR, 5'10", 175 lbs. Deb: 4/12/11 F

YEAR	TM/L	G	AB	R	H	2B	3B	HR	RBI	BB	SO	AVG	OBP	SLG	PRO+	BR/A	SB	CS	SBR	FA	FR	G/POS	TPR
1911	Phi-A	7	19	1	2	1	0	0				.105	.105	.158	-27	-3	0			.900	1	/O-6	-0.3
	StL-A	123	443	53	115	17	8	2	62	43		.260	.328	.348	92	-5	18			.929	13	*O-117/1-5	0.2
	Yr	130	462	54	117	18	8	2	64	43		.253	.320	.340	87	-8	18			.928	13	*O-123/1-5	-0.1
1912	StL-A	108	360	32	77	10	2	1	36	34		.214	.284	.261	58	-19	17			.972	11	*O-100	-1.4
Total	2	238	822	86	194	28	10	3	100	77		.236	.304	.305	75	-28	35			.947	24	O-223/1-5	-1.5

■ BERT HOGG
Hogg, Wilbert George "Sonny" b: 4/21/13, Detroit, Mich. d: 11/5/73, Detroit, Mich. BR/TR, 5'11.5", 162 lbs. Deb: 6/1/34

YEAR	TM/L	G	AB	R	H	2B	3B	HR	RBI	BB	SO	AVG	OBP	SLG	PRO+	BR/A	SB	CS	SBR	FA	FR	G/POS	TPR
1934	Bro-N	2	1	0	0	0	0	0	0	0	0	.000	.000	.000	-99	-0	0			.000	0	/3-1	0.0

■ GEORGE HOGRIEVER
Hogriever, George C. b: 3/17/1869, Cincinnati, Ohio d: 1/26/61, Appleton, Wis. BR/TR, 5'8", 160 lbs. Deb: 4/24/1895

YEAR	TM/L	G	AB	R	H	2B	3B	HR	RBI	BB	SO	AVG	OBP	SLG	PRO+	BR/A	SB	CS	SBR	FA	FR	G/POS	TPR
1895	Cin-N	69	239	61	65	8	7	2	34	36	17	.272	.374	.389	93	-2	41			.934	2	O-66/2-3	-0.4
1901	Mil-A	54	221	25	52	10	2	0	16	30		.235	.329	.299	79	-5	7			.901	2	O-54	-0.7
Total	2	123	460	86	117	18	9	2	50	66	17	.254	.353	.346	87	-7	48			.920	4	O-120/2-3	-1.1

■ BILL HOHMAN
Hohman, William Henry b: 11/27/03, Brooklyn, Md. d: 10/29/68, Baltimore, Md. BR/TR, 6', 178 lbs. Deb: 8/24/27

YEAR	TM/L	G	AB	R	H	2B	3B	HR	RBI	BB	SO	AVG	OBP	SLG	PRO+	BR/A	SB	CS	SBR	FA	FR	G/POS	TPR
1927	Phi-N	7	18	1	5	0	0	0	2	3		.278	.350	.278	69	-1	0			.917	-0	/O-6	-0.1

■ EDDIE HOHNHORST
Hohnhorst, Edward Hicks b: 1/31/1885, Kentucky d: 3/28/16, Covington, Ky. BL/TL, 6'1", 175 lbs. Deb: 9/10/10

YEAR	TM/L	G	AB	R	H	2B	3B	HR	RBI	BB	SO	AVG	OBP	SLG	PRO+	BR/A	SB	CS	SBR	FA	FR	G/POS	TPR
1910	Cle-A	18	63	8	20	3	1	0	6	4		.317	.358	.397	135	2	3			.972	-1	1-18	0.1
1912	Cle-A	15	54	5	11	1	0	0	2	2		.204	.232	.222	29	-5	5			.963	-1	1-15	-0.6
Total	2	33	117	13	31	4	1	0	8	6		.265	.301	.316	83	-3	8			.968	-2	/1-33	-0.5

■ CHRIS HOILES
Hoiles, Christopher Allen b: 3/20/65, Bowling Green, O. BR/TR, 6', 195 lbs. Deb: 4/25/89

YEAR	TM/L	G	AB	R	H	2B	3B	HR	RBI	BB	SO	AVG	OBP	SLG	PRO+	BR/A	SB	CS	SBR	FA	FR	G/POS	TPR
1989	Bal-A	6	9	0	1	1	0	0	1	1	3	.111	.200	.222	19	-1	0	0	0	1.000	1	/C-3,D-3	0.0
1990	Bal-A	23	63	7	12	3	0	1	6	5	12	.190	.250	.286	51	-4	0	0	0	1.000	-1	/C-7,1-6,D	-0.5
1991	Bal-A	107	341	36	83	15	0	11	31	29	61	.243	.305	.384	93	-4	0	2	-1	.998	-14	C-89,D-13/1	-1.4
1992	Bal-A	96	310	49	85	10	1	20	40	55	60	.274	.387	.506	145	19	0	2	-1	.994	-10	C-95/D-1	1.4
1993	Bal-A	126	419	80	130	28	0	29	82	69	94	.310	.419	.585	160	37	1	1	-0	.993	-1	*C-124/D-2	4.1
1994	Bal-A	99	332	45	82	10	0	19	53	63	73	.247	.375	.449	105	3	2	0	1	.989	6	C-98	1.4
Total	6	457	1474	217	393	67	1	80	213	222	303	.267	.369	.476	124	50	3	5	-2	.994	-19	C-416/D-26,1	5.0

■ RAY HOLBERT
Holbert, Ray Arthur b: 9/25/70, Torrance, Cal. BR/TR, 6', 170 lbs. Deb: 5/2/94

YEAR	TM/L	G	AB	R	H	2B	3B	HR	RBI	BB	SO	AVG	OBP	SLG	PRO+	BR/A	SB	CS	SBR	FA	FR	G/POS	TPR
1994	SD-N	5	5	1	1	0	0	0	0	0	4	.200	.200	.200	5	-1	0	0	0	.000	0	/S-1	-0.1

■ BILL HOLBERT
Holbert, William Henry b: 3/14/1855, Baltimore, Md. d: 3/20/35, Laurel, Md. BR/TR, Deb: 9/5/1876 MU

YEAR	TM/L	G	AB	R	H	2B	3B	HR	RBI	BB	SO	AVG	OBP	SLG	PRO+	BR/A	SB	CS	SBR	FA	FR	G/POS	TPR
1876	Lou-N	12	43	3	11	0	0	0	5	0	3	.256	.256	.256	60	-2				.843	7	C-12	0.5
1878	Mil-N	45	173	10	32	0	0	0	12	3	14	.185	.199	.197	28	-13				.818	7	O-30,C-21	-0.7
1879	Syr-N	59	229	11	46	0	0	0	21	1	20	.201	.204	.201	39	-14				.897	-1	*C-56/O-4M	-1.2
	Tro-N	4	15	1	4	0	0	0	2	0	1	.267	.267	.267	82	-0				.893	1	/C-4	0.0
	Yr	63	244	12	50	0	0	0	23	1	21	.205	.207	.205	41	-14				.897	0	C-60/O-4	-1.2
1880	Tro-N	60	212	18	40	5	1	0	8	9	18	.189	.222	.222	48	-11				.911	12	*C-58/O-3	0.1
1881	Tro-N	46	180	16	49	3	0	0	14	3	13	.272	.284	.289	77	-5				.918	7	C-43/O-3	0.3
1882	Tro-N	71	251	24	46	9	0	0	23	11	22	.183	.218	.203	38	-16				.892	16	C-58,3-12/O	0.1
1883	NY-a	73	299	26	71	9	1	0		1		.237	.240	.274	62	-13				.920	35	*C-68/O-5,2	2.3
1884	*NY-a	65	255	28	53	5	0	0		7		.208	.235	.227	53	-13				.920	21	C-59/O-5,S	1.2
1885	NY-a	56	202	13	35	3	0	0		8		.173	.205	.188	27	-16				.900	12	C-39,O-13/3	0.0
1886	NY-a	48	171	8	35	0	0	0		6		.205	.232	.251	54	-9	4			.922	19	C-45/O-3,S	1.3
1887	NY-a	69	255	20	58	4	3	0		7		.227	.248	.267	46	-19	12			.894	2	C-60/1-8,S2	-1.0
1888	Bro-a	15	50	4	6	1	0	0	1	2		.120	.170	.140	-0	-6	0			.926	2	C-15	-0.2
Total	12	623	2335	182	486	41	7	0	86	58	91	.208	.228	.232	47	-138	16			.907	140	C-538/O-69,31S2	2.7

■ SAMMY HOLBROOK
Holbrook, James Marbury b: 7/17/10, Meridian, Miss. d: 4/10/91, Jackson, Miss. BR/TR, 5'11", 189 lbs. Deb: 4/25/35

YEAR	TM/L	G	AB	R	H	2B	3B	HR	RBI	BB	SO	AVG	OBP	SLG	PRO+	BR/A	SB	CS	SBR	FA	FR	G/POS	TPR
1935	Was-A	52	135	20	35	2	2	2	25	30	16	.259	.408	.348	101	2	0	0	0	.952	-11	C-47	-0.7

YEAR	TM/L	G	AB	R	H	2B	3B	HR	RBI	BB	SO	AVG	OBP	SLG	PRO+	BR/A	SB	CS	SBR	FA	FR	G/POS	TPR
■ **JOE HOLDEN**				Holden, Joseph Francis "Socks" b: 6/4/13, St.Clair, Pa. BL/TR, 5'8", 175 lbs. Deb: 6/14/34																			
1934	Phi-N	10	14	1	1	0	0	0	0	0	2	.071	.071	.071	-54	-3	0			1.000	2	/C-6	-0.1
1935	Phi-N	6	9	0	1	0	0	0	0	0	3	.111	.111	.111	-36	-2	1			1.000	-1	/C-4	-0.2
1936	Phi-N	1	1	0	0	0	0	0	0	0	0	.000	.000	.000	-91	-0	0			.000	0	H	0.0
Total	3	17	24	1	2	0	0	0	0	0	5	.083	.083	.083	-49	-5	1			1.000	2	/C-10	-0.3
■ **BILL HOLDEN**				Holden, William Paul b: 9/7/1889, Birmingham, Ala. d: 9/14/71, Pensacola, Fla. BR/TR, 6', 170 lbs. Deb: 9/11/13																			
1913	NY-A	18	53	6	16	3	1	0	8	8	5	.302	.393	.396	131	2	0			.977	3	O-16	0.4
1914	NY-A	50	165	12	30	3	3	0	12	16	26	.182	.254	.224	44	-11	2	4	-2	.981	-1	O-45	-1.8
	Cin-N	11	28	2	6	0	0	0	1	3	5	.214	.290	.214	49	-2	0			1.000	-2	O-10	-0.4
Total	2	79	246	20	52	6	3	0	21	27	36	.211	.289	.260	64	-11	2	4		.981	0	/O-71	-1.8
■ **JIM HOLDSWORTH**			Holdsworth, James "Long Jim" b: 7/14/1850, New York, N.Y. d: 3/22/18, New York, N.Y. BR/TR, Deb: 5/14/1872																				
1872	Cle-n	22	111	19	33	5	1	0	11	1	2	.297	.304	.360	110	2						*S-21	0.1
	Eck-n	2	7	1	2	0	0	0	0	0	0	.286	.286	.286	90	0						/S-2	0.0
	Yr	24	118	20	35	5	1	0	11	1	2	.297	.303	.356	109	2						S-23	0.1
1873	Mut-n	53	233	46	75	6	8	0	27	0	3	.322	.322	.416	116	4						*S-53	0.2
1874	Phi-n	57	286	60	97	8	9	0		0	1	.339	.341	.430	139	11						3-31,S-23/O	0.8
1875	Mut-n	71	325	45	91	11	1	0		0	1	.280	.282	.320	102	-1						O-45,S-26	-0.1
1876	NY-N	52	241	23	64	3	2	0	19	1	2	.266	.269	.295	101	1				.902	1	*O-49/2-3	0.1
1877	Har-N	55	260	26	66	5	2	0	20	2	8	.254	.260	.288	81	-5				.833	-3	*O-55	-0.9
1882	Tro-N	1	3	0	0	0	0	0	0	0	1	.000	.000	.000	-99	-1				1.000	1	/O-1	0.0
1884	Ind-a	5	18	1	2	0	0	0		0	2	.111	.200	.111	4	-2				.929	1	/O-5	0.0
Total	4 n	205	962	171	298	30	19	0	38	3	5	.310	.312	.380	118	17						S-125/O-49,3	1.0
Total	4	113	522	50	132	8	4	0	39	5	11	.253	.260	.284	85	-6				.875	0	O-110/2-3	-0.8
■ **WALTER HOLKE**			Holke, Walter Henry "Union Man" b: 12/25/1892, St.Louis, Mo. d: 10/12/54, St.Louis, Mo. BB/TL, 6'1.5", 185 lbs. Deb: 10/6/14 C																				
1914	NY-N	2	6	0	2	0	0	0	0	0	0	.333	.333	.333	102	-0	0			.950	0	/1-2	0.0
1916	NY-N	34	111	16	39	4	2	0	13	6	16	.351	.390	.423	158	7	10			.997	-0	1-34	0.7
1917	*NY-N	153	527	55	146	12	7	2	55	34	54	.277	.327	.338	107	4	13			.989	-5	*1-153	-0.7
1918	NY-N	88	326	38	82	17	4	1	27	10	26	.252	.276	.337	88	-6	10			.990	5	1-88	-0.5
1919	Bos-N	137	518	48	151	14	6	0	48	21	25	.292	.325	.342	105	2	19			.993	6	*1-136	0.4
1920	Bos-N	144	551	50	162	15	11	3	64	28	31	.294	.329	.377	107	4	4	11	-5	.991	-3	*1-143	-0.8
1921	Bos-N	150	579	60	151	15	10	3	63	17	41	.261	.284	.337	67	-28	8	11	-4	**.997**	3	*1-150	-3.4
1922	Bos-N	105	395	35	115	9	4	0	46	14	23	.291	.317	.334	71	-17	6	8	-3	.993	-4	*1-105	-2.7
1923	Phi-N	147	562	64	175	31	4	7	70	16	37	.311	.330	.418	86	-13	7	9	-3	.991	-1	*1-146/P-1	-2.4
1924	Phi-N	148	563	60	169	23	6	0	64	25	33	.300	.330	.394	83	-14	3	8	-4	.993	4	*1-148	-2.4
1925	Phi-N	39	86	11	21	5	0	1	17	3	6	.244	.270	.337	50	-7	0	0	0	.994	1	1-23	-0.6
	Cin-N	65	232	24	65	8	4	1	20	17	12	.280	.329	.362	78	-8	1	3	-2	.997	1	1-65	-1.1
	Yr	104	318	35	86	13	4	2	37	20	18	.270	.314	.355	69	-15	1	3	-2	.996	2	1-88	-1.7
Total	11	1212	4456	464	1278	153	58	24	487	191	304	.287	.318	.363	89	-74	81	50		.993	7	*1-1193/P-1	-13.5
■ **BILL HOLLAHAN**			Hollahan, William James "Happy" b: 11/22/1896, New York, N.Y. d: 11/27/65, New York, N.Y. BR/TR, 5'8", 165 lbs. Deb: 9/27/20																				
1920	Was-A	3	4	0	1	0	0	0	1	1	2	.250	.400	.250	77	-0	1	0	0	1.000	0	/3-3	0.1
■ **DUTCH HOLLAND**			Holland, Robert Clyde b: 10/12/03, Middlesex, N.C. d: 6/16/67, Lumberton, N.C. BR/TR, 6'1", 190 lbs. Deb: 8/16/32																				
1932	Bos-N	39	156	15	46	11	1	1	18	12	20	.295	.345	.397	103	1	0			.990	2	O-39	0.0
1933	Bos-N	13	31	3	8	3	0	0	3	3	8	.258	.324	.355	102	0	1			.867	1	/O-7	-0.2
1934	Cle-A	50	128	19	32	12	1	2	13	13	11	.250	.319	.406	85	-3	0	0	0	.957	-4	O-31	-0.8
Total	3	102	315	37	86	26	2	3	34	28	39	.273	.332	.397	95	-3	1	0		.969	-3	/O-77	-1.0
■ **WILL HOLLAND**			Holland, Willard A. b: Georgetown, Del. d: 7/19/30, Philadelphia, Pa. 5'10", 180 lbs. Deb: 7/10/1889																				
1889	Bal-a	40	143	13	27	1	2	0	16	9	28	.189	.247	.224	34	-13	4			.853	-15	S-39/O-1	-2.2
■ **GARY HOLLE**			Holle, Gary Charles b: 8/11/54, Albany, N.Y. BR/TL, 6'6", 210 lbs. Deb: 6/2/79																				
1979	Tex-A	5	6	0	1	1	0	0	1	0	1	.167	.286	.333	67	-0	0	0	0	1.000	-0	/1-1	-0.1
■ **BUG HOLLIDAY**			Holliday, James Wear b: 2/8/1867, St.Louis, Mo. d: 2/15/10, Cincinnati, Ohio BR/TR, 5'11", 151 lbs. Deb: 4/17/1889 U																				
1889	Cin-a	135	563	107	181	28	7	**19**	104	43	59	.321	.372	.497	142	27	46			.923	-7	*O-135	1.4
1890	Cin-N	131	518	93	140	18	14	4	75	49	36	.270	.341	.382	111	7	50			.948	-8	*O-131	0.0
1891	Cin-N	111	442	74	141	21	10	9	84	37	28	.319	.376	.473	145	24	30			.939	-8	*O-111	1.1
1892	Cin-N	152	602	114	176	23	16	**13**	91	57	39	.292	.355	.449	145	30	43			.933	-4	*O-152/P-1	1.8
1893	Cin-N	126	500	108	155	24	10	5	89	73	22	.310	.401	.428	117	13	32			.944	-10	*O-125/1-1	-0.3
1894	Cin-N	121	511	119	190	24	7	13	119	64	30	.372	.420	.523	121	16	29			.914	-8	*O-119/1-1	0.6
1895	Cin-N	32	127	25	38	9	2	0	20	10	3	.299	.350	.402	90	-2	6			.940	-4	O-32	-0.7
1896	Cin-N	29	84	17	27	4	0	0	8	9	4	.321	.394	.369	95	-0	1			.925	-2	O-16/1-5,SP	-0.3
1897	Cin-N	61	195	50	61	9	4	2	20	27		.313	.399	.431	112	3	6			.940	-6	O-42/S-4,21	-0.5
1898	Cin-N	30	106	21	25	2	1	0	7	14		.236	.325	.274	67	-4	5			.969	-2	O-28	-0.8
Total	10	928	3648	728	1134	162	71	65	617	359	211	.311	.376	.448	125	114	248			.935	-45	O-891/1-10,S2P	2.3
■ **HOLLY HOLLINGSHEAD**		Hollingshead, John Samuel (a.k.a. Samuel John Holly) b: 1/17/1853, Washington, D.C. d: 10/6/26, Washington, D.C. Deb: 4/20/1872 M																					
1872	Nat-n	9	46	12	15	0	1	0	5	1	0	.326	.340	.370	102	-1						/2-9	-0.1
1873	Was-n	30	136	25	35	1	3	0	19	0	6	.257	.257	.309	68	-5						O-30/2-2	-0.3
1875	Was-n	19	81	7	20	0	2	0		0		.247	.247	.296	90	-1						O-19,M	0.0
Total	3 n	58	263	44	70	1	6	0		1		.266	.269	.316	81	-6						/O-49,2-11	-0.4
■ **DAVE HOLLINS**			Hollins, David Michael b: 5/25/66, Buffalo, N.Y. BB/TR, 6'1", 195 lbs. Deb: 4/12/90																				
1990	Phi-N	72	114	14	21	0	0	5	15	10	28	.184	.256	.316	57	-7	0	0	0	.932	-1	3-30/1-1	-0.9
1991	Phi-N	56	151	18	45	10	2	6	21	17	26	.298	.380	.510	150	10	1	1	-0	.922	-3	3-36/1-6	0.6
1992	Phi-N	156	586	104	158	28	4	27	93	76	110	.270	.372	.469	137	30	9	6	-1	.954	-20	*3-156/1-1	1.0
1993	*Phi-N★	143	543	104	148	30	4	18	93	85	109	.273	.376	.442	120	17	2	3	-1	.914	-29	*3-143	-1.2
1994	Phi-N	44	162	28	36	7	1	4	26	23	32	.222	.333	.352	80	-4	1	0	0	.887	-15	3-43/O-1	-1.9
Total	5	471	1556	268	408	75	11	60	248	211	305	.262	.362	.440	120	46	13	10	-2	.930	-68	3-408/1-8,O	-2.4
■ **STAN HOLLMIG**			Hollmig, Stanley Ernest "Hondo" b: 1/2/26, Fredericksburg, Tex d: 12/4/81, San Antonio, Tex. BR/TR, 6'2.5", 190 lbs. Deb: 4/19/49																				
1949	Phi-N	81	251	28	64	11	6	2	26	20	43	.255	.315	.371	85	-6	1			.958	-6	O-66	-1.4
1950	Phi-N	11	12	1	3	2	0	0	1	0	3	.250	.250	.417	73	-1	0	0	0	1.000	-1	/O-3	-0.1
1951	Phi-N	2	2	0	0	0	0	0	0	0	0	.000	.000	.000	-99	-1	0	0	0	.000	0	H	-0.1
Total	3	94	265	29	67	13	6	2	26	20	46	.253	.310	.370	84	-7	1	0		.959	-6	/O-69	-1.6
■ **CHARLIE HOLLOCHER**		Hollocher, Charles Jacob b: 6/11/1896, St.Louis, Mo. d: 8/14/40, Frontenac, Mo. BL/TR, 5'7", 154 lbs. Deb: 4/16/18																					
1918	*Chi-N	131	509	72	**161**	23	6	2	38	47	30	.316	.379	.397	133	21	26			.929	-19	*S-131	0.8
1919	Chi-N	115	430	51	116	14	5	3	26	44	19	.270	.347	.347	108	6	16			.941	6	*S-115	2.0
1920	Chi-N	80	301	53	96	9	0	0	22	41	15	.319	.406	.389	126	12	20	14	-2	.954	9	S-80	2.7
1921	Chi-N	140	558	71	161	28	8	3	37	43	13	.289	.342	.384	91	-6	5	16	-8	**.963**	3	*S-137	0.2

YEAR	TM/L	G	AB	R	H	2B	3B	HR	RBI	BB	SO	AVG	OBP	SLG	PRO+	BR/A	SB	CS	SBR	FA	FR	G/POS	TPR
1922	Chi-N	152	592	90	201	37	8	3	69	58	5	.340	.403	.444	116	16	19	29	-12	**.965**	-5	*S-152	1.3
1923	Chi-N	66	260	46	89	14	2	1	28	26	5	.342	.410	.423	120	9	9	10	-3	.963	-9	S-65	0.3
1924	Chi-N	76	286	28	70	12	4	2	21	18	7	.245	.292	.336	67	-14	4	11	-5	.969	-4	S-71	-0.8
Total	7	760	2936	411	894	145	35	14	241	277	94	.304	.370	.392	110	44	99	80		.954	-13	S-751	6.5

■ ED HOLLY
Holly, Edward William (b: Edward William Ruthlavy) b: 7/6/1879, Chicago, Ill. d: 11/27/73, Williamsport, Pa. BR/TR, 5'10", 165 lbs. Deb: 7/18/06

YEAR	TM/L	G	AB	R	H	2B	3B	HR	RBI	BB	SO	AVG	OBP	SLG	PRO+	BR/A	SB	CS	SBR	FA	FR	G/POS	TPR
1906	StL-N	10	34	1	2	0	0	0	7	5		.059	.179	.059	-27	-5	0			.939	-3	S-10	-0.8
1907	StL-N	150	545	55	125	18	3	1	40	36		.229	.283	.279	79	-14	16			.927	11	*S-147/2-3	0.0
1914	Pit-F	100	350	28	86	9	4	0	26	17	52	.246	.281	.294	49	-27	14			.942	-2	S-94/O-2,2	-2.3
1915	Pit-F	16	42	8	11	2	0	0	5	5	6	.262	.354	.310	79	-1	3			.865	-4	S-11/3-3	-0.5
Total	4	276	971	92	224	29	7	1	78	63	58	.231	.282	.278	64	-47	33			.931	2	S-262/2-4,3O	-3.6

■ WATTIE HOLM
Holm, Roscoe Albert b: 12/28/01, Peterson, Iowa d: 5/19/50, Everly, Iowa BR/TR, 5'9.5", 160 lbs. Deb: 4/15/24

YEAR	TM/L	G	AB	R	H	2B	3B	HR	RBI	BB	SO	AVG	OBP	SLG	PRO+	BR/A	SB	CS	SBR	FA	FR	G/POS	TPR
1924	StL-N	81	293	40	86	10	4	0	23	8	16	.294	.317	.355	81	-8	1	4	-2	.988	2	O-64/C-9,3	-1.3
1925	StL-N	13	58	10	12	1	1	0	2	3	1	.207	.246	.259	28	-6	1	0	0	.976	2	O-13	-0.5
1926	*StL-N	55	144	18	41	5	1	0	21	18	14	.285	.364	.333	85	-2	3			.962	-3	O-39	-0.8
1927	StL-N	110	419	55	120	27	8	3	66	24	29	.286	.327	.411	93	-5	4			.967	-8	O-97/3-9	-1.8
1928	*StL-N	102	386	61	107	24	6	3	47	32	17	.277	.334	.394	88	-7	1			.918	-10	3-83/O-7	-1.3
1929	StL-N	64	176	21	41	5	6	0	14	12	8	.233	.282	.330	50	-14	1			.944	3	O-44/3-1	-1.3
1932	StL-N	11	17	2	3	1	0	0	1	3	1	.176	.333	.235	55	-1	0			1.000	0	/O-4	-0.1
Total	7	436	1493	207	410	73	26	6	174	100	86	.275	.322	.370	81	-44	11	4		.970	-15	O-268/3-97,C	-7.1

■ BILLY HOLM
Holm, William Frederick Henry b: 7/21/12, Chicago, Ill. d: 7/27/77, East Chicago, Ind BR/TR, 5'10.5", 168 lbs. Deb: 9/24/43

YEAR	TM/L	G	AB	R	H	2B	3B	HR	RBI	BB	SO	AVG	OBP	SLG	PRO+	BR/A	SB	CS	SBR	FA	FR	G/POS	TPR
1943	Chi-N	7	15	0	1	0	0	0	0	2	4	.067	.176	.067	-29	-2	0			1.000	1	/C-7	-0.1
1944	Chi-N	54	132	10	18	2	0	0	6	16	19	.136	.235	.152	10	-15	1			.979	-2	C-50	-1.6
1945	Bos-A	58	135	12	25	2	1	0	9	23	17	.185	.317	.215	54	-7	1	1	-0	.980	-4	C-57	-0.9
Total	3	119	282	22	44	4	1	0	15	41	40	.156	.272	.177	30	-25	2	1		.981	-4	C-114	-2.6

■ GARY HOLMAN
Holman, Gary Richard b: 1/25/44, Long Beach, Cal. BL/TL, 6'1", 200 lbs. Deb: 6/26/68

YEAR	TM/L	G	AB	R	H	2B	3B	HR	RBI	BB	SO	AVG	OBP	SLG	PRO+	BR/A	SB	CS	SBR	FA	FR	G/POS	TPR
1968	Was-A	75	85	10	25	5	1	0	7	13	15	.294	.388	.376	137	4	0	0		1.000	2	1-33,O-10	0.6
1969	Was-A	41	31	1	5	1	0	0	2	4	7	.161	.257	.194	29	-3	0	0	0	1.000	-1	1-11/O-3	-0.5
Total	2	116	116	11	30	6	1	0	9	17	22	.259	.353	.328	107	1	0	0	0	1.000	1	/1-44,O-13	0.1

■ FRED HOLMES
Holmes, Frederick C. b: 7/1/1878, Chicago, Ill. d: 2/13/56, Norwood Park, Ill. BR/TR, Deb: 8/23/03

YEAR	TM/L	G	AB	R	H	2B	3B	HR	RBI	BB	SO	AVG	OBP	SLG	PRO+	BR/A	SB	CS	SBR	FA	FR	G/POS	TPR
1903	NY-A	1	0	0	0	0	0	0	0	1		—	1.000	—	207	0	0			.833	-0	/1-1	0.0
1904	Chi-N	1	3	1	1	1	0	0	0	0	1	.333	.333	.667	206	0	0			1.000	0	/C-1	0.0
Total	2	2	3	1	1	1	0	0	0	1	1	.333	.500	.667	255	1	0			1.000	-0	/C-1,1-1	0.0

■ DUCKY HOLMES
Holmes, Howard Elbert b: 7/8/1883, Dayton, Ohio d: 9/18/45, Dayton, Ohio BR/TR, 5'10", 160 lbs. Deb: 4/18/06

YEAR	TM/L	G	AB	R	H	2B	3B	HR	RBI	BB	SO	AVG	OBP	SLG	PRO+	BR/A	SB	CS	SBR	FA	FR	G/POS	TPR
1906	StL-N	9	27	2	5	0	0	0	2	2		.185	.267	.185	43	-2	0			.979	-1	/C-9	-0.2

■ DUCKY HOLMES
Holmes, James William b: 1/28/1869, Des Moines, Iowa d: 8/6/32, Truro, Iowa BL/TR, 5'6", 170 lbs. Deb: 8/8/1895

YEAR	TM/L	G	AB	R	H	2B	3B	HR	RBI	BB	SO	AVG	OBP	SLG	PRO+	BR/A	SB	CS	SBR	FA	FR	G/POS	TPR
1895	Lou-N	40	161	33	60	10	2	3	20	12	9	.373	.426	.516	152	13	9			.780	-11	O-29/S-8,3P	0.0
1896	Lou-N	47	141	22	38	3	2	0	18	13	5	.270	.360	.319	83	-3	8			.790	-7	O-33/P-2,S2	-1.0
1897	Lou-N	2	4	0	0	0	0	0	0	1		.000	.200	.000	-46	-1	0			1.000	1	/S-1	0.0
	NY-N	79	306	51	82	8	6	1	44	18		.268	.317	.343	76	-11	30			.904	-7	O-77/S-1	-2.1
	Yr	81	310	51	82	8	6	1	44	19		.265	.315	.339	75	-12	30			.904	-6	O-77/S-2	-2.1
1898	StL-N	23	101	9	24	1	1	0	0	2		.238	.260	.267	50	-7	4			.900	2	O-22	-0.6
	Bal-N	113	442	54	126	10	9	1	64	23		.285	.333	.355	96	-3	25			.935	4	*O-113	-0.7
	Yr	136	543	63	150	11	10	1	64	25		.276	.320	.339	87	-10	29			.930	6	*O-135	-1.3
1899	Bal-N	138	553	80	177	31	7	4	66	39		.320	.381	.423	114	10	50			.927	6	*O-138	0.5
1901	Det-A	131	537	90	158	28	10	4	62	37		.294	.347	.406	103	1	35			.907	-2	*O-131	-0.9
1902	Det-A	92	362	50	93	15	4	2	33	28		.257	.319	.337	80	-9	16			.950	6	O-92	-0.9
1903	Was-A	21	71	13	16	3	1	1	8	5		.225	.286	.338	85	-1	10			.912	1	O-14/3-4,2	-0.1
	Chi-A	86	344	53	96	7	5	0	18	25		.279	.335	.328	104	3	25			.965	2	O-82/3-3	0.0
	Yr	107	415	66	112	10	6	1	26	30		.270	.327	.330	101	1	35			.956	3	O-96/3-7,2	-0.1
1904	Chi-A	68	251	42	78	11	9	1	19	14		.311	.354	.438	156	15	13			.975	2	O-63	1.5
1905	Chi-A	92	328	42	66	15	2	0	22	19		.201	.258	.250	67	-12	11			.936	-1	O-89	-2.0
Total	10	932	3601	539	1014	142	58	17	374	236	14	.282	.337	.367	99	-5	236			.924	-5	O-883/3-11,SP2	-6.3

■ TOMMY HOLMES
Holmes, Thomas Francis "Kelly" b: 3/29/17, Brooklyn, N.Y. BL/TL, 5'10", 180 lbs. Deb: 4/14/42 M

YEAR	TM/L	G	AB	R	H	2B	3B	HR	RBI	BB	SO	AVG	OBP	SLG	PRO+	BR/A	SB	CS	SBR	FA	FR	G/POS	TPR
1942	Bos-N	141	558	56	155	24	4	4	41	64	10	.278	.353	.357	110	8	2			.990	15	*O-140	1.7
1943	Bos-N	152	629	75	170	33	10	5	41	58	20	.270	.334	.378	107	5	7			.993	8	*O-152	0.5
1944	Bos-N	155	631	93	195	42	6	13	73	61	11	.309	.372	.456	127	22	4			.991	6	*O-155	2.0
1945	Bos-N†	154	636	125	**224**	**47**	6	**28**	117	70	9	.352	.420	**.577**	175	62	15			.983	1	*O-154	**5.4**
1946	Bos-N	149	568	80	176	35	6	9	79	58	14	.310	.377	.424	126	19	7			.987	8	*O-146	2.1
1947	Bos-N	150	618	90	**191**	33	3	9	53	44	16	.309	.360	.416	108	7	3			.989	10	*O-147	0.8
1948	*Bos-N★	139	585	85	190	35	7	6	61	46	20	.325	.375	.439	122	17	1			.983	4	*O-137	1.3
1949	Bos-N	117	380	47	101	20	4	8	59	39	6	.266	.337	.403	103	1	1			.987	5	*O-103	0.1
1950	Bos-N	105	322	44	96	20	1	9	51	33	8	.298	.370	.450	122	10	0			1.000	-0	O-88	0.6
1951	Bos-N	27	29	1	5	0	0	0	5	3	4	.172	.250	.241	35	-3	0	0	0	1.000	-1	/O-3,M	-0.4
1952	*Bro-N	31	36	2	4	1	0	0	1	4	4	.111	.200	.139	-4	-5	0	0	0	1.000	-1	/O-6	-0.6
Total	11	1320	4992	698	1507	292	47	88	581	480	122	.302	.366	.432	122	144	40	0		.989	53	*O-1231	13.5

■ RED HOLT
Holt, James Emmett Madison b: 7/25/1894, Dayton, Tenn. d: 2/2/61, Birmingham, Ala. BL/TL, 5'11", 175 lbs. Deb: 9/5/25

YEAR	TM/L	G	AB	R	H	2B	3B	HR	RBI	BB	SO	AVG	OBP	SLG	PRO+	BR/A	SB	CS	SBR	FA	FR	G/POS	TPR
1925	Phi-A	27	88	13	24	7	0	1	8	12	9	.273	.360	.386	84	-2	0	0	0	.986	0	1-25	-0.3

■ JIM HOLT
Holt, James William b: 5/27/44, Graham, N.C. BL/TR, 6', 195 lbs. Deb: 4/17/68

YEAR	TM/L	G	AB	R	H	2B	3B	HR	RBI	BB	SO	AVG	OBP	SLG	PRO+	BR/A	SB	CS	SBR	FA	FR	G/POS	TPR
1968	Min-A	70	106	9	22	0	0	0	8	4	20	.208	.236	.245	44	-7	0	1	-1	.973	-5	O-38/1-1	-1.6
1969	Min-A	12	14	3	5	0	0	1	2	0	4	.357	.357	.571	153	1	0	0	0	1.000	-2	/O-5,1-1	-0.1
1970	*Min-A	142	319	37	85	9	3	6	40	17	32	.266	.304	.342	77	-10	3	1	0	.995	-11	*O-130/1-2	-2.6
1971	Min-A	126	340	35	88	11	3	1	29	16	28	.259	.294	.318	71	-13	5	1	1	.986	-5	*O-106/1-3	-2.3
1972	Min-A	10	27	6	12	1	0	0	6	0	1	.444	.444	.593	197	3	0	0	0	.917	-3	/O-7,1-1	0.3
1973	Min-A	132	441	52	131	25	3	11	58	29	43	.297	.343	.442	115	8	0	3	-2	.990	5	*O-102,1-33	0.4
1974	Min-A	79	197	24	50	11	0	0	16	14	16	.254	.307	.310	75	-6	0	0	0	.996	5	1-67/O-5	-0.5
	*Oak-A	30	42	1	6	0	0	0	0	1	9	.143	.182	.143	-6	-6	0	0	0	1.000	1	1-17/D-3	-0.5
	Yr	109	239	25	56	11	0	0	16	15	25	.234	.285	.280	62	-11	0	0	0	.996	6	1-84/O-5,D	-1.0
1975	*Oak-A	102	123	7	27	3	0	2	16	11	11	.220	.294	.293	68	-5	0	0	0	.991	6	1-52/O-2,CD	-0.6
1976	Oak-A	4	7	0	2	0	0	0	1	1	2	.286	.375	.571	182	1	0	0	0	.000	0	/D-2	0.1
Total	9	707	1616	174	428	64	10	19	177	93	166	.265	.308	.352	84	-35	8	6	-1	.988	-11	O-395,1-177/DC	-7.4

■ ROGER HOLT
Holt, Roger Boyd b: 4/8/56, Daytona Beach, Fla. BB/TR, 5'11", 165 lbs. Deb: 10/4/80

YEAR	TM/L	G	AB	R	H	2B	3B	HR	RBI	BB	SO	AVG	OBP	SLG	PRO+	BR/A	SB	CS	SBR	FA	FR	G/POS	TPR
1980	NY-A	2	6	0	1	0	0	0	1	1	2	.167	.286	.167	28	-1	0	0	0	1.000	1	/2-2	0.0

■ MARTY HONAN
Honan, Martin Weldon b: 4/1871, Chicago, Ill. d: 8/20/08, Chicago, Ill. Deb: 10/3/1890

YEAR	TM/L	G	AB	R	H	2B	3B	HR	RBI	BB	SO	AVG	OBP	SLG	PRO+	BR/A	SB	CS	SBR	FA	FR	G/POS	TPR
1890	Chi-N	1	3	0	0	0	0	0	1	0	2	.000	.000	.000	-96	-1	0			.857	-0	/C-1	-0.1

YEAR	TM/L	G	AB	R	H	2B	3B	HR	RBI	BB	SO	AVG	OBP	SLG	PRO+	BR/A	SB	CS	SBR	FA	FR	G/POS	TPR
1891	Chi-N	5	12	1	2	0	1	0	3	1	3	.167	.231	.333	64	-1	0			.963	2	/C-5	0.1
Total	2	6	15	1	2	0	1	0	4	1	5	.133	.188	.267	32	-1	0			.941	1	/C-6	0.0

■ ABIE HOOD
Hood, Albie Larrison   b: 1/31/03, Sanford, N.C.   d: 10/14/88, Chesapeake, Va.   BL/TR, 5'7", 152 lbs.   Deb: 7/15/25

YEAR	TM/L	G	AB	R	H	2B	3B	HR	RBI	BB	SO	AVG	OBP	SLG	PRO+	BR/A	SB	CS	SBR	FA	FR	G/POS	TPR
1925	Bos-N	5	21	2	6	2	0	1	2	1	0	.286	.318	.524	122	0	0	0	0	.920	-4	/2-5	-0.3

■ WALLY HOOD
Hood, Wallace James Sr.   b: 2/9/1895, Whittier, Cal.   d: 5/2/65, Hollywood, Cal.   BR/TR, 5'11.5", 160 lbs.   Deb: 4/15/20   F

YEAR	TM/L	G	AB	R	H	2B	3B	HR	RBI	BB	SO	AVG	OBP	SLG	PRO+	BR/A	SB	CS	SBR	FA	FR	G/POS	TPR
1920	Bro-N	7	14	4	2	1	0	0	1	4	4	.143	.333	.214	58	-1	2	0	1	.944	1	/O-5	0.1
	Pit-N	2	1	1	0	0	0	0	0	1	0	.000	.500	.000	50	-1	1	0	0	.000	0	H	0.0
	Yr	9	15	5	2	1	0	0	1	5	4	.133	.350	.200	59	-1	3	0	1	.944	1	/O-5	0.1
1921	Bro-N	56	65	16	17	1	2	1	4	9	14	.262	.360	.385	94	-0	2	2	-1	.957	-6	O-20	-0.7
1922	Bro-N	2	0	2	0	0	0	0	0	0	0	—	—	—	—		0	0	0	.000	0	R	0.0
Total	3	67	80	23	19	2	2	1	5	14	18	.237	.358	.350	88	-1	5	2	0	.951	-4	/O-25	-0.6

■ ALEX HOOKS
Hooks, Alexander Marcus   b: 8/29/06, Edgewood, Tex.   d: 6/19/93, Edgewood, Tex.   BL/TL, 6'1", 183 lbs.   Deb: 4/17/35

YEAR	TM/L	G	AB	R	H	2B	3B	HR	RBI	BB	SO	AVG	OBP	SLG	PRO+	BR/A	SB	CS	SBR	FA	FR	G/POS	TPR
1935	Phi-A	15	44	4	10	3	0	0	4	3	10	.227	.277	.295	48	-3	0	0	0	1.000	0	1-10	-0.4

■ HARRY HOOPER
Hooper, Harry Bartholomew   b: 8/24/1887, Bell Station, Cal.   d: 12/18/74, Santa Cruz, Cal.   BL/TR, 5'10", 168 lbs.   Deb: 4/16/09   H

YEAR	TM/L	G	AB	R	H	2B	3B	HR	RBI	BB	SO	AVG	OBP	SLG	PRO+	BR/A	SB	CS	SBR	FA	FR	G/POS	TPR
1909	Bos-A	81	255	29	72	3	4	0	12	16		.282	.337	.325	107	2	15			.952	4	O-74	0.4
1910	Bos-A	155	584	81	156	9	10	2	27	62		.267	.346	.327	108	7	40			.938	11	*O-155	1.1
1911	Bos-A	130	524	93	163	20	6	4	45	73		.311	.399	.395	123	19	38			.954	6	*O-130	1.7
1912	*Bos-A	147	590	98	143	20	12	2	53	66		.242	.326	.327	83	-13	29			.964	2	*O-147	-1.9
1913	Bos-A	148	586	100	169	29	12	4	40	60	51	.288	.359	.399	119	14	26			.968	9	*O-147/P-1	1.7
1914	Bos-A	142	530	85	137	23	15	1	41	58	47	.258	.336	.364	110	6	19	14	-3	.973	11	*O-140	0.9
1915	*Bos-A	149	566	90	133	20	13	2	51	89	36	.235	.342	.327	103	4	22	20	-5	.972	11	*O-149	0.3
1916	Bos-A	151	575	75	156	20	11	1	37	80	35	.271	.361	.350	113	11	27	11	2	.966	8	*O-151	1.4
1917	Bos-A	151	559	89	143	21	11	3	45	80	40	.256	.355	.349	116	13	21			.971	-1	*O-151	0.4
1918	*Bos-A	126	474	81	137	26	13	1	44	75	25	.289	.391	.405	143	26	24			.963	-0	*O-126	2.1
1919	Bos-A	128	491	76	131	25	6	3	49	79	28	.267	.374	.360	113	12	23			.979	10	*O-128	1.3
1920	Bos-A	139	536	91	167	30	17	7	53	88	27	.312	.411	.470	139	32	16	18	-6	.963	7	*O-139	2.2
1921	Chi-A	108	419	74	137	26	5	8	58	55	21	.327	.406	.470	125	17	13	7	-0	.975	-3	*O-108	0.5
1922	Chi-A	152	602	111	183	35	8	11	80	68	33	.304	.379	.444	114	13	16	12	-2	.962	7	*O-149	0.7
1923	Chi-A	145	576	87	166	32	4	10	65	68	22	.288	.370	.410	106	6	18	18	-5	.960	-4	*O-143	-1.3
1924	Chi-A	130	476	107	156	27	6	10	62	66	32	.328	.413	.481	134	25	16	13	-3	.986	11	*O-123	2.3
1925	Chi-A	127	442	62	117	23	5	6	55	54	21	.265	.351	.380	90	-7	12	8	-1	.976	4	*O-124	-1.1
Total	17	2309	8785	1429	2466	389	160	75	817	1136	412	.281	.368	.387	114	188	375	121		.966	91	*O-2284/P-1	12.7

■ MIKE HOOPER
Hooper, Michael H.   b: 2/7/1850, Baltimore, Md.   d: 12/1/17, Baltimore, Md.   5'6", 165 lbs.   Deb: 6/27/1873

YEAR	TM/L	G	AB	R	H	2B	3B	HR	RBI	BB	SO	AVG	OBP	SLG	PRO+	BR/A	SB	CS	SBR	FA	FR	G/POS	TPR
1873	Mar-n	3	14	3	3	0	0	0	0	0	0	.214	.214	.214	35	-1						/O-2,C-1	-0.1

■ CHARLIE HOOVER
Hoover, Charles E.   b: 9/21/1865, Mound City, Ill.   BL/TR, 5'8",   Deb: 10/9/1888

YEAR	TM/L	G	AB	R	H	2B	3B	HR	RBI	BB	SO	AVG	OBP	SLG	PRO+	BR/A	SB	CS	SBR	FA	FR	G/POS	TPR
1888	KC-a	3	10	0	3	0	0	1	0	1	0	.300	.300	.300	87	-0	0			.857	0	/C-3	0.0
1889	KC-a	71	258	44	64	2	5	1	25	29	38	.248	.329	.306	77	-8	9			.916	-4	C-66/3-4,O	-0.5
Total	2	74	268	44	67	2	5	1	26	29	38	.250	.328	.306	77	-8	9			.913	-4	/C-69,3-4,O	-0.5

■ JOE HOOVER
Hoover, Robert Joseph   b: 4/15/15, Brawley, Cal.   d: 9/2/65, Los Angeles, Cal.   BR/TR, 5'11", 175 lbs.   Deb: 4/21/43

YEAR	TM/L	G	AB	R	H	2B	3B	HR	RBI	BB	SO	AVG	OBP	SLG	PRO+	BR/A	SB	CS	SBR	FA	FR	G/POS	TPR
1943	Det-A	144	575	78	140	15	8	4	38	36	101	.243	.289	.318	72	-21	6	5	-1	.944	-6	*S-144	-1.9
1944	Det-A	120	441	67	104	20	2	0	29	35	66	.236	.301	.290	66	-19	7	10	-4	.932	15	*S-119/2-1	0.2
1945	*Det-A	74	222	33	57	10	5	1	17	21	35	.257	.324	.360	92	-2	6	2	1	.944	-7	S-68	-0.4
Total	3	338	1238	178	301	45	15	5	84	92	202	.243	.300	.316	73	-43	19	17	-5	.939	35	S-331/2-1	-2.1

■ BUSTER HOOVER
Hoover, William J.   b: 1863, Philadelphia, Pa.   BR/TR, 6'1", 178 lbs.   Deb: 4/17/1884

YEAR	TM/L	G	AB	R	H	2B	3B	HR	RBI	BB	SO	AVG	OBP	SLG	PRO+	BR/A	SB	CS	SBR	FA	FR	G/POS	TPR
1884	Phi-U	63	275	76	100	20	8	0		12		.364	.390	.495	150	19				.780	-1	O-37,S-15/123	1.5
	Phi-N	10	42	6	8	1	0	1	4	4	9	.190	.261	.286	75	-1				.929	-1	O-10	-0.2
1886	Bal-a	40	157	25	34	2	6	0		16		.217	.297	.306	91	-1	15			.839	-1	O-40	-0.3
1892	Cin-N	14	51	7	9	0	0	0	2	5	4	.176	.250	.176	30	-4	1			.966	1	O-14	-0.4
Total	3	127	525	114	151	23	14	1	6	37	13	.288	.337	.390	116	12	16			.840	-3	O-101/S-15,213	0.6

■ DON HOPKINS
Hopkins, Donald   b: 1/9/52, West Point, Miss.   BL/TR, 6', 175 lbs.   Deb: 4/8/75

YEAR	TM/L	G	AB	R	H	2B	3B	HR	RBI	BB	SO	AVG	OBP	SLG	PRO+	BR/A	SB	CS	SBR	FA	FR	G/POS	TPR
1975	*Oak-A	82	6	25	1	0	0	0	0	2	0	.167	.375	.167	59	-0	21	9	1	1.000	-2	D-20/O-5R	-0.2
1976	Oak-A	3	0	0	0	0	0	0	0	0	0	—	—	—	—	0	0	1	-1	.000	0	R	-0.1
Total	2	85	6	25	1	0	0	0	0	2	0	.167	.375	.167	59	-0	21	10	0	1.000	-2	/D-20,O-5	-0.3

■ GAIL HOPKINS
Hopkins, Gail Eason   b: 2/19/43, Tulsa, Okla.   BL/TR, 5'10", 200 lbs.   Deb: 6/29/68

YEAR	TM/L	G	AB	R	H	2B	3B	HR	RBI	BB	SO	AVG	OBP	SLG	PRO+	BR/A	SB	CS	SBR	FA	FR	G/POS	TPR
1968	Chi-A	29	37	4	8	2	0	0	2	6	3	.216	.326	.270	81	-1	0	0	0	1.000	-1	/1-7	-0.2
1969	Chi-A	124	373	52	99	13	3	8	46	50	28	.265	.354	.381	100	1	2	1	0	.994	-3	*1-101	-1.0
1970	Chi-A	116	287	32	82	8	1	6	29	28	19	.286	.351	.383	99	-0	0	0	0	.987	-2	1-77/C-8	-0.8
1971	KC-A	103	295	35	82	16	1	9	47	37	13	.278	.366	.431	126	11	3	1	0	.990	3	1-83	0.6
1972	KC-A	53	71	1	15	2	0	0	5	7	4	.211	.282	.239	56	-4	0	0	0	.990	-2	1-13/3-1	-0.7
1973	KC-A	74	138	17	34	6	1	2	16	29	15	.246	.385	.348	100	1	2	2	-1	1.000	0	D-36,1-10	0.0
1974	LA-N	15	18	1	4	0	0	0	0	3	1	.222	.333	.222	60	-1	0	0	0	1.000	1	/C-2,1-2	-0.1
Total	7	514	1219	142	324	47	6	25	145	160	83	.266	.355	.376	103	8	6	4	-1	.991	-4	1-293/D-36,C3	-2.1

■ BUCK HOPKINS
Hopkins, John Winton "Sis"   b: 1/3/1883, Grafton, Va.   d: 10/2/29, Phoebus, Va.   BL/TL, 5'10", 165 lbs.   Deb: 7/22/07

YEAR	TM/L	G	AB	R	H	2B	3B	HR	RBI	BB	SO	AVG	OBP	SLG	PRO+	BR/A	SB	CS	SBR	FA	FR	G/POS	TPR
1907	StL-N	15	44	7	6	3	0	0	3	10		.136	.333	.205	71	-1	7			.875	-2	O-15	-0.6

■ MARTY HOPKINS
Hopkins, Meredith Hilliard   b: 2/22/07, Wolfe City, Tex.   d: 11/20/63, Dallas, Tex.   BR/TR, 5'11", 175 lbs.   Deb: 4/17/34

YEAR	TM/L	G	AB	R	H	2B	3B	HR	RBI	BB	SO	AVG	OBP	SLG	PRO+	BR/A	SB	CS	SBR	FA	FR	G/POS	TPR
1934	Phi-N	10	25	6	3	0	0	0	7	5		.120	.313	.200	36	-2	0			1.000	-1	/3-9	-0.3
	Chi-A	67	210	22	45	7	0	2	28	42	26	.214	.348	.276	61	-11	0	3	-2	.957	4	3-63	-0.6
1935	Chi-A	59	144	20	32	3	0	2	17	36	23	.222	.378	.285	72	-5	1	0	0	.960	-7	3-49/2-5	-0.9
Total	2	136	379	48	80	12	0	4	48	85	54	.211	.357	.274	63	-18	1	3		.960	-4	3-121/2-5	-1.8

■ MIKE HOPKINS
Hopkins, Michael Joseph "Skinner"   b: 11/1/1872, Glasgow, Scotland   d: 2/5/52, Pittsburgh, Pa.   BR/TR, 5'8", 160 lbs.   Deb: 8/24/02

YEAR	TM/L	G	AB	R	H	2B	3B	HR	RBI	BB	SO	AVG	OBP	SLG	PRO+	BR/A	SB	CS	SBR	FA	FR	G/POS	TPR
1902	Pit-N	1	2	0	2	0	0	0	1	0		1.000	1.000	1.500	647	1	0			1.000	0	/C-1	0.1

■ JOHNNY HOPP
Hopp, John Leonard "Hippity"   b: 7/18/16, Hastings, Neb.   BL/TL, 5'10", 175 lbs.   Deb: 9/18/39   C

YEAR	TM/L	G	AB	R	H	2B	3B	HR	RBI	BB	SO	AVG	OBP	SLG	PRO+	BR/A	SB	CS	SBR	FA	FR	G/POS	TPR
1939	StL-N	6	4	1	2	1	0	0	2	1	1	.500	.600	.750	246	1	0			1.000	0	/1-2	0.1
1940	StL-N	80	152	24	41	7	4	1	14	9	21	.270	.315	.388	88	-3	3			.967	-2	O-39,1-10	-0.6
1941	StL-N	134	445	83	135	25	11	4	50	50	63	.303	.378	.436	121	12	15			.982	1	O-91,1-39	0.6
1942	*StL-N	95	314	41	81	16	7	3	37	36	40	.258	.334	.382	102	1	14			.983	-4	1-88	-0.9
1943	*StL-N	91	241	33	54	10	2	2	25	24	22	.224	.297	.307	71	-9	4			.950	-2	O-52,1-27	-1.5
1944	*StL-N	139	527	106	177	35	9	11	72	58	47	.336	.404	.499	150	35	15			.997	-10	*O-131/1-6	1.9
1945	StL-N	124	446	67	129	18	3	8	44	49	24	.289	.363	.395	108	5	14			.980	-7	*O-104,1-15	-0.7
1946	Bos-N★	129	445	71	148	23	8	3	48	34	34	.333	.386	.440	133	19	21			.981	-1	1-68,O-58	1.2
1947	Bos-N	134	430	74	124	20	7	3	32	58	30	.288	.376	.358	98	1	13			.980	-6	*O-125	-1.1
1948	Pit-N	120	392	64	109	15	12	1	31	40	25	.278	.345	.385	95	-2	5			1.000	1	O-80,1-25	-0.6

YEAR	TM/L	G	AB	R	H	2B	3B	HR	RBI	BB	SO	AVG	OBP	SLG	PRO+	BR/A	SB	CS	SBR	FA	FR	G/POS	TPR
1949	Pit-N	20	55	5	12	3	1	0	3	7	3	.218	.306	.309	64	-3	0			.929	-1	/O-7,1-6	-0.4
	Bro-N	8	14	0	0	0	0	0	0	0	3	.000	.000	.000	-96	-4	0			1.000	1	/O-4,1-2	-0.3
	Pit-N	85	316	50	106	11	4	5	36	30	26	.335	.393	.443	121	10	9			.994	-0	1-71/O-9	0.8
	Yr	113	385	55	118	14	5	5	39	37	32	.306	.367	.408	105	3	9			.990	-0	1-79,O-20	0.1
1950	Pit-N	106	318	51	108	24	5	8	47	43	17	.340	.420	.522	141	20	7			.990	-6	1-70/O-7	1.2
	*NY-A	19	27	9	9	2	1	1	8	8	1	.333	.486	.593	180	4	0	1	-1	1.000	-1	1-12/O-6	0.2
1951	*NY-A	46	63	10	13	1	0	2	4	9	11	.206	.306	.317	71	-3	2	0	1	.992	-1	1-25	-0.4
1952	NY-A	15	25	4	4	0	0	0	2	2	3	.160	.250	.160	17	-3	2	0	1	1.000	1	1-12	-0.2
	Det-A	42	46	5	10	1	0	0	3	6	7	.217	.308	.239	53	-3	0	0	0	1.000	-1	/O-4,1-1	-0.4
	Yr	57	71	9	14	1	0	0	5	8	10	.197	.287	.211	41	-5	2	0	1	1.000	-0	1-13/O-4	-0.6
Total	14	1393	4260	698	1262	216	74	46	458	464	378	.296	.368	.414	113	79	128	1		.985	-36	O-717,1-479	-1.1

■ SHAGS HORAN
Horan, Joseph Patrick b: 9/6/1895, St.Louis, Mo. d: 2/13/69, Torrance, Cal. BR/TR, 5'10", 170 lbs. Deb: 7/14/24

YEAR	TM/L	G	AB	R	H	2B	3B	HR	RBI	BB	SO	AVG	OBP	SLG	PRO+	BR/A	SB	CS	SBR	FA	FR	G/POS	TPR
1924	NY-A	22	31	4	9	1	0	0	7	1	5	.290	.313	.323	64	-2	0	0	0	1.000	-4	O-14	-0.6

■ SAM HORN
Horn, Samuel Lee b: 11/2/63, Dallas, Tex. BL/TL, 6'5", 250 lbs. Deb: 7/25/87

YEAR	TM/L	G	AB	R	H	2B	3B	HR	RBI	BB	SO	AVG	OBP	SLG	PRO+	BR/A	SB	CS	SBR	FA	FR	G/POS	TPR
1987	Bos-A	46	158	31	44	7	0	14	34	17	55	.278	.356	.589	141	9	0	1	-1	.000	0	D-40	0.7
1988	Bos-A	24	61	4	9	0	0	2	8	11	20	.148	.278	.246	46	-4	0	0	0	.000	0	D-16	-0.5
1989	Bos-A	33	54	1	8	2	0	0	4	8	16	.148	.258	.185	25	-5	0	0	0	1.000	0	D-14/1-2	-0.6
1990	Bal-A	79	246	30	61	13	0	14	45	32	62	.248	.335	.472	127	8	0	0	0	.970	-0	D-63,1-10	0.5
1991	Bal-A	121	317	45	74	16	0	23	61	41	99	.233	.327	.502	131	12	0	0	0	.000	0	*D-102	0.8
1992	Bal-A	63	162	13	38	10	1	5	19	21	60	.235	.326	.401	100	0	0	0	0	.000	0	D-46	-0.2
1993	Cle-A	12	33	8	15	1	0	4	8	1	5	.455	.486	.848	252	7	0	0	0	.000	0	D-11	0.6
Total	7	378	1031	132	249	49	1	62	179	131	317	.242	.331	.471	120	27	0	1	-1	.972	-0	D-292/1-12	1.3

■ BOB HORNER
Horner, James Robert b: 8/6/57, Junction City, Kan. BR/TR, 6'1", 210 lbs. Deb: 6/16/78

YEAR	TM/L	G	AB	R	H	2B	3B	HR	RBI	BB	SO	AVG	OBP	SLG	PRO+	BR/A	SB	CS	SBR	FA	FR	G/POS	TPR
1978	Atl-N	89	323	50	86	17	1	23	63	24	42	.266	.321	.539	123	8	0	0	0	.956	6	3-89	1.3
1979	Atl-N	121	487	66	153	15	1	33	98	22	74	.314	.348	.552	132	19	0	2	-1	.930	-7	3-82,1-45	0.8
1980	Atl-N	124	463	81	124	14	1	35	89	27	50	.268	.310	.529	126	13	3	1	0	.935	5	*3-121/1-1	1.7
1981	Atl-N	79	300	42	83	10	0	15	42	32	39	.277	.348	.460	125	9	2	3	-1	.935	-15	3-79	-0.9
1982	*Atl-N★	140	499	85	130	24	0	32	97	66	75	.261	.351	.501	131	20	3	5	-2	.970	-17	*3-137	-0.3
1983	Atl-N	104	386	75	117	25	1	20	68	50	63	.303	.384	.528	140	21	4	2	0	.958	-13	*3-104/1-1	0.7
1984	Atl-N	32	113	15	31	8	0	3	19	14	17	.274	.354	.425	110	2	0	0	0	.965	-1	3-32	0.1
1985	Atl-N	130	483	61	129	25	3	27	89	50	57	.267	.337	.499	123	14	1	1	0	1.000	-10	1-87,3-40	-0.3
1986	Atl-N	141	517	70	141	22	0	27	87	52	72	.273	.342	.472	116	10	1	4	-2	.995	2	*1-139	0.0
1988	StL-N	60	206	15	53	9	1	3	33	32	23	.257	.360	.354	105	2	0	0	0	.990	-1	1-57	-0.3
Total	10	1020	3777	560	1047	169	8	218	685	369	512	.277	.344	.499	125	117	14	18	-7	.946	-50	3-684,1-330	2.8

■ ROGERS HORNSBY
Hornsby, Rogers "Rajah" b: 4/27/1896, Winters, Tex. d: 1/5/63, Chicago, Ill. BR/TR, 5'11", 175 lbs. Deb: 9/10/15 MCH

YEAR	TM/L	G	AB	R	H	2B	3B	HR	RBI	BB	SO	AVG	OBP	SLG	PRO+	BR/A	SB	CS	SBR	FA	FR	G/POS	TPR
1915	StL-N	18	57	5	14	2	0	0	4	2	6	.246	.271	.281	67	-2	0	2	-1	.922	1	S-18	-0.2
1916	StL-N	139	495	63	155	17	15	6	65	40	63	.313	.369	.444	150	29	17			.928	-2	3-83,S-45,1/2	3.5
1917	StL-N	145	523	86	171	24	17	8	66	45	34	.327	.385	.484	170	42	17			.939	21	*S-144	7.7
1918	StL-N	115	416	51	117	19	11	5	60	40	43	.281	.349	.416	138	18	8			.933	10	*S-109/O-3	3.6
1919	StL-N	138	512	68	163	15	9	8	71	48	41	.318	.384	.430	154	34	17			.933	2	3-72,S-37,2/1	4.5
1920	StL-N	149	589	96	218	44	20	9	94	60	50	.370	.431	.559	190	68	12	15	-5	.962	11	*2-149	8.1
1921	StL-N	154	592	131	235	44	18	21	126	60	48	.397	.458	.639	191	78	13	13	-4	.969	-3	*2-142/O-6,S31	7.1
1922	StL-N	154	623	141	250	46	14	42	152	65	50	.401	.459	.722	210	99	17	12	-2	.967	-7	*2-154	8.5
1923	StL-N	107	424	89	163	32	10	17	83	55	29	.384	.459	.627	188	54	3	7	-3	.962	-17	2-96,1-10	3.3
1924	StL-N	143	536	121	227	43	14	25	94	89	32	.424	.507	.696	223	97	5	12	-6	.965	-4	*2-143	8.5
1925	StL-N	138	504	133	203	41	10	39	143	83	39	.403	.489	.756	208	83	5	3	-0	.954	-20	*2-136,M	6.0
1926	*StL-N	134	527	96	167	34	5	11	93	61	39	.317	.388	.463	123	18	3			.962	-29	*2-134,M	-0.8
1927	NY-N	155	568	133	205	32	9	26	125	86	38	.361	.448	.586	176	63	9			.972	3	*2-155,M	6.9
1928	Bos-N	140	486	99	188	42	7	21	94	107	41	.387	.498	.632	204	80	5			.973	-24	*2-140,M	5.8
1929	*Chi-N	156	602	156	229	47	8	39	149	87	65	.380	.459	.679	178	74	2			.973	1	*2-156	7.2
1930	Chi-N	42	104	15	32	5	1	2	18	12	12	.308	.385	.433	96	-0	0			.916	-3	2-25,M	-0.2
1931	Chi-N	100	357	64	118	37	1	16	90	56	23	.331	.421	.574	162	32	1			.951	-15	2-69,3-26M	2.3
1932	Chi-N	19	58	10	13	2	0	1	7	10	4	.224	.357	.310	82	-1	0			1.000	-4	O-10/3-6M	-0.5
1933	StL-N	46	83	9	27	6	0	2	21	12	6	.325	.423	.470	147	6	1			.967	-7	2-17	-0.1
	StL-A	11	9	2	3	1	0	1	2	2	1	.333	.455	.778	208	1	0	0	0	.000	0	HM	0.1
1934	StL-A	24	23	2	7	2	0	1	11	7	4	.304	.484	.522	147	2	0	0	0	1.000	0	/3-1,O-1M	0.2
1935	StL-A	10	24	1	5	3	0	0	3	3	6	.208	.296	.333	60	-1	0	0	0	1.000	0	/1-3,2-1,3M	-0.2
1936	StL-A	2	5	1	2	0	0	0	2	1	0	.400	.500	.400	121	0	0	0	0	1.000	-0	/1-1,M	0.0
1937	StL-A	20	56	7	18	3	0	1	11	7	5	.321	.397	.429	107	1	0	0	0	.947	-5	2-17,M	-0.2
Total	23	2259	8173	1579	2930	541	169	301	1584	1038	679	.358	.434	.577	176	874	135	64		.965	-91	*2-1561,S-356,3/10	81.1

■ JOE HORNUNG
Hornung, Michael Joseph "Ubbo Ubbo" b: 6/12/1857, Carthage, N.Y. d: 10/30/31, Howard Beach, N.Y. BR/TR, 5'8.5", 164 lbs. Deb: 5/1/1879 U

YEAR	TM/L	G	AB	R	H	2B	3B	HR	RBI	BB	SO	AVG	OBP	SLG	PRO+	BR/A	SB	CS	SBR	FA	FR	G/POS	TPR
1879	Buf-N	78	319	46	85	18	7	0	38	2	27	.266	.266	.367	105	1				.844	-2	*O-77/1-1	-0.4
1880	Buf-N	85	342	47	91	8	11	1	42	8	29	.266	.283	.363	115	5				.874	-0	*O-67,1-18/2P	0.1
1881	Bos-N	83	324	40	78	12	8	2	25	5	25	.241	.252	.346	90	-4				.948	12	*O-83	0.6
1882	Bos-N	85	388	67	117	14	11	1	50	2	25	.302	.305	.402	124	10				.932	11	*O-84/1-1	1.8
1883	Bos-N	98	446	107	124	25	13	8	66	8	54	.278	.291	.446	117	8				.936	7	*O-98/3-1	1.2
1884	Bos-N	115	518	119	139	27	10	7	51	17	80	.268	.292	.400	116	8				.916	3	*O-110/1-6	0.8
1885	Bos-N	25	109	14	22	4	1	1	7	1	20	.202	.209	.284	61	-5				.919	-3	O-25	-0.8
1886	Bos-N	94	424	67	109	12	2	2	40	10	62	.257	.274	.309	80	-10	16			.948	7	*O-94	-0.5
1887	Bos-N	98	437	85	118	10	6	5	49	17	28	.270	.302	.355	82	-11	41			.935	13	*O-98	0.0
1888	Bos-N	107	431	61	103	11	7	3	53	16	39	.239	.269	.318	85	-8	29			.947	-8	*O-107	-1.9
1889	Bal-a	135	533	73	122	13	9	1	78	22	72	.229	.259	.293	59	-30	34			.913	11	*O-134/3-1	-1.9
1890	NY-N	120	513	62	122	18	5	0	65	12	37	.238	.258	.292	60	-28	39			.931	-3	O-77,1-36/3S	-0.5
Total	12	1123	4784	788	1230	172	90	31	564	120	498	.257	.277	.350	91	-64	159			.922	49	*O-1054/1-62,32SP	-4.1

■ TONY HORTON
Horton, Anthony Darrin b: 12/6/44, Santa Monica, Cal. BR/TR, 6'3", 210 lbs. Deb: 7/31/64

YEAR	TM/L	G	AB	R	H	2B	3B	HR	RBI	BB	SO	AVG	OBP	SLG	PRO+	BR/A	SB	CS	SBR	FA	FR	G/POS	TPR
1964	Bos-A	36	126	9	28	5	1	2	6	3	20	.222	.240	.286	44	-10	0	0	0	1.000	1	O-24/1-8	-1.1
1965	Bos-A	60	163	23	48	8	1	7	23	18	36	.294	.365	.485	131	7	0	2	-1	.980	-1	1-44	0.2
1966	Bos-A	6	22	0	3	0	0	0	2	0	5	.136	.136	.136	-19	-3	0	0	0	1.000	1	/1-6	-0.3
1967	Bos-A	21	39	2	12	3	0	0	9	0	5	.308	.308	.385	96	-0	0	0	0	.929	-1	/1-6	-0.2
	Cle-A	106	363	35	102	13	4	10	44	18	52	.281	.322	.421	117	7	3	0	0	.991	-6	1-94	-0.4
	Yr	127	402	37	114	16	4	10	53	18	57	.284	.321	.418	114	6	3	0	0	.987	-6	*1-100	-0.6
1968	Cle-A	133	477	57	119	29	4	14	59	34	56	.249	.304	.411	117	4	0	0	0	.992	-4	*1-128	-0.6
1969	Cle-A	159	625	77	174	25	4	27	93	37	91	.278	.321	.461	113	9	0	3	-1	.989	-0	*1-157	-0.6
1970	Cle-A	115	413	48	111	19	3	17	59	30	54	.269	.321	.453	107	3	3	2	-0	.994	3	*1-112	-0.4
Total	7	636	2228	251	597	102	15	76	297	140	319	.268	.315	.430	109	18	6	7	-2	.990	-8	1-555/O-24	-3.4

■ WILLIE HORTON
Horton, Willie Watterson b: 10/18/42, Arno, Va. BR/TR, 5'11", 209 lbs. Deb: 9/10/63 C

YEAR	TM/L	G	AB	R	H	2B	3B	HR	RBI	BB	SO	AVG	OBP	SLG	PRO+	BR/A	SB	CS	SBR	FA	FR	G/POS	TPR
1963	Det-A	15	43	6	14	2	1	1	4	0	8	.326	.326	.488	120	1	2	0	1	1.000	-1	/O-9	0.0

YEAR	TM/L	G	AB	R	H	2B	3B	HR	RBI	BB	SO	AVG	OBP	SLG	PRO+	BR/A	SB	CS	SBR	FA	FR	G/POS	TPR
1964	Det-A	25	80	6	13	1	3	1	10	11	20	.162	.272	.287	55	-5	0	0	0	.943	-2	O-23	-0.8
1965	Det-A★	143	512	69	140	20	2	29	104	48	101	.273	.343	.490	132	21	5	9	-4	.988	5	*O-141/3-1	1.6
1966	Det-A	146	526	72	138	22	6	27	100	44	103	.262	.323	.481	125	15	1	1	-0	.979	-4	*O-137	0.6
1967	Det-A	122	401	47	110	20	3	19	67	36	80	.274	.340	.481	137	17	0	0	0	.971	-0	*O-110	1.3
1968	*Det-A★	143	512	68	146	20	2	36	85	49	110	.285	.357	.543	165	38	0	3	-2	.973	-0	*O-139	3.4
1969	Det-A	141	508	66	133	17	1	28	91	52	93	.262	.334	.465	116	10	3	3	-1	.972	9	*O-136	1.0
1970	Det-A★	96	371	53	113	18	2	17	69	28	43	.305	.357	.501	133	15	0	1	-1	.982	5	O-96	1.6
1971	Det-A	119	450	64	130	25	1	22	72	37	75	.289	.352	.496	133	18	1	5	-3	.963	-10	*O-118	-0.1
1972	*Det-A	108	333	44	77	9	5	11	36	27	47	.231	.295	.387	99	-1	0	0	0	1.000	-10	O-98	-1.8
1973	Det-A★	111	411	42	130	19	3	17	53	23	57	.316	.363	.501	132	16	1	4	-1	.942	-10	*O-107/D-1	0.0
1974	Det-A	72	238	32	71	8	1	15	47	21	36	.298	.363	.529	149	14	0	1	-1	.947	-4	O-64/D-1	0.8
1975	Det-A	159	615	62	169	13	1	25	92	44	109	.275	.323	.421	104	2	1	2	-1	.000	0	*D-159	-0.3
1976	Det-A	114	401	40	105	17	0	14	56	49	63	.262	.345	.409	116	8	0	0	0	.000	0	*D-105	0.6
1977	Det-A	1	4	0	1	0	0	0	0	0	0	.250	.250	.250	35	-0	0	0	0	1.000	0	/O-1	-0.1
	Tex-A	139	519	55	150	23	3	15	75	42	117	.289	.342	.432	108	6	2	3	-1	.938	-1	*D-128,O-10	-0.1
	Yr	140	523	55	151	23	3	15	75	42	117	.289	.342	.430	108	5	2	3	-1	.941	-2	*D-128,O-11	-0.2
1978	Cle-A	50	169	15	42	7	0	5	22	15	25	.249	.314	.379	95	-1	3	0	1	.000	0	D-48	-0.2
	Oak-A	32	102	11	32	8	0	3	19	9	15	.314	.369	.480	145	6	0	1	-1	.333	-1	D-27/O-1	0.4
	Tor-A	33	122	12	25	6	0	3	19	4	29	.205	.230	.328	54	-8	0	0	0	.000	0	D-30	-0.9
	Yr	115	393	38	99	21	0	11	60	28	69	.252	.303	.389	95	-4	3	1	0	.333	-1	*D-105/O-1	-0.7
1979	Sea-A	162	646	77	180	19	5	29	106	42	112	.279	.327	.458	107	5	1	1	-0	.000	0	*D-162	-0.1
1980	Sea-A	97	335	32	74	10	1	8	36	39	70	.221	.310	.328	74	-11	0	4	-2	.000	0	D-92	-1.7
Total	18	2028	7298	873	1993	284	40	325	1163	620	1313	.273	.335	.457	119	166	20	38	-17	.972	-24	*O-1190,D-753/3	5.2

■ STEVE HOSEY
Hosey, Steven Bernard b: 4/2/69, Oakland, Cal. BR/TR, 6'3", 215 lbs. Deb: 8/29/92

YEAR	TM/L	G	AB	R	H	2B	3B	HR	RBI	BB	SO	AVG	OBP	SLG	PRO+	BR/A	SB	CS	SBR	FA	FR	G/POS	TPR
1992	SF-N	21	56	6	14	1	0	1	6	0	15	.250	.250	.321	64	-3	1	1	-0	.960	-2	O-18	-0.6
1993	SF-N	3	2	0	1	1	0	0	1	1	1	.500	.667	1.000	350	1	0	0	0	.000	-0	/O-1	0.0
Total	2	24	58	6	15	2	0	1	7	1	16	.259	.271	.345	77	-2	1	1	-0	.960	-3	/O-19	-0.6

■ TIM HOSLEY
Hosley, Timothy Kenneth b: 5/10/47, Spartanburg, S.C. BR/TR, 5'10", 195 lbs. Deb: 9/8/70

YEAR	TM/L	G	AB	R	H	2B	3B	HR	RBI	BB	SO	AVG	OBP	SLG	PRO+	BR/A	SB	CS	SBR	FA	FR	G/POS	TPR
1970	Det-A	7	12	1	2	0	0	1	2	0	6	.167	.167	.417	55	-1	0	0	0	1.000	2	/C-4	0.1
1971	Det-A	7	16	2	3	0	0	2	6	0	1	.188	.188	.563	102	-0	0	0	0	1.000	-0	/C-4,1-1	0.0
1973	Oak-A	13	14	3	3	0	0	0	2	2	3	.214	.313	.214	53	-1	0	0	0	.952	-1	C-13	-0.2
1974	Oak-A	11	7	3	2	0	0	0	1	1	2	.286	.375	.286	99	0	0	0	0	1.000	0	/C-8,1-1	0.0
1975	Chi-N	62	141	22	36	7	0	6	20	27	25	.255	.382	.433	120	5	1	1	-0	.968	-2	C-53	0.4
1976	Oak-A	37	55	4	9	2	0	1	4	8	12	.164	.270	.255	56	-3	0	0	0	.968	-1	C-37	-0.3
	Chi-N	1	1	0	0	0	0	0	0	0	0	.000	.000	.000	-92	-0	0	0	0	.000	0	H	0.0
1977	Oak-A	39	78	5	15	0	0	1	10	16	13	.192	.337	.231	59	-4	0	0	0	.955	3	C-19,D-12/1	-0.1
1978	Oak-A	13	23	1	7	2	0	0	3	1	6	.304	.360	.391	117	1	0	0	0	.962	-0	/C-6,D-1	0.1
1981	Oak-A	18	21	2	2	0	0	1	5	2	5	.095	.174	.238	19	-2	0	0	0	.750	-0	/1-1,D-4	-0.3
Total	9	208	368	43	79	11	0	12	53	57	73	.215	.326	.342	87	-5	1	1	-0	.968	0	C-144/D-17,1	-0.3

■ CHUCK HOSTETLER
Hostetler, Charles Cloyd b: 9/22/03, McClellandtown, Pa. d: 2/18/71, Fort Collins, Colo BL/TR, 6', 175 lbs. Deb: 4/18/44

YEAR	TM/L	G	AB	R	H	2B	3B	HR	RBI	BB	SO	AVG	OBP	SLG	PRO+	BR/A	SB	CS	SBR	FA	FR	G/POS	TPR
1944	Det-A	90	265	42	79	9	2	0	20	21	31	.298	.350	.347	94	-2	4	4	-1	.985	0	O-65	-0.6
1945	*Det-A	42	44	3	7	3	0	0	2	7	8	.159	.275	.227	43	-3	0	0	0	.889	-3	/O-8	-0.6
Total	2	132	309	45	86	12	2	0	22	28	39	.278	.338	.330	87	-5	4	4	-1	.979	-2	/O-73	-1.2

■ DAVE HOSTETLER
Hostetler, David Alan b: 3/27/56, Pasadena, Cal. BR/TR, 6'4", 215 lbs. Deb: 9/15/81

YEAR	TM/L	G	AB	R	H	2B	3B	HR	RBI	BB	SO	AVG	OBP	SLG	PRO+	BR/A	SB	CS	SBR	FA	FR	G/POS	TPR
1981	Mon-N	5	6	1	3	0	0	1	1	0	2	.500	.500	1.000	314	2	0	0	0	1.000	-0	/1-2	0.1
1982	Tex-A	113	418	53	97	12	3	22	67	42	113	.232	.304	.433	105	1	2	2	-1	.990	-11	*1-109/D-3	-1.6
1983	Tex-A	94	304	31	67	9	2	11	46	42	103	.220	.325	.372	93	-2	0	2	-1	1.000	-0	D-88/1-2	-0.7
1984	Tex-A	37	82	7	18	2	1	3	10	13	27	.220	.326	.378	91	-1	0	0	0	1.000	-1	1-14,D-13	-0.1
1988	Pit-N	6	8	0	2	0	0	0	0	0	3	.250	.250	.250	45	-1	0	0	0	.944	-0	/1-4,C-1	-0.1
Total	5	255	818	92	187	23	6	37	124	97	248	.229	.315	.407	100	-1	2	4	-2	.990	-11	1-131,D-104/C	-2.4

■ PETE HOTALING
Hotaling, Peter James "Monkey" b: 12/16/1856, Mohawk, N.Y. d: 7/3/28, Cleveland, Ohio BL/TR, 5'8", 166 lbs. Deb: 5/1/1879

YEAR	TM/L	G	AB	R	H	2B	3B	HR	RBI	BB	SO	AVG	OBP	SLG	PRO+	BR/A	SB	CS	SBR	FA	FR	G/POS	TPR
1879	Cin-N	81	369	64	103	20	9	1	27	12	17	.279	.302	.390	133	13				.843	-0	*O-69/C-8,23	0.9
1880	Cle-N	78	325	40	78	17	8	0	41	10	30	.240	.263	.342	105	2				.896	-2	*O-78/C-2	-0.3
1881	Wor-N	77	317	51	98	15	3	1	35	18	12	.309	.346	.385	123	8				.862	-3	*O-74/C-3	0.3
1882	Bos-N	84	378	64	98	16	5	0	28	16	21	.259	.289	.328	97	-1				.865	2	*O-84	0.1
1883	Cle-N	100	417	54	108	20	8	0	30	12	31	.259	.280	.345	90	-5				.829	1	*O-100	-0.4
1884	Cle-N	102	408	69	99	16	6	3	27	28	50	.243	.291	.333	93	-4				.849	-1	*O-102/2-1	-0.6
1885	Bro-a	94	370	73	95	9	5	1		49		.257	.350	.316	111	7				.893	0	*O-94	0.4
1887	Cle-a	126	505	108	151	28	13	3		53		.299	.373	.424	126	19	43			.903	1	*O-126	1.4
1888	Cle-a	98	403	67	101	7	6	0	55	26		.251	.307	.298	97	-1	35			.878	-9	*O-98	-1.1
Total	9	840	3492	590	931	148	63	9	243	224	161	.267	.314	.353	108	38	78			.869	-11	O-825/C-13,23	0.7

■ KEN HOTTMAN
Hottman, Kenneth Roger b: 5/7/48, Stockton, Cal. BR/TR, 5'11", 190 lbs. Deb: 9/11/71

YEAR	TM/L	G	AB	R	H	2B	3B	HR	RBI	BB	SO	AVG	OBP	SLG	PRO+	BR/A	SB	CS	SBR	FA	FR	G/POS	TPR
1971	Chi-A	6	16	1	2	0	0	0	0	1	2	.125	.176	.125	-13	-2	0	0	0	1.000	-1	/O-5	-0.4

■ SADIE HOUCK
Houck, Sargent Perry b: 3/1856, Washington, D.C. d: 5/26/19, Washington, D.C. BR/TR, 5'7", 151 lbs. Deb: 5/1/1879

YEAR	TM/L	G	AB	R	H	2B	3B	HR	RBI	BB	SO	AVG	OBP	SLG	PRO+	BR/A	SB	CS	SBR	FA	FR	G/POS	TPR
1879	Bos-N	80	356	69	95	24	9	2	49	4	11	.267	.275	.402	117	6				.814	-8	O-47,S-33	-0.2
1880	Bos-N	12	47	2	7	0	0	0	2	0	6	.149	.149	.149	1	-5				.786	-1	O-12	-0.6
	Pro-N	49	184	27	37	7	7	1	22	3	6	.201	.214	.332	85	-3				.873	-1	O-49	-0.5
	Yr	61	231	29	44	7	7	1	24	3	12	.190	.201	.294	68	-7				.855	-3	O-61	-1.1
1881	Det-N	75	308	43	86	16	6	1	36	6	6	.279	.293	.380	106	1				.868	1	*S-75	0.6
1883	Det-N	101	416	52	105	18	12	0	40	9	18	.252	.268	.353	91	-4				.852	5	*S-101	0.3
1884	Phi-a	108	472	93	140	19	14	0		7		.297	.318	.396	124	10				**.893**	23	*S-108/2-1	3.1
1885	Phi-a	93	388	74	99	10	9	0		10		.255	.286	.327	88	-7				.863	22	*S-93	1.5
1886	Bal-a	61	260	29	50	8	1	0		4		.192	.196	.231	41	-18	25			.849	-5	S-55/2-5,O	-2.0
	Was-N	52	195	14	42	3	0	0	14	2	28	.215	.223	.231	41	-14	4			.858	1	S-51/2-1	-1.2
1887	NY-a	10	33	3	5	1	0	0		3		.152	.243	.182	20	-3	2			.831	4	S-10/2-1	0.1
Total	8	641	2659	406	666	106	58	4	163	48	75	.250	.269	.338	91	-35	31			.863	39	S-526,O-109/2	1.1

■ RALPH HOUK
Houk, Ralph George "Major" b: 8/9/19, Lawrence, Kan. BR/TR, 5'11", 193 lbs. Deb: 4/26/47 MC

YEAR	TM/L	G	AB	R	H	2B	3B	HR	RBI	BB	SO	AVG	OBP	SLG	PRO+	BR/A	SB	CS	SBR	FA	FR	G/POS	TPR
1947	*NY-A	41	92	7	25	3	1	0	12	11	5	.272	.356	.326	91	-1	0	0	0	.987	2	C-41	0.3
1948	NY-A	14	29	3	8	2	0	0	3	2	0	.276	.276	.345	65	-2	0	0	0	1.000	5	C-14	0.1
1949	NY-A	5	7	0	4	0	0	0	1	0	1	.571	.571	.571	203	1	0	0	0	.889	-1	/C-5	0.1
1950	NY-A	10	9	0	1	1	0	0	1	0	2	.111	.111	.222	-17	-2	0	0	0	.929	1	/C-9	-0.1
1951	NY-A	3	5	0	1	0	0	0	0	0	0	.200	.200	.200	9	-1	0	0	0	1.000	-1	/C-3	-0.1
1952	*NY-A	9	6	0	2	0	0	0	0	1	0	.333	.429	.333	121	-0	0	0	0	.917	1	/C-9	0.1
1953	NY-A	9	9	2	2	0	0	0	3	0	1	.222	.222	.222	21	-1	0	0	0	1.000	-0	/C-8	-0.1
1954	NY-A	1	1	0	0	0	0	0	0	0	0	.000	.000	.000	-99	-0	0	0	0	.000	0	H	0.0
Total	8	91	158	12	43	6	1	0	20	12	10	.272	.327	.323	79	-5	0	0	0	.981	6	/C-89	0.5

YEAR	TM/L	G	AB	R	H	2B	3B	HR	RBI	BB	SO	AVG	OBP	SLG	PRO+	BR/A	SB	CS	SBR	FA	FR	G/POS	TPR

■ FRANK HOUSE   House, Henry Franklin "Pig"   b: 2/18/30, Bessemer, Ala.   BL/TR, 6'1.5", 190 lbs.   Deb: 7/21/50

YEAR	TM/L	G	AB	R	H	2B	3B	HR	RBI	BB	SO	AVG	OBP	SLG	PRO+	BR/A	SB	CS	SBR	FA	FR	G/POS	TPR
1950	Det-A	5	5	1	2	1	0	0	0	0	1	.400	.400	.600	148	0	0	0	0	1.000	0	/C-5	0.0
1951	Det-A	18	41	3	9	2	0	1	4	6	2	.220	.319	.341	78	-1	1	1	-0	.957	1	C-18	0.0
1954	Det-A	114	352	35	88	12	1	9	38	31	34	.250	.313	.366	87	-7	2	1	-0	.992	-1	*C-107	-0.3
1955	Det-A	102	328	37	85	11	1	15	53	22	25	.259	.312	.436	102	-1	0	0	0	.987	2	C-93	0.4
1956	Det-A	94	321	44	77	6	2	10	44	21	19	.240	.293	.364	72	-14	1	1	-0	.986	-6	C-88	-1.7
1957	Det-A	106	348	31	90	9	0	7	36	35	26	.259	.328	.345	82	-8	1	1	-0	.997	9	C-97	0.4
1958	KC-A	76	202	16	51	6	3	4	24	12	13	.252	.298	.371	81	-5	1	0	0	.992	-7	C-55	-1.0
1959	KC-A	98	347	32	82	14	3	1	30	20	23	.236	.282	.303	59	-19	0	3	-2	.982	-8	C-95	-2.5
1960	Cin-N	23	28	0	5	2	0	0	3	0	2	.179	.179	.250	16	-3	0	0	0	1.000	1	/C-8	-0.2
1961	Det-A	17	22	3	5	1	1	0	3	4	2	.227	.346	.364	87	-0	0	0	0	.974	-1	C-14	-0.1
Total	10	653	1994	202	494	64	11	47	235	151	147	.248	.304	.362	80	-60	6	7	-2	.988	-10	C-580	-5.0

■ CHARLIE HOUSEHOLDER   Householder, Charles F.   b: 1856, Harrisburg, Pa.   BR/TR, 5'7", 150 lbs.   Deb: 4/20/1884

YEAR	TM/L	G	AB	R	H	2B	3B	HR	RBI	BB	SO	AVG	OBP	SLG	PRO+	BR/A	SB	CS	SBR	FA	FR	G/POS	TPR
1884	CP-U	83	310	32	74	12	5	1		12		.239	.267	.319	59	-18				.796	-6	3-41,O-40/SP	-2.1

■ CHARLIE HOUSEHOLDER   Householder, Charles W.   b: 1856, Harrisburg, Pa.   d: 12/26/08, Harrisburg, Pa.   BL/TL, 5'11", 158 lbs.   Deb: 5/2/1882

YEAR	TM/L	G	AB	R	H	2B	3B	HR	RBI	BB	SO	AVG	OBP	SLG	PRO+	BR/A	SB	CS	SBR	FA	FR	G/POS	TPR
1882	Bal-a	74	307	42	78	10	7	1		4		.254	.264	.342	111	4				.971	3	*1-74/C-3	-0.2
1884	Bro-a	76	273	28	66	15	3	3		12		.242	.279	.352	104	1				.959	-5	1-40,C-31/O2	-0.5
Total	2	150	580	70	144	25	10	4		16		.248	.271	.347	108	5				.967	-2	1-114/C-34,O2	-0.7

■ ED HOUSEHOLDER   Householder, Edward H.   b: 10/12/1869, Pittsburgh, Pa.   d: 7/3/24, Los Angeles, Cal.   Deb: 4/17/03

YEAR	TM/L	G	AB	R	H	2B	3B	HR	RBI	BB	SO	AVG	OBP	SLG	PRO+	BR/A	SB	CS	SBR	FA	FR	G/POS	TPR
1903	Bro-N	12	43	5	9	0	0	0	9	2		.209	.244	.209	31	-4	3			.967	1	O-12	-0.4

■ PAUL HOUSEHOLDER   Householder, Paul Wesley   b: 9/4/58, Columbus, Ohio   BB/TR, 6', 180 lbs.   Deb: 8/26/80

YEAR	TM/L	G	AB	R	H	2B	3B	HR	RBI	BB	SO	AVG	OBP	SLG	PRO+	BR/A	SB	CS	SBR	FA	FR	G/POS	TPR
1980	Cin-N	20	45	3	11	1	1	0	7	1	13	.244	.261	.311	59	-3	1	0	0	1.000	-1	O-14	-0.4
1981	Cin-N	23	69	12	19	4	0	2	9	10	16	.275	.367	.420	121	-3	2	3	1	1.000	-1	O-19	0.1
1982	Cin-N	138	417	40	88	11	5	9	34	30	77	.211	.267	.326	64	-21	17	11	-2	.992	6	*O-131	-2.0
1983	Cin-N	123	380	40	97	24	4	6	43	44	60	.255	.336	.387	96	-2	12	12	-4	.991	-1	*O-112	-0.9
1984	Cin-N	14	12	3	1	1	0	0	0	3	3	.083	.267	.167	23	-1	1	1	-0	1.000	-2	O-10	-0.2
	StL-N	13	14	1	2	0	0	0	0	0	3	.143	.143	.143	-20	-2	0	0	0	1.000	-3	/O-8	-0.6
	Yr	27	26	4	3	1	0	0	0	3	6	.115	.207	.154	3	-3	1	1	-0	1.000	-5	O-18	-1.0
1985	Mil-A	95	299	41	77	15	0	11	34	27	60	.258	.321	.418	101	-0	1	2	-1	.986	-1	O-91/D-3	-0.5
1986	Mil-A	26	78	4	17	3	1	0	16	7	16	.218	.291	.321	64	-4	1	2	-1	1.000	1	O-22/D-3	-0.8
1987	Hou-N	14	12	2	1	1	0	0	1	4	2	.083	.313	.167	33	-1	0	0	0	1.000	-2	/O-7	-0.3
Total	8	466	1326	146	313	60	11	29	144	126	250	.236	.305	.363	83	-31	36	29	-7	.991	-7	O-414/D-6	-5.8

■ JOHN HOUSEMAN   Houseman, John Franklin   b: 1/10/1870, Holland   d: 11/4/22, Chicago, Ill.   160 lbs.   Deb: 9/11/1894

YEAR	TM/L	G	AB	R	H	2B	3B	HR	RBI	BB	SO	AVG	OBP	SLG	PRO+	BR/A	SB	CS	SBR	FA	FR	G/POS	TPR
1894	Chi-N	4	15	5	6	3	1	0	4	5	3	.400	.571	.733	202	3	2			.950	-0	/S-3,2-1	0.2
1897	StL-N	80	278	34	68	6	6	0	21	28		.245	.329	.309	70	-11	16			.918	-3	2-41,O-33/S3	-1.2
Total	2	84	293	39	74	9	7	0	25	33	3	.253	.344	.331	79	-8	18			.916	-3	2-42,O-33,S3	-1.0

■ BEN HOUSER   Houser, Benjamin Franklin   b: 11/30/1883, Shenandoah, Pa.   d: 1/15/52, Augusta, Maine   BL/TL, 6'1", 185 lbs.   Deb: 5/2/10

YEAR	TM/L	G	AB	R	H	2B	3B	HR	RBI	BB	SO	AVG	OBP	SLG	PRO+	BR/A	SB	CS	SBR	FA	FR	G/POS	TPR
1910	Phi-A	34	69	9	13	3	2	0	7	7		.188	.263	.290	74	-2	0			1.000	-2	1-26	-0.3
1911	Bos-N	20	71	11	18	1	0	1	9	8	6	.254	.329	.310	73	-2	2			.988	0	1-20	-0.2
1912	Bos-N	108	332	38	95	17	3	8	52	22	29	.286	.332	.428	105	1	1			.986	-3	1-83	-0.3
Total	3	162	472	58	126	21	5	9	68	37	35	.267	.322	.390	96	-4	3			.989	-3	1-129	-0.8

■ WAYNE HOUSIE   Housie, Wayne Tyrone   b: 5/20/65, Hampton, Va.   BB/TR, 5'9", 165 lbs.   Deb: 9/17/91

YEAR	TM/L	G	AB	R	H	2B	3B	HR	RBI	BB	SO	AVG	OBP	SLG	PRO+	BR/A	SB	CS	SBR	FA	FR	G/POS	TPR
1991	Bos-A	11	8	2	2	1	0	0	0	1	3	.250	.333	.375	91	-0	1	0	0	1.000	-1	/O-4,D-2	-0.1
1993	NY-N	18	16	2	3	1	0	0	1	1	1	.188	.235	.250	30	-2	0	0	0	.000	-1	/O-2	-0.2
Total	2	29	24	4	5	2	0	0	1	2	4	.208	.269	.292	51	-2	1	0	0	1.000	-2	/O-6,D-2	-0.3

■ LEFTY HOUTZ   Houtz, Fred Fritz   b: 9/4/1875, Connersville, Ind.   d: 2/15/59, Wapakoneta, Ohio   BL/TL, 5'10", 170 lbs.   Deb: 7/23/1899

YEAR	TM/L	G	AB	R	H	2B	3B	HR	RBI	BB	SO	AVG	OBP	SLG	PRO+	BR/A	SB	CS	SBR	FA	FR	G/POS	TPR
1899	Cin-N	5	17	1	4	0	1	0	0	4		.235	.381	.353	100	0	1			1.000	4	/O-5	0.4

■ STEVE HOVLEY   Hovley, Stephen Eugene   b: 12/18/44, Ventura, Cal.   BL/TL, 5'10", 188 lbs.   Deb: 6/26/69

YEAR	TM/L	G	AB	R	H	2B	3B	HR	RBI	BB	SO	AVG	OBP	SLG	PRO+	BR/A	SB	CS	SBR	FA	FR	G/POS	TPR
1969	Sea-A	91	329	41	91	14	3	3	20	30	84	.277	.339	.365	98	-1	10	4	1	.989	7	O-84	0.2
1970	Mil-A	40	135	17	38	9	0	0	16	17	11	.281	.366	.348	97	-0	5	1	1	.958	-2	O-38	-0.3
	Oak-A	72	100	8	19	1	0	0	1	5	11	.190	.229	.200	20	-11	3	0	1	1.000	-6	O-42	-1.8
	Yr	112	235	25	57	10	0	0	17	22	22	.243	.310	.285	67	-10	8	1	2	.977	-8	O-80	-2.1
1971	Oak-A	24	27	3	3	0	2	0	3	7	9	.111	.314	.185	45	-2	2	0	1	1.000	-1	O-11	-0.2
1972	KC-A	105	196	24	53	5	1	3	24	24	29	.270	.353	.352	111	3	3	3	-1	.982	-5	O-68	-0.5
1973	KC-A	104	232	29	59	8	1	2	24	33	34	.254	.347	.323	83	-4	6	4	-1	.975	-10	O-79,D-15	-1.8
Total	5	436	1019	122	263	39	5	8	88	116	128	.258	.336	.330	88	-14	29	12	2	.982	-16	O-322/D-15	-4.4

■ CHRIS HOWARD   Howard, Christopher Hugh   b: 2/27/66, San Diego, Cal.   BR/TR, 6'2", 200 lbs.   Deb: 9/15/91

YEAR	TM/L	G	AB	R	H	2B	3B	HR	RBI	BB	SO	AVG	OBP	SLG	PRO+	BR/A	SB	CS	SBR	FA	FR	G/POS	TPR
1991	Sea-A	9	6	1	1	1	0	0	0	1	2	.167	.286	.333	71	-0	0	0	0	1.000	1	/C-9	0.1
1993	Sea-A	4	1	0	0	0	0	0	0	0	0	.000	.000	.000	-99	-0	0	0	0	1.000	1	/C-4	0.0
1994	Sea-A	9	25	2	5	1	0	0	2	1	6	.200	.259	.240	29	-3	0	0	0	1.000	-3	/C-9	-0.5
Total	3	22	32	3	6	2	0	0	2	2	8	.188	.257	.250	33	-3	0	0	0	1.000	-1	/C-22	-0.4

■ DAVE HOWARD   Howard, David Austin "Del"   b: 5/1/1889, Washington, D.C.   d: 1/26/56, Dallas, Tex.   BR/TR, 5'11", 165 lbs.   Deb: 5/8/12

YEAR	TM/L	G	AB	R	H	2B	3B	HR	RBI	BB	SO	AVG	OBP	SLG	PRO+	BR/A	SB	CS	SBR	FA	FR	G/POS	TPR
1912	Was-A	1	0	1	0	0	0	0	0	0		—	—	—	—	0	0			.000	-0	R	0.0
1915	Bro-F	24	36	5	8	1	0	0	1	1	8	.222	.243	.250	32	-4	0			.925	3	2-12/O-2,S3	-0.1
Total	2	25	36	6	8	1	0	0	1	1	8	.222	.243	.250	32	-4	0			.925	3	/2-12,O-2,3S	-0.1

■ DAVID HOWARD   Howard, David Wayne   b: 2/26/67, Sarasota, Fla.   BB/TR, 6', 165 lbs.   Deb: 4/14/91   F

YEAR	TM/L	G	AB	R	H	2B	3B	HR	RBI	BB	SO	AVG	OBP	SLG	PRO+	BR/A	SB	CS	SBR	FA	FR	G/POS	TPR
1991	KC-A	94	236	20	51	7	0	1	17	16	45	.216	.269	.258	46	-17	3	2	-0	.962	19	S-63,2-26/30D	0.6
1992	KC-A	74	219	19	49	6	2	1	18	15	43	.224	.274	.283	55	-13	3	4	-2	.976	-3	S-74/O-2	-1.3
1993	KC-A	15	24	5	8	0	1	0	2	2	5	.333	.385	.417	109	0	1	0	0	.927	2	/2-7,S-3,3O	0.2
1994	KC-A	46	83	9	19	4	0	1	13	11	23	.229	.319	.313	59	-5	3	2	-0	1.000	8	3-25,S-15/2OPD	0.3
Total	4	229	562	53	127	17	3	3	50	44	116	.226	.283	.283	55	-35	10	8	-2	.971	26	S-155/2-36,3ODP	-0.2

■ DOUG HOWARD   Howard, Douglas Lynn   b: 2/6/48, Salt Lake City, Utah   BR/TR, 6'3", 185 lbs.   Deb: 9/6/72

YEAR	TM/L	G	AB	R	H	2B	3B	HR	RBI	BB	SO	AVG	OBP	SLG	PRO+	BR/A	SB	CS	SBR	FA	FR	G/POS	TPR
1972	Cal-A	11	38	4	10	1	0	0	2	1	3	.263	.300	.289	81	-1	0	0	0	1.000	-1	/O-8,1-1,3	-0.2
1973	Cal-A	8	21	2	2	0	0	0	1	1	6	.095	.136	.095	-37	-4	0	0	0	1.000	1	/O-6,1-1,3	-0.5
1974	Cal-A	22	39	5	9	1	0	0	5	2	1	.231	.268	.282	62	-2	1	0	0	1.000	-2	/O-8,1-5,D	-0.4
1975	StL-N	17	29	1	6	0	0	1	0	1	7	.207	.207	.310	41	-2	0	0	0	1.000	1	/1-7	-0.1
1976	Cle-A	39	90	7	19	4	0	0	13	3	13	.211	.245	.256	47	-6	1	1	-0	.991	1	1-32/O-2,D	-0.7
Total	5	97	217	19	46	5	1	1	22	7	30	.212	.236	.268	48	-15	2	1	0	.994	-1	/1-46,O-24,D3	-1.9

■ ELSTON HOWARD   Howard, Elston Gene   b: 2/23/29, St.Louis, Mo.   d: 12/14/80, New York, N.Y.   BR/TR, 6'2", 200 lbs.   Deb: 4/14/55   C

YEAR	TM/L	G	AB	R	H	2B	3B	HR	RBI	BB	SO	AVG	OBP	SLG	PRO+	BR/A	SB	CS	SBR	FA	FR	G/POS	TPR
1955	*NY-A	97	279	33	81	8	7	10	43	20	38	.290	.340	.477	120	6	0	0	0	.978	3	O-75/C-9	0.5
1956	*NY-A	98	290	35	76	8	5	34	21	30		.262	.314	.362	81	-9	0	0	-1	.990	-5	O-65,C-26	-1.5
1957	*NY-A☆	110	356	33	90	13	4	8	44	16	43	.253	.285	.379	81	-11	2	5	-2	.961	-12	O-71,C-32/1	-2.8

YEAR	TM/L	G	AB	R	H	2B	3B	HR	RBI	BB	SO	AVG	OBP	SLG	PRO+	BR/A	SB	CS	SBR	FA	FR	G/POS	TPR
1958	*NY-A☆	103	376	45	118	19	5	11	66	22	60	.314	.352	.479	131	14	1	1	-0	.997	2	C-67,O-24/1	1.9
1959	NY-A☆	125	443	59	121	24	6	18	73	20	57	.273	.309	.476	116	7	0	1	-1	.985	-2	1-50,C-43,O	0.2
1960	*NY-A★	107	323	29	79	11	3	6	39	28	43	.245	.305	.353	82	-9	3	0	1	.987	2	C-91/O-1	-0.1
1961	*NY-A★	129	446	64	155	17	5	21	77	28	65	.348	.390	.549	156	33	1	3	-2	.993	7	*C-111/1-9	4.2
1962	*NY-A★	136	494	63	138	23	5	21	91	31	76	.279	.323	.474	115	8	1	1	-0	.995	-1	*C-129	1.2
1963	*NY-A★	135	487	75	140	21	6	28	85	35	68	.287	.343	.528	141	25	0	0	0	.994	-3	*C-132	2.7
1964	*NY-A★	150	550	63	172	27	3	15	84	48	73	.313	.371	.455	127	20	1	1	-0	**.998**	11	*C-146	3.9
1965	NY-A☆	110	391	38	91	15	1	9	45	24	65	.233	.279	.345	77	-13	0	0	0	.991	-5	C-95/1-5,O	-1.3
1966	NY-A	126	410	38	105	19	2	6	35	37	65	.256	.319	.356	97	-1	0	0	0	.985	-4	*C-100,1-13	0.0
1967	NY-A	66	199	13	39	6	0	3	17	12	36	.196	.249	.271	56	-11	0	0	0	.984	-1	C-48/1-1	-1.0
	*Bos-A	42	116	9	17	3	0	1	11	9	24	.147	.214	.198	21	-11	0	0	0	.996	2	C-41	-0.8
	Yr	108	315	22	56	9	0	4	28	21	60	.178	.236	.244	42	-23	0	0	0	.990	1	C-89/1-1	-1.8
1968	Bos-A	71	203	22	49	4	0	5	18	22	45	.241	.319	.335	92	-2	1	1	0	.995	-3	C-68	-0.1
Total	14	1605	5363	619	1471	218	50	167	762	373	786	.274	.325	.427	108	48	9	14	-6	.993	-9	*C-1138,O-265/1	7.0

■ FRANK HOWARD

Howard, Frank Oliver "Hondo" or "The Capital Punisher" b: 8/8/36, Columbus, Ohio BR/TR, 6'7", 255 lbs. Deb: 9/10/58 MC

YEAR	TM/L	G	AB	R	H	2B	3B	HR	RBI	BB	SO	AVG	OBP	SLG	PRO+	BR/A	SB	CS	SBR	FA	FR	G/POS	TPR
1958	LA-N	8	29	3	7	1	0	1	2	1	11	.241	.267	.379	66	-1	0	0	0	1.000	0	/O-8	-0.2
1959	LA-N	9	21	2	3	0	1	1	6	2	9	.143	.217	.381	52	-2	0	0	0	1.000	0	/O-6	-0.2
1960	LA-N	117	448	54	120	15	2	23	77	32	108	.268	.321	.464	105	2	0	1	-1	.984	-2	*O-115/1-4	-0.7
1961	LA-N	92	267	36	79	12	2	15	45	21	50	.296	.349	.517	116	5	0	1	-1	.934	-4	O-65/1-7	-0.3
1962	LA-N	141	493	80	146	25	6	31	119	39	108	.296	.349	.560	148	30	1	0	0	.972	2	*O-131	2.5
1963	*LA-N	123	417	58	114	16	1	28	64	33	116	.273	.333	.518	151	25	1	2	-1	.960	-1	*O-111	1.9
1964	LA-N	134	433	60	98	13	2	24	69	51	113	.226	.308	.432	114	7	1	0	0	.979	-7	*O-122	-0.5
1965	Was-A	149	516	53	149	22	6	21	84	55	112	.289	.360	.477	138	25	0	0	0	.981	-8	*O-138	1.2
1966	Was-A	146	493	52	137	19	4	18	71	53	104	.278	.349	.442	127	17	1	1	-0	.982	-2	*O-135	0.9
1967	Was-A	149	519	71	133	20	2	36	89	60	155	.256	.339	.511	154	33	0	1	-1	.986	-7	*O-141/1-4	2.1
1968	Was-A★	158	598	79	164	28	3	**44**	106	54	141	.274	.340	**.552**	172	49	0	0	0	.955	2	*O-107,1-55	4.6
1969	Was-A★	161	592	111	175	17	2	48	111	102	96	.296	.403	.574	180	64	1	0	0	.974	-18	*O-114,1-70	3.7
1970	Was-A★	161	566	90	160	15	1	**44**	**126**	**132**	125	.283	.420	.546	173	61	1	2	-1	.973	-9	*O-120,1-48	4.2
1971	Was-A★	153	549	60	153	25	2	26	83	77	121	.279	.369	.474	146	33	1	0	0	.993	3	*O-100,1-68	2.8
1972	Tex-A	95	287	28	70	9	0	9	31	42	55	.244	.342	.369	117	7	1	0	0	.981	-6	1-66,O-21	-0.6
	Det-A	14	33	1	8	1	0	1	7	4	8	.242	.324	.364	101	0	0	0	0	.952	-1	1-10/O-1	-0.1
	Yr	109	320	29	78	10	0	10	38	46	63	.244	.341	.369	115	7	1	0	0	.978	-7	1-76,O-22	-0.7
1973	Det-A	85	227	26	58	9	1	12	29	24	28	.256	.327	.463	113	3	0	1	-1	.923	-1	D-76/1-2	0.0
Total	16	1895	6488	864	1774	245	35	382	1119	782	1460	.273	.355	.499	143	357	8	9	-3	.975	-57	*O-1435,1-334/D	21.3

■ DEL HOWARD

Howard, George Elmer b: 12/24/1877, Kenney, Ill. d: 12/24/56, Seattle, Wash. BL/TR, 6', 180 lbs. Deb: 4/15/05 F

YEAR	TM/L	G	AB	R	H	2B	3B	HR	RBI	BB	SO	AVG	OBP	SLG	PRO+	BR/A	SB	CS	SBR	FA	FR	G/POS	TPR
1905	Pit-N	123	435	56	127	18	5	2	63	27		.292	.345	.370	110	5	19			.978	-7	1-90,O-28/P	-0.6
1906	Bos-N	147	545	46	142	19	8	1	54	26		.261	.306	.330	101	-1	17			.911	-12	O-87,2-45,S/1	-1.8
1907	Bos-N	50	187	20	51	4	2	1	13	11		.273	.330	.332	108	2	11			.969	-3	O-45/2-3	-0.3
	*Chi-N	51	148	10	34	2	2	0	13	6		.230	.269	.270	65	-6	3			.972	-4	1-33/O-8	-1.2
	Yr	101	335	30	85	6	4	1	26	17		.254	.304	.304	88	-5	14			.961	-6	O-53,1-33/2	-1.5
1908	*Chi-N	96	315	42	88	7	3	1	26	23		.279	.338	.330	109	3	11			.965	-5	O-81/1-5	-0.6
1909	Chi-N	69	203	25	40	4	2	1	24	18		.197	.282	.251	64	-8	6			.980	0	1-57	-1.0
Total	5	536	1833	199	482	54	22	6	193	111		.263	.318	.326	98	-5	67			.946	-30	O-249,1-187/2SP	-5.5

■ IVON HOWARD

Howard, Ivon Chester b: 10/12/1882, Kenney, Ill. d: 3/30/67, Medford, Ore. BB/TR, 5'10", 170 lbs. Deb: 4/25/14 F

YEAR	TM/L	G	AB	R	H	2B	3B	HR	RBI	BB	SO	AVG	OBP	SLG	PRO+	BR/A	SB	CS	SBR	FA	FR	G/POS	TPR
1914	StL-A	81	209	21	51	6	2	0	20	28	42	.244	.342	.292	94	-0	14	10	2	.936	-7	3-34,1-28/OS	-1.0
1915	StL-A	113	324	43	90	10	7	2	43	43	48	.278	.368	.370	126	11	29	12	2	.992	5	1-48,3-23,O/2S	1.7
1916	Cle-A	81	246	20	46	11	5	0	23	30	34	.187	.298	.272	68	-9	9			.970	7	2-65/1-7	-0.1
1917	Cle-A	27	39	7	4	0	0	0	0	3	5	.103	.167	.103	-17	-5	1			.833	2	/3-6,2-4,O	-0.4
Total	4	302	818	91	191	27	14	2	86	104	129	.233	.331	.308	92	-4	53	22		.990	6	/1-83,2-71,3OS	0.2

■ LARRY HOWARD

Howard, Lawrence Rayford b: 6/6/45, Columbus, Ohio BR/TR, 6'3", 200 lbs. Deb: 8/9/70

YEAR	TM/L	G	AB	R	H	2B	3B	HR	RBI	BB	SO	AVG	OBP	SLG	PRO+	BR/A	SB	CS	SBR	FA	FR	G/POS	TPR
1970	Hou-N	31	88	11	27	6	0	2	16	10	23	.307	.378	.443	124	3	0	0	0	.993	-5	C-26/1-2,O	-0.1
1971	Hou-N	24	64	6	15	3	0	2	14	3	17	.234	.269	.375	83	-2	0	1	-1	.992	2	C-22	0.1
1972	Hou-N	54	157	16	35	7	0	2	13	17	30	.223	.299	.306	74	-5	0	0	0	.980	0	C-53/O-1	-0.4
1973	Hou-N	20	48	3	8	0	0	0	4	5	12	.167	.245	.229	32	-4	0	0	0	.989	-1	C-20	-0.5
	Atl-N	4	8	0	1	0	0	0		2	3	.125	.300	.125	20	-1	0	0	0	1.000	-0	/C-2	-0.1
	Yr	24	56	3	9	0	0	0	4	7	15	.161	.254	.214	31	-5	0	0	0	.990	-1	C-22	-0.6
Total	4	133	365	36	86	19	0	6	47	37	85	.236	.306	.337	81	-9	0	1	-1	.986	-4	C-123/O-2,1	-1.0

■ MIKE HOWARD

Howard, Michael Fredric b: 4/2/58, Seattle, Wash. BB/TR, 6'2", 185 lbs. Deb: 9/12/81

YEAR	TM/L	G	AB	R	H	2B	3B	HR	RBI	BB	SO	AVG	OBP	SLG	PRO+	BR/A	SB	CS	SBR	FA	FR	G/POS	TPR
1981	NY-N	14	24	4	4	1	0	0	3	4	6	.167	.286	.208	43	-2	2	0	1	.952	-1	O-14	-0.2
1982	NY-N	33	39	5	7	0	0	1	3	6	7	.179	.304	.256	59	-2	2	0	1	1.000	-3	O-22/2-3	-0.4
1983	NY-N	1	3	0	1	0	0	0	1	0	1	.333	.333	.333	86	-0	0	0	0	.000	-0	/O-1	0.0
Total	3	48	66	9	12	1	0	1	7	10	14	.182	.299	.242	54	-4	4	0	1	.980	-4	/O-37,2-3	-0.6

■ PAUL HOWARD

Howard, Paul Joseph "Del" b: 5/20/1884, Boston, Mass. d: 8/29/68, Miami, Fla. BR/TR, 5'8", 170 lbs. Deb: 9/16/09

YEAR	TM/L	G	AB	R	H	2B	3B	HR	RBI	BB	SO	AVG	OBP	SLG	PRO+	BR/A	SB	CS	SBR	FA	FR	G/POS	TPR
1909	Bos-A	6	15	2	3	1	0	0		2	3	.200	.368	.267	99	0		0		1.000	-1	/O-6	-0.1

■ STEVE HOWARD

Howard, Steven Bernard b: 12/7/63, Oakland, Cal. BR/TR, 6'2", 205 lbs. Deb: 6/16/90

YEAR	TM/L	G	AB	R	H	2B	3B	HR	RBI	BB	SO	AVG	OBP	SLG	PRO+	BR/A	SB	CS	SBR	FA	FR	G/POS	TPR
1990	Oak-A	21	52	5	12	4	0	0	1	4	17	.231	.286	.308	69	-2	0	0	0	.933	-4	O-14/D-7	-0.7

■ THOMAS HOWARD

Howard, Thomas Sylvester b: 12/11/64, Middletown, Ohio BB/TR, 6'2", 200 lbs. Deb: 7/3/90

YEAR	TM/L	G	AB	R	H	2B	3B	HR	RBI	BB	SO	AVG	OBP	SLG	PRO+	BR/A	SB	CS	SBR	FA	FR	G/POS	TPR
1990	SD-N	20	44	4	12	2	0	0	0	1	11	.273	.318	.318	61	-2	0	1	-1	.950	-2	O-13	-0.5
1991	SD-N	106	281	30	70	12	3	4	22	24	57	.249	.310	.356	84	-6	10	7	-1	.995	3	O-86	-0.6
1992	SD-N	5	3	1	1	0	0	0	0	0	0	.333	.333	.333	88	-0	0	0	0	.000	0	/H	0.0
	Cle-A	117	358	36	99	15	2	2	32	17	60	.277	.309	.346	85	-8	15	8	-0	.990	-7	O-97/D-2	-1.7
1993	Cle-A	74	178	26	42	7	3	0	23	12	42	.236	.284	.326	64	-9	5	1	1	.977	-3	O-47/D-7	-1.2
	Cin-N	38	141	22	39	8	3	4	13	12	21	.277	.333	.461	110	2	5	6	-2	.987	2	O-37	0.1
1994	Cin-N	83	178	24	47	11	0	5	24	10	30	.264	.303	.410	84	-5	4	2	0	.965	-5	O-57	-1.0
Total	5	443	1183	143	310	55	8	18	114	75	221	.262	.307	.368	84	-28	39	25	-3	.985	-12	O-337/D-9	-4.9

■ WILBUR HOWARD

Howard, Wilbur Leon b: 1/8/49, Lowell, N.C. BB/TR, 6'2", 175 lbs. Deb: 9/4/73

YEAR	TM/L	G	AB	R	H	2B	3B	HR	RBI	BB	SO	AVG	OBP	SLG	PRO+	BR/A	SB	CS	SBR	FA	FR	G/POS	TPR
1973	Mil-A	16	39	3	8	0	0	0	1	2	10	.205	.244	.205	28	-4	0	1	-1	.969	2	O-12/D-1	-0.2
1974	Hou-N	64	111	19	24	4	0	2	5	6	18	.216	.250	.306	57	-7	4	5	-2	1.000	-4	O-50	-1.5
1975	Hou-N	121	392	62	111	16	8	0	21	21	67	.283	.325	.365	98	-3	32	11	3	.995	1	O-95	-0.2
1976	Hou-N	94	191	26	42	7	2	1	19	8	28	.220	.247	.293	58	-11	7	5	-1	.961	-8	O-63/2-2	-2.3
1977	Hou-N	87	187	22	48	5	3	0	13	5	30	.257	.276	.321	65	-10	11	1	3	.990	-4	O-62/2-4	-1.3
1978	Hou-N	84	148	17	34	4	1	0	13	5	22	.230	.269	.291	61	-8	6	2	1	1.000	-7	O-38/C-3,2	-1.7
Total	6	466	1068	149	267	37	11	6	71	45	175	.250	.284	.322	73	-42	60	25	2	.987	-20	O-320/2-7,CD	-7.2

■ JIM HOWARTH

Howarth, James Eugene b: 3/7/47, Biloxi, Miss. BL/TL, 5'11", 175 lbs. Deb: 9/5/71

YEAR	TM/L	G	AB	R	H	2B	3B	HR	RBI	BB	SO	AVG	OBP	SLG	PRO+	BR/A	SB	CS	SBR	FA	FR	G/POS	TPR
1971	SF-N	7	13	3	3	1	0	0	2	3	3	.231	.375	.308	97	0	0	0	0	1.000	-1	/O-6	-0.1

YEAR	TM/L	G	AB	R	H	2B	3B	HR	RBI	BB	SO	AVG	OBP	SLG	PRO+	BR/A	SB	CS	SBR	FA	FR	G/POS	TPR
1972	SF-N	74	119	16	28	4	0	1	7	16	18	.235	.326	.294	76	-3	3	2	-0	1.000	-3	O-25/1-4	-0.9
1973	SF-N	65	90	8	18	1	1	0	7	7	8	.200	.258	.233	36	-8	0	0	0	1.000	-5	O-33/1-1	-1.4
1974	SF-N	6	4	0	0	0	0	0	0	0	0	.000	.000	.000	-96	-1	0	0	0	.000	-0	/O-1	-0.1
Total	4	152	226	27	49	6	1	1	16	26	29	.217	.298	.265	58	-12	3	2	-0	1.000	-9	/O-65,1-5	-2.5

■ ART HOWE
Howe, Arthur Henry b: 12/15/46, Pittsburgh, Pa. BR/TR, 6'2", 190 lbs. Deb: 7/10/74 MC

YEAR	TM/L	G	AB	R	H	2B	3B	HR	RBI	BB	SO	AVG	OBP	SLG	PRO+	BR/A	SB	CS	SBR	FA	FR	G/POS	TPR
1974	*Pit-N	29	74	10	18	4	1	1	5	9	13	.243	.325	.365	96	-0	0	0	0	.937	4	3-20/S-2	0.3
1975	Pit-N	63	146	13	25	9	0	1	10	15	15	.171	.248	.253	40	-12	1	0	0	.938	3	3-42/S-3	-0.9
1976	Hou-N	21	29	0	4	1	0	0	6	6	6	.138	.286	.172	35	-2	0	0	0	.938	2	/3-8,2-2	-0.1
1977	Hou-N	125	413	44	109	23	7	8	58	41	60	.264	.338	.412	110	5	0	1	-1	.985	6	2-96,3-19,S	1.7
1978	Hou-N	119	420	46	123	33	3	7	55	34	41	.293	.347	.436	127	14	2	3	-1	.977	-4	*2-107,3-11/1	1.7
1979	Hou-N	118	355	32	88	15	2	6	33	36	37	.248	.319	.352	88	-6	3	1	0	.991	6	2-68,3-59/1	0.3
1980	*Hou-N	110	321	34	91	12	5	10	46	34	29	.283	.354	.445	132	13	1	0	0	.986	1	1-77,3-25/S2	1.1
1981	*Hou-N	103	361	43	107	22	4	3	36	41	23	.296	.368	.404	125	12	1	3	-2	.966	5	3-98/1-2	1.5
1982	Hou-N	110	365	29	87	15	1	5	38	41	45	.238	.317	.326	87	-6	2	0	1	.972	5	3-72,1-35	-0.2
1984	StL-N	89	139	17	30	5	0	2	12	18	18	.216	.306	.295	71	-5	0	2	-1	.979	8	3-45,1-11/2S	0.1
1985	StL-N	4	3	0	0	0	0	0	0	0	0	.000	.000	.000	-99	-1	0	0	0	1.000	0	/1-1,3-1	-0.1
Total	11	891	2626	268	682	139	23	43	293	275	287	.260	.332	.379	103	10	10	10	-3	.965	38	3-400,2-284,1/S	5.4

■ SHORTY HOWE
Howe, John b: New York, N.Y. Deb: 6/17/1890

YEAR	TM/L	G	AB	R	H	2B	3B	HR	RBI	BB	SO	AVG	OBP	SLG	PRO+	BR/A	SB	CS	SBR	FA	FR	G/POS	TPR
1890	NY-N	19	64	4	11	3	0	0	3	2	1	.172	.221	.172	15	-7	3			.887	3	2-18/3-1	-0.2
1893	NY-N	1	5	1	3	0	0	0	2	0	0	.600	.600	.600	219	1	1			.400	-1	/3-1	0.0
Total	2	20	69	5	14	3	0	0	5	2	1	.203	.247	.203	30	-6	4			.400	2	/2-18,3-2	-0.2

■ HARRY HOWELL
Howell, Henry Harry b: 11/14/1876, New Jersey d: 5/22/56, Spokane, Wash. BR/TR, 5'9" Deb: 10/10/1898 U

YEAR	TM/L	G	AB	R	H	2B	3B	HR	RBI	BB	SO	AVG	OBP	SLG	PRO+	BR/A	SB	CS	SBR	FA	FR	G/POS	TPR
1898	Bro-N	2	8	1	2	0	0	0	1	1		.250	.333	.250	68	-0	0			1.000	0	/P-2	0.0
1899	Bal-N	28	82	4	12	2	2	0	3	3		.146	.195	.220	13	-10	0			.940	1	P-28	0.0
1900	*Bro-N	22	42	6	12	2	0	1	6	6		.286	.388	.405	112	1	1			.949	1	P-21	0.0
1901	Bal-A	53	188	26	41	10	5	2	26	5		.218	.242	.356	62	-11	6			.905	-3	P-37/O-9,S12	-0.5
1902	Bal-A	96	347	42	93	16	11	2	42	18		.268	.312	.395	91	-5	7			.951	-9	P-26,2-26,O3S/1	-1.6
1903	NY-A	40	106	14	23	3	2	1	12	5		.217	.259	.311	66	-4	1			1.000	1	P-25/3-7,S12	-0.4
1904	StL-A	36	113	9	25	5	2	1	6	4		.221	.261	.327	91	-2	0			.971	9	P-34	0.0
1905	StL-A	42	135	9	26	6	1	0	10	3		.193	.216	.289	63	-6	0			.966	18	P-38/O-3	-0.1
1906	StL-A	35	103	5	13	3	1	0	6	9		.126	.174	.175	10	-11	2			.934	7	P-35	0.0
1907	StL-A	44	114	12	27	5	0	2	7	7		.237	.281	.333	96	-1	2			.982	9	P-42/O-2	0.1
1908	StL-A	41	120	10	22	7	0	1	9	4		.183	.210	.267	54	-6	0			.961	0	P-41	0.0
1909	StL-A	18	34	5	6	1	0	0	3	2		.176	.222	.206	38	-2	0			.938	1	P-10/3-7,O	0.0
1910	StL-A	1	2	0	0	0	0	0	0	0		.000	.000	.000	-99	-0	0			1.000	0	/P-1	0.0
Total	13	458	1394	143	302	60	25	11	131	64		.217	.257	.319	69	-59	19			.958	36	P-340/O-33,32S1	-2.5

■ DIXIE HOWELL
Howell, Homer Elliott b: 4/24/20, Louisville, Ky. d: 10/5/90, Binghamton, N.Y. BR/TR, 5'11", 195 lbs. Deb: 5/6/47

YEAR	TM/L	G	AB	R	H	2B	3B	HR	RBI	BB	SO	AVG	OBP	SLG	PRO+	BR/A	SB	CS	SBR	FA	FR	G/POS	TPR
1947	Pit-N	76	214	23	59	11	0	4	25	27	34	.276	.357	.383	94	-1	1			.974	-3	C-74	0.0
1949	Cin-N	64	172	17	42	6	1	2	18	8	21	.244	.286	.326	63	-9	0			.987	5	C-56	-0.1
1950	Cin-N	82	224	30	50	9	1	2	22	32	31	.223	.326	.299	65	-11	0			.986	-4	C-81	-1.1
1951	Cin-N	77	207	22	52	6	1	2	18	15	34	.251	.302	.319	66	-10	0	2	-1	.987	4	C-73	-0.5
1952	Cin-N	17	37	4	7	1	1	2	4	3	9	.189	.250	.432	86	-1	0	0	0	.981	1	C-16	0.0
1953	Bro-N	1	1	0	0	0	0	0	0	0	0	.000	.000	.000	-98	-0	0	0	0	.000	0	H	0.0
1955	Bro-N	16	42	2	11	4	0	0	5	1	7	.262	.279	.357	66	-2	0	0	0	.981	-2	C-13	-0.3
1956	Bro-N	7	13	0	3	0	0	0	1	1	3	.231	.286	.385	72	-1	1	0	0	1.000	-0	/C-6	-0.1
Total	8	340	910	98	224	39	4	12	93	87	140	.246	.315	.337	73	-35	1	2		.984	2	C-319	-2.1

■ JACK HOWELL
Howell, Jack Robert b: 8/18/61, Tucson, Ariz. BL/TR, 6', 185 lbs. Deb: 5/20/85

YEAR	TM/L	G	AB	R	H	2B	3B	HR	RBI	BB	SO	AVG	OBP	SLG	PRO+	BR/A	SB	CS	SBR	FA	FR	G/POS	TPR
1985	Cal-A	43	137	19	27	4	0	5	18	16	33	.197	.281	.336	68	-6	1	1	-0	.931	-1	3-42	-0.8
1986	*Cal-A	63	151	26	41	14	2	4	21	19	28	.272	.353	.470	123	5	2	0	1	.977	-1	3-39/O-8,D	0.4
1987	Cal-A	138	449	64	110	18	5	23	64	57	118	.245	.333	.461	111	7	4	3	-1	.987	-8	O-89,3-48,2	-0.5
1988	Cal-A	154	500	59	127	32	2	16	63	46	130	.254	.324	.422	110	6	2	6	-3	.953	-20	*3-152/O-2	-1.8
1989	Cal-A	144	474	56	108	19	4	20	52	52	125	.228	.308	.411	103	1	0	3	-2	.974	23	*3-142/O-4	2.3
1990	Cal-A	105	316	35	72	19	1	8	33	46	61	.228	.328	.370	97	-1	3	0	1	.939	7	3-102/1-1,S	0.8
1991	Cal-A	32	81	11	17	2	0	2	7	11	11	.210	.304	.309	70	-3	1	1	-0	.968	-2	2-12/3-8,01D	-0.2
	SD-N	58	160	24	33	3	1	6	16	18	33	.206	.287	.350	76	-5	0	0	0	.985	6	3-54	0.1
Total	7	737	2268	294	535	111	15	84	274	265	539	.236	.319	.409	101	3	13	14	-5	.961	7	3-587,O-108/21DS	0.3

■ RED HOWELL
Howell, Murray Donald "Porky" b: 1/29/09, Atlanta, Ga. d: 10/1/50, Travelers Rest, S.C BR/TR, 6', 215 lbs. Deb: 4/24/41

YEAR	TM/L	G	AB	R	H	2B	3B	HR	RBI	BB	SO	AVG	OBP	SLG	PRO+	BR/A	SB	CS	SBR	FA	FR	G/POS	TPR
1941	Cle-A	11	7	0	2	0	0	0	4	2	4	.286	.545	.286	132	1	0	0	0	.000	0	H	0.1

■ PAT HOWELL
Howell, Patrick O'Neal b: 8/31/68, Mobile, Ala. BB/TR, 5'11", 155 lbs. Deb: 7/10/92

YEAR	TM/L	G	AB	R	H	2B	3B	HR	RBI	BB	SO	AVG	OBP	SLG	PRO+	BR/A	SB	CS	SBR	FA	FR	G/POS	TPR
1992	NY-N	31	75	9	14	1	0	0	1	2	15	.187	.218	.200	19	-8	4	2	0	1.000	-0	O-28	-1.0

■ ROY HOWELL
Howell, Roy Lee b: 12/18/53, Lompoc, Cal. BL/TR, 6'1", 190 lbs. Deb: 9/9/74

YEAR	TM/L	G	AB	R	H	2B	3B	HR	RBI	BB	SO	AVG	OBP	SLG	PRO+	BR/A	SB	CS	SBR	FA	FR	G/POS	TPR
1974	Tex-A	13	44	2	11	1	0	1	3	2	10	.250	.283	.341	81	-1	0	0	0	.906	-2	3-12	-0.3
1975	Tex-A	125	383	43	96	15	2	10	51	39	79	.251	.325	.379	99	-1	2	2	-1	.933	-7	*3-115/D-5	-0.8
1976	Tex-A	140	491	55	124	28	2	8	53	30	106	.253	.297	.367	92	-6	1	0	0	.926	-8	*3-130/D-8	-1.5
1977	Tex-A	7	17	0	0	0	0	0	2	2	4	.000	.105	.000	-68	-4	0	0	0	1.000	-0	/O-2,1-1,3D	-0.4
	Tor-A	96	364	41	115	17	1	10	44	42	76	.316	.388	.451	126	14	4	1	0	.953	-7	3-87/D-8	0.7
	Yr	103	381	41	115	17	1	10	44	44	80	.302	.376	.430	117	10	4	1	0	.954	-7	3-88,D-10/O1	0.3
1978	Tor-A★	140	551	67	149	28	3	8	61	44	78	.270	.326	.376	95	-4	0	1	-1	.950	11	*3-131/O-5,D	0.4
1979	Tor-A	138	511	60	126	28	4	15	72	42	91	.247	.311	.405	90	-4	1	4	-2	.952	-1	*3-133/O-4	-1.2
1980	Tor-A	142	528	51	142	28	9	10	57	50	92	.269	.338	.413	100	0	0	0	0	.958	-18	*3-138/D-2	-2.0
1981	*Mil-A	76	244	37	58	13	1	6	33	23	39	.238	.309	.373	101	-0	0	0	0	.958	-6	3-53,D-13/1O	-1.2
1982	*Mil-A	98	300	31	78	11	2	4	38	21	39	.260	.308	.350	86	-6	0	2	-1	.933	-1	D-84/1-4,O	-1.2
1983	Mil-A	69	194	23	54	9	6	4	25	15	29	.278	.330	.448	121	5	1	3	-2	.960	-1	D-54/1-2	0.2
1984	Mil-A	68	164	12	38	5	1	4	20	8	28	.232	.284	.348	77	-5	1	1	-4	.907	1	3-46/1-4,D	-0.5
Total	11	1112	3791	422	991	183	31	80	454	318	675	.261	.322	.389	97	-17	9	14		.944	-22	3-846,D-189/1O	-7.4

■ BILL HOWERTON
Howerton, William Ray "Hopalong" b: 12/12/21, Lompoc, Cal. BL/TR, 5'11", 185 lbs. Deb: 9/11/49

YEAR	TM/L	G	AB	R	H	2B	3B	HR	RBI	BB	SO	AVG	OBP	SLG	PRO+	BR/A	SB	CS	SBR	FA	FR	G/POS	TPR
1949	StL-N	9	13	1	4	1	0	0	1	0	0	.308	.308	.385	81	-0	0			.900	-1	/O-6	-0.2
1950	StL-N	110	313	50	88	20	8	10	59	47	60	.281	.375	.492	120	9	0			.969	-11	O-94	-0.5
1951	StL-N	24	65	10	17	4	1	1	4	10	12	.262	.360	.400	104	1	0	1	-1	.949	1	O-17	0.0
	Pit-N	80	219	29	60	12	2	11	37	26	44	.274	.351	.498	122	6	1	0	0	.950	-8	O-53/3-4	-0.3
	Yr	104	284	39	77	16	3	12	41	36	56	.271	.353	.475	118	7	1	1	-1	.950	-8	O-70/3-4	-0.3
1952	Pit-N	13	25	3	8	1	1	0	4	6	5	.320	.452	.440	144	2	0			.900	-2	/O-5,3-1	0.0
	NY-N	11	15	2	1	1	0	0	1	3	4	.067	.222	.133	1	-2	0			.900	-0	/O-3	-0.2
	Yr	24	40	5	9	2	1	0	5	9	9	.225	.367	.325	92	-0	0			.938	-2	/O-8,3-1	-0.2
Total	4	247	650	95	178	39	12	22	106	92	125	.274	.364	.472	117	16	1	1		.958	-22	O-178/3-5	-1.2

YEAR	TM/L	G	AB	R	H	2B	3B	HR	RBI	BB	SO	AVG	OBP	SLG	PRO+	BR/A	SB	CS	SBR	FA	FR	G/POS	TPR

■ DANN HOWITT   Howitt, Dann Paul John   b: 2/13/64, Battle Creek, Mich.   BL/TR, 6'5", 205 lbs.   Deb: 9/15/89

YEAR	TM/L	G	AB	R	H	2B	3B	HR	RBI	BB	SO	AVG	OBP	SLG	PRO+	BR/A	SB	CS	SBR	FA	FR	G/POS	TPR
1989	Oak-A	3	3	0	0	0	0	0	0	0	2	.000	.000	.000	-99	-1	0	0	0	1.000	-1	/1-1,O-1	-0.1
1990	Oak-A	14	22	3	3	0	1	0	1	3	12	.136	.240	.227	33	-2	0	0	0	1.000	-2	O-11/1-5,3	-0.4
1991	Oak-A	21	42	5	7	1	0	1	3	1	12	.167	.186	.262	24	-4	0	0	0	1.000	-1	O-20/1-1	-0.9
1992	Oak-A	22	48	1	6	0	0	1	2	5	4	.125	.208	.188	12	-6	0	0	0	.951	1	O-19/1-4,D	-0.6
	Sea-A	13	37	6	10	4	1	1	8	3	5	.270	.325	.514	131	1	1	1	-0	1.000	0	O-11	0.2
	Yr	35	85	7	16	4	1	2	10	8	9	.188	.258	.329	66	-4	1	1	-0	.970	2	O-30/1-4,D	-0.4
1993	Sea-A	32	76	6	16	3	1	2	8	4	18	.211	.250	.355	60	-5	0	0	0	1.000	-5	O-29/D-2	-1.0
1994	Chi-A	10	14	4	5	3	0	0	1	0	7	.357	.400	.571	148	1	0	0	0	1.000	-2	/O-7,1-4	-0.1
Total	6	115	242	25	47	11	3	5	22	17	60	.194	.247	.326	57	-15	1	1	-0	.987	-12	/O-98,1-15,D3	-2.9

■ DAN HOWLEY   Howley, Daniel Philip "Howling Dan" or "Dapper Dan"   b: 10/16/1885, Weymouth, Mass.   d: 3/10/44, Weymouth, Mass.   BR/TR, 6', 187 lbs.   Deb: 5/15/13   MC

YEAR	TM/L	G	AB	R	H	2B	3B	HR	RBI	BB	SO	AVG	OBP	SLG	PRO+	BR/A	SB	CS	SBR	FA	FR	G/POS	TPR
1913	Phi-N	26	32	5	4	2	0	0	2	4	4	.125	.222	.188	17	-3	3			.954	1	C-22	-0.2

■ DICK HOWSER   Howser, Richard Dalton   b: 5/14/36, Miami, Fla.   d: 6/17/87, Kansas City, Mo.   BR/TR, 5'8", 155 lbs.   Deb: 4/11/61   MC

YEAR	TM/L	G	AB	R	H	2B	3B	HR	RBI	BB	SO	AVG	OBP	SLG	PRO+	BR/A	SB	CS	SBR	FA	FR	G/POS	TPR
1961	KC-A★	158	611	108	171	29	6	3	45	92	38	.280	.379	.362	97	1	37	9	6	.950	-17	*S-157	0.3
1962	KC-A	83	286	53	68	8	3	6	34	38	8	.238	.329	.350	79	-8	19	2	5	.962	-8	S-72	-0.5
1963	KC-A	15	41	4	8	0	1	0	1	7	3	.195	.313	.195	44	-3	0	0	0	.957	-4	S-10	-0.6
	Cle-A	49	162	25	40	5	0	1	10	22	18	.247	.337	.296	80	-4	9	3	1	.950	-17	S-44	-1.7
	Yr	64	203	29	48	5	1	1	11	29	21	.236	.332	.276	72	-7	9	3	1	.951	-20	S-54	-2.3
1964	Cle-A	162	637	101	163	23	4	3	52	76	39	.256	.337	.319	84	-11	20	7	2	.974	5	*S-162	0.6
1965	Cle-A	107	307	47	72	8	2	1	6	57	25	.235	.356	.283	83	-4	17	4	3	.977	-6	S-73,2-17	-0.1
1966	Cle-A	67	140	18	32	9	1	2	4	15	23	.229	.303	.350	87	-2	2	4	-2	.986	-7	2-26,S-26	-0.8
1967	NY-A	63	149	18	40	6	0	0	10	25	15	.268	.381	.309	110	3	1	4	-2	.990	-6	2-22,3-12/S	-0.4
1968	NY-A	85	150	24	23	2	1	0	3	35	17	.153	.321	.180	57	-6	0	1	-1	.982	5	2-29/3-2,S	0.0
Total	8	789	2483	398	617	90	17	16	165	367	186	.248	.348	.318	86	-34	105	34	11	.963	-56	S-548/2-94,3	-3.2

■ DUMMY HOY   Hoy, William Ellsworth   b: 5/23/1862, Houcktown, Ohio   d: 12/15/61, Cincinnati, Ohio   BL/TR, 5'4", 148 lbs.   Deb: 4/20/1888

YEAR	TM/L	G	AB	R	H	2B	3B	HR	RBI	BB	SO	AVG	OBP	SLG	PRO+	BR/A	SB	CS	SBR	FA	FR	G/POS	TPR
1888	Was-N	136	503	77	138	10	8	2	29	69	48	.274	.374	.338	136	25	**82**			.897	7	*O-136	2.7
1889	Was-N	127	507	98	139	11	6	0	39	75	30	.274	.374	.320	101	6	35			.890	-4	*O-127	-0.1
1890	Buf-P	122	493	107	147	17	8	1	53	94	36	.298	.418	.371	122	23	39			.912	6	*O-122/2-1	2.0
1891	StL-a	141	567	136	165	14	5	5	66	**119**	25	.291	.424	.360	108	7	59			.909	-1	*O-141	0.2
1892	Was-N	152	593	108	166	19	8	3	75	86	23	.280	.375	.354	124	21	60			.884	-12	*O-152	0.2
1893	Was-N	130	564	106	138	12	6	0	45	66	9	.245	.337	.287	68	-23	48			.892	-1	*O-130	-2.5
1894	Cin-N	126	495	114	148	22	13	6	70	87	18	.299	.416	.426	100	2	27			.896	3	*O-126	-0.3
1895	Cin-N	107	429	93	119	21	12	3	55	52	8	.277	.363	.403	94	-5	50			.883	-3	*O-107	-1.3
1896	Cin-N	121	443	120	132	23	7	4	57	65	13	.298	.403	.409	107	6	50			.946	5	*O-120	0.1
1897	Cin-N	128	497	87	145	24	6	2	42	54		.292	.375	.376	92	-5	37			.934	7	*O-128	-0.6
1898	Lou-N	148	582	104	177	15	16	6	66	49		.304	.367	.416	126	19	37			.946	6	*O-148	1.3
1899	Lou-N	154	633	116	194	17	13	5	49	61		.306	.376	.398	113	12	32			.927	-6	*O-154	-0.5
1901	Chi-A	132	527	112	155	28	11	2	60	**86**		.294	.407	.400	128	25	27			.958	2	*O-132	1.5
1902	Cin-N	72	279	48	81	15	2	2	20	41		.290	.389	.380	125	10	11			.933	-5	O-72	0.0
Total	14	1796	7112	1426	2044	248	121	40	726	1004	**210**	.287	.386	.373	109	123	594			.915	2	*O-1795/2-1	2.7

■ KENT HRBEK   Hrbek, Kent Alan   b: 5/21/60, Minneapolis, Minn.   BL/TR, 6'4", 235 lbs.   Deb: 8/24/81

YEAR	TM/L	G	AB	R	H	2B	3B	HR	RBI	BB	SO	AVG	OBP	SLG	PRO+	BR/A	SB	CS	SBR	FA	FR	G/POS	TPR
1981	Min-A	24	67	5	16	5	0	1	7	5	9	.239	.301	.358	84	-1	0	0	0	1.000	-2	1-13/D-8	-0.4
1982	Min-A★	140	532	82	160	21	4	23	92	54	80	.301	.365	.485	128	20	3	1	0	.993	-0	*1-138/D-2	1.2
1983	Min-A	141	515	75	153	41	5	16	84	57	71	.297	.370	.489	130	21	4	6	-2	.990	-6	*1-137/D-1	0.8
1984	Min-A	149	559	80	174	31	3	27	107	65	87	.311	.387	.522	142	32	1	1	-0	.990	-6	*1-156/D-2	1.7
1985	Min-A	158	593	78	165	31	2	21	93	67	87	.278	.353	.444	110	9	1	1	-0	.995	1	*1-158/D-2	0.0
1986	Min-A	149	550	85	147	27	1	29	91	71	81	.267	.357	.478	122	17	2	2	-1	.992	-2	*1-147/D-1	0.3
1987	*Min-A	143	477	85	136	20	1	34	90	84	60	.285	.392	.545	140	29	5	2	0	.996	-10	*1-137/D-1	0.9
1988	Min-A	143	510	75	159	31	0	25	76	67	54	.312	.392	.520	149	34	0	3	-2	.997	-6	*1-105,D-37	1.6
1989	Min-A	109	375	59	102	17	0	25	84	53	35	.272	.364	.517	136	18	3	0	1	.995	1	1-89,D-18	1.2
1990	Min-A	143	492	61	141	26	0	22	79	69	45	.287	.382	.474	129	20	5	2	-0	**.997**	1	*1-120,D-20/3	1.2
1991	*Min-A	132	462	72	131	20	1	20	89	67	48	.284	.374	.461	124	16	4	4	-1	.994	4	*1-128	1.0
1992	Min-A	112	394	52	96	20	0	15	58	71	56	.244	.359	.409	111	7	5	2	0	.997	-1	*1-104/D-8	0.5
1993	Min-A	123	392	60	95	11	1	25	83	71	57	.242	.360	.467	120	12	4	2	0	.995	-3	*1-115/D-2	0.5
1994	Min-A	81	274	34	74	11	0	10	53	37	28	.270	.359	.420	100	0	0	0	0	.997	-2	1-72/D-4	-0.7
Total	14	1747	6192	903	1749	312	18	293	1086	838	798	.282	.370	.481	127	233	37	26	-5	.994	-21	*1-1609,D-106/3	9.3

■ WALT HRINIAK   Hriniak, Walter John   b: 5/22/43, Natick, Mass.   BL/TR, 5'11", 180 lbs.   Deb: 9/10/68   C

YEAR	TM/L	G	AB	R	H	2B	3B	HR	RBI	BB	SO	AVG	OBP	SLG	PRO+	BR/A	SB	CS	SBR	FA	FR	G/POS	TPR
1968	Atl-N	9	26	0	9	0	0	0	3	0	3	.346	.346	.346	108	0	0	0	0	.967	3	/C-9	0.4
1969	Atl-N	7	7	0	1	0	0	0	0	2	1	.143	.333	.143	38	-0	0	0	0	1.000	-1	/C-6	-0.1
	SD-N	31	66	4	15	0	0	0	1	8	11	.227	.329	.227	61	-3	0	0	0	.981	-2	C-19	-0.4
	Yr	38	73	4	16	0	0	0	1	10	12	.219	.329	.219	58	-4	0	0	0	.982	-3	/C-25	-0.5
Total	2	47	99	4	25	0	0	0	4	10	15	.253	.333	.253	71	-3	0	0	0	.977	-0	/C-34	-0.1

■ AL HUBBARD   Hubbard, Allen (a.k.a. Al West For 1 Game In 1883)   b: 12/9/1860, Westfield, Mass.   d: 12/14/30, Newton, Mass.   Deb: 9/13/1883

YEAR	TM/L	G	AB	R	H	2B	3B	HR	RBI	BB	SO	AVG	OBP	SLG	PRO+	BR/A	SB	CS	SBR	FA	FR	G/POS	TPR
1883	Phi-a	2	6	2	2	0	0	0		1		.333	.429	.333	138	0				.750	-0	/S-1,C-1	0.0

■ GLENN HUBBARD   Hubbard, Glenn Dee   b: 9/25/57, Hahn Air Force Base, Germany   BR/TR, 5'7", 180 lbs.   Deb: 7/14/78

YEAR	TM/L	G	AB	R	H	2B	3B	HR	RBI	BB	SO	AVG	OBP	SLG	PRO+	BR/A	SB	CS	SBR	FA	FR	G/POS	TPR
1978	Atl-N	44	163	15	42	4	0	2	13	10	20	.258	.309	.319	68	-7	2	1	0	.979	3	2-44	0.0
1979	Atl-N	97	325	34	75	12	0	3	29	27	43	.231	.292	.295	56	-19	0	6	-4	.968	5	2-91	-1.3
1980	Atl-N	117	431	55	107	21	3	9	43	49	69	.248	.325	.374	91	-5	7	5	-1	.978	19	*2-117	2.2
1981	Atl-N	99	361	39	85	13	5	6	33	33	59	.235	.303	.349	82	-8	4	2	0	.991	-4	2-98	-0.7
1982	*Atl-N	145	532	75	132	25	1	9	59	59	62	.248	.327	.350	86	-9	4	3	-1	.983	20	*2-144	1.8
1983	Atl-N★	148	517	65	136	24	6	12	70	55	71	.263	.339	.402	97	-2	3	8	-4	.985	22	*2-148	2.4
1984	Atl-N	120	397	53	93	27	2	9	43	55	61	.234	.333	.380	93	-3	4	1	1	.988	20	*2-117	2.2
1985	Atl-N	142	439	51	102	21	0	5	39	56	54	.232	.325	.314	75	-13	4	3	-1	.989	**62**	*2-140	5.4
1986	Atl-N	143	408	42	94	16	1	4	36	66	74	.230	.343	.304	76	-11	3	2	-0	.976	**41**	*2-142	3.5
1987	Atl-N	141	443	69	117	33	2	5	38	77	57	.264	.380	.381	98	-1	1	1	-0	.986	**28**	*2-139	3.5
1988	*Oak-A	105	294	35	75	12	2	3	33	33	50	.255	.336	.340	87	-2	1	3	-2	.987	4	*2-104/D-1	0.4
1989	Oak-A	53	131	12	26	6	0	3	12	19	20	.198	.300	.313	76	-4	2	0	1	.968	10	*2-48/D-3	0.8
Total	12	1354	4441	545	1084	214	22	70	448	539	640	.244	.330	.349	85	-83	35	35	-11	.983	229	*2-1332/D-4	20.2

■ TRENIDAD HUBBARD   Hubbard, Trenidad Aviel (b: Trent Hubbard)   b: 5/11/64, Chicago, Ill.   BR/TR, 5'8", 180 lbs.   Deb: 7/7/94

YEAR	TM/L	G	AB	R	H	2B	3B	HR	RBI	BB	SO	AVG	OBP	SLG	PRO+	BR/A	SB	CS	SBR	FA	FR	G/POS	TPR
1994	Col-N	18	25	3	7	1	1	1	3	3	4	.280	.357	.520	107	0	0	0	0	1.000	-1	/O-5	-0.1

■ KEN HUBBS   Hubbs, Kenneth Douglas   b: 12/23/41, Riverside, Cal.   d: 2/13/64, Provo, Utah   BR/TR, 6'2", 175 lbs.   Deb: 9/10/61

YEAR	TM/L	G	AB	R	H	2B	3B	HR	RBI	BB	SO	AVG	OBP	SLG	PRO+	BR/A	SB	CS	SBR	FA	FR	G/POS	TPR
1961	Chi-N	10	28	4	5	1	1	1	2	0	8	.179	.179	.393	46	-2	0	0	0	1.000	-2	/2-8	-0.3
1962	Chi-N	160	661	90	172	24	9	5	49	35	129	.260	.300	.346	71	-28	3	7	-3	.983	4	*2-159	-1.0
1963	Chi-N	154	566	54	133	19	3	8	47	39	93	.235	.287	.322	71	-21	8	9	-3	.974	20	*2-152	1.1
Total	3	324	1255	148	310	44	13	14	98	74	230	.247	.292	.336	70	-51	11	16	-6	.979	23	2-319	-0.2

YEAR	TM/L	G	AB	R	H	2B	3B	HR	RBI	BB	SO	AVG	OBP	SLG	PRO+	BR/A	SB	CS	SBR	FA	FR	G/POS	TPR

■ CLARENCE HUBER   Huber, Clarence Bill "Gilly"   b: 10/27/1896, Tyler, Tex.   d: 2/22/65, Laredo, Tex.   BR/TR, 5'10", 165 lbs.   Deb: 9/17/20

1920	Det-A	11	42	4	9	2	1	0	5	0	5	.214	.214	.310	39	-4	0	0	0	.907	2	3-11	-0.1
1921	Det-A	1	0	0	0	0	0	0	0	0	0	—	—	—	—	0	0	0	0	1.000	-0	/3-1	0.0
1925	Phi-N	124	436	46	124	28	5	5	54	17	33	.284	.311	.406	75	-17	3	5	-2	.947	-9	*3-120	-1.9
1926	Phi-N	118	376	45	92	17	7	1	34	42	29	.245	.324	.335	74	-13	9			.956	8	*3-115	0.1
Total	4	254	854	95	225	47	13	6	93	59	67	.263	.313	.370	73	-35	12	5		.948	1	3-247	-1.9

■ OTTO HUBER   Huber, Otto   b: 3/12/14, Garfield, N.J.   d: 4/9/89, Passaic, N.J.   BR/TR, 5'10", 165 lbs.   Deb: 6/10/39

1939	Bos-N	11	22	2	6	1	0	0	3	0	1	.273	.273	.318	63	-1	0			1.000	-0	/2-4,3-4	-0.1

■ DAVE HUDGENS   Hudgens, David Mark   b: 12/5/56, Oroville, Cal.   BL/TL, 6'2", 210 lbs.   Deb: 9/4/83

1983	Oak-A	6	7	0	1	0	0	0	0	0	3	.143	.143	.143	-22	-1	0	0	0	1.000	-0	/1-3,D-1	-0.1

■ JIMMY HUDGENS   Hudgens, James Price   b: 8/24/02, Newburg, Mo.   d: 8/26/55, St.Louis, Mo.   BL/TR, 6', 180 lbs.   Deb: 9/14/23

1923	StL-N	6	12	2	3	1	0	0	0	3	3	.250	.400	.333	97	0	0	0	0	1.000	1	/1-3,2-1	0.1
1925	Cin-N	3	7	0	3	1	1	0	0	1	1	.429	.500	.857	245	2	0	0	0	1.000	0	/1-3	0.1
1926	Cin-N	17	20	2	5	1	0	0	1	1	0	.250	.286	.300	59	-1	0	0	0	1.000	0	/1-6	-0.1
Total	3	26	39	4	11	3	1	0	1	5	4	.282	.364	.410	107	0	0	0		1.000	1	/1-12,2-1	0.1

■ REX HUDLER   Hudler, Rex Allen   b: 9/2/60, Tempe, Ariz.   BR/TR, 6'1", 180 lbs.   Deb: 9/9/84

1984	NY-A	9	7	2	1	1	0	0	0	1	5	.143	.333	.286	76	-0	0	0	0	1.000	0	/2-9	0.0
1985	NY-A	20	51	4	8	0	1	0	1	1	9	.157	.173	.196	1	-7	0	1	-1	.977	7	2-16/1-1,S	0.0
1986	Bal-A	14	1	1	0	0	0	0	0	0	0	.000	.000	.000	-99	-0	1	0	0	.800	1	2-13/3-1	0.1
1988	Mon-N	77	216	38	59	14	2	4	14	10	34	.273	.305	.412	100	-1	29	7	5	.978	-1	2-41,S-27/O	0.6
1989	Mon-N	92	155	21	38	7	0	6	13	6	23	.245	.278	.406	92	-2	15	4	2	.958	-14	2-38,O-23,S	-1.4
1990	Mon-N	4	3	1	1	0	0	0	0	0	1	.333	.333	.333	87	-0	0	0	0	.000	0	/H	0.0
	StL-N	89	217	30	61	11	2	7	22	12	31	.281	.325	.447	110	2	18	10	-1	.979	0	O-45,2-10/13S	0.1
	Yr	93	220	31	62	11	2	7	22	12	32	.282	.325	.445	109	2	18	10	-1	.979	0	O-45,2-10/13S	0.1
1991	StL-N	101	207	21	47	10	2	1	15	10	29	.227	.263	.309	60	-11	12	8	-1	.981	-3	O-58,1-12/2	-1.8
1992	StL-N	61	98	17	24	4	0	3	5	2	23	.245	.267	.378	83	-3	2	6	-3	.957	-8	2-16,O-12/1	-1.4
1994	Cal-A	56	124	17	37	8	0	8	20	6	28	.298	.331	.556	120	3	2	2	-1	.971	-2	2-22,O-18/31D	0.1
Total	9	523	1079	152	276	55	7	29	90	48	183	.256	.291	.400	89	-19	79	38	1	.969	-20	2-170,O-160/S13D	-3.7

■ JOHNNY HUDSON   Hudson, John Wilson "Mr. Chips"   b: 6/30/12, Bryan, Tex.   d: 11/7/70, Bryan, Tex.   BR/TR, 5'10", 160 lbs.   Deb: 6/20/36

1936	Bro-N	6	12	1	2	0	0	0	0	2	1	.167	.286	.167	24	-1	0			.889	-1	/S-4,2-1	-0.2
1937	Bro-N	13	27	3	5	4	0	0	2	3	9	.185	.267	.333	61	-2	0			.867	-4	S-11/2-1	-0.5
1938	Bro-N	135	498	59	130	21	5	2	37	39	76	.261	.315	.335	77	-15	7			.963	-4	*2-132/S-3	-1.2
1939	Bro-N	109	343	46	87	17	3	2	32	30	36	.254	.317	.338	74	-13	5			.959	-18	S-50,2-45/3	-2.4
1940	Bro-N	85	179	13	39	4	3	0	19	9	26	.218	.255	.274	43	-14	2			.921	-8	S-38,2-27/3	-1.0
1941	Chi-N	50	99	8	20	4	0	0	6	3	15	.202	.225	.242	33	-9	3			.907	-1	S-17,2-13,3	-0.8
1945	NY-N	28	11	8	0	0	0	0	0	1	1	.000	.083	.000	-75	-3	0			.875	3	/3-5,2-2	0.0
Total	7	426	1169	138	283	50	11	4	96	87	164	.242	.296	.314	65	-56	17			.962	-25	2-221,S-123/3	-6.1

■ FRANK HUELSMAN   Huelsman, Frank Elmer   b: 6/5/1874, St.Louis, Mo.   d: 6/9/59, Affton, Mo.   BR/TR, 6'2", 210 lbs.   Deb: 10/3/1897

1897	StL-N	2	7	0	2	1	0	0	0	0	0	.286	.286	.429	89	-0	0			.000	-1	/O-2	-0.1
1904	Chi-A	3	6	0	1	1	0	0	0	0	0	.167	.167	.333	58	-0	0			.000	-1	/O-1	-0.1
	Det-A	4	18	1	6	1	0	0	4	1	1	.333	.368	.389	144	1	0			1.000	-1	/O-4	0.0
	Chi-A	1	1	0	0	0	0	0	0	0	0	.000	.000	.000	-99	-0	0			.000	0	H	0.0
	StL-A	20	68	6	15	2	1	0	1	6	1	.221	.303	.279	90	-1	0			1.000	-3	O-18	-0.5
	Was-A	84	303	21	75	19	4	2	30	24		.248	.313	.356	113	5	6			.960	-3	O-84	-0.4
	Yr	112	396	28	97	23	5	2	35	31		.245	.311	.343	110	5	7			.960	-8	*O-107	-1.0
1905	Was-A	121	421	48	114	28	8	3	62	31		.271	.333	.397	136	17	11			.929	-9	*O-116	0.3
Total	3	235	824	76	213	52	13	5	97	62		.258	.322	.371	123	21	18			.941	-18	O-225	-0.8

■ MIKE HUFF   Huff, Michael Kale   b: 8/11/63, Honolulu, Hawaii   BR/TR, 6'1", 180 lbs.   Deb: 8/7/89

1989	LA-N	12	25	4	5	1	0	1	2	3	6	.200	.310	.360	93	-0	0	1	-1	1.000	-0	/O-9	-0.1
1991	Cle-A	51	146	28	35	6	1	2	10	25	30	.240	.366	.336	95	0	11	2	2	.990	-3	O-48/2-2	-0.2
	Chi-A	51	97	14	26	4	1	1	15	12	18	.268	.360	.361	103	1	3	2	-0	.986	-11	O-48/2-2,D	-1.1
	Yr	102	243	42	61	10	2	3	25	37	48	.251	.364	.346	98	1	14	4	2	.988	-14	O-96/2-4,D	-1.3
1992	Chi-A	60	115	13	24	5	0	0	8	10	24	.209	.278	.252	50	-8	1	2	-1	1.000	-10	O-56/D-1	-2.0
1993	Chi-A	43	44	4	8	2	0	0	6	9	15	.182	.333	.295	72	-1	1	0	0	1.000	-12	O-43	-1.3
1994	Tor-A	80	207	31	63	15	3	3	25	27	27	.304	.392	.449	115	6	2	1	0	.992	-6	O-76	-0.2
Total	5	297	634	94	161	33	5	8	66	86	120	.254	.354	.360	94	-3	18	8	1	.993	-42	O-280/2-4,D	-4.9

■ BEN HUFFMAN   Huffman, Benjamin Franklin   b: 6/26/14, Rileyville, Va.   BL/TR, 5'11.5", 175 lbs.   Deb: 4/23/37

1937	StL-A	76	176	18	48	9	0	1	24	10	7	.273	.323	.341	67	-9	1	0	0	.970	-8	C-42	-1.3

■ ED HUG   Hug, Edward Ambrose   b: 7/14/1880, Fayetteville, O.   d: 5/11/53, Cincinnati, Ohio   BR/TR,   Deb: 7/6/03

1903	Bro-N	1	0	0	0	0	0	0	1			—	1.000	—	199	0	0			.000	0	/C-1	0.0

■ MILLER HUGGINS   Huggins, Miller James "Hug" or "Mighty Mite"
b: 3/27/1879, Cincinnati, Ohio   d: 9/25/29, New York, N.Y.   BB/TR, 5'6.5", 140 lbs.   Deb: 4/15/04   MH

1904	Cin-N	140	491	96	129	12	7	2	30	88		.263	.377	.328	108	8	13			.945	1	*2-140	1.4
1905	Cin-N	149	564	117	154	11	8	1	38	103		.273	.392	.326	103	7	27			.945	**36**	*2-149	4.5
1906	Cin-N	146	545	81	159	11	7	0	26	71		.292	.376	.338	118	14	41			.948	22	*2-146	4.0
1907	Cin-N	156	561	64	139	12	4	1	31	83		.248	.346	.289	95	0	28			.961	0	*2-156	-0.1
1908	Cin-N	135	498	65	119	14	5	0	23	58		.239	.321	.287	97	0	30			.959	4	*2-135	0.3
1909	Cin-N	57	159	18	34	3	1	0	6	28		.214	.335	.245	81	-2	11			.933	4	2-31,3-15	-0.1
1910	StL-N	151	547	101	145	15	6	1	36	116	46	.265	.399	.320	114	18	34			.963	3	*2-151	1.9
1911	StL-N	138	509	106	133	19	2	1	24	96	52	.261	.385	.312	99	5	37			.961	11	*2-136	1.3
1912	StL-N	120	431	82	131	15	4	0	29	87	31	.304	.422	.357	117	16	35			.943	-7	*2-114	0.6
1913	StL-N	121	382	74	109	12	0	0	27	92	49	.285	**.432**	.317	117	17	23			**.977**	0	*2-113,M	1.6
1914	StL-N	148	509	85	134	17	4	1	24	105	63	.263	.396	.318	115	16	32			.964	-5	*2-147,M	1.2
1915	StL-N	107	353	57	85	5	2	1	24	74	68	.241	.377	.283	101	5	13	12	-3	.957	4	*2-105,M	0.7
1916	StL-N	18	18	9	2	3	0	0	0	2	3	.333	.500	.333	159	1	1			1.000	0	/2-7,M	0.6
Total	13	1586	5558	948	1474	146	50	9	318	1003	312	.265	.382	.314	107	105	324	12		.956	77	*2-1530/3-15	18.2

■ ED HUGHES   Hughes, Edward J.   b: 10/5/1880, Chicago, Ill.   d: 10/11/27, McHenry, Ill.   BR/TR, 6'1", 180 lbs.   Deb: 8/29/02   F

1902	Chi-A	1	4	0	1	0	0	0	0			.250	.250	.250	41	-0	0			.778	0	/C-1	0.0
1905	Bos-A	6	14	2	3	0	0	0	2	0		.214	.214	.214	36	-1	0			.500	-2	/P-6	0.0
1906	Bos-A	2	3	0	0	0	0	0	0			.000	.000	.000	-99	-1	0			.750	-0	/P-2	0.0
Total	3	9	21	2	4	0	0	0	2	0		.190	.190	.190	17	-2	0			.571	-2	/P-8,C-1	0.0

■ JOE HUGHES   Hughes, Joseph Thompson   b: 2/21/1880, Pardoe, Pa.   d: 3/13/51, Cleveland, Ohio   BR/TR, 5'10", 165 lbs.   Deb: 8/30/02

1902	Chi-N	1	3	0	0	0	0	0	0	0	0	.000	.000	.000	-99	-1	0			.000	-0	/O-1	-0.1

YEAR	TM/L	G	AB	R	H	2B	3B	HR	RBI	BB	SO	AVG	OBP	SLG	PRO+	BR/A	SB	CS	SBR	FA	FR	G/POS	TPR
■ KEITH HUGHES	Hughes, Keith Wills b: 9/12/63, Bryn Mawr, Pa. BL/TL, 6'3", 210 lbs. Deb: 5/19/87																						
1987	NY-A	4	4	0	0	0	0	0	0	0	2	.000	.000	.000	-99	-1	0	0	0	.000	0	/H	-0.1
	Phi-N	37	76	8	20	2	0	0	10	7	11	.263	.333	.289	65	-4	0	0	0	.963	-2	O-19	-0.6
1988	Bal-A	41	108	10	21	4	2	2	14	16	21	.194	.298	.324	76	-3	1	0	0	.969	2	O-31/D-1	-0.2
1990	NY-N	8	9	0	0	0	0	0	0	0	4	.000	.000	.000	-99	-2	0	0	0	1.000	-1	/O-5	-0.4
1993	Cin-N	3	4	0	0	0	0	0	0	0	0	.000	.000	.000	-99	-1	0	0	0	.000	-1	/O-2	-0.2
Total	4	93	201	18	41	6	2	2	24	23	44	.204	.289	.284	57	-12	1	0	0	.969	-2	/O-57,D-1	-1.5
■ ROY HUGHES	Hughes, Roy John "Jeep" or "Sage" b: 1/11/11, Cincinnati, Ohio BR/TR, 5'10.5", 167 lbs. Deb: 4/16/35																						
1935	Cle-A	82	266	40	78	15	3	0	14	18	17	.293	.340	.372	83	-7	13	3	2	.987	-1	2-40,S-29/3	-0.1
1936	Cle-A	152	638	112	188	35	9	0	63	57	40	.295	.356	.378	81	-19	20	9	1	.973	5	*2-152	-0.2
1937	Cle-A	104	346	57	96	12	6	1	40	40	22	.277	.352	.355	78	-11	11	6	-0	.939	12	3-58,2-32	0.4
1938	StL-A	58	96	16	27	3	0	2	13	12	11	.281	.361	.375	85	-2	3	0	1	.957	4	2-21/3-5,S	0.4
1939	StL-A	17	23	6	2	0	0	0	1	4	4	.087	.222	.087	-18	-4	0	0	0	1.000	1	/2-6,S-1	-0.3
	Phi-N	65	237	22	54	5	1	1	16	21	18	.228	.291	.270	53	-15	4			.984	-1	2-65	-1.2
1940	Phi-N	1	0	0	0	0	0	0	0	0	0	—	—	—	—	0	0			1.000	-0	/2-1	0.0
1944	Chi-N	126	478	86	137	16	1	1	28	35	30	.287	.337	.351	94	-3	16			.951	11	3-66,S-52	1.3
1945	*Chi-N	69	222	34	58	8	1	0	8	16	18	.261	.311	.306	73	-8	6			.931	-8	S-36,2-21/31	-1.2
1946	Phi-N	89	276	23	65	11	1	0	22	19	15	.236	.287	.283	64	-13	7			.942	-12	S-34,3-31/21	-2.5
Total	9	763	2582	396	705	105	27	5	205	222	175	.273	.332	.340	78	-83	80	18		.980	12	2-345,3-170,S/1	-3.4
■ TERRY HUGHES	Hughes, Terry Wayne b: 5/13/49, Spartanburg, S.C. BR/TR, 6'1", 185 lbs. Deb: 9/2/70																						
1970	Chi-N	2	3	0	1	0	0	0	0	0	0	.333	.333	.333	71	-0	0	0	0	1.000	-0	/3-1,O-1	0.0
1973	StL-N	11	14	1	3	1	0	0	1	1	4	.214	.267	.286	53	-1	0	0	0	1.000	0	/3-5,1-1	-0.1
1974	Bos-A	41	69	5	14	2	0	1	6	6	18	.203	.286	.275	58	-4	0	0	0	.958	4	3-36/D-1	0.0
Total	3	54	86	6	18	3	0	1	7	7	22	.209	.284	.279	58	-5	0	0	0	.961	3	/3-42,D-1,1O	-0.1
■ TOM HUGHES	Hughes, Thomas Franklin b: 8/6/07, Emmet, Ark. d: 8/10/89, Beaumont, Tex. BL/TR, 6'1", 190 lbs. Deb: 9/9/30																						
1930	Det-A	17	59	8	22	2	3	0	5	4	8	.373	.413	.508	130	3	0	1	-1	.897	-3	O-16	-0.2
■ BILL HUGHES	Hughes, William R. b: 11/25/1866, Blandensville, Ill. d: 8/25/43, Santa Ana, Cal. BL/TL, Deb: 9/28/1884																						
1884	Was-U	14	49	5	6	0	0	0		2		.122	.157	.122	-24	-8				.955	0	/1-9,O-6	-0.8
1885	Phi-a	4	16	3	3	1	1	0		1		.188	.278	.375	99	-0				1.000	-0	/O-2,P-2	0.0
Total	2	18	65	8	9	1	1	0		3		.138	.188	.185	6	-8				.813	-0	/1-9,O-8,P	-0.8
■ EMIL HUHN	Huhn, Emil Hugo "Hap" b: 3/10/1892, North Vernon, Ind. d: 9/5/25, Camden, S.C. BR/TR, 6', 180 lbs. Deb: 4/10/15																						
1915	New-F	124	415	34	94	18	1	1	41	28	40	.227	.279	.282	53	-29	13			.985	-2	*1-101,C-16	-3.5
1916	Cin-N	37	94	4	24	3	2	0	3	2	11	.255	.271	.330	86	-2	0			.989	1	C-18,1-14/O	-0.1
1917	Cin-N	23	51	2	10	1	2	0	3	2	5	.196	.226	.294	62	-3	1			.969	-2	C-15/1-1	-0.4
Total	3	184	560	40	128	22	5	1	47	32	56	.229	.273	.291	59	-33	14			.986	-3	1-116/C-49,O	-4.0
■ TIM HULETT	Hulett, Timothy Craig b: 1/12/60, Springfield, Ill. BR/TR, 6', 185 lbs. Deb: 9/15/83																						
1983	Chi-A	6	5	0	1	0	0	0	0	0	0	.200	.200	.200	10	-1	1	0	0	.875	2	/2-6	0.1
1984	Chi-A	8	7	1	0	0	0	0	0	1	4	.000	.125	.000	-59	-2	1	0	0	1.000	4	/3-4,2-3	0.3
1985	Chi-A	141	395	52	106	19	4	5	37	30	81	.268	.326	.375	88	-6	6	4	-1	.924	8	*3-115,2-28/O	0.1
1986	Chi-A	150	520	53	120	16	5	17	44	21	91	.231	.262	.379	70	-23	4	1	1	.951	-6	3-89,2-66	-2.7
1987	Chi-A	68	240	20	52	10	0	7	28	10	41	.217	.248	.346	54	-16	0	1	-1	.953	-3	3-61/2-8	-2.0
1989	Bal-A	33	97	12	27	5	0	3	18	10	17	.278	.346	.423	119	2	0	0	0	.976	-5	2-23,3-11	-0.2
1990	Bal-A	53	153	16	39	7	1	3	16	15	41	.255	.321	.373	97	-1	1	0	0	.961	6	3-24,2-16/D	0.6
1991	Bal-A	79	206	29	42	9	0	7	18	13	49	.204	.255	.350	68	-10	0	1	-1	.976	-8	3-39,2-26,D/S	-1.8
1992	Bal-A	57	142	11	41	7	2	2	21	10	31	.289	.340	.408	106	1	0	1	-1	.935	10	3-27,D-13,2/S	1.0
1993	Bal-A	85	260	40	78	15	0	2	23	23	56	.300	.364	.381	96	-1	1	2	-1	.963	19	3-75/S-8,2D	1.7
1994	Bal-A	36	92	11	21	2	1	2	15	12	24	.228	.317	.337	65	-5	0	0	0	.992	13	2-23/3-9,S	0.8
Total	11	716	2117	245	527	90	13	48	220	145	435	.249	.300	.372	80	-61	14	11	-2	.947	40	3-454,2-213/DSO	-2.1
■ BILLY HULEN	Hulen, William Franklin b: 3/12/1870, Dixon, Cal. d: 10/2/47, Santa Rosa, Cal. BL/TL, 5'8", 148 lbs. Deb: 5/2/1896																						
1896	Phi-N	88	339	87	90	18	7	0	38	55	20	.265	.368	.360	93	-2	23			.874	-21	S-73,O-12/2	-1.8
1899	Was-N	19	68	10	10	1	0	0	3	10		.147	.256	.162	16	-8	5			.902	-4	S-19	-0.9
Total	2	107	407	97	100	19	7	0	41	65	20	.246	.350	.327	81	-9	28			.880	-25	/S-92,O-12,2	-2.7
■ DAVID HULSE	Hulse, David Lindsey b: 2/25/68, San Angelo, Tex. BL/TL, 5'11", 170 lbs. Deb: 8/11/92																						
1992	Tex-A	32	92	14	28	4	0	0	2	3	18	.304	.326	.348	92	-1	3	1	0	.984	-4	O-31/D-1	-0.5
1993	Tex-A	114	407	71	118	9	10	1	29	26	57	.290	.334	.369	92	-5	29	9	3	.988	-6	*O-112/D-2	-0.9
1994	Tex-A	77	310	58	79	8	4	1	19	21	53	.255	.306	.316	65	-16	18	2	4	.978	-4	O-76/D-1	-1.6
Total	3	223	809	143	225	21	14	2	50	50	128	.278	.323	.346	82	-22	50	12	8	.984	-13	O-219/D-4	-3.0
■ RUDY HULSWITT	Hulswitt, Rudolph Edward b: 2/23/1877, Newport, Ky. d: 1/16/50, Louisville, Ky. BR/TR, 5'8.5", 165 lbs. Deb: 6/16/1899 C																						
1899	Lou-N	1	0	0	0	0	0	0	0	0	0	—	—	—	—	0	0			.333	-1	/S-1	-0.1
1902	Phi-N	128	497	59	135	11	7	0	38	30		.272	.316	.322	97	-2	12			.917	8	*S-125/3-3	1.4
1903	Phi-N	138	519	56	128	22	9	1	58	28		.247	.288	.329	78	-16	10			.906	-3	*S-138	-1.3
1904	Phi-N	113	406	36	99	11	4	1	36	16		.244	.276	.298	80	-10	8			.912	-13	*S-113	-2.1
1908	Cin-N	119	386	27	88	5	7	1	28	30		.228	.287	.285	85	-7	7			.936	-6	*S-118/2-1	-1.2
1909	StL-N	82	289	21	81	7	2	0	29	19		.280	.329	.329	111	3	7			.930	-6	S-65,2-12	-0.2
1910	StL-N	63	133	9	33	7	2	0	14	13	10	.248	.320	.331	93	-1	5			.854	-13	S-30/2-2	-1.4
Total	7	644	2230	208	564	64	32	3	203	136	10	.253	.299	.314	89	-33	49			.915	-32	S-590/2-15,3	-4.9
■ JOHN HUMMEL	Hummel, John Edwin "Silent John" b: 4/4/1883, Bloomsburg, Pa. d: 5/18/59, Springfield, Mass. BR/TR, 5'11", 160 lbs. Deb: 9/12/05																						
1905	Bro-N	30	109	19	29	3	4	0	7	9		.266	.322	.367	114	2	6			.962	0	2-30	0.2
1906	Bro-N	97	286	20	57	6	4	1	21	36		.199	.289	.259	77	-7	10			.953	1	2-50,O-21,1	-0.8
1907	Bro-N	107	342	41	80	12	3	3	31	26		.234	.294	.313	98	-2	8			.951	13	2-44,O-33,1/S	1.0
1908	Bro-N	154	594	51	143	11	12	4	41	34		.241	.284	.320	97	-4	20			.973	6	O-95,2-43/S1	0.0
1909	Bro-N	146	542	54	152	15	9	4	52	22		.280	.314	.363	113	5	16			.987	-17	1-54,2-38,SO	-1.4
1910	Bro-N	153	578	67	141	21	13	5	74	57	81	.244	.314	.351	97	-4	21			**.965**	-14	*2-153	-2.2
1911	Bro-N	137	477	54	129	21	11	5	58	67	66	.270	.360	.392	115	10	16			**.972**	-5	*2-127/1-4,S	0.2
1912	Bro-N	122	411	55	116	21	7	5	54	49	55	.282	.359	.404	113	7	7			.969	-15	2-58,O-44,1	-1.1
1913	Bro-N	67	198	20	48	7	7	2	24	13	23	.242	.292	.379	88	-4	4			.938	-1	O-28,S-17/12	-0.4
1914	Bro-N	73	208	25	55	8	9	0	20	16	25	.264	.317	.389	107	1	5			.982	-2	1-36,O-19/2S	-0.2
1915	Bro-N	53	100	6	23	2	3	0	8	6	11	.230	.274	.310	75	-3	1	1	-0	1.000	-4	O-21,1-11/S	-0.9
1918	NY-A	22	61	9	18	1	2	0	6	2	12	.295	.317	.377	135	3	3			.960	-3	O-15/1-3,2	-0.1
Total	12	1161	3906	421	991	128	84	29	394	346	269	.254	.316	.352	103	5	117	1		.963	-39	2-548,O-293,1/S	-5.7
■ AL HUMPHREY	Humphrey, Albert b: 2/28/1886, Ashtabula, Ohio d: 5/13/61, Ashtabula, Ohio BL/TR, 5'11", 180 lbs. Deb: 9/1/11																						
1911	Bro-N	8	27	4	5	0	0	0	0	3	7	.185	.267	.185	29	-3	0			.923	-2	/O-8	-0.5

YEAR	TM/L	G	AB	R	H	2B	3B	HR	RBI	BB	SO	AVG	OBP	SLG	PRO+	BR/A	SB	CS	SBR	FA	FR	G/POS	TPR

■ TERRY HUMPHREY   Humphrey, Terryal Gene   b: 8/4/49, Chickasha, Okla.   BR/TR, 6'3", 190 lbs.   Deb: 9/5/71

1971	Mon-N	9	26	1	5	1	0	0	1	0	4	.192	.192	.231	19	-3	0	0	0	.981	2	/C-9	0.0
1972	Mon-N	69	215	13	40	8	0	1	9	16	38	.186	.249	.237	38	-17	4	1	1	.986	-3	C-65	-1.9
1973	Mon-N	43	90	5	15	2	0	1	9	5	16	.167	.211	.222	19	-10	0	1	-1	1.000	5	C-35	-0.5
1974	Mon-N	20	52	3	10	3	0	0	3	4	9	.192	.250	.250	38	-4	0	0	0	.990	6	C-17	0.2
1975	Det-A	18	41	0	10	0	0	0	1	2	6	.244	.279	.244	47	-3	0	0	0	1.000	1	C-18	-0.1
1976	Cal-A	71	196	17	48	10	0	1	19	13	30	.245	.308	.311	87	-3	0	1	-1	.980	1	C-71	-0.1
1977	Cal-A	123	304	17	69	11	0	2	34	21	58	.227	.286	.283	58	-18	1	1	0	.989	-0	*C-123	-1.5
1978	Cal-A	53	114	11	25	4	1	1	9	6	12	.219	.270	.298	62	-6	0	1	-1	.978	11	C-52/2-1,3	0.5
1979	Cal-A	9	17	2	1	0	0	0	0	1	2	.059	.111	.059	-55	-4	0	0	0	.983	6	/C-9	0.2
Total	9	415	1055	69	223	39	1	6	85	68	175	.211	.268	.267	51	-67	5	5	-2	.986	28	C-399/3-1,2	-3.2

■ MIKE HUMPHREYS   Humphreys, Michael Butler   b: 4/10/67, Dallas, Tex.   BR/TR, 6', 185 lbs.   Deb: 7/29/91

1991	NY-A	25	40	9	8	0	0	0	3	9	7	.200	.347	.200	55	-2	2	0	1	1.000	-2	/O-9,3-6,D	-0.3
1992	NY-A	4	10	0	1	0	0	0	0	0	1	.100	.100	.100	-44	-2	0	0	0	1.000	1	/O-2,D-1	-0.1
1993	NY-A	25	35	6	6	2	1	1	6	4	11	.171	.256	.371	69	-2	2	1	0	1.000	-7	O-21/D-3	-0.9
Total	3	54	85	15	15	2	1	1	9	13	19	.176	.286	.259	51	-6	4	1	1	1.000	-8	/O-32,D-11,3	-1.3

■ JOHN HUMPHRIES   Humphries, John Henry   b: 11/12/1861, N.Gower, Ont., Can.   d: 11/29/33, Salinas, Cal.   BL/TL, 6', 185 lbs.   Deb: 7/7/1883

1883	NY-N	29	107	5	12	1	0	0	4	1	22	.112	.120	.121	-26	-16				.815	-5	C-20,O-12	-1.8
1884	Was-a	49	193	23	34	2	0	0		9		.176	.217	.187	37	-12				.890	-6	C-35,O-12/1	-1.4
	NY-N	20	64	6	6	0	0	0	2	9	19	.094	.205	.094	-2	-7				.896	11	C-20	0.4
Total	2	98	364	34	52	3	0	0	6	19	41	.143	.188	.151	9	-35				.876	-0	/C-75,O-24,1	-2.8

■ RANDY HUNDLEY   Hundley, Cecil Randolph   b: 6/1/42, Martinsville, Va.   BR/TR, 6', 175 lbs.   Deb: 9/27/64   FC

1964	SF-N	2	1	1	0	0	0	0	0	0	1	.000	.000	.000	-98	-0	0	0	0	.000	0	/C-2	0.0
1965	SF-N	6	15	0	1	0	0	0	0	0	4	.067	.067	.067	-61	-3	0	0	0	1.000	4	/C-6	0.1
1966	Chi-N	149	526	50	124	22	3	19	63	35	113	.236	.287	.397	87	-10	1	3	-2	.986	-11	*C-149	-1.4
1967	Chi-N	152	539	68	144	25	3	14	60	44	75	.267	.325	.403	102	1	2	4	-2	.996	-12	*C-152	-0.4
1968	Chi-N	160	553	41	125	18	4	7	65	39	69	.226	.282	.311	73	-18	1	0	0	.995	-13	*C-160	-2.3
1969	Chi-N★	151	522	67	133	15	1	18	64	61	90	.255	.336	.391	91	-6	2	3	-1	.992	12	*C-151	1.3
1970	Chi-N	73	250	13	61	5	0	7	36	16	52	.244	.289	.348	62	-14	0	1	-1	.990	-1	C-73	-1.1
1971	Chi-N	9	21	1	7	1	0	0	2	0	2	.333	.333	.381	89	-0	0	0	0	.979	3	/C-8	0.3
1972	Chi-N	114	357	23	78	12	0	5	30	22	62	.218	.264	.294	53	-22	1	0	0	**.995**	7	*C-113	-1.1
1973	Chi-N	124	368	35	83	11	1	10	43	30	51	.226	.284	.342	68	-16	5	6	-2	.993	11	*C-122	-0.3
1974	Min-A	32	88	2	17	2	0	3	4	12		.193	.228	.216	27	-8	0	0	0	.965	1	C-28	-0.6
1975	SD-N	74	180	7	37	5	1	2	14	19	29	.206	.285	.278	60	-10	0	0	0	.970	1	C-51	-0.8
1976	Chi-N	13	18	3	3	2	0	0	1	1	4	.167	.211	.278	35	-2	0	0	0	.923	-0	/C-9	-0.2
1977	Chi-N	2	4	0	0	0	0	0	0	0	1	.000	.000	.000	-90	-1	0	0	0	1.000	0	/C-2	-0.1
Total	14	1061	3442	311	813	118	13	82	381	271	565	.236	.294	.350	76	-109	12	17	-7	.990	2	*C-1026	-6.6

■ TODD HUNDLEY   Hundley, Todd Randolph   b: 5/27/69, Martinsville, Va.   BB/TR, 5'11", 170 lbs.   Deb: 5/18/90   F

1990	NY-N	36	67	8	14	6	0	0	2	6	18	.209	.274	.299	58	-4	0	0	0	.988	2	C-36	-0.1
1991	NY-N	21	60	5	8	0	1	1	7	6	14	.133	.224	.217	25	-6	0	0	0	1.000	-6	C-20	-1.2
1992	NY-N	123	358	32	75	17	0	7	32	19	76	.209	.257	.316	62	-19	3	0	1	.996	2	*C-121	-1.0
1993	NY-N	130	417	40	95	17	2	11	53	23	62	.228	.271	.357	68	-20	1	1	-0	.988	-7	*C-123	-2.1
1994	NY-N	91	291	45	69	10	1	16	42	25	73	.237	.304	.443	91	-5	2	1	0	.990	-3	C-82	-0.3
Total	5	401	1193	130	261	50	4	35	136	79	243	.219	.273	.355	70	-53	6	2	1	.992	-11	C-382	-4.7

■ BERNIE HUNGLING   Hungling, Bernard Herman "Bud"   b: 3/5/1896, Dayton, Ohio   d: 3/30/68, Dayton, Ohio   BR/TR, 6'2", 180 lbs.   Deb: 4/14/22

1922	Bro-N	39	102	9	23	1	2	1	13	6	20	.225	.269	.304	48	-8	2	0	1	.968	1	C-36	-0.4
1923	Bro-N	2	4	0	0	0	0	0	0	0	2	.000	.000	.000	-99	-1	0	1	-1	.667	-1	/C-1	-0.2
1930	StL-A	10	31	4	10	2	0	0	2	5	3	.323	.417	.387	102	0	0	1	-1	1.000	-4	C-10	-0.3
Total	3	51	137	13	33	3	2	1	15	11	25	.241	.297	.314	57	-9	2	2	-1	.968	-3	/C-47	-0.9

■ BILL HUNNEFIELD   Hunnefield, William Fenton "Wild Bill"   b: 1/5/1899, Dedham, Mass.   d: 8/28/76, Nantucket, Mass.   BB/TR, 5'10", 165 lbs.   Deb: 4/17/26

1926	Chi-A	131	470	81	129	26	4	3	48	37	28	.274	.329	.366	84	-12	24	9	2	.931	-8	S-98,3-17,2	-0.7
1927	Chi-A	112	365	45	104	25	1	2	36	25	24	.285	.332	.375	85	-8	15	13	-3	.933	-20	S-79,2-17/3	-2.3
1928	Chi-A	94	333	42	98	8	3	2	24	26	24	.294	.351	.354	87	-6	16	6	1	.967	-12	2-82/S-3,3	-1.4
1929	Chi-A	47	127	13	23	5	0	0	9	7	3	.181	.224	.220	15	-16	5	2	0	.969	-4	2-29/3-4,S	-1.8
1930	Chi-A	31	81	11	22	2	0	1	5	4	10	.272	.314	.333	67	-4	1	1	-0	.932	-11	S-22/1-1	-1.2
1931	Cle-A	21	71	13	17	4	1	0	4	9	4	.239	.325	.324	67	-3	3	1	0	.853	-10	S-21/2-1	-1.0
	Bos-N	11	21	2	6	0	0	0	1	0	2	.286	.286	.286	56	-1	0			.864	2	/3-5,2-4	0.1
	NY-N	64	196	23	53	5	0	1	17	9	16	.270	.302	.311	67	-9	3			.951	-5	2-56/S-5	-1.1
	Yr	75	217	25	59	5	0	1	18	9	18	.272	.301	.309	66	-10	3			.951	-3	2-60/3-5,S	-1.0
Total	6	511	1664	230	452	75	9	9	144	117	111	.272	.322	.344	76	-60	67	32		.925	-67	S-230,2-204/31	-9.4

■ RANDY HUNT   Hunt, James Randall   b: 1/3/60, Prattville, Ala.   BR/TR, 6', 185 lbs.   Deb: 6/4/85

1985	StL-N	14	19	1	3	0	0	0	0	1	6	.158	.158	.158	-12	-3	0	1	-1	1.000	1	C-13	-0.2
1986	Mon-N	21	48	4	10	0	0	2	6	4	15	.208	.283	.333	70	-2	0	0	0	.960	6	C-21	0.5
Total	2	35	67	5	13	0	0	2	6	5	21	.194	.250	.284	48	-5	0	1	-1	.967	7	/C-34	0.3

■ KEN HUNT   Hunt, Kenneth Lawrence   b: 7/13/34, Grand Forks, N.Dak   BR/TR, 6'1", 205 lbs.   Deb: 9/10/59

1959	NY-A	6	12	2	4	1	0	0	1	0	3	.333	.333	.417	108	0	0	0	0	1.000	0	/O-5	0.0
1960	NY-A	25	22	4	6	2	0	0	1	4	4	.273	.407	.364	117	1	0	0	0	.957	-6	O-24	-0.5
1961	LA-A	149	479	70	122	29	3	25	84	49	120	.255	.329	.484	103	-0	8	2	1	.950	-6	*O-134/2-1	-1.2
1962	LA-A	13	11	4	2	0	0	0	1	1	5	.182	.250	.455	88	-0	1	0	0	.867	1	/1-3	-0.1
1963	LA-A	59	142	17	26	6	1	5	16	15	49	.183	.261	.345	72	-6	2	1	0	.972	-6	O-50	-1.6
	Was-A	7	20	1	4	0	0	1	4	2	6	.200	.273	.350	73	-1	0	0	0	1.000	0	/O-5	-0.1
	Yr	66	162	18	30	6	1	6	20	17	55	.185	.263	.346	73	-6	2	1	0	.976	-6	O-55	-1.7
1964	Was-A	51	96	9	13	4	0	2	6	14	35	.135	.245	.208	28	-9	0	1	-1	1.000	-2	O-37	-1.4
Total	6	310	782	107	177	42	4	33	111	85	222	.226	.306	.417	89	-15	9	4	0	.964	-21	O-255/1-3,2	-4.9

■ JOEL HUNT   Hunt, Oliver Joel "Jodie"   b: 10/11/05, Texico, N.Mex.   d: 7/24/78, Teague, Tex.   BR/TR, 5'10", 165 lbs.   Deb: 4/27/31

1931	StL-N	4	1	2	0	0	0	0	0	0	1	.000	.000	.000	-96	-0	0			.000	-1	/O-1	-0.1
1932	StL-N	12	21	0	4	1	0	0	3	4	3	.190	.320	.238	51	-1	0			1.000	0	/O-5	-0.1
Total	2	16	22	2	4	1	0	0	3	4	4	.182	.308	.227	45	-2	0			1.000	0	/O-6	-0.2

■ DICK HUNT   Hunt, Richard M.   b: 1847, New York   d: 11/20/1895, Brooklyn, N.Y.   5'9", 145 lbs.   Deb: 5/7/1872

1872	Eck-n	11	48	11	15	4	0	0	5	1	0	.313	.327	.396	143	0						/O-8,2-3	0.2

■ RON HUNT   Hunt, Ronald Kenneth   b: 2/23/41, St.Louis, Mo.   BR/TR, 6', 186 lbs.   Deb: 4/16/63

1963	NY-N	143	533	64	145	28	4	10	42	40	50	.272	.338	.396	109	6	5	4	-1	.967	2	*2-142/3-1	2.3
1964	NY-N★	127	475	59	144	19	6	6	42	29	30	.303	.357	.406	117	11	5	2	1	.979	-8	*2-109,3-12	1.4
1965	NY-N	57	196	21	47	12	1	1	10	14	19	.240	.310	.327	82	-4	2	7	-4	.979	-5	2-46/3-6	-0.9

YEAR	TM/L	G	AB	R	H	2B	3B	HR	RBI	BB	SO	AVG	OBP	SLG	PRO+	BR/A	SB	CS	SBR	FA	FR	G/POS	TPR
1966	NY-N★	132	479	63	138	19	2	3	33	41	34	.288	.358	.355	101	2	8	10	-4	.970	7	*2-123/S-1,3	1.5
1967	LA-N	110	388	44	102	17	3	3	33	39	24	.263	.346	.345	107	4	2	1	0	.980	-16	2-90/3-8	-0.6
1968	SF-N	148	529	79	132	19	0	2	28	78	41	.250	.372	.297	103	7	6	6	-2	.972	-17	*2-147	-0.3
1969	SF-N	128	478	72	125	23	3	3	41	51	47	.262	.363	.341	100	3	9	2	2	.979	-9	*2-125/3-1	0.6
1970	SF-N	117	367	70	103	17	1	6	41	44	29	.281	.396	.381	111	9	1	2	-1	.968	-28	2-85,3-16	-1.4
1971	Mon-N	152	520	89	145	20	3	5	38	58	41	.279	.403	.358	116	17	5	7	-3	.979	-9	*2-133,3-19	1.7
1972	Mon-N	129	443	56	112	20	0	0	18	51	29	.253	.363	.298	88	-3	9	2	2	.982	-7	*2-122/3-5	-0.2
1973	Mon-N	113	401	61	124	14	0	0	18	52	19	.309	.419	.344	110	10	10	7	-1	.982	-21	*2-102,3-14	-0.7
1974	Mon-N	115	403	66	108	15	0	0	26	55	17	.268	.375	.305	87	-4	2	5	-2	.941	-14	3-75,2-31/S	-2.0
	StL-N	12	23	1	4	0	0	0	0	3	2	.174	.321	.174	42	-2	0	0	0	1.000	-1	/2-5	-0.3
	Yr	127	426	67	112	15	0	0	26	58	19	.263	.372	.298	85	-5	2	5	-2	.941	-16	3-75,2-36/S	-2.3
Total	12	1483	5235	745	1429	223	23	39	370	555	382	.273	.369	.347	104	57	65	55	-14	.976	-126	*2-1260,3-158/S	1.1

■ BRIAN HUNTER
Hunter, Brian Lee b: 3/5/71, Portland, Ore. BR/TR, 6'4", 180 lbs. Deb: 6/27/94

YEAR	TM/L	G	AB	R	H	2B	3B	HR	RBI	BB	SO	AVG	OBP	SLG	PRO+	BR/A	SB	CS	SBR	FA	FR	G/POS	TPR
1994	Hou-N	6	24	2	6	1	0	0	0	1	6	.250	.280	.292	50	-2	2	1	0	.938	1	/O-6	-0.1

■ BRIAN HUNTER
Hunter, Brian Ronald b: 3/4/68, Torrance, Cal. BR/TL, 6', 195 lbs. Deb: 5/31/91

YEAR	TM/L	G	AB	R	H	2B	3B	HR	RBI	BB	SO	AVG	OBP	SLG	PRO+	BR/A	SB	CS	SBR	FA	FR	G/POS	TPR
1991	*Atl-N	97	271	32	68	16	1	12	50	17	48	.251	.298	.450	101	-1	0	2	-1	.988	-4	1-85/O-6	-1.1
1992	*Atl-N	102	238	34	57	13	2	14	41	21	50	.239	.301	.487	113	3	1	2	-1	.997	3	1-92/O-6	0.1
1993	Atl-N	37	80	4	11	3	1	0	8	2	15	.138	.159	.200	-5	-12	0	0	0	.994	0	1-29/O-2	-1.3
1994	Pit-N	76	233	28	53	15	1	11	47	15	55	.227	.274	.442	83	-7	0	0	0	.991	-1	1-59/O-5	-1.2
	Cin-N	9	23	6	7	1	0	4	10	2	1	.304	.360	.870	209	3	0	0	0	1.000	-0	/O-5,1-1	0.3
	Yr	85	256	34	60	16	1	15	57	17	56	.234	.282	.480	94	-4	0	0	0	.991	-1	1-60,O-10	-0.9
Total	4	321	845	104	196	48	5	41	156	57	169	.232	.281	.446	92	-13	1	4	-2	.992	-2	1-266/O-24	-3.2

■ EDDIE HUNTER
Hunter, Edison Franklin b: 2/6/05, Bellevue, Ky. d: 3/14/67, Colerain, Ohio BR/TR, 5'7.5", 150 lbs. Deb: 8/5/33

YEAR	TM/L	G	AB	R	H	2B	3B	HR	RBI	BB	SO	AVG	OBP	SLG	PRO+	BR/A	SB	CS	SBR	FA	FR	G/POS	TPR
1933	Cin-N	1	0	0	0	0	0	0	0	0	0	—	—	—	—	0	0	0	0	.000	0	/3-1	0.0

■ NEWT HUNTER
Hunter, Frederick Creighton b: 1/5/1880, Chillicothe, Ohio d: 10/26/63, Columbus, Ohio BR/TR, 6', 180 lbs. Deb: 4/12/11 C

YEAR	TM/L	G	AB	R	H	2B	3B	HR	RBI	BB	SO	AVG	OBP	SLG	PRO+	BR/A	SB	CS	SBR	FA	FR	G/POS	TPR
1911	Pit-N	65	209	35	53	10	6	2	24	25	43	.254	.345	.388	101	0	9			.989	-2	1-61	-0.2

■ GEORGE HUNTER
Hunter, George Henry b: 7/8/1887, Buffalo, N.Y. d: 1/11/68, Harrisburg, Pa. BB/TL, 5'8.5", 165 lbs. Deb: 5/4/09 F

YEAR	TM/L	G	AB	R	H	2B	3B	HR	RBI	BB	SO	AVG	OBP	SLG	PRO+	BR/A	SB	CS	SBR	FA	FR	G/POS	TPR
1909	Bro-N	44	123	8	28	7	0	0		8	9	.228	.286	.285	80	-3	1			.871	-4	O-23,P-16	-0.8
1910	Bro-N	1	0	0	0	0	0	0		0	0	—	—	—	—	0	0			.000	-0	/O-1	0.0
Total	2	45	123	8	28	7	0	0		8	9	.228	.286	.285	80	-3	1			.871	-5	O-24,P-16	-0.8

■ BILLY HUNTER
Hunter, Gordon William b: 6/4/28, Punxsutawney, Pa. BR/TR, 6', 180 lbs. Deb: 4/14/53 MC

YEAR	TM/L	G	AB	R	H	2B	3B	HR	RBI	BB	SO	AVG	OBP	SLG	PRO+	BR/A	SB	CS	SBR	FA	FR	G/POS	TPR
1953	StL-A★	154	567	50	124	18	1	1	37	24	45	.219	.253	.259	38	-50	3	1	0	.970	15	*S-152	-2.4
1954	Bal-A	125	411	28	100	9	5	2	27	21	38	.243	.283	.304	66	-21	5	4	-1	.948	1	*S-124	-1.2
1955	NY-A	98	255	14	58	7	1	3	20	15	18	.227	.270	.298	54	-17	9	2	2	.958	1	S-98	-0.8
1956	NY-A	39	75	8	21	3	4	0	11	2	4	.280	.299	.427	93	-1	1	1	-1	1.000	10	S-32/3-4	0.9
1957	KC-A	116	319	39	61	10	4	8	29	27	43	.191	.261	.323	58	-19	1	2	-1	.974	-5	2-64,S-35,3	-1.9
1958	KC-A	22	58	6	9	1	1	2	11	5	7	.155	.222	.310	44	-5	1	1	-0	.933	-3	S-12/2-8,3	-0.6
	Cle-A	76	190	21	37	10	2	0	9	17	37	.195	.264	.268	48	-14	4	1	1	.948	1	S-75/3-2	-0.7
	Yr	98	248	27	46	11	3	2	20	22	44	.185	.255	.278	47	-18	5	2	0	.946	-3	S-87/2-8,3	-1.3
Total	6	630	1875	166	410	58	18	16	144	111	192	.219	.265	.294	53	-126	23	12	-0	.958	19	S-528/2-72,3	-6.7

■ BUDDY HUNTER
Hunter, Harold James b: 8/9/47, Omaha, Neb. BR/TR, 5'10", 170 lbs. Deb: 7/1/71

YEAR	TM/L	G	AB	R	H	2B	3B	HR	RBI	BB	SO	AVG	OBP	SLG	PRO+	BR/A	SB	CS	SBR	FA	FR	G/POS	TPR
1971	Bos-A	8	9	2	2	1	0	0	0	2	1	.222	.364	.333	92	-0	0	0	0	1.000	1	/2-6	0.1
1973	Bos-A	13	7	3	3	1	0	0	2	3	1	.429	.636	.571	229	2	0	0	0	1.000	3	/3-3,2-2,D	0.5
1975	Bos-A	1	1	0	0	0	0	0	0	0	0	.000	.000	.000	-92	-0	0	0	0	.750	0	/2-1	0.0
Total	3	22	17	5	5	2	0	0	2	5	2	.294	.478	.412	144	1	0	0	0	.968	5	/2-9,3-3,D	0.6

■ HERB HUNTER
Hunter, Herbert Harrison b: 12/25/1896, Boston, Mass. d: 7/25/70, Orlando, Fla. BL/TR, 6'0.5", 165 lbs. Deb: 4/29/16

YEAR	TM/L	G	AB	R	H	2B	3B	HR	RBI	BB	SO	AVG	OBP	SLG	PRO+	BR/A	SB	CS	SBR	FA	FR	G/POS	TPR
1916	NY-N	21	28	3	7	0	0	1	4	0	5	.250	.250	.357	90	-1	0			1.000	0	/3-6,1-2	0.0
	Chi-N	2	4	0	0	0	0	0	0	0	0	.000	.000	.000	-90	-1	0			.750	0	/3-1	-0.1
	Yr	23	32	3	7	0	0	1	4	0	5	.219	.219	.313	65	-1	0			.941	1	/3-7,1-2	-0.1
1917	Chi-N	3	3	0	0	0	0	0	0	0	0	.000	.000	.000	-93	-1	0			1.000	0	/2-1,3-1	0.0
1920	Bos-A	4	12	2	1	0	0	0	0	1	1	.083	.154	.083	-38	-2	0	0	0	.857	-1	/O-4	-0.3
1921	StL-N	9	2	3	0	0	0	0	0	0	0	.000	.333	.000	-4	-0	0	3	-2	1.000	0	/1-1	-0.2
Total	4	39	49	8	8	0	0	1	4	2	6	.163	.196	.224	24	-5	0	3		.905	0	/3-8,O-4,12	-0.6

■ LEM HUNTER
Hunter, Robert Lemuel b: 1/16/1863, Warren, Ohio d: 11/9/56, W.Lafayette, Ohio Deb: 9/1/1883

YEAR	TM/L	G	AB	R	H	2B	3B	HR	RBI	BB	SO	AVG	OBP	SLG	PRO+	BR/A	SB	CS	SBR	FA	FR	G/POS	TPR
1883	Cle-N	1	4	1	1	0	0	0	0	0	2	.250	.250	.250	53		0			.000	-1	/O-1,P-1	0.0

■ BILL HUNTER
Hunter, William Ellsworth b: 7/8/1887, Buffalo, N.Y. d: 4/10/34, Buffalo, N.Y. BL/TL, 5'7.5", 155 lbs. Deb: 8/6/12 F

YEAR	TM/L	G	AB	R	H	2B	3B	HR	RBI	BB	SO	AVG	OBP	SLG	PRO+	BR/A	SB	CS	SBR	FA	FR	G/POS	TPR
1912	Cle-A	21	55	6	9	2	0	0		2	10	.164	.303	.200	43	-4	0			1.000	-0	O-16	-0.5

■ BILL HUNTER
Hunter, William Robert b: 1855, St.Thomas, Ont., Can. 5'7.5", 160 lbs. Deb: 5/2/1884

YEAR	TM/L	G	AB	R	H	2B	3B	HR	RBI	BB	SO	AVG	OBP	SLG	PRO+	BR/A	SB	CS	SBR	FA	FR	G/POS	TPR
1884	Lou-a	2	7	1	1	0	0	0		0		.143	.143	.143	-7	-1				.667	-2	/C-2	-0.3

■ STEVE HUNTZ
Huntz, Stephen Michael b: 12/3/45, Cleveland, Ohio BB/TR, 6'1", 204 lbs. Deb: 9/19/67

YEAR	TM/L	G	AB	R	H	2B	3B	HR	RBI	BB	SO	AVG	OBP	SLG	PRO+	BR/A	SB	CS	SBR	FA	FR	G/POS	TPR
1967	StL-N	3	6	1	1	0	0	0	0	1	2	.167	.286	.167	33	-0	0	0	0	1.000	-1	/2-2	-0.2
1969	StL-N	71	139	13	27	4	0	3	13	27	34	.194	.325	.288	73	-4	0	0	0	.945	-6	S-52,2-12/3	-0.6
1970	SD-N	106	352	54	77	8	0	11	37	66	69	.219	.344	.335	86	-5	0	3	-2	.958	-12	S-57,3-51	-1.3
1971	Chi-N	35	86	10	18	3	1	2	6	7	9	.209	.269	.337	69	-4	1	0	0	1.000	-1	/2-14/S-7,3	-0.3
1975	SD-N	22	53	3	8	0	0	0	4	7	8	.151	.250	.226	35	-5	0	0	0	.939	1	3-16/2-2	-0.4
Total	5	237	636	81	131	19	1	16	60	108	122	.206	.322	.314	76	-19	1	3	-2	.955	-18	S-116/3-79,2	-2.8

■ DAVE HUPPERT
Huppert, David Blain b: 4/1/57, South Gate, Cal. BR/TR, 6'1", 190 lbs. Deb: 9/15/83

YEAR	TM/L	G	AB	R	H	2B	3B	HR	RBI	BB	SO	AVG	OBP	SLG	PRO+	BR/A	SB	CS	SBR	FA	FR	G/POS	TPR
1983	Bal-A	2	0	0	0	0	0	0	0	0	0	—	—	—	—	0	0	0	0	1.000	0	/C-2	0.0
1985	Mil-A	15	21	1	1	0	0	0	2	0	7	.048	.130	.048	-49	-4	0	0	0	.960	2	C-15	-0.2
Total	2	17	21	1	1	0	0	0	2	0	7	.048	.130	.048	-49	-4	0	0	0	.962	3	/C-17	-0.2

■ CLINT HURDLE
Hurdle, Clinton Merrick b: 7/30/57, Big Rapids, Mich. BL/TR, 6'3", 195 lbs. Deb: 9/18/77

YEAR	TM/L	G	AB	R	H	2B	3B	HR	RBI	BB	SO	AVG	OBP	SLG	PRO+	BR/A	SB	CS	SBR	FA	FR	G/POS	TPR
1977	KC-A	9	26	5	8	0	0	2	7	2	7	.308	.357	.538	139	1	0	0	0	1.000	-0	/O-9	0.1
1978	*KC-A	133	417	48	110	25	5	7	56	56	84	.264	.352	.398	108	5	1	3	-2	.958	-11	O-78,1-52/3D	-1.3
1979	KC-A	59	171	16	41	10	3	3	30	28	24	.240	.350	.386	96	-0	0	1	-1	.968	-3	O-50/3-1,D	-0.6
1980	*KC-A	130	395	50	116	31	2	10	60	34	61	.294	.353	.458	119	10	0	1	-1	.960	-3	*O-126	0.3
1981	*KC-A	28	76	12	25	3	1	4	15	13	10	.329	.427	.553	182	8	0	0	0	1.000	1	O-28	0.8
1982	Cin-N	19	34	2	7	1	0	1	2	2	6	.206	.270	.235	42	-3	0	1	-1	.950	-2	O-17	-0.6
1983	NY-N	13	33	3	6	2	0	0	2	1	10	.182	.229	.242	31	-3	0	0	0	.800	-2	/3-9,O-1	-0.5
1985	NY-N	43	82	7	16	4	0	3	15	12	16	.195	.313	.354	88	-1	0	0	0	1.000	-2	C-17,O-10	-0.3
1986	StL-N	78	154	18	30	5	1	3	15	26	38	.195	.315	.299	71	-6	0	0	0	.994	-2	1-39,O-10/C3	-1.0
1987	NY-N	3	3	1	1	0	0	0	0	0	1	.333	.333	.333	82	-0	0	0	0	1.000	-0	/1-1	0.0
Total	10	515	1391	162	360	81	12	32	193	176	261	.259	.345	.403	106	12	1	6	-3	.965	-23	O-329/1-92,C3D	-3.1

YEAR	TM/L	G	AB	R	H	2B	3B	HR	RBI	BB	SO	AVG	OBP	SLG	PRO+	BR/A	SB	CS	SBR	FA	FR	G/POS	TPR
■ **JERRY HURLEY**	Hurley, Jeremiah b: 4/1875, New York, N.Y. d: 12/27/19, New York, N.Y. BR/TR, Deb: 9/23/01																						
1901	Cin-N	9	21	1	1	0	0	0	0	0	1	.048	.130	.048	-51	-4	1			.938	1	/C-7	-0.3
1907	Bro-N	1	2	0	0	0	0	0	0	0	1	.000	.333	.000	5	-0	0			1.000	-0	/C-1	0.0
Total	2	10	23	1	1	0	0	0	0	0	2	.043	.154	.043	-44	-4	1			.943	1	/C-8	-0.3
■ **JERRY HURLEY**	Hurley, Jeremiah Joseph b: 6/15/1863, Boston, Mass. d: 9/17/50, Boston, Mass. BR/TR, 6', 190 lbs. Deb: 5/1/1889																						
1889	Bos-N	1	4	0	0	0	0	0	0	0	0	.000	.000	.000	-94	-1	0			.000	-1	/O-1,C-1	-0.2
1890	Pit-P	8	22	5	6	1	0	0	2	2	5	.273	.333	.318	81	-1	0			.906	-0	/C-7,O-1	0.0
1891	Cin-a	24	66	10	14	3	2	0	6	12	13	.212	.333	.318	80	-2	2			.862	-3	C-24/O-1,1	-0.3
Total	3	33	92	15	20	4	2	0	8	14	18	.217	.321	.304	72	-3	2			.870	-5	/C-32,O-3,1	-0.5
■ **DICK HURLEY**	Hurley, William H. b: 1847, Honesdale, Pa. 5'7", 160 lbs. Deb: 4/18/1872																						
1872	Oly-n	2	7	0	0	0	0	0	0	0	0	.000	.000	.000	-99	-2						/O-2	-0.1
■ **DON HURST**	Hurst, Frank O'Donnell b: 8/12/05, Maysville, Ky. d: 12/6/52, Los Angeles, Cal. BL/TL, 6', 215 lbs. Deb: 5/13/28																						
1928	Phi-N	107	396	73	113	23	4	19	64	68	40	.285	.391	.508	129	17	3			.989	4	*1-104	1.2
1929	Phi-N	154	589	100	179	29	4	31	125	80	36	.304	.390	.525	117	15	10			.985	5	*1-154	0.4
1930	Phi-N	119	391	78	128	19	3	17	78	46	22	.327	.401	.522	113	8	6			.984	-3	1-96/O-7	-0.4
1931	Phi-N	137	489	63	149	37	5	11	91	64	28	.305	.386	.468	119	14	8			.986	11	*1-135	1.2
1932	Phi-N	150	579	109	196	41	4	24	143	65	27	.339	.412	.547	139	32	10			.993	-3	*1-150	1.7
1933	Phi-N	147	550	58	147	27	8	8	76	48	32	.267	.327	.389	92	-6	3			.985	7	*1-142	-1.3
1934	Phi-N	40	130	16	34	9	0	2	21	12	7	.262	.324	.377	77	-4	1			.994	-1	1-34	-0.8
	Chi-N	51	151	13	30	5	0	3	12	8	18	.199	.239	.291	42	-13	0			.986	-2	1-48	-1.8
	Yr	91	281	29	64	14	0	5	33	20	25	.228	.279	.331	60	-16	1			.990	-3	1-82	-2.6
Total	7	905	3275	510	976	190	28	115	610	391	210	.298	.375	.478	113	63	41			.987	19	1-863/O-7	0.2
■ **BUTCH HUSKEY**	Huskey, Robert Leon b: 11/10/71, Anadarko, Okla. BR/TR, 6'3", 244 lbs. Deb: 9/8/93																						
1993	NY-N	13	41	2	6	1	0	0	3	1	13	.146	.167	.171	-10	-6	0	0	0	.923	3	3-13	-0.3
■ **JEFF HUSON**	Huson, Jeffrey Kent b: 8/15/64, Scottsdale, Ariz. BL/TR, 6'3", 180 lbs. Deb: 9/2/88																						
1988	Mon-N	20	42	7	13	2	0	0	3	4	3	.310	.370	.357	105	0	2	1	0	.932	1	S-15/2-2,3O	0.2
1989	Mon-N	32	74	1	12	5	0	0	2	6	6	.162	.225	.230	30	-7	3	0	1	.886	4	S-20/2-9,3	-0.1
1990	Tex-A	145	396	57	95	12	2	0	28	46	54	.240	.322	.280	70	-15	12	4	1	.960	-13	*S-119,3-36,2	-1.9
1991	Tex-A	119	268	36	57	8	3	2	26	39	32	.213	.313	.287	68	-11	8	3	1	.965	-0	*S-116/2-2,3	-0.3
1992	Tex-A	123	318	49	83	14	3	4	24	41	43	.261	.347	.362	102	2	18	6	2	.968	-9	S-82,2-47/OD	0.0
1993	Tex-A	23	45	3	6	1	1	0	2	0	10	.133	.133	.200	-12	-7	0	0	0	.909	5	S-12/2-5,3D	-0.1
Total	6	462	1143	153	266	42	9	6	85	136	148	.233	.316	.301	74	-37	43	14	5	.956	-12	S-364/2-77,3DO	-2.2
■ **CARL HUSTA**	Husta, Carl Lawrence "Sox" b: 4/8/02, Egg Harbor, N.J. d: 11/6/51, Kingston, N.Y. BR/TR, 5'11", 176 lbs. Deb: 9/24/25																						
1925	Phi-A	6	22	3	3	0	0	0	2	2	3	.136	.208	.136	-11	-4	0	0	0	.976	2	/S-6	-0.1
■ **HARRY HUSTON**	Huston, Harry Emanuel Kress b: 10/14/1883, Bellefontaine, O. d: 10/13/69, Blackwell, Okla. BR/TR, 5'9", 168 lbs. Deb: 9/3/06																						
1906	Phi-N	2	4	0	0	0	0	0	0	0	1	.000	.200	.000	-37	-1	0			1.000	-0	/C-2	-0.1
■ **WARREN HUSTON**	Huston, Warren Llewellyn b: 10/31/13, Newtonville, Mass. BR/TR, 6', 170 lbs. Deb: 6/24/37																						
1937	Phi-A	38	54	5	7	3	0	0	3	2	9	.130	.161	.185	-13	-10	0	1	-1	.918	8	2-16,S-15/3	-0.1
1944	Bos-N	33	55	7	11	1	0	0	1	8	5	.200	.313	.218	49	-3	0			.979	3	3-20/2-5,S	0.0
Total	2	71	109	12	18	4	0	0	4	10	14	.165	.242	.202	19	-13	0	1		.964	11	/3-22,2-21,S	-0.1
■ **JOE HUTCHESON**	Hutcheson, Joseph Johnson "Slug" or "Poodles" b: 2/5/05, Springtown, Tex. d: 2/23/93, Tyler, Tex. BL/TR, 6'2", 200 lbs. Deb: 7/8/33																						
1933	Bro-N	55	184	19	43	4	1	6	21	15	13	.234	.295	.364	91	-1	0			.989	1	O-45	-0.4
■ **ED HUTCHINSON**	Hutchinson, Edwin Forrest b: 5/19/1867, Pittsburgh, Pa. d: 7/19/34, Colfax, Cal. BL/TR, 5'11", 175 lbs. Deb: 6/17/1890																						
1890	Chi-N	4	17	0	1	1	0	0	0	0	0	.059	.059	.118	-47	-3	0			1.000	6	/2-4	0.2
■ **FRED HUTCHINSON**	Hutchinson, Frederick Charles b: 8/12/19, Seattle, Wash. d: 11/12/64, Bradenton, Fla. BL/TR, 6'2", 200 lbs. Deb: 5/2/39 M																						
1939	Det-A	13	34	5	13	1	0	0	6	2	0	.382	.417	.412	105	0	0	0	0	1.000	-0	P-13	0.0
1940	*Det-A	17	30	1	8	1	0	0	2	0	0	.267	.267	.300	43	-3	0	0	0	.900	0	P-17	0.0
1941	Det-A	2	2	0	0	0	0	0	0	0	2	.000	.000	.000	-91	-1	0	0	0	.000	0	H	-0.1
1946	Det-A	40	89	11	28	4	0	0	13	6	1	.315	.358	.360	95	-0	0	0	0	.983	3	P-28	0.0
1947	Det-A	56	106	8	32	5	2	2	15	6	6	.302	.339	.443	113	1	2	0	1	.982	2	P-33	0.0
1948	Det-A	76	112	11	23	1	0	1	12	22	8	.205	.341	.241	55	-6	3	0	1	1.000	3	P-33	0.0
1949	Det-A	38	73	12	18	2	1	0	7	8	5	.247	.329	.301	67	-3	1	0	0	.983	2	P-33	0.0
1950	Det-A	44	95	15	31	7	0	0	20	12	3	.326	.407	.400	104	1	0	0	0	.944	2	P-39	0.0
1951	Det-A★	47	85	7	16	2	0	0	7	7	4	.188	.250	.212	26	-9	0	1	-1	.939	2	P-31	0.0
1952	Det-A	17	18	0	1	0	0	0	1	0	0	.056	.190	.056	-29	-3	0	0	0	1.000	2	P-12,M	0.0
1953	Det-A	4	6	1	1	0	0	0	0	0	1	.167	.167	.667	118	0	0	0	0	1.000	-0	/P-3,1-1M	0.0
Total	11	354	650	71	171	23	3	4	83	66	30	.263	.334	.326	75	-22	6	1	1	.970	15	P-242/1-1	-0.1
■ **ROY HUTSON**	Hutson, Roy Lee b: 2/27/02, Luray, Mo. d: 5/20/57, LaMesa, Cal. BL/TR, 5'9", 165 lbs. Deb: 9/20/25																						
1925	Bro-N	7	8	1	4	0	0	0	1	1	1	.500	.556	.500	177	1	0	0	0	1.000	-1	/O-4	0.0
■ **JIM HUTTO**	Hutto, James Neamon b: 10/17/47, Norfolk, Va. BR/TR, 5'11", 195 lbs. Deb: 4/17/70																						
1970	Phi-N	57	92	7	17	2	0	3	12	5	20	.185	.227	.304	42	-8	0	0	0	1.000	-3	O-22,1-12/C3	-1.2
1975	Bal-A	4	5	0	0	0	0	0	0	0	2	.000	.000	.000	-99	-1	0	0	0	1.000	-0	/C-3	-0.1
Total	2	61	97	7	17	2	0	3	12	5	22	.175	.216	.289	35	-9	0	0	0	1.000	-3	/O-22,1-12,C3	-1.3
■ **TOM HUTTON**	Hutton, Thomas George b: 4/20/46, Los Angeles, Cal. BL/TL, 5'11", 180 lbs. Deb: 9/16/66																						
1966	LA-N	3	2	0	0	0	0	0	0	0	0	.000	.000	.000	-99	-1	0	0	0	1.000	-0	/1-3	-0.1
1969	LA-N	16	48	2	13	0	0	0	4	5	7	.271	.340	.271	78	-1	0	0	0	.993	4	1-16	0.2
1972	Phi-N	134	381	40	99	16	2	4	38	56	24	.260	.355	.344	97	0	5	8	-3	.992	1	1-87,O-48	-1.1
1973	Phi-N	106	247	31	65	11	0	5	29	32	31	.263	.348	.368	96	-1	3	1	0	.998	4	1-71	0.0
1974	Phi-N	96	208	32	50	6	3	4	33	30	13	.240	.336	.356	90	-2	2	2	-1	.996	-3	1-39,O-33	-0.9
1975	Phi-N	113	165	24	41	6	0	3	24	27	10	.248	.354	.339	90	-2	2	5	-2	.994	3	1-71,O-12	-0.4
1976	*Phi-N	95	124	15	25	5	1	1	13	27	11	.202	.344	.282	77	-3	1	2	-1	1.000	1	1-72/O-1	-0.2
1977	*Phi-N	107	81	12	25	3	0	2	11	12	10	.309	.398	.420	114	2	1	1	-0	.993	7	1-73/O-9	0.2
1978	Tor-A	64	173	19	44	9	0	2	9	19	11	.254	.328	.341	87	-3	1	2	-1	1.000	-5	O-55/1-9	-1.1
	Mon-N	39	59	4	12	3	0	0	5	10	5	.203	.319	.254	63	-3	0	0	0	1.000	1	1-17/O-5	-0.7
1979	Mon-N	86	83	14	21	2	1	1	13	10	7	.253	.330	.337	84	-2	0	0	0	1.000	1	1-25/O-9	-0.1
1980	Mon-N	62	55	2	12	2	0	0	5	4	10	.218	.271	.255	47	-4	0	0	0	1.000	-2	/1-7,O-4,P	-0.6
1981	Mon-N	31	29	1	3	0	0	0	2	2	1	.103	.161	.103	-23	-5	0	0	0	1.000	-0	/1-9,O-2	-0.6
Total	12	952	1655	196	410	63	7	22	186	234	140	.248	.341	.334	87	-22	15	21	-8	.995	5	1-499,O-178/P	-5.4
■ **HAM HYATT**	Hyatt, Robert Hamilton b: 11/1/1884, Buncombe Co., N.C. d: 9/11/63, Liberty Lake, Wash. BL/TR, 6'1", 185 lbs. Deb: 4/15/09																						
1909	*Pit-N	49	67	9	20	3	4	0	7	3		.299	.329	.463	134	2	1			.933	3	/O-6,1-2	0.5
1910	Pit-N	74	175	19	46	5	6	1	30	8	14	.263	.306	.377	94	-2	3			.986	-2	1-38/O-4	-0.4

YEAR	TM/L	G	AB	R	H	2B	3B	HR	RBI	BB	SO	AVG	OBP	SLG	PRO+	BR/A	SB	CS	SBR	FA	FR	G/POS	TPR
1912	Pit-N	46	97	13	28	3	1	0	22	6	8	.289	.330	.340	85	-2	2			.955	-2	O-15/1-3	-0.5
1913	Pit-N	63	81	8	27	6	2	4	16	3	8	.333	.372	.605	184	8	0			1.000	-2	/1-5,O-5	0.7
1914	Pit-N	74	79	2	17	3	1	1	15	7	14	.215	.295	.316	86	-1	1			.980	-2	/1-7,C-1	-0.4
1915	StL-N	106	295	23	79	8	9	2	46	28	24	.268	.337	.376	116	6	3	3	-1	.991	-6	1-64,O-25	-0.4
1918	NY-A	53	131	11	30	8	0	2	10	8	8	.229	.273	.336	82	-4	1			1.000	-1	O-25/1-5	-0.7
Total	7	465	925	85	247	36	23	10	146	63	<u>76</u>	.267	.321	.388	108	6	11	3		.989	-11	1-124/O-80,C	-1.2

■ TIM HYERS
Hyers, Timothy James b: 10/3/71, Atlanta, Ga. BL/TL, 6'1", 185 lbs. Deb: 4/4/94

YEAR	TM/L	G	AB	R	H	2B	3B	HR	RBI	BB	SO	AVG	OBP	SLG	PRO+	BR/A	SB	CS	SBR	FA	FR	G/POS	TPR
1994	SD-N	52	118	13	30	3	0	0	7	9	15	.254	.307	.280	55	-8	3	0	1	.986	0	1-41/O-2	-0.9

■ JIM HYNDMAN
Hyndman, James William b: 7/1865, Ontario, Canada Deb: 7/23/1886

YEAR	TM/L	G	AB	R	H	2B	3B	HR	RBI	BB	SO	AVG	OBP	SLG	PRO+	BR/A	SB	CS	SBR	FA	FR	G/POS	TPR
1886	Phi-a	1	4	0	0	0	0	0	0			.000	.000	.000	-99	-1	0			1.000	0	/O-1,P-1	-0.1

■ PAT HYNES
Hynes, Patrick J. b: 3/12/1884, St.Louis, Mo. d: 3/12/07, St.Louis, Mo. TL , Deb: 9/27/03

YEAR	TM/L	G	AB	R	H	2B	3B	HR	RBI	BB	SO	AVG	OBP	SLG	PRO+	BR/A	SB	CS	SBR	FA	FR	G/POS	TPR
1903	StL-N	1	3	0	0	0	0	0	0			.000	.000	.000	-99	-1	0			.500	-1	/P-1	0.0
1904	StL-N	66	254	23	60	7	3	0	15	3		.236	.248	.287	74	-8	3			.901	-12	O-63/P-5	-2.5
Total	2	67	257	23	60	7	3	0	15	3		.233	.245	.284	71	-9	3			.857	-12	/O-63,P-6	-2.5

■ PETE INCAVIGLIA
Incaviglia, Peter Joseph b: 4/2/64, Pebble Beach, Cal. BR/TR, 6'1", 225 lbs. Deb: 4/8/86

YEAR	TM/L	G	AB	R	H	2B	3B	HR	RBI	BB	SO	AVG	OBP	SLG	PRO+	BR/A	SB	CS	SBR	FA	FR	G/POS	TPR
1986	Tex-A	153	540	82	135	21	2	30	88	55	185	.250	.324	.463	108	5	3	2	-0	.921	-11	*O-114,D-36	-1.0
1987	Tex-A	139	509	85	138	26	4	27	80	48	168	.271	.335	.497	116	11	9	3	1	.945	-3	*O-132/D-6	0.4
1988	Tex-A	116	418	59	104	19	3	22	54	39	153	.249	.323	.467	116	8	6	4	-1	.989	6	O-93,D-21	1.0
1989	Tex-A	133	453	48	107	27	4	21	81	32	136	.236	.295	.453	106	2	5	7	-3	.973	-3	*O-125/D-5	-0.7
1990	Tex-A	153	529	59	123	27	0	24	85	45	146	.233	.304	.420	100	-1	3	4	-2	.974	-0	*O-145/D-2	-0.7
1991	Det-A	97	337	38	72	12	1	11	38	36	92	.214	.291	.353	76	-11	1	3	-2	.973	2	O-54,D-41	-1.4
1992	Hou-N	113	349	31	93	22	1	11	44	25	99	.266	.321	.430	116	6	2	2	-1	.970	4	O-98	0.8
1993	*Phi-N	116	368	60	101	16	3	24	89	21	82	.274	.324	.530	126	11	1	1	-0	.971	-2	O-97	0.7
1994	Phi-N	80	244	28	56	10	1	13	32	16	71	.230	.280	.439	84	-7	1	0	0	.979	-2	O-63	-1.0
Total	9	1100	3747	490	929	180	19	183	591	317	1132	.248	.313	.453	107	24	31	26	-6	.966	-11	O-921,D-111	-1.9

■ ALEXIS INFANTE
Infante, Fermin Alexis (Carpio) b: 12/4/61, Barquisimeto, Venez. BR/TR, 5'10", 175 lbs. Deb: 9/27/87

YEAR	TM/L	G	AB	R	H	2B	3B	HR	RBI	BB	SO	AVG	OBP	SLG	PRO+	BR/A	SB	CS	SBR	FA	FR	G/POS	TPR
1987	Tor-A	1	0	0	0	0	0	0	0	0	0	—		—		0	0	0	0	.000	0	/R	0.0
1988	Tor-A	19	15	7	3	0	0	0	0	2	4	.200	.294	.200	41	-1	0	0	0	.909	1	/3-9,S-2,D	0.0
1989	Tor-A	20	12	1	2	0	0	0	0	0	1	.167	.167	.167	-6	-2	1	0	0	1.000	4	/S-9,3-4,2D	0.3
1990	Atl-N	20	28	3	1	1	0	0	0	0	7	.036	.069	.071	-58	-6	0	0	0	.964	4	2-10/3-4,S	-0.2
Total	4	60	55	11	6	1	0	0	0	2	12	.109	.155	.127	-20	-9	1	0	0	.933	9	/3-17,S-14,2D	0.1

■ SCOTTY INGERTON
Ingerton, William John b: 4/19/1886, Peninsula, Ohio d: 6/15/56, Cleveland, Ohio BR/TR, 6'1", 172 lbs. Deb: 4/12/11

YEAR	TM/L	G	AB	R	H	2B	3B	HR	RBI	BB	SO	AVG	OBP	SLG	PRO+	BR/A	SB	CS	SBR	FA	FR	G/POS	TPR
1911	Bos-N	136	521	63	130	24	4	5	61	39	68	.250	.304	.340	74	-20	6			.942	18	3-58,O-43,12/S	-0.3

■ CHARLIE INGRAHAM
Ingraham, Charles W. b: 4/8/1860, Illinois d: 2/18/06, Chicago, Ill. 5'11", 170 lbs. Deb: 7/4/1883

YEAR	TM/L	G	AB	R	H	2B	3B	HR	RBI	BB	SO	AVG	OBP	SLG	PRO+	BR/A	SB	CS	SBR	FA	FR	G/POS	TPR
1883	Bal-a	1	4	0	1	0	0	0				.250	.250	.250	60	-0				.833	-1	/C-1	-0.1

■ GAREY INGRAM
Ingram, Garey Lamar b: 7/25/70, Columbus, Ga. BR/TR, 5'11", 180 lbs. Deb: 5/15/94

YEAR	TM/L	G	AB	R	H	2B	3B	HR	RBI	BB	SO	AVG	OBP	SLG	PRO+	BR/A	SB	CS	SBR	FA	FR	G/POS	TPR
1994	LA-N	26	78	10	22	1	0	3	8	7	22	.282	.341	.410	101	-0	0	0	0	.982	6	2-23	0.6

■ MEL INGRAM
Ingram, Melvin David b: 7/4/04, Asheville, N.C. d: 10/28/79, Medford, Ore. BR/TR, 5'11.5", 175 lbs. Deb: 7/24/29

YEAR	TM/L	G	AB	R	H	2B	3B	HR	RBI	BB	SO	AVG	OBP	SLG	PRO+	BR/A	SB	CS	SBR	FA	FR	G/POS	TPR
1929	Pit-N	3	0	1	0	0	0	0	0	0	0	—		—		—	0			.000	0	R	0.0

■ RICCARDO INGRAM
Ingram, Riccardo Benay b: 9/10/66, Douglas, Ga. BR/TR, 6', 205 lbs. Deb: 6/26/94

YEAR	TM/L	G	AB	R	H	2B	3B	HR	RBI	BB	SO	AVG	OBP	SLG	PRO+	BR/A	SB	CS	SBR	FA	FR	G/POS	TPR
1994	Det-A	12	23	3	5	0	0	0	2	1	2	.217	.250	.217	22	-3	0	1	-1	1.000	-0	/O-8,D-1	-0.3

■ DANE IORG
Iorg, Dane Charles b: 5/11/50, Eureka, Cal. BL/TR, 6', 180 lbs. Deb: 4/9/77 F

YEAR	TM/L	G	AB	R	H	2B	3B	HR	RBI	BB	SO	AVG	OBP	SLG	PRO+	BR/A	SB	CS	SBR	FA	FR	G/POS	TPR
1977	Phi-N	12	30	3	5	1	0	0	2	1	3	.167	.194	.200	6	-4	0	0	0	.986	-0	/1-9	-0.5
	StL-N	30	32	2	10	1	0	0	4	5	4	.313	.405	.344	105	1	0	1	-1	.875	-2	/O-7	-0.2
	Yr	42	62	5	15	2	0	0	6	6	7	.242	.309	.274	58	-4	0	1	-1	.986	-2	/1-9,O-7	-0.7
1978	StL-N	35	85	6	23	4	1	0	4	4	10	.271	.303	.341	81	-2	0	0	0	1.000	0	O-25	-0.3
1979	StL-N	79	179	12	52	11	1	1	21	12	28	.291	.339	.380	95	-1	1	2	-0	.964	-6	O-39,1-10	-1.0
1980	StL-N	105	251	33	76	23	1	3	36	20	34	.303	.354	.438	116	5	1	1	-0	.991	-3	O-63/1-5,3	-0.1
1981	StL-N	75	217	23	71	11	2	2	39	7	9	.327	.348	.424	115	4	2	0	1	.963	-11	O-57/1-8,3	-0.9
1982	*StL-N	102	238	17	70	14	1	0	34	23	23	.294	.356	.361	100	0	1	3	-0	.971	-5	O-63,1-10/3	-0.7
1983	StL-N	58	116	6	31	9	1	0	11	10	11	.267	.331	.362	92	-1	1	0	0	.974	-3	O-22,1-11	-0.5
1984	StL-N	15	28	3	4	2	0	0	3	2	6	.143	.200	.214	17	-3	0	0	0	1.000	-1	/1-6,O-5	-0.4
	*KC-A	78	235	27	60	16	2	5	30	13	15	.255	.294	.404	90	-4	0	3	-1	.995	-4	1-43,O-22/3D	-1.1
1985	*KC-A	64	130	7	29	9	1	1	21	11	18	.223	.268	.331	63	-7	0	1	-1	1.000	-5	O-32/1-2,3D	-1.3
1986	SD-N	90	106	10	24	2	1	2	11	2	21	.226	.241	.321	55	-7	0	0	0	1.000	-1	1-10/3-6,OP	-0.9
Total	10	743	1647	149	455	103	11	14	216	107	180	.276	.321	.378	92	-19	5	7	-3	.977	-41	O-338,1-114/3DP	-7.9

■ GARTH IORG
Iorg, Garth Ray b: 10/12/54, Arcata, Cal. BR/TR, 5'11", 170 lbs. Deb: 4/9/78 F

YEAR	TM/L	G	AB	R	H	2B	3B	HR	RBI	BB	SO	AVG	OBP	SLG	PRO+	BR/A	SB	CS	SBR	FA	FR	G/POS	TPR
1978	Tor-A	19	49	3	8	0	0	0	3	3	4	.163	.226	.163	11	-6	0	0	0	.966	4	2-18	-0.1
1980	Tor-A	80	222	24	55	10	1	2	14	12	39	.248	.286	.329	65	-11	2	1	0	.988	8	2-32,3-20,01/SD	-0.2
1981	Tor-A	70	215	17	52	11	0	0	10	7	31	.242	.269	.293	58	-12	2	3	-1	.963	-0	2-46,3-17/S1D	-1.1
1982	Tor-A	129	417	45	119	20	5	1	36	12	38	.285	.312	.365	78	-13	4	3	-0	.946	-4	*3-100,2-30/D	-1.8
1983	Tor-A	122	375	40	103	22	5	2	39	13	45	.275	.301	.376	80	-11	7	0	2	.976	-3	3-85,2-39/S	-1.1
1984	Tor-A	121	247	24	56	10	3	1	25	5	16	.227	.245	.304	49	-17	1	3	-2	.945	1	*3-112/2-7,SD	-1.8
1985	*Tor-A	131	288	33	90	22	1	7	37	21	26	.313	.366	.469	122	8	3	6	-3	.951	11	*3-104,2-23	1.6
1986	Tor-A	137	327	30	85	19	1	3	44	20	47	.260	.305	.352	76	-11	4	0	1	.955	-15	3-90,2-52/S	-2.4
1987	Tor-A	122	310	35	65	11	0	4	30	21	52	.210	.264	.284	45	-25	2	1	0	.982	-13	2-91,3-28/D	-3.4
Total	9	931	2450	251	633	125	16	20	238	114	298	.258	.294	.347	72	-96	23	17	-3	.955	-12	3-556,2-338/O1DS	-10.3

■ HAPPY IOTT
Iott, Frederick "Happy Jack" or "Biddo" (b: Frederick Hoyot)
b: 7/7/1876, Houlton, Me. d: 2/17/41, Island Falls, Me. BR/TR, 5'10", 175 lbs. Deb: 9/16/03

YEAR	TM/L	G	AB	R	H	2B	3B	HR	RBI	BB	SO	AVG	OBP	SLG	PRO+	BR/A	SB	CS	SBR	FA	FR	G/POS	TPR
1903	Cle-A	3	10	1	2	0	0	0	0	0		.200	.333	.200	64	-0	1			.875	-0	/O-3	-0.1

■ HAL IRELAN
Irelan, Harold "Grump" b: 8/5/1890, Burnettsville, Ind. d: 7/16/44, Carmel, Ind. BB/TR, 5'7", 165 lbs. Deb: 4/23/14

YEAR	TM/L	G	AB	R	H	2B	3B	HR	RBI	BB	SO	AVG	OBP	SLG	PRO+	BR/A	SB	CS	SBR	FA	FR	G/POS	TPR
1914	Phi-N	67	165	16	39	8	1	0	16	21	22	.236	.326	.303	82	-3	3			.909	11	2-44/S-3,13	0.8

■ TIM IRELAND
Ireland, Timothy Neal b: 3/14/53, Oakland, Cal. BR/TR, 6', 180 lbs. Deb: 9/20/81

YEAR	TM/L	G	AB	R	H	2B	3B	HR	RBI	BB	SO	AVG	OBP	SLG	PRO+	BR/A	SB	CS	SBR	FA	FR	G/POS	TPR
1981	KC-A	4	0	1	0	0	0	0	0	0	0	—		—		0	0	1	-1	1.000	-0	/1-4	-0.1
1982	KC-A	7	7	2	1	0	0	0	0	1	1	.143	.250	.143	11	-1	0	0	0	1.000	0	/2-4,O-2,3	-0.1
Total	2	11	7	3	1	0	0	0	0	1	1	.143	.250	.143	11	-1	0	1	-1	1.000	0	/2-4,1-4,O3	-0.2

■ MONTE IRVIN
Irvin, Monford b: 2/25/19, Columbia, Ala. BR/TR, 6'1", 195 lbs. Deb: 7/8/49 H

YEAR	TM/L	G	AB	R	H	2B	3B	HR	RBI	BB	SO	AVG	OBP	SLG	PRO+	BR/A	SB	CS	SBR	FA	FR	G/POS	TPR
1949	NY-N	36	76	7	17	2	1	0	7	11	11	.224	.366	.316	84	-1	0			1.000	0	O-10/1-5,3	-0.1
1950	NY-N	110	374	61	112	19	5	15	66	52	41	.299	.392	.497	131	18	3			.979	5	1-59,O-49/3	1.8
1951	*NY-N	151	558	94	174	19	11	24	**121**	89	44	.312	.415	.514	147	40	12	2	2	.996	11	*O-112,1-39	4.6
1952	NY-N†	46	126	10	39	2	1	4	21	10	11	.310	.365	.437	120	3	0	1	-1	1.000	-2	O-32	0.0

YEAR	TM/L	G	AB	R	H	2B	3B	HR	RBI	BB	SO	AVG	OBP	SLG	PRO+	BR/A	SB	CS	SBR	FA	FR	G/POS	TPR
1953	NY-N	124	444	72	146	21	5	21	97	55	34	.329	.406	.541	142	28	2	0	1	.973	8	*O-113	3.0
1954	*NY-N	135	432	62	113	13	3	19	64	70	23	.262	.367	.438	108	6	7	4	-0	.976	4	*O-128/1-1,3	0.5
1955	NY-N	51	150	16	38	7	1	1	17	17	15	.253	.341	.333	80	-4	3	0	1	.961	-1	O-45	-0.4
1956	Chi-N	111	339	44	92	13	3	15	50	41	41	.271	.350	.460	118	8	1	0	0	.991	11	O-96	1.5
Total	8	764	2499	366	731	97	31	99	443	351	220	.293	.385	.475	126	98	28	7		.983	38	O-585,1-104/3	10.9

■ ED IRVIN
Irvin, William Edward b: 1882, Philadelphia, Pa. d: 2/18/16, Philadelphia, Pa. BR/TR Deb: 5/18/12

YEAR	TM/L	G	AB	R	H	2B	3B	HR	RBI	BB	SO	AVG	OBP	SLG	PRO+	BR/A	SB	CS	SBR	FA	FR	G/POS	TPR
1912	Det-A	1	3	0	2	0	2	0	0	0	0	.667	.667	2.000	675	2	0			.500	-1	/3-1	0.1

■ ARTHUR IRWIN
Irwin, Arthur Albert "Doc" or "Sandy" b: 2/14/1858, Toronto, Ont., Can. d: 7/16/21, Atlantic Ocean BL/TR, 5'8.5", 158 lbs. Deb: 5/1/1880 FMU

YEAR	TM/L	G	AB	R	H	2B	3B	HR	RBI	BB	SO	AVG	OBP	SLG	PRO+	BR/A	SB	CS	SBR	FA	FR	G/POS	TPR
1880	Wor-N	85	352	53	91	19	4	1	35	11	27	.259	.281	.344	102	-1				.895	31	*S-82/3-3,C	**3.4**
1881	Wor-N	50	206	27	55	8	2	0	24	7	4	.267	.291	.325	88	-3				.851	-8	S-50	-0.7
1882	Wor-N	84	333	30	73	12	4	0	30	14	34	.219	.251	.279	68	-12				.837	21	3-51,S-33	1.0
1883	Pro-N	98	406	67	116	22	7	0	44	12	38	.286	.306	.374	103	1				.856	-7	*S-94/2-4	-0.4
1884	*Pro-N	102	404	73	97	14	3	2	44	28	52	.240	.289	.304	89	-4				.881	-6	*S-102/P-1	-0.8
1885	Pro-N	59	218	16	39	2	1	0	14	14	29	.179	.228	.197	40	-14				.875	4	S-58/3-1,2	-0.8
1886	Phi-N	101	373	51	87	6	6	0	34	35	39	.233	.299	.282	77	-10	24			.891	4	*S-100/3-1	-0.4
1887	Phi-N	100	374	65	95	14	8	2	56	48	26	.254	.344	.350	88	-6	19			.892	-10	*S-100	-1.2
1888	Phi-N	125	448	51	98	12	4	0	28	33	56	.219	.277	.263	69	-15	19			.900	12	*S-122/2-3	0.0
1889	Phi-N	18	73	9	16	5	0	0	10	6	6	.219	.278	.288	54	-5	6			.845	-6	S-18	-0.9
	Was-N	85	313	49	73	10	5	0	32	42	37	.233	.326	.297	80	-7	9			.895	12	S-85/P-1,2M	0.8
	Yr	103	386	58	89	15	5	0	42	48	43	.231	.317	.295	74	-12	15			.888	6	*S-103/P-1,2	-0.1
1890	Bos-P	96	354	60	92	17	1	0	45	57	29	.260	.364	.314	77	-11	16			.878	3	*S-96	-0.3
1891	Bos-a	6	17	1	2	0	0	0	0	2	1	.118	.286	.118	16	-2	0			.778	-1	/S-6,M	-0.2
1894	Phi-N	1	0	0	0	0	0	0	0	0	0	—	—	—	—	0	0			.000	0	/S-1,M	0.0
Total	13	1010	3871	552	934	141	45	5	396	309	378	.241	.299	.305	81	-88	93			.881	49	S-947/3-56,2PC	-0.5

■ CHARLIE IRWIN
Irwin, Charles Edwin b: 2/15/1869, Clinton, Ill. d: 9/21/25, Chicago, Ill. BL/TR, 5'10", 160 lbs. Deb: 9/3/1893

YEAR	TM/L	G	AB	R	H	2B	3B	HR	RBI	BB	SO	AVG	OBP	SLG	PRO+	BR/A	SB	CS	SBR	FA	FR	G/POS	TPR
1893	Chi-N	21	82	14	25	6	2	0	13	10	1	.305	.394	.427	120	3	4			.910	-1	S-21	0.2
1894	Chi-N	128	498	84	144	24	9	8	95	63	23	.289	.379	.422	88	-11	35			.822	14	3-67,S-61	-1.4
1895	Chi-N	3	10	4	2	0	0	0	0	2	1	.200	.333	.200	37	-1	0			.900	-2	/S-3	-0.2
1896	Cin-N	127	476	77	141	16	6	1	67	26	17	.296	.338	.361	79	-16	31			**.931**	7	*3-127	-0.5
1897	Cin-N	134	505	89	146	26	6	0	74	47		.289	.360	.364	88	-11	27			.940	6	*3-134	-1.1
1898	Cin-N	136	501	77	120	14	5	3	55	31		.240	.297	.305	68	-22	18			.940	14	*3-136	-0.7
1899	Cin-N	90	314	42	73	4	8	1	52	26		.232	.295	.306	64	-16	26			.909	-13	3-78/S-6,21	-2.6
1900	Cin-N	87	333	59	91	15	6	1	44	14		.273	.314	.363	89	-6	9			.931	-11	3-61,S-16/O2	-1.4
1901	Cin-N	67	260	25	62	12	2	0	25	14		.238	.285	.300	75	-9	13			.893	4	3-67	-0.4
	Bro-N	65	242	25	52	13	2	0	20	14		.215	.269	.285	59	-13	4			.956	-2	3-65	-1.4
	Yr	132	502	50	114	25	4	0	45	28		.227	.277	.293	67	-21	17			.921	2	*3-132	-1.8
1902	Bro-N	131	458	59	125	14	0	2	63	30		.273	.346	.317	104	4	13			.927	-10	*3-130/S-1	-0.6
Total	10	989	3679	555	981	144	46	16	488	286	42	.267	.330	.344	82	-97	180			.921	-31	3-865,S-108/O21	-10.1

■ JOHN IRWIN
Irwin, John b: 7/21/1861, Toronto, Ont., Can d: 2/28/34, Boston, Mass. BL/TR, 5'10", 168 lbs. Deb: 5/31/1882 F

YEAR	TM/L	G	AB	R	H	2B	3B	HR	RBI	BB	SO	AVG	OBP	SLG	PRO+	BR/A	SB	CS	SBR	FA	FR	G/POS	TPR
1882	Wor-N	1	4	0	0	0	0	0	0	0	2	.000	.000	.000	-98	-1				.636	-1	/1-1	-0.2
1884	Bos-U	105	432	81	101	22	6	1		15		.234	.260	.319	57	-26				.780	4	*3-105	-1.9
1886	Phi-a	3	13	4	3	1	0	0		0		.231	.231	.308	67	-1				.714	-1	/S-2,3-1	-0.2
1887	Was-N	8	31	6	11	2	0	2	3	6		.355	.429	.613	196	4	6			.875	-2	/S-5,3-4	0.2
1888	Was-N	37	126	14	28	5	2	0	8	5	18	.222	.263	.294	82	-2	15			.860	-1	S-27,3-10	-0.3
1889	Was-N	58	228	42	66	11	4	0	25	25	14	.289	.370	.373	115	6	10			.868	0	3-58	0.7
1890	Buf-P	77	308	62	72	11	4	0	34	43	19	.234	.335	.295	75	-9	18			.883	4	3-64,1-12/2	-0.2
1891	Bos-a	19	72	6	16	2	2	0	15	6	9	.222	.282	.306	69	-3	6			.882	-6	O-17/3-2,S	-0.3
	Lou-a	14	55	7	15	1	1	0	7	5	6	.273	.344	.327	93	-0	1			.795	-7	3-14	-0.6
	Yr	33	127	13	31	3	3	0	22	11	15	.244	.309	.315	80	-4	7			.882	-6	O-17,3-16/S	-0.9
Total	8	322	1269	222	312	55	19	3	92	102	74	.246	.308	.326	80	-32	56			.829	-4	3-258/S-35,O12	-2.8

■ TOMMY IRWIN
Irwin, Thomas Andrew b: 12/20/12, Altoona, Pa. BR/TR, 5'11", 165 lbs. Deb: 10/1/38

YEAR	TM/L	G	AB	R	H	2B	3B	HR	RBI	BB	SO	AVG	OBP	SLG	PRO+	BR/A	SB	CS	SBR	FA	FR	G/POS	TPR
1938	Cle-A	3	9	1	1	0	0	0	0	3	1	.111	.333	.111	16	-1	0	0	0	1.000	-0	/S-3	-0.1

■ WALT IRWIN
Irwin, Walter Kingsley b: 9/23/1897, Henrietta, Pa. d: 8/18/76, Spring Lake, Mich. BR/TR, 5'10.5", 170 lbs. Deb: 4/24/21

YEAR	TM/L	G	AB	R	H	2B	3B	HR	RBI	BB	SO	AVG	OBP	SLG	PRO+	BR/A	SB	CS	SBR	FA	FR	G/POS	TPR
1921	StL-N	4	1	1	0	0	0	0	0	0	1	.000	.000	.000	-99	-0	0			.000	0	H	0.0

■ ORLANDO ISALES
Isales, Orlando (Pizarro) b: 12/22/59, Santurce, P.R. BR/TR, 5'9", 175 lbs. Deb: 9/11/80

YEAR	TM/L	G	AB	R	H	2B	3B	HR	RBI	BB	SO	AVG	OBP	SLG	PRO+	BR/A	SB	CS	SBR	FA	FR	G/POS	TPR
1980	Phi-N	3	5	1	2	0	1	0	3	1	0	.400	.500	.800	244	1	0	0	0	1.000	-0	/O-2	0.1

■ FRANK ISBELL
Isbell, William Frank "Bald Eagle" b: 8/21/1875, Delevan, N.Y. d: 7/15/41, Wichita, Kan. BL/TR, 5'11", 190 lbs. Deb: 5/1/1898

YEAR	TM/L	G	AB	R	H	2B	3B	HR	RBI	BB	SO	AVG	OBP	SLG	PRO+	BR/A	SB	CS	SBR	FA	FR	G/POS	TPR
1898	Chi-N	45	159	17	37	4	0	0	8	3		.233	.252	.258	46	-11	3			.956	-7	O-28,P-13/32S	-1.6
1901	Chi-A	137	556	93	143	15	8	3	70	36		.257	.311	.329	79	-15	**52**			.980	13	*1-137/2-2,PS3	-0.3
1902	Chi-A	137	515	62	130	14	4	4	59	14		.252	.276	.318	68	-23	38			.986	10	*1-133/S-4,PC	-1.5
1903	Chi-A	138	546	52	132	25	9	2	59	12		.242	.266	.332	82	-13	26			.984	7	*1-117,3-19/2SO	-0.8
1904	Chi-A	96	314	27	66	10	4	1	34	16		.210	.255	.271	69	-11	19			.986	0	1-57,2-27/OS	-1.3
1905	Chi-A	94	341	55	101	21	11	2	45	15		.296	.335	.440	151	18	15			.964	-2	2-43,O-41/1S	1.6
1906	*Chi-A	143	549	71	153	18	11	0	57	30		.279	.324	.352	115	8	37			.949	-22	*2-132,O-14/PC	-1.5
1907	Chi-A	125	486	60	118	19	7	0	41	22		.243	.281	.311	92	-6	22			.957	9	2-119/O-5,PS	0.2
1908	Chi-A	84	320	31	79	15	3	1	49	19		.247	.297	.322	103	1	18			.990	2	1-65,2-18	0.1
1909	Chi-A	120	433	33	97	16	6	0	33	23		.224	.265	.291	79	-12	23			.994	1	*1-101/O-9,2	-1.3
Total	10	1119	4219	501	1056	158	62	13	455	190		.250	.289	.326	89	-64	253			.980	12	1-619,2-351,O/3PSC	-6.4

■ MIKE IVIE
Ivie, Michael Wilson b: 8/8/52, Atlanta, Ga. BR/TR, 6'3", 205 lbs. Deb: 9/4/71

YEAR	TM/L	G	AB	R	H	2B	3B	HR	RBI	BB	SO	AVG	OBP	SLG	PRO+	BR/A	SB	CS	SBR	FA	FR	G/POS	TPR
1971	SD-N	6	17	0	8	0	0	0	3	1	0	.471	.526	.471	198	2	0	0	0	1.000	-2	/C-6	0.1
1974	SD-N	12	34	1	3	0	0	1	3	2	8	.088	.139	.176	-13	-5	0	0	0	.986	-0	1-11	-0.6
1975	SD-N	111	377	36	94	16	2	8	46	20	63	.249	.294	.366	88	-8	4	4	-1	.989	-5	1-78,3-61/C	-1.9
1976	SD-N	140	405	51	118	19	5	7	70	30	44	.291	.348	.415	126	12	6	6	-2	.995	-5	*1-135/C-2,3	0.4
1977	SD-N	134	489	66	133	29	2	9	66	39	57	.272	.328	.395	104	1	3	2	-0	.992	-5	*1-105,3-25	-1.1
1978	SF-N	117	318	34	98	14	3	11	55	27	45	.308	.366	.475	139	16	3	0	1	.995	-10	1-76,O-22	0.2
1979	SF-N	133	402	58	115	18	3	27	89	47	80	.286	.362	.547	155	29	5	1	1	.995	-6	1-98/O-24/32	1.9
1980	SF-N	79	286	21	69	16	1	4	25	19	40	.241	.289	.346	78	-9	1	2	-1	.993	-6	1-72	-2.2
1981	SF-N	7	17	1	5	2	0	0	3	0	1	.294	.294	.412	100	-0	0	0	0	1.000	1	/1-5	-0.1
	Hou-N	19	42	2	10	3	0	0	6	2	11	.238	.273	.310	68	-2	0	1	-1	.989	2	1-10	-0.1
	Yr	26	59	3	15	5	0	0	9	2	12	.254	.279	.339	78	-2	0	1	-1	.992	3	1-15	-0.1
1982	Hou-N	7	6	0	2	0	0	0	1	0		.333	.429	.333	125	0	0	0	0	.000	0	/H	0.0
	Det-A	80	259	35	60	12	1	14	38	24	51	.232	.302	.448	102	0	0	0	0	.000	0	D-79	-0.3
1983	Det-A	12	42	4	9	4	0	0	3	1		.214	.250	.310	54	-0	0	0	0	1.000	0	1-12	-0.4
Total	11	857	2694	309	724	133	17	81	411	214	402	.269	.326	.421	102	33	22	16	-3	.993	-31	1-602/3-92,DOC2	-4.0

YEAR	TM/L	G	AB	R	H	2B	3B	HR	RBI	BB	SO	AVG	OBP	SLG	PRO+	BR/A	SB	CS	SBR	FA	FR	G/POS	TPR

■ HANK IZQUIERDO Izquierdo, Enrique Roberto (Valdes) b: 3/20/31, Matanzas, Cuba BR/TR, 5'11", 175 lbs. Deb: 8/9/67

1967	Min-A	16	26	4	7	2	0	0	2	1	2	.269	.296	.346	83	-1	0	0	0	.986	3	C-16	0.3

■ RAY JABLONSKI Jablonski, Raymond Leo "Jabbo" b: 12/17/26, Chicago, Ill. d: 11/25/85, Chicago, Ill. BR/TR, 5'10", 183 lbs. Deb: 4/14/53

1953	StL-N	157	604	64	162	23	5	21	112	34	61	.268	.308	.427	89	-11	2	2	-1	.932	-16	*3-157	-3.0
1954	StL-N★	152	611	80	181	33	3	12	104	49	42	.296	.350	.419	99	-1	9	4	0	.925	-7	3-149/1-1	-1.1
1955	Cin-N	74	221	28	53	9	0	9	28	13	35	.240	.291	.403	77	-8	0	1	-1	.872	-10	3-28,O-28	-2.0
1956	Cin-N	130	407	42	104	25	1	15	66	37	57	.256	.328	.432	96	-2	2	4	-2	.970	-25	*3-127/2-1	-2.9
1957	NY-N	107	305	37	88	15	1	9	57	31	47	.289	.354	.433	110	5	0	2	-1	.941	-3	3-70/1-6,O	0.2
1958	SF-N	82	230	28	53	15	1	12	46	17	50	.230	.289	.461	97	-2	2	0	1	.946	-8	3-57	-0.9
1959	StL-N	60	87	11	22	4	0	3	14	8	19	.253	.316	.402	84	-2	1	0	0	.900	-3	3-19/S-1	-0.5
	KC-A	25	65	4	17	1	0	2	8	3	11	.262	.294	.369	79	-2	0	0	0	.947	-3	3-17	-0.5
1960	KC-A	21	32	3	7	1	0	0	3	4	8	.219	.306	.250	52	-2	0	0	0	.944	0	/3-6	-0.2
Total	8	808	2562	297	687	126	11	83	438	196	330	.268	.324	.423	94	-26	16	13	-3	.936	-75	3-630/O-29,1S2	-10.9

■ FRED JACKLITSCH Jacklitsch, Frederick Lawrence b: 5/24/1876, Brooklyn, N.Y. d: 7/18/37, Brooklyn, N.Y. BR/TR, 5'9", 180 lbs. Deb: 6/6/00

1900	Phi-N	5	11	0	2	1	0	0	3	0		.182	.182	.273	25	-1	0			1.000	-2	/C-3	-0.2
1901	Phi-N	33	120	14	30	4	3	0	24	12		.250	.328	.333	90	-1	2			.971	-1	C-30/3-1	0.1
1902	Phi-N	38	114	8	23	4*	0	0	8	9		.202	.278	.237	59	-5	2			.927	-9	C-29/O-1	-1.2
1903	Bro-N	60	176	31	47	8	3	1	21	33		.267	.389	.364	118	6	4			.975	-9	C-53/2-1,O	0.3
1904	Bro-N	26	77	8	18	3	1	0	8	7		.234	.322	.299	94	-0	7			.957	-7	1-11/2-8,C	-0.7
1905	NY-A	1	3	1	0	0	0	0	1	1		.000	.250	.000	-17	-0	0			1.000	-0	/C-1	0.0
1907	Phi-N	73	202	19	43	7	0	0	17	27		.213	.312	.248	76	-4	7			.984	11	C-58/1-6,O	1.3
1908	Phi-N	37	86	6	19	3	0	0	7	14		.221	.337	.256	87	-1	3			.976	3	C-30	0.6
1909	Phi-N	20	32	6	10	1	1	0	1	10		.313	.476	.406	173	4	1			.964	-2	C-11/2-1	0.3
1910	Phi-N	25	51	7	10	3	0	0	2	5	9	.196	.268	.255	51	-3	0			.989	5	C-13/1-2,23	0.3
1914	Bal-F	122	337	40	93	21	4	2	48	52	66	.276	.380	.380	93	-2	7			**.988**	2	*C-118	1.1
1915	Bal-F	49	135	20	32	9	0	2	13	31	25	.237	.387	.348	94	0	2			.992	-5	C-45/S-1	-0.3
1917	Bos-N	1	0	0	0	0	0	0	0	0	0	—	—	—	—	0	0			1.000	-0	/C-1	0.0
Total	13	490	1344	160	327	64	12	5	153	201	100	.243	.349	.320	91	-8	35			.978	-14	C-397/1-19,2O3S	1.6

■ CHARLIE JACKSON Jackson, Charles Herbert "Lefty" b: 2/7/1894, Granite City, Ill. d: 5/27/68, Radford, Va. BL/TL, 5'9", 150 lbs. Deb: 8/20/15

1915	Chi-A	1	1	0	0	0	0	0	0	0	1	.000	.000	.000	-97	-0	0			.000	0	H	0.0
1917	Pit-N	41	121	7	29	3	2	0	1	10	22	.240	.303	.298	82	-2	4			.986	0	O-36	-0.4
Total	2	42	122	7	29	3	2	0	1	10	23	.238	.301	.295	80	-3	4			.986	0	/O-36	-0.4

■ CHUCK JACKSON Jackson, Charles Leo b: 3/19/63, Seattle, Wash. BR/TR, 6' ", 185 lbs. Deb: 5/26/87

1987	Hou-N	35	71	3	15	3	0	1	6	7	19	.211	.282	.296	55	-5	1	1	-0	.957	-1	3-16,O-13/S	-0.6
1988	Hou-N	46	83	7	19	5	1	1	8	7	16	.229	.289	.349	86	-2	1	1	-0	.908	1	3-32/S-3,O	-0.1
1994	Tex-A	1	2	0	0	0	0	0	0	0	0	.000	.000	.000	-99	-1	0	0	0	.000	0	/3-1	-0.1
Total	3	82	156	10	34	8	1	2	14	14	35	.218	.282	.321	69	-7	2	2	-1	.928	0	/3-49,O-16,S	-0.8

■ DARRIN JACKSON Jackson, Darrin Jay b: 8/22/62, Los Angeles, Cal. BR/TR, 6'1", 170 lbs. Deb: 6/17/85

1985	Chi-N	5	11	0	1	0	0	0	0	0	3	.091	.091	.091	-44	-2	0	0	0	1.000	-1	/O-4	-0.3
1987	Chi-N	7	5	2	4	1	0	0	0	0	0	.800	.800	1.000	359	2	0	0	0	1.000	-2	/O-5	0.0
1988	Chi-N	100	188	29	50	11	3	6	20	5	28	.266	.289	.452	105	0	4	1	1	.983	-10	O-74	-1.1
1989	Chi-N	45	83	7	19	4	0	1	8	6	17	.229	.281	.313	65	-4	1	2	-1	.970	-1	O-39	-0.7
	SD-N	25	87	10	18	3	0	3	12	7	17	.207	.266	.345	73	-3	0	2	-1	.954	2	O-24	-0.3
	Yr	70	170	17	37	7	0	4	20	13	34	.218	.273	.329	68	-7	1	4	-2	.962	1	O-63	-1.0
1990	SD-N	58	113	10	29	3	0	3	9	5	24	.257	.288	.363	77	-4	3	0	1	.985	-5	O-39	-0.9
1991	SD-N	122	359	51	94	12	1	21	49	27	66	.262	.317	.476	117	7	5	3	-0	.992	7	O-98/P-1	1.2
1992	SD-N	155	587	72	146	23	5	17	70	26	106	.249	.285	.392	88	-11	14	3	2	.996	24	*O-153	1.4
1993	Tor-A	46	176	15	38	8	0	5	19	8	53	.216	.250	.347	58	-11	0	2	-1	.989	-2	O-46	-1.4
	NY-N	31	87	4	17	1	0	1	7	2	22	.195	.213	.241	22	-10	0	0	0	1.000	3	O-26	-0.8
1994	Chi-A	104	369	43	115	17	3	10	51	27	56	.312	.363	.455	110	6	7	1	2	.996	0	*O-102	0.5
Total	9	698	2065	243	531	83	12	67	245	113	392	.257	.299	.406	91	-30	34	14	2	.990	15	O-610/P-1	-2.4

■ GEORGE JACKSON Jackson, George Christopher "Hickory" b: 10/14/1882, Springfield, Mo. d: 11/25/72, Cleburne, Tex. BR/TR, 6'0.5", 180 lbs. Deb: 8/2/11

1911	Bos-N	39	147	28	51	11	2	0	25	12	21	.347	.404	.449	128	5	12			.929	-2	O-39	0.1
1912	Bos-N	110	397	55	104	13	5	4	48	38	72	.262	.342	.350	88	-6	22			.943	2	*O-107	-1.0
1913	Bos-N	3	10	2	3	0	0	0	0	0	2	.300	.300	.300	70	-0	0			.875	0	/O-3	0.0
Total	3	152	554	85	158	24	7	4	73	50	95	.285	.357	.375	98	-1	34			.938	-0	O-149	-0.9

■ HENRY JACKSON Jackson, Henry Everett b: 6/23/1861, Union City, Ind. d: 9/14/32, Chicago, Ill. BR/TR, 6'2", 185 lbs. Deb: 9/13/1887

1887	Ind-N	10	38	1	10	1	0	0	3	0	12	.263	.263	.289	55	-2	2			.933	-1	1-10	-0.4

■ JIM JACKSON Jackson, James Benner b: 11/28/1877, Philadelphia, Pa. d: 10/9/55, Philadelphia, Pa. BR/TR, Deb: 4/26/01

1901	Bal-A	99	364	42	91	17	3	2	50	20		.250	.291	.330	69	-16	11			**.971**	3	O-96	-1.9
1902	NY-N	35	110	14	20	5	1	0	13	15		.182	.280	.245	63	-4	6			.897	-2	O-34	-1.0
1905	Cle-A	109	426	59	109	12	4	2	31	34		.256	.317	.317	100	0	15			.950	4	*O-106/3-3	-0.1
1906	Cle-A	105	374	44	80	13	2	0	38	38		.214	.290	.259	73	-10	25			.975	-6	*O-104	-2.3
Total	4	348	1274	159	300	47	10	4	132	107		.235	.298	.297	80	-31	57			.959	-1	O-340/3-3	-5.3

■ JOE JACKSON Jackson, Joseph Jefferson "Shoeless Joe" b: 7/16/1889, Pickens Co., S.C. d: 12/5/51, Greenville, S.C. BL/TR, 6'1", 200 lbs. Deb: 8/25/08

1908	Phi-A	5	23	0	3	0	0	0	3	0		.130	.130	.130	-14	-3	0			.875	-1	/O-5	-0.4
1909	Phi-A	5	17	3	3	0	0	0	3	1		.176	.222	.176	26	-1	0			.833	-1	/O-4	-0.2
1910	Cle-A	20	75	15	29	2	5	1	11	8		.387	.446	.587	220	10	4			.977	0	/O-20	1.0
1911	Cle-A	147	571	126	233	45	19	7	83	56		.408	**.468**	.590	192	70	41			.958	8	*O-147	6.8
1912	Cle-A	154	572	121	**226**	44	**26**	3	90	54		.395	.458	.579	190	66	35			.950	13	*O-150	6.9
1913	Cle-A	148	528	109	**197**	**39**	17	7	71	80	26	.373	.460	**.551**	190	**62**	26			.930	2	*O-148	6.0
1914	Cle-A	122	453	61	153	22	13	3	53	41	34	.338	.399	.464	153	28	22	15	-2	.967	2	*O-119	2.5
1915	Cle-A	83	303	42	99	16	9	3	45	28	11	.327	.389	.469	154	19	10	10	-3	.961	-4	O-49,1-30	1.0
	Chi-A	45	158	21	43	4	5	2	36	24	12	.272	.378	.399	129	6	6	10	-4	.947	-2	O-46	-0.2
	Yr	128	461	63	142	20	14	5	81	52	23	.308	.385	.445	145	25	16	20	-7	.953	-5	O-95,1-30	0.8
1916	Chi-A	155	592	91	202	40	**21**	3	78	46	25	.341	.393	.495	165	44	24	14	-1	.975	-1	*O-155	3.6
1917	*Chi-A	146	538	91	162	20	17	5	75	57	25	.301	.375	.429	142	27	13			.984	9	*O-145	3.1
1918	Chi-A	17	65	9	23	2	2	1	20	8	1	.354	.425	.492	175	6	3			1.000	-0	O-17	0.5
1919	*Chi-A	139	516	79	181	31	14	7	96	60	10	.351	.422	.506	159	41	9			.967	-4	*O-139	2.9
1920	Chi-A	146	570	105	218	42	**20**	12	121	56	14	.382	.444	.589	172	58	9	12	-5	.965	-1	*O-146	4.0
Total	13	1332	4981	873	1772	307	168	54	785	519	158	.356	.423	.517	169	433	202	61		.962	23	*O-1289/1-30	37.5

■ KEN JACKSON Jackson, Kenneth Bernard b: 8/21/63, Shreveport, La. BR/TR, 5'9", 170 lbs. Deb: 9/12/87

1987	Phi-N	8	16	1	4	1	0	0	1	4		.250	.333	.375	85	-0	0	0	0	.955	-1	/S-8	-0.1

YEAR	TM/L	G	AB	R	H	2B	3B	HR	RBI	BB	SO	AVG	OBP	SLG	PRO+	BR/A	SB	CS	SBR	FA	FR	G/POS	TPR

■ LOU JACKSON Jackson, Louis Clarence b: 7/26/35, Riverton, La. d: 5/27/69, Tokyo, Japan BL/TR, 5'10", 168 lbs. Deb: 7/23/58

1958	Chi-N	24	35	5	6	2	1	1	6	1	9	.171	.194	.371	46	-3	0	1	-1	1.000	-4	O-12	-0.8
1959	Chi-N	6	4	2	1	0	0	0	1	0	2	.250	.250	.250	34	-0	0	0	0	.000	0	H	0.0
1964	Bal-A	4	8	0	3	0	0	0	0	0	2	.375	.375	.375	110	0	0	0	0	1.000	1	/O-1	0.1
Total	3	34	47	7	10	2	1	1	7	1	13	.213	.229	.362	55	-3	0	1	-1	1.000	-4	O-13	-0.7

■ RANDY JACKSON Jackson, Ransom Joseph "Handsome Ransom" b: 2/10/26, Little Rock, Ark. BR/TR, 6'1.5", 180 lbs. Deb: 5/2/50

1950	Chi-N	34	111	13	25	4	3	3	6	7	25	.225	.271	.396	74	-5	4			.911	-4	3-27	-0.9
1951	Chi-N	145	557	78	153	24	6	16	76	47	44	.275	.332	.425	101	-1	14	3	2	.956	8	*3-143	0.8
1952	Chi-N	116	379	44	88	8	5	9	34	27	42	.232	.285	.351	75	-14	6	5	-1	.958	-3	*3-104/O-1	-2.0
1953	Chi-N	139	498	61	142	22	8	19	66	42	61	.285	.341	.476	108	5	8	4	0	.949	3	*3-133	0.5
1954	Chi-N★	126	484	77	132	17	6	19	67	44	55	.273	.336	.450	102	0	2	1	0	.955	-1	*3-124	-0.3
1955	Chi-N★	138	499	73	132	13	7	21	70	58	58	.265	.342	.445	107	5	0	2	-1	.949	-13	*3-134	-1.0
1956	*Bro-N	101	307	37	84	15	7	8	53	28	38	.274	.338	.446	101	0	2	1	0	.993	21	3-80	2.3
1957	Bro-N	48	131	7	26	1	0	2	16	9	20	.198	.250	.252	32	-12	0	0	0	.976	-2	3-34	-1.5
1958	LA-N	35	65	8	12	3	0	1	4	5	10	.185	.243	.277	36	-6	0	0	0	.964	7	3-17	0.1
	Cle-A	29	91	7	22	3	1	4	13	3	18	.242	.266	.429	90	-2	0	0	0	.901	5	3-24	0.4
1959	Cle-A	3	7	0	1	0	0	0	0	0	1	.143	.143	.143	-22	-1	0	0	0	1.000	-0	/3-2	-0.2
	Chi-N	41	74	7	18	5	1	1	10	11	10	.243	.341	.378	92	-1	0	0	0	.941	-3	3-22/O-1	-0.3
Total	10	955	3203	412	835	115	44	103	415	281	382	.261	.322	.421	94	-31	36	16		.955	18	3-844/O-2	-2.1

■ REGGIE JACKSON Jackson, Reginald Martinez b: 5/18/46, Wyncote, Pa. BL/TL, 6', 200 lbs. Deb: 6/9/67 H

1967	KC-A	35	118	13	21	4	4	1	6	10	46	.178	.271	.305	72	-4	1	1	-0	.933	-2	O-34	-0.9
1968	Oak-A	154	553	82	138	13	6	29	74	50	171	.250	.317	.452	138	23	14	4	2	.959	8	*O-151	2.8
1969	Oak-A★	152	549	123	151	36	3	47	118	114	142	.275	.410	.608	190	68	13	5	1	.964	5	*O-150	6.6
1970	Oak-A	149	426	57	101	21	2	23	66	75	135	.237	.361	.458	129	18	26	17	-2	.956	-11	*O-142	-0.2
1971	*Oak-A★	150	567	87	157	29	3	32	80	63	161	.277	.355	.508	145	32	16	10	-1	.977	9	*O-145	3.4
1972	*Oak-A★	135	499	72	132	25	2	25	75	59	125	.265	.352	.473	152	31	9	8	-2	.971	2	*O-135	2.7
1973	*Oak-A★	151	539	99	158	28	2	32	117	76	111	.293	.387	.531	165	46	22	8	2	.971	4	*O-145/D-3	4.6
1974	*Oak-A★	148	506	90	146	25	1	29	93	86	105	.289	.396	.514	171	48	25	5	5	.968	9	*O-127,D-19	5.6
1975	*Oak-A★	157	593	91	150	39	3	36	104	67	133	.253	.332	.511	138	27	17	8	0	.965	9	*O-147/D-9	3.0
1976	Bal-A	134	498	84	138	27	2	27	91	54	108	.277	.353	.502	158	34	28	7	4	.964	-2	*O-121,D-11	3.7
1977	*NY-A★	146	525	93	150	39	2	32	110	74	129	.286	.377	.550	151	37	17	3	-1	.949	-1	*O-127,D-18	3.3
1978	*NY-A†	139	511	82	140	13	5	27	97	58	133	.274	.358	.477	136	24	14	11	-2	.986	3	*O-125/D-3	1.9
1979	NY-A★	131	465	78	138	24	2	29	89	65	107	.297	.385	.544	151	33	9	8	-2	.986	7	*O-125/D-3	3.1
1980	*NY-A★	143	514	94	154	22	4	41	111	83	122	.300	.399	.597	172	51	1	2	-1	.962	-2	O-94,D-46	4.2
1981	*NY-A★	94	334	33	79	17	1	15	54	46	82	.237	.331	.428	119	8	0	3	-2	.974	-4	O-61,D-33	0.3
1982	*Cal-A★	153	530	92	146	17	1	39	101	85	156	.275	.378	.532	147	35	4	5	-2	.972	-18	*O-139/D-5	1.2
1983	Cal-A†	116	397	43	77	14	1	14	49	52	140	.194	.294	.340	74	-14	0	2	-1	.986	-5	D-62,O-47	-2.3
1984	Cal-A	143	525	67	117	17	2	25	81	55	141	.223	.300	.406	94	-5	8	4	0	1.000	-4	*D-134/O-3	-0.9
1985	Cal-A	143	460	64	116	27	0	27	85	78	138	.252	.362	.487	130	20	1	2	-1	.944	-9	O-81,D-52	0.7
1986	*Cal-A	132	419	65	101	12	2	18	58	92	115	.241	.381	.408	116	13	1	1	-0	.833	-0	*D-121/O-4	1.0
1987	Oak-A	115	336	42	74	14	1	15	43	33	97	.220	.298	.402	89	-6	2	1	0	1.000	-2	D-79,O-20	-1.0
Total	21	2820	9864	1551	2584	463	49	563	1702	1375	2597	.262	.358	.490	140	519	228	115	-1	.967	8	*O-2102,D-630	42.8

■ SONNY JACKSON Jackson, Roland Thomas b: 7/9/44, Washington, D.C. BL/TR, 5'9", 155 lbs. Deb: 9/27/63 C

1963	Hou-N	1	3	0	0	0	0	0	0	0	1	.000	.000	.000	-99	-1	0	0	0	.833	1	/S-1	0.0
1964	Hou-N	9	23	3	8	1	0	0	1	2	3	.348	.400	.391	131	1	1	0	0	.870	-4	/S-7	-0.2
1965	Hou-N	10	23	1	3	0	0	0	0	1	1	.130	.167	.130	-16	-4	1	1	-0	.969	-1	/S-8,3-1	-0.4
1966	Hou-N	150	596	80	174	6	5	3	25	42	53	.292	.342	.334	95	-3	49	14	6	.951	-13	*S-150	0.4
1967	Hou-N	129	520	67	123	18	3	0	25	36	45	.237	.286	.283	66	-23	22	9	1	.943	-8	*S-128	-1.9
1968	Atl-N	105	358	37	81	8	2	1	19	25	35	.226	.282	.268	66	-14	16	6	1	.952	-17	S-99	-2.4
1969	*Atl-N	98	318	41	76	3	5	1	27	35	33	.239	.318	.289	71	-11	12	7	-1	.961	-23	S-97	-2.6
1970	Atl-N	103	328	60	85	14	3	0	20	45	27	.259	.350	.320	76	-10	11	4	1	.933	-23	S-87	-2.1
1971	Atl-N	149	547	58	141	20	5	2	25	35	45	.258	.304	.324	73	-19	7	6	-2	.980	3	*O-145	-2.7
1972	Atl-N	60	126	20	30	6	3	0	8	7	9	.238	.278	.333	67	-6	1	0	0	.976	-5	S-17,O-10/3	-1.0
1973	Atl-N	117	206	29	43	7	2	0	12	22	13	.209	.288	.252	47	-14	5	3	0	.981	-14	O-56,S-36	-2.7
1974	Atl-N	5	7	0	3	0	0	0	0	0	0	.429	.429	.429	134	-0	0	1	-1	1.000	-0	/O-1	-0.1
Total	12	936	3055	396	767	81	28	7	162	250	265	.251	.300	.303	73	-104	126	51	7	.949	-104	S-630,O-212/3	-15.6

■ RON JACKSON Jackson, Ronald Harris b: 10/22/33, Kalamazoo, Mich. BR/TR, 6'7", 225 lbs. Deb: 6/15/54

1954	Chi-A	40	93	10	26	4	0	4	10	6	20	.280	.337	.452	111	1	2	1	0	.988	-3	1-35	-0.3
1955	Chi-A	40	74	10	15	1	1	2	7	8	22	.203	.280	.324	61	-4	1	0	0	.988	-1	1-29	-0.6
1956	Chi-A	22	56	7	12	3	0	1	4	10	13	.214	.333	.321	73	-2	1	0	0	1.000	1	1-19	-0.2
1957	Chi-A	13	60	4	19	3	0	2	8	1	12	.317	.328	.467	114	1	0	0	0	.992	-1	1-13	-0.1
1958	Chi-A	61	146	19	34	4	0	7	21	18	46	.233	.325	.404	101	0	2	0	0	.997	-2	1-38	-0.3
1959	Chi-A	10	14	3	3	0	0	1	2	1	0	.214	.313	.500	121	0	0	0	0	1.000	-0	/1-5	0.0
1960	Bos-A	10	31	1	7	3	0	0	0	1	6	.226	.250	.290	44	-2	0	0	0	.973	-0	/1-9	-0.3
Total	7	196	474	54	116	18	1	17	52	45	119	.245	.317	.395	92	-6	6	1	0	.992	-6	1-148	-1.8

■ RON JACKSON Jackson, Ronnie Damien b: 5/9/53, Birmingham, Ala. BR/TR, 6', 205 lbs. Deb: 9/12/75

1975	Cal-A	13	39	2	9	2	0	2	6	2	10	.231	.268	.282	60	-2	1	1	-0	.947	-0	/O-9,3-3,D	-0.3
1976	Cal-A	127	410	44	93	18	3	8	40	30	58	.227	.291	.344	91	-6	5	4	-1	.950	1	*3-114/2-7,OD	-0.7
1977	Cal-A	106	292	38	71	15	2	6	28	24	42	.243	.303	.390	91	-4	3	2	-0	.990	2	1-75,3-31/OD	-0.6
1978	Cal-A	105	387	49	115	18	6	6	57	16	51	.297	.340	.421	117	8	2	3	-1	.994	-3	1-75,3-31/OD	0.1
1979	Min-A	159	583	85	158	40	6	14	68	51	59	.271	.339	.429	102	1	3	1	0	.994	11	*1-157/S-1,3O	0.3
1980	Min-A	131	396	48	105	29	3	5	42	28	41	.265	.319	.391	87	-7	1	8	-5	.991	-1	*1-119,O-15/3D	-1.9
1981	Min-A	54	175	17	46	9	2	3	20	10	15	.263	.306	.383	91	-1	5	2	-1	.988	1	1-36/O-7,3D	-0.4
	Det-A	31	95	12	27	8	1	2	18	8	11	.284	.340	.421	114	2	4	1	1	1.000	-1	1-29	0.0
	Yr	85	270	29	73	17	1	5	40	18	26	.270	.318	.396	99	-1	6	3	0	.993	1	1-65/O-7,D3	-0.4
1982	*Cal-A	53	142	15	47	6	0	2	19	10	12	.331	.383	.415	119	4	0	1	-0	.994	0	1-37/3-9	0.2
1983	Cal-A	102	348	41	80	16	1	8	39	27	33	.230	.291	.351	76	-12	2	2	-1	.957	-2	3-38,1-35,DO	-1.4
1984	Cal-A	33	91	5	15	2	1	0	5	7	13	.165	.224	.209	21	-10	0	2	-0	.990	-0	1-21/3-9,O	-1.1
	Bal-A	12	28	0	8	2	0	0	2	0	4	.286	.286	.357	78	-1	0	0	0	.960	2	3-10	-0.1
	Yr	45	119	5	23	4	1	0	7	7	17	.193	.238	.244	34	-11	0	2	-0	.990	1	1-21,3-19/O	-1.1
Total	10	926	2986	356	774	165	22	56	342	213	329	.259	.316	.385	94	-29	23	27	-9	.993	14	1-552,3-250/OD2S	-6.1

■ SAM JACKSON Jackson, Samuel b: 3/24/1849, Ripon, England d: 8/4/1893, Clifton Springs, N.Y. BR/TR, 5'5", 160 lbs. Deb: 5/16/1871

1871	Bos-n	16	76	17	17	5	3	0	11	1	4	.224	.234	.368	67	-4	0					2-14/O-1	-0.3
1872	Atl-n	3	12	0	2	1	0	0	0	0	0	.167	.167	.250	23	-1						/O-3	-0.1
Total	2 n	19	88	17	19	6	3	0	11	1	4	.216	.225	.352	61	-5						/2-14,O-4	-0.4

■ TRAVIS JACKSON Jackson, Travis Calvin "Stonewall" b: 11/2/03, Waldo, Ark. d: 7/27/87, Waldo, Ark. BR/TR, 5'10.5", 160 lbs. Deb: 9/27/22 CH

1922	NY-N	3	8	1	0	0	0	0	0	0	2	.000	.000	.000	-99	-2	0	0	0	.909	0	/S-3	-0.2

YEAR	TM/L	G	AB	R	H	2B	3B	HR	RBI	BB	SO	AVG	OBP	SLG	PRO+	BR/A	SB	CS	SBR	FA	FR	G/POS	TPR
1923	*NY-N	96	327	45	90	12	7	4	37	22	40	.275	.321	.391	88	-6	3	3	-1	.943	-3	S-60,3-31/2	-0.3
1924	*NY-N	151	596	81	180	26	8	11	76	21	56	.302	.326	.428	103	1	6	7	-2	.937	-0	*S-151	1.5
1925	NY-N	112	411	51	117	15	2	9	59	24	43	.285	.327	.397	87	-9	8	3	1	.941	5	*S-110	0.8
1926	NY-N	111	385	64	126	24	8	8	51	20	26	.327	.362	.494	130	14	2			.962	1	*S-108/O-1	2.6
1927	NY-N	127	469	67	149	29	4	14	98	32	30	.318	.363	.486	126	16	8			.952	28	*S-124/3-2	5.4
1928	NY-N	150	537	73	145	35	6	14	77	56	46	.270	.339	.436	101	-1	8			.952	28	*S-149	4.3
1929	NY-N	149	551	92	162	21	12	21	94	64	56	.294	.367	.490	111	8	10			**.969**	19	*S-149	4.1
1930	NY-N	116	431	70	146	27	8	13	82	32	25	.339	.386	.529	121	14	6			.956	11	*S-115	3.3
1931	NY-N	145	555	65	172	26	10	5	71	36	23	.310	.353	.420	110	7	13			**.970**	10	*S-145	3.1
1932	NY-N	52	195	23	50	17	1	4	38	13	16	.256	.310	.415	95	-2	1			.925	-5	S-52	-0.2
1933	*NY-N	53	122	11	30	5	0	1	12	8	11	.246	.292	.287	67	-5	2			.890	7	S-21,3-21	0.4
1934	NY-N★	137	523	75	140	26	7	16	101	37	71	.268	.316	.436	102	-0	1			.945	12	*S-130/3-9	1.9
1935	NY-N	128	511	74	154	20	12	9	80	29	64	.301	.340	.440	110	6	3			.947	-7	*3-128	0.4
1936	*NY-N	126	465	41	107	8	1	7	53	18	56	.230	.260	.297	50	-33	0			.952	-1	*3-116/S-9	-2.9
Total	15	1656	6086	833	1768	291	86	135	929	412	565	.291	.337	.433	102	7	71	13		.952	104	*S-1326,3-307/O2	24.2

■ BO JACKSON
Jackson, Vincent Edward   b: 11/30/62, Bessemer, Ala.   BR/TR, 6'1", 225 lbs.   Deb: 9/2/86

YEAR	TM/L	G	AB	R	H	2B	3B	HR	RBI	BB	SO	AVG	OBP	SLG	PRO+	BR/A	SB	CS	SBR	FA	FR	G/POS	TPR
1986	KC-A	25	82	9	17	2	1	2	9	7	34	.207	.286	.329	66	-4	3	1	0	.886	-3	O-23/D-1	-0.7
1987	KC-A	116	396	46	93	17	2	22	53	30	158	.235	.297	.455	93	-5	10	4	1	.955	-7	*O-113/D-1	-1.5
1988	KC-A	124	439	63	108	16	4	25	68	25	146	.246	.288	.472	108	2	27	6	5	.973	6	*O-121/D-2	1.0
1989	KC-A★	135	515	86	132	15	6	32	105	39	172	.256	.312	.495	125	14	26	9	2	.967	7	*O-110,D-24	2.1
1990	KC-A	111	405	74	110	16	1	28	78	44	128	.272	.346	.523	142	21	15	9	-1	.952	8	O-97,D-10	2.6
1991	Chi-A	23	71	8	16	4	0	3	14	12	25	.225	.337	.408	108	1	0	1	-1	.000	0	D-21	-0.1
1993	*Chi-A	85	284	32	66	9	0	16	45	23	106	.232	.290	.433	94	-4	0	2	-1	.989	3	O-47,D-36	-0.5
1994	Cal-A	75	201	23	56	7	0	13	43	20	72	.279	.347	.507	113	3	1	0	0	.964	-2	O-46/D-9	0.1
Total	8	694	2393	341	598	86	14	141	415	200	841	.250	.311	.474	112	29	82	32	5	.962	12	O-557,D-104	3.0

■ BILL JACKSON
Jackson, William Riley   b: 4/4/1881, Pittsburgh, Pa.   d: 9/24/58, Peoria, Ill.   BL/TL, 5'11.5", 160 lbs.   Deb: 4/30/14

YEAR	TM/L	G	AB	R	H	2B	3B	HR	RBI	BB	SO	AVG	OBP	SLG	PRO+	BR/A	SB	CS	SBR	FA	FR	G/POS	TPR
1914	Chi-F	26	25	2	1	0	0	0	1	3	5	.040	.143	.040	-54	-6	0			.917	0	/O-6,1-4	-0.6
1915	Chi-F	50	98	15	16	1	0	1	12	14	15	.163	.268	.204	29	-10	3			.983	0	1-36/O-1	-1.2
Total	2	76	123	17	17	1	0	1	13	17	20	.138	.243	.171	12	-16	3			.984	0	/1-40,O-7	-1.8

■ SPOOK JACOBS
Jacobs, Forrest Vandergrift   b: 11/4/25, Cheswold, Del.   BR/TR, 5'8.5", 155 lbs.   Deb: 4/13/54

YEAR	TM/L	G	AB	R	H	2B	3B	HR	RBI	BB	SO	AVG	OBP	SLG	PRO+	BR/A	SB	CS	SBR	FA	FR	G/POS	TPR
1954	Phi-A	132	508	63	131	11	1	0	26	60	22	.258	.336	.283	71	-18	17	3	3	.974	-19	*2-131	-2.7
1955	KC-A	13	23	7	6	0	0	0	1	3	0	.261	.370	.261	71	-1	1	2	-1	1.000	-3	/2-7	-0.4
1956	KC-A	32	97	13	21	3	0	0	5	15	5	.216	.321	.247	52	-6	4	1	1	.968	-4	2-31	-0.7
	Pit-N	11	37	4	6	2	0	0	1	2	5	.162	.225	.216	20	-4	0	2	-1	.926	-4	2-11	-0.9
Total	3	188	665	87	164	16	1	0	33	80	32	.247	.329	.274	65	-30	22	8	2	.971	-29	2-180	-4.7

■ JAKE JACOBS
Jacobs, Lamar Gary   b: 6/9/37, Youngstown, Ohio   BR/TR, 6', 175 lbs.   Deb: 9/13/60

YEAR	TM/L	G	AB	R	H	2B	3B	HR	RBI	BB	SO	AVG	OBP	SLG	PRO+	BR/A	SB	CS	SBR	FA	FR	G/POS	TPR
1960	Was-A	6	2	0	0	0	0	0	0	0	0	.000	.000	.000	-99	-1	0	0	0	.000	0	H	-0.1
1961	Min-A	4	8	0	2	0	0	0	0	0	2	.250	.250	.250	32	-1	0	0	0	1.000	-1	/O-3	-0.2
Total	2	10	10	0	2	0	0	0	0	0	2	.200	.200	.200	7	-1	0	0	0	1.000	-1	/O-3	-0.3

■ MIKE JACOBS
Jacobs, Morris Elmore   b: 12/1877, Louisville, Ky.   d: 3/21/49, Louisville, Ky.   Deb: 7/16/02

YEAR	TM/L	G	AB	R	H	2B	3B	HR	RBI	BB	SO	AVG	OBP	SLG	PRO+	BR/A	SB	CS	SBR	FA	FR	G/POS	TPR
1902	Chi-N	5	19	1	4	0	0	0	2	0		.211	.211	.211	31	-2	0			.880	-2	/S-5	-0.3

■ OTTO JACOBS
Jacobs, Otto Albert   b: 4/19/1889, Chicago, Ill.   d: 11/19/55, Chicago, Ill.   BR/TR, 5'9", 180 lbs.   Deb: 6/13/18

YEAR	TM/L	G	AB	R	H	2B	3B	HR	RBI	BB	SO	AVG	OBP	SLG	PRO+	BR/A	SB	CS	SBR	FA	FR	G/POS	TPR
1918	Chi-A	29	73	4	15	3	1	0	3	5	8	.205	.256	.274	59	-4	0			.955	-4	C-21	-0.7

■ RAY JACOBS
Jacobs, Raymond F.   b: 1/2/02, Salt Lake City, Utah   d: 4/5/52, Los Angeles, Cal.   BR/TR, 6', 160 lbs.   Deb: 4/20/28

YEAR	TM/L	G	AB	R	H	2B	3B	HR	RBI	BB	SO	AVG	OBP	SLG	PRO+	BR/A	SB	CS	SBR	FA	FR	G/POS	TPR
1928	Chi-N	2	5	0	0	0	0	0	0	0	0	.000	.000	.000	-99	-1	0			.000	0	H	-0.1

■ MERWIN JACOBSON
Jacobson, Merwin John William "Jake"   b: 3/7/1894, New Britain, Conn.   d: 1/13/78, Baltimore, Md.   BL/TL, 5'11.5", 165 lbs.   Deb: 9/8/15

YEAR	TM/L	G	AB	R	H	2B	3B	HR	RBI	BB	SO	AVG	OBP	SLG	PRO+	BR/A	SB	CS	SBR	FA	FR	G/POS	TPR
1915	NY-N	8	24	0	2	0	0	0	0	1	5	.083	.120	.083	-40	-4	0			.909	1	/O-5	-0.5
1916	Chi-N	4	13	2	3	0	0	0	0	1		.231	.286	.231	54	-1	2			1.000	0	/O-4	-0.1
1926	Bro-N	110	288	41	71	9	2	0	23	36	28	.247	.330	.292	70	-11	5			.975	-3	O-86	-1.9
1927	Bro-N	11	6	4	0	0	0	0	1	0	1	.000	.000	.000	-99	-2	0			1.000	-1	/O-3	-0.3
Total	4	133	331	47	76	9	2	0	24	38	34	.230	.309	.269	59	-18	7			.973	-4	/O-98	-2.8

■ BABY DOLL JACOBSON
Jacobson, William Chester   b: 8/16/1890, Cable, Ill.   d: 1/16/77, Orion, Ill.   BR/TR, 6'3", 215 lbs.   Deb: 4/14/15

YEAR	TM/L	G	AB	R	H	2B	3B	HR	RBI	BB	SO	AVG	OBP	SLG	PRO+	BR/A	SB	CS	SBR	FA	FR	G/POS	TPR
1915	Det-A	37	65	5	14	6	2	0	4	5	14	.215	.282	.369	90	-1	0	2	-1	.983	-2	1-10/O-7	-0.6
	StL-A	34	115	13	24	6	1	1	9	10	26	.209	.295	.304	82	-3	3	3	-1	.981	-1	O-32	-0.7
	Yr	71	180	18	38	12	3	1	13	15	40	.211	.290	.328	84	-4	3	5	-2	.984	-4	O-39,1-10	-1.3
1917	StL-A	148	529	53	131	23	7	4	55	31	67	.248	.294	.340	97	-4	10			.975	7	*O-131,1-11	-0.5
1919	StL-A	120	455	70	147	31	8	4	51	24	47	.323	.362	.453	125	13	9			.949	1	*O-106/1-8	0.7
1920	StL-A	154	609	97	216	34	14	9	122	46	37	.355	.402	.501	134	29	11	7	-1	.979	11	*O-154/1-1	2.6
1921	StL-A	151	599	90	211	38	14	5	90	42	30	.352	.398	.487	118	15	8	8	-2	.982	5	*O-142,1-11	0.7
1922	StL-A	145	555	88	176	22	16	9	102	46	36	.317	.379	.463	114	11	19	6	-2	.969	6	*O-137/1-7	0.7
1923	StL-A	147	592	76	183	29	6	8	81	29	27	.309	.343	.419	95	-6	6	6	-2	.974	8	*O-146	-1.0
1924	StL-A	152	579	103	184	41	12	19	97	35	45	.318	.361	.528	120	13	6	8	-3	.986	16	*O-152	1.5
1925	StL-A	142	540	103	184	30	9	15	76	45	26	.341	.392	.513	122	16	8	11	-4	.965	1	*O-139	0.4
1926	StL-A	50	182	18	52	15	1	2	21	9	14	.286	.319	.412	86	-5	1	2	-1	.964	-6	O-50	-1.5
	Bos-A	98	394	44	120	36	1	6	69	22	22	.305	.344	.447	109	3	4	1	1	.980	-8	O-98	-1.1
	Yr	148	576	62	172	51	2	8	90	31	36	.299	.337	.436	101	-2	5	3	-0	.975	-15	*O-148	-2.6
1927	Bos-A	45	155	11	38	9	3	0	24	5	12	.245	.278	.342	61	-9	1	0	0	.979	1	O-39	-1.0
	Cle-A	32	103	13	26	5	0	1	13	6	4	.252	.300	.301	56	-7	0	0	0	.932	-1	O-31	-0.9
	Phi-A	17	35	3	8	3	0	0	5	0	1	.229	.229	.400	57	-2	0	0	0	1.000	-5	O-14	-0.8
	Yr	94	293	27	72	17	3	1	42	11	9	.246	.280	.334	59	-19	1	0	0	.959	-5	O-84	-2.7
Total	11	1472	5507	787	1714	328	94	83	819	355	410	.311	.357	.450	111	63	86	54		.973	29	*O-1378/1-48	-1.5

■ BROOK JACOBY
Jacoby, Brook Wallace   b: 11/23/59, Philadelphia, Pa.   BR/TR, 5'11", 195 lbs.   Deb: 9/13/81

YEAR	TM/L	G	AB	R	H	2B	3B	HR	RBI	BB	SO	AVG	OBP	SLG	PRO+	BR/A	SB	CS	SBR	FA	FR	G/POS	TPR
1981	Atl-N	11	10	0	2	0	0	0	0	0	3	.200	.200	.200	13	-2	0	0	0	1.000	2	/3-3	0.1
1983	Atl-N	4	8	0	0	0	0	0	0	0	1	.000	.000	.000	-93	-2	0	0	0	1.000	0	/3-2	-0.3
1984	Cle-A	126	439	64	116	19	3	7	40	32	73	.264	.319	.369	88	-7	3	2	-0	.951	-20	*3-126/S-1	-2.9
1985	Cle-A	161	606	72	166	26	3	20	87	48	120	.274	.327	.426	105	3	2	3	-1	.958	-7	*3-161/2-1	-0.7
1986	Cle-A★	158	583	83	168	30	4	17	80	56	137	.288	.351	.441	116	13	2	1	0	.941	-13	*3-158	-0.3
1987	Cle-A	155	540	73	162	26	4	32	69	75	73	.300	.388	.541	142	33	2	3	-1	.946	-7	*3-144/1-7,D	2.1
1988	Cle-A	152	552	59	133	25	0	9	49	48	101	.241	.303	.335	76	-17	2	1	0	.975	4	*3-151	-1.9
1989	Cle-A	147	519	49	141	26	5	13	64	62	90	.272	.353	.416	114	10	2	5	-2	.955	-10	*3-144/D-3	-0.1
1990	Cle-A★	155	553	77	162	24	4	14	75	63	58	.293	.367	.427	122	17	1	4	-2	.981	-12	*3-155	-0.2
1991	Cle-A	66	231	14	54	19	4	4	24	16	32	.234	.289	.333	71	-9	0	1	-1	.988	-0	1-55,3-15	-1.3
	Oak-A	56	188	14	40	12	0	0	20	11	22	.213	.260	.277	51	-13	2	0	1	.982	-8	3-52/1-3	-2.1
	Yr	122	419	28	94	21	4	4	44	27	54	.224	.276	.308	63	-22	2	1	0	.987	-8	3-67,1-58	-3.4

YEAR	TM/L	G	AB	R	H	2B	3B	HR	RBI	BB	SO	AVG	OBP	SLG	PRO+	BR/A	SB	CS	SBR	FA	FR	G/POS	TPR
1992	Cle-A	120	291	30	76	7	0	4	36	28	54	.261	.328	.326	85	-5	0	3	-2	.957	3	*3-111,1-10	-0.5
Total	11	1311	4520	535	1220	204	24	120	545	439	764	.270	.337	.405	104	22	16	25	-10	.958	-71	*3-1166,1-153/D2S	-8.1

■ HARRY JACOBY
Jacoby, Harry   b: Philadelphia, Pa.   Deb: 5/2/1882

YEAR	TM/L	G	AB	R	H	2B	3B	HR	RBI	BB	SO	AVG	OBP	SLG	PRO+	BR/A	SB	CS	SBR	FA	FR	G/POS	TPR
1882	Bal-a	31	121	17	21	1	1	1		7		.174	.219	.223	53	-5				.776	8	3-19,O-13	0.3
1885	Bal-a	11	43	4	6	2	0	0		2		.140	.178	.186	15	-4				.896	-8	2-11	-1.1
Total	2	42	164	21	27	3	1	1		9		.165	.208	.213	43	-9				.776	-0	/3-19,O-13,2	-0.8

■ JOHN JAHA
Jaha, John Emil   b: 5/27/66, Portland, Ore.   BR/TR, 6'1", 195 lbs.   Deb: 7/9/92

YEAR	TM/L	G	AB	R	H	2B	3B	HR	RBI	BB	SO	AVG	OBP	SLG	PRO+	BR/A	SB	CS	SBR	FA	FR	G/POS	TPR
1992	Mil-A	47	133	17	30	3	1	2	10	12	30	.226	.299	.308	72	-5	10	0	3	1.000	-0	1-38/O-1,D	-0.4
1993	Mil-A	153	515	78	136	21	0	19	70	51	109	.264	.340	.416	103	2	13	9	-2	.992	9	*1-150/2-1,3	-0.3
1994	Mil-A	84	291	45	70	14	0	12	39	32	75	.241	.336	.412	90	-4	3	3	-1	.989	-1	1-73,D-11	-1.2
Total	3	284	939	140	236	38	1	33	119	95	214	.251	.333	.399	95	-7	26	12	1	.992	7	1-261/D-19,32O	-1.9

■ ART JAHN
Jahn, Arthur Charles   b: 12/2/1895, Struble, Iowa   d: 1/9/48, Little Rock, Ark.   BR/TR, 6', 180 lbs.   Deb: 7/2/25

YEAR	TM/L	G	AB	R	H	2B	3B	HR	RBI	BB	SO	AVG	OBP	SLG	PRO+	BR/A	SB	CS	SBR	FA	FR	G/POS	TPR
1925	Chi-N	58	226	30	68	10	8	0	37	11	20	.301	.336	.416	90	-4	2	2	-1	.985	2	O-58	-0.6
1928	NY-N	10	29	4	8	1	0	1	7	2	5	.276	.323	.414	91	-0	0			1.000	1	/O-8	0.0
	Phi-N	36	94	8	21	4	0	0	11	4	11	.223	.270	.266	39	-8	0			.978	-4	O-29	-1.4
	Yr	46	123	15	29	5	0	1	18	6	16	.236	.282	.301	51	-9	0			.985	-3	O-37	-1.4
Total	2	104	349	45	97	15	8	1	55	17	36	.278	.317	.375	76	-13	2	2		.985	-2	/O-95	-2.0

■ ART JAMES
James, Arthur   b: 8/2/52, Detroit, Mich.   BL/TL, 6', 170 lbs.   Deb: 4/10/75

YEAR	TM/L	G	AB	R	H	2B	3B	HR	RBI	BB	SO	AVG	OBP	SLG	PRO+	BR/A	SB	CS	SBR	FA	FR	G/POS	TPR
1975	Det-A	11	40	2	9	2	0	0	1	1	3	.225	.244	.275	44	-3	1	2	-1	1.000	2	O-11	-0.3

■ BERT JAMES
James, Berton Hulon "Jesse"   b: 7/7/1886, Coopertown, Tenn.   d: 1/2/59, Adairville, Ky.   BL/TR, 5'11", 175 lbs.   Deb: 9/18/09

YEAR	TM/L	G	AB	R	H	2B	3B	HR	RBI	BB	SO	AVG	OBP	SLG	PRO+	BR/A	SB	CS	SBR	FA	FR	G/POS	TPR
1909	StL-N	6	21	1	6	0	0	0	4			.286	.400	.286	120	1	1			.909	0	/O-6	0.1

■ CHARLIE JAMES
James, Charles Wesley   b: 12/22/37, St.Louis, Mo.   BR/TR, 6'1", 195 lbs.   Deb: 8/2/60

YEAR	TM/L	G	AB	R	H	2B	3B	HR	RBI	BB	SO	AVG	OBP	SLG	PRO+	BR/A	SB	CS	SBR	FA	FR	G/POS	TPR
1960	StL-N	43	50	5	9	1	0	2	5	1	12	.180	.196	.320	35	-5	0	0	0	.917	-10	O-37	-1.6
1961	StL-N	108	349	43	89	19	2	4	44	15	59	.255	.292	.355	64	-18	2	2	-1	.962	-6	O-90	-3.0
1962	StL-N	129	388	50	107	13	4	8	59	10	58	.276	.301	.392	77	-13	3	4	-2	.988	-10	*O-116	-3.0
1963	StL-N	116	347	34	93	14	2	10	45	10	64	.268	.292	.406	91	-5	2	1	0	.994	-5	*O-101	-1.0
1964	*StL-N	88	233	24	52	9	1	5	17	11	58	.223	.261	.335	61	-12	0	1	0	.963	-3	O-60	-1.9
1965	Cin-N	26	39	2	8	0	0	0	2	1	9	.205	.225	.205	21	-4	0	0	0	.909	-1	/O-7	-0.5
Total	6	510	1406	158	358	56	9	29	172	48	260	.255	.284	.369	71	-57	7	8		.976	-29	O-411	-11.0

■ CLEO JAMES
James, Cleo Joel   b: 8/31/40, Clarksdale, Miss.   BR/TR, 5'10", 176 lbs.   Deb: 4/15/68

YEAR	TM/L	G	AB	R	H	2B	3B	HR	RBI	BB	SO	AVG	OBP	SLG	PRO+	BR/A	SB	CS	SBR	FA	FR	G/POS	TPR
1968	LA-N	10	10	2	2	1	0	0	0	0	6	.200	.200	.300	52	-1	0	0	0	1.000	-0	/O-2	-0.1
1970	Chi-N	100	176	33	37	7	2	3	14	17	24	.210	.298	.324	59	-10	5	0	2	1.000	-10	O-90	-2.1
1971	Chi-N	54	150	25	43	7	0	2	13	10	16	.287	.355	.373	93	-1	6	2	1	.979	-1	O-48/3-2	-0.4
1973	Chi-N	44	45	9	5	0	0	0	0	1	6	.111	.130	.111	-30	-8	5	0	2	.960	-4	O-22	-1.1
Total	4	208	381	69	87	15	2	5	27	28	52	.228	.300	.318	63	-20	16	2	4	.988	-15	O-162/3-2	-3.7

■ DION JAMES
James, Dion   b: 11/9/62, Philadelphia, Pa.   BL/TL, 6'1", 170 lbs.   Deb: 9/16/83

YEAR	TM/L	G	AB	R	H	2B	3B	HR	RBI	BB	SO	AVG	OBP	SLG	PRO+	BR/A	SB	CS	SBR	FA	FR	G/POS	TPR
1983	Mil-A	11	20	1	2	0	0	0	1	2	2	.100	.182	.100	-22	-3	1	0	1	1.000	-3	/O-9,D-2	-0.7
1984	Mil-A	128	387	52	114	19	5	1	30	32	41	.295	.353	.377	106	4	10	10	-3	.989	-1	*O-118	-0.4
1985	Mil-A	18	49	5	11	1	0	0	3	6	6	.224	.309	.245	54	-3	0	0	0	1.000	-2	O-11/D-3	-0.5
1987	Atl-N	134	494	80	154	37	6	10	61	70	63	.312	.399	.472	124	19	10	8	-2	.996	1	*O-126	1.3
1988	Atl-N	132	386	46	99	17	5	3	30	58	59	.256	.355	.350	98	1	9	9	-3	.987	-12	*O-120	-1.9
1989	Atl-N	63	170	15	44	7	0	1	11	25	23	.259	.357	.318	92	-1	1	3	-2	1.000	-0	O-46/1-8	-0.4
	Cle-A	71	245	26	75	11	0	4	29	24	26	.306	.368	.400	114	5	1	4	-2	.976	-7	O-37,D-27/1	0.2
1990	Cle-A	87	248	28	68	15	2	1	22	27	23	.274	.348	.363	99	-0	5	3	-0	.996	-5	1-35,O-33,D	-0.8
1992	NY-A	67	145	24	38	8	0	3	17	22	15	.262	.363	.379	109	2	1	0	0	1.000	-8	O-46/D-5	-0.6
1993	NY-A	115	343	62	114	21	2	7	36	31	31	.332	.391	.466	134	17	0	0	0	.966	-14	*O-103/1-1,D	0.0
Total	9	826	2487	339	719	136	20	30	240	297	289	.289	.367	.396	110	41	38	37	-11	.986	-45	O-649/D-48,1	-3.8

■ CHRIS JAMES
James, Donald Chris   b: 10/4/62, Rusk, Tex.   BR/TR, 6'1", 195 lbs.   Deb: 4/23/86

YEAR	TM/L	G	AB	R	H	2B	3B	HR	RBI	BB	SO	AVG	OBP	SLG	PRO+	BR/A	SB	CS	SBR	FA	FR	G/POS	TPR
1986	Phi-N	16	46	5	13	3	0	1	5	1	13	.283	.298	.413	91	-1	0	0	0	1.000	-1	O-11	-0.2
1987	Phi-N	115	358	48	105	20	6	17	54	27	67	.293	.346	.525	123	11	3	1	0	.990	-2	*O-108	0.6
1988	Phi-N	150	566	57	137	24	1	19	66	31	73	.242	.285	.389	90	-9	7	4	-0	.989	-4	*O-116/3-31	-1.8
1989	Phi-N	45	179	14	37	4	0	2	19	4	23	.207	.224	.263	39	-14	3	1	0	.985	-1	O-37,3-11	-1.8
	SD-N	87	303	41	80	13	2	11	46	22	45	.264	.316	.429	111	3	2	1	0	.987	-0	O-79/3-6	0.1
	Yr	132	482	55	117	17	2	13	65	26	68	.243	.283	.367	84	-11	5	2	0	.986	-1	*O-116,3-17	-1.7
1990	Cle-A	140	528	62	158	32	4	12	70	31	71	.299	.343	.443	119	12	4	3	-1	1.000	0	*D-124,O-14	0.7
1991	Cle-A	115	437	31	104	16	2	5	41	18	61	.238	.275	.318	63	-22	3	4	-2	1.000	0	D-60,O-39,1	-2.8
1992	SF-N	111	248	25	60	10	4	5	32	14	45	.242	.288	.375	91	-4	2	3	-1	.974	1	O-62	-0.6
1993	Hou-N	65	129	19	33	10	1	6	19	15	34	.256	.338	.488	122	4	2	0	1	.958	3	O-34	0.6
	Tex-A	8	31	5	11	1	0	3	7	3	6	.355	.412	.677	195	4	0	0	0	1.000	-1	/O-7	0.3
1994	Tex-A	52	133	28	34	8	4	7	19	20	38	.256	.365	.534	137	7	0	0	0	1.000	-6	O-48	0.0
Total	9	904	2958	335	772	141	24	88	378	186	476	.261	.309	.414	99	-9	26	17		.987	-11	O-555,D-184/31	-4.9

■ SKIP JAMES
James, Philip Robert   b: 10/21/49, Elmhurst, Ill.   BL/TL, 6', 185 lbs.   Deb: 9/12/77

YEAR	TM/L	G	AB	R	H	2B	3B	HR	RBI	BB	SO	AVG	OBP	SLG	PRO+	BR/A	SB	CS	SBR	FA	FR	G/POS	TPR
1977	SF-N	10	15	3	4	1	0	0	3	3	3	.267	.353	.333	86	-0	0	0	0	1.000	1	/1-9	0.0
1978	SF-N	41	21	5	2	1	0	0	3	4	5	.095	.240	.143	10	-3	1	0	0	1.000	2	1-27	-0.1
Total	2	51	36	8	6	2	0	0	6	6	8	.167	.286	.222	42	-3	1	0	0	1.000	3	/1-36	-0.1

■ BERNIE JAMES
James, Robert Byrne   b: 9/2/05, Angleton, Tex.   d: 8/1/94, San Antonio, Tex.   BB/TR, 5'9.5", 150 lbs.   Deb: 5/6/29

YEAR	TM/L	G	AB	R	H	2B	3B	HR	RBI	BB	SO	AVG	OBP	SLG	PRO+	BR/A	SB	CS	SBR	FA	FR	G/POS	TPR
1929	Bos-N	46	101	12	31	3	2	0	9	9	13	.307	.369	.376	89	-2	3			.940	-9	2-32/O-1	-0.9
1930	Bos-N	8	11	1	2	1	0	0	1	0	1	.182	.182	.273	8	-2	0			.941	0	/2-7	-0.1
1933	NY-N	60	125	22	28	5	1	1	10	8	12	.224	.271	.280	58	-7	5			.948	2	2-26/S-6,3	-0.3
Total	3	114	237	35	61	9	3	1	20	17	26	.257	.310	.321	70	-10	8			.944	-7	/2-65,S-6,3O	-1.3

■ CHARLIE JAMIESON
Jamieson, Charles Devine "Cuckoo"   b: 2/7/1893, Paterson, N.J.   d: 10/27/69, Paterson, N.J.   BL/TL, 5'8.5", 165 lbs.   Deb: 9/20/15

YEAR	TM/L	G	AB	R	H	2B	3B	HR	RBI	BB	SO	AVG	OBP	SLG	PRO+	BR/A	SB	CS	SBR	FA	FR	G/POS	TPR
1915	Was-A	17	68	9	19	3	2	0	7	6	9	.279	.338	.382	113	1	0			1.000	4	O-17	0.4
1916	Was-A	64	145	16	36	4	0	0	13	18	18	.248	.331	.276	83	-2	5			.913	-4	O-41/1-4,P	-0.9
1917	Was-A	20	35	4	6	2	0	0	2	6	5	.171	.293	.229	60	-2	0			.875	-2	/O-9,P-1	-0.4
	Phi-A	85	345	41	92	6	2	0	27	37	36	.267	.341	.296	96	-1	8			.937	-2	O-83	-0.8
	Yr	105	380	45	98	8	2	0	29	43	41	.258	.336	.289	92	-2	8			.930	-4	O-92/P-1	-1.2
1918	Phi-A	110	416	50	84	11	2	0	11	54	30	.202	.297	.238	61	-18	11			.970	-0	*O-102/P-5	-2.7
1919	Cle-A	26	17	3	6	2	1	0	2	3	2	.353	.353	.588	153	1	2			.750	-1	/P-4,O-3	0.0
1920	*Cle-A	108	370	69	118	7	7	1	40	41	26	.319	.388	.411	108	5	2	9	-5	.966	-3	O-98/1-4	-0.8
1921	Cle-A	140	536	94	166	33	10	1	46	67	27	.310	.387	.414	103	4	8	4	0	.974	-6	*O-137	-1.1
1922	Cle-A	145	567	87	183	29	11	3	57	54	22	.323	.388	.429	112	11	15	9	-1	.978	-3	*O-144/P-2	-0.2
1923	Cle-A	152	644	130	**222**	36	12	2	51	80	37	.345	.422	.447	129	30	18	14	1	.974	8	*O-152	2.4
1924	Cle-A	143	594	80	213	34	4	0	54	47	15	.359	.407	.458	121	19	21	12	-3	.974	4	*O-139	1.2
1925	Cle-A	138	557	109	165	24	5	4	42	72	26	.296	.380	.379	92	-5	14	18	-7	.955	7	*O-135	-1.2

YEAR	TM/L	G	AB	R	H	2B	3B	HR	RBI	BB	SO	AVG	OBP	SLG	PRO+	BR/A	SB	CS	SBR	FA	FR	G/POS	TPR
1926	Cle-A	143	555	89	166	33	7	2	45	53	22	.299	.361	.395	96	-3	9	7	-2	.960	-0	*O-143	-1.4
1927	Cle-A	127	489	73	151	23	6	0	36	64	14	.309	.394	.380	101	4	7	9	-3	.969	5	*O-127	-0.3
1928	Cle-A	112	433	63	133	18	4	1	37	56	20	.307	.388	.374	100	2	3	12	-6	.984	20	*O-111	0.8
1929	Cle-A	102	364	56	106	22	1	0	26	50	12	.291	.378	.357	87	-5	2	13	-7	.980	-2	O-93	-1.9
1930	Cle-A	103	366	64	110	22	1	1	52	36	20	.301	.368	.374	85	-7	5	2	0	.955	-5	O-95	-1.7
1931	Cle-A	28	43	7	13	2	1	0	4	5	1	.302	.375	.395	97	-0	1	1	-0	.833	-2	/O-7	-0.2
1932	Cle-A	16	16	0	1	0	0	0	0	2	3	.063	.211	.125	-10	-3	0	0	0	1.000	-0	/O-2	-0.2
Total	18	1779	6560	1062	1990	322	80	18	552	748	345	.303	.378	.385	101	31	131	110		.967	19	*O-1638/P-13,1	-9.0

■ VIC JANOWICZ
Janowicz, Victor Felix b: 2/26/30, Elyria, Ohio BR/TR, 5'9", 185 lbs. Deb: 5/31/53

YEAR	TM/L	G	AB	R	H	2B	3B	HR	RBI	BB	SO	AVG	OBP	SLG	PRO+	BR/A	SB	CS	SBR	FA	FR	G/POS	TPR
1953	Pit-N	42	123	10	31	3	1	2	8	5	31	.252	.287	.341	63	-7	0	1	-1	.937	-12	C-35	-1.7
1954	Pit-N	41	73	10	11	3	0	0	2	7	23	.151	.235	.192	13	-9	0	0	0	.904	1	3-18/O-1	-0.9
Total	2	83	196	20	42	6	1	2	10	12	54	.214	.267	.286	44	-16	0	1	-1	.937	-11	/C-35,3-18,O	-2.6

■ RAY JANSEN
Jansen, Raymond William b: 1/16/1889, St.Louis, Mo. d: 3/19/34, St.Louis, Mo. BR/TR, 5'11", 155 lbs. Deb: 9/30/10

YEAR	TM/L	G	AB	R	H	2B	3B	HR	RBI	BB	SO	AVG	OBP	SLG	PRO+	BR/A	SB	CS	SBR	FA	FR	G/POS	TPR
1910	StL-A	1	5	0	4	0	0	0	0	0		.800	.800	.800	428	2	0			.700	0	/3-1	0.2

■ HEINIE JANTZEN
Jantzen, Walter C. b: 4/9/1890, Chicago, Ill. d: 4/1/48, Hines, Ill. BR/TR, 5'11.5", 170 lbs. Deb: 6/29/12

YEAR	TM/L	G	AB	R	H	2B	3B	HR	RBI	BB	SO	AVG	OBP	SLG	PRO+	BR/A	SB	CS	SBR	FA	FR	G/POS	TPR
1912	StL-A	31	119	10	22	0	1	1	8	4		.185	.218	.227	28	-11	3			1.000	3	O-31	-1.0

■ HAL JANVRIN
Janvrin, Harold Chandler "Childe Harold" b: 8/27/1892, Haverhill, Mass. d: 3/1/62, Boston, Mass. BR/TR, 5'11.5", 168 lbs. Deb: 7/9/11

YEAR	TM/L	G	AB	R	H	2B	3B	HR	RBI	BB	SO	AVG	OBP	SLG	PRO+	BR/A	SB	CS	SBR	FA	FR	G/POS	TPR
1911	Bos-A	9	27	2	4	1	0	0	1	3		.148	.258	.185	25	-3	0			.733	-1	/3-5,1-4	-0.5
1913	Bos-A	87	276	18	57	5	1	3	25	23	27	.207	.272	.264	56	-16	17			.923	-10	S-48,3-19/21	-2.4
1914	Bos-A	145	492	65	117	18	6	1	51	38	50	.238	.296	.305	81	-12	29	20	-3	.919	-22	2-59,1-57,S/3	-4.2
1915	*Bos-A	99	316	41	85	9	1	0	37	14	27	.269	.317	.304	88	-5	8	14	-6	.917	-20	S-64,3-20/2	-2.8
1916	*Bos-A	117	310	32	69	11	4	0	26	32	32	.223	.299	.284	75	-9	6			.921	-19	S-59,2-39/13	-2.7
1917	Bos-A	55	127	21	25	3	0	0	8	11	13	.197	.266	.220	49	-8	2			.940	1	2-38,S-10/1	-0.5
1919	Was-A	61	208	17	37	4	1	1	13	19	17	.178	.253	.221	34	-18	8			.927	-27	2-56/S-2	-4.6
	StL-N	7	14	1	3	1	0	0	1	2	2	.214	.313	.286	86	-0	0			1.000	-0	/2-2,S-1,3	-0.2
1920	StL-N	87	270	33	74	8	4	1	28	17	19	.274	.317	.344	93	-3	5	6	-2	.926	-2	S-27,1-25,O/2	-0.8
1921	StL-N	18	32	5	9	1	0	0	5	1	0	.281	.303	.313	65	-2	1	0	0	.968	0	/1-9,2-1	-0.1
	Bro-N	44	92	8	18	4	0	0	14	7	6	.196	.253	.239	30	-9	3	1	0	.922	-4	S-17,2-10/130	-1.2
	Yr	62	124	13	27	5	0	0	19	8	6	.218	.265	.258	38	-11	4	1	1	.922	-3	1-17,S-17,2/30	-1.3
1922	Bro-N	30	57	9	17	3	1	0	1	4	4	.298	.344	.386	89	-1	0	0	0	.889	-4	2-15/S-4,310	-0.4
Total	10	759	2221	250	515	68	18	6	210	171	197	.232	.292	.287	70	-85	79	41		.907	-110	S-252,2-242,1/30	-20.4

■ ROY JARVIS
Jarvis, Leroy Gilbert b: 6/27/26, Shawnee, Okla. d: 1/13/90, Oklahoma City, Okla. BR/TR, 5'9", 160 lbs. Deb: 4/30/44

YEAR	TM/L	G	AB	R	H	2B	3B	HR	RBI	BB	SO	AVG	OBP	SLG	PRO+	BR/A	SB	CS	SBR	FA	FR	G/POS	TPR
1944	Bro-N	1	1	0	0	0	0	0	0	0	1	.000	.000	.000	-99	-0	0			1.000	-0	/C-1	0.0
1946	Pit-N	2	4	0	1	0	0	0	0	1	1	.250	.400	.250	84	-0	0			.800	-0	/C-1	0.0
1947	Pit-N	18	45	4	7	1	0	1	4	6	5	.156	.255	.244	32	-4	0			.967	-0	C-15	-0.4
Total	3	21	50	4	8	1	0	1	4	7	7	.160	.263	.240	34	-5	0			.955	-1	/C-17	-0.4

■ PAUL JATA
Jata, Paul b: 9/4/49, Astoria, N.Y. BR/TR, 6'1", 190 lbs. Deb: 4/19/72

YEAR	TM/L	G	AB	R	H	2B	3B	HR	RBI	BB	SO	AVG	OBP	SLG	PRO+	BR/A	SB	CS	SBR	FA	FR	G/POS	TPR
1972	Det-A	32	74	8	17	2	0	0	3	7	14	.230	.296	.257	64	-3	0	1	-1	.991	-1	1-12,O-10/C	-0.7

■ AL JAVIER
Javier, Ignacio Alfredo (b: Ignacio Alfredo Wilkes (Javier)) b: 2/4/54, San Pedro De Macoris, D.R. BR/TR, 5'11", 170 lbs. Deb: 9/9/76

YEAR	TM/L	G	AB	R	H	2B	3B	HR	RBI	BB	SO	AVG	OBP	SLG	PRO+	BR/A	SB	CS	SBR	FA	FR	G/POS	TPR
1976	Hou-N	8	24	1	5	0	0	0	0	2	5	.208	.269	.208	41	-2	0	0	0	1.000	-0	/O-7	-0.4

■ JULIAN JAVIER
Javier, Manuel Julian (Liranzo) b: 8/9/36, San Francisco De Macoris, D.R. BR/TR, 6'1", 175 lbs. Deb: 5/28/60 F

YEAR	TM/L	G	AB	R	H	2B	3B	HR	RBI	BB	SO	AVG	OBP	SLG	PRO+	BR/A	SB	CS	SBR	FA	FR	G/POS	TPR
1960	StL-N	119	451	55	107	19	8	4	21	21	72	.237	.273	.341	62	-24	19	4	3	.962	5	*2-119	-0.5
1961	StL-N	113	445	58	124	14	3	2	41	30	51	.279	.327	.337	70	-19	11	4	1	.966	-0	*2-113	-0.6
1962	StL-N	155	598	97	157	25	5	7	39	47	73	.263	.317	.356	73	-22	26	9	2	.977	1	*2-151/S-4	-0.4
1963	StL-N★	161	609	82	160	27	9	9	46	24	86	.263	.297	.381	86	-12	18	10	-1	.969	-14	*2-161	-1.2
1964	*StL-N	155	535	66	129	19	5	12	65	30	82	.241	.283	.363	74	-19	9	7	-2	.966	-7	*2-154	-1.6
1965	StL-N	77	229	34	52	6	4	2	23	8	44	.227	.262	.314	56	-13	5	5	-2	.975	-2	2-69	-1.6
1966	StL-N	147	460	52	105	13	5	7	31	26	63	.228	.271	.324	64	-22	11	5	0	.981	-6	*2-145	-1.2
1967	*StL-N	140	520	68	146	16	3	14	64	25	92	.281	.315	.404	106	2	6	7	-2	.965	-19	*2-138	-1.1
1968	*StL-N★	139	519	54	135	25	4	4	52	24	61	.260	.294	.347	93	-5	10	3	1	.976	-24	*2-139	-2.3
1969	StL-N	143	493	59	139	28	2	10	42	40	74	.282	.337	.408	107	5	8	4	0	.967	-18	*2-141	-0.2
1970	StL-N	139	513	62	129	16	3	2	42	24	70	.251	.286	.306	58	-31	6	4	-1	.980	13	*2-137	-0.8
1971	StL-N	90	259	32	67	9	4	3	28	9	33	.259	.289	.347	76	-8	5	1	1	.978	2	2-80/3-1	-0.1
1972	*Cin-N	44	91	3	19	2	0	2	12	6	11	.209	.258	.297	61	-5	1	0	0	.896	-3	3-19/2-5,1	-0.4
Total	13	1622	5722	722	1469	216	55	78	506	314	812	.257	.298	.355	78	-174	135	63	3	.972	-68	*2-1552/3-20,S1	-12.4

■ STAN JAVIER
Javier, Stanley Julian Antonio (De Javier) b: 1/9/64, San Francisco De Macoris, D.R. BB/TR, 6', 185 lbs. Deb: 4/15/84 F

YEAR	TM/L	G	AB	R	H	2B	3B	HR	RBI	BB	SO	AVG	OBP	SLG	PRO+	BR/A	SB	CS	SBR	FA	FR	G/POS	TPR
1984	NY-A	7	7	1	1	0	0	0	0	0	1	.143	.143	.143	-22	-1	0	0	0	1.000	-2	/O-5	-0.3
1986	Oak-A	59	114	13	23	8	0	0	8	16	27	.202	.305	.272	63	-6	8	0	2	1.000	-1	O-51/D-2	-0.5
1987	Oak-A	81	151	22	28	3	1	2	9	19	33	.185	.276	.258	46	-12	3	2	-0	.983	-9	O-71/1-6,D	-2.2
1988	*Oak-A	125	397	49	102	13	3	2	35	32	63	.257	.316	.320	81	-10	20	1	5	.980	-13	*O-115/1-4,D	-2.1
1989	*Oak-A	112	310	42	77	12	3	1	28	31	45	.248	.319	.316	82	-7	12	2	5	.991	-8	O-107/1-1,2	-1.4
1990	Oak-A	19	33	4	8	0	2	0	3	6	6	.242	.306	.364	90	-0	0	0	0	1.000	-2	O-13/D-2	-0.3
	LA-N	104	276	56	84	9	4	3	24	19	44	.304	.387	.399	120	9	15	7	0	1.000	6	O-87	0.9
1991	LA-N	121	176	21	36	5	3	1	11	16	36	.205	.271	.284	57	-10	7	1	2	.986	-14	O-69/1-2	-2.4
1992	LA-N	56	58	6	11	3	0	1	5	6	11	.190	.277	.293	63	-3	1	2	-1	1.000	-7	O-27	-1.2
	Phi-N	74	276	36	72	14	1	0	24	31	43	.261	.340	.319	88	-3	17	1	5	.986	13	O-74	1.3
	Yr	130	334	42	83	17	1	1	29	37	54	.249	.329	.314	84	-6	18	3	4	.987	5	*O-101	0.1
1993	Cal-A	92	237	33	69	10	4	3	28	27	33	.291	.366	.405	104	2	12	2	2	.981	-11	O-64,1-12/2D	-0.9
1994	Oak-A	109	419	75	114	23	0	10	44	49	76	.272	.351	.399	101	2	24	7	3	.986	-0	*O-108/1-1,3	0.2
Total	10	959	2454	358	625	100	21	23	219	267	418	.255	.330	.341	87	-40	119	25	21	.988	-52	O-791/1-26,D23	-8.9

■ TEX JEANES
Jeanes, Ernest Lee b: 12/19/1900, Maypearl, Tex. d: 4/5/73, Longview, Tex. BR/TR, 6', 176 lbs. Deb: 4/20/21

YEAR	TM/L	G	AB	R	H	2B	3B	HR	RBI	BB	SO	AVG	OBP	SLG	PRO+	BR/A	SB	CS	SBR	FA	FR	G/POS	TPR
1921	Cle-A	5	3	2	2	0	0	0	0	1	0	.667	.750	1.000	338	1	0	0	0	1.000	-1	/O-5	0.0
1922	Cle-A	1	1	0	0	0	0	0	0	1	0	.000	.500	.000	39	-1	0	0	0	.000	-1	/P-1,O-1	0.0
1925	Was-A	15	19	2	5	1	0	1	4	3	2	.263	.364	.474	113	0	1	0	0	1.000	-5	O-13	-0.5
1926	Was-A	21	30	6	7	0	0	0	1	0	5	.233	.233	.300	39	-3	0	0	0	1.000	-3	O-14	-0.6
1927	NY-N	11	20	5	6	0	0	0	2	2	0	.300	.364	.300	79	-0	0			1.000	1	/O-6,P-1	0.0
Total	5	53	73	15	20	1	0	1	11	7	7	.274	.338	.370	85	-2	1	0		1.000	-9	/O-39,P-2	-1.1

■ HAL JEFFCOAT
Jeffcoat, Harold Bentley b: 9/6/24, W.Columbia, S.C. BR/TR, 5'10.5", 185 lbs. Deb: 4/20/48 F

YEAR	TM/L	G	AB	R	H	2B	3B	HR	RBI	BB	SO	AVG	OBP	SLG	PRO+	BR/A	SB	CS	SBR	FA	FR	G/POS	TPR
1948	Chi-N	134	473	53	132	16	4	4	42	24	68	.279	.315	.355	85	-11	8			.976	9	*O-119	-0.9
1949	Chi-N	108	363	43	89	18	6	2	26	20	48	.245	.286	.344	70	-16	12			.963	7	*O-101	-1.4
1950	Chi-N	66	179	21	42	13	1	2	18	6	23	.235	.259	.352	60	-11	5			.967	-3	O-53	-1.6
1951	Chi-N	113	278	44	76	20	2	4	27	16	23	.273	.315	.403	90	-4	8	4	0	.989	-2	O-87	-0.8
1952	Chi-N	102	297	29	65	17	3	4	30	15	40	.219	.259	.330	61	-16	7	2	1	.996	3	O-95	-1.6
1953	Chi-N	106	183	22	43	3	1	4	22	21	26	.235	.314	.328	66	-9	5	0		.973	-17	*O-100	-2.6

YEAR	TM/L	G	AB	R	H	2B	3B	HR	RBI	BB	SO	AVG	OBP	SLG	PRO+	BR/A	SB	CS	SBR	FA	FR	G/POS	TPR
1954	Chi-N	56	31	13	8	2	1	1	6	1	7	.258	.281	.484	94	-0	2	0	1	.889	-1	P-43/O-3	-0.1
1955	Chi-N	52	23	3	4	0	0	1	1	2	9	.174	.240	.304	43	-2	0	0	0	.903	1	P-50	0.0
1956	Cin-N	49	54	5	8	2	0	0	5	3	20	.148	.193	.185	2	-7	0	1	-1	.969	3	P-38	0.0
1957	Cin-N	53	69	13	14	3	1	4	11	5	20	.203	.267	.449	82	-2	0	0	0	.958	-1	P-37	0.0
1958	Cin-N	50	9	2	5	0	0	0	0	1	2	.556	.600	.556	198	1	0	0	0	1.000	2	P-49/O-1	0.0
1959	Cin-N	17	1	1	1	1	0	0	0	0	0	1.000	1.000	2.000	655	1	0	0	0	1.000	0	P-17	0.0
	StL-N	12	3	0	0	0	0	0	0	0	3	.000	.000	.000	-94	-1	0	0	0	1.000	0	P-11	0.0
	Yr	29	4	1	1	1	0	0	0	0	3	.250	.250	.500	90	-0	0	0	0	1.000	0	P-28	0.0
Total	12	918	1963	249	487	95	18	26	188	114	289	.248	.291	.355	73	-78	49	7		.978	0	O-559,P-245	-9.0

■ GREGG JEFFERIES
Jefferies, Gregory Scott   b: 8/1/67, Burlingame, Cal.   BB/TR, 5'11", 175 lbs.   Deb: 9/6/87

YEAR	TM/L	G	AB	R	H	2B	3B	HR	RBI	BB	SO	AVG	OBP	SLG	PRO+	BR/A	SB	CS	SBR	FA	FR	G/POS	TPR
1987	NY-N	6	6	0	3	1	0	0	2	0	0	.500	.500	.667	217	1	0	0	0	.000	0	/H	0.1
1988	*NY-N	29	109	19	35	8	2	6	17	8	10	.321	.368	.596	181	11	5	1	1	.979	-3	3-20,2-10	0.9
1989	NY-N	141	508	72	131	28	2	12	56	39	46	.258	.317	.392	107	3	21	6	3	.975	-31	*2-123,3-20	-2.3
1990	NY-N	153	604	96	171	**40**	3	15	68	46	40	.283	.339	.434	111	8	11	2	2	.976	-9	2-118,3-34	0.4
1991	NY-N	136	486	59	132	19	2	9	62	47	38	.272	.338	.374	101	1	26	5	5	.982	-16	2-77,3-51	-0.9
1992	KC-A	152	604	66	172	36	3	10	75	43	29	.285	.333	.404	103	1	19	9	0	.939	-2	*3-146/2-1,D	0.0
1993	StL-N★	142	544	89	186	24	3	16	83	62	32	.342	.411	.485	142	34	46	9	8	.993	-11	*1-140/2-1	1.9
1994	StL-N★	103	397	52	129	27	1	12	55	45	26	.325	.395	.489	134	20	12	5	1	.993	-9	*1-102	0.3
Total	8	862	3258	453	959	183	16	80	418	290	221	.294	.355	.434	118	80	140	37	20	.977	-82	2-330,3-271,1/D	0.4

■ REGGIE JEFFERSON
Jefferson, Reginald Jirod   b: 9/25/68, Tallahassee, Fla.   BB/TL, 6'4", 210 lbs.   Deb: 5/18/91

YEAR	TM/L	G	AB	R	H	2B	3B	HR	RBI	BB	SO	AVG	OBP	SLG	PRO+	BR/A	SB	CS	SBR	FA	FR	G/POS	TPR
1991	Cin-N	5	7	1	1	0	0	1	1	1	2	.143	.250	.571	120	0	0	0	0	1.000	0	/1-2	0.0
	Cle-A	26	101	10	20	3	0	2	12	3	22	.198	.221	.287	39	-8	0	0	0	.993	1	1-26	-0.8
1992	Cle-A	24	89	8	30	6	2	1	6	1	17	.337	.352	.483	134	4	0	0	0	.993	1	1-15/D-7	0.3
1993	Cle-A	113	366	35	91	11	2	10	34	28	78	.249	.311	.372	83	-9	1	3	-2	.976	-0	D-88,1-15	-1.6
1994	Sea-A	63	162	24	53	11	0	8	32	17	32	.327	.394	.543	136	9	0	0	0	.981	1	D-32,1-13/O	0.6
Total	4	231	725	78	195	31	4	22	85	50	151	.269	.322	.414	96	-5	1	3	-2	.988	3	D-127/1-71,O	-1.5

■ STAN JEFFERSON
Jefferson, Stanley   b: 12/4/62, New York, N.Y.   BB/TR, 5'11", 175 lbs.   Deb: 9/7/86

YEAR	TM/L	G	AB	R	H	2B	3B	HR	RBI	BB	SO	AVG	OBP	SLG	PRO+	BR/A	SB	CS	SBR	FA	FR	G/POS	TPR
1986	NY-N	14	24	6	5	1	0	1	3	2	8	.208	.296	.375	86	-0	0	0	0	1.000	-1	/O-7	-0.1
1987	SD-N	116	422	59	97	8	7	8	29	39	92	.230	.298	.339	71	-18	34	11	4	.987	-10	*O-107	-2.8
1988	SD-N	49	111	16	16	1	2	1	4	9	22	.144	.215	.216	25	-11	5	1	0	1.000	-4	O-38	-1.7
1989	NY-A	10	12	1	1	0	0	0	1	0	4	.083	.083	.083	-54	-2	1	1	0	1.000	-3	/O-7,D-1	-0.6
	Bal-A	35	127	19	33	7	0	4	20	4	22	.260	.288	.409	97	-1	9	3	1	.988	-2	O-32/D-2	0.1
	Yr	45	139	20	34	7	0	4	21	4	26	.245	.271	.381	84	-4	10	4	1	.988	-2	O-39/D-3	-0.5
1990	Bal-A	10	19	1	0	0	0	0	0	2	8	.000	.095	.000	-74	-2	1	0	0	1.000	-2	/O-5,D-1	-0.6
	Cle-A	49	98	21	27	8	0	2	10	8	18	.276	.343	.418	112	2	8	4	0	.985	0	O-34/D-5	0.1
	Yr	59	117	22	27	8	0	2	10	10	26	.231	.302	.350	83	-3	9	4	0	.987	-2	O-39/D-6	-0.5
1991	Cin-N	13	19	2	1	0	0	0	0	1	3	.053	.100	.053	-54	-4	2	0	1	1.000	0	/O-5	-0.5
Total	6	296	832	125	180	25	9	16	67	65	177	.216	.279	.326	66	-40	60	20	6	.990	-20	O-235/D-9	-6.1

■ IRV JEFFRIES
Jeffries, Irvine Franklin   b: 9/10/05, Louisville, Ky.   d: 6/8/82, Louisville, Ky.   BR/TR, 5'10", 175 lbs.   Deb: 4/30/30

YEAR	TM/L	G	AB	R	H	2B	3B	HR	RBI	BB	SO	AVG	OBP	SLG	PRO+	BR/A	SB	CS	SBR	FA	FR	G/POS	TPR
1930	Chi-A	40	97	14	23	3	0	2	11	3	2	.237	.275	.330	54	-7	1	2	-1	.976	-3	3-20,S-13	-0.8
1931	Chi-A	79	223	29	50	10	0	2	16	14	9	.224	.270	.296	52	-16	3	0	1	.949	2	3-61/2-6,SO	-0.9
1934	Phi-N	56	175	28	43	6	0	4	19	15	10	.246	.305	.349	66	-9	2			.962	4	2-52/3-1	-0.2
Total	3	175	495	71	116	19	0	8	46	32	21	.234	.284	.321	58	-32	6	2		.955	3	/3-82,2-58,SO	-1.9

■ CHRIS JELIC
Jelic, Christopher John   b: 12/16/63, Bethlehem, Pa.   BR/TR, 5'11", 180 lbs.   Deb: 9/30/90

YEAR	TM/L	G	AB	R	H	2B	3B	HR	RBI	BB	SO	AVG	OBP	SLG	PRO+	BR/A	SB	CS	SBR	FA	FR	G/POS	TPR
1990	NY-N	4	11	2	1	0	0	1	0	1	3	.091	.091	.364	19	-1	0	0	0	1.000	-1	/O-4	-0.3

■ FRANK JELINCICH
Jelincich, Frank Anthony "Jelly"   b: 9/3/19, San Jose, Cal.   BR/TR, 6'2", 198 lbs.   Deb: 9/6/41

YEAR	TM/L	G	AB	R	H	2B	3B	HR	RBI	BB	SO	AVG	OBP	SLG	PRO+	BR/A	SB	CS	SBR	FA	FR	G/POS	TPR
1941	Chi-N	4	8	0	1	0	0	0	2	1	2	.125	.222	.125	-1	-1	0			1.000	-1	/O-2	-0.2

■ GREG JELKS
Jelks, Gregory Dion   b: 8/16/61, Cherokee, Ala.   BR/TR, 6'2", 190 lbs.   Deb: 8/20/87

YEAR	TM/L	G	AB	R	H	2B	3B	HR	RBI	BB	SO	AVG	OBP	SLG	PRO+	BR/A	SB	CS	SBR	FA	FR	G/POS	TPR
1987	Phi-N	10	11	2	1	1	0	0	0	3	4	.091	.286	.182	26	-1	0			.750	0	/3-4,1-2,O	-0.1

■ STEVE JELTZ
Jeltz, Larry Steven   b: 5/28/59, Paris, France   BB/TR, 5'11", 180 lbs.   Deb: 7/17/83

YEAR	TM/L	G	AB	R	H	2B	3B	HR	RBI	BB	SO	AVG	OBP	SLG	PRO+	BR/A	SB	CS	SBR	FA	FR	G/POS	TPR
1983	Phi-N	13	8	0	1	0	1	0	1	1	2	.125	.222	.375	63	-0	0	0	0	1.000	1	/2-4,S-2,3	0.0
1984	Phi-N	28	68	7	14	0	1	1	7	7	11	.206	.280	.279	57	-4	2	1	0	.992	11	S-27/3-1	1.0
1985	Phi-N	89	196	17	37	4	1	0	12	26	55	.189	.284	.219	41	-15	1	1	-0	.958	6	S-86	-0.3
1986	Phi-N	145	439	44	96	11	4	0	36	65	97	.219	.321	.262	60	-22	6	3	0	.967	-2	*S-141	-1.1
1987	Phi-N	114	293	37	68	9	6	0	12	39	54	.232	.324	.304	66	-14	1	2	-1	.971	3	*S-114/O-1	-0.3
1988	Phi-N	148	379	39	71	11	4	0	27	59	58	.187	.297	.237	54	-21	3	0	1	.976	-1	*S-148	-1.1
1989	Phi-N	116	263	28	64	7	3	4	25	45	44	.243	.356	.338	99	-5	1	4	2	.985	-1	S-63,3-30,2/O	0.7
1990	KC-A	74	103	11	16	4	0	0	10	6	21	.155	.202	.194	11	-12	1	1	-0	.977	9	2-34,S-23,O/3D	-0.3
Total	8	727	1749	183	367	46	20	5	130	248	342	.210	.309	.268	61	-86	18	10	-1	.971	28	S-604/2-61,3OD	-1.4

■ JOHN JENKINS
Jenkins, John Robert   b: 7/7/1896, Bosworth, Mo.   d: 8/3/68, Columbia, Mo.   BR/TR, 5'8", 160 lbs.   Deb: 8/5/22

YEAR	TM/L	G	AB	R	H	2B	3B	HR	RBI	BB	SO	AVG	OBP	SLG	PRO+	BR/A	SB	CS	SBR	FA	FR	G/POS	TPR
1922	Chi-A	5	3	0	0	0	0	0	1	0	2	.000	.000	.000	-99	-1	0	0	0	.000	-0	/2-1,S-1	-0.1

■ JOE JENKINS
Jenkins, Joseph Daniel   b: 10/12/1890, Shelbyville, Tenn.   d: 6/21/74, Fresno, Cal.   BR/TR, 5'11", 170 lbs.   Deb: 4/30/14

YEAR	TM/L	G	AB	R	H	2B	3B	HR	RBI	BB	SO	AVG	OBP	SLG	PRO+	BR/A	SB	CS	SBR	FA	FR	G/POS	TPR
1914	StL-A	19	32	0	4	1	1	0	1	1	11	.125	.152	.219	12	-4	2			.931	-4	/C-9	-0.8
1917	Chi-A	10	9	0	1	0	0	0	2	0	5	.111	.111	.111	-32	-1	0			.000	0	/C-1	-0.2
1919	Chi-A	11	19	0	3	1	0	0	1	1	1	.158	.200	.211	15	-2	1			.824	-2	/C-4	-0.4
Total	3	40	60	0	8	2	1	0	3	2	17	.133	.161	.200	6	-7	3			.891	-6	/C-14	-1.4

■ TOM JENKINS
Jenkins, Thomas Griffith "Tut"   b: 4/10/1898, Camden, Ala.   d: 5/3/79, Weymouth, Mass.   BL/TR, 6'1.5", 174 lbs.   Deb: 9/15/25

YEAR	TM/L	G	AB	R	H	2B	3B	HR	RBI	BB	SO	AVG	OBP	SLG	PRO+	BR/A	SB	CS	SBR	FA	FR	G/POS	TPR
1925	Bos-A	15	64	9	19	4	0	0	5	3	4	.297	.338	.359	77	-2	1			.938	-2	O-15	-0.5
1926	Bos-A	21	50	3	9	2	1	0	6	3	7	.180	.226	.240	22	-6	1			1.000	-1	O-13	-0.8
	Phi-A	6	23	3	4	2	0	0	0	0	2	.174	.174	.261	12	-3	0			1.000	0	/O-6	-0.3
	Yr	27	73	6	13	4	1	0	6	3	9	.178	.211	.247	19	-9	1			1.000	-1	O-19	-1.1
1929	StL-A	21	22	1	4	1	0	0	4	8	1	.182	.308	.273	49	-2	1			1.000	-1	/O-3	-0.3
1930	StL-A	2	8	1	2	1	0	0	2	0	0	.250	.250	.625	110	-0	0			1.000	0	/O-2	0.0
1931	StL-A	81	230	20	61	7	2	3	25	17	25	.265	.316	.352	73	-9	1	3	-2	.952	-4	O-58	-1.7
1932	StL-A	25	62	5	20	1	0	0	5	1	6	.323	.333	.339	70	-3	0			.939	2	O-12	-0.2
Total	6	171	459	42	119	14	6	3	44	28	53	.259	.303	.336	64	-25	3	3	-2	.958	-6	O-109	-3.8

■ ALAMAZOO JENNINGS
Jennings, Alfred Gorden   b: 11/30/1850, Newport, Ky.   d: 11/2/1894, Cincinnati, Ohio   Deb: 8/15/1878   U

YEAR	TM/L	G	AB	R	H	2B	3B	HR	RBI	BB	SO	AVG	OBP	SLG	PRO+	BR/A	SB	CS	SBR	FA	FR	G/POS	TPR
1878	Mil-N	1	2	0	0	0	0	0	0	0	1	.000	.333	.000	16	-0				.429	-2	/C-1	-0.2

■ HUGHIE JENNINGS
Jennings, Hugh Ambrose "Ee-Yah"   b: 4/2/1869, Pittston, Pa.   d: 2/1/28, Scranton, Pa.   BR/TR, 5'8.5", 165 lbs.   Deb: 6/1/1891   MCH

YEAR	TM/L	G	AB	R	H	2B	3B	HR	RBI	BB	SO	AVG	OBP	SLG	PRO+	BR/A	SB	CS	SBR	FA	FR	G/POS	TPR
1891	Lou-a	90	360	53	105	10	8	1	58	17	36	.292	.339	.372	105	1	12			.894	7	S-70,1-17/3	1.0
1892	Lou-N	152	594	65	132	16	4	2	61	30	30	.222	.270	.273	70	-22	28			.907	15	*S-152	0.0
1893	Lou-N	23	88	6	12	3	0	0	9	3	3	.136	.174	.170	-9	-14	0			.899	6	S-23	-0.6
	Bal-N	16	55	6	14	0	0	1	6	4	3	.255	.339	.309	71	-2	0			.886	-2	S-15/O-1	-0.3

YEAR	TM/L	G	AB	R	H	2B	3B	HR	RBI	BB	SO	AVG	OBP	SLG	PRO+	BR/A	SB	CS	SBR	FA	FR	G/POS	TPR
	Yr	39	143	12	26	3	0	1	15	7	6	.182	.240	.224	25	-16	0			.895	4	S-38/O-1	-0.9
1894	*Bal-N	128	501	134	168	28	16	4	109	37	17	.335	.411	.479	109	7	37			.928	33	*S-128	3.6
1895	*Bal-N	131	529	159	204	41	7	4	125	24	17	.386	.444	.512	142	34	53			.940	36	*S-131	6.0
1896	*Bal-N	130	521	125	209	27	9	0	121	19	11	.401	.472	.488	151	42	70			.928	34	*S-130	6.7
1897	*Bal-N	117	439	133	156	26	9	2	79	42		.355	.463	.469	146	35	60			.933	27	*S-116	5.4
1898	Bal-N	143	534	135	175	25	11	1	87	78		.328	.454	.421	149	42	28			.929	-0	S-115,2-27/O	4.5
1899	Bro-N	16	41	7	7	0	2	0	6	9		.171	.346	.268	68	-1	4			.825	-6	S-11/1-4	-0.6
	Bal-N	2	8	2	3	0	2	0	2	0		.375	.375	.875	227	1	0			1.000	-1	/2-2	0.0
	Bro-N	51	175	35	57	3	8	0	34	13		.326	.424	.434	133	9	14			.987	-1	1-46/2-1,S	0.7
	Yr	69	224	44	67	3	12	0	42	22		.299	.408	.420	124	9	18			.985	-8	1-50,S-12/2	0.1
1900	*Bro-N	115	441	61	120	18	6	1	69	31		.272	.348	.347	87	-8	31			.982	5	*1-112/2-2	-0.3
1901	Phi-N	82	302	38	79	21	2	1	39	25		.262	.342	.354	100	1	13			.979	-3	1-80/2-1,S	-0.3
1902	Phi-N	78	290	32	79	13	4	1	32	14		.272	.330	.355	111	4	8			.983	2	1-69/S-5,2	0.5
1903	Bro-N	6	17	2	4	0	0	0	1	1		.235	.316	.235	60	-1	1			1.000	0	/O-4	-0.1
1907	Det-A	1	4	0	1	1	0	0	0	0		.250	.250	.500	133	0	0			.750	-1	/2-1,S-1M	-0.1
1909	Det-A	2	4	1	2	0	0	0	2	0		.500	.500	.500	207	0	0			1.000	0	/1-2,M	0.1
1912	Det-A	1	1	0	0	0	0	0	0	0		.000	.000	.000	-99	-0	0			.000	0	HM	0.0
1918	Det-A	1	0	0	0	0	0	0	0	0	0						0			1.000	0	/1-1,M	0.0
Total	17	1285	4904	994	1527	232	88	18	840	347	117	.311	.390	.406	117	127	359			.922	150	S-899,1-331/203	26.2

■ DOUG JENNINGS
Jennings, James Douglas b: 9/30/64, Atlanta, Ga. BL/TL, 5'10", 175 lbs. Deb: 4/8/88

YEAR	TM/L	G	AB	R	H	2B	3B	HR	RBI	BB	SO	AVG	OBP	SLG	PRO+	BR/A	SB	CS	SBR	FA	FR	G/POS	TPR
1988	Oak-A	71	101	9	21	6	0	1	15	21	28	.208	.355	.297	88	-1	0	1	-1	1.000	-3	O-23,1-14/D	-0.5
1989	Oak-A	4	4	0	0	0	0	0	0	0	2	.000	.000	.000	-99	-1	0	0	0	1.000	-1	/O-3	-0.2
1990	*Oak-A	64	156	19	30	7	2	2	14	17	48	.192	.280	.301	65	-7	0	3	-2	.984	-8	O-45/1-4,D	-1.9
1991	Oak-A	8	9	0	1	0	0	0	0	2	2	.111	.273	.111	11	-1	0	1	-1	1.000	-1	/O-6	-0.2
1993	Chi-N	42	52	8	13	3	1	2	8	3	10	.250	.316	.462	107	0	0	0	0	1.000	-1	1-10	-0.1
Total	5	189	322	36	65	16	3	5	37	43	90	.202	.307	.317	76	-10	0	5	-3	.991	-13	/O-77,1-28,D	-2.9

■ BILL JENNINGS
Jennings, William Lee b: 9/28/25, St.Louis, Mo. BR/TR, 6'2", 175 lbs. Deb: 7/19/51

YEAR	TM/L	G	AB	R	H	2B	3B	HR	RBI	BB	SO	AVG	OBP	SLG	PRO+	BR/A	SB	CS	SBR	FA	FR	G/POS	TPR
1951	StL-A	64	195	20	35	10	2	0	13	26	42	.179	.276	.251	42	-16	1	0	0	.953	-5	S-64	-1.6

■ WOODY JENSEN
Jensen, Forrest Docenus b: 8/11/07, Bremerton, Wash. BL/TL, 5'10.5", 160 lbs. Deb: 4/20/31

YEAR	TM/L	G	AB	R	H	2B	3B	HR	RBI	BB	SO	AVG	OBP	SLG	PRO+	BR/A	SB	CS	SBR	FA	FR	G/POS	TPR
1931	Pit-N	73	267	43	65	5	4	3	17	10	18	.243	.276	.326	62	-15	4			.974	5	O-67	-1.4
1932	Pit-N	7	5	2	0	0	0	0	0	0	2	.000	.000	.000	-99	-1	0			.000	-1	/O-1	-0.2
1933	Pit-N	70	196	29	58	7	3	0	15	8	2	.296	.330	.362	98	-1	1			.980	-0	O-40	-0.3
1934	Pit-N	88	283	34	82	13	4	0	27	4	13	.290	.304	.364	76	-10	2			.993	-3	O-66	-1.4
1935	Pit-N	143	627	97	203	28	7	8	62	15	14	.324	.344	.429	103	2	9			.977	-4	*O-140	-0.7
1936	Pit-N	153	696	98	197	34	10	10	58	16	19	.283	.305	.404	87	-14	2			.975	-5	*O-153	-2.0
1937	Pit-N	124	509	77	142	23	9	5	45	15	29	.279	.301	.389	86	-11	2			.963	-0	*O-120	-1.6
1938	Pit-N	68	125	12	25	4	0	0	10	1	3	.200	.213	.232	22	-13	0			.900	-11	O-38	-2.6
1939	Pit-N	12	12	0	2	0	0	0	1	0	0	.167	.167	.167	-10	-2	0			1.000	-1	/O-3	-0.3
Total	9	738	2720	392	774	114	37	26	235	69	100	.285	.307	.382	84	-66	20			.972	-13	O-628	-10.5

■ JACKIE JENSEN
Jensen, Jack Eugene b: 3/9/27, San Francisco, Cal. d: 7/14/82, Charlottesville, Va. BR/TR, 5'11", 190 lbs. Deb: 4/18/50

YEAR	TM/L	G	AB	R	H	2B	3B	HR	RBI	BB	SO	AVG	OBP	SLG	PRO+	BR/A	SB	CS	SBR	FA	FR	G/POS	TPR
1950	*NY-A	45	70	13	12	2	2	1	5	7	8	.171	.247	.300	41	-7	4	0	1	.947	-4	O-23	-1.0
1951	NY-A	56	168	30	50	8	1	8	25	18	18	.298	.369	.500	138	8	8	2	1	.974	1	O-48	0.8
1952	NY-A	7	19	3	2	1	1	0	2	4	4	.105	.261	.263	49	-1	1	0	0	1.000	-1	/O-5	-0.3
	Was-A★	144	570	80	163	29	5	10	80	63	40	.286	.360	.407	117	13	17	6	2	.977	6	*O-143	1.5
	Yr	151	589	83	165	30	6	10	82	67	44	.280	.357	.402	115	12	18	6	2	.978	5	*O-148	1.2
1953	Was-A	147	552	87	147	32	8	10	84	73	51	.266	.357	.408	109	7	18	8	1	.983	-4	*O-146	-0.2
1954	Bos-A	152	580	92	160	25	7	25	117	79	52	.276	.365	.472	115	11	22	7	2	.986	-7	*O-151	0.0
1955	Bos-A★	152	574	95	158	27	6	26	116	89	63	.275	.375	.479	118	14	16	7	1	.977	1	*O-150	0.9
1956	Bos-A	151	578	80	182	23	11	20	97	89	63	.315	.407	.497	123	19	11	3	2	.962	2	*O-151	1.4
1957	Bos-A	145	544	82	153	29	2	23	103	75	66	.281	.370	.469	121	16	8	5	-1	.960	4	*O-144	1.2
1958	Bos-A★	154	548	83	157	31	0	35	122	99	65	.286	.398	.535	144	35	9	4	0	.981	3	*O-153	3.1
1959	Bos-A	148	535	101	148	31	0	28	112	88	67	.277	.379	.492	131	24	20	5	3	.982	15	*O-146	3.4
1961	Bos-A	137	498	64	131	21	2	13	66	66	69	.263	.353	.392	96	-2	9	3	2	.986	11	*O-131	0.0
Total	11	1438	5236	810	1463	259	45	199	929	750	546	.279	.372	.460	119	138	143	55	10	.977	28	*O-1391	10.8

■ DAN JESSEE
Jessee, Daniel Edward b: 2/22/01, Olive Hill, Ky. d: 4/30/70, Venice, Fla. BL/TR, 5'10", 165 lbs. Deb: 8/14/29

YEAR	TM/L	G	AB	R	H	2B	3B	HR	RBI	BB	SO	AVG	OBP	SLG	PRO+	BR/A	SB	CS	SBR	FA	FR	G/POS	TPR
1929	Cle-A	1	0	0	0	0	0	0	0	0	0					0	0	0	0	.000	0	R	0.0

■ GARRY JESTADT
Jestadt, Garry Arthur b: 3/19/47, Chicago, Ill. BR/TR, 6'2", 188 lbs. Deb: 9/17/69

YEAR	TM/L	G	AB	R	H	2B	3B	HR	RBI	BB	SO	AVG	OBP	SLG	PRO+	BR/A	SB	CS	SBR	FA	FR	G/POS	TPR
1969	Mon-N	6	6	1	0	0	0	0	0	0	0	.000	.000	.000	-99	-2	0	0	0	.667	-0	/S-1	-0.2
1971	Chi-N	3	3	0	0	0	0	0	0	0	0	.000	.000	.000	-87	-1	0	0	0	.000	0	/3-1	-0.1
	SD-N	75	189	17	55	13	0	0	13	11	24	.291	.330	.360	102	0	1	3	-2	.935	11	3-49,2-23/S	1.1
	Yr	78	192	17	55	13	0	0	13	11	24	.286	.325	.354	98	-1	1	3	-2	.935	11	3-50,2-23/S	1.0
1972	SD-N	92	256	15	63	5	1	6	22	13	21	.246	.283	.344	83	-7	0	0	0	.944	-17	2-48,3-25/S	-2.4
Total	3	176	454	33	118	18	1	6	36	24	45	.260	.297	.344	87	-9	1	3	-2	.942	-7	/3-75,2-71,S	-1.6

■ JOHNNY JETER
Jeter, John b: 10/24/44, Shreveport, La. BR/TR, 6'1", 180 lbs. Deb: 6/14/69 F

YEAR	TM/L	G	AB	R	H	2B	3B	HR	RBI	BB	SO	AVG	OBP	SLG	PRO+	BR/A	SB	CS	SBR	FA	FR	G/POS	TPR
1969	Pit-N	28	29	7	9	1	1	1	6	3	15	.310	.375	.517	151	2	1	1	-0	1.000	-4	O-20	-0.2
1970	*Pit-N	85	126	27	30	3	2	2	12	13	34	.238	.314	.341	77	-4	9	5	-0	1.000	-8	O-56	-1.4
1971	SD-N	18	75	8	24	4	0	1	3	2	16	.320	.338	.413	120	2	2	0	1	.967	4	O-17	0.6
1972	SD-N	110	326	25	72	4	3	7	21	18	92	.221	.266	.316	70	-14	11	5	0	.987	1	O-91	-1.8
1973	Chi-A	89	300	38	72	14	4	7	26	9	74	.240	.262	.383	77	-10	4	3	-1	.955	-3	O-72/D-3	-1.8
1974	Cle-A	6	17	3	6	1	0	0	1	1	6	.353	.389	.412	132	1	1	2	-1	.833	-1	/O-6	-0.2
Total	6	336	873	108	213	27	10	18	69	46	237	.244	.284	.360	82	-24	28	16	-1	.975	-11	O-262/D-3	-4.8

■ SHAWN JETER
Jeter, Shawn Darrell b: 6/28/66, Shreveport, La. BL/TR, 6'2", 185 lbs. Deb: 6/13/92 F

YEAR	TM/L	G	AB	R	H	2B	3B	HR	RBI	BB	SO	AVG	OBP	SLG	PRO+	BR/A	SB	CS	SBR	FA	FR	G/POS	TPR
1992	Chi-A	13	18	1	2	0	0	0	0	0	7	.111	.111	.111	-38	-3	0	0	0	.909	-2	/O-8,D-3	-0.5

■ SAM JETHROE
Jethroe, Samuel "Jet" b: 1/20/22, E.St.Louis, Ill. BB/TR, 6'1", 178 lbs. Deb: 4/18/50

YEAR	TM/L	G	AB	R	H	2B	3B	HR	RBI	BB	SO	AVG	OBP	SLG	PRO+	BR/A	SB	CS	SBR	FA	FR	G/POS	TPR
1950	Bos-N	141	582	100	159	28	8	18	58	52	93	.273	.338	.442	110	7	35			.969	8	*O-141	0.9
1951	Bos-N	148	572	101	160	29	10	18	65	57	88	.280	.356	.460	127	20	35	5	8	.974	7	*O-140	2.9
1952	Bos-N	151	608	79	141	23	7	13	58	68	112	.232	.318	.357	90	-8	28	9	3	.970	4	*O-151	-0.8
1954	Pit-N	2	1	0	0	0	0	0	0	0	0	.000	.000	.000	-99	-0	0	0	0	1.000	-0	/O-1	-0.1
Total	4	442	1763	280	460	80	25	49	181	177	293	.261	.337	.418	108	18	98	14		.971	19	O-433	2.9

■ NAT JEWETT
Jewett, Nathan W. b: 12/25/1842, New York, N.Y. d: 2/23/14, Bronx, N.Y. 5'6", 137 lbs. Deb: 7/4/1872

YEAR	TM/L	G	AB	R	H	2B	3B	HR	RBI	BB	SO	AVG	OBP	SLG	PRO+	BR/A	SB	CS	SBR	FA	FR	G/POS	TPR
1872	Eck-n	2	8	1	1	0	0	0	0	0	0	.125	.125	.125	-27	-1						/C-2	-0.1

■ HOUSTON JIMENEZ
Jimenez, Alfonso (Gonzalez) b: 10/30/57, Navojoa, Mexico BR/TR, 5'8", 144 lbs. Deb: 6/13/83

YEAR	TM/L	G	AB	R	H	2B	3B	HR	RBI	BB	SO	AVG	OBP	SLG	PRO+	BR/A	SB	CS	SBR	FA	FR	G/POS	TPR
1983	Min-A	36	86	5	15	5	1	0	9	4	11	.174	.211	.256	27	-9	0	1	-1	.969	4	S-36	-0.3
1984	Min-A	108	298	28	60	11	1	0	19	15	34	.201	.240	.245	33	-27	0	1	-1	.959	-5	*S-107	-2.4

YEAR	TM/L	G	AB	R	H	2B	3B	HR	RBI	BB	SO	AVG	OBP	SLG	PRO+	BR/A	SB	CS	SBR	FA	FR	G/POS	TPR
1987	Pit-N	5	6	0	0	0	0	0	0	0	1	2	.000	.143	.000	-58	-1	0	0	0	1.000	1	/2-2,S-2	0.0
1988	Cle-A	9	21	1	1	0	0	0	0	1	0	2	.048	.048	.048	-71	-5	0	0	0	.973	6	/2-7,S-2	0.1
Total	4	158	411	34	76	16	2	0	29	20	49	.185	.223	.234	25	-42	0	2	-1	.962	7	S-147/2-9	-2.6

■ ELVIO JIMENEZ
Jimenez, Felix Elvio (Rivera) b: 1/6/40, San Pedro De Macoris, D.R. BR/TR, 5'9", 170 lbs. Deb: 10/4/64 F

YEAR	TM/L	G	AB	R	H	2B	3B	HR	RBI	BB	SO	AVG	OBP	SLG	PRO+	BR/A	SB	CS	SBR	FA	FR	G/POS	TPR
1964	NY-A	1	6	0	2	0	0	0	0	0	0	.333	.333	.333	85	-0	0	0	0	1.000	0	/O-1	0.0

■ MANNY JIMENEZ
Jimenez, Manuel Emilio (Rivera) b: 11/19/38, San Pedro De Macoris, D.R. BL/TR, 6'1", 195 lbs. Deb: 4/11/62 F

YEAR	TM/L	G	AB	R	H	2B	3B	HR	RBI	BB	SO	AVG	OBP	SLG	PRO+	BR/A	SB	CS	SBR	FA	FR	G/POS	TPR
1962	KC-A	139	479	48	144	24	2	11	69	31	34	.301	.357	.428	105	4	0	1	-1	.985	-5	*O-122	-0.9
1963	KC-A	60	157	12	44	9	0	0	15	16	14	.280	.365	.338	93	-1	0	1	-1	.960	1	O-40	-0.2
1964	KC-A	95	204	19	46	7	0	12	38	15	24	.225	.295	.436	97	-1	0	0	0	.939	-4	O-49	-0.7
1966	KC-A	13	35	1	4	0	1	0	1	6	4	.114	.244	.171	22	-3	0	0	0	.909	-2	O-12	-0.7
1967	Pit-N	50	56	3	14	2	0	2	10	1	4	.250	.276	.393	89	-1	0	0	0	1.000	-1	/O-6	-0.3
1968	Pit-N	66	66	7	20	1	1	1	11	6	15	.303	.403	.394	142	4	0	0	0	.857	-1	/O-5	0.3
1969	Chi-N	6	6	0	1	0	0	0	0	0	2	.167	.167	.167	-6	-1	0	0	0	.000	0	H	-0.1
Total	7	429	1003	90	273	43	4	26	144	75	97	.272	.339	.401	100	0	0	2	-1	.966	-11	O-234	-2.6

■ TOMMY JOHNS
Johns, Thomas Pearce b: 9/7/1851, Baltimore, Md. d: 4/13/27, Baltimore, Md. Deb: 5/14/1873

YEAR	TM/L	G	AB	R	H	2B	3B	HR	RBI	BB	SO	AVG	OBP	SLG	PRO+	BR/A	SB	CS	SBR	FA	FR	G/POS	TPR
1873	Mar-n	1	4	0	0	0	0	0	0	0	0	.000	.000	.000	-99	-1						/O-1	-0.1

■ PETE JOHNS
Johns, William R. b: 1/17/1889, Cleveland, Ohio d: 8/9/64, Cleveland, Ohio BR/TR, 5'10", 165 lbs. Deb: 8/25/15

YEAR	TM/L	G	AB	R	H	2B	3B	HR	RBI	BB	SO	AVG	OBP	SLG	PRO+	BR/A	SB	CS	SBR	FA	FR	G/POS	TPR
1915	Chi-A	28	100	7	21	2	1	0	11	8	11	.210	.275	.250	56	-6	2	7	-4	.943	4	3-28	-0.5
1918	StL-A	46	89	5	16	1	1	0	11	4	6	.180	.215	.213	30	-8	0			.990	-1	1-10/S-4,302	-1.1
Total	2	74	189	12	37	3	2	0	22	12	17	.196	.248	.233	44	-13	2	7		.929	2	/3-32,1-10,OS2	-1.6

■ ABBIE JOHNSON
Johnson, Albert L. b: 7/26/1872, London, Ont., Can. 5'9.5", 165 lbs. Deb: 9/1/1896

YEAR	TM/L	G	AB	R	H	2B	3B	HR	RBI	BB	SO	AVG	OBP	SLG	PRO+	BR/A	SB	CS	SBR	FA	FR	G/POS	TPR
1896	Lou-N	25	87	10	20	2	1	0	14	4	6	.230	.264	.276	44	-7	0			.937	-5	2-25	-0.9
1897	Lou-N	48	161	16	39	6	1	0	23	13		.242	.303	.292	59	-9	2			.879	-11	2-33,S-12	-1.6
Total	2	73	248	26	59	8	2	0	37	17	6	.238	.289	.286	54	-16	2			.903	-15	/2-58,S-12	-2.5

■ ALEX JOHNSON
Johnson, Alexander b: 12/7/42, Helena, Ark. BR/TR, 6', 205 lbs. Deb: 7/25/64

YEAR	TM/L	G	AB	R	H	2B	3B	HR	RBI	BB	SO	AVG	OBP	SLG	PRO+	BR/A	SB	CS	SBR	FA	FR	G/POS	TPR
1964	Phi-N	43	109	18	33	7	1	4	18	6	26	.303	.345	.495	135	5	1	2	-1	.980	-1	O-35	0.2
1965	Phi-N	97	262	27	77	9	3	8	28	15	60	.294	.337	.443	120	6	4	4	-1	.966	-5	O-82	-0.2
1966	StL-N	25	86	7	16	0	1	2	6	5	18	.186	.231	.279	41	-7	1	1	-0	.962	-1	O-22	-1.0
1967	StL-N	81	175	20	39	9	2	1	12	9	26	.223	.273	.314	68	-7	1	0	-0	.970	0	O-57	-1.0
1968	Cin-N	149	603	79	188	32	6	2	58	26	71	.312	.343	.395	114	10	16	6	1	.947	5	*O-140	0.9
1969	Cin-N	139	523	86	165	18	4	17	88	25	69	.315	.357	.463	122	14	11	8	-2	.927	1	*O-132	0.7
1970	Cal-A★	156	614	85	202	26	6	14	86	35	68	.329	.372	.459	133	26	17	2	4	.959	5	*O-156	2.7
1971	Cal-A	65	242	19	63	8	0	2	21	15	34	.260	.309	.318	84	-6	5	2	0	.926	-6	O-61	-1.5
1972	Cle-A	108	356	31	85	10	1	8	37	22	40	.239	.285	.340	83	-8	6	8	-3	.955	-5	O-95	-2.4
1973	Tex-A	158	624	62	179	26	3	8	68	32	82	.287	.324	.377	101	-1	10	5	0	.987	1	*D-116,O-41	-0.4
1974	Tex-A	114	453	57	132	14	3	4	41	28	59	.291	.338	.362	104	2	20	9	1	.956	0	O-81,D-32	0.4
	NY-A	10	28	3	6	1	0	1	2	0	3	.214	.214	.357	64	-1	0	0	0	.000	-0	/O-1,D-4	-0.2
	Yr	124	481	60	138	15	3	5	43	28	62	.287	.331	.362	102	1	20	9	1	.956	5	O-82,D-36	0.2
1975	NY-A	52	119	15	31	5	1	1	15	7	21	.261	.302	.345	85	-3	2	3	-1	1.000	1	D-28/O-7	-0.6
1976	Det-A	125	429	41	115	15	2	6	45	19	49	.268	.302	.354	88	-7	14	10	-2	.954	-3	O-90,D-19	-1.8
Total	13	1322	4623	550	1331	180	33	78	525	244	626	.288	.329	.392	105	23	113	63	-4	.953	-5	O-1000,D-199	-4.2

■ TONY JOHNSON
Johnson, Anthony Clair b: 6/23/56, Memphis, Tenn. BR/TR, 6'3", 145 lbs. Deb: 9/28/81

YEAR	TM/L	G	AB	R	H	2B	3B	HR	RBI	BB	SO	AVG	OBP	SLG	PRO+	BR/A	SB	CS	SBR	FA	FR	G/POS	TPR
1981	Mon-N	2	1	0	0	0	0	0	0	0	0	.000	.000	.000	-99	-0	0	0	0	.000	-0	/O-1	-0.1
1982	Tor-A	70	98	17	23	2	1	3	14	11	26	.235	.312	.367	79	-3	3	13	-7	.979	-2	O-28,D-28	-1.4
Total	2	72	99	17	23	2	1	3	14	11	26	.232	.309	.364	77	-3	3	13	-7	.979	-3	/O-29,D-28	-1.5

■ BOB JOHNSON
Johnson, Bobby Earl b: 7/31/59, Dallas, Tex. BR/TR, 6'3", 195 lbs. Deb: 9/1/81

YEAR	TM/L	G	AB	R	H	2B	3B	HR	RBI	BB	SO	AVG	OBP	SLG	PRO+	BR/A	SB	CS	SBR	FA	FR	G/POS	TPR
1981	Tex-A	6	18	2	5	0	0	2	4	1	3	.278	.316	.611	171	1	0	0	0	1.000	-1	/C-5,1-1	0.1
1982	Tex-A	20	56	4	7	2	0	2	7	3	22	.125	.183	.268	23	-6	0	1	-1	1.000	0	C-14/1-3	-0.6
1983	Tex-A	72	175	18	37	6	1	5	16	16	55	.211	.281	.343	72	-7	3	0	1	1.000	3	C-62,1-10	-0.1
Total	3	98	249	24	49	8	1	9	27	20	80	.197	.262	.345	68	-12	3	1		1.000		/C-81,1-14	-0.6

■ BRIAN JOHNSON
Johnson, Brian David b: 1/8/68, Oakland, Cal. BR/TR, 6'2", 210 lbs. Deb: 4/5/94

YEAR	TM/L	G	AB	R	H	2B	3B	HR	RBI	BB	SO	AVG	OBP	SLG	PRO+	BR/A	SB	CS	SBR	FA	FR	G/POS	TPR
1994	SD-N	36	93	7	23	4	1	3	16	5	21	.247	.286	.409	79	-3	0	0	0	1.000	2	C-24/1-5	0.0

■ CALEB JOHNSON
Johnson, Caleb Clark b: 5/23/1844, Fulton, Ill. d: 3/7/25, Sterling, Ill. Deb: 5/24/1871

YEAR	TM/L	G	AB	R	H	2B	3B	HR	RBI	BB	SO	AVG	OBP	SLG	PRO+	BR/A	SB	CS	SBR	FA	FR	G/POS	TPR
1871	Cle-n	16	67	10	15	1	0	0	7	0	1	.224	.224	.239	35	-5	1					/2-8,O-7,S	-0.4

■ CHARLIE JOHNSON
Johnson, Charles Cleveland "Home Run" b: 3/12/1885, Slatington, Pa. d: 8/28/40, Marcus Hook, Pa. BL/TL, 5'9", 150 lbs. Deb: 9/21/08

YEAR	TM/L	G	AB	R	H	2B	3B	HR	RBI	BB	SO	AVG	OBP	SLG	PRO+	BR/A	SB	CS	SBR	FA	FR	G/POS	TPR
1908	Phi-N	6	16	2	4	0	1	0	2	1		.250	.333	.375	122	0	0			1.000	-0	/O-4	0.0

■ CHARLES JOHNSON
Johnson, Charles Edward b: 7/20/71, Fort Pierce, Fla. BR/TR, 6'2", 215 lbs. Deb: 5/6/94

YEAR	TM/L	G	AB	R	H	2B	3B	HR	RBI	BB	SO	AVG	OBP	SLG	PRO+	BR/A	SB	CS	SBR	FA	FR	G/POS	TPR
1994	Fla-N	4	11	5	5	1	0	1	4	1	4	.455	.500	.818	224	2	0	0	0	1.000	0	/C-4	0.2

■ CLIFF JOHNSON
Johnson, Clifford b: 7/22/47, San Antonio, Tex. BR/TR, 6'4", 225 lbs. Deb: 9/13/72

YEAR	TM/L	G	AB	R	H	2B	3B	HR	RBI	BB	SO	AVG	OBP	SLG	PRO+	BR/A	SB	CS	SBR	FA	FR	G/POS	TPR
1972	Hou-N	5	4	0	1	0	0	0	0	0	0	.250	.500	.250	121	0	0	0	0	1.000	1	/C-1	0.1
1973	Hou-N	7	20	6	6	2	0	2	6	1	7	.300	.364	.700	189	2	0	0	0	1.000	-0	/1-5	0.2
1974	Hou-N	83	171	26	39	4	1	10	29	33	45	.228	.362	.439	129	7	0	1	-1	.978	-4	C-28,1-21	0.3
1975	Hou-N	122	340	52	94	16	1	20	65	46	64	.276	.371	.506	152	23	1	0	0	.991	-7	1-47,C-41/O	1.0
1976	Hou-N	108	318	36	72	21	2	10	49	62	59	.226	.359	.399	126	12	0	1	-1	.977	-12	C-66,O-20,1	0.1
1977	Hou-N	51	144	22	43	8	0	10	23	23	30	.299	.409	.563	173	15	0	1	-1	.946	-0	O-34,1-10	1.2
	*NY-A	56	142	24	42	8	0	12	31	20	23	.296	.405	.606	173	15	0	1	-1	1.000	3	D-25,C-15,1	1.5
1978	*NY-A	76	174	20	32	9	1	6	19	30	32	.184	.307	.351	87	-3	0	0	0	.975	0	D-39,C-22/1	-0.4
1979	NY-A	28	64	11	17	6	0	2	6	10	7	.266	.365	.453	122	2	0	0	0	1.000	0	D-22/C-4	0.1
	Cle-A	72	240	37	65	10	0	18	61	24	39	.271	.349	.538	135	11	2	0	0	.000	-0	D-62/C-1	0.9
	Yr	100	304	48	82	16	0	20	67	34	46	.270	.353	.520	132	13	2	0	0	1.000	0	D-84/C-5	0.9
1980	Cle-A	54	174	25	40	3	1	6	28	25	30	.230	.327	.362	88	-3	0	1	-1	.000	0	D-45	-0.5
	Chi-N	68	196	28	46	0	0	10	34	29	35	.235	.336	.429	104	1	0	0	0	.992	-6	1-46/O-3,C	-0.8
1981	*Oak-A	84	273	40	71	8	0	17	59	28	60	.260	.336	.476	138	13	5	3	-0	1.000	1	D-68/1-9	0.9
1982	Oak-A	73	214	19	51	10	0	7	31	26	41	.238	.326	.383	98	-0	1	2	-1	.987	1	D-48,1-11	-0.3
1983	Tor-A	142	407	59	108	23	1	22	76	67	69	.265	.376	.489	128	17	0	1	-1	1.000	0	*D-130/1-6	1.1
1984	Tor-A	127	359	51	109	23	1	16	61	50	62	.304	.393	.507	142	21	0	1	-1	1.000	-1	*D-109/1-2	1.7
1985	Tex-A	82	296	31	76	17	1	12	56	31	44	.257	.333	.443	109	3	0	0	0	.000	0	D-82	-0.2
	*Tor-A	24	73	4	20	0	0	1	10	9	15	.274	.354	.315	83	-1	0	0	0	.947	-1	D-21/1-3	-0.2
	Yr	106	369	35	96	17	1	13	66	40	59	.260	.337	.417	104	2	0	0	0	.947	-1	*D-103/1-3	0.0
1986	Tor-A	107	336	48	84	12	1	15	55	52	57	.250	.357	.426	109	5	0	0	0	1.000	0	D-95/1-1	0.3
Total	15	1369	3945	539	1016	188	10	196	699	568	719	.258	.358	.459	129	141	9	12	-5	.993	-33	D-746,1-189,C/O	7.4

YEAR	TM/L	G	AB	R	H	2B	3B	HR	RBI	BB	SO	AVG	OBP	SLG	PRO+	BR/A	SB	CS	SBR	FA	FR	G/POS	TPR

■ DARRELL JOHNSON

Johnson, Darrell Dean b: 8/25/28, Horace, Neb. BR/TR, 6'1", 180 lbs. Deb: 4/20/52 MC

YEAR	TM/L	G	AB	R	H	2B	3B	HR	RBI	BB	SO	AVG	OBP	SLG	PRO+	BR/A	SB	CS	SBR	FA	FR	G/POS	TPR
1952	StL-A	29	78	9	22	2	1	0	9	11	4	.282	.371	.333	94	-0	0	0	0	.990	1	C-22	0.2
	Chi-A	22	37	3	4	0	0	0	1	5	9	.108	.214	.108	-8	-5	1	0	0	.955	5	C-21	0.0
	Yr	51	115	12	26	2	1	0	10	16	13	.226	.321	.261	62	-5	1	0	0	.974	6	C-43	0.2
1957	NY-A	21	46	4	10	1	0	1	8	3	10	.217	.280	.304	61	-3	0	0	0	1.000	4	C-20	0.2
1958	NY-A	5	16	1	4	0	0	0	0	0	2	.250	.250	.250	39	-1	0	0	0	1.000	1	/C-4	0.0
1960	StL-N	8	2	0	0	0	0	0	0	1	0	.000	.333	.000	1	-0	0	0	0	1.000	1	/C-8	0.1
1961	Phi-N	21	61	4	14	1	0	0	3	3	8	.230	.277	.246	41	-5	0	0	0	.982	2	C-21	-0.2
	*Cin-N	20	54	3	17	2	0	1	6	1	2	.315	.327	.407	92	-1	0	0	0	1.000	4	C-20	0.4
	Yr	41	115	7	31	3	0	1	9	4	10	.270	.300	.322	65	-6	0	0	0	.991	6	C-41	0.2
1962	Cin-N	2	4	0	0	0	0	0	0	2	0	.000	.333	.000	-2	-0	0	0	0	1.000	2	/C-2	0.1
	Bal-A	6	22	0	4	0	0	0	1	0	4	.182	.182	.182	-2	-3	0	0	0	1.000	-1	/C-6	-0.4
Total	6	134	320	24	75	6	1	2	28	26	39	.234	.296	.278	57	-19	1	0	0	.988	20	C-124	0.4

■ DAVEY JOHNSON

Johnson, David Allen b: 1/30/43, Orlando, Fla. BR/TR, 6'1", 180 lbs. Deb: 4/13/65 M

YEAR	TM/L	G	AB	R	H	2B	3B	HR	RBI	BB	SO	AVG	OBP	SLG	PRO+	BR/A	SB	CS	SBR	FA	FR	G/POS	TPR
1965	Bal-A	20	47	5	8	3	0	0	1	5	6	.170	.250	.234	38	-4	3	0	1	.929	3	/3-9,2-3,S	0.0
1966	*Bal-A	131	501	45	129	20	3	7	56	31	64	.257	.302	.351	88	-8	3	4	-2	.971	2	*2-126/S-3	0.2
1967	Bal-A	148	510	62	126	30	3	10	64	59	82	.247	.330	.376	109	6	4	5	-2	.981	0	*2-144/3-3	1.6
1968	Bal-A★	145	504	50	122	24	4	9	56	44	80	.242	.309	.359	102	1	7	3	0	.978	4	*2-127,S-34	1.6
1969	*Bal-A†	142	511	52	143	34	1	7	57	57	52	.280	.356	.391	108	6	3	4	-2	.984	-3	*2-142/S-2	1.3
1970	*Bal-A★	149	530	68	149	27	1	10	53	66	68	.281	.361	.392	106	6	2	1	0	.990	1	*2-149/S-2	1.9
1971	*Bal-A	142	510	67	144	26	1	18	72	51	55	.282	.353	.443	125	17	3	1	0	.984	-1	*2-140	3.0
1972	Bal-A	118	376	31	83	22	3	5	32	52	68	.221	.322	.335	93	-2	1	1	-0	.990	10	*2-116	1.6
1973	Atl-N★	157	559	84	151	25	0	43	99	81	93	.270	.371	.546	140	30	5	3	-0	.966	-3	*2-156	3.7
1974	Atl-N	136	454	56	114	18	0	15	62	75	59	.251	.361	.390	105	5	1	2	-1	.993	7	1-73,2-71	1.0
1975	Atl-N	1	1	0	1	1	0	0	1	0	0	1.000	1.000	2.000	691	1	0	0	0	.000	0	H	0.1
1977	*Phi-N	78	156	23	50	9	1	8	36	23	20	.321	.414	.545	148	11	1	1	-0	1.000	-2	1-43/2-9,3	0.8
1978	Phi-N	44	89	14	17	2	0	2	14	10	19	.191	.287	.281	59	-5	0	0	0	.930	-6	2-15/3-9,1	-1.1
	Chi-N	24	49	5	15	1	1	2	6	5	9	.306	.393	.490	130	2	0	0	0	.839	-3	3-12	-0.1
	Yr	68	138	19	32	3	1	4	20	15	28	.232	.325	.355	86	-2	0	0	0	.844	-9	3-21,2-15/1	-1.2
Total	13	1435	4797	564	1252	242	18	136	609	559	675	.261	.343	.404	110	66	33	25	-5	.980	10	*2-1198,1-123/S3	15.6

■ DERON JOHNSON

Johnson, Deron Roger b: 7/17/38, San Diego, Cal. d: 4/23/92, Poway, Cal. BR/TR, 6'2", 209 lbs. Deb: 9/20/60 C

YEAR	TM/L	G	AB	R	H	2B	3B	HR	RBI	BB	SO	AVG	OBP	SLG	PRO+	BR/A	SB	CS	SBR	FA	FR	G/POS	TPR
1960	NY-A	6	4	0	2	1	0	0	0	0	0	.500	.500	.750	247	1	0	0	0	.750	0	/3-5	0.1
1961	NY-A	13	19	1	2	0	0	0	2	2	5	.105	.190	.105	-20	-3	0	0	0	1.000	0	/3-8	-0.1
	KC-A	83	283	31	61	11	3	8	42	14	44	.216	.255	.360	61	-16	0	1	-1	.948	3	O-59,3-19/1	-1.8
	Yr	96	302	32	63	11	3	8	44	16	49	.209	.251	.344	57	-19	0	1	-1	.948	5	O-59,3-27/1	-1.9
1962	KC-A	17	19	1	2	1	0	0	0	3	8	.105	.227	.158	6	-3	0	0	0	1.000	-1	/1-2,3-2,O	-0.4
1964	Cin-N	140	477	63	130	24	4	21	79	37	98	.273	.328	.472	118	10	4	3	-1	.990	3	*1-131,O-10/3	0.7
1965	Cin-N	159	616	92	177	30	7	32	130	52	97	.287	.345	.515	129	23	0	4	-2	.948	-12	*3-159	0.5
1966	Cin-N	142	505	75	130	25	3	24	81	39	87	.257	.313	.461	103	1	2	1	0	.980	-8	*O-106,1-71,3	-1.5
1967	Cin-N	108	361	39	81	18	1	13	53	22	104	.224	.273	.388	78	-11	0	1	-1	.997	-4	1-81,3-24	-2.2
1968	Atl-N	127	342	29	71	11	1	8	33	35	79	.208	.287	.316	81	-8	0	1	-1	.996	-4	1-97,3-21	-1.8
1969	Phi-N	138	475	51	121	19	4	17	80	60	111	.255	.338	.419	114	9	4	2	0	1.000	-14	O-72,3-50,1	-1.0
1970	Phi-N	159	574	66	147	28	3	27	93	72	132	.256	.339	.456	114	10	0	0	0	.995	-11	*1-154/3-3	-1.3
1971	Phi-N	158	582	74	154	29	0	34	95	72	146	.265	.348	.490	135	26	0	1	-1	.995	-4	*1-136,3-22	0.9
1972	Phi-N	96	230	19	49	4	1	9	31	26	69	.213	.301	.357	84	-5	0	1	-1	.982	-4	1-62	-1.5
1973	Phi-N	12	36	3	6	2	0	1	5	5	10	.167	.286	.306	62	-2	0	0	0	.976	-0	1-10	-0.3
	*Oak-A	131	464	61	114	14	2	19	81	59	116	.246	.332	.407	113	8	0	1	-1	.994	-3	*D-107,1-23	0.0
1974	Oak-A	50	174	16	34	1	2	7	23	11	37	.195	.243	.345	72	-7	1	0	0	.991	-2	1-28,D-23	-1.2
	Mil-A	49	152	14	23	3	0	6	18	21	41	.151	.254	.289	56	-9	1	0	0	.833	-0	D-46/1-2	-1.1
	Bos-A	11	25	0	3	0	0	0	2	0	6	.120	.120	.120	-29	-4	0	0	0	.000	0	/D-8	-0.5
	Yr	110	351	30	60	4	2	13	43	32	84	.171	.240	.305	57	-20	2	0	1	.983	-3	D-69,1-30/H	-2.8
1975	Chi-A	148	555	66	129	25	1	18	72	48	117	.232	.295	.378	88	-10	0	1	-1	.994	-4	D-93,1-55	-2.2
	Bos-A	3	10	2	6	0	0	1	3	2	0	.600	.667	.900	313	3	0	0	0	1.000	-1	/1-2,D-1	0.2
	Yr	151	565	68	135	25	1	19	75	50	117	.239	.302	.388	92	-7	0	1	-1	.994	-5	D-94,1-57	-2.0
1976	Bos-A	15	38	3	5	1	1	0	5	0	11	.132	.233	.211	27	-4	0	0	0	1.000	0	/1-5,D-9	-0.4
Total	16	1765	5941	706	1447	247	33	245	923	585	1318	.244	.313	.420	102	9	11	18	-8	.993	-63	1-880,3-332,DO	-14.9

■ DON JOHNSON

Johnson, Donald Spore "Pep" b: 12/7/11, Chicago, Ill. BR/TR, 6', 170 lbs. Deb: 9/26/43 F

YEAR	TM/L	G	AB	R	H	2B	3B	HR	RBI	BB	SO	AVG	OBP	SLG	PRO+	BR/A	SB	CS	SBR	FA	FR	G/POS	TPR
1943	Chi-N	10	42	5	8	2	0	0	1	2	4	.190	.227	.238	35	-4	0			.957	3	2-10	0.0
1944	Chi-N☆	154	608	50	169	37	1	2	71	28	48	.278	.311	.352	87	-12	8			.947	1	*2-154	-0.3
1945	*Chi-N†	138	557	94	168	23	2	2	58	32	34	.302	.343	.361	98	-2	9			.975	10	*2-138	1.7
1946	Chi-N	83	314	37	76	10	1	1	19	26	39	.242	.306	.290	71	-12	6			.981	-10	2-83	-1.7
1947	Chi-N	120	402	33	104	17	2	3	26	24	45	.259	.302	.333	71	-17	2			.970	-4	*2-108/3-6	-1.4
1948	Chi-N	6	12	0	3	0	0	0	0	0	1	.250	.250	.250	37	-1	1			1.000	1	/2-2,3-2	-0.3
Total	6	511	1935	219	528	89	6	8	175	112	171	.273	.315	.337	83	-48	26			.966	-2	2-495/3-8	-2.0

■ ED JOHNSON

Johnson, Edwin Cyril b: 3/31/1899, Morganfield, Ky. d: 7/3/75, Morganfield, Ky. BL/TR, 5'9", 160 lbs. Deb: 9/26/20

YEAR	TM/L	G	AB	R	H	2B	3B	HR	RBI	BB	SO	AVG	OBP	SLG	PRO+	BR/A	SB	CS	SBR	FA	FR	G/POS	TPR
1920	Was-A	4	13	1	3	0	0	0	2	3	2	.231	.375	.231	65	-0	0	0	0	.625	-1	/O-4	-0.1

■ ELMER JOHNSON

Johnson, Elmer Ellsworth "Hickory" b: 6/12/1884, Beard, Ind. d: 10/31/66, Hollywood, Fla. BR/TR, 5'9", 185 lbs. Deb: 4/24/14

YEAR	TM/L	G	AB	R	H	2B	3B	HR	RBI	BB	SO	AVG	OBP	SLG	PRO+	BR/A	SB	CS	SBR	FA	FR	G/POS	TPR
1914	NY-N	11	12	0	2	1	0	0	0	1	3	.167	.231	.250	44	-1	0			.947	-1	C-11	-0.2

■ ERIK JOHNSON

Johnson, Erik Anthony b: 10/11/65, Oakland, Cal. BR/TR, 5'11", 175 lbs. Deb: 7/8/93

YEAR	TM/L	G	AB	R	H	2B	3B	HR	RBI	BB	SO	AVG	OBP	SLG	PRO+	BR/A	SB	CS	SBR	FA	FR	G/POS	TPR
1993	SF-N	4	5	1	2	2	0	0	0	0	1	.400	.400	.800	219	1	0	0	0	1.000	-1	/2-2,3-1,S	0.0
1994	SF-N	5	13	0	2	0	0	0	0	0	4	.154	.154	.154	-20	-2	0	0	0	1.000	1	/2-2,S-1	-0.1
Total	2	9	18	1	4	2	0	0	0	0	5	.222	.222	.333	45	-2	0	0	0	1.000	-0	/2-4,S-2,3	-0.1

■ ERNIE JOHNSON

Johnson, Ernest Rudolph b: 4/29/1888, Chicago, Ill. d: 5/1/52, Monrovia, Cal. BL/TR, 5'9", 151 lbs. Deb: 8/5/12 F

YEAR	TM/L	G	AB	R	H	2B	3B	HR	RBI	BB	SO	AVG	OBP	SLG	PRO+	BR/A	SB	CS	SBR	FA	FR	G/POS	TPR
1912	Chi-A	21	42	7	11	0	1	0	5	1		.262	.279	.310	70	-2	0			.984	3	S-16	0.2
1915	StL-F	152	512	58	123	18	10	7	67	46	35	.240	.305	.355	73	-21	32			.942	18	*S-152	1.0
1916	StL-A	74	236	29	54	9	3	0	19	30	23	.229	.323	.292	89	-2	13			.936	-8	S-60,3-12	-0.8
1917	StL-A	80	199	28	49	6	2	2	20	12	16	.246	.296	.327	93	-2	13			.924	11	S-39,2-18,3	1.2
1918	StL-A	29	34	7	9	1	0	0	0	6	2	.265	.286	.294	77	-1	4			.821	-2	S-11/3-1	-0.3
1921	Chi-A	142	613	93	181	28	7	1	51	29	24	.295	.328	.369	78	-21	22	13	-1	.947	18	*S-141	0.9
1922	Chi-A	144	603	85	153	17	3	0	56	40	30	.254	.304	.292	56	-38	21	18	-5	.952	2	*S-141	-2.6
1923	Chi-A	12	53	5	10	2	0	0	3	3	5	.189	.246	.226	25	-6	2	1	0	.922	-6	S-12	-0.5
	*NY-A	19	38	6	17	1	1	0	8	1	1	.447	.462	.605	176	4	0	0	0	.977	-1	S-15/3-1	0.4
	Yr	31	91	11	27	3	1	0	11	4	6	.297	.333	.385	88	-2	2	1	0	.944	-1	S-27/3-1	-0.1
1924	NY-A	64	119	24	42	4	8	3	12	11	7	.353	.412	.597	158	10	1	6	-3	.955	-1	2-27/S-9,3	0.5
1925	NY-A	76	170	30	48	5	1	5	17	12	9	.282	.315	.412	85	-5	6	3	0	.955	-10	2-34,S-28/3	-1.2
Total	10	813	2619	372	697	91	36	19	256	181	153	.266	.317	.350	78	-84	114	41		.944	29	S-624/2-79,3	-1.2

YEAR	TM/L	G	AB	R	H	2B	3B	HR	RBI	BB	SO	AVG	OBP	SLG	PRO+	BR/A	SB	CS	SBR	FA	FR	G/POS	TPR

■ FRANK JOHNSON Johnson, Frank Herbert b: 7/22/42, ElPaso, Tex. BR/TR, 6'1", 155 lbs. Deb: 9/7/66

1966	SF-N	15	32	2	7	0	0	0	0	2	7	.219	.265	.219	35	-3	0	1	-1	1.000	-3	O-13	-0.8
1967	SF-N	8	10	3	3	0	0	0	0	1	2	.300	.364	.300	93	-0	0	0	0	.889	-0	/O-3	0.0
1968	SF-N	67	174	11	33	2	0	1	7	12	23	.190	.246	.218	40	-12	1	0	0	.944	3	3-36/O-8,S2	-1.0
1969	SF-N	7	10	2	1	0	0	0	0	0	1	.100	.100	.100	-45	-2	0	0	0	1.000	-1	/O-7	-0.3
1970	SF-N	67	161	25	44	1	2	3	31	19	18	.273	.357	.360	94	-1	1	1	-0	.979	-2	O-33,1-27	-0.6
1971	SF-N	32	49	4	4	1	0	0	5	3	9	.082	.135	.102	-33	-9	0	0	0	.975	-3	/1-9,O-4	-1.3
Total	6	196	436	47	92	4	2	4	43	37	60	.211	.277	.257	52	-26	2	2	-1	.979	-6	/O-68,1-36,3S2	-4.0

■ HOWARD JOHNSON Johnson, Howard Michael b: 11/29/60, Clearwater, Fla. BB/TR, 5'11", 178 lbs. Deb: 4/14/82

1982	Det-A	54	155	23	49	5	0	4	14	16	30	.316	.384	.426	122	5	7	4	-0	.901	-9	3-33,D-10/O	-0.5
1983	Det-A	27	66	11	14	0	0	3	5	7	10	.212	.297	.348	79	-2	0	0	0	.851	-6	3-21/D-2	-0.8
1984	*Det-A	116	355	43	88	14	1	12	50	40	67	.248	.326	.394	99	-0	10	6	-1	.944	-18	*3-108/S-9,10D	-2.0
1985	NY-N	126	389	38	94	18	4	11	46	34	78	.242	.303	.393	96	-3	6	4	-1	.941	-13	3-113/S-7,O	-1.8
1986	NY-N	88	220	30	54	14	0	10	39	31	64	.245	.341	.445	119	5	8	1	2	.903	-2	3-45,S-34/O	0.7
1987	NY-N	157	554	93	147	22	1	36	99	83	113	.265	.366	.504	135	27	32	10	4	.938	-18	*3-140,S-38/O	1.3
1988	*NY-N	148	495	85	114	21	1	24	68	86	104	.230	.348	.422	126	18	23	7	3	.951	-14	*3-131/S-52	1.0
1989	NY-N★	153	571	**104**	164	41	3	36	101	77	126	.287	.373	.559	171	51	41	8	8	.910	-33	*3-143,S-31	3.0
1990	NY-N	154	590	89	144	37	3	23	90	69	100	.244	.323	.434	107	4	34	8	5	.913	-5	3-92,S-73	1.1
1991	NY-N★	156	564	108	146	34	4	**38**	**117**	78	120	.259	.350	.535	147	33	30	16	-1	.927	-4	*3-104,O-30,S	3.2
1992	NY-N	100	350	48	78	19	0	7	43	55	79	.223	.332	.337	91	-3	22	5	4	.981	-4	O-98	-0.6
1993	NY-N	72	235	32	56	8	2	7	26	43	43	.238	.356	.379	98	-0	6	4	-1	.944	5	3-67	0.5
1994	Col-N	93	227	30	48	10	2	10	40	39	73	.211	.327	.405	77	-8	11	3	2	.979	-2	O-62/1-1	-1.0
Total	13	1444	4771	734	1196	243	21	221	738	658	1007	.251	.343	.449	120	128	230	76	23	.929	-121	3-997,S-272,O/D1	4.1

■ SPUD JOHNSON Johnson, John Ralph b: 1860, Canada BL/TL, 5'9", 175 lbs. Deb: 4/18/1889

1889	Col-a	116	459	91	130	14	10	2	79	39	47	.283	.355	.370	112	9	34			.879	-11	O-69,3-44/1S	-0.2
1890	Col-a	135	538	106	186	23	18	1		48		.346	.409	.461	168	46	43			.926	-16	*O-135	2.2
1891	Cle-N	80	327	49	84	8	3	1	46	22	23	.257	.319	.309	80	-9	16			.872	-5	O-79/1-1	-1.4
Total	3	331	1324	246	400	45	31	4	125	109	70	.302	.368	.392	125	46	93			.899	-32	O-283/3-44,1S	0.6

■ LANCE JOHNSON Johnson, Kenneth Lance b: 7/6/63, Cincinnati, Ohio BL/TL, 5'10", 160 lbs. Deb: 7/10/87

1987	*StL-N	33	59	4	13	2	1	0	7	4	6	.220	.270	.288	47	-4	6	1	1	.931	-6	O-25	-0.9
1988	Chi-A	33	124	11	23	4	1	0	6	6	11	.185	.223	.234	28	-12	6	2	1	.970	-4	O-31/D-1	-1.7
1989	Chi-A	50	180	28	54	8	2	0	16	17	24	.300	.360	.367	108	2	16	3	3	.983	0	O-45/D-1	0.4
1990	Chi-A	151	541	76	154	18	9	1	51	33	45	.285	.327	.357	93	-5	36	22	-2	.973	-2	*O-148/D-1	-1.3
1991	Chi-A	159	588	72	161	14	**13**	0	49	26	58	.274	.306	.342	81	-16	26	11	1	.995	13	*O-157	-0.5
1992	Chi-A	157	567	67	158	15	**12**	3	47	34	33	.279	.321	.363	92	-6	41	14	4	.987	6	*O-157	0.3
1993	*Chi-A	147	540	75	168	18	**14**	0	47	36	33	.311	.354	.396	104	3	35	7	6	.980	16	*O-146	2.1
1994	Chi-A	106	412	56	114	11	14	3	54	26	23	.277	.323	.393	84	-10	26	6	4	1.000	13	*O-103/D-1	0.5
Total	8	836	3011	389	845	90	66	7	277	182	233	.281	.323	.361	88	-49	192	66	18	.985	39	O-812/D-4	-1.1

■ LAMAR JOHNSON Johnson, Lamar b: 9/2/50, Bessemer, Ala. BR/TR, 6'2", 225 lbs. Deb: 5/18/74

1974	Chi-A	10	29	1	10	0	0	0	2	0	3	.345	.345	.345	100	-0	0	0	0	1.000	-0	/1-7,D-3	-0.1
1975	Chi-A	8	30	2	6	3	0	1	1	1	5	.200	.226	.400	73	-1	0	0	0	.960	-1	/1-6,D-2	-0.3
1976	Chi-A	82	222	29	71	11	1	4	33	19	37	.320	.379	.432	136	10	2	1	0	.983	-1	D-35,1-34/O	0.7
1977	Chi-A	118	374	52	113	12	5	18	65	24	53	.302	.344	.505	128	13	1	1	-0	.990	1	D-68,1-45	1.0
1978	Chi-A	148	498	52	136	23	2	8	72	43	46	.273	.333	.376	98	-1	6	5	-1	.992	2	*1-108,D-36	-0.8
1979	Chi-A	133	479	60	148	29	1	12	74	41	56	.309	.366	.449	118	12	8	2	1	.987	-1	1-94,D-37	0.6
1980	Chi-A	147	541	51	150	26	3	13	81	47	53	.277	.335	.409	103	2	2	3	-1	.990	2	1-80,D-66	-0.4
1981	Chi-A	41	134	10	37	7	0	1	15	5	14	.276	.302	.351	89	-2	0	2	-1	.989	-1	1-36/D-2	-0.8
1982	Tex-A	105	324	37	84	11	0	7	38	31	40	.259	.326	.358	92	-3	3	5	-2	.982	-2	D-77,1-12	-1.1
Total	9	792	2631	294	755	122	12	64	381	211	307	.287	.342	.415	109	30	22	19	-5	.989	-1	1-422,D-326/O	-1.2

■ LARRY JOHNSON Johnson, Larry Doby b: 8/17/50, Cleveland, Ohio BR/TR, 6', 185 lbs. Deb: 10/3/72

1972	Cle-A	1	2	0	1	0	0	0	0	0	1	.500	.500	.500	192	0	0	0	0	1.000	0	/C-1	0.1
1974	Cle-A	1	0	1	0	0	0	0	0	0	0	—	—	—	—	0	0	0	0	.000	0	R	0.0
1975	Mon-N	1	3	0	1	1	0	0	1	1	1	.333	.500	.667	212	1	0	0	0	1.000	-0	/C-1	0.0
1976	Mon-N	6	13	0	2	1	0	0	0	0	5	.154	.154	.231	8	-2	0	0	0	1.000	1	/C-5	-0.1
1978	Chi-A	3	8	0	1	0	0	0	0	0	0	.125	.222	.125	0	-1	0	0	0	.857	-0	/C-2,D-1	-0.2
Total	5	12	26	1	5	2	0	0	1	2	8	.192	.250	.269	46	-2	0	0	0	.975	-1	/C-9,D-1	-0.2

■ LOU JOHNSON Johnson, Louis Brown "Slick" b: 9/22/34, Lexington, Ky. BR/TR, 5'11", 175 lbs. Deb: 4/17/60

1960	Chi-N	34	68	6	14	2	1	0	5	1	19	.206	.270	.265	48	-5	3	1	0	1.000	1	O-25	-0.4
1961	LA-A	1	0	0	0	0	0	0	0	0	0	—	—	—	—	0	0	0	0	.000	-0	/O-1	0.0
1962	Mil-N	61	117	22	33	4	5	2	13	11	27	.282	.349	.453	116	3	6	1	1	1.000	-9	O-55	-0.7
1965	*LA-N	131	468	57	121	24	1	12	58	24	81	.259	.317	.391	105	-3	15	6	1	.985	-3	*O-128	-0.6
1966	*LA-N	152	526	71	143	20	2	17	73	21	75	.272	.317	.414	110	5	8	10	-4	.985	-2	*O-148	-0.7
1967	LA-N	104	330	39	89	14	1	11	41	24	52	.270	.332	.418	124	9	4	3	-1	.976	2	O-91	0.7
1968	Chi-N	62	205	14	50	14	3	1	14	6	23	.244	.289	.356	87	-3	3	1	0	.970	-4	O-57	-1.2
	Cle-A	65	202	25	52	11	1	5	23	9	24	.257	.302	.396	112	2	6	1	1	.989	-5	O-57	0.2
1969	Cal-A	67	133	10	27	8	0	0	9	10	19	.203	.274	.263	53	-8	5	1	1	.935	-5	O-44	-1.5
Total	8	677	2049	244	529	97	14	48	232	110	320	.258	.313	.389	103	5	50	24	1	.981	-19	O-606	-4.2

■ OTIS JOHNSON Johnson, Otis L. b: 11/5/1883, Fowler, Ind. d: 11/9/15, Johnson City, N.Y. BB/TR, 5'9", 185 lbs. Deb: 4/12/11

| 1911 | NY-A | 71 | 209 | 21 | 49 | 9 | 6 | 3 | 36 | 39 | | .234 | .363 | .378 | 100 | 1 | 12 | | | .907 | -9 | S-47,2-15/3 | -0.6 |

■ PAUL JOHNSON Johnson, Paul Oscar b: 9/2/1896, N.Grosvenor Dale, Conn. d: 2/14/73, McAllen, Tex. BR/TR, 5'8", 160 lbs. Deb: 9/13/20

1920	Phi-A	18	72	6	15	0	0	0	5	4	8	.208	.250	.208	22	-8	1	1	-0	.933	-3	O-18	-1.2
1921	Phi-A	48	127	17	40	6	2	1	10	9	17	.315	.360	.417	97	-1	0	2	-1	.969	-5	O-32	-0.8
Total	2	66	199	23	55	6	2	1	15	13	25	.276	.321	.342	71	-9	1	3	-2	.958	-7	/O-50	-2.0

■ RANDY JOHNSON Johnson, Randall Glenn b: 6/10/56, Escondido, Cal. BR/TR, 6'1", 190 lbs. Deb: 4/27/82

1982	Atl-N	27	46	5	11	0	0	0	6	6	4	.239	.352	.348	93	0	0	1	-1	.955	5	2-13/3-4	0.5
1983	Atl-N	86	144	22	36	3	0	1	17	20	27	.250	.345	.292	73	-5	1	3	-2	.991	10	3-53/2-4	0.4
1984	Atl-N	91	294	28	82	13	0	5	30	21	21	.279	.329	.374	91	-4	4	7	-3	.939	5	3-81	-0.3
Total	3	204	484	55	129	21	0	6	53	47	52	.267	.336	.347	85	-8	5	11	-5	.956	20	3-138/2-17	0.6

■ RANDY JOHNSON Johnson, Randall Stuart b: 8/15/58, Miami, Fla. BL/TL, 6'2", 195 lbs. Deb: 7/5/80

1980	Chi-A	12	20	0	4	0	0	0	3	2	5	.200	.304	.200	41	-1	0	0	0	.000	-0	/1-1,O-1,D	-0.2
1982	Min-A	89	234	26	58	10	0	10	33	30	46	.248	.333	.419	102	1	0	0	0	1.000	-0	D-67/O-2	-0.2
Total	2	101	254	26	62	10	0	10	36	32	50	.244	.331	.402	98	-1	0	0	0	1.000	-1	/D-71,O-3,1	-0.4

■ FOOTER JOHNSON Johnson, Richard Allan "Treads" b: 2/15/32, Dayton, Ohio BL/TL, 5'11", 175 lbs. Deb: 6/22/58

| 1958 | Chi-N | 8 | 5 | 1 | 0 | 0 | 0 | 0 | 0 | 0 | 1 | .000 | .000 | .000 | -99 | -1 | 0 | 0 | 0 | .000 | 0 | H | -0.1 |

YEAR	TM/L	G	AB	R	H	2B	3B	HR	RBI	BB	SO	AVG	OBP	SLG	PRO+	BR/A	SB	CS	SBR	FA	FR	G/POS	TPR

■ BOB JOHNSON
Johnson, Robert Lee "Indian Bob" b: 11/26/06, Pryor, Okla. d: 7/6/82, Tacoma, Wash. BR/TR, 6′, 180 lbs. Deb: 4/12/33 F

YEAR	TM/L	G	AB	R	H	2B	3B	HR	RBI	BB	SO	AVG	OBP	SLG	PRO+	BR/A	SB	CS	SBR	FA	FR	G/POS	TPR
1933	Phi-A	142	535	103	155	44	4	21	93	85	74	.290	.387	.505	133	26	8	3	1	.952	2	*O-142	1.9
1934	Phi-A	141	547	111	168	26	6	34	92	58	60	.307	.375	.563	144	33	12	8	-1	.967	10	*O-139	3.3
1935	Phi-A★	147	582	103	174	29	5	28	109	78	76	.299	.384	.510	130	25	2	4	-2	.946	4	*O-147	2.1
1936	Phi-A	153	566	91	165	29	14	25	121	88	71	.292	.389	.525	126	22	6	6	-2	.962	3	*O-131,2-22/1	1.7
1937	Phi-A	138	477	91	146	32	6	25	108	98	65	.306	.425	.556	148	37	9	7	-2	.976	9	*O-133/2-2	3.6
1938	Phi-A★	152	563	114	176	27	9	30	113	87	73	.313	.406	.552	142	36	9	8	-2	.963	10	*O-150/2-3,3	3.5
1939	Phi-A☆	150	544	115	184	30	9	23	114	99	59	.338	.440	.553	156	49	15	5	2	.967	7	*O-150/2-1	4.7
1940	Phi-A☆	138	512	93	137	25	4	31	103	83	64	.268	.374	.514	130	23	8	2	1	.962	5	*O-136	2.1
1941	Phi-A	149	552	98	152	30	8	22	107	95	75	.275	.385	.478	130	25	6	4	-1	.990	7	*O-122,1-28	2.1
1942	Phi-A★	149	550	78	160	35	7	13	80	82	61	.291	.384	.451	135	26	3	2	-0	.963	5	*O-149	2.4
1943	Was-A★	117	438	65	116	22	8	7	63	64	50	.265	.362	.400	127	16	11	5	0	.996	9	O-88,3-19,1	2.2
1944	Bos-A★	144	525	106	170	40	8	17	106	95	67	.324	**.431**	.528	**175**	**54**	2	7	-4	.977	4	*O-142	4.9
1945	Bos-A†	143	529	71	148	27	7	12	74	63	56	.280	.358	.425	124	16	5	3	-0	.975	3	*O-140	1.1
Total	13	1863	6920	1239	2051	396	95	288	1283	1075	851	.296	.393	.506	139	387	96	64	-10	.968	79	*O-1769/1-39,23	35.6

■ BOB JOHNSON
Johnson, Robert Wallace b: 3/4/36, Omaha, Neb. BR/TR, 5′10″, 175 lbs. Deb: 4/19/60

YEAR	TM/L	G	AB	R	H	2B	3B	HR	RBI	BB	SO	AVG	OBP	SLG	PRO+	BR/A	SB	CS	SBR	FA	FR	G/POS	TPR
1960	KC-A	76	146	12	30	4	0	1	9	19	23	.205	.301	.253	51	-10	2	0	1	.947	12	S-30,2-27,3	0.6
1961	Was-A	61	224	27	66	13	1	6	28	19	26	.295	.352	.442	113	4	4	2	0	.956	-2	S-57/2-2,3	0.6
1962	Was-A	135	466	58	134	20	2	12	43	32	50	.288	.335	.416	102	0	9	6	-1	.944	-4	3-72,S-50/2O	0.1
1963	Bal-A	82	254	34	75	10	0	8	32	18	35	.295	.347	.429	120	7	5	1	1	.987	-2	2-50/1-8,S3	1.0
1964	Bal-A	93	210	18	52	8	2	3	29	9	37	.248	.282	.348	74	-8	1	0	0	.964	-12	S-18,1-15,2/3O	-1.9
1965	Bal-A	87	273	36	66	13	2	5	27	15	34	.242	.284	.359	80	-8	1	0	0	.996	-11	1-34,S-23,3/2	-1.9
1966	Bal-A	71	157	13	34	5	0	1	10	12	24	.217	.276	.268	58	-8	1	1	-1	.966	0	2-20,1-17/3	-0.9
1967	Bal-A	4	3	1	1	0	0	0	0	1	1	.333	.500	.333	152	0	0	0	0	.000	0	H	0.0
	NY-N	90	230	26	80	8	3	5	27	12	29	.348	.380	.474	145	13	1	1	-0	.987	-7	2-39,1-23,S/3	0.8
1968	Cin-N	16	15	2	4	0	0	0	1	1	2	.267	.313	.267	71	-0	0	0	0	.500	-1	/S-2,1-1	-0.1
	Atl-N	59	187	15	49	5	1	0	11	10	20	.262	.299	.299	80	-5	0	0	0	.948	1	3-48/2-4	-0.3
	Yr	75	202	17	53	5	1	0	12	11	22	.262	.300	.297	79	-5	0	0	0	.948	1	3-48/2-4,S1	-0.4
1969	StL-N	19	29	1	6	0	0	1	2	2	4	.207	.258	.310	58	-2	0	0	0	.833	-1	/3-4,1-1	-0.3
	Oak-A	51	67	5	23	1	0	1	9	3	4	.343	.380	.403	125	2	0	0	0	1.000	0	/1-7,2-2	0.2
1970	Oak-A	30	46	6	8	1	0	1	2	3	2	.174	.240	.261	39	-4	2	1	0	.952	1	/3-6,1-1	-0.3
Total	11	874	2307	254	628	88	11	44	230	156	291	.272	.321	.377	95	-18	24	12	0	.956	-26	S-201,2-167,31/O	-2.4

■ RON JOHNSON
Johnson, Ronald David b: 3/23/56, Long Beach, Cal. BR/TR, 6′3″, 215 lbs. Deb: 9/12/82

YEAR	TM/L	G	AB	R	H	2B	3B	HR	RBI	BB	SO	AVG	OBP	SLG	PRO+	BR/A	SB	CS	SBR	FA	FR	G/POS	TPR
1982	KC-A	8	14	2	4	2	0	0	4	0	3	.286	.444	.429	141	1	0	0	0	.976	-0	/1-7	0.0
1983	KC-A	9	27	2	7	0	0	0	1	3	1	.259	.333	.259	66	-1	0	0	0	.971	-1	/1-7,C-2	-0.3
1984	Mon-N	5	5	0	1	0	0	0	1	0	2	.200	.200	.200	13	-1	0	0	0	1.000	-1	/1-2,O-1	-0.1
Total	3	22	46	4	12	2	0	0	2	7	6	.261	.358	.304	85	-1	0	0	0	.974	-2	/1-16,C-2,O	-0.4

■ RONDIN JOHNSON
Johnson, Rondin Allen b: 12/16/58, Bremerton, Wash. BB/TR, 5′10″, 160 lbs. Deb: 9/3/86

YEAR	TM/L	G	AB	R	H	2B	3B	HR	RBI	BB	SO	AVG	OBP	SLG	PRO+	BR/A	SB	CS	SBR	FA	FR	G/POS	TPR
1986	KC-A	11	31	1	8	0	1	0	2	0	3	.258	.258	.323	56	-2	0	0	0	1.000	4	2-11	0.2

■ ROY JOHNSON
Johnson, Roy Cleveland b: 2/23/03, Pryor, Okla. d: 9/10/73, Tacoma, Wash. BL/TR, 5′9″, 175 lbs. Deb: 4/18/29 F

YEAR	TM/L	G	AB	R	H	2B	3B	HR	RBI	BB	SO	AVG	OBP	SLG	PRO+	BR/A	SB	CS	SBR	FA	FR	G/POS	TPR
1929	Det-A	148	640	128	201	**45**	14	10	69	67	60	.314	.379	.475	118	17	20	15	-3	.928	14	*O-146	1.7
1930	Det-A	125	462	84	127	30	13	2	35	40	46	.275	.333	.409	85	-11	17	10	-1	.936	4	*O-118	-1.4
1931	Det-A	151	621	107	173	37	**19**	8	55	72	51	.279	.355	.438	104	3	33	21	-3	.960	15	*O-150	0.5
1932	Det-A	49	195	33	49	14	2	3	22	20	26	.251	.324	.390	81	-6	7	2	1	.929	-4	O-48	-0.7
	Bos-A	94	349	70	104	24	4	11	47	44	41	.298	.378	.484	125	13	13	4	2	.930	-6	O-85	0.3
	Yr	143	544	103	153	38	6	14	69	64	67	.281	.359	.450	109	7	20	6	2	.930	-5	*O-133	-0.4
1933	Bos-A	133	483	88	151	30	7	10	95	55	36	.313	.387	.466	126	19	13	10	-2	.922	4	*O-125	1.3
1934	Bos-A	143	569	85	182	43	10	7	119	54	36	.320	.379	.467	109	7	11	5	0	.948	-3	*O-137	-0.2
1935	Bos-A	145	553	70	174	33	9	3	66	74	34	.315	.398	.423	105	6	11	12	-4	.944	-2	*O-142	-0.4
1936	*NY-A	63	147	21	39	8	2	1	19	21	14	.265	.361	.367	83	-4	3	1	0	.944	0	O-33	-0.4
1937	NY-A	12	51	5	15	3	0	0	6	3	2	.294	.333	.353	73	-2	1	0	0	.840	-2	O-12	-0.4
	Bos-N	85	260	24	72	8	3	3	22	38	29	.277	.369	.365	110	5	5			.965	-1	O-63/3-1	0.2
1938	Bos-N	7	29	2	5	0	0	0	1	1	5	.172	.200	.172	4	-1				.769	-2	/O-7	-0.6
Total	10	1155	4359	717	1292	275	83	58	556	489	380	.296	.369	.437	107	43	135	80		.938	22	*O-1066/3-1	-0.1

■ ROY JOHNSON
Johnson, Roy Edward b: 6/27/59, Parkin, Ark. BL/TL, 6′4″, 205 lbs. Deb: 7/3/82

YEAR	TM/L	G	AB	R	H	2B	3B	HR	RBI	BB	SO	AVG	OBP	SLG	PRO+	BR/A	SB	CS	SBR	FA	FR	G/POS	TPR
1982	Mon-N	17	32	2	7	2	0	0	2	1	6	.219	.242	.281	45	-2	0	0	0	1.000	-2	O-11	-0.5
1984	Mon-N	16	33	2	5	2	0	1	2	7	10	.152	.300	.303	73	-1	1	0	0	.938	-1	O-10	-0.2
1985	Mon-N	3	5	0	0	0	0	0	0	0	3	.000	.000	.000	-99	-1	0	0	0	.000	-1	/O-3	-0.3
Total	3	36	70	4	12	4	0	1	4	8	19	.171	.256	.271	49	-5	1	0	0	.971	-4	/O-24	-1.0

■ STAN JOHNSON
Johnson, Stanley Lucius b: 2/12/37, Dallas, Tex. BL/TL, 5′10″, 180 lbs. Deb: 9/18/60

YEAR	TM/L	G	AB	R	H	2B	3B	HR	RBI	BB	SO	AVG	OBP	SLG	PRO+	BR/A	SB	CS	SBR	FA	FR	G/POS	TPR
1960	Chi-A	5	6	1	1	0	0	1	0	1	1	.167	.167	.667	116	0	0	1	-1	1.000	-1	/O-2	-0.1
1961	KC-A	3	3	1	0	0	0	0	1	2	1	.000	.400	.000	17	-0	0	0	0	.000	-1	/O-2	-0.1
Total	2	8	9	2	1	0	0	1	1	2	2	.111	.273	.444	89	-0	0	1	-1	1.000	-2	/O-4	-0.2

■ TIM JOHNSON
Johnson, Timothy Evald b: 7/22/49, Grand Forks, N.D. BL/TR, 6′1″, 170 lbs. Deb: 4/24/73 C

YEAR	TM/L	G	AB	R	H	2B	3B	HR	RBI	BB	SO	AVG	OBP	SLG	PRO+	BR/A	SB	CS	SBR	FA	FR	G/POS	TPR
1973	Mil-A	136	465	30	99	10	2	0	32	29	93	.213	.261	.243	44	-35	6	3	0	.962	-18	*S-135	-3.7
1974	Mil-A	93	245	25	60	7	7	0	25	11	48	.245	.280	.331	76	-8	4	3	-1	.970	-2	S-64,2-26/3OD	-0.3
1975	Mil-A	38	85	6	12	1	0	0	2	6	17	.141	.198	.153	0	-11	3	0	1	1.000	1	2-11,3-11,S/1D	-0.8
1976	Mil-A	105	273	25	75	4	3	0	14	19	32	.275	.327	.311	89	-3	4	1	1	.980	-18	*2-100,3-17/1S	-1.7
1977	Mil-A	30	33	5	2	1	0	0	2	5	10	.061	.184	.091	-22	-6	0	0	0	.929	3	2-10/S-6,3OD	-0.2
1978	Mil-A	3	3	1	0	0	0	0	0	2	0	.000	.400	.000	22	-0	0	0	0	1.000	-1	/S-2	-0.1
	Tor-A	68	79	9	19	2	0	0	3	8	16	.241	.318	.266	65	-3	0	0	-1	.975	5	S-49,2-13	0.4
	Yr	71	82	10	19	2	0	0	3	10	16	.232	.323	.256	63	-4	0	0	-1	.975	4	S-51,2-13	0.3
1979	Tor-A	43	86	6	16	2	1	0	8	8	15	.186	.255	.233	32	-9	1	1	0	.958	2	2-25/3-9,1	-0.2
Total	7	516	1269	116	283	27	13	0	84	88	231	.223	.276	.265	55	-75	18	9	0	.965	-25	S-267,2-185/31DO	-6.6

■ WALLACE JOHNSON
Johnson, Wallace Darnell b: 12/25/56, Gary, Ind. BB/TR, 5′11″, 185 lbs. Deb: 9/8/81

YEAR	TM/L	G	AB	R	H	2B	3B	HR	RBI	BB	SO	AVG	OBP	SLG	PRO+	BR/A	SB	CS	SBR	FA	FR	G/POS	TPR
1981	*Mon-N	11	9	1	2	1	0	0	3	1	1	.222	.300	.444	108	0	1	1	-0	1.000	1	/2-1	0.1
1982	Mon-N	36	57	5	11	2	0	0	5	5	5	.193	.258	.263	45	-4	4	1	1	.952	-6	2-13	-0.9
1983	Mon-N	3	2	1	1	0	0	0	0	0	0	.500	.667	.500	229	1	0	0	0	.000	0	/H	0.1
	SF-N	7	8	0	1	0	0	0	1	0	6	.125	.125	.125	-32	-1	0	0	0	1.000	-1	/2-1	-0.1
	Yr	10	10	1	2	0	0	0	1	0	6	.200	.273	.200	34	-1	0	0	0	1.000	-1	/2-1	-0.0
1984	Mon-N	17	24	3	5	0	0	0	2	3	1	.208	.345	.208	61	-1	0	0	0	.968	-1	/1-4	-0.1
1986	Mon-N	61	127	13	36	3	1	1	10	7	9	.283	.321	.346	85	-3	6	3	0	.991	-0	1-27	-0.5
1987	Mon-N	75	85	7	21	5	0	1	14	7	6	.247	.304	.341	69	-4	5	0	2	.972	-1	/1-9	-0.4
1988	Mon-N	86	94	3	29	5	1	0	12	2	15	.309	.387	.383	116	2	0	2	-1	.989	1	1-13/2-1	0.2
1989	Mon-N	85	114	9	31	3	1	2	17	7	12	.272	.314	.368	93	1	0	1	0	.972	-1	1-18	-0.4

YEAR	TM/L	G	AB	R	H	2B	3B	HR	RBI	BB	SO	AVG	OBP	SLG	PRO+	BR/A	SB	CS	SBR	FA	FR	G/POS	TPR
1990	Mon-N	47	49	6	8	1	0	1	5	7	6	.163	.281	.245	48	-3	1	0	0	1.000	-1	/1-7	-0.5
Total	9	428	569	52	145	17	6	5	59	52	58	.255	.318	.332	81	-15	19	7	2	.983	-7	/1-78,2-16	-2.5

■ WALTER JOHNSON

Johnson, Walter Perry "Barney" or "The Big Train"   b: 11/6/1887, Humboldt, Kan.   d: 12/10/46, Washington, D.C.   BR/TR, 6'1", 200 lbs.   Deb: 8/2/07   MH

YEAR	TM/L	G	AB	R	H	2B	3B	HR	RBI	BB	SO	AVG	OBP	SLG	PRO+	BR/A	SB	CS	SBR	FA	FR	G/POS	TPR
1907	Was-A	14	36	3	4	0	1	0	1	1		.111	.135	.167	-4	-4	0			.893	-2	P-14	0.0
1908	Was-A	36	79	7	13	3	2	0	5	6		.165	.250	.253	69	-3	0			.938	-4	P-36	0.0
1909	Was-A	40	101	6	13	3	0	1	6	1		.129	.137	.188	3	-11	0			.926	-2	P-40	0.0
1910	Was-A	45	137	14	24	6	1	2	12	4		.175	.199	.277	51	-8	2			.950	-1	P-45	0.0
1911	Was-A	42	128	18	30	5	3	1	15	0		.234	.234	.344	62	-7	1			.965	4	P-40	0.0
1912	Was-A	55	144	16	38	6	4	2	20	7		.264	.298	.403	99	-1	2			.964	1	P-50	0.0
1913	Was-A	54	134	12	35	5	6	2	14	5	14	.261	.293	.433	109	0	2			1.000	-0	P-48/O-1	0.0
1914	Was-A	55	136	23	30	4	1	3	16	10	27	.221	.274	.331	79	-4	2	1	0	.964	2	P-51/O-1	-0.1
1915	Was-A	64	147	14	34	7	4	2	17	8	34	.231	.276	.374	93	-2	0	2	-1	.951	0	P-47/O-4	-0.2
1916	Was-A	58	142	13	32	2	4	1	7	11	28	.225	.286	.317	82	-4	0			.937	-5	P-48	0.0
1917	Was-A	57	130	15	33	12	1	0	15	9	30	.254	.312	.362	107	1	1			1.000	-1	P-47	0.0
1918	Was-A	65	150	10	40	4	4	1	18	9	18	.267	.321	.367	109	1	2			.988	-3	P-39/O-4	0.0
1919	Was-A	56	125	13	24	1	3	1	8	12	17	.192	.263	.272	51	-8	1			.988	-0	P-39/O-3	-0.1
1920	Was-A	33	64	6	17	1	3	1	7	3	10	.266	.299	.422	92	-1	0	0	0	.971	-1	P-21	0.0
1921	Was-A	38	111	10	30	7	0	0	10	6	14	.270	.308	.333	67	-6	0	0	0	.982	-3	P-35	0.0
1922	Was-A	43	108	8	22	3	0	1	15	2	12	.204	.218	.259	25	-12	0	0	0	1.000	-1	P-41	0.0
1923	Was-A	42	93	11	18	3	0	0	13	4	15	.194	.227	.290	37	-9	0	0	0	.970	-2	P-42	0.0
1924	*Was-A	39	113	18	32	9	0	1	14	3	11	.283	.308	.389	82	-4	0	0	0	1.000	-1	P-38	0.0
1925	*Was-A	36	97	12	42	6	1	2	20	3	6	.433	.455	.577	164	9	0	1	-1	1.000	-4	P-30	0.0
1926	Was-A	35	103	6	20	5	0	1	12	3	11	.194	.217	.272	28	-11	0	0	0	.980	-5	P-33	0.0
1927	Was-A	26	46	6	16	2	0	2	10	3	4	.348	.388	.522	136	2	0	0	0	1.000	0	P-18	0.0
Total	21	933	2324	241	547	94	41	24	255	110	251	.235	.274	.342	76	-84	13	4		.969	-25	P-802/O-13	-0.4

■ BILL JOHNSON

Johnson, William F. "Sleepy Bill"   b: 9/1862, New Jersey   d: 7/17/42, Chester, Pa.   BL/TL, 140 lbs.   Deb: 6/27/1884

YEAR	TM/L	G	AB	R	H	2B	3B	HR	RBI	BB	SO	AVG	OBP	SLG	PRO+	BR/A	SB	CS	SBR	FA	FR	G/POS	TPR
1884	Phi-U	1	4	0	0	0	0	0		0	0	.000	.000	.000	-99	-1				.000	-0	/O-1	-0.1
1887	Ind-N	11	42	3	8	0	0	0	3	0	6	.190	.209	.190	12	-5	5			.765	-2	O-11	-0.6
1890	Bal-a	24	95	15	28	2	3	0		7		.295	.350	.379	110	1	8			.865	2	O-24	0.2
1891	Bal-a	129	480	101	130	13	14	2	79	89	55	.271	.389	.369	116	13	32			.877	6	*O-129	1.2
1892	Bal-N	4	15	2	2	0	0	0	2	2	0	.133	.235	.133	12	-2	0			.667	-1	/O-4	-0.3
Total	5	169	636	121	168	15	17	2	84	98	61	.264	.368	.351	105	6	45			.867	5	O-169	0.4

■ BILL JOHNSON

Johnson, William Lawrence   b: 10/18/1892, Chicago, Ill.   d: 11/3/50, Los Angeles, Cal.   BL/TR, 5'11", 170 lbs.   Deb: 9/22/16

YEAR	TM/L	G	AB	R	H	2B	3B	HR	RBI	BB	SO	AVG	OBP	SLG	PRO+	BR/A	SB	CS	SBR	FA	FR	G/POS	TPR
1916	Phi-A	4	15	1	4	1	0	0	1	0	4	.267	.267	.333	84	-0	0			1.000	-1	/O-4	-0.2
1917	Phi-A	48	109	7	19	2	2	1	8	8	14	.174	.237	.257	51	-7	4			.900	-3	O-30	-1.2
Total	2	52	124	8	23	3	2	1	9	8	18	.185	.241	.266	55	-7	4			.909	-4	/O-34	-1.4

■ BILLY JOHNSON

Johnson, William Russell "Bull"   b: 8/30/18, Montclair, N.J.   BR/TR, 5'10", 180 lbs.   Deb: 4/22/43

YEAR	TM/L	G	AB	R	H	2B	3B	HR	RBI	BB	SO	AVG	OBP	SLG	PRO+	BR/A	SB	CS	SBR	FA	FR	G/POS	TPR
1943	*NY-A	155	592	70	166	24	6	5	94	53	30	.280	.344	.367	107	5	3	5	-2	.966	12	*3-155	1.8
1946	NY-A	85	296	51	77	14	5	4	35	31	42	.260	.334	.382	98	-1	1	0	0	.955	7	3-74	0.8
1947	*NY-A★	132	494	67	141	19	8	10	95	44	43	.285	.351	.417	114	8	1	2	-1	.952	-17	*3-132	-0.9
1948	NY-A	127	496	59	131	20	6	12	64	41	30	.294	.358	.446	114	8	0	0	0	.947	6	*3-118	1.2
1949	*NY-A	113	329	48	82	11	3	8	56	48	44	.249	.348	.374	91	-4	1	0	0	.951	-2	3-81,1-21/2	-0.8
1950	*NY-A	108	327	44	85	16	2	6	40	42	30	.260	.346	.376	87	-6	1	0	0	.958	-1	*3-100/1-5	-0.8
1951	NY-A	15	40	5	12	3	0	0	4	7	0	.300	.404	.375	116	1	0	1	-1	.960	-3	3-13	-0.2
	StL-N	124	442	52	116	23	1	14	64	46	49	.262	.340	.414	101	1	5	3	-0	.976	11	*3-124	1.0
1952	StL-N	94	282	23	71	10	2	2	34	34	21	.252	.339	.323	84	-5	1	0	0	.951	2	3-89	-0.5
1953	StL-N	11	5	0	1	0	0	0	1	1	1	.200	.333	.400	90	-0	0	0	0	1.000	2	3-11	0.2
Total	9	964	3253	419	882	141	33	61	487	347	290	.271	.346	.391	100	6	13	11	-3	.959	18	3-897/1-26,2	1.8

■ GREGORY JOHNSTON

Johnston, Gregory Bernard   b: 2/12/55, Los Angeles, Cal.   BL/TL, 6', 175 lbs.   Deb: 7/27/79

YEAR	TM/L	G	AB	R	H	2B	3B	HR	RBI	BB	SO	AVG	OBP	SLG	PRO+	BR/A	SB	CS	SBR	FA	FR	G/POS	TPR
1979	SF-N	42	74	5	15	2	0	1	7	2	17	.203	.224	.270	37	-7	0	0	0	.966	-1	O-17	-0.9
1980	Min-A	14	27	3	5	3	0	0	1	2	4	.185	.241	.296	43	-2	0	0	0	1.000	-3	O-14	-0.5
1981	Min-A	7	16	2	2	0	0	0	0	2	5	.125	.222	.125	2	-2	0	0	0	1.000	0	/O-6	-0.2
Total	3	63	117	10	22	5	0	1	8	6	26	.188	.228	.256	33	-11	0	0	0	.985	-4	/O-37	-1.6

■ JIMMY JOHNSTON

Johnston, James Harle   b: 12/10/1889, Cleveland, Tenn.   d: 2/14/67, Chattanooga, Tenn.   BR/TR, 5'10", 160 lbs.   Deb: 5/3/11   FC

YEAR	TM/L	G	AB	R	H	2B	3B	HR	RBI	BB	SO	AVG	OBP	SLG	PRO+	BR/A	SB	CS	SBR	FA	FR	G/POS	TPR
1911	Chi-A	1	2	0	0	0	0	0		2	0	.000	.000	.000	-99	-1	0			1.000	-0	/O-1	-0.1
1914	Chi-N	50	101	9	23	3	2	1	8	4	9	.228	.264	.327	76	-3	3			.929	4	O-28/2-4	0.0
1916	*Bro-N	118	425	58	107	13	8	1	26	35	38	.252	.313	.327	94	-3	22	19	-5	.964	7	*O-106	-0.7
1917	Bro-N	103	330	33	89	10	4	0	25	23	28	.270	.321	.324	96	-1	16			.958	4	O-66,1-14/S23	-0.2
1918	Bro-N	123	484	54	136	16	8	0	27	33	31	.281	.328	.347	106	-3	22			.956	9	O-96,1-21/32	0.5
1919	Bro-N	117	405	56	114	11	4	1	23	29	26	.281	.334	.336	100	0	11			.960	-6	2-87,O-14/1S	-0.2
1920	*Bro-N	155	635	87	185	17	12	1	52	43	23	.291	.338	.361	98	-2	19	15	-3	.934	-6	*3-146/O-7,S	-0.4
1921	Bro-N	152	624	104	203	41	14	5	56	45	26	.325	.372	.460	115	13	28	16	-1	.935	8	*3-150/S-3	3.0
1922	Bro-N	138	567	110	181	20	7	4	49	38	17	.319	.364	.400	98	-1	18	9	0	.947	2	2-62,S-50,3	1.3
1923	Bro-N	151	625	111	203	29	11	4	60	53	15	.325	.378	.426	115	14	16	13	-3	.948	19	2-84,S-52,3	3.6
1924	Bro-N	86	315	51	94	11	2	2	29	27	10	.298	.356	.365	97	-1	5	6	-2	.939	-4	S-63,3-10/1O	0.1
1925	Bro-N	123	431	63	128	13	3	2	43	45	15	.297	.369	.355	88	-6	7	5	-1	.886	-23	3-81,O-20/1S	-2.4
1926	Bos-N	23	57	6	14	1	0	1	5	10	3	.246	.358	.316	91	-0	2			.865	-4	3-14/2-2,O	-0.3
	NY-N	37	69	11	16	0	0	0	5	6	5	.232	.293	.232	43	-5	0			1.000	-5	O-14	-1.1
	Yr	60	126	18	30	1	0	1	10	16	8	.238	.324	.270	64	-6	2			1.000	-1	O-15,3-14/2	-1.4
Total	13	1377	5070	754	1493	185	75	22	410	391	246	.294	.347	.374	100	7	169	83		.926	10	3-448,O-354,2S/1	3.1

■ JOHNNY JOHNSTON

Johnston, John Thomas   b: 3/28/1890, Longview, Tex.   d: 3/7/40, San Diego, Cal.   BL/TR, 5'11", 172 lbs.   Deb: 4/10/13

YEAR	TM/L	G	AB	R	H	2B	3B	HR	RBI	BB	SO	AVG	OBP	SLG	PRO+	BR/A	SB	CS	SBR	FA	FR	G/POS	TPR
1913	StL-A	111	380	37	85	14	4	2	27	42	51	.224	.308	.297	79	-10	11			.965	12	*O-107	-0.3

■ REX JOHNSTON

Johnston, Rex David   b: 11/8/37, Colton, Cal.   BB/TR, 6'1.5", 202 lbs.   Deb: 4/15/64

YEAR	TM/L	G	AB	R	H	2B	3B	HR	RBI	BB	SO	AVG	OBP	SLG	PRO+	BR/A	SB	CS	SBR	FA	FR	G/POS	TPR
1964	Pit-N	14	7	1	0	0	0	0	0	3	0	.000	.300	.000	-7	-1	0	0	0	1.000	-2	/O-8	-0.3

■ DICK JOHNSTON

Johnston, Richard Frederick   b: 4/6/1863, Kingston, N.Y.   d: 4/4/34, Detroit, Mich.   BR/TR, 5'8", 155 lbs.   Deb: 8/12/1884

YEAR	TM/L	G	AB	R	H	2B	3B	HR	RBI	BB	SO	AVG	OBP	SLG	PRO+	BR/A	SB	CS	SBR	FA	FR	G/POS	TPR
1884	Ric-a	39	146	23	41	5	5	2		2		.281	.291	.425	132	5				.865	9	O-37/S-2	1.1
1885	Bos-N	26	111	17	26	6	3	1	23	0	15	.234	.234	.369	96	-1				.842	1	O-26	0.0
1886	Bos-N	109	413	48	99	18	9	5	57	3	70	.240	.245	.334	78	-12	11			.892	17	*O-109	0.2
1887	Bos-N	127	507	87	131	13	20	5	77	16	35	.258	.281	.393	85	-12	52			.933	25	*O-127	0.9
1888	Bos-N	135	585	102	173	31	18	12	68	15	33	.296	.314	.472	145	27	35			.898	7	*O-135	2.9
1889	Bos-N	132	539	80	123	16	4	5	67	41	60	.228	.285	.301	60	-31	34			.917	-7	*O-132	-3.6
1890	Bos-P	2	9	0	1	0	0	0		0		.111	.111	.111	-38	-2	0			.800	-1	/O-2	-0.1
	NY-P	77	306	37	74	9	7	1	43	18	25	.242	.288	.327	59	-20	7			.897	3	O-76/S-2	-1.6
	Yr	79	315	37	75	9	7	1	43	18	26	.238	.284	.321	56	-22	7			.894	3	O-78/S-2	-1.7

YEAR	TM/L	G	AB	R	H	2B	3B	HR	RBI	BB	SO	AVG	OBP	SLG	PRO+	BR/A	SB	CS	SBR	FA	FR	G/POS	TPR
1891	Cin-a	99	376	59	83	11	2	6	51	38	44	.221	.301	.309	68	-18	12			.895	-1	*O-99	-1.9
Total	8	746	2992	453	751	109	68	33	386	133	283	.251	.285	.366	87	-63	151			.903	54	O-743/S-4	-2.1

■ DOC JOHNSTON
Johnston, Wheeler Roger b: 9/9/1887, Cleveland, Tenn. d: 2/17/61, Chattanooga, Tenn. BL/TL, 6', 170 lbs. Deb: 10/3/09 F

YEAR	TM/L	G	AB	R	H	2B	3B	HR	RBI	BB	SO	AVG	OBP	SLG	PRO+	BR/A	SB	CS	SBR	FA	FR	G/POS	TPR
1909	Cin-N	3	10	1	0	0	0	0	1	0		.000	.000	.000	-99	-2	0			1.000	0	/1-3	-0.2
1912	Cle-A	43	164	22	46	7	4	1	11	11		.280	.326	.390	101	-0	8			.991	-2	1-41	-0.3
1913	Cle-A	133	530	74	135	19	12	2	39	35	65	.255	.309	.347	89	-8	19			.989	-1	*1-133	-1.1
1914	Cle-A	103	340	43	83	15	1	0	23	28	46	.244	.311	.294	79	-9	14	9	-1	.987	-7	1-90/O-2	-2.1
1915	Pit-N	147	543	71	144	19	12	5	64	38	40	.265	.328	.372	113	8	26	17	-2	.991	-12	*1-147	-1.1
1916	Pit-N	114	404	33	86	10	10	0	39	20	42	.213	.262	.287	68	-16	17			.987	-2	*1-110	-2.5
1918	Cle-A	74	273	30	62	12	2	0	25	26	19	.227	.301	.286	70	-10	12			.989	-3	1-73	-1.8
1919	Cle-A	102	331	42	101	17	3	1	33	25	18	.305	.359	.384	102	1	21			.984	-3	1-98	-0.6
1920	*Cle-A	147	535	68	156	24	10	2	71	28	32	.292	.333	.385	87	-11	13	7	-0	.992	-1	*1-147	-1.5
1921	Cle-A	118	384	53	114	20	7	2	46	29	15	.297	.353	.401	90	-6	2	9	-5	.988	-1	*1-116	-1.3
1922	Phi-A	71	260	41	65	11	7	1	29	24	15	.250	.316	.358	73	-10	7	6	-2	.990	-5	1-65	-2.0
Total	11	1055	3774	478	992	154	68	14	381	264	292	.263	.319	.351	88	-63	139	48		.989	-37	*1-1023/O-2	-14.5

■ FRED JOHNSTON
Johnston, Wilfred Ivy b: 7/9/1899, Charlotte, N.C. d: 7/14/59, Tyler, Tex. BR/TR, 5'11.5", 170 lbs. Deb: 6/29/24

YEAR	TM/L	G	AB	R	H	2B	3B	HR	RBI	BB	SO	AVG	OBP	SLG	PRO+	BR/A	SB	CS	SBR	FA	FR	G/POS	TPR
1924	Bro-N	4	4	1	1	0	0	0	0	0	1	.250	.250	.250	35	-0	0	0	0	.667	0	/2-1,3-1	0.0

■ JAY JOHNSTONE
Johnstone, John William b: 11/20/45, Manchester, Conn. BL/TR, 6'1", 175 lbs. Deb: 7/30/66

YEAR	TM/L	G	AB	R	H	2B	3B	HR	RBI	BB	SO	AVG	OBP	SLG	PRO+	BR/A	SB	CS	SBR	FA	FR	G/POS	TPR
1966	Cal-A	61	254	35	67	12	4	3	17	11	36	.264	.297	.378	95	-2	3	3	-1	.975	-2	O-61	-0.8
1967	Cal-A	79	230	18	48	7	1	2	10	5	37	.209	.226	.274	49	-15	3	2	-0	.973	2	O-63	-1.8
1968	Cal-A	41	115	11	30	4	1	0	3	7	15	.261	.303	.313	90	-2	2	1	0	.984	2	O-29	-0.1
1969	Cal-A	148	540	64	146	20	5	10	59	38	75	.270	.324	.381	102	-0	3	9	-5	.983	12	*O-144	0.0
1970	Cal-A	119	320	34	76	10	5	11	39	24	53	.237	.293	.403	93	-4	1	0	0	.981	-1	*O-100	-1.0
1971	Chi-A	124	388	53	101	14	1	16	40	38	50	.260	.331	.425	109	4	10	5	0	.968	-3	*O-119	-0.4
1972	Chi-A	113	261	27	49	9	0	4	17	25	42	.188	.259	.268	56	-14	2	1	0	.988	-12	O-97	-3.3
1973	Oak-A	23	28	1	3	1	0	0	3	2	4	.107	.167	.143	-13	-4	0	1	-1	1.000	-2	/O-7,2-2,D	-0.7
1974	Phi-N	64	200	30	59	10	4	6	30	24	28	.295	.371	.475	130	8	5	5	-2	.968	-7	O-59	-0.3
1975	Phi-N	122	350	50	115	19	2	7	54	42	39	.329	.401	.454	132	16	7	3	0	.976	-2	*O-101	1.1
1976	*Phi-N	129	440	62	140	38	4	5	53	41	39	.318	.379	.457	132	19	5	5	-2	.982	8	*O-122/1-6	2.1
1977	*Phi-N	112	363	64	103	18	4	15	59	38	38	.284	.355	.479	116	8	3	7	-3	1.000	3	O-91,1-19	0.3
1978	Phi-N	35	56	3	10	2	0	0	4	6	9	.179	.258	.214	33	-5	0	2	-1	.988	1	/1-8,O-7	-0.9
	*NY-A	36	65	6	17	0	0	1	6	4	10	.262	.333	.308	83	-1	0	1	-1	1.000	-3	O-22/D-5	-0.5
1979	NY-A	23	48	7	10	1	0	1	7	2	7	.208	.240	.292	44	-4	1	0	0	1.000	-2	O-19	-0.6
	SD-N	75	201	10	59	8	2	0	32	18	21	.294	.352	.353	99	-4	1	3	-2	.985	-3	O-45,1-22	-0.7
1980	LA-N	109	251	31	77	15	2	2	20	24	29	.307	.372	.406	119	7	3	2	0	.965	1	O-61	0.6
1981	*LA-N	61	83	8	17	3	0	1	7	6	13	.205	.267	.349	76	-3	0	0	-1	.957	-0	O-16/1-2	-0.4
1982	LA-N	21	13	1	1	1	0	0	2	5	2	.077	.333	.154	41	-1	0	0	-1	.000	0	H	-0.2
	Chi-N	98	269	39	67	13	1	10	43	40	41	.249	.346	.416	109	4	0	2	-1	.982	1	O-86	-0.1
	Yr	119	282	40	68	14	1	10	45	45	43	.241	.346	.404	107	3	0	2	-1	.982	1	O-86	0.1
1983	Chi-N	86	140	16	36	7	0	6	22	20	24	.257	.362	.436	115	3	1	1	-0	.935	-4	O-44	-0.2
1984	Chi-N	52	73	8	21	2	2	0	3	7	18	.288	.350	.370	94	-0	0	0	0	1.000	-4	O-15	-0.5
1985	*LA-N	17	15	0	2	1	0	0	2	1	2	.133	.188	.200	9	-2	0	0	0	.000	0	H	-0.2
Total	20	1748	4703	578	1254	215	38	102	531	429	632	.267	.331	.394	103	10	50	54	-17	.979	-17	*O-1308/1-57,D2	-8.4

■ STAN JOK
Jok, Stanley Edward "Tucker" b: 5/3/26, Buffalo, N.Y. d: 3/6/72, Buffalo, N.Y. BR/TR, 6', 190 lbs. Deb: 4/13/54

YEAR	TM/L	G	AB	R	H	2B	3B	HR	RBI	BB	SO	AVG	OBP	SLG	PRO+	BR/A	SB	CS	SBR	FA	FR	G/POS	TPR
1954	Phi-N	3	3	0	0	0	0	0	0	0	2	.000	.000	.000	-99	-1	0	0	0	.000	0	H	-0.1
	Chi-A	3	12	1	2	0	0	0	2	0	2	.167	.231	.167	10	-1	0	0	0	1.000	-0	/3-3	-0.2
1955	Chi-A	6	4	3	1	0	0	1	2	1	1	.250	.400	1.000	260	1	0	0	0	.857	1	/3-3,O-1	0.1
Total	2	12	19	4	3	0	0	1	4	2	5	.158	.238	.316	47	-2	0	0	0	.941	0	/3-6,O-1	-0.2

■ SMEAD JOLLEY
Jolley, Smead Powell "Guinea" or "Smudge" b: 1/14/02, Wesson, Ark. d: 11/17/91, Alameda, Cal. BL/TR, 6'3.5", 210 lbs. Deb: 4/17/30

YEAR	TM/L	G	AB	R	H	2B	3B	HR	RBI	BB	SO	AVG	OBP	SLG	PRO+	BR/A	SB	CS	SBR	FA	FR	G/POS	TPR
1930	Chi-A	152	616	76	193	38	12	16	114	28	52	.313	.346	.492	114	10	3	1	0	.950	-3	*O-151	-0.3
1931	Chi-A	54	110	5	33	11	0	3	28	7	4	.300	.353	.482	125	3	0	0	0	.857	-5	O-23	-0.2
1932	Chi-A	12	42	5	15	3	0	0	7	3	0	.357	.413	.429	127	2	1	0	0	.923	-2	O-11	-0.1
	Bos-A	137	531	57	164	27	5	18	99	27	29	.309	.345	.480	115	9	0	5	-3	.943	-5	*O-126/C-5	-0.6
	Yr	149	573	60	179	30	5	18	106	30	29	.312	.350	.476	116	11	1	5	-3	.942	-8	*O-137/C-5	-0.7
1933	Bos-A	118	411	47	116	32	4	9	65	24	20	.282	.325	.445	103	-0	1	1	-0	.955	-4	*O-102	-0.9
Total	4	473	1710	188	521	111	21	46	313	89	105	.305	.343	.475	112	24	5	7	-3	.944	-19	O-413/C-5	-2.1

■ JONES
Jones Deb: 5/14/1873

YEAR	TM/L	G	AB	R	H	2B	3B	HR	RBI	BB	SO	AVG	OBP	SLG	PRO+	BR/A	SB	CS	SBR	FA	FR	G/POS	TPR
1873	Mar-n	1	4	0	3	1	0	0	0	0	0	.750	.750	1.000	535	2						/O-1	0.1
1874	Bal-n	2	7	0	1	0	0	0		0		.143	.143	.143	-9	-1						/C-1,O-1	-0.1
Total	2 n	3	11	0	4	1	0	0				.364	.364	.455	166	1						/O-2,C-1	0.0

■ JONES
Jones b: Johnstown, Pa. Deb: 7/14/1884

YEAR	TM/L	G	AB	R	H	2B	3B	HR	RBI	BB	SO	AVG	OBP	SLG	PRO+	BR/A	SB	CS	SBR	FA	FR	G/POS	TPR
1884	Was-a	4	17	2	5	0	0	0		1		.294	.333	.294	120	0				1.000	-0	/O-4	0.0

■ JONES
Jones Deb: 4/30/1885

YEAR	TM/L	G	AB	R	H	2B	3B	HR	RBI	BB	SO	AVG	OBP	SLG	PRO+	BR/A	SB	CS	SBR	FA	FR	G/POS	TPR
1885	NY-a	1	4	0	1	0	0	0				.250	.250	.250	63	-0				1.000	1	/3-1	0.1

■ CHARLIE JONES
Jones, Charles C. "Casey" b: 6/2/1876, Butler, Pa. d: 4/2/47, Two Harbors, Minn. BR/TR, 6'1", Deb: 5/3/01

YEAR	TM/L	G	AB	R	H	2B	3B	HR	RBI	BB	SO	AVG	OBP	SLG	PRO+	BR/A	SB	CS	SBR	FA	FR	G/POS	TPR
1901	Bos-A	10	41	6	6	2	0	0	6	1		.146	.167	.195	0	-6	2			.929	-2	O-10	-0.8
1904	Chi-A	5	17	2	4	0	1	0	1	1		.235	.278	.353	103	0	0			1.000	1	/O-5	0.1
1905	Was-A	142	544	68	113	18	4	2	41	31		.208	.254	.267	68	-20	24			.971	16	*O-142	-1.2
1906	Was-A	131	497	56	120	11	11	3	42	24		.241	.283	.326	95	-4	34			.961	-8	*O-128/2-1	-0.3
1907	Was-A	121	437	48	116	14	10	0	37	22		.265	.304	.343	115	6	26			.967	-1	*O-111/2-5,1S	0.1
1908	StL-A	74	263	37	61	11	2	0	17	14		.232	.279	.289	84	-5	14			.963	-1	O-72	-1.0
Total	6	483	1799	217	420	56	28	5	144	93		.233	.276	.304	87	-29	100			.966	20	O-468/2-6,1S	-3.1

■ CHARLIE JONES
Jones, Charles F. b: New York, N.Y. Deb: 6/28/1884

YEAR	TM/L	G	AB	R	H	2B	3B	HR	RBI	BB	SO	AVG	OBP	SLG	PRO+	BR/A	SB	CS	SBR	FA	FR	G/POS	TPR
1884	Bro-a	25	90	10	16	1	0	0		5		.178	.221	.189	35	-6				.871	-7	2-13,3-11/O	-1.2

■ CHARLEY JONES
Jones, Charles Wesley "Baby" (b: Benjamin Wesley Rippay) b: 4/30/1850, Alamance Co., N.C. BR/TR, 5'11.5", 202 lbs. Deb: 5/4/1875 U

YEAR	TM/L	G	AB	R	H	2B	3B	HR	RBI	BB	SO	AVG	OBP	SLG	PRO+	BR/A	SB	CS	SBR	FA	FR	G/POS	TPR
1875	Wes-n	12	47	5	13	2	4	0		0		.277	.277	.489	151	2						O-12	0.2
	Har-n	1	4	1	0	0	0	0		0		.000	.000	.000	-95	-1						/O-1	-0.1
	Yr	13	51	6	13	2	4	0		0		.255	.255	.451	132	1						O-13	0.1
1876	Cin-N	64	276	40	79	17	4	4	38	7	17	.286	.304	.420	162	19				.857	3	*O-64	1.8
1877	Cin-N	17	69	16	21	3	1	1	10	4	8	.304	.342	.478	175	6				.920	1	1-10/O-8	0.6
	Chi-N	2	8	1	3	0	0	0	2	1	0	.375	.444	.500	176	1				1.000	1	O-2	0.1
	Yr	38	163	36	51	8	7	1	26	10	17	.313	.353	.466	175	14				.838	10	O-38	2.0
																							2.7
1878	Cin-N	61	261	50	81	11	7	3	39	4	17	.310	.321	.441	163	17				.896	6	*O-61	1.9

YEAR	TM/L	G	AB	R	H	2B	3B	HR	RBI	BB	SO	AVG	OBP	SLG	PRO+	BR/A	SB	CS	SBR	FA	FR	G/POS	TPR
1879	Bos-N	83	355	**85**	112	22	10	9	62	29	38	.315	.367	.510	182	31				**.933**	12	*O-83	3.5
1880	Bos-N	66	280	44	84	15	3	5	37	11	27	.300	.326	.429	159	17				.826	-4	*O-66	1.0
1883	Cin-a	90	391	84	115	15	12	10		20		.294	.328	.471	146	18				.876	2	*O-90	1.7
1884	Cin-a	112	472	117	148	19	17	7		37		.314	**.376**	.470	166	34				.887	3	*O-112	3.1
1885	Cin-a	112	487	108	157	19	17	5		21		.322	.362	.462	156	29				.891	12	*O-112	3.4
1886	Cin-a	127	500	87	135	22	10	6		61		.270	.356	.390	130	17	3			.879	3	*O-127	1.5
1887	Cin-a	41	153	28	48	7	4	2		19		.314	.400	.451	134	7	7			.900	-0	O-41	0.5
	NY-a	62	247	30	63	11	3	3		12		.255	.306	.360	89	-4	8			.917	4	O-62/P-2,1	-0.1
	Yr	103	400	58	111	18	7	5		31		.278	.343	.395	107	4	15			.910	4	*O-103/P-2,1	0.4
1888	KC-a	6	25	2	4	0	1	0		5	1	.160	.192	.240	36	-2	1			.750	-1	/O-6	-0.3
Total	11	881	3687	728	1101	170	98	56	219	237	124	.299	.347	.443	150	206	19			.882	51	O-872/1-11,P	20.7

■ CHRIS JONES
Jones, Christopher Carlos b: 12/16/65, Utica, N.Y. BR/TR, 6'2", 205 lbs. Deb: 4/21/91

YEAR	TM/L	G	AB	R	H	2B	3B	HR	RBI	BB	SO	AVG	OBP	SLG	PRO+	BR/A	SB	CS	SBR	FA	FR	G/POS	TPR
1991	Cin-N	52	89	14	26	1	2	2	6	2	11	.292	.308	.416	98	-1	2	1	0	1.000	-5	O-26	-0.6
1992	Hou-N	54	63	7	12	1	0	1	4	7	21	.190	.271	.302	65	-3	3	0	1	.931	-13	O-43	-1.7
1993	Col-N	86	209	29	57	11	4	6	31	10	48	.273	.306	.450	85	-5	9	4	0	.983	-9	O-70	-1.5
1994	Col-N	21	40	6	12	2	1	0	2	2	14	.300	.333	.400	77	-1	0	1	-1	.941	-5	O-14	-0.7
Total	4	213	401	56	107	16	8	9	43	21	114	.267	.303	.414	84	-10	14	6	1	.974	-33	O-153	-4.5

■ CHRIS JONES
Jones, Christopher Dale b: 7/13/57, Los Angeles, Cal. BL/TL, 6', 183 lbs. Deb: 6/8/85

YEAR	TM/L	G	AB	R	H	2B	3B	HR	RBI	BB	SO	AVG	OBP	SLG	PRO+	BR/A	SB	CS	SBR	FA	FR	G/POS	TPR
1985	Hou-N	31	25	0	5	0	0	0	1	3	7	.200	.286	.200	39	-2	0	0	0	1.000	-3	O-15	-0.6
1986	SF-N	3	1	0	0	0	0	0	0	0	0	.000	.000	.000	-99	-0	1	0	0	.000	0	/H	0.0
Total	2	34	26	0	5	0	0	0	1	3	7	.192	.276	.192	34	-2	1	0	0	1.000	-3	/O-15	-0.6

■ CLARENCE JONES
Jones, Clarence Woodrow b: 11/7/41, Zanesville, Ohio BL/TL, 6'2", 185 lbs. Deb: 4/20/67 C

YEAR	TM/L	G	AB	R	H	2B	3B	HR	RBI	BB	SO	AVG	OBP	SLG	PRO+	BR/A	SB	CS	SBR	FA	FR	G/POS	TPR
1967	Chi-N	53	135	13	34	7	0	2	16	14	33	.252	.322	.348	88	-2	0	0	0	.978	-4	O-31,1-13	-0.9
1968	Chi-N	5	2	0	0	0	0	0	0	2	1	.000	.500	.000	56	-0	0	0	0	1.000	-0	/1-1	0.0
Total	2	58	137	13	34	7	0	2	16	16	34	.248	.327	.343	88	-2	0	0	0	.979	-4	/O-31,1-14	-0.9

■ CLEON JONES
Jones, Cleon Joseph b: 8/4/42, Plateau, Ala. BR/TL, 6', 200 lbs. Deb: 9/14/63

YEAR	TM/L	G	AB	R	H	2B	3B	HR	RBI	BB	SO	AVG	OBP	SLG	PRO+	BR/A	SB	CS	SBR	FA	FR	G/POS	TPR
1963	NY-N	6	15	1	2	0	0	0	1	0	4	.133	.133	.133	-23	-2	0	0	0	1.000	-1	/O-5	-0.4
1965	NY-N	30	74	2	11	1	0	1	9	2	23	.149	.171	.203	5	-9	1	0	0	1.000	-1	O-23	-1.2
1966	NY-N	139	495	74	136	16	4	8	57	30	62	.275	.320	.372	94	-4	16	8	0	.979	-2	*O-129	-1.3
1967	NY-N	129	411	46	101	10	5	5	30	19	57	.246	.286	.331	77	-13	12	2	2	.977	-6	O-115	-2.4
1968	NY-N	147	509	63	151	29	4	14	55	31	98	.297	.343	.452	136	21	23	12	-0	.963	-10	*O-139	0.5
1969	*NY-N★	137	483	92	164	25	4	12	75	64	60	.340	.424	.482	150	35	16	8	0	.991	8	*O-122,1-15	3.7
1970	NY-N	134	506	71	140	25	8	10	63	57	87	.277	.356	.417	106	5	12	3	2	.981	12	O-130	1.2
1971	NY-N	136	505	63	161	24	6	14	69	53	87	.319	.386	.473	144	29	6	5	-1	.981	7	*O-132	3.0
1972	NY-N	106	375	39	92	15	1	5	52	30	83	.245	.308	.331	84	-8	1	6	-3	.986	-1	O-84,1-20	-1.9
1973	*NY-N	92	339	36	88	13	0	11	48	28	51	.260	.322	.395	99	-1	1	1	-0	.967	1	O-92	-0.5
1974	NY-N	124	461	62	130	23	1	13	60	38	79	.282	.345	.421	115	8	3	3	-1	.970	-1	O-120	0.5
1975	NY-N	21	50	2	12	1	0	0		3	6	.240	.283	.260	54	-3	0	0	0	1.000	-3	O-12	-0.7
1976	Chi-A	12	40	2	8	1	0	0		3	2	.200	.304	.225	56	-2	0	0	0	1.000	-2	/O-8,D-3	-0.5
Total	13	1213	4263	565	1196	183	33	93	524	360	702	.281	.342	.404	111	56	91	48	-2	.978	-0	*O-1111/1-35,D	-0.0

■ COBE JONES
Jones, Coburn Dyas b: 8/21/07, Denver, Colo. d: 6/3/69, Denver, Colo. BB/TR, 5'7", 155 lbs. Deb: 9/27/28

YEAR	TM/L	G	AB	R	H	2B	3B	HR	RBI	BB	SO	AVG	OBP	SLG	PRO+	BR/A	SB	CS	SBR	FA	FR	G/POS	TPR
1928	Pit-N	1	2	0	1	0	0	0	0	0	0	.500	.500	.500	156	0	0			1.000	-0	/S-1	0.0
1929	Pit-N	25	63	6	16	5	1	0	4	1	5	.254	.266	.365	53	-5	1			.919	-8	S-15	-1.0
Total	2	26	65	6	17	5	1	0	4	1	5	.262	.273	.369	56	-5	1			.921	-8	/S-16	-1.0

■ DARRYL JONES
Jones, Darryl Lee b: 6/5/51, Meadville, Pa. BR/TR, 5'10", 175 lbs. Deb: 6/6/79 F

YEAR	TM/L	G	AB	R	H	2B	3B	HR	RBI	BB	SO	AVG	OBP	SLG	PRO+	BR/A	SB	CS	SBR	FA	FR	G/POS	TPR
1979	NY-A	18	47	6	12	5	1	0	6	2	7	.255	.286	.404	86	-1	0	0	0	1.000	-1	D-15/O-2	-0.2

■ DAVY JONES
Jones, David Jefferson "Kangaroo" b: 6/30/1880, Cambria, Wis. d: 3/31/72, Mankato, Minn. BL/TR, 5'10", 165 lbs. Deb: 9/15/01

YEAR	TM/L	G	AB	R	H	2B	3B	HR	RBI	BB	SO	AVG	OBP	SLG	PRO+	BR/A	SB	CS	SBR	FA	FR	G/POS	TPR
1901	Mil-A	14	52	12	9	0	0	3		5	11	.173	.328	.346	91	-0	4			.911	1	O-14	0.0
1902	StL-A	15	49	4	11	1	1	0		3	6	.224	.309	.286	67	-2	5			.973	5	O-15	0.1
	Chi-N	64	243	41	74	12	3	0		14	38	.305	.399	.379	144	15	12			.955	-1	O-64	1.0
1903	Chi-N	130	497	64	140	18	3	1		62	53	.282	.352	.336	99	1	15			.970	0	*O-130	-0.6
1904	Chi-N	98	336	44	82	11	5	3		39	41	.244	.330	.333	105	3	14			.932	-10	O-97	-1.3
1906	Det-A	84	323	41	84	12	2	0		24	41	.260	.347	.310	103	3	21			.981	-0	O-83	0.3
1907	*Det-A	126	491	101	134	10	6	0		27	60	.273	.357	.318	111	9	30			.971	13	*O-125	1.8
1908	*Det-A	56	121	17	25	2	1	0		10	13	.207	.284	.240	68	-4	11			.960	2	O-32	-0.3
1909	*Det-A	69	204	44	57	2	2	0		10	28	.279	.369	.309	110	4	12			.982	-2	O-57	-0.1
1910	Det-A	113	377	77	100	6	6	0		24	51	.265	.362	.313	105	4	25			.956	1	O-101	0.0
1911	Det-A	98	341	78	93	10	0	0		19	41	.273	.354	.302	80	-8	25			.950	-1	O-92	-1.4
1912	Det-A	99	316	54	93	5	2	0		24	38	.294	.370	.332	106	2	16			.962	-1	O-81	-0.2
1913	Chi-A	12	21	2	6	0	0	0		0	9	0	.286	.500	.286	132	2	1		.867	-1	/O-9	0.1
1914	Pit-F	97	352	58	96	9	8	2		24	42	16	.273	.355	.361	86	-6	15	.970	8	O-93	-0.3
1915	Pit-F	14	49	6	16	0	1	0		4	6		.327	.400	.367	107	1	1	.926	-1	O-11	-0.1
Total	14	1089	3772	643	1020	98	40	9	289	478	16	.270	.356	.325	101	22	207			.962	18	*O-1006	-1.0

■ FIELDER JONES
Jones, Fielder Allison b: 8/13/1871, Shinglehouse, Pa. d: 3/13/34, Portland, Ore. BL/TR, 5'11", 180 lbs. Deb: 4/18/1896 M

YEAR	TM/L	G	AB	R	H	2B	3B	HR	RBI	BB	SO	AVG	OBP	SLG	PRO+	BR/A	SB	CS	SBR	FA	FR	G/POS	TPR
1896	Bro-N	104	395	82	140	10	8	3	46	48	15	.354	.427	.443	137	24	18			.928	-4	O-103	1.0
1897	Bro-N	135	548	134	172	15	10	1	49	61		.314	.392	.383	111	12	48			.941	4	*O-135	0.5
1898	Bro-N	146	596	89	181	15	9	1	69	46		.304	.362	.364	108	7	36			.946	-7	*O-144/S-2	-1.0
1899	Bro-N	102	365	75	104	8	2	2	38	54		.285	.390	.334	97	2	18			.946	-3	O-96	-0.8
1900	*Bro-N	136	552	106	171	26	4	4	54	57		.310	.383	.393	108	7	33			.957	0	*O-136	-0.3
1901	Chi-A	133	521	120	162	16	3	2	65	84		.311	.412	.365	120	20	38			.937	1	*O-133	1.0
1902	Chi-A	135	532	98	171	16	5	0	54	57		.321	.390	.370	117	15	33			.972	13	*O-135	1.8
1903	Chi-A	136	530	71	152	18	5	0	45	47		.287	.348	.340	112	9	21			**.985**	0	*O-136	0.1
1904	Chi-A	149	547	72	133	14	5	3	42	53		.243	.316	.303	100	2	25			.977	5	*O-149,M	-0.3
1905	Chi-A	153	568	91	139	17	12	2	38	73		.245	.335	.327	115	12	20			.970	-1	*O-153,M	1.3
1906	*Chi-A	144	496	77	114	22	4	2	34	83		.230	.346	.302	106	8	26			**.988**	8	*O-144,M	1.0
1907	Chi-A	154	559	72	146	18	1	0	47	67		.261	.345	.297	109	9	17			.973	2	*O-154,M	0.5
1908	Chi-A	149	529	92	134	11	7	1	50	86		.253	.366	.306	121	17	26			.968	-2	*O-149,M	1.1
1914	StL-F	5	3	0	1	0	0	0	0	1	0	.333	.500	.333	113	0	0			.000	0	HM	0.0
1915	StL-F	7	6	1	0	0	0	0	0	0	0	.000	.000	.000	-95	-2	0			1.000	-1	/O-3,M	-0.3
Total	15	1788	6747	1180	1920	206	75	21	631	817	15	.285	.368	.347	112	142	359			.964	24	*O-1770/S-2	5.6

■ FRANK JONES
Jones, Frank M. b: 8/25/1858, Princeton, Ill. d: 2/4/36, Marietta, Ohio BL Deb: 7/2/1884

YEAR	TM/L	G	AB	R	H	2B	3B	HR	RBI	BB	SO	AVG	OBP	SLG	PRO+	BR/A	SB	CS	SBR	FA	FR	G/POS	TPR
1884	Det-N	2	8	0	1	0	0	0		0	1	.125	.125	.125	-22	-1				.667	-1	/S-1,O-1	-0.2

■ DEACON JONES
Jones, Grover William b: 4/18/34, White Plains, N.Y. BL/TR, 5'10", 185 lbs. Deb: 9/8/62 C

YEAR	TM/L	G	AB	R	H	2B	3B	HR	RBI	BB	SO	AVG	OBP	SLG	PRO+	BR/A	SB	CS	SBR	FA	FR	G/POS	TPR
1962	Chi-A	18	28	3	9	2	0	0	8	4	6	.321	.406	.393	117	1	0	0	0	.962	-0	/1-6	0.0
1963	Chi-A	17	16	4	3	0	1	1	2	2	2	.188	.316	.500	127	1	0	0	0	1.000	0	/1-1	0.1

YEAR	TM/L	G	AB	R	H	2B	3B	HR	RBI	BB	SO	AVG	OBP	SLG	PRO+	BR/A	SB	CS	SBR	FA	FR	G/POS	TPR
1966	Chi-A	5	5	0	2	0	0	0	0	0	0	.400	.400	.400	140	0	0	0	0	.000	0	H	0.0
Total	3	40	49	7	14	2	1	1	10	6	8	.286	.375	.429	122	2	0	0	0	.966	-0	/1-7	0.1

■ HAL JONES
Jones, Harold Marion   b: 4/9/36, Louisiana, Mo.   BR/TR, 6'2", 194 lbs.   Deb: 4/25/61

YEAR	TM/L	G	AB	R	H	2B	3B	HR	RBI	BB	SO	AVG	OBP	SLG	PRO+	BR/A	SB	CS	SBR	FA	FR	G/POS	TPR
1961	Cle-A	12	35	2	6	1	0	2	4	2	12	.171	.216	.343	48	-3	0	0	0	.974	-2	1-10	-0.5
1962	Cle-A	5	16	2	5	1	0	0	1	0	4	.313	.353	.375	99	-0	0	0	0	.969	0	/1-4	0.0
Total	2	17	51	4	11	1	0	2	5	2	16	.216	.259	.353	64	-3	0	0	0	.973	-2	/1-14	-0.5

■ HENRY JONES
Jones, Henry Monroe "Baldy"   b: 5/10/1857, New York   d: 5/31/55, Manistee, Mich.   BB, 5'6", 149 lbs.   Deb: 8/20/1884

YEAR	TM/L	G	AB	R	H	2B	3B	HR	RBI	BB	SO	AVG	OBP	SLG	PRO+	BR/A	SB	CS	SBR	FA	FR	G/POS	TPR
1884	Det-N	34	127	24	28	3	1	0	3	16	18	.220	.308	.260	86	-1				.897	-2	2-16,O-11/S	-0.3

■ HOWIE JONES
Jones, Howard "Cotton" (b: Howard Painter)   b: 3/1/1897, Irwin, Pa.   d: 7/15/72, Jeannette, Pa.   BL/TL, 5'11", 165 lbs.   Deb: 9/5/21

YEAR	TM/L	G	AB	R	H	2B	3B	HR	RBI	BB	SO	AVG	OBP	SLG	PRO+	BR/A	SB	CS	SBR	FA	FR	G/POS	TPR
1921	StL-N	3	2	0	0	0	0	0	0	0	1	.000	.000	.000	-99	-1	0	0	0	.000	-1	/O-1	-0.1

■ DALTON JONES
Jones, James Dalton   b: 12/10/43, McComb, Miss.   BL/TR, 6'1", 180 lbs.   Deb: 4/17/64

YEAR	TM/L	G	AB	R	H	2B	3B	HR	RBI	BB	SO	AVG	OBP	SLG	PRO+	BR/A	SB	CS	SBR	FA	FR	G/POS	TPR
1964	Bos-A	118	374	37	86	16	4	6	39	22	38	.230	.275	.342	67	-17	6	3	0	.959	-8	2-85/S-1,3	-1.9
1965	Bos-A	112	367	41	99	13	5	5	37	28	45	.270	.325	.373	92	-4	8	1	2	.930	-3	3-81/2-8	-0.7
1966	Bos-A	115	252	26	59	11	5	4	23	22	27	.234	.303	.365	83	-6	1	2	-1	.962	-15	2-70/3-3	-1.9
1967	*Bos-A	89	159	18	46	6	2	3	25	11	23	.289	.335	.409	110	2	0	1	-1	.912	-4	3-30,2-19/1	-0.3
1968	Bos-A	111	354	38	83	13	0	5	29	17	53	.234	.272	.314	72	-12	1	1	-0	.996	-6	1-56,2-26/3	-2.5
1969	Bos-A	111	336	50	74	18	3	3	33	39	36	.220	.305	.318	71	-13	1	1	-0	.992	-1	1-81/3-9,2	-2.1
1970	Det-A	89	191	29	42	7	0	6	21	33	33	.220	.338	.351	90	-2	1	1	-0	.985	-3	2-35,3-18,1	-0.4
1971	Det-A	83	138	15	35	5	0	5	11	9	21	.254	.304	.399	94	-1	1	3	-2	1.000	-7	O-16,3-13/12	-1.1
1972	Det-A	7	7	0	0	0	0	0	0	0	2	.000	.000	.000	-97	-2	0	0	0	.000	-0	H	-0.2
	Tex-A	72	151	14	24	2	0	4	19	10	31	.159	.211	.252	39	-12	1	0	0	.979	-7	3-23,2-17/1O	-2.1
	Yr	79	158	14	24	2	0	4	19	10	33	.152	.202	.241	33	-14	1	0	0	.979	-7	3-23,2-17/1O	-2.3
Total	9	907	2329	268	548	91	19	41	237	191	309	.235	.296	.343	79	-66	20	13	-2	.967	-54	2-262,3-186,1/OS	-13.2

■ JAKE JONES
Jones, James Murrell   b: 11/23/20, Epps, La.   BR/TR, 6'3", 197 lbs.   Deb: 9/20/41

YEAR	TM/L	G	AB	R	H	2B	3B	HR	RBI	BB	SO	AVG	OBP	SLG	PRO+	BR/A	SB	CS	SBR	FA	FR	G/POS	TPR
1941	Chi-A	3	11	0	0	0	0	0	0	0	4	.000	.000	.000	-99	-3	0	0	0	1.000	-1	/1-3	-0.4
1942	Chi-A	7	20	2	3	1	0	0	0	2	2	.150	.227	.200	21	-2	1	0	0	.961	-1	/1-5	-0.3
1946	Chi-A	24	79	10	21	5	1	3	13	2	13	.266	.284	.468	112	0	0	0	0	.986	-3	1-20	-0.4
1947	Chi-A	45	171	15	41	7	1	3	20	13	25	.240	.297	.345	81	-5	1	0	0	.988	-1	1-43	-0.7
	Bos-A	109	404	50	95	14	3	16	76	41	60	.235	.310	.403	91	-6	5	4	-1	.991	-2	*1-109	-1.4
	Yr	154	575	65	136	21	4	19	96	54	85	.237	.306	.386	88	-11	6	4	-1	.990	-3	*1-152	-2.1
1948	Bos-A	36	105	3	21	4	0	1	8	11	26	.200	.276	.267	43	-9	1	0	0	.993	2	1-31	-0.6
Total	5	224	790	80	181	31	5	23	117	69	130	.229	.294	.368	80	-25	8	4	0	.989	-6	1-211	-3.8

■ JIM JONES
Jones, James Tilford "Sheriff"   b: 12/25/1876, London, Ky.   d: 5/6/53, London, Ky.   BR/TR, 5'10", 162 lbs.   Deb: 6/29/1897

YEAR	TM/L	G	AB	R	H	2B	3B	HR	RBI	BB	SO	AVG	OBP	SLG	PRO+	BR/A	SB	CS	SBR	FA	FR	G/POS	TPR
1897	Lou-N	2	4	1	1	0	0	0	1	0		.250	.400	.500	141	0	0			.000	-0	/P-1	0.0
1901	NY-N	21	91	10	19	4	3	0	5	4		.209	.250	.319	67	-4	2			.900	1	O-20/P-1	-0.5
1902	NY-N	67	249	16	59	11	1	0	19	13		.237	.275	.289	75	-8	7			.897	-1	O-67	-1.4
Total	3	90	344	28	79	16	4	0	24	18		.230	.270	.299	73	-12	9			.898	-0	/O-87,P-2	-1.9

■ JEFF JONES
Jones, Jeffrey Raymond   b: 10/22/57, Philadelphia, Pa.   BR/TR, 6'2", 200 lbs.   Deb: 4/4/83

YEAR	TM/L	G	AB	R	H	2B	3B	HR	RBI	BB	SO	AVG	OBP	SLG	PRO+	BR/A	SB	CS	SBR	FA	FR	G/POS	TPR
1983	Cin-N	16	44	6	10	3	0	0	5	11	13	.227	.393	.295	90	1	2	0	1	1.000	1	O-13/1-1	0.1

■ BINKY JONES
Jones, John Joseph   b: 7/11/1899, St.Louis, Mo.   d: 5/13/61, St.Louis, Mo.   BR/TR, 5'9", 154 lbs.   Deb: 4/15/24

YEAR	TM/L	G	AB	R	H	2B	3B	HR	RBI	BB	SO	AVG	OBP	SLG	PRO+	BR/A	SB	CS	SBR	FA	FR	G/POS	TPR
1924	Bro-N	10	37	0	4	1	0	0	2	0	3	.108	.108	.135	-36	-7	0	0	0	.898	-1	S-10	-0.7

■ JOHN JONES
Jones, John William "Skins"   b: 5/13/01, Coatesville, Pa.   d: 11/3/56, Baltimore, Md.   BL/TL, 5'11", 185 lbs.   Deb: 9/26/23

YEAR	TM/L	G	AB	R	H	2B	3B	HR	RBI	BB	SO	AVG	OBP	SLG	PRO+	BR/A	SB	CS	SBR	FA	FR	G/POS	TPR
1923	Phi-A	1	4	0	1	0	0	0	0	0	1	.250	.250	.250	31	-0	0	0	0	1.000	0	/O-1	0.0
1932	Phi-A	4	6	0	1	0	0	0	0	0	3	.167	.167	.167	-13	-1	0	0	0	1.000	-0	/O-1	-0.1
Total	2	5	10	0	2	0	0	0	1	0	4	.200	.200	.200	4	-1	0	0	0	1.000	0	/O-2	-0.1

■ CHIPPER JONES
Jones, Larry Wayne   b: 4/24/72, DeLand, Fla.   BB/TR, 6'3", 185 lbs.   Deb: 9/11/93

YEAR	TM/L	G	AB	R	H	2B	3B	HR	RBI	BB	SO	AVG	OBP	SLG	PRO+	BR/A	SB	CS	SBR	FA	FR	G/POS	TPR
1993	Atl-N	8	3	2	2	1	0	0	0	1	1	.667	.750	1.000	360	1	0	0	0	1.000	1	/S-3	0.2

■ LYNN JONES
Jones, Lynn Morris   b: 1/1/53, Meadville, Pa.   BR/TR, 5'9", 175 lbs.   Deb: 4/13/79   FC

YEAR	TM/L	G	AB	R	H	2B	3B	HR	RBI	BB	SO	AVG	OBP	SLG	PRO+	BR/A	SB	CS	SBR	FA	FR	G/POS	TPR
1979	Det-A	95	213	33	63	8	0	4	26	17	22	.296	.351	.390	96	-1	9	6	-1	.980	-10	O-84	-1.4
1980	Det-A	30	55	9	14	2	2	0	6	10	5	.255	.369	.364	99	0	1	0	0	1.000	-2	O-17/D-6	-0.1
1981	Det-A	71	174	19	45	5	0	2	19	18	10	.259	.332	.322	86	-3	1	2	-1	.989	-4	O-60/D-4	-1.0
1982	Det-A	58	139	15	31	3	1	0	14	7	14	.223	.260	.259	43	-11	0	2	-1	1.000	-5	O-56/D-1	-1.8
1983	Det-A	49	64	9	17	1	2	0	6	3	6	.266	.299	.344	78	-2	1	0	0	.968	-7	O-31/D-6	-0.9
1984	*KC-A	47	103	11	31	6	0	1	10	4	9	.301	.333	.388	98	-0	1	3	-2	.962	-12	O-45	-1.5
1985	*KC-A	110	152	12	32	7	0	0	9	8	15	.211	.264	.257	43	-12	0	1	-1	.983	-24	*O-100/D-2	-3.8
1986	KC-A	67	47	1	6	2	0	0	1	6	5	.128	.226	.170	10	-6	0	0	0	.971	-21	O-62/2-1,D	-2.7
Total	8	527	947	109	239	34	5	7	91	73	86	.252	.310	.321	73	-34	13	14	-5	.983	-84	O-455/D-22,2	-13.2

■ MACK JONES
Jones, Mack "Mack The Knife"   b: 11/6/38, Atlanta, Ga.   BL/TR, 6'1", 180 lbs.   Deb: 7/13/61

YEAR	TM/L	G	AB	R	H	2B	3B	HR	RBI	BB	SO	AVG	OBP	SLG	PRO+	BR/A	SB	CS	SBR	FA	FR	G/POS	TPR
1961	Mil-N	28	104	13	24	3	2	0	12	12	28	.231	.322	.298	70	-4	4	4	-1	1.000	-2	O-26	-0.9
1962	Mil-N	91	333	51	85	17	4	10	36	44	100	.255	.354	.420	110	5	5	1	1	.973	-8	O-91	-0.7
1963	Mil-N	93	228	36	50	11	4	3	22	26	59	.219	.318	.342	91	-2	8	4	-0	.978	-8	O-80	-1.4
1965	Mil-N	143	504	78	132	18	7	31	75	29	122	.262	.314	.510	127	16	8	2	1	.980	-10	*O-133	0.1
1966	Atl-N	118	417	60	110	14	1	23	66	39	85	.264	.338	.468	120	11	16	10	-1	.981	-3	*O-112/1-1	0.2
1967	Atl-N	140	454	72	115	23	4	17	50	64	108	.253	.357	.434	127	17	10	6	-1	.985	2	*O-126	1.3
1968	Cin-N	103	234	40	59	9	1	10	34	28	46	.252	.345	.427	123	7	2	3	-1	.988	-8	O-60	-0.6
1969	Mon-N	135	455	73	123	23	5	22	79	67	110	.270	.382	.488	142	27	6	7	-2	.959	7	*O-129	2.5
1970	Mon-N	108	271	51	65	11	3	14	32	59	74	.240	.399	.458	129	14	5	3	-0	.968	-4	O-87	0.5
1971	Mon-N	43	91	11	15	3	0	3	9	15	24	.165	.296	.297	68	-4	1	0	0	.952	-2	O-27	-0.6
Total	10	1002	3091	485	778	132	31	133	415	383	756	.252	.349	.444	120	86	65	40	-5	.976	-35	O-871/1-1	0.4

■ RED JONES
Jones, Maurice Morris   b: 11/2/14, Timpson, Tex.   d: 6/30/75, Lincoln, Cal.   BL/TR, 6'3", 190 lbs.   Deb: 4/16/40

YEAR	TM/L	G	AB	R	H	2B	3B	HR	RBI	BB	SO	AVG	OBP	SLG	PRO+	BR/A	SB	CS	SBR	FA	FR	G/POS	TPR
1940	StL-N	12	11	0	1	0	0	0	1	1	2	.091	.167	.091	-26	-2	0	0	0	1.000	-0	/O-1	-0.2

■ RICKY JONES
Jones, Ricky Miron   b: 6/4/58, Tupelo, Miss.   BR/TR, 6'3", 186 lbs.   Deb: 9/3/86

YEAR	TM/L	G	AB	R	H	2B	3B	HR	RBI	BB	SO	AVG	OBP	SLG	PRO+	BR/A	SB	CS	SBR	FA	FR	G/POS	TPR
1986	Bal-A	16	33	2	6	2	0	0	4	6	8	.182	.308	.242	53	-2	0	0	0	1.000	7	2-11/3-6	0.5

■ BOB JONES
Jones, Robert Oliver   b: 10/11/49, Elkton, Md.   BL/TL, 6'2", 195 lbs.   Deb: 10/1/74

YEAR	TM/L	G	AB	R	H	2B	3B	HR	RBI	BB	SO	AVG	OBP	SLG	PRO+	BR/A	SB	CS	SBR	FA	FR	G/POS	TPR
1974	Tex-A	2	5	0	0	0	0	0	0	0	0	.000	.000	.000	-99	-1	0	0	0	1.000	0	/O-2	-0.1
1975	Tex-A	9	11	2	1	0	0	0	0	3	3	.091	.286	.091	11	-1	0	0	0	1.000	-1	/O-5,D-1	-0.2
1976	Cal-A	78	166	22	35	6	0	6	17	14	30	.211	.276	.355	90	-3	3	0	1	.990	-5	O-62/D-2	-0.9
1977	Cal-A	14	17	3	3	0	0	1	3	4	5	.176	.333	.353	91	-0	0	0	0	1.000	0	/D-6	0.0
1981	Tex-A	10	34	4	9	1	0	3	7	1	7	.265	.286	.559	146	2	0	1	-1	1.000	3	O-10	0.4
1983	Tex-A	41	72	5	16	4	0	1	6	5	17	.222	.291	.319	69	-3	0	0	-1	1.000	-0	O-11,D-11/1	-0.5
1984	Tex-A	64	143	14	37	4	0	4	22	10	19	.259	.312	.371	85	-3	1	1	-0	1.000	-0	O-22,1-15/D	-0.5

YEAR	TM/L	G	AB	R	H	2B	3B	HR	RBI	BB	SO	AVG	OBP	SLG	PRO+	BR/A	SB	CS	SBR	FA	FR	G/POS	TPR
1985	Tex-A	83	134	14	30	2	0	5	23	11	30	.224	.288	.351	73	-5	1	0	0	1.000	-7	O-30,D-10/1	-1.3
1986	Tex-A	13	21	1	2	0	0	0	3	2	5	.095	.174	.095	-24	-4	0	0	0	.909	-2	/O-9,1-2	-0.6
Total	9	314	603	65	133	17	0	20	86	50	117	.221	.286	.348	78	-18	5	4	-1	.992	-11	O-151/D-34,1	-3.7

■ BOB JONES
Jones, Robert Walter "Ducky" b: 12/2/1889, Clayton, Cal. d: 8/30/64, San Diego, Cal. BL/TR, 6', 170 lbs. Deb: 4/11/17

YEAR	TM/L	G	AB	R	H	2B	3B	HR	RBI	BB	SO	AVG	OBP	SLG	PRO+	BR/A	SB	CS	SBR	FA	FR	G/POS	TPR
1917	Det-A	46	77	16	12	1	2	0	2	4	8	.156	.198	.221	28	-7	3			.938	-1	2-18/3-8	-0.8
1918	Det-A	74	287	43	79	14	4	0	21	17	16	.275	.320	.352	107	1	7			.947	-8	3-63/1-6,O	-0.7
1919	Det-A	127	439	37	114	18	6	1	57	34	39	.260	.314	.335	84	-10	11			.944	-24	*3-127	-3.0
1920	Det-A	81	265	35	66	6	3	1	18	22	13	.249	.309	.306	65	-13	3	4	-2	.942	-5	3-67/2-5,S	-1.6
1921	Det-A	141	554	82	168	23	9	1	72	37	24	.303	.348	.383	87	-11	8	9	-3	.950	10	*3-141	0.6
1922	Det-A	124	455	65	117	10	6	3	44	36	18	.257	.314	.325	69	-21	8	5	-1	.962	11	*3-119	-0.2
1923	Det-A	100	372	51	93	15	4	1	40	29	13	.250	.306	.320	66	-19	7	6	-2	.954	5	3-97	-0.7
1924	Det-A	110	393	52	107	27	4	0	47	20	20	.272	.308	.361	73	-17	1	5	-3	.956	-2	*3-106	-1.3
1925	Det-A	50	148	18	35	6	0	0	15	9	5	.236	.280	.277	42	-13	1	1	-0	.985	9	3-46	-0.2
Total	9	853	2990	399	791	120	38	7	316	208	156	.265	.314	.337	75	-109	49	<u>30</u>		.953	-5	3-774/2-23,1SO	-7.9

■ RON JONES
Jones, Ronald Glen b: 6/11/64, Seguin, Tex. BL/TR, 5'10", 195 lbs. Deb: 8/26/88

YEAR	TM/L	G	AB	R	H	2B	3B	HR	RBI	BB	SO	AVG	OBP	SLG	PRO+	BR/A	SB	CS	SBR	FA	FR	G/POS	TPR
1988	Phi-N	33	124	15	36	6	1	8	26	2	14	.290	.302	.548	136	5	0	0	0	1.000	2	O-32	0.7
1989	Phi-N	12	31	7	9	0	0	2	4	9	1	.290	.450	.484	167	3	1	0	0	1.000	2	O-12	0.5
1990	Phi-N	24	58	5	16	2	0	3	7	9	9	.276	.373	.466	130	2	0	1	-1	1.000	-1	O-16	0.1
1991	Phi-N	28	26	0	4	2	0	0	3	2	9	.154	.214	.231	25	-3	0	0	0	.000	0	H	-0.4
Total	4	97	239	27	65	10	1	13	40	22	33	.272	.333	.485	128	8	1	1	-0	1.000	3	/O-60	0.9

■ ROSS JONES
Jones, Ross A. b: 1/14/60, Miami, Fla. BR/TR, 6'2", 185 lbs. Deb: 4/2/84

YEAR	TM/L	G	AB	R	H	2B	3B	HR	RBI	BB	SO	AVG	OBP	SLG	PRO+	BR/A	SB	CS	SBR	FA	FR	G/POS	TPR
1984	NY-N	17	10	2	1	1	0	0	1	3	4	.100	.308	.200	46	-1	0	0	0	.833	1	/S-6,2-1,3	0.1
1986	Sea-A	11	21	0	2	0	0	0	0	0	4	.095	.095	.095	-48	-4	0	1	-1	1.000	1	/S-4,2-3,3D	-0.4
1987	KC-A	39	114	10	29	4	2	0	10	5	15	.254	.290	.325	62	-6	1	0	0	.974	1	S-36/2-3	-0.2
Total	3	67	145	12	32	5	2	0	11	8	23	.221	.266	.283	46	-11	1	1	-0	.971	3	/S-46,2-7,3D	-0.5

■ RUPPERT JONES
Jones, Ruppert Sanderson b: 3/12/55, Dallas, Tex. BL/TL, 5'10", 175 lbs. Deb: 8/1/76

YEAR	TM/L	G	AB	R	H	2B	3B	HR	RBI	BB	SO	AVG	OBP	SLG	PRO+	BR/A	SB	CS	SBR	FA	FR	G/POS	TPR
1976	KC-A	28	51	9	11	1	1	1	7	3	16	.216	.259	.333	72	-2	0	2	-1	1.000	-5	O-17/D-3	-0.9
1977	Sea-A★	160	597	85	157	26	8	24	76	55	120	.263	.327	.454	111	8	13	9	-2	.981	26	*O-155/D-4	2.2
1978	Sea-A	129	472	48	111	24	3	6	46	55	85	.235	.315	.337	84	-10	22	6	3	.985	16	*O-128	0.4
1979	Sea-A	162	622	109	166	29	9	21	78	85	78	.267	.358	.444	113	12	33	12	3	.989	14	*O-161	2.1
1980	NY-A	83	328	38	73	11	3	9	42	34	50	.223	.301	.357	81	-9	18	8	1	.988	9	O-82	-0.3
1981	SD-N	105	397	53	99	34	1	4	39	43	66	.249	.323	.370	104	1	7	9	-3	.993	10	*O-104	0.5
1982	SD-N★	116	424	69	120	20	2	12	61	62	90	.283	.376	.425	130	18	18	15	-4	.984	8	*O-114	2.1
1983	SD-N	133	335	42	78	12	3	12	49	35	58	.233	.305	.394	96	-3	11	11	-3	.981	-2	*O-111/1-5	-1.2
1984	*Det-A	79	215	26	61	12	1	12	37	21	47	.284	.347	.516	136	10	2	4	-2	1.000	-5	O-73/D-2	0.2
1985	Cal-A	125	389	66	90	17	2	21	67	57	82	.231	.330	.447	111	6	7	4	-0	.995	10	O-73,D-43	1.2
1986	*Cal-A	126	393	73	90	21	3	17	49	64	87	.229	.341	.427	109	6	10	3	1	.981	-12	*O-121	-0.9
1987	Cal-A	85	192	25	47	8	2	8	28	20	38	.245	.316	.432	99	-1	2	1	0	.965	-15	O-66/D-3	-1.6
Total	12	1331	4415	643	1103	215	38	147	579	534	817	.250	.332	.416	106	37	143	84	-8	.986	51	*O-1205/D-55,1	3.8

■ JACK JONES
Jones, Ryerson L. "Ri" or "Angel Sleeves" b: Cincinnati, Ohio TR , Deb: 8/13/1883

YEAR	TM/L	G	AB	R	H	2B	3B	HR	RBI	BB	SO	AVG	OBP	SLG	PRO+	BR/A	SB	CS	SBR	FA	FR	G/POS	TPR
1883	Lou-a	2	7	1	0	0	0	0		0		.000	.000	.000	-99	-2				.500	-1	/O-2,S-1	-0.2
1884	Cin-U	69	272	36	71	5	1	2		12		.261	.285	.309	59	-16				.858	2	S-41,2-19,3	-1.2
Total	2	71	279	37	71	5	1	2		12		.254	.285	.301	56	-17				.857	1	/S-42,2-19,3O	-1.4

■ TOM JONES
Jones, Thomas b: 1/22/1877, Honesdale, Pa. d: 6/21/23, Danville, Pa. BR/TR, 6'1", 195 lbs. Deb: 8/25/02

YEAR	TM/L	G	AB	R	H	2B	3B	HR	RBI	BB	SO	AVG	OBP	SLG	PRO+	BR/A	SB	CS	SBR	FA	FR	G/POS	TPR
1902	Bal-A	37	159	22	45	8	4	0	14	2		.283	.292	.384	83	-4	1			.955	-2	1-37/2-1	-0.6
1904	StL-A	156	625	53	152	15	10	2	68	15		.243	.270	.309	88	-10	16			.988	0	*1-134,2-23/O	-1.4
1905	StL-A	135	504	44	122	16	2	0	48	30		.242	.290	.282	86	-8	5			.985	7	*1-135	-0.6
1906	StL-A	144	539	51	136	22	6	0	30	24		.252	.290	.315	94	-5	27			.985	11	*1-143	0.1
1907	StL-A	155	549	53	137	17	3	0	34	34		.250	.298	.291	88	-7	24			.983	2	*1-155	-1.1
1908	StL-A	155	549	43	135	14	2	1	50	30		.246	.290	.284	86	-8	18			.986	-2	*1-155	-1.5
1909	StL-A	97	337	30	84	9	3	0	29	18		.249	.299	.294	94	-3	13			.989	7	1-95/3-2	0.4
	*Det-A	44	153	13	43	9	0	0	18	5		.281	.317	.340	103	0	9			.984	2	1-44	0.2
	Yr	141	490	43	127	18	3	0	47	23		.259	.305	.308	97	-2	22			.988	9	*1-139/3-2	0.6
1910	Det-A	135	432	32	110	12	4	1	45	35		.255	.325	.308	92	-4	22			.985	-4	*1-135	-0.8
Total	8	1058	3847	341	964	122	34	4	336	193		.251	.294	.303	90	-49	135			.984	22	*1-1033/2-24,O3	-5.3

■ TRACY JONES
Jones, Tracy Donald b: 3/31/61, Hawthorne, Cal. BR/TR, 6'3", 220 lbs. Deb: 4/7/86

YEAR	TM/L	G	AB	R	H	2B	3B	HR	RBI	BB	SO	AVG	OBP	SLG	PRO+	BR/A	SB	CS	SBR	FA	FR	G/POS	TPR
1986	Cin-N	46	86	16	30	3	0	2	10	9	5	.349	.411	.453	132	4	7	1	2	1.000	-0	O-24/1-2	0.5
1987	Cin-N	117	359	53	104	17	3	10	44	23	40	.290	.338	.437	99	-1	31	8	5	.990	-3	O-95	-0.3
1988	Cin-N	37	83	9	19	1	0	1	9	8	6	.229	.304	.277	65	-3	9	0	3	.955	-2	O-25	-0.4
	Mon-N	53	141	20	47	5	1	2	15	12	12	.333	.390	.426	128	5	9	6	-1	1.000	-8	O-43	-0.5
	Yr	90	224	29	66	6	1	3	24	20	18	.295	.358	.371	105	2	18	6	2	.980	-10	O-68	-0.9
1989	SF-N	40	97	5	18	4	0	0	12	5	14	.186	.233	.227	33	-8	2	1	-0	1.000	-8	O-30	-1.9
	Det-A	46	158	17	41	10	0	3	26	16	16	.259	.331	.380	102	1	1	1	-0	.986	-1	O-36/D-8	-0.2
1990	Det-A	50	118	15	27	4	1	4	9	6	13	.229	.283	.381	84	-3	1	1	-0	.952	-2	O-27,D-20	-0.6
	Sea-A	25	86	8	26	4	0	2	15	3	12	.302	.341	.419	110	1	0	1	-1	1.000	-1	O-18/D-5	-0.1
	Yr	75	204	23	53	8	1	6	24	9	25	.260	.307	.397	95	-2	1	2	-1	.973	-3	O-45,D-25	-0.7
1991	Sea-A	79	175	30	44	8	1	3	24	18	22	.251	.325	.360	89	-2	2	0	1	1.000	-5	D-37,O-36	-0.9
Total	6	493	1303	173	356	56	6	27	164	100	140	.273	.331	.388	96	-7	62	19	7	.988	-31	O-334/D-70,1	-4.4

■ NIPPY JONES
Jones, Vernal Leroy b: 6/29/25, Los Angeles, Cal. BR/TR, 6'1", 185 lbs. Deb: 6/8/46

YEAR	TM/L	G	AB	R	H	2B	3B	HR	RBI	BB	SO	AVG	OBP	SLG	PRO+	BR/A	SB	CS	SBR	FA	FR	G/POS	TPR
1946	*StL-N	16	12	3	4	0	0	0	1	2	2	.333	.429	.333	113	-0	0			.800	1	/2-3	0.1
1947	StL-N	23	73	6	18	4	0	1	5	2	10	.247	.267	.342	58	-5	0			.935	-2	2-13/O-2	-0.5
1948	StL-N	132	481	58	122	21	9	10	81	36	45	.254	.307	.397	84	-12	2			.986	-9	*1-128	-2.2
1949	StL-N	110	380	51	114	20	8	6	62	16	20	.300	.330	.426	97	-3	1			.984	-8	1-98	-1.1
1950	StL-N	13	26	0	6	1	0	0	6	3	1	.231	.310	.269	52	-2	0			.983	1	/1-8	-0.2
1951	StL-N	80	300	20	79	12	3	6	41	9	13	.263	.287	.333	66	-15	1	2	-1	.991	-1	1-71	-2.0
1952	Phi-N	8	30	3	5	0	0	1	5	0	4	.167	.167	.267	19	-3	0			.976	0	/1-8	-0.3
1957	*Mil-N	30	79	5	21	2	1	2	7	3	6	.266	.293	.392	88	-2	0	0	0	.994	-0	1-20/O-1	-0.3
Total	8	412	1381	146	369	60	12	25	209	71	102	.267	.304	.382	81	-40	4	<u>2</u>		.987	-19	1-333/2-16,O	-6.5

■ BILL JONES
Jones, William b: Syracuse, N.Y. Deb: 5/17/1882

YEAR	TM/L	G	AB	R	H	2B	3B	HR	RBI	BB	SO	AVG	OBP	SLG	PRO+	BR/A	SB	CS	SBR	FA	FR	G/POS	TPR
1882	Bal-a	4	15	1	1	0	0	0				.067	.067	.067	-59	-2				1.000	0	/O-2,C-2	-0.2
1884	Phi-U	4	14	2	2	0	0	0		1		.143	.200	.143	-6	-2				.862	0	/C-4,O-1	-0.1
Total	2	8	29	3	3	0	0	0		1		.103	.133	.103	-30	-4				.857	1	/C-6,O-3	-0.3

■ BILL JONES
Jones, William Dennis "Midget" b: 4/8/1887, Hartland, N.B., Can. d: 10/10/46, Boston, Mass. BL/TR, 5'6.5", 157 lbs. Deb: 6/20/11

YEAR	TM/L	G	AB	R	H	2B	3B	HR	RBI	BB	SO	AVG	OBP	SLG	PRO+	BR/A	SB	CS	SBR	FA	FR	G/POS	TPR
1911	Bos-N	24	51	6	11	2	1	0	3	15	7	.216	.394	.294	87	-0	1			.867	-1	O-18	-0.2

YEAR	TM/L	G	AB	R	H	2B	3B	HR	RBI	BB	SO	AVG	OBP	SLG	PRO+	BR/A	SB	CS	SBR	FA	FR	G/POS	TPR
1912	Bos-N	3	2	0	1	0	0	0	2	0	1	.500	.500	.500	171	0	0			.000	0	H	0.0
Total	2	27	53	6	12	2	1	0	5	15	8	.226	.397	.302	89	-0	1			.867	-1	/O-18	-0.2

■ TEX JONES
Jones, William Roderick b: 8/4/1885, Marion, Kan. d: 2/26/38, Wichita, Kan. BR/TR, 6′, 192 lbs. Deb: 4/13/11

YEAR	TM/L	G	AB	R	H	2B	3B	HR	RBI	BB	SO	AVG	OBP	SLG	PRO+	BR/A	SB	CS	SBR	FA	FR	G/POS	TPR
1911	Chi-A	9	31	4	6	1	0	0	4	3		.194	.265	.226	39	-3	1			1.000	3	/1-9	0.0

■ TIM JONES
Jones, William Timothy b: 12/1/62, Sumter, S.C. BL/TR, 5′10″, 172 lbs. Deb: 7/26/88

YEAR	TM/L	G	AB	R	H	2B	3B	HR	RBI	BB	SO	AVG	OBP	SLG	PRO+	BR/A	SB	CS	SBR	FA	FR	G/POS	TPR
1988	StL-N	31	52	2	14	0	0	0	3	4	10	.269	.321	.269	70	-2	4	1	1	.955	5	/S-9,2-8,3	0.4
1989	StL-N	42	75	11	22	6	0	0	7	7	8	.293	.361	.373	107	1	1	0	0	1.000	-2	2-12,S-12/3CO	0.0
1990	StL-N	67	128	9	28	7	1	0	12	12	20	.219	.291	.313	66	-6	3	4	-2	.944	3	S-29,2-19/3P	-0.4
1991	StL-N	16	24	1	4	2	0	0	2	2	6	.167	.231	.250	35	-2	0	1	-1	1.000	-2	S-14/2-4	-0.5
1992	StL-N	67	145	9	29	4	0	0	3	11	29	.200	.256	.228	39	-11	5	2	0	.972	2	S-34,2-28/3O	-0.8
1993	StL-N	29	61	13	16	6	0	1	1	9	8	.262	.366	.361	97	0	2	2	-1	.975	5	S-21/2-7	0.6
Total	6	252	485	45	113	25	1	1	28	45	81	.233	.302	.295	68	-20	15	10	-2	.964	9	S-119/2-78,30PC	-0.7

■ WILLIE JONES
Jones, Willie Edward "Puddin' Head" b: 8/16/25, Dillon, S.C. d: 10/18/83, Cincinnati, Ohio BR/TR, 6′1″, 192 lbs. Deb: 9/10/47

YEAR	TM/L	G	AB	R	H	2B	3B	HR	RBI	BB	SO	AVG	OBP	SLG	PRO+	BR/A	SB	CS	SBR	FA	FR	G/POS	TPR
1947	Phi-N	18	62	5	14	1	0	0	10	7	0	.226	.304	.258	53	-4	2			.909	2	3-17	-0.2
1948	Phi-N	17	60	9	20	2	0	2	9	3	5	.333	.365	.467	126	2	0			.926	2	3-17	0.4
1949	Phi-N	149	532	71	130	35	1	19	77	65	66	.244	.333	.421	102	0	3			.948	-4	3-145	-0.6
1950	*Phi-N★	157	610	100	163	28	6	25	88	61	40	.267	.337	.456	108	6	5			.954	-6	*3-157	-0.3
1951	Phi-N★	148	564	79	161	28	5	22	81	60	47	.285	.358	.470	123	17	6	2	1	.966	-9	*3-147	0.8
1952	Phi-N	147	541	60	135	12	3	18	72	53	36	.250	.323	.383	96	-3	5	3	-0	.969	4	*3-147	-0.3
1953	Phi-N	149	481	61	108	16	2	19	70	85	45	.225	.342	.385	90	-6	1	1	-0	.975	-3	*3-147	-1.2
1954	Phi-N	142	535	64	145	28	3	12	56	61	54	.271	.346	.402	94	-4	4	1	1	.968	-2	*3-141	-0.9
1955	Phi-N	146	516	65	133	20	3	16	81	77	51	.258	.357	.401	103	4	6	2	1	.960	-13	*3-146	-0.9
1956	Phi-N	149	520	88	144	20	4	17	78	92	49	.277	.387	.429	121	19	5	4	-1	.973	1	*3-149	2.1
1957	Phi-N	133	440	58	96	19	2	9	47	69	41	.218	.313	.332	76	-14	1	0		.966	-7	*3-126	-1.9
1958	Phi-N	118	398	52	108	15	1	14	60	49	45	.271	.354	.420	105	4	1	2	-1	.967	-13	*3-110/1-1	-1.0
1959	Phi-N	47	160	23	43	9	1	7	24	19	14	.269	.346	.469	113	3	0	0	0	.975	-3	3-46	0.0
	Cle-A	11	18	1	4	1	0	0	1	1	3	.222	.263	.278	51	-1	0	0	0	.929	2	/3-4	0.0
	Cin-N	72	233	33	58	12	1	7	31	28	26	.249	.332	.399	91	-3	0	2	-1	.966	-3	3-68	-0.7
1960	Cin-N	79	149	16	40	7	0	3	27	31	16	.268	.394	.376	110	4	1	0		.962	-3	3-46/2-1	0.0
1961	Cin-N	9	7	1	0	0	0	0	2	0	3	.000	.222	.000	-34	-1	0	0		.000	-0	/3-1	-0.2
Total	15	1691	5826	786	1502	252	33	190	812	755	541	.258	.345	.410	102	20	40	17		.963	-55	*3-1614/2-1,1	-4.9

■ BUBBER JONNARD
Jonnard, Clarence James b: 11/23/1897, Nashville, Tenn. d: 8/23/77, New York, N.Y. BR/TR, 6′1″, 185 lbs. Deb: 10/1/20 FC

YEAR	TM/L	G	AB	R	H	2B	3B	HR	RBI	BB	SO	AVG	OBP	SLG	PRO+	BR/A	SB	CS	SBR	FA	FR	G/POS	TPR
1920	Chi-A	2	5	0	0	0	0	0	0	0	1	.000	.000	.000	-99	-1	0	0	0	.857	0	/C-1	-0.1
1922	Pit-N	10	21	4	5	0	1	0	2	2	4	.238	.304	.333	64	-1	0	0	0	.974	2	C-10	0.1
1926	Phi-N	19	34	3	4	1	0	0	2	3	4	.118	.189	.147	-8	-5	0			.949	0	C-15	-0.4
1927	Phi-N	53	143	18	42	6	0	0	14	7	7	.294	.327	.336	77	-5	0			.967	-9	C-41	-1.1
1929	StL-N	18	31	1	3	0	0	0	2	0	6	.097	.097	.097	-51	-7	0			.957	1	C-18	-0.5
1935	Phi-N	1	1	0	0	0	0	0	0	0	1	.000	.000	.000	-91	-0	0			1.000	-0	/C-1	0.0
Total	6	103	235	26	54	7	1	0	20	12	23	.230	.267	.268	41	-20	0	0	0	.960	-5	/C-86	-2.0

■ EDDIE JOOST
Joost, Edwin David b: 6/5/16, San Francisco, Cal BR/TR, 6′, 175 lbs. Deb: 9/11/36 M

YEAR	TM/L	G	AB	R	H	2B	3B	HR	RBI	BB	SO	AVG	OBP	SLG	PRO+	BR/A	SB	CS	SBR	FA	FR	G/POS	TPR
1936	Cin-N	13	26	1	4	1	0	0	1	2	5	.154	.214	.192	11	-3	0			.947	-1	/S-7,2-5	-0.4
1937	Cin-N	6	12	0	1	0	0	0	0	0	4	.083	.083	.083	-57	-3	0			.875	0	/2-6	-0.2
1939	Cin-N	42	143	23	36	6	3	0	14	12	15	.252	.310	.336	73	-5	1			.957	-3	2-32/S-6	-0.6
1940	*Cin-N	88	278	24	60	7	2	1	24	32	40	.216	.301	.266	57	-15	4			.960	-1	S-78/2-7,3	-0.9
1941	Cin-N	152	537	67	136	25	4	4	40	69	59	.253	.340	.337	91	-5	9			.942	-6	*S-147/2-4,13	0.0
1942	Cin-N	142	562	65	126	30	3	6	41	62	57	.224	.307	.320	84	-11	9			.933	-10	*S-130,2-15	-1.4
1943	Bos-N	124	421	34	78	16	3	2	20	68	80	.185	.299	.252	61	-20	5			.945	13	3-67,2-60/S	-0.3
1945	Bos-N	35	141	16	35	7	1	0	9	13	7	.248	.312	.312	73	-5	0			.945	-7	2-19,3-16	-1.1
1947	Phi-A	151	540	76	111	22	3	13	64	114	110	.206	.348	.330	87	-6	6	6	-2	.956	-1	*S-151	-0.3
1948	Phi-A	135	509	99	127	22	2	16	55	119	91	.250	.393	.395	110	11	2	4	-2	.973	5	*S-135	2.1
1949	Phi-A★	144	525	128	138	25	3	23	81	149	80	.263	.429	.453	138	36	2	1	0	.969	8	*S-144	5.2
1950	Phi-A	131	476	79	111	12	3	18	58	103	64	.233	.373	.384	96	-1	5	1	1	.956	-7	*S-131	0.3
1951	Phi-A	140	553	107	160	28	5	19	78	106	70	.289	.409	.461	132	28	10	8	-2	.974	4	*S-140	3.9
1952	Phi-A☆	146	540	94	132	26	3	20	75	122	94	.244	.388	.415	116	16	5	8	-3	.962	-7	*S-146	1.7
1953	Phi-A	51	177	39	44	6	0	6	15	45	24	.249	.401	.384	109	4	3	2	-0	.958	-6	S-51	0.2
1954	Phi-A	19	47	7	17	3	0	1	9	10	10	.362	.474	.489	163	5	0	1	-1	.963	-3	/S-9,3-5,2M	0.2
1955	Bos-A	55	119	15	23	2	0	5	17	17	21	.193	.299	.336	65	-6	0	0		.932	5	S-20,2-17/3	0.1
Total	17	1574	5606	874	1339	238	35	134	601	1043	827	.239	.361	.366	99	18	61	31		.958	-20	*S-1296,2-166/31	8.4

■ DUTCH JORDAN
Jordan, Adolf Otto b: 1/5/1880, Pittsburgh, Pa. d: 12/23/72, W.Allegheny, Pa. BR/TR, 5′10″, 185 lbs. Deb: 4/25/03

YEAR	TM/L	G	AB	R	H	2B	3B	HR	RBI	BB	SO	AVG	OBP	SLG	PRO+	BR/A	SB	CS	SBR	FA	FR	G/POS	TPR
1903	Bro-N	78	267	27	63	11	1	0	21	19		.236	.289	.285	66	-12	9			.928	-14	2-54,3-18/O1	-2.3
1904	Bro-N	87	252	21	45	10	2	0	19	13		.179	.225	.234	43	-17	7			.958	-17	2-70,3-11/1	-3.5
Total	2	165	519	48	108	21	3	0	40	32		.208	.258	.260	55	-29	16			.945	-31	2-124/3-29,1O	-5.8

■ BUCK JORDAN
Jordan, Baxter Byerly b: 1/16/07, Cooleemee, N.C. d: 3/18/93, Salisbury, N.C. BL/TR, 6′, 170 lbs. Deb: 9/15/27

YEAR	TM/L	G	AB	R	H	2B	3B	HR	RBI	BB	SO	AVG	OBP	SLG	PRO+	BR/A	SB	CS	SBR	FA	FR	G/POS	TPR
1927	NY-N	5	5	0	1	0	0	0	0	0	3	.200	.200	.200	7	-1	0			.000	0	H	-0.1
1929	NY-N	2	2	1	1	0	0	0	0	0	0	.500	.500	1.000	262	0	0			1.000	-0	/1-1	0.0
1931	Was-A	9	18	3	4	2	0	0	1	1	3	.222	.263	.333	56	-1	0	0	0	.978	-1	/1-7	-0.2
1932	Bos-N	49	212	27	68	12	3	2	29	4	5	.321	.333	.434	109	2	1			.991	-1	1-49	-0.3
1933	Bos-N	152	588	77	168	29	9	4	46	34	22	.286	.327	.386	112	7	4			.991	-3	*1-150	-1.1
1934	Bos-N	124	489	68	152	26	9	2	58	35	19	.311	.358	.413	114	9	3			.989	-3	*1-117	-0.4
1935	Bos-N	130	470	62	131	24	5	0	35	19	17	.279	.307	.383	91	-7	3			.983	1	1-95/3-8,O	-1.6
1936	Bos-N	138	555	81	179	27	5	3	66	45	22	.323	.375	.405	118	14	2			.993	1	*1-136	0.2
1937	Bos-N	8	8	1	2	0	0	0	0	0	0	.250	.250	.250	40	-1	0			.000	0	H	-0.1
	Cin-N	98	316	45	89	14	3	1	28	25	14	.282	.334	.354	92	-4	6			.989	-2	1-76	-1.4
	Yr	106	324	46	91	14	3	1	28	25	14	.281	.332	.352	91	-4	6			.989	-2	1-76	-1.5
1938	Cin-N	9	7	0	2	0	0	0	0	2	0	.286	.444	.286	107	0	0			.000	0	H	0.0
	Phi-N	87	310	31	93	18	1	0	18	17	4	.300	.336	.365	95	-2	1			.973	-4	3-58,1-17	-0.7
	Yr	96	317	31	95	18	1	0	18	19	4	.300	.339	.363	96	-2	1			.973	-4	3-58,1-17	-0.7
Total	10	811	2980	396	890	153	35	17	281	182	109	.299	.340	.391	106	18	20	0		.990	-12	1-648/3-66,O	-5.7

■ BRIAN JORDAN
Jordan, Brian O'Neal b: 3/29/67, Baltimore, Md. BR/TR, 6′1″, 205 lbs. Deb: 4/8/92

YEAR	TM/L	G	AB	R	H	2B	3B	HR	RBI	BB	SO	AVG	OBP	SLG	PRO+	BR/A	SB	CS	SBR	FA	FR	G/POS	TPR
1992	StL-N	55	193	17	40	9	4	5	22	10	48	.207	.250	.373	77	-7	7	2	1	.991	-1	O-53	-0.8
1993	StL-N	67	223	33	69	10	6	10	44	12	35	.309	.346	.543	139	11	6	6	-2	.973	-3	O-65	0.5
1994	StL-N	53	178	14	46	8	2	5	15	16	40	.258	.323	.410	93	-2	4	3	-1	.991	5	O-46/1-1	0.2
Total	3	175	594	64	155	27	12	20	81	38	123	.261	.312	.448	106	2	17	11	-2	.984	2	O-164/1-1	-0.1

■ SLATS JORDAN
Jordan, Clarence Veasey b: 9/26/1879, Baltimore, Md. d: 12/7/53, Catonsville, Md. BL/TL, 6′1″, 190 lbs. Deb: 9/28/01

YEAR	TM/L	G	AB	R	H	2B	3B	HR	RBI	BB	SO	AVG	OBP	SLG	PRO+	BR/A	SB	CS	SBR	FA	FR	G/POS	TPR
1901	Bal-A	1	3	0	0	0	0	0	0	0	0	.000	.000	.000	-96	-1	0			.867	-1	/1-1	-0.1

YEAR	TM/L	G	AB	R	H	2B	3B	HR	RBI	BB	SO	AVG	OBP	SLG	PRO+	BR/A	SB	CS	SBR	FA	FR	G/POS	TPR
1902	Bal-A	1	4	0	0	0	0	0	0	0	0	.000	.000	.000	-96	-1	0			.000	-0	/O-1	-0.1
Total	2	2	7	0	0	0	0	0	0	0	0	.000	.000	.000	-96	-2	0			—	-1	/O-1,1-1	-0.2

■ JIMMY JORDAN Jordan, James William "Lord" b: 1/13/08, Tucapau, S.C. d: 12/4/57, Gastonia, N.C. BR/TR, 5'9", 157 lbs. Deb: 4/20/33

YEAR	TM/L	G	AB	R	H	2B	3B	HR	RBI	BB	SO	AVG	OBP	SLG	PRO+	BR/A	SB	CS	SBR	FA	FR	G/POS	TPR
1933	Bro-N	70	211	16	54	12	1	0	17	4	6	.256	.270	.322	71	-8	3			.969	12	S-51,2-11	0.7
1934	Bro-N	97	369	34	98	17	2	0	43	9	32	.266	.285	.322	66	-19	1			.956	-13	S-51,2-41/3	-2.6
1935	Bro-N	94	295	26	82	7	0	0	30	9	17	.278	.302	.302	64	-15	3			.983	27	2-46,S-28/3	1.6
1936	Bro-N	115	398	26	93	15	1	2	28	15	21	.234	.262	.291	48	-29	1			.970	-17	2-98/S-9,3	-3.9
Total	4	376	1273	102	327	51	4	2	118	37	76	.257	.279	.308	60	-71	8			.969	8	2-196,S-139/3	-4.2

■ MIKE JORDAN Jordan, Michael Henry "Mitty" b: 2/7/1863, Lawrence, Mass. d: 9/25/40, Lawrence, Mass. 5'7.5", 155 lbs. Deb: 8/21/1890

YEAR	TM/L	G	AB	R	H	2B	3B	HR	RBI	BB	SO	AVG	OBP	SLG	PRO+	BR/A	SB	CS	SBR	FA	FR	G/POS	TPR
1890	Pit-N	37	125	8	12	1	0	0	6	15	19	.096	.210	.104	-9	-17	5			.947	2	O-37	-1.4

■ RICKY JORDAN Jordan, Paul Scott b: 5/26/65, Richmond, Cal. BR/TR, 6'5", 210 lbs. Deb: 7/17/88

YEAR	TM/L	G	AB	R	H	2B	3B	HR	RBI	BB	SO	AVG	OBP	SLG	PRO+	BR/A	SB	CS	SBR	FA	FR	G/POS	TPR
1988	Phi-N	69	273	41	84	15	1	11	43	7	39	.308	.325	.491	128	9	1	1	-0	.992	-5	1-69	-0.3
1989	Phi-N	144	523	63	149	22	3	12	75	23	62	.285	.321	.407	107	3	4	3	-1	.993	-11	*1-140	-2.1
1990	Phi-N	92	324	32	78	21	0	5	44	13	39	.241	.281	.352	73	-13	2	0	1	.995	-8	1-84	-2.7
1991	Phi-N	101	301	38	82	21	3	9	49	14	49	.272	.309	.452	113	4	0	2	-1	.987	-6	1-72	-0.8
1992	Phi-N	94	276	33	84	19	0	4	34	5	44	.304	.317	.417	106	1	3	0	1	.995	-6	1-54,O-11	-0.8
1993	*Phi-N	90	159	21	46	4	1	5	18	4	32	.289	.327	.421	100	-0	0	0	0	.990	-5	1-33	-0.8
1994	Phi-N	72	220	29	62	14	2	8	37	6	32	.282	.304	.473	100	-1	0	0	0	.993	-8	1-49	-1.3
Total	7	662	2076	257	585	116	10	54	300	76	297	.282	.312	.425	104	3	10	6	-1	.992	-49	1-501/O-11	-8.8

■ SCOTT JORDAN Jordan, Scott Allan b: 5/27/63, Waco, Tex. BR/TR, 6', 175 lbs. Deb: 9/2/88

YEAR	TM/L	G	AB	R	H	2B	3B	HR	RBI	BB	SO	AVG	OBP	SLG	PRO+	BR/A	SB	CS	SBR	FA	FR	G/POS	TPR
1988	Cle-A	7	9	0	1	0	0	0	1	0	3	.111	.111	.111	-37	-2	0	0	0	1.000	-1	/O-6	-0.3

■ TOM JORDAN Jordan, Thomas Jefferson b: 9/5/19, Lawton, Okla. BR/TR, 6'1.5", 195 lbs. Deb: 9/4/44

YEAR	TM/L	G	AB	R	H	2B	3B	HR	RBI	BB	SO	AVG	OBP	SLG	PRO+	BR/A	SB	CS	SBR	FA	FR	G/POS	TPR
1944	Chi-A	14	45	2	12	1	1	0	3	1	0	.267	.283	.333	77	-2	0	0	0	.947	-1	C-14	-0.2
1946	Chi-A	10	15	1	4	2	1	0	1	0	0	.267	.267	.533	124	1	0	0	0	1.000	1	/C-2	0.1
	Cle-A	14	35	2	7	1	0	1	3	3	1	.200	.263	.314	65	-2	1	1	-0	.974	-6	C-13	-0.8
	Yr	24	50	3	11	3	1	1	3	3	2	.220	.264	.380	83	-2	1	1	-0	.980	-5	C-15	-0.7
1948	StL-A	1	1	0	0	0	0	0	0	0	0	.000	.000	.000	-97	-0	0	0	0	.000	-0	H	0.0
Total	3	39	96	5	23	4	2	1	6	4	2	.240	.270	.354	78	-3	1	1	-0	.963	-6	/C-29	-0.9

■ TIM JORDAN Jordan, Timothy Joseph b: 2/14/1879, New York, N.Y. d: 9/13/49, Bronx, N.Y. BL/TL, 6'1", 170 lbs. Deb: 8/10/01

YEAR	TM/L	G	AB	R	H	2B	3B	HR	RBI	BB	SO	AVG	OBP	SLG	PRO+	BR/A	SB	CS	SBR	FA	FR	G/POS	TPR
1901	Was-A	6	20	2	4	1	0	0	2	0	3	.200	.304	.250	56	-1	0			.941	-1	/1-6	-0.2
1903	NY-A	2	8	2	1	0	0	0	0	0	0	.125	.125	.125	-23	-1	0			.889	-1	/1-2	-0.2
1906	Bro-N	129	450	67	118	20	8	**12**	78	59		.262	.352	.422	153	27	16			.978	-9	*1-126	1.5
1907	Bro-N	147	485	43	133	15	8	4	53	74		.274	.371	.363	141	25	10			.980	-6	*1-143	1.8
1908	Bro-N	148	515	58	127	18	5	**12**	60	59		.247	.328	.371	128	16	9			.982	-15	*1-146	-0.2
1909	Bro-N	103	330	41	90	20	3	3	36	59		.273	.386	.379	142	19	13			.983	-9	1-95	1.0
1910	Bro-N	5	5	1	1	0	0	1	3	0	2	.200	.200	.800	195	0	0			.000	-0	H	0.0
Total	7	540	1813	220	474	74	24	32	232	254	2	.261	.355	.382	139	86	48			.980	-40	1-518	3.7

■ ART JORGENS Jorgens, Arndt Ludwig b: 5/18/05, Modum, Norway d: 3/1/80, Wilmette, Ill. BR/TR, 5'9", 160 lbs. Deb: 4/26/29 F

YEAR	TM/L	G	AB	R	H	2B	3B	HR	RBI	BB	SO	AVG	OBP	SLG	PRO+	BR/A	SB	CS	SBR	FA	FR	G/POS	TPR
1929	NY-A	18	34	6	11	3	0	0	4	6	7	.324	.425	.412	125	2	0	2	-1	.979	-0	C-15	0.1
1930	NY-A	16	30	7	11	3	0	0	1	2	4	.367	.406	.467	126	1	0	0	0	.960	-0	C-16	0.2
1931	NY-A	46	100	12	27	1	2	0	14	9	3	.270	.330	.320	76	-3	0	0	-1	.962	-1	C-40	-0.3
1932	NY-A	56	151	13	33	7	1	2	19	14	11	.219	.285	.318	59	-10	0	0	0	.967	0	C-56	-0.6
1933	NY-A	21	50	9	11	3	0	2	13	12	3	.220	.371	.400	111	1	1	0	0	.982	1	C-19	0.4
1934	NY-A	58	183	14	38	6	1	0	20	23	24	.208	.296	.251	45	-15	2	0	1	.984	6	C-56	-0.5
1935	NY-A	36	84	6	20	2	0	0	8	12	10	.238	.333	.262	59	-5	0	0	0	1.000	6	C-33	0.2
1936	NY-A	31	66	5	18	3	1	0	5	2	3	.273	.294	.348	60	-4	0	0	0	.990	3	C-30	-0.1
1937	NY-A	13	23	3	3	1	0	0	3	2	5	.130	.200	.174	-5	-4	1	0	0	1.000	6	C-11	-0.3
1938	NY-A	9	17	3	4	2	0	0	2	0	4	.235	.350	.353	77	-1	0	0	0	.923	1	/C-8	0.0
1939	NY-A	3	0	1	0	0	0	0	0	0	0	—	—	—	—	0	0	0	0	1.000	0	/C-2	0.0
Total	11	307	738	79	176	31	5	4	89	85	73	.238	.317	.310	66	-37	3	3	-1	.978	17	C-286	-0.9

■ PINKY JORGENSEN Jorgensen, Carl b: 11/21/14, Laton, Cal. BR/TR, 6'1", 195 lbs. Deb: 9/14/37

YEAR	TM/L	G	AB	R	H	2B	3B	HR	RBI	BB	SO	AVG	OBP	SLG	PRO+	BR/A	SB	CS	SBR	FA	FR	G/POS	TPR
1937	Cin-N	6	14	1	4	0	0	0	1	1	2	.286	.333	.286	73	-0				.875	0	/O-4	-0.1

■ SPIDER JORGENSEN Jorgensen, John Donald b: 11/3/19, Folsom, Cal. BL/TR, 5'9", 155 lbs. Deb: 4/15/47

YEAR	TM/L	G	AB	R	H	2B	3B	HR	RBI	BB	SO	AVG	OBP	SLG	PRO+	BR/A	SB	CS	SBR	FA	FR	G/POS	TPR
1947	*Bro-N	129	441	57	121	29	8	5	67	58	45	.274	.360	.410	100	1	4			.949	-5	*3-128	-0.3
1948	Bro-N	31	90	15	27	6	2	1	13	16	13	.300	.411	.444	127	4	1			.887	-6	3-24	-0.6
1949	*Bro-N	53	134	15	36	5	1	1	14	23	13	.269	.376	.343	90	-1	0			.946	-5	3-36	-0.6
1950	Bro-N	2	2	0	0	0	0	0	1	1	0	.000	.333	.000	-4	-0	0			1.000	-0	/3-1	0.0
	NY-N	24	37	5	5	0	0	0	4	5	2	.135	.238	.135	1	-5	0			.913	1	/3-5	-0.4
	Yr	26	39	5	5	0	0	0	5	6	2	.128	.244	.128	1	-6	0			.917	1	/3-6	-0.4
1951	NY-N	28	51	5	12	0	2	0	8	3	2	.235	.291	.353	72	-2	0	0	0	1.000	-2	O-11/3-1	-0.5
Total	5	267	755	97	201	40	11	9	107	106	75	.266	.359	.384	95	-4	5	0		.940	-17	3-195/O-11	-2.1

■ MIKE JORGENSEN Jorgensen, Michael b: 8/16/48, Passaic, N.J. BL/TL, 6', 195 lbs. Deb: 9/10/68

YEAR	TM/L	G	AB	R	H	2B	3B	HR	RBI	BB	SO	AVG	OBP	SLG	PRO+	BR/A	SB	CS	SBR	FA	FR	G/POS	TPR
1968	NY-N	8	14	0	2	1	0	0	0	0	0	.143	.143	.214	6	-0	0	0	0	1.000	-0	/1-4	-0.2
1970	NY-N	76	87	15	17	3	1	3	4	10	23	.195	.278	.356	69	-4	2	2	-1	.992	3	1-50,O-10	-0.3
1971	NY-N	45	118	16	26	1	1	5	11	11	24	.220	.303	.373	92	-1	1	2	-1	.951	-2	O-31/1-1	-0.6
1972	Mon-N	113	372	48	86	12	3	13	47	53	75	.231	.333	.384	102	1	12	13	-4	.995	3	1-76,O-28	-1.1
1973	Mon-N	138	413	49	95	16	2	9	47	64	49	.230	.338	.344	86	-6	16	7	1	**.995**	4	*1-123,O-11	-1.1
1974	Mon-N	131	287	45	89	16	1	11	59	70	39	.310	.448	.488	153	24	5	5	-2	.998	-1	1-91,O-29	2.5
1975	Mon-N	144	445	58	116	18	0	18	67	79	75	.261	.380	.422	117	13	3	3	-1	.994	3	*1-133/O-6	0.7
1976	Mon-N	125	343	36	87	13	0	6	23	52	48	.254	.352	.344	94	-1	7	1	2	.989	1	1-81,O-41	-0.5
1977	Mon-N	19	20	3	4	1	0	0	1	0	4	.200	.304	.250	52	-1	0	0	0	1.000	1	/1-5	0.0
	Oak-A	66	203	18	50	4	1	8	32	25	44	.246	.335	.394	99	0	3	3	-0	.989	1	1-48,O-20/D	-0.3
1978	Tex-A	96	97	20	19	0	0	1	9	18	10	.196	.322	.258	65	-4	1	0	1	.994	-0	1-78/O-9,D	0.1
1979	Tex-A	90	157	21	35	7	0	6	16	14	29	.223	.295	.382	82	-4	0	0	0	.988	2	1-60,O-20	-0.6
1980	NY-N	119	321	43	82	11	0	7	43	46	55	.255	.349	.355	100	1	3	3	-2	.995	-1	1-72,O-31	-0.7
1981	NY-N	86	122	8	25	5	2	3	15	12	24	.205	.276	.352	79	-4	0	0	0	.991	1	1-40,O-19	-0.4
1982	NY-N	120	114	16	29	6	0	2	14	21	24	.254	.370	.360	106	-1	2	0	-1	.991	-3	1-56,O-16	-0.1
1983	NY-N	38	24	5	6	1	0	1	3	2	6	.250	.333	.500	129	-1	0	0	0	1.000	1	1-19	0.1
	Atl-N	57	48	5	12	1	0	0	8	8	8	.250	.357	.333	86	-1	0	0	-1	1.000	1	1-19/O-6	-0.1
	Yr	95	72	10	18	2	0	1	11	10	12	.250	.349	.389	100	-1	0	0	-1	1.000	2	1-38/O-6	0.0
1984	Atl-N	31	26	4	7	1	0	0	5	3	6	.269	.355	.308	91	-1				1.000		/1-8,O-4	-0.1
	StL-N	59	98	5	24	4	0	1	12	10	17	.245	.315	.357	91	-1				.991	1	1-39	-0.1
	Yr	90	124	9	31	4	0	1	17	13	23	.250	.321	.347	87	-2				.992	-0	1-47/O-4	-0.4
1985	*StL-N	72	112	14	22	6	0	0	11	31	27	.196	.375	.250	79	-1	2	1	0	.994	-2	*1-49/O-2	-0.6
Total	17	1633	3421	429	833	132	13	95	426	532	589	.243	.349	.373	100	10	58	44	-9	.994	21	*1-1052,O-283/D	-3.6

YEAR	TM/L	G	AB	R	H	2B	3B	HR	RBI	BB	SO	AVG	OBP	SLG	PRO+	BR/A	SB	CS	SBR	FA	FR	G/POS	TPR

■ **TERRY JORGENSEN** Jorgensen, Terry Allen b: 9/2/66, Kewaunee, Wis. BR/TR, 6'4", 208 lbs. Deb: 9/10/89

1989	Min-A	10	23	1	4	1	0	0	4	5	11	.174	.296	.217	44	-2	0	0	0	.958	3	/3-9	0.2
1992	Min-A	22	58	5	18	1	0	0	5	3	11	.310	.355	.328	89	-1	1	2	-1	1.000	2	1-13/3-9,S	0.0
1993	Min-A	59	152	15	34	7	0	1	12	10	21	.224	.282	.289	51	-11	1	0	0	.982	8	3-45/1-9,S	-0.2
Total	3	91	233	21	56	9	0	1	19	17	37	.240	.295	.292	60	-13	2	2	-1	.975	13	/3-63,1-22,S	0.0

■ **FELIX JOSE** Jose, Domingo Felix Andujar (b: Domingo Felix Andujar (Jose)) b: 5/2/65, Santo Domingo, D.R. BB/TR, 6'1", 190 lbs. Deb: 9/2/88

1988	Oak-A	8	6	2	2	1	0	0	1	0	1	.333	.333	.500	135	0	1	0	0	1.000	-1	/O-6	0.0
1989	Oak-A	20	57	3	11	2	0	0	5	4	13	.193	.246	.228	36	-5	0	1	0	.974	-0	O-19	-0.6
1990	Oak-A	101	341	42	90	12	0	8	39	16	65	.264	.307	.370	92	-4	8	2	1	.977	0	O-92/D-7	-0.5
	StL-N	25	85	12	23	4	1	3	13	8	16	.271	.333	.447	112	1	4	4	-1	1.000	-0	O-23	-0.2
1991	StL-N★	154	568	69	173	40	6	8	77	50	113	.305	.363	.438	123	18	20	12	-1	.990	4	*O-153	1.8
1992	StL-N	131	509	62	150	22	3	14	75	40	100	.295	.347	.432	123	15	28	12	-1	.979	11	*O-127	2.6
1993	KC-A	149	499	64	126	24	3	6	43	36	95	.253	.304	.349	71	-21	31	13	2	.972	-10	*O-144/D-1	-3.2
1994	KC-A	99	366	56	111	28	1	11	55	35	75	.303	.364	.475	106	3	10	12	-4	.980	2	O-98	-0.1
Total	7	687	2431	310	686	133	14	50	308	189	478	.282	.336	.410	103	6	102	56	-3	.981	4	O-662/D-8	-0.2

■ **RICK JOSEPH** Joseph, Ricardo Emelindo (Harrigan) b: 8/24/39, San Pedro De Macoris, D.R. d: 9/8/79, Santiago, D.R. BR/TR, 6'1", 195 lbs. Deb: 6/18/64

1964	KC-A	17	54	3	12	2	0	0	3	11	.222	.263	.259	45	-4	0	0	1	.981	-1	1-12/3-3	-0.7
1967	Phi-N	17	41	4	9	2	0	1	5	4	10	.220	.289	.341	79	-1	0	0	0	1.000	1	1-13	0.0
1968	Phi-N	66	155	20	34	5	0	3	12	16	35	.219	.297	.310	82	-3	0	0	-1	.992	1	1-30,3-14/O	-0.6
1969	Phi-N	99	264	35	72	15	0	6	37	22	57	.273	.331	.398	106	2	2	1	0	.956	7	3-58,1-17/2	0.8
1970	Phi-N	71	119	7	27	2	1	3	10	6	28	.227	.264	.336	61	-7	0	0	0	.917	-5	O-12,1-10/3	-1.3
Total	5	270	633	69	154	26	1	13	65	51	141	.243	.302	.349	85	-13	2	3	-1	.933	2	/3-84,1-82,O2	-1.8

■ **DUANE JOSEPHSON** Josephson, Duane Charles b: 6/3/42, New Hampton, Iowa BR/TR, 6', 195 lbs. Deb: 9/15/65

1965	Chi-A	4	9	2	1	0	0	0	0	2	4	.111	.273	.111	14	-1	0	0	0	1.000	1	/C-4	0.0
1966	Chi-A	11	38	3	9	1	0	0	3	3	3	.237	.293	.263	65	-2	0	0	0	.974	-6	C-11	0.2
1967	Chi-A	62	189	11	45	5	1	1	9	6	24	.238	.262	.291	65	-9	0	3	-2	1.000	-6	C-59	-1.4
1968	Chi-A★	128	434	35	107	16	6	6	45	18	52	.247	.286	.353	92	-5	2	4	-2	.990	12	*C-122	1.5
1969	Chi-A	52	162	19	39	6	2	1	20	13	17	.241	.301	.321	71	-6	0	0	-1	.984	-1	C-47	-0.5
1970	Chi-A	96	285	28	90	12	1	4	41	24	28	.316	.375	.407	111	5	0	1	-1	.985	-11	C-84	-0.3
1971	Bos-A	91	306	38	75	14	1	10	39	22	35	.245	.296	.395	88	-6	2	0	1	.989	-4	C-87	-0.7
1972	Bos-A	26	82	11	22	4	1	1	7	4	11	.268	.310	.378	99	-0	0	0	-1	.980	-1	1-16/C-6	-0.4
Total	8	470	1505	147	388	58	12	23	164	92	174	.258	.305	.358	89	-24	4	10	-5	.989	-7	C-420/1-16	-1.6

■ **VON JOSHUA** Joshua, Von Everett b: 5/1/48, Oakland, Cal. BL/TL, 5'10", 170 lbs. Deb: 9/2/69

1969	LA-N	14	8	0	2	0	0	0	0	0	2	.250	.250	.250	43	-1	1	0	0	.800	-2	/O-8	-0.3
1970	LA-N	72	109	23	29	1	3	1	8	6	24	.266	.304	.358	80	-3	2	2	-1	.941	-8	O-41	-1.3
1971	LA-N	11	7	2	0	0	0	0	0	0	1	.000	.000	.000	-99	-2	0	0	0	1.000	-1	/O-5	-0.3
1973	LA-N	75	159	19	40	4	1	2	17	9	29	.252	.292	.327	74	-6	7	2	1	.984	-5	O-46	-1.2
1974	*LA-N	81	124	11	29	5	1	1	16	7	17	.234	.280	.315	69	-5	3	2	-0	.943	-4	O-35	-1.6
1975	SF-N	129	507	75	161	25	10	7	43	32	75	.318	.359	.448	118	11	20	10	0	**.993**	6	*O-117	1.3
1976	SF-N	42	156	13	41	5	2	0	2	4	20	.263	.281	.321	68	-7	1	3	-2	.948	-3	O-35	-1.3
	Mil-A	107	423	44	113	13	5	5	28	18	58	.267	.297	.357	93	-5	8	10	-4	.982	6	*O-105/D-1	-0.8
1977	Mil-A	144	536	58	140	25	7	9	49	21	74	.261	.289	.384	82	-15	12	9	-2	.970	-6	*O-140	-2.8
1979	LA-N	94	142	22	40	7	1	3	14	7	23	.282	.315	.408	97	-1	1	1	0	.967	-9	O-46	-1.1
1980	SD-N	53	63	8	15	2	1	2	7	5	15	.238	.294	.397	97	-1	0	1	-1	1.000	0	O-12/1-2	-0.3
Total	10	822	2234	277	610	87	31	30	184	108	338	.273	.307	.380	91	-34	55	40	-8	.975	-31	O-590/1-2,D	-9.7

■ **TED JOURDAN** Jourdan, Theodore Charles b: 9/5/1895, New Orleans, La. d: 9/23/61, New Orleans, La. BL/TL, 6', 175 lbs. Deb: 9/18/16

1916	Chi-A	3	2	0	0	0	0	0	0	1	1	.000	.333	.000	1	-0	2			.000	0	H	0.0
1917	Chi-A	17	34	2	5	0	0	0	2	1	3	.147	.171	.206	15	-4	0			.973	-0	1-14	-0.5
1918	Chi-A	7	10	1	1	0	0	0	1	0	0	.100	.100	.100	-39	-2	0			1.000	-0	/1-2	-0.2
1920	Chi-A	48	150	16	36	5	2	0	8	17	17	.240	.337	.300	70	-6	3	2	-0	.982	-4	1-40	-1.1
Total	4	75	196	19	42	5	2	0	11	19	21	.214	.300	.270	56	-11	5	2		.981	-4	/1-56	-1.8

■ **POP JOY** Joy, Aloysius C. b: 6/11/1860, Washington, D.C. d: 6/28/37, Washington, D.C. Deb: 6/3/1884

| 1884 | Was-U | 36 | 130 | 12 | 28 | 0 | 0 | 0 | | 2 | | .215 | .227 | .215 | 22 | -14 | | | | .966 | 0 | 1-36 | -1.6 |

■ **JOYCE** Joyce Deb: 8/14/1886

| 1886 | Was-N | 1 | 0 | 0 | 0 | | | | | 0 | 0 | — | — | — | — | 0 | 0 | | | .000 | -0 | /O-1 | 0.0 |

■ **BILL JOYCE** Joyce, William Michael "Scrappy Bill" b: 9/21/1865, St.Louis, Mo. d: 5/8/41, St.Louis, Mo. BL/TR, 5'11", 185 lbs. Deb: 4/19/1890 M

1890	Bro-P	133	489	121	123	18	18	1	78	**123**	77	.252	.413	.368	103	6	43			.811	-11	*3-133	0.0
1891	Bos-a	65	243	76	75	9	15	3	51	63	27	.309	.460	.506	179	29	36			.849	-1	3-64/1-1	2.6
1892	Bro-N	97	372	89	91	15	12	6	45	82	55	.245	.392	.398	144	25	23			.862	-19	3-94/O-3	0.8
1894	Was-N	99	355	103	126	25	14	17	89	87	33	.355	.496	.648	**180**	51	21			.866	-3	*3-99	3.7
1895	Was-N	126	474	110	148	25	13	17	95	**96**	54	.312	.442	.527	151	40	29			.844	-9	*3-126	2.7
1896	Was-N	81	310	85	97	16	10	8	51	67	20	.313	.454	.506	153	28	32			.888	-7	3-48,2-33	2.0
	NY-N	49	165	36	61	9	2	5	43	34	14	.370	.500	.539	179	22	13			.883	-0	3-49,M	2.0
	Yr	130	475	121	158	25	12	**13**	94	101	34	.333	.470	.518	162	50	45			.885	-7	3-97,2-33	4.0
1897	NY-N	109	388	109	118	15	13	3	64	78		.304	.441	.433	135	26	33			.852	1	*3-106/1-2M	2.8
1898	NY-N	145	508	91	131	20	9	10	91	88		.258	.386	.392	127	22	34			.966	8	*1-130,3-14/2M	2.8
Total	8	904	3304	820	970	152	106	70	607	718	**280**	.294	.435	.467	144	249	264			.851	-41	3-733,1-133/2O	19.0

■ **WALLY JOYNER** Joyner, Wallace Keith b: 6/16/62, Atlanta, Ga. BL/TL, 6'2", 190 lbs. Deb: 4/8/86

1986	*Cal-A★	154	593	82	172	27	3	22	100	57	58	.290	.354	.457	120	16	5	2	0	.989	9	*1-152	1.4
1987	Cal-A	149	564	100	161	33	1	34	117	72	64	.285	.371	.528	140	32	8	2	1	.993	-7	*1-149	1.5
1988	Cal-A	158	597	81	176	31	2	13	85	55	51	.295	.359	.419	120	17	8	2	1	.995	6	*1-156	1.7
1989	Cal-A	159	593	78	167	30	2	16	79	46	58	.282	.340	.420	115	11	3	2	-0	**.997**	-4	*1-159	-0.6
1990	Cal-A	83	310	35	83	15	0	8	41	41	34	.268	.355	.394	111	5	2	1	0	.995	2	1-83	0.1
1991	Cal-A	143	551	79	166	34	3	21	96	52	66	.301	.363	.488	133	24	2	0	1	.994	-1	*1-141	1.6
1992	KC-A	149	572	66	154	36	2	9	66	55	50	.269	.338	.386	100	-0	11	5	0	.993	14	*1-145/D-4	0.4
1993	KC-A	141	497	83	145	36	3	15	65	66	67	.292	.378	.467	119	14	5	9	-4	.994	21	*1-140	1.8
1994	KC-A	97	363	52	113	20	3	8	57	47	43	.311	.390	.449	107	4	3	2	-0	.991	3	1-86,D-11	-0.1
Total	9	1233	4640	656	1337	262	19	146	706	491	491	.288	.360	.447	119	124	47	25	-1	.994	50	*1-1211/D-15	7.8

■ **FRANK JUDE** Jude, Frank b: 1884, Libby, Minn. d: 5/4/61, Brownsville, Tex. BR/TR, 5'7", 150 lbs. Deb: 7/9/06

| 1906 | Cin-N | 80 | 308 | 31 | 64 | 6 | 4 | 1 | 31 | 16 | | .208 | .261 | .263 | 61 | -14 | 7 | | | .965 | -3 | O-80 | -2.4 |

■ **JOE JUDGE** Judge, Joseph Ignatius b: 5/25/1894, Brooklyn, N.Y. d: 3/11/63, Washington, D.C. BL/TL, 5'8.5", 155 lbs. Deb: 9/20/15 C

1915	Was-A	12	41	7	17	2	0	0	9	4	6	.415	.500	.463	185	5	2	3	-1	.990	-1	1-10/O-2	0.3
1916	Was-A	103	336	42	74	10	8	0	28	54	44	.220	.333	.298	91	-2	18			.986	4	*1-103	-0.2
1917	Was-A	102	393	62	112	15	15	2	30	50	40	.285	.369	.415	141	19	17			.988	-1	*1-100	1.6

YEAR	TM/L	G	AB	R	H	2B	3B	HR	RBI	BB	SO	AVG	OBP	SLG	PRO+	BR/A	SB	CS	SBR	FA	FR	G/POS	TPR
1918	Was-A	130	502	56	131	23	7	1	46	49	32	.261	.332	.341	105	2	20			.985	2	*1-130	-0.1
1919	Was-A	135	521	83	150	33	12	2	31	81	35	.288	.386	.409	124	19	23			.988	-4	*1-133	1.1
1920	Was-A	126	493	103	164	19	15	5	51	65	34	.333	.416	.462	136	28	12	12	-4	.992	-8	*1-124	1.3
1921	Was-A	153	622	87	187	26	11	7	72	68	35	.301	.372	.412	105	5	21	6	3	.996	-3	*1-152	0.1
1922	Was-A	148	591	84	174	32	15	10	81	50	20	.294	.355	.450	114	11	5	15	-8	.996	3	*1-147	0.0
1923	Was-A	113	405	56	127	24	6	2	63	58	20	.314	.406	.417	123	16	11	7	-1	.993	8	*1-112	1.6
1924	*Was-A	140	516	71	167	38	9	3	79	53	21	.324	.393	.450	121	16	13	8	-1	.994	-2	*1-140	0.4
1925	*Was-A	112	376	65	118	31	5	8	66	55	21	.314	.406	.487	128	17	7	12	-5	.993	8	*1-109	0.9
1926	Was-A	134	453	70	132	25	11	7	92	53	25	.291	.367	.442	113	8	7	5	-1	.994	10	*1-128	0.9
1927	Was-A	137	522	68	161	29	11	2	71	45	22	.308	.366	.418	104	3	10	5	0	.996	-6	*1-136	-1.1
1928	Was-A	153	542	78	166	31	10	3	93	80	19	.306	.396	.417	115	14	16	4	2	.996	1	*1-149	0.4
1929	Was-A	143	543	83	171	35	8	6	71	73	33	.315	.397	.442	115	14	12	5	1	.996	3	*1-142	0.3
1930	Was-A	126	442	83	144	29	11	10	80	60	29	.326	.410	.509	131	22	13	6	0	.998	2	*1-117	1.2
1931	Was-A	35	74	11	21	3	0	0	9	8	8	.284	.354	.324	79	-2	0	0	0	.994	1	1-15	-0.2
1932	Was-A	82	291	45	75	16	3	3	29	37	19	.258	.343	.364	84	-6	3	3	-1	.997	1	1-78	-1.1
1933	Bro-N	42	112	7	24	2	1	0	9	7	10	.214	.261	.250	48	-7	1			.989	0	1-28	-1.1
	Bos-A	35	108	20	32	8	1	0	22	13	4	.296	.372	.389	103	1	2	1	0	1.000	-0	1-29	-0.2
1934	Bos-A	10	15	3	5	2	0	0	2	2	1	.333	.412	.467	118	0	0	0	0	1.000	0	/1-2	0.0
Total	20	2171	7898	1184	2352	433	159	71	1034	965	478	.298	.378	.420	115	182	213	92		.993	13	*1-2084/O-2	6.1

■ WALLY JUDNICH
Judnich, Walter Franklin b: 1/24/17, San Francisco, Cal d: 7/12/71, Glendale, Cal. BL/TL, 6'1", 205 lbs. Deb: 4/16/40

YEAR	TM/L	G	AB	R	H	2B	3B	HR	RBI	BB	SO	AVG	OBP	SLG	PRO+	BR/A	SB	CS	SBR	FA	FR	G/POS	TPR
1940	StL-A	137	519	97	157	27	7	24	89	54	71	.303	.368	.520	125	18	5	5	-1	.989	-1	*O-133	0.9
1941	StL-A	146	546	90	155	40	6	14	83	80	45	.284	.377	.456	116	13	5	5	-2	.980	3	*O-140	0.5
1942	StL-A	132	457	78	143	22	6	17	82	74	41	.313	.413	.499	153	34	3	2	-0	.991	-2	*O-122	2.5
1946	StL-A	142	511	60	134	23	4	15	72	60	54	.262	.340	.411	104	2	0	4	-2	.995	11	*O-137	0.5
1947	StL-A	144	500	58	129	24	3	18	64	60	62	.258	.338	.426	109	5	2	5	-2	.989	-6	*1-129,O-15	-0.9
1948	*Cle-A	79	218	36	56	13	3	2	29	56	23	.257	.411	.372	112	7	2	3	-1	.970	-8	O-49,1-20	-0.5
1949	Pit-N	10	35	5	8	1	0	0	1	1	2	.229	.250	.257	35	-3	0			1.000	1	/O-8	-0.2
Total	7	790	2786	424	782	150	29	90	420	385	298	.281	.369	.452	119	75	20	24		.988	-2	O-604,1-149	2.8

■ LYLE JUDY
Judy, Lyle Leroy "Punch" b: 11/15/13, Lawrenceville, Ill d: 1/15/91, Ormond Beach, Fla. BR/TR, 5'10", 150 lbs. Deb: 9/17/35

YEAR	TM/L	G	AB	R	H	2B	3B	HR	RBI	BB	SO	AVG	OBP	SLG	PRO+	BR/A	SB	CS	SBR	FA	FR	G/POS	TPR
1935	StL-N	8	11	2	0	0	0	0	2	2	2	.000	.154	.000	-53	-2	2			1.000	1	/2-5	-0.2

■ RED JUELICH
Juelich, John Samuel b: 9/20/16, St.Louis, Mo. d: 12/25/70, St.Louis, Mo. BR/TR, 5'11.5", 170 lbs. Deb: 5/30/39

YEAR	TM/L	G	AB	R	H	2B	3B	HR	RBI	BB	SO	AVG	OBP	SLG	PRO+	BR/A	SB	CS	SBR	FA	FR	G/POS	TPR
1939	Pit-N	17	46	5	11	0	2	0	4	2	4	.239	.271	.326	61	-3	0			.935	-5	2-10/3-2	-0.8

■ GEORGE JUMONVILLE
Jumonville, George Benedict b: 5/16/17, Mobile, Ala. BR/TR, 6', 175 lbs. Deb: 9/13/40

YEAR	TM/L	G	AB	R	H	2B	3B	HR	RBI	BB	SO	AVG	OBP	SLG	PRO+	BR/A	SB	CS	SBR	FA	FR	G/POS	TPR
1940	Phi-N	11	34	0	3	0	0	0	1	6	6	.088	.139	.088	-38	-6	0			.952	-4	S-10/3-1	-1.0
1941	Phi-N	6	7	1	3	0	0	1	2	0	0	.429	.429	.857	266	1	0			1.000	1	/2-1,S-1	0.2
Total	2	17	41	1	6	0	0	1	2	1	6	.146	.186	.220	12	-5	0			.953	-4	/S-11,2-1,3	-0.8

■ ED JURAK
Jurak, Edward James b: 10/24/57, Los Angeles, Cal. BR/TR, 6'2", 185 lbs. Deb: 6/30/82

YEAR	TM/L	G	AB	R	H	2B	3B	HR	RBI	BB	SO	AVG	OBP	SLG	PRO+	BR/A	SB	CS	SBR	FA	FR	G/POS	TPR
1982	Bos-A	12	21	3	7	0	0	0	7	2	4	.333	.391	.333	96	-0	0	0	0	.923	2	3-11/O-1	0.1
1983	Bos-A	75	159	19	44	8	4	0	18	18	25	.277	.354	.377	95	-1	1	2	-1	.943	9	S-38,1-19,3/2D	0.8
1984	Bos-A	47	66	6	16	3	1	1	7	12	12	.242	.359	.364	96	-0	0	2	-1	1.000	5	1-19,2-14/3S	0.3
1985	Bos-A	26	13	4	3	0	0	0	0	1	3	.231	.286	.231	42	-1	0	0	0	.833	-4	/3-7,S-3,10D	0.2
1988	Oak-N	3	1	1	0	0	0	0	0	0	0	.000	.000	.000	-99	-0	0	0	0	.000	-0	/3-1,D-1	0.0
1989	SF-N	30	42	2	10	0	0	0	1	5	5	.238	.319	.238	63	-2	0	0	0	.875	-2	/S-6,3-5,201	-0.4
Total	6	193	302	35	80	11	5	1	33	38	49	.265	.349	.344	88	-4	1	4	-2	.941	17	/S-49,3-45,12D0	1.0

■ BILLY JURGES
Jurges, William Frederick b: 5/9/08, Bronx, N.Y. BR/TR, 5'11", 175 lbs. Deb: 5/4/31 MC

YEAR	TM/L	G	AB	R	H	2B	3B	HR	RBI	BB	SO	AVG	OBP	SLG	PRO+	BR/A	SB	CS	SBR	FA	FR	G/POS	TPR
1931	Chi-N	88	293	34	59	15	5	0	23	25	41	.201	.264	.287	47	-22	2			.963	11	3-54,2-33/S	-0.6
1932	*Chi-N	115	396	40	100	24	4	2	52	19	26	.253	.288	.348	71	-16	1			.964	32	*S-108/3-5	2.4
1933	Chi-N	143	487	49	131	17	6	5	50	26	39	.269	.313	.359	92	-6	3			.958	20	*S-143	2.6
1934	Chi-N	100	358	43	88	15	2	8	33	19	34	.246	.289	.366	76	-13	1			.966	14	S-98	0.7
1935	*Chi-N	146	519	69	125	33	1	1	59	42	39	.241	.304	.314	66	-24	3			.964	30	*S-146	1.3
1936	Chi-N	118	429	51	120	25	1	1	42	23	25	.280	.321	.350	79	-13	4			.960	17	*S-116	1.1
1937	Chi-N☆	129	450	53	134	18	10	1	65	42	41	.298	.365	.389	101	2	2			.975	-7	*S-128	0.3
1938	*Chi-N	137	465	53	114	18	3	1	47	58	53	.245	.335	.303	75	-14	3			.953	-0	*S-136	-0.4
1939	NY-N☆	138	543	84	155	21	11	6	63	47	34	.285	.349	.398	99	-0	3			.965	15	*S-137	2.7
1940	NY-N†	63	214	23	54	3	3	2	36	25	14	.252	.347	.322	85	-3	2			.967	-1	S-63	0.1
1941	NY-N	134	471	50	138	25	2	5	61	47	36	.293	.361	.386	108	6	3			.957	7	*S-134	2.3
1942	NY-N	127	464	45	119	7	2	3	30	43	42	.256	.324	.289	79	-11	1			.978	7	*S-124	0.4
1943	NY-N	136	481	46	110	8	2	4	29	53	38	.229	.310	.279	70	-17	2			.955	1	S-99,3-28	-1.0
1944	NY-N	85	246	28	52	2	1	1	23	29	20	.211	.279	.240	47	-17	4			.961	-1	3-61,S-10/2	-1.7
1945	NY-N	61	176	22	57	3	1	3	24	24	11	.324	.400	.403	123	6	2			.937	2	3-44/S-8	1.0
1946	Chi-N	82	221	26	49	9	2	0	17	43	28	.222	.351	.281	82	-3	3			.976	-3	S-73/3-7,2	-0.3
1947	Chi-N	14	40	5	8	2	0	1	2	9	9	.200	.347	.325	83	-1	0			.925	-4	S-14	-0.4
Total	17	1816	6253	721	1613	245	55	43	656	568	530	.258	.325	.335	82	-147	36			.964	140	*S-1540,3-199/2	10.5

■ JOE JUST
Just, Joseph Erwin (b: Joseph Erwin Juszczak) b: 1/8/16, Milwaukee, Wis. BR/TR, 5'11", 185 lbs. Deb: 5/13/44

YEAR	TM/L	G	AB	R	H	2B	3B	HR	RBI	BB	SO	AVG	OBP	SLG	PRO+	BR/A	SB	CS	SBR	FA	FR	G/POS	TPR
1944	Cin-N	11	11	0	2	0	0	0	0	0	2	.182	.250	.182	24	-1	0			.923	0	C-10	-0.1
1945	Cin-N	14	34	2	5	0	0	0	2	4	7	.147	.237	.147	8	-4	0			.947	-2	C-14	-0.5
Total	2	25	45	2	7	0	0	0	2	4	9	.156	.240	.156	12	-5	0			.941	-1	/C-24	-0.6

■ DAVID JUSTICE
Justice, David Christopher b: 4/14/66, Cincinnati, Ohio BL/TL, 6'3", 195 lbs. Deb: 5/24/89

YEAR	TM/L	G	AB	R	H	2B	3B	HR	RBI	BB	SO	AVG	OBP	SLG	PRO+	BR/A	SB	CS	SBR	FA	FR	G/POS	TPR
1989	Atl-N	16	51	7	12	3	0	1	3	3	9	.235	.291	.353	81	-1	2	1	0	1.000	-1	O-16	-0.3
1990	Atl-N	127	439	76	124	23	2	28	78	64	92	.282	.374	.535	139	23	11	6	-0	.981	-2	1-69,O-61	1.5
1991	*Atl-N	109	396	67	109	25	1	21	87	65	81	.275	.381	.503	138	21	8	8	-2	.968	5	*O-106	2.2
1992	*Atl-N	144	484	78	124	19	5	21	72	79	85	.256	.363	.446	121	14	2	4	-2	.976	14	*O-140	2.5
1993	*Atl-N★	157	585	90	158	15	4	40	120	78	90	.270	.359	.515	129	24	3	5	-2	.985	9	*O-157	2.7
1994	Atl-N★	104	352	61	110	16	2	19	59	69	45	.313	.428	.531	148	27	2	4	-2	.947	2	*O-102	2.5
Total	6	657	2307	379	637	101	14	130	419	358	402	.276	.376	.501	133	109	28	28	-8	.972	27	O-582/1-69	11.1

■ SKIP JUTZE
Jutze, Alfred Henry b: 5/28/46, Queens, N.Y. BR/TR, 5'11", 195 lbs. Deb: 9/1/72

YEAR	TM/L	G	AB	R	H	2B	3B	HR	RBI	BB	SO	AVG	OBP	SLG	PRO+	BR/A	SB	CS	SBR	FA	FR	G/POS	TPR
1972	StL-N	21	71	1	17	2	0	0	5	1	16	.239	.250	.268	48	-5	0	1	-1	.964	0	C-17	-0.5
1973	Hou-N	90	278	18	62	6	0	0	18	19	37	.223	.275	.245	45	-20	0	1	-1	.984	-6	C-86	-2.5
1974	Hou-N	8	13	0	3	0	0	0	1	1	1	.231	.286	.231	48	-1	0	0	0	1.000	-0	/C-7	-0.1
1975	Hou-N	51	93	9	21	3	0	0	6	6	16	.226	.242	.247	39	-8	1	0	0	.988	3	C-47	-0.3
1976	Hou-N	42	92	7	14	2	3	0	6	4	16	.152	.188	.239	22	-10	0	0	0	.986	2	C-42	-0.8
1977	Sea-A	42	109	10	24	1	0	3	15	7	12	.220	.267	.321	60	-6	0	4	-2	.984	-2	C-40	-1.0
Total	6	254	656	45	141	14	3	3	51	34	86	.215	.255	.259	44	-50	1	6	-4	.983	-3	C-239	-5.2

■ HERB JUUL
Juul, Herbert Victor b: 2/2/1886, Chicago, Ill. d: 11/14/28, Chicago, Ill. BL/TL, 5'11", 150 lbs. Deb: 7/11/11

YEAR	TM/L	G	AB	R	H	2B	3B	HR	RBI	BB	SO	AVG	OBP	SLG	PRO+	BR/A	SB	CS	SBR	FA	FR	G/POS	TPR
1911	Cin-N	2	2	0	0	0	0	0	0	0	0	.000	.000	.000	-99	-1	0			.000	-0	/P-1	0.0

YEAR	TM/L	G	AB	R	H	2B	3B	HR	RBI	BB	SO	AVG	OBP	SLG	PRO+	BR/A	SB	CS	SBR	FA	FR	G/POS	TPR

■ JIM KAAT　Kaat, James Lee　b: 11/7/38, Zeeland, Mich.　BL/TL, 6'4", 217 lbs.　Deb: 8/2/59　C

1959	Was-A	3	1	0	0	0	0	0	0	0	1	.000	.000	.000	-99	-0	0	0	0	1.000	0	/P-3	0.0
1960	Was-A	13	14	0	2	0	0	0	0	0	6	.143	.143	.143	-23	-2	0	0	0	1.000	0	P-13	0.0
1961	Min-A	47	63	10	15	3	1	0	1	4	13	.238	.294	.317	60	-4	0	0	0	.968	3	P-36	0.0
1962	Min-A☆	48	100	9	18	3	1	1	10	8	40	.180	.241	.260	33	-9	0	0	0	.967	6	P-39	0.0
1963	Min-A	36	61	2	8	1	0	1	8	2	19	.131	.185	.197	7	-8	0	0	0	.984	4	P-31	0.0
1964	Min-A	46	83	11	14	1	0	3	11	11	31	.169	.266	.289	54	-5	0	0	0	.928	3	P-36	0.0
1965	*Min-A	56	93	6	23	4	0	1	9	3	29	.247	.271	.323	65	-4	2	0	1	.929	3	P-45	0.0
1966	Min-A★	47	118	12	23	2	1	2	13	5	41	.195	.228	.280	42	-9	0	0	0	.956	0	P-41	0.0
1967	Min-A	45	99	7	17	3	1	1	4	7	26	.172	.226	.253	38	-8	0	0	0	.952	1	P-42	0.0
1968	Min-A	36	77	7	12	3	0	0	5	2	18	.156	.177	.195	12	-8	0	0	0	.976	-0	P-30	0.0
1969	Min-A	43	87	8	18	8	0	2	10	4	20	.207	.250	.368	69	-4	0	0	0	.826	-3	P-40	0.0
1970	*Min-A	56	76	17	15	1	0	1	8	6	20	.197	.265	.250	42	-6	0	0	0	.935	-2	P-45	0.0
1971	Min-A	54	93	6	15	3	0	0	5	2	16	.161	.179	.194	5	-12	2	0	1	.982	-0	P-39	0.0
1972	Min-A	24	45	3	13	3	0	2	4	1	16	.289	.304	.489	127	1	0	1	-1	.923	-0	P-15	0.0
1973	Min-A	31	0	1	0	0	0	0	0	0	0	—	—	—	—	0	0	0	0	.969	-1	P-29	0.0
	Chi-A	7	0	0	0	0	0	0	0	0	0	—	—	—	—	0	0	0	0	1.000	-0	/P-7	0.0
	Yr	38	0	0	0	0	0	0	0	0	0	—	—	—	—	0	0	0	0	.973	-2	P-36	0.0
1974	Chi-A	42	1	0	0	0	0	0	0	0	0	.000	.000	.000	-98	-0	0	0	0	.959	-2	P-42	0.0
1975	Chi-A★	43	0	0	0	0	0	0	0	0	0	—	—	—	—	0	0	0	0	.982	-2	P-43	0.0
1976	*Phi-N	42	79	4	14	3	1	1	8	2	24	.177	.198	.278	33	-7	0	0	0	.949	-3	P-38	0.0
1977	Phi-N	36	53	4	10	3	0	0	2	2	12	.189	.218	.245	23	-6	0	0	0	.897	-2	P-35	0.0
1978	Phi-N	26	48	4	7	1	0	0	4	0	15	.146	.163	.167	-8	-7	0	0	0	1.000	-2	P-26	0.0
1979	Phi-N	3	1	0	0	0	0	0	0	0	1	.000	.500	.000	47	0	0	0	0	1.000	-0	/P-3	0.0
	NY-A	40	0	0	0	0	0	0	0	0	0	—	—	—	—	0	0	0	0	.909	-1	P-40	0.0
1980	NY-A	4	0	0	0	0	0	0	0	0	0	—	—	—	—	0	0	0	0	.800	1	P-4	0.0
	StL-N	49	35	4	5	1	0	1	2	2	13	.143	.189	.257	23	-4	1	0	0	.952	-2	P-49	0.0
1981	StL-N	41	8	2	3	1	0	0	2	1	0	.375	.444	.500	163	1	0	0	0	.895	1	P-41	0.0
1982	*StL-N	62	12	0	0	0	0	0	0	1	4	.000	.077	.000	-76	-3	0	0	0	.917	1	P-62	0.0
1983	StL-N	24	4	0	0	0	0	0	0	0	2	.000	.000	.000	-99	-1	0	0	0	.889	0	P-24	0.0
Total	25	1004	1251	117	232	44	5	16	106	63	367	.185	.229	.267	38	-104	5	1	1	.947	6	P-898	0.0

■ JACK KADING　Kading, John Frederick　b: 11/17/1884, Waukesha, Wis.　d: 6/2/64, Chicago, Ill.　BR/TR, 6'3", 190 lbs.　Deb: 9/12/10

1910	Pit-N	8	23	5	7	2	1	0	4	4	5	.304	.407	.478	149	1	0			1.000	1	/1-8	0.3
1914	Chi-F	3	3	0	0	0	0	0	0	0	0	.000	.000	.000	-99	-1	0			.000	0	H	-0.1
Total	2	11	26	5	7	2	1	0	4	4	5	.269	.367	.423	121	1	0			1.000	1	/1-8	0.2

■ JAKE KAFORA　Kafora, Frank Jacob "Tomatoes"　b: 10/16/1888, Chicago, Ill.　d: 3/23/28, Chicago, Ill.　BR/TR, 6', 180 lbs.　Deb: 10/5/13

1913	Pit-N	1	1	0	0	0	0	0	0	0	1	.000	.500	.000	52	0	0			1.000	-1	/C-1	-0.1
1914	Pit-N	21	23	2	3	0	0	0	0	0	6	.130	.200	.130	-1	-3	0			1.000	-1	C-17	-0.4
Total	2	22	24	3	3	0	0	0	0	0	7	.125	.222	.125	4	-3	0			1.000	-2	/C-18	-0.5

■ IKE KAHDOT　Kahdot, Isaac Leonard "Chief"　b: 10/22/01, Georgetown, Okla.　BR/TR, 5'5", 145 lbs.　Deb: 9/5/22

| 1922 | Cle-A | 4 | 2 | 0 | 0 | 0 | 0 | 0 | 0 | 0 | 1 | .000 | .000 | .000 | -99 | -1 | 0 | 0 | 0 | 1.000 | 1 | /3-2 | 0.0 |

■ NICK KAHL　Kahl, Nicholas Alexander　b: 4/10/1879, Coulterville, Ill.　d: 7/13/59, Sparta, Ill.　BR/TR, 5'9", 185 lbs.　Deb: 5/2/05

| 1905 | Cle-A | 40 | 135 | 16 | 29 | 4 | 1 | 0 | 21 | 4 | | .215 | .248 | .259 | 60 | -6 | 1 | | | .948 | 0 | 2-32/S-1,O | -0.6 |

■ BOB KAHLE　Kahle, Robert Wayne　b: 11/23/15, Newcastle, Ind.　d: 12/16/88, Inglewood, Cal.　BR/TR, 6', 170 lbs.　Deb: 4/21/38

| 1938 | Bos-N | 8 | 3 | 2 | 1 | 0 | 0 | 0 | 0 | 0 | 0 | .333 | .333 | .333 | 93 | -0 | 0 | | | .000 | 0 | H | 0.0 |

■ OWEN KAHN　Kahn, Owen Earle "Jack"　b: 6/5/05, Richmond, Va.　d: 1/17/81, Richmond, Va.　BR/TR, 5'11", 160 lbs.　Deb: 5/24/30

| 1930 | Bos-N | 1 | 0 | 1 | 0 | 0 | 0 | 0 | 0 | 0 | 0 | — | — | — | — | 0 | 0 | | | .000 | 0 | R | 0.0 |

■ MIKE KAHOE　Kahoe, Michael Joseph　b: 9/3/1873, Yellow Springs, O　d: 5/14/49, Akron, Ohio　BR/TR, 6', 185 lbs.　Deb: 9/22/1895

1895	Cin-N	3	4	0	0	0	0	0	0	0	0	.000	.000	.000	-96	-1	0			1.000	-1	/C-3	-0.1
1899	Cin-N	14	42	2	7	1	1	0	4	0		.167	.167	.238	10	-5	1			.957	4	C-13	-0.1
1900	Cin-N	52	175	18	33	3	3	1	9	4		.189	.215	.257	31	-17	3			.963	5	C-51/S-1	-0.7
1901	Cin-N	4	13	0	4	0	0	0	0	1		.308	.357	.308	100	0	0			1.000	-2	/C-4	-0.2
	Chi-N	67	237	21	53	12	2	1	21	8		.224	.249	.304	62	-12	5			.974	9	C-63/1-6	0.3
	Yr	71	250	21	57	12	2	1	21	9		.228	.255	.304	64	-12	5			.974	7	C-67/1-6	0.1
1902	Chi-N	7	18	0	4	1	0	0	2	0		.222	.222	.278	56	-1	0			.875	-1	/C-4,3-2,S	-0.1
	StL-A	55	197	21	48	9	2	2	28	6		.244	.270	.340	69	-9	4			.967	-0	C-53	-0.3
1903	StL-A	77	244	26	46	7	5	0	23	11		.189	.227	.258	46	-16	1			.971	-3	C-71/O-2	-1.2
1904	StL-A	72	236	9	51	6	1	0	12	8		.216	.242	.250	59	-11	4			.968	1	C-69	-0.3
1905	Phi-N	16	51	2	13	2	0	0	4	1		.255	.269	.294	70	-2	1			.975	0	C-15	-0.1
1907	Chi-N	5	10	0	4	0	0	0	1	0		.400	.400	.400	142	0	0			1.000	-1	/C-3,1-1	-0.1
	Was-A	17	47	3	9	1	0	0	1	0		.191	.191	.213	31	-4	0			.976	1	C-15	-0.2
1908	Was-A	17	27	1	5	1	0	0	1	0		.185	.185	.222	35	-2	0			.983	4	C-11	0.3
1909	Was-A	4	8	0	1	0	0	0	0	0		.125	.125	.125	-22	-1	2			.867	-0	/C-3	-0.1
Total	11	410	1309	103	278	43	14	4	105	39	0	.212	.237	.276	52	-81	21			.968	15	C-378/1-7,O3S	-2.9

■ AL KAISER　Kaiser, Alfred Edward "Deerfoot"　b: 8/3/1886, Cincinnati, Ohio　d: 4/11/69, Cincinnati, Ohio　BR/TR, 5'9", 165 lbs.　Deb: 4/18/11

1911	Chi-N	26	84	16	21	0	0	7	7	12	.250	.308	.369	89	-2	6			.905	-3	O-22	-0.6
	Bos-N	66	197	20	40	5	2	2	15	10	26	.203	.249	.279	44	-15	4			.922	-6	O-58	-2.4
	Yr	92	281	36	61	5	2	2	22	17	38	.217	.267	.306	57	-17	10			.918	-9	O-80	-3.0
1912	Bos-N	4	13	0	0	0	0	0	0	0	3	.000	.000	.000	-98	-4	0			.900	0	O-4	-0.4
1914	Ind-F	59	187	22	43	10	0	1	16	17	41	.230	.301	.299	50	-14	6			.918	-3	O-50/1-1	-2.0
Total	3	155	481	58	104	15	7	3	38	34	82	.216	.274	.295	50	-34	16			.917	-12	O-134/1-1	-5.4

■ JOHN KALAHAN　Kalahan, John Joseph　b: 9/30/1878, Philadelphia, Pa.　d: 6/20/52, Philadelphia, Pa.　BR/TR, 6', 165 lbs.　Deb: 9/29/03

| 1903 | Phi-A | 1 | 5 | 0 | 0 | 0 | 0 | 0 | 0 | 0 | 0 | .000 | .000 | .000 | -96 | -1 | 0 | | | 1.000 | -1 | /C-1 | -0.2 |

■ CHARLIE KALBFUS　Kalbfus, Charles Henry "Skinny"　b: 12/28/1864, Washington, D.C.　d: 11/18/41, Washington, D.C.　BR/TR, 5'11", 145 lbs.　Deb: 4/18/1884

| 1884 | Was-U | 1 | 5 | 1 | 1 | 0 | 0 | 0 | | 0 | | .200 | .200 | .200 | 9 | -1 | | | | .000 | -1 | /O-1 | -0.1 |

■ FRANK KALIN　Kalin, Frank Bruno "Fats" (b: Frank Bruno Kalinkiewicz)
b: 10/3/17, Steubenville, Ohio　d: 1/12/75, Weirton, W.Va.　BR/TR, 6', 200 lbs.　Deb: 9/25/40

1940	Pit-N	3	3	0	0	0	0	0	1	2	1	.000	.400	.000	19	-0	0			.667	-1	/O-2	-0.1
1943	Chi-A	4	4	0	0	0	0	0	0	0	1	.000	.000	.000	-99	-1	0	0	0	.000	0	H	-0.1
Total	2	7	7	0	0	0	0	0	1	2	2	.000	.222	.000	-34	-1	0	0	0	.667	-1	/O-2	-0.2

■ AL KALINE　Kaline, Albert William　b: 12/19/34, Baltimore, Md.　BR/TR, 6'2", 180 lbs.　Deb: 6/25/53　H

| 1953 | Det-A | 30 | 28 | 9 | 7 | 0 | 0 | 1 | 2 | 1 | 5 | .250 | .300 | .357 | 78 | -1 | 1 | 0 | 0 | 1.000 | -7 | O-20 | -0.8 |
| 1954 | Det-A | 138 | 504 | 42 | 139 | 18 | 3 | 4 | 43 | 22 | 45 | .276 | .306 | .347 | 80 | -15 | 9 | 5 | -0 | .971 | 11 | *O-135 | -1.1 |

YEAR	TM/L	G	AB	R	H	2B	3B	HR	RBI	BB	SO	AVG	OBP	SLG	PRO+	BR/A	SB	CS	SBR	FA	FR	G/POS	TPR
1955	Det-A★	152	588	121	**200**	24	8	27	102	82	57	**.340**	.425	.546	163	53	6	8	-3	.979	7	*O-152	5.0
1956	Det-A★	153	617	96	194	32	10	27	128	70	55	.314	.385	.530	139	33	7	1	2	.984	17	*O-153	4.2
1957	Det-A★	149	577	83	170	29	4	23	90	43	38	.295	.347	.478	120	14	11	9	-2	.985	7	*O-145	1.1
1958	Det-A★	146	543	84	170	34	7	16	85	54	47	.313	.377	.490	127	20	7	4	-0	.994	23	*O-145	3.6
1959	Det-A★	136	511	86	167	19	2	27	94	72	42	.327	.414	**.530**	149	36	10	4	1	.989	11	*O-136	4.0
1960	Det-A★	147	551	77	153	29	4	15	68	65	47	.278	.357	.426	108	7	19	4	3	.987	9	*O-142	1.2
1961	Det-A★	153	586	116	190	**41**	7	19	82	66	42	.324	.396	.515	138	32	14	1	4	.990	12	*O-147/3-1	3.8
1962	Det-A★	100	398	78	121	16	6	29	94	47	39	.304	.379	.593	152	28	4	0	1	.983	12	*O-100	3.4
1963	Det-A★	145	551	89	172	24	3	27	101	54	48	.312	.378	.514	142	31	6	4	-1	.992	-2	*O-140	2.1
1964	Det-A†	146	525	77	154	31	5	17	68	75	51	.293	.385	.469	134	26	4	1	1	.990	11	*O-136	3.2
1965	Det-A★	125	399	72	112	18	2	18	72	72	49	.281	.391	.471	142	24	6	0	2	.985	-4	*O-112/3-1	1.8
1966	Det-A★	142	479	85	138	29	1	29	88	81	66	.288	.396	.534	161	40	5	5	-2	**.993**	12	*O-136	3.9
1967	Det-A†	131	458	94	141	28	2	25	78	83	47	.308	.415	.541	176	46	8	2	1	.983	8	*O-130	5.2
1968	*Det-A	102	327	49	94	14	1	10	53	55	39	.287	.395	.428	145	20	6	4	-1	.978	-1	O-74,1-22	1.5
1969	Det-A	131	456	74	124	17	0	21	69	54	61	.272	.350	.447	117	10	1	2	-1	.966	1	O-118/1-9	0.3
1970	Det-A	131	467	64	130	24	4	16	71	77	49	.278	.382	.450	127	19	2	2	-1	.988	1	O-91,1-52	1.2
1971	Det-A★	133	405	69	119	19	2	15	54	82	57	.294	.421	.462	144	28	4	6	-2	**1.000**	-6	*O-129/1-5	1.4
1972	*Det-A	106	278	46	87	11	2	10	32	28	33	.313	.380	.475	148	17	1	0	0	.991	-6	O-84,1-11	0.8
1973	Det-A	91	310	40	79	13	0	10	45	29	28	.255	.325	.394	95	-2	4	1	-1	1.000	-5	O-63,1-36	-1.2
1974	Det-A★	147	558	71	146	28	2	13	64	65	75	.262	.340	.389	105	4	2	2	-1	.000	0	*D-146	0.0
Total	22	2834	10116	1622	3007	498	75	399	1583	1277	1020	.297	.379	.480	134	468	137	65	2	.986	103	*O-2488,D-146,1/3	44.6

■ WILLIE KAMM
Kamm, William Edward   b: 2/2/1900, San Francisco, Cal.   d: 12/21/88, Belmont, Cal.   BR/TR, 5'10.5", 170 lbs.   Deb: 4/18/23

YEAR	TM/L	G	AB	R	H	2B	3B	HR	RBI	BB	SO	AVG	OBP	SLG	PRO+	BR/A	SB	CS	SBR	FA	FR	G/POS	TPR
1923	Chi-A	149	544	57	159	39	9	6	87	62	82	.292	.366	.430	110	8	18	13	-2	.960	8	*3-149	2.5
1924	Chi-A	147	528	58	134	28	6	6	93	64	59	.254	.337	.364	83	-14	10	9	-2	**.971**	8	*3-146	0.3
1925	Chi-A	152	509	82	142	32	4	6	83	**90**	36	.279	.391	.393	105	7	11	13	-5	**.957**	-0	*3-152	1.2
1926	Chi-A	143	480	63	141	24	10	0	62	77	24	.294	.396	.385	108	9	12	4	1	**.978**	14	*3-142	3.1
1927	Chi-A	148	540	85	146	32	13	0	59	70	18	.270	.354	.378	92	-5	8	9	-3	**.972**	1	*3-146	-0.1
1928	Chi-A	155	552	70	170	30	12	1	84	73	22	.308	.391	.411	112	12	17	9	-0	**.977**	-3	*3-155	1.7
1929	Chi-A	147	523	72	140	33	6	3	63	75	23	.268	.363	.371	90	-6	12	5	1	**.978**	4	*3-145	0.4
1930	Chi-A	112	331	49	89	21	6	3	47	51	20	.269	.368	.396	97	-0	5	4	-1	.939	15	*3-106	1.7
1931	Chi-A	18	59	9	15	4	1	0	9	7	6	.254	.333	.356	86	-1	1	1	-0	.938	2	3-18	0.1
	Cle-A	114	410	68	121	31	4	0	66	64	13	.295	.392	.390	100	2	13	9	-2	.947	1	*3-114	0.8
	Yr	132	469	77	136	35	5	0	75	71	19	.290	.384	.386	99	1	14	10	-2	.945	3	*3-132	0.9
1932	Cle-A	148	524	76	150	34	9	3	83	75	36	.286	.379	.403	96	-2	6	3	0	.967	7	*3-148	1.4
1933	Cle-A	133	447	59	126	17	2	1	47	54	27	.282	.359	.336	81	-10	6	3	0	**.984**	1	*3-131	-0.2
1934	Cle-A	121	386	52	104	23	3	0	42	62	38	.269	.372	.345	84	-7	7	1	2	**.978**	11	*3-118	1.0
1935	Cle-A	6	18	2	6	0	0	0	1	0	1	.333	.333	.333	72	-1	0	1	-0	.875	-2	/3-4	-0.3
Total	13	1693	5851	802	1643	348	85	29	826	824	405	.281	.372	.384	97	-8	126	84	-13	.967	65	*3-1674	13.6

■ ALEX KAMPOURIS
Kampouris, Alexis William   b: 11/13/12, Sacramento, Cal.   d: 5/29/93, Sacramento, Cal.   BR/TR, 5'8", 155 lbs.   Deb: 7/31/34

YEAR	TM/L	G	AB	R	H	2B	3B	HR	RBI	BB	SO	AVG	OBP	SLG	PRO+	BR/A	SB	CS	SBR	FA	FR	G/POS	TPR
1934	Cin-N	19	66	6	13	1	0	0	3	3	18	.197	.254	.212	27	-7	2			.946	-1	2-16	-0.7
1935	Cin-N	148	499	46	123	26	5	7	62	32	84	.246	.295	.361	77	-17	8			.957	-1	*2-141/S-6	-0.7
1936	Cin-N	122	355	43	85	10	4	5	46	24	46	.239	.289	.332	72	-15	3			.969	28	*2-119/O-1	1.9
1937	Cin-N	146	458	62	114	21	4	17	71	60	65	.249	.342	.424	112	8	2			.961	3	*2-146	2.0
1938	Cin-N	21	74	13	19	1	0	2	7	10	13	.257	.353	.351	97	-0	0			.973	-2	2-21	0.1
	NY-N	82	268	35	66	9	1	5	37	27	50	.246	.318	.343	81	-7	0			.972	13	2-79	1.1
	Yr	103	342	48	85	10	1	7	44	37	63	.249	.325	.345	84	-7	0			.972	14	*2-100	1.2
1939	NY-N	74	201	23	50	12	2	5	29	30	41	.249	.349	.403	101	1	0			.973	10	2-62,3-11	1.3
1941	Bro-N	16	51	8	16	4	2	2	9	11	8	.314	.444	.588	181	6	0			.987	0	2-15	0.7
1942	Bro-N	10	21	3	5	2	1	0	3	0	4	.238	.238	.429	92	-0	0			.970	2	/2-9	0.2
1943	Bro-N	19	44	9	10	4	1	0	4	17	6	.227	.452	.364	136	4	0			.946	-1	2-18	0.3
	Was-A	51	145	24	30	4	2	0	13	30	25	.207	.361	.276	91	0	7	1	2	.936	-3	3-33,2-10/O	-0.1
Total	9	708	2182	272	531	94	20	45	284	244	360	.243	.325	.367	91	-28	22	1		.964	50	2-636/3-44,SO	6.1

■ FRANK KANE
Kane, Francis Thomas "Sugar" (a.k.a. Frank Thomas Kiley In 1915)   b: 3/9/1895, Whitman, Mass.   d: 12/2/62, Brockton, Mass.   BL/TR, 5'11.5", 175 lbs.   Deb: 9/13/15

YEAR	TM/L	G	AB	R	H	2B	3B	HR	RBI	BB	SO	AVG	OBP	SLG	PRO+	BR/A	SB	CS	SBR	FA	FR	G/POS	TPR
1915	Bro-F	3	10	2	2	0	1	0	2	0	0	.200	.200	.400	59	-1	0			1.000	1	/O-2	0.0
1919	NY-A	1	1	0	0	0	0	0	0	0	0	.000	.000	.000	-99	-0	0			.000	0	H	0.0
Total	2	4	11	2	2	0	1	0	2	0	0	.182	.182	.364	45	-1	0			1.000	1	/O-2	0.0

■ JIM KANE
Kane, James Joseph "Shamus"   b: 11/27/1881, Scranton, Pa.   d: 10/2/47, Omaha, Neb.   BL/TL, 6'2", 225 lbs.   Deb: 4/21/08

YEAR	TM/L	G	AB	R	H	2B	3B	HR	RBI	BB	SO	AVG	OBP	SLG	PRO+	BR/A	SB	CS	SBR	FA	FR	G/POS	TPR
1908	Pit-N	55	145	16	35	3	3	0	22	12		.241	.299	.303	93	-1	5			.966	-2	1-40	-0.4

■ JOHN KANE
Kane, John Francis   b: 9/24/1882, Chicago, Ill.   d: 1/28/34, St.Anthony, Idaho   BR/TR, 5'6", 138 lbs.   Deb: 4/11/07

YEAR	TM/L	G	AB	R	H	2B	3B	HR	RBI	BB	SO	AVG	OBP	SLG	PRO+	BR/A	SB	CS	SBR	FA	FR	G/POS	TPR
1907	Cin-N	79	262	40	65	9	4	3	19	22		.248	.325	.347	106	2	20			.959	-1	O-42,3-25/S2	0.1
1908	Cin-N	130	455	61	97	11	7	3	23	43		.213	.299	.288	90	-4	30			**.981**	4	*O-127/2-1	-0.6
1909	Chi-N	20	45	6	4	1	0	0	5	2		.089	.146	.111	-20	-6	1			.917	3	/O-8,S-3,32	-0.4
1910	*Chi-N	32	62	11	15	0	0	1	12	9	10	.242	.338	.290	84	-1	2			1.000	-7	O-18/2-6,3S	-0.8
Total	4	261	824	118	181	21	11	7	59	76	10	.220	.303	.297	89	-9	53			.975	-0	O-195/3-32,2S	-1.7

■ JOHN KANE
Kane, John Francis   b: 2/19/1900, Chicago, Ill.   d: 7/25/56, Chicago, Ill.   BB/TR, 5'10.5", 162 lbs.   Deb: 9/3/25

YEAR	TM/L	G	AB	R	H	2B	3B	HR	RBI	BB	SO	AVG	OBP	SLG	PRO+	BR/A	SB	CS	SBR	FA	FR	G/POS	TPR
1925	Chi-A	14	56	6	10	1	0	0	3	0	3	.179	.193	.196	-1	-9	0	0	0	.935	1	/S-8,2-6	-0.6

■ TOM KANE
Kane, Thomas Joseph "Sugar"   b: 12/15/06, Chicago, Ill.   d: 11/26/73, Chicago, Ill.   BR/TR, 5'10.5", 160 lbs.   Deb: 8/3/38

YEAR	TM/L	G	AB	R	H	2B	3B	HR	RBI	BB	SO	AVG	OBP	SLG	PRO+	BR/A	SB	CS	SBR	FA	FR	G/POS	TPR
1938	Bos-N	2	2	0	0	0	0	0	0	0	0	.000	.500	.000	53	0	0			1.000	-1	/2-2	-0.1

■ JERRY KANE
Kane, William Jeremiah   b: 4/1869, Baltimore, Md.   d: 6/16/49, E.St.Louis, Ill.   BR/TR, 6', 175 lbs.   Deb: 5/2/1890

YEAR	TM/L	G	AB	R	H	2B	3B	HR	RBI	BB	SO	AVG	OBP	SLG	PRO+	BR/A	SB	CS	SBR	FA	FR	G/POS	TPR
1890	StL-a	8	25	3	5	0	0	0	2	0		.200	.259	.200	31	-2	0			.907	-1	/1-5,C-4	-0.3

■ ROD KANEHL
Kanehl, Roderick Edwin "Hot Rod"   b: 4/1/34, Wichita, Kan.   BR/TR, 6'1", 180 lbs.   Deb: 4/15/62

YEAR	TM/L	G	AB	R	H	2B	3B	HR	RBI	BB	SO	AVG	OBP	SLG	PRO+	BR/A	SB	CS	SBR	FA	FR	G/POS	TPR
1962	NY-N	133	351	52	87	10	2	4	27	23	36	.248	.296	.322	65	-17	8	6	-1	.944	15	2-62,3-30,O/1S	0.1
1963	NY-N	109	191	26	46	6	0	1	9	5	26	.241	.268	.288	59	-10	6	3	0	.974	-7	O-58,3-13,2/1	-1.9
1964	NY-N	98	254	25	59	7	1	1	11	7	18	.232	.256	.280	52	-16	3	1	0	.988	19	2-34,O-25,3/1	0.4
Total	3	340	796	103	192	23	3	6	47	35	80	.241	.277	.300	60	-44	17	10	-1	.950	27	2-108,O-103/31S	-1.4

■ HEINIE KAPPEL
Kappel, Henry   b: 9/1863, Philadelphia, Pa.   d: 8/27/05, Philadelphia, Pa.   BR/TR, 5'8", 160 lbs.   Deb: 5/22/1887 F

YEAR	TM/L	G	AB	R	H	2B	3B	HR	RBI	BB	SO	AVG	OBP	SLG	PRO+	BR/A	SB	CS	SBR	FA	FR	G/POS	TPR
1887	Cin-a	23	78	11	22	3	2	0		2		.282	.309	.372	87	-2	3			.667	-3	/3-9,O-7,2S	-0.4
1888	Cin-a	36	143	18	37	4	4	1	15	2		.259	.274	.364	98	-1	20			.790	-12	S-25,2-10/3	-1.2
1889	Col-a	46	173	25	47	7	5	3	21	21	28	.272	.354	.422	127	6	10			.791	-2	S-23,3-23	0.5
Total	3	105	394	54	106	14	11	4	36	25	28	.269	.318	.391	109	3	33			.796	-17	/S-49,3-33,2O	-1.1

■ JOE KAPPEL
Kappel, Joseph   b: 4/27/1857, Philadelphia, Pa.   d: 7/8/29, Philadelphia, Pa.   BR, 5'11", 175 lbs.   Deb: 5/26/1884 F

YEAR	TM/L	G	AB	R	H	2B	3B	HR	RBI	BB	SO	AVG	OBP	SLG	PRO+	BR/A	SB	CS	SBR	FA	FR	G/POS	TPR
1884	Phi-N	4	15	1	1	0	0	0	0	0	2	.067	.067	.067	-61	-3				.727	-3	/C-4	-0.5

YEAR	TM/L	G	AB	R	H	2B	3B	HR	RBI	BB	SO	AVG	OBP	SLG	PRO+	BR/A	SB	CS	SBR	FA	FR	G/POS	TPR
1890	Phi-a	56	208	29	50	8	1	1		20		.240	.310	.303	83	-5	12			.851	-5	O-23,S-18,3/C2	-0.8
Total	2	60	223	30	51	8	1	1	0	20	2	.229	.295	.287	74	-7	12			.773	-8	/O-23,S-18,3C2	-1.3

■ RON KARKOVICE   Karkovice, Ronald Joseph b: 8/8/63, Union, N.J.   BR/TR, 6'1", 215 lbs.   Deb: 8/17/86

YEAR	TM/L	G	AB	R	H	2B	3B	HR	RBI	BB	SO	AVG	OBP	SLG	PRO+	BR/A	SB	CS	SBR	FA	FR	G/POS	TPR
1986	Chi-A	37	97	13	24	7	0	4	9	3	37	.247	.318	.443	101	-0	1	0	0	.996	14	C-37	1.6
1987	Chi-A	39	85	7	6	0	0	2	7	7	40	.071	.160	.141	-19	-15	3	0	1	.982	10	C-37/D-1	-0.2
1988	Chi-A	46	115	10	20	4	0	3	9	7	30	.174	.228	.287	43	-9	4	2	0	.995	9	C-46	0.2
1989	Chi-A	71	182	21	48	9	2	3	24	10	56	.264	.309	.385	97	-1	0	0	0	.986	17	C-68/D-2	1.9
1990	Chi-A	68	183	30	45	10	0	6	20	16	52	.246	.310	.399	99	-1	2	0	1	.994	6	C-69/O-1	0.9
1991	Chi-A	75	167	25	41	13	0	5	22	15	42	.246	.311	.413	101	-0	0	0	0	.988	11	C-69/O-1	1.4
1992	Chi-A	123	342	39	81	12	1	13	50	30	89	.237	.304	.392	95	-3	10	4	1	.990	5	*C-119/O-1	0.8
1993	*Chi-A	128	403	60	92	17	1	20	54	29	126	.228	.290	.424	91	-7	2	2	-1	.994	14	*C-127	1.3
1994	Chi-A	77	207	33	44	9	1	11	29	36	68	.213	.329	.425	93	-2	0	3	-2	.993	-3	C-76	-0.3
Total	9	664	1781	238	401	81	5	67	228	159	540	.225	.295	.389	86	-38	22	11	0	.991	82	C-643/D-5,O	7.6

■ BILL KARLON   Karlon, William John "Hank" b: 1/21/09, Palmer, Mass.   d: 12/7/64, Ware, Mass.   BR/TR, 6'1", 190 lbs.   Deb: 4/28/30

YEAR	TM/L	G	AB	R	H	2B	3B	HR	RBI	BB	SO	AVG	OBP	SLG	PRO+	BR/A	SB	CS	SBR	FA	FR	G/POS	TPR
1930	NY-A	2	5	0	0	0	0	0		0		.000	.000	.000	-99	-2	0	0	0		-0	/O-1	-0.2

■ MARTY KAROW   Karow, Martin Gregory (b: Martin Gregory Karowsky) b: 7/18/04, Braddock, Pa.   d: 4/27/86, Bryan, Texas   BR/TR, 5'10.5", 170 lbs.   Deb: 6/21/27

YEAR	TM/L	G	AB	R	H	2B	3B	HR	RBI	BB	SO	AVG	OBP	SLG	PRO+	BR/A	SB	CS	SBR	FA	FR	G/POS	TPR
1927	Bos-A	6	10	0	2	1	0	0	2	0	0	.200	.200	.300	29	-1	0	0	0	1.000	-1	/S-3,3-2	-0.1

■ ERIC KARROS   Karros, Eric Peter b: 11/4/67, Hackensack, N.J.   BR/TR, 6'4", 205 lbs.   Deb: 9/1/91

YEAR	TM/L	G	AB	R	H	2B	3B	HR	RBI	BB	SO	AVG	OBP	SLG	PRO+	BR/A	SB	CS	SBR	FA	FR	G/POS	TPR
1991	LA-N	14	14	0	1	1	0	0	1	1	6	.071	.133	.143	-23	-2	0	0	0	1.000	0	1-10	-0.3
1992	LA-N	149	545	63	140	30	1	20	88	37	103	.257	.307	.426	107	3	2	4	-2	.993	11	*1-143	0.3
1993	LA-N	158	619	74	153	27	2	23	80	34	82	.247	.289	.409	89	-12	0	1	-1	.992	15	*1-157	-1.0
1994	LA-N	111	406	51	108	21	1	14	46	29	53	.266	.318	.426	98	-3	2	0	1	.991	16	*1-109	0.5
Total	4	432	1584	188	402	79	4	57	215	101	244	.254	.301	.417	96	-14	4	5	-2	.992	42	1-419	-0.5

■ JOHN KARST   Karst, John Gottlieb "King" b: 10/15/1893, Philadelphia, Pa.   d: 5/21/76, Cape May Court House, N.J.   BL/TR, 5'11.5", 175 lbs.   Deb: 10/6/15

YEAR	TM/L	G	AB	R	H	2B	3B	HR	RBI	BB	SO	AVG	OBP	SLG	PRO+	BR/A	SB	CS	SBR	FA	FR	G/POS	TPR
1915	Bro-N	1	0	0	0	0	0	0	0	0	0	—	—	—	—	—	0	0	0	1.000	0	/3-1	0.0

■ EDDIE KASKO   Kasko, Edward Michael b: 6/27/32, Linden, N.J.   BR/TR, 6', 180 lbs.   Deb: 4/18/57   M

YEAR	TM/L	G	AB	R	H	2B	3B	HR	RBI	BB	SO	AVG	OBP	SLG	PRO+	BR/A	SB	CS	SBR	FA	FR	G/POS	TPR
1957	StL-N	134	479	59	131	16	5	1	35	33	53	.273	.320	.334	75	-16	6	1	1	.961	-7	*3-120,S-13/2	-2.0
1958	StL-N	104	259	20	57	8	1	2	22	21	25	.220	.279	.282	47	-19	1	2	-1	.961	6	S-77,2-12/3	-0.8
1959	Cin-N	118	329	39	93	14	1	2	31	14	38	.283	.312	.350	74	-12	2	2	-1	.976	12	S-84,3-31/2	0.6
1960	Cin-N	126	479	56	140	21	1	6	51	46	37	.292	.362	.378	101	2	9	9	-3	.966	3	3-86,2-33,S	0.3
1961	*Cin-N★	126	469	64	127	22	1	2	27	32	36	.271	.323	.335	74	-17	4	3	-1	.964	-18	*S-112,3-12/2	-2.6
1962	Cin-N	134	533	74	148	26	2	4	41	35	44	.278	.328	.356	81	-14	3	3	-1	.941	-8	*3-114,S-21	-2.0
1963	Cin-N	76	199	25	48	9	0	3	10	21	29	.241	.314	.332	83	-4	0	2	-1	.959	-1	3-48,S-15/2	-0.5
1964	Hou-N	133	448	45	109	16	1	0	22	37	52	.243	.302	.283	70	-17	4	6	-2	.978	10	*S-128/3-2	-0.1
1965	Hou-N	68	215	18	53	7	1	1	10	11	20	.247	.296	.302	74	-8	1	3	-2	.976	-10	S-59/3-2	-1.7
1966	Bos-A	58	136	11	29	7	0	1	12	15	19	.213	.291	.287	61	-7	1	0	0	.976	8	S-20,3-10/2	0.3
Total	10	1077	3546	411	935	146	13	22	261	265	353	.264	.318	.331	76	-112	31	31	-9	.971	-9	S-544,3-426/2	-8.5

■ RAY KATT   Katt, Raymond Frederick b: 5/9/27, New Braunfels, Tex.   BR/TR, 6'2", 200 lbs.   Deb: 9/16/52   C

YEAR	TM/L	G	AB	R	H	2B	3B	HR	RBI	BB	SO	AVG	OBP	SLG	PRO+	BR/A	SB	CS	SBR	FA	FR	G/POS	TPR
1952	NY-N	9	27	4	6	0	0	1	1	1	5	.222	.250	.222	32	-2	0	0	0	1.000	1	/C-8	-0.1
1953	NY-N	8	29	2	5	1	0	0	1	1	3	.172	.200	.207	6	-4	0	0	0	.975	-1	/C-8	-0.4
1954	NY-N	86	200	26	51	7	1	9	33	19	29	.255	.320	.435	94	-2	1	0	0	.973	-7	C-82	-0.6
1955	NY-N	124	326	27	70	7	2	7	28	22	38	.215	.269	.313	54	-22	0	0	0	.987	-8	*C-122	-2.6
1956	NY-N	37	101	10	23	4	0	7	14	6	16	.228	.278	.475	98	-1	0	1	-1	.978	-4	C-37	-0.5
	StL-N	47	158	11	41	4	0	6	20	6	24	.259	.291	.399	83	-4	0	1	-1	.984	-2	C-47	-0.5
	Yr	84	259	21	64	8	0	13	34	12	40	.247	.286	.429	89	-5	0	2	-1	.982	-1	C-84	-0.5
1957	NY-N	72	165	11	38	3	1	2	17	15	35	.230	.302	.297	62	-9	1	0	0	.981	-6	C-68	-1.3
1958	StL-N	19	41	1	7	1	0	1	4	4	6	.171	.244	.268	34	-4	0	0	0	.971	0	C-14	-0.3
1959	StL-N	15	24	0	7	2	0	0	2	0	8	.292	.292	.375	71	-1	0	0	0	.976	0	C-14	-0.1
Total	8	417	1071	92	248	29	4	32	120	74	164	.232	.285	.356	69	-49	2	2	-1	.981	-22	C-400	-5.9

■ BENNY KAUFF   Kauff, Benjamin Michael b: 1/5/1890, Pomeroy, Ohio   d: 11/17/61, Columbus, Ohio   BL/TL, 5'8", 157 lbs.   Deb: 4/20/12

YEAR	TM/L	G	AB	R	H	2B	3B	HR	RBI	BB	SO	AVG	OBP	SLG	PRO+	BR/A	SB	CS	SBR	FA	FR	G/POS	TPR
1912	NY-A	5	11	4	3	0	0	0		2	3	.273	.429	.273	96	0	1			1.000	-1	/O-4	-0.1
1914	Ind-F	154	571	120	211	44	13	8	95	72	55	.370	.447	.534	138	34	75			.953	16	*O-154	4.4
1915	Bro-F	136	483	92	165	23	11	12	83	85	50	.342	.446	.509	156	42	55			.959	15	*O-136	5.3
1916	NY-N	154	552	71	146	22	15	9	74	68	65	.264	.348	.408	139	26	40	26	-4	.962	2	*O-154	1.9
1917	*NY-N	153	559	89	172	22	4	5	68	59	54	.308	.379	.388	140	28	30			.976	-4	*O-153	1.7
1918	NY-N	67	270	41	85	19	4	2	39	16	30	.315	.355	.437	144	13	9			.952	-1	O-67	1.0
1919	NY-N	135	491	73	136	27	10	10	67	39	45	.277	.334	.422	128	15	21			.950	-3	*O-134	0.4
1920	NY-N	55	157	31	43	12	3	0	26	25	14	.274	.380	.446	138	8	3	7	-3	.960	-1	O-51	0.2
Total	8	859	3094	521	961	169	57	49	454	367	313	.311	.389	.450	141	167	234	33		.960	23	O-853	14.8

■ DICK KAUFFMAN   Kauffman, Howard Richard b: 6/22/1888, E.Lewisburg, Pa.   d: 4/16/48, Mifflinburg, Pa.   BB/TR, 6'3", 190 lbs.   Deb: 9/17/14

YEAR	TM/L	G	AB	R	H	2B	3B	HR	RBI	BB	SO	AVG	OBP	SLG	PRO+	BR/A	SB	CS	SBR	FA	FR	G/POS	TPR
1914	StL-A	7	15	1	4	1	0	0	0	3		.267	.267	.333	83	-0				.967	-1	/1-7	-0.2
1915	StL-A	37	124	9	32	8	2	0	14	5	27	.258	.298	.355	99	-1	0	3	-2	.984	-1	1-32/O-1	-0.5
Total	2	44	139	10	36	9	2	0	16	5	30	.259	.295	.353	97	-1	0	3		.982	-2	/1-39,O-1	-0.7

■ TONY KAUFMANN   Kaufmann, Anthony Charles b: 12/16/1900, Chicago, Ill.   d: 6/4/82, Elgin, Ill.   BR/TR, 5'11", 165 lbs.   Deb: 9/23/21   C

YEAR	TM/L	G	AB	R	H	2B	3B	HR	RBI	BB	SO	AVG	OBP	SLG	PRO+	BR/A	SB	CS	SBR	FA	FR	G/POS	TPR
1921	Chi-N	2	5	0	2	1	0	0	0	1		.400	.400	.600	161	0	0	0	0	1.000	-1	/P-2	0.0
1922	Chi-N	38	45	4	9	2	1	1	4	2	14	.200	.234	.356	49	-4	0	0	0	.933	-1	/P-37	0.0
1923	Chi-N	33	74	10	16	2	0	2	10	7	17	.216	.284	.324	60	-4	0	0	0	.962	-1	P-33	0.0
1924	Chi-N	35	76	6	24	5	0	1	14	3	10	.316	.342	.421	102	0	0	0	0	.981	-1	P-34	0.0
1925	Chi-N	31	78	8	15	7	0	2	13	2	17	.192	.213	.359	42	-7	0	0	0	.981	-0	P-31	0.0
1926	Chi-N	30	60	9	15	2	0	1	7	2	10	.250	.274	.333	62	-3	1			1.000	-2	P-26	0.0
1927	Chi-N	9	16	2	5	0	0	1	4	4	4	.313	.450	.500	154	1	0	0	0	1.000	2	/P-9	0.0
	Phi-N	8	7	1	1	0	0	0	2	0	1	.143	.143	.571	83	-0	0	0	0	1.000	-1	/P-5,O-1	0.0
	StL-N	1	0	0	0	0	0	0	0	0	0	—	—	—	—	-0	0	0	0	.000	-0	/P-1	0.0
	Yr	18	23	3	6	0	0	2	8	4	5	.261	.370	.522	136	1	0	0	0	1.000	1	P-15/O-1	0.0
1928	StL-N	5	0	0	0	0	0	0	0	0	0	—	—	—	—	-0	0	0	0	1.000	-0	/P-4	0.0
1929	NY-N	39	32	18	1	0	0	0	1	6	4	.031	.184	.031	-43	-7	3			.964	-4	O-16	-1.0
1930	StL-N	2	3	1	1	0	0	0	0	1		.333	.500	.333	103	0	0	0	0	1.000	-0	/P-2	0.0
1931	StL-N	20	18	1	2	0	0	0	1	1	1	.111	.158	.111	-26	-3	0	0	0	.929	-1	/P-15,O-1	-0.1
1935	StL-N	7	0	2	0	0	0	0	0	0	0	—	—	—	—	-0	0	0	0	1.000	0	/P-3	0.0
Total	12	260	414	62	91	19	1	9	57	28	82	.220	.269	.336	57	-27	4	0		.972	-9	P-202/O-18	-1.1

■ CHARLIE KAVANAGH   Kavanagh, Charles Hugh "Silk" b: 6/9/1893, Chicago, Ill.   d: 9/6/73, Reedsburg, Wis.   BR/TR, 5'9", 165 lbs.   Deb: 6/11/14

YEAR	TM/L	G	AB	R	H	2B	3B	HR	RBI	BB	SO	AVG	OBP	SLG	PRO+	BR/A	SB	CS	SBR	FA	FR	G/POS	TPR
1914	Chi-A	6	5	0	1	0	0	0	0		2	.200	.333	.200	62	-0	0			.000	0	H	0.0

■ LEO KAVANAGH   Kavanagh, Leo Daniel b: 8/9/1894, Chicago, Ill.   d: 8/10/50, Chicago, Ill.   BR/TR, 5'9", 180 lbs.   Deb: 4/22/14

YEAR	TM/L	G	AB	R	H	2B	3B	HR	RBI	BB	SO	AVG	OBP	SLG	PRO+	BR/A	SB	CS	SBR	FA	FR	G/POS	TPR
1914	Chi-F	5	11	0	3	0	0	0	1	1	0	.273	.333	.273	62	-1	0			1.000	-1	/S-5	-0.1

■ MARTY KAVANAGH

Kavanagh, Martin Joseph b: 6/13/1891, Harrison, N.J. d: 7/28/60, Eloise, Mich. BR/TR, 6', 187 lbs. Deb: 4/18/14

YEAR	TM/L	G	AB	R	H	2B	3B	HR	RBI	BB	SO	AVG	OBP	SLG	PRO+	BR/A	SB	CS	SBR	FA	FR	G/POS	TPR
1914	Det-A	128	439	60	109	21	6	4	35	41	42	.248	.318	.351	98	-2	16	14	-4	.929	-7	*2-115/1-4	-1.5
1915	Det-A	113	332	55	98	14	13	4	49	42	44	.295	.378	.452	141	16	8	8	-2	.987	-15	1-44,2-42/SO3	-0.2
1916	Det-A	58	78	6	11	4	0	0	5	9	15	.141	.239	.192	29	-7	0			1.000	0	O-11/2-2,3	-0.8
	Cle-A	19	44	4	11	2	1	1	10	2	5	.250	.283	.409	102	-0	0			.894	-2	/2-9,1-1,3	0.0
	Yr	77	122	10	22	6	1	1	15	11	20	.180	.254	.270	55	-7	0			1.000	0	O-11,2-11/31	-0.8
1917	Cle-A	14	14	1	0	0	0	0	0	3	2	.000	.176	.000	-43	-2	0			1.000	0	/O-2	-0.2
1918	Cle-A	13	38	4	8	2	0	0	6	7	7	.211	.348	.263	77	-1	1			.967	-1	1-12	-0.3
	StL-N	12	44	6	8	1	0	1	8	3	1	.182	.234	.273	56	-2	1			1.000	-2	/O-8,2-4	-0.5
	Det-A	13	44	2	12	3	0	0	9	11	6	.273	.418	.341	135	3	0			.964	-1	1-12	0.1
Total 5		370	1033	138	257	47	20	10	122	118	122	.249	.330	.362	104	4	26	22		.926	-26	2-172/1-73,O3S	-3.4

■ KAVANAUGH

Kavanaugh Deb: 9/11/1872

YEAR	TM/L	G	AB	R	H	2B	3B	HR	RBI	BB	SO	AVG	OBP	SLG	PRO+	BR/A	SB	CS	SBR	FA	FR	G/POS	TPR
1872	Eck-n	5	22	3	6	1	0	0	2	0	0	.273	.273	.318	96	0						/1-4,O-1	0.0

■ BILL KAY

Kay, Walter Brocton "King Bill" b: 2/14/1878, New Castle, Va. d: 12/3/45, Roanoke, Va. BL/TR, 6'2", 180 lbs. Deb: 8/12/07

YEAR	TM/L	G	AB	R	H	2B	3B	HR	RBI	BB	SO	AVG	OBP	SLG	PRO+	BR/A	SB	CS	SBR	FA	FR	G/POS	TPR
1907	Was-A	25	60	8	20	1	1	0	7	0		.333	.333	.383	139	2	0			1.000	-0	O-12	0.2

■ EDDIE KAZAK

Kazak, Edward Terrance (b: Edward Terrance Tkaczuk) b: 7/18/20, Steubenville, O. BR/TR, 6', 175 lbs. Deb: 9/29/48

YEAR	TM/L	G	AB	R	H	2B	3B	HR	RBI	BB	SO	AVG	OBP	SLG	PRO+	BR/A	SB	CS	SBR	FA	FR	G/POS	TPR
1948	StL-N	6	22	1	6	3	0	0	2	0	2	.273	.273	.409	78	-1	0			.900	1	/3-6	0.0
1949	StL-N★	92	326	43	99	15	3	6	42	29	17	.304	.362	.423	105	2	0			.926	-4	3-80/2-5	-0.2
1950	StL-N	93	207	21	53	2	2	5	23	18	19	.256	.319	.357	74	-8	0			.936	1	3-48	-0.7
1951	StL-N	11	33	2	6	2	0	0	4	5	5	.182	.289	.242	44	-3	0	0	0	.933	-1	3-10	-0.4
1952	StL-N	3	2	1	0	0	0	0	0	0	0	.000	.000	.000	-99	-1	0	0	0	1.000	0	/3-1	0.0
	Cin-N	13	15	1	1	0	1	0	0	0	2	.067	.067	.200	-29	-3	0	0	0	.667	-0	/3-3,1-1	-0.3
	Yr	16	17	2	1	0	1	0	0	0	2	.059	.059	.176	-37	-3	0	0	0	.750	-0	/3-4,1-1	-0.3
Total 5		218	605	69	165	22	6	11	71	52	45	.273	.332	.383	87	-12		0		.927	-3	3-148/2-5,1	-1.6

■ TED KAZANSKI

Kazanski, Theodore Stanley b: 1/25/34, Hamtramck, Mich. BR/TR, 6'1", 175 lbs. Deb: 6/25/53

YEAR	TM/L	G	AB	R	H	2B	3B	HR	RBI	BB	SO	AVG	OBP	SLG	PRO+	BR/A	SB	CS	SBR	FA	FR	G/POS	TPR
1953	Phi-N	95	360	39	78	17	5	2	27	26	53	.217	.275	.308	52	-26	1	1	-0	.949	-19	S-95	-3.8
1954	Phi-N	39	104	7	14	2	0	1	8	4	14	.135	.167	.183	-9	-17	0	1	-1	.945	-7	S-38	-2.2
1955	Phi-N	9	12	1	1	0	0	1	1	1	1	.083	.154	.333	25	-1	0	0	0	1.000	1	/S-4,3-4	-0.1
1956	Phi-N	117	379	35	80	11	1	4	34	20	41	.211	.253	.277	43	-31	0	2	-1	.979	-10	*2-116/S-1	-3.5
1957	Phi-N	62	185	15	49	7	1	3	11	17	20	.265	.327	.362	88	-3	1	1	-0	.968	-3	3-36,2-22/S	-0.4
1958	Phi-N	95	289	21	66	12	3	3	35	22	34	.228	.292	.315	62	-16	2	3	-1	.988	-13	2-59,S-22,3	-2.6
Total 6		417	1329	118	288	49	9	14	116	90	163	.217	.270	.299	51	-94	4	8	-4	.981	-51	2-197,S-163/3	-12.6

■ BOB KEARNEY

Kearney, Robert Henry b: 10/3/56, San Antonio, Tex. BR/TR, 6', 190 lbs. Deb: 9/25/79

YEAR	TM/L	G	AB	R	H	2B	3B	HR	RBI	BB	SO	AVG	OBP	SLG	PRO+	BR/A	SB	CS	SBR	FA	FR	G/POS	TPR
1979	SF-N	2	0	0	0	0	0	0	0	1	0	—	1.000	—	211	0	0	0	0	.000	0	/C-1	0.0
1981	Oak-A	1	0	0	0	0	0	0	0	0	0	—	—	—	—	0	0	0	0	.000	0	/C-1	0.0
1982	Oak-A	22	71	7	12	3	0	0	5	3	10	.169	.224	.211	21	-8	0	0	0	.970	5	C-22	-0.2
1983	Oak-A	108	298	33	76	11	0	8	32	21	50	.255	.313	.372	93	-3	1	4	-2	.982	5	*C-101/D-3	0.4
1984	Sea-A	133	431	39	97	24	1	7	43	18	72	.225	.259	.334	64	-22	7	5	-1	.988	5	*C-133	-1.2
1985	Sea-A	108	305	24	74	14	1	6	27	11	59	.243	.278	.354	71	-12	1	1	-0	**.995**	6	*C-108	-0.2
1986	Sea-A	81	204	23	49	10	0	6	25	12	35	.240	.282	.377	77	-7	0	2	-1	.989	14	C-79	1.0
1987	Sea-A	24	47	5	8	4	1	0	1	1	9	.170	.188	.298	25	-5	0	0	0	.981	6	C-24	0.2
Total 8		479	1356	131	316	66	3	27	133	67	235	.233	.275	.346	70	-57	9	12	-5	.987	41	C-469/D-3	-0.0

■ TEDDY KEARNS

Kearns, Edward Joseph b: 1/1/1900, Trenton, N.J. d: 12/21/49, Trenton, N.J. BR/TR, 5'11", 180 lbs. Deb: 10/1/20

YEAR	TM/L	G	AB	R	H	2B	3B	HR	RBI	BB	SO	AVG	OBP	SLG	PRO+	BR/A	SB	CS	SBR	FA	FR	G/POS	TPR
1920	Phi-A	1	1	0	0	0	0	0	0	0	0	.000	.000	.000	-99	-0	0	0	0	.000	0	H	0.0
1924	Chi-N	4	16	0	4	0	1	0	1	1	1	.250	.294	.375	72	-1	0	0	0	1.000	-0	/1-4	-0.1
1925	Chi-N	3	2	0	1	0	0	0	0	0	0	.500	.500	.500	154	-0	0	0	0	1.000	-0	/1-3	0.0
Total 3		8	19	0	5	0	1	0	1	1	1	.263	.300	.368	76	-1	0	0	0	1.000	-0	/1-7	-0.1

■ TOM KEARNS

Kearns, Thomas J. "Dasher" b: 11/9/1859, Rochester, N.Y. d: 12/7/38, Buffalo, N.Y. BR/TR, 5'7", 160 lbs. Deb: 8/26/1880

YEAR	TM/L	G	AB	R	H	2B	3B	HR	RBI	BB	SO	AVG	OBP	SLG	PRO+	BR/A	SB	CS	SBR	FA	FR	G/POS	TPR
1880	Buf-N	2	7	0	0	0	0	0	0	0	0	.000	.000	.000	-98	-1				.667	-1	/C-2	-0.3
1882	Det-N	4	13	2	4	2	0	0	1	0	4	.308	.308	.462	143	1				.733	-3	/2-4	-0.2
1884	Det-N	21	79	9	16	0	1	0	7	2	10	.203	.222	.228	45	-5				.810	-10	2-21	-1.3
Total 3		27	99	11	20	2	1	0	8	2	14	.202	.218	.242	48	-6				.801	-14	/2-25,C-2	-1.8

■ EDDIE KEARSE

Kearse, Edward Paul "Truck" b: 2/23/16, San Francisco, Cal. d: 7/15/68, Eureka, Cal. BR/TR, 6'1", 195 lbs. Deb: 6/13/42

YEAR	TM/L	G	AB	R	H	2B	3B	HR	RBI	BB	SO	AVG	OBP	SLG	PRO+	BR/A	SB	CS	SBR	FA	FR	G/POS	TPR
1942	NY-A	11	26	2	5	0	0	0	2	3	1	.192	.276	.192	34	-2	1	0	0	1.000	3	C-11	0.2

■ CHICK KEATING

Keating, Walter Francis b: 8/8/1891, Philadelphia, Pa. d: 7/13/59, Philadelphia, Pa. BR/TR, 5'9.5", 155 lbs. Deb: 9/26/13

YEAR	TM/L	G	AB	R	H	2B	3B	HR	RBI	BB	SO	AVG	OBP	SLG	PRO+	BR/A	SB	CS	SBR	FA	FR	G/POS	TPR
1913	Chi-N	2	5	0	1	1	0	0	0	0	1	.200	.200	.400	69	-0	0			1.000	-1	/S-2	-0.1
1914	Chi-N	20	30	3	3	0	1	0	0	6	9	.100	.250	.167	25	-3	0			.951	0	S-14	-0.2
1915	Chi-N	4	8	1	0	0	0	0	0	0	3	.000	.000	.000	-99	-2	1			.750	-5	/S-2	-0.2
1926	Phi-N	4	2	0	0	0	0	0	0	0	0	.000	.000	.000	-95	-1	0			1.000	-0	/2-2,S-2,3	-0.1
Total 4		30	45	4	4	1	1	0	0	6	13	.089	.196	.156	4	-5	1			.903	-1	/S-20,2-2,3	-0.6

■ GREG KEATLEY

Keatley, Gregory Steven b: 9/12/53, Princeton, W.Va. BR/TR, 6'2", 200 lbs. Deb: 9/27/81

YEAR	TM/L	G	AB	R	H	2B	3B	HR	RBI	BB	SO	AVG	OBP	SLG	PRO+	BR/A	SB	CS	SBR	FA	FR	G/POS	TPR
1981	KC-A	2	0	0	0	0	0	0	0	0	0	—	—	—	—	—	0	0	0	1.000	0	/C-2	0.0

■ PAT KEEDY

Keedy, Charles Patrick b: 1/10/58, Birmingham, Ala. BR/TR, 6'4", 205 lbs. Deb: 9/10/85

YEAR	TM/L	G	AB	R	H	2B	3B	HR	RBI	BB	SO	AVG	OBP	SLG	PRO+	BR/A	SB	CS	SBR	FA	FR	G/POS	TPR
1985	Cal-A	3	4	1	2	1	0	1	1	0	0	.500	.500	1.500	424	2	0	1	-1	.000	-0	/3-2,O-1	0.1
1987	Chi-A	17	41	6	7	1	0	2	2	2	14	.171	.209	.341	42	-4	1	0	0	.943	4	3-11/1-2,2SOD	0.1
1989	Cle-A	9	14	3	3	2	0	0	1	2	5	.214	.313	.357	87	-0	0	0	0	1.000	-0	/O-3,3-2,1SD	0.0
Total 3		29	59	10	12	4	0	3	4	4	19	.203	.254	.424	77	-2	1	1	-0	.929	3	/3-15,O-5,1DS2	0.2

■ WILLIE KEELER

Keeler, William Henry "Wee Willie" (b: William Henry O'Kelleher)
b: 3/3/1872, Brooklyn, N.Y. d: 1/1/23, Brooklyn, N.Y. BL/TL, 5'4.5", 140 lbs. Deb: 9/30/1892 H

YEAR	TM/L	G	AB	R	H	2B	3B	HR	RBI	BB	SO	AVG	OBP	SLG	PRO+	BR/A	SB	CS	SBR	FA	FR	G/POS	TPR
1892	NY-N	14	53	7	17	3	0	0		2	5	.321	.368	.377	128	2	5			.878	-3	3-14	-0.1
1893	NY-N	7	24	5	8	2	1	1	7	5	1	.333	.448	.625	183	3	3			.667	-5	/O-3,2-2,S	-0.2
	Bro-N	20	80	14	25	1	1		9	4	4	.313	.353	.387	101	0	2			.833	-1	3-12/O-8	0.0
	Yr	27	104	19	33	3	2	2	16	9	5	.317	.377	.442	121	3	5			.833	-6	3-12,O-11/2S	-0.3
1894	*Bal-N	129	590	165	219	27	22	5	94	40	6	.371	.427	.517	121	20	32			.938	3	*O-128/2-1	1.1
1895	*Bal-N	131	565	162	213	24	15	4	78	37	12	.377	.429	.494	134	28	47			.946	0	*O-131	1.4
1896	*Bal-N	126	544	153	210	22	13	4	82	37	9	.386	.432	.496	142	33	67			.969	6	*O-126	2.4
1897	*Bal-N	129	564	145	**239**	27	19	0	74	35		**.424**	.464	.539	164	52	64			.970	-2	*O-129	3.4
1898	Bal-N	129	561	126	**216**	7	2	1	44	31		**.385**	.420	.410	136	26	28			.961	0	*O-128/3-1	1.6
1899	Bro-N	141	570	**140**	216	12	13	1	61	37		.379	.425	.451	137	30	45			.979	-2	*O-141	1.5
1900	*Bro-N	136	563	106	**204**	13	12	4	68	30		.362	.402	.449	127	19	41			.940	5	*O-136/2-1	1.3
1901	Bro-N	136	595	123	202	18	12	2	43	21		.339	.369	.420	125	18	23			**.985**	-6	*O-125,3-10/2	0.3
1902	Bro-N	133	559	86	186	20	5	0	38	21		.333	.365	.386	131	19	19			**.978**	2	*O-133	1.3
1903	NY-A	132	512	95	160	14	7	0	32	32		.313	.368	.367	114	10	24			.935	-9	*O-128/3-4	-0.8

YEAR	TM/L	G	AB	R	H	2B	3B	HR	RBI	BB	SO	AVG	OBP	SLG	PRO+	BR/A	SB	CS	SBR	FA	FR	G/POS	TPR
1904	NY-A	143	543	78	186	14	8	2	40	35		.343	.390	.409	146	28	21			.935	-3	*O-142	1.9
1905	NY-A	149	560	81	169	14	4	4	38	43		.302	.357	.363	115	9	19			.968	-4	*O-137,2-12/3	-0.1
1906	NY-A	152	592	96	180	8	3	2	33	40		.304	.353	.338	106	4	23			.987	-2	*O-152	-0.6
1907	NY-A	107	423	50	99	5	2	0	17	15		.234	.265	.255	61	-19	7			.969	-3	*O-107	-2.9
1908	NY-A	91	323	38	85	3	1	1	14	31		.263	.337	.288	102	2	14			.936	-1	O-88	-0.3
1909	NY-A	99	360	44	95	7	5	1	32	24		.264	.327	.319	104	2	10			.968	-5	O-95	-0.8
1910	NY-N	19	10	5	3	0	0	0	0	3	1	.300	.462	.300	123	1	1			1.000	-1	/O-2	0.0
Total	19	2123	8591	1719	2932	241	145	33	810	524	36	.341	.388	.415	125	286	495			.960	-30	*O-2039/3-44,2S	10.3

■ BOB KEELY
Keely, Robert William b: 8/22/09, St.Louis, Mo. BR/TR, 6', 175 lbs. Deb: 7/25/44 C

YEAR	TM/L	G	AB	R	H	2B	3B	HR	RBI	BB	SO	AVG	OBP	SLG	PRO+	BR/A	SB	CS	SBR	FA	FR	G/POS	TPR
1944	StL-N	1	0	0	0	0	0	0	0	0	0	—	—	—		0	0			1.000	-0	/C-1	0.0
1945	StL-N	1	1	0	0	0	0	0	0	0	0	.000	.000	.000	-98	-0	0			1.000	-0	/C-1	0.0
Total	2	2	1	0	0	0	0	0	0	0	0	.000	.000	.000	-98	-0	0			1.000	-0	/C-2	0.0

■ BILL KEEN
Keen, William Brown "Buster" b: 8/16/1892, Oglethorpe, Ga. d: 7/16/47, South Point, Ohio BR/TR, 6', 181 lbs. Deb: 8/8/11

YEAR	TM/L	G	AB	R	H	2B	3B	HR	RBI	BB	SO	AVG	OBP	SLG	PRO+	BR/A	SB	CS	SBR	FA	FR	G/POS	TPR
1911	Pit-N	6	7	0	0	0	0	0	0	1	4	.000	.125	.000	-62	-2	0			1.000	-0	/1-1	-0.2

■ JIM KEENAN
Keenan, James William b: 2/10/1858, New Haven, Conn. d: 9/21/26, Cincinnati, Ohio BR/TR, 5'10", 186 lbs. Deb: 5/17/1875

YEAR	TM/L	G	AB	R	H	2B	3B	HR	RBI	BB	SO	AVG	OBP	SLG	PRO+	BR/A	SB	CS	SBR	FA	FR	G/POS	TPR
1875	NH-n	4	13	1	1	0	0	0		0		.077	.077	.077	-53	-2						/3-2,C-1	-0.2
1880	Buf-N	2	7	1	1	0	0	0	0	1	1	.143	.250	.143	36	-0				.947	3	/C-2	0.2
1882	Pit-a	25	96	10	21	7	0	1		1		.219	.227	.323	87	-1				.906	1	C-22/O-3,S	0.1
1884	Ind-a	68	249	36	73	14	4	3	16			.293	.343	.418	151	14				.923	-2	C-59/1-6,OSP	1.5
1885	Cin-a	36	132	16	35	2	2	1	8			.265	.307	.333	100	-0				.926	-1	C-33/1-4,P	0.1
1886	Cin-a	44	148	31	40	4	3	3	18			.270	.357	.399	132	6	0			.915	3	C-30/O-7,31P	0.7
1887	Cin-a	47	174	19	44	4	1	0	11			.253	.301	.287	63	-9	7			.934	9	C-38,1-11	0.2
1888	Cin-a	85	313	38	73	9	8	1	40	22		.233	.294	.323	93	-3	9			.946	3	C-69,1-16	0.4
1889	Cin-a	87	300	52	86	10	11	6	60	48	35	.287	.395	.453	137	15	18			.962	1	C-66,1-21/3	1.8
1890	Cin-N	54	202	21	28	3	2	0	19	19	36	.139	.216	.223	28	-19	5			.950	2	C-50/1-2,O3	-0.9
1891	Cin-N	75	252	30	51	7	5	4	33	33	39	.202	.302	.317	80	-6	2			.974	-4	1-41,C-34/3	-0.8
Total	10	523	1873	254	452	61	36	22	152	177	111	.241	.314	.348	99	-4	41			.935	14	C-403,1-105/O3PS	3.3

■ GEORGE KEERL
Keerl, George Henry b: 4/10/1847, Baltimore, Md. d: 9/13/23, Menominee, Mich. BR/TR, 5'7", 145 lbs. Deb: 5/5/1875

YEAR	TM/L	G	AB	R	H	2B	3B	HR	RBI	BB	SO	AVG	OBP	SLG	PRO+	BR/A	SB	CS	SBR	FA	FR	G/POS	TPR
1875	Chi-n	6	23	2	3	0	0	0		0		.130	.130	.130	-9	-2						/2-6	-0.2

■ JIM KEESEY
Keesey, James Ward b: 10/27/02, Perryville, Md. d: 9/5/51, Boise, Idaho BR/TR, 6'0.5", 170 lbs. Deb: 9/6/25

YEAR	TM/L	G	AB	R	H	2B	3B	HR	RBI	BB	SO	AVG	OBP	SLG	PRO+	BR/A	SB	CS	SBR	FA	FR	G/POS	TPR
1925	Phi-A	5	5	1	2	0	0	0	1	0	2	.400	.400	.400	97	-0	0	0	0	1.000	-0	/1-2	0.0
1930	Phi-A	11	12	2	3	1	0	0	2	1	2	.250	.308	.333	60	-1	0	0	0	.909	-0	/1-3	-0.1
Total	2	16	17	3	5	1	0	0	3	1	4	.294	.333	.353	71	-1	0	0	0	.923	-1	/1-5	-0.1

■ BILL KEISTER
Keister, William Hoffman "Wagon Tongue" b: 8/17/1874, Baltimore, Md. d: 8/19/24, Baltimore, Md. BL/TR, 5'5.5", 168 lbs. Deb: 5/20/1896

YEAR	TM/L	G	AB	R	H	2B	3B	HR	RBI	BB	SO	AVG	OBP	SLG	PRO+	BR/A	SB	CS	SBR	FA	FR	G/POS	TPR
1896	Bal-N	15	58	8	14	3	0	0	5	3	5	.241	.302	.293	56	-4	4			.923	-5	/2-8,3-6	-0.7
1898	Bos-N	10	30	5	5	2	0	0	4	0		.167	.167	.233	14	-3	0			1.000	1	/S-4,2-4,O	-0.2
1899	Bal-N	136	523	96	172	22	16	3	73	16		.329	.368	.449	117	10	33			.895	-30	S-90,2-46/O	-1.0
1900	StL-N	126	497	78	149	26	10	1	72	25		.300	.347	.398	106	3	32			.927	-23	*2-116/S-7,3	-1.3
1901	Bal-A	115	442	78	145	20	21	2	93	18		.328	.365	.482	128	15	24			.851	-23	*S-112	0.1
1902	Was-A	119	483	82	145	33	9	9	90	14		.300	.329	.462	117	8	27			.912	-4	O-65,2-40,3/S	0.2
1903	Phi-N	100	400	53	128	27	7	3	63	14		.320	.352	.445	131	14	11			.940	3	*O-100	1.1
Total	7	621	2433	400	758	133	63	18	400	90	5	.312	.349	.440	116	43	131			.870	-80	S-215,2-214,0/3	-1.8

■ MICKEY KELIHER
Keliher, Maurice Michael b: 1/11/1890, Washington, D.C. d: 9/7/30, Washington, D.C. BL/TL, 6', 175 lbs. Deb: 9/9/11

YEAR	TM/L	G	AB	R	H	2B	3B	HR	RBI	BB	SO	AVG	OBP	SLG	PRO+	BR/A	SB	CS	SBR	FA	FR	G/POS	TPR
1911	Pit-N	3	7	0	0	0	0	0	0	0	5	.000	.000	.000	-96	-2	0			.875	-0	/1-3	-0.2
1912	Pit-N	2	0	1	0	0	0	0	0	0	0	—	—	—		0	0			.000	0	R	0.0
Total	2	5	7	1	0	0	0	0	0	0	5	.000	.000	.000	-96	-2	0			.875	-0	/1-3	-0.2

■ SKEETER KELL
Kell, Everett Lee b: 10/11/29, Swifton, Ark. BR/TR, 5'9", 160 lbs. Deb: 4/19/52 F

YEAR	TM/L	G	AB	R	H	2B	3B	HR	RBI	BB	SO	AVG	OBP	SLG	PRO+	BR/A	SB	CS	SBR	FA	FR	G/POS	TPR
1952	Phi-A	75	213	24	47	8	3	0	17	14	18	.221	.275	.286	53	-14	5	1	1	.963	-5	2-68	-1.5

■ GEORGE KELL
Kell, George Clyde b: 8/23/22, Swifton, Ark. BR/TR, 5'9", 175 lbs. Deb: 9/28/43 FH

YEAR	TM/L	G	AB	R	H	2B	3B	HR	RBI	BB	SO	AVG	OBP	SLG	PRO+	BR/A	SB	CS	SBR	FA	FR	G/POS	TPR
1943	Phi-A	1	5	1	1	0	1	0	1	0	0	.200	.200	.600	131	0	0	0	0	1.000	0	/3-1	0.0
1944	Phi-A	139	514	51	138	15	3	0	44	22	23	.268	.300	.309	75	-17	5	2	0	.958	-5	*3-139	-2.1
1945	Phi-A	147	567	50	154	30	3	4	56	27	15	.272	.306	.356	92	-8	2	0	1	**.964**	22	*3-147	2.0
1946	Phi-A	26	87	3	26	6	1	0	11	10	6	.299	.378	.391	116	2	0	0	0	.979	3	3-26	0.6
	Det-A	105	434	67	142	19	6	4	41	30	14	.327	.371	.440	119	10	3	2	-0	.984	5	*3-105/1-1	1.8
	Yr	131	521	70	168	25	10	4	52	40	20	.322	.372	.432	118	12	3	2	-0	**.983**	8	*3-131/1-1	2.4
1947	Det-A★	152	588	75	188	29	5	5	93	61	16	.320	.387	.412	118	16	9	11	-4	.962	18	*3-152	3.1
1948	Det-A☆	92	368	47	112	24	3	2	44	33	15	.304	.369	.402	102	1	2	2	-1	.969	-8	3-92	-0.8
1949	Det-A★	134	522	97	179	38	9	3	59	71	13	**.343**	.424	.467	136	28	7	5	-1	.975	1	*3-134	2.5
1950	Det-A★	157	641	114	218	56	6	8	101	66	18	.340	.403	.484	122	21	3	3	-1	**.982**	-3	*3-157	1.4
1951	Det-A★	147	598	92	191	36	3	2	59	61	18	.319	.386	.400	112	12	10	3	-1	**.960**	9	*3-147	2.0
1952	Det-A	39	152	11	45	8	0	1	17	15	13	.296	.359	.368	102	1	0	1	-1	.959	-2	3-39	-0.3
	Bos-A†	75	276	41	88	15	2	6	40	31	10	.319	.390	.453	124	9	0	1	-1	.959	-7	3-73	0.1
	Yr	114	428	52	133	23	2	7	57	46	23	.311	.379	.423	117	10	0	2	-1	.959	-9	3-112	-0.2
1953	Bos-A★	134	460	68	141	41	2	12	73	52	22	.307	.383	.483	126	17	5	2	0	**.972**	-14	*3-124/O-7	0.0
1954	Bos-A	26	93	15	24	3	0	0	10	10	3	.258	.361	.290	72	-3	0	0	0	.920	-3	3-25	-0.7
	Chi-A†	71	233	25	66	10	0	5	48	18	12	.283	.335	.391	95	-2	1	1	-0	.996	-11	1-32,3-31/O	-1.7
	Yr	97	326	40	90	13	0	5	58	33	15	.276	.343	.362	88	-5	1	1	-0	.936	-14	3-56,1-32/O	-2.4
1955	Chi-A	128	429	44	134	24	1	8	81	51	36	.312	.393	.429	118	12	2	2	-1	**.976**	-19	*3-105,1-24/O	-0.9
1956	Chi-A	21	80	7	25	5	0	1	11	8	6	.313	.375	.412	106	1	0	0	0	1.000	-4	3-18/1-4	-0.3
	Bal-A★	102	345	40	90	17	2	8	37	25	31	.261	.316	.391	93	-5	0	1	-1	.974	-7	*3-97/1-2,2	-1.1
	Yr	123	425	52	115	22	2	9	48	33	37	.271	.328	.395	96	-4	0	1	-1	**.978**	-11	*3-115/1-6,2	-1.4
1957	Bal-A★	99	310	28	92	9	0	9	44	25	16	.297	.353	.413	116	6	2	0	1	.979	-4	3-80,1-22	0.3
Total	15	1795	6702	881	2054	385	50	78	870	621	287	.306	.368	.414	111	100	51	36	-6	.969	-29	*3-1692/1-85,O2	5.9

■ DUKE KELLEHER
Kelleher, Albert Aloysius b: 9/30/1893, New York, N.Y. d: 9/28/47, Staten Island, N.Y. TR, Deb: 8/18/16

YEAR	TM/L	G	AB	R	H	2B	3B	HR	RBI	BB	SO	AVG	OBP	SLG	PRO+	BR/A	SB	CS	SBR	FA	FR	G/POS	TPR
1916	NY-N	1	0	0	0	0	0	0	0	0	0	—	—	—		0	0			.000	0	/C-1	0.0

■ FRANKIE KELLEHER
Kelleher, Francis Eugene b: 8/22/16, San Francisco, Cal d: 4/13/79, Stockton, Cal. BR/TR, 6'1", 195 lbs. Deb: 7/18/42

YEAR	TM/L	G	AB	R	H	2B	3B	HR	RBI	BB	SO	AVG	OBP	SLG	PRO+	BR/A	SB	CS	SBR	FA	FR	G/POS	TPR
1942	Cin-N	38	110	13	20	3	1	3	12	16	20	.182	.286	.309	74	-4	0			.986	0	O-30	-0.5
1943	Cin-N	9	10	1	0	0	0	0	0	2	0	.000	.167	.000	-51	-2	0			1.000	0	/O-1	-0.2
Total	2	47	120	14	20	3	1	3	12	18	20	.167	.275	.283	64	-6	0			.986	0	/O-31	-0.7

■ JOHN KELLEHER
Kelleher, John Patrick b: 9/13/1893, Brookline, Mass. d: 8/21/60, Brighton, Mass. BR/TR, 5'11", 150 lbs. Deb: 7/31/12

YEAR	TM/L	G	AB	R	H	2B	3B	HR	RBI	BB	SO	AVG	OBP	SLG	PRO+	BR/A	SB	CS	SBR	FA	FR	G/POS	TPR
1912	StL-N	8	12	0	4	1	0	0		0	2	.333	.333	.417	107	0	0			1.000	1	/3-3	0.1
1916	Bro-N	2	3	0	0	0	0	0	0	0	0	.000	.000	.000	-97	-1	0			1.000	-1	/S-1,3-1	-0.2
1921	Chi-N	95	301	31	93	11	7	4	47	16	16	.309	.346	.432	104	2	2	5	-2	.947	3	3-37,2-27,1S/O	0.6
1922	Chi-N	63	193	23	50	7	1	0	20	15	14	.259	.316	.306	60	-11	3	7	-3	.932	4	3-46/S-7,1	-0.6

YEAR	TM/L	G	AB	R	H	2B	3B	HR	RBI	BB	SO	AVG	OBP	SLG	PRO+	BR/A	SB	CS	SBR	FA	FR	G/POS	TPR
1923	Chi-N	66	193	27	59	10	0	6	21	14	9	.306	.353	.451	110	2	2	4	-2	.975	-7	1-22,S-14,3/2	-0.5
1924	Bos-N	1	1	0	0	0	0	0	0	0	1	.000	.000	.000	-99	-0	0	0	0	.000	0	H	0.0
Total	6	235	703	81	206	29	8	10	89	45	42	.293	.337	.400	92	-8	9	16		.924	-0	/3-98,1-37,2SO	-0.6

■ MICK KELLEHER
Kelleher, Michael Dennis b: 7/25/47, Seattle, Wash. BR/TR, 5'9", 176 lbs. Deb: 9/1/72 C

YEAR	TM/L	G	AB	R	H	2B	3B	HR	RBI	BB	SO	AVG	OBP	SLG	PRO+	BR/A	SB	CS	SBR	FA	FR	G/POS	TPR
1972	StL-N	23	63	5	10	2	1	0	1	6	15	.159	.232	.222	30	-6	0	0	0	.984	5	S-23	0.2
1973	StL-N	43	38	4	7	2	0	0	2	4	11	.184	.279	.237	44	-3	0	0	0	.955	9	S-42	0.8
1974	Hou-N	19	57	4	9	0	0	0	2	5	10	.158	.226	.158	9	-7	1	1	-0	.944	4	S-18	-0.1
1975	StL-N	7	4	0	0	0	0	0	0	0	1	.000	.000	.000	-97	-1	0	0	0	.909	2	/S-7	0.1
1976	Chi-N	124	337	28	77	12	1	0	22	15	32	.228	.266	.270	48	-23	0	4	-2	.980	12	*S-101,3-22/2	-0.3
1977	Chi-N	63	122	14	28	5	2	0	11	9	12	.230	.288	.303	53	-8	0	0	0	.976	18	2-40,S-14/3	1.3
1978	Chi-N	68	95	8	24	1	0	0	6	7	11	.253	.304	.263	53	-6	4	1	1	1.000	18	3-37,2-17,S	1.4
1979	Chi-N	73	142	14	36	4	1	0	10	7	9	.254	.288	.296	57	-8	2	0	1	.966	22	3-32,2-29,S	1.6
1980	Chi-N	105	96	12	14	1	0	0	4	9	17	.146	.219	.177	11	-11	1	3	-2	.974	25	2-57,3-31,S	1.5
1981	Det-A	61	77	10	17	4	0	0	6	7	10	.221	.286	.273	59	-4	0	0	0	.930	6	3-39,2-11/S	0.3
1982	Det-A	2	0	0	0	0	0	0	0	0	0	.000	.000	.000	-99	-0	0	0	0	1.000	-0	/2-1,3-1	-0.1
	Cal-A	34	49	9	8	1	0	0	1	5	5	.163	.255	.184	23	-5	1	1	-0	.965	7	S-28/3-6	0.3
	Yr	36	50	9	8	1	0	0	1	5	5	.160	.250	.180	20	-5	1	1	-0	.965	7	S-28/3-7,2	0.2
Total	11	622	1081	108	230	32	6	0	65	74	133	.213	.268	.253	43	-82	9	10	-3	.976	128	S-283,3-169,2	7.0

■ CHARLIE KELLER
Keller, Charles Ernest "King Kong" b: 9/12/16, Middletown, Md. d: 5/23/90, Frederick, Md. BL/TR, 5'10", 190 lbs. Deb: 4/22/39 F

YEAR	TM/L	G	AB	R	H	2B	3B	HR	RBI	BB	SO	AVG	OBP	SLG	PRO+	BR/A	SB	CS	SBR	FA	FR	G/POS	TPR
1939	*NY-A	111	398	87	133	21	6	11	83	81	49	.334	.447	.500	144	30	6	3	0	.969	-3	*O-105	2.2
1940	NY-A★	138	500	102	143	18	15	21	93	106	65	.286	.411	.508	142	34	8	2	1	.967	2	*O-136	2.8
1941	*NY-A★	140	507	102	151	24	10	33	122	102	65	.298	.416	.580	163	47	6	4	-1	.980	4	*O-137	4.1
1942	*NY-A	152	544	106	159	24	9	26	108	114	61	.292	.417	.513	164	49	14	2	3	.985	-0	*O-152	4.4
1943	*NY-A†	141	512	97	139	15	11	31	86	106	60	.271	.396	.525	167	45	7	5	-1	.994	4	*O-141	4.3
1945	NY-A	44	163	26	49	7	4	10	34	31	21	.301	.434	.577	178	16	0	2	-1	1.000	4	O-44	1.7
1946	NY-A	150	538	98	148	29	10	30	101	113	101	.275	.405	.533	158	44	1	4	-2	.979	-1	*O-149	3.5
1947	NY-A†	45	151	36	36	6	1	13	36	41	18	.238	.404	.550	165	14	0	0	0	.967	-2	O-43	1.0
1948	NY-A	83	247	41	66	15	2	6	44	41	25	.267	.373	.417	111	4	1	1	-0	.977	-5	O-66	-0.4
1949	NY-A	60	116	17	29	4	1	3	16	25	15	.250	.392	.379	104	2	2	0	1	.976	-6	O-31	-0.5
1950	Det-A	50	51	7	16	1	3	2	16	13	6	.314	.453	.569	155	5	0	0	0	1.000	-1	/O-6	0.3
1951	Det-A	54	62	6	16	2	0	3	21	11	12	.258	.370	.435	117	2	0	0	0	1.000	1	/O-8	0.2
1952	NY-A	2	1	0	0	0	0	0	0	0	1	.000	.000	.000	-99	-0	0	0	0	.000	-0	/O-1	-0.1
Total	13	1170	3790	725	1085	166	72	189	760	784	499	.286	.410	.518	152	293	45	23	-0	.980	-4	*O-1019	23.5

■ HAL KELLER
Keller, Harold Kefauver b: 7/7/27, Middletown, Md. BL/TR, 6'1", 200 lbs. Deb: 9/13/49 F

YEAR	TM/L	G	AB	R	H	2B	3B	HR	RBI	BB	SO	AVG	OBP	SLG	PRO+	BR/A	SB	CS	SBR	FA	FR	G/POS	TPR
1949	Was-A	3	3	1	1	0	0	0	0	0	0	.333	.333	.333	79	-0	0	0	0	.000	0	H	0.0
1950	Was-A	11	28	1	6	3	0	1	5	2	2	.214	.267	.429	79	-1	0	0	0	1.000	-2	/C-8	-0.2
1952	Was-A	11	23	2	4	2	0	0	0	1	1	.174	.208	.261	31	-2	0	0	0	.967	-0	C-11	-0.2
Total	3	25	54	4	11	5	0	1	5	3	3	.204	.246	.352	60	-4	0	0	0	.982	-2	/C-19	-0.4

■ FRANK KELLERT
Kellert, Frank William b: 7/6/24, Oklahoma City, Okla. d: 11/19/76, Oklahoma City, Okla. BR/TR, 6'2.5", 185 lbs. Deb: 4/18/53

YEAR	TM/L	G	AB	R	H	2B	3B	HR	RBI	BB	SO	AVG	OBP	SLG	PRO+	BR/A	SB	CS	SBR	FA	FR	G/POS	TPR
1953	StL-A	2	4	0	0	0	0	0	0	0	0	.000	.000	.000	-98	-1	0	0	0	1.000	-0	/1-1	-0.1
1954	Bal-A	10	34	3	7	2	0	0	1	5	4	.206	.308	.265	62	-2	0	0	0	1.000	-1	/1-9	-0.4
1955	*Bro-N	39	80	12	26	4	2	4	19	9	10	.325	.393	.575	149	2	0	1	0	.983	-0	1-22	0.4
1956	Chi-N	71	129	10	24	3	1	4	17	12	22	.186	.255	.318	54	-9	0	0	0	.991	3	1-27	-0.8
Total	4	122	247	25	57	9	3	8	37	26	36	.231	.304	.389	85	-6	0	1	-1	.990	1	/1-59	-0.9

■ RED KELLETT
Kellett, Donald Stafford b: 7/15/09, Brooklyn, N.Y. d: 11/3/70, Ft.Lauderdale, Fla. BR/TR, 6', 185 lbs. Deb: 7/2/34

YEAR	TM/L	G	AB	R	H	2B	3B	HR	RBI	BB	SO	AVG	OBP	SLG	PRO+	BR/A	SB	CS	SBR	FA	FR	G/POS	TPR
1934	Bos-A	9	9	0	0	0	0	0	0	1	5	.000	.100	.000	-68	-2	0	0	0	.778	1	/S-4,2-2,3	-0.1

■ JOE KELLEY
Kelley, Joseph James b: 12/9/1871, Cambridge, Mass. d: 8/14/43, Baltimore, Md. BR/TR, 5'11", 190 lbs. Deb: 7/27/1891 MCH

YEAR	TM/L	G	AB	R	H	2B	3B	HR	RBI	BB	SO	AVG	OBP	SLG	PRO+	BR/A	SB	CS	SBR	FA	FR	G/POS	TPR
1891	Bos-N	12	45	7	11	1	1	0	3	2	7	.244	.277	.311	63	-2	0			.852	-1	O-12	-0.3
1892	Pit-N	56	205	26	49	7	7	0	28	17	21	.239	.297	.341	93	-2	8			.919	2	O-56	-0.4
	Bal-N	10	33	3	7	0	0	0	4	4	7	.212	.316	.212	59	-1	2			.824	-3	O-10	-0.3
	Yr	66	238	29	56	7	7	0	32	21	28	.235	.300	.324	88	-4	10			.908	-1	O-66	-0.7
1893	Bal-N	125	502	120	153	27	16	9	76	77	44	.305	.401	.476	131	22	33			.940	7	*O-125	1.9
1894	*Bal-N	129	507	165	199	48	20	6	111	107	36	.393	.502	.602	158	53	46			.951	2	*O-129	3.5
1895	*Bal-N	131	518	148	189	26	19	10	134	77	29	.365	.456	.546	154	43	54			.964	11	*O-131	3.5
1896	*Bal-N	131	519	148	189	31	19	8	100	91	19	.364	.469	.543	164	53	87			.958	4	*O-131	3.8
1897	*Bal-N	131	505	113	183	31	9	5	118	70		.362	.447	.489	147	37	44			.959	-2	*O-122/S-3,3	2.2
1898	Bal-N	124	464	71	149	18	15	2	110	56		.321	.398	.438	137	23	24			.969	1	*O-122/3-2	1.4
1899	Bro-N	143	538	108	175	21	14	6	93	70		.325	.410	.450	133	26	31			.977	8	*O-143	2.0
1900	*Bro-N	121	454	90	145	23	17	6	91	53		.319	.398	.485	135	21	26			.959	1	O-77,1-32,3	1.4
1901	Bro-N	120	492	77	151	22	12	4	65	40		.307	.363	.425	124	15	18			.975	7	*1-115/3-5	1.9
1902	Bal-A	60	222	50	69	17	7	1	34	34		.311	.405	.464	134	11	12			.973	-0	O-48/3-8,1	0.7
	Cin-N	40	156	24	50	9	2	1	12	15		.321	.380	.423	135	6	3			.971	3	O-20,2-10/3SM	0.9
1903	Cin-N	105	383	85	121	22	4	3	45	51		.316	.402	.418	120	10	18			.947	-7	O-67,S-12,2/31M	0.1
1904	Cin-N	123	449	75	126	21	13	0	63	49		.281	.359	.385	119	10	15			.988	0	*1-117/O-6,2M	0.8
1905	Cin-N	90	321	43	89	7	6	1	37	27		.277	.346	.346	96	-2	8			.974	-3	O-85/1-2M	-0.1
1906	Cin-N	129	465	43	106	19	11	1	53	44		.228	.300	.323	90	-6	9			.966	-5	*O-122/1-3,S3	-1.9
1908	Bos-N	73	228	25	59	8	2	2	17	27		.259	.342	.338	119	6	5			.938	-4	O-51,1-11M	-0.1
Total	17	1853	7006	1421	2220	358	194	65	1194	911	163	.317	.402	.451	132	321	443			.955	20	*O-1465,1-291/32S	20.2

■ MIKE KELLEY
Kelley, Michael Joseph b: 12/2/1875, Templeton, Mass. d: 6/6/55, Minneapolis, Minn. BR/TR, 6', 210 lbs. Deb: 7/15/1899

YEAR	TM/L	G	AB	R	H	2B	3B	HR	RBI	BB	SO	AVG	OBP	SLG	PRO+	BR/A	SB	CS	SBR	FA	FR	G/POS	TPR
1899	Lou-N	76	282	48	68	11	2	3	33	21		.241	.307	.326	74	-10	6			.974	-0	1-76	-0.9

■ FRANK KELLIHER
Kelliher, Francis Mortimer "Yucka" b: 5/23/1899, Somerville, Mass. d: 3/4/56, Somerville, Mass. BL/TL, 5'9.5", 175 lbs. Deb: 9/19/19

YEAR	TM/L	G	AB	R	H	2B	3B	HR	RBI	BB	SO	AVG	OBP	SLG	PRO+	BR/A	SB	CS	SBR	FA	FR	G/POS	TPR
1919	Was-A	1	1	0	0	0	0	0	0	0	0	.000	.000	.000	-99	-0	0			.000	0	H	0.0

■ NATE KELLOGG
Kellogg, Nathaniel Monroe b: 9/28/1858, Rochester, Iowa d: 15, 5'9", 175 lbs. Deb: 8/27/1885

YEAR	TM/L	G	AB	R	H	2B	3B	HR	RBI	BB	SO	AVG	OBP	SLG	PRO+	BR/A	SB	CS	SBR	FA	FR	G/POS	TPR
1885	Det-N	5	17	4	2	1	0	0	0	1	5	.118	.167	.176	11	-2				.783	-2	/S-5	-0.3

■ BILL KELLOGG
Kellogg, William Dearstyne b: 5/25/1884, Albany, N.Y. d: 12/12/71, Baltimore, Md. BR/TR, 5'10", 153 lbs. Deb: 4/14/14

YEAR	TM/L	G	AB	R	H	2B	3B	HR	RBI	BB	SO	AVG	OBP	SLG	PRO+	BR/A	SB	CS	SBR	FA	FR	G/POS	TPR
1914	Cin-N	71	126	14	22	0	1	0	7	14	28	.175	.262	.190	34	-10	7			.988	-1	1-38,2-11/O3	-1.2

■ RED KELLY
Kelly, Albert Michael b: 11/15/1884, Union, Ill. d: 2/4/61, Zephyrhills, Fla. BR/TR, 5'11.5", 165 lbs. Deb: 6/18/10

YEAR	TM/L	G	AB	R	H	2B	3B	HR	RBI	BB	SO	AVG	OBP	SLG	PRO+	BR/A	SB	CS	SBR	FA	FR	G/POS	TPR
1910	Chi-A	14	45	6	7	0	1	0	1	7		.156	.296	.200	58	-2	0			1.000	-1	O-14	-0.4

■ CHARLIE KELLY
Kelly, Charles H. Deb: 6/14/1883

YEAR	TM/L	G	AB	R	H	2B	3B	HR	RBI	BB	SO	AVG	OBP	SLG	PRO+	BR/A	SB	CS	SBR	FA	FR	G/POS	TPR
1883	Phi-N	2	7	1	1	0	0	0			3	.143	.143	.429	71	-0				.700	0	/3-2	0.0
1886	Phi-a	1	3	0	0	0	0	0	0	0	0	.000	.000	.000	-99	-1	0			.333	-1	/S-1	-0.2
Total	2	3	10	1	1	0	0	0			3	.100	.100	.300						.700	-1	/3-2,S-1	-0.2

YEAR	TM/L	G	AB	R	H	2B	3B	HR	RBI	BB	SO	AVG	OBP	SLG	PRO+	BR/A	SB	CS	SBR	FA	FR	G/POS	TPR

■ **PAT KELLY**   Kelly, Dale Patrick b: 8/27/55, Santa Maria, Cal. BR/TR, 6'3", 210 lbs. Deb: 5/28/80

YEAR	TM/L	G	AB	R	H	2B	3B	HR	RBI	BB	SO	AVG	OBP	SLG	PRO+	BR/A	SB	CS	SBR	FA	FR	G/POS	TPR
1980	Tor-A	3	7	0	2	0	0	0	0	0	4	.286	.286	.286	55	-0	0	0	0	1.000	1	/C-3	0.1

■ **GEORGE KELLY**   Kelly, George Lange "Highpockets" b: 9/10/1895, San Francisco, Cal. d: 10/13/84, Burlingame, Cal. BR/TR, 6'4", 190 lbs. Deb: 8/18/15 FCH

YEAR	TM/L	G	AB	R	H	2B	3B	HR	RBI	BB	SO	AVG	OBP	SLG	PRO+	BR/A	SB	CS	SBR	FA	FR	G/POS	TPR
1915	NY-N	17	38	2	6	0	0	1	4	1	9	.158	.179	.237	27	-3	0	1	-1	.983	-0	/1-9,O-4	-0.5
1916	NY-N	49	76	4	12	2	1	0	3	6	24	.158	.220	.211	34	-6	1			.981	-3	1-13,O-12/3	-1.1
1917	NY-N	11	7	0	0	0	0	0	0	0	3	.000	.000	.000	-99	-2	0			1.000	-1	/O-4,P-1,12	-0.2
	Pit-N	8	23	2	2	0	1	0	1	9	.087	.125	.174	-9	-3	0			.971	-1	/1-8	-0.5
	Yr	19	30	2	2	0	1	0	0	1	12	.067	.097	.133	-30	-5	0			.972	-1	/1-9,O-4,P2	-0.7
1919	NY-N	32	107	12	31	6	2	1	14	3	15	.290	.315	.411	119	2	1			.994	-3	1-32	-0.2
1920	NY-N	155	590	69	157	22	11	11	94	41	92	.266	.320	.397	106	4	6	16	-8	.994	4	*1-155	-0.4
1921	*NY-N	149	587	95	181	42	9	23	122	40	73	.308	.356	.528	131	23	4	12	-6	.990	12	*1-149	2.5
1922	*NY-N	151	592	96	194	33	8	17	107	30	65	.328	.363	.497	119	14	12	3	2	.993	10	*1-151	1.8
1923	*NY-N	145	560	82	172	23	5	16	103	47	64	.307	.362	.452	115	11	14	7	0	.993	-6	*1-145	-0.2
1924	*NY-N	144	571	91	185	37	9	21	136	38	52	.324	.371	.531	143	32	7	2	1	.993	-1	*1-125,O-14/23	2.3
1925	NY-N	147	586	87	181	29	3	20	99	35	54	.309	.350	.471	112	9	5	2	0	.981	18	*2-108,1-25,O	2.4
1926	NY-N	136	499	70	151	24	4	13	80	36	52	.303	.352	.445	115	9	4			.993	8	*1-114,2-18	1.1
1927	Cin-N	61	222	27	60	16	4	5	21	11	23	.270	.308	.446	103	0	1			.992	-3	1-49,2-13/O	-0.6
1928	Cin-N	116	402	46	119	33	7	3	58	28	35	.296	.345	.435	104	2	2			.991	9	1-99,O-13	0.2
1929	Cin-N	147	577	73	169	45	9	5	103	33	61	.293	.332	.428	91	-10	7			.993	4	*1-147	-1.9
1930	Cin-N	51	188	18	54	10	1	5	35	7	20	.287	.313	.431	81	-6	1			.993	2	1-50	-0.9
	Chi-N	39	166	22	55	6	1	3	19	7	16	.331	.362	.434	91	-2	0			.998	4	1-39	-0.2
	Yr	90	354	40	109	16	2	8	54	14	36	.308	.336	.432	86	-9	1			.995	5	1-89	-1.1
1932	Bro-N	64	202	23	49	9	1	4	22	22	27	.243	.317	.356	82	-5	0			.984	-2	1-62/O-1	-1.1
Total	16	1622	5993	819	1778	337	76	148	1020	386	694	.297	.342	.452	110	68	65	43		.992	51	*1-1373,2-145/O3P	2.5

■ **PAT KELLY**   Kelly, Harold Patrick b: 7/30/44, Philadelphia, Pa. BL/TL, 6'1", 185 lbs. Deb: 9/6/67

YEAR	TM/L	G	AB	R	H	2B	3B	HR	RBI	BB	SO	AVG	OBP	SLG	PRO+	BR/A	SB	CS	SBR	FA	FR	G/POS	TPR
1967	Min-A	8	1	1	0	0	0	0	0	0	1	.000	.000	.000	-93	-0	0	0	0	.000	0	H	0.0
1968	Min-A	12	35	2	4	2	0	1	2	3	10	.114	.205	.257	37	-3	0	2	-1	.955	0	O-10	-0.5
1969	KC-A	112	417	61	110	20	4	8	32	49	70	.264	.348	.388	105	3	40	13	4	.980	12	*O-107	1.4
1970	KC-A	136	452	56	106	16	1	6	38	76	105	.235	.347	.314	84	-8	34	16	1	.963	11	*O-118	-0.2
1971	Chi-A	67	213	32	62	6	3	3	22	36	29	.291	.396	.390	119	7	14	9	-1	.991	-1	*O-61	0.4
1972	Chi-A	119	402	57	105	14	7	5	24	55	69	.261	.356	.368	113	8	32	9	4	.968	-2	*O-109	0.6
1973	Chi-A★	144	550	77	154	24	5	1	44	54	91	.280	.358	.347	96	-1	22	15	-2	.978	2	*O-141/D-1	-0.8
1974	Chi-A	122	424	60	119	16	3	4	21	46	58	.281	.354	.361	103	3	18	11	-1	.976	-5	D-67,O-53	-0.7
1975	Chi-A	133	471	73	129	21	7	9	45	58	69	.274	.356	.406	113	9	18	10	-1	.991	-3	O-115,D-14	0.1
1976	Chi-A	107	311	42	79	20	5	3	34	45	45	.254	.354	.386	116	7	15	7	0	.950	-4	D-63,O-26	0.2
1977	Bal-A	120	360	50	92	13	0	10	49	53	75	.256	.357	.375	106	5	25	7	3	.984	-14	*O-109/D-1	-1.0
1978	Bal-A	100	274	38	75	12	1	11	40	34	58	.274	.358	.445	133	12	10	8	-2	.969	-4	O-80/D-2	0.1
1979	*Bal-A	68	153	25	44	11	0	9	25	20	25	.288	.374	.536	147	10	4	5	-2	1.000	-3	O-24,D-18	0.4
1980	Bal-A	89	200	38	52	10	1	3	26	34	54	.260	.368	.365	102	2	16	2	4	1.000	-3	O-36,D-30	0.1
1981	Cle-A	48	75	8	16	4	0	1	6	14	19	.213	.337	.307	88	-1	2	4	-2	1.000	-2	D-18/O-8	-0.6
Total	15	1385	4338	620	1147	189	35	76	418	588	768	.264	.356	.377	107	54	250	118	4	.978	-15	O-997,D-214	-0.5

■ **JIM KELLY**   Kelly, James Robert (Also Played Under Real Name Of Robert John Taggert In 1918) b: 2/1/1884, Bloomfield, N.J. d: 4/10/61, Kingsport, Tenn. BL/TR, 5'10.5", 180 lbs. Deb: 4/26/14

YEAR	TM/L	G	AB	R	H	2B	3B	HR	RBI	BB	SO	AVG	OBP	SLG	PRO+	BR/A	SB	CS	SBR	FA	FR	G/POS	TPR
1914	Pit-N	32	44	4	10	2	1	0	3	2	3	.227	.261	.318	75	-2	0			1.000	0	/O-7	-0.2
1915	Pit-F	148	524	68	154	12	17	4	50	35	46	.294	.340	.405	100	-2	38			.952	14	*O-148	0.5
1918	Bos-N	35	146	19	48	1	4	0	4	9	9	.329	.376	.390	140	7	4			.955	1	O-35	0.6
Total	3	215	714	91	212	15	22	4	57	46	58	.297	.343	.396	106	3	42			.954	15	O-190	0.9

■ **TOM KELLY**   Kelly, Jay Thomas b: 8/15/50, Graceville, Minn. BL/TL, 5'11", 188 lbs. Deb: 5/11/75 M

YEAR	TM/L	G	AB	R	H	2B	3B	HR	RBI	BB	SO	AVG	OBP	SLG	PRO+	BR/A	SB	CS	SBR	FA	FR	G/POS	TPR
1975	Min-A	49	127	11	23	5	0	1	11	15	22	.181	.268	.244	44	-9	0	0	0	.985	1	1-43/O-2	-1.0

■ **JOHN KELLY**   Kelly, John B. b: 3/13/1879, Clifton Heights, Pa. d: 3/19/44, Baltimore, Md. 5'9", 165 lbs. Deb: 4/11/07

YEAR	TM/L	G	AB	R	H	2B	3B	HR	RBI	BB	SO	AVG	OBP	SLG	PRO+	BR/A	SB	CS	SBR	FA	FR	G/POS	TPR
1907	StL-N	53	197	12	37	5	0	0	6	13		.188	.245	.213	45	-12	7			.968	-1	O-52	-1.7

■ **JOHN KELLY**   Kelly, John Francis "Honest John" or "Father" b: 3/3/1859, Paterson, N.J. d: 4/13/08, Paterson, N.J. BR/TR, 6', 185 lbs. Deb: 5/1/1882

YEAR	TM/L	G	AB	R	H	2B	3B	HR	RBI	BB	SO	AVG	OBP	SLG	PRO+	BR/A	SB	CS	SBR	FA	FR	G/POS	TPR
1882	Cle-N	30	104	6	14	2	0	0		5	1	24	.135	.143	.154	-5	-12				.800	-14	C-30	-2.3
1883	Bal-a	48	202	18	46	9	2	0		3		.228	.239	.292	68	-7				.803	-17	C-38,O-13	-2.0
	Phi-N	1	3	0	0	0	0	0		0	2	.000	.000	.000	-99	-1				1.000	1	/O-1	0.0
1884	Cin-U	38	142	23	40	5	1	0		6		.282	.311	.352	74	-5				.865	-1	C-37/O-2	-0.3
	Was-U	4	14	1	5	1	0	0		0		.357	.357	.429	116	0				.967	1	/C-3,O-1	0.1
	Yr	42	156	24	45	6	1	1		6		.288	.315	.359	77	-5				.874	-1	C-40/O-3	-0.2
Total	3	121	465	48	105	17	3	1	5	10	26	.226	.242	.282	56	-25				.834	-31	C-108/O-17	-4.5

■ **KICK KELLY**   Kelly, John O. "Diamond John" b: 10/31/1856, New York, N.Y. d: 3/27/26, Malba, N.Y. 6'0.5", 185 lbs. Deb: 5/1/1879 MU

YEAR	TM/L	G	AB	R	H	2B	3B	HR	RBI	BB	SO	AVG	OBP	SLG	PRO+	BR/A	SB	CS	SBR	FA	FR	G/POS	TPR
1879	Syr-N	10	36	4	4	1	0	0		0	6	.111	.111	.139	-20	-4				.827	-1	/C-8,1-2	-0.5
	Tro-N	6	22	1	5	0	0	0		0	1	.227	.227	.227	54	-1				.789	-3	/C-3,O-2,3	-0.3
	Yr	16	58	5	9	1	0	0		0	7	.155	.155	.172	9	-5				.817	-4	C-11/1-2,O3	-0.8

■ **JOE KELLY**   Kelly, Joseph Henry b: 9/23/1886, Weir City, Kan. d: 8/16/77, St.Joseph, Mo. BR/TR, 5'10", 175 lbs. Deb: 4/14/14

YEAR	TM/L	G	AB	R	H	2B	3B	HR	RBI	BB	SO	AVG	OBP	SLG	PRO+	BR/A	SB	CS	SBR	FA	FR	G/POS	TPR
1914	Pit-N	141	508	47	113	19	9	1	48	39	59	.222	.283	.301	77	-15	21			.946	4	*O-139	-1.9
1916	Chi-N	54	169	18	43	7	1	2	15	9	16	.254	.296	.343	87	-3	10			.953	-1	O-46	-0.7
1917	Bos-N	116	445	41	99	9	8	3	36	26	45	.222	.268	.299	78	-12	21			.946	14	*O-116	-0.6
1918	Bos-N	47	155	20	36	2	4	0	15	6	12	.232	.265	.297	74	-5	12			.933	0	O-45	-0.8
1919	Bos-N	18	64	3	9	1	0	0	3	0	11	.141	.154	.156	-7	-8	2			.943	-1	O-16	-1.1
Total	5	376	1341	129	300	38	22	6	117	80	143	.224	.272	.298	75	-44	66			.945	16	O-362	-5.1

■ **JOE KELLY**   Kelly, Joseph James b: 4/23/1900, New York, N.Y. d: 11/24/67, Lynbrook, N.Y. BL/TL, 6', 180 lbs. Deb: 4/13/26

YEAR	TM/L	G	AB	R	H	2B	3B	HR	RBI	BB	SO	AVG	OBP	SLG	PRO+	BR/A	SB	CS	SBR	FA	FR	G/POS	TPR
1926	Chi-N	65	176	16	59	15	3	0	32	7	11	.335	.361	.455	117	4	0			.953	-5	O-39	-0.3
1928	Chi-N	32	52	3	11	1	0	1	7	1	3	.212	.255	.288	42	-4	0			.974	0	1-10	-0.5
Total	2	97	228	19	70	16	3	1	39	8	14	.307	.336	.417	100	-1	0			.953	-4	/O-39,1-10	-0.8

■ **KING KELLY**   Kelly, Michael Joseph b: 12/31/1857, Troy, N.Y. d: 11/8/1894, Boston, Mass. BR/TR, 5'10", 170 lbs. Deb: 5/1/1878 MH

YEAR	TM/L	G	AB	R	H	2B	3B	HR	RBI	BB	SO	AVG	OBP	SLG	PRO+	BR/A	SB	CS	SBR	FA	FR	G/POS	TPR
1878	Cin-N	60	237	29	67	7	1	0	27	7	7	.283	.303	.321	116	5				.765	-5	*O-47,C-17/3	1.3
1879	Cin-N	77	345	78	120	20	12	2	47	8	14	.348	.363	.493	188	32				.832	12	3-33,O-29,C/2	3.9
1880	Chi-N	84	344	72	100	17	9	1	60	12	22	.291	.315	.401	133	11				.779	-3	*O-64,C-17,3/S2P	0.7
1881	Chi-N	82	353	84	114	27	3	2	55	16	14	.323	.352	.433	139	15				.841	-0	*O-72,C-11/3	1.3
1882	Chi-N	84	377	81	115	37	4	1	55	10	27	.305	.323	.432	134	13				.810	-1	S-42,O-38,C/31	1.3
1883	Chi-N	98	428	92	109	28	10	3	61	16	35	.255	.282	.388	95	-4				.813	3	*O-82,C-38/23P	0.0
1884	Chi-N	108	452	120	160	28	5	13	95	46	24	.354	.414	.524	178	39				.794	-5	O-63,C-28,S3/1P	3.1
1885	*Chi-N	107	438	124	126	24	7	9	75	46	24	.288	.355	.456	135	14				.867	3	O-69,C-37/231	1.8
1886	*Chi-N	118	451	155	175	32	11	4	79	83	33	.388	.483	.534	182	44	53			.811	3	O-56,C-53/132S	4.5
1887	Bos-N	116	484	120	156	34	11	8	63	55	40	.322	.393	.488	143	29	84			.856	-11	O-61,2-30,C/PS3M	1.7

YEAR	TM/L	G	AB	R	H	2B	3B	HR	RBI	BB	SO	AVG	OBP	SLG	PRO+	BR/A	SB	CS	SBR	FA	FR	G/POS	TPR
1888	Bos-N	107	440	85	140	22	11	9	71	31	39	.318	.368	.480	166	32	56			.905	-3	C-76,O-34	3.4
1889	Bos-N	125	507	120	149	41	5	9	78	65	40	.294	.376	.448	122	14	68			.848	-9	*O-113,C-23	0.3
1890	Bos-P	89	340	83	111	18	6	4	66	52	22	.326	.419	.450	124	12	51			.915	-3	C-56,S-27/O13PM	1.1
1891	Cin-a	82	283	56	84	15	7	1	53	51	28	.297	.408	.410	123	9	22			.904	14	C-66/3-8,O21PS	2.3
	Bos-a	4	15	2	4	0	0	1	4	0	2	.267	.267	.467	111	-0	1			.950	-1	/C-4	0.0
	Yr	86	298	58	88	15	7	2	57	51	30	.295	.402	.413	123	9	23			.906	13	C-70/3-8,O21PS	2.3
	Bos-N	16	52	7	12	1	0	0	5	6	10	.231	.322	.250	60	-3	6			.844	-5	C-11/O-6	-0.6
1892	*Bos-N	78	281	40	53	7	0	2	41	39	31	.189	.287	.235	54	-16	24			.912	0	C-72/O-2,31P	-0.9
1893	NY-N	20	67	9	18	1	0	0	15	6	5	.269	.329	.284	63	-3	3			.895	-4	C-17/O-1	-0.5
Total	16	1455	5894	1357	1813	359	102	69	950	549	417	.308	.368	.438	136	241	368			.820	1	O-750,C-583/3S21P	24.7

■ MIKE KELLY
Kelly, Michael Raymond b: 6/2/70, Los Angeles, Cal. BR/TR, 6'4", 195 lbs. Deb: 4/5/94

YEAR	TM/L	G	AB	R	H	2B	3B	HR	RBI	BB	SO	AVG	OBP	SLG	PRO+	BR/A	SB	CS	SBR	FA	FR	G/POS	TPR
1994	Atl-N	30	77	14	21	10	1	2	9	2	17	.273	.300	.506	105	-5	0	0	1	-1	.962	-5	O-25	-0.5

■ PAT KELLY
Kelly, Patrick Franklin b: 10/14/67, Philadelphia, Pa. BR/TR, 6', 180 lbs. Deb: 5/20/91

YEAR	TM/L	G	AB	R	H	2B	3B	HR	RBI	BB	SO	AVG	OBP	SLG	PRO+	BR/A	SB	CS	SBR	FA	FR	G/POS	TPR
1991	NY-A	96	298	35	72	12	4	3	23	15	52	.242	.289	.339	73	-11	12	1	3	.926	7	3-80,2-19	-0.1
1992	NY-A	106	318	38	72	22	2	7	27	25	72	.226	.303	.374	89	-5	8	5	-1	.978	6	*2-101/D-1	0.3
1993	NY-A	127	406	49	111	24	1	7	51	24	68	.273	.322	.389	93	-5	14	11	-2	.978	9	*2-125	0.5
1994	NY-A	93	286	35	80	21	2	3	41	19	51	.280	.335	.399	95	-2	6	5	-1	.978	1	2-93	-0.1
Total	4	422	1308	157	335	79	9	20	142	83	243	.256	.313	.376	88	-23	40	22	-1	.978	23	2-338/3-80,D	0.6

■ SPEED KELLY
Kelly, Robert Brown b: 8/19/1884, Bryan, Ohio d: 5/6/49, Goshen, Ind. BR/TR, 6'2", 185 lbs. Deb: 7/13/09

YEAR	TM/L	G	AB	R	H	2B	3B	HR	RBI	BB	SO	AVG	OBP	SLG	PRO+	BR/A	SB	CS	SBR	FA	FR	G/POS	TPR
1909	Was-A	17	42	3	6	2	1	0	1	3		.143	.200	.238	40	-3	1			.852	-1	3-10/2-3,O	-0.5

■ ROBERTO KELLY
Kelly, Roberto Conrado (Gray) "Bobby" b: 10/1/64, Panama City, Pan. BR/TR, 6'4", 185 lbs. Deb: 7/29/87

YEAR	TM/L	G	AB	R	H	2B	3B	HR	RBI	BB	SO	AVG	OBP	SLG	PRO+	BR/A	SB	CS	SBR	FA	FR	G/POS	TPR
1987	NY-A	23	52	12	14	3	0	1	7	5	15	.269	.333	.385	91	-1	9	3	1	.955	-0	O-17/D-2	0.0
1988	NY-A	38	77	9	19	4	1	1	7	3	15	.247	.275	.364	78	-2	5	2	0	.986	-2	O-30/D-3	-0.4
1989	NY-A	137	441	65	133	18	3	9	48	41	89	.302	.369	.417	123	14	35	12	3	.984	7	*O-137	2.1
1990	NY-A	162	641	85	183	32	4	15	61	33	148	.285	.324	.418	106	3	42	17	2	.988	8	*O-160/D-1	1.0
1991	NY-A	126	486	68	130	22	2	20	69	45	77	.267	.336	.444	114	8	32	9	4	.986	7	*O-125	1.3
1992	NY-A★	152	580	81	158	31	2	10	66	41	96	.272	.325	.384	99	-2	28	5	5	.983	10	*O-146	1.0
1993	Cin-N★	78	320	44	102	17	3	9	35	17	43	.319	.357	.475	120	9	21	5	3	.995	5	O-77	1.5
1994	Cin-N	47	179	29	54	8	0	3	21	11	35	.302	.352	.397	96	-1	9	8	-2	.992	9	O-47	-0.1
	Atl-N	63	255	44	73	15	3	6	24	24	36	.286	.348	.439	103	1	10	3	1	.985	-2	O-63	-0.1
	Yr	110	434	73	127	23	3	9	45	35	71	.293	.350	.422	100	0	19	11	-1	.988	1	*O-110	-0.2
Total	8	826	3031	437	866	150	18	74	338	220	554	.286	.339	.420	108	29	191	64	19	.986	33	O-802/D-6	6.3

■ VAN KELLY
Kelly, Van Howard b: 3/18/46, Charlotte, N.C. BL/TR, 5'11", 180 lbs. Deb: 6/13/69

YEAR	TM/L	G	AB	R	H	2B	3B	HR	RBI	BB	SO	AVG	OBP	SLG	PRO+	BR/A	SB	CS	SBR	FA	FR	G/POS	TPR
1969	SD-N	73	209	16	51	7	1	3	15	12	24	.244	.285	.330	75	-8	0	1	-1	.971	-3	3-49,2-10	-1.2
1970	SD-N	38	89	9	15	3	0	1	9	15	21	.169	.288	.236	44	-7	0	1	-1	.971	1	3-27/2-1	-0.7
Total	2	111	298	25	66	10	1	4	24	27	45	.221	.286	.302	65	-14	0	2	-1	.971	-3	/3-76,2-11	-1.9

■ BILL KELLY
Kelly, William Henry "Big Bill" b: 12/28/1898, Syracuse, N.Y. d: 4/8/90, Syracuse, N.Y. BR/TR, 6', 190 lbs. Deb: 9/6/20

YEAR	TM/L	G	AB	R	H	2B	3B	HR	RBI	BB	SO	AVG	OBP	SLG	PRO+	BR/A	SB	CS	SBR	FA	FR	G/POS	TPR
1920	Phi-A	9	13	0	3	1	0	0	0	0	2	.231	.231	.308	41	-1	0	0	0	1.000	0	/1-2	-0.1
1928	Phi-N	23	71	6	12	1	1	0	5	7	20	.169	.244	.211	19	-8	0			.991	1	1-23	-0.9
Total	2	32	84	6	15	2	1	0	5	7	22	.179	.242	.226	22	-10	0	0		.992	2	1-25	-1.0

■ BILL KELLY
Kelly, William J. b: New York, N.Y. Deb: 5/4/1871

YEAR	TM/L	G	AB	R	H	2B	3B	HR	RBI	BB	SO	AVG	OBP	SLG	PRO+	BR/A	SB	CS	SBR	FA	FR	G/POS	TPR
1871	Kek-n	18	67	16	15	1	1	0	7	6	1	.224	.288	.269	60	-3	0					O-17/1-1	-0.2

■ BILLY KELLY
Kelly, William Joseph b: 5/1/1886, Baltimore, Md. d: 6/3/40, Detroit, Mich. BR/TR, 6'0.5", 183 lbs. Deb: 5/2/10

YEAR	TM/L	G	AB	R	H	2B	3B	HR	RBI	BB	SO	AVG	OBP	SLG	PRO+	BR/A	SB	CS	SBR	FA	FR	G/POS	TPR
1910	StL-N	2	2	1	0	0	0	0	0	1	0	.000	.333	.000	-1	-0	0			.000	0	/C-1	0.0
1911	Pit-N	6	8	0	1	0	0	0	0	0	2	.125	.125	.125	-29	-1	0			1.000	1	/C-1	0.0
1912	Pit-N	48	132	20	42	3	2	1	11	2	16	.318	.328	.394	99	-1	8			.990	-9	C-39	-0.6
1913	Pit-N	48	82	11	22	2	2	0	9	2	12	.268	.302	.341	87	-2	1			.960	-4	C-40	0.4
Total	4	104	224	32	65	5	4	1	20	5	30	.290	.312	.362	89	-4	9			.977	-5	/C-81	-0.2

■ BILLY KELSEY
Kelsey, George William b: 8/24/1881, Covington, Ohio d: 4/25/68, Springfield, Ohio BR/TR, 5'10", 150 lbs. Deb: 10/4/07

YEAR	TM/L	G	AB	R	H	2B	3B	HR	RBI	BB	SO	AVG	OBP	SLG	PRO+	BR/A	SB	CS	SBR	FA	FR	G/POS	TPR
1907	Pit-N	2	5	1	2	0	0	0	0	0	0	.400	.400	.400	149	0	0			1.000	-1	/C-2	0.0

■ KEN KELTNER
Keltner, Kenneth Frederick "Butch" b: 10/31/16, Milwaukee, Wis. d: 12/12/91, New Berlin, Wis. BR/TR, 6', 190 lbs. Deb: 10/2/37

YEAR	TM/L	G	AB	R	H	2B	3B	HR	RBI	BB	SO	AVG	OBP	SLG	PRO+	BR/A	SB	CS	SBR	FA	FR	G/POS	TPR
1937	Cle-A	1	1	0	0	0	0	0	0	1	0	.000	.000	.000	-99	-0	0	0	0	1.000	0	/3-1	0.0
1938	Cle-A	149	576	86	159	31	9	26	113	33	75	.276	.319	.497	103	-2	4	3	-1	.956	-10	*3-149	-0.9
1939	Cle-A	154	587	84	191	35	11	13	97	51	41	.325	.379	.489	125	20	6	6	-2	.974	-6	*3-154	2.4
1940	Cle-A★	149	543	67	138	24	10	15	77	51	56	.254	.322	.418	93	-7	10	5	0	.953	-6	*3-148	-0.9
1941	Cle-A★	149	581	83	156	31	13	23	84	51	56	.269	.330	.485	119	12	2	2	-1	.971	23	*3-149	3.5
1942	Cle-A★	152	624	72	179	34	4	6	78	20	36	.287	.312	.383	101	-3	4	3	-1	.945	16	*3-151	1.4
1943	Cle-A★	110	427	47	111	31	3	4	39	36	20	.260	.317	.375	109	3	2	2	-1	.969	-5	*3-107	1.0
1944	Cle-A★	149	573	74	169	41	9	13	91	53	29	.295	.355	.466	139	26	4	3	-1	.968	15	*3-149	4.4
1946	Cle-A★	116	398	47	96	17	1	13	45	30	38	.241	.294	.387	95	-5	0	3	-2	.965	-2	*3-112	-0.7
1947	Cle-A	151	541	49	139	29	3	11	76	59	45	.257	.331	.383	101	-0	5	4	-1	.972	-9	*3-150	-1.0
1948	*Cle-A★	153	558	91	166	24	4	31	119	89	52	.297	.395	.522	146	36	2	1	0	.969	-9	*3-153	3.3
1949	Cle-A	80	246	35	57	9	2	8	30	38	26	.232	.335	.382	91	-4	0	1	-1	.980	-1	3-69	-0.7
1950	Bos-A	13	28	2	9	2	0	0	2	3	6	.321	.387	.393	91	-0	0	0	0	.947	-2	/3-8,1-1	-0.2
Total	13	1526	5683	737	1570	308	69	163	852	514	480	.276	.338	.441	113	75	39	33	-8	.965	36	*3-1500/1-1	11.6

■ JOHN KELTY
Kelty, John James "Chief" b: 6/1866, Jersey City, N.J. 5'10", 175 lbs. Deb: 4/19/1890

YEAR	TM/L	G	AB	R	H	2B	3B	HR	RBI	BB	SO	AVG	OBP	SLG	PRO+	BR/A	SB	CS	SBR	FA	FR	G/POS	TPR
1890	Pit-N	59	207	24	49	10	1	1	27	22	42	.237	.322	.319	98	0	10			.898	-3	O-59	-0.4

■ BILL KEMMER
Kemmer, William Edward (b: William Edward Kemmerer) b: 11/15/1873, Pennsylvania d: 6/8/45, Washington, D.C. BR/TR, 6'2", Deb: 6/3/1895

YEAR	TM/L	G	AB	R	H	2B	3B	HR	RBI	BB	SO	AVG	OBP	SLG	PRO+	BR/A	SB	CS	SBR	FA	FR	G/POS	TPR
1895	Lou-N	11	38	5	7	0	0	1	3	2	4	.184	.225	.263	27	-4	0			.809	2	/3-9,1-2	-0.1

■ RUDY KEMMLER
Kemmler, Rudolph (b: Rudolph Kemler) b: 1860, Chicago, Ill. d: 6/20/09, Chicago, Ill. BR/TR, Deb: 7/26/1879

YEAR	TM/L	G	AB	R	H	2B	3B	HR	RBI	BB	SO	AVG	OBP	SLG	PRO+	BR/A	SB	CS	SBR	FA	FR	G/POS	TPR
1879	Pro-N	2	7	0	1	0	0	0	0	0		.143	.143	.143	-6	-1				.833	2	/C-2	0.1
1881	Cle-N	1	3	0	0	0	0	0	0	0	1	.000	.000	.000	-99	-1				1.000	1	/C-1	0.0
1882	Cin-a	3	11	0	1	1	0	0			1	.091	.091	.182	-10	-1				.909	-1	C-3,O-1	-0.2
	Pit-a	24	99	7	25	4	0	0			1	.253	.260	.293	90	-1				.920	3	C-23/O-1	0.2
	Yr	27	110	7	26	5	0	0			1	.236	.243	.282	79	-2				.919	1	C-26/O-2	0.0
1883	Col-a	84	318	27	66	6	2	0			13	.208	.239	.239	59	-13				.872	-9	*C-82/O-2	-1.5
1884	Col-a	61	211	28	42	3	3	0			15	.199	.252	.242	67	-7				.906	-19	C-58/1-2,O	-2.0
1885	Pit-a	18	64	2	13	2	1	0			2	.203	.239	.266	60	-3				.870	-3	C-18	-0.3
1886	StL-a	35	123	13	17	2	0	0			8	.138	.197	.154	10	-13	0			.914	4	C-32/1-3	-0.5
1889	Col-a	8	26	2	3	0	0	0			2	.115	.207	.115	-8	-4				.930	1	C-28	-0.2
Total	8	236	862	79	168	18	6	0	0	42	5	.195	.234	.230	52	-42	0			.894	-22	C-227/1-5,O	-4.4

YEAR	TM/L	G	AB	R	H	2B	3B	HR	RBI	BB	SO	AVG	OBP	SLG	PRO+	BR/A	SB	CS	SBR	FA	FR	G/POS	TPR

■ STEVE KEMP   Kemp, Steven F   b: 8/7/54, San Angelo, Tex.   BL/TL, 6′, 195 lbs.   Deb: 4/7/77

YEAR	TM/L	G	AB	R	H	2B	3B	HR	RBI	BB	SO	AVG	OBP	SLG	PRO+	BR/A	SB	CS	SBR	FA	FR	G/POS	TPR
1977	Det-A	151	552	75	142	29	4	18	88	71	93	.257	.347	.422	103	3	3	3	-1	.981	-3	*O-148	-0.7
1978	Det-A	159	582	75	161	18	4	15	79	97	87	.277	.381	.399	116	16	2	3	-1	.977	8	*O-157	1.6
1979	Det-A★	134	490	88	156	26	3	26	105	68	70	.318	.404	.543	148	34	5	6	-2	.976	6	*O-120,D-11	3.1
1980	Det-A	135	508	88	149	23	4	21	101	69	64	.293	.382	.474	130	22	5	1	1	.995	6	O-85,D-46	2.4
1981	Det-A	105	372	52	103	18	4	9	49	70	48	.277	.393	.419	129	17	9	3	1	.986	3	O-92,D-12	1.7
1982	Chi-A	160	580	91	166	23	1	19	98	89	83	.286	.384	.428	123	21	7	7	-2	.976	-7	*O-154/D-2	0.8
1983	NY-A	109	373	53	90	17	3	12	49	41	37	.241	.320	.399	100	-0	1	0	0	.987	1	*O-101/D-2	-0.2
1984	NY-A	94	313	37	91	12	1	7	41	40	54	.291	.373	.403	119	9	4	1	1	.972	-2	O-75,D-12	0.5
1985	Pit-N	92	236	19	59	13	2	2	21	25	54	.250	.322	.347	88	-4	1	0	0	1.000	-1	O-63	-0.6
1986	Pit-N	13	16	1	3	0	0	1	1	4	6	.188	.350	.375	98	0	1	0	0	1.000	0	/O-4	0.1
1988	Tex-A	16	36	2	8	0	0	0	2	2	9	.222	.263	.222	36	-3	1	0	0	1.000	-2	/O-5,1-1,D	-0.4
Total	11	1168	4058	581	1128	179	25	130	634	576	605	.278	.370	.431	119	115	39	24	-3	.982	10	*O-1004/D-92,1	8.3

■ FRED KENDALL   Kendall, Fred Lyn   b: 1/31/49, Torrance, Cal.   BR/TR, 6′1″, 190 lbs.   Deb: 9/8/69

YEAR	TM/L	G	AB	R	H	2B	3B	HR	RBI	BB	SO	AVG	OBP	SLG	PRO+	BR/A	SB	CS	SBR	FA	FR	G/POS	TPR
1969	SD-N	10	26	2	4	0	0	0	2	5	.154	.214	.154	5	-3	0	0	0	1.000	-1	/C-9	-0.4
1970	SD-N	4	9	0	0	0	0	0	1	0	0	.000	.000	.000	-99	-3	0	0	0	1.000	-1	/C-2,1-1,O	-0.4
1971	SD-N	49	111	2	19	1	0	1	7	7	16	.171	.220	.207	23	-11	1	0	0	1.000	1	C-39/1-1,3	-1.0
1972	SD-N	91	273	18	59	3	4	6	18	11	42	.216	.249	.322	66	-14	0	0	0	.995	3	C-82/1-1	-0.9
1973	SD-N	145	507	39	143	22	3	10	59	30	35	.282	.323	.396	107	3	3	1	0	.984	-17	*C-138	-0.8
1974	SD-N	141	424	32	98	15	2	8	45	49	33	.231	.311	.333	84	-10	0	1	-1	.983	-23	*C-133	-3.0
1975	SD-N	103	286	16	57	12	1	0	24	26	28	.199	.266	.248	46	-21	0	1	-1	.977	-8	C-85	-2.7
1976	SD-N	146	456	30	112	17	0	2	39	36	42	.246	.305	.296	77	-14	1	1	-0	.994	-19	*C-146	-3.1
1977	Cle-A	103	317	18	79	13	1	3	39	16	27	.249	.287	.325	69	-14	0	1	-1	.991	-13	*C-102/D-1	-2.5
1978	Bos-A	20	41	3	8	1	0	0	4	1	5	.195	.214	.220	20	-4	0	0	0	1.000	1	1-13/C-5,D	-0.2
1979	SD-N	46	102	8	17	2	0	1	6	11	7	.167	.248	.216	29	-10	0	0	0	.977	5	C-40/1-2	-0.5
1980	SD-N	19	24	2	7	0	0	0	2	0	3	.292	.292	.292	67	-1	0	0	0	.938	0	C-14/1-1	-0.1
Total	12	877	2576	170	603	86	11	31	244	189	240	.234	.288	.312	72	-102	5	5	-2	.987	-71	C-795/1-19,D30	-15.6

■ AL KENDERS   Kenders, Albert Daniel George   b: 4/4/37, Barrington, N.J.   BR/TR, 6′, 185 lbs.   Deb: 8/14/61

YEAR	TM/L	G	AB	R	H	2B	3B	HR	RBI	BB	SO	AVG	OBP	SLG	PRO+	BR/A	SB	CS	SBR	FA	FR	G/POS	TPR
1961	Phi-N	10	23	0	4	1	0	0	1	1	0	.174	.208	.217	13	-3	0	0	0	1.000	-2	C-10	-0.4

■ EDDIE KENNA   Kenna, Edward Aloysius "Scrap Iron"   b: 9/30/1897, San Francisco, Cal.   d: 8/21/72, San Francisco, Cal   BR/TR, 5′7.5″, 150 lbs.   Deb: 6/2/28

YEAR	TM/L	G	AB	R	H	2B	3B	HR	RBI	BB	SO	AVG	OBP	SLG	PRO+	BR/A	SB	CS	SBR	FA	FR	G/POS	TPR
1928	Was-A	41	118	14	35	4	2	1	20	14	8	.297	.376	.390	102	1	5	-3	.942	-3	C-33	-0.2

■ ED KENNEDY   Kennedy, Edward   b: 4/1/1856, Carbondale, Pa.   d: 5/20/05, New York, N.Y.   Deb: 5/1/1883

YEAR	TM/L	G	AB	R	H	2B	3B	HR	RBI	BB	SO	AVG	OBP	SLG	PRO+	BR/A	SB	CS	SBR	FA	FR	G/POS	TPR
1883	NY-a	94	356	57	78	6	7	2			17	.219	.255	.292	72	-11				.884	-7	*O-94	-1.7
1884	*NY-a	103	378	49	72	6	4	1			16	.190	.225	.225	49	-20				.915	6	*O-100/S-1,2C	-1.5
1885	NY-a	96	349	35	71	8	4	2			12	.203	.238	.266	64	-13				.841	2	*O-96	-1.3
1886	Bro-a	6	22	1	4	0	0	0			2	.182	.250	.182	36	-2	1			.909	-1	/O-6	-0.2
Total	4	299	1105	142	225	20	13	5			47	.204	.239	.259	61	-47	1			.878	-0	O-296/C-1,2S	-4.7

■ JIM KENNEDY   Kennedy, James Earl   b: 11/1/46, Tulsa, Okla.   BL/TR, 5′9″, 160 lbs.   Deb: 6/14/70   F

YEAR	TM/L	G	AB	R	H	2B	3B	HR	RBI	BB	SO	AVG	OBP	SLG	PRO+	BR/A	SB	CS	SBR	FA	FR	G/POS	TPR
1970	StL-N	12	24	1	3	0	0	0	0	0	0	.125	.125	.125	-32	-4	0	0	0	.909	1	/S-7,2-5	-0.3

■ JOHN KENNEDY   Kennedy, John Edward   b: 5/29/41, Chicago, Ill.   BR/TR, 6′, 185 lbs.   Deb: 9/5/62

YEAR	TM/L	G	AB	R	H	2B	3B	HR	RBI	BB	SO	AVG	OBP	SLG	PRO+	BR/A	SB	CS	SBR	FA	FR	G/POS	TPR
1962	Was-A	14	42	6	11	0	1	1	2	2	7	.262	.295	.381	81	-1	0	1	-1	.974	0	/S-9,3-2	-0.1
1963	Was-A	36	62	3	11	1	1	0	4	6	22	.177	.261	.226	38	-5	2	0	1	.954	6	3-26/S-2	0.2
1964	Was-A	148	482	55	111	16	4	7	35	29	119	.230	.281	.324	68	-21	3	3	-1	.941	9	*3-106,S-49/2	-1.2
1965	*LA-N	104	105	12	18	3	0	1	5	8	33	.171	.243	.229	36	-9	1	0	0	.971	11	3-95/S-5	0.2
1966	*LA-N	125	274	15	55	9	2	3	24	10	64	.201	.242	.281	49	-20	1	2	-1	.965	13	3-87/S-28,2	-0.6
1967	NY-A	78	179	22	35	4	0	1	17	17	35	.196	.269	.235	52	-10	2	1	0	.915	7	S-36,3-34/2	-0.1
1969	Sea-A	61	128	18	30	3	1	4	14	14	25	.234	.315	.367	92	-2	4	0	1	.916	-4	S-33,3-23	-0.2
1970	Mil-A	25	55	8	14	2	0	2	6	5	9	.255	.317	.400	96	-0	0	1	-1	.921	-1	2-16/3-5,S1	-0.1
	Bos-A	43	129	15	33	7	1	4	17	6	14	.256	.294	.419	88	-2	0	0	0	.960	3	3-33/2-2	0.0
	Yr	68	184	23	47	9	1	6	23	11	23	.255	.301	.413	91	-3	0	1	-1	.962	1	3-38,2-18/S1	-0.1
1971	Bos-A	74	272	41	75	12	5	5	22	14	42	.276	.321	.412	99	-1	1	1	-0	.974	-18	2-37,S-33/3	-1.3
1972	Bos-A	71	212	22	52	11	1	2	22	18	40	.245	.313	.335	88	-3	0	0	0	.962	-6	2-32,S-27,3	-0.5
1973	Bos-A	67	155	17	28	9	1	1	16	12	45	.181	.249	.271	44	-12	0	0	0	.980	7	2-31,3-24/D	-0.3
1974	Bos-A	10	15	3	2	0	0	1	1	1	6	.133	.188	.333	44	-1	0	0	0	.778	-1	/2-6,3-4	0.0
Total	12	856	2110	237	475	77	17	32	185	142	461	.225	.282	.323	70	-87	14	10	-2	.953	26	3-455,S-226,2/D1	-4.2

■ JOHN KENNEDY   Kennedy, John Irvin   b: 10/12/26, Jacksonville, Fla.   BR/TR, 5′10″, 175 lbs.   Deb: 4/22/57

YEAR	TM/L	G	AB	R	H	2B	3B	HR	RBI	BB	SO	AVG	OBP	SLG	PRO+	BR/A	SB	CS	SBR	FA	FR	G/POS	TPR
1957	Phi-N	5	2	1	0	0	0	0	0	0	1	.000	.000	.000	-99	-1	0	0	0	.500	0	/3-2	0.0

■ JUNIOR KENNEDY   Kennedy, Junior Raymond   b: 8/9/50, Fort Gibson, Okla.   BR/TR, 6′, 185 lbs.   Deb: 8/9/74   F

YEAR	TM/L	G	AB	R	H	2B	3B	HR	RBI	BB	SO	AVG	OBP	SLG	PRO+	BR/A	SB	CS	SBR	FA	FR	G/POS	TPR
1974	Cin-N	22	19	2	3	0	0	0	6	6	4	.158	.360	.158	49	-1	0	0	0	.909	-1	2-17/3-5	-0.2
1978	Cin-N	89	157	22	40	2	2	0	11	31	28	.255	.381	.293	91	-0	4	1	1	.979	13	2-71/3-4	1.7
1979	Cin-N	83	220	29	60	7	0	1	17	28	31	.273	.355	.318	85	-4	4	3	-1	.980	-1	2-59/S-5,3	-0.1
1980	Cin-N	104	337	31	88	16	3	1	34	36	34	.261	.332	.335	87	-5	3	1	0	.988	2	*2-103	0.3
1981	Cin-N	27	44	5	11	1	0	0	5	1	5	.250	.267	.273	52	-3	0	0	0	.980	2	2-16/3-5	0.0
1982	Chi-N	105	242	22	53	3	1	2	25	21	34	.219	.281	.264	52	-15	1	4	-2	.978	13	2-71,S-28/3	0.0
1983	Chi-N	17	22	3	3	0	0	0	3	1	6	.136	.174	.136	-12	-3	0	0	0	1.000	2	/2-7,3-4,S	-0.1
Total	7	447	1041	114	258	29	6	4	95	124	142	.248	.328	.299	75	-31	12	9	-2	.982	30	2-344/S-34,3	1.6

■ DOC KENNEDY   Kennedy, Michael Joseph   b: 8/11/1853, Brooklyn, N.Y.   d: 5/23/20, Grove, N.Y.   BR/TR, 5′9.5″, 185 lbs.   Deb: 5/1/1879

YEAR	TM/L	G	AB	R	H	2B	3B	HR	RBI	BB	SO	AVG	OBP	SLG	PRO+	BR/A	SB	CS	SBR	FA	FR	G/POS	TPR
1879	Cle-N	49	193	19	56	8	2	1	18	2	10	.290	.297	.368	119	4				.891	3	C-46/1-4	0.8
1880	Cle-N	66	250	26	50	10	1	0	18	5	12	.200	.216	.248	58	-10				.899	-1	*C-65/O-2	-1.0
1881	Cle-N	39	150	19	47	7	1	0	15	5	13	.313	.335	.373	129	5				.920	5	C-35/O-3,3	1.0
1882	Cle-N	1	3	0	1	0	0	0	0	1	0	.333	.500	.333	180	0				.857	3	/C-1	0.3
1883	Buf-N	5	19	3	6	0	0	0	2	2	2	.316	.381	.316	113	0				.583	-2	/O-4,1-1	-0.1
Total	5	160	615	67	160	25	4	1	53	15	37	.260	.278	.319	98	-1				.901	9	C-147/O-9,13	1.0

■ RAY KENNEDY   Kennedy, Raymond Lincoln   b: 5/19/1895, Pittsburgh, Pa.   d: 1/18/69, Casselberry, Fla.   BR/TR, 5′9″, 165 lbs.   Deb: 9/8/16

YEAR	TM/L	G	AB	R	H	2B	3B	HR	RBI	BB	SO	AVG	OBP	SLG	PRO+	BR/A	SB	CS	SBR	FA	FR	G/POS	TPR
1916	StL-A	1	1	0	0	0	0	0	0	0	0	.000	.000	.000	-99	-0	0	0	0	.000	0	H	0.0

■ BOB KENNEDY   Kennedy, Robert Daniel   b: 8/18/20, Chicago, Ill.   BR/TR, 6′2″, 193 lbs.   Deb: 9/14/39   FMC

YEAR	TM/L	G	AB	R	H	2B	3B	HR	RBI	BB	SO	AVG	OBP	SLG	PRO+	BR/A	SB	CS	SBR	FA	FR	G/POS	TPR
1939	Chi-A	3	8	0	2	0	0	0	1	0	0	.250	.250	.250	27	-1	0	0	0	.750	-1	/3-2	-0.2
1940	Chi-A	154	606	74	153	23	3	3	52	42	58	.252	.301	.315	59	-36	3	7	-3	.938	-3	*3-154	-3.8
1941	Chi-A	76	257	16	53	9	3	1	29	17	23	.206	.255	.276	41	-22	5	5	-0	.934	3	3-71	-1.7
1942	Chi-A	113	412	37	95	18	5	0	38	22	41	.231	.270	.299	61	-22	11	7	-1	.956	4	3-96,O-16	-1.9
1946	Chi-A	113	411	43	106	13	5	3	34	24	42	.258	.300	.350	85	-10	6	8	-3	.965	4	O-75,3-29	-1.2
1947	Chi-A	115	428	47	112	19	3	6	48	18	38	.262	.291	.362	84	-11	3	4	-2	.968	-3	*O-106/3-1	-2.2
1948	Chi-A	30	113	4	28	9	1	0	14	4	17	.248	.274	.336	64	-6	2	0	0	.970	-0	O-30	-0.9
	*Cle-A	66	73	10	22	3	2	0	6	4	9	.301	.338	.397	98	-1	0	0	0	1.000	-13	O-50/2-8,2,1	-1.4

YEAR	TM/L	G	AB	R	H	2B	3B	HR	RBI	BB	SO	AVG	OBP	SLG	PRO+	BR/A	SB	CS	SBR	FA	FR	G/POS	TPR
	Yr	96	186	14	50	11	3	0	19	8	23	.269	.299	.360	77	-7	0	2	-1	.981	-13	O-80/2-2,1	-2.3
1949	Cle-A	121	424	49	117	23	5	9	57	37	40	.276	.334	.417	100	-2	5	5	-2	.990	3	O-98,3-21	-0.6
1950	Cle-A	146	540	79	157	27	5	9	54	53	31	.291	.355	.409	99	-2	3	4	-2	.987	1	*O-144	-0.8
1951	Cle-A	108	321	30	79	15	4	7	29	34	33	.246	.320	.383	95	-3	4	2	0	.968	-1	*O-106	-0.7
1952	Cle-A	22	40	6	12	3	1	0	12	9	5	.300	.429	.425	148	3	1	0	0	1.000	0	O-13/3-3	0.3
1953	Cle-A	100	161	22	38	5	0	3	22	19	11	.236	.320	.323	76	-5	0	2	-1	1.000	-21	O-89	-3.0
1954	Cle-A	1	0	0	0	0	0	0	0	0	0	—	—	—	—	0	0	0	0	.000	-0	/O-1	0.0
	Bal-A	106	323	37	81	13	2	6	45	28	43	.251	.311	.359	90	-6	2	1	0	.938	-6	3-71,O-21	-1.5
	Yr	107	323	37	81	13	2	6	45	28	43	.251	.311	.359	90	-6	2	1	0	.938	-7	3-71,O-22	-1.5
1955	Bal-A	26	70	10	10	1	0	0	5	10	10	.143	.250	.157	12	-9	0	1	-1	1.000	-1	O-14/1-6,3	-1.1
	Chi-A	83	214	28	65	10	2	9	43	16	16	.304	.352	.495	122	6	0	2	-1	.938	-13	3-55,O-20/1	-0.9
	Yr	109	284	38	75	11	2	9	48	26	26	.264	.326	.412	97	-2	0	3	-2	.938	-13	3-56,O-34/1	-2.0
1956	Chi-A	8	13	0	1	0	0	0	0	2	4	.077	.200	.077	-24	-2	0	0	0	1.000	-1	/3-6	-0.3
	Det-A	69	177	17	41	5	0	4	22	24	19	.232	.330	.328	74	-6	2	2	-1	.931	-3	O-29,3-27	-1.0
	Yr	77	190	17	42	5	0	4	22	26	23	.221	.321	.311	67	-9	2	2	-1	.909	-4	3-33,O-29	-1.3
1957	Chi-A	4	2	0	0	0	0	0	0	0	1	.000	.000	.000	-99	-1	0	0	0	.000	0	H	-0.1
	Bro-N	19	31	5	4	1	0	1	4	1	5	.129	.156	.258	8	-4	0	0	0	1.000	-4	/O-9,3-3	-0.9
Total	16	1483	4624	514	1176	196	41	63	514	364	443	.254	.310	.355	80	-142	45	50	-17	.978	-55	O-821,3-540/12	-23.9

■ SNAPPER KENNEDY
Kennedy, Sherman Montgomery b: 11/1/1878, Conneaut, Ohio d: 8/15/45, Pasadena, Tex. BB/TR, 5'10", 165 lbs. Deb: 5/1/02

YEAR	TM/L	G	AB	R	H	2B	3B	HR	RBI	BB	SO	AVG	OBP	SLG	PRO+	BR/A	SB	CS	SBR	FA	FR	G/POS	TPR
1902	Chi-N	1	5	0	0	0	0	0	0	0		.000	.000	.000	-99	-1	0			1.000	1	/O-1	-0.1

■ TERRY KENNEDY
Kennedy, Terrence Edward b: 6/4/56, Euclid, Ohio BL/TR, 6'3", 220 lbs. Deb: 9/4/78 F

YEAR	TM/L	G	AB	R	H	2B	3B	HR	RBI	BB	SO	AVG	OBP	SLG	PRO+	BR/A	SB	CS	SBR	FA	FR	G/POS	TPR
1978	StL-N	10	29	0	5	0	0	0	2	4	3	.172	.273	.172	27	-3	0	0	0	.980	0	C-10	-0.3
1979	StL-N	33	109	11	31	7	0	2	17	6	20	.284	.322	.404	96	-1	0	0	0	.993	-4	C-32	-0.4
1980	StL-N	84	248	28	63	12	3	4	34	28	34	.254	.330	.375	93	-2	0	0	0	.967	-3	C-41,O-28	-0.5
1981	SD-N★	101	382	32	115	24	1	2	41	22	53	.301	.342	.385	114	6	0	2	-1	.964	-8	*C-100	0.0
1982	SD-N	153	562	75	166	42	1	21	97	26	91	.295	.332	.486	133	21	1	0	0	.990	-18	*C-139,1-12	0.8
1983	SD-N☆	149	549	47	156	27	2	17	98	51	89	.284	.347	.434	119	13	1	3	-2	.986	-8	*C-143/1-4	1.0
1984	*SD-N	148	530	54	127	16	1	14	57	33	99	.240	.287	.353	79	-16	1	2	-1	.982	-14	*C-147	-2.6
1985	SD-N★	143	532	54	139	27	1	10	74	31	102	.261	.302	.372	89	-9	0	0	0	.986	0	*C-140/1-5	-0.2
1986	SD-N	141	432	46	114	22	1	12	57	37	74	.264	.325	.403	102	0	0	3	-2	.990	-0	*C-123	0.6
1987	Bal-A★	143	512	51	128	13	1	18	62	35	112	.250	.299	.385	82	-14	1	0	0	.993	-16	*C-142	-1.9
1988	Bal-A	85	265	20	60	10	0	3	16	15	54	.226	.270	.298	61	-14	0	0	0	.994	-8	C-79	-1.7
1989	*SF-N	125	355	19	85	15	0	5	34	35	56	.239	.308	.324	83	-8	1	2	-1	.986	-3	*C-121/1-2	-0.7
1990	SF-N	107	303	25	84	22	0	2	26	31	38	.277	.344	.370	100	0	1	2	-1	.991	-12	*C-103	-0.8
1991	SF-N	69	171	12	40	7	1	3	13	11	31	.234	.284	.339	77	-6	0	0	0	.978	-3	C-58/1-2	-0.7
Total	14	1491	4979	474	1313	244	12	113	628	365	855	.264	.316	.386	97	-31	6	15	-7	.985	-100	*C-1378/O-28,1	-7.4

■ ED KENNEDY
Kennedy, William Edward b: 4/5/1861, Bellevue, Ky. d: 12/22/12, Cheyenne, Wyoming BR/TR, 5'7", 160 lbs. Deb: 5/17/1884

YEAR	TM/L	G	AB	R	H	2B	3B	HR	RBI	BB	SO	AVG	OBP	SLG	PRO+	BR/A	SB	CS	SBR	FA	FR	G/POS	TPR
1884	Cin-U	13	48	6	10	1	1	0		1		.208	.224	.271	31	-5				.857	0	/3-8,S-4,O	-0.4

■ JERRY KENNEY
Kenney, Gerald T b: 6/30/45, St.Louis, Mo. BL/TR, 6'1", 170 lbs. Deb: 9/5/67

YEAR	TM/L	G	AB	R	H	2B	3B	HR	RBI	BB	SO	AVG	OBP	SLG	PRO+	BR/A	SB	CS	SBR	FA	FR	G/POS	TPR
1967	NY-A	20	58	4	18	2	0	1	5	10	8	.310	.412	.397	145	4	2	1	0	.952	-4	S-18	0.2
1969	NY-A	130	447	49	115	14	2	2	34	48	36	.257	.331	.311	83	-9	25	14	-1	.975	11	3-83,O-31,S	0.1
1970	NY-A	140	404	46	78	10	7	4	35	52	44	.193	.285	.282	60	-22	20	6	2	.960	15	*3-135/2-2	-0.6
1971	NY-A	120	325	50	85	10	3	0	20	56	38	.262	.372	.311	101	3	9	8	-2	.953	11	*3-109/S-5,1	1.2
1972	NY-A	50	119	16	25	2	0	0	7	16	13	.210	.304	.227	62	-5	3	0	1	.969	5	S-45/3-1	0.6
1973	Cle-A	5	16	0	4	0	1	0	2	2	0	.250	.333	.375	97	-0	0	0	0	1.000	-2	/2-5	-0.1
Total	6	465	1369	165	325	38	13	7	103	184	139	.237	.329	.299	82	-30	59	29	0	.962	36	3-328/S-78,021	1.4

■ JOHN KENNEY
Kenney, John Deb: 5/2/1872

YEAR	TM/L	G	AB	R	H	2B	3B	HR	RBI	BB	SO	AVG	OBP	SLG	PRO+	BR/A	SB	CS	SBR	FA	FR	G/POS	TPR
1872	Atl-n	5	19	0	0	0	0	0	1	0	1	.000	.000	.000	-85	-4						/2-3,O-2	-0.3

■ JEFF KENT
Kent, Jeffrey Franklin b: 3/7/68, Bellflower, Cal. BR/TR, 6'1", 185 lbs. Deb: 4/12/92

YEAR	TM/L	G	AB	R	H	2B	3B	HR	RBI	BB	SO	AVG	OBP	SLG	PRO+	BR/A	SB	CS	SBR	FA	FR	G/POS	TPR
1992	Tor-A	65	192	36	46	13	1	8	35	20	47	.240	.330	.443	110	2	2	1	0	.915	-3	3-49,2-17/1	-0.1
	NY-N	37	113	16	27	8	1	3	15	7	29	.239	.289	.407	97	-1	0	2	-1	.980	8	2-34/3-1,S	0.7
1993	NY-N	140	496	65	134	24	0	21	80	30	88	.270	.322	.446	104	2	4	4	-1	.969	-19	*2-127,3-12/S	-1.5
1994	NY-N	107	415	53	121	24	5	14	68	23	84	.292	.344	.475	110	5	1	4	-2	.976	0	*2-107	0.6
Total	3	349	1216	170	328	69	7	46	198	80	248	.270	.328	.451	106	8	7	11	-5	.974	-14	2-285/3-62,S1	-0.3

■ DICK KENWORTHY
Kenworthy, Richard Lee b: 4/1/41, Red Oak, Iowa BR/TR, 5'9", 170 lbs. Deb: 9/8/62

YEAR	TM/L	G	AB	R	H	2B	3B	HR	RBI	BB	SO	AVG	OBP	SLG	PRO+	BR/A	SB	CS	SBR	FA	FR	G/POS	TPR
1962	Chi-A	3	4	0	0	0	0	0	0	0	3	.000	.000	.000	-99	-1	0	0	0	1.000	1	/2-2	0.0
1964	Chi-A	2	2	0	0	0	0	0	0	0	1	.000	.000	.000	-99	-1	0	0	0	.000	0	H	-0.1
1965	Chi-A	3	1	0	0	0	0	0	0	1	0	.000	.667	.000	113	0	0	0	0	.000	0	H	0.0
1966	Chi-A	9	25	1	5	0	0	0	0	0	6	.200	.200	.200	16	-3	0	0	0	.875	-3	/3-6	-0.6
1967	Chi-A	50	97	9	22	4	1	4	11	4	17	.227	.260	.412	101	-0	0	2	-1	.971	1	3-35	-0.1
1968	Chi-A	58	122	2	27	2	0	0	2	5	21	.221	.252	.238	49	-8	0	1	0	.938	4	3-38	-0.4
Total	6	125	251	12	54	6	1	4	13	10	42	.215	.251	.295	63	-12	0	3	-2	.948	4	/3-79,2-2	-1.2

■ DUKE KENWORTHY
Kenworthy, William Jennings "Iron Duke" b: 7/4/1886, Cambridge, Ohio d: 9/21/50, Eureka, Cal. BB/TR, 5'7", 165 lbs. Deb: 8/28/12

YEAR	TM/L	G	AB	R	H	2B	3B	HR	RBI	BB	SO	AVG	OBP	SLG	PRO+	BR/A	SB	CS	SBR	FA	FR	G/POS	TPR
1912	Was-A	12	38	6	9	1	0	0				.237	.293	.263	59	-0	3			1.000	-0	O-12	-0.3
1914	KC-F	146	545	93	173	40	14	15	91	36	44	.317	.354	.525	136	25	37			.952	21	*2-145	4.6
1915	KC-F	122	396	59	118	30	7	3	52	28	32	.298	.355	.432	115	7	20			.936	-7	2-108/O-7	0.0
1917	StL-A	5	10	1	1	0	0	0	1	1	1	.100	.182	.100	-14	-1	1			.889	1	/2-4	0.0
Total	4	285	989	159	301	71	21	18	146	67	77	.304	.360	.473	123	28	61			.945	14	2-257/O-19	4.3

■ JOE KEOUGH
Keough, Joseph William b: 1/7/46, Pomona, Cal. BL/TL, 6', 185 lbs. Deb: 8/7/68 F

YEAR	TM/L	G	AB	R	H	2B	3B	HR	RBI	BB	SO	AVG	OBP	SLG	PRO+	BR/A	SB	CS	SBR	FA	FR	G/POS	TPR
1968	Oak-A	34	98	7	21	2	1	2	18	8	11	.214	.274	.316	82	-2	1	0	0	.962	1	O-29/1-1	-0.3
1969	KC-A	70	166	17	31	2	0	0	7	13	13	.187	.254	.199	28	-16	1	0	0	1.000	-3	O-49/1-1	-2.2
1970	KC-A	57	183	28	59	6	2	4	21	23	18	.322	.398	.443	132	8	1	1	-0	.985	2	O-34,1-18	0.7
1971	KC-A	110	351	34	87	14	2	3	30	35	26	.248	.318	.325	83	-8	0	6	-4	.982	-6	*O-100	-2.4
1972	KC-A	56	64	8	14	2	0	0	5	8	7	.219	.324	.250	73	-2	2	0	1	1.000	-3	O-16	-0.5
1973	Chi-A	5	1	1	0	0	0	0	0	0	0	.000	.000	.000	-97	-0	0	0	0	.000	0	H	0.0
Total	6	332	863	95	212	26	5	9	81	87	75	.246	.318	.319	82	-19	9	9	-4	.984	-9	O-228/1-20	-4.7

■ MARTY KEOUGH
Keough, Richard Martin b: 4/14/35, Oakland, Cal. BL/TL, 6', 180 lbs. Deb: 4/21/56 F

YEAR	TM/L	G	AB	R	H	2B	3B	HR	RBI	BB	SO	AVG	OBP	SLG	PRO+	BR/A	SB	CS	SBR	FA	FR	G/POS	TPR
1956	Bos-A	3	2	1	0	0	0	0	1	0	0	.000	.333	.000	-5	-0	0	0	0	.000	0	H	0.0
1957	Bos-A	9	17	1	1	0	0	0	0	4	3	.059	.238	.059	-14	-3	0	0	0	1.000	0	/O-7	-0.3
1958	Bos-A	68	118	21	26	3	3	1	9	7	29	.220	.264	.322	57	-7	1	1	0	.974	-5	O-25/1-2	-1.4
1959	Bos-A	96	251	40	61	13	5	7	27	26	40	.243	.321	.418	97	-1	3	1	0	.993	-1	O-69/1-3	-0.6
1960	Bos-A	38	105	15	26	6	1	2	9	8	16	.248	.301	.352	73	-4	2	1	0	1.000	-4	O-29	-0.5
	Cle-A	65	149	19	37	5	0	3	11	9	23	.248	.296	.342	74	-6	3	4	-2	.986	4	O-42	-1.3
	Yr	103	254	34	63	11	1	5	20	17	39	.248	.298	.346	74	-10	5	5	-2	.992	-3	O-71	-1.8
1961	Was-A	135	390	57	97	18	9	9	34	32	60	.249	.309	.410	92	-6	12	5	1	.978	2	*O-100,1-10	-0.9

YEAR	TM/L	G	AB	R	H	2B	3B	HR	RBI	BB	SO	AVG	OBP	SLG	PRO+	BR/A	SB	CS	SBR	FA	FR	G/POS	TPR
1962	Cin-N	111	230	34	64	8	2	7	27	21	31	.278	.349	.422	102	1	3	1	0	.968	-5	O-71,1-29	-0.8
1963	Cin-N	95	172	21	39	8	2	6	21	25	37	.227	.338	.401	109	2	1	4	-2	.992	-3	1-46,O-28	-0.5
1964	Cin-N	109	276	29	71	9	1	9	28	22	58	.257	.314	.395	95	-2	1	2	-1	.991	-6	O-81/1-4	-1.2
1965	Cin-N	62	43	14	5	0	0	0	3	3	14	.116	.191	.116	-10	-6	0	0	0	.988	-1	1-32/O-4	-0.7
1966	Atl-N	17	17	1	1	0	0	0	1	1	6	.059	.111	.059	-50	-3	0	0	0	1.000	-2	/1-4,O-3	-0.6
	Chi-N	33	26	3	6	1	0	0	5	5	9	.231	.375	.269	82	-0	1	0	0	1.000	-2	/O-5	-0.2
	Yr	50	43	4	7	1	0	0	6	6	15	.163	.280	.186	32	-4	1	0	0	.667	-3	/O-8,1-4	-0.8
Total	11	841	1796	256	434	71	23	43	176	164	318	.242	.311	.379	86	-35	26	19	-4	.984	-25	O-464,1-130	-9.0

■ JOHN KERINS
Kerins, John Nelson b: 7/15/1858, Indianapolis, Ind d: 9/8/19, Louisville, Ky. BR/TR, 5'10", 177 lbs. Deb: 5/1/1884 MU

YEAR	TM/L	G	AB	R	H	2B	3B	HR	RBI	BB	SO	AVG	OBP	SLG	PRO+	BR/A	SB	CS	SBR	FA	FR	G/POS	TPR
1884	Ind-a	94	364	58	78	10	3	6		6			.214	.229	.308	76	-10				.972	6	*1-87/C-5,O3	-1.3
1885	Lou-a	112	456	65	111	9	16	3		20			.243	.281	.353	100	-1				.947	3	*1-96,C-19/O3	-0.6
1886	Lou-a	120	487	113	131	19	9	4	66				.269	.360	.370	122	12	26			.933	39	C-65,1-47/OS	4.6
1887	Lou-a	112	476	101	140	18	19	5		38			.294	.349	.443	118	9	49			.970	25	1-74,C-35/O	2.4
1888	Lou-a	83	319	38	75	11	4	2	41	25			.235	.297	.313	98	-0	16			.844	2	O-47,C-33/132M	-1.2
1889	Lou-a	2	9	2	3	1	0	0	3	0	1		.333	.333	.444	123	0	0			.500	-1	/O-2,C-1	-0.1
	Bal-a	16	53	7	15	2	0	0	12	2	4		.283	.321	.321	82	-1	2			.981	-2	/1-9,C-4,OS	-0.3
	Yr	18	62	9	18	3	0	0	15	2	5		.290	.323	.339	87	-1	2			.981	-2	/1-9,C-5,OS	-0.4
1890	StL-a	18	63	8	8	2	0	0		8			.127	.225	.159	12	-7	2			.968	1	1-17/C-1M	-0.6
Total	7	557	2227	392	561	72	51	20	56	165	5	.252	.308	.357	102	2	95			.963	73	1-334,C-163/O3S2	4.4

■ ORIE KERLIN
Kerlin, Orie Milton "Cy" b: 1/23/1891, Summerfield, La. d: 10/29/74, Shreveport, La. BL/TR, 5'7", 149 lbs. Deb: 6/6/15

YEAR	TM/L	G	AB	R	H	2B	3B	HR	RBI	BB	SO	AVG	OBP	SLG	PRO+	BR/A	SB	CS	SBR	FA	FR	G/POS	TPR
1915	Pit-F	3	1	0	0	0	0	0	0	0	0	.000	.000	.000	-99	-0				.000	-0	/C-3	0.0

■ BILL KERN
Kern, William George b: 2/28/33, Coplay, Pa. BR/TR, 6'2", 184 lbs. Deb: 9/19/62

YEAR	TM/L	G	AB	R	H	2B	3B	HR	RBI	BB	SO	AVG	OBP	SLG	PRO+	BR/A	SB	CS	SBR	FA	FR	G/POS	TPR
1962	KC-A	8	16	1	4	0	0	1	1	0	3	.250	.250	.438	77	-1	0	0	0	1.000	1	/O-3	0.0

■ JOE KERNAN
Kernan, Joseph b: Baltimore, Md. Deb: 4/14/1873

YEAR	TM/L	G	AB	R	H	2B	3B	HR	RBI	BB	SO	AVG	OBP	SLG	PRO+	BR/A	SB	CS	SBR	FA	FR	G/POS	TPR
1873	Mar-n	2	8	1	3	0	0	0	1	0	0	.375	.375	.375	158	1						/2-1,O-1	0.0

■ GEORGE KERNEK
Kernek, George Boyd b: 1/12/40, Holdenville, Okla. BL/TL, 6'3", 170 lbs. Deb: 9/5/65

YEAR	TM/L	G	AB	R	H	2B	3B	HR	RBI	BB	SO	AVG	OBP	SLG	PRO+	BR/A	SB	CS	SBR	FA	FR	G/POS	TPR
1965	StL-N	10	31	6	9	3	1	0	3	2	4	.290	.333	.452	109	0	0	0	0	.972	-0	/1-7	0.0
1966	StL-N	20	50	5	12	0	1	0	3	4	9	.240	.309	.280	65	-2	1	0	0	.984	-0	1-16	-0.3
Total	2	30	81	11	21	3	2	0	6	6	13	.259	.318	.346	82	-2	1	0	0	.980	-0	/1-23	-0.3

■ RUSS KERNS
Kerns, Russell Eldon b: 11/10/20, Fremont, Ohio BL/TR, 6', 188 lbs. Deb: 8/18/45

YEAR	TM/L	G	AB	R	H	2B	3B	HR	RBI	BB	SO	AVG	OBP	SLG	PRO+	BR/A	SB	CS	SBR	FA	FR	G/POS	TPR
1945	Det-A	1	1	0	0	0	0	0	0	0	0	.000	.000	.000	-94	-0	0	0	0	.000	0	H	0.0

■ JOHN KERR
Kerr, John Francis b: 11/26/1898, San Francisco, Cal. d: 10/19/93, Long Beach, Cal. BR/TR, 5'8", 158 lbs. Deb: 5/1/23

YEAR	TM/L	G	AB	R	H	2B	3B	HR	RBI	BB	SO	AVG	OBP	SLG	PRO+	BR/A	SB	CS	SBR	FA	FR	G/POS	TPR
1923	Det-A	19	42	4	9	1	0	0	1	4	5	.214	.283	.238	39	-4	0	0	0	.877	4	S-15	0.1
1924	Det-A	17	11	3	3	0	0	0	1	0	0	.273	.273	.273	42	-1	0	0	0	.000	-0	/3-3,O-2	-0.1
1929	Chi-A	127	419	50	108	20	4	1	39	31	24	.258	.310	.332	66	-21	9	8	-2	.971	24	*2-122/S-1	0.6
1930	Chi-A	70	266	37	77	11	6	3	27	21	23	.289	.351	.410	95	-2	4	2	0	.980	2	2-52/S-20	0.3
1931	Chi-A	128	444	51	119	17	2	2	50	35	22	.268	.324	.329	77	-15	9	3	1	.968	1	*2-117/3-7,S	0.1
1932	Was-A	51	132	14	36	6	0	0	15	13	3	.273	.338	.333	75	-5	3	2	-0	.954	-1	2-17,S-14/3	-0.3
1933	*Was-A	28	40	5	8	0	0	0	3	2	2	.200	.256	.200	22	-4	0	0	0	.966	3	2-16/3-1	-0.1
1934	Was-A	31	103	8	28	4	0	0	12	9	13	.272	.324	.311	67	-5	1	1	-0	.971	10	3-17,2-13	0.5
Total	8	471	1457	172	388	59	13	6	145	115	92	.266	.323	.337	73	-57	26	16	-2	.970	48	2-337/S-51,3O	1.1

■ DOC KERR
Kerr, John Jonas b: 1/17/1882, Dellroy, Ohio d: 6/9/37, Baltimore, Md. BB/TR, 5'10.5", 190 lbs. Deb: 4/22/14

YEAR	TM/L	G	AB	R	H	2B	3B	HR	RBI	BB	SO	AVG	OBP	SLG	PRO+	BR/A	SB	CS	SBR	FA	FR	G/POS	TPR
1914	Pit-F	42	71	3	17	4	2	1	7	10	13	.239	.333	.394	89	-1	0			.970	1	C-18	0.1
	Bal-F	14	34	4	9	1	1	0	1	1	6	.265	.286	.353	63	-2	1			.979	5	C-13/1-1	0.4
	Yr	56	105	7	26	5	3	1	8	11	19	.248	.314	.381	81	-3	1			.974	5	C-31/1-1	0.5
1915	Bal-F	3	6	1	2	0	0	0	0	1	0	.333	.429	.333	102	0	0			1.000	-1	/C-2,1-1	-0.1
Total	2	59	111	8	28	5	3	1	8	12	19	.252	.325	.378	82	-3	1			.975	4	/C-33,1-2	0.4

■ BUDDY KERR
Kerr, John Joseph b: 11/6/22, Astoria, N.Y. BR/TR, 6'2", 180 lbs. Deb: 9/8/43

YEAR	TM/L	G	AB	R	H	2B	3B	HR	RBI	BB	SO	AVG	OBP	SLG	PRO+	BR/A	SB	CS	SBR	FA	FR	G/POS	TPR
1943	NY-N	27	98	14	28	3	0	2	12	8	9	.286	.352	.378	110	1	1			.955	5	S-27	0.8
1944	NY-N	150	548	68	146	31	4	9	63	37	32	.266	.316	.387	97	-3	14			.954	17	*S-149	2.6
1945	NY-N	149	546	53	136	20	3	4	40	41	34	.249	.304	.319	72	-21	5			.964	28	*S-148	1.9
1946	NY-N	138	497	50	124	20	3	6	40	53	31	.249	.324	.338	87	-8	7			.982	6	*S-126,3-18	0.6
1947	NY-N	138	547	73	157	23	5	7	49	36	49	.287	.331	.386	89	-9	2			.977	12	*S-138	1.0
1948	NY-N★	144	496	41	119	16	4	0	46	56	36	.240	.317	.288	64	-23	9			.967	3	*S-143	-1.2
1949	NY-N	90	220	16	46	4	0	0	19	21	23	.209	.284	.227	39	-19	0			.959	6	S-89	-0.8
1950	Bos-N	155	507	45	115	24	6	2	46	50	50	.227	.296	.310	64	-27	0			.965	6	*S-155	-1.3
1951	Bos-N	69	118	12	32	4	0	1	18	22	20	.186	.328	.227	41	-14	0			.969	13	S-63/2-5	0.3
Total	9	1067	3631	378	903	145	25	31	333	324	280	.249	.312	.328	76	-123	38	0		.967	92	*S-1038/3-18,2	3.9

■ MEL KERR
Kerr, John Melville b: 5/22/03, Souris, Man., Can. d: 8/9/80, Vero Beach, Fla. BL/TL, 5'11.5", 155 lbs. Deb: 9/16/25 C

YEAR	TM/L	G	AB	R	H	2B	3B	HR	RBI	BB	SO	AVG	OBP	SLG	PRO+	BR/A	SB	CS	SBR	FA	FR	G/POS	TPR
1925	Chi-N	1	0	1	0	0	0	0	0	0	0	—	—	—	—	0	0	0	0	.000	0	R	0.0

■ DAN KERWIN
Kerwin, Daniel Patrick (b: Daniel Patrick Kervin) b: 7/9/1879, Philadelphia, Pa. d: 7/13/60, Philadelphia, Pa. BL/TL, 5'9", 164 lbs. Deb: 9/27/03

YEAR	TM/L	G	AB	R	H	2B	3B	HR	RBI	BB	SO	AVG	OBP	SLG	PRO+	BR/A	SB	CS	SBR	FA	FR	G/POS	TPR
1903	Cin-N	2	6	1	4	1	0	0	1	2		.667	.778	.833	323	2	0			.500	-1	/O-2	0.1

■ DON KESSINGER
Kessinger, Donald Eulon b: 7/17/42, Forrest City, Ark. BB/TR, 6'1", 175 lbs. Deb: 9/7/64 FM

YEAR	TM/L	G	AB	R	H	2B	3B	HR	RBI	BB	SO	AVG	OBP	SLG	PRO+	BR/A	SB	CS	SBR	FA	FR	G/POS	TPR
1964	Chi-N	4	12	1	2	0	0	0	0	0	1	.167	.167	.167	-6	-2	0	0	0	1.000	-1	/S-4	-0.3
1965	Chi-N	106	309	19	62	4	3	0	14	20	44	.201	.254	.233	37	-25	1	2	-1	.948	21	*S-105	0.1
1966	Chi-N	150	533	50	146	8	2	1	43	26	46	.274	.308	.302	70	-21	13	7	-0	.951	-10	*S-148	-1.9
1967	Chi-N	145	580	61	134	10	7	0	42	33	80	.231	.277	.272	55	-33	6	13	-6	.973	-3	*S-143	-3.1
1968	Chi-N★	160	655	63	157	14	7	1	32	38	86	.240	.283	.287	67	-25	9	9	-3	.962	18	*S-159	0.8
1969	Chi-N★	158	664	109	181	38	6	4	53	61	70	.273	.335	.366	85	-13	11	8	-2	.976	25	*S-157	2.9
1970	Chi-N★	154	631	100	168	21	14	1	39	66	59	.266	.338	.349	75	-22	12	6	-0	.972	9	*S-154	0.6
1971	Chi-N★	155	617	77	159	18	6	2	38	52	54	.258	.318	.316	70	-24	15	8	-0	.966	4	*S-154	0.0
1972	Chi-N★	149	577	77	158	20	6	1	39	67	42	.274	.351	.334	87	-8	8	7	-2	.965	8	*S-146	2.0
1973	Chi-N	160	577	52	151	22	3	0	43	57	44	.262	.328	.310	72	-20	6	6	-2	.964	17	*S-158	1.6
1974	Chi-N★	153	599	83	155	20	7	1	42	62	54	.259	.332	.321	80	-15	7	7	-2	.958	2	*S-150	0.5
1975	Chi-N	154	601	77	146	26	10	6	46	68	47	.243	.321	.319	75	-19	4	7	-1	.967	-2	*S-140,3-13	-1.0
1976	StL-N	145	502	55	120	22	6	1	40	61	51	.239	.323	.313	80	-12	3	0	1	.969	-4	*S-113,2-31/3	0.0
1977	StL-N	59	134	14	32	4	0	0	7	14	26	.239	.311	.269	58	-8	0	2	-2	.978	2	S-26,2-24/3	-0.2
	Chi-A	39	119	12	28	3	2	0	11	13	7	.235	.311	.294	66	-5	2	1	0	.959	-4	S-21,2-13/3	-0.7
1978	Chi-A	131	431	35	110	18	1	1	31	36	34	.255	.313	.309	75	-14	2	4	-2	.974	-19	*S-123/2-9	-2.0
1979	Chi-A	56	114	12	29	1	0	0	7	10	12	.254	.267	.282	48	-8	1	0	1	.975	-4	S-54/1-1,2	-0.3
Total	16	2078	7651	899	1931	254	80	14	527	684	759	.252	.316	.312	72	-274	100	85	-21	.966	61	*S-1955/2-78,31	-1.1

■ KEITH KESSINGER
Kessinger, Robert Keith b: 2/19/67, Forest City, Ark. BB/TR, 6'2", 185 lbs. Deb: 9/15/93 F

YEAR	TM/L	G	AB	R	H	2B	3B	HR	RBI	BB	SO	AVG	OBP	SLG	PRO+	BR/A	SB	CS	SBR	FA	FR	G/POS	TPR
1993	Cin-N	11	27	4	7	1	0	1	3	4	4	.259	.355	.407	103	0	0	0	0	.935	-1	S-11	0.0

YEAR	TM/L	G	AB	R	H	2B	3B	HR	RBI	BB	SO	AVG	OBP	SLG	PRO+	BR/A	SB	CS	SBR	FA	FR	G/POS	TPR

■ HENRY KESSLER   Kessler, Henry "Lucky" b: 1847, Brooklyn, N.Y. d: 1/9/1900, Franklin, Pa. BR/TR, 5'10", 144 lbs. Deb: 8/4/1873

1873	Atl-n	1	5	0	1	0	0	0	1	0	0	.200	.200	.200	20	-0						/1-1	0.0
1874	Atl-n	14	57	8	16	2	0	0		0		.281	.281	.316	101	0						/C-8,2-4,O3	0.0
1875	Atl-n	25	104	17	26	2	0	0		1		.250	.257	.269	94	0						S-18/O-6,C2	0.0
1876	Cin-N	59	248	26	64	5	0	0	11	7	10	.258	.278	.278	100	2				.788	-8	S-46,O-16	-0.6
1877	Cin-N	6	20	0	2	0	0	0	0	2	1	.100	.182	.100	-10	-2				.500	-5	/C-5,1-1	-0.7
Total	3 n	40	166	25	43	4	0	0	1	1		.259	.263	.283	94	0						/S-18,C-9,O231	0.0
Total	2	65	268	26	66	5	0	0	11	9	11	.246	.271	.265	91	-1				.788	-14	/S-46,O-16,C1	-1.3

■ FRED KETCHUM   Ketchum, Frederick L. b: 7/27/1875, Elmira, N.Y. d: 3/12/08, Cortland, N.Y. BL/TR, 5'8", 157 lbs. Deb: 9/12/1899

1899	Lou-N	15	61	13	18	1	0	0	5	0		.295	.306	.311	70	-3	2			1.000	-4	O-15	-0.7
1901	Phi-A	5	22	5	5	0	0	0	2	0		.227	.227	.227	25	-2	0			.875	-1	/O-5	-0.3
Total	2	20	83	18	23	1	0	0	7	0		.277	.286	.289	58	-5	2			.960	-5	/O-20	-1.0

■ PHIL KETTER   Ketter, Philip (b: Philip Ketterer) 4/13/1884, St.Louis, Mo. d: 4/9/65, St.Louis, Mo. TR , Deb: 5/23/12

| 1912 | StL-A | 2 | 6 | 1 | 2 | 0 | 0 | 0 | 0 | 0 | | .333 | .333 | .333 | 94 | -0 | 0 | | | 1.000 | -1 | /C-2 | -0.1 |

■ SAM KHALIFA   Khalifa, Sam b: 12/5/63, Fontana, Cal. BR/TR, 5'11", 170 lbs. Deb: 6/25/85

1985	Pit-N	95	320	30	76	14	3	2	31	34	56	.237	.311	.319	77	-9	5	2	0	.967	13	S-95	1.3
1986	Pit-N	64	151	8	28	6	0	0	4	19	28	.185	.276	.225	39	-12	0	2	-1	.961	14	S-60/2-6	0.5
1987	Pit-N	5	17	1	3	0	0	0	2	0	2	.176	.176	.176	-6	-3	0	0	0	.917	-5	/S-5	-0.7
Total	3	164	488	39	107	20	3	2	37	53	86	.219	.296	.285	62	-24	5	4	-1	.964	22	S-160/2-6	1.1

■ HOD KIBBIE   Kibbie, Horace Kent b: 7/18/03, Ft.Worth, Tex. d: 10/19/75, Ft.Worth, Tex. BR/TR, 5'10", 150 lbs. Deb: 6/13/25

| 1925 | Bos-N | 11 | 41 | 5 | 11 | 0 | 0 | 0 | 2 | 5 | 6 | .268 | .348 | .317 | 78 | -1 | 0 | 0 | 0 | .904 | -0 | /2-8,S-3 | -0.1 |

■ JACK KIBBLE   Kibble, John Westly "Happy" b: 1/2/1892, Seatonville, Ill. d: 12/13/69, Roundup, Mont. BB/TR, 5'9.5", 154 lbs. Deb: 9/10/12

| 1912 | Cle-A | 5 | 8 | 1 | 0 | 0 | 0 | 0 | 0 | 0 | 0 | .000 | .111 | .000 | -65 | -2 | 0 | 0 | 0 | 1.000 | 4 | /3-4,2-1 | 0.2 |

■ STEVE KIEFER   Kiefer, Steven George b: 10/18/60, Chicago, Ill. BR/TR, 6'1", 180 lbs. Deb: 9/3/84 F

1984	Oak-A	23	40	7	7	1	2	0	2	2	10	.175	.214	.300	43	-3	2	1	0	.904	1	S-17/3-2,D	-0.2
1985	Oak-A	40	66	8	13	1	1	1	10	1	18	.197	.209	.288	37	-6	0	0	0	.881	3	3-34/D-2	-0.3
1986	Mil-A	2	6	0	0	0	0	0	0	0	4	.000	.000	.000	-97	-2	0	0	0	1.000	0	/S-2	0.1
1987	Mil-A	28	99	17	20	4	0	5	17	7	28	.202	.262	.394	69	-5	0	0	0	.966	-3	3-26/2-4	-0.7
1988	Mil-A	7	10	2	3	1	0	1	2	3	4	.300	.462	.700	219	2	0	0	0	1.000	-1	/2-4,3-4	0.1
1989	NY-A	5	8	0	1	0	0	0	0	0	5	.125	.125	.125	-30	-1	0	0	0	1.000	-1	/3-5	-0.3
Total	6	105	229	34	44	7	3	7	30	12	68	.192	.239	.341	56	-15	2	1	0	.920	1	/3-71,S-19,2D	-1.3

■ BILL KIENZLE   Kienzle, William H. b: Philadelphia, Pa. BL/TL, Deb: 9/15/1882

1882	Phi-a	9	33	8	11	3	2	0		5		.333	.421	.545	200	3				.842	-1	/O-9	0.2
1884	Phi-U	67	299	76	76	13	8	0		21		.254	.303	.351	83	-6				.772	-2	O-67	-0.9
Total	2	76	332	84	87	16	10	0		26		.262	.316	.370	95	-3				.781	-8	/O-76	-0.7

■ PETE KILDUFF   Kilduff, Peter John b: 4/4/1893, Weir City, Kan. d: 2/14/30, Pittsburg, Kan. BR/TR, 5'7", 155 lbs. Deb: 4/18/17

1917	NY-N	31	78	12	16	3	0	1	12	4	11	.205	.253	.282	66	-3	2			.954	-2	2-21/S-5,3	-0.5
	Chi-N	56	202	23	56	9	5	0	15	12	19	.277	.324	.371	105	1	11			.920	-14	S-51/2-5	-1.2
	Yr	87	280	35	72	12	5	1	27	16	30	.257	.304	.346	96	-2	13			.917	-16	S-56,2-26/3	-1.7
1918	Chi-N	30	93	7	19	2	2	0	13	7	7	.204	.267	.269	62	-4	1			.935	-3	2-30	-0.6
1919	Chi-N	31	88	5	24	4	2	0	8	10	5	.273	.360	.364	117	2	1			.974	-4	3-14/2-8,S	-0.1
	Bro-N	32	73	9	22	3	1	0	8	12	11	.301	.407	.370	132	4	5			.862	-4	3-26/2-1	0.1
	Yr	63	161	14	46	7	3	0	16	22	16	.286	.382	.366	124	6	6			.903	-8	3-40/2-9,S	0.0
1920	*Bro-N	141	478	62	130	26	8	0	58	58	43	.272	.351	.360	101	2	9	-5		.967	8	*2-134/3-5	1.0
1921	Bro-N	107	372	45	107	15	10	3	45	31	36	.288	.344	.406	94	-3	6	6	-2	.963	13	*2-105/3-1	1.1
Total	5	428	1384	163	374	62	28	4	159	134	132	.270	.338	.364	98	-2	28	15		.963	-7	2-304/S-63,3	-0.2

■ JOHN KILEY   Kiley, John Frederick b: 7/1/1859, Dedham, Mass. d: 12/18/40, Norwood, Mass. BL/TL, 5'7", 147 lbs. Deb: 5/1/1884

1884	Was-a	14	56	9	12	2	2	0		3		.214	.267	.321	103	0				.571	-4	O-14	-0.3
1891	Bos-N	1	2	0	0	0	0	0		1	1	.000	.500	.000	45	0				1.000	0	/P-1	0.0
Total	2	15	58	9	12	2	2	0	0	4	1	.207	.281	.310	102	0				.571	-4	/O-14,P-1	-0.3

■ PAT KILHULLEN   Kilhullen, Joseph Isadore b: 8/10/1890, Carbondale, Pa. d: 11/2/22, Oakland, Cal. BR/TR, 5'9", 175 lbs. Deb: 6/10/14

| 1914 | Pit-N | 1 | 1 | 0 | 0 | 0 | 0 | 0 | 0 | 0 | 0 | .000 | .000 | .000 | -99 | -0 | 0 | | | .000 | 0 | /C-1 | 0.0 |

■ HARMON KILLEBREW   Killebrew, Harmon Clayton "Killer" b: 6/29/36, Payette, Idaho BR/TR, 5'11", 213 lbs. Deb: 6/23/54 H

1954	Was-A	9	13	1	4	1	0	0	3	2	3	.308	.400	.385	122	0	0	0	0	1.000	-2	/2-3	-0.2
1955	Was-A	38	80	12	16	1	0	4	7	9	31	.200	.281	.363	76	-3	0	0	0	.935	5	3-23/2-3	0.2
1956	Was-A	44	99	10	22	2	0	5	13	10	39	.222	.294	.394	80	-3	0	0	0	.951	-0	3-20/2-4	-0.3
1957	Was-A	9	31	4	9	2	0	2	5	2	8	.290	.333	.548	139	1	0	0	0	.947	-1	/3-7,2-1	0.1
1958	Was-A	13	31	2	6	0	0	0	0	0	12	.194	.219	.194	15	-4	0	0	0	1.000	0	/3-9	-0.4
1959	Was-A★	153	546	98	132	20	2	**42**	105	90	116	.242	.356	.516	137	28	3	2	0	.938	-8	*3-150/O-4	2.0
1960	Was-A	124	442	84	122	19	1	31	80	71	106	.276	.377	.534	145	28	1	0	0	.987	-9	1-71,3-65	1.3
1961	Min-A★	150	541	94	156	20	7	46	122	107	109	.288	.409	.606	159	46	1	2	-1	.987	-10	*1-119,3-45/O	2.6
1962	Min-A	155	552	85	134	21	1	**48**	126	106	142	.243	.369	.545	137	29	1	4	0	.967	-10	*O-151/1-4	0.9
1963	Min-A	142	515	88	133	18	0	**45**	96	72	105	.258	.353	**.555**	147	32	0	0	0	.987	-3	*O-137	2.2
1964	Min-A★	158	577	95	156	11	1	**49**	111	93	135	.270	.377	.548	153	42	0	0	0	.971	-7	*O-157	2.9
1965	*Min-A★	113	401	78	108	16	1	25	75	72	69	.269	.386	.501	144	25	0	0	0	.988	-9	1-72,3-44/O	1.2
1966	Min-A★	162	569	89	160	27	1	39	110	**103**	98	.281	.393	.538	155	42	0	2	-1	.951	-17	*3-107,1-42,O	2.0
1967	Min-A★	163	547	105	147	24	1	**44**	113	**131**	111	.269	.413	.558	170	52	1	0	0	.992	-8	1-160/3-3	3.8
1968	Min-A★	100	295	40	62	7	2	17	40	70	70	.210	.365	.420	131	13	0	0	0	.994	-9	1-77,3-11	1.3
1969	*Min-A★	162	555	106	153	20	2	**49**	**140**	**145**	84	.276	**.430**	.584	177	63	8	2	1	.929	-21	*3-105,1-80	3.9
1970	*Min-A★	157	527	96	143	20	1	41	113	128	84	.271	.416	.546	161	48	0	3	-2	.948	-29	*3-138,1-28	1.4
1971	Min-A★	147	500	61	127	19	1	28	**119**	**114**	96	.254	.393	.464	137	28	3	2	-0	.997	-15	1-90,3-64	0.4
1972	Min-A	139	433	53	100	13	2	26	74	94	91	.231	.369	.450	136	22	0	1	-1	.992	11	*1-130	2.5
1973	Min-A	69	248	29	60	9	1	5	32	41	59	.242	.352	.347	94	-1	0	0	0	.998	4	1-57/D-9	-0.1
1974	Min-A	122	333	28	74	7	0	13	54	45	61	.222	.315	.360	90	-4	0	0	0	.992	2	D-57,1-33	-0.6
1975	KC-A	106	312	25	62	13	0	14	44	54	70	.199	.319	.375	93	-3	1	2	-1	1.000	-1	D-92/1-6	-0.7
Total	22	2435	8147	1283	2086	290	24	573	1584	1559	1699	.256	.379	.509	142	482	19	18	-5	.992	-123	1-969,3-791,OD/2	26.4

■ RED KILLEFER   Killefer, Wade Hampton b: 4/13/1884, Bloomingdale, Mich d: 9/4/58, Los Angeles, Cal. BR/TR, 5'9", 175 lbs. Deb: 9/16/07 F

1907	Det-A	1	4	0	0	0	0	0	0	0	0	.000	.000	.000	-97	-1	0			1.000	0	/O-1	-0.1
1908	Det-A	28	75	9	16	1	0	0	11	3		.213	.253	.227	54	-4	4			.956	-2	2-16/S-7,3	-1.1
1909	Det-A	23	61	6	17	2	2	1	4	3		.279	.343	.426	137	2	2			.912	-1	2-17/O-1	0.1
	Was-A	40	121	11	21	1	0	0	5	13		.174	.265	.182	43	-7	4			.957	-3	O-24/3-6,C2S	-1.2
	Yr	63	182	17	38	3	2	1	9	16		.209	.291	.264	76	-4	6			.957	-4	O-25,2-20/3CS	-1.1
1910	Was-A	106	345	35	79	17	1	0	24	29		.229	.318	.284	93	-1	17			.940	-5	2-88,O-12	-0.9

YEAR	TM/L	G	AB	R	H	2B	3B	HR	RBI	BB	SO	AVG	OBP	SLG	PRO+	BR/A	SB	CS	SBR	FA	FR	G/POS	TPR
1914	Cin-N	42	141	16	39	6	1	0	12	20	18	.277	.386	.333	111	3	11			.968	-4	O-37/2-5,3	-0.3
1915	Cin-N	155	555	75	151	25	11	1	41	38	33	.272	.340	.362	110	8	12	18	-7	.970	5	*O-150/1-2	-0.3
1916	Cin-N	70	234	29	57	9	1	1	18	21	8	.244	.327	.303	96	-0	7			.966	-2	O-68	-0.6
	NY-N	2	1	0	1	0	0	0	1	1	0	1.000	1.000	1.000	544	1	0			.000	0	H	0.1
	Yr	72	235	29	58	9	1	1	19	22	8	.247	.332	.306	99	1	7			.966	-2	O-68	-0.5
Total	7	467	1537	181	381	61	16	3	116	128	59	.248	.328	.314	98	0	57	18		.965	-16	O-293,2-129/3SC1	-4.3

■ BILL KILLEFER
Killefer, William Lavier "Reindeer Bill"
b: 10/10/1887, Bloomingdale, Mich d: 7/3/60, Elsmere, Del. BR/TR, 5'10.5", 200 lbs. Deb: 9/13/09 FMC

YEAR	TM/L	G	AB	R	H	2B	3B	HR	RBI	BB	SO	AVG	OBP	SLG	PRO+	BR/A	SB	CS	SBR	FA	FR	G/POS	TPR
1909	StL-A	11	29	0	4	0	0	0	1	0		.138	.138	.138	-14	-4	2			.905	2	C-11	-0.1
1910	StL-A	74	193	14	24	2	2	0	7	12		.124	.184	.155	7	-21	0			.938	12	C-73	-0.3
1911	Phi-N	6	16	3	3	0	0	0	2	0	2	.188	.188	.188	5	-2	0			.975	2	/C-6	0.0
1912	Phi-N	85	268	18	60	6	3	1	21	4	14	.224	.241	.280	40	-23	6			.973	17	C-85	0.2
1913	Phi-N	120	360	25	88	14	3	0	24	4	17	.244	.255	.300	56	-21	2			.988	13	*C-118/1-1	0.2
1914	Phi-N	98	299	27	70	10	1	0	27	8	17	.234	.261	.274	56	-17	3			.978	18	C-90	0.9
1915	*Phi-N	105	320	26	76	9	2	0	24	18	14	.237	.287	.278	70	-11	5	3	-0	.972	14	*C-104	1.1
1916	Phi-N	97	286	22	62	5	4	3	27	8	14	.217	.246	.294	63	-13	2			.985	-1	*C-91	-0.8
1917	Phi-N	125	409	28	112	12	0	0	31	15	21	.274	.306	.303	84	-8	4			.984	10	*C-120/O-1	1.3
1918	*Chi-N	104	331	30	77	10	3	0	22	17	10	.233	.276	.281	68	-13	5			.982	9	*C-104	0.6
1919	Chi-N	103	315	17	90	10	2	0	22	15	8	.286	.322	.330	96	-2	5			.987	17	*C-100	2.6
1920	Chi-N	62	191	16	42	7	1	0	16	8	5	.220	.280	.267	56	-10	2	2	-1	.977	18	C-61	1.2
1921	Chi-N	45	133	11	43	1	0	0	16	4	4	.323	.357	.331	83	-3	3	3	-1	.964	-1	C-42,M	-0.3
Total	13	1035	3150	237	751	86	21	4	240	113	126	.238	.273	.283	63	-147	39	8		.976	131	*C-1005/O-1,1	6.6

■ GENE KIMBALL
Kimball, Eugene Boynton b: 8/31/1850, Rochester, N.Y. d: 8/2/1882, Rochester, N.Y. 5'10", 160 lbs. Deb: 5/4/1871

YEAR	TM/L	G	AB	R	H	2B	3B	HR	RBI	BB	SO	AVG	OBP	SLG	PRO+	BR/A	SB	CS	SBR	FA	FR	G/POS	TPR
1871	Cle-n	29	131	18	25	1	0	0	9	3	2	.191	.209	.198	19	-12	5					2-17/S-6,O	-0.9

■ DICK KIMBLE
Kimble, Richard Lewis b: 7/27/15, Buchtel, Ohio BL/TR, 5'9", 160 lbs. Deb: 8/20/45

YEAR	TM/L	G	AB	R	H	2B	3B	HR	RBI	BB	SO	AVG	OBP	SLG	PRO+	BR/A	SB	CS	SBR	FA	FR	G/POS	TPR
1945	Was-A	20	49	5	12	1	1	0	1	5	2	.245	.315	.306	88	-1	0	0	0	.950	-3	S-15	-0.3

■ BRUCE KIMM
Kimm, Bruce Edward b: 6/29/51, Cedar Rapids, Iowa BR/TR, 5'11", 175 lbs. Deb: 5/4/76 C

YEAR	TM/L	G	AB	R	H	2B	3B	HR	RBI	BB	SO	AVG	OBP	SLG	PRO+	BR/A	SB	CS	SBR	FA	FR	G/POS	TPR
1976	Det-A	63	152	13	40	8	0	1	6	15	20	.263	.329	.336	91	-1	4	3	-1	.970	4	C-61/D-2	0.4
1977	Det-A	14	25	2	2	1	0	0	1	0	4	.080	.115	.120	-34	-5	0	1	-1	.958	3	C-12/D-2	-0.2
1979	Chi-N	9	11	0	1	0	0	0	0	0	0	.091	.091	.091	-46	-2	0	1	-1	.969	2	/C-9	-0.1
1980	Chi-A	100	251	20	61	10	1	0	19	17	26	.243	.290	.291	60	-13	1	3	-2	.985	-1	C-98	-1.4
Total	4	186	439	35	104	19	1	1	26	32	50	.237	.290	.292	62	-22	5	8	-3	.977	8	C-180/D-4	-1.3

■ WALLY KIMMICK
Kimmick, Walter Lyons b: 5/30/1897, Turtle Creek, Pa. d: 7/24/89, Boswell, Pa. BR/TR, 5'11", 174 lbs. Deb: 9/13/19

YEAR	TM/L	G	AB	R	H	2B	3B	HR	RBI	BB	SO	AVG	OBP	SLG	PRO+	BR/A	SB	CS	SBR	FA	FR	G/POS	TPR
1919	StL-N	2	1	1	0	0	0	0	0	1	0	.000	.500	.000	61	0	1			1.000	0	/S-1	0.0
1921	Cin-N	3	6	0	1	0	0	0	1	0	1	.167	.167	.167	-12	-1	0	0	0	.667	-0	/3-2	-0.1
1922	Cin-N	39	89	11	22	2	1	0	12	3	12	.247	.272	.292	46	-7	0	0	0	.965	2	S-30/2-3,3	-0.3
1923	Cin-N	29	80	11	18	2	1	0	6	5	15	.225	.271	.275	45	-6	3	0	1	.972	8	2-17/3-4,S	0.3
1925	Phi-N	70	141	16	43	3	2	1	10	22	26	.305	.399	.376	91	-1	0	3	-2	.904	-3	S-28,3-21,2	-0.3
1926	Phi-N	20	28	0	6	2	1	0	2	3	7	.214	.290	.357	70	-1	0			1.000	-2	/1-5,S-4,32	-0.3
Total	6	163	345	39	90	9	5	1	31	34	61	.261	.327	.325	67	-17	4	3		.933	4	/S-64,2-34,31	-0.7

■ JERRY KINDALL
Kindall, Gerald Donald "Slim" b: 5/27/35, St.Paul, Minn. BR/TR, 6'2.5", 175 lbs. Deb: 7/1/56

YEAR	TM/L	G	AB	R	H	2B	3B	HR	RBI	BB	SO	AVG	OBP	SLG	PRO+	BR/A	SB	CS	SBR	FA	FR	G/POS	TPR
1956	Chi-N	32	55	7	9	1	1	0	0	6	17	.164	.246	.218	27	-6	1	0	0	.956	2	S-18	-0.2
1957	Chi-N	72	181	18	29	3	0	6	12	8	48	.160	.196	.276	25	-19	1	0	0	.920	-4	2-28,3-19/S	-2.1
1958	Chi-N	3	6	0	1	1	0	0	0	0	3	.167	.167	.333	29	-1	0	0	0	1.000	1	/2-3	0.1
1960	Chi-N	89	246	17	59	16	2	2	23	5	52	.240	.255	.346	63	-13	4	3	-1	.966	14	2-82/S-2	0.7
1961	Chi-N	96	310	37	75	22	3	9	44	18	89	.242	.288	.419	84	-8	2	2	-1	.950	7	2-50,S-47	0.6
1962	Cle-A	154	530	51	123	21	1	13	55	45	107	.232	.292	.349	74	-20	4	3	-1	.978	21	*2-154	1.6
1963	Cle-A	86	234	27	48	4	1	5	20	18	71	.205	.268	.295	58	-13	3	1	0	.958	5	S-46,2-37/1	-0.5
1964	Cle-A	23	25	5	9	1	0	2	2	2	7	.360	.407	.640	188	3	0	0	0	.989	3	1-23	0.6
	Min-A	62	128	8	19	2	0	1	6	7	44	.148	.199	.188	8	-16	0	0	0	.969	5	2-51/S-7,1	-0.9
	Yr	85	153	13	28	3	0	3	8	9	51	.183	.233	.261	37	-13	0	0	0	.969	8	2-51,1-24/S	-0.3
1965	Min-A	125	342	41	67	12	1	6	36	36	97	.196	.278	.289	59	-18	2	2	-1	.963	-1	*2-106,3-10/S	-1.2
Total	9	742	2057	211	439	83	9	44	198	145	535	.213	.268	.327	62	-111	17	11	-2	.967	50	2-511,S-136/31	-1.3

■ RALPH KINER
Kiner, Ralph McPherran b: 10/27/22, Santa Rita, N.Mex. BR/TR, 6'2", 195 lbs. Deb: 4/16/46 H

YEAR	TM/L	G	AB	R	H	2B	3B	HR	RBI	BB	SO	AVG	OBP	SLG	PRO+	BR/A	SB	CS	SBR	FA	FR	G/POS	TPR
1946	Pit-N	144	502	63	124	17	3	23	81	74	109	.247	.345	.430	116	10	3			.969	1	*O-140	0.5
1947	Pit-N	152	565	118	177	23	4	51	127	98	81	.313	.417	.639	172	57	1			.983	13	*O-152	6.0
1948	Pit-N★	156	555	104	147	19	5	40	123	112	61	.265	.391	.533	145	36	1			.975	7	*O-154	3.4
1949	Pit-N★	152	549	116	170	19	5	54	127	117	61	.310	.432	.658	183	66	6			.979	-1	*O-152	5.6
1950	Pit-N★	150	547	112	149	21	6	47	118	122	79	.272	.408	.590	154	44	2			.965	-3	*O-150	3.4
1951	Pit-N★	151	531	124	164	31	6	42	109	137	57	.309	.452	.627	182	67	2	1	0	.967	-5	O-94,1-58	5.4
1952	Pit-N☆	149	516	90	126	17	2	37	87	110	77	.244	.384	.500	140	30	3	0	1	.970	-6	*O-149	1.9
1953	Pit-N	41	148	27	40	6	1	7	29	25	21	.270	.383	.466	121	5	1	0	0	1.000	1	O-41	0.4
	Chi-N★	117	414	73	117	14	2	28	87	75	67	.283	.394	.529	135	22	1	1	-0	.964	-4	*O-116	1.3
	Yr	158	562	100	157	20	3	35	116	100	88	.279	.391	.512	131	27	2	1	0	.973	-3	*O-157	1.7
1954	Chi-N	147	557	88	159	36	5	22	73	76	90	.285	.373	.487	121	17	2	0	1	.971	-0	*O-147	1.1
1955	Cle-A	113	321	56	78	13	0	18	54	65	46	.243	.370	.452	116	8	0	0	0	.986	-5	O-87	-0.1
Total	10	1472	5205	971	1451	216	39	369	1015	1011	749	.279	.398	.548	148	363	22	2		.974	-2	*O-1382/1-58	28.9

■ CHICK KING
King, Charles Gilbert b: 11/10/30, Paris, Tenn. BR/TR, 6'2", 190 lbs. Deb: 8/27/54

YEAR	TM/L	G	AB	R	H	2B	3B	HR	RBI	BB	SO	AVG	OBP	SLG	PRO+	BR/A	SB	CS	SBR	FA	FR	G/POS	TPR
1954	Det-A	11	28	4	6	0	1	0	3	3	8	.214	.290	.286	59	-2	0	0	0	.958	1	/O-7	-0.1
1955	Det-A	7	21	3	5	0	0	0	0	2	2	.238	.273	.238	39	-2	0	0	0	.923	-0	/O-6	-0.2
1956	Det-A	7	9	0	2	0	0	0	0	0	1	.222	.300	.222	40	-1	0	0	0	.800	1	/O-4	-0.2
1958	Chi-N	8	8	1	2	0	0	0	1	3	1	.250	.455	.250	95	0	0	0	0	1.000	-2	/O-7	-0.2
1959	Chi-N	7	3	0	0	0	0	0	0	0	1	.000	.000	.000	-99	-1	0	0	0	1.000	-0	/O-1	-0.1
	StL-N	5	7	3	3	0	0	0	1	0	2	.429	.429	.429	121	0	0	0	0	1.000	-0	/O-4	0.0
	Yr	12	10	3	3	0	0	0	1	0	3	.300	.300	.300	59	-1	0	0	0	1.000	-0	/O-5	-0.1
Total	5	45	76	11	18	0	1	0	5	8	18	.237	.310	.263	56	-5	0	0	0	.947	-3	/O-29	-0.8

■ LEE KING
King, Edward Lee b: 3/28/1894, Waltham, Mass. d: 9/7/38, Newton Center, Mass. BR/TR, 5'10", 160 lbs. Deb: 6/24/16

YEAR	TM/L	G	AB	R	H	2B	3B	HR	RBI	BB	SO	AVG	OBP	SLG	PRO+	BR/A	SB	CS	SBR	FA	FR	G/POS	TPR
1916	Phi-A	42	144	13	27	1	2	0	8	7	15	.188	.230	.222	38	-11	4			1.000	-10	O-22,S-11/32	-2.5
1919	Bos-N	2	1	0	0	0	0	0	0	0	0	.000	.000	.000	-99	-0	0			.000	0	H	0.0
Total	2	44	145	13	27	1	2	0	8	7	15	.186	.229	.221	37	-12	4			1.000	-10	/O-22,S-11,32	-2.5

■ HAL KING
King, Harold b: 2/1/44, Oviedo, Fla. BL/TR, 6'1", 200 lbs. Deb: 9/6/67

YEAR	TM/L	G	AB	R	H	2B	3B	HR	RBI	BB	SO	AVG	OBP	SLG	PRO+	BR/A	SB	CS	SBR	FA	FR	G/POS	TPR
1967	Hou-N	15	44	2	11	2	0	2	6	9	9	.250	.283	.364	87	-1	0	0	0	1.000	-2	C-11	-0.3
1968	Hou-N	27	55	4	8	2	1	0	2	16	16	.145	.242	.218	40	-4	0	0	0	.968	-4	C-19	-0.8
1970	Atl-N	89	204	29	53	8	0	11	30	32	41	.260	.366	.461	113	4	0	1	0	.985	-11	C-62	-0.4
1971	Atl-N	86	198	14	41	9	0	5	19	29	43	.207	.320	.328	79	-5	0	0	0	.983	-2	C-60	-0.5

YEAR	TM/L	G	AB	R	H	2B	3B	HR	RBI	BB	SO	AVG	OBP	SLG	PRO+	BR/A	SB	CS	SBR	FA	FR	G/POS	TPR
1972	Tex-A	50	122	12	22	5	0	4	12	25	35	.180	.333	.320	99	1	0	0	0	.970	-7	C-38	-0.6
1973	*Cin-N	35	43	5	8	0	0	4	10	6	10	.186	.286	.465	110	0	0	0	0	1.000	-1	/C-9	0.0
1974	Cin-N	20	17	1	3	1	0	0	3	3	4	.176	.300	.235	52	-1	0	0	0	1.000	0	/C-5	-0.1
Total	7	322	683	67	146	26	3	24	82	104	158	.214	.325	.366	93	-6	1	0	0	.982	-26	C-204	-2.7

■ JIM KING   King, James Hubert b: 8/27/32, Elkins, Ark. BL/TR, 6′, 185 lbs. Deb: 4/17/55

YEAR	TM/L	G	AB	R	H	2B	3B	HR	RBI	BB	SO	AVG	OBP	SLG	PRO+	BR/A	SB	CS	SBR	FA	FR	G/POS	TPR
1955	Chi-N	113	301	43	77	12	3	11	45	24	39	.256	.315	.425	95	-3	2	1	0	.990	5	O-93	-0.1
1956	Chi-N	118	317	32	79	13	2	15	54	30	40	.249	.316	.445	103	1	1	2	-1	.990	14	O-82	1.0
1957	StL-N	22	35	1	11	0	0	0	2	4	2	.314	.385	.314	89	-0	0	0	0	1.000	-2	/O-8	-0.3
1958	SF-N	34	56	8	12	2	1	2	8	10	8	.214	.343	.393	96	-0	0	1	-1	1.000	-2	O-15	-0.3
1961	Was-A	110	263	43	71	12	1	11	46	38	45	.270	.366	.449	118	7	4	0	1	.980	-6	O-91/C-1	-0.2
1962	Was-A	132	333	39	81	15	0	11	35	55	37	.243	.355	.387	101	2	4	2	0	.979	2	*O-101	-0.1
1963	Was-A	136	459	61	106	16	5	24	62	45	43	.231	.301	.444	106	2	3	0	1	.987	1	*O-123	-0.2
1964	Was-A	134	415	46	100	15	1	18	56	55	65	.241	.337	.412	108	5	3	1	0	.973	8	*O-121	0.8
1965	Was-A	120	258	46	55	10	2	14	49	44	50	.213	.339	.430	119	7	1	0	0	.993	9	O-88	0.3
1966	Was-A	117	310	41	77	14	2	10	30	38	41	.248	.330	.403	111	4	4	0	1	.987	0	O-85	0.3
1967	Was-A	47	100	16	21	2	1	2	12	15	13	.210	.331	.300	91	-1	1	1	-0	.962	-3	O-31/C-1	-0.5
	Chi-A	23	50	2	6	1	0	0	2	4	16	.120	.185	.140	-3	-6	0	0	0	1.000	-0	O-12	-1.0
	Cle-A	19	21	2	3	0	0	0	0	1	2	.143	.182	.143	-3	-3	0	0	0	1.000	-0	/O-1	-0.3
	Yr	89	171	14	30	3	1	2	14	20	31	.175	.273	.234	53	-10	1	1	-0	.971	-5	O-44/C-1	-1.8
Total	11	1125	2918	374	699	112	19	117	401	363	401	.240	.328	.411	104	15	23	8	2	.984	13	O-851/C-2	-0.6

■ JEFF KING   King, Jeffrey Wayne b: 12/26/64, Marion, Ind. BR/TR, 6′1″, 175 lbs. Deb: 6/2/89

YEAR	TM/L	G	AB	R	H	2B	3B	HR	RBI	BB	SO	AVG	OBP	SLG	PRO+	BR/A	SB	CS	SBR	FA	FR	G/POS	TPR
1989	Pit-N	75	215	31	42	13	3	5	19	20	34	.195	.270	.353	80	-6	4	2	0	.995	-2	1-46,3-13/2S	-1.2
1990	*Pit-N	127	371	46	91	17	1	14	53	21	50	.245	.288	.410	93	-5	3	3	-1	.938	16	*3-115/1-1	1.1
1991	Pit-N	33	109	16	26	1	1	4	18	14	15	.239	.331	.376	100	0	3	1	0	.975	1	3-33	0.1
1992	*Pit-N	130	480	56	111	21	2	14	65	27	56	.231	.275	.371	82	-13	4	6	-2	.953	-4	3-73,1-32,2/SO	-2.2
1993	Pit-N	158	611	82	180	35	3	9	98	59	54	.295	.361	.406	105	5	8	6	-1	.964	21	*3-156/2-2,S	2.5
1994	Pit-N	94	339	36	89	23	0	5	42	30	38	.263	.322	.375	81	-9	3	2	-0	.955	11	3-91/2-1	0.2
Total	6	617	2125	267	539	110	10	51	295	171	247	.254	.312	.387	91	-28	25	20	-4	.955	43	3-481/1-79,2SO	0.5

■ LEE KING   King, Lee b: 12/26/1892, Hundred, W.Va. d: 9/16/67, Shinnston, W.Va. BR/TR, 5′8″, 160 lbs. Deb: 9/20/16

YEAR	TM/L	G	AB	R	H	2B	3B	HR	RBI	BB	SO	AVG	OBP	SLG	PRO+	BR/A	SB	CS	SBR	FA	FR	G/POS	TPR
1916	Pit-N	8	18	0	2	0	0	0	1	0	7	.111	.111	.111	-31	-3	0			.714	-1	/O-8	-0.5
1917	Pit-N	111	381	32	95	14	5	1	35	15	58	.249	.281	.320	81	-9	8			.968	9	*O-102	-0.6
1918	Pit-N	36	112	9	26	3	2	1	11	11	15	.232	.301	.321	87	-2	3			.909	-8	O-36	-1.3
1919	NY-N	21	20	5	2	1	0	0	1	1	6	.100	.143	.150	-12	-3	0			.667	-3	/O-7	-0.6
1920	NY-N	93	261	32	72	11	4	7	42	21	38	.276	.335	.429	120	6	3	7	-3	.951	-11	O-84	-1.4
1921	NY-N	39	94	17	21	4	2	0	7	13	6	.223	.324	.309	68	-4	0	2	-1	.921	-5	O-35/1-1	-1.2
	Phi-N	64	216	25	58	19	4	4	32	8	37	.269	.298	.449	88	-5	1	4	-2	.911	-2	O-57	-1.3
	Yr	103	310	42	79	23	6	4	39	21	43	.255	.306	.406	83	-8	1	6	-3	.914	-7	O-92/1-1	-2.5
1922	Phi-N	19	53	8	12	5	1	2	13	8	6	.226	.328	.472	95	-1	0	1	0	.946	0	O-15	-0.2
	*NY-N	20	34	6	6	3	0	0	2	5	2	.176	.282	.265	41	-3	1	0	0	1.000	0	/1-5,O-5	-0.3
	Yr	39	87	14	18	8	1	2	15	13	8	.207	.310	.391	76	-3	1	0	0	.961	-0	O-20/1-5	-0.5
Total	7	411	1189	134	294	60	18	15	144	82	175	.247	.299	.366	87	-22	16	13		.940	-21	O-349/1-6	-7.4

■ LYNN KING   King, Lynn Paul "Dig" b: 11/28/07, Villisca, Iowa d: 5/11/72, Atlantic, Iowa BL/TR, 5′9″, 165 lbs. Deb: 9/21/35

YEAR	TM/L	G	AB	R	H	2B	3B	HR	RBI	BB	SO	AVG	OBP	SLG	PRO+	BR/A	SB	CS	SBR	FA	FR	G/POS	TPR
1935	StL-N	8	22	6	4	0	0	0	4	1	2	.182	.308	.182	34	-2	2			1.000	2	/O-6	0.0
1936	StL-N	78	100	12	19	2	1	0	10	9	14	.190	.257	.230	32	-9	2			.984	-4	O-34	-1.4
1939	StL-N	89	85	10	20	2	0	0	11	15	3	.235	.350	.259	62	-4	2			.982	-10	O-44	-1.4
Total	3	175	207	28	43	4	1	0	28	18	28	.208	.302	.237	45	-15	6			.986	-12	/O-84	-2.8

■ MART KING   King, Marshal Ney b: 12/1849, Troy, N.Y. d: 10/19/11, Troy, N.Y. TR , 5′9.5″, 176 lbs. Deb: 5/8/1871

YEAR	TM/L	G	AB	R	H	2B	3B	HR	RBI	BB	SO	AVG	OBP	SLG	PRO+	BR/A	SB	CS	SBR	FA	FR	G/POS	TPR
1871	Chi-n	20	101	23	21	1	0	2	16	8	1	.208	.266	.277	51	-8	5					O-10/C-7,S	-0.5
1872	Tro-n	3	11	0	0	0	0	0	1	0	1	.000	.000	.000	-99	-2						O-3	-0.2
Total	2 n	23	112	23	21	1	0	2	17	8	2	.188	.242	.250	39	-10						/O-13,C-7, S	-0.7

■ SAM KING   King, Samuel Warren b: 5/17/1852, Peabody, Mass. d: 8/11/22, Peabody, Mass. TL , 6′, Deb: 5/1/1884

YEAR	TM/L	G	AB	R	H	2B	3B	HR	RBI	BB	SO	AVG	OBP	SLG	PRO+	BR/A	SB	CS	SBR	FA	FR	G/POS	TPR
1884	Was-a	12	45	3	8	2	0	0		1		.178	.213	.222	48	-2				.912	-1	1-12	-0.5

■ STEVE KING   King, Stephen F. b: 1842, Troy, N.Y. d: 7/8/1895, Troy, N.Y. 5′9″, 175 lbs. Deb: 5/9/1871

YEAR	TM/L	G	AB	R	H	2B	3B	HR	RBI	BB	SO	AVG	OBP	SLG	PRO+	BR/A	SB	CS	SBR	FA	FR	G/POS	TPR
1871	Tro-n	29	144	45	57	10	6	0	34	1	1	.396	.400	.549	167	12	3					*O-29	0.8
1872	Tro-n	25	129	33	40	9	1	0	21	1	2	.310	.315	.395	116	2						O-25	0.2
Total	2 n	54	273	78	97	19	7	0	55	2	3	.355	.360	.476	144	14						/O-54	1.0

■ WES KINGDON   Kingdon, Westcott William b: 7/4/1900, Los Angeles, Cal. d: 4/19/75, Capistrano, Cal. BR/TR, 5′8″, 148 lbs. Deb: 6/12/32

YEAR	TM/L	G	AB	R	H	2B	3B	HR	RBI	BB	SO	AVG	OBP	SLG	PRO+	BR/A	SB	CS	SBR	FA	FR	G/POS	TPR
1932	Was-A	18	34	10	11	3	1	0	3	5	2	.324	.410	.471	129	2	0	0	0	.929	-2	/3-8,S-4	0.1

■ MIKE KINGERY   Kingery, Michael Scott b: 3/29/61, St.James, Minn. BL/TL, 6′, 180 lbs. Deb: 7/7/86

YEAR	TM/L	G	AB	R	H	2B	3B	HR	RBI	BB	SO	AVG	OBP	SLG	PRO+	BR/A	SB	CS	SBR	FA	FR	G/POS	TPR
1986	KC-A	62	209	25	54	8	5	3	14	12	30	.258	.299	.388	83	-5	7	3	0	.973	-3	O-59	-1.0
1987	Sea-A	120	354	38	99	25	4	9	52	27	43	.280	.334	.449	100	-0	7	9	-3	.992	10	*O-114/D-4	0.3
1988	Sea-A	57	123	21	25	6	0	1	9	19	23	.203	.315	.276	64	-5	3	1	0	.989	-1	O-44,1-10	-0.7
1989	Sea-A	31	76	14	17	3	0	2	6	7	14	.224	.289	.342	75	-3	1	1	-0	1.000	3	O-23	-0.1
1990	SF-N	105	207	24	61	7	1	0	24	12	19	.295	.336	.338	89	-3	6	1	1	.978	-12	O-95	-1.5
1991	SF-N	91	110	13	20	2	2	0	8	15	21	.182	.280	.236	48	-7	1	0	0	.975	-7	O-38/1-6	-1.5
1992	Oak-A	12	28	3	3	0	0	0	1	1	3	.107	.138	.107	-32	-5	0	0	0	1.000	-2	O-10	-0.8
1994	Col-N	105	301	56	105	27	8	4	41	30	26	.349	.411	.532	123	10	5	7	-3	.979	-5	O-98/1-1	0.1
Total	8	583	1408	194	384	78	20	19	155	123	179	.273	.334	.397	92	-19	30	22	-4	.984	-18	O-481/1-17,D	-5.2

■ DAVE KINGMAN   Kingman, David Arthur b: 12/21/48, Pendleton, Ore. BR/TR, 6′6″, 210 lbs. Deb: 7/30/71

YEAR	TM/L	G	AB	R	H	2B	3B	HR	RBI	BB	SO	AVG	OBP	SLG	PRO+	BR/A	SB	CS	SBR	FA	FR	G/POS	TPR
1971	*SF-N	41	115	17	32	10	2	6	24	9	35	.278	.336	.557	151	7	5	0	2	.981	-4	1-20,O-14	0.3
1972	SF-N	135	472	65	106	17	4	29	83	51	140	.225	.306	.462	114	7	16	6	1	.932	3	3-59,1-56,O	0.6
1973	SF-N	112	305	54	62	10	1	24	55	41	122	.203	.302	.479	109	2	8	5	-1	.910	2	3-60,1-46/P	0.3
1974	SF-N	121	350	41	78	18	2	18	55	37	125	.223	.303	.440	101	-1	8	8	-2	.983	2	1-91,3-21/O	-0.7
1975	NY-N	134	502	65	116	22	1	36	88	34	153	.231	.285	.494	119	11	7	5	-1	.958	5	O-71,1-58,3	0.4
1976	NY-N★	123	474	70	113	14	1	37	86	28	135	.238	.288	.506	130	13	7	4	-0	.959	3	*O-111,1-16	1.2
1977	NY-N	58	211	22	44	7	0	9	28	13	66	.209	.264	.370	71	-10	3	2	-0	.974	-2	O-45,1-17	-1.5
	SD-N	56	168	16	40	4	0	11	39	12	48	.238	.297	.488	119	3	2	3	-1	.964	2	O-28,1-13/3	0.2
	Yr	114	379	38	84	16	0	20	67	25	114	.222	.279	.422	92	-7	5	5	-0	.970	-0	O-73,1-30/3	-1.3
	Cal-A	10	36	4	7	2	0	2	4	1	16	.194	.237	.417	77	-1	0	0	0	.974	-1	/1-8,O-2	-0.3
	NY-A	8	24	5	6	0	0	4	7	2	13	.250	.333	.833	208	3	0	1	-1	1.000	0	/D-6	0.2
	Yr	18	60	9	13	2	0	6	11	3	29	.217	.277	.583	131	2	0	1	-1	.974	-1	/1-8,H-6,O	-0.1
1978	Chi-N	119	395	65	105	17	4	28	79	39	111	.266	.341	.542	128	13	3	4	-2	.978	5	*O-100/1-6	0.8
1979	Chi-N†	145	532	97	153	19	5	**48**	115	45	131	.288	.348	**.613**	143	28	4	2	0	.954	5	*O-139	2.8
1980	Chi-N★	81	255	31	71	8	0	18	57	21	44	.278	.328	.522	126	6	1	2	-1	.941	1	O-61/1-2	0.6
1981	NY-N	100	353	40	78	11	3	22	59	55	105	.221	.328	.456	122	10	6	0	1	.974	-6	1-56,O-48	0.2

YEAR	TM/L	G	AB	R	H	2B	3B	HR	RBI	BB	SO	AVG	OBP	SLG	PRO+	BR/A	SB	CS	SBR	FA	FR	G/POS	TPR
1982	NY-N	149	535	80	109	9	1	**37**	99	59	156	.204	.288	.432	99	-3	4	0	1	.986	-14	*1-143	-2.4
1983	NY-N	100	248	25	49	7	0	13	29	22	57	.198	.266	.383	79	-8	2	1	0	.994	-5	1-50/O-5	-1.7
1984	Oak-A	147	549	68	147	23	1	35	118	44	119	.268	.324	.505	136	24	2	1	0	1.000	-2	*D-139/1-9	1.8
1985	Oak-A	158	592	66	141	16	0	30	91	62	114	.238	.313	.417	105	3	3	2	-0	1.000	-1	*D-149/1-9	-0.2
1986	Oak-A	144	561	70	118	19	0	35	94	33	126	.210	.258	.431	90	-11	3	3	-1	.895	-1	*D-140/1-3	-1.6
Total	16	1941	6677	901	1575	240	25	442	1210	608	1816	.236	.305	.478	115	94	85	49	-4	.957	-11	O-648,1-603,D3/P	1.0

■ **HARRY KINGMAN**   Kingman, Henry Lees   b: 4/3/1892, Tientsin, China   d: 12/27/82, Oakland, Cal.   BL/TL, 6'1.5", 165 lbs.   Deb: 7/1/14

YEAR	TM/L	G	AB	R	H	2B	3B	HR	RBI	BB	SO	AVG	OBP	SLG	PRO+	BR/A	SB	CS	SBR	FA	FR	G/POS	TPR
1914	NY-A	4	3	0	0	0	0	0	0	1	2	.000	.250	.000	-24	-0	0			1.000	-0	/1-1	-0.1

■ **WALT KINLOCK**   Kinlock, Walter   b: 1878, St.Joseph, Mo.   Deb: 8/1/1895

| 1895 | StL-N | 1 | 3 | 0 | 1 | 0 | 0 | 0 | 0 | 0 | 2 | .333 | .333 | .333 | 73 | -0 | 0 | | | 1.000 | 1 | /3-1 | 0.0 |

■ **BOB KINSELLA**   Kinsella, Robert Francis "Red"   b: 1/5/1899, Springfield, Ill.   d: 12/30/51, Los Angeles, Cal.   BL/TR, 5'9.5", 165 lbs.   Deb: 9/20/19

1919	NY-N	3	9	1	2	0	0	0	0	0	3	.222	.222	.222	34	-1	1			.500	-2	/O-3	-0.3
1920	NY-N	1	3	0	1	0	0	0	1	0	2	.333	.333	.333	93	-0	0	0	0	.500	-1	/O-1	-0.1
Total	2	4	12	1	3	0	0	0	1	0	5	.250	.250	.250	49	-1	1	0		.500	-2	/O-4	-0.4

■ **KINSLER**   Kinsler   b: Staten Island, N.Y.   Deb: 6/8/1893

| 1893 | NY-N | 1 | 3 | 0 | 0 | 0 | 0 | 0 | 0 | 1 | 1 | .000 | .250 | .000 | -31 | -1 | 0 | | | 1.000 | -0 | /O-1 | -0.1 |

■ **TOM KINSLOW**   Kinslow, Thomas F.   b: 1/12/1866, Washington, D.C.   d: 2/22/01, Washington, D.C.   BR/TR, 5'10", 160 lbs.   Deb: 6/4/1886

1886	Was-N	3	8	1	2	0	0	0	1	0	1	.250	.250	.250	56	-0	0			1.000	-0	/C-3	0.0
1887	NY-a	2	6	0	0					0	0	.000	.000	.000	-99	-2	0			1.000	-0	/C-2	-0.1
1890	Bro-P	64	242	30	64	11	6	4	46	10	22	.264	.299	.409	83	-8	2			.909	11	C-64	0.7
1891	Bro-N	61	228	22	54	6	0	0	33	9	22	.237	.266	.263	55	-13	3			.922	-9	C-61	-1.5
1892	Bro-N	66	246	37	75	6	11	2	40	13	16	.305	.342	.443	142	11	4			.933	5	C-66	1.9
1893	Bro-N	78	312	38	76	8	4	4	45	11	13	.244	.272	.333	63	-18	4			.932	-2	C-76/O-2	-1.1
1894	Bro-N	62	223	39	68	5	6	2	41	20	11	.305	.362	.408	92	-3	4			.907	-9	C-61/1-1	-0.4
1895	Pit-N	19	62	10	14	2	0	0	5	2	2	.226	.250	.258	33	-6	1			.962	-2	C-18	-0.5
1896	Lou-N	8	25	4	7	0	1	0	7	1	5	.280	.308	.360	79	-1	0			.810	-2	/C-5,1-1	-0.2
1898	Was-N	3	9	0	1	0	0	0	0	0		.111	.111	.111	-36	-2	0			.800	-1	/C-3,1-1	-0.2
	StL-N	14	53	5	15	2	1	0	4	1		.283	.309	.358	89	-1	0			.925	1	C-14	0.1
	Yr	17	62	5	16	2	1	0	4	1		.258	.281	.323	72	-3	0			.909	0	C-17/1-1	-0.1
Total	10	380	1414	186	376	40	29	12	222	67	92	.266	.301	.361	81	-43	18			.923	-7	C-373/1-3,O	-1.3

■ **WALT KINZIE**   Kinzie, Walter Harris   b: 3/1858, Kansas   d: 11/5/09,   BR, 5'10.5", 161 lbs.   Deb: 7/17/1882

1882	Det-N	13	53	5	5	0	1	0	2	0	8	.094	.094	.132	-28	-7				.852	-4	S-13	-1.0
1884	Chi-N	19	82	4	13	3	0	2	8	0	13	.159	.159	.268	29	-7				.831	-3	S-17/3-2	-0.8
	StL-a	2	9	0	1	0	0	0	0			.111	.111	.111	-26	-1				.727	-3	/2-2	-0.4
Total	2	34	144	9	19	3	1	2	10	0	21	.132	.132	.208	6	-15				.840	-9	/S-30,2-3,3	-2.2

■ **ED KIPPERT**   Kippert, Edward August "Kickapoo"   b: 1/3/1880, Detroit, Mich.   d: 6/3/60, Detroit, Mich.   BR/TR, 5'10.5", 180 lbs.   Deb: 4/14/14

| 1914 | Cin-N | 2 | 2 | 0 | 0 | 0 | 0 | 0 | 0 | 0 | 0 | .000 | .000 | .000 | -97 | -0 | 0 | | | 1.000 | -1 | /O-2 | -0.1 |

■ **JIM KIRBY**   Kirby, James Herschel   b: 5/5/23, Nashville, Tenn.   BR/TR, 5'11", 175 lbs.   Deb: 5/1/49

| 1949 | Chi-N | 3 | 2 | 0 | 1 | 0 | 0 | 0 | 0 | 0 | 0 | .500 | .500 | .500 | 174 | 0 | 0 | | | .000 | 0 | H | 0.0 |

■ **LA RUE KIRBY**   Kirby, La Rue   b: 12/30/1889, Eureka, Mich.   d: 6/10/61, Lansing, Mich.   BB/TR, 6', 185 lbs.   Deb: 8/7/12

1912	NY-N	3	5	1	1	0	0	0	0	0	0	.200	.200	.400	60	-0	0			1.000	0	/P-3	0.0
1914	StL-F	52	195	21	48	6	3	2	18	14	30	.246	.303	.338	63	-11	5			.973	2	O-50	-1.2
1915	StL-F	61	178	15	38	7	2	0	16	17	31	.213	.282	.275	47	-13	3			.969	-3	O-52/P-1	-2.0
Total	3	116	378	37	87	14	5	2	34	31	61	.230	.292	.310	55	-25	8			.971	-1	O-102/P-4	-3.2

■ **WAYNE KIRBY**   Kirby, Wayne Leonard   b: 1/22/64, Williamsburg, Va.   BL/TR, 5'10", 185 lbs.   Deb: 9/12/91

1991	Cle-A	21	43	4	9	2	0	0	5	2	6	.209	.244	.256	38	-4	1	2	-1	1.000	-1	O-21	-0.6
1992	Cle-A	21	18	9	3	1	0	1	1	3	2	.167	.286	.389	89	-0	0	3	-2	1.000	-0	/O-2,D-4	-0.2
1993	Cle-A	131	458	71	123	19	5	6	60	37	58	.269	.327	.371	88	-8	17	5	2	.983	13	*O-123/D-5	0.4
1994	Cle-A	78	191	33	56	6	0	5	23	13	30	.293	.341	.403	87	-4	11	4	1	.959	-11	O-68/D-2	-1.4
Total	4	251	710	117	191	28	5	12	89	55	96	.269	.325	.373	85	-16	29	14	0	.979	1	O-214/D-11	-1.8

■ **TOM KIRK**   Kirk, Thomas Daniel   b: 9/27/27, Philadelphia, Pa.   d: 8/1/74, Philadelphia, Pa.   BL/TL, 5'10.5", 182 lbs.   Deb: 6/24/47

| 1947 | Phi-A | 1 | 1 | 0 | 0 | 0 | 0 | 0 | 0 | 0 | 0 | .000 | .000 | .000 | -98 | -0 | 0 | 0 | 0 | .000 | 0 | H | 0.0 |

■ **JAY KIRKE**   Kirke, Judson Fabian   b: 6/16/1888, Fleischmanns, N.Y   d: 8/31/68, New Orleans, La.   BL/TR, 6', 195 lbs.   Deb: 9/28/10

1910	Det-A	8	25	3	5	1	0	0	3	1		.200	.231	.240	44	-2	1			.917	-3	/2-7,O-1	-0.5
1911	Bos-N	20	89	9	32	5	5	0	12	2	6	.360	.380	.528	142	4	3			.929	-1	O-14/1-3,2S3	0.3
1912	Bos-N	103	359	53	115	11	4	4	62	9	46	.320	.339	.407	102	-1	7			.903	-2	O-72,3-14/S1	-0.5
1913	Bos-N	18	38	3	9	2	0	0	3	1	6	.237	.293	.289	65	-2	0			.923	2	O-13	0.0
1914	Cle-A	67	242	18	66	10	2	1	25	7	30	.273	.296	.343	89	-4	5	10	-5	.974	-0	O-42,1-18	-1.2
1915	Cle-A	87	339	35	105	19	2	2	40	14	21	.310	.346	.395	120	6	5	6	-2	.986	-1	1-87	0.2
1918	NY-N	17	56	1	14	1	0	0	3	1	3	.250	.263	.268	63	-3	0			.978	1	1-16	-0.3
Total	7	320	1148	122	346	49	13	7	148	35	112	.301	.328	.385	103	-0	21	16		.927	-4	O-142,1-125/32S	-2.0

■ **WILLIE KIRKLAND**   Kirkland, Willie Charles   b: 2/17/34, Siluria, Ala.   BL/TR, 6'1", 206 lbs.   Deb: 4/15/58

1958	SF-N	122	418	48	108	25	6	14	56	43	69	.258	.335	.447	107	4	3	2	-0	.961	-0	*O-115	-0.3
1959	SF-N	126	463	64	126	22	4	22	68	42	84	.272	.337	.475	116	9	5	3	-0	.969	1	*O-117	0.4
1960	SF-N	146	515	59	130	21	10	21	65	44	86	.252	.316	.454	115	8	12	7	-1	.978	4	*O-143	0.4
1961	Cle-A	146	525	84	136	22	5	27	95	48	77	.259	.324	.474	113	7	7	0	2	.974	8	*O-138	1.0
1962	Cle-A	137	419	50	84	9	4	21	72	43	62	.200	.275	.377	76	-16	9	1	2	.972	6	*O-125	-2.0
1963	Cle-A	127	427	51	98	13	2	15	47	45	99	.230	.304	.375	90	-6	8	1	1	.984	7	*O-112	-0.4
1964	Bal-A	66	150	14	30	5	0	3	22	17	26	.200	.286	.293	62	-8	3	2	-0	.989	0	O-58	-1.0
	Was-A	32	102	8	22	6	0	5	13	6	30	.216	.252	.422	86	-2	0	0	-0	.907	-3	O-27	-0.7
	Yr	98	252	22	52	11	0	8	35	23	56	.206	.275	.345	72	-10	3	2	-0	.964	-3	O-85	-1.7
1965	Was-A	123	312	38	72	9	1	14	54	19	65	.231	.275	.401	91	-5	3	2	-0	.987	-6	O-92	-1.6
1966	Was-A	124	163	21	31	2	1	6	17	16	50	.190	.260	.325	68	-7	2	0	1	.983	-12	O-68	-2.1
Total	9	1149	3494	443	837	134	29	148	509	323	648	.240	.307	.422	99	-15	52	19	4	.974	-2	O-995	-6.3

■ **ED KIRKPATRICK**   Kirkpatrick, Edgar Leon   b: 10/8/44, Spokane, Wash.   BL/TR, 5'11.5", 195 lbs.   Deb: 9/13/62

1962	LA-A	3	6	0	0	0	0	0	0	0	0	.000	.000	.000	-99	-2	0	0	0	1.000	1	/C-1	-0.1
1963	LA-A	34	77	4	15	5	0	2	7	6	19	.195	.262	.338	71	-3	1	0	0	.986	-0	C-14,O-10	-0.3
1964	LA-A	75	219	20	53	13	3	2	22	23	30	.242	.320	.356	97	-1	2	2	-1	.969	-2	O-63	-0.7
1965	Cal-A	19	73	8	19	5	0	3	8	3	9	.260	.289	.452	110	1	1	0	0	.969	1	O-19	-0.1
1966	Cal-A	117	312	31	60	7	4	9	44	51	67	.192	.315	.327	87	-4	7	4	0	.994	-6	*O-102/1-3	-1.6
1967	Cal-A	3	8	0	0	0	0	0	0	0	0	.000	.000	.000	-99	-2	0	0	0	1.000	-2	/C-2,O-1	-0.5
1968	Cal-A	89	161	23	37	4	0	1	15	25	32	.230	.337	.273	90	-1	1	3	-2	.982	-5	O-45/C-4,1	-1.1

YEAR	TM/L	G	AB	R	H	2B	3B	HR	RBI	BB	SO	AVG	OBP	SLG	PRO+	BR/A	SB	CS	SBR	FA	FR	G/POS	TPR
1969	KC-A	120	315	40	81	11	4	14	49	43	42	.257	.352	.451	122	9	3	5	-2	.995	8	O-82/C-8,132	1.2
1970	KC-A	134	424	59	97	17	2	18	62	55	65	.229	.319	.406	98	-1	4	4	-1	.978	-8	C-89,O-19,1	-0.9
1971	KC-A	120	365	46	80	12	1	9	46	48	60	.219	.313	.332	83	-8	3	4	-2	.992	-1	O-61,C-59	-1.1
1972	KC-A	113	364	43	100	15	1	9	43	51	50	.275	.368	.396	128	14	3	5	-2	.991	-5	*C-108/1-1	1.3
1973	KC-A	126	429	61	113	24	3	6	45	46	48	.263	.336	.375	93	-4	3	7	-3	.990	-5	*O-108,C-14/D	-1.7
1974	*Pit-N	116	271	32	67	9	0	6	38	51	30	.247	.370	.347	105	4	1	2	-1	.993	-4	1-59,O-14/C	-0.5
1975	*Pit-N	89	144	15	34	5	0	5	16	18	22	.236	.321	.375	93	-1	1	0	0	1.000	-1	1-28,O-14	-0.3
1976	Pit-N	83	146	14	34	9	0	0	16	14	15	.233	.300	.295	69	-6	1	0	0	.990	-1	1-25/O-9,3	-0.8
1977	Pit-N	21	28	5	4	2	0	1	4	8	6	.143	.333	.321	75	-1	1	0	0	.972	-1	1-10/O-2,3	-0.2
	Tex-A	20	48	2	9	1	0	0	3	4	11	.188	.250	.208	26	-5	2	0	1	1.000	1	/O-6,1-3,CD	-0.4
	Mil-A	29	77	8	21	4	0	0	6	10	8	.273	.364	.325	89	-1	0	1	-1	.973	-2	O-22/3-1,D	-0.4
	Yr	49	125	10	30	5	0	0	9	14	19	.240	.321	.280	65	-6	2	1	0	.980	-2	O-28/D-8,1C3	-0.8
Total	16	1311	3467	411	824	143	18	85	424	456	518	.238	.330	.363	97	-12	34	39	-13	.989	-32	O-577,C-306,1/D32	-8.2

■ ENOS KIRKPATRICK   Kirkpatrick, Enos Claire   b: 12/8/1885, Pittsburgh, Pa.   d: 4/14/64, Pittsburgh, Pa.   BR/TR, 5'10", 175 lbs.   Deb: 8/24/12

YEAR	TM/L	G	AB	R	H	2B	3B	HR	RBI	BB	SO	AVG	OBP	SLG	PRO+	BR/A	SB	CS	SBR	FA	FR	G/POS	TPR
1912	Bro-N	32	94	13	18	1	1	0	6	9	15	.191	.269	.223	37	-8	5			.968	6	3-29/S-3	-0.2
1913	Bro-N	48	89	13	22	4	1	1	5	3	18	.247	.287	.348	79	-3	5			.897	-1	S-10/1-8,23	-0.4
1914	Bal-F	55	174	22	44	7	2	2	16	18	30	.253	.330	.351	74	-7	10			.932	-5	3-36,S-11/O1	-1.0
1915	Bal-F	68	171	22	41	8	2	0	19	24	15	.240	.337	.310	71	-6	12			.911	-3	3-28,2-21/1S	-0.8
Total	4	203	528	70	125	20	6	3	46	54	78	.237	.315	.314	68	-24	32			.936	-2	/3-97,S-29,210	-2.4

■ JOE KIRRENE   Kirrene, Joseph John   b: 10/4/31, San Francisco, Cal.   BR/TR, 6'2", 195 lbs.   Deb: 10/1/50

YEAR	TM/L	G	AB	R	H	2B	3B	HR	RBI	BB	SO	AVG	OBP	SLG	PRO+	BR/A	SB	CS	SBR	FA	FR	G/POS	TPR
1950	Chi-A	1	4	0	1	0	0	0	0	0	1	.250	.250	.250	29	-0	0	0	0	1.000	-1	/3-1	-0.1
1954	Chi-A	9	23	4	7	1	0	0	4	5	2	.304	.448	.348	116	1	1	0	0	.947	-2	/3-9	-0.1
Total	2	10	27	4	8	1	0	0	4	5	3	.296	.424	.333	105	1	1	0	0	.952	-3	/3-10	-0.2

■ ERNIE KISH   Kish, Ernest Alexander   b: 2/6/18, Washington, D.C.   d: 12/21/93, Kirtland, Ohio   BL/TR, 5'9.5", 170 lbs.   Deb: 7/29/45

YEAR	TM/L	G	AB	R	H	2B	3B	HR	RBI	BB	SO	AVG	OBP	SLG	PRO+	BR/A	SB	CS	SBR	FA	FR	G/POS	TPR
1945	Phi-A	43	110	10	27	5	1	0	10	9	9	.245	.320	.309	83	-2	0	3	-2	.932	-4	O-30	-1.0

■ BILL KISSINGER   Kissinger, William Francis "Shang"   b: 8/15/1871, Dayton, Ky.   d: 4/20/29, Cincinnati, Ohio   BR/TR, 185 lbs.   Deb: 5/30/1895

YEAR	TM/L	G	AB	R	H	2B	3B	HR	RBI	BB	SO	AVG	OBP	SLG	PRO+	BR/A	SB	CS	SBR	FA	FR	G/POS	TPR
1895	Bal-N	2	5	1	1	0	0	0	0	0	1	.200	.200	.200	3	-1	0			1.000	-0	/P-2	0.0
	StL-N	33	97	8	24	6	1	0	8	0	11	.247	.247	.330	49	-8	1			.975	-5	P-24/S-4,O3	-0.6
	Yr	35	102	9	25	6	1	0	8	0	12	.245	.245	.324	46	-9	1			.976	-5	P-26/S-4,O3	-0.6
1896	StL-N	23	73	8	22	4	0	0	12	0	1	.301	.301	.356	76	-3	0			.906	0	P-20/O-3,3	-0.2
1897	StL-N	14	39	7	13	3	2	0	6	3		.333	.381	.513	137	2	0			.786	-2	/O-7,P-7	-0.1
Total	3	72	214	24	60	13	3	0	26	3	<u>16</u>	.280	.290	.369	73	-9	1			.935	-6	/P-53,O-14,S3	-0.9

■ CHRIS KITSOS   Kitsos, Christopher Anestos   b: 2/11/28, New York, N.Y.   BB/TR, 5'9", 165 lbs.   Deb: 4/21/54

YEAR	TM/L	G	AB	R	H	2B	3B	HR	RBI	BB	SO	AVG	OBP	SLG	PRO+	BR/A	SB	CS	SBR	FA	FR	G/POS	TPR
1954	Chi-N	1	0	0	0	0	0	0	0	0	0	—	—	—	—	0	0	0	0	1.000	0	/S-1	0.0

■ RON KITTLE   Kittle, Ronald Dale   b: 1/5/58, Gary, Indiana   BR/TR, 6'4", 220 lbs.   Deb: 9/2/82

YEAR	TM/L	G	AB	R	H	2B	3B	HR	RBI	BB	SO	AVG	OBP	SLG	PRO+	BR/A	SB	CS	SBR	FA	FR	G/POS	TPR
1982	Chi-A	20	29	3	7	2	0	1	7	3	12	.241	.313	.414	97	-0	0	0	0	1.000	-2	/O-5,D-3	-0.2
1983	*Chi-A★	145	520	75	132	19	3	35	100	39	150	.254	.316	.504	117	10	8	3	1	.964	-9	*O-139/D-2	-0.3
1984	Chi-A	139	466	67	100	15	0	32	74	49	137	.215	.298	.453	100	-2	3	6	-3	.972	3	*O-124/D-7	-0.5
1985	Chi-A	116	379	51	87	12	0	26	58	31	92	.230	.296	.467	101	-1	1	4	-2	.989	-3	O-57,D-57	-0.8
1986	Chi-A	86	296	34	63	11	0	17	48	28	87	.213	.287	.422	87	-6	2	1	0	1.000	2	D-62,O-19	-0.6
	NY-A	30	80	8	19	2	0	4	12	7	23	.237	.299	.412	92	-1	2	0	1	1.000	0	D-24/O-1	-0.1
	Yr	116	376	42	82	13	0	21	60	35	110	.218	.290	.420	89	-7	4	1	1	1.000	2	D-86,O-21	-0.7
1987	NY-A	59	159	21	44	5	0	12	28	10	36	.277	.324	.535	123	5	0	1	-1	1.000	1	D-49/O-2	0.3
1988	Cle-A	75	225	31	58	8	0	18	43	16	65	.258	.329	.533	134	9	0	0	0	.000	0	D-63	0.8
1989	Chi-A	51	169	26	51	10	0	11	37	22	42	.302	.385	.556	166	15	0	1	-1	.982	-3	1-27,D-17/O	0.8
1990	Chi-A	83	277	29	68	14	0	16	43	24	77	.245	.313	.469	118	6	0	0	0	.987	-4	D-54,1-25	-0.2
	Bal-A	22	61	4	10	2	0	2	3	2	14	.164	.203	.295	39	-5	0	0	0	1.000	-1	D-13/1-5	-0.7
	Yr	105	338	33	78	16	0	18	46	26	91	.231	.293	.438	104	0	0	0	0	.989	-5	D-67,1-30	-0.9
1991	Chi-A	17	47	7	9	0	0	2	7	5	9	.191	.296	.319	72	-2	0	0	0	.982	-1	1-15	-0.4
Total	10	843	2708	356	648	100	3	176	460	236	744	.239	.309	.473	110	28	16	16	-5	.974	-17	O-353,D-351/1	-1.9

■ MALACHI KITTRIDGE   Kittridge, Malachi Jeddidah "Jeddidah"   b: 10/12/1869, Clinton, Mass.   d: 6/23/28, Gary, Ind.   BR/TR, 5'7", 170 lbs.   Deb: 4/19/1890   M

YEAR	TM/L	G	AB	R	H	2B	3B	HR	RBI	BB	SO	AVG	OBP	SLG	PRO+	BR/A	SB	CS	SBR	FA	FR	G/POS	TPR
1890	Chi-N	96	333	46	67	8	3	3	35	39	55	.201	.287	.270	60	-17	7			.944	2	*C-96	-0.6
1891	Chi-N	79	296	26	62	8	5	2	27	17	28	.209	.252	.291	58	-17	4			.940	-0	C-79	-0.4
1892	Chi-N	69	229	19	41	5	0	0	10	11	27	.179	.217	.201	26	-21	2			.946	15	C-69	-0.1
1893	Chi-N	70	255	32	59	9	5	2	30	17	15	.231	.279	.329	62	-15	3			.939	6	C-70	-0.3
1894	Chi-N	51	168	36	53	8	2	0	23	26	20	.315	.407	.387	88	-3	2			.925	2	C-51	0.3
1895	Chi-N	60	212	30	48	6	3	2	29	16	9	.226	.284	.325	54	-16	6			.976	-2	C-59	-1.0
1896	Chi-N	65	215	17	48	4	1	1	19	14	14	.223	.274	.265	41	-19	6			.962	1	C-64/P-1	-0.9
1897	Chi-N	79	262	25	53	5	5	1	30	22		.202	.264	.271	40	-24	9			.952	3	C-79	-1.0
1898	Lou-N	86	287	27	70	8	5	1	31	15		.244	.281	.317	73	-11	9			.944	-11	C-86	-1.3
1899	Lou-N	45	129	11	26	2	1	0	12	26		.202	.340	.233	58	-6	3			.974	7	C-43	0.4
	Was-N	44	133	14	20	3	0	0	11	10		.150	.215	.173	7	-17	2			.949	4	C-43	-0.9
	Yr	89	262	25	46	5	1	0	23	36		.176	.280	.202	33	-23	5			.961	11	C-86	-0.5
1901	Bos-N	114	381	24	96	14	2	0	40	32		.252	.312	.304	72	-14	2			**.984**	12	*C-113	1.0
1902	Bos-N	80	255	18	60	7	0	2	30	24		.235	.304	.286	81	-5	4			.981	6	C-72	0.2
1903	Bos-N	32	99	10	21	2	0	0	6	11		.212	.291	.232	52	-6	1			.981	5	C-30	0.2
	Was-A	60	192	8	41	7	1	0	16	10		.214	.252	.245	49	-12	1			.978	-3	C-60	-0.9
1904	Was-A	81	265	11	64	7	0	0	24	8		.242	.266	.268	70	-9	2			.982	1	C-79,M	0.0
1905	Was-A	77	238	16	39	8	0	0	14	15		.164	.213	.197	32	-18	1			.978	4	C-76	-0.7
1906	Was-A	22	68	5	13	0	0	0	3	1		.191	.203	.191	25	-6	0			.946	-2	C-22	-0.2
	Cle-A	5	10	0	1	0	0	0	0	0		.100	.100	.100	-38	-2	0			.938	-1	/C-5	-0.2
	Yr	27	78	5	14	0	0	0	3	1		.179	.190	.179	16	-8	0			.945	-3	C-27	-0.9
Total	16	1215	4027	375	882	108	31	17	390	314	<u>166</u>	.219	.277	.274	56	-236	64			.961	47	*C-1196/P-1	-6.7

■ BOBBY KLAUS   Klaus, Robert Francis   b: 12/27/37, Spring Grove, Ill.   BR/TR, 5'10", 170 lbs.   Deb: 4/21/64   F

YEAR	TM/L	G	AB	R	H	2B	3B	HR	RBI	BB	SO	AVG	OBP	SLG	PRO+	BR/A	SB	CS	SBR	FA	FR	G/POS	TPR
1964	Cin-N	40	93	10	17	5	1	2	6	4	13	.183	.216	.323	48	-7	1	0	0	.972	4	2-18,3-11/S	-0.2
	NY-N	56	209	25	51	8	3	2	11	25	30	.244	.325	.340	90	-2	3	4	-2	.986	-4	2-25,3-28/S	-0.6
	Yr	96	302	35	68	13	4	4	17	29	43	.225	.293	.334	76	-9	4	4	-1	.981	0	2-43,3-39/S	-0.8
1965	NY-N	119	288	30	55	12	0	2	12	45	49	.191	.302	.253	61	-14	1	6	-3	.968	15	2-72,S-28,3	0.3
Total	2	215	590	65	123	25	4	6	29	74	92	.208	.298	.295	69	-23	5	10	-5	.973	16	2-115/3-64,S	-0.5

■ BILLY KLAUS   Klaus, William Joseph   b: 12/9/28, Fox Lake, Ill.   BL/TR, 5'10", 165 lbs.   Deb: 4/16/52   F

YEAR	TM/L	G	AB	R	H	2B	3B	HR	RBI	BB	SO	AVG	OBP	SLG	PRO+	BR/A	SB	CS	SBR	FA	FR	G/POS	TPR
1952	Bos-N	7	4	0	0	0	0	0	0	1	0	.000	.200	.000	-42	-1	0	0	0	.500	-1	/S-4	-0.2
1953	Mil-N	2	2	1	0	0	0	0	0	0	1	.000	.000	.000	-99	-1	0	0	0	.000	0	H	-0.1
1955	Bos-A	135	541	83	153	26	5	7	60	60	44	.283	.354	.377	89	-8	6	10	0	.955	-7	*S-126/3-8	-0.3
1956	Bos-A	135	520	91	141	25	7	5	59	90	43	.271	.380	.387	92	-5	1	10	2	.945	-4	3-106,S-26	-0.5
1957	Bos-A	127	477	76	120	18	3	6	42	55	53	.252	.329	.369	85	-9	3	3	1	.961	11	*S-118	1.5
1958	Bos-A	61	88	5	14	4	0	1	7	5	16	.159	.204	.239	20	-10	0	0	0	.883	-6	S-27	-1.6

YEAR	TM/L	G	AB	R	H	2B	3B	HR	RBI	BB	SO	AVG	OBP	SLG	PRO+	BR/A	SB	CS	SBR	FA	FR	G/POS	TPR
1959	Bal-A	104	321	33	80	11	0	3	25	51	38	.249	.352	.312	86	-4	2	4	-2	.970	-12	S-59,3-49/2	-1.4
1960	Bal-A	46	43	8	9	2	0	1	6	9	9	.209	.346	.326	84	-1	0	0	0	.960	8	2-30,S-12/3	0.8
1961	Was-A	91	251	26	57	8	2	7	30	30	34	.227	.314	.359	81	-7	2	2	-1	.961	-5	3-51,S-18/2O	-1.0
1962	Phi-N	102	248	30	51	8	2	4	20	29	43	.206	.291	.302	61	-13	1	1	-0	.983	-6	3-53,S-30,2	-1.7
1963	Phi-N	11	18	1	1	0	0	0	1	0	4	.056	.105	.056	-53	-4	0	0	0	1.000	-2	/S-5,3-3	-0.6
Total	11	821	2513	357	626	106	15	40	250	331	285	.249	.337	.351	82	-62	14	7	0	.955	-24	S-425,3-272/2O	-5.1

■ **OLLIE KLEE**   Klee, Ollie Chester "Babe" b: 5/20/1900, Piqua, Ohio d: 2/9/77, Toledo, Ohio BL/TL, 5'9.5", 160 lbs. Deb: 8/10/25

YEAR	TM/L	G	AB	R	H	2B	3B	HR	RBI	BB	SO	AVG	OBP	SLG	PRO+	BR/A	SB	CS	SBR	FA	FR	G/POS	TPR
1925	Cin-N	3	1	0	0	0	0	0	0	0	1	.000	.000	.000	-99	-0	0	0	0	.000	-1	/O-1	-0.1

■ **CHUCK KLEIN**   Klein, Charles Herbert b: 10/7/04, Indianapolis, Ind. d: 3/28/58, Indianapolis, Ind. BL/TR, 6', 185 lbs. Deb: 7/30/28 CH

YEAR	TM/L	G	AB	R	H	2B	3B	HR	RBI	BB	SO	AVG	OBP	SLG	PRO+	BR/A	SB	CS	SBR	FA	FR	G/POS	TPR
1928	Phi-N	64	253	41	91	14	4	11	34	14	22	.360	.396	.577	146	16	0			.978	1	O-63	1.2
1929	Phi-N	149	616	126	219	45	6	43	145	54	61	.356	.407	.657	149	44	5			.966	-2	*O-149	2.9
1930	Phi-N	156	648	158	250	59	8	40	170	54	50	.386	.436	.687	155	55	4			.960	23	*O-156	5.8
1931	Phi-N	148	594	121	200	34	10	31	121	59	49	.337	.398	.584	149	39	7			.971	-5	*O-148	2.4
1932	Phi-N	154	650	152	226	50	15	38	137	60	49	.348	.404	.646	158	51	20			.960	9	*O-154	4.9
1933	Phi-N★	152	606	101	223	44	7	28	120	56	36	.368	.422	.602	168	52	15			.986	9	*O-152	5.5
1934	Chi-N★	115	435	78	131	27	2	20	80	47	38	.301	.372	.510	136	22	3			.962	-3	*O-110	1.4
1935	*Chi-N	119	434	71	127	14	4	21	73	41	42	.293	.355	.488	123	14	4			.958	-1	*O-111	0.8
1936	Chi-N	29	109	19	32	5	0	5	18	16	14	.294	.384	.477	128	4	0			.917	1	O-29	0.4
	Phi-N	117	492	83	152	30	7	20	86	33	45	.309	.352	.520	120	12	6			.930	-4	*O-117	0.2
	Yr	146	601	102	184	35	7	25	104	49	59	.306	.358	.512	122	16	6			.927	-4	*O-146	0.6
1937	Phi-N	115	406	74	132	20	2	15	57	39	21	.325	.386	.495	127	15	3			.949	-4	*O-102	0.8
1938	Phi-N	129	458	53	113	22	2	8	61	38	30	.247	.304	.356	83	-11	7			.960	-3	*O-119	-1.8
1939	Phi-N	25	47	8	9	2	1	1	9	10	4	.191	.333	.340	84	-1	1			1.000	-0	O-11/1-1	-0.1
	Pit-N	85	270	37	81	16	4	11	47	26	17	.300	.361	.511	134	12	1			.951	-2	O-66	0.8
	Yr	110	317	45	90	18	5	12	56	36	21	.284	.357	.486	127	11	2			.958	-2	O-77/1-1	0.7
1940	Phi-N	116	354	39	77	16	2	7	37	44	30	.218	.304	.333	79	-10	2			.984	-3	O-96	-1.8
1941	Phi-N	50	73	6	9	0	0	1	3	10	6	.123	.229	.164	12	-8	0			.958	-1	O-14	-1.0
1942	Phi-N	14	14	0	1	0	0	0	0	0	2	.071	.071	.071	-61	-3	0			.000	0	H	-0.3
1943	Phi-N	12	20	0	2	0	0	0	3	0	3	.100	.100	.100	-44	-4	1			.000	-1	/O-2	-0.5
1944	Phi-N	4	7	1	1	0	0	0	0	0	2	.143	.143	.143	-20	-1	0			1.000	1	/O-1	-0.1
Total	17	1753	6486	1168	2076	398	74	300	1201	601	521	.320	.379	.543	135	298	79			.962	16	*O-1600/1-1	21.5

■ **LOU KLEIN**   Klein, Louis Frank b: 10/22/18, New Orleans, La. d: 6/20/76, Metairie, La. BR/TR, 5'11", 170 lbs. Deb: 4/21/43 MC

YEAR	TM/L	G	AB	R	H	2B	3B	HR	RBI	BB	SO	AVG	OBP	SLG	PRO+	BR/A	SB	CS	SBR	FA	FR	G/POS	TPR
1943	*StL-N	154	627	91	180	28	14	7	62	50	70	.287	.342	.410	112	8	9			.973	-19	*2-126,S-51	-0.1
1945	StL-N	19	57	12	13	4	1	1	6	14	9	.228	.389	.386	113	2	0			.929	-2	/S-7,O-7,32	0.2
1946	StL-N	23	93	12	18	3	0	1	4	9	7	.194	.265	.258	47	-7	1			.975	-3	2-23	-0.9
1949	StL-N	58	114	25	25	6	0	2	12	22	20	.219	.355	.325	80	-3	0			.890	-4	S-21/2-9,3	-0.5
1951	Cle-A	2	2	0	0	0	0	0	0	0	1	.000	.000	.000	-99	-1	0	0	0	.000	0	H	-0.1
	Phi-A	49	144	22	33	7	0	5	17	10	12	.229	.279	.382	76	-6	0	0	0	.975	-4	2-42	-0.8
	Yr	51	146	22	33	7	0	5	17	10	13	.226	.276	.377	74	-6	0	0	0	.975	-4	2-42	-0.9
Total	5	305	1037	162	269	48	15	16	101	105	119	.259	.330	.381	97	-6	10	0		.975	-30	2-202/S-79,3O	-2.2

■ **RED KLEINOW**   Kleinow, John Peter b: 7/20/1879, Milwaukee, Wis. d: 10/9/29, New York, N.Y. BR/TR, 5'10", 165 lbs. Deb: 5/3/04

YEAR	TM/L	G	AB	R	H	2B	3B	HR	RBI	BB	SO	AVG	OBP	SLG	PRO+	BR/A	SB	CS	SBR	FA	FR	G/POS	TPR
1904	NY-A	68	209	12	43	8	4	0	16	15		.206	.259	.282	68	-8	4			.966	-6	C-62/3-2,O	-0.8
1905	NY-A	88	253	23	56	6	3	1	24	20		.221	.284	.281	71	-8	7			.978	-8	C-83/1-3	-0.9
1906	NY-A	96	268	30	59	9	3	0	31	24		.220	.287	.276	69	-9	8			.972	-1	C-95/1-1	-0.2
1907	NY-A	90	269	30	71	6	4	0	26	24		.264	.327	.316	97	-1	5			.967	-13	C-86/1-1	-0.7
1908	NY-A	96	279	16	47	3	2	1	13	22		.168	.237	.204	43	-17	5			.973	-4	C-89/2-2	-1.6
1909	NY-A	78	206	24	47	11	4	0	15	25		.228	.315	.320	100	0	7			.966	-3	C-77	0.4
1910	NY-A	6	12	2	5	0	0	0	2	1		.417	.462	.417	166	1	2			1.000	0	/C-5	0.1
	Bos-A	50	147	9	22	1	0	1	8	20		.150	.251	.177	34	-11	3			.968	4	C-49	-0.2
	Yr	56	159	11	27	1	0	1	10	21		.170	.267	.195	44	-10	4			.970	4	C-54	-0.1
1911	Bos-A	8	14	0	3	0	0	0	0	0		.214	.313	.214	48	-1	1			1.000	0	/C-8	0.0
	Phi-N	4	8	0	1	1	0	0	1	0		.125	.125	.250	4	-1	0			1.000	-0	/C-4	-0.1
Total	8	584	1665	146	354	45	20	3	135	153	1	.213	.282	.269	71	-54	42			.971	-31	C-558/1-5,230	-4.0

■ **RYAN KLESKO**   Klesko, Ryan Anthony b: 6/12/71, Westminster, Cal. BL/TL, 6'3", 220 lbs. Deb: 9/12/92

YEAR	TM/L	G	AB	R	H	2B	3B	HR	RBI	BB	SO	AVG	OBP	SLG	PRO+	BR/A	SB	CS	SBR	FA	FR	G/POS	TPR
1992	Atl-N	13	14	0	0	0	0	0	1	0	5	.000	.067	.000	-75	-3	0	0	0	1.000	-1	/1-5	-0.4
1993	Atl-N	22	17	3	6	1	0	2	5	3	4	.353	.450	.765	216	3	0	0	0	1.000	-1	/1-3,O-2	0.2
1994	Atl-N	92	245	42	68	13	3	17	47	26	48	.278	.349	.563	133	11	1	0	0	.921	-11	O-74/1-6	-0.1
Total	3	127	276	45	74	14	3	19	53	29	57	.268	.342	.547	128	10	1	0	0	.921	-12	/O-76,1-14	-0.3

■ **JAY KLEVEN**   Kleven, Jay Allen b: 12/2/49, Oakland, Cal. BR/TR, 6'2", 190 lbs. Deb: 6/20/76

YEAR	TM/L	G	AB	R	H	2B	3B	HR	RBI	BB	SO	AVG	OBP	SLG	PRO+	BR/A	SB	CS	SBR	FA	FR	G/POS	TPR
1976	NY-N	2	5	0	1	0	0	0	2	0	1	.200	.200	.200	15	-1	0	0	0	1.000	0	/C-2	0.0

■ **LOU KLIMCHOCK**   Klimchock, Louis Stephen b: 10/15/39, Hostetter, Pa. BL/TR, 5'11", 180 lbs. Deb: 9/27/58

YEAR	TM/L	G	AB	R	H	2B	3B	HR	RBI	BB	SO	AVG	OBP	SLG	PRO+	BR/A	SB	CS	SBR	FA	FR	G/POS	TPR
1958	KC-A	2	10	2	2	0	0	1	1	0	1	.200	.200	.500	84	-0	0	0	0	1.000	-1	/2-2	-0.1
1959	KC-A	17	66	10	18	0	0	4	13	1	6	.273	.284	.470	101	-0	0	0	0	.949	-4	2-16	-0.3
1960	KC-A	10	10	0	3	0	0	0	0	0	0	.300	.300	.300	62	-1	0	0	0	.000	0	/2-1	-0.1
1961	KC-A	57	121	8	26	4	1	1	16	5	13	.215	.246	.289	42	-10	0	0	0	.976	-5	1-11/O-7,32	-1.7
1962	Mil-N	8	8	0	0	0	0	0	0	0	2	.000	.000	.000	-99	-2	0	0	0	.000	0	H	-0.2
1963	Was-A	9	14	1	2	0	0	0	2	0	1	.143	.143	.143	-20	-2	0	0	0	1.000	1	/2-3	-0.1
	Mil-N	24	46	6	9	1	0	0	1	0	12	.196	.196	.217	19	-5	0	1	-1	.988	0	1-12	-0.6
1964	Mil-N	10	21	3	7	2	0	0	2	1	2	.333	.364	.429	121	1	0	0	0	1.000	-3	/3-4,2-2	-0.2
1965	Mil-N	34	39	3	3	0	0	0	3	2	8	.077	.122	.077	-42	-7	0	0	0	.923	1	/1-4	-0.7
1966	NY-N	5	5	0	0	0	0	0	0	0	3	.000	.000	.000	-99	-1	0	0	0	.000	0	H	-0.1
1968	Cle-A	11	15	0	2	0	0	0	3	1	0	.133	.188	.133	-2	-2	0	0	0	.500	-3	/3-4,1-1,2	-0.5
1969	Cle-A	90	258	26	74	13	2	6	26	18	14	.287	.333	.422	107	2	0	0	0	.934	-16	1-56,2-21/C	-1.3
1970	Cle-A	41	56	5	9	0	0	1	5	2	5	.161	.217	.214	18	-6	0	0	0	1.000	-1	/1-5,2-5	-0.7
Total	12	318	669	64	155	21	3	13	69	31	71	.232	.267	.330	63	-35	0	1	-1	.906	-30	/3-70,2-52,10C	-6.6

■ **BOBBY KLINE**   Kline, John Robert b: 1/27/29, St.Petersburg, Fla BR/TR, 6', 179 lbs. Deb: 4/11/55

YEAR	TM/L	G	AB	R	H	2B	3B	HR	RBI	BB	SO	AVG	OBP	SLG	PRO+	BR/A	SB	CS	SBR	FA	FR	G/POS	TPR
1955	Was-A	77	140	12	31	5	0	0	9	11	27	.221	.288	.257	50	-10	0	0	0	.943	13	S-69/2-4,3P	0.7

■ **JOHNNY KLING**   Kling, John "Noisy" b: 2/25/1875, Kansas City, Mo. d: 1/31/47, Kansas City, Mo. BR/TR, 5'9.5", 160 lbs. Deb: 9/11/00 FM

YEAR	TM/L	G	AB	R	H	2B	3B	HR	RBI	BB	SO	AVG	OBP	SLG	PRO+	BR/A	SB	CS	SBR	FA	FR	G/POS	TPR
1900	Chi-N	15	51	8	15	3	1	0	7	2		.294	.321	.392	100	-0				.901	-2	C-15	-0.1
1901	Chi-N	74	256	26	70	6	3	0	21	9		.273	.301	.320	83	-6	8			.952	-10	C-69/1-1,O	-0.9
1902	Chi-N	114	431	49	123	19	3	0	57	29		.285	.330	.343	111	5	24			.974	6	*C-112/S-1	2.4
1903	Chi-N	132	491	67	146	29	13	3	68	22		.297	.330	.428	119	9	23			.969	2	*C-132	2.3
1904	Chi-N	123	452	41	110	18	0	2	46	16		.243	.271	.296	75	-14	7			.974	-11	*C-104,O-10/1	-1.5
1905	Chi-N	111	380	26	83	8	6	1	52	28		.218	.272	.279	62	-18	13			.966	0	*C-106/O-4,1	-0.7
1906	*Chi-N	107	343	45	107	15	8	2	46	23		.312	.357	.420	134	12	14			.982	5	C-96/O-3	2.9
1907	*Chi-N	104	334	44	95	15	8	1	43	27		.284	.342	.386	120	7	9			.987	6	C-98/1-2	2.5

YEAR	TM/L	G	AB	R	H	2B	3B	HR	RBI	BB	SO	AVG	OBP	SLG	PRO+	BR/A	SB	CS	SBR	FA	FR	G/POS	TPR
1908	*Chi-N	126	424	51	117	23	5	4	59	21		.276	.315	.382	117	7	16			.979	2	*C-117/O-6,1	2.2
1910	*Chi-N	91	297	31	80	17	2	2	32	37	27	.269	.354	.360	109	4	3			.979	-5	C-86	0.8
1911	Chi-N	27	80	8	14	3	2	1	5	8	14	.175	.250	.300	53	-5	1			.969	5	C-25	0.2
	Bos-N	75	241	32	54	8	1	2	24	30	29	.224	.310	.290	63	-12	0			.951	-5	C-71/3-1	-1.0
	Yr	102	321	40	68	11	3	3	29	38	43	.212	.295	.293	61	-17	1			.956	-0	C-96/3-1	-0.8
1912	Bos-N	81	252	26	80	10	3	2	30	15	30	.317	.356	.405	106	2	3			.958	5	C-74,M	1.3
1913	Cin-N	80	209	20	57	7	6	0	23	14	30	.273	.318	.364	95	-2	2			.975	7	C-63	1.1
Total	13	1260	4241	474	1151	181	61	20	513	281	114	.271	.318	.357	100	-11	123			.971	3	*C-1168/O-24,13S	11.5

■ RUDY KLING
Kling, Rudolph A. b: 3/23/1870, St.Louis, Mo. d: 3/14/37, St.Louis, Mo. BR/TR, 5'10", 178 lbs. Deb: 9/21/02

YEAR	TM/L	G	AB	R	H	2B	3B	HR	RBI	BB	SO	AVG	OBP	SLG	PRO+	BR/A	SB	CS	SBR	FA	FR	G/POS	TPR
1902	StL-N	4	10	1	2	0	0	0	0	4		.200	.429	.200	99	0	1			.842	-2	/S-4	-0.1

■ JOE KLINGER
Klinger, Joseph John b: 8/2/02, Canonsburg, Pa. d: 7/31/60, Little Rock, Ark. BR/TR, 6', 190 lbs. Deb: 9/13/27

YEAR	TM/L	G	AB	R	H	2B	3B	HR	RBI	BB	SO	AVG	OBP	SLG	PRO+	BR/A	SB	CS	SBR	FA	FR	G/POS	TPR
1927	NY-N	3	5	0	2	0	0	0	0	0	2	.400	.400	.400	115	0	0			1.000	0	/O-1	0.0
1930	Chi-A	4	8	0	3	0	0	0	1	0	0	.375	.375	.375	94	-0	0	0	0	1.000	-1	/C-2,1-2	-0.1
Total	2	7	13	0	5	0	0	0	1	0	2	.385	.385	.385	102	-0	0	0	0	1.000	-1	/1-2,C-2,O	-0.1

■ NAP KLOZA
Kloza, John Clarence b: 9/7/03, Poland d: 6/11/62, Milwaukee, Wis. BR/TR, 5'11", 180 lbs. Deb: 8/16/31

YEAR	TM/L	G	AB	R	H	2B	3B	HR	RBI	BB	SO	AVG	OBP	SLG	PRO+	BR/A	SB	CS	SBR	FA	FR	G/POS	TPR
1931	StL-A	3	7	1	1	0	0	0	0	1	4	.143	.250	.143	5	-1	0	0	0	1.000	-0	/O-3	-0.1
1932	StL-A	19	13	4	2	0	1	0	2	4	4	.154	.353	.308	69	-1	0	0	0	1.000	-1	/O-3	-0.2
Total	2	22	20	5	3	0	1	0	2	5	8	.150	.320	.250	48	-1	0	0	0	1.000	-2	/O-6	-0.3

■ JOE KLUGMANN
Klugmann, Joe b: 3/26/1895, St.Louis, Mo. d: 7/18/51, Moberly, Mo. BR/TR, 5'11", 175 lbs. Deb: 9/23/21

YEAR	TM/L	G	AB	R	H	2B	3B	HR	RBI	BB	SO	AVG	OBP	SLG	PRO+	BR/A	SB	CS	SBR	FA	FR	G/POS	TPR
1921	Chi-N	6	21	3	6	0	0	0	2	1	2	.286	.348	.286	69	-1	0	1	-1	.969	0	/2-5	-0.1
1922	Chi-N	2	2	0	0	0	0	0	0	0	0	.000	.000	.000	-98	-1	0	0	0	1.000	1	/2-2	0.0
1924	Bro-N	31	79	7	13	2	1	0	3	2	9	.165	.185	.215	7	-10	0	0	0	.929	-1	2-28/S-1	-1.2
1925	Cle-A	38	85	12	28	9	2	0	12	8	4	.329	.387	.482	119	2	3	1	0	.959	-3	2-29/1-4,3	0.0
Total	4	77	187	22	47	11	3	0	17	11	15	.251	.296	.342	67	-10	3	2	-0	.947	-3	/2-64,1-4,3S	-1.3

■ ELMER KLUMPP
Klumpp, Elmer Edward b: 8/26/06, St.Louis, Mo. BR/TR, 6', 184 lbs. Deb: 4/17/34

YEAR	TM/L	G	AB	R	H	2B	3B	HR	RBI	BB	SO	AVG	OBP	SLG	PRO+	BR/A	SB	CS	SBR	FA	FR	G/POS	TPR
1934	Was-A	12	15	2	2	0	0	0	0	0	1	.133	.188	.133	-17	-3	0	0	0	.889	-1	C-11	-0.3
1937	Bro-N	5	11	0	1	0	0	0	2	1	4	.091	.167	.091	-28	-2	0	0	0	1.000	1	/C-3	-0.1
Total	2	17	26	2	3	0	0	0	2	1	5	.115	.179	.115	-21	-5	0	0		.943	-0	/C-14	-0.4

■ BILLY KLUSMAN
Klusman, William F. b: 3/24/1865, Cincinnati, Ohio d: 6/24/07, Cincinnati, Ohio BR/TR, 5'10.5", 185 lbs. Deb: 6/21/1888

YEAR	TM/L	G	AB	R	H	2B	3B	HR	RBI	BB	SO	AVG	OBP	SLG	PRO+	BR/A	SB	CS	SBR	FA	FR	G/POS	TPR
1888	Bos-N	28	107	9	18	4	0	2	11	5	13	.168	.205	.262	47	-6	3			.914	-9	2-28	-1.4
1890	StL-a	15	65	9	18	4	1	1		1		.277	.288	.415	94	-1	1			.896	-3	2-15	-0.3
Total	2	43	172	18	36	8	1	3	11	6	13	.209	.236	.320	67	-8	4			.908	-12	/2-43	-1.7

■ TED KLUSZEWSKI
Kluszewski, Theodore Bernard "Big Klu" b: 9/10/24, Argo, Ill. d: 3/29/88, Cincinnati, Ohio BL/TL, 6'2", 225 lbs. Deb: 4/18/47 C

YEAR	TM/L	G	AB	R	H	2B	3B	HR	RBI	BB	SO	AVG	OBP	SLG	PRO+	BR/A	SB	CS	SBR	FA	FR	G/POS	TPR
1947	Cin-N	9	10	1	1	0	0	0	2	1	2	.100	.182	.100	-23	-2	0			1.000	-0	/1-2	-0.2
1948	Cin-N	113	379	49	104	23	4	12	57	18	32	.274	.307	.451	107	1	1			.990	1	1-98	0.2
1949	Cin-N	136	531	63	164	26	2	8	68	19	24	.309	.333	.411	97	-3	3			.989	-7	*1-134	-1.1
1950	Cin-N	134	538	76	165	37	0	25	111	33	28	.307	.348	.511	123	16	3			.987	-11	*1-131	0.1
1951	Cin-N	154	607	74	157	35	2	13	77	35	38	.259	.301	.387	83	-16	6	2	1	.997	-6	*1-154	-2.9
1952	Cin-N	135	497	62	159	24	11	16	86	47	28	.320	.383	.509	146	30	3	3	-1	.993	-10	*1-133	1.5
1953	Cin-N★	149	570	97	180	25	0	40	108	55	34	.316	.380	.570	142	34	2	0	1	.995	-18	*1-147	1.1
1954	Cin-N★	149	573	104	187	28	3	**49**	**141**	78	35	.326	.410	.642	165	53	0	2	-1	**.996**	-4	*1-149	4.0
1955	Cin-N★	153	612	116	**192**	25	0	47	113	66	40	.314	.384	.585	144	38	1	1	-0	**.995**	-9	*1-153	1.9
1956	Cin-N★	138	517	91	156	14	1	35	102	49	31	.302	.366	.536	130	21	1	0	0	.990	-5	*1-131	0.8
1957	Cin-N	69	127	12	34	7	0	6	21	5	5	.268	.301	.465	95	-1	0	0	0	.989	0	1-23	-0.3
1958	Pit-N	100	301	29	88	13	4	4	37	26	16	.292	.351	.402	101	1	0	0	0	.994	-5	1-72	-0.9
1959	Pit-N	60	122	11	32	10	1	2	17	5	14	.262	.291	.410	85	-3	0	0	0	1.000	-1	1-20	-0.5
	*Chi-A	31	101	11	30	2	1	2	10	9	10	.297	.355	.396	107	1	0	1	-1	1.000	-2	1-29	-0.4
1960	Chi-A	81	181	20	53	9	0	5	39	22	10	.293	.369	.425	116	4	0	1	-1	.997	-2	1-39	-0.1
1961	LA-A	107	263	32	64	12	0	15	39	24	23	.243	.307	.460	91	-4	0	0	0	.989	-5	1-66	-1.4
Total	15	1718	5929	848	1766	290	29	279	1028	492	365	.298	.354	.498	122	169	20	10		.993	-82	*1-1481	1.8

■ MICKEY KLUTTS
Klutts, Gene Ellis b: 9/20/54, Montebello, Cal. BR/TR, 5'11", 189 lbs. Deb: 7/7/76

YEAR	TM/L	G	AB	R	H	2B	3B	HR	RBI	BB	SO	AVG	OBP	SLG	PRO+	BR/A	SB	CS	SBR	FA	FR	G/POS	TPR
1976	NY-A	2	3	0	0	0	0	0	0	0	1	.000	.000	.000	-99	-1	0	0	0	.875	0	/S-2	0.0
1977	NY-A	5	15	3	4	1	0	1	4	2	1	.267	.389	.533	150	1	0	1	-1	1.000	2	/3-4,S-1	0.3
1978	NY-A	1	2	1	2	1	0	0	1	0	0	1.000	1.000	1.500	608	2	0	0	0	.750	-3	/3-1	0.2
1979	Oak-A	24	73	3	14	2	1	1	4	7	20	.192	.262	.288	51	-5	0	0	-1	.882	-4	S-10/2-8,3	-0.8
1980	Oak-A	75	197	20	53	14	0	4	21	13	41	.269	.314	.401	102	-0	1	4	-2	.947	-6	3-62/S-8,2D	-0.9
1981	*Oak-A	15	46	9	17	0	0	5	11	2	9	.370	.396	.696	220	7	0	0	0	.957	-5	3-14	0.2
1982	Oak-A	55	157	10	28	8	0	0	14	9	18	.178	.223	.229	26	-16	0	0	0	.946	-3	3-49	-2.0
1983	Tor-A	22	43	3	11	0	0	3	5	1	11	.256	.289	.465	98	-0	0	1	-1	1.000	-3	3-17/D-2	-0.4
Total	8	199	536	49	129	26	1	14	59	34	101	.241	.290	.371	84	-13	1	7	-4	.948	-18	3-153/S-21,2D	-3.4

■ CLYDE KLUTTZ
Kluttz, Clyde Franklin b: 12/12/17, Rockwell, N.C. d: 5/12/79, Salisbury, N.C. BR/TR, 6', 198 lbs. Deb: 4/20/42

YEAR	TM/L	G	AB	R	H	2B	3B	HR	RBI	BB	SO	AVG	OBP	SLG	PRO+	BR/A	SB	CS	SBR	FA	FR	G/POS	TPR
1942	Bos-N	72	210	21	56	10	1	1	31	7	13	.267	.294	.338	86	-4	0			.979	0	C-57	0.0
1943	Bos-N	66	207	13	51	7	0	0	20	15	9	.246	.297	.280	68	-8	0			.973	2	C-55	-0.2
1944	Bos-N	81	229	20	64	12	2	2	19	13	14	.279	.318	.376	91	-3	0			.980	4	C-58	0.4
1945	Bos-N	25	81	9	24	4	1	0	10	2	6	.296	.313	.370	89	-1	0			.987	-0	C-19	-0.1
	NY-N	73	222	25	62	14	0	4	21	15	10	.279	.331	.396	100	-1	1			.978	-4	C-62	-0.3
	Yr	98	303	34	86	18	1	4	31	17	16	.284	.326	.389	97	-2	1			.981	-6	C-76	-0.4
1946	NY-N	5	8	0	3	0	0	0	1	0	1	.375	.375	.375	112	0	0			.857	-1	/C-2	0.0
	StL-N	52	136	8	36	7	0	0	14	10	10	.265	.315	.316	76	-4	0			.980	2	C-49	0.0
	Yr	57	144	8	39	7	0	0	15	10	11	.271	.318	.319	78	-4	0			.976	1	C-51	0.0
1947	Pit-N	73	232	26	70	9	2	6	42	17	18	.302	.355	.435	106	2	1			.987	3	C-69	0.9
1948	Pit-N	94	271	26	60	12	2	4	20	20	19	.221	.275	.325	61	-15	3			.978	0	C-91	-1.0
1951	StL-A	4	4	2	2	1	0	0	1	0	0	.500	.600	.750	256	1	0	0	0	1.000	1	/C-1	0.2
	Was-A	53	159	15	49	9	0	1	22	20	8	.308	.389	.384	111	3	0			.968	-7	C-46	-0.2
	Yr	57	163	17	51	10	0	1	23	21	8	.313	.395	.393	115	4	0	0		.976	-6	C-47	-0.0
1952	Was-A	58	144	7	33	5	0	1	11	12	11	.229	.293	.285	58	-7	0			.979	-1	C-52	-0.6
Total	9	656	1903	172	510	90	8	19	212	132	119	.268	.318	.354	86	-39	5	0		.978	-3	C-556	0.0

■ JOE KMAK
Kmak, Joseph Robert b: 5/3/63, Napa, Cal. BR/TR, 6', 185 lbs. Deb: 4/6/93

YEAR	TM/L	G	AB	R	H	2B	3B	HR	RBI	BB	SO	AVG	OBP	SLG	PRO+	BR/A	SB	CS	SBR	FA	FR	G/POS	TPR
1993	Mil-A	51	110	9	24	5	0	0	7	14	13	.218	.317	.264	59	-6	2	1		1.000	1	C-50	-0.2

■ OTTO KNABE
Knabe, Franz Otto "Dutch" b: 6/12/1884, Carrick, Pa. d: 5/17/61, Philadelphia, Pa. BR/TR, 5'8", 175 lbs. Deb: 10/3/05 M

YEAR	TM/L	G	AB	R	H	2B	3B	HR	RBI	BB	SO	AVG	OBP	SLG	PRO+	BR/A	SB	CS	SBR	FA	FR	G/POS	TPR
1905	Pit-N	3	10	0	3	1	0	0	2		3	.300	.462	.400	154	1	0			.786	0	/3-3	0.1
1907	Phi-N	129	444	67	113	16	9	1	34		52	.255	.339	.338	114	8	18			.960	1	*2-121/O-5	0.9
1908	Phi-N	151	555	63	121	26	8	0	27		49	.218	.290	.294	84	-10	27			.969	11	*2-151	0.0
1909	Phi-N	113	402	40	94	13	3	0	34		35	.234	.308	.281	82	-8	9			.938	7	*2-110/O-1	-0.3

YEAR	TM/L	G	AB	R	H	2B	3B	HR	RBI	BB	SO	AVG	OBP	SLG	PRO+	BR/A	SB	CS	SBR	FA	FR	G/POS	TPR
1910	Phi-N	137	510	73	133	18	6	1	44	47	42	.261	.327	.325	87	-8	15			.954	14	*2-136	0.3
1911	Phi-N	142	528	99	125	15	6	1	42	94	35	.237	.352	.294	80	-10	23			.950	4	*2-142	-1.0
1912	Phi-N	126	426	56	120	11	4	0	46	55	20	.282	.366	.326	85	-7	16			.952	1	*2-123	-0.9
1913	Phi-N	148	571	70	150	25	7	2	53	45	26	.263	.320	.342	85	-11	14			.959	12	*2-148	-0.2
1914	Bal-F	147	469	45	106	26	2	2	42	53	28	.226	.307	.303	57	-30	10			.956	1	*2-144,M	-3.1
1915	Bal-F	103	320	38	81	16	2	1	25	37	16	.253	.334	.325	74	-11	7			.975	7	2-94/O-1M	-0.3
1916	Pit-N	28	89	4	17	3	1	0	9	6	6	.191	.258	.247	55	-5	1			.962	-0	2-28	-0.5
	Chi-N	51	145	17	40	8	0	0	7	9	18	.276	.327	.331	92	-1	3			.939	6	2-42/S-1,3O	0.6
	Yr	79	234	21	57	11	1	0	16	15	24	.244	.300	.299	79	-6	4			.948	5	2-70/S-1,3O	0.1
Total	11	1278	4469	572	1103	178	48	8	365	485	191	.247	.325	.313	83	-92	143			.957	64	*2-1239/O-8,3S	-4.4

■ COTTON KNAUPP
Knaupp, Henry Antone b: 8/13/1889, San Antonio, Tex. d: 7/6/67, New Orleans, La. BR/TR, 5'9", 165 lbs. Deb: 8/30/10

YEAR	TM/L	G	AB	R	H	2B	3B	HR	RBI	BB	SO	AVG	OBP	SLG	PRO+	BR/A	SB	CS	SBR	FA	FR	G/POS	TPR
1910	Cle-A	18	59	3	14	3	1	0	11	8		.237	.338	.322	105	1	1			.884	-8	S-18	-0.8
1911	Cle-A	13	39	2	4	1	0	0	0	0		.103	.103	.128	-35	-7	3			.964	2	S-13	-0.5
Total	2	31	98	5	18	4	1	0	11	8		.184	.252	.245	48	-6	4			.913	-6	/S-31	-1.3

■ ALAN KNICELY
Knicely, Alan Lee b: 5/19/55, Harrisonburg, Va. BR/TR, 6'0.5", 194 lbs. Deb: 8/12/79

YEAR	TM/L	G	AB	R	H	2B	3B	HR	RBI	BB	SO	AVG	OBP	SLG	PRO+	BR/A	SB	CS	SBR	FA	FR	G/POS	TPR
1979	Hou-N	7	6	0	0	0	0	0	0	2	3	.000	.250	.000	-27	-1	0	0	0	1.000	-2	/C-3,3-1	-0.3
1980	Hou-N	1	1	0	0	0	0	0	0	0	1	.000	.000	.000	-99	-0	0	0	0	.000	0	/H	0.0
1981	Hou-N	3	7	2	4	0	0	2	2	0	1	.571	.571	1.429	477	3	0	0	0	1.000	0	/C-2,O-1	0.3
1982	Hou-N	59	133	10	25	2	0	2	12	14	30	.188	.270	.248	50	-9	0	1	-1	.977	-9	C-23,O-16/3	-1.9
1983	Cin-N	59	98	11	22	3	0	2	10	16	28	.224	.333	.316	78	-2	0	2	-1	1.000	-2	C-31/O-8,1	-0.5
1984	Cin-N	10	29	0	4	0	0	0	5	3	6	.138	.219	.138	2	-4	0	0	0	.984	0	/1-8,C-1	-0.4
1985	Cin-N	48	158	17	40	9	0	5	26	16	34	.253	.326	.405	98	-0	0	0	0	.968	-14	C-46	-1.3
	Phi-N	7	7	0	0	0	0	0	0	0	4	.000	.000	.000	-97	-2	0	0	0	1.000	-0	/1-1	-0.2
	Yr	55	165	17	40	9	0	5	26	16	38	.242	.313	.388	91	-2	0	0	0	.968	-14	C-46/1-1	-1.5
1986	StL-N	34	82	8	16	3	0	1	6	17	21	.195	.333	.268	68	-3	1	1	-0	.995	-1	1-29/C-2	-0.9
Total	8	228	521	48	111	17	0	12	61	68	128	.213	.306	.315	73	-19	1	4	-2	.979	-26	C-108/1-40,O3	-4.9

■ AUSTIN KNICKERBOCKER
Knickerbocker, Austin Jay b: 10/15/18, Bangall, N.Y. BR/TR, 5'11", 185 lbs. Deb: 4/19/47

YEAR	TM/L	G	AB	R	H	2B	3B	HR	RBI	BB	SO	AVG	OBP	SLG	PRO+	BR/A	SB	CS	SBR	FA	FR	G/POS	TPR
1947	Phi-A	21	48	8	12	3	2	0	2	3	4	.250	.294	.396	89	-1	0	1	-1	.943	0	O-14	-0.2

■ BILL KNICKERBOCKER
Knickerbocker, William Hart b: 12/29/11, Los Angeles, Cal. d: 9/8/63, Sebastopol, Cal. BR/TR, 5'11", 170 lbs. Deb: 4/12/33

YEAR	TM/L	G	AB	R	H	2B	3B	HR	RBI	BB	SO	AVG	OBP	SLG	PRO+	BR/A	SB	CS	SBR	FA	FR	G/POS	TPR
1933	Cle-A	80	279	20	63	16	3	2	32	11	30	.226	.255	.326	51	-21	1	4	-2	.939	2	S-80	-1.5
1934	Cle-A	146	593	82	188	32	5	4	67	25	40	.317	.347	.408	93	-8	6	6	-2	.962	-7	*S-146	-0.7
1935	Cle-A	132	540	77	161	34	5	0	55	27	31	.298	.332	.380	82	-15	2	12	-7	.956	9	*S-128	-0.5
1936	Cle-A	155	618	81	182	35	3	8	73	56	30	.294	.354	.400	85	-15	5	14	-7	.952	-1	*S-155	-1.1
1937	StL-A	121	491	53	128	29	5	4	61	30	32	.261	.303	.365	67	-26	3	2	-0	.958	-13	*S-115/2-6	-2.9
1938	NY-A	46	128	15	32	8	3	1	21	11	10	.250	.309	.383	73	-6	0	0	0	.982	-2	2-34/S-3	-0.5
1939	NY-A	6	13	2	2	1	0	0	1	0	0	.154	.154	.231	-3	-2	0	0	0	1.000	2	/2-2,S-2	0.0
1940	NY-A	45	124	17	30	8	1	1	10	14	8	.242	.333	.347	80	-4	1	1	-0	.985	-1	S-19,3-17	-0.4
1941	Chi-A	89	343	51	84	23	2	1	29	41	27	.245	.329	.385	89	-6	6	5	-1	.970	-17	2-88	-1.7
1942	Phi-A	87	289	25	73	12	0	1	19	29	30	.253	.323	.304	77	-8	1	2	-1	.964	-12	2-81/S-1	-1.7
Total	10	907	3418	423	943	198	27	28	368	244	238	.276	.326	.374	79	-109	25	46	-20	.955	-42	S-649,2-211/3	-11.0

■ LON KNIGHT
Knight, Alonzo P. b: 6/16/1853, Philadelphia, Pa. d: 4/23/32, Philadelphia, Pa. BR/TR, 5'11.5", 165 lbs. Deb: 9/4/1875 MU

YEAR	TM/L	G	AB	R	H	2B	3B	HR	RBI	BB	SO	AVG	OBP	SLG	PRO+	BR/A	SB	CS	SBR	FA	FR	G/POS	TPR
1875	Ath-n	13	47	4	6	2	0	0		0		.128	.128	.170	2	-5						P-13	0.0
1876	Phi-N	55	240	32	60	9	3	0	24	2	2	.250	.256	.313	89	-3				.804	-7	P-34,1-13/O2	-0.6
1880	Wor-N	49	201	31	48	11	3	0	21	5	8	.239	.257	.323	88	-3				.863	5	O-49	0.0
1881	Det-N	83	340	67	92	16	3	1	52	23	21	.271	.317	.344	104	1				.890	1	*O-82/2-1,1	0.1
1882	Det-N	86	347	39	72	12	6	0	24	16	21	.207	.242	.277	66	-13				.867	1	*O-84/1-2	-1.1
1883	Phi-a	97	429	98	108	23	9	1		21		.252	.287	.354	97	-3				.858	0	*O-93/3-3,2M	-0.3
1884	Phi-a	108	484	94	131	18	12	1		10		.271	.287	.364	104	0				.911	11	*O-108/P-2,1M	0.8
1885	Phi-a	29	119	17	25	1	1	0		9		.210	.271	.235	58	-6				.921	4	O-29/P-1	-0.2
	Pro-N	25	81	8	13	1	0	0	8	11	17	.160	.261	.173	44	-4				.957	1	O-25/P-1	-0.4
Total	7	532	2241	386	549	91	37	3	129	97	69	.245	.277	.323	90	-30				.887	17	O-479/P-38,123	-1.7

■ RAY KNIGHT
Knight, Charles Ray b: 12/28/52, Albany, Ga. BR/TR, 6'2", 190 lbs. Deb: 9/10/74 C

YEAR	TM/L	G	AB	R	H	2B	3B	HR	RBI	BB	SO	AVG	OBP	SLG	PRO+	BR/A	SB	CS	SBR	FA	FR	G/POS	TPR
1974	Cin-N	14	11	1	2	1	0	0	2	1	2	.182	.250	.273	47	-1	0	0	0	1.000	1	3-14	0.0
1977	Cin-N	80	92	8	24	5	1	1	13	9	16	.261	.327	.370	85	-2	1	1	-0	.941	4	3-37,2-17/OS	0.3
1978	Cin-N	83	65	7	13	3	0	1	4	3	13	.200	.235	.292	47	-5	0	0	0	.868	5	3-60/2-4,O1S	0.0
1979	*Cin-N	150	551	64	175	37	4	10	79	38	57	.318	.365	.454	121	16	4	4	-1	.962	-15	*3-149	-0.2
1980	Cin-N★	162	618	71	163	39	7	14	78	36	62	.264	.309	.417	101	-1	1	2	-1	.969	-15	*3-162	-2.1
1981	Cin-N	106	386	43	100	23	1	6	34	33	51	.259	.324	.370	95	-3	2	4	-2	.957	-13	*3-105	-2.2
1982	Hou-N★	158	609	72	179	36	6	6	70	48	58	.294	.350	.402	119	14	2	5	-2	.990	-2	1-96,3-67	0.3
1983	Hou-N	145	507	43	154	36	4	9	70	42	62	.304	.362	.444	130	19	0	3	-2	.993	-11	*1-143	-0.1
1984	Hou-N	88	278	15	62	10	0	2	29	14	30	.223	.263	.281	57	-17	0	3	-2	.946	-2	3-54,1-24	-2.4
	NY-N	27	93	13	26	4	0	1	6	7	13	.280	.337	.355	96	-0	0	0	0	.962	-4	3-27/1-3	-0.5
	Yr	115	371	28	88	14	0	3	35	21	43	.237	.282	.299	67	-17	0	3	-2	.951	-6	3-81,1-27	-2.9
1985	NY-N	90	271	22	59	12	0	6	36	13	32	.218	.256	.328	64	-14	1	1	-0	.958	-11	3-73/2-2,1	-2.7
1986	*NY-N	137	486	51	145	24	2	11	76	40	63	.298	.357	.424	118	11	2	1	0	.948	-11	*3-132/1-1	-0.2
1987	Bal-A	150	563	46	144	24	0	14	65	39	90	.256	.311	.373	82	-15	1	1	-0	.956	10	*3-130,D-14/1	-0.7
1988	Det-A	105	299	34	65	12	2	3	33	20	30	.217	.273	.301	63	-15	1	1	-0	.991	-3	1-64,D-25,3/O	-2.4
Total	13	1495	4829	490	1311	266	27	84	595	343	579	.271	.325	.390	99	-11	14	25	-11	.957	-67	*3-1021,1-339/D2OS	-12.9

■ JOHN KNIGHT
Knight, John Wesley "Schoolboy" b: 10/6/1885, Philadelphia, Pa. d: 12/19/65, Walnut Creek, Cal. BR/TR, 6'2.5", 180 lbs. Deb: 4/14/05

YEAR	TM/L	G	AB	R	H	2B	3B	HR	RBI	BB	SO	AVG	OBP	SLG	PRO+	BR/A	SB	CS	SBR	FA	FR	G/POS	TPR
1905	Phi-A	88	325	28	66	12	1	3	29	9		.203	.227	.274	58	-16	4			.895	-28	S-79/3-4	-4.8
1906	Phi-A	74	253	29	49	7	2	3	20	19		.194	.250	.273	62	-11	6			.922	1	3-67/2-7	-0.9
1907	Phi-A	40	139	6	29	7	1	0	12	10		.209	.272	.273	72	-4	7			.862	-0	3-40	-0.4
	Bos-A	98	360	31	78	9	3	2	29	19		.217	.256	.275	70	-13	8			.924	8	3-92/2-4	-0.2
	Yr	138	499	37	107	16	4	2	41	29		.214	.260	.275	71	-17	9			.906	8	*3-132/2-4	-0.6
1909	NY-A	116	360	46	85	8	5	0	40	37		.236	.311	.286	88	-4	15			.901	1	S-77,1-19,2	-0.3
1910	NY-A	117	414	58	129	25	4	3	45	34		.312	.372	.413	138	17	23			.929	-1	S-79,1-23/230	2.2
1911	NY-A	132	470	69	126	16	7	3	62	42		.268	.342	.351	88	-8	18			.907	8	S-82,1-27,2/3	0.0
1912	Was-A	32	93	10	15	2	1	0	9	16		.161	.284	.204	40	-7	4			.926	-5	2-27/1-5	-1.2
1913	NY-A	70	250	24	59	10	0	0	24	25	27	.236	.310	.276	72	-9	7			.980	8	1-50,2-21	-0.2
Total	8	767	2664	301	636	96	24	14	270	211	27	.239	.300	.309	84	-55	86			.909	-14	S-317,3-208,12/O	-5.8

■ JOE KNIGHT
Knight, Joseph William "Quiet Joe" b: 9/28/1859, Port Stanley, Ont., Canada d: 10/16/38, Lynhurst, Ont., Canada BL/TL, 5'11", 185 lbs. Deb: 5/16/1884

YEAR	TM/L	G	AB	R	H	2B	3B	HR	RBI	BB	SO	AVG	OBP	SLG	PRO+	BR/A	SB	CS	SBR	FA	FR	G/POS	TPR
1884	Phi-N	6	24	2	6	3	0	0	2	0	2	.250	.250	.375	98	-0				.789	-0	/P-6	0.0
1890	Cin-N	127	481	67	150	26	8	4	67	38	31	.312	.367	.424	131	18	17			.925	-6	*O-127	0.6
Total	2	133	505	69	156	29	8	4	69	38	33	.309	.362	.422	130	18	17			.925	-6	O-127/P-6	0.6

YEAR	TM/L	G	AB	R	H	2B	3B	HR	RBI	BB	SO	AVG	OBP	SLG	PRO+	BR/A	SB	CS	SBR	FA	FR	G/POS	TPR

■ PETE KNISELY   Knisely, Peter Cole   b: 8/11/1887, Waynesburg, Pa.   d: 7/1/48, Brownsville, Pa.   BR/TR, 5'9", 185 lbs.   Deb: 9/4/12

1912	Cin-N	21	67	10	22	7	3	0	7	4	5	.328	.375	.522	148	4	3			.939	-2	O-13/2-3,S	0.1
1913	Chi-N	2	2	0	0	0	0	0	0	0	1	.000	.000	.000	-99	-1	0			.000	0	H	-0.1
1914	Chi-N	37	69	5	9	0	1	0	5	5	6	.130	.200	.159	7	-8	0			.975	2	O-17	-0.7
1915	Chi-N	64	134	12	33	9	0	0	17	15	18	.246	.331	.313	95	-0	1	2	-1	.940	-7	O-33/2-9	-1.1
Total	4	124	272	27	64	16	4	0	29	24	30	.235	.307	.324	86	-5	4	2		.951	-7	/O-63,2-12,S	-1.8

■ CHUCK KNOBLAUCH   Knoblauch, Edward Charles   b: 7/7/68, Houston, Tex.   BR/TR, 5'9", 175 lbs.   Deb: 4/9/91

1991	*Min-A	151	565	78	159	24	6	1	50	59	40	.281	.354	.350	91	-5	25	5	5	.975	-1	*2-148/S-2	0.2
1992	Min-A★	155	600	104	178	19	6	2	56	88	60	.297	.391	.358	108	10	34	13	2	.992	-16	*2-154/S-1,D	0.0
1993	Min-A	153	602	82	167	27	4	2	41	65	44	.277	.357	.346	89	-7	29	11	2	.988	-5	*2-148/S-6,O	-0.5
1994	Min-A★	109	445	85	139	**45**	3	5	51	41	56	.312	.383	.461	116	12	35	6	7	**.994**	-23	*2-109/S-1	-0.2
Total	4	568	2212	349	643	115	19	10	198	253	200	.291	.371	.373	100	10	123	35	16	.986	-45	2-559/S-10,OD	-0.5

■ MIKE KNODE   Knode, Kenneth Thomson   b: 11/8/1895, Westminster, Md.   d: 12/20/80, South Bend, Ind.   BR/TR, 5'10", 160 lbs.   Deb: 6/28/20   F

| 1920 | StL-N | 42 | 65 | 11 | 15 | 1 | 1 | 0 | 12 | 5 | 6 | .231 | .306 | .277 | 71 | -2 | 0 | 1 | -1 | .824 | -0 | /O-9,2-4,S3 | -0.4 |

■ RAY KNODE   Knode, Robert Troxell "Bob"   b: 1/28/01, Westminster, Md.   d: 4/13/82, Battle Creek, Mich   BL/TL, 5'10", 160 lbs.   Deb: 6/30/23   F

1923	Cle-A	22	38	7	11	0	0	2	4	2	4	.289	.325	.447	102	-0	1	0	0	.992	0	1-21	0.0
1924	Cle-A	11	37	6	9	1	0	0	4	3	0	.243	.300	.270	47	-3	2	1	0	.992	1	1-10	-0.2
1925	Cle-A	45	108	13	27	5	0	0	11	10	4	.250	.314	.296	55	-7	3	3	-1	.990	1	1-34	-0.9
1926	Cle-A	31	24	6	8	1	1	0	4	3	4	.333	.407	.458	124	1	0	0	0	.984	1	1-11	0.1
Total	4	109	207	32	55	7	1	2	23	18	12	.266	.324	.338	70	-9	6	4	-1	.990	2	/1-76	-1.0

■ PUNCH KNOLL   Knoll, Charles Elmer   b: 10/7/1881, Evansville, Ind.   d: 2/8/60, Evansville, Ind.   BR/TR, 5'7.5", 170 lbs.   Deb: 4/27/05

| 1905 | Was-A | 79 | 244 | 24 | 52 | 10 | 5 | 0 | 29 | 9 | | .213 | .247 | .295 | 75 | -8 | 3 | | | .937 | 2 | O-63/C-5,1 | -0.9 |

■ BOBBY KNOOP   Knoop, Robert Frank   b: 10/18/38, Sioux City, Iowa   BR/TR, 6'1", 170 lbs.   Deb: 4/13/64   MC

1964	LA-A	162	486	42	105	8	1	7	38	46	109	.216	.291	.280	66	-23	3	2	-0	.978	**37**	*2-161	2.8
1965	Cal-A	142	465	47	125	24	4	7	43	31	101	.269	.315	.383	99	-1	3	2	-0	.971	13	*2-142	2.5
1966	Cal-A★	161	590	54	137	18	**11**	17	72	43	144	.232	.285	.386	94	-6	1	5	-3	**.981**	17	*2-161	2.0
1967	Cal-A	159	511	51	125	18	5	9	38	44	136	.245	.306	.352	98	-2	2	2	-1	.986	1	*2-159	1.0
1968	Cal-A	152	494	48	123	20	4	3	39	35	128	.249	.303	.324	93	-5	3	2	-0	.981	16	*2-151	2.2
1969	Cal-A	27	71	5	14	1	0	1	6	13	16	.197	.321	.254	66	-3	1	3	-2	.977	2	2-27	-0.1
	Chi-A	104	345	34	79	14	1	6	41	35	68	.229	.304	.328	73	-12	2	0	1	.985	23	*2-104	2.0
	Yr	131	416	39	93	15	1	7	47	48	84	.224	.307	.315	72	-15	3	3	-1	.984	25	*2-131	1.9
1970	Chi-A	130	402	34	92	13	2	5	36	34	79	.229	.292	.308	63	-20	0	1	-1	.984	**35**	*2-126	2.5
1971	KC-A	72	161	14	33	8	1	1	11	15	36	.205	.273	.286	59	-9	1	0	0	.968	-1	2-52/3-1	-0.6
1972	KC-A	44	97	8	23	5	0	0	7	9	16	.237	.302	.289	77	-3	0	0	0	.972	8	2-33/3-4	0.7
Total	9	1153	3622	337	856	129	29	56	331	305	833	.236	.298	.334	83	-84	16	17	-5	.980	150	*2-1116/3-5	15.0

■ RANDY KNORR   Knorr, Randy Duane   b: 11/12/68, San Gabriel, Cal.   BR/TR, 6'2", 205 lbs.   Deb: 9/5/91

1991	Tor-A	3	1	0	0	0	0	0	0	1	1	.000	.500	.000	49	-0	0	0	0	1.000	1	/C-3	0.1
1992	Tor-A	8	19	1	5	0	0	1	2	1	5	.263	.300	.421	96	-0	0	0	0	1.000	1	/C-8	0.1
1993	*Tor-A	39	101	11	25	3	2	4	20	9	29	.248	.309	.436	97	-1	0	0	0	1.000	-1	C-39	0.0
1994	Tor-A	40	124	20	30	2	0	7	19	10	35	.242	.304	.427	85	-3	0	0	0	.993	-0	C-40	-0.1
Total	4	90	245	32	60	5	2	12	41	21	70	.245	.307	.429	91	-4	0	0	0	.996	1	/C-90	0.1

■ GEORGE KNOTHE   Knothe, George Bertram   b: 1/12/1898, Bayonne, N.J.   d: 7/3/81, Dover, N.J.   BR/TR, 5'10", 165 lbs.   Deb: 4/25/32   F

| 1932 | Phi-N | 6 | 12 | 2 | 1 | 0 | 0 | 0 | 0 | 0 | 0 | .083 | .083 | .167 | -31 | -2 | 0 | | | .923 | -1 | /2-5 | -0.3 |

■ FRITZ KNOTHE   Knothe, Wilfred Edgar   b: 5/1/03, Passaic, N.J.   d: 3/27/63, Passaic, N.J.   BR/TR, 5'10.5", 180 lbs.   Deb: 4/12/32   F

1932	Bos-N	89	344	45	82	19	1	1	36	39	37	.238	.318	.308	72	-13	5			.947	-3	3-87	-1.0
1933	Bos-N	44	158	15	36	5	2	1	6	13	25	.228	.291	.304	76	-5	1			.978	-7	3-33/S-9	-1.0
	Phi-N	41	113	10	17	2	0	0	11	6	19	.150	.193	.168	3	-14	2			.949	15	3-32/2-4	0.3
	Yr	85	271	25	53	7	2	1	17	19	44	.196	.251	.247	42	-20	3			.961	8	3-65/S-9,2	-0.7
Total	2	174	615	70	135	26	3	2	53	58	81	.220	.289	.281	59	-32	8			.953	5	3-152/S-9,2	-1.7

■ JOE KNOTTS   Knotts, Joseph Steven   b: 3/3/1884, Greensboro, Pa.   d: 9/15/50, Philadelphia, Pa.   BR/TR,   Deb: 9/18/07

| 1907 | Bos-N | 3 | 8 | 0 | 0 | 0 | 0 | 0 | 0 | 0 | 1 | .000 | .111 | .000 | -65 | -2 | 0 | | | 1.000 | -0 | /C-3 | -0.2 |

■ ED KNOUFF   Knouff, Edward "Fred"   b: 6/1868, Philadelphia, Pa.   d: 9/14/1900, Philadelphia, Pa.   BR/TR, 210 lbs.   Deb: 7/1/1885

1885	Phi-a	14	48	5	9	0	0	0		2		.188	.220	.188	28	-4				.867	1	P-14/O-1	0.0
1886	Bal-a	1	3	0	0	0	0	0		0		.000	.250	.000	-20	-0	0			1.000	1	/P-1	0.0
1887	Bal-a	9	31	4	9	0	0	0		1		.290	.313	.290	73	-1	1			.889	-1	/P-9,O-3	-0.1
	StL-a	15	56	4	10	1	2	0		1		.179	.207	.268	29	-6	1			.800	-2	/O-9,P-6	-0.4
	Yr	24	87	8	19	1	2	0		2		.218	.244	.276	43	-7	2			.897	-3	P-15,O-12	-0.5
1888	StL-a	9	31	1	3	0	0	0	1	0	1	.097	.200	.097	-3	-4	1			.842	-2	/P-9	0.0
	Cle-a	2	6	0	1	0	0	0	0	1		.167	.286	.333	101	0	0			1.000	1	P-2,2-1	0.0
	Yr	11	37	1	4	0	0	0	1	1	4	.108	.214	.135	12	-4	1			.880	-1	P-11/2-1	0.0
1889	Phi-a	3	12	2	3	1	0	0	2	1	1	.250	.308	.333	84	-0	1			1.000	1	/P-3	0.0
Total	5	53	187	16	35	3	2	0	3	9	1	.187	.236	.225	35	-3	4			.891	-3	/P-44,O-13,2	-0.5

■ JAKE KNOWDELL   Knowdell, Jacob Augustus   b: 7/27/1840, Brooklyn, N.Y.   5'7.5", 148 lbs.   Deb: 6/20/1874

1874	Atl-n	23	84	8	12	1	1	0		2		.143	.163	.179	10	-8						C-20/O-3	-0.6
1875	Atl-n	43	161	17	32	3	0	0		2		.199	.209	.217	55	-6						C-33/S-8,O	-0.4
1878	Mil-N	4	14	2	3	1	0	0	2	0	3	.214	.214	.286	59	-1				.875	-2	/C-2,O-1,S	-0.3
Total	2 n	66	245	25	44	4	1	0		4		.180	.193	.204	38	-14						/C-53,S-8,O	-1.0

■ JIMMY KNOWLES   Knowles, James "Darby"   b: 9/1856, Toronto, Ont., Can.   d: 2/11/12, Jersey City, N.J.   5'9", 160 lbs.   Deb: 5/2/1884

1884	Pit-a	46	182	19	42	5	7	0		5		.231	.259	.335	91	-0				.961	-0	1-46	-0.7
	Bro-a	41	153	19	36	5	1	1		3		.235	.255	.301	80	-3				.953	1	1-30,3-11	-0.6
	Yr	87	335	38	78	10	8	1		8		.233	.257	.319	86	-5				.958	1	1-76,3-11	-1.3
1886	Was-N	115	443	43	94	16	11	3	35	15	73	.212	.238	.318	72	-15	20			.899	**28**	2-62,3-53	1.5
1887	NY-a	16	60	12	15	1	1	0		1		.250	.262	.300	59	-3	6			.934	-3	2-16/3-1	-0.5
1890	Roc-a	123	491	83	138	12	8	5		59		.281	.359	.369	124	16	55			.881	7	*3-123	2.4
1892	NY-N	16	59	9	9	1	0	0	7	6	8	.153	.231	.169	22	-5	2			.792	-5	3-15/S-1	-0.9
Total	5	357	1388	185	334	40	28	9	42	89	81	.241	.288	.329	91	-13	83			.861	28	3-203/2-78,1S	1.2

■ ANDY KNOX   Knox, Andrew Jackson "Dasher"   b: 1/6/1864, Philadelphia, Pa.   d: 9/14/40, Philadelphia, Pa.   BR/TR,   Deb: 9/19/1890

| 1890 | Phi-a | 21 | 75 | 6 | 19 | 3 | 0 | 0 | | 3 | | .253 | .333 | .293 | 87 | -1 | | | | .963 | -2 | 1-21 | -0.3 |

■ CLIFF KNOX   Knox, Clifford Hiram "Bud"   b: 1/7/02, Coalville, Iowa   d: 9/24/65, Oskaloosa, Iowa   BB/TR, 5'11.5", 178 lbs.   Deb: 7/1/24

| 1924 | Pit-N | 6 | 18 | 1 | 4 | 1 | 0 | 0 | 2 | 2 | 0 | .222 | .300 | .222 | 41 | -1 | 0 | 0 | 0 | .917 | 2 | /C-6 | 0.1 |

YEAR	TM/L	G	AB	R	H	2B	3B	HR	RBI	BB	SO	AVG	OBP	SLG	PRO+	BR/A	SB	CS	SBR	FA	FR	G/POS	TPR

■ JOHN KNOX
Knox, John Clinton b: 7/26/48, Newark, N.J. BL/TR, 6', 170 lbs. Deb: 8/1/72

YEAR	TM/L	G	AB	R	H	2B	3B	HR	RBI	BB	SO	AVG	OBP	SLG	PRO+	BR/A	SB	CS	SBR	FA	FR	G/POS	TPR
1972	*Det-A	14	13	1	1	0	0	0	1	2	0	.077	.143	.154	-11	-2	0	0	0	1.000	4	/2-4	0.2
1973	Det-A	12	32	1	9	1	0	0	3	3	3	.281	.343	.313	80	-1	1	1	-0	1.000	-3	/2-9	-0.3
1974	Det-A	55	88	11	27	1	1	0	6	6	13	.307	.351	.341	96	-0	5	4	-1	.956	8	2-33/3-1,D	0.7
1975	Det-A	43	86	8	23	1	0	0	2	9	9	.267	.344	.279	74	-2	1	2	-1	.980	-1	2-23/3-3,D	-0.4
Total	4	124	219	21	60	4	1	0	11	20	27	.274	.335	.301	79	-5	7	7	-2	.973	8	/2-69,D-5,3	0.2

■ NICK KOBACK
Koback, Nicholas Nicholie b: 7/19/35, Hartford, Conn. BR/TR, 6', 187 lbs. Deb: 7/29/53

YEAR	TM/L	G	AB	R	H	2B	3B	HR	RBI	BB	SO	AVG	OBP	SLG	PRO+	BR/A	SB	CS	SBR	FA	FR	G/POS	TPR
1953	Pit-N	7	16	1	2	0	1	0	0	1	4	.125	.176	.250	10	-2	0	0	0	1.000	-3	/C-6	-0.5
1954	Pit-N	4	10	0	0	0	0	0	0	0	8	.000	.000	.000	-99	-3	0	0	0	1.000	0	/C-4	-0.3
1955	Pit-N	5	7	0	2	0	0	0	0	0	1	.286	.286	.286	53	-0	0	0	0	1.000	0	/C-2	0.0
Total	3	16	33	1	4	0	1	0	0	1	13	.121	.147	.182	-15	-6	0	0	0	1.000	-3	/C-12	-0.8

■ BARNEY KOCH
Koch, Barnett b: 3/23/23, Campbell, Neb. d: 6/6/87, Tacoma, Wash. BR/TR, 5'8", 140 lbs. Deb: 7/23/44

YEAR	TM/L	G	AB	R	H	2B	3B	HR	RBI	BB	SO	AVG	OBP	SLG	PRO+	BR/A	SB	CS	SBR	FA	FR	G/POS	TPR
1944	Bro-N	33	96	11	21	2	0	0	1	3	9	.219	.242	.240	37	-8	0			.956	-6	2-29/S-1	-1.3

■ BRAD KOCHER
Kocher, Bradley Wilson b: 1/16/1888, White Haven, Pa. d: 1/13/65, White Haven, Pa. BR/TR, 5'11", 188 lbs. Deb: 4/24/12

YEAR	TM/L	G	AB	R	H	2B	3B	HR	RBI	BB	SO	AVG	OBP	SLG	PRO+	BR/A	SB	CS	SBR	FA	FR	G/POS	TPR
1912	Det-A	29	63	5	13	3	1	0	9	2		.206	.231	.286	49	-4	0			.904	-5	C-24	-0.6
1915	NY-N	4	11	3	5	0	1	0	2	0	1	.455	.455	.636	243	2	0			1.000	-1	/C-3	0.1
1916	NY-N	34	65	1	7	2	0	0	1	2	10	.108	.134	.138	-17	-9	0			.978	-7	C-30	-1.7
Total	3	67	139	9	25	5	2	0	12	4	11	.180	.203	.245	34	-12	0			.943	-11	C-57	-2.2

■ PETE KOEGEL
Koegel, Peter John b: 7/31/47, Mineola, N.Y. BR/TR, 6'6.5", 230 lbs. Deb: 9/1/70

YEAR	TM/L	G	AB	R	H	2B	3B	HR	RBI	BB	SO	AVG	OBP	SLG	PRO+	BR/A	SB	CS	SBR	FA	FR	G/POS	TPR
1970	Mil-A	7	8	2	2	0	0	1	1	1	3	.250	.333	.625	157	1	0	0	0	1.000	-0	/O-1	0.0
1971	Mil-A	2	3	0	0	0	0	0	0	2	2	.000	.400	.000	22	-0	0	0	0	1.000	-0	/1-1	0.0
	Phi-N	12	26	1	6	1	0	0	3	2	7	.231	.286	.269	58	-1	0	0	0	1.000	-1	/C-7,O-1	-0.2
1972	Phi-N	41	49	3	7	2	0	0	1	6	16	.143	.236	.184	20	-5	0	0	0	1.000	-2	/1-8,C-5,3O	-0.8
Total	3	62	86	6	15	3	0	1	5	11	28	.174	.268	.244	45	-6	0	0	0	.971	-3	/C-12,1-9,3O	-1.0

■ BEN KOEHLER
Koehler, Benard James b: 1/26/1877, Schoerndorn, Germany d: 5/21/61, South Bend, Ind. BR/TR, 5'10.5", 175 lbs. Deb: 4/23/05

YEAR	TM/L	G	AB	R	H	2B	3B	HR	RBI	BB	SO	AVG	OBP	SLG	PRO+	BR/A	SB	CS	SBR	FA	FR	G/POS	TPR
1905	StL-A	142	536	55	127	14	6	2	47	32		.237	.285	.297	89	-7	22			.969	6	*O-124,1-12/2	-0.9
1906	StL-A	66	186	27	41	1	1	0	15	24		.220	.322	.237	79	-3	9			.957	-4	O-52/2-7,S3	-1.0
Total	2	208	722	82	168	15	7	2	62	56		.233	.295	.281	87	-10	31			.966	1	0-176/2-13,13S	-1.9

■ PIP KOEHLER
Koehler, Horace Levering b: 1/16/02, Gilbert, Pa. d: 12/8/86, Tacoma, Wash. BR/TR, 5'10", 165 lbs. Deb: 4/22/25

YEAR	TM/L	G	AB	R	H	2B	3B	HR	RBI	BB	SO	AVG	OBP	SLG	PRO+	BR/A	SB	CS	SBR	FA	FR	G/POS	TPR
1925	NY-N	12	2	1	0	0	0	0	0	0	1	.000	.000	.000	-99	-1	0	0	0	1.000	-1	/O-3	-0.1

■ BRIAN KOELLING
Koelling, Brian Wayne b: 6/11/69, Cincinnati, Ohio BR/TR, 6'1", 185 lbs. Deb: 8/21/93

YEAR	TM/L	G	AB	R	H	2B	3B	HR	RBI	BB	SO	AVG	OBP	SLG	PRO+	BR/A	SB	CS	SBR	FA	FR	G/POS	TPR
1993	Cin-N	7	15	1	1	0	0	0	2	2	2	.067	.125	.067	-47	-3	0	0	0	.941	1	/2-3,S-2	-0.2

■ LEN KOENECKE
Koenecke, Leonard George b: 1/18/04, Baraboo, Wis. d: 9/17/35, Toronto, Ont., Can BL/TR, 5'11", 180 lbs. Deb: 4/12/32

YEAR	TM/L	G	AB	R	H	2B	3B	HR	RBI	BB	SO	AVG	OBP	SLG	PRO+	BR/A	SB	CS	SBR	FA	FR	G/POS	TPR
1932	NY-N	42	137	33	35	5	4	1	14	11	13	.255	.320	.380	89	-2	3			.924	-5	O-35	-0.9
1934	Bro-N	123	460	79	147	31	7	14	73	70	38	.320	.411	.509	152	36	8			.994	2	*O-121	3.1
1935	Bro-N	100	325	43	92	13	4	4	27	43	45	.283	.369	.372	102	2	0			.966	-4	O-91	-0.5
Total	3	265	922	155	274	49	9	19	114	124	96	.297	.383	.441	125	36	11			.976	-7	O-247	1.7

■ MARK KOENIG
Koenig, Mark Anthony b: 7/19/04, San Francisco, Cal. d: 4/22/93, Willows, Cal. BB/TR, 6', 180 lbs. Deb: 9/8/25

YEAR	TM/L	G	AB	R	H	2B	3B	HR	RBI	BB	SO	AVG	OBP	SLG	PRO+	BR/A	SB	CS	SBR	FA	FR	G/POS	TPR
1925	NY-A	28	110	14	23	6	1	0	4	5	4	.209	.243	.282	34	-12	0	1	-1	.944	-3	S-28	-1.1
1926	*NY-A	147	617	93	167	26	8	5	62	43	37	.271	.319	.363	79	-21	4	3	-1	.931	-0	*S-141	-0.6
1927	*NY-A	123	526	99	150	20	11	3	62	25	21	.285	.320	.382	84	-14	3	2	-0	.936	14	*S-122	1.2
1928	*NY-A	132	533	89	170	19	10	4	63	32	19	.319	.360	.415	106	4	3	5	-2	.923	-20	*S-125	-0.3
1929	NY-A	116	373	44	109	27	5	3	41	23	17	.292	.335	.416	99	-2	1	1	-0	.911	-13	S-61,3-37/2	-0.7
1930	NY-A	21	74	9	17	5	0	0	9	6	5	.230	.296	.297	53	-5	0	0	0	.905	2	S-19	-0.1
	Det-A	76	267	37	64	9	2	1	16	20	15	.240	.295	.300	50	-20	2	0	1	.922	-14	S-70/P-2,3O	-2.4
	Yr	97	341	46	81	14	2	1	25	26	20	.238	.295	.299	51	-25	2	0	1	.918	-13	S-89/P-2,3O	-2.5
1931	Det-A	106	364	33	92	24	4	1	39	14	12	.253	.282	.349	63	-20	8	2	1	.955	-22	2-55,S-35/P	-3.4
1932	*Chi-N	33	102	15	36	7	3	3	11	3	5	.353	.377	.510	137	5	0			.932	-10	S-31	1.7
1933	Chi-N	80	218	32	62	12	1	3	25	15	9	.284	.330	.390	105	1	5			.922	5	3-37,S-26/2	1.0
1934	Cin-N	151	633	60	172	26	6	1	67	15	24	.272	.289	.336	68	-29	5			.930	6	3-64,S-58,2/1	-1.6
1935	NY-N	107	396	40	112	12	0	3	37	13	18	.283	.306	.336	74	-15	0			.968	-11	2-64,S-21,3	-1.9
1936	*NY-N	42	58	7	16	4	0	1	7	8	4	.276	.373	.397	109	1	0			.905	-1	S-10/2-8,3	0.0
Total	12	1162	4271	572	1190	195	49	28	443	222	190	.279	.316	.367	81	-126	31	14		.927	-50	S-747,3-158,2/P10	-8.2

■ HENRY KOHLER
Kohler, Henry C. b: 5/5/1852, Baltimore, Md. d: 8/27/34, Baltimore, Md. Deb: 7/12/1871

YEAR	TM/L	G	AB	R	H	2B	3B	HR	RBI	BB	SO	AVG	OBP	SLG	PRO+	BR/A	SB	CS	SBR	FA	FR	G/POS	TPR
1871	Kek-n	3	12	1	2	1	0	0	1	0	0	.167	.167	.250	17	-1	0					/1-2,3-1	-0.1
1873	Mar-n	6	25	2	3	3	0	0	0	0	0	.120	.120	.240	4	-3						/3-5,C-1,1	-0.2
1874	Bal-n	2	4	0	0	0	0	0	0			.000	.000	.000	-99	-1						/1-1	-0.1
Total	3 n	11	41	2	5	4	0	0				.122	.122	.220	-2	-5						/3-6,1-4,C	-0.4

■ DICK KOKOS
Kokos, Richard Jerome (b: Richard Jerome Kokoszka) b: 2/28/28, Chicago, Ill. d: 4/9/86, Chicago, Ill. BL/TL, 5'8.5", 170 lbs. Deb: 7/8/48

YEAR	TM/L	G	AB	R	H	2B	3B	HR	RBI	BB	SO	AVG	OBP	SLG	PRO+	BR/A	SB	CS	SBR	FA	FR	G/POS	TPR
1948	StL-A	71	258	40	77	15	3	4	40	28	32	.298	.374	.426	110	3	4	3	-1	.964	-1	O-71	-0.1
1949	StL-A	143	501	80	131	28	1	23	77	66	91	.261	.351	.459	109	4	3	5	-2	.981	8	*O-138	0.3
1950	StL-A	143	490	77	128	27	5	18	67	88	73	.261	.375	.447	106	4	8	8	-2	.970	9	*O-127	0.5
1953	StL-A	107	299	41	72	12	0	13	38	56	53	.241	.361	.411	106	3	0	5	-3	.963	-1	O-83	-0.4
1954	Bal-A	11	10	1	2	0	0	1	1	4	3	.200	.429	.500	166	1	0	0	0	1.000	0	/O-1	0.1
Total	5	475	1558	239	410	82	9	59	223	242	252	.263	.365	.441	108	16	15	21	-8	.971	16	O-420	0.4

■ GARY KOLB
Kolb, Gary Alan b: 3/13/40, Rock Falls, Ill. BL/TR, 6', 195 lbs. Deb: 9/7/60

YEAR	TM/L	G	AB	R	H	2B	3B	HR	RBI	BB	SO	AVG	OBP	SLG	PRO+	BR/A	SB	CS	SBR	FA	FR	G/POS	TPR
1960	StL-N	9	3	1	0	0	0	0	0	0	0	.000	.000	.000	-92	-1	0	0	0	1.000	-0	/O-2	-0.1
1962	StL-N	6	14	1	5	0	0	0	0	1	3	.357	.400	.357	96	-0	0	0	0	1.000	-1	/O-6	-0.1
1963	StL-N	75	96	23	26	1	5	3	10	22	26	.271	.407	.479	141	6	2	1	0	.981	-11	O-58/C-1,3	-0.7
1964	Mil-N	36	64	7	12	1	0	0	6	6	10	.188	.257	.203	31	-6	3	2	-0	1.000	-0	O-14/3-7,2C	-1.3
1965	Mil-N	24	27	3	7	1	0	0	1	1	6	.259	.286	.259	54	-2	0	0	0	1.000	-3	O-13	-0.5
	NY-N	40	90	8	15	2	0	1	7	3	28	.167	.194	.222	17	-10	1	0	0	.976	-1	O-29/1-1,3	-1.2
	Yr	64	117	11	22	3	0	1	8	4	34	.188	.215	.231	26	-11	3	0	1	.981	-4	O-42/1-1,3	-1.7
1968	Pit-N	74	119	16	26	9	1	0	6	11	17	.218	.285	.319	82	-3	2	1	0	.900	-25	O-25,C-10/32	-0.6
1969	Pit-N	29	37	4	3	1	0	0	0	2	14	.081	.128	.108	-34	-7	0	0	0	1.000	0	/C-7	-0.7
Total	7	293	450	63	94	9	6	6	29	46	104	.209	.282	.296	65	-21	10	4	1	.965	-23	0-147/C-20,321	-5.2

■ DON KOLLOWAY
Kolloway, Donald Martin "Butch" or "Cab" b: 8/4/18, Posen, Ill. d: 6/30/94, Blue Island, Ill. BR/TR, 6'3", 200 lbs. Deb: 9/16/40

YEAR	TM/L	G	AB	R	H	2B	3B	HR	RBI	BB	SO	AVG	OBP	SLG	PRO+	BR/A	SB	CS	SBR	FA	FR	G/POS	TPR
1940	Chi-A	10	40	5	9	1	0	0	3	0	3	.225	.225	.250	23	-5	1	0	0	.922	4	2-10	-0.5
1941	Chi-A	71	280	33	76	8	3	3	24	6	12	.271	.292	.354	71	-13	11	4	1	.955	-7	2-62/1-4	-1.6
1942	Chi-A	147	601	72	164	**40**	4	3	60	20	39	.273	.311	.368	92	-8	16	14	-4	.966	-9	*2-116,1-33	-1.6
1943	Chi-A	85	348	29	75	14	4	0	33	9	30	.216	.235	.287	53	-22	11	7	-1	.968	-1	2-85	-2.1
1946	Chi-A	123	482	45	135	23	4	0	29	22	29	.280	.293	.363	86	-12	14	6	1	.972	3	2-90,3-31	-0.1

YEAR	TM/L	G	AB	R	H	2B	3B	HR	RBI	BB	SO	AVG	OBP	SLG	PRO+	BR/A	SB	CS	SBR	FA	FR	G/POS	TPR
1947	Chi-A	124	485	49	135	25	4	2	35	17	34	.278	.303	.359	87	-11	11	4	1	.962	5	2-99,1-11/3	0.1
1948	Chi-A	119	417	60	114	14	4	6	38	18	18	.273	.303	.369	81	-13	2	4	-2	.966	11	2-83,3-18	0.0
1949	Chi-A	4	4	0	0	0	0	0	0	0	1	.000	.000	.000	-99	-1	0	0	0	.000	0	/3-2	-0.1
	Det-A	126	483	71	142	19	3	2	47	49	25	.294	.361	.358	91	-6	7	7	-2	.956	-21	2-62,1-57/3	-2.6
	Yr	130	487	71	142	19	3	2	47	49	26	.292	.359	.355	89	-7	7	7	-2	.956	-21	2-62,1-57/3	-2.7
1950	Det-A	125	467	55	135	20	4	6	62	29	28	.289	.331	.388	81	-15	1	3	-2	.989	3	*1-118/2-1	-1.5
1951	Det-A	78	212	28	54	7	0	1	17	15	12	.255	.307	.302	65	-10	2	3	-1	.992	6	1-59	-0.8
1952	Det-A	65	173	19	42	9	0	2	21	7	19	.243	.280	.329	69	-8	0	2	-1	.979	4	1-32/2-8	-1.1
1953	Phi-A	2	1	0	0	0	0	0	0	0	1	.000	.000	.000	-96	-0	0	0	0	.000	0	/3-1	0.0
Total	12	1079	3993	466	1081	180	30	29	393	189	251	.271	.305	.353	80	-124	76	54	-10	.964	-13	2-616,1-314/3	-11.8

■ KARL KOLSETH
Kolseth, Karl Dickey "Koley" b: 12/25/1892, Cambridge, Mass. d: 5/3/56, Cumberland, Md. BL/TR, 6', 182 lbs. Deb: 9/30/15

YEAR	TM/L	G	AB	R	H	2B	3B	HR	RBI	BB	SO	AVG	OBP	SLG	PRO+	BR/A	SB	CS	SBR	FA	FR	G/POS	TPR
1915	Bal-F	6	23	1	6	1	1	0	1	1	0	.261	.292	.391	79	-1	0			.915	-2	/1-6	-0.3

■ FRED KOMMERS
Kommers, Frederick Raymond "Bugs" b: 3/31/1886, Chicago, Ill. d: 6/14/43, Chicago, Ill. BL/TR, 6', 175 lbs. Deb: 6/25/13

YEAR	TM/L	G	AB	R	H	2B	3B	HR	RBI	BB	SO	AVG	OBP	SLG	PRO+	BR/A	SB	CS	SBR	FA	FR	G/POS	TPR
1913	Pit-N	40	155	14	36	5	4	0	22	10	29	.232	.279	.316	73	-6	1			.979	-2	O-40	-1.0
1914	StL-F	76	244	33	75	9	8	3	41	24	36	.307	.376	.447	107	3	7			.908	-2	O-67	-0.2
	Bal-F	16	42	5	9	1	0	1	1	7	7	.214	.340	.310	67	-2	0			.938	-2	O-12	-0.5
	Yr	92	286	38	84	10	8	4	42	31	43	.294	.371	.427	101	1	7			.911	-4	O-79	-0.7
Total	2	132	441	52	120	15	12	4	64	41	72	.272	.340	.388	93	-5	8			.938	-6	O-119	-1.7

■ BRAD KOMMINSK
Komminsk, Brad Lynn b: 4/4/61, Lima, Ohio BR/TR, 6'2", 205 lbs. Deb: 9/28/83

YEAR	TM/L	G	AB	R	H	2B	3B	HR	RBI	BB	SO	AVG	OBP	SLG	PRO+	BR/A	SB	CS	SBR	FA	FR	G/POS	TPR
1983	Atl-N	19	36	2	8	2	0	0	4	5	9	.222	.317	.278	62	-2	0	0	0	.944	-1	O-13	-0.3
1984	Atl-N	90	301	37	61	10	0	8	36	29	77	.203	.277	.316	62	-15	18	8	1	.993	-2	O-80	-2.1
1985	Atl-N	106	300	52	68	12	3	4	21	38	71	.227	.316	.327	75	-9	10	8	-2	.959	-4	O-92	-1.9
1986	Atl-N	5	5	1	2	0	0	0	1	0	1	.400	.400	.400	115	0	1	0	-1	1.000	-0	/3-2,O-2	-0.1
1987	Mil-A	7	15	0	1	0	0	0	0	1	7	.067	.125	.067	-46	-3	1	0	0	1.000	-0	/O-5,D-1	-0.3
1989	Cle-A	71	198	27	47	8	2	8	33	24	55	.237	.323	.419	106	1	8	2	1	.995	3	O-68	0.4
1990	SF-N	8	5	2	1	0	0	0	0	1	2	.200	.333	.200	52	-0	0	0	0	1.000	-3	/O-7	-0.3
	Bal-A	46	101	18	24	4	0	3	8	14	29	.238	.342	.366	101	0	1	1	-0	1.000	-5	O-40/D-2	-0.5
1991	Oak-A	24	25	1	3	1	0	0	2	2	9	.120	.185	.160	-4	-4	1	0	0	1.000	-6	O-22	-0.9
Total	8	376	986	140	215	37	5	23	105	114	258	.218	.303	.336	75	-31	39	20	-0	.984	-17	O-329/D-3,3	-6.0

■ ED KONETCHY
Konetchy, Edward Joseph "Big Ed" b: 9/3/1885, LaCrosse, Wis. d: 5/27/47, Ft.Worth, Tex. BR/TR, 6'2.5", 195 lbs. Deb: 6/29/07

YEAR	TM/L	G	AB	R	H	2B	3B	HR	RBI	BB	SO	AVG	OBP	SLG	PRO+	BR/A	SB	CS	SBR	FA	FR	G/POS	TPR
1907	StL-N	91	331	34	83	11	8	3	30	26		.251	.317	.360	116	5	13			.975	4	1-91	0.8
1908	StL-N	154	545	46	135	19	12	5	50	38		.248	.309	.354	117	9	16			.986	11	*1-154	2.0
1909	StL-N	152	576	88	165	23	14	4	80	65		.286	.366	.396	145	31	25			.985	5	*1-152	3.7
1910	StL-N	144	520	87	157	23	16	3	78	78	59	.302	.397	.425	145	32	18			**.991**	8	*1-144/P-1	**4.1**
1911	StL-N	158	571	90	165	**38**	13	6	88	81	63	.289	.384	.433	132	25	27			**.991**	-6	*1-158	1.9
1912	StL-N	143	538	81	169	26	13	8	82	62	66	.314	.389	.455	134	25	25			.991	6	*1-142/O-1	2.8
1913	StL-N	140	504	75	139	18	17	3	68	53	41	.276	.353	.427	124	15	27			**.995**	7	*1-140/P-1	2.2
1914	Pit-N	154	563	56	140	23	9	4	51	32	48	.249	.291	.343	92	-8	20			**.995**	5	*1-154	-0.7
1915	Pit-F	152	576	79	181	31	18	10	93	41	52	.314	.363	.483	126	18	27			**.994**	-0	*1-152	1.5
1916	Bos-N	158	566	76	147	29	13	3	70	43	46	.260	.320	.373	117	11	13			.990	9	*1-158	1.5
1917	Bos-N	130	474	56	129	19	13	2	54	36	40	.272	.330	.380	125	13	16			**.994**	2	*1-129	1.1
1918	Bos-N	119	437	33	103	15	5	2	56	32	35	.236	.291	.307	86	-8	5			**.992**	-2	*1-112/O-6,P	-1.6
1919	Bos-N	132	486	46	145	24	9	1	47	29	39	.298	.342	.391	117	10	14			**.994**	7	*1-132	1.3
1920	*Bro-N	131	497	62	153	22	12	5	63	33	18	.308	.352	.431	120	12	3	2	-0	.990	1	*1-130	1.0
1921	Bro-N	55	197	25	53	6	5	3	23	19	21	.269	.336	.396	90	-3	3	3	-1	.987	-1	1-54	-0.6
	Phi-N	72	268	38	86	17	4	8	59	21	17	.321	.379	.504	122	8	3	0	1	.986	6	1-71	1.3
	Yr	127	465	63	139	23	9	11	82	40	38	.299	.361	.458	109	6	6	3	0	.986	6	*1-125	0.7
Total	15	2085	7649	972	2150	344	181	75	992	689	545	.281	.346	.403	121	196	255	5		.990	59	*1-2073/O-7,P	22.3

■ MIKE KONNICK
Konnick, Michael Aloysius b: 1/13/1889, Glen Lyon, Pa. d: 7/9/71, Wilkes-Barre, Pa. BR/TR, 5'9", 180 lbs. Deb: 10/3/09

YEAR	TM/L	G	AB	R	H	2B	3B	HR	RBI	BB	SO	AVG	OBP	SLG	PRO+	BR/A	SB	CS	SBR	FA	FR	G/POS	TPR
1909	Cin-N	2	5	0	2	1	0	0	1	0		.400	.400	.600	211	1	0			1.000	-1	/C-2	0.0
1910	Cin-N	1	3	0	0	0	0	0	0	1	0	.000	.250	.000	-27	-0	0			1.000	-1	/S-1	-0.1
Total	2	3	8	0	2	1	0	0	1	1	0	.250	.333	.375	117	0	0			1.000	-1	/C-2,S-1	-0.1

■ BRUCE KONOPKA
Konopka, Bruno Bruce b: 9/16/19, Hammond, Ind. BL/TL, 6'2", 190 lbs. Deb: 6/7/42

YEAR	TM/L	G	AB	R	H	2B	3B	HR	RBI	BB	SO	AVG	OBP	SLG	PRO+	BR/A	SB	CS	SBR	FA	FR	G/POS	TPR
1942	Phi-A	5	10	2	3	0	0	0	1	1	0	.300	.364	.300	88	-0	0	0	0	1.000	-0	/1-3	0.0
1943	Phi-A	2	2	0	0	0	0	0	0	0	0	.000	.000	.000	-99	-0	0	0	0	.000	0	H	-0.1
1946	Phi-A	38	93	7	22	4	1	0	9	4	8	.237	.268	.301	59	-5	0	0	0	.994	1	1-20/O-1	-0.6
Total	3	45	105	9	25	4	1	0	10	5	9	.238	.273	.295	59	-6	0	0	0	.995	1	/1-23,O-1	-0.7

■ HARRY KOONS
Koons, Henry M. b: 1863, Philadelphia, Pa. BR/TR, 5'8", 174 lbs. Deb: 4/17/1884

YEAR	TM/L	G	AB	R	H	2B	3B	HR	RBI	BB	SO	AVG	OBP	SLG	PRO+	BR/A	SB	CS	SBR	FA	FR	G/POS	TPR
1884	Alt-U	21	78	8	18	2	1	0		2		.231	.250	.282	44	-6				.866	5	3-21/C-1	-0.1
	CP-U	1	3	0	0	0	0	0		0		.000	.000	.000	-99	-1				.000	0	/3-1	-0.1
	Yr	22	81	8	18	2	1	0		2		.222	.241	.272	39	-7				.866	5	3-22/C-1	-0.2

■ GEORGE KOPACZ
Kopacz, George Felix "Sonny" b: 2/26/41, Chicago, Ill. BL/TL, 6'1", 195 lbs. Deb: 9/18/66

YEAR	TM/L	G	AB	R	H	2B	3B	HR	RBI	BB	SO	AVG	OBP	SLG	PRO+	BR/A	SB	CS	SBR	FA	FR	G/POS	TPR
1966	Atl-N	6	9	1	0	0	0	0	0	0	5	.000	.100	.000	-68	-2	0	0	0	.909	-1	/1-2	-0.3
1970	Pit-N	10	16	1	3	0	0	0	0	0	5	.188	.188	.188	1	-2	0	0	0	1.000	-1	/1-3	-0.3
Total	2	16	25	2	3	0	0	0	0	0	10	.120	.154	.120	-25	-4	0	0	0	.964	-2	/1-5	-0.6

■ WALLY KOPF
Kopf, Walter Henry b: 7/10/1899, Stonington, Conn. d: 4/30/79, Hamilton Co., Ohio BB/TR, 5'11", 168 lbs. Deb: 10/1/21 F

YEAR	TM/L	G	AB	R	H	2B	3B	HR	RBI	BB	SO	AVG	OBP	SLG	PRO+	BR/A	SB	CS	SBR	FA	FR	G/POS	TPR
1921	NY-N	2	3	0	1	0	0	0	1	1	1	.333	.500	.333	125	0	0	0	0	1.000	2	/3-2	0.2

■ LARRY KOPF
Kopf, William Lorenz (a.k.a. Fred Brady In 1913) b: 11/3/1890, Bristol, Conn. d: 10/15/86, Anderson Twp., O. BB/TR, 5'9", 160 lbs. Deb: 9/2/13 F

YEAR	TM/L	G	AB	R	H	2B	3B	HR	RBI	BB	SO	AVG	OBP	SLG	PRO+	BR/A	SB	CS	SBR	FA	FR	G/POS	TPR
1913	Cle-A	6	10	2	3	1	0	0	1	0	1	.300	.300	.400	102	-0	0			.923	2	/2-4,3-1	0.2
1914	Phi-A	37	69	8	13	2	2	0	12	8	14	.188	.300	.275	76	-2	6			.899	1	S-13/3-8,2	0.3
1915	Phi-A	118	386	39	87	10	2	1	33	41	45	.225	.314	.269	77	-10	5	9	-4	.920	-8	S-74,3-42/2	-1.5
1916	Cin-N	11	40	2	11	2	0	0	5	1		.275	.293	.325	92	-1	1			.942	-2	S-11	-0.3
1917	Cin-N	148	573	81	146	19	8	2	26	28	48	.255	.297	.326	95	-5	17			.916	-11	*S-145	-1.0
1919	*Cin-N	135	503	51	136	18	5	0	58	28	27	.270	.313	.326	95	-4	18			.943	-34	*S-135	-3.4
1920	Cin-N	126	458	56	112	15	6	0	59	35	24	.245	.305	.303	76	-13	14	13	-4	.929	-33	*S-123/2-4,3O	-4.3
1921	Cin-N	107	367	39	80	8	3	1	25	43	29	.218	.310	.264	56	-22	3	14	-8	.947	-15	S-93/2-4,3O	-3.6
1922	Bos-N	126	466	59	124	6	5	1	37	45	22	.266	.332	.298	67	-22	8	9	-3	.944	-14	2-78,S-33,3	-3.1
1923	Bos-N	39	138	15	38	1	0	0	10	13	6	.275	.338	.312	75	-5	3	2		.905	-9	S-37/2-4	-0.7
Total	10	853	3010	349	750	84	30	5	266	242	214	.249	.312	.302	78	-82	72	48		.928	-122	S-664/2-99,3O	-17.7

■ MERLIN KOPP
Kopp, Merlin Henry "Manny" b: 1/2/1892, Toledo, Ohio d: 5/6/60, Sacramento, Cal. BB/TR, 5'8", 158 lbs. Deb: 8/2/15

YEAR	TM/L	G	AB	R	H	2B	3B	HR	RBI	BB	SO	AVG	OBP	SLG	PRO+	BR/A	SB	CS	SBR	FA	FR	G/POS	TPR
1915	Was-A	16	32	2	8	0	0	0	5	0		.250	.351	.250	79	-1	1			.933	-1	/O-9	-0.2
1918	Phi-A	96	363	60	85	7	7	0	18	42	55	.234	.320	.292	84	-6	22			.972	12	O-96	0.0
1919	Phi-A	75	235	34	53	2	4	1	12	42	43	.226	.348	.281	77	-6	16			.924	-2	O-65	-1.3
Total	3	187	630	96	146	9	11	1	30	89	105	.232	.332	.286	81	-12	39			.953	8	O-170	-1.5

YEAR	TM/L	G	AB	R	H	2B	3B	HR	RBI	BB	SO	AVG	OBP	SLG	PRO+	BR/A	SB	CS	SBR	FA	FR	G/POS	TPR

■ **JOE KOPPE**   Koppe, Joseph (b: Joseph Kopchia) b: 10/19/30, Detroit, Mich.   BR/TR, 5'10", 165 lbs.   Deb: 8/9/58

1958	Mil-N	16	9	3	4	0	0	0	0	1	1	.444	.500	.444	167	1	0	0	0	.833	5	/S-3	0.6
1959	Phi-N	126	422	68	110	18	7	7	28	41	80	.261	.329	.386	88	-7	7	7	-2	.954	5	*S-113,2-11	0.6
1960	Phi-N	58	170	13	29	6	1	1	13	23	47	.171	.273	.235	41	-14	3	2	-0	.956	-12	S-55/3-2	-2.3
1961	Phi-N	6	3	1	0	0	0	0	0	0	0	.000	.000	.000	-99	-1	0	0	0	.800	0	/S-5	-0.1
	LA-A	91	338	46	85	12	2	5	40	45	77	.251	.341	.343	75	-12	3	3	-1	.947	-6	S-88/2-3,3	-1.0
1962	LA-A	128	375	47	85	16	0	4	40	73	84	.227	.356	.301	81	-7	2	1	0	.957	4	*S-118/2-5,3	0.8
1963	LA-A	76	143	11	30	4	1	1	12	9	30	.210	.261	.273	53	-9	0	0	0	.962	8	S-19,3-18,2/O	0.0
1964	LA-A	54	113	10	29	4	1	0	6	14	16	.257	.339	.310	91	-1	0	0	0	.945	15	S-31,2-13/3	1.6
1965	Cal-A	23	33	3	7	1	0	1	2	3	10	.212	.278	.333	75	-1	1	0	0	.979	9	2-10/S-4,3	0.9
Total	8	578	1606	202	379	61	12	19	141	209	345	.236	.327	.324	76	-50	16	13	-3	.952	29	S-436/2-56,3O	1.1

■ **GEORGE KOPSHAW**   Kopshaw, George Karl b: 7/5/1895, Passaic, N.J. d: 12/26/34, Lynchburg, Va.   BR/TR, 5'11.5", 176 lbs.   Deb: 8/4/23

| 1923 | StL-N | 2 | 5 | 1 | 1 | 1 | 0 | 0 | 0 | 0 | 1 | .200 | .200 | .400 | 56 | -0 | 0 | 0 | 0 | 1.000 | -1 | /C-1 | -0.1 |

■ **STEVE KORCHECK**   Korcheck, Stephen Joseph "Hoss" b: 8/11/32, McClellandtown, Pa.   BR/TR, 6'1", 205 lbs.   Deb: 9/6/54

1954	Was-A	2	7	0	1	0	0	0	0	0	2	.143	.143	.143	-23	-1	0	0	0	.857	-1	/C-2	-0.2
1955	Was-A	13	36	3	10	2	0	0	2	0	5	.278	.297	.333	73	-1	0	0	0	1.000	1	C-12	0.0
1958	Was-A	21	51	6	4	2	1	0	1	1	16	.078	.096	.157	-32	-9	0	0	0	.975	0	C-20	-0.9
1959	Was-A	22	51	3	8	2	0	0	4	5	13	.157	.197	.196	19	-6	0	0	0	.974	6	C-22	0.1
Total	4	58	145	12	23	6	1	0	7	6	36	.159	.197	.214	13	-18	0	0	0	.976	7	/C-56	-1.0

■ **ART KORES**   Kores, Arthur Emil "Dutch" b: 7/22/1886, Milwaukee, Wis. d: 3/26/74, Milwaukee, Wis.   BR/TR, 5'9", 167 lbs.   Deb: 7/24/15

| 1915 | StL-F | 60 | 201 | 18 | 47 | 9 | 2 | 1 | 22 | 21 | 13 | .234 | .306 | .313 | 63 | -11 | 6 | | | .960 | 19 | 3-60 | 1.2 |

■ **ANDY KOSCO**   Kosco, Andrew John b: 10/5/41, Youngstown, Ohio   BR/TR, 6'3", 207 lbs.   Deb: 8/13/65

1965	Min-A	23	55	3	13	4	0	1	6	1	15	.236	.250	.364	69	-2	0	0	0	1.000	0	O-14/1-2	-0.3
1966	Min-A	57	158	11	35	5	0	2	13	7	31	.222	.255	.291	53	-10	0	1	-1	.986	-1	O-40/1-5	-1.4
1967	Min-A	9	28	4	4	1	0	0	4	2	4	.143	.200	.179	12	-3	0	0	0	.923	-0	/O-7	-0.4
1968	NY-A	131	466	47	112	19	1	15	59	16	71	.240	.270	.382	99	-1	2	2	-1	.960	3	O-95,1-28	-0.9
1969	LA-N	120	424	51	105	13	2	19	74	21	66	.248	.285	.422	103	-1	0	1	-1	.981	-6	*O-109/1-3	-1.5
1970	LA-N	74	224	21	51	12	0	8	27	1	40	.228	.231	.388	66	-12	1	1	-0	.981	-2	O-58/1-1	-1.7
1971	Mil-A	98	264	27	60	6	2	10	39	24	57	.227	.292	.379	90	-4	1	3	-2	.988	-3	O-45,1-29,3	-1.3
1972	Cal-A	49	142	15	34	4	2	6	13	5	13	.239	.270	.423	110	1	0	0	0	.985	0	O-36	0.0
	Bos-A	17	47	5	10	2	1	3	6	2	9	.213	.260	.489	113	1	0	0	0	1.000	1	O-12	0.0
	Yr	66	189	20	44	6	3	9	19	7	32	.233	.268	.439	111	1	0	0	0	.988	1	O-48	0.0
1973	*Cin-N	47	118	17	33	7	0	9	21	13	26	.280	.351	.568	159	9	0	0	0	1.000	-5	O-36/1-1	0.2
1974	Cin-N	33	37	3	7	2	0	0	5	7	8	.189	.318	.243	59	-2	0	0	0	.846	-2	/3-8,O-1	-0.4
Total	10	658	1963	204	464	75	8	73	267	99	350	.236	.275	.394	92	-28	5	8	-3	.979	-16	O-453/1-69,3	-7.7

■ **CLEM KOSHOREK**   Koshorek, Clement John "Scooter" b: 6/20/25, Royal Oak, Mich. d: 9/8/91, Royal Oak, Mich.   BR/TR, 5'4.5", 165 lbs.   Deb: 4/15/52

1952	Pit-N	98	322	27	84	17	0	0	15	26	39	.261	.320	.314	74	-11	4	7	-3	.949	1	S-33,2-27,3	-1.0
1953	Pit-N	1	1	0	0	0	0	0	0	0	1	.000	.000	.000	-99	-0	0	0	0	.000	0	H	0.0
Total	2	99	323	27	84	17	0	0	15	26	40	.260	.319	.313	74	-11	4	7	-3	.949	1	/S-33,2-27,3	-1.0

■ **KEVIN KOSLOFSKI**   Koslofski, Kevin Craig b: 9/24/66, Decatur, Ill.   BL/TR, 5'8", 165 lbs.   Deb: 6/28/92

1992	KC-A	55	133	20	33	0	2	3	13	12	23	.248	.315	.346	83	-3	2	1	0	.991	-0	O-52	-0.5
1993	KC-A	15	26	4	7	0	0	1	2	4	5	.269	.387	.385	102	-0	0	1	-1	1.000	-0	O-13/D-1	-0.1
1994	KC-A	2	4	2	1	0	0	0	0	2	1	.250	.500	.250	94	-0	0	0	0	.750	0	/O-2	0.0
Total	3	72	163	26	41	0	2	4	15	18	29	.252	.333	.350	87	-3	2	2	-1	.986	-1	/O-67,D-1	-0.6

■ **MIKE KOSMAN**   Kosman, Michael Thomas b: 12/10/17, Hamtramck, Mich.   BR/TR, 5'9", 160 lbs.   Deb: 4/20/44

| 1944 | Cin-N | 1 | 0 | 0 | 0 | 0 | 0 | 0 | 0 | 0 | 0 | — | — | — | — | — | 0 | 0 | 0 | .000 | 0 | R | 0.0 |

■ **FRED KOSTER**   Koster, Frederick Charles "Fritz" b: 12/21/05, Louisville, Ky. d: 4/24/79, St.Matthews, Ky.   BL/TL, 5'10.5", 165 lbs.   Deb: 4/27/31

| 1931 | Phi-N | 76 | 151 | 21 | 34 | 2 | 2 | 0 | 8 | 14 | 21 | .225 | .291 | .265 | 47 | -11 | 4 | | | .923 | -4 | O-41 | -1.7 |

■ **FRANK KOSTRO**   Kostro, Frank Jerry b: 8/4/37, Windber, Pa.   BR/TR, 6'2", 190 lbs.   Deb: 9/2/62

1962	Det-A	16	41	5	11	3	0	0	3	1	6	.268	.286	.341	66	-2	0	0	0	.967	1	3-11	-0.1
1963	Det-A	31	52	4	12	1	0	0	0	9	13	.231	.344	.250	67	-2	0	0	0	.929	-1	/3-6,1-3,O	-0.3
	LA-A	43	99	6	22	2	1	2	10	6	17	.222	.267	.323	68	-4	0	0	0	.960	-2	3-19/1-5,O	-0.7
	Yr	74	151	10	34	3	1	2	10	15	30	.225	.295	.298	68	-6	0	0	0	.953	-3	3-25/1-8,O	-1.0
1964	Min-A	59	103	10	28	5	0	3	12	4	21	.272	.306	.408	96	-1	0	0	0	.912	-3	3-12/2-7,O1	-0.4
1965	Min-A	20	31	2	5	0	0	0	1	4	5	.161	.257	.226	37	-3	0	0	0	.923	-1	/2-7,3-6,O	-0.3
1967	Min-A	32	31	4	10	0	0	0	2	3	2	.323	.382	.323	102	0	0	0	0	1.000	-1	/O-3,3-1	-0.1
1968	Min-A	63	108	9	26	4	1	0	9	6	20	.241	.281	.296	71	-4	0	0	0	1.000	-1	O-24/1-5	-0.7
1969	Min-A	2	2	0	0	0	0	0	0	0	1	.000	.000	.000	-98	-1	0	0	0	.000	0	H	-0.1
Total	7	266	467	40	114	17	2	5	37	33	85	.244	.295	.321	74	-16	0	0	0	.926	-8	/3-55,O-37,21	-2.7

■ **ERNIE KOY**   Koy, Ernest Anyz "Chief" b: 9/17/09, Sealy, Tex.   BR/TR, 6', 200 lbs.   Deb: 4/19/38

1938	Bro-N	142	521	78	156	29	13	11	76	38	76	.299	.352	.468	121	14	15			.984	-1	*O-135/3-1	0.8
1939	Bro-N	125	425	57	118	37	5	8	67	39	64	.278	.338	.445	105	2	11			.962	-0	*O-114	-0.2
1940	Bro-N	24	48	9	11	2	1	1	8	3	3	.229	.275	.375	73	-2	1			1.000	-4	O-19	-0.6
	StL-N	93	348	44	108	19	5	8	52	28	59	.310	.368	.463	121	10	12			.970	-3	O-91	0.3
	Yr	117	396	53	119	21	6	9	60	31	62	.301	.357	.452	115	8	13			.973	-6	*O-110	-0.3
1941	StL-N	13	40	5	8	1	0	2	4	1	8	.200	.220	.375	61	-2	0			1.000	-2	O-12	-0.5
	Cin-N	67	204	24	51	11	2	2	27	14	22	.250	.301	.353	84	-5	1			.990	-1	O-49	-1.0
	Yr	80	244	29	59	12	2	4	31	15	30	.242	.288	.357	80	-7	1			.991	-3	O-61	-1.5
1942	Cin-N	3	2	0	0	0	0	0	0	0	2	.000	.000	.000	-99	-0	0			.000	0	H	-0.1
	Phi-N	91	258	21	63	9	3	4	26	14	50	.244	.283	.349	89	-5	0			.981	-9	O-78	-1.8
	Yr	94	260	21	63	9	3	4	26	14	52	.242	.281	.346	87	-5	0			.981	-9	O-78	-1.9
Total	5	558	1846	238	515	108	29	36	260	137	284	.279	.332	.427	107	11	40			.977	-20	O-498/3-1	-3.1

■ **AL KOZAR**   Kozar, Albert Kenneth b: 7/5/21, McKees Rocks, Pa.   BR/TR, 5'9.5", 173 lbs.   Deb: 4/19/48

1948	Was-A	150	577	61	144	25	8	1	58	66	52	.250	.327	.326	76	-20	4	2	0	.967	-21	*2-149	-3.1
1949	Was-A	105	350	46	94	15	2	4	31	25	23	.269	.321	.357	81	-11	2	1	0	.977	-7	*2-102	-1.4
1950	Was-A	20	55	7	11	1	0	0	3	5	8	.200	.267	.218	27	-6	0	0	0	.962	-0	2-15	-0.6
	Chi-A	10	10	4	3	0	0	1	2	0	3	.300	.300	.600	129	0	0	0	0	1.000	3	/2-4,3-1	0.3
	Yr	30	65	11	14	1	0	1	5	5	11	.215	.271	.277	42	-6	0	0	0	.968	2	2-19/3-1	-0.3
Total	3	285	992	118	252	41	10	6	94	96	86	.254	.321	.334	76	-37	6	3	0	.971	-26	2-270/3-1	-4.8

■ **JOE KRACHER**   Kracher, Joseph Peter "Jug" b: 11/4/15, Philadelphia, Pa. d: 12/24/81, San Angelo, Tex.   BR/TR, 5'11", 185 lbs.   Deb: 9/17/39

| 1939 | Phi-N | 5 | 5 | 1 | 1 | 0 | 0 | 0 | 0 | 2 | 1 | .200 | .429 | .200 | 76 | 0 | 0 | 0 | 0 | 1.000 | -1 | /C-2 | -0.1 |

YEAR	TM/L	G	AB	R	H	2B	3B	HR	RBI	BB	SO	AVG	OBP	SLG	PRO+	BR/A	SB	CS	SBR	FA	FR	G/POS	TPR

■ **CLARENCE KRAFT** Kraft, Clarence Otto "Big Boy" b: 6/9/1887, Evansville, Ind. d: 3/26/58, Fort Worth, Tex. BR/TR, 6′, 190 lbs. Deb: 5/1/14

1914	Bos-N	3	3	0	1	0	0	0	0	0	1	.333	.333	.333	99	-0	0			1.000	0	/1-1	0.0

■ **ED KRANEPOOL** Kranepool, Edward Emil b: 11/8/44, New York, N.Y. BL/TL, 6′3″, 215 lbs. Deb: 9/22/62

1962	NY-N	3	6	0	1	1	0	0	0	0	1	.167	.167	.333	30	-1	0	0	0	1.000	1	/1-3	0.0
1963	NY-N	86	273	22	57	12	2	2	14	18	50	.209	.258	.289	56	-15	4	2	0	.954	-2	O-55,1-20	-2.3
1964	NY-N	119	420	47	108	19	4	10	45	32	50	.257	.313	.393	100	-1	0	1	-1	.991	3	*1-104/O-6	-0.4
1965	NY-N☆	153	525	44	133	24	4	10	53	39	71	.253	.307	.371	94	-5	1	4	-2	.992	-2	*1-147	-1.8
1966	NY-N	146	464	51	118	15	2	16	57	41	66	.254	.319	.399	100	-0	1	1	-0	.992	5	*1-132,O-11	-0.4
1967	NY-N	141	469	37	126	17	1	10	54	37	51	.269	.323	.373	100	0	0	4	-2	.992	4	*1-139	-0.7
1968	NY-N	127	373	29	86	13	1	3	20	19	39	.231	.272	.295	70	-14	0	3	-2	.994	1	*1-113/O-2	-2.2
1969	*NY-N	112	353	36	84	9	2	11	49	37	32	.238	.310	.368	88	-6	3	2	-0	.993	3	*1-106/O-2	-1.2
1970	NY-N	43	47	2	8	0	0	0	3	5	2	.170	.250	.170	24	-6	0	0	0	1.000	0	/1-8	-0.6
1971	NY-N	122	421	61	118	20	4	14	58	38	33	.280	.341	.447	123	12	0	4	-2	.998	-3	*1-108,O-11	-0.3
1972	NY-N	122	327	28	88	15	1	8	34	34	35	.269	.340	.394	111	5	1	0		.996	-1	*1-108/O-1	-0.4
1973	*NY-N	100	284	28	68	12	2	1	35	30	28	.239	.312	.306	73	-10	1	0		.998	-0	1-51,O-32	-1.5
1974	NY-N	94	217	20	65	11	1	4	24	18	14	.300	.353	.415	116	4	1	0		.977	-6	O-33,1-24	-0.4
1975	NY-N	106	325	42	105	16	0	4	43	27	21	.323	.375	.409	123	10	1	1	-0	.997	-6	1-82/O-4	0.4
1976	NY-N	123	415	47	121	17	1	10	49	35	38	.292	.343	.410	121	10	1	0		.996	-6	1-86,O-31	-0.2
1977	NY-N	108	281	28	79	17	0	10	40	23	20	.281	.336	.448	113	4	1	4	-2	.984	-1	O-42,1-41	-0.2
1978	NY-N	66	81	7	17	2	0	3	19	8	12	.210	.289	.346	79	-2	0	0	0	1.000	-2	O-12/1-3	-0.5
1979	NY-N	82	155	7	36	5	0	2	17	13	18	.232	.296	.303	66	-7	0	1	-1	1.000	0	1-29/O-8	-1.0
Total	18	1853	5436	536	1418	225	25	118	614	454	581	.261	.319	.377	97	-21	15	27	-12	.994	-1	*1-1304,O-250	-13.7

■ **CHARLIE KRAUSE** Krause, Charles b: 10/2/1873, Detroit, Mich. d: 3/30/48, Eloise, Mich. TR , Deb: 7/27/01

1901	Cin-N	1	4	0	1	0	0	0				.250	.250	.250	48	-0	0			.000	0	/2-1	0.0

■ **DANNY KRAVITZ** Kravitz, Daniel "Dusty" or "Beak" b: 12/21/30, Lopez, Pa. BL/TR, 5′11″, 195 lbs. Deb: 4/17/56

1956	Pit-N	32	68	6	18	2	2	2	10	5	9	.265	.315	.441	103	0	1	1	-0	.944	0	C-26/3-2	0.1
1957	Pit-N	19	41	2	6	1	0	0	4	2	10	.146	.186	.171	-3	-6	0	0	0	1.000	0	C-15	-0.5
1958	Pit-N	45	100	9	24	3	2	1	5	11	10	.240	.315	.340	76	-3	0	0	0	.967	-6	C-37	-0.8
1959	Pit-N	52	162	18	41	9	1	3	21	5	14	.253	.275	.377	72	-7	0	1	-1	.986	-1	C-45	-0.6
1960	Pit-N	8	6	0	0	0	0	0	0	1	2	.000	.143	.000	-57	-1	0	0	0	1.000	-0	/C-1	-0.1
	KC-A	59	175	17	41	7	2	4	14	11	19	.234	.280	.366	73	-7	0	0	0	.971	-4	C-47	-0.8
Total	5	215	552	52	130	22	7	10	54	35	64	.236	.281	.355	70	-25	1	2	-1	.973	-10	C-171/3-2	-2.7

■ **MIKE KREEVICH** Kreevich, Michael Andreas b: 6/10/08, Mt.Olive, Ill. d: 4/25/94, Pana, Ill. BR/TR, 5′7.5″, 168 lbs. Deb: 9/7/31

1931	Chi-N	5	12	0	2	0	0	0	0	0	6	.167	.167	.167	-10	-2	1			1.000	-0	/O-4	-0.2
1935	Chi-N	6	23	3	10	2	0	0	2	1	0	.435	.458	.522	149	2	1	1	-0	1.000	-2	/3-6	-0.1
1936	Chi-A	137	550	99	169	32	11	5	69	61	46	.307	.378	.433	96	-3	10	5	0	.964	-2	*O-133	-0.9
1937	Chi-A	144	583	94	176	29	16	12	73	43	45	.302	.350	.468	104	2	10	1	2	.988	7	*O-138	0.6
1938	Chi-A★	129	489	73	146	26	12	6	73	55	23	.297	.371	.436	99	-1	13	5	1	.975	4	*O-127	0.0
1939	Chi-A	145	541	85	175	30	8	6	77	59	40	.323	.390	.436	108	8	23	10	1	.975	16	*O-139/3-4	1.8
1940	Chi-A	144	582	86	154	27	10	8	55	34	49	.265	.305	.387	77	-21	15	7	0	.982	12	*O-144	-1.6
1941	Chi-A	121	436	44	101	16	8	0	37	35	26	.232	.289	.305	58	-27	17	5	2	.994	0	*O-113	-3.1
1942	Phi-A	116	444	57	113	19	1	1	30	47	31	.255	.326	.309	79	-11	7	9	-3	.981	4	*O-107	-1.7
1943	StL-A	60	161	24	41	6	0	0	10	26	13	.255	.358	.292	89	-1	4	1		.993	5	O-51	0.2
1944	*StL-A	105	402	55	121	15	6	5	44	27	24	.301	.348	.405	108	4	3	3	-1	.986	-1	*O-100	-0.3
1945	StL-A	84	295	34	70	11	1	2	21	37	27	.237	.322	.302	78	-8	4	1	1	.991	4	O-81	-0.8
	Was-A	45	158	22	44	8	2	1	23	21	9	.278	.363	.373	124	5	7	5	-1	.971	-2	O-40	0.0
	Yr	129	453	56	114	19	3	3	44	58	36	.252	.337	.327	92	-3	11	6	-0	.985	2	*O-121	-0.8
Total	12	1241	4676	676	1321	221	75	45	514	446	339	.283	.346	.391	92	-54	115	53		.982	46	*O-1177/3-10	-6.1

■ **CHARLIE KREHMEYER** Krehmeyer, Charles L. b: 7/5/1863, St.Louis, Mo. d: 2/10/26, St.Louis, Mo. BL/TL, Deb: 7/8/1884

1884	StL-a	21	70	3	16	0	1	0		2		.229	.250	.257	64	-3				.619	-5	O-15/C-7,1	-0.7
1885	Lou-a	4	31	4	7	1	1	0		1		.226	.250	.323	80	-1				.909	-1	/C-4,O-2,1	-0.2
	StL-N	1	3	0	0	0	0	0	0	0	2	.000	.000	.000	-99	-1				.429	-2	/C-1	-0.2
Total	2	29	104	7	23	1	2	0	0	3	2	.221	.243	.269	64	-4				.571	-7	/O-17,C-12,1	-1.1

■ **MICKEY KREITNER** Kreitner, Albert Joseph b: 10/10/22, Nashville, Tenn. BR/TR, 6′3″, 190 lbs. Deb: 9/28/43

1943	Chi-N	3	8	0	3	0	0	0	2	1	2	.375	.444	.375	140	0	0			1.000	-1	/C-3	0.0
1944	Chi-N	39	85	3	13	2	0	0	1	8	16	.153	.234	.176	17	-9	0			.992	-1	C-39	-0.9
Total	2	42	93	3	16	2	0	0	3	9	18	.172	.252	.194	27	-9	0			.992	-1	/C-42	-0.9

■ **RALPH KREITZ** Kreitz, Ralph Wesley "Red" b: 11/13/1885, Plum Creek, Neb. d: 7/20/41, Portland, Ore. BR/TR, 5′9.5″, 175 lbs. Deb: 8/1/11

1911	Chi-A	7	17	0	4	1	0	0	2	1		.235	.316	.294	73	-1	0			1.000	-3	/C-7	-0.3

■ **JIMMY KREMERS** Kremers, James Edward b: 10/8/65, Little Rock, Ark. BL/TR, 6′3″, 205 lbs. Deb: 6/5/90

1990	Atl-N	29	73	7	8	1	1	1	2	6	27	.110	.177	.192	1	-10	0	0	0	.992	-3	C-27	-1.3

■ **WAYNE KRENCHICKI** Krenchicki, Wayne Richard b: 9/17/54, Trenton, N.J. BL/TR, 6′1″, 180 lbs. Deb: 6/15/79

1979	Bal-A	16	21	1	4	1	0	0	0	0	0	.190	.190	.238	15	-2	0	0	0	.875	1	/3-7,2-6	-0.1
1980	Bal-A	9	14	1	2	0	0	0	0	1	3	.143	.200	.143	-4	-2	0	0	0	1.000	0	/S-6,2-1,D	-0.2
1981	Bal-A	33	56	7	12	4	0	0	6	4	9	.214	.267	.286	59	-3	0	0	0	.964	4	S-16/2-7,3D	0.3
1982	Cin-N	94	187	19	53	6	1	2	21	13	23	.283	.330	.358	91	-2	5	3	-0	.955	7	3-70/2-9	0.4
1983	Cin-N	51	77	6	21	2	0	0	11	8	4	.273	.349	.299	78	-2	0	0	0	.980	1	3-39/2-1	-0.1
	Det-A	59	133	18	37	7	0	1	16	11	27	.278	.338	.353	93	-1	0	1	-1	.934	-8	3-48/2-6,S1	-0.9
1984	Cin-N	97	181	18	54	9	2	6	22	19	23	.298	.365	.470	127	6	0	1	-1	.967	3	3-62/1-3,2	0.7
1985	Cin-N	90	173	16	47	9	4	0	25	28	20	.272	.373	.393	109	3	0	0	0	.967	-3	3-52/2-3	0.7
1986	Mon-N	101	221	21	53	2	2	6	23	22	32	.240	.309	.312	72	-8	2	4	-2	.991	3	1-41,3-24/2O	-1.2
Total	8	550	1063	107	283	44	5	15	124	106	141	.266	.334	.359	92	-11	7	8	-3	.955	14	3-308/1-47,2SDO	-0.2

■ **CHUCK KRESS** Kress, Charles Steven b: 12/9/21, Philadelphia, Pa. BL/TL, 6′, 190 lbs. Deb: 4/16/47

1947	Cin-N	11	27	4	4	0	0	0	6	6	4	.148	.303	.148	23	-3	0			.983	1	/1-8	-0.2
1949	Cin-N	27	29	3	6	3	0	0	3	3	5	.207	.281	.310	58	-2	0			.974	-0	1-16	-0.2
	Chi-A	97	353	45	98	17	6	1	44	39	44	.278	.349	.368	93	-4	6	7	-2	.994	-0	1-95	-0.7
1950	Chi-A	8	6	0	0	0	0	0	0	0	0	.000	.000	.000	-99	-2	0	0	0	1.000	-0	/1-2	-0.2
1954	Det-A	24	37	4	7	0	1	0	3	1	4	.189	.211	.243	24	-4	0	1	-1	.971	-4	/1-7,O-1	-0.5
	Bro-N	13	12	1	1	0	0	0	2	0	2	.083	.083	.083	-55	-3	0	0	0	.500	-3	/1-1	-0.3
Total	4	175	466	57	116	20	7	1	52	49	59	.249	.320	.328	74	-18	6	8		.990	-5	1-129/O-1	-2.1

■ **RED KRESS** Kress, Ralph b: 1/2/07, Columbia, Cal. d: 11/29/62, Los Angeles, Cal. BR/TR, 5′11.5″, 165 lbs. Deb: 9/24/27 C

1927	StL-A	7	23	3	7	2	1	1	3	3	3	.304	.385	.609	150	2	1			.974	1	/S-7	0.3
1928	StL-A	150	560	78	153	26	10	3	81	48	70	.273	.332	.371	82	-15	5	4	-3	.929	-17	*S-150	-1.4
1929	StL-A	147	557	82	170	38	4	9	107	52	54	.305	.366	.436	102	1	5	8	-3	.946	-2	*S-146	1.3

YEAR	TM/L	G	AB	R	H	2B	3B	HR	RBI	BB	SO	AVG	OBP	SLG	PRO+	BR/A	SB	CS	SBR	FA	FR	G/POS	TPR
1930	StL-A	154	614	94	192	43	8	16	112	50	56	.313	.366	.487	110	9	3	12	-6	.938	-12	*S-123,3-31	0.6
1931	StL-A	150	605	87	188	46	8	16	114	46	48	.311	.360	.493	118	14	3	16	-9	.936	-11	3-84,O-40,S1	-0.2
1932	StL-A	14	52	2	9	0	1	2	9	4	6	.173	.232	.327	41	-5	1	1	-0	.909	2	3-14	-0.2
	Chi-A	135	515	83	147	42	4	9	57	47	36	.285	.346	.435	108	5	6	3	-0	.956	11	O-64,S-53,3/1	1.6
	Yr	149	567	85	156	42	5	11	66	51	42	.275	.336	.425	101	-1	7	4	-0	.956	13	O-64,S-53,3/1	1.4
1933	Chi-A	129	467	47	116	20	5	10	78	37	40	.248	.304	.377	83	-13	4	4	-1	.978	-4	*1-111/O-8	-2.8
1934	Chi-A	8	14	3	4	0	0	0	1	3	3	.286	.412	.286	80	-0	0	0	0	1.000	-4	/2-3	-0.4
	Was-A	56	171	18	39	4	3	4	24	17	19	.228	.298	.357	71	-8	3	0	1	.993	-2	1-30,O-10/2S3	-1.1
	Yr	64	185	21	43	4	3	4	25	20	22	.232	.307	.351	72	-8	3	0	1	.993	-6	1-30,O-10/2S3	-1.5
1935	Was-A	84	252	32	75	13	4	2	42	25	16	.298	.361	.405	101	-0	3	3	-1	.964	17	S-53/1-5,PO2	1.7
1936	Was-A	109	391	51	111	20	6	8	51	39	25	.284	.349	.427	96	-4	6	0	2	.927	9	S-64,2-33/1	1.2
1938	StL-A	150	566	74	171	33	3	7	79	69	47	.302	.378	.408	97	-1	5	4	-1	.965	-15	*S-150	-0.5
1939	StL-A	13	43	5	12	1	0	0	8	6	2	.279	.367	.302	72	-2	1	0	0	.933	-3	S-13	-0.3
	Det-A	51	157	19	38	7	0	1	22	17	16	.242	.316	.306	55	-10	2	1	0	.959	-3	S-25,2-16/3	-0.5
	Yr	64	200	24	50	8	0	1	30	23	18	.250	.327	.305	59	-12	3	1	0	.951	-1	S-38,2-16/3	-0.8
1940	Det-A	33	99	13	22	3	1	1	11	10	12	.222	.294	.303	50	-7	0	0	0	.924	9	3-17,S-12	0.2
1946	NY-N	1	1	0	0	0	0	0	0	1	0	.000	.500	.000	48	-0	0			1.000	1	/P-1	0.0
Total	14	1391	5087	691	1454	298	58	89	799	474	453	.286	.347	.420	96	-35	47	56		.944	-16	S-835,3-170,10/2P	-0.5

■ CHAD KREUTER
Kreuter, Chadden Michael b: 8/26/64, Greenbrae, Cal. BB/TR, 6'2", 190 lbs. Deb: 9/14/88

YEAR	TM/L	G	AB	R	H	2B	3B	HR	RBI	BB	SO	AVG	OBP	SLG	PRO+	BR/A	SB	CS	SBR	FA	FR	G/POS	TPR
1988	Tex-A	16	51	3	14	2	1	1	5	7	13	.275	.362	.412	113	1	0	0	0	.990	2	C-16	0.4
1989	Tex-A	87	158	16	24	3	0	5	9	27	40	.152	.276	.266	52	-10	0	1	-1	.992	12	C-85	0.4
1990	Tex-A	22	22	2	1	1	0	0	2	8	9	.045	.300	.091	14	-2	0	0	0	.977	-1	C-20/D-1	-0.3
1991	Tex-A	3	4	0	0	0	0	0	0	0	1	.000	.000	.000	-99	-1	0	0	0	1.000	-1	/C-1	-0.1
1992	Det-A	67	190	22	48	9	0	2	16	20	38	.253	.324	.332	83	-4	0	1	-1	.983	5	C-62/D-1	0.3
1993	Det-A	119	374	59	107	23	3	15	51	49	92	.286	.373	.484	129	16	2	1	0	.988	3	*C-112/1-1,D	2.3
1994	Det-A	65	170	17	38	8	0	1	19	28	36	.224	.333	.288	63	-9	0	1	-1	.987	-0	C-64/1-1,O	-0.8
Total	7	379	969	119	232	46	4	24	102	139	229	.239	.337	.369	92	-9	2	4	-2	.988	17	C-360/D-4,1O	2.2

■ PAUL KRICHELL
Krichell, Paul Bernard b: 12/19/1882, New York, N.Y. d: 6/4/57, New York, N.Y. BR/TR, 5'7", 150 lbs. Deb: 5/12/11

YEAR	TM/L	G	AB	R	H	2B	3B	HR	RBI	BB	SO	AVG	OBP	SLG	PRO+	BR/A	SB	CS	SBR	FA	FR	G/POS	TPR
1911	StL-A	28	82	6	19	3	0	0	8	4		.232	.276	.268	54	-5	2			.943	-2	C-25	-0.4
1912	StL-A	59	161	19	35	6	0	0	8	19		.217	.304	.255	62	-7	2			.959	-1	C-59	-0.3
Total	2	87	243	25	54	9	0	0	16	23		.222	.295	.259	60	-12	4			.955	-3	/C-84	-0.7

■ BILL KRIEG
Krieg, William Frederick b: 1/29/1859, Petersburg, Ill. d: 3/25/30, Chillicothe, Ill. BR/TR, 5'8", 180 lbs. Deb: 4/20/1884

YEAR	TM/L	G	AB	R	H	2B	3B	HR	RBI	BB	SO	AVG	OBP	SLG	PRO+	BR/A	SB	CS	SBR	FA	FR	G/POS	TPR
1884	CP-U	71	279	35	69	15	4	0		11		.247	.276	.330	64	-14				.932	15	C-53,O-20/S1	0.4
1885	Chi-N	1	3	0	0	0	0	0	0	0	2	.000	.000	.000	-87	-1				.800	2	/O-1	0.1
	Bro-a	17	60	7	9	4	0	1		2		.150	.177	.267	39	-4				.910	-4	C-12/1-5	-0.7
1886	Was-N	27	98	11	25	6	3	1	15	3	12	.255	.277	.408	113	1	2			.975	-1	1-27	-0.3
1887	Was-N	25	95	9	24	4	1	2	17	7	5	.253	.311	.379	95	-1	2			.973	-3	1-16/O-9	-0.4
Total	4	141	535	62	127	29	8	4	32	23	19	.237	.270	.344	74	-18	4			.929	9	/C-65,1-49,OS	-0.9

■ KRIEGER
Krieger Deb: 7/28/1884

YEAR	TM/L	G	AB	R	H	2B	3B	HR	RBI	BB	SO	AVG	OBP	SLG	PRO+	BR/A	SB	CS	SBR	FA	FR	G/POS	TPR
1884	KC-U	1	3	0	0	0	0	0		0		.000	.000	.000	-99	-1				.000	-1	/O-1,P-1	-0.1

■ JOHN KRONER
Kroner, John Harold b: 11/13/08, St.Louis, Mo. d: 8/26/68, St.Louis, Mo. BR/TR, 6', 185 lbs. Deb: 9/29/35

YEAR	TM/L	G	AB	R	H	2B	3B	HR	RBI	BB	SO	AVG	OBP	SLG	PRO+	BR/A	SB	CS	SBR	FA	FR	G/POS	TPR
1935	Bos-A	2	4	1	1	0	0	0	0	1		.250	.400	.250	67	-0	0	0	0	1.000	-1	/3-2	-0.1
1936	Bos-A	84	298	40	87	17	8	4	62	26	24	.292	.349	.443	89	-6	2	3	-1	.964	-2	2-38,3-28,S/O	-0.4
1937	Cle-A	86	283	29	67	14	1	2	26	22	25	.237	.292	.314	52	-21	1	1	-0	.969	-2	2-64,3-11	-1.9
1938	Cle-A	51	117	13	29	16	0	1	17	19	6	.248	.353	.410	92	-1	0	1	-1	.974	12	2-31/1-7,3S	1.0
Total	4	223	702	83	184	47	9	7	105	68	56	.262	.327	.385	75	-29	3	5	-2	.968	6	2-133/3-44,S1O	-1.4

■ MIKE KRSNICH
Krsnich, Michael b: 9/24/31, W.Allis, Wis. BR/TR, 6'1", 190 lbs. Deb: 4/23/60 F

YEAR	TM/L	G	AB	R	H	2B	3B	HR	RBI	BB	SO	AVG	OBP	SLG	PRO+	BR/A	SB	CS	SBR	FA	FR	G/POS	TPR
1960	Mil-N	4	9	0	3	1	0	0	2	0	0	.333	.333	.444	120	-0	0	0	0	1.000	-0	/O-3	0.0
1962	Mil-N	11	12	0	1	1	0	0	2	0	4	.083	.083	.167	-36	-2	0	0	0	1.000	-0	/O-3,1-1,3	-0.3
Total	2	15	21	0	4	2	0	0	4	0	4	.190	.190	.286	28	-2	0	0	0	1.000	-0	/O-6,3-1,1	-0.3

■ ROCKY KRSNICH
Krsnich, Rocco Peter b: 8/5/27, W.Allis, Wis. BR/TR, 6'1", 174 lbs. Deb: 9/13/49 F

YEAR	TM/L	G	AB	R	H	2B	3B	HR	RBI	BB	SO	AVG	OBP	SLG	PRO+	BR/A	SB	CS	SBR	FA	FR	G/POS	TPR
1949	Chi-A	16	55	7	12	3	1	1	9	6	4	.218	.295	.364	76	-2	0	1	-1	.935	4	3-16	0.0
1952	Chi-A	40	91	11	21	7	2	1	15	12	9	.231	.327	.385	97	-0	0	0	0	.959	11	3-37	1.0
1953	Chi-A	64	129	9	26	8	0	1	14	12	11	.202	.270	.287	49	-9	0	2	-1	.929	8	3-57	-0.2
Total	3	120	275	27	59	18	3	3	38	30	24	.215	.294	.335	70	-12	0	3	-2	.942	23	3-110	0.8

■ OTTO KRUEGER
Krueger, Arthur William "Oom Paul" b: 9/17/1876, Chicago, Ill. d: 2/20/61, St.Louis, Mo. BR/TR, 5'7", 165 lbs. Deb: 9/16/1899

YEAR	TM/L	G	AB	R	H	2B	3B	HR	RBI	BB	SO	AVG	OBP	SLG	PRO+	BR/A	SB	CS	SBR	FA	FR	G/POS	TPR
1899	Cle-N	13	44	4	10	1	0	0	2	8		.227	.358	.250	73	-1	1			.763	-2	/3-9,S-2,2	-0.3
1900	StL-N	12	35	8	14	3	2	1	3	10		.400	.543	.686	240	8	0			.852	-6	2-12	0.2
1901	StL-N	142	520	77	143	16	12	2	79	50		.275	.353	.363	114	11	19			.881	-9	*3-142	0.3
1902	StL-N	128	467	55	124	7	8	0	46	29		.266	.313	.315	97	-2	14			.897	-5	*S-107,3-18	0.6
1903	Pit-N	80	256	42	63	6	8	1	28	21		.246	.323	.344	87	-4	5			.884	-5	S-29,O-28,3/2	-0.9
1904	Pit-N	86	268	34	52	6	2	1	26	29		.194	.242	.243	61	-12	8			.905	-5	O-33,S-32,3	-1.9
1905	Phi-N	46	114	10	21	1	1	0	12	13		.184	.273	.211	47	-7	1			.930	-9	S-23/O-6,3	-1.7
Total	7	507	1704	230	427	40	33	5	196	160		.251	.326	.322	94	-7	48			.902	-36	S-193,3-193/O2	-3.7

■ ERNIE KRUEGER
Krueger, Ernest George b: 12/27/1890, Chicago, Ill. d: 4/22/76, Waukegan, Ill. BR/TR, 5'10.5", 185 lbs. Deb: 8/4/13

YEAR	TM/L	G	AB	R	H	2B	3B	HR	RBI	BB	SO	AVG	OBP	SLG	PRO+	BR/A	SB	CS	SBR	FA	FR	G/POS	TPR
1913	Cle-A	5	6	0	0	0	0	0	0	0	2	.000	.000	.000	-97	-1				1.000	-0	/C-4	-0.2
1915	NY-A	10	29	3	5	1	0	0	0	0	5	.172	.200	.207	22	-3	0	1	-1	.905	-4	/C-8	-0.7
1917	NY-N	8	10	0	0	0	0	0	0	0	0	.000	.000	.000	-99	-1	0			.857	-2	/C-5	-0.5
	Bro-N	31	81	10	22	2	2	1	6	5	7	.272	.330	.383	115	1				.979	1	C-23	0.5
	Yr	39	91	10	22	2	2	1	6	5	11	.242	.296	.341	94	-1	1			.973	-1	C-28	0.0
1918	Bro-N	30	87	4	25	4	2	0	7	4	9	.287	.319	.379	113	1				.986	6	C-23	0.9
1919	Bro-N	80	226	24	56	7	4	5	36	19	25	.248	.312	.381	105	1	2			.963	5	C-66	1.4
1920	*Bro-N	52	146	21	42	4	3	1	17	16	13	.288	.358	.363	104	1	2	0	1	.959	-4	C-46	0.1
1921	Bro-N	65	163	18	43	11	4	3	20	14	12	.264	.322	.436	95	-1	2	2	-1	.969	-2	C-52	-0.1
1925	Cin-N	37	88	7	27	4	0	1	7	6	8	.307	.351	.386	90	-1	1	2	-1	.946	-4	C-30	-0.4
Total	8	318	836	87	220	33	14	11	93	64	85	.263	.319	.376	97	-4	12	5		.964	-3	C-257	1.0

■ CHRIS KRUG
Krug, Everett Ben b: 12/25/39, Los Angeles, Cal. BR/TR, 6'4", 200 lbs. Deb: 5/30/65 C

YEAR	TM/L	G	AB	R	H	2B	3B	HR	RBI	BB	SO	AVG	OBP	SLG	PRO+	BR/A	SB	CS	SBR	FA	FR	G/POS	TPR
1965	Chi-N	60	169	16	34	5	0	5	24	13	52	.201	.262	.320	61	-9	0	1	-1	.980	1	C-58	-0.6
1966	Chi-N	11	28	1	6	1	0	0	1	3	8	.214	.241	.250	36	-2	0	0	0	1.000	3	C-10	0.1
1969	SD-N	8	17	0	1	0	0	0	0	1	6	.059	.111	.059	-53	-2	0	0	0	.938	-1	/C-7	-0.4
Total	3	79	214	17	41	6	0	5	25	15	66	.192	.248	.290	50	-15	0	1	-1	.980	3	/C-75	-0.9

■ GENE KRUG
Krug, Gary Eugene b: 2/12/55, Garden City, Kan. BL/TL, 6'4", 225 lbs. Deb: 4/29/81

YEAR	TM/L	G	AB	R	H	2B	3B	HR	RBI	BB	SO	AVG	OBP	SLG	PRO+	BR/A	SB	CS	SBR	FA	FR	G/POS	TPR
1981	Chi-N	7	5	0	2	0	0	0	0	1	1	.400	.500	.400	151	0	0	0	0	.000	0	/H	0.0

YEAR	TM/L	G	AB	R	H	2B	3B	HR	RBI	BB	SO	AVG	OBP	SLG	PRO+	BR/A	SB	CS	SBR	FA	FR	G/POS	TPR

■ HENRY KRUG
Krug, Henry Charles b: 12/4/1876, San Francisco, Cal. d: 1/14/08, San Francisco, Cal BR/TR, Deb: 7/26/02

| 1902 | Phi-N | 53 | 198 | 20 | 45 | 3 | 3 | 0 | 14 | 7 | | .227 | .261 | .273 | 65 | -9 | 2 | | | .947 | -7 | O-28,2-13/S3 | -1.7 |

■ MARTY KRUG
Krug, Martin John b: 9/10/1888, Koblenz, Germany d: 6/27/66, Glendale, Cal. BR/TR, 5'9", 165 lbs. Deb: 5/29/12

1912	Bos-A	24	39	6	12	2	1	0	7	5		.308	.386	.410	122	1	2			.895	-2	/S-13,2-4	0.0
1922	Chi-N	127	450	67	124	23	4	4	60	43	43	.276	.343	.371	82	-11	7	9	-3	.937	-6	*3-104,2-23/S	-1.1
Total	2	151	489	73	136	25	5	4	67	48	43	.278	.346	.374	85	-10	9	9		.910	-8	3-104/2-27,S	-1.1

■ ART KRUGER
Kruger, Arthur T. b: 3/16/1881, San Antonio, Tex. d: 11/28/49, Honda, Cal. BR/TR, 6', 185 lbs. Deb: 4/11/07

1907	Cin-N	100	317	25	74	10	9	0	28	18		.233	.285	.322	87	-6	10			.972	0	O-96	-1.0
1910	Cle-A	47	168	14	26	4	2	0	10	15		.155	.237	.202	37	-12	10			.947	2	O-47	-1.4
	Bos-N	1	1	0	0	0	0	0	0	0		.000	.000	.000	-96	-0	0			.000	0	H	0.0
	Cle-A	15	55	5	12	2	1	0	4	5		.218	.295	.291	82	-1	2			.974	2	O-15	0.0
1914	KC-F	122	441	45	114	24	7	4	47	23	59	.259	.297	.372	76	-18	11			.963	-7	*O-120	-3.2
1915	KC-F	80	240	24	57	9	2	2	26	12	29	.237	.277	.317	61	-14	5			.984	0	O-66	-1.8
Total	4	365	1222	113	283	49	21	6	115	73	88	.232	.281	.321	70	-52	38			.968	-2	O-344	-7.4

■ JOHN KRUK
Kruk, John Martin b: 2/9/61, Charleston, W.Va. BL/TL, 5'10", 200 lbs. Deb: 4/7/86

1986	SD-N	122	278	33	86	16	2	4	38	45	58	.309	.406	.424	132	14	2	4	-2	.981	-5	O-74/1-9	0.5
1987	SD-N	138	447	72	140	14	2	20	91	73	93	.313	.410	.488	142	29	18	10	-1	.996	3	*1-101,O-29	2.3
1988	SD-N	120	378	54	91	17	1	9	44	80	68	.241	.373	.362	114	10	5	3	-0	.995	-2	1-63,O-55	0.2
1989	SD-N	31	76	7	14	0	0	3	6	17	14	.184	.333	.303	83	-1	0	0	-0	.962	1	O-27	0.0
	Phi-N	81	281	46	93	13	6	5	38	27	39	.331	.390	.473	146	17	3	0	1	.983	-4	O-72/1-7	1.2
	Yr	112	357	53	107	13	6	8	44	44	53	.300	.377	.437	132	15	3	0	1	.977	-3	O-99/1-7	1.2
1990	Phi-N	142	443	52	129	25	8	7	67	69	70	.291	.387	.431	125	17	10	5	0	.986	-5	O-87,1-61	0.7
1991	Phi-N☆	152	538	84	158	27	6	21	92	67	100	.294	.373	.483	141	29	7	0	2	.997	-1	*1-102,O-52	2.4
1992	Phi-N★	144	507	86	164	30	4	10	70	92	88	.323	.428	.458	151	39	3	5	-2	.993	-12	*1-121,O-35	1.8
1993	*Phi-N★	150	535	100	169	33	5	14	85	111	87	.316	.433	.475	145	40	6	2	-1	.993	-11	*1-144	1.7
1994	Phi-N	75	255	35	77	17	0	5	38	42	51	.302	.401	.427	117	8	4	1	1	.995	-1	1-69	0.2
Total	9	1155	3738	569	1121	192	34	98	569	623	668	.300	.400	.448	135	202	58	30	-1	.995	-37	1-677,O-431	11.0

■ DICK KRYHOSKI
Kryhoski, Richard David b: 3/24/25, Leonia, N.J. BL/TL, 6'2", 200 lbs. Deb: 4/19/49

1949	NY-A	54	177	18	52	10	3	1	27	9	17	.294	.335	.401	94	-2	2	4	-2	.983	-1	1-51	-0.5
1950	Det-A	53	169	20	37	10	0	4	19	8	11	.219	.258	.349	53	-13	0	1	-1	.991	-0	1-47	-1.4
1951	Det-A	119	421	58	121	19	4	12	57	28	29	.287	.333	.437	107	2	1	2	-1	.991	3	*1-112	-0.1
1952	StL-A	111	342	38	83	13	1	11	42	23	42	.243	.296	.383	86	-8	2	0	1	.989	-5	1-86	-1.6
1953	StL-A	104	338	35	94	18	4	16	50	26	33	.278	.333	.497	119	7	0	0	-3	.992	5	1-88	0.6
1954	Bal-A	100	300	32	78	13	2	1	34	19	24	.260	.308	.327	80	-9	0	0	0	.992	3	1-69	-1.0
1955	KC-A	28	47	2	10	2	0	0	2	6	7	.213	.302	.255	50	-3	0	1	-1	.988	0	1-14	-0.4
Total	7	569	1794	203	475	85	14	45	231	119	163	.265	.315	.403	93	-26	5	13	-6	.990	5	1-467	-4.4

■ TONY KUBEK
Kubek, Anthony Christopher b: 10/12/36, Milwaukee, Wis. BL/TR, 6'3", 191 lbs. Deb: 4/20/57

1957	*NY-A	127	431	56	128	21	3	3	39	24	48	.297	.338	.381	98	-2	6	6	-2	.938	1	O-50,S-41,3/2	-0.2
1958	*NY-A☆	138	559	66	148	21	1	2	48	25	57	.265	.297	.317	72	-22	5	4	-1	.961	20	*S-134/O-3,12	0.9
1959	NY-A★	132	512	67	143	25	7	6	51	24	46	.279	.314	.391	95	-5	3	3	-1	.968	-1	S-67,O-53,3/2	-0.3
1960	NY-A	147	568	77	155	25	3	14	62	31	42	.273	.314	.401	98	-4	3	0	1	.968	-4	*S-136,O-29	0.3
1961	*NY-A★	153	617	84	170	38	6	8	46	27	60	.276	.307	.395	91	-10	1	3	0	.959	13	*S-145	1.3
1962	*NY-A	45	169	28	53	6	1	4	17	12	17	.314	.359	.432	115	3	2	1	0	.954	5	S-35/O-6	1.2
1963	*NY-A	135	557	72	143	21	3	7	44	28	68	.257	.295	.343	79	-16	4	2	0	.980	10	*S-132/O-1	0.3
1964	NY-A	106	415	46	95	16	3	8	31	26	55	.229	.276	.340	69	-18	4	1	-1	.978	4	S-99	-0.6
1965	NY-A	109	339	26	74	5	3	5	35	20	48	.218	.262	.295	58	-19	1	3	-2	.964	-10	S-93/O-3,1	-2.6
Total	9	1092	4167	522	1109	178	30	57	373	217	441	.266	.305	.364	85	-92	29	23	-5	.967	39	S-882,O-145/321	0.3

■ TED KUBIAK
Kubiak, Theodore Rodger b: 5/12/42, New Brunswick, N.J. BB/TR, 6', 175 lbs. Deb: 4/14/67

1967	KC-A	53	102	6	16	2	1	0	5	12	20	.157	.246	.196	33	-8	0	0	0	.984	-3	S-20,2-10/3	-1.1
1968	Oak-A	48	120	10	30	5	2	0	8	8	18	.250	.308	.325	96	-1	1	1	-0	.929	-3	2-24,S-12	-0.2
1969	Oak-A	92	305	38	76	9	1	2	27	25	35	.249	.308	.305	75	-10	2	0	1	.976	-0	S-42,2-33	-0.3
1970	Mil-A	158	540	63	136	9	6	4	41	72	51	.252	.340	.313	81	-12	4	9	-4	.989	-17	2-91,S-73	-1.9
1971	Mil-A	89	260	26	59	6	5	3	17	41	31	.227	.332	.323	87	-3	0	5	-3	.971	-3	2-48,S-39	-0.1
	StL-N	32	72	8	18	3	2	1	10	11	12	.250	.349	.389	105	1	1	0	0	.959	-4	S-17,2-14	-0.1
1972	Tex-A	46	116	5	26	3	0	0	7	12	12	.224	.302	.250	69	-4	0	1	-1	.990	-3	2-25,S-15/3	-0.6
	*Oak-A	51	94	14	17	4	1	0	8	9	11	.181	.280	.245	51	-6	0	0	-0	.988	2	2-49/3-1	-0.2
	Yr	97	210	19	43	7	1	0	15	21	23	.205	.280	.248	61	-10	0	1	-1	.989	-1	2-74,S-15/3	-0.8
1973	*Oak-A	106	182	15	40	6	1	3	17	12	19	.220	.268	.313	67	-9	1	1	-0	.973	6	2-83,S-26/3	0.1
1974	Oak-A	99	220	22	46	3	0	0	18	18	15	.209	.269	.223	46	-15	1	1	-0	.995	-9	2-71,S-19,3/D	-2.2
1975	Oak-A	20	28	2	7	1	0	0	4	2	2	.250	.300	.286	68	-1	0	0	0	1.000	2	/S-7,3-7,2	0.2
	SD-N	87	196	13	44	5	0	0	14	24	18	.224	.309	.250	60	-10	0	1	-1	.954	1	3-64,2-11/1	-0.9
1976	SD-N	96	212	16	50	5	2	0	26	25	28	.236	.316	.278	76	-6	0	2	-2	.971	-9	3-27,2-25/S1	-1.7
Total	10	977	2447	236	565	61	21	13	202	271	272	.231	.309	.289	73	-85	13	22	-9	.981	-39	2-490,S-276,3/1D	-9.0

■ JACK KUBISZYN
Kubiszyn, John Henry b: 12/19/36, Buffalo, N.Y. BR/TR, 5'11", 170 lbs. Deb: 4/23/61

1961	Cle-A	25	42	4	9	0	0	0	0	2	5	.214	.250	.214	26	-4	0	0	0	1.000	3	/3-8,S-7,2	-0.1
1962	Cle-A	25	59	3	10	2	0	1	2	5	7	.169	.234	.254	32	-6	0	0	0	.964	2	S-18/3-1	-0.2
Total	2	50	101	7	19	2	0	1	2	7	12	.188	.241	.238	30	-10	0	0	0	.969	5	/S-25,3-9,2	-0.3

■ GIL KUBSKI
Kubski, Gilbert Thomas b: 10/12/54, Longview, Tex. BL/TR, 6'3", 185 lbs. Deb: 9/2/80

| 1980 | Cal-A | 22 | 63 | 11 | 16 | 3 | 0 | 0 | 6 | 6 | 10 | .254 | .319 | .302 | 73 | -2 | 1 | 1 | -0 | 1.000 | 1 | O-20 | -0.3 |

■ STEVE KUCZEK
Kuczek, Stanislaw Leo b: 12/28/24, Amsterdam, N.Y. BR/TR, 6', 160 lbs. Deb: 9/29/49

| 1949 | Bos-N | 1 | 1 | 0 | 1 | 1 | 0 | 0 | 0 | 0 | 0 | 1.000 | 1.000 | 2.000 | 723 | 1 | 0 | | | .000 | 0 | H | 0.1 |

■ BILL KUEHNE
Kuehne, William J. (b: William J. Knelme) b: 10/24/1858, Leipzig, Germany d: 10/27/21, Sulphur Springs, O BR/TR, 185 lbs. Deb: 5/1/1883

1883	Col-a	95	374	38	85	8	14	1		2		.227	.231	.332	86	-5				.833	-5	*3-69,2-18/SO	-0.9
1884	Col-a	110	415	48	98	13	16	5		9		.236	.254	.381	113	6				.881	11	*3-110	1.6
1885	Pit-a	104	411	54	93	9	19	0		15		.226	.257	.341	89	-6				.865	-1	*3-97/S-7	-0.5
1886	Pit-a	117	481	73	98	16	17	1		19		.204	.237	.314	72	-17	26			.899	-1	O-54,3-47,1	-1.8
1887	Pit-N	102	402	68	120	18	15	1	41	14	39	.299	.324	.425	113	6	17			.883	-13	*S-91/3-4,1O	-0.2
1888	Pit-N	138	524	60	123	22	11	3	62	9	68	.235	.250	.336	93	-5	34			.910	0	3-75,S-63	-0.2
1889	Pit-N	97	390	43	96	20	5	5	57	9	36	.246	.263	.362	82	-12	15			.885	-1	3-75,O-13/2S1	-0.9
1890	Pit-P	126	528	66	126	21	12	5	73	28	37	.239	.277	.352	74	-22	21			.850	6	*3-126	-0.9
1891	Col-a	68	261	32	56	9	0	2	22	10	22	.215	.244	.272	50	-18	21			.885	-2	3-68	-1.5
	Lou-a	41	159	28	44	3	1	0	18	8	13	.277	.315	.327	85	-4	10			.904	-1	3-41	0.1
	Yr	109	420	60	100	12	1	2	40	18	35	.238	.271	.293	64	-21	31			.893	-3	*3-109	-1.4
1892	Lou-N	76	287	22	48	9	1	0	36	13	36	.167	.203	.216	29	-25	6			.874	-3	3-76	-2.4
	StL-N	6	24	1	5	0	0	0	2	0	3	.208	.208	.208	25	-2				.895	1	/3-5,S-1	-0.2

YEAR	TM/L	G	AB	R	H	2B	3B	HR	RBI	BB	SO	AVG	OBP	SLG	PRO+	BR/A	SB	CS	SBR	FA	FR	G/POS	TPR
	Cin-N	6	24	3	5	1	0	1	4	1	5	.208	.240	.375	87	-1	0			.941	2	/3-4,2-2	0.1
	StL-N	1	4	0	0	0	0	0	0	0	1	.000	.000	.000	-99	-1	0			1.000	1	/3-1	0.0
	Yr	89	339	26	57	6	5	1	40	14	45	.168	.203	.224	32	-29	7			.880	-0	3-86/2-2,S	-2.5
Total	10	1087	4284	536	996	145	115	25	313	137	260	.232	.258	.338	82	-105	151			.876	-4	3-798,S-171/021	-8.0

■ HARVEY KUENN
Kuenn, Harvey Edward b: 12/4/30, W.Allis, Wis. d: 2/28/88, Peoria, Ariz. BR/TR, 6'2", 190 lbs. Deb: 9/6/52 MC

YEAR	TM/L	G	AB	R	H	2B	3B	HR	RBI	BB	SO	AVG	OBP	SLG	PRO+	BR/A	SB	CS	SBR	FA	FR	G/POS	TPR
1952	Det-A	19	80	2	26	2	2	0	8	2	1	.325	.349	.400	107	1	2	1	0	.962	2	S-19	0.4
1953	Det-A★	155	679	94	209	33	7	2	48	50	31	.308	.356	.386	101	1	6	5	-1	.973	-21	*S-155	-0.9
1954	Det-A☆	155	656	81	201	28	6	5	48	29	13	.306	.337	.390	100	-1	9	9	-3	.966	-3	*S-155	1.2
1955	Det-A★	145	620	101	190	38	5	8	62	40	27	.306	.349	.423	109	6	8	3	1	.956	-28	*S-141	-0.9
1956	Det-A★	146	591	96	196	32	7	12	88	55	34	.332	.391	.470	126	22	9	5	-0	.968	-20	*S-141/O-1	1.4
1957	Det-A★	151	624	74	173	30	6	9	44	47	28	.277	.328	.388	92	-7	5	8	-3	.955	-49	*S-136,3-17/1	-4.8
1958	Det-A☆	139	561	73	179	39	3	8	54	51	34	.319	.376	.442	116	13	5	10	-5	.984	15	*O-138	1.6
1959	Det-A★	139	561	99	198	42	7	9	71	48	37	.353	.405	.501	140	31	7	2	1	.988	1	*O-137	2.5
1960	Cle-A★	126	474	65	146	24	0	9	54	55	25	.308	.381	.416	119	14	3	0	1	.966	1	*O-119/3-5	1.0
1961	SF-N	131	471	60	125	22	4	5	46	47	34	.265	.333	.361	87	-8	5	4	-1	.988	-7	O-93,3-32/S	-2.1
1962	*SF-N	130	487	73	148	23	5	10	68	49	37	.304	.369	.433	116	12	3	6	-3	.970	-9	*O-105,3-30	-0.5
1963	SF-N	120	417	61	121	13	2	6	31	44	38	.290	.361	.374	113	8	2	1	0	.975	-30	O-64,3-53	-2.7
1964	SF-N	111	351	42	92	16	2	4	22	35	32	.262	.331	.353	91	-4	0	1	-1	.952	-13	O-88,1-11/3	-2.3
1965	SF-N	23	59	4	14	0	0	0	6	10	3	.237	.357	.237	69	-2	3	1	0	1.000	-1	O-14/1-7	-0.4
	Chi-N	54	120	11	26	5	0	0	6	22	13	.217	.338	.258	69	-4	1	0	0	.975	-3	O-35/1-1	-0.8
	Yr	77	179	15	40	5	0	0	12	32	16	.223	.342	.251	69	-6	4	1	1	.981	-4	O-49/1-8	-1.2
1966	Chi-N	3	3	0	1	0	0	0	0	0	1	.333	.333	.333	85	-0	0	0	0	.000	0	/O-1	0.0
	Phi-N	86	159	15	47	9	0	0	15	10	16	.296	.337	.352	92	-2	0	0	0	1.000	-6	O-31,1-13/3	-1.0
	Yr	89	162	15	48	9	0	0	15	10	17	.296	.337	.352	92	-2	0	0	0	1.000	-7	O-32,1-13/3	-1.0
Total	15	1833	6913	951	2092	356	56	87	671	594	404	.303	.359	.408	108	80	68	56	-13	.978	-163	O-826,S-748,3/1	-8.3

■ JOE KUHEL
Kuhel, Joseph Anthony b: 6/25/06, Cleveland, Ohio d: 2/26/84, Kansas City, Kan. BL/TL, 6', 180 lbs. Deb: 7/31/30 M

YEAR	TM/L	G	AB	R	H	2B	3B	HR	RBI	BB	SO	AVG	OBP	SLG	PRO+	BR/A	SB	CS	SBR	FA	FR	G/POS	TPR
1930	Was-A	18	63	9	18	3	3	0	17	5	6	.286	.348	.429	95	-1	1	0	0	.981	-1	1-16	-0.2
1931	Was-A	139	524	70	141	34	8	8	85	47	45	.269	.335	.410	94	-5	7	5	-1	.991	-7	*1-139	-2.4
1932	Was-A	101	347	52	101	21	5	4	52	32	19	.291	.353	.415	99	-0	5	2	0	.994	-2	1-85	-0.8
1933	*Was-A	153	602	89	194	34	10	11	107	59	48	.322	.385	.467	126	22	17	8	0	.996	-7	*1-153	0.1
1934	Was-A	63	263	49	76	12	3	3	25	30	14	.289	.364	.392	99	-0	2	7	-4	.994	-4	1-63	-1.3
1935	Was-A	151	633	99	165	25	9	2	74	78	44	.261	.345	.338	80	-17	5	4	-1	.991	0	*1-151	-3.3
1936	Was-A	149	588	107	189	42	8	16	118	64	30	.321	.390	.502	120	23	15	7	0	.993	-2	*1-149	0.6
1937	Was-A	136	547	73	155	24	11	6	61	63	39	.283	.357	.400	95	-4	6	3	0	.993	3	*1-136	-1.6
1938	Chi-A	117	412	67	110	27	4	8	51	72	35	.267	.376	.410	95	-2	9	7	-2	.988	-7	*1-111	-2.2
1939	Chi-A	139	546	107	164	24	9	15	56	64	51	.300	.376	.460	110	8	18	5	2	.992	-4	*1-136	-0.7
1940	Chi-A	155	603	111	169	28	8	27	94	87	59	.280	.374	.488	120	18	12	5	1	.988	-5	*1-155	-0.1
1941	Chi-A	153	600	99	150	39	5	12	63	70	55	.250	.331	.392	92	-8	20	5	3	.994	-1	*1-151	-1.6
1942	Chi-A	115	413	60	103	14	4	4	52	60	22	.249	.347	.332	94	-2	22	9	1	.991	-4	*1-112	-1.2
1943	Chi-A	153	531	55	113	21	1	5	46	76	45	.213	.324	.284	77	-13	14	8	-1	.995	1	*1-153	-2.4
1944	Was-A	139	518	90	144	26	7	4	51	68	40	.278	.364	.378	117	13	11	6	-0	.987	-2	*1-138	0.4
1945	Was-A	142	533	73	152	29	13	2	75	79	31	.285	.378	.400	137	27	10	5	0	.989	-6	*1-141	1.2
1946	Was-A	14	20	2	3	0	0	0	2	5	2	.150	.320	.150	36	-1	0	0	0	1.000	0	/1-5	-0.2
	Chi-A	64	238	24	65	9	3	4	20	21	24	.273	.335	.387	105	1	4	4	-1	.994	-2	1-63	-0.6
	Yr	78	258	26	68	9	3	4	22	26	26	.264	.333	.368	100	-0	4	4	-1	.994	-2	1-68	-0.8
1947	Chi-A	3	3	0	0	0	0	0	0	0	3	.000	.000	.000	-99	-1	0	0	0	.000	0	H	-0.1
Total	18	2104	7984	1236	2212	412	111	131	1049	980	612	.277	.359	.406	104	56	178	90	-1	.992	-48	*1-2057	-16.4

■ KENNY KUHN
Kuhn, Kenneth Harold b: 3/20/37, Louisville, Ky. BL/TR, 5'10.5", 175 lbs. Deb: 7/7/55

YEAR	TM/L	G	AB	R	H	2B	3B	HR	RBI	BB	SO	AVG	OBP	SLG	PRO+	BR/A	SB	CS	SBR	FA	FR	G/POS	TPR
1955	Cle-A	4	6	0	2	0	0	0	0	1	0	.333	.429	.333	103	1	0	1	0	1.000	-2	/S-4	-0.1
1956	Cle-A	27	22	7	6	1	0	0	2	0	4	.273	.273	.318	54	-1	0	1	-1	1.000	-1	S-17/2-5	0.0
1957	Cle-A	40	53	5	9	0	0	0	5	4	9	.170	.228	.170	10	-6	0	0	0	.974	-3	2-14/3-2,S	-0.9
Total	3	71	81	12	17	1	0	0	7	5	13	.210	.256	.222	30	-8	0	2	-1	.963	-3	/S-22,2-19,3	-1.0

■ WALT KUHN
Kuhn, Walter Charles "Red" b: 2/2/1884, Fresno, Cal. d: 6/14/35, Fresno, Cal. BR/TR, 5'7", 162 lbs. Deb: 4/18/12

YEAR	TM/L	G	AB	R	H	2B	3B	HR	RBI	BB	SO	AVG	OBP	SLG	PRO+	BR/A	SB	CS	SBR	FA	FR	G/POS	TPR
1912	Chi-A	76	178	16	36	7	0	0	10	20		.202	.286	.242	53	-10	5			.966	9	C-75/2-1	0.4
1913	Chi-A	26	50	5	8	1	0	0	5	13	8	.160	.333	.180	52	-2	1			.980	-2	C-24	-0.3
1914	Chi-A	17	40	4	11	1	0	0	0	8	11	.275	.396	.300	111	1	2	3	-1	.987	-1	C-16	0.0
Total	3	119	268	25	55	9	0	0	15	41	19	.205	.313	.239	62	-12	8	3		.971	6	C-115/2-1	0.1

■ CHARLIE KUHNS
Kuhns, Charles B. b: 10/27/1877, Freeport, Pa. d: 7/15/22, Pittsburgh, Pa. 5'9", 160 lbs. Deb: 6/4/1897

YEAR	TM/L	G	AB	R	H	2B	3B	HR	RBI	BB	SO	AVG	OBP	SLG	PRO+	BR/A	SB	CS	SBR	FA	FR	G/POS	TPR
1897	Pit-N	1	3	0	0	0	0	0	0	0	1	.000	.250	.000	-32	-1	0			.667	0	/3-1	0.0
1899	Bos-N	7	18	2	5	0	0	0	3	2		.278	.350	.278	67	-1	0			.813	-1	/S-3,3-3	-0.1
Total	2	8	21	2	5	0	0	0	3	3		.238	.333	.238	53	-1	0			.733	-1	/3-4,S-3	-0.1

■ DUANE KUIPER
Kuiper, Duane Eugene b: 6/19/50, Racine, Wis. BL/TR, 6', 175 lbs. Deb: 9/9/74

YEAR	TM/L	G	AB	R	H	2B	3B	HR	RBI	BB	SO	AVG	OBP	SLG	PRO+	BR/A	SB	CS	SBR	FA	FR	G/POS	TPR
1974	Cle-A	10	22	7	11	2	0	0	4	2	2	.500	.542	.591	228	4	1	1	-0	1.000	1	/2-8	0.5
1975	Cle-A	90	346	42	101	11	1	0	25	30	24	.292	.362	.329	97	-0	19	18	-5	.972	-14	2-87/D-1	-1.5
1976	Cle-A	135	506	47	133	13	6	0	37	30	42	.263	.305	.312	82	-12	10	17	-7	.987	20	*2-128/1-5,D	0.9
1977	Cle-A	148	610	62	169	15	5	1	50	37	55	.277	.326	.333	83	-14	11	11	-3	.985	2	*2-148	-0.5
1978	Cle-A	149	547	52	155	18	6	1	43	19	35	.283	.312	.338	84	-12	4	9	-4	.979	-19	*2-149	-2.5
1979	Cle-A	140	479	46	122	9	5	0	39	37	27	.255	.313	.294	65	-23	4	9	-4	.988	-4	*2-140	-2.1
1980	Cle-A	42	149	10	42	6	0	0	9	13	8	.282	.340	.315	80	-4	0	1	-1	.995	-8	2-42	-0.9
1981	Cle-A	72	206	15	53	6	0	0	14	8	13	.257	.285	.286	66	-9	1	1	-0	.983	-5	2-72	-1.1
1982	SF-N	107	218	26	61	9	1	0	17	32	24	.280	.377	.330	100	1	2	2	-1	.978	-7	2-51	-0.4
1983	SF-N	72	176	14	44	2	2	0	14	27	13	.250	.356	.284	82	-3	0	1	-1	.988	-9	2-64	-1.0
1984	SF-N	83	115	8	23	1	0	0	11	12	12	.200	.276	.209	39	-9	0	1	-1	.969	6	2-31/1-1	-0.3
1985	SF-N	9	5	0	3	0	0	0	0	1	0	.600	.667	.600	270	1	0	0	0	.000	0	/H	0.1
Total	12	1057	3379	329	917	91	29	1	263	248	255	.271	.326	.316	81	-79	52	71	-27	.983	-36	2-920/1-6,D	-8.8

■ JEFF KUNKEL
Kunkel, Jeffrey William b: 3/25/62, W.Palm Beach, Fla. BR/TR, 6'2", 180 lbs. Deb: 7/23/84 F

YEAR	TM/L	G	AB	R	H	2B	3B	HR	RBI	BB	SO	AVG	OBP	SLG	PRO+	BR/A	SB	CS	SBR	FA	FR	G/POS	TPR
1984	Tex-A	50	142	13	29	2	3	3	7	2	35	.204	.221	.324	47	-10	4	3	-1	.922	-1	S-48/D-1	-0.9
1985	Tex-A	2	4	1	1	0	0	0	0	0	2	.250	.250	.250	37	-0	0	0	0	1.000	1	/S-2	0.1
1986	Tex-A	8	13	3	3	0	0	1	2	0	3	.231	.231	.462	81	-0	0	0	0	.769	0	/S-5,D-1	-0.1
1987	Tex-A	15	32	1	7	0	1	0	2	0	10	.219	.242	.313	46	-3	0	1	-1	.955	0	2-10/3-3,01SD	-0.1
1988	Tex-A	55	154	14	35	8	3	2	15	4	35	.227	.252	.357	67	-7	0	1	-1	.949	1	2-28,S-19,3/OPD	0.0
1989	Tex-A	108	293	39	79	21	2	8	29	20	75	.270	.323	.437	110	3	3	2	-0	.936	2	S-59,0-30/23PD	0.8
1990	Tex-A	99	200	17	34	11	1	3	17	11	66	.170	.221	.280	39	-17	2	1	0	.958	-1	S-67,3-15,2/OD	-0.4
1992	Chi-N	20	52	0	4	2	0	1	1	0	8	.138	.138	.207	-3	-4	0	0	0	1.000	4	/S-6,2-3,O	0.0
Total	8	357	867	88	192	44	9	18	73	37	234	.221	.260	.355	69	-38	9	8	-2	.940	22	S-207/2-62,03DP1	-0.6

■ RUSTY KUNTZ
Kuntz, Russell Jay b: 2/4/55, Orange, Cal. BR/TR, 6'3", 190 lbs. Deb: 9/1/79 C

YEAR	TM/L	G	AB	R	H	2B	3B	HR	RBI	BB	SO	AVG	OBP	SLG	PRO+	BR/A	SB	CS	SBR	FA	FR	G/POS	TPR
1979	Chi-A	5	11	0	1	0	0	0	0	2	6	.091	.231	.091	-9	-2	0	0	0	1.000	-1	/O-5	-0.1

YEAR	TM/L	G	AB	R	H	2B	3B	HR	RBI	BB	SO	AVG	OBP	SLG	PRO+	BR/A	SB	CS	SBR	FA	FR	G/POS	TPR
1980	Chi-A	36	62	5	14	4	0	0	3	5	13	.226	.284	.290	58	-4	1	0	0	.979	-5	O-34	-0.9
1981	Chi-A	67	55	15	14	2	0	0	4	6	8	.255	.339	.291	85	-1	1	0	0	1.000	-13	O-51/D-5	-1.5
1982	Chi-A	21	26	4	5	1	0	0	3	2	8	.192	.250	.231	33	-2	0	0	0	1.000	-7	O-21	-1.0
1983	Chi-A	28	42	6	11	1	0	0	1	6	13	.262	.354	.286	76	-1	1	0	0	.976	-6	O-27/D-1	-0.7
	Min-A	31	100	13	19	3	0	3	5	12	28	.190	.277	.310	59	-6	0	0	0	.986	0	O-30	-0.7
	Yr	59	142	19	30	4	0	3	6	18	41	.211	.300	.303	64	-7	1	0	0	.982	-6	O-57/D-1	-1.4
1984	*Det-A	84	140	32	40	12	0	2	22	25	28	.286	.398	.414	126	6	2	2	-1	.987	-16	O-67,D-10	-1.2
1985	Det-A	5	5	0	0	0	0	0	0	2	2	.000	.286	.000	-13	-1	0	1	-1	1.000	-0	/1-1,D-3	-0.2
Total	7	277	441	75	104	23	0	5	38	60	106	.236	.330	.322	81	-10	5	3	-0	.988	-46	O-235/D-19,1	-6.3

■ WHITEY KUROWSKI
Kurowski, George John   b: 4/19/18, Reading, Pa.   BR/TR, 5'11", 193 lbs.   Deb: 9/23/41

YEAR	TM/L	G	AB	R	H	2B	3B	HR	RBI	BB	SO	AVG	OBP	SLG	PRO+	BR/A	SB	CS	SBR	FA	FR	G/POS	TPR
1941	StL-N	5	9	1	3	2	0	0	2	0	2	.333	.400	.556	157	1	0			1.000	-1	/3-4	0.0
1942	*StL-N	115	366	51	93	17	3	9	42	33	60	.254	.326	.391	102	0	7			.944	9	*3-104/S-1,O	1.1
1943	*StL-N☆	139	522	69	150	24	8	13	70	31	54	.287	.330	.439	116	8	3			.952	1	*3-137/S-2	1.2
1944	*StL-N★	149	555	95	150	25	7	20	87	58	40	.270	.341	.449	119	13	2			.965	4	*3-146/2-9,S	1.8
1945	StL-N†	133	511	84	165	27	3	21	102	45	45	.323	.383	.511	144	28	1			.964	2	*3-131/S-6	3.3
1946	*StL-N★	142	519	76	156	32	5	14	89	72	47	.301	.391	.462	136	25	2			.966	0	*3-138	2.9
1947	StL-N★	146	513	108	159	27	6	27	104	87	56	.310	.420	.544	148	37	4			.954	-14	*3-141	2.3
1948	StL-N	77	220	34	47	8	0	2	33	42	28	.214	.352	.277	68	-8	0			.939	-11	3-65	-2.0
1949	StL-N	10	14	0	2	0	0	0	0	1	0	.143	.200	.143	-6	-2	0			1.000	-0	/3-2	-0.3
Total	9	916	3229	518	925	162	32	106	529	369	332	.286	.366	.455	124	102	19			.957	-10	3-868/S-10,2O	10.3

■ CRAIG KUSICK
Kusick, Craig Robert   b: 9/30/48, Milwaukee, Wis.   BR/TR, 6'3", 232 lbs.   Deb: 9/8/73

YEAR	TM/L	G	AB	R	H	2B	3B	HR	RBI	BB	SO	AVG	OBP	SLG	PRO+	BR/A	SB	CS	SBR	FA	FR	G/POS	TPR
1973	Min-A	15	48	4	12	2	0	4	7	9		.250	.357	.292	81	-1	0	0	0	.989	-1	1-11/O-2,D	-0.3
1974	Min-A	76	201	36	48	7	1	8	26	35	36	.239	.354	.403	113	4	0	0	0	.996	4	1-75	0.4
1975	Min-A	57	156	14	37	8	0	6	27	21	23	.237	.346	.404	109	2	0	0	0	.990	1	1-51	0.0
1976	Min-A	109	266	33	69	13	0	11	36	35	44	.259	.348	.432	124	8	5	1	1	.977	3	D-79,1-23	0.9
1977	Min-A	115	268	34	68	12	0	12	45	49	60	.254	.375	.433	121	9	3	1	0	.972	-2	D-85,1-23	0.5
1978	Min-A	77	191	23	33	3	2	4	20	37	38	.173	.310	.272	64	-8	3	2	-0	.987	2	D-35,1-27/O	-1.0
1979	Min-A	24	54	8	13	4	0	3	6	3	11	.241	.281	.481	97	-0	0	0	0	1.000	0	D-12/1-8	-0.1
	Tor-A	24	54	3	11	1	0	2	7	7	7	.204	.306	.333	72	-2	0	0	0	.978	1	1-20/P-1,D	-0.2
	Yr	48	108	11	24	5	0	5	13	10	18	.222	.294	.407	85	-3	0	0	0	.983	1	1-28,D-13/P	-0.3
Total	7	497	1238	155	291	50	3	46	171	194	228	.235	.345	.392	105	12	11	4	1	.988	9	1-238,D-214/OP	0.2

■ ART KUSNYER
Kusnyer, Arthur William   b: 12/19/45, Akron, Ohio   BR/TR, 6'2", 198 lbs.   Deb: 9/21/70   C

YEAR	TM/L	G	AB	R	H	2B	3B	HR	RBI	BB	SO	AVG	OBP	SLG	PRO+	BR/A	SB	CS	SBR	FA	FR	G/POS	TPR
1970	Chi-A	4	10	0	1	0	0	0	0	0	4	.100	.100	.100	-43	-2	0	0	0	.941	1	/C-3	-0.1
1971	Cal-A	6	13	0	2	0	0	0	0	0	3	.154	.154	.154	-14	-2	0	0	0	.958	1	/C-6	-0.1
1972	Cal-A	64	179	13	37	2	1	2	13	16	33	.207	.276	.263	64	-8	0	0	0	.975	-3	C-63	-0.9
1973	Cal-A	41	64	5	8	2	0	0	3	2	12	.125	.152	.156	-14	-10	0	1	-1	.979	1	C-41	-0.9
1976	Mil-A	15	34	2	4	1	0	0	3	1	5	.118	.167	.147	-8	-5	1	0	0	.938	-1	C-14	-0.5
1978	KC-A	9	13	1	3	1	0	1	2	2	4	.231	.333	.538	138	1	0	0	0	.946	3	/C-9	0.4
Total	6	139	313	21	55	6	1	3	21	21	61	.176	.232	.230	37	-26	1	1	-0	.970	2	C-136	-2.1

■ JUL KUSTUS
Kustus, Joseph J. "Joe" or "Kul"   b: 9/5/1882, Detroit, Mich.   d: 4/27/16, Eloise, Mich.   BR/TR, 5'10",   Deb: 4/17/09

YEAR	TM/L	G	AB	R	H	2B	3B	HR	RBI	BB	SO	AVG	OBP	SLG	PRO+	BR/A	SB	CS	SBR	FA	FR	G/POS	TPR
1909	Bro-N	53	173	12	25	5	0	1	11	11		.145	.204	.191	23	-16	9			.951	0	O-50	-1.9

■ RANDY KUTCHER
Kutcher, Randy Scott   b: 4/20/60, Anchorage, Alaska   BR/TR, 5'11", 175 lbs.   Deb: 6/19/86

YEAR	TM/L	G	AB	R	H	2B	3B	HR	RBI	BB	SO	AVG	OBP	SLG	PRO+	BR/A	SB	CS	SBR	FA	FR	G/POS	TPR
1986	SF-N	71	186	28	44	9	1	7	16	11	41	.237	.279	.409	92	-3	6	5	-1	.990	-1	O-51,S-13/32	-0.6
1987	SF-N	14	16	7	3	1	1	0	1	1	5	.188	.235	.375	61	-1	1	0	0	1.000	1	/O-6,2-2,3S	0.0
1988	Bos-A	19	12	2	2	1	0	0	0	0	2	.167	.167	.250	14	-1	0	1	-1	1.000	-0	/O-7,3-2,D	-0.2
1989	Bos-A	77	160	28	36	10	3	2	18	11	46	.225	.275	.363	74	-6	3	0	1	.982	-3	O-57/3-6,CD	-0.9
1990	*Bos-A	63	74	18	17	4	1	1	5	13	18	.230	.345	.351	91	-1	3	3	-1	1.000	-0	O-34,3-11/2D	-0.2
Total	5	244	448	83	102	25	6	10	40	36	112	.228	.285	.377	82	-12	13	9	-2	.989	-3	0-155/3-25,DS2C	-1.9

■ JOE KUTINA
Kutina, Joseph Peter   b: 1/16/1885, Chicago, Ill.   d: 4/13/45, Chicago, Ill.   BR/TR, 6'2", 205 lbs.   Deb: 9/6/11

YEAR	TM/L	G	AB	R	H	2B	3B	HR	RBI	BB	SO	AVG	OBP	SLG	PRO+	BR/A	SB	CS	SBR	FA	FR	G/POS	TPR
1911	StL-A	26	101	12	26	6	2	3	15	2		.257	.279	.446	105	-0	2			.981	-1	1-26	-0.1
1912	StL-A	69	205	18	42	9	3	1	18	13		.205	.262	.293	61	-11	0			.985	-3	1-51/O-1	-1.5
Total	2	95	306	30	68	15	5	4	33	15		.222	.268	.343	76	-11	2			.984	-4	/1-77,O-1	-1.6

■ AL KVASNAK
Kvasnak, Alexander   b: 1/11/21, Sagamore, Pa.   BR/TR, 6'1", 170 lbs.   Deb: 4/15/42

YEAR	TM/L	G	AB	R	H	2B	3B	HR	RBI	BB	SO	AVG	OBP	SLG	PRO+	BR/A	SB	CS	SBR	FA	FR	G/POS	TPR
1942	Was-A	5	11	3	2	0	0	0	0	2	1	.182	.308	.182	40	-1	0	0	0	1.000	-0	/O-3	-0.1

■ ANDY KYLE
Kyle, Andrew Ewing   b: 10/29/1889, Toronto, Ont., Can.   d: 9/6/71, Toronto, Ont., Can.   BL/TL, 5'8", 160 lbs.   Deb: 9/7/12

YEAR	TM/L	G	AB	R	H	2B	3B	HR	RBI	BB	SO	AVG	OBP	SLG	PRO+	BR/A	SB	CS	SBR	FA	FR	G/POS	TPR
1912	Cin-N	9	21	3	7	1	0	0	4	4	2	.333	.440	.381	129	1	0			1.000	0	/O-7	0.1

■ CHET LAABS
Laabs, Chester Peter   b: 4/30/12, Milwaukee, Wis.   d: 1/26/83, Warren, Mich.   BR/TR, 5'8", 175 lbs.   Deb: 5/5/37

YEAR	TM/L	G	AB	R	H	2B	3B	HR	RBI	BB	SO	AVG	OBP	SLG	PRO+	BR/A	SB	CS	SBR	FA	FR	G/POS	TPR
1937	Det-A	72	242	31	58	13	5	8	37	24	66	.240	.308	.434	83	-8	6	2	1	.971	-7	O-62	-1.5
1938	Det-A	64	211	26	50	7	3	7	37	15	52	.237	.288	.398	66	-12	3	2	-0	.971	-1	O-53	-1.4
1939	Det-A	5	16	1	5	1	1	0	2	2	0	.313	.389	.500	117	0	0	0	0	.933	1	/O-5	0.1
	StL-A	95	317	52	95	20	5	10	62	33	62	.300	.368	.489	115	6	4	1	0	.972	-4	O-79	0.3
	Yr	100	333	53	100	21	6	10	64	35	62	.300	.369	.489	115	7	4	1	1	.969	1	O-84	0.4
1940	StL-A	105	218	32	59	11	5	10	40	34	59	.271	.372	.505	122	7	3	3	-0	.969	-7	O-63	-0.3
1941	StL-A	118	392	64	109	23	6	15	59	51	59	.278	.361	.482	117	9	5	2	0	.982	-2	*O-100	0.2
1942	StL-A	144	520	90	143	21	7	27	99	88	88	.275	.380	.498	144	30	0	3	-2	.970	-4	*O-139	1.7
1943	StL-A★	151	580	83	145	27	7	17	85	73	105	.250	.338	.409	115	11	5	7	-3	.976	2	*O-150	0.2
1944	*StL-A	66	201	28	47	10	2	5	23	29	33	.234	.330	.378	96	-1	3	1	0	1.000	-2	O-55	-0.5
1945	StL-A	35	109	15	26	4	3	1	8	16	17	.239	.352	.358	101	1	0	0	0	.986	-4	O-35	-0.5
1946	StL-A	80	264	40	69	13	0	16	52	20	50	.261	.316	.492	111	5	3	1	0	.987	1	O-72	0.3
1947	Phi-A	15	32	5	7	1	0	1	5	4	4	.219	.306	.344	79	-1	0	0	0	1.000	-0	/O-7	-0.1
Total	11	950	3102	467	813	151	44	117	509	389	595	.262	.346	.452	113	47	32	22	-4	.977	-21	O-820	-1.5

■ COCO LABOY
Laboy, Jose Alberto   b: 7/3/39, Ponce, P.R.   BR/TR, 5'10", 170 lbs.   Deb: 4/8/69

YEAR	TM/L	G	AB	R	H	2B	3B	HR	RBI	BB	SO	AVG	OBP	SLG	PRO+	BR/A	SB	CS	SBR	FA	FR	G/POS	TPR
1969	Mon-N	157	562	53	145	29	1	18	83	40	96	.258	.312	.409	100	-1	0	2	-1	.944	4	*3-156	0.1
1970	Mon-N	137	432	37	86	26	1	5	53	31	81	.199	.256	.299	48	-33	0	2	-1	.946	-4	*3-132/2-3	-3.9
1971	Mon-N	76	151	10	38	4	0	1	14	11	19	.252	.302	.298	70	-6	0	1	-1	.937	1	3-65/2-2	-0.6
1972	Mon-N	28	69	6	18	2	0	3	14	10	16	.261	.354	.420	117	-2	0	0	0	.980	-2	3-24/2-3,S	-0.2
1973	Mon-N	22	33	2	4	1	0	1	2	5	8	.121	.237	.242	32	-3	0	0	0	.889	1	3-20/2-1	-0.2
Total	5	420	1247	108	291	62	2	28	166	97	220	.233	.292	.354	77	-41	0	5	-3	.944	-0	3-397/2-9,S	-4.6

■ CANDY LaCHANCE
LaChance, George Joseph   b: 2/15/1870, Waterbury, Conn.   d: 8/18/32, Waterville, Conn.   BB/TR, 6'1", 183 lbs.   Deb: 8/15/1893

YEAR	TM/L	G	AB	R	H	2B	3B	HR	RBI	BB	SO	AVG	OBP	SLG	PRO+	BR/A	SB	CS	SBR	FA	FR	G/POS	TPR
1893	Bro-N	11	35	1	6	1	0	0	6	2	12	.171	.237	.200	17	-4	0			.654	-6	/C-6,O-5	-0.8
1894	Bro-N	68	257	48	83	13	8	5	52	16	32	.323	.365	.494	114	5	20			.979	-8	1-56,C-10/O	-0.2
1895	Bro-N	127	536	99	167	22	8	8	108	29	48	.312	.356	.427	110	7	37			.983	-6	*1-125/O-3	0.3
1896	Bro-N	89	348	60	99	10	13	5	58	23	32	.284	.331	.448	111	3	17			.986	-3	*1-89	0.1
1897	Bro-N	126	520	86	160	28	16	8	90	15		.308	.333	.446	111	5	26			.978	-4	*1-126	0.1

YEAR	TM/L	G	AB	R	H	2B	3B	HR	RBI	BB	SO	AVG	OBP	SLG	PRO+	BR/A	SB	CS	SBR	FA	FR	G/POS	TPR
1898	Bro-N	136	526	62	130	23	7	5	65	31		.247	.299	.346	85	-12	23			.988	-20	1-74,S-48,O	-2.9
1899	Bal-N	125	472	65	145	23	10	1	75	21		.307	.350	.405	101	-1	31			.984	-7	*1-125	-0.6
1901	Cle-A	133	548	81	166	22	9	1	75	7		.303	.314	.381	96	-5	11			.979	-3	*1-133	-0.8
1902	Bos-A	138	541	60	151	13	4	6	56	18		.279	.309	.351	80	-15	8			.983	-11	*1-138	-2.8
1903	*Bos-A	141	522	60	134	22	6	1	53	28		.257	.303	.328	85	-10	12			.984	-11	*1-141	-2.4
1904	Bos-A	157	573	55	130	19	5	1	47	23		.227	.265	.283	69	-20	7			**.992**	-14	*1-157	-4.2
1905	Bos-A	12	41	1	6	1	0	0	5	6		.146	.255	.171	36	-3	0			.988	-0	1-12	-0.4
Total	12	1263	4919	678	1377	197	86	39	690	219	124	.280	.318	.379	93	-49	192			.984	-93	*1-1176/S-48,OC	-14.6

■ RENE LACHEMANN
Lachemann, Rene George   b: 5/4/45, Los Angeles, Cal.   BR/TR, 6', 198 lbs.   Deb: 5/4/65   FMC

YEAR	TM/L	G	AB	R	H	2B	3B	HR	RBI	BB	SO	AVG	OBP	SLG	PRO+	BR/A	SB	CS	SBR	FA	FR	G/POS	TPR
1965	KC-A	92	216	20	49	7	1	9	29	12	57	.227	.268	.394	87	-5	0	0	0	.980	2	C-75	0.1
1966	KC-A	7	5	0	1	1	0	0	0	0	1	.200	.200	.400	70	-0	0	0	0	1.000	1	/C-6	0.1
1968	Oak-A	19	60	3	9	1	0	0	4	1	11	.150	.177	.167	5	-7	0	0	0	.967	-6	C-16	-1.5
Total	3	118	281	23	59	9	1	9	33	13	69	.210	.247	.345	70	-12	0	0	0	.978	-3	/C-97	-1.3

■ PETE LaCOCK
LaCock, Ralph Pierre   b: 1/17/52, Burbank, Cal.   BL/TL, 6'3", 210 lbs.   Deb: 9/6/72

YEAR	TM/L	G	AB	R	H	2B	3B	HR	RBI	BB	SO	AVG	OBP	SLG	PRO+	BR/A	SB	CS	SBR	FA	FR	G/POS	TPR
1972	Chi-N	5	6	3	3	0	0	0	4	0	1	.500	.500	.500	167	1	1	0	0	1.000	-1	/O-3	0.0
1973	Chi-N	11	16	1	4	1	0	0	3	1	2	.250	.294	.313	63	-1	0	0	0	1.000	-0	/O-5	-0.1
1974	Chi-N	35	110	9	20	4	1	1	8	12	16	.182	.268	.264	47	-8	0	0	0	.974	1	O-22,1-11	-0.9
1975	Chi-N	106	249	30	57	8	1	6	30	37	27	.229	.339	.341	82	-5	0	2	-1	.988	1	1-53,O-26	-1.0
1976	Chi-N	106	244	34	54	9	2	8	28	42	37	.221	.338	.373	93	-2	1	4	-2	.975	-4	1-54,O-19	-1.3
1977	*KC-A	88	218	25	66	12	1	3	29	15	25	.303	.350	.408	105	2	2	1	0	.990	1	1-29,D-26,O	0.1
1978	KC-A	118	322	44	95	21	2	5	48	21	27	.295	.338	.419	109	3	1	0	0	.993	-6	*1-106	-0.7
1979	KC-A	132	408	54	113	25	4	3	56	37	26	.277	.339	.380	92	-4	2	1	0	**.997**	1	*1-108,D-16	-1.0
1980	*KC-A	114	156	14	32	6	0	1	18	17	10	.205	.287	.263	51	-10	1	0	0	.997	-3	1-86,O-29	-1.5
Total	9	715	1729	214	444	86	11	27	224	182	171	.257	.329	.366	89	-25	8	8	-2	.991	-9	1-447,O-116/D	-6.4

■ LEE LACY
Lacy, Leondaus   b: 4/10/48, Longview, Tex.   BR/TR, 6'1", 175 lbs.   Deb: 6/30/72

YEAR	TM/L	G	AB	R	H	2B	3B	HR	RBI	BB	SO	AVG	OBP	SLG	PRO+	BR/A	SB	CS	SBR	FA	FR	G/POS	TPR
1972	LA-N	60	243	34	63	7	3	0	12	19	37	.259	.313	.313	80	-6	5	3	-0	.973	-8	2-58	-1.2
1973	LA-N	57	135	14	28	2	0	0	8	15	34	.207	.287	.222	45	-10	2	3	-1	.965	1	2-41	-1.0
1974	*LA-N	48	78	13	22	6	0	0	8	2	14	.282	.300	.359	87	-2	2	0	1	.968	2	2-34/3-1	0.2
1975	LA-N	101	306	44	96	11	5	7	40	22	29	.314	.360	.451	129	11	5	9	-4	.935	-4	2-43,O-43/S	0.2
1976	Atl-N	50	180	25	49	4	2	3	20	6	12	.272	.299	.367	83	-4	2	2	-1	.969	-10	2-44/O-5,3	-1.4
	LA-N	53	158	17	42	7	1	0	14	16	13	.266	.333	.323	88	-2	1	-2	-1	.979	1	O-37/3-3,2	-0.4
	Yr	103	338	42	91	11	3	3	34	22	25	.269	.316	.346	86	-6	3	4	-2	.970	-10	2-46,O-42/3	-1.8
1977	*LA-N	75	169	28	45	7	0	6	21	10	21	.266	.307	.414	92	-2	4	0	1	1.000	-13	O-32,2-22,3	-1.3
1978	*LA-N	103	245	29	64	16	4	13	40	27	30	.261	.333	.518	136	11	7	4	-0	.971	-5	O-44,2-24/3S	0.5
1979	*Pit-N	84	182	17	45	9	3	5	15	22	36	.247	.332	.412	97	-1	6	1	1	.973	-2	O-41/2-5	-0.5
1980	Pit-N	109	278	45	93	20	4	7	33	28	33	.335	.399	.511	150	19	18	9	0	.984	5	O-88/3-3	2.2
1981	Pit-N	78	213	31	57	11	4	2	10	11	29	.268	.307	.385	92	-3	24	3	5	.977	3	O-63/3-1	0.5
1982	Pit-N	121	359	66	112	16	3	5	31	32	57	.312	.370	.415	116	8	40	15	3	.965	-8	*O-113/3-2	0.0
1983	Pit-N	108	288	40	87	12	3	4	13	22	36	.302	.352	.406	107	3	31	13	2	1.000	-8	O-98	-0.6
1984	Pit-N	138	474	66	152	26	3	12	70	32	61	.321	.364	.464	131	18	21	11	-0	**.996**	4	*O-127/2-2	2.0
1985	Bal-A	121	492	69	144	22	4	9	48	39	95	.293	.347	.409	109	6	10	3	1	.984	4	*O-115/D-5	0.7
1986	Bal-A	130	491	77	141	18	0	11	47	37	71	.287	.337	.391	99	-1	4	6	-2	.992	6	*O-120/D-3	-0.1
1987	Bal-A	87	258	35	63	13	3	7	28	32	49	.244	.328	.399	94	-2	3	2	-0	.973	2	O-80/D-4	-0.3
Total	16	1523	4549	650	1303	207	42	91	458	372	657	.286	.342	.410	108	43	185	86	4	.983	-31	*O-1006,2-275/3DS	-0.3

■ GUY LACY
Lacy, Osceola Guy   b: 6/12/1897, Cleveland, Tenn.   d: 11/19/53, Cleveland, Tenn.   BR/TR, 5'11.5", 170 lbs.   Deb: 5/7/26

YEAR	TM/L	G	AB	R	H	2B	3B	HR	RBI	BB	SO	AVG	OBP	SLG	PRO+	BR/A	SB	CS	SBR	FA	FR	G/POS	TPR
1926	Cle-A	13	24	2	4	0	0	1	2	2	2	.167	.259	.292	43	-2	0	0	0	.976	1	2-11/3-2	-0.1

■ HI LADD
Ladd, Arthur Clifford   b: 2/9/1870, Willimantic, Conn.   d: 5/7/48, Cranston, R.I.   BL/TR, 6'4", 180 lbs.   Deb: 7/12/1898

YEAR	TM/L	G	AB	R	H	2B	3B	HR	RBI	BB	SO	AVG	OBP	SLG	PRO+	BR/A	SB	CS	SBR	FA	FR	G/POS	TPR
1898	Pit-N	1	1	0	0	0	0	0	0	0		.000	.000	.000	-99	-0	0			.000	0	H	0.0
	Bos-N	1	4	1	1	0	0	0	0	0		.250	.250	.250	41	-0	0			1.000	-0	/O-1	0.0
	Yr	2	5	1	1	0	0	0	0	0		.200	.200	.200	14	-1	0			1.000	-0	/O-1	0.0

■ STEVE LADEW
Ladew, Stephen   b: St.Louis, Mo.   Deb: 9/27/1889

YEAR	TM/L	G	AB	R	H	2B	3B	HR	RBI	BB	SO	AVG	OBP	SLG	PRO+	BR/A	SB	CS	SBR	FA	FR	G/POS	TPR
1889	KC-a	2	4	0	0	0	0	0		0	3	.000	.000	.000	-95	-1	0			1.000	-0	/O-1,P-1	-0.1

■ JOE LAFATA
Lafata, Joseph Joseph   b: 8/3/21, Detroit, Mich.   BL/TL, 6', 163 lbs.   Deb: 4/17/47

YEAR	TM/L	G	AB	R	H	2B	3B	HR	RBI	BB	SO	AVG	OBP	SLG	PRO+	BR/A	SB	CS	SBR	FA	FR	G/POS	TPR
1947	NY-N	62	95	13	21	1	0	2	18	15	18	.221	.333	.295	68	-4	1			.974	-1	O-19/1-2	-0.6
1948	NY-N	1	1	0	0	0	0	0	0	0	1	.000	.000	.000	-99	-0	0			.000	0	H	0.0
1949	NY-N	64	140	18	33	2	2	3	16	9	23	.236	.282	.343	67	-7	1			.984	-4	1-47	-1.1
Total	3	127	236	31	54	3	2	5	34	24	42	.229	.303	.322	67	-11	2			.985	-5	/1-49,O-19	-1.7

■ FLIP LAFFERTY
Lafferty, Frank Bernard   b: 5/4/1854, Scranton, Pa.   d: 2/8/10, Wilmington, Del.   TR ,   Deb: 9/15/1876

YEAR	TM/L	G	AB	R	H	2B	3B	HR	RBI	BB	SO	AVG	OBP	SLG	PRO+	BR/A	SB	CS	SBR	FA	FR	G/POS	TPR
1876	Phi-N	1	3	0	0	0	0	0	0	0	0	.000	.000	.000	-99	-1				.750	0	/P-1	0.0
1877	Lou-N	4	17	2	1	1	0	0	0	0	4	.059	.059	.118	-39	-3				.750	-1	/O-4	-0.4
Total	2	5	20	2	1	1	0	0	0	0	4	.050	.050	.100	-46	-3				.750	-1	/O-4,P-1	-0.4

■ TY LaFOREST
LaForest, Byron Joseph   b: 4/18/17, Edmundston, N.B., Canada   d: 5/5/47, Arlington, Mass.   BR/TR, 5'9", 165 lbs.   Deb: 8/4/45

YEAR	TM/L	G	AB	R	H	2B	3B	HR	RBI	BB	SO	AVG	OBP	SLG	PRO+	BR/A	SB	CS	SBR	FA	FR	G/POS	TPR
1945	Bos-A	52	204	25	51	7	4	2	16	10	35	.250	.285	.353	83	-5	4	4	-1	.966	1	3-45/O-5	-0.5

■ ROGER LaFRANCOIS
LaFrancois, Roger Victor   b: 8/2/54, Norwich, Conn.   BL/TR, 6'2", 215 lbs.   Deb: 5/27/82

YEAR	TM/L	G	AB	R	H	2B	3B	HR	RBI	BB	SO	AVG	OBP	SLG	PRO+	BR/A	SB	CS	SBR	FA	FR	G/POS	TPR
1982	Bos-A	8	10	1	4	1	0	0	0	0	1	.400	.400	.500	137	0	0	0	0	1.000	-0	/C-8	0.0

■ MIKE LAGA
Laga, Michael Russell   b: 6/14/60, Ridgewood, N.J.   BL/TL, 6'2", 210 lbs.   Deb: 9/1/82

YEAR	TM/L	G	AB	R	H	2B	3B	HR	RBI	BB	SO	AVG	OBP	SLG	PRO+	BR/A	SB	CS	SBR	FA	FR	G/POS	TPR
1982	Det-A	27	88	6	23	9	0	3	11	4	23	.261	.293	.466	104	0	1	0	0	.994	-2	1-19/D-8	-0.3
1983	Det-A	12	21	2	4	0	0	0	2	1	9	.190	.227	.190	17	-2	0	0	0	1.000	0	/1-5,D-6	-0.3
1984	Det-A	9	11	1	6	0	0	0	1	1	4	.545	.583	.545	216	2	0	0	0	1.000	0	/1-4,D-4	0.2
1985	Det-A	9	36	3	6	1	0	2	6	0	9	.167	.167	.361	40	-3	0	0	0	.974	1	/1-4,D-5	-0.3
1986	Det-A	15	45	6	9	1	0	3	8	5	13	.200	.280	.422	88	-1	0	0	0	1.000	-0	1-12/D-2	-0.2
	StL-N	18	46	7	10	4	0	3	8	5	18	.217	.308	.500	120	1	0	0	0	1.000	2	1-16	0.2
1987	StL-N	17	29	4	4	1	0	1	4	2	7	.138	.194	.276	22	-3	0	0	0	.973	1	1-12	-0.3
1988	StL-N	41	100	5	13	0	0	1	4	2	21	.130	.147	.160	-12	-14	0	0	0	1.000	1	1-37	-1.7
1989	SF-N	17	20	1	4	1	0	1	7	1	6	.200	.238	.400	82	-1	0	0	0	1.000	-0	/1-4	-0.1
1990	SF-N	23	27	4	5	1	0	2	4	1	7	.185	.241	.444	88	-1	0	0	0	1.000	1	1-10	0.0
Total	9	188	423	39	84	18	0	16	55	22	115	.199	.242	.355	63	-22	1	0	0	.996	2	1-123/D-25	-2.7

■ JOE LAHOUD
Lahoud, Joseph Michael   b: 4/14/47, Danbury, Conn.   BL/TL, 6', 202 lbs.   Deb: 4/10/68

YEAR	TM/L	G	AB	R	H	2B	3B	HR	RBI	BB	SO	AVG	OBP	SLG	PRO+	BR/A	SB	CS	SBR	FA	FR	G/POS	TPR
1968	Bos-A	29	78	5	19	1	0	6	16	16	16	.244	.330	.244	71	-2	0	2	-1	.926	-3	O-25	-0.9
1969	Bos-A	101	218	32	41	5	0	9	21	40	43	.188	.317	.335	78	-6	2	1	0	.979	-7	O-66/1-1	-1.7
1970	Bos-A	17	49	6	12	1	0	2	5	7	6	.245	.339	.388	93	-0	0	0	0	.963	2	O-13	0.1
1971	Bos-A	107	256	39	55	9	3	14	32	40	45	.215	.330	.438	108	3	2	2	-0	.993	0	O-69	0.2
1972	Mil-A	111	316	35	75	8	1	12	34	45	54	.237	.332	.399	119	8	3	6	-2	.974	-2	O-97	0.0
1973	Mil-A	96	225	29	46	9	0	12	26	27	36	.204	.304	.311	75	-7	5	5	-2	1.000	2	D-41,O-40	-0.9

YEAR	TM/L	G	AB	R	H	2B	3B	HR	RBI	BB	SO	AVG	OBP	SLG	PRO+	BR/A	SB	CS	SBR	FA	FR	G/POS	TPR
1974	Cal-A	127	325	46	88	16	3	13	44	47	57	.271	.368	.458	145	19	4	5	-2	.976	-6	*O-106,D-10	0.8
1975	Cal-A	76	192	21	41	6	2	6	33	48	33	.214	.373	.359	116	6	2	1	0	1.000	-3	D-35,O-29	0.2
1976	Cal-A	42	96	8	17	4	0	0	4	18	16	.177	.319	.219	63	-4	0	0	0	.962	-2	O-26/D-3	-0.7
	Tex-A	38	89	10	20	3	1	1	5	10	16	.225	.303	.315	79	-2	1	0	0	1.000	-2	D-22/O-5	-0.4
	Yr	80	185	18	37	7	1	1	9	28	32	.200	.312	.265	72	-6	1	0	0	.964	-4	O-31,D-25	-1.1
1977	*KC-A	34	65	8	17	5	0	2	8	11	16	.262	.368	.431	116	2	1	0	0	.952	-1	O-15/D-4	0.1
1978	KC-A	13	16	0	2	0	0	0	0	1	1	.125	.125	.125	-29	-3	0	0	0	.000	-0	/O-1,D-1	-0.3
Total	11	791	1925	239	429	68	12	65	218	309	339	.223	.335	.372	103	14	20	20	-6	.979	-19	O-492,D-116/1	-3.5

■ DICK LAJESKIE
Lajeskie, Richard Edward   b: 1/8/26, Passaic, N.J.   d: 8/15/76, Ramsey, N.J.   BR/TR, 5'11", 175 lbs.   Deb: 9/10/46

YEAR	TM/L	G	AB	R	H	2B	3B	HR	RBI	BB	SO	AVG	OBP	SLG	PRO+	BR/A	SB	CS	SBR	FA	FR	G/POS	TPR
1946	NY-N	6	10	3	2	0	0	0	0	3	2	.200	.429	.200	81	0				.964	5	/2-4	0.5

■ NAP LAJOIE
Lajoie, Napoleon "Larry"   b: 9/5/1874, Woonsocket, R.I.   d: 2/7/59, Daytona Beach, Fla.   BR/TR, 6'1", 195 lbs.   Deb: 8/12/1896   MH

YEAR	TM/L	G	AB	R	H	2B	3B	HR	RBI	BB	SO	AVG	OBP	SLG	PRO+	BR/A	SB	CS	SBR	FA	FR	G/POS	TPR
1896	Phi-N	39	175	36	57	12	7	4	42	1	11	.326	.330	.543	129	5	7			.995	-3	1-39	0.2
1897	Phi-N	127	545	107	197	40	23	9	127	15		.361	.392	.569	156	39	20			.984	-6	*1-108,O-19/3	2.8
1898	Phi-N	147	608	113	197	43	11	6	127	21		.324	.354	.461	139	26	25			.949	-1	*2-146/1-1	3.2
1899	Phi-N	77	312	70	118	19	9	6	70	12		.378	.419	.554	172	29	13			.954	23	2-67/O-5	4.9
1900	Phi-N	102	451	95	152	33	12	7	92	10		.337	.362	.510	140	21	22			.954	30	*2-102/3-1	5.0
1901	Phi-A	131	544	145	232	48	14	14	125	24		.426	.463	.643	196	67	27			.960	29	*2-119,S-12	8.9
1902	Phi-A	1	4	0	1	0	0	0	1	0		.250	.250	.250	37	-0	1			1.000	-0	/2-1	-0.1
	Cle-A	86	348	81	132	35	5	7	64	19		.379	.421	.569	180	36	19			.974	30	2-86	6.3
	Yr	87	352	81	133	35	5	7	65	19		.378	.419	.565	178	36	20			.974	29	2-87	6.2
1903	Cle-A	125	485	90	167	41	11	7	93	24		.344	.379	.518	170	39	21			.955	40	*2-122/1-1,3	8.4
1904	Cle-A	140	553	92	208	49	15	6	102	27		.376	.413	.552	205	64	29			.962	-1	2-95,S-44/1	7.2
1905	Cle-A	65	249	29	82	12	2	2	41	17		.329	.377	.418	150	14	11			.991	9	2-59/1-5M	2.5
1906	Cle-A	152	602	88	214	48	9	0	91	30		.355	.392	.465	170	46	20			.973	32	*2-130,3-15/SM	8.5
1907	Cle-A	137	509	53	152	30	6	2	63	30		.299	.345	.393	134	18	24			.969	45	*2-128/1-9M	6.6
1908	Cle-A	157	581	77	168	32	6	2	74	47		.289	.352	.375	136	23	15			.964	49	*2-156/1-1M	7.8
1909	Cle-A	128	469	56	152	33	7	1	47	35		.324	.378	.431	149	26	13			.959	19	*2-120/1-8M	4.6
1910	Cle-A	159	591	94	227	51	7	4	76	60		.384	.445	.514	198	66	26			.966	15	*2-149,1-10	8.5
1911	Cle-A	90	315	36	115	20	1	2	60	26		.365	.420	.454	142	18	13			.990	-7	1-41,2-37	1.0
1912	Cle-A	117	448	66	165	34	4	0	90	28		.368	.414	.462	146	26	18			.959	5	2-97,1-20	2.7
1913	Cle-A	137	465	66	156	25	2	1	68	33	17	.335	.398	.404	131	19	17			.970	9	*2-126	2.8
1914	Cle-A	121	419	37	108	14	3	0	50	32	15	.258	.313	.305	83	-9	14	15	-5	.959	6	2-80,1-31	-1.0
1915	Phi-A	129	490	40	137	24	5	1	61	11	16	.280	.301	.355	100	-3	10	6	-1	.962	14	*2-110,S-10/13	1.3
1916	Phi-A	113	426	33	105	14	4	2	35	14	26	.246	.272	.312	79	-13	15			.973	30	*2-105/1-5,O	2.2
Total	21	2480	9589	1504	3242	657	163	83	1599	516	85	.338	.380	.467	150	558	380	21		.963	367	*2-2035,1-286/SO3	94.3

■ EDDIE LAKE
Lake, Edward Erving "Sparky"   b: 3/18/16, Antioch, Cal.   BR/TR, 5'7", 160 lbs.   Deb: 9/26/39

YEAR	TM/L	G	AB	R	H	2B	3B	HR	RBI	BB	SO	AVG	OBP	SLG	PRO+	BR/A	SB	CS	SBR	FA	FR	G/POS	TPR
1939	StL-N	2	4	0	1	0	0	0	0	1	0	.250	.400	.250	74	-0	0			.857	-1	/S-2	-0.1
1940	StL-N	32	66	12	14	3	0	2	7	12	17	.212	.342	.348	86	-1	1			.957	-7	2-17/S-6	-0.7
1941	StL-N	45	76	9	8	2	0	0	0	15	22	.105	.253	.132	10	-9	3			.903	6	S-15,3-15/2	-0.2
1943	Bos-A	75	216	26	43	10	0	3	16	47	35	.199	.345	.287	84	-2	3	6	-3	.961	3	S-63	0.3
1944	Bos-A	57	126	21	26	5	0	0	8	23	22	.206	.329	.246	66	-5	5	2	0	.927	-5	S-41/P-6,23	-0.7
1945	Bos-A	133	473	81	132	27	1	11	51	106	81	.279	.412	.410	136	27	9	7	-2	.948	19	*S-130/2-1	5.7
1946	Det-A	155	587	105	149	24	1	8	31	103	69	.254	.369	.339	93	-2	15	9	-1	.947	-21	*S-155	-1.6
1947	Det-A	158	602	96	127	19	6	12	46	120	54	.211	.343	.322	83	-11	11	10	-3	.943	-29	*S-158	-3.6
1948	Det-A	64	198	51	52	6	0	2	18	57	20	.263	.427	.323	99	3	3	3	-1	.972	-3	2-45,3-17	0.2
1949	Det-A	94	240	38	47	9	1	1	15	61	33	.196	.359	.254	63	-10	2	8	-4	.959	-10	S-38,2-19,3	-2.1
1950	Det-A	20	7	3	0	0	0	0	1	1	3	.000	.125	.000	-64	-2	0	0	0	.000	0	/S-1,3-1	-0.2
Total	11	835	2595	442	599	105	9	39	193	546	312	.231	.366	.323	91	-11	52	45		.947	-48	S-609/2-90,3P	-3.0

■ FRED LAKE
Lake, Frederick Lovett   b: 10/16/1866, Nova Scotia, Can.   d: 11/24/31, Boston, Mass.   BR/TR, 5'10", 170 lbs.   Deb: 5/7/1891   M

YEAR	TM/L	G	AB	R	H	2B	3B	HR	RBI	BB	SO	AVG	OBP	SLG	PRO+	BR/A	SB	CS	SBR	FA	FR	G/POS	TPR
1891	Bos-N	5	7	1	1	0	0	0	0	2	4	.143	.333	.143	36	-1	0			1.000	-0	/C-4,O-1	-0.1
1894	Lou-N	16	42	8	12	2	0	1	10	11	6	.286	.474	.405	122	-1	0			.864	-3	/2-6,S-5,C	0.0
1897	*Bos-N	19	62	2	15	4	0	0	5	1		.242	.254	.306	45	-5	2			.970	-1	C-18	-0.4
1898	Pit-N	5	13	1	1	0	0	0	1	2		.077	.200	.077	-20	-2	0			1.000	-0	/1-3	-0.2
1910	Bos-N	3	1	0	0	0	0	0	0	1	0	.000	.500	.000	46	0	0			.000	-0	HM	0.0
Total	5	48	125	12	29	6	0	1	16	17	10	.232	.342	.304	68	-5	4			.930	-5	/C-27,2-6,S10	-0.7

■ STEVE LAKE
Lake, Steven Michael   b: 3/14/57, Inglewood, Cal.   BR/TR, 6'1", 190 lbs.   Deb: 4/9/83

YEAR	TM/L	G	AB	R	H	2B	3B	HR	RBI	BB	SO	AVG	OBP	SLG	PRO+	BR/A	SB	CS	SBR	FA	FR	G/POS	TPR
1983	Chi-N	38	85	9	22	4	1	1	7	2	6	.259	.284	.365	75	-3	0	0	0	1.000	4	C-32	0.2
1984	*Chi-N	25	54	4	12	4	0	2	7	0	7	.222	.236	.407	71	-2	0	0	0	.955	0	C-24	-0.1
1985	Chi-N	58	119	5	18	2	0	1	11	3	21	.151	.179	.193	4	-15	1	0	0	.995	9	C-55	-0.8
1986	Chi-N	10	19	4	8	1	0	0	4	1	2	.421	.450	.474	144	1	0	0	0	1.000	-0	C-10	0.1
	StL-N	26	49	4	12	1	0	2	10	2	5	.245	.275	.388	81	-1	0	0	0	.976	1	C-26	0.0
	Yr	36	68	8	20	2	0	2	14	3	7	.294	.324	.412	100	-0	0	0	0	.983	1	C-36	0.1
1987	*StL-N	74	179	19	45	7	2	2	19	10	18	.251	.291	.346	67	-9	0	0	0	.996	-2	C-59	-0.7
1988	StL-N	36	54	5	15	3	0	1	4	3	15	.278	.339	.389	107	1	0	0	0	.983	-1	C-19	0.1
1989	Phi-N	58	155	9	39	5	1	2	14	12	20	.252	.305	.335	83	-3	0	0	0	.990	3	C-55	-0.2
1990	Phi-N	29	80	4	20	2	0	0	6	3	12	.250	.286	.275	55	-5	0	0	0	.993	-4	C-28	-0.2
1991	Phi-N	58	158	12	36	4	1	1	11	2	26	.228	.237	.285	47	-11	0	0	0	.993	2	C-58	-0.7
1992	Phi-N	20	53	3	13	2	0	1	2	1	8	.245	.259	.340	69	-2	0	0	0	.975	0	C-17	-0.2
1993	Chi-N	44	120	11	27	6	0	5	13	4	19	.225	.250	.400	72	-5	0	0	0	.985	1	C-41	-0.2
Total	11	476	1125	89	267	41	5	18	108	43	159	.237	.269	.331	64	-56	1	0	0	.989	18	C-424	-2.1

■ AL LAKEMAN
Lakeman, Albert Wesley "Moose"   b: 12/31/18, Cincinnati, Ohio   d: 5/25/76, Spartanburg, S.C.   BR/TR, 6'2", 195 lbs.   Deb: 4/19/42   C

YEAR	TM/L	G	AB	R	H	2B	3B	HR	RBI	BB	SO	AVG	OBP	SLG	PRO+	BR/A	SB	CS	SBR	FA	FR	G/POS	TPR
1942	Cin-N	20	38	0	6	2	0	0	2	3	10	.158	.238	.184	24	-4	0			.970	3	C-17	0.0
1943	Cin-N	22	55	5	14	2	1	0	6	3	11	.255	.293	.327	80	-2	0			1.000	0	C-21	-0.2
1944	Cin-N	1	1	0	0	0	0	0	0	0	1	.000	.000	.000	-99	-0	0			.000	0	H	0.0
1945	Cin-N	76	258	22	66	9	4	8	31	17	45	.256	.304	.415	101	-1	0			.963	-11	C-74	-0.7
1946	Cin-N	23	30	0	4	0	0	0	4	2	7	.133	.188	.133	-9	-4	0			1.000	-0	/C-6	-0.5
1947	Cin-N	2	2	0	0	0	0	0	0	1	0	.000	.000	.000	-99	-1	0			.000	0	H	-0.1
	Phi-N	55	182	11	29	3	0	6	19	5	39	.159	.186	.275	22	-21	0			.995	-5	1-29,C-23	-2.6
	Yr	57	184	11	29	3	0	6	19	5	39	.158	.184	.272	20	-22	0			.995	-5	1-29,C-23	-2.7
1948	Phi-N	32	68	2	11	2	1	0	4	5	22	.162	.219	.235	23	-7	0			1.000	-2	C-22/P-1	-0.8
1949	Bos-N	3	6	0	1	0	0	0	0	1	0	.167	.286	.167	26	-1	0			1.000	1	/1-2	-0.1
1954	Det-A	5	6	0	0	0	0	0	0	0	1	.000	.000	.000	-99	-2	0	0	0	1.000	-0	/C-4	-0.1
Total	9	239	646	40	131	17	5	15	66	36	137	.203	.248	.314	55	-42	0	0		.974	-16	C-167/1-31,P	-5.0

■ TIM LAKER
Laker, Timothy John   b: 11/27/69, Encino, Cal.   BR/TR, 6'3", 195 lbs.   Deb: 8/18/92

YEAR	TM/L	G	AB	R	H	2B	3B	HR	RBI	BB	SO	AVG	OBP	SLG	PRO+	BR/A	SB	CS	SBR	FA	FR	G/POS	TPR
1992	Mon-N	28	46	8	10	3	0	0	4	2	14	.217	.250	.283	51	-3	1	1	-0	.991	5	C-28	0.3
1993	Mon-N	43	86	3	17	2	0	0	7	2	16	.198	.225	.244	24	-9	2	0	1	.987	2	C-43	-0.5
Total	2	71	132	11	27	5	1	0	11	4	30	.205	.234	.258	33	-12	3	1	0	.989	7	/C-71	-0.2

YEAR	TM/L	G	AB	R	H	2B	3B	HR	RBI	BB	SO	AVG	OBP	SLG	PRO+	BR/A	SB	CS	SBR	FA	FR	G/POS	TPR

■ DAN LALLY
Lally, Daniel J. b: 8/12/1867, Jersey City, N.J. d: 4/14/36, Milwaukee, Wis. BR/TR, 5'11.5", 210 lbs. Deb: 8/19/1891

1891	Pit-N	41	143	24	32	6	2	1	17	16	20	.224	.319	.315	87	-2	0			.839	-7	O-41	-0.9
1897	StL-N	87	355	56	99	15	5	2	42	9		.279	.310	.366	80	-12	12			.897	2	O-84/1-3	-1.3
Total	2	128	498	80	131	21	7	3	59	25	20	.263	.313	.351	82	-14	12			.886	-4	O-125/1-3	-2.2

■ RAY LAMANNO
Lamanno, Raymond Simond b: 11/17/19, Oakland, Cal. d: 2/9/94, Berkeley, Cal. BR/TR, 6', 185 lbs. Deb: 9/11/41

1941	Cin-N	1	0	0	0	0	0	0	0	0	0	—	1.000	—	197	0	0			1.000	-0	/C-1	0.0
1942	Cin-N	111	371	40	98	12	2	12	43	31	54	.264	.324	.404	113	5	0			.978	-11	*C-104	0.2
1946	Cin-N★	85	239	18	58	12	0	1	30	11	26	.243	.285	.305	70	-10	0			.974	2	C-61	-0.5
1947	Cin-N	118	413	33	106	21	3	5	50	28	39	.257	.307	.358	77	-15	0			.986	9	*C-109	0.1
1948	Cin-N	127	385	31	93	12	0	0	27	48	32	.242	.329	.273	67	-16	2			.978	-11	*C-125	-2.0
Total	5	442	1408	122	355	57	5	18	150	118	151	.252	.314	.338	82	-36	2			.980	-11	C-400	-2.2

■ BILL LAMAR
Lamar, William Harmong "Good Time Bill" b: 3/21/1897, Rockville, Md. d: 5/24/70, Rockport, Mass. BL/TR, 6'1", 185 lbs. Deb: 9/19/17

1917	NY-A	11	41	2	10	0	0	0	3	0	2	.244	.244	.244	48	-3	1			1.000	0	O-11	-0.3
1918	NY-A	28	110	12	25	3	0	0	2	6	2	.227	.267	.255	56	-6	2			.884	-2	O-27	-1.1
1919	NY-A	11	16	1	3	1	0	0	0	2	1	.188	.278	.250	48	-1	1			1.000	-1	/O-3,1-1	-0.2
	Bos-A	48	148	18	43	5	1	0	14	5	9	.291	.314	.338	88	-3	3			.922	-1	O-36	-0.8
	Yr	59	164	19	46	6	1	0	14	7	10	.280	.310	.329	83	-4	4			.926	-3	O-39/1-1	-1.0
1920	*Bro-N	24	44	5	12	4	0	0	4	0	1	.273	.273	.364	79	-1	0	0	0	1.000	-3	O-12	-0.5
1921	Bro-N	3	3	2	1	0	0	0	0	0	0	.333	.333	.333	74	-0	0	0	0	.000	-1	/O-1	-0.1
1924	Phi-A	87	367	68	121	22	5	7	48	18	21	.330	.361	.474	113	5	8	8	-2	.971	0	O-87	0.1
1925	Phi-A	138	568	85	202	39	8	3	77	21	17	.356	.379	.468	107	4	2	6	-3	.953	4	*O-131	-0.3
1926	Phi-A	116	419	62	119	17	6	5	50	18	15	.284	.315	.389	78	-15	4	5	-2	.954	-3	*O-107	-2.6
1927	Phi-A	84	324	48	97	23	3	4	47	16	10	.299	.334	.426	91	-5	4	8	-4	.952	-3	O-79	-1.6
Total	9	550	2040	303	633	114	23	19	245	86	78	.310	.339	.417	94	-24	25	27		.952	-7	O-494/1-1	-7.4

■ LAYMON LAMB
Lamb, Laymon Raymond b: 3/17/1895, Lincoln, Neb. d: 10/5/55, Fayetteville, Ark. BR/TR, 5'7", 150 lbs. Deb: 9/14/20

1920	StL-A	9	24	4	9	2	0	0	4	0	7	.375	.375	.458	116	1	0	0	1	1.000	-2	/O-7	-0.1
1921	StL-A	45	134	18	34	9	2	1	17	4	12	.254	.281	.373	62	-8	0	0	0	.942	-9	3-25/2-7,O	-1.5
Total	2	54	158	22	43	11	2	1	21	4	19	.272	.294	.386	72	-8	0	0	1	1.000	-11	/3-25,O-13,2	-1.6

■ PETE LAMER
Lamer, Pierre b: 12/1873, New York, N.Y. d: 10/24/31, Brooklyn, N.Y. TR, 5'10", 170 lbs. Deb: 9/10/02

1902	Chi-N	2	9	2	2	0	0	0	0	0		.222	.222	.222	38	-1	0			.857	-0	/C-2	-0.1
1907	Cin-N	1	2	0	0	0	0	0	0	0		.000	.000	.000	-96	-0	0			1.000	-0	/C-1	-0.1
Total	2	3	11	2	2	0	0	0	0	0		.182	.182	.182	13	-1	0			.867	-1	/C-3	-0.2

■ GENE LAMONT
Lamont, Gene William b: 12/25/46, Rockford, Ill. BL/TR, 6'1", 195 lbs. Deb: 9/2/70 MC

1970	Det-A	15	44	3	13	3	1	1	4	2	9	.295	.340	.477	122	1	0	0	0	1.000	1	C-15	0.3
1971	Det-A	7	15	2	1	0	0	0	1	0	5	.067	.067	.067	-60	-3	0	0	0	.952	2	/C-7	-0.1
1972	Det-A	1	0	0	0	0	0	0	0	0	0	—	—	—	—	0	0	0	0	1.000	-0	/C-1	0.0
1974	Det-A	60	92	9	20	4	0	3	8	7	19	.217	.273	.359	78	-3	0	0	0	.974	8	C-60	0.7
1975	Det-A	4	8	1	3	1	0	0	1	0	2	.375	.375	.500	139	0	1	0	0	.944	1	/C-4	0.2
Total	5	87	159	15	37	8	1	4	14	9	35	.233	.278	.371	80	-4	1	0	0	.977	12	/C-87	1.1

■ BOBBY LaMOTTE
LaMotte, Robert Eugene b: 2/15/1898, Savannah, Ga. d: 11/2/70, Chatham, Ga. BR/TR, 5'11", 160 lbs. Deb: 9/1/20

1920	Was-A	4	3	0	0	0	0	0	0	1	1	.000	.250	.000	-31	-1	0	0	0	.750	0	/S-1,3-1	0.0
1921	Was-A	16	41	5	8	0	0	0	2	5	0	.195	.283	.195	25	-5	0	0	0	.940	2	S-12	-0.2
1922	Was-A	68	214	22	54	10	2	1	23	15	21	.252	.307	.332	70	-10	6	1	1	.954	8	3-62/S-6	0.4
1925	StL-A	97	356	61	97	20	4	2	51	34	22	.272	.338	.368	75	-14	5	5	-2	.926	2	S-93/3-3	-0.3
1926	StL-A	36	79	11	16	4	0	0	9	11	6	.203	.300	.329	61	-5	0	0	0	.919	-2	S-30/3-1	-0.4
Total	5	221	693	99	175	34	9	3	85	66	50	.253	.320	.341	69	-33	11	6	-0	.927	10	S-142/3-67	-0.5

■ KEITH LAMPARD
Lampard, Christopher Keith b: 12/20/45, Warrington, England BL/TR, 6'2", 197 lbs. Deb: 9/15/69

1969	Hou-N	9	12	2	3	0	0	1	2	0	3	.250	.250	.500	108	0	0	0	0	1.000	1	/O-1	0.1
1970	Hou-N	53	72	8	17	8	1	0	5	5	24	.236	.295	.375	82	-2	0	0	0	1.000	-1	O-16/1-2	-0.3
Total	2	62	84	10	20	8	1	1	7	5	27	.238	.289	.393	85	-2	0	0	0	1.000	1	/O-17,1-2	-0.2

■ TOM LAMPKIN
Lampkin, Thomas Michael b: 3/4/64, Cincinnati, Ohio BL/TR, 5'11", 180 lbs. Deb: 9/10/88

1988	Cle-A	4	4	0	0	0	0	0	0	0	1	.000	.200	.000	-38	-1	0	0	0	1.000	-1	/C-3	-0.2
1990	SD-N	26	63	4	14	0	1	1	4	4	9	.222	.269	.302	56	-4	0	1	-1	.971	1	C-20	-0.3
1991	SD-N	38	58	4	11	3	1	0	3	3	9	.190	.230	.276	40	-5	0	0	0	1.000	0	C-11	-0.4
1992	SD-N	9	17	3	4	0	0	0	0	6	1	.235	.458	.235	100	1	2	0	1	1.000	-2	/C-7,O-1	0.0
1993	Mil-A	73	162	22	32	8	0	4	25	20	26	.198	.286	.321	64	-8	7	3	0	.978	-4	C-60/O-3,D	-0.9
Total	5	150	304	33	61	11	2	5	32	34	45	.201	.283	.299	59	-17	9	4	0	.981	-5	C-101/O-4,D	-1.8

■ RICK LANCELLOTTI
Lancellotti, Richard Anthony b: 7/5/56, Providence, R.I. BL/TL, 6'3", 195 lbs. Deb: 8/27/82

1982	SD-N	17	39	2	7	2	0	0	4	2	8	.179	.220	.231	28	-4	0	0	0	1.000	-2	/1-7,O-3	-0.6
1986	SF-N	15	18	2	4	0	0	2	6	0	7	.222	.222	.556	113	0	0	0	0	1.000	1	/1-1,O-1	0.1
1990	Bos-A	4	8	0	0	0	0	0	1	0	3	.000	.000	.000	-96	-2	0	0	0	1.000	-1	/1-2	-0.2
Total	3	36	65	4	11	2	0	2	11	2	18	.169	.194	.292	35	-6	0	0	0	1.000	-0	/1-10,O-4	-0.7

■ GROVER LAND
Land, Grover Cleveland b: 9/22/1884, Frankfort, Ky. d: 7/22/58, Phoenix, Ariz. BR/TR, 6', 190 lbs. Deb: 9/2/08 C

1908	Cle-A	8	16	1	3	0	0	0	2	0		.188	.188	.188	22	-1	0			.955	-1	/C-8	-0.3
1909	Cle-A	1	4	0	2	0	0	0	1	0		.500	.500	.500	207	0	0			1.000	0	/C-1	0.1
1910	Cle-A	34	111	4	23	0	0	0	7	2		.207	.228	.207	36	-8	1			.982	5	C-33	-0.1
1911	Cle-A	35	107	6	15	1	2	0	10	3		.140	.164	.187	-2	-15	2			.961	1	C-34/1-1	-1.1
1913	Cle-A	17	47	3	11	1	0	0	9	4	1	.234	.321	.255	67	-2	1			.924	1	C-17	0.0
1914	Bro-F	102	335	24	92	6	2	0	29	12	23	.275	.306	.304	59	-20	7			.970	-0	C-97	-1.2
1915	Bro-F	96	290	25	75	13	2	0	22	6	20	.259	.279	.317	60	-17	3			.960	-6	C-81	-1.9
Total	7	293	910	62	221	21	6	0	80	27	44	.243	.271	.279	50	-64	14			.964	-2	C-271/1-1	-4.5

■ DOC LAND
Land, William Gilbert (b: Doc Burrell Land) b: 5/14/03, Binnsville, Miss. d: 4/14/86, Livingston, Ala. BL/TL, 5'11", 165 lbs. Deb: 10/6/29

| 1929 | Was-A | 1 | 3 | 0 | 0 | 0 | 0 | 0 | 0 | 1 | 0 | .000 | .250 | .000 | -30 | -1 | 0 | 0 | 0 | 1.000 | -0 | /O-1 | -0.1 |

■ KEN LANDENBERGER
Landenberger, Kenneth Henry "Red" b: 7/29/28, Lyndhurst, Ohio d: 7/28/60, Cleveland, Ohio BL/TL, 6'3", 200 lbs. Deb: 9/20/52

| 1952 | Chi-A | 2 | 5 | 0 | 1 | 0 | 0 | 0 | 0 | 0 | 2 | .200 | .200 | .200 | 11 | -1 | 0 | 0 | 0 | 1.000 | 0 | /1-1 | 0.0 |

■ RAFAEL LANDESTOY
Landestoy, Rafael Silvialdo (Santana) b: 5/28/53, Bani, D.R. BB/TR, 5'10", 165 lbs. Deb: 8/27/77 C

1977	*LA-N	15	18	6	5	0	0	0	3	2		.278	.381	.278	80	-0	2	0	1	1.000	3	/2-8,S-3	0.3
1978	Hou-N	59	218	18	58	5	1	0	9	8	23	.266	.292	.298	70	-9	7	4	-0	.980	-13	S-50/O-3,2	-1.8
1979	Hou-N	129	282	33	76	9	6	0	30	29	24	.270	.340	.344	92	-3	13	4	2	.971	-2	*2-114/S-3	0.2
1980	*Hou-N	149	393	40	97	13	8	1	27	31	37	.247	.307	.328	84	-9	23	12	-0	.991	-6	2-94,S-65/3	-0.7
1981	Hou-N	35	74	6	11	1	0	0	4	16	9	.149	.300	.189	43	-5	4	1	1	.966	-4	2-31	-0.8
	Cin-N	12	11	2	2	0	0	0	1	0	0	.182	.250	.182	24	-1	0	0	0	1.000	-0	/2-3	-0.1

YEAR	TM/L	G	AB	R	H	2B	3B	HR	RBI	BB	SO	AVG	OBP	SLG	PRO+	BR/A	SB	CS	SBR	FA	FR	G/POS	TPR
	Yr	47	85	8	13	1	1	0	5	17	9	.153	.294	.188	40	-6	5	1	1	.967	-5	2-34	-0.9
1982	Cin-N	73	111	11	21	3	0	1	9	8	14	.189	.250	.243	38	-9	2	0	1	1.000	4	3-21,2-16/OS	-0.5
1983	Cin-N	7	5	0	0	0	0	0	0	0	0	.000	.000	.000	-97	-1	0	0	0	1.000	-1	/1-2,3-1,O	-0.2
	*LA-N	64	64	6	11	1	1	1	1	3	8	.172	.209	.266	31	-6	0	2	-1	1.000	2	2-14,3-10,O/S	-0.5
	Yr	71	69	6	11	1	1	1	1	3	8	.159	.194	.246	21	-7	0	2	-1	1.000	1	2-14,3-11,0/1S	-0.7
1984	LA-N	53	54	10	10	0	0	1	2	1	6	.185	.200	.241	24	-6	2	1	0	.886	1	2-14,3-11/O	-0.4
Total	8	596	1230	134	291	32	17	4	83	100	123	.237	.297	.300	70	-50	54	24	2	.976	-17	2-296,S-124/301	-4.5

■ JIM LANDIS

Landis, James Henry b: 3/9/34, Fresno, Cal. BR/TR, 6'1", 180 lbs. Deb: 4/16/57

YEAR	TM/L	G	AB	R	H	2B	3B	HR	RBI	BB	SO	AVG	OBP	SLG	PRO+	BR/A	SB	CS	SBR	FA	FR	G/POS	TPR
1957	Chi-A	96	274	38	58	11	3	2	16	45	61	.212	.329	.296	72	-10	14	4	2	.985	4	O-90	-0.9
1958	Chi-A	142	523	72	145	23	7	15	64	52	80	.277	.352	.434	117	12	19	7	2	.986	6	*O-142	1.2
1959	*Chi-A	149	515	78	140	26	7	5	60	78	68	.272	.376	.379	109	10	20	9	1	.993	16	*O-148	1.8
1960	Chi-A	148	494	89	125	25	6	10	49	80	84	.253	.367	.389	106	6	23	6	3	.985	13	*O-147	1.5
1961	Chi-A	140	534	87	151	18	8	22	85	65	71	.283	.365	.470	123	18	19	5	3	.988	19	*O-139	3.1
1962	Chi-A★	149	534	82	122	21	6	15	61	80	105	.228	.339	.375	92	-5	19	7	2	.995	10	*O-144	-0.2
1963	Chi-A	133	396	56	89	6	6	13	45	47	75	.225	.316	.369	93	-3	8	6	-1	.993	1	*O-124	-1.0
1964	Chi-A	106	298	30	62	8	4	1	18	36	64	.208	.306	.272	64	-14	5	0	2	.995	-4	*O-101	-2.1
1965	KC-A	118	364	46	87	15	1	3	36	57	84	.239	.347	.310	90	-3	8	3	1	.985	6	*O-108	-0.2
1966	Cle-A	85	158	23	35	5	1	3	14	20	25	.222	.317	.323	84	-3	2	1	0	1.000	-11	O-61	-1.7
1967	Det-A	25	48	4	10	0	0	2	4	7	12	.208	.309	.333	87	-1	0	2	-1	.952	0	O-22	-0.3
	Bos-A	5	7	1	1	0	0	1	1	1	3	.143	.250	.571	126	0	0	0	0	1.000	-1	/O-5	-0.1
	Yr	30	55	5	11	0	0	3	5	8	15	.200	.302	.364	92	-0	0	2	-1	.960	-1	O-17	-0.3
	Hou-N	50	143	19	36	11	1	1	14	20	35	.252	.348	.364	107	2	2	1	0	1.000	-1	O-44	-0.1
Total	11	1346	4288	625	1061	169	50	93	467	588	767	.247	.346	.375	100	10	139	51	11	.989	58	*O-1265	1.1

■ KEN LANDREAUX

Landreaux, Kenneth Francis b: 12/22/54, Los Angeles, Cal. BL/TR, 5'10", 165 lbs. Deb: 9/11/77

YEAR	TM/L	G	AB	R	H	2B	3B	HR	RBI	BB	SO	AVG	OBP	SLG	PRO+	BR/A	SB	CS	SBR	FA	FR	G/POS	TPR
1977	Cal-A	23	76	6	19	5	1	0	5	5	15	.250	.296	.342	76	-3	1	1	-0	.970	5	O-22	0.1
1978	Cal-A	93	260	37	58	7	5	5	23	20	20	.223	.284	.346	79	-8	7	3	0	.986	-7	O-83/D-1	-1.8
1979	Min-A	151	564	81	172	27	5	15	83	37	57	.305	.352	.450	110	8	10	3	1	.981	-8	*O-147	-0.6
1980	Min-A★	129	484	56	136	23	11	7	62	39	42	.281	.337	.417	98	-2	8	6	-1	.976	-9	*O-120/D-6	-1.7
1981	*LA-N	99	390	48	98	16	4	7	41	25	42	.251	.298	.367	91	-6	18	4	3	1.000	-4	*O-95	-1.1
1982	LA-N	129	461	71	131	23	7	7	50	39	54	.284	.345	.410	113	8	31	10	3	.986	2	*O-117	1.1
1983	*LA-N	141	481	63	135	25	3	17	66	34	52	.281	.331	.451	115	8	30	11	2	.990	-2	*O-137	0.5
1984	LA-N	134	438	39	110	11	5	11	47	29	35	.251	.299	.374	89	-7	10	9	-2	.986	-16	*O-129	-3.1
1985	*LA-N	147	482	70	129	26	2	12	50	33	37	.268	.316	.405	103	1	15	5	2	.975	-7	*O-140	-1.0
1986	LA-N	103	283	34	74	13	2	4	29	22	39	.261	.317	.364	94	-3	10	5	0	.955	-5	O-85	-1.1
1987	LA-N	115	182	17	37	4	0	6	23	16	28	.203	.271	.324	58	-11	5	3	-0	.951	-6	O-63	-1.9
Total	11	1264	4101	522	1099	180	45	91	479	299	421	.268	.321	.400	99	-15	145	60	8	.981	-57	*O-1138/D-7	-10.6

■ HOBIE LANDRITH

Landrith, Hobert Neal b: 3/16/30, Decatur, Ill. BL/TR, 5'10", 170 lbs. Deb: 7/30/50 C

YEAR	TM/L	G	AB	R	H	2B	3B	HR	RBI	BB	SO	AVG	OBP	SLG	PRO+	BR/A	SB	CS	SBR	FA	FR	G/POS	TPR
1950	Cin-N	4	14	1	3	0	0	0	2	1	1	.214	.313	.214	41	-1	0			1.000	-1	/C-4	-0.2
1951	Cin-N	4	13	3	5	1	0	0	0	1	1	.385	.429	.462	137	1	0	0	0	1.000	1	/C-4	0.2
1952	Cin-N	15	50	1	13	4	0	0	4	0	4	.260	.260	.340	65	-2	0	1	-1	1.000	0	C-14	-0.2
1953	Cin-N	52	154	15	37	3	1	3	16	12	8	.240	.299	.331	64	-8	2	0	1	.985	4	C-47	-0.5
1954	Cin-N	48	81	12	16	0	0	5	14	18	14	.198	.343	.383	86	-1	1	0	0	.986	4	C-42	0.4
1955	Cin-N	43	87	9	22	3	0	4	7	10	14	.253	.330	.425	93	-1	0	1	-1	1.000	4	C-27	0.3
1956	Chi-N	111	312	22	69	10	3	4	32	39	38	.221	.310	.311	69	-13	0	2	-1	.975	-3	C-99	-1.3
1957	StL-N	75	214	18	52	6	0	3	26	25	27	.243	.322	.313	70	-8	2	1	-1	.987	5	C-67	-0.2
1958	StL-N	70	144	9	31	4	0	3	13	26	21	.215	.335	.306	68	-6	0	1	-1	.992	2	C-45	-0.2
1959	SF-N	109	283	30	71	14	0	3	29	43	23	.251	.350	.332	85	-5	0	4	-2	.992	7	*C-109	0.5
1960	SF-N	71	190	18	46	10	0	1	20	23	11	.242	.324	.311	79	-5	1	1	-0	.966	-5	C-70	-0.7
1961	SF-N	43	71	11	17	4	0	2	10	12	7	.239	.349	.380	97	-0	0	0	0	.985	2	C-30	0.2
1962	NY-N	23	45	6	13	0	0	1	7	8	3	.289	.396	.422	118	1	0	0	0	.968	-1	C-21	0.1
	Bal-A	60	167	18	37	4	1	4	17	19	9	.222	.305	.329	75	-6	0	0	0	.982	5	C-60	0.1
1963	Bal-A	2	1	0	0	0	0	0	0	0	0	.000	.000	.000	-99	-0	0	0	0	1.000	-0	/C-1	0.0
	Was-A	42	103	6	18	3	0	1	7	15	12	.175	.280	.233	46	-7	0	0	0	.978	2	C-37	-0.5
	Yr	44	104	6	18	3	0	1	7	15	12	.173	.277	.231	44	-7	0	0	0	.978	2	C-38	-0.5
Total	14	772	1929	179	450	69	5	34	203	253	188	.233	.323	.327	76	-63	5	12		.983	22	C-677	-2.0

■ CED LANDRUM

Landrum, Cedric Bernard b: 9/3/63, Butler, Ala. BL/TR, 5'7", 167 lbs. Deb: 5/28/91

YEAR	TM/L	G	AB	R	H	2B	3B	HR	RBI	BB	SO	AVG	OBP	SLG	PRO+	BR/A	SB	CS	SBR	FA	FR	G/POS	TPR
1991	Chi-N	56	86	28	20	2	1	0	6	10	18	.233	.313	.279	65	-4	27	5	5	.968	-9	O-44	-0.9
1993	NY-N	22	19	2	5	1	0	0	1	0	5	.263	.263	.316	55	-1	0	0	0	.000	-1	/O-3	-0.2
Total	2	78	105	30	25	3	1	0	7	10	23	.238	.304	.286	63	-5	27	5	5	.968	-11	/O-47	-1.1

■ DON LANDRUM

Landrum, Donald Leroy b: 2/16/36, Santa Rosa, Cal. BL/TR, 6', 180 lbs. Deb: 9/28/57

YEAR	TM/L	G	AB	R	H	2B	3B	HR	RBI	BB	SO	AVG	OBP	SLG	PRO+	BR/A	SB	CS	SBR	FA	FR	G/POS	TPR
1957	Phi-N	2	7	1	1	1	0	0	0	2	1	.143	.333	.286	71	-0	0	0	0	1.000	1	/O-2	0.0
1960	StL-N	13	49	7	12	0	1	2	3	4	6	.245	.315	.408	88	-1	3	0	1	1.000	-0	O-13	-0.1
1961	StL-N	28	66	5	11	2	0	0	3	5	14	.167	.225	.242	22	-7	1	0	0	1.000	-3	O-25/2-1	-1.1
1962	StL-N	32	35	11	11	0	0	0	3	4	2	.314	.385	.314	82	-1	2	0	1	1.000	-6	O-26	-0.7
	Chi-N	83	238	29	67	5	2	1	15	30	31	.282	.369	.332	87	-3	9	2	2	.969	-1	O-59	-0.6
	Yr	115	273	40	78	5	2	1	18	34	33	.286	.371	.330	85	-4	11	2	2	.973	-7	O-85	-1.3
1963	Chi-N	84	227	27	55	4	1	1	10	13	42	.242	.295	.282	64	-10	6	3	0	.972	-4	O-57	-1.9
1964	Chi-N	11	11	2	0	0	0	0	0	1	2	.000	.083	.000	-71	-2	0	0	0	1.000	1	/O-1	-0.2
1965	Chi-N	131	425	60	96	20	4	6	34	36	84	.226	.301	.334	77	-13	14	8	-1	.988	1	*O-115	-1.8
1966	SF-N	72	102	9	19	4	0	1	7	9	18	.186	.259	.255	42	-8	1	1	-0	.968	-5	O-54	-1.5
Total	8	456	1160	151	272	36	8	12	75	104	200	.234	.308	.310	69	-45	36	14	2	.982	-16	O-352/2-1	-7.9

■ JESSE LANDRUM

Landrum, Jesse Glenn b: 7/31/12, Crockett, Tex. d: 6/27/83, Beaumont, Tex. BR/TR, 5'11.5", 175 lbs. Deb: 4/26/38

YEAR	TM/L	G	AB	R	H	2B	3B	HR	RBI	BB	SO	AVG	OBP	SLG	PRO+	BR/A	SB	CS	SBR	FA	FR	G/POS	TPR
1938	Chi-A	4	6	0	0	0	0	0	1	0	2	.000	.000	.000	-98	-2	0	0	0	1.000	-1	/2-3	-0.2

■ TITO LANDRUM

Landrum, Terry Lee b: 10/25/54, Joplin, Mo. BR/TR, 5'11", 175 lbs. Deb: 7/23/80

YEAR	TM/L	G	AB	R	H	2B	3B	HR	RBI	BB	SO	AVG	OBP	SLG	PRO+	BR/A	SB	CS	SBR	FA	FR	G/POS	TPR
1980	StL-N	35	77	6	19	2	2	0	7	6	17	.247	.310	.325	75	-3	3	2	-0	.976	-5	O-29	-0.9
1981	StL-N	81	119	13	31	5	4	0	10	6	14	.261	.302	.370	87	-2	4	2	0	1.000	-13	O-67	-1.8
1982	StL-N	79	72	12	20	3	0	2	14	8	18	.278	.358	.403	111	1	0	1	-1	1.000	5	O-56	0.5
1983	StL-N	6	5	0	1	0	1	0	1	0	2	.200	.333	.600	154	0	1	0	0	1.000	-2	/O-5	-0.1
	*Bal-A	26	42	8	13	2	0	1	4	1	11	.310	.326	.429	108	0	0	2	-1	1.000	-6	O-26	-0.2
1984	StL-N	105	173	21	47	9	1	3	26	10	27	.272	.311	.387	98	-1	3	4	-2	.979	-21	O-88	-2.7
1985	*StL-N	85	161	21	45	8	2	4	21	19	30	.280	.356	.429	119	4	1	4	-2	1.000	-11	O-73	-1.0
1986	StL-N	96	205	24	43	7	1	2	17	20	41	.210	.283	.283	57	-12	1	4	-2	.993	-4	O-23/1-1	-1.8
1987	StL-N	30	50	5	10	1	0	1	4	3	16	.200	.298	.320	39	-4	1	0	-0	1.000	-4	O-31	-0.7
	LA-N	51	67	8	16	3	0	1	6	7	14	.239	.282	.328	63	-4	1	0	-1	.971	-5	O-31	-0.9
	Yr	81	117	13	26	4	0	1	10	10	30	.222	.289	.282	53	-7	2	0	-1	.987	-7	O-54/1-1	-1.6
1988	Bal-A	13	24	2	3	0	1	0	4	2	6	.125	.250	.208	31	-2	0	0	0	1.000	-0	O-12/D-1	-0.5
Total	9	607	995	120	248	40	12	13	111	85	196	.249	.312	.353	84	-22	17	18	-6	.992	-65	O-488/D-1,1	-10.6

YEAR	TM/L	G	AB	R	H	2B	3B	HR	RBI	BB	SO	AVG	OBP	SLG	PRO+	BR/A	SB	CS	SBR	FA	FR	G/POS	TPR
■ CHAPPY LANE			Lane, George M.		b: Pittsburgh, Pa.			BR , 165 lbs.			Deb: 5/16/1882												
1882	Pit-a	57	214	26	38	8	2	3		5		.178	.196	.276	60	-8				.974	5	1-43,O-13/C	-0.7
1884	Tol-a	57	215	26	49	9	5	1		2		.228	.242	.330	82	-5				.948	4	1-46/O-9,3C	-0.6
Total	2	114	429	52	87	17	7	4		7		.203	.219	.303	72	-13				.961	9	/1-89,O-22,C3	-1.3
■ HUNTER LANE			Lane, James Hunter "Dodo"		b: 7/20/1900, Pulaski, Tenn.			BR/TR, 5'11", 165 lbs.			Deb: 5/13/24												
1924	Bos-N	7	15	0	1	0	0	0	0	1	1	.067	.125	.067	-49	-3	0	0	0	.909	-1	/3-4,2-1	-0.4
■ MARVIN LANE			Lane, Marvin		b: 1/18/50, Sandersville, Ga.			BR/TR, 5'11", 180 lbs.			Deb: 9/4/71												
1971	Det-A	8	14	0	2	0	0	0	1	1	3	.143	.143	.143	-1	-2	0	0	0	1.000	-1	/O-6	-0.3
1972	Det-A	8	6	2	0	0	0	0	0	0	1	.000	.000	.000	-97	-1	0	0	0	1.000	-1	/O-3	-0.2
1973	Det-A	6	8	2	2	0	0	1	2	2	2	.250	.400	.625	173	1	0	0	0	1.000	-1	/O-4	0.0
1974	Det-A	50	103	16	24	4	1	2	9	19	24	.233	.352	.350	99	0	2	0	1	.986	-3	O-46/D-1	-0.3
1976	Det-A	18	48	3	9	1	0	0	5	6	11	.188	.278	.208	42	-3	0	0	0	.960	-2	O-15	-0.6
Total	5	90	179	23	37	5	1	3	17	28	42	.207	.314	.296	74	-5	2	0	1	.983	-8	/O-74,D-1	-1.4
■ DICK LANE			Lane, Richard Harrison		b: 6/28/27, Highland Park, Mich.			BR/TR, 5'11", 178 lbs.			Deb: 6/20/49												
1949	Chi-A	12	42	4	5	0	0	0	4	5	3	.119	.213	.119	-11	-7	0	1	-1	1.000	1	O-11	-0.7
■ DON LANG			Lang, Donald Charles		b: 3/15/15, Selma, Cal.			BR/TR, 6', 175 lbs.			Deb: 7/4/38												
1938	Cin-N	21	50	5	13	3	1	1	11	2	7	.260	.288	.420	95	-1	0			.976	2	3-15/2-1,S	0.1
1948	StL-N	117	323	30	87	14	1	4	31	47	38	.269	.364	.356	90	-3	2			.964	9	3-95/2-2	0.5
Total	2	138	373	35	100	17	2	5	42	49	45	.268	.355	.365	91	-4	2			.966	10	3-110/2-3,S	0.6
■ BILL LANGE			Lange, William Alexander "Little Eva"		b: 6/6/1871, San Francisco, Cal.		d: 7/23/50, San Francisco, Cal.		BR/TR, 6'1.5", 190 lbs.			Deb: 4/27/1893											
1893	Chi-N	117	469	92	132	8	7	8	88	52	20	.281	.358	.380	97	-2	47			.888	2	2-57,O-40/3SC	0.1
1894	Chi-N	111	442	84	145	16	6	6	90	56	18	.328	.405	.446	100	-0	65			.910	4	*O-109/S-2,3	-0.3
1895	Chi-N	123	478	120	186	27	16	10	98	55	24	.389	.456	.575	155	38	67			.924	10	*O-123	3.1
1896	Chi-N	122	469	114	153	21	16	4	92	65	24	.326	.414	.465	126	19	84			.932	10	*O-121/C-1	1.6
1897	Chi-N	118	479	119	163	24	14	5	83	48		.340	.406	.480	128	19	**73**			.946	2	*O-118	1.1
1898	Chi-N	113	442	79	141	16	11	5	69	36		.319	.377	.439	134	18	22			.970	10	*O-111/1-2	1.9
1899	Chi-N	107	416	81	135	21	7	1	58	38		.325	.382	.416	122	13	41			.976	12	O-94,1-14	1.6
Total	7	811	3195	689	1055	133	80	39	578	350	86	.330	.401	.459	124	105	399			.942	50	O-716/2-57,1S3C	9.1
■ SAM LANGFORD			Langford, Elton		b: 5/21/1899, Briggs, Tex.		d: 7/31/93, Plainview, Tex.		BL/TR, 6', 180 lbs.			Deb: 4/13/26											
1926	Bos-A	1	1	0	0	0	0	0	0	0	0	.000	.000	.000	-99	-0	0	0	0	.000	0	H	0.0
1927	Cle-A	20	67	10	18	5	0	1	7	5	7	.269	.347	.388	90	-1	0	1	-1	1.000	-2	O-20	-0.5
1928	Cle-A	110	427	50	118	17	8	4	50	21	35	.276	.312	.382	81	-13	3	7	-3	.972	-8	*O-107	-3.1
Total	3	131	495	61	136	22	8	5	57	26	42	.275	.316	.382	81	-14	3	8	-4	.976	-11	O-127	-3.6
■ BOB LANGSFORD			Langsford, Robert William (b: Robert Hugo Lankswert)		b: 8/5/1865, Louisville, Ky.		d: 1/10/07, Louisville, Ky.		BR/TR,			Deb: 6/18/1899											
1899	Lou-N	1	4	0	0	0	0	0	0	0		.000	.000	.000	-99	-1	0			1.000	-0	/S-1	-0.1
■ HAL LANIER			Lanier, Harold Clifton		b: 7/4/42, Denton, N.C.		BR/TR, 6'2", 180 lbs.		Deb: 6/18/64	FMC													
1964	SF-N	98	383	40	105	16	3	2	28	5	44	.274	.284	.347	75	-13	2	1	0	.979	10	2-98/S-3	0.6
1965	SF-N	159	522	41	118	15	9	0	39	21	67	.226	.256	.289	52	-33	2	1	0	.976	-5	*2-158/S-1	-2.7
1966	SF-N	149	459	37	106	14	2	3	37	16	49	.231	.257	.290	50	-31	1	0	0	.991	28	*2-112,S-41	0.8
1967	SF-N	151	525	37	112	16	3	0	42	16	61	.213	.239	.255	42	-39	2	2	-1	.974	29	*S-137,2-34	0.2
1968	SF-N	151	486	37	100	14	1	0	27	12	57	.206	.225	.239	39	-36	2	2	-1	**.979**	14	*S-150	-0.8
1969	SF-N	150	495	37	113	9	1	0	35	25	68	.228	.265	.251	46	-36	0	1	-1	.969	**29**	*S-150	0.8
1970	SF-N	134	438	33	101	13	1	2	41	21	41	.231	.266	.279	47	-33	1	2	-1	.967	13	*S-130/2-4,1	-0.7
1971	*SF-N	109	206	21	48	8	0	1	13	15	26	.233	.285	.286	63	-10	0	0	0	.957	5	3-83,2-13/S1	-0.4
1972	NY-A	60	103	5	22	3	0	0	6	2	13	.214	.236	.243	44	-7	1	2	-1	.973	4	3-47/S-9,2	0.1
1973	NY-A	35	86	9	18	3	0	0	5	3	10	.209	.244	.244	39	-7	0	0	0	.960	1	S-26/2-8,3	-0.4
Total	10	1196	3703	297	843	111	20	8	273	136	436	.228	.256	.275	50	-245	11	11	-3	.971	132	S-655,2-430,3/1	-2.5
■ RIMP LANIER			Lanier, Lorenzo		b: 10/19/48, Tuskegee, Ala.		BL/TR, 5'8", 150 lbs.			Deb: 9/11/71													
1971	Pit-N	6	4	0	0	0	0	0	0	1	1	.000	.200	.000	-39	-1	0	0	0	.000	0	H	-0.1
■ RAY LANKFORD			Lankford, Raymond Lewis		b: 6/5/67, Los Angeles, Cal.		BL/TL, 5'11", 180 lbs.			Deb: 8/21/90													
1990	StL-N	39	126	12	36	10	1	3	12	13	27	.286	.353	.452	119	3	8	2	1	.989	2	O-35	0.6
1991	StL-N	151	566	83	142	23	**15**	9	69	41	114	.251	.303	.392	93	-6	44	20	1	.984	11	*O-149	0.3
1992	StL-N	153	598	87	175	40	6	20	86	72	147	.293	.373	.480	144	35	42	24	-2	.996	10	*O-153	4.3
1993	StL-N	127	407	64	97	17	3	7	45	81	111	.238	.366	.346	95	0	14	14	-4	.978	3	*O-121	-0.4
1994	StL-N	109	416	89	111	25	5	19	57	58	113	.267	.362	.488	121	14	11	10	-3	.978	3	*O-104	1.2
Total	5	579	2113	335	561	115	30	58	269	265	512	.265	.351	.431	115	46	119	70	-6	.985	29	O-562	6.0
■ RED LANNING			Lanning, Lester Alfred		b: 5/13/1895, Harvard, Ill.		d: 6/13/62, Bristol, Conn.		BL/TL, 5'9", 165 lbs.			Deb: 6/20/16											
1916	Phi-A	19	33	5	6	2	0	0	1	10	9	.182	.372	.242	89	0	0			.909	-4	/O-9,P-6	-0.4
■ CARNEY LANSFORD			Lansford, Carney Ray		b: 2/7/57, San Jose, Cal.		BR/TR, 6'2", 195 lbs.		Deb: 4/8/78	F													
1978	Cal-A	121	453	63	133	23	2	8	52	31	67	.294	.344	.406	115	8	20	9	1	.942	-26	*3-117/S-2,D	-1.9
1979	*Cal-A	157	654	114	188	30	5	19	79	39	115	.287	.330	.436	108	6	20	8	1	**.983**	-24	*3-157	-1.8
1980	Cal-A	151	602	87	157	27	3	15	80	50	93	.261	.317	.390	95	-5	14	5	1	.955	-24	*3-150	-3.0
1981	Bos-A	102	399	61	134	23	3	4	52	34	28	**.336**	.391	.439	131	16	15	10	-2	.951	-0	3-86,D-16	1.3
1982	Bos-A	128	482	65	145	28	4	11	63	46	48	.301	.364	.444	114	9	9	4	0	.968	-13	*3-114,D-13	-0.6
1983	Oak-A	80	299	43	92	16	2	10	45	22	33	.308	.361	.475	136	14	8	4	-8	.957	-5	3-78/S-1	0.4
1984	Oak-A	151	597	70	179	31	5	14	74	40	62	.300	.347	.439	124	18	9	3	1	.957	-8	*3-151	0.9
1985	Oak-A	98	401	51	111	18	2	13	46	18	27	.277	.314	.429	109	4	2	3	-1	.976	-32	3-97	-3.1
1986	Oak-A	151	591	80	168	16	4	19	72	39	51	.284	.334	.421	112	9	16	7	1	.982	-18	*3-100,1-60/2D	-1.5
1987	Oak-A	151	554	89	160	27	4	19	76	60	44	.289	.368	.455	125	20	27	8	3	**.980**	-3	*3-142,1-17/D	1.7
1988	*Oak-A★	150	556	80	155	20	2	7	57	35	35	.279	.329	.360	96	-3	29	8	4	**.979**	-12	*3-143/1-9,2D	-1.2
1989	*Oak-A	148	551	81	185	28	2	2	52	51	25	.336	.401	.405	132	26	37	15	2	.957	-26	*3-136,1-15/D	0.2
1990	Oak-A	134	507	58	136	15	1	3	50	45	50	.268	.335	.320	88	-7	16	14	-4	**.970**	-21	*3-126/1-5,D	-3.2
1991	Oak-A	5	16	0	1	0	0	0	1	0	2	.063	.063	.063	-69	-2	1	0	0	1.000	-1	/3-4,D-1	-0.5
1992	*Oak-A	135	496	65	130	30	1	7	75	43	39	.262	.330	.369	101	-0	7	2	1	.965	-23	*3-119,1-18/SD	-2.3
Total	15	1862	7158	1007	2074	332	40	151	874	553	719	.290	.346	.411	112	112	224	104	5	.966	-235	*3-1720,1-124/DS2	-14.6
■ JODY LANSFORD			Lansford, Joseph Dale		b: 1/15/61, San Jose, Cal.		BR/TR, 6'5", 225 lbs.		Deb: 7/31/82	F													
1982	SD-N	13	22	6	4	0	0	0	3	6	4	.182	.357	.182	58	-1	0	1	-1	.986	-1	/1-9	-0.3
1983	SD-N	12	8	1	2	0	0	0	2	0	3	.250	.250	.625	140	-0	0	0	0	1.000	0	/1-8	0.0
Total	2	25	30	7	6	0	0	0	5	6	7	.200	.333	.300	82	-1	0	1	-1	.988	-1	/1-17	-0.3
■ MIKE LANSING			Lansing, Michael Thomas		b: 4/3/68, Rawlins, Wyo.		BR/TR, 6', 180 lbs.		Deb: 4/7/93														
1993	Mon-N	141	491	64	141	29	1	3	45	46	56	.287	.354	.369	90	-6	23	5	4	.942	6	3-81,S-51,2	0.8

YEAR	TM/L	G	AB	R	H	2B	3B	HR	RBI	BB	SO	AVG	OBP	SLG	PRO+	BR/A	SB	CS	SBR	FA	FR	G/POS	TPR
1994	Mon-N	106	394	44	105	21	2	5	35	30	37	.266	.329	.368	80	-11	12	8	-1	.983	1	2-82,3-27,S	-0.8
Total	2	247	885	108	246	50	3	8	80	76	93	.278	.343	.368	85	-17	35	13	3	.947	7	3-108,2-107/S	0.0

■ PETE LAPAN
Lapan, Peter Nelson b: 6/25/1891, Easthampton, Mass d: 1/5/53, Norwalk, Cal. BR/TR, 5'7", 165 lbs. Deb: 9/16/22

YEAR	TM/L	G	AB	R	H	2B	3B	HR	RBI	BB	SO	AVG	OBP	SLG	PRO+	BR/A	SB	CS	SBR	FA	FR	G/POS	TPR
1922	Was-A	11	34	7	11	0	1	0	6	3	4	.324	.378	.441	119	1	1	0	0	.958	-0	C-11	0.2
1923	Was-A	2	2	0	0	0	0	0	0	0	0	.000	.000	.000	-99	-1	0	0	0	.000	0	H	-0.1
Total	2	13	36	7	11	1	0	1	6	3	4	.306	.359	.417	107	0	1	0	0	.958	-0	/C-11	0.1

■ RALPH LaPOINTE
LaPointe, Ralph Robert b: 1/8/22, Winooski, Vt. d: 9/13/67, Burlington, Vt. BR/TR, 5'11", 185 lbs. Deb: 4/15/47

YEAR	TM/L	G	AB	R	H	2B	3B	HR	RBI	BB	SO	AVG	OBP	SLG	PRO+	BR/A	SB	CS	SBR	FA	FR	G/POS	TPR
1947	Phi-N	56	211	33	65	7	0	1	15	17	15	.308	.362	.355	95	-1	8			.956	-10	S-54	-0.8
1948	StL-N	87	222	27	50	3	0	0	15	18	19	.225	.283	.239	40	-18	1			.965	8	2-44,S-25/3	-0.7
Total	2	143	433	60	115	10	0	1	30	35	34	.266	.322	.296	66	-19	9			.955	-2	/S-79,2-44,3	-1.5

■ FRANK LaPORTE
LaPorte, Frank Breyfogle "Pot" b: 2/6/1880, Uhrichsville, Ohio d: 9/25/39, Newcomerstown, O. BR/TR, 5'8", 175 lbs. Deb: 9/29/05

YEAR	TM/L	G	AB	R	H	2B	3B	HR	RBI	BB	SO	AVG	OBP	SLG	PRO+	BR/A	SB	CS	SBR	FA	FR	G/POS	TPR
1905	NY-A	11	40	4	16	1	0	1	12	1		.400	.415	.500	170	3	1			.918	-3	2-11	0.0
1906	NY-A	123	454	60	120	23	9	2	54	22		.264	.300	.368	99	-2	10			.904	-5	*3-114/2-5,O	-0.4
1907	NY-A	130	470	56	127	20	11	0	48	27		.270	.317	.360	107	3	10			.896	-10	3-64,O-63/1	-0.9
1908	Bos-A	62	156	14	37	1	3	0	15	12		.237	.296	.282	86	-2	3			.950	10	2-27,3-12/O	0.8
	NY-A	39	145	7	38	3	4	1	15	8		.262	.301	.359	113	2	3			.934	-3	2-26,O-11	-0.3
	Yr	101	301	21	75	4	7	1	30	20		.249	.298	.319	98	-1	6			.942	6	2-53,O-16,3	0.5
1909	NY-A	89	309	35	92	19	3	0	31	18		.298	.340	.379	126	8	5			.938	-15	2-83	-1.0
1910	NY-A	124	432	43	114	14	6	2	67	33		.264	.321	.338	100	-0	16			.959	-11	2-79,O-23,3	-1.5
1911	StL-A	136	507	71	159	37	12	2	82	34		.314	.361	.446	130	18	4			.950	-6	*2-133/3-3	0.9
1912	StL-A	80	266	32	83	11	4	1	38	20		.312	.367	.395	122	7	7			.944	-3	2-39,O-32	0.2
	Was-A	40	136	13	42	9	1	0	17	12		.309	.365	.390	115	3	3			.939	3	2-37	0.4
	Yr	120	402	45	125	20	5	1	55	32		.311	.366	.393	120	10	10			.941	0	2-76,O-32	0.6
1913	Was-A	79	242	25	61	6	4	0	18	17	16	.252	.309	.306	78	-7	10			.952	3	3-46,2-13,O	-0.4
1914	Ind-F	133	505	86	157	27	12	4	**107**	36	36	.311	.361	.436	95	-4	15			.956	6	*2-132	0.1
1915	New-F	148	550	55	139	28	10	2	56	48	33	.253	.314	.351	82	-16	14			.960	5	*2-146	-0.9
Total	11	1194	4212	501	1185	198	79	15	560	288	85	.281	.331	.377	104	12	101			.952	-30	2-731,3-254,O/1	-3.0

■ JACK LAPP
Lapp, John Walker b: 9/10/1884, Frazer, Pa. d: 2/6/20, Philadelphia, Pa. BL/TR, 5'8", Deb: 9/11/08

YEAR	TM/L	G	AB	R	H	2B	3B	HR	RBI	BB	SO	AVG	OBP	SLG	PRO+	BR/A	SB	CS	SBR	FA	FR	G/POS	TPR
1908	Phi-A	13	35	4	5	0	1	0	1	5		.143	.268	.200	49	-2	0			.947	-3	C-13	-0.4
1909	Phi-A	21	56	8	19	3	1	0	10	3		.339	.373	.429	150	3	1			.938	1	C-19	0.6
1910	*Phi-A	71	192	18	45	4	3	0	17	20		.234	.310	.286	88	-2	0			.980	6	C-63	1.1
1911	*Phi-A	68	167	35	59	10	3	1	26	24		.353	.435	.467	154	13	4			.972	-6	C-57/1-4	1.2
1912	Phi-A	91	281	26	82	15	6	1	35	19		.292	.337	.399	114	4	3			.958	-14	C-83	-0.2
1913	*Phi-A	82	238	23	54	4	4	1	20	37	26	.227	.336	.290	85	-3	1			.968	-14	C-78/1-1	-1.1
1914	*Phi-A	69	199	22	46	7	2	0	19	31	14	.231	.338	.286	91	-1	1	4	-2	.977	-7	C-67	-0.4
1915	Phi-A	112	312	26	85	16	5	2	31	30	29	.272	.340	.375	118	6	5	2	0	.967	-4	C-89,1-12	0.9
1916	Chi-A	40	101	6	21	0	1	0	7	8	10	.208	.266	.228	48	-6	1			.989	-0	C-34	-0.5
Total	9	567	1581	168	416	59	26	5	166	177	79	.263	.340	.343	105	12	16	6		.969	-39	C-503/1-17	1.2

■ NORM LARKER
Larker, Norman Howard John b: 12/27/30, Beaver Meadows, Pa. BL/TL, 6', 200 lbs. Deb: 4/15/58

YEAR	TM/L	G	AB	R	H	2B	3B	HR	RBI	BB	SO	AVG	OBP	SLG	PRO+	BR/A	SB	CS	SBR	FA	FR	G/POS	TPR
1958	LA-N	99	253	32	70	16	5	4	29	29	21	.277	.358	.427	103	2	1	1	-0	.985	-2	O-43,1-35	-0.4
1959	*LA-N	108	311	37	90	14	1	8	49	26	25	.289	.348	.418	96	-2	0	1	-1	.990	4	1-55,O-30	-0.3
1960	LA-N★	133	440	56	142	26	3	5	78	36	24	.323	.375	.430	112	8	1	0	0	.993	4	*1-119/O-2	0.3
1961	LA-N	97	282	29	76	16	1	5	38	24	22	.270	.329	.387	82	-7	0	0	0	.995	2	1-86/O-1	-1.2
1962	Hou-N	147	506	58	133	19	5	9	63	70	47	.263	.360	.374	105	5	1	1	-0	.991	6	*1-135/O-6	0.2
1963	Mil-N	64	147	15	26	6	0	1	14	24	24	.177	.301	.238	58	-7	0	2	-1	.992	4	1-42	-0.6
	SF-N	19	14	0	1	0	0	0	0	2	2	.071	.188	.071	-22	-2	0	0	0	.929	-0	1-11	-0.3
	Yr	83	161	15	27	6	0	1	14	26	26	.168	.291	.224	51	-9	0	2	-1	.987	4	1-53	-0.9
Total	6	667	1953	227	538	97	15	32	271	211	165	.275	.351	.390	97	-3	3	5	-2	.991	17	1-483/O-82	-2.3

■ BARRY LARKIN
Larkin, Barry Louis b: 4/28/64, Cincinnati, Ohio BR/TR, 6', 185 lbs. Deb: 8/13/86

YEAR	TM/L	G	AB	R	H	2B	3B	HR	RBI	BB	SO	AVG	OBP	SLG	PRO+	BR/A	SB	CS	SBR	FA	FR	G/POS	TPR
1986	Cin-N	41	159	27	45	4	3	3	19	9	21	.283	.321	.403	94	-1	8	0	2	.976	-0	S-36/2-3	0.4
1987	Cin-N	125	439	64	107	16	2	12	43	36	52	.244	.308	.371	76	-16	21	6	3	.965	-0	*S-119	-0.3
1988	Cin-N★	151	588	91	174	32	5	12	56	41	24	.296	.350	.429	118	13	40	7	6	.960	10	*S-148	4.5
1989	Cin-N☆	97	325	47	111	14	4	4	36	20	23	.342	.383	.446	132	13	10	5	0	.976	16	S-82	3.8
1990	*Cin-N	158	614	85	185	25	6	7	67	49	49	.301	.360	.396	103	4	30	5	6	.977	20	*S-156	4.3
1991	Cin-N★	123	464	88	140	27	4	20	69	55	64	.302	.379	.506	141	26	24	6	4	.976	18	*S-119	5.8
1992	Cin-N	140	533	76	162	32	6	12	78	63	58	.304	.382	.454	132	24	15	4	2	.983	8	*S-140	4.7
1993	Cin-N★	100	384	57	121	20	3	8	51	51	33	.315	.394	.445	125	15	14	1	4	.965	-6	S-99	2.1
1994	Cin-N†	110	427	78	119	23	5	9	52	64	52	.279	.373	.419	107	6	26	2	7	**.980**	2	*S-110	2.3
Total	9	1045	3933	613	1164	193	38	87	471	388	382	.296	.364	.431	115	83	188	36	35	.973	68	*S-1009/2-3	27.6

■ ED LARKIN
Larkin, Edward Francis b: 7/1/1885, Wyalusing, Pa. d: 3/28/34, Wyalusing, Pa. BR/TR, 5'8", Deb: 10/2/09

YEAR	TM/L	G	AB	R	H	2B	3B	HR	RBI	BB	SO	AVG	OBP	SLG	PRO+	BR/A	SB	CS	SBR	FA	FR	G/POS	TPR
1909	Phi-A	2	6	0	1	0	0	0	1	1		.167	.286	.167	42	-0				.769	-2	/C-2	-0.2

■ GENE LARKIN
Larkin, Eugene Thomas b: 10/24/62, Flushing, N.Y. BB/TR, 6'3", 212 lbs. Deb: 5/21/87

YEAR	TM/L	G	AB	R	H	2B	3B	HR	RBI	BB	SO	AVG	OBP	SLG	PRO+	BR/A	SB	CS	SBR	FA	FR	G/POS	TPR
1987	*Min-A	85	233	23	62	11	2	4	28	25	31	.266	.342	.382	89	-3	1	4	-2	.989	-2	D-40,1-26	-1.0
1988	Min-A	149	505	56	135	30	2	8	70	68	55	.267	.371	.382	108	8	3	2	-0	.994	-5	D-86,1-60	-0.4
1989	Min-A	136	446	61	119	25	1	6	46	54	57	.267	.358	.368	98	0	5	2	0	.992	-7	1-67,D-41,O	-1.3
1990	Min-A	119	401	46	108	26	4	5	42	42	55	.269	.346	.392	99	0	5	3	-0	1.000	-2	O-47,D-43,1	-0.7
1991	*Min-A	98	255	34	73	14	1	2	19	30	21	.286	.364	.373	99	1	2	3	-1	.968	-10	O-47,1-39/23D	-1.4
1992	Min-A	115	337	38	83	18	1	6	42	28	43	.246	.312	.359	85	-7	7	2	1	.992	-6	1-55,O-43/D	-1.1
1993	Min-A	56	144	17	38	7	1	1	19	21	16	.264	.365	.347	92	-1	0	1	-1	1.000	-8	O-28,1-18/3D	-1.1
Total	7	758	2321	275	618	131	12	32	266	268	278	.266	.352	.374	97	-2	23	17	-3	.992	-40	1-293,D-221,O/32	-7.6

■ TERRY LARKIN
Larkin, Frank S. d: 9/16/1894, Brooklyn, N.Y. BR/TR, Deb: 5/20/1876

YEAR	TM/L	G	AB	R	H	2B	3B	HR	RBI	BB	SO	AVG	OBP	SLG	PRO+	BR/A	SB	CS	SBR	FA	FR	G/POS	TPR
1876	NY-N	1	4	0	0	0	0	0	0	0	0	.000	.000	.000	-99	-1				.500	-0	/P-1	0.0
1877	Har-N	58	228	28	52	6	5	1	18	5	23	.228	.245	.311	83	-4				.885	-1	*P-56/3-2,2	0.0
1878	Chi-N	58	226	33	65	9	4	0	32	**17**	17	.288	.337	.363	122	5				.858	-4	*P-56/O-1,3	0.1
1879	Chi-N	60	228	26	50	12	2	0	18	8	24	.219	.246	.289	71	-7				.918	-7	*P-58/O-3	-0.1
1880	Tro-N	6	20	1	3	1	0	0	1	3	4	.150	.261	.200	56	-1				1.000	-0	/P-5,O-2,S	-0.1
1884	Was-U	17	70	11	17	0	0	0		4		.243	.284	.243	46	-5				.726	-4	3-17	-0.8
	Ric-a	40	139	17	28	1	4	0		9		.201	.265	.266	75	-3				.907	-2	2-40	-0.2
Total	6	240	915	116	215	29	15	1	69	46	68	.235	.274	.303	84	-16				.884	-16	P-176/2-41,3OS	-1.1

■ HENRY LARKIN
Larkin, Henry E. "Ted" b: 1/12/1860, Reading, Pa. d: 1/31/42, Reading, Pa. BR/TR, 5'10", 175 lbs. Deb: 5/1/1884 M

YEAR	TM/L	G	AB	R	H	2B	3B	HR	RBI	BB	SO	AVG	OBP	SLG	PRO+	BR/A	SB	CS	SBR	FA	FR	G/POS	TPR
1884	Phi-a	85	326	59	90	21	9	3		15		.276	.324	.423	133	11				.856	-7	*O-85/2-2	0.2
1885	Phi-a	108	453	114	149	**37**	14	8		26		.329	.372	.525	171	34				.882	12	O-108	3.8
1886	Phi-a	139	565	133	180	**36**	16	2		59		.319	**.390**	.450	161	40	32			.866	5	*O-139	3.6
1887	Phi-a	126	497	105	154	22	12	3		48		.310	.380	.421	123	16	37			.895	3	O-93,1-23,2	1.2
1888	Phi-a	135	546	92	147	28	12	7	101	33		.269	.326	.403	134	20	20			.967	-8	*1-122,2-14	0.1

YEAR	TM/L	G	AB	R	H	2B	3B	HR	RBI	BB	SO	AVG	OBP	SLG	PRO+	BR/A	SB	CS	SBR	FA	FR	G/POS	TPR
1889	Phi-a	133	516	105	164	23	12	3	74	83	41	.318	.428	.426	145	36	11			.973	-4	*1-131/3-1,2	1.9
1890	Cle-P	125	506	93	168	32	15	5	112	65	18	.332	.420	.484	154	42	5			.978	-8	*1-125/O-1M	2.1
1891	Phi-a	133	526	94	147	27	14	10	93	66	56	.279	.376	.441	130	19	2			.974	-5	*1-111,O-23	0.6
1892	Was-N	119	464	76	130	13	7	8	96	39	21	.280	.346	.390	126	14	21			.969	1	*1-117/O-2	0.9
1893	Was-N	81	319	54	101	20	3	4	73	50	5	.317	.422	.436	131	17	1			.963	-9	1-81	0.5
Total	10	1184	4718	925	1430	259	114	53	549	484	141	.303	.380	.440	141	248	129			.971	-21	1-710,O-451/23	14.9

■ BOB LARMORE
Larmore, Robert McKahan "Red" b: 12/6/1896, Anderson, Ind. d: 1/15/64, St.Louis, Mo. BR/TR, 5'10.5", 185 lbs. Deb: 5/14/18

YEAR	TM/L	G	AB	R	H	2B	3B	HR	RBI	BB	SO	AVG	OBP	SLG	PRO+	BR/A	SB	CS	SBR	FA	FR	G/POS	TPR
1918	StL-N	4	7	0	2	0	0	0	1	0	2	.286	.286	.286	77	-0	0			.778	-1	/S-2	-0.1

■ SAM LaROQUE
LaRoque, Samuel H. J. b: 2/26/1864, St.Mathias, Que., Canada TR , 5'11", 190 lbs. Deb: 7/30/1888

YEAR	TM/L	G	AB	R	H	2B	3B	HR	RBI	BB	SO	AVG	OBP	SLG	PRO+	BR/A	SB	CS	SBR	FA	FR	G/POS	TPR
1888	Det-N	2	9	1	4	0	0	0	2	1	1	.444	.500	.444	203	1	0			.789	0	/2-2	0.1
1890	Pit-N	111	434	59	105	20	4	1	40	35	29	.242	.316	.313	95	-2	27			.925	-10	2-78,S-31/1O	-0.5
1891	Pit-N	1	4	0	0	0	0	0	0	0	1	.000	.000	.000	-99	-1	0			.714	0	/3-1	-0.1
	Lou-a	10	35	6	11	2	1	1	8	5	8	.314	.429	.514	172	3	1			.875	-3	2-10/1-1	0.0
Total	3	124	482	66	120	22	5	2	50	41	39	.249	.326	.328	101	1	28			.916	-13	/2-90,S-31,130	-0.5

■ VIC LaROSE
LaRose, Victor Raymond b: 12/23/44, Los Angeles, Cal. BR/TR, 5'11", 180 lbs. Deb: 9/13/68

YEAR	TM/L	G	AB	R	H	2B	3B	HR	RBI	BB	SO	AVG	OBP	SLG	PRO+	BR/A	SB	CS	SBR	FA	FR	G/POS	TPR
1968	Chi-N	4	2	0	0	0	0	0	0	0	1	.000	.333	.000	6	-0	0	0	0	1.000	1	/2-2,S-2	0.1

■ HARRY LaROSS
LaRoss, Harry Raymond "Spike" b: 1/2/1888, Easton, Pa. d: 3/22/54, Chicago, Ill. BR/TR, 5'11.5", 170 lbs. Deb: 6/24/14

YEAR	TM/L	G	AB	R	H	2B	3B	HR	RBI	BB	SO	AVG	OBP	SLG	PRO+	BR/A	SB	CS	SBR	FA	FR	G/POS	TPR
1914	Cin-N	22	48	7	11	1	0	0	5	2	10	.229	.260	.250	50	-3	4			.739	-6	O-20	-1.0

■ SWEDE LARSEN
Larsen, Erling Adeli b: 11/15/13, Jersey City, N.J. BR/TR, 5'11", 170 lbs. Deb: 6/17/36

YEAR	TM/L	G	AB	R	H	2B	3B	HR	RBI	BB	SO	AVG	OBP	SLG	PRO+	BR/A	SB	CS	SBR	FA	FR	G/POS	TPR
1936	Bos-N	3	1	0	0	0	0	0	0	0	0	.000	.000	.000	-99	-0	0			1.000	-0	/2-2	-0.1

■ TONY LaRUSSA
LaRussa, Anthony b: 10/4/44, Tampa, Fla. BR/TR, 6'1", 190 lbs. Deb: 5/10/63 MC

YEAR	TM/L	G	AB	R	H	2B	3B	HR	RBI	BB	SO	AVG	OBP	SLG	PRO+	BR/A	SB	CS	SBR	FA	FR	G/POS	TPR
1963	KC-A	34	44	4	11	1	1	0	1	7	12	.250	.353	.318	85	-1	0	0	0	.957	2	S-14/2-3	0.2
1968	Oak-A	5	3	0	1	0	0	0	0	0	0	.333	.333	.333	108	0	0	0	0	.000	0	H	0.0
1969	Oak-A	8	8	0	0	0	0	0	0	0	1	.000	.000	.000	-99	-2	0	0	0	.000	0	H	-0.2
1970	Oak-A	52	106	6	21	4	1	0	6	15	19	.198	.303	.255	57	-6	0	0	0	.969	-1	2-44	-0.4
1971	Oak-A	23	8	3	0	0	0	0	0	0	4	.000	.000	.000	-99	-2	0	0	0	.833	4	/2-7,S-4,3	0.2
	Atl-N	9	7	1	2	0	0	0	0	1	1	.286	.375	.286	84	-0	0	0	0	.933	0	/2-9	0.1
1973	Chi-N	1	0	1	0	0	0	0	0	0	0	—	—	—	—	0	0	0	0	.000	0	R	0.0
Total	6	132	176	15	35	5	2	0	7	23	37	.199	.295	.250	54	-11	0	0	0	.963	6	/2-63,S-18,3	-0.1

■ AL LARY
Lary, Alfred Allen b: 9/26/29, Northport, Ala. BR/TR, 6'3", 185 lbs. Deb: 9/6/54 F

YEAR	TM/L	G	AB	R	H	2B	3B	HR	RBI	BB	SO	AVG	OBP	SLG	PRO+	BR/A	SB	CS	SBR	FA	FR	G/POS	TPR
1954	Chi-N	2	2	0	1	0	0	0	0	0	1	.500	.500	.500	160	0	0	0	0	1.000	0	/P-1	0.0
1955	Chi-N	4	0	1	0	0	0	0	0	0	0					0	0	0	0	.000	0	R	0.0
1962	Chi-N	23	6	1	1	0	0	0	0	2	1	.167	.375	.167	49	-0	0	0	0	.857	-0	P-15	0.0
Total	3	29	8	2	2	0	0	0	0	2	2	.250	.400	.250	75	-0	0	0	0	.889	-0	/P-16	0.0

■ LYN LARY
Lary, Lynford Hobart "Broadway" b: 1/28/06, Armona, Cal. d: 1/9/73, Downey, Cal. BR/TR, 6', 165 lbs. Deb: 5/11/29

YEAR	TM/L	G	AB	R	H	2B	3B	HR	RBI	BB	SO	AVG	OBP	SLG	PRO+	BR/A	SB	CS	SBR	FA	FR	G/POS	TPR
1929	NY-A	80	236	48	73	9	2	5	26	24	15	.309	.381	.428	115	6	4	1	1	.943	5	3-55,S-14/2	1.4
1930	NY-A	117	464	93	134	20	8	3	52	45	40	.289	.357	.386	92	-5	14	2	3	.940	-8	*S-113	0.3
1931	NY-A	155	610	100	171	35	9	10	107	88	54	.280	.376	.416	115	15	13	10	-2	.946	9	*S-155	3.4
1932	NY-A	91	280	56	65	14	4	3	39	52	28	.232	.358	.343	87	-4	9	3	1	.941	2	S-80/1-5,230	0.5
1933	NY-A	52	127	25	28	3	3	0	13	28	17	.220	.361	.291	79	-3	2	1	0	.938	2	3-28,S-16/1O	0.1
1934	NY-A	1	0	0	0	0	0	0	0	1	0	—	1.000	—	189	0	0	0	0	.800	-0	/1-1	0.0
	Bos-A	129	419	58	101	20	4	2	54	66	51	.241	.344	.322	68	-19	12	5	1	.965	-5	*S-129	-1.5
	Yr	130	419	58	101	20	4	2	54	67	51	.241	.346	.322	68	-19	12	5	1	.965	-5	*S-129/1-1	-1.5
1935	Was-A	39	103	8	20	4	0	0	7	12	10	.194	.278	.233	35	-10	3	0	1	.953	-4	S-30	-1.1
	StL-A	93	371	78	107	25	7	2	35	64	43	.288	.396	.410	104	4	25	4	5	.962	13	S-93	2.5
	Yr	132	474	86	127	29	7	2	42	76	53	.268	.371	.371	90	-5	28	4	6	.960	9	*S-123	1.4
1936	StL-A	155	619	112	179	30	6	2	52	117	54	.289	.404	.367	89	-6	37	9	6	.956	-5	*S-155	0.6
1937	Cle-A	156	644	110	187	46	7	8	77	88	64	.290	.378	.421	100	2	18	8	1	.963	6	*S-156	1.7
1938	Cle-A	141	568	94	152	36	4	3	51	88	65	.268	.366	.361	84	-12	23	6	3	.964	-0	*S-141	0.2
1939	Cle-A	3	2	0	0	0	0	0	0	1	1	.000	.000	.000	-99	-0	0	0	0	.000	-1	/S-2	-0.1
	Bro-N	29	31	7	5	1	0	0	1	12	6	.161	.409	.258	80	-0	1			.947	1	S-12/3-7	0.2
	StL-N	34	75	11	14	3	0	0	9	16	15	.187	.330	.227	49	-5	1			.961	-6	S-30/3-3	-0.8
	Yr	63	106	18	19	4	1	0	10	28	21	.179	.356	.236	59	-5	2			.958	-4	S-42,3-10	-0.6
1940	StL-A	27	54	5	3	1	0	0	1	5	9	.056	.136	.111	-35	-9	1			.952	3	S-12/2-1	-0.9
Total	12	1302	4603	805	1239	247	56	38	526	705	470	.269	.369	.372	90	-47	162	49		.956	11	*S-1138/3-95,120	6.5

■ DON LASSETTER
Lassetter, Donald O'Neal b: 3/27/33, Newnan, Ga. BR/TR, 6'3", 200 lbs. Deb: 9/21/57

YEAR	TM/L	G	AB	R	H	2B	3B	HR	RBI	BB	SO	AVG	OBP	SLG	PRO+	BR/A	SB	CS	SBR	FA	FR	G/POS	TPR
1957	StL-N	4	13	2	2	0	1	0	0	1	3	.154	.214	.308	37	-1	0	0	0	1.000	1	/O-3	-0.1

■ JUICE LATHAM
Latham, George Warren "Jumbo" b: 9/6/1852, Utica, N.Y. d: 5/26/14, Utica, N.Y. BR/TR, 5'8", 164 lbs. Deb: 4/19/1875 M

YEAR	TM/L	G	AB	R	H	2B	3B	HR	RBI	BB	SO	AVG	OBP	SLG	PRO+	BR/A	SB	CS	SBR	FA	FR	G/POS	TPR
1875	Bos-n	16	77	23	21	4	1	0				.273	.273	.351	110	1						1-16	0.0
	NH-n	20	76	6	15	1	0	0		0		.197	.197	.211	47	-3						1-13/S-4,3M	-0.3
	Yr	36	153	29	36	5	1	0		0		.235	.235	.281	82	-2						1-29/S-4,3	-0.3
1877	Lou-N	59	278	42	81	10	6	0	22	5	6	.291	.304	.371	94	-5				.950	2	*1-59	-0.3
1882	Phi-a	74	323	47	92	10	2	0		10		.285	.306	.328	102	-1				.972	-0	*1-74,M	-0.9
1883	Lou-a	88	368	60	92	7	6	0		12		.250	.274	.302	92	-2				.956	-3	*1-67,2-14/S	-1.0
1884	Lou-a	77	308	31	52	3	3	0		8		.169	.197	.198	31	-22				.961	3	*1-76/3-1	-2.7
Total	4	298	1277	180	317	30	17	0	22	35	6	.248	.270	.298	82	-30				.960	1	1-276/2-14,S3	-4.9

■ ARLIE LATHAM
Latham, Walter Arlington "The Freshest Man On Earth"
b: 3/15/1860, W.Lebanon, N.H. d: 11/29/52, Garden City, N.Y. BR/TR, 5'8", 150 lbs. Deb: 7/5/1880 MUC

YEAR	TM/L	G	AB	R	H	2B	3B	HR	RBI	BB	SO	AVG	OBP	SLG	PRO+	BR/A	SB	CS	SBR	FA	FR	G/POS	TPR
1880	Buf-N	22	79	9	10	3	1	0	3	1	8	.127	.138	.190	10	-7				.887	-2	S-12,O-10/C	-0.8
1883	StL-a	98	406	86	96	12	7	0		18		.236	.236	.300	79	-11				.866	22	*3-98/C-1	0.9
1884	StL-a	110	474	115	130	17	12	1		19		.274	.311	.367	116	7				.864	40	*3-110/C-1	4.3
1885	*StL-a	110	485	84	100	15	3	1		18		.206	.242	.256	55	-26				.875	1	*3-109/C-2	-2.1
1886	*StL-a	134	578	152	174	18	8	0		55		.301	.368	.374	127	17	60			.827	1	*3-133/2-1	1.8
1887	*StL-a	136	627	163	198	35	10	2		45		.316	.366	.413	106	0	129			.877	2	*3-132/2-5,C	0.4
1888	*StL-a	133	570	119	151	19	5	2	31	43		.265	.325	.326	98	-4	109			.882	3	*3-133/S-1	0.1
1889	StL-a	118	512	110	126	13	3	1	49	42	30	.246	.317	.307	69	-24	69			.883	9	*3-116/2-3	-0.9
1890	Chi-P	52	214	47	49	7	2	1	20	22	22	.229	.310	.294	59	-13	32			.880	3	3-52	-0.6
	Cin-N	41	164	35	41	6	2	0	15	23	18	.250	.346	.311	92	-1	20			.853	5	3-41/O-1	0.5
1891	Cin-N	135	533	119	145	20	10	7	53	74	35	.272	.372	.386	120	15	87			.879	20	*3-135/C-1	3.7
1892	Cin-N	152	622	111	148	20	4	4	60	54	54	.238	.310	.283	81	-13	66			.883	-5	*3-142/2-9,O	-1.2
1893	Cin-N	127	531	101	150	18	6	2	49	62	20	.282	.368	.350	89	-7	57			.892	-11	*3-127	-1.3
1894	Cin-N	129	524	129	164	23	6	6	60	60	24	.313	.393	.403	99	-9	59			.860	-10	*3-127/2-2	-1.5
1895	Cin-N	112	460	93	143	14	6	2	69	42	25	.311	.375	.380	91	-6	48			.861	-16	*3-108/1-3,2	-1.6
1896	StL-N	8	35	3	7	0	0	0	5	4	3	.200	.282	.200	29	-3	2			.744	-1	/3-8,M	-0.4

YEAR	TM/L	G	AB	R	H	2B	3B	HR	RBI	BB	SO	AVG	OBP	SLG	PRO+	BR/A	SB	CS	SBR	FA	FR	G/POS	TPR
1899	Was-N	6	6	1	1	0	0	0	0	0	1	.167	.286	.167	26	-1	0			1.000	-0	/O-1,2-1	-0.1
1909	NY-N	4	2	1	0	0	0	0	0	0	0	.000	.000	.000	-99	-0	1			1.000	1	/2-2	0.0
Total	17	1627	6822	1478	1833	245	85	27	398	589	239	.269	.334	.341	91	-84	739			.870	60	*3-1571/2-24,OSC1	1.2

■ CHICK LATHERS
Lathers, Charles Ten Eyck b: 10/22/1888, Detroit, Mich. d: 7/26/71, Petoskey, Mich. BL/TR, 6', 180 lbs. Deb: 5/1/10

YEAR	TM/L	G	AB	R	H	2B	3B	HR	RBI	BB	SO	AVG	OBP	SLG	PRO+	BR/A	SB	CS	SBR	FA	FR	G/POS	TPR
1910	Det-A	41	82	4	19	2	0	0	3	8		.232	.300	.256	70	-3	0			.926	5	3-14/2-7,S	0.2
1911	Det-A	29	45	5	10	1	0	0	4	5		.222	.314	.244	54	-3	0			.867	-3	/2-9,3-8,S1	-0.5
Total	2	70	127	9	29	3	0	0	7	13		.228	.305	.252	64	-5	0			.933	2	/3-22,2-16,S1	-0.3

■ TACKS LATIMER
Latimer, Clifford Wesley b: 11/30/1877, Loveland, Ohio d: 4/24/36, Loveland, Ohio BR/TR, 6', 160 lbs. Deb: 10/1/1898

YEAR	TM/L	G	AB	R	H	2B	3B	HR	RBI	BB	SO	AVG	OBP	SLG	PRO+	BR/A	SB	CS	SBR	FA	FR	G/POS	TPR
1898	NY-N	5	17	1	5	1	0	0				.294	.294	.353	88	-0				.889	-1	/C-4,O-2	-0.1
1899	Lou-N	9	29	3	8	1	0	0	4	2		.276	.323	.310	74	-1	1			.980	3	/C-8,1-1	0.2
1900	Pit-N	4	12	1	4	1	0	0	2	0		.333	.333	.417	106	-0	0			.947	0	/C-4	0.0
1901	Bal-A	1	4	0	1	0	0	0	0	0		.250	.250	.250	37	-0	0			1.000	0	/C-1	-0.1
1902	Bro-N	8	24	0	1	0	0	0	0	0		.042	.042	.042	-74	-5	0			.947	-0	/C-8	-0.5
Total	5	27	86	5	19	3	0	0	7	2		.221	.239	.256	41	-7	1			.949	2	/C-25,O-2,1	-0.5

■ CHARLIE LAU
Lau, Charles Richard b: 4/12/33, Romulus, Mich. d: 3/18/84, Key Colony Beach, Fla. BL/TR, 6', 190 lbs. Deb: 9/12/56 C

YEAR	TM/L	G	AB	R	H	2B	3B	HR	RBI	BB	SO	AVG	OBP	SLG	PRO+	BR/A	SB	CS	SBR	FA	FR	G/POS	TPR
1956	Det-A	3	9	1	2	0	0	0	0	0	1	.222	.222	.222	18	-1	0	0	0	1.000	1	/C-3	0.0
1958	Det-A	30	68	8	10	1	2	0	6	12	15	.147	.293	.221	41	-5	0	0	0	.985	1	C-27	-0.4
1959	Det-A	2	6	0	1	0	0	0	0	0	2	.167	.167	.167	-8	-1	0	0	0	1.000	1	C-2	0.0
1960	Mil-N	21	53	4	10	2	0	0	2	6	10	.189	.271	.226	41	-4	0	0	0	1.000	5	C-16	0.1
1961	Mil-N	28	82	3	17	5	0	0	5	14	10	.207	.330	.268	65	-4	1	1	-0	.968	-3	C-25	-0.6
	Bal-A	17	47	3	8	0	0	1	4	1	3	.170	.188	.234	12	-6	0	0	0	.990	-5	C-17	-0.1
1962	Bal-A	81	197	21	58	11	2	6	37	7	11	.294	.322	.462	115	3	1	0	0	.996	-5	C-56	0.0
1963	Bal-A	29	48	4	9	2	0	0	6	1	5	.188	.204	.229	22	-5	0	0	0	.964	1	/C-8	-0.4
	KC-A	62	187	15	55	11	0	3	26	14	17	.294	.343	.401	102	1	1	0	0	.982	-11	C-50	-0.8
	Yr	91	235	19	64	13	0	3	32	15	22	.272	.316	.366	88	-4	1	0	0	.979	-9	C-58	-1.2
1964	KC-A	43	118	11	32	7	1	2	9	10	18	.271	.328	.398	98	-0	0	0	0	.990	-6	C-35	-0.5
	Bal-A	62	158	16	41	15	1	1	14	17	27	.259	.335	.386	100	0	0	0	0	.992	-3	C-47	-0.1
	Yr	105	276	27	73	22	2	3	23	27	45	.264	.332	.391	99	-0	0	0	0	.991	-9	C-82	-0.6
1965	Bal-A	68	132	15	39	5	2	2	18	17	18	.295	.376	.409	120	4	0	0	0	.989	-6	C-35	0.0
1966	Bal-A	18	12	1	6	2	1	0	5	4	1	.500	.625	.833	320	4	0	0	0	.000	0	H	0.4
1967	Bal-A	11	8	0	1	0	0	0	3	4	2	.125	.300	.250	65	-0	0	0	0	.000	0	H	-0.1
	Atl-N	52	45	3	9	1	0	1	5	4	9	.200	.265	.289	59	-2	0	0	0	.000	0	H	-0.3
Total	11	527	1170	105	298	63	6	16	140	109	150	.255	.321	.365	89	-17	3	1	0	.988	-21	C-321	-2.7

■ BILLY LAUDER
Lauder, William b: 2/23/1874, New York, N.Y. d: 5/20/33, Norwalk, Conn. BR/TR, 5'10", 160 lbs. Deb: 6/25/1898 C

YEAR	TM/L	G	AB	R	H	2B	3B	HR	RBI	BB	SO	AVG	OBP	SLG	PRO+	BR/A	SB	CS	SBR	FA	FR	G/POS	TPR
1898	Phi-N	97	361	42	95	14	7	2	67	19		.263	.300	.357	92	-5	6			.866	-17	3-97	-2.0
1899	Phi-N	151	583	74	156	17	6	3	90	34		.268	.310	.333	79	-18	15			.893	-14	*3-151	-2.7
1901	Phi-A	2	8	1	1	0	0	0	0	0		.125	.125	.125	-29	-1	0			.833	1	/3-2	-0.1
1902	NY-N	125	482	41	114	20	1	1	44	10		.237	.252	.288	67	-20	19			.907	3	*3-121/O-4	-1.8
1903	NY-N	108	395	52	111	13	0	0	53	14		.281	.307	.314	74	-14	19			.908	-7	*3-108	-1.8
Total	5	483	1829	210	477	64	14	6	254	77		.261	.292	.321	77	-58	59			.894	-33	3-479/O-4	-8.4

■ TIM LAUDNER
Laudner, Timothy Jon b: 6/7/58, Mason City, Iowa BR/TR, 6'3", 212 lbs. Deb: 8/28/81

YEAR	TM/L	G	AB	R	H	2B	3B	HR	RBI	BB	SO	AVG	OBP	SLG	PRO+	BR/A	SB	CS	SBR	FA	FR	G/POS	TPR
1981	Min-A	14	43	4	7	2	0	2	5	3	17	.163	.234	.349	62	-2	0	0	0	1.000	-1	C-12/D-2	-0.3
1982	Min-A	93	306	37	78	19	1	7	33	34	74	.255	.329	.392	95	-2	0	2	-1	.976	-15	C-93	-1.4
1983	Min-A	62	168	20	31	9	0	6	18	15	49	.185	.251	.345	60	-10	0	0	0	.986	6	C-57/D-4	-0.2
1984	Min-A	87	262	31	54	16	1	10	35	18	78	.206	.260	.389	73	-10	0	0	0	.978	9	C-81/D-2	0.2
1985	Min-A	72	164	16	39	5	0	7	19	12	45	.238	.294	.396	82	-4	0	1	-1	.969	-4	C-68/1-1	-0.7
1986	Min-A	76	193	21	47	10	0	10	29	24	56	.244	.336	.451	109	2	1	0	0	.984	-15	C-68	-0.8
1987	*Min-A	113	288	30	55	7	1	16	43	23	80	.191	.253	.389	65	-16	1	0	0	.987	-8	*C-101/1-7,D	-1.7
1988	Min-A★	117	375	38	94	18	1	13	54	36	89	.251	.318	.408	99	-1	0	0	0	.992	0	*C-109/1-3,D	0.7
1989	Min-A	100	239	24	53	11	1	6	27	25	65	.222	.295	.351	76	-8	1	0	0	.991	0	C-68,D-19,1	-0.5
Total	9	734	2038	221	458	97	5	77	263	190	553	.225	.293	.391	83	-50	3	3	-1	.984	-27	C-657/D-33,1	-4.7

■ CHUCK LAUER
Lauer, John Charles b: 1865, Pittsburgh, Pa. TR , Deb: 7/17/1884

YEAR	TM/L	G	AB	R	H	2B	3B	HR	RBI	BB	SO	AVG	OBP	SLG	PRO+	BR/A	SB	CS	SBR	FA	FR	G/POS	TPR
1884	Pit-a	13	44	5	5	0	0	0		0		.114	.114	.114	-25	-6				.938	-1	O-10/P-3,1	-0.5
1889	Pit-N	4	16	2	3	0	0	0	1	0	5	.188	.188	.188	5	-2	0			.815	1	/C-3,O-1	-0.1
1890	Chi-N	2	8	1	2	1	0	0	2	0	0	.250	.250	.375	78	-0	0			.833	0	/C-2	0.0
Total	3	19	68	8	10	1	0	0	3	0	5	.147	.147	.162	-5	-8	0			.944	-0	/O-11,C-5,P1	-0.6

■ BEN LAUGHLIN
Laughlin, Benjamin Deb: 4/28/1873

YEAR	TM/L	G	AB	R	H	2B	3B	HR	RBI	BB	SO	AVG	OBP	SLG	PRO+	BR/A	SB	CS	SBR	FA	FR	G/POS	TPR
1873	Res-n	12	50	3	12	1	0	0	6	0	0	.240	.240	.260	51	-3						2-12	-0.3

■ BILL LAUTERBORN
Lauterborn, William Bernard b: 6/9/1879, Hornell, N.Y. d: 4/19/65, Andover, N.Y. BR/TR, 5'6", 140 lbs. Deb: 9/20/04

YEAR	TM/L	G	AB	R	H	2B	3B	HR	RBI	BB	SO	AVG	OBP	SLG	PRO+	BR/A	SB	CS	SBR	FA	FR	G/POS	TPR
1904	Bos-N	20	69	7	19	2	0	0	2	1		.275	.286	.304	85	-1	1			.943	-3	2-20	-0.4
1905	Bos-N	67	200	11	37	1	1	0	9	12		.185	.238	.200	32	-17	1			.843	-7	3-29,2-23/SO	-2.4
Total	2	87	269	18	56	3	1	0	11	13		.208	.250	.227	45	-18	2			.929	-10	/2-43,3-29,SO	-2.8

■ COOKIE LAVAGETTO
Lavagetto, Harry Arthur b: 12/1/12, Oakland, Cal. d: 8/10/90, Orinda, Cal. BR/TR, 6', 170 lbs. Deb: 4/17/34 MC

YEAR	TM/L	G	AB	R	H	2B	3B	HR	RBI	BB	SO	AVG	OBP	SLG	PRO+	BR/A	SB	CS	SBR	FA	FR	G/POS	TPR
1934	Pit-N	87	304	41	67	16	3	3	46	32	39	.220	.295	.322	64	-16	6			.961	-14	2-83	-2.4
1935	Pit-N	78	231	27	67	9	4	0	19	18	15	.290	.341	.364	87	-4	1			.951	-11	2-42,3-15	-1.2
1936	Pit-N	60	197	21	48	15	2	2	26	15	13	.244	.300	.371	78	-6	0			.951	-7	2-37,3-13/S	-0.5
1937	Bro-N	149	503	64	142	26	6	8	70	74	41	.282	.375	.406	110	9	13			.949	-7	*2-100,3-45	1.0
1938	Bro-N☆	137	487	68	133	34	6	6	79	68	31	.273	.364	.405	109	7	15			.929	-11	*3-132/2-4	-0.2
1939	Bro-N☆	153	587	93	176	28	5	10	87	78	30	.300	.387	.416	112	12	14			.948	-5	*3-149	0.9
1940	Bro-N★	118	448	56	115	21	3	4	43	70	32	.257	.361	.344	90	-4	4			.932	-14	*3-116	-1.5
1941	*Bro-N★	132	441	75	122	24	7	1	78	80	21	.277	.388	.370	109	9	7			.938	-20	*3-120	-0.9
1946	Bro-N	88	242	36	57	9	1	3	27	38	17	.236	.339	.318	86	-3	3			.927	-5	3-67	-0.8
1947	*Bro-N	41	69	6	18	1	0	3	11	12	5	.261	.370	.406	102	0	0			.961	3	3-18/1-3	0.3
Total	10	1043	3509	487	945	183	37	40	486	485	244	.269	.360	.377	98	4	63			.936	-85	3-675,2-266/1S	-5.3

■ MIKE LaVALLIERE
LaValliere, Michael Eugene b: 8/18/60, Charlotte, N.C. BL/TR, 5'9", 190 lbs. Deb: 9/9/84

YEAR	TM/L	G	AB	R	H	2B	3B	HR	RBI	BB	SO	AVG	OBP	SLG	PRO+	BR/A	SB	CS	SBR	FA	FR	G/POS	TPR
1984	Phi-N	6	7	0	0	0	0	0	0	2	0	.000	.222	.000	-32	-1	0	0	0	1.000	2	/C-6	0.1
1985	StL-N	12	34	2	5	1	0	0	6	7	3	.147	.293	.176	34	-3	0	0	0	1.000	-2	C-12	-0.4
1986	StL-N	110	303	18	71	10	2	3	30	36	37	.234	.318	.310	74	-10	0	1	-1	.988	2	*C-108	-0.3
1987	Pit-N	121	340	33	102	19	0	1	36	43	32	.300	.380	.365	98	1	0	0	0	.992	8	*C-112	1.5
1988	Pit-N	120	352	24	92	18	0	2	47	50	34	.261	.356	.330	99	2	3	2	-0	.987	-0	*C-114	1.0
1989	Pit-N	68	190	15	60	10	0	2	23	29	24	.316	.406	.400	136	10	0	2	-1	.991	-7	C-65	0.6
1990	*Pit-N	96	279	27	72	15	0	3	31	44	20	.258	.363	.344	99	1	0	3	-2	.995	-4	C-95	0.2
1991	*Pit-N	108	336	25	97	11	2	3	41	33	27	.289	.356	.360	103	2	2	1	0	**.998**	2	*C-105	1.1
1992	*Pit-N	95	293	22	75	13	2	2	29	44	21	.256	.355	.328	95	-0	0	1	-1	.994	-1	C-92/3-1	0.2
1993	Pit-N	1	5	0	1	0	0	0	0	0	0	.200	.200	.200	7	-1	0	0	0	1.000	1	/C-1	0.0

YEAR	TM/L	G	AB	R	H	2B	3B	HR	RBI	BB	SO	AVG	OBP	SLG	PRO+	BR/A	SB	CS	SBR	FA	FR	G/POS	TPR
	*Chi-A	37	97	6	25	2	0	0	8	4	14	.258	.287	.278	54	-6	0	1	-1	1.000	4	C-37	-0.1
1994	Chi-A	59	139	6	39	4	0	1	24	20	15	.281	.375	.331	85	-2	0	2	-1	.991	5	C-57	0.3
Total	11	833	2375	178	639	103	5	17	275	312	229	.269	.356	.338	95	-7	5	15	-8	.992	15	C-804/3-1	4.7

■ DOC LAVAN
Lavan, John Leonard (b: John Leonard Laven) b: 10/28/1890, Grand Rapids, Mich d: 5/29/52, Detroit, Mich. BR/TR, 5'8.5", 151 lbs. Deb: 6/22/13

YEAR	TM/L	G	AB	R	H	2B	3B	HR	RBI	BB	SO	AVG	OBP	SLG	PRO+	BR/A	SB	CS	SBR	FA	FR	G/POS	TPR
1913	StL-A	46	149	8	21	2	1	0	4	10	46	.141	.210	.168	11	-17	3			.899	-5	S-46	-1.9
	Phi-A	5	14	1	1	0	1	0	1	0	0	.071	.071	.214	-17	-2	0			1.000	0	/S-5	-0.2
	Yr	51	163	9	22	2	2	0	5	10	46	.135	.199	.172	9	-19	3			.906	-5	S-51	-2.1
1914	StL-A	75	239	21	63	7	4	1	21	17	39	.264	.318	.339	101	-0	6	12	-5	.916	-12	S-74	-1.3
1915	StL-A	157	514	44	112	17	7	1	48	42	83	.218	.281	.284	72	-19	13	19	-8	.913	5	*S-157	-1.0
1916	StL-A	110	343	32	81	13	1	0	19	32	38	.236	.305	.280	80	-9	7			.950	**34**	*S-106	3.4
1917	StL-A	118	355	19	85	8	5	0	30	19	34	.239	.284	.290	78	-10	5			.923	12	*S-110/2-7	0.7
1918	Was-A	117	464	44	129	17	2	0	45	14	21	.278	.302	.323	90	-8	12			.917	-10	*S-117/O-1	-1.4
1919	StL-N	100	356	25	86	12	2	1	25	11	30	.242	.264	.295	72	-13	4			.929	9	S-99	0.2
1920	StL-N	142	516	52	149	21	10	1	63	19	38	.289	.318	.374	102	-0	11	14	-5	.942	16	*S-138	2.4
1921	StL-N	150	560	58	145	23	11	2	82	23	30	.259	.291	.350	70	-25	7	7	-2	.950	**19**	*S-150	0.6
1922	StL-N	89	264	24	60	8	1	0	27	13	10	.227	.271	.265	41	-23	3	1	0	.937	15	S-82/3-5	-0.1
1923	StL-N	50	111	10	22	6	0	1	12	9	7	.198	.264	.279	44	-9	0	3	-2	.924	1	S-40/3-4,12	-0.7
1924	StL-N	4	6	0	0	0	0	0	0	0	0	.000	.000	.000	-99	-2	0	0	0	1.000	2	/2-2,S-2	0.0
Total	12	1163	3891	338	954	134	45	7	377	209	376	.245	.288	.308	75	-137	71	56		.930	86	*S-1126/2-10,310	0.7

■ ART LaVIGNE
LaVigne, Arthur David b: 1/26/1885, Worcester, Mass. d: 7/18/50, Worcester, Mass. BR/TR, 5'10", 162 lbs. Deb: 4/24/14

YEAR	TM/L	G	AB	R	H	2B	3B	HR	RBI	BB	SO	AVG	OBP	SLG	PRO+	BR/A	SB	CS	SBR	FA	FR	G/POS	TPR
1914	Buf-F	51	90	10	14	2	0	0	4	7	25	.156	.216	.178	3	-13	0			.967	6	C-34/1-3	-0.5

■ JOHNNY LAVIN
Lavin, John b: Troy, N.Y. 5'11", 175 lbs. Deb: 9/10/1884

YEAR	TM/L	G	AB	R	H	2B	3B	HR	RBI	BB	SO	AVG	OBP	SLG	PRO+	BR/A	SB	CS	SBR	FA	FR	G/POS	TPR
1884	StL-a	16	52	9	11	2	0	0			3	.212	.268	.250	68	-2				.750	-3	O-16	-0.5

■ RUDY LAW
Law, Rudy Karl b: 10/7/56, Waco, Tex. BL/TL, 6'1", 165 lbs. Deb: 9/12/78

YEAR	TM/L	G	AB	R	H	2B	3B	HR	RBI	BB	SO	AVG	OBP	SLG	PRO+	BR/A	SB	CS	SBR	FA	FR	G/POS	TPR
1978	LA-N	11	12	2	3	0	0	0	1	1	2	.250	.308	.250	58	-1	3	1	0	1.000	-2	/O-6	-0.3
1980	LA-N	128	388	55	101	5	4	1	23	23	27	.260	.307	.302	72	-14	40	13	4	.988	-1	*O-106	-1.6
1982	Chi-A	121	336	55	107	15	8	3	32	23	41	.318	.362	.438	118	8	36	10	5	.973	-5	O-94/D-3	0.6
1983	*Chi-A	141	501	95	142	20	7	3	34	42	36	.283	.341	.369	92	-5	77	12	16	**.994**	-4	*O-132/D-3	0.4
1984	Chi-A	136	487	68	122	14	7	6	37	39	42	.251	.310	.345	77	-15	29	17	-2	.985	-2	*O-130	-2.3
1985	Chi-A	125	390	62	101	21	6	4	36	27	40	.259	.312	.374	84	-9	29	6	5	.987	-5	*O-120/D-3	-1.2
1986	KC-A	87	307	42	80	26	5	1	36	29	22	.261	.328	.388	92	-3	14	6	1	.987	-8	O-77/D-2	-1.3
Total	7	749	2421	379	656	101	37	18	199	184	210	.271	.326	.366	88	-38	228	65	29	.986	-27	O-665/D-11	-5.7

■ VANCE LAW
Law, Vance Aaron b: 10/1/56, Boise, Idaho BR/TR, 6'2", 190 lbs. Deb: 6/1/80 F

YEAR	TM/L	G	AB	R	H	2B	3B	HR	RBI	BB	SO	AVG	OBP	SLG	PRO+	BR/A	SB	CS	SBR	FA	FR	G/POS	TPR
1980	Pit-N	25	74	11	17	2	2	0	3	3	7	.230	.260	.311	58	-4	2	0	1	.964	-3	2-11/S-8,3	-0.6
1981	Pit-N	30	67	1	9	0	1	0	3	2	15	.134	.159	.164	-8	-9	1	1	-0	1.000	5	2-19/S-7,3	-0.4
1982	Chi-A	114	359	40	101	20	1	5	54	26	46	.281	.332	.384	96	-2	4	2	0	.953	-3	S-85,3-39,2/O	0.1
1983	*Chi-A	145	408	55	99	21	5	4	42	51	56	.243	.328	.348	83	-9	3	1	0	.966	5	*3-139/2-3,SOD	-0.5
1984	Chi-A	151	481	60	121	18	2	17	59	41	75	.252	.312	.403	92	-6	4	1	1	.955	-12	*3-137,2-22/OS	-1.9
1985	Mon-N	147	519	75	138	30	6	10	52	86	96	.266	.372	.405	124	19	6	5	-1	.985	-1	*2-126,1-20,3/O	2.2
1986	Mon-N	112	360	37	81	17	2	5	44	37	66	.225	.299	.325	73	-13	3	5	-2	.993	17	2-94,1-20,3/PO	0.5
1987	Mon-N	133	436	52	119	27	1	12	56	51	62	.273	.349	.422	100	0	8	5	-1	.980	-9	*2-106,3-22,1/P	-0.3
1988	Chi-N★	151	556	73	163	29	2	11	78	55	79	.293	.360	.412	116	12	1	4	-2	.953	-12	3-150/O-1	-0.3
1989	*Chi-N	130	408	38	96	22	3	7	42	38	73	.235	.300	.355	81	-10	2	2	-1	.949	-18	3-119/O-1	-3.1
1991	Oak-A	74	134	11	28	7	1	0	9	18	27	.209	.303	.276	65	-6	0	0	0	.951	-6	3-67/S-3,O1P	-1.2
Total	11	1212	3802	453	972	193	26	71	442	408	602	.256	.329	.369	94	-28	34	26	-5	.956	-37	3-700,2-391,S/1OPDD	-5.8

■ GARLAND LAWING
Lawing, Garland Frederick "Knobby" b: 8/29/19, Gastonia, N.C. BR/TR, 6'1", 180 lbs. Deb: 5/29/46

YEAR	TM/L	G	AB	R	H	2B	3B	HR	RBI	BB	SO	AVG	OBP	SLG	PRO+	BR/A	SB	CS	SBR	FA	FR	G/POS	TPR
1946	Cin-N	2	3	0	0	0	0	0	0	0	0	.000	.000	.000	-99	-1	0			.000	-1	/O-1	-0.1
	NY-N	8	12	2	2	0	0	0	0	0	3	.167	.167	.167	-5	-2	0			1.000	-1	/O-4	-0.3
	Yr	10	15	2	2	0	0	0	0	0	5	.133	.133	.133	-24	-2	0			1.000	-1	/O-5	-0.4

■ TOM LAWLESS
Lawless, Thomas James b: 12/19/56, Erie, Pa. BR/TR, 5'11", 170 lbs. Deb: 7/15/82

YEAR	TM/L	G	AB	R	H	2B	3B	HR	RBI	BB	SO	AVG	OBP	SLG	PRO+	BR/A	SB	CS	SBR	FA	FR	G/POS	TPR
1982	Cin-N	49	165	19	35	6	0	0	4	9	30	.212	.253	.248	40	-13	16	5	2	.978	7	2-47	-0.2
1984	Cin-N	43	80	10	20	2	0	1	2	8	12	.250	.318	.313	74	-3	6	3	0	1.000	-3	2-23/3-6	-0.5
	Mon-N	11	17	1	3	1	0	0	0	0	4	.176	.176	.235	15	-2	1	0	0	1.000	0	/2-9	-0.1
	Yr	54	97	11	23	3	0	1	2	8	16	.237	.295	.299	66	-4	7	3	0	1.000	-3	2-32/3-6	-0.6
1985	*StL-N	47	58	8	12	3	1	0	8	5	4	.207	.270	.293	58	-3	2	1	0	.971	9	3-13,2-11	0.6
1986	StL-N	46	39	5	11	1	0	0	3	2	8	.282	.317	.308	74	-1	8	1	2	.875	3	3-12/2-7,O	0.3
1987	*StL-N	19	25	5	2	1	0	0	0	3	5	.080	.179	.120	-19	-4	2	0	1	1.000	-1	/2-7,3-3,O	-0.5
1988	StL-N	54	65	9	10	2	1	0	3	7	9	.154	.236	.262	42	-5	6	0	2	1.000	2	3-24/O-6,21	-0.2
1989	Tor-A	59	70	20	16	1	0	0	3	7	12	.229	.299	.243	55	-4	12	1	3	1.000	0	O-16,3-12,D/2C	0.0
1990	Tor-A	15	12	1	1	0	0	0	1	0	1	.083	.083	.083	-52	-2	0	2	-1	.800	1	/3-4,O-2,2D	-0.1
Total	8	343	531	78	110	17	2	2	24	41	85	.207	.264	.258	46	-38	53	13	8	.988	20	2-117/3-74,ODC1	-0.7

■ MIKE LAWLOR
Lawlor, Michael H. b: 3/11/1854, Troy, N.Y. d: 8/3/18, Troy, N.Y. TR, 6', 180 lbs. Deb: 5/27/1880

YEAR	TM/L	G	AB	R	H	2B	3B	HR	RBI	BB	SO	AVG	OBP	SLG	PRO+	BR/A	SB	CS	SBR	FA	FR	G/POS	TPR
1880	Tro-N	4	9	1	1	0	0	0		0	1	.111	.200	.111	8	-1				.867	1	/C-4	0.0
1884	Was-U	2	7	0	0	0	0	0		0	0	.000	.000	.000	-99	-2				1.000	1	/C-2	-0.1
Total	2	6	16	1	1	0	0	0		0	1	1	.063	.118	.063	-42	-3				.920	2	/C-6	-0.1

■ JIM LAWRENCE
Lawrence, James Ross b: 2/12/39, Hamilton, Ont., Can. BL/TR, 6'1", 185 lbs. Deb: 5/30/63

YEAR	TM/L	G	AB	R	H	2B	3B	HR	RBI	BB	SO	AVG	OBP	SLG	PRO+	BR/A	SB	CS	SBR	FA	FR	G/POS	TPR
1963	Cle-A	2	0	0	0	0	0	0	0	0	0	—	—	—	—	0	0	0		.750	0	/C-2	0.0

■ BILL LAWRENCE
Lawrence, William Henry b: 3/11/06, San Mateo, Cal. BR/TR, 6'4", 194 lbs. Deb: 4/13/32

YEAR	TM/L	G	AB	R	H	2B	3B	HR	RBI	BB	SO	AVG	OBP	SLG	PRO+	BR/A	SB	CS	SBR	FA	FR	G/POS	TPR
1932	Det-A	25	46	10	10	1	0	0	3	5	5	.217	.294	.239	38	-4	0	2	-1	1.000	2	O-15	-0.4

■ OTIS LAWRY
Lawry, Otis Carroll "Rabbit" b: 11/1/1893, Fairfield, Me. d: 10/23/65, China, Maine BL/TR, 5'8", 133 lbs. Deb: 6/28/16

YEAR	TM/L	G	AB	R	H	2B	3B	HR	RBI	BB	SO	AVG	OBP	SLG	PRO+	BR/A	SB	CS	SBR	FA	FR	G/POS	TPR
1916	Phi-A	41	123	10	25	1	0	0	4	9	21	.203	.263	.203	42	-9	4			.905	-10	2-29/O-5	-2.0
1917	Phi-A	30	55	7	9	1	0	0	1	2	9	.164	.193	.182	15	-6	1			.921	-3	2-17/O-1	-0.9
Total	2	71	178	17	34	2	0	0	5	11	30	.191	.242	.197	34	-14	5			.911	-13	/2-46,O-6	-2.9

■ MARCUS LAWTON
Lawton, Marcus Dwayne b: 8/18/65, Gulfport, Miss. BB/TR, 6'1", 160 lbs. Deb: 8/11/89

YEAR	TM/L	G	AB	R	H	2B	3B	HR	RBI	BB	SO	AVG	OBP	SLG	PRO+	BR/A	SB	CS	SBR	FA	FR	G/POS	TPR
1989	NY-A	10	14	1	3	0	0	0	0	0	3	.214	.214	.214	21	-1	1	0	0	.818	-2	/O-8,D-1	-0.3

■ GENE LAYDEN
Layden, Eugene Francis b: 3/14/1894, Pittsburgh, Pa. d: 12/12/84, Pittsburgh, Pa. BL/TL, 5'10", 160 lbs. Deb: 7/29/15

YEAR	TM/L	G	AB	R	H	2B	3B	HR	RBI	BB	SO	AVG	OBP	SLG	PRO+	BR/A	SB	CS	SBR	FA	FR	G/POS	TPR
1915	NY-A	3	7	2	2	0	0	0	0	0	1	.286	.286	.286	71	-0	0	1	-1	.750	-1	/O-2	-0.2

■ PETE LAYDON
Laydon, Peter John b: 12/30/19, Dallas, Tex. d: 7/18/82, Edna, Tex. BR/TR, 5'11", 185 lbs. Deb: 4/28/48

YEAR	TM/L	G	AB	R	H	2B	3B	HR	RBI	BB	SO	AVG	OBP	SLG	PRO+	BR/A	SB	CS	SBR	FA	FR	G/POS	TPR
1948	StL-N	41	104	11	26	2	1	0	4	6	12	.250	.297	.288	55	-7	4	2	0	.973	-1	O-30	-0.9

■ HERMAN LAYNE
Layne, Herman b: 2/13/01, New Haven, W.Va. d: 8/27/73, Gallipolis, Ohio BR/TR, 5'11", 165 lbs. Deb: 4/16/27

YEAR	TM/L	G	AB	R	H	2B	3B	HR	RBI	BB	SO	AVG	OBP	SLG	PRO+	BR/A	SB	CS	SBR	FA	FR	G/POS	TPR
1927	Pit-N	11	6	3	0	0	0	0	0	1	0	.000	.143	.000	-55	-1	0			.000	-1	/O-2	-0.3

YEAR	TM/L	G	AB	R	H	2B	3B	HR	RBI	BB	SO	AVG	OBP	SLG	PRO+	BR/A	SB	CS	SBR	FA	FR	G/POS	TPR

■ HILLIS LAYNE Layne, Ivoria Hillis "Tony" b: 2/23/18, Whitwell, Tenn. BL/TR, 6', 170 lbs. Deb: 9/16/41

1941	Was-A	13	50	8	14	2	0	0	6	4	5	.280	.333	.320	77	-2	1	1	-0	.953	0	3-13	-0.1
1944	Was-A	33	87	6	17	2	0	0	8	6	10	.195	.263	.218	40	-7	2	0	1	.949	1	3-18/2-3	-0.5
1945	Was-A	61	147	23	44	5	4	1	14	10	7	.299	.352	.408	132	5	0	1	-1	.956	-5	3-33	0.1
Total	3	107	284	37	75	9	4	1	28	20	22	.264	.321	.335	92	-3	3	2	-0	.953	-3	/3-64,2-3	-0.5

■ LES LAYTON Layton, Lester Lee b: 11/18/21, Nardin, Okla. BR/TR, 6', 165 lbs. Deb: 4/24/48

| 1948 | NY-N | 63 | 91 | 14 | 21 | 4 | 4 | 2 | 12 | 6 | 21 | .231 | .286 | .429 | 90 | -2 | 1 | | | .951 | -1 | O-20 | -0.3 |

■ JOHNNY LAZOR Lazor, John Paul b: 9/9/12, Taylor, Wash. BL/TR, 5'9.5", 180 lbs. Deb: 4/22/43

1943	Bos-A	83	208	21	47	10	2	0	13	21	25	.226	.297	.293	72	-7	5	6	-2	.979	-3	O-63	-1.6
1944	Bos-A	16	24	0	2	1	0	0	0	1	0	.083	.120	.125	-30	-4	0	0	0	1.000	0	/O-6,C-1	-0.4
1945	Bos-A	101	335	35	104	19	2	5	45	18	17	.310	.346	.424	120	7	3	2	-0	.961	-8	O-81	-0.6
1946	Bos-A	23	29	1	4	0	0	1	4	2	11	.138	.194	.241	20	-3	0	0	0	1.000	-1	/O-7	-0.6
Total	4	223	596	57	157	30	4	6	62	42	53	.263	.312	.357	92	-7	8	8	-2	.971	-13	O-157/C-1	-3.2

■ TONY LAZZERI Lazzeri, Anthony Michael "Poosh 'Em Up Tony" b: 12/6/03, San Francisco, Cal. d: 8/6/46, San Francisco, Cal. BR/TR, 5'11.5", 170 lbs. Deb: 4/13/26 CH

1926	*NY-A	155	589	79	162	28	14	18	114	54	96	.275	.338	.462	109	4	16	7	1	.961	-20	*2-149/S-5,3	-1.0
1927	*NY-A	153	570	92	176	29	8	18	102	69	82	.309	.383	.482	127	22	22	14	-2	.971	5	*2-113,S-38/3	3.1
1928	*NY-A	116	404	62	134	30	11	10	82	43	50	.332	.397	.535	148	27	15	5	2	.956	-11	*2-110	2.0
1929	NY-A	147	545	101	193	37	11	18	106	68	45	.354	.429	.561	164	52	9	10	-3	.969	-4	*2-147	4.8
1930	NY-A	143	571	109	173	34	15	9	121	60	62	.303	.372	.462	115	13	4	4	-1	.971	6	2-77,3-60/S10	2.3
1931	NY-A	135	484	67	129	27	7	8	83	79	80	.267	.371	.401	109	8	18	9	0	.958	-3	2-90,3-39	1.1
1932	*NY-A	142	510	79	153	28	16	15	113	82	64	.300	.399	.506	140	31	11	11	-3	.978	6	*2-134/3-5	3.8
1933	NY-A☆	139	523	94	154	22	12	18	104	73	62	.294	.383	.486	137	28	15	7	0	.968	-14	*2-138	2.1
1934	NY-A	123	438	59	117	24	6	14	67	71	64	.267	.369	.445	117	11	11	1	3	.976	-13	2-92,3-30	0.7
1935	NY-A	130	477	72	130	18	6	13	83	63	75	.273	.361	.417	107	5	11	5	0	.970	-21	*2-118/S-9	-0.6
1936	*NY-A	150	537	82	154	29	6	14	109	97	65	.287	.397	.441	110	11	8	5	-1	.968	-32	*2-148/S-2	-0.9
1937	*NY-A	126	446	56	109	21	3	14	70	71	76	.244	.348	.399	87	-9	7	1	2	.966	-8	*2-125	-0.6
1938	*Chi-N	54	120	21	32	5	0	5	23	22	30	.267	.380	.433	120	4	0			.946	-8	S-25/3-7,2O	-0.2
1939	Bro-N	14	39	6	11	2	0	3	6	10	7	.282	.451	.564	165	4	1			.914	0	2-11/3-2	0.5
	NY-N	13	44	7	13	0	0	1	8	7	6	.295	.392	.364	103	1	0			.889	-2	3-13	-0.2
	Yr	27	83	13	24	2	0	4	14	17	13	.289	.422	.458	133	5	1			.897	-2	3-15,2-11	0.3
Total	14	1740	6297	986	1840	334	115	178	1191	869	864	.292	.380	.467	122	213	148	79		.967	-119	*2-1456,3-166/SO1	16.9

■ FREDDY LEACH Leach, Frederick b: 11/23/1897, Springfield, Mo. d: 12/10/81, Hagerman, Idaho BL/TR, 5'11", 183 lbs. Deb: 5/24/23

1923	Phi-N	52	104	5	27	4	0	1	16	3	14	.260	.280	.327	54	-7	1	2	-1	.950	-6	O-26	-1.5
1924	Phi-N	8	28	6	13	2	1	2	7	2	1	.464	.500	.821	221	5	0	0	0	1.000	-1	/O-7	0.3
1925	Phi-N	65	292	47	91	15	4	5	28	5	21	.312	.323	.442	86	-7	1	2	-1	.952	-2	O-65	-1.4
1926	Phi-N	129	492	73	162	29	7	11	71	16	33	.329	.352	.484	117	10	6			.979	-5	*O-123	0.2
1927	Phi-N	140	536	69	164	30	4	12	83	21	32	.306	.342	.444	108	4	2			.981	14	*O-140	0.9
1928	Phi-N	145	588	83	179	36	11	13	96	30	36	.304	.342	.469	107	4	4			.978	11	*O-120,1-25	0.4
1929	NY-N	113	411	74	119	22	6	8	47	17	14	.290	.324	.431	85	-11	10			.974	-12	*O-95	-2.7
1930	NY-N	126	544	90	178	19	13	13	71	22	25	.327	.361	.482	104	2	3			.978	-3	*O-124	-0.8
1931	NY-N	129	515	75	159	30	5	6	61	29	9	.309	.348	.421	109	5	4			.976	-4	*O-125	-0.7
1932	Bos-N	84	223	21	55	9	2	1	29	18	10	.247	.306	.318	71	-9	1			.977	-2	O-50	-1.4
Total	10	991	3733	543	1147	196	53	72	509	163	189	.307	.341	.446	101	-4	32	4		.975	-5	O-875/1-25	-6.7

■ RICK LEACH Leach, Richard Max b: 5/4/57, Ann Arbor, Mich. BL/TL, 6', 195 lbs. Deb: 4/30/81

1981	Det-A	54	83	9	16	3	1	1	11	16	15	.193	.323	.289	75	-2	0	1	-1	1.000	-1	1-32,O-15/D	-0.6
1982	Det-A	82	218	23	52	7	2	3	12	21	29	.239	.305	.330	74	-8	4	0	1	.995	-1	1-56,O-14/D	-1.0
1983	Det-A	99	242	22	60	17	0	3	26	19	21	.248	.305	.355	83	-6	2	2	-1	.994	3	1-73,O-13/D	-0.7
1984	Tor-A	65	88	11	23	6	2	0	7	8	14	.261	.323	.375	89	-1	0	0	0	1.000	-1	O-23,1-15/PD	-0.3
1985	Tor-A	16	35	2	7	0	1	0	1	3	9	.200	.263	.257	42	-3	0	0	0	.987	-0	1-10/O-4	-0.3
1986	Tor-A	110	246	35	76	14	1	5	39	13	24	.309	.344	.435	108	2	0	1	-1	.978	-8	D-42,O-39/1	-0.7
1987	Tor-A	98	195	26	55	13	1	3	25	25	25	.282	.372	.405	104	2	0	1	-1	.981	-6	O-43,D-30/1	-0.6
1988	Tor-A	87	199	21	55	13	1	0	23	18	27	.276	.336	.352	93	-2	0	1	-1	1.000	-4	O-49,D-25/1	-0.8
1989	Tex-A	110	239	32	65	14	1	1	23	32	33	.272	.360	.351	100	1	2	1	0	.951	-4	D-44,O-41/1	-0.5
1990	SF-N	78	174	24	51	13	0	2	16	21	20	.293	.372	.402	117	5	0	2	-1	.989	-3	O-52/1-7	-0.1
Total	10	799	1719	205	460	100	10	18	183	176	217	.268	.338	.369	94	-11	8	8	-2	.983	-26	O-293,1-213,D/P	-5.7

■ TOMMY LEACH Leach, Thomas William b: 11/4/1877, French Creek, N.Y. d: 9/29/69, Haines City, Fla. BR/TR, 5'6.5", 150 lbs. Deb: 9/28/1898

1898	Lou-N	3	10	0	1	0	0	0	0	0		.100	.100	.100	-43	-2	0			.727	-0	/3-3,2-1	-0.2
1899	Lou-N	106	406	75	117	10	6	5	57	37		.288	.349	.379	100	-0	19			.908	1	3-80,S-25/2	0.3
1900	*Pit-N	51	160	20	34	1	2	1	16	21		.213	.304	.262	57	-9	8			.864	1	3-31/S-8,2O	-0.7
1901	Pit-N	98	374	64	114	12	13	2	44	20		.305	.347	.422	119	8	16			.903	9	3-92/S-4	1.7
1902	Pit-N	135	514	97	143	14	22	6	85	45		.278	.341	.426	132	18	25			.926	13	*3-134	3.3
1903	*Pit-N	127	507	97	151	16	17	7	87	40		.298	.352	.438	121	12	22			.879	7	*3-127	1.9
1904	Pit-N	146	579	92	149	15	12	6	56	45		.257	.316	.373	98	-1	23			.907	36	*3-146	4.1
1905	Pit-N	131	499	71	128	10	14	3	53	37		.257	.309	.345	92	-6	17			.988	11	O-71,3-58/2S	0.5
1906	Pit-N	133	476	66	136	10	7	1	39	33		.286	.333	.342	106	3	21			.929	2	3-65,O-60/S	0.4
1907	Pit-N	149	547	102	166	19	12	4	43	40		.303	.352	.404	135	20	43			.980	11	*O-111,3-33/S2	3.1
1908	Pit-N	152	583	93	151	24	16	5	43	54		.259	.324	.381	125	15	24			.937	-4	*3-150/O-2	1.9
1909	*Pit-N	151	587	126	153	29	6	6	43	66		.261	.337	.368	110	6	27			.969	3	*O-138,3-13	0.4
1910	Pit-N	135	529	83	143	24	5	4	52	38	62	.270	.319	.357	92	-7	18			.966	9	*O-131/S-2,2	-0.5
1911	Pit-N	108	386	60	92	12	6	3	43	46	50	.238	.323	.324	78	-11	19			.987	2	O-89,S-13/3	-1.3
1912	Pit-N	28	97	24	29	4	2	0	19	12	9	.299	.376	.381	109	2	6			.986	4	O-24	0.4
	Chi-N	82	265	50	64	10	3	2	32	55	20	.242	.378	.325	93	-2	14			.975	5	O-73/3-4	0.2
	Yr	110	362	74	93	14	5	2	51	67	29	.257	.377	.340	97	-2	20			.978	9	O-97/3-4	0.6
1913	Chi-N	131	456	99	131	23	10	6	32	77	44	.287	.391	.421	132	21	21			.990	3	*O-121/3-2	1.9
1914	Chi-N	153	577	80	152	24	3	4	46	79	50	.263	.353	.373	116	13	16			.968	3	*O-136,3-16	1.8
1915	Cin-N	107	335	42	75	7	5	0	17	56	38	.224	.338	.275	85	-4	20	14	-2	.959	-4	O-96	-1.6
1918	Pit-N	30	72	14	14	2	1	0	8	5	5	.194	.363	.306	101	1	2			.952	-2	O-23/S-3	-0.2
Total	19	2156	7959	1355	2143	266	172	63	810	820	278	.269	.340	.370	108	79	361	14		.975	114	*O-1079,3-955/S2	17.4

■ DAN LEAHY Leahy, Daniel C. b: 8/8/1870, Knoxville, Tenn. d: 12/30/03, Knoxville, Tenn. Deb: 9/2/1896

| 1896 | Phi-N | 2 | 6 | 0 | 2 | 1 | 0 | 0 | 1 | 1 | 2 | .333 | .429 | .500 | 146 | 0 | 0 | | | .857 | 1 | /S-2 | 0.1 |

■ TOM LEAHY Leahy, Thomas Joseph b: 6/2/1869, New Haven, Conn. d: 6/11/51, New Haven, Conn. TR, 168 lbs. Deb: 5/18/1897

1897	Pit-N	24	92	10	24	3	3	0	12	7		.261	.320	.359	82	-3	3			.935	-3	O-13/C-6,3	-0.5
	Was-N	19	52	12	20	2	1	0	7	9		.385	.529	.462	164	6	6			.727	-4	O-10/3-5,2C	0.2
	Yr	43	144	22	44	5	4	0	19	16		.306	.405	.396	114	4	9			.881	-7	O-23,3-11/C2	-0.3
1898	Was-N	15	55	10	10	2	0	0	8	5		.182	.297	.218	48	-3	6			.913	0	3-12/2-3	-0.3

YEAR	TM/L	G	AB	R	H	2B	3B	HR	RBI	BB	SO	AVG	OBP	SLG	PRO+	BR/A	SB	CS	SBR	FA	FR	G/POS	TPR
1901	Mil-A	33	99	18	24	6	2	0	10	11		.242	.348	.343	97	0	3			.941	-5	C-28/O-2,2	-0.2
	Phi-A	5	15	1	5	1	0	0	1	1		.333	.375	.400	110	0	0			1.000	-1	/O-2,C-1,S	0.0
	Yr	38	114	19	29	7	2	0	11	12		.254	.351	.351	99	0	3			.944	-6	C-29/O-4,2S	-0.2
1905	StL-N	35	97	3	22	1	3	0	7	8		.227	.286	.299	77	-3	0			.946	-9	C-29	-0.9
Total	4	131	410	54	105	15	9	0	42	44		.256	.348	.337	93	-2	18			.942	-21	/C-65,O-27,32S	-1.7

■ FRED LEAR Lear, Frederick Francis "King" b: 4/7/1894, New York, N.Y. d: 10/13/55, E.Orange, N.J. BR/TR, 6'0.5", 180 lbs. Deb: 6/7/15

YEAR	TM/L	G	AB	R	H	2B	3B	HR	RBI	BB	SO	AVG	OBP	SLG	PRO+	BR/A	SB	CS	SBR	FA	FR	G/POS	TPR
1915	Phi-A	2	2	0	0	0	0	0	0	0	2	.000	.000	.000	-99	-0	0			.600	-0	/3-2	-0.1
1918	Chi-N	2	1	0	0	0	0	0	0	1	0	.000	.500	.000	56	0	0			.000	0	H	0.0
1919	Chi-N	40	76	8	17	3	1	1	11	8	11	.224	.306	.329	90	-1	2			.990	-1	/1-9,2-9,S	-0.3
1920	NY-N	31	87	12	22	0	1	1	7	8	15	.253	.323	.310	83	-2	0	2	-1	.951	-3	3-24/2-1	-0.5
Total	4	75	166	20	39	3	2	2	18	17	28	.235	.314	.313	85	-3	2	2		.924	-5	/3-26,2-10,1S	-0.9

■ BILL LEARD Leard, William Wallace "Wild Bill" b: 10/14/1885, Oneida, N.Y. d: 1/15/70, San Francisco, Cal BR/TR, 5'10", 155 lbs. Deb: 7/21/17

YEAR	TM/L	G	AB	R	H	2B	3B	HR	RBI	BB	SO	AVG	OBP	SLG	PRO+	BR/A	SB	CS	SBR	FA	FR	G/POS	TPR
1917	Bro-N	3	3	0	0	0	0	0	0	0	1	.000	.000	.000	-97	-1	0			.000	-1	/2-1	-0.1

■ JACK LEARY Leary, John J. b: 1858, New Haven, Conn. TL, 5'11", 186 lbs. Deb: 8/21/1880

YEAR	TM/L	G	AB	R	H	2B	3B	HR	RBI	BB	SO	AVG	OBP	SLG	PRO+	BR/A	SB	CS	SBR	FA	FR	G/POS	TPR
1880	Bos-N	1	3	1	0	0	0	0	0	1	0	.000	.250	.000	-7	-0				1.000	1	/O-1,P-1	0.0
1881	Det-N	3	11	2	3	1	1	0	4	1	1	.273	.333	.545	165	1				.833	-0	/O-2,P-2	0.1
1882	Pit-a	60	257	32	75	7	3	1		5		.292	.305	.354	128	7				.759	-14	3-33,O-27/P12	-0.6
	Bal-a	4	18	3	4	1	0	0		0		.222	.222	.278	73	-0				.900	-0	/P-3,O-1	0.0
	Yr	64	275	35	79	8	3	1		5		.287	.300	.349	124	7				.759	-14	3-33,O-28/P12	-0.6
1883	Lou-a	40	165	16	31	1	3	3		2		.188	.198	.285	58	-7				.816	-1	S-40	-0.7
	Bal-a	3	11	1	2	0	2	0		0		.182	.182	.545	122	0				.727	-1	/2-3	-0.1
	Yr	43	176	17	33	1	5	3		2		.188	.197	.301	62	-7				.816	-2	S-40/2-3	-0.8
1884	Alt-U	8	33	1	3	0	0	0		1		.091	.118	.091	-42	-6				.692	-2	/O-6,P-3,3	-0.6
	CP-U	10	40	0	7	1	0	0		0		.175	.175	.200	2	-5				.840	1	/2-4,3-3,OP	-0.3
	Yr	18	73	1	10	1	0	0		1		.137	.149	.151	-18	-12				.625	-1	/O-9,P-5,32	-0.9
Total	5	129	538	56	125	11	9	4		10	1	.232	.246	.309	81	-11				.725	-17	/S-40,O-40,3P21	-2.2

■ JOHN LEARY Leary, John Louis "Jack" b: 5/2/1891, Waltham, Mass. d: 8/18/61, Waltham, Mass. BR/TR, 5'11.5", 180 lbs. Deb: 4/14/14

YEAR	TM/L	G	AB	R	H	2B	3B	HR	RBI	BB	SO	AVG	OBP	SLG	PRO+	BR/A	SB	CS	SBR	FA	FR	G/POS	TPR
1914	StL-A	144	533	35	141	28	7	0	45	10	71	.265	.282	.343	91	-9	9	15	-6	.987	-4	*1-130,C-15	-2.4
1915	StL-A	75	227	19	55	10	0	0	15	5	36	.242	.268	.286	68	-10	2	4	-2	.985	-2	1-53,C-11	-1.5
Total	2	219	760	54	196	38	7	0	60	15	107	.258	.278	.326	85	-19	11	19	-8	.987	-7	1-183/C-26	-3.9

■ HAL LEATHERS Leathers, Harold Langford "Chuck" b: 12/2/1898, Selma, Cal. d: 4/12/77, Modesto, Cal. BL/TR, 5'8", 152 lbs. Deb: 9/13/20

YEAR	TM/L	G	AB	R	H	2B	3B	HR	RBI	BB	SO	AVG	OBP	SLG	PRO+	BR/A	SB	CS	SBR	FA	FR	G/POS	TPR
1920	Chi-N	9	23	3	7	1	0	1	1	1	1	.304	.333	.478	129	1	0	1	0	.825	-1	/S-6,2-3	0.1

■ EMIL LEBER Leber, Emil Bohmiel b: 5/15/1881, Cleveland, Ohio d: 11/6/24, Cleveland, Ohio BR/TR, 5'11", 170 lbs. Deb: 9/2/05

YEAR	TM/L	G	AB	R	H	2B	3B	HR	RBI	BB	SO	AVG	OBP	SLG	PRO+	BR/A	SB	CS	SBR	FA	FR	G/POS	TPR
1905	Cle-A	2	6	1	0	0	0	0	0	1		.000	.143	.000	-53	-1	0			1.000	-0	/3-2	-0.1

■ BEVO LeBOURVEAU LeBourveau, De Witt Wiley b: 8/24/1894, Dana, Cal. d: 12/9/47, Nevada City, Cal. BL/TR, 5'11", 175 lbs. Deb: 9/9/19

YEAR	TM/L	G	AB	R	H	2B	3B	HR	RBI	BB	SO	AVG	OBP	SLG	PRO+	BR/A	SB	CS	SBR	FA	FR	G/POS	TPR
1919	Phi-N	17	63	4	17	0	0	0	0	10	8	.270	.370	.270	88	-0	2			1.000	2	O-15	0.1
1920	Phi-N	84	261	29	67	7	2	3	12	11	36	.257	.295	.333	76	-8	9	6	-1	.949	3	O-72	-1.2
1921	Phi-N	93	281	42	83	12	5	6	35	29	51	.295	.361	.438	102	1	4	5	-2	.911	-8	O-76	-1.4
1922	Phi-N	74	167	24	45	8	3	2	20	24	29	.269	.368	.389	87	-3	0	3	-2	.920	-3	O-42	-1.0
1929	Phi-A	12	16	1	5	0	1	0	2	5	1	.313	.476	.438	132	1	0	1	-1	1.000	0	/O-3	0.0
Total	5	280	788	100	217	27	11	11	69	79	125	.275	.345	.379	91	-9	15	15		.935	-7	O-208	-3.5

■ MIKE LEDWITH Ledwith, Michael b: Brooklyn, N.Y. d: 1/2/29, Bronx, N.Y. Deb: 8/19/1874

YEAR	TM/L	G	AB	R	H	2B	3B	HR	RBI	BB	SO	AVG	OBP	SLG	PRO+	BR/A	SB	CS	SBR	FA	FR	G/POS	TPR
1874	Atl-n	1	4	1	1	0	0	0		0		.250	.250	.250	68	-0						/C-1	0.0

■ CLIFF LEE Lee, Clifford Walker b: 8/4/1896, Lexington, Neb. d: 8/25/80, Denver, Colo. BR/TR, 6'1", 175 lbs. Deb: 5/15/19

YEAR	TM/L	G	AB	R	H	2B	3B	HR	RBI	BB	SO	AVG	OBP	SLG	PRO+	BR/A	SB	CS	SBR	FA	FR	G/POS	TPR
1919	Pit-N	42	112	5	22	2	4	0	2	6	8	.196	.237	.286	55	-6	2			.962	-11	C-28/O-6	-1.7
1920	Pit-N	37	76	9	18	2	2	0	8	4	14	.237	.275	.316	67	-3	0	1	-1	.974	0	C-19/O-2	-0.3
1921	Phi-N	88	286	31	88	14	4	4	29	13	34	.308	.338	.427	94	-3	5	2	0	.987	-7	1-48,O-27/C	-1.2
1922	Phi-N	122	422	65	136	29	6	17	77	32	43	.322	.371	.540	121	11	2	3	-1	.967	-5	O-89,1-18/3	-0.1
1923	Phi-N	107	355	54	114	20	4	11	47	20	39	.321	.357	.493	110	3	3	3	-1	.959	-11	O-83,1-16	-1.3
1924	Phi-N	21	56	4	14	3	2	1	7	2	5	.250	.276	.429	77	-2	0	1	-1	1.000	-1	O-13/1-4	-0.4
	Cin-N	6	6	1	2	1	0	0	2	0	2	.333	.333	.500	122	0	0	0	0	.000	-0	/O-1	0.0
	Yr	27	62	5	16	4	2	1	9	2	7	.258	.281	.435	82	-2	0	1	-1	1.000	-1	O-14/1-4	-0.4
1925	Cle-A	77	230	43	74	15	6	4	42	21	33	.322	.378	.491	118	6	2	1	0	.951	-3	O-70	-0.1
1926	Cle-A	21	40	4	7	1	0	1	2	6	8	.175	.283	.275	45	-3	0	0	0	1.000	-0	/O-9,C-3	-0.4
Total	8	521	1583	216	475	87	28	38	216	104	186	.300	.344	.462	103	2	14	11		.960	-36	O-300/1-86,C3	-5.5

■ DEREK LEE Lee, Derek Gerald b: 7/28/66, Chicago, Ill. BL/TR, 6'1", 200 lbs. Deb: 6/27/93

YEAR	TM/L	G	AB	R	H	2B	3B	HR	RBI	BB	SO	AVG	OBP	SLG	PRO+	BR/A	SB	CS	SBR	FA	FR	G/POS	TPR
1993	Min-A	15	33	3	5	1	0	0	4	1	4	.152	.176	.182	-4	-5	0	0	0	1.000	-2	O-13	-0.7

■ DUD LEE Lee, Ernest Dudley (a.k.a. Ernest Dudley In 1920-21) b: 8/22/1899, Denver, Colo. d: 1/7/71, Denver, Colo. BL/TR, 5'9", 150 lbs. Deb: 10/3/20

YEAR	TM/L	G	AB	R	H	2B	3B	HR	RBI	BB	SO	AVG	OBP	SLG	PRO+	BR/A	SB	CS	SBR	FA	FR	G/POS	TPR
1920	StL-A	1	2	2	2	0	0	0	1	0	0	1.000	1.000	1.000	418	1	0	0	0	.333	-2	/S-1	0.0
1921	StL-A	72	180	18	30	4	2	0	11	14	34	.167	.235	.211	14	-24	1	1	-0	.922	-5	S-31,2-30/3	-1.5
1924	Bos-A	94	288	36	73	9	4	0	29	40	17	.253	.350	.313	72	-11	8	4	0	.937	-8	S-90	-0.9
1925	Bos-A	84	255	22	57	3	2	0	19	34	19	.224	.315	.275	51	-19	2	3	-1	.924	17	S-84	0.4
1926	Bos-A	2	7	2	1	0	0	0	0	0	0	.143	.250	.143	4	-1	0	0	0	1.000	-1	/S-2	-0.2
Total	5	253	732	80	163	20	9	0	60	88	70	.223	.311	.275	50	-54	12	8	-1	.928	12	S-208/2-30,3	-2.2

■ HAL LEE Lee, Harold Burnham "Sheriff" b: 2/15/05, Ludlow, Miss. d: 9/4/89, Pascagoula, Miss. BR/TR, 5'11", 180 lbs. Deb: 4/19/30

YEAR	TM/L	G	AB	R	H	2B	3B	HR	RBI	BB	SO	AVG	OBP	SLG	PRO+	BR/A	SB	CS	SBR	FA	FR	G/POS	TPR
1930	Bro-N	22	37	5	6	0	0	1	4	4	5	.162	.244	.243	19	-5	0			1.000	-1	O-12	-0.6
1931	Phi-N	44	131	13	29	10	0	2	12	10	18	.221	.282	.344	62	-7	0			.967	-1	O-38	-1.1
1932	Phi-N	149	595	76	180	42	10	18	85	36	45	.303	.343	.497	110	7	6			.965	11	*O-148	0.8
1933	Phi-N	46	167	25	48	12	2	0	12	18	13	.287	.360	.383	100	0	1			.981	-1	O-45	-0.1
	Bos-N	88	312	32	69	15	9	1	28	18	26	.221	.266	.337	77	-10	1			.977	2	O-87	-1.4
	Yr	134	479	57	117	27	11	1	40	36	39	.244	.300	.353	87	-9	2			.978	3	*O-132	-1.5
1934	Bos-N	139	521	70	152	23	6	8	79	47	43	.292	.353	.405	111	8	3			.985	5	*O-128/2-4	0.7
1935	Bos-N	112	422	49	128	18	6	3	39	18	25	.303	.333	.374	98	-2	0			.962	6	*O-110	-0.1
1936	Bos-N	152	565	46	143	24	7	3	64	52	50	.253	.318	.336	82	-15	4			.973	-6	*O-150	-2.6
Total	7	752	2750	316	755	144	40	33	323	203	225	.275	.326	.392	95	-25	15			.973	16	O-718/2-4	-4.4

■ LEONIDAS LEE Lee, Leonidas Pyrrhus (b: Leonidas Pyrrhus Funkhouser) b: 12/13/1860, St.Louis, Mo. d: 6/11/12, Hendersonville, N.C. Deb: 7/17/1877

YEAR	TM/L	G	AB	R	H	2B	3B	HR	RBI	BB	SO	AVG	OBP	SLG	PRO+	BR/A	SB	CS	SBR	FA	FR	G/POS	TPR
1877	StL-N	4	18	0	5	0	0	0	0	1		.278	.278	.333	97	-0				.667	-2	/O-4,S-1	-0.2

■ LERON LEE Lee, Leron b: 3/4/48, Bakersfield, Cal. BL/TR, 6', 196 lbs. Deb: 9/5/69

YEAR	TM/L	G	AB	R	H	2B	3B	HR	RBI	BB	SO	AVG	OBP	SLG	PRO+	BR/A	SB	CS	SBR	FA	FR	G/POS	TPR
1969	StL-N	7	23	3	5	1	0	0	0	1	6	.217	.308	.261	60	-0	0	0	0	1.000	-0	/O-7	-0.2
1970	StL-N	121	264	28	60	13	1	6	23	24	66	.227	.294	.352	71	-11	5	1	1	.969	-5	O-77	-1.8
1971	StL-N	25	28	3	5	3	0	1	2	4	12	.179	.281	.321	68	-1	0	1	-1	.800	-3	/O-8	-0.5
	SD-N	79	256	29	70	20	2	4	21	18	45	.273	.321	.414	115	4	4	5	-2	.920	-4	O-68	-0.5

YEAR	TM/L	G	AB	R	H	2B	3B	HR	RBI	BB	SO	AVG	OBP	SLG	PRO+	BR/A	SB	CS	SBR	FA	FR	G/POS	TPR
	Yr	104	284	32	75	21	2	5	23	22	57	.264	.317	.405	108	2	4	6	-2	.914	-6	O-76	-1.0
1972	SD-N	101	370	50	111	23	7	12	47	29	58	.300	.356	.497	151	23	2	5	-2	.975	4	O-96	2.1
1973	SD-N	118	333	36	79	7	2	3	30	33	61	.237	.308	.297	74	-12	4	0	1	.970	4	O-84	-1.2
1974	Cle-A	79	232	18	54	13	0	5	25	15	42	.233	.279	.353	82	-6	3	2	-0	.958	4	O-62/D-2	-0.6
1975	Cle-A	13	23	3	3	1	0	0	0	2	5	.130	.231	.174	16	-3	1	0	0	1.000	-1	/O-5,D-3	-0.3
	LA-N	48	43	2	11	4	0	0	2	3	9	.256	.304	.349	85	-1	0	0	0	1.000	0	/O-4	-0.3
1976	LA-N	23	45	1	6	0	1	0	2	2	9	.133	.170	.178	-1	-6	0	0	0	1.000	-2	O-10	-0.9
Total	8	614	1617	173	404	83	13	31	152	133	315	.250	.309	.375	95	-15	19	14	-3	.962	-5	O-421/D-5	-4.2

■ MANUEL LEE
Lee, Manuel Lora "Manny" (b: Manuel Lora (Lee))   b: 6/17/65, San Pedro De Macoris, D.R.   BB/TR, 5'9", 151 lbs.   Deb: 4/10/85

YEAR	TM/L	G	AB	R	H	2B	3B	HR	RBI	BB	SO	AVG	OBP	SLG	PRO+	BR/A	SB	CS	SBR	FA	FR	G/POS	TPR
1985	*Tor-A	64	40	9	8	0	0	0	2	2	9	.200	.238	.200	21	-4	1	4	-2	.971	19	2-38/S-8,3D	1.2
1986	Tor-A	35	78	8	16	0	1	1	7	4	10	.205	.244	.269	39	-7	0	1	-1	.990	4	2-29/S-5/3	-0.3
1987	Tor-A	56	121	14	31	2	3	1	11	6	13	.256	.291	.347	67	-6	2	0	1	.966	12	2-27,S-26/D	0.8
1988	Tor-A	116	381	38	111	16	3	2	38	26	64	.291	.337	.365	96	-2	3	3	-1	.988	10	2-98,S-23/3D	1.2
1989	*Tor-A	99	300	27	78	9	2	3	34	20	60	.260	.306	.333	82	-7	4	2	0	.985	-2	2-40,S-28,3D/O	-0.6
1990	Tor-A	117	391	45	95	12	4	6	41	26	90	.243	.290	.340	74	-14	3	1	0	.993	-10	*2-112/S-9	-2.1
1991	*Tor-A	138	445	41	104	18	3	0	29	24	107	.234	.276	.288	54	-28	7	2	1	.967	-28	*S-138	-4.5
1992	*Tor-A	128	396	49	104	10	1	3	39	50	73	.263	.345	.316	83	-8	6	2	1	.987	-18	*S-128	-1.6
1993	Tex-A	73	205	31	45	3	1	1	12	22	39	.220	.301	.259	54	-13	2	4	-2	.968	5	S-72/D-1	-0.5
1994	Tex-A	95	335	41	93	18	2	2	38	21	66	.278	.320	.361	81	-10	3	1	0	.967	4	S-85,2-13	0.1
Total	10	921	2692	303	685	88	20	19	249	201	531	.254	.307	.323	73	-98	31	20	-3	.972	-4	S-522,2-357/3DO	-6.3

■ TERRY LEE
Lee, Terry James   b: 3/13/62, San Francisco, Cal.   BR/TR, 6'5", 215 lbs.   Deb: 9/3/90

YEAR	TM/L	G	AB	R	H	2B	3B	HR	RBI	BB	SO	AVG	OBP	SLG	PRO+	BR/A	SB	CS	SBR	FA	FR	G/POS	TPR
1990	Cin-N	12	19	1	4	1	0	0	3	2	2	.211	.286	.263	50	-1	0	0	0	1.000	0	/1-6	-0.1
1991	Cin-N	3	6	0	0	0	0	0	0	0	2	.000	.000	.000	-96	-2	0	0	0	1.000	0	/1-2	0.0
Total	2	15	25	1	4	1	0	0	3	2	4	.160	.222	.200	17	-3	0	0	0	1.000	0	/1-8	-0.1

■ BILLY LEE
Lee, William Joseph   b: 1/9/1892, Bayonne, N.J.   d: 1/6/84, West Hazelton, Pa.   BR/TR, 5'9", 165 lbs.   Deb: 4/15/15

YEAR	TM/L	G	AB	R	H	2B	3B	HR	RBI	BB	SO	AVG	OBP	SLG	PRO+	BR/A	SB	CS	SBR	FA	FR	G/POS	TPR
1915	StL-A	18	59	2	11	1	0	0	4	6	5	.186	.262	.203	41	-4	1	1	-0	1.000	2	O-15/3-1	-0.3
1916	StL-A	7	11	1	2	0	0	0	0	1	1	.182	.250	.182	31	-1	0			1.000	-1	/O-4	-0.2
Total	2	25	70	3	13	1	0	0	4	7	6	.186	.260	.200	39	-5	1	1		1.000	2	/O-19,3-1	-0.5

■ WATTY LEE
Lee, Wyatt Arnold   b: 8/12/1879, Lynch Station, Va.   d: 3/6/36, Washington, D.C.   BL/TL, 5'10.5", 171 lbs.   Deb: 4/30/01

YEAR	TM/L	G	AB	R	H	2B	3B	HR	RBI	BB	SO	AVG	OBP	SLG	PRO+	BR/A	SB	CS	SBR	FA	FR	G/POS	TPR
1901	Was-A	43	129	15	33	6	3	0	12	7		.256	.304	.349	82	-3	0			.948	0	P-36/O-7	-0.2
1902	Was-A	109	391	61	100	21	5	4	45	33		.256	.319	.366	89	-6	8			.916	0	O-96,P-13	-1.1
1903	Was-A	75	231	17	48	8	4	0	13	18		.208	.265	.277	62	-11	5			.930	7	O-47,P-22	-0.6
1904	Pit-N	8	12	1	4	0	1	0	0	0		.333	.333	.500	152	1	0			.889	0	/P-5	0.0
Total	4	235	763	94	185	35	13	4	70	58		.242	.300	.338	80	-20	13			.917	8	O-150/P-76	-1.9

■ GENE LEEK
Leek, Eugene Harold   b: 7/15/36, San Diego, Cal.   BR/TR, 6', 185 lbs.   Deb: 4/22/59

YEAR	TM/L	G	AB	R	H	2B	3B	HR	RBI	BB	SO	AVG	OBP	SLG	PRO+	BR/A	SB	CS	SBR	FA	FR	G/POS	TPR
1959	Cle-A	13	36	7	8	3	0	1	5	2	7	.222	.263	.389	80	-1	0	0	0	.955	-2	3-13/S-1	-0.3
1961	LA-A	57	199	16	45	9	1	5	20	7	54	.226	.260	.357	57	-13	0	1	-1	.958	18	3-49/S-7,O	0.6
1962	LA-A	7	14	0	2	0	0	0	0	0	6	.143	.143	.143	-24	-2	0	0	0	1.000	0	/3-4	-0.2
Total	3	77	249	23	55	12	1	6	25	9	67	.221	.254	.349	55	-16	0	1	-1	.959	16	/3-66,S-8,O	0.1

■ DAVE LEEPER
Leeper, David Dale   b: 10/30/59, Santa Ana, Cal.   BL/TL, 5'11", 170 lbs.   Deb: 9/10/84

YEAR	TM/L	G	AB	R	H	2B	3B	HR	RBI	BB	SO	AVG	OBP	SLG	PRO+	BR/A	SB	CS	SBR	FA	FR	G/POS	TPR
1984	KC-A	4	6	1	0	0	0	0	0	0	1	.000	.000	.000	-99	-2	0	0	0	1.000	-0	/O-2,D-1	-0.2
1985	KC-A	15	34	1	3	0	0	0	4	1	4	.088	.114	.088	-43	-7	0	0	0	.929	-1	/O-8	-0.8
Total	2	19	40	2	3	0	0	0	4	1	4	.075	.098	.075	-52	-8	0	0	0	.944	-1	/O-10,D-1	-1.0

■ GEORGE LEES
Lees, George Edward   b: 2/2/1895, Bethlehem, Pa.   d: 1/2/80, Harrisburg, Pa.   BR/TR, 5'9", 150 lbs.   Deb: 5/7/21

YEAR	TM/L	G	AB	R	H	2B	3B	HR	RBI	BB	SO	AVG	OBP	SLG	PRO+	BR/A	SB	CS	SBR	FA	FR	G/POS	TPR
1921	Chi-A	20	42	3	9	2	0	0	4	0	3	.214	.214	.262	21	-5	0	1	-1	.951	-2	C-16	-0.7

■ JIM LEFEBVRE
Lefebvre, James Kenneth   b: 1/7/42, Inglewood, Cal.   BB/TR, 6', 185 lbs.   Deb: 4/12/65   MC

YEAR	TM/L	G	AB	R	H	2B	3B	HR	RBI	BB	SO	AVG	OBP	SLG	PRO+	BR/A	SB	CS	SBR	FA	FR	G/POS	TPR
1965	*LA-N	157	544	57	136	21	4	12	69	71	92	.250	.339	.369	106	5	3	5	-2	.970	-12	*2-156	0.5
1966	*LA-N★	152	544	69	149	23	3	24	74	48	72	.274	.336	.460	129	19	1	1	-0	.980	-11	*2-119,3-40	1.7
1967	LA-N	136	494	51	129	18	5	8	50	44	64	.261	.325	.366	106	3	1	5	-3	.955	6	3-92,2-34/1	-0.8
1968	LA-N	84	286	23	69	12	1	5	31	26	55	.241	.307	.343	102	0	0	0	0	.978	-10	2-62,3-16/O1	-0.8
1969	LA-N	95	275	29	65	15	2	4	44	48	37	.236	.352	.349	104	3	2	1	0	.985	1	3-44,2-37/1	0.7
1970	LA-N	109	314	33	79	15	1	4	44	29	42	.252	.317	.344	81	-9	1	1	-0	.988	-4	2-70,3-21/1	-0.8
1971	LA-N	119	388	40	95	14	2	12	68	39	55	.245	.317	.384	104	1	0	2	-1	.988	-17	*2-102/3-7	-0.9
1972	LA-N	70	169	11	34	5	0	5	24	17	30	.201	.274	.337	75	-6	0	0	0	.987	-4	2-33,3-11	-0.6
Total	8	922	3014	313	756	126	18	74	404	322	447	.251	.326	.378	105	18	8	15	-7	.979	-48	2-613,3-231/1O	0.6

■ JOE LEFEBVRE
Lefebvre, Joseph Henry   b: 2/22/56, Concord, N.H.   BL/TR, 5'10", 175 lbs.   Deb: 5/22/80

YEAR	TM/L	G	AB	R	H	2B	3B	HR	RBI	BB	SO	AVG	OBP	SLG	PRO+	BR/A	SB	CS	SBR	FA	FR	G/POS	TPR
1980	*NY-A	74	150	26	34	1	1	8	21	27	30	.227	.345	.407	107	2	0	0	0	.975	-14	O-71	-1.4
1981	SD-N	86	246	31	63	13	4	8	31	35	33	.256	.353	.439	133	11	6	4	-1	.994	4	O-84	1.3
1982	SD-N	102	239	25	57	9	0	4	21	18	50	.238	.295	.326	78	-8	0	0	0	.972	-17	3-39,O-36/C	-2.8
1983	SD-N	18	20	1	5	0	0	0	1	2	3	.250	.318	.250	61	-1	0	0	0	1.000	-2	/O-6,3-4,C	-0.3
	*Phi-N	101	258	34	80	20	6	8	38	31	46	.310	.390	.543	158	20	5	3	-0	.990	-9	O-74/3-9,C	0.6
	Yr	119	278	35	85	20	6	8	39	33	49	.306	.385	.522	151	19	5	3	-0	.990	-11	O-80,3-13/C	0.2
1984	Phi-N	52	160	22	40	9	3	3	18	23	37	.250	.351	.363	99	1	0	4	-1	.966	0	O-47/3-1	-0.2
1986	Phi-N	14	18	0	2	0	0	0	0	3	5	.111	.238	.111	-1	-2	0	0	0	1.000	-0	/O-3	-0.4
Total	6	447	1091	139	281	52	13	31	130	139	204	.258	.346	.414	115	22	11	9	-2	.986	-37	O-321/3-53,C	-2.8

■ BILL LEFEBVRE
Lefebvre, Wilfred Henry "Lefty"   b: 11/11/15, Natick, R.I.   BL/TL, 5'11.5", 180 lbs.   Deb: 6/10/38

YEAR	TM/L	G	AB	R	H	2B	3B	HR	RBI	BB	SO	AVG	OBP	SLG	PRO+	BR/A	SB	CS	SBR	FA	FR	G/POS	TPR
1938	Bos-A	1	1	1	1	0	0	1	1	0	0	1.000	1.000	4.000	1048	1	0	0	0	.000	-0	/P-1	0.0
1939	Bos-A	7	10	3	3	0	0	0	1	2	2	.300	.417	.300	83	-0	0	0	0	1.000	-1	/P-5	0.0
1943	Was-A	7	14	0	4	3	0	0	1	0	0	.286	.286	.500	148	1	0	0	0	1.000	-0	/P-6	0.0
1944	Was-A	60	62	4	16	2	2	0	8	12	9	.258	.378	.355	115	2	0	0	0	.933	-0	P-24/1-2	0.0
Total	4	75	87	8	24	5	2	1	11	15	11	.276	.382	.414	129	4	0	0	0	.960	-1	/P-36,1-2	0.0

■ AL LEFEVRE
Lefevre, Alfredo Modesto   b: 9/16/1898, New York, N.Y.   d: 1/21/82, Glen Cove, N.Y.   BR/TR, 5'10.5", 160 lbs.   Deb: 6/28/20

YEAR	TM/L	G	AB	R	H	2B	3B	HR	RBI	BB	SO	AVG	OBP	SLG	PRO+	BR/A	SB	CS	SBR	FA	FR	G/POS	TPR
1920	NY-N	17	27	5	4	0	1	0	0	0	13	.148	.148	.222	5	-3	0	0	0	1.000	3	/S-9,2-6,3	0.0

■ WADE LEFLER
Lefler, Wade Hampton   b: 6/5/1896, Cooleemee, N.C.   d: 3/6/81, Hickory, N.C.   BL/TL, 5'11", 162 lbs.   Deb: 4/16/24

YEAR	TM/L	G	AB	R	H	2B	3B	HR	RBI	BB	SO	AVG	OBP	SLG	PRO+	BR/A	SB	CS	SBR	FA	FR	G/POS	TPR
1924	Bos-N	1	1	0	0	0	0	0	0	0	1	.000	.000	.000	-99	-0	0	0	0	.000	0	H	0.0
	Was-A	5	8	0	5	3	0	0	4	0	0	.625	.625	1.000	325	2	0	0	0	1.000	-0	/O-1	0.2
Total	1	6	9	0	5	3	0	0	4	0	1	.556	.556	.889	279	2	0	0	0	1.000	-0	/O-1	0.2

■ RON LeFLORE
LeFlore, Ronald   b: 6/16/48, Detroit, Mich.   BR/TR, 6', 200 lbs.   Deb: 8/1/74

YEAR	TM/L	G	AB	R	H	2B	3B	HR	RBI	BB	SO	AVG	OBP	SLG	PRO+	BR/A	SB	CS	SBR	FA	FR	G/POS	TPR
1974	Det-A	59	254	37	66	8	1	2	13	13	58	.260	.304	.323	78	-7	23	9	2	.935	3	O-59	-0.6
1975	Det-A	136	550	66	142	13	6	8	37	33	139	.258	.303	.347	80	-15	28	20	-4	.973	6	*O-134	-1.9
1976	Det-A★	135	544	93	172	23	8	4	39	51	111	.316	.377	.410	125	18	58	20	5	.973	16	*O-132/D-1	3.5
1977	Det-A	154	652	100	212	30	10	16	57	37	121	.325	.365	.475	121	18	39	19	0	.972	2	*O-152	1.3
1978	Det-A	155	666	126	198	30	3	12	62	65	104	.297	.363	.405	113	12	68	16	11	.976	9	*O-155	2.6

YEAR	TM/L	G	AB	R	H	2B	3B	HR	RBI	BB	SO	AVG	OBP	SLG	PRO+	BR/A	SB	CS	SBR	FA	FR	G/POS	TPR
1979	Det-A	148	600	110	180	22	10	9	57	52	95	.300	.356	.415	104	4	78	14	15	.990	4	*O-113,D-34	1.6
1980	Mon-N	139	521	95	134	21	11	4	39	62	99	.257	.337	.363	95	-2	**97**	19	**18**	.957	6	*O-130	1.6
1981	Chi-A	82	337	46	83	10	4	0	24	28	70	.246	.306	.300	77	-10	36	11	4	.960	-1	O-82	-0.9
1982	Chi-A	91	334	58	96	15	4	4	25	22	91	.287	.331	.392	98	-1	28	14	0	.939	-4	O-83/D-2	-0.7
Total	9	1099	4458	731	1283	172	57	59	353	363	888	.288	.344	.392	103	16	455	142	51	.968	41	*O-1040/D-37	6.5

■ LOU LEGETT
Legett, Louis Alfred "Doc" b: 6/1/01, New Orleans, La. d: 3/6/88, New Orleans, La. BR/TR, 5'10", 166 lbs. Deb: 5/8/29

YEAR	TM/L	G	AB	R	H	2B	3B	HR	RBI	BB	SO	AVG	OBP	SLG	PRO+	BR/A	SB	CS	SBR	FA	FR	G/POS	TPR
1929	Bos-N	39	81	7	13	2	0	0	6	3	18	.160	.190	.185	-7	-14	2			.914	-1	C-28	-1.2
1933	Bos-A	8	5	1	1	1	0	0	1	0	0	.200	.200	.400	56	-0	0	0	0	1.000	1	/C-2	0.0
1934	Bos-A	19	38	4	11	0	0	0	1	2	4	.289	.325	.289	56	-2	0	0	0	.977	-0	C-17	-0.2
1935	Bos-A	2	0	1	0	0	0	0	0	0	0	—	—	—			0	0	0	.000	0	R	0.0
Total	4	68	124	13	25	3	0	0	8	5	22	.202	.233	.226	16	-16	2	0		.938	-1	/C-47	-1.4

■ GREG LEGG
Legg, Gregory Lynn b: 4/21/60, San Jose, Cal. BR/TR, 6'1", 185 lbs. Deb: 4/18/86

YEAR	TM/L	G	AB	R	H	2B	3B	HR	RBI	BB	SO	AVG	OBP	SLG	PRO+	BR/A	SB	CS	SBR	FA	FR	G/POS	TPR
1986	Phi-N	11	20	2	9	1	0	0	1	0	3	.450	.450	.500	156	1	0	0	0	.941	2	/2-4,S-1	0.4
1987	Phi-N	3	2	1	0	0	0	0	0	0	0	.000	.000	.000	-97	-1	0	0	0	1.000	-0	/2-1,S-1,3	-0.1
Total	2	14	22	3	9	1	0	0	1	0	3	.409	.409	.455	132	1	0	0	0	.952	2	/2-5,S-2,3	0.3

■ MIKE LEHANE
Lehane, Michael Patrick b: 4/15/1865, New York, N.Y. BR, 6'1.5", 180 lbs. Deb: 4/26/1884

YEAR	TM/L	G	AB	R	H	2B	3B	HR	RBI	BB	SO	AVG	OBP	SLG	PRO+	BR/A	SB	CS	SBR	FA	FR	G/POS	TPR
1884	Was-U	3	12	1	4	2	0	0				.333	.333	.500	128	0				.688	-1	/S-3,O-1,3	0.0
1890	Col-a	140	512	54	108	19	5	0			43	.211	.276	.268	65	-23	13			**.982**	10	*1-140	-1.8
1891	Col-a	137	511	59	110	12	7	1	52	34	77	.215	.268	.272	58	-29	16			**.981**	7	*1-137	-2.5
Total	3	280	1035	114	222	33	12	1	52	77	77	.214	.273	.272	62	-51	29			.982	16	1-277/S-3,3O	-4.3

■ PAUL LEHNER
Lehner, Paul Eugene "Peanuts" or "Gulliver" b: 7/1/20, Dolomite, Ala. d: 12/27/67, Birmingham, Ala. BL/TL, 5'9", 165 lbs. Deb: 9/10/46

YEAR	TM/L	G	AB	R	H	2B	3B	HR	RBI	BB	SO	AVG	OBP	SLG	PRO+	BR/A	SB	CS	SBR	FA	FR	G/POS	TPR
1946	StL-A	16	45	6	10	1	2	0	5	1	5	.222	.239	.333	56	-3	0	0	0	.941	-3	O-12	-0.7
1947	StL-A	135	483	59	120	25	9	7	48	28	29	.248	.294	.381	85	-12	5	5	-2	.980	-6	*O-127	-2.7
1948	StL-A	103	333	23	92	15	4	2	46	30	19	.276	.336	.363	84	-8	0	2	-1	.974	-4	O-89/1-2	-2.0
1949	StL-A	104	297	25	68	13	0	3	37	16	20	.229	.271	.303	50	-23	0	2	-1	.987	2	O-56,1-18	-2.5
1950	Phi-A	114	427	48	132	17	5	9	52	32	33	.309	.357	.436	104	1	1	1	-0	.981	6	*O-101	0.3
1951	Phi-A	9	28	1	4	1	0	0	1	1	1	.143	.172	.179	-5	-4	0	0	0	1.000	1	/O-6	-0.3
	Chi-A	23	72	9	15	3	1	0	3	10	4	.208	.305	.278	60	-4	0	0	0	.980	-4	O-20	-0.8
	StL-A	21	67	2	9	5	0	1	2	6	5	.134	.205	.254	23	-8	0	1	-1	1.000	-1	O-18	-1.0
	Cle-A	12	13	2	3	0	0	0	1	1	2	.231	.286	.231	43	-1	0	0	0	1.000	-0	/O-1	-0.1
	Yr	65	180	14	31	9	1	1	7	18	12	.172	.247	.250	35	-17	0	1	-1	.991	-4	O-45	-2.2
1952	Bos-A	3	3	0	2	0	0	0	2	2	0	.667	.800	.667	288	1	0	0	0	1.000	-0	/O-2	0.1
Total	7	540	1768	175	455	80	21	22	197	127	118	.257	.309	.364	78	-60	6	11	-5	.981	-11	O-432/1-20	-9.7

■ CLARENCE LEHR
Lehr, Clarence Emanuel "King" b: 5/16/1886, Escanaba, Mich. d: 1/31/48, Detroit, Mich. BR/TR, 5'11", 165 lbs. Deb: 5/18/11

YEAR	TM/L	G	AB	R	H	2B	3B	HR	RBI	BB	SO	AVG	OBP	SLG	PRO+	BR/A	SB	CS	SBR	FA	FR	G/POS	TPR
1911	Phi-N	23	27	2	4	0	0	0	2	0	7	.148	.148	.148	-17	-4	0			1.000	-1	/O-5,2-4,S	-0.5

■ HANK LEIBER
Leiber, Henry Edward b: 1/17/11, Phoenix, Ariz. d: 11/8/93, Tucson, Ariz. BR/TR, 6'1.5", 205 lbs. Deb: 4/16/33

YEAR	TM/L	G	AB	R	H	2B	3B	HR	RBI	BB	SO	AVG	OBP	SLG	PRO+	BR/A	SB	CS	SBR	FA	FR	G/POS	TPR
1933	NY-N	6	10	1	2	0	0	0	0	2	2	.200	.200	.200	15	-1	0			1.000	1	/O-1	0.0
1934	NY-N	63	187	17	45	5	3	2	25	4	13	.241	.257	.332	58	-12	1			.971	-6	O-51	-1.9
1935	NY-N	154	613	110	203	37	4	22	107	48	29	.331	.389	.512	143	36	0			.965	-15	*O-154	1.5
1936	*NY-N	101	337	44	94	19	7	9	67	37	41	.279	.352	.457	118	8	1			.961	-7	O-86/1-1	-0.3
1937	*NY-N	51	184	24	54	7	3	4	32	15	27	.293	.347	.429	108	2	1			.988	-7	O-46	-0.6
1938	NY-N★	98	360	50	97	18	4	12	65	31	45	.269	.327	.442	109	3	0			.974	-9	O-89	-0.8
1939	Chi-N	112	365	65	113	16	1	24	88	59	42	.310	.411	.556	155	29	1			.977	4	O-98	2.9
1940	Chi-N†	117	440	68	133	24	2	17	86	45	68	.302	.371	.482	136	21	1			.985	-6	*O-103,1-12	0.9
1941	Chi-N†	53	162	20	35	5	0	7	25	16	25	.216	.291	.377	90	-3	0			.964	-5	O-29,1-15	-1.0
1942	NY-N	58	147	11	32	6	0	4	23	19	27	.218	.315	.340	91	-1	0			.990	-0	O-41/P-1	-0.4
Total	10	813	2805	410	808	137	24	101	518	274	319	.288	.356	.462	122	83	5			.973	-49	O-698/1-28,P	0.3

■ NEMO LEIBOLD
Leibold, Harry Loran b: 2/17/1892, Butler, Ind. d: 2/4/77, Detroit, Mich. BL/TR, 5'6.5", 157 lbs. Deb: 4/12/13

YEAR	TM/L	G	AB	R	H	2B	3B	HR	RBI	BB	SO	AVG	OBP	SLG	PRO+	BR/A	SB	CS	SBR	FA	FR	G/POS	TPR
1913	Cle-A	93	286	37	74	11	6	0	12	21	43	.259	.309	.339	87	-5	16			.945	-0	O-74	-1.0
1914	Cle-A	115	402	46	106	13	3	0	32	54	56	.264	.354	.311	96	-0	12	14	-5	.931	9	*O-107	-0.1
1915	Cle-A	57	207	28	53	5	4	0	4	24	16	.256	.339	.319	95	-1	5	3	-0	.969	9	O-52	0.6
	Chi-A	36	74	10	17	1	0	0	11	15	11	.230	.360	.243	78	-1	1	3	-2	1.000	5	O-22	0.1
	Yr	93	281	38	70	6	4	0	15	39	27	.249	.345	.299	91	-2	6	6	-2	.978	14	O-74	0.7
1916	Chi-A	45	82	5	20	1	2	0	13	7	7	.244	.303	.305	82	-2	7			1.000	-5	O-24	-0.8
1917	*Chi-A	125	428	59	101	12	6	0	29	74	34	.236	.350	.292	94	-0	27			.961	-1	*O-122	-0.8
1918	Chi-A	116	440	57	110	14	7	0	31	63	32	.250	.344	.314	97	-0	13			.979	8	*O-114	0.2
1919	*Chi-A	122	434	81	131	18	2	0	26	72	30	.302	.404	.353	113	11	17			.928	7	*O-122	1.0
1920	Chi-A	108	413	61	91	16	3	1	28	55	30	.220	.316	.281	59	-23	7	15	-7	.977	5	*O-105	-3.2
1921	Bos-A	123	467	88	143	26	6	0	31	41	27	.306	.363	.388	94	-4	13	7	-0	.949	4	*O-117	-0.8
1922	Bos-A	81	271	42	70	8	1	1	18	41	14	.258	.360	.306	76	-8	1	6	-3	.966	6	O-71	-1.0
1923	Bos-A	12	18	1	2	0	0	0	0	1	2	.111	.158	.111	-28	-3	0	1	-1	.909	-3	O-10	-0.7
	Was-A	95	315	68	96	13	4	1	22	53	16	.305	.408	.381	114	9	7	6	-2	.980	1	O-84	0.4
	Yr	107	333	69	98	13	4	1	22	54	18	.294	.396	.366	106	5	7	7	-2	.977	-2	O-94	-0.3
1924	*Was-A	84	246	41	72	6	4	0	20	42	10	.293	.398	.350	97	-1	7	5	-1	.994	-3	O-70	-0.6
1925	*Was-A	56	84	14	23	1	1	0	7	8	7	.274	.337	.310	66	-4	1	0		.972	-6	O-26/3-1	-1.0
Total	13	1268	4167	638	1109	145	49	3	284	571	335	.266	.357	.327	91	-30	134	60		.961	38	*O-1120/3-1	-7.7

■ ELMER LEIFER
Leifer, Elmer Edwin b: 5/23/1893, Clarington, Ohio d: 9/26/48, Everett, Wash. BL/TR, 5'9.5", 170 lbs. Deb: 9/7/21

YEAR	TM/L	G	AB	R	H	2B	3B	HR	RBI	BB	SO	AVG	OBP	SLG	PRO+	BR/A	SB	CS	SBR	FA	FR	G/POS	TPR
1921	Chi-A	9	10	0	3	0	0	0	1	0	4	.300	.300	.300	54	-1	0	0	0	1.000	-1	/3-1,O-1	-0.1

■ JOHN LEIGHTON
Leighton, John Atkinson b: 10/4/1861, Peabody, Mass. d: 10/31/56, Lynn, Mass. 5'11", 170 lbs. Deb: 7/12/1890

YEAR	TM/L	G	AB	R	H	2B	3B	HR	RBI	BB	SO	AVG	OBP	SLG	PRO+	BR/A	SB	CS	SBR	FA	FR	G/POS	TPR
1890	Syr-a	7	27	6	8	2	0	0		3		.296	.367	.370	131	1	2			.938	-0	/O-7	0.0

■ BILL LEINHAUSER
Leinhauser, William Charles b: 11/4/1893, Philadelphia, Pa. d: 4/14/78, Elkins Park, Pa. BR/TR, 5'10", 150 lbs. Deb: 5/18/12

YEAR	TM/L	G	AB	R	H	2B	3B	HR	RBI	BB	SO	AVG	OBP	SLG	PRO+	BR/A	SB	CS	SBR	FA	FR	G/POS	TPR
1912	Det-A	1	4	0	0	0	0	0	0	0		.000	.000	.000	-99	-1	0			1.000	0	/O-1	-0.1

■ ED LEIP
Leip, Edgar Ellsworth b: 11/29/10, Trenton, N.J. d: 11/24/83, Zephyrhills, Fla. BR/TR, 5'9", 160 lbs. Deb: 9/16/39

YEAR	TM/L	G	AB	R	H	2B	3B	HR	RBI	BB	SO	AVG	OBP	SLG	PRO+	BR/A	SB	CS	SBR	FA	FR	G/POS	TPR
1939	Was-A	9	32	4	11	1	0	0	2	2	4	.344	.382	.375	102	0	0	1	-1	.951	-1	/2-8	-0.1
1940	Pit-N	3	5	2	1	0	0	0	1	0	0	.200	.200	.200	11	-1	0			1.000	-0	/2-2	-0.1
1941	Pit-N	15	25	1	5	0	2	0	3	1	2	.200	.231	.360	65	-1	1			.889	-0	/2-7,3-1	0.1
1942	Pit-N	3	0	0	0	0	0	0	0	0	0	—	—	—		0	0			.000	0	R	0.0
Total	4	30	62	7	17	1	2	0	5	3	6	.274	.308	.355	80	-2	1	1		.931	0	/2-17,3-1	-0.1

■ SCOTT LEIUS
Leius, Scott Thomas b: 9/24/65, Yonkers, N.Y. BR/TR, 6'3", 180 lbs. Deb: 9/3/90

YEAR	TM/L	G	AB	R	H	2B	3B	HR	RBI	BB	SO	AVG	OBP	SLG	PRO+	BR/A	SB	CS	SBR	FA	FR	G/POS	TPR
1990	Min-A	14	25	4	6	1	0	1	2	2	6	.240	.296	.400	87	-0	0	0	0	1.000	3	S-12/3-1	0.3
1991	*Min-A	109	199	35	57	7	2	5	20	30	35	.286	.380	.417	115	5	5	5	-2	.953	-2	3-79,S-19/O	0.3
1992	Min-A	129	409	50	102	18	2	2	35	34	61	.249	.309	.318	73	-14	6	5	-1	.955	4	*3-125,S-10	-1.1
1993	Min-A	10	18	4	3	0	0	0	2	2	4	.167	.250	.167	14	-2	0	0	0	.947	4	/S-9	0.2

YEAR	TM/L	G	AB	R	H	2B	3B	HR	RBI	BB	SO	AVG	OBP	SLG	PRO+	BR/A	SB	CS	SBR	FA	FR	G/POS	TPR
1994	Min-A	97	350	57	86	16	1	14	49	37	58	.246	.320	.417	88	-7	2	4	-2	.969	-1	3-95/S-2	-0.9
Total	5	359	1001	150	254	42	5	22	110	105	160	.254	.326	.372	86	-19	13	14	-5	.959	8	3-300/S-52,O	-1.2

■ FRANK LEJA
Leja, Frank John   b: 2/7/36, Holyoke, Mass.   d: 5/3/91, Boston, Mass.   BL/TL, 6'4", 205 lbs.   Deb: 5/1/54

YEAR	TM/L	G	AB	R	H	2B	3B	HR	RBI	BB	SO	AVG	OBP	SLG	PRO+	BR/A	SB	CS	SBR	FA	FR	G/POS	TPR
1954	NY-A	12	5	2	1	0	0	0	0	0	1	.200	.200	.200	10	-1	0	0	0	1.000	0	/1-6	-0.1
1955	NY-A	7	2	1	0	0	0	0	0	0	1	.000	.000	.000	-99	-1	0	0	0	1.000	0	/1-2	-0.1
1962	LA-A	7	16	0	0	0	0	0	0	1	6	.000	.059	.000	-85	-4	0	0	0	.953	-0	/1-4	-0.5
Total	3	26	23	3	1	0	0	0	0	1	8	.043	.083	.043	-67	-5	0	0	0	.958	-0	/1-12	-0.7

■ LARRY LeJEUNE
LeJeune, Sheldon Aldenbert   b: 7/22/1885, Chicago, Ill.   d: 4/21/52, Eloise, Mich.   BR/TR, 6', 185 lbs.   Deb: 5/10/11

YEAR	TM/L	G	AB	R	H	2B	3B	HR	RBI	BB	SO	AVG	OBP	SLG	PRO+	BR/A	SB	CS	SBR	FA	FR	G/POS	TPR
1911	Bro-N	6	19	2	3	0	0	0	2	2	8	.158	.238	.158	12	-2	2			.818	-2	/O-6	-0.5
1915	Pit-N	18	65	4	11	0	1	0	2	2	7	.169	.206	.200	23	-6	4	3	-1	.940	2	O-18	-0.6
Total	2	24	84	6	14	0	1	0	4	4	15	.167	.213	.190	21	-8	6	3		.918	1	/O-24	-1.1

■ DON LeJOHN
LeJohn, Donald Everett   b: 5/13/34, Daisytown, Pa.   BR/TR, 5'10", 175 lbs.   Deb: 6/30/65

YEAR	TM/L	G	AB	R	H	2B	3B	HR	RBI	BB	SO	AVG	OBP	SLG	PRO+	BR/A	SB	CS	SBR	FA	FR	G/POS	TPR
1965	*LA-N	34	78	2	20	2	0	0	7	5	13	.256	.301	.282	70	-1	0	1	-1	.959	1	3-26	-0.4

■ JACK LELIVELT
Lelivelt, John Frank   b: 11/14/1885, Chicago, Ill.   d: 1/20/41, Seattle, Wash.   BL/TL, 5'11", 175 lbs.   Deb: 6/24/09   F

YEAR	TM/L	G	AB	R	H	2B	3B	HR	RBI	BB	SO	AVG	OBP	SLG	PRO+	BR/A	SB	CS	SBR	FA	FR	G/POS	TPR
1909	Was-A	91	318	25	93	8	6	0	24	19		.292	.334	.355	124	8	8			.970	8	O-91	1.4
1910	Was-A	110	347	40	92	10	3	0	33	40		.265	.343	.311	110	5	20			.964	4	O-86/1-7	0.6
1911	Was-A	72	225	29	72	12	4	0	22	22		.320	.386	.409	124	8	7			.939	4	O-49/1-7	0.8
1912	NY-A	36	149	12	54	6	7	2	23	4		.362	.383	.537	153	9	7			.963	-1	O-36	0.6
1913	NY-A	18	28	2	6	0	1	0	4	2	2	.214	.267	.286	61	-1	1			1.000	1	/O-5	-0.1
	Cle-A	23	23	0	9	2	0	0	7	0	3	.391	.391	.478	150	1	1			.000	-1	/O-1	0.1
	Yr	41	51	2	15	2	1	0	11	2	5	.294	.321	.373	101	-0	2			1.000	1	/O-6	0.0
1914	Cle-A	34	64	6	21	5	1	0	13	2	10	.328	.348	.438	131	2	2	3	-1	.933	-3	O-13/1-1	-0.3
Total	6	384	1154	114	347	43	22	2	126	89	15	.301	.353	.381	124	31	46	3		.962	13	O-281/1-15	3.1

■ JOHNNIE LeMASTER
LeMaster, Johnnie Lee   b: 6/19/54, Portsmouth, Ohio   BR/TR, 6'2", 167 lbs.   Deb: 9/2/75

YEAR	TM/L	G	AB	R	H	2B	3B	HR	RBI	BB	SO	AVG	OBP	SLG	PRO+	BR/A	SB	CS	SBR	FA	FR	G/POS	TPR
1975	SF-N	22	74	4	14	4	0	2	9	4	15	.189	.241	.324	53	-5	2	1	0	.967	-1	S-22	-0.4
1976	SF-N	33	100	9	21	3	2	0	9	2	21	.210	.225	.280	42	-8	2	0	1	.937	11	S-31	0.7
1977	SF-N	68	134	13	20	5	1	0	8	13	27	.149	.224	.201	15	-16	2	1	0	.934	7	S-54/3-2	-0.5
1978	SF-N	101	272	23	64	18	3	1	14	21	45	.235	.293	.335	78	-9	6	6	-2	.966	3	S-96/2-2	0.2
1979	SF-N	108	343	42	87	11	2	3	29	23	55	.254	.304	.324	77	-12	9	5	-0	.959	0	*S-106	-0.1
1980	SF-N	135	405	33	87	16	6	3	31	25	57	.215	.260	.306	59	-23	0	1	-1	.957	-14	*S-134	-2.5
1981	SF-N	104	324	27	82	9	1	0	28	24	46	.253	.307	.287	70	-12	3	7	-3	.964	-8	*S-103	-1.5
1982	SF-N	130	436	34	94	14	1	2	30	31	78	.216	.268	.266	50	-29	13	4	2	.963	-8	*S-130	-2.5
1983	SF-N	141	534	81	128	16	1	6	30	60	96	.240	.319	.307	77	-16	39	19	2	.964	-22	*S-139	-2.6
1984	SF-N	132	451	46	98	13	2	4	32	31	97	.217	.268	.282	56	-27	17	5	2	.964	4	*S-129	-0.9
1985	SF-N	12	16	1	0	0	0	0	0	1	5	.000	.059	.000	-86	-4	0	0	0	.955	-1	S-10	-0.5
	Cle-A	11	20	0	3	0	0	0	2	0	6	.150	.150	.150	-18	-3	0	1	-1	.949	3	S-10	0.0
	Pit-N	22	58	4	9	0	0	1	6	5	12	.155	.222	.207	21	-6	1	0		.983	13	S-21	0.9
1987	Oak-A	20	24	3	2	0	0	0	1	1	4	.083	.120	.083	-48	-5	0	1	-1	1.000	5	/3-8,S-7,2D	0.0
Total	12	1039	3191	320	709	109	19	22	229	241	564	.222	.278	.289	60	-174	94	51	-2	.961	-9	S-992/3-10,2D	-9.7

■ STEVE LEMBO
Lembo, Stephen Neal   b: 11/13/26, Brooklyn, N.Y.   d: 12/4/89, Flushing, N.Y.   BR/TR, 6'1", 185 lbs.   Deb: 9/16/50

YEAR	TM/L	G	AB	R	H	2B	3B	HR	RBI	BB	SO	AVG	OBP	SLG	PRO+	BR/A	SB	CS	SBR	FA	FR	G/POS	TPR
1950	Bro-N	5	6	0	1	0	0	0	0	1	0	.167	.286	.167	22	-1	0			1.000	2	/C-5	0.2
1952	Bro-N	2	5	0	1	0	0	0	1	0	1	.200	.200	.200	11	-1	0	0	0	1.000	1	/C-2	0.0
Total	2	7	11	0	2	0	0	0	1	1	1	.182	.250	.182	18	-1	0	0	0	1.000	3	/C-7	0.2

■ MARK LEMKE
Lemke, Mark Alan   b: 8/13/65, Utica, N.Y.   BB/TR, 5'10", 167 lbs.   Deb: 9/17/88

YEAR	TM/L	G	AB	R	H	2B	3B	HR	RBI	BB	SO	AVG	OBP	SLG	PRO+	BR/A	SB	CS	SBR	FA	FR	G/POS	TPR
1988	Atl-N	16	58	8	13	4	0	0	2	4	5	.224	.274	.293	60	-3	0	2	-1	.970	4	2-16	0.1
1989	Atl-N	14	55	4	10	2	1	2	10	5	7	.182	.250	.364	72	-2	0	1	-1	1.000	-2	2-14	-0.4
1990	Atl-N	102	239	22	54	13	0	0	21	21	22	.226	.288	.280	54	-15	0	1	-1	.989	23	3-45,2-44/S	0.9
1991	*Atl-N	136	269	36	63	11	2	2	23	29	27	.234	.308	.312	71	-10	1	2	-1	.978	13	*2-110,3-15	0.4
1992	*Atl-N	155	427	38	97	7	4	6	26	50	39	.227	.308	.304	70	-16	0	3	-2	.984	-10	*2-145,3-13	-2.7
1993	*Atl-N	151	493	52	124	19	2	7	49	65	50	.252	.339	.341	82	-11	1	2	-1	.982	6	*2-150	-0.2
1994	Atl-N	104	350	40	103	15	0	3	31	38	37	.294	.363	.363	90	-4	0	3	-2	.994	7	*2-103	0.4
Total	7	678	1891	200	464	71	9	20	162	212	187	.245	.321	.324	75	-61	2	14	-8	.985	42	2-582/3-73,S	-1.5

■ CHET LEMON
Lemon, Chester Earl   b: 2/12/55, Jackson, Miss.   BR/TR, 6', 195 lbs.   Deb: 9/9/75

YEAR	TM/L	G	AB	R	H	2B	3B	HR	RBI	BB	SO	AVG	OBP	SLG	PRO+	BR/A	SB	CS	SBR	FA	FR	G/POS	TPR
1975	Chi-A	9	35	2	9	2	0	0	1	2	6	.257	.297	.314	72	-1	1	0	0	.923	-4	/3-6,O-1,D	-0.5
1976	Chi-A	132	451	46	111	15	5	4	38	28	65	.246	.300	.328	83	-10	13	7	-0	.992	11	*O-131	-0.4
1977	Chi-A	150	553	99	151	38	4	19	67	52	88	.273	.347	.459	118	13	8	7	-2	.978	**35**	*O-149	4.0
1978	Chi-A★	105	357	51	107	24	6	13	55	39	46	.300	.381	.510	147	22	5	9	-4	.983	14	O-95,D-10	2.8
1979	Chi-A★	148	556	79	177	**44**	2	17	86	56	68	.318	.394	.496	138	31	7	11	-5	.977	9	*O-147	2.8
1980	Chi-A	147	514	76	150	32	6	11	51	71	56	.292	.390	.442	128	22	6	6	-2	.981	2	*O-139/2-1,D	1.6
1981	Chi-A	94	328	50	99	23	6	9	50	33	48	.302	.388	.491	155	24	5	8	-3	.984	2	O-93	2.0
1982	Det-A	125	436	75	116	20	1	19	52	56	69	.266	.369	.447	122	15	1	4	-2	.984	1	*O-121/D-1	1.0
1983	Det-A	145	491	78	125	21	5	24	69	54	70	.255	.352	.464	126	18	0	7	-4	.988	11	*O-145	2.0
1984	*Det-A★	141	509	77	146	34	6	20	76	51	83	.287	.360	.495	135	24	5	5	-2	.995	11	*O-140/D-1	3.3
1985	Det-A	145	517	69	137	28	4	18	68	45	93	.265	.336	.439	111	7	0	2	-1	.990	11	*O-144	1.2
1986	Det-A	126	403	45	101	21	3	12	53	39	53	.251	.329	.407	99	-0	2	1	-0	.985	3	*O-124	-0.1
1987	*Det-A	146	470	75	130	30	3	20	75	70	82	.277	.380	.481	132	23	0	0	0	.992	3	*O-145	2.0
1988	Det-A	144	512	67	135	29	4	17	64	59	65	.264	.348	.436	123	16	1	2	-1	.974	4	*O-111,D-13	1.5
1989	Det-A	127	414	45	98	19	2	7	47	46	71	.237	.325	.343	90	-4	1	5	-3	.985	-6	*O-111,D-13	-1.7
1990	Det-A	104	322	39	83	16	4	5	32	48	61	.258	.361	.379	106	4	3	2	-0	.973	6	O-96/D-6	0.8
Total	16	1988	6868	973	1875	396	61	215	884	749	1024	.273	.357	.442	121	203	58	76	-28	.984	116	*O-1925/D-39,32	22.3

■ JIM LEMON
Lemon, James Robert   b: 3/23/28, Covington, Va.   BR/TR, 6'4", 200 lbs.   Deb: 8/20/50   MC

YEAR	TM/L	G	AB	R	H	2B	3B	HR	RBI	BB	SO	AVG	OBP	SLG	PRO+	BR/A	SB	CS	SBR	FA	FR	G/POS	TPR
1950	Cle-A	12	34	4	6	1	0	1	1	3	12	.176	.243	.294	38	-3	0	0	0	.824	-2	O-10	-0.5
1953	Cle-A	16	46	5	8	1	0	1	5	3	15	.174	.224	.261	32	-5	0	0	0	.913	-1	O-11/1-2	-0.6
1954	Was-A	37	128	12	30	2	3	2	13	9	34	.234	.285	.344	76	-5	0	0	0	.951	-5	O-33	-1.0
1955	Was-A	10	25	3	5	2	0	1	3	3	4	.200	.286	.400	88	-1	0	0	0	.923	-0	/O-6	-0.1
1956	Was-A	146	538	77	146	21	**11**	27	96	65	138	.271	.352	.502	123	16	2	4	-2	.963	8	*O-141	1.4
1957	Was-A	137	518	58	147	23	6	17	64	49	94	.284	.349	.450	118	12	1	7	-4	.971	-3	*O-131/1-3	-0.3
1958	Was-A	142	501	65	123	15	9	26	75	50	120	.246	.315	.467	114	8	2	4	-2	.978	-6	*O-137	-0.1
1959	Was-A	147	531	73	148	18	3	33	100	46	99	.279	.337	.510	130	20	5	2	0	.969	-3	*O-142	1.6
1960	Was-A★	148	528	81	142	10	1	38	100	67	114	.269	.359	.508	133	23	2	1	0	.960	-1	*O-145	1.6
1961	Min-A	129	423	57	109	26	1	14	52	44	98	.258	.333	.423	95	-3	1	1	-0	.940	-6	*O-120	-1.6
1962	Min-A	12	17	1	3	0	0	1	5	3	9	.176	.300	.353	72	-1	0	0	0	1.000	-1	/O-3	-0.2
1963	Min-A	7	17	0	2	0	0	0	1	0	4	.118	.118	.118	-18	-3	0	0	0	1.000	-1	/O-4	-0.4
	Phi-N	31	59	6	16	2	0	2	6	8	13	.271	.358	.407	121	2	0	0	0	.963	-2	O-18	0.0
	Chi-A	36	80	4	16	3	1	1	8	12	32	.200	.304	.262	62	-4	0	0	0	.979	-3	1-25	-0.8
Total	12	1010	3445	446	901	121	35	164	529	363	787	.262	.335	.460	114	57	13	18	-7	.961	-12	O-901/1-30	-1.0

YEAR	TM/L	G	AB	R	H	2B	3B	HR	RBI	BB	SO	AVG	OBP	SLG	PRO+	BR/A	SB	CS	SBR	FA	FR	G/POS	TPR

■ BOB LEMON   Lemon, Robert Granville   b: 9/22/20, San Bernardino, Cal.   BL/TR, 6', 185 lbs.   Deb: 9/9/41   MCH

YEAR	TM/L	G	AB	R	H	2B	3B	HR	RBI	BB	SO	AVG	OBP	SLG	PRO+	BR/A	SB	CS	SBR	FA	FR	G/POS	TPR
1941	Cle-A	5	4	0	1	0	0	0	0	0	1	.250	.250	.250	34	-0	0	0	0	1.000	0	/3-1	0.0
1942	Cle-A	5	5	0	0	0	0	0	0	0	3	.000	.000	.000	-99	-1	0	0	0	.500	0	/3-1	-0.1
1946	Cle-A	55	89	9	16	3	0	1	4	7	18	.180	.240	.247	39	-8	0	1	-1	.976	0	P-32,O-12	-0.3
1947	Cle-A	47	56	11	18	4	3	2	5	6	9	.321	.387	.607	179	5	0	0	0	.983	4	P-37/O-2	-0.1
1948	*Cle-A☆	52	119	20	34	9	0	5	21	8	23	.286	.331	.487	119	2	0	0	0	.965	8	P-43	0.0
1949	Cle-A★	46	108	17	29	6	2	7	19	10	20	.269	.331	.556	135	4	0	0	0	.963	6	P-37	0.0
1950	Cle-A★	72	136	21	37	9	1	6	26	13	25	.272	.340	.485	113	2	0	0	0	.957	5	P-44	0.0
1951	Cle-A★	56	102	11	21	4	1	3	13	9	22	.206	.270	.353	72	-5	0	0	0	.976	4	P-42	0.0
1952	Cle-A★	54	124	14	28	5	0	2	9	4	21	.226	.250	.315	60	-7	0	0	0	.982	7	P-42	0.0
1953	Cle-A	51	112	12	26	9	1	2	17	7	20	.232	.277	.384	79	-4	2	0	1	.972	8	P-41	0.0
1954	*Cle-A★	40	98	11	21	4	1	2	10	6	24	.214	.260	.337	61	-6	0	0	0	.963	4	P-36	0.0
1955	Cle-A	49	78	11	19	0	0	1	9	13	16	.244	.352	.282	69	-3	0	0	0	.983	2	P-35	0.0
1956	Cle-A	43	93	8	18	0	0	5	12	9	21	.194	.272	.355	63	-5	0	0	0	.934	4	P-39	0.0
1957	Cle-A	25	46	2	3	1	0	1	1	0	14	.065	.065	.152	-43	-9	0	0	0	1.000	3	P-21	0.0
1958	Cle-A	15	13	1	3	0	0	0	1	1	4	.231	.286	.231	45	-1	0	0	0	1.000	1	P-11	0.0
Total	15	615	1183	148	274	54	9	37	147	93	241	.232	.289	.386	82	-36	2	1	0	.969	62	P-460/O-14,3	-0.5

■ DON LENHARDT   Lenhardt, Donald Eugene "Footsie"   b: 10/4/22, Alton, Ill.   BR/TR, 6'3", 190 lbs.   Deb: 4/18/50   C

YEAR	TM/L	G	AB	R	H	2B	3B	HR	RBI	BB	SO	AVG	OBP	SLG	PRO+	BR/A	SB	CS	SBR	FA	FR	G/POS	TPR
1950	StL-A	139	480	75	131	22	6	22	81	90	94	.273	.390	.481	118	13	3	2	-0	.988	-12	1-86,O-39,3	-0.2
1951	StL-A	31	103	9	27	3	0	5	18	6	13	.262	.303	.437	95	-1	1	0	0	.982	-2	O-27/1-1	-0.4
	Chi-A	64	199	23	53	9	1	10	45	24	25	.266	.351	.472	124	6	1	1	-0	.983	-2	O-53/1-2	0.2
	Yr	95	302	32	80	12	1	15	63	30	38	.265	.335	.460	114	5	2	1	0	.983	-4	O-80/1-3	-0.2
1952	Bos-A	30	105	18	31	4	0	7	24	15	18	.295	.383	.533	142	6	0	1	-1	.981	-2	O-27	0.2
	Det-A	45	144	18	27	2	1	3	13	28	18	.188	.320	.278	67	-6	0	1	-1	.989	3	O-43	-0.5
	StL-A	18	48	5	13	4	1	1	5	4	8	.271	.327	.458	114	1	0	0	0	1.000	0	O-11/1-2	0.0
	Yr	93	297	41	71	10	2	11	42	47	44	.239	.343	.397	102	1	0	2	-1	.988	2	O-81/1-2	-0.3
1953	StL-A	97	303	37	96	15	0	10	35	41	41	.317	.400	.465	131	14	1	2	-1	.969	2	O-77/3-6	1.2
1954	Bal-A	13	33	2	5	1	0	0	1	3	9	.152	.222	.182	12	-4	0	0	0	1.000	-1	/O-7,1-2	-0.5
	Bos-A	44	66	5	18	4	0	3	17	3	9	.273	.314	.470	101	-0	0	0	0	1.000	-3	O-13/3-1	-0.4
	Yr	57	99	7	23	5	0	3	18	6	18	.232	.283	.374	74	-4	0	0	0	1.000	-4	O-20/1-2,3	-0.9
Total	5	481	1481	192	401	64	9	61	239	214	235	.271	.365	.450	114	28	6	7	-2	.980	-15	O-297/1-93,3	-0.4

■ PATRICK LENNON   Lennon, Patrick Orlando   b: 4/27/68, Whiteville, N.C.   BR/TR, 6'2", 200 lbs.   Deb: 9/15/91

YEAR	TM/L	G	AB	R	H	2B	3B	HR	RBI	BB	SO	AVG	OBP	SLG	PRO+	BR/A	SB	CS	SBR	FA	FR	G/POS	TPR
1991	Sea-A	9	8	2	1	1	0	0	1	3	1	.125	.364	.250	73	-0	0	0	0	1.000	0	/O-1,D-5	0.0
1992	Sea-A	1	2	0	0	0	0	0	0	0	0	.000	.000	.000	-99	-1	0	0	0	1.000	-0	/1-1	-0.1
Total	2	10	10	2	1	1	0	0	1	3	1	.100	.308	.200	44	-1	0	0	0	1.000	-0	/D-5,1-1,O	-0.1

■ BOB LENNON   Lennon, Robert Albert "Arch"   b: 9/15/28, Brooklyn, N.Y.   BL/TL, 6', 200 lbs.   Deb: 9/9/54

YEAR	TM/L	G	AB	R	H	2B	3B	HR	RBI	BB	SO	AVG	OBP	SLG	PRO+	BR/A	SB	CS	SBR	FA	FR	G/POS	TPR
1954	NY-N	3	3	0	0	0	0	0	0	0	0	.000	.000	.000	-99	-1	0	0	0	.000	0	H	-0.1
1956	NY-N	26	55	3	10	1	0	1	4	17	.182	.237	.200	19	-6	0	0	0	.885	-4	O-21	-1.2
1957	Chi-N	9	21	2	3	1	0	1	3	1	9	.143	.182	.333	35	-2	0	0	0	1.000	-1	/O-4	-0.4
Total	3	38	79	5	13	2	0	1	4	5	26	.165	.214	.228	19	-9	0	0	0	.900	-6	/O-25	-1.7

■ BILL LENNON   Lennon, William F.   b: 1848, Brooklyn, N.Y.   5'7", 145 lbs.   Deb: 5/4/1871   MU

YEAR	TM/L	G	AB	R	H	2B	3B	HR	RBI	BB	SO	AVG	OBP	SLG	PRO+	BR/A	SB	CS	SBR	FA	FR	G/POS	TPR
1871	Kek-n	12	48	5	11	3	0	0	5	1	0	.229	.245	.292	52	-3	1					C-12,M	-0.2
1872	Nat-n	11	55	11	12	2	0	0	5	0	0	.218	.218	.255	39	-5						C-11	-0.4
1873	Mar-n	5	19	2	4	1	0	0	0	0	0	.211	.211	.263	50	-1						/1-4,C-1,3	-0.1
Total	3 n	28	122	18	27	6	0	0	10	1		.221	.228	.270	45	-9						/C-24,1-4,3	-0.7

■ ED LENNOX   Lennox, James Edgar "Eggie"   b: 11/3/1885, Camden, N.J.   d: 10/26/39, Camden, N.J.   BR/TR, 5'10", 174 lbs.   Deb: 8/8/06

YEAR	TM/L	G	AB	R	H	2B	3B	HR	RBI	BB	SO	AVG	OBP	SLG	PRO+	BR/A	SB	CS	SBR	FA	FR	G/POS	TPR
1906	Phi-A	6	17	1	1	1	0	0	1			.059	.111	.118	-28	-2	0			.909	5	/3-6	0.3
1909	Bro-N	126	435	33	114	18	9	2	44	47		.262	.337	.359	120	10	11			.959	-3	*3-121	1.2
1910	Bro-N	110	367	19	95	19	4	3	32	36	39	.259	.333	.357	104	2	7			.950	-16	*3-100	-1.2
1912	Chi-N	27	81	13	19	4	1	0	16	12	10	.235	.347	.346	90	-1	1			.934	-5	3-24	-0.6
1914	Pit-F	124	430	71	134	25	10	11	84	71	38	.312	.414	.493	135	24	19			.954	-15	*3-123	1.3
1915	Pit-F	55	53	1	16	3	1	1	9	7	12	.302	.383	.453	124	2	0			1.000	2	/3-3	0.5
Total	6	448	1383	138	379	70	25	18	185	174	99	.274	.361	.400	118	34	38			.953	-32	3-377	1.5

■ JIM LENTINE   Lentine, James Matthew   b: 7/16/54, Los Angeles, Cal.   BR/TR, 6', 175 lbs.   Deb: 9/3/78

YEAR	TM/L	G	AB	R	H	2B	3B	HR	RBI	BB	SO	AVG	OBP	SLG	PRO+	BR/A	SB	CS	SBR	FA	FR	G/POS	TPR
1978	StL-N	8	11	1	2	0	0	0	1	0	0	.182	.250	.182	23	-1	1	0	0	1.000	-0	/O-3	-0.1
1979	StL-N	11	23	2	9	1	0	0	1	3	6	.391	.462	.435	145	2	0	1	-1	1.000	-0	/O-8	0.1
1980	StL-N	9	10	1	1	0	0	0	1	0	2	.100	.100	.100	-43	-2	0	0	0	1.000	-2	/O-6	-0.4
	Det-A	67	161	19	42	8	1	1	17	28	30	.261	.377	.342	96	0	2	1	0	.963	-3	O-55/D-9	-0.4
Total	3	95	205	23	54	9	1	1	20	31	38	.263	.368	.332	92	-1	3	2	-0	.969	-5	/O-72,D-9	-0.8

■ EDDIE LEON   Leon, Eduardo Antonio   b: 8/11/46, Tucson, Ariz.   BR/TR, 6', 175 lbs.   Deb: 9/9/68

YEAR	TM/L	G	AB	R	H	2B	3B	HR	RBI	BB	SO	AVG	OBP	SLG	PRO+	BR/A	SB	CS	SBR	FA	FR	G/POS	TPR
1968	Cle-A	6	1	0	0	0	0	0	0	0	1	.000	.000	.000	-99	-0	0	0	0	1.000	3	/S-6	0.3
1969	Cle-A	64	213	20	51	6	3	0	19	19	37	.239	.302	.310	69	-9	2	2	-1	.952	9	S-64	0.6
1970	Cle-A	152	549	58	136	20	4	10	56	47	89	.248	.309	.353	78	-16	1	2	-1	.982	8	*2-141,S-23/3	0.5
1971	Cle-A	131	429	35	112	12	2	4	35	34	69	.261	.317	.326	76	-13	3	5	-2	.983	0	*2-107,S-24	-0.4
1972	Cle-A	89	225	14	45	2	1	4	16	20	47	.200	.268	.271	59	-11	0	2	-1	.993	-1	2-36,S-35	-0.8
1973	Chi-A	127	399	37	91	10	3	3	30	34	103	.228	.294	.291	63	-19	1	5	-3	.972	-2	*S-122/2-3	-0.9
1974	Chi-A	31	46	1	5	1	0	0	3	2	12	.109	.146	.130	-20	-7	0	0	0	.962	8	S-21/2-7,3D	0.3
1975	NY-A	1	0	0	0	0	0	0	0	0	0	—	—	—	—	0	0	0	0	1.000	0	/S-1	0.0
Total	8	601	1862	165	440	51	10	24	159	156	358	.236	.298	.313	69	-76	7	16	-8	.963	25	S-296,2-294/3D	-0.4

■ LEONARD   Leonard   Deb: 9/12/1892

YEAR	TM/L	G	AB	R	H	2B	3B	HR	RBI	BB	SO	AVG	OBP	SLG	PRO+	BR/A	SB	CS	SBR	FA	FR	G/POS	TPR
1892	StL-N	1	0	0	0	0	0	0	0	0	1	—	1.000	—	219	0	1			.000	-0	/O-1	0.0

■ ANDY LEONARD   Leonard, Andrew Jackson   b: 6/1/1846, County Cavan, Ireland   d: 8/21/03, Boston, Mass.   BR/TR, 5'7", 168 lbs.   Deb: 5/5/1871

YEAR	TM/L	G	AB	R	H	2B	3B	HR	RBI	BB	SO	AVG	OBP	SLG	PRO+	BR/A	SB	CS	SBR	FA	FR	G/POS	TPR
1871	Oly-n	31	148	33	43	8	3	0	30	3	1	.291	.305	.385	102	1	14					*2-20,O-10/S	0.0
1872	Bos-n	46	243	59	84	8	2	2	44	0	2	.346	.346	.420	128	6						*O-37/3-6,2	0.4
1873	Bos-n	58	302	81	95	12	6	0	58	4	0	.315	.324	.394	102	-2						*O-45,2-12/13	-0.2
1874	Bos-n	71	340	68	109	18	4	0		2		.321	.325	.397	122	6						*O-51,S-11/2	0.5
1875	Bos-n	80	394	87	127	14	6	1		1		.322	.324	.396	143	15						*O-73/S-3,32	1.3
1876	Bos-N	64	303	53	85	10	2	0	27	4	6	.281	.290	.327	103	1				.925	-1	O-35,2-30	-0.8
1877	Bos-N	58	272	46	78	5	0	0	27	5	5	.287	.300	.305	88	-4				.875	-4	O-37,S-21	-0.8
1878	Bos-N	60	262	41	68	8	5	0	16	3	19	.260	.268	.328	88	-4				.777	-7	/O-60	-1.3
1880	Cin-N	33	133	15	28	3	0	1	17	8	11	.211	.255	.256	75	-3				.833	-12	S-23,3-10	-1.3
Total	5 n	286	1427	328	458	60	21	3	132	10	3	.321	.326	.399	121	26						O-216/2-45,S31	2.0
Total	4	215	970	155	259	26	7	1	87	20	41	.267	.282	.311	91	-11				.856	-23	O-132/S-44,23	-3.4

■ JEFFREY LEONARD   Leonard, Jeffrey   b: 9/22/55, Philadelphia, Pa.   BR/TR, 6'2", 200 lbs.   Deb: 9/2/77

YEAR	TM/L	G	AB	R	H	2B	3B	HR	RBI	BB	SO	AVG	OBP	SLG	PRO+	BR/A	SB	CS	SBR	FA	FR	G/POS	TPR
1977	LA-N	11	10	1	3	0	1	0	2	1	4	.300	.364	.500	130	0	0	0	0	1.000	-2	O-10	-0.2

YEAR	TM/L	G	AB	R	H	2B	3B	HR	RBI	BB	SO	AVG	OBP	SLG	PRO+	BR/A	SB	CS	SBR	FA	FR	G/POS	TPR
1978	Hou-N	8	26	2	10	2	0	0	4	1	2	.385	.407	.462	154	2	0	1	-1	1.000	1	/O-8	0.2
1979	Hou-N	134	411	47	119	15	5	0	47	46	68	.290	.364	.350	102	2	23	10	1	.959	-7	*O-123	-0.8
1980	*Hou-N	88	216	29	46	7	5	3	20	19	46	.213	.277	.333	75	-8	4	1	1	.979	-2	O-56,1-11	-1.3
1981	Hou-N	7	18	1	3	1	1	0	3	0	4	.167	.167	.333	41	-2	1	0	1	1.000	-0	/1-2,O-2	-0.2
	SF-N	37	127	20	39	11	3	4	26	12	21	.307	.371	.535	158	9	4	2	0	1.000	2	O-28/1-5	1.1
	Yr	44	145	21	42	12	4	4	29	12	25	.290	.348	.510	145	8	5	2	0	1.000	2	O-30/1-7	0.9
1982	SF-N	80	278	32	72	16	1	9	49	19	65	.259	.311	.421	103	0	18	5	2	.958	-5	O-74/1-1	-0.4
1983	SF-N	139	516	74	144	17	7	21	87	35	116	.279	.326	.461	120	11	26	7	4	.975	8	*O-136	1.9
1984	SF-N	136	514	76	155	27	4	21	86	47	123	.302	.360	.484	140	26	17	7	1	.970	6	*O-131	3.0
1985	SF-N	133	507	49	122	20	3	17	62	21	107	.241	.272	.393	88	-11	11	6	-0	.977	3	*O-126	-1.3
1986	SF-N	89	341	48	95	11	3	6	42	20	62	.279	.324	.381	99	-1	16	3	3	.970	3	O-87	0.2
1987	*SF-N★	131	503	70	141	29	4	19	63	21	68	.280	.312	.467	108	3	16	7	1	.966	-4	O-127	-0.4
1988	SF-N	44	160	12	41	8	1	2	20	9	24	.256	.296	.356	90	-2	7	5	-1	.987	-3	O-43	-0.8
	Mil-A	94	374	45	88	19	0	8	44	16	68	.235	.272	.350	72	-14	10	4	1	.985	3	O-91/D-2	-1.4
1989	Sea-A★	150	566	69	144	20	1	24	93	38	125	.254	.307	.420	100	-2	6	1	1	.982	7	*D-123,O-26	-0.3
1990	Sea-A	134	478	39	120	20	0	10	75	37	97	.251	.309	.356	84	-10	4	2	0	.983	-8	O-79,D-48	-2.2
Total	14	1415	5045	614	1342	223	37	144	723	342	1000	.266	.316	.411	103	3	163	61	12	.974	-3	*O-1147,D-173/1	-2.9

■ **JOE LEONARD**   Leonard, Joseph Howard   b: 11/15/1894, W.Chicago, Ill.   d: 5/1/20, Washington, D.C.   BL/TR   5'7.5", 156 lbs.   Deb: 5/7/14

YEAR	TM/L	G	AB	R	H	2B	3B	HR	RBI	BB	SO	AVG	OBP	SLG	PRO+	BR/A	SB	CS	SBR	FA	FR	G/POS	TPR
1914	Pit-N	53	126	17	25	2	2	0	4	12	21	.198	.268	.246	56	-7	4			.909	-8	3-38/S-1	-1.5
1916	Cle-A	3	2	1	0	0	0	0	0	0	1	.000	.000	.000	-94	-0	0			1.000	0	/2-1	0.0
	Was-A	42	168	20	46	7	0	0	14	22	23	.274	.358	.315	103	1	4			.952	-8	3-42	-0.5
	Yr	45	170	21	46	7	0	0	14	22	24	.271	.354	.312	101	1	4			.952	-7	3-42/2-1	-0.5
1917	Was-A	99	297	30	57	6	7	0	23	45	40	.192	.302	.259	72	-9	6			.925	-2	3-68,1-19/SO	-1.2
1919	Was-A	71	198	26	51	8	3	2	20	20	28	.258	.329	.359	94	-3	3			.944	-9	2-28,3-25/1O	-1.0
1920	Was-A	1	0	0	0	0	0	0	0	0	0	—	—	—			0	0	0	.000	-0	R	0.0
Total	5	269	791	94	179	23	12	2	61	99	113	.226	.315	.293	82	-16	17	0		.937	-27	3-173/2-29,1OS	-4.2

■ **MARK LEONARD**   Leonard, Mark David   b: 8/14/64, Mountain View, Cal.   BL/TR   6'1", 195 lbs.   Deb: 7/21/90

YEAR	TM/L	G	AB	R	H	2B	3B	HR	RBI	BB	SO	AVG	OBP	SLG	PRO+	BR/A	SB	CS	SBR	FA	FR	G/POS	TPR
1990	SF-N	11	17	3	3	1	0	1	2	3	8	.176	.300	.412	97	-0	0	0	0	1.000	-1	/O-7	-0.1
1991	SF-N	64	129	14	31	7	1	2	14	12	25	.240	.310	.357	90	-2	0	1	-1	1.000	-6	O-34	-0.9
1992	SF-N	55	128	13	30	7	0	4	16	16	31	.234	.333	.383	108	2	0	1	-1	.984	0	O-37	0.1
1993	Bal-A	10	15	1	1	1	0	0	3	3	7	.067	.222	.133	-2	-2	0	0	0	.833	-1	/O-4,D-3	-0.3
1994	SF-N	14	11	2	4	1	1	0	2	3	2	.364	.500	.636	201	2	0	0	0	1.000	-1	/O-2	0.1
Total	5	154	300	33	69	17	2	7	37	37	73	.230	.323	.370	94	-1	0	2	-1	.984	-8	/O-84,D-3	-1.1

■ **JOHN LEOVICH**   Leovich, John Joseph   b: 5/5/18, Portland, Ore.   BR/TR   6'0.5", 200 lbs.   Deb: 5/1/41

YEAR	TM/L	G	AB	R	H	2B	3B	HR	RBI	BB	SO	AVG	OBP	SLG	PRO+	BR/A	SB	CS	SBR	FA	FR	G/POS	TPR
1941	Phi-A	1	2	0	1	0	0	0	0	0	0	.500	.500	1.000	296	1	0	0	0	.000	-0	/C-1	0.0

■ **TED LEPCIO**   Lepcio, Thaddeus Stanley   b: 7/28/30, Utica, N.Y.   BR/TR   5'10", 177 lbs.   Deb: 4/15/52

YEAR	TM/L	G	AB	R	H	2B	3B	HR	RBI	BB	SO	AVG	OBP	SLG	PRO+	BR/A	SB	CS	SBR	FA	FR	G/POS	TPR
1952	Bos-A	84	274	34	72	17	2	5	26	24	41	.263	.329	.394	93	-3	3	3	-1	.972	8	2-57,3-25/S	0.6
1953	Bos-A	66	161	17	38	4	2	4	11	17	24	.236	.313	.360	77	-5	0	0	0	.981	17	2-34,S-20,3	1.4
1954	Bos-A	116	398	42	102	19	4	8	45	42	62	.256	.332	.384	86	-8	3	4	-2	.971	16	2-80,3-24,S	1.2
1955	Bos-A	51	134	19	31	9	0	6	15	12	36	.231	.313	.433	91	-2	1	1	-0	.943	6	3-45	0.3
1956	Bos-A	83	284	34	74	10	0	15	51	30	77	.261	.338	.454	96	-3	1	3	-2	.966	7	2-57,3-22	0.8
1957	Bos-A	79	232	24	56	10	2	9	37	29	61	.241	.328	.418	97	-1	0	0	0	.976	9	2-68	1.3
1958	Bos-A	50	136	10	27	3	0	6	14	12	47	.199	.268	.353	65	-7	1	1	-1	.980	-3	2-40	-0.8
1959	Bos-A	3	3	1	1	1	0	0	1	0	2	.333	.333	.667	160	0	0	0	0	1.000	0	/2-1	0.0
	Det-A	76	215	25	60	8	0	7	24	17	49	.279	.332	.414	98	-1	2	0	1	.951	-6	S-35,2-24,3	-0.2
	Yr	79	218	26	61	9	0	7	25	17	51	.280	.332	.417	99	-1	2	0	1	.951	-6	S-35,2-25,3	-0.2
1960	Phi-N	69	141	16	32	7	0	2	8	17	41	.227	.319	.319	75	-4	0	3	-2	.942	-5	3-50,S-14/2	-1.1
1961	Chi-A	5	2	0	0	0	0	0	0	1	0	.000	.333	.000	-2	-0	0	0	0	.000	-0	/3-1	0.0
	Min-A	47	112	11	19	3	1	7	19	8	31	.170	.231	.402	62	-7	1	0	0	.919	2	3-35,2-22/S	-0.3
	Yr	52	114	11	19	3	1	7	19	9	31	.167	.234	.395	62	-7	1	0	0	.895	2	3-36,2-22/S	-0.3
Total	10	729	2092	233	512	91	11	69	251	209	471	.245	.319	.398	87	-41	11	15	-6	.972	51	2-388,3-224/S	3.2

■ **PETE LePINE**   LePine, Louis Joseph   b: 9/5/1876, Montreal, Que., Can   d: 12/3/49, Woonsocket, R.I.   BL/TL   Deb: 7/21/02

YEAR	TM/L	G	AB	R	H	2B	3B	HR	RBI	BB	SO	AVG	OBP	SLG	PRO+	BR/A	SB	CS	SBR	FA	FR	G/POS	TPR
1902	Det-A	30	96	8	20	3	2	1	19	8		.208	.276	.313	62	-5	1			1.000	-2	O-19/1-8	-0.7

■ **DON LEPPERT**   Leppert, Don Eugene "Tiger"   b: 11/20/30, Memphis, Tenn.   BL/TR   5'8", 175 lbs.   Deb: 4/11/55

YEAR	TM/L	G	AB	R	H	2B	3B	HR	RBI	BB	SO	AVG	OBP	SLG	PRO+	BR/A	SB	CS	SBR	FA	FR	G/POS	TPR
1955	Bal-A	40	70	6	8	0	1	0	2	9	10	.114	.215	.143	-2	-10	1	1	-0	.937	-7	2-35	-1.7

■ **DON LEPPERT**   Leppert, Donald George   b: 10/19/31, Indianapolis, Ind.   BR/TR   6'2", 220 lbs.   Deb: 6/18/61   C

YEAR	TM/L	G	AB	R	H	2B	3B	HR	RBI	BB	SO	AVG	OBP	SLG	PRO+	BR/A	SB	CS	SBR	FA	FR	G/POS	TPR
1961	Pit-N	22	60	6	16	2	1	3	5	1	11	.267	.279	.483	97	1	0	0	0	.968	1	C-21	0.1
1962	Pit-N	45	139	14	37	6	1	3	18	12	21	.266	.329	.388	92	-2	0	1	-1	.989	4	C-44	0.3
1963	Was-A☆	73	211	20	50	11	0	6	24	20	29	.237	.306	.374	90	-3	0	0	0	.984	-8	C-60	-0.9
1964	Was-A	50	122	6	19	3	0	3	12	11	32	.156	.226	.254	33	-11	0	0	0	.990	1	C-43	-0.9
Total	4	190	532	46	122	22	2	15	59	44	93	.229	.291	.363	78	-16	0	1	-1	.985	-2	C-168	-1.4

■ **DUTCH LERCHEN**   Lerchen, Bertram Roe   b: 4/4/1889, Detroit, Mich.   d: 1/7/62, Detroit, Mich.   BR/TR   5'8", 160 lbs.   Deb: 8/14/10   F

YEAR	TM/L	G	AB	R	H	2B	3B	HR	RBI	BB	SO	AVG	OBP	SLG	PRO+	BR/A	SB	CS	SBR	FA	FR	G/POS	TPR
1910	Bos-A	6	15	1	0	0	0	0	0	0	1	.000	.063	.000	-78	-3	0			.929	-3	/S-6	-0.8

■ **GEORGE LERCHEN**   Lerchen, George Edward   b: 12/1/22, Detroit, Mich.   BB/TR   5'11", 175 lbs.   Deb: 4/15/52   F

YEAR	TM/L	G	AB	R	H	2B	3B	HR	RBI	BB	SO	AVG	OBP	SLG	PRO+	BR/A	SB	CS	SBR	FA	FR	G/POS	TPR
1952	Det-A	14	32	1	5	1	0	1	3	7	10	.156	.308	.281	64	-1	0	0	0	1.000	-0	/O-7	-0.2
1953	Cin-N	22	17	2	5	1	0	0	2	5	6	.294	.455	.353	113	1	0	0	0	1.000	-0	/O-1	0.0
Total	2	36	49	3	10	2	0	1	5	12	16	.204	.361	.306	82	-1	0	0	0	1.000	-0	/O-8	-0.2

■ **WALT LERIAN**   Lerian, Walter Irvin "Peck"   b: 2/10/03, Baltimore, Md.   d: 10/22/29, Baltimore, Md.   BR/TR   5'11", 170 lbs.   Deb: 4/16/28

YEAR	TM/L	G	AB	R	H	2B	3B	HR	RBI	BB	SO	AVG	OBP	SLG	PRO+	BR/A	SB	CS	SBR	FA	FR	G/POS	TPR
1928	Phi-N	96	239	28	65	16	2	2	25	41	29	.272	.385	.381	97	1	1			.977	-3	C-74	0.4
1929	Phi-N	105	273	28	61	13	2	6	25	53	37	.223	.354	.352	71	-12	0			.986	1	*C-103	-0.3
Total	2	201	512	56	126	29	4	8	50	94	66	.246	.368	.365	83	-11	1			.982	-1	C-177	0.1

■ **ROY LESLIE**   Leslie, Roy Reid   b: 8/23/1894, Bailey, Tex.   d: 4/9/72, Sherman, Tex.   BR/TR   6'1", 175 lbs.   Deb: 9/6/17

YEAR	TM/L	G	AB	R	H	2B	3B	HR	RBI	BB	SO	AVG	OBP	SLG	PRO+	BR/A	SB	CS	SBR	FA	FR	G/POS	TPR
1917	Chi-N	7	19	1	4	0	0	1	1	1	5	.211	.250	.211	39	-1	1			.969	-0	/1-6	-0.2
1919	StL-N	12	24	2	5	1	0	0	4	4	3	.208	.321	.250	78	-0	0			.957	-0	/1-9	-0.1
1922	Phi-N	141	513	44	139	23	2	6	50	37	49	.271	.320	.359	68	-25	3	7	-3	.990	-4	*1-139	-3.6
Total	3	160	556	47	148	24	2	6	55	42	57	.266	.318	.349	68	-27	4	7		.988	-4	1-154	-3.9

■ **SAM LESLIE**   Leslie, Samuel Andrew "Sambo"   b: 7/26/05, Moss Point, Miss.   d: 1/21/79, Pascagoula, Miss.   BL/TL   6', 192 lbs.   Deb: 10/6/29

YEAR	TM/L	G	AB	R	H	2B	3B	HR	RBI	BB	SO	AVG	OBP	SLG	PRO+	BR/A	SB	CS	SBR	FA	FR	G/POS	TPR
1929	NY-N	1	1	0	0	0	0	0	0	0	0	.000	.000	.000	-99	-0	0			1.000	-0	/O-1	-0.1
1930	NY-N	2	2	0	1	0	0	0	0	0	0	.500	.500	.500	146	-0	0					H	0.0
1931	NY-N	53	53	11	16	4	0	3	5	1	2	.302	.315	.547	131	2	3			1.000	0	/1-6	0.2
1932	NY-N	77	75	5	22	4	0	1	15	2	5	.293	.329	.387	94	-1	0			1.000	-0	/1-2	-0.1
1933	NY-N	40	137	21	44	12	1	3	27	12	9	.321	.380	.518	157	10	0			.990	-0	1-35	0.7
	Bro-N	96	364	41	104	11	4	5	46	23	14	.286	.340	.379	123	5	1			.982	-6	1-95	-1.2
	Yr	136	501	62	148	23	7	8	73	35	23	.295	.351	.417	123	15	1			.984	-6	*1-130	-0.5

YEAR	TM/L	G	AB	R	H	2B	3B	HR	RBI	BB	SO	AVG	OBP	SLG	PRO+	BR/A	SB	CS	SBR	FA	FR	G/POS	TPR
1934	Bro-N	146	546	75	181	29	6	9	102	69	34	.332	.409	.456	138	32	5			.993	5	*1-138	2.4
1935	Bro-N	142	520	72	160	30	7	5	93	55	19	.308	.379	.421	117	14	4			.989	-0	*1-138	0.0
1936	*NY-N	117	417	49	123	19	5	6	54	23	16	.295	.335	.408	100	-1	0			.991	0	1-99	-1.0
1937	*NY-N	72	191	25	59	7	2	3	30	20	12	.309	.380	.414	114	4	1			.990	3	1-44	0.2
1938	NY-N	76	154	12	39	7	1	1	16	11	6	.253	.307	.331	75	-5	0			.988	-3	1-32	-1.1
Total	10	822	2460	311	749	123	28	36	389	216	118	.304	.366	.421	117	60	14			.989	-2	1-589/O-1	0.0

■ CHARLIE LETCHAS
Letchas, Charlie b: 10/3/15, Thomasville, Ga. BR/TR, 5'10", 150 lbs. Deb: 9/16/39

YEAR	TM/L	G	AB	R	H	2B	3B	HR	RBI	BB	SO	AVG	OBP	SLG	PRO+	BR/A	SB	CS	SBR	FA	FR	G/POS	TPR
1939	Phi-N	12	44	2	10	2	0	1	3	1	2	.227	.244	.341	57	-3	0			.933	-1	2-12	-0.3
1941	Was-A	2	8	0	1	0	0	0	1	1	1	.125	.222	.125	-6	-1	0	0	0	.800	1	2-2	-0.2
1944	Phi-N	116	396	29	94	8	0	0	33	32	27	.237	.298	.258	59	-21	0			.968	6	2-47,3-32,S	-1.0
1946	Phi-N	6	13	1	3	0	0	0	0	1	1	.231	.286	.231	49	-1	0			1.000	1	/2-4	-0.1
Total	4	136	461	32	108	10	0	1	37	35	31	.234	.291	.262	58	-26	0	0		.959	5	/2-65,3-32,S	-1.5

■ TOM LETCHER
Letcher, Frederick Thomas b: 1/1868, Ohio BL , Deb: 9/27/1891

YEAR	TM/L	G	AB	R	H	2B	3B	HR	RBI	BB	SO	AVG	OBP	SLG	PRO+	BR/A	SB	CS	SBR	FA	FR	G/POS	TPR
1891	Mil-a	6	21	3	4	1	0	0	2	0	1	.190	.190	.238	19	-2	1			.857	0	/O-6	-0.2

■ LEUTZ
Leutz Deb: 5/7/1872

YEAR	TM/L	G	AB	R	H	2B	3B	HR	RBI	BB	SO	AVG	OBP	SLG	PRO+	BR/A	SB	CS	SBR	FA	FR	G/POS	TPR
1872	Eck-n	4	13	2	1	0	0	0	0	0	0	.077	.077	.077	-62	-2						/C-4	-0.2

■ JESSE LEVAN
Levan, Jesse Roy b: 7/15/26, Reading, Pa. BL/TR, 6', 172 lbs. Deb: 9/27/47

YEAR	TM/L	G	AB	R	H	2B	3B	HR	RBI	BB	SO	AVG	OBP	SLG	PRO+	BR/A	SB	CS	SBR	FA	FR	G/POS	TPR
1947	Phi-N	2	9	3	4	0	0	0	1	0	0	.444	.444	.444	142	1	0			1.000	-1	/O-2	0.0
1954	Was-A	7	10	1	3	0	0	0	0	0	0	.300	.300	.300	68	-0	0	0	0	.000	-0	/3-4,1-1	-0.1
1955	Was-A	16	16	1	3	0	0	1	4	0	2	.188	.188	.375	51	-1	0	0	0	.000	0	H	-0.1
Total	3	25	35	5	10	0	0	1	5	0	2	.286	.286	.371	80	-1	0	0		—	-1	/3-4,O-2,1	-0.2

■ JIM LEVEY
Levey, James Julius b: 9/13/06, Pittsburgh, Pa. d: 3/14/70, Dallas, Tex. BB/TR, 5'10.5", 154 lbs. Deb: 9/17/30

YEAR	TM/L	G	AB	R	H	2B	3B	HR	RBI	BB	SO	AVG	OBP	SLG	PRO+	BR/A	SB	CS	SBR	FA	FR	G/POS	TPR
1930	StL-A	8	37	7	9	2	0	0	3	3	2	.243	.300	.297	50	-3	0	0	0	.958	2	/S-8	0.0
1931	StL-A	139	498	53	104	19	2	5	38	35	83	.209	.264	.285	43	-42	13	8	-1	.920	-10	*S-139	-3.8
1932	StL-A	152	568	59	159	30	8	4	63	21	48	.280	.310	.382	74	-23	6	4	-1	.939	-18	*S-152	-2.7
1933	StL-A	141	529	43	103	10	4	2	36	26	68	.195	.237	.240	25	-57	4	6	-2	.945	-6	*S-138	-5.4
Total	4	440	1632	162	375	61	14	11	140	85	201	.230	.272	.305	48	-125	23	18	-4	.936	-33	S-437	-11.9

■ CHARLIE LEVIS
Levis, Charles H. b: 6/21/1860, St.Louis, Mo. d: 10/16/26, St.Louis, Mo. BR , Deb: 4/17/1884

YEAR	TM/L	G	AB	R	H	2B	3B	HR	RBI	BB	SO	AVG	OBP	SLG	PRO+	BR/A	SB	CS	SBR	FA	FR	G/POS	TPR
1884	Bal-U	87	373	59	85	11	4	6		3		.228	.234	.327	46	-29				.955	-0	*1-87	-3.6
	Was-U	1	3	0	0	0	0	0		0		.000	.000	.000	-99	-1				1.000	0	/1-1	-0.1
	Yr	88	376	59	85	11	4	6		3		.226	.232	.324	45	-30				.955	-0	1-88	-3.7
	Ind-a	3	10	0	2	0	0	0		0		.200	.200	.200	32	-1				1.000	0	/1-3	-0.1
1885	Bal-a	1	4	2	1	0	0	0		0		.250	.400	.250	110	-0				.889	0	/1-1	0.0
Total	2	92	390	61	88	11	4	6		3		.226	.234	.321	45	-31				.956	-0	/1-92	-3.8

■ JESSE LEVIS
Levis, Jesse b: 4/14/68, Philadelphia, Pa. BL/TR, 5'9", 180 lbs. Deb: 4/24/92

YEAR	TM/L	G	AB	R	H	2B	3B	HR	RBI	BB	SO	AVG	OBP	SLG	PRO+	BR/A	SB	CS	SBR	FA	FR	G/POS	TPR
1992	Cle-A	28	43	2	12	4	0	1	3	0	5	.279	.279	.442	101	-0	0	0	0	.985	1	C-21/D-1	0.1
1993	Cle-A	31	63	7	11	2	0	0	4	2	10	.175	.200	.206	9	-8	0	0	0	.991	1	C-29	-0.6
1994	Cle-A	1	1	0	1	0	0	0	0	0	0	1.000	1.000	1.000	400	0	0	0	0	.000	0	/H	0.0
Total	3	60	107	9	24	6	0	1	7	2	15	.224	.239	.308	49	-8	0	0	0	.989	2	/C-50,D-1	-0.5

■ ED LEVY
Levy, Edward Clarence (b: Edward Clarence Whitner) b: 10/28/16, Birmingham, Ala. BR/TR, 6'5.5", 190 lbs. Deb: 4/16/40

YEAR	TM/L	G	AB	R	H	2B	3B	HR	RBI	BB	SO	AVG	OBP	SLG	PRO+	BR/A	SB	CS	SBR	FA	FR	G/POS	TPR
1940	Phi-N	1	0	0	0	0	0	0	0	0	0	.000	.000	.000	-99		0			0	0	H	0.0
1942	NY-A	13	41	5	5	0	0	0	3	4	5	.122	.200	.122	-9	-6	1	0	0	.992	2	1-13	-0.5
1944	NY-A	40	153	12	37	11	2	4	29	6	19	.242	.270	.418	92	-3	1	1	-0	.962	-1	O-36	-0.6
Total	3	54	195	17	42	11	2	4	32	10	24	.215	.254	.354	70	-9	2	1		.962	0	/O-36,1-13	-1.1

■ LEWIS
Lewis b: Brooklyn, N.Y. Deb: 7/12/1890

YEAR	TM/L	G	AB	R	H	2B	3B	HR	RBI	BB	SO	AVG	OBP	SLG	PRO+	BR/A	SB	CS	SBR	FA	FR	G/POS	TPR
1890	Buf-P	1	5	1	1	0	0	0	0	0	0	.200	.200	.200	8	-1	0			.000	0	/O-1,P-1	-0.1

■ ALLAN LEWIS
Lewis, Allan Sydney "The Panamanian Express" b: 12/12/41, Colon, Panama BB/TR, 6', 170 lbs. Deb: 4/11/67

YEAR	TM/L	G	AB	R	H	2B	3B	HR	RBI	BB	SO	AVG	OBP	SLG	PRO+	BR/A	SB	CS	SBR	FA	FR	G/POS	TPR
1967	KC-A	34	6	7	1	0	0	0	0	0	3	.167	.167	.167	-1	-1	14	5	1	.000	-0	H	0.0
1968	Oak-A	26	4	9	1	0	0	0	0	1	0	.250	.400	.250	105	0	8	4	0	.000	-0	/O-1	0.0
1969	Oak-A	12	1	2	0	0	0	0	0	0	0	.000	.000	.000	-99	-0	0	0	0	.000	0	H	0.0
1970	Oak-A	25	8	8	2	0	0	1	1	0	0	.250	.250	.625	139	0	7	1	2	1.000	-0	/O-2	0.2
1972	*Oak-A	24	10	5	2	1	0	0	2	0	1	.200	.200	.300	50	-1	8	3	1	.900	-1	/O-6	-0.1
1973	*Oak-A	35	0	16	0	0	0	0	0	0	0	—	—	—		0	7	4	-0	1.000	-0	/O-1,D-6	-0.1
Total	6	156	29	47	6	1	0	1	3	1	4	.207	.233	.345	69	-1	44	17	3	.923	-2	/O-10,D-6	0.0

■ DARREN LEWIS
Lewis, Darren Joel b: 8/28/67, Berkeley, Cal. BR/TR, 6', 180 lbs. Deb: 8/21/90

YEAR	TM/L	G	AB	R	H	2B	3B	HR	RBI	BB	SO	AVG	OBP	SLG	PRO+	BR/A	SB	CS	SBR	FA	FR	G/POS	TPR
1990	Oak-A	25	35	4	8	0	0	1	7	4	.229	.372	.229	75	-1	2	0	1	1.000	-5	O-23/D-2	-0.5
1991	SF-N	72	222	41	55	5	3	1	15	36	30	.248	.358	.311	93	-1	13	7	-0	1.000	3	O-68	0.1
1992	SF-N	100	320	38	74	8	1	1	18	29	46	.231	.297	.272	66	-14	28	8	4	1.000	0	O-94	-1.3
1993	SF-N	136	522	84	132	17	7	2	48	30	40	.253	.302	.324	70	-22	46	15	5	**1.000**	8	*O-131	-1.2
1994	SF-N	114	451	70	116	15	9	4	29	53	50	.257	.341	.357	85	-9	30	13	1	**.993**	3	*O-113	-0.7
Total	5	447	1550	237	385	45	20	8	111	155	170	.248	.323	.319	77	-47	119	43	10	.998	3	O-429/D-2	-3.6

■ FRED LEWIS
Lewis, Frederick Miller b: 10/13/1858, Buffalo, N.Y. d: 6/5/45, Utica, N.Y. BB/TR, 5'10.5", 194 lbs. Deb: 7/2/1881

YEAR	TM/L	G	AB	R	H	2B	3B	HR	RBI	BB	SO	AVG	OBP	SLG	PRO+	BR/A	SB	CS	SBR	FA	FR	G/POS	TPR
1881	Bos-N	27	114	17	25	6	0	0	9	7	5	.219	.264	.272	72	-3				.837	-2	O-27	-0.6
1883	Phi-N	38	160	21	40	7	0	0	18	4	13	.250	.268	.294	78	-4				.814	1	O-38	-0.3
	StL-a	49	209	37	63	8	4	1		1		.301	.305	.392	116	3				.848	-0	O-49	0.2
1884	StL-a	73	300	59	97	25	3	0		16		.323	.366	.427	152	17				.853	3	O-73	1.6
	StL-U	8	30	6	9	1	0	0		3		.300	.364	.333	88	-0				.909	-2	/O-8	-0.2
1885	StL-N	45	181	12	53	9	0	1	27	9	10	.293	.326	.359	130	6				.957	7	O-45	1.1
1886	Cin-a	77	324	72	103	14	6	2		20		.318	.365	.417	140	14	8			.884	-2	O-76/3-1	0.9
Total	5	317	1318	224	390	70	13	4	54	60	28	.296	.330	.378	123	32	8			.866	4	O-316/3-1	2.7

■ DUFFY LEWIS
Lewis, George Edward b: 4/18/1888, San Francisco, Cal d: 6/17/79, Salem, N.H. BL/TL, 5'10.5", 165 lbs. Deb: 4/16/10 C

YEAR	TM/L	G	AB	R	H	2B	3B	HR	RBI	BB	SO	AVG	OBP	SLG	PRO+	BR/A	SB	CS	SBR	FA	FR	G/POS	TPR
1910	Bos-A	151	541	64	153	29	4	8	68	32		.283	.328	.407	127	14	10			.944	10	*O-149	1.9
1911	Bos-A	130	469	64	144	32	4	7	86	25		.307	.355	.437	122	12	11			.939	5	*O-125	1.0
1912	*Bos-A	154	581	85	165	36	9	6	109	52		.284	.346	.408	110	5	9			.947	7	*O-154	0.4
1913	Bos-A	149	551	54	164	31	12	0	90	30	55	.298	.336	.397	112	6	12			.960	11	*O-142/P-1,3	1.1
1914	Bos-A	146	510	53	142	37	9	2	79	57	41	.278	.357	.398	127	16	22	31	-12	.952	-2	*O-142	-0.4
1915	*Bos-A	152	557	69	162	31	7	2	76	45	63	.291	.348	.382	122	14	14	7	0	.952	-7	*O-152	-0.1
1916	*Bos-A	152	563	56	151	29	5	1	56	33	56	.268	.313	.343	97	-4	16			.970	-1	*O-151	-1.4
1917	Bos-A	150	553	55	167	29	9	1	65	29	54	.302	.342	.392	125	14	8			.972	4	*O-150	1.1
1919	NY-A	141	559	60	152	23	4	7	89	17	42	.272	.293	.365	84	-14	8			.985	-6	*O-141	-3.2
1920	NY-A	107	365	34	99	8	1	4	61	24	32	.271	.320	.332	70	-9	2	8	-4	.961	-2	O-99	-2.9
1921	Was-A	27	102	11	19	4	1	0	14	8	10	.186	.252	.245	29	-11	1	1	-0	.980	-2	O-27	-1.5
Total	11	1459	5351	612	1518	289	68	38	793	352	353	.284	.333	.384	108	36	113	47		.959	16	*O-1432/3-1,P	-4.0

YEAR	TM/L	G	AB	R	H	2B	3B	HR	RBI	BB	SO	AVG	OBP	SLG	PRO+	BR/A	SB	CS	SBR	FA	FR	G/POS	TPR

■ JACK LEWIS
Lewis, John David b: 2/12/1884, Pittsburgh, Pa. d: 2/25/56, Steubenville, Ohio BR/TR, 5'8", 158 lbs. Deb: 9/16/11

1911	Bos-A	18	59	7	16	0	0	0	6	7		.271	.368	.271	80	-1	2			.931	-2	2-18	-0.3
1914	Pit-F	117	394	32	92	14	5	1	48	17	46	.234	.276	.302	50	-30	9			.949	9	*2-115/S-1	-2.3
1915	Pit-F	82	231	24	61	6	5	0	26	8	31	.264	.292	.333	68	-11	7			.962	-2	2-45,S-11/O13	-1.4
Total	3	217	684	63	169	20	10	1	80	32	77	.247	.290	.310	59	-42	18			.951	5	2-178/S-12,O13	-4.0

■ BUDDY LEWIS
Lewis, John Kelly b: 8/10/16, Gastonia, N.C. BL/TR, 6'1", 175 lbs. Deb: 9/16/35

1935	Was-A	8	28	0	3	0	0	0	2	0	5	.107	.107	.107	-46	-6	0	0	0	.941	-0	/3-6	-0.6
1936	Was-A	143	601	100	175	21	13	6	67	47	46	.291	.347	.399	89	-12	6	6	-2	.933	5	*3-139	-0.3
1937	Was-A	156	668	107	210	32	6	10	79	52	44	.314	.367	.425	104	3	11	5	0	.938	-19	*3-156	-1.0
1938	Was-A★	151	656	122	194	35	9	12	91	58	35	.296	.354	.431	103	1	17	9	-0	.912	-0	*3-151	0.2
1939	Was-A	140	536	87	171	23	**16**	10	75	72	27	.319	.402	.478	134	28	10	9	-2	.933	14	*3-134	3.7
1940	Was-A	148	600	101	190	38	6	6	63	74	36	.317	.393	.443	124	23	15	10	-2	.960	-1	*O-112,3-36	1.5
1941	Was-A	149	569	97	169	29	11	9	72	82	30	.297	.386	.434	122	19	10	7	-1	.972	3	O-96,3-49	1.6
1945	Was-A	69	258	42	86	14	7	2	37	37	15	.333	.423	.465	172	25	1	2	-1	.981	4	O-69	2.5
1946	Was-A	150	582	82	170	28	13	7	45	59	26	.292	.359	.421	125	18	5	3	-0	.970	4	*O-145	1.6
1947	Was-A★	140	506	67	132	15	4	6	48	51	27	.261	.330	.342	89	-7	6	6	-2	.968	1	O-130	-1.6
1949	Was-A	95	257	25	63	14	4	3	28	41	12	.245	.355	.366	93	-2	2	2	-1	.979	-0	O-67	-0.6
Total	11	1349	5261	830	1563	249	93	71	607	573	303	.297	.368	.420	112	90	83	59	-11	.927	11	3-671,O-619	7.0

■ JOHNNY LEWIS
Lewis, Johnny Joe b: 8/10/39, Greenville, Ala. BL/TR, 6'1", 189 lbs. Deb: 4/14/64 C

1964	StL-N	40	94	10	22	2	2	7	13	23	.234	.327	.362	86	-2	2	2	-1	.966	-1	O-36	-0.4
1965	NY-N	148	477	64	117	15	3	15	45	59	117	.245	.332	.384	105	3	4	7	-3	.975	1	*O-142	-0.5
1966	NY-N	65	166	21	32	6	1	5	20	21	43	.193	.283	.331	72	-6	2	0	1	.988	-3	O-49	-1.1
1967	NY-N	13	34	2	4	1	0	0	2	2	11	.118	.167	.147	-10	-5	0	0	0	1.000	-0	O-10	-0.6
Total	4	266	771	97	175	24	6	22	74	95	194	.227	.314	.359	90	-9	8	9	-3	.977	-3	O-237	-2.6

■ MARK LEWIS
Lewis, Mark David b: 11/30/69, Hamilton, Ohio BR/TR, 6'1", 190 lbs. Deb: 4/26/91

1991	Cle-A	84	314	29	83	15	1	0	30	15	45	.264	.298	.318	70	-13	2	2	-1	.966	-14	2-50,S-36	-2.4
1992	Cle-A	122	413	44	109	21	0	5	30	25	69	.264	.311	.351	87	-8	4	5	-2	.954	-9	*S-121/3-1	-1.1
1993	Cle-A	14	52	6	13	2	0	1	5	0	7	.250	.250	.346	59	-3	3	0	1	.964	-3	S-13	-0.4
1994	Cle-A	20	73	6	15	5	0	1	8	2	13	.205	.227	.315	36	-7	1	0	0	.902	-7	S-13/3-6,2	-1.2
Total	4	240	852	85	220	43	1	7	73	42	134	.258	.295	.336	74	-31	10	7	-1	.958	-34	S-183/2-51,3	-5.1

■ PHIL LEWIS
Lewis, Philip b: 10/7/1883, Pittsburgh, Pa. d: 8/8/59, Port Wentworth, Ga. BR/TR, 6', 195 lbs. Deb: 4/14/05

1905	Bro-N	118	433	32	110	9	2	3	33	16		.254	.282	.305	81	-11	16			.904	-6	*S-118	-1.6
1906	Bro-N	136	452	40	110	8	4	0	37	43		.243	.309	.279	90	-5	14			.922	-22	*S-135	-2.6
1907	Bro-N	136	475	52	118	11	1	0	30	23		.248	.286	.276	83	-11	16			.938	-20	*S-136	-3.2
1908	Bro-N	118	415	22	91	5	6	1	30	13		.219	.243	.267	66	-17	9			.943	-7	*S-116	-2.6
Total	4	508	1775	146	429	33	13	4	130	95		.242	.281	.282	80	-44	55			.926	-55	S-505	-10.0

■ BILL LEWIS
Lewis, William Henry "Buddy" b: 10/15/04, Ripley, Tenn. d: 10/24/77, Memphis, Tenn. BR/TR, 5'9", 165 lbs. Deb: 6/3/33

1933	StL-N	15	35	8	14	1	0	1	8	2	3	.400	.432	.514	161	3	0			1.000	1	/C-8	0.4
1935	Bos-N	6	4	1	0	0	0	0	0	1	1	.000	.200	.000	-45	-1	0			.000	0	/C-1	-0.1
1936	Bos-N	29	62	11	19	2	0	0	3	12	7	.306	.419	.339	113	2	0			.967	-4	C-21	-0.1
Total	3	50	101	20	33	3	0	1	11	15	11	.327	.414	.386	124	4	0			.981	-3	/C-30	0.2

■ JIM LEYRITZ
Leyritz, James Joseph b: 12/27/63, Lakewood, Ohio BR/TR, 6', 190 lbs. Deb: 6/8/90

1990	NY-A	92	303	28	78	13	1	5	25	27	51	.257	.332	.356	92	-3	2	3	-1	.929	-19	3-69,O-14,C	-2.3
1991	NY-A	32	77	8	14	3	0	0	4	13	15	.182	.300	.221	46	-5	0	1	-1	.909	-8	3-18/C-5,1D	-1.4
1992	NY-A	63	144	17	37	6	0	7	26	14	22	.257	.348	.444	121	4	0	1	-1	.990	4	D-31,C-18/13O2	0.6
1993	NY-A	95	259	43	80	14	0	14	53	37	59	.309	.411	.525	155	21	0	0	0	.993	-6	1-29,O-28,DC	1.2
1994	NY-A	75	249	47	66	12	0	17	58	35	61	.265	.369	.518	134	13	0	0	0	1.000	-4	C-37,D-25,1	0.9
Total	5	357	1032	143	275	48	1	43	166	126	208	.266	.361	.440	119	30	2	5	-2	.927	-33	/3-89,C-83,D1O2	-1.0

■ CARLOS LEZCANO
Lezcano, Carlos Manuel (Rubio) b: 9/30/55, Arecibo, P.R. BR/TR, 6'2", 185 lbs. Deb: 4/10/80

1980	Chi-N	42	88	15	18	4	1	3	12	11	29	.205	.300	.375	81	-2	1	2	-1	.948	-4	O-39	-0.8
1981	Chi-N	7	14	1	1	0	0	0	2	0	4	.071	.071	.071	-57	-3	0	0	0	1.000	-1	/O-5	-0.4
Total	2	49	102	16	19	4	1	3	14	11	33	.186	.272	.333	64	-5	1	2	-1	.952	-4	/O-44	-1.2

■ SIXTO LEZCANO
Lezcano, Sixto Joaquin (Curras) b: 11/28/53, Arecibo, P.R. BR/TR, 5'11", 175 lbs. Deb: 9/10/74

1974	Mil-A	15	54	5	13	2	0	2	9	4	9	.241	.293	.389	95	-0	1	1	-0	.972	2	O-15	0.1
1975	Mil-A	134	429	55	106	19	3	11	43	46	93	.247	.326	.382	99	-1	5	5	-2	.977	-3	*O-129/D-2	-1.0
1976	Mil-A	145	513	53	146	19	5	7	56	51	112	.285	.352	.382	117	11	14	10	-2	.973	8	*O-142/D-3	1.3
1977	Mil-A	109	400	50	109	21	4	21	49	52	78	.273	.359	.503	132	18	6	5	-1	.988	13	*O-108	2.4
1978	Mil-A	132	442	62	129	21	4	15	61	64	83	.292	.383	.459	135	22	3	3	-1	.979	10	*O-127/D-3	2.6
1979	Mil-A	138	473	84	152	29	3	28	101	77	74	.321	.420	.573	165	45	4	3	-0	.986	4	*O-135	4.0
1980	Mil-A	112	411	51	94	19	3	18	55	39	75	.229	.300	.421	98	-2	1	1	-0	.983	6	*O-108/D-4	-0.1
1981	StL-N	72	214	26	57	8	2	5	28	40	40	.266	.382	.393	117	6	0	1	-1	.973	-4	O-65	0.0
1982	SD-N	138	470	73	136	26	6	16	84	78	69	.289	.393	.472	149	33	2	1	-0	.990	16	*O-134	4.6
1983	SD-N	97	317	41	74	11	2	8	49	47	66	.233	.334	.356	95	-2	0	0	0	.968	-5	O-91	0.1
	*Phi-N	18	39	8	11	1	0	1	7	5	9	.282	.364	.308	89	-0	1	0	0	1.000	-1	O-15	-0.1
	Yr	115	356	49	85	12	2	8	56	52	75	.239	.337	.351	94	-2	1	0	0	.971	-5	O-106	0.0
1984	Phi-N	109	256	36	71	6	2	14	40	38	43	.277	.371	.480	135	12	0	1	-1	.981	-1	O-87	0.9
1985	Pit-N	72	116	16	24	2	0	3	9	35	17	.207	.395	.302	98	2	0	0	0	.967	-2	O-40	-0.1
Total	12	1291	4134	560	1122	184	34	148	591	576	768	.271	.363	.440	125	143	37	31	-8	.980	52	*O-1196/D-12	14.7

■ STEVE LIBBY
Libby, Stephen Augustus b: 12/8/1853, Scarborough, Me. d: 3/31/35, Milford, Conn. 6'1.5", 168 lbs. Deb: 5/10/1879

| 1879 | Buf-N | 1 | 2 | 0 | 0 | 0 | 0 | 0 | 0 | 0 | 1 | .000 | .000 | .000 | -98 | -0 | | | | 1.000 | 0 | /1-1 | 0.0 |

■ AL LIBKE
Libke, Albert Walter b: 9/12/18, Tacoma, Wash. BL/TR, 6'4", 215 lbs. Deb: 4/19/45

1945	Cin-N	130	449	41	127	23	5	4	53	34	62	.283	.336	.383	102	0	6			.963	2	*O-108/P-4,1	-0.4
1946	Cin-N	124	431	32	109	22	1	5	42	43	50	.253	.322	.343	92	-5	0			.972	-5	*O-115/P-1	-1.6
Total	2	254	880	73	236	45	6	9	95	77	112	.268	.329	.364	97	-5	6			.967	-3	O-223/P-5,1	-2.0

■ FRANKIE LIBRAN
Libran, Francisco (Rosas) b: 5/6/48, Mayaguez, P.R. BR/TR, 6', 168 lbs. Deb: 9/3/69

| 1969 | SD-N | 10 | 10 | 1 | 1 | 1 | 0 | 0 | 1 | 1 | 2 | .100 | .182 | .200 | 7 | -1 | 0 | 0 | 0 | 1.000 | 1 | /S-9 | 0.0 |

■ JOHN LICKERT
Lickert, John Wilbur b: 4/4/60, Pittsburgh, Pa. BR/TR, 5'11", 175 lbs. Deb: 9/19/81

| 1981 | Bos-A | 1 | 0 | 0 | 0 | 0 | 0 | 0 | 0 | 0 | 0 | — | — | — | — | | 0 | | | 1.000 | -0 | /C-1 | 0.0 |

■ DAVE LIDDELL
Liddell, David Alexander (b: b: 6/15/66, Los Angeles, Cal. BR/TR, 6', 190 lbs. Deb: 6/3/90

| 1990 | NY-N | 1 | 1 | 1 | 1 | 0 | 0 | 0 | 1 | 0 | 0 | 1.000 | 1.000 | 1.000 | 453 | | 0 | 0 | 0 | 1.000 | -0 | /C-1 | 0.0 |

■ MIKE LIEBERTHAL
Lieberthal, Michael Scott b: 1/18/72, Glendale, Cal. BR/TR, 6', 170 lbs. Deb: 6/30/94

| 1994 | Phi-N | 24 | 79 | 6 | 21 | 3 | 1 | 1 | 5 | 3 | 5 | .266 | .301 | .367 | 74 | -3 | 0 | 0 | 0 | .969 | -3 | C-22 | -0.5 |

YEAR	TM/L	G	AB	R	H	2B	3B	HR	RBI	BB	SO	AVG	OBP	SLG	PRO+	BR/A	SB	CS	SBR	FA	FR	G/POS	TPR

■ **FRED LIESE**   Liese, Frederick Richard b: 10/7/1885, Wisconsin d: 6/30/67, Los Angeles, Cal. BL/TL, 5'8", 150 lbs. Deb: 4/14/10

| 1910 | Bos-N | 5 | 4 | 0 | 0 | 0 | 0 | 0 | 0 | 1 | 2 | .000 | .200 | .000 | -39 | -1 | 0 | | | .000 | 0 | H | -0.1 |

■ **GENE LILLARD**   Lillard, Robert Eugene b: 11/12/13, Santa Barbara, Cal d: 4/12/91, Goleta, Cal. BR/TR, 5'10.5", 178 lbs. Deb: 5/8/36 F

1936	Chi-N	19	34	6	7	1	0	0	2	3	8	.206	.270	.235	36	-3	0			.947	-1	/S-4,3-3	-0.3
1939	Chi-N	23	10	3	1	0	0	0	0	6	3	.100	.438	.100	51	-0	0			1.000	0	P-20	0.0
1940	StL-N	2	0	0	0	0	0	0	0	0	0	—	—	—	—	0	0			1.000	0	/P-2	0.0
Total	3	44	44	9	8	1	0	0	2	9	11	.182	.321	.205	43	-3	0			1.000	-1	/P-22,S-4,3	-0.3

■ **BILL LILLARD**   Lillard, William Beverly b: 1/10/18, Goleta, Cal. BR/TR, 5'10", 170 lbs. Deb: 9/11/39 F

1939	Phi-A	7	19	4	6	1	0	0	1	3	1	.316	.409	.368	102	0	0	0	0	.974	2	/S-7	0.3
1940	Phi-A	73	206	26	49	8	2	1	21	28	28	.238	.332	.311	69	-9	0	1	-1	.921	-18	S-69/2-1	-2.1
Total	2	80	225	30	55	9	2	1	22	31	29	.244	.339	.316	72	-9	0	1	-1	.927	-16	/S-76,2-1	-1.8

■ **JIM LILLIE**   Lillie, James J. "Grasshopper" (b: James J. Lilly) b: 7/27/1861, New Haven, Conn. d: 11/9/1890, Kansas City, Mo. Deb: 5/17/1883

1883	Buf-N	50	201	25	47	7	3	1	29	1	31	.234	.238	.313	64	-9				.835	-7	O-47/P-3,CS32	-1.4
1884	Buf-N	114	471	68	105	12	5	3	53	5	71	.223	.231	.289	60	-22				.852	16	*O-114/P-2	-0.8
1885	Buf-N	112	430	49	107	13	3	2	30	6	39	.249	.259	.307	80	-11				.862	0	*O-112/S-3,-1	-1.3
1886	KC-N	114	416	37	73	9	0	0	22	11	80	.175	.197	.197	19	-41	13			.884	11	*O-114/P-1	-3.0
Total	4	390	1518	179	332	41	11	6	134	23	221	.219	.230	.272	54	-82	13			.863	21	O-387/P-6,SC123D	-6.5

■ **BOB LILLIS**   Lillis, Robert Perry b: 6/2/30, Altadena, Cal. BR/TR, 5'11", 160 lbs. Deb: 8/30/58 MC

1958	LA-N	20	69	10	27	3	1	1	5	4	2	.391	.432	.507	143	4	1	2	-1	.964	-3	S-19	0.2
1959	LA-N	30	48	7	11	2	0	0	2	3	4	.229	.275	.271	43	-4	0	0	0	.919	8	S-20	0.5
1960	LA-N	48	60	6	16	4	0	0	6	2	6	.267	.290	.333	66	-3	2	0	1	.982	15	S-23,3-14/2	1.3
1961	LA-N	19	9	0	1	0	0	0	1	1	1	.111	.200	.111	-13	-1	0	0	0	1.000	1	3-12/2-1,S	0.0
	StL-N	86	230	24	50	4	0	0	21	7	13	.217	.247	.235	26	-24	3	3	-1	.928	2	S-56,2-24	-1.8
	Yr	105	239	24	51	4	0	0	22	8	14	.213	.245	.230	25	-25	3	3	-1	.924	3	S-57,2-25,3	-1.8
1962	Hou-N	129	457	38	114	12	4	1	30	28	23	.249	.293	.300	64	-24	7	3	0	.972	9	S-99,2-33/3	-0.4
1963	Hou-N	147	469	31	93	13	1	1	19	15	35	.198	.230	.237	37	-39	3	4	-2	.957	-5	*S-124,2-19/3	-4.0
1964	Hou-N	109	332	31	89	11	2	0	17	11	10	.268	.292	.313	75	-12	4	9	-4	.995	1	2-52,S-43,3	-1.0
1965	Hou-N	124	408	34	90	12	1	0	20	20	10	.221	.267	.255	51	-27	2	2	-1	.968	-12	*S-104/3-9,2	-3.5
1966	Hou-N	68	164	14	38	6	0	0	11	7	4	.232	.263	.268	52	-11	1	1	-0	.951	-9	2-35,S-18/3	-1.8
1967	Hou-N	37	82	3	20	1	0	0	5	1	8	.244	.253	.256	48	-6	0	1	-1	.947	3	S-23/2-3,3	-0.2
Total	10	817	2328	198	549	68	9	3	137	99	116	.236	.271	.277	54	-145	23	25	-8	.959	8	S-530,2-174/3	-10.7

■ **LOU LIMMER**   Limmer, Louis b: 3/10/25, New York, N.Y. BL/TL, 6'2", 190 lbs. Deb: 4/22/51

1951	Phi-A	94	214	25	34	9	1	5	30	28	40	.159	.256	.280	44	-17	1	0	0	.988	2	1-58	-1.7
1954	Phi-A	115	316	41	73	10	3	14	32	35	37	.231	.308	.415	96	-3	2	3	-1	.988	2	1-79	-0.6
Total	2	209	530	66	107	19	4	19	62	63	77	.202	.287	.360	75	-20	3	3	-1	.988	4	1-137	-2.3

■ **RUFINO LINARES**   Linares, Rufino (b: Rufino De La Cruz (Linares)) b: 2/28/51, San Pedro De Macoris, D.R. BR/TR, 6', 170 lbs. Deb: 4/10/81

1981	Atl-N	78	253	27	67	9	2	5	25	9	28	.265	.290	.375	85	-6	8	4	0	.963	3	O-60	-0.5
1982	Atl-N	77	191	28	57	7	1	2	17	7	29	.298	.327	.377	92	-2	5	2	0	1.000	0	O-53	-0.3
1984	Atl-N	34	58	4	12	3	0	1	10	6	12	.207	.281	.310	62	-3	0	0	0	.958	1	O-13	-0.3
1985	Cal-A	18	43	7	11	2	0	3	11	2	5	.256	.289	.512	114	1	2	0	1	1.000	-1	D-14/O-2	0.0
Total	4	207	545	66	147	21	3	11	63	24	74	.270	.302	.380	88	-10	15	6	1	.977	4	O-128/D-14	-1.1

■ **CARL LIND**   Lind, Henry Carl "Hooks" b: 9/19/03, New Orleans, La. d: 8/2/46, New York, N.Y. BR/TR, 6', 160 lbs. Deb: 9/14/27

1927	Cle-A	12	37	2	5	0	0	0	1	5	7	.135	.256	.135	4	-5	1	0	0	.969	2	2-11/S-1	-0.3
1928	Cle-A	154	650	102	191	42	4	1	54	36	48	.294	.331	.375	84	-15	8	5	-1	.960	4	*2-154	-0.7
1929	Cle-A	66	225	19	54	8	1	0	13	13	17	.240	.282	.284	44	-19	0	2	-1	.957	16	2-64/3-1	-0.1
1930	Cle-A	24	69	8	17	3	0	0	6	3	7	.246	.278	.290	43	-6	0	1	-1	.940	11	S-22/2-2	0.5
Total	4	256	981	131	267	53	5	1	74	57	79	.272	.313	.339	69	-45	9	8	-2	.960	33	2-231/S-23,3	-0.6

■ **JACK LIND**   Lind, Jackson Hugh b: 6/8/46, Denver, Col. BB/TR, 6', 170 lbs. Deb: 9/10/74

1974	Mil-A	9	17	4	4	2	0	0	1	3	2	.235	.350	.353	103	0	0	0	0	1.000	-0	/S-5,2-4	0.1
1975	Mil-A	17	20	1	1	0	0	0	0	2	12	.050	.136	.050	-45	-4	1	0	0	.919	5	/S-9,3-6,1	0.2
Total	2	26	37	5	5	2	0	0	1	5	14	.135	.238	.189	23	-4	1	0	0	.943	5	/S-14,3-6,21	0.3

■ **JOSE LIND**   Lind, Jose (Salgado) "Chico" b: 5/1/64, Toa Baja, P.R. BR/TR, 5'11", 170 lbs. Deb: 8/28/87

1987	Pit-N	35	143	21	46	8	4	0	11	8	12	.322	.358	.434	108	1	2	1	0	.995	6	2-35	0.9
1988	Pit-N	154	611	82	160	24	4	2	49	42	75	.262	.309	.324	83	-13	15	4	2	.987	3	*2-153	-0.2
1989	Pit-N	153	578	52	134	21	3	2	48	39	64	.232	.283	.289	66	-26	15	1	4	.976	-14	*2-151	-3.3
1990	*Pit-N	152	514	46	134	28	5	1	48	35	52	.261	.309	.340	82	-13	8	0	1	.991	17	*2-152	0.9
1991	*Pit-N	150	502	53	133	16	6	3	54	30	56	.265	.309	.339	83	-11	7	4	-0	.989	23	*2-149	1.5
1992	*Pit-N	135	468	38	110	14	1	0	39	26	29	.235	.277	.269	56	-27	3	1	0	**.992**	12	*2-134	-1.3
1993	KC-A	136	431	33	107	13	2	0	37	13	36	.248	.274	.288	48	-31	3	2	0	**.994**	-4	*2-136	-3.1
1994	KC-A	85	290	34	78	16	2	1	31	16	34	.269	.307	.348	63	-16	9	5	0	.988	2	2-84/D-1	-1.1
Total	8	1000	3537	359	902	140	27	9	317	209	358	.255	.298	.318	71	-137	62	18	6	.988	44	2-994/D-1	-5.7

■ **EM LINDBECK**   Lindbeck, Emerit Desmond b: 8/27/35, Kewanee, Ill. BL/TR, 6', 185 lbs. Deb: 4/22/60

| 1960 | Det-A | 2 | 1 | 0 | 0 | 0 | 0 | 0 | 0 | 1 | 0 | .000 | .500 | .000 | 46 | -0 | 0 | 0 | 0 | .000 | 0 | H | 0.0 |

■ **JOHNNY LINDELL**   Lindell, John Harlan b: 8/30/16, Greeley, Colo. d: 8/27/85, Newport Beach, Cal. BR/TR, 6'4.5", 217 lbs. Deb: 4/18/41

1941	NY-A	1	1	0	0	0	0	0	0	0	0	.000	.000	.000	-99	-0	0	0	0	.000	0	H	0.0
1942	NY-A	27	24	1	6	1	0	0	4	0	5	.250	.250	.292	53	-2	0	0	0	.923	-0	P-23	0.0
1943	*NY-A☆	122	441	53	108	17	**12**	4	51	51	55	.245	.329	.365	102	1	2	5	-2	.966	-2	*O-122	-1.0
1944	NY-A	149	594	91	178	33	**16**	18	103	44	56	.300	.351	.500	137	25	5	4	-1	.986	9	*O-149	2.7
1945	NY-A	41	159	26	45	6	3	1	20	17	10	.283	.363	.377	110	2	4	1	0	.982	0	O-41	0.0
1946	NY-A	102	332	41	86	10	5	10	40	32	47	.259	.328	.410	104	1	4	1	-1	.982	-0	O-74,1-14	-0.3
1947	*NY-A	127	476	66	131	18	7	11	67	32	70	.275	.322	.412	104	1	1	2	-1	.978	7	*O-118	0.1
1948	NY-A	88	309	58	98	17	2	13	55	35	50	.317	.387	.511	139	16	0	0	0	.994	2	O-79	1.3
1949	*NY-A	78	211	33	51	10	0	6	27	35	37	.242	.350	.374	92	-3	3	0	1	.983	-6	O-65	-1.0
1950	NY-A	7	21	0	4	0	0	0	2	4	2	.190	.320	.190	34	-2	0	0	0	.857	-2	/O-6	-0.4
	StL-N	36	113	16	21	5	0	1	15	11	24	.186	.287	.398	74	-5	0	0	0	.984	-2	O-33	-0.8
1953	Pit-N	58	91	11	26	6	1	4	15	16	15	.286	.404	.505	136	5	0	0	0	.962	2	P-27/1-2	0.0
	Phi-N	11	18	3	7	1	0	0	2	6	2	.389	.542	.444	162	2	0	0	0	1.000	-1	/P-5,O-2	0.0
	Yr	69	109	14	33	7	1	4	17	22	17	.303	.429	.495	141	8	0	0	0	.964	2	P-32/1-2,O	0.0
1954	Phi-N	7	5	0	1	0	0	0	0	0	2	.200	.429	.200	70	-0	0	0	0	.000	0	H	0.0
Total	12	854	2795	401	762	124	48	72	404	289	366	.273	.344	.429	113	43	17	13		.980	7	O-689/P-55,1	0.6

■ **JIM LINDEMAN**   Lindeman, James William b: 1/10/62, Evanston, Ill. BR/TR, 6'1", 200 lbs. Deb: 9/3/86

| 1986 | StL-N | 19 | 55 | 7 | 14 | 1 | 0 | 1 | 6 | 2 | 10 | .255 | .281 | .327 | 68 | -3 | 1 | 1 | -0 | .992 | -1 | 1-17/3-1,O | -0.5 |
| 1987 | *StL-N | 75 | 207 | 20 | 43 | 13 | 0 | 8 | 28 | 11 | 56 | .208 | .258 | .386 | 67 | -11 | 3 | 1 | 0 | .976 | -1 | O-49,1-20 | -1.3 |

YEAR	TM/L	G	AB	R	H	2B	3B	HR	RBI	BB	SO	AVG	OBP	SLG	PRO+	BR/A	SB	CS	SBR	FA	FR	G/POS	TPR
1988	StL-N	17	43	3	9	1	0	2	7	2	9	.209	.244	.372	74	-2	0	0	0	.941	-2	O-12/1-3	-0.4
1989	StL-N	73	45	8	5	1	0	0	2	3	18	.111	.167	.133	-13	-7	0	0	0	.989	0	1-42/O-5	-0.7
1990	Det-A	12	32	5	7	1	0	2	8	2	13	.219	.265	.438	92	-1	0	0	0	1.000	-1	D-10/1-1,O	-0.2
1991	Phi-N	65	95	13	32	5	0	0	12	13	14	.337	.417	.389	129	4	0	1	-1	1.000	-5	O-30/1-1	-0.2
1992	Phi-N	29	39	6	10	1	0	1	6	3	11	.256	.310	.359	89	-1	0	0	0	1.000	-3	/O-9	-0.4
1993	Hou-N	9	23	2	8	3	0	0	0	0	7	.348	.348	.478	123	1	0	0	0	1.000	1	/1-9	0.1
1994	NY-N	52	137	18	37	8	1	7	20	6	35	.270	.306	.496	104	0	0	0	0	.948	-3	O-33/1-4	-0.4
Total	9	351	676	82	165	34	1	21	89	42	173	.244	.292	.391	83	-17	4	3	-1	.970	-14	O-140/1-97,D3	-4.0

■ BOB LINDEMANN
Lindemann, John Frederick Mann b: 6/5/1881, Philadelphia, Pa. d: 12/19/51, Williamsport, Pa. BB/TR, 6', 175 lbs. Deb: 8/28/01

YEAR	TM/L	G	AB	R	H	2B	3B	HR	RBI	BB	SO	AVG	OBP	SLG	PRO+	BR/A	SB	CS	SBR	FA	FR	G/POS	TPR
1901	Phi-A	3	9	0	1	0	0	0	0	0	0	.111	.111	.111	-37	-2	0			.600	-0	/O-3	-0.2

■ WALT LINDEN
Linden, Walter Charles b: 3/27/24, Chicago, Ill. BR/TR, 6'1", 190 lbs. Deb: 4/30/50

YEAR	TM/L	G	AB	R	H	2B	3B	HR	RBI	BB	SO	AVG	OBP	SLG	PRO+	BR/A	SB	CS	SBR	FA	FR	G/POS	TPR
1950	Bos-N	3	5	0	2	1	0	0	0	1	0	.400	.500	.600	201	1	0			1.000	-1	/C-3	0.0

■ CHRIS LINDSAY
Lindsay, Christian Haller "Pinky" or "The Crab" b: 7/24/1878, Moon Township, Beaver County, Pa. d: 1/25/41, Cleveland, Ohio BR/TR, 6', 190 lbs. Deb: 7/6/05

YEAR	TM/L	G	AB	R	H	2B	3B	HR	RBI	BB	SO	AVG	OBP	SLG	PRO+	BR/A	SB	CS	SBR	FA	FR	G/POS	TPR
1905	Det-A	88	329	38	88	14	1	0	31	18		.267	.315	.316	100	-0	10			.978	-0	1-88	-0.4
1906	Det-A	141	499	59	112	16	2	0	33	45		.224	.293	.265	73	-15	18			.977	-8	*1-122,2-17/3	-2.9
Total	2	229	828	97	200	30	3	0	64	63		.242	.301	.285	83	-15	28			.978	-8	1-210/2-17,3	-3.3

■ BILL LINDSAY
Lindsay, William Gibbons b: 2/24/1881, Madison, N.C. d: 7/14/63, Greensboro, N.C. BL/TR, 5'10.5", 165 lbs. Deb: 6/21/11

YEAR	TM/L	G	AB	R	H	2B	3B	HR	RBI	BB	SO	AVG	OBP	SLG	PRO+	BR/A	SB	CS	SBR	FA	FR	G/POS	TPR
1911	Cle-A	19	66	6	16	2	0	0	5	1		.242	.265	.273	49	-5	2			.883	2	3-15/2-1	-0.2

■ DOUG LINDSEY
Lindsey, Michael Douglas b: 9/22/67, Austin, Tex. BR/TR, 6'2", 200 lbs. Deb: 10/6/91

YEAR	TM/L	G	AB	R	H	2B	3B	HR	RBI	BB	SO	AVG	OBP	SLG	PRO+	BR/A	SB	CS	SBR	FA	FR	G/POS	TPR
1991	Phi-N	1	3	0	0	0	0	0	0	0	3	.000	.000	.000	-99	-1	0	0	0	1.000	0	/C-1	-0.1
1993	Phi-N	2	2	0	1	0	0	0	0	0	1	.500	.500	.500	171	0	0	0	0	1.000	-0	/C-2	0.0
	Chi-A	2	1	0	0	0	0	0	0	0	0	.000	.000	.000	-99	0	0	0	0	1.000	0	/C-2	0.0
Total	2	5	6	0	1	0	0	0	0	0	4	.167	.167	.167	-8	-1	0	0	0	1.000	1	/C-5	-0.1

■ BILL LINDSEY
Lindsey, William Donald b: 4/12/60, Staten Island, N.Y. BR/TR, 6'3", 195 lbs. Deb: 7/18/87

YEAR	TM/L	G	AB	R	H	2B	3B	HR	RBI	BB	SO	AVG	OBP	SLG	PRO+	BR/A	SB	CS	SBR	FA	FR	G/POS	TPR
1987	Chi-A	9	16	2	3	0	0	0	1	0	3	.188	.188	.188	-0	-2	0	0	0	1.000	2	/C-9	0.0

■ CHUCK LINDSTROM
Lindstrom, Charles William b: 9/7/36, Chicago, Ill. BR/TR, 5'11", 175 lbs. Deb: 9/28/58 F

YEAR	TM/L	G	AB	R	H	2B	3B	HR	RBI	BB	SO	AVG	OBP	SLG	PRO+	BR/A	SB	CS	SBR	FA	FR	G/POS	TPR
1958	Chi-A	1	1	1	1	0	1	0	1	1	0	1.000	1.000	3.000	975	1	0	0	0	1.000	-0	/C-1	0.1

■ FREDDY LINDSTROM
Lindstrom, Frederick Charles (b: Frederick Anthony Lindstrom) b: 11/21/05, Chicago, Ill. d: 10/4/81, Chicago, Ill. BR/TR, 5'11", 170 lbs. Deb: 4/15/24 FH

YEAR	TM/L	G	AB	R	H	2B	3B	HR	RBI	BB	SO	AVG	OBP	SLG	PRO+	BR/A	SB	CS	SBR	FA	FR	G/POS	TPR
1924	*NY-N	52	79	19	20	3	1	0	4	6	10	.253	.314	.316	71	-3	3	1	0	.911	7	2-23,3-11	0.5
1925	NY-N	104	356	43	102	15	12	4	33	22	20	.287	.332	.430	97	-3	5	9	-4	.957	-1	3-96/2-1,S	-0.1
1926	NY-N	140	543	90	164	19	9	9	76	39	21	.302	.351	.420	108	5	11			.962	-3	*3-138/O-1	1.1
1927	NY-N	138	562	107	172	36	8	7	58	40	40	.306	.354	.436	111	8	10			.968	1	3-87,O-51	1.0
1928	NY-N	153	646	99	231	39	9	14	107	25	21	.358	.383	.511	131	27	15			.958	15	*3-153	4.8
1929	NY-N	130	549	99	175	23	6	15	91	30	28	.319	.354	.464	101	-0	10			.966	7	*3-128	1.1
1930	NY-N	148	609	127	231	39	7	22	106	48	33	.379	.425	.575	142	41	15			.953	6	*3-148	4.8
1931	NY-N	78	303	38	91	12	6	5	36	26	12	.300	.356	.429	113	5	5			.975	-7	O-73/2-4	-0.6
1932	NY-N	144	595	83	161	26	5	15	92	27	28	.271	.303	.407	91	-9	6			.982	9	*O-128,3-15	-1.6
1933	Pit-N	138	538	70	167	39	10	5	55	33	22	.310	.350	.448	127	18	1			.988	11	*O-130	2.3
1934	Pit-N	97	383	59	111	24	4	4	49	23	21	.290	.333	.405	94	-3	1			.990	1	O-92	-0.6
1935	*Chi-N	90	342	49	94	22	4	3	62	10	13	.275	.297	.389	82	-9	1			.979	-2	O-50,3-33	-1.1
1936	Bro-N	26	106	12	28	4	0	0	10	5	7	.264	.297	.302	61	-6	1			.982	-0	O-26	-0.5
Total	13	1438	5611	895	1747	301	81	103	779	334	276	.311	.351	.449	110	71	84	10		.959	37	3-809,O-551/2S	11.1

■ CARL LINHART
Linhart, Carl James b: 12/14/29, Zborov, Czech. BL/TR, 5'11", 184 lbs. Deb: 8/2/52

YEAR	TM/L	G	AB	R	H	2B	3B	HR	RBI	BB	SO	AVG	OBP	SLG	PRO+	BR/A	SB	CS	SBR	FA	FR	G/POS	TPR
1952	Det-A	3	2	0	0	0	0	0	0	0	0	.000	.000	.000	-99	-1	0	0	0	.000	0	H	-0.1

■ BOB LINTON
Linton, Claud Clarence b: 4/18/03, Emerson, Ark. d: 4/3/80, Destin, Fla. BL/TR, 6', 185 lbs. Deb: 4/26/29

YEAR	TM/L	G	AB	R	H	2B	3B	HR	RBI	BB	SO	AVG	OBP	SLG	PRO+	BR/A	SB	CS	SBR	FA	FR	G/POS	TPR
1929	Pit-N	17	18	0	2	0	0	0	1	1	2	.111	.158	.111	-31	-4	0			1.000	0	/C-8	-0.3

■ LARRY LINTZ
Lintz, Larry b: 10/10/49, Martinez, Cal. BB/TR, 5'9", 150 lbs. Deb: 7/14/73

YEAR	TM/L	G	AB	R	H	2B	3B	HR	RBI	BB	SO	AVG	OBP	SLG	PRO+	BR/A	SB	CS	SBR	FA	FR	G/POS	TPR
1973	Mon-N	52	116	20	29	1	0	0	3	17	18	.250	.351	.259	69	-4	12	4	1	.945	2	2-34,S-15	0.2
1974	Mon-N	113	319	60	76	10	1	0	20	44	50	.238	.334	.276	68	-12	50	7	11	.961	-13	2-67,S-31/3	-0.8
1975	Mon-N	46	132	18	26	0	0	0	3	23	18	.197	.316	.197	43	-9	17	9	-0	.970	-6	2-39/S-2	-1.4
	StL-N	27	18	6	5	1	0	0	1	3	2	.278	.381	.333	96	0	4	0	1	.889	9	/2-6,S-6	1.0
	Yr	73	150	24	31	1	0	0	4	26	20	.207	.324	.213	49	-9	21	9	1	.963	3	2-45/S-8	-0.4
1976	Oak-A	68	1	21	0	0	0	0	0	2	0	.000	.667	.000	111	0	31	11	3	1.000	-0	D-19/2-5,O	0.3
1977	Oak-A	41	30	11	4	0	0	0	0	8	13	.133	.333	.167	42	-2	13	5	1	1.000	11	2-28/S-2,3D	1.0
1978	Cle-A	3	0	1	0	0	0	0	0	0	0	—	—	—	—	0	1	2	-1	.000	0	R	-0.1
Total	6	350	616	137	140	13	1	0	27	97	101	.227	.336	.252	63	-27	128	38	16	.962	3	2-179/S-56,DO3	0.2

■ PHIL LINZ
Linz, Philip Francis b: 6/4/39, Baltimore, Md. BR/TR, 6'1", 180 lbs. Deb: 4/13/62

YEAR	TM/L	G	AB	R	H	2B	3B	HR	RBI	BB	SO	AVG	OBP	SLG	PRO+	BR/A	SB	CS	SBR	FA	FR	G/POS	TPR
1962	NY-A	71	129	28	37	8	0	1	14	6	17	.287	.319	.372	88	-2	6	2	1	.937	-3	S-21/3-8,2O	-0.3
1963	*NY-A	72	186	22	50	9	0	2	12	15	18	.269	.330	.349	91	-2	1	6	-3	.963	1	S-22,3-13/O/2	-0.3
1964	*NY-A	112	368	63	92	21	3	5	25	43	61	.250	.332	.364	92	-3	3	4	-2	.952	11	S-55,3-41/2O	1.0
1965	NY-A	99	285	37	59	12	1	2	16	30	33	.207	.283	.277	60	-15	2	1	0	.954	11	S-71/3-4,O2	0.1
1966	Phi-N	40	70	4	14	3	0	0	6	2	14	.200	.222	.243	29	-7	0	0	0	.971	-3	3-14/S-6,2	-0.6
1967	Phi-N	23	18	4	4	2	0	1	5	2	1	.222	.300	.500	124	0	0	0	0	.833	-1	/S-7,3-1	-0.1
	NY-N	24	58	8	12	2	0	0	1	4	10	.207	.270	.241	48	-4	0	0	0	.964	-2	2-11/S-8,3O	-0.6
	Yr	47	76	12	16	4	0	1	6	6	11	.211	.277	.303	66	-3	0	0	0	.963	-4	S-15,2-11/3O	-0.7
1968	NY-N	78	258	19	54	7	0	0	17	10	41	.209	.244	.236	45	-17	1	0	0	.968	-12	2-71	-2.9
Total	7	519	1372	185	322	64	4	11	96	112	195	.235	.296	.311	72	-49	13	13	-4	.952	6	S-190,2-102/3O	-3.7

■ JOHNNY LIPON
Lipon, John Joseph "Skids" b: 11/10/22, Martins Ferry, O. BR/TR, 6', 175 lbs. Deb: 8/16/42 MC

YEAR	TM/L	G	AB	R	H	2B	3B	HR	RBI	BB	SO	AVG	OBP	SLG	PRO+	BR/A	SB	CS	SBR	FA	FR	G/POS	TPR
1942	Det-A	34	131	5	25	2	0	0	9	7	7	.191	.232	.206	22	-14	1	3	-2	.945	7	S-34	-0.6
1946	Det-A	14	20	4	6	0	0	0	1	5	3	.300	.440	.300	103	0	0	0	0	.933	3	/S-8,3-1	0.4
1948	Det-A	121	458	65	133	18	8	5	52	68	22	.290	.384	.397	105	5	4	4	-1	.970	-12	*S-117/2-1,3	-0.1
1949	Det-A	127	439	57	110	14	6	3	59	75	24	.251	.362	.330	84	-8	2	4	-2	.965	4	*S-120	0.2
1950	Det-A	147	601	104	176	27	6	2	63	81	26	.293	.378	.368	89	-8	9	6	-1	.958	9	*S-147	1.1
1951	Det-A	129	487	56	129	15	1	0	38	49	27	.265	.335	.300	72	-18	7	6	-2	.949	-13	*S-125	-2.3
1952	Det-A	39	136	17	30	4	2	0	12	16	6	.221	.303	.279	62	-7	3	1	0	.978	-3	S-39	-0.6
	Bos-A	79	234	25	48	8	1	0	18	32	20	.205	.301	.248	50	-15	1	1	-0	.982	14	S-69/3-7	0.4
	Yr	118	370	42	78	12	3	0	30	48	26	.211	.301	.259	54	-22	4	2	0	.981	12	*S-108/3-7	-0.2
1953	Bos-A	60	145	18	31	7	0	0	13	14	16	.214	.283	.262	46	-11	1	0	0	.951	4	S-58	-0.4
	StL-A	7	9	0	2	0	0	0	1	0	1	.222	.222	.222	20	-1	0	0	0	1.000	-1	/3-6,2-1	-0.2
	Yr	67	154	18	33	7	0	0	14	14	17	.214	.280	.260	44	-12	1	0	0	.951	3	S-58/3-6,2	-0.6

YEAR	TM/L	G	AB	R	H	2B	3B	HR	RBI	BB	SO	AVG	OBP	SLG	PRO+	BR/A	SB	CS	SBR	FA	FR	G/POS	TPR
1954	Cin-N	1	1	0	0	0	0	0	0	0	0	.000	.000	.000	-97	-0				.000	0	H	0.0
Total	9	758	2661	351	690	95	24	10	266	347	152	.259	.346	.324	77	-77	28	25	-7	.961	13	S-717/3-15,2	-2.1

■ NIG LIPSCOMB
Lipscomb, Gerard   b: 2/24/11, Rutherfordton, N.C   d: 2/27/78, Huntersville, N.C.   BR/TR, 6', 175 lbs.   Deb: 4/23/37

YEAR	TM/L	G	AB	R	H	2B	3B	HR	RBI	BB	SO	AVG	OBP	SLG	PRO+	BR/A	SB	CS	SBR	FA	FR	G/POS	TPR
1937	StL-A	36	96	11	31	9	1	0	8	11	10	.323	.398	.438	110	1	0	0	0	.963	2	2-27/P-3,3	0.6

■ BOB LIPSKI
Lipski, Robert Peter   b: 7/7/38, Scranton, Pa.   BL/TR, 6'1", 180 lbs.   Deb: 4/28/63

YEAR	TM/L	G	AB	R	H	2B	3B	HR	RBI	BB	SO	AVG	OBP	SLG	PRO+	BR/A	SB	CS	SBR	FA	FR	G/POS	TPR
1963	Cle-A	2	1	0	0	0	0	0	0	0	1	.000	.000	.000	-99	-0	0	0	0	1.000	0	/C-2	0.0

■ NELSON LIRIANO
Liriano, Nelson Arturo (Bonilla)   b: 6/3/64, Santo Domingo, D.R.   BB/TR, 5'10", 172 lbs.   Deb: 8/25/87

YEAR	TM/L	G	AB	R	H	2B	3B	HR	RBI	BB	SO	AVG	OBP	SLG	PRO+	BR/A	SB	CS	SBR	FA	FR	G/POS	TPR
1987	Tor-A	37	158	29	38	6	2	2	10	16	22	.241	.310	.342	71	-6	13	2	3	.995	3	2-37	0.1
1988	Tor-A	99	276	36	73	6	2	3	23	11	40	.264	.298	.333	76	-9	12	5	1	.961	-13	2-80,D-11/3	-1.9
1989	*Tor-A	132	418	51	110	26	3	5	53	43	51	.263	.335	.376	102	1	16	7	1	.980	-18	*2-122/D-5	-1.2
1990	Tor-A	50	170	16	36	7	2	1	15	16	20	.212	.283	.294	61	-9	3	5	-2	.983	-12	2-49	-2.3
	Min-A	53	185	30	47	5	7	0	13	22	24	.254	.333	.357	87	-3	5	2	0	.968	-15	2-50/S-1,D	-1.8
	Yr	103	355	46	83	12	9	1	28	38	44	.234	.310	.327	75	-12	8	7	-2	.975	-28	2-99/D-2,S	-4.1
1991	KC-A	10	22	5	9	0	0	0	1	0	2	.409	.409	.409	127	1	1	1	-1	1.000	1	2-10	0.1
1993	Col-N	48	151	28	46	6	3	2	15	18	22	.305	.379	.424	98	-0	6	4	-1	.975	-13	S-35,2-16/3	-1.1
1994	Col-N	87	255	39	65	17	5	3	31	42	44	.255	.360	.396	83	-6	0	2	-1	.973	-5	2-79/S-3,3	-1.0
Total	7	516	1635	234	424	73	24	16	161	168	225	.259	.330	.363	86	-32	55	28	-0	.976	-74	2-443/S-39,D3	-9.1

■ JOE LIS
Lis, Joseph Anthony   b: 8/15/46, Somerville, N.J.   BR/TR, 6', 195 lbs.   Deb: 9/5/70

YEAR	TM/L	G	AB	R	H	2B	3B	HR	RBI	BB	SO	AVG	OBP	SLG	PRO+	BR/A	SB	CS	SBR	FA	FR	G/POS	TPR
1970	Phi-N	13	37	1	7	2	0	1	4	5	11	.189	.286	.324	65	-2	0	0	0	.947	0	/O-9	-0.2
1971	Phi-N	59	123	16	26	6	0	6	10	16	43	.211	.312	.407	102	0	0	1	-1	.978	-3	O-35	-0.5
1972	Phi-N	62	140	13	34	6	0	6	18	30	34	.243	.380	.414	122	5	0	1	-1	.996	1	1-30,O-14	0.3
1973	Min-A	103	253	37	62	11	1	9	25	28	66	.245	.327	.403	101	0	0	1	-1	.987	2	1-96/D-1	-0.4
1974	Min-A	24	41	5	8	0	0	0	3	5	12	.195	.298	.195	42	-3	0	0	0	.992	0	1-18	-0.4
	Cle-A	57	109	15	22	3	0	6	16	14	30	.202	.293	.394	97	-1	1	0	0	1.000	-0	1-31/3-9,OD	-0.2
	Yr	81	150	20	30	3	0	6	19	19	42	.200	.294	.340	82	-4	1	0	0	.997	-0	1-49/3-9,DO	-0.6
1975	Cle-A	9	13	4	4	2	0	2	8	3	3	.308	.471	.923	286	3	0	0	0	1.000	-0	/1-8,D-1	0.3
1976	Cle-A	20	51	4	16	1	0	2	7	8	8	.314	.407	.451	153	4	0	0	0	1.000	-0	1-17/D-1	0.3
1977	Sea-A	9	13	1	3	0	0	0	1	2	5	.231	.286	.231	43	-1	0	0	0	1.000	-1	/1-4,C-1	-0.2
Total	8	356	780	96	182	31	1	32	92	110	209	.233	.334	.399	105	6	1	3	-2	.992	-1	1-204/O-59,D3C	-1.0

■ RICK LISI
Lisi, Riccardo Patrick Emilio   b: 3/17/56, Halifax, N.S., Can.   BR/TR, 6', 175 lbs.   Deb: 5/9/81

YEAR	TM/L	G	AB	R	H	2B	3B	HR	RBI	BB	SO	AVG	OBP	SLG	PRO+	BR/A	SB	CS	SBR	FA	FR	G/POS	TPR
1981	Tex-A	9	16	6	5	0	0	0	4	3	0	.313	.450	.313	130	1	0	1	-1	1.000	-2	/O-8	-0.2

■ PAT LISTACH
Listach, Patrick Alan   b: 9/12/67, Natchitoches, La.   BB/TR, 5'9", 170 lbs.   Deb: 4/8/92

YEAR	TM/L	G	AB	R	H	2B	3B	HR	RBI	BB	SO	AVG	OBP	SLG	PRO+	BR/A	SB	CS	SBR	FA	FR	G/POS	TPR
1992	Mil-A	149	579	93	168	19	6	1	47	55	124	.290	.353	.349	99	1	54	18	5	.966	-7	*S-148/2-1,O	1.0
1993	Mil-A	98	356	50	87	15	1	3	30	37	70	.244	.321	.317	73	-13	18	9	0	.975	-16	S-95/O-6	-2.1
1994	Mil-A	16	54	8	16	3	0	0	2	3	8	.296	.333	.352	75	-2	2	1	0	.958	-0	S-16	-0.1
Total	3	263	989	151	271	37	7	4	79	95	202	.274	.340	.338	88	-14	74	28	5	.969	-23	S-259/O-7,2	-1.2

■ PETE LISTER
Lister, Morris Elmer   b: 7/21/1881, Savanna, Ill.   d: 3/27/47, St.Petersburg, Fla   BR/TR,   Deb: 9/14/07

YEAR	TM/L	G	AB	R	H	2B	3B	HR	RBI	BB	SO	AVG	OBP	SLG	PRO+	BR/A	SB	CS	SBR	FA	FR	G/POS	TPR
1907	Cle-A	22	65	5	18	2	0	0	4	3		.277	.319	.308	99	-0	2			.974	-1	1-22	-0.2

■ SCOTT LITTLE
Little, Dennis Scott   b: 1/19/63, E.St.Louis, Ill.   BR/TR, 6', 198 lbs.   Deb: 7/27/89

YEAR	TM/L	G	AB	R	H	2B	3B	HR	RBI	BB	SO	AVG	OBP	SLG	PRO+	BR/A	SB	CS	SBR	FA	FR	G/POS	TPR
1989	Pit-N	3	4	0	1	0	0	0	0	0	0	.250	.250	.250	45	-0	0	0	0	1.000	0	/O-1	0.1

■ HARRY LITTLE
Little, Harry A.   b: St.Louis, Mo.   TR,   Deb: 7/16/1877

YEAR	TM/L	G	AB	R	H	2B	3B	HR	RBI	BB	SO	AVG	OBP	SLG	PRO+	BR/A	SB	CS	SBR	FA	FR	G/POS	TPR
1877	StL-N	3	12	2	2	0	0	0	0	1	6	.167	.231	.167	29	-1				1.000	-0	/O-3	-0.1
	Lou-N	1	3	0	0	0	0	0	0	1	1	.000	.250	.000	-13	-0				.857	0	/2-1	0.0
	Yr	4	15	2	2	0	0	0	0	2	7	.133	.235	.133	19	-1				1.000	-0	/O-3,2-1	-0.1

■ BRYAN LITTLE
Little, Richard Bryan "Twig"   b: 10/8/59, Houston, Tex.   BB/TR, 5'10", 160 lbs.   Deb: 7/29/82

YEAR	TM/L	G	AB	R	H	2B	3B	HR	RBI	BB	SO	AVG	OBP	SLG	PRO+	BR/A	SB	CS	SBR	FA	FR	G/POS	TPR
1982	Mon-N	29	42	6	9	0	0	0	3	4	6	.214	.283	.214	40	-3	2	1	0	1.000	-2	2-16,S-10	-0.5
1983	Mon-N	106	350	48	91	15	3	1	36	50	22	.260	.356	.329	91	-2	4	5	-2	.968	-32	S-66,2-51	-3.0
1984	Mon-N	85	266	31	65	11	1	0	9	34	19	.244	.332	.293	81	-6	2	3	-1	.982	-22	2-77/S-2	-2.8
1985	Chi-A	73	188	35	47	9	1	2	27	26	21	.250	.350	.340	87	-3	0	1	-1	.989	-6	2-68/3-2,S	-0.7
1986	Chi-A	20	35	3	6	1	0	0	2	4	4	.171	.256	.200	25	-4	0	0	0	1.000	0	2-12/S-7,3	-0.3
	NY-A	14	41	3	8	1	0	0	0	2	7	.195	.233	.220	24	-4	0	0	0	.975	5	2-14	0.1
	Yr	34	76	6	14	2	0	0	2	6	11	.184	.244	.211	25	-8	0	0	0	.983	6	2-26/S-7,3	-0.2
Total	5	327	922	126	226	37	5	3	77	120	79	.245	.336	.306	80	-22	8	10	-4	.987	-56	2-238/S-86,3	-7.2

■ JACK LITTLE
Little, William Arthur   b: 3/12/1891, Mart, Tex.   d: 7/27/61, Dallas, Tex.   BR/TR, 5'11", 175 lbs.   Deb: 7/2/12

YEAR	TM/L	G	AB	R	H	2B	3B	HR	RBI	BB	SO	AVG	OBP	SLG	PRO+	BR/A	SB	CS	SBR	FA	FR	G/POS	TPR
1912	NY-A	3	12	2	3	0	0	0	0	1		.250	.357	.250	70	-0	2			1.000	0	/O-3	0.0

■ DENNIS LITTLEJOHN
Littlejohn, Dennis Gerald   b: 10/4/54, Santa Monica, Cal.   BR/TR, 6'2", 200 lbs.   Deb: 7/9/78

YEAR	TM/L	G	AB	R	H	2B	3B	HR	RBI	BB	SO	AVG	OBP	SLG	PRO+	BR/A	SB	CS	SBR	FA	FR	G/POS	TPR
1978	SF-N	2	0	0	0	0	0	0	0	0	0	—	—	—		0	0	0	0	.000	0	/C-2	0.0
1979	SF-N	63	193	15	38	6	1	1	13	21	46	.197	.276	.254	49	-14	0	0	0	.986	5	C-63	-0.6
1980	SF-N	13	29	2	7	1	0	0	2	7	7	.241	.389	.276	91	0	0	0	0	.983	2	C-10	0.2
Total	3	78	222	17	45	7	1	1	15	28	53	.203	.292	.257	55	-14	0	0	0	.985	7	/C-75	-0.4

■ LARRY LITTLETON
Littleton, Larry Marvin   b: 4/3/54, Charlotte, N.C.   BR/TR, 6'1", 185 lbs.   Deb: 4/12/81

YEAR	TM/L	G	AB	R	H	2B	3B	HR	RBI	BB	SO	AVG	OBP	SLG	PRO+	BR/A	SB	CS	SBR	FA	FR	G/POS	TPR
1981	Cle-A	26	23	2	0	0	0	0	1	3	6	.000	.115	.000	-65	-5	0	0	0	1.000	-10	O-24	-1.6

■ GREG LITTON
Litton, Jon Gregory   b: 7/13/64, New Orleans, La.   BR/TR, 6', 175 lbs.   Deb: 5/2/89

YEAR	TM/L	G	AB	R	H	2B	3B	HR	RBI	BB	SO	AVG	OBP	SLG	PRO+	BR/A	SB	CS	SBR	FA	FR	G/POS	TPR
1989	*SF-N	71	143	12	36	5	3	4	17	7	29	.252	.291	.413	102	-0	0	2	-1	.953	-5	3-34,2-15/SOC	-0.6
1990	SF-N	93	204	17	50	9	1	1	24	11	45	.245	.287	.314	68	-9	1	0	0	.985	-11	O-56,2-18/S3	-2.1
1991	SF-N	59	127	13	23	7	1	1	15	11	25	.181	.252	.276	50	-9	0	2	-1	.989	-2	1-15,2-15,3/SOCP	-1.2
1992	SF-N	68	140	9	32	5	0	4	15	11	33	.229	.285	.350	84	-3	0	1	-1	.992	-3	2-31,3-10/1SO	-0.7
1993	Sea-A	72	174	25	52	17	0	3	25	18	30	.299	.368	.448	116	4	0	1	-1	1.000	1	O-22,2-17,1D/3S	0.3
1994	Bos-A	11	21	2	2	0	0	0	1	0	5	.095	.095	.095	-48	-5	0	0	0	1.000	0	/2-4,1-3,3D	-0.1
Total	6	374	809	78	195	43	5	13	97	58	167	.241	.295	.355	81	-22	1	6	-3	.997	-18	2-100/O-91,31SDCP	-4.6

■ JACK LITTRELL
Littrell, Jack Napier   b: 1/22/29, Louisville, Ky.   BR/TR, 6', 179 lbs.   Deb: 4/19/52

YEAR	TM/L	G	AB	R	H	2B	3B	HR	RBI	BB	SO	AVG	OBP	SLG	PRO+	BR/A	SB	CS	SBR	FA	FR	G/POS	TPR
1952	Phi-A	4	2	0	0	0	0	0	0	1	2	.000	.333	.000	-2	-0	0	0	0	1.000	0	/S-2,3-1	0.0
1954	Phi-A	9	30	7	9	2	0	1	3	6	3	.300	.417	.467	141	2	1	0	0	.976	-1	/S-9	0.2
1955	KC-A	37	70	7	14	0	1	0	1	4	12	.200	.243	.229	27	-7	0	0	0	.947	0	S-22/1-6,2	-0.6
1957	Chi-N	61	153	8	29	4	1	1	13	9	43	.190	.235	.261	34	-14	0	0	0	.944	1	S-47/2-6,3	-0.9
Total	4	111	255	22	52	6	3	2	17	20	60	.204	.262	.275	45	-20	1	0	0	.949	0	/S-80,2-10,13	-1.3

■ DANNY LITWHILER
Litwhiler, Daniel Webster   b: 8/31/16, Ringtown, Pa.   BR/TR, 5'10.5", 198 lbs.   Deb: 4/25/40   C

YEAR	TM/L	G	AB	R	H	2B	3B	HR	RBI	BB	SO	AVG	OBP	SLG	PRO+	BR/A	SB	CS	SBR	FA	FR	G/POS	TPR
1940	Phi-N	36	142	10	49	2	2	5	17	3	17	.345	.363	.493	139	7	1			.986	1	O-34	0.6
1941	Phi-N	151	590	72	180	29	6	18	66	39	43	.305	.345	.466	134	23	1			.964	17	O-150	3.2
1942	Phi-N★	151	591	59	160	25	9	9	56	27	42	.271	.310	.389	109	4	2			**1.000**	-2	*O-151	-0.6

YEAR	TM/L	G	AB	R	H	2B	3B	HR	RBI	BB	SO	AVG	OBP	SLG	PRO+	BR/A	SB	CS	SBR	FA	FR	G/POS	TPR
1943	Phi-N	36	139	23	36	6	0	5	17	11	14	.259	.313	.410	113	1	1			.989	5	O-34	0.5
	*StL-N	80	258	40	72	14	3	7	31	19	31	.279	.333	.438	117	5	1			1.000	1	O-70	0.3
	Yr	116	397	63	108	20	3	12	48	30	45	.272	.326	.428	115	6	2			.996	6	*O-104	0.8
1944	*StL-N	140	492	53	130	25	5	15	82	37	56	.264	.328	.427	109	5	2			.974	-1	*O-136	-0.2
1946	StL-N	6	5	0	0	0	0	0	0	1	1	.000	.167	.000	-49	-1	0			.000	0	H	-0.1
	Bos-N	79	247	29	72	12	2	8	38	19	23	.291	.347	.453	125	7	1			.985	-3	O-65/3-2	0.1
	Yr	85	252	29	72	12	2	8	38	20	24	.286	.343	.444	121	6	1			.985	-3	O-65/3-2	0.0
1947	Bos-N	91	226	38	59	5	2	7	31	25	43	.261	.337	.394	96	-2	1			.976	-6	O-66	-1.0
1948	Bos-N	13	33	0	9	2	0	0	6	4	2	.273	.385	.333	97	0	0			1.000	2	/O-8	0.1
	Cin-N	106	338	51	93	19	2	14	44	48	41	.275	.365	.467	128	13	1			.988	2	O-83,3-15	1.1
	Yr	119	371	51	102	21	2	14	50	52	43	.275	.367	.456	125	13	1			.990	4	O-91,3-15	1.2
1949	Cin-N	102	292	35	85	18	1	11	48	44	42	.291	.384	.473	127	12	0			.987	-5	O-82/3-3	0.3
1950	Cin-N	54	112	15	29	4	0	6	12	20	21	.259	.371	.455	116	3	0			.958	-3	O-29	-0.1
1951	Cin-N	12	29	3	8	1	0	2	3	2	5	.276	.323	.517	120	1	0	0	0	.933	-1	/O-7	0.0
Total	11	1057	3494	428	982	162	32	107	451	299	377	.281	.342	.438	119	78	11	0		.982	9	O-915/3-20	4.2

■ PADDY LIVINGSTON
Livingston, Patrick Joseph b: 1/14/1880, Cleveland, Ohio d: 9/19/77, Cleveland, Ohio BR/TR, 5'8", 197 lbs. Deb: 9/2/01

YEAR	TM/L	G	AB	R	H	2B	3B	HR	RBI	BB	SO	AVG	OBP	SLG	PRO+	BR/A	SB	CS	SBR	FA	FR	G/POS	TPR
1901	Cle-A	1	2	0	0	0	0	0	0	0		.000	.333	.000	-2	-0	0			1.000	-1	/C-1	-0.1
1906	Cin-N	50	139	8	22	1	4	0	8	12		.158	.259	.223	48	-8	0			.960	3	C-47	-0.1
1909	Phi-A	64	175	15	41	6	4	0	15	15		.234	.323	.314	99	0	4			.969	9	C-64	1.7
1910	Phi-A	37	120	11	25	4	3	0	9	6		.208	.264	.292	75	-4	2			.968	4	C-37	0.4
1911	Phi-A	27	71	9	17	4	0	0	8	7		.239	.316	.296	72	-3	1			.977	5	C-26	0.4
1912	Cle-A	20	47	5	11	2	1	0	3	1		.234	.280	.319	69	-2	0			.976	0	C-14	-0.1
1917	StL-N	7	20	0	4	0	0	0	2	0		.200	.200	.200	23	-2	2			1.000	1	/C-6	-0.1
Total	7	206	574	48	120	17	12	0	45	41	1	.209	.287	.280	73	-18	9			.969	21	C-195	2.1

■ MICKEY LIVINGSTON
Livingston, Thompson Orville b: 11/15/14, Newberry, S.C. d: 4/3/83, Newberry, S.C. BR/TR, 6'1.5", 185 lbs. Deb: 9/17/38

YEAR	TM/L	G	AB	R	H	2B	3B	HR	RBI	BB	SO	AVG	OBP	SLG	PRO+	BR/A	SB	CS	SBR	FA	FR	G/POS	TPR
1938	Was-A	2	4	0	3	2	0	0		0	1	.750	.750	1.250	421	2	0			.667	-1	/C-2	0.1
1941	Phi-N	95	207	16	42	6	1	0	18	20	38	.203	.276	.242	49	-14	2			.974	-1	C-71/1-1	-1.0
1942	Phi-N	89	239	20	49	6	1	2	22	25	20	.205	.283	.264	64	-11	0			.987	-6	C-78/1-6	-1.2
1943	Phi-N	84	265	25	66	9	2	3	18	19	18	.249	.304	.332	87	-5	1			.988	-2	C-84/1-2	-0.1
	Chi-N	36	111	11	29	5	1	4	16	12	8	.261	.333	.432	122	3	1			1.000	-1	C-31/1-4	0.4
	Yr	120	376	36	95	14	3	7	34	31	26	.253	.313	.362	98	-2	2			.991	-3	*C-115/1-6	0.3
1945	*Chi-N	71	224	19	57	4	2	2	23	19	6	.254	.324	.317	80	-6	2			.990	-1	C-68/1-1	-0.2
1946	Chi-N	66	176	14	45	14	0	2	20	20	19	.256	.338	.369	103	1	0			.981	-2	C-56	0.5
1947	Chi-N	19	33	2	7	2	0	0	3	1	5	.212	.235	.273	36	-3	0			1.000	-0	/C-7	-0.3
	NY-N	5	6	0	1	0	0	0	0	1	2	.167	.286	.167	23	-1	0			.800	0	/C-1	0.0
	Yr	24	39	2	8	2	0	0	3	2	7	.205	.244	.256	34	-4	0			.970	-1	/C-8	-0.3
1948	NY-N	45	99	9	21	4	1	2	12	21	11	.212	.350	.333	85	-1	1			.980	-1	C-42	0.0
1949	NY-N	19	57	6	17	4	1	2	6	2	8	.298	.333	.544	132	2	0			.985	1	C-19	0.2
	Bos-N	28	64	6	15	2	1	0	6	3	5	.234	.290	.297	61	-4	0			.977	1	C-22	-0.2
	Yr	47	121	12	32	4	1	4	18	5	13	.264	.310	.413	95	-1	0			.980	-1	C-41	-0.3
1951	Bro-N	2	5	0	2	0	0	0	2	1	0	.400	.500	.400	142	0	0	0	0	1.000	-0	/C-2	0.0
Total	10	561	1490	128	354	56	9	19	153	144	141	.238	.310	.326	82	-37	7	0		.984	-11	C-483/1-14	-1.8

■ SCOTT LIVINGSTONE
Livingstone, Scott Louis b: 7/15/65, Dallas, Tex. BL/TR, 6', 190 lbs. Deb: 7/19/91

YEAR	TM/L	G	AB	R	H	2B	3B	HR	RBI	BB	SO	AVG	OBP	SLG	PRO+	BR/A	SB	CS	SBR	FA	FR	G/POS	TPR
1991	Det-A	44	127	19	37	5	0	2	11	10	25	.291	.343	.378	98	-0	2	1	0	.980	1	3-43	0.0
1992	Det-A	117	354	43	100	21	0	4	46	21	36	.282	.323	.376	95	-3	1	3	-2	.962	-6	*3-112	-1.1
1993	Det-A	98	304	39	89	10	2	2	39	19	32	.293	.334	.359	87	-6	1	3	-2	.955	-3	3-62,D-32	-1.1
1994	Det-A	15	23	0	5	1	0	0	1	1	4	.217	.250	.261	32	-2	0	0	0	1.000	0	/1-5,3-1,D	-0.2
	SD-N	57	180	11	49	12	1	2	10	6	22	.272	.296	.383	76	-7	2	2	-1	.942	-1	3-50	-0.8
Total	4	331	988	112	280	49	3	10	107	57	119	.283	.322	.369	88	-18	6	9	-4	.960	-8	3-268/D-37,1	-3.2

■ ABEL LIZOTTE
Lizotte, Abel b: 4/13/1870, Lewiston, Me. d: 12/4/26, Wilkes-Barre, Pa. 5'8", 174 lbs. Deb: 9/17/1896

YEAR	TM/L	G	AB	R	H	2B	3B	HR	RBI	BB	SO	AVG	OBP	SLG	PRO+	BR/A	SB	CS	SBR	FA	FR	G/POS	TPR
1896	Pit-N	7	29	3	3	0	0	0	3	2	2	.103	.161	.103	-31	-5	1			.952	1	/1-7	-0.4

■ WINSTON LLENAS
Llenas, Winston Enriquillo (Davila) b: 9/23/43, Santiago, D.R. BR/TR, 5'10", 165 lbs. Deb: 8/15/68 C

YEAR	TM/L	G	AB	R	H	2B	3B	HR	RBI	BB	SO	AVG	OBP	SLG	PRO+	BR/A	SB	CS	SBR	FA	FR	G/POS	TPR
1968	Cal-A	16	39	5	5	1	0	0	2	2	5	.128	.190	.154	6	-4	0	0	0	.800	-3	/3-9	-0.9
1969	Cal-A	34	47	4	8	2	0	0	2	2	10	.170	.204	.213	18	-5	0	0	0	.929	-2	/3-9	-0.8
1972	Cal-A	44	64	3	17	3	0	0	7	3	8	.266	.299	.313	87	-1	0	0	0	.950	-1	3-10/2-2,O	-0.3
1973	Cal-A	78	130	16	35	1	0	1	25	10	16	.269	.326	.300	84	-3	0	0	0	1.000	-4	2-20,3-11/OD	-0.6
1974	Cal-A	72	138	16	36	6	0	2	17	11	19	.261	.315	.348	96	-1	0	0	0	1.000	-8	O-32,2-15/D/3	-1.0
1975	Cal-A	56	113	6	21	4	0	0	10	10	11	.186	.252	.221	37	-9	0	1	-1	1.000	-3	2-12,0-10/13D	-0.6
Total	6	300	531	50	122	17	0	3	61	38	69	.230	.284	.279	66	-24	0	1	-1	1.000	-13	/2-49,O-48,3D1	-4.2

■ MIKE LOAN
Loan, William Joseph b: 9/27/1894, Philadelphia, Pa. d: 11/21/66, Springfield, Pa. BR/TR, 5'11", 185 lbs. Deb: 9/18/12

YEAR	TM/L	G	AB	R	H	2B	3B	HR	RBI	BB	SO	AVG	OBP	SLG	PRO+	BR/A	SB	CS	SBR	FA	FR	G/POS	TPR
1912	Phi-N	1	2	1	1	0	0	0	0	0	0	.500	.500	.500	163	0	0			1.000	-1	/C-1	0.0

■ BOB LOANE
Loane, Robert Kenneth b: 8/6/14, Berkeley, Cal. BR/TR, 6', 190 lbs. Deb: 7/29/39

YEAR	TM/L	G	AB	R	H	2B	3B	HR	RBI	BB	SO	AVG	OBP	SLG	PRO+	BR/A	SB	CS	SBR	FA	FR	G/POS	TPR
1939	Was-A	3	9	2	0	0	0	0	1	4	4	.000	.308	.000	-16	-1	0	0	0	.909	-1	/O-3	0.0
1940	Bos-N	13	22	4	5	3	0	0	1	2	5	.227	.292	.364	84	-1	2			1.000	0	O-10	0.0
Total	2	16	31	6	5	3	0	0	2	6	9	.161	.297	.258	54	-2	2	0		.969	-1	/O-13	0.0

■ FRANK LOBERT
Lobert, Frank John b: 11/26/1883, Williamsport, Pa. d: 5/29/32, Pittsburgh, Pa. BR/TR, 6', 180 lbs. Deb: 6/6/14 F

YEAR	TM/L	G	AB	R	H	2B	3B	HR	RBI	BB	SO	AVG	OBP	SLG	PRO+	BR/A	SB	CS	SBR	FA	FR	G/POS	TPR
1914	Bal-F	11	30	3	6	0	1	0	2	0	0	.200	.200	.267	20	-4	0			.870	-2	/3-7,2-1	-0.5

■ HANS LOBERT
Lobert, John Bernard "Honus" b: 10/18/1881, Wilmington, Del. d: 9/14/68, Philadelphia, Pa. BR/TR, 5'9", 170 lbs. Deb: 9/21/03 FMC

YEAR	TM/L	G	AB	R	H	2B	3B	HR	RBI	BB	SO	AVG	OBP	SLG	PRO+	BR/A	SB	CS	SBR	FA	FR	G/POS	TPR
1903	Pit-N	5	13	1	1	1	0	0	0	1		.077	.143	.154	-15	-2	1			.778	-1	/3-3,2-1,S	-0.3
1905	Chi-N	14	46	7	9	2	0	0	1	3		.196	.260	.239	47	-3	4			.918	0	3-13/O-1	-0.3
1906	Cin-N	79	268	39	83	5	5	0	19	19		.310	.366	.366	123	7	20			.959	-11	3-35,S-31,2/O	-0.2
1907	Cin-N	148	537	61	132	9	12	1	41	37		.246	.299	.313	88	-8	30			.941	-18	*S-142/3-5	-2.5
1908	Cin-N	155	570	71	167	17	18	4	63	46		.293	.348	.407	145	27	47			.921	-26	3-99,S-35,O	0.6
1909	Cin-N	122	425	50	90	13	5	4	52	48		.212	.304	.294	86	-6	30			.921	-14	3-122	-1.7
1910	Cin-N	93	314	43	97	6	6	3	40	30	9	.309	.369	.395	128	11	41			.932	-2	3-90	1.2
1911	Phi-N	147	541	94	154	20	9	9	72	66	31	.285	.368	.405	115	11	40			.954	-17	*3-147	-0.4
1912	Phi-N	65	257	37	84	12	5	2	33	19	13	.327	.373	.436	113	4	13			.976	-13	3-64	-0.9
1913	Phi-N	150	573	98	172	28	11	7	55	42	34	.300	.353	.424	117	11	41			.974	-15	*3-145/S-3,2	-0.2
1914	Phi-N	135	505	83	139	24	5	1	52	49	32	.275	.343	.349	99	-0	31			.943	-26	*3-133/S-2	-2.3
1915	NY-N	106	386	46	97	18	4	0	38	25	24	.251	.304	.319	94	-3	14	15	-5	.950	-5	*3-103	-1.0
1916	NY-N	48	76	6	17	3	0	1	6	11	5	.224	.272	.316	84	-2	2			.961	-2	3-20	0.1
1917	NY-N	50	52	4	10	1	0	1	5	5	5	.192	.276	.269	70	-2	1			.906	2	3-21	0.0
Total	14	1317	4563	640	1252	159	82	32	482	395	156	.274	.337	.366	109	46	316	15		.944	-142	3-1000,S-214/O2	-7.9

■ HARRY LOCHHEAD
Lochhead, Robert Henry b: 3/29/1876, Stockton, Cal. d: 8/22/09, Stockton, Cal. BR/TR, 5'11", 172 lbs. Deb: 4/16/1899

YEAR	TM/L	G	AB	R	H	2B	3B	HR	RBI	BB	SO	AVG	OBP	SLG	PRO+	BR/A	SB	CS	SBR	FA	FR	G/POS	TPR
1899	Cle-N	148	541	52	129	7	1	1	43	21		.238	.280	.261	52	-35	23			.909	2	*S-146/2-1,P	-2.0

YEAR	TM/L	G	AB	R	H	2B	3B	HR	RBI	BB	SO	AVG	OBP	SLG	PRO+	BR/A	SB	CS	SBR	FA	FR	G/POS	TPR
1901	Det-A	1	4	2	2	0	0	0	0	0	0	.500	.600	.500	198	1	0			.857	-0	/S-1	0.0
	Phi-A	9	34	3	3	0	0	0	2	3		.088	.162	.088	-28	-6	0			.757	-8	/S-9	-1.3
	Yr	10	38	5	5	0	0	0	2	3		.132	.214	.132	-3	-5	0			.773	-9	S-10	-1.3
Total	2	158	579	57	134	7	1	1	45	24		.231	.275	.252	48	-40	23			.903	-7	S-156/P-1,2	-3.3

■ DON LOCK   Lock, Don Wilson b: 7/27/36, Wichita, Kan.   BR/TR, 6'2", 202 lbs.   Deb: 7/17/62

YEAR	TM/L	G	AB	R	H	2B	3B	HR	RBI	BB	SO	AVG	OBP	SLG	PRO+	BR/A	SB	CS	SBR	FA	FR	G/POS	TPR
1962	Was-A	71	225	30	57	6	2	12	37	30	63	.253	.341	.458	114	4	4	5	-2	.973	3	O-67	0.1
1963	Was-A	149	531	71	134	20	1	27	82	70	151	.252	.342	.446	119	14	7	3	0	.980	15	*O-146	2.2
1964	Was-A	152	512	73	127	17	4	28	80	79	137	.248	.350	.461	124	17	4	2	0	.987	13	*O-149	2.4
1965	Was-A	143	418	52	90	15	1	16	39	57	115	.215	.317	.371	96	-2	1	3	-2	.969	2	*O-136	-0.7
1966	Was-A	138	386	52	90	13	1	16	48	57	126	.233	.335	.396	110	6	2	6	-3	.977	7	*O-136	0.5
1967	Phi-N	112	313	46	79	13	1	14	51	43	98	.252	.352	.435	123	10	9	5	-0	.973	-2	O-97	0.4
1968	Phi-N	99	248	27	52	7	2	8	34	26	64	.210	.285	.351	90	-3	3	4	-2	.955	-5	O-78	-1.5
1969	Phi-N	4	4	0	0	0	0	0	0	0	1	.000	.000	.000	-99	-1	0	0	0			/O-1	-0.1
	Bos-A	53	58	8	13	1	0	1	2	11	21	.224	.348	.293	77	-1	0	1	-1	1.000	-6	O-28/1-4	-0.9
Total	8	921	2695	359	642	92	12	122	373	373	776	.238	.334	.417	111	43	30	29	-8	.976	27	O-831/1-4	2.4

■ MARSHALL LOCKE   Locke, Marshall b: Indianapolis, Ind.   Deb: 7/5/1884

YEAR	TM/L	G	AB	R	H	2B	3B	HR	RBI	BB	SO	AVG	OBP	SLG	PRO+	BR/A	SB	CS	SBR	FA	FR	G/POS	TPR
1884	Ind-a	7	29	5	7	0	1	0		0		.241	.241	.310	81	-1				.800	-1	/O-7	-0.2

■ KEITH LOCKHART   Lockhart, Keith Virgil b: 11/10/64, Whittier, Cal.   BL/TR, 5'10", 170 lbs.   Deb: 4/5/94

YEAR	TM/L	G	AB	R	H	2B	3B	HR	RBI	BB	SO	AVG	OBP	SLG	PRO+	BR/A	SB	CS	SBR	FA	FR	G/POS	TPR
1994	SD-N	27	43	4	9	0	0	2	6	4	10	.209	.292	.349	67	-2	1	0	0	1.000	-1	3-13/2-5,SO	-0.3

■ GENE LOCKLEAR   Locklear, Gene b: 7/19/49, Lumberton, N.C.   BL/TR, 5'10", 165 lbs.   Deb: 4/5/73

YEAR	TM/L	G	AB	R	H	2B	3B	HR	RBI	BB	SO	AVG	OBP	SLG	PRO+	BR/A	SB	CS	SBR	FA	FR	G/POS	TPR
1973	Cin-N	29	26	6	5	0	0	0	2	5		.192	.276	.192	34	-2	0	0	0	1.000	-1	/O-5	-0.4
	SD-N	67	154	20	37	6	1	3	25	21	22	.240	.331	.351	97	-1	9	4	0	.952	2	O-37	0.0
	Yr	96	180	26	42	6	1	3	25	23	27	.233	.324	.328	89	-3	9	4	0	.954	1	O-42	-0.4
1974	SD-N	39	74	7	20	3	2	1	3	4	12	.270	.308	.405	103	-0	0	1	-1	1.000	1	O-12	-0.1
1975	SD-N	100	237	31	76	11	1	5	27	22	26	.321	.381	.439	135	11	4	2	0	.970	-1	O-51	0.9
1976	SD-N	43	67	9	15	3	0	0	8	4	15	.224	.268	.269	57	-4	0	0	0	.952	-1	O-11	-0.5
	NY-A	13	32	2	7	1	0	0	1	2	7	.219	.265	.250	52	-2	0	0	0	1.000	-1	/O-3,D-6	-0.3
1977	NY-A	1	5	1	3	0	0	0	2	0	0	.600	.600	.600	231	1	0	0	0	.667	-0	/O-1	0.1
Total	5	292	595	76	163	24	4	9	66	55	87	.274	.337	.373	105	3	13	7	0	.962	-0	O-120/D-6	-0.3

■ STU LOCKLIN   Locklin, Stuart Carlton b: 7/22/28, Appleton, Wis.   BL/TL, 6'1.5", 190 lbs.   Deb: 6/23/55

YEAR	TM/L	G	AB	R	H	2B	3B	HR	RBI	BB	SO	AVG	OBP	SLG	PRO+	BR/A	SB	CS	SBR	FA	FR	G/POS	TPR
1955	Cle-A	16	18	4	3	1	0	0	0	3	4	.167	.286	.222	37	-2	0	0	0	1.000	-3	/O-7	-0.4
1956	Cle-A	9	6	0	1	0	0	0	0	0	1	.167	.167	.167	-12	-1	0	0	0	1.000	-0	/O-1	-0.1
Total	2	25	24	4	4	1	0	0	0	3	5	.167	.259	.208	26	-3	0	0	0	1.000	-3	/O-8	-0.5

■ WHITEY LOCKMAN   Lockman, Carroll Walter b: 7/25/26, Lowell, N.C.   BL/TR, 6'1", 175 lbs.   Deb: 7/5/45   MC

YEAR	TM/L	G	AB	R	H	2B	3B	HR	RBI	BB	SO	AVG	OBP	SLG	PRO+	BR/A	SB	CS	SBR	FA	FR	G/POS	TPR
1945	NY-N	32	129	16	44	9	0	3	18	13	10	.341	.410	.481	145	8	1			.961	-4	O-32	0.2
1947	NY-N	2	2	0	1	0	0	0	1	0	0	.500	.500	.500	165	0	0			.000	0	H	0.0
1948	NY-N	146	584	117	167	24	10	18	59	68	63	.286	.361	.454	119	15	8			.987	7	*O-144	1.4
1949	NY-N	151	617	97	186	32	7	11	65	62	31	.301	.368	.429	113	12	12			.973	4	*O-151	0.9
1950	NY-N	129	532	72	157	28	5	6	52	42	29	.295	.349	.400	96	-3	1			.978	9	*O-128	0.1
1951	*NY-N	153	614	85	173	27	7	12	73	50	32	.282	.339	.407	99	-1	4	5	-2	.986	4	*1-119,O-34	-0.6
1952	NY-N★	154	606	99	176	17	4	13	58	67	52	.290	.363	.396	110	9	2	4	-2	.992	3	*1-154	0.4
1953	NY-N	150	607	85	179	22	4	9	61	52	36	.295	.351	.389	91	-7	3	4	-2	.989	7	*1-120,O-30	-0.8
1954	*NY-N	148	570	73	143	17	3	16	60	59	31	.251	.321	.375	80	-17	2	2	-1	.987	-8	*1-145/O-2	-3.2
1955	NY-N	147	576	76	157	19	0	15	49	39	34	.273	.322	.384	86	-12	3	3	-1	.983	-4	O-81,1-68	-2.4
1956	NY-N	48	169	13	46	7	1	1	10	16	17	.272	.335	.343	83	-4	0	2	-1	.960	-1	O-39/1-7	-0.8
	StL-N	70	193	14	48	0	2	0	10	18	8	.249	.313	.269	59	-11	2	2	-1	.955	-8	O-57/1-2	-2.3
	Yr	118	362	27	94	7	3	1	20	34	25	.260	.323	.304	70	-14	2	4	-2	.957	-8	O-96/1-9	-3.1
1957	NY-N	133	456	51	113	9	4	7	30	39	19	.248	.310	.331	73	-17	5	5	-2	.991	-6	*1-102,O-27	-3.3
1958	SF-N	92	122	15	29	7	0	2	7	13	8	.238	.311	.328	71	-5	0	0	0	1.000	-11	O-25,2-15/1	-1.6
1959	Bal-A	38	69	7	15	1	1	0	2	8	4	.217	.299	.261	56	-4	0	0	0	.992	-4	1-22/2-5,O	-0.8
	Cin-N	52	84	10	22	5	1	0	7	4	6	.262	.295	.345	68	-4	0	0	0	.971	0	1-20/2-6,3O	-0.4
1960	Cin-N	21	10	0	2	1	0	0	1	2	3	.200	.385	.500	138	1	0	0	0	1.000	0	/1-5	0.1
Total	15	1666	5940	836	1658	222	49	114	563	552	383	.279	.342	.391	95	-40	43	27		.989	-9	1-771,O-752/23	-13.1

■ SKIP LOCKWOOD   Lockwood, Claude Edward b: 8/17/46, Boston, Mass.   BR/TR, 6', 190 lbs.   Deb: 4/23/65

YEAR	TM/L	G	AB	R	H	2B	3B	HR	RBI	BB	SO	AVG	OBP	SLG	PRO+	BR/A	SB	CS	SBR	FA	FR	G/POS	TPR
1965	KC-A	42	33	4	4	0	0	0	0	7	11	.121	.293	.121	23	-3	0	0	0	1.000	2	/3-7	-0.1
1969	Sea-A	6	7	0	0	0	0	0	0	0	2	.000	.000	.000	-99	-2	0	0	0	1.000	0	/P-6	0.0
1970	Mil-A	27	53	2	12	1	0	1	2	1	11	.226	.241	.302	48	-4	0	0	0	.970	-1	P-27	0.0
1971	Mil-A	36	62	2	5	1	0	1	4	5	20	.081	.149	.145	-17	-10	0	0	0	1.000	-3	P-33	0.0
1972	Mil-A	31	53	3	7	0	0	0	0	3	12	.132	.193	.132	-2	-7	0	1	-1	.958	-3	P-29	0.0
1973	Mil-A	37	0	0	0	0	0	0	0	0	0	—	—	—	—		0	0	0	.944	-3	P-37	0.0
1974	Cal-A	37	0	0	0	0	0	0	0	0	0	—	—	—	—	0	0	0	0	1.000	-0	P-37	0.0
1975	NY-N	24	6	0	1	0	0	0	0	0	1	.167	.167	.167	-8	-1	0	0	0	.800	-1	P-24	0.0
1976	NY-N	56	6	2	6	1	0	0	2	2	3	.333	.400	.389	132	1	0	1	-1	.867	-2	P-56	0.0
1977	NY-N	63	15	1	3	1	0	0	1	0	1	.200	.200	.200	8	-2	0	0	0	.875	-2	P-63	0.0
1978	NY-N	57	11	1	2	1	0	1	1	0	5	.182	.182	.545	100	-0	0	0	0	.900	-2	P-57	0.0
1979	NY-N	28	2	0	0	0	0	0	0	0	0	.000	.000	.000	-99	-1	0	0	0	.800	-1	P-27	0.0
1980	Bos-A	24	0	0	0	0	0	0	0	0	0	—	—	—	—		0	0	0	1.000	-1	P-24	0.0
Total	13	468	260	15	40	4	0	3	11	18	66	.154	.214	.204	19	-28	0	2	-1	.947	-11	P-420/3-7	-0.1

■ MILO LOCKWOOD   Lockwood, Milo Hathaway b: 4/7/1858, Solon, Ohio   d: 10/9/1897, Economy, Pa.   5'10", 160 lbs.   Deb: 4/17/1884

YEAR	TM/L	G	AB	R	H	2B	3B	HR	RBI	BB	SO	AVG	OBP	SLG	PRO+	BR/A	SB	CS	SBR	FA	FR	G/POS	TPR
1884	Was-U	20	67	9	14	1	0	0		8		.209	.293	.224	44	-5				.773	2	O-11,P-11/3	-0.2

■ DARIO LODIGIANI   Lodigiani, Dario Antonio b: 6/6/16, San Francisco, Cal   BR/TR, 5'8", 150 lbs.   Deb: 4/18/38   C

YEAR	TM/L	G	AB	R	H	2B	3B	HR	RBI	BB	SO	AVG	OBP	SLG	PRO+	BR/A	SB	CS	SBR	FA	FR	G/POS	TPR
1938	Phi-A	93	325	36	91	15	1	6	44	34	25	.280	.361	.388	90	-5	3	0	1	.953	-6	2-80,3-13	-0.5
1939	Phi-A	121	393	46	102	22	4	6	44	42	18	.260	.337	.382	85	-9	2	0	0	.944	2	3-89,2-28	-0.4
1940	Phi-A	1	1	0	0	0	0	0	0	0	0	.000	.000	.000	-99	-0	0	0	0	.000	0	H	0.0
1941	Chi-A	87	322	39	77	19	2	4	40	31	19	.239	.316	.348	76	-11	0	0	0	.962	6	3-86	-0.5
1942	Chi-A	59	168	9	47	7	0	0	15	18	10	.280	.353	.321	92	-1	3	4	-2	.944	6	3-43/2-7	0.4
1946	Chi-A	44	155	12	38	8	0	0	13	16	14	.245	.324	.297	77	-4	4	0	1	.935	-5	3-44	-0.8
Total	6	405	1364	142	355	71	7	16	156	141	86	.260	.338	.358	84	-31	12	8	-1	.947	3	3-275,2-115	-1.8

■ GEORGE LOEPP   Loepp, George Herbert b: 9/11/01, Detroit, Mich.   d: 9/4/67, Los Angeles, Cal.   BR/TR, 5'11", 170 lbs.   Deb: 8/29/28

YEAR	TM/L	G	AB	R	H	2B	3B	HR	RBI	BB	SO	AVG	OBP	SLG	PRO+	BR/A	SB	CS	SBR	FA	FR	G/POS	TPR
1928	Bos-A	15	51	6	9	3	1	0	3	5	12	.176	.250	.275	38	-5	0	0	0	.949	-0	O-14	-0.6
1930	Was-A	50	134	23	37	7	1	0	14	20	9	.276	.382	.343	85	-2	6	4	-2	.958	-5	O-48	-1.1
Total	2	65	185	29	46	10	2	0	17	25	21	.249	.347	.324	73	-7	6	4	-2	.956	-6	/O-62	-1.7

■ KENNY LOFTON   Lofton, Kenneth b: 5/31/67, E.Chicago, Ind.   BL/TL, 6', 180 lbs.   Deb: 9/14/91

YEAR	TM/L	G	AB	R	H	2B	3B	HR	RBI	BB	SO	AVG	OBP	SLG	PRO+	BR/A	SB	CS	SBR	FA	FR	G/POS	TPR
1991	Hou-N	20	74	9	15	1	0	0	0	5	19	.203	.253	.216	35	-6	2	1	0	.977	0	O-20	-0.7

YEAR	TM/L	G	AB	R	H	2B	3B	HR	RBI	BB	SO	AVG	OBP	SLG	PRO+	BR/A	SB	CS	SBR	FA	FR	G/POS	TPR
1992	Cle-A	148	576	96	164	15	8	5	42	68	54	.285	.362	.365	106	6	**66**	12	**13**	.982	17	*O-143	3.3
1993	Cle-A	148	569	116	185	28	8	1	42	81	83	.325	.410	.408	121	21	**70**	14	**13**	.979	13	*O-146	4.1
1994	Cle-A★	112	459	105	**160**	32	9	12	57	52	56	.349	.417	.536	137	26	**60**	12	**11**	.993	8	*O-112	3.8
Total	4	428	1678	326	524	76	25	18	141	206	212	.312	.389	.420	118	47	198	39	36	.983	37	O-421	10.5

■ DICK LOFTUS
Loftus, Richard Joseph b: 3/7/01, Concord, Mass. d: 1/21/72, Concord, Mass. BL/TR, 6', 155 lbs. Deb: 4/20/24

YEAR	TM/L	G	AB	R	H	2B	3B	HR	RBI	BB	SO	AVG	OBP	SLG	PRO+	BR/A	SB	CS	SBR	FA	FR	G/POS	TPR
1924	Bro-N	46	81	18	22	6	0	0	8	7	2	.272	.330	.346	84	-2	1	0	0	1.000	-3	O-29/1-1	-0.6
1925	Bro-N	51	131	16	31	6	0	0	13	5	5	.237	.275	.282	44	-11	2	0	1	.977	1	O-38	-1.1
Total	2	97	212	34	53	12	0	0	21	12	7	.250	.296	.307	59	-13	3	0	1	.985	-2	/O-67,1-1	-1.7

■ TOM LOFTUS
Loftus, Thomas Joseph b: 11/15/1856, St.Louis, Mo. d: 4/16/10, Dubuque, Iowa BR, 168 lbs. Deb: 8/17/1877 M

YEAR	TM/L	G	AB	R	H	2B	3B	HR	RBI	BB	SO	AVG	OBP	SLG	PRO+	BR/A	SB	CS	SBR	FA	FR	G/POS	TPR
1877	StL-N	3	11	2	2	0	0	0	0	0	1	.182	.182	.182	16	-1				.778	2	/O-3	0.0
1883	StL-a	6	22	1	4	0	0	0		0	2	.182	.250	.182	39	-1				.882	0	/O-6	-0.1
Total	2	9	33	3	6	0	0	0	0	2	1	.182	.229	.182	32	-2				.846	2	/O-9	-0.1

■ JOHNNY LOGAN
Logan, John "Yatcha" b: 3/23/27, Endicott, N.Y. BR/TR, 5'11", 175 lbs. Deb: 4/17/51

YEAR	TM/L	G	AB	R	H	2B	3B	HR	RBI	BB	SO	AVG	OBP	SLG	PRO+	BR/A	SB	CS	SBR	FA	FR	G/POS	TPR
1951	Bos-N	62	169	14	37	7	1	0	16	18	13	.219	.298	.272	59	-10	0	0	0	.958	4	S-58	-0.2
1952	Bos-N	117	456	56	129	21	3	4	42	31	33	.283	.334	.368	98	-2	1	2	-1	**.972**	18	*S-117	2.4
1953	Mil-N	150	611	100	167	27	8	11	73	41	33	.273	.326	.398	93	-7	2	2	-1	**.975**	21	*S-150	2.3
1954	Mil-N	154	560	66	154	17	7	8	66	51	51	.275	.342	.373	92	-7	2	2	-1	**.969**	14	*S-154	2.1
1955	Mil-N★	154	595	95	177	**37**	5	13	83	58	58	.297	.364	.442	118	16	3	3	-1	.963	8	*S-154	3.5
1956	Mil-N	148	545	69	153	27	5	15	46	46	49	.281	.342	.431	113	9	3	0	1	.968	3	*S-148	2.6
1957	*Mil-N☆	129	494	59	135	19	7	10	49	31	49	.273	.321	.401	100	-2	5	0	2	.960	24	*S-129	3.6
1958	*Mil-N★	145	530	54	120	20	0	11	53	40	57	.226	.287	.326	68	-26	1	3	-2	.959	10	*S-144	-0.4
1959	Mil-N☆	138	459	59	137	17	0	13	50	57	45	.291	.372	.411	118	13	1	3	-2	.975	-3	*S-138	2.0
1960	Mil-N	136	482	52	118	14	4	7	42	43	40	.245	.309	.334	82	-12	1	1	-0	.956	2	*S-136	0.0
1961	Mil-N	18	19	0	2	1	0	0	1	1	3	.105	.150	.158	-19	-3	0	0	0	1.000	-0	/S-2	-0.4
	Pit-N	27	52	5	12	4	0	0	5	2	8	.231	.286	.308	57	-3	0	0	0	1.000	-0	/3-7,S-6	-0.6
	Yr	45	71	5	14	5	0	0	6	5	11	.197	.250	.268	38	-6	0	0	0	.964	0	/S-8,3-7	0.2
1962	Pit-N	44	80	7	24	3	0	1	12	7	6	.300	.356	.375	96	-0	0	0	0	.980	2	3-19	0.2
1963	Pit-N	81	181	15	42	2	1	0	9	23	27	.232	.325	.254	69	-6	0	0	0	.920	2	S-44/3-4	-0.2
Total	13	1503	5244	651	1407	216	41	93	547	451	472	.268	.331	.378	95	-41	19	13	-2	.965	105	*S-1380/3-30	17.3

■ PETE LOHMAN
Lohman, George F. b: 10/21/1864, Lake Elmo, Minn. d: 11/21/28, Los Angeles, Cal. Deb: 5/11/1891

YEAR	TM/L	G	AB	R	H	2B	3B	HR	RBI	BB	SO	AVG	OBP	SLG	PRO+	BR/A	SB	CS	SBR	FA	FR	G/POS	TPR
1891	Was-a	32	109	18	21	1	4	1	11	16	17	.193	.302	.303	76	-3	1			.914	-3	C-21/O-8,3S2	-0.4

■ HOWARD LOHR
Lohr, Howard Sylvester b: 6/3/1892, Philadelphia, Pa. d: 6/9/77, Philadelphia, Pa. BR/TR, 6', 165 lbs. Deb: 6/17/14

YEAR	TM/L	G	AB	R	H	2B	3B	HR	RBI	BB	SO	AVG	OBP	SLG	PRO+	BR/A	SB	CS	SBR	FA	FR	G/POS	TPR
1914	Cin-N	18	47	6	10	1	1	0	7	0	8	.213	.213	.277	44	-3	2			.926	-3	O-17	-0.8
1916	Cle-A	3	7	0	1	0	0	0	1	0	1	.143	.143	.143	-13	-1	1			1.000	-1	/O-3	-0.2
Total	2	21	54	6	11	1	1	0	8	0	9	.204	.204	.259	36	-4	3			.933	-4	/O-20	-1.0

■ JACK LOHRKE
Lohrke, Jack Wayne "Lucky" b: 2/25/24, Los Angeles, Cal. BR/TR, 6', 180 lbs. Deb: 4/18/47

YEAR	TM/L	G	AB	R	H	2B	3B	HR	RBI	BB	SO	AVG	OBP	SLG	PRO+	BR/A	SB	CS	SBR	FA	FR	G/POS	TPR
1947	NY-N	112	329	44	79	12	4	11	35	46	29	.240	.337	.401	95	-3	3			.939	-2	*3-111	-0.4
1948	NY-N	97	280	35	70	15	1	5	31	30	30	.250	.323	.364	85	-6	3			.898	-2	3-50,2-36	-0.6
1949	NY-N	55	180	32	48	11	4	5	22	16	12	.267	.333	.456	110	2	3			.969	4	2-23,3-19,S	0.7
1950	NY-N	30	43	4	8	0	0	0	4	4	8	.186	.255	.186	18	-5				.958	0	3-16/2-1	-0.5
1951	*NY-N	23	40	1	8	0	0	1	3	10	2	.200	.360	.275	73	-1	0	0	0	.943	1	3-17/S-1	-0.2
1952	Phi-N	25	29	4	6	0	0	0	1	4	3	.207	.303	.207	44	-2	1	0	0	1.000	1	/S-5,3-3,2	-0.1
1953	Phi-N	12	13	3	2	0	0	0	0	1	2	.154	.214	.154	-2	-2	0	0	0	.750	1	/2-2,S-2,3	-0.1
Total	7	354	914	125	221	38	9	22	96	111	86	.242	.327	.375	87	-17	9	0		.928	2	3-217/2-63,S	-1.2

■ ALBERTO LOIS
Lois, Alberto (b: Alberto Louis (Pie)) b: 5/6/56, Hato Mayor, D.R. BR/TR, 5'9", 175 lbs. Deb: 9/8/78

YEAR	TM/L	G	AB	R	H	2B	3B	HR	RBI	BB	SO	AVG	OBP	SLG	PRO+	BR/A	SB	CS	SBR	FA	FR	G/POS	TPR
1978	Pit-N	3	4	0	1	0	1	0	0	0	1	.250	.250	.750	163	0	0	0	0	1.000	-0	/O-2	0.0
1979	Pit-N	11	0	6	0	0	0	0	0	0	0	—	—	—	—		0	1	1	-0	.000	0	/R	-0.1
Total	2	14	4	6	1	0	1	0	0	0	1	.250	.250	.750	163	0	1	1	-0	1.000	-0	/O-2	-0.1

■ RON LOLICH
Lolich, Ronald John b: 9/19/46, Portland, Ore. BR/TR, 6'1", 185 lbs. Deb: 7/18/71

YEAR	TM/L	G	AB	R	H	2B	3B	HR	RBI	BB	SO	AVG	OBP	SLG	PRO+	BR/A	SB	CS	SBR	FA	FR	G/POS	TPR
1971	Chi-A	2	8	0	1	0	0	0	0	0	2	.125	.125	.250	4	-1	0	0	0	1.000	-1	/O-2	-0.2
1972	Cle-A	24	80	4	15	1	0	2	8	4	20	.188	.226	.275	47	-5	0	0	0	1.000	-1	O-22	-0.8
1973	Cle-A	61	140	16	32	7	0	2	15	7	27	.229	.265	.321	63	-7	0	2	-1	.909	-4	O-32,D-12	-1.4
Total	3	87	228	20	48	9	0	4	23	11	49	.211	.247	.303	56	-13	0	2	-1	.953	-5	/O-56,D-12	-2.4

■ SHERM LOLLAR
Lollar, John Sherman b: 8/23/24, Durham, Ark. d: 9/24/77, Springfield, Mo. BR/TR, 6'1", 185 lbs. Deb: 4/20/46 C

YEAR	TM/L	G	AB	R	H	2B	3B	HR	RBI	BB	SO	AVG	OBP	SLG	PRO+	BR/A	SB	CS	SBR	FA	FR	G/POS	TPR
1946	Cle-A	28	62	7	15	6	0	1	9	5	9	.242	.299	.387	97	-3	0	1	-1	.990	-3	C-24	-0.4
1947	*NY-A	11	32	4	7	0	1	1	6	1	5	.219	.242	.375	71	-1	0	1	-1	1.000	1	/C-9	-0.1
1948	NY-A	22	38	0	8	0	0	0	4	1	6	.211	.231	.211	18	-4	0	0	0	.976	1	C-10	-0.3
1949	StL-A	109	284	28	74	9	1	8	49	32	22	.261	.340	.384	88	-6	0	1	-1	.988	-3	C-93	-0.5
1950	StL-A	126	396	55	111	22	3	13	65	64	25	.280	.391	.449	110	7	2	0	1	.981	-5	*C-109	0.7
1951	StL-A	98	310	44	78	21	0	8	44	43	26	.252	.350	.397	99	-0	1	0	0	**.995**	-2	*C-85/3-1	0.2
1952	Chi-A	132	375	35	90	15	0	13	50	54	34	.240	.354	.384	104	3	1	0	0	.989	-2	*C-120	0.7
1953	Chi-A	113	334	46	96	19	0	8	54	47	29	.287	.388	.416	114	8	1	0	0	**.994**	1	*C-107/1-1	1.1
1954	Chi-A☆	107	316	31	77	13	0	7	34	37	28	.244	.336	.351	85	-6	3	0	1	.993	-3	C-93	-0.5
1955	Chi-A	138	426	67	111	13	1	16	61	68	34	.261	.375	.408	108	6	2	2	-1	**.995**	10	*C-136	2.0
1956	Chi-A★	136	450	55	132	28	2	11	75	58	34	.293	.387	.438	116	12	2	0	1	**.993**	4	*C-132	2.0
1957	Chi-A	101	351	33	90	11	2	11	70	36	24	.256	.346	.393	101	1	2	0	1	.998	-2	*C-96	0.4
1958	Chi-A☆	127	421	53	115	16	0	20	84	57	37	.273	.370	.454	128	17	4	3	-1	.987	2	*C-116	2.6
1959	*Chi-A★	140	505	63	134	22	3	22	84	55	49	.265	.348	.451	119	13	4	3	-1	.993	10	*C-122,1-24	2.8
1960	Chi-A★	129	421	43	106	23	0	7	46	42	39	.252	.331	.356	87	-7	2	0	1	**.995**	-2	*C-123	-0.2
1961	Chi-A	116	337	38	95	10	1	7	41	37	22	.282	.363	.380	100	-0	0	0	0	**.998**	-10	*C-107	-0.3
1962	Chi-A	84	220	17	59	12	0	2	26	32	23	.268	.369	.350	95	-0	1	0	0	.991	-8	C-66	-0.6
1963	Chi-A	35	73	4	17	4	0	0	6	8	7	.233	.317	.288	72	-2	0	0	0	.981	-2	C-23/1-2	-0.4
Total	18	1752	5351	623	1415	244	14	155	808	671	453	.264	.359	.402	104	40	20	10	-2	.992	-16	*C-1571/1-27,3	9.2

■ DOUG LOMAN
Loman, Douglas Edward b: 5/9/58, Bakersfield, Cal. BL/TL, 5'11", 185 lbs. Deb: 9/3/84

YEAR	TM/L	G	AB	R	H	2B	3B	HR	RBI	BB	SO	AVG	OBP	SLG	PRO+	BR/A	SB	CS	SBR	FA	FR	G/POS	TPR
1984	Mil-A	23	76	13	21	4	0	2	12	15	7	.276	.402	.408	130	4	0	2	-1	.967	3	O-23	0.5
1985	Mil-A	24	66	10	14	3	2	0	7	4	12	.212	.224	.318	47	-5	0	0	0	1.000	1	O-20	-0.4
Total	2	47	142	23	35	7	2	2	19	19	19	.246	.327	.366	93	-1	0	2	-1	.981	4	/O-43	0.1

■ ERNIE LOMBARDI
Lombardi, Ernesto Natali "Schnozz" or "Bocci" b: 4/6/08, Oakland, Cal. d: 9/26/77, Santa Cruz, Cal. BR/TR, 6'3", 230 lbs. Deb: 4/15/31 H

YEAR	TM/L	G	AB	R	H	2B	3B	HR	RBI	BB	SO	AVG	OBP	SLG	PRO+	BR/A	SB	CS	SBR	FA	FR	G/POS	TPR
1931	Bro-N	73	182	20	54	7	4	4	23	12	12	.297	.340	.412	102	1	0			.984	3	C-50	0.6
1932	Cin-N	118	413	43	125	22	9	11	68	41	19	.303	.371	.479	131	18	0			.963	-11	*C-110	1.3
1933	Cin-N	107	350	30	99	21	1	4	47	16	17	.283	.322	.383	102	0	0			.972	-16	C-95	-1.0
1934	Cin-N	132	417	42	127	19	4	9	62	16	16	.305	.331	.434	107	3	0			.989	-3	*C-111	0.5
1935	Cin-N	120	332	36	114	23	3	12	64	16	19	.343	.379	.539	148	21	1			.983	-6	*C-82	1.9
1936	Cin-N☆	121	387	42	129	23	2	12	68	19	16	.333	.375	.496	142	21	1			.962	-13	*C-105	1.2

YEAR	TM/L	G	AB	R	H	2B	3B	HR	RBI	BB	SO	AVG	OBP	SLG	PRO+	BR/A	SB	CS	SBR	FA	FR	G/POS	TPR
1937	Cin-N☆	120	368	41	123	22	1	9	59	14	17	.334	.362	.473	132	14	1			.973	-18	C-90	0.2
1938	Cin-N★	129	489	60	167	30	1	19	95	40	14	**.342**	.391	.524	154	34	0			.985	-3	*C-123	3.8
1939	*Cin-N★	130	450	43	129	26	2	20	85	35	19	.287	.342	.487	120	11	0			.984	4	*C-120	2.1
1940	*Cin-N★	109	376	50	120	22	0	14	74	31	14	.319	.382	.489	137	19	0			.989	-4	*C-101	2.2
1941	Cin-N	117	398	33	105	12	1	10	60	36	14	.264	.325	.374	96	-2	1			.983	-1	*C-116	0.6
1942	Bos-N★	105	309	32	102	14	0	11	46	37	12	**.330**	.403	.482	162	24	1			.980	-16	C-85	1.5
1943	NY-N★	104	295	19	90	7	0	10	51	16	11	.305	.347	.431	123	8	1			.971	-14	C-73	-0.1
1944	NY-N	117	373	37	95	13	0	10	58	33	25	.255	.317	.370	93	-4	0			.968	-15	*C-100	-1.3
1945	NY-N†	115	368	46	113	7	1	19	70	43	11	.307	.387	.486	140	20	0			.983	2	C-96	2.7
1946	NY-N	88	238	19	69	4	1	12	39	18	24	.290	.347	.466	129	8	0			.978	1	C-63	1.3
1947	NY-N	48	110	8	31	5	0	4	21	7	9	.282	.325	.436	100	-0	0			.980	-3	C-24	-0.2
Total	17	1853	5855	601	1792	277	27	190	990	430	262	.306	.358	.460	126	195	8			.979	-113	*C-1544	17.3

■ PHIL LOMBARDI
Lombardi, Phillip Arden b: 2/20/63, Abilene, Tex. BR/TR, 6'2", 200 lbs. Deb: 4/26/86

YEAR	TM/L	G	AB	R	H	2B	3B	HR	RBI	BB	SO	AVG	OBP	SLG	PRO+	BR/A	SB	CS	SBR	FA	FR	G/POS	TPR
1986	NY-A	20	36	6	10	3	0	2	6	4	7	.278	.366	.528	141	2	0	0	0	.867	-1	/O-8,C-3	0.1
1987	NY-A	5	8	0	1	0	0	0	0	0	2	.125	.125	.125	-34	-2	0	0	0	1.000	-0	/C-3	-0.2
1989	NY-N	18	48	4	11	1	0	1	3	5	8	.229	.302	.313	80	-1	0	0	0	.980	-1	C-16/1-1	-0.2
Total	3	43	92	10	22	4	0	3	9	9	17	.239	.314	.380	95	-1	0	0	0	.975	-2	/C-22,O-8,1	-0.3

■ STEVE LOMBARDOZZI
Lombardozzi, Stephen Paul b: 4/26/60, Malden, Mass. BR/TR, 6', 175 lbs. Deb: 7/12/85

YEAR	TM/L	G	AB	R	H	2B	3B	HR	RBI	BB	SO	AVG	OBP	SLG	PRO+	BR/A	SB	CS	SBR	FA	FR	G/POS	TPR
1985	Min-A	28	54	10	20	4	1	0	6	6	6	.370	.433	.481	142	3	3	2	-0	.982	11	2-26	1.4
1986	Min-A	156	453	53	103	20	5	8	33	52	76	.227	.308	.347	76	-15	3	1	0	**.991**	-3	*2-155	-1.2
1987	*Min-A	136	432	51	103	19	3	8	38	33	66	.238	.299	.352	69	-19	5	1	1	.977	-1	*2-133	-1.2
1988	Min-A	103	287	34	60	15	2	3	27	35	48	.209	.299	.307	68	-12	2	5	-2	.986	-7	2-90,S-12/3	-1.8
1989	Hou-N	21	37	5	8	3	1	1	3	4	9	.216	.293	.432	109	0	0	0	0	.922	0	2-18/3-1	0.1
1990	Hou-N	2	1	0	0	0	0	0	0	0	1	.000	.500	.000	52	0	0	0	0	.000	0	/H	0.0
Total	6	446	1264	153	294	61	12	20	107	131	206	.233	.308	.347	76	-42	13	9	-2	.983	0	2-422/S-12,3	-2.7

■ WALTER LONERGAN
Lonergan, Walter E. b: 9/22/1885, Boston, Mass. d: 1/23/58, Lexington, Mass. BR/TR, 5'7", 156 lbs. Deb: 8/17/11

YEAR	TM/L	G	AB	R	H	2B	3B	HR	RBI	BB	SO	AVG	OBP	SLG	PRO+	BR/A	SB	CS	SBR	FA	FR	G/POS	TPR
1911	Bos-A	10	26	2	7	0	0	0	1	1		.269	.296	.269	59	-1	1			.935	-1	/2-7,S-1,3	-0.2

■ DAN LONG
Long, Daniel W. b: 8/27/1867, Boston, Mass. d: 4/30/29, Sausalito, Cal. Deb: 8/29/1888

YEAR	TM/L	G	AB	R	H	2B	3B	HR	RBI	BB	SO	AVG	OBP	SLG	PRO+	BR/A	SB	CS	SBR	FA	FR	G/POS	TPR
1888	Lou-a	1	2	0	0	0	0	0	0	1		.000	.333	.000	11	-0	0			.000	-0	/O-1	0.0
1890	Bal-a	21	77	19	12	0	0	0		14		.156	.301	.156	33	-6	16			.939	-1	O-21	-0.6
Total	2	22	79	19	12	0	0	0	0	15		.152	.302	.152	33	-6	16			.939	-1	/O-22	-0.6

■ HERMAN LONG
Long, Herman C. "Germany" or "Flying Dutchman" b: 4/13/1866, Chicago, Ill. d: 9/17/09, Denver, Colo. BL/TR, 5'8.5", 160 lbs. Deb: 4/17/1889

YEAR	TM/L	G	AB	R	H	2B	3B	HR	RBI	BB	SO	AVG	OBP	SLG	PRO+	BR/A	SB	CS	SBR	FA	FR	G/POS	TPR
1889	KC-a	136	574	137	158	32	6	3	60	64	63	.275	.358	.368	101	-0	89			.874	32	*S-128/2-8,O	3.3
1890	Bos-N	101	431	95	108	15	3	6	52	40	34	.251	.320	.355	90	-8	49			.898	11	*S-101	0.8
1891	Bos-N	139	577	129	163	21	12	9	76	80	51	.282	.377	.407	115	9	60			.902	15	*S-139	2.8
1892	*Bos-N	151	646	115	181	33	6	6	78	44	36	.280	.334	.378	105	1	57			.889	14	*S-141,O-12/3	1.9
1893	Bos-N	128	552	**149**	159	22	6	6	58	73	32	.288	.376	.382	94	-6	38			.883	16	*S-123/2-5	1.3
1894	Bos-N	104	475	136	154	28	11	12	79	35	17	.324	.375	.505	103	-2	24			.885	3	*S-98/O-5,2	0.5
1895	Bos-N	124	535	109	169	23	10	9	75	31	12	.316	.357	.447	99	-5	35			.891	-7	*S-122/2-2	-0.5
1896	Bos-N	120	501	105	172	26	8	6	100	26	16	.343	.382	.463	115	*9	36			.897	10	*S-120	1.9
1897	*Bos-N	107	450	89	145	32	7	3	69	23		.322	.358	.444	105	0	22			.905	-3	*S-107/O-1	0.0
1898	Bos-N	144	589	99	156	21	10	6	99	39		.265	.311	.365	89	-11	20			.923	1	*S-142/2-2	-0.3
1899	Bos-N	145	578	91	153	30	8	6	100	45		.265	.321	.375	83	-17	20			.929	-10	*S-143/1-2	-1.4
1900	Bos-N	125	486	80	127	19	4	**12**	66	44		.261	.325	.391	86	-12	26			.937	-6	*S-125	-0.8
1901	Bos-N	138	518	54	112	14	6	3	68	25		.216	.254	.284	51	-34	20			**.946**	-3	*S-138	-2.5
1902	Bos-N	120	439	40	101	11	0	2	44	31		.230	.282	.269	69	-16	24			**.946**	23	*S-107,2-13	1.5
1903	NY-A	22	80	6	15	3	0	0	8	2		.188	.207	.225	28	-7	3			.889	-5	S-22	-1.1
	Det-A	69	239	21	53	12	0	0	23	10		.222	.256	.272	60	-12	11			.879	-5	S-38,2-31	-0.9
	Yr	91	319	27	68	15	0	0	31	12		.213	.244	.260	52	-19	14			.883	-4	S-60,2-31	-2.0
1904	Phi-N	1	4	0	1	0	0	0	0	0		.250	.250	.250	56	-0	0			.889	1	/2-1	0.1
Total	16	1874	7674	1455	2127	342	97	91	1055	612	**261**	.277	.335	.383	93	-109	534			.906	94	*S-1794/2-65,O13	6.6

■ JIMMIE LONG
Long, James Albert b: 6/29/1898, Ft.Dodge, Iowa d: 9/14/70, Ft.Dodge, Iowa BR/TR, 5'11", 160 lbs. Deb: 9/12/22

YEAR	TM/L	G	AB	R	H	2B	3B	HR	RBI	BB	SO	AVG	OBP	SLG	PRO+	BR/A	SB	CS	SBR	FA	FR	G/POS	TPR
1922	Chi-A	3	3	0	0	0	0	0	1	0		.000	.250	.000	-30	-1	0	0	0	1.000	-1	/C-2	-0.1

■ JIM LONG
Long, James M. b: 11/15/1862, Louisville, Ky. d: 12/12/32, Louisville, Ky. Deb: 8/9/1891

YEAR	TM/L	G	AB	R	H	2B	3B	HR	RBI	BB	SO	AVG	OBP	SLG	PRO+	BR/A	SB	CS	SBR	FA	FR	G/POS	TPR
1891	Lou-a	6	25	5	6	0	0	0	4	3	6	.240	.367	.240	75	-0	1			.857	1	/O-6	0.0
1893	Bal-N	55	226	31	48	8	1	2	25	16	27	.212	.276	.283	48	-18	23			.893	-1	O-55	-1.8
Total	2	61	251	36	54	8	1	2	29	19	33	.215	.286	.279	51	-18	24			.890	-0	/O-61	-1.8

■ JEOFF LONG
Long, Jeoffrey Keith b: 10/9/41, Covington, Ky. BR/TR, 6'1", 200 lbs. Deb: 7/31/63

YEAR	TM/L	G	AB	R	H	2B	3B	HR	RBI	BB	SO	AVG	OBP	SLG	PRO+	BR/A	SB	CS	SBR	FA	FR	G/POS	TPR
1963	StL-N	5	5	0	1	0	0	0	0	1		.200	.200	.200	14	-1	0	0	0	.000	-0	H	-0.1
1964	StL-N	28	43	5	10	1	0	1	4	6	18	.233	.340	.326	81	-1	0	0	0	.833	-2	/O-4,1-3	-0.3
	Chi-A	23	35	0	5	0	0	0	5	4	15	.143	.231	.143	7	-4	0	0	0	1.000	-1	/1-5,O-5	-0.5
Total	2	56	83	5	16	1	0	1	9	10	34	.193	.287	.241	48	-6	0	0	0	.750	-2	/O-9,1-8	-0.9

■ DALE LONG
Long, Richard Dale b: 2/6/26, Springfield, Mo. d: 1/27/91, Palm Coast, Fla. BL/TL, 6'4", 210 lbs. Deb: 4/21/51 C

YEAR	TM/L	G	AB	R	H	2B	3B	HR	RBI	BB	SO	AVG	OBP	SLG	PRO+	BR/A	SB	CS	SBR	FA	FR	G/POS	TPR
1951	Pit-N	10	12	1	2	0	0	1	0	3		.167	.167	.417	50	-1	0	0	0	1.000	-0	/1-1	-0.1
	StL-A	34	105	11	25	5	1	2	11	10	22	.238	.310	.362	79	-3	0	0	0	.988	-1	1-28/O-1	-0.5
1955	Pit-N	131	419	59	122	19	**13**	16	79	48	72	.291	.365	.513	132	19	0	1	-1	.988	6	*1-119	1.7
1956	Pit-N★	148	517	64	136	20	7	27	91	54	85	.263	.333	.485	119	13	1	0	0	.982	-3	*1-138	0.1
1957	Pit-N	7	22	0	4	1	0	0	5	4	10	.182	.308	.227	48	-2	0	0	0	1.000	-0	/1-7	-0.2
	Chi-N	123	397	55	121	19	0	21	62	52	63	.305	.387	.511	141	23	1	1	-0	.995	-1	*1-104	1.6
	Yr	130	419	55	125	20	0	21	67	56	73	.298	.382	.496	136	22	1	1	-0	.995	-1	*1-111	1.4
1958	Chi-N	142	480	68	130	26	4	20	75	66	64	.271	.361	.467	119	13	0	0	0	.992	-2	*1-137/C-2	0.4
1959	Chi-N	110	296	34	70	10	3	14	37	31	53	.236	.309	.432	96	-3	0	0	0	.985	-2	1-85	-0.9
1960	SF-N	37	54	4	9	0	0	3	6	7	7	.167	.262	.333	66	-3	0	0	0	1.000	-0	1-10	-0.3
	*NY-A	26	41	6	15	3	1	3	10	5	6	.366	.435	.707	216	6	0	0	0	.988	-1	1-11	0.5
1961	Was-A	123	377	52	94	20	4	17	49	39	41	.249	.321	.459	107	3	0	0	0	.983	-5	1-95	-1.0
1962	Was-A	67	191	17	46	0	0	4	24	18	22	.241	.310	.346	77	-6	5	1	1	.996	-0	1-51	-0.9
	*NY-A	41	94	12	28	4	0	4	17	18	9	.298	.411	.468	140	6	0	0	0	.992	1	1-31	0.6
	Yr	108	285	29	74	12	0	8	41	36	31	.260	.345	.386	98	-0	6	1	1	.995	1	1-82	-0.3
1963	NY-A	14	15	1	3	0	0	0	3	1	3	.200	.250	.200	28	-1	0	0	0	.917	-1	/1-2	-0.2
Total	10	1013	3020	384	805	135	33	132	467	353	460	.267	.345	.464	116	65	10	3	1	.988	-7	1-819/C-2,O	0.8

■ TOM LONG
Long, Thomas Augustus b: 6/1/1890, Mitchum, Ala. d: 6/15/72, Mobile, Ala. BR/TR, 5'10.5", 165 lbs. Deb: 9/11/11

YEAR	TM/L	G	AB	R	H	2B	3B	HR	RBI	BB	SO	AVG	OBP	SLG	PRO+	BR/A	SB	CS	SBR	FA	FR	G/POS	TPR
1911	Was-A	14	48	1	11	3	0	0	5	1		.229	.245	.292	50	-3	4			.875	-2	O-13	-0.6
1912	Was-A	1	0	0	0	0	0	0	0	0		.000	.000	.000	-99	-0	0			.000	0	H	0.0
1915	StL-N	140	507	61	149	21	**25**	2	61	31	50	.294	.339	.446	137	20	19	15	-3	.927	-4	*O-136	0.8
1916	StL-N	119	403	37	118	11	10	1	33	10	43	.293	.312	.377	112	4	21	14	-2	.945	-8	*O-106	-1.3

YEAR	TM/L	G	AB	R	H	2B	3B	HR	RBI	BB	SO	AVG	OBP	SLG	PRO+	BR/A	SB	CS	SBR	FA	FR	G/POS	TPR
1917	StL-N	144	530	49	123	12	14	3	41	37	44	.232	.285	.325	89	-8	21			.919	-19	*O-137	-4.0
Total	5	418	1489	148	401	47	49	6	140	79	137	.269	.309	.379	110	13	65	29		.928	-33	O-392	-5.1

■ TONY LONGMIRE
Longmire, Anthony Eugene b: 8/12/68, Vallejo, Cal. BL/TR, 6'1", 197 lbs. Deb: 9/3/93

YEAR	TM/L	G	AB	R	H	2B	3B	HR	RBI	BB	SO	AVG	OBP	SLG	PRO+	BR/A	SB	CS	SBR	FA	FR	G/POS	TPR
1993	*Phi-N	11	13	1	3	0	0	0	1	0	1	.231	.231	.231	24	-1	0	0	0	1.000	0	/O-2	-0.1
1994	Phi-N	69	139	10	33	11	0	0	17	10	27	.237	.293	.317	60	-8	2	1	0	.941	0	O-32	-1.1
Total	2	80	152	11	36	11	0	0	18	10	28	.237	.288	.309	57	-10	2	1	0	.945	-2	/O-34	-1.2

■ JOE LONNETT
Lonnett, Joseph Paul b: 2/7/27, Beaver Falls, Pa. BR/TR, 5'10", 180 lbs. Deb: 4/22/56 C

YEAR	TM/L	G	AB	R	H	2B	3B	HR	RBI	BB	SO	AVG	OBP	SLG	PRO+	BR/A	SB	CS	SBR	FA	FR	G/POS	TPR
1956	Phi-N	16	22	2	4	0	0	0	2	7		.182	.250	.182	19	-2	0	0	0	1.000	0	/C-7	-0.2
1957	Phi-N	67	160	12	27	5	0	5	15	22	39	.169	.273	.294	54	-10	0	0	0	.997	5	C-65	-0.3
1958	Phi-N	17	50	0	7	2	0	0	2	2	11	.140	.173	.180	-6	-8	0	0	0	.988	2	C-15	-0.5
1959	Phi-N	43	93	8	16	1	0	1	10	14	17	.172	.287	.215	36	-8	0	1	-1	.983	-6	C-43	-1.3
Total	4	143	325	22	54	8	0	6	27	40	74	.166	.262	.246	37	-29	0	1	-1	.992	1	C-130	-2.3

■ BRUCE LOOK
Look, Bruce Michael b: 6/9/43, Lansing, Mich. BL/TR, 5'11", 183 lbs. Deb: 4/17/68 F

YEAR	TM/L	G	AB	R	H	2B	3B	HR	RBI	BB	SO	AVG	OBP	SLG	PRO+	BR/A	SB	CS	SBR	FA	FR	G/POS	TPR
1968	Min-A	59	118	7	29	4	0	0	9	20	24	.246	.355	.280	90	-1	0	1	-1	.996	2	C-41	0.3

■ DEAN LOOK
Look, Dean Zachary b: 7/23/37, Lansing, Mich. BR/TR, 5'11", 185 lbs. Deb: 9/22/61 F

YEAR	TM/L	G	AB	R	H	2B	3B	HR	RBI	BB	SO	AVG	OBP	SLG	PRO+	BR/A	SB	CS	SBR	FA	FR	G/POS	TPR
1961	Chi-A	3	6	0	0	0	0	0	0	0	1	.000	.000	.000	-99	-2	0	0	0	1.000	-0	/O-1	-0.2

■ STAN LOPATA
Lopata, Stanley Edward "Stash" b: 9/12/25, Delray, Mich. BR/TR, 6'2", 210 lbs. Deb: 9/19/48

YEAR	TM/L	G	AB	R	H	2B	3B	HR	RBI	BB	SO	AVG	OBP	SLG	PRO+	BR/A	SB	CS	SBR	FA	FR	G/POS	TPR
1948	Phi-N	6	15	2	2	1	0	0	2	0	4	.133	.133	.200	-11	-2	0			1.000	0	/C-4	-0.2
1949	Phi-N	83	240	31	65	9	2	8	27	21	44	.271	.330	.425	104	1	1			.973	-3	C-58	0.1
1950	*Phi-N	58	129	10	27	2	1	1	11	22	25	.209	.325	.279	61	-7	1			.974	1	C-51	-0.4
1951	Phi-N	3	5	0	0	0	0	0	0	0	0	.000	.000	.000	-99	-1	0	0	0	1.000	0	/C-1	-0.1
1952	Phi-N	57	179	25	49	9	1	4	27	36	33	.274	.395	.402	123	7	1	1	-0	.987	6	C-55	1.6
1953	Phi-N	81	234	34	56	12	3	8	31	28	39	.239	.321	.419	91	-3	3	1	0	.987	4	C-80	0.5
1954	Phi-N	86	259	42	75	14	5	14	42	33	37	.290	.372	.544	136	13	1	3	-2	.989	9	C-75/1-1	2.3
1955	Phi-N★	99	303	49	82	9	3	22	58	58	62	.271	.391	.538	146	21	4	1	1	.995	4	C-66,1-24	2.6
1956	Phi-N☆	146	535	96	143	33	7	32	95	75	93	.267	.358	.535	138	28	5	2	0	.982	-18	*C-102,1-39	1.3
1957	Phi-N	116	388	50	92	18	2	18	67	56	81	.237	.335	.433	108	4	2	2	-1	.988	-9	*C-108	-0.1
1958	Phi-N	86	258	36	64	9	0	9	33	60	63	.248	.394	.388	109	6	0	1	-1	.987	-9	C-80	0.1
1959	Mil-N	25	48	0	5	0	0	0	4	3	13	.104	.157	.104	-31	-9	0	0	0	1.000	-3	C-11/1-2	-1.2
1960	Mil-N	7	8	0	1	0	0	0	1	0	3	.125	.222	.125	-2	-1	0	0	0	.944	1	/C-4	0.0
Total	13	853	2601	375	661	116	25	116	397	393	497	.254	.354	.452	115	56	18	11		.986	-15	C-695/1-66	6.5

■ DAVEY LOPES
Lopes, David Earl b: 5/3/45, E.Providence, R.I. BR/TR, 5'9", 170 lbs. Deb: 9/22/72 C

YEAR	TM/L	G	AB	R	H	2B	3B	HR	RBI	BB	SO	AVG	OBP	SLG	PRO+	BR/A	SB	CS	SBR	FA	FR	G/POS	TPR
1972	LA-N	11	42	6	9	4	0	1	7	6	.214	.327	.310	84	-1	4	0	1	.964	-2	2-11	-0.1
1973	LA-N	142	535	77	147	13	5	6	37	62	77	.275	.355	.351	101	2	36	16	1	.984	-13	*2-135/O-5,S3	-0.2
1974	*LA-N	145	530	95	141	26	3	10	35	66	71	.266	.352	.383	110	8	59	18	7	.965	-22	*2-143	0.0
1975	LA-N	155	618	108	162	24	6	8	41	91	93	.262	.359	.359	104	6	77	12	16	.979	-23	*2-137,O-24,S	0.6
1976	LA-N	117	427	72	103	17	7	4	20	56	49	.241	.335	.342	94	-2	63	10	13	.964	-20	*2-100,O-19	-0.4
1977	*LA-N	134	502	85	142	19	5	11	53	73	69	.283	.376	.406	110	4	47	12	7	.979	8	*2-130	3.4
1978	*LA-N★	151	587	93	163	25	4	17	58	71	70	.278	.356	.421	117	13	45	4	11	.974	3	*2-147/O-2	4.0
1979	LA-N★	153	582	109	154	20	6	28	73	97	88	.265	.373	.464	129	25	44	4	11	.981	-34	*2-152	1.2
1980	LA-N★	141	553	79	139	15	3	10	49	58	71	.251	.324	.344	88	-8	23	7	3	.980	-16	*2-140	-1.3
1981	*LA-N	58	214	35	44	2	0	5	17	22	35	.206	.289	.285	66	-10	20	2	5	.993	-4	2-55	-0.5
1982	Oak-A	128	450	58	109	19	3	11	42	40	51	.242	.305	.371	89	-8	28	12	1	.977	-19	*2-125/O-6	-1.9
1983	Oak-A	147	494	64	137	13	4	17	67	51	61	.277	.347	.423	118	12	22	4	4	.983	-38	*2-123,D-12/O3	-1.7
1984	Oak-A	72	230	32	59	11	1	9	36	31	36	.257	.347	.430	122	7	12	0	4	.965	-8	O-42,2-17/3D	0.2
	*Chi-N	16	17	5	4	1	0	0	6	5		.235	.435	.294	99	0	3	0	1	1.000	0	/O-9,2-2	-0.1
1985	Chi-N	99	275	52	78	10	0	11	44	46	37	.284	.386	.444	118	8	47	4	12	.991	-12	O-79/3-4,2	0.6
1986	Chi-N	59	157	38	47	8	2	6	22	31	16	.299	.421	.490	140	10	17	6	2	.902	-4	3-32,O-22	0.6
	*Hou-N	37	98	11	23	2	1	1	13	12	9	.235	.318	.306	75	-3	8	2	1	1.000	5	O-19/3-5	0.2
	Yr	96	255	49	70	10	3	7	35	43	25	.275	.383	.420	117	7	25	8	3	1.000	1	O-41,3-37	0.8
1987	Hou-N	47	43	4	10	2	0	1	6	13	8	.233	.411	.349	108	1	2	1	0	.857	-1	/O-5	0.0
Total	16	1812	6354	1023	1671	232	50	155	614	833	852	.263	.351	.388	107	69	557	114	99	.977	-201	*2-1418,O-239/3DS	4.6

■ AL LOPEZ
Lopez, Alfonso Ramon b: 8/20/08, Tampa, Fla. BR/TR, 5'11", 165 lbs. Deb: 9/27/28 MH

YEAR	TM/L	G	AB	R	H	2B	3B	HR	RBI	BB	SO	AVG	OBP	SLG	PRO+	BR/A	SB	CS	SBR	FA	FR	G/POS	TPR
1928	Bro-N	3	12	0	0	0	0	0	0	0	0	.000	.000	.000	-99	-4	0			1.000	-2	/C-3	-0.5
1930	Bro-N	128	421	60	130	20	4	6	57	33	35	.309	.362	.418	89	-7	3			.983	5	*C-126	0.7
1931	Bro-N	111	360	38	97	13	4	0	40	28	33	.269	.324	.328	76	-12	1			.977	-8	*C-105	-1.2
1932	Bro-N	126	404	44	111	18	6	1	43	34	35	.275	.331	.356	87	-7	3			.976	-2	*C-125	-0.2
1933	Bro-N	126	372	39	112	11	4	3	41	21	39	.301	.338	.376	108	4	10			.991	18	*C-124/2-1	3.0
1934	Bro-N★	140	439	58	120	23	2	7	54	49	44	.273	.349	.383	101	1	2			.982	-7	*C-137/2-2,3	0.1
1935	Bro-N	128	379	50	95	12	4	3	39	35	36	.251	.316	.327	75	-13	2			.980	6	*C-126	-0.1
1936	Bos-N	128	426	46	103	12	5	7	50	41	41	.242	.311	.343	81	-12	1			.975	10	*C-127/1-1	0.4
1937	Bos-N	105	334	31	68	11	1	3	38	35	57	.204	.281	.269	55	-21	3			.984	3	*C-102	-0.7
1938	Bos-N	71	236	19	63	6	1	1	14	11	24	.267	.305	.314	78	-8	5			.989	3	C-71	-0.1
1939	Bos-N	131	412	32	104	22	3	8	49	40	45	.252	.319	.369	91	-6	0			.986	3	*C-129	0.3
1940	Bos-N	36	119	20	35	3	1	2	17	6	8	.294	.328	.387	102	-0	1			.987	2	C-36	0.4
	Pit-N	59	174	15	45	6	2	1	24	13	13	.259	.310	.333	78	-5	5			.992	4	C-59	0.2
	Yr	95	293	35	80	9	3	3	41	19	21	.273	.317	.355	87	-5	6			.990	6	C-95	0.6
1941	Pit-N★	114	317	33	84	9	1	5	43	31	23	.265	.330	.347	91	-3	0			.980	-0	*C-114	0.5
1942	Pit-N	103	289	17	74	8	2	1	26	34	17	.256	.338	.308	88	-3	0			.995	6	*C-99	0.9
1943	Pit-N	118	372	40	98	9	4	1	39	44	25	.263	.341	.317	88	-5	2			.991	9	*C-116/3-1	1.3
1944	Pit-N	115	331	27	76	12	1	1	34	34	24	.230	.303	.281	62	-16	4			.984	4	*C-115	-0.6
1945	Pit-N	91	243	22	53	8	0	0	18	35	12	.218	.317	.251	57	-13	1			.992	8	C-91	-0.1
1946	Pit-N	56	150	13	46	2	0	1	12	23	14	.307	.399	.340	108	3	1			.985	1	C-56	0.7
1947	Cle-A	61	126	9	33	1	0	0	14	9	13	.262	.311	.270	64	-6	1	1	-0	1.000	0	C-57	-0.4
Total	19	1950	5916	613	1547	206	43	51	652	556	538	.261	.326	.337	83	-133	46	1		.985	67	*C-1918/3-3,21	4.6

■ ART LOPEZ
Lopez, Arturo (Rodriguez) b: 6/8/37, Mayaguez, P.R. BL/TL, 5'9", 170 lbs. Deb: 4/12/65

YEAR	TM/L	G	AB	R	H	2B	3B	HR	RBI	BB	SO	AVG	OBP	SLG	PRO+	BR/A	SB	CS	SBR	FA	FR	G/POS	TPR
1965	NY-A	38	49	5	7	0	0	0	0	1	6	.143	.160	.143	-13	-7	0	0	0	.958	-2	O-16	-1.0

■ CARLOS LOPEZ
Lopez, Carlos Antonio (Morales) b: 9/27/50, Mazatlan, Mexico BR/TR, 6', 190 lbs. Deb: 9/17/76

YEAR	TM/L	G	AB	R	H	2B	3B	HR	RBI	BB	SO	AVG	OBP	SLG	PRO+	BR/A	SB	CS	SBR	FA	FR	G/POS	TPR
1976	Cal-A	9	10	1	0	0	0	0	2	3	.000	.167	.000	-52	-2	2	0	1	1.000	-1	/O-4,D-1	-0.3
1977	Sea-A	99	297	39	84	18	1	8	34	14	61	.283	.322	.431	104	1	16	4	2	.972	3	O-90/D-2	0.3
1978	Bal-A	129	193	21	46	6	0	4	20	9	34	.238	.276	.332	75	-7	5	7	-3	.988	-25	*O-114/D-1	-3.8
Total	3	237	500	61	130	24	1	12	54	25	98	.260	.301	.384	90	-8	23	11	0	.979	-23	O-208/D-4	-3.8

■ HECTOR LOPEZ
Lopez, Hector Headley (Swainson) b: 7/9/29, Colon, Panama BR/TR, 5'11", 182 lbs. Deb: 5/12/55

YEAR	TM/L	G	AB	R	H	2B	3B	HR	RBI	BB	SO	AVG	OBP	SLG	PRO+	BR/A	SB	CS	SBR	FA	FR	G/POS	TPR
1955	KC-A	128	483	50	140	15	2	15	68	33	58	.290	.339	.422	103	0	1	4	-2	.936	15	3-93,2-36	1.6
1956	KC-A	151	561	91	153	27	3	18	69	63	73	.273	.349	.428	104	2	4	5	-2	.940	1	*3-121,O-20/2S	0.3

YEAR	TM/L	G	AB	R	H	2B	3B	HR	RBI	BB	SO	AVG	OBP	SLG	PRO+	BR/A	SB	CS	SBR	FA	FR	G/POS	TPR
1957	KC-A	121	391	51	115	19	4	11	35	41	66	.294	.361	.448	118	9	1	6	-3	.937	4	*3-111/2-4,O	1.3
1958	KC-A	151	564	84	147	28	4	17	73	49	61	.261	.322	.415	99	-1	2	2	-1	.974	6	2-96,3-55/SO	1.2
1959	KC-A	35	135	22	38	10	3	6	24	8	23	.281	.324	.533	129	5	1	0	0	.933	-12	2-33	-0.4
	NY-A	112	406	60	115	16	2	16	69	28	54	.283	.339	.451	119	9	3	1	0	.926	-5	3-76,O-35	0.3
	Yr	147	541	82	153	26	5	22	93	36	77	.283	.336	.471	122	14	4	1	1	.926	-17	3-76,O-35,2	-0.1
1960	*NY-A	131	408	66	116	14	6	9	42	46	64	.284	.362	.414	116	9	1	1	-0	.976	-0	O-106/2-5,3	0.4
1961	*NY-A	93	243	27	54	7	2	3	22	24	38	.222	.295	.305	64	-13	1	0	0	.977	1	O-72	-1.5
1962	*NY-A	106	335	45	92	19	1	6	48	33	53	.275	.340	.391	99	-0	0	1	-1	.984	3	O-84/2-1,3	-0.2
1963	*NY-A	130	433	54	108	13	4	14	52	35	71	.249	.306	.395	95	-3	1	2	-1	.957	-3	*O-124/2-1	-1.4
1964	*NY-A	127	285	34	74	9	3	10	34	24	54	.260	.319	.418	101	0	1	1	-0	.971	-13	*O-103/3-1	-1.7
1965	NY-A	111	283	25	74	12	2	7	39	26	61	.261	.326	.392	104	0	0	0	0	.942	-8	O-75/1-2	-1.0
1966	NY-A	54	117	14	25	4	1	4	16	8	20	.214	.270	.368	84	-3	0	0	0	.936	-2	O-29	-0.7
Total	12	1450	4644	623	1251	193	37	136	591	418	696	.269	.333	.415	104	17	16	23	-9	.967	-13	O-652,3-459,2/S1	-1.8

■ JAVY LOPEZ
Lopez, Javier Torres b: 11/5/70, Ponce, P.R. BR/TR, 6'3", 185 lbs. Deb: 9/18/92

YEAR	TM/L	G	AB	R	H	2B	3B	HR	RBI	BB	SO	AVG	OBP	SLG	PRO+	BR/A	SB	CS	SBR	FA	FR	G/POS	TPR
1992	*Atl-N	9	16	3	6	2	0	0	2	0	1	.375	.375	.500	137	1	0	0	0	1.000	1	/C-9	0.2
1993	Atl-N	8	16	1	6	1	1	1	2	0	2	.375	.412	.750	201	2	0	0	0	.975	2	/C-7	0.4
1994	Atl-N	80	277	27	68	9	0	13	35	17	61	.245	.301	.419	85	-7	0	2	-1	.995	2	C-75	-0.2
Total	3	97	309	31	80	12	1	14	39	17	64	.259	.310	.440	93	-4	0	2	-1	.994	5	/C-91	0.4

■ LUIS LOPEZ
Lopez, Luis Antonio b: 9/1/64, Brooklyn, N.Y. BR/TR, 6'1", 190 lbs. Deb: 9/14/90

YEAR	TM/L	G	AB	R	H	2B	3B	HR	RBI	BB	SO	AVG	OBP	SLG	PRO+	BR/A	SB	CS	SBR	FA	FR	G/POS	TPR
1990	LA-N	6	6	0	0	0	0	0	0	0	2	.000	.000	.000	-99	-2	0	0	0	1.000	-0	/1-1	-0.2
1991	Cle-A	35	82	7	18	4	1	0	7	4	7	.220	.264	.293	54	-5	0	0	0	1.000	-2	C-12,1-10/30D	-0.8
Total	2	41	88	7	18	4	1	0	7	4	9	.205	.247	.273	43	-7	0	0	0	.977	-2	/C-12,1-11,DO3	-1.0

■ LUIS LOPEZ
Lopez, Luis Manuel (Santos) b: 9/4/70, Cidra, P.R. BB/TR, 5'11", 175 lbs. Deb: 9/7/93

YEAR	TM/L	G	AB	R	H	2B	3B	HR	RBI	BB	SO	AVG	OBP	SLG	PRO+	BR/A	SB	CS	SBR	FA	FR	G/POS	TPR
1993	SD-N	17	43	1	5	1	0	0	0	0	8	.116	.116	.140	-31	-8	0	0	0	.983	3	2-15	-0.5
1994	SD-N	77	235	29	65	16	1	2	20	15	39	.277	.328	.379	84	-5	3	2	-0	.941	2	S-43,2-29/3	0.0
Total	2	94	278	30	70	17	1	2	21	15	47	.252	.297	.342	67	-13	3	2	-0	.974	5	/2-44,S-43,3	-0.5

■ BRIS LORD
Lord, Bristol Robotham "The Human Eyeball" b: 9/21/1883, Upland, Pa. d: 11/13/64, Annapolis, Md. BR/TR, 5'9", 185 lbs. Deb: 4/21/05

YEAR	TM/L	G	AB	R	H	2B	3B	HR	RBI	BB	SO	AVG	OBP	SLG	PRO+	BR/A	SB	CS	SBR	FA	FR	G/POS	TPR
1905	*Phi-A	66	238	38	57	14	0	0	13	14		.239	.285	.298	83	-5	3			.963	0	O-61	-0.8
1906	Phi-A	118	434	50	101	13	7	1	44	27		.233	.281	.302	80	-10	12			.941	-2	*O-115	-2.0
1907	Phi-A	57	170	12	31	3	0	1	11	14		.182	.249	.218	48	-10	2			.951	-2	O-53/P-1	-1.5
1909	Cle-A	69	249	26	67	7	3	1	25	8		.269	.295	.333	94	-5	10			.992	6	O-67	0.1
1910	Cle-A	58	210	23	46	8	7	0	17	12		.219	.268	.324	84	-5	4			.958	4	O-56	-0.4
	*Phi-A	70	279	53	78	13	11	1	20	23		.280	.337	.416	137	11	6			.980	4	O-70	1.2
	Yr	128	489	76	124	21	18	1	37	35		.254	.307	.376	114	6	10			.972	8	*O-126	0.8
1911	*Phi-A	134	574	92	178	37	11	3	55	35		.310	.355	.429	120	14	15			.963	8	*O-132	1.4
1912	Phi-A	97	378	63	90	12	9	0	25	34		.238	.309	.317	82	-9	15			.942	-0	O-97	-1.4
1913	Bos-N	73	235	22	59	12	1	6	26	8	22	.251	.276	.387	86	-5	7			.914	-10	O-62	-1.9
Total	8	742	2767	379	707	119	49	13	236	175	22	.256	.304	.348	95	-22	74			.957	8	O-713/P-1	-5.3

■ HARRY LORD
Lord, Harry Donald b: 3/8/1882, Porter, Me. d: 8/9/48, Westbrook, Maine BL/TR, 5'10.5", 165 lbs. Deb: 9/25/07 M

YEAR	TM/L	G	AB	R	H	2B	3B	HR	RBI	BB	SO	AVG	OBP	SLG	PRO+	BR/A	SB	CS	SBR	FA	FR	G/POS	TPR
1907	Bos-A	10	38	4	6	1	0	0	3	1		.158	.179	.184	16	-4	1			.919	0	3-10	-0.3
1908	Bos-A	145	560	61	145	15	6	2	37	22		.259	.297	.318	97	-3	23			.902	-10	*3-144	-0.8
1909	Bos-A	136	534	86	166	12	7	0	31	20		.311	.345	.360	120	11	36			.929	-7	*3-134	1.0
1910	Bos-A	77	288	26	72	5	5	1	32	14		.250	.294	.313	88	-5	17			.927	-5	3-70/S-1	-0.9
	Chi-A	44	165	26	49	6	3	0	10	14		.297	.352	.370	132	6	17			.952	-11	3-44	-0.4
	Yr	121	453	51	121	11	8	1	42	28		.267	.315	.333	103	1	34			.935	-16	*3-114/S-1	-1.3
1911	Chi-A	141	561	103	180	18	18	3	61	32		.321	.364	.433	126	18	43			.941	-17	*3-138	0.3
1912	Chi-A	151	570	81	152	19	12	5	54	52		.267	.333	.368	104	2	28			.895	-27	*3-106,O-45	-2.6
1913	Chi-A	150	547	62	144	18	12	1	42	45	39	.263	.327	.346	98	-2	24			.924	-31	*3-150	-3.4
1914	Chi-A	21	69	8	13	1	1	1	3	5	3	.188	.243	.275	57	-4	2	2	-1	.933	-6	3-19/O-1	-1.1
1915	Buf-F	97	359	50	97	12	4	1	21	21	15	.270	.311	.345	74	-14	15			.946	-14	3-92/O-1M	-2.6
Total	9	972	3691	506	1024	107	70	14	294	226	57	.277	.326	.356	103	6	206	2		.924	-126	3-907/O-47,S	-10.8

■ CARLTON LORD
Lord, William Carlton b: 1/7/1900, Philadelphia, Pa. d: 8/15/47, Chester, Pa. BR/TR, 5'11", 170 lbs. Deb: 7/12/23

YEAR	TM/L	G	AB	R	H	2B	3B	HR	RBI	BB	SO	AVG	OBP	SLG	PRO+	BR/A	SB	CS	SBR	FA	FR	G/POS	TPR
1923	Phi-N	17	47	3	11	2	0	0	2	2	3	.234	.265	.277	39	-4	0	1	-1	.833	-1	3-14	-0.4

■ SCOTT LOUCKS
Loucks, Scott Gregory b: 11/11/56, Anchorage, Alaska BR/TR, 6', 178 lbs. Deb: 9/1/80

YEAR	TM/L	G	AB	R	H	2B	3B	HR	RBI	BB	SO	AVG	OBP	SLG	PRO+	BR/A	SB	CS	SBR	FA	FR	G/POS	TPR
1980	Hou-N	8	3	4	1	0	0	0	0	0	2	.333	.333	.333	94	0	0	0	0	1.000	-2	/O-4	-0.2
1981	Hou-N	10	7	2	4	0	0	0	0	1	3	.571	.625	.571	254	2	1	0	0	1.000	-2	/O-5	0.0
1982	Hou-N	44	49	6	11	2	0	0	3	3	17	.224	.269	.265	54	-3	4	1	1	.978	-7	O-37	-1.0
1983	Hou-N	7	14	2	3	0	0	0	1		4	.214	.267	.214	37	-1	2	2	-1	1.000	0	/O-6	-0.2
1985	Pit-N	4	7	1	2	2	0	0	1	2	2	.286	.444	.571	184	1	0	0	0	1.000	0	/O-4	0.0
Total	5	73	80	15	21	4	0	0	4	7	28	.262	.322	.313	83	-2	7	3	0	.985	-10	/O-56	-1.4

■ BALDY LOUDEN
Louden, William P. b: 8/27/1885, Piedmont, W.Va. d: 12/8/35, Piedmont, W.Va. BR/TR, 5'11", 175 lbs. Deb: 9/13/07

YEAR	TM/L	G	AB	R	H	2B	3B	HR	RBI	BB	SO	AVG	OBP	SLG	PRO+	BR/A	SB	CS	SBR	FA	FR	G/POS	TPR
1907	NY-A	4	9	4	1	0	0	0	0	1		.111	.273	.111	21	-1	1			.750	1	/3-3	0.0
1912	Det-A	122	403	57	97	12	4	1	36	58		.241	.352	.298	89	-3	28			.951	23	2-87,3-26/S	1.8
1913	Det-A	76	191	28	46	4	5	0	23	24	22	.241	.344	.314	94	-1	6			.906	-2	2-30,3-26/SO	0.0
1914	Buf-F	126	431	73	135	11	4	6	63	52	41	.313	.391	.399	103	3	35			.931	-18	*S-115	-0.5
1915	Buf-F	141	469	67	132	18	5	4	48	64	45	.281	.372	.367	96	-1	30			.978	14	2-88,S-27,3	1.8
1916	Cin-N	134	439	38	96	16	4	1	32	54	54	.219	.313	.280	85	-6	12			**.968**	17	*2-108,S-23	1.8
Total	6	603	1942	267	507	61	22	12	202	254	162	.261	.355	.334	94	-7	112			.961	37	2-313,S-176/3O	4.9

■ CHARLIE LOUDENSLAGER
Loudenslager, Charles Edward b: 5/21/1881, Baltimore, Md. d: 10/31/33, Baltimore, Md. TR, 5'9", 186 lbs. Deb: 4/15/04

YEAR	TM/L	G	AB	R	H	2B	3B	HR	RBI	BB	SO	AVG	OBP	SLG	PRO+	BR/A	SB	CS	SBR	FA	FR	G/POS	TPR
1904	Bro-N	1	2	0	0	0	0	0	0	0	0	.000	.000	.000	-99	-0	0			1.000	-1	/2-1	-0.1

■ BILL LOUGHLIN
Loughlin, William H. b: Baltimore, Md. Deb: 5/9/1883

YEAR	TM/L	G	AB	R	H	2B	3B	HR	RBI	BB	SO	AVG	OBP	SLG	PRO+	BR/A	SB	CS	SBR	FA	FR	G/POS	TPR
1883	Bal-a	1	5	0	2	0	0	0		0		.400	.400	.400	154	0				.000	-0	/O-1	0.0

■ LOUGHRAN
Loughran b: New York, N.Y. Deb: 6/6/1884

YEAR	TM/L	G	AB	R	H	2B	3B	HR	RBI	BB	SO	AVG	OBP	SLG	PRO+	BR/A	SB	CS	SBR	FA	FR	G/POS	TPR
1884	NY-N	9	29	4	3	1	1	0	3	7	11	.103	.278	.207	54	-1				.857	-3	/C-9,O-1	-0.3

■ TOM LOVELACE
Lovelace, Thomas Rivers b: 10/19/1897, Wolfe City, Tex. d: 7/12/79, Dallas, Tex. BR/TR, 5'11", 170 lbs. Deb: 9/23/22

YEAR	TM/L	G	AB	R	H	2B	3B	HR	RBI	BB	SO	AVG	OBP	SLG	PRO+	BR/A	SB	CS	SBR	FA	FR	G/POS	TPR
1922	Pit-N	1	1	0	0	0	0	0	0	0	0	.000	.000	.000	-99	-0	0	0	0		0	H	0.0

■ LEN LOVETT
Lovett, Leonard Walker b: 7/17/1852, Lancaster Co., Pa d: 11/18/22, Newark, Del. BR/TR, Deb: 8/4/1873

YEAR	TM/L	G	AB	R	H	2B	3B	HR	RBI	BB	SO	AVG	OBP	SLG	PRO+	BR/A	SB	CS	SBR	FA	FR	G/POS	TPR
1873	Res-n	1	5	1	2	0	0	0	1	0		.400	.400	.400	148	0						/P-1	0.0
1875	Cen-n	6	21	2	5	1	0	0		1		.238	.273	.286	102	0						/O-5	0.0
Total	2 n	7	26	3	7	1	0	0		1		.269	.296	.308	112	0						/O-5,P-1	0.0

■ MEM LOVETT
Lovett, Merritt Marwood b: 6/15/12, Chicago, Ill. BR/TR, 5'9.5", 165 lbs. Deb: 9/4/33

YEAR	TM/L	G	AB	R	H	2B	3B	HR	RBI	BB	SO	AVG	OBP	SLG	PRO+	BR/A	SB	CS	SBR	FA	FR	G/POS	TPR
1933	Chi-A	1	1	0	0	0	0	0	0	0	0	.000	.000	.000	-99	-0	0	0	0	.000	0	H	0.0

YEAR	TM/L	G	AB	R	H	2B	3B	HR	RBI	BB	SO	AVG	OBP	SLG	PRO+	BR/A	SB	CS	SBR	FA	FR	G/POS	TPR

■ JAY LOVIGLIO   Loviglio, John Paul b: 5/30/56, Freeport, N.Y. BR/TR, 5'9", 160 lbs. Deb: 9/2/80

1980	Phi-N	16	5	7	0	0	0	0	1	0	1	.000	.167	.000	-47	-1	1	2	-1	1.000	1	/2-1	-0.1
1981	Chi-A	14	15	5	4	0	0	0	2	1	1	.267	.313	.267	70	-1	2	2	-1	.786	3	/3-4,2-3,D	0.2
1982	Chi-A	15	31	5	6	0	0	0	2	1	4	.194	.219	.194	14	-4	2	1	0	.964	4	2-13/D-2	0.1
1983	Chi-N	1	1	0	0	0	0	0	0	0	1	.000	.000	.000	-95	-0	0	0	0	.000	0	/H	0.0
Total	4	46	52	17	10	0	0	0	4	3	6	.192	.236	.192	21	-5	5	5	-2	.971	9	/2-17,D-4,3	0.2

■ JOE LOVITTO   Lovitto, Joseph b: 1/6/51, San Pedro, Cal. BB/TR, 6', 185 lbs. Deb: 4/15/72

1972	Tex-A	117	330	23	74	9	1	1	19	37	54	.224	.306	.267	75	-10	13	11	-3	.976	4	*O-103	-1.5
1973	Tex-A	26	44	3	6	1	0	0	5	7	15	.136	.224	.159	10	-5	1	0	0	.898	1	3-20/O-3	-0.4
1974	Tex-A	113	283	27	63	9	3	2	26	25	36	.223	.286	.297	69	-11	6	8	-3	.972	-12	*O-107/1-5	-3.2
1975	Tex-A	50	106	17	22	3	0	1	8	13	16	.208	.294	.264	59	-5	2	2	-1	.985	-6	O-38/1-2,CD	-1.4
Total	4	306	763	70	165	22	4	4	53	80	113	.216	.292	.271	67	-31	22	21	-6	.975	-14	O-251/3-20,1DC	-6.5

■ TOREY LOVULLO   Lovullo, Salvatore Anthony b: 7/25/65, Santa Monica, Cal. BB/TR, 6'1", 185 lbs. Deb: 9/10/88

1988	Det-A	12	21	2	8	1	1	1	2	1	2	.381	.409	.667	204	3	0	0	0	1.000	-0	/2-9,3-3	0.3
1989	Det-A	29	87	8	10	2	0	1	4	14	20	.115	.238	.172	18	-9	0	0	0	1.000	-3	1-18,3-11	-1.4
1991	NY-A	22	51	0	9	2	0	0	2	5	7	.176	.250	.216	30	-5	0	0	0	.940	0	3-22	-0.5
1993	Cal-A	116	367	42	92	20	0	6	30	36	49	.251	.319	.354	78	-11	7	6	-2	.981	-24	2-91,3-14/SO1D	-3.4
1994	Sea-A	36	72	9	16	5	0	2	7	9	13	.222	.309	.375	74	-3	1	0	0	1.000	3	2-20/3-5,D	0.1
Total	5	215	598	61	135	30	1	10	45	65	91	.226	.303	.329	69	-26	8	6	-1	.984	-24	2-120/3-55,1SDO	-4.9

■ FLETCHER LOW   Low, Fletcher b: 4/7/1893, Essex, Mass. d: 6/6/73, Hanover, N.H. BR/TR, 5'10.5", 175 lbs. Deb: 10/7/15

| 1915 | Bos-N | 1 | 4 | 1 | 1 | 0 | 1 | 0 | 1 | 0 | 0 | .250 | .250 | .750 | 207 | -0 | 0 | 0 | | 1.000 | -0 | /3-1 | 0.0 |

■ CHARLIE LOWE   Lowe, Charles b: Baltimore, Md. Deb: 9/28/1872

| 1872 | Atl-n | 7 | 32 | 1 | 5 | 0 | 0 | 0 | 2 | 0 | 2 | .156 | .156 | .156 | -3 | -4 | | | | | | /2-6 | -0.3 |

■ DICK LOWE   Lowe, Richard Alvern b: 1/28/1854, Evansville, Wis. d: 6/28/22, Janesville, Wis. Deb: 6/26/1884

| 1884 | Det-N | 1 | 3 | 0 | 1 | 0 | 0 | 0 | 0 | 0 | 1 | .333 | .333 | .333 | 117 | -0 | 0 | | | .125 | -3 | /C-1 | -0.2 |

■ BOBBY LOWE   Lowe, Robert Lincoln "Link" b: 7/10/1868, Pittsburgh, Pa. d: 12/8/51, Detroit, Mich. BR/TR, 5'10", 150 lbs. Deb: 4/19/1890 M

1890	Bos-N	52	207	35	58	13	2	2	21	26	32	.280	.366	.391	112	3	15			.951	-9	S-24,O-15,3	-0.4
1891	Bos-N	125	497	92	129	19	5	6	74	53	54	.260	.342	.354	92	-7	43			.927	-6	*O-107,2-17/S3P	-1.5
1892	*Bos-N	124	475	79	115	16	7	3	57	37	46	.242	.308	.324	84	-11	36			.928	13	O-90,3-14,S2	0.0
1893	Bos-N	126	526	130	157	19	5	14	89	55	29	.298	.369	.433	105	0	22			.936	1	*2-121/S-5	0.4
1894	Bos-N	133	613	158	212	34	11	17	115	50	25	.346	.401	.520	112	8	23			.927	-6	*2-130/S-2,3	0.6
1895	Bos-N	99	412	101	122	12	7	7	62	40	16	.296	.370	.410	94	-5	24			.954	15	*2-99	1.2
1896	Bos-N	73	305	59	98	11	4	2	48	20	11	.321	.371	.403	98	-1	15			.965	25	2-73	2.3
1897	*Bos-N	123	499	87	154	24	8	5	106	32		.309	.355	.419	98	-4	16			.952	-4	*2-123	-0.1
1898	Bos-N	147	559	65	152	11	7	4	94	29		.272	.311	.338	82	-15	12			.958	16	*2-145/S-2	1.0
1899	Bos-N	152	559	81	152	5	9	4	88	35		.272	.316	.335	72	-24	17			.954	7	*2-148/S-4	-1.1
1900	Bos-N	127	474	65	132	11	5	3	71	26		.278	.323	.342	74	-18	15			.951	-7	*2-127	-1.8
1901	Bos-N	129	491	47	125	11	1	3	47	17		.255	.284	.299	63	-24	22			.912	-5	*3-111,2-18	-2.7
1902	Chi-N	119	472	41	116	13	3	0	31	11		.246	.270	.286	74	-16	16			.957	26	*2-117/3-2	1.5
1903	Chi-N	32	105	14	28	5	3	0	15	4		.267	.319	.371	99	-0	5			.948	4	2-22/1-6,3	0.4
1904	Pit-N	1	1	0	0	0	0	0	0	0		.000	.000	.000	-97	-0	0			.000	0	H	0.0
	Det-A	140	506	47	105	14	6	0	40	17		.208	.236	.259	58	-25	15			.964	-2	*2-140,M	-2.4
1905	Det-A	58	181	17	35	7	2	0	9	13		.193	.255	.254	61	-8	3			.980	-1	O-24,3-22/2S1	-1.0
1906	Det-A	41	145	11	30	3	0	1	12	4		.207	.233	.248	49	-9	3			.915	8	S-19,2-17/3	0.0
1907	Det-A	17	37	2	9	2	0	0	5	4		.243	.317	.297	93	-0	0			.870	-4	3-10/O-4,S	-0.5
Total	18	1818	7064	1131	1929	230	85	71	984	473	213	.273	.325	.360	86	-157	302			.950	70	*2-1313,O-240,3/S1P	-4.1

■ JOHN LOWENSTEIN   Lowenstein, John Lee b: 1/27/47, Wolf Point, Mont. BL/TR, 6', 175 lbs. Deb: 9/2/70

1970	Cle-A	17	43	5	11	3	1	1	6	1	9	.256	.273	.442	89	-1	1	0	0	1.000	4	2-10/3-2,OS	0.4
1971	Cle-A	58	140	15	26	5	0	4	9	16	28	.186	.269	.307	58	-8	1	5	-3	.986	-6	2-29,O-18/S	-1.6
1972	Cle-A	68	151	16	32	8	1	6	21	20	43	.212	.304	.397	104	1	2	4	-2	1.000	-2	O-58/1-2	-0.6
1973	Cle-A	98	305	42	89	16	1	6	40	23	41	.292	.341	.410	109	3	5	3	-0	.931	-10	O-51,2-25/31D	-0.7
1974	Cle-A	140	508	65	123	14	2	8	48	53	85	.242	.316	.325	85	-9	36	17	1	.986	-1	*O-100,3-28,1/2	-1.5
1975	Cle-A	91	265	37	64	5	1	12	33	28	28	.242	.314	.404	102	0	15	10	-2	.983	-5	O-36,D-31/32	-0.9
1976	Cle-A	93	229	33	47	8	2	2	14	25	35	.205	.283	.284	67	-9	11	8	-2	.972	-5	O-61/D-11/1	-2.0
1977	Cle-A	81	149	24	36	6	1	4	12	21	29	.242	.335	.376	97	-0	1	8	-5	1.000	-3	O-39,D-19/1	-1.0
1978	Tex-A	77	176	28	39	8	3	5	21	37	29	.222	.363	.386	110	4	16	3	3	.926	-9	3-25,D-21,O	-0.4
1979	*Bal-A	97	197	33	50	8	2	11	34	30	37	.254	.355	.482	128	8	16	4	2	.992	-8	O-72/1-1,3D	0.0
1980	Bal-A	104	196	38	61	8	0	4	27	32	29	.311	.408	.413	127	9	7	3	0	.992	-11	O-91/D-3	-0.4
1981	Bal-A	83	189	19	47	7	0	6	20	22	32	.249	.330	.381	105	1	7	6	-2	.990	-12	O-73/D-4	-1.5
1982	Bal-A	122	322	69	103	15	2	24	66	54	59	.320	.419	.602	177	35	7	6	-2	1.000	-7	*O-111	2.4
1983	*Bal-A	122	310	52	87	13	2	15	60	49	55	.281	.381	.481	138	17	2	1	0	.982	-11	*O-107/2-1,D	0.3
1984	Bal-A	105	270	34	64	13	0	8	28	33	54	.237	.322	.374	94	-2	1	0	0	.971	-8	O-67,D-22/1	-1.2
1985	Bal-A	12	26	0	2	0	0	0	2	2	3	.077	.143	.077	-39	-5	0	0	0	1.000	-0	/O-4,D-6	-0.5
Total	16	1368	3476	510	881	137	18	116	441	446	596	.253	.340	.403	108	43	128	78	-8	.984	-96	O-906,D-125/321S	-9.2

■ PEANUTS LOWREY   Lowrey, Harry Lee b: 8/27/18, Culver City, Cal. d: 7/2/86, Inglewood, Cal. BR/TR, 5'8.5", 170 lbs. Deb: 4/14/42 C

1942	Chi-N	27	58	4	11	0	0	1	4	4	4	.190	.242	.241	43	-4	0			.978	-1	O-19	-0.6
1943	Chi-N	130	480	59	140	25	12	1	63	35	24	.292	.340	.400	115	8	13			.982	14	*O-113,S-16/2	1.7
1945	*Chi-N	143	523	72	148	22	7	7	89	48	27	.283	.343	.392	106	4	11			.987	6	*O-138/S-2	0.0
1946	Chi-N★	144	540	75	139	24	5	4	54	56	22	.257	.328	.343	92	-6	10			.979	8	*O-126,3-20	-0.3
1947	Chi-N	115	448	56	126	17	5	5	37	38	26	.281	.339	.375	93	-5	2			.945	9	3-91,O-25/2	0.4
1948	Chi-N	129	435	47	128	12	3	2	54	34	31	.294	.347	.349	93	-4	2			.983	-1	*O-103/3-9,2S	-1.1
1949	Chi-N	38	111	18	30	5	0	2	10	9	8	.270	.325	.369	88	-2	3			.966	-4	O-31/3-1	-0.8
	Cin-N	89	309	48	85	16	2	2	25	37	11	.275	.354	.359	91	-3	1			.995	8	O-78	0.1
	Yr	127	420	66	115	21	2	4	35	46	19	.274	.347	.362	90	-5	4			.989	5	*O-109/3-1	-0.7
1950	Cin-N	91	264	34	60	14	0	1	11	36	7	.227	.320	.292	62	-14	0			.987	1	O-72/2-1	-1.5
	StL-N	17	56	10	15	0	1	0	4	6	1	.268	.349	.321	74	-2	0			1.000	1	/2-6,3-5,O	-0.1
	Yr	108	320	44	75	14	1	1	15	42	8	.234	.325	.297	64	-16	0			.982	2	O-76/2-7,3	-1.6
1951	StL-N	114	370	52	112	19	5	5	40	35	12	.303	.366	.422	111	6	0	1	-1	.983	-5	O-85,3-11/2	0.1
1952	StL-N	132	374	48	107	18	2	1	48	34	13	.286	.352	.353	96	-1	3	2	-0	.978	-9	*O-106/3-6	-1.5
1953	StL-N	104	182	26	49	9	2	5	27	15	21	.269	.325	.423	93	-2	1	0		1.000	-10	O-38,2-10/3	-1.2
1954	StL-N	74	61	6	7	3	0	0	7	8		.115	.229	.197	12	-8	0	0		1.000	-5	O-12	-1.3
1955	Phi-N	54	106	9	20	4	0	0	8	7	10	.189	.239	.226	25	-11	2	0	1	.973	-6	O-28/2-2,1	-1.7
Total	13	1401	4317	564	1177	186	45	37	479	403	226	.273	.336	.362	92	-45	48	3		.983	9	O-978,3-144/2S1	-7.8

■ DWIGHT LOWRY   Lowry, Dwight (b: Dwight Lowery) b: 10/23/57, Lumberton, N.C. BL/TR, 6'3", 210 lbs. Deb: 4/3/84

| 1984 | Det-A | 32 | 45 | 8 | 11 | 2 | 0 | 2 | 7 | 3 | 11 | .244 | .292 | .422 | 95 | -0 | 0 | 0 | 0 | 1.000 | 5 | C-31 | 0.5 |
| 1986 | Det-A | 56 | 150 | 21 | 46 | 4 | 0 | 3 | 18 | 17 | 19 | .307 | .392 | .393 | 115 | 4 | 0 | 0 | 0 | .992 | -1 | C-55/1-1,O | 0.6 |

YEAR	TM/L	G	AB	R	H	2B	3B	HR	RBI	BB	SO	AVG	OBP	SLG	PRO+	BR/A	SB	CS	SBR	FA	FR	G/POS	TPR
1987	Det-A	13	25	0	5	2	0	0	1	0	6	.200	.200	.280	27	-3	0	0	0	1.000	1	C-12/1-1	-0.2
1988	Min-A	7	7	0	0	0	0	0	0	0	2	.000	.000	.000	-97	-2	0	0	0	1.000	2	/C-5,D-6	0.0
Total	4	108	227	29	62	8	0	5	26	20	38	.273	.343	.374	96	-1	0	0	0	.995	7	C-103/D-6,1O	0.9

■ JOHN LOWRY
Lowry, John D. b: Baltimore, Md.   Deb: 6/12/1875

YEAR	TM/L	G	AB	R	H	2B	3B	HR	RBI	BB	SO	AVG	OBP	SLG	PRO+	BR/A	SB	CS	SBR	FA	FR	G/POS	TPR
1875	Was-n	6	21	2	3	0	0	0			1	.143	.182	.143	14	-2						/O-5	-0.1

■ WILLIE LOZADO
Lozado, William b: 5/12/59, New York, N.Y. BR/TR, 6', 166 lbs. Deb: 7/16/84

YEAR	TM/L	G	AB	R	H	2B	3B	HR	RBI	BB	SO	AVG	OBP	SLG	PRO+	BR/A	SB	CS	SBR	FA	FR	G/POS	TPR
1984	Mil-A	43	107	15	29	8	2	1	20	12	23	.271	.345	.411	113	2	0	3	-2	.925	-1	3-36/S-6,2D	-0.1

■ STEVE LUBRATICH
Lubratich, Steven George b: 5/1/55, Oakland, Cal. BR/TR, 6', 170 lbs. Deb: 9/27/81

YEAR	TM/L	G	AB	R	H	2B	3B	HR	RBI	BB	SO	AVG	OBP	SLG	PRO+	BR/A	SB	CS	SBR	FA	FR	G/POS	TPR
1981	Cal-A	7	21	2	3	1	0	0	2	0	2	.143	.143	.190	-5	-3	1	0		1.000	2	/3-6	-0.1
1983	Cal-A	57	156	12	34	9	0	0	7	4	17	.218	.237	.276	41	-13	0	1	-1	.949	16	S-23,3-22,2	0.5
Total	2	64	177	14	37	10	0	0	8	4	19	.209	.227	.266	36	-15	1	1	-0	.988	18	/3-28,S-23,2	0.4

■ HAL LUBY
Luby, Hugh Max b: 6/13/13, Blackfoot, Idaho d: 5/4/86, Eugene, Ore. BR/TR, 5'10", 185 lbs. Deb: 9/10/36

YEAR	TM/L	G	AB	R	H	2B	3B	HR	RBI	BB	SO	AVG	OBP	SLG	PRO+	BR/A	SB	CS	SBR	FA	FR	G/POS	TPR
1936	Phi-A	9	38	3	7	1	0	0	3	0	7	.184	.205	.211	3	-6	2	0	1	.880	-4	/2-9	-0.8
1944	NY-N	111	323	30	82	10	2	2	35	52	15	.254	.364	.316	93	-1	2			.943	16	3-65,2-45/1	1.9
Total	2	120	361	33	89	11	2	2	38	52	22	.247	.349	.305	83	-7	4	0		.954	12	/3-65,2-54,1	1.1

■ JOHNNY LUCADELLO
Lucadello, John b: 2/22/19, Thurber, Tex. BB/TR, 5'11", 160 lbs. Deb: 9/24/38

YEAR	TM/L	G	AB	R	H	2B	3B	HR	RBI	BB	SO	AVG	OBP	SLG	PRO+	BR/A	SB	CS	SBR	FA	FR	G/POS	TPR
1938	StL-A	7	20	1	3	1	0	0	0	0	0	.150	.150	.200	-13	-4	0	0	0	.909	-1	/3-6	-0.5
1939	StL-A	9	30	0	7	2	0	0	4	2	4	.233	.281	.300	48	-2	0	0	0	.912	-4	/2-7	-0.6
1940	StL-A	17	63	15	20	4	2	0	10	6	4	.317	.394	.540	137	3	1	0	0	.968	0	2-16	0.5
1941	StL-A	107	351	58	98	22	4	2	31	48	23	.279	.366	.382	95	-2	5	2	0	.962	-16	2-70,S-12/3O	-1.1
1946	StL-A	87	210	21	52	7	1	1	15	36	20	.248	.358	.305	82	-4	0	1	-1	.942	-7	3-37,2-19	-1.0
1947	NY-A	12	12	0	1	0	0	0	0	1	5	.083	.154	.083	-33	-2	0	0	0	1.000	-2	/2-5	-0.4
Total	6	239	686	95	181	36	7	5	60	93	56	.264	.353	.359	88	-10	6	3	0	.965	-29	2-117/3-49,SO	-3.1

■ RED LUCAS
Lucas, Charles Frederick "The Nashville Narcissus" b: 4/28/02, Columbia, Tenn. d: 7/9/86, Nashville, Tenn. BL/TR, 5'9.5", 170 lbs. Deb: 4/19/23

YEAR	TM/L	G	AB	R	H	2B	3B	HR	RBI	BB	SO	AVG	OBP	SLG	PRO+	BR/A	SB	CS	SBR	FA	FR	G/POS	TPR
1923	NY-N	3	2	0	0	0	0	0	0	0	1	.000	.000	.000	-99	-1	0	0	0	1.000	1	/P-3	0.0
1924	Bos-N	33	33	5	11	1	0	0	5	1	4	.333	.353	.364	96	-0	0	0	0	1.000	1	P-27/3-2	0.0
1925	Bos-N	6	20	1	3	0	0	0	2	2	4	.150	.227	.150	-2	-3	0	0	0	.968	0	/2-6	-0.3
1926	Cin-N	66	76	15	23	4	4	0	14	10	13	.303	.384	.461	130	3	0			1.000	-1	P-39/2-1	0.0
1927	Cin-N	80	150	14	47	5	2	0	28	12	10	.313	.368	.373	102	1	0			.983	-6	P-37/2-5,SO	-0.4
1928	Cin-N	39	73	8	23	2	1	0	7	4	6	.315	.351	.370	90	-1	0			1.000	-0	P-27	0.0
1929	Cin-N	76	140	15	41	6	0	0	13	13	15	.293	.353	.336	75	-5	1			.949	0	P-32	0.0
1930	Cin-N	80	113	18	38	4	1	2	19	17	4	.336	.423	.442	115	4	0			1.000	-3	P-33	0.0
1931	Cin-N	97	153	15	43	4	0	0	17	12	9	.281	.333	.307	78	-4	0			.984	1	P-29	0.0
1932	Cin-N	76	150	13	43	11	2	0	19	10	9	.287	.335	.387	97	-1	0			.973	-0	P-31	0.0
1933	Cin-N	75	122	14	35	6	1	1	15	12	6	.287	.356	.377	111	2	0			1.000	0	P-29	0.0
1934	Pit-N	68	105	11	23	5	1	0	8	6	16	.219	.261	.286	45	-8	1			.939	-3	P-29	0.0
1935	Pit-N	47	66	6	21	6	0	0	10	7	11	.318	.392	.409	112	1	0			.968	-1	P-20	0.0
1936	Pit-N	69	108	11	26	4	1	0	14	8	17	.241	.293	.296	58	-6	0			.976	-1	P-27	0.0
1937	Pit-N	59	82	8	22	3	0	0	17	7	6	.268	.326	.305	72	-3	0			1.000	-2	P-20	0.0
1938	Pit-N	33	46	1	5	0	0	0	2	3	2	.109	.163	.109	-24	-8	0			1.000	-1	P-13	0.0
Total	16	907	1439	155	404	61	13	3	190	124	133	.281	.340	.347	84	-29	2	0		.981	-14	P-396/2-12,S3O	-0.7

■ FRED LUCAS
Lucas, Frederick Warrington "Fritz" b: 1/19/03, Vineland, N.J. d: 3/11/87, Cambridge, Md. BR/TR, 5'10", 165 lbs. Deb: 7/15/35

YEAR	TM/L	G	AB	R	H	2B	3B	HR	RBI	BB	SO	AVG	OBP	SLG	PRO+	BR/A	SB	CS	SBR	FA	FR	G/POS	TPR
1935	Phi-N	20	34	1	9	0	0	0	2	3	6	.265	.324	.265	55	-2	0			.944	-2	O-10	-0.4

■ JOHNNY LUCAS
Lucas, John Charles "Buster" b: 2/10/03, Glen Carbon, Ill. d: 10/31/70, Maryville, Ill. BR/TL, 5'10", 186 lbs. Deb: 4/15/31

YEAR	TM/L	G	AB	R	H	2B	3B	HR	RBI	BB	SO	AVG	OBP	SLG	PRO+	BR/A	SB	CS	SBR	FA	FR	G/POS	TPR
1931	Bos-A	3	2	0	0	0	0	0	0	0	1	.000	.000	.000	-99	-1	0	0	0	.000	-1	/O-2	-0.2
1932	Bos-A	1	1	0	0	0	0	0	0	0	0	.000	.000	.000	-99	-0	0	0	0	.000	0	H	0.0
Total	2	4	3	0	0	0	0	0	0	0	1	.000	.000	.000	-99	-1	0	0	0	—	0	/O-2	-0.2

■ FRANK LUCE
Luce, Frank Edward b: 12/6/1896, Spencer, Ohio d: 2/3/42, Milwaukee, Wis. BL/TR, 5'11", 180 lbs. Deb: 9/17/23

YEAR	TM/L	G	AB	R	H	2B	3B	HR	RBI	BB	SO	AVG	OBP	SLG	PRO+	BR/A	SB	CS	SBR	FA	FR	G/POS	TPR
1923	Pit-N	9	12	2	6	0	0	0	3	2	2	.500	.571	.500	181	2	2	1	0	1.000	-2	/O-5	0.0

■ JOE LUCEY
Lucey, Joseph Earl "Scootch" b: 3/27/1897, Holyoke, Mass. d: 7/30/80, Holyoke, Mass. BR/TR, 6', 168 lbs. Deb: 7/6/20

YEAR	TM/L	G	AB	R	H	2B	3B	HR	RBI	BB	SO	AVG	OBP	SLG	PRO+	BR/A	SB	CS	SBR	FA	FR	G/POS	TPR
1920	NY-A	3	3	0	0	0	0	0	0	0	0	.000	.000	.000	-97	-1	0	0	0	1.000	0	/2-1,S-1	0.0
1925	Bos-A	10	15	0	2	0	0	0	0	0	4	.133	.133	.133	-32	-3	0	0	0	.889	-1	/P-7,S-3	-0.3
Total	2	13	18	0	2	0	0	0	0	0	4	.111	.111	.111	-43	-4	0	0	0	.778	-0	/P-7,S-4,2	-0.3

■ FRED LUDERUS
Luderus, Frederick William b: 9/12/1885, Milwaukee, Wis. d: 1/5/61, Three Lakes, Wis. BL/TR, 5'11.5", 185 lbs. Deb: 9/23/09

YEAR	TM/L	G	AB	R	H	2B	3B	HR	RBI	BB	SO	AVG	OBP	SLG	PRO+	BR/A	SB	CS	SBR	FA	FR	G/POS	TPR
1909	Chi-N	11	37	8	11	1	1	1	9	3		.297	.366	.459	152	2	0			.950	-2	1-11	0.1
1910	Chi-N	24	54	5	11	1	1	0	3	4	3	.204	.259	.259	52	-3	0			.975	-0	1-17	-0.4
	Phi-N	21	68	10	20	5	2	0	14	9	5	.294	.385	.426	132	3	2			.985	1	1-19	0.4
	Yr	45	122	15	31	6	3	0	17	13	8	.254	.331	.352	98	-0	2			.981	0	1-36	0.0
1911	Phi-N	146	551	69	166	24	11	16	99	40	76	.301	.353	.472	128	18	6			.985	-2	*1-146	1.6
1912	Phi-N	148	572	77	147	31	5	10	69	44	65	.257	.318	.381	85	-14	8			.990	10	*1-146	-0.6
1913	Phi-N	155	588	67	154	32	7	18	86	34	51	.262	.304	.432	105	-0	3			.984	-1	*1-155	0.0
1914	Phi-N	121	443	55	110	16	5	12	55	33	31	.248	.308	.388	100	-2	2			.975	-1	*1-121	-0.3
1915	*Phi-N	141	499	55	157	36	7	7	62	42	36	.315	.376	.457	150	29	9	7	-2	.993	10	*1-141	3.8
1916	Phi-N	146	508	52	143	26	3	5	53	41	32	.281	.341	.374	115	9	8			.982	-2	*1-146	0.3
1917	Phi-N	154	522	57	136	24	4	5	72	65	35	.261	.349	.351	110	8	5			.991	5	*1-154	0.8
1918	Phi-N	125	468	54	135	23	2	5	67	42	33	.288	.351	.378	115	8	4			.988	7	*1-125	1.1
1919	Phi-N	138	509	60	149	30	6	5	49	54	48	.293	.365	.405	123	15	6			.985	10	*1-138	2.2
1920	Phi-N	16	32	1	5	0	0	0	2	5	6	.156	.229	.219	28	-3	0	1	-1	.983	0	/1-7	-0.4
Total	12	1346	4851	570	1344	251	54	84	642	414	421	.277	.340	.403	113	72	55	8		.986	39	*1-1326	8.6

■ BILL LUDWIG
Ludwig, William Lawrence b: 5/27/1882, Louisville, Ky. d: 9/5/47, Louisville, Ky. BR/TR, Deb: 4/16/08

YEAR	TM/L	G	AB	R	H	2B	3B	HR	RBI	BB	SO	AVG	OBP	SLG	PRO+	BR/A	SB	CS	SBR	FA	FR	G/POS	TPR
1908	StL-N	66	187	15	34	2	2	0	8	16		.182	.246	.214	50	-10	3			.952	-3	C-62	-1.0

■ ROY LUEBBE
Luebbe, Roy John b: 9/17/1900, Parkersburg, Iowa d: 8/21/85, Papillion, Neb. BB/TR, 6', 175 lbs. Deb: 8/22/25

YEAR	TM/L	G	AB	R	H	2B	3B	HR	RBI	BB	SO	AVG	OBP	SLG	PRO+	BR/A	SB	CS	SBR	FA	FR	G/POS	TPR
1925	NY-A	8	15	1	0	0	0	0	3	2	6	.000	.118	.000	-69	-4	0	0	0	1.000	1	/C-8	-0.2

■ HENRY LUFF
Luff, Henry T. b: 9/14/1856, Philadelphia, Pa. d: 10/11/16, Philadelphia, Pa. 5'11", 175 lbs. Deb: 4/21/1875

YEAR	TM/L	G	AB	R	H	2B	3B	HR	RBI	BB	SO	AVG	OBP	SLG	PRO+	BR/A	SB	CS	SBR	FA	FR	G/POS	TPR
1875	NH-n	38	165	15	46	11	3	2			0	.279	.279	.418	158	10						3-26/P-10,O	0.8
1882	Det-N	3	11	1	3	2	0	0	1	0	0	.273	.273	.455	129	0				.667	-1	/2-3,O-1	-0.1
	Cin-a	28	120	16	28	2	2	0			2	.233	.246	.283	74	-4				.922	-2	1-27/O-1	-0.8
1883	Lou-a	6	23	1	4	0	0	0			2	.174	.174	.174	13	-2				.868	-1	1-4,O-2	-0.3
1884	Phi-U	26	111	9	30	4	2	0			4	.270	.296	.342	79	-3				.733	-3	O-12/1-6,32	-0.6
	KC-U	5	19	0	1	0	0	0				.053	.100	.053	-66	-4				.444	-4	/3-4,O-4	-0.8
	Yr	31	130	9	31	4	2	0			5	.238	.267	.300	59	-7				.706	-7	O-16/3-9,12	-1.4
Total	3	68	284	27	66	8	4	0	1	7	0	.232	.251	.289	64	-13				.911	-12	/1-37,O-20,32	-2.6

YEAR	TM/L	G	AB	R	H	2B	3B	HR	RBI	BB	SO	AVG	OBP	SLG	PRO+	BR/A	SB	CS	SBR	FA	FR	G/POS	TPR

■ EDDIE LUKON   Lukon, Edward Paul "Mongoose" b: 8/5/20, Burgettstown, Pa.   BL/TL, 5'10", 168 lbs.   Deb: 8/6/41

1941	Cin-N	23	86	6	23	3	0	3	6	6	6	.267	.315	.302	74	-3	1			.980	2	O-22	-0.2
1945	Cin-N	2	8	1	1	0	0	0	0	0	1	.125	.125	.125	-31	-1	0			1.000	0	/O-2	-0.2
1946	Cin-N	102	312	31	78	8	8	12	34	26	29	.250	.310	.442	116	4	3			.985	2	O-83	0.3
1947	Cin-N	86	200	26	41	6	1	11	33	28	36	.205	.306	.410	89	-4	0			1.000	-2	O-55	-0.8
Total	4	213	606	64	143	17	9	23	70	60	72	.236	.307	.408	99	-4	4			.989	3	O-162	-0.9

■ MIKE LUM   Lum, Michael Ken-Wai b: 10/27/45, Honolulu, Hawaii   BL/TL, 6', 180 lbs.   Deb: 9/12/67   C

1967	Atl-N	9	26	1	6	0	0	0	1	1	4	.231	.259	.231	42	-2	0	1	-1	.944	1	/O-6	-0.2
1968	Atl-N	122	232	22	52	7	3	3	21	14	35	.224	.280	.319	79	-6	3	5	-2	.976	-9	O-95	-2.4
1969	*Atl-N	121	168	20	45	8	0	1	22	16	18	.268	.332	.333	86	-3	0	0	0	.992	-8	O-89	-1.3
1970	Atl-N	123	291	25	74	17	2	7	28	17	43	.254	.307	.399	83	-8	3	2	-0	.988	-3	O-98	-1.5
1971	Atl-N	145	454	56	122	14	1	13	55	47	63	.269	.344	.390	101	1	0	3	-2	.990	9	*O-125/1-1	0.3
1972	Atl-N	123	369	40	84	14	2	9	38	50	52	.228	.325	.350	84	-7	1	4	-2	.976	4	*O-109/1-2	-1.0
1973	Atl-N	138	513	74	151	26	6	16	82	41	89	.294	.354	.462	116	10	2	5	-2	.991	-3	1-84,O-64	-0.4
1974	Atl-N	106	361	50	84	11	2	11	50	45	49	.233	.321	.366	88	-6	0	2	-1	.994	-5	1-60,O-50	-1.9
1975	Atl-N	124	364	32	83	8	2	8	36	39	38	.228	.303	.327	72	-14	2	4	-2	.992	-1	1-60,O-38	-2.3
1976	*Cin-N	84	136	15	31	5	1	3	20	22	24	.228	.340	.346	93	-1	0	1	-1	1.000	-6	O-38	-1.0
1977	Cin-N	81	125	14	20	1	0	5	16	9	33	.160	.222	.288	35	-12	2	0	1	1.000	-3	O-24/1-8	-1.5
1978	Cin-N	86	146	15	39	7	1	6	23	22	18	.267	.363	.452	126	5	0	0	0	.987	-1	O-43/1-7	0.3
1979	Atl-N	111	217	27	54	6	0	6	27	18	34	.249	.306	.359	75	-7	0	2	-1	.998	-3	1-51/O-3	-0.9
1980	Atl-N	93	83	7	17	3	0	0	5	18	19	.205	.347	.241	65	-3	0	0	0	1.000	-3	O-19,1-10	-0.7
1981	Atl-N	10	11	1	1	0	0	0	0	2	2	.091	.231	.091	-6	-1	0	0	0	1.000	0	/O-1	-0.1
	Chi-N	41	58	5	14	1	0	2	7	5	5	.241	.313	.362	87	-1	0	0	0	.923	-4	O-14/1-1	-0.6
	Yr	51	69	6	15	1	0	2	7	7	7	.217	.299	.319	72	-2	0	0	0	.938	-4	O-15/1-1	-0.7
Total	15	1517	3554	404	877	128	20	90	431	366	506	.247	.322	.370	89	-54	13	29	-14	.986	-29	O-816,1-284	-15.2

■ HARRY LUMLEY   Lumley, Harry G "Judge" b: 9/29/1880, Forest City, Pa.   d: 5/22/38, Binghamton, N.Y.   BL/TL, 5'10", 183 lbs.   Deb: 4/14/04   M

1904	Bro-N	150	577	79	161	23	**18**	9	78	41		.279	.331	.428	137	23	30			.955	4	*O-150	1.9
1905	Bro-N	130	505	50	148	19	10	7	47	36		.293	.340	.412	134	19	22			.912	-1	*O-129	1.2
1906	Bro-N	133	484	72	157	23	12	9	61	48		.324	.386	**.477**	184	45	35			.949	-1	*O-131	4.3
1907	Bro-N	127	454	47	121	23	11	9	66	31		.267	.316	.425	144	19	18			.959	-4	*O-118	1.2
1908	Bro-N	127	440	36	95	13	12	4	39	29		.216	.266	.327	93	-5	4			.955	-5	*O-116	-1.8
1909	Bro-N	55	172	13	43	8	3	0	14	16		.250	.314	.331	104	1	1			.948	2	O-52,M	0.0
1910	Bro-N	8	21	3	3	0	0	0	0	3	6	.143	.280	.143	25	-2	0			.833	-1	/O-4	-0.3
Total	7	730	2653	300	728	109	66	38	305	204	6	.274	.328	.408	135	99	110			.946	-5	O-700	6.5

■ JERRY LUMPE   Lumpe, Jerry Dean b: 6/2/33, Lincoln, Mo.   BL/TR, 6'2", 185 lbs.   Deb: 4/17/56   C

1956	NY-A	20	62	12	16	3	0	0	4	5	11	.258	.313	.306	66	-3	1	1	-0	.916	3	S-17/3-1	0.1
1957	*NY-A	40	103	15	35	6	2	0	11	9	13	.340	.393	.437	128	4	2	2	-1	.956	-2	3-30/S-18	0.2
1958	*NY-A	81	232	34	59	8	4	3	32	23	21	.254	.324	.362	92	-3	1	2	-1	.943	5	3-65/S-5	0.1
1959	NY-A	18	45	2	10	0	0	0	2	6	7	.222	.314	.222	52	-3	0	0	0	1.000	2	3-12/S-4,2	0.0
	KC-A	108	403	47	98	11	5	3	28	41	32	.243	.313	.318	72	-15	2	1	0	.986	-10	2-61,S-56/3	-1.6
	Yr	126	448	49	108	11	5	3	30	47	39	.241	.313	.308	70	-17	2	1	0	.987	-8	2-62,S-60,3	-1.6
1960	KC-A	146	574	69	156	19	3	8	53	48	49	.272	.328	.357	85	-12	1	1	-0	.982	-7	*2-134,S-15	-0.5
1961	KC-A	148	569	81	167	29	9	3	54	48	39	.293	.351	.392	96	-3	1	0	0	.979	16	*2-147	2.9
1962	KC-A	156	641	89	193	34	10	10	83	44	38	.301	.346	.432	103	2	0	2	-1	.986	-4	*2-156/S-2	1.4
1963	KC-A	157	595	75	161	26	7	5	59	58	44	.271	.335	.363	91	-6	3	2	0	.988	2	*2-155	1.1
1964	Det-A☆	158	624	75	160	21	6	6	46	50	61	.256	.314	.338	80	-16	2	1	0	.983	-21	*2-158	-2.6
1965	Det-A	145	502	72	129	15	3	4	39	56	34	.257	.335	.323	87	-7	7	0	2	.985	-18	*2-139	-1.2
1966	Det-A	113	385	30	89	14	3	1	26	24	44	.231	.276	.291	62	-19	0	3	-2	.991	-6	2-95	-2.2
1967	Det-A	81	177	19	41	4	0	1	17	16	18	.232	.295	.322	80	-4	0	0	0	.963	-3	2-54/3-6	-0.5
Total	12	1371	4912	620	1314	190	52	47	454	428	411	.268	.327	.356	87	-84	20	15	-3	.984	-44	*2-1100,3-118,S	-2.8

■ DON LUND   Lund, Donald Andrew b: 5/18/23, Detroit, Mich.   BR/TR, 6', 200 lbs.   Deb: 7/3/45   C

1945	Bro-N	4	3	0	0	0	0	0	0	1	1	.000	.250	.000	-27	-0	0			.000	0	H	0.0
1947	Bro-N	11	20	5	6	2	0	2	5	3	7	.300	.391	.700	178	2	0			1.000	0	/O-5	0.2
1948	Bro-N	27	69	9	13	4	0	1	5	5	16	.188	.243	.290	42	-6	1			.977	-2	O-25	-0.8
	StL-A	63	161	21	40	7	4	3	25	10	17	.248	.305	.398	84	-5	0	0	0	1.000	-4	O-45	-1.1
1949	Det-A	2	2	0	0	0	0	0	0	0	1	.000	.000	.000	-99	-1	0	0	0	.000	0	H	-0.1
1952	Det-A	8	23	1	7	0	0	0	1	3	3	.304	.385	.304	93	-0	0	1	-1	1.000	0	/O-7	-0.1
1953	Det-A	131	421	51	108	21	4	9	47	39	65	.257	.323	.390	93	-5	3	3	-1	.980	1	*O-123	-0.9
1954	Det-A	35	54	4	7	2	0	0	3	4	3	.130	.190	.167	-2	-8	1	0	0	.971	-8	O-31	-1.6
Total	7	281	753	91	181	36	8	15	86	65	113	.240	.305	.369	81	-22	5	4		.983	-12	O-236	-4.4

■ GORDY LUND   Lund, Gordon Thomas b: 2/23/41, Iron Mountain, Mich   BR/TR, 5'11", 170 lbs.   Deb: 8/1/67

1967	Cle-A	3	8	1	2	1	0	0	0	2	2	.250	.250	.375	82	-0	0	0		.667	-2	/S-2	-0.2
1969	Sea-A	20	38	4	10	0	0	0	1	5	7	.263	.349	.263	75	-1	1	1	-0	.927	-1	S-17/2-1,3	-0.1
Total	2	23	46	5	12	1	0	0	1	5	9	.261	.333	.283	76	-1	1	1	-0	.902	-2	/S-19,3-1,2	-0.3

■ TOM LUNDSTEDT   Lundstedt, Thomas Robert b: 4/10/49, Davenport, Iowa   BB/TR, 6'4", 195 lbs.   Deb: 8/31/73

1973	Chi-N	4	5	0	0	0	0	0	0	0	1	.000	.000	.000	-93	-1	0	0	0	1.000	1	/C-4	-0.1
1974	Chi-N	22	32	1	3	0	0	0	0	5	7	.094	.216	.094	-11	-5	0	0	0	.987	2	C-22	-0.3
1975	Min-A	18	28	2	3	0	0	1	4	5	5	.107	.219	.107	-5	-4	0	0	0	1.000	1	C-14/D-2	-0.2
Total	3	44	65	3	6	0	0	1	4	9	13	.092	.203	.092	-14	-10	0	0	0	.993	4	/C-40,D-2	-0.6

■ HARRY LUNTE   Lunte, Harry August b: 9/15/1892, St.Louis, Mo.   d: 7/27/65, St.Louis, Mo.   BR/TR, 5'11.5", 165 lbs.   Deb: 5/19/19

1919	Cle-A	26	77	2	15	2	0	0	2	1	7	.195	.215	.221	21	-8	0			.935	-2	S-24	-1.0
1920	*Cle-A	23	71	6	14	0	0	0	7	5	6	.197	.250	.197	19	-8	0	1	-1	.979	3	S-21/2-2	-0.4
Total	2	49	148	8	29	2	0	0	9	6	13	.196	.232	.209	20	-16	0	1		.955	1	/S-45,2-2	-1.4

■ TONY LUPIEN   Lupien, Ulysses John b: 4/23/17, Chelmsford, Mass.   BL/TL, 5'10.5", 185 lbs.   Deb: 9/12/40

1940	Bos-A	10	19	5	9	3	2	0	4	1	0	.474	.500	.842	232	4	0	0	0	1.000	-0	/1-8	0.3
1942	Bos-A	128	463	63	130	25	7	3	70	50	20	.281	.351	.384	103	2	10	12	-4	.992	-7	*1-121	-1.7
1943	Bos-A	154	608	65	155	21	9	4	47	54	23	.255	.317	.339	90	-8	16	9	-1	.993	4	*1-153	-1.5
1944	Phi-N	153	597	82	169	23	9	5	52	56	29	.283	.347	.377	107	6	18			.992	1	*1-151	-0.1
1945	Phi-N	15	54	1	17	1	0	0	3	6	0	.315	.383	.333	103	1	2			1.000	3	1-15	0.2
1948	Chi-A	154	617	69	152	19	3	6	54	74	38	.246	.327	.316	74	-23	11	7	-1	.993	-4	*1-154	-2.8
Total	6	614	2358	285	632	92	30	18	230	241	111	.268	.337	.355	94	-19	57	28		.993	-4	1-602	-5.6

■ AL LUPLOW   Luplow, Alvin David b: 3/13/39, Saginaw, Mich.   BL/TR, 5'11", 180 lbs.   Deb: 9/16/61

1961	Cle-A	5	18	0	1	0	0	0	2	1	6	.056	.150	.056	-44	-4	0	0	0	1.000	2	/O-5	-0.3
1962	Cle-A	97	318	54	88	15	3	14	45	36	44	.277	.361	.475	127	12	1	0	0	.960	-3	O-86	0.5
1963	Cle-A	100	295	34	69	6	2	7	27	33	62	.234	.317	.339	85	-6	4	4	-1	.994	3	O-85	-0.8
1964	Cle-A	19	18	1	2	0	0	0	0	1	8	.111	.158	.111	-24	-3	0	0	0	1.000	-1	/O-5	-0.4

YEAR	TM/L	G	AB	R	H	2B	3B	HR	RBI	BB	SO	AVG	OBP	SLG	PRO+	BR/A	SB	CS	SBR	FA	FR	G/POS	TPR
1965	Cle-A	53	45	3	6	2	0	1	4	3	14	.133	.188	.244	22	-5	0	1	-1	1.000	-2	/O-6	-0.7
1966	NY-N	111	334	31	84	9	1	7	31	38	46	.251	.332	.347	91	-3	2	6	-3	.987	-12	*O-101	-2.4
1967	NY-N	41	112	11	23	1	0	3	9	8	19	.205	.264	.295	61	-6	0	0	0	.966	-4	O-33	-1.2
	Pit-N	55	103	13	19	1	0	1	8	6	14	.184	.236	.223	32	-9	1	0	0	.961	3	O-25	-0.8
	Yr	96	215	24	42	2	0	4	17	14	33	.195	.251	.260	47	-15	1	0	0	.963	-1	O-58	-2.0
Total	7	481	1243	147	292	34	6	33	125	127	213	.235	.312	.352	85	-23	8	11	-4	.977	-14	O-346	-6.1

■ SCOTT LUSADER
Lusader, Scott Edward b: 9/30/64, Chicago, Ill. BL/TL, 5'10", 165 lbs. Deb: 9/1/87

YEAR	TM/L	G	AB	R	H	2B	3B	HR	RBI	BB	SO	AVG	OBP	SLG	PRO+	BR/A	SB	CS	SBR	FA	FR	G/POS	TPR
1987	Det-A	23	47	8	15	3	1	1	8	5	7	.319	.385	.489	135	2	1	0	0	.967	-5	O-22/D-1	-0.2
1988	Det-A	16	16	3	1	0	0	1	3	1	4	.063	.118	.250	-0	-2	0	0	0	1.000	-1	O-4	-0.4
1989	Det-A	40	103	15	26	4	0	1	8	9	21	.252	.313	.320	81	-3	3	0	1	.933	-6	O-33/D-1	-0.8
1990	Det-A	45	87	13	21	2	0	2	16	12	8	.241	.333	.333	86	-1	0	0	0	.982	-7	O-42/D-2	-0.9
1991	NY-A	11	7	2	1	0	0	0	1	1	3	.143	.250	.143	12	-1	1	1	-1	1.000	-1	/O-4,D-1	-0.3
Total	5	135	260	41	64	9	1	5	36	28	43	.246	.319	.346	86	-5	4	1	1	.961	-20	O-105/D-5	-2.6

■ ERNIE LUSH
Lush, Ernest Benjamin b: 10/31/1884, Bridgeport, Conn. d: 2/26/37, Detroit, Mich. BR/TL, Deb: 4/20/10 F

YEAR	TM/L	G	AB	R	H	2B	3B	HR	RBI	BB	SO	AVG	OBP	SLG	PRO+	BR/A	SB	CS	SBR	FA	FR	G/POS	TPR
1910	StL-N	1	4	0	0	0	0	0	0	0	1	.000	.200	.000	-42	-1				1.000	-0	/O-1	-0.1

■ JOHNNY LUSH
Lush, John Charles b: 10/8/1885, Williamsport, Pa. d: 11/18/46, Beverly Hills, Cal BL/TL, 5'9.5", 165 lbs. Deb: 4/22/04

YEAR	TM/L	G	AB	R	H	2B	3B	HR	RBI	BB	SO	AVG	OBP	SLG	PRO+	BR/A	SB	CS	SBR	FA	FR	G/POS	TPR
1904	Phi-N	106	369	39	102	22	3	2	42	27		.276	.336	.369	122	9	12			.950	-10	1-62,O-33/P	-0.5
1905	Phi-N	6	16	3	5	0	0	0	1	1		.313	.389	.313	114	0	0			.667	-1	/O-3,P-2	-0.1
1906	Phi-N	76	212	28	56	7	1	0	15	14		.264	.310	.307	92	-2	6			.907	5	P-37,O-22/1	0.0
1907	Phi-N	17	40	4	8	1	1	0	5	1		.200	.220	.275	56	-2	1			1.000	0	/P-8,O-4	-0.2
	StL-N	27	82	6	23	2	3	0	5	5		.280	.322	.378	123	2	4			.917	-1	P-20/O-7	-0.3
	Yr	44	122	11	31	3	4	0	10	6		.254	.289	.344	101	-0	5			.941	-3	P-28,O-11	-0.5
1908	StL-N	45	89	7	15	2	0	0	2	7		.169	.229	.191	36	-6	1			.926	0	P-38	0.0
1909	StL-N	45	92	11	22	5	0	0	14	6		.239	.293	.293	87	-2	2			.945	-1	P-34/O-3	-0.1
1910	StL-N	47	93	8	21	1	3	0	10	8	11	.226	.287	.301	74	-3	2			.928	-2	P-36	0.0
Total	7	369	993	107	252	40	11	2	94	69	11	.254	.307	.322	98	-4	28			.926	-12	P-182/O-72,1	-1.2

■ BILLY LUSH
Lush, William Lucas b: 11/10/1873, Bridgeport, Conn. d: 8/28/51, Hawthorne, N.Y. BB/TR, 5'8", 165 lbs. Deb: 9/3/1895 F

YEAR	TM/L	G	AB	R	H	2B	3B	HR	RBI	BB	SO	AVG	OBP	SLG	PRO+	BR/A	SB	CS	SBR	FA	FR	G/POS	TPR
1895	Was-N	5	18	2	6	0	0	0	2	2	1	.333	.400	.333	92	-0	0			.692	-1	/O-5	-0.1
1896	Was-N	97	352	74	87	9	11	4	45	66	49	.247	.369	.369	95	-1	28			.885	-2	*O-91/2-3	-0.9
1897	Was-N	3	12	1	0	0	0	0	0	2		.000	.143	.000	-61	-3	0			1.000	1	/O-3	-0.2
1901	Bos-N	7	22	5	2	1	1	0	3	3		.185	.267	.264	58	-2	0			.960	3	/O-7	0.0
1902	Bos-N	120	413	68	92	8	1	2	19	76		.223	.346	.262	87	-2	30			.952	11	*O-116/3-1	0.0
1903	Det-A	119	423	71	116	18	14	1	33	70		.274	.379	.390	135	21	14			.968	12	*O-101,3-12/2S	2.8
1904	Cle-A	138	477	76	123	13	8	1	50	72		.258	.359	.325	118	13	12			.959	3	*O-138	0.9
Total	7	489	1722	294	429	49	35	8	152	291	50	.249	.360	.332	107	27	84			.943	24	O-461/3-13,2S	2.6

■ CHARLIE LUSKEY
Luskey, Charles Melton b: 4/6/1876, Washington, D.C. d: 12/20/62, Bethesda, Md. BR/TR, 5'7", 165 lbs. Deb: 9/12/01

YEAR	TM/L	G	AB	R	H	2B	3B	HR	RBI	BB	SO	AVG	OBP	SLG	PRO+	BR/A	SB	CS	SBR	FA	FR	G/POS	TPR
1901	Was-A	11	41	8	8	3	1	0	3	2		.195	.233	.317	52	-3	0			.818	-1	/O-8,C-3	-0.4

■ LUKE LUTENBERG
Lutenberg, Charles William b: 10/4/1864, Quincy, Ill. d: 12/24/38, Quincy, Ill. BR/TR, 6'2", 225 lbs. Deb: 7/7/1894

YEAR	TM/L	G	AB	R	H	2B	3B	HR	RBI	BB	SO	AVG	OBP	SLG	PRO+	BR/A	SB	CS	SBR	FA	FR	G/POS	TPR
1894	Lou-N	69	250	42	48	10	4	0	23	23	21	.192	.284	.264	35	-27	4			.977	1	1-67/2-2	-1.9

■ LYLE LUTTRELL
Luttrell, Lyle Kenneth b: 2/22/30, Bloomington, Ill. d: 7/11/84, Chattanooga, Tenn BR/TR, 6', 180 lbs. Deb: 5/15/56

YEAR	TM/L	G	AB	R	H	2B	3B	HR	RBI	BB	SO	AVG	OBP	SLG	PRO+	BR/A	SB	CS	SBR	FA	FR	G/POS	TPR
1956	Was-A	38	122	17	23	5	3	2	9	8	19	.189	.256	.328	53	-9	5	1	1	.939	-7	S-37	-1.1
1957	Was-A	19	45	4	9	4	0	0	5	3	8	.200	.250	.289	47	-3	0	0	0	.927	-5	S-17	-0.8
Total	2	57	167	21	32	9	3	2	14	11	27	.192	.254	.317	52	-12	5	1	1	.936	-12	/S-54	-1.9

■ RED LUTZ
Lutz, Louis William b: 12/17/1898, Cincinnati, Ohio d: 2/22/84, Cincinnati, Ohio BR/TR, 5'10", 170 lbs. Deb: 5/31/22

YEAR	TM/L	G	AB	R	H	2B	3B	HR	RBI	BB	SO	AVG	OBP	SLG	PRO+	BR/A	SB	CS	SBR	FA	FR	G/POS	TPR
1922	Cin-N	1	1	0	1	1	0	0	0	0	0	1.000	1.000	2.000	669	1	0	0	0	.000	0	/C-1	0.1

■ JOE LUTZ
Lutz, Rollin Joseph b: 2/18/25, Keokuk, Iowa BL/TL, 6', 195 lbs. Deb: 4/17/51 C

YEAR	TM/L	G	AB	R	H	2B	3B	HR	RBI	BB	SO	AVG	OBP	SLG	PRO+	BR/A	SB	CS	SBR	FA	FR	G/POS	TPR
1951	StL-A	14	36	7	6	0	1	0	2	6	9	.167	.286	.222	38	-3	0	0	0	1.000	-1	1-11	-0.5

■ RUBE LUTZKE
Lutzke, Walter John b: 11/17/1897, Milwaukee, Wis. d: 3/6/38, Granville, Wis. BR/TR, 5'11", 175 lbs. Deb: 4/18/23

YEAR	TM/L	G	AB	R	H	2B	3B	HR	RBI	BB	SO	AVG	OBP	SLG	PRO+	BR/A	SB	CS	SBR	FA	FR	G/POS	TPR
1923	Cle-A	143	511	71	131	20	6	3	65	59	57	.256	.338	.337	78	-16	9	6	-1	.940	20	*3-143	1.6
1924	Cle-A	106	341	37	83	18	3	0	42	38	46	.243	.328	.314	65	-17	4	0	1	.947	19	*3-103/2-3	1.0
1925	Cle-A	81	238	31	52	9	0	1	16	26	29	.218	.295	.269	44	-20	2	4	-2	.936	-1	3-69,2-10	-1.7
1926	Cle-A	142	475	42	124	28	6	0	59	34	35	.261	.313	.345	71	-21	6	3	0	.960	-1	*3-142	-1.2
1927	Cle-A	100	311	35	78	12	3	0	41	22	29	.251	.307	.309	60	-19	2	1	0	.938	6	3-98	-0.8
Total	5	572	1876	216	468	87	18	4	223	179	196	.249	.319	.321	66	-93	23	14	-2	.945	45	3-555/2-13	-1.1

■ GREG LUZINSKI
Luzinski, Gregory Michael b: 11/22/50, Chicago, Ill. BR/TR, 6'1", 225 lbs. Deb: 9/9/70 C

YEAR	TM/L	G	AB	R	H	2B	3B	HR	RBI	BB	SO	AVG	OBP	SLG	PRO+	BR/A	SB	CS	SBR	FA	FR	G/POS	TPR
1970	Phi-N	8	12	0	2	0	0	0	0	3	5	.167	.333	.167	39	-1	0	1	-1	1.000	1	/1-3	-0.1
1971	Phi-N	28	100	13	30	8	0	3	15	12	32	.300	.386	.470	141	6	2	0	1	.996	6	1-28	1.1
1972	Phi-N	150	563	66	158	33	5	18	68	42	114	.281	.334	.453	119	12	0	4	-2	.960	1	*O-145/1-2	0.4
1973	Phi-N	161	610	76	174	26	4	29	97	51	135	.285	.347	.484	125	19	3	3	-1	.993	-2	*O-159	0.9
1974	Phi-N	85	302	29	82	14	1	7	48	29	76	.272	.335	.394	99	-0	3	0	1	.981	-2	O-82	0.3
1975	Phi-N★	161	596	85	179	35	3	34	120	89	151	.300	.398	.540	152	43	3	6	-3	.966	-7	*O-159	2.8
1976	*Phi-N★	149	533	74	162	28	1	21	95	50	107	.304	.375	.478	137	26	1	2	-1	.964	-8	*O-144	1.2
1977	*Phi-N★	149	554	99	171	35	4	39	130	80	140	.309	.399	.594	155	43	3	2	-0	.964	-5	*O-148	3.2
1978	*Phi-N★	155	540	85	143	32	2	35	101	100	135	.265	.390	.526	152	40	8	7	-2	.984	-7	*O-154	2.6
1979	Phi-N	137	452	47	114	23	1	18	81	56	103	.252	.347	.427	107	5	3	3	-1	.946	-15	*O-125	-1.7
1980	*Phi-N	106	368	44	84	19	1	19	56	60	100	.228	.346	.440	112	6	3	0	1	.993	-12	*O-105	-0.9
1981	Chi-A	104	378	55	100	15	1	21	62	58	80	.265	.367	.476	144	22	1	1	-0	.000	0	*D-103	1.9
1982	Chi-A	159	583	87	170	37	1	18	102	89	120	.292	.391	.451	130	27	2	1	-0	.000	0	*D-156	2.1
1983	*Chi-A	144	502	73	128	26	1	32	95	70	117	.255	.358	.502	129	20	2	1	-0	1.000	0	*D-139/1-2	1.5
1984	Chi-A	125	412	47	98	13	0	13	58	56	80	.238	.333	.364	89	-5	2	1	1	1.000	0	*D-114	1.5
Total	15	1821	6505	880	1795	344	24	307	1128	845	1495	.276	.366	.478	129	262	37	31	-8	.972	-40	*O-1221,D-512/1	14.6

■ MITCH LYDEN
Lyden, Mitchell Scott b: 12/14/64, Portland, Ore. BR/TR, 6'3", 225 lbs. Deb: 6/16/93

YEAR	TM/L	G	AB	R	H	2B	3B	HR	RBI	BB	SO	AVG	OBP	SLG	PRO+	BR/A	SB	CS	SBR	FA	FR	G/POS	TPR
1993	Fla-N	6	10	2	3	0	0	1	1	0	3	.300	.300	.600	127	0	0	0	0	1.000	-1	/C-2	-0.1

■ SCOTT LYDY
Lydy, Donald Scott b: 10/26/68, Mesa, Ariz. BR/TR, 6'5", 195 lbs. Deb: 5/18/93

YEAR	TM/L	G	AB	R	H	2B	3B	HR	RBI	BB	SO	AVG	OBP	SLG	PRO+	BR/A	SB	CS	SBR	FA	FR	G/POS	TPR
1993	Oak-A	41	102	11	23	5	0	2	7	8	39	.225	.288	.333	71	-4	2	0	1	.958	-2	O-38/D-2	-0.6

■ JERRY LYNCH
Lynch, Gerald Thomas b: 7/17/30, Bay City, Mich. BL/TR, 6'1", 189 lbs. Deb: 4/15/54

YEAR	TM/L	G	AB	R	H	2B	3B	HR	RBI	BB	SO	AVG	OBP	SLG	PRO+	BR/A	SB	CS	SBR	FA	FR	G/POS	TPR
1954	Pit-N	98	284	27	68	4	5	8	36	20	43	.239	.292	.373	73	-12	2	2	-1	.965	-4	O-83	-2.0
1955	Pit-N	88	282	43	80	18	6	5	28	22	33	.284	.336	.433	106	2	2	2	-1	.950	-2	O-71/C-2	-0.4
1956	Pit-N	19	19	1	3	1	0	0	2	1	4	.158	.200	.263	24	-2	0	0	0	1.000	-1	/O-1	-0.2
1957	Cin-N	67	124	11	32	4	1	4	13	6	18	.258	.292	.403	79	-4	0	0	0	1.000	-2	O-24/C-2	-0.7
1958	Cin-N	122	420	58	131	20	5	16	68	18	54	.312	.340	.498	112	8	1	4	-2	.970	-7	*O-101	-0.8
1959	Cin-N	117	379	49	102	16	3	17	58	29	50	.269	.323	.462	103	1	2	0	1	.979	2	O-98	-0.2

YEAR	TM/L	G	AB	R	H	2B	3B	HR	RBI	BB	SO	AVG	OBP	SLG	PRO+	BR/A	SB	CS	SBR	FA	FR	G/POS	TPR
1960	Cin-N	102	159	23	46	8	2	6	27	16	25	.289	.358	.478	124	5	0	0	0	.913	-4	O-32	0.0
1961	*Cin-N	96	181	33	57	13	2	13	50	27	25	.315	.407	.624	166	17	2	2	-1	.948	-4	O-44	1.0
1962	Cin-N	114	288	41	81	15	4	12	57	24	38	.281	.339	.486	115	5	3	3	-1	.970	-0	O-73	0.0
1963	Cin-N	22	32	5	8	3	0	2	9	1	5	.250	.294	.531	129	1	0	0	0	1.000	-1	/O-7	-0.1
	Pit-N	88	237	26	63	6	3	10	36	22	28	.266	.331	.443	120	6	0	1	-1	.960	-6	O-64	-0.4
	Yr	110	269	31	71	9	3	12	45	23	33	.264	.327	.454	121	7	0	1	-1	.962	-7	O-71	-0.5
1964	Pit-N	114	297	35	81	14	2	16	66	26	57	.273	.333	.495	130	11	0	1	-1	.983	-13	O-78	-0.6
1965	Pit-N	73	121	7	34	1	0	5	16	8	26	.281	.331	.413	108	1	0	2	-1	.903	-3	O-26	-0.5
1966	Pit-N	64	56	5	12	1	0	1	6	4	10	.214	.267	.286	54	-3	0	0	0	1.000	-0	/O-4	-0.4
Total	13	1184	2879	364	798	123	34	115	470	224	416	.277	.331	.463	110	34	12	17	-7	.964	-46	O-706/C-4	-5.3

■ HENRY LYNCH
Lynch, Henry W.   b: 4/8/1866, Worcester, Mass.   d: 11/23/25, Worcester, Mass.   5'7", 143 lbs.   Deb: 9/21/1893

YEAR	TM/L	G	AB	R	H	2B	3B	HR	RBI	BB	SO	AVG	OBP	SLG	PRO+	BR/A	SB	CS	SBR	FA	FR	G/POS	TPR
1893	Chi-N	4	14	0	3	2	0	0	2	1	1	.214	.267	.357	66	-1	0			.833	-1	/O-4	-0.2

■ DANNY LYNCH
Lynch, Matt Dan "Dummy"   b: 2/7/26, Dallas, Tex.   d: 6/30/78, Plano, Tex.   BR/TR, 5'11", 174 lbs.   Deb: 9/14/48

YEAR	TM/L	G	AB	R	H	2B	3B	HR	RBI	BB	SO	AVG	OBP	SLG	PRO+	BR/A	SB	CS	SBR	FA	FR	G/POS	TPR
1948	Chi-N	7	7	3	2	0	0	1	1	1	1	.286	.375	.714	197	1	0			1.000	0	/2-1	0.1

■ MIKE LYNCH
Lynch, Michael Joseph   b: 9/10/1875, St.Paul, Minn.   d: 4/1/47, Jennings Lodge, Ore   TR, 5'10", 155 lbs.   Deb: 4/24/02

YEAR	TM/L	G	AB	R	H	2B	3B	HR	RBI	BB	SO	AVG	OBP	SLG	PRO+	BR/A	SB	CS	SBR	FA	FR	G/POS	TPR
1902	Chi-N	7	28	4	4	0	0	0	0	2		.143	.200	.143	6	-3	0			.929	-1	/O-7	-0.5

■ TOM LYNCH
Lynch, Thomas James   b: 4/3/1860, Bennington, Vt.   d: 3/28/55, Cohoes, N.Y.   BL/TR, 5'10.5", 170 lbs.   Deb: 8/18/1884   U

YEAR	TM/L	G	AB	R	H	2B	3B	HR	RBI	BB	SO	AVG	OBP	SLG	PRO+	BR/A	SB	CS	SBR	FA	FR	G/POS	TPR
1884	Wil-U	16	58	6	16	3	1	0			5	.276	.333	.362	86	-1				.846	-3	/C-8,O-8,1	-0.3
	Phi-N	13	48	7	15	4	2	0	3	4	5	.313	.365	.479	171	4				.860	-2	/C-7,O-7	0.3
1885	Phi-N	13	53	7	10	3	0	0	1	10	3	.189	.317	.245	86	-0				.838	3	O-13	0.2
Total	2	42	159	20	41	10	3	0	4	19	8	.258	.337	.358	110	3				.887	-2	/O-28,C-15,1	0.2

■ WALT LYNCH
Lynch, Walter Edward "Jabber"   b: 4/15/1897, Buffalo, N.Y.   d: 12/21/76, Daytona Beach, Fla   TR, 6', 176 lbs.   Deb: 7/8/22

YEAR	TM/L	G	AB	R	H	2B	3B	HR	RBI	BB	SO	AVG	OBP	SLG	PRO+	BR/A	SB	CS	SBR	FA	FR	G/POS	TPR
1922	Bos-A	3	2	1	1	0	0	0	0	0	0	.500	.500	.500	163	0	0	0	0	1.000	0	/C-3	0.0

■ BYRD LYNN
Lynn, Byrd "Birdie"   b: 3/13/1889, Unionville, Ill.   d: 2/5/40, Napa, Cal.   BR/TR, 5'11", 165 lbs.   Deb: 4/16/16

YEAR	TM/L	G	AB	R	H	2B	3B	HR	RBI	BB	SO	AVG	OBP	SLG	PRO+	BR/A	SB	CS	SBR	FA	FR	G/POS	TPR
1916	Chi-A	31	40	4	9	1	0	0	3	4	7	.225	.311	.250	68	-1	2			.952	8	C-13	0.8
1917	*Chi-A	35	72	7	16	2	0	0	5	7	11	.222	.300	.250	67	-3	1			.959	-2	C-29	-0.3
1918	Chi-A	5	8	0	2	0	0	0	0	2	1	.250	.400	.250	95	0	0			1.000	-1	/C-4	-0.1
1919	*Chi-A	29	66	4	15	4	0	0	4	4	9	.227	.271	.288	57	-4	0			.982	1	C-28	-0.2
1920	Chi-A	16	25	0	8	2	1	0	3	1	3	.320	.346	.480	117	0	0	0	0	1.000	-1	C-14	0.0
Total	5	116	211	15	50	9	1	0	15	18	31	.237	.303	.289	72	-7	3	0		.969	5	/C-88	0.2

■ FRED LYNN
Lynn, Fredric Michael   b: 2/3/52, Chicago, Ill.   BL/TL, 6'1", 190 lbs.   Deb: 9/5/74

YEAR	TM/L	G	AB	R	H	2B	3B	HR	RBI	BB	SO	AVG	OBP	SLG	PRO+	BR/A	SB	CS	SBR	FA	FR	G/POS	TPR
1974	Bos-A	15	43	5	18	2	2	2	10	6	6	.419	.500	.698	226	7	0	0	0	1.000	-0	O-12/D-1	0.6
1975	*Bos-A★	145	528	103	175	47	7	21	105	62	90	.331	.405	.566	158	40	10	5	0	.983	13	*O-144	4.7
1976	Bos-A★	132	507	76	159	32	8	10	65	48	67	.314	.374	.467	130	18	14	9	-1	.984	14	*O-128/D-5	2.6
1977	Bos-A★	129	497	81	129	29	5	18	76	51	63	.260	.332	.447	98	-2	2	3	-1	.994	8	*O-125/D-1	-0.1
1978	Bos-A★	150	541	75	161	33	3	22	82	75	50	.298	.384	.492	131	22	3	6	-3	.984	8	*O-149	2.1
1979	Bos-A★	147	531	116	177	42	1	39	122	82	79	.333	.426	.637	173	55	2	2	-1	.987	7	*O-143	5.2
1980	Bos-A★	110	415	67	125	32	3	12	61	58	39	.301	.387	.480	129	18	12	0	4	.994	9	*O-110	2.5
1981	Cal-A★	76	256	28	56	8	1	5	31	38	42	.219	.327	.316	86	-4	1	2	-1	.978	1	O-69	-0.6
1982	*Cal-A★	138	472	89	141	38	1	21	86	58	72	.299	.379	.517	143	28	7	8	-3	.991	-3	*O-133	1.9
1983	Cal-A★	117	437	56	119	20	3	22	74	55	83	.272	.356	.483	130	18	2	2	-1	.993	-2	*O-113/D-2	1.2
1984	Cal-A	142	517	84	140	28	4	23	79	77	97	.271	.367	.474	132	23	2	2	-1	.982	-10	*O-140	0.9
1985	Bal-A	124	448	59	118	12	1	23	68	53	100	.263	.343	.449	118	11	7	3	0	.994	2	*O-123	0.9
1986	Bal-A	112	397	67	114	13	1	23	67	53	59	.287	.374	.490	137	21	2	2	-1	.984	-4	*O-107/D-1	1.3
1987	Bal-A	111	396	49	100	24	0	23	60	39	72	.253	.321	.487	113	6	3	7	-3	.991	-3	*O-101/D-8	-0.3
1988	Bal-A	87	301	37	76	13	1	18	37	28	66	.252	.316	.482	123	8	2	2	-1	.991	0	O-83/D-2	0.6
	Det-A	27	90	9	20	1	0	7	19	5	16	.222	.271	.467	106	0	0	0	0	1.000	0	O-22/D-3	0.0
	Yr	114	391	46	96	14	1	25	56	33	82	.246	.306	.478	120	8	2	2	-1	.992	1	*O-105/D-5	0.6
1989	Det-A	117	353	44	85	11	1	11	46	47	71	.241	.332	.371	100	1	1	1	-0	.992	-1	O-68,D-46	-0.3
1990	SD-N	90	196	18	47	3	1	6	23	24	44	.240	.320	.357	85	-4	2	0	1	1.000	-4	O-55	-0.9
Total	17	1969	6925	1063	1960	388	43	306	1111	857	1116	.283	.364	.484	129	266	72	54	-11	.988	35	*O-1825/D-69	22.3

■ JERRY LYNN
Lynn, Jerome Edward   b: 4/14/16, Scranton, Pa.   d: 9/25/72, Scranton, Pa.   BR/TR, 5'10", 164 lbs.   Deb: 9/19/37

YEAR	TM/L	G	AB	R	H	2B	3B	HR	RBI	BB	SO	AVG	OBP	SLG	PRO+	BR/A	SB	CS	SBR	FA	FR	G/POS	TPR
1937	Was-A	1	3	0	2	1	0	0	0	0	0	.667	.667	1.000	329	1	0	0	0	1.000	1	/2-1	0.2

■ RUSS LYON
Lyon, Russell Mayo   b: 6/26/13, Ball Ground, Ga.   d: 12/24/75, Charleston, S.C.   BR/TR, 6'1", 230 lbs.   Deb: 4/21/44

YEAR	TM/L	G	AB	R	H	2B	3B	HR	RBI	BB	SO	AVG	OBP	SLG	PRO+	BR/A	SB	CS	SBR	FA	FR	G/POS	TPR
1944	Cle-A	7	11	1	2	0	0	0	1	1	1	.182	.250	.182	25	-1	0	0	0	.909	0	/C-3	-0.1

■ BARRY LYONS
Lyons, Barry Stephen   b: 6/3/60, Biloxi, Miss.   BR/TR, 6'1", 205 lbs.   Deb: 4/19/86

YEAR	TM/L	G	AB	R	H	2B	3B	HR	RBI	BB	SO	AVG	OBP	SLG	PRO+	BR/A	SB	CS	SBR	FA	FR	G/POS	TPR
1986	NY-N	6	9	1	0	0	0	0	2	1	2	.000	.100	.000	-72	-2	0	0	0	.941	0	/C-3	-0.2
1987	NY-N	53	130	15	33	4	1	4	24	8	24	.254	.307	.392	88	-3	0	0	0	.984	0	C-49	0.0
1988	NY-N	50	91	5	21	7	1	0	11	3	12	.231	.255	.330	70	-4	0	0	0	.979	-2	C-32/1-1	-0.5
1989	NY-N	79	235	15	58	13	1	3	27	11	28	.247	.286	.340	82	-6	0	1	-1	.980	1	C-76	-0.2
1990	NY-N	24	80	8	19	0	0	2	9	2	7	.237	.265	.313	58	-5	0	0	0	.980	3	C-23	0.0
	LA-N	3	5	1	1	0	0	1	2	0	1	.200	.200	.800	166	0	0	0	0	1.000	-1	/C-2	0.0
	Yr	27	85	9	20	0	0	3	9	2	10	.235	.261	.341	65	-5	0	0	0	.980	3	C-25	0.0
1991	LA-N	9	9	0	0	0	0	0	0	0	2	.000	.000	.000	-99	-2	0	0	0	1.000	-1	/C-6	-0.1
	Cal-A	2	5	0	1	0	0	0	0	0	0	.200	.200	.200	11	-1	0	0	0	1.000	0	/1-2	-0.1
Total	6	226	564	45	133	24	2	10	73	25	78	.236	.274	.339	73	-22	0	1	-1	.980	3	C-191/1-3	-1.1

■ DENNY LYONS
Lyons, Dennis Patrick Aloysius   b: 3/12/1866, Cincinnati, Ohio   d: 1/2/29, W.Covington, Ky.   BR/TR, 5'10", 185 lbs.   Deb: 9/18/1885

YEAR	TM/L	G	AB	R	H	2B	3B	HR	RBI	BB	SO	AVG	OBP	SLG	PRO+	BR/A	SB	CS	SBR	FA	FR	G/POS	TPR
1885	Pro-N	4	16	3	2	1	0	0	1	0	3	.125	.125	.188	-0	-2				.824	-0	/3-4	-0.2
1886	Phi-a	32	123	22	26	3	1	0		8		.211	.281	.252	67	-5	7			.807	-7	3-32	-0.9
1887	Phi-a	137	570	128	209	43	14	6		47		.367	.421	.523	162	47	73			.866	-6	*3-137	3.5
1888	Phi-a	111	456	93	135	22	5	6	83	41		.296	.363	.406	147	25	39			.878	-13	*3-111	1.2
1889	Phi-a	131	510	135	168	36	4	9	82	79	44	.329	.426	.469	157	41	10			.860	9	3-130/1-1	4.5
1890	Phi-a	88	339	79	120	29	5	7		57		.354	.461	.531	197	44	21			.909	9	3-88	4.8
1891	StL-a	120	451	124	142	24	3	11	84	88	58	.315	.445	.455	137	22	9			.871	-6	*3-120	1.8
1892	NY-N	108	389	71	100	16	7	8	51	59	36	.257	.359	.396	130	15	11			.871	-6	*3-108	1.3
1893	Pit-N	131	490	103	150	19	16	3	105	97	29	.306	.430	.429	131	27	19			.918	-5	*3-131	2.8
1894	Pit-N	71	254	51	82	14	4	4	50	42	12	.323	.427	.457	114	8	14			.898	7	3-71	1.1
1895	StL-N	33	129	24	38	6	0	2	25	14	5	.295	.377	.388	99	0	3			.894	-5	3-33	-0.3
1896	Pit-N	118	436	77	134	25	6	4	71	67	25	.307	.406	.420	123	17	13			.893	-15	*3-116	-0.2
1897	Pit-N	37	131	22	27	6	4	2	17	22		.206	.346	.359	89	-1	5			.989	-1	1-35/3-2	-0.2
Total	13	1121	4294	932	1333	244	69	62	569	621	212	.310	.407	.443	139	237	224			.882	-27	*3-1083/1-36	19.8

■ ED LYONS
Lyons, Edward Hoyte "Mouse"   b: 5/12/23, Winston-Salem, N.C   BR/TR, 5'9", 165 lbs.   Deb: 9/15/47   C

YEAR	TM/L	G	AB	R	H	2B	3B	HR	RBI	BB	SO	AVG	OBP	SLG	PRO+	BR/A	SB	CS	SBR	FA	FR	G/POS	TPR
1947	Was-A	7	26	2	4	0	0	0	0	2	2	.154	.214	.154	3	-3	0	0	0	1.000	4	/2-7	0.1

YEAR	TM/L	G	AB	R	H	2B	3B	HR	RBI	BB	SO	AVG	OBP	SLG	PRO+	BR/A	SB	CS	SBR	FA	FR	G/POS	TPR

■ HARRY LYONS   Lyons, Harry P.   b: 3/25/1866, Chester, Pa.   d: 6/30/12, Mauricetown, N.J.   BR/TR, 5'10.5", 157 lbs.   Deb: 8/29/1887

YEAR	TM/L	G	AB	R	H	2B	3B	HR	RBI	BB	SO	AVG	OBP	SLG	PRO+	BR/A	SB	CS	SBR	FA	FR	G/POS	TPR
1887	Phi-N	1	4	0	0	0	0	0	0	1	0	.000	.200	.000	-38	-1	0			.500	-0	/O-1	-0.1
	*StL-a	2	8	2	1	0	0	0		0	0	.125	.125	.125	-27	-1	2			1.000	1	/2-1,O-1	-0.1
1888	*StL-a	123	499	66	97	10	5	4	63	20		.194	.230	.259	51	-30	36			.891	6	*O-122/3-2,S2	-2.6
1889	NY-N	5	20	1	2	0	0	0	2	2	0	.100	.182	.200	7	-3	0			1.000	-1	/O-5	-0.3
1890	Roc-a	133	584	83	152	11	11	3		27		.260	.294	.332	91	-9	47			.920	11	*O-132/3-2,CP	-0.2
1892	NY-N	96	411	67	98	5	2	0	53	33	29	.238	.297	.260	70	-14	25			.910	3	O-96	-1.5
1893	NY-N	47	187	27	51	5	2	0	21	14	6	.273	.323	.321	71	-8	10			.917	2	O-47	-0.6
Total	6	407	1713	246	401	31	21	7	139	97	35	.234	.277	.289	69	-66	120			.908	21	O-404/3-4,2PCS	-5.4

■ PAT LYONS   Lyons, Patrick Jerry   b: 3/1860, Canada   d: 1/20/14, Springfield, Ohio   TR ,   Deb: 7/21/1890

YEAR	TM/L	G	AB	R	H	2B	3B	HR	RBI	BB	SO	AVG	OBP	SLG	PRO+	BR/A	SB	CS	SBR	FA	FR	G/POS	TPR
1890	Cle-N	11	38	2	2	1	0	0	1	4	4	.053	.143	.079	-36	-7	0			.839	-5	2-11	-1.0

■ STEVE LYONS   Lyons, Stephen John   b: 6/3/60, Tacoma, Wash.   BL/TR, 6'3", 192 lbs.   Deb: 4/15/85

YEAR	TM/L	G	AB	R	H	2B	3B	HR	RBI	BB	SO	AVG	OBP	SLG	PRO+	BR/A	SB	CS	SBR	FA	FR	G/POS	TPR
1985	Bos-A	133	371	52	98	14	3	5	30	32	64	.264	.324	.358	83	-8	12	9	-2	.973	-8	*O-114/3-1,SD	-2.1
1986	Bos-A	59	124	20	31	7	2	1	14	12	23	.250	.316	.363	84	-3	2	3	-1	.972	-5	O-55	-1.0
	Chi-A	42	123	10	25	2	1	0	6	7	24	.203	.252	.236	33	-11	2	3	-1	.987	1	O-35/3-3,1D	-1.2
	Yr	101	247	30	56	9	3	1	20	19	47	.227	.285	.300	58	-14	4	6	-2	.978	-4	O-90/3-3,1D	-2.2
1987	Chi-A	76	193	26	54	11	1	1	19	12	37	.280	.322	.363	79	-6	3	1	0	.971	11	3-51,O-15/2D	0.4
1988	Chi-A	146	472	59	127	28	3	5	45	32	59	.269	.317	.373	93	-5	1	2	-1	.927	10	*3-128,O-14/2C1	0.3
1989	Chi-A	140	443	51	117	21	3	2	50	35	68	.264	.319	.339	88	-7	9	6	-1	.982	-8	2-70,1-40,30/SCD	-1.7
1990	Chi-A	94	146	22	28	6	1	1	11	10	41	.192	.248	.267	45	-11	1	0	0	.991	-1	1-61,2-15/O3SDP	-1.4
1991	Bos-A	87	212	15	51	10	1	4	17	11	35	.241	.278	.354	70	-9	10	3	1	1.000	0	O-45,2-16,3/1SDP	-0.8
1992	Atl-N	11	14	0	1	0	1	0	1	0	4	.071	.071	.214	-21	-2	0	0	0	1.000	-2	/O-6,2-2	-0.4
	Mon-N	16	13	2	3	0	0	0	1	1	3	.231	.286	.231	48	-1	1	2	-1	1.000	-2	/O-8,1-1	-0.4
	Yr	27	27	2	4	0	1	0	2	1	7	.148	.179	.222	13	-3	1	2	-1	1.000	-3	O-14/2-2,1	-0.8
	Bos-A	21	28	3	7	0	1	0	2	2	1	.250	.300	.321	69	-1	1	1	-1	1.000	-0	/1-8,O-5,2D	-0.2
1993	Bos-A	28	23	4	3	1	0	0	0	2	5	.130	.200	.174	1	-3	1	2	-1	1.000	-1	O-10/2-9,C13D	-0.5
Total	9	853	2162	264	545	100	17	19	196	156	364	.252	.304	.340	77	-67	42	32	-7	.979	-4	O-334,3-229,21/DSCF	-9.0

■ TERRY LYONS   Lyons, Terence Hilbert   b: 12/14/08, New Holland, Ohio   d: 9/9/59, Dayton, Ohio   BR/TR, 6'0.5", 165 lbs.   Deb: 4/19/29

YEAR	TM/L	G	AB	R	H	2B	3B	HR	RBI	BB	SO	AVG	OBP	SLG	PRO+	BR/A	SB	CS	SBR	FA	FR	G/POS	TPR
1929	Phi-N	1	0	0	0	0	0	0	0	0	0	—	—	—	—	0	0			.000	0	/1-1	0.0

■ TED LYONS   Lyons, Theodore Amar   b: 12/28/1900, Lake Charles, La.   d: 7/25/86, Sulphur, La.   BB/TR, 5'11", 200 lbs.   Deb: 7/2/23   MCH

YEAR	TM/L	G	AB	R	H	2B	3B	HR	RBI	BB	SO	AVG	OBP	SLG	PRO+	BR/A	SB	CS	SBR	FA	FR	G/POS	TPR
1923	Chi-A	9	5	0	1	0	0	0	1	1	3	.200	.333	.200	43	-0	0	0	0	1.000	1	/P-9	0.0
1924	Chi-A	41	77	10	17	0	1	0	6	5	13	.221	.277	.247	37	-7	0	0	0	.902	-3	P-41	0.0
1925	Chi-A	43	97	6	18	3	0	0	7	3	13	.186	.218	.216	11	-13	0	0	0	.957	0	P-43	0.0
1926	Chi-A	41	104	7	22	1	1	0	3	1	10	.212	.219	.240	20	-12	0	0	0	.955	4	P-39	0.0
1927	Chi-A	41	110	16	28	6	2	1	9	6	17	.255	.293	.373	74	-5	0	0	0	.979	0	P-39	0.0
1928	Chi-A	49	91	10	23	2	0	0	8	1	9	.253	.261	.275	41	-8	0	0	0	.920	2	P-39	0.0
1929	Chi-A	40	91	7	20	4	0	0	11	9	13	.220	.290	.264	44	-8	0	0	0	.946	2	P-37/O-1	0.0
1930	Chi-A	57	122	20	38	6	3	1	15	2	18	.311	.323	.434	93	-2	0	0	0	.938	3	P-42	0.0
1931	Chi-A	42	33	6	5	0	0	0	3	2	1	.152	.200	.152	-7	-5	0	0	0	.957	-1	P-22	0.0
1932	Chi-A	49	73	11	19	2	1	1	10	4	10	.260	.308	.356	76	-3	0	0	0	.964	-1	P-33	0.0
1933	Chi-A	51	91	11	26	2	1	1	11	4	6	.286	.316	.363	83	-2	0	1	-1	.983	0	P-36	0.0
1934	Chi-A	50	97	9	20	4	0	1	16	3	19	.206	.245	.278	34	-10	0	0	0	.939	2	P-30	0.0
1935	Chi-A	29	82	5	18	4	0	0	6	3	4	.220	.256	.268	35	-8	0	0	0	**1.000**	1	P-23	0.0
1936	Chi-A	26	70	2	11	0	0	0	5	5	12	.157	.213	.157	-7	-12	0	0	0	**1.000**	1	P-26	0.0
1937	Chi-A	23	57	6	12	0	0	0	3	9	14	.211	.318	.211	36	-5	0	0	0	**1.000**	0	P-22	0.0
1938	Chi-A	24	72	9	14	2	0	0	4	2	9	.194	.216	.222	10	-10	0	0	0	.982	2	P-23	0.0
1939	Chi-A☆	21	61	5	18	3	0	0	8	5	7	.295	.348	.344	76	-2	0	0	0	.912	-1	P-21	0.0
1940	Chi-A	22	75	4	18	4	0	0	7	2	7	.240	.260	.293	43	-6	0	0	0	.923	-2	P-22	0.0
1941	Chi-A	22	74	8	20	2	0	0	6	2	6	.270	.289	.297	56	-5	0	0	0	.981	1	P-22	0.0
1942	Chi-A	20	67	10	16	4	0	0	10	3	7	.239	.282	.299	65	-3	0	0	0	.980	1	P-20	0.0
1946	Chi-A	5	14	0	0	0	0	0	0	1	3	.000	.067	.000	-83	-3	0	0	0	1.000	0	/P-5,M	0.0
Total	21	705	1563	162	364	49	9	5	149	73	201	.233	.270	.285	44	-130	0	1	-1	.958	11	P-594/O-1	0.0

■ BILL LYONS   Lyons, William Allen   b: 4/26/58, Alton, Ill.   BR/TR, 6'1", 175 lbs.   Deb: 7/20/83

YEAR	TM/L	G	AB	R	H	2B	3B	HR	RBI	BB	SO	AVG	OBP	SLG	PRO+	BR/A	SB	CS	SBR	FA	FR	G/POS	TPR
1983	StL-N	42	60	3	10	1	1	0	3	1	11	.167	.180	.217	10	-7	3	2	-0	.985	2	2-23/3-8,S	-0.5
1984	StL-N	46	73	13	16	3	0	0	3	9	13	.219	.305	.260	62	-3	3	1	0	.991	14	2-25,S-11/3	1.2
Total	2	88	133	16	26	4	1	0	6	10	24	.195	.252	.241	39	-11	6	3	0	.989	16	/2-48,S-13,3	0.7

■ DAD LYTLE   Lytle, Edward Benson "Pop"   b: 3/10/1862, Racine, Wis.   d: 12/21/50, Long Beach, Cal.   BR/TR, 5'11", 160 lbs.   Deb: 8/11/1890

YEAR	TM/L	G	AB	R	H	2B	3B	HR	RBI	BB	SO	AVG	OBP	SLG	PRO+	BR/A	SB	CS	SBR	FA	FR	G/POS	TPR
1890	Chi-N	1	4	1	0	0	0	0	0	0	1	.000	.000	.000	-96	-1	0			1.000	1	/O-1	0.0
	Pit-N	15	55	2	8	1	0	0	0	8	9	.145	.254	.164	25	-5	0			.837	-6	/2-8,O-7	-1.0
	Yr	16	59	3	8	1	0	0	0	8	10	.136	.239	.153	16	-6	0			.824	-5	/O-8,2-8	-1.0

■ JIM LYTTLE   Lyttle, James Lawrence   b: 5/20/46, Hamilton, Ohio   BL/TR, 6', 186 lbs.   Deb: 5/17/69

YEAR	TM/L	G	AB	R	H	2B	3B	HR	RBI	BB	SO	AVG	OBP	SLG	PRO+	BR/A	SB	CS	SBR	FA	FR	G/POS	TPR
1969	NY-A	28	83	7	15	4	0	0	4	4	19	.181	.218	.229	26	-8	1	1	-1	.983	1	O-28	-1.0
1970	NY-A	87	126	20	39	7	1	3	14	10	26	.310	.360	.452	129	5	3	6	-3	.989	-9	O-70	-0.9
1971	NY-A	49	86	7	17	5	0	1	7	8	18	.198	.274	.291	64	-4	0	2	-1	1.000	-3	O-29	-1.0
1972	Chi-A	44	82	8	19	5	2	0	5	1	28	.232	.241	.341	70	-3	0	1	-1	1.000	-2	O-21	-0.7
1973	Mon-N	49	116	12	30	5	1	4	19	9	14	.259	.312	.422	98	-1	0	2	-1	.974	2	O-36	-0.1
1974	Mon-N	25	9	1	3	0	0	0	2	1	3	.333	.400	.333	101	0	0	0	0	1.000	-6	O-18	-0.6
1975	Mon-N	44	55	7	15	4	0	0	6	13	6	.273	.412	.345	107	1	0	1	-1	1.000	-3	O-16	-0.3
1976	Mon-N	42	85	6	23	4	1	1	8	7	13	.271	.326	.376	95	-1	0	0	0	.977	-3	O-29	-0.4
	LA-N	23	68	3	15	3	0	0	5	8	12	.221	.303	.265	63	-3	0	1	0	1.000	4	O-18	0.0
	Yr	65	153	9	38	7	1	1	13	15	25	.248	.315	.327	81	-4	0	1	-1	.990	1	O-47	-0.4
Total	8	391	710	71	176	37	5	9	70	61	139	.248	.308	.352	86	-14	4	15	-8	.988	-18	O-265	-5.0

■ KEVIN MAAS   Maas, Kevin Christian   b: 1/20/65, Castro Valley, Cal.   BL/TL, 6'3", 195 lbs.   Deb: 6/29/90

YEAR	TM/L	G	AB	R	H	2B	3B	HR	RBI	BB	SO	AVG	OBP	SLG	PRO+	BR/A	SB	CS	SBR	FA	FR	G/POS	TPR
1990	NY-A	79	254	42	64	9	0	21	41	43	76	.252	.367	.535	149	17	1	2	-1	.983	-3	1-57,D-18	0.8
1991	NY-A	148	500	69	110	14	1	23	63	83	128	.220	.333	.390	100	1	5	1	1	.983	-1	*D-109,1-36	-0.6
1992	NY-A	98	286	35	71	12	0	11	35	25	63	.248	.309	.406	99	-1	3	1	0	.986	3	D-62,1-22	-0.7
1993	NY-A	59	151	20	31	4	0	9	25	24	32	.205	.318	.411	97	-1	1	1	-0	.984	-1	D-31,1-17	-0.4
Total	4	384	1191	166	276	39	1	64	164	175	299	.232	.334	.427	110	16	10	5	0	.983	-8	D-220,1-132	-0.9

■ JOHN MABRY   Mabry, John Steven   b: 10/17/70, Wilmington, Del.   BL/TR, 6'4", 195 lbs.   Deb: 4/23/94

YEAR	TM/L	G	AB	R	H	2B	3B	HR	RBI	BB	SO	AVG	OBP	SLG	PRO+	BR/A	SB	CS	SBR	FA	FR	G/POS	TPR
1994	StL-N	6	23	2	7	3	0	0	3	2	4	.304	.360	.435	110	0	0	0	0	1.000	1	/O-6	0.1

■ HARVEY MacDONALD   Mac Donald, Harvey Forsyth   b: 5/18/1898, New York, N.Y.   d: 10/4/65, Manoa, Pa.   BL/TL, 5'11", 170 lbs.   Deb: 6/12/28

YEAR	TM/L	G	AB	R	H	2B	3B	HR	RBI	BB	SO	AVG	OBP	SLG	PRO+	BR/A	SB	CS	SBR	FA	FR	G/POS	TPR
1928	Phi-N	13	16	0	4	0	0	0	2	3		.250	.333	.250	53	-1	0			1.000	-0	/O-2	-0.1

■ MACEY   Macey   b: Columbus, Ohio   Deb: 10/2/1890

YEAR	TM/L	G	AB	R	H	2B	3B	HR	RBI	BB	SO	AVG	OBP	SLG	PRO+	BR/A	SB	CS	SBR	FA	FR	G/POS	TPR
1890	Phi-a	1	1	0	0	0	0	0	0		0	.000	.000	.000	-99	-0	0			1.000	-1	/C-1	-0.1

YEAR	TM/L	G	AB	R	H	2B	3B	HR	RBI	BB	SO	AVG	OBP	SLG	PRO+	BR/A	SB	CS	SBR	FA	FR	G/POS	TPR

■ MIKE MACFARLANE
Macfarlane, Michael Andrew　b: 4/12/64, Stockton, Cal.　BR/TR, 6'1", 200 lbs.　Deb: 7/23/87

1987	KC-A	8	19	0	4	1	0	0	3	2	2	.211	.286	.263	46	-1	0	0	0	1.000	-1	/C-8	-0.2
1988	KC-A	70	211	25	56	15	0	4	26	21	37	.265	.335	.393	102	1	0	0	0	.994	-15	C-68	-0.9
1989	KC-A	69	157	13	35	6	0	2	19	7	27	.223	.265	.299	59	-9	0	0	0	.996	2	C-59/D-4	-0.4
1990	KC-A	124	400	37	102	24	4	6	58	25	69	.255	.310	.380	94	-4	1	0	0	.991	-19	*C-112/D-5	-1.7
1991	KC-A	84	267	34	74	18	2	13	41	17	52	.277	.334	.506	128	9	1	0	0	.993	-12	C-69/D-4	0.2
1992	KC-A	129	402	51	94	28	3	17	48	30	89	.234	.311	.445	107	2	1	5	-3	.993	-1	*C-104/D-13	0.4
1993	KC-A	117	388	55	106	27	0	20	67	40	83	.273	.365	.497	122	12	2	5	-2	.985	3	*C-114	1.8
1994	KC-A	92	314	53	80	17	3	14	47	35	71	.255	.362	.462	102	1	1	0	0	.993	5	C-81/D-8	1.0
Total	8	693	2158	268	551	136	12	76	309	177	430	.255	.330	.435	105	11	6	10	-4	.991	-38	C-615/D-34	0.2

■ ED MacGAMWELL
Mac Gamwell, Edward M.　b: 1/10/1879, Buffalo, N.Y.　d: 5/26/24, Albany, N.Y.　BL/TL,　Deb: 4/14/05

1905	Bro-N	4	16	0	4	0	0	0	0	1		.250	.294	.250	68	-1	0			.951	-1	/1-4	-0.1

■ KEN MACHA
Macha, Kenneth Edward　b: 9/29/50, Monroeville, Pa.　BR/TR, 6'2", 217 lbs.　Deb: 9/14/74　FC

1974	Pit-N	5	5	1	3	1	0	0	1	0	0	.600	.600	.600	300	1	0	0	0	1.000	-0	/C-1	0.1
1977	Pit-N	35	95	2	26	4	0	0	11	6	17	.274	.317	.316	68	-4	1	1	-0	.964	-5	3-17,1-11/O	-1.0
1978	Pit-N	29	52	5	11	1	1	0	5	12	10	.212	.359	.269	75	-1	2	0	1	.970	-3	3-21	-0.4
1979	Mon-N	25	36	8	10	3	1	0	4	2	9	.278	.333	.417	104	0	0	0	0	1.000	-1	3-13/1-2,OC	0.1
1980	Mon-N	49	107	10	31	5	1	1	8	11	17	.290	.361	.383	108	1	0	2	-1	.910	-5	3-33/1-2,CO	-0.6
1981	Tor-A	37	85	4	17	2	0	0	6	8	15	.200	.269	.224	41	-6	1	1	-0	.892	-1	3-19,1-16/CD	-0.9
Total	6	180	380	30	98	16	3	1	35	39	68	.258	.330	.324	80	-9	4	4	-1	.938	-13	3-103/1-31,OCD	-2.7

■ MIKE MACHA
Macha, Michael William　b: 2/17/54, Victoria, Tex.　BR/TR, 5'11", 180 lbs.　Deb: 4/20/79　F

1979	Atl-N	6	13	2	2	0	0	0	1	1	5	.154	.214	.154	2	-2	0	0	0	.769	0	/3-3	-0.1
1980	Tor-A	5	8	0	0	0	0	0	0	0	1	.000	.000	.000	-96	-2	0	0	0	.778	1	/3-2,C-1	-0.2
Total	2	11	21	2	2	0	0	0	1	1	6	.095	.136	.095	-33	-4	0	0	0	.773	1	/3-5,C-1	-0.3

■ DAVE MACHEMER
Machemer, David Ritchie　b: 5/24/51, St.Joseph, Mo.　BR/TR, 5'11.5", 180 lbs.　Deb: 6/21/78

1978	Cal-A	10	22	6	6	1	0	1	2	2	1	.273	.333	.455	124	1	0	1	-1	1.000	-2	/2-5,3-3,S	-0.2
1979	Det-A	19	26	8	5	1	0	0	2	3	2	.192	.276	.231	37	-2	0	3	-2	.972	4	2-11/O-1	0.0
Total	2	29	48	14	11	2	0	1	4	5	3	.229	.302	.333	74	-2	0	4	-2	.978	2	/2-16,3-3,OS	-0.2

■ CONNIE MACK
Mack, Cornelius Alexander "The Tall Tactician" (b: Cornelius Alexander McGillicuddy)
b: 12/22/1862, E.Brookfield, Mass　d: 2/8/56, Philadelphia, Pa.　BR/TR, 6'1", 150 lbs.　Deb: 9/11/1886　FMH

1886	Was-N	10	36	4	13	2	1	0	5	2		.361	.361	.472	161	2	0			.957	9	C-10	1.1
1887	Was-N	82	314	35	63	6	1	0	20	8	17	.201	.228	.226	28	-30	26			.906	3	C-76/O-5,2	-1.7
1888	Was-N	85	300	49	56	5	6	3	29	17	18	.187	.249	.273	70	-9	31			.916	5	C-79/O-4,S1	0.3
1889	Was-N	98	386	51	113	16	1	0	42	15	12	.293	.333	.339	94	-3	26			.891	5	C-45,O-34,1	0.3
1890	Buf-P	123	503	95	134	15	12	0	53	47	13	.266	.353	.344	94	-1	16			.925	-11	*C-112/O-9,1	-0.2
1891	Pit-N	75	280	43	60	10	0	0	29	19	11	.214	.286	.250	58	-14	4			.926	9	C-72/1-3	0.0
1892	Pit-N	97	346	39	84	9	4	1	31	21	22	.243	.298	.301	81	-8	11			.951	24	C-92/O-3,1	2.0
1893	Pit-N	37	133	22	38	3	1	0	15	10	9	.286	.358	.323	83	-3	4			.941	5	C-37	0.5
1894	Pit-N	69	228	32	57	7	1	1	21	20	14	.250	.321	.303	52	-18	8			.947	5	C-69,M	-0.5
1895	Pit-N	14	49	12	15	2	0	0	4	7	1	.306	.404	.347	100	-1	1			.962	-2	C-12/1-1M	0.0
1896	Pit-N	33	120	9	26	4	1	0	16	5	8	.217	.248	.267	37	-11	0			.974	1	1-28/C-5M	-0.8
Total	11	723	2695	391	659	79	28	5	265	169	127	.245	.305	.300	72	-95	127			.927	53	C-609/1-61,O2S	1.0

■ DENNY MACK
Mack, Dennis Joseph (b: Dennis Joseph McGee)　b: 1851, Easton, Pa.　d: 4/10/1888, Wilkes-Barre, Pa.　BR/TR, 5'7", 164 lbs.　Deb: 5/6/1871　MU

1871	Rok-n	25	122	34	30	7	1	0	17	8	7	.246	.292	.320	79	-2	12					*1-23/P-3,S	0.0
1872	Ath-n	47	205	68	59	9	1	0	34	23	9	.288	.360	.341	116	5						1-24,S-22	0.4
1873	Phi-n	48	205	55	60	5	0	0	19	15	9	.293	.341	.317	92	-2						*1-42/O-4,S2	0.2
1874	Phi-n	56	248	48	51	7	4	0		1		.206	.209	.266	48	-15						*1-56	-1.1
1876	StL-N	48	180	32	39	5	0	0	7	11	5	.217	.262	.261	79	-3				.886	-8	S-41/2-5,O	-1.0
1880	Buf-N	17	59	5	12	0	0	0	3	5	2	.203	.266	.203	60	-2				.940	-2	S-16/2-1	-0.3
1882	Lou-a	72	264	41	48	3	1	0		16		.182	.229	.201	49	-13				.898	-3	S-49,2-24/OM	-1.2
1883	Pit-a	60	224	26	44	5	3	0		13		.196	.241	.246	60	-9				.844	4	S-38,1-25/2	-0.6
Total	4 n	176	780	205	200	28	6	0	70	47	25	.256	.299	.308	83	-14						1-145/S-26,OP2	-0.7
Total	4	197	727	104	143	13	4	0	10	45	12	.197	.244	.230	60	-27				.886	-8	S-144/2-31,1O	-3.1

■ EARLE MACK
Mack, Earle Thaddeus (b: Earle Thaddeus McGillicuddy)
b: 2/1/1890, Spencer, Mass.　d: 2/4/67, Upper Darby Township, Pa.　BL/TR, 5'8", 140 lbs.　Deb: 10/5/10　FMC

1910	Phi-A	1	4	0	2	0	1	0	0	0		.500	.500	1.000	372	1	0			1.000	-1	/C-1	0.1
1911	Phi-A	2	4	0	0	0	0	0	0	0		.000	.000	.000	-99	-1	0			.000	0	/3-2	-0.1
1914	Phi-A	2	8	0	0	0	0	0	1	0	0	.000	.000	.000	-99	-2	1			1.000	0	/1-2	-0.2
Total	3	5	16	0	2	0	1	0	1	0	0	.125	.125	.250	11	-2	1			1.000	-1	/1-2,3-2,C	-0.2

■ REDDY MACK
Mack, Joseph (b: Joseph McNamara)　b: 5/2/1866, Ireland　d: 12/30/16, Newport, Ky.　Deb: 9/16/1885

1885	Lou-a	11	41	7	10	1	0	0		2		.244	.295	.268	79	-1				.885	0	2-11	0.0
1886	Lou-a	137	483	82	118	23	11	1		68		.244	.342	.344	109	5	13			.900	6	*2-137	1.5
1887	Lou-a	128	478	117	147	23	8	1		83		.308	.415	.356	124	19	22			.912	5	*2-128	2.3
1888	Lou-a	112	446	77	97	13	5	3	34	52		.217	.320	.289	98	2	18			.907	4	*2-112	0.9
1889	Bal-a	136	519	84	125	24	7	1	87	60	69	.241	.329	.320	84	-11	23			.897	-11	*2-135/O-1	-1.2
1890	Bal-a	26	95	14	27	3	5	0		10		.284	.370	.421	127	3	7			.932	1	2-26	0.4
Total	6	550	2062	381	524	87	36	6	121	275	69	.254	.352	.340	104	18	83			.905	5	2-549/O-1	3.9

■ JOE MACK
Mack, Joe John (b: Joseph John Maciarz)　b: 1/4/12, Chicago, Ill.　BB/TL, 5'11.5", 185 lbs.　Deb: 4/17/45

1945	Bos-N	66	260	30	60	13	1	3	44	34	39	.231	.320	.323	79	-7	1			.991	0	1-65	-1.1

■ QUINN MACK
Mack, Quinn David　b: 9/11/65, Los Angeles, Cal.　BL/TL, 5'10", 185 lbs.　Deb: 6/16/94　F

1994	Sea-A	5	21	1	5	3	0	0	2	1	3	.238	.273	.381	65	-1	2	0	1	1.000	-0	/O-4,D-1	-0.1

■ RAY MACK
Mack, Raymond James (b: Raymond James Mickovsky)　b: 8/31/16, Cleveland, Ohio　d: 5/7/69, Bucyrus, Ohio　BR/TR, 6', 200 lbs.　Deb: 9/9/38

1938	Cle-A	2	6	2	2	0	1	0	2	0	1	.333	.333	.667	147	0	0	0	0	1.000	2	/2-2	0.2
1939	Cle-A	36	112	12	17	4	1	1	6	12	19	.152	.240	.232	22	-14	0	2	-1	.976	2	2-34/3-1	-1.0
1940	Cle-A★	146	530	60	150	21	5	12	69	51	77	.283	.346	.409	98	-2	4	2	0	.965	-9	*2-146	-0.1
1941	Cle-A	145	500	54	114	22	4	9	44	54	66	.228	.303	.342	74	-20	8	4	0	.970	-5	*2-145	-1.4
1942	Cle-A	143	481	43	108	14	6	4	45	41	51	.225	.288	.291	67	-22	9	3	1	.969	-4	*2-143	-1.7
1943	Cle-A	153	545	56	120	25	2	7	62	47	61	.220	.285	.312	79	-16	8	3	1	.967	-2	*2-153	-1.0
1944	Cle-A	83	284	24	66	15	3	0	29	28	45	.232	.301	.306	77	-9	4	1	1	.951	10	2-83	0.7
1946	Cle-A	61	171	13	35	6	2	1	9	23	27	.205	.299	.281	67	-8	2	2	-0	.970	-4	2-61	-0.4
1947	NY-A	1	0	0	0	0	0	0	0	0	0	—	—	—		0	0	0	0	.000	0	R	0.0
	Chi-N	21	78	9	17	6	0	2	12	5	15	.218	.274	.372	73	-3	0			.965	7	2-21	0.5
Total	9	791	2707	273	629	113	24	34	278	261	365	.232	.301	.330	76	-93	35	17		.966	3	2-788/3-1	-4.2

YEAR	TM/L	G	AB	R	H	2B	3B	HR	RBI	BB	SO	AVG	OBP	SLG	PRO+	BR/A	SB	CS	SBR	FA	FR	G/POS	TPR

■ **SHANE MACK** Mack, Shane Lee b: 12/7/63, Los Angeles, Cal. BR/TR, 6' ", 185 lbs. Deb: 5/25/87 F

1987	SD-N	105	238	28	57	11	3	4	25	18	47	.239	.301	.361	77	-8	4	6	-2	.982	-8	O-91	-2.0
1988	SD-N	56	119	13	29	3	0	0	12	14	21	.244	.338	.269	78	-3	5	1	1	.983	-3	O-55	-0.6
1990	Min-A	125	313	50	102	10	4	8	44	29	69	.326	.392	.460	129	13	13	4	2	.988	1	*O-109/D-4	1.3
1991	*Min-A	143	442	79	137	27	8	18	74	34	79	.310	.367	.529	139	22	13	9	-2	.977	-9	*O-140/D-1	0.9
1992	Min-A	156	600	101	189	31	6	16	75	64	106	.315	.395	.467	136	30	26	14	-1	.988	1	*O-155	2.8
1993	Min-A	128	503	66	139	30	4	10	61	41	76	.276	.336	.412	99	-1	15	5	2	.986	14	*O-128	1.1
1994	Min-A	81	303	55	101	21	2	15	61	32	51	.333	.408	.564	147	22	4	1	1	.990	1	O-75/D-4	1.9
Total	7	794	2518	392	754	133	27	71	352	232	449	.299	.368	.458	122	74	80	40	0	.985	-3	O-753/D-9	5.4

■ **PETE MACKANIN** Mackanin, Peter b: 8/1/51, Chicago, Ill. BR/TR, 6'2", 190 lbs. Deb: 7/3/73

1973	Tex-A	44	90	3	9	2	0	0	2	4	26	.100	.147	.122	-24	-15	0	0	0	.947	2	S-33,3-10	-1.1
1974	Tex-A	2	6	0	1	0	1	0	0	0	2	.167	.167	.500	88	-0	0	0	0	1.000	2	/S-2	0.2
1975	Mon-N	130	448	59	101	19	6	12	44	31	99	.225	.279	.375	77	-16	11	5	0	.966	18	*2-127/S-1,3	1.0
1976	Mon-N	114	380	36	85	15	2	8	33	15	66	.224	.257	.337	65	-19	6	2	1	.965	-2	*2-100/3-8,SO	-1.5
1977	Mon-N	55	85	9	19	2	2	1	6	4	17	.224	.258	.329	58	-5	3	1	0	1.000	3	/2-9,S-8,3O	-0.1
1978	Phi-N	5	8	0	2	0	0	0	1	0	4	.250	.250	.250	40	-1	0	0	0	1.000	0	/1-1,3-1	-0.1
1979	Phi-N	13	9	2	1	0	0	1	2	1	2	.111	.200	.444	69	-0	0	0	0	1.000	0	/2-2,S-2,3	0.2
1980	Min-A	108	319	31	85	18	0	4	35	14	34	.266	.297	.361	74	-12	6	2	1	.968	16	2-71,S-30/13D	1.0
1981	Min-A	77	225	21	52	7	1	4	18	7	40	.231	.258	.324	63	-11	1	2	-1	.980	-5	2-31,S-28,1/3D	-1.4
Total	9	548	1570	161	355	63	12	30	141	76	290	.226	.265	.339	65	-79	27	12	1	.968	36	2-340,S-107/31DO	-1.8

■ **ERIC MacKENZIE** Mac Kenzie, Eric Hugh b: 8/29/32, Glendon, Alt., Can. BL/TR, 6', 185 lbs. Deb: 4/23/55

| 1955 | KC-A | 1 | 1 | 0 | 0 | 0 | 0 | 0 | 0 | 0 | 0 | .000 | .000 | .000 | -99 | -0 | 0 | 0 | 0 | .000 | 0 | /C-1 | 0.0 |

■ **GORDON MacKENZIE** Mac Kenzie, Henry Gordon b: 7/9/37, St.Petersburg, Fla BR/TR, 5'11", 175 lbs. Deb: 8/13/61 C

| 1961 | KC-A | 11 | 24 | 1 | 3 | 0 | 0 | 0 | 1 | 6 | .125 | .160 | .125 | -22 | -4 | 0 | 0 | 0 | 1.000 | -1 | /C-7 | -0.4 |

■ **FELIX MACKIEWICZ** Mackiewicz, Felix Thaddeus b: 11/20/17, Chicago, Ill. d: 12/20/93, Olivette, Mo. BR/TR, 6'2", 195 lbs. Deb: 9/7/41

1941	Phi-A	5	14	3	4	0	0	1	0	1	0	.286	.333	.429	103	0	0	0	0	1.000	0	/O-3	-0.1
1942	Phi-A	6	14	3	3	2	0	0	2	0	4	.214	.214	.357	59	-1	0	0	0	1.000	0	/O-3	-0.1
1943	Phi-A	9	16	1	1	0	0	0	0	2	8	.063	.167	.063	-32	-3	0	0	0	1.000	0	/O-3	-0.3
1945	Cle-A	120	359	42	98	14	7	2	37	44	41	.273	.356	.368	115	7	5	5	-2	.987	5	*O-112	0.6
1946	Cle-A	78	258	35	67	15	4	0	16	16	32	.260	.305	.349	88	-5	5	1	1	.983	-2	O-72	-1.0
1947	Cle-A	2	5	0	0	0	0	0	0	0	0	.000	.000	.000	-99	-1	0	0	0	1.000	0	/O-2	-0.2
	Was-A	3	6	1	1	1	0	0	0	0	1	.167	.167	.333	38	-1	0	0	0	1.000	-1	/O-3	-0.2
	Yr	5	11	1	1	1	0	0	0	0	3	.091	.091	.182	-26	-2	0	0	0	1.000	-1	/O-5	-0.4
Total	6	223	672	85	174	32	12	2	55	63	88	.259	.325	.351	97	-3	10	6	-1	.986	2	O-198	-1.3

■ **STEVE MACKO** Macko, Steven Joseph b: 9/6/54, Burlington, Iowa d: 11/15/81, Arlington, Tex. BL/TR, 5'10", 160 lbs. Deb: 8/18/79

1979	Chi-N	19	40	2	9	1	0	0	3	4	8	.225	.295	.250	46	-3	0	0	0	1.000	4	2-10/3-4	0.2
1980	Chi-N	6	20	2	6	2	0	0	2	0	3	.300	.300	.400	87	-0	0	0	0	1.000	1	/S-3,3-2,2	0.1
Total	2	25	60	4	15	3	0	0	5	4	11	.250	.297	.300	59	-3	0	0	0	1.000	6	/2-11,3-6,S	0.3

■ **LONNIE MACLIN** Maclin, Lonnie Lee b: 2/17/67, Clayton, Mo. BL/TL, 5'11", 185 lbs. Deb: 9/7/93

| 1993 | StL-N | 12 | 13 | 2 | 1 | 0 | 0 | 0 | 1 | 0 | 5 | .077 | .077 | .077 | -60 | -3 | 1 | 0 | 0 | 1.000 | -2 | /O-5 | -0.4 |

■ **MAX MACON** Macon, Max Cullen b: 10/14/15, Pensacola, Fla. d: 8/5/89, Jupiter, Fla. BL/TL, 6'3", 175 lbs. Deb: 4/21/38

1938	StL-N	46	36	5	11	0	0	0	3	2	4	.306	.342	.306	75	-1	0			.946	0	P-38/O-1	0.0
1940	Bro-N	2	1	0	1	0	0	0	0	0	0	1.000	1.000	1.000	427	0	0			.000	-0	/P-2	0.0
1942	Bro-N	26	43	4	12	2	1	0	1	2	4	.279	.311	.372	98	-0	1			.960	-0	P-14	0.0
1943	Bro-N	45	55	7	9	0	0	0	6	0	1	.164	.164	.164	-5	-7	1			1.000	0	P-25/1-3	-0.2
1944	Bos-N	106	366	38	100	15	3	3	36	12	23	.273	.296	.355	79	-11	7			.977	-2	1-72,O-22/P	-1.8
1947	Bos-N	1	1	0	0	0	0	0	0	0	0	.000	.000	.000	-99	-0	0			1.000	0	/P-1	0.0
Total	6	226	502	54	133	17	4	3	46	16	32	.265	.288	.333	72	-19	9			.965	-2	/P-81,1-75,O	-2.0

■ **WADDY MacPHEE** Mac Phee, Walter Scott b: 12/23/1899, Brooklyn, N.Y. d: 1/20/80, Charlotte, N.C. BR/TR, 5'8", 140 lbs. Deb: 9/27/22

| 1922 | NY-N | 2 | 7 | 2 | 2 | 0 | 0 | 0 | 0 | 1 | 0 | .286 | .375 | .571 | 140 | 0 | 0 | | | .889 | 1 | /3-2 | 0.1 |

■ **JIMMY MACULLAR** Macullar, James F. "Little Mac" b: 1/16/1855, Boston, Mass. d: 4/8/24, Baltimore, Md. BR/TL, 5'6", 155 lbs. Deb: 5/5/1879 MU

1879	Syr-N	64	246	24	52	9	0	0	13	3	27	.211	.221	.248	61	-9				.864	1	S-37,O-26/23M	-0.7
1882	Cin-a	79	299	44	70	6	6	0		1	14	.234	.268	.294	85	-5				.922	-1	*O-79	-0.5
1883	Cin-a	14	48	4	8	2	0	0		0	4	.167	.231	.208	40	-3				.900	-4	O-14/S-1	-0.6
1884	Bal-a	107	360	73	73	16	6	4		36		.203	.290	.314	93	-2				.866	1	*S-107	0.0
1885	Bal-a	100	320	52	61	7	6	3		49		.191	.306	.278	87	-3				.877	-1	*S-98/O-2,P	-0.1
1886	Bal-a	85	268	49	55	7	1	0		49		.205	.332	.239	82	-2	23			.852	-10	S-82/O-2,2P	-1.0
Total	6	449	1541	246	319	47	19	7	13	155	27	.207	.285	.276	83	-25	23			.865	-11	S-325,O-123/2P3	-2.9

■ **GENE MADDEN** Madden, Eugene b: 6/5/1890, Elm Grove, W.Va. d: 4/6/49, Utica, N.Y. BL/TR, 5'10", 155 lbs. Deb: 4/20/16

| 1916 | Pit-N | 1 | 1 | 0 | 0 | 0 | 0 | 0 | 0 | 0 | 0 | .000 | .000 | .000 | -99 | -0 | 0 | | | .000 | 0 | H | 0.0 |

■ **FRANK MADDEN** Madden, Francis A. "Red" b: 10/17/1892, Pittsburgh, Pa. d: 4/30/52, Pittsburgh, Pa. Deb: 7/4/14

| 1914 | Pit-F | 2 | 2 | 0 | 1 | 0 | 0 | 0 | 1 | 0 | 0 | .500 | .500 | .500 | 161 | 0 | 0 | | | .000 | 0 | /C-1 | 0.0 |

■ **BUNNY MADDEN** Madden, Thomas Francis b: 9/14/1882, Boston, Mass. d: 1/20/54, Cambridge, Mass. BR/TR, 5'10", 190 lbs. Deb: 6/3/09

1909	Bos-A	10	17	0	4	0	0	0	3	0	0	.235	.235	.235	48	-1	0			.941	1	/C-7	0.1
1910	Bos-A	14	35	4	13	3	0	0	4	3	0	.371	.436	.457	175	3	0			.938	-3	C-12	0.1
1911	Bos-A	4	15	2	3	0	0	0	2	2	0	.200	.294	.200	39	-1	0			1.000	-2	/C-4	-0.3
	Phi-N	28	76	4	21	1	1	0	4	0	13	.276	.276	.316	65	-4	0			.924	3	C-22	0.1
Total	3	56	143	10	41	4	1	0	11	5	13	.287	.315	.329	87	-3	0			.935	-1	/C-45	-0.0

■ **TOMMY MADDEN** Madden, Thomas Joseph b: 7/31/1883, Philadelphia, Pa. d: 7/26/30, Philadelphia, Pa. BL/TL, 5'11", 160 lbs. Deb: 9/10/06

1906	Bos-N	4	15	1	4	0	0	0	0	0	1	.267	.313	.267	83	-0	0			1.000	-0	/O-4	-0.1
1910	NY-A	1	1	0	0	0	0	0	0	0	0	.000	.000	.000	-95	-0	0			.000	-0	H	-0.1
Total	2	5	16	1	4	0	0	0	0	0	1	.250	.294	.250	71	-1	0			1.000	-1	/O-4	-0.2

■ **CLARENCE MADDERN** Maddern, Clarence James b: 9/26/21, Bisbee, Ariz. d: 8/9/86, Tucson, Ariz. BR/TR, 6'1", 185 lbs. Deb: 9/19/46

1946	Chi-N	3	3	0	0	0	0	0	0	1	0	.000	.250	.000	-27	-0	0			1.000	-0	/O-2	-0.1
1948	Chi-N	80	214	16	54	12	1	4	27	10	25	.252	.301	.374	85	-5	0			.981	-2	O-55	-1.0
1949	Chi-N	10	9	1	3	0	0	0	2	2	0	.333	.455	.667	202	1	0			1.000	-0	/1-1	0.2
1951	Cle-A	11	12	0	2	0	0	0	0	0	1	.167	.167	.167	-10	-2	0			.667	-0	/O-1	-0.2
Total	4	104	238	17	59	12	1	5	29	12	26	.248	.301	.370	84	-6	0			.973	-2	/O-58,1-1	-1.1

■ **ELLIOTT MADDOX** Maddox, Elliott b: 12/21/47, East Orange, N.J. BR/TR, 5'11", 181 lbs. Deb: 4/7/70

| 1970 | Det-A | 109 | 258 | 30 | 64 | 13 | 4 | 3 | 24 | 30 | 42 | .248 | .333 | .364 | 92 | -3 | 2 | 3 | -1 | .919 | 0 | 3-40,O-37,S/2 | -0.5 |
| 1971 | Was-A | 128 | 258 | 38 | 56 | 8 | 2 | 1 | 18 | 51 | 42 | .217 | .346 | .275 | 83 | -4 | 10 | 4 | 1 | .990 | -3 | *O-103,3-12 | -1.0 |

YEAR	TM/L	G	AB	R	H	2B	3B	HR	RBI	BB	SO	AVG	OBP	SLG	PRO+	BR/A	SB	CS	SBR	FA	FR	G/POS	TPR
1972	Tex-A	98	294	40	74	7	2	0	10	49	53	.252	.362	.289	100	2	20	10	0	.990	4	O-94	0.2
1973	Tex-A	100	172	24	41	1	0	1	17	29	28	.238	.358	.262	80	-3	5	4	-1	.981	-7	O-89/3-7,D	-1.4
1974	NY-A	137	466	75	141	26	2	3	45	69	48	.303	.397	.386	130	21	6	5	-1	.986	9	*O-135/2-2,3	2.4
1975	NY-A	55	218	36	67	10	3	1	23	21	24	.307	.386	.394	124	8	9	3	1	1.000	8	O-55/2-1	1.5
1976	*NY-A	18	46	4	10	2	0	0	3	4	3	.217	.280	.261	60	-2	0	1	-1	1.000	-1	O-13/D-2	-0.4
1977	Bal-A	49	107	14	28	7	0	2	9	13	9	.262	.363	.383	110	2	2	2	-1	.990	-4	O-45/3-1	-0.4
1978	NY-N	119	389	43	100	18	2	2	39	71	38	.257	.374	.329	102	4	2	11	-6	.988	-3	O-79,3-43/1	-0.9
1979	NY-N	86	224	21	60	13	0	1	12	20	27	.268	.336	.339	88	-3	3	2	0	.985	-1	O-65,3-11	-0.7
1980	NY-N	130	411	35	101	16	1	4	34	52	44	.246	.339	.319	87	-6	1	9	-5	.956	-3	*3-115/O-4,1	-1.6
Total	11	1029	2843	360	742	121	16	18	234	409	358	.261	.361	.334	100	17	60	54	-14	.989	-1	O-719,3-230/S21D	-2.8

■ GARRY MADDOX
Maddox, Garry Lee   b: 9/1/49, Cincinnati, Ohio   BR/TR, 6'3", 184 lbs.   Deb: 4/25/72

YEAR	TM/L	G	AB	R	H	2B	3B	HR	RBI	BB	SO	AVG	OBP	SLG	PRO+	BR/A	SB	CS	SBR	FA	FR	G/POS	TPR
1972	SF-N	125	458	62	122	26	7	12	58	14	97	.266	.294	.432	103	-1	13	6	0	.979	4	*O-121	-0.2
1973	SF-N	144	587	81	187	30	10	11	76	24	73	.319	.352	.460	118	13	24	10	1	.969	8	*O-140	1.6
1974	SF-N	135	538	74	153	31	3	8	50	29	64	.284	.325	.398	97	-4	21	9	1	.986	7	*O-131	-0.2
1975	SF-N	17	52	4	7	1	0	1	4	6	3	.135	.237	.212	24	-5	1	1	-0	1.000	3	O-13	-0.3
	Phi-N	99	374	50	109	25	8	4	46	36	54	.291	.361	.433	115	8	24	3	5	.983	18	O-97	2.7
	Yr	116	426	54	116	26	8	5	50	42	57	.272	.346	.406	104	2	25	4	5	.985	21	O-110	2.4
1976	*Phi-N	146	531	75	175	37	6	6	68	42	59	.330	.383	.456	133	23	29	12	2	.989	24	*O-144	4.5
1977	*Phi-N	139	571	85	167	27	10	14	74	24	58	.292	.326	.448	101	-1	22	6	3	.977	14	*O-138	1.1
1978	*Phi-N	155	598	62	172	34	3	11	68	39	89	.288	.333	.410	106	3	33	7	6	.983	21	*O-154	2.4
1979	Phi-N	148	548	70	154	28	6	13	61	17	71	.281	.308	.425	95	-6	26	13	0	.996	27	*O-140	1.6
1980	*Phi-N	143	549	59	142	31	3	11	73	18	52	.259	.282	.386	80	-16	25	5	0	.976	14	*O-143	-0.3
1981	Phi-N	94	323	37	85	7	1	5	40	17	42	.263	.302	.337	78	-10	9	4	0	.977	9	O-94	-0.3
1982	Phi-N	119	412	39	117	27	2	8	61	12	32	.284	.304	.417	98	-3	7	5	-1	.992	7	*O-111	0.1
1983	*Phi-N	97	324	27	89	14	2	4	32	17	31	.275	.313	.367	89	-5	7	6	-2	.977	-0	O-95	-1.0
1984	Phi-N	77	241	29	68	11	0	5	19	13	29	.282	.319	.390	97	-1	2	3	-0	1.000	0	O-69	-0.4
1985	Phi-N	105	218	22	52	8	1	4	23	13	26	.239	.284	.339	72	-8	4	2	0	.980	-12	O-94	-2.4
1986	Phi-N	6	7	1	3	0	0	0	1	2	1	.429	.556	.429	169	1	0	1	-1	1.000	-1	/O-3	-0.1
Total	15	1749	6331	777	1802	337	62	117	754	323	781	.285	.323	.413	100	-11	248	92	19	.983	142	*O-1687	8.8

■ JERRY MADDOX
Maddox, Jerry Glenn   b: 7/28/53, Whittier, Cal.   BR/TR, 6'2", 200 lbs.   Deb: 6/3/78

YEAR	TM/L	G	AB	R	H	2B	3B	HR	RBI	BB	SO	AVG	OBP	SLG	PRO+	BR/A	SB	CS	SBR	FA	FR	G/POS	TPR
1978	Atl-N	7	14	1	3	0	0	0	1	1	2	.214	.267	.214	32	-1	0	0		.909	-0	/3-5	-0.2

■ ART MADISON
Madison, Arthur   b: 1/14/1872, Clarksburg, Mass.   d: 1/27/33, N.Adams, Mass.   BR/TR, 5'9", 165 lbs.   Deb: 9/9/1895

YEAR	TM/L	G	AB	R	H	2B	3B	HR	RBI	BB	SO	AVG	OBP	SLG	PRO+	BR/A	SB	CS	SBR	FA	FR	G/POS	TPR
1895	Phi-N	11	34	6	12	3	0	0	8	1	1	.353	.371	.441	109	0	4			.955	-1	/S-6,2-3,3	0.0
1899	Pit-N	42	118	20	32	2	4	0	19	11		.271	.338	.356	91	-1	1			.953	-5	2-19,S-15/3	-0.4
Total	2	53	152	26	44	5	4	0	27	12	1	.289	.345	.375	95	-1	5			.926	-6	/2-22,S-21,3	-0.4

■ SCOTTI MADISON
Madison, Charles Scott   b: 9/12/59, Pensacola, Fla.   BB/TR, 5'11", 195 lbs.   Deb: 7/6/85

YEAR	TM/L	G	AB	R	H	2B	3B	HR	RBI	BB	SO	AVG	OBP	SLG	PRO+	BR/A	SB	CS	SBR	FA	FR	G/POS	TPR
1985	Det-A	6	11	0	0	0	0	0	1	2	0	.000	.154	.000	-54	-2	0	0	0	1.000	-0	/C-1,D-3	-0.2
1986	Det-A	2	7	0	0	0	0	0	1	0	3	.000	.000	.000	-99	-2	0	0		.667	-1	/3-1,D-1	-0.3
1987	KC-A	7	15	4	4	3	0	0	0	1	5	.267	.313	.467	100	-0	0	0	0	1.000	-1	/1-4,C-3	-0.1
1988	KC-A	16	35	4	6	2	0	0	2	4	5	.171	.256	.229	37	-3	1	0	0	1.000	-2	/C-4,O-3,1D	-0.4
1989	Cin-N	40	98	13	17	7	0	1	7	8	9	.173	.243	.276	46	-7	0	1	-1	1.000	2	3-26	-0.5
Total	5	71	166	21	27	12	0	1	11	15	22	.163	.236	.253	37	-14	1	1	-0	.985	-1	/3-27,D-8,C10	-1.5

■ ED MADJESKI
Madjeski, Edward William (b: Edward William Majewski)   b: 7/24/09, Far Rockaway, N.Y   BR/TR, 5'11", 178 lbs.   Deb: 5/2/32

YEAR	TM/L	G	AB	R	H	2B	3B	HR	RBI	BB	SO	AVG	OBP	SLG	PRO+	BR/A	SB	CS	SBR	FA	FR	G/POS	TPR
1932	Phi-A	17	35	4	8	0	0	0	3	3	6	.229	.289	.229	35	-3	0	0		1.000	2	/C-8	-0.1
1933	Phi-A	51	142	17	40	4	0	0	17	4	21	.282	.301	.310	62	-8	0	0		.958	-4	C-41	-0.9
1934	Phi-A	8	8	1	3	1	0	0	2	0	1	.375	.375	.500	129	0	0	0		.000	-1	/C-1	0.0
	Chi-A	85	281	36	62	14	2	5	32	14	31	.221	.260	.338	52	-21	2	0	1	.973	2	C-79	-1.4
	Yr	93	289	37	65	15	2	5	34	14	32	.225	.263	.343	54	-21	2	0	1	.971	2	C-80	-1.4
1937	NY-N	5	15	0	3	0	0	0	2	0	2	.200	.200	.200	9	-2	0			1.000	-2	/C-5	-0.4
Total	4	166	481	58	116	19	2	5	56	21	61	.241	.274	.320	53	-34	2	0		.970	-2	C-134	-2.8

■ BILL MADLOCK
Madlock, Bill   b: 1/2/51, Memphis, Tenn.   BR/TR, 5'11", 185 lbs.   Deb: 9/7/73

YEAR	TM/L	G	AB	R	H	2B	3B	HR	RBI	BB	SO	AVG	OBP	SLG	PRO+	BR/A	SB	CS	SBR	FA	FR	G/POS	TPR
1973	Tex-A	21	77	16	27	5	3	1	5	7	9	.351	.412	.532	171	7	3	2	-0	.918	-6	3-21	0.1
1974	Chi-N	128	453	65	142	21	5	9	54	42	39	.313	.378	.442	124	11	7	7	-1	.946	-12	*3-121	0.1
1975	Chi-N★	130	514	77	182	29	7	7	64	42	34	.354	.406	.479	139	27	9	7	-2	.943	-11	*3-128	1.5
1976	Chi-N	142	514	68	174	36	1	15	84	56	27	.339	.415	.500	146	32	15	11	-2	.961	-20	*3-136	0.9
1977	SF-N	140	533	70	161	28	1	12	46	43	33	.302	.361	.426	111	8	13	10	-2	.949	-17	*3-126/2-6	-1.2
1978	SF-N	122	447	76	138	26	3	15	44	48	39	.309	.380	.481	145	26	16	5	2	.974	-24	*2-114/1-3	1.3
1979	SF-N	69	249	37	65	9	2	7	41	18	19	.261	.311	.398	99	-2	11	3	2	.976	-14	2-63/1-5	-1.0
	*Pit-N	85	311	48	102	17	3	7	44	34	22	.328	.396	.469	129	13	21	8	2	.969	-6	3-85	0.8
	Yr	154	560	85	167	26	5	14	85	52	41	.298	.359	.438	117	13	32	11	3	.969	-20	3-85,2-63/1	-0.2
1980	Pit-N	137	494	62	137	22	4	10	53	45	33	.277	.343	.399	105	3	16	10	-1	.955	-17	*3-127,1-12	-1.8
1981	Pit-N★	82	279	35	95	23	1	6	45	34	17	.341	.418	.495	153	20	18	6	2	.956	-4	3-78	1.8
1982	Pit-N	154	568	92	181	33	3	19	95	48	39	.319	.376	.488	136	27	18	6	2	.952	-6	*3-146/1-3	1.9
1983	Pit-N★	130	473	68	153	21	0	12	68	49	24	.323	.389	.444	127	18	3	4	-2	.958	-14	*3-126	0.2
1984	Pit-N	103	403	38	102	16	0	4	44	26	20	.253	.300	.323	75	-14	3	1	0	.942	-13	3-98/1-1	-2.4
1985	Pit-N	110	399	49	100	23	1	10	41	39	42	.251	.325	.388	100	-0	3	3	-1	.940	-16	3-98,1-12	-2.0
	*LA-N	34	114	20	41	4	0	2	15	10	11	.360	.425	.447	149	8	7	1	2	.948	3	3-32	1.2
	Yr	144	513	69	141	27	1	12	56	49	53	.275	.347	.402	110	6	10	4	1	.943	-13	*3-130,1-12	-0.8
1986	LA-N	111	379	38	106	17	0	10	60	30	43	.280	.341	.404	112	6	3	3	-1	.910	-8	*3-101/1-2	-0.6
1987	LA-N	21	61	5	11	1	0	1	7	6	5	.180	.265	.344	61	-4	0	0	0	.912	-4	3-16/1-1	-0.8
	*Det-A	87	326	56	91	17	0	14	50	28	45	.279	.354	.460	119	9	3	4	-0	.989	-2	D-64,1-22/3	0.3
Total	15	1806	6594	920	2008	348	34	163	860	605	510	.305	.369	.442	123	200	174	90	-2	.948	-185	*3-1440,2-183/D1	0.3

■ SAL MADRID
Madrid, Salvador   b: 6/9/20, ElPaso, Tex.   d: 2/24/77, Ft.Wayne, Ind.   BR/TR, 5'9", 165 lbs.   Deb: 9/17/47

YEAR	TM/L	G	AB	R	H	2B	3B	HR	RBI	BB	SO	AVG	OBP	SLG	PRO+	BR/A	SB	CS	SBR	FA	FR	G/POS	TPR
1947	Chi-N	8	24	0	3	1	0	0	1	1	6	.125	.160	.167	-14	-4	0			.956	4	/S-8	0.0

■ DAVE MAGADAN
Magadan, David Joseph   b: 9/30/62, Tampa, Fla.   BL/TR, 6'3", 190 lbs.   Deb: 9/7/86

YEAR	TM/L	G	AB	R	H	2B	3B	HR	RBI	BB	SO	AVG	OBP	SLG	PRO+	BR/A	SB	CS	SBR	FA	FR	G/POS	TPR
1986	NY-N	10	18	3	8	0	0	0	3	3	1	.444	.524	.444	175	2	0	0		1.000	1	/1-9	0.3
1987	NY-N	85	192	21	61	13	1	3	24	22	22	.318	.388	.443	126	8	0	0		.981	3	3-50,1-13	0.9
1988	*NY-N	112	314	39	87	15	0	1	35	60	39	.277	.396	.334	117	11	0	1	-1	.988	-1	1-71,3-48	0.4
1989	NY-N	127	374	47	107	22	3	4	41	49	37	.286	.370	.393	124	13	1	0	0	.991	3	1-87,3-28	1.0
1990	NY-N	144	451	74	148	28	6	6	72	74	55	.328	.425	.457	143	30	2	1	0	.998	3	*1-113,3-19	2.5
1991	NY-N	124	418	58	108	23	0	4	51	83	50	.258	.384	.342	106	8	1	1	-0	.996	2	*1-122	0.1
1992	NY-N	99	321	33	91	9	1	3	28	56	44	.283	.390	.346	111	8	1	0	-1	.941	-13	3-93/1-2	-0.5
1993	Fla-N	66	227	22	65	12	0	4	29	44	30	.286	.404	.392	108	5	0	0	0	.961	1	3-63/1-2	0.5
	Sea-A	71	228	27	59	11	0	1	21	36	33	.259	.360	.320	83	-4	2	0		.991	-1	1-41,3-27/D	-0.7
1994	Fla-N	74	211	30	58	7	0	1	17	39	25	.275	.390	.322	84	-3	0	0		.958	-5	3-48,1-16	-0.9
Total	9	912	2754	354	792	140	11	27	321	466	336	.288	.392	.376	115	76	7	4	-0	.994	-7	1-476,3-376/D	3.6

YEAR	TM/L	G	AB	R	H	2B	3B	HR	RBI	BB	SO	AVG	OBP	SLG	PRO+	BR/A	SB	CS	SBR	FA	FR	G/POS	TPR

■ EVER MAGALLANES   Magallanes, Everado (Espinoza)   b: 11/6/65, Chihuahua, Mexico   BL/TR, 5'10", 165 lbs.   Deb: 5/17/91

1991	Cle-A	3	2	0	0	0	0	0	0	1	1	.000	.333	.000	1	-0	0	0	0	1.000	-1	/S-2	-0.1

■ LEE MAGEE   Magee, Leo Christopher (b: Leopold Christopher Hoernschemeyer)   b: 6/4/1889, Cincinnati, Ohio   d: 3/14/66, Columbus, Ohio   BB/TR, 5'11", 165 lbs.   Deb: 7/4/11   M

1911	StL-N	26	69	9	18	1	1	0	8	8	8	.261	.338	.304	82	-1	4			.975	-2	2-18/S-3	-0.4
1912	StL-N	128	458	60	133	13	8	0	40	39	29	.290	.347	.354	94	-3	16			.956	7	O-85,2-23/1S	-0.1
1913	StL-N	137	531	54	142	13	7	2	31	34	30	.267	.314	.330	85	-11	23			.982	13	*O-108,2-22/1S	-0.3
1914	StL-N	142	529	59	150	23	4	2	40	42	24	.284	.337	.353	107	4	36			.970	5	*O-102,1-39/2	0.4
1915	Bro-F	121	452	87	146	19	10	4	49	22	19	.323	.366	.436	112	6	34			.937	-1	*2-115/1-2M	0.7
1916	NY-A	131	510	57	131	18	4	3	45	50	31	.257	.324	.325	93	-4	29	25	-6	.975	5	*O-128/2-2	-1.4
1917	NY-A	51	173	17	38	4	1	0	8	13	18	.220	.278	.254	62	-8	3			.938	-8	O-50	-2.1
	StL-A	36	112	11	19	1	0	0	4	6	6	.170	.212	.179	20	-11	3			.971	6	3-20/2-6,1O	-0.5
	Yr	87	285	28	57	5	1	0	12	19	24	.200	.252	.225	46	-18	6			.938	-2	O-51,3-20/21	-2.6
1918	Cin-N	119	459	61	133	22	13	0	28	28	19	.290	.331	.394	123	11	19			.956	9	*2-114/3-3	3.0
1919	Bro-N	45	181	16	43	7	2	0	7	5	8	.238	.262	.298	67	-8	5			.938	-1	2-36/3-9	-0.7
	Chi-N	79	267	36	78	12	4	1	17	18	16	.292	.339	.378	115	5	14			.978	-6	O-45,S-13,3/2	-0.4
	Yr	124	448	52	121	19	6	1	24	23	24	.270	.309	.346	96	-3	19			.978	-7	O-45,2-43,3S	-1.1
Total	9	1015	3741	467	1031	133	54	12	277	265	208	.276	.325	.350	97	-20	186	25		.969	27	O-519,2-349/13S	-1.8

■ SHERRY MAGEE   Magee, Sherwood Robert   b: 8/6/1884, Clarendon, Pa.   d: 3/13/29, Philadelphia, Pa.   BR/TR, 5'11", 179 lbs.   Deb: 6/29/04   U

1904	Phi-N	95	364	51	101	15	12	3	57	14		.277	.308	.409	125	9	11			.921	5	O-94/1-1	0.8
1905	Phi-N	155	603	100	180	24	17	5	98	44		.299	.354	.420	135	25	48			.963	10	*O-155	2.8
1906	Phi-N	154	563	77	159	36	8	6	67	52		.282	.348	.407	135	22	55			.982	11	*O-154	2.8
1907	Phi-N	140	503	75	165	28	12	4	**85**	53		.328	.396	.455	169	40	46			.978	7	*O-139	4.6
1908	Phi-N	143	508	79	144	30	16	2	57	49		.283	.359	.417	143	25	40			.970	2	*O-142	2.3
1909	Phi-N	143	522	60	141	33	14	2	66	43		.270	.339	.398	128	16	38			.970	-6	*O-143	0.4
1910	Phi-N	154	519	**110**	172	39	17	6	**123**	94	36	**.331**	**.445**	**.507**	172	51	49			.974	-13	*O-154	3.2
1911	Phi-N	121	445	79	128	32	5	15	94	49	33	.288	.366	.483	135	19	22			**.981**	3	*O-120	1.6
1912	Phi-N	132	464	79	142	25	9	6	66	55	54	.306	.388	.438	118	12	30			.963	-11	*O-124/1-6	-0.6
1913	Phi-N	138	470	92	144	36	6	11	70	38	36	.306	.369	.479	136	21	23			.968	-10	*O-123/1-4	0.6
1914	Phi-N	146	544	96	171	**39**	11	15	**103**	55	42	.314	.380	**.509**	154	34	25			.940	2	O-67,S-39,1/2	4.5
1915	Bos-N	156	571	72	160	34	12	6	87	54	39	.280	.350	.392	130	21	15	12	-3	.981	15	*O-135,1-21	2.9
1916	Bos-N	122	419	44	101	17	5	3	54	44	52	.241	.322	.327	104	3	10			.978	-5	*O-120/1-2,S	-1.0
1917	Bos-N	72	246	24	63	8	4	0	29	13	23	.256	.302	.333	100	-0	7			.954	2	O-65/1-2	-0.3
	Cin-N	45	137	17	44	8	4	0	23	16	7	.321	.400	.438	164	11	4			.989	4	O-41/1-2	1.4
	Yr	117	383	41	107	16	8	1	52	29	30	.279	.338	.371	124	10	11			.967	6	*O-106/1-4	1.1
1918	Cin-N	115	400	46	119	15	13	2	**76**	37	18	.298	.360	.415	142	20	14			.981	-2	1-66,O-38/2	1.5
1919	*Cin-N	56	163	11	35	6	1	0	21	26	19	.215	.337	.264	84	-2	4			.990	-3	O-47/2-1,3	-0.9
Total	16	2087	7441	1112	2169	425	166	83	1176	736	359	.291	.364	.427	137	324	441	12		.970	16	*O-1861,1-136/S23	26.6

■ HARL MAGGERT   Maggert, Harl Vestin   b: 2/13/1883, Cromwell, Ind.   d: 1/7/63, Fresno, Cal.   BL/TR, 5'8", 155 lbs.   Deb: 9/4/07   F

1907	Pit-N	3	6	1	0	0	0	0	0	2		.000	.250	.000	-21	-1	1			1.000	0	/O-2	-0.1
1912	Phi-A	74	242	39	62	8	6	1	13	36		.256	.357	.351	107	3	10			.939	-6	O-61	-0.6
Total	2	77	248	40	62	8	6	1	13	38		.250	.354	.343	104	2	11			.942	-6	/O-63	-0.7

■ HARL MAGGERT   Maggert, Harl Warren   b: 5/4/14, Los Angeles, Cal.   d: 7/10/86, Citrus Heights, Cal.   BR/TR, 6', 190 lbs.   Deb: 4/19/38   F

1938	Bos-N	66	89	12	25	3	0	3	19	10	20	.281	.354	.416	123	3				.944	-9	O-10/3-8	0.2

■ STUBBY MAGNER   Magner, Edmund Burke   b: 2/20/1888, Kalamazoo, Mich.   d: 9/6/56, Chillicothe, Ohio   BR/TR, 5'3", 135 lbs.   Deb: 7/12/11

1911	NY-A	13	33	3	7	0	0	0	4	4		.212	.297	.212	40	-3	1			.970	-0	/S-6,2-5	-0.3

■ JOHN MAGNER   Magner, John T.   b: 1855, St.Louis, Mo.   Deb: 7/14/1879   U

1879	Cin-N	1	4	0	0	0	0	0	1	0	1	.000	.000	.000	-99	-1				.500	-0	/O-1	-0.1

■ GEORGE MAGOON   Magoon, George Henry "Maggie" or "Topsy"   b: 3/27/1875, St.Albans, Maine   d: 12/6/43, Rochester, N.H.   BR/TR, 5'10", 160 lbs.   Deb: 6/29/1898

1898	Bro-N	93	343	35	77	7	0	2	39	30		.224	.293	.254	57	-19	7			.925	13	S-93	-0.1
1899	Bal-N	62	207	26	53	8	3	0	31	26		.256	.353	.324	82	-5	7			.923	5	S-62	0.5
	Chi-N	59	189	24	43	5	1	0	21	24		.228	.333	.265	67	-7	5			.896	6	S-59	0.3
	Yr	121	396	50	96	13	4	0	52	50		.242	.344	.295	75	-12	12			.909	12	*S-121	0.8
1901	Cin-N	127	460	47	116	16	7	1	53	52		.252	.331	.324	97	-1	15			.919	-20	*S-112,2-15	-1.1
1902	Cin-N	45	162	29	44	9	2	0	23	13		.272	.344	.352	105	1	7			.930	4	2-41/S-3	0.7
1903	Cin-N	42	139	6	30	4	0	0	9	19		.216	.314	.259	58	-8	2			.971	5	2-32/3-9	-0.2
	Chi-A	94	334	32	76	11	3	0	25	30		.228	.303	.278	79	-8	4			.936	-21	2-94	-2.6
Total	5	522	1834	199	439	62	16	2	201	194		.239	.321	.294	78	-45	47			.916	-8	S-329,2-182/3	-2.5

■ TOM MAGRANN   Magrann, Thomas Joseph   b: 12/9/63, Hollywood, Fla.   BR/TR, 6'3", 177 lbs.   Deb: 9/7/89

1989	Cle-A	9	10	0	0	0	0	0	0	0	4	.000	.000	.000	-98	-3	0	0	0	1.000	3	/C-9	0.1

■ FREDDIE MAGUIRE   Maguire, Frederick Edward   b: 5/10/1899, Roxbury, Mass.   d: 11/3/61, Boston, Mass.   BR/TR, 5'11", 155 lbs.   Deb: 9/22/22

1922	NY-N	5	12	4	4	0	0	0	1	0	1	.333	.333	.333	72	-0	1	0		.944	2	/2-3	0.1
1923	*NY-N	41	30	11	6	1	0	0	2	2	4	.200	.250	.233	29	-3	1	0		.881	12	2-16/3-1	0.9
1928	Chi-N	140	574	67	160	24	7	1	41	25	38	.279	.312	.350	74	-22	6			.976	**51**	*2-138	3.1
1929	Bos-N	138	496	54	125	26	8	0	41	19	40	.252	.284	.337	55	-36	8			.971	8	*2-138/S-1	-2.0
1930	Bos-N	146	516	54	138	21	5	0	52	20	22	.267	.297	.328	53	-40	4			.969	-4	*2-146	-3.2
1931	Bos-N	148	492	36	112	18	2	0	26	16	26	.228	.259	.272	45	-39	3			**.976**	9	*2-148	-2.1
Total	6	618	2120	226	545	90	22	1	163	82	131	.257	.289	.322	57	-140	23	0		.971	77	2-589/S-1,3	-3.2

■ JACK MAGUIRE   Maguire, Jack   b: 2/5/25, St.Louis, Mo.   BR/TR, 5'11", 165 lbs.   Deb: 4/18/50

1950	NY-N	29	40	3	7	0	0	0	3	3	13	.175	.233	.225	21	-5	0			1.000	1	/O-9,1-2	-0.3
1951	NY-N	16	20	6	8	1	1	1	4	2	2	.400	.455	.700	204	3	0	0	0	1.000	-0	/O-8	0.2
	Pit-N	8	5	1	0	0	0	0	0	1	0	.000	.167	.000	-50	-1	0	0	0	1.000	1	/2-1,3-1	0.0
	Yr	24	25	7	8	1	1	1	4	3	2	.320	.393	.560	151	2	0	0	0	1.000	0	/O-8,2-1,3	0.2
	StL-A	41	127	15	31	2	1	1	14	12	21	.244	.309	.299	63	-6	1	0		.969	-0	O-26/3-5,2	-0.7
Total	2	94	192	25	46	3	2	2	21	18	36	.240	.305	.318	66	-9	1	0		.979	0	/O-43,3-6,21	-0.8

■ JIM MAHADY   Mahady, James Bernard   b: 4/22/01, Cortland, N.Y.   d: 8/9/36, Cortland, N.Y.   BR/TR, 5'11", 170 lbs.   Deb: 10/2/21

1921	NY-N	1	0	0	0	0	0	0	0	0	0	—	—	—	—	0	0	0	0	1.000	0	/2-1	0.0

■ ART MAHAN   Mahan, Arthur Leo   b: 6/8/13, Somerville, Mass.   BL/TL, 5'11", 178 lbs.   Deb: 4/30/40

1940	Phi-N	146	544	55	133	24	5	2	39	40	37	.244	.297	.318	73	-21	4			.992	4	*1-145/P-1	-3.1

■ FRANK MAHAR   Mahar, Frank Edward   b: 12/4/1878, Natick, Mass.   d: 12/5/61, Somerville, Mass.   TR, 5'10.5",   Deb: 8/29/02

1902	Phi-A	1	1	0	0	0	0	0	0	0		.000	.000	.000	-99	-0	0			1.000	0	H	0.0

YEAR	TM/L	G	AB	R	H	2B	3B	HR	RBI	BB	SO	AVG	OBP	SLG	PRO+	BR/A	SB	CS	SBR	FA	FR	G/POS	TPR

■ BILLY MAHARG   Maharg, William Joseph   b: 3/19/1881, Philadelphia, Pa.   d: 11/20/53, Philadelphia, Pa.   BR/TR, 5′4.5″, 155 lbs.   Deb: 5/18/12

1912	Det-A	1	1	0	0	0	0	0	0	0	0	.000	.000	.000	-99	-0	0			1.000	1	/3-1	0.0
1916	Phi-N	1	1	0	0	0	0	0	0	0	0	.000	.000	.000	-97	-0	0			.000	-0	/O-1	-0.1
Total	2	2	2	0	0	0	0	0	0	0	0	.000	.000	.000	-99	-0	0			—	0	/O-1,3-1	-0.1

■ TOM MAHER   Maher, Thomas Francis   b: 7/6/1870, Philadelphia, Pa.   d: 8/25/29, Philadelphia, Pa.   Deb: 4/24/02

1902	Phi-N	1	0	0	0	0	0	0	0	0	0	—	—	—	—		0			.000	0	R	0.0

■ GREG MAHLBERG   Mahlberg, Gregory John   b: 8/8/52, Milwaukee, Wis.   BR/TR, 5′10″, 180 lbs.   Deb: 9/24/78

1978	Tex-A	1	1	0	0	0	0	0	0	0	0	.000	.000	.000	-99	-0	0	0	0	1.000	0	/C-1	0.0
1979	Tex-A	7	17	2	2	0	0	1	1	2	4	.118	.211	.294	35	-2	0	0	0	1.000	-2	/C-7	-0.3
Total	2	8	18	2	2	0	0	1	1	2	4	.111	.200	.278	28	-2	0	0	0	1.000	-2	/C-8	-0.3

■ DAN MAHONEY   Mahoney, Daniel J.   b: 3/20/1864, Springfield, Mass.   d: 2/1/04, Springfield, Mass.   BR/TR, 5′9.5″, 165 lbs.   Deb: 8/20/1892

1892	Cin-N	5	21	1	4	0	1	0	1	1	4	.190	.227	.286	56	-1	0			.943	2	/C-5	0.1
1895	Was-N	6	12	2	2	0	0	0	1	0	0	.167	.167	.167	-14	-2	0			1.000	-1	/C-2,1-1	-0.2
Total	2	11	33	3	6	0	1	0	2	1	4	.182	.206	.242	28	-3	0			.949	1	/C-7,1-1	-0.1

■ DANNY MAHONEY   Mahoney, Daniel Joseph   b: 9/6/1888, Haverhill, Mass.   d: 9/28/60, Utica, N.Y.   BR/TR, 5′6.5″, 145 lbs.   Deb: 5/15/11

1911	Cin-N	1	0	0	0	0	0	0	0	0	0	—	—	—	—		0			.000	0	R	0.0

■ MIKE MAHONEY   Mahoney, George W. "Big Mike"   b: 12/5/1873, Boston, Mass.   d: 1/3/40, Boston, Mass.   BR, 6′4″, 220 lbs.   Deb: 5/18/1897

1897	Bos-N	2	2	1	1	0	0	0	1	0		.500	.500	.500	155	0	0			1.000	0	/C-1,P-1	0.0
1898	StL-N	2	7	0	0	0	0	0	0	0	0	.000	.000	.000	-98	-2	0			.920	-0	/1-2	-0.2
Total	2	4	9	1	1	0	0	0	1	0		.111	.111	.111	-36	-2	0			.920	-0	/1-2,P-1,C	-0.2

■ JIM MAHONEY   Mahoney, James Thomas "Moe"   b: 5/26/34, Englewood, N.J.   BR/TR, 6′, 175 lbs.   Deb: 7/28/59   C

1959	Bos-A	31	23	10	3	0	0	1	4	3	7	.130	.231	.261	33	-2	0	0	0	.940	10	S-30	0.9
1961	Was-A	43	108	10	26	0	1	0	6	5	23	.241	.274	.259	44	-8	1	2	-1	.968	12	S-31/2-2	0.4
1962	Cle-A	41	74	12	18	4	0	3	5	3	14	.243	.273	.419	86	-2	0	0	0	.964	8	S-23/2-8,3	0.8
1965	Hou-N	5	5	0	1	0	0	0	0	0	3	.200	.200	.200	14	-1	0	0	0	1.000	0	/S-5	0.0
Total	4	120	210	32	48	4	1	4	15	11	47	.229	.267	.314	57	-13	1	2	-1	.962	31	/S-89,2-10,3	2.1

■ BOB MAIER   Maier, Robert Phillip   b: 9/5/15, Dunellen, N.J.   d: 8/4/93, S.Plainfield, N.J.   BR/TR, 5′8″, 180 lbs.   Deb: 4/17/45

1945	*Det-A	132	486	58	128	25	7	1	34	38	32	.263	.317	.350	88	-8	7	11	-5	.936	-13	*3-124/O-5	-2.4

■ EMIL MAILHO   Mailho, Emil Pierre "Lefty"   b: 12/16/09, Berkeley, Cal.   BL/TL, 5′10″, 165 lbs.   Deb: 4/14/36

1936	Phi-A	21	18	5	1	0	0	0	0	5	3	.056	.261	.056	-18	-3	0	0	0	1.000	-0	/O-1	-0.3

■ CHARLIE MAISEL   Maisel, Charles Louis   b: 4/21/1894, Catonsville, Md.   d: 8/25/53, Baltimore, Md.   BR/TR, 6′,   Deb: 10/2/15

1915	Bal-F	1	4	0	0	0	0	0	0	0	0	.000	.000	.000	-97	-1	0			1.000	0	/C-1	-0.1

■ FRITZ MAISEL   Maisel, Frederick Charles "Flash"   b: 12/23/1889, Catonsville, Md.   d: 4/22/67, Baltimore, Md.   BR/TR, 5′7.5″, 170 lbs.   Deb: 8/11/13   F

1913	NY-A	51	187	33	48	4	3	0	12	34	20	.257	.371	.310	99	1	25			.950	-5	3-51	-0.3
1914	NY-A	150	548	78	131	23	9	2	47	76	69	.239	.334	.325	98	-8	**74**	17	**12**	.928	-18	*3-148	-0.1
1915	NY-A	135	530	77	149	16	6	4	46	48	35	.281	.342	.357	109	5	51	12	**8**	.940	-9	*3-134	1.0
1916	NY-A	53	158	18	36	5	0	0	7	20	18	.228	.318	.259	72	-5	4			.980	-5	O-26,3-11/2	-1.2
1917	NY-A	113	404	46	80	4	4	0	20	36	18	.198	.267	.228	51	-23	29			.967	-1	*2-100/3-7	-2.2
1918	StL-A	90	284	43	66	4	2	0	16	46	17	.232	.341	.261	84	-3	11			.949	-4	3-79/O-1	-0.6
Total	6	592	2111	295	510	56	24	6	148	260	177	.242	.327	.299	88	-25	194	29		.938	-43	3-430,2-104/O	-3.4

■ GEORGE MAISEL   Maisel, George John   b: 3/12/1892, Catonsville, Md.   d: 11/20/68, Baltimore, Md.   BR/TR, 5′10.5″, 180 lbs.   Deb: 5/1/13   F

1913	StL-A	11	18	2	3	2	0	0	1	1	7	.167	.211	.278	44	-1	0			.833	-2	/O-5	-0.4
1916	Det-A	8	5	2	0	0	0	0	0	2		.000	.000	.000	-97	-1	0			.857	2	/3-3	0.1
1921	Chi-N	111	393	54	122	7	2	0	43	11	13	.310	.334	.338	78	-12	17	7	1	.978	0	*O-108	-1.8
1922	Chi-N	38	84	9	16	1	1	0	6	8	2	.190	.261	.226	26	-9	1	3	-2	1.000	-2	O-26	-1.4
Total	4	168	500	67	141	10	3	0	50	20	24	.282	.314	.314	66	-23	18	10		.979	-2	O-139/3-3	-3.5

■ HANK MAJESKI   Majeski, Henry "Heeney"   b: 12/13/16, Staten Island, N.Y.   d: 8/9/91, Staten Island, N.Y.   BR/TR, 5′9″, 180 lbs.   Deb: 5/17/39

1939	Bos-N	106	367	35	100	16	1	7	54	18	30	.272	.310	.379	91	-6	2			.945	12	3-99	0.7
1940	Bos-N	3	3	0	0	0	0	0	0	0	0	.000	.000	.000	-99	-1	0			.000	0	H	-0.1
1941	Bos-N	19	55	5	8	5	0	0	3	1	13	.145	.161	.236	11	-7	0			.911	1	3-11	-0.6
1946	NY-A	8	12	1	1	0	1	0	0	0	3	.083	.083	.250	-9	-2	0	0	0	.750	-1	/3-2	-0.3
	Phi-A	78	264	25	66	14	3	1	25	26	13	.250	.320	.337	84	-6	3	2	-0	.967	8	3-72	0.3
	Yr	86	276	26	67	14	4	1	25	26	16	.243	.310	.333	80	-7	3	2	-0	.964	7	3-74	0.0
1947	Phi-A	141	479	54	134	26	5	8	72	53	31	.280	.358	.405	110	6	1	0	0	**.988**	7	*3-134/S-4,2	1.5
1948	Phi-A	148	590	88	183	41	4	12	120	48	43	.310	.368	.454	118	13	2	1	0	**.975**	1	*3-142/S-8	1.3
1949	Phi-A	114	448	62	124	26	5	9	67	29	23	.277	.326	.417	99	-3	0	1	-1	.957	-4	*3-113	-1.0
1950	Chi-A	122	414	47	128	18	2	6	46	42	34	.309	.377	.406	103	2	1	4	-2	.970	10	3-112	0.8
1951	Chi-A	12	35	4	9	4	0	0	6	1	0	.257	.278	.371	76	-1	0	0	0	.950	-0	/3-9	-0.2
	Phi-A	89	323	41	92	19	4	5	42	35	24	.285	.358	.415	106	3	1	2	-1	.974	14	3-88	1.4
	Yr	101	358	45	101	23	4	5	48	36	24	.282	.351	.411	104	1	1	2	-1	.972	14	3-97	1.2
1952	Phi-A	34	117	14	30	2	2	1	20	19	10	.256	.365	.359	96	-0	1	1	-1	.976	4	3-34	0.3
	Cle-A	36	54	7	16	2	0	0	9	7	7	.296	.377	.333	106	1	0	0	0	.913	-0	3-11/2-3	0.0
	Yr	70	171	21	46	4	2	2	29	26	17	.269	.369	.351	101	1	1	1	-1	.966	3	3-45/2-3	0.3
1953	Cle-A	50	50	6	15	1	0	2	12	3	8	.300	.352	.440	116	1	0	0	0	1.000	-2	2-10/3-7,O	-0.1
1954	*Cle-A	57	121	10	34	4	0	3	17	7	14	.281	.320	.388	92	-2	0	0	0	.990	4	2-25,3-10	0.4
1955	Cle-A	36	48	3	9	2	0	2	8	6	6	.188	.328	.354	80	-1	0	0	0	1.000	-2	/3-9,2-4	-0.3
	Bal-A	16	41	2	7	1	0	0	2	2	4	.171	.209	.195	10	-5	0	0	0	1.000	-3	3-8,2-5	-0.9
	Yr	52	89	5	16	3	0	2	10	8	10	.180	.277	.281	50	-6	0	0	0	1.000	-5	3-17/2-9	-1.2
Total	13	1069	3421	404	956	181	27	57	501	299	260	.279	.342	.398	100	-9	10	11		.968	49	3-861/2-48,SO	3.2

■ MIKE MAKSUDIAN   Maksudian, Michael Bryant   b: 5/28/66, Belleville, Ill.   BL/TR, 5′11″, 220 lbs.   Deb: 9/2/92

1992	Tor-A	3	3	0	0	0	0	0	0	0	0	.000	.000	.000	-96	-1	0	0	0	.000	0	/1-1	-0.1
1993	Min-A	5	12	2	2	1	0	0	2	4	2	.167	.375	.250	71	-1	0	0	0	1.000	1	/1-4,3-1	0.0
1994	Chi-N	26	26	6	7	2	0	0	4	10	6	.269	.472	.346	121	2	0	1	-1	1.000	-0	/1-3,C-2,3	0.1
Total	3	34	41	8	9	3	0	0	6	14	6	.220	.418	.293	93	1	0	1	-1	1.000	1	/1-8,3-3,C	0.0

■ CHARLIE MALAY   Malay, Charles Francis   b: 6/13/1879, Brooklyn, N.Y.   d: 9/18/49, Brooklyn, N.Y.   BB/TR, 5′11.5″, 175 lbs.   Deb: 4/24/05   F

1905	Bro-N	102	349	33	88	7	2	1	31	22		.252	.300	.292	83	-7	13			.932	-9	2-75,O-25/S	-1.8

■ JOE MALAY   Malay, Joseph Charles   b: 10/25/05, Brooklyn, N.Y.   d: 3/19/89, Bridgeport, Conn.   BL/TL, 6′, 175 lbs.   Deb: 9/7/33   F

1933	NY-N	8	24	0	3	0	0	0	2	0	0	.125	.125	.125	-29	-4	0			1.000	2	/1-8	-0.3
1935	NY-N	1	1	0	1	0	0	0	0	0	0	1.000	1.000	1.000	447	0	0			.000	0	H	0.0
Total	2	9	25	0	4	0	0	0	2	0	0	.160	.160	.160	-9	-3	0			1.000	2	/1-8	-0.3

YEAR	TM/L	G	AB	R	H	2B	3B	HR	RBI	BB	SO	AVG	OBP	SLG	PRO+	BR/A	SB	CS	SBR	FA	FR	G/POS	TPR

■ CANDY MALDONADO
Maldonado, Candido (Guadarrama) b: 9/5/60, Humacao, P.R. BR/TR, 6', 190 lbs. Deb: 9/7/81

1981	LA-N	11	12	0	1	0	0	0	0	0	5	.083	.083	.083	-55	-2	0	0	0	1.000	-2	/O-9	-0.5
1982	LA-N	6	4	0	0	0	0	0	0	0	1	.000	.200	.000	-41	-1	0	0	0	1.000	-1	/O-3	-0.1
1983	*LA-N	42	62	5	12	1	1	1	6	5	14	.194	.254	.290	51	-4	0	0	0	1.000	-8	O-33	-1.3
1984	LA-N	116	254	25	68	14	0	5	28	19	29	.268	.321	.382	98	-1	0	3	-2	.955	-16	*O-102/3-4	-2.2
1985	*LA-N	121	213	20	48	7	1	5	19	19	40	.225	.289	.338	77	-7	1	1	-0	.984	-22	*O-113	-3.3
1986	SF-N	133	405	49	102	31	3	18	85	20	77	.252	.292	.477	114	5	4	4	-1	.983	-4	*O-101/3-1	-0.3
1987	*SF-N	118	442	69	129	28	4	20	85	34	78	.292	.351	.509	131	18	8	8	-2	.973	-6	*O-116	0.6
1988	SF-N	142	499	53	127	23	1	12	68	37	89	.255	.315	.377	102	1	6	5	-1	.962	-6	*O-139	-0.8
1989	*SF-N	129	345	39	75	23	0	9	41	37	69	.217	.299	.362	91	-5	4	1	1	.974	-6	*O-116	-1.3
1990	Cle-A	155	590	76	161	32	2	22	95	49	134	.273	.334	.446	117	12	3	5	-2	.993	7	*O-134,D-20	1.3
1991	Mil-A	34	111	11	23	6	0	5	20	13	23	.207	.290	.396	90	-2	1	0	0	.976	-2	O-24	-0.4
	*Tor-A	52	177	26	49	9	0	7	28	23	53	.277	.379	.446	123	6	3	0	1	.990	0	O-52/D-9	0.6
	Yr	86	288	37	72	15	0	12	48	36	76	.250	.345	.427	111	5	4	0	1	.986	-2	O-76/D-9	0.2
1992	*Tor-A	137	489	64	133	25	4	20	66	59	112	.272	.359	.462	123	15	2	2	-1	.978	5	*O-132/D-4	1.7
1993	Chi-N	70	140	8	26	5	0	3	15	13	40	.186	.260	.286	47	-11	0	0	0	.914	-5	O-41	-1.7
	Cle-A	28	81	11	20	2	0	5	20	11	18	.247	.337	.457	112	1	0	1	-1	.976	-3	O-26/D-2	-0.3
1994	Cle-A	42	92	11	18	5	1	5	12	19	31	.196	.333	.435	92	-1	1	1	-0	1.000	-1	D-25/O-5	-0.3
Total	14	1336	3916	470	992	211	17	137	588	359	814	.253	.322	.421	106	23	33	31	-9	.976	-66	*O-1146/D-60,3	-8.3

■ JIM MALER
Maler, James Michael b: 8/16/58, New York, N.Y. BR/TR, 6'4", 230 lbs. Deb: 9/3/81

1981	Sea-A	12	23	1	8	1	0	0	2	2	1	.348	.423	.391	131	1	1	0	0	1.000	-0	/1-5,D-2	0.1
1982	Sea-A	64	221	18	50	8	3	4	26	12	35	.226	.275	.344	67	-10	0	0	0	.991	3	1-57/D-5	-1.0
1983	Sea-A	26	66	5	12	1	0	1	3	5	11	.182	.260	.242	38	-6	0	3	-2	1.000	0	1-19/D-5	-0.8
Total	3	102	310	24	70	10	3	5	31	19	47	.226	.284	.326	65	-15	1	3	-2	.994	3	/1-81,D-12	-1.7

■ TONY MALINOSKY
Malinosky, Anthony Francis b: 10/5/09, Collinsville, Ill. BR/TR, 5'10.5", 165 lbs. Deb: 4/26/37

| 1937 | Bro-N | 35 | 79 | 7 | 18 | 2 | 0 | 0 | 3 | 9 | 11 | .228 | .307 | .253 | 53 | -5 | 0 | | | .833 | -9 | 3-13,S-11 | -1.4 |

■ BOBBY MALKMUS
Malkmus, Robert Edward b: 7/4/31, Newark, N.J. BR/TR, 5'9", 180 lbs. Deb: 6/1/57

1957	Mil-N	13	22	6	2	0	1	0	3	3	3	.091	.200	.182	4	-3	0	0	0	.972	4	/2-7	0.1
1958	Was-A	41	70	5	13	2	1	0	3	4	15	.186	.230	.243	31	-7	0	0	0	.964	8	2-26/3-2,S	0.2
1959	Was-A	6	0	0	0	0	0	0	0	0	0	—	—	—	—	0	0	0	0	.000	0	R	0.0
1960	Phi-N	79	133	16	28	4	1	1	12	11	28	.211	.271	.278	51	-9	2	2	-1	1.000	1	S-29,2-23,3	-0.1
1961	Phi-N	121	342	39	79	8	2	7	31	20	43	.231	.277	.327	61	-20	1	3	-2	.988	16	2-58,S-34,3	0.3
1962	Phi-N	8	5	3	1	1	0	0	0	1	1	.200	.200	.400	58	-0	0	0	0	1.000	2	/S-1	0.2
Total	6	268	572	69	123	15	5	8	46	38	90	.215	.266	.301	53	-39	3	5	-2	.982	36	2-114/S-65,3	0.7

■ JERRY MALLETT
Mallett, Gerald Gordon b: 9/18/35, Bonne Terre, Mo. BR/TR, 6'5", 208 lbs. Deb: 9/19/59

| 1959 | Bos-A | 4 | 15 | 1 | 4 | 0 | 0 | 0 | 1 | 1 | 3 | .267 | .313 | .267 | 58 | -1 | 0 | 0 | 0 | 1.000 | 3 | /O-4 | 0.2 |

■ LES MALLON
Mallon, Leslie Clyde b: 11/21/05, Sweetwater, Tex. d: 4/17/91, Granbury, Tex. BR/TR, 5'8", 160 lbs. Deb: 4/14/31

1931	Phi-N	122	375	41	116	19	2	1	45	29	40	.309	.359	.379	91	-4	0			.956	6	2-97/1-5,S3	0.8
1932	Phi-N	103	347	44	90	16	0	5	31	28	28	.259	.318	.349	71	-14	1			.955	-31	2-88/3-5	-4.1
1934	Bos-N	42	166	23	49	6	1	0	18	15	12	.295	.354	.343	95	-1	0			.967	-4	2-42	-0.3
1935	Bos-N	116	412	48	113	24	2	2	25	28	37	.274	.322	.357	89	-7	3			.975	-14	2-73,3-36/O	-1.3
Total	4	383	1300	156	368	65	5	8	119	100	117	.283	.336	.359	85	-26	4			.962	-43	2-300/3-44,1SO	-4.9

■ BEN MALLONEE
Mallonee, Howard Bennett "Lefty" b: 3/31/1894, Baltimore, Md. d: 2/19/78, Baltimore, Md. BL/TL, 5'6", 150 lbs. Deb: 9/14/21

| 1921 | Phi-A | 7 | 25 | 2 | 6 | 1 | 0 | 0 | 4 | 1 | 2 | .240 | .269 | .280 | 40 | -2 | 1 | 0 | 0 | 1.000 | 0 | /O-6 | -0.2 |

■ JULE MALLONEE
Mallonee, Julius Norris b: 4/4/1900, Charlotte, N.C. d: 12/26/34, Charlotte, N.C. BL/TR, 6'2", 180 lbs. Deb: 8/4/25

| 1925 | Chi-A | 2 | 3 | 1 | 0 | 0 | 0 | 0 | 0 | 1 | 0 | .000 | .250 | .000 | -34 | -1 | 0 | 0 | 0 | 1.000 | -0 | /O-1 | -0.1 |

■ JIM MALLORY
Mallory, James Baugh "Sunny Jim" b: 9/1/18, Lawrenceville, Va. BR/TR, 6'1", 170 lbs. Deb: 9/8/40

1940	Was-A	4	12	2	2	0	0	0	1	1	1	.167	.231	.167	5	-2	0	0	0	1.000	1	/O-3	-0.1
1945	StL-N	13	43	3	10	2	0	0	5	0	2	.233	.233	.279	41	-4	0			.923	-2	O-11	-0.6
	NY-N	37	94	10	28	1	0	0	9	6	7	.298	.340	.309	80	-2	1			.979	-0	O-21	-0.4
	Yr	50	137	13	38	3	0	0	14	6	9	.277	.308	.299	68	-6	1			.959	-2	O-32	-1.0
Total	2	54	149	15	40	3	0	0	14	7	10	.268	.301	.289	63	-8	1	0		.964	-1	/O-35	-1.1

■ SHELDON MALLORY
Mallory, Sheldon b: 7/16/53, Argo, Ill. BL/TL, 6'2", 175 lbs. Deb: 4/10/77

| 1977 | Oak-A | 64 | 126 | 19 | 27 | 4 | 1 | 0 | 5 | 11 | 18 | .214 | .293 | .262 | 53 | -8 | 12 | 5 | 1 | .977 | -3 | O-45/1-4,D | -1.2 |

■ HARRY MALMBERG
Malmberg, Harry William "Swede" b: 7/31/26, Fairfield, Ala. d: 10/29/76, San Francisco, Cal BR/TR, 6'1", 170 lbs. Deb: 4/12/55 C

| 1955 | Det-A | 67 | 208 | 25 | 45 | 5 | 2 | 0 | 19 | 29 | 19 | .216 | .312 | .260 | 56 | -12 | 0 | 1 | -1 | .985 | 6 | 2-65 | -0.2 |

■ EDDIE MALONE
Malone, Edward Russell b: 6/16/20, Chicago, Ill. BR/TR, 5'10", 175 lbs. Deb: 7/17/49

1949	Chi-A	55	170	17	46	7	2	1	16	29	19	.271	.377	.353	97	-0	2	1	0	.990	-3	C-51	0.0
1950	Chi-A	31	71	2	16	2	0	0	10	10	8	.225	.321	.254	50	-5	0	0	0	1.000	2	C-21	-0.2
Total	2	86	241	19	62	9	2	1	26	39	27	.257	.361	.324	83	-5	2	1	0	.993	-2	/C-72	-0.2

■ FERGY MALONE
Malone, Ferguson G. b: 1842, Ireland d: 1/1/05, Seattle, Wash. BR/TL, 5'8", 156 lbs. Deb: 6/3/1871 MU

1871	Ath-n	27	134	33	46	7	1	1	33	9	4	.343	.385	.433	136	7	9					*C-27	0.4
1872	Ath-n	41	213	46	61	6	2	0	39	4	5	.286	.300	.333	94	-1						C-21,1-18	0.0
1873	Phi-n	53	259	59	75	11	2	0	42	14	7	.290	.326	.347	95	-2						*C-53/S-1M	-0.1
1874	Chi-n	47	222	32	55	5	0	0		5		.248	.264	.270	70	-7						*C-47,M	-0.5
1875	Phi-n	29	122	15	28	2	1	0		1		.230	.236	.262	69	-4						1-21/C-4,O	-0.3
1876	Phi-N	22	96	14	22	2	0	0	6	0	1	.229	.229	.250	60	-4				.777	-2	C-20/O-3,S	-0.5
1884	Phi-U	1	4	0	1	0	0	0		0		.250	.250	.250	39	-0				.818	-1	/C-1,M	-0.1
Total	5 n	197	950	185	265	31	6	1	114	33	16	.279	.303	.327	92	-8						C-152/1-39,OS	-0.5
Total	2	23	100	14	23	2	0	0		0	1	.230	.230	.250	59	-4				.780		/C-21,O-3,S	-0.6

■ LEW MALONE
Malone, Lewis Aloysius b: 3/13/1897, Baltimore, Md. d: 2/17/72, Brooklyn, N.Y. BR/TR, 5'11", 175 lbs. Deb: 5/31/15

1915	Phi-A	76	201	17	41	4	4	1	17	21	40	.204	.283	.279	70	-8	7	1	2	.919	-4	2-43,3-12/OS	-1.0
1916	Phi-A	5	4	1	0	0	0	0	0	0	2	.000	.200	.000	-42	-1	0			1.000	-0	/S-1	-0.1
1917	Bro-N	1	0	1	0	0	0	0	0	0	0	—	—	—	—	0	0			.000	0	R	0.0
1919	Bro-N	51	162	9	33	7	3	0	11	6	18	.204	.232	.284	54	-9	1			.934	-7	3-47/2-2,S	-1.6
Total	4	133	367	28	74	11	7	1	28	28	60	.202	.260	.278	62	-18	8	1		.910	-11	/3-59,2-45,SO	-2.7

■ JOHN MALONEY
Maloney, John Deb: 9/15/1876

1876	NY-N	2	7	1	2	0	1	0	0	0	1	.286	.286	.571	206	1				.800	-0	/O-2	0.0
1877	Har-N	1	4	0	1	0	0	0	0	0	0	.250	.250	.250	65	-0				.250	-1	/O-1	-0.1
Total	2	3	11	1	3	0	1	0	0	0	1	.273	.273	.455	152	1				.556	-1	/O-3	-0.1

YEAR TM/L	G	AB	R	H	2B	3B	HR	RBI	BB	SO	AVG	OBP	SLG	PRO+	BR/A	SB	CS	SBR	FA	FR	G/POS	TPR

■ PAT MALONEY
Maloney, Patrick William b: 1/19/1888, Grosvenor Dale, Conn. d: 6/27/79, Pawtucket, R.I. BR/TR, 6', 150 lbs. Deb: 6/19/12

YEAR TM/L	G	AB	R	H	2B	3B	HR	RBI	BB	SO	AVG	OBP	SLG	PRO+	BR/A	SB	CS	SBR	FA	FR	G/POS	TPR
1912 NY-A	25	79	9	17	1	0	0	4	6		.215	.279	.228	43	-6	3			.926	2	O-20	-0.4

■ BILLY MALONEY
Maloney, William Alphonse b: 6/5/1878, Lewiston, Me. d: 9/2/60, Breckenridge, Tex. BL/TR, 5'10", 177 lbs. Deb: 5/2/01

YEAR TM/L	G	AB	R	H	2B	3B	HR	RBI	BB	SO	AVG	OBP	SLG	PRO+	BR/A	SB	CS	SBR	FA	FR	G/POS	TPR
1901 Mil-A	86	290	42	85	3	4	0	22	7		.293	.328	.331	87	-5	11			.952	9	C-72/O-8	0.9
1902 StL-A	30	112	8	23	3	0	0	11	6		.205	.258	.232	37	-9	0			.906	-4	O-23/C-7	-1.4
Cin-N	27	89	13	22	4	0	1	7	2		.247	.272	.326	77	-3	8			.848	-3	O-18/C-7	-0.6
1905 Chi-N	145	558	78	145	17	14	2	56	43		.260	.325	.351	98	-2	59			.954	3	*O-145	-0.6
1906 Bro-N	151	566	71	125	15	7	0	32	49		.221	.286	.272	80	-13	38			.966	11	*O-151	-1.1
1907 Bro-N	144	502	51	115	7	10	0	32	31		.229	.287	.283	86	-9	25			.967	5	*O-144	-1.1
1908 Bro-N	113	359	31	70	5	7	3	17	24		.195	.255	.273	71	-12	14			.947	4	*O-107/C-4	-1.4
Total 6	696	2476	294	585	54	42	6	177	162		.236	.294	.299	83	-53	155			.954	25	O-596/C-90	-5.3

■ FRANK MALZONE
Malzone, Frank James b: 2/28/30, Bronx, N.Y. BR/TR, 5'10", 180 lbs. Deb: 9/17/55

YEAR TM/L	G	AB	R	H	2B	3B	HR	RBI	BB	SO	AVG	OBP	SLG	PRO+	BR/A	SB	CS	SBR	FA	FR	G/POS	TPR
1955 Bos-A	6	20	2	7	1	0	0	1	1	3	.350	.381	.400	101	0	0	0	0	1.000	2	/3-4	0.2
1956 Bos-A	27	103	15	17	3	1	2	11	9	8	.165	.232	.272	29	-11	1	0	0	.931	1	3-26	-0.9
1957 Bos-A★	153	634	82	185	31	5	15	103	31	41	.292	.326	.427	98	-3	2	1	0	.954	14	*3-153	1.5
1958 Bos-A★	155	627	76	185	30	2	15	87	33	53	.295	.334	.421	100	-1	1	3	-2	.950	17	*3-155	1.6
1959 Bos-A★	154	604	90	169	34	2	19	92	42	58	.280	.328	.437	103	1	6	0	2	.953	8	*3-154	1.1
1960 Bos-A★	152	595	60	161	30	2	14	79	36	42	.271	.317	.398	89	-10	2	3	-1	.948	-0	*3-151	-0.5
1961 Bos-A	151	590	74	157	21	4	14	87	44	49	.266	.318	.386	85	-13	1	3	-2	.950	-5	*3-149	-1.8
1962 Bos-A	156	619	74	175	20	3	21	95	35	43	.283	.321	.426	96	-5	0	1	-1	.967	5	*3-156	0.1
1963 Bos-A★	151	580	66	169	25	2	15	71	31	45	.291	.331	.419	105	3	0	2	-1	.964	4	*3-148	0.6
1964 Bos-A☆	148	537	62	142	19	0	13	56	37	43	.264	.314	.372	86	-10	0	0	0	.959	-0	*3-143	-1.3
1965 Bos-A	106	364	40	87	20	0	3	34	28	38	.239	.295	.319	70	-14	1	1	-0	.969	-3	3-96	-2.1
1966 Cal-A	82	155	6	32	5	0	2	12	6	11	.206	.255	.277	54	-9	0	0	0	.925	-1	3-35	-1.2
Total 12	1441	5428	647	1486	239	21	133	728	337	434	.274	.318	.399	91	-71	14	14	-4	.955	47	*3-1370	-2.7

■ GUS MANCUSO
Mancuso, August Rodney "Blackie" b: 12/5/05, Galveston, Tex. d: 10/26/84, Houston, Tex. BR/TR, 5'10", 185 lbs. Deb: 4/30/28 FC

YEAR TM/L	G	AB	R	H	2B	3B	HR	RBI	BB	SO	AVG	OBP	SLG	PRO+	BR/A	SB	CS	SBR	FA	FR	G/POS	TPR
1928 StL-N	11	38	2	7	1	0	0	3	0	5	.184	.184	.237	9	-5	0			.984	4	C-11	0.0
1930 *StL-N	76	227	39	83	17	2	7	59	18	16	.366	.415	.551	127	10	1			.969	1	C-61	1.4
1931 *StL-N	67	187	13	49	16	1	1	23	18	13	.262	.327	.374	85	-4	2			.972	6	C-56	0.6
1932 StL-N	103	310	25	88	23	1	5	43	30	15	.284	.347	.413	100	1	0			.977	8	C-82	1.3
1933 *NY-N	144	481	39	127	17	2	6	56	48	21	.264	.331	.345	95	-2	0			.972	2	*C-142	0.8
1934 NY-N	122	383	32	94	14	0	7	46	27	19	.245	.295	.337	70	-16	0			.977	6	*C-122	-0.4
1935 NY-N★	128	447	33	133	18	2	5	56	30	16	.298	.342	.380	95	-3	1			.972	-5	*C-126	-0.1
1936 *NY-N	139	519	55	156	21	3	9	63	39	28	.301	.351	.405	104	3	0			.977	8	*C-138	1.4
1937 *NY-N★	86	287	30	80	17	1	4	39	17	20	.279	.319	.387	90	-4	1			.982	16	C-81	1.5
1938 NY-N	52	158	19	55	8	2	0	15	17	13	.348	.411	.437	132	8	0			.977	4	C-44	1.4
1939 Chi-N	80	251	17	58	10	0	2	17	24	19	.231	.298	.295	59	-14	0			.981	5	C-76	-0.6
1940 Bro-N	60	144	16	33	8	0	0	16	13	7	.229	.293	.285	56	-8	0			.982	7	C-56	0.1
1941 StL-N	106	328	25	75	13	1	2	37	37	19	.229	.309	.293	66	-14	0			.989	11	*C-105	0.4
1942 StL-N	5	13	0	1	0	0	0	1	0	0	.077	.077	.077	-51	-2	0			.917	-1	/C-3	-0.4
NY-N	39	109	4	21	1	1	0	8	14	7	.193	.285	.220	48	-7	1			.982	3	C-38	-0.2
Yr	44	122	4	22	1	1	0	9	14	7	.180	.265	.205	38	-9	1			.977	1	C-41	-0.6
1943 NY-N	94	252	11	50	5	0	2	20	28	16	.198	.284	.242	52	-15	0			.974	-0	C-77	-1.1
1944 NY-N	78	195	15	49	4	1	1	25	30	20	.251	.351	.297	84	-3	0			.976	5	C-72	0.5
1945 Phi-N	70	176	11	35	5	0	0	16	28	10	.199	.309	.227	52	-11	2			.988	1	C-70	-0.7
Total 17	1460	4505	386	1194	197	16	53	543	418	264	.265	.328	.351	85	-89	8			.977	75	*C-1360	5.9

■ FRANK MANCUSO
Mancuso, Frank Octavius b: 5/23/18, Houston, Tex. BR/TR, 6', 195 lbs. Deb: 4/18/44 F

YEAR TM/L	G	AB	R	H	2B	3B	HR	RBI	BB	SO	AVG	OBP	SLG	PRO+	BR/A	SB	CS	SBR	FA	FR	G/POS	TPR
1944 *StL-A	88	244	19	50	11	0	1	24	20	32	.205	.271	.262	50	-16	1	0	0	.953	-6	C-87	-1.8
1945 StL-A	119	365	39	98	13	3	1	38	46	44	.268	.354	.329	94	-2	0	2	-1	.989	-6	*C-115	-0.2
1946 StL-A	87	262	22	63	8	3	3	23	30	31	.240	.323	.328	78	-7	1	0	0	.973	-18	C-85	-2.1
1947 Was-A	43	131	5	30	5	1	0	13	5	11	.229	.257	.282	51	-9	0	0	0	.958	-4	C-35	-1.1
Total 4	337	1002	85	241	37	7	5	98	101	118	.241	.314	.306	74	-34	2	2	-1	.972	-34	C-322	-5.2

■ CARL MANDA
Manda, Carl Alan b: 11/16/1888, Little River, Kan. d: 3/9/83, Artesia, N.Mex. BR/TR, 5'10", 170 lbs. Deb: 9/11/14

YEAR TM/L	G	AB	R	H	2B	3B	HR	RBI	BB	SO	AVG	OBP	SLG	PRO+	BR/A	SB	CS	SBR	FA	FR	G/POS	TPR
1914 Chi-A	9	15	2	4	0	0	0	1	3	3	.267	.389	.267	99	0	1			.971	4	/2-7	0.5

■ JIM MANGAN
Mangan, James Daniel b: 9/24/29, San Francisco, Cal. BR/TR, 5'10", 190 lbs. Deb: 4/16/52

YEAR TM/L	G	AB	R	H	2B	3B	HR	RBI	BB	SO	AVG	OBP	SLG	PRO+	BR/A	SB	CS	SBR	FA	FR	G/POS	TPR
1952 Pit-N	11	13	1	2	0	0	0	2	1	3	.154	.214	.154	4	-2	0	0	0	.833	-1	/C-4	-0.2
1954 Pit-N	14	26	2	5	0	0	0	2	4	9	.192	.300	.192	32	-2	0	0	0	1.000	0	/C-7	-0.2
1956 NY-N	20	20	2	2	0	0	0	1	4	6	.100	.250	.100	-1	-3	0	0	0	1.000	0	C-15	-0.2
Total 3	45	59	5	9	0	0	0	5	9	18	.153	.265	.153	15	-7	0	0	0	.985	-0	/C-26	-0.6

■ ANGEL MANGUAL
Mangual, Angel Luis (Guilbe) b: 3/19/47, Juana Diaz, P.R. BR/TR, 5'10", 180 lbs. Deb: 9/15/69 F

YEAR TM/L	G	AB	R	H	2B	3B	HR	RBI	BB	SO	AVG	OBP	SLG	PRO+	BR/A	SB	CS	SBR	FA	FR	G/POS	TPR
1969 Pit-N	6	4	1	1	1	0	0	0	0	0	.250	.250	.500	108	-1	0	0	0	.000	-1	/O-3	-0.1
1971 *Oak-A	94	287	32	82	8	1	4	30	17	27	.286	.326	.362	97	-2	1	4	-2	.988	-2	O-81	-1.0
1972 *Oak-A	91	272	19	67	13	2	5	32	14	48	.246	.286	.364	97	-2	0	1	-1	.971	3	O-74	-0.3
1973 *Oak-A	74	192	20	43	4	1	3	13	9	34	.224	.259	.302	61	-11	1	1	-0	.947	-5	O-50,D-14/12	-1.9
1974 *Oak-A	115	321	36	85	14	4	9	43	17	59	.233	.267	.367	87	-8	3	0	1	.961	-7	O-74,D-37/3	-1.9
1975 Oak-A	62	109	13	24	0	1	0	6	3	18	.220	.241	.275	47	-8	0	1	-1	.978	-9	O-39,D-15	-1.9
1976 Oak-A	8	12	0	2	1	0	0	0	1	1	.167	.167	.250	22	-1	0	1	-1	1.000	-2	/O-7	-0.4
Total 7	450	1241	122	304	44	8	22	125	59	187	.245	.280	.346	83	-32	5	8	-3	.969	-23	O-328/D-66,132	-7.5

■ PEPE MANGUAL
Mangual, Jose Manuel (Guilbe) b: 5/23/52, Ponce, P.R. BR/TR, 5'10", 165 lbs. Deb: 9/6/72 F

YEAR TM/L	G	AB	R	H	2B	3B	HR	RBI	BB	SO	AVG	OBP	SLG	PRO+	BR/A	SB	CS	SBR	FA	FR	G/POS	TPR
1972 Mon-N	8	11	2	3	0	0	0	0	1	5	.273	.333	.273	73	-0	0	1	-1	1.000	-1	/O-3	-0.2
1973 Mon-N	33	62	9	11	2	1	3	7	6	18	.177	.250	.387	71	-3	2	4	-2	.966	-3	O-22	-0.9
1974 Mon-N	23	61	10	19	3	0	0	4	5	15	.311	.364	.361	98	-0	5	0	2	1.000	-6	O-22	-0.6
1975 Mon-N	140	514	84	126	16	2	9	45	74	115	.245	.345	.337	86	-8	33	11	3	.972	-4	*O-138	-1.5
1976 Mon-N	66	215	34	56	9	1	3	16	50	49	.260	.404	.353	112	7	17	7	1	.968	1	O-62	0.4
NY-N	41	102	15	19	5	2	1	9	10	32	.186	.259	.304	63	-5	7	3	0	.985	-2	O-38	-0.9
Yr	107	317	49	75	14	3	4	25	60	81	.237	.361	.338	99	2	24	10	1	.973	-3	*O-100	-0.5
1977 NY-N	8	7	1	1	0	0	0	2	1	4	.143	.250	.143	-9	-1	0	0	0	.833	-1	/O-4	-0.2
Total 6	319	972	155	235	35	6	16	83	147	238	.242	.345	.340	89	-11	64	26	4	.972	-18	O-289	-3.9

■ GEORGE MANGUS
Mangus, George Graham b: 5/22/1890, Red Creek, N.Y. d: 8/10/33, Rutland, Mass. BL/TR, 5'11.5", 165 lbs. Deb: 8/20/12

YEAR TM/L	G	AB	R	H	2B	3B	HR	RBI	BB	SO	AVG	OBP	SLG	PRO+	BR/A	SB	CS	SBR	FA	FR	G/POS	TPR
1912 Phi-N	10	25	2	5	3	0	0	3	1	6	.200	.231	.320	47	-2	0			.750	-1	/O-5	-0.4

■ CLYDE MANION
Manion, Clyde Jennings "Pete" b: 10/30/1896, Jefferson City, Mo d: 9/4/67, Detroit, Mich. BR/TR, 5'11", 175 lbs. Deb: 5/5/20

YEAR TM/L	G	AB	R	H	2B	3B	HR	RBI	BB	SO	AVG	OBP	SLG	PRO+	BR/A	SB	CS	SBR	FA	FR	G/POS	TPR
1920 Det-A	32	80	4	22	4	1	0	8	4	7	.275	.318	.350	79	-3	0	0	0	.940	-2	C-30	-0.3
1921 Det-A	12	10	0	2	0	0	0	2	2	2	.200	.385	.200	53	-1	0	0	0	1.000	1	/C-3	0.0
1922 Det-A	42	69	9	19	4	1	0	12	4	6	.275	.315	.362	79	-2	0	0	0	.932	-2	C-22/1-1	-0.4
1923 Det-A	23	22	3	3	1	0	0	1	4	4	.136	.208	.136	-8	-3	0	0	0	.857	-0	/C-3,1-1	-0.4

YEAR	TM/L	G	AB	R	H	2B	3B	HR	RBI	BB	SO	AVG	OBP	SLG	PRO+	BR/A	SB	CS	SBR	FA	FR	G/POS	TPR
1924	Det-A	14	13	1	3	0	0	0	2	1	1	.231	.286	.231	35	-1	0	0	0	.750	-1	/C-3,1-1	-0.2
1926	Det-A	75	176	15	35	4	0	0	14	24	16	.199	.295	.222	36	-16	1	1	-0	.972	-0	C-74	-1.3
1927	Det-A	1	0	0	0	0	0	0	0	1	0	—	1.000	—	174	0	0			.000	0	H	0.0
1928	StL-A	76	243	25	55	5	1	2	31	15	18	.226	.274	.280	44	-20	3	0	1	.980	12	C-71	-0.1
1929	StL-A	35	111	16	27	2	0	0	11	15	3	.243	.342	.261	53	-7	1	0	0	.976	5	C-34	0.1
1930	StL-A	57	148	12	32	4	0	0	11	24	17	.216	.326	.243	45	-12	0	1	-1	.985	11	C-56	0.3
1932	Cin-N	49	135	7	28	4	0	0	12	14	16	.207	.282	.237	43	-11	0			.970	4	C-47	-0.4
1933	Cin-N	36	84	3	14	1	0	0	3	8	7	.167	.239	.179	21	-8	0			.981	4	C-34	-0.3
1934	Cin-N	25	54	4	10	0	0	0	4	4	7	.185	.241	.185	16	-6	0			1.000	3	C-24	-0.3
Total	13	477	1145	96	250	25	3	3	112	118	102	.218	.293	.253	45	-90	5	3		.973	33	C-401/1-3	-3.3

■ PHIL MANKOWSKI   Mankowski, Philip Anthony b: 1/9/53, Buffalo, N.Y.   BL/TR, 6', 180 lbs.   Deb: 8/30/76

YEAR	TM/L	G	AB	R	H	2B	3B	HR	RBI	BB	SO	AVG	OBP	SLG	PRO+	BR/A	SB	CS	SBR	FA	FR	G/POS	TPR
1976	Det-A	24	85	9	23	2	1	1	4	4	8	.271	.303	.353	88	-1	0	0	0	.971	2	3-23	0.1
1977	Det-A	94	286	21	79	7	3	3	27	16	41	.276	.319	.353	79	-8	1	2	-1	.964	13	3-85/2-1	0.3
1978	Det-A	88	222	28	61	8	0	4	20	22	28	.275	.344	.365	97	-0	2	3	-1	.972	-1	3-80/D-1	-0.3
1979	Det-A	42	99	11	22	4	0	0	8	10	16	.222	.294	.263	50	-7	0	0	0	.963	-1	3-36	-0.8
1980	NY-N	8	12	1	2	1	0	0	1	2	4	.167	.286	.250	52	-1	0	0	0	.571	-1	/3-3	-0.2
1982	NY-N	13	35	2	8	1	0	0	4	1	6	.229	.250	.257	42	-3	0	1	-1	.957	-1	3-13	-0.4
Total	6	269	739	72	195	23	4	8	64	55	103	.264	.318	.338	79	-20	3	6	-3	.962	12	3-240/D-1,2	-1.3

■ CHARLIE MANLOVE   Manlove, Charles Henry Weeks "Chick" b: 10/8/1862, Philadelphia, Pa.   d: 2/12/52, Altoona, Pa.   BR/TR, 5'9", 165 lbs.   Deb: 5/31/1884

YEAR	TM/L	G	AB	R	H	2B	3B	HR	RBI	BB	SO	AVG	OBP	SLG	PRO+	BR/A	SB	CS	SBR	FA	FR	G/POS	TPR
1884	Alt-U	2	7	1	3	0	0	0		0	0	.429	.429	.429	132	0				1.000	-1	/C-1,O-1	-0.1
	NY-N	3	10	0	0	0	0	0		0	4	.000	.000	.000	-98	-2				.833	-1	/C-3,O-1	-0.3
Total	1	5	17	1	3	0	0	0		0	4	.176	.176	.176	4	-2				.880	-2	/C-4,O-2	-0.4

■ GARTH MANN   Mann, Ben Garth "Red" b: 11/16/15, Brandon, Tex.   d: 9/11/80, Italy, Tex.   BR/TR, 6', 155 lbs.   Deb: 5/14/44

YEAR	TM/L	G	AB	R	H	2B	3B	HR	RBI	BB	SO	AVG	OBP	SLG	PRO+	BR/A	SB	CS	SBR	FA	FR	G/POS	TPR
1944	Chi-N	1	0	1	0	0	0	0	0	0	0	—	—	—		0	0			.000	0	R	0.0

■ FRED MANN   Mann, Fred J. b: 4/1/1858, Sutton, Vt.   d: 4/6/16, Springfield, Mass.   BL, 5'10.5", 178 lbs.   Deb: 5/1/1882

YEAR	TM/L	G	AB	R	H	2B	3B	HR	RBI	BB	SO	AVG	OBP	SLG	PRO+	BR/A	SB	CS	SBR	FA	FR	G/POS	TPR
1882	Wor-N	19	77	12	18	5	0	0	7	2	15	.234	.253	.299	74	-2				.703	-6	3-18/1-1	-0.8
	Phi-a	29	121	13	28	7	4	0		4		.231	.256	.355	93	-2				.798	-10	3-29	-1.1
1883	Col-a	96	394	61	98	18	13	1		18		.249	.282	.368	117	8				.854	-3	*O-82/1-9,3S	0.4
1884	Col-a	99	366	70	101	12	18	7		25		.276	.341	.464	174	31				.857	-6	*O-97/2-2	2.1
1885	Pit-a	99	391	60	99	17	6	0		31		.253	.318	.327	106	4				.908	-8	*O-97/3-3	-0.6
1886	Pit-a	116	440	85	110	16	14	2		45		.250	.335	.364	119	11	26			.878	-3	*O-116	0.4
1887	Cle-a	64	259	45	80	15	7	2		23		.309	.385	.444	135	13	25			.879	1	O-64	1.0
	Phi-a	55	229	42	63	14	6	0		15		.275	.336	.389	102	-0	16			.916	-4	O-55	-0.4
	Yr	119	488	87	143	29	13	2		38		.293	.362	.418	119	13	41			.896	-3	*O-119	0.6
Total	6	577	2277	388	597	104	68	12	7	163	15	.262	.323	.383	122	63	67			.881	-39	O-511/3-56,12S	1.0

■ JOHNNY MANN   Mann, John Leo b: 2/4/1898, Fontanet, Ind.   d: 3/31/77, Terre Haute, Ind.   BR/TR, 5'11", 160 lbs.   Deb: 4/18/28

YEAR	TM/L	G	AB	R	H	2B	3B	HR	RBI	BB	SO	AVG	OBP	SLG	PRO+	BR/A	SB	CS	SBR	FA	FR	G/POS	TPR
1928	Chi-A	6	6	0	2	0	0	0	1	0		.333	.429	.333	104	0	0	0	0	1.000	0	/3-2	0.0

■ KELLY MANN   Mann, Kelly John b: 8/17/67, Santa Monica, Cal.   BR/TR, 6'3", 215 lbs.   Deb: 9/4/89

YEAR	TM/L	G	AB	R	H	2B	3B	HR	RBI	BB	SO	AVG	OBP	SLG	PRO+	BR/A	SB	CS	SBR	FA	FR	G/POS	TPR
1989	Atl-N	7	24	1	5	0	0	1	6			.208	.240	.292	50	-2	0	0	0	1.000	2	/C-7	0.1
1990	Atl-N	11	28	2	4	1	0	1	2	0	6	.143	.143	.286	14	-3	0	0	0	1.000	-1	C-10	-0.4
Total	2	18	52	3	9	3	0	1	2	0	12	.173	.189	.288	30	-5	0	0	0	1.000	1	/C-17	-0.3

■ LES MANN   Mann, Leslie "Major" b: 11/18/1893, Lincoln, Neb.   d: 1/14/62, Pasadena, Cal.   BR/TR, 5'9", 172 lbs.   Deb: 4/30/13

YEAR	TM/L	G	AB	R	H	2B	3B	HR	RBI	BB	SO	AVG	OBP	SLG	PRO+	BR/A	SB	CS	SBR	FA	FR	G/POS	TPR
1913	Bos-N	120	407	54	103	24	7	3	51	18	73	.253	.291	.369	86	-9	7			.960	-2	*O-120	-1.6
1914	*Bos-N	126	389	44	96	16	11	4	40	24	50	.247	.292	.375	99	-2	9			.952	13	*O-123	0.7
1915	Chi-F	135	470	74	144	12	**19**	4	58	36	40	.306	.357	.438	119	10	18			.969	5	*O-130/S-1	1.0
1916	Chi-N	127	415	46	113	13	9	2	29	19	31	.272	.307	.361	95	-3	11	7	-1	.972	-8	*O-115	-1.9
1917	Chi-N	117	444	63	121	19	10	1	44	27	46	.273	.316	.367	101	-0	14			.953	0	*O-116	-0.7
1918	*Chi-N	129	489	69	141	27	7	2	55	38	45	.288	.342	.384	119	10	21			.961	-3	*O-129	-0.7
1919	Chi-N	80	299	31	68	8	8	1	22	11	29	.227	.257	.318	72	-11	12			.982	2	O-78	-1.7
	Bos-N	40	145	15	41	6	4	3	20	9	14	.283	.329	.441	136	6	7			.929	3	O-40	0.6
	Yr	120	444	46	109	14	12	4	42	20	43	.245	.281	.358	92	-5	19			.962	4	*O-118	-1.1
1920	Bos-N	115	424	48	117	7	8	3	32	38	42	.276	.341	.351	104	3	7	7	-2	.980	3	*O-110	-0.5
1921	StL-N	97	256	57	84	12	7	7	30	23	28	.328	.384	.512	140	14	5	5	-2	.969	0	O-79	0.8
1922	StL-N	84	147	42	51	14	1	2	20	16	12	.347	.415	.497	141	9	0	1	-1	.978	-11	O-57	-0.5
1923	StL-N	38	89	20	33	5	5	5	11	9	5	.371	.434	.640	184	11	0	0	0	.979	-3	O-26	0.6
	Cin-N	8	1	1	0	0	0	0	0	0	0	.000	.000	.000	-99	-0	0			.000	0	H	0.0
	Yr	46	90	21	33	5	5	5	11	9	5	.367	.430	.633	181	10	0			.979	-3	O-26	0.6
1924	Bos-N	32	102	13	28	7	4	0	10	8	10	.275	.333	.422	105	1	1	0	0	1.000	2	O-28	0.1
1925	Bos-N	60	184	27	63	11	4	2	20	5	11	.342	.373	.478	127	7	6	1	1	.992	-2	O-57	0.3
1926	Bos-N	50	129	23	39	8	2	1	20	9	9	.302	.348	.419	116	2	5			.966	-6	O-46	-0.6
1927	Bos-N	29	66	8	17	3	1	0	6	8	3	.258	.338	.333	87	-1	2			.955	-2	O-24	-0.4
	NY-N	29	67	13	22	4	1	2	10	8	7	.328	.400	.507	142	4	2			1.000	-4	O-22	-0.1
	Yr	58	133	21	39	7	2	2	16	16	10	.293	.369	.421	116	3	4			.973	-6	O-46	-0.5
1928	NY-N	82	193	29	51	7	1	2	25	18	9	.264	.330	.342	76	-7	2			.952	-19	O-68	-2.8
Total	16	1498	4716	677	1332	203	106	44	503	324	464	.282	.332	.398	108	43	129	21		.966	-32	*O-1368/S-1	-6.7

■ JIM MANNING   Manning, James H. b: 1/31/1862, Fall River, Mass.   d: 10/22/29, Edinburg, Tex.   BB/TR, 5'7", 157 lbs.   Deb: 5/16/1884   M

YEAR	TM/L	G	AB	R	H	2B	3B	HR	RBI	BB	SO	AVG	OBP	SLG	PRO+	BR/A	SB	CS	SBR	FA	FR	G/POS	TPR
1884	Bos-N	89	345	52	83	8	6	2	35	19	47	.241	.280	.316	88	-5				.878	1	O-73/S-9,23	-0.4
1885	Bos-N	84	306	34	63	8	9	2	27	19	36	.206	.252	.310	84	-5				.898	9	*O-83/S-1	0.2
	Det-N	20	78	15	21	4	0	1	9	4	10	.269	.305	.359	114	1				.802	-7	S-20	-0.5
	Yr	104	384	49	84	12	9	3	36	23	46	.219	.263	.320	90	-4				.898	3	O-83,S-21	-0.3
1886	Det-N	26	97	14	18	2	3	0	7	6	10	.186	.233	.268	51	-6	7			.947	-1	O-26/S-1	-0.7
1887	Det-N	13	52	5	10	1	0	0	3	5	4	.192	.276	.212	36	-4	3			.867	-4	O-10/S-3	-0.8
1889	KC-a	132	506	68	103	16	7	3	68	54	61	.204	.281	.281	61	-27	58			.927	-3	O-69,2-63/S3	-3.0
Total	5	364	1384	188	298	39	25	8	149	107	168	.215	.278	.297	73	-46	68			.903	-11	O-261/2-72,S3	-5.2

■ JACK MANNING   Manning, John E. b: 12/20/1853, Braintree, Mass.   d: 8/15/29, Boston, Mass.   BR/TR, 5'8.5", 158 lbs.   Deb: 4/23/1873   M

YEAR	TM/L	G	AB	R	H	2B	3B	HR	RBI	BB	SO	AVG	OBP	SLG	PRO+	BR/A	SB	CS	SBR	FA	FR	G/POS	TPR
1873	Bos-n	32	159	29	43	5	2	0	22	1	11	.270	.275	.327	71	-7						1-29/O-5	-0.4
1874	Bal-n	42	168	33	59	10	1	0		3		.351	.363	.423	150	9						P-22,2-20/S	0.6
	Har-n	1	5	1	1	0	0	0		0		.200	.200	.200	26	-0						/3-1	0.0
	Yr	43	173	34	60	10	1	0		3		.347	.358	.416	146	9						P-22,2-20/S3	0.6
1875	Bos-n	77	343	71	94	8	2	1		2		.274	.278	.318	102	-0						*O-58,P-27,13	0.3
1876	Bos-N	70	288	52	76	9	7	5	25	7	5	.264	.281	.330	101	-0				.777	-5	*O-56,P-34/S2	-0.5
1877	Cin-N	57	252	47	80	16	7	0	36	5	6	.317	.331	.437	157	16				.742	-13	S-26,1-17,OP/2M	-0.9
1878	Bos-N	60	248	40	63	10	4	0	23	10	6	.254	.283	.302	86	-4				.753	-13	*O-59/P-3	-1.9
1880	Cin-N	48	190	20	41	6	3	2	17	7	15	.216	.244	.311	87	-2				.798	-3	O-47/1-1	-0.6
1881	Buf-N	1	1	0	0	0	0	0	0	0	0	.000	.000	.000	-99	-0				1.000	0	/O-1	0.0
1883	Phi-N	98	420	60	112	31	5	0	37	20	37	.267	.300	.364	110	6				.853	10	*O-98	1.3

YEAR	TM/L	G	AB	R	H	2B	3B	HR	RBI	BB	SO	AVG	OBP	SLG	PRO+	BR/A	SB	CS	SBR	FA	FR	G/POS	TPR
1884	Phi-N	104	424	71	115	29	4	5	52	40	67	.271	.334	.394	134	18				.847	-1	*O-104	1.3
1885	Phi-N	107	445	61	114	24	4	3	40	37	27	.256	.313	.348	116	9				.896	-6	*O-107	0.0
1886	Bal-a	137	556	78	124	18	7	1		50		.223	.291	.286	83	-10	24			.887	-10	*O-137	-2.0
Total	3 n	152	675	134	197	23	5	1	92	6	11	.292	.298	.345	105	2	1					/O-63,P-49,12S3	0.5
Total	9	682	2824	430	725	147	31	13	230	176	173	.257	.301	.345	108	33	24			.844	-40	O-621/P-47,S12	-2.2

■ RICK MANNING
Manning, Richard Eugene b: 9/2/54, Niagara Falls, N.Y. BL/TR, 6'1", 180 lbs. Deb: 5/23/75

YEAR	TM/L	G	AB	R	H	2B	3B	HR	RBI	BB	SO	AVG	OBP	SLG	PRO+	BR/A	SB	CS	SBR	FA	FR	G/POS	TPR
1975	Cle-A	120	480	69	137	16	5	3	35	44	62	.285	.348	.358	100	1	19	11	-1	.974	13	*O-118/D-1	0.8
1976	Cle-A	138	552	73	161	24	7	6	43	41	75	.292	.341	.393	116	10	16	10	-1	.987	8	*O-136	1.2
1977	Cle-A	68	252	33	57	7	3	5	18	21	35	.226	.286	.337	71	-10	9	5	-0	.990	5	O-68	-0.8
1978	Cle-A	148	566	65	149	27	3	3	50	38	62	.263	.311	.337	83	-13	12	12	-4	.995	5	*O-144	-1.8
1979	Cle-A	144	560	67	145	12	2	3	51	55	48	.259	.326	.304	71	-21	30	8	4	.986	15	*O-141	-0.8
1980	Cle-A	140	471	55	110	17	4	3	52	63	66	.234	.326	.306	74	-15	12	6	0	.990	8	*O-139	-1.3
1981	Cle-A	103	360	47	88	15	3	4	33	40	57	.244	.320	.336	90	-4	25	3	6	.987	13	*O-103	1.2
1982	Cle-A	152	562	71	152	18	2	8	44	54	60	.270	.334	.352	89	-7	12	8	-1	.978	6	*O-152	-0.7
1983	Cle-A	50	194	20	54	6	0	1	10	12	22	.278	.320	.325	75	-6	7	3	0	.987	3	O-50	-0.4
	Mil-A	108	375	40	86	14	4	3	33	26	40	.229	.281	.312	68	-17	11	2	2	.991	6	*O-108	-1.2
	Yr	158	569	60	140	20	4	4	43	38	62	.246	.294	.316	71	-23	18	5	2	.990	9	*O-158	-1.6
1984	Mil-A	119	341	53	85	10	5	7	31	34	32	.249	.319	.370	94	-3	5	7	-3	.987	-14	*O-114/D-1	-2.2
1985	Mil-A	79	216	19	47	9	1	2	18	14	19	.218	.265	.296	54	-14	1	0	0	.976	-6	O-74/D-2	-2.1
1986	Mil-A	89	205	31	52	7	3	8	27	17	20	.254	.314	.434	98	-1	5	3	-0	.988	-5	O-83/D-5	-0.8
1987	Mil-A	97	114	21	26	7	1	0	13	12	18	.228	.302	.307	60	-6	4	0	1	.958	-19	O-78/D-2	-2.4
Total	13	1555	5248	664	1349	189	43	56	458	471	616	.257	.319	.341	84	-108	168	78	4	.985	40	*O-1508/D-11	-11.3

■ TIM MANNING
Manning, Timothy Edward b: 12/3/1853, Henley-On-The- Thames, England d: 6/11/34, Oak Park, Ill. BR/TR, 5'10", 170 lbs. Deb: 5/1/1882

YEAR	TM/L	G	AB	R	H	2B	3B	HR	RBI	BB	SO	AVG	OBP	SLG	PRO+	BR/A	SB	CS	SBR	FA	FR	G/POS	TPR
1882	Pro-N	21	76	7	8	0	0	0		8	13	.105	.160	.105	-13	-9				.787	-10	S-17/C-4	-1.8
1883	Bal-a	35	121	23	26	5	0	0			14	.215	.296	.256	77	-3				.913	3	2-35	0.1
1884	Bal-a	91	341	49	70	14	5	2			26	.205	.275	.293	82	-6				.907	-2	*2-91	-0.6
1885	Bal-a	43	157	17	32	8	1	0			10	.204	.265	.268	70	-5				.919	3	2-41/3-3	-0.1
	Pro-N	10	35	3	2	1	0	0	0	1	11	.057	.083	.086	-47	-6				.854	-3	S-10	-0.8
Total	4	200	730	99	138	28	6	2	8	56	24	.189	.256	.252	63	-29				.911	-9	2-167/S-27,C3	-3.2

■ DON MANNO
Manno, Donald D. b: 5/15/15, Williamsport, Pa. BR/TR, 6'1", 190 lbs. Deb: 9/22/40

YEAR	TM/L	G	AB	R	H	2B	3B	HR	RBI	BB	SO	AVG	OBP	SLG	PRO+	BR/A	SB	CS	SBR	FA	FR	G/POS	TPR
1940	Bos-N	3	7	1	2	0	0	1	4	0	2	.286	.286	.714	177	1	0			1.000	0	/O-2	0.1
1941	Bos-N	22	30	2	5	1	0	0	4	3	7	.167	.242	.200	27	-3	0			1.000	-1	/O-5,3-3,1	-0.5
Total	2	25	37	3	7	1	0	1	8	3	9	.189	.250	.297	56	-2	0			1.000	-1	/O-7,3-3,1	-0.4

■ FRED MANRIQUE
Manrique, Fred Eloy (Reyes) b: 11/5/61, Edo Bolivar, Venez. BR/TR, 6'1", 175 lbs. Deb: 8/23/81

YEAR	TM/L	G	AB	R	H	2B	3B	HR	RBI	BB	SO	AVG	OBP	SLG	PRO+	BR/A	SB	CS	SBR	FA	FR	G/POS	TPR
1981	Tor-A	14	28	1	4	0	0	0	1	0	12	.143	.172	.143	-8	-4	0	1	-1	.949	3	S-11/3-2,D	-0.1
1984	Tor-A	10	9	0	3	0	0	0	1	0	1	.333	.333	.333	82	-0	0	0	0	.938	3	/2-9,D-1	0.2
1985	Mon-N	9	13	5	4	1	1	1	1	1	3	.308	.357	.769	219	2	0	0	0	1.000	2	/2-2,S-2,3	0.4
1986	StL-N	13	17	2	3	0	0	1	1	1	1	.176	.222	.353	57	-1	1	0	0	1.000	-2	/3-4,2-1	-0.2
1987	Chi-A	115	298	30	77	13	3	4	29	19	69	.258	.305	.362	74	-11	5	3	-0	.984	19	2-92,S-23/D	1.1
1988	Chi-A	140	345	43	81	10	6	5	37	21	54	.235	.285	.342	75	-12	6	5	-1	.985	12	*2-129,S-12/D	0.4
1989	Chi-A	65	187	23	56	13	1	2	30	8	30	.299	.335	.412	112	3	0	4	-2	.961	-5	2-57/S-2,3	-0.3
	Tex-A	54	191	23	55	12	0	2	22	9	33	.288	.320	.382	96	-1	4	1	1	.963	-11	S-37,2-17/3D	-0.9
	Yr	119	378	46	111	25	1	4	52	17	63	.294	.327	.397	104	1	4	5	-2	.952	-16	2-74,S-39/3D	-1.2
1990	Min-A	69	228	22	54	10	0	5	29	4	35	.237	.256	.346	63	-12	2	0	1	.974	-10	2-67/D-1	-2.0
1991	Oak-A	9	21	2	3	0	0	0	0	2	1	.143	.217	.143	2	-3	0	0	0	.955	-0	/S-7,2-2	-0.3
Total	9	498	1337	151	340	59	11	20	151	65	239	.254	.293	.360	79	-40	18	14	-3	.976	11	2-376/S-94,3D	-1.7

■ JOHN MANSELL
Mansell, John b: 1861, Auburn, N.Y. d: 2/20/25, Romulus, N.Y. BL , 5'10", 168 lbs. Deb: 5/9/1882 F

YEAR	TM/L	G	AB	R	H	2B	3B	HR	RBI	BB	SO	AVG	OBP	SLG	PRO+	BR/A	SB	CS	SBR	FA	FR	G/POS	TPR
1882	Phi-a	31	126	17	30	3	1	0		4		.238	.262	.278	73	-4				.791	-4	O-31	-0.7

■ MIKE MANSELL
Mansell, Michael R. b: 1/15/1858, Auburn, N.Y. d: 12/4/02, Auburn, N.Y. BL , 5'11", 175 lbs. Deb: 5/1/1879 F

YEAR	TM/L	G	AB	R	H	2B	3B	HR	RBI	BB	SO	AVG	OBP	SLG	PRO+	BR/A	SB	CS	SBR	FA	FR	G/POS	TPR
1879	Syr-N	67	242	24	52	4	2	1	13	5	45	.215	.231	.260	69	-7				.881	15	*O-67	0.5
1880	Cin-N	53	187	22	36	6	2	2	12	4	37	.193	.209	.278	64	-7				.865	12	O-53	0.4
1882	Pit-a	79	347	59	96	18	16	2		7		.277	.291	.438	150	17				.829	3	*O-79	1.8
1883	Pit-a	96	412	90	106	12	13	3		25		.257	.300	.371	120	10				.883	4	*O-96	1.1
1884	Pit-a	27	100	15	14	0	3	1		7		.140	.204	.230	41	-6				.796	-1	O-27	-0.8
	Phi-a	20	70	6	14	1	1	0		5		.200	.253	.243	59	-3				.762	-1	O-20	-0.4
	Ric-a	29	113	21	34	2	5	0		8		.301	.363	.407	153	7				.763	-5	O-29	0.1
	Yr	76	283	42	62	3	9	1		20		.219	.280	.304	89	-2				.775	-7	O-76	-1.1
Total	5	371	1471	237	352	43	42	9	25	61	82	.239	.271	.344	106	11				.854	26	O-371	2.7

■ TOM MANSELL
Mansell, Thomas E. "Brick" b: 1/1/1855, Auburn, N.Y. d: 10/6/34, Auburn, N.Y. BL/TL, 5'8", 160 lbs. Deb: 5/1/1879 F

YEAR	TM/L	G	AB	R	H	2B	3B	HR	RBI	BB	SO	AVG	OBP	SLG	PRO+	BR/A	SB	CS	SBR	FA	FR	G/POS	TPR
1879	Tro-N	40	177	29	43	6	0	0	11	3	9	.243	.256	.277	81	-3				.742	-6	O-40	-1.1
	Syr-N	1	4	0	1	0	0	0	0	0	0	.250	.250	.250	74	-0				1.000	-0	/O-1	0.0
	Yr	41	181	29	44	6	0	0	11	3	9	.243	.255	.276	81	-3				.747	-6	O-41	-1.1
1883	Det-N	34	131	22	29	4	1	0	10	8	13	.221	.266	.267	66	-5				.758	-2	O-34/P-1	-0.6
	StL-a	28	112	23	45	8	1	0		7		.402	.437	.491	188	10				.786	-6	O-28	0.4
1884	Cin-a	65	266	49	66	4	6	0		15		.248	.301	.308	95	-2				.752	-11	O-65	-1.3
	Col-a	23	77	9	15	1	3	0		6		.195	.262	.286	85	-1				.667	-4	O-23	-0.5
	Yr	88	343	58	81	5	9	0		21		.236	.292	.303	93	-2				.739	-15	O-88	-1.8
Total	3	191	767	132	199	23	11	0	21	39	22	.259	.300	.318	100	-0				.751	-28	O-191/P-1	-3.1

■ FELIX MANTILLA
Mantilla, Felix (Lamela) b: 7/29/34, Isabela, P.R. BR/TR, 6', 160 lbs. Deb: 6/21/56

YEAR	TM/L	G	AB	R	H	2B	3B	HR	RBI	BB	SO	AVG	OBP	SLG	PRO+	BR/A	SB	CS	SBR	FA	FR	G/POS	TPR
1956	Mil-N	35	53	9	15	1	1	0	3	1	8	.283	.309	.340	79	-2	0	1	-1	1.000	9	S-15/3-3	0.8
1957	*Mil-N	71	182	28	43	9	1	4	21	14	34	.236	.298	.363	82	-5	2	0	1	.931	6	S-35,2-13/3O	0.5
1958	*Mil-N	85	226	37	50	5	1	7	19	20	20	.221	.285	.345	72	-10	2	0	1	.987	-6	O-43,2-21/S3	-1.6
1959	Mil-N	103	251	26	54	5	0	3	19	16	31	.215	.268	.271	48	-19	6	1	1	.970	4	2-60,S-23/3O	-0.9
1960	Mil-N	63	148	21	38	7	0	3	11	7	16	.257	.295	.365	86	-3	3	1	0	.956	-12	2-26,S-25/O	-1.3
1961	Mil-N	45	93	13	20	3	0	5	10	16	16	.215	.289	.280	58	-6	1	1	-0	.933	-3	S-19,2-10,O/3	-0.9
1962	NY-N	141	466	54	128	17	4	11	59	37	51	.275	.335	.399	94	-4	3	3	-0	.948	-7	3-95,S-25,2	-0.7
1963	Bos-A	66	178	27	56	8	0	6	15	20	14	.315	.384	.461	131	8	2	1	0	.965	-5	S-27,O-11/2	0.5
1964	Bos-A	133	425	69	123	20	1	30	64	41	46	.289	.357	.553	142	23	0	1	-1	.984	-6	O-48,2-45/3S	2.0
1965	Bos-A★	150	534	60	147	17	2	18	92	79	84	.275	.371	.416	118	15	7	3	0	.976	-22	*2-123,O-27/1	0.3
1966	Hou-N	77	151	16	33	5	0	6	22	11	32	.219	.280	.371	85	-4	1	0	0	.990	-2	1-14,3-14/2O	-0.6
Total	11	969	2707	360	707	97	10	89	330	256	352	.261	.331	.403	100	-6	27	10	2	.977	-44	2-326,S-180,O3/1	-1.9

■ MICKEY MANTLE
Mantle, Mickey Charles "The Commerce Comet" b: 10/20/31, Spavinaw, Okla. BB/TR, 5'11", 198 lbs. Deb: 4/17/51 CH

YEAR	TM/L	G	AB	R	H	2B	3B	HR	RBI	BB	SO	AVG	OBP	SLG	PRO+	BR/A	SB	CS	SBR	FA	FR	G/POS	TPR
1951	*NY-A	96	341	61	91	11	5	13	65	43	74	.267	.349	.443	117	7	8	7	-2	.959	-6	O-86	-0.3
1952	*NY-A☆	142	549	94	171	37	7	23	87	75	111	.311	.394	.530	166	47	4	1	1	.968	3	*O-141/3-1	4.6
1953	*NY-A★	127	461	105	136	24	3	21	92	79	90	.295	.398	.497	145	30	8	4	0	.982	1	*O-121/S-1	2.7
1954	NY-A★	146	543	129	163	17	12	27	102	102	107	.300	.411	.525	160	47	5	2	0	.975	-1	*O-144/S-4,2	4.1

YEAR	TM/L	G	AB	R	H	2B	3B	HR	RBI	BB	SO	AVG	OBP	SLG	PRO+	BR/A	SB	CS	SBR	FA	FR	G/POS	TPR
1955	*NY-A★	147	517	121	158	25	**11**	**37**	99	**113**	97	.306	**.433**	**.611**	**181**	61	8	1	2	.995	8	*O-145/S-2	**6.3**
1956	*NY-A★	150	533	**132**	188	22	5	**52**	**130**	112	99	**.353**	.467	**.705**	**213**	**89**	10	1	2	.990	8	*O-144	**8.7**
1957	*NY-A★	144	474	**121**	173	28	6	34	94	**146**	75	.365	.515	.665	223	**91**	16	3	3	.979	0	*O-139	**8.6**
1958	*NY-A★	150	519	**127**	158	21	1	**42**	97	**129**	120	.304	.445	.592	**189**	69	18	3	4	.977	-1	*O-150	**6.5**
1959	NY-A★	144	541	104	154	23	4	31	75	93	126	.285	.392	.514	152	40	21	3	5	**.995**	8	*O-143	**4.5**
1960	*NY-A★	153	527	**119**	145	17	6	**40**	94	111	125	.275	.402	.558	166	51	14	3	2	.991	-1	*O-150	**4.4**
1961	*NY-A★	153	514	**132**	163	16	6	54	128	**126**	112	.317	.452	**.687**	210	84	12	1	3	.983	4	*O-150	**8.0**
1962	*NY-A★	123	377	96	121	15	1	30	89	**122**	78	.321	**.488**	**.605**	198	61	9	0	3	.978	-6	*O-117	**5.0**
1963	*NY-A†	65	172	40	54	8	0	15	35	40	32	.314	.443	.622	197	24	2	1	0	.990	-2	O-52	2.0
1964	*NY-A★	143	465	92	141	25	2	35	111	99	102	.303	**.426**	.591	**177**	51	6	3	0	.978	-13	*O-132	3.3
1965	NY-A†	122	361	44	92	12	1	19	46	73	76	.255	.380	.452	136	19	4	1	1	.966	-4	*O-108	1.2
1966	NY-A	108	333	40	96	12	1	23	56	57	76	.288	.392	.538	171	31	1	1	-0	1.000	-7	O-97	2.1
1967	NY-A★	144	440	63	108	17	0	22	55	107	113	.245	.394	.434	150	32	1	1	-0	.993	0	*1-131	2.7
1968	NY-A★	144	435	57	103	14	1	18	54	106	97	.237	.387	.398	143	28	6	2	1	.988	-3	*1-131	1.7
Total	18	2401	8102	1677	2415	344	72	536	1509	1733	1710	.298	.423	.557	173	863	153	38	23	.982	-9	*O-2019,1-262/S23	76.1

■ JEFF MANTO
Manto, Jeffrey Paul b: 8/23/64, Bristol, Pa. BR/TR, 6'3", 210 lbs. Deb: 6/7/90

YEAR	TM/L	G	AB	R	H	2B	3B	HR	RBI	BB	SO	AVG	OBP	SLG	PRO+	BR/A	SB	CS	SBR	FA	FR	G/POS	TPR
1990	Cle-A	30	76	12	17	5	1	2	14	21	18	.224	.392	.395	121	3	0	1	-1	.990	1	1-25/3-5	0.2
1991	Cle-A	47	128	15	27	7	0	2	13	14	22	.211	.308	.313	72	-5	2	0	1	.929	1	3-32,1-14/CO	-0.3
1993	Phi-N	8	18	0	1	0	0	0	0	0	3	.056	.105	.056	-56	-4	0	0	0	1.000	-0	/3-6,S-1	-0.4
Total	3	85	222	27	45	12	1	4	27	35	43	.203	.324	.320	79	-6	2	1	0	.943	3	/3-43,1-39,CSO	-0.5

■ CHUCK MANUEL
Manuel, Charles Fuqua b: 1/4/44, Northfork, W.Va. BL/TR, 6'4", 200 lbs. Deb: 4/8/69 C

YEAR	TM/L	G	AB	R	H	2B	3B	HR	RBI	BB	SO	AVG	OBP	SLG	PRO+	BR/A	SB	CS	SBR	FA	FR	G/POS	TPR
1969	*Min-A	83	164	14	34	6	0	2	24	28	33	.207	.323	.280	69	-6	1	0	0	.967	-6	O-46	-1.4
1970	*Min-A	59	64	4	12	0	0	1	7	6	17	.188	.268	.234	39	-5	0	0	0	1.000	-3	O-11	-0.8
1971	Min-A	18	16	1	2	1	0	0	1	1	8	.125	.176	.188	3	-2	0	0	0	.000	-0	/O-1	-0.3
1972	Min-A	63	122	6	25	5	0	1	8	4	16	.205	.236	.270	48	-8	0	0	0	.977	-1	O-28	-1.1
1974	LA-N	4	3	0	1	0	0	0	1	1	0	.333	.500	.333	142	0	0	0	0	.000	0	H	0.0
1975	LA-N	15	15	0	2	0	0	0	2	0	3	.133	.133	.133	-27	-3	0	0	0	.000	0	H	-0.3
Total	6	242	384	25	76	12	0	4	43	40	77	.198	.277	.260	52	-24	1	0	0	.973	-9	/O-86	-3.9

■ JERRY MANUEL
Manuel, Jerry b: 12/23/53, Hahira, Ga. BB/TR, 6', 165 lbs. Deb: 9/18/75 C

YEAR	TM/L	G	AB	R	H	2B	3B	HR	RBI	BB	SO	AVG	OBP	SLG	PRO+	BR/A	SB	CS	SBR	FA	FR	G/POS	TPR
1975	Det-A	6	18	0	1	0	0	0	0	0	4	.056	.056	.056	-66	-4	0	0	0	.944	3	/2-6	-0.1
1976	Det-A	54	43	4	6	1	0	0	2	3	9	.140	.213	.163	11	-5	1	0	0	.921	10	2-47/S-4,D	0.7
1980	Mon-N	7	6	0	0	0	0	0	0	0	2	.000	.000	.000	-99	-2	0	0	0	.941	3	/S-7	0.1
1981	*Mon-N	27	55	10	11	5	0	3	10	6	11	.200	.279	.455	104	-0	0	0	0	.987	-0	2-23/S-2	0.0
1982	SD-N	2	5	0	1	0	1	0	1	1	0	.200	.333	.600	165	0	0	0	0	1.000	1	/2-1,S-1,3	-0.1
Total	5	96	127	14	19	6	1	3	13	10	26	.150	.217	.283	42	-10	1	0	0	.949	14	2-77,S-14,3D	0.6

■ FRANK MANUSH
Manush, Frank Benjamin b: 9/18/1883, Tuscumbia, Ala. d: 1/5/65, Laguna Beach, Cal. BR/TR, 5'10.5", 175 lbs. Deb: 8/31/08 F

YEAR	TM/L	G	AB	R	H	2B	3B	HR	RBI	BB	SO	AVG	OBP	SLG	PRO+	BR/A	SB	CS	SBR	FA	FR	G/POS	TPR
1908	Phi-A	23	77	6	12	2	1	0	2	3		.156	.188	.208	27	-6	2			.933	-5	3-20/2-2	-1.2

■ HEINIE MANUSH
Manush, Henry Emmett b: 7/20/01, Tuscumbia, Ala. d: 5/12/71, Sarasota, Fla. BL/TL, 6'1", 200 lbs. Deb: 4/20/23 FCH

YEAR	TM/L	G	AB	R	H	2B	3B	HR	RBI	BB	SO	AVG	OBP	SLG	PRO+	BR/A	SB	CS	SBR	FA	FR	G/POS	TPR
1923	Det-A	109	308	59	103	20	5	4	54	20	21	.334	.406	.471	133	15	3	5	-2	.953	-4	O-79	0.4
1924	Det-A	120	422	83	122	24	8	9	68	27	30	.289	.355	.448	108	3	14	5	1	.979	-6	*O-106/1-1	-0.8
1925	Det-A	99	278	46	84	14	3	5	47	24	21	.302	.362	.428	101	0	8	3	1	.982	-5	O-73	-0.8
1926	Det-A	136	498	95	188	35	8	14	86	31	28	**.378**	.421	.564	153	37	11	5	0	.967	-4	*O-120	2.4
1927	Det-A	151	593	102	177	31	18	6	90	47	29	.298	.354	.442	104	2	12	8	-1	.971	-3	*O-149	-1.1
1928	StL-A	154	638	104	**241**	**47**	20	13	108	39	14	.378	.414	.575	153	46	17	5	2	.992	2	*O-154	3.8
1929	StL-A	142	574	85	204	**45**	10	6	81	43	24	.355	.401	.500	126	22	9	8	-2	.987	-2	*O-141	0.7
1930	StL-A	49	198	26	65	16	4	2	29	5	7	.328	.345	.480	103	0	3	1	0	.990	-2	O-48	-0.1
	Was-A	88	356	74	129	33	8	7	65	26	17	.362	.406	.559	141	22	4	3	-1	.988	-2	O-86	1.2
	Yr	137	554	100	194	49	12	9	94	31	24	.350	.385	.531	128	22	7	4	-0	.989	1	*O-134	1.1
1931	Was-A	146	616	110	189	41	11	6	70	36	27	.307	.351	.438	106	4	3	3	-1	.977	-11	*O-143	-1.6
1932	Was-A	149	625	121	214	41	14	14	116	36	29	.342	.383	.520	133	29	7	2	1	.988	-2	*O-146	1.8
1933	*Was-A	153	658	115	**221**	32	**17**	5	95	36	18	.336	.372	.459	120	18	6	3	1	.982	-2	*O-150	0.7
1934	Was-A★	137	556	88	194	42	11	11	89	36	23	.349	.392	.523	140	30	7	3	0	.980	-0	*O-131	2.3
1935	Was-A	119	479	68	131	26	9	4	56	35	17	.273	.328	.390	88	-10	2	0	1	.985	3	*O-111	-1.0
1936	Bos-A	82	313	43	91	15	5	0	45	17	11	.291	.329	.371	69	-16	1	3	-2	.966	-8	O-72	-2.5
1937	Bro-N	132	466	57	155	25	7	4	73	40	24	.333	.389	.442	123	16	6			.970	-12	*O-123	0.0
1938	Bro-N	17	51	9	12	3	1	0	6	5	4	.235	.304	.333	73	-2	1			1.000	1	O-12	-0.1
	Pit-N	15	13	2	4	1	1	0	4	2	0	.308	.400	.538	155	1	0			.000	0	H	0.1
	Yr	32	64	11	16	4	2	0	10	7	4	.250	.324	.375	90	-1	1			1.000	1	O-12	0.0
1939	Pit-N	10	12	0	0	0	0	0	0	1	1	.000	.077	.000	-79	-3	0			1.000	-0	/O-1	-0.3
Total	17	2008	7654	1287	2524	491	160	110	1183	506	345	.330	.377	.479	121	214	114	<u>58</u>		.979	-50	*O-1845/1-1	5.1

■ KIRT MANWARING
Manwaring, Kirt Dean b: 7/15/65, Elmira, N.Y. BR/TR, 5'11", 185 lbs. Deb: 9/15/87

YEAR	TM/L	G	AB	R	H	2B	3B	HR	RBI	BB	SO	AVG	OBP	SLG	PRO+	BR/A	SB	CS	SBR	FA	FR	G/POS	TPR
1987	SF-N	6	7	0	1	0	0	0	0	0	1	.143	.250	.143	8	-1	0	0	0	.909	-1	/C-6	-0.2
1988	SF-N	40	116	12	29	7	0	1	15	2	21	.250	.281	.336	80	-3	0	1	-1	.979	-2	C-40	-0.4
1989	*SF-N	85	200	14	42	4	2	0	18	11	28	.210	.265	.250	49	-13	2	1	0	.982	-0	C-81	-1.1
1990	SF-N	8	13	0	2	0	1	0	1	0	3	.154	.154	.308	25	-1	0	0	0	1.000	2	/C-8	-0.1
1991	SF-N	67	178	16	40	9	0	0	19	9	22	.225	.274	.275	57	-10	1	1	-0	.988	1	C-67	-0.6
1992	SF-N	109	349	24	85	10	5	4	26	29	42	.244	.311	.335	88	-6	2	1	0	.994	1	*C-108	0.0
1993	SF-N	130	432	48	119	15	1	5	49	41	76	.275	.340	.350	90	-5	1	3	-2	**.998**	-1	*C-130	-0.5
1994	SF-N	97	316	30	79	17	1	1	29	25	50	.250	.311	.320	67	-15	1	1	0	.993	5	C-97	-0.5
Total	8	542	1611	144	397	62	10	11	157	117	243	.246	.307	.318	75	-55	7	8	-3	.992	5	C-537	-2.7

■ CLIFF MAPES
Mapes, Clifford Franklin b: 3/13/22, Sutherland, Neb. BL/TR, 6'3", 205 lbs. Deb: 4/20/48

YEAR	TM/L	G	AB	R	H	2B	3B	HR	RBI	BB	SO	AVG	OBP	SLG	PRO+	BR/A	SB	CS	SBR	FA	FR	G/POS	TPR
1948	NY-A	53	88	19	22	11	1	1	12	6	13	.250	.298	.432	94	-2	1	1	-0	.958	1	O-21	-0.1
1949	*NY-A	111	304	56	75	13	3	7	38	58	50	.247	.369	.458	98	0	6	0	2	.976	3	*O-108	0.0
1950	*NY-A	108	356	60	88	14	6	12	61	47	61	.247	.338	.421	96	-3	1	6	-3	.950	-7	O-102	-1.7
1951	NY-A	45	51	6	11	3	1	2	8	4	14	.216	.273	.431	92	-1	0	0	0	1.000	-9	O-34	-1.0
	StL-A	56	201	32	55	7	2	7	30	26	33	.274	.360	.433	110	3	0	1	-1	.983	-1	O-53	-0.1
	Yr	101	252	38	66	10	3	9	38	30	47	.262	.343	.433	109	2	0	1	-1	.986	-10	O-87	-1.1
1952	Det-A	86	193	26	38	7	0	9	23	27	42	.197	.295	.373	84	-5	0	1	-1	.967	-10	O-63	-1.8
Total	5	459	1193	199	289	55	13	38	172	168	213	.242	.338	.406	97	-8	8	9	-3	.969	-23	O-381	-4.7

■ HOWARD MAPLE
Maple, Howard Albert "Mape" b: 7/20/03, Adrian, Mo. d: 11/9/70, Portland, Ore. BL/TR, 5'7", 175 lbs. Deb: 5/19/32

YEAR	TM/L	G	AB	R	H	2B	3B	HR	RBI	BB	SO	AVG	OBP	SLG	PRO+	BR/A	SB	CS	SBR	FA	FR	G/POS	TPR
1932	Was-A	44	41	6	10	0	1	0	7	7	7	.244	.367	.293	74	-1	0	0	0	1.000	-3	C-41	-0.3

■ GEORGE MAPPES
Mappes, George Richard "Dick" b: 12/25/1865, St.Louis, Mo. d: 2/20/34, St.Louis, Mo. Deb: 9/23/1885

YEAR	TM/L	G	AB	R	H	2B	3B	HR	RBI	BB	SO	AVG	OBP	SLG	PRO+	BR/A	SB	CS	SBR	FA	FR	G/POS	TPR
1885	Bal-a	6	19	2	4	0	1	0		1		.211	.250	.316	79	-0				.875	-2	/2-6	-0.2
1886	StL-N	6	14	1	2	0	0	0	0	1	5	.143	.200	.143	6	-2	0			1.000	-1	/C-3,3-2,2	-0.2
Total	2	12	33	3	6	0	1	0	<u>0</u>	2	<u>5</u>	.182	.229	.242	48	-2	0			.848	-3	/2-7,C-3,3	-0.4

YEAR	TM/L	G	AB	R	H	2B	3B	HR	RBI	BB	SO	AVG	OBP	SLG	PRO+	BR/A	SB	CS	SBR	FA	FR	G/POS	TPR

■ RABBIT MARANVILLE   Maranville, Walter James Vincent   b: 11/11/1891, Springfield, Mass.   d: 1/5/54, New York, N.Y.   BR/TR, 5'5", 155 lbs.   Deb: 9/10/12   MH

1912	Bos-N	26	86	8	18	2	0	0	8	9	14	.209	.292	.233	44	-6	1			.929	5	S-26	0.1
1913	Bos-N	143	571	68	141	13	8	2	48	68	62	.247	.330	.308	81	-12	25			.949	15	*S-143	1.7
1914	*Bos-N	156	586	74	144	23	6	4	78	45	56	.246	.306	.326	88	-9	28			.938	52	*S-156	**5.9**
1915	Bos-N	149	509	51	124	23	6	2	43	45	65	.244	.308	.324	96	-3	18	12	-2	.941	21	*S-149	3.1
1916	Bos-N	155	604	79	142	16	13	4	38	50	69	.235	.296	.325	94	-5	32	15	1	**.947**	22	*S-155	3.0
1917	Bos-N	142	561	69	146	19	13	3	43	40	47	.260	.312	.357	111	6	27			.947	14	*S-142	3.0
1918	Bos-N	11	38	3	12	1	0	0	3	4	0	.316	.381	.368	134	2	0			.932	2	S-11	0.4
1919	Bos-N	131	480	44	128	18	10	5	43	36	23	.267	.319	.377	113	7	12			.941	29	*S-131	**4.7**
1920	Bos-N	134	493	48	131	19	15	1	43	28	24	.266	.305	.371	98	-3	14	11	-2	.948	14	*S-133	2.1
1921	Pit-N	153	612	90	180	25	12	1	70	47	38	.294	.347	.379	90	-8	25	12	0	.962	-11	*S-153	-0.4
1922	Pit-N	155	672	115	198	26	15	0	63	61	43	.295	.355	.378	88	-11	24	13	-1	.961	11	*S-138,2-18	1.4
1923	Pit-N	141	581	78	161	19	9	1	41	42	34	.277	.327	.346	76	-20	14	11	-2	**.965**	12	*S-141	0.4
1924	Pit-N	152	594	62	158	33	20	2	71	35	53	.266	.307	.399	86	-13	18	14	-3	**.973**	4	*2-152	-1.0
1925	Chi-N	75	266	37	62	10	3	0	23	29	20	.233	.308	.293	54	-18	6	5	-1	.955	4	S-74,M	-0.7
1926	Bro-N	78	234	32	55	8	5	0	24	26	24	.235	.312	.312	69	-10	7			.948	10	S-60,2-18	0.6
1927	StL-N	9	29	0	7	1	0	0	0	2	2	.241	.290	.276	51	-2	0			.962	3	/S-9	0.2
1928	*StL-N	112	366	40	88	14	10	1	34	36	27	.240	.310	.342	69	-17	3			.969	-5	*S-112/2-2	-0.9
1929	Bos-N	146	560	87	159	26	10	0	55	47	33	.284	.344	.366	79	-18	13			.961	20	*S-145/2-1	1.8
1930	Bos-N	142	558	85	157	26	8	2	43	48	23	.281	.344	.367	75	-22	9			**.965**	-13	*S-138/3-4	-1.7
1931	Bos-N	145	562	69	146	22	5	0	33	56	34	.260	.329	.317	77	-17	9			.949	-24	*S-137,2-11	-2.7
1932	Bos-N	149	571	67	134	20	4	0	37	46	28	.235	.295	.284	59	-32	4			**.975**	6	*2-149	-1.9
1933	Bos-N	143	478	46	104	15	4	0	38	36	34	.218	.274	.266	59	-25	2			.971	-27	*2-142	-4.7
1935	Bos-N	23	67	3	10	2	0	0	5	3	3	.149	.186	.179	-2	-10	0			.963	-5	2-20	-1.3
Total	23	2670	10078	1255	2605	380	177	28	884	839	756	.258	.318	.340	82	-246	291	93		.952	158	*S-2153,2-513/3	13.1

■ JOHNNY MARCUM   Marcum, John Alfred "Footsie"   b: 9/9/09, Campbellsburg, Ky.   d: 9/10/84, Louisville, Ky.   BL/TR, 5'11", 197 lbs.   Deb: 9/7/33

1933	Phi-A	5	12	2	2	0	0	0	2	0	1	.167	.286	.167	22	-1	0	0	0	1.000	0	/P-5	0.0
1934	Phi-A	58	112	10	30	4	0	1	13	3	5	.268	.287	.330	61	-7	0	1	-1	.949	-0	P-37	0.0
1935	Phi-A	64	119	13	37	2	1	2	17	9	5	.311	.359	.395	96	-1	0	0	0	.896	-3	P-39	0.0
1936	Bos-A	48	88	6	18	3	0	2	7	3	5	.205	.231	.307	30	-10	0	0	0	.950	0	P-31	0.0
1937	Bos-A	51	86	12	23	8	0	0	13	7	4	.267	.323	.360	69	-4	0	0	0	.981	1	P-37	0.0
1938	Bos-A	19	37	3	5	0	0	0	3	6	9	.135	.256	.135	1	-6	0	0	0	1.000	-1	P-15	0.0
1939	StL-A	16	22	3	10	1	0	0	5	1	2	.455	.478	.500	147	2	0	0	0	1.000	-0	P-12	0.0
	Chi-N	38	57	7	16	0	0	0	12	5	1	.281	.339	.281	58	-3	0	0	0	.941	-1	P-19	0.0
	Yr	54	79	10	26	1	0	0	17	6	3	.329	.376	.342	83	-2	0	0	0	.962	-1	P-31	0.0
Total	7	299	533	56	141	18	1	5	70	36	32	.265	.311	.330	62	-30	0	1	-1	.953	-4	P-195	0.0

■ RED MARION   Marion, John Wyeth   b: 3/14/14, Richburg, S.C.   d: 3/13/75, San Jose, Cal.   BR/TR, 6'2", 175 lbs.   Deb: 9/16/35   F

1935	Was-A	4	11	1	2	1	0	1	0	2	0	.182	.182	.545	85	-0	0	0	0	.833	-0	/O-3	-0.1
1943	Was-A	14	17	2	3	0	0	0	1	3	1	.176	.300	.176	42	-1	0	0	0	1.000	-1	/O-4	-0.2
Total	2	18	28	3	5	1	0	1	2	3	1	.179	.258	.321	63	-1	0	0	0	.923	-1	/O-7	-0.3

■ MARTY MARION   Marion, Martin Whiteford "Slats" or "The Octopus"   b: 12/1/17, Richburg, S.C.   BR/TR, 6'2", 170 lbs.   Deb: 4/16/40   FMC

1940	StL-N	125	435	44	121	18	1	3	46	21	34	.278	.311	.345	76	-14	9			.949	-6	*S-125	-1.1
1941	StL-N	155	547	50	138	22	3	3	58	42	48	.252	.308	.320	72	-20	8			.954	7	*S-155	-0.2
1942	*StL-N	147	485	66	134	**38**	5	0	54	48	50	.276	.343	.375	102	1	8			.960	7	*S-147	1.9
1943	*StL-N★	129	418	38	117	15	3	1	52	32	37	.280	.334	.337	90	-5	1			.970	25	*S-128	3.1
1944	*StL-N★	144	506	50	135	26	2	6	63	43	50	.267	.324	.362	91	-6	1			**.972**	5	*S-144	1.0
1945	StL-N†	123	430	63	119	27	5	1	59	39	39	.277	.340	.370	95	-3	2			.967	-2	*S-122	0.5
1946	*StL-N★	146	498	51	116	29	4	3	46	59	53	.233	.318	.325	79	-13	1			**.973**	19	*S-145	1.5
1947	StL-N★	149	540	57	147	19	6	4	74	44	59	.272	.334	.352	79	-16	3			**.981**	20	*S-141	1.1
1948	StL-N†	144	567	70	143	26	4	4	43	37	54	.252	.298	.333	67	-27	4			**.974**	9	*S-142	-0.9
1949	StL-N☆	134	515	61	140	31	2	5	70	42	42	.272	.323	.369	81	-14	0			.976	17	*S-134	1.2
1950	StL-N	106	372	36	92	10	2	4	40	44	55	.247	.327	.317	67	-17	1			.978	-1	*S-101	-1.0
1952	StL-A	67	186	16	46	11	0	2	19	19	17	.247	.320	.339	81	-5	0	2	-1	.980	-7	S-63,M	-0.9
1953	StL-A	3	7	0	0	0	0	0	0	0	0	.000	.000	.000	-98	-2	0	0	0	1.000	-1	/3-2,M	-0.4
Total	13	1572	5506	602	1448	272	37	36	624	470	537	.263	.323	.345	81	-140	35	2		.969	92	*S-1547/3-2	5.8

■ ROGER MARIS   Maris, Roger Eugene (b: Roger Eugene Maras)   b: 9/10/34, Hibbing, Minn.   d: 12/14/85, Houston, Tex.   BL/TR, 6', 204 lbs.   Deb: 4/16/57

1957	Cle-A	116	358	61	84	9	5	14	51	60	79	.235	.346	.405	106	3	8	4	0	.975	5	*O-112	0.3
1958	Cle-A	51	182	26	41	5	1	9	27	17	33	.225	.291	.412	94	-2	4	2	0	.967	5	O-47	-1.2
	KC-A	99	401	61	99	14	3	19	53	28	52	.247	.299	.439	99	-2	0	0	0	.975	-4	O-99	-1.2
	Yr	150	583	87	140	19	4	28	80	45	85	.240	.297	.431	97	-4	4	2	0	.972	1	*O-146	-1.2
1959	KC-A★	122	433	69	118	21	7	16	72	58	53	.273	.362	.464	123	14	2	1	0	.975	6	*O-117	1.5
1960	*NY-A★	136	499	98	141	18	7	39	**112**	70	65	.283	.374	**.581**	164	42	2	2	-1	.985	3	*O-131	3.8
1961	*NY-A★	161	590	**132**	159	16	4	**61**	**142**	94	67	.269	.376	.620	170	57	0	0	0	.968	-11	*O-160	3.5
1962	*NY-A★	157	590	92	151	34	1	33	100	87	78	.256	.357	.485	128	23	1	0	0	.991	-4	*O-154	1.0
1963	*NY-A	90	312	53	84	14	1	23	53	35	40	.269	.347	.542	146	18	1	0	0	.988	0	O-86	1.7
1964	*NY-A	141	513	86	144	12	2	26	71	62	78	.281	.365	.464	127	19	3	0	1	.996	-0	*O-137	1.4
1965	NY-A	46	155	22	37	7	0	8	27	29	29	.239	.359	.439	126	6	0	0	0	.971	-2	O-43	-0.1
1966	NY-A	119	348	37	81	9	2	13	43	36	60	.233	.310	.382	101	0	0	0	0	.993	-7	O-95	-1.1
1967	*StL-N	125	410	64	107	18	7	9	55	52	61	.261	.350	.405	117	10	0	0	0	.991	0	*O-118	0.6
1968	*StL-N	100	310	25	79	18	2	5	45	24	38	.255	.310	.374	106	2	0	0	0	.983	3	O-84	0.0
Total	12	1463	5101	826	1325	195	42	275	851	652	733	.260	.348	.476	128	191	21	9		.982	-3	*O-1383	11.7

■ GENE MARKLAND   Markland, Cleneth Eugene "Mousey"   b: 12/26/19, Detroit, Mich.   BR/TR, 5'10", 160 lbs.   Deb: 4/25/50

| 1950 | Phi-A | 5 | 8 | 2 | 1 | 0 | 0 | 0 | 3 | 0 | .125 | .364 | .125 | 30 | -1 | 0 | 0 | 0 | 1.000 | 0 | /2-5 | -0.1 |

■ HAL MARNIE   Marnie, Harry Sylvester   b: 7/6/18, Philadelphia, Pa.   BR/TR, 6'1", 178 lbs.   Deb: 9/15/40

1940	Phi-N	11	34	4	6	0	0	0	4	4	2	.176	.263	.176	24	-3	0			.984	6	2-11	0.3
1941	Phi-N	61	158	12	38	3	1	0	11	13	25	.241	.298	.297	71	-6	0			.990	5	2-39,S-16/3	0.2
1942	Phi-N	24	30	3	5	0	0	0	0	1	2	.167	.194	.167	6	-4	1			.971	8	2-11/S-7,3	0.5
Total	3	96	222	19	49	3	3	0	15	18	29	.221	.279	.261	55	-13	1			.987	19	/2-61,S-23,3	1.0

■ FRED MAROLEWSKI   Marolewski, Fred Daniel "Fritz"   b: 10/6/28, Chicago, Ill.   BR/TR, 6'2.5", 205 lbs.   Deb: 9/19/53

| 1953 | StL-N | 1 | 0 | 0 | 0 | 0 | 0 | 0 | 0 | 0 | 0 | — | — | — | — | 0 | 0 | 0 | 0 | .000 | 0 | /1-1 | 0.0 |

■ OLLIE MARQUARDT   Marquardt, Albert Ludwig   b: 9/22/02, Toledo, Ohio   d: 2/7/68, Port Clinton, Ohio   BR/TR, 5'9", 156 lbs.   Deb: 4/14/31

| 1931 | Bos-A | 17 | 39 | 4 | 7 | 1 | 0 | 0 | 2 | 3 | 4 | .179 | .238 | .205 | 18 | -5 | 0 | 1 | -1 | .946 | -3 | 2-13/S-1,3 | -0.7 |

■ GONZALO MARQUEZ   Marquez, Gonzalo Enrique (Moya)   b: 3/31/46, Carupano, Venez.   d: 12/20/84, Valencia, Venez.   BL/TL, 5'11", 180 lbs.   Deb: 8/11/72

1972	*Oak-A	23	21	2	8	0	0	0	4	3	4	.381	.480	.381	167	2	1	1	-0	.929	0	/1-2	0.2
1973	Oak-A	23	25	1	6	1	0	0	2	0	4	.240	.240	.280	49	-2	0	0	0	.000	-1	/2-2,1-1,OD	-0.3
	Chi-N	19	58	5	13	2	0	1	4	3	4	.224	.274	.310	57	-3	0	0	0	.994	2	1-18	-0.2

YEAR	TM/L	G	AB	R	H	2B	3B	HR	RBI	BB	SO	AVG	OBP	SLG	PRO+	BR/A	SB	CS	SBR	FA	FR	G/POS	TPR
1974	Chi-N	11	11	1	0	0	0	0	0	1	2	.000	.083	.000	-72	-3	0	0	0	1.000	-0	/1-1	-0.3
Total	3	76	115	9	27	3	0	1	10	7	14	.235	.290	.287	62	-6	1	1	-0	.989	1	/1-22,2-2,DO	-0.6

■ **LUIS MARQUEZ**   Marquez, Luis Angel (Sanchez) "Canena" b: 10/28/25, Aguadilla, P.R. d: 3/1/88, Aguadilla, P.R. BR/TR, 5'10.5", 174 lbs. Deb: 4/18/51

1951	Bos-N	68	122	19	24	5	1	0	11	10	20	.197	.274	.254	46	-9	4	4	-1	1.000	-2	O-43	-1.4
1954	Chi-N	17	12	2	1	0	0	0	0	2	4	.083	.214	.083	-19	-2	3	0	1	1.000	-4	O-14	-0.6
	Pit-N	14	9	3	1	0	0	0	0	4	0	.111	.385	.111	37	-1	0	0	0	1.000	-1	/O-4	-0.2
	Yr	31	21	5	2	0	0	0	0	6	4	.095	.296	.095	7	-3	3	0	1	1.000	-5	O-18	-0.8
Total	2	99	143	24	26	5	1	0	11	16	24	.182	.278	.231	40	-12	7	4	-0	1.000	-7	/O-61	-2.2

■ **BOB MARQUIS**   Marquis, Robert Rudolph b: 12/23/24, Oklahoma City, Okla. BL/TL, 6'1", 170 lbs. Deb: 4/17/53

1953	Cin-N	40	44	9	12	1	1	2	3	4	11	.273	.333	.477	107	0	0	0	0	.905	-2	O-10	-0.2

■ **ROGER MARQUIS**   Marquis, Roger Julian "Noonie" b: 4/5/37, Holyoke, Mass. BL/TL, 6', 190 lbs. Deb: 9/25/55

1955	Bal-A	1	1	0	0	0	0	0	0	0	0	.000	.000	.000	-99	-0	0	0	0	.000	-0	/O-1	-0.1

■ **LEFTY MARR**   Marr, Charles W. b: 9/19/1862, Cincinnati, Ohio d: 1/11/12, New Britain, Conn. BL/TL, Deb: 10/3/1886

1886	Cin-a	8	29	2	8	1	1	0		0	1	.276	.323	.379	116	0	1			.696	-1	/O-8	-0.1
1889	Col-a	139	546	110	167	26	15	1	75	87	32	.306	.407	.414	141	34	29			.856	12	3-66,O-47,S/1C	4.1
1890	Cin-N	130	527	91	157	17	12	1	73	46	29	.298	.361	.381	117	11	44			.930	-11	O-64,3-63/S	0.0
1891	Cin-N	72	286	32	74	9	7	0	32	25	15	.259	.323	.339	92	-3	16			.835	-10	O-72	-1.4
	Cin-a	14	57	9	11	1	0	0	4	7	4	.193	.281	.211	38	-5	2			.923	-1	O-14	-0.5
Total	4	363	1445	244	417	54	35	2	184	166	80	.289	.368	.379	118	38	92			.853	-10	O-205,3-129/S1C	2.1

■ **ORESTE MARRERO**   Marrero, Oreste Vilato (Vazquez) b: 10/31/69, Bayamon, P.R. BL/TL, 6', 195 lbs. Deb: 8/12/93

1993	Mon-N	32	81	10	17	5	1	1	4	11	21	.210	.326	.333	74	-3	1	3	-2	.991	-0	1-32	-0.7

■ **WILLIAM MARRIOTT**   Marriott, William Earl b: 4/18/1893, Pratt, Kan. d: 8/11/69, Berkeley, Cal. BL/TR, 6', 170 lbs. Deb: 9/6/17

1917	Chi-N	3	6	0	0	0	0	0	0	0	1	.000	.000	.000	-93	-1	0			.667	-0	/O-1	-0.2
1920	Chi-N	14	43	7	12	4	2	0	5	6	5	.279	.367	.465	135	2	1	1	-0	.892	-4	2-14	-0.2
1921	Chi-N	30	38	3	12	1	1	0	7	4	1	.316	.381	.395	105	0	0	1	-1	.826	-1	/2-6,S-1,3O	-0.1
1925	Bos-N	103	370	37	99	9	1	4	40	28	26	.268	.322	.365	67	-18	3	8	-4	.928	3	3-89/O-1	-1.2
1926	Bro-N	109	360	39	96	13	9	3	42	17	20	.267	.303	.378	84	-9	12			.927	-8	*3-104	-1.1
1927	Bro-N	6	9	0	1	0	1	0	1	2	2	.111	.273	.333	61	-1	0			.889	1	/3-2	0.0
Total	6	265	826	86	220	27	14	4	95	57	55	.266	.317	.347	78	-27	16	10		.925	-9	3-196/2-20,OS	-2.8

■ **ARMANDO MARSANS**   Marsans, Armando b: 10/3/1887, Matanzas, Cuba d: 9/3/60, Havana, Cuba BR/TR, 5'10", 157 lbs. Deb: 7/4/11

1911	Cin-N	58	138	17	36	2	2	0	11	15	11	.261	.346	.304	86	-2	11			.968	-5	O-34/1-1,3	-0.9
1912	Cin-N	110	416	59	132	19	7	1	38	20	17	.317	.353	.404	110	5	35			.975	-5	O-98/1-6	-0.3
1913	Cin-N	118	435	49	129	7	6	0	38	17	25	.297	.327	.340	91	-5	37			.963	-5	O-94,1-22/3S	-1.5
1914	Cin-N	36	124	16	37	3	0	0	22	14	6	.298	.374	.323	105	1	13			.916	1	O-36	0.1
	StL-F	9	40	5	14	0	2	0	2	3	0	.350	.395	.450	113	1	4			.927	0	/2-7,S-2	0.1
1915	StL-F	36	124	16	22	3	0	0	6	14	5	.177	.261	.202	23	-13	5			.975	3	O-35	-1.3
1916	StL-A	151	528	51	134	12	1	1	60	57	41	.254	.333	.286	91	-5	46	26	-2	.977	5	*O-150	-1.0
1917	StL-A	75	257	31	59	12	0	0	20	20	6	.230	.285	.276	74	-8	11			.963	-4	O-67/3-5,2	-1.8
	NY-A	25	88	10	20	4	0	0	15	8	3	.227	.292	.273	72	-3	6			.974	3	O-25	-0.1
	Yr	100	345	41	79	16	0	0	35	28	9	.229	.287	.275	73	-11	17			.967	-1	O-92/3-5,2	-1.9
1918	NY-A	37	123	13	29	5	1	0	9	5	3	.236	.266	.293	67	-5	3			.943	-6	O-36	-1.5
Total	8	655	2273	267	612	67	19	2	221	173	117	.269	.325	.318	88	-35	171	26		.967	-11	O-575/1-29,23S	-8.2

■ **FRED MARSH**   Marsh, Fred Francis b: 1/5/24, Valley Falls, Kan. BR/TR, 5'10", 180 lbs. Deb: 4/19/49

1949	Cle-A	1	0	0	0	0	0	0	0	0	0	—	—	—	—	0	0	0	0	.000	0	R	0.0
1951	StL-A	130	445	44	108	21	4	4	43	36	56	.243	.299	.335	69	-20	4	4	-1	.928	3	*3-117/S-3,2	-1.9
1952	StL-A	11	24	3	5	1	0	0	1	5	4	.208	.345	.250	65	-1	0	1	-1	.963	2	/2-9,S-3	0.1
	Was-A	9	24	1	1	0	0	0	1	1	4	.042	.080	.042	-68	-5	0	0	0	1.000	0	/2-5,O-2	-0.8
	StL-A	76	223	25	64	8	1	2	26	22	29	.287	.351	.359	95	-1	3	2	-0	.945	-15	S-57,3-21	-1.4
	Yr	96	271	29	70	9	1	2	28	28	37	.258	.328	.321	79	-7	3	3	-1	.945	-15	S-60,3-21,2/O	-2.1
1953	Chi-A	67	95	22	19	2	1	1	2	13	26	.200	.303	.274	55	-6	0	3	-2	.940	7	3-32,S-17/12	-0.1
1954	Chi-A	62	98	21	30	5	2	0	4	9	16	.306	.364	.398	105	1	4	2	0	.975	18	3-36/S-3,1O	1.9
1955	Bal-A	89	303	30	66	7	1	2	19	35	33	.218	.301	.267	58	-18	1	2	-1	.983	-15	2-76,S-18,S	-2.9
1956	Bal-A	20	24	2	3	0	0	0	4	3	3	.125	.250	.125	2	-3	1	0	0	.929	0	/S-8,3-8,2	-0.2
Total	7	465	1236	148	296	43	8	10	96	125	171	.239	.310	.311	69	-54	13	14	-5	.928	-2	3-232,S-107/210	-5.3

■ **TOM MARSH**   Marsh, Thomas Owen b: 12/27/65, Toledo, Ohio BR/TR, 6'2", 180 lbs. Deb: 6/5/92

1992	Phi-N	42	125	7	25	3	2	2	16	2	23	.200	.219	.304	47	-9	0	1	-1	.971	-1	O-35	-1.2
1994	Phi-N	8	18	3	5	1	1	0	3	1	1	.278	.316	.444	96	-0	0	0	0	.889	-1	/O-7	-0.1
Total	2	50	143	10	30	4	3	2	19	3	24	.210	.231	.322	53	-9	0	1	-1	.961	-2	/O-42	-1.3

■ **CHARLIE MARSHALL**   Marshall, Charles Anthony (b: Charles Anthony Marczlewicz) b: 8/28/19, Wilmington, Del. BR/TR, 5'10.5", 178 lbs. Deb: 6/14/41

1941	StL-N	1	0	0	0	0	0	0	0	0	0	—	—	—			0			1.000	-0	/C-1	0.0

■ **DAVE MARSHALL**   Marshall, David Lewis b: 1/14/43, Artesia, Cal. BL/TR, 6'1", 190 lbs. Deb: 9/7/67

1967	SF-N	1	0	0	0	0	0	0	0	0	0	—	—	—			0	0	0	.000	0	R	0.0
1968	SF-N	76	174	17	46	5	1	6	16	20	37	.264	.344	.322	101	1	2	1	0	.924	-6	O-50	-0.8
1969	SF-N	110	267	32	62	7	1	2	33	40	68	.232	.343	.288	80	-6	1	8	-5	.956	-10	O-87	-2.5
1970	NY-N	92	189	21	46	10	1	6	29	17	43	.243	.306	.402	88	-4	4	1	1	.973	-1	O-43	-0.6
1971	NY-N	100	214	28	51	9	1	3	21	26	54	.238	.326	.332	88	-3	3	1	0	.989	-4	O-64	-0.9
1972	NY-N	72	156	21	39	5	0	4	11	22	28	.250	.346	.359	103	1	3	3	-1	.972	-3	O-42	-0.5
1973	SD-N	39	49	4	14	5	0	0	4	8	9	.286	.397	.388	128	2	0	1	-1	1.000	-1	/O-8	0.1
Total	7	490	1049	123	258	41	4	16	114	133	239	.246	.336	.338	92	-8	13	15	-5	.966	-24	O-294	-5.2

■ **ED MARSHALL**   Marshall, Edward Herbert b: 6/4/06, New Albany, Miss. BR/TR, 5'11", 150 lbs. Deb: 9/28/29

1929	NY-N	5	15	6	6	2	0	0	2	1	0	.400	.438	.533	140	1	0			1.000	-2	/2-5	-0.1
1930	NY-N	78	223	33	69	5	3	0	21	13	9	.309	.350	.359	73	-9	0			.947	-3	S-45,2-17/3	-0.6
1931	NY-N	68	194	15	39	6	2	0	10	8	8	.201	.233	.253	31	-19	1			.956	-4	2-47,S-11/3	-1.2
1932	NY-N	68	226	18	56	8	1	0	28	6	11	.248	.270	.292	52	-15	0			.922	-3	S-63	-1.2
Total	4	219	658	72	170	21	6	0	61	28	28	.258	.291	.309	56	-42	1			.931	-4	S-119/2-69,3	-3.1

■ **JOE MARSHALL**   Marshall, Joseph Hanley "Home Run Joe" b: 2/19/1876, Audubon, Minn. d: 9/11/31, Santa Monica, Cal BR/TR, Deb: 9/7/03

1903	Pit-N	10	23	2	6	1	2	0	2	0		.261	.261	.478	106	-0	4			1.000	-4	/S-3,O-3,2	-0.4
1906	StL-N	33	95	2	15	1	2	0	7	6		.158	.216	.211	34	-7	0			.903	-1	O-23/1-4	-1.1
Total	2	43	118	4	21	2	4	0	9	6		.178	.224	.263	50	-7	4			.903	-5	/O-26,1-4,S2	-1.5

■ **KEITH MARSHALL**   Marshall, Keith Alan b: 7/2/51, San Francisco, Cal. BR/TR, 6'2", 175 lbs. Deb: 4/7/73

1973	KC-A	8	9	0	2	1	0	0	3	1	4	.222	.300	.333	73	-0	0	0	0	1.000	-3	/O-8	-0.3

YEAR	TM/L	G	AB	R	H	2B	3B	HR	RBI	BB	SO	AVG	OBP	SLG	PRO+	BR/A	SB	CS	SBR	FA	FR	G/POS	TPR
■ MIKE MARSHALL			Marshall, Michael Allen b: 1/12/60, Libertyville, Ill. BR/TR, 6'5", 220 lbs. Deb: 9/7/81																				
1981	*LA-N	14	25	2	5	3	0	0	1	1	4	.200	.259	.320	66	-1	0	0	0	1.000	-1	/1-3,3-3,O	-0.2
1982	LA-N	49	95	10	23	3	0	5	9	13	23	.242	.339	.432	117	2	2	0	1	1.000	-4	O-19,1-13	-0.2
1983	*LA-N	140	465	47	132	17	1	17	65	43	127	.284	.351	.434	117	10	7	3	0	.976	-7	*O-109,1-33	-0.1
1984	LA-N☆	134	495	68	127	27	0	21	65	40	93	.257	.316	.438	111	6	4	3	-1	.981	-4	*O-118,1-15	0.5
1985	*LA-N	135	518	72	152	27	2	28	95	37	137	.293	.344	.515	141	26	3	10	-5	.991	-0	*O-125/1-7	1.7
1986	LA-N	103	330	47	77	11	0	19	53	27	90	.233	.299	.439	109	2	4	4	-1	.963	-2	O-97	-0.4
1987	LA-N	104	402	45	118	19	0	16	72	18	79	.294	.330	.460	109	4	0	5	-3	.987	-6	*O-102	-0.8
1988	*LA-N	144	542	63	150	27	2	20	82	24	93	.277	.316	.445	120	11	4	1	1	.966	-5	O-90,1-53	0.4
1989	LA-N	105	377	41	98	21	1	11	42	33	78	.260	.328	.408	111	5	2	5	-2	.978	-2	O-102	-0.2
1990	NY-N	53	163	24	39	8	1	6	27	7	40	.239	.283	.411	89	-3	0	2	-1	.993	-1	1-42/O-1	-0.8
	*Bos-A	30	112	10	32	6	1	4	12	4	26	.286	.316	.464	111	1	0	0	0	1.000	1	D-14/1-8,O	0.1
1991	Bos-A	22	62	4	18	4	0	1	7	0	19	.290	.290	.403	86	-1	0	0	0	.979	-3	/1-5,O-4,D	-0.4
	Cal-A	2	7	0	0	0	0	0	0	0	1	.000	.000	.000	-99	-2	0	0	0	1.000	0	/1-1,D-1	-0.2
	Yr	24	69	4	18	4	0	1	7	0	20	.261	.261	.362	67	-3	0	0	0	.984	-2	/D-8,1-6,O	-0.6
Total	11	1035	3593	433	971	173	8	148	530	247	810	.270	.324	.446	115	60	26	33	-12	.978	-21	O-777,1-180/D3	-0.6
■ MAX MARSHALL			Marshall, Milo Max b: 9/18/13, Shenandoah, Iowa BL/TR, 6'1", 180 lbs. Deb: 5/10/42																				
1942	Cin-N	131	530	49	135	17	6	7	43	34	38	.255	.301	.349	90	-8	4			.976	-10	*O-129	-2.7
1943	Cin-N	132	508	55	120	11	8	4	39	34	52	.236	.287	.313	74	-18	8			.981	-5	*O-129	-3.2
1944	Cin-N	66	229	36	56	13	2	4	23	21	10	.245	.308	.371	94	-2	3			.965	2	O-59	-0.4
Total	3	329	1267	140	311	41	16	15	105	89	100	.245	.297	.339	84	-28	15			.975	-14	O-317	-6.3
■ JIM MARSHALL			Marshall, Rufus James b: 5/25/31, Danville, Ill. BL/TL, 6'1", 190 lbs. Deb: 4/15/58 MC																				
1958	Bal-A	85	191	17	41	4	3	5	19	18	30	.215	.282	.346	76	-7	3	2	-0	1.000	-5	1-52/O-8	-1.5
	Chi-N	26	81	12	22	2	0	5	11	12	13	.272	.372	.481	126	3	1	0	0	.992	-4	1-15,O-11	-0.1
1959	Chi-N	108	294	39	74	10	1	11	40	33	39	.252	.327	.405	95	-2	0	1	-1	.997	1	1-72/O-8	-0.7
1960	SF-N	75	118	19	28	2	2	2	13	17	24	.237	.333	.339	90	-1	0	1	-1	.968	-3	1-28/O-6	-0.2
1961	SF-N	44	36	5	8	0	0	1	7	3	8	.222	.282	.306	58	-2	0	0	0	1.000	-0	/1-4,O-2	-0.2
1962	NY-N	17	32	6	11	1	0	3	4	3	6	.344	.400	.656	175	3	0	0	0	1.000	-0	/1-5,O-1	0.3
	Pit-N	55	100	13	22	5	1	2	12	15	19	.220	.322	.350	80	-3	1	0	0	1.000	1	1-26	-0.3
	Yr	72	132	19	33	6	1	5	16	18	25	.250	.340	.424	103	1	1	0	0	1.000	1	1-31/O-1	0.0
Total	5	410	852	111	206	24	7	29	106	101	139	.242	.323	.388	93	-9	5	4	-1	.994	-10	1-202/O-36	-3.2
■ WILLARD MARSHALL			Marshall, Willard Warren b: 2/8/21, Richmond, Va. BL/TR, 6'1", 205 lbs. Deb: 4/14/42																				
1942	NY-N★	116	401	41	103	9	2	11	59	26	20	.257	.307	.372	98	-2	1			.975	-0	*O-107	-0.9
1946	NY-N	131	510	63	144	18	3	13	48	33	29	.282	.327	.406	107	3	3			.978	2	*O-125	-0.2
1947	NY-N★	155	587	102	171	19	6	36	107	67	30	.291	.366	.528	134	26	3			.972	12	*O-155	2.9
1948	NY-N	143	537	72	146	21	8	14	86	64	34	.272	.350	.419	107	5	2			.983	5	*O-142	0.1
1949	NY-N★	141	499	81	153	19	3	12	70	78	20	.307	.401	.429	123	19	4			.974	6	*O-138	1.8
1950	Bos-N	105	298	38	70	10	2	5	40	36	5	.235	.319	.332	77	-10	1			.958	1	O-85	-1.2
1951	Bos-N	136	469	65	132	24	7	11	62	48	18	.281	.351	.433	118	11	0	3	-2	1.000	-8	*O-136	-0.3
1952	Bos-N	21	66	5	15	4	1	2	11	4	4	.227	.271	.409	89	-1	0	0	0	.938	1	O-16	-0.1
	Cin-N	107	397	52	106	23	1	8	46	37	21	.267	.333	.390	100	-0	0	1	-1	.985	2	*O-105	-0.3
	Yr	128	463	57	121	27	2	10	57	41	25	.261	.324	.393	99	-1	0	1	-1	.979	3	*O-121	-0.4
1953	Cin-N	122	357	51	95	14	6	17	62	41	28	.266	.342	.482	111	5	0	0	0	.995	5	O-95	0.8
1954	Chi-A	47	71	7	18	2	0	1	7	11	9	.254	.354	.324	84	-1	0	0	0	.960	-7	O-29	-0.9
1955	Chi-A	22	41	6	7	0	0	0	6	13	1	.171	.370	.171	48	-2	0	0	0	.957	-1	O-12	-0.4
Total	11	1246	4233	583	1160	163	39	130	604	458	219	.274	.347	.423	109	51	14	4		.979	20	*O-1145	1.3
■ BILL MARSHALL			Marshall, William Henry b: 2/14/11, Dorchester, Mass. d: 5/5/77, Sacramento, Cal. BR/TR, 5'8.5", 156 lbs. Deb: 6/20/31																				
1931	Bos-A	1	0	1	0	0	0	0	0	0	0	—	—	—			0	0	0	.000	0	R	0.0
1934	Cin-N	6	8	0	1	0	0	0	0	0	2	.125	.125	.125	-34	-1	0	0	0	.875	1	/2-2	-0.1
Total	2	7	8	1	1	0	0	0	0	0	2	.125	.125	.125	-34	-1	0	0	0	.875	1	/2-2	-0.1
■ DOC MARSHALL			Marshall, William Riddle b: 9/22/1875, Butler, Pa. d: 12/11/59, Clinton, Ill. BR/TR, 6', 185 lbs. Deb: 4/15/04																				
1904	Phi-N	8	20	1	2	0	0	0	1	0		.100	.100	.100	-40	-3	0			.944	2	/C-7	-0.1
	NY-N	1	0	0	0	0	0	0	0	0		—	—	—			0			.000	0	/C-1	0.0
	Bos-N	13	43	3	9	0	1	0	2	2		.209	.244	.256	56	-2	2			.955	1	C-10/O-1	0.0
	NY-N	10	17	3	6	1	0	0	2	1		.353	.389	.412	141	1	0			.917	2	/C-2,O-2,2	0.3
	Yr	32	80	7	17	1	1	0	5	3		.213	.241	.250	52	-5	2			.945	5	C-20/O-3,2	0.2
1906	NY-N	38	102	8	17	3	2	0	7	7		.167	.234	.235	45	-7	7			1.000	-2	O-16,C-13/1	-0.9
	StL-N	39	123	6	34	4	1	0	10	6		.276	.315	.325	104	0	1			.961	9	C-38	1.4
	Yr	77	225	14	51	7	3	0	17	13		.227	.278	.284	76	-7	8			.969	7	C-51,O-16/1	0.5
1907	StL-N	84	268	19	54	8	2	2	18	12		.201	.246	.269	64	-12	2			.952	5	C-83	0.1
1908	StL-N	6	14	0	1	0	0	0	1	0		.071	.071	.071	-57	-2	0			1.000	2	/C-6	0.0
	Chi-N	12	20	4	6	0	1	0	3	0		.300	.300	.400	118	0	0			1.000	5	/C-4,O-3	0.6
	Yr	18	34	4	7	0	1	0	4	0		.206	.206	.265	49	-2	0			1.000	7	C-10/O-3	0.6
1909	Bro-N	50	149	7	30	7	1	0	10	6		.201	.232	.262	55	-8	3			.968	-5	C-49/O-1	-1.1
Total	5	261	756	51	159	23	8	2	54	34		.210	.251	.270	64	-34	15			.960	19	C-213/O-23,12	0.3
■ DOC MARTEL			Martel, Leon Alphonse "Marty" b: 1/29/1883, Weymouth, Mass. d: 10/11/47, Washington, D.C. BR/TR, 6', 185 lbs. Deb: 7/6/09																				
1909	Phi-N	24	41	1	11	3	1	0	7	4		.268	.333	.390	123	1	0			.974	4	C-12	0.7
1910	Bos-N	10	31	0	4	0	0	0	1	2	3	.129	.182	.129	-9	-4	0			.980	-0	1-10	-0.5
Total	2	34	72	1	15	3	1	0	8	6	3	.208	.269	.278	64	-3	0			.974	4	/C-12,1-10	0.2
■ AL MARTIN			Martin, Albert (a.k.a. Albert May in 1872) Deb: 5/7/1872																				
1872	Eck-n	4	18	2	5	0	0	0	2	0	0	.278	.278	.278	84	-0						/2-4	0.0
1874	Atl-n	7	30	1	4	0	0	0		0	0	.133	.133	.133	-17	-4						/2-6,O-1	-0.3
1875	Atl-n	6	26	1	3	0	0	0		0	0	.115	.115	.115	-23	-3						/O-6	-0.3
Total	3 n	17	74	4	12	0	0	0		0	0	.162	.162	.162	34							/2-10,O-7	-0.6
■ ALBERT MARTIN			Martin, Albert Lee b: 11/24/67, West Covina, Cal. BL/TL, 6'2", 220 lbs. Deb: 7/28/92																				
1992	Pit-N	12	12	1	2	1	0	0	2	0	5	.167	.167	.333	39	-1	0	0	0	1.000	-2	/O-7	-0.3
1993	Pit-N	143	480	85	135	26	8	18	64	42	122	.281	.340	.481	117	11	16	9	-1	.975	-10	*O-136	-0.3
1994	Pit-N	82	276	48	79	12	4	9	33	34	56	.286	.369	.457	114	6	15	6	1	.979	2	O-77	0.8
Total	3	237	768	134	216	38	13	27	99	76	183	.281	.348	.470	115	16	31	15	-4	.977	-9	O-220	0.2
■ BILLY MARTIN			Martin, Alfred Manuel b: 5/16/28, Berkeley, Cal. d: 12/25/89, Johnson City, N.Y. BR/TR, 5'11.5", 165 lbs. Deb: 4/18/50 MC																				
1950	NY-A	34	36	10	9	1	0	1	8	3	3	.250	.308	.361	73	-2	0	0	0	.976	-1	2-22/3-1	-0.2
1951	*NY-A	51	58	10	15	1	2	0	2	4	9	.259	.328	.345	85	-1	0	1	-1	.988	16	2-23/S-6,3O	1.4
1952	*NY-A	109	363	32	97	13	3	3	33	22	31	.267	.323	.344	91	-5	3	6	-3	.984	18	*2-107	1.6
1953	*NY-A	149	587	72	151	24	6	15	75	43	56	.257	.314	.395	94	-4	6	7	-2	.985	-1	*2-146,S-18	-0.3
1955	*NY-A	20	70	8	21	4	1	0	9	7	9	.300	.364	.371	100	0	1	0	0	.977	1	2-17/S-3	0.2
1956	*NY-A★	121	458	76	121	24	5	9	49	30	56	.264	.314	.397	90	-9	7	3	0	.980	-14	*2-105,3-16	-1.4

YEAR	TM/L	G	AB	R	H	2B	3B	HR	RBI	BB	SO	AVG	OBP	SLG	PRO+	BR/A	SB	CS	SBR	FA	FR	G/POS	TPR
1957	NY-A	43	145	12	35	5	2	1	12	3	14	.241	.262	.324	60	-8	2	1	0	.947	-3	2-26,3-13	-1.0
	KC-A	73	265	33	68	9	3	9	27	12	20	.257	.296	.415	91	-4	7	1	2	.987	-20	2-52,3-20/S	-1.9
	Yr	116	410	45	103	14	5	10	39	15	34	.251	.284	.383	80	-12	9	2	2	.973	-23	2-78,3-33/S	-2.9
1958	Det-A	131	498	56	127	19	1	7	42	16	62	.255	.282	.339	65	-24	5	3	-0	.958	-18	S-88,3-41	-3.5
1959	Cle-A	73	242	37	63	7	0	9	24	8	18	.260	.292	.401	92	-4	0	2	-1	.997	-11	2-67/3-4	-1.1
1960	Cin-N	103	317	34	78	17	1	3	16	27	34	.246	.305	.334	74	-11	0	1	-1	.975	-13	2-97	-1.7
1961	Mil-N	6	6	1	0	0	0	0	0	0	1	.000	.000	.000	-99	-2	0	0	0	.000	0	H	-0.2
	Min-A	108	374	44	92	15	5	6	36	13	42	.246	.277	.361	65	-19	3	2	-0	.963	-15	*2-105/S-1	-2.4
Total	11	1021	3419	425	877	137	28	64	333	188	355	.257	.301	.369	81	-96	34	29	-7	.980	-61	2-767,S-118/3O	-10.5

■ PHONNEY MARTIN
Martin, Alphonse Case b: 8/4/1845, New York, N.Y.   d: 5/24/33, Hollis, N.Y.   5'7", 148 lbs.   Deb: 4/26/1872

YEAR	TM/L	G	AB	R	H	2B	3B	HR	RBI	BB	SO	AVG	OBP	SLG	PRO+	BR/A	SB	CS	SBR	FA	FR	G/POS	TPR
1872	Tro-n	25	120	27	34	3	1	0	14	0	1	.283	.283	.325	86	-2						O-23/P-8	0.0
	Eck-n	18	79	12	14	0	0	0	9	1	2	.177	.188	.177	15	-7						P-10/O-8	-0.1
	Yr	43	199	39	48	3	1	0	23	1	3	.241	.245	.266	61	-8						O-31/P-18	-0.1
1873	Mut-n	31	139	12	30	2	0	0	14	0	4	.216	.216	.230	32	-11						O-30/P-6	-0.6
Total	2 n	74	338	51	78	5	1	0	37	1	7	.231	.233	.251	48	-20						/O-61,P-24	-0.7

■ BABE MARTIN
Martin, Boris Michael (b: Boris Michael Martinovich)   b: 3/28/20, Seattle, Wash.   BR/TR, 5'11.5", 194 lbs.   Deb: 9/25/44

YEAR	TM/L	G	AB	R	H	2B	3B	HR	RBI	BB	SO	AVG	OBP	SLG	PRO+	BR/A	SB	CS	SBR	FA	FR	G/POS	TPR
1944	StL-A	2	4	0	3	1	0	0	1	0	0	.750	.750	1.000	376	1	0	0	0	1.000	-0	/O-1	0.1
1945	StL-A	54	185	13	37	5	2	2	16	11	24	.200	.245	.281	50	-12	0	1	-1	.992	6	O-48/1-6	-1.0
1946	StL-A	3	9	0	2	0	0	0	1	1	2	.222	.300	.222	45	-1	0	0	0	1.000	1	/C-2	0.0
1948	Bos-A	4	4	0	2	0	0	0	0	0	1	.500	.500	.500	158	0	0	0	0	.000	0	/C-1	0.0
1949	Bos-A	2	2	0	0	0	0	0	0	0	0	.000	.000	.000	-93	-0	0	0	0	.000	0	/C-1	-0.1
1953	StL-A	4	2	0	0	0	0	0	0	1	0	.000	.333	.000	-4	-0	0	0	0	.000	0	/C-1	0.0
Total	6	69	206	13	44	6	2	2	18	13	27	.214	.260	.291	56	-12	0	1	-1	.992	6	/O-49,1-6,C	-1.0

■ FRANK MARTIN
Martin, Frank   b: 2/28/1879, Chicago, Ill.   d: 9/30/24, Chicago, Ill.   Deb: 6/30/1897

YEAR	TM/L	G	AB	R	H	2B	3B	HR	RBI	BB	SO	AVG	OBP	SLG	PRO+	BR/A	SB	CS	SBR	FA	FR	G/POS	TPR
1897	Lou-N	2	8	1	2	0	0	0	0	0		.250	.250	.250	33	-1	0			.813	0	/2-2	0.0
1898	Chi-N	1	4	0	0	0	0	0	0	0		.000	.000	.000	-99	-1	0			1.000	0	/2-1	-0.1
1899	NY-N	17	54	5	14	2	0	0	1	2		.259	.298	.296	66	-3	0			.824	3	3-17	-0.1
Total	3	20	66	6	16	2	0	0	1	2		.242	.275	.273	52	-4	0			.870	3	/3-17,2-3	-0.1

■ HERSH MARTIN
Martin, Hershel Ray   b: 9/19/09, Birmingham, Ala.   d: 11/17/80, Cuba, Mo.   BB/TR, 6'2", 190 lbs.   Deb: 4/23/37

YEAR	TM/L	G	AB	R	H	2B	3B	HR	RBI	BB	SO	AVG	OBP	SLG	PRO+	BR/A	SB	CS	SBR	FA	FR	G/POS	TPR
1937	Phi-N	141	579	102	164	35	7	8	49	69	66	.283	.362	.409	101	1	11			.978	5	*O-139	0.2
1938	Phi-N☆	120	466	58	139	36	6	3	39	34	48	.298	.347	.421	113	8	8			.965	1	*O-116	0.5
1939	Phi-N	111	393	59	111	28	5	1	22	42	27	.282	.355	.387	102	2	4			.976	11	O-95	0.9
1940	Phi-N	33	83	10	21	6	1	0	5	9	9	.253	.326	.349	90	-1	1			.979	-0	O-23	-0.2
1944	NY-A	85	328	49	99	12	4	9	47	34	26	.302	.371	.445	128	12	5	2	0	.964	3	O-80	1.1
1945	NY-A	117	408	53	109	18	6	7	53	65	31	.267	.368	.392	115	9	4	1	1	.984	3	*O-102	0.8
Total	6	607	2257	331	643	135	29	28	215	253	207	.285	.359	.408	109	31	33	3		.974	23	O-555	3.3

■ JERRY MARTIN
Martin, Jerry Lindsey   b: 5/11/49, Columbia, S.C.   BR/TR, 6'1", 195 lbs.   Deb: 9/7/74   F

YEAR	TM/L	G	AB	R	H	2B	3B	HR	RBI	BB	SO	AVG	OBP	SLG	PRO+	BR/A	SB	CS	SBR	FA	FR	G/POS	TPR
1974	Phi-N	13	14	2	3	1	0	0	1	1	5	.214	.267	.286	52	-1	0	0	0	1.000	-3	O-11	-0.5
1975	Phi-N	57	113	15	24	7	1	2	11	11	16	.212	.288	.345	72	-4	2	2	-1	.979	-3	O-49	-1.0
1976	*Phi-N	130	121	30	30	7	0	2	15	7	28	.248	.289	.355	80	-3	3	2	-0	.975	-30	*O-110/1-1	-3.7
1977	*Phi-N	116	215	34	56	16	3	6	28	18	42	.260	.329	.447	101	0	6	4	-1	.984	-19	*O-106/1-1	-2.2
1978	*Phi-N	128	266	40	72	13	4	9	36	28	65	.271	.342	.451	119	6	9	5	-0	.987	-15	*O-112	-1.3
1979	Chi-N	150	534	74	145	34	3	19	73	38	85	.272	.323	.453	100	-1	2	4	-2	.981	-2	*O-144	-1.1
1980	Chi-N	141	494	57	112	22	2	23	73	38	107	.227	.285	.419	88	-10	8	3	1	.978	-12	*O-129	-2.7
1981	SF-N	72	241	23	58	5	3	4	25	21	52	.241	.309	.336	85	-5	6	2	1	.993	-4	O-64	-1.1
1982	KC-A	147	519	52	138	22	1	15	65	38	138	.266	.318	.399	95	-4	1	1	-0	.980	4	*O-142/D-3	-0.4
1983	KC-A	13	44	4	14	2	0	2	13	1	7	.318	.333	.500	125	1	1	0	0	.957	-2	O-13	0.0
1984	NY-N	51	91	6	14	1	0	3	5	6	29	.154	.206	.264	32	-9	0	0	0	1.000	-1	O-30/1-3	-1.1
Total	11	1018	2652	337	666	130	17	85	345	207	574	.251	.309	.409	93	-29	38	23	-2	.982	-87	O-910/1-5,D	-15.1

■ JACK MARTIN
Martin, John Christopher   b: 4/19/1887, Plainfield, N.J.   d: 7/4/80, Plainfield, N.J.   BR/TR, 5'9", 159 lbs.   Deb: 4/25/12

YEAR	TM/L	G	AB	R	H	2B	3B	HR	RBI	BB	SO	AVG	OBP	SLG	PRO+	BR/A	SB	CS	SBR	FA	FR	G/POS	TPR
1912	NY-A	71	231	30	52	6	1	0	17	37		.225	.347	.260	70	-7	14			.898	3	S-65/3-4,2	0.1
1914	Bos-N	33	85	10	18	2	0	0	5	6	7	.212	.264	.235	49	-5	0			.949	0	3-26/1-1,2	-0.5
	Phi-N	83	292	26	74	5	3	0	21	27	29	.253	.319	.291	77	-8	6			.930	-3	S-83	-0.4
	Yr	116	377	36	92	7	3	0	26	33	36	.244	.307	.279	71	-13	6			.930	-3	S-83,3-26/12	-0.9
Total	2	187	608	66	144	13	4	0	43	70	36	.237	.323	.271	71	-21	20			.915	-0	S-148/3-30,21	-0.8

■ PEPPER MARTIN
Martin, John Leonard Roosevelt "The Wild Horse Of The Osage"
b: 2/29/04, Temple, Okla.   d: 3/5/65, McAlester, Okla.   BR/TR, 5'8", 170 lbs.   Deb: 4/16/28   C

YEAR	TM/L	G	AB	R	H	2B	3B	HR	RBI	BB	SO	AVG	OBP	SLG	PRO+	BR/A	SB	CS	SBR	FA	FR	G/POS	TPR
1928	*StL-N	39	13	11	4	0	0	0	1	1	2	.308	.400	.308	86	-0	2			1.000	-2	/O-4	-0.2
1930	StL-N	6	1	5	0	0	0	0	0	0	0	.000	.000	.000	-97	-0	0			.000	0	H	0.0
1931	*StL-N	123	413	68	124	32	8	7	75	30	40	.300	.351	.467	114	7	16			.967	0	*O-110	0.1
1932	StL-N	85	323	47	77	19	6	4	34	30	31	.238	.305	.372	79	-10	9			.976	-1	O-69,3-15	-1.4
1933	StL-N★	145	599	122	189	36	12	8	57	67	46	.316	.387	.456	133	27	26			.943	-3	*3-145	3.5
1934	*StL-N★	110	454	74	131	25	11	5	49	32	41	.289	.337	.425	96	-3	23			.936	-5	*3-107/P-1	-0.3
1935	StL-N★	135	539	121	161	41	6	9	54	34	58	.299	.341	.447	106	4	20			.904	-14	*3-114,O-16	-0.7
1936	StL-N	143	572	121	177	36	11	11	76	58	66	.309	.373	.469	126	20	23			.976	-10	*O-127,3-15/P	0.5
1937	StL-N☆	98	339	60	103	27	8	5	38	33	50	.304	.366	.475	124	11	9			.973	11	O-82/3-5	1.9
1938	StL-N	91	269	34	79	18	2	2	38	18	34	.294	.340	.398	97	-1	4			.986	-3	O-62/3-4	-0.6
1939	StL-N	88	281	48	86	17	7	3	37	30	35	.306	.375	.448	113	6	6			.975	-4	O-51,3-22	0.0
1940	StL-N	86	228	28	72	15	4	3	39	22	24	.316	.398	.456	122	7	6			.974	-3	O-63/3-2	0.2
1944	StL-N	40	86	15	24	4	0	2	4	15	11	.279	.386	.395	118	3	2			.980	-4	O-29	-0.2
Total	13	1189	4117	754	1227	270	75	59	501	369	438	.298	.358	.443	112	70	146			.973	-36	O-613,3-429/P	2.8

■ J. C. MARTIN
Martin, Joseph Clifton   b: 12/13/36, Axton, Va.   BL/TR, 6'2", 200 lbs.   Deb: 9/10/59   C

YEAR	TM/L	G	AB	R	H	2B	3B	HR	RBI	BB	SO	AVG	OBP	SLG	PRO+	BR/A	SB	CS	SBR	FA	FR	G/POS	TPR
1959	Chi-A	3	4	0	1	0	0	0	0	0	1	.250	.250	.250	38	-0	0	0	0	.667	-0	/3-2	0.0
1960	Chi-A	7	20	0	2	1	0	0	2	0	3	.100	.100	.150	-34	-4	0	0	0	1.000	-0	/3-5,1-1	-0.4
1961	Chi-A	110	274	26	63	8	3	5	32	21	31	.230	.290	.336	68	-13	1	2	-1	.988	9	1-60,3-36	-0.7
1962	Chi-A	18	26	0	2	0	0	0	2	0	3	.077	.077	.077	-59	-6	0	0	0	1.000	-1	/C-6,1-1,3	-0.6
1963	Chi-A	105	259	25	53	11	1	5	28	26	35	.205	.280	.313	67	-11	0	0	0	.983	14	C-98/1-3,3	0.6
1964	Chi-A	122	294	23	58	10	1	4	22	16	30	.197	.244	.279	46	-22	0	0	0	.986	8	*C-120	-1.0
1965	Chi-A	119	230	21	60	12	0	2	21	24	29	.261	.336	.339	98	-0	2	1	0	.982	1	*C-112/1-4,3	0.4
1966	Chi-A	67	157	13	40	5	3	2	20	14	24	.255	.320	.363	103	0	0	0	0	.982	-1	C-63	0.3
1967	Chi-A	101	252	22	59	12	1	2	32	30	41	.234	.318	.337	97	-1	4	4	-1	.987	7	*C-96/1-1	0.6
1968	NY-N	78	244	20	55	9	2	3	31	21	31	.225	.300	.316	84	-4	0	0	0	.994	-3	C-53,1-14	-0.6
1969	*NY-N	66	177	12	37	5	1	4	21	12	32	.209	.259	.316	59	-10	0	0	0	.996	-6	C-48/1-2	-1.5
1970	Chi-N	40	77	11	12	1	0	1	4	20	10	.156	.337	.208	44	-6	0	0	0	.983	2	C-36/1-3	-0.3
1971	Chi-N	47	125	13	33	5	0	4	17	12	16	.264	.338	.352	84	-3	1	0	0	.996	2	C-43/O-1	0.1
1972	Chi-N	25	50	3	12	3	0	0	7	5	9	.240	.309	.300	67	-2	0	0	0	.970	-3	C-17	-0.5
Total	14	908	2189	189	487	82	12	32	230	201	299	.222	.293	.315	72	-81	9	8	-2	.987	26	C-692/1-89,3O	-3.6

YEAR	TM/L	G	AB	R	H	2B	3B	HR	RBI	BB	SO	AVG	OBP	SLG	PRO+	BR/A	SB	CS	SBR	FA	FR	G/POS	TPR

■ MIKE MARTIN   Martin, Joseph Michael   b: 12/3/58, Portland, Ore.   BL/TR, 6'2", 193 lbs.   Deb: 8/15/86

| 1986 | Chi-N | 8 | 13 | 1 | 1 | 0 | 0 | 0 | 2 | 4 | .077 | .200 | .154 | -1 | -2 | 0 | 0 | 0 | 1.000 | 0 | /C-8 | -0.2 |

■ JOE MARTIN   Martin, Joseph Samuel "Silent Joe"   b: 1/1/1876, Hollidaysburg, Pa.   d: 5/25/64, Altoona, Pa.   BL/TR, 5'9.5", 155 lbs.   Deb: 4/28/03

1903	Was-A	35	119	11	27	4	5	0	7	5		.227	.258	.345	78	-3	2			.892	-3	2-15,3-13/O	-0.8
	StL-A	44	173	18	37	6	4	0	7	6		.214	.249	.295	64	-8	2			.983	-3	O-38/2-6,3	-1.4
	Yr	79	292	29	64	10	9	0	14	11		.219	.252	.315	70	-11	2			.959	-8	O-45,2-21,3	-2.2

■ NORBERTO MARTIN   Martin, Norberto Edonal (McDonald)   b: 12/10/66, San Pedro De Macoris, D.R.   BR/TR, 5'10", 175 lbs.   Deb: 9/20/93

1993	Chi-A	8	14	3	5	0	0	0	2	1	1	.357	.400	.357	108	0	0	0	0	.957	3	/2-5,D-1	0.3
1994	Chi-A	45	131	19	36	7	1	1	16	9	16	.275	.321	.366	78	-4	4	2	0	.982	-6	2-28/S-6,3OD	-0.8
Total	2	53	145	22	41	7	1	1	18	10	17	.283	.329	.366	80	-4	4	2	0	.978	-3	/2-33,S-6,3OD	-0.5

■ STU MARTIN   Martin, Stuart McGuire   b: 11/17/13, Rich Square, N.C.   BL/TR, 6', 155 lbs.   Deb: 4/14/36

1936	StL-N☆	92	332	63	99	21	4	6	41	29	27	.298	.356	.440	114	6	17			.949	-13	2-83/S-3	-0.1
1937	StL-N	90	223	34	58	6	1	1	17	32	18	.260	.353	.309	80	-5	3			.946	-6	2-48/1-9,S	-0.9
1938	StL-N	114	417	54	116	26	2	1	27	30	28	.278	.328	.357	84	-9	4			.967	-10	2-99	-1.3
1939	StL-N	120	425	60	114	26	7	3	30	33	40	.268	.325	.384	85	-9	4			.977	-3	*2-107/1-1	-0.7
1940	StL-N	112	369	45	88	12	6	4	32	33	35	.238	.301	.336	71	-14	4			.972	-25	3-73,2-33	-3.8
1941	Pit-N	88	233	37	71	13	2	0	19	10	17	.305	.341	.378	103	1	4			.972	-4	2-53/3-2,1	0.0
1942	Pit-N	42	120	16	27	4	2	1	12	8	10	.225	.273	.317	71	-5	1			.979	-11	2-30/1-1,S	-1.5
1943	Chi-N	64	118	13	26	4	0	0	5	15	10	.220	.308	.254	64	-5	1			.980	1	2-22/3-8,1	-0.3
Total	8	722	2237	322	599	112	24	16	183	190	185	.268	.327	.361	86	-41	36			.966	-71	2-475/3-83,1S	-8.6

■ GENE MARTIN   Martin, Thomas Eugene   b: 1/12/47, Americus, Ga.   BL/TR, 6'0.5", 190 lbs.   Deb: 7/28/68

| 1968 | Was-A | 9 | 11 | 1 | 4 | 1 | 0 | 1 | 1 | 0 | 1 | .364 | .364 | .727 | 232 | 2 | 0 | 0 | 0 | .000 | -1 | /O-2 | 0.1 |

■ BILLY MARTIN   Martin, William Lloyd   b: 2/13/1894, Washington, D.C.   d: 9/14/49, Arlington, Va.   BR/TR, 5'8.5", 170 lbs.   Deb: 10/6/14

| 1914 | Bos-N | 1 | 3 | 0 | 0 | 0 | 0 | 0 | 0 | 0 | 0 | .000 | .000 | .000 | -99 | -1 | 0 | | | .500 | -1 | /S-1 | -0.2 |

■ JOE MARTIN   Martin, William Joseph "Smokey Joe"   b: 8/28/11, Seymour, Mo.   d: 9/28/60, Buffalo, N.Y.   BR/TR, 5'11.5", 181 lbs.   Deb: 5/5/36

1936	NY-N	7	15	0	4	1	0	0	2	0	4	.267	.313	.333	75	-1	0	0	0	1.000	1	/3-7	0.0
1938	Chi-A	1	0	0	0	0	0	0	0	0	0	—	—	—	—	0	0	0	0	.000	0	R	0.0
Total	2	8	15	0	4	1	0	0	2	0	4	.267	.313	.333	75	-1	0	0	0	1.000	1	/3-7	0.0

■ CARLOS MARTINEZ   Martinez, Carlos Alberto Escobar (b: Carlos Alberto Escobar (Martinez))   b: 8/11/64, LaGuaira, Venez.   BR/TR, 6'5", 175 lbs.   Deb: 9/2/88

1988	Chi-A	17	55	5	9	1	0	0	0	0	12	.164	.164	.182	-3	-7	1	0	0	.909	3	3-15/D-2	-0.5
1989	Chi-A	109	350	44	105	22	0	5	32	21	57	.300	.341	.406	112	5	4	1	1	.912	-6	3-68,1-34,O/D	-0.2
1990	Chi-A	92	272	18	61	6	5	4	24	10	40	.224	.252	.327	62	-15	0	4	-2	.988	-1	1-82/O-1,D	-2.9
1991	Cle-A	72	257	22	73	14	0	5	30	10	43	.284	.316	.397	95	-2	3	2	-0	.968	-4	D-41,1-31	-1.0
1992	Cle-A	69	228	23	60	9	1	5	35	7	21	.263	.288	.377	87	-5	1	2	-1	.996	-5	1-37,3-28/D	-1.3
1993	Cle-A	80	262	26	64	10	0	5	31	20	29	.244	.298	.340	71	-11	1	1	-0	.934	-9	3-35,1-22,D	-2.2
Total	6	439	1424	138	372	62	6	24	152	68	202	.261	.297	.364	83	-35	10	10	-3	.986	-27	1-206,3-146/DO	-8.1

■ CARMELO MARTINEZ   Martinez, Carmelo (Salgado)   b: 7/28/60, Dorado, P.R.   BR/TR, 6'2", 220 lbs.   Deb: 8/22/83

1983	Chi-N	29	89	8	23	3	6	6	16	4	19	.258	.290	.494	108	0	0	0	0	.992	-0	1-26/3-1,O	-0.1
1984	*SD-N	149	488	64	122	28	2	13	66	68	82	.250	.346	.395	108	6	1	3	-2	.976	21	*O-142/1-2	2.2
1985	SD-N	150	514	64	130	28	1	21	72	87	82	.253	.364	.434	124	18	0	4	-2	.978	13	*O-150/1-3	2.5
1986	SD-N	113	244	28	58	10	0	9	25	35	46	.238	.336	.389	101	1	1	1	-0	.978	-0	O-60,1-26/3	-0.2
1987	SD-N	139	447	59	122	21	2	15	70	70	82	.273	.375	.430	117	12	5	5	-2	.968	-3	O-78,1-65	0.1
1988	SD-N	121	365	48	86	12	0	18	65	35	57	.236	.303	.416	106	2	1	1	-0	.993	10	O-64,1-41	0.7
1989	SD-N	111	267	23	59	12	2	6	39	32	54	.221	.304	.348	86	-5	0	0	0	.982	5	O-65,1-32	-0.7
1990	Phi-N	71	198	23	48	8	0	8	31	29	37	.242	.339	.404	104	1	2	1	0	.994	-2	1-43,O-20	-0.4
	*Pit-N	12	19	3	4	1	0	2	4	1	5	.211	.250	.579	126	0	0	0	0	1.000	0	/1-5,O-2	0.1
	Yr	83	217	26	52	9	0	10	35	30	42	.240	.332	.419	106	2	2	1	0	.995	-2	1-48,O-22	-0.3
1991	Pit-N	11	16	1	4	0	0	0	1	2	2	.250	.294	.250	55	-1	0	0	0	.945	-1	/1-8	-0.2
	KC-A	44	121	17	25	6	0	4	17	27	25	.207	.351	.355	96	1	1	0	-1	.991	4	1-43/D-1	0.1
	Cin-N	53	138	12	32	5	0	6	19	15	37	.232	.307	.399	93	-1	1	0	0	.985	0	1-25,O-16	-0.3
Total	9	1003	2906	350	713	134	7	108	424	404	528	.245	.340	.408	108	35	10	16	-7	.980	41	O-598,1-319/3D	3.8

■ TINO MARTINEZ   Martinez, Constantino   b: 12/7/67, Tampa, Fla.   BL/TR, 6'2", 205 lbs.   Deb: 8/20/90

1990	Sea-A	24	68	4	15	4	0	0	5	9	9	.221	.312	.279	66	-3	0	0	0	1.000	0	1-23	-0.4
1991	Sea-A	36	112	11	23	2	0	4	9	11	24	.205	.276	.330	67	-5	0	0	0	.993	2	1-29/D-5	-0.5
1992	Sea-A	136	460	53	118	19	2	16	66	42	77	.257	.321	.411	103	1	2	1	0	.995	1	1-78,D-47	-0.5
1993	Sea-A	109	408	48	108	25	1	17	60	45	56	.265	.345	.456	112	6	0	3	-2	.997	-3	*1-103/D-6	-0.7
1994	Sea-A	97	329	42	86	21	0	20	61	29	52	.261	.323	.508	108	2	1	2	-1	.997	-2	1-82/D-8	-0.7
Total	5	402	1377	158	350	71	3	57	201	136	218	.254	.325	.434	102	2	3	6	-3	.996	-2	1-315/D-66	-2.8

■ DAVE MARTINEZ   Martinez, David   b: 9/26/64, New York, N.Y.   BL/TL, 5'10", 150 lbs.   Deb: 6/15/86

1986	Chi-N	53	108	13	15	1	1	1	7	6	22	.139	.191	.194	6	-14	4	2	0	.988	-4	O-46	-1.9
1987	Chi-N	142	459	70	134	18	8	8	36	57	96	.292	.373	.418	105	5	16	8	0	.980	1	*O-139	0.2
1988	Chi-N	75	256	27	65	10	1	4	34	21	46	.254	.315	.348	86	-4	7	3	0	.970	-1	O-72	-0.7
	Mon-N	63	191	24	49	3	5	2	12	17	48	.257	.317	.356	89	-3	16	6	1	.992	-5	O-60	-0.8
	Yr	138	447	51	114	13	6	6	46	38	94	.255	.316	.351	87	-7	23	9	1	.979	-5	*O-132	-1.5
1989	Mon-N	126	361	41	99	16	7	3	27	27	57	.274	.325	.382	100	0	23	4	5	.967	-18	*O-118	-0.3
1990	Mon-N	118	391	60	109	13	5	11	39	24	48	.279	.322	.422	107	2	13	11	-3	.989	-3	*O-108/P-1	-0.5
1991	Mon-N	124	396	47	117	18	5	7	42	20	54	.295	.334	.419	112	5	16	7	1	.982	-1	*O-112	0.4
1992	Cin-N	135	393	47	100	20	5	3	31	42	54	.254	.326	.354	90	-5	12	8	-1	.991	-4	*O-111,1-21	-1.4
1993	SF-N	91	241	28	58	12	1	5	27	27	39	.241	.317	.361	84	-6	6	3	0	.993	-5	O-73	-1.2
1994	SF-N	97	235	23	58	9	3	4	27	21	22	.247	.314	.362	78	-8	3	4	-2	1.000	-5	O-58,1-25	-1.6
Total	9	1024	3031	380	804	120	41	48	282	262	486	.265	.326	.379	93	-26	116	56	1	.984	-43	O-897/1-46,P	-9.3

■ DOMINGO MARTINEZ   Martinez, Domingo Emilio (La Fontaine)   b: 8/4/67, Santo Domingo, D.R.   BR/TR, 6'2", 215 lbs.   Deb: 9/11/92

1992	Tor-A	7	8	2	5	0	0	1	3	0	1	.625	.625	1.000	333	2	0	0	0	1.000	-1	/1-7	0.2
1993	Tor-A	8	14	2	4	0	0	1	3	1	7	.286	.333	.500	120	1	0	0	0	1.000	1	/1-7,3-1	0.1
Total	2	15	22	4	9	0	0	2	6	1	8	.409	.435	.682	196	3	0	0	0	1.000	0	/1-14,3-1	0.3

■ EDGAR MARTINEZ   Martinez, Edgar   b: 1/2/63, New York, N.Y.   BR/TR, 6', 175 lbs.   Deb: 9/12/87

1987	Sea-A	13	43	6	16	5	2	0	5	2	5	.372	.413	.581	152	3	0	0	0	1.000	1	3-12/D-1	0.4
1988	Sea-A	14	32	0	9	4	0	0	5	4	7	.281	.361	.406	110	0	0	0	0	.929	-4	3-13	-0.4
1989	Sea-A	65	171	20	41	5	0	2	20	17	26	.240	.319	.304	75	-5	2	1	-0	.916	6	3-61	-1.2
1990	Sea-A	144	487	71	147	27	2	11	49	74	62	.302	.399	.433	131	23	1	4	-2	.928	-1	*3-143/D-2	2.1
1991	Sea-A	150	544	98	167	35	1	14	52	84	72	.307	.407	.452	137	31	0	3	-2	.962	3	*3-144/D-2	3.2
1992	Sea-A★	135	528	100	181	46	3	18	73	54	61	.343	.408	.544	164	44	14	4	2	.943	1	*3-103,D-28/1	4.6

YEAR	TM/L	G	AB	R	H	2B	3B	HR	RBI	BB	SO	AVG	OBP	SLG	PRO+	BR/A	SB	CS	SBR	FA	FR	G/POS	TPR
1993	Sea-A	42	135	20	32	7	0	4	13	28	19	.237	.368	.378	100	1	0	0	0	.889	-4	D-24,3-16	-0.4
1994	Sea-A	89	326	47	93	23	1	13	51	53	42	.285	.390	.482	121	11	6	2	1	.950	6	3-64,D-23	1.5
Total	8	652	2266	362	686	152	9	62	268	316	294	.303	.394	.460	132	109	23	14	-2	.946	-5	3-556/D-80,1	9.8

■ TONY MARTINEZ　　Martinez, Gabriel Antonio (Diaz)　b: 3/18/40, Perico, Cuba　d: 8/24/91, Miami, Fla.　BR/TR, 5'10", 165 lbs.　Deb: 4/9/63

YEAR	TM/L	G	AB	R	H	2B	3B	HR	RBI	BB	SO	AVG	OBP	SLG	PRO+	BR/A	SB	CS	SBR	FA	FR	G/POS	TPR
1963	Cle-A	43	141	10	22	4	0	0	8	5	18	.156	.185	.184	4	-18	1	1	-0	.961	-6	S-41	-2.4
1964	Cle-A	9	14	1	3	1	0	0	2	0	2	.214	.214	.286	38	-1	0	1	-1	1.000	4	/2-4,S-1	0.2
1965	Cle-A	4	3	0	0	0	0	0	0	0	0	.000	.000	.000	-99	-1	0	0	0	.000	0	H	-0.1
1966	Cle-A	17	17	2	5	0	0	0	0	1	6	.294	.333	.294	82	-0	1	1	-0	.833	1	/S-5,2-4	0.1
Total	4	73	175	13	30	5	0	0	10	6	26	.171	.199	.200	13	-20	2	3	-1	.958	-1	/S-47,2-8	-2.2

■ BUCK MARTINEZ　　Martinez, John Albert　b: 11/7/48, Redding, Cal.　BR/TR, 5'10", 190 lbs.　Deb: 6/18/69

YEAR	TM/L	G	AB	R	H	2B	3B	HR	RBI	BB	SO	AVG	OBP	SLG	PRO+	BR/A	SB	CS	SBR	FA	FR	G/POS	TPR
1969	KC-A	72	205	14	47	6	1	4	23	8	25	.229	.258	.327	62	-11	0	0	0	.972	-1	C-55/O-1	-1.0
1970	KC-A	6	9	1	1	0	0	0	0	2	1	.111	.273	.111	10	-1	0	0	0	.958	2	/C-5	0.1
1971	KC-A	22	46	3	7	2	0	0	1	5	9	.152	.235	.196	23	-5	0	1	-1	.968	2	C-21	-0.3
1973	KC-A	14	32	2	8	1	0	1	6	4	5	.250	.333	.375	92	-0	0	0	0	.966	-1	C-14	-0.1
1974	KC-A	43	107	10	23	3	1	1	8	14	19	.215	.317	.290	71	-4	0	1	-1	.977	1	C-38	-0.2
1975	KC-A	80	226	15	51	9	2	3	23	21	28	.226	.294	.323	72	-8	1	0	0	.980	-0	C-79	-0.5
1976	*KC-A	95	267	24	61	13	3	5	34	16	45	.228	.272	.356	82	-7	0	0	0	.991	5	C-94	0.1
1977	KC-A	29	80	3	18	4	0	1	9	3	12	.225	.253	.313	53	-5	0	1	-1	.993	3	C-28	-0.3
1978	Mil-A	89	256	26	56	10	1	4	20	14	42	.219	.259	.277	51	-17	1	1	-0	.978	-3	C-89	-1.9
1979	Mil-A	69	196	17	53	8	0	4	26	8	25	.270	.299	.372	80	-6	0	1	-1	.967	-2	C-68/P-1	-0.6
1980	Mil-A	76	219	16	49	9	0	3	17	12	33	.224	.267	.306	58	-13	1	0	0	.985	11	C-76	0.1
1981	Tor-A	45	128	13	29	8	1	4	21	11	16	.227	.293	.398	92	-2	1	0	0	.991	2	C-45	0.2
1982	Tor-A	96	260	26	63	17	0	10	37	24	34	.242	.306	.423	90	-4	1	1	-0	.988	6	C-93	0.4
1983	Tor-A	88	221	27	56	14	0	10	33	29	39	.253	.340	.452	109	3	0	1	-1	.989	-3	C-85	0.2
1984	Tor-A	102	232	24	51	13	1	5	37	29	49	.220	.311	.349	80	-6	0	3	-2	.995	-4	C-98/D-1	-0.9
1985	Tor-A	42	99	11	16	3	0	4	14	10	12	.162	.245	.313	50	-7	0	0	0	.988	4	C-42	-0.2
1986	Tor-A	81	160	13	29	8	0	2	12	20	25	.181	.272	.269	47	-12	0	0	0	.994	-1	C-78/D-1	-1.0
Total	17	1049	2743	245	618	128	10	58	321	230	419	.225	.287	.343	73	-105	5	10	-5	.984	19	*C-1008/D-2,PO	-5.9

■ JOSE MARTINEZ　　Martinez, Jose (Azcuiz)　b: 7/26/41, Cardenas, Cuba　BR/TR, 5'10", 190 lbs.　Deb: 6/18/69　C

YEAR	TM/L	G	AB	R	H	2B	3B	HR	RBI	BB	SO	AVG	OBP	SLG	PRO+	BR/A	SB	CS	SBR	FA	FR	G/POS	TPR
1969	Pit-N	77	168	20	45	6	0	1	16	9	32	.268	.309	.321	78	-5	1	3	-2	.975	10	2-42,S-20/3O	0.7
1970	Pit-N	19	20	1	1	0	0	0	0	1	5	.050	.095	.050	-61	-5	0	0	0	1.000	3	/3-7,2-4,S	-0.1
Total	2	96	188	21	46	6	0	1	16	10	37	.245	.286	.293	63	-9	1	3	-2	.966	13	/2-46,S-21,3O	0.6

■ MARTY MARTINEZ　　Martinez, Orlando (Oliva)　b: 8/23/41, Havana, Cuba　BB/TR, 6'1", 175 lbs.　Deb: 5/2/62　MC

YEAR	TM/L	G	AB	R	H	2B	3B	HR	RBI	BB	SO	AVG	OBP	SLG	PRO+	BR/A	SB	CS	SBR	FA	FR	G/POS	TPR
1962	Min-A	37	18	13	3	0	1	0	3	3	4	.167	.286	.278	51	-1	0	0	0	.920	8	S-11/3-1	0.7
1967	Atl-N	44	73	14	21	2	1	0	5	11	11	.288	.388	.342	112	2	0	1	-1	.920	4	S-25/2-9,C31	0.8
1968	Atl-N	113	356	34	82	5	3	0	12	29	28	.230	.292	.261	67	-14	6	6	-2	.955	-5	S-54,3-37,2C	-1.6
1969	Hou-N	78	198	14	61	5	4	0	15	10	21	.308	.341	.374	102	0	0	0	0	1.000	-9	O-21,S-17,3/CP2	-0.8
1970	Hou-N	75	150	12	33	3	0	0	12	9	22	.220	.264	.240	38	-13	1	0	0	.990	-6	S-29,3-10/C2	-1.6
1971	Hou-N	32	62	4	16	3	1	0	4	3	6	.258	.292	.339	80	-2	1	0	0	.968	1	/2-9,S-7,13	0.0
1972	StL-N	9	7	0	3	0	0	0	2	0	1	.429	.429	.429	146	0	0	0	0	1.000	0	/S-3,2-2,3	0.1
	Oak-A	22	40	3	5	0	0	0	1	3	6	.125	.186	.125	-7	-5	0	0	0	.944	-5	2-17/S-6,3	-0.1
	Tex-A	26	41	3	6	1	1	0	3	2	8	.146	.186	.220	21	-4	0	1	-1	.944	-2	/S-5,3-4,2	-0.7
	Yr	48	81	6	11	1	1	0	4	5	14	.136	.186	.173	8	-9	0	1	-1	.946	2	2-18,S-11/3	-0.8
Total	7	436	945	97	230	19	11	0	57	70	107	.243	.298	.287	70	-37	7	8	-3	.950	-5	S-157/3-74,2CO1P	-3.2

■ CHITO MARTINEZ　　Martinez, Reyenaldo Ignacio　b: 12/19/65, Belize City, British Honduras (Belize)　BL/TL, 5'10", 180 lbs.　Deb: 7/5/91

YEAR	TM/L	G	AB	R	H	2B	3B	HR	RBI	BB	SO	AVG	OBP	SLG	PRO+	BR/A	SB	CS	SBR	FA	FR	G/POS	TPR
1991	Bal-A	67	216	32	58	12	1	13	33	11	51	.269	.304	.514	127	6	1	1	-0	.982	2	O-54/1-1,D	0.7
1992	Bal-A	83	198	26	53	10	1	5	25	31	47	.268	.372	.404	114	5	0	1	-1	.973	1	O-52/D-4	0.5
1993	Bal-A	8	15	0	0	0	0	0	0	4	4	.000	.211	.000	-37	-3	0	0	0	1.000	-2	/O-5,D-2	-0.5
Total	3	158	429	58	111	22	2	18	58	46	102	.259	.333	.445	115	8	1	2	-1	.978	2	O-111/D-10,1	0.7

■ HECTOR MARTINEZ　　Martinez, Rodolfo Hector (Santos)　b: 5/11/39, Las Villas, Cuba　BR/TR, 5'10", 160 lbs.　Deb: 9/30/62

YEAR	TM/L	G	AB	R	H	2B	3B	HR	RBI	BB	SO	AVG	OBP	SLG	PRO+	BR/A	SB	CS	SBR	FA	FR	G/POS	TPR
1962	KC-A	1	1	0	0	0	0	0	0	0	1	.000	.000	.000	-96	-0	0	0	0	.000	0	H	0.0
1963	KC-A	6	14	2	4	0	0	1	3	1	3	.286	.375	.500	135	1	0	1	-1	1.000	0	/O-3	0.0
Total	2	7	15	2	4	0	0	1	3	1	4	.267	.353	.467	120	0	0	1	-1	1.000	0	/O-3	0.0

■ TED MARTINEZ　　Martinez, Teodoro Noel (Encarnacion)　b: 12/10/47, Central Barahona, D.R.　BR/TR, 6', 165 lbs.　Deb: 7/18/70

YEAR	TM/L	G	AB	R	H	2B	3B	HR	RBI	BB	SO	AVG	OBP	SLG	PRO+	BR/A	SB	CS	SBR	FA	FR	G/POS	TPR
1970	NY-N	4	16	0	1	0	0	0	0	0	3	.063	.063	.063	-66	-4	0	0	0	1.000	1	/2-4,S-1	-0.3
1971	NY-N	38	125	16	36	5	2	1	10	4	22	.288	.326	.384	102	0	6	0	2	.976	-7	S-23,2-13/3O	-0.2
1972	NY-N	103	330	22	74	5	5	1	19	12	49	.224	.254	.279	52	-21	7	4	-0	.994	1	2-47,S-42,O/3	-1.5
1973	*NY-N	92	263	34	67	11	0	1	14	13	38	.255	.295	.308	68	-11	3	5	-2	.941	-4	S-44,O-21,3/2	-1.4
1974	NY-N	116	334	32	73	15	7	2	43	14	40	.219	.250	.323	61	-19	3	2	-0	.952	14	S-75,3-12,2O	0.2
1975	StL-N	16	21	1	4	2	0	0	2	0	2	.190	.190	.286	30	-2	1	0	-1	1.000	-1	/O-7,2-2,S3	-0.4
	*Oak-A	86	87	7	15	0	0	0	3	2	9	.172	.200	.172	6	-11	1	1	-0	.955	4	S-45,2-31,3	-0.5
1977	LA-N	67	137	21	41	6	1	1	10	2	20	.299	.309	.380	84	-3	3	4	-2	.992	14	2-27,S-13,3	1.1
1978	LA-N	54	55	13	14	1	0	1	5	4	14	.255	.317	.327	80	-1	3	2	-0	.912	10	S-17,3-16,2	1.0
1979	LA-N	81	112	19	30	5	1	0	2	4	16	.268	.293	.330	71	-5	3	2	-0	.769	-0	3-23,S-21,2	-0.4
Total	9	657	1480	165	355	50	16	7	108	55	213	.240	.271	.309	62	-77	29	20	-3	.956	31	S-282,2-168/3O	-2.4

■ JOE MARTY　　Marty, Joseph Anton　b: 9/1/13, Sacramento, Cal.　d: 10/4/84, Sacramento, Cal.　BR/TR, 6', 182 lbs.　Deb: 4/22/37

YEAR	TM/L	G	AB	R	H	2B	3B	HR	RBI	BB	SO	AVG	OBP	SLG	PRO+	BR/A	SB	CS	SBR	FA	FR	G/POS	TPR
1937	Chi-N	88	290	41	84	17	2	5	44	28	30	.290	.356	.414	104	2	3			.976	-2	O-84	-0.3
1938	*Chi-N	76	235	32	57	8	3	7	35	18	26	.243	.305	.391	88	-4	0			.987	-4	O-68	-1.0
1939	Chi-N	23	76	6	10	1	0	2	10	4	13	.132	.175	.224	6	-10	2			.933	2	O-21	-1.3
	Phi-N	91	299	32	76	12	6	9	44	24	27	.254	.310	.425	98	-2	1			.974	3	O-79/P-1	-0.2
	Yr	114	375	38	86	13	6	11	54	28	40	.229	.283	.384	79	-13	3			.968	1	*O-100/P-1	-1.5
1940	Phi-N	123	455	52	123	21	8	13	50	17	50	.270	.298	.437	105	0	2			.974	2	*O-118	-0.3
1941	Phi-N	137	477	60	128	19	3	8	39	51	41	.268	.344	.371	105	4	6			.964	-6	*O-132	-1.1
Total	5	538	1832	223	478	78	22	44	222	142	187	.261	.318	.400	97	-11	14			.972	-9	O-502/P-1	-4.2

■ BOB MARTYN　　Martyn, Robert Gordon　b: 8/15/30, Weiser, Idaho　BL/TR, 6', 176 lbs.　Deb: 6/18/57

YEAR	TM/L	G	AB	R	H	2B	3B	HR	RBI	BB	SO	AVG	OBP	SLG	PRO+	BR/A	SB	CS	SBR	FA	FR	G/POS	TPR
1957	KC-A	58	131	10	35	2	1	2	12	11	20	.267	.324	.366	87	-2	1	3	-2	.976	-3	O-49	-1.0
1958	KC-A	95	226	25	59	10	7	2	23	26	36	.261	.337	.394	99	-0	1	4	-2	.967	-5	O-63	-1.0
1959	KC-A	1	1	0	0	0	0	0	0	0	0	.000	.000	.000	-98	-0	0	0	0	.000	0	R	0.0
Total	3	154	358	35	94	12	11	3	35	37	56	.263	.332	.383	94	-2	2	7	-4	.970	-8	O-112	-2.0

■ GARY MARTZ　　Martz, Gary Arthur　b: 1/10/51, Spokane, Wash.　BR/TR, 6'4", 210 lbs.　Deb: 7/8/75

YEAR	TM/L	G	AB	R	H	2B	3B	HR	RBI	BB	SO	AVG	OBP	SLG	PRO+	BR/A	SB	CS	SBR	FA	FR	G/POS	TPR
1975	KC-A	1	1	0	0	0	0	0	0	0	0	.000	.000	.000	-97	-0	0	0	0	1.000	-0	/O-1	-0.1

■ JOHN MARZANO　　Marzano, John Robert　b: 2/14/63, Philadelphia, Pa.　BR/TR, 5'11", 197 lbs.　Deb: 7/31/87

YEAR	TM/L	G	AB	R	H	2B	3B	HR	RBI	BB	SO	AVG	OBP	SLG	PRO+	BR/A	SB	CS	SBR	FA	FR	G/POS	TPR
1987	Bos-A	52	168	20	41	11	0	5	24	7	41	.244	.287	.399	77	-6	0	1	-1	.986	1	C-52	-0.2
1988	Bos-A	10	29	3	4	1	0	0	1	1	3	.138	.167	.172	-5	-4	0	0	0	1.000	5	C-10	0.2

YEAR	TM/L	G	AB	R	H	2B	3B	HR	RBI	BB	SO	AVG	OBP	SLG	PRO+	BR/A	SB	CS	SBR	FA	FR	G/POS	TPR
1989	Bos-A	7	18	5	8	3	0	1	3	0	2	.444	.444	.778	224	3	0	0	0	1.000	-0	/C-7	0.3
1990	Bos-A	32	83	8	20	4	0	0	6	5	10	.241	.284	.289	58	-5	0	1	-1	1.000	4	C-32	0.1
1991	Bos-A	49	114	10	30	8	0	0	9	1	16	.263	.276	.333	64	-6	0	0	0	.985	-2	C-48	-0.6
1992	Bos-A	19	50	4	4	2	1	0	1	2	12	.080	.132	.160	-17	-8	0	0	0	.968	0	C-18/D-1	-0.7
Total	6	169	462	50	107	29	1	6	44	16	84	.232	.265	.338	61	-25	0	2	-1	.988	8	C-167/D-1	-0.9

■ CLYDE MASHORE   Mashore, Clyde Wayne b: 5/29/45, Concord, Cal. BR/TR, 5'11", 184 lbs. Deb: 7/11/69

YEAR	TM/L	G	AB	R	H	2B	3B	HR	RBI	BB	SO	AVG	OBP	SLG	PRO+	BR/A	SB	CS	SBR	FA	FR	G/POS	TPR
1969	Cin-N	2	1	1	0	0	0	0	0	0	0	.000	.000	.000	-95	-0	0	0	0	.000	0	H	0.0
1970	Mon-N	13	25	2	4	0	0	1	3	4	11	.160	.276	.280	49	-2	0	0	0	1.000	-2	O-10	-0.4
1971	Mon-N	66	114	20	22	5	0	1	7	10	22	.193	.258	.263	48	-8	1	0	0	.967	-11	O-47/3-1	-2.2
1972	Mon-N	93	176	23	40	7	1	3	23	14	41	.227	.284	.330	73	-6	6	1	1	.988	-13	O-74	-2.2
1973	Mon-N	67	103	12	21	3	0	3	14	15	28	.204	.305	.320	71	-4	4	3	-1	.958	-3	O-44/2-1	-0.9
Total	5	241	419	58	87	15	1	8	47	43	102	.208	.281	.305	64	-20	11	4	1	.974	-28	O-175/2-1,3	-5.7

■ PHIL MASI   Masi, Philip Samuel b: 1/6/16, Chicago, Ill. d: 3/29/90, Mt.Prospect, Ill. BR/TR, 5'10", 180 lbs. Deb: 4/23/39

YEAR	TM/L	G	AB	R	H	2B	3B	HR	RBI	BB	SO	AVG	OBP	SLG	PRO+	BR/A	SB	CS	SBR	FA	FR	G/POS	TPR
1939	Bos-N	46	114	14	29	7	2	1	14	9	15	.254	.315	.377	92	-2	0			.960	-3	C-42	-0.3
1940	Bos-N	63	138	11	27	4	1	1	14	14	14	.196	.270	.261	50	-10	0			.966	-1	C-52	-0.7
1941	Bos-N	87	180	17	40	8	2	3	18	16	13	.222	.286	.339	79	-6	4			.978	-7	C-83	-0.8
1942	Bos-N	57	87	14	19	3	1	0	9	12	4	.218	.313	.276	74	-3	2			.961	2	C-39/O-4	0.1
1943	Bos-N	80	238	27	65	9	1	2	28	27	20	.273	.347	.345	102	1	7			.991	-6	C-73	0.0
1944	Bos-N	89	251	33	69	13	5	3	23	31	20	.275	.355	.402	108	3	4			.977	-6	C-63,1-12/3	0.6
1945	Bos-N†	114	371	55	101	25	4	7	46	42	32	.272	.348	.418	112	5	9			.980	1	C-95/1-7	1.1
1946	Bos-N★	133	397	52	106	17	5	3	62	55	41	.267	.358	.358	102	2	5			.981	-5	*C-124	0.4
1947	Bos-N★	126	411	54	125	22	4	9	50	47	27	.304	.377	.443	120	12	7			.989	-6	*C-123	1.4
1948	*Bos-N★	113	376	43	95	19	0	5	44	35	26	.253	.318	.343	80	-10	2			.988	1	*C-109	-0.2
1949	Bos-N	37	105	13	22	2	0	0	6	14	10	.210	.303	.229	47	-8	1			.993	-2	C-37	-0.7
	Pit-N	48	135	16	37	6	1	2	13	17	16	.274	.355	.378	94	-1	1			.994	-2	C-44/1-2	0.0
	Yr	85	240	29	59	8	1	2	19	31	26	.246	.332	.313	74	-8	2			.994	-3	C-81/1-2	-0.7
1950	Chi-A	122	377	38	105	17	2	7	55	49	36	.279	.366	.390	96	-2	2	1	0	.996	-1	*C-114	0.2
1951	Chi-A	84	225	24	61	11	2	4	28	32	27	.271	.367	.391	107	3	1	0	0	.979	-0	C-78	0.6
1952	Chi-A	30	63	9	16	1	1	0	7	10	10	.254	.356	.302	84	-1	0	0	0	.956	0	C-25	-0.7
Total	14	1229	3468	420	917	164	31	47	417	410	311	.264	.344	.370	97	-14	45	1		.983	-27	*C-1101/1-21,O3	1.7

■ HARRY MASKREY   Maskrey, Harry H. b: 12/21/1861, Mercer, Pa. d: 8/17/30, Mercer, Pa. Deb: 9/21/1882 F

YEAR	TM/L	G	AB	R	H	2B	3B	HR	RBI	BB	SO	AVG	OBP	SLG	PRO+	BR/A	SB	CS	SBR	FA	FR	G/POS	TPR
1882	Lou-a	1	4	0	0	0	0	0		0		.000	.000	.000	-99	-1				.000	-1	/O-1	-0.1

■ LEECH MASKREY   Maskrey, Samuel Leech b: 2/11/1854, Mercer, Pa. d: 4/1/22, Mercer, Pa. BR/TR, 5'8", 150 lbs. Deb: 5/2/1882 F

YEAR	TM/L	G	AB	R	H	2B	3B	HR	RBI	BB	SO	AVG	OBP	SLG	PRO+	BR/A	SB	CS	SBR	FA	FR	G/POS	TPR
1882	Lou-a	76	288	30	65	14	2	0		9		.226	.249	.288	85	-4				.902	-1	*O-76/2-1	-0.4
1883	Lou-a	96	361	50	73	13	8	1		10		.202	.224	.291	69	-11				.914	9	*O-96/S-1	-0.2
1884	Lou-a	105	412	48	103	13	4	0		17		.250	.281	.301	94	-2				.896	2	*O-103/3-3,S	-0.2
1885	Lou-a	109	423	54	97	8	11	1		19		.229	.269	.307	82	-9				.899	-3	*O-108/3-3	-1.3
1886	Lou-a	5	19	1	3	1	0	0		1		.158	.200	.211	27	-2	0			.800	-1	/O-5	-0.3
	Cin-a	27	98	7	19	3	1	0		5		.194	.240	.245	51	-6	4			.926	1	O-26/3-2	-0.5
	Yr	32	117	8	22	4	1	0		6		.188	.234	.239	47	-7	4			.915	-0	O-31/3-2	-0.8
Total	5	418	1601	190	360	52	26	2		61		.225	.256	.294	80	-33	4			.904	7	O-414/3-8,S2	-2.9

■ CHARLIE MASON   Mason, Charles E. b: 6/25/1853, New Orleans, La. d: 10/21/36, Philadelphia, Pa. BR/TR, 175 lbs. Deb: 4/26/1875 M

YEAR	TM/L	G	AB	R	H	2B	3B	HR	RBI	BB	SO	AVG	OBP	SLG	PRO+	BR/A	SB	CS	SBR	FA	FR	G/POS	TPR
1875	Cen-n	12	47	5	11	1	0	0		0		.234	.234	.255	75	-1						/O-10,1-2	-0.1
	Was-n	8	34	2	3	0	0	0		0		.088	.088	.088	-40	-5						/O-7,P-1	-0.4
	Yr	20	81	7	14	1	0	0		0		.173	.173	.185	25	-6						O-17/1-2,P	-0.5
1883	Phi-a	1	2	0	1	0	0	0		0		.500	.500	.500	207	0				.000	-0	/O-1	0.0

■ DON MASON   Mason, Donald Stetson b: 12/20/44, Boston, Mass. BL/TR, 5'11", 160 lbs. Deb: 4/14/66

YEAR	TM/L	G	AB	R	H	2B	3B	HR	RBI	BB	SO	AVG	OBP	SLG	PRO+	BR/A	SB	CS	SBR	FA	FR	G/POS	TPR
1966	SF-N	42	25	8	3	0	0	1	1	0	2	.120	.120	.240	-3	-3	0	1	-1	.905	5	/2-9	0.1
1967	SF-N	4	3	0	0	0	0	0	0	0	0	.000	.000	.000	-99	-1	0	0	0	1.000	1	/2-2	0.0
1968	SF-N	10	19	3	3	0	0	0	1	1	4	.158	.200	.158	9	-2	1	1	-0	1.000	-1	/2-5,S-4,3	-0.4
1969	SF-N	104	250	43	57	4	2	0	13	36	29	.228	.325	.260	67	-10	1	5	-3	.956	10	2-51,3-21/S	0.1
1970	SF-N	46	36	4	5	0	0	0	1	5	7	.139	.244	.139	5	-5	0	0	0	.950	2	2-14	-0.3
1971	SD-N	113	344	43	73	12	1	2	11	27	35	.212	.270	.270	57	-20	6	4	-1	.965	-12	2-90/3-3	-2.7
1972	SD-N	9	11	1	2	0	0	0	0	1	1	.182	.250	.182	26	-1	0	0	0	.692	-0	/2-3	-0.1
1973	SD-N	8	8	0	0	0	0	0	0	0	2	.000	.000	.000	-99	-2	0	0	0	.750	1	/2-1	-0.2
Total	8	336	696	102	143	16	3	3	27	70	80	.205	.278	.250	52	-44	8	11	-4	.955	5	2-175/3-26,S	-3.5

■ JIM MASON   Mason, James Percy b: 8/14/50, Mobile, Ala. BL/TR, 6'2", 190 lbs. Deb: 9/26/71

YEAR	TM/L	G	AB	R	H	2B	3B	HR	RBI	BB	SO	AVG	OBP	SLG	PRO+	BR/A	SB	CS	SBR	FA	FR	G/POS	TPR
1971	Was-A	3	9	0	3	0	0	0	0	1	3	.333	.400	.333	116	0	0	0	0	.955	2	/S-3	0.3
1972	Tex-A	46	147	10	29	3	0	0	10	9	39	.197	.248	.218	41	-11	0	0	0	.948	-6	S-32,3-10	-1.4
1973	Tex-A	92	238	23	49	7	2	3	19	23	48	.206	.276	.290	62	-12	0	1	-1	.947	4	S-74,2-19/3	0.4
1974	NY-A	152	440	41	110	18	6	5	37	35	87	.250	.305	.352	91	-6	1	2	-1	.964	-4	*S-152	0.8
1975	NY-A	94	223	17	34	3	2	2	16	22	49	.152	.229	.211	26	-22	0	2	-1	.955	-10	S-93/2-1	-2.6
1976	*NY-A	93	217	17	39	7	1	1	14	9	37	.180	.212	.235	31	-19	0	0	0	.966	7	S-93	-0.9
1977	Tor-A	22	79	10	13	3	0	2	7	10	.165	.233	.203	20	-9	1	1	-0	.971	-5	S-22	-1.2
	Tex-A	36	55	9	12	3	0	1	7	6	10	.218	.295	.327	69	-2	0	0	0	.976	7	S-32/3-1,D	0.6
	Yr	58	134	19	25	6	0	1	9	13	20	.187	.259	.254	40	-11	1	1	-0	.973	3	S-54/3-1,D	-0.6
1978	Tex-A	55	105	10	20	4	0	0	3	5	17	.190	.227	.229	28	-10	0	1	-0	.938	1	S-42,3-11/2D	-0.7
1979	Mon-N	40	71	3	13	5	1	0	6	7	16	.183	.256	.282	47	-5	0	2	-1	.966	0	S-33/3-6	-0.4
Total	9	633	1584	140	322	53	12	12	114	124	316	.203	.262	.275	54	-95	2	8	-4	.959	2	S-576/3-29,2D	-4.6

■ GORDON MASSA   Massa, Gordon Richard "Moose" or "Duke" b: 9/2/35, Cincinnati, Ohio BL/TR, 6'3", 210 lbs. Deb: 9/24/57

YEAR	TM/L	G	AB	R	H	2B	3B	HR	RBI	BB	SO	AVG	OBP	SLG	PRO+	BR/A	SB	CS	SBR	FA	FR	G/POS	TPR
1957	Chi-N	6	15	2	7	1	0	0	3	4	3	.467	.579	.533	205	3	0	0	0	1.000	-3	/C-6	0.0
1958	Chi-N	2	2	0	0	0	0	0	0	0	2	.000	.000	.000	-99	-1	0	0	0	.000	0	H	-0.1
Total	2	8	17	2	7	1	0	0	3	4	5	.412	.524	.471	172	2	0	0	0	1.000	-3	/C-6	-0.1

■ ROY MASSEY   Massey, Roy Hardee "Red" b: 10/9/1890, Sevierville, Tenn. d: 6/23/54, Atlanta, Ga. BL/TR, 5'11", 170 lbs. Deb: 4/16/18

YEAR	TM/L	G	AB	R	H	2B	3B	HR	RBI	BB	SO	AVG	OBP	SLG	PRO+	BR/A	SB	CS	SBR	FA	FR	G/POS	TPR
1918	Bos-N	66	203	20	59	7	0	0	18	23	20	.291	.363	.340	120	5	1			.954	-3	O-45/3-2,1S	0.0

■ BILL MASSEY   Massey, William Harry "Big Bill" b: 1/1871, Philadelphia, Pa. d: 10/9/40, Manila, Philippines BR , 5'11", 168 lbs. Deb: 9/18/1894

YEAR	TM/L	G	AB	R	H	2B	3B	HR	RBI	BB	SO	AVG	OBP	SLG	PRO+	BR/A	SB	CS	SBR	FA	FR	G/POS	TPR
1894	Cin-N	13	53	7	15	5	0	3	5	3	2	.283	.321	.340	57	-4	0			.991	-1	1-10/2-2,3	-0.4

■ MIKE MASSEY   Massey, William Herbert b: 9/28/1893, Galveston, Tex. d: 10/17/71, Shreveport, La. BB/TR, 6', 195 lbs. Deb: 4/12/17

YEAR	TM/L	G	AB	R	H	2B	3B	HR	RBI	BB	SO	AVG	OBP	SLG	PRO+	BR/A	SB	CS	SBR	FA	FR	G/POS	TPR
1917	Bos-N	31	91	12	18	0	0	0	2	15	15	.198	.318	.198	63	-3	2			.900	-8	2-25	-1.1

■ VICTOR MATA   Mata, Victor Jose (Abreu) b: 6/17/61, Santiago, D.R. BR/TR, 6'1", 165 lbs. Deb: 7/22/84

YEAR	TM/L	G	AB	R	H	2B	3B	HR	RBI	BB	SO	AVG	OBP	SLG	PRO+	BR/A	SB	CS	SBR	FA	FR	G/POS	TPR
1984	NY-A	30	70	8	23	5	0	1	6	0	12	.329	.338	.443	119	1	1	1	-0	.942	-6	O-28	-0.5
1985	NY-A	6	7	1	1	0	0	0	0	0	0	.143	.143	.143	-22	0	0	0	0	1.000	-2	/O-3	-0.3
Total	2	36	77	9	24	5	0	1	6	0	12	.312	.321	.416	106	0	1	1	-0	.943	-7	/O-31	-0.8

YEAR	TM/L	G	AB	R	H	2B	3B	HR	RBI	BB	SO	AVG	OBP	SLG	PRO+	BR/A	SB	CS	SBR	FA	FR	G/POS	TPR

■ TOM MATCHICK   Matchick, John Thomas b: 9/7/43, Hazleton, Pa.   BL/TR, 6', 175 lbs.   Deb: 9/2/67

YEAR	TM/L	G	AB	R	H	2B	3B	HR	RBI	BB	SO	AVG	OBP	SLG	PRO+	BR/A	SB	CS	SBR	FA	FR	G/POS	TPR
1967	Det-A	8	6	1	1	0	0	0	0	0	2	.167	.167	.167	-1	-1	0	0	0	1.000	0	/S-1	-0.1
1968	*Det-A	80	227	18	46	6	2	3	14	10	46	.203	.249	.286	60	-11	0	2	-1	.950	-14	S-59,2-13/1	-2.4
1969	Det-A	94	298	25	72	11	2	0	32	15	51	.242	.278	.292	57	-17	3	0	1	.972	-7	2-47,3-27/S1	-2.0
1970	Bos-A	10	14	2	1	0	0	0	0	2	2	.071	.188	.071	-24	-2	0	1	-1	1.000	-1	/3-2,2-1,S	-0.4
	KC-A	55	158	11	31	3	2	0	11	5	23	.196	.226	.241	29	-15	0	0	1	.985	13	S-43,2-10/3	0.2
	Yr	65	172	13	32	3	2	0	11	7	25	.186	.222	.227	24	-18	0	1	-1	.985	12	S-44,2-11/3	-0.2
1971	Mil-A	42	114	6	25	1	0	1	7	7	23	.219	.264	.254	48	-8	3	2	-0	.979	1	3-41/2-1	-0.8
1972	Bal-A	3	9	0	2	0	0	0	0	0	1	.222	.222	.222	32	-1	0	1	-0	.857	-1	/3-3	-0.2
Total	6	292	826	63	178	21	6	4	64	39	148	.215	.255	.270	49	-55	6	6	-2	.967	-8	S-110/3-74,21	-5.7

■ MIKE MATHENY   Matheny, Michael Scott b: 9/22/70, Columbus, Ohio   BR/TR, 6'3", 205 lbs.   Deb: 4/7/94

YEAR	TM/L	G	AB	R	H	2B	3B	HR	RBI	BB	SO	AVG	OBP	SLG	PRO+	BR/A	SB	CS	SBR	FA	FR	G/POS	TPR
1994	Mil-A	28	53	3	12	3	0	1	2	3	13	.226	.293	.340	61	-3	0	1	-1	.989	3	C-27	0.0

■ JOE MATHES   Mathes, Joseph John b: 7/28/1891, Milwaukee, Wis.   d: 12/21/78, St.Louis, Mo.   BB/TR, 6'0.5", 180 lbs.   Deb: 9/19/12

YEAR	TM/L	G	AB	R	H	2B	3B	HR	RBI	BB	SO	AVG	OBP	SLG	PRO+	BR/A	SB	CS	SBR	FA	FR	G/POS	TPR
1912	Phi-A	4	14	0	2	0	0	0	0	0	0	.143	.200	.143	-2	-2	0			.889	-1	/3-4	-0.3
1914	StL-F	26	85	10	25	3	0	0	6	9	11	.294	.362	.329	76	-3	1			.938	-4	2-23	-0.7
1916	Bos-N	2	0	0	0	0	0	0	0	0	0	—	—	—	—	0	0			.000	-1	/2-2	-0.1
Total	3	32	99	10	27	3	0	0	6	9	11	.273	.339	.303	67	-4	1			.921	-6	/2-25,3-4	-1.1

■ EDDIE MATHEWS   Mathews, Edwin Lee b: 10/13/31, Texarkana, Tex.   BL/TR, 6'1", 200 lbs.   Deb: 4/15/52   MCH

YEAR	TM/L	G	AB	R	H	2B	3B	HR	RBI	BB	SO	AVG	OBP	SLG	PRO+	BR/A	SB	CS	SBR	FA	FR	G/POS	TPR
1952	Bos-N	145	528	80	128	23	5	25	58	59	115	.242	.320	.447	114	8	6	4	-1	.957	-10	*3-142	-0.5
1953	Mil-N★	157	579	110	175	31	8	47	135	99	83	.302	.406	.627	175	64	1	3	-2	.939	3	*3-157	5.8
1954	Mil-N	138	476	96	138	21	4	40	103	113	61	.290	.428	.603	177	57	10	3	1	.966	-2	*3-127,O-10	5.2
1955	Mil-N★	141	499	108	144	23	5	41	101	109	98	.289	.417	.601	175	56	3	4	-2	.952	-4	*3-137	4.9
1956	*Mil-N☆	151	552	103	150	21	2	37	95	91	86	.272	.376	.518	146	36	6	0	2	.944	-12	*3-150	2.8
1957	*Mil-N★	148	572	109	167	28	9	32	94	90	79	.292	.388	.540	157	47	3	1	0	.964	-2	*3-147	4.8
1958	*Mil-N☆	149	546	97	137	18	1	31	77	85	85	.251	.354	.458	123	18	5	0	2	.955	5	*3-149	2.6
1959	Mil-N★	148	594	118	182	16	8	46	114	80	71	.306	.391	.593	172	59	2	1	0	.961	3	*3-148	6.2
1960	Mil-N★	153	548	108	152	19	7	39	124	111	113	.277	.401	.551	170	55	7	3	0	.950	-13	*3-153	4.2
1961	Mil-N★	152	572	103	175	23	6	32	91	93	95	.306	.405	.535	156	48	12	7	-1	.961	-6	*3-151	4.2
1962	Mil-N★	152	536	106	142	25	6	29	90	101	90	.265	.383	.496	138	30	4	2	0	.964	2	*3-140/1-7	3.3
1963	Mil-N	158	547	82	144	27	4	23	84	124	119	.263	.400	.453	147	39	3	4	-2	.968	15	*3-121,O-42	5.3
1964	Mil-N	141	502	83	117	19	1	23	74	85	100	.233	.345	.412	112	9	2	2	-1	.962	-3	*3-128/1-7	0.9
1965	Mil-N	156	546	77	137	23	0	32	95	73	110	.251	.342	.469	125	18	1	0	0	.956	9	*3-153	2.6
1966	Atl-N	134	452	72	113	21	4	16	53	63	82	.250	.342	.420	109	6	1	1	-0	.946	-2	*3-127	0.1
1967	Hou-N	101	328	39	78	13	2	10	38	48	65	.238	.337	.381	109	4	2	4	-2	.987	-4	1-79,3-24	-0.7
	Det-A	36	108	14	25	3	0	6	19	15	23	.231	.336	.426	121	3	0	0	0	.933	-2	3-21,1-13	0.0
1968	*Det-A	31	52	4	11	0	0	3	8	5	12	.212	.281	.385	97	-0	0	0	0	.974	-1	/1-6,3-6	-0.1
Total	17	2391	8537	1509	2315	354	72	512	1453	1444	1487	.271	.378	.509	145	559	68	39	-3	.956	-20	*3-2181,1-112/O	51.6

■ NELSON MATHEWS   Mathews, Nelson Elmer b: 7/21/41, Columbia, Ill.   BR/TR, 6'4", 195 lbs.   Deb: 9/9/60

YEAR	TM/L	G	AB	R	H	2B	3B	HR	RBI	BB	SO	AVG	OBP	SLG	PRO+	BR/A	SB	CS	SBR	FA	FR	G/POS	TPR
1960	Chi-N	3	8	1	2	0	0	0	0	0	2	.250	.250	.250	38	-1	0	0	0	1.000	0	/O-2	-0.1
1961	Chi-N	3	9	0	1	0	0	0	0	0	2	.111	.111	.111	-40	-2	0	0	0	1.000	0	/O-2	-0.2
1962	Chi-N	15	49	5	15	2	0	2	13	5	4	.306	.393	.469	126	2	3	3	-1	.962	-2	O-14	-0.2
1963	Chi-N	61	155	12	24	3	2	4	10	16	48	.155	.234	.277	44	-11	3	4	-2	.979	-2	O-46	-1.9
1964	KC-A	157	573	58	137	27	5	14	60	43	143	.239	.293	.377	82	-14	2	3	-1	.968	9	*O-154	-1.4
1965	KC-A	67	184	17	39	7	2	2	15	24	49	.212	.303	.359	89	-3	0	2	-1	.981	-2	O-57	-0.9
Total	6	306	978	93	218	39	14	22	98	88	248	.223	.289	.359	78	-29	8	12	-5	.972	4	O-275	-4.7

■ BOBBY MATHEWS   Mathews, Robert T. b: 11/21/1851, Baltimore, Md.   d: 4/17/1898, Baltimore, Md.   BR/TR, 5'5.5", 140 lbs.   Deb: 5/4/1871   U

YEAR	TM/L	G	AB	R	H	2B	3B	HR	RBI	BB	SO	AVG	OBP	SLG	PRO+	BR/A	SB	CS	SBR	FA	FR	G/POS	TPR
1871	Kek-n	19	89	15	24	3	1	0	10	2	0	.270	.286	.326	74	-3	2					P-19	0.0
1872	Bal-n	50	221	35	50	2	1	0	21	3	2	.226	.237	.244	46	-14						*P-49/O-3,3	0.4
1873	Mut-n	52	223	40	43	4	3	0	13	10	3	.193	.227	.238	37	-17						*P-52/O-5	0.6
1874	Mut-n	65	297	47	70	8	1	0		4		.236	.246	.269	62	-13						*P-65	0.0
1875	Mut-n	70	268	23	47	5	2	0		0		.175	.175	.209	31	-19						*P-70	0.0
1876	NY-N	56	218	19	40	4	1	0	9	3	2	.183	.195	.211	40	-12				.810	-6	*P-56/O-1	0.0
1877	Cin-N	15	59	5	10	0	0	0	0	1	2	.169	.183	.169	13	-5				.862	-3	P-15/O-1,S	-0.2
1879	Pro-N	43	173	25	35	2	0	1	10	7	12	.202	.233	.231	55	-8				.956	-5	P-27,O-21/3	-0.9
1881	Pro-N	16	57	6	11	1	0	0	4	5	6	.193	.258	.211	50	-3				.810	-3	P-14/O-5	-0.2
	Bos-N	19	71	2	12	2	0	0	4	0	5	.169	.169	.197	15	-7				.818	-4	O-18/P-5	-0.9
	Yr	35	128	8	23	3	0	0	8	5	11	.180	.211	.203	32	-10				.811	-7	O-23,P-19	-1.1
1882	Bos-N	45	169	17	38	6	0	0	13	8	18	.225	.260	.260	67	-6				.867	-10	P-34,O-13/S	-0.6
1883	Phi-a	45	167	15	31	2	0	0		5		.186	.209	.198	29	-13				.874	-2	P-44/O-3	0.1
1884	Phi-a	49	184	26	34	5	1	0		7		.185	.215	.223	40	-12				.775	-4	P-49/O-1	0.0
1885	Phi-a	48	179	22	30	3	0	0		10		.168	.212	.184	24	-16				.881	-0	P-48/O-1	0.0
1886	Phi-a	24	88	16	21	3	0	0		3		.239	.264	.273	67	-3	1			.843	-0	P-24/O-1	-0.1
1887	Phi-a	7	25	5	5	0	0	0		4		.200	.310	.200	44	-2	0			.889	-7	/P-7	0.0
Total	5 n	256	1098	160	234	22	8	0	44	19	5	.213	.226	.248	47	-66	4					P-255/O-8,3	1.0
Total	10	367	1390	158	267	28	2	1	40	53	45	.192	.222	.217	42	-87	1			.845	-30	P-323/O-65,3S	-2.9

■ JIMMY MATHISON   Mathison, James Michael Ignatius b: 11/11/1878, Baltimore, Md.   d: 7/4/11, Baltimore, Md.   TR,   Deb: 8/29/02

YEAR	TM/L	G	AB	R	H	2B	3B	HR	RBI	BB	SO	AVG	OBP	SLG	PRO+	BR/A	SB	CS	SBR	FA	FR	G/POS	TPR
1902	Bal-A	29	91	12	24	2	1	0	7	9		.264	.368	.308	85	-1	2			.889	-3	3-28/S-1	-0.3

■ JOHN MATIAS   Matias, John Roy b: 8/15/44, Honolulu, Hawaii   BL/TL, 5'11", 170 lbs.   Deb: 4/7/70

YEAR	TM/L	G	AB	R	H	2B	3B	HR	RBI	BB	SO	AVG	OBP	SLG	PRO+	BR/A	SB	CS	SBR	FA	FR	G/POS	TPR
1970	Chi-A	58	117	7	22	2	0	2	6	3	22	.188	.215	.256	28	-11	1	0	0	.941	-4	O-22,1-18	-1.8

■ FRANCISCO MATOS   Matos, Francisco Aguirre (Mancebo) b: 7/23/69, Santo Domingo, D.R.   BR/TR, 6'1", 160 lbs.   Deb: 7/17/94

YEAR	TM/L	G	AB	R	H	2B	3B	HR	RBI	BB	SO	AVG	OBP	SLG	PRO+	BR/A	SB	CS	SBR	FA	FR	G/POS	TPR
1994	Oak-A	14	28	1	7	1	0	0	2	1	2	.250	.276	.286	49	-2	1	0	0	.925	1	2-12	-0.1

■ C. V. MATTERSON   Matterson, C. V. b: Ohio   Deb: 6/13/1884

YEAR	TM/L	G	AB	R	H	2B	3B	HR	RBI	BB	SO	AVG	OBP	SLG	PRO+	BR/A	SB	CS	SBR	FA	FR	G/POS	TPR
1884	StL-U	1	4	0	0	0	0	0	0			.000	.000	.000	-97	-1				.000	-1	/O-1,P-1	-0.1

■ GARY MATTHEWS   Matthews, Gary Nathaniel b: 7/5/50, San Fernando, Cal.   BR/TR, 6'3", 190 lbs.   Deb: 9/6/72

YEAR	TM/L	G	AB	R	H	2B	3B	HR	RBI	BB	SO	AVG	OBP	SLG	PRO+	BR/A	SB	CS	SBR	FA	FR	G/POS	TPR
1972	SF-N	20	62	11	18	1	1	4	14	7	13	.290	.362	.532	149	4	0	1	-1	.971	-1	O-19	0.2
1973	SF-N	148	540	74	162	22	10	12	58	58	83	.300	.369	.444	119	15	17	5	2	.983	6	*O-145	1.7
1974	SF-N	154	561	87	161	27	6	16	82	70	69	.287	.369	.442	120	16	11	9	2	.970	5	*O-151	1.2
1975	SF-N	116	425	79	119	22	3	12	58	65	93	.280	.378	.431	119	12	13	4	2	.967	8	*O-113	1.8
1976	SF-N	156	587	79	164	28	4	20	84	75	94	.279	.362	.443	124	19	12	5	1	.975	-3	*O-156	1.1
1977	Atl-N	148	555	89	157	25	5	17	64	67	90	.283	.362	.438	101	1	22	8	2	.965	2	*O-145	0.6
1978	Atl-N	129	474	75	135	20	5	18	62	61	92	.285	.369	.462	118	11	8	7	-2	.969	2	*O-127	0.6
1979	Atl-N★	156	631	97	192	34	5	27	90	60	75	.304	.365	.502	125	21	18	6	2	.974	1	*O-156	1.7
1980	Atl-N	135	571	79	159	19	7	19	75	42	93	.278	.328	.419	104	2	11	6	-0	.964	-3	*O-143	-0.6
1981	*Phi-N	101	359	62	108	21	3	9	67	59	42	.301	.404	.451	136	19	15	5	3	.963	1	*O-100	2.2
1982	Phi-N	162	616	89	173	31	1	19	83	66	87	.281	.352	.427	114	12	21	4	4	.966	3	*O-162	1.5

YEAR	TM/L	G	AB	R	H	2B	3B	HR	RBI	BB	SO	AVG	OBP	SLG	PRO+	BR/A	SB	CS	SBR	FA	FR	G/POS	TPR
1983	*Phi-N	132	446	66	115	18	2	10	50	69	81	.258	.357	.374	104	4	13	9	-2	.974	-1	*O-122	-0.3
1984	*Chi-N	147	491	101	143	21	2	14	82	**103**	97	.291	**.417**	.428	126	22	17	8	0	.955	-4	*O-145	1.4
1985	Chi-N	97	298	45	70	12	0	13	40	59	64	.235	.365	.406	104	3	2	0	1	.977	-2	O-85	-0.1
1986	Chi-N	123	370	49	96	16	1	21	46	60	59	.259	.363	.478	121	11	3	2	-0	.940	-8	*O-105	-0.1
1987	Chi-N	44	42	3	11	3	0	1	8	4	11	.262	.326	.333	72	-2	0	0	0	1.000	-0	/O-2	-0.2
	Sea-A	45	119	10	28	1	0	3	15	15	22	.235	.321	.319	67	-5	0	1	-1	1.000	0	D-39	-0.7
Total	16	2033	7147	1083	2011	319	51	234	978	940	1125	.281	.367	.439	116	164	183	74	11	.968	12	*O-1876/D-39	12.0

■ BOB MATTHEWS
Matthews, Robert   b: Camden, N.J.   Deb: 9/25/1891

YEAR	TM/L	G	AB	R	H	2B	3B	HR	RBI	BB	SO	AVG	OBP	SLG	PRO+	BR/A	SB	CS	SBR	FA	FR	G/POS	TPR
1891	Phi-a	1	3	1	1	0	0	0	0	0	1	.333	.600	.333	163	1				.000	-0	/O-1	0.0

■ WID MATTHEWS
Matthews, Wid Curry "Matty"   b: 10/20/1896, Raleigh, Ill   d: 10/5/65, Hollywood, Cal.   BL/TL, 5'8.5", 155 lbs.   Deb: 4/18/23

YEAR	TM/L	G	AB	R	H	2B	3B	HR	RBI	BB	SO	AVG	OBP	SLG	PRO+	BR/A	SB	CS	SBR	FA	FR	G/POS	TPR
1923	Phi-A	129	485	52	133	11	6	1	25	50	27	.274	.343	.328	76	-16	16	16	-5	.947	-8	*O-127	-3.6
1924	Was-A	53	169	25	51	10	4	0	13	11	4	.302	.355	.408	100	-0	3	8	-4	.985	5	O-44	-0.2
1925	Was-A	10	9	2	4	0	0	0	1	0	1	.444	.444	.444	129	0	0	0	0	1.000	-0	/O-1	0.0
Total	3	192	663	79	188	21	10	1	39	61	32	.284	.348	.350	83	-16	19	24	-9	.957	-4	O-172	-3.8

■ STEVE MATTHIAS
Matthias, Stephen J.   b: 1860, Mitchellville, Md.   BR/TR, 5'8", 160 lbs.   Deb: 4/20/1884

YEAR	TM/L	G	AB	R	H	2B	3B	HR	RBI	BB	SO	AVG	OBP	SLG	PRO+	BR/A	SB	CS	SBR	FA	FR	G/POS	TPR
1884	CP-U	37	142	24	39	7	1	0		5		.275	.299	.338	73	-5				.840	2	S-36/O-2	-0.2

■ BOBBY MATTICK
Mattick, Robert James   b: 12/5/15, Sioux City, Iowa   BR/TR, 5'11", 178 lbs.   Deb: 5/5/38   FM

YEAR	TM/L	G	AB	R	H	2B	3B	HR	RBI	BB	SO	AVG	OBP	SLG	PRO+	BR/A	SB	CS	SBR	FA	FR	G/POS	TPR
1938	Chi-N	1	1	0	1	0	0	0	1	0	0	1.000	1.000	1.000	439	0	0			.000	0	/S-1	0.0
1939	Chi-N	51	178	16	51	12	1	0	23	6	19	.287	.314	.365	80	-5	1			.927	7	S-48	0.6
1940	Chi-N	128	441	30	96	15	0	0	33	19	33	.218	.250	.252	39	-36	5			.946	10	*S-126/3-1	-1.6
1941	Cin-N	20	60	8	11	3	0	0	7	8	7	.183	.279	.233	45	-4	1			.982	-2	S-12/3-5,2	-0.5
1942	Cin-N	6	10	0	2	1	0	0	0	0	1	.200	.200	.300	45	-1	0			1.000	1	/S-3	0.1
Total	5	206	690	54	161	31	1	0	64	33	60	.233	.269	.281	52	-46	7			.943	17	S-190/3-6,2	-1.4

■ WALLY MATTICK
Mattick, Walter Joseph "Chink"   b: 3/12/1887, St.Louis, Mo.   d: 11/5/68, Los Altos, Cal.   BR/TR, 5'10", 180 lbs.   Deb: 4/11/12   F

YEAR	TM/L	G	AB	R	H	2B	3B	HR	RBI	BB	SO	AVG	OBP	SLG	PRO+	BR/A	SB	CS	SBR	FA	FR	G/POS	TPR
1912	Chi-A	90	285	45	74	7	9	1	35	27		.260	.334	.358	101	0	15			.982	-3	O-79	-0.7
1913	Chi-A	71	207	15	39	8	1	0	11	18	16	.188	.253	.237	44	-15	3			.977	2	O-64	-1.7
1918	StL-N	8	14	0	2	0	0	0	1	2	3	.143	.333	.143	49	-1	0			1.000	0	/O-3	0.0
Total	3	169	506	60	115	15	10	1	47	47	19	.227	.302	.302	77	-15	18			.980	-1	O-146	-2.4

■ MIKE MATTIMORE
Mattimore, Michael Joseph   b: 1859, Renovo, Pa.   d: 4/28/31, Butte, Mont.   BL/TL, 5'8.5", 160 lbs.   Deb: 5/3/1887

YEAR	TM/L	G	AB	R	H	2B	3B	HR	RBI	BB	SO	AVG	OBP	SLG	PRO+	BR/A	SB	CS	SBR	FA	FR	G/POS	TPR
1887	NY-N	8	32	5	8	1	0	0	4	0	6	.250	.250	.281	50	-2	1			.889	-1	/P-7,O-2	0.0
1888	Phi-a	41	142	22	38	6	5	0	12	12		.268	.333	.380	129	5	16			.915	5	P-26,O-16	0.2
1889	Phi-a	23	73	10	17	1	2	1	8	9	7	.233	.333	.342	94	-0	6			.944	-3	O-12/1-7,P	-0.3
	KC-a	19	75	6	12	1	1	0	5	3	16	.160	.192	.200	11	-9	0			.844	-2	O-19/P-1	-0.9
	Yr	42	148	16	29	2	3	1	13	12	23	.196	.265	.270	52	-10	6			.873	-5	O-31/1-7,P	-1.2
1890	Bro-a	33	129	14	17	1	1	0		16		.132	.238	.155	17	-13	11			.887	-6	P-19,O-14	-0.9
Total	4	124	451	57	92	10	9	1	29	40	29	.204	.278	.273	64	-20	34			.853	-7	/O-63,P-58,1	-1.9

■ DON MATTINGLY
Mattingly, Donald Arthur   b: 4/20/61, Evansville, Ind.   BL/TL, 6', 175 lbs.   Deb: 9/8/82

YEAR	TM/L	G	AB	R	H	2B	3B	HR	RBI	BB	SO	AVG	OBP	SLG	PRO+	BR/A	SB	CS	SBR	FA	FR	G/POS	TPR
1982	NY-A	7	12	0	2	0	0	0	1	0	1	.167	.167	.167	-8	-2	0	0	0	1.000	1	/O-6,1-1	-0.1
1983	NY-A	91	279	34	79	15	4	4	32	21	31	.283	.336	.409	108	3	0	0	0	.974	-10	O-48,1-42/2	-1.1
1984	NY-A★	153	603	91	**207**	**44**	2	23	110	41	33	**.343**	.386	.537	**159**	46	1	1	-0	**.996**	13	*1-133,O-19	4.9
1985	NY-A★	159	652	107	211	48	3	35	**145**	56	41	.324	.379	.567	159	51	2	2	-1	**.995**	-11	*1-159	2.8
1986	NY-A★	162	677	117	**238**	**53**	2	31	113	53	35	.352	.399	**.573**	163	57	0	0	0	**.996**	-7	*1-160/3-3,D	3.7
1987	NY-A★	141	569	93	186	38	2	30	115	51	38	.327	.383	.559	147	38	1	4	-2	**.996**	-4	*1-140/D-1	2.0
1988	NY-A★	144	599	94	186	37	0	18	88	41	29	.311	.358	.462	129	22	0	1	0	.993	-4	*1-143/O-1,D	0.6
1989	NY-A★	158	631	79	191	37	2	23	113	51	30	.303	.356	.477	134	27	3	0	1	.995	-5	*1-145,D-17/O	1.1
1990	NY-A	102	394	40	101	16	0	5	42	28	20	.256	.311	.335	80	-10	1	0	0	.997	6	1-89,D-13/O	-1.2
1991	NY-A	152	587	64	169	35	0	9	68	46	42	.288	.344	.394	103	3	2	0	1	.996	-4	*1-127,D-22	-1.0
1992	NY-A	157	640	89	184	40	0	14	86	39	43	.287	.329	.416	108	5	3	0	1	**.997**	7	*1-143,D-15	0.3
1993	NY-A	134	530	78	154	27	2	17	86	61	42	.291	.366	.445	121	16	0	0	0	**.998**	-2	*1-130/D-5	0.3
1994	NY-A	97	372	62	113	20	1	6	51	60	24	.304	.400	.411	118	12	0	0	0	.998	3	1-97	0.6
Total	13	1657	6545	948	2021	410	18	215	1050	548	409	.309	.364	.475	131	268	14	7	0	.996	-18	*1-1509/O-76,D32	12.9

■ RALPH MATTIS
Mattis, Ralph "Matty"   b: 8/24/1890, Roxborough, Pa.   d: 9/13/60, Williamsport, Pa.   BR/TR, 5'11", 172 lbs.   Deb: 4/22/14

YEAR	TM/L	G	AB	R	H	2B	3B	HR	RBI	BB	SO	AVG	OBP	SLG	PRO+	BR/A	SB	CS	SBR	FA	FR	G/POS	TPR
1914	Pit-F	36	85	14	21	4	1	0	8	9	11	.247	.326	.318	68	-4	2			.938	2	O-24	-0.3

■ CLOY MATTOX
Mattox, Cloy Mitchell "Monk"   b: 11/24/02, Leesville, Va.   d: 8/3/85, Danville, Va.   BL/TR, 5'8", 168 lbs.   Deb: 9/1/29   F

YEAR	TM/L	G	AB	R	H	2B	3B	HR	RBI	BB	SO	AVG	OBP	SLG	PRO+	BR/A	SB	CS	SBR	FA	FR	G/POS	TPR
1929	Phi-A	3	6	0	1	0	0	0	0	1	1	.167	.286	.167	19	-1	0	0	0	.875	-0	/C-3	-0.1

■ JIM MATTOX
Mattox, James Powell   b: 12/17/1896, Leesville, Va.   d: 10/12/73, Myrtle Beach, S.C.   BL/TR, 5'9.5", 168 lbs.   Deb: 4/30/22   F

YEAR	TM/L	G	AB	R	H	2B	3B	HR	RBI	BB	SO	AVG	OBP	SLG	PRO+	BR/A	SB	CS	SBR	FA	FR	G/POS	TPR
1922	Pit-N	29	51	11	15	1	1	0	3	1	3	.294	.308	.353	69	-2	0	0	0	.984	1	C-21	0.0
1923	Pit-N	22	32	4	6	1	1	0	1	0	5	.188	.235	.281	35	-3	0	0	0	.960	1	C-8	-0.2
Total	2	51	83	15	21	2	2	0	4	1	8	.253	.279	.325	56	-5	0	0	0	.978	2	/C-29	-0.2

■ LEN MATUSZEK
Matuszek, Leonard James   b: 9/27/54, Toledo, Ohio   BL/TR, 6'2", 195 lbs.   Deb: 9/3/81

YEAR	TM/L	G	AB	R	H	2B	3B	HR	RBI	BB	SO	AVG	OBP	SLG	PRO+	BR/A	SB	CS	SBR	FA	FR	G/POS	TPR
1981	Phi-N	13	11	1	3	1	0	0	1	3	1	.273	.429	.364	121	1	0	1	-1	1.000	2	/1-1,3-1	0.1
1982	Phi-N	25	39	1	3	0	0	1	3	1	10	.077	.122	.103	-36	-7	0	1	-1	.750	-2	/3-8,1-3	-1.1
1983	Phi-N	28	80	12	22	6	1	4	16	4	14	.275	.310	.525	129	2	0	1	-1	1.000	-1	1-21	0.0
1984	Phi-N	101	262	40	65	17	1	12	43	39	54	.248	.354	.458	125	9	4	3	-1	.990	-1	1-81/O-1	0.8
1985	Tor-A	62	151	23	32	6	2	2	15	11	24	.212	.265	.318	57	-9	2	1	0	1.000	0	D-54/1-5	-1.0
	*LA-N	43	63	10	14	2	1	3	13	8	14	.222	.319	.429	111	1	0	1	-1	1.000	-1	O-17,1-10/3	-0.2
1986	LA-N	91	199	26	52	7	0	9	28	21	47	.261	.335	.432	118	4	2	2	-1	1.000	-4	O-37,1-31	-0.3
1987	LA-N	16	15	0	1	0	0	0	1	1	4	.067	.125	.067	-49	-3	0	0	0	1.000	0	/1-3	-0.3
Total	7	379	820	113	192	40	4	30	119	88	168	.234	.314	.405	99	-2	8	10	-4	.990	-2	1-155/O-55,D3	-2.0

■ GENE MAUCH
Mauch, Gene William "Skip"   b: 11/18/25, Salina, Kan.   BR/TR, 5'10", 165 lbs.   Deb: 4/18/44   M

YEAR	TM/L	G	AB	R	H	2B	3B	HR	RBI	BB	SO	AVG	OBP	SLG	PRO+	BR/A	SB	CS	SBR	FA	FR	G/POS	TPR
1944	Bro-N	5	15	2	2	1	0	0	2	2	3	.133	.235	.200	24	-2	0			1.000	-2	/S-5	-0.3
1947	Pit-N	16	30	8	9	0	0	0	1	7	6	.300	.432	.300	95	0	0			.963	-1	/2-6,S-4	-0.1
1948	Bro-N	12	13	1	2	0	0	0	0	1	4	.154	.214	.154	1	-2	0			.950	1	/2-7,S-1	-0.2
	Chi-N	53	138	18	28	3	2	1	7	26	10	.203	.329	.275	68	-5	1			.925	-6	2-26,S-19	-0.9
	Yr	65	151	19	30	3	2	1	7	27	14	.199	.320	.265	62	-7	1			.929	-5	2-33,S-20	-0.9
1949	Chi-N	72	150	15	37	5	1	2	7	21	15	.247	.339	.333	83	-3	3			.971	12	2-25,S-19/3	1.0
1950	Bos-N	48	121	17	28	5	0	1	15	14	9	.231	.316	.298	67	-6	1			.968	-1	2-28/3-7,S	-0.5
1951	Bos-N	19	20	5	2	0	0	0	1	7	4	.100	.333	.100	24	-2	0			1.000	-0	S-10/3-3,2	-0.2
1952	StL-N	7	3	0	0	0	0	0	0	0	1	.000	.250	.000	-25	-0	0			.500	1	/S-2	-0.1
1956	Bos-A	7	25	4	8	0	0	0	1	3	3	.320	.393	.320	80	-1	0			.935	-2	/2-6	-0.2
1957	Bos-A	65	222	23	60	10	3	2	28	22	26	.270	.339	.369	88	-3	1			.962	-10	2-58	-0.8
Total	9	304	737	93	176	25	5	7	62	104	82	.239	.335	.312	75	-23	6	0		.958	-10	2-158/S-65,3	-2.1

YEAR	TM/L	G	AB	R	H	2B	3B	HR	RBI	BB	SO	AVG	OBP	SLG	PRO+	BR/A	SB	CS	SBR	FA	FR	G/POS	TPR

■ AL MAUL   Maul, Albert Joseph "Smiling Al"   b: 10/9/1865, Philadelphia, Pa.   d: 5/3/58, Philadelphia, Pa.   BR/TR, 6', 175 lbs.   Deb: 6/20/1884

YEAR	TM/L	G	AB	R	H	2B	3B	HR	RBI	BB	SO	AVG	OBP	SLG	PRO+	BR/A	SB	CS	SBR	FA	FR	G/POS	TPR
1884	Phi-U	1	4	0	0	0	0	0	0	0	0	.000	.000	.000	-99	-1				1.000	-0	/P-1	0.0
1887	Phi-N	16	56	15	17	2	2	1	4	15	10	.304	.451	.464	146	4	5			.897	2	/O-8,P-7,1	0.3
1888	Pit-N	74	259	21	54	9	4	0	31	21	45	.208	.276	.274	82	-4	9			.975	-1	1-38,O-34/P	-0.9
1889	Pit-N	68	257	37	71	6	6	4	44	29	41	.276	.356	.393	121	8	18			.946	11	O-64/P-6	1.3
1890	Pit-P	45	162	31	42	6	2	0	21	22	12	.259	.348	.321	86	-2	5			.904	4	P-30,O-15/S	-0.1
1891	Pit-N	47	149	15	28	2	4	0	14	20	28	.188	.284	.255	59	-7	4			.877	-2	O-40/P-8	-0.9
1893	Was-N	44	134	10	34	8	4	0	12	33	14	.254	.405	.373	110	4	1			.889	1	P-37/O-7	0.1
1894	Was-N	42	125	23	30	3	3	2	20	14	11	.240	.349	.360	74	-5	1			.877	2	P-29,O-12	-0.1
1895	Was-N	22	72	9	18	5	2	0	16	6	7	.250	.308	.375	76	-3	0			.933	1	P-16/O-4	-0.1
1896	Was-N	8	28	6	8	1	1	0	5	3	2	.286	.355	.393	97	-0	0			.923	-1	/P-8	0.0
1897	Was-N	1	1	0	0	0	0	0		0	0	.000	.000	.000	-99	-0	0			1.000	0	/P-1	0.0
	Bal-N	2	3	0	1	0	0	0		0	0	.333	.333	.333	76	-0	0			1.000	-0	/P-2	0.0
	Yr	3	4	0	1	0	0	0		0	0	.250	.250	.250	32	-0	0			1.000	-0	/P-3	0.0
1898	Bal-N	29	93	21	19	3	2	0	10	16		.204	.338	.280	75	-3	1			.978	-5	P-28/O-1	0.0
1899	Bro-N	4	11	2	3	0	0	0	0	1		.273	.333	.273	66	-0	0			.900	0	/P-4	0.0
1900	Phi-N	5	15	2	3	0	0	0	1	2		.200	.294	.200	38	-1	0			.917	0	/P-5	0.0
1901	NY-N	3	8	1	3	0	0	0	1	0		.375	.375	.375	122	0	0			1.000	0	/P-3	0.0
Total	15	411	1377	193	331	45	30	7	179	182	170	.240	.336	.332	91	-12	44			.910	13	P-188,O-185/1S	-0.4

■ MARK MAULDIN   Mauldin, Marshall Reese   b: 11/5/14, Atlanta, Ga.   d: 9/2/90, Union City, Ga.   BR/TR, 5'11", 170 lbs.   Deb: 9/10/34

YEAR	TM/L	G	AB	R	H	2B	3B	HR	RBI	BB	SO	AVG	OBP	SLG	PRO+	BR/A	SB	CS	SBR	FA	FR	G/POS	TPR
1934	Chi-A	10	38	3	10	2	0	1	3	0	3	.263	.263	.395	66	-2	0	0	0	.906	-0	3-10	-0.2

■ ROB MAURER   Maurer, Robert John   b: 1/7/67, Evansville, Ind.   BL/TL, 6'3", 210 lbs.   Deb: 9/8/91

YEAR	TM/L	G	AB	R	H	2B	3B	HR	RBI	BB	SO	AVG	OBP	SLG	PRO+	BR/A	SB	CS	SBR	FA	FR	G/POS	TPR
1991	Tex-A	13	16	0	1	1	0	0	2	2	6	.063	.211	.125	-5	-2	0	0	0	1.000	1	/1-4,D-2	-0.1
1992	Tex-A	8	9	1	2	0	0	0	1	1	2	.222	.300	.222	50	-1	0	0	0	1.000	0	/1-3,D-1	0.0
Total	2	21	25	1	3	1	0	0	3	3	8	.120	.241	.160	14	-3	0	0	0	1.000	1	/1-7,D-3	-0.1

■ CARMEN MAURO   Mauro, Carmen Louis   b: 11/10/26, St.Paul, Minn.   BL/TR, 6', 167 lbs.   Deb: 10/1/48

YEAR	TM/L	G	AB	R	H	2B	3B	HR	RBI	BB	SO	AVG	OBP	SLG	PRO+	BR/A	SB	CS	SBR	FA	FR	G/POS	TPR
1948	Chi-N	3	5	2	1	0	0	1	1	2	0	.200	.429	.800	235	1	0			1.000	1	/O-2	0.1
1950	Chi-N	62	185	19	42	4	3	1	10	13	31	.227	.285	.297	54	-12	3			.946	-3	O-49	-1.8
1951	Chi-N	13	29	3	5	1	0	0	3	2	6	.172	.250	.207	24	-3	0	0	0	.900	1	O-6	-0.3
1953	Bro-N	8	9	1	0	0	0	0	0	0	4	.000	.000	.000	-98	-3	0	0	0	1.000	-0	/O-1	-0.3
	Was-A	17	23	1	4	0	1	0	2	1	3	.174	.208	.261	27	-2	0	0	0	1.000	-0	/O-6	-0.3
	Phi-A	64	165	14	44	4	4	0	17	19	21	.267	.342	.339	81	-4	3	4	-2	.969	-1	O-49/3-1	-0.8
	Yr	81	188	15	48	4	5	0	19	20	24	.255	.327	.330	76	-6	3	4	-2	.971	-1	O-55/3-1	-1.1
Total	4	167	416	40	96	9	8	2	33	37	65	.231	.298	.305	61	-23	6	4		.958	-4	O-113/3-1	-3.4

■ BOB MAVIS   Mavis, Robert Henry   b: 4/8/18, Milwaukee, Wis.   BL/TR, 5'7", 160 lbs.   Deb: 9/17/49

YEAR	TM/L	G	AB	R	H	2B	3B	HR	RBI	BB	SO	AVG	OBP	SLG	PRO+	BR/A	SB	CS	SBR	FA	FR	G/POS	TPR
1949	Det-A	1	0	0	0	0	0	0	0	0	0	—	—	—		0	0	0	0	.000	0	R	0.0

■ DAL MAXVILL   Maxvill, Charles Dallan   b: 2/18/39, Granite City, Ill.   BR/TR, 5'11", 160 lbs.   Deb: 6/10/62   C

YEAR	TM/L	G	AB	R	H	2B	3B	HR	RBI	BB	SO	AVG	OBP	SLG	PRO+	BR/A	SB	CS	SBR	FA	FR	G/POS	TPR
1962	StL-N	79	189	20	42	3	1	1	18	17	39	.222	.290	.265	46	-14	1	2	-1	.962	-2	S-76/3-1	-1.2
1963	StL-N	53	51	12	12	2	0	0	3	6	11	.235	.316	.275	66	-2	0	0	0	.974	7	S-24/2-9,3	0.6
1964	*StL-N	37	26	4	6	0	0	0	4	0	7	.231	.231	.231	28	-2	1	0	0	.972	6	2-15,S-13/3O	0.4
1965	StL-N	68	89	10	12	2	2	0	10	7	15	.135	.206	.202	14	-10	0	0	0	.993	13	2-49,S-12	0.5
1966	StL-N	134	394	25	96	14	3	0	24	37	61	.244	.312	.294	69	-15	3	0	1	.967	24	*S-128/2-5,O	2.1
1967	*StL-N	152	476	37	108	14	4	1	41	48	66	.227	.299	.279	67	-19	0	2	-1	.974	3	*S-148/2-7	-0.4
1968	*StL-N	151	459	51	116	8	5	1	24	52	71	.253	.330	.298	91	-3	0	2	-1	.969	-9	*S-151	0.2
1969	StL-N	132	372	27	65	10	2	2	32	44	52	.175	.264	.228	39	-30	1	1	-0	.969	21	*S-131	0.4
1970	StL-N	152	399	35	80	5	2	0	28	51	56	.201	.291	.223	39	-33	0	0	0	**.982**	**38**	*S-136,2-22	1.9
1971	StL-N	142	356	31	80	10	2	0	24	43	45	.225	.310	.258	60	-17	1	2	-1	.979	**29**	*S-140	2.6
1972	StL-N	105	276	22	61	6	1	2	23	31	47	.221	.300	.261	61	-13	0	1	-1	.980	9	S-95,2-11	0.7
	*Oak-A	27	36	2	9	1	0	0	1	1	11	.250	.270	.278	67	-2	0	1	-1	.983	4	2-24/S-4	0.3
1973	Oak-A	29	19	0	4	0	0	0	1	1	3	.211	.250	.211	33	-2	0	0	0	.966	4	S-18,2-11/3	0.2
	Pit-N	74	217	19	41	4	3	0	17	22	40	.189	.264	.235	40	-17	0	0	0	.971	4	S-74	-0.5
1974	Pit-N	8	22	3	4	0	0	0	0	0	8	.182	.250	.182	23	-2	0	0	0	.946	1	/S-8	-0.1
	*Oak-A	60	52	3	10	0	0	0	2	8	10	.192	.300	.192	47	-3	0	0	0	1.000	9	2-30,S-29/3	0.8
1975	Oak-A	20	10	1	2	0	0	0	0	0	5	.200	.200	.200	14	-1	0	0	0	.955	2	S-20/2-2	0.2
Total	14	1423	3443	302	748	79	24	6	252	370	538	.217	.295	.259	57	-188	7	11	-5	.973	160	*S-1207,2-185/3O	8.7

■ CHARLIE MAXWELL   Maxwell, Charles Richard "Smokey"   b: 4/8/27, Lawton, Mich.   BL/TL, 5'11", 185 lbs.   Deb: 9/20/50

YEAR	TM/L	G	AB	R	H	2B	3B	HR	RBI	BB	SO	AVG	OBP	SLG	PRO+	BR/A	SB	CS	SBR	FA	FR	G/POS	TPR
1950	Bos-A	3	8	1	0	0	0	0	0	0	3	.000	.111	.000	-63	-2	0	0	0	1.000	1	/O-2	-0.1
1951	Bos-A	49	80	8	15	1	0	3	12	9	18	.188	.270	.313	52	-6	0	1	-1	.926	-1	O-13	-0.8
1952	Bos-A	8	15	0	1	1	0	0	0	3	11	.067	.222	.133	0	-2	0	0	0	.966	2	/1-3,O-3	-0.1
1954	Bos-A	74	104	9	26	4	1	0	5	12	21	.250	.328	.308	67	-4	3	0	1	1.000	-7	O-27	-1.2
1955	Bal-A	4	4	0	0	0	0	0	0	0	1	.000	.000	.000	-99	-1	0	0	0	.000	0	H	-0.1
	Det-A	55	109	19	29	7	1	7	18	18	20	.266	.328	.541	134	9	0	0	0	.967	2	O-26/1-2	0.5
	Yr	59	113	19	29	7	1	7	18	18	21	.257	.317	.522	126	3	0	0	0	.967	2	O-26/1-2	0.4
1956	Det-A☆	141	500	96	163	14	3	28	87	79	74	.326	.420	.534	150	37	1	1	-0	.987	13	*O-136	4.2
1957	Det-A★	138	492	75	136	23	3	24	82	76	84	.276	.378	.482	130	21	3	2	-0	**.997**	14	*O-137	2.8
1958	Det-A	131	397	56	108	14	3	13	65	64	54	.272	.373	.426	111	7	6	1	0	.986	-1	*O-114,1-14	0.1
1959	Det-A	145	518	81	130	12	2	31	95	81	91	.251	.359	.461	117	13	0	2	-1	.986	10	*O-136	1.5
1960	Det-A	134	482	70	114	16	5	24	81	58	75	.237	.326	.440	102	1	5	0	2	**.996**	8	*O-120	0.4
1961	Det-A	79	131	11	30	4	2	5	18	20	24	.229	.336	.405	94	-1	0	0	0	.965	2	O-25	-0.1
1962	Det-A	30	67	5	13	2	0	1	9	9	10	.194	.280	.269	47	-5	0	0	0	.966	-1	O-15/1-1	-0.6
	Chi-A	69	206	30	61	8	3	9	43	34	32	.296	.396	.495	139	12	0	0	0	.990	-1	O-56/1-6	0.8
	Yr	99	273	35	74	10	3	10	52	42	42	.271	.362	.440	115	7	0	0	0	.985	-1	O-71/1-7	0.2
1963	Chi-A	71	130	17	30	4	2	3	17	31	27	.231	.379	.362	111	3	0	0	0	1.000	-4	O-24,1-17	-0.2
1964	Chi-A	2	2	0	0	0	0	0	0	0	0	.000	.000	.000	-99	-1	0	0	0	.000	0	H	-0.1
Total	14	1133	3245	478	856	110	26	148	532	484	545	.264	.363	.451	116	77	18	7		.988	37	O-834/1-43	7.0

■ CARLOS MAY   May, Carlos   b: 5/17/48, Birmingham, Ala.   BL/TR, 6', 215 lbs.   Deb: 9/6/68   F

YEAR	TM/L	G	AB	R	H	2B	3B	HR	RBI	BB	SO	AVG	OBP	SLG	PRO+	BR/A	SB	CS	SBR	FA	FR	G/POS	TPR
1968	Chi-A	17	67	4	12	1	0	0	1	3	15	.179	.214	.194	24	-6	0	0	0	.960	-2	O-17	-1.0
1969	Chi-A★	100	367	62	103	18	2	18	62	56	66	.281	.387	.488	137	19	1	4	-2	.982	-1	*O-100	1.0
1970	Chi-A	150	555	83	158	28	4	12	68	79	96	.285	.377	.414	114	12	12	5	1	.991	1	*O-141/1-7	0.6
1971	Chi-A	141	500	64	147	21	7	7	70	62	61	.294	.399	.406	119	14	16	7	1	.986	-5	*1-130/O-9	-0.3
1972	Chi-A☆	148	523	83	161	26	3	12	68	79	70	.308	.408	.438	149	35	23	14	-2	.983	-1	*O-145/1-5	2.9
1973	Chi-A	149	553	62	148	20	5	20	96	53	73	.268	.337	.412	106	4	8	6	1	.992	1	D-75,O-70/1	-0.1
1974	Chi-A	149	551	66	137	19	2	8	58	46	76	.249	.308	.334	82	-12	8	9	-3	.988	6	*O-129,D-13	-1.6
1975	Chi-A	128	454	55	123	19	2	8	53	67	46	.271	.375	.374	111	9	8	4	1	.988	-5	1-63,O-46,D	0.1
1976	Chi-A	20	63	7	11	2	0	0	3	9	15	.175	.278	.206	43	-4	4	0	1	1.000		D-10/O-9	-0.5
	*NY-A	87	288	38	80	11	3	6	40	34	32	.278	.364	.361	114	5	1	1	-0	.950	0	D-71/O-7,1	0.4
	Yr	107	351	45	91	13	2	6	43	43	37	.259	.348	.333	101	2	5	1	1	.970	-1	D-81/O-16/1	-0.1

YEAR	TM/L	G	AB	R	H	2B	3B	HR	RBI	BB	SO	AVG	OBP	SLG	PRO+	BR/A	SB	CS	SBR	FA	FR	G/POS	TPR
1977	NY-A	65	181	21	41	7	1	2	16	17	24	.227	.296	.309	66	-8	0	0	0	1.000	-1	D-53/O-4	-1.1
	Cal-A	11	18	0	6	0	0	0	1	5	1	.333	.478	.333	131	1	0	0	0	1.000	0	/1-3,D-1	0.1
	Yr	76	199	21	47	7	1	2	17	22	25	.236	.315	.312	73	-7	0	0	0	1.000	-1	D-54/O-4,1	-1.0
Total	10	1165	4120	545	1127	172	23	90	536	512	565	.274	.360	.392	111	70	85	53	-6	.984	-1	O-677,D-242,1	0.7

■ DAVE MAY   May, David La France   b: 12/23/43, New Castle, Del.   BL/TR, 5′10.5″, 186 lbs.   Deb: 7/28/67   F

YEAR	TM/L	G	AB	R	H	2B	3B	HR	RBI	BB	SO	AVG	OBP	SLG	PRO+	BR/A	SB	CS	SBR	FA	FR	G/POS	TPR
1967	Bal-A	36	85	12	20	1	1	1	7	6	13	.235	.286	.306	75	-3	0	0	0	.969	-0	O-19	-0.4
1968	Bal-A	84	152	15	29	6	3	0	7	19	27	.191	.285	.270	69	-5	3	3	-1	.984	-11	O-61	-2.2
1969	*Bal-A	78	120	8	29	6	0	3	10	9	23	.242	.305	.367	86	-2	2	1	0	.940	-4	O-40	-0.8
1970	Bal-A	25	31	6	6	0	1	1	6	4	4	.194	.286	.355	75	-1	0	0	0	1.000	-0	/O-9	-0.4
	Mil-A	100	342	36	82	8	1	7	31	44	56	.240	.330	.330	82	-8	8	6	-1	.989	8	O-99	-0.6
	Yr	125	373	42	88	8	2	8	37	48	60	.236	.326	.332	81	-9	8	6	-1	.989	6	*O-108	-1.0
1971	Mil-A	144	501	74	139	20	3	16	65	50	59	.277	.347	.425	119	12	15	9	-1	.975	10	*O-142	1.6
1972	Mil-A	143	500	49	119	20	2	9	45	47	56	.238	.307	.340	94	-4	11	13	-5	.985	15	*O-138	0.0
1973	Mil-A★	156	624	96	189	23	4	25	93	44	78	.303	.354	.473	134	26	6	7	-2	.979	3	*O-152/D-2	2.0
1974	Mil-A	135	477	56	108	15	1	10	42	28	73	.226	.274	.325	72	-18	4	3	-1	.989	-3	*O-121/D-8	-2.8
1975	Atl-N	82	203	28	56	8	0	12	40	25	27	.276	.361	.493	130	8	1	1	-0	.964	-1	O-53	0.5
1976	Atl-N	105	214	27	46	5	3	3	20	26	31	.215	.303	.308	69	-8	5	1	1	.972	-0	O-60	-1.0
1977	Tex-A	120	340	46	82	14	1	7	42	32	43	.241	.314	.350	80	-9	4	3	-1	.969	-4	*O-111/D-5	-1.8
1978	Mil-A	39	77	9	15	4	0	2	11	9	10	.195	.295	.325	74	-3	0	0	0	.944	-2	O-16/D-8	-0.3
	Pit-N	5	4	0	0	0	0	0	0	1	1	.000	.200	.000	-38	-1	1	0	0	.000	0	H	-0.1
Total	12	1252	3670	462	920	130	20	96	422	344	501	.251	.320	.375	97	-16	60	47	-10	.978	10	*O-1021/D-23	-6.3

■ DERRICK MAY   May, Derrick Brant   b: 7/14/68, Rochester, N.Y.   BL/TR, 6′4″, 210 lbs.   Deb: 9/6/90   F

YEAR	TM/L	G	AB	R	H	2B	3B	HR	RBI	BB	SO	AVG	OBP	SLG	PRO+	BR/A	SB	CS	SBR	FA	FR	G/POS	TPR
1990	Chi-N	17	61	8	15	3	0	1	11	2	7	.246	.270	.344	63	-3	1	0	0	.972	5	O-17	-0.3
1991	Chi-N	15	22	4	5	2	0	1	3	2	1	.227	.292	.455	102	-0	0	0	0	1.000	0	/O-7	0.0
1992	Chi-N	124	351	33	96	11	0	8	45	14	40	.274	.307	.373	89	-5	5	3	-0	.969	-11	O-108	-1.9
1993	Chi-N	128	465	62	137	25	2	10	77	31	41	.295	.340	.422	104	2	10	3	1	.970	1	*O-122	0.2
1994	Chi-N	100	345	43	98	19	2	8	51	30	34	.284	.341	.420	100	-0	3	2	0	.994	2	O-92	0.2
Total	5	384	1244	150	351	60	4	28	187	79	123	.282	.327	.404	97	-7	19	8	1	.977	-7	O-346	-2.0

■ JERRY MAY   May, Jerry Lee   b: 12/14/43, Staunton, Va.   BR/TR, 6′2.5″, 195 lbs.   Deb: 9/19/64

YEAR	TM/L	G	AB	R	H	2B	3B	HR	RBI	BB	SO	AVG	OBP	SLG	PRO+	BR/A	SB	CS	SBR	FA	FR	G/POS	TPR
1964	Pit-N	11	31	1	8	0	0	0	3	3	9	.258	.324	.258	66	-1	0	0	0	.988	4	C-11	0.3
1965	Pit-N	4	2	0	1	0	0	0	1	0	0	.500	.500	.500	182	0	0	0	0	1.000	-0	/C-4	0.0
1966	Pit-N	42	52	6	13	4	0	1	2	2	15	.250	.291	.385	86	-1	0	1	0	.984	8	C-41	0.7
1967	Pit-N	110	325	23	88	13	2	3	22	36	55	.271	.349	.351	100	1	0	0	0	.993	-0	*C-110	0.7
1968	Pit-N	137	416	26	91	15	2	1	33	41	80	.219	.293	.272	72	-14	0	0	0	.988	4	*C-135	-0.1
1969	Pit-N	62	190	21	44	8	0	7	23	9	53	.232	.274	.384	84	-5	1	1	-0	.994	-5	C-52	-0.8
1970	Pit-N	51	139	13	29	4	2	1	16	21	25	.209	.317	.288	65	-7	0	0	0	.994	13	C-45	0.8
1971	KC-A	71	218	16	55	13	2	1	24	27	37	.252	.335	.344	93	-1	0	0	0	.997	0	C-71	0.1
1972	KC-A	53	116	10	22	5	1	1	4	14	13	.190	.277	.276	65	-5	0	0	0	.979	-1	C-41	-0.5
1973	KC-A	11	30	4	4	1	1	0	2	3	5	.133	.235	.233	30	-3	0	0	0	.940	-2	C-11	-0.4
	NY-N	4	8	0	2	0	0	0	0	1	1	.250	.333	.250	65	-0	0	0	0	1.000	-1	/C-4	-0.1
Total	10	556	1527	120	357	63	10	15	130	157	293	.234	.310	.318	81	-35	1	2	-1	.990	21	C-525	0.7

■ LEE MAY   May, Lee Andrew   b: 3/23/43, Birmingham, Ala.   BR/TR, 6′3″, 205 lbs.   Deb: 9/1/65   FC

YEAR	TM/L	G	AB	R	H	2B	3B	HR	RBI	BB	SO	AVG	OBP	SLG	PRO+	BR/A	SB	CS	SBR	FA	FR	G/POS	TPR
1965	Cin-N	5	4	1	0	0	0	0	0	0	1	.000	.000	.000	-94	-1	0	0	0	.000	0	H	-0.1
1966	Cin-N	25	75	14	25	5	1	2	10	0	14	.333	.333	.507	119	2	0	1	-1	.972	-1	1-16	-0.1
1967	Cin-N	127	438	54	116	29	2	12	57	19	80	.265	.310	.422	97	-3	4	8	-4	.994	2	1-81,O-48	-1.2
1968	Cin-N	146	559	78	162	32	1	22	80	34	100	.290	.337	.469	132	20	4	7	-3	.996	0	*1-122,O-33	0.8
1969	Cin-N★	158	607	85	169	32	3	38	110	45	142	.278	.334	.529	132	23	5	4	-1	.993	0	*1-156/O-7	0.9
1970	*Cin-N	153	605	78	153	34	2	34	94	38	125	.253	.299	.484	106	1	1	1	-0	.993	0	*1-153	-1.2
1971	Cin-N★	147	553	85	154	17	3	39	98	42	135	.278	.334	.532	145	29	3	0	1	.994	-7	*1-143	1.1
1972	Hou-N★	148	592	87	168	31	2	29	98	52	145	.284	.344	.490	137	27	3	1	0	.996	-3	*1-146	1.2
1973	Hou-N	148	545	65	147	24	3	28	105	34	122	.270	.315	.479	117	10	1	0	0	.993	-3	*1-144	-0.5
1974	Hou-N	152	556	59	149	26	0	24	85	17	97	.268	.298	.444	110	3	1	0	0	.994	0	*1-145	-0.5
1975	Bal-A	146	580	67	152	28	3	20	99	36	91	.262	.311	.424	113	7	1	2	-1	.993	3	*1-144/D-2	0.0
1976	Bal-A	148	530	61	137	17	4	25	**109**	41	104	.258	.315	.447	130	17	4	1	1	.996	0	1-94,D-52	1.0
1977	Bal-A	150	585	75	148	16	2	27	99	38	119	.253	.299	.426	101	-2	2	2	-1	.995	-7	*1-110,D-39	-1.7
1978	Bal-A	148	556	56	137	16	1	25	80	31	110	.246	.287	.414	101	-2	5	2	0	.973	-0	*D-140/1-4	-0.7
1979	*Bal-A	124	456	59	116	15	0	19	69	28	100	.254	.299	.412	93	-6	3	4	-2	.913	-1	*D-117/1-2	-1.2
1980	Bal-A	78	222	20	54	10	2	7	31	15	53	.243	.291	.401	88	-4	2	0	0	1.000	0	D-58/1-7	-0.6
1981	*KC-A	26	55	3	16	3	0	0	8	3	14	.291	.328	.345	95	-0	0	1	-1	1.000	-1	/1-8,D-4	-0.2
1982	KC-A	42	91	12	28	5	2	3	12	4	18	.308	.340	.505	147	6	0	0	0	.989	-2	1-32/D-2	0.3
Total	18	2071	7609	959	2031	340	31	354	1244	487	1570	.267	.315	.459	116	126	39	35	-9	.994	-19	*1-1507,D-414/O	-2.7

■ PINKY MAY   May, Merrill Glend   b: 1/18/11, Laconia, Ind.   BR/TR, 5′11.5″, 165 lbs.   Deb: 4/21/39   F

YEAR	TM/L	G	AB	R	H	2B	3B	HR	RBI	BB	SO	AVG	OBP	SLG	PRO+	BR/A	SB	CS	SBR	FA	FR	G/POS	TPR
1939	Phi-N	135	464	49	133	27	3	2	62	41	20	.287	.346	.371	95	-3	4			**.956**	8	*3-132	0.7
1940	Phi-N★	136	501	59	147	24	2	1	48	58	33	.293	.371	.355	105	6	2			.954	13	*3-135/S-1	2.1
1941	Phi-N	142	490	46	131	17	4	0	39	55	30	.267	.344	.318	91	-5	2			**.972**	25	*3-140	2.4
1942	Phi-N	115	345	25	82	15	0	0	18	51	17	.238	.338	.281	86	-4	3			.963	17	*3-107	1.5
1943	Phi-N	137	415	31	117	19	2	1	48	56	21	.282	.369	.345	111	8	2			**.963**	11	*3-132	2.2
Total	5	665	2215	210	610	102	11	4	215	261	121	.275	.354	.337	98	2	13			.962	74	3-646/S-1	8.9

■ MILT MAY   May, Milton Scott   b: 8/1/50, Gary, Ind.   BL/TR, 6′, 190 lbs.   Deb: 9/8/70   FC

YEAR	TM/L	G	AB	R	H	2B	3B	HR	RBI	BB	SO	AVG	OBP	SLG	PRO+	BR/A	SB	CS	SBR	FA	FR	G/POS	TPR
1970	Pit-N	5	4	1	2	1	0	0	2	0	0	.500	.600	.750	265	1	0	0	0	.000	0	H	0.1
1971	*Pit-N	49	126	15	35	1	0	6	25	9	16	.278	.324	.429	113	2	0	0	0	1.000	3	C-31	0.6
1972	*Pit-N	57	139	12	39	10	0	0	14	10	13	.281	.329	.353	96	-1	0	0	0	.985	2	C-33	0.5
1973	Pit-N	101	283	29	76	8	1	7	31	34	26	.269	.351	.378	105	2	0	1	-1	.973	-6	C-79	-0.1
1974	Hou-N	127	405	47	117	17	4	7	54	39	33	.289	.353	.402	116	8	0	1	-1	**.993**	2	*C-116	1.5
1975	Hou-N	111	386	29	93	15	1	4	52	26	41	.241	.289	.316	73	-15	1	2	-1	.986	1	*C-102	-1.1
1976	Det-A	6	25	2	7	1	0	0	1	0	1	.280	.280	.320	73	-1	0	0	0	1.000	1	/C-6	0.0
1977	Det-A	115	397	32	99	9	3	12	46	26	31	.249	.296	.378	78	-13	0	0	0	.986	7	C-111	-0.3
1978	Det-A	105	352	24	88	9	0	10	37	27	26	.250	.307	.361	85	-7	0	0	0	.979	1	C-94	-0.4
1979	Det-A	6	11	1	3	1	0	0	3	1	1	.273	.333	.455	107	-0	0	0	0	1.000	1	/C-5	0.1
	Chi-A	65	202	23	51	13	0	7	28	14	27	.252	.307	.421	94	-2	0	0	0	.981	1	C-65	0.1
	Yr	71	213	24	54	15	0	7	31	15	28	.254	.309	.423	95	-2	0	0	0	.982	2	C-70	0.2
1980	SF-N	111	358	27	93	18	0	5	25	28	40	.260	.310	.366	90	-5	0	1	-1	.986	-4	C-103	-0.7
1981	SF-N	97	316	20	98	17	0	2	33	34	29	.310	.377	.383	118	8	1	4	-2	.989	-1	C-93	0.9
1982	SF-N	114	395	29	104	19	0	9	39	28	38	.263	.312	.380	93	-4	0	1	-1	.987	-1	C-110	-0.2
1983	SF-N	66	186	18	46	6	0	6	20	21	23	.247	.324	.376	96	-1	2	0	1	.981	-2	C-56	-0.1
	Pit-N	7	12	0	3	0	0	0	0	1	1	.250	.308	.250	55	-1	0	0	0	1.000	2	/C-4	0.1
	Yr	73	198	18	49	6	0	6	20	22	24	.247	.323	.369	94	-2	2	0	1	.983	0	C-60	0.0

YEAR	TM/L	G	AB	R	H	2B	3B	HR	RBI	BB	SO	AVG	OBP	SLG	PRO+	BR/A	SB	CS	SBR	FA	FR	G/POS	TPR
1984	Pit-N	50	96	4	17	3	0	1	8	10	15	.177	.255	.240	40	-8	0	0	-1	.993	5	C-26	-0.3
Total	15	1192	3693	313	971	147	11	77	443	305	361	.263	.321	.371	93	-37	4	13	-7	.986	14	*C-1034	0.7

◼ JOHN MAYBERRY
Mayberry, John Claiborn b: 2/18/49, Detroit, Mich. BL/TL, 6'3", 220 lbs. Deb: 9/10/68 C

YEAR	TM/L	G	AB	R	H	2B	3B	HR	RBI	BB	SO	AVG	OBP	SLG	PRO+	BR/A	SB	CS	SBR	FA	FR	G/POS	TPR
1968	Hou-N	4	9	0	0	0	0	0	0	0	2	.000	.100	.000	-69	-2	0	0	0	1.000	-0	/1-2	-0.3
1969	Hou-N	5	4	0	0	0	0	0	0	1	1	.000	.200	.000	-41	-1	0	0	0	.000	0	H	-0.1
1970	Hou-N	50	148	23	32	3	2	5	14	21	33	.216	.322	.365	87	-3	1	1	-0	.995	3	1-45	-0.3
1971	Hou-N	46	137	16	25	0	1	7	14	13	32	.182	.263	.350	74	-5	0	0	0	.997	-3	1-37	-1.2
1972	KC-A★	149	503	65	150	24	3	25	100	78	74	.298	.396	.507	168	43	0	2	-1	**.995**	-0	*1-146	3.3
1973	KC-A★	152	510	87	142	20	2	26	100	**122**	79	.278	**.420**	.478	141	33	3	0	1	.994	-5	*1-149/D-1	1.7
1974	KC-A★	126	427	63	100	13	1	22	69	77	72	.234	.359	.424	118	11	4	2	0	.990	-2	*1-106,D-16	0.2
1975	KC-A	156	554	95	161	38	1	34	106	**119**	73	.291	.419	.547	**167**	53	5	3	-0	.988	3	*1-131,D-27	4.6
1976	*KC-A	161	594	76	138	22	2	13	95	82	73	.232	.327	.342	95	-2	3	2	-0	.996	3	*1-160/D-2	-1.7
1977	*KC-A	153	543	73	125	22	1	23	82	83	86	.230	.340	.401	100	1	1	3	-2	**.995**	-6	*1-145/D-8	-1.5
1978	Tor-A	152	515	51	129	15	2	22	70	60	57	.250	.333	.416	107	5	1	2	-1	.993	-14	*1-139/D-7	-1.9
1979	Tor-A	137	464	61	127	22	1	21	74	69	60	.274	.374	.461	122	16	1	1	-0	.995	-8	*1-135	-0.1
1980	Tor-A	149	501	62	124	19	2	30	82	77	80	.248	.351	.473	118	13	0	0	0	.994	-4	*1-136/D-8	0.0
1981	Tor-A	94	290	34	72	6	1	17	43	44	45	.248	.363	.452	125	10	1	1	-0	.993	-6	1-80,D-10	-0.1
1982	Tor-A	17	33	7	9	0	0	2	3	7	5	.273	.415	.455	127	1	0	0	0	1.000	-1	D-13/1-4	0.0
	NY-A	69	215	20	45	7	0	8	27	28	38	.209	.315	.353	84	-4	0	0	0	.996	-4	1-63/D-4	-1.1
	Yr	86	248	27	54	7	0	10	30	35	43	.218	.329	.367	90	-3	0	0	0	.996	-4	1-67,D-17	-1.1
Total	15	1620	5447	733	1379	211	19	255	879	881	810	.253	.363	.439	122	170	20	17	-4	.994	-49	*1-1478/D-96	1.5

◼ LEE MAYE
Maye, Arthur Lee b: 12/11/34, Tuscaloosa, Ala. BL/TR, 6'2", 190 lbs. Deb: 7/17/59

YEAR	TM/L	G	AB	R	H	2B	3B	HR	RBI	BB	SO	AVG	OBP	SLG	PRO+	BR/A	SB	CS	SBR	FA	FR	G/POS	TPR
1959	Mil-N	51	140	17	42	5	1	4	16	7	26	.300	.338	.436	114	2	2	2	-1	.976	1	O-44	0.0
1960	Mil-N	41	83	14	25	6	0	0	2	7	21	.301	.363	.373	110	1	5	0	2	.968	-1	O-19	0.1
1961	Mil-N	110	373	68	101	11	5	14	41	36	50	.271	.340	.440	112	6	10	1	2	.972	-2	O-96	0.0
1962	Mil-N	99	349	40	85	10	0	10	41	25	58	.244	.296	.358	77	-12	9	3	1	.977	3	O-94	-1.6
1963	Mil-N	124	442	67	120	22	7	11	34	36	52	.271	.331	.428	118	10	14	2	3	.983	-8	*O-111	-0.2
1964	Mil-N	153	588	96	179	**44**	5	10	74	34	54	.304	.347	.447	121	16	5	10	-5	.961	-1	*O-135/3-5	0.3
1965	Mil-N	15	53	8	16	2	0	2	7	2	6	.302	.339	.453	120	1	0	0	0	.962	1	O-13	0.2
	Hou-N	108	415	38	104	17	7	3	36	20	37	.251	.287	.347	83	-11	1	5	-3	.953	3	*O-103	-1.6
	Yr	123	468	46	120	19	7	5	43	22	43	.256	.293	.359	88	-9	1	5	-3	.954	4	*O-116	-1.4
1966	Hou-N	115	358	38	103	12	4	9	36	20	26	.288	.327	.419	113	5	4	3	-1	.949	-1	O-97	-0.1
1967	Cle-A	115	297	43	77	20	4	9	27	26	47	.259	.321	.444	123	8	3	3	-1	.981	-10	O-77/2-1	-0.7
1968	Cle-A	109	299	20	84	13	2	4	26	15	24	.281	.317	.378	112	3	0	0	0	.984	1	O-80/1-1	0.0
1969	Cle-A	43	108	9	27	5	0	1	15	8	15	.250	.308	.324	74	-4	1	0	0	.982	1	O-28	-0.4
	Was-A	71	238	41	69	9	3	9	26	20	25	.290	.345	.466	132	9	1	3	-2	.944	-6	O-65	-0.2
	Yr	114	346	50	96	14	3	10	41	28	40	.277	.333	.422	112	5	2	3	-1	.957	-5	O-93	-0.6
1970	Was-A	96	255	28	67	12	1	7	30	21	32	.263	.321	.400	103	0	4	2	0	1.000	-8	O-68/3-1	-1.1
	Chi-A	6	6	0	1	0	0	0	1	0	1	.167	.167	.167	-8	-1	0	0	0	.000	0	H	-0.1
	Yr	102	261	28	68	12	1	7	31	21	33	.261	.318	.395	100	-1	4	2	0	1.000	-8	O-68/3-1	-1.2
1971	Chi-A	32	44	6	9	2	0	1	7	5	7	.205	.286	.318	69	-2	0	0	0	1.000	-1	O-10	-0.3
Total	13	1288	4048	533	1109	190	39	94	419	282	481	.274	.324	.410	108	32	59	34	-3	.970	-31	*O-1040/3-6,12	-5.7

◼ ED MAYER
Mayer, Edward H. b: 8/16/1866, Marshall, Ill. d: 5/18/13, Chicago, Ill. 5'8.5", 155 lbs. Deb: 4/19/1890

YEAR	TM/L	G	AB	R	H	2B	3B	HR	RBI	BB	SO	AVG	OBP	SLG	PRO+	BR/A	SB	CS	SBR	FA	FR	G/POS	TPR
1890	Phi-N	117	484	49	117	25	5	1	70	22	36	.242	.286	.320	75	-17	20			.878	-4	*3-114/O-4	-1.5
1891	Phi-N	68	268	24	50	2	4	0	31	14	29	.187	.238	.224	34	-23	7			.895	-6	3-31,O-29/S2	-2.5
Total	2	185	752	73	167	27	9	1	101	36	65	.222	.269	.286	60	-40	27			.882	-10	3-145/O-33,S2	-4.0

◼ SAM MAYER
Mayer, Samuel Frankel (b: Samuel Frankel Erskine) b: 2/28/1893, Atlanta, Ga. d: 7/1/62, Atlanta, Ga. BR/TL, 5'10", 164 lbs. Deb: 9/14/15 F

YEAR	TM/L	G	AB	R	H	2B	3B	HR	RBI	BB	SO	AVG	OBP	SLG	PRO+	BR/A	SB	CS	SBR	FA	FR	G/POS	TPR
1915	Was-A	11	29	5	7	0	0	1	4	4	2	.241	.333	.345	101	0	1	2	-1	1.000	-0	/O-9,P-1,1	-0.1

◼ WALLY MAYER
Mayer, Walter A. b: 7/8/1890, Cincinnati, Ohio d: 11/18/51, Minneapolis, Minn. BR/TR, 5'11", 168 lbs. Deb: 9/28/11

YEAR	TM/L	G	AB	R	H	2B	3B	HR	RBI	BB	SO	AVG	OBP	SLG	PRO+	BR/A	SB	CS	SBR	FA	FR	G/POS	TPR
1911	Chi-A	1	3	0	0	0	0	0	0	0	0	.000	.400	.000	16	-0	0			.900	-1	/C-1	-0.1
1912	Chi-A	9	9	1	0	0	0	0	0	0	1	.000	.000	.000	-73	-2	0			1.000	-0	/C-6	-0.2
1914	Chi-A	40	85	7	14	3	1	0	5	14	23	.165	.290	.224	55	-4	1	1	-0	.968	5	C-33/3-1	0.3
1915	Chi-A	22	54	3	12	3	1	0	5	5	8	.222	.288	.315	78	-2	0	2	-1	.990	-1	C-20	-0.3
1917	Bos-A	4	12	2	2	0	0	0	0	5	2	.167	.412	.167	78	0	0			.964	2	/C-4	0.2
1918	Bos-A	26	49	7	11	4	0	0	5	7	7	.224	.321	.306	91	-0	0			.964	-1	C-23	0.0
1919	StL-A	30	62	2	14	4	1	0	5	6	11	.226	.314	.323	77	-2	0			.959	6	C-25	0.5
Total	7	132	274	22	53	14	4	0	20	42	51	.193	.303	.266	68	-10	1	3		.969	10	C-112/3-1	0.4

◼ PADDY MAYES
Mayes, Adair Bushyhead b: 3/17/1885, Locust Grove, Okla. d: 5/28/62, Fayetteville, Ark. BL/TR, 5'11", 160 lbs. Deb: 6/11/11

YEAR	TM/L	G	AB	R	H	2B	3B	HR	RBI	BB	SO	AVG	OBP	SLG	PRO+	BR/A	SB	CS	SBR	FA	FR	G/POS	TPR
1911	Phi-N	5	5	1	0	0	0	0	0	1	2	.000	.286	.000	-17	-1	0			1.000	-0	/O-2	-0.1

◼ BUSTER MAYNARD
Maynard, James Walter b: 3/25/13, Henderson, N.C. d: 9/7/77, Durham, N.C. BR/TR, 5'11", 170 lbs. Deb: 9/17/40

YEAR	TM/L	G	AB	R	H	2B	3B	HR	RBI	BB	SO	AVG	OBP	SLG	PRO+	BR/A	SB	CS	SBR	FA	FR	G/POS	TPR
1940	NY-N	7	29	6	8	2	2	1	2	2	6	.276	.323	.586	145	2				.929	-1	/O-7	0.0
1942	NY-N	89	190	17	47	4	1	4	32	19	19	.247	.319	.342	93	-2	3			.982	-0	O-58,3-10/2	-0.4
1943	NY-N	121	393	43	81	8	2	9	32	24	27	.206	.252	.305	60	-21	3			.965	-6	O-74,3-22	-3.4
1946	NY-N	7	4	2	0	0	0	0	0	1	1	.000	.200	.000	-41	-1				.750	-1	/O-3	-0.2
Total	4	224	616	68	136	14	5	14	66	46	53	.221	.276	.328	74	-22	6			.967	-8	O-142/3-32,2	-4.0

◼ CHICK MAYNARD
Maynard, Le Roy Evans b: 11/2/1896, Turners Falls, Mass. d: 1/31/57, Bangor, Maine BL/TR, 5'9", 150 lbs. Deb: 6/27/22

YEAR	TM/L	G	AB	R	H	2B	3B	HR	RBI	BB	SO	AVG	OBP	SLG	PRO+	BR/A	SB	CS	SBR	FA	FR	G/POS	TPR
1922	Bos-A	12	24	1	3	0	0	0	0	3	2	.125	.222	.125	-8	-4	0	1	-1	.872	-2	S-12	-0.6

◼ BRENT MAYNE
Mayne, Brent Danem b: 4/19/68, Loma Linda, Cal. BL/TR, 6'1", 195 lbs. Deb: 9/18/90

YEAR	TM/L	G	AB	R	H	2B	3B	HR	RBI	BB	SO	AVG	OBP	SLG	PRO+	BR/A	SB	CS	SBR	FA	FR	G/POS	TPR
1990	KC-A	5	13	2	3	0	0	0	1	3	3	.231	.375	.231	74	-0	0	1	-1	.970	1	/C-5	0.0
1991	KC-A	85	231	22	58	8	0	3	31	23	42	.251	.319	.325	78	-7	2	4	-2	.987	4	C-80/D-1	0.0
1992	KC-A	82	213	16	48	10	0	0	18	11	26	.225	.263	.272	49	-15	0	4	-2	.990	6	C-62/3-8,D	-1.2
1993	KC-A	71	205	22	52	9	1	2	22	18	31	.254	.317	.337	72	-8	3	2	-0	.995	6	C-68/D-1	0.1
1994	KC-A	46	144	19	37	5	1	2	20	14	27	.257	.323	.347	67	-7	1	0	0	.996	7	C-42/D-3	0.2
Total	5	289	806	81	198	32	2	7	92	69	129	.246	.306	.316	67	-36	6	11	-5	.991	20	C-257/3-8,D	-0.9

◼ EDDIE MAYO
Mayo, Edward Joseph "Hotshot" (b: Edward Joseph Mayoski) b: 4/15/10, Holyoke, Mass. BL/TR, 5'11", 178 lbs. Deb: 5/29/36 C

YEAR	TM/L	G	AB	R	H	2B	3B	HR	RBI	BB	SO	AVG	OBP	SLG	PRO+	BR/A	SB	CS	SBR	FA	FR	G/POS	TPR
1936	*NY-N	46	141	11	28	4	1	1	8	11	12	.199	.257	.262	40	-12	0			.981	5	3-40	-0.6
1937	Bos-N	65	172	19	39	6	1	1	18	15	20	.227	.293	.291	65	-9	1			.956	-4	3-50	-1.1
1938	Bos-N	8	14	2	3	0	0	1	4	1	0	.214	.267	.429	98	-0	0			.923	2	/3-6,S-2	0.1
1943	Phi-A	128	471	49	103	10	1	0	28	34	32	.219	.278	.244	54	-27	2	0	1	**.976**	-3	*3-123	-3.0
1944	Det-A	154	607	76	151	18	5	5	63	57	23	.249	.317	.313	76	-18	9	13	-5	.978	**29**	*2-143,S-11	1.6
1945	*Det-A†	134	501	71	143	24	3	10	54	47	29	.285	.347	.405	111	6	7	7	-2	**.980**	18	*2-124	3.1
1946	Det-A	51	202	21	51	9	2	0	22	14	12	.252	.301	.317	68	-9	1			.965	-11	2-49	-1.6
1947	Det-A	142	535	66	149	28	4	6	48	48	26	.279	.338	.379	96	-3	3	7	-3	.983	-23	*2-142	-2.1
1948	Det-A	106	370	35	92	20	1	2	42	30	19	.249	.310	.324	67	-18	1	9	-5	.975	-10	2-86,3-10	-2.7
Total	9	834	3013	350	759	119	16	26	287	257	175	.252	.313	.328	78	-89	29	38		.978	3	2-544,3-229/S	-6.3

YEAR	TM/L	G	AB	R	H	2B	3B	HR	RBI	BB	SO	AVG	OBP	SLG	PRO+	BR/A	SB	CS	SBR	FA	FR	G/POS	TPR

■ JACKIE MAYO   Mayo, John Lewis b: 7/26/25, Litchfield, Ill. BL/TR, 6'1", 190 lbs. Deb: 9/19/48

1948	Phi-N	12	35	7	8	2	1	0	3	7	7	.229	.386	.343	101	0	1			1.000	1	O-11	0.1
1949	Phi-N	45	39	3	5	0	0	0	2	4	5	.128	.209	.128	-8	-6	0			.889	-7	O-25	-1.3
1950	*Phi-N	18	36	1	8	3	0	0	3	2	5	.222	.263	.306	50	-3	0			.958	-3	O-15	-0.5
1951	Phi-N	9	7	1	1	0	0	0	0	0	0	.143	.143	.143	-23	-1	0	0	0	1.000	-2	/O-5	-0.3
1952	Phi-N	50	119	13	29	5	0	1	4	12	17	.244	.313	.311	74	-4	1	3	-2	1.000	4	O-27/1-6	-0.3
1953	Phi-N	5	4	0	0	0	0	0	0	0	1	.000	.000	.000	-99	-1	0	0	0	.000	-0	/O-1	-0.2
Total	6	139	240	25	51	10	1	1	12	25	35	.213	.292	.275	56	-15	2	3		.972	-7	/O-84,1-6	-2.5

■ WILLIE MAYS   Mays, Willie Howard "Say Hey" b: 5/6/31, Westfield, Ala. BR/TR, 5'11", 180 lbs. Deb: 5/25/51 CH

1951	*NY-N	121	464	59	127	22	5	20	68	57	60	.274	.356	.472	120	12	7	4	-0	.976	11	*O-121	1.9
1952	NY-N	34	127	17	30	2	4	4	23	16	17	.236	.326	.409	102	0	4	1	1	.991	8	O-34	0.7
1954	*NY-N★	151	565	119	195	33	**13**	41	110	66	57	**.345**	.415	**.667**	176	**61**	8	5	-1	.985	16	*O-151	**6.7**
1955	NY-N★	152	580	123	185	18	**13**	**51**	127	79	60	.319	.404	**.659**	176	**62**	24	4	5	.982	**20**	*O-152	**7.7**
1956	NY-N★	152	578	101	171	27	8	36	84	68	65	.296	.371	.557	146	37	**40**	10	6	.979	12	*O-152	4.7
1957	NY-N★	152	585	112	195	26	**20**	35	97	76	62	.333	.411	**.626**	174	**61**	38	19	0	.980	11	*O-150	6.3
1958	SF-N★	152	600	**121**	208	33	11	29	96	78	56	.347	.423	.583	167	58	31	6	6	.980	17	*O-151	7.2
1959	SF-N★	151	575	125	180	43	5	34	104	65	58	.313	.385	.583	157	45	27	4	6	.984	7	*O-147	5.0
1960	SF-N★	153	595	107	**190**	29	12	29	103	61	70	.319	.386	.555	164	51	25	10	2	.981	14	*O-152	5.9
1961	SF-N★	154	572	**129**	176	32	3	40	123	81	77	.308	.395	.584	162	50	18	9	0	.980	10	*O-153	5.0
1962	*SF-N★	162	621	130	189	36	5	**49**	141	78	85	.304	.385	.615	167	56	18	2	4	.991	14	*O-161	**6.4**
1963	SF-N★	157	596	115	187	32	7	38	103	66	83	.314	.384	.582	176	57	8	3	1	.981	13	*O-157/S-1	6.6
1964	SF-N★	157	578	121	171	21	9	**47**	111	82	72	.296	.384	**.607**	171	54	19	5	3	.984	14	*O-155/1-1,S3	6.5
1965	SF-N★	157	558	118	177	21	3	**52**	112	76	71	.317	**.399**	**.645**	184	**61**	9	4	0	.983	16	*O-151	**7.3**
1966	SF-N★	152	552	99	159	29	4	37	103	70	81	.288	.370	.556	149	36	5	1	1	.982	12	*O-150	4.3
1967	SF-N★	141	486	83	128	22	2	22	70	51	92	.263	.336	.453	125	15	6	0	2	.976	-2	*O-134	1.0
1968	SF-N★	148	498	84	144	20	5	23	79	67	81	.289	.376	.488	158	36	12	6	0	.978	0	*O-142/1-1	3.3
1969	SF-N★	117	403	64	114	17	3	13	58	49	71	.283	.365	.437	126	14	6	2	1	.976	-7	*O-108/1-1	0.2
1970	SF-N★	139	478	94	139	15	2	28	83	79	90	.291	.395	.506	141	29	5	0	2	.975	-2	*O-129/1-5	2.6
1971	*SF-N★	136	417	82	113	24	5	18	61	**112**	123	.271	**.429**	.482	160	39	23	3	5	.970	-2	O-84,1-48	3.6
1972	SF-N	19	49	8	9	2	0	0	3	17	5	.184	.394	.224	79	-0	3	0	1	1.000	-1	O-14	-0.1
	NY-N★	69	195	27	52	9	1	8	19	43	43	.267	.402	.446	144	13	1	5	-3	.974	-5	O-49,1-11	0.8
	Yr	88	244	35	61	11	1	8	22	60	48	.250	.400	.402	131	13	4	5	-2	.979	-5	O-63,1-11	0.7
1973	*NY-N★	66	209	24	44	10	0	6	25	27	47	.211	.304	.344	81	-6	1	0	0	.991	-5	O-45,1-17	-1.4
Total	22	2992	10881	2062	3283	523	140	660	1903	1464	1526	.302	.387	.557		844	338	103	40	.981	180	*O-2842/1-84,S3	92.2

■ BILL MAZEROSKI   Mazeroski, William Stanley "Maz" b: 9/5/36, Wheeling, W.Va. BR/TR, 5'11.5", 183 lbs. Deb: 7/7/56 C

1956	Pit-N	81	255	30	62	8	1	3	14	18	24	.243	.293	.318	66	-12	0	0	0	.981	11	2-81	0.5
1957	Pit-N	148	526	59	149	27	7	8	54	27	49	.283	.319	.407	96	-4	3	3	-1	.978	4	*2-144	1.1
1958	Pit-N★	152	567	69	156	24	6	19	68	25	71	.275	.309	.439	98	-4	1	1	-0	.980	19	*2-152	2.5
1959	Pit-N	135	493	50	119	15	6	7	59	29	54	.241	.285	.339	66	-25	1	3	-1	.981	-9	*2-133	-2.5
1960	*Pit-N★	151	538	58	147	21	5	11	64	40	50	.273	.325	.392	95	-4	4	0	1	**.989**	25	*2-151	3.8
1961	Pit-N	152	558	71	148	21	2	13	59	26	55	.265	.302	.380	79	-17	2	1	0	.975	31	*2-152	2.9
1962	Pit-N★	159	572	55	155	24	9	14	81	37	47	.271	.318	.418	95	-5	0	3	-2	.985	41	*2-159	5.0
1963	Pit-N†	142	534	43	131	22	3	8	52	32	46	.245	.288	.343	80	-14	2	0	1	.984	57	*2-138	6.0
1964	Pit-N☆	162	601	66	161	22	8	10	64	29	52	.268	.302	.381	91	-8	1	1	-0	.975	34	*2-162	4.1
1965	Pit-N	130	494	52	134	17	1	6	54	18	34	.271	.300	.346	81	-13	2	1	0	**.988**	26	*2-127	2.5
1966	Pit-N	162	621	56	163	22	7	16	82	31	62	.262	.299	.398	91	-8	4	3	-1	**.992**	41	*2-162	4.5
1967	Pit-N★	163	639	62	167	25	3	9	77	30	55	.261	.294	.352	84	-14	1	2	-1	.981	17	*2-163	1.4
1968	Pit-N	143	506	36	127	18	2	3	42	38	38	.251	.306	.312	87	-8	3	4	-2	.981	26	*2-142	2.8
1969	Pit-N	67	227	13	52	7	1	3	25	22	16	.229	.303	.308	73	-8	1	1	-0	.988	14	2-65	1.1
1970	*Pit-N	112	367	29	84	14	0	7	39	27	40	.229	.285	.324	64	-19	2	1	0	.987	24	*2-102	1.3
1971	*Pit-N	70	193	17	49	3	1	1	16	15	8	.254	.308	.295	72	-7	0	0	0	.986	-1	2-46/3-7	-0.5
1972	*Pit-N	34	64	3	12	4	0	0	3	3	5	.188	.224	.250	35	-6	0	0	0	.986	3	2-15/3-3	-0.2
Total	17	2163	7755	769	2016	294	62	138	853	447	706	.260	.302	.367		84	-176	27	23	-6	.983	362	*2-2094/3-10	36.3

■ MEL MAZZERA   Mazzera, Melvin Leonard "Mike" b: 1/31/14, Stockton, Cal. BL/TL, 5'11", 180 lbs. Deb: 9/9/35

1935	StL-A	12	30	4	7	2	0	1	2	4	9	.233	.324	.400	82	-1	0	0	0	.950	-1	O-10	-0.2
1937	StL-A	7	7	1	2	2	0	0	2	0	2	.286	.286	.571	110	0	0	0	0	.000	0	H	0.0
1938	StL-A	86	204	33	57	8	2	6	29	12	25	.279	.329	.426	88	-5	1	1	-0	.976	-1	O-47	-0.7
1939	StL-A	33	110	21	33	5	2	3	22	10	20	.300	.364	.464	108	1	0	0	0	.983	0	O-25	0.0
1940	Phi-A	69	156	16	37	5	4	0	13	19	15	.237	.320	.321	80	-4	1			.985	-4	O-42,1-11	-1.0
Total	5	207	507	75	136	22	8	10	66	45	71	.268	.333	.402	90	-8	2	1		.978	-6	O-124/1-11	-1.9

■ LEE MAZZILLI   Mazzilli, Lee Louis b: 3/25/55, New York, N.Y. BB/TR, 6'1", 185 lbs. Deb: 9/7/76

1976	NY-N	24	77	9	15	3	0	2	7	14	10	.195	.326	.299	83	-1	5	4	-1	.983	2	O-23	-0.1
1977	NY-N	159	537	66	134	24	3	6	46	72	72	.250	.342	.339	87	-8	22	15	-2	.992	11	*O-156	-0.5
1978	NY-N	148	542	78	148	28	5	16	61	69	82	.273	.356	.432	124	17	20	13	-2	.987	14	*O-144	2.4
1979	NY-N★	158	597	78	181	34	4	15	79	93	74	.303	.397	.449	135	32	34	12	3	.989	8	*O-143,1-15	3.7
1980	NY-N	152	578	82	162	31	4	16	76	82	92	.280	.373	.431	127	23	41	15	3	.983	1	1-92,O-66	2.0
1981	NY-N	95	324	36	74	14	5	6	34	46	53	.228	.328	.358	96	-1	17	7	1	.970	-4	O-89	-0.4
1982	Tex-A	58	195	23	47	8	0	4	17	28	26	.241	.339	.344	93	-1	11	6	-0	.945	-3	O-26,D-24	-0.6
	NY-A	37	128	20	34	2	0	6	17	15	15	.266	.347	.422	112	2	2	3	-1	.995	-3	1-23/O-2,D	-0.3
	Yr	95	323	43	81	10	0	10	34	43	41	.251	.342	.375	100	1	13	9	-2	.949	-6	D-33,O-28,1	-0.9
1983	Pit-N	109	246	37	59	9	0	5	24	49	43	.240	.370	.337	95	0	15	5	2	.985	0	O-57/1-7	0.0
1984	Pit-N	111	266	37	63	11	1	4	21	40	42	.237	.339	.331	89	-3	8	1	2	.989	-0	O-74/1-5	-1.1
1985	Pit-N	92	117	20	33	8	0	1	9	29	17	.282	.425	.376	127	6	4	1	1	.986	-1	1-19/O-5	0.5
1986	Pit-N	61	93	18	21	2	1	1	8	26	25	.226	.395	.301	93	4	1	1	0	1.000	-3	O-18/1-7	-0.4
	*NY-N	39	58	10	16	3	0	2	7	12	11	.276	.417	.431	138	4	3	1	-0	1.000	1	O-10/1-8	0.2
	Yr	100	151	28	37	5	1	3	15	38	36	.245	.403	.351	109	4	4	1	-1	.986	-4	O-28,1-15	-0.2
1987	NY-N	88	124	26	38	8	1	3	24	21	14	.306	.407	.460	136	7	3	0	-0	1.000	5	O-25,1-13	0.0
1988	*NY-N	68	116	9	17	2	0	0	12	16	16	.147	.233	.164	16	-12	4	1	-1	1.000	-4	O-18/1-16	-1.9
1989	NY-N	48	60	10	11	2	0	2	7	17	19	.183	.364	.317	101	1	3	0	1	.889	-0	O-10/1-8	-0.3
	*Tor-A	28	66	12	15	3	0	4	11	17	16	.227	.400	.455	143	5	2	0	1	.944	-1	D-19/1-2,O	0.4
Total	14	1475	4124	571	1068	191	24	93	460	642	627	.259	.361	.385		109	70	197	90	5	.986	4	O-868,1-215/D	3.6

■ JIMMY McALEER   McAleer, James Robert "Loafer" b: 7/10/1864, Youngstown, Ohio d: 4/29/31, Youngstown, Ohio BR/TR, 6', 175 lbs. Deb: 4/24/1889 M

1889	Cle-N	110	447	69	105	6	6	1	35	30	49	.235	.289	.282	76	-23	37			.955	-9	*O-110	-1.5
1890	Cle-P	86	341	58	91	8	7	1	42	37	33	.267	.340	.340	89	-4	21			.940	11	O-86	0.3
1891	Cle-N	136	565	97	134	16	11	1	61	49	47	.237	.304	.310	76	-19	51			.924	5	*O-136	-1.6
1892	*Cle-N	149	571	92	136	26	7	4	70	63	54	.238	.318	.329	92	-6	40			.948	12	*O-149	-0.1
1893	Cle-N	91	350	63	83	5	1	2	41	35	21	.237	.310	.277	65	-14	32			.928	4	O-91	-2.0
1894	Cle-N	64	253	36	73	15	1	2	40	13	11	.289	.331	.379	68	-14	14			.953	3	O-64	-1.2
1895	*Cle-N	131	528	84	143	17	2	0	68	38	37	.271	.327	.311	61	-31	32			.934	3	*O-131	-3.2

YEAR	TM/L	G	AB	R	H	2B	3B	HR	RBI	BB	SO	AVG	OBP	SLG	PRO+	BR/A	SB	CS	SBR	FA	FR	G/POS	TPR
1896	*Cle-N	116	455	70	131	16	4	1	54	47	32	.288	.361	.347	82	-11	24			.958	7	*O-116	-1.2
1897	Cle-N	24	91	6	20	2	0	0	10	7		.220	.283	.242	37	-8	4			.947	-1	O-24	-0.9
1898	Cle-N	106	366	47	87	3	0	0	48	46		.238	.331	.246	67	-13	7			.965	3	*O-104/2-2	-1.7
1901	Cle-A	3	7	0	1	0	0	0	0	0		.143	.143	.143	-22	-1	0			1.000	-1	/O-2,P-1,3M	-0.2
1902	StL-A	2	3	0	2	0	0	0	0	0		.667	.667	.667	274	1	0			.000	-1	/O-2,M	0.0
1907	StL-A	2	0	0	0	0	0	0	0	0		—	—	—			0			.000	0	RM	0.0
Total	13	1020	3977	619	1006	114	39	12	469	365	290	.253	.322	.310	72	-154	262			.944	54	*O-1015/2-2,3P	-13.3

■ JACK McALEESE
McAleese, John James b: 1877, Sharon, Pa. d: 11/15/50, New York, N.Y. BR/TR, 5'8", Deb: 8/10/01

YEAR	TM/L	G	AB	R	H	2B	3B	HR	RBI	BB	SO	AVG	OBP	SLG	PRO+	BR/A	SB	CS	SBR	FA	FR	G/POS	TPR
1901	Chi-A	1	1	0	0	0	0	0	0	0		.000	.000	.000	-99	-0	0			1.000	0	/P-1	0.0
1909	StL-A	85	267	33	57	7	0	0	12	32		.213	.318	.240	82	-3	18			.910	-3	O-79/3-2	-1.1
Total	2	86	268	33	57	7	0	0	12	32		.213	.317	.239	82	-4	18			.910	-3	/O-79,3-2,P	-1.1

■ BILL McALLESTER
McAllester, William Lusk b: 12/29/1888, Chattanooga, Tenn. d: 3/3/70, Chattanooga, Tenn. BR/TR, 5'11.5", 170 lbs. Deb: 5/2/13

YEAR	TM/L	G	AB	R	H	2B	3B	HR	RBI	BB	SO	AVG	OBP	SLG	PRO+	BR/A	SB	CS	SBR	FA	FR	G/POS	TPR
1913	StL-A	49	85	3	13	4	0	0	6	11	12	.153	.250	.200	33	-7	2			.908	-4	C-39	-0.9

■ SPORT McALLISTER
McAllister, Lewis William b: 7/23/1874, Austin, Miss. d: 7/17/62, Wyandotte, Mich. BB/TR, 5'11", 180 lbs. Deb: 8/7/1896

YEAR	TM/L	G	AB	R	H	2B	3B	HR	RBI	BB	SO	AVG	OBP	SLG	PRO+	BR/A	SB	CS	SBR	FA	FR	G/POS	TPR
1896	Cle-N	8	27	2	6	2	0	0	1	0	2	.222	.250	.296	41	-2	1			.500	-6	/O-4,C-2,P	-0.8
1897	Cle-N	43	137	23	30	5	1	0	11	12		.219	.287	.270	45	-11	3			.894	-6	O-28/S-4,P1C2	-1.6
1898	Cle-N	17	57	8	13	3	1	0	9	5		.228	.290	.316	75	-2	0			.941	1	/P-9,O-8	0.0
1899	Cle-N	113	418	29	99	6	8	1	31	19		.237	.273	.297	61	-23	5			.943	-15	O-79,C-17/31SP2	-3.8
1901	Det-A	90	306	45	92	9	4	3	57	15		.301	.344	.386	97	-2	17			.898	-19	C-35,1-28,O3/S	-1.6
1902	Det-A	21	67	8	14	1	0	1	8	2		.209	.243	.269	41	-5	0			1.000	-0	/1-5,S-5,2C3O	-0.5
	Bal-A	3	11	0	1	0	0	0	1	1		.091	.167	.091	-26	-2	0			.923	-1	/2-2,1-1	-0.2
	Det-A	45	162	11	34	4	2	0	24	3		.210	.229	.259	34	-14	1			.991	-1	1-21,O-11/C3S	-1.5
	Yr	69	240	19	49	5	2	1	33	6		.204	.230	.254	33	-22	1			.992	-1	1-27,O-12/CS32D	-2.2
1903	Det-A	78	265	31	69	8	2	0	22	10		.260	.297	.306	84	-5	5			.888	-7	S-46,C-18/O31	-0.9
Total	7	418	1450	157	358	38	18	5	164	67	2	.247	.287	.308	67	-68	32			.914	-55	O-147/C-83,1S3P2	-10.9

■ JIM McANANY
McAnany, James b: 9/4/36, Los Angeles, Cal. BR/TR, 5'10", 196 lbs. Deb: 9/19/58

YEAR	TM/L	G	AB	R	H	2B	3B	HR	RBI	BB	SO	AVG	OBP	SLG	PRO+	BR/A	SB	CS	SBR	FA	FR	G/POS	TPR
1958	Chi-A	5	13	0	0	0	0	0	0	0	5	.000	.000	.000	-99	-4	0	0	0	1.000	1	/O-3	-0.3
1959	*Chi-A	67	210	22	58	9	3	0	27	19	26	.276	.339	.348	90	-3	2	1	0	.966	-1	O-67	-0.6
1960	Chi-A	3	2	0	0	0	0	0	0	0	0	.000	.000	.000	-99	-1	0	0	0	.000	0	H	-0.1
1961	Chi-N	11	10	1	3	1	0	0	0	1	3	.300	.364	.400	101	-0	0	0	0	.000	-0	/O-1	0.0
1962	Chi-N	7	6	0	0	0	0	0	0	1	2	.000	.143	.000	-56	-1	0	0	0	.000	0	H	-0.1
Total	5	93	241	23	61	10	3	0	27	21	38	.253	.316	.320	75	-8	2	1	0	.968	-1	/O-71	-1.1

■ BUB McATEE
McAtee, Michael James "Butch" b: 3/1845, Troy, N.Y. d: 10/18/1876, Troy, N.Y. TR, 5'9", 160 lbs. Deb: 5/8/1871

YEAR	TM/L	G	AB	R	H	2B	3B	HR	RBI	BB	SO	AVG	OBP	SLG	PRO+	BR/A	SB	CS	SBR	FA	FR	G/POS	TPR
1871	Chi-n	26	135	34	37	8	2	0	10	5	2	.274	.300	.363	81	-5	5					*1-26	-0.3
1872	Tro-n	25	130	30	29	4	1	0	15	1	2	.223	.229	.269	52	-7						1-25	-0.5
Total	2 n	51	265	64	66	12	3	0	25	6	4	.249	.266	.317	68	-12						/1-51	-0.8

■ IKE McAULEY
McAuley, James Earl b: 8/19/1891, Wichita, Kan. d: 4/6/28, Des Moines, Iowa BR/TR, 5'9.5", 150 lbs. Deb: 9/10/14

YEAR	TM/L	G	AB	R	H	2B	3B	HR	RBI	BB	SO	AVG	OBP	SLG	PRO+	BR/A	SB	CS	SBR	FA	FR	G/POS	TPR
1914	Pit-N	15	24	3	3	0	0	0	0	0	8	.125	.125	.125	-27	-4	0			.900	1	/S-5,3-3,2	-0.3
1915	Pit-N	5	15	0	2	1	0	0	0	0	6	.133	.133	.200	0	-2	0			.917	-3	/S-5	-0.5
1916	Pit-N	4	8	1	2	0	0	0	1	0	1	.250	.250	.250	53	-0	0			.938	1	/S-4	-0.3
1917	StL-N	3	7	0	2	0	0	0	1	0	1	.286	.286	.286	78	-0	0			.833	-2	/S-3	-0.3
1925	Chi-N	37	125	10	35	7	2	0	11	11	12	.280	.343	.368	80	-2	1	0	0	.949	-8	S-37	-0.7
Total	5	64	179	14	44	8	2	0	13	11	28	.246	.293	.313	62	-10	1	0	0	.940	-12	/S-54,3-3,2	-1.8

■ GENE McAULIFFE
McAuliffe, Eugene Leo b: 2/28/1872, Randolph, Mass. d: 4/29/53, Randolph, Mass. BR/TR, 6'1", 180 lbs. Deb: 8/17/04

YEAR	TM/L	G	AB	R	H	2B	3B	HR	RBI	BB	SO	AVG	OBP	SLG	PRO+	BR/A	SB	CS	SBR	FA	FR	G/POS	TPR
1904	Bos-N	1	2	0	1	0	0	0	0	0		.500	.500	.500	217	-0				.667	-0	/C-1	0.0

■ DICK McAULIFFE
McAuliffe, Richard John b: 11/29/39, Hartford, Conn. BL/TR, 5'11", 176 lbs. Deb: 9/17/60

YEAR	TM/L	G	AB	R	H	2B	3B	HR	RBI	BB	SO	AVG	OBP	SLG	PRO+	BR/A	SB	CS	SBR	FA	FR	G/POS	TPR
1960	Det-A	8	27	2	7	0	1	0	1	2	6	.259	.310	.333	72	-1	0	0	0	.884	1	/S-7	0.1
1961	Det-A	80	285	36	73	12	4	6	33	24	39	.256	.323	.389	87	-6	2	3	-1	.933	-29	S-55,3-22	-3.1
1962	Det-A	139	471	50	124	20	5	12	63	64	76	.263	.351	.403	99	0	4	2	0	.965	-21	2-70,3-49,S	-1.2
1963	Det-A	150	568	77	149	18	6	13	61	64	75	.262	.337	.384	98	-1	11	5	0	.963	-24	*S-133,2-15	-1.4
1964	Det-A	162	557	85	134	18	7	24	66	77	96	.241	.336	.427	109	7	8	5	-1	.958	-8	*S-160	1.1
1965	*Det-A★	113	404	61	105	13	6	15	54	49	62	.260	.343	.433	118	10	6	9	-4	.956	-15	*S-112	-0.2
1966	Det-A★	124	430	83	118	16	8	23	56	66	80	.274	.375	.509	148	28	5	7	-3	.964	-11	*S-105,3-15	2.5
1967	Det-A★	153	557	92	133	16	7	22	65	105	118	.239	.366	.411	126	21	6	5	-1	.965	-14	*2-145,S-43	1.9
1968	*Det-A	151	570	95	142	24	10	16	56	82	99	.249	.346	.411	125	18	8	7	-2	.986	-20	*2-148/S-5	0.7
1969	Det-A	74	271	49	71	10	5	11	33	47	41	.262	.371	.458	125	10	2	5	-2	.976	-0	2-72	1.4
1970	Det-A	146	530	73	124	21	1	12	50	101	62	.234	.360	.345	95	-0	5	6	-2	.975	-6	*2-127,S-15,3	0.4
1971	Det-A	128	477	67	99	16	6	18	57	53	67	.208	.293	.379	86	-10	4	1	1	.987	7	*2-123/S-7	0.9
1972	*Det-A	122	408	47	98	16	3	8	30	59	59	.240	.339	.353	103	3	0	3	-3	.975	-7	*2-116/S-3,3	0.2
1973	Det-A	106	343	39	94	18	1	12	47	49	52	.274	.366	.437	118	9	0	4	-2	.986	5	*2-102/S-2,D	1.7
1974	Bos-A	100	272	32	57	13	1	5	24	39	40	.210	.311	.320	76	-8	2	0	1	.971	-4	2-53,3-40/SD	-1.4
1975	Bos-A	7	15	0	2	0	0	0	1	1	2	.133	.188	.133	-7	-2	0	0	0	.769	-2	/3-7	-0.4
Total	16	1763	6185	888	1530	231	71	197	697	882	974	.247	.344	.403	108	78	63	59	-17	.977	-150	2-971,S-666,3/D	3.2

■ GEORGE McAVOY
McAvoy, George H. Deb: 7/17/14

YEAR	TM/L	G	AB	R	H	2B	3B	HR	RBI	BB	SO	AVG	OBP	SLG	PRO+	BR/A	SB	CS	SBR	FA	FR	G/POS	TPR
1914	Phi-N	1	1	0	0	0	0	0	0	0	0	.000	.000	.000	-94	-0	0			.000	0	H	0.0

■ WICKEY McAVOY
McAvoy, James Eugene b: 10/22/1894, Rochester, N.Y. d: 7/6/73, Rochester, N.Y. BR/TR, 5'11", 172 lbs. Deb: 9/29/13

YEAR	TM/L	G	AB	R	H	2B	3B	HR	RBI	BB	SO	AVG	OBP	SLG	PRO+	BR/A	SB	CS	SBR	FA	FR	G/POS	TPR
1913	Phi-A	4	9	0	1	0	0	0	0	0	4	.111	.200	.111	-9	-1	0			1.000	1	/C-4	0.0
1914	Phi-A	8	16	1	2	0	1	0	0	0		.125	.125	.250	13	-2	0			.971	1	/C-8	-0.1
1915	Phi-A	68	184	12	35	7	2	0	6	11	32	.190	.236	.250	47	-13	0	2	-1	.931	5	C-64	-0.5
1917	Phi-A	10	24	1	6	3	0	0	4	0	3	.250	.250	.417	105	-0	0			.955	3	/C-8	0.4
1918	Phi-A	83	271	14	66	5	3	0	32	13	23	.244	.283	.284	70	-10	5			.960	5	C-74/P-1,1O	0.1
1919	Phi-A	62	170	10	24	3	0	1	11	14	21	.141	.207	.194	13	-20	1			.973	-1	C-57	-1.9
Total	6	235	674	38	134	18	8	1	53	38	87	.199	.245	.254	47	-46	6	2		.954	13	C-215/O-1,1P	-2.0

■ ALGIE McBRIDE
McBride, Algernon Griggs b: 5/23/1869, Washington, D.C. d: 1/10/56, Georgetown, Ohio BL/TL, 5'9", 152 lbs. Deb: 5/12/1896

YEAR	TM/L	G	AB	R	H	2B	3B	HR	RBI	BB	SO	AVG	OBP	SLG	PRO+	BR/A	SB	CS	SBR	FA	FR	G/POS	TPR
1896	Chi-N	9	29	2	7	1	1	1	7	7	3	.241	.389	.448	116	1	0			.917	0	/O-9	0.0
1898	Cin-N	120	486	94	147	14	12	2	43	51		.302	.383	.393	114	9	16			.959	7	*O-120	0.8
1899	Cin-N	64	251	57	87	12	5	1	23	30		.347	.431	.446	138	15	5			.950	-2	O-64	0.7
1900	Cin-N	112	436	59	120	15	8	4	59	25		.275	.320	.374	94	-5	12			.915	-9	*O-110	-2.0
1901	Cin-N	30	123	19	29	7	0	2	18	7		.236	.282	.341	86	-3	0			.968	-2	O-28	-0.7
	NY-N	68	264	27	74	11	3	2	29	12		.280	.317	.383	95	-2	3			.948	-4	O-65	-1.0
	Yr	98	387	46	103	18	3	4	47	19		.266	.306	.344	92	-4	3			.956	-6	O-93	-1.7
Total	5	403	1589	258	464	60	26	12	179	132	3	.292	.356	.385	108	15	36			.946	-10	O-396	-2.2

■ BAKE McBRIDE
McBride, Arnold Ray b: 2/3/49, Fulton, Mo. BL/TR, 6'2", 190 lbs. Deb: 7/26/73

YEAR	TM/L	G	AB	R	H	2B	3B	HR	RBI	BB	SO	AVG	OBP	SLG	PRO+	BR/A	SB	CS	SBR	FA	FR	G/POS	TPR
1973	StL-N	40	63	8	19	3	0	0	5	4	10	.302	.362	.349	98	0	0	1	-1	.976	1	O-17	-0.1

YEAR	TM/L	G	AB	R	H	2B	3B	HR	RBI	BB	SO	AVG	OBP	SLG	PRO+	BR/A	SB	CS	SBR	FA	FR	G/POS	TPR
1974	StL-N	150	559	81	173	19	5	6	56	43	57	.309	.372	.394	115	12	30	11	2	.990	14	*O-144	2.3
1975	StL-N	116	413	70	124	10	9	5	36	34	52	.300	.355	.404	107	4	26	8	3	.990	7	*O-107	1.0
1976	StL-N☆	72	272	40	91	13	4	3	24	18	28	.335	.389	.445	135	12	10	5	0	.981	9	O-66	2.0
1977	StL-N	43	122	21	32	5	1	4	20	7	19	.262	.302	.418	93	-2	9	3	1	1.000	-5	O-33	-0.7
	*Phi-N	85	280	55	95	20	5	11	41	25	25	.339	.399	.564	149	19	27	4	6	.986	1	O-73	2.2
	Yr	128	402	76	127	25	6	15	61	32	44	.316	.371	.520	133	18	36	7	7	.990	-4	*O-106	1.5
1978	*Phi-N	122	472	68	127	20	4	10	49	28	68	.269	.317	.392	96	-3	28	3	7	**.996**	1	*O-119	0.3
1979	Phi-N	151	582	82	163	16	12	12	60	41	77	.280	.332	.411	98	-2	25	14	-1	.989	15	*O-147	0.6
1980	*Phi-N	137	554	68	171	33	10	9	87	26	58	.309	.345	.453	115	10	13	10	-2	.990	6	*O-133	0.9
1981	*Phi-N	58	221	26	60	17	1	2	21	11	25	.271	.306	.385	91	-3	5	0	2	.987	-4	O-56	-0.8
1982	Cle-A	27	85	8	31	3	3	0	13	2	12	.365	.379	.471	132	4	2	2	-1	1.000	-2	O-22	0.0
1983	Cle-A	70	230	21	67	8	1	1	18	9	26	.291	.321	.348	81	-6	8	2	1	.977	0	O-46,D-15	-0.7
Total	11	1071	3853	548	1153	167	55	63	430	248	457	.299	.348	.420	109	45	183	63	17	.989	46	O-963/D-15	7.0

■ GEORGE McBRIDE
McBride, George Florian b: 11/20/1880, Milwaukee, Wis. d: 7/2/73, Milwaukee, Wis. BR/TR, 5'11", 170 lbs. Deb: 9/12/01 MC

YEAR	TM/L	G	AB	R	H	2B	3B	HR	RBI	BB	SO	AVG	OBP	SLG	PRO+	BR/A	SB	CS	SBR	FA	FR	G/POS	TPR
1901	Mil-A	3	12	0	2	0	0	0	0	1		.167	.231	.167	12	-1	0			1.000	-1	/S-3	-0.2
1905	Pit-N	27	87	9	19	4	0	0	7	6		.218	.277	.264	60	-4	2			.902	4	3-17/S-8	-0.8
	StL-N	81	281	22	61	1	2	2	34	14		.217	.264	.256	57	-15	10			.938	-2	S-80/1-1	-1.6
	Yr	108	368	31	80	5	2	2	41	20		.217	.267	.258	58	-19	12			.935	-6	S-88,3-17/1	-2.4
1906	StL-N	90	313	24	53	8	2	0	13	17		.169	.215	.208	33	-25	5			.944	9	S-90	-1.5
1908	Was-A	155	518	47	120	10	6	0	34	41		.232	.292	.274	92	-4	12			.948	33	*S-155	3.5
1909	Was-A	156	504	38	118	16	0	0	34	36		.234	.294	.266	81	-10	17			**.935**	11	*S-156	0.4
1910	Was-A	154	514	54	118	19	4	1	55	61		.230	.321	.288	95	-1	11			.939	27	*S-154	3.5
1911	Was-A	154	557	58	131	11	4	0	59	52		.235	.312	.269	64	-26	15			.941	24	*S-154	0.8
1912	Was-A	152	521	56	118	13	7	1	52	38		.226	.288	.284	63	-25	17			**.941**	31	*S-152	1.9
1913	Was-A	150	499	52	107	18	7	1	52	43	46	.214	.286	.285	66	-22	12			**.960**	11	*S-150	0.4
1914	Was-A	156	503	49	102	12	4	0	24	43	70	.203	.274	.243	53	-28	12	14	-5	**.958**	12	*S-156	-0.9
1915	Was-A	146	476	54	97	8	6	1	30	29	60	.204	.251	.252	50	-31	10	5	0	**.968**	9	*S-146	-1.1
1916	Was-A	139	466	36	106	15	4	1	36	23	58	.227	.271	.283	67	-20	8			.957	13	*S-139	0.1
1917	Was-A	50	141	6	27	3	0	0	9	10	17	.191	.265	.213	46	-9	1			.943	-1	S-41/3-6,2	-0.9
1918	Was-A	18	53	2	7	0	0	0	1	0	11	.132	.132	.132	-21	-8	1			.986	1	S-14/2-2	-0.6
1919	Was-A	15	40	3	8	1	1	0	4	3	6	.200	.256	.275	49	-3	0			.932	1	S-15	-0.2
1920	Was-A	13	41	6	9	1	0	0	3	2	3	.220	.256	.244	34	-4	0			.966	-3	S-13	-0.6
Total	16	1659	5526	516	1203	140	47	7	447	419	271	.218	.281	.264	65	-236	133	19		.948	170	*S-1626/3-23,21	2.2

■ JOHN McBRIDE
McBride, John F. Deb: 10/12/1890

YEAR	TM/L	G	AB	R	H	2B	3B	HR	RBI	BB	SO	AVG	OBP	SLG	PRO+	BR/A	SB	CS	SBR	FA	FR	G/POS	TPR
1890	Phi-a	1	2	0	0	0	0	0	0	0		.000	.000	.000	-99	-1	0			1.000	1	/O-1	0.0

■ TOM McBRIDE
McBride, Thomas Raymond b: 11/2/14, Bonham, Tex. BR/TR, 6', 190 lbs. Deb: 4/23/43

YEAR	TM/L	G	AB	R	H	2B	3B	HR	RBI	BB	SO	AVG	OBP	SLG	PRO+	BR/A	SB	CS	SBR	FA	FR	G/POS	TPR
1943	Bos-A	26	96	11	23	3	1	0	7	7	3	.240	.291	.292	70	-4	2	0	1	.984	0	O-24	-0.5
1944	Bos-A	71	216	29	53	7	3	0	24	8	13	.245	.276	.306	67	-10	4	0	1	.992	-1	O-57/1-5	-1.2
1945	Bos-A	100	344	38	105	11	7	1	47	26	17	.305	.354	.387	112	5	2	2	-1	.984	-0	O-81,1-11	-0.1
1946	*Bos-A	61	153	21	46	5	2	0	19	9	6	.301	.340	.359	90	-2	0	1	-1	1.000	-7	O-43	-1.2
1947	Bos-A	2	5	0	1	0	0	0	0	0	0	.200	.200	.200	11	-1	0	0	0	1.000	1	/O-1	0.0
	Was-A	56	166	19	45	4	2	0	15	15	9	.271	.331	.319	84	-4	3	1	0	.972	-4	O-51/3-1	-1.0
	Yr	58	171	19	46	4	2	0	15	15	9	.269	.328	.316	81	-4	3	1	0	.973	-3	O-52/3-1	-1.0
1948	Was-A	92	206	22	53	9	1	1	29	28	15	.257	.346	.325	81	-5	2	2	-1	.983	2	O-55	-0.6
Total	6	408	1186	140	326	39	16	2	141	93	63	.275	.328	.340	88	-20	13	6	0	.985	-9	O-312/1-16,3	-4.6

■ SWAT McCABE
McCabe, James Arthur b: 11/20/1881, Towanda, Pa. d: 12/9/44, Bristol, Conn. BL/TR, 5'10", Deb: 9/23/09

YEAR	TM/L	G	AB	R	H	2B	3B	HR	RBI	BB	SO	AVG	OBP	SLG	PRO+	BR/A	SB	CS	SBR	FA	FR	G/POS	TPR
1909	Cin-N	3	11	2	6	1	0	0	0	0		.545	.545	.636	269	2	1			.625	-1	/O-3	0.1
1910	Cin-N	13	35	3	9	1	0	0	5	1	2	.257	.297	.286	73	-1	0			1.000	1	/O-9	-0.1
Total	2	16	46	5	15	2	0	0	5	1	2	.326	.354	.370	118	1	1			.875	-1	/O-12	0.0

■ JOE McCABE
McCabe, Joseph Robert b: 8/27/38, Indianapolis, Ind. BR/TR, 6', 190 lbs. Deb: 4/18/64

YEAR	TM/L	G	AB	R	H	2B	3B	HR	RBI	BB	SO	AVG	OBP	SLG	PRO+	BR/A	SB	CS	SBR	FA	FR	G/POS	TPR
1964	Min-A	14	19	1	3	0	0	0	2	0	8	.158	.158	.158	-12	-2	0	0	0	1.000	0	C-12	-0.2
1965	Was-A	14	27	1	5	0	0	1	5	4	13	.185	.290	.296	68	-1	1	0	0	.972	-3	C-11	-0.3
Total	2	28	46	2	8	0	0	1	7	4	21	.174	.240	.239	36	-4	1	0	0	.986	-2	/C-23	-0.5

■ BILL McCABE
McCabe, William Francis b: 10/28/1892, Chicago, Ill. d: 9/2/66, Chicago, Ill. BB/TR, 5'9.5", 180 lbs. Deb: 4/16/18

YEAR	TM/L	G	AB	R	H	2B	3B	HR	RBI	BB	SO	AVG	OBP	SLG	PRO+	BR/A	SB	CS	SBR	FA	FR	G/POS	TPR
1918	*Chi-N	29	45	9	8	0	1	0	5	4	7	.178	.245	.222	42	-3	2			.939	5	2-13/O-4	0.3
1919	Chi-N	33	84	8	13	3	1	0	5	9	15	.155	.253	.214	41	-6	3			.950	-1	O-20/S-4,3	-0.9
1920	Chi-N	3	2	1	1	0	0	0	0	0	0	.500	.500	.500	184	0	0	0	0	.000	0	H	
	*Bro-N	41	68	10	10	0	0	0	3	2	6	.147	.171	.147	-8	-9	1	2	-1	.882	4	S-13/O-6,23	-0.7
	Yr	44	70	11	11	0	0	0	3	2	6	.157	.181	.157	-2	-9	1	2	-1	.882	4	S-13/O-6,23	-0.7
Total	3	106	199	28	32	3	2	0	13	15	28	.161	.227	.196	26	-18	6	2		.943	8	/O-30,S-17,23	-1.3

■ HARRY McCAFFERY
McCaffery, Harry Charles b: 11/25/1858, St.Louis, Mo. d: 4/19/28, St.Louis, Mo. BR/TR, 5'10.5", 185 lbs. Deb: 6/15/1882 U

YEAR	TM/L	G	AB	R	H	2B	3B	HR	RBI	BB	SO	AVG	OBP	SLG	PRO+	BR/A	SB	CS	SBR	FA	FR	G/POS	TPR
1882	Lou-a	1	4	1	1	0	0	0		0		.250	.250	.250	73	-0				1.000	0	/2-1	-0.1
	StL-a	38	153	23	42	8	6	0		3		.275	.288	.405	127	4				.891	4	O-23/2-8,31	0.7
	Yr	39	157	24	43	8	6	0		3		.274	.287	.401	125	4				.891	3	O-23/2-9,31	0.6
1883	StL-a	5	18	0	1	0	0	0		1		.056	.105	.056	-44	-3				.889	1	/O-5	-0.2
1885	Cin-a	1	5	0	0	0	0	0		0		.000	.000	.000	-98	-1				.000	-0	/P-1	0.0
Total	3	45	180	24	44	8	6	0		4		.244	.261	.356	101	-0				.891	4	/O-28,2-9,3P1	0.4

■ SPARROW McCAFFREY
McCaffrey, Charles P. b: 1868, Philadelphia, Pa. d: 4/29/1894, Philadelphia, Pa. 120 lbs. Deb: 8/13/1889

YEAR	TM/L	G	AB	R	H	2B	3B	HR	RBI	BB	SO	AVG	OBP	SLG	PRO+	BR/A	SB	CS	SBR	FA	FR	G/POS	TPR
1889	Col-a	2	1	1	1	0	0	0	0	1	0	1.000	1.000	1.000	495	1	0			.000	0	/C-2	0.1

■ BRIAN McCALL
McCall, Brian Allen "Bam" b: 1/25/43, Kentfield, Cal. BL/TL, 5'10", 170 lbs. Deb: 9/18/62

YEAR	TM/L	G	AB	R	H	2B	3B	HR	RBI	BB	SO	AVG	OBP	SLG	PRO+	BR/A	SB	CS	SBR	FA	FR	G/POS	TPR
1962	Chi-A	4	8	2	3	0	0	2	3	0	2	.375	.375	1.125	287	2	0	0	0	1.000	0	/O-1	0.2
1963	Chi-A	3	7	1	0	0	0	0	0	1	2	.000	.125	.000	-62	-2	0	0	0	1.000	-0	/O-2	-0.2
Total	2	7	15	3	3	0	0	2	3	1	4	.200	.250	.600	126	0	0	0	0	1.000	-0	/O-3	-0.0

■ JACK McCANDLESS
McCandless, Scott Cook b: 5/5/1891, Pittsburgh, Pa. d: 8/17/61, Pittsburgh, Pa. BL/TR, 6', 170 lbs. Deb: 9/10/14

YEAR	TM/L	G	AB	R	H	2B	3B	HR	RBI	BB	SO	AVG	OBP	SLG	PRO+	BR/A	SB	CS	SBR	FA	FR	G/POS	TPR
1914	Bal-F	11	31	5	8	1	0	0	3	0		.258	.343	.323	71	-1	0			1.000	-0	/O-8	-0.2
1915	Bal-F	117	406	47	87	6	7	5	34	41	99	.214	.296	.300	58	-24	9			.945	3	*O-105	-2.9
Total	2	128	437	52	95	6	8	5	35	44	99	.217	.299	.302	59	-26	9			.948	3	O-113	-3.1

■ EMMETT McCANN
McCann, Robert Emmett b: 3/4/02, Philadelphia, Pa. d: 4/15/37, Philadelphia, Pa. BR/TR, 5'11", 150 lbs. Deb: 4/19/20

YEAR	TM/L	G	AB	R	H	2B	3B	HR	RBI	BB	SO	AVG	OBP	SLG	PRO+	BR/A	SB	CS	SBR	FA	FR	G/POS	TPR
1920	Phi-A	13	34	4	9	1	1	0	2	3	1	.265	.342	.353	84	-1	0			.907	-0	S-11	-0.1
1921	Phi-A	52	157	15	35	5	0	0	15	4	6	.223	.242	.255	27	-17	2	1	0	.949	0	S-32/3-9,21	-1.4
1926	Bos-A	6	3	0	0	0	0	0	0	1	1	.000	.250	.000	-32	-1	0			1.000	-0	/S-1,3-1	-0.1
Total	3	71	194	19	44	6	1	0	18	8	8	.227	.261	.268	36	-19	2	1		.939	-1	/S-44,3-10,21	-1.6

■ ROGER McCARDELL
McCardell, Roger Morton b: 8/29/32, Gorsuch Mills, Md. BR/TR, 6', 200 lbs. Deb: 5/8/59

YEAR	TM/L	G	AB	R	H	2B	3B	HR	RBI	BB	SO	AVG	OBP	SLG	PRO+	BR/A	SB	CS	SBR	FA	FR	G/POS	TPR
1959	SF-N	4	4	0	0	0	0	0	0	0	0	.000	.000	.000	-99	-1	0	0	0	1.000	0	/C-3	-0.1

■ BILL McCARREN
McCarren, William Joseph   b: 11/4/1895, Fortenia, Pa.   d: 9/11/83, Denver, Colo.   BR/TR, 5'11.5", 170 lbs.   Deb: 5/4/23

YEAR	TM/L	G	AB	R	H	2B	3B	HR	RBI	BB	SO	AVG	OBP	SLG	PRO+	BR/A	SB	CS	SBR	FA	FR	G/POS	TPR
1923	Bro-N	69	216	28	53	10	1	3	27	22	39	.245	.326	.343	79	-6	0	1	-1	.927	-2	3-66/O-1	-0.3

■ ALEX McCARTHY
McCarthy, Alexander George   b: 5/12/1888, Chicago, Ill.   d: 3/12/78, Salisbury, Md.   BR/TR, 5'9", 150 lbs.   Deb: 10/7/10

YEAR	TM/L	G	AB	R	H	2B	3B	HR	RBI	BB	SO	AVG	OBP	SLG	PRO+	BR/A	SB	CS	SBR	FA	FR	G/POS	TPR
1910	Pit-N	3	12	1	1	0	1	0	0	0	2	.083	.083	.250	-3	-2	0			.875	0	/S-3	-0.2
1911	Pit-N	50	150	18	36	5	1	2	31	14	24	.240	.305	.327	74	-6	4			.981	-1	S-33,2-11/3O	-0.4
1912	Pit-N	111	401	53	111	12	4	1	41	30	26	.277	.332	.334	84	-9	8			.962	3	*2-105/3-4	-0.8
1913	Pit-N	31	74	7	15	5	0	0	10	7	7	.203	.298	.270	66	-3	1			.902	-2	S-12,3-12/2	-0.5
1914	Pit-N	57	173	14	26	0	1	1	14	6	17	.150	.192	.179	11	-19	2			.975	11	3-36,2-10/S	-0.7
1915	Pit-N	21	49	3	10	0	1	0	3	5	10	.204	.291	.245	64	-2	1	2	-1	.950	1	/2-9,S-5,31	-0.2
	Chi-N	23	72	4	19	3	0	1	6	5	7	.264	.329	.347	105	0	2	3	-1	.972	11	2-12,3-12/S	1.2
	Yr	44	121	7	29	3	1	1	9	10	17	.240	.313	.306	88	-1	3	5	-2	.964	12	2-21,3-16/S1	1.0
1916	Chi-N	37	107	10	26	2	3	0	6	11	7	.243	.341	.318	93	-0	1			.931	-2	2-34/S-3	-0.2
	Pit-N	50	146	11	29	3	0	0	3	15	10	.199	.282	.219	54	-7	3			.955	-5	S-39/2-7,3	-1.2
	Yr	87	253	21	55	5	3	0	9	26	17	.217	.308	.261	72	-7	4			.951	-7	S-42,2-41/3	-1.4
1917	Pit-N	49	151	15	33	4	0	0	8	11	13	.219	.276	.245	58	-7	1			.964	7	3-26,2-13/S	0.1
Total	8	432	1335	136	306	34	11	5	122	104	123	.229	.295	.282	67	-55	23	5		.957	23	2-207,S-111,3/10	-2.9

■ JERRY McCARTHY
McCarthy, Jerome Francis   b: 5/23/23, Brooklyn, N.Y.   d: 10/3/65, Oceanside, N.Y.   BL/TL, 6'1", 205 lbs.   Deb: 6/19/48

YEAR	TM/L	G	AB	R	H	2B	3B	HR	RBI	BB	SO	AVG	OBP	SLG	PRO+	BR/A	SB	CS	SBR	FA	FR	G/POS	TPR
1948	StL-A	2	3	0	1	0	0	0	0	0	0	.333	.333	.333	76	-0	0	0	0	.600	-1	/1-2	-0.1

■ JACK McCARTHY
McCarthy, John Arthur   b: 3/26/1869, Gilbertville, Mass   d: 9/11/31, Chicago, Ill.   BL/TL, 5'9", 155 lbs.   Deb: 8/3/1893

YEAR	TM/L	G	AB	R	H	2B	3B	HR	RBI	BB	SO	AVG	OBP	SLG	PRO+	BR/A	SB	CS	SBR	FA	FR	G/POS	TPR
1893	Cin-N	49	195	28	55	8	3	0	22	22	7	.282	.355	.354	86	-4	6			.887	-1	O-47/1-2	-0.6
1894	Cin-N	40	167	29	45	9	1	0	21	17	6	.269	.348	.335	63	-10	3			.895	2	O-25,1-15	-0.8
1898	Pit-N	137	537	75	155	13	12	4	78	34		.289	.336	.380	107	4	7			.935	4	*O-137	-0.3
1899	Pit-N	138	560	108	171	22	17	3	67	39		.305	.355	.421	113	8	28			.961	-5	*O-138	-0.7
1900	Chi-N	124	503	68	148	16	7	0	48	24		.294	.329	.354	92	-6	22			.944	-1	*O-123	-1.5
1901	Cle-A	86	343	60	110	14	7	0	32	30		.321	.382	.402	123	12	9			.949	-1	O-86	0.4
1902	Cle-A	95	359	45	102	31	5	0	41	24		.284	.329	.398	105	2	12			.944	-5	O-95	-0.9
1903	Cle-A	108	415	47	110	20	8	0	43	19		.265	.299	.352	96	-2	15			.964	-3	*O-108	-1.3
	Chi-N	24	101	11	28	5	0	0	14	4		.277	.305	.327	82	-3	8			.947	-3	O-24	-0.7
1904	Chi-N	115	432	36	114	14	2	0	51	23		.264	.307	.306	89	-6	14			.961	-5	*O-115	-1.8
1905	Chi-N	59	170	16	47	4	3	0	14	10		.276	.320	.335	92	-2	8			.986	2	O-37/1-6	-0.2
1906	Bro-N	91	322	23	98	13	1	0	35	20		.304	.347	.351	128	9	9			.924	3	O-86	0.8
1907	Bro-N	25	91	4	20	2	0	0	8	2		.220	.237	.242	54	-5	4			1.000	-4	O-25	-1.2
Total	12	1091	4195	550	1203	171	66	7	474	268	13	.287	.333	.364	100	-3	145			.946	-17	*O-1046/1-23	-8.8

■ JOHNNY McCARTHY
McCarthy, John Joseph   b: 1/7/10, Chicago, Ill.   d: 9/13/73, Mundelein, Ill.   BL/TL, 6'1.5", 185 lbs.   Deb: 9/2/34

YEAR	TM/L	G	AB	R	H	2B	3B	HR	RBI	BB	SO	AVG	OBP	SLG	PRO+	BR/A	SB	CS	SBR	FA	FR	G/POS	TPR
1934	Bro-N	17	39	7	7	2	0	1	5	2	2	.179	.220	.308	42	-3	0			.961	1	1-13	-0.3
1935	Bro-N	22	48	9	12	1	1	0	4	2	9	.250	.280	.313	60	-3	1			.982	-1	1-19	-0.7
1936	NY-N	4	16	1	7	0	0	1	2	0	1	.438	.438	.625	185	2	1			.981	1	/1-4	0.3
1937	*NY-N	114	420	53	117	19	3	10	65	24	37	.279	.322	.410	96	-3	2			.987	2	*1-110	-1.3
1938	NY-N	134	470	55	128	13	4	8	59	39	28	.272	.329	.368	91	-6	3			.993	-3	*1-125	-2.4
1939	NY-N	50	80	12	21	6	1	1	11	3	8	.262	.298	.400	85	-2	0			1.000	-4	1-12/O-4,P	-0.7
1940	NY-N	51	67	6	16	4	0	0	5	2	8	.239	.261	.299	53	-4	0			1.000	1	/1-6	-0.4
1941	NY-N	14	40	1	13	3	0	0	12	3	0	.325	.372	.400	115	1	0			.987	0	/1-8,O-1	0.1
1943	Bos-N	78	313	32	95	24	6	2	33	10	19	.304	.327	.438	122	7	1			.996	1	1-78	0.3
1946	Bos-N	2	7	0	1	0	0	0	1	2	0	.143	.333	.143	37	-0	0			1.000	-1	/1-2	-0.1
1948	NY-N	56	57	6	15	0	1	2	9	3	2	.263	.300	.404	88	-1	0			.966	-0	/1-6	-0.2
Total	11	542	1557	182	432	72	16	25	209	90	114	.277	.319	.392	95	-14	8			.990	-5	1-383/O-5,P	-5.4

■ JOE McCARTHY
McCarthy, Joseph N.   b: 12/25/1881, Syracuse, N.Y.   d: 1/12/37, Syracuse, N.Y.   BR/TR,   Deb: 9/27/05

YEAR	TM/L	G	AB	R	H	2B	3B	HR	RBI	BB	SO	AVG	OBP	SLG	PRO+	BR/A	SB	CS	SBR	FA	FR	G/POS	TPR
1905	NY-A	1	2	0	0	0	0	0	0	0	0	.000	.000	.000	-90	-0	0			1.000	0	/C-1	0.0
1906	StL-N	15	37	3	9	2	0	0	2	2	2	.243	.282	.297	84	-1	0			.984	0	C-15	0.0
Total	2	16	39	3	9	2	0	0	2	2	2	.231	.268	.282	74	-1	0			.985	-0	/C-16	0.0

■ TOMMY McCARTHY
McCarthy, Thomas Francis Michael   b: 7/24/1863, Boston, Mass.   d: 8/5/22, Boston, Mass.   BR/TR, 5'7", 170 lbs.   Deb: 7/10/1884 MH

YEAR	TM/L	G	AB	R	H	2B	3B	HR	RBI	BB	SO	AVG	OBP	SLG	PRO+	BR/A	SB	CS	SBR	FA	FR	G/POS	TPR
1884	Bos-U	53	209	37	45	2	2	0		6		.215	.237	.244	32	-19				.794	-2	O-48/P-7	-1.9
1885	Bos-N	40	148	16	27	2	0	0	11	5	25	.182	.209	.196	33	-11	3			.865	3	O-40	-0.8
1886	Phi-N	8	27	6	5	2	1	0	3	2		.185	.241	.333	73	-1	1			.818	-1	/O-8,P-1	-0.2
1887	Phi-N	18	70	7	13	4	0	0	6	2	5	.186	.219	.243	27	-7	15			.818	-9	/O-8,2-5,S3	-1.4
1888	*StL-a	131	511	107	140	20	3	1	68	38		.274	.328	.331	100	-2	93			.932	30	*O-131/P-2	2.2
1889	StL-a	140	604	136	176	24	7	2	63	46	26	.291	.348	.364	91	-12	57			.893	14	*O-140/2-2,P	-0.1
1890	StL-a	133	548	137	192	28	9	6		66		.350	.430	.467	144	27	**83**			.893	7	*O-102,3-32/2M	2.8
1891	StL-a	136	578	127	179	21	6	8	95	50	19	.310	.375	.408	108	1	37			.895	-1	*O-113,2-14,S/3P	-0.2
1892	*Bos-N	152	603	119	146	19	5	4	63	93	29	.242	.347	.310	91	-6	53			.883	2	*O-152	-1.0
1893	Bos-N	116	462	107	160	28	6	5	111	64		.346	.429	.465	128	18	46			.902	3	*O-108/2-7,S	1.3
1894	Bos-N	127	539	118	188	21	8	13	126	59	17	.349	.419	.490	110	7	43			.904	11	*O-127/S-2,2P	0.7
1895	Bos-N	117	452	90	131	13	2	2	73	72	12	.290	.391	.341	83	-10	18			.885	-10	*O-109/2-9	-2.3
1896	Bro-N	104	377	62	94	8	4	3	47	34	17	.249	.316	.316	71	-15	22			.920	-2	*O-103	-2.2
Total	13	1275	5128	1069	1496	192	53	44	666	537	163	.292	.364	.376	99	-31	468			.897	45	*O-1189/2-39,3SP	-3.1

■ BILL McCARTHY
McCarthy, William John   b: 2/14/1886, Boston, Mass.   d: 2/4/28, Washington, D.C.   TR,   Deb: 6/5/05

YEAR	TM/L	G	AB	R	H	2B	3B	HR	RBI	BB	SO	AVG	OBP	SLG	PRO+	BR/A	SB	CS	SBR	FA	FR	G/POS	TPR
1905	Bos-N	1	3	0	0	0	0	0	0	0	0	.000	.000	.000	-99	-1	0			.667	-0	/C-1	-0.1
1907	Cin-N	3	8	1	1	0	0	0	0	0	0	.125	.125	.125	-21	-1	0			1.000	-1	/C-3	-0.2
Total	2	4	11	1	1	0	0	0	0	0	0	.091	.091	.091	-43	-2	0			.842	-1	/C-4	-0.3

■ FRANK McCARTON
McCarton, Francis   b: 10/6/1854, Middletown, Conn.   d: 6/17/07, New York, N.Y.   Deb: 4/26/1872

YEAR	TM/L	G	AB	R	H	2B	3B	HR	RBI	BB	SO	AVG	OBP	SLG	PRO+	BR/A	SB	CS	SBR	FA	FR	G/POS	TPR
1872	Man-n	19	83	19	31	5	0	0	9	1	3	.373	.381	.434	159	6						O-19	0.5

■ DAVID McCARTY
McCarty, David Andrew   b: 11/23/69, Houston, Tex.   BR/TL, 6'5", 215 lbs.   Deb: 5/17/93

YEAR	TM/L	G	AB	R	H	2B	3B	HR	RBI	BB	SO	AVG	OBP	SLG	PRO+	BR/A	SB	CS	SBR	FA	FR	G/POS	TPR
1993	Min-A	98	350	36	75	15	2	2	21	19	80	.214	.257	.286	45	-27	2	6	-3	.960	5	O-67,1-36/D	-2.8
1994	Min-A	44	131	21	34	8	2	1	12	7	32	.260	.322	.374	79	-4	2	1	0	.981	1	1-32,O-14	-0.5
Total	2	142	481	57	109	23	4	3	33	26	112	.227	.275	.310	55	-31	4	7	-3	.964	6	/O-81,1-68,D	-3.3

■ LEW McCARTY
McCarty, George Lewis   b: 11/17/1888, Milton, Pa.   d: 6/9/30, Reading, Pa.   BR/TR, 5'11.5", 192 lbs.   Deb: 8/30/13

YEAR	TM/L	G	AB	R	H	2B	3B	HR	RBI	BB	SO	AVG	OBP	SLG	PRO+	BR/A	SB	CS	SBR	FA	FR	G/POS	TPR
1913	Bro-N	9	26	1	6	0	0	0	2	2	2	.231	.286	.231	47	-2	0			1.000	0	/C-9	-0.1
1914	Bro-N	90	284	20	72	14	2	1	30	14	22	.254	.293	.327	83	-7	1			.970	1	C-84	0.1
1915	Bro-N	84	276	19	66	9	4	0	19	7	23	.239	.261	.301	68	-11	7	4	-0	.969	-8	C-81	-1.5
1916	Bro-N	55	150	17	47	6	1	0	13	14	16	.313	.383	.367	127	5	4			.985	-4	C-27,1-17	0.4
	NY-N	25	68	6	27	3	4	0	9	7	9	.397	.453	.559	222	10	0			.993	0	C-24	1.3
	Yr	80	218	23	74	9	5	0	22	21	25	.339	.405	.427	155	15	4			.989	-3	C-51,1-17	1.7
1917	*NY-N	56	162	15	40	3	2	2	19	14	6	.247	.311	.327	99	-0	1			.979	-3	C-54	0.1
1918	NY-N	86	257	16	69	7	3	0	24	18	13	.268	.321	.319	97	-1	2			.975	-7	C-75	-0.2
1919	NY-N	85	210	17	59	8	1	0	21	18	15	.281	.341	.371	115	4	2			.970	-8	C-59	0.1

YEAR	TM/L	G	AB	R	H	2B	3B	HR	RBI	BB	SO	AVG	OBP	SLG	PRO+	BR/A	SB	CS	SBR	FA	FR	G/POS	TPR
1920	NY-N	36	38	2	5	0	0	0	0	4	2	.132	.214	.132	1	-5	2	0	1	1.000	2	/C-5	-0.2
	StL-N	5	7	0	2	0	0	0	0	5	0	.286	.583	.286	160	1	0	0	0	1.000	-1	/C-3	0.1
	Yr	41	45	2	7	0	0	0	0	9	2	.156	.296	.156	33	-3	2	0	1	1.000	1	/C-8	-0.1
1921	StL-N	1	1	0	0	0	0	0	0	0	1	.000	.000	.000	-99	-0	0	0	0	.000	0	H	0.0
Total	9	532	1479	113	393	47	20	5	137	102	109	.266	.318	.335	97	-5	20	4		.975	-28	C-421/1-17	0.1

■ TIM McCARVER
McCarver, James Timothy   b: 10/16/41, Memphis, Tenn.   BL/TR, 6'1", 195 lbs.   Deb: 9/10/59

YEAR	TM/L	G	AB	R	H	2B	3B	HR	RBI	BB	SO	AVG	OBP	SLG	PRO+	BR/A	SB	CS	SBR	FA	FR	G/POS	TPR
1959	StL-N	8	24	3	4	1	0	0	2	1	2	.167	.231	.208	17	-3	0	0	0	.971	-2	/C-6	-0.5
1960	StL-N	10	10	3	2	0	0	0	0	0	2	.200	.200	.200	9	-1	0	0	0	1.000	-0	/C-5	-0.1
1961	StL-N	22	67	5	16	2	1	1	6	0	5	.239	.239	.343	47	-5	0	0	0	.969	-2	C-20	-0.6
1963	StL-N	127	405	39	117	12	7	4	51	27	43	.289	.336	.383	97	-1	5	2	0	.994	-0	*C-126	0.3
1964	*StL-N	143	465	53	134	19	3	9	52	40	44	.288	.346	.400	101	1	2	0	1	.987	-9	*C-137	-0.2
1965	StL-N	113	409	48	113	17	2	11	48	31	26	.276	.329	.408	97	-2	5	1	1	.995	-4	*C-111	0.1
1966	StL-N★	150	543	50	149	19	13	12	68	36	38	.274	.322	.424	105	3	9	5	3	.992	-4	*C-148	0.8
1967	*StL-N★	138	471	68	139	26	3	14	69	54	32	.295	.374	.452	137	23	8	8	-2	.997	4	*C-130	3.4
1968	*StL-N	128	434	35	110	15	6	5	48	26	31	.253	.297	.350	95	-3	4	3	-1	.986	3	*C-109	0.8
1969	StL-N	138	515	46	134	27	3	7	51	49	26	.260	.327	.365	93	-5	4	9	-4	.986	9	*C-136	0.8
1970	Phi-N	44	164	16	47	11	1	4	14	14	10	.287	.346	.439	112	2	2	2	-1	.991	0	C-44	0.4
1971	Phi-N	134	474	51	132	20	5	8	46	43	26	.278	.340	.392	107	4	5	3	-0	.985	-8	*C-125	0.1
1972	Phi-N	45	152	14	36	8	0	2	14	17	15	.237	.322	.329	83	-3	1	2	-1	.989	-3	C-40	-0.6
	Mon-N	77	239	19	60	5	1	5	20	19	14	.251	.309	.343	84	-5	4	4	-1	.990	1	C-45,O-14/3	-0.5
	Yr	122	391	33	96	13	1	7	34	36	29	.246	.314	.338	83	-8	5	6	-2	.990	-3	C-85,O-14/3	-1.1
1973	StL-N	130	331	30	88	16	4	3	49	38	31	.266	.345	.366	97	-1	2	0	1	.986	-6	1-77,C-11	-1.2
1974	StL-N	74	106	13	23	0	1	0	11	22	6	.217	.366	.236	72	-3	0	1	-1	.969	-1	C-21/1-6	-0.4
	Bos-A	11	28	3	7	1	0	0	1	4	1	.250	.344	.286	77	-1	1	0	0	1.000	1	/C-8,D-2	0.1
1975	Bos-A	12	21	1	8	2	1	0	3	1	3	.381	.409	.571	161	2	0	0	0	.957	-0	/C-7,1-1	0.2
	Phi-N	47	59	6	15	2	0	1	7	14	7	.254	.397	.339	102	1	0	0	0	.984	1	C-10/1-1	0.2
1976	*Phi-N	90	155	26	43	11	2	3	29	35	14	.277	.414	.432	136	9	2	1	0	1.000	5	C-41/1-2	1.6
1977	*Phi-N	93	169	28	54	13	2	6	30	28	11	.320	.422	.527	146	12	3	5	-2	.988	2	C-42/1-3	1.2
1978	*Phi-N	90	146	18	36	9	1	1	14	28	24	.247	.375	.342	101	1	2	2	-1	.995	2	C-34,1-11	0.3
1979	Phi-N	79	137	13	33	5	1	1	12	19	12	.241	.338	.314	76	-4	0	0	0	.989	3	C-31/O-1	0.0
1980	Phi-N	6	5	2	1	1	0	0	2	1	0	.200	.333	.400	98	-0	0	0	0	1.000	-0	/1-2	0.0
Total	21	1909	5529	590	1501	242	57	97	645	548	422	.271	.340	.388	102	23	61	49	-11	.990	-9	*C-1387,1-103/O3D	6.2

■ AL McCAULEY
McCauley, Allen A.   b: 3/4/1863, Indianapolis, Ind.   d: 8/24/17, Wayne Twnshp., Ind   BL/TL, 6', 180 lbs.   Deb: 6/21/1884

YEAR	TM/L	G	AB	R	H	2B	3B	HR	RBI	BB	SO	AVG	OBP	SLG	PRO+	BR/A	SB	CS	SBR	FA	FR	G/POS	TPR
1884	Ind-a	17	53	7	10	0	1	0	12			.189	.358	.226	97	1				1.000	0	P-10/1-5,O	-0.2
1890	Phi-N	112	418	63	102	25	7	1	42	57	38	.244	.346	.344	99	0	8			.973	-6	*1-116	-1.1
1891	Was-N	59	206	36	58	5	8	1	31	30	13	.282	.378	.398	128	8	9			.969	-2	1-59	0.3
Total	3	188	677	106	170	30	16	2	73	99	51	.251	.357	.352	107	9	17			.971	-7	1-180/P-10,O	-1.0

■ JIM McCAULEY
McCauley, James A.   b: 3/24/1863, Stanley, N.Y.   d: 9/14/30, Canandaigua, N.Y.   BL/TR, 6', 180 lbs.   Deb: 9/17/1884

YEAR	TM/L	G	AB	R	H	2B	3B	HR	RBI	BB	SO	AVG	OBP	SLG	PRO+	BR/A	SB	CS	SBR	FA	FR	G/POS	TPR
1884	StL-a	1	2	0	0	0	0	0	0			.000	.000	.000	-97	-0				.818	1	/C-1	0.1
1885	Buf-N	24	84	4	15	2	1	0	7	11	12	.179	.274	.226	61	-3				.936	-1	C-21/O-4	-0.2
	Chi-N	3	6	1	1	0	0	0	0	2	3	.167	.375	.167	70	-0				.800	-3	/C-2,O-2	-0.3
	Yr	27	90	5	16	2	1	0	7	13	15	.178	.282	.222	62	-3				.927	-3	C-23/O-6	-0.5
1886	Bro-a	11	30	5	7	1	0	0	11			.233	.439	.267	122	2	2			.846	-1	C-11	0.2
Total	3	39	122	10	23	3	1	0	7	24	15	.189	.322	.230	76	-2	2			.893	-3	/C-35,O-6	-0.6

◪ PAT McCAULEY
McCauley, Patrick M.   b: 6/10/1870, Ware, Mass.   d: 1/23/17, Newark, N.J.   TR, 5'10.5", 156 lbs.   Deb: 9/5/1893

YEAR	TM/L	G	AB	R	H	2B	3B	HR	RBI	BB	SO	AVG	OBP	SLG	PRO+	BR/A	SB	CS	SBR	FA	FR	G/POS	TPR
1893	StL-N	5	16	0	1	0	0	0	0	0	1	.063	.063	.063	-67	-4	0			.808	1	/C-5	-0.2
1896	Was-N	26	84	14	21	3	0	3	11	7	8	.250	.315	.393	86	-2	3			.917	0	C-24/O-1	0.0
1903	NY-A	6	19	0	1	0	0	0	1	0		.053	.053	.053	-64	-4	0			.920	-2	/C-6	-0.6
Total	3	37	119	14	23	3	0	3	12	7	9	.193	.244	.294	44	-10	3			.900	-2	/C-35,O-1	-0.8

■ BILL McCAULEY
McCauley, William H.   b: 12/20/1869, Washington, D.C.   d: 1/27/26, Washington, D.C.   Deb: 8/31/1895

YEAR	TM/L	G	AB	R	H	2B	3B	HR	RBI	BB	SO	AVG	OBP	SLG	PRO+	BR/A	SB	CS	SBR	FA	FR	G/POS	TPR
1895	Was-N	1	2	0	0	0	0	0	0	0	0	.000	.000	.000	-99	-1	0			.714	0	/S-1	0.0

■ HARRY McCHESNEY
McChesney, Harry Vincent "Pud"   b: 6/1/1880, Pittsburgh, Pa.   d: 8/11/60, Pittsburgh, Pa.   BR/TR, 5'9", 165 lbs.   Deb: 9/17/04

YEAR	TM/L	G	AB	R	H	2B	3B	HR	RBI	BB	SO	AVG	OBP	SLG	PRO+	BR/A	SB	CS	SBR	FA	FR	G/POS	TPR
1904	Chi-N	22	88	9	23	6	2	0	11	4		.261	.293	.375	106	0	2			.967	-2	O-22	-0.3

■ PETE McCLANAHAN
McClanahan, Robert Hugh   b: 10/24/06, Coldspring, Tex.   d: 10/28/87, Mont Belvieu, Tex.   BR/TR, 5'9", 170 lbs.   Deb: 4/24/31

YEAR	TM/L	G	AB	R	H	2B	3B	HR	RBI	BB	SO	AVG	OBP	SLG	PRO+	BR/A	SB	CS	SBR	FA	FR	G/POS	TPR
1931	Pit-N	7	4	2	2	0	0	0	0	0	0	.500	.667	.500	220	1	0			.000	0	H	0.1

■ HARVEY McCLELLAN
McClellan, Harvey McDowell "Little Mac"   b: 12/22/1894, Cynthiana, Ky.   d: 11/6/25, Cynthiana, Ky.   BR/TR, 5'9.5", 143 lbs.   Deb: 5/31/19

YEAR	TM/L	G	AB	R	H	2B	3B	HR	RBI	BB	SO	AVG	OBP	SLG	PRO+	BR/A	SB	CS	SBR	FA	FR	G/POS	TPR
1919	Chi-A	7	12	2	4	0	0	0	1	1	1	.333	.385	.333	102	0	0			1.000	0	/3-3,S-2	0.1
1920	Chi-A	10	18	4	6	1	1	0	5	4	1	.333	.455	.500	153	2	2	0	1	.917	-3	/S-4,3-2	-0.1
1921	Chi-A	63	196	20	35	4	1	1	14	14	18	.179	.237	.224	18	-24	2	3	-1	.968	18	2-21,S-15,O/3	-0.6
1922	Chi-A	91	301	28	68	17	3	2	28	16	32	.226	.272	.322	55	-21	3	2	-0	.971	-5	3-71/S-8,2O	-1.9
1923	Chi-A	141	550	67	129	29	3	1	41	27	44	.235	.270	.304	52	-40	14	11	-2	.958	-18	*S-139/2-2	-4.6
1924	Chi-A	32	85	9	15	3	0	0	9	6	7	.176	.239	.212	17	-11	2	0	1	.938	3	S-21/2-7,3O	-0.5
Total	6	344	1162	130	257	54	8	4	98	68	103	.221	.267	.292	46	-94	23	16		.952	-4	S-189/3-82,2O	-7.6

■ BILL McCLELLAN
McClellan, William Henry   b: 3/22/1856, Chicago, Ill.   d: 7/3/29, Chicago, Ill.   BL/TL, 156 lbs.   Deb: 5/20/1878

YEAR	TM/L	G	AB	R	H	2B	3B	HR	RBI	BB	SO	AVG	OBP	SLG	PRO+	BR/A	SB	CS	SBR	FA	FR	G/POS	TPR
1878	Chi-N	48	205	26	46	6	1	0	29	2	13	.224	.232	.263	59	-9				.866	-9	*2-42/S-5,O	-1.4
1881	Pro-N	68	259	30	43	3	1	0	16	15	21	.166	.212	.185	26	-21				.855	-8	S-50,O-17/2	-2.5
1883	Phi-N	80	326	42	75	21	4	1	33	19	18	.230	.272	.328	89	-3				.849	5	*S-78/O-2,3	0.3
1884	Phi-N	111	450	71	116	13	2	3	33	28	43	.258	.301	.316	99	1				.852	-12	*S-111/O-1	-0.9
1885	Bro-a	112	464	85	124	22	7	0	28			.267	.317	.345	108	5				.837	-5	3-57,2-55	-0.1
1886	Bro-a	141	595	131	152	33	9	1	56			.255	.322	.346	108	5	43			.907	-7	*2-141	0.4
1887	Bro-a	136	548	109	144	24	6	1	80			.263	.363	.334	94	-2	70			.879	-23	*2-136	-1.7
1888	Bro-a	74	278	33	57	7	3	0	21	40		.205	.307	.252	80	-4	13			.905	-7	2-56,O-18	-0.9
	Cle-a	22	72	6	16	0	0	0	5	6		.222	.282	.222	64	-3	6			.875	-4	O-15/2-5,S	-0.6
	Yr	96	350	39	73	7	3	0	26	46		.209	.302	.246	77	-7	19			.897	-11	2-61,O-33/S	-1.5
Total	8	792	3197	533	773	129	33	6	137	274	95	.242	.305	.308	90	-31	132			.893	-68	2-436,S-246/3O	-7.0

■ LLOYD McCLENDON
McClendon, Lloyd Glenn   b: 1/11/59, Gary, Ind.   BR/TR, 5'11", 195 lbs.   Deb: 4/6/87

YEAR	TM/L	G	AB	R	H	2B	3B	HR	RBI	BB	SO	AVG	OBP	SLG	PRO+	BR/A	SB	CS	SBR	FA	FR	G/POS	TPR
1987	Cin-N	45	72	8	15	5	0	2	13	4	15	.208	.250	.361	57	-5	1	0	0	.981	-2	C-12/1-5,3O	-0.6
1988	Cin-N	72	137	9	30	4	0	3	14	15	22	.219	.305	.314	75	-4	4	0	1	1.000	-3	C-23,O-17,1/3	-0.6
1989	*Chi-N	92	259	47	74	12	1	12	40	37	31	.286	.377	.479	133	12	6	4	-1	.962	-7	O-45,1-28/3C	0.1
1990	Chi-N	49	107	5	17	3	0	1	10	14	21	.159	.256	.215	29	-10	1	0	0	.980	1	O-23/C-8,1	-1.0
	Pit-N	4	3	1	1	0	0	1	2	0	1	.333	.333	1.333	349	1	0	0	0	.000	0	/O-1	0.1
	Yr	53	110	6	18	3	0	2	12	14	22	.164	.258	.245	37	-9	1	0	0	.980	1	O-24/C-8,1	-0.9
1991	*Pit-N	85	163	24	47	7	0	7	24	18	23	.288	.366	.460	133	7	2	1	0	.966	-7	O-32,1-22/C	-0.2
1992	*Pit-N	84	190	26	48	8	1	3	28	28	24	.253	.355	.353	102	1	3	5	-2	.964	-7	O-60,1-18	-0.9
1993	Pit-N	88	181	21	40	11	1	2	19	23	17	.221	.309	.326	70	-7	0	3	-2	.967	-9	O-61/1-6	-2.0

YEAR	TM/L	G	AB	R	H	2B	3B	HR	RBI	BB	SO	AVG	OBP	SLG	PRO+	BR/A	SB	CS	SBR	FA	FR	G/POS	TPR
1994	Pit-N	51	92	9	22	4	0	4	12	4	11	.239	.278	.413	77	-3	0	1	-1	.967	-2	O-20/1-2	-0.6
Total	8	570	1204	150	294	54	3	35	154	143	165	.244	.328	.381	94	-9	15	12	-3	.966	-36	O-260,1-101/C3	-5.7

■ JEFF McCLESKEY
McCleskey, Jefferson Lamar b: 11/6/1891, Americus, Ga. d: 5/11/71, Americus, Ga. BL/TR, 5'11", 160 lbs. Deb: 9/8/13

YEAR	TM/L	G	AB	R	H	2B	3B	HR	RBI	BB	SO	AVG	OBP	SLG	PRO+	BR/A	SB	CS	SBR	FA	FR	G/POS	TPR
1913	Bos-N	2	3	0	0	0	0	0	0	1	0	.000	.250	.000	-25	-0	0			.750	-0	/3-2	-0.1

■ McCLOSKEY
McCloskey b: Brooklyn, N.Y. Deb: 5/25/1875

YEAR	TM/L	G	AB	R	H	2B	3B	HR	RBI	BB	SO	AVG	OBP	SLG	PRO+	BR/A	SB	CS	SBR	FA	FR	G/POS	TPR
1875	Was-n	11	40	1	7	0	0	0		1		.175	.195	.175	30	-3						C-10	-0.2

■ BILL McCLOSKEY
McCloskey, William George b: 5/1854, Pennsylvania 5'8", 155 lbs. Deb: 8/18/1884

YEAR	TM/L	G	AB	R	H	2B	3B	HR	RBI	BB	SO	AVG	OBP	SLG	PRO+	BR/A	SB	CS	SBR	FA	FR	G/POS	TPR
1884	Wil-U	9	30	0	3	0	0	0		0		.100	.100	.100	-44	-6				.588	1	/O-5,C-5	-0.4

■ HAL McCLURE
McClure, Harold Murray "Mac" b: 8/8/1859, Lewisburg, Pa. d: 3/1/19, Lewisburg, Pa. BR/TR, 6', 165 lbs. Deb: 5/10/1882

YEAR	TM/L	G	AB	R	H	2B	3B	HR	RBI	BB	SO	AVG	OBP	SLG	PRO+	BR/A	SB	CS	SBR	FA	FR	G/POS	TPR
1882	Bos-N	2	6	1	2	0	0	0	0	0	1	.333	.333	.333	115	0				.750	-0	/O-2	0.0

■ LARRY McCLURE
McClure, Lawrence Ledwith b: 10/3/1885, Wayne, W.Va. d: 8/31/49, Huntington, W.Va. BR/TR, 5'6.5", 130 lbs. Deb: 7/26/10

YEAR	TM/L	G	AB	R	H	2B	3B	HR	RBI	BB	SO	AVG	OBP	SLG	PRO+	BR/A	SB	CS	SBR	FA	FR	G/POS	TPR
1910	NY-A	1	1	0	0	0	0	0	0	0	0	.000	.000	.000	-95	-0	0			.000	0	/O-1	0.0

■ AMBY McCONNELL
McConnell, Ambrose Moses b: 4/29/1883, N.Pownal, Vt. d: 5/20/42, Utica, N.Y. BL/TR, 5'7", 150 lbs. Deb: 4/17/08

YEAR	TM/L	G	AB	R	H	2B	3B	HR	RBI	BB	SO	AVG	OBP	SLG	PRO+	BR/A	SB	CS	SBR	FA	FR	G/POS	TPR
1908	Bos-A	140	502	77	140	10	6	2	43	38		.279	.343	.335	117	10	31			.939	-20	*2-126/S-3	-1.2
1909	Bos-A	121	453	61	108	7	8	0	36	34		.238	.300	.289	84	-8	26			.954	14	*2-121	0.5
1910	Bos-A	11	35	6	6	0	0	0	1	5		.171	.310	.171	50	-2	4			.959	-1	2-10	-0.3
	Chi-A	33	120	13	33	2	3	0	5	7		.275	.320	.342	112	1	4			.952	-1	2-32	0.0
	Yr	44	155	19	39	2	3	0	6	12		.252	.318	.303	97	-0	8			.954	-2	2-42	-0.3
1911	Chi-A	104	396	45	111	11	5	1	34	23		.280	.331	.341	90	-5	7			.973	-7	*2-103	-1.4
Total	4	409	1506	202	398	30	22	3	119	107		.264	.324	.319	98	-3	72			.954	-14	2-392/S-3	-2.4

■ GEORGE McCONNELL
McConnell, George Neely "Slats" b: 9/16/1877, Shelbyville, Tenn. d: 5/10/64, Chattanooga, Tenn. BR/TR, 6'3", 190 lbs. Deb: 4/13/09

YEAR	TM/L	G	AB	R	H	2B	3B	HR	RBI	BB	SO	AVG	OBP	SLG	PRO+	BR/A	SB	CS	SBR	FA	FR	G/POS	TPR
1909	NY-A	13	43	4	9	0	1	0	5	1		.209	.227	.256	52	-2	1			.964	2	1-11/P-2	-0.2
1912	NY-A	42	91	11	27	4	2	0	8	4		.297	.333	.385	99	-0	0			.913	5	P-23/1-2	0.0
1913	NY-A	39	67	4	12	2	0	0	2	0	11	.179	.179	.209	13	-7	0			.965	5	P-35/1-1	0.0
1914	Chi-N	1	2	0	0	0	0	0	0	0	1	.000	.000	.000	-99	-0	0			1.000	0	/P-1	0.0
1915	Chi-F	53	125	14	31	6	2	1	18	0	16	.248	.254	.352	65	-7	2			.974	3	P-44	0.0
1916	Chi-N	28	57	2	9	0	0	0	0	2	4	.158	.200	.158	10	-6	0			.952	2	P-28	0.0
Total	6	176	385	35	88	12	5	1	33	7	32	.229	.248	.294	54	-24	3			.953	16	P-133/1-14	-0.2

■ SAM McCONNELL
McConnell, Samuel Faulkner b: 6/8/1895, Philadelphia, Pa. d: 6/27/81, Phoenixville, Pa. BL/TR, 5'6.5", 150 lbs. Deb: 4/19/15

YEAR	TM/L	G	AB	R	H	2B	3B	HR	RBI	BB	SO	AVG	OBP	SLG	PRO+	BR/A	SB	CS	SBR	FA	FR	G/POS	TPR
1915	Phi-A	6	11	1	2	1	0	0	0	1	3	.182	.250	.273	58	-1	0			.842	2	/3-5	0.1

■ DON McCORMACK
McCormack, Donald Ross b: 9/18/55, Omak, Wash. BR/TR, 6'3", 205 lbs. Deb: 9/30/80

YEAR	TM/L	G	AB	R	H	2B	3B	HR	RBI	BB	SO	AVG	OBP	SLG	PRO+	BR/A	SB	CS	SBR	FA	FR	G/POS	TPR
1980	Phi-N	2	1	0	1	0	0	0	0	0	0	1.000	1.000	1.000	436	0	0	0	0	1.000	1	/C-2	0.1
1981	Phi-N	3	4	0	1	0	0	0	0	0	1	.250	.250	.250	40	-0	0	0	0	1.000	0	/C-3	0.0
Total	2	5	5	0	2	0	0	0	0	0	1	.400	.400	.400	121	0	0	0	0	1.000	1	/C-5	0.1

■ FRANK McCORMICK
McCormick, Frank Andrew "Buck" b: 6/9/11, New York, N.Y. d: 11/21/82, Manhasset, N.Y. BR/TR, 6'4", 205 lbs. Deb: 9/11/34 C

YEAR	TM/L	G	AB	R	H	2B	3B	HR	RBI	BB	SO	AVG	OBP	SLG	PRO+	BR/A	SB	CS	SBR	FA	FR	G/POS	TPR
1934	Cin-N	12	16	1	5	2	1	0	5	0	1	.313	.313	.563	132	1	0			.941	-1	/1-2	0.0
1937	Cin-N	24	83	5	27	5	0	0	9	2	4	.325	.341	.386	102	0	1			1.000	1	1-20/2-4,O	-0.2
1938	Cin-N★	151	640	89	**209**	40	4	5	106	18	17	.327	.348	.425	115	11	1			.995	-3	*1-151	-1.0
1939	*Cin-N★	156	630	99	**209**	41	4	18	**128**	40	16	.332	.374	.495	131	26	1			**.996**	2	*1-156	1.0
1940	*Cin-N★	155	618	93	191	**44**	3	19	127	52	26	.309	.367	.482	131	25	2			**.995**	1	*1-155	1.1
1941	Cin-N★	154	603	77	162	31	5	17	97	40	13	.269	.318	.421	107	3	2			**.995**	1	*1-154	-0.8
1942	Cin-N★	145	564	58	156	24	0	13	89	45	18	.277	.332	.388	111	6	1			.993	6	*1-144	0.3
1943	Cin-N†	126	472	56	143	28	0	8	56	29	15	.303	.345	.413	120	10	2			.995	3	*1-120	0.8
1944	Cin-N☆	153	581	85	177	37	3	20	102	57	17	.305	.371	.482	144	32	7			.992	12	*1-153	3.7
1945	Cin-N†	152	580	68	160	33	0	10	81	56	22	.276	.345	.384	105	4	6			.994	5	*1-151	-0.1
1946	Phi-N★	135	504	46	143	20	2	11	66	36	21	.284	.333	.397	110	4	2			**.999**	4	*1-134	0.1
1947	Phi-N	15	40	7	9	2	0	1	8	3	2	.225	.279	.350	69	-2	0			.989	-1	1-12	-0.3
	Bos-N	81	212	24	75	18	2	2	43	11	8	.354	.386	.486	133	9	2			.996	-1	1-46	0.7
	Yr	96	252	31	84	20	2	3	51	14	10	.333	.368	.464	123	7	2			.995	-2	1-58	0.4
1948	*Bos-N	75	180	14	45	9	2	4	34	10	9	.250	.289	.389	84	-5	0			.987	3	1-50	-0.3
Total	13	1534	5723	722	1711	334	26	128	951	399	189	.299	.348	.434	118	125	27			.995	31	*1-1448/2-4,O	5.0

■ MOOSE McCORMICK
McCormick, Harry Elwood b: 2/28/1881, Philadelphia, Pa. d: 7/9/62, Lewisburg, Pa. BL/TL, 5'11", 180 lbs. Deb: 4/14/04

YEAR	TM/L	G	AB	R	H	2B	3B	HR	RBI	BB	SO	AVG	OBP	SLG	PRO+	BR/A	SB	CS	SBR	FA	FR	G/POS	TPR
1904	NY-N	59	203	28	54	9	5	1	26	13		.266	.323	.374	110	2	13			.916	-5	O-55	-0.6
	Pit-N	66	238	25	69	10	6	2	23	13		.290	.332	.408	124	6	6			.940	-6	O-66	-0.4
	Yr	125	441	53	123	19	11	3	49	26		.279	.328	.392	118	8	19			.928	-11	*O-121	-1.0
1908	Phi-N	11	22	0	2	0	0	0	2	2		.091	.167	.091	-17	-3	0			1.000	0	/O-5	-0.4
	NY-N	73	252	31	76	16	3	0	32	4		.302	.315	.389	119	4	6			.901	-11	O-65	-1.1
	Yr	84	274	31	78	16	3	0	34	6		.285	.308	.365	108	1	6			.910	-11	O-70	-1.5
1909	NY-N	110	413	68	120	21	8	3	27	49		.291	.373	.402	138	19	4			.924	-14	*O-110	0.1
1912	*NY-N	42	39	4	13	4	1	0	8	6	9	.333	.422	.487	144	2	1			.667	-3	/O-6,1-1	0.0
1913	*NY-N	57	80	9	22	2	3	0	15	5	13	.275	.318	.375	97	-1	0			.909	-2	O-15	-0.3
Total	5	418	1247	165	356	62	26	6	133	92	22	.285	.340	.391	122	30	30			.920	-40	O-322/1-1	-2.7

■ JIM McCORMICK
McCormick, James Ambrose b: 11/2/1868, Spencer, Mass. d: 2/1/48, Saco, Maine BR/TR, 6'1", 160 lbs. Deb: 9/10/1892

YEAR	TM/L	G	AB	R	H	2B	3B	HR	RBI	BB	SO	AVG	OBP	SLG	PRO+	BR/A	SB	CS	SBR	FA	FR	G/POS	TPR
1892	StL-N	3	11	0	0	0	0	0	0	1	5	.000	.083	.000	-78	-2	0			1.000	-0	/2-2,3-1	-0.2

■ JERRY McCORMICK
McCormick, John b: Philadelphia, Pa. d: 9/19/05, Philadelphia, Pa. Deb: 5/1/1883

YEAR	TM/L	G	AB	R	H	2B	3B	HR	RBI	BB	SO	AVG	OBP	SLG	PRO+	BR/A	SB	CS	SBR	FA	FR	G/POS	TPR
1883	Bal-a	93	389	40	102	16	6	0		2		.262	.266	.334	89	-6				.799	1	*3-93	-0.5
1884	Phi-U	67	295	41	84	12	6	0		4		.285	.294	.339	77	-9				.811	14	3-54/2-5,0SP	0.4
	Was-U	42	157	23	34	8	2	0		1		.217	.222	.293	40	-13				.792	-6	3-38/S-4	-1.7
	Yr	109	452	64	118	20	4	0		5		.261	.269	.323	64	-22				**.806**	8	3-92/S-7,20P	-1.3
Total	2	202	841	104	220	36	10	0		7		.262	.268	.328	75	-28				.802	9	3-185/S-7,02P	-1.8

■ MIKE McCORMICK
McCormick, Michael J. "Kid" or "Dude" b: 5/1883, Scotland d: 11/18/53, Jersey City, N.J. BR/TR, 5'3", 155 lbs. Deb: 4/14/04

YEAR	TM/L	G	AB	R	H	2B	3B	HR	RBI	BB	SO	AVG	OBP	SLG	PRO+	BR/A	SB	CS	SBR	FA	FR	G/POS	TPR
1904	Bro-N	105	347	28	64	5	4	0	27	43		.184	.278	.222	56	-16	22			**.914**	-3	*3-104/2-1	-1.7

■ MIKE McCORMICK
McCormick, Myron Winthrop b: 5/6/17, Angels Camp, Cal. d: 4/14/76, Ventura, Cal. BR/TR, 6', 200 lbs. Deb: 4/16/40

YEAR	TM/L	G	AB	R	H	2B	3B	HR	RBI	BB	SO	AVG	OBP	SLG	PRO+	BR/A	SB	CS	SBR	FA	FR	G/POS	TPR
1940	*Cin-N	110	417	48	125	20	0	1	30	13	36	.300	.326	.355	87	-8	8			.986	6	*O-107	-0.6
1941	Cin-N	110	369	52	106	17	3	4	31	30	24	.287	.341	.382	103	1	4			.976	7	*O-101	0.3
1942	Cin-N	40	135	18	32	2	1	1	11	13	7	.237	.304	.319	82	-3	0			.990	1	O-38	-0.4
1943	Cin-N	4	15	0	2	0	0	0	1	0	0	.133	.235	.133	8	-2	0			.909	-0	/O-4	-0.3
1946	Cin-N	23	74	10	16	2	0	0	5	8	4	.216	.293	.243	55	-4	0			1.000	1	O-21	-0.5
	Bos-N	59	164	23	43	6	2	1	16	11	7	.262	.309	.341	83	-4	0			.973	-2	O-48	-0.8
	Yr	82	238	33	59	8	2	1	21	19	11	.248	.304	.311	75	-8	0			.982	-1	O-69	-1.3
1947	Bos-N	92	284	42	81	13	7	3	36	20	21	.285	.332	.412	99	-1	1			.981	-12	O-79	-1.6

YEAR	TM/L	G	AB	R	H	2B	3B	HR	RBI	BB	SO	AVG	OBP	SLG	PRO+	BR/A	SB	CS	SBR	FA	FR	G/POS	TPR
1948	*Bos-N	115	343	45	104	22	7	1	39	32	34	.303	.363	.417	112	6	1			.975	-11	*O-100	-1.0
1949	*Bro-N	55	139	17	29	5	1	2	14	14	12	.209	.281	.302	54	-9	1			1.000	-6	O-49	-1.7
1950	NY-N	4	4	0	0	0	0	0	0	0	2	.000	.000	.000	-99	-1	0			.000	0	H	-0.1
	Chi-A	55	138	16	32	4	3	0	10	16	6	.232	.312	.304	60	-8	0	1	-1	.982	-1	O-44	-1.1
1951	Was-A	81	243	31	70	9	3	1	23	29	20	.288	.364	.362	98	0	1	2	-1	.966	1	O-62	-0.2
Total	10	748	2325	302	640	100	29	14	215	188	173	.275	.330	.361	90	-33	16	3		.980	-14	O-653	-8.0

■ BARRY McCORMICK
McCormick, William J. b: 12/25/1874, Maysville, Ky. d: 1/28/56, Cincinnati, Ohio TR, 5'9", Deb: 9/25/1895 U

YEAR	TM/L	G	AB	R	H	2B	3B	HR	RBI	BB	SO	AVG	OBP	SLG	PRO+	BR/A	SB	CS	SBR	FA	FR	G/POS	TPR
1895	Lou-N	3	12	2	3	0	1	0	0	0		.250	.250	.417	75	-1	1			1.000	-2	/S-2,2-1	-0.2
1896	Chi-N	45	168	22	37	3	1	1	23	14	30	.220	.280	.268	43	-14	9			.835	-5	3-35/S-6,2O	-1.6
1897	Chi-N	101	419	87	112	8	10	2	55	33		.267	.324	.348	75	-16	44			.851	-2	3-56,S-46/2	-1.4
1898	Chi-N	137	530	76	131	15	9	2	78	47		.247	.314	.321	82	-12	15			.888	4	*3-136/S-1,2	-0.7
1899	Chi-N	102	376	48	97	15	2	2	52	25		.258	.311	.324	76	-12	14			.941	5	2-99/S-3	-0.1
1900	Chi-N	110	379	35	83	13	5	3	48	38		.219	.292	.303	67	-17	8			.907	-9	S-84,3-21/2	-1.7
1901	Chi-N	115	427	45	100	15	6	1	32	31		.234	.288	.304	75	-14	12			.911	0	*S-112/3-3	-0.5
1902	StL-A	139	504	55	124	14	4	3	51	37		.246	.304	.308	71	-19	10			.905	-11	*3-132/S-7,O	-2.8
1903	StL-A	61	207	13	45	6	1	1	16	18		.217	.283	.271	69	-7	5			.969	-4	2-28,3-28/S	-1.0
	Was-A	63	219	14	47	10	2	0	23	10		.215	.255	.279	59	-11	3			.960	8	2-63	0.0
	Yr	124	426	27	92	16	3	1	39	28		.216	.269	.275	64	-18	8			.962	4	2-91,3-28/S	-1.0
1904	Was-A	113	404	36	88	11	1	0	39	27		.218	.274	.250	67	-14	9			.938	-1	*2-113	-1.4
Total	10	989	3645	433	867	110	42	15	417	280	30	.238	.297	.303	71	-139	130			.885	-17	3-411,2-314,S/O	-11.4

■ BARNEY McCOSKY
McCosky, William Barney b: 4/11/17, Coal Run, Pa. BL/TR, 6'1", 184 lbs. Deb: 4/18/39

YEAR	TM/L	G	AB	R	H	2B	3B	HR	RBI	BB	SO	AVG	OBP	SLG	PRO+	BR/A	SB	CS	SBR	FA	FR	G/POS	TPR
1939	Det-A	147	611	120	190	33	14	4	58	70	45	.311	.384	.430	100	1	20	4	4	.986	9	*O-145	0.8
1940	*Det-A	143	589	123	200	39	19	4	57	67	41	.340	.408	.491	120	18	13	9	-2	.983	-1	*O-141	0.8
1941	Det-A	127	494	80	160	25	8	3	55	61	33	.324	.401	.425	108	7	8	3	1	.985	5	*O-122	0.5
1942	Det-A	154	600	75	176	28	11	7	50	68	37	.293	.365	.412	109	7	11	5	0	.981	5	*O-154	0.3
1946	Det-A	25	91	11	18	5	0	1	11	17	9	.198	.324	.286	67	-4	0	0	0	.966	-1	O-24	-0.6
	Phi-A	92	308	33	109	17	4	1	34	43	13	.354	.433	.445	146	21	2	2	-1	.981	-4	O-85	1.3
	Yr	117	399	44	127	22	4	2	45	60	22	.318	.407	.409	127	17	2	2	-1	.978	-4	*O-109	0.7
1947	Phi-A	137	546	77	179	22	7	1	52	57	29	.328	.395	.399	119	16	1	4	-2	.983	4	*O-136	1.1
1948	Phi-A	135	515	95	168	21	5	0	46	68	22	.326	.405	.386	111	11	1	3	-2	.990	-3	*O-134	-0.1
1950	Phi-A	66	179	19	43	10	1	0	11	22	12	.240	.323	.307	63	-10	0	0	0	.987	-5	O-42	-1.6
1951	Phi-A	12	27	4	8	2	0	1	1	3	4	.296	.367	.481	125	1	0	0	0	1.000	-1	/O-7	-0.2
	Cin-N	25	50	2	16	2	1	1	11	4	2	.320	.370	.460	120	1	0	0	0	1.000	-3	O-11	-0.2
	Cle-A	31	61	8	13	3	0	0	2	8	5	.213	.304	.262	57	-4	1	0	0	1.000	-1	O-16	-0.5
1952	Cle-A	54	80	14	17	4	1	1	6	8	5	.213	.284	.325	74	-3	0	1	-0	.944	-5	O-19	-1.0
1953	Cle-A	22	21	3	4	3	0	0	3	1	4	.190	.227	.333	51	-2	0	0	0	.000	0	H	-0.2
Total	11	1170	4172	664	1301	214	71	24	397	497	261	.312	.386	.414	109	62	58	31	-1	.984	-1	*O-1036	0.6

■ WILLIE McCOVEY
McCovey, Willie Lee "Stretch" b: 1/10/38, Mobile, Ala. BL/TL, 6'4", 210 lbs. Deb: 7/30/59 H

YEAR	TM/L	G	AB	R	H	2B	3B	HR	RBI	BB	SO	AVG	OBP	SLG	PRO+	BR/A	SB	CS	SBR	FA	FR	G/POS	TPR
1959	SF-N	52	192	32	68	9	5	13	38	22	35	.354	.431	.656	189	24	2	0	1	.989	-2	1-51	2.0
1960	SF-N	101	260	37	62	15	3	13	51	45	53	.238	.351	.469	130	11	1	1	-0	.985	-3	1-71	0.2
1961	SF-N	106	328	59	89	12	3	18	50	37	60	.271	.354	.491	126	12	1	2	-1	.985	-2	1-84	0.3
1962	*SF-N	91	229	41	67	6	1	20	54	29	35	.293	.372	.590	156	17	3	3	-1	.976	-2	O-57,1-17	1.1
1963	SF-N★	152	564	103	158	19	5	44	102	50	119	.280	.350	.566	161	42	1	1	-0	.942	3	*O-135,1-23	3.9
1964	SF-N	130	364	55	80	14	1	18	54	61	73	.220	.340	.412	108	5	2	1	0	.935	-6	O-83,1-26	-0.6
1965	SF-N	160	540	93	149	17	4	39	92	88	118	.276	.383	.539	152	39	0	4	-2	.991	-3	*1-156	2.7
1966	SF-N★	150	502	85	148	26	6	36	96	76	100	.295	.394	.586	163	44	2	1	0	.984	-3	*1-145	3.3
1967	SF-N	135	456	73	126	17	4	31	91	71	110	.276	.381	.535	162	37	3	3	-1	.989	1	*1-127	3.1
1968	SF-N★	148	523	81	153	16	4	36	105	72	71	.293	.383	.545	176	49	4	2	0	.985	-3	*1-146	4.6
1969	SF-N★	149	491	101	157	26	2	45	126	121	66	.320	.458	.656	212	79	0	0	0	.992	-6	*1-148	6.3
1970	*SF-N★	152	495	98	143	39	2	39	126	137	75	.289	.446	.612	183	64	0	0	0	.989	13	*1-146	6.2
1971	*SF-N	105	329	45	91	13	0	18	70	64	57	.277	.401	.480	151	24	0	2	-1	.983	-2	1-95	1.4
1972	SF-N	81	263	30	56	8	0	14	35	38	45	.213	.317	.403	102	1	0	0	0	.986	-5	1-74	-1.2
1973	SF-N	130	383	52	102	14	3	29	75	105	78	.266	.425	.546	161	35	1	0	0	.988	1	*1-117	2.8
1974	SD-N	128	344	53	87	19	1	22	63	96	76	.253	.417	.506	164	34	1	0	0	.987	-6	*1-104	2.2
1975	SD-N	122	413	43	104	17	0	23	68	57	80	.252	.347	.460	130	16	1	0	0	.986	-1	*1-115	0.9
1976	SD-N	71	202	20	41	9	0	7	36	21	39	.203	.281	.351	86	-5	0	0	0	.991	5	1-51	-0.4
	Oak-A	11	24	0	5	0	0	0	0	3	4	.208	.296	.208	52	-1	0	0	0	.000	0	/D-9	-0.2
1977	SF-N	141	478	54	134	21	0	28	86	67	106	.280	.369	.500	131	21	3	0	1	.989	-7	*1-136	0.7
1978	SF-N	108	351	32	80	19	2	12	64	36	57	.228	.300	.396	97	-3	1	0	0	.987	-4	1-97	-1.2
1979	SF-N	117	353	34	88	9	0	15	57	36	70	.249	.321	.402	103	0	0	1	-0	.987	-1	1-89	-0.7
1980	SF-N	48	113	8	23	8	0	1	16	13	23	.204	.291	.301	67	-5	0	0	0	.992	-2	1-27	-0.9
Total	22	2588	8197	1229	2211	353	46	521	1555	1345	1550	.270	.377	.515	148	540	26	22	-5	.987	-30	*1-2045,O-275/D	36.5

■ ART McCOY
McCoy, Arthur Gray b: 7/1864, Danville, Pa. d: 3/22/04, Danville, Pa. 168 lbs. Deb: 7/8/1889

YEAR	TM/L	G	AB	R	H	2B	3B	HR	RBI	BB	SO	AVG	OBP	SLG	PRO+	BR/A	SB	CS	SBR	FA	FR	G/POS	TPR
1889	Was-N	2	6	0	0	0	0	0	0	2	1	.000	.250	.000	-29	-1	0			.889	-2	/2-2	-0.2

■ BENNY McCOY
McCoy, Benjamin Jenison b: 11/9/15, Jenison, Mich. BL/TR, 5'9", 170 lbs. Deb: 9/14/38

YEAR	TM/L	G	AB	R	H	2B	3B	HR	RBI	BB	SO	AVG	OBP	SLG	PRO+	BR/A	SB	CS	SBR	FA	FR	G/POS	TPR
1938	Det-A	7	15	2	3	1	0	0	0	1	2	.200	.250	.267	28	-2	0	0	0	.963	2	/2-6,3-1	0.1
1939	Det-A	55	192	38	58	13	6	1	33	29	26	.302	.394	.448	107	2	3	1	0	.958	-2	2-34,S-16	0.4
1940	Phi-A	134	490	56	126	26	5	7	62	65	44	.257	.345	.373	88	-8	2	2	-1	.951	-16	*2-130/3-1	-1.5
1941	Phi-A	141	517	86	140	12	7	8	61	95	50	.271	.384	.368	102	-5	3	3	-1	.963	-13	*2-135	0.1
Total	4	337	1214	182	327	52	18	16	156	190	122	.269	.369	.381	97	-2	8	6	-1	.957	-28	2-305/S-16,3	-0.9

■ TOMMY McCRAW
McCraw, Tommy Lee b: 11/21/40, Malvern, Ark. BL/TL, 6', 183 lbs. Deb: 6/4/63 C

YEAR	TM/L	G	AB	R	H	2B	3B	HR	RBI	BB	SO	AVG	OBP	SLG	PRO+	BR/A	SB	CS	SBR	FA	FR	G/POS	TPR
1963	Chi-A	102	280	38	71	11	3	6	33	21	46	.254	.313	.379	94	-2	15	4	2	.993	-1	1-97	-0.5
1964	Chi-A	125	368	47	96	11	5	6	36	32	65	.261	.327	.367	95	-2	15	7	0	.992	-7	1-84,O-36	-1.4
1965	Chi-A	133	273	38	65	12	1	5	21	25	48	.238	.309	.344	91	-4	12	7	-1	.993	-8	1-72,O-64	-1.6
1966	Chi-A	151	389	49	89	16	4	5	48	29	40	.229	.291	.329	83	-9	20	11	-1	.990	-2	*1-121,O-41	-1.9
1967	Chi-A	125	453	55	107	18	3	11	45	33	55	.236	.290	.362	95	-4	24	10	1	.991	11	*1-123/O-6	0.1
1968	Chi-A	136	477	51	112	16	12	9	44	36	58	.235	.295	.375	101	-0	20	5	3	.986	2	*1-135	-0.5
1969	Chi-A	93	240	21	62	12	2	2	25	21	24	.258	.326	.350	85	-5	1	3	-2	.989	-10	1-44,O-41	-2.1
1970	Chi-A	129	332	39	73	11	2	6	31	21	50	.220	.275	.319	61	-18	12	3	0	.987	-3	1-59,O-49	-2.6
1971	Was-A	122	207	33	44	6	4	7	25	19	38	.213	.294	.382	96	-2	12	3	0	.958	-9	O-60,1-30	-1.6
1972	Cle-A	129	391	43	101	13	5	7	33	41	47	.258	.335	.371	106	2	4	12	-10	1.000	-1	O-84,1-38	-0.7
1973	Cal-A	99	264	25	70	7	0	3	24	30	42	.265	.345	.326	97	-0	3	2	-0	1.000	2	O-34,1-25/D	-0.2
1974	Cal-A	56	119	21	34	7	0	3	17	12	13	.286	.351	.429	131	5	2	1	0	1.000	2	1-29,O-12/D	0.5
	Cle-A	45	112	17	34	9	0	3	17	5	34	.304	.339	.455	128	4	5	2	0	.990	2	1-38/O-1	0.3
	Yr	101	231	38	68	16	0	6	34	17	24	.294	.345	.442	130	8	7	3	0	.994	4	1-67,O-13/D	0.8
1975	Cle-A	23	51	7	14	1	1	2	5	7	7	.275	.362	.451	129	2	4	1	1	1.000	-2	1-16/O-3	0.0
Total	13	1468	3956	484	972	150	42	75	404	332	544	.246	.311	.362	94	-33	143	68	2	.991	-22	1-911,O-431/D	-12.2

YEAR	TM/L	G	AB	R	H	2B	3B	HR	RBI	BB	SO	AVG	OBP	SLG	PRO+	BR/A	SB	CS	SBR	FA	FR	G/POS	TPR

■ RODNEY McCRAY   McCray, Rodney Duncan   b: 9/13/63, Detroit, Mich.   BR/TR, 5'10", 175 lbs.   Deb: 4/30/90

1990	Chi-A	32	6	8	0	0	0	0	1	0	4	.000	.143	.000	-58	-1	6	0	2	1.000	-5	O-13/D-7	-0.4
1991	Chi-A	17	7	2	2	0	0	0	0	0	2	.286	.286	.286	60	-0	1	1	-0	1.000	-2	/O-8,D-6	-0.2
1992	NY-N	18	1	3	1	0	0	0	1	0	0	1.000	1.000	1.000	475	0	2	0	1	1.000	-4	O-13	-0.3
Total	3	67	14	13	3	0	0	0	1	0	6	.214	.267	.214	36	-1	9	1	2	1.000	-10	/O-34,D-13	-0.9

■ FRANK McCREA   McCrea, Francis William   b: 9/6/1896, Jersey City, N.J.   d: 2/25/81, Dover, N.J.   BR/TR, 5'9", 155 lbs.   Deb: 9/26/25

1925	Cle-A	1	5	1	1	0	0	0	0	0	0	.200	.200	.200	2	-1	0	0	0	1.000	-1	/C-1	-0.1

■ JUDGE McCREDIE   McCredie, Walter Henry   b: 11/29/1876, Manchester, Iowa   d: 7/29/34, Portland, Ore.   BL/TR, 6'2", 195 lbs.   Deb: 4/20/03

1903	Bro-N	56	213	40	69	5	0	0	20	24		.324	.397	.347	116	6	10			.925	-4	O-56	-0.2

■ TOM McCREERY   McCreery, Thomas Livingston   b: 10/19/1874, Beaver, Pa.   d: 7/3/41, Beaver, Pa.   BB/TR, 5'11", 180 lbs.   Deb: 6/8/1895

1895	Lou-N	31	108	18	35	3	1	0	10	8	15	.324	.376	.370	99	0	3			.875	-6	O-18/P-8,S31	-0.7
1896	Lou-N	115	441	87	155	23	21	7	65	42	58	.351	.409	.546	157	35	26			.916	1	*O-111/2-1,P	2.2
1897	Lou-N	89	338	55	96	5	6	4	40	38		.284	.356	.370	98	-2	13			.856	-5	*O-89	-1.2
	NY-N	49	177	36	53	8	5	1	27	22		.299	.380	.418	114	4	15			.900	-2	O-45/2-3	-0.1
	Yr	138	515	91	149	13	11	5	67	60		.289	.365	.386	101	2	28			.869	-7	*O-134/2-3	-1.3
1898	NY-N	35	121	15	24	4	3	1	17	19		.198	.307	.306	78	-3	3			.820	-5	O-35	-1.0
	Pit-N	53	190	33	59	5	7	2	20	26		.311	.394	.442	142	11	3			.934	-1	O-51	0.6
	Yr	88	311	48	83	9	10	3	37	45		.267	.360	.389	117	8	6			.901	-6	O-86	-0.4
1899	Pit-N	118	455	76	147	21	9	2	64	47		.323	.390	.422	123	15	11			.911	-7	O-97/S-9,2	0.1
1900	Pit-N	43	132	20	29	4	3	1	13	16		.220	.304	.318	71	-5	7			.887	2	O-35/P-1	-0.5
1901	Bro-N	91	335	47	97	11	14	3	53	32		.290	.355	.433	124	10	13			.947	4	O-82/1-4,S	0.8
1902	Bro-N	112	430	49	105	8	4	4	57	29		.244	.295	.309	86	-8	16			.979	-1	*1-108/O-4	-1.1
1903	Bro-N	40	141	13	37	5	2	0	10	20		.262	.354	.326	97	0	5			.892	-2	O-38	-0.4
	Bos-N	23	83	15	18	2	1	1	10	9		.217	.293	.301	72	-3	6			.900	0	O-23	-0.4
	Yr	63	224	28	55	7	3	1	20	29		.246	.332	.317	88	-3	11			.896	-2	O-61	-0.8
Total	9	799	2951	464	855	99	76	26	386	308	<u>73</u>	.290	.359	.401	113	54	116			.905	-22	O-628,1-113/S2P3	-1.7

■ FRANK McCUE   McCue, Frank Aloysius   b: 10/4/1898, Chicago, Ill.   d: 7/5/53, Chicago, Ill.   BB/TR, 5'9", 150 lbs.   Deb: 9/15/22

1922	Phi-A	2	5	0	0	0	0	0	0	0	0	.000	.000	.000	-97	-1	0	0	0	.000	0	/3-2	-0.1

■ CLYDE McCULLOUGH   McCullough, Clyde Edward   b: 3/4/17, Nashville, Tenn.   d: 9/18/82, San Francisco, Cal.   BR/TR, 5'11.5", 180 lbs.   Deb: 4/28/40   C

1940	Chi-N	9	26	4	4	1	0	0	1	5	5	.154	.290	.192	36	-2	0			1.000	3	/C-7	0.1
1941	Chi-N	125	418	41	95	9	2	9	53	34	67	.227	.289	.323	75	-15	5			.982	-8	*C-119	-1.3
1942	Chi-N	109	337	39	95	22	1	5	31	25	47	.282	.331	.398	117	6	7			.980	-1	C-97	1.4
1943	Chi-N	87	266	20	63	5	2	2	23	24	33	.237	.302	.293	73	-9	6			.977	-16	C-81	-2.1
1946	Chi-N	95	307	38	88	18	5	4	34	22	39	.287	.338	.417	116	5	2			.991	-2	C-89	0.8
1947	Chi-N	86	234	25	59	12	4	3	30	20	20	.252	.314	.376	86	-5	1			.984	7	C-64	0.5
1948	Chi-N☆	69	172	10	36	4	2	1	7	15	25	.209	.273	.273	50	-12	0			.973	5	C-51	-0.5
1949	Pit-N	91	241	30	57	9	3	4	21	24	30	.237	.316	.349	76	-8	1			.985	8	C-90	0.4
1950	Pit-N	103	279	28	71	16	4	6	34	31	35	.254	.340	.405	92	-3	3			.985	-8	*C-100	-0.7
1951	Pit-N	92	259	26	77	9	2	8	39	27	31	.297	.366	.440	113	5	2	0	1	.988	10	C-87	1.8
1952	Pit-N	66	172	10	40	5	1	1	15	10	18	.233	.283	.291	58	-10	0	1	-1	.981	7	C-61/1-1	-0.1
1953	Chi-N☆	77	229	21	59	3	2	6	23	15	23	.258	.303	.367	72	-10	0	0	0	.987	-3	C-73	-1.0
1954	Chi-N	31	81	9	21	7	0	3	17	5	5	.259	.310	.457	96	-1	0	0	0	.981	-2	C-26/3-3	-0.1
1955	Chi-N	44	81	7	16	0	0	0	10	8	15	.198	.278	.198	29	-8	0	0	0	.989	7	C-37	0.0
1956	Chi-N	14	19	1	4	1	0	0	1	0	5	.211	.211	.263	27	-2	0	0	0	1.000	1	/C-7	-0.1
Total	15	1098	3121	308	785	121	28	52	339	265	398	.252	.314	.358	85	-69	27	<u>1</u>		.984	7	C-989/3-3,1	-0.9

■ HARRY McCURDY   McCurdy, Harry Henry "Hank"   b: 9/15/1899, Stevens Point, Wis.   d: 7/21/72, Houston, Tex.   BL/TR, 5'11", 187 lbs.   Deb: 7/4/22

1922	StL-N	13	27	3	8	2	0	5	5	1	5	.296	.321	.519	119	1	0	0	0	.967	-1	/C-9,1-2	0.0
1923	StL-N	67	185	17	49	11	2	0	15	11	11	.265	.306	.346	79	-7	3	1	0	.969	-7	C-58	-1.1
1926	Chi-A	44	86	16	28	7	2	1	11	6	10	.326	.370	.488	127	3	0	1	-1	.974	-4	C-25/1-8	0.0
1927	Chi-A	86	262	34	75	19	3	1	27	32	24	.286	.366	.393	99	-0	6	4	-1	.972	-3	C-82	0.2
1928	Chi-A	49	103	12	27	10	0	2	13	8	15	.262	.315	.417	92	-2	1	3	-2	.964	-4	C-34	-0.4
1930	Phi-N	80	148	23	49	8	2	1	26	15	12	.331	.393	.419	90	-2	0			.966	-5	C-41	-0.4
1931	Phi-N	66	150	21	43	9	1	0	25	23	16	.287	.382	.367	95	-0	2			.968	-1	C-45	0.1
1932	Phi-N	62	136	13	32	6	1	1	14	17	13	.235	.325	.316	65	-6	0			.974	-1	C-42	-0.5
1933	Phi-N	73	54	9	15	1	0	2	12	16	6	.278	.451	.407	130	3	0			.000	0	/C-2	0.3
1934	Cin-N	3	6	0	0	0	0	0	0	0	0	.000	.000	.000	-99	-2	0			1.000	0	/1-1	-0.1
Total	10	543	1157	148	326	71	12	9	148	129	108	.282	.355	.387	92	-13	12	<u>9</u>		.970	-24	C-338/1-11	-1.9

■ TERRY McDANIEL   McDaniel, Terrence Keith   b: 12/6/66, Kansas City, Mo.   BR/TR, 5'9", 205 lbs.   Deb: 8/31/91

1991	NY-N	23	29	3	6	1	0	0	2	1	11	.207	.233	.241	34	-3	2	0	1	1.000	-3	O-14	-0.5

■ RAY McDAVID   McDavid, Ray Darnell   b: 7/20/71, San Diego, Cal.   BL/TR, 6'3", 190 lbs.   Deb: 7/15/94

1994	SD-N	9	28	2	7	1	0	0	4	2	10	.250	.276	.286	47	-2	1	0	0	1.000	-0	/O-7	-0.2

■ RED McDERMOTT   McDermott, Frank A.   b: 11/12/1889, Philadelphia, Pa.   d: 9/11/64, Philadelphia, Pa.   BR/TR, 5'6", 150 lbs.   Deb: 8/6/12

1912	Det-A	5	15	2	4	1	0	0	0	0		.267	.313	.333	87	-0	1			1.000	-0	/O-5	-0.1

■ JOE McDERMOTT   McDermott, Joseph   Deb: 5/4/1871

1871	Kek-n	2	8	3	2	0	0	0	1	1	1	.250	.333	.250	69	-0	1					/O-2	0.0
1872	Eck-n	7	33	3	9	3	0	0	3	1	2	.273	.294	.364	119	1						/P-7	0.0
Total	2 n	9	41	6	11	3	0	0	<u>4</u>	2	<u>3</u>	.268	.302	.341	107	1						/P-7,O-2	0.0

■ MICKEY McDERMOTT   McDermott, Maurice Joseph "Maury"   b: 8/29/28, Poughkeepsie, N.Y.   BL/TL, 6'2", 170 lbs.   Deb: 4/24/48   C

1948	Bos-A	7	8	2	3	1	0	0	0	0	0	.375	.375	.500	125	0	0	0	0	1.000	1	/P-7	0.0
1949	Bos-A	12	33	3	7	3	0	0	6	3	6	.212	.278	.303	50	-2	0	0	0	.941	-0	P-12	0.0
1950	Bos-A	39	44	11	16	5	0	0	12	9	3	.364	.472	.477	131	2	0	0	0	.938	1	P-38	0.0
1951	Bos-A	43	66	8	18	1	1	1	6	3	14	.273	.314	.364	76	-2	0	1	-1	.950	1	P-34	0.0
1952	Bos-A	36	62	10	14	1	1	1	7	4	11	.226	.273	.323	60	-3	0	0	0	.944	-0	P-30	0.0
1953	Bos-A	45	93	9	28	8	1	0	13	2	16	.301	.316	.419	92	-1	1	0	0	.957	1	P-32	0.0
1954	Was-A	54	95	7	19	4	0	0	4	7	12	.200	.255	.232	36	-9	0	0	0	.955	1	P-30	0.0
1955	Was-A	70	95	10	25	4	0	1	10	6	16	.263	.314	.337	79	-3	1	0	0	.943	1	P-31	0.0
1956	*NY-A	46	52	4	11	0	0	0	6	5	6	.212	.317	.269	58	-3	0	0	0	1.000	-0	P-23	0.0
1957	KC-A	58	49	6	12	1	0	4	7	9	16	.245	.362	.510	133	2	0	0	0	.960	-1	P-29/1-2	0.0
1958	Det-A	4	3	0	1	0	0	0	0	0	0	.333	.333	.333	78	-0	0	0	0	.000	-0	/P-2	0.0
1961	StL-N	22	14	1	1	0	0	0	1	1	5	.071	.071	.143	-41	-3	0	0	0	1.000	-0	/P-19	0.0
	KC-A	7	5	0	1	1	0	0	1	0	0	.200	.333	.400	93	-0	0			.500	0	/P-4	0.0
Total	12	443	619	71	156	29	2	9	74	52	112	.252	.312	.349	76	-22	1	2	-1	.951	4	P-291/1-2	0.0

YEAR	TM/L	G	AB	R	H	2B	3B	HR	RBI	BB	SO	AVG	OBP	SLG	PRO+	BR/A	SB	CS	SBR	FA	FR	G/POS	TPR

■ TERRY McDERMOTT McDermott, Terrence Michael b: 3/20/51, Rockville Cen., N.Y BR/TR, 6'3", 205 lbs. Deb: 9/12/72

| 1972 | LA-N | 9 | 23 | 2 | 3 | 0 | 0 | 0 | 0 | 2 | 8 | .130 | .200 | .130 | -5 | -3 | 0 | 0 | 0 | 1.000 | -1 | /1-7 | -0.5 |

■ SANDY McDERMOTT McDermott, Thomas Nathaniel b: 3/15/1856, Zanesville, Ohio d: 11/23/22, Mansfield, Ohio Deb: 6/18/1885

| 1885 | Bal-a | 1 | 0 | 0 | 0 | 0 | 0 | 0 | 0 | | | — | — | — | — | 0 | | | | .000 | 0 | /2-1 | 0.0 |

■ McDONALD McDonald Deb: 5/18/1872

| 1872 | Eck-n | 1 | 4 | 0 | 0 | 0 | 0 | 0 | 0 | 0 | 0 | .000 | .000 | .000 | -99 | -1 | | | | | | /S-1 | -0.1 |

■ TEX McDONALD McDonald, Charles E. (b: Charles C. Crabtree) b: 1/31/1891, Farmersville, Tex. d: 3/31/43, Houston, Tex. BL/TR, 5'10", 160 lbs. Deb: 4/11/12

1912	Cin-N	61	140	16	36	3	4	1	15	13	24	.257	.329	.357	90	-2	5			.915	-9	S-42	-0.7
1913	Cin-N	11	10	1	3	0	0	0	2	0	1	.300	.300	.300	72	-0	0			.000	0	/S-1	0.0
	Bos-N	62	145	24	52	4	4	0	18	15	17	.359	.422	.441	144	9	4			.869	-1	3-31/2-6,O	0.8
	Yr	73	155	25	55	4	4	0	20	15	18	.355	.415	.432	140	8	4			.869	-1	3-31/2-6,SO	0.8
1914	Pit-F	67	223	27	71	16	7	3	29	13	23	.318	.361	.493	121	6	9			.925	-3	O-29,2-27/S	0.2
	Buf-F	69	250	32	74	13	6	3	32	20	26	.296	.353	.432	100	-0	11			.953	-3	O-61,2-10	-0.6
	Yr	136	473	59	145	29	13	6	61	33	49	.307	.357	.461	110	5	20			.943	-6	O-90,2-37/S	-0.4
1915	Buf-F	87	251	31	68	9	6	6	39	27	34	.271	.346	.426	104	1	5			.924	-7	O-65	-0.9
Total	4	357	1019	131	304	45	27	13	135	88	125	.298	.359	.434	110	12	34			.936	-22	O-156/S-48,23	-1.2

■ JACK McDONALD McDonald, Daniel b: 1847, Brooklyn, N.Y. d: 11/23/1880, Brooklyn, N.Y. 5'11", 154 lbs. Deb: 5/2/1872

| 1872 | Atl-n | 15 | 61 | 9 | 15 | 4 | 1 | 0 | 5 | 0 | 1 | .246 | .246 | .344 | 68 | -3 | | | | | | O-14 | -0.2 |

■ DAVE McDONALD McDonald, David Bruce b: 5/20/43, New Albany, Ind. BL/TR, 6'3", 215 lbs. Deb: 9/15/69

1969	NY-A	9	23	0	5	1	0	0	2	5	7	.217	.280	.261	54	-1	0	1	-1	.960	-1	/1-7	-0.3
1971	Mon-N	24	39	3	4	2	0	1	4	1	12	.103	.186	.231	17	-4	0	0	0	.983	-1	/1-8,O-1	-0.6
Total	2	33	62	3	9	3	0	1	6	6	19	.145	.221	.242	31	-6	0	1	-1	.972	-1	/1-15,O-1	-0.9

■ ED McDONALD McDonald, Edward C. b: 10/28/1886, Albany, N.Y. d: 3/11/46, Albany, N.Y. BR/TR, 6', 180 lbs. Deb: 8/5/11

1911	Bos-N	54	175	28	36	7	3	1	21	40	39	.206	.359	.297	78	-4	11			.955	-6	3-53/S-1	-0.9
1912	Bos-N	121	459	70	119	23	6	2	34	70	91	.259	.363	.349	94	-2	22			.940	-2	*3-118	-0.3
1913	Chi-N	1	0	0	0	0	0	0	0	0	0	—	—	—	—	-0	0			.000	0	R	0.0
Total	3	176	634	98	155	30	9	3	55	110	130	.244	.362	.334	89	-6	33			.945	-7	3-171/S-1	-1.2

■ JIM McDONALD McDonald, James b: Philadelphia, Pa. BR/TR, 6', 180 lbs. Deb: 6/2/02

| 1902 | NY-N | 2 | 9 | 0 | 3 | 0 | 0 | 0 | 1 | 0 | | .333 | .333 | .333 | 107 | 0 | 0 | | | 1.000 | -0 | /O-2 | -0.1 |

■ JIM McDONALD McDonald, James A. b: 8/6/1860, San Francisco, Cal. d: 9/14/14, San Francisco, Cal. Deb: 6/20/1884

1884	Was-U	2	6	0	1	0	0	0	0			.167	.167	.167	-9	-1				.700	-1	/C-1,O-1	-0.2
	Pit-a	38	145	11	23	3	0	0		0	2	.159	.170	.179	14	-13				.795	-6	3-22,O-15/2	-1.9
1885	Buf-N	5	14	0	0	0	0	0	0	0	4	.000	.000	.000	-97	-3				.875	2	/S-4,O-1	-0.1
Total	2	45	165	11	24	3	0	0	0	2	4	.145	.156	.164	3	-17				.848	-6	/3-22,O-17,S2C	-2.2

■ JOE McDONALD McDonald, Malcolm Joseph b: 4/9/1888, Texas d: 5/30/63, Baytown, Tex. BR/TR, 5'11", 175 lbs. Deb: 9/6/10

| 1910 | StL-A | 10 | 32 | 4 | 5 | 0 | 0 | 0 | 1 | 1 | | .156 | .182 | .156 | 6 | -3 | 0 | | | .821 | -3 | 3-10 | -0.7 |

■ JIM McDONNELL McDonnell, James William "Mack" b: 8/15/22, Gagetown, Mich. BL/TR, 5'11", 165 lbs. Deb: 9/23/43

1943	Cle-A	2	1	1	0	0	0	0	0	2	1	.000	.667	.000	108	0	0	0	0	1.000	-0	/C-1	0.0
1944	Cle-A	20	43	5	10	0	0	0	4	4	3	.233	.298	.233	55	-2	0	0	0	.900	-2	C-13	-0.4
1945	Cle-A	28	51	3	10	2	0	0	8	2	4	.196	.226	.235	36	-4	0	0	0	.980	8	C-23	0.5
Total	3	50	95	9	20	2	0	0	12	8	8	.211	.272	.232	48	-6	0	0	0	.953	6	/C-37	0.1

■ ED McDONOUGH McDonough, Edward Sebastian b: 9/11/1886, Elgin, Ill. d: 9/2/26, Elgin, Ill. BR/TR, 6', 160 lbs. Deb: 8/3/09

1909	Phi-N	1	1	0	0	0	0	0	0	0		.000	.000	.000	-99	-0	0			1.000	0	/C-1	0.0
1910	Phi-N	5	9	1	1	0	0	0	0	0	1	.111	.111	.111	-34	-2	0			1.000	-1	/C-4	-0.2
Total	2	6	10	1	1	0	0	0	0	0	1	.100	.100	.100	-40	-2	0			1.000	-1	/C-5	-0.2

■ GIL McDOUGALD McDougald, Gilbert James b: 5/19/28, San Francisco, Cal BR/TR, 6'1", 180 lbs. Deb: 4/20/51

1951	*NY-A	131	402	72	123	23	4	14	63	56	54	.306	.396	.488	143	25	14	5	1	.949	-16	3-82,2-55	1.2
1952	*NY-A	152	555	65	146	16	5	11	78	57	73	.263	.336	.369	102	1	6	5	-1	.968	12	*3-117,2-38	1.2
1953	*NY-A	141	541	82	154	27	7	10	83	60	65	.285	.361	.416	113	10	3	4	-2	.953	6	*3-136,2-26	1.2
1954	NY-A	126	394	66	102	22	2	12	48	62	64	.259	.367	.416	118	11	3	4	-2	.989	1	2-92,3-35	1.6
1955	*NY-A	141	533	79	152	10	8	13	53	65	59	.285	.365	.407	109	7	6	4	-1	.985	19	*2-126,3-17	3.5
1956	*NY-A☆	120	438	79	136	13	3	13	56	68	59	.311	.407	.443	128	20	3	8	-4	.970	3	S-92,2-31/3	2.8
1957	*NY-A★	141	539	87	156	25	9	13	62	59	71	.289	.364	.442	121	16	2	6	-2	.976	15	*S-121,2-21/3	4.2
1958	*NY-A★	138	503	69	126	19	1	14	65	59	75	.250	.333	.376	98	-1	6	2	1	.977	-2	*2-115,S-19	0.6
1959	NY-A★	127	434	44	109	16	8	4	34	35	40	.251	.311	.353	85	-9	0	3	-2	.989	8	2-53,S-52,3	0.5
1960	*NY-A	119	337	54	87	16	4	8	34	38	45	.258	.339	.401	105	2	2	4	-2	.945	-3	3-84,2-42	0.0
Total	10	1336	4676	697	1291	187	51	112	576	559	623	.276	.358	.410	112	81	45	44	-13	.984	42	2-599,3-508,S	16.8

■ ODDIBE McDOWELL McDowell, Oddibe b: 8/25/62, Hollywood, Fla. BL/TL, 5'9", 165 lbs. Deb: 5/19/85

1985	Tex-A	111	406	63	97	14	5	18	42	36	85	.239	.306	.431	98	-2	25	7	3	.993	10	*O-103/D-4	0.8
1986	Tex-A	154	572	105	152	24	7	18	49	65	112	.266	.342	.427	105	4	33	15	1	.991	3	*O-148/D-1	0.3
1987	Tex-A	128	407	65	98	26	4	14	52	51	99	.241	.325	.428	97	-2	24	2	6	.989	-2	*O-125	-0.1
1988	Tex-A	120	437	55	108	19	5	6	37	41	89	.247	.315	.355	85	-9	33	10	4	.989	-3	*O-113/D-3	-1.2
1989	Cle-A	69	239	33	53	5	2	3	22	25	36	.222	.298	.297	67	-10	12	5	1	.992	4	O-64/D-2	-1.0
	Atl-N	76	280	56	85	18	4	7	24	27	37	.304	.365	.471	134	12	15	10	-2	.978	5	O-68	1.4
1990	Atl-N	113	305	47	74	14	0	7	25	21	53	.243	.296	.357	74	-11	13	2	3	.971	-6	O-72	-1.6
1994	Tex-A	59	183	34	48	5	1	1	15	28	39	.262	.360	.317	83	-4	14	2	3	.983	-4	O-53/D-2	-0.5
Total	7	830	2829	458	715	125	28	74	266	294	550	.253	.325	.395	95	-21	169	53	19	.987	5	O-746/D-12	-1.9

■ PRYOR McELVEEN McElveen, Pryor Mynatt "Humpty" b: 11/5/1881, Atlanta, Ga. d: 10/27/51, Pleasant Hill, Tenn. BR/TR, 5'10", 168 lbs. Deb: 4/26/09

1909	Bro-N	81	258	22	51	8	3	1	25	14		.198	.242	.271	61	-13	6			.938	-4	3-37,O-13,S/12	-1.8
1910	Bro-N	74	213	19	48	8	3	1	26	22	47	.225	.307	.305	81	-5	6			.943	-5	3-54/S-6,2C	-0.9
1911	Bro-N	16	31	1	6	0	0	0	5	0	3	.194	.194	.194	9	-4	0			.929	-1	/2-5,S-1	-0.5
Total	3	171	502	42	105	16	4	4	56	36	50	.209	.268	.281	67	-22	12			.941	-10	/3-91,S-17,201C	-3.2

■ LEE McELWEE McElwee, Leland Stanford b: 5/23/1894, LaMesa, Cal. d: 2/8/57, Union, Maine BR/TR, 5'10.5", 160 lbs. Deb: 7/3/16

| 1916 | Phi-N | 54 | 155 | 9 | 41 | 3 | 0 | 0 | 10 | 8 | 17 | .265 | .301 | .284 | 79 | -4 | 0 | | | .883 | -2 | 3-30/O-9,21S | -0.6 |

■ FRANK McELYEA McElyea, Frank b: 8/4/18, Hawthorne Twsp., Ill. d: 4/19/87, Evansville, Ill. BR/TR, 6'6", 221 lbs. Deb: 9/10/42

| 1942 | Bos-N | 7 | 4 | 2 | 0 | 0 | 0 | 0 | 0 | 0 | 0 | .000 | .000 | .000 | -99 | -0 | 0 | | | 1.000 | -0 | /O-1 | -0.1 |

■ GUY McFADDEN McFadden, Guy G. b: 9/3/1872, Topeka, Kan. d: 3/10/11, Topeka, Kan. Deb: 8/24/1895

| 1895 | StL-N | 4 | 14 | 1 | 3 | 0 | 0 | 0 | 2 | 0 | 2 | .214 | .214 | .214 | 11 | -2 | 0 | | | .968 | -1 | /1-4 | -0.2 |

YEAR	TM/L	G	AB	R	H	2B	3B	HR	RBI	BB	SO	AVG	OBP	SLG	PRO+	BR/A	SB	CS	SBR	FA	FR	G/POS	TPR

■ LEON McFADDEN   McFadden, Leon   b: 4/26/44, Little Rock, Ark.   BR/TR, 6'2", 195 lbs.   Deb: 9/6/68

1968	Hou-N	16	47	2	13	1	0	0	1	6	10	.277	.358	.298	101	0	1	0	0	.968	-1	S-16	0.2
1969	Hou-N	44	74	3	13	2	0	0	3	4	9	.176	.218	.203	19	-8	1	2	-1	.944	-3	O-17/S-8	-1.2
1970	Hou-N	2	0	0	0	0	0	0	0	0	0	—	—	—	—	0	0	0	0	.000	0	R	0.0
Total	3	62	121	5	26	3	0	0	4	10	19	.215	.275	.240	50	-8	2	2	-1	.966	-4	/S-24,O-17	-1.0

■ ALEX McFARLAN   McFarlan, Alexander Shepherd   b: 11/11/1866, Kentucky   d: 3/2/39, Peewee Valley, Ky.   Deb: 6/19/1892   F

1892	Lou-N	14	42	2	7	0	0	0	1	8	11	.167	.300	.167	46	-2	1			.773	-3	O-12/2-2	-0.5

■ CHRIS McFARLAND   McFarland, Christopher   b: 8/17/1861, Fall River, Mass.   d: 5/24/18, New Bedford, Mass.   5'9", 170 lbs.   Deb: 4/19/1884

1884	Bal-U	3	14	2	3	1	0	0				.214	.214	.286	31	-1				.571	-1	/O-3,P-1	-0.2

■ ED McFARLAND   McFarland, Edward William   b: 8/3/1874, Cleveland, Ohio   d: 11/28/59, Cleveland, Ohio   BR/TR, 5'10", 180 lbs.   Deb: 7/7/1893

1893	Cle-N	8	22	5	9	2	1	0	6	1	2	.409	.458	.591	168	2	0			1.000	-4	/O-5,3-2,C	-0.1
1896	StL-N	83	290	48	70	13	4	3	36	15	17	.241	.281	.345	67	-15	7			.961	8	C-80/O-2	0.2
1897	StL-N	31	107	14	35	5	2	1	17	8		.327	.374	.439	116	2	2			.965	2	C-23/1-3,O2	0.6
	Phi-N	38	130	18	29	3	5	1	16	14		.223	.308	.346	74	-5	2			.951	-2	C-37	-0.2
	Yr	69	237	32	64	8	7	2	33	22		.270	.337	.388	93	-3	4			.957	0	C-60/1-3,O2	0.4
1898	Phi-N	121	429	65	121	21	5	3	71	44		.282	.352	.375	113	8	4			.960	-1	*C-121	1.7
1899	Phi-N	96	324	59	108	22	9	2	57	36		.333	.403	.475	146	21	9			.968	13	C-94	3.7
1900	Phi-N	94	344	50	105	14	8	0	38	29		.305	.364	.392	110	5	9			**.963**	-3	C-93/3-1	0.9
1901	Phi-N	74	295	33	84	14	2	1	32	18		.285	.326	.356	96	-2	11			.970	2	C-74	0.8
1902	Chi-A	75	246	29	56	9	2	1	25	19		.228	.291	.293	65	-11	8			.967	1	C-69/O-2,1	-0.3
1903	Chi-A	61	201	15	42	7	2	1	19	14		.209	.264	.279	66	-8	3			.968	-0	C-56/1-1	-0.3
1904	Chi-A	50	160	22	44	11	3	0	20	17		.275	.348	.381	136	7	2			.975	-11	C-49	0.1
1905	Chi-A	80	250	24	70	13	4	0	31	23		.280	.345	.364	130	9	5			.973	6	C-70	2.4
1906	*Chi-A	12	23	0	4	1	0	0	3	3		.174	.269	.217	54	-1	0			.973	-1	/C-7	-0.1
1907	Chi-A	52	138	11	39	9	1	0	8	12		.283	.340	.362	128	4	3			.972	-1	C-43	0.7
1908	Bos-N	19	48	5	10	2	1	0	4	3		.208	.224	.292	66	-2	0			.978	4	C-13	0.3
Total	14	894	3007	398	826	146	49	13	383	254	<u>19</u>	.275	.335	.369	104	13	65			.967	14	C-830/O-12,132	10.4

■ HERM McFARLAND   McFarland, Hermas Walter   b: 3/11/1870, Des Moines, Iowa   d: 9/21/35, Richmond, Va.   BL/TR, 5'6", 150 lbs.   Deb: 4/21/1896

1896	Lou-N	30	110	11	21	4	1	1	12	9	14	.191	.252	.273	40	-10	4			.833	-3	O-28/C-1	-1.3
1898	Cin-N	19	64	10	18	1	3	0	11	7		.281	.361	.391	108	1	3			.968	-2	O-17	-0.3
1901	Chi-A	132	473	83	130	21	9	4	59	75		.275	.384	.383	116	14	33			.946	5	*O-132	0.8
1902	Chi-A	7	27	5	5	0	0	0	4	2		.185	.241	.185	20	-3	1			1.000	-0	/O-7	-0.4
	Bal-A	61	242	54	78	19	6	3	36	36		.322	.418	.488	144	16	10			.965	6	O-61	1.7
	Yr	68	269	59	83	19	6	3	40	38		.309	.402	.457	133	13	11			.967	6	O-68	1.3
1903	NY-A	103	362	41	88	16	9	5	45	46		.243	.333	.378	106	3	13			.939	-3	*O-103	-0.6
Total	5	352	1278	204	340	61	28	13	167	175	<u>14</u>	.266	.362	.388	110	21	64			.941	2	O-348/C-1	-0.1

■ HOWIE McFARLAND   McFarland, Howard Alexander   b: 3/7/11, ElReno, Okla.   BR/TR, 6', 175 lbs.   Deb: 7/16/45

1945	Was-A	6	11	0	1	0	0	0	2	0	3	.091	.091	.091	-52	-2	0	0	0	1.000	-0	/O-3	-0.3

■ ORLANDO McFARLANE   McFarlane, Orlando Dejesus (Quesada)   b: 6/28/38, Oriente, Cuba   BR/TR, 6', 180 lbs.   Deb: 4/23/62

1962	Pit-N	8	23	0	2	0	0	0	1	1	4	.087	.125	.087	-42	-5	0	0	0	1.000	2	/C-8	-0.2
1964	Pit-N	37	78	5	19	5	0	0	1	4	27	.244	.280	.308	66	-4	0	0	0	.983	-6	C-35/O-1	-0.9
1966	Det-A	49	138	16	35	7	0	5	13	9	46	.254	.304	.413	102	0	0	0	0	.991	-2	C-33	0.0
1967	Cal-A	12	22	0	5	0	0	0	3	1	7	.227	.261	.227	47	-1	0	0	0	.935	-1	/C-6	-0.2
1968	Cal-A	18	31	1	9	0	0	0	2	5	9	.290	.389	.290	112	1	0	0	0	.977	-0	/C-9	0.1
Total	5	124	292	22	70	12	0	5	20	20	93	.240	.291	.332	78	-9	0	0	0	.985	-8	/C-91,O-1	-1.2

■ PATSY McGAFFIGAN   McGaffigan, Mark Andrew   b: 9/12/1888, Carlyle, Ill.   d: 12/22/40, Carlyle, Ill.   BR/TR, 5'8", 140 lbs.   Deb: 4/16/17

1917	Phi-N	19	60	5	10	1	0	0	6	0	7	.167	.167	.183	7	-7	1			.920	-1	S-17/O-1	-0.7
1918	Phi-N	54	192	17	39	3	2	1	8	16	23	.203	.268	.255	56	-10	3			.948	-12	2-53/S-1	-2.1
Total	2	73	252	22	49	4	2	1	14	16	30	.194	.245	.238	45	-16	4			.923	-12	/2-53,S-18,O	-2.8

■ EDDIE McGAH   McGah, Edward Joseph   b: 9/30/21, Oakland, Cal.   BR/TR, 6', 183 lbs.   Deb: 4/26/46

1946	Bos-A	15	37	2	8	1	1	0	7	1	7	.216	.341	.297	75	-1	0	0	0	.981	-2	C-14	-0.3
1947	Bos-A	9	14	1	0	0	0	0	2	3	0	.000	.176	.000	-45	-3	0	0	0	.964	2	/C-7	-0.1
Total	2	24	51	3	8	1	1	0	3	10	7	.157	.295	.216	41	-4	0	0	0	.975	-0	/C-21	-0.4

■ AMBROSE McGANN   McGann, Ambrose   b: Baltimore, Md.   Deb: 5/2/1895

1895	Lou-N	20	73	9	21	5	2	0	9	8	6	.288	.358	.411	105	1	6			.852	-2	/S-8,3-6,O	-0.1

■ DAN McGANN   McGann, Dennis Lawrence "Cap"   b: 7/15/1871, Shelbyville, Ky.   d: 12/13/10, Louisville, Ky.   BB/TR, 6', 190 lbs.   Deb: 8/8/1896

1896	Bos-N	43	171	25	55	6	7	2	30	12	10	.322	.383	.474	118	4	2			.905	-17	2-43	-0.9
1898	Bal-N	145	535	99	161	18	8	5	106	53		.301	.404	.393	126	22	33			.983	2	*1-145	2.1
1899	Bro-N	63	214	49	52	11	4	2	32	21		.243	.362	.360	96	-0	16			.985	2	1-61	0.1
	Was-N	76	280	65	96	9	8	5	58	14		.343	.410	.486	147	18	11			.990	2	1-76	1.8
	Yr	139	494	114	148	20	12	7	90	35		.300	.389	.431	124	18	27			**.988**	4	*1-137	1.9
1900	StL-N	121	444	79	132	10	9	4	58	32		.297	.376	.387	112	5	26			**.990**	-1	*1-121/2-1	0.6
1901	StL-N	103	423	73	115	15	9	6	56	16		.272	.333	.392	116	8	17			.984	-3	*1-103	0.4
1902	Bal-A	68	250	40	79	10	8	0	42	19		.316	.378	.420	116	6	17			.987	3	1-68	0.7
	NY-N	61	227	25	68	5	7	0	21	12		.300	.356	.383	129	8	12			.981	2	1-61	0.9
1903	NY-N	129	482	75	130	21	6	3	50	32		.270	.331	.357	92	-5	36			**.988**	-0	*1-129	-0.7
1904	NY-N	141	517	81	148	22	6	6	71	36		.286	.354	.387	123	14	42			**.991**	3	*1-141	1.5
1905	*NY-N	136	491	88	147	23	14	5	75	55		.299	.391	.434	143	27	22			**.991**	5	*1-136	2.9
1906	NY-N	134	451	62	107	14	8	0	37	60		.237	.344	.304	100	2	30			**.995**	3	*1-133	0.2
1907	NY-N	81	262	29	78	9	1	2	36	29		.298	.383	.363	129	10	9			**.994**	5	1-81	1.5
1908	Bos-N	135	475	52	115	22	5	2	55	38		.240	.321	.291	97	0	9			.988	5	*1-133	0.3
Total	12	1436	5222	842	1482	181	100	42	727	429	<u>10</u>	.284	.364	.381	117	122	282			.989	10	*1-1376/2-53	11.4

■ CHIPPY McGARR   McGarr, James B.   b: 5/10/1863, Worcester, Mass.   d: 6/4/04, Worcester, Mass.   BR/TR, 5'7", 168 lbs.   Deb: 7/11/1884   U

1884	CP-U	19	70	10	11	2	0	0		0		.157	.157	.186	-7	-10				.905	-6	2-13/O-6	-1.5
1886	Phi-a	71	267	41	71	9	3	2		9		.266	.295	.345	99	-1	17			.850	1	S-71	0.0
1887	Phi-a	137	536	93	158	23	6	1		23		.295	.326	.366	93	-6	84			.875	-1	*S-137	-0.5
1888	StL-a	34	132	17	31	1	0	0	13	6		.235	.268	.242	58	-7	25			.895	-3	2-33/S-1	-0.7
1889	KC-a	25	108	22	31	5	0	0	16	6	11	.287	.330	.315	79	-3	12			.857	-2	3-11/O-6,2S	-0.4
	Bal-a	3	7	1	1	0	0	0	1	1		.143	.250	.143	13	-1	0			.583	-2	/S-3	-0.2
	Yr	28	115	23	32	5	0	0	16	7	12	.278	.325	.304	76	-4	12			.857	-4	3-11/O-6,S2	-0.6
1890	Bos-N	121	487	68	115	12	7	1	51	34	38	.236	.291	.296	66	-23	39			**.933**	-2	3-115/S-5,O	-1.8
1893	Cle-N	63	249	38	77	12	0	0	28	20	15	.309	.363	.357	86	-5	24			.886	0	3-63	-0.3
1894	Cle-N	128	523	94	144	24	6	2	74	28	29	.275	.316	.356	59	-36	31			.902	-7	*3-128	-3.3
1895	*Cle-N	112	419	85	111	14	2	2	59	34	33	.265	.322	.322	63	-24	19			.870	-5	*3-108/2-4	-2.3

YEAR	TM/L	G	AB	R	H	2B	3B	HR	RBI	BB	SO	AVG	OBP	SLG	PRO+	BR/A	SB	CS	SBR	FA	FR	G/POS	TPR
1896	*Cle-N	113	455	68	122	16	4	1	53	22	30	.268	.302	.327	62	-26	16			.924	-7	*3-113/C-1	-2.6
Total	10	826	3253	537	872	116	28	9	294	183	157	.268	.310	.329	70	-144	267			.903	-33	3-538,S-220/2OC	-13.6

■ JIM McGARR
McGarr, James Vincent "Reds" b: 11/9/1888, Philadelphia, Pa. d: 7/21/81, Miami, Fla. BR/TR, 5'9.5", 170 lbs. Deb: 5/18/12

YEAR	TM/L	G	AB	R	H	2B	3B	HR	RBI	BB	SO	AVG	OBP	SLG	PRO+	BR/A	SB	CS	SBR	FA	FR	G/POS	TPR
1912	Det-A	1	4	0	0	0	0	0	0	0	0	.000	.000	.000	-99	-1	0			.800	-0	/2-1	-0.2

■ DAN McGARVEY
McGarvey, Daniel Francis b: 12/2/1887, Philadelphia, Pa. d: 3/7/47, Philadelphia, Pa. Deb: 5/18/12

YEAR	TM/L	G	AB	R	H	2B	3B	HR	RBI	BB	SO	AVG	OBP	SLG	PRO+	BR/A	SB	CS	SBR	FA	FR	G/POS	TPR
1912	Det-A	1	3	0	0	0	0	0	0	0	1	.000	.400	.000	18	-0	0			.667	0	/O-1	0.0

■ JACK McGEACHY
McGeachy, John Charles b: 5/23/1864, Clinton, Mass. d: 4/5/30, Cambridge, Mass. BR/TR, 5'8", 165 lbs. Deb: 6/17/1886

YEAR	TM/L	G	AB	R	H	2B	3B	HR	RBI	BB	SO	AVG	OBP	SLG	PRO+	BR/A	SB	CS	SBR	FA	FR	G/POS	TPR
1886	Det-N	6	27	3	9	0	1	0	4	0	3	.333	.333	.407	121	1	2			.875	-1	/O-6	0.0
	StL-N	59	226	31	46	12	3	2	24	1	37	.204	.207	.310	59	-11	8			.880	2	O-55/2-2,3	-1.0
	Yr	65	253	34	55	12	4	2	28	1	40	.217	.220	.320	66	-10	10			.880	1	O-61/2-2,3	-1.0
1887	Ind-N	99	405	49	109	17	3	1	56	5	16	.269	.280	.333	72	-15	27			.894	7	*O-98/3-1,P	-0.9
1888	Ind-N	118	452	45	99	15	2	0	30	5	21	.219	.231	.261	56	-23	49			.932	5	*O-117/S-1,P	-2.1
1889	Ind-N	131	532	83	142	32	1	2	63	9	39	.267	.282	.342	73	-22	37			.918	9	*O-131/P-3	-1.4
1890	Bro-P	104	443	84	108	24	4	1	65	19	12	.244	.278	.323	57	-30	21			.906	-1	*O-104	-2.8
1891	Phi-a	50	201	24	46	4	3	2	13	6	12	.229	.255	.308	59	-12	9			.920	2	O-50	-1.0
	Bos-a	41	178	26	45	2	1	1	21	12	8	.253	.304	.292	72	-7	11			.910	-4	O-41	-1.1
	Yr	91	379	50	91	6	4	3	34	18	20	.240	.278	.301	65	-19	20			.916	-2	O-91	-2.1
Total	6	608	2464	345	604	106	18	9	276	57	148	.245	.265	.314	65	-120	164			.909	18	O-602/P-5,32S	-10.3

■ MIKE McGEARY
McGeary, Michael Henry b: 1851, Philadelphia, Pa. BR/TR, 5'7", 138 lbs. Deb: 5/9/1871 M

YEAR	TM/L	G	AB	R	H	2B	3B	HR	RBI	BB	SO	AVG	OBP	SLG	PRO+	BR/A	SB	CS	SBR	FA	FR	G/POS	TPR
1871	Tro-n	29	148	42	39	4	0	0	12	6	0	.264	.292	.291	67	-6	**20**					*C-26/S-3	-0.4
1872	Ath-n	47	226	68	81	9	2	0	35	2	1	.358	.364	.416	139	10						C-25,S-20/O	0.6
1873	Ath-n	52	275	63	83	9	1	0	30	1	1	.302	.304	.342	84	-7						*S-44,C-13/3	-0.8
1874	Ath-n	54	270	61	87	11	2	0			2	.322	.327	.378	114	2						S-26,C-24/O	0.1
1875	Phi-n	68	309	71	89	6	2	0			1	.288	.290	.320	107	1						3-24,23,S/OCM	0.0
1876	StL-N	61	276	48	72	3	0	0	30	2	1	.261	.266	.272	84	-4				.889	5	*2-56/C-5,O3	0.1
1877	StL-N	57	258	35	65	3	2	0	20	2	6	.252	.258	.279	73	-7				.883	7	2-39,3-19	0.1
1879	Pro-N	85	374	62	103	7	2	0	35	5	13	.275	.285	.305	96	-2				.884	1	*2-73,3-12	0.5
1880	Pro-N	18	59	5	8	0	0	0	1	0	6	.136	.136	.136	-8	-6				.887	3	3-17/2-2,SM	-0.3
	Cle-N	31	111	14	28	2	1	0	6	4	3	.252	.278	.288	94	-1				.887	-4	3-29/O-2	-0.4
	Yr	49	170	19	36	2	1	0	7	4	9	.212	.230	.235	60	-7				.887	-1	3-46/2-2,OS	-0.7
1881	Cle-N	11	41	1	9	0	0	0	5	0	6	.220	.220	.220	41	-3				.724	-7	3-11,M	-0.9
1882	Det-N	34	133	14	19	4	1	0	2	2	20	.143	.156	.188	10	-13				.928	8	S-33/2-3	-0.3
Total	5 n	250	1228	305	379	39	7	0	77	12	2	.309	.315	.352	103	-1						S-111/C-89,32O	-0.5
Total	6	297	1252	179	304	19	6	0	99	15	55	.243	.252	.268	72	-35				.885	13	2-173/3-89,SCO	-1.2

■ DAN McGEE
McGee, Daniel Aloysius b: 9/29/11, New York, N.Y. d: 12/4/91, Lakehurst, N.J. BR/TR, 5'8.5", 152 lbs. Deb: 7/14/34

YEAR	TM/L	G	AB	R	H	2B	3B	HR	RBI	BB	SO	AVG	OBP	SLG	PRO+	BR/A	SB	CS	SBR	FA	FR	G/POS	TPR
1934	Bos-N	7	22	2	3	0	0	0	1	3	6	.136	.240	.136	4	-3	0			.951	3	/S-7	0.0

■ FRANK McGEE
McGee, Francis De Sales b: 4/28/1899, Columbus, Ohio d: 1/30/34, Columbus, Ohio BR/TR, 5'11.5", 175 lbs. Deb: 9/19/25

YEAR	TM/L	G	AB	R	H	2B	3B	HR	RBI	BB	SO	AVG	OBP	SLG	PRO+	BR/A	SB	CS	SBR	FA	FR	G/POS	TPR
1925	Was-A	2	3	0	0	0	0	0	0	0	1	.000	.000	.000	-99	-1	0	0	0	1.000	0	/1-2	-0.1

■ PAT McGEE
McGee, Patrick b: Philadelphia, Pa. d: 6/21/1889, New York, N.Y. Deb: 9/24/1874

YEAR	TM/L	G	AB	R	H	2B	3B	HR	RBI	BB	SO	AVG	OBP	SLG	PRO+	BR/A	SB	CS	SBR	FA	FR	G/POS	TPR
1874	Atl-n	16	65	4	11	2	0	0		0		.169	.169	.200	19	-5						O-15/S-2,2	-0.4
1875	Mut-n	25	94	4	16	3	0	0				.170	.170	.202	27	-7						O-25	-0.6
	Atl-n	18	63	3	9	4	1	0			1	.143	.156	.238	39	-3						O-13/2-5	-0.3
	Yr	43	157	7	25	7	1	0			1	.159	.165	.217	31	-10						O-38/2-5	-0.9
Total	2 n	59	222	11	36	9	1	0			1	.162	.166	.212	28	-15						/O-53,2-6,S	-1.3

■ WILLIE McGEE
McGee, Willie Dean b: 11/2/58, San Francisco, Cal. BB/TR, 6'1", 175 lbs. Deb: 5/10/82

YEAR	TM/L	G	AB	R	H	2B	3B	HR	RBI	BB	SO	AVG	OBP	SLG	PRO+	BR/A	SB	CS	SBR	FA	FR	G/POS	TPR
1982	*StL-N	123	422	43	125	12	8	4	56	12	58	.296	.319	.391	97	-3	24	12	0	.958	-9	*O-117	-1.6
1983	StL-N★	147	601	75	172	22	8	5	75	26	98	.286	.316	.374	90	-9	39	8	7	.987	8	*O-145	0.2
1984	StL-N	145	571	82	166	19	11	6	50	29	80	.291	.326	.394	104	2	43	10	7	.985	11	*O-141	1.6
1985	*StL-N★	152	612	114	**216**	26	**18**	10	82	34	86	**.353**	.387	.503	148	33	56	16	7	.978	13	*O-149	5.4
1986	StL-N	124	497	65	127	22	7	7	48	37	82	.256	.308	.370	87	-10	19	16	-4	**.991**	15	*O-121	-0.2
1987	*StL-N★	153	620	76	177	37	11	11	105	24	90	.285	.314	.434	94	-7	16	4	2	.981	8	*O-152/S-1	-0.1
1988	StL-N★	137	562	73	164	24	6	3	50	32	84	.292	.331	.372	100	2	41	6	9	.975	10	*O-135	1.6
1989	StL-N	58	199	23	47	10	2	3	17	10	34	.236	.276	.352	76	-7	8	6	-1	.976	2	O-47	-0.8
1990	StL-N	125	501	76	168	32	5	3	62	38	86	**.335**	.383	.437	125	17	28	9	3	.957	16	*O-124	3.4
	*Oak-A	29	113	23	31	3	2	0	15	10	18	.274	.333	.336	91	-1	3	0	1	.986	1	O-28/D-1	0.0
1991	SF-N	131	497	67	155	30	3	4	43	34	74	.312	.358	.408	119	12	17	9	-0	.978	-2	*O-128	0.7
1992	SF-N	138	474	56	141	20	2	1	36	29	88	.297	.339	.354	102	1	13	4	2	.976	3	*O-119	0.4
1993	SF-N	130	475	53	143	28	1	4	46	38	67	.301	.354	.389	102	2	10	9	-2	.979	3	*O-126	-0.3
1994	SF-N	45	156	19	44	3	0	5	23	15	24	.282	.345	.397	96	-1	3	0	1	.988	0	*O-44	
Total	13	1637	6300	845	1876	288	84	66	708	368	969	.298	.338	.402	105	35	320	109	31	.978	76	*O-1574/D-1,S	10.3

■ DAN McGEEHAN
McGeehan, Daniel De Sales b: 6/7/1885, Jeddo, Pa. d: 7/12/55, Hazleton, Pa. BR/TR, 5'6", 135 lbs. Deb: 4/22/11 F

YEAR	TM/L	G	AB	R	H	2B	3B	HR	RBI	BB	SO	AVG	OBP	SLG	PRO+	BR/A	SB	CS	SBR	FA	FR	G/POS	TPR
1911	StL-N	3	9	0	2	0	0	0	1	0	1	.222	.222	.222	25	-1	0			.818	-1	/2-3	-0.2

■ ED McGHEE
McGhee, Warren Edward b: 9/29/24, Perry, Ark. d: 2/13/86, Memphis, Tenn. BR/TR, 5'11", 170 lbs. Deb: 9/20/50

YEAR	TM/L	G	AB	R	H	2B	3B	HR	RBI	BB	SO	AVG	OBP	SLG	PRO+	BR/A	SB	CS	SBR	FA	FR	G/POS	TPR
1950	Chi-A	3	6	0	1	0	1	0	0	0	1	.167	.167	.500	67	-0	0			1.000	-0	/O-1	-0.1
1953	Phi-A	104	358	36	94	11	4	1	29	32	43	.263	.328	.324	74	-13	4	3	-1	.982	7	O-99	-1.0
1954	Phi-A	21	53	5	11	2	0	0	9	4	8	.208	.263	.358	69	-3	0	1	-1	.933	1	O-13	-0.3
	Chi-A	42	75	12	17	1	0	0	5	12	8	.227	.333	.240	57	-4	5	1	-2	.982	-3	O-34	-0.7
	Yr	63	128	17	28	3	0	0	14	16	16	.219	.306	.289	62	-7	5	1		.960	-3	O-47	-1.0
1955	Chi-A	26	13	6	1	0	0	0	0	6	1	.077	.368	.077	24	-1	2	1	0	.923	-6	O-17	-0.7
Total	4	196	505	59	124	14	5	3	43	54	61	.246	.322	.311	70	-21	11	5	0	.975	-2	O-164	-2.8

■ BILL McGHEE
McGhee, William Mac "Fibber" b: 9/5/08, Shawmut, Ala. d: 3/84, Decatur.Ga. BL/TL, 5'10.5", 185 lbs. Deb: 7/5/44

YEAR	TM/L	G	AB	R	H	2B	3B	HR	RBI	BB	SO	AVG	OBP	SLG	PRO+	BR/A	SB	CS	SBR	FA	FR	G/POS	TPR
1944	Phi-A	77	287	27	83	12	0	1	19	21	20	.289	.335	.341	96	-2	2	1	0	.989	-0	1-75	-0.6
1945	Phi-A	93	250	24	63	6	1	0	19	24	16	.252	.320	.284	76	-7	3	2	-1	.989	-5	O-48/1-8	-1.6
Total	2	170	537	51	146	18	1	1	38	45	36	.272	.329	.315	87	-9	5	3	-0	.990	-5	/1-83,O-48	-2.2

■ BILL McGILVRAY
McGilvray, William Alexander "Big Bill" b: 4/29/1883, Portland, Ore. d: 5/23/52, Denver, Colo. BL/TL, 6', 160 lbs. Deb: 4/17/08

YEAR	TM/L	G	AB	R	H	2B	3B	HR	RBI	BB	SO	AVG	OBP	SLG	PRO+	BR/A	SB	CS	SBR	FA	FR	G/POS	TPR
1908	Cin-N	2	2	0	0	0	0	0	0	0	0	.000	.000	.000	-99	-0	0			.000	0	H	-0.1

■ TIM McGINLEY
McGinley, Timothy S. b: Philadelphia, Pa. d: 11/2/1899, Oakland, Cal. 5'9.5", 155 lbs. Deb: 4/30/1875

YEAR	TM/L	G	AB	R	H	2B	3B	HR	RBI	BB	SO	AVG	OBP	SLG	PRO+	BR/A	SB	CS	SBR	FA	FR	G/POS	TPR
1875	Cen-n	13	51	5	13	1	1	0		1		.255	.269	.314	110	1						C-12/O-1	0.1
	NH-n	32	130	13	36	3	1	0		1		.277	.282	.315	122	3						C-33	0.4
	Yr	45	181	18	49	4	2	0		2		.271	.279	.315	118	4						C-45/O-1	0.5
1876	Bos-N	9	40	5	6	1	0	0	2	0	1	.150	.150	.150	0	-4				.600	-3	/O-6,C-3	-0.7

YEAR	TM/L	G	AB	R	H	2B	3B	HR	RBI	BB	SO	AVG	OBP	SLG	PRO+	BR/A	SB	CS	SBR	FA	FR	G/POS	TPR

■ FRANK McGINN McGinn, Frank J. b: 1869, Cincinnati, Ohio d: 11/19/1897, Cincinnati, Ohio Deb: 6/9/1890

| 1890 | Pit-N | 1 | 4 | 0 | 0 | 0 | 0 | 0 | 0 | 0 | 2 | .000 | .000 | .000 | -99 | -1 | 0 | | | 1.000 | -0 | /O-1 | -0.1 |

■ RUSS McGINNIS McGinnis, Russell Brent b: 6/18/63, Coffeyville, Kan. BR/TR, 6'3", 225 lbs. Deb: 6/3/92

| 1992 | Tex-A | 14 | 33 | 2 | 8 | 4 | 0 | 0 | 4 | 3 | 7 | .242 | .306 | .364 | 90 | -0 | 0 | 0 | 0 | 1.000 | -3 | C-10/1-2,3 | -0.4 |

■ JOHN McGLONE McGlone, John T. b: 1864, Brooklyn, N.Y. d: 11/24/27, Brooklyn, N.Y. 5'10", 165 lbs. Deb: 10/7/1886

1886	Was-N	4	15	2	1	0	0	0	1	0	3	.067	.067	.067	-63	-3	0			.846	-1	/3-4	-0.4
1887	Cle-a	21	79	14	20	2	1	0		7		.253	.337	.304	82	-1	15			.854	1	3-21	0.0
1888	Cle-a	55	203	22	37	1	3	1	22	16		.182	.249	.232	56	-9	26			.787	-6	3-48/O-7	-1.4
Total	3	80	297	38	58	3	4	1	23	23	3	.195	.265	.242	58	-14	41			.810	-7	/3-73,O-7	-1.8

■ ART McGOVERN McGovern, Arthur John b: 2/27/1882, St.John, N.B., Can. d: 11/14/15, Thornton, R.I. BR/TR, 5'10", 160 lbs. Deb: 4/21/05

| 1905 | Bos-A | 15 | 44 | 1 | 5 | 1 | 0 | 0 | 4 | | | .114 | .204 | .136 | 9 | -4 | 0 | | | .951 | -4 | C-15 | -0.7 |

■ BEAUTY McGOWAN McGowan, Frank Bernard b: 11/8/01, Branford, Conn. d: 5/6/82, Hamden, Conn. BL/TR, 5'11", 190 lbs. Deb: 4/12/22

1922	Phi-A	99	300	36	69	10	5	1	20	40	46	.230	.323	.307	63	-16	6	5	-1	.965	9	O-82	-1.4
1923	Phi-A	95	287	41	73	9	1	1	19	36	25	.254	.340	.303	69	-12	4	3	-1	.971	-0	O-79	-1.7
1928	StL-A	47	168	35	61	13	4	2	18	16	15	.363	.406	.524	143	11	2	1	0	.962	-1	O-47	0.6
1929	StL-A	125	441	62	112	26	6	2	51	61	34	.254	.346	.354	78	-14	5	2	0	.975	7	*O-117	-1.4
1937	Bos-N	9	12	0	1	0	0	0	0	1	2	.083	.154	.083	-37	-2	0			1.000	-1	/O-2	-0.3
Total	5	375	1208	174	316	58	16	6	108	154	122	.262	.347	.351	80	-33	17	11		.970	14	O-327	-4.2

■ JOHN McGRAW McGraw, John Joseph "Mugsy" or "Little Napoleon" b: 4/7/1873, Truxton, N.Y. d: 2/25/34, New Rochelle, N.Y. BL/TR, 5'7", 155 lbs. Deb: 8/26/1891 MH

1891	Bal-a	33	115	17	31	3	5	0	14	12	17	.270	.359	.383	111	2	4			.811	-15	S-21/O-9,2	-1.0
1892	Bal-N	79	286	41	77	13	2	1	26	32	21	.269	.355	.339	107	3	15			.897	1	O-34,2-34/S3	0.4
1893	Bal-N	127	480	123	154	9	10	5	64	101	11	.321	.454	.412	129	27	38			.894	-23	*S-117,O-11	0.7
1894	*Bal-N	124	512	156	174	18	14	1	92	91	12	.340	.451	.436	110	13	78			.892	-2	*3-118/2-6	0.9
1895	*Bal-N	96	388	110	143	13	6	2	48	60	9	.369	.459	.448	131	21	61			.878	9	*3-95/2-1	2.6
1896	*Bal-N	23	77	20	25	2	2	0	14	11	4	.325	.422	.403	116	2	13			.833	-2	3-18/1-1	0.1
1897	*Bal-N	106	391	90	127	15	3	0	48	99		.325	.471	.379	126	24	44			.886	-13	*3-105	1.2
1898	Bal-N	143	515	**143**	176	8	10	0	53	**112**		.342	.475	.396	148	43	43			.900	-12	*3-137/O-3	3.0
1899	Bal-N	117	399	**140**	156	13	3	1	33	**124**		.391	**.547**	.446	165	50	73			.945	2	*3-117,M	4.8
1900	StL-N	99	334	84	115	10	4	2	33	85		.344	**.505**	.416	157	37	29			.909	-9	*3-99	2.5
1901	Bal-A	73	232	71	81	14	9	0	28	61		.349	.508	.487	169	28	24			.890	-20	3-69,M	0.8
1902	Bal-A	20	63	14	18	3	2	1	3	17		.286	.451	.444	143	5	5			.864	-8	3-19,M	-0.3
	NY-N	35	107	13	25	0	0	0	5	26		.234	.401	.234	97	2	7			.926	-3	S-34,M	0.2
1903	NY-N	12	11	2	3	0	0	0	1	1		.273	.467	.273	108	0	1			.000	-2	/2-2,0-2,S3M	-0.2
1904	NY-N	5	12	0	4	0	0	0	0	3		.333	.467	.333	142	1	0			.947	3	/2-2,S-2M	0.4
1905	NY-N	3	0	0	0	0	0	0	0	0		—	—	—	—		0			.000	-2	/O-1,M	0.0
1906	NY-N	4	2	0	0	0	0	0	0	0		.000	.333	.000	4	-0	0			.000	0	/3-1,M	0.0
Total	16	1099	3924	1024	1309	121	70	13	462	836	74	.334	.466	.410	135	258	436			.898	-92	3-782,S-183/O21	16.1

■ FRED McGRIFF McGriff, Frederick Stanley b: 10/31/63, Tampa, Fla. BL/TL, 6'3", 215 lbs. Deb: 5/17/86

1986	Tor-A	3	5	1	1	0	0	0	0	0	2	.200	.200	.200	9	-1	0	0	0	1.000	-0	/1-1,D-2	-0.1
1987	Tor-A	107	295	58	73	16	0	20	43	60	104	.247	.376	.505	128	13	3	2	-0	.983	-1	D-90,1-14	0.7
1988	Tor-A	154	536	100	151	35	4	34	82	79	149	.282	.378	.552	156	40	6	1	1	.997	-5	*1-153	2.3
1989	*Tor-A	161	551	98	148	27	3	**36**	92	119	132	.269	.402	.525	**162**	**49**	7	4	-0	.989	-1	*1-159/D-2	3.5
1990	Tor-A	153	557	91	167	21	1	35	88	94	108	.300	.403	.530	156	43	5	3	-0	.996	9	*1-147/D-6	4.1
1991	SD-N	153	528	84	147	19	1	31	106	105	135	.278	.400	.494	146	35	4	1	1	.990	-11	*1-153	1.5
1992	SD-N★	152	531	79	152	30	4	**35**	104	96	108	.286	.396	.556	166	46	8	6	-1	.991	-1	*1-151	3.5
1993	SD-N	83	302	52	83	11	1	18	46	42	55	.275	.365	.497	126	11	4	3	-1	.983	-6	1-83	-0.2
	*Atl-N	68	255	59	79	18	1	19	55	34	51	.310	.393	.612	163	22	1	0	0	.992	-1	1-66	1.6
	Yr	151	557	111	162	29	2	37	101	76	106	.291	.378	.549	143	33	5	3	-0	.987	-7	*1-149	1.4
1994	Atl-N★	113	424	81	135	25	1	34	94	50	76	.318	.392	.623	159	36	7	3	0	.994	-5	*1-112	2.1
Total	9	1147	3984	703	1136	202	16	262	710	679	920	.285	.391	.541	153	296	45	23	-0	.992	-22	*1-1039,D-100	19.0

■ TERRY McGRIFF McGriff, Terence Roy b: 9/23/63, Fort Pierce, Fla. BR/TR, 6'2", 190 lbs. Deb: 7/11/87

1987	Cin-N	34	89	6	20	3	0	2	11	8	17	.225	.289	.326	60	-5	0	0	0	.983	4	C-33	0.0
1988	Cin-N	35	96	9	19	3	0	1	4	12	31	.198	.287	.260	56	-5	1	0	0	.990	3	C-32	0.0
1989	Cin-N	6	11	1	3	0	0	0	2	2	3	.273	.385	.273	88	-0	0	0	0	.929	1	/C-6	0.1
1990	Cin-N	2	4	0	0	0	0	0	0	0	0	.000	.000	.000	-96	-1	0	0	0	1.000	1	/C-1	0.0
	Hou-N	4	5	0	0	0	0	0	0	0	0	.000	.000	.000	-99	-1	0	0	0	.900	1	/C-4	-0.1
	Yr	6	9	0	0	0	0	0	0	0	0	.000	.000	.000	-99	-2	0	0	0	.938	2	/C-5	-0.1
1993	Fla-N	3	7	0	0	0	0	0	0	1	2	.000	.125	.000	-60	-2	0	0	0	1.000	-0	/C-3	-0.2
1994	StL-N	42	114	10	25	6	0	0	13	13	11	.219	.310	.272	56	-7	0	0	0	.991	1	C-39	-0.3
Total	6	126	326	26	67	12	0	3	30	36	65	.206	.288	.270	51	-22	1	0	0	.985	11	C-118	-0.5

■ MARK McGRILLIS McGrillis, Mark A. b: 10/22/1872, Philadelphia, Pa. d: 5/16/35, Philadelphia, Pa. Deb: 9/17/1892

| 1892 | StL-N | 1 | 3 | 0 | 0 | 0 | 0 | 0 | 0 | 0 | 1 | .000 | .000 | .000 | -99 | -1 | 0 | | | 1.000 | -0 | /3-1 | -0.1 |

■ JOE McGUCKIN McGuckin, Joseph W. b: 3/13/1862, Paterson, N.J. d: 12/31/03, Yonkers, N.Y. 5'8.5", 160 lbs. Deb: 8/27/1890

| 1890 | Bal-a | 11 | 37 | 2 | 4 | 0 | 0 | 0 | | 6 | | .108 | .250 | .108 | 6 | -4 | 3 | | | .962 | 3 | O-11 | -0.1 |

■ JOHN McGUINNESS McGuinness, John James b: 1857, Ireland d: 12/19/16, Binghamton, N.Y. Deb: 5/6/1876

1876	NY-N	1	4	0	0	0	0	0	0	0	0	.000	.000	.000	-99	-1				.500	-2	/2-1,C-1	-0.2
1879	Syr-N	12	51	7	15	1	1	0	4	0	0	.294	.294	.353	126	1				.928	-1	1-12	0.1
1884	Phi-U	53	220	25	52	8	1	0		5		.236	.253	.282	49	-15				.959	-4	1-48/2-5,S	-1.9
Total	3	66	275	32	67	9	2	0	4	5	6	.244	.257	.291	59	-15				.954	-2	/1-60,2-6,SC	-2.0

■ JIM McGUIRE McGuire, James A. b: 2/4/1875, Dunkirk, N.Y. d: 1/26/17, Buffalo, N.Y. TR, Deb: 9/10/01

| 1901 | Cle-A | 18 | 69 | 4 | 16 | 2 | 0 | 0 | 3 | 0 | | .232 | .232 | .261 | 38 | -6 | 0 | | | .913 | 1 | S-18 | -0.3 |

■ DEACON McGUIRE McGuire, James Thomas b: 11/18/1863, Youngstown, Ohio d: 10/31/36, Duck Lake, Mich. BR/TR, 6'1", 185 lbs. Deb: 6/21/1884 MC

1884	Tol-a	45	151	12	28	7	0	1		5		.185	.217	.252	51	-8				.906	-8	C-41/O-4,S	-1.2
1885	Det-N	34	121	11	23	4	2	0	5	5	23	.190	.222	.256	54	-6				.920	14	C-31/O-3	1.0
1886	Phi-N	50	167	25	33	7	1	2	18	19	25	.198	.280	.287	72	-5	2			.899	-6	C-49/O-1	-0.5
1887	Phi-N	41	150	22	46	6	6	2	23	11	8	.307	.362	.467	122	4	3			.884	-1	C-41	0.6
1888	Phi-N	12	51	7	17	4	0	2	11	4	9	.333	.382	.490	168	4	0			.800	-5	C-10/3-2	-0.1
	Det-N	3	13	0	0	0	0	0	0	0	4	.000	.000	.000	-99	-3	0			.810	-2	/C-3	-0.5
	Yr	15	64	7	17	4	0	2	11	4	13	.266	.309	.391	117	1	0			.802	-7	C-13/3-2	-0.6
	Cle-a	26	94	15	24	1	3	0	11	13	7	.255	.333	.362	126	3	2			.891	-1	C-17/1-6,O	0.3
1890	Roc-a	87	331	46	99	16	6	0	66	21		.299	.356	.408	135	14	8			.938	8	C-71,1-15/OP	2.4
1891	Was-a	114	413	55	125	22	10	3	66	43	34	.303	.382	.426	137	20	10			.911	-12	*C-98,O-18/31	1.5

YEAR	TM/L	G	AB	R	H	2B	3B	HR	RBI	BB	SO	AVG	OBP	SLG	PRO+	BR/A	SB	CS	SBR	FA	FR	G/POS	TPR
1892	Was-N	97	315	46	73	14	4	4	43	61	48	.232	.360	.340	115	8	7			.936	-1	C-89/1-8,O	1.2
1893	Was-N	63	237	29	62	14	3	1	26	26	12	.262	.342	.359	89	-4	3			.889	-5	C-50,1-12	-0.5
1894	Was-N	104	425	67	130	18	6	6	78	33	19	.306	.366	.419	92	-6	11			.918	-1	*C-104	0.2
1895	Was-N	132	533	89	179	30	8	10	97	40	18	.336	.388	.478	124	18	16			.936	11	*C-132/S-1	3.3
1896	Was-N	108	389	60	125	25	3	2	70	30	14	.321	.379	.416	110	5	12			.936	-1	*C-98/1-1	1.3
1897	Was-N	93	327	51	112	17	7	4	53	21		.343	.386	.474	127	12	9			.947	8	C-73/1-6	2.3
1898	Was-N	131	489	59	131	18	3	1	57	24		.268	.310	.323	82	-12	10			.967	4	C-93,1-37M	0.0
1899	Was-N	59	199	25	54	3	1	1	12	16		.271	.335	.312	79	-5	3			.973	-4	C-56/1-1	-0.5
	Bro-N	46	157	22	50	12	4	0	23	12		.318	.385	.446	125	5	4			.971	2	C-46	1.0
	Yr	105	356	47	104	15	5	1	35	28		.292	.357	.371	99	0	7			.972	-2	*C-102/1-1	0.5
1900	*Bro-N	71	241	20	69	15	2	0	34	19		.286	.348	.365	91	-3	2			.952	-6	C-69	-0.3
1901	Bro-N	85	301	28	89	16	4	0	40	18		.296	.342	.375	105	2	4			.960	-5	C-81/1-3	0.6
1902	Det-A	73	229	27	52	14	1	2	23	24		.227	.300	.323	71	-9	0			.952	-5	C-70	-0.6
1903	Det-A	72	248	15	62	12	1	0	21	19		.250	.306	.306	87	-4	3			.960	-6	C-69/1-1	-0.2
1904	NY-A	101	322	17	67	12	2	0	20	27		.208	.276	.258	66	-12	2			.970	13	C-97/1-1	1.3
1905	NY-A	72	228	9	50	7	2	0	33	18		.219	.291	.268	69	-8	3			.975	-6	C-71	-0.7
1906	NY-A	51	144	11	43	5	0	0	14	12		.299	.365	.333	108	2	3			.962	-1	C-49/1-1	0.5
1907	NY-A	1	1	0	0	0	0	0	0	0		.000	.000	.000	-93	-0	0			1.000	1	/C-1	0.0
	Bos-A	6	4	1	3	0	0	1	1	0		.750	.750	1.500	620	2	0			.000		HM	0.2
	Yr	7	5	1	3	0	0	1	1	0		.600	.600	1.200	470	2	0			1.000	1	/C-1	0.2
1908	Bos-A	1	1	0	0	0	0	0	0	0		.000	.000	.000	-97	-0	0			.000		HM	0.0
	Cle-A	1	4	0	1	1	0	0	2	0		.250	.250	.500	142	-0	0			1.000	-0	/1-1	0.0
	Yr	2	5	0	1	1	0	0	2	0		.200	.200	.400	93	-0	0			1.000	-0	/1-1	0.0
1910	Cle-N	1	3	0	1	0	0	0	0	0		.333	.500	.333	159	0	0			1.000	-1	/C-1,M	-0.1
1912	Det-N	1	2	1	1	0	0	0	0	0		.500	.500	.500	192	0	0			.714	0	/C-1	0.1
Total	26	1781	6290	770	1749	300	79	45	787	515	214	.278	.341	.372	101	15	117			.938	-16	*C-1611/1-94,03SP	12.6

■ MICKEY McGUIRE
McGuire, M C Adolphus b: 1/18/41, Dayton, Ohio BR/TR, 5'10", 170 lbs. Deb: 9/7/62

1962	Bal-A	6	4	0	0	0	0	0	0	0	0	.000	.000	.000	-99	-1	0	0	0	1.000	-0	/S-5	-0.1
1967	Bal-A	10	17	2	4	0	0	0	2	0	2	.235	.235	.235	40	-1	0	0	0	1.000	-2	/2-4	-0.4
Total	2	16	21	2	4	0	0	0	2	0	2	.190	.190	.190	11	-2	0	0	0	1.000	-3	/S-5,2-4	-0.5

■ BILL McGUIRE
McGuire, William Patrick b: 2/14/64, Omaha, Neb. BR/TR, 6'3", 205 lbs. Deb: 8/2/88

1988	Sea-A	9	16	1	3	0	0	0	2	3	2	.188	.316	.188	43	-1	0	0	0	1.000	-0	/C-9	-0.1
1989	Sea-A	14	28	2	5	0	0	1	4	2	6	.179	.233	.286	44	-2	0	0	0	1.000	4	C-14	0.3
Total	2	23	44	3	8	0	0	1	6	5	8	.182	.265	.250	44	-3	0	0	0	1.000	4	/C-23	0.2

■ BILL McGUNNIGLE
McGunnigle, William Henry "Gunner" b: 1/1/1855, Boston, Mass. d: 3/9/1899, Brockton, Mass. BR/TR, 5'9", 155 lbs. Deb: 5/2/1879 M

1879	Buf-N	47	171	22	30	0	0	0	5	5	24	.175	.199	.187	27	-13				.918	1	O-34,P-14	-1.0
1880	Buf-N	7	22	0	4	0	0	0	1	0	4	.182	.182	.182	23	-2				1.000	-2	/P-5,O-3	-0.2
	Wor-N	1	4	0	0	0	0	0	0	0	2	.000	.000	.000	-92	-1				1.000	-1	/O-1	-0.2
	Yr	8	26	0	4	0	0	0	1	0	6	.154	.154	.154	5	-3				1.000	-2	/P-5,O-4	-0.4
1882	Cle-N	1	5	2	1	0	1	0	6	5	1	.200	.200	.200	30	-0				.000	-1	/O-1	-0.1
Total	3	56	202	24	35	0	1	0			31	.173	.193	.183	25	-16				.900	-1	/O-39,P-19	-1.5

■ MARK McGWIRE
McGwire, Mark David b: 10/1/63, Pomona, Cal. BR/TR, 6'5", 225 lbs. Deb: 8/22/86

1986	Oak-A	18	53	10	10	1	0	3	9	4	18	.189	.259	.377	76	-2	0	1	-1	.833	-3	3-16	-0.6
1987	Oak-A★	151	557	97	161	28	4	49	118	71	131	.289	.374	.618	168	53	1	1	-0	.992	-7	*1-145/3-8,O	3.3
1988	*Oak-A★	155	550	87	143	22	1	32	99	76	117	.260	.354	.478	135	26	0	0	0	.993	-8	*1-154/O-1	0.6
1989	*Oak-A★	143	490	74	113	17	0	33	95	83	94	.231	.345	.467	132	21	1	1	-0	.995	7	*1-141/D-2	1.6
1990	*Oak-A★	156	523	87	123	16	0	39	108	110	116	.235	.375	.489	146	35	2	1	0	.997	-5	*1-154/D-2	1.8
1991	Oak-A†	154	483	62	97	22	0	22	75	93	116	.201	.333	.383	103	4	2	1	0	.997	2	*1-152	-0.4
1992	*Oak-A★	139	467	87	125	22	0	42	104	90	105	.268	.391	.585	180	50	0	1	-1	.995	-10	*1-139	3.1
1993	Oak-A	27	84	16	28	6	0	9	24	21	19	.333	.472	.726	231	16	0	1	-1	1.000	1	1-25	1.2
1994	Oak-A	47	135	26	34	3	0	9	25	37	40	.252	.413	.474	139	10	0	0	0	.988	-2	1-40/D-5	0.4
Total	9	990	3342	546	834	137	5	238	657	585	756	.250	.366	.507	145	213	6	7	-2	.995	-26	1-950/3-24,DO	11.0

■ JIM McHALE
McHale, James Bernard "J.B." b: 12/17/1875, Miners Mills, Pa. d: 6/17/59, Los Angeles, Cal. BR/TR, 5'11", 165 lbs. Deb: 4/14/08

1908	Bos-A	21	67	9	15	2	2	0	7	4		.224	.278	.313	90	-1	4			.970	-2	O-19	-0.4

■ JOHN McHALE
McHale, John Joseph b: 9/21/21, Detroit, Mich. BL/TR, 6', 200 lbs. Deb: 5/28/43

1943	Det-A	4	3	0	0	0	0	0	0	1	1	.000	.250	.000	-23	-0	0	0	0	.000	0	H	0.0
1944	Det-A	1	1	0	0	0	0	0	0	0	0	.000	.000	.000	-95	-0	0	0	0	.000	0	H	0.0
1945	*Det-A	19	14	0	2	0	0	0	1	1	4	.143	.250	.143	14	-1	0	0	0	1.000	0	/1-3	-0.1
1947	Det-A	39	95	10	20	1	0	3	11	7	24	.211	.265	.316	59	-6	1	1	-0	.995	-1	1-25	-0.8
1948	Det-A	1	1	0	0	0	0	0	0	0	0	.000	.000	.000	-97	-0	0	0	0	.000	0	H	0.0
Total	5	64	114	10	22	1	0	3	12	9	29	.193	.258	.281	49	-8	1	1	-0	.995	-1	/1-28	-0.9

■ BOB McHALE
McHale, Robert Emmet "Rabbit" b: 2/25/1872, Michigan Bluff, Cal. d: 6/9/52, Sacramento, Cal. Deb: 5/9/1898

1898	Was-N	11	33	5	6	2	0	0	7	1		.182	.270	.242	47	-2	1			.900	-1	/O-9,S-1,1	-0.4

■ AUSTIN McHENRY
McHenry, Austin Bush "Mac" b: 9/22/1895, Wrightsville, O. d: 11/27/22, Jefferson, Ohio BR/TR, 5'11", 152 lbs. Deb: 6/22/18

1918	StL-N	80	272	32	71	12	6	1	29	21	24	.261	.319	.360	111	3	8			.952	2	O-80	0.0
1919	StL-N	110	371	41	106	19	11	1	47	19	57	.286	.322	.404	125	10	7			.985	1	*O-103	0.4
1920	StL-N	137	504	66	142	19	11	10	65	25	73	.282	.316	.423	115	7	8	11	-4	.952	2	*O-133	-0.4
1921	StL-N	152	574	92	201	37	8	17	102	38	48	.350	.393	.531	145	36	10	20	-9	.965	7	*O-152	2.3
1922	StL-N	64	238	31	72	18	3	5	43	14	27	.303	.344	.466	112	3	2	2	-1	.935	7	O-61	0.5
Total	5	543	1959	262	592	105	39	34	286	117	229	.302	.343	.448	126	59	35	33		.960	18	O-529	2.8

■ VANCE McHENRY
McHenry, Vance Loren b: 7/10/56, Chico, Cal. BR/TR, 5'9", 165 lbs. Deb: 8/13/81

1981	Sea-A	15	18	3	4	0	0	0	2	1	1	.222	.263	.222	39	-1	0	0	0	.893	0	S-13/D-1	-0.1
1982	Sea-A	3	1	0	0	0	0	0	0	0	0	.000	.000	.000	-97	-0	0	0	0	.500	0	/S-1,D-1	-0.1
Total	2	18	19	3	4	0	0	0	2	1	1	.211	.250	.211	32	-2	0	0	0	.867	-0	/S-14,D-2	-0.2

■ IRISH McILVEEN
McIlveen, Henry Cooke b: 7/27/1880, Belfast, Ireland d: 10/18/60, Lorain, Ohio BL/TL, 5'11.5", 180 lbs. Deb: 7/10/06

1906	Pit-N	5	5	1	2	0	0	0				.400	.400	.400	143	0				1.000	0	/P-2	0.0
1908	NY-A	44	169	17	36	3	3	0	8	14		.213	.277	.266	76	-4	6			.949	0	O-44	-0.7
1909	NY-A	4	3	0	0	0	0	0	0	1		.000	.250	.000	-20	-0	0			.000	0	H	0.0
Total	3	53	177	18	38	3	3	0	8	15		.215	.280	.266	76	-4	6			.949	0	/O-44,P-2	-0.7

■ STUFFY McINNIS
McInnis, John Phalen "Jack" b: 9/19/1890, Gloucester, Mass. d: 2/16/60, Ipswich, Mass. BR/TR, 5'9.5", 162 lbs. Deb: 4/12/09 M

1909	Phi-A	19	46	4	11	0	0	0				.239	.286	.304	85	-1	0			.886	4	S-14	0.4
1910	Phi-A	38	73	10	22	2	4	0	12	7		.301	.363	.438	152	4	3			.927	-5	S-17/2-5,3O	0.0
1911	*Phi-A	126	468	76	150	20	6	3	77	25		.321	.361	.425	121	12	23			.982	-15	1-97,S-24	-0.1
1912	Phi-A	153	568	83	186	25	13	3	101	49		.327	.384	.433	138	28	27			.984	3	*1-153	2.8

YEAR	TM/L	G	AB	R	H	2B	3B	HR	RBI	BB	SO	AVG	OBP	SLG	PRO+	BR/A	SB	CS	SBR	FA	FR	G/POS	TPR
1913	*Phi-A	148	543	79	176	30	4	4	90	45	31	.324	.382	.416	137	24	16			.992	-2	*1-148	2.3
1914	*Phi-A	149	576	74	181	12	8	1	95	19	27	.314	.341	.368	118	10	25	19	-4	.995	0	*1-149	0.3
1915	Phi-A	119	456	44	143	14	4	0	49	14	17	.314	.337	.362	113	5	8	8	-2	.989	5	*1-119	0.5
1916	Phi-A	140	512	42	151	25	3	1	60	25	19	.295	.331	.361	114	6	7			.992	7	*1-140	0.8
1917	Phi-A	150	567	50	172	19	4	0	44	33	19	.303	.342	.351	113	7	18			.993	2	*1-150	0.4
1918	*Bos-A	117	423	40	115	11	5	0	56	19	10	.272	.306	.322	91	-6	10			.992	4	1-94,3-23	-0.6
1919	Bos-A	120	440	32	134	12	5	1	58	23	11	.305	.341	.361	103	1	8			.995	3	*1-118	-0.1
1920	Bos-A	148	559	50	166	21	3	2	71	18	19	.297	.321	.356	83	-15	6	11	-5	.996	-1	*1-148	-2.4
1921	Bos-A	152	584	72	179	31	10	0	76	21	9	.307	.335	.394	88	-12	2	4	-2	.999	4	*1-152	-1.3
1922	Cle-A	142	537	58	164	28	7	1	78	15	9	.305	.325	.389	85	-13	1	5	-3	.997	-5	*1-140	-2.6
1923	Bos-N	154	607	70	191	23	9	2	95	26	12	.315	.343	.392	97	-3	7	8	-3	.991	4	*1-154	-1.0
1924	Bos-N	146	581	57	169	23	7	1	59	15	6	.291	.311	.360	83	-15	9	3	1	.994	7	*1-146	-1.7
1925	*Pit-N	59	155	19	57	10	4	0	24	17	1	.368	.437	.484	126	7	1	1	-0	.993	1	1-46	0.5
1926	Pit-N	47	127	12	38	6	1	0	13	7	3	.299	.336	.362	83	-3	1			.988	-1	1-40	-0.6
1927	Phi-N	1	0	0	0	0	0	0	0	0	0	—	—	—	—	—	0			1.000	-0	/1-1,M	
Total	19	2128	7822	872	2405	312	101	20	1062	380	189	.307	.343	.381	106	35	172	59		.993	17	*1-1995/S-55,320	-2.4

■ TIM McINTOSH
McIntosh, Timothy Allen b: 3/21/65, Minneapolis, Minn. BR/TR, 5'11", 195 lbs. Deb: 9/3/90

YEAR	TM/L	G	AB	R	H	2B	3B	HR	RBI	BB	SO	AVG	OBP	SLG	PRO+	BR/A	SB	CS	SBR	FA	FR	G/POS	TPR
1990	Mil-A	5	5	1	1	0	0	1	1	0	2	.200	.200	.800	168	-0	0	0	0	.875	-0	/C-4	0.0
1991	Mil-A	7	11	2	4	1	0	1	1	0	4	.364	.364	.727	199	1	0	0	0	.000	-2	/O-4,1-1,D	0.0
1992	Mil-A	35	77	7	14	3	0	0	6	3	9	.182	.232	.221	28	-7	1	3	-2	.983	1	C-14,O-10/1D	-0.8
1993	Mil-A	1	0	0	0	0	0	0	0	0	0	—	—	—			0			.000	0	/C-1	0.0
	Mon-N	20	21	2	2	1	0	0	2	0	7	.095	.095	.143	-36	-4	0	0	0	1.000	-3	/O-7,C-5	-0.7
Total	4	68	114	12	21	5	0	2	10	3	22	.184	.218	.281	38	-10	1	3	-2	.973	-4	/C-24,O-21,1D	-1.5

■ MATTY McINTYRE
McIntyre, Matthew W. b: 6/12/1880, Stonington, Conn. d: 4/2/20, Detroit, Mich. BL/TL, 5'11", 175 lbs. Deb: 7/3/01

YEAR	TM/L	G	AB	R	H	2B	3B	HR	RBI	BB	SO	AVG	OBP	SLG	PRO+	BR/A	SB	CS	SBR	FA	FR	G/POS	TPR
1901	Phi-A	82	308	38	85	12	4	0	46	30		.276	.346	.341	87	-5	11			.921	-3	O-82	-1.2
1904	Det-A	152	578	74	146	11	10	2	46	44		.253	.310	.317	101	1	11			.959	12	*O-152	0.5
1905	Det-A	131	495	59	130	21	5	0	30	48		.263	.330	.325	107	5	9			.968	16	*O-131	1.6
1906	Det-A	133	493	63	128	19	11	0	39	56		.260	.338	.343	110	7	29			.982	12	*O-133	1.3
1907	Det-A	20	81	6	23	1	1	0	9	7		.284	.341	.321	107	1	3			1.000	3	O-20	0.3
1908	*Det-A	151	569	105	168	24	13	0	28	83		.295	.392	.383	146	32	20			.977	16	*O-151	4.7
1909	*Det-A	125	476	65	116	18	9	1	34	54		.244	.325	.326	101	1	13			.975	-0	*O-122	-0.4
1910	Det-A	83	305	40	72	15	5	0	25	39		.236	.323	.318	94	-2	4			.946	4	O-77	-0.2
1911	Chi-A	146	569	102	184	19	11	1	52	64		.323	.397	.401	127	22	17			.948	-2	O-146	1.2
1912	Chi-A	49	84	10	14	0	0	0	10	14		.167	.300	.167	36	-6	3			1.000	-1	O-25	-0.8
Total	10	1072	3958	562	1066	140	69	4	319	439		.269	.346	.343	110	57	120			.964	56	*O-1039	7.0

■ OTTO McIVOR
McIvor, Edward Otto b: 7/26/1884, Greenville, Tex. d: 5/4/54, Dallas, Tex. BB/TL, 5'11.5", 175 lbs. Deb: 4/18/11

YEAR	TM/L	G	AB	R	H	2B	3B	HR	RBI	BB	SO	AVG	OBP	SLG	PRO+	BR/A	SB	CS	SBR	FA	FR	G/POS	TPR
1911	StL-N	30	62	11	14	2	1	1	9	9	14	.226	.333	.339	91	-1	0			.926	-3	O-17	-0.5

■ DAVE McKAY
McKay, David Lawrence b: 3/14/50, Vancouver, B.C., Can BB/TR, 6'1", 195 lbs. Deb: 8/22/75 C

YEAR	TM/L	G	AB	R	H	2B	3B	HR	RBI	BB	SO	AVG	OBP	SLG	PRO+	BR/A	SB	CS	SBR	FA	FR	G/POS	TPR
1975	Min-A	33	125	8	32	4	1	2	16	6	14	.256	.295	.352	81	-3	1	1	-0	.923	2	3-33	-0.2
1976	Min-A	45	138	8	28	2	0	0	8	9	27	.203	.272	.217	43	-10	1	2	-1	.911	-1	3-41/S-2,D	-1.6
1977	Tor-A	95	274	18	54	4	3	3	22	7	51	.197	.223	.266	32	-26	2	1	0	.968	7	2-40,3-32,S/D	-1.6
1978	Tor-A	145	504	59	120	20	8	7	45	20	91	.238	.269	.351	71	-20	4	4	-1	.984	-7	*2-140/S-3,3D	-1.8
1979	Tor-A	47	156	19	34	9	0	0	12	7	19	.218	.256	.276	43	-12	1	1	-0	.974	6	2-46/3-2	-0.6
1980	Oak-A	123	295	29	72	16	1	1	29	10	57	.244	.283	.315	68	-13	1	1	-0	.977	-6	2-62,3-54,S	-1.6
1981	*Oak-A	79	224	25	59	11	1	4	21	16	43	.263	.318	.375	104	1	4	1	-0	.926	-4	3-43,2-38/S	-0.1
1982	Oak-A	78	212	25	42	4	1	4	17	11	35	.198	.238	.283	44	-17	6	2	-1	.968	-3	2-59,3-16/S	-1.7
Total	8	645	1928	191	441	70	15	21	170	86	337	.229	.268	.313	62	-101	20	12	-1	.976	-6	2-385,3-223/SD	-8.6

■ ED McKEAN
McKean, Edwin John "Mack" b: 6/6/1864, Grafton, Ohio d: 8/16/19, Cleveland, Ohio BR/TR, 5'9", 160 lbs. Deb: 4/16/1887

YEAR	TM/L	G	AB	R	H	2B	3B	HR	RBI	BB	SO	AVG	OBP	SLG	PRO+	BR/A	SB	CS	SBR	FA	FR	G/POS	TPR
1887	Cle-a	132	539	97	154	16	13	2		60		.286	.358	.375	108	7	76			.847	-8	*S-123/2-8,O	0.1
1888	Cle-a	131	548	94	164	21	15	6	68	28		.299	.340	.425	149	28	52			.909	3	S-78,O-48/23	3.0
1889	Cle-N	123	500	88	159	22	8	4	75	42	25	.318	.375	.418	124	16	35			.907	6	*S-122/2-1	2.5
1890	Cle-N	136	530	95	157	15	14	7	61	87	25	.296	.401	.417	141	31	23			.903	-18	*S-134/2-3	1.9
1891	Cle-N	141	603	115	170	13	12	6	69	64	19	.282	.352	.373	107	4	14			.887	-12	*S-141	0.1
1892	*Cle-N	129	531	76	139	14	10	0	93	49	28	.262	.325	.326	93	-5	19			.862	-45	*S-129	-4.1
1893	Cle-N	125	545	103	169	29	24	4	133	50	14	.310	.372	.473	117	9	16			.902	-4	*S-125	1.0
1894	Cle-N	130	554	116	198	30	15	8	128	49	12	.357	.412	.509	116	13	33			.905	-21	*S-130	0.3
1895	*Cle-N	131	565	131	193	32	17	8	119	45	25	.342	.397	.501	123	17	12			.909	-19	*S-131	0.3
1896	*Cle-N	133	571	100	193	29	12	7	112	45	9	.338	.388	.468	118	13	13			.915	-33	*S-133	-1.3
1897	Cle-N	125	523	83	143	21	14	2	78	40		.273	.330	.379	82	-15	11			.920	-30	*S-125	-3.6
1898	Cle-N	151	604	89	172	23	1	9	94	56		.285	.346	.371	107	5	11			.932	-36	*S-151	-2.2
1899	StL-N	67	277	40	72	7	3	3	40	20		.260	.310	.339	76	-10	4			.886	-17	S-42,1-15,2	-2.1
Total	13	1654	6890	1227	2083	272	158	66	1070	635	157	.302	.364	.416	114	115	323			.900	-232	*S-1564/O-52,213	-4.4

■ BILL McKECHNIE
McKechnie, William Boyd "Deacon" b: 8/7/1886, Wilkinsburg, Pa. d: 10/29/65, Bradenton, Fla. BB/TR, 5'10", 160 lbs. Deb: 9/8/07 MCH

YEAR	TM/L	G	AB	R	H	2B	3B	HR	RBI	BB	SO	AVG	OBP	SLG	PRO+	BR/A	SB	CS	SBR	FA	FR	G/POS	TPR
1907	Pit-N	3	8	0	1	0	0	0	0	0	0	.125	.125	.125	-21	-1	0			1.000	-0	/3-2,2-1	-0.2
1910	Pit-N	71	212	23	46	1	2	0	12	11	23	.217	.256	.241	42	-16	4			.971	8	2-36,S-14/31	-0.8
1911	Pit-N	104	321	40	73	8	7	2	37	28	18	.227	.293	.315	68	-15	9			.975	-0	1-57,2-17,S/3	-1.5
1912	Pit-N	24	73	8	18	0	1	0	4	4	5	.247	.286	.274	54	-5	2			.978	3	3-13/S-4,21	-0.3
1913	Bos-N	1	4	1	0	0	0	0	0	0	1	.000	.200	.000	-39	-1	0			1.000	0	/O-1	-0.1
	NY-A	45	112	7	15	0	0	0	8	8	17	.134	.198	.134	-2	-14	2			.950	5	2-28/S-7,3	-1.0
1914	Ind-F	149	570	107	173	24	6	2	38	53	36	.304	.368	.377	84	-12	47			.939	23	*3-149	1.6
1915	New-F	127	451	49	113	22	5	1	43	41	31	.251	.316	.328	77	-16	28			.956	9	*3-117/O-1M	-1.0
1916	NY-N	71	260	22	64	9	1	0	17	7	20	.246	.269	.288	75	-8	7			.940	-3	3-71	-1.1
	Cin-N	37	130	4	36	3	0	0	10	3	12	.277	.293	.300	84	-3	4			.960	-4	3-35	-0.6
	Yr	108	390	26	100	12	1	0	27	10	32	.256	.277	.292	78	-11	11			.947	-8	3-106	-1.7
1917	Cin-N	48	134	11	34	3	1	0	15	7	7	.254	.296	.291	84	-3	5			.943	-7	2-26,S-13/3	-0.9
1918	Pit-N	126	435	34	111	13	9	2	43	24	22	.255	.297	.340	91	-5	12			.966	-1	*3-126	-0.4
1920	Pit-N	40	133	13	29	3	1	1	13	4	7	.218	.241	.278	47	-9	7	4	-0	.943	-1	3-20,S-10/21	-1.0
Total	11	846	2843	319	713	86	33	8	240	190	199	.251	.301	.313	72	-108	127	4		.952	22	3-553,2-117/1SO	-7.3

■ FRANK McKEE
McKee, Frank b: Philadelphia, Pa. Deb: 6/11/1884

YEAR	TM/L	G	AB	R	H	2B	3B	HR	RBI	BB	SO	AVG	OBP	SLG	PRO+	BR/A	SB	CS	SBR	FA	FR	G/POS	TPR
1884	Was-U	4	17	2	3	0	0	0		1		.176	.222	.176	10	-2				.200	-2	/O-3,3-2,C	-0.3

■ RED McKEE
McKee, Raymond Ellis b: 7/20/1890, Shawnee, Ohio d: 8/5/72, Saginaw, Mich. BL/TR, 5'11", 180 lbs. Deb: 4/19/13

YEAR	TM/L	G	AB	R	H	2B	3B	HR	RBI	BB	SO	AVG	OBP	SLG	PRO+	BR/A	SB	CS	SBR	FA	FR	G/POS	TPR
1913	Det-A	68	187	18	53	3	4	1	20	21	21	.283	.359	.358	112	3	7			.950	-5	C-62	0.4
1914	Det-A	34	64	7	12	1	1	0	8	14	16	.188	.342	.234	71	-2	1	2	-1	.964	-6	C-27	-0.7
1915	Det-A	55	106	10	29	5	0	1	17	13	16	.274	.353	.349	105	1	1			.954	-6	C-35	-0.3
1916	Det-A	32	76	3	16	1	2	0	4	6	11	.211	.268	.276	61	-4	0			.955	-5	C-26	-0.7
Total	4	189	433	38	110	10	7	2	49	54	64	.254	.339	.323	95	-1	9	2		.954	-22	C-150	-1.3

YEAR	TM/L	G	AB	R	H	2B	3B	HR	RBI	BB	SO	AVG	OBP	SLG	PRO+	BR/A	SB	CS	SBR	FA	FR	G/POS	TPR
■ JIM McKEEVER	McKeever, James b: 4/19/1861, St.John, N.B., Can. d: 8/19/1897, Boston, Mass. Deb: 4/17/1884																						
1884	Bos-U	16	66	13	9	0	0	0		0		.136	.136	.136	-26	-11				.869	-6	C-12/O-4	-1.4
■ JOHN McKELVEY	McKelvey, John Wellington b: 8/27/1847, Rochester, N.Y. d: 5/31/44, Rochester, N.Y. BR/TR, 5'7.5", 175 lbs. Deb: 4/21/1875																						
1875	NH-n	43	187	26	43	4	1	0	4			.230	.246	.262	87	-1						O-39/3-4	-0.1
■ RUSS McKELVY	McKelvy, Russell Errett b: 9/8/1856, Meadville, Pa. d: 10/19/15, Omaha, Neb. BR/TR, Deb: 5/1/1878																						
1878	Ind-N	63	253	33	57	4	3	2	36	5	38	.225	.240	.289	84	-4				.846	6	*O-62/P-4	-0.1
1882	Pit-a	1	4	0	0	0	0	0		0		.000	.000	.000	-99	-1				.000	-0	/O-1	-0.1
Total	2	64	257	33	57	4	3	2	36	5	38	.222	.237	.284	81	-4				.846	5	/O-63,P-4	-0.2
■ ED McKENNA	McKenna, Edward J. b: St.Louis, Mo. Deb: 7/29/1874																						
1874	Phi-n	1	4	0	0	0	0	0		0		.000	.000	.000	-97	-1						/1-1	-0.1
1877	StL-N	1	5	0	1	0	0	0	0	0	1	.200	.200	.200	28	-0				1.000	-0	/O-1	-0.1
1884	Was-U	32	117	19	22	1	0	0		0	4	.188	.215	.197	13	-14				.876	-14	C-23,O-10/3	-2.3
Total	2	33	122	19	23	1	0	0	0	4	1	.189	.214	.197	13	-14				.556	-14	/C-23,O-11,3	-2.4
■ DAVE McKEOUGH	McKeough, David J. b: 12/1/1863, Utica, N.Y. d: 7/11/01, Utica, N.Y. 5'7", 158 lbs. Deb: 4/22/1890																						
1890	Roc-a	62	218	38	49	5	0	0		29		.225	.316	.248	72	-6	14			.929	-4	C-47,S-13/23	-0.5
1891	Phi-a	15	54	4	14	1	1	0		3	8	.259	.355	.315	89	-1	0			.854	-4	C-14/S-1	-0.3
Total	2	77	272	42	63	6	1	0	3	37	6	.232	.324	.261	75	-7	14			.912	-9	/C-61,S-14,23	-0.8
■ RICH McKINNEY	McKinney, Charles Richard b: 11/22/46, Piqua, Ohio BR/TR, 5'11", 185 lbs. Deb: 6/26/70																						
1970	Chi-A	43	119	12	20	5	0	4	17	11	25	.168	.244	.311	50	-8	3	2	-0	.931	2	3-23,S-11	-0.6
1971	Chi-A	114	369	35	100	11	2	8	46	35	37	.271	.337	.377	99	-0	0	0	0	.968	-9	2-67,O-25/3	-0.6
1972	NY-A	37	121	10	26	2	0	1	7	7	13	.215	.258	.256	55	-7	1	0	0	.917	-3	3-33	-1.1
1973	Oak-A	48	65	9	16	3	0	1	7	7	4	.246	.319	.338	90	-1	0	0	0	.900	-1	3-17/2-7,OD	-0.1
1974	Oak-A	5	7	0	1	0	0	0	0	0	0	.143	.143	.143	-19	-1	0	0	0	1.000	-2	/2-3	-0.4
1975	Oak-A	8	7	0	1	0	0	0	2	1	2	.143	.250	.143	14	-1	0	0	0	1.000	-0	/1-1,D-2	-0.1
1977	Oak-A	86	198	13	35	7	0	6	21	16	43	.177	.238	.303	47	-15	0	1	-1	.978	-4	1-32,D-18/3O2	-2.2
Total	7	341	886	79	199	28	2	20	100	77	124	.225	.289	.328	73	-33	4	3	-1	.911	-17	/3-85,2-80,1ODS	-5.1
■ BOB McKINNEY	McKinney, Robert Francis b: 10/4/1875, McSherrystown, Pa. d: 8/19/46, Hanover, Pa. BR/TR, 5'7", 165 lbs. Deb: 7/23/01																						
1901	Phi-A	2	2	0	0	0	0	0	0	0		.000	.000	.000	-96	-1	0			.000	-1	/2-1,3-1	-0.2
■ ALEX McKINNON	McKinnon, Alexander J. b: 8/14/1856, Boston, Mass. d: 7/24/1887, Charlestown, Mass BR , 5'11.5", 170 lbs. Deb: 5/1/1884 M																						
1884	NY-N	116	470	66	128	21	12	4	73	8	62	.272	.285	.394	108	3				.955	-2	*1-116	-1.1
1885	StL-N	100	411	42	121	21	6	1	44	8	31	.294	.308	.382	130	13				.978	-2	*1-100,M	-0.1
1886	StL-N	122	491	75	148	24	7	8	72	21	23	.301	.330	.428	138	21	10			.963	-6	*1-119/O-3	0.1
1887	Pit-N	48	200	26	68	16	4	1	30	8	9	.340	.365	.475	140	10	6			.977	3	1-48	0.7
Total	4	386	1572	209	465	82	29	14	219	45	125	.296	.315	.412	127	48	16			.967	-7	1-383/O-3	-0.4
■ JIM McKNIGHT	McKnight, James Arthur b: 6/1/36, Bee Branch, Ark. d: 2/24/94, Van Buren County, Ark. BR/TR, 6'1", 185 lbs. Deb: 9/22/60 F																						
1960	Chi-N	3	6	0	2	0	0	0	1	0	1	.333	.333	.333	84	-0	0	0	0	.667	-2	/2-1,O-1	-0.2
1962	Chi-N	60	85	6	19	0	1	0	5	2	13	.224	.241	.247	30	-8	0	0	0	.955	3	/3-9,O-5,2	-0.6
Total	2	63	91	6	21	0	1	0	6	2	14	.231	.247	.253	34	-8	0	0	0	.875	1	/3-9,O-6,2	-0.8
■ JEFF McKNIGHT	McKnight, Jefferson Alan b: 2/18/63, Conway, Ark. BB/TR, 6', 170 lbs. Deb: 6/6/89 F																						
1989	NY-N	6	12	2	3	0	0	0	2	1		.250	.357	.250	80	-0	0	0	0	1.000	-3	/2-4,1-1,3S	-0.3
1990	Bal-A	29	75	11	15	2	0	1	4	5	17	.200	.259	.267	49	-5	0	0	0	1.000	-3	1-15/O-8,2SD	-0.9
1991	Bal-A	16	41	2	7	1	0	0	2	2	7	.171	.209	.195	13	-5	1	0	0	1.000	-0	/O-7,1-2,D	-0.5
1992	NY-N	31	85	10	23	3	1	2	13	2	8	.271	.287	.400	94	-1	0	1	-1	.980	-3	2-14/1-9,3SO	-0.5
1993	NY-N	105	164	19	42	3	1	2	13	13	31	.256	.315	.323	72	-6	0	0	0	.943	-7	S-29,2-15,1/3C	-1.2
1994	NY-N	31	27	1	4	1	0	0	2	4	12	.148	.258	.185	18	-3	0	0	0	1.000	-0	/1-2	-0.3
Total	6	218	404	45	94	10	2	5	34	28	76	.233	.286	.304	63	-21	1	1	-0	.996	-16	/1-39,2-38,SO3DC	-3.7
■ ED McLANE	McLane, Edward Cameron b: 8/20/1881, Weston, Mass. d: 8/21/75, Baltimore, Md. 5'10", 179 lbs. Deb: 10/6/07																						
1907	Bro-N	1	2	0	0	0	0	0	0	0		.000	.333	.000	5	-0	0			.333	-1	/O-1	-0.1
■ ART McLARNEY	McLarney, Arthur James b: 12/20/08, Ft.Worden, Wash. d: 12/20/84, Seattle, Wash. BB/TR, 6', 168 lbs. Deb: 8/23/32																						
1932	NY-N	9	23	2	3	1	0	0	3	1	3	.130	.167	.174	-8	-4	0			1.000	-1	/S-7	-0.4
■ POLLY McLARRY	McLarry, Howard Zell b: 3/25/1891, Leonard, Tex. d: 11/4/71, Bonham, Tex. BL/TR, 6', 185 lbs. Deb: 9/2/12																						
1912	Chi-A	2	2	0	0	0	0	0	0	0		.000	.000	.000	-99	-1	0			.000	0	H	-0.1
1915	Chi-N	68	127	16	25	3	0	1	12	14	20	.197	.277	.244	58	-6	2	2	-1	.957	3	2-21,1-18	-0.4
Total	2	70	129	16	25	3	0	1	12	14	20	.194	.273	.240	56	-7	2	2		.957	3	/2-21,1-18	-0.5
■ BARNEY McLAUGHLIN	McLaughlin, Bernard b: 1857, Ireland d: 2/13/21, Lowell, Mass. BR/TR, Deb: 8/2/1884 F																						
1884	KC-U	42	162	15	37	7	3	0		9		.228	.269	.309	65	-8				.762	-4	O-24,2-12/PS	-1.0
1887	Phi-N	50	205	26	45	8	3	1	26	11	27	.220	.263	.302	53	-13	2			.879	-11	2-50	-2.0
1890	Syr-a	86	329	43	87	8	1	2		47		.264	.360	.313	110	7	13			.902	-12	S-86	0.0
Total	3	178	696	84	169	23	7	3	26	67	27	.243	.312	.309	82	-14	15			.900	-27	/S-88,2-62,OP	-3.0
■ FRANK McLAUGHLIN	McLaughlin, Francis Edward b: 6/19/1856, Lowell, Mass. d: 4/5/17, Lowell, Mass. BR/TR, 5'9", 160 lbs. Deb: 8/9/1882 F																						
1882	Wor-N	15	55	7	12	0	2	1	4	0	11	.218	.218	.345	76	-2				.760	-3	S-14/O-1	-0.4
1883	Pit-a	29	114	15	25	2	0	1		6		.219	.258	.263	72	-3				.802	-1	S-25/O-4,2P	-0.3
1884	Cin-U	16	67	10	16	4	1	2		1		.239	.261	.418	76	-3				.740	-7	S-16	-0.8
	CP-U	15	67	11	16	4	1	0		1		.239	.250	.328	56	-4				.888	6	2-14/S-1,O	0.2
	KC-U	32	123	17	28	11	0	1		9		.228	.280	.341	78	-4				.847	-9	2-10,0-10/3SP	-1.1
	Yr	63	257	38	60	19	2	3		12		.233	.268	.358	72	-10				.873	-10	2-24,S-22,0/3P	-1.7
Total	3	107	426	60	97	21	4	5	4	18	11	.228	.259	.331	72	-15				.769	-15	/S-61,2-26,O3P	-2.4
■ JAMES McLAUGHLIN	McLaughlin, James b: San Francisco, Cal. Deb: 5/3/1884																						
1884	Was-U	10	37	3	7	3	0	0		0		.189	.189	.270	24	-4				.696	-3	/S-9,3-1	-0.6
■ KID McLAUGHLIN	McLaughlin, James Anson "Sunshine" b: 4/12/1888, Randolph, N.Y. d: 11/13/34, Allegany, N.Y. BL/TR, 5'8.5", 158 lbs. Deb: 6/30/14																						
1914	Cin-N	3	2	1	0	0	0	0	0	0		.000	.000	.000	-97	-0	0			1.000	-1	/O-2	-0.1
■ JIM McLAUGHLIN	McLaughlin, James Robert b: 1/3/02, St.Louis, Mo. d: 12/18/68, Mount Vernon, Ill. BR/TR, 5'8.5", 168 lbs. Deb: 4/18/32																						
1932	StL-A	1	1	0	0	0	0	0	0	0		.000	.000	.000	-95	-0	0	0	0	.000	-0	/3-1	0.0
■ TOM McLAUGHLIN	McLaughlin, Thomas b: 3/28/1860, Louisville, Ky. d: 7/21/21, Louisville, Ky. TR , Deb: 7/17/1883																						
1883	Lou-a	42	146	16	28	1	2	0		5		.192	.219	.226	47	-8				.844	4	S-19,O-17/132	-0.4
1884	Lou-a	98	335	41	67	11	6	0		22		.200	.262	.269	77	-7				.892	19	*S-94/3-4,2	1.1
1885	Lou-a	112	411	49	87	13	9	2		15		.212	.245	.302	72	-13				.883	1	*2-93,S-19	-0.8
1886	NY-a	74	250	27	34	3	1	0		26		.136	.220	.156	19	-22	13			.886	7	S-63,2-10/O	-1.2

YEAR	TM/L	G	AB	R	H	2B	3B	HR	RBI	BB	SO	AVG	OBP	SLG	PRO+	BR/A	SB	CS	SBR	FA	FR	G/POS	TPR
1891	Was-a	14	41	9	11	0	0	1	3	7	6	.268	.400	.317	111	1	3			.871	-0	S-14	0.2
Total	5	340	1183	142	227	28	19	2	3	75	6	.192	.247	.253	61	-49	16			.886	30	S-209,2-106/O31	-1.1

■ RALPH McLAURIN
McLaurin, Ralph Edgar b: 5/23/1885, Kissimmee, Fla. d: 2/11/43, McColl, S.C.   Deb: 9/5/08

YEAR	TM/L	G	AB	R	H	2B	3B	HR	RBI	BB	SO	AVG	OBP	SLG	PRO+	BR/A	SB	CS	SBR	FA	FR	G/POS	TPR
1908	StL-N	8	22	2	5	0	0	0	0	0	0	.227	.227	.227	47	-1	0			.875	-0	/O-6	-0.2

■ LARRY McLEAN
McLean, John Bannerman b: 7/18/1881, Fredericton, N.B., Canada d: 3/24/21, Boston, Mass. BR/TR, 6'5", 228 lbs. Deb: 4/26/01

YEAR	TM/L	G	AB	R	H	2B	3B	HR	RBI	BB	SO	AVG	OBP	SLG	PRO+	BR/A	SB	CS	SBR	FA	FR	G/POS	TPR
1901	Bos-A	9	19	4	4	1	0	0	2	0		.211	.211	.263	31	-2	1			1.000	0	/1-5	-0.1
1903	Chi-N	1	4	0	0	0	0	0	1	1		.000	.000	.000	-42	-1	0			.889	-0	/C-1	-0.1
1904	StL-N	27	84	5	14	2	1	0	4	4		.167	.205	.214	31	-7	1			.954	-2	C-24	-0.7
1906	Cin-N	12	35	3	7	2	0	0	2	4		.200	.282	.257	65	-1	0			.954	-2	C-12	-0.2
1907	Cin-N	113	374	35	108	9	9	0	54	13		.289	.313	.361	107	1	4			.975	-3	C-89,1-13	0.7
1908	Cin-N	99	309	24	67	9	4	1	28	15		.217	.258	.282	74	-10	2			.963	-6	C-69,1-19	-1.1
1909	Cin-N	95	324	26	83	12	2	2	36	21		.256	.307	.324	97	-2	1			.978	-6	C-95	0.1
1910	Cin-N	127	423	27	126	14	7	2	71	26	23	.298	.340	.378	114	6	4			.983	-4	*C-119	1.4
1911	Cin-N	107	328	24	94	7	2	0	34	20	18	.287	.330	.320	85	-7	1			.968	-8	C-98	1.0
1912	Cin-N	102	333	17	81	15	1	1	27	18	15	.243	.284	.303	63	-18	1			.973	-2	C-98	-1.0
1913	StL-N	48	152	7	41	9	0	0	12	6	9	.270	.297	.329	80	-4	0			.981	-8	C-42	-0.9
	*NY-N	30	75	3	24	4	0	0	9	4	4	.320	.354	.373	107	1	1			.953	-4	C-28	-0.1
	Yr	78	227	10	65	13	0	0	21	10	13	.286	.316	.344	89	-4	1			.970	-12	C-70	-1.0
1914	NY-N	79	154	8	40	6	0	0	14	4	9	.260	.283	.299	76	-5	4			.973	-4	C-74	-0.5
1915	NY-N	13	33	0	5	0	0	0	4	0	1	.152	.152	.152	-9	-4	0			.985	2	C-12	-0.2
Total	13	862	2647	183	694	90	26	6	298	136	79	.262	.301	.323	86	-53	20			.973	-29	C-761/1-37	-1.7

■ MARK McLEMORE
McLemore, Mark Tremell b: 10/4/64, San Diego, Cal. BB/TR, 5'11", 195 lbs. Deb: 9/13/86

YEAR	TM/L	G	AB	R	H	2B	3B	HR	RBI	BB	SO	AVG	OBP	SLG	PRO+	BR/A	SB	CS	SBR	FA	FR	G/POS	TPR
1986	Cal-A	5	4	0	0	0	0	0	0	1	2	.000	.000	.000	-40	-1	0	1	-1	1.000	4	/2-2	0.2
1987	Cal-A	138	433	61	102	13	3	3	41	48	72	.236	.312	.300	66	-20	25	8	3	.974	-5	*2-132/S-6,D	-1.6
1988	Cal-A	77	233	38	56	11	2	2	16	25	28	.240	.314	.330	83	-5	13	7	-0	.979	7	2-63/3-5,D	0.4
1989	Cal-A	32	103	12	25	3	1	0	14	7	19	.243	.297	.291	68	-4	6	1	1	.966	3	2-27/D-1	0.0
1990	Cal-A	20	48	4	7	2	0	0	2	4	9	.146	.212	.188	13	-6	1	0	0	1.000	-1	/2-8,S-8,D	-0.6
	Cle-A	8	12	2	2	0	0	0	0	0	6	.167	.167	.167	-7	-2	0	0	0	1.000	3	/3-4,2-3,D	0.1
	Yr	28	60	6	9	2	0	0	2	4	15	.150	.203	.183	9	-7	1	0	0	1.000	2	2-11/S-8,3D	-0.5
1991	Hou-N	21	61	6	9	1	0	0	2	6	13	.148	.224	.164	11	-7	0	1	-1	.975	1	2-19	-0.7
1992	Bal-A	101	228	40	56	7	2	0	27	21	26	.246	.309	.294	68	-9	11	5	0	.978	9	2-70,D-17	0.1
1993	Bal-A	148	581	81	165	27	5	4	72	64	92	.284	.356	.368	91	-6	21	15	-3	.987	12	*O-124,2-25/3D	0.1
1994	Bal-A	104	343	44	88	11	1	3	29	51	50	.257	.354	.321	71	-13	20	5	3	.981	-3	2-96/O-7	-1.0
Total	9	654	2046	288	510	75	14	12	203	227	317	.249	.325	.317	73	-74	97	43		.979	28	2-445,0-131/DS3	-3.1

■ RALPH McLEOD
McLeod, Ralph Alton b: 10/19/16, N.Quincy, Mass. BL/TL, 6', 170 lbs. Deb: 9/14/38

YEAR	TM/L	G	AB	R	H	2B	3B	HR	RBI	BB	SO	AVG	OBP	SLG	PRO+	BR/A	SB	CS	SBR	FA	FR	G/POS	TPR
1938	Bos-N	6	7	1	2	1	0	0	0	2		.286	.286	.429	105	-0				1.000	-0	/O-1	0.0

■ JIM McLEOD
McLeod, Soule James b: 9/12/08, Jones, La. d: 8/3/81, Little Rock, Ark. BR/TR, 6', 187 lbs. Deb: 5/22/30

YEAR	TM/L	G	AB	R	H	2B	3B	HR	RBI	BB	SO	AVG	OBP	SLG	PRO+	BR/A	SB	CS	SBR	FA	FR	G/POS	TPR
1930	Was-A	18	34	3	9	1	0	0	1	1	5	.265	.306	.294	53	-2	1	1	-0	1.000	-1	3-10/S-7	-0.2
1932	Was-A	7	0	1	0	0	0	0	0	1	0	—	1.000	—	183	0	0	0	0	1.000	0	/S-1	0.1
1933	Phi-N	67	232	20	45	6	1	0	15	12	25	.194	.237	.228	30	-21	1			.914	-6	3-67/S-1	-2.5
Total	3	92	266	24	54	7	1	0	16	14	30	.203	.248	.237	33	-23	2	1		.922	-6	/3-77,S-9	-2.6

■ JACK McMAHON
McMahon, John Henry b: 10/15/1869, Waterbury, Conn. d: 12/30/1894, Bridgeport, Conn. BR/TL, 5'10", 165 lbs. Deb: 8/8/1892

YEAR	TM/L	G	AB	R	H	2B	3B	HR	RBI	BB	SO	AVG	OBP	SLG	PRO+	BR/A	SB	CS	SBR	FA	FR	G/POS	TPR
1892	NY-N	40	147	21	33	5	7	1	24	10	9	.224	.281	.374	99	-1	3			.973	-2	1-36/C-5	-0.4
1893	NY-N	11	30	5	10	2	1	0	4	2	0	.333	.375	.467	123	1	0			.891	-1	C-11	0.0
Total	2	51	177	26	43	7	8	1	28	12	9	.243	.295	.390	103	-0	3			.900	-3	/1-36,C-16	-0.4

■ FRANK McMANUS
McManus, Francis E. b: 9/21/1875, Lawrence, Mass. d: 9/1/23, Syracuse, N.Y. TR, 5'10", Deb: 9/14/1899

YEAR	TM/L	G	AB	R	H	2B	3B	HR	RBI	BB	SO	AVG	OBP	SLG	PRO+	BR/A	SB	CS	SBR	FA	FR	G/POS	TPR
1899	Was-N	7	21	3	8	1	0	0	2	2		.381	.435	.429	139	1	3			.931	0	/C-7	0.2
1903	Bro-N	2	7	0	0	0	0	0	0	0		.000	.000	.000	-99	-2	0			.929	1	/C-2	-0.1
1904	Det-A	1	0	0	0	0	0	0	0	0		—	—	—			0			.000	0	/C-1	0.0
	NY-A	4	7	0	0	0	0	0	0	0		.000	.000	.000	-96	-2	0			.900	-1	/C-4	-0.3
	Yr	5	7	0	0	0	0	0	0	0		.000	.000	.000	-97	-2	0			.900	-1	/C-5	-0.3
Total	3	14	35	3	8	1	0	0	2	2		.229	.270	.257	50	-2	3			.925	-0	/C-14	-0.2

■ JIM McMANUS
McManus, James Michael b: 7/20/36, Brookline, Mass. BL/TL, 6'4", 215 lbs. Deb: 9/21/60

YEAR	TM/L	G	AB	R	H	2B	3B	HR	RBI	BB	SO	AVG	OBP	SLG	PRO+	BR/A	SB	CS	SBR	FA	FR	G/POS	TPR
1960	KC-A	5	13	3	4	0	0	1	2	1	2	.308	.357	.538	138	1	0	0	0	1.000	-0	/1-3	0.0

■ MARTY McMANUS
McManus, Martin Joseph b: 3/14/1900, Chicago, Ill. d: 2/18/66, St.Louis, Mo. BR/TR, 5'10.5", 160 lbs. Deb: 9/26/20 M

YEAR	TM/L	G	AB	R	H	2B	3B	HR	RBI	BB	SO	AVG	OBP	SLG	PRO+	BR/A	SB	CS	SBR	FA	FR	G/POS	TPR
1920	StL-A	1	3	0	1	0	0	0	1	0	0	.333	.333	1.000	237	-0	0			.667	-2	/3-1	0.0
1921	StL-A	121	412	49	107	19	8	3	64	27	30	.260	.308	.367	68	-21	5	3	-0	.952	-11	2-96,3-13/1S	-2.7
1922	StL-A	154	606	88	189	34	11	11	109	38	41	.312	.358	.459	108	6	9	6	-1	.964	3	*2-153/1-1	1.1
1923	StL-A	154	582	86	180	35	10	15	94	49	50	.309	.367	.481	116	11	14	10	-2	.960	-1	*2-133,1-20	0.8
1924	StL-A	123	442	71	147	23	5	9	80	55	40	.333	.409	.441	112	9	13	9	-2	.972	7	*2-119	1.5
1925	StL-A	154	587	108	169	**44**	8	13	90	73	69	.288	.371	.457	104	2	5	11	-5	.967	4	*2-154/O-1	0.3
1926	StL-A	149	549	102	156	30	10	9	68	55	62	.284	.350	.424	97	-4	5	7	-3	.958	15	3-84,2-61/1	1.5
1927	Det-A	108	369	60	99	19	7	9	69	34	38	.268	.332	.431	95	-4	8	7	-2	.960	-2	S-39,2-35,3/1	-0.1
1928	Det-A	139	500	78	144	37	5	8	73	51	32	.288	.355	.430	104	2	11	13	-5	.955	6	3-92,1-45/S	1.4
1929	Det-A	154	599	99	168	32	8	18	90	60	52	.280	.347	.451	103	2	16	11	-2	.972	6	*3-150/S-8	1.4
1930	Det-A	132	484	74	155	40	4	9	89	59	28	.320	.396	.475	118	14	**23**	8	2	**.966**	4	*3-130/S-3,1	2.6
1931	Det-A	107	362	39	98	17	3	5	53	49	22	.271	.361	.359	87	-6	7	3	0	.950	13	3-79,2-21/1	1.2
	Bos-A	17	62	8	18	4	1	0	9	8	1	.290	.371	.403	110	1	1	1	-0	1.000	8	3-11/2-7	0.9
	Yr	124	424	47	116	21	3	4	62	57	23	.274	.362	.366	90	-5	8	4	0	.956	21	3-90,2-28/1	2.1
1932	Bos-A	93	302	39	71	19	4	5	24	36	30	.235	.317	.374	80	-9	1	2	-1	.969	6	2-49,3-30/S1M	0.0
1933	Bos-A	106	366	51	104	30	4	3	36	49	21	.284	.369	.413	108	5	3	0	1	.957	-5	3-76,2-26/1M	0.6
1934	Bos-N	119	435	56	120	18	0	8	47	32	42	.276	.330	.372	95	-4	5			.964	-5	2-73,3-37	-0.3
Total	15	1831	6660	1008	1926	401	88	120	996	675	558	.289	.357	.430	101	5	126	91		.965	44	2-927,3-725/1SO	8.8

■ JIMMY McMATH
McMath, Jimmy Lee b: 8/10/49, Tuscaloosa, Ala. BL/TL, 6'1.5", 195 lbs. Deb: 9/7/68

YEAR	TM/L	G	AB	R	H	2B	3B	HR	RBI	BB	SO	AVG	OBP	SLG	PRO+	BR/A	SB	CS	SBR	FA	FR	G/POS	TPR
1968	Chi-N	6	14	0	2	0	0	0	2	0	6	.143	.143	.143	-13	-2	0	0	0	1.000	-0	/O-3	-0.2

■ GEORGE McMILLAN
McMillan, George A. "Reddy" b: Evansville, Ind. 5'8", 175 lbs. Deb: 8/11/1890

YEAR	TM/L	G	AB	R	H	2B	3B	HR	RBI	BB	SO	AVG	OBP	SLG	PRO+	BR/A	SB	CS	SBR	FA	FR	G/POS	TPR
1890	NY-N	10	35	4	5	0	0	0	1	7	4	.143	.286	.143	26	-3	1			.800	-1	O-10	-0.4

■ NORM McMILLAN
McMillan, Norman Alexis "Bub" b: 10/5/1895, Latta, S.C. d: 9/28/69, Marion, S.C. BR/TR, 6', 175 lbs. Deb: 4/12/22

YEAR	TM/L	G	AB	R	H	2B	3B	HR	RBI	BB	SO	AVG	OBP	SLG	PRO+	BR/A	SB	CS	SBR	FA	FR	G/POS	TPR
1922	*NY-A	33	78	7	20	11	2	0	11	6	10	.256	.310	.321	63	-4	1	1		.921	-8	O-26/3-5	-1.2
1923	Bos-A	131	459	37	116	24	5	0	42	28	44	.253	.299	.327	64	-25	13	5	1	.942	12	3-67,2-34,S	-0.2
1924	StL-A	76	201	25	56	12	2	0	27	12	17	.279	.332	.358	73	-8	6	4	-1	.966	-3	2-37,3-19/S1	-1.0
1928	Chi-N	49	123	11	27	2	2	1	12	13	19	.220	.299	.293	56	-8	0			.977	-1	2-19,3-18	-0.7
1929	*Chi-N	124	495	77	134	35	5	5	55	36	43	.271	.324	.392	76	-19	13			.944	6	*3-120	-0.8
Total	5	413	1356	157	353	74	16	6	147	95	133	.260	.313	.352	69	-64	36	10		.944	7	3-229/2-90,SO1	-3.9

YEAR	TM/L	G	AB	R	H	2B	3B	HR	RBI	BB	SO	AVG	OBP	SLG	PRO+	BR/A	SB	CS	SBR	FA	FR	G/POS	TPR

■ **ROY McMILLAN**   McMillan, Roy David b: 7/17/30, Bonham, Tex.   BR/TR, 5′11″, 170 lbs.   Deb: 4/17/51 MC

YEAR	TM/L	G	AB	R	H	2B	3B	HR	RBI	BB	SO	AVG	OBP	SLG	PRO+	BR/A	SB	CS	SBR	FA	FR	G/POS	TPR
1951	Cin-N	85	199	21	42	4	0	1	8	17	26	.211	.273	.246	40	-17	0	0	0	.963	5	S-54,3-12/2	-0.9
1952	Cin-N	154	540	60	132	32	2	7	57	45	81	.244	.306	.350	82	-14	4	5	-2	.971	11	*S-154	0.7
1953	Cin-N	155	557	51	130	15	4	5	43	43	52	.233	.290	.302	54	-37	2	4	-2	.972	14	*S-155	-1.4
1954	Cin-N	154	588	86	147	21	2	4	42	47	54	.250	.311	.313	61	-33	4	2	0	.959	6	*S-154	-1.4
1955	Cin-N	151	470	50	126	21	2	1	37	66	33	.268	.366	.328	81	-10	4	4	-1	.969	17	*S-150	1.8
1956	Cin-N★	150	479	51	126	16	7	3	62	76	54	.263	.370	.344	88	-5	4	3	-1	**.975**	30	*S-150	3.7
1957	Cin-N★	151	448	50	122	25	5	1	55	66	44	.272	.373	.357	91	-3	5	1	1	**.977**	-8	*S-151	0.4
1958	Cin-N	145	393	48	90	18	3	1	25	47	33	.229	.313	.298	60	-22	5	2	0	**.980**	4	*S-145	-0.6
1959	Cin-N	79	246	38	65	14	2	9	24	27	27	.264	.347	.447	106	2	0	2	-1	.974	-7	S-73	0.0
1960	Cin-N	124	399	42	94	12	2	10	42	35	40	.236	.304	.351	77	-12	2	0	1	.964	-13	*S-116,2-10	-1.7
1961	Mil-N	154	505	42	111	16	0	7	48	61	86	.220	.309	.293	65	-25	2	4	-2	**.975**	-0	*S-154	-1.4
1962	Mil-N	137	468	66	115	13	0	12	41	60	53	.246	.338	.350	87	-7	2	2	-1	.972	1	*S-135	0.5
1963	Mil-N	100	320	35	80	10	1	4	29	17	25	.250	.292	.325	78	-9	1	5	-3	.979	7	S-94	0.2
1964	Mil-N	8	13	1	4	0	0	0	2	0	2	.308	.308	.308	73	-0	1	0	0	.933	-1	/S-8	-0.1
	NY-N	113	379	30	80	8	2	1	25	14	16	.211	.247	.251	42	-29	3	1	0	.976	-1	*S-111	-2.3
	Yr	121	392	31	84	8	2	1	27	14	18	.214	.249	.253	43	-30	4	1	1	.975	-2	*S-119	-2.4
1965	NY-N	157	528	44	128	19	2	1	42	24	60	.242	.281	.292	64	-26	1	0	0	.964	-4	*S-153	-2.0
1966	NY-N	76	220	24	47	9	1	1	12	20	25	.214	.285	.277	59	-12	1	1	-0	.975	-6	S-71	-0.1
Total	16	2093	6752	739	1639	253	35	68	594	665	711	.243	.316	.321	72	-259	41	36	-9	.972	66	*S-2028/3-12,2	-4.6

■ **TOM McMILLAN**   McMillan, Thomas Erwin b: 9/13/51, Richmond, Va.   BR/TR, 5′9″, 165 lbs.   Deb: 9/17/77

YEAR	TM/L	G	AB	R	H	2B	3B	HR	RBI	BB	SO	AVG	OBP	SLG	PRO+	BR/A	SB	CS	SBR	FA	FR	G/POS	TPR
1977	Sea-A	2	5	0	0	0	0	0	0	0	0	.000	.000	.000	-99	-1	0	0	0	1.000	-0	/S-2	-0.2

■ **TOMMY McMILLAN**   McMillan, Thomas Law "Rebel" b: 4/18/1888, Pittston, Pa. d: 7/15/66, Orlando, Fla.   BR/TR, 5′5″, 130 lbs.   Deb: 8/19/08

YEAR	TM/L	G	AB	R	H	2B	3B	HR	RBI	BB	SO	AVG	OBP	SLG	PRO+	BR/A	SB	CS	SBR	FA	FR	G/POS	TPR
1908	Bro-N	43	147	9	35	3	0	0	3	9		.238	.296	.259	80	-3	5			.873	-5	S-29,O-14	-0.9
1909	Bro-N	108	373	18	79	15	1	0	24	20		.212	.254	.257	61	-18	11			.914	-10	*S-105/2-2,3	-2.9
1910	Bro-N	23	74	2	13	1	0	0	2	6	10	.176	.237	.189	26	-7	4			.898	-1	S-23	-0.8
	Cin-N	82	248	20	46	0	3	0	13	31	23	.185	.281	.210	46	-16	7			.927	10	S-82	-0.4
	Yr	105	322	22	59	1	3	0	15	37	33	.183	.271	.205	41	-23	11			.921	8	*S-105	-1.2
1912	NY-A	41	149	24	34	2	0	0	12	15		.228	.303	.242	53	-9	18			.948	-8	S-41	-1.3
Total	4	297	991	73	207	21	4	0	54	81	33	.209	.273	.238	56	-53	45			.917	-14	S-280/O-14,23	-6.3

■ **HUGH McMULLEN**   McMullen, Hugh Raphael b: 12/16/01, LaCygne, Kan. d: 5/23/86, Whittier, Cal.   BB/TR, 6′1″, 180 lbs.   Deb: 9/19/25

YEAR	TM/L	G	AB	R	H	2B	3B	HR	RBI	BB	SO	AVG	OBP	SLG	PRO+	BR/A	SB	CS	SBR	FA	FR	G/POS	TPR
1925	NY-N	5	15	1	2	1	0	0	0	3		.133	.133	.200	-17	-3	0	0	0	1.000	-0	/C-5	-0.4
1926	NY-N	57	91	5	17	2	0	0	6	2	18	.187	.204	.209	11	-11	1			.942	-0	C-56	-0.9
1928	Was-A	1	1	0	0	0	0	0	0	0	1	.000	.000	.000	-99	-0	0			.000	0	H	0.0
1929	Cin-N	1	1	0	0	0	0	0	0	0	0	.000	.000	.000	-99	-0	0			1.000	0	/C-1	0.0
Total	4	64	108	6	19	3	0	0	6	2	22	.176	.191	.204	5	-15	1	0		.947	-2	/C-62	-1.3

■ **KEN McMULLEN**   McMullen, Kenneth Lee b: 6/1/42, Oxnard, Cal.   BR/TR, 6′3″, 195 lbs.   Deb: 9/17/62

YEAR	TM/L	G	AB	R	H	2B	3B	HR	RBI	BB	SO	AVG	OBP	SLG	PRO+	BR/A	SB	CS	SBR	FA	FR	G/POS	TPR
1962	LA-N	6	11	0	3	0	0	0	0	0	3	.273	.273	.273	50	-1	0	0	0	1.000	-0	/O-2	-0.1
1963	LA-N	79	233	16	55	9	0	5	28	20	46	.236	.299	.339	89	-4	1	2	-1	.933	6	3-71/2-1,O	0.2
1964	LA-N	24	67	3	14	0	0	1	2	3	7	.209	.243	.254	43	-5	0	1	-1	.991	-3	1-13/3-4,O	-1.0
1965	Was-A	150	555	75	146	18	6	18	54	47	90	.263	.325	.414	110	7	2	0	1	.954	6	*3-142/O-8,1	1.0
1966	Was-A	147	524	48	122	19	4	13	54	44	89	.233	.292	.359	87	-9	3	1	0	.951	-1	*3-141/1-8,O	-1.4
1967	Was-A	146	563	73	138	22	2	16	67	46	84	.245	.303	.377	104	1	5	3	-0	.965	12	*3-145	1.3
1968	Was-A	151	557	66	138	11	2	20	62	63	66	.248	.327	.382	118	12	1	3	0	.962	5	*3-145,S-11	1.9
1969	Was-A	158	562	83	153	25	2	19	87	70	103	.272	.354	.425	123	17	4	5	-2	.976	19	*3-154	3.6
1970	Was-A	15	59	5	12	2	0	0	3	5	10	.203	.266	.237	42	-5	0	0	0	.971	6	3-15	0.1
	Cal-A	124	422	50	98	9	3	14	61	59	81	.232	.331	.367	96	-2	1	0	0	.959	9	*3-122	0.6
	Yr	139	481	55	110	11	3	14	64	64	91	.229	.323	.351	89	-7	1	0	0	.960	15	*3-137	0.7
1971	Cal-A	160	593	63	148	19	2	21	68	53	74	.250	.314	.395	107	3	1	1	-0	.966	-1	*3-158	0.1
1972	Cal-A	137	472	36	127	18	1	9	34	48	59	.247	.297	.369	118	9	1	2	-1	.970	2	*3-137	0.6
1973	LA-N	42	85	6	21	5	0	5	18	7	12	.247	.297	.482	118	4	0	0	0	.922	5	3-24	0.6
1974	*LA-N	44	60	5	15	1	0	3	12	2	12	.250	.274	.417	95	-1	0	0	0	1.000	-1	/3-7,2-3	-0.1
1975	LA-N	39	46	4	11	1	0	2	14	7	12	.239	.340	.435	119	1	0	0	0	1.000	1	3-11/1-3	0.2
1976	Oak-A	98	186	20	41	6	2	5	23	22	33	.220	.306	.355	97	-1	1	1	-0	.952	-1	*3-35,1-26,D/O2	-0.5
1977	Mil-A	63	136	15	31	7	1	5	19	15	33	.228	.305	.404	91	-2	0	0	0	.978	2	D-29,1-11/3	-0.2
Total	16	1583	5131	568	1273	172	26	156	606	510	815	.248	.318	.383	105	23	20	19	-5	.961	66	*3-1318/1-62,DOS2	7.3

■ **FRED McMULLIN**   McMullin, Frederick William b: 10/13/1891, Scammon, Kan. d: 11/21/52, Los Angeles, Cal.   BR/TR, 5′11″, 170 lbs.   Deb: 8/27/14

YEAR	TM/L	G	AB	R	H	2B	3B	HR	RBI	BB	SO	AVG	OBP	SLG	PRO+	BR/A	SB	CS	SBR	FA	FR	G/POS	TPR
1914	Det-A	1	1	0	0	0	0	0	0	0	1	.000	.000	.000	-97	-0	0			.667	0	/S-1	0.0
1916	Chi-A	68	187	8	48	3	0	0	10	19	30	.257	.332	.273	81	-4	9			.950	-4	3-63/S-2,2	-0.6
1917	*Chi-A	59	194	35	46	2	1	0	12	27	17	.237	.339	.258	81	-3	9			.932	-13	3-52/S-2	-1.7
1918	Chi-A	70	235	32	65	7	0	1	16	25	26	.277	.356	.319	103	2	7			.941	-2	3-69/2-1	0.2
1919	*Chi-A	60	170	31	50	8	4	0	19	11	18	.294	.355	.388	108	2	4			.931	-0	3-46/2-5	0.3
1920	Chi-A	46	127	14	25	1	4	0	13	9	13	.197	.255	.268	39	-11	1	1	-0	.962	-5	3-29/2-3,S	-1.5
Total	6	304	914	120	234	21	9	1	70	91	105	.256	.333	.302	85	-15	30	1		.942	-24	3-259/2-10,S	-3.3

■ **JOHN McMULLIN**   McMullin, John F. "Lefty" b: 1848, Philadelphia, Pa. d: 4/11/1881, Philadelphia, Pa.   BR/TL, 5′9″, 160 lbs.   Deb: 5/9/1871

YEAR	TM/L	G	AB	R	H	2B	3B	HR	RBI	BB	SO	AVG	OBP	SLG	PRO+	BR/A	SB	CS	SBR	FA	FR	G/POS	TPR
1871	Tro-n	29	136	38	38	0	5	0	32	8	6	.279	.319	.353	92	-1	11					*P-29	0.0
1872	Mut-n	54	237	48	60	7	1	0	24	11	6	.253	.286	.291	83	-3						*O-53/P-3	0.1
1873	Ath-n	52	227	54	62	8	1	0	29	8	4	.273	.298	.317	76	-8						*O-51/P-1	-0.3
1874	Ath-n	55	262	61	89	10	2	2		7		.340	.357	.416	134	8						*O-54/C-1	0.7
1875	Phi-n	54	223	34	56	9	4	2		5		.251	.268	.354	109	1						*O-53/P-4	0.2
Total	5 n	244	1085	235	305	34	13	4		39		.281	.306	.347	100	-3						O-211/P-37,C	0.7

■ **CARL McNABB**   McNabb, Carl Mac "Skinny" b: 1/25/17, Stevenson, Ala.   BR/TR, 5′9″, 155 lbs.   Deb: 4/20/45

YEAR	TM/L	G	AB	R	H	2B	3B	HR	RBI	BB	SO	AVG	OBP	SLG	PRO+	BR/A	SB	CS	SBR	FA	FR	G/POS	TPR
1945	Det-A	1	1	0	0	0	0	0	0	0	1	.000	.000	.000	-94	-0	0	0	0	.000	0	H	0.0

■ **ERIC McNAIR**   McNair, Donald Eric "Boob" b: 4/12/09, Meridian, Miss. d: 3/11/49, Meridian, Miss.   BR/TR, 5′8″, 160 lbs.   Deb: 9/20/29

YEAR	TM/L	G	AB	R	H	2B	3B	HR	RBI	BB	SO	AVG	OBP	SLG	PRO+	BR/A	SB	CS	SBR	FA	FR	G/POS	TPR
1929	Phi-A	4	8	2	4	1	0	0	3	0	0	.500	.500	.625	181	1	1	0	0	1.000	-0	/S-4	0.1
1930	*Phi-A	78	237	27	63	12	2	0	34	9	19	.266	.296	.333	57	-16	5	2	0	.915	-7	S-31,3-29/2O	-1.7
1931	*Phi-A	79	280	41	76	10	1	5	33	11	19	.271	.306	.368	72	-12	1	4	-2	.915	-6	3-47,2-16,S	-1.4
1932	Phi-A	135	554	87	158	**47**	3	18	95	28	29	.285	.323	.478	101	-2	8	4	0	.953	-7	*S-133	0.2
1933	Phi-A	89	310	57	81	15	4	7	48	15	32	.261	.302	.403	84	-8	2	1	0	.966	-2	S-46,2-27	-0.5
1934	Phi-A	151	599	80	168	20	4	17	82	35	42	.280	.321	.412	91	-10	7	8	-3	.951	4	*S-151	0.0
1935	Phi-A	137	526	55	142	22	4	4	57	35	33	.270	.319	.342	72	-22	3	7	-3	.955	-21	*S-121,3-11/1	-3.8
1936	Bos-A	128	494	68	141	36	2	4	74	27	34	.285	.323	.391	73	-22	2	7	-3	.966	-12	S-84,2-35,3	-2.5
1937	Bos-A	126	455	60	133	29	4	12	76	30	33	.292	.340	.453	94	-5	10	7	-1	.969	-6	*2-106/S-9,31	-0.4
1938	Bos-A	46	96	8	15	1	1	0	7	3	9	.156	.182	.188	-7	-16	1	0	0	.870	-4	S-15,2-14/3	-1.2
1939	Chi-A	129	479	62	155	18	5	7	82	38	41	.324	.375	.426	102	-3	3	3	-0	.937	-5	*3-103,2-19/S	0.7
1940	Chi-A	66	251	26	57	13	1	7	31	12	26	.227	.265	.371	62	-15	1	7	-4	.958	-17	2-65/3-1	-3.1

YEAR	TM/L	G	AB	R	H	2B	3B	HR	RBI	BB	SO	AVG	OBP	SLG	PRO+	BR/A	SB	CS	SBR	FA	FR	G/POS	TPR
1941	Det-A	23	59	5	11	1	0	0	3	4	4	.186	.250	.203	19	-7	0	0	0	.970	-2	3-11/S-3	-0.9
1942	Det-A	26	68	5	11	2	0	1	4	3	5	.162	.197	.235	20	-7	0	1	-1	.881	-8	S-21	-1.5
	Phi-A	34	103	8	25	2	0	0	4	11	5	.243	.316	.262	64	-5	1	0	0	.952	-6	S-29/2-1	-0.9
	Yr	60	171	13	36	4	0	1	8	14	10	.211	.270	.251	46	-12	1	1	-0	.927	-13	S-50/2-1	-2.4
Total	14	1251	4519	592	1240	229	29	82	633	261	328	.274	.318	.392	80	-146	58	54	-15	.949	-83	S-669,2-288,3/10	-16.9

■ MIKE McNALLY
McNally, Michael Joseph "Minooka Mike" b: 9/9/1892, Minooka, Pa. d: 5/29/65, Bethlehem, Pa. BR/TR, 5'11", 150 lbs. Deb: 4/21/15

YEAR	TM/L	G	AB	R	H	2B	3B	HR	RBI	BB	SO	AVG	OBP	SLG	PRO+	BR/A	SB	CS	SBR	FA	FR	G/POS	TPR
1915	Bos-A	23	53	7	8	0	1	0	3	9	7	.151	.196	.189	16	-6	0	2	-1	.891	1	3-18/2-5	-0.6
1916	*Bos-A	87	135	28	23	0	0	0	9	10	19	.170	.228	.170	20	-13	9			.964	7	2-35,3-14/SO	-0.6
1917	Bos-A	42	50	9	15	1	0	0	2	6	3	.300	.375	.320	113	1	3			.935	6	3-14/S-9,2	0.8
1919	Bos-A	33	42	10	11	4	0	0	6	1	2	.262	.279	.357	83	-1	4			.950	9	S-11,3-11/2	0.9
1920	Bos-A	93	312	42	80	5	1	0	23	31	24	.256	.326	.279	64	-15	13	10	-2	.930	-9	2-76/S-8,1	-2.3
1921	*NY-A	71	215	36	56	4	2	1	24	14	15	.260	.306	.312	57	-14	5	6	-2	.974	18	3-49,2-16	0.5
1922	*NY-A	52	143	20	36	2	2	0	18	16	14	.252	.331	.294	63	-7	3	0	1	.983	-0	3-34/2-9,S1	-0.4
1923	NY-A	30	38	5	8	0	0	0	1	3	4	.211	.268	.211	27	-4	2	0	1	1.000	-0	S-13/3-7,2	-0.3
1924	NY-A	49	69	11	17	0	0	0	2	7	5	.246	.316	.246	46	-5	1	1	-0	.985	10	2-25,3-13/S	0.4
1925	Was-A	12	21	1	3	0	0	0	0	1	4	.143	.182	.143	-17	-4	0	0	0	1.000	1	/3-7,S-2,2	-0.3
Total	10	492	1078	169	257	16	6	1	85	92	97	.238	.299	.267	54	-69	40	19		.946	41	2-181,3-167/S10	-1.9

■ JIM McNAMARA
McNamara, James Patrick b: 6/10/65, Nashua, N.H. BL/TR, 6'4", 210 lbs. Deb: 4/9/92

YEAR	TM/L	G	AB	R	H	2B	3B	HR	RBI	BB	SO	AVG	OBP	SLG	PRO+	BR/A	SB	CS	SBR	FA	FR	G/POS	TPR
1992	SF-N	30	74	6	16	1	0	1	9	6	25	.216	.275	.270	58	-4	0	0	0	.993	-0	C-30	-0.3
1993	SF-N	4	7	0	1	0	0	0	1	0	1	.143	.143	.143	-24	-1	0	0	0	1.000	-0	/C-4	-0.1
Total	2	34	81	6	17	1	0	1	10	6	26	.210	.264	.259	51	-5	0	0	0	.993	-0	/C-34	-0.4

■ GEORGE McNAMARA
McNamara, George Francis b: 1/11/01, Chicago, Ill. d: 6/12/90, Hinsdale, Ill. BL/TR, 6', 175 lbs. Deb: 9/28/22

YEAR	TM/L	G	AB	R	H	2B	3B	HR	RBI	BB	SO	AVG	OBP	SLG	PRO+	BR/A	SB	CS	SBR	FA	FR	G/POS	TPR
1922	Was-A	3	11	3	3	0	0	0	1	1	2	.273	.333	.273	63	-1	0	0	0	1.000	-1	/O-3	-0.1

■ DINNY McNAMARA
McNamara, John Raymond b: 9/16/05, Lexington, Mass. d: 12/20/63, Arlington, Mass. BL/TR, 5'9", 165 lbs. Deb: 7/2/27

YEAR	TM/L	G	AB	R	H	2B	3B	HR	RBI	BB	SO	AVG	OBP	SLG	PRO+	BR/A	SB	CS	SBR	FA	FR	G/POS	TPR
1927	Bos-N	11	9	3	0	0	0	0	0	0	3	.000	.000	.000	-99	-3	0			1.000	0	/O-3	-0.2
1928	Bos-N	9	4	2	1	0	0	0	0	0	1	.250	.250	.250	33	-0	0			1.000	0	/O-3	-0.1
Total	2	20	13	5	1	0	0	0	0	0	4	.077	.077	.077	-63	-3	0			1.000	0	/O-6	-0.3

■ BOB McNAMARA
McNamara, Robert Maxey b: 9/19/16, Denver, Colo. BR/TR, 5'10", 170 lbs. Deb: 5/27/39

YEAR	TM/L	G	AB	R	H	2B	3B	HR	RBI	BB	SO	AVG	OBP	SLG	PRO+	BR/A	SB	CS	SBR	FA	FR	G/POS	TPR
1939	Phi-A	9	9	0	2	1	0	0	3	1	1	.222	.300	.333	63	-1	0	0	0	1.000	0	/3-5,S-2,12	0.0

■ TOM McNAMARA
McNamara, Thomas Henry b: 11/5/1895, Roxbury, Mass. d: 5/5/74, Danvers, Mass. BR/TR, 6'2", 200 lbs. Deb: 6/25/22

YEAR	TM/L	G	AB	R	H	2B	3B	HR	RBI	BB	SO	AVG	OBP	SLG	PRO+	BR/A	SB	CS	SBR	FA	FR	G/POS	TPR
1922	Pit-N	1	1	0	0	0	0	0	0	0	0	.000	.000	.000	-99	-0	0			.000	0	H	0.0

■ RUSTY McNEALY
McNealy, Robert Lee b: 8/12/58, Sacramento, Cal. BL/TL, 5'8", 160 lbs. Deb: 9/4/83

YEAR	TM/L	G	AB	R	H	2B	3B	HR	RBI	BB	SO	AVG	OBP	SLG	PRO+	BR/A	SB	CS	SBR	FA	FR	G/POS	TPR
1983	Oak-A	15	4	5	0	0	0	0	0	0	0	.000	.000	.000	-99	-1	0	1	-1	1.000	-2	/O-5,D-7	-0.4

■ EARL McNEELY
McNeely, George Earl b: 5/12/1898, Sacramento, Cal. d: 7/16/71, Sacramento, Cal. BR/TR, 5'9", 155 lbs. Deb: 8/9/24 C

YEAR	TM/L	G	AB	R	H	2B	3B	HR	RBI	BB	SO	AVG	OBP	SLG	PRO+	BR/A	SB	CS	SBR	FA	FR	G/POS	TPR
1924	*Was-A	43	179	31	59	5	6	0	15	5	21	.330	.355	.425	104	0	3	1	0	.973	-2	O-42	-0.4
1925	*Was-A	122	385	76	110	14	2	3	37	48	54	.286	.378	.356	89	-5	15	16	-5	.975	-2	*O-112/1-1	-1.7
1926	Was-A	124	442	84	134	20	12	0	48	44	28	.303	.373	.403	105	4	18	6	2	.969	-0	*O-118	-0.2
1927	Was-A	73	185	40	51	10	4	0	16	11	13	.276	.320	.373	80	-6	11	4	1	.977	-7	O-47/1-4	-1.4
1928	StL-A	127	496	66	117	27	7	0	44	37	39	.236	.299	.319	61	-29	8	6	-1	.984	7	*O-120	-3.0
1929	StL-A	69	230	27	56	8	1	1	18	7	13	.243	.272	.300	45	-19	2	1	0	.980	-7	O-62	-2.8
1930	StL-A	76	235	33	64	19	1	0	20	22	14	.272	.340	.362	75	-9	8	3	1	.939	-7	O-38,1-27	-1.8
1931	StL-A	49	102	12	23	4	0	0	15	9	5	.225	.288	.265	45	-8	4	4	-1	.969	-5	O-37/1-1	-1.5
Total	8	683	2254	369	614	107	33	4	213	183	187	.272	.335	.354	78	-71	69	41	-4	.974	-21	O-576/1-33	-12.8

■ JEFF McNEELY
McNeely, Jeffrey Lavern b: 10/18/69, Monroe, N.C. BR/TR, 6'2", 190 lbs. Deb: 9/5/93

YEAR	TM/L	G	AB	R	H	2B	3B	HR	RBI	BB	SO	AVG	OBP	SLG	PRO+	BR/A	SB	CS	SBR	FA	FR	G/POS	TPR
1993	Bos-A	21	37	10	11	1	1	0	1	7	9	.297	.409	.378	106	1	6	0	2	.913	-3	O-13/D-3	0.0

■ NORM McNEIL
McNeil, Norman Francis b: 10/22/1892, Chicago, Ill. d: 4/11/42, Buffalo, N.Y. BR/TR, 5'11", 180 lbs. Deb: 6/21/19

YEAR	TM/L	G	AB	R	H	2B	3B	HR	RBI	BB	SO	AVG	OBP	SLG	PRO+	BR/A	SB	CS	SBR	FA	FR	G/POS	TPR
1919	Bos-A	5	9	0	3	0	0	0	1	1	0	.333	.400	.333	113	0	0			.818	-2	/C-5	-0.1

■ JERRY McNERTNEY
McNertney, Gerald Edward b: 8/7/36, Boone, Iowa BR/TR, 6'1", 195 lbs. Deb: 4/16/64 C

YEAR	TM/L	G	AB	R	H	2B	3B	HR	RBI	BB	SO	AVG	OBP	SLG	PRO+	BR/A	SB	CS	SBR	FA	FR	G/POS	TPR
1964	Chi-A	73	186	16	40	5	0	3	23	19	24	.215	.298	.290	66	-8	0	0	0	.987	8	C-69	0.2
1966	Chi-A	44	59	3	13	0	0	0	1	7	6	.220	.303	.220	57	-3	1	1	-0	.969	5	C-37	0.3
1967	Chi-A	56	123	8	28	6	0	0	13	6	14	.228	.275	.350	87	-2	0	0	0	.996	13	C-52	1.4
1968	Chi-A	74	169	18	37	4	1	3	18	18	29	.219	.302	.308	84	-3	0	0	0	.985	13	C-64/1-1	1.6
1969	Sea-A	128	410	39	99	18	1	8	55	29	63	.241	.292	.349	80	-12	1	0	0	.988	2	*C-122	-0.4
1970	Mil-A	111	296	27	72	11	1	6	22	22	33	.243	.304	.348	79	-9	1	4	-2	.984	-9	C-94,1-13	-1.7
1971	StL-N	56	128	15	37	4	2	4	22	12	14	.289	.350	.445	119	3	0	0	0	.985	-3	C-36	0.2
1972	StL-N	39	48	3	10	3	1	0	5	6	16	.208	.296	.313	74	-2	0	0	0	.982	2	C-10	0.0
1973	Pit-N	9	4	0	1	0	0	0	0	0	0	.250	.250	.250	40	-1	0	0	0	1.000	1	/C-9	0.1
Total	9	590	1423	129	337	51	6	27	163	119	199	.237	.301	.338	81	-36	3	5	-2	.987	33	C-493/1-14	1.7

■ PAT McNULTY
McNulty, Patrick Howard b: 2/27/1899, Cleveland, Ohio d: 5/4/63, Hollywood, Cal. BL/TR, 5'11", 160 lbs. Deb: 9/5/22

YEAR	TM/L	G	AB	R	H	2B	3B	HR	RBI	BB	SO	AVG	OBP	SLG	PRO+	BR/A	SB	CS	SBR	FA	FR	G/POS	TPR
1922	Cle-A	22	59	10	16	2	1	0	5	9	5	.271	.368	.339	85	-1	4	1	1	.956	-3	O-22	-0.5
1924	Cle-A	101	291	46	78	13	5	0	26	33	22	.268	.347	.347	78	-9	10	7	-1	.961	-4	O-75	-1.8
1925	Cle-A	118	373	70	117	18	2	6	43	47	23	.314	.392	.421	105	4	7	7	-2	.965	-2	*O-111	-0.5
1926	Cle-A	48	56	3	14	2	1	0	6	5	9	.250	.311	.321	65	-3	0	1	-2	.909	-2	/O-9	-0.5
1927	Cle-A	19	41	3	13	1	0	0	4	4	3	.317	.378	.341	87	-1	1	2	-1	.906	-1	O-12	-0.2
Total	5	308	820	132	238	36	9	6	84	98	62	.290	.368	.378	91	-10	22	18	-4	.957	-11	O-229	-3.5

■ BILL McNULTY
McNulty, William Francis b: 8/29/46, Sacramento, Cal. BR/TR, 6'4", 205 lbs. Deb: 7/9/69

YEAR	TM/L	G	AB	R	H	2B	3B	HR	RBI	BB	SO	AVG	OBP	SLG	PRO+	BR/A	SB	CS	SBR	FA	FR	G/POS	TPR
1969	Oak-A	5	17	0	0	0	0	0	0	0	10	.000	.000	.000	-99	-5	0	0	0	1.000	1	/O-5	-0.4
1972	Oak-A	4	10	0	1	0	0	0	0	2	1	.100	.250	.100	7	-2	0	0	0	.800	-2	/3-3	-0.3
Total	2	9	27	0	1	0	0	0	0	2	11	.037	.103	.037	-61	-6	0	0	0	1.000	-0	/O-5,3-3	-0.7

■ BID McPHEE
McPhee, John Alexander b: 11/1/1859, Massena, N.Y. d: 1/3/43, San Diego, Cal. BR/TR, 5'8", 152 lbs. Deb: 5/2/1882 M

YEAR	TM/L	G	AB	R	H	2B	3B	HR	RBI	BB	SO	AVG	OBP	SLG	PRO+	BR/A	SB	CS	SBR	FA	FR	G/POS	TPR
1882	Cin-a	78	311	43	71	8	7	1	11			.228	.255	.309	84	-6				**.920**	-1	*2-78	-0.5
1883	Cin-a	96	367	61	90	10	10	2	18			.245	.281	.343	95	-3				**.928**	3	*2-96	0.1
1884	Cin-a	112	450	107	125	8	7	5	27			.278	.327	.360	118	8				.924	16	*2-112	2.4
1885	Cin-a	110	431	78	114	12	4	0	19			.265	.306	.311	94	-3				**.936**	6	*2-110	0.6
1886	Cin-a	140	560	139	150	23	12	8	59			.268	.343	.395	127	16	40			**.939**	31	*2-140	4.6
1887	Cin-a	129	540	137	156	20	19	2	55			.289	.360	.407	111	8	95			.924	26	*2-129	3.0
1888	Cin-a	111	458	88	110	12	10	4	51	43		.240	.312	.336	102	0	54			**.940**	31	*2-111	3.3
1889	Cin-a	135	540	109	145	25	7	5	57	60	29	.269	.346	.369	100	-0	63			**.946**	41	*2-135/3-1	4.0
1890	Cin-N	132	528	125	135	16	22	3	39	82	26	.256	.358	.369	119	14	55			.942	30	*2-132	4.5
1891	Cin-N	138	562	107	144	14	16	6	38	74	35	.256	.345	.370	107	6	33			**.954**	23	*2-138	3.1
1892	Cin-N	144	573	111	157	19	12	4	60	84	48	.274	.373	.370	127	22	44			.948	25	*2-144	4.5
1893	Cin-N	127	491	101	138	17	11	3	68	94	20	.281	.401	.379	105	7	25			.954	34	*2-127	3.5

YEAR	TM/L	G	AB	R	H	2B	3B	HR	RBI	BB	SO	AVG	OBP	SLG	PRO+	BR/A	SB	CS	SBR	FA	FR	G/POS	TPR
1894	Cin-N	126	474	107	144	21	9	5	88	90	23	.304	.420	.418	99	2	33			.945	31	*2-126	2.9
1895	Cin-N	115	432	107	129	24	12	1	75	73	30	.299	.409	.417	109	8	30			.955	15	*2-115	2.3
1896	Cin-N	117	433	81	132	18	7	1	87	51	18	.305	.391	.386	99	-0	48			**.978**	6	*2-117	1.0
1897	Cin-N	81	282	45	85	13	7	1	39	35		.301	.386	.408	103	1	9			.966	12	2-81	1.5
1898	Cin-N	133	486	72	121	26	9	1	60	66		.249	.341	.346	91	-6	21			.956	-12	*2-130/O-3	-0.9
1899	Cin-N	111	373	60	104	17	7	1	65	40		.279	.360	.370	98	-0	18			.955	-4	*2-105/O-1	0.2
Total	18	2135	8291	1678	2250	303	188	53	727	981	229	.271	.355	.372	106	72	568			.944	314	*2-2126/O-4,3	40.1

■ MART McQUAID
McQuaid, Mortimer Martin b: 6/28/1861, Chicago, Ill. d: 3/5/28, Chicago, Ill. Deb: 8/15/1891

YEAR	TM/L	G	AB	R	H	2B	3B	HR	RBI	BB	SO	AVG	OBP	SLG	PRO+	BR/A	SB	CS	SBR	FA	FR	G/POS	TPR
1891	StL-a	4	11	1	4	2	0	0	1	0	1	.364	.364	.545	139	0	1			1.000	-1	/2-3,O-1	0.0
1898	Was-N	1	4	0	0	0	0	0	0	0		.000	.000	.000	-99	-1	0			.333	-1	/O-1	-0.2
Total	2	5	15	1	4	2	0	0	1	0	1	.267	.267	.400	81	-1	1			.333	-1	/2-3,O-2	-0.2

■ JERRY McQUAIG
McQuaig, Gerald Joseph b: 1/31/12, Douglas, Ga. BR/TR, 5'11", 183 lbs. Deb: 8/25/34

YEAR	TM/L	G	AB	R	H	2B	3B	HR	RBI	BB	SO	AVG	OBP	SLG	PRO+	BR/A	SB	CS	SBR	FA	FR	G/POS	TPR
1934	Phi-A	7	16	2	1	0	0	0	1	2	4	.063	.167	.063	-40	-3	0	0	0	.889	-1	/O-6	-0.5

■ MOX McQUERY
McQuery, William Thomas b: 6/28/1861, Garrard Co., Ky. d: 6/12/1900, Cincinnati, Ohio 6'4", Deb: 8/20/1884

YEAR	TM/L	G	AB	R	H	2B	3B	HR	RBI	BB	SO	AVG	OBP	SLG	PRO+	BR/A	SB	CS	SBR	FA	FR	G/POS	TPR
1884	Cin-U	35	132	31	37	5	0	2		8		.280	.321	.364	80	-4				.978	1	1-35	-0.6
1885	Det-N	70	278	34	76	15	4	3	30	8	29	.273	.294	.388	119	5				.976	5	1-69/O-1	0.2
1886	KC-N	122	449	62	111	27	4	4	38	36	44	.247	.303	.352	93	-5	4			.969	-1	*1-122	-1.7
1890	Syr-a	122	461	64	142	17	6	2		53		.308	.383	.384	141	25	26			.972	-1	*1-122	1.5
1891	Was-a	68	261	40	63	9	4	2	37	18	19	.241	.305	.330	85	-5	3			.977	1	1-68	-0.7
Total	5	417	1581	231	429	73	18	13	105	123	92	.271	.327	.365	108	16	33			.973	7	1-416/O-1	-1.3

■ GLENN McQUILLEN
McQuillen, Glenn Richard "Red" b: 4/19/15, Strasburg, Va. d: 6/8/89, Gardenville, Md. BR/TR, 6', 198 lbs. Deb: 6/16/38

YEAR	TM/L	G	AB	R	H	2B	3B	HR	RBI	BB	SO	AVG	OBP	SLG	PRO+	BR/A	SB	CS	SBR	FA	FR	G/POS	TPR
1938	StL-A	43	116	14	33	4	0	0	13	4	12	.284	.308	.319	57	-8	0	1	-1	.971	-0	O-30	-0.8
1941	StL-A	7	21	4	7	2	1	0	3	1	2	.333	.364	.524	128	1	0	1	-1	.933	-0	/O-6	0.0
1942	StL-A	100	339	40	96	15	12	3	47	10	17	.283	.306	.425	103	-1	1	1	-0	.969	-5	O-77	-1.1
1946	StL-A	59	166	24	40	3	3	1	12	19	18	.241	.319	.313	73	-6	0	0	0	.977	-2	O-48	-1.1
1947	StL-A	1	1	0	0	0	0	0	0	0	0	.000	.000	.000	-98	-0	0	0	0	.000	0	H	0.0
Total	5	210	643	82	176	24	16	4	75	34	49	.274	.311	.379	87	-14	1	5	-3	.970	-7	O-161	-3.0

■ GEORGE McQUINN
McQuinn, George Hartley b: 5/29/10, Arlington, Va. d: 12/24/78, Alexandria, Va. BL/TL, 5'11", 165 lbs. Deb: 4/14/36

YEAR	TM/L	G	AB	R	H	2B	3B	HR	RBI	BB	SO	AVG	OBP	SLG	PRO+	BR/A	SB	CS	SBR	FA	FR	G/POS	TPR
1936	Cin-N	38	134	5	27	3	4	0	13	10	22	.201	.262	.284	50	-10				.992	1	1-38	-1.3
1938	StL-A	148	602	100	195	42	7	12	82	58	49	.324	.384	.477	115	13	4	5	-2	.992	-0	*1-148	-0.6
1939	StL-A☆	154	617	101	195	37	13	20	94	65	42	.316	.383	.515	125	22	6	5	-1	.993	10	*1-154	1.3
1940	StL-A	151	594	78	166	39	10	16	84	57	58	.279	.343	.460	104	2	3	3	-1	**.992**	10	*1-150	-0.3
1941	StL-A	130	495	93	147	28	4	18	80	74	30	.297	.388	.479	124	18	5	4	-1	**.995**	8	*1-125	1.5
1942	StL-A☆	145	554	86	145	32	5	12	78	60	77	.262	.335	.403	105	3	1	1	-0	.991	1	*1-144	-0.5
1943	StL-A	125	449	53	109	19	2	12	74	56	65	.243	.327	.374	103	1	4	3	-1	.992	2	*1-122	-0.4
1944	*StL-A★	146	516	83	129	26	3	11	72	85	74	.250	.357	.376	103	4	4	3	-1	**.994**	-5	*1-146	-1.0
1945	StL-A†	139	483	69	134	31	3	7	61	65	51	.277	.364	.398	115	10	1	1	-0	.991	4	*1-136	0.5
1946	Phi-A	136	484	47	109	23	6	3	35	64	62	.225	.317	.316	78	-14	4	2	-0	.988	-1	*1-134	-1.9
1947	*NY-A★	144	517	84	157	24	3	13	80	78	66	.304	.395	.437	132	24	0	2	-1	.994	-3	*1-142	1.7
1948	NY-A★	94	302	33	75	11	4	11	41	40	38	.248	.336	.421	102	-0	0	2	-1	.993	-1	1-90	-0.3
Total	12	1550	5747	832	1588	315	64	135	794	712	634	.276	.357	.424	109	73	32	31		.992	31	*1-1529	-1.3

■ BRIAN McRAE
McRae, Brian Wesley b: 8/27/67, Bradenton, Fla. BB/TR, 6', 175 lbs. Deb: 8/7/90 F

YEAR	TM/L	G	AB	R	H	2B	3B	HR	RBI	BB	SO	AVG	OBP	SLG	PRO+	BR/A	SB	CS	SBR	FA	FR	G/POS	TPR
1990	KC-A	46	168	21	48	8	3	2	23	9	29	.286	.322	.405	104	0	4	3	-1	1.000	4	O-45	0.2
1991	KC-A	152	629	86	164	28	9	8	64	24	99	.261	.290	.372	81	-17	20	11	-1	.993	8	*O-150	-1.4
1992	KC-A	149	533	63	119	23	5	4	52	42	88	.223	.287	.308	65	-25	18	5	2	.993	10	*O-148	-1.6
1993	KC-A	153	627	78	177	28	9	12	69	37	105	.282	.326	.413	92	-8	23	14	-2	.983	5	*O-153	-0.8
1994	KC-A	114	436	71	119	22	6	4	40	54	67	.273	.361	.372	84	-9	28	8	4	.988	-6	*O-110/D-4	-1.3
Total	5	614	2393	319	627	109	32	30	248	166	388	.262	.315	.372	83	-60	93	41	3	.990	20	O-606/D-4	-4.9

■ HAL McRAE
McRae, Harold Abraham b: 7/10/45, Avon Park, Fla. BR/TR, 5'11", 180 lbs. Deb: 7/11/68 FCM

YEAR	TM/L	G	AB	R	H	2B	3B	HR	RBI	BB	SO	AVG	OBP	SLG	PRO+	BR/A	SB	CS	SBR	FA	FR	G/POS	TPR
1968	Cin-N	17	51	1	10	1	0	0	2	4	14	.196	.255	.216	40	-4	1	1	-0	.926	-4	2-16	-0.8
1970	*Cin-N	70	165	18	41	6	1	8	23	15	23	.248	.315	.442	100	-1	0	2	-1	.981	-5	O-46/3-6,2	-0.9
1971	Cin-N	99	337	39	89	24	2	9	34	11	35	.264	.291	.427	103	-0	3	2	-0	.966	-1	O-91	-0.6
1972	*Cin-N	61	97	9	27	4	0	5	26	2	10	.278	.307	.474	126	3	0	0	0	.867	-6	O-12,3-11	-0.4
1973	KC-A	106	338	36	79	18	3	9	50	34	38	.234	.315	.385	89	-5	2	2	-1	.963	-4	O-64,D-37/3	-1.3
1974	KC-A	148	539	71	167	36	4	15	88	54	68	.310	.378	.475	136	25	11	8	-2	.950	2	D-90,O-56/3	2.2
1975	KC-A★	126	480	58	147	38	6	5	71	47	47	.306	.373	.442	126	17	11	8	-2	.986	-1	*O-114,D-12/3	0.9
1976	*KC-A★	149	527	75	175	34	5	8	73	64	43	.332	**.412**	.461	154	**38**	22	12	-1	.970	-0	*D-117,O-31	3.4
1977	*KC-A	162	641	104	191	**54**	11	21	92	59	43	.298	.369	.515	137	32	18	14	-3	.958	4	*D-116,O-46	2.7
1978	*KC-A	156	623	90	170	39	5	16	72	51	62	.273	.334	.429	113	7	17	8	0	1.000	0	*D-153/O-3	0.3
1979	*KC-A	101	393	55	113	32	4	10	74	38	46	.288	.356	.466	117	9	5	4	-1	.000	0	*D-100	0.5
1980	*KC-A	124	489	73	145	39	5	14	83	29	56	.297	.346	.483	123	14	10	2	2	1.000	-1	*D-110/O-9	1.1
1981	*KC-A	101	389	38	106	23	2	7	36	34	52	.272	.334	.396	111	5	3	4	-2	.909	0	D-97/O-4	0.0
1982	KC-A★	159	613	91	189	**46**	8	27	**133**	55	61	.308	.370	.542	146	38	4	0	-0	.500	-0	*D-158/O-1	3.0
1983	*KC-A	157	589	84	183	41	6	12	82	50	68	.311	.374	.462	128	23	2	3	-1	.000	0	*D-156	1.6
1984	*KC-A	106	317	30	96	13	4	3	42	34	47	.303	.372	.397	112	6	3	4	-2	.000	0	D-94	0.2
1985	*KC-A	112	320	41	83	19	0	14	70	44	45	.259	.351	.450	117	8	0	1	-1	.000	0	*D-106	0.5
1986	KC-A	112	278	22	70	14	0	7	37	18	39	.252	.300	.378	81	-8	0	0	0	.000	0	D-75	-0.9
1987	KC-A	18	32	5	10	3	0	1	9	5	1	.313	.405	.500	135	2	0	0	0	.000	0	/D-7	0.1
Total	19	2084	7218	940	2091	484	66	191	1097	648	779	.290	.355	.454	122	210	109	78	-14	.966	-15	*D-1428,O-477/32	11.6

■ McREMER
McRemer Deb: 6/20/1884

YEAR	TM/L	G	AB	R	H	2B	3B	HR	RBI	BB	SO	AVG	OBP	SLG	PRO+	BR/A	SB	CS	SBR	FA	FR	G/POS	TPR
1884	Was-U	1	3	0	0	0	0	0		0		.000	.000	.000	-99	-1				1.000	0	/O-1	-0.1

■ KEVIN McREYNOLDS
McReynolds, Walter Kevin b: 10/16/59, Little Rock, Ark. BR/TR, 6'1", 210 lbs. Deb: 6/2/83

YEAR	TM/L	G	AB	R	H	2B	3B	HR	RBI	BB	SO	AVG	OBP	SLG	PRO+	BR/A	SB	CS	SBR	FA	FR	G/POS	TPR
1983	SD-N	39	140	15	31	3	1	4	14	12	29	.221	.283	.343	75	-5	2	1	0	.989	0	O-38	-0.7
1984	*SD-N	147	525	68	146	26	6	20	75	34	69	.278	.322	.465	119	11	3	6	-3	.991	18	*O-143	2.3
1985	SD-N	152	564	61	132	24	4	15	75	43	81	.234	.292	.371	85	-12	4	0	1	.993	23	*O-150	0.7
1986	SD-N	158	560	89	161	31	6	26	96	66	83	.287	.364	.504	140	29	8	6	-1	.977	-14	*O-154	1.0
1987	NY-N	151	590	86	163	32	5	29	95	39	70	.276	.322	.495	119	13	14	1	4	.987	9	*O-150	2.0
1988	*NY-N	147	552	82	159	30	2	27	99	38	56	.288	.338	.496	144	28	21	0	6	.985	10	*O-147	4.3
1989	NY-N	148	545	74	148	25	3	22	85	46	74	.272	.329	.450	127	17	15	7	0	.969	15	*O-145	3.0
1990	NY-N	147	521	75	140	23	1	24	82	71	61	.269	.353	.455	122	16	9	5	0	.988	5	*O-144	2.0
1991	NY-N	143	522	65	135	32	1	16	74	49	46	.259	.325	.416	108	4	6	6	-2	.993	2	*O-141	0.1
1992	KC-A	109	373	45	92	25	0	13	49	67	48	.247	.361	.418	115	9	7	1	2	.986	-3	*O-106/D-1	0.5
1993	KC-A	110	351	44	86	22	4	11	42	37	56	.245	.319	.425	92	-5	2	2	0	.990	0	*O-104/D-1	-0.7
1994	NY-N	51	180	23	46	11	2	4	21	20	34	.256	.330	.406	90	-3	2	0	1	1.000	0	O-47	0.1
Total	12	1502	5423	727	1439	284	35	211	807	522	707	.265	.331	.447	116	102	93	32	9	.987	68	*O-1469/D-2	14.4

YEAR	TM/L	G	AB	R	H	2B	3B	HR	RBI	BB	SO	AVG	OBP	SLG	PRO+	BR/A	SB	CS	SBR	FA	FR	G/POS	TPR

■ PETE McSHANNIC McShannic, Peter Robert b: 3/20/1864, Pittsburgh, Pa. d: 11/30/46, Toledo, Ohio BB/TR, 5'7", 190 lbs. Deb: 9/15/1888

1888	Pit-N	26	98	5	19	1	0	0	5	1	9	.194	.218	.204	38	-7	3			.907	-0	3-26	-0.6

■ TRICK McSORLEY McSorley, John Bernard b: 12/6/1858, St.Louis, Mo. d: 2/9/36, St.Louis, Mo. BR/TR, 5'4", 142 lbs. Deb: 5/6/1875

1875	RS-n	15	52	4	11	0	0	0			0	.212	.212	.212	52	-2						/3-8,O-6	-0.2
1884	Tol-a	21	68	12	17	1	0	0			3	.250	.282	.265	77	-2				.974	1	1-16/O-5,3P	-0.2
1885	StL-N	2	6	2	3	1	0	0	1	2	1	.500	.625	.667	340	2				.400	-2	/3-2	0.0
1886	StL-a	5	20	1	3	3	0	0		1		.150	.150	.300	38	-2	0			.765	-3	/S-5	-0.4
Total	3	28	94	15	23	5	0	0	1	5	1	.245	.283	.298	85	-1	0			.400	-4	/1-16,S-5,03P	-0.6

■ PAUL McSWEENEY McSweeney, Paul A. b: 4/3/1867, St.Louis, Mo. d: 8/12/51, St.Louis, Mo. Deb: 9/20/1891

| 1891 | StL-a | 3 | 12 | 2 | 3 | 1 | 0 | 0 | 2 | 0 | 0 | .250 | .308 | .333 | 73 | -1 | 1 | | | .643 | -2 | /2-3,3-1 | -0.2 |

■ JIM McTAMANY McTamany, James Edward b: 7/1/1863, Philadelphia, Pa. d: 4/16/16, Lenni, Pa. BR/TR, 5'8", 190 lbs. Deb: 8/15/1885

1885	Bro-a	35	131	21	36	7	2	1			9	.275	.321	.382	121	3				.896	-5	O-35	-0.3
1886	Bro-a	111	418	86	106	23	10	2			54	.254	.353	.371	126	14	18			.893	14	*O-111	2.2
1887	Bro-a	134	520	123	134	22	10	1			76	.258	.353	.344	97	1	66			.918	8	*O-134	0.5
1888	KC-a	130	516	94	127	12	6	4	41	67		.246	.345	.331	110	7	55			.913	6	*O-130	0.8
1889	Col-a	139	529	113	146	21	7	4	52	116	66	.276	.407	.365	127	27	40			.902	-5	*O-139	1.5
1890	Col-a	125	466	**140**	120	27	7	1		**112**		.258	.405	.352	132	27	43			.940	2	*O-125	2.2
1891	Col-a	81	304	59	76	17	9	3	35	58	48	.250	.374	.395	127	13	20			.929	-3	O-81	0.6
	Phi-a	58	218	57	49	6	3	3	21	43	44	.225	.365	.321	94	-1	13			.901	0	O-58	-0.2
	Yr	139	522	116	125	23	12	6	56	101	92	.239	.370	.364	112	12	33			.917	-2	*O-139	0.4
Total	7	813	3102	693	794	135	58	19	149	535	158	.256	.373	.355	117	91	255			.913	16	O-813	7.3

■ BILL McTIGUE McTigue, William Patrick "Rebel" b: 1/3/1891, Nashville, Tenn. d: 5/8/20, Nashville, Tenn. BL/TL, 6'1.5", 175 lbs. Deb: 5/2/11

1911	Bos-N	14	12	1	1	1	0	0	0	0	5	.083	.083	.167	-28	-2	0			.875	-1	P-14	0.0
1912	Bos-N	10	13	2	1	0	0	0	1	1	5	.077	.143	.077	-38	-2	0			1.000	1	P-10	0.0
1913	Bos-N	1	0	0	0	0	0	0	0	0	0	—	—	—	—	—	0			.000	0	R	0.0
1916	Det-A	3	1	0	0	0	0	0	0	0	0	.000	.000	.000	-97	-0	0			1.000	0	/P-3	0.0
Total	4	28	26	3	2	1	0	0	1	1	10	.077	.111	.115	-36	-5	0			.957	0	/P-27	0.0

■ CAL McVEY McVey, Calvin Alexander b: 8/30/1850, Montrose, Iowa d: 8/20/26, San Francisco, Cal BR/TR, 5'9", 170 lbs. Deb: 5/5/1871 M

1871	Bos-n	29	153	43	**66**	9	5	0	43	1	2	.431	.435	.556	177	14	6					*C-28/O-1	0.9
1872	Bos-n	46	237	56	73	11	3	0	41	0	1	.308	.308	.380	105	-0						*C-40/O-9	0.0
1873	Bal-n	38	192	49	73	8	5	3	33	3	2	.380	.390	.521	166	15						C-25/O-6,S213M	1.1
1874	Bos-n	70	341	**91**	**124**	22	4	4			0	.364	.364	.487	159	20						*O-55,C-15	1.6
1875	Bos-n	82	389	88	137	**33**	9	3			1	.352	.354	**.506**	187	32						*1-54,O-17,C/P	2.7
1876	Chi-N	63	308	62	107	15	0	1	53	2	4	.347	.352	.406	136	9				.959	4	*1-55,P-11/CO3	0.9
1877	Chi-N	60	266	58	98	9	7	0	36	8	11	.368	.387	.455	147	12				.859	-13	*C-40,3-17,P/21	0.0
1878	Cin-N	61	271	43	83	10	4	2	28	5	10	.306	.319	.395	147	14				.814	-10	*3-61/C-3M	0.6
1879	Cin-N	81	354	64	105	18	6	0	55	8	13	.297	.312	.381	134	13				.946	-7	*1-72/O-7,P3CM	0.3
Total	5 n	265	1312	327	473	83	26	10	117	5	5	.361	.363	.486	160	80						C-119/O-88,1S2P3D	6.3
Total	4	265	1199	227	393	52	17	3	172	23	38	.328	.340	.407	140	48				.951	-26	1-128/3-80,CPO2	1.8

■ GEORGE McVEY McVey, George W. b: 9/16/1865, Port Jervis, N.Y. d: 5/3/1896, Quincy, Ill. BR/TR, 6'1", 185 lbs. Deb: 9/19/1885

| 1885 | Bro-a | 6 | 21 | 2 | 3 | 0 | 0 | 0 | 2 | | | .143 | .217 | .143 | 15 | -2 | | | | .967 | -0 | /1-3,C-3 | -0.2 |

■ BILL McWILLIAMS McWilliams, William Henry b: 11/28/10, Dubuque, Iowa BR/TR, 6', 185 lbs. Deb: 7/8/31

| 1931 | Bos-A | 2 | 2 | 0 | 0 | 0 | 0 | 0 | 0 | 1 | 1 | .000 | .000 | .000 | -99 | -1 | 0 | 0 | 0 | .000 | 0 | H | -0.1 |

■ BOB MEACHAM Meacham, Robert Andrew b: 8/25/60, Los Angeles, Cal. BB/TR, 6'1", 180 lbs. Deb: 6/30/83

1983	NY-A	22	51	5	12	2	0	0	4	4	10	.235	.304	.275	63	-2	8	0	2	.929	9	S-18/3-4	1.0
1984	NY-A	99	360	62	91	13	4	2	25	32	70	.253	.319	.328	83	-8	9	5	-0	.955	-12	S-96/2-2	-1.1
1985	NY-A	156	481	70	105	16	2	1	47	54	102	.218	.304	.266	59	-26	25	7	3	.963	-17	*S-155	-2.4
1986	NY-A	56	161	19	36	7	1	0	10	17	39	.224	.309	.280	62	-8	3	6	-3	.948	-5	S-56	-1.0
1987	NY-A	77	203	28	55	11	1	5	21	19	33	.271	.351	.409	102	1	6	5	-1	.961	-1	S-56,2-25/D	0.3
1988	NY-A	47	115	18	25	9	0	0	7	14	22	.217	.313	.296	72	-4	7	1	2	.959	-7	S-24,2-21/3	-0.8
Total	6	457	1371	202	324	58	8	8	114	140	276	.236	.316	.308	73	-47	58	24	3	.957	-32	S-405/2-48,3D	-4.0

■ CHARLIE MEAD Mead, Charles Richard b: 4/9/21, Vermilion, Alt., Canada BL/TR, 6'1.5", 185 lbs. Deb: 8/28/43

1943	NY-N	37	146	9	40	6	1	1	13	10	15	.274	.321	.349	93	-2	3			.976	1	O-37	-0.3
1944	NY-N	39	78	5	14	1	0	1	8	5	7	.179	.229	.231	30	-7	0			.981	2	O-23	-0.7
1945	NY-N	11	37	4	10	1	0	1	6	5	2	.270	.357	.378	103	0	0			.962	1	O-11	0.1
Total	3	87	261	18	64	8	1	3	27	20	24	.245	.299	.318	75	-9	3			.975	3	/O-71	-0.9

■ LOUIE MEADOWS Meadows, Michael Ray b: 4/29/61, Maysville, N.C. BL/TL, 5'11", 190 lbs. Deb: 7/3/86

1986	Hou-N	6	6	1	2	0	0	0	0	0	0	.333	.333	.333	87	-0	1	0	0	.000	-0	/O-1	0.0
1988	Hou-N	35	42	5	8	1	0	2	6	3	6	.190	.190	.381	95	-0	4	2	0	1.000	0	/O-10	0.0
1989	Hou-N	31	51	5	9	0	0	3	10	1	14	.176	.192	.353	55	-3	1	2	-1	1.000	-4	O-14/1-1	-0.9
1990	Hou-N	15	14	3	2	0	0	0	0	2	2	.143	.250	.143	11	-2	0	0	0	1.000	-2	/O-9	-0.4
	Phi-N	15	14	1	1	0	0	0	0	1	2	.071	.133	.071	-42	-2	0	0	0	1.000	-0	/O-4	-0.5
	Yr	30	28	4	3	0	0	0	0	3	6	.107	.194	.107	-15	-4	0	0	0	1.000	-4	O-13	-0.9
Total	4	102	127	15	22	0	1	5	13	10	28	.173	.234	.307	54	-8	6	4	-1	1.000	-9	/O-38,1-1	-1.8

■ PAT MEANEY Meaney, Patrick J. b: 7/1871, Philadelphia, Pa. d: 10/20/22, Philadelphia, Pa. BR/TL, Deb: 5/18/12

| 1912 | Det-A | 1 | 2 | 0 | 0 | 0 | 0 | 0 | 0 | 0 | 1 | .000 | .500 | .000 | 48 | 0 | 0 | | | .833 | -0 | /S-1 | 0.0 |

■ CHARLIE MEARA Meara, Charles Edward "Goggy" b: 4/13/1891, New York, N.Y. d: 2/8/62, Bronx, N.Y. BL/TR, 5'10", 160 lbs. Deb: 6/1/14

| 1914 | NY-A | 4 | 7 | 2 | 2 | 0 | 0 | 0 | 1 | 2 | 2 | .286 | .444 | .286 | 120 | 0 | 0 | 1 | -1 | 1.000 | -0 | /O-3 | -0.1 |

■ PAT MEARES Meares, Patrick James b: 9/6/68, Salina, Kan. BR/TR, 6', 185 lbs. Deb: 5/5/93

1993	Min-A	111	346	33	87	14	3	0	33	7	52	.251	.268	.309	55	-22	4	5	-2	.961	-1	*S-111	-1.7
1994	Min-A	80	229	29	61	12	1	2	24	14	50	.266	.314	.354	72	-10	5	1	1	.963	2	S-79	-0.1
Total	2	191	575	62	148	26	4	2	57	21	102	.257	.287	.327	62	-32	9	6	-1	.962	1	S-190	-1.8

■ RAY MEDEIROS Medeiros, Ray Antone "Pep" b: 5/9/26, Oakland, Cal. BR/TR, 5'10", 163 lbs. Deb: 4/25/45

| 1945 | Cin-N | 1 | 0 | 0 | 0 | 0 | 0 | 0 | 0 | 0 | 0 | | | | | 0 | 0 | | | .000 | 0 | R | 0.0 |

■ LUIS MEDINA Medina, Luis Main b: 3/26/63, Santa Monica, Cal. BR/TL, 6'4", 200 lbs. Deb: 9/2/88

1988	Cle-A	16	51	10	13	0	0	6	8	2	18	.255	.309	.608	146	3	0	0	0	1.000	-0	1-16	0.1
1989	Cle-A	30	83	8	17	1	0	4	8	6	35	.205	.258	.361	72	-3	0	1	-1	.500	-1	D-25/O-3,1	-0.6
1991	Cle-A	5	16	0	1	0	0	0	0	1	7	.063	.118	.063	-48	-3	0	0	0	.000	0	/D-5	-0.4
Total	3	51	150	18	31	1	0	10	16	9	60	.207	.261	.453	85	-3	0	1	-1	1.000	-2	/D-30,1-17,O	-0.9

YEAR	TM/L	G	AB	R	H	2B	3B	HR	RBI	BB	SO	AVG	OBP	SLG	PRO+	BR/A	SB	CS	SBR	FA	FR	G/POS	TPR

■ JOE MEDWICK
Medwick, Joseph Michael "Ducky" or "Muscles" b: 11/24/11, Carteret, N.J. d: 3/21/75, St.Petersburg, Fla BR/TR, 5'10", 187 lbs. Deb: 9/2/32 H

1932	StL-N	26	106	13	37	12	1	2	12	2	10	.349	.367	.538	136	5	3			.970	0	O-26	0.4
1933	StL-N	148	595	92	182	40	10	18	98	26	56	.306	.337	.497	129	20	5			.980	8	*O-147	2.1
1934	*StL-N★	149	620	110	198	40	**18**	18	106	21	83	.319	.343	.529	122	16	3			.960	4	*O-149	1.4
1935	StL-N★	154	634	132	224	46	13	23	126	30	59	.353	.386	.576	149	41	4			.965	3	*O-154	3.6
1936	StL-N★	155	636	115	**223**	**64**	13	18	**138**	34	33	.351	.387	.577	157	47	3			.985	14	*O-155	5.3
1937	StL-N★	156	633	111	237	56	10	**31**	154	41	50	**.374**	**.414**	**.641**	179	66	4			**.988**	4	*O-156	**6.2**
1938	StL-N★	146	590	100	190	**47**	8	21	**122**	42	41	.322	.369	.536	138	29	0			.974	8	*O-144	3.2
1939	StL-N★	150	606	98	201	48	8	14	117	45	44	.332	.380	.507	128	23	6			.976	5	*O-149	2.2
1940	StL-N	37	158	21	48	12	0	3	20	6	8	.304	.329	.437	104	0	0			.988	-0	O-37	-0.2
	Bro-N★	106	423	62	127	18	12	14	66	26	28	.300	.345	.499	123	11	2			.980	5	*O-103	1.2
	Yr	143	581	83	175	30	12	17	86	32	36	.301	.341	.482	118	12	2			.982	5	*O-140	1.0
1941	*Bro-N★	133	538	100	171	33	10	18	88	38	35	.318	.364	.517	140	26	2			.983	1	*O-131	2.0
1942	Bro-N★	142	553	69	166	37	4	4	96	32	25	.300	.338	.403	115	9	2			.990	-3	*O-140	-0.1
1943	Bro-N	48	173	13	47	10	0	0	25	10	8	.272	.315	.329	86	-3	1			.971	-5	O-42	-1.1
	NY-N	78	324	41	91	20	3	5	45	9	14	.281	.300	.407	103	-1	0			.988	5	O-74/1-3	0.0
	Yr	126	497	54	138	30	3	5	70	19	22	.278	.306	.380	97	-4	1			.983	-0	*O-116/1-3	-1.1
1944	NY-N★	128	490	64	165	24	3	7	85	38	24	.337	.386	.441	133	21	2			.993	8	*O-122	2.3
1945	NY-N	26	92	14	28	4	0	3	11	2	2	.304	.319	.446	110	1	2			.979	-1	O-23	-0.1
	Bos-N	66	218	17	62	13	0	0	26	12	12	.284	.325	.344	85	-4	3			1.000	1	O-38,1-15	-0.7
	Yr	92	310	31	90	17	0	3	37	14	14	.290	.323	.374	93	-4	5			.992	0	O-61,1-15	-0.8
1946	Bro-N	41	77	7	24	4	0	2	18	6	5	.312	.369	.442	128	3	0			1.000	-3	O-18/1-1	-0.1
1947	StL-N	75	150	19	46	12	0	4	28	16	12	.307	.373	.467	117	4	0			1.000	-5	O-43	-0.3
1948	StL-N	20	19	0	4	0	0	0	2	1	2	.211	.250	.211	24	-2	0			.000	-0	/O-1	-0.2
Total	17	1984	7635	1198	2471	540	113	205	1383	437	551	.324	.362	.505	133	310	42			.980	49	*O-1852/1-19	27.1

■ TOMMY MEE
Mee, Thomas William "Judge" b: 3/18/1890, Chicago, Ill. d: 5/16/81, Chicago, Ill. BR/TR, 5'8", 165 lbs. Deb: 6/14/10

1910	StL-A	8	19	1	3	2	0	0	1	0		.158	.158	.263	34	-2	0			.828	-1	/S-6,2-1,3	-0.3

■ DAD MEEK
Meek, Frank J. b: 3/14/1867, St.Louis, Mo. d: 12/22/22, St.Louis, Mo. Deb: 5/10/1889

1889	StL-a	2	2	2	1	0	0	0	1	0	0	.500	.500	.500	164	0	1			.667	0	/C-2	0.0
1890	StL-a	4	16	3	5	0	0	0		0	0	.313	.313	.313	74	-1	1			.913	3	/C-4	0.2
Total	2	6	18	5	6	0	0	0	1	0	0	.333	.333	.333	84	-1	2			.898	3	/C-6	0.2

■ SAMMY MEEKS
Meeks, Samuel Mack b: 4/23/23, Anderson, S.C. BR/TR, 5'9", 160 lbs. Deb: 4/29/48

1948	Was-A	24	33	4	4	1	0	0	2	1	12	.121	.147	.152	-21	-6	0	0	0	.939	-0	S-10/2-1	-0.6
1949	Cin-N	16	36	10	11	2	0	2	6	2	6	.306	.342	.528	128	1	1			1.000	5	/2-8,S-3	0.7
1950	Cin-N	39	95	7	27	5	0	1	8	6	14	.284	.327	.368	82	-2	1			.951	-4	S-29/3-2	-0.5
1951	Cin-N	23	35	4	8	0	0	0	2	0	4	.229	.229	.229	23	-4	1	0	0	.929	-1	/3-4,S-1	-0.5
Total	4	102	199	25	50	8	0	3	18	9	36	.251	.284	.337	64	-11	3	0		.953	0	/S-43,2-9,3	-0.9

■ DUTCH MEIER
Meier, Arthur Ernst b: 3/30/1879, St.Louis, Mo. d: 3/23/48, Chicago, Ill. BR/TR, 5'10", 175 lbs. Deb: 5/12/06

1906	Pit-N	82	273	32	70	11	4	0	16	13		.256	.298	.326	90	-4	4			.975	-12	O-52,S-17	-1.9

■ DAVE MEIER
Meier, David Keith b: 8/8/59, Helena, Mont. BR/TR, 6', 185 lbs. Deb: 4/3/84

1984	Min-A	59	147	18	35	8	1	0	13	6	9	.238	.273	.306	57	-9	0	1	-1	.978	-4	O-50/3-1,D	-1.4
1985	Min-A	71	104	15	27	6	0	1	8	18	12	.260	.374	.346	93	-0	0	6	-4	.987	-9	O-63/D-3	-1.4
1987	Tex-A	13	21	4	6	1	0	0	0	0	4	.286	.286	.333	63	-1	0	0	0	.917	-1	/O-8	-0.2
1988	Chi-N	2	5	0	2	0	0	0	1	0	1	.400	.400	.400	125	0	0	0	0	1.000	-1	/3-1	-0.1
Total	4	145	277	37	70	15	1	1	22	24	26	.253	.317	.325	73	-10	0	7	-4	.978	-15	O-121/D-7,3	-3.1

■ WALT MEINERT
Meinert, Walter Henry b: 12/11/1890, New York, N.Y. d: 11/9/58, Decatur, Ill. BL/TL, 5'7.5", 150 lbs. Deb: 9/6/13

1913	StL-A	4	8	1	3	0	0	0	0	1	3	.375	.444	.375	144	1	1			1.000	-0	/O-2	0.0

■ FRANK MEINKE
Meinke, Frank Louis b: 10/18/1863, Chicago, Ill. d: 11/8/31, Chicago, Ill. BR , 5'10.5", 172 lbs. Deb: 5/1/1884 F

1884	Det-N	92	341	28	56	5	7	6	24	6	89	.164	.179	.273	42	-22				.839	-3	S-51,P-35/O32	-1.3
1885	Det-N	1	3	0	0	0	0	0	0	0	1	.000	.000	.000	-99	-1				1.000	-0	/O-1,P-1	0.0
Total	2	93	344	28	56	5	7	6	24	6	90	.163	.177	.270	41	-22				1.000	-3	/S-51,P-36,O23	-1.3

■ BOB MEINKE
Meinke, Robert Bernard b: 6/25/1887, Chicago, Ill. d: 12/29/52, Chicago, Ill. BR/TR, 5'10", 135 lbs. Deb: 8/22/10 F

1910	Cin-N	2	1	0	0	0	0	0	0	1	0	.000	.500	.000	51	0	0			1.000	1	/S-2	0.1

■ GEORGE MEISTER
Meister, George B. b: 6/5/1864, Dorzbach, Germany d: 8/24/08, Pittsburgh, Pa. Deb: 8/15/1884

1884	Tol-a	34	119	9	23	6	0	0	3			.193	.244	.244	58	-5				.817	-9	3-34	-1.4

■ JOHN MEISTER
Meister, John F. b: 5/10/1863, Allentown, Pa. d: 1/17/23, Philadelphia, Pa. 5'8", 175 lbs. Deb: 8/24/1886

1886	NY-a	45	186	35	44	7	3	2		4		.237	.253	.339	89	-3	1			.906	-8	2-45	-0.8
1887	NY-a	39	157	24	35	6	2	1		16		.223	.303	.306	73	-5	9			.930	-9	O-22,2-14/3S	-1.2
Total	2	84	343	59	79	13	5	3		20		.230	.277	.324	81	-8	10			.905	-17	/2-59,O-22,3S	-2.0

■ KARL MEISTER
Meister, Karl Daniel "Dutch" b: 5/15/1891, Marietta, Ohio d: 8/15/67, Marietta, Ohio BR/TR, 6', 178 lbs. Deb: 8/10/13

1913	Cin-N	4	7	1	2	1	0	0	0	0	4	.286	.286	.429	103	-0	0			.667	-2	/O-4	-0.2

■ MOXIE MEIXELL
Meixell, Merton Merrill b: 10/18/1887, Lake Crystal, Minn d: 8/17/82, Los Angeles, Cal. BL/TR, 5'10", 168 lbs. Deb: 7/7/12

1912	Cle-A	3	2	0	1	0	0	0	0	0		.500	.500	.500	181	0	0			.000	0	/O-1	0.0

■ ROBERTO MEJIA
Mejia, Roberto Antonio (Diaz) b: 4/14/72, Hato Mayor, D.R. BR/TR, 5'11", 160 lbs. Deb: 7/15/93

1993	Col-N	65	229	31	53	14	5	5	20	13	63	.231	.276	.402	68	-11	4	1	1	.963	7	2-65	-0.2
1994	Col-N	38	116	11	28	8	1	4	14	15	33	.241	.328	.431	82	-3	3	1	0	.959	-3	2-34	-0.4
Total	2	103	345	42	81	22	6	9	34	28	96	.235	.294	.412	73	-15	7	2	1	.961	4	/2-99	-0.6

■ ROMAN MEJIAS
Mejias, Roman (Gomez) b: 8/9/30, Abreus, Las Villas, Cuba BR/TR, 6', 175 lbs. Deb: 4/13/55

1955	Pit-N	71	167	14	36	8	1	3	21	9	13	.216	.256	.329	55	-11	1	3	-2	.926	-0	O-44	-1.5
1957	Pit-N	58	142	12	39	7	4	2	15	6	13	.275	.309	.423	97	-1	2	2	-1	1.000	-2	O-42	-0.5
1958	Pit-N	76	157	17	42	3	2	5	19	2	27	.268	.281	.408	82	-5	2	0	1	.973	-1	O-57	-0.7
1959	Pit-N	96	276	28	65	6	1	7	28	21	48	.236	.301	.341	71	-11	1	2	-1	.970	-0	O-85	-1.6
1960	Pit-N	3	1	0	0	0	0	0	0	0	1	.000	.000	.000	-99	-0	0	0	0	.000	0	H	0.0
1961	Pit-N	4	1	1	0	0	0	0	0	0	1	.000	.000	.000	-99	-0	0	0	0	1.000	-1	/O-2	-0.1
1962	Hou-N	146	566	82	162	12	3	24	76	30	83	.286	.329	.445	114	9	12	4	1	.946	-4	*O-142	-0.3
1963	Bos-A	111	357	43	81	18	0	11	39	14	36	.227	.262	.370	72	-14	4	1	1	.973	2	O-86	-1.6
1964	Bos-A	62	101	14	24	3	1	2	4	7	16	.238	.294	.347	74	-4	0	0	0	.962	-3	O-37	-0.8
Total	9	627	1768	212	449	57	12	54	202	89	238	.254	.296	.391	86	-38	22	12	-1	.963	-8	O-495	-7.1

■ SAM MEJIAS
Mejias, Samuel Elias b: 5/9/52, Santiago, D.R. BR/TR, 6', 170 lbs. Deb: 9/6/76 C

1976	StL-N	18	21	1	3	1	0	0	0	2	2	.143	.217	.190	16	-2	2	0	1	1.000	-3	O-17	-0.5
1977	Mon-N	74	101	14	23	4	1	3	8	2	17	.228	.243	.376	65	-5	1	0	0	.966	-12	O-56	-1.9

YEAR	TM/L	G	AB	R	H	2B	3B	HR	RBI	BB	SO	AVG	OBP	SLG	PRO+	BR/A	SB	CS	SBR	FA	FR	G/POS	TPR
1978	Mon-N	67	56	9	13	1	0	0	6	2	5	.232	.259	.250	43	-4	0	0	0	.949	-14	O-52/P-1	-2.0
1979	Chi-N	31	11	4	2	0	0	0	0	2	5	.182	.308	.182	34	-1	0	0	0	.875	-8	O-23	-0.9
	Cin-N	7	2	1	1	0	0	0	0	0	0	.500	.500	.500	173	0	0	0	0	1.000	-2	/O-5	-0.2
	Yr	38	13	5	3	0	0	0	0	2	5	.231	.333	.231	53	-1	0	0	0	.889	-10	O-28	-1.1
1980	Cin-N	71	108	16	30	5	1	1	10	6	13	.278	.322	.370	93	-1	4	2	0	.989	-13	O-67	-1.7
1981	Cin-N	66	49	6	14	2	0	0	7	2	9	.286	.314	.327	80	-1	1	0	0	.972	-16	O-58	-1.9
Total	6	334	348	51	86	13	2	4	31	16	51	.247	.282	.330	69	-15	8	2	1	.973	-68	O-278/P-1	-9.1

■ DUTCH MELE   Mele, Albert Ernest b: 1/11/15, New York, N.Y. d: 2/12/75, Hollywood, Fla. BL/TL, 6'0.5", 195 lbs. Deb: 9/14/37

YEAR	TM/L	G	AB	R	H	2B	3B	HR	RBI	BB	SO	AVG	OBP	SLG	PRO+	BR/A	SB	CS	SBR	FA	FR	G/POS	TPR
1937	Cin-N	6	14	1	2	1	0	0	1	1	1	.143	.200	.214	13	-2	0			1.000	-2	/O-5	-0.4

■ SAM MELE   Mele, Sabath Anthony b: 1/21/23, Astoria, N.Y. BR/TR, 6'1", 187 lbs. Deb: 4/15/47 MC

YEAR	TM/L	G	AB	R	H	2B	3B	HR	RBI	BB	SO	AVG	OBP	SLG	PRO+	BR/A	SB	CS	SBR	FA	FR	G/POS	TPR
1947	Bos-A	123	453	71	137	14	8	12	73	37	35	.302	.356	.448	114	8	0	3	-2	.992	-3	*O-116/1-1	-0.3
1948	Bos-A	66	180	25	42	12	1	2	25	13	21	.233	.292	.344	66	-9	1	1	-0	.971	-4	O-55	-1.6
1949	Bos-A	18	46	1	9	1	1	0	7	7	14	.196	.302	.261	46	-4	2	0	1	.955	-0	O-11	-0.4
	Was-A	78	264	21	64	12	2	3	25	17	34	.242	.288	.337	67	-14	2	1	0	.966	-8	O-63,1-11	-2.5
	Yr	96	310	22	73	13	3	3	32	24	48	.235	.290	.326	63	-18	4	1	1	.964	-9	O-74,1-11	-2.9
1950	Was-A	126	435	57	119	21	6	12	86	51	40	.274	.351	.432	105	2	2	0	1	.990	-5	O-99,1-16	-0.7
1951	Was-A	143	558	58	153	**36**	7	5	94	32	31	.274	.315	.391	92	-9	2	3	-1	.993	3	*O-124,1-15	-1.2
1952	Was-A	9	28	2	12	3	0	2	10	1	2	.429	.448	.750	237	5	0	0	0	.917	-1	/O-7	0.3
	Chi-A	123	423	46	105	18	2	14	59	48	40	.248	.328	.400	101	-0	1	2	-1	1.000	-6	*O-112/1-3	-1.2
	Yr	132	451	48	117	21	2	16	69	49	42	.259	.335	.421	109	4	1	2	-1	.994	-7	*O-119/1-3	-0.9
1953	Chi-A	140	481	64	132	26	8	12	82	58	47	.274	.353	.437	109	5	3	1	0	.996	-8	*O-138/1-2	-0.7
1954	Bal-A	72	230	17	55	9	4	5	32	18	26	.239	.294	.378	90	-5	1	0	0	.962	-4	O-62	-1.1
	Bos-A	42	132	22	42	6	0	7	23	12	12	.318	.384	.523	132	5	0	1	-1	.994	-4	1-22,O-13	-0.1
	Yr	114	362	39	97	15	4	12	55	30	38	.268	.327	.431	107	2	1	1	-0	.961	-8	O-75,1-22	-1.2
1955	Bos-A	14	31	1	4	2	0	0	1	0	7	.129	.129	.194	-13	-5	1	0	0	1.000	2	/O-7	-0.3
	Cin-N	35	62	4	13	1	0	2	7	5	13	.210	.279	.323	56	-4	0	1	-1	.960	-4	O-13/1-1	-0.6
1956	Cle-A	57	114	17	29	7	0	4	20	12	20	.254	.325	.421	94	-1	0	1	-1	.969	-0	O-20/1-8	-0.3
Total	10	1046	3437	406	916	168	39	80	544	311	342	.267	.329	.408	97	-26	15	14	-4	.985	-39	O-840/1-79	-10.7

■ FRANCISCO MELENDEZ   Melendez, Francisco Javier (Villegas) b: 1/25/64, Rio Piedras, P.R. BL/TL, 6', 190 lbs. Deb: 8/26/84

YEAR	TM/L	G	AB	R	H	2B	3B	HR	RBI	BB	SO	AVG	OBP	SLG	PRO+	BR/A	SB	CS	SBR	FA	FR	G/POS	TPR
1984	Phi-N	21	23	0	3	0	0	0	2	1	5	.130	.167	.130	-15	-3	0	0	0	1.000	1	1-10	-0.3
1986	Phi-N	9	8	0	2	0	0	0	0	0	0	.250	.250	.250	37	-1	0	0	0	1.000	-0	/1-2	-0.1
1987	SF-N	12	16	2	5	0	0	0	1	0	3	.313	.313	.500	117	0	0	0	0	1.000	-1	/1-5	0.0
1988	SF-N	23	26	1	5	0	0	0	3	3	2	.192	.276	.192	38	-2	0	0	0	1.000	-1	/1-6,O-1	-0.4
1989	Bal-A	9	11	1	3	0	0	0	3	1	2	.273	.333	.273	75	-0	0	0	0	1.000	-1	/1-5	0.0
Total	5	74	84	4	18	0	0	1	9	5	14	.214	.258	.250	43	-6	0	0	0	1.000	-1	/1-28,O-1	-0.8

■ LUIS MELENDEZ   Melendez, Luis Antonio (Santana) b: 8/11/49, Aibonito, P.R. BR/TR, 6', 165 lbs. Deb: 9/7/70

YEAR	TM/L	G	AB	R	H	2B	3B	HR	RBI	BB	SO	AVG	OBP	SLG	PRO+	BR/A	SB	CS	SBR	FA	FR	G/POS	TPR
1970	StL-N	21	70	11	21	1	0	0	8	2	12	.300	.319	.314	69	-3	3	0	1	1.000	1	O-18	-0.2
1971	StL-N	88	173	25	39	3	1	0	11	24	29	.225	.320	.254	62	-8	2	0	1	.959	-10	O-66	-2.0
1972	StL-N	118	332	32	79	11	3	5	28	25	34	.238	.293	.334	79	-10	5	4	-1	.959	-6	*O-105	-2.3
1973	StL-N	121	341	35	91	18	1	2	35	27	50	.267	.321	.343	84	-7	2	7	-4	.990	2	O-95	-1.3
1974	StL-N	83	124	15	27	4	3	0	8	11	9	.218	.287	.298	64	-6	2	2	-1	.977	-8	O-46/S-1	-1.6
1975	StL-N	110	291	33	77	8	5	2	27	16	25	.265	.303	.347	77	-9	2	3	-0	.983	-6	O-89	-1.9
1976	StL-N	20	24	0	3	0	0	0	0	0	3	.125	.125	.125	-29	-4	0	0	0	1.000	-1	/O-8	-0.5
	SD-N	72	119	15	29	5	0	0	5	3	12	.244	.262	.286	60	-7	1	1	-0	.988	-12	O-60	-2.2
	Yr	92	143	15	32	5	0	0	5	3	15	.224	.240	.259	44	-11	1	1	-0	.990	-13	O-68	-2.7
1977	SD-N	8	3	1	0	0	0	0	0	0	0	.000	.000	.000	-29	-1	0	0	0	1.000	-1	/O-2	-0.1
Total	8	641	1477	167	366	50	13	9	122	109	175	.248	.300	.318	73	-54	18	16	-4	.977	-40	O-489/S-1	-12.1

■ SKI MELILLO   Melillo, Oscar Donald "Spinach" b: 8/4/1899, Chicago, Ill. d: 11/14/63, Chicago, Ill. BR/TR, 5'8", 150 lbs. Deb: 4/18/26 C

YEAR	TM/L	G	AB	R	H	2B	3B	HR	RBI	BB	SO	AVG	OBP	SLG	PRO+	BR/A	SB	CS	SBR	FA	FR	G/POS	TPR
1926	StL-A	99	385	54	98	18	5	1	30	32	31	.255	.315	.335	66	-19	6	7	-2	.965	8	2-88,3-11	-1.0
1927	StL-A	107	356	45	80	18	2	0	26	25	28	.225	.276	.287	45	-30	3	6	-3	.935	-2	*2-101	-3.0
1928	StL-A	51	132	9	25	2	0	0	9	9	11	.189	.241	.205	18	-16	2	1	-0	.961	4	2-28,3-19	-1.1
1929	StL-A	141	494	57	146	17	10	5	67	29	30	.296	.337	.401	86	-11	11	6	-0	.973	23	*2-141	1.6
1930	StL-A	149	574	62	147	30	10	5	59	23	44	.256	.287	.369	63	-34	15	9	-1	.979	**27**	*2-148	-2.4
1931	StL-A	151	617	88	189	34	11	2	75	37	29	.306	.346	.407	94	-6	7	11	-5	.968	**33**	*2-151	2.9
1932	StL-A	154	612	71	148	19	11	3	66	36	42	.242	.286	.324	54	-42	6	6	-2	.981	11	*2-153	-2.4
1933	StL-A	132	496	50	145	23	6	3	79	29	18	.292	.333	.381	83	-12	12	10	-2	**.991**	23	*2-130	1.5
1934	StL-A	144	552	54	133	19	2	1	55	28	27	.241	.279	.297	45	-46	4	6	-2	**.981**	18	*2-141	-2.0
1935	StL-A	19	62	8	13	3	0	0	5	8	4	.210	.300	.258	43	-5	0	0	0	.970	-2	2-18	-0.3
	Bos-A	106	400	45	104	13	2	1	39	38	22	.260	.327	.310	61	-22	3	2	-0	.973	18	2-105	0.3
	Yr	125	462	53	117	16	2	1	44	46	26	.253	.324	.303	59	-27	3	2	-0	.973	19	*2-123	0.0
1936	Bos-A	98	327	39	74	12	4	0	32	28	16	.226	.287	.287	40	-31	1	0	0	.980	-8	2-93	-2.9
1937	Bos-A	26	56	8	14	2	0	0	6	5	4	.250	.311	.286	50	-4	0	1	-1	.939	-2	2-19/S-2,3	-0.7
Total	12	1377	5063	590	1316	210	64	22	548	327	306	.260	.306	.340	64	-279	69	65	-18	.973	151	*2-1316/3-32,S	-7.1

■ JOE MELLANA   Mellana, Joseph Peter b: 3/11/05, Oakland, Cal. d: 11/1/69, Larkspur, Cal. BR/TR, 5'10", 180 lbs. Deb: 9/21/27

YEAR	TM/L	G	AB	R	H	2B	3B	HR	RBI	BB	SO	AVG	OBP	SLG	PRO+	BR/A	SB	CS	SBR	FA	FR	G/POS	TPR
1927	Phi-A	4	7	1	2	0	0	0	0	0	1	.286	.286	.286	46	-1	0	0	0	.889	2	/3-2	0.1

■ BILL MELLOR   Mellor, William Harpin b: 6/6/1874, Camden, N.J. d: 11/5/40, Bridgeton, R.I. BR/TR, 6', 190 lbs. Deb: 7/28/02

YEAR	TM/L	G	AB	R	H	2B	3B	HR	RBI	BB	SO	AVG	OBP	SLG	PRO+	BR/A	SB	CS	SBR	FA	FR	G/POS	TPR
1902	Bal-A	10	36	4	13	3	0	0	5	3		.361	.410	.444	131	2	1			.978	-1	1-10	0.0

■ PAUL MELOAN   Meloan, Paul B. "Molly" b: 8/23/1888, Paynesville, Mo. d: 2/11/50, Taft, Cal. BR/TL, 5'10.5", 175 lbs. Deb: 8/2/10

YEAR	TM/L	G	AB	R	H	2B	3B	HR	RBI	BB	SO	AVG	OBP	SLG	PRO+	BR/A	SB	CS	SBR	FA	FR	G/POS	TPR
1910	Chi-A	65	222	23	54	6	6	0	23	17		.243	.314	.324	104	1	4			.948	3	O-65	0.2
1911	Chi-A	1	3	0	1	0	0	0	1	0		.333	.333	.333	89	-0	0			.000	-1	/O-1	-0.1
	StL-A	64	206	30	54	11	2	3	14	15		.262	.318	.379	98	-1	7			.904	-6	O-54	-1.0
	Yr	65	209	30	55	11	2	3	15	15		.263	.319	.378	98	-1	7			.893	-6	O-55	-1.1
Total	2	130	431	53	109	17	8	3	38	32		.253	.316	.350	101	-0	11			.923	-3	O-120	-0.9

■ DAVE MELTON   Melton, David Olin b: 10/3/28, Pampa, Tex. BR/TR, 6', 185 lbs. Deb: 4/17/56

YEAR	TM/L	G	AB	R	H	2B	3B	HR	RBI	BB	SO	AVG	OBP	SLG	PRO+	BR/A	SB	CS	SBR	FA	FR	G/POS	TPR
1956	KC-A	3	3	0	1	0	0	0	0	0	0	.333	.333	.333	76	-0	0	0	0	1.000	-1	/O-3	-0.1
1958	KC-A	9	6	0	0	0	0	0	0	0	5	.000	.000	.000	-98	-2	0	0	0	1.000	-0	/O-2	-0.2
Total	2	12	9	0	1	0	0	0	0	0	5	.111	.111	.111	-39	-2	0	0	0	1.000	-1	/O-5	-0.3

■ BILL MELTON   Melton, William Edwin b: 7/7/45, Gulfport, Miss. BR/TR, 6'2", 200 lbs. Deb: 5/4/68

YEAR	TM/L	G	AB	R	H	2B	3B	HR	RBI	BB	SO	AVG	OBP	SLG	PRO+	BR/A	SB	CS	SBR	FA	FR	G/POS	TPR
1968	Chi-A	34	109	5	29	8	2	0	16	10	32	.266	.328	.394	117	2	1	1	-0	.968	3	3-33	0.6
1969	Chi-A	157	556	67	142	26	2	23	87	56	106	.255	.329	.433	106	4	1	2	-1	.952	7	*3-148,O-11	1.0
1970	Chi-A	141	514	74	135	15	1	33	96	56	107	.263	.345	.488	123	15	2	4	-2	1.000	9	O-71,3-70	1.8
1971	Chi-A☆	150	543	72	146	18	2	**33**	86	61	87	.269	.354	.492	133	23	3	3	-1	.968	27	*3-148	5.1
1972	Chi-A	57	208	22	51	9	0	7	30	23	31	.245	.320	.370	103	1	1	1	-0	.935	3	3-56	0.3
1973	Chi-A	152	560	83	155	29	1	20	87	75	66	.277	.364	.439	121	16	4	4	-1	.953	14	*3-151/D-1	2.9
1974	Chi-A	136	495	63	120	17	0	21	63	59	60	.242	.329	.404	107	5	3	2	-0	.939	-3	*3-123,D-11	0.0

YEAR	TM/L	G	AB	R	H	2B	3B	HR	RBI	BB	SO	AVG	OBP	SLG	PRO+	BR/A	SB	CS	SBR	FA	FR	G/POS	TPR
1975	Chi-A	149	512	62	123	16	0	15	70	78	106	.240	.349	.359	99	2	5	4	-1	.945	1	*3-138,D-11	0.1
1976	Cal-A	118	341	31	71	17	3	6	42	44	53	.208	.302	.328	90	-4	2	0	1	.992	-3	D-51,1-30,3	-1.1
1977	Cle-A	50	133	17	32	11	0	0	14	17	21	.241	.336	.323	83	-3	1	3	-2	1.000	1	1-15,D-14,3	-0.5
Total	10	1144	3971	496	1004	162	9	160	591	479	669	.253	.340	.419	112	61	23	24	-8	.949	57	3-901/D-88,O1	10.2

■ BOB MELVIN
Melvin, Robert Paul b: 10/28/61, Palo Alto, Cal. BR/TR, 6'4", 205 lbs. Deb: 5/25/85

YEAR	TM/L	G	AB	R	H	2B	3B	HR	RBI	BB	SO	AVG	OBP	SLG	PRO+	BR/A	SB	CS	SBR	FA	FR	G/POS	TPR
1985	Det-A	41	82	10	18	4	1	0	4	3	21	.220	.247	.293	47	-6	0	0	0	.989	8	C-41	0.3
1986	SF-N	89	268	24	60	14	2	5	25	15	69	.224	.265	.347	71	-12	3	2	-0	.988	7	C-84/3-1	0.0
1987	*SF-N	84	246	31	49	8	0	11	31	17	44	.199	.251	.366	64	-14	0	4	-2	.998	4	C-78/1-1	-0.8
1988	SF-N	92	273	23	64	13	1	8	27	13	46	.234	.269	.377	87	-6	0	2	-1	.984	-8	C-89/1-1	-1.0
1989	Bal-A	85	278	22	67	10	1	1	32	15	53	.241	.280	.295	64	-13	1	4	-2	.991	-9	C-75/D-9	-2.1
1990	Bal-A	93	301	30	73	14	1	5	37	11	53	.243	.269	.346	73	-12	0	1	-1	.997	1	C-76,D-10/1	-0.8
1991	Bal-A	79	228	11	57	10	0	1	23	11	46	.250	.285	.307	66	-11	0	0	0	.998	6	C-72/D-4	-0.1
1992	KC-A	32	70	5	22	5	0	0	6	5	13	.314	.360	.386	106	1	0	0	0	1.000	-0	C-21/1-3	0.1
1993	Bos-A	77	176	13	39	7	0	3	23	7	44	.222	.255	.313	49	-13	0	0	0	.994	-7	C-76/1-1	-1.7
1994	NY-A	9	14	2	4	0	0	1	3	0	3	.286	.286	.500	104	-0	0	0	0	1.000	-1	/C-4,1-4,D	-0.1
	Chi-A	11	19	3	3	0	0	0	1	1	4	.158	.200	.158	-6	-3	0	0	0	1.000	2	C-11	-0.1
	Yr	20	33	5	7	0	0	1	4	1	7	.212	.235	.303	39	-3	0	0	0	1.000	1	C-15/1-4,D	-0.2
Total	10	692	1955	174	456	85	6	35	212	98	396	.233	.270	.337	69	-88	4	13	-7	.993	3	C-627/D-24,13	-6.3

■ MINNIE MENDOZA
Mendoza, Cristobal Rigoberto (Carreras) b: 11/16/33, Ceiba Del Agua, Cuba BR/TR, 6', 180 lbs. Deb: 4/9/70 C

YEAR	TM/L	G	AB	R	H	2B	3B	HR	RBI	BB	SO	AVG	OBP	SLG	PRO+	BR/A	SB	CS	SBR	FA	FR	G/POS	TPR
1970	Min-A	16	16	2	3	0	0	0	2	0	1	.188	.188	.188	4	-2	0	0	0	1.000	0	/3-5,2-4	-0.2

■ MARIO MENDOZA
Mendoza, Mario (Aizpuru) b: 12/26/50, Chihuahua, Mex. BR/TR, 5'11", 187 lbs. Deb: 4/26/74

YEAR	TM/L	G	AB	R	H	2B	3B	HR	RBI	BB	SO	AVG	OBP	SLG	PRO+	BR/A	SB	CS	SBR	FA	FR	G/POS	TPR
1974	*Pit-N	91	163	10	36	1	2	0	15	8	35	.221	.262	.252	46	-12	1	1	-0	.964	5	S-87	-0.1
1975	Pit-N	56	50	8	9	1	0	0	2	3	17	.180	.226	.200	19	-5	0	0	0	.952	8	S-53/3-1	0.4
1976	Pit-N	50	92	6	17	5	0	0	12	4	15	.185	.219	.239	30	-9	0	1	-1	.967	12	S-45/3-2,2	0.6
1977	Pit-N	70	81	5	16	3	0	0	4	3	10	.198	.226	.235	23	-9	0	0	0	.928	12	S-45,3-19/P	0.5
1978	Pit-N	57	55	5	12	1	0	1	3	2	9	.218	.283	.291	58	-3	3	1	0	.980	9	2-21,3-18,S	0.8
1979	Sea-A	148	373	26	74	10	3	1	29	9	62	.198	.219	.249	26	-39	0	3	0	.968	28	*S-148	0.2
1980	Sea-A	114	277	27	68	6	3	2	14	16	42	.245	.287	.310	63	-14	3	4	-2	.959	12	*S-114	0.6
1981	Tex-A	88	229	18	53	6	1	0	22	7	25	.231	.257	.266	54	-14	2	1	0	.970	3	S-88	-0.3
1982	Tex-A	12	17	1	2	0	0	0	0	0	4	.118	.118	.118	-37	-3	0	0	0	.882	2	S-12/D-1	-0.1
Total	9	686	1337	106	287	33	9	4	101	52	219	.215	.247	.262	41	-108	12	8	-1	.961	91	S-606/3-40,2DP	2.6

■ MIKE MENDOZA
Mendoza, Michael Joseph b: 11/26/55, Inglewood, Cal. BR/TR, 6'5", 215 lbs. Deb: 9/7/79

YEAR	TM/L	G	AB	R	H	2B	3B	HR	RBI	BB	SO	AVG	OBP	SLG	PRO+	BR/A	SB	CS	SBR	FA	FR	G/POS	TPR
1979	Hou-N	2	0	0	0	0	0	0	0	0	0					0	0	0	0	.000	0	/P-1	0.0

■ JOCK MENEFEE
Menefee, John b: 1/15/1868, Rowlesburg, W.Va. d: 3/11/53, Belle Vernon, Pa. BR/TR, 6', 165 lbs. Deb: 8/17/1892

YEAR	TM/L	G	AB	R	H	2B	3B	HR	RBI	BB	SO	AVG	OBP	SLG	PRO+	BR/A	SB	CS	SBR	FA	FR	G/POS	TPR
1892	Pit-N	2	3	0	0	0	0	0	0	0	0	.000	.000	.000	-99	-1	0			1.000	0	/O-1,P-1	-0.1
1893	Lou-N	22	73	10	20	2	1	0	12	13	5	.274	.391	.329	100	1	2			.913	3	P-15/O-7	0.1
1894	Lou-N	29	79	7	13	1	0	0	4	8	7	.165	.250	.177	5	-12	2			.940	2	P-28/2-1	0.0
	Pit-N	13	47	6	12	1	2	0	7	3	3	.255	.300	.362	60	-3	2			.909	2	P-13	0.0
	Yr	42	126	13	25	2	2	0	11	11	10	.198	.268	.246	26	-15	4			.928	4	P-41/2-1	0.0
1895	Pit-N	2	0	0	0	0	0	0	0	0	0	—	—	—	0		0			.667	0	/P-2	0.0
1898	NY-N	1	5	0	0	0	0	0	0	0	0	.000	.000	.000	-99	-1	0			.750	0	/P-1	0.0
1900	Chi-N	17	46	5	5	0	0	0	4	2		.109	.180	.109	-20	-7	0			.889	-2	P-16	0.0
1901	Chi-N	48	152	19	39	5	3	0	13	8		.257	.327	.329	94	-1	4			.913	-2	O-24,P-21/12	-0.3
1902	Chi-N	65	216	24	50	4	1	0	15	15		.231	.303	.259	76	-5	4			.952	-4	O-23,P-22,1/32	-0.8
1903	Chi-N	22	64	3	13	3	0	0	2	3		.203	.239	.250	40	-5	0			.896	3	P-20/1-2	-0.1
Total	9	221	685	74	152	16	7	0	57	52	15	.222	.295	.266	60	-35	14			.918	5	P-139/O-55,123	-1.2

■ DENIS MENKE
Menke, Denis John b: 7/21/40, Algona, Iowa BR/TR, 6', 190 lbs. Deb: 4/14/62 C

YEAR	TM/L	G	AB	R	H	2B	3B	HR	RBI	BB	SO	AVG	OBP	SLG	PRO+	BR/A	SB	CS	SBR	FA	FR	G/POS	TPR
1962	Mil-N	50	146	12	28	3	1	2	16	16	38	.192	.280	.267	49	-10	0	1	-1	.980	5	2-20,3-15/S10	-0.4
1963	Mil-N	146	518	58	121	16	4	11	50	37	106	.234	.292	.344	83	-11	6	7	-2	.976	12	S-82,3-51,2/10	0.6
1964	Mil-N	151	505	79	143	29	5	20	65	68	77	.283	.373	.479	137	26	4	2	0	.964	3	*S-141,2-15/3	4.0
1965	Mil-N	71	181	16	44	13	1	4	18	18	38	.243	.315	.392	97	-1	1	3	-2	.967	-7	S-54/1-8,3	-0.7
1966	Atl-N	138	454	55	114	20	4	15	60	71	87	.251	.360	.412	112	9	0	7	-4	.955	-22	*S-106,3-39/1	-0.9
1967	Atl-N	129	418	37	95	14	3	7	39	65	62	.227	.335	.325	91	-3	5	7	-3	.965	-23	*S-124/3-3	-1.8
1968	Hou-N	150	542	56	135	23	6	6	56	64	81	.249	.335	.347	107	6	5	8	-3	.982	-17	*2-119,S-35/13	-0.5
1969	Hou-N★	154	553	72	149	25	5	10	90	87	91	.269	.373	.387	115	14	2	7	-4	.956	-9	*S-131,2-23/13	1.7
1970	Hou-N★	154	562	82	171	26	6	13	92	82	80	.304	.398	.441	130	26	6	5	-1	.954	-16	*S-133,2-21/130	2.2
1971	Hou-N	146	475	57	117	26	3	1	43	59	68	.246	.332	.320	88	-6	4	5	-2	.997	-19	*1-101,3-32,S/2	-1.9
1972	*Cin-N	140	447	41	104	19	2	9	50	58	76	.233	.327	.345	97	-1	0	1	-1	.955	1	*3-130,1-11	-0.3
1973	*Cin-N	139	241	38	46	10	0	3	26	69	53	.191	.375	.270	86	-1	1	1	-0	.966	16	*3-123/S-7,21	1.6
1974	Hou-N	32	39	2	4	0	0	0	1	4	10	.103	.213	.138	-1	-4	0	0	0	1.000	3	1-12/3-7,2S	0.1
Total	13	1598	5071	605	1270	225	40	101	606	698	853	.250	.346	.370	104	44	34	54	-22	.961	-58	S-841,3-420,21/O	3.9

■ MIKE MENOSKY
Menosky, Michael William "Leaping Mike" b: 10/16/1894, Glen Campbell, Pa. d: 4/11/83, Detroit, Mich. BL/TR, 5'10", 163 lbs. Deb: 4/18/14

YEAR	TM/L	G	AB	R	H	2B	3B	HR	RBI	BB	SO	AVG	OBP	SLG	PRO+	BR/A	SB	CS	SBR	FA	FR	G/POS	TPR
1914	Pit-F	68	140	26	37	4	1	2	9	16	30	.264	.352	.350	83	-3	5			.942	-3	O-41	-0.8
1915	Pit-F	17	21	3	2	0	0	0	1	2	0	.095	.208	.095	-17	-3	2			.917	-2	/O-9	-0.6
1916	Was-A	11	37	5	6	1	1	0	3	1	10	.162	.184	.243	29	-3	1			.952	1	/O-9	-0.3
1917	Was-A	114	322	46	83	12	10	1	34	45	55	.258	.359	.366	123	10	22			.982	9	O-94	1.4
1919	Was-A	116	342	62	98	15	3	6	39	44	46	.287	.379	.401	120	10	13			.979	0	*O-103	0.4
1920	Bos-A	141	532	80	158	24	9	3	64	65	52	.297	.383	.393	111	10	23	19	-5	.961	-3	*O-141	-0.7
1921	Bos-A	133	477	71	143	18	5	3	45	60	45	.300	.388	.377	99	2	12	6	0	.970	-4	*O-133	-1.1
1922	Bos-A	126	406	61	115	16	5	3	32	40	33	.283	.355	.369	90	-5	9	5	-0	.977	6	*O-103	-0.7
1923	Bos-A	84	188	22	43	8	4	0	25	22	19	.229	.310	.314	64	-10	3	6	-3	.920	-2	O-49	-1.2
Total	9	810	2465	382	685	98	38	18	252	295	290	.278	.364	.370	100	7	90	36		.967	7	O-682	-3.6

■ ED MENSOR
Mensor, Edward "The Midget" b: 11/7/1886, Woodville, Ore. d: 4/20/70, Salem, Ore. BB/TR, 5'6", 145 lbs. Deb: 7/15/12

YEAR	TM/L	G	AB	R	H	2B	3B	HR	RBI	BB	SO	AVG	OBP	SLG	PRO+	BR/A	SB	CS	SBR	FA	FR	G/POS	TPR
1912	Pit-N	39	99	19	26	3	2	0	1	23	12	.263	.402	.333	104	2	10			.955	-2	O-32	-0.2
1913	Pit-N	44	56	9	10	1	0	0	1	8	13	.179	.292	.196	43	-4	2			.971	-1	O-18/2-1,S	-0.5
1914	Pit-N	44	89	15	18	2	1	1	6	22	13	.202	.372	.281	99	1	2			.969	2	O-25	0.2
Total	3	127	244	43	54	6	3	1	8	53	38	.221	.367	.283	89	-1	14			.964	-1	/O-75,S-1,2	-0.5

■ TED MENZE
Menze, Theodore Charles b: 11/4/1897, St.Louis, Mo. d: 12/23/69, St.Louis, Mo. BR/TR, 5'9", 172 lbs. Deb: 4/23/18

YEAR	TM/L	G	AB	R	H	2B	3B	HR	RBI	BB	SO	AVG	OBP	SLG	PRO+	BR/A	SB	CS	SBR	FA	FR	G/POS	TPR
1918	StL-N	1	3	0	0	0	0	0	0	0	2	.000	.000	.000	-99	-1	0			1.000	-0	/O-1	-0.1

■ RUDY MEOLI
Meoli, Rudolph Bartholomew b: 5/1/51, Troy, N.Y. BL/TR, 5'9", 165 lbs. Deb: 9/9/71

YEAR	TM/L	G	AB	R	H	2B	3B	HR	RBI	BB	SO	AVG	OBP	SLG	PRO+	BR/A	SB	CS	SBR	FA	FR	G/POS	TPR
1971	Cal-A	7	3	0	0	0	0	0	0	0	0	.000	.000	.000	-99	-1	0			.000	0	H	-0.1
1973	Cal-A	120	305	36	68	12	1	2	23	31	38	.223	.295	.289	70	-12	2	4	-2	.933	-2	S-95,3-13/2	-0.5
1974	Cal-A	36	90	9	22	2	0	0	3	8	10	.244	.306	.267	70	-3	2	4	-2	.946	-1	3-20/S-8,12	-0.3
1975	Cal-A	70	126	12	27	4	1	0	6	15	20	.214	.298	.246	59	-6	1	0	0	.976	5	S-28,3-15,2/D	-0.3
1978	Chi-N	47	29	10	3	0	1	0	2	6	4	.103	.257	.172	20	-3	1	0	0	.900	6	/2-6,3-5	0.4

YEAR	TM/L	G	AB	R	H	2B	3B	HR	RBI	BB	SO	AVG	OBP	SLG	PRO+	BR/A	SB	CS	SBR	FA	FR	G/POS	TPR
1979	Phi-N	30	73	2	13	4	1	0	6	9	15	.178	.268	.260	43	-6	2	0	1	.984	3	S-16,2-15/3	0.0
Total	6	310	626	69	133	20	4	2	40	69	88	.212	.291	.267	61	-31	10	8	-2	.944	10	S-147/3-54,2D1	-0.8

■ ORLANDO MERCADO   Mercado, Orlando (Rodriguez) b: 11/7/61, Arecibo, P.R. BR/TR, 6', 195 lbs. Deb: 9/13/82

YEAR	TM/L	G	AB	R	H	2B	3B	HR	RBI	BB	SO	AVG	OBP	SLG	PRO+	BR/A	SB	CS	SBR	FA	FR	G/POS	TPR
1982	Sea-A	9	17	1	2	0	0	1	6	0	5	.118	.118	.294	8	-2	0	0	0	1.000	1	/C-8	-0.1
1983	Sea-A	66	178	10	35	11	2	1	16	14	27	.197	.259	.298	51	-12	2	2	-1	.995	4	C-65	-0.6
1984	Sea-A	30	78	5	17	3	1	0	5	4	12	.218	.265	.282	52	-5	1	0	0	.992	-6	C-29	-1.0
1986	Tex-A	46	102	7	24	1	1	1	7	6	13	.235	.284	.294	56	-6	0	1	-1	.996	16	C-45	1.1
1987	Det-A	10	22	2	3	0	0	0	1	2	0	.136	.208	.136	-6	-3	0	0	0	.980	3	C-10	0.0
	LA-N	7	5	1	3	1	0	0	1	1	1	.600	.667	.800	294	2	0	0	0	1.000	0	/C-7	0.2
1988	Oak-A	16	24	3	3	0	0	1	1	3	8	.125	.222	.250	33	-2	0	0	0	.959	1	C-16	-0.1
1989	Min-A	19	38	1	4	0	0	0	1	4	4	.105	.190	.105	-14	-6	1	0	0	1.000	4	C-19	-0.1
1990	NY-N	42	90	10	19	1	0	3	7	8	11	.211	.290	.322	68	-4	0	0	0	.991	2	C-40	-0.1
	Mon-N	8	8	0	2	0	0	0	0	0	1	.250	.250	.250	39	-1	0	0	0	1.000	3	/C-8	0.2
	Yr	50	98	10	21	1	0	3	7	8	12	.214	.287	.316	66	-5	0	0	0	.992	4	C-48	0.1
Total	8	253	562	40	112	17	4	7	45	42	82	.199	.261	.281	48	-40	4	3	-1	.993	27	C-247	-0.5

■ ORLANDO MERCED   Merced, Orlando Luis (Villanueva) b: 11/2/66, Hato Rey, P.R. BB/TR, 6', 180 lbs. Deb: 6/27/90

YEAR	TM/L	G	AB	R	H	2B	3B	HR	RBI	BB	SO	AVG	OBP	SLG	PRO+	BR/A	SB	CS	SBR	FA	FR	G/POS	TPR
1990	Pit-N	25	24	3	5	1	0	0	1	0	9	.208	.240	.250	36	-2	0	0	0	.000	-0	/C-1,O-1	-0.3
1991	*Pit-N	120	411	83	113	17	2	10	50	64	81	.275	.374	.399	119	12	8	4	0	.988	-8	*1-105/O-7	-0.2
1992	*Pit-N	134	405	50	100	28	5	6	60	52	63	.247	.336	.385	105	3	5	4	-1	.995	0	*1-114,O-17	-0.5
1993	Pit-N	137	447	68	140	26	4	8	70	77	64	.313	.415	.443	130	23	3	3	-1	.965	3	*O-109,1-42	2.0
1994	Pit-N	108	386	48	105	21	3	9	51	42	58	.272	.345	.412	97	-2	4	1	1	.981	-9	O-68,1-55	-1.5
Total	5	524	1673	252	463	93	14	33	231	236	275	.277	.368	.408	112	34	20	12	-1	.992	-14	1-316,O-202/C	-0.5

■ HENRY MERCEDES   Mercedes, Henry Felipe (Perez) b: 7/23/69, Santo Domingo, D.R. BR/TR, 5'11", 185 lbs. Deb: 4/22/92

YEAR	TM/L	G	AB	R	H	2B	3B	HR	RBI	BB	SO	AVG	OBP	SLG	PRO+	BR/A	SB	CS	SBR	FA	FR	G/POS	TPR
1992	Oak-A	9	5	1	4	0	1	0	1	0	1	.800	.800	1.200	479	2	0	0	0	.875	-0	/C-9	0.2
1993	Oak-A	20	47	5	10	2	0	0	3	2	15	.213	.260	.255	42	-4	1	1	-0	.987	-0	C-18/D-1	-0.4
Total	2	29	52	6	14	2	1	0	4	2	16	.269	.309	.346	81	-2	1	1	-0	.976	-0	/C-27,D-1	-0.2

■ LUIS MERCEDES   Mercedes, Luis Roberto (Santana) b: 2/15/68, San Pedro De Macoris, D.R. BR/TR, 6', 180 lbs. Deb: 9/8/91

YEAR	TM/L	G	AB	R	H	2B	3B	HR	RBI	BB	SO	AVG	OBP	SLG	PRO+	BR/A	SB	CS	SBR	FA	FR	G/POS	TPR
1991	Bal-A	19	54	10	11	2	0	0	2	4	9	.204	.259	.241	41	-4	0	0	0	1.000	-2	O-15/D-1	-0.7
1992	Bal-A	23	50	7	7	2	0	0	4	8	9	.140	.271	.180	28	-5	0	1	-1	.956	2	O-16/D-7	-0.3
1993	Bal-A	10	24	1	7	2	0	0	0	5	4	.292	.414	.375	109	1	1	1	-0	1.000	-0	/O-8,D-2	0.0
	SF-N	18	25	1	4	0	1	0	3	1	3	.160	.250	.240	33	-2	0	1	-1	1.000	-1	/O-5	-0.4
Total	3	70	153	19	29	6	1	0	9	18	25	.190	.287	.242	47	-11	1	3	-2	.976	-2	/O-44,D-10	-1.4

■ WIN MERCER   Mercer, George Barclay b: 6/20/1874, Chester, W.Va. d: 1/12/03, San Francisco, Cal BR/TR, 5'7", 140 lbs. Deb: 4/21/1894

YEAR	TM/L	G	AB	R	H	2B	3B	HR	RBI	BB	SO	AVG	OBP	SLG	PRO+	BR/A	SB	CS	SBR	FA	FR	G/POS	TPR
1894	Was-N	53	164	29	48	5	2	2	29	9	20	.293	.329	.384	74	-7	9			.944	2	P-50/O-4	-0.1
1895	Was-N	63	196	26	50	9	1	1	26	12	32	.255	.308	.327	65	-11	7			.874	-8	P-43/S-7,O32	-0.8
1896	Was-N	49	156	23	38	1	1	1	14	9	18	.244	.302	.282	54	-10	9			.856	1	P-46/O-1	0.0
1897	Was-N	49	135	22	43	2	5	0	19	6		.319	.367	.407	102	0	7			.865	-1	P-46	0.0
1898	Was-N	80	249	38	80	3	5	2	25	18		.321	.369	.398	120	6	14			.863	-9	P-33,S-23,O/32	-0.4
1899	Was-N	108	375	73	112	6	7	1	35	32		.299	.360	.360	99	0	16			.846	-14	3-62,P-23,O/S1	-1.6
1900	NY-N	76	248	32	73	4	0	0	27	26		.294	.366	.310	92	-1	15			.931	-2	P-33,3-19,O/S2	-0.4
1901	Was-A	51	140	26	42	7	2	0	16	23		.300	.402	.379	119	5	10			.944	-2	P-24,O-16/1S3	-0.1
1902	Det-A	35	100	8	18	2	0	0	6	6		.180	.226	.200	19	-11	1			.935	4	P-35	0.0
Total	9	564	1763	277	504	39	23	7	197	141	70	.286	.345	.346	88	-29	88			.903	-29	P-333/3-90,OS12	-3.4

■ JOHN MERCER   Mercer, John Locke b: 6/22/1892, Taylortown, La. d: 12/22/82, Shreveport, La. BL/TL, 5'10.5", 155 lbs. Deb: 6/25/12

YEAR	TM/L	G	AB	R	H	2B	3B	HR	RBI	BB	SO	AVG	OBP	SLG	PRO+	BR/A	SB	CS	SBR	FA	FR	G/POS	TPR
1912	StL-N	1	1	0	0	0	0	0	0	0	0	.000	.000	.000	-99	-0	0			.500	-0	/1-1	-0.1

■ ANDY MERCHANT   Merchant, James Anderson b: 8/30/50, Mobile, Ala. BL/TR, 5'11", 185 lbs. Deb: 9/28/75

YEAR	TM/L	G	AB	R	H	2B	3B	HR	RBI	BB	SO	AVG	OBP	SLG	PRO+	BR/A	SB	CS	SBR	FA	FR	G/POS	TPR
1975	Bos-A	1	4	1	2	0	0	0	0	1	0	.500	.600	.500	197	1	0	0	0	1.000	-1	/C-1	0.0
1976	Bos-A	2	2	0	0	0	0	0	0	0	2	.000	.000	.000	-89	-0	0	0	0	1.000	-0	/C-1	-0.1
Total	2	3	6	1	2	0	0	0	0	1	2	.333	.429	.333	109	0	0	0	0	1.000	-1	/C-2	-0.1

■ ART MEREWETHER   Merewether, Arthur Francis "Merry" b: 7/1/02, E.Providence, R.I. BR/TR, 5'9.5", 155 lbs. Deb: 7/10/22

YEAR	TM/L	G	AB	R	H	2B	3B	HR	RBI	BB	SO	AVG	OBP	SLG	PRO+	BR/A	SB	CS	SBR	FA	FR	G/POS	TPR
1922	Pit-N	1	1	0	0	0	0	0	0	0	0	.000	.000	.000	-99	-0	0	0	0	.000	0	H	0.0

■ FRED MERKLE   Merkle, Frederick Charles b: 12/20/1888, Watertown, Wis. d: 3/2/56, Daytona Beach, Fla. BR/TR, 6'1", 190 lbs. Deb: 9/21/07 C

YEAR	TM/L	G	AB	R	H	2B	3B	HR	RBI	BB	SO	AVG	OBP	SLG	PRO+	BR/A	SB	CS	SBR	FA	FR	G/POS	TPR
1907	NY-N	15	47	0	12	1	0	0	5	1		.255	.271	.277	69	-2	0			.949	-1	1-15	-0.4
1908	NY-N	38	41	6	11	2	1	1	7	4		.268	.333	.439	140	2	0			1.000	-2	1-11/O-5,23	-0.1
1909	NY-N	79	236	15	45	9	1	0	20	16		.191	.245	.237	49	-14	8			.976	-3	1-70/2-1	-2.0
1910	NY-N	144	506	75	148	35	14	4	70	44	59	.292	.353	.441	131	18	23			.981	1	*1-144	1.9
1911	*NY-N	149	541	80	153	24	10	12	84	43	60	.283	.342	.431	112	7	49			.985	15	*1-148	2.1
1912	*NY-N	129	479	82	148	22	6	11	84	42	70	.309	.374	.449	121	13	37			.980	-1	*1-129	1.0
1913	*NY-N	153	563	78	147	30	13	3	69	41	60	.261	.315	.371	95	-5	35			.986	-4	*1-153	-1.1
1914	NY-N	146	512	71	132	25	7	7	63	52	80	.258	.327	.375	112	7	23			.990	3	*1-146	0.8
1915	NY-N	140	505	52	151	25	3	4	62	36	39	.299	.348	.384	129	16	20	15	-3	.989	-1	*1-110,O-30	1.0
1916	NY-N	112	401	45	95	19	3	7	44	33	46	.237	.308	.352	108	3	17			.984	0	*1-112	-0.1
	*Bro-N	23	69	6	16	1	0	0	2	7	4	.232	.312	.246	70	-2	2			.992	-1	1-15/O-4	-0.4
	Yr	135	470	51	111	20	3	7	46	40	50	.236	.308	.336	102	1	19			.985	-1	*1-127/O-4	-0.5
1917	Bro-N	2	8	1	1	0	0	0	0	1	1	.125	.250	.250	13	-1	0			1.000	0	/1-2	-0.1
	Chi-N	146	549	65	146	30	9	3	57	42	60	.266	.323	.370	104	2	13			.983	-3	*1-140/O-6	-0.7
	Yr	148	557	66	147	31	9	3	57	42	61	.264	.320	.368	103	1	13			.983	-3	*1-142/O-6	-0.8
1918	*Chi-N	129	482	55	143	25	5	3	65	35	36	.297	.349	.388	122	12	21			.990	1	*1-129	0.9
1919	Chi-N	133	498	52	133	20	6	3	62	33	35	.267	.315	.349	99	-1	20			.985	-10	*1-132/2-1	-1.7
1920	Chi-N	92	330	33	94	20	4	3	38	24	32	.285	.335	.397	108	3	5	3	-2	.985	-0	1-85/O-1	-0.1
1925	NY-A	7	13	4	5	1	0	0	1	1	1	.385	.429	.462	128	1	1	0	0	1.000	0	/1-5	0.0
1926	NY-A	1	0	0	0	0	0	0	0	0	0	.000	.000	.000	-99	-0	0	0	0	1.000	0	/1-1	-0.1
Total	16	1638	5782	720	1580	290	82	60	733	454	583	.273	.331	.383	109	58	272	20		.985	-5	*1-1547/O-46,23	0.9

■ ED MERRILL   Merrill, Edward Mason b: 5/1860, Kentucky d: 8/18/24, Chicago, Ill. 5'11", 176 lbs. Deb: 5/5/1882

YEAR	TM/L	G	AB	R	H	2B	3B	HR	RBI	BB	SO	AVG	OBP	SLG	PRO+	BR/A	SB	CS	SBR	FA	FR	G/POS	TPR
1882	Lou-a	1	0	0	0	0	0	0	0			—	—	—		0				.000	0	/O-1	0.0
	Wor-N	2	8	0	1	0	0	0	4	0	1	.125	.125	.125	-19	-1				.714	-1	/3-2	-0.1
1884	Ind-a	55	196	14	35	3	1	0	6			.179	.207	.204	35	-13				.900	-4	2-55	-1.5
Total	2	58	204	14	36	3	1	0	4	6	1	.176	.204	.201	33	-14				.900	-5	/2-55,3-2,O	-1.6

■ LLOYD MERRIMAN   Merriman, Lloyd Archer "Citation" b: 8/2/24, Clovis, Cal. BL/TL, 6', 195 lbs. Deb: 4/24/49

YEAR	TM/L	G	AB	R	H	2B	3B	HR	RBI	BB	SO	AVG	OBP	SLG	PRO+	BR/A	SB	CS	SBR	FA	FR	G/POS	TPR
1949	Cin-N	103	287	35	66	12	5	4	26	21	36	.230	.285	.348	68	-14	-1			.969	-1	O-86	-1.7
1950	Cin-N	92	298	44	77	15	3	2	31	30	23	.258	.330	.349	79	-9	6			.989	-4	O-84	-1.6
1951	Cin-N	114	359	34	87	23	2	5	36	31	34	.242	.303	.359	76	-12	8	4	0	.997	9	*O-102	-0.7
1954	Cin-N	73	112	12	30	8	1	0	16	23	10	.268	.406	.357	98	1	3	0	1	.981	-1	O-25	0.0
1955	Chi-N	1	1	0	0	0	0	0	0	0	0	.000	.000	.000	-97	-0	0	0	0	.000	0	H	0.0

YEAR	TM/L	G	AB	R	H	2B	3B	HR	RBI	BB	SO	AVG	OBP	SLG	PRO+	BR/A	SB	CS	SBR	FA	FR	G/POS	TPR
	Chi-N	72	145	15	31	6	1	1	8	21	21	.214	.313	.290	62	-8	1	0	0	.977	-6	O-47	-1.5
Total	5	455	1202	140	291	64	12	12	117	126	124	.242	.317	.345	75	-42	20	4		.985	-2	O-344	-5.5

■ GEORGE MERRITT
Merritt, George Washington   b: 4/14/1880, Paterson, N.J.   d: 2/21/38, Memphis, Tenn.   TR , 6', 160 lbs.   Deb: 9/6/01

YEAR	TM/L	G	AB	R	H	2B	3B	HR	RBI	BB	SO	AVG	OBP	SLG	PRO+	BR/A	SB	CS	SBR	FA	FR	G/POS	TPR
1901	Pit-N	4	11	2	3	0	1	0	0	0		.273	.385	.455	139	1	1			1.000	-0	/P-3	0.0
1902	Pit-N	2	9	2	3	1	0	0	2	0		.333	.333	.444	135	0	1			1.000	1	/O-2	0.1
1903	Pit-N	9	27	4	4	0	1	0	3	2		.148	.233	.222	29	-3	1			.889	-2	/O-7,P-1	-0.4
Total	3	15	47	8	10	1	2	0	5	2		.213	.288	.319	74	-2	1			.929	-1	/O-9,P-4	-0.3

■ HERM MERRITT
Merritt, Herman G.   b: 11/12/1900, Independence, Kan.   d: 5/26/27, Kansas City, Mo.   BR/TR,   Deb: 8/24/21

YEAR	TM/L	G	AB	R	H	2B	3B	HR	RBI	BB	SO	AVG	OBP	SLG	PRO+	BR/A	SB	CS	SBR	FA	FR	G/POS	TPR
1921	Det-A	20	46	3	17	1	2	0	6	1	5	.370	.396	.478	123	2	1	0	0	.882	-6	S-17	-0.3

■ JOHN MERRITT
Merritt, John Howard   b: 10/12/1894, Tupelo, Miss.   d: 11/3/55, Tupelo, Miss.   BR/TL, 5'11", 170 lbs.   Deb: 9/27/13

YEAR	TM/L	G	AB	R	H	2B	3B	HR	RBI	BB	SO	AVG	OBP	SLG	PRO+	BR/A	SB	CS	SBR	FA	FR	G/POS	TPR
1913	NY-N	1	0	0	0	0	0	0	0	0	0	—	—	—	—	-0				.000	-0	/O-1	0.0

■ BILL MERRITT
Merritt, William Henry   b: 7/30/1870, Lowell, Mass.   d: 11/17/37, Lowell, Mass.   BR/TR, 5'7", 160 lbs.   Deb: 8/8/1891

YEAR	TM/L	G	AB	R	H	2B	3B	HR	RBI	BB	SO	AVG	OBP	SLG	PRO+	BR/A	SB	CS	SBR	FA	FR	G/POS	TPR
1891	Chi-N	11	42	4	9	1	0	0	4	2	2	.214	.250	.238	42	-3	0			.955	-3	C-11/1-1	-0.5
1892	Lou-N	46	168	22	33	4	2	1	13	11	15	.196	.246	.262	58	-9	3			.940	-3	C-46	-0.8
1893	Bos-N	39	141	30	49	6	3	3	26	13	13	.348	.403	.496	128	5	3			.945	-4	C-37/O-2	0.3
1894	Bos-N	10	26	3	6	1	0	0	6	8	0	.231	.412	.269	62	-1	0			.881	-3	/C-8,O-1	0.0
	Pit-N	36	109	18	30	1	2	1	18	15	7	.275	.363	.349	73	-4	2			.952	-1	C-28/1-4,O	-0.2
	Cin-N	29	113	17	37	6	1	1	21	9	3	.327	.387	.425	92	-2	1			.953	-3	C-24/3-3,1O	-0.2
	Yr	75	248	38	73	8	3	2	45	32	10	.294	.379	.375	81	-7	6			.941	-3	C-60/1-5,O3	-0.4
1895	Cin-N	22	79	9	14	2	0	0	12	6	5	.177	.235	.203	13	-10	2			.955	-1	C-20/2-1	-0.8
	Pit-N	67	239	32	68	5	1	0	27	18	16	.285	.340	.314	73	-9	2			.935	-2	C-63/1-2	-0.4
	Yr	89	318	41	82	7	1	0	39	24	21	.258	.314	.286	57	-20	4			.939	-3	C-83/1-2,2	-1.2
1896	Pit-N	77	282	26	82	8	2	1	42	18	10	.291	.336	.344	83	-7	3			.941	-2	C-62/3-5,21S	0.2
1897	Pit-N	62	209	21	55	6	1	1	26	9		.263	.297	.316	64	-11	2			.946	-4	C-53/1-7	-0.8
1899	Bos-N	1	2	0	0	0	0	0	0	0		.000	.333	.000	-5	-0	0			1.000	0	/C-1	0.0
Total	8	400	1410	182	383	40	12	8	195	109	<u>71</u>	.272	.327	.334	75	-52	21			.942	-19	C-353/1-18,302S	-3.2

■ JACK MERSON
Merson, John Warren   b: 1/17/22, Elkridge, Md.   BR/TR, 5'11", 175 lbs.   Deb: 9/14/51

YEAR	TM/L	G	AB	R	H	2B	3B	HR	RBI	BB	SO	AVG	OBP	SLG	PRO+	BR/A	SB	CS	SBR	FA	FR	G/POS	TPR
1951	Pit-N	13	50	6	18	2	2	1	14	1	7	.360	.373	.540	138	2	0	0	0	.987	2	2-13	0.5
1952	Pit-N	111	398	41	98	20	2	5	38	22	38	.246	.287	.344	72	-15	1	1	-0	.978	-6	2-81,3-27	-1.9
1953	Bos-A	1	4	0	0	0	0	0	0	0	0	.000	.000	.000	-95	-1	0	0	0	.875	0	/2-1	-0.1
Total	3	125	452	47	116	22	4	6	52	23	45	.257	.294	.363	78	-14	1	1	-0	.978	-3	/2-95,3-27	-1.5

■ SAM MERTES
Mertes, Samuel Blair "Sandow"   b: 8/6/1872, San Francisco, Cal.   d: 3/11/45, San Francisco, Cal   BR/TR, 5'10", 185 lbs.   Deb: 6/30/1896

YEAR	TM/L	G	AB	R	H	2B	3B	HR	RBI	BB	SO	AVG	OBP	SLG	PRO+	BR/A	SB	CS	SBR	FA	FR	G/POS	TPR
1896	Phi-N	37	143	20	34	4	4	0	14	8	10	.238	.288	.322	61	-8	19			.907	-1	O-35/S-1,2	-1.0
1898	Chi-N	83	269	45	80	4	8	1	47	34		.297	.388	.383	121	9	27			.880	-2	O-60,S-14/21	0.7
1899	Chi-N	117	426	83	127	13	16	9	81	33		.298	.349	.467	126	13	45			.923	-1	*O-108/1-3,S	0.4
1900	Chi-N	127	481	72	142	25	4	7	60	42		.295	.356	.407	114	9	38			.923	-5	O-88,1-33/S	-0.2
1901	Chi-A	137	545	94	151	16	17	5	98	52		.277	.347	.396	108	7	46			.940	-6	*2-132/O-5	0.5
1902	Chi-A	129	497	60	140	23	7	1	79	37		.282	.334	.362	97	-2	46			.922	6	*O-120/S-5,CP123	-0.3
1903	NY-N	138	517	100	145	**32**	14	7	**104**	61		.280	.360	.437	122	14	45			**.973**	8	*O-137/C-1,1	1.3
1904	NY-N	148	532	83	147	28	11	4	78	54		.276	.346	.393	123	14	47			.956	-1	*O-147/S-1	0.5
1905	*NY-N	150	551	81	154	27	17	5	108	56		.279	.351	.417	126	17	52			.960	-11	*O-150	-0.1
1906	NY-N	71	253	37	60	9	6	1	33	29		.237	.323	.332	102	1	21			.970	1	O-71	-0.1
	StL-N	53	191	20	47	7	4	0	19	16		.246	.304	.325	100	-0	10			.890	-6	O-53	-1.0
	Yr	124	444	57	107	16	10	1	52	45		.241	.315	.329	101	1	31			.938	-5	*O-124	-1.1
Total	10	1190	4405	695	1227	188	108	40	721	422	<u>10</u>	.279	.346	.398	113	73	396			.938	-14	O-974,2-138/1SC3P	0.7

■ LENNIE MERULLO
Merullo, Leonard Richard   b: 5/5/17, Boston, Mass.   BR/TR, 5'11", 168 lbs.   Deb: 9/12/41   F

YEAR	TM/L	G	AB	R	H	2B	3B	HR	RBI	BB	SO	AVG	OBP	SLG	PRO+	BR/A	SB	CS	SBR	FA	FR	G/POS	TPR
1941	Chi-N	7	17	3	6	1	0	0	1	2	0	.353	.421	.412	140	1	1			.968	2	/S-7	0.3
1942	Chi-N	143	515	53	132	23	3	2	37	35	45	.256	.310	.324	89	-8	14			.946	-1	*S-143	0.0
1943	Chi-N	129	453	37	115	18	3	1	25	26	42	.254	.297	.313	78	-14	7			.940	-12	*S-125	-1.8
1944	Chi-N	66	193	20	41	8	1	1	16	16	18	.212	.276	.280	57	-11	3			.937	-4	S-56/1-1	-0.5
1945	*Chi-N	121	394	40	94	18	0	2	37	31	30	.239	.297	.299	68	-17	7			.948	-4	*S-118	-1.3
1946	Chi-N	65	126	14	19	8	0	0	7	11	13	.151	.219	.214	24	-13	2			.946	18	S-44	0.7
1947	Chi-N	108	373	24	90	16	1	0	29	15	26	.241	.274	.290	52	-26	4			.949	7	*S-108	-1.4
Total	7	639	2071	191	497	92	8	6	152	136	174	.240	.291	.301	69	-88	38			.945	11	S-601/1-1	-4.0

■ MATT MERULLO
Merullo, Matthew Bates   b: 8/4/65, Winchester, Mass.   BL/TR, 6'2", 200 lbs.   Deb: 4/12/89   F

YEAR	TM/L	G	AB	R	H	2B	3B	HR	RBI	BB	SO	AVG	OBP	SLG	PRO+	BR/A	SB	CS	SBR	FA	FR	G/POS	TPR
1989	Chi-A	31	81	5	18	1	0	1	8	6	14	.222	.276	.272	56	-5	0	1	-1	.973	-4	C-27/D-1	-0.8
1991	Chi-A	80	140	8	32	1	0	5	21	9	18	.229	.275	.343	72	-6	0	0	0	.989	-1	C-27,1-16/D	-0.6
1992	Chi-A	24	50	3	9	1	1	0	3	1	8	.180	.212	.240	27	-5	0	0	0	.971	-1	C-16/D-1	-0.5
1993	Chi-A	8	20	1	1	0	0	0	0	0	1	.050	.050	.050	-75	-5	0	0	0	.000	-0	/D-6	-0.5
1994	Cle-A	4	10	1	1	0	0	0	0	2	1	.100	.250	.100	-5	-2	0	0	0	.957	-0	/C-4	-0.1
Total	5	147	301	18	61	3	1	6	32	18	42	.203	.250	.279	47	-22	0	1	-1	.976	-6	/C-74,1-16,D	-2.5

■ STEVE MESNER
Mesner, Stephan Mathias   b: 1/13/18, Los Angeles, Cal.   d: 4/6/81, San Diego, Cal.   BR/TR, 5'9", 178 lbs.   Deb: 9/23/38

YEAR	TM/L	G	AB	R	H	2B	3B	HR	RBI	BB	SO	AVG	OBP	SLG	PRO+	BR/A	SB	CS	SBR	FA	FR	G/POS	TPR
1938	Chi-N	2	4	2	1	0	0	0	0	1	1	.250	.400	.250	80	-0	0			.667	-1	/S-1	-0.1
1939	Chi-N	17	43	7	12	4	0	0	6	3	4	.279	.340	.372	90	-1	0			.927	-1	S-12/2-1,3	0.2
1941	StL-N	24	69	8	10	1	0	0	10	5	6	.145	.203	.159	3	-9	0			.958	5	3-22	-0.3
1943	Cin-N	137	504	53	137	26	1	0	52	26	20	.272	.309	.327	85	-11	6			.944	1	*3-130	-0.9
1944	Cin-N	121	414	31	100	17	4	1	47	34	20	.242	.301	.309	75	-14	1			.951	-7	*3-120	-2.1
1945	Cin-N	150	540	52	137	19	1	1	52	52	18	.254	.322	.298	74	-18	4			.971	12	*3-148/2-3	-0.2
Total	6	451	1574	153	397	67	6	2	167	121	69	.252	.308	.306	75	-52	11			.956	10	3-421/S-13,2	-3.4

■ BOBBY MESSENGER
Messenger, Charles Walter   b: 3/19/1884, Bangor, Me.   d: 7/10/51, Bath, Maine   BB/TR, 5'10.5", 165 lbs.   Deb: 8/30/09

YEAR	TM/L	G	AB	R	H	2B	3B	HR	RBI	BB	SO	AVG	OBP	SLG	PRO+	BR/A	SB	CS	SBR	FA	FR	G/POS	TPR
1909	Chi-A	31	112	18	19	1	1	0	0	13		.170	.268	.196	49	-6	7			.950	-2	O-31	-1.0
1910	Chi-A	9	26	7	6	0	1	0	4	4		.231	.375	.308	119	1	3			.846	-0	/O-8	0.0
1911	Chi-A	13	17	4	2	0	0	0	0	3		.118	.250	.235	37	-1	0			.875	-1	/O-4	-0.2
1914	StL-A	1	2	0	0	0	0	0	0	0		.000	.000	.000	-99	-0	0			.000	-0	/O-1	-0.1
Total	4	54	157	29	27	1	3	0	4	20	<u>0</u>	.172	.282	.217	57	-7	10			.918	-3	/O-44	-1.3

■ TOM MESSITT
Messitt, Thomas John   b: 7/27/1874, Frankfort, Pa.   d: 9/22/34, Chicago, Ill.   5'9", 177 lbs.   Deb: 9/14/1899

YEAR	TM/L	G	AB	R	H	2B	3B	HR	RBI	BB	SO	AVG	OBP	SLG	PRO+	BR/A	SB	CS	SBR	FA	FR	G/POS	TPR
1899	Lou-N	3	11	0	1	0	0	0	0	0		.091	.091	.091	-50	-2	0			1.000	1	/C-3	-0.1

■ AL METCALF
Metcalf, Al   b: Brooklyn, N.Y.   Deb: 5/27/1875

YEAR	TM/L	G	AB	R	H	2B	3B	HR	RBI	BB	SO	AVG	OBP	SLG	PRO+	BR/A	SB	CS	SBR	FA	FR	G/POS	TPR
1875	Mut-n	8	31	2	7	0	0	0		1		.226	.250	.226	62	-1						/3-4,O-2,S	-0.1

■ SCAT METHA
Metha, Frank Joseph   b: 12/13/13, Los Angeles, Cal.   d: 3/2/75, Fountain Valley, Cal.   BR/TR, 5'11", 165 lbs.   Deb: 4/22/40

YEAR	TM/L	G	AB	R	H	2B	3B	HR	RBI	BB	SO	AVG	OBP	SLG	PRO+	BR/A	SB	CS	SBR	FA	FR	G/POS	TPR
1940	Det-A	26	37	6	9	0	1	0	3	2	8	.243	.282	.297	46	-3	0	1	-1	.960	4	2-10/3-6	0.0

YEAR	TM/L	G	AB	R	H	2B	3B	HR	RBI	BB	SO	AVG	OBP	SLG	PRO+	BR/A	SB	CS	SBR	FA	FR	G/POS	TPR

■ BUD METHENY   Metheny, Arthur Beauregard b: 6/1/15, St.Louis, Mo.   BL/TL, 5'11", 190 lbs.   Deb: 4/27/43

YEAR	TM/L	G	AB	R	H	2B	3B	HR	RBI	BB	SO	AVG	OBP	SLG	PRO+	BR/A	SB	CS	SBR	FA	FR	G/POS	TPR
1943	*NY-A	103	360	51	94	18	2	9	36	39	34	.261	.333	.397	113	5	2	3	-1	.963	-12	O-91	-1.4
1944	NY-A	137	518	72	124	16	1	14	67	56	57	.239	.316	.355	89	-8	5	5	-2	.956	-8	*O-132	-2.6
1945	NY-A	133	509	64	126	18	2	8	53	54	31	.248	.325	.338	88	-7	5	2	0	.984	-6	*O-128	-2.2
1946	NY-A	3	3	0	0	0	0	0	0	0	0	.000	.000	.000	-99	-1	0	0	0	.000	0	H	-0.1
Total	4	376	1390	187	344	52	5	31	156	149	122	.247	.323	.359	94	-11	12	10	-2	.968	-26	O-351	-6.3

■ CATFISH METKOVICH   Metkovich, George Michael b: 10/8/21, Angels Camp, Cal.   BL/TL, 6'1", 185 lbs.   Deb: 7/16/43

YEAR	TM/L	G	AB	R	H	2B	3B	HR	RBI	BB	SO	AVG	OBP	SLG	PRO+	BR/A	SB	CS	SBR	FA	FR	G/POS	TPR
1943	Bos-A	78	321	34	79	14	4	5	27	19	38	.246	.294	.361	90	-5	1	3	-2	.955	-3	O-76/1-2	-1.5
1944	Bos-A	134	549	94	152	28	8	9	59	31	57	.277	.319	.406	108	3	13	4	2	.962	5	O-82,1-50	0.3
1945	Bos-A	138	539	65	140	26	3	5	62	51	70	.260	.331	.347	94	-4	19	6	2	.985	-4	1-97,O-42	-1.6
1946	*Bos-A	86	281	42	69	15	2	4	25	36	39	.246	.333	.356	88	-4	8	3	1	.948	-11	O-81	-1.9
1947	Cle-A	126	473	68	120	22	7	5	40	32	51	.254	.302	.362	86	-11	5	3	-0	.989	1	*O-119/1-1	-1.7
1949	Chi-A	93	338	50	80	9	4	5	45	41	24	.237	.321	.331	75	-13	5	4	-1	.968	-7	O-87	-2.5
1951	Pit-N	120	423	51	124	21	3	3	40	28	23	.293	.338	.378	90	-6	3	2	-0	.994	1	O-69,1-37	-0.9
1952	Pit-N	125	373	41	101	18	3	7	41	32	29	.271	.335	.391	98	-1	5	2	0	.988	-7	1-72,O-33	-1.1
1953	Pit-N	26	41	5	6	0	1	1	7	6	3	.146	.255	.268	37	-4	0	0	0	1.000	-1	/1-5,O-4	-0.5
	Chi-N	61	124	19	29	9	0	2	12	16	10	.234	.326	.355	76	-4	2	1	0	1.000	-5	O-38/1-7	-1.0
	Yr	87	165	24	35	9	1	3	19	22	13	.212	.309	.333	66	-8	2	1	0	1.000	-6	O-42,1-12	-1.5
1954	Mil-N	68	123	7	34	5	1	1	15	15	15	.276	.360	.358	94	-1	0	0	0	1.000	1	1-18,O-13	-0.1
Total	10	1055	3585	476	934	167	36	47	373	307	359	.261	.323	.367	91	-49	61	28	2	.976	-28	O-644,1-289	-12.5

■ CHARLIE METRO   Metro, Charles (b: Charles Moreskonich) b: 4/28/19, Nanty Glo, Pa.   BR/TR, 5'11.5", 178 lbs.   Deb: 5/4/43   MC

YEAR	TM/L	G	AB	R	H	2B	3B	HR	RBI	BB	SO	AVG	OBP	SLG	PRO+	BR/A	SB	CS	SBR	FA	FR	G/POS	TPR
1943	Det-A	44	40	12	8	0	0	0	2	3	6	.200	.256	.200	32	-3	1	1	-0	.966	-2	O-14	-0.6
1944	Det-A	38	78	8	15	0	1	0	5	3	10	.192	.222	.218	25	-8	1	0	0	1.000	-2	O-20	-1.0
	Phi-A	24	40	4	4	0	0	0	1	7	6	.100	.234	.100	-3	-5	0	0	0	1.000	-1	O-11/3-5,2	-0.7
	Yr	62	118	12	19	0	1	0	6	10	16	.161	.227	.178	16	-13	1	0	0	1.000	-2	O-31/3-5,2	-1.7
1945	Phi-A	65	200	18	42	10	1	3	15	23	33	.210	.291	.315	76	-6	1	1	-0	.972	-5	O-57	-0.5
Total	3	171	358	42	69	10	2	3	23	36	55	.193	.266	.257	51	-22	3	2	-0	.980	-9	O-102/3-5,2	-3.8

■ LENNY METZ   Metz, Leonard Raymond b: 7/6/1899, Louisville, Colo.   d: 2/24/53, Denver, Colo.   BR/TR, 5'10.5", 170 lbs.   Deb: 9/11/23

YEAR	TM/L	G	AB	R	H	2B	3B	HR	RBI	BB	SO	AVG	OBP	SLG	PRO+	BR/A	SB	CS	SBR	FA	FR	G/POS	TPR
1923	Phi-N	12	37	4	8	0	0	0	3	4	3	.216	.310	.216	37	-3	0	0	0	.969	1	/2-6,S-6	-0.2
1924	Phi-N	7	7	1	2	0	0	0	1	1	0	.286	.375	.286	71	-0	0	0	0	.846	0	/S-6	0.0
1925	Phi-N	11	14	1	0	0	0	0	0	0	2	.000	.000	.000	-92	-4	0	0	0	1.000	2	/S-9,2-2	-0.2
Total	3	30	58	6	10	0	0	0	4	5	5	.172	.250	.172	11	-8	0	0	0	.951	3	/S-21,2-8	-0.4

■ ROGER METZGER   Metzger, Roger Henry b: 10/10/47, Fredericksburg, Tex   BB/TR, 6', 165 lbs.   Deb: 6/16/70

YEAR	TM/L	G	AB	R	H	2B	3B	HR	RBI	BB	SO	AVG	OBP	SLG	PRO+	BR/A	SB	CS	SBR	FA	FR	G/POS	TPR
1970	Chi-N	1	2	0	0	0	0	0	0	0	0	.000	.000	.000	-89	-1	0	0	0	.833	1	/S-1	0.1
1971	Hou-N	150	562	64	132	14	11	0	26	44	50	.235	.295	.299	70	-22	15	6	1	.977	-5	*S-148	-0.7
1972	Hou-N	153	641	84	142	12	3	2	38	60	71	.222	.289	.259	58	-34	23	9	2	.971	5	*S-153	-0.7
1973	Hou-N	154	580	67	145	11	14	1	35	39	70	.250	.301	.322	73	-21	10	4	1	**.982**	-19	*S-149	-2.1
1974	Hou-N	143	572	66	145	18	10	0	30	37	73	.253	.299	.320	76	-19	9	7	-2	.976	-11	*S-143	-1.3
1975	Hou-N	127	450	54	102	7	9	2	26	41	39	.227	.291	.296	68	-20	4	5	-2	.977	11	*S-126	0.2
1976	Hou-N	152	481	37	101	13	8	0	29	52	63	.210	.287	.270	65	-23	1	1	-0	**.986**	-3	*S-150/2-2	-0.9
1977	Hou-N	97	269	24	50	9	6	0	16	32	24	.186	.272	.264	49	-20	2	0	1	.973	-4	S-96/2-1	-1.4
1978	Hou-N	45	123	11	27	4	1	0	6	12	9	.220	.289	.268	61	-6	2	1	-0	.964	-4	S-42/2-1	-0.6
	SF-N	75	235	17	61	6	1	0	17	12	17	.260	.296	.294	68	-10	8	1	2	.974	-12	S-74	-1.3
	Yr	120	358	28	88	10	2	0	23	24	26	.246	.293	.285	66	-17	8	1	1	.970	-16	S-116/2-1	-1.9
1979	SF-N	94	259	24	65	7	8	0	31	23	31	.251	.312	.340	83	-6	11	3	2	.956	3	S-78,2-10/3	0.6
1980	SF-N	28	27	5	2	0	0	0	0	3	2	.074	.167	.074	-31	-5	0	0	0	.971	3	S-13/2-1	-0.2
Total	11	1219	4201	453	972	101	71	5	254	355	449	.231	.293	.293	67	-188	83	36	3	.976	-36	*S-1173/2-15,3	-8.3

■ WILLIAM METZIG   Metzig, William Andrew b: 12/4/18, Ft.Dodge, Iowa   BR/TR, 6'1", 180 lbs.   Deb: 9/19/44

YEAR	TM/L	G	AB	R	H	2B	3B	HR	RBI	BB	SO	AVG	OBP	SLG	PRO+	BR/A	SB	CS	SBR	FA	FR	G/POS	TPR
1944	Chi-A	5	16	1	2	0	0	0	1	1	4	.125	.176	.125	-13	-2	0	0	0	1.000	2	/2-5	0.0

■ ALEX METZLER   Metzler, Alexander b: 1/4/03, Fresno, Cal.   d: 11/30/73, Fresno, Cal.   BL/TR, 5'9", 167 lbs.   Deb: 9/16/25

YEAR	TM/L	G	AB	R	H	2B	3B	HR	RBI	BB	SO	AVG	OBP	SLG	PRO+	BR/A	SB	CS	SBR	FA	FR	G/POS	TPR
1925	Chi-N	9	38	2	7	2	0	0	2	3	7	.184	.244	.237	23	-4	0	0	0	1.000	2	/O-9	-0.3
1926	Phi-A	20	67	8	16	3	0	0	12	7	5	.239	.311	.284	53	-5	1	0	0	1.000	2	O-17	-0.4
1927	Chi-A	134	543	87	173	29	11	3	61	61	39	.319	.396	.429	117	15	15	11	-2	.965	16	*O-134	1.9
1928	Chi-A	139	464	71	141	18	14	3	55	77	30	.304	.410	.422	121	17	16	8	0	.968	-4	*O-134	0.5
1929	Chi-A	146	568	80	156	23	13	2	49	80	45	.275	.367	.371	92	-5	9	5	-0	.960	1	*O-142	-1.3
1930	Chi-A	56	79	12	14	4	0	0	5	11	6	.177	.278	.228	31	-8	0	2	-1	.969	-5	O-27	-1.4
	StL-A	56	209	30	54	6	3	1	23	21	12	.258	.326	.330	65	-11	5	1	0	.951	-5	O-56	-1.8
	Yr	112	288	42	68	10	3	1	28	32	18	.236	.313	.302	57	-19	5	3	-0	.955	-10	O-83	-3.2
Total	6	560	1968	290	561	85	41	9	207	260	144	.285	.374	.384	97	-0	46	27	-2	.965	6	O-519	-2.8

■ HENSLEY MEULENS   Meulens, Hensley Filemon Acasio "Bam-Bam" b: 6/23/67, Curacao, Neth.Antilles   BR/TR, 6'4", 200 lbs.   Deb: 8/23/89

YEAR	TM/L	G	AB	R	H	2B	3B	HR	RBI	BB	SO	AVG	OBP	SLG	PRO+	BR/A	SB	CS	SBR	FA	FR	G/POS	TPR
1989	NY-A	8	28	2	5	0	0	1	2	8	14	.179	.233	.179	18	-3	0	1	-1	.875	2	/3-8	-0.1
1990	NY-A	23	83	12	20	7	0	3	10	9	25	.241	.337	.434	113	1	1	0	0	.963	3	O-23	0.4
1991	NY-A	96	288	37	64	8	1	6	29	18	97	.222	.277	.319	64	-14	3	0	1	.967	2	O-73,D-13/1	-1.4
1992	NY-A	2	5	1	3	0	0	1	1	1	0	.600	.667	1.200	416	2	0	0	0	1.000	0	/3-2	0.2
1993	NY-A	30	53	8	9	1	1	2	5	8	19	.170	.279	.340	67	-3	0	1	-1	1.000	-4	O-24/1-3,3	-0.8
Total	5	159	457	60	101	16	2	12	46	38	149	.221	.291	.344	75	-16	4	2	0	.970	3	O-120/D-13,31	-1.7

■ IRISH MEUSEL   Meusel, Emil Frederick b: 6/9/1893, Oakland, Cal.   d: 3/1/63, Long Beach, Cal.   BR/TR, 5'11.5", 178 lbs.   Deb: 10/1/14   FC

YEAR	TM/L	G	AB	R	H	2B	3B	HR	RBI	BB	SO	AVG	OBP	SLG	PRO+	BR/A	SB	CS	SBR	FA	FR	G/POS	TPR
1914	Was-A	1	2	0	0	0	0	0	0	0	0	.000	.000	.000	-96	-0	0			1.000	-0	/O-1	-0.1
1918	Phi-N	124	473	48	132	25	6	4	62	30	21	.279	.323	.383	108	3	18			.972	8	*O-120/2-4	0.6
1919	Phi-N	135	521	69	159	26	7	5	59	15	15	.305	.327	.411	113	7	24			.968	-2	*O-128	-0.4
1920	Phi-N	138	518	75	160	27	8	14	69	32	27	.309	.349	.473	129	17	17	11	-2	.929	-5	*O-129/1-3	0.2
1921	Phi-N	84	343	59	121	21	7	12	51	18	17	.353	.385	.560	136	17	8	4	0	.929	2	O-84	1.2
	*NY-N	62	243	37	80	12	6	2	36	15	12	.329	.373	.453	117	6	5	9	-4	.971	-1	O-62	-0.3
	Yr	146	586	96	201	33	13	14	87	33	29	.343	.380	.515	129	23	13	13	-4	.947	1	*O-146	0.9
1922	*NY-N	154	617	100	204	28	17	16	132	35	33	.331	.369	.509	123	19	12	10	-2	.980	-9	*O-154	-0.3
1923	*NY-N	146	595	102	177	22	14	19	**125**	38	16	.297	.341	.477	115	10	8	2	0	.949	-8	*O-145	-0.9
1924	*NY-N	139	549	75	170	26	8	6	102	30	14	.310	.351	.423	109	7	11	7	-1	.967	-7	*O-138	-1.0
1925	NY-N	135	516	82	169	35	8	21	111	26	11	.328	.363	.548	135	24	5	4	-1	.959	1	*O-126	1.4
1926	NY-N	129	449	51	131	16	5	6	65	16	16	.292	.322	.432	103	-0	5			.958	-5	*O-112	-0.3
1927	Bro-N	42	74	7	18	3	1	1	7	11	5	.243	.341	.351	85	-1	0			1.000	-0	O-17	-0.3
Total	11	1289	4900	701	1521	250	93	106	819	269	199	.310	.348	.464	118	107	113	53		.959	-25	*O-1216/2-4,1	-1.2

■ BOB MEUSEL   Meusel, Robert William "Long Bob" b: 7/19/1896, San Jose, Cal.   d: 11/28/77, Downey, Cal.   BR/TR, 6'3", 190 lbs.   Deb: 4/14/20   F

YEAR	TM/L	G	AB	R	H	2B	3B	HR	RBI	BB	SO	AVG	OBP	SLG	PRO+	BR/A	SB	CS	SBR	FA	FR	G/POS	TPR
1920	NY-A	119	460	75	151	40	7	11	83	20	72	.328	.359	.517	126	14	4	4	-1	.947	-10	O-64,3-45/1	0.0
1921	*NY-A	149	598	104	190	40	16	24	135	34	88	.318	.356	.559	128	20	17	6	2	.934	5	*O-147	1.5
1922	*NY-A	121	473	61	151	26	11	16	84	40	58	.319	.376	.522	129	18	13	8	-1	.950	-5	*O-121	0.9
1923	*NY-A	132	460	59	144	29	10	9	91	31	52	.313	.359	.478	117	9	13	15	-5	.953	-7	*O-121	-1.0

YEAR	TM/L	G	AB	R	H	2B	3B	HR	RBI	BB	SO	AVG	OBP	SLG	PRO+	BR/A	SB	CS	SBR	FA	FR	G/POS	TPR
1924	NY-A	143	579	93	188	40	11	12	120	32	43	.325	.365	.494	120	14	26	14	-1	.951	-7	*O-143/3-2	-0.3
1925	NY-A	156	624	101	181	34	12	**33**	**138**	54	55	.290	.348	.542	125	18	13	14	-5	.985	-9	*O-131,3-27	-0.2
1926	*NY-A	108	413	73	130	22	3	12	81	37	32	.315	.373	.470	120	11	16	17	-5	.960	-6	*O-107	-0.7
1927	*NY-A	135	516	75	174	47	9	8	103	45	58	.337	.393	.510	137	27	24	10	1	.950	-4	*O-131	1.5
1928	*NY-A	131	518	77	154	45	5	11	113	39	56	.297	.349	.467	116	10	6	9	-4	.975	4	*O-131	0.2
1929	NY-A	100	391	46	102	15	3	10	57	17	42	.261	.292	.391	79	-14	1	5	-3	.968	3	O-96	-1.9
1930	Cin-N	113	443	62	128	30	8	10	62	26	63	.289	.330	.460	93	-7	9			.962	-4	*O-112	-1.7
Total	11	1407	5475	826	1693	368	95	156	1067	375	619	.309	.356	.497	119	121	142	102		.958	-3	*O-1304/3-74,1	-1.7

■ BENNY MEYER

Meyer, Bernhard "Earache" b: 1/1/1888, Hematite, Mo. d: 2/6/74, Festus, Mo. BR/TR, 5'9", 170 lbs. Deb: 4/9/13 C

YEAR	TM/L	G	AB	R	H	2B	3B	HR	RBI	BB	SO	AVG	OBP	SLG	PRO+	BR/A	SB	CS	SBR	FA	FR	G/POS	TPR
1913	Bro-N	38	87	12	17	0	1	1	10	10	14	.195	.278	.253	51	-5	8			.943	-2	O-26/C-1	-0.9
1914	Bal-F	143	500	76	152	18	10	5	40	71	53	.304	.395	.410	105	6	23			.916	-11	*O-132/S-4	-1.0
1915	Bal-F	35	120	20	29	2	0	0	5	37	13	.242	.424	.258	82	-0	6			.931	-3	O-34	-0.6
	Buf-F	93	333	37	77	8	6	1	29	40	37	.231	.316	.300	64	-17	9			.947	-6	O-88	-3.0
	Yr	128	453	57	106	10	6	1	34	77	50	.234	.348	.289	70	-17	15			.943	-10	*O-122	-3.6
1925	Phi-N	1	1	1	1	1	0	0	0	0	0	1.000	1.000	2.000	594	1	0	0	0	.000	0	/2-1	0.1
Total	4	310	1041	146	276	29	17	7	84	158	117	.265	.365	.346	86	-15	46	0		.931	-22	O-280/S-4,2C	-5.4

■ DAN MEYER

Meyer, Daniel Thomas b: 8/3/52, Hamilton, Ohio BL/TR, 5'11", 180 lbs. Deb: 9/14/74

YEAR	TM/L	G	AB	R	H	2B	3B	HR	RBI	BB	SO	AVG	OBP	SLG	PRO+	BR/A	SB	CS	SBR	FA	FR	G/POS	TPR
1974	Det-A	13	50	5	10	1	1	3	7	1	1	.200	.231	.440	86	-1	1	0	0	.967	1	O-12	-0.1
1975	Det-A	122	470	56	111	17	3	8	47	26	25	.236	.279	.336	70	-19	8	3	1	.950	-0	O-74,1-46	-2.6
1976	Det-A	105	294	37	74	8	4	2	16	17	22	.252	.293	.327	78	-8	10	0	3	.988	-4	O-47,1-19/D	-1.3
1977	Sea-A	159	582	75	159	24	4	22	90	43	51	.273	.324	.442	107	5	11	8	-2	.992	1	*1-159	-0.6
1978	Sea-A	123	444	38	101	18	1	8	56	24	39	.227	.267	.327	66	-21	7	3	0	.989	-2	*1-121/O-2,D	-3.0
1979	Sea-A	144	525	72	146	21	7	20	74	29	35	.278	.321	.459	106	3	11	7	-1	.936	-14	*3-101,O-31,1	-1.4
1980	Sea-A	146	531	56	146	25	6	11	71	31	42	.275	.316	.407	96	-4	8	4	0	.961	-10	*O-123/3-5,1D	-1.9
1981	Sea-A	83	252	26	66	10	1	3	22	10	16	.262	.293	.345	80	-7	4	3	-1	.961	2	3-49,O-14/1D	-1.1
1982	Oak-A	120	383	28	92	17	3	8	59	18	33	.240	.274	.363	77	-13	1	1	-0	.990	-3	1-58,D-38,O	-2.2
1983	Oak-A	69	169	15	32	9	0	1	13	19	11	.189	.271	.260	50	-11	0	0	0	.987	-6	1-41,D-12,O/3	-2.0
1984	Oak-A	20	22	1	7	3	1	0	4	0	2	.318	.318	.545	143	1	0	0	0	.944	0	/1-3,D-1	0.1
1985	Oak-A	14	12	2	0	0	0	0	0	1	0	.000	.077	.000	-83	-3	0	0	0	.000	-0	/3-1,O-1,D	-0.4
Total	12	1118	3734	411	944	153	31	86	459	219	277	.253	.296	.379	86	-80	61	29	1	.991	-38	1-469,O-326,3/D	-16.5

■ GEORGE MEYER

Meyer, George Francis b: 8/3/09, Chicago, Ill. d: 1/3/92, Hoffman Estates, Ill. BR/TR, 5'9", 160 lbs. Deb: 9/3/38

YEAR	TM/L	G	AB	R	H	2B	3B	HR	RBI	BB	SO	AVG	OBP	SLG	PRO+	BR/A	SB	CS	SBR	FA	FR	G/POS	TPR
1938	Chi-A	24	81	10	24	2	2	0	9	11	17	.296	.387	.370	89	-1	3	1	0	.967	6	2-24	0.6

■ DUTCH MEYER

Meyer, Lambert Dalton b: 10/6/15, Waco, Tex. BR/TR, 5'10.5", 181 lbs. Deb: 6/23/37

YEAR	TM/L	G	AB	R	H	2B	3B	HR	RBI	BB	SO	AVG	OBP	SLG	PRO+	BR/A	SB	CS	SBR	FA	FR	G/POS	TPR
1937	Chi-N	1	0	0	0	0	0	0	0	0	0	—	—	—	—	0	0			.000	0	R	0.0
1940	Det-A	23	58	12	15	3	0	0	6	4	10	.259	.317	.310	58	-4	2	0	-1	.960	0	2-21	-0.2
1941	Det-A	46	153	12	29	9	1	1	14	8	13	.190	.230	.281	31	-16	1	1	-0	.972	6	2-40	-0.7
1942	Det-A	14	52	5	17	3	0	2	9	4	4	.327	.386	.500	137	2	0	1	-1	.989	6	2-14	0.9
1945	Cle-A	130	524	71	153	29	8	7	48	40	32	.292	.342	.418	125	15	4	4	-2	.978	-32	*2-130	-1.2
1946	Cle-A	72	207	13	48	5	3	0	16	26	16	.232	.321	.285	75	-7	0	1	-1	.977	-13	2-64	-1.8
Total	6	286	994	113	262	49	12	10	93	82	75	.264	.322	.367	94	-9	5	7		.977	-32	2-269	-3.0

■ LEO MEYER

Meyer, Leo b: 3/29/1888, Iowa d: 9/2/68, Smyrna, Del. TR, Deb: 9/27/09

YEAR	TM/L	G	AB	R	H	2B	3B	HR	RBI	BB	SO	AVG	OBP	SLG	PRO+	BR/A	SB	CS	SBR	FA	FR	G/POS	TPR
1909	Bro-N	7	23	1	3	0	0	0	2	0	2	.130	.200	.130	3	-3	0			.882	2	/S-7	-0.1

■ SCOTT MEYER

Meyer, Scott William b: 8/19/57, Evergreen Park, Ill BR/TR, 6'1", 195 lbs. Deb: 9/10/78

YEAR	TM/L	G	AB	R	H	2B	3B	HR	RBI	BB	SO	AVG	OBP	SLG	PRO+	BR/A	SB	CS	SBR	FA	FR	G/POS	TPR
1978	Oak-A	8	9	1	1	1	0	0	0	1	4	.111	.111	.222	-9	-1	0	0	0	1.000	-1	/C-7	-0.2

■ JOEY MEYER

Meyer, Tanner Joe b: 5/10/62, Honolulu, Hawaii BR/TR, 6'3", 260 lbs. Deb: 4/4/88

YEAR	TM/L	G	AB	R	H	2B	3B	HR	RBI	BB	SO	AVG	OBP	SLG	PRO+	BR/A	SB	CS	SBR	FA	FR	G/POS	TPR
1988	Mil-A	103	327	22	86	18	0	11	45	23	88	.263	.313	.419	102	0	0	1	-1	.986	-0	D-66,1-33	-0.4
1989	Mil-A	53	147	13	33	6	0	7	29	12	36	.224	.283	.408	93	-2	1	0	0	.982	-1	D-31,1-18	-0.4
Total	2	156	474	35	119	24	0	18	74	35	124	.251	.304	.416	100	-2	1	1	-0	.984	-1	/D-97,1-51	-0.8

■ BILLY MEYER

Meyer, William Adam b: 1/14/1892, Knoxville, Tenn. d: 3/31/57, Knoxville, Tenn. BR/TR, 5'9.5", 170 lbs. Deb: 9/6/13 M

YEAR	TM/L	G	AB	R	H	2B	3B	HR	RBI	BB	SO	AVG	OBP	SLG	PRO+	BR/A	SB	CS	SBR	FA	FR	G/POS	TPR
1913	Chi-A	1	1	0	1	0	0	0	0	0	0	1.000	1.000	1.000	490	0	0			.857	1	/C-1	0.1
1916	Phi-A	50	138	6	32	2	2	1	12	8	11	.232	.274	.297	75	-5	3			.961	7	C-48	0.6
1917	Phi-A	62	162	9	38	5	1	0	9	7	14	.235	.271	.278	68	-7	0			.962	9	C-55	0.7
Total	3	113	301	15	71	7	3	1	21	15	25	.236	.274	.289	73	-11	3			.960	18	C-104	1.4

■ LEVI MEYERLE

Meyerle, Levi Samuel "Long Levi" b: 7/1845, Philadelphia, Pa. d: 11/4/21, Philadelphia, Pa. BR/TR, 6'1", 177 lbs. Deb: 5/20/1871

YEAR	TM/L	G	AB	R	H	2B	3B	HR	RBI	BB	SO	AVG	OBP	SLG	PRO+	BR/A	SB	CS	SBR	FA	FR	G/POS	TPR
1871	Ath-n	26	130	45	64	9	3	**4**	40	2	1	**.492**	**.500**	**.700**	243	23	4					*3-26/P-1	**1.4**
1872	Ath-n	27	146	31	48	7	6	1	31	0	1	.329	.329	.479	145	7						O-25/S-1,3	0.6
1873	Phi-n	48	238	53	83	14	4	3	56	2	0	.349	.354	.479	138	10						*3-48/S-1	0.7
1874	Chi-n	53	253	66	102	20	0	1		3		**.403**	**.410**	.494	185	23						2-26,3-14/OS	**1.7**
1875	Phi-n	68	300	55	96	13	9	1		0		.320	.320	.433	152	14						2-32,3-21,1	1.1
1876	Phi-N	55	256	46	87	12	8	0	34	3	2	.340	.347	.449	165	17				.791	-3	*3-49/O-3,2P	1.3
1877	Cin-N	27	107	11	35	7	2	0	15	0	4	.327	.327	.430	154	6				.822	6	S-18,2-12/O	0.7
1884	Phi-U	3	11	0	1	1	0	0	0	0	0	.091	.091	.182	-30	-2				.789	-1	/1-2,O-1	-0.1
Total	5 n	222	1067	250	393	63	22	10	127	7	2	.368	.372	.497	167	77						3-110/2-58,O1SP	5.5
Total	3	85	374	57	123	20	10	0	49	3	6	.329	.334	.436	155	21				.891	-4	/3-49,S-18,2O1P	1.7

■ HENRY MEYERS

Meyers, Henry L. b: 1860, Philadelphia, Pa. d: 6/28/1898, Harrisburg, Pa. Deb: 8/30/1890

YEAR	TM/L	G	AB	R	H	2B	3B	HR	RBI	BB	SO	AVG	OBP	SLG	PRO+	BR/A	SB	CS	SBR	FA	FR	G/POS	TPR
1890	Phi-a	5	19	2	3	0	0	0		1		.158	.238	.158	17	-2	2			.684	-3	/3-5	-0.4

■ CHIEF MEYERS

Meyers, John Tortes b: 7/29/1880, Riverside, Cal. d: 7/25/71, San Bernardino, Cal. BR/TR, 5'11", 194 lbs. Deb: 4/16/09

YEAR	TM/L	G	AB	R	H	2B	3B	HR	RBI	BB	SO	AVG	OBP	SLG	PRO+	BR/A	SB	CS	SBR	FA	FR	G/POS	TPR
1909	NY-N	90	220	15	61	10	5	1	30	22		.277	.359	.382	128	7	3			.963	2	C-64	1.6
1910	NY-N	127	365	25	104	18	0	1	62	40	18	.285	.362	.342	106	4	5			.969	5	*C-117	2.0
1911	*NY-N	133	391	48	130	18	9	1	61	25	33	.332	.392	.432	126	14	7			.979	-3	*C-128	2.2
1912	*NY-N	126	371	60	133	16	5	6	54	47	20	.358	.441	.477	147	26	8			.973	-10	*C-122	2.7
1913	*NY-N	120	378	37	118	18	5	3	47	37	22	.312	.387	.410	127	14	7			.967	1	*C-116	2.6
1914	NY-N	134	381	33	109	13	5	1	55	34	25	.286	.357	.354	116	8	4			.970	-12	*C-128	0.0
1915	NY-N	110	289	24	67	10	5	1	26	26	15	.232	.311	.311	94	-2	4	4	-1	**.986**	-4	C-96	0.6
1916	*Bro-N	80	239	21	59	10	3	0	21	26	15	.247	.336	.314	97	0	2			.984	7	C-74	1.5
1917	Bro-N	47	132	8	28	3	0	0	9	13	7	.212	.283	.235	58	-6	4			.974	-6	C-44	-1.0
	Bos-N	25	68	5	17	4	4	0	4	4	1	.250	.311	.426	133	2	0			1.000	7	C-24	1.2
	Yr	72	200	13	45	7	4	0	13	17	11	.225	.292	.300	82	-4	4			.984	1	C-68	0.2
Total	9	992	2834	276	826	120	41	14	363	274	162	.291	.367	.378	117	67	44	4		.974	-14	C-911	13.4

■ LOU MEYERS

Meyers, Lewis Henry "Crazy Horse" b: 12/9/1859, Cincinnati, Ohio d: 11/30/20, Cincinnati, Ohio BR/TR, 5'11", 165 lbs. Deb: 5/10/1884

YEAR	TM/L	G	AB	R	H	2B	3B	HR	RBI	BB	SO	AVG	OBP	SLG	PRO+	BR/A	SB	CS	SBR	FA	FR	G/POS	TPR
1884	Cin-U	2	3	1	0	0	0	0		0	1	.000	.250	.000	-24	-1				.667	-2	/C-2,O-1	-0.2

■ MICKEY MICELOTTA

Micelotta, Robert Peter b: 10/20/28, Corona, N.Y. BR/TR, 5'11", 185 lbs. Deb: 4/20/54

YEAR	TM/L	G	AB	R	H	2B	3B	HR	RBI	BB	SO	AVG	OBP	SLG	PRO+	BR/A	SB	CS	SBR	FA	FR	G/POS	TPR
1954	Phi-N	13	3	2	0	0	0	0	0	1	1	.000	.250	.000	-28	-1	0	0	0	1.000	0	/S-1	0.0

YEAR	TM/L	G	AB	R	H	2B	3B	HR	RBI	BB	SO	AVG	OBP	SLG	PRO+	BR/A	SB	CS	SBR	FA	FR	G/POS	TPR
1955	Phi-N	4	4	0	0	0	0	0	0	0	0	.000	.000	.000	-99	-1	0	0	0	1.000	0	/S-2	-0.1
Total	2	17	7	2	0	0	0	0	0	1	1	.000	.125	.000	-64	-2	0	0	0	1.000	1	/S-3	-0.1

■ GENE MICHAEL
Michael, Eugene Richard "Stick" b: 6/2/38, Kent, Ohio BB/TR, 6'2", 183 lbs. Deb: 7/15/66 MC

YEAR	TM/L	G	AB	R	H	2B	3B	HR	RBI	BB	SO	AVG	OBP	SLG	PRO+	BR/A	SB	CS	SBR	FA	FR	G/POS	TPR
1966	Pit-N	30	33	9	5	2	1	0	2	0	7	.152	.152	.273	15	-4	0	0	0	.903	5	/S-8,2-2,3	0.2
1967	LA-N	98	223	20	45	3	1	0	7	11	30	.202	.246	.224	39	-18	1	3	-2	.950	5	S-83	-1.0
1968	NY-A	61	116	8	23	3	0	1	8	2	23	.198	.218	.250	43	-8	3	2	-0	.939	-1	S-43/P-1	-0.7
1969	NY-A	119	412	41	112	24	4	2	31	43	56	.272	.342	.364	101	1	7	4	-0	.968	-1	*S-118	1.3
1970	NY-A	134	435	42	93	10	-1	2	38	50	93	.214	.295	.255	56	-26	3	1	0	.957	2	*S-123/3-4,2	-0.9
1971	NY-A	139	456	36	102	15	0	3	35	48	64	.224	.302	.276	69	-18	3	3	-1	.973	17	*S-136	1.6
1972	NY-A	126	391	29	91	7	4	1	32	32	45	.233	.292	.279	73	-13	4	2	0	.969	24	*S-121	3.0
1973	NY-A	129	418	30	94	11	1	3	47	26	51	.225	.270	.278	56	-24	1	3	-2	.965	5	*S-129	-0.5
1974	NY-A	81	177	19	46	9	0	0	13	14	24	.260	.314	.311	83	-4	0	0	0	.970	5	2-45,S-39/3	-1.0
1975	Det-N	56	145	15	31	2	0	3	13	8	28	.214	.255	.290	51	-9	0	0	0	.938	-4	S-44/2-7,3	-1.0
Total	10	973	2806	249	642	86	12	15	226	234	421	.229	.290	.284	66	-124	22	18	-4	.962	55	S-844/2-57,3P	2.5

■ CASS MICHAELS
Michaels, Casimir Eugene (Played In 1943 Under Real Name Of Casimir Eugene Kwietniewski)
b: 3/4/26, Detroit, Mich. d: 11/12/82, Grosse Pointe, Mich. BR/TR, 5'11", 175 lbs. Deb: 8/19/43

YEAR	TM/L	G	AB	R	H	2B	3B	HR	RBI	BB	SO	AVG	OBP	SLG	PRO+	BR/A	SB	CS	SBR	FA	FR	G/POS	TPR
1943	Chi-A	2	7	0	0	0	0	0	0	0	0	.000	.000	.000	-99	-2	0	0	0	1.000	-1	/3-2	-0.4
1944	Chi-A	27	68	4	12	4	1	0	5	2	5	.176	.200	.265	33	-6	0	0	0	.930	6	S-21/3-3	0.1
1945	Chi-A	129	445	47	109	8	5	2	54	37	28	.245	.307	.299	78	-12	8	7	-2	.936	10	*S-126/2-1	0.6
1946	Chi-A	91	291	37	75	8	0	1	22	29	36	.258	.333	.296	80	-7	9	3	1	.957	3	2-66,3-13/S	0.1
1947	Chi-A	110	355	31	97	15	4	3	34	39	28	.273	.350	.363	102	1	10	5	0	.982	11	2-60,3-44/S	1.7
1948	Chi-A	145	484	47	120	12	6	5	56	69	42	.248	.344	.329	82	-11	8	2	1	.957	13	S-85,2-55/O	1.0
1949	Chi-A★	154	561	73	173	27	9	6	83	101	50	.308	.417	.421	126	25	5	7	-3	.976	12	*2-154	3.9
1950	Chi-A	36	138	21	43	6	3	4	19	13	8	.312	.375	.486	122	4	0	0	0	.964	-6	2-35	-0.1
	Was-A★	106	388	48	97	8	4	4	47	55	39	.250	.345	.322	75	-14	2	3	-1	.975	8	*2-104	-0.3
	Yr	142	526	69	140	14	7	8	66	68	47	.266	.352	.365	88	-9	2	3	-1	.972	2	*2-139	-0.4
1951	Was-A	138	485	59	125	20	4	4	45	61	41	.258	.342	.340	86	-8	1	1	-0	.964	-23	*2-128	-2.6
1952	Was-A	22	86	10	20	4	1	0	7	7	15	.233	.290	.337	77	-3	0	0	0	.977	1	2-22	-0.1
	StL-A	55	166	21	44	8	2	3	25	23	16	.265	.354	.392	104	1	1	0	0	.916	-0	3-42/2-8	0.1
	Phi-A	55	200	22	50	4	5	1	18	23	11	.250	.330	.335	80	-5	3	0	1	.993	-13	2-55	-1.5
	Yr	132	452	53	114	16	8	5	50	53	42	.252	.332	.356	89	-7	4	0	1	.989	-13	2-85,3-42	-1.5
1953	Phi-A	117	411	53	103	10	0	12	42	51	56	.251	.335	.363	85	-8	7	0	2	.970	-11	*2-110	-1.1
1954	Chi-A	101	282	35	74	13	2	7	44	56	31	.262	.392	.397	113	7	10	4	1	.958	-4	3-91/2-2	0.2
Total	12	1288	4367	508	1142	147	46	53	501	566	406	.262	.349	.353	92	-39	64	32	0	.973	3	2-800,S-240,3/O	1.6

■ RALPH MICHAELS
Michaels, Ralph Joseph b: 5/3/02, Etna, Pa. d: 8/5/88, Monroeville, Pa. BR/TR, 5'10.5", 178 lbs. Deb: 4/16/24

YEAR	TM/L	G	AB	R	H	2B	3B	HR	RBI	BB	SO	AVG	OBP	SLG	PRO+	BR/A	SB	CS	SBR	FA	FR	G/POS	TPR
1924	Chi-N	8	11	0	4	0	0	0	2	0	1	.364	.364	.364	95	-0	0	0	0	.929	1	/S-4	0.1
1925	Chi-N	22	50	10	14	1	0	0	6	6	9	.280	.357	.300	69	-2	1	0	0	.975	3	3-15/1-1,2S	0.2
1926	Chi-N	2	0	1	0	0	0	0	0	0	0	—	—	—	—	0	0			.000	0	H	0.0
Total	3	32	61	11	18	1	0	0	8	6	10	.295	.358	.311	73	-2	1	0		.933	3	/3-15,S-5,21	0.3

■ ED MICKELSON
Mickelson, Edward Allen b: 9/9/26, Ottawa, Ill. BR/TR, 6'3", 205 lbs. Deb: 9/18/50

YEAR	TM/L	G	AB	R	H	2B	3B	HR	RBI	BB	SO	AVG	OBP	SLG	PRO+	BR/A	SB	CS	SBR	FA	FR	G/POS	TPR
1950	StL-N	5	10	1	1	0	0	0	0	2	3	.100	.250	.100	-4	-1	0			1.000	1	/1-4	-0.1
1953	StL-A	7	15	1	2	1	0	0	2	2	6	.133	.235	.200	18	-2	0	0	0	1.000	0	/1-3	-0.2
1957	Chi-N	6	12	0	0	0	0	0	1	0	4	.000	.000	.000	-99	-3	0	0	0	1.000	1	/1-2	-0.3
Total	3	18	37	2	3	1	0	0	3	4	13	.081	.171	.108	-23	-7	0	0		1.000	2	/1-9	-0.6

■ EZRA MIDKIFF
Midkiff, Ezra Millington "Salt Rock" b: 11/13/1882, Salt Rock, W.Va. d: 3/20/57, Huntington, W.Va. BL/TR, 5'10", 180 lbs. Deb: 10/5/09

YEAR	TM/L	G	AB	R	H	2B	3B	HR	RBI	BB	SO	AVG	OBP	SLG	PRO+	BR/A	SB	CS	SBR	FA	FR	G/POS	TPR
1909	Cin-N	1	2	0	0	0	0	0	0	0		.000	.000	.000	-99	-0	0			.000	-1	/3-1	-0.1
1912	NY-A	21	86	9	21	1	0	0	9	7		.244	.301	.256	56	-5	4			.901	2	3-21	-0.3
1913	NY-A	83	284	22	56	9	1	0	14	12	33	.197	.232	.236	37	-23	9			.957	18	3-76/S-4,2	-0.5
Total	3	105	372	31	77	10	1	0	23	19	33	.207	.247	.239	41	-28	13			.942	18	/3-98,S-4,2	-0.9

■ ED MIERKOWICZ
Mierkowicz, Edward Frank "Butch" or "Mouse" b: 3/6/24, Wyandotte, Mich. BR/TR, 6'4", 205 lbs. Deb: 8/31/45

YEAR	TM/L	G	AB	R	H	2B	3B	HR	RBI	BB	SO	AVG	OBP	SLG	PRO+	BR/A	SB	CS	SBR	FA	FR	G/POS	TPR
1945	*Det-A	10	15	0	2	2	0	0	2	1	3	.133	.188	.267	29	-1	0			1.000	-1	/O-6	-0.3
1947	Det-A	21	42	6	8	1	0	1	1	1	12	.190	.209	.286	36	-4	1	0	0	.947	-1	O-10	-0.5
1948	Det-A	3	5	0	1	0	0	0	1	2	2	.200	.429	.200	69	-0	0	0	0	1.000	0	/O-1	0.0
1950	StL-N	1	1	0	0	0	0	0	0	0	1	.000	.000	.000	-95	-0	0			.000	0	H	0.0
Total	4	35	63	6	11	3	0	2	4	4	18	.175	.224	.270	36	-6	1	0		.968	-2	/O-17	-0.8

■ MATT MIESKE
Mieske, Matthew Todd b: 2/13/68, Midland, Mich. BR/TR, 6', 185 lbs. Deb: 5/3/93

YEAR	TM/L	G	AB	R	H	2B	3B	HR	RBI	BB	SO	AVG	OBP	SLG	PRO+	BR/A	SB	CS	SBR	FA	FR	G/POS	TPR
1993	Mil-A	23	58	9	14	0	0	3	7	4	14	.241	.290	.397	84	-2	0	2	-1	.935	-2	O-22	-0.5
1994	Mil-A	84	259	39	67	13	1	10	38	21	62	.259	.342	.432	90	-4	3	5	-2	.976	-3	O-80/D-1	-1.0
Total	2	107	317	48	81	13	1	13	45	25	76	.256	.316	.426	89	-6	3	7	-3	.967	-5	O-102/D-1	-1.5

■ LARRY MIGGINS
Miggins, Lawrence Edward "Irish" b: 8/20/25, Bronx, N.Y. BR/TR, 6'4", 198 lbs. Deb: 10/3/48

YEAR	TM/L	G	AB	R	H	2B	3B	HR	RBI	BB	SO	AVG	OBP	SLG	PRO+	BR/A	SB	CS	SBR	FA	FR	G/POS	TPR
1948	StL-N	1	1	1	0	0	0	0	0	0	0	.000	.000	.000	-95	-0	0			.000	0	H	0.0
1952	StL-N	42	96	7	22	5	1	2	10	3	19	.229	.253	.365	69	-4	0	1	-1	.967	-4	O-25/1-1	-1.1
Total	2	43	97	8	22	5	1	2	10	3	19	.227	.250	.361	67	-5	0	1		.967	-4	/O-25,1-1	-1.1

■ JOHN MIHALIC
Mihalic, John Michael b: 11/13/11, Cleveland, Ohio d: 4/24/87, Ft.Oglethorpe, Ga. BR/TR, 5'11", 172 lbs. Deb: 9/18/35

YEAR	TM/L	G	AB	R	H	2B	3B	HR	RBI	BB	SO	AVG	OBP	SLG	PRO+	BR/A	SB	CS	SBR	FA	FR	G/POS	TPR
1935	Was-A	6	22	4	5	3	0	0	6	2	3	.227	.292	.364	71	-1	1	0	0	.966	-1	/S-6	-0.1
1936	Was-A	25	88	15	21	2	1	0	8	14	14	.239	.343	.284	60	-5	2	1	0	.972	1	2-25	-0.2
1937	Was-A	38	107	13	27	5	2	0	8	17	9	.252	.355	.336	79	-3	2	1	0	.981	4	2-28/S-3	0.3
Total	3	69	217	32	53	10	3	0	22	33	26	.244	.344	.318	70	-9	5	2	0	.977	4	/2-53,S-9	0.0

■ EDDIE MIKSIS
Miksis, Edward Thomas b: 9/11/26, Burlington, N.J. BR/TR, 6'0.5", 185 lbs. Deb: 6/17/44

YEAR	TM/L	G	AB	R	H	2B	3B	HR	RBI	BB	SO	AVG	OBP	SLG	PRO+	BR/A	SB	CS	SBR	FA	FR	G/POS	TPR
1944	Bro-N	26	91	12	20	2	0	0	11	6	11	.220	.268	.242	45	-7	4			.896	-4	3-15,S-10	-1.0
1946	Bro-N	23	48	3	7	0	0	0	5	3	3	.146	.212	.146	2	-6	0			.970	0	3-13/2-1	-0.6
1947	*Bro-N	45	86	18	23	1	0	4	10	9	8	.267	.337	.419	96	-1	0			1.000	3	2-13,O-11/3S	0.3
1948	Bro-N	86	221	28	47	7	1	2	16	19	27	.213	.278	.281	50	-15	5			.967	4	2-54,3-22/S	-1.0
1949	*Bro-N	50	113	17	25	5	0	1	6	7	8	.221	.267	.292	48	-8	3			.978	6	3-29/S-4,21	-0.3
1950	Bro-N	51	76	13	19	2	1	2	10	5	10	.250	.296	.382	75	-3	3			.964	5	2-15,S-15/3	0.3
1951	Bro-N	19	10	6	2	1	0	0	0	1	2	.200	.333	.300	70	-0	0	0	0	1.000	0	/3-6,2-1	0.2
	Chi-N	102	421	48	112	13	3	4	35	33	36	.266	.319	.340	76	-14	11	5	0	.969	5	*2-102	-0.6
	Yr	121	431	54	114	14	3	4	35	34	38	.265	.320	.339	76	-14	11	5	0	.969	5	*2-103/3-6	-0.4
1952	Chi-N	93	383	44	89	20	1	2	19	20	32	.232	.272	.305	59	-21	4	4	-1	.950	-13	2-54,S-40	-3.1
1953	Chi-N	142	577	61	145	17	6	8	39	33	59	.251	.293	.343	64	-31	13	4	2	.954	-13	2-92,S-53	-3.3
1954	Chi-N	38	99	9	20	3	0	1	9	5	12	.202	.225	.293	33	-10	1	0	0	.961	4	2-21/3-2,O	-0.4
1955	Chi-N	131	481	52	113	14	2	9	41	32	55	.235	.283	.328	62	-27	3	6	-3	**.989**	5	*O-111,3-18	-3.0
1956	Chi-N	114	356	54	85	10	3	9	27	32	40	.239	.303	.360	79	-11	4	2	0	.975	-3	3-48,O-33,2/S	-1.4
1957	StL-N	49	38	3	8	0	0	2	2	7	7	.211	.333	.289	68	-2	0	0	0	1.000	-11	O-31	-1.3
	Bal-A	1	1	0	0	0	0	0	0	0	0	.000	.000	.000	-99	-0	0	0	0	.000	0	H	0.0

YEAR	TM/L	G	AB	R	H	2B	3B	HR	RBI	BB	SO	AVG	OBP	SLG	PRO+	BR/A	SB	CS	SBR	FA	FR	G/POS	TPR
1958	Bal-A	3	2	0	0	0	0	0	0	0	1	.000	.000	.000	-99	-1	0	0	0	.000	0	/S-1	-0.1
	Cin-N	69	50	15	7	0	0	0	4	5	5	.140	.218	.140	-2	-7	1	1	-0	1.000	-4	O-32,3-14/2S1	-1.2
Total	14	1042	3053	383	722	95	17	44	228	215	313	.236	.288	.322	62	-164	52	22		.962	-17	2-382,O-219,3S/1	-16.5

■ HORACE MILAN
Milan, Horace Robert b: 4/7/1894, Linden, Tenn. d: 6/29/55, Texarkana, Ark. BR/TR, 5'9", 175 lbs. Deb: 8/29/15 F

YEAR	TM/L	G	AB	R	H	2B	3B	HR	RBI	BB	SO	AVG	OBP	SLG	PRO+	BR/A	SB	CS	SBR	FA	FR	G/POS	TPR
1915	Was-A	11	27	6	11	1	1	0	7	8	7	.407	.543	.519	214	5	2			1.000	-3	O-10	0.2
1917	Was-A	31	73	8	21	3	1	0	9	4	9	.288	.342	.356	114	1	4			.932	-4	O-23	-0.4
Total	2	42	100	14	32	4	2	0	16	12	16	.320	.404	.400	144	6	6			.944	-6	/O-33	-0.2

■ CLYDE MILAN
Milan, Jesse Clyde "Deerfoot" b: 3/25/1887, Linden, Tenn. d: 3/3/53, Orlando, Fla. BL/TR, 5'9", 168 lbs. Deb: 8/19/07 FMC

YEAR	TM/L	G	AB	R	H	2B	3B	HR	RBI	BB	SO	AVG	OBP	SLG	PRO+	BR/A	SB	CS	SBR	FA	FR	G/POS	TPR
1907	Was-A	48	183	22	51	3	3	0	9	8		.279	.323	.328	117	3	8			.929	4	O-47	0.6
1908	Was-A	130	485	55	116	10	12	1	32	38		.239	.304	.315	110	5	29			.959	9	*O-122	1.1
1909	Was-A	130	400	36	80	12	4	1	15	31		.200	.268	.257	69	-14	10			.972	5	*O-120	-1.6
1910	Was-A	142	531	89	148	17	6	0	16	71		.279	.379	.333	129	22	44			.946	11	*O-142	2.9
1911	Was-A	154	616	109	194	24	8	3	35	74		.315	.395	.394	116	21	58			.957	11	*O-154	2.3
1912	Was-A	154	601	105	184	19	11	1	79	63		.306	.377	.379	116	13	88			.935	4	*O-154	1.3
1913	Was-A	154	579	92	174	18	9	3	54	58	25	.301	.367	.378	116	12	75			.932	-7	*O-154	-0.3
1914	Was-A	115	437	63	129	19	11	1	39	32	26	.295	.346	.396	118	8	38	21	-1	.949	-4	*O-113	-0.2
1915	Was-A	153	573	83	165	13	7	2	66	53	32	.288	.353	.346	107	5	40	19	1	.946	-0	*O-151	-0.2
1916	Was-A	150	565	58	154	14	3	1	45	56	31	.273	.343	.313	98	-0	34	21	-2	.961	17	*O-149	0.7
1917	Was-A	155	579	60	170	15	4	0	48	58	26	.294	.364	.333	114	11	20			.962	-5	*O-153	-0.2
1918	Was-A	128	503	56	146	18	5	0	56	36	14	.290	.344	.346	110	5	26			.972	2	*O-124	0.1
1919	Was-A	88	321	43	92	12	6	0	37	40	16	.287	.371	.361	107	4	11			.953	-3	O-86	-0.5
1920	Was-A	126	506	70	163	22	5	3	41	28	12	.322	.364	.403	106	4	10	12	-4	.971	8	*O-123	-0.2
1921	Was-A	113	406	55	117	19	11	1	40	37	13	.288	.351	.397	95	-4	4	5	-2	.931	2	O-99	-1.0
1922	Was-A	42	74	8	17	5	0	0	5	2	2	.230	.250	.297	44	-6	0	0	0	1.000	1	O-12,M	-0.6
Total	16	1982	7359	1004	2100	240	105	17	617	685	197	.285	.353	.353	109	92	495	78		.953	58	*O-1903	4.2

■ LARRY MILBOURNE
Milbourne, Lawrence William b: 2/14/51, Port Norris, N.J. BB/TR, 6', 165 lbs. Deb: 4/6/74

YEAR	TM/L	G	AB	R	H	2B	3B	HR	RBI	BB	SO	AVG	OBP	SLG	PRO+	BR/A	SB	CS	SBR	FA	FR	G/POS	TPR
1974	Hou-N	112	136	31	38	2	1	0	9	10	14	.279	.329	.309	83	-3	6	2	1	.974	17	2-87/S-8,O	1.7
1975	Hou-N	73	151	17	32	1	2	1	9	6	14	.212	.247	.265	45	-12	1	2	-1	.968	10	2-43,S-22	0.0
1976	Hou-N	59	145	22	36	4	0	0	7	14	10	.248	.319	.276	77	-4	6	1	1	.965	-1	2-32	-0.2
1977	Sea-A	86	242	24	53	10	0	2	21	6	21	.219	.244	.285	44	-19	3	1	0	.982	4	2-41,S-40/3D	-0.9
1978	Sea-A	93	234	31	53	6	2	2	20	9	6	.226	.255	.295	55	-14	5	7	-3	.989	16	3-32,S-23,2D	0.1
1979	Sea-A	123	356	40	99	13	4	2	26	19	20	.278	.315	.354	79	-11	5	3	-0	.981	-17	S-65,2-49,3	-2.0
1980	Sea-A	106	258	31	68	6	6	0	26	19	13	.264	.317	.333	78	-8	7	6	-2	.976	0	2-38,S-34/3D	-0.4
1981	*NY-A	61	163	24	51	7	2	1	12	9	14	.313	.353	.399	118	4	2	0	1	.955	-7	S-39,2-14/3D	0.2
1982	NY-A	14	27	2	4	1	0	0	0	1	4	.148	.179	.185	0	-4	0	1	-1	.917	1	/S-9,2-3,3	-0.3
	Min-A	29	98	9	23	1	1	0	1	7	8	.235	.286	.265	51	-6	1	1	-0	.981	-10	2-26	-1.6
	Cle-A	82	291	29	80	11	4	2	25	12	20	.275	.308	.361	83	-7	2	5	-2	.981	-6	2-63,S-21/3D	-1.1
	Yr	125	416	40	107	13	5	2	26	20	32	.257	.295	.327	70	-17	3	7	-3	.979	-15	2-92,S-30,3/D	-3.0
1983	Phi-N	41	66	3	16	0	1	0	4	4	7	.242	.286	.273	56	-4	2	1	-0	.963	1	2-27/S-8,3	-0.3
	NY-A	31	70	5	14	4	0	0	2	5	10	.200	.263	.257	46	-5	1	1	-0	1.000	0	2-19/S-6,3	-0.1
1984	Sea-A	79	211	22	56	5	1	1	22	12	16	.265	.305	.313	72	-8	0	2	-1	.900	-9	3-40,2-14/SD	-1.8
Total	11	989	2448	290	623	71	24	11	184	133	176	.254	.295	.317	70	-101	41	33	-8	.974	1	2-471,S-280,3/DO	-6.7

■ DON MILES
Miles, Donald Ray b: 3/13/36, Indianapolis, Ind. BL/TR, 6'1", 210 lbs. Deb: 9/9/58

YEAR	TM/L	G	AB	R	H	2B	3B	HR	RBI	BB	SO	AVG	OBP	SLG	PRO+	BR/A	SB	CS	SBR	FA	FR	G/POS	TPR
1958	LA-N	8	22	2	4	0	0	0	0	0	6	.182	.217	.182	7	-3	0	0	0	1.000	2	/O-5	-0.2

■ DEE MILES
Miles, Wilson Daniel b: 2/15/09, Kellerman, Ala. d: 11/2/76, Birmingham, Ala. BL/TR, 6', 175 lbs. Deb: 7/7/35

YEAR	TM/L	G	AB	R	H	2B	3B	HR	RBI	BB	SO	AVG	OBP	SLG	PRO+	BR/A	SB	CS	SBR	FA	FR	G/POS	TPR
1935	Was-A	60	215	28	57	5	2	0	29	7	13	.265	.291	.307	57	-14	6	4	-1	.970	2	O-45	-1.3
1936	Was-A	25	59	8	14	1	2	0	7	1	5	.237	.250	.322	43	-6	0	1	-1	.958	0	O-10	-0.6
1939	Phi-A	106	320	49	96	17	6	1	37	15	17	.300	.331	.400	88	-7	3	4	-2	.968	-7	O-77	-1.6
1940	Phi-A	88	236	26	71	9	6	1	23	8	18	.301	.327	.403	90	-4	1	1	-0	.945	-1	O-50	-0.8
1941	Phi-A	80	170	14	53	7	1	0	15	4	8	.312	.331	.365	86	-4	0	1	-1	1.000	0	O-35	-0.6
1942	Phi-A	99	346	41	94	12	5	0	22	12	10	.272	.300	.335	79	-11	5	3	-0	.984	5	O-81	-1.9
1943	Bos-A	45	121	9	26	2	2	0	10	3	3	.215	.234	.264	45	-9	0	2	-1	.968	-1	O-25	-1.3
Total	7	503	1467	175	411	53	24	2	143	50	74	.280	.306	.353	76	-53	15	16	-5	.971	-10	O-323	-8.1

■ MIKE MILEY
Miley, Michael Wilfred b: 3/30/53, Yazoo City, Miss. d: 1/6/77, Baton Rouge, La. BB/TR, 6'1", 185 lbs. Deb: 7/6/75

YEAR	TM/L	G	AB	R	H	2B	3B	HR	RBI	BB	SO	AVG	OBP	SLG	PRO+	BR/A	SB	CS	SBR	FA	FR	G/POS	TPR
1975	Cal-A	70	224	17	39	3	2	4	26	16	54	.174	.232	.259	42	-18	0	1	-1	.939	-9	S-70	-2.1
1976	Cal-A	14	38	4	7	2	0	0	4	4	8	.184	.262	.237	50	-2	1	0	0	.981	-2	S-14	-0.2
Total	2	84	262	21	46	5	2	4	30	20	62	.176	.237	.256	43	-20	1	1	-0	.945	-11	/S-84	-2.3

■ FELIX MILLAN
Millan, Felix Bernardo (Martinez) b: 8/21/43, Yabucoa, P.R. BR/TR, 5'11", 172 lbs. Deb: 6/2/66

YEAR	TM/L	G	AB	R	H	2B	3B	HR	RBI	BB	SO	AVG	OBP	SLG	PRO+	BR/A	SB	CS	SBR	FA	FR	G/POS	TPR
1966	Atl-N	37	91	20	25	6	0	0	3	2	6	.275	.290	.341	74	-3	3	1	0	.973	-2	2-25/S-1,3	-0.4
1967	Atl-N	41	136	13	32	3	3	2	6	4	10	.235	.268	.346	75	-5	0	3	-2	.972	3	2-41	-0.1
1968	Atl-N	149	570	49	165	22	2	1	33	22	26	.289	.323	.340	99	-1	6	6	-2	.980	3	*2-145	1.0
1969	*Atl-N★	162	652	98	174	23	5	6	57	34	35	.267	.311	.345	83	-15	14	3	2	**.980**	-16	*2-162	-1.6
1970	Atl-N†	142	590	100	183	25	2		37	35	35	.310	.354	.380	91	-7	16	5	2	.979	-19	*2-142	-1.2
1971	Atl-N★	143	577	65	167	20	8	2	45	37	22	.289	.333	.362	92	-6	11	7	-1	.982	6	*2-141	1.2
1972	Atl-N	125	498	46	128	19	3	1	38	23	28	.257	.294	.313	66	-22	6	4	-1	.987	-16	*2-120	-3.5
1973	*NY-N	153	638	82	185	23	4	3	37	35	22	.290	.333	.353	91	-7	2	1	-1	.989	-4	*2-153	-0.3
1974	NY-N	136	518	50	139	15	2	1	33	31	14	.268	.320	.311	78	-15	5	1	1	.979	-20	*2-134	-2.9
1975	NY-N	162	676	81	191	37	2	1	56	36	28	.283	.330	.348	92	-8	1	6	-3	.972	-25	*2-162	-2.8
1976	NY-N	139	531	55	150	25	2	1	35	41	19	.282	.342	.343	101	1	2	4	-2	.977	-24	*2-136	-1.8
1977	NY-N	91	314	40	78	11	2	2	21	18	9	.248	.296	.315	67	-15	1	1	-0	.977	-16	2-89	-2.6
Total	12	1480	5791	699	1617	229	38	22	403	318	242	.279	.324	.343	87	-103	67	43	-6	.980	-129	*2-1450/3-1,S	-15.0

■ FRANK MILLARD
Millard, Frank E. b: 7/4/1865, E.St.Louis, Ill. d: 7/4/1892, Galveston, Tex. Deb: 5/4/1890

YEAR	TM/L	G	AB	R	H	2B	3B	HR	RBI	BB	SO	AVG	OBP	SLG	PRO+	BR/A	SB	CS	SBR	FA	FR	G/POS	TPR
1890	StL-a	1	1	0	0	0	0	0		1		.000	.500	.000	42	0				.625	1	/2-1	0.0

■ DUSTY MILLER
Miller, Charles Bradley b: 9/10/1868, Oil City, Pa. d: 9/3/45, Memphis, Tenn. BL/TR, 5'11.5", 170 lbs. Deb: 9/23/1889

YEAR	TM/L	G	AB	R	H	2B	3B	HR	RBI	BB	SO	AVG	OBP	SLG	PRO+	BR/A	SB	CS	SBR	FA	FR	G/POS	TPR
1889	Bal-a	11	40	4	6	1	1	0	6	2	11	.150	.209	.225	23	-4	3			.636	-7	/S-8,O-3	-1.0
1890	StL-a	26	96	17	21	5	3	1		8		.219	.279	.365	78	-4	3			.872	3	O-24/S-3	-0.2
1895	Cin-N	132	529	103	177	31	16	10	112	33	34	.335	.378	.510	123	14	43			.937	11	*O-132	1.2
1896	Cin-N	125	504	91	162	38	12	4	93	33	30	.321	.368	.468	112	6	76			.902	-2	*O-125	-0.5
1897	Cin-N	119	440	83	139	27	1	4	70	48		.316	.393	.409	105	3	29			.929	2	*O-119	-0.3
1898	Cin-N	152	586	99	175	24	12	3	90	38		.299	.351	.396	106	3	32			.929	8	*O-152	0.0
1899	Cin-N	80	323	44	81	12	5	0	37	9		.251	.278	.319	62	-18	18			.927	7	O-80	-1.5
	StL-N	10	39	3	8	1	0	0	9	3		.205	.279	.231	40	-3	1			.875	-1	O-10	-0.5
	Yr	90	362	47	89	13	5	0	40	12		.246	.278	.309	60	-21	19			.921	6	O-90	-2.0
Total	7	655	2557	444	769	139	50	22	411	174	75	.301	.352	.420	102	-3	206			.923	21	O-645/S-11	-2.8

YEAR	TM/L	G	AB	R	H	2B	3B	HR	RBI	BB	SO	AVG	OBP	SLG	PRO+	BR/A	SB	CS	SBR	FA	FR	G/POS	TPR

■ BRUCE MILLER
Miller, Charles Bruce b: 3/4/47, Fort Wayne, Ind.   BR/TR, 6'1", 185 lbs.   Deb: 8/4/73

YEAR	TM/L	G	AB	R	H	2B	3B	HR	RBI	BB	SO	AVG	OBP	SLG	PRO+	BR/A	SB	CS	SBR	FA	FR	G/POS	TPR
1973	SF-N	12	21	1	3	0	0	0	2	2	3	.143	.217	.143	2	-3	0	0	0	.900	1	/3-4,2-3,S	-0.2
1974	SF-N	73	198	19	55	7	1	0	16	11	15	.278	.319	.323	76	-6	1	1	-0	.938	13	3-41,S-13/2	0.8
1975	SF-N	99	309	22	74	6	3	1	31	15	26	.239	.277	.288	55	-19	0	1	-1	.949	10	3-68,2-21/S	-0.9
1976	SF-N	12	25	1	4	1	0	0	2	2	5	.160	.222	.200	20	-3	0	0	0	.920	-1	/2-8,3-2	-0.4
Total	4	196	553	43	136	14	4	1	51	30	49	.246	.287	.291	59	-30	1	2	-1	.944	22	3-115/2-41,S	-0.7

■ CHARLIE MILLER
Miller, Charles Elmer b: 1/4/1892, Warrensburg, Mo.   d: 4/23/72, Warrensburg, Mo.   TR,   Deb: 9/18/12

YEAR	TM/L	G	AB	R	H	2B	3B	HR	RBI	BB	SO	AVG	OBP	SLG	PRO+	BR/A	SB	CS	SBR	FA	FR	G/POS	TPR
1912	StL-A	1	2	0	0	0	0	0	0	0		.000	.000	.000	-99	-1	0			1.000	-0	/S-1	-0.1

■ CHARLIE MILLER
Miller, Charles Hess b: 12/30/1877, Conestoga, Pa.   d: 1/13/51, Millersville, Pa.   BR/TR, 6', 190 lbs.   Deb: 10/2/15

YEAR	TM/L	G	AB	R	H	2B	3B	HR	RBI	BB	SO	AVG	OBP	SLG	PRO+	BR/A	SB	CS	SBR	FA	FR	G/POS	TPR
1915	Bal-F	1	1	0	0	0	0	0	0	0	0	.000	.000	.000	-97	-0	0			.000	0	H	0.0

■ CHUCK MILLER
Miller, Charles Marion b: 9/18/1889, Woodville, Ohio   d: 6/16/61, Houston, Tex.   BL/TL, 5'8.5", 155 lbs.   Deb: 9/19/13

YEAR	TM/L	G	AB	R	H	2B	3B	HR	RBI	BB	SO	AVG	OBP	SLG	PRO+	BR/A	SB	CS	SBR	FA	FR	G/POS	TPR
1913	StL-N	4	12	0	2	0	0	0	1	0	2	.167	.167	.167	-5	-2	0			1.000	-1	/O-3	-0.3
1914	StL-N	36	36	4	7	1	0	0	2	3	9	.194	.256	.222	43	-2	2			1.000	-3	O-14	-0.6
Total	2	40	48	4	9	1	0	0	3	3	11	.188	.235	.208	31	-4	2			1.000	-4	/O-17	-0.9

■ DUSTY MILLER
Miller, Dakin Evans b: 9/3/1876, Malvern, Iowa   d: 4/19/50, Stockton, Cal.   BL/TR, 5'10", 175 lbs.   Deb: 4/17/02

YEAR	TM/L	G	AB	R	H	2B	3B	HR	RBI	BB	SO	AVG	OBP	SLG	PRO+	BR/A	SB	CS	SBR	FA	FR	G/POS	TPR
1902	Chi-N	51	187	17	46	4	1	0	13	7		.246	.299	.278	80	-4	10			.955	1	O-51	-0.7

■ DARRELL MILLER
Miller, Darrell Keith b: 2/26/58, Washington, D.C.   BR/TR, 6'2", 200 lbs.   Deb: 8/14/84

YEAR	TM/L	G	AB	R	H	2B	3B	HR	RBI	BB	SO	AVG	OBP	SLG	PRO+	BR/A	SB	CS	SBR	FA	FR	G/POS	TPR
1984	Cal-A	17	41	5	7	0	0	0	1	4	9	.171	.244	.171	17	-5	0	0	0	.990	-1	1-16/O-1	-0.6
1985	Cal-A	51	48	8	18	2	1	2	7	1	10	.375	.400	.583	166	4	0	1	-1	.952	-11	O-45/C-1,3D	-0.7
1986	Cal-A	33	57	6	13	2	1	0	4	4	8	.228	.279	.298	58	-3	0	0	0	1.000	-10	C-23,O-10/D	-1.3
1987	Cal-A	53	108	14	26	5	0	4	16	9	13	.241	.311	.398	89	-2	1	0		.984	-6	C-33,O-18/3D	-0.6
1988	Cal-A	70	140	21	31	4	1	2	7	9	29	.221	.292	.307	70	-6	2	1	0	.987	3	C-53,O-8,D	0.0
Total	5	224	394	54	95	13	3	8	35	27	69	.241	.303	.350	80	-11	3	2	-0	.987	-25	/C-97,O-95,1D3	-3.2

■ BING MILLER
Miller, Edmund John b: 8/30/1894, Vinton, Iowa   d: 5/7/66, Philadelphia, Pa.   BR/TR, 6', 185 lbs.   Deb: 4/16/21   FC

YEAR	TM/L	G	AB	R	H	2B	3B	HR	RBI	BB	SO	AVG	OBP	SLG	PRO+	BR/A	SB	CS	SBR	FA	FR	G/POS	TPR
1921	Was-A	114	420	57	121	28	8	9	71	25	50	.288	.334	.457	105	1	3	4	-2	.945	2	*O-109	-0.6
1922	Phi-A	143	535	90	179	29	12	21	90	24	42	.335	.371	.551	134	24	10	10	-3	.977	5	*O-139	1.5
1923	Phi-A	123	458	68	137	25	4	12	64	27	34	.299	.344	.450	106	2	9	3	1	.978	-1	*O-119	-0.5
1924	Phi-A	113	398	62	136	22	4	6	62	12	24	.342	.376	.462	114	7	11	5	0	.973	-2	O-94/1-7	-0.1
1925	Phi-A	124	474	78	151	29	10	10	81	19	14	.319	.355	.485	105	1	11	6	-0	.975	-10	*O-115,1-12	-1.6
1926	Phi-A	38	110	13	32	6	2	2	13	11	6	.291	.355	.436	100	-0	4	1	1	1.000	-5	O-34/1-1	-0.6
	StL-A	94	353	60	117	27	5	4	50	22	12	.331	.382	.470	116	8	7	9	-3	.939	4	O-94	0.2
	Yr	132	463	73	149	33	7	6	63	33	18	.322	.375	.462	112	7	11	10	-3	.950	-1	O-128/1-1	-0.4
1927	StL-A	143	492	83	160	32	7	5	75	30	26	.325	.375	.449	109	6	8	7	-2	.970	4	*O-126	0.1
1928	Phi-A	139	510	76	168	34	7	8	85	27	24	.329	.372	.471	117	12	10	6	-1	.968	0	*O-133	0.3
1929	*Phi-A	147	556	84	186	32	16	8	93	40	25	.335	.383	.493	120	15	24	9	2	.970	6	*O-145	1.3
1930	*Phi-A	154	585	89	177	38	7	9	100	47	22	.303	.357	.438	96	-4	13	13	-4	.976	5	*O-154	-1.2
1931	*Phi-A	137	534	75	150	43	5	8	77	36	16	.281	.338	.425	94	-6	5	3	-0	.987	6	*O-137	-0.9
1932	Phi-A	95	305	40	90	17	4	7	58	20	11	.295	.343	.446	99	-1	7	3	0	.979	1	O-84	-0.4
1933	Phi-A	67	120	22	33	7	1	2	17	12	7	.275	.344	.400	96	-1	4	2	0	1.000	-6	O-30/1-6	-0.8
1934	Phi-A	81	177	22	43	10	2	1	22	16	14	.243	.309	.339	70	-8	1	0	0	1.000	-3	O-46	-1.2
1935	Bos-A	78	138	18	42	8	1	3	26	10	8	.304	.356	.442	99	-1	0	1	-1	.962	-2	O-29	-0.4
1936	Bos-A	30	47	9	14	2	1	1	6	5	5	.298	.377	.447	97	-0	0	0	0	1.000	-3	O-13	-0.3
Total	16	1820	6212	946	1936	389	96	116	990	383	340	.312	.359	.461	108	54	127	82	-11	.971	4	*O-1601/1-26	-5.2

■ EDDIE MILLER
Miller, Edward Lee b: 6/29/57, San Pablo, Cal.   BB/TR, 5'9", 175 lbs.   Deb: 9/5/77

YEAR	TM/L	G	AB	R	H	2B	3B	HR	RBI	BB	SO	AVG	OBP	SLG	PRO+	BR/A	SB	CS	SBR	FA	FR	G/POS	TPR
1977	Tex-A	17	6	7	2	0	0	0	1	1	1	.333	.429	.333	110	0	3	1	0	1.000	-0	/O-2,D-3	0.0
1978	Atl-N	6	21	5	3	1	0	0	2	2	4	.143	.250	.190	29	-2	3	0	1	1.000	-1	/O-5	-0.2
1979	Atl-N	27	113	12	35	1	0	0	5	5	24	.310	.350	.319	78	-3	15	2	3	.988	3	O-27	0.2
1980	Atl-N	11	19	3	3	0	0	0	0	0	5	.158	.158	.158	-11	-3	1	2	-1	1.000	-3	/O-9	-0.8
1981	Atl-N	50	134	29	31	3	1	0	7	7	20	.231	.285	.269	56	-8	23	5	4	.985	-1	O-36	-0.7
1982	Det-A	14	25	3	1	0	0	0	0	4	4	.040	.250	.040	-14	-4	0	3	-2	1.000	-0	/O-8,D-1	-0.6
1984	SD-N	13	14	4	4	0	1	1	2	0	4	.286	.286	.643	155	1	4	0	1	1.000	-1	/O-8	0.1
Total	7	138	332	63	79	5	2	1	17	19	71	.238	.297	.274	57	-18	49	13	7	.989	-4	/O-95,D-4	-2.0

■ EDDIE MILLER
Miller, Edward Robert "Eppie" b: 11/26/16, Pittsburgh, Pa.   BR/TR, 5'9", 180 lbs.   Deb: 9/9/36

YEAR	TM/L	G	AB	R	H	2B	3B	HR	RBI	BB	SO	AVG	OBP	SLG	PRO+	BR/A	SB	CS	SBR	FA	FR	G/POS	TPR
1936	Cin-N	5	10	0	1	0	0	0	0	1	1	.100	.182	.100	-24	-2	0			.938	-0	/S-4,2-1	-0.2
1937	Cin-N	36	60	3	9	3	1	0	5	3	8	.150	.190	.233	15	-7	0			.926	7	S-30/3-4	0.1
1939	Bos-N	77	296	32	79	12	2	4	31	16	21	.267	.315	.361	88	-6	4			.970	12	S-77	1.3
1940	Bos-N★	151	569	78	157	33	3	14	79	41	43	.276	.330	.418	111	7	8			.970	15	*S-151	3.5
1941	Bos-N★	154	585	54	140	27	3	6	68	35	72	.239	.288	.326	76	-20	8			.966	12	*S-154	0.4
1942	Bos-N★	142	534	47	130	28	2	6	47	22	40	.243	.279	.337	81	-15	11			.983	4	*S-142	-0.2
1943	Cin-N★	154	576	49	129	26	4	2	71	33	43	.224	.270	.293	64	-28	8			.979	27	*S-154	1.1
1944	Cin-N†	155	536	48	112	21	5	4	55	41	41	.209	.269	.289	59	-30	9			.971	12	*S-155	-0.5
1945	Cin-N	115	421	46	100	27	2	13	49	18	42	.238	.275	.404	89	-9	4			.975	5	*S-115	0.5
1946	Cin-N†	91	299	30	58	10	0	6	36	25	34	.194	.258	.288	57	-18	5			.970	24	S-88	1.1
1947	Cin-N†	151	545	69	146	38	4	19	87	49	40	.268	.333	.457	109	5	5			.972	-5	*S-151	0.7
1948	Phi-N	130	468	45	115	20	1	14	61	19	40	.246	.281	.382	99	-15	1			.966	-14	*S-122	-2.2
1949	Phi-N	85	266	21	55	10	1	6	29	29	21	.207	.294	.320	66	-13	1			.986	-10	2-82/S-1	-2.0
1950	StL-N	64	172	17	39	8	0	3	22	19	21	.227	.307	.326	64	-9	0			.980	14	S-51/2-1	0.8
Total	14	1510	5337	539	1270	263	28	97	640	351	465	.238	.290	.352	80	-160	64			.972	102	*S-1395/2-84,3	4.4

■ ED MILLER
Miller, Edwin J. "Big Ed" b: 11/24/1888, Annville, Pa.   d: 4/17/80, S.Lebanon Twsp, Pa   BR/TR, 6', 180 lbs.   Deb: 6/29/12

YEAR	TM/L	G	AB	R	H	2B	3B	HR	RBI	BB	SO	AVG	OBP	SLG	PRO+	BR/A	SB	CS	SBR	FA	FR	G/POS	TPR
1912	StL-A	13	46	4	9	1	0	0	5	2		.196	.245	.217	34	-4	1			.951	-4	/1-8,S-5	-0.8
1914	StL-A	41	58	8	8	0	1	0	4	4	13	.138	.219	.172	18	-6	1	3	-2	.981	-2	/1-8,2-5,O3	-1.0
1918	Cle-A	32	96	9	22	4	3	0	3	12	10	.229	.321	.333	89	-1	2			.977	1	1-22/O-4	-0.2
Total	3	86	200	21	39	5	4	0	12	18	23	.195	.275	.260	58	-11	4	3		.972	-5	/1-38,O-9,2S3	-2.0

■ ELMER MILLER
Miller, Elmer b: 7/28/1890, Sandusky, Ohio   d: 11/28/44, Beloit, Wis.   BR/TR, 6', 175 lbs.   Deb: 4/26/12

YEAR	TM/L	G	AB	R	H	2B	3B	HR	RBI	BB	SO	AVG	OBP	SLG	PRO+	BR/A	SB	CS	SBR	FA	FR	G/POS	TPR
1912	StL-N	12	37	5	7	1	0	0	3	4	9	.189	.268	.216	34	-3	1			1.000	0	O-11	-0.4
1915	NY-A	26	83	4	12	1	0	0	3	4	14	.145	.193	.157	5	-10	0			.955	-4	O-26	-1.7
1916	NY-A	43	152	12	34	3	2	1	18	11	18	.224	.280	.289	70	-6	8			.969	-3	O-42	-0.3
1917	NY-A	114	379	43	95	11	3	3	35	40	44	.251	.336	.319	99	1	11			.961	-6	O-112	-1.2
1918	NY-A	67	202	18	49	9	2	1	22	19	17	.243	.317	.322	91	-0	2			.947	-4	O-62	-0.2
1921	*NY-A	56	242	41	72	9	8	4	36	19	16	.298	.356	.450	102	0	2	2	-1	.947	3	O-56	-0.1
1922	NY-A	51	172	31	46	7	3	3	18	11	12	.267	.311	.384	79	-6	2	3	-1	.982	-5	O-51	-1.2
	Bos-A	44	147	16	28	2	3	4	16	5	11	.190	.222	.327	42	-13	3	1	-0	.957	1	O-35	-1.6
	Yr	95	319	47	74	9	5	7	34	16	23	.232	.271	.357	62	-19	5	4	-1	.970	-2	O-86	-2.8
Total	7	413	1414	170	343	43	20	16	151	113	140	.243	.307	.335	80	-40	29	6		.960	-0	O-395	-6.7

YEAR	TM/L	G	AB	R	H	2B	3B	HR	RBI	BB	SO	AVG	OBP	SLG	PRO+	BR/A	SB	CS	SBR	FA	FR	G/POS	TPR

■ **ELMER MILLER**   Miller, Elmer Joseph "Lefty"   b: 4/17/03, Detroit, Mich.   d: 1/8/87, Corona, Cal.   BL/TL, 5'11", 189 lbs.   Deb: 6/21/29

1929	Phi-N	31	38	3	9	1	0	1	4	1	5	.237	.256	.342	44	-3	0			.750	2	/P-8,O-4	-0.1

■ **KOHLY MILLER**   Miller, Frank E.   b: 1/1874, Philadelphia, Pa.   d: 3/29/51, Reading, Pa.   Deb: 9/16/1892

1892	Was-N	1	3	0	0	0	0	0	0	0	1	.000	.000	.000	-99	-1	0			.400	-1	/S-1	-0.2
	StL-N	1	4	0	0	0	0	0	0	0		.000	.000	.000	-99	-1	0			.500	-1	/3-1	-0.2
	Yr	2	7	0	0	0	0	0	0	0	1	.000	.000	.000	-99	-2	0			.400	-2	/S-1,3-1	-0.4
1897	Phi-N	3	11	2	2	0	0	0	1	2		.182	.308	.182	32	-1	0			.857	-2	/2-3	-0.3
Total	2	5	18	2	2	0	0	0	1	2	1	.111	.200	.111	-13	-3	0			.857	-5	/2-3,3-1,S	-0.7

■ **GEORGE MILLER**   Miller, George C.   b: 2/19/1853, Newport, Ky.   d: 7/24/29, Norwood, Ohio   BR/TR, 5'5", 160 lbs.   Deb: 9/6/1877

1877	Cin-N	11	37	4	6	1	0	0	3	5	2	.162	.262	.189	50	-1				.918	0	C-11	-0.1
1884	Cin-a	6	20	6	5	1	1	0		1		.250	.318	.400	127	1				.975	2	/C-6	0.3
Total	2	17	57	10	11	2	1	0	3	6	2	.193	.281	.263	79	-1				.938	2	/C-17	0.2

■ **DOGGIE MILLER**   Miller, George Frederick "Foghorn" or "Calliope"   b: 8/15/1864, Brooklyn, N.Y.   d: 4/6/09, Brooklyn, N.Y.   BR/TR, 5'6", 145 lbs.   Deb: 5/1/1884   M

1884	Pit-a	89	347	46	78	10	2	0		13		.225	.257	.265	69	-12				.798	-5	O-49,C-36/32	-1.3
1885	Pit-a	42	166	19	27	3	1	0		4		.163	.182	.193	19	-15				.893	-5	C-33/O-6,S3	-1.5
1886	Pit-a	83	317	70	80	15	1	2		43		.252	.348	.325	110	5	35			.918	-22	C-61,O-23/2	-0.9
1887	Pit-N	87	342	58	83	17	4	1	34	35	13	.243	.317	.325	83	-6	33			.928	-22	C-73,O-14/3	-1.9
1888	Pit-N	103	404	50	112	17	5	0	36	18	16	.277	.319	.344	121	10	27			.908	-15	C-68,O-32/3	0.0
1889	Pit-N	104	422	77	113	25	3	6	56	31	11	.268	.321	.384	107	3	16			.889	-5	C-76,O-27/3	0.4
1890	Pit-N	138	549	85	150	24	3	4	66	66	11	.273	.357	.350	120	17	32			.850	1	3-88,O-25,SC/2	2.0
1891	Pit-N	135	548	80	156	19	6	4	57	59	26	.285	.357	.363	113	10	35			.938	-16	C-41,S-37,30/1	0.1
1892	Pit-N	149	623	103	158	15	12	2	59	69	14	.254	.335	.326	100	1	28			.906	-11	O-76,C-63,S/3	-0.7
1893	Pit-N	41	154	23	28	6	1	0	17	17	8	.182	.268	.234	39	-13	3			.916	-0	C-40	-0.8
1894	StL-N	127	481	93	163	9	11	3	86	58	9	.339	.414	.453	109	9	17			.832	-14	3-52,C-41,21/OSM	-2.7
1895	StL-N	121	490	81	143	15	4	5	74	25	12	.292	.334	.369	82	-13	18			.829	-23	3-46,C-46,O/S1	-1.4
1896	Lou-N	98	324	54	89	17	4	1	33	27	9	.275	.334	.361	87	-6	16			.922	-16	C-48,2-25/O31S	-8.7
Total	13	1317	5167	839	1380	192	57	33	518	467	129	.267	.333	.345	97	-12	260			.918	-153	C-636,O-309,3/S21	-8.7

■ **HUGHIE MILLER**   Miller, Hugh Stanley "Cotton"   b: 12/28/1887, St.Louis, Mo.   d: 12/24/45, Jefferson Barracks, Mo.   BR/TR, 6'1.5", 175 lbs.   Deb: 6/18/11

1911	Phi-N	1	0	0	0	0	0	0	0	0		—	—	—			0			.000	0	R	0.0
1914	StL-F	132	490	51	109	20	5	0	46	27	57	.222	.264	.284	40	-44	4			.990	0	*1-130	-5.0
1915	StL-F	7	6	0	3	1	0	0	3	0	0	.500	.500	.667	200	1	0			1.000	-0	/1-6	0.1
Total	3	140	496	51	112	21	5	0	49	27	57	.226	.267	.288	42	-43	4			.990	-0	1-136	-4.9

■ **JAKE MILLER**   Miller, Jacob George (b: Jacob George Munzing)   b: 12/1/1895, Baltimore, Md.   d: 8/24/74, Towson, Md.   BR/TR, 5'10", 170 lbs.   Deb: 7/16/22

1922	Pit-N	3	11	0	1	0	0	0	0	2		.091	.231	.091	-14	-2	1	0	0	.889	0	/O-3	-0.2

■ **HACK MILLER**   Miller, James Eldridge   b: 2/13/13, Celeste, Tex.   d: 11/21/66, Dallas, Tex.   BR/TR, 5'11.5", 215 lbs.   Deb: 4/18/44

1944	Det-A	5	5	1	1	0	0	1	3	1	1	.200	.333	.800	207	1	0	0	0	1.000	0	/C-5	0.1
1945	Det-A	2	4	0	3	0	0	0	1	0		.750	.750	.750	315	1	0	0	0	1.000	-0	/C-2	0.1
Total	2	7	9	1	4	0	0	1	4	1	1	.444	.500	.778	250	2	0	0	0	1.000	-0	/C-7	0.2

■ **JIM MILLER**   Miller, James McCurdy "Rabbit"   b: 10/2/1880, Pittsburgh, Pa.   d: 2/7/37, Pittsburgh, Pa.   BR/TR, 5'8", 165 lbs.   Deb: 9/9/01

1901	NY-N	18	58	3	8	0	0	0	3	6		.138	.219	.138	5	-7	1			.936	-2	2-18	-0.8

■ **JOHN MILLER**   Miller, John Allen   b: 3/14/44, Alhambra, Cal.   BR/TR, 5'11", 195 lbs.   Deb: 9/11/66

1966	NY-A	6	23	1	2	0	0	1	2	0	9	.087	.087	.217	-16	-3	0	0	0	1.000	-1	/1-3,O-3	-0.5
1969	LA-N	26	38	3	8	1	0	1	1	2	9	.211	.250	.316	62	-2	0	0	0	1.000	-2	/O-6,1-5,32	-0.5
Total	2	32	61	4	10	1	0	2	3	2	18	.164	.190	.279	33	-6	0	0	0	1.000	-3	/O-9,1-8,32	-1.0

■ **DOTS MILLER**   Miller, John Barney   b: 9/9/1886, Kearny, N.J.   d: 9/5/23, Saranac Lake, N.Y.   BR/TR, 5'11.5", 170 lbs.   Deb: 4/16/09

1909	*Pit-N	151	560	71	156	31	13	3	87	39		.279	.329	.396	115	8	14			.953	-11	*2-150	-0.7
1910	Pit-N	120	444	45	101	13	10	1	48	33	41	.227	.284	.309	69	-19	11			.946	-19	*2-119/1-1,S	-4.2
1911	Pit-N	137	470	82	126	17	8	6	78	51	48	.268	.348	.377	99	-1	17			.943	-6	*2-129	-1.0
1912	Pit-N	148	567	74	156	33	12	4	87	37	45	.275	.324	.397	98	-4	18			.985	1	*1-147	-0.5
1913	Pit-N	154	580	75	158	24	20	7	90	37	52	.272	.317	.419	114	8	20			.985	-4	*1-150/S-3	0.2
1914	StL-N	155	573	67	166	27	10	4	88	34	52	.290	.339	.393	119	12	16			.993	0	1-91,S-60/2	1.6
1915	StL-N	150	553	73	146	17	10	2	72	43	48	.264	.324	.342	101	1	27	19	-3	.991	4	1-94,2-55/3S	0.2
1916	StL-N	143	505	47	120	22	7	1	46	40	49	.238	.300	.315	89	-6	18			.993	-3	1-93,2-38,S/3	-0.6
1917	StL-N	148	544	61	135	15	9	2	45	33	52	.248	.295	.320	91	-6	14			.960	19	2-92,1-46,S	1.7
1919	StL-N	101	346	38	80	10	4	1	24	13	23	.231	.265	.292	72	-13	6			.981	2	1-68,2-28	-1.4
1920	Phi-N	98	343	41	87	12	2	1	27	16	17	.254	.289	.309	68	-14	13	6	0	.948	-9	2-59,3-17,S/10	-2.1
1921	Phi-N	84	320	37	95	11	3	0	23	15	27	.297	.330	.350	74	-11	3	5	-2	.940	1	3-41,1-38/2	-1.1
Total	12	1589	5805	711	1526	232	108	32	715	391	454	.263	.314	.357	95	-46	177	30		.988	-21	1-737,2-681,S/30	-8.0

■ **JOE MILLER**   Miller, Joseph A.   b: 2/17/1861, Baltimore, Md.   d: 4/23/28, Wheeling, W.Va.   BR, 5'9.5", 165 lbs.   Deb: 5/1/1884

1884	Tol-a	105	423	46	101	12	8	1		26		.239	.284	.312	91	-4				.864	1	*S-105	-0.2
1885	Lou-a	98	339	44	62	9	5	0		28		.183	.249	.239	55	-17				.891	3	*S-79,3-11/2	-1.1
Total	2	203	762	90	163	21	13	1		54		.214	.269	.280	75	-21				.876	4	S-184/3-11,2	-1.3

■ **JOE MILLER**   Miller, Joseph Wick   b: 7/24/1850, Germany   d: 8/30/1891, White Bear Lake, Minn.   5'10.5", 169 lbs.   Deb: 6/26/1872   M

1872	Nat-n	1	4	0	1	0	0	0	0	0	0	.250	.250	.250	47	-0						/1-1,M	0.0
1875	Wes-n	13	50	4	6	1	0	0		0		.120	.120	.140	-10	-5						2-13	-0.5
	Chi-n	15	53	1	8	0	0	0		0		.151	.151	.151	5	-5						2-14/O-2	-0.4
	Yr	28	103	5	14	1	0	0		0		.136	.136	.146	-3	-10						2-27/O-2	-0.9
Total	2 n	29	107	5	15	1	0	0		0		.140	.140	.150	-0	-11						/2-27,O-2,1	-0.9

■ **KEITH MILLER**   Miller, Keith Alan   b: 6/12/63, Midland, Mich.   BR/TR, 5'11", 180 lbs.   Deb: 6/16/87

1987	NY-N	25	51	14	19	2	2	0	1	2	6	.373	.407	.490	144	3	8	1	2	.967	2	2-16	0.7
1988	NY-N	40	70	9	15	1	1	1	5	6	10	.214	.276	.300	69	-3	0	5	-3	.946	-7	2-16/S-8,3O	-1.4
1989	NY-N	57	143	15	33	7	0	1	7	5	27	.231	.262	.301	63	-7	6	0	2	.967	-4	2-23,O-14/S3	-0.9
1990	NY-N	88	233	42	60	8	0	1	12	23	46	.258	.329	.305	76	-7	16	3	3	.980	5	O-61,2-11/S	0.0
1991	NY-N	98	275	41	77	22	1	4	23	23	44	.280	.347	.411	113	5	14	4	2	.972	3	2-60,O-28/3S	0.8
1992	KC-A	106	416	57	118	24	4	4	38	31	46	.284	.354	.389	105	3	16	6	1	.971	-20	2-93,O-16/D	-1.4
1993	KC-A	37	108	9	18	3	0	0	3	8	19	.167	.231	.194	15	-13	3	1	0	.889	-6	3-21,O-4,2D	-1.8
1994	KC-A	5	15	1	2	0	0	0			3	.133	.133	.133	-29	-3	0	0	0	1.000	1	/O-4,3-2	-0.2
Total	8	456	1311	188	342	67	8	11	89	98	201	.261	.324	.349	87	-21	63	20	7	.969	-28	2-222,O-128/3SD	-4.2

■ **ED MILLER**   Miller, L. Edward   b: Tecumseh, Mich.   Deb: 7/18/1884

1884	Tol-a	8	24	2	6	0	0	0		1		.250	.280	.250	72	-1				.615	-1	/O-8	-0.1

YEAR	TM/L	G	AB	R	H	2B	3B	HR	RBI	BB	SO	AVG	OBP	SLG	PRO+	BR/A	SB	CS	SBR	FA	FR	G/POS	TPR

■ HACK MILLER   Miller, Lawrence H.   b: 1/1/1894, New York, N.Y.   d: 9/17/71, Oakland, Cal.   BR/TR, 5'9", 195 lbs.   Deb: 9/22/16

1916	Bro-N	3	3	0	1	0	1	0	1	1	1	.333	.500	1.000	345	1	0			1.000	-1	/O-3	0.0
1918	*Bos-A	12	29	2	8	2	0	0	4	0	4	.276	.276	.345	89	-1	0			1.000	-3	O-10	-0.4
1922	Chi-N	122	466	61	164	28	5	12	78	26	39	.352	.389	.511	128	18	3	3	-1	.959	-3	*O-116	0.6
1923	Chi-N	135	485	74	146	24	2	20	88	27	39	.301	.343	.482	116	9	6	5	-1	.978	6	*O-129	0.4
1924	Chi-N	53	131	17	44	8	1	4	25	8	11	.336	.379	.504	133	6	0	1	-1	.948	-4	O-32	0.0
1925	Chi-N	24	86	10	24	3	2	2	9	2	9	.279	.303	.430	84	-2	0	1	-1	.878	-3	O-21	-0.7
Total	6	349	1200	164	387	65	11	38	205	64	103	.322	.361	.490	120	31	10	9		.962	-8	O-311	-0.1

■ LEMMIE MILLER   Miller, Lemmie Earl   b: 6/2/60, Dallas, Tex.   BR/TR, 6'1", 190 lbs.   Deb: 5/22/84

| 1984 | LA-N | 8 | 12 | 1 | 2 | 0 | 0 | 0 | 0 | 1 | 2 | .167 | .231 | .167 | 13 | -1 | 0 | 0 | 0 | 1.000 | -1 | /O-5 | -0.3 |

■ OTTO MILLER   Miller, Lowell Otto "Moonie"   b: 6/1/1889, Minden, Neb.   d: 3/29/62, Brooklyn, N.Y.   BR/TR, 6', 196 lbs.   Deb: 7/16/10   C

1910	Bro-N	31	66	5	11	3	0	0	2	2	19	.167	.203	.212	22	-7	1			.987	9	C-28	0.4
1911	Bro-N	25	62	7	13	2	2	0	8	0	4	.210	.210	.306	46	-5	2			.927	-3	C-22	-0.6
1912	Bro-N	98	316	35	88	18	1	1	31	18	50	.278	.325	.351	88	-6	11			.975	13	C-94	1.6
1913	Bro-N	104	320	26	87	11	7	0	26	10	31	.272	.294	.350	81	-9	7			.971	14	*C-103/1-1	1.4
1914	Bro-N	54	169	17	39	6	1	0	9	7	20	.231	.261	.278	59	-9	0			.964	0	C-50/1-1	-0.5
1915	Bro-N	84	254	20	57	4	6	0	25	6	26	.224	.245	.287	60	-13	3			.981	8	C-83	0.2
1916	*Bro-N	73	216	16	55	9	2	1	17	7	29	.255	.281	.329	85	-4	6			.968	4	C-69	0.5
1917	Bro-N	92	274	19	63	9	4	1	17	14	29	.230	.272	.288	70	-10	5			.979	1	C-91	-0.2
1918	Bro-N	75	228	8	44	6	1	0	8	9	20	.193	.230	.228	40	-16	1			.972	-4	C-62/1-1	-0.8
1919	Bro-N	51	164	18	37	5	0	0	5	7	14	.226	.257	.256	53	-9	2			.966	2	C-51	-0.3
1920	*Bro-N	90	301	16	87	9	2	0	33	9	18	.289	.312	.332	82	-7	0	5	-3	**.986**	-2	C-89	-0.6
1921	Bro-N	91	286	22	67	8	6	1	27	9	26	.234	.257	.315	50	-21	2	1	0	.972	9	C-91	-0.7
1922	Bro-N	59	180	20	47	11	1	1	23	6	13	.261	.285	.350	63	-10	0			.968	3	C-57	-0.4
Total	13	927	2836	229	695	97	33	5	231	104	301	.245	.275	.308	67	-125	40	6		.973	62	C-890/1-3	-0.4

■ KEITH MILLER   Miller, Neal Keith   b: 3/7/63, Dallas, Tex.   BB/TR, 5'11", 175 lbs.   Deb: 4/23/88

1988	Phi-N	47	48	4	8	0	0	0	6	5	13	.167	.245	.229	36	-4	0	0	0	1.000	-3	/O-4,3-3,S	-0.8
1989	Phi-N	8	10	0	3	1	0	0	0	0	3	.300	.300	.400	98	-0	0	0	0	1.000	-1	/O-2	-0.1
Total	2	55	58	4	11	4	0	0	6	5	16	.190	.254	.259	47	-4	0	0	0	1.000	-4	/O-6,3-3,S	-0.9

■ NORM MILLER   Miller, Norman Calvin   b: 2/5/46, Los Angeles, Cal.   BL/TR, 5'11", 195 lbs.   Deb: 9/11/65

1965	Hou-N	11	15	2	3	0	1	0	1	1	7	.200	.250	.333	67	-1	0	0	0	1.000	-0	/O-2	-0.1
1966	Hou-N	11	34	1	5	0	0	1	3	2	8	.147	.194	.235	20	-4	0	0	0	1.000	-4	/O-8,3-2	-0.4
1967	Hou-N	64	190	15	39	9	3	1	14	19	42	.205	.278	.300	68	-8	2	0	1	.967	1	O-53	-1.0
1968	Hou-N	79	257	35	61	18	2	6	28	22	48	.237	.310	.393	112	3	6	5	-1	.971	-3	O-74	-0.5
1969	Hou-N	119	409	58	108	21	4	4	50	47	77	.264	.350	.364	102	3	2	4	-1	.984	-1	*O-114	-0.7
1970	Hou-N	90	226	29	54	9	0	4	29	41	33	.239	.358	.332	90	-2	3	1	0	.947	-5	O-72/C-1	-0.9
1971	Hou-N	45	74	5	19	5	0	2	5	6	13	.257	.313	.405	105	-0	2	0	0	1.000	-5	O-20/C-1	-0.5
1972	Hou-N	67	107	18	26	4	0	4	13	13	23	.243	.331	.393	107	1	1	0	0	1.000	-4	O-29	-0.4
1973	Hou-N	3	3	0	0	0	0	0	0	0	0	.000	.000	.000	-99	-1	0	0	0	.000	-0	/O-1	-0.1
	Atl-N	9	8	2	3	1	0	1	6	3	3	.375	.545	.875	267	2	0	0	0	.667	-0	/O-1	0.2
	Yr	12	11	2	3	1	0	1	6	3	3	.273	.429	.636	181	1	0	0	0	.667	-1	/O-2	0.1
1974	Atl-N	42	41	1	7	1	0	1	5	7	9	.171	.292	.268	55	-2	0	0	0	1.000	-1	/O-4	-0.3
Total	10	540	1364	166	325	68	10	24	159	160	265	.238	.325	.356	95	-9	16	10	-1	.972	-18	O-378/C-2,3	-4.7

■ ORLANDO MILLER   Miller, Orlando Salmon (Dixon)   b: 1/13/69, Changuinola, Pan.   BR/TR, 6'1", 180 lbs.   Deb: 7/8/94

| 1994 | Hou-N | 16 | 40 | 3 | 13 | 0 | 1 | 2 | 9 | 2 | 12 | .325 | .386 | .525 | 138 | 2 | 1 | 0 | 0 | 1.000 | -1 | S-11/2-3 | 0.2 |

■ OTTO MILLER   Miller, Otis Louis   b: 2/2/01, Belleville, Ill.   d: 7/26/59, Belleville, Ill.   BR/TR, 5'10.5", 168 lbs.   Deb: 4/17/27

1927	StL-A	51	76	8	17	5	0	0	8	8	5	.224	.306	.289	53	-5	0	1	-1	.938	-4	S-35,3-11	-0.8
1930	Bos-A	112	370	49	106	22	5	0	40	26	21	.286	.333	.373	82	-10	2	4	-2	.948	-6	3-83,2-15	-1.1
1931	Bos-A	107	389	38	106	12	1	0	43	15	20	.272	.301	.308	64	-21	1	1	-0	.953	-1	3-75,2-25	-1.5
1932	Bos-A	2	2	0	0	0	0	0	0	0	0	.000	.000	.000	-99	-1	0	0	0	.000	0	H	-0.1
Total	4	272	837	95	229	39	6	0	91	49	46	.274	.315	.335	71	-36	3	6	-3	.949	-11	3-169/2-40,S	-3.5

■ RALPH MILLER   Miller, Ralph Joseph   b: 2/29/1896, Ft.Wayne, Ind.   d: 3/18/39, Ft.Wayne, Ind.   BR/TR, 6', 190 lbs.   Deb: 4/14/20

1920	Phi-N	97	338	28	74	14	1	0	28	11	32	.219	.246	.266	45	-24	3	4	-2	.940	0	3-91/1-3,SO	-2.3
1921	Phi-N	57	204	19	62	10	0	3	26	6	10	.304	.327	.397	84	-5	3	5	-2	.910	0	S-46,3-10	-0.2
1924	*Was-A	9	15	1	2	0	0	0	0	1	1	.133	.188	.133	-17	-3	0	0	0	.941	0	/2-3	-0.2
Total	3	163	557	48	138	24	1	3	54	18	43	.248	.274	.311	59	-31	6	9	-4	.927	1	3-101/S-48,210	-2.7

■ RAY MILLER   Miller, Raymond Peter   b: 2/12/1888, Pittsburgh, Pa.   d: 4/7/27, Pittsburgh, Pa.   BL/TL, 5'10", 168 lbs.   Deb: 4/14/17

1917	Cle-A	19	21	1	4	1	0	0	2	8	3	.190	.414	.238	92	0	0			1.000	1	/1-4	0.2
	Pit-N	6	27	1	4	1	0	0	0	2	3	.148	.207	.185	20	-3	0			1.000	0	/1-6	-0.3
Total	1	25	48	2	8	2	0	0	2	10	6	.167	.310	.208	56	-2	0			1.000	2	/1-10	-0.1

■ RICK MILLER   Miller, Richard Alan   b: 4/19/48, Grand Rapids, Mich.   BL/TL, 6', 185 lbs.   Deb: 9/4/71

1971	Bos-A	15	33	9	11	5	0	1	7	8	8	.333	.463	.576	180	4	0	2	-1	.969	1	O-14	0.3
1972	Bos-A	89	98	13	21	4	1	3	15	11	27	.214	.294	.367	91	-1	0	2	-1	.967	-11	O-75	-1.7
1973	Bos-A	143	441	65	115	17	7	6	43	51	59	.261	.341	.372	95	-2	12	7	-1	.978	-4	*O-137	-1.3
1974	Bos-A	114	280	41	73	8	1	5	22	37	47	.261	.347	.350	94	-1	13	2	3	.989	2	*O-105	0.2
1975	*Bos-A	77	108	21	21	2	1	0	15	21	20	.194	.326	.231	55	-6	3	2	-0	.981	-8	O-65	-1.6
1976	Bos-A	105	269	40	76	15	3	0	27	34	47	.283	.363	.361	100	1	11	10	-3	.991	5	O-82/D-4	0.0
1977	Bos-A	86	189	34	48	9	3	0	24	22	30	.254	.341	.333	76	-6	11	5	0	.992	-7	O-79/D-1	-1.5
1978	Cal-A	132	475	66	125	25	4	1	37	54	70	.263	.343	.339	96	-1	3	13	-7	.989	15	*O-129	0.2
1979	*Cal-A	120	427	60	125	15	5	2	28	50	69	.293	.368	.365	102	3	5	4	-1	.989	10	*O-117	0.7
1980	Cal-A	129	412	52	113	14	3	2	38	48	71	.274	.351	.397	92	-3	7	3	0	.984	5	*O-118	-0.2
1981	Bos-A	97	316	38	92	17	2	2	33	28	36	.291	.351	.377	103	3	3	5	-2	.987	-3	O-95	-0.7
1982	Bos-A	135	409	50	104	18	2	4	38	40	41	.254	.324	.325	75	-14	5	6	-2	.983	-6	*O-127	-2.5
1983	Bos-A	104	262	41	75	10	2	2	21	28	30	.286	.357	.363	92	-2	3	3	-1	.993	0	O-66/1-2,D	-0.5
1984	Bos-A	95	123	17	32	5	1	0	12	17	22	.260	.350	.317	82	-2	1	1	0	.974	-7	O-31/1-8	-1.1
1985	Bos-A	41	45	5	15	2	0	0	9	5	6	.333	.400	.378	110	1	1	0	0	1.000	-2	/O-8,D-4	-0.1
Total	15	1482	3887	552	1046	161	35	28	369	454	583	.269	.348	.350	92	-29	78	65	-16	.986	-10	*O-1248/D-11,1	-10.0

■ ROD MILLER   Miller, Rodney Carter   b: 1/16/40, Portland, Ore.   BL/TR, 5'10", 160 lbs.   Deb: 9/28/57

| 1957 | Bro-N | 1 | 1 | 0 | 0 | 0 | 0 | 0 | 0 | 0 | 1 | .000 | .000 | .000 | -91 | -0 | 0 | 0 | 0 | .000 | 0 | H | 0.0 |

■ DOC MILLER   Miller, Roy Oscar   b: 2/4/1883, Chatham, Ontario, Canada   d: 7/31/38, Jersey City, N.J.   BL/TL, 5'10.5", 170 lbs.   Deb: 5/4/10

1910	Chi-N	1	1	0	0	0	0	0	0	0	0	.000	.000	.000	-99	-0	0			.000	0	H	0.0
	Bos-N	130	482	48	138	27	4	3	55	33	52	.286	.333	.378	102	-0	17			.951	-12	*O-130	-1.9
	Yr	131	483	48	138	27	4	3	55	33	52	.286	.333	.377	102	-0	17			.951	-12	*O-130	-1.9
1911	Bos-N	146	577	69	**192**	36	3	7	91	43	43	.333	.379	.442	120	13	32			.961	2	*O-146	0.8

YEAR	TM/L	G	AB	R	H	2B	3B	HR	RBI	BB	SO	AVG	OBP	SLG	PRO+	BR/A	SB	CS	SBR	FA	FR	G/POS	TPR
1912	Bos-N	51	201	26	47	8	1	2	24	14	17	.234	.287	.313	63	-11	6			.948	3	O-50	-1.1
	Phi-N	67	177	24	51	12	5	0	21	9	13	.288	.323	.412	94	-2	3			.986	2	O-40	-0.2
	Yr	118	378	50	98	20	6	2	45	23	30	.259	.303	.360	78	-13	9			.964	5	O-90	-1.3
1913	Phi-N	69	87	9	30	6	0	0	11	6	6	.345	.400	.414	127	3	2			.800	-4	O-12	-0.1
1914	Cin-N	93	192	30	49	7	2	0	33	16	18	.255	.313	.313	83	-4	4			.976	-4	O-47	-1.1
Total	5	557	1717	184	507	96	15	12	235	121	149	.295	.343	.390	102	-0	64			.958	-13	O-425	-3.6

■ RUDY MILLER
Miller, Rudel Charles   b: 7/12/1900, Kalamazoo, Mich.   d: 1/22/94, Kalamazoo, Mich.   BR/TR, 6'1", 180 lbs.   Deb: 9/19/29

YEAR	TM/L	G	AB	R	H	2B	3B	HR	RBI	BB	SO	AVG	OBP	SLG	PRO+	BR/A	SB	CS	SBR	FA	FR	G/POS	TPR
1929	Phi-A	2	4	1	1	0	0	0	1	3	0	.250	.571	.250	115	0	0	0	0	.750	-0	/3-2	0.0

■ TOM MILLER
Miller, Thomas P. "Reddy"   b: Philadelphia, Pa.   d: 5/29/1876, Philadelphia, Pa.   Deb: 10/24/1874

YEAR	TM/L	G	AB	R	H	2B	3B	HR	RBI	BB	SO	AVG	OBP	SLG	PRO+	BR/A	SB	CS	SBR	FA	FR	G/POS	TPR
1874	Ath-n	4	16	1	8	0	0	0		0		.500	.500	.500	202	2						C-4	0.1
1875	StL-n	55	212	17	34	2	0	0		2		.160	.168	.170	19	-16						*C-52/3-3	-1.2
Total	2 n	59	228	18	42	2	0	0		2		.184	.191	.193	35	-14						/C-56,3-3	-1.1

■ TOM MILLER
Miller, Thomas Royall   b: 7/5/1897, Powhatan Court House, Va.   d: 8/13/80, Richmond, Va.   BL/TR, 5'11", 180 lbs.   Deb: 7/29/18

YEAR	TM/L	G	AB	R	H	2B	3B	HR	RBI	BB	SO	AVG	OBP	SLG	PRO+	BR/A	SB	CS	SBR	FA	FR	G/POS	TPR
1918	Bos-N	2	2	0	0	0	0	0	0	0	0	.000	.000	.000	-99	-0	1			.000	0	H	-0.1
1919	Bos-N	7	6	2	2	0	0	0	0	0	1	.333	.333	.333	105	0	0			.000	0	H	0.0
Total	2	9	8	2	2	0	0	0	0	0	1	.250	.250	.250	53	0	1				0	-0,-0	-0.1

■ WARD MILLER
Miller, Ward Taylor "Windy" or "Grump"   b: 7/5/1884, Mt.Carroll, Ill.   d: 9/4/58, Dixon, Ill.   BL/TR, 5'11", 177 lbs.   Deb: 4/14/09

YEAR	TM/L	G	AB	R	H	2B	3B	HR	RBI	BB	SO	AVG	OBP	SLG	PRO+	BR/A	SB	CS	SBR	FA	FR	G/POS	TPR
1909	Pit-N	15	56	2	8	0	1	0	4	4		.143	.213	.179	20	-5	2			.967	-1	O-14	-0.8
	Cin-N	43	113	17	35	3	1	0	4	6		.310	.345	.354	118	2	9			.981	-7	O-26	-0.6
	Yr	58	169	19	43	3	2	0	8	10		.254	.300	.296	84	-3	11			.976	-8	O-40	-1.4
1910	Cin-N	81	126	21	30	6	0	0	10	22	13	.238	.356	.286	92	-0	10			.944	2	O-64	0.0
1912	Chi-N	86	241	45	74	11	4	0	22	26	18	.307	.377	.386	109	4	11			.943	-8	O-64	-0.8
1913	Chi-N	80	203	23	48	5	7	1	16	34	33	.236	.349	.345	98	1	13			.980	3	O-63	0.2
1914	StL-F	121	402	49	118	17	7	4	50	59	36	.294	.397	.400	102	3	18			.953	10	*O-111	0.9
1915	StL-F	154	536	80	164	19	9	1	63	79	39	.306	.400	.381	104	7	33			.963	3	*O-154	0.2
1916	StL-A	146	485	72	129	17	5	1	50	72	76	.266	.371	.328	116	13	25	21	-5	.943	-5	*O-136	-0.6
1917	StL-A	43	82	13	17	1	1	1	2	16	15	.207	.350	.280	96	0	7			.966	-4	O-25	-0.5
Total	8	769	2244	322	623	79	35	8	221	318	230	.278	.375	.355	104	24	128	21		.957	-8	O-619	-2.0

■ WARREN MILLER
Miller, Warren Lemuel "Gitz"   b: 7/14/1885, Philadelphia, Pa.   d: 8/12/56, Philadelphia, Pa.   BL/TL, 5'10", 160 lbs.   Deb: 7/29/09

YEAR	TM/L	G	AB	R	H	2B	3B	HR	RBI	BB	SO	AVG	OBP	SLG	PRO+	BR/A	SB	CS	SBR	FA	FR	G/POS	TPR
1909	Was-A	26	51	5	11	0	0	0	1	4		.216	.216	.216	57	-2	0			1.000	-1	O-15	-0.5
1911	Was-A	21	34	3	5	0	0	0	0	0		.147	.147	.147	-18	-5	0			.778	-2	/O-9	-0.7
Total	2	47	85	8	16	0	0	0	1	4		.188	.225	.188	25	-8	0			.931	-3	/O-24	-1.2

■ BILL MILLER
Miller, William Alexander   b: 5/23/1879, Germany   d: 9/8/57, Ashtabula, Ohio   BL/TL, 6'2", 170 lbs.   Deb: 8/23/02

YEAR	TM/L	G	AB	R	H	2B	3B	HR	RBI	BB	SO	AVG	OBP	SLG	PRO+	BR/A	SB	CS	SBR	FA	FR	G/POS	TPR
1902	Pit-N	1	5	0	1	0	0	0	2	0		.200	.200	.200	23	-0	0			.000	-0	/O-1	-0.1

■ JOE MILLETTE
Millette, Joseph Anthony   b: 8/12/66, Walnut Creek, Cal.   BR/TR, 6'1", 180 lbs.   Deb: 7/16/92

YEAR	TM/L	G	AB	R	H	2B	3B	HR	RBI	BB	SO	AVG	OBP	SLG	PRO+	BR/A	SB	CS	SBR	FA	FR	G/POS	TPR
1992	Phi-N	33	78	5	16	0	0	0	2	5	10	.205	.271	.205	37	-6	1	0	0	.974	10	S-26/3-3,2	0.6
1993	Phi-N	10	10	3	2	0	0	0	2	1	2	.200	.273	.200	29	-1	0	0	0	1.000	3	/S-7,3-3	0.3
Total	2	43	88	8	18	0	0	0	4	6	12	.205	.271	.205	36	-7	1	0	0	.978	13	/S-33,3-6,2	0.9

■ WALLY MILLIES
Millies, Walter Louis   b: 10/18/06, Chicago, Ill.   BR/TR, 5'10.5", 170 lbs.   Deb: 9/23/34

YEAR	TM/L	G	AB	R	H	2B	3B	HR	RBI	BB	SO	AVG	OBP	SLG	PRO+	BR/A	SB	CS	SBR	FA	FR	G/POS	TPR
1934	Bro-N	2	7	0	0	0	0	0	0	0	0	.000	.000	.000	-99	-2	0			1.000	1	/C-2	-0.1
1936	Was-A	74	215	26	67	10	2	0	25	11	8	.312	.345	.377	83	-6	1	0	0	.968	1	C-72	-0.2
1937	Was-A	59	179	21	40	7	1	0	28	9	15	.223	.261	.274	36	-18	1	0	0	.971	2	C-56	-1.2
1939	Phi-N	84	205	12	48	3	0	0	12	9	5	.234	.267	.249	41	-17	0			.964	-7	C-84	-2.1
1940	Phi-N	26	43	1	3	0	0	0	0	6	3	.070	.149	.070	-39	-8	0			.958	2	C-24	-0.5
1941	Phi-N	1	2	0	0	0	0	0	0	0	1	.000	.000	.000	-99	-1	0			.800	0	/C-1	0.0
Total	6	246	651	60	158	20	3	0	65	33	32	.243	.280	.283	47	-51	2	0		.966	-2	C-239	-4.1

■ JOCKO MILLIGAN
Milligan, John   b: 8/8/1861, Philadelphia, Pa.   d: 8/29/23, Philadelphia, Pa.   BR/TR, 6', 192 lbs.   Deb: 5/1/1884

YEAR	TM/L	G	AB	R	H	2B	3B	HR	RBI	BB	SO	AVG	OBP	SLG	PRO+	BR/A	SB	CS	SBR	FA	FR	G/POS	TPR
1884	Phi-a	66	268	39	77	20	3	3		8		.287	.308	.418	127	6				**.939**	13	C-65/O-1	2.3
1885	Phi-a	67	265	35	71	15	4	2		7		.268	.289	.377	103	-0				.935	11	C-61/1-6,O	1.4
1886	Phi-a	75	301	52	76	17	3	5		21		.252	.301	.379	111	3	18			.919	5	C-40,1-29/O3	0.7
1887	Phi-a	95	377	54	114	27	4	2		21		.302	.344	.411	110	4	8			.966	3	1-50,C-47/O	0.5
1888	*StL-a	63	219	19	55	6	2	5	37	17		.251	.311	.365	105	-0	3			.941	8	C-58/1-5	1.1
1889	StL-a	72	273	53	100	30	2	12	76	16	19	.366	.408	.623	170	21	2			.933	14	C-66/1-9	3.3
1890	Phi-P	62	234	38	69	9	3	3	57	19	19	.295	.363	.397	101	-0	2			.893	4	C-59/1-3	0.7
1891	Phi-a	118	455	75	138	**35**	12	11	106	56	51	.303	.397	.505	153	30	2			.939	0	C-87,1-32	3.1
1892	Was-N	88	323	40	89	20	9	4	43	26	24	.276	.335	.430	135	12	2			.947	5	C-59,1-28	1.9
1893	Bal-N	24	102	19	25	5	2	1	19	5	7	.245	.294	.363	73	-5	2			.981	1	1-22/C-1	-0.3
	NY-N	42	147	16	34	5	6	1	25	14	13	.231	.302	.367	77	-6	2			.934	14	C-42	0.9
	Yr	66	249	35	59	10	8	2	44	19	20	.237	.299	.365	76	-10	4			.932	15	C-43,1-22	0.6
Total	10	772	2964	440	848	189	50	49	363	210	133	.286	.341	.433	122	65	41			.930	78	C-585,1-184/O3	15.6

■ RANDY MILLIGAN
Milligan, Randy Andre   b: 11/27/61, San Diego, Cal.   BR/TR, 6'2", 230 lbs.   Deb: 9/12/87

YEAR	TM/L	G	AB	R	H	2B	3B	HR	RBI	BB	SO	AVG	OBP	SLG	PRO+	BR/A	SB	CS	SBR	FA	FR	G/POS	TPR
1987	NY-N	3	1	0	0	0	0	0	0	1	1	.000	.500	.000	49	0	0	0	0	.000	0	/H	0.0
1988	Pit-N	40	82	10	18	5	0	3	8	20	24	.220	.379	.390	123	3	1	2	-1	.987	-1	1-25/O-2	0.0
1989	Bal-A	124	365	56	98	23	5	12	45	74	75	.268	.396	.458	144	24	9	5	-0	.995	2	*1-117/D-1	1.7
1990	Bal-A	109	362	64	96	20	1	20	60	88	68	.265	.412	.492	157	31	6	3	0	.990	4	1-98/D-9	2.9
1991	Bal-A	141	483	57	127	17	2	16	70	84	108	.263	.374	.406	121	16	0	5	-3	.990	3	*1-106,D-25/O	0.8
1992	Bal-A	137	462	71	111	21	1	11	53	106	81	.240	.386	.361	108	10	0	1	-1	.994	-6	*1-129/D-6	-0.6
1993	Cin-N	83	234	30	64	11	1	6	29	46	49	.274	.395	.406	115	7	0	2	-1	.994	-1	1-61/O-9	0.6
	Cle-A	19	47	7	20	7	0	1	7	14	4	.426	.557	.574	206	8	0	0	0	1.000	-1	1-18/D-1	0.6
1994	Mon-N	47	82	10	19	2	0	1	12	14	21	.232	.344	.329	75	-3	0	0	0	.978	2	1-33	-0.2
Total	8	703	2118	305	553	106	10	70	284	447	431	.261	.393	.420	127	97	16	18	-6	.992	9	1-587/D-42,O	5.8

■ JACK MILLS
Mills, Abbott Paige   b: 10/23/1889, S.Williamstown, Mass.   d: 6/3/73, Washington, D.C.   BL/TR, 6', 165 lbs.   Deb: 7/1/11

YEAR	TM/L	G	AB	R	H	2B	3B	HR	RBI	BB	SO	AVG	OBP	SLG	PRO+	BR/A	SB	CS	SBR	FA	FR	G/POS	TPR
1911	Cle-A	13	17	5	5	0	0	0	1	1		.294	.368	.294	85	-0	1			1.000	2	/3-7	0.1

■ CHARLIE MILLS
Mills, Charles   b: Brooklyn, N.Y.   d: 4/10/1874, Brooklyn, N.Y.   6',   Deb: 5/18/1871   U

YEAR	TM/L	G	AB	R	H	2B	3B	HR	RBI	BB	SO	AVG	OBP	SLG	PRO+	BR/A	SB	CS	SBR	FA	FR	G/POS	TPR
1871	Mut-n	32	146	27	36	4	3	0	22	1	0	.247	.252	.315	68	-5	2					*C-28/O-3,2	-0.3
1872	Mut-n	6	31	6	4	0	0	0	2	0	1	.129	.129	.129	-22	-4						/O-5,C-2	-0.3
Total	2 n	38	177	33	40	4	3	0	24	1		.226	.230	.282	53	-9						/C-30,O-8,2	-0.6

■ BUSTER MILLS
Mills, Colonel Buster "Bus"   b: 9/16/08, Ranger, Tex.   d: 12/1/91, Arlington, Tex.   BR/TR, 5'11.5", 195 lbs.   Deb: 4/18/34   MC

YEAR	TM/L	G	AB	R	H	2B	3B	HR	RBI	BB	SO	AVG	OBP	SLG	PRO+	BR/A	SB	CS	SBR	FA	FR	G/POS	TPR
1934	StL-N	29	72	7	17	4	1	1	8	4	11	.236	.295	.361	70	-3	0			1.000	-0	O-18	-0.4
1935	Bro-N	17	56	12	12	2	1	1	7	5	11	.214	.323	.339	80	-1	0			.971	-2	O-17	-0.4
1937	Bos-N	123	505	85	149	25	8	7	58	46	41	.295	.361	.418	92	-6	11	8	-2	.946	-5	*O-120	-1.5
1938	StL-A	123	466	66	133	24	4	3	46	43	46	.285	.350	.373	81	-13	7	8	-3	.964	3	*O-113	-1.5
1940	NY-A	34	63	10	25	3	1	1	15	7	5	.397	.457	.587	176	7	0	0	0	1.000	-2	O-14	0.4

YEAR	TM/L	G	AB	R	H	2B	3B	HR	RBI	BB	SO	AVG	OBP	SLG	PRO+	BR/A	SB	CS	SBR	FA	FR	G/POS	TPR
1942	Cle-A	80	195	19	54	4	2	1	26	23	18	.277	.353	.333	99	0	5	4	-1	.973	2	O-53	-0.1
1946	Cle-A	9	22	1	6	0	0	0	3	3	5	.273	.360	.273	84	-0	0	1	-1	1.000	-0	/O-6	-0.2
Total	7	415	1379	200	396	62	19	14	163	131	137	.287	.355	.390	91	-17	23	21		.964	-5	O-341	-3.7

■ EVERETT MILLS
Mills, Everett b: 1/20/1845, Newark, N.J. d: 6/22/08, Newark, N.J. 6'1", 174 lbs. Deb: 5/5/1871 M

YEAR	TM/L	G	AB	R	H	2B	3B	HR	RBI	BB	SO	AVG	OBP	SLG	PRO+	BR/A	SB	CS	SBR	FA	FR	G/POS	TPR
1871	Oly-n	32	157	38	43	6	4	1	24	3	1	.274	.287	.382	95	-0	2					*1-32	0.1
1872	Bal-n	55	267	55	76	13	3	0	35	3	2	.285	.293	.356	94	-3						*1-53,M	-0.1
1873	Bal-n	54	263	64	87	16	6	0	57	2	1	.331	.336	.437	126	8						*1-53/O-1	0.8
1874	Har-n	53	241	40	70	6	2	0		6		.290	.308	.332	99	-1						*1-53	-0.1
1875	Har-n	80	341	59	91	10	4	1		0		.267	.267	.328	100	-1						*1-78	-0.2
1876	Har-n	63	254	28	66	8	1	0	23	1	3	.260	.263	.299	80	-6				.939	-2	*1-63	-0.9
Total	5 n	274	1269	256	367	51	19	2	116	14	4	.289	.297	.364	103	2						1-269/O-1	0.5

■ FRANK MILLS
Mills, Frank Le Moyne b: 5/13/1895, Knoxville, Ohio d: 8/31/83, Youngstown, Ohio BL/TR, 6', 180 lbs. Deb: 9/22/14

YEAR	TM/L	G	AB	R	H	2B	3B	HR	RBI	BB	SO	AVG	OBP	SLG	PRO+	BR/A	SB	CS	SBR	FA	FR	G/POS	TPR
1914	Cle-A	4	8	0	1	0	0	0	0	1	2	.125	.222	.125	4	-1	0			.900	-1	/C-2	-0.2

■ BRAD MILLS
Mills, James Bradley b: 1/19/57, Exeter, Cal. BL/TR, 6', 195 lbs. Deb: 6/8/80

YEAR	TM/L	G	AB	R	H	2B	3B	HR	RBI	BB	SO	AVG	OBP	SLG	PRO+	BR/A	SB	CS	SBR	FA	FR	G/POS	TPR
1980	Mon-N	21	60	1	18	1	0	0	8	5	6	.300	.354	.317	88	-1	0	1	-1	.977	-1	3-18	-0.3
1981	*Mon-N	17	21	3	5	1	0	0	1	2	1	.238	.304	.286	67	-1	0	0	0	1.000	0	/3-7,2-2	-0.1
1982	Mon-N	54	67	6	15	3	0	0	2	5	11	.224	.278	.313	64	-3	0	0	0	.867	-3	3-13	-0.7
1983	Mon-N	14	20	1	5	0	0	0	1	2	3	.250	.318	.250	60	-1	0	0	0	1.000	-1	/3-3,1-1	-0.2
Total	4	106	168	11	43	5	0	0	12	14	21	.256	.313	.304	73	-6	0	1	-1	.959	-5	/3-41,2-2,1	-1.3

■ RUPERT MILLS
Mills, Rupert Frank b: 10/12/1892, Newark, N.J. d: 7/20/29, Lake Hopatcong, N.J. BR/TR, 6'2", 185 lbs. Deb: 6/23/15

YEAR	TM/L	G	AB	R	H	2B	3B	HR	RBI	BB	SO	AVG	OBP	SLG	PRO+	BR/A	SB	CS	SBR	FA	FR	G/POS	TPR
1915	New-F	41	134	12	27	5	1	0	16	6	21	.201	.241	.254	34	-13	6			.976	0	1-37	-1.5

■ BILL MILLS
Mills, William Henry b: 11/2/20, Boston, Mass. BR/TR, 5'10", 175 lbs. Deb: 5/19/44

YEAR	TM/L	G	AB	R	H	2B	3B	HR	RBI	BB	SO	AVG	OBP	SLG	PRO+	BR/A	SB	CS	SBR	FA	FR	G/POS	TPR
1944	Phi-A	5	4	0	1	0	0	0	0	1	1	.250	.400	.250	89	0	0	0	0	.000	0	/C-1	0.0

■ PETE MILNE
Milne, William James b: 4/10/25, Mobile, Ala. BL/TR, 6'1", 180 lbs. Deb: 9/15/48

YEAR	TM/L	G	AB	R	H	2B	3B	HR	RBI	BB	SO	AVG	OBP	SLG	PRO+	BR/A	SB	CS	SBR	FA	FR	G/POS	TPR
1948	NY-N	12	27	0	6	0	1	0	2	1	6	.222	.250	.296	47	-2	0			.867	-2	/O-9	-0.5
1949	NY-N	31	29	5	7	1	0	1	6	3	6	.241	.313	.379	85	-1	0			1.000	-0	/O-1	-0.1
1950	NY-N	4	4	1	1	0	1	0	1	0	1	.250	.250	.750	151	0	0			.000	0	H	0.0
Total	3	47	60	6	14	1	2	1	9	4	13	.233	.281	.367	73	-2	0			.882	-2	/O-10	-0.6

■ BRIAN MILNER
Milner, Brian Tate b: 11/17/59, Fort Worth, Tex. BR/TR, 6'2", 200 lbs. Deb: 6/23/78

YEAR	TM/L	G	AB	R	H	2B	3B	HR	RBI	BB	SO	AVG	OBP	SLG	PRO+	BR/A	SB	CS	SBR	FA	FR	G/POS	TPR
1978	Tor-A	2	9	3	4	0	1	0	2	0	1	.444	.444	.667	204	1	0	0	0	.800	-3	/C-2	-0.1

■ EDDIE MILNER
Milner, Eddie James b: 5/21/55, Columbus, Ohio BL/TL, 5'11", 173 lbs. Deb: 9/2/80

YEAR	TM/L	G	AB	R	H	2B	3B	HR	RBI	BB	SO	AVG	OBP	SLG	PRO+	BR/A	SB	CS	SBR	FA	FR	G/POS	TPR
1980	Cin-N	6	3	1	0	0	0	0	0	0	0	.000	.000	.000	-99	-1	0	0	0	.000	0	/H	-0.1
1981	Cin-N	8	5	0	1	1	0	0	1	1	1	.200	.333	.400	106	0	0	0	0	1.000	-1	/O-4	-0.1
1982	Cin-N	113	407	61	109	23	5	4	31	41	40	.268	.338	.378	98	-1	18	12	-2	.987	-3	*O-107	-0.8
1983	Cin-N	146	502	77	131	23	6	9	33	68	60	.261	.350	.384	100	1	41	12	5	.990	20	*O-139	2.2
1984	Cin-N	117	336	44	78	8	4	7	29	51	50	.232	.337	.342	87	-5	21	13	-2	.983	10	*O-108	0.1
1985	Cin-N	145	453	82	115	19	7	3	33	61	31	.254	.344	.347	89	-5	35	13	3	.983	15	*O-135	0.9
1986	Cin-N	145	424	70	110	22	6	15	47	36	56	.259	.317	.446	104	1	18	11	-1	.990	7	*O-127	0.3
1987	*SF-N	101	214	38	54	14	0	4	19	24	33	.252	.328	.374	90	-3	10	9	-2	.993	-9	O-84	-1.7
1988	Cin-N	23	51	3	9	1	0	0	2	4	9	.176	.236	.196	24	-5	2	2	-1	.968	-0	O-15	-0.7
Total	9	804	2395	376	607	111	28	42	195	286	280	.253	.335	.376	94	-17	145	72	0	.987	38	O-719	0.1

■ JOHN MILNER
Milner, John David "The Hammer" b: 12/28/49, Atlanta, Ga. BL/TL, 6', 185 lbs. Deb: 9/15/71

YEAR	TM/L	G	AB	R	H	2B	3B	HR	RBI	BB	SO	AVG	OBP	SLG	PRO+	BR/A	SB	CS	SBR	FA	FR	G/POS	TPR
1971	NY-N	9	18	1	3	0	0	0	0	0	3	.167	.167	.222	9	-2	0	0	0	1.000	1	/O-3	-0.1
1972	NY-N	117	362	52	86	12	2	17	38	51	74	.238	.340	.423	118	9	2	1	0	.965	3	O-91,1-10	0.8
1973	*NY-N	129	451	69	108	12	3	23	72	62	84	.239	.333	.432	112	7	1	1	-0	.989	-7	1-95,O-29	-0.9
1974	NY-N	137	507	70	128	19	0	20	63	66	77	.252	.339	.408	110	6	10	2	2	.994	-0	*1-133	-0.2
1975	NY-N	91	220	24	42	11	0	7	29	33	22	.191	.302	.336	81	-6	1	1	-0	.985	6	O-31,1-29	-0.3
1976	NY-N	127	443	56	120	25	4	15	78	65	53	.271	.364	.447	137	22	0	7	-4	.985	4	*O-112,1-12	1.7
1977	NY-N	131	388	43	99	20	3	12	57	61	55	.255	.356	.415	111	7	6	2	1	.994	-1	1-87,O-22	0.1
1978	Pit-N	108	295	39	80	17	0	8	38	34	25	.271	.347	.390	101	1	5	0	2	1.000	-2	O-69,1-28	-0.3
1979	*Pit-N	128	326	52	90	9	4	16	60	53	37	.276	.379	.475	126	12	3	5	-2	.958	-2	1-70,O-11	0.4
1980	Pit-N	114	238	31	58	6	0	8	34	52	29	.244	.379	.370	108	5	2	2	-1	.991	-5	1-70,O-11	-0.5
1981	Pit-N	34	59	6	14	1	0	2	9	5	3	.237	.297	.356	82	-1	0	0	0	.980	-2	/1-8,O-8	-0.5
	*Mon-N	31	76	6	18	5	0	3	9	12	6	.237	.341	.421	114	1	0	1	-1	.978	1	1-21	0.1
	Yr	65	135	12	32	6	0	5	18	17	9	.237	.322	.393	100	-0	0	1	-1	.979	-1	1-29/O-8	-0.4
1982	Mon-N	26	28	1	3	0	0	0	2	4	2	.107	.219	.107	-6	-4	0	0	0	1.000	0	/1-5	-0.4
	Pit-N	33	25	5	6	2	0	2	8	6	3	.240	.406	.560	163	2	1	0	0	1.000	0	/1-1	0.3
	Yr	59	53	6	9	2	0	2	10	10	5	.170	.313	.321	76	-2	1	0	0	1.000	0	/1-6	-0.1
Total	12	1215	3436	455	855	140	16	131	498	504	473	.249	.347	.413	112	59	31	22	-4	.991	-4	1-547,O-440	0.2

■ MIKE MILOSEVICH
Milosevich, Michael "Mollie" b: 1/13/15, Zeigler, Ill. d: 2/3/66, E.Chicago, Ind. BR/TR, 5'10.5", 172 lbs. Deb: 4/30/44

YEAR	TM/L	G	AB	R	H	2B	3B	HR	RBI	BB	SO	AVG	OBP	SLG	PRO+	BR/A	SB	CS	SBR	FA	FR	G/POS	TPR
1944	NY-A	94	312	27	77	11	4	0	32	30	37	.247	.313	.308	75	-10	1	2	-1	.954	7	S-91	0.3
1945	NY-A	30	69	5	15	2	0	0	7	6	6	.217	.289	.246	54	-4	0	0	0	.957	1	S-22/2-1	-0.2
Total	2	124	381	32	92	13	4	0	39	36	43	.241	.309	.297	71	-14	1	2	-1	.954	8	S-113/2-1	0.1

■ DON MINCHER
Mincher, Donald Ray b: 6/24/38, Huntsville, Ala. BL/TR, 6'3", 213 lbs. Deb: 4/18/60

YEAR	TM/L	G	AB	R	H	2B	3B	HR	RBI	BB	SO	AVG	OBP	SLG	PRO+	BR/A	SB	CS	SBR	FA	FR	G/POS	TPR
1960	Was-A	27	79	10	19	4	1	2	5	11	11	.241	.333	.392	96	-0	0	1	-1	.977	-4	1-20	-0.7
1961	Min-A	35	101	18	19	5	1	5	11	22	11	.188	.333	.406	91	-1	0	1	-1	.969	-2	1-29	-0.6
1962	Min-A	86	121	20	29	1	1	9	29	34	24	.240	.406	.488	134	7	0	0	0	.978	-1	1-25	0.4
1963	Min-A	82	225	41	58	8	0	17	42	30	51	.258	.353	.520	138	11	0	0	0	.983	-5	1-60	0.4
1964	Min-A	120	287	45	68	12	4	23	56	27	51	.237	.303	.547	130	10	0	0	0	.992	-0	1-76	0.7
1965	*Min-A	128	346	43	87	17	3	22	65	49	73	.251	.348	.509	134	15	1	3	-2	.992	-5	1-99/O-1	0.4
1966	Min-A	139	431	53	108	30	0	14	62	58	68	.251	.342	.418	110	6	3	2	0	.992	3	*1-130	0.1
1967	Cal-A★	147	487	81	133	23	3	25	76	69	69	.273	.368	.487	157	35	0	3	-2	.994	-2	*1-142/O-1	2.4
1968	Cal-A	120	399	35	94	12	1	13	48	43	65	.236	.316	.368	111	5	0	2	-1	.991	-3	*1-113	-0.9
1969	Sea-A★	140	427	53	105	14	0	25	78	78	69	.246	.369	.454	131	19	10	11	-4	.995	-5	*1-122	1.4
1970	Oak-A	140	463	62	114	18	0	27	74	56	71	.246	.331	.460	120	11	5	4	-4	.990	2	*1-137	0.1
1971	Oak-A	28	92	9	22	6	1	2	8	20	14	.239	.375	.391	120	3	1	1	-0	.996	1	1-27	0.3
	Was-A	100	323	35	94	15	1	10	45	53	52	.291	.394	.437	143	20	2	1	0	.990	3	1-88	1.6
	Yr	128	415	44	116	21	2	12	53	73	66	.280	.390	.427	138	23	3	2	0	.991	4	*1-115	1.9
1972	Tex-A	61	191	23	45	10	0	6	39	46	23	.236	.389	.382	136	11	2	1	0	.994	6	1-59	1.4
	*Oak-A	47	54	2	8	1	0	0	5	10	16	.148	.281	.167	37	-4	0	2	-1	.988	-1	1-11	-0.7
	Yr	108	245	25	53	11	0	6	44	56	39	.216	.366	.335	115	7	2	3	-1	.993	5	1-70	0.7
Total	13	1400	4026	530	1003	176	16	200	643	606	668	.249	.351	.450	127	149	24	32	-12	.990	2	*1-1138/O-2	6.3

■ ED MINCHER
Mincher, Edward John b: Baltimore, Md. Deb: 5/4/1871

YEAR	TM/L	G	AB	R	H	2B	3B	HR	RBI	BB	SO	AVG	OBP	SLG	PRO+	BR/A	SB	CS	SBR	FA	FR	G/POS	TPR
1871	Kek-n	9	36	4	8	0	0	0	5	0	0	.222	.222	.222	28	-3	1					/O-9	-0.2

YEAR	TM/L	G	AB	R	H	2B	3B	HR	RBI	BB	SO	AVG	OBP	SLG	PRO+	BR/A	SB	CS	SBR	FA	FR	G/POS	TPR
1872	Nat-n	11	54	4	5	0	0	0	3	0	1	.093	.093	.093	-37	-9						O-11	-0.6
Total	2 n	20	90	8	13	0	0	0	8	0	1	.144	.144	.144	-12	-13						/O-20	-0.8

■ DAN MINNEHAN
Minnehan, Daniel Joseph   b: 11/28/1865, Troy, N.Y.   d: 8/8/29, Troy, N.Y.   BR/TR, 5'10", 145 lbs.   Deb: 9/20/1895

YEAR	TM/L	G	AB	R	H	2B	3B	HR	RBI	BB	SO	AVG	OBP	SLG	PRO+	BR/A	SB	CS	SBR	FA	FR	G/POS	TPR
1895	Lou-N	8	34	6	13	0	0	0	6	1	1	.382	.400	.382	109	1	0			.920	-0	/3-7,O-2	0.0

■ MINNIE MINOSO
Minoso, Saturnino Orestes Armas (Arrieta)   b: 11/29/22, Havana, Cuba   BR/TR, 5'10", 175 lbs.   Deb: 4/19/49   C

YEAR	TM/L	G	AB	R	H	2B	3B	HR	RBI	BB	SO	AVG	OBP	SLG	PRO+	BR/A	SB	CS	SBR	FA	FR	G/POS	TPR
1949	Cle-A	9	16	2	3	0	0	1	1	2	2	.188	.350	.375	94	-0	0	1	-1	1.000	-1	/O-7	-0.2
1951	Cle-A	8	14	3	6	2	0	0	2	1	1	.429	.529	.571	209	2	0	0	0	.952	-0	/1-7	0.2
	Chi-A★	138	516	109	167	32	14	10	74	71	41	.324	.419	.498	150	38	31	10	3	.961	-12	O-82,3-68/S	2.6
	Yr	146	530	112	173	34	**14**	10	76	72	42	.326	.422	.500	152	41	**31**	10	4	.961	-12	O-82,3-68/1S	2.8
1952	Chi-A★	147	569	96	160	24	9	13	61	71	46	.281	.375	.424	121	17	**22**	16	-3	.979	4	*O-143/3-9,S	1.2
1953	Chi-A★	151	556	104	174	24	8	15	104	74	43	.313	.410	.466	132	27	**25**	16	-2	.967	5	*O-147,3-10	2.5
1954	Chi-A★	153	568	119	182	29	**18**	19	116	77	46	.320	.416	**.535**	154	43	18	11	-1	.978	13	*O-146/3-9	5.0
1955	Chi-A	139	517	79	149	26	7	10	70	76	43	.288	.390	.424	115	13	19	8	1	.971	12	*O-138/3-2	2.0
1956	Chi-A	151	545	106	172	29	**11**	21	88	86	40	.316	.430	.525	149	42	12	6	0	.974	3	*O-148/3-8,1	3.6
1957	Chi-A★	153	568	96	176	**36**	5	12	103	79	54	.310	.413	.454	136	32	18	15	-4	.984	6	*O-152/3-1	2.6
1958	Cle-A	149	556	94	168	25	2	24	80	59	53	.302	.384	.484	141	32	14	14	-4	.975	13	*O-147/3-1	3.3
1959	Cle-A	148	570	92	172	32	0	21	92	54	46	.302	.379	.468	136	29	8	10	-4	.985	16	*O-148	3.4
1960	Chi-A★	154	591	89	**184**	32	4	20	105	52	63	.311	.380	.481	132	27	17	13	-3	.980	5	*O-154	2.0
1961	Chi-A	152	540	91	151	28	3	14	82	67	46	.280	.376	.420	114	13	9	4	0	.956	3	*O-147	0.8
1962	StL-N	39	97	14	19	5	0	1	10	7	17	.196	.271	.278	44	-8	4	0	1	.972	-1	O-27	-0.9
1963	Was-A	109	315	38	72	12	2	4	30	33	38	.229	.317	.317	79	-8	8	6	-1	.955	-5	O-74/3-8	-1.9
1964	Chi-A	30	31	4	7	0	0	1	5	5	3	.226	.351	.323	91	-0	0	0	0	1.000	0	/O-5	0.0
1976	Chi-A	3	8	0	1	0	0	0	0	0	0	.125	.125	.125	-27	-1	0	0	0	.000	0	/D-3	-0.1
1980	Chi-A	2	2	0	0	0	0	0	0	0	0	.000	.000	.000	-99	-1	0	0	0	.000	0	/H	-0.1
Total	17	1835	6579	1136	1963	336	83	186	1023	814	584	.298	.391	.459	130	297	205	130	-16	.974	62	*O-1665,3-116/1DS	26.0

■ WILLY MIRANDA
Miranda, Guillermo (Perez)   b: 5/24/26, Velasco, Cuba   BB/TR, 5'9.5", 150 lbs.   Deb: 5/6/51

YEAR	TM/L	G	AB	R	H	2B	3B	HR	RBI	BB	SO	AVG	OBP	SLG	PRO+	BR/A	SB	CS	SBR	FA	FR	G/POS	TPR
1951	Was-A	7	9	2	4	0	0	0	0	0	0	.444	.444	.444	143	1	0	0	0	.818	-0	/S-2,1-1	0.0
1952	Chi-A	12	8	1	2	1	0	0	0	3	0	.250	.455	.375	131	1	0	0	0	1.000	4	/S-4,3-4,2	0.5
	StL-A	7	11	2	1	0	1	0	1	3	1	.091	.286	.273	54	-1	0	0	0	.900	-1	/S-7	-0.1
	Chi-A	58	142	13	31	3	1	0	7	10	14	.218	.275	.254	47	-10	1	0	0	.975	11	S-50/2-1,3	0.4
	Yr	77	161	16	34	4	2	0	8	16	15	.211	.287	.261	52	-10	1	0	0	.970	14	S-61/3-5,2	0.8
1953	StL-A	17	6	2	1	0	0	0	0	1	1	.167	.286	.167	24	-1	1	1	-0	.933	3	/S-3,6	0.3
	NY-A	48	58	12	13	0	0	1	5	5	10	.224	.286	.276	54	-4	1	1	-0	.984	17	S-45	1.4
	Yr	65	64	14	14	0	0	1	5	6	11	.219	.286	.266	51	-4	2	2	-1	.979	20	S-53/3-6	1.7
1954	NY-A	92	116	12	29	4	2	1	12	10	11	.250	.310	.345	82	-3	0	3	-2	.948	16	S-88/2-4,3	1.5
1955	Bal-A	153	487	42	124	12	6	1	38	42	58	.255	.315	.310	74	-19	4	3	-1	.958	19	*S-153/2-1	1.2
1956	Bal-A	148	461	38	100	16	4	2	34	46	73	.217	.288	.282	55	-31	3	6	-3	.962	-4	*S-147	-2.0
1957	Bal-A	115	314	29	61	3	0	0	20	24	42	.194	.251	.204	28	-31	2	1	0	.966	-3	*S-115	-2.6
1958	Bal-A	102	214	15	43	6	0	1	8	14	25	.201	.250	.243	38	-18	1	1	-0	.962	-2	*S-102	-1.4
1959	Bal-A	65	88	8	14	5	0	0	7	7	16	.159	.221	.216	21	-10	0	0	0	.974	22	S-47,3-11/2	1.4
Total	9	824	1914	176	423	50	14	6	132	165	250	.221	.284	.271	54	-126	13	16	-6	.962	88	S-768/3-23,21	0.6

■ JOHN MISSE
Misse, John Beverly   b: 5/30/1885, Highland, Kan.   d: 3/18/70, St.Joseph, Mo.   BR/TR, 5'8", 150 lbs.   Deb: 5/26/14

YEAR	TM/L	G	AB	R	H	2B	3B	HR	RBI	BB	SO	AVG	OBP	SLG	PRO+	BR/A	SB	CS	SBR	FA	FR	G/POS	TPR
1914	StL-F	99	306	28	60	8	1	0	22	36	52	.196	.281	.229	31	-31	3			.948	14	2-50,S-48/3	-1.4

■ CLARENCE MITCHELL
Mitchell, Clarence Elmer   b: 2/22/1891, Franklin, Neb.   d: 11/6/63, Grand Island, Neb.   BL/TL, 5'11.5", 190 lbs.   Deb: 6/2/11   C

YEAR	TM/L	G	AB	R	H	2B	3B	HR	RBI	BB	SO	AVG	OBP	SLG	PRO+	BR/A	SB	CS	SBR	FA	FR	G/POS	TPR
1911	Det-A	5	4	2	2	0	0	0	0	0	1	.500	.600	.500	198	1	0			1.000	-1	/P-5	0.0
1916	Cin-N	56	117	11	28	2	1	0	11	4	6	.239	.264	.274	67	-5	1			.985	-2	P-29/1-9,O	-0.5
1917	Cin-N	47	90	13	25	3	0	0	5	5	5	.278	.316	.311	97	-0	0			.982	-0	P-32/1-6,O	-0.1
1918	Bro-N	10	24	2	6	1	1	0	2	0	3	.250	.250	.375	90	-0	0			.750	-2	/O-6,1-2,P	-0.4
1919	Bro-N	34	49	7	18	1	0	1	2	4	4	.367	.415	.449	156	3	0			.976	1	P-23	0.0
1920	*Bro-N	55	107	9	25	2	2	0	11	8	9	.234	.287	.290	64	-5	0			1.000	1	P-19,1-11/O	-0.4
1921	Bro-N	46	91	11	24	5	0	0	12	5	7	.264	.316	.319	66	-4	3	1	0	.945	3	P-37/1-4	0.0
1922	Bro-N	56	155	21	45	6	3	3	28	19	6	.290	.371	.426	106	2	0	0	0	.992	3	1-42/P-5	0.2
1923	Phi-N	53	78	10	21	3	2	1	9	4	11	.269	.305	.397	75	-3	0	0	0	.988	-3	P-29	0.0
1924	Phi-N	69	102	7	26	3	0	0	13	2	7	.255	.276	.284	45	-8	1	0	0	**1.000**	3	P-30	0.0
1925	Phi-N	52	92	7	18	2	0	0	13	5	9	.196	.237	.217	16	-12	2	0	1	**1.000**	4	P-32/1-2	0.0
1926	Phi-N	39	78	8	19	4	0	0	6	5	5	.244	.289	.295	55	-5	0			.986	0	P-28/1-4	0.0
1927	Phi-N	18	42	5	10	1	0	1	6	2	1	.238	.273	.357	67	-2	0			.963	1	P-13	0.0
1928	Phi-N	5	4	0	1	0	0	0	0	0	0	.250	.250	.250	30	-0	0			1.000	0	/P-3	0.0
	*StL-N	19	56	0	7	1	0	0	1	0	3	.125	.125	.143	-30	-11	0			.982	2	P-19	0.0
	Yr	24	60	0	8	1	0	0	1	0	3	.133	.133	.150	-26	-11	0			.983	3	P-22	0.0
1929	StL-N	26	66	9	18	3	1	0	9	4	6	.273	.314	.348	63	-4	1			.974	-1	P-25	0.0
1930	StL-N	1	2	0	1	0	0	0	0	0	0	.500	.500	.500	138	0	0			.000	-0	/P-1	0.0
	NY-N	24	47	9	12	1	0	0	1	1	5	.255	.271	.277	33	-5	0			1.000	0	P-24	0.0
	Yr	25	49	9	13	1	0	0	1	1	5	.265	.288	.286	38	-5	0			1.000	2	P-25	0.0
1931	NY-N	27	73	5	16	2	0	1	4	2	4	.219	.240	.288	42	-6	0			.885	-2	P-27	0.0
1932	NY-N	8	10	2	2	0	0	0	0	1	1	.200	.273	.200	30	-1	0			.833	-1	/P-8	0.0
Total	18	650	1287	138	324	41	10	7	133	72	92	.252	.293	.315	64	-65	9	1		.972	14	P-390/1-80,O	-1.2

■ FRED MITCHELL
Mitchell, Frederick Francis (b: Frederick Francis Yapp)   b: 6/5/1878, Cambridge, Mass.   d: 10/13/70, Newton, Mass.   BR/TR, 5'9.5", 185 lbs.   Deb: 4/27/01   MC

YEAR	TM/L	G	AB	R	H	2B	3B	HR	RBI	BB	SO	AVG	OBP	SLG	PRO+	BR/A	SB	CS	SBR	FA	FR	G/POS	TPR
1901	Bos-A	20	44	5	7	0	2	0	4	2		.159	.196	.250	23	-5	0			.875	-0	P-17/2-2,S	-0.1
1902	Bos-A	1	1	0	0	0	0	0	0	0		.000	.000	.000	-97	-0	0			.667	0	/P-1	0.0
	Phi-A	19	48	7	9	1	1	0	3	1		.188	.204	.250	24	-5	1			.942	-2	P-18/O-1	-0.1
	Yr	20	49	7	9	1	1	0	3	1		.184	.200	.245	22	-5	1			.927	-2	P-19/O-1	-0.1
1903	Phi-N	29	95	11	19	4	0	0	10	0		.200	.200	.242	27	-9	0			.857	-3	P-28	-0.2
1904	Phi-N	25	82	9	17	3	1	0	3	5		.207	.253	.268	63	-4	1			.981	3	P-13/1-9,3O	-0.2
	Bro-N	8	24	3	7	1	1	0	6	1		.292	.346	.417	139	1	0			.906	1	/P-8	0.0
	Yr	33	106	12	24	4	2	0	9	6		.226	.274	.302	80	-3	1			.952	4	P-21/1-9,3O	-0.2
1905	Bro-N	27	79	4	15	0	0	0	8	4		.190	.238	.190	30	-7	0			.881	-2	P-12/1-7,3SO	-0.7
1910	NY-A	68	196	16	45	7	2	0	18	9		.230	.274	.286	71	-7	6			.968	-15	C-62	-1.8
1913	Bos-N	4	3	0	1	0	0	0	0	0		.333	.333	.333	89	-0	0			.000	0	H	0.0
Total	7	201	572	55	120	16	7	0	52	22	2	.210	.245	.262	52	-35	8			.904	-14	/P-97,C-62,130S2	-2.9

■ JOHNNY MITCHELL
Mitchell, John Franklin   b: 8/9/1894, Detroit, Mich.   d: 11/4/65, Birmingham, Mich.   BB/TR, 5'8", 155 lbs.   Deb: 5/21/21

YEAR	TM/L	G	AB	R	H	2B	3B	HR	RBI	BB	SO	AVG	OBP	SLG	PRO+	BR/A	SB	CS	SBR	FA	FR	G/POS	TPR
1921	NY-A	13	42	4	11	1	0	0	4	4	4	.262	.326	.286	56	-3	1	0	0	.958	-6	/S-7,2-5	-0.7
1922	NY-A	4	4	1	0	0	0	0	0	1	1	.000	.000	.000	-98	-1	0	0	0	1.000	-1	/S-4	-0.2
	Bos-A	59	203	20	51	4	1	0	8	16	17	.251	.304	.296	61	-11	1	2	-5	.962	-5	S-58	-1.1
	Yr	63	207	21	51	4	1	0	8	16	18	.246	.313	.290	58	-12	1	2	-5	.963	-6	S-62	-1.3
1923	Bos-A	92	347	40	78	15	4	0	19	34	18	.225	.296	.291	55	-23	7	11	-5	.961	-0	S-87/2-5	-1.9

YEAR	TM/L	G	AB	R	H	2B	3B	HR	RBI	BB	SO	AVG	OBP	SLG	PRO+	BR/A	SB	CS	SBR	FA	FR	G/POS	TPR
1924	Bro-N	64	243	42	64	10	0	1	16	37	22	.263	.361	.317	86	-3	3	1	0	.951	-1	S-64	0.4
1925	Bro-N	97	336	45	84	8	3	0	18	28	19	.250	.308	.292	55	-22	2	0	1	.947	-4	S-90	-1.5
Total	5	329	1175	152	288	38	8	2	63	119	81	.245	.317	.296	62	-63	14	14	-4	.955	-16	S-310/2-10	-5.0

■ KEITH MITCHELL
Mitchell, Keith Alexander b: 8/6/69, San Diego, Cal. BR/TR, 5'10", 180 lbs. Deb: 7/23/91

YEAR	TM/L	G	AB	R	H	2B	3B	HR	RBI	BB	SO	AVG	OBP	SLG	PRO+	BR/A	SB	CS	SBR	FA	FR	G/POS	TPR
1991	*Atl-N	48	66	11	21	0	0	2	5	8	12	.318	.392	.409	118	2	3	1	0	.970	-7	O-34	-0.5
1994	Sea-A	46	128	21	29	2	0	5	15	18	22	.227	.327	.359	75	-5	0	0	0	.980	-7	O-38/D-6	-1.1
Total	2	94	194	32	50	2	0	7	20	26	34	.258	.348	.376	89	-3	3	1	0	.976	-13	/O-72,D-6	-1.6

■ KEVIN MITCHELL
Mitchell, Kevin Darnell b: 1/13/62, San Diego, Cal. BR/TR, 5'11", 210 lbs. Deb: 9/4/84

YEAR	TM/L	G	AB	R	H	2B	3B	HR	RBI	BB	SO	AVG	OBP	SLG	PRO+	BR/A	SB	CS	SBR	FA	FR	G/POS	TPR
1984	NY-N	7	14	0	3	0	0	0	1	0	3	.214	.214	.214	21	-1	0	1	-1	.833	-1	/3-5	-0.3
1986	*NY-N	108	328	51	91	22	2	12	43	33	61	.277	.345	.466	125	10	3	3	-1	.983	-11	O-68,S-24/31	-0.1
1987	SD-N	62	196	19	48	7	1	7	26	20	38	.245	.315	.398	91	-3	0	0	0	.945	4	3-51/O-3	0.0
	*SF-N	69	268	49	82	13	1	15	44	28	50	.306	.376	.530	144	16	9	6	-1	.962	-5	3-68/O-3,S	0.9
	Yr	131	464	68	130	20	2	22	70	48	88	.280	.350	.474	121	13	9	6	-1	.954	-2	*3-119/O-6,S	0.9
1988	SF-N	148	505	60	127	25	7	19	80	48	85	.251	.323	.442	123	13	5	5	-2	.943	-5	*3-102,O-40	0.5
1989	*SF-N★	154	543	100	158	34	6	**47**	**125**	87	115	.291	.392	**.635**	**194**	**66**	3	4	-2	.978	7	*O-147/3-2	**7.0**
1990	SF-N★	140	524	90	152	24	2	35	93	58	87	.290	.363	.544	151	35	4	7	-3	.971	7	*O-138	3.6
1991	SF-N	113	371	52	95	13	1	27	69	43	57	.256	.341	.515	142	20	2	3	-1	.970	3	*O-100/1-1	2.0
1992	Sea-A	99	360	48	103	24	0	9	67	35	46	.286	.354	.428	117	8	0	1	-1	1.000	-0	O-69,D-26	0.5
1993	Cin-N	93	323	56	110	21	3	19	64	25	48	.341	.390	.601	160	26	1	0	0	.957	1	O-87	2.6
1994	Cin-N	95	310	57	101	18	1	30	77	59	62	.326	.438	.681	187	41	2	0	-1	.972	4	O-89/1-1	4.2
Total	10	1088	3742	582	1070	201	24	220	689	436	652	.286	.364	.529	147	231	29	31	-10	.972	3	O-744,3-235/DS1	20.9

■ DALE MITCHELL
Mitchell, Loren Dale b: 8/23/21, Colony, Okla. d: 1/5/87, Tulsa, Okla. BL/TL, 6'1", 195 lbs. Deb: 9/15/46

YEAR	TM/L	G	AB	R	H	2B	3B	HR	RBI	BB	SO	AVG	OBP	SLG	PRO+	BR/A	SB	CS	SBR	FA	FR	G/POS	TPR
1946	Cle-A	11	44	7	19	3	0	0	5	1	2	.432	.444	.500	175	4	1	0	0	1.000	-0	O-11	0.4
1947	Cle-A	123	493	69	156	16	10	1	34	23	14	.316	.347	.396	109	4	2	5	-2	.977	-9	*O-115	-1.4
1948	*Cle-A	141	608	82	204	30	8	4	56	45	17	.336	.383	.431	119	16	13	18	-7	**.991**	4	*O-140	0.4
1949	Cle-A★	149	640	81	**203**	16	**23**	3	56	43	11	.317	.360	.428	110	7	10	3	1	**.994**	4	*O-149	0.3
1950	Cle-A	130	506	81	156	27	5	3	49	67	21	.308	.390	.399	106	6	3	7	-3	.972	-11	*O-127	-1.3
1951	Cle-A	134	510	83	148	21	7	11	62	53	16	.290	.358	.424	117	11	7	7	-2	.992	-6	*O-124	-0.1
1952	Cle-A★	134	511	61	165	26	3	5	58	52	9	.323	.387	.415	132	22	6	6	-2	.992	-5	*O-128	1.0
1953	Cle-A	134	500	76	150	26	4	13	60	42	20	.300	.354	.446	118	11	3	1	0	.970	-6	*O-125	0.1
1954	*Cle-A	53	60	6	17	1	0	1	6	9	1	.283	.377	.350	98	0	0	0	0	.889	-1	/O-6,1-1	-0.1
1955	Cle-A	61	58	4	15	2	1	0	10	4	3	.259	.306	.328	68	-3	0	0	0	1.000	-1	/1-8,O-3	-0.4
1956	Cle-A	38	30	2	4	0	0	0	6	7	2	.133	.297	.133	17	-3	0	0	0	.000	-0	/O-1	-0.4
	*Bro-N	19	24	3	7	1	0	0	1	0	3	.292	.292	.333	63	-1	0	0	0	1.000	-0	/O-2	-0.2
Total	11	1127	3984	555	1244	169	61	41	403	346	119	.312	.368	.416	114	74	45	47	-15	.985	-32	O-931/1-9	-1.7

■ MIKE MITCHELL
Mitchell, Michael Francis b: 12/12/1879, Springfield, Ohio d: 7/16/61, Phoenix, Ariz. BR/TR, 6'1", 185 lbs. Deb: 4/11/07

YEAR	TM/L	G	AB	R	H	2B	3B	HR	RBI	BB	SO	AVG	OBP	SLG	PRO+	BR/A	SB	CS	SBR	FA	FR	G/POS	TPR
1907	Cin-N	148	558	64	163	17	12	3	47	37		.292	.339	.382	121	12	17			.962	22	*O-146/1-2	3.2
1908	Cin-N	119	406	41	90	9	6	1	37	46		.222	.304	.281	89	-4	18			.959	1	*O-118/1-1	-0.9
1909	Cin-N	145	523	83	162	17	**17**	4	86	57		.310	.378	.430	152	31	37			.962	6	*O-145/1-1	3.4
1910	Cin-N	156	583	79	167	16	**18**	5	88	59	56	.286	.356	.401	126	18	35			.958	-3	*O-149/1-7	0.8
1911	Cin-N	142	529	74	154	22	22	2	84	44	34	.291	.348	.427	121	12	35			.971	11	*O-140	1.6
1912	Cin-N	147	552	60	156	14	13	4	78	41	43	.283	.333	.377	97	-4	23			.947	-0	*O-144	-1.1
1913	Chi-N	82	279	37	73	11	6	4	35	32	33	.262	.340	.387	107	3	15			.941	4	O-82	0.3
	Pit-N	54	199	25	54	8	2	1	16	14	15	.271	.319	.347	94	-2	8			.946	7	O-54	0.3
	Yr	136	478	62	127	19	8	5	51	46	48	.266	.331	.370	102	1	23			.943	11	*O-136	0.6
1914	Pit-N	76	273	31	64	11	5	2	23	16	16	.234	.279	.333	86	-6	5			.984	9	O-76	0.0
	Was-A	55	193	20	55	5	3	1	20	22	19	.285	.361	.358	112	3	9	7	-2	.957	4	O-53	0.4
Total	8	1124	4095	514	1138	130	104	27	514	368	216	.278	.340	.380	114	64	202	7		.959	61	*O-1107/1-11	8.0

■ BOBBY MITCHELL
Mitchell, Robert McKasha b: 2/6/1856, Cincinnati, Ohio d: 5/1/33, Springfield, Ohio BL/TL, 5'5", 135 lbs. Deb: 9/6/1877

YEAR	TM/L	G	AB	R	H	2B	3B	HR	RBI	BB	SO	AVG	OBP	SLG	PRO+	BR/A	SB	CS	SBR	FA	FR	G/POS	TPR
1877	Cin-N	13	49	5	10	3	0	0	5	1		.204	.224	.265	59	-2				.920	-1	P-12/O-2	-0.1
1878	Cin-N	13	49	4	12	0	0	0	8	1	4	.245	.260	.245	74	-1				.944	0	/P-9,S-2,O	0.0
1879	Cle-N	30	109	11	16	2	0	0	6	0	14	.147	.147	.202	14	-10				.714	-6	P-23/O-9	-0.5
1882	StL-a	1	4	0	0	0	0	0	0	0	0	.000	.000	.000	-96	-1				.000	-1	/O-1,P-1	-0.1
Total	4	57	211	20	38	5	2	0	19	2	20	.180	.188	.223	35	-14				.811	-7	/P-45,O-13,S	-0.7

■ BOBBY MITCHELL
Mitchell, Robert Van b: 4/7/55, Salt Lake City, Utah BL/TL, 5'10", 170 lbs. Deb: 9/1/80

YEAR	TM/L	G	AB	R	H	2B	3B	HR	RBI	BB	SO	AVG	OBP	SLG	PRO+	BR/A	SB	CS	SBR	FA	FR	G/POS	TPR
1980	LA-N	9	3	1	1	0	0	0	0	1	0	.333	.500	.333	139	0	0	0	0	1.000	-3	/O-8	-0.3
1981	LA-N	10	8	0	1	0	0	0	0	1	4	.125	.222	.125	1	-1	0	0	0	1.000	-3	/O-7	-0.4
1982	Min-A	124	454	48	113	11	6	2	28	54	53	.249	.331	.313	76	-13	8	9	-3	.997	14	*O-121	-0.6
1983	Min-A	59	152	26	35	4	2	1	15	28	21	.230	.354	.303	80	-3	1	1	-0	.990	-3	O-44	-0.8
Total	4	202	617	75	150	15	8	3	43	84	78	.243	.337	.308	76	-17	9	10	-3	.996	5	O-180	-2.1

■ BOBBY MITCHELL
Mitchell, Robert Vance b: 10/22/43, Norristown, Pa. BR/TR, 6'4", 190 lbs. Deb: 7/5/70

YEAR	TM/L	G	AB	R	H	2B	3B	HR	RBI	BB	SO	AVG	OBP	SLG	PRO+	BR/A	SB	CS	SBR	FA	FR	G/POS	TPR
1970	NY-A	10	22	1	5	2	0	0	4	2	3	.227	.320	.318	81	-1	0	2	-1	1.000	1	/O-7	-0.1
1971	Mil-A	35	55	7	10	1	1	2	6	6	18	.182	.262	.345	72	-2	0	2	-1	.974	1	O-19	-0.4
1973	Mil-A	47	130	12	29	6	0	5	20	5	32	.223	.252	.385	79	-4	4	1	1	.960	-4	O-20,D-19	-0.9
1974	Mil-A	88	173	27	42	6	2	5	20	18	46	.243	.318	.387	103	0	7	6	-2	.969	-5	D-53,O-26	-0.8
1975	Mil-A	93	229	39	57	14	3	9	41	25	69	.249	.323	.454	117	0	3	4	-2	.992	-4	O-72,D-11	-0.3
Total	5	273	609	86	143	29	6	21	91	56	168	.235	.301	.406	100	-2	14	15	-5	.984	-11	O-144/D-83	-2.5

■ RALPH MITTERLING
Mitterling, Ralph "Sarge" b: 4/19/1890, Freeburg, Pa. d: 1/22/56, Pittsburgh, Pa. BR/TR, 5'10", 165 lbs. Deb: 7/7/16

YEAR	TM/L	G	AB	R	H	2B	3B	HR	RBI	BB	SO	AVG	OBP	SLG	PRO+	BR/A	SB	CS	SBR	FA	FR	G/POS	TPR
1916	Phi-A	13	39	1	6	0	0	0	2	3	6	.154	.214	.154	11	-4	0			.944	-2	O-12	-0.8

■ GEORGE MITTERWALD
Mitterwald, George Eugene b: 6/7/45, Berkeley, Cal. BR/TR, 6'2", 206 lbs. Deb: 9/15/66 C

YEAR	TM/L	G	AB	R	H	2B	3B	HR	RBI	BB	SO	AVG	OBP	SLG	PRO+	BR/A	SB	CS	SBR	FA	FR	G/POS	TPR
1966	Min-A	3	5	1	1	0	0	0	0	0	0	.200	.200	.200	14	-1	0	0	0	1.000	1	/C-3	0.0
1968	Min-A	11	34	1	7	1	0	0	1	3	8	.206	.270	.235	52	-2	0	0	0	.961	0	C-10	-0.1
1969	*Min-A	69	187	18	48	8	0	5	13	17	47	.257	.329	.380	96	-1	0	1	-1	.987	11	C-63/O-1	1.2
1970	*Min-A	117	369	36	82	12	2	15	46	34	84	.222	.291	.388	84	-9	3	5	-2	.996	24	*C-117	2.0
1971	Min-A	125	388	38	97	13	1	13	44	39	104	.250	.319	.389	97	-2	3	4	-1	.986	-10	*C-120	-0.9
1972	Min-A	64	163	12	30	4	1	1	8	9	37	.184	.227	.239	37	-13	0	1	-1	.984	6	C-61	-0.6
1973	Min-A	125	432	50	112	15	0	16	64	39	111	.259	.328	.405	101	1	3	3	-2	.992	-1	*C-122/D-3	0.5
1974	Chi-N	78	215	17	54	7	0	7	28	18	42	.251	.315	.381	90	-3	1	3	-2	.974	-4	C-68	-0.6
1975	Chi-N	84	200	19	44	4	3	5	26	19	42	.220	.288	.345	72	-8	0	0	0	.976	-1	C-59,1-10	-0.8
1976	Chi-N	101	303	19	65	7	0	5	28	16	63	.215	.254	.287	49	-20	1	1	0	.981	6	C-64,1-25	-2.2
1977	Chi-N	110	349	40	83	22	0	9	43	28	69	.238	.296	.378	72	-15	1	2	-1	.989	12	*C-109/1-1	0.1
Total	11	887	2645	251	623	93	7	76	301	222	607	.236	.298	.362	80	-73	14	17	-6	.987	40	C-796/1-36,DO	-1.4

■ JOHNNY MIZE
Mize, John Robert "The Big Cat" b: 1/7/13, Demorest, Ga. d: 6/2/93, Demorest, Ga. BL/TR, 6'2", 215 lbs. Deb: 4/16/36 CH

YEAR	TM/L	G	AB	R	H	2B	3B	HR	RBI	BB	SO	AVG	OBP	SLG	PRO+	BR/A	SB	CS	SBR	FA	FR	G/POS	TPR
1936	StL-N	126	414	76	136	30	8	19	93	50	32	.329	.402	.577	162	35	1			.994	1	1-97/O-8	2.5
1937	StL-N★	145	560	103	204	40	7	25	113	56	57	.364	.427	.595	171	55	2			.988	-13	*1-144	2.5

YEAR	TM/L	G	AB	R	H	2B	3B	HR	RBI	BB	SO	AVG	OBP	SLG	PRO+	BR/A	SB	CS	SBR	FA	FR	G/POS	TPR
1938	StL-N	149	531	85	179	34	16	27	102	74	47	.337	.422	.614	172	52	0			.989	-2	*1-140	3.4
1939	StL-N★	153	564	104	197	44	14	28	108	92	49	.349	.444	.626	174	60	0			.987	-4	*1-152	3.9
1940	StL-N★	155	579	111	182	31	13	43	137	82	49	.314	.404	.636	173	56	7			.990	-7	*1-153	3.4
1941	StL-N★	126	473	67	150	39	8	16	100	70	45	.317	.406	.535	153	34	4			.994	3	*1-122	2.8
1942	NY-N★	142	541	97	165	25	7	26	110	60	39	.305	.380	.521	161	40	3			.995	-3	*1-138	3.0
1946	NY-N★	101	377	70	127	18	3	22	70	62	26	.337	.437	.576	185	43	3			.989	5	*1-101	4.4
1947	NY-N★	154	586	137	177	26	2	51	138	74	42	.302	.384	.614	160	48	2			.996	4	*1-154	4.9
1948	NY-N★	152	560	110	162	26	4	40	125	94	37	.289	.395	.564	156	44	4			.991	4	*1-152	4.6
1949	NY-N★	106	388	59	102	15	0	18	62	50	19	.263	.351	.441	111	6	1			.994	2	*1-101	0.7
	*NY-A	13	23	4	6	1	0	1	2	4	2	.261	.393	.435	119	1	0	0	0	.980	-2	/1-6	0.0
1950	*NY-A	90	274	43	76	12	0	25	72	29	24	.277	.351	.595	143	14	0	1	-1	.996	-3	1-72	0.8
1951	*NY-A	113	332	37	86	14	1	10	49	36	24	.259	.339	.398	102	1	1	0	0	.994	-4	1-93	-0.7
1952	*NY-A	78	137	9	36	9	0	4	29	11	15	.263	.327	.416	112	2	0	0	0	.987	1	1-27	0.1
1953	*NY-A★	81	104	6	26	3	0	4	27	12	17	.250	.339	.394	101	0	0	0	0	1.000	0	1-15	-0.1
Total	15	1884	6443	1118	2011	367	83	359	1337	856	524	.312	.397	.562	157	490	28	1		.992	-14	*1-1667/O-8	36.2

■ JOHN MIZEROCK
Mizerock, John Joseph b: 12/8/60, Punxsutawney, Pa. BL/TR, 5'11", 190 lbs. Deb: 4/12/83

YEAR	TM/L	G	AB	R	H	2B	3B	HR	RBI	BB	SO	AVG	OBP	SLG	PRO+	BR/A	SB	CS	SBR	FA	FR	G/POS	TPR
1983	Hou-N	33	85	8	13	4	1	1	10	12	15	.153	.265	.259	49	-6	0	0	0	.967	1	C-33	-0.4
1985	Hou-N	15	38	6	9	4	0	0	6	2	8	.237	.293	.342	79	-1	0	0	0	.966	3	C-15	0.3
1986	Hou-N	44	81	9	15	1	1	1	6	24	16	.185	.377	.259	81	-1	0	0	0	.987	4	C-42	0.5
1989	Atl-N	11	27	1	6	0	0	0	2	0	3	.222	.222	.222	27	-3	0	0	0	1.000	0	C-11	-0.2
Total	4	103	231	24	43	9	2	2	24	38	42	.186	.309	.268	64	-10	0	0	0	.979	8	C-101	0.2

■ BILL MIZEUR
Mizeur, William Francis "Bad Bill" b: 6/22/1897, Nokomis, Ill. d: 8/27/76, Decatur, Ill. BL/TR, 6', 180 lbs. Deb: 9/30/23

YEAR	TM/L	G	AB	R	H	2B	3B	HR	RBI	BB	SO	AVG	OBP	SLG	PRO+	BR/A	SB	CS	SBR	FA	FR	G/POS	TPR
1923	StL-A	1	1	0	0	0	0	0	0	0	0	.000	.000	.000	-95	-0	0	0	0	.000	0	H	0.0
1924	StL-A	1	1	0	0	0	0	0	0	0	0	.000	.000	.000	-94	-0	0	0	0	.000	0	H	0.0
Total	2	2	2	0	0	0	0	0	0	0	0	.000	.000	.000	-94	-1	0				0	-0,-0	0.0

■ DAVE MOATES
Moates, David Allan b: 1/30/48, Great Lakes, Ill. BL/TL, 5'9", 163 lbs. Deb: 9/21/74

YEAR	TM/L	G	AB	R	H	2B	3B	HR	RBI	BB	SO	AVG	OBP	SLG	PRO+	BR/A	SB	CS	SBR	FA	FR	G/POS	TPR
1974	Tex-A	1	0	0	0	0	0	0	0	0	0	—	—	—	—	0	0	0	0	.000	0	R	0.0
1975	Tex-A	54	175	21	48	9	0	3	14	13	15	.274	.324	.377	99	-1	9	2	2	.984	1	O-51/D-1	0.0
1976	Tex-A	85	137	21	33	7	1	0	13	11	18	.241	.297	.307	75	-4	6	3	0	.991	-10	O-66/D-7	-1.7
Total	3	140	312	42	81	16	1	3	27	24	33	.260	.313	.346	88	-5	15	5	2	.987	-9	O-117/D-8	-1.7

■ DANNY MOELLER
Moeller, Daniel Edward b: 3/23/1885, DeWitt, Iowa d: 4/14/51, Florence, Ala. BB/TR, 5'11", 165 lbs. Deb: 9/24/07

YEAR	TM/L	G	AB	R	H	2B	3B	HR	RBI	BB	SO	AVG	OBP	SLG	PRO+	BR/A	SB	CS	SBR	FA	FR	G/POS	TPR
1907	Pit-N	11	42	4	12	1	1	0	3	4		.286	.348	.357	119	1	2			.800	-1	O-11	-0.2
1908	Pit-N	36	109	14	21	3	1	0	9	9		.193	.254	.239	57	-5	4			.950	-5	O-27	-1.3
1912	Was-A	132	519	90	143	26	10	6	46	52		.276	.346	.399	112	7	30			.944	10	*O-132	1.0
1913	Was-A	153	589	88	139	15	10	5	42	72	103	.236	.322	.321	86	-9	62			.926	6	*O-153	-1.1
1914	Was-A	151	571	83	143	19	10	1	45	71	89	.250	.341	.324	96	-1	26	25	-7	.930	-1	*O-150	-1.8
1915	Was-A	118	438	65	99	11	10	2	23	59	63	.226	.319	.311	87	-7	32	10	4	.952	-3	*O-116	-1.2
1916	Was-A	78	240	30	59	8	1	1	23	30	35	.246	.335	.300	92	-2	13			.963	2	O-63	-0.4
	Cle-A	25	30	5	2	0	0	0	1	5	6	.067	.200	.067	-19	-4	2			1.000	-2	/O-8,2-1	-0.7
	Yr	103	270	35	61	8	1	1	24	35	41	.226	.319	.274	78	-6	15			.966	-1	O-71/2-1	-1.1
Total	7	704	2538	379	618	83	43	15	192	302	296	.243	.328	.328	93	-20	171	35		.938	5	O-660/2-1	-5.7

■ JOE MOFFETT
Moffett, Joseph W. b: 6/1859, Wheeling, W.Va. 6', 179 lbs. Deb: 5/6/1884 F

YEAR	TM/L	G	AB	R	H	2B	3B	HR	RBI	BB	SO	AVG	OBP	SLG	PRO+	BR/A	SB	CS	SBR	FA	FR	G/POS	TPR
1884	Tol-a	56	204	17	41	5	3	0		2		.201	.209	.255	49	-12				.957	-5	1-38,3-11/2O	-2.0

■ SAM MOFFETT
Moffett, Samuel R. b: 3/14/1857, Wheeling, W.Va. d: 5/5/07, Butte, Mont. BR/TR, 6', 175 lbs. Deb: 5/15/1884 F

YEAR	TM/L	G	AB	R	H	2B	3B	HR	RBI	BB	SO	AVG	OBP	SLG	PRO+	BR/A	SB	CS	SBR	FA	FR	G/POS	TPR
1884	Cle-N	67	256	26	47	12	2	0	15	8	56	.184	.208	.246	41	-17				.827	6	O-42,P-24/132	-0.8
1887	Ind-N	11	41	6	5	1	0	0	1	1	6	.122	.143	.146	-20	-7	2			.857	-3	/P-6,O-5	-0.4
1888	Ind-N	10	35	6	4	0	0	0	0	5	4	.114	.225	.114	11	-3	0			.750	-1	/P-7,O-3	-0.2
Total	3	88	332	38	56	13	2	0	16	14	66	.169	.202	.220	30	-27	2			.821	1	/O-50,P-37,123	-1.4

■ JOHN MOHARDT
Mohardt, John Henry b: 1/21/1898, Pittsburgh, Pa. d: 11/24/61, LaJolla, Cal. BR/TR, 5'10", 165 lbs. Deb: 4/15/22

YEAR	TM/L	G	AB	R	H	2B	3B	HR	RBI	BB	SO	AVG	OBP	SLG	PRO+	BR/A	SB	CS	SBR	FA	FR	G/POS	TPR
1922	Det-A	5	1	2	1	0	0	0	0	0	1	1.000	1.000	1.000	436	1	0	1	-1	1.000	-1	/O-3	-0.1

■ KID MOHLER
Mohler, Ernest Follette b: 12/13/1874, Oneida, Ill. d: 11/4/61, San Francisco, Cal. BR/TL, 5'4.5", 145 lbs. Deb: 9/29/1894

YEAR	TM/L	G	AB	R	H	2B	3B	HR	RBI	BB	SO	AVG	OBP	SLG	PRO+	BR/A	SB	CS	SBR	FA	FR	G/POS	TPR
1894	Was-N	3	9	0	1	0	0	0	0	2	4	.111	.273	.111	-5	-2	0			.952	2	/2-3	0.0

■ JOHNNY MOKAN
Mokan, John Leo b: 9/23/1895, Buffalo, N.Y. d: 2/10/85, Buffalo, N.Y. BR/TR, 5'7", 165 lbs. Deb: 4/15/21

YEAR	TM/L	G	AB	R	H	2B	3B	HR	RBI	BB	SO	AVG	OBP	SLG	PRO+	BR/A	SB	CS	SBR	FA	FR	G/POS	TPR
1921	Pit-N	19	52	7	14	3	2	0	9	5	3	.269	.333	.404	92	-1	0	0	0	.946	5	O-15	-0.1
1922	Pit-N	31	89	9	23	3	1	0	8	9	3	.258	.327	.315	65	-4	0	1	-1	.903	-4	O-23	-1.0
	Phi-N	47	151	20	38	7	1	3	27	16	25	.252	.327	.371	73	-6	1	0	0	.905	-6	O-37/3-2	-1.4
	Yr	78	240	29	61	10	2	3	35	25	28	.254	.327	.350	70	-11	1	1	-0	.905	-10	O-60/3-2	-2.4
1923	Phi-N	113	400	76	125	23	3	10	48	53	31	.313	.401	.460	113	8	6	11	-5	.969	7	*O-105/3-1	0.4
1924	Phi-N	96	366	50	95	15	1	7	44	30	27	.260	.321	.363	74	-14	7	5	0	.986	-0	O-94	-2.1
1925	Phi-N	75	209	30	69	11	2	6	42	27	9	.330	.417	.488	120	7	3	5	-2	.984	-12	O-68	-1.1
1926	Phi-N	127	456	68	138	23	5	6	62	41	35	.303	.365	.414	104	3	4			.967	-8	*O-123	-1.3
1927	Phi-N	74	213	22	61	13	2	0	33	25	21	.286	.361	.366	94	-1	5			.962	-9	O-63	-1.4
Total	7	582	1936	282	563	98	17	32	273	206	150	.291	.364	.409	97	-8	26	22		.966	-32	O-528/3-3	-8.0

■ FENTON MOLE
Mole, Fenton Le Roy "Muscles" b: 6/14/25, San Leandro, Cal. BL/TL, 6'1.5", 200 lbs. Deb: 9/1/49

YEAR	TM/L	G	AB	R	H	2B	3B	HR	RBI	BB	SO	AVG	OBP	SLG	PRO+	BR/A	SB	CS	SBR	FA	FR	G/POS	TPR
1949	NY-A	10	27	2	5	2	1	0	2	5	3	.185	.267	.333	58	-2	0	0	0	1.000	1	/1-8	-0.1

■ BOB MOLINARO
Molinaro, Robert Joseph b: 5/21/50, Newark, N.J. BL/TR, 6', 190 lbs. Deb: 9/18/75

YEAR	TM/L	G	AB	R	H	2B	3B	HR	RBI	BB	SO	AVG	OBP	SLG	PRO+	BR/A	SB	CS	SBR	FA	FR	G/POS	TPR
1975	Det-A	6	19	2	5	1	0	1	0	1	0	.263	.300	.368	84	-0	0	0	0	1.000	-0	/O-6	-0.1
1977	Det-A	4	4	0	1	1	0	0	0	0	2	.250	.250	.500	94	-0	0	0	0	.000	-0	H	0.0
	Chi-A	1	2	0	1	0	0	0	0	0	0	.500	.500	.500	174	-0	1	0	0	1.000	-0	/O-1	0.0
	Yr	5	6	0	2	1	0	0	0	0	2	.333	.333	.500	119	0	1	0	0	1.000	-0	/O-1	0.0
1978	Chi-A	105	286	39	75	5	5	6	27	19	12	.262	.315	.378	93	-3	22	6	3	1.000	-7	O-62,D-32	-1.1
1979	Bal-A	8	6	0	0	0	0	0	0	1	3	.000	.143	.000	-60	-1	1	0	0	1.000	-1	/O-5	-0.2
1980	Chi-A	119	344	48	100	16	4	5	36	26	29	.291	.353	.404	107	4	18	7	1	1.000	-0	O-49,D-47	-0.1
1981	Chi-A	47	42	7	11	1	1	0	9	6	4	.262	.392	.405	133	2	1	0	0	1.000	0	/O-2,D-4	0.2
1982	Chi-N	65	66	6	13	1	0	1	12	6	5	.197	.264	.258	45	-5	1	1	0	1.000	-1	/O-4	-0.7
	Phi-N	19	14	0	4	0	0	0	2	3	1	.286	.412	.286	96	0	1	0	0	1.000	0	/O-4	0.0
	Yr	84	80	6	17	1	0	1	14	9	6	.213	.292	.262	55	-5	2	1	0	1.000	-1	/O-8	-0.7
1983	Phi-N	19	18	1	2	1	0	0	3	3	3	.111	.111	.333	19	-2	0	0	0	1.000	0	/D-1	-0.3
	Det-A	8	2	0	0	0	0	0	0	1	1	.000	.333	.000	1	-0	1	1	-0	.000	-0	/O-1	-0.1
Total	8	401	803	106	212	25	11	14	90	65	57	.264	.328	.375	95	-6	46	15	5	.980	-12	O-129/D-84	-2.4

■ PAUL MOLITOR
Molitor, Paul Leo b: 8/22/56, St.Paul, Minn. BR/TR, 6', 185 lbs. Deb: 4/7/78

YEAR	TM/L	G	AB	R	H	2B	3B	HR	RBI	BB	SO	AVG	OBP	SLG	PRO+	BR/A	SB	CS	SBR	FA	FR	G/POS	TPR
1978	Mil-A	125	521	73	142	26	4	6	45	19	54	.273	.303	.372	89	-9	30	12	2	.976	-5	2-91,S-31/3D	-0.1
1979	Mil-A	140	584	88	188	27	16	9	62	48	48	.322	.375	.469	126	21	33	13	2	.979	1	*2-122,S-10/D	3.3
1980	Mil-A†	111	450	81	137	29	2	9	37	48	48	.304	.375	.438	126	17	34	7	6	.971	-2	2-91,S-12/3D	2.8

YEAR	TM/L	G	AB	R	H	2B	3B	HR	RBI	BB	SO	AVG	OBP	SLG	PRO+	BR/A	SB	CS	SBR	FA	FR	G/POS	TPR
1981	*Mil-A	64	251	45	67	11	0	2	19	25	29	.267	.341	.335	100	1	10	6	-1	.976	2	O-46,D-16	-0.1
1982	*Mil-A	160	666	**136**	201	26	8	19	71	69	93	.302	.368	.450	132	29	41	9	7	.942	-1	*3-150/S-4,D	3.1
1983	Mil-A	152	608	95	164	28	6	15	47	59	74	.270	.336	.410	113	10	41	8	8	.966	2	*3-146/D-2	1.7
1984	Mil-A	13	46	3	10	1	0	0	6	2	8	.217	.250	.239	38	-4	1	0	0	.933	4	/3-7,D-4	0.0
1985	Mil-A★	140	576	93	171	28	3	10	48	54	80	.297	.358	.408	110	8	21	7	3	.953	-2	*3-135/D-4	0.6
1986	Mil-A	105	437	62	123	24	6	9	55	40	81	.281	.342	.426	104	2	20	5	3	.944	2	3-91,D-10/O	0.5
1987	Mil-A	118	465	114	164	41	5	16	75	69	67	.353	.438	.566	159	42	45	10	8	.947	-10	D-58,3-41,2	3.5
1988	Mil-A★	154	609	115	190	34	6	13	60	71	54	.312	.386	.452	132	28	41	10	6	.941	-8	*3-105,D-49/2	2.4
1989	Mil-A	155	615	84	194	35	4	11	56	64	67	.315	.384	.439	133	28	27	11	2	.950	4	*3-112,D-28,2	3.4
1990	Mil-A	103	418	64	119	27	6	12	45	37	51	.285	.344	.464	125	13	18	3	4	.988	-1	2-60,1-37/3D	1.4
1991	Mil-A	158	665	**133**	**216**	32	**13**	17	75	77	62	.325	.400	.489	148	45	19	8	1	.986	-1	*D-112,1-46	3.6
1992	Mil-A★	158	609	89	195	36	7	12	89	73	66	.320	.396	.461	142	36	31	6	6	.996	-4	*D-108,1-48	3.1
1993	*Tor-A	160	636	121	**211**	37	5	22	111	77	71	.332	.406	.509	144	40	22	4	4	.985	-1	*D-137,1-23	3.5
1994	Tor-A★	115	454	86	155	30	4	14	75	55	48	.341	.414	.518	137	20	20	6	1	1.000	5	*D-110/1-5	2.5
Total	17	2131	8610	1482	2647	472	95	196	976	887	1001	.307	.375	.453	128	333	454	119	65	.950	-21	3-791,D-665,21/SO	35.2

■ FRED MOLLENKAMP
Mollenkamp, Frederick Henry b: 3/15/1890, Cincinnati, Ohio d: 11/1/48, Cincinnati, Ohio Deb: 8/29/14

YEAR	TM/L	G	AB	R	H	2B	3B	HR	RBI	BB	SO	AVG	OBP	SLG	PRO+	BR/A	SB	CS	SBR	FA	FR	G/POS	TPR
1914	Phi-N	3	8	0	1	0	0	0	0	2	0	.125	.300	.125	26	-1	0			1.000	2	/1-3	0.1

■ FRITZ MOLLWITZ
Mollwitz, Frederick August b: 6/16/1890, Coburg, Germany d: 10/3/67, Bradenton, Fla. BR/TR, 6'2", 170 lbs. Deb: 9/26/13

YEAR	TM/L	G	AB	R	H	2B	3B	HR	RBI	BB	SO	AVG	OBP	SLG	PRO+	BR/A	SB	CS	SBR	FA	FR	G/POS	TPR
1913	Chi-N	2	7	1	3	0	0	0	0	0	0	.429	.429	.429	145	0	0			1.000	0	/1-2	0.0
1914	Chi-N	13	20	0	3	0	0	0	1	0	3	.150	.150	.150	-11	-3	1			.962	-1	/1-4,O-1	-0.4
	Cin-N	32	111	12	18	2	0	0	5	3	9	.162	.198	.180	12	-12	2			.991	1	1-32	-1.3
	Yr	45	131	12	21	2	0	0	6	3	12	.160	.191	.176	9	-15	3			.989	0	1-36/O-1	-1.7
1915	Cin-N	153	525	36	136	21	3	1	51	15	49	.259	.281	.316	79	-14	19	11	-1	**.996**	0	*1-153	-2.1
1916	Cin-N	65	183	12	41	4	4	0	16	5	12	.224	.245	.290	65	-8	6			.981	-1	1-54	-1.2
	Chi-N	33	71	1	19	2	0	0	11	7	6	.268	.333	.296	85	-1	4			.976	-1	1-19/O-6	-0.3
	Yr	98	254	13	60	6	4	0	27	12	18	.236	.271	.291	71	-9	10			.980	-2	1-73/O-6	-1.5
1917	Pit-N	36	140	15	36	4	1	0	12	8	8	.257	.297	.300	81	-3	4			.994	-1	1-36/2-1	-0.6
1918	Pit-N	119	432	43	116	12	7	0	45	23	24	.269	.305	.329	90	-6	23			.990	-0	*1-119	-1.2
1919	Pit-N	56	168	11	29	2	4	0	12	15	18	.173	.249	.232	43	-11	9			.994	-3	1-53/O-1	-1.8
	StL-N	25	83	7	19	3	0	0	5	7	3	.229	.289	.265	71	-3	2			.994	1	1-25	-0.3
	Yr	81	251	18	48	5	4	0	17	22	21	.191	.262	.243	52	-14	11			.994	-3	1-78/O-1	-2.1
Total	7	534	1740	138	420	50	19	1	158	83	132	.241	.278	.294	72	-61	70	11		.991	-6	1-497/O-8,2	-9.2

■ BLAS MONACO
Monaco, Blas b: 11/16/15, San Antonio, Tex. BB/TR, 5'11", 170 lbs. Deb: 8/18/37

YEAR	TM/L	G	AB	R	H	2B	3B	HR	RBI	BB	SO	AVG	OBP	SLG	PRO+	BR/A	SB	CS	SBR	FA	FR	G/POS	TPR
1937	Cle-A	5	7	0	2	0	1	0	2	0	2	.286	.375	.571	134	0	0	0	0	1.000	0	/2-3	0.1
1946	Cle-A	12	6	2	0	0	0	0	0	1	1	.000	.143	.000	-62	-1	0	0	0	.000	0	H	-0.1
Total	2	17	13	2	2	0	1	0	2	1	3	.154	.267	.308	53	-1	0	0	0	1.000	0	/2-3	0.0

■ FREDDIE MONCEWICZ
Moncewicz, Frederick Alfred b: 9/1/03, Brockton, Mass. d: 4/23/69, Brockton, Mass. BR/TR, 5'8.5", 175 lbs. Deb: 6/19/28

YEAR	TM/L	G	AB	R	H	2B	3B	HR	RBI	BB	SO	AVG	OBP	SLG	PRO+	BR/A	SB	CS	SBR	FA	FR	G/POS	TPR
1928	Bos-A	3	1	0	0	0	0	0	0	0	1	.000	.000	.000	-99	-0	0	0	0	1.000	0	/S-2	0.0

■ ALEX MONCHAK
Monchak, Alex b: 12/22/19, Bayonne, N.J. BR/TR, 6', 180 lbs. Deb: 6/22/40 C

YEAR	TM/L	G	AB	R	H	2B	3B	HR	RBI	BB	SO	AVG	OBP	SLG	PRO+	BR/A	SB	CS	SBR	FA	FR	G/POS	TPR
1940	Phi-N	19	14	1	2	0	0	0	0	0	6	.143	.143	.143	-22	-2	1			.833	0	/S-9,2-1	-0.2

■ RICK MONDAY
Monday, Robert James b: 11/20/45, Batesville, Ark. BL/TL, 6'3", 200 lbs. Deb: 9/3/66

YEAR	TM/L	G	AB	R	H	2B	3B	HR	RBI	BB	SO	AVG	OBP	SLG	PRO+	BR/A	SB	CS	SBR	FA	FR	G/POS	TPR
1966	KC-A	17	41	4	4	1	1	0	2	6	16	.098	.213	.171	12	-5	1	1	-0	.964	-1	O-15	-0.7
1967	KC-A	124	406	52	102	14	6	14	58	42	107	.251	.324	.419	122	10	3	6	-3	.972	15	*O-113	1.9
1968	Oak-A★	148	482	56	132	24	7	8	49	72	143	.274	.373	.402	142	26	14	6	1	.978	-0	*O-144	2.2
1969	Oak-A	122	399	57	108	17	4	12	54	72	100	.271	.389	.424	133	20	12	3	2	.964	-2	*O-119	1.5
1970	Oak-A	112	376	63	109	19	7	10	37	58	99	.290	.388	.457	137	20	17	11	-2	.981	1	*O-109	1.5
1971	*Oak-A	116	355	53	87	9	3	18	56	49	93	.245	.337	.439	121	9	6	9	-4	.984	-0	*O-111	0.1
1972	Chi-N	138	434	68	108	22	5	11	42	78	102	.249	.365	.399	105	5	12	9	-2	**.996**	-6	*O-134	-0.9
1973	Chi-N	149	554	93	148	24	5	26	56	92	124	.267	.372	.469	123	18	5	12	-6	.973	1	*O-148	0.7
1974	Chi-N	142	538	84	158	19	7	20	58	70	94	.294	.377	.467	130	22	7	9	-3	.984	2	*O-139	1.5
1975	Chi-N	136	491	89	131	29	4	17	60	83	95	.267	.374	.446	121	15	8	3	1	.973	1	*O-131	1.2
1976	Chi-N	137	534	107	145	20	5	32	77	60	125	.272	.347	.507	129	26	5	9	-4	.993	7	*O-103,1-32	1.6
1977	*LA-N	118	392	47	90	13	1	15	48	60	109	.230	.332	.383	91	-4	2	4	-2	.991	-11	*O-115/1-3	-2.2
1978	*LA-N★	119	342	54	87	14	1	19	57	49	100	.254	.349	.468	127	12	2	4	-2	.995	-11	*O-103/1-1	-0.5
1979	LA-N	12	33	2	10	0	0	0	2	5	6	.303	.395	.303	94	0	0	0	0	.964	-0	O-10	0.0
1980	LA-N	96	194	35	52	7	1	10	25	28	49	.268	.363	.469	133	9	2	2	-1	.969	-7	O-50	-0.1
1981	*LA-N	66	130	24	41	1	2	11	25	24	42	.315	.426	.608	198	17	1	2	-1	.962	-6	O-41	1.0
1982	*LA-N	104	210	37	54	6	4	11	42	39	51	.257	.376	.481	142	12	2	1	0	.943	-7	O-57/1-4	0.4
1983	*LA-N	99	178	21	44	7	1	6	20	29	42	.247	.353	.399	108	3	0	0	0	.969	-4	O-44/1-4	-0.3
1984	LA-N	31	47	4	9	2	0	1	7	8	16	.191	.309	.298	72	-2	0	0	0	.987	-1	1-10/O-2	-0.4
Total	19	1986	6136	950	1619	248	64	241	775	924	1513	.264	.362	.443	124	207	98	91	-25	.979	-29	*O-1688/1-54	8.5

■ RAUL MONDESI
Mondesi, Raul Ramon (Avelino) b: 3/12/71, San Cristobal, D.R. BR/TR, 5'11", 202 lbs. Deb: 7/19/93

YEAR	TM/L	G	AB	R	H	2B	3B	HR	RBI	BB	SO	AVG	OBP	SLG	PRO+	BR/A	SB	CS	SBR	FA	FR	G/POS	TPR
1993	LA-N	42	86	13	25	3	1	4	10	4	16	.291	.322	.488	120	2	4	1	0	.951	-5	O-40	-0.2
1994	LA-N	112	434	63	133	27	8	16	56	16	78	.306	.334	.516	125	13	11	8	-2	.965	2	*O-112	1.1
Total	2	154	520	76	158	30	9	20	66	20	94	.304	.332	.512	124	15	15	9	-1	.962	-3	O-152	0.9

■ DON MONEY
Money, Donald Wayne "Brooks" b: 6/7/47, Washington, D.C. BR/TR, 6'1", 190 lbs. Deb: 4/10/68

YEAR	TM/L	G	AB	R	H	2B	3B	HR	RBI	BB	SO	AVG	OBP	SLG	PRO+	BR/A	SB	CS	SBR	FA	FR	G/POS	TPR
1968	Phi-N	4	13	1	3	2	0	0	2	2	4	.231	.333	.385	115	0	0	1	-1	1.000	-1	/S-4	-0.1
1969	Phi-N	127	450	41	103	22	2	6	42	43	83	.229	.298	.327	77	-14	1	3	-2	.969	17	*S-126	1.6
1970	Phi-N	120	447	66	132	25	4	14	66	43	68	.295	.366	.463	124	15	4	7	-3	.961	11	*3-119/S-2	2.2
1971	Phi-N	121	439	40	98	22	8	7	38	31	80	.223	.279	.358	79	-13	4	1	1	.953	5	3-68,O-40,2	-0.8
1972	Phi-N	152	536	54	119	16	2	15	52	41	92	.222	.280	.343	74	-19	5	7	-3	**.978**	20	*3-151/S-2	-0.3
1973	Mil-A	145	556	75	158	28	2	11	61	53	53	.284	.350	.401	113	10	22	5	4	.971	-23	*3-124,S-21	-0.8
1974	Mil-A☆	159	629	85	178	32	3	15	65	62	80	.283	.349	.415	120	16	19	6	2	**.989**	-10	*3-157/2-1,D	0.8
1975	Mil-A	109	405	58	112	16	1	15	43	31	51	.277	.333	.432	114	7	7	9	-3	.951	-21	3-99/S-7	-1.8
1976	Mil-A★	117	439	51	117	18	4	12	62	47	50	.267	.337	.408	120	11	6	5	-1	.958	-3	*3-103,D-10/S	0.4
1977	Mil-A†	152	570	86	159	28	3	25	83	57	70	.279	.352	.470	122	17	8	5	-1	.981	-3	*2-116,O-23,3/D	2.0
1978	Mil-A★	137	518	88	152	30	2	14	54	48	70	.293	.361	.440	124	16	3	0	1	.994	-2	1-61,2-36,3D/S	1.4
1979	Mil-A	92	350	52	83	20	1	6	38	40	47	.237	.319	.351	81	-9	1	0	0	1.000	0	D-33,3-26,12	-1.2
1980	Mil-A	86	289	39	74	17	1	17	46	40	36	.256	.348	.498	133	13	0	0	0	.940	2	3-55,1-14,D/2	1.1
1981	*Mil-A	60	185	17	40	7	0	2	14	19	27	.216	.293	.286	71	-7	0	0	0	.977	-5	3-56/1-1,D	-1.3
1982	*Mil-A	96	275	40	78	14	3	16	55	32	38	.284	.360	.531	152	15	0	0	0	.923	5	D-66,3-16,1/2	1.8
1983	Mil-A	43	114	5	17	5	0	1	8	11	17	.149	.224	.219	24	-12	0	0	0	.980	4	D-28,3-11/1	-1.3
Total	16	1720	6215	798	1623	302	36	176	729	600	866	.261	.330	.406	106	49	80	51	-7	.968	-7	*3-1025,2-192,DS1/O	4.1

■ FRANK MONROE
Monroe, Frank W. b: Hamilton, Ohio Deb: 7/18/1884

YEAR	TM/L	G	AB	R	H	2B	3B	HR	RBI	BB	SO	AVG	OBP	SLG	PRO+	BR/A	SB	CS	SBR	FA	FR	G/POS	TPR
1884	Ind-a	2	8	1	0	0	0	0	0		0	.000	.000	.000	-99	-2				1.000	-1	/O-1,C-1	-0.3

YEAR	TM/L	G	AB	R	H	2B	3B	HR	RBI	BB	SO	AVG	OBP	SLG	PRO+	BR/A	SB	CS	SBR	FA	FR	G/POS	TPR

■ JOHN MONROE   Monroe, John Allen b: 8/24/1898, Farmersville, Tex. d: 6/19/56, Conroe, Tex. BL/TR, 5'10", 160 lbs. Deb: 4/16/21

YEAR	TM/L	G	AB	R	H	2B	3B	HR	RBI	BB	SO	AVG	OBP	SLG	PRO+	BR/A	SB	CS	SBR	FA	FR	G/POS	TPR
1921	NY-N	19	21	4	3	0	0	1	3	3	6	.143	.280	.286	50	-2	0	0	0	.846	2	/2-8,S-1	0.0
	Phi-N	41	133	13	38	4	2	1	8	11	9	.286	.345	.368	82	-3	2	2	-1	.938	5	2-28/3-9	0.3
	Yr	60	154	17	41	4	2	2	11	14	15	.266	.335	.357	79	-4	2	2	-1	.920	7	2-36/3-9,S	0.3

■ ED MONTAGUE   Montague, Edward Francis b: 7/24/05, San Francisco, Cal. d: 6/17/88, Daly City, Cal. BR/TR, 5'10", 165 lbs. Deb: 5/14/28

YEAR	TM/L	G	AB	R	H	2B	3B	HR	RBI	BB	SO	AVG	OBP	SLG	PRO+	BR/A	SB	CS	SBR	FA	FR	G/POS	TPR
1928	Cle-A	32	51	12	12	0	1	0	3	6	7	.235	.339	.275	62	-3	0	0	0	.914	5	S-15/3-9	0.4
1930	Cle-A	58	179	37	47	5	2	1	16	37	38	.263	.392	.330	82	-3	1	5	-3	.917	-15	S-46,3-13	-1.4
1931	Cle-A	64	193	27	55	8	3	1	26	21	22	.285	.358	.373	87	-3	3	4	-2	.924	16	S-64	1.5
1932	Cle-A	66	192	29	47	5	1	0	24	21	24	.245	.326	.281	55	-12	3	3	-1	.891	-13	S-57,3-11	-2.1
Total	4	220	615	105	161	18	7	2	69	85	91	.262	.357	.324	74	-21	7	12	-5	.912	-7	S-182/3-33	-1.6

■ WILLIE MONTANEZ   Montanez, Guillermo (Naranjo) b: 4/1/48, Catano, P.R. BL/TL, 6'1", 193 lbs. Deb: 4/12/66

YEAR	TM/L	G	AB	R	H	2B	3B	HR	RBI	BB	SO	AVG	OBP	SLG	PRO+	BR/A	SB	CS	SBR	FA	FR	G/POS	TPR
1966	Cal-A	8	2	0	0	0	0	0	0	0	2	.000	.000	.000	-99	-1	1	0	0	1.000	0	/1-2	0.0
1970	Phi-N	18	25	3	6	0	0	0	3	1	4	.240	.269	.240	39	-2	0	0	0	1.000	-1	O-10/1-5	-0.3
1971	Phi-N	158	599	78	153	27	6	30	99	67	105	.255	.333	.471	126	19	4	7	-3	.972	5	*O-158/1-9	1.3
1972	Phi-N	147	531	60	131	39	3	13	64	58	108	.247	.322	.405	103	2	1	3	-2	.985	14	*O-130,1-14	0.8
1973	Phi-N	146	552	69	145	16	5	11	65	46	80	.263	.326	.370	90	-7	2	6	-3	.994	-6	1-99,O-51	-2.7
1974	Phi-N	143	527	55	160	33	1	7	79	32	57	.304	.347	.410	107	4	3	6	-3	.992	-1	*1-137/O-1	-1.0
1975	Phi-N	21	84	9	24	8	0	2	16	4	12	.286	.318	.452	108	0	1	0	0	.990	2	1-21	0.1
	SF-N	135	518	52	158	26	2	8	85	45	50	.305	.365	.409	110	7	5	3	-0	.994	-1	*1-134	-0.3
	Yr	156	602	61	182	34	2	10	101	49	62	.302	.359	.415	110	8	6	3	0	.993	0	*1-155	-0.2
1976	SF-N	60	230	22	71	15	2	2	20	15	15	.309	.354	.417	115	4	2	1	0	.989	4	1-58	0.4
	Atl-N	103	420	52	135	14	0	9	64	21	32	.321	.354	.419	112	6	0	4	-2	.986	-6	*1-103	-1.0
	Yr	163	650	74	206	29	2	11	84	36	47	.317	.354	.418	113	10	2	5	-2	.987	-1	*1-161	-0.6
1977	Atl-N★	136	544	70	156	31	1	20	68	35	60	.287	.330	.458	97	-3	1	1	-0	.992	-4	*1-134	-1.6
1978	NY-N	159	609	66	156	32	0	17	96	60	92	.256	.324	.392	103	3	9	4	0	.995	3	*1-158	-0.6
1979	NY-N	109	410	36	96	19	0	5	47	25	48	.234	.280	.317	65	-21	0	1	-1	.989	1	*1-108	-2.6
	Tex-A	38	144	19	46	6	0	8	24	8	14	.319	.359	.528	137	7	0	1	-1	.995	1	1-19,D-17	0.6
1980	SD-N	128	481	39	132	12	4	6	63	36	52	.274	.329	.353	96	-3	3	4	-2	.994	1	*1-124	-1.1
	Mon-N	14	19	1	4	0	0	0	1	3	3	.211	.318	.211	50	-1	0	1	-1	1.000	0	/1-4	-0.2
	Yr	142	500	40	136	12	4	6	64	39	55	.272	.328	.348	94	-4	3	5	-2	.994	1	*1-128	-1.3
1981	Mon-N	26	62	6	11	0	1	0	5	4	9	.177	.227	.210	24	-6	0	1	-1	.992	1	1-16	-0.6
	Pit-N	29	38	2	10	0	0	1	1	1	2	.263	.282	.342	74	-1	0	0	0	1.000	-1	1-11	-0.3
	Yr	55	100	8	21	0	1	1	6	5	11	.210	.248	.260	43	-7	0	1	-1	.995	0	1-27	-0.9
1982	Pit-N	36	32	4	9	1	0	0	1	3	3	.281	.343	.313	82	-1	0	0	0	1.000	0	/1-2,O-2	-0.1
	Phi-N	18	16	0	1	0	0	0	1	1	3	.063	.118	.063	-47	-3	0	0	0	1.000	1	/1-6	-0.3
	Yr	54	48	4	10	1	0	0	2	4	6	.208	.269	.229	40	-4	0	0	0	1.000	1	/1-8,O-2	-0.4
Total	14	1632	5843	645	1604	279	25	139	802	465	751	.275	.331	.402	101	1	32	42	-16	.992	15	*1-1164,O-352/D	-9.5

■ RENE MONTEAGUDO   Monteagudo, Rene (Miranda) b: 3/12/16, Havana, Cuba d: 9/14/73, Hialeah, Fla. BL/TL, 5'7", 165 lbs. Deb: 9/6/38 F

YEAR	TM/L	G	AB	R	H	2B	3B	HR	RBI	BB	SO	AVG	OBP	SLG	PRO+	BR/A	SB	CS	SBR	FA	FR	G/POS	TPR
1938	Was-A	5	6	0	3	0	0	0	1	0	0	.500	.500	.500	162	1	0	0	0	1.000	-1	/P-5	0.0
1940	Was-A	27	33	4	6	1	1	0	1	1	4	.182	.206	.273	24	-4	0	0	0	.941	-1	P-27	0.0
1944	Was-A	10	38	2	11	2	0	0	4	0	1	.289	.289	.342	84	-1	0	0	0	.929	-1	/O-9	-0.3
1945	Phi-N	114	193	26	58	6	0	0	15	28	7	.301	.389	.332	104	3	2			.918	-1	O-35,P-14	0.0
Total	4	156	270	32	78	9	1	0	21	29	12	.289	.358	.330	94	-2	2	0		.889	-4	/P-46,O-44	-0.3

■ FELIPE MONTEMAYOR   Montemayor, Felipe Angel "Monty" b: 2/7/30, Monterrey, Mexico BL/TR, 6'2", 185 lbs. Deb: 4/14/53

YEAR	TM/L	G	AB	R	H	2B	3B	HR	RBI	BB	SO	AVG	OBP	SLG	PRO+	BR/A	SB	CS	SBR	FA	FR	G/POS	TPR
1953	Pit-N	28	55	5	6	4	0	0	2	4	13	.109	.210	.182	3	-8	0	0	0	1.000	1	O-12	-0.7
1955	Pit-N	36	95	10	20	1	3	2	8	18	24	.211	.342	.347	85	-2	1	0	0	.957	-5	O-28	-0.8
Total	2	64	150	15	26	5	3	2	10	22	37	.173	.295	.287	55	-10	1	0	0	.974	-5	/O-40	-1.5

■ AL MONTGOMERY   Montgomery, Alvin Atlas b: 7/3/20, Loving, N.Mex. d: 4/26/42, Waverly, Va. BR/TR, 5'10.5", 185 lbs. Deb: 6/20/41

YEAR	TM/L	G	AB	R	H	2B	3B	HR	RBI	BB	SO	AVG	OBP	SLG	PRO+	BR/A	SB	CS	SBR	FA	FR	G/POS	TPR
1941	Bos-N	42	52	4	10	1	0	0	4	9	8	.192	.323	.212	55	-3	0			.976	-6	C-30	-0.8

■ BOB MONTGOMERY   Montgomery, Robert Edward b: 4/16/44, Nashville, Tenn. BR/TR, 6'1", 203 lbs. Deb: 9/6/70

YEAR	TM/L	G	AB	R	H	2B	3B	HR	RBI	BB	SO	AVG	OBP	SLG	PRO+	BR/A	SB	CS	SBR	FA	FR	G/POS	TPR
1970	Bos-A	22	78	8	14	2	0	1	4	6	20	.179	.247	.244	33	-7	0	0	0	.981	0	C-22	-0.6
1971	Bos-A	67	205	19	49	11	2	2	24	16	43	.239	.304	.341	77	-6	1	0	0	.989	-3	C-66	-0.7
1972	Bos-A	24	77	7	22	1	0	2	7	3	17	.286	.313	.377	99	-0	0	0	0	.985	-2	C-22	-0.2
1973	Bos-A	34	128	18	41	6	2	7	25	7	36	.320	.356	.563	146	7	0	0	0	.974	1	C-33	0.9
1974	Bos-A	88	254	26	64	10	0	4	38	13	50	.252	.291	.339	75	-8	3	0	1	.977	-6	C-79/D-5	-1.1
1975	*Bos-A	62	195	16	44	10	1	2	26	4	37	.226	.245	.318	53	-12	1	1	-0	.987	-5	C-53/1-6,D	-1.6
1976	Bos-A	31	93	10	23	3	1	3	13	5	20	.247	.286	.398	88	-2	0	1	-1	.983	-1	C-30/D-1	-0.2
1977	Bos-A	17	40	6	12	2	0	2	7	4	9	.300	.378	.500	123	1	0	0	0	.982	-0	C-15	0.1
1978	Bos-A	10	29	2	7	1	0	0	5	2	12	.241	.290	.345	70	-1	0	0	0	.976	0	C-10	-0.1
1979	Bos-A	32	86	13	30	4	0	4	24	1	24	.349	.378	.419	109	1	0	0	0	.984	-4	C-31	-0.2
Total	10	387	1185	125	306	50	8	23	156	64	268	.258	.300	.372	83	-28	6	2	1	.983	-19	C-361/D-9,1	-3.7

■ CHARLIE MONTOYO   Montoyo, Jose Carlos (Diaz) b: 10/17/65, Florida, P.R. BR/TR, 5'10", 170 lbs. Deb: 9/7/93

YEAR	TM/L	G	AB	R	H	2B	3B	HR	RBI	BB	SO	AVG	OBP	SLG	PRO+	BR/A	SB	CS	SBR	FA	FR	G/POS	TPR
1993	Mon-N	4	5	1	2	1	0	0	3	0	0	.400	.400	.600	157	0	0	0	0	.000	0	/2-3	0.0

■ AL MONTREUIL   Montreuil, Allan Arthur b: 8/23/43, New Orleans, La. BR/TR, 5'5", 158 lbs. Deb: 9/1/72

YEAR	TM/L	G	AB	R	H	2B	3B	HR	RBI	BB	SO	AVG	OBP	SLG	PRO+	BR/A	SB	CS	SBR	FA	FR	G/POS	TPR
1972	Chi-N	5	11	0	1	0	0	0	0	0	4	.091	.167	.091	-23	-2	0	0	0	1.000	0	/2-5	-0.2

■ DAN MONZON   Monzon, Daniel Francisco b: 5/17/46, Bronx, N.Y. BR/TR, 5'10", 182 lbs. Deb: 4/25/72

YEAR	TM/L	G	AB	R	H	2B	3B	HR	RBI	BB	SO	AVG	OBP	SLG	PRO+	BR/A	SB	CS	SBR	FA	FR	G/POS	TPR
1972	Min-A	55	55	13	15	1	0	0	5	8	12	.273	.365	.291	92	-0	1	0	0	.977	9	2-13/3-5,SO	1.1
1973	Min-A	39	76	10	17	1	1	0	4	11	9	.224	.330	.263	66	-3	1	0	0	.968	9	2-17,3-14/O	0.7
Total	2	94	131	23	32	2	1	0	9	19	21	.244	.344	.275	77	-3	2	0	1	.971	18	/2-30,3-19,SO	1.8

■ JOE MOOCK   Moock, Joseph Geoffrey b: 3/12/44, Plaquemine, La. BL/TR, 6'1", 180 lbs. Deb: 9/1/67

YEAR	TM/L	G	AB	R	H	2B	3B	HR	RBI	BB	SO	AVG	OBP	SLG	PRO+	BR/A	SB	CS	SBR	FA	FR	G/POS	TPR
1967	NY-N	13	40	2	9	2	0	0	5	0	7	.225	.225	.275	43	-3	0	0	0	.917	2	3-12	-0.2

■ GEORGE MOOLIC   Moolic, George Henry "Prunes" b: 3/12/1865, Lawrence, Mass. d: 2/19/15, Methuen, Mass. BR/TR, 5'7", 145 lbs. Deb: 5/1/1886

YEAR	TM/L	G	AB	R	H	2B	3B	HR	RBI	BB	SO	AVG	OBP	SLG	PRO+	BR/A	SB	CS	SBR	FA	FR	G/POS	TPR
1886	Chi-N	16	56	9	8	3	0	0	2	2	17	.143	.172	.196	10	-6	0			.945	3	C-15/O-2	-0.2

■ WALLY MOON   Moon, Wallace Wade b: 4/3/30, Bay, Ark. BL/TR, 6', 175 lbs. Deb: 4/13/54 C

YEAR	TM/L	G	AB	R	H	2B	3B	HR	RBI	BB	SO	AVG	OBP	SLG	PRO+	BR/A	SB	CS	SBR	FA	FR	G/POS	TPR
1954	StL-N	151	635	106	193	29	9	12	76	71	73	.304	.375	.435	109	10	18	10	-1	.978	2	*O-148	0.4
1955	StL-N	152	593	86	175	24	8	19	76	47	65	.295	.350	.459	113	10	11	11	-3	.975	-9	*O-100,1-51	-1.0
1956	StL-N	149	540	86	161	22	11	16	68	80	65	.298	.390	.469	129	24	12	9	-2	.988	0	O-97,1-52	1.5
1957	StL-N★	142	516	86	152	28	5	24	73	62	57	.295	.371	.508	131	22	5	6	-2	.966	-9	*O-133	0.4
1958	StL-N	108	290	36	69	10	3	7	38	47	30	.238	.344	.366	85	-5	2	3	-1	.984	-8	O-82	-1.9
1959	*LA-N★	145	543	93	164	26	11	19	74	81	64	.302	.396	.495	126	22	15	6	1	.983	-4	*O-143/1-1	1.2
1960	LA-N	138	469	74	140	21	6	13	69	67	63	.299	.387	.452	121	15	6	10	-4	.986	-4	*O-127	0.9
1961	LA-N	134	463	79	152	25	8	17	88	89	79	.328	**.438**	.505	137	28	7	5	-5	.970	-9	*O-133	1.1
1962	LA-N	95	244	36	59	9	1	4	31	30	33	.242	.327	.336	84	-5	5	2	0	.981	-2	O-36,1-32	-1.1

YEAR	TM/L	G	AB	R	H	2B	3B	HR	RBI	BB	SO	AVG	OBP	SLG	PRO+	BR/A	SB	CS	SBR	FA	FR	G/POS	TPR
1963	LA-N	122	343	41	90	13	2	8	48	45	43	.262	.350	.382	119	9	5	5	-2	.962	-13	O-96	-1.1
1964	LA-N	68	118	8	26	2	1	2	9	12	22	.220	.292	.305	74	-4	1	1	-0	1.000	-1	O-23	-0.7
1965	*LA-N	53	89	6	18	3	0	1	11	13	22	.202	.304	.270	67	-4	2	0	1	1.000	-2	O-23	-0.7
Total	12	1457	4843	737	1399	212	60	142	661	644	591	.289	.374	.445	117	123	89	68	-14	.978	-50	*O-1141,1-136	-1.0

■ AL MOORE
Moore, Albert James b: 8/4/02, Brooklyn, N.Y. d: 11/29/74, AtSea N.Y.To P.R BR/TR, 5'10", 174 lbs. Deb: 9/27/25

YEAR	TM/L	G	AB	R	H	2B	3B	HR	RBI	BB	SO	AVG	OBP	SLG	PRO+	BR/A	SB	CS	SBR	FA	FR	G/POS	TPR
1925	NY-N	2	8	0	1	0	0	0	0	1	2	.125	.222	.125	-9	-1	0	1	-1	1.000	-0	/O-2	-0.2
1926	NY-N	28	81	12	18	4	0	0	10	5	7	.222	.267	.272	46	-6	2			.966	3	O-20	-0.5
Total	2	30	89	12	19	4	0	0	10	6	9	.213	.263	.258	41	-7	2	1		.968	3	/O-22	-0.7

■ JUNIOR MOORE
Moore, Alvin Earl b: 1/25/53, Waskom, Tex. BR/TR, 5'11", 185 lbs. Deb: 8/2/76

YEAR	TM/L	G	AB	R	H	2B	3B	HR	RBI	BB	SO	AVG	OBP	SLG	PRO+	BR/A	SB	CS	SBR	FA	FR	G/POS	TPR
1976	Atl-N	20	26	1	7	1	0	0	2	4	4	.269	.387	.308	93	0	0	0	0	.929	1	/3-6,2-1,O	0.1
1977	Atl-N	112	361	41	94	9	3	5	34	33	29	.260	.324	.343	71	-15	4	5	-2	.942	-4	*3-104/2-1	-2.2
1978	Chi-A	24	65	8	19	0	1	0	4	6	7	.292	.352	.323	90	-1	1	1	-0	.857	-2	D-12/3-6,O	-0.0
1979	Chi-A	88	201	24	53	6	2	1	23	12	20	.264	.305	.328	71	-8	0	2	-1	.966	-9	O-61,D-10/2	-2.0
1980	Chi-A	45	121	9	31	4	1	1	9	7	11	.256	.297	.331	72	-5	0	2	-1	.929	-2	3-34/O-3,1D	-0.9
Total	5	289	774	83	204	20	7	7	73	62	71	.264	.320	.335	73	-28	5	10	-5	.936	-14	3-150/O-70,D21	-5.2

■ ANSE MOORE
Moore, Anselm Winn b: 9/22/17, Delhi, La. BL/TR, 6'1", 190 lbs. Deb: 4/17/46

YEAR	TM/L	G	AB	R	H	2B	3B	HR	RBI	BB	SO	AVG	OBP	SLG	PRO+	BR/A	SB	CS	SBR	FA	FR	G/POS	TPR
1946	Det-A	51	134	16	28	4	0	1	8	12	9	.209	.279	.261	48	-9	1	1	-0	.971	1	O-32	-1.1

■ ARCHIE MOORE
Moore, Archie Francis b: 8/30/41, Upper Darby, Pa. BL/TL, 6'2", 190 lbs. Deb: 4/20/64

YEAR	TM/L	G	AB	R	H	2B	3B	HR	RBI	BB	SO	AVG	OBP	SLG	PRO+	BR/A	SB	CS	SBR	FA	FR	G/POS	TPR
1964	NY-A	31	23	4	4	2	0	0	1	2	9	.174	.240	.261	39	-2	0	0	0	1.000	-2	/O-8,1-7	-0.4
1965	NY-A	9	17	1	7	2	0	1	4	4	4	.412	.524	.706	248	4	0	0	0	.889	-0	/O-5	0.3
Total	2	40	40	5	11	4	0	1	5	6	13	.275	.370	.450	128	2	0	0	0	.929	-2	/O-13,1-7	-0.1

■ CHARLEY MOORE
Moore, Charles Wesley b: 12/1/1884, Jackson Co., Ind. d: 7/29/70, Portland, Ore. BR/TR, 5'10", 160 lbs. Deb: 4/16/12

YEAR	TM/L	G	AB	R	H	2B	3B	HR	RBI	BB	SO	AVG	OBP	SLG	PRO+	BR/A	SB	CS	SBR	FA	FR	G/POS	TPR
1912	Chi-N	5	9	2	2	0	1	0	2	0	1	.222	.222	.444	80	-0	0			.800	1	/S-2,2-1,3	0.0

■ CHARLIE MOORE
Moore, Charles William b: 6/21/53, Birmingham, Ala. BR/TR, 5'11", 180 lbs. Deb: 9/8/73

YEAR	TM/L	G	AB	R	H	2B	3B	HR	RBI	BB	SO	AVG	OBP	SLG	PRO+	BR/A	SB	CS	SBR	FA	FR	G/POS	TPR
1973	Mil-A	8	27	0	5	0	1	0	3	2	4	.185	.241	.259	42	-2	0	0	0	.981	3	/C-8	0.1
1974	Mil-A	72	204	17	50	10	4	0	19	21	34	.245	.316	.333	87	-3	3	4	-2	.985	3	C-61/D-6	-0.6
1975	Mil-A	73	241	26	70	20	1	1	29	17	31	.290	.337	.394	106	1	1	5	-3	.960	-6	C-47,O-22/D	-0.6
1976	Mil-A	87	241	33	46	7	4	3	16	43	45	.191	.316	.290	80	-5	1	2	-1	.969	-3	C-49,O-28/3D	-0.9
1977	Mil-A	138	375	42	93	15	6	5	45	31	39	.248	.307	.360	81	-10	1	7	-4	.980	-7	*C-137	-1.7
1978	Mil-A	96	268	30	72	7	1	5	31	12	24	.269	.300	.358	84	-6	4	2	0	.983	-2	C-95	-0.6
1979	Mil-A	111	337	45	101	16	2	5	38	29	32	.300	.357	.404	105	3	8	5	-1	.979	9	*C-106	1.4
1980	Mil-A	111	320	42	93	13	2	2	30	24	28	.291	.340	.363	96	-2	10	5	0	.989	-15	*C-105	-1.3
1981	*Mil-A	48	156	16	47	8	3	1	9	12	13	.301	.351	.410	125	5	1	4	-2	.970	-0	C-34/O-8,D	-0.2
1982	*Mil-A	133	456	53	116	22	4	6	45	29	42	.254	.300	.360	86	-10	2	10	-5	.988	5	*O-115,C-20/2	-1.2
1983	Mil-A	151	529	65	150	27	6	2	49	55	42	.284	.355	.369	108	7	11	4	1	.978	0	*O-150/C-7,D	0.3
1984	Mil-A	70	188	13	44	7	1	2	17	10	26	.234	.276	.314	66	-9	2	3	-1	.984	-3	O-61/C-7	-1.6
1985	Mil-A	105	349	35	81	13	4	0	31	27	53	.232	.289	.292	60	-19	4	0	1	.977	5	*C-102/O-3	-0.8
1986	Mil-A	80	235	24	61	12	3	3	39	21	38	.260	.320	.374	86	-5	5	5	-2	.992	13	C-72/O-4,2D	1.0
1987	Tor-A	51	107	15	23	10	1	1	7	13	12	.215	.306	.355	73	-4	0	0	0	.984	6	C-44/O-5	0.4
Total	15	1334	4033	456	1052	187	43	36	408	346	470	.261	.321	.355	89	-59	51	57	-19	.980	9	C-894,O-396/D23	-5.2

■ DEE MOORE
Moore, D C b: 4/6/14, Hedley, Tex. BR/TR, 5'11", 190 lbs. Deb: 9/12/36

YEAR	TM/L	G	AB	R	H	2B	3B	HR	RBI	BB	SO	AVG	OBP	SLG	PRO+	BR/A	SB	CS	SBR	FA	FR	G/POS	TPR
1936	Cin-N	6	10	4	4	2	1	0	1	0	3	.400	.400	.800	230	2	0			1.000	-0	/P-2,C-1	0.0
1937	Cin-N	7	13	2	1	0	0	0	0	1	2	.077	.200	.077	-23	-2	0			.931	2	/C-6	0.0
1943	Bro-N	37	79	8	20	3	0	0	12	11	8	.253	.344	.291	84	-1	1			.982	-6	C-15/3-9	-0.7
	Phi-N	37	113	13	27	4	1	1	8	15	8	.239	.328	.319	91	-1	0			.960	-0	C-21/O-6,31	-0.0
	Yr	74	192	21	47	7	1	1	20	26	16	.245	.335	.307	88	-2	1			.968	-7	C-36,3-14/O1	-0.7
1946	Phi-N	11	13	2	1	0	0	0	1	7	3	.077	.400	.077	41	-0	0			1.000	0	/C-6,1-2	-0.0
Total	4	98	228	29	53	9	2	1	22	34	24	.232	.335	.303	85	-3	1			.962	-5	/C-49,3-14,01P	-0.7

■ GENE MOORE
Moore, Eugene Jr. "Rowdy" b: 8/26/09, Lancaster, Tex. d: 3/12/78, Jackson, Miss. BL/TL, 5'11", 175 lbs. Deb: 9/19/31 F

YEAR	TM/L	G	AB	R	H	2B	3B	HR	RBI	BB	SO	AVG	OBP	SLG	PRO+	BR/A	SB	CS	SBR	FA	FR	G/POS	TPR
1931	Cin-N	4	14	2	2	1	0	0	1	0	0	.143	.143	.214	-6	-2	0			1.000	0	/O-3	-0.2
1933	StL-N	11	38	6	15	3	2	0	8	4	10	.395	.452	.579	183	4	1			.967	0	/O-10	0.4
1934	StL-N	9	18	2	5	1	0	0	1	2	2	.278	.350	.333	79	-0	0			.923	1	/O-3	0.0
1935	StL-N	3	3	0	0	0	0	0	0	0	1	.000	.000	.000	-96	-1	0			.000	0	H	-0.1
1936	Bos-N	151	637	91	185	38	12	13	67	40	80	.290	.335	.449	117	12	6			.977	15	*O-151	2.0
1937	Bos-N☆	148	561	88	159	29	10	16	70	61	79	.283	.358	.456	132	23	11			.978	14	*O-148	3.1
1938	Bos-N	54	180	27	49	8	3	3	19	16	20	.272	.338	.400	114	3	1			.981	1	O-47	0.2
1939	Bro-N	107	306	45	69	13	6	3	39	40	50	.225	.315	.337	73	-12	4			.961	-6	O-86/1-1	-2.1
1940	Bro-N	10	26	3	7	2	0	0	2	1	3	.269	.296	.346	72	-1	0			1.000	-1	/O-6	-0.2
	Bos-N	103	363	46	106	24	1	5	39	25	32	.292	.338	.405	110	4	2			.986	6	O-94	0.6
	Yr	113	389	49	113	26	1	5	41	26	35	.290	.335	.401	107	3	2			.986	5	*O-100	0.4
1941	Bos-N	129	397	42	108	17	8	5	43	45	37	.272	.349	.393	114	7	5			.968	4	*O-110	0.5
1942	Was-A	1	2	0	0	0	0	0	0	0	0	.000	.000	.000	-99	-0	0	0		.000	0	/O-1	-0.1
1943	Was-A	92	254	41	68	14	2	0	39	19	29	.268	.321	.370	106	1	0	2	-1	.985	0	O-57/1-1	-0.3
1944	*StL-A	110	390	56	93	13	6	6	58	24	37	.238	.284	.349	76	-13	0	5	-3	.968	2	O-98/1-1	-2.1
1945	StL-A	110	354	48	92	16	2	5	50	40	26	.260	.337	.359	97	-1	1	3	-2	.970	-3	*O-100	-1.2
Total	14	1042	3543	497	958	179	53	58	436	317	401	.270	.333	.400	105	24	31	10		.975	32	O-914/1-3	0.5

■ FERDIE MOORE
Moore, Ferdinand Depage b: 2/21/1896, Camden, N.J. d: 5/6/47, Atlantic City, N.J. Deb: 10/2/14

YEAR	TM/L	G	AB	R	H	2B	3B	HR	RBI	BB	SO	AVG	OBP	SLG	PRO+	BR/A	SB	CS	SBR	FA	FR	G/POS	TPR
1914	Phi-A	2	4	1	2	0	0	0	1	0	2	.500	.500	.500	209	0	0			.895	-1	/1-2	0.0

■ GARY MOORE
Moore, Gary Douglas b: 2/24/45, Tulsa, Okla. BR/TL, 5'10", 175 lbs. Deb: 5/3/70

YEAR	TM/L	G	AB	R	H	2B	3B	HR	RBI	BB	SO	AVG	OBP	SLG	PRO+	BR/A	SB	CS	SBR	FA	FR	G/POS	TPR
1970	LA-N	7	16	2	3	0	2	0	0	0	1	.188	.188	.438	65	-1	1	0	0	1.000	-1	/O-5,1-1	-0.2

■ EDDIE MOORE
Moore, Graham Edward b: 1/18/1899, Barlow, Ky. d: 2/10/76, Ft.Myers, Fla. BR/TR, 5'7", 165 lbs. Deb: 9/25/23

YEAR	TM/L	G	AB	R	H	2B	3B	HR	RBI	BB	SO	AVG	OBP	SLG	PRO+	BR/A	SB	CS	SBR	FA	FR	G/POS	TPR
1923	Pit-N	6	26	6	7	1	0	0	1	2	3	.269	.321	.308	65	-1	1	0	0	.923	-5	/S-6	-0.5
1924	Pit-N	72	209	47	75	8	4	2	13	27	12	.359	.437	.464	139	13	6	7	-2	.988	4	O-35,3-13/2	1.3
1925	*Pit-N	142	547	106	163	29	8	6	77	73	26	.298	.383	.413	99	-1	19	7	2	.952	-6	*2-122,O-15/3	-0.4
1926	Pit-N	43	132	19	30	8	1	0	19	12	6	.227	.292	.303	57	-8	3			.911	-11	2-24/3-9,S	-1.8
	Bos-N	54	184	17	49	3	2	0	15	16	12	.266	.325	.304	77	-6	6			.973	-3	2-39,S-14/3	-0.7
	Yr	97	316	36	79	11	3	0	34	28	18	.250	.311	.304	68	-14	9			.950	-14	2-63,S-15,3	-2.5
1927	Bos-N	112	411	53	124	14	4	1	32	39	17	.302	.364	.363	103	3	5			.947	3	3-52,2-39,O/S	0.3
1928	Bos-N	68	215	27	51	9	0	2	18	19	12	.237	.299	.307	62	-12	7			.958	6	O-54/2-1	-1.0
1929	Bro-N	111	402	48	119	18	6	0	48	44	16	.296	.370	.371	86	-8	3			.955	-18	2-74,S-36/O3	-1.6
1930	Bro-N	76	196	24	55	13	1	1	20	21	7	.281	.356	.372	77	-7	1			.991	3	2-23,O-23,S/3	-0.2
1932	NY-N	37	106	9	23	8	0	0	9	10	13	.264	.340	.333	84	-2	1			.930	3	S-21/3-6,2	0.3
1934	Cle-A	27	65	4	10	2	0	0	8	10	4	.154	.267	.185	18	-8	0			.932	5	2-18/3-3,S	-0.6
Total	10	748	2474	360	706	108	26	13	257	272	121	.285	.359	.366	89	-37	52	14		.956	-29	2-349,O-145/S3	-4.9

YEAR	TM/L	G	AB	R	H	2B	3B	HR	RBI	BB	SO	AVG	OBP	SLG	PRO+	BR/A	SB	CS	SBR	FA	FR	G/POS	TPR

■ HARRY MOORE   Moore, Henry S.   Deb: 4/17/1884

| 1884 | Was-U | 111 | 461 | 77 | 155 | 23 | 5 | 1 | | 19 | | .336 | .363 | .414 | 114 | 10 | | | | .820 | -9 | *O-105/S-8 | -0.1 |

■ JACKIE MOORE   Moore, Jackie Spencer   b: 2/19/39, Jay, Fla.   BR/TR, 6', 180 lbs.   Deb: 4/18/65   MC

| 1965 | Det-A | 21 | 53 | 2 | 5 | 0 | 0 | 0 | 2 | 6 | 12 | .094 | .186 | .094 | -17 | -8 | 0 | 0 | 0 | .985 | 4 | C-20 | -0.4 |

■ JIMMY MOORE   Moore, James William   b: 4/24/03, Paris, Tenn.   d: 3/7/86, Memphis, Tenn.   BR/TR, 6'0.5", 187 lbs.   Deb: 8/31/30

1930	Chi-A	16	39	4	8	2	0	0	2	6	3	.205	.326	.256	52	-3	0	0	0	.900	0	O-11	-0.3
	*Phi-A	15	50	10	19	3	0	2	12	2	4	.380	.404	.560	136	3	1	1	-0	.958	-0	O-13	0.1
	Yr	31	89	14	27	5	0	2	14	8	7	.303	.367	.427	100	0	1	1	-0	.932	-0	O-24	-0.2
1931	*Phi-A	49	143	18	32	5	1	2	21	11	13	.224	.284	.315	54	-10	0	1	-1	.973	0	O-36	-1.2
Total	2	80	232	32	59	10	1	4	35	19	20	.254	.316	.358	71	-10	1	2	-1	.958	0	/O-60	-1.4

■ JERRIE MOORE   Moore, Jeremiah S.   b: Detroit, Mich.   d: 9/26/1890, Wayne, Mich.   BL, 5'11", 170 lbs.   Deb: 4/17/1884

1884	Alt-U	20	80	10	25	3	1	1		0		.313	.313	.412	94	-1				.800	-8	C-12/O-9	-0.7
	Cle-N	9	30	1	6	0	0	0	10	0	5	.200	.200	.200	25	-3				.887	-1	/C-9	-0.3
1885	Det-N	6	23	2	4	1	0	0	0	1	3	.174	.208	.217	38	-2				.800	-3	/C-6	-0.4
Total	2	35	133	13	35	4	1	1	10	1	8	.263	.269	.331	71	-5				.830	-12	/C-27,O-9	-1.4

■ JOHNNY MOORE   Moore, John Francis   b: 3/23/02, Waterville, Conn.   d: 4/4/91, Bradenton, Fla.   BL/TR, 5'10.5", 175 lbs.   Deb: 9/15/28

1928	Chi-N	4	4	0	0	0	0	0	0	0	0	.000	.000	.000	-99	-1	0			.000	0	H	-0.1
1929	Chi-N	37	63	13	18	1	0	2	8	4	6	.286	.338	.397	81	-2	0			.971	-0	O-15	-0.3
1931	Chi-N	39	104	19	25	3	1	2	16	7	5	.240	.288	.346	69	-5	1			.964	1	O-22	-0.5
1932	*Chi-N	119	443	59	135	24	5	13	64	22	38	.305	.342	.470	117	9	4			.983	1	*O-109	0.3
1933	Cin-N	135	514	60	135	19	5	1	44	29	16	.263	.306	.325	81	-12	4			.974	5	*O-132	-1.6
1934	Cin-N	16	42	5	8	1	0	0	5	3	2	.190	.244	.262	36	-4	0			1.000	0	O-10	-0.4
	Phi-N	116	458	68	157	34	6	11	93	40	18	.343	.397	.515	125	16	7			.981	7	O-115	1.7
	Yr	132	500	73	165	35	7	11	98	43	20	.330	.384	.494	120	13	7			.983	6	*O-125	1.3
1935	Phi-N	153	600	84	194	33	3	19	93	45	50	.323	.375	.483	117	14	4			.973	-10	*O-150	-0.1
1936	Phi-N	124	472	85	155	24	3	16	68	26	22	.328	.365	.494	117	10	1			.948	-8	*O-112	-0.2
1937	Phi-N	96	307	46	98	16	2	9	59	18	18	.319	.357	.472	114	5	2			.943	-2	O-72	0.0
1945	Chi-N	7	6	0	1	0	0	0	2	1	1	.167	.286	.167	28	-1	0			.000	0	H	-0.1
Total	10	846	3013	439	926	155	26	73	452	195	176	.307	.352	.449	109	30	23			.970	-7	O-737	-1.3

■ JO-JO MOORE   Moore, Joseph Gregg "The Gause Ghost"   b: 12/25/08, Gause, Tex.   BL/TR, 5'11", 155 lbs.   Deb: 9/17/30

1930	NY-N	3	5	1	1	0	0	0	0	0	1	.200	.200	.200	-3	-1	0			1.000	-0	/O-1	-0.1
1931	NY-N	4	8	0	2	1	0	0	3	0	1	.250	.250	.375	68	-0	0			1.000	0	/O-1	-0.1
1932	NY-N	86	361	53	110	15	2	2	27	20	18	.305	.341	.374	94	-3	4			.982	-4	O-86	-1.2
1933	*NY-N	132	524	56	153	16	5	0	42	21	27	.292	.323	.342	91	-6	4			.966	3	*O-132	-1.0
1934	NY-N†	139	580	106	192	37	4	15	61	31	23	.331	.370	.486	130	24	5			.954	-10	*O-131	0.8
1935	NY-N★	155	681	108	201	28	9	15	71	53	24	.295	.353	.429	111	10	5			.972	2	*O-155	0.6
1936	*NY-N☆	152	649	110	205	29	9	7	63	37	27	.316	.358	.421	110	9	2			.981	8	*O-149	1.0
1937	*NY-N★	142	580	89	180	37	10	6	57	46	37	.310	.364	.440	116	13	7			.975	-7	*O-140	0.1
1938	NY-N☆	125	506	76	153	23	6	11	56	22	27	.302	.335	.437	110	5	2			.978	-5	*O-114	-0.3
1939	NY-N	138	562	80	151	23	2	10	47	45	17	.269	.324	.370	85	-12	5			.986	3	*O-136	-1.4
1940	NY-N★	138	543	83	150	33	4	6	46	43	30	.276	.337	.385	98	-1	7			.982	-1	*O-133	-1.0
1941	NY-N	121	428	47	117	16	2	7	40	30	15	.273	.322	.369	93	-5	4			.972	-4	*O-116	-1.6
Total	12	1335	5427	809	1615	258	53	79	513	348	247	.298	.344	.408	105	33	46			.975	-14	*O-1294	-4.2

■ KELVIN MOORE   Moore, Kelvin Orlando   b: 9/26/57, Leroy, Ala.   BR/TL, 6'1", 195 lbs.   Deb: 8/28/81

1981	*Oak-A	14	47	5	12	0	1	1	3	5	15	.255	.327	.362	103	0	1	0	0	1.000	-1	1-13	-0.1
1982	Oak-A	21	67	6	15	1	1	2	6	3	23	.224	.257	.358	70	-3	0	1	-1	.971	-2	1-20	-0.6
1983	Oak-A	41	124	12	26	4	0	5	16	10	39	.210	.274	.363	78	-4	2	4	-2	.994	-3	1-40	-1.1
Total	3	76	238	23	53	5	2	8	25	18	77	.223	.280	.361	81	-7	3	5	-2	.989	-5	/1-73	-1.8

■ MOLLY MOORE   Moore, Maurice   d: 2/24/1881, New York, N.Y.   Deb: 6/30/1875

| 1875 | Atl-n | 22 | 88 | 5 | 20 | 5 | 0 | 0 | | 0 | | .227 | .227 | .284 | 87 | -1 | | | | | | S-14/1-6,3 | -0.1 |

■ RANDY MOORE   Moore, Randolph Edward   b: 6/21/06, Naples, Tex.   d: 6/12/92, Mt.Pleasant, Tex.   BL/TR, 6', 185 lbs.   Deb: 4/12/27

1927	Chi-A	6	15	0	0	0	0	0	0	0	2	.000	.000	.000	-99	-4	0	0	0	1.000	1	/O-4	-0.4
1928	Chi-A	24	61	6	13	4	1	0	5	3	5	.213	.250	.311	47	-5	0	1	-1	.946	0	O-16	-0.6
1930	Bos-N	83	191	24	55	9	0	2	34	10	13	.288	.323	.366	69	-10	3			.986	-2	O-34,3-13	-1.2
1931	Bos-N	83	192	19	50	8	1	3	34	13	3	.260	.311	.359	83	-5	1			.952	0	O-29,3-22/2	-0.5
1932	Bos-N	107	351	41	103	21	2	3	43	15	11	.293	.322	.390	94	-3	1			.987	-7	O-41,3-31,1/C	-1.3
1933	Bos-N	135	497	64	150	23	7	8	70	40	16	.302	.356	.425	133	20	3			.979	-0	*O-122,1-10	1.3
1934	Bos-N	123	422	55	120	21	2	7	64	40	16	.284	.346	.393	105	3	2			.965	-2	O-72,3-37	-0.4
1935	Bos-N	125	407	42	112	20	4	4	42	26	16	.275	.319	.373	93	-5	1			.950	0	O-78,1-21	-1.0
1936	Bro-N	42	88	4	21	3	0	0	14	8	1	.239	.302	.273	55	-5	0			.964	-4	O-21	-1.0
1937	Bro-N	13	22	3	3	1	0	0	2	3	2	.136	.240	.182	16	-3	0			.889	1	O-10	-0.2
	StL-N	8	7	0	0	0	0	0	0	0	0	.000	.000	.000	-98	-2	0			.000	0	/O-1	-0.2
	Yr	21	29	3	3	1	0	0	2	3	2	.103	.188	.138	-10	-4	0			.889	-0	C-10/O-1	-0.4
Total	10	749	2253	258	627	110	17	27	308	158	85	.278	.326	.378	95	-19	11	1		.969	-15	O-418/1-90,3C2	-5.5

■ BOBBY MOORE   Moore, Robert Vincent   b: 10/27/65, Cincinnati, Ohio   BR/TR, 5'9", 165 lbs.   Deb: 9/5/91

| 1991 | KC-A | 18 | 14 | 3 | 5 | 1 | 0 | 0 | 3 | 0 | 1 | .357 | .400 | .429 | 129 | -4 | 1 | 3 | 2 | -0 | 1.000 | -4 | O-13 | -0.4 |

■ TERRY MOORE   Moore, Terry Bluford   b: 5/27/12, Vernon, Ala.   BR/TR, 5'11", 195 lbs.   Deb: 4/16/35   MC

1935	StL-N	119	456	63	131	34	3	6	53	15	40	.287	.314	.414	90	-7	13			.984	14	*O-117	0.3
1936	StL-N	143	590	85	156	39	4	5	47	37	52	.264	.309	.369	82	-16	9			.977	22	*O-133	0.1
1937	StL-N	115	461	76	123	17	3	5	43	32	41	.267	.317	.349	79	-13	13			.988	14	*O-106	-0.3
1938	StL-N	94	312	49	85	21	3	4	21	46	19	.272	.366	.397	104	3	9			.987	9	O-75/3-6	0.9
1939	StL-N★	130	417	65	123	25	2	17	77	43	38	.295	.362	.487	119	10	6			**.994**	11	*O-121/P-1	1.7
1940	StL-N★	136	537	92	163	33	4	17	64	42	44	.304	.356	.475	121	14	18			.987	17	*O-133	2.4
1941	StL-N★	122	493	86	145	26	4	6	68	52	31	.294	.364	.400	108	5	3			.984	7	*O-121	0.5
1942	*StL-N★	130	489	80	141	26	3	6	49	56	26	.288	.364	.391	112	8	10			.986	-3	*O-126/3-1	-0.1
1946	*StL-N	91	278	32	73	14	1	3	28	18	26	.263	.312	.353	85	-6	0			.982	1	O-66	-0.8
1947	StL-N	127	460	61	130	17	1	7	45	38	39	.283	.339	.370	84	-10	1			.983	6	*O-120	-1.5
1948	StL-N	91	207	30	48	11	0	4	18	27	12	.232	.321	.343	75	-7	0			.993	-10	O-71	-2.0
Total	11	1298	4700	719	1318	263	28	80	513	406	368	.280	.340	.399	98	-18	82			.985	83	*O-1189/3-7,P	1.2

■ SCRAPPY MOORE   Moore, William Allen   b: 12/16/1892, St.Louis, Mo.   d: 10/13/64, Little Rock, Ark.   BR/TR, 5'8", 153 lbs.   Deb: 6/21/17

| 1917 | StL-A | 4 | 8 | 1 | 1 | 0 | 0 | 0 | 1 | 0 | 1 | .125 | .222 | .125 | 6 | -1 | 0 | | | .750 | 0 | /3-2 | -0.1 |

■ BILL MOORE   Moore, William Henry "Willie"   b: 12/12/01, Kansas City, Mo.   d: 5/24/72, Kansas City, Mo.   BL/TR, 5'11", 170 lbs.   Deb: 9/7/26

| 1926 | Bos-A | 5 | 18 | 2 | 3 | 0 | 0 | 0 | 0 | 2 | 2 | .167 | .167 | .167 | -13 | -3 | 0 | 0 | 0 | 1.000 | 0 | /C-5 | -0.2 |

YEAR	TM/L	G	AB	R	H	2B	3B	HR	RBI	BB	SO	AVG	OBP	SLG	PRO+	BR/A	SB	CS	SBR	FA	FR	G/POS	TPR
1927	Bos-A	44	69	7	15	2	0	0	4	13	8	.217	.341	.246	56	-4	0	0	0	.938	2	C-42	0.0
Total	2	49	87	9	18	2	0	0	4	13	10	.207	.310	.230	43	-7	0	0	0	.946	2	/C-47	-0.2

■ BILL MOORE
Moore, William Ross b: 10/10/60, Los Angeles, Cal. BR/TL, 6'1", 185 lbs. Deb: 7/19/86

YEAR	TM/L	G	AB	R	H	2B	3B	HR	RBI	BB	SO	AVG	OBP	SLG	PRO+	BR/A	SB	CS	SBR	FA	FR	G/POS	TPR
1986	Mon-N	6	12	0	2	0	0	0	0	0	4	.167	.167	.167	-8	-2	0	0	0	1.000	-1	/1-3,O-1	-0.3

■ ANDRES MORA
Mora, Andres (Ibarra) b: 5/25/55, Rio Bravo, Mex. BR/TR, 6', 180 lbs. Deb: 4/13/76

YEAR	TM/L	G	AB	R	H	2B	3B	HR	RBI	BB	SO	AVG	OBP	SLG	PRO+	BR/A	SB	CS	SBR	FA	FR	G/POS	TPR
1976	Bal-A	73	220	18	48	11	0	6	25	13	49	.218	.262	.350	83	-6	1	0	0	.951	-2	D-34,O-31	-1.0
1977	Bal-A	77	233	32	57	8	2	13	44	5	53	.245	.264	.464	100	-2	0	0	0	1.000	-9	O-57/3-1,D	-1.3
1978	Bal-A	76	229	21	49	8	0	8	14	13	47	.214	.259	.354	75	-9	0	1	-1	.978	1	O-69/D-1	-1.1
1980	Cle-A	9	18	0	2	0	0	0	0	0	0	.111	.111	.111	-39	-3	0	0	0	1.000	0	/O-3	-0.4
Total	4	235	700	71	156	27	2	27	83	31	149	.223	.258	.383	83	-19	1	1	-0	.978	-10	O-160/D-40,3	-3.8

■ JOSE MORALES
Morales, Jose Manuel (Hernandez) b: 12/30/44, Frederiksted, V.I. BR/TR, 6', 195 lbs. Deb: 8/13/73 C

YEAR	TM/L	G	AB	R	H	2B	3B	HR	RBI	BB	SO	AVG	OBP	SLG	PRO+	BR/A	SB	CS	SBR	FA	FR	G/POS	TPR
1973	Oak-A	6	14	0	4	1	0	0	1	1	5	.286	.333	.357	100	0	0	1	-1	.000	0	/D-3	-0.1
	Mon-N	5	5	0	2	0	0	0	0	0	0	.400	.400	.400	118	0	0	0	0	.000	0	H	0.0
1974	Mon-N	25	26	3	7	4	0	1	5	1	7	.269	.296	.538	123	1	0	0	0	.800	-1	/C-2	0.0
1975	Mon-N	93	163	18	49	6	1	2	24	14	21	.301	.356	.387	102	0	0	2	-1	.983	4	1-27/O-6,C	0.2
1976	Mon-N	104	158	12	50	11	0	4	37	7	20	.316	.337	.462	120	3	0	0	0	.977	1	1-21,C-12	0.4
1977	Mon-N	65	74	3	15	4	1	1	9	5	12	.203	.253	.324	55	-5	0	0	0	1.000	-2	/C-8,1-8	-0.7
1978	Min-A	101	242	22	76	13	1	2	38	20	35	.314	.369	.401	114	5	0	1	-1	.000	0	D-77/C-1,1O	0.2
1979	Min-A	92	191	21	51	5	1	2	27	14	27	.267	.324	.335	75	-6	0	0	0	1.000	0	D-77/1-1	-0.9
1980	Min-A	97	241	36	73	17	2	8	36	22	19	.303	.364	.490	123	7	0	0	0	1.000	-1	D-86/C-2,1	0.4
1981	Bal-A	38	86	6	21	3	0	2	14	3	13	.244	.270	.349	77	-3	0	0	0	1.000	-0	D-22/1-3	-0.4
1982	Bal-A	3	3	0	0	0	0	0	0	0	0	.000	.000	.000	-99	-1	0	0	0	.000	0	/H	-0.1
	LA-N	35	30	1	9	1	0	1	8	4	8	.300	.382	.433	131	1	0	0	0	.000	0	H	0.0
1983	*LA-N	47	53	4	15	3	0	3	8	1	11	.283	.296	.509	120	1	0	0	0	.951	-0	/1-4	0.1
1984	LA-N	22	19	0	3	0	0	0	0	1	2	.158	.200	.158	2	-2	0	0	0	.000	0	H	-0.3
Total	12	733	1305	126	375	68	6	26	207	89	182	.287	.336	.408	102	1	0	4	-2	.981	0	D-265/1-67,CO	-1.2

■ JERRY MORALES
Morales, Julio Ruben (Torres) b: 2/18/49, Yabucao, P.R. BR/TR, 5'10", 175 lbs. Deb: 9/5/69

YEAR	TM/L	G	AB	R	H	2B	3B	HR	RBI	BB	SO	AVG	OBP	SLG	PRO+	BR/A	SB	CS	SBR	FA	FR	G/POS	TPR
1969	SD-N	19	41	5	8	2	0	1	6	5	7	.195	.283	.317	71	-2	0	2	-1	1.000	-1	O-19	-0.4
1970	SD-N	28	58	6	9	0	1	1	4	3	11	.155	.197	.241	17	-7	0	0	0	.926	-5	O-26	-1.3
1971	SD-N	12	17	1	2	0	0	0	1	2	2	.118	.211	.118	-5	-2	1	0	0	1.000	-1	/O-7	-0.4
1972	SD-N	115	347	38	83	15	7	4	18	35	54	.239	.309	.357	96	-3	4	6	-2	.987	4	O-96/3-4	-0.6
1973	SD-N	122	388	47	109	23	2	9	34	27	55	.281	.328	.420	115	6	6	5	-1	.991	5	*O-100	0.1
1974	Chi-N	151	534	70	146	21	7	15	82	46	63	.273	.333	.423	106	3	2	12	-7	.975	-7	*O-143	-1.6
1975	Chi-N	153	578	62	156	21	0	12	91	50	65	.270	.333	.369	91	-7	3	7	-3	.979	0	*O-151	-1.7
1976	Chi-N	140	537	66	147	17	0	16	67	41	49	.274	.325	.395	95	-4	3	8	-4	.983	3	*O-136	-1.1
1977	Chi-N★	136	490	56	142	34	5	11	69	43	75	.290	.350	.447	101	0	0	3	-2	.985	-7	*O-128	-1.4
1978	StL-N	130	457	44	109	19	8	4	46	33	44	.239	.291	.341	77	-15	4	4	-1	.977	-0	*O-126	-2.3
1979	Det-A	129	440	50	93	23	1	14	56	30	56	.211	.265	.364	65	-23	10	4	1	.986	-9	*O-119/D-7	-3.5
1980	NY-N	94	193	19	49	7	1	3	30	13	31	.254	.304	.347	84	-4	2	1	-1	.973	-7	O-63	-1.5
1981	Chi-N	84	245	27	70	6	2	1	25	22	29	.286	.347	.339	91	-2	1	1	-0	.986	-6	O-72	-1.1
1982	Chi-N	65	116	14	33	2	2	4	30	9	7	.284	.336	.440	112	2	1	2	-1	1.000	-5	O-41	-0.5
1983	Chi-N	63	87	11	17	9	0	0	11	7	19	.195	.255	.299	51	-6	0	0	0	1.000	-6	O-29	-1.1
Total	15	1441	4528	516	1173	199	36	95	570	366	567	.259	.316	.382	91	-64	37	57	-23	.983	-44	*O-1256/D-7,3	-18.6

■ RICH MORALES
Morales, Richard Angelo b: 9/20/43, San Francisco, Cal. BR/TR, 5'11", 170 lbs. Deb: 8/8/67 C

YEAR	TM/L	G	AB	R	H	2B	3B	HR	RBI	BB	SO	AVG	OBP	SLG	PRO+	BR/A	SB	CS	SBR	FA	FR	G/POS	TPR
1967	Chi-A	8	10	0	0	0	0	0	0	0	2	.000	.000	.000	-99	-2	0	0	0	.944	2	/S-7	-0.1
1968	Chi-A	10	29	2	5	0	0	0	0	2	5	.172	.226	.172	22	-3	0	0	0	.966	3	/S-7,2-5	0.0
1969	Chi-A	55	121	12	26	0	1	0	6	7	18	.215	.269	.231	39	-10	1	0	0	.976	10	2-38,S-13/3	0.4
1970	Chi-A	62	112	6	18	2	0	1	2	9	16	.161	.230	.205	20	-12	1	0	0	.967	-4	S-24,3-20,2	-0.4
1971	Chi-A	84	185	19	45	8	0	2	14	22	26	.243	.336	.319	84	-3	2	3	-1	.976	-1	S-57,3-18/2O	0.0
1972	Chi-A	110	287	24	59	7	1	2	20	19	49	.206	.262	.258	54	-16	2	3	-1	.968	-1	S-86,2-16,3	-0.9
1973	Chi-A	7	4	1	0	0	0	0	1	1	0	.000	.000	.000	-38	-1	0	0	0	1.000	1	/3-5,2-2	0.0
	SD-N	90	244	9	40	6	1	0	16	27	36	.164	.247	.197	27	-24	0	1	-1	.988	22	2-79,S-10	0.2
1974	SD-N	54	61	8	12	3	0	1	5	8	6	.197	.290	.295	67	-3	1	0	0	.933	7	S-29,2-18/31	0.6
Total	8	480	1053	81	205	26	3	6	64	95	159	.195	.268	.242	46	-74	7	7	-2	.970	47	S-233,2-173/310	-0.2

■ CHARLIE MORAN
Moran, Charles Barthell "Uncle Charlie" b: 2/22/1878, Nashville, Tenn. d: 6/14/49, Horse Cave, Ky. BR/TR, 5'8", 180 lbs. Deb: 9/9/03 U

YEAR	TM/L	G	AB	R	H	2B	3B	HR	RBI	BB	SO	AVG	OBP	SLG	PRO+	BR/A	SB	CS	SBR	FA	FR	G/POS	TPR
1903	StL-N	4	14	2	6	0	0	0	1	0		.429	.429	.429	149	1	1			1.000	-1	/P-3,S-1	0.0
1908	StL-N	21	63	2	11	1	2	0	2	0		.175	.175	.254	38	-5	0			.903	-3	C-16	-0.7
Total	2	25	77	4	17	1	2	0	3	0		.221	.221	.286	61	-4	1			.903	-4	/C-16,P-3,S	-0.7

■ CHARLES MORAN
Moran, Charles Vincent b: 3/26/1879, Washington, D.C. d: 4/11/34, Washington, D.C. TR, Deb: 4/29/03

YEAR	TM/L	G	AB	R	H	2B	3B	HR	RBI	BB	SO	AVG	OBP	SLG	PRO+	BR/A	SB	CS	SBR	FA	FR	G/POS	TPR
1903	Was-A	98	373	41	84	14	5	1	24	33		.225	.297	.298	77	-10	8			.943	5	S-96/2-2	0.0
1904	Was-A	62	243	27	54	10	0	0	7	23		.222	.289	.263	77	-6	7			.919	-13	S-61/3-1	-2.0
	StL-A	82	272	15	47	3	1	0	14	25		.173	.242	.191	40	-18	2			.937	-3	3-81/O-1	-2.0
	Yr	144	515	42	101	13	1	0	21	48		.196	.265	.225	58	-23	9			.938	-16	3-82,S-61/O	-4.0
1905	StL-A	27	82	6	16	1	0	0	5	10		.195	.290	.207	62	-3	3			.954	-4	2-20/3-5	-0.8
Total	3	269	970	89	201	28	6	1	50	91		.207	.279	.252	66	-36	20			.935	-15	S-157/3-87,2O	-4.8

■ HERBIE MORAN
Moran, John Herbert b: 2/16/1884, Costello, Pa. d: 9/21/54, Clarkson, N.Y. BL/TR, 5'5", 150 lbs. Deb: 4/16/08

YEAR	TM/L	G	AB	R	H	2B	3B	HR	RBI	BB	SO	AVG	OBP	SLG	PRO+	BR/A	SB	CS	SBR	FA	FR	G/POS	TPR
1908	Phi-A	19	59	4	9	0	0	0	4	6		.153	.242	.153	27	-4	1			.952	1	O-19	-0.5
	Bos-N	8	29	3	8	0	0	0	2	2		.276	.364	.276	106	0	1			1.000	2	/O-8	0.3
1909	Bos-N	8	31	8	7	1	0	0	0	5		.226	.333	.258	80	-1	0			1.000	-1	/O-8	-0.1
1910	Bos-N	20	67	11	8	0	0	0	3	14		.119	.280	.119	17	-7	6			.958	-4	O-20	-0.4
1912	Bro-N	130	508	77	140	18	10	1	40	69	38	.276	.368	.356	102	4	28			.961	8	*O-129	0.5
1913	Bro-N	132	515	71	137	15	5	0	26	45	29	.266	.333	.315	83	-10	21			.950	1	*O-129	-1.4
1914	Cin-N	107	395	43	93	10	5	1	35	41	29	.235	.312	.294	78	-10	26			.954	-5	*O-107	-2.2
	*Bos-N	41	154	24	41	3	1	0	4	17	11	.266	.347	.299	93	-1	4			.940	-8	O-41	-1.1
	Yr	148	549	67	134	13	6	1	39	58	40	.244	.322	.295	82	-11	30			.950	-13	*O-148	-3.3
1915	Bos-N	130	419	59	84	13	5	0	21	66	41	.200	.320	.255	79	-8	16	10	-1	.964	-6	*O-123	-2.2
Total	7	595	2177	300	527	60	26	2	135	264	162	.242	.332	.296	83	-35	103	10		.957	-2	O-584	-7.1

■ PAT MORAN
Moran, Patrick Joseph b: 2/7/1876, Fitchburg, Mass. d: 3/7/24, Orlando, Fla. BR/TR, 5'10", 180 lbs. Deb: 5/15/01 M

YEAR	TM/L	G	AB	R	H	2B	3B	HR	RBI	BB	SO	AVG	OBP	SLG	PRO+	BR/A	SB	CS	SBR	FA	FR	G/POS	TPR
1901	Bos-N	52	180	12	38	5	1	2	18	3		.211	.228	.283	44	-13	3			.973	-5	C-28,1-13/3SO2	-1.6
1902	Bos-N	80	251	22	60	5	5	3	24	17		.239	.303	.311	88	-3	6			.982	1	C-71/1-3,O	0.5
1903	Bos-N	109	389	40	102	25	5	7	54	29		.262	.331	.406	114	6	8			.967	19	*C-107/1-1	3.5
1904	Bos-N	113	398	26	90	11	3	4	34	18		.226	.267	.299	77	-11	10			.957	4	C-72,3-39/1	0.2
1905	Bos-N	85	267	22	64	11	5	2	22	8		.240	.270	.341	83	-7	3			.986	13	C-78	1.4
1906	*Chi-N	70	226	19	57	13	1	0	35	7		.252	.281	.319	82	-6	6			.979	3	C-61	0.4
1907	*Chi-N	65	198	8	45	9	1	0	14	10		.227	.271	.278	68	-8	6			.973	-5	C-59	-0.2
1908	Chi-N	50	150	12	39	5	1	0	12	13		.260	.323	.307	97	-0	6			.968	1	C-45	0.5

YEAR	TM/L	G	AB	R	H	2B	3B	HR	RBI	BB	SO	AVG	OBP	SLG	PRO+	BR/A	SB	CS	SBR	FA	FR	G/POS	TPR
1909	Chi-N	77	246	18	54	11	1	1	23	16		.220	.278	.285	73	-8	2			.984	1	C-74	0.0
1910	Phi-N	68	199	13	47	7	1	0	11	17	16	.236	.306	.281	69	-8	6			.989	0	C-56	-0.2
1911	Phi-N	34	103	2	19	3	0	0	8	3	13	.184	.208	.214	18	-11	0			.984	-1	C-32	-1.0
1912	Phi-N	13	26	1	3	1	0	0	1	1	7	.115	.148	.154	-16	-4	0			.955	-2	C-13	-0.5
1913	Phi-N	1	1	0	0	0	0	0	0	0	0	.000	.000	.000	-96	-0	0			.000	0	H	0.0
1914	Phi-N	1	0	0	0	0	0	0	1	0	0	—	—	—		-0	0			.000	0	/C-1	0.0
Total	14	818	2634	198	618	102	24	18	262	142	36	.235	.283	.312	78	-74	55			.976	34	C-697/3-43,1OS2	3.0

■ AL MORAN
Moran, Richard Alan   b: 12/5/38, Detroit, Mich.   BR/TR, 6'1.5", 190 lbs.   Deb: 4/9/63

YEAR	TM/L	G	AB	R	H	2B	3B	HR	RBI	BB	SO	AVG	OBP	SLG	PRO+	BR/A	SB	CS	SBR	FA	FR	G/POS	TPR
1963	NY-N	119	331	26	64	5	2	1	23	36	60	.193	.274	.230	46	-22	3	7	-3	.951	6	*S-116/3-1	-1.3
1964	NY-N	16	22	2	5	0	0	0	4	2	2	.227	.292	.227	50	-1	0	0	0	.957	4	S-15/3-1	0.3
Total	2	135	353	28	69	5	2	1	27	38	62	.195	.276	.229	46	-23	3	7	-3	.951	10	S-131/3-2	-1.0

■ ROY MORAN
Moran, Roy Ellis "Deedle"   b: 9/17/1884, Vincennes, Ind.   d: 7/18/66, Atlanta, Ga.   BR/TR, 5'8", 155 lbs.   Deb: 9/3/12

YEAR	TM/L	G	AB	R	H	2B	3B	HR	RBI	BB	SO	AVG	OBP	SLG	PRO+	BR/A	SB	CS	SBR	FA	FR	G/POS	TPR
1912	Was-A	7	13	1	2	0	0	0		0	8	.154	.476	.154	82	1	3			.889	-0	/O-6	0.0

■ BILL MORAN
Moran, William L.   b: 10/10/1869, Joliet, Ill.   d: 4/8/16, Joliet, Ill.   175 lbs.   Deb: 5/7/1892

YEAR	TM/L	G	AB	R	H	2B	3B	HR	RBI	BB	SO	AVG	OBP	SLG	PRO+	BR/A	SB	CS	SBR	FA	FR	G/POS	TPR
1892	StL-N	24	81	2	11	1	0	0	5	2	12	.136	.157	.148	-8	-11	0			.891	-4	C-22/O-2	-1.3
1895	Chi-N	15	55	8	9	2	1	1	9	3	2	.164	.220	.291	29	-6	2			.827	-2	C-15	-0.5
Total	2	39	136	10	20	3	1	1	14	5	14	.147	.183	.206	10	-17	2			.866	-6	/C-37,O-2	-1.8

■ BILLY MORAN
Moran, William Nelson   b: 11/27/33, Montgomery, Ala.   BR/TR, 5'11", 185 lbs.   Deb: 4/15/58

YEAR	TM/L	G	AB	R	H	2B	3B	HR	RBI	BB	SO	AVG	OBP	SLG	PRO+	BR/A	SB	CS	SBR	FA	FR	G/POS	TPR
1958	Cle-A	115	257	26	58	11	0	1	18	13	23	.226	.263	.280	51	-17	3	2	-0	.960	13	2-74,S-38	0.0
1959	Cle-A	11	17	1	5	0	0	0	2	0	1	.294	.294	.294	64	-1	0	0	0	1.000	-1	/2-6,S-5	-0.1
1961	LA-A	54	173	17	45	7	1	2	22	17	16	.260	.330	.347	73	-7	0	0	0	.966	-5	/2-51/S-2	-0.6
1962	LA-A★	160	659	90	186	25	3	17	74	39	80	.282	.326	.407	99	-2	5	1	1	.986	19	*2-160	3.4
1963	LA-A	153	597	67	164	29	5	7	65	31	57	.275	.314	.375	98	-3	1	1	-0	.973	15	*2-151	2.7
1964	LA-A	50	198	26	53	10	1	0	11	13	20	.268	.316	.328	88	-4	1	3	-2	.929	-7	3-47/2-3,S	-1.3
	Cle-A	69	151	14	31	6	0	1	10	18	16	.205	.294	.265	57	-8	0	1	-1	.972	3	3-42,2-15/1	-0.6
	Yr	119	349	40	84	16	1	1	21	31	36	.241	.306	.301	73	-12	1	4	-2	.947	-4	3-89,2-18/1S	-1.9
1965	Cle-A	22	24	1	3	0	0	0	0	2	5	.125	.222	.125	1	-3	0	0	0	1.000	1	/2-7,S-1	-0.2
Total	7	634	2076	242	545	88	10	28	202	133	218	.263	.310	.355	85	-45	10	8	-2	.976	39	2-467/3-89,S1	3.3

■ MICKEY MORANDINI
Morandini, Michael Robert   b: 4/22/66, Kittanning, Pa.   BL/TR, 5'11", 170 lbs.   Deb: 9/1/90

YEAR	TM/L	G	AB	R	H	2B	3B	HR	RBI	BB	SO	AVG	OBP	SLG	PRO+	BR/A	SB	CS	SBR	FA	FR	G/POS	TPR
1990	Phi-N	25	79	9	19	4	0	1	3	6	19	.241	.294	.329	71	-3	3	0	1	.990	1	2-25	-0.1
1991	Phi-N	98	325	38	81	11	4	1	20	29	45	.249	.315	.317	79	-9	13	2	3	.986	8	2-97	0.4
1992	Phi-N	127	422	47	112	8	8	3	30	25	64	.265	.306	.344	84	-9	8	3	1	.991	11	*2-124/S-3	0.6
1993	*Phi-N	120	425	57	105	19	9	3	33	34	73	.247	.310	.355	79	-13	13	2	3	.990	-1	*2-111	-0.8
1994	Phi-N	87	274	40	80	16	5	2	26	34	33	.292	.378	.409	106	4	10	5	0	.985	4	2-79	0.9
Total	5	457	1525	191	397	58	26	10	112	128	234	.260	.322	.352	85	-30	47	12	7	.989	23	2-436/S-3	1.0

■ MIKE MORDECAI
Mordecai, Michael Howard   b: 12/13/67, Birmingham, Ala.   BB/TR, 5'11", 175 lbs.   Deb: 5/8/94

YEAR	TM/L	G	AB	R	H	2B	3B	HR	RBI	BB	SO	AVG	OBP	SLG	PRO+	BR/A	SB	CS	SBR	FA	FR	G/POS	TPR
1994	Atl-N	4	4	1	1	0	0	1	3	1	0	.250	.400	1.000	249	1	0	0	0	1.000	-0	/S-4	0.1

■ RAY MOREHART
Morehart, Raymond Anderson   b: 12/2/1899, Near Abner, Tex.   d: 1/13/89, Dallas, Tex.   BL/TR, 5'9", 157 lbs.   Deb: 8/9/24

YEAR	TM/L	G	AB	R	H	2B	3B	HR	RBI	BB	SO	AVG	OBP	SLG	PRO+	BR/A	SB	CS	SBR	FA	FR	G/POS	TPR
1924	Chi-A	31	100	10	20	4	2	0	8	17	7	.200	.316	.280	56	-6	3	1	0	.873	-12	S-27/2-2	-1.4
1926	Chi-A	73	192	27	61	10	3	0	21	11	15	.318	.358	.401	101	0	3	11	-6	.950	-5	2-48	-0.9
1927	NY-A	73	195	45	50	7	2	1	20	29	18	.256	.353	.328	80	-5	4	4	-1	.945	4	2-53	-0.1
Total	3	177	487	82	131	21	7	1	49	57	40	.269	.347	.347	83	-11	10	16	-7	.946	-13	2-103/S-27	-2.4

■ DANNY MOREJON
Morejon, Daniel (Torres)   b: 7/21/30, Havana, Cuba   BR/TR, 6'1", 175 lbs.   Deb: 7/11/58

YEAR	TM/L	G	AB	R	H	2B	3B	HR	RBI	BB	SO	AVG	OBP	SLG	PRO+	BR/A	SB	CS	SBR	FA	FR	G/POS	TPR
1958	Cin-N	12	26	4	5	0	0	0	1	9	2	.192	.400	.192	60	-1	1	0	0	1.000	-2	O-11	-0.4

■ KEITH MORELAND
Moreland, Bobby Keith   b: 5/2/54, Dallas, Tex.   BR/TR, 6', 200 lbs.   Deb: 10/1/78

YEAR	TM/L	G	AB	R	H	2B	3B	HR	RBI	BB	SO	AVG	OBP	SLG	PRO+	BR/A	SB	CS	SBR	FA	FR	G/POS	TPR
1978	Phi-N	1	2	0	0	0	0	0	0	0	0	.000	.000	.000	-99	-1	0	0	0	1.000	0	/C-1	0.0
1979	Phi-N	14	48	3	18	3	2	0	8	3	5	.375	.412	.521	148	3	0	0	0	1.000	-0	C-13	0.3
1980	*Phi-N	62	159	13	50	8	0	4	29	8	14	.314	.347	.440	112	2	3	1	0	.967	-1	C-39/3-4,O	0.3
1981	*Phi-N	61	196	16	50	7	0	6	37	15	13	.255	.311	.383	92	-2	1	2	-1	.982	-7	C-50/3-7,1O	-1.0
1982	Chi-N	138	476	50	124	17	2	15	68	46	71	.261	.330	.399	100	0	0	6	-4	.989	-21	O-86,C-44/3	-2.7
1983	Chi-N	154	533	76	161	30	3	16	70	68	73	.302	.384	.460	127	20	0	3	-2	.976	-6	*O-151/C-3	0.9
1984	*Chi-N	140	495	59	138	17	3	16	80	34	71	.279	.329	.422	101	-0	1	4	-2	.976	-7	*O-103,1-29/3C	-1.5
1985	Chi-N	161	587	74	180	30	3	14	106	68	58	.307	.380	.440	116	13	12	3	0	.976	-9	*O-148,1-12,3/C	0.1
1986	Chi-N	156	586	72	159	30	0	12	79	53	48	.271	.332	.384	90	-8	3	6	-3	.980	-9	*O-121,3-24,C1	-2.5
1987	Chi-N	153	563	63	150	29	1	27	88	39	66	.266	.314	.465	99	-2	3	3	-1	.934	4	*3-150/1-1	-0.1
1988	SD-N	143	511	40	131	23	0	5	64	40	51	.256	.310	.331	86	-9	2	3	-1	.994	-5	1-73,O-64/3	-2.3
1989	Det-A	90	318	34	95	16	0	5	35	27	33	.299	.357	.396	115	6	3	2	-0	1.000	-6	D-51,1-31,3/C	-0.4
	Bal-A	33	107	11	23	4	0	1	10	4	12	.215	.243	.280	49	-7	0	0	0	.000	0	D-29	-0.8
	Yr	123	425	45	118	20	0	6	45	31	45	.278	.330	.367	99	-1	3	2	-0	1.000	-6	D-80,1-31,3/C	-1.2
Total	12	1306	4581	511	1279	214	14	121	674	405	515	.279	.339	.411	103	15	28	33	-11	.979	-65	O-677,3-220,C1/D	-9.7

■ HARRY MORELOCK
Morelock, A. Harry   b: 11/1869, Philadelphia, Pa.   Deb: 8/21/1891

YEAR	TM/L	G	AB	R	H	2B	3B	HR	RBI	BB	SO	AVG	OBP	SLG	PRO+	BR/A	SB	CS	SBR	FA	FR	G/POS	TPR
1891	Phi-N	4	14	1	1	0	0	0	3	3		.071	.235	.071	-9	-2	0			.824	-4	/S-4	-0.5
1892	Phi-N	1	3	0	0	0	0	0	0	1	0	.000	.250	.000	-23	-0	0			.600	-1	/3-1	-0.1
Total	2	5	17	1	1	0	0	0	4	3	.059	.238	.059	-11	-2	0			.824	-4	/S-4,3-1	-0.6

■ JOSE MORENO
Moreno, Jose De Los Santos (b: Jose De Los Santos Mauricio (Moreno))   b: 11/1/57, Santo Domingo, D.R.   BB/TR, 6', 175 lbs.   Deb: 5/24/80

YEAR	TM/L	G	AB	R	H	2B	3B	HR	RBI	BB	SO	AVG	OBP	SLG	PRO+	BR/A	SB	CS	SBR	FA	FR	G/POS	TPR
1980	NY-N	37	46	6	9	2	1	2	9	3	12	.196	.245	.413	83	-1	1	0	0	.917	0	/2-4,3-4	-0.1
1981	SD-N	34	48	5	11	2	0	0	6	1	8	.229	.245	.271	50	-1	4	1	1	1.000	0	/O-9,2-1	-0.3
1982	Cal-A	11	3	3	0	0	0	0	0	2	0	.000	.400	.000	21	-0	0	2	-1	1.000	1	/2-2,D-1	0.0
Total	3	82	97	14	20	4	1	2	15	6	20	.206	.252	.330	66	-5	5	3	-0	.947	1	/O-9,2-7,3D	-0.4

■ OMAR MORENO
Moreno, Omar Renan (Quintero)   b: 10/24/52, Puerto Armuelles, Panama   BL/TL, 6'2", 180 lbs.   Deb: 9/6/75

YEAR	TM/L	G	AB	R	H	2B	3B	HR	RBI	BB	SO	AVG	OBP	SLG	PRO+	BR/A	SB	CS	SBR	FA	FR	G/POS	TPR
1975	Pit-N	6	6	1	1	0	0	0	0	1	1	.167	.286	.167	28	-1	1	0	0	.000	-1	/O-1	-0.1
1976	Pit-N	48	122	24	33	4	1	2	12	16	24	.270	.360	.369	106	1	15	5	2	.960	-1	O-42	0.1
1977	Pit-N	150	492	69	118	19	9	7	34	38	102	.240	.296	.358	72	-20	53	16	6	.977	8	*O-147	-1.0
1978	Pit-N	155	515	95	121	15	7	2	33	81	104	.235	.342	.303	78	-12	71	22	8	.984	17	*O-152	0.7
1979	*Pit-N	162	695	110	196	21	12	8	69	51	104	.282	.334	.381	90	-9	77	21	11	.975	23	*O-162	1.8
1980	Pit-N	162	676	87	168	20	13	2	36	57	101	.249	.309	.325	76	-21	96	33	4	.990	27	*O-162	0.9
1981	Pit-N	103	434	62	120	18	8	1	35	26	76	.276	.322	.362	91	-5	39	14	3	.997	10	*O-103	0.4
1982	Pit-N	158	645	82	158	18	9	3	44	44	121	.245	.294	.315	80	-27	60	26	2	.983	13	*O-157	-1.7
1983	Hou-N	97	405	48	98	12	2	1	25	22	72	.242	.283	.326	73	-16	30	13	1	.977	9	O-97	-0.9
	NY-A	48	152	17	38	9	1	1	17	8	31	.250	.287	.342	75	-5	7	3	0	.992	-0	O-48	-0.6
1984	NY-A	117	355	37	92	12	6	4	38	18	48	.259	.297	.361	84	-8	20	11	-1	.985	-3	*O-108/D-1	-0.9
1985	NY-A	34	66	12	13	4	1	1	0	4	16	.197	.209	.333	40	-4	1	0	-0	1.000	0	O-26/D-1	-0.6
	KC-A	24	70	9	17	1	3	2	16	3	8	.243	.284	.429	91	-1	1	2	-1	1.000	-3	O-21	-0.6
	Yr	58	136	21	30	5	4	3	16	4	24	.221	.248	.382	70	-6	1	2	-1	1.000	-3	O-47/D-1	-1.2

YEAR	TM/L	G	AB	R	H	2B	3B	HR	RBI	BB	SO	AVG	OBP	SLG	PRO+	BR/A	SB	CS	SBR	FA	FR	G/POS	TPR
1986	Atl-N	118	359	46	84	18	6	4	27	21	77	.234	.276	.351	68	-16	17	16	-5	.970	-3	O-97	-2.7
Total	12	1382	4992	699	1257	171	87	37	386	387	885	.252	.308	.343	79	-146	487	182	37	.982	103	*O-1323/D-2	-5.3

■ CHET MORGAN
Morgan, Chester Collins "Chick" b: 6/6/10, Cleveland, Miss. d: 9/20/91, Pasadena, Tex. BL/TR, 5'9", 160 lbs. Deb: 4/19/35

YEAR	TM/L	G	AB	R	H	2B	3B	HR	RBI	BB	SO	AVG	OBP	SLG	PRO+	BR/A	SB	CS	SBR	FA	FR	G/POS	TPR
1935	Det-A	14	23	2	4	1	0	0	1	5	0	.174	.321	.217	43	-2	0	0	0	.909	-0	/O-4	-0.2
1938	Det-A	74	306	50	87	6	1	0	27	20	12	.284	.330	.310	58	-19	5	6	-2	.980	0	O-74	-2.2
Total	2	88	329	52	91	7	1	0	28	25	12	.277	.329	.304	57	-21	5	6	-2	.977	0	/O-78	-2.4

■ ED MORGAN
Morgan, Edward Carre b: 5/22/04, Cairo, Ill. d: 4/9/80, New Orleans, La. BR/TR, 6'0.5", 180 lbs. Deb: 4/11/28

YEAR	TM/L	G	AB	R	H	2B	3B	HR	RBI	BB	SO	AVG	OBP	SLG	PRO+	BR/A	SB	CS	SBR	FA	FR	G/POS	TPR
1928	Cle-A	76	265	42	83	24	6	4	54	21	17	.313	.366	.494	123	8	5	5	-2	.968	1	1-36,O-21,3	0.4
1929	Cle-A	93	318	60	101	19	10	3	37	37	24	.318	.392	.469	116	8	8	4	-3	.908	-11	O-80	-0.8
1930	Cle-A	150	584	122	204	47	11	26	136	62	66	.349	.413	.601	148	41	8	4	0	.987	-3	*1-129,O-19	2.2
1931	Cle-A	131	462	87	162	33	4	11	86	83	46	.351	.451	.511	144	33	4	5	-2	.984	2	*1-117/3-3	2.1
1932	Cle-A	144	532	96	156	32	7	4	68	94	44	.293	.402	.402	102	5	7	6	-2	.985	-8	*1-142/3-1	-1.5
1933	Cle-A	39	121	10	32	3	3	1	13	7	9	.264	.305	.364	73	-5	1	1	-0	.997	2	1-32/O-1	-0.6
1934	Bos-A	138	528	95	141	28	4	3	79	81	46	.267	.367	.352	80	-14	7	1	2	.988	-7	*1-137	-3.0
Total	7	771	2810	512	879	186	45	52	473	385	252	.313	.398	.467	117	76	36	25	-4	.986	-23	1-593,O-121/3	-1.2

■ EDDIE MORGAN
Morgan, Edwin Willis "Pepper" b: 11/19/14, Brady Lake, Ohio d: 6/27/82, Lakewood, Ohio BL/TL, 5'10", 160 lbs. Deb: 4/14/36

YEAR	TM/L	G	AB	R	H	2B	3B	HR	RBI	BB	SO	AVG	OBP	SLG	PRO+	BR/A	SB	CS	SBR	FA	FR	G/POS	TPR
1936	StL-N	8	18	4	5	0	0	1	3	2	4	.278	.350	.444	113	0	0			.889	-0	/O-4	0.0
1937	Bro-N	31	48	4	9	3	0	0	5	9	7	.188	.316	.250	55	-3	0			.984	-3	/1-7,O-7	-0.6
Total	2	39	66	8	14	3	0	1	8	11	11	.212	.325	.303	70	-2	0			.842	-3	/O-11,1-7	-0.6

■ BILL MORGAN
Morgan, Henry William b: 10/1857, Washington, D.C. Deb: 5/4/1875

YEAR	TM/L	G	AB	R	H	2B	3B	HR	RBI	BB	SO	AVG	OBP	SLG	PRO+	BR/A	SB	CS	SBR	FA	FR	G/POS	TPR
1875	RS-n	19	69	11	18	4	0	0			5	.261	.311	.319	131	3						/O-8,P-7,3	0.2
1878	Mil-N	14	56	2	11	0	0	0	5	3	9	.196	.237	.196	41	-4				.769	-6	O-13/3-3,2	-0.9
1882	Pit-a	17	66	10	17	2	1	0			4	.258	.300	.318	114	1				.688	-8	O-11/C-7	-0.6
1884	Ric-a	6	20	0	2	0	0	0			1	.100	.143	.100	-20	-3				.850	-2	/C-3,O-2,2	-0.4
	Bal-U	2	9	1	2	0	0	0			1	.222	.300	.222	40	-1				.909	0	/C-1,2-1,O	-0.1
Total	3	39	151	13	32	2	1	0	5	9	9	.212	.256	.238	62	-6				.743	-16	/O-27,C-11,23	-2.0

■ RED MORGAN
Morgan, James Edward b: 10/6/1883, Neola, Iowa d: 3/25/81, New York, N.Y. TR, Deb: 6/20/06

YEAR	TM/L	G	AB	R	H	2B	3B	HR	RBI	BB	SO	AVG	OBP	SLG	PRO+	BR/A	SB	CS	SBR	FA	FR	G/POS	TPR
1906	Bos-A	88	307	20	66	6	1	3	21	16		.215	.270	.264	67	-11	7			.866	-13	3-88	-2.4

■ JOE MORGAN
Morgan, Joe Leonard b: 9/19/43, Bonham, Tex. BL/TR, 5'7", 160 lbs. Deb: 9/21/63 H

YEAR	TM/L	G	AB	R	H	2B	3B	HR	RBI	BB	SO	AVG	OBP	SLG	PRO+	BR/A	SB	CS	SBR	FA	FR	G/POS	TPR
1963	Hou-N	8	25	5	6	0	1	0	3	5	5	.240	.367	.320	106	1	0	0		.909	-3	/2-7	-0.1
1964	Hou-N	10	37	4	7	0	0	0	0	6	7	.189	.302	.189	44	-3	0	1	-1	.949	-0	2-10	-0.3
1965	Hou-N	157	601	100	163	22	12	14	40	97	77	.271	.375	.418	132	28	20	9	1	.969	-2	*2-157	4.3
1966	Hou-N†	122	425	60	121	14	8	5	42	89	43	.285	.412	.391	134	25	11	8	-2	.965	-16	*2-117	1.6
1967	Hou-N	133	494	73	136	27	11	6	42	81	51	.275	.380	.411	131	22	29	5	6	.979	-5	*2-130/O-1	3.4
1968	Hou-N	10	20	6	5	0	1	0	0	7	4	.250	.444	.350	144	2	3	0	1	.882	-4	/2-5,O-1	-0.1
1969	Hou-N	147	535	94	126	18	5	15	43	110	74	.236	.387	.372	110	11	49	14	6	.972	-4	*2-132,O-14	2.5
1970	Hou-N	144	548	102	147	28	9	8	52	102	55	.268	.384	.396	114	15	42	13	5	.979	11	*2-142	4.1
1971	Hou-N	160	583	87	149	27	11	13	56	88	52	.256	.354	.407	118	15	40	8	7	.986	-3	*2-157	3.5
1972	*Cin-N★	149	552	122	161	23	4	16	73	115	44	.292	.419	.435	152	44	58	17	1	.990	-7	*2-149	5.5
1973	*Cin-N★	157	576	116	167	35	2	26	82	111	61	.290	.408	.493	157	48	67	15	11	.990	-8	*2-154	6.1
1974	*Cin-N★	149	512	107	150	31	3	22	67	120	69	.293	.430	.494	160	47	58	12	10	.982	-13	*2-142	5.2
1975	*Cin-N★	146	498	107	163	27	6	17	94	132	52	.327	.471	.508	169	55	67	10	14	.986	-7	*2-142	7.1
1976	*Cin-N★	141	472	113	151	30	5	27	111	114	41	.320	.453	.576	186	58	60	9	13	.993	-18	*2-133	5.8
1977	*Cin-N★	153	521	113	150	21	6	22	78	117	58	.288	.420	.478	138	33	49	10	9	.993	-18	*2-151	3.5
1978	Cin-N★	132	441	68	104	27	0	13	75	79	40	.236	.354	.385	107	6	19	5	3	.980	-31	*2-124	-1.4
1979	*Cin-N★	127	436	70	109	26	1	9	32	93	45	.250	.383	.376	107	8	28	6	5	.980	-13	*2-121	0.8
1980	*Hou-N	141	461	66	112	17	5	11	49	93	47	.243	.370	.373	117	14	24	6	4	.988	-12	*2-130	1.4
1981	SF-N	90	308	47	74	16	1	8	31	66	37	.240	.374	.377	116	9	14	5	1	.991	-11	2-87	0.5
1982	SF-N	134	463	68	134	19	4	14	61	85	60	.289	.402	.438	135	25	24	4	5	.989	-6	*2-120/3-3	3.1
1983	*Phi-N	123	404	72	93	20	1	16	59	89	54	.230	.374	.403	117	12	18	2	4	.971	-2	*2-117	2.1
1984	Oak-A	116	365	50	89	21	0	6	43	66	39	.244	.361	.351	105	5	8	3	1	.977	-31	*2-100/D-5	-2.3
Total	22	2649	9277	1650	2517	449	96	268	1133	1865	1015	.271	.395	.427	133	478	689	162	110	.981	-206	*2-2527/O-16,D3	56.3

■ JOE MORGAN
Morgan, Joseph Michael b: 11/19/30, Walpole, Mass. BL/TR, 5'10", 170 lbs. Deb: 4/14/59 MC

YEAR	TM/L	G	AB	R	H	2B	3B	HR	RBI	BB	SO	AVG	OBP	SLG	PRO+	BR/A	SB	CS	SBR	FA	FR	G/POS	TPR
1959	Mil-N	13	23	2	5	1	0	0	1	2	4	.217	.280	.261	49	-1	0	0	0	.913	-2	/2-7	-0.4
	KC-A	20	21	2	4	2	0	0	3	3	7	.190	.292	.286	58	-1	0	0	0	1.000	-1	/3-2	-0.2
1960	Phi-N	26	83	5	11	2	2	0	2	6	11	.133	.191	.205	8	-11	0	0	0	.971	1	3-24	-1.0
	Cle-A	22	47	6	14	2	0	2	4	6	4	.298	.377	.468	131	2	0	0	0	.889	-2	3-12/O-2	-1.0
1961	Cle-A	4	10	0	2	0	0	0	0	1	3	.200	.273	.200	29	-1	0	0	0	1.000	0	/O-2	-0.1
1964	StL-N	3	3	0	0	0	0	0	0	0	0	.000	.000	.000	-92	-1	0	0	0	.000	0	H	-0.1
Total	4	88	187	15	36	5	2	2	10	18	31	.193	.263	.283	49	-13	0	0	0	.944	-3	/3-38,2-7,O	-1.8

■ RAY MORGAN
Morgan, Raymond Caryll b: 6/14/1889, Baltimore, Md. d: 2/15/40, Baltimore, Md. BR/TR, 5'8.5", 155 lbs. Deb: 8/7/11

YEAR	TM/L	G	AB	R	H	2B	3B	HR	RBI	BB	SO	AVG	OBP	SLG	PRO+	BR/A	SB	CS	SBR	FA	FR	G/POS	TPR
1911	Was-A	25	89	11	19	2	0	0	5	4		.213	.247	.236	36	-8	2			.900	-3	3-25	-1.1
1912	Was-A	81	273	40	65	10	7	1	30	29		.238	.318	.337	87	-5	11			.939	-7	2-76/S-4,3	-1.3
1913	Was-A	138	481	58	131	19	8	0	57	68	63	.272	.369	.345	107	7	19			.950	-6	*2-134/S-4	-0.1
1914	Was-A	147	491	50	126	22	4	1	49	62	34	.257	.352	.340	104	4	24	17	-3	.948	-9	*2-146	-1.0
1915	Was-A	62	193	21	45	5	4	0	21	30	15	.233	.342	.301	91	-1	6	5	-1	.965	-4	2-57/S-2,3	-0.6
1916	Was-A	99	315	41	84	12	4	1	29	59	29	.267	.398	.340	123	13	14			.957	-17	2-82/S-9,13	-0.1
1917	Was-A	101	338	32	90	9	1	1	33	40	29	.266	.348	.308	101	1	7			.961	-8	2-95/3-3	-0.2
1918	Was-A	88	300	25	70	11	1	0	30	28	14	.233	.311	.277	79	-7	4			.959	-5	2-80/O-2	-0.8
Total	8	741	2480	278	630	90	33	4	254	320	184	.254	.348	.322	98	4	87	22		.953	-58	2-670/3-32,S10	-5.2

■ BOBBY MORGAN
Morgan, Robert Morris b: 6/29/26, Oklahoma City, Okla. BR/TR, 5'9", 175 lbs. Deb: 4/18/50

YEAR	TM/L	G	AB	R	H	2B	3B	HR	RBI	BB	SO	AVG	OBP	SLG	PRO+	BR/A	SB	CS	SBR	FA	FR	G/POS	TPR
1950	Bro-N	67	199	38	45	10	3	7	21	32	43	.226	.342	.412	95	-1	0			.969	6	3-52,S-10	0.5
1952	*Bro-N	76	191	36	45	8	0	7	16	46	35	.236	.392	.387	115	6	2	2	-1	.968	3	3-60/2-5,S	0.8
1953	*Bro-N	69	196	35	51	6	2	7	33	33	47	.260	.370	.418	103	1	2	2	-1	.920	-2	3-36,S-21	0.3
1954	Phi-N	135	455	58	119	25	2	14	50	70	68	.262	.360	.418	102	2	3	1	0	.954	-22	*S-129/3-8,2	-0.9
1955	Phi-N	136	483	61	112	20	2	10	49	73	72	.232	.333	.344	81	-12	6	4	-1	.980	-13	2-88,S-41/31	-1.6
1956	Phi-N	8	25	1	5	0	0	0	1	6	4	.200	.355	.200	56	-1	0	0	0	.857	1	/3-5,2-3	-0.0
	StL-N	61	113	14	22	7	0	3	20	15	24	.195	.289	.336	67	-5	0	2	-1	.980	1	2-13,3-11/S	-0.5
	Yr	69	138	15	27	7	0	3	21	21	28	.196	.302	.312	65	-7	0	2	-1	.877	1	3-16,2-16/S	-0.5
1957	Phi-N	2	0	0	0	0	0	0	—	—	—						0	0	0	1.000	0	2-1	0.0
	Chi-N	125	425	43	88	20	2	5	27	52	87	.207	.295	.299	61	-23	5	0		.976	8	*2-116,3-12	-0.5
	Yr	127	425	43	88	20	2	5	27	52	87	.207	.295	.299	61	-23	5	0		.976	8	*2-117,3-12	-0.5
1958	Chi-N	1	0	0	0	0	0	0				.000	.000	.000	-99	-0	0	0		.000	0	H	0.0
Total	8	671	2088	286	487	96	11	53	217	327	381	.233	.339	.366	88	-33	18	11		.978	-18	2-231,S-211,3/1	-2.2

YEAR	TM/L	G	AB	R	H	2B	3B	HR	RBI	BB	SO	AVG	OBP	SLG	PRO+	BR/A	SB	CS	SBR	FA	FR	G/POS	TPR

■ VERN MORGAN   Morgan, Vernon Thomas   b: 8/8/28, Emporia, Va.   d: 11/8/75, Minneapolis, Minn.   BL/TR, 6'1", 190 lbs.   Deb: 8/10/54   C

1954	Chi-N	24	64	3	15	2	0	0	2	1	10	.234	.246	.266	33	-6	0	0	0	.895	-4	3-15	-1.1
1955	Chi-N	7	7	1	1	0	0	0	1	3	4	.143	.400	.143	52	-0	0	0	0	.667	-1	/3-2	-0.1
Total	2	31	71	4	16	2	0	0	3	4	14	.225	.267	.254	36	-7	0	0	0	.864	-5	/3-17	-1.2

■ BILL MORGAN   Morgan, William   Deb: 8/6/1883

1883	Pit-a	32	114	12	18	2	1	0		7		.158	.207	.193	31	-8				.825	-2	S-21/O-6,C2	-0.8
1884	Was-a	45	162	8	28	1	1	0		8		.173	.216	.191	39	-10				.781	-5	O-31,C-12/2S	-1.3
Total	2	77	276	20	46	3	2	0		15		.167	.212	.192	35	-18				.771	-6	/O-37,S-23,C2	-2.1

■ MOE MORHARDT   Morhardt, Meredith Goodwin   b: 1/16/37, Manchester, Conn.   BL/TL, 6'1", 185 lbs.   Deb: 9/7/61

1961	Chi-N	7	18	3	5	0	0	0	1	3	5	.278	.381	.278	78	-0	0	0	0	.962	-1	/1-7	-0.2
1962	Chi-N	18	16	1	2	0	0	0	2	2	8	.125	.222	.125	-4	-2	0	0	0	.000	0	H	-0.2
Total	2	25	34	4	7	0	0	0	3	5	13	.206	.308	.206	39	-3	0	0	0	.962	-1	/1-7	-0.4

■ ED MORIARTY   Moriarty, Edward Jerome   b: 10/12/12, Holyoke, Mass.   d: 9/29/91, Holyoke, Mass.   BR/TR, 5'10.5", 180 lbs.   Deb: 6/21/35

1935	Bos-N	8	34	4	11	2	1	1	1	0	6	.324	.324	.529	136	1	0			.923	-4	/2-8	-0.2
1936	Bos-N	6	6	1	1	0	0	0	0	0	1	.167	.167	.167	-11	-1	0			.000	0	H	-0.1
Total	2	14	40	5	12	2	1	1	1	0	7	.300	.300	.475	114	0	0			.923	-4	/2-8	-0.3

■ GENE MORIARITY   Moriarity, Eugene John   b: 1/5/1865, Holyoke, Mass.   BL/TL, 5'8", 130 lbs.   Deb: 6/18/1884

1884	Bos-N	4	16	1	1	0	0	0	0	0	8	.063	.063	.063	-61	-3				.714	-1	/O-4	-0.3
	Ind-a	10	37	4	8	0	2	0		0		.216	.216	.324	76	-1				.769	-1	/O-7,P-2,3	-0.2
1885	Det-N	11	39	1	1	1	0	0	0	0	10	.026	.050	.051	-75	-7				.905	2	/O-6,3-4,SP	-0.5
1892	StL-N	47	177	20	31	4	1	3	19	4	37	.175	.207	.260	43	-13	7			.820	2	O-47	-1.2
Total	3	72	269	26	41	5	3	3	19	4	55	.152	.174	.227	24	-24	7			.822	2	/O-64,3-5,PS	-2.2

■ GEORGE MORIARTY   Moriarty, George Joseph   b: 6/7/1884, Chicago, Ill.   d: 4/8/64, Miami, Fla.   BR/TR, 6', 185 lbs.   Deb: 9/27/03   FMU

1903	Chi-N	1	5	1	0	0	0	0	0	0		.000	.000	.000	-99	-1	0			1.000	-0	/3-1	-0.2
1904	Chi-N	4	13	0	0	0	0	0	0	1		.000	.071	.000	-77	-3	0			.778	-2	/3-2,O-2	-0.3
1906	NY-A	65	197	22	46	7	7	0	23	17		.234	.298	.340	90	-3	8			.912	3	3-39,O-15/12	-0.1
1907	NY-A	126	437	51	121	16	5	0	43	25		.277	.320	.336	101	0	28			.899	-9	3-91,1-22/O2S	-0.8
1908	NY-A	101	348	25	82	12	1	0	27	11		.236	.269	.276	76	-9	22			.976	0	1-52,3-28,O/2	-0.2
1909	*Det-A	133	473	43	129	4	1	39	24			.273	.309	.338	100	-1	34			**.939**	2	*3-106,1-24	0.5
1910	Det-A	136	490	53	123	24	3	2	60	33		.251	.308	.324	92	-5	33			.927	-1	*3-134	-0.3
1911	Det-A	130	478	51	116	20	4	1	60	27		.243	.287	.308	63	-25	28			.929	-4	*3-129/1-1	-2.7
1912	Det-A	105	375	38	93	23	1	0	54	26		.248	.316	.315	83	-8	27			.987	-8	1-71,3-33	-1.7
1913	Det-A	105	347	29	83	5	2	0	30	24	25	.239	.302	.265	67	-14	33			.938	-3	3-94/O-7	-1.7
1914	Det-A	132	465	56	118	19	5	1	40	39	27	.254	.318	.323	90	-6	34	15	1	.956	17	*3-126/1-3	1.8
1915	Det-A	31	38	2	8	1	0	0	0	5	7	.211	.318	.237	63	-2	1	1	-0	.875	-0	3-12/1-1,2O	0.1
1916	Chi-A	7	5	1	1	0	0	0	0	0		.200	.429	.200	88	0	1			1.000	1	/1-1,3-1	0.1
Total	13	1076	3671	372	920	147	32	5	376	234	59	.251	.303	.312	84	-77	248	16		.931	5	3-796,1-180/O2S	-5.8

■ BILL MORIARTY   Moriarty, William Joseph   b: 8/1883, Chicago, Ill.   d: 12/25/16, Elgin, Ill.   BR/TR, 6'2", 180 lbs.   Deb: 4/29/09   F

1909	Cin-N	6	20	1	4	1	0	0	1	0		.200	.200	.250	40	-1	2			.944	0	/S-6	-0.1

■ BILL MORLEY   Morley, William M. (b: William Morley Jennings)   b: 1/23/1890, Holland, Mich.   d: 5/14/85, Lubbock, Tex.   BR/TR, 5'11", 170 lbs.   Deb: 9/8/13

1913	Was-A	2	3	0	0	0	0	0	0	0	0	.000	.000	.000	-98	-1	0			.000	0	/2-1	-0.1

■ RUSS MORMAN   Morman, Russell Lee   b: 4/28/62, Independence, Mo.   BR/TR, 6'4", 215 lbs.   Deb: 8/3/86

1986	Chi-A	49	159	18	40	5	0	4	17	16	36	.252	.328	.358	84	-3	1	0	0	.989	-3	1-47	-0.9
1988	Chi-A	40	75	8	18	2	0	3	3	3	17	.240	.269	.267	51	-5	0	0	0	.981	-3	1-22,O-10/D	-0.9
1989	Chi-A	37	58	5	13	2	0	0	6	6	16	.224	.297	.259	59	-3	1	0	0	.988	1	1-35/D-1	-0.3
1990	KC-A	12	37	5	10	4	2	1	3	3	3	.270	.325	.568	147	2	0	0	0	1.000	0	/O-8,1-3,D	0.1
1991	KC-A	12	23	1	6	0	0	0	1	1	5	.261	.292	.261	54	-1	0	0	0	1.000	0	/1-8,O-2,D	-0.2
1994	Fla-N	13	33	2	7	0	1	1	2	2	9	.212	.278	.364	62	-2	0	0	0	.987	2	/1-8	-0.1
Total	6	163	385	39	94	13	3	6	34	31	86	.244	.305	.340	76	-12	2	0	0	.989	-5	1-123/O-20,D	-2.3

■ JEFF MORONKO   Moronko, Jeffrey Robert   b: 8/17/59, Houston, Tex.   BR/TR, 6'2", 190 lbs.   Deb: 9/1/84

1984	Cle-A	7	19	1	3	1	0	0	3	3	5	.158	.273	.211	35	-2	0			.895	-0	/3-6,D-1	-0.2
1987	NY-A	7	11	0	1	0	0	0	0	0	2	.091	.167	.091	-29	-2	0	0	0	1.000	-0	/3-3,S-2,O	-0.2
Total	2	14	30	1	4	1	0	0	3	3	7	.133	.235	.167	12	-4	0	0	0	.926	-0	/3-9,O-2,SD	-0.4

■ JOHN MORRILL   Morrill, John Francis "Honest John"   b: 2/19/1855, Boston, Mass.   d: 4/2/32, Boston, Mass.   BR/TR, 5'10.5", 155 lbs.   Deb: 4/24/1876   M

1876	Bos-N	66	278	38	73	5	2	0	26	3	5	.263	.269	.295	87	-4				.857	7	2-37,C-23/O1	0.3
1877	Bos-N	61	242	47	73	5	1	0	28	6	15	.302	.319	.331	101	0				.864	-9	3-30,1-18,O/2	-0.8
1878	Bos-N	60	233	26	56	5	1	0	23	5	16	.240	.256	.270	68	-9				.957	-1	*1-59/O-1,3	-0.8
1879	Bos-N	84	348	56	98	18	5	0	49	14	32	.282	.309	.362	118	6				.878	3	3-51,1-33	0.8
1880	Bos-N	86	342	51	81	16	8	2	44	11	37	.237	.261	.348	108	3				.966	0	1-46,3-40/P	0.0
1881	Bos-N	81	311	47	90	19	3	1	39	12	30	.289	.316	.379	123	8				.969	9	*1-74/2-4,P3	1.0
1882	Bos-N	83	349	73	101	19	11	2	54	18	29	.289	.324	.424	137	14				.964	-3	*1-76/S-3,2O3PM	0.3
1883	Bos-N	97	404	83	129	33	16	6	68	15	68	.319	.344	.525	155	25				**.974**	-1	*1-81/O-7,3S2PM	1.4
1884	Bos-N	111	438	80	114	19	7	3	61	30	87	.260	.308	.356	109	5				.971	3	*1-91,2-17/P3OM	0.5
1885	Bos-N	111	394	74	89	20	7	4	44	64	78	.226	.334	.343	124	14				.969	2	*1-92,3-17/3M	0.5
1886	Bos-N	117	430	86	106	25	6	7	69	56	81	.247	.333	.381	121	13	9			.895	-3	S-55,1-42,2/PM	0.6
1887	Bos-N	127	504	79	141	32	6	12	81	37	86	.280	.330	.438	112	7	19			.984	4	*1-127,M	-0.2
1888	Bos-N	135	486	60	96	18	7	4	39	55	68	.198	.282	.288	81	-9	21			.979	9	*1-133/2-2M	-1.3
1889	Was-N	44	146	20	27	5	1	2	16	30	23	.185	.328	.260	70	-5	12			.980	1	1-40/3-3,2PM	-0.7
1890	Bos-P	2	7	1	1	0	0	0	2	1	1	.143	.333	.143	28	-1	0			.750	-1	/S-1,1-1	-0.1
Total	15	1265	4912	821	1275	239	80	43	643	358	656	.260	.310	.367	111	68	61			.971	22	1-916,3-138,2/SOCP	0.8

■ DOYT MORRIS   Morris, Doyt Theodore   b: 7/15/16, Stanley, N.C.   d: 7/4/84, Gastonia, N.C.   BR/TR, 6'4", 195 lbs.   Deb: 6/6/37

1937	Phi-A	6	13	0	2	0	0	0	0	0	0	.154	.154	.154	-23	-2	0	0	0	1.000	-0	/O-3	-0.2

■ E. MORRIS   Morris, E.   b: Trenton, N.J.   Deb: 9/11/1884

1884	Bal-U	1	3	0	0	0	0	0		0		.000	.000	.000	-91	-1				.500	-1	/O-1,P-1	-0.1

■ JOHN MORRIS   Morris, John Daniel   b: 2/23/61, N.Bellmore, N.Y.   BL/TR, 6'1", 185 lbs.   Deb: 8/5/86

1986	StL-N	39	100	8	24	0	1	1	14	7	15	.240	.290	.290	61	-5	6	2	1	.986	-1	O-31	-0.7
1987	*StL-N	101	157	22	41	6	4	3	23	11	22	.261	.314	.408	88	-3	5	2	0	.989	-15	O-74	-1.8
1988	StL-N	20	38	3	11	2	0	1	3	1	7	.289	.308	.395	99	-0	0	0	0	.857	-3	O-16	-0.6
1989	StL-N	96	117	8	28	4	1	2	14	4	22	.239	.264	.342	70	-5	1	0	0	1.000	-13	O-51	-1.9
1990	StL-N	18	18	0	2	0	0	0	0	3	6	.111	.238	.111	-1	-2	0	0	0	1.000	-2	/O-6	-0.4
1991	Phi-N	85	127	15	28	2	1	6	11	12	25	.220	.293	.276	61	-6	2	0	1	.974	-10	O-57	-1.8

YEAR	TM/L	G	AB	R	H	2B	3B	HR	RBI	BB	SO	AVG	OBP	SLG	PRO+	BR/A	SB	CS	SBR	FA	FR	G/POS	TPR
1992	Cal-A	43	57	4	11	1	0	1	3	4	11	.193	.258	.263	46	-4	1	0	0	1.000	-3	O-14/D-6	-0.7
Total	7	402	614	60	145	15	8	8	63	42	108	.236	.288	.326	69	-26	15	4	2	.981	-49	O-249/D-6	-7.9

■ WALTER MORRIS
Morris, John Walter   b: 1/31/1880, Rockwall, Tex.   d: 8/2/61, Dallas, Tex.   BR/TR, 5'11",   Deb: 8/31/08

YEAR	TM/L	G	AB	R	H	2B	3B	HR	RBI	BB	SO	AVG	OBP	SLG	PRO+	BR/A	SB	CS	SBR	FA	FR	G/POS	TPR
1908	StL-N	23	73	1	13	1	1	0	2	0		.178	.178	.219	28	-6	1			.938	4	S-23	-0.2

■ P. MORRIS
Morris, P.   b: Rockford, Ill.   Deb: 5/14/1884

YEAR	TM/L	G	AB	R	H	2B	3B	HR	RBI	BB	SO	AVG	OBP	SLG	PRO+	BR/A	SB	CS	SBR	FA	FR	G/POS	TPR
1884	Was-U	1	3	0	0	0	0	0		0		.000	.000	.000	-99	-1				.750	0	/S-1	-0.1

■ HAL MORRIS
Morris, William Harold   b: 4/9/65, Fort Rucker, Ala.   BL/TL, 6'3", 200 lbs.   Deb: 7/29/88

YEAR	TM/L	G	AB	R	H	2B	3B	HR	RBI	BB	SO	AVG	OBP	SLG	PRO+	BR/A	SB	CS	SBR	FA	FR	G/POS	TPR
1988	NY-A	15	20	1	2	0	0	0	0	0	9	.100	.100	.100	-44	-4	0	0	0	1.000	-1	/O-4,D-1	-0.5
1989	NY-A	15	18	2	5	0	0	0	4	1	4	.278	.316	.278	69	-1	0	0	0	1.000	-2	/O-5,1-2,D	-0.2
1990	*Cin-N	107	309	50	105	22	3	7	36	21	32	.340	.384	.498	135	14	9	3	1	.995	-0	1-80/O-6	0.9
1991	Cin-N	136	478	72	152	33	1	14	59	46	61	.318	.379	.479	135	22	10	4	1	.992	4	*1-128/O-1	1.9
1992	Cin-N	115	395	41	107	21	3	6	53	45	53	.271	.348	.385	105	3	6	6	-2	**.999**	5	*1-109	-0.1
1993	Cin-N	101	379	48	120	18	0	7	49	34	51	.317	.376	.420	112	7	2	2	-1	.994	3	1-98	0.2
1994	Cin-N	112	436	60	146	30	4	10	78	34	62	.335	.389	.491	129	18	6	2	1	**.994**	1	*1-112	1.1
Total	7	601	2035	274	637	124	11	44	279	181	272	.313	.372	.450	121	61	33	17	-0	.995	11	1-529/O-16,D	3.3

■ JIM MORRISON
Morrison, James Forrest   b: 9/23/52, Pensacola, Fla.   BR/TR, 5'11", 182 lbs.   Deb: 9/18/77

YEAR	TM/L	G	AB	R	H	2B	3B	HR	RBI	BB	SO	AVG	OBP	SLG	PRO+	BR/A	SB	CS	SBR	FA	FR	G/POS	TPR
1977	Phi-N	5	7	3	3	0	0	0	1	1	1	.429	.500	.429	145	1	0	0	0	.875	1	/3-5	0.1
1978	*Phi-N	53	108	12	17	1	1	3	10	10	21	.157	.235	.269	40	-9	1	1	-0	.968	13	2-31/3-3,O	0.6
1979	Chi-A	67	240	38	66	14	0	14	35	15	48	.275	.328	.508	122	6	11	3	2	.982	0	2-48,3-29	1.0
1980	Chi-A	162	604	66	171	40	0	15	57	36	74	.283	.332	.424	106	4	9	6	-1	.969	-3	*2-161/S-1,D	1.1
1981	Chi-A	90	290	27	68	8	1	10	34	10	29	.234	.265	.372	84	-7	3	2	-0	.956	8	3-87/2-1,D	-0.2
1982	Chi-A	51	166	17	37	7	3	7	19	13	15	.223	.279	.428	91	-3	0	1	-1	.914	-14	3-50/D-1	-1.9
	Pit-N	44	86	10	24	4	1	4	15	5	14	.279	.319	.488	119	2	2	0	1	.964	2	3-26/O-2,2S	0.4
1983	Pit-N	66	158	16	48	7	2	6	25	9	25	.304	.349	.487	126	5	2	6	-3	.973	5	2-28,3-26/S	0.6
1984	Pit-N	100	304	38	87	14	2	11	45	20	52	.286	.332	.454	119	7	0	1	-1	.938	0	3-61,2-26/S1	0.7
1985	Pit-N	92	244	17	62	10	0	4	22	8	44	.254	.281	.344	75	-9	3	0	1	.961	1	3-59,2-15/O	-0.8
1986	Pit-N	154	537	58	147	35	4	23	88	47	88	.274	.337	.482	120	13	9	8	-2	.946	-13	*3-151/2-1,S	-0.5
1987	Pit-N	96	348	41	92	22	1	9	46	27	57	.264	.319	.411	91	-5	8	5	-1	.975	1	3-82,S-17/2	-0.4
	*Det-A	34	117	15	24	1	1	4	19	2	26	.205	.225	.333	47	-9	2	1	-0	.962	3	3-16/2-3,SO1D	-0.6
1988	Det-A	24	74	7	16	5	0	0	6	0	14	.216	.216	.284	40	-6	0	2	-1	1.000	-0	D-14/1-4,3OS	-0.8
	Atl-N	51	92	6	14	2	0	2	13	10	13	.152	.235	.239	35	-8	0	1	-1	.933	0	3-20/O-4,P	-0.9
Total	12	1089	3375	371	876	170	16	112	435	213	521	.260	.308	.419	98	-18	50	37	-7	.949	1	3-619,2-324/SDO1PD	-1.6

■ JON MORRISON
Morrison, Jonathan W.   b: 1859, London, Ontario, Canada   5'9.5", 167 lbs.   Deb: 8/1/1884

YEAR	TM/L	G	AB	R	H	2B	3B	HR	RBI	BB	SO	AVG	OBP	SLG	PRO+	BR/A	SB	CS	SBR	FA	FR	G/POS	TPR
1884	Ind-a	44	182	26	48	6	8	1		7		.264	.306	.401	132	6				.784	3	O-44	0.7
1887	NY-a	9	34	7	4	0	0	0		6		.118	.268	.118	10	-4	0			.600	-4	/O-9	-0.7
Total	2	53	216	33	52	6	8	1		13		.241	.299	.356	110	3	0			.756	-1	/O-53	0.0

■ TOM MORRISON
Morrison, Thomas J.   b: 1875, St.Louis, Mo.   5'3", 145 lbs.   Deb: 9/18/1895

YEAR	TM/L	G	AB	R	H	2B	3B	HR	RBI	BB	SO	AVG	OBP	SLG	PRO+	BR/A	SB	CS	SBR	FA	FR	G/POS	TPR
1895	Lou-N	6	22	3	6	0	2	0	4	1	1	.273	.304	.455	100	-0	0			1.000	-3	/S-3,3-3	-0.2
1896	Lou-N	8	27	3	4	1	0	0	0	4	4	.148	.258	.185	19	-3	0			.864	-1	/3-5,O-2,S	-0.3
Total	2	14	49	6	10	1	2	0	4	5	5	.204	.278	.306	55	-3	0			.839	-3	/3-8,S-4,O	-0.5

■ JACK MORRISSEY
Morrissey, John Albert "King"   b: 5/2/1876, Lansing, Mich.   d: 10/30/36, Lansing, Mich.   BB/TR, 5'10", 160 lbs.   Deb: 9/18/02

YEAR	TM/L	G	AB	R	H	2B	3B	HR	RBI	BB	SO	AVG	OBP	SLG	PRO+	BR/A	SB	CS	SBR	FA	FR	G/POS	TPR
1902	Cin-N	12	39	5	11	1	1	0	3	4		.282	.349	.359	108	-2	0			.941	-2	2-11/O-1	-0.1
1903	Cin-N	29	89	14	22	1	0	0	9	14		.247	.350	.258	67	-4	3			.922	-10	2-17/O-8,S	-1.3
Total	2	41	128	19	33	2	1	0	12	18		.258	.349	.289	78	-3	3			.930	-12	/2-28,O-9,S	-1.4

■ JOHN MORRISSEY
Morrissey, John J.   b: 12/30/1856, Janesville, Wis.   d: 4/29/1884, Janesville, Wis.   Deb: 5/2/1881   F

YEAR	TM/L	G	AB	R	H	2B	3B	HR	RBI	BB	SO	AVG	OBP	SLG	PRO+	BR/A	SB	CS	SBR	FA	FR	G/POS	TPR
1881	Buf-N	12	47	3	10	2	0	0	3	0	3	.213	.213	.255	47	-3				.865	-2	3-12	-0.4
1882	Det-N	2	7	1	2	0	0	0	0	0	0	.286	.286	.286	84	-0				.714	-1	/3-2	-0.1
Total	2	14	54	4	12	2	0	0	3	0	5	.222	.222	.259	52	-3				.841	-3	/3-14	-0.5

■ JO-JO MORRISSEY
Morrissey, Joseph Anselm   b: 1/16/04, Warren, R.I.   d: 5/2/50, Worcester, Mass.   BR/TR, 6'1.5", 178 lbs.   Deb: 4/12/32

YEAR	TM/L	G	AB	R	H	2B	3B	HR	RBI	BB	SO	AVG	OBP	SLG	PRO+	BR/A	SB	CS	SBR	FA	FR	G/POS	TPR
1932	Cin-N	89	269	15	65	10	1	0	13	14	15	.242	.282	.286	55	-17	2			.967	8	S-45,2-42,3/O	-0.4
1933	Cin-N	148	534	43	123	20	0	0	26	20	22	.230	.261	.268	52	-33	5			.964	-9	2-88,S-63,3	-3.5
1936	Chi-A	17	38	3	7	1	0	0	6	2	3	.184	.225	.211	8	-6	0	0	0	.895	0	/3-9,S-4,2	-0.4
Total	3	254	841	61	195	31	1	0	45	36	40	.232	.266	.271	51	-56	7	0		.971	-0	2-131,S-112/3O	-4.3

■ TOM MORRISSEY
Morrissey, Thomas J.   b: 1861, Janesville, Wis.   d: 9/23/41, Janesville, Wis.   5'11", 180 lbs.   Deb: 9/27/1884   F

YEAR	TM/L	G	AB	R	H	2B	3B	HR	RBI	BB	SO	AVG	OBP	SLG	PRO+	BR/A	SB	CS	SBR	FA	FR	G/POS	TPR
1884	Mil-U	12	47	3	8	2	0	0				.170	.170	.213	6	-8				.710	-1	3-12	-0.8

■ BUD MORSE
Morse, Newell Obediah   b: 9/4/04, Berkeley, Cal.   d: 4/6/87, Sparks, Nev.   BL/TR, 5'9", 150 lbs.   Deb: 9/14/29

YEAR	TM/L	G	AB	R	H	2B	3B	HR	RBI	BB	SO	AVG	OBP	SLG	PRO+	BR/A	SB	CS	SBR	FA	FR	G/POS	TPR
1929	Phi-A	8	27	1	2	0	0	0	0	0	2	.074	.074	.074	-60	-6	0	0	0	.975	2	/2-8	-0.4

■ HAP MORSE
Morse, Peter Raymond "Pete"   b: 12/6/1886, St.Paul, Minn.   d: 6/19/74, St.Paul, Minn.   BR/TR, 5'8", 160 lbs.   Deb: 4/18/11

YEAR	TM/L	G	AB	R	H	2B	3B	HR	RBI	BB	SO	AVG	OBP	SLG	PRO+	BR/A	SB	CS	SBR	FA	FR	G/POS	TPR
1911	StL-N	4	8	0	0	0	0	0	0	1		.000	.111	.000	-70	-2	0			.750	-0	/S-2,O-1	-0.2

■ CHARLIE MORTON
Morton, Charles Hazen   b: 10/12/1854, Kingsville, Ohio   d: 12/9/21, Massillon, Ohio   BR/TR, 150 lbs.   Deb: 5/2/1882   MU

YEAR	TM/L	G	AB	R	H	2B	3B	HR	RBI	BB	SO	AVG	OBP	SLG	PRO+	BR/A	SB	CS	SBR	FA	FR	G/POS	TPR
1882	Pit-a	25	103	12	29	0	3	0		5		.282	.315	.340	127	3				.816	-1	O-25/3-3,S	0.4
	StL-a	9	32	2	2	0	1	0		2		.063	.118	.125	-17	-4				.708	-4	/2-7,O-3	-0.8
	Yr	34	135	14	31	0	4	0		7		.230	.268	.289	90	-1				.821	-3	O-28/2-7,3S	-0.4
1884	Tol-a	32	111	11	18	6	2	0		7		.162	.212	.252	49	-6				.861	-1	3-16,O-15/P2M	-0.5
1885	Det-N	22	79	9	14	1	2	0	3	5	10	.177	.226	.241	51	-4				.750	2	3-18/S-4M	-0.2
Total	3	88	325	34	63	7	8	0	3	19	10	.194	.238	.265	66	-11				.841	-3	/O-43,3-37,2SP	-1.1

■ GUY MORTON
Morton, Guy Jr. "Moose"   b: 11/4/30, Tuscaloosa, Ala.   BR/TR, 6'2", 200 lbs.   Deb: 9/17/54   F

YEAR	TM/L	G	AB	R	H	2B	3B	HR	RBI	BB	SO	AVG	OBP	SLG	PRO+	BR/A	SB	CS	SBR	FA	FR	G/POS	TPR
1954	Bos-A	1	1	0	0	0	0	0	0	0	1	.000	.000	.000	-90	-0	0	0	0	.000	0	H	0.0

■ BUBBA MORTON
Morton, Wycliffe Nathaniel   b: 12/13/31, Washington, D.C.   BR/TR, 5'10.5", 180 lbs.   Deb: 4/19/61

YEAR	TM/L	G	AB	R	H	2B	3B	HR	RBI	BB	SO	AVG	OBP	SLG	PRO+	BR/A	SB	CS	SBR	FA	FR	G/POS	TPR
1961	Det-A	77	108	26	31	5	1	2	19	9	25	.287	.347	.407	98	-0	3	1	0	.952	-4	O-30	-0.5
1962	Det-A	90	195	30	51	6	3	4	17	32	32	.262	.366	.385	99	0	1	1	-0	.991	-2	O-62/1-3	-0.4
1963	Det-A	6	11	2	1	0	0	0	2	2	1	.091	.231	.091	-5	-2	0	0	0	.875	-0	/O-3	-0.4
	Mil-N	15	28	1	5	0	0	0	2	2	3	.179	.258	.179	28	-2	0	0	0	1.000	-1	/O-9	-0.4
1966	Cal-A	15	50	4	11	1	0	0	4	2	6	.220	.250	.240	43	-4	1	1	-0	1.000	0	O-14	-0.5
1967	Cal-A	80	201	23	63	9	3	0	32	22	29	.313	.387	.388	135	9	5	3	-2	1.000	-6	O-61	-0.1
1968	Cal-A	81	163	13	44	6	1	0	18	14	18	.270	.343	.325	107	2	4	2	-0	.985	-4	O-50/3-1	-0.5
1969	Cal-A	87	172	19	42	10	0	7	32	28	29	.244	.360	.436	128	7	0	0	-0	1.000	-0	O-49/1-1	0.5
Total	7	451	928	117	248	37	8	14	128	111	143	.267	.352	.370	106	10	7	7	-2	.988	-17	O-278/1-4,3	-2.1

■ WALT MORYN
Moryn, Walter Joseph "Moose"   b: 4/12/26, St.Paul, Minn.   BL/TR, 6'2", 205 lbs.   Deb: 6/29/54

YEAR	TM/L	G	AB	R	H	2B	3B	HR	RBI	BB	SO	AVG	OBP	SLG	PRO+	BR/A	SB	CS	SBR	FA	FR	G/POS	TPR
1954	Bro-N	48	91	16	25	4	2	2	14	7	11	.275	.333	.429	94	-1	0	0	0	.881	-0	O-20	-0.2

YEAR	TM/L	G	AB	R	H	2B	3B	HR	RBI	BB	SO	AVG	OBP	SLG	PRO+	BR/A	SB	CS	SBR	FA	FR	G/POS	TPR
1955	Bro-N	11	19	3	5	1	0	1	3	5	4	.263	.417	.474	132	1	0	0	0	.833	-2	/O-7	-0.1
1956	Chi-N	147	529	69	151	27	3	23	67	50	67	.285	.351	.478	122	16	4	2	0	.983	10	*O-141	1.9
1957	Chi-N	149	568	76	164	33	0	19	88	50	90	.289	.349	.447	114	11	0	2	-1	.960	7	*O-147	0.9
1958	Chi-N☆	143	512	77	135	26	7	26	77	62	83	.264	.352	.494	123	16	1	2	-1	.978	5	*O-141	1.3
1959	Chi-N	117	381	41	89	14	1	14	48	44	66	.234	.318	.386	87	-7	0	0	0	.989	0	*O-104	-1.2
1960	Chi-N	38	109	12	32	4	0	2	11	13	19	.294	.369	.385	108	2	2	1	0	.964	0	O-30	0.1
	StL-N	75	200	24	49	4	3	11	35	17	38	.245	.304	.460	97	-1	0	0	0	.990	-3	O-62	-0.7
	Yr	113	309	36	81	8	3	13	46	30	57	.262	.327	.434	101	0	2	1	0	.981	-3	O-92	-0.6
1961	StL-N	17	32	0	4	2	0	0	2	1	5	.125	.152	.188	-10	-5	0	0	0	.889	-1	/O-7	-0.7
	Pit-N	40	65	6	13	1	0	3	9	2	10	.200	.235	.354	53	-5	0	0	0	.950	1	O-11	-0.4
	Yr	57	97	6	17	3	0	3	11	3	15	.175	.208	.299	31	-10	0	0	0	.931	-0	O-18	-1.1
Total	8	785	2506	324	667	116	16	101	354	251	393	.266	.338	.446	108	27	7	7	-2	.972	17	O-670	0.9

■ ROSS MOSCHITTO
Moschitto, Rosaire Allen b: 2/15/45, Fresno, Cal. BR/TR, 6'2", 175 lbs. Deb: 4/15/65

YEAR	TM/L	G	AB	R	H	2B	3B	HR	RBI	BB	SO	AVG	OBP	SLG	PRO+	BR/A	SB	CS	SBR	FA	FR	G/POS	TPR
1965	NY-A	96	27	12	5	0	0	1	3	0	12	.185	.185	.296	35	-2	0	0	0	.941	-26	O-89	-3.1
1967	NY-A	14	9	1	1	0	0	0	0	1	2	.111	.200	.111	-6	-1	0	0	0	1.000	-2	/O-8	-0.4
Total	2	110	36	13	6	0	0	1	3	1	14	.167	.189	.250	25	-4	0	0	0	.944	-28	/O-97	-3.5

■ LLOYD MOSEBY
Moseby, Lloyd Anthony b: 11/5/59, Portland, Ark. BL/TR, 6'3", 200 lbs. Deb: 5/24/80

YEAR	TM/L	G	AB	R	H	2B	3B	HR	RBI	BB	SO	AVG	OBP	SLG	PRO+	BR/A	SB	CS	SBR	FA	FR	G/POS	TPR
1980	Tor-A	114	389	44	89	24	1	9	46	25	85	.229	.282	.365	73	-15	4	6	-2	.982	6	*O-104/D-6	-1.6
1981	Tor-A	100	378	36	88	16	2	9	43	24	86	.233	.280	.357	78	-12	11	8	-2	.989	3	*O-100	-1.5
1982	Tor-A	147	487	51	115	20	9	9	52	33	106	.236	.295	.370	74	-18	11	7	-1	.992	-1	*O-145	-2.3
1983	Tor-A	151	539	104	170	31	7	18	81	51	85	.315	.380	.499	132	23	27	8	3	.983	10	*O-147	3.2
1984	Tor-A	158	592	97	166	28	**15**	18	92	78	122	.280	.372	.470	126	22	39	9	6	.990	17	*O-156	4.0
1985	*Tor-A	152	584	92	151	30	7	18	70	76	91	.259	.348	.426	108	7	37	15	2	.980	1	*O-152	0.5
1986	Tor-A★	152	589	89	149	24	5	21	86	64	122	.253	.332	.418	100	0	32	11	3	.983	3	*O-147/D-3	0.1
1987	Tor-A	155	592	106	167	27	4	26	96	70	124	.282	.360	.473	116	14	39	7	8	.980	-8	*O-153/D-2	0.8
1988	Tor-A	128	472	77	113	17	7	10	42	70	93	.239	.345	.369	99	1	31	8	5	.984	-6	*O-125/D-1	-0.4
1989	*Tor-A	135	502	72	111	25	3	11	43	56	101	.221	.307	.349	86	-9	24	7	3	.986	-3	*O-120,D-14	-1.4
1990	Det-A	122	431	64	107	16	5	14	51	48	77	.248	.331	.406	104	2	17	5	2	.983	8	*O-116/D-4	1.0
1991	Det-A	74	260	37	68	15	1	6	35	21	43	.262	.324	.396	97	-1	8	1	2	.955	-1	O-64/D-7	-0.2
Total	12	1588	5815	869	1494	273	66	169	737	616	1135	.257	.334	.414	102	15	280	92	29	.984	28	*O-1529/D-37	2.2

■ ARNIE MOSER
Moser, Arnold Robert b: 8/9/15, Houston, Tex. BR/TR, 5'11", 165 lbs. Deb: 6/20/37

YEAR	TM/L	G	AB	R	H	2B	3B	HR	RBI	BB	SO	AVG	OBP	SLG	PRO+	BR/A	SB	CS	SBR	FA	FR	G/POS	TPR
1937	Cin-N	5	5	0	0	0	0	0	0	0	2	.000	.000	.000	-99	-1	0			.000	0	H	-0.1

■ JERRY MOSES
Moses, Gerald Braheen b: 8/9/46, Yazoo City, Miss. BR/TR, 6'3", 210 lbs. Deb: 5/9/65

YEAR	TM/L	G	AB	R	H	2B	3B	HR	RBI	BB	SO	AVG	OBP	SLG	PRO+	BR/A	SB	CS	SBR	FA	FR	G/POS	TPR
1965	Bos-A	4	4	1	1	0	0	1	1	0	2	.250	.250	1.000	224	1	0	0	0	.000	0	H	0.1
1968	Bos-A	6	18	2	6	0	0	2	4	1	4	.333	.368	.667	196	2	0	1	-1	.963	-3	/C-6	-0.1
1969	Bos-A	53	135	13	41	9	1	4	17	5	23	.304	.333	.474	117	3	0	1	-1	.981	-5	C-36	-0.2
1970	Bos-A☆	92	315	26	83	18	1	6	35	21	45	.263	.314	.384	85	-7	1	1	-0	.990	2	C-88/O-1	0.0
1971	Cal-A	69	181	12	41	8	2	4	15	10	34	.227	.267	.359	82	-5	0	0	0	.977	5	C-63/O-1	-0.1
1972	Cle-A	52	141	9	31	3	0	4	14	11	29	.220	.290	.326	81	-3	0	0	0	.982	1	C-39/1-3	-0.2
1973	NY-A	21	59	5	15	2	0	0	3	2	6	.254	.279	.288	62	-3	0	0	0	1.000	5	C-17/D-1	0.2
1974	Det-A	74	198	19	47	6	3	4	19	11	38	.237	.284	.359	81	-5	0	1	-1	.985	0	C-74	-0.3
1975	SD-N	13	19	1	3	2	0	0	1	2	3	.158	.238	.263	42	-2	0	0	0	.900	-1	/C-5	-0.2
	Chi-A	2	2	1	1	0	1	0	0	0	0	.500	.500	1.500	441	1	0	0	0	1.000	-0	/1-1,D-1	0.1
Total	9	386	1072	89	269	48	8	25	109	63	184	.251	.297	.381	89	-19	1	4	-2	.984	3	C-328/1-4,DO	-0.5

■ JOHN MOSES
Moses, John William b: 8/9/57, Los Angeles, Cal. BB/TL, 5'10", 170 lbs. Deb: 8/23/82

YEAR	TM/L	G	AB	R	H	2B	3B	HR	RBI	BB	SO	AVG	OBP	SLG	PRO+	BR/A	SB	CS	SBR	FA	FR	G/POS	TPR
1982	Sea-A	22	44	7	14	5	1	1	3	4	5	.318	.375	.545	145	3	5	1	1	.947	-4	O-19	-0.1
1983	Sea-A	93	130	19	27	4	1	0	6	12	20	.208	.280	.254	46	-9	11	5	0	.979	-9	O-71,D-10	-1.9
1984	Sea-A	19	35	3	12	1	1	0	2	0	5	.343	.395	.429	129	1	1	0	0	1.000	-4	O-19/D-1	-0.3
1985	Sea-A	33	62	4	12	0	0	0	3	2	8	.194	.219	.194	14	-7	5	2	0	1.000	-7	O-29	-1.5
1986	Sea-A	103	399	56	102	16	3	3	34	34	65	.256	.314	.333	76	-13	25	18	-3	.987	2	O-93/1-7,D	-1.8
1987	Sea-A	116	390	58	96	16	4	3	38	29	49	.246	.303	.331	65	-20	23	15	-2	.987	-2	*O-100/1-16,D	-2.7
1988	Min-A	105	206	33	65	10	2	2	12	15	21	.316	.368	.422	117	5	11	6	0	1.000	-14	O-82/D-2	-1.1
1989	Min-A	129	242	33	68	12	3	1	31	19	23	.281	.336	.368	92	-2	14	7	0	.988	-24	*O-108/1-2,PD	-2.8
1990	Min-A	115	172	26	38	3	1	1	14	19	19	.221	.306	.267	58	-9	2	3	-1	1.000	-17	O-85,D-10/1P	-3.0
1991	Det-A	13	21	5	1	1	0	0	1	2	7	.048	.130	.095	-36	-4	4	0	1	1.000	-2	O-12	-0.5
1992	Sea-A	21	22	3	3	1	0	0	1	5	4	.136	.296	.182	37	-2	0	0	0	1.000	-4	O-18/D-1	-0.6
Total	11	769	1723	247	438	69	17	11	145	143	226	.254	.315	.333	75	-58	101	57	-4	.990	-86	O-636/D-36,1P	-16.2

■ WALLY MOSES
Moses, Wallace b: 10/8/10, Uvalda, Ga. d: 10/10/90, Vidalia, Ga. BL/TL, 5'10", 160 lbs. Deb: 4/17/35 C

YEAR	TM/L	G	AB	R	H	2B	3B	HR	RBI	BB	SO	AVG	OBP	SLG	PRO+	BR/A	SB	CS	SBR	FA	FR	G/POS	TPR
1935	Phi-A	85	345	60	112	21	3	5	35	25	18	.325	.375	.446	113	6	3	4	-2	.943	0	O-80	0.2
1936	Phi-A	146	585	98	202	35	11	7	66	62	32	.345	.410	.479	121	20	12	6	0	.974	3	*O-144	1.5
1937	Phi-A☆	154	649	113	208	48	13	25	86	54	38	.320	.374	.550	132	28	9	7	-2	.958	6	*O-154	2.5
1938	Phi-A	142	589	86	181	29	8	8	49	58	31	.307	.369	.424	101	1	15	5	2	.966	5	*O-139	0.2
1939	Phi-A	115	437	68	134	28	7	3	33	44	23	.307	.370	.423	105	3	7	4	-0	.965	-1	*O-103	-0.1
1940	Phi-A	142	537	91	166	41	9	9	50	75	44	.309	.396	.469	126	22	6	4	-1	.974	4	*O-133	1.8
1941	Phi-A	116	438	78	132	31	4	3	35	62	27	.301	.388	.418	116	12	3	3	-1	.975	4	*O-109	1.3
1942	Chi-A	146	577	73	156	28	4	7	49	74	27	.270	.353	.369	106	5	16	10	-1	.980	7	*O-145	0.3
1943	Chi-A	150	599	82	147	22	**12**	3	48	55	47	.245	.310	.337	89	-9	56	14	8	.979	9	*O-148	0.0
1944	Chi-A	136	535	82	150	26	9	3	34	52	22	.280	.345	.379	108	6	21	7	2	.975	-2	*O-134	-0.1
1945	Chi-A†	140	569	79	168	**35**	15	2	50	69	33	.295	.373	.420	134	25	11	5	0	.977	9	*O-139	2.7
1946	Chi-A	56	168	20	46	9	1	4	16	17	20	.274	.344	.411	115	3	2	2	-1	1.000	-1	O-36	0.0
	*Bos-A	48	175	23	36	11	3	2	17	14	15	.206	.268	.337	65	-9	2	4	-1	.979	1	O-44	-1.3
	Yr	104	343	43	82	20	4	6	33	31	35	.239	.306	.373	88	-6	4	6	-2	.989	-0	O-80	-1.3
1947	Bos-A	90	255	32	70	18	2	2	27	27	16	.275	.344	.384	95	-2	3	0	1	.974	-3	O-58	-0.7
1948	Bos-A	78	189	26	49	12	1	2	29	21	19	.259	.340	.365	83	-5	5	0	2	.981	1	O-45	-0.4
1949	Phi-A	110	308	49	85	19	3	1	25	51	19	.276	.381	.367	102	2	1	3	-2	.983	-3	O-92	-0.6
1950	Phi-A	88	265	47	70	16	5	2	21	40	17	.264	.365	.385	94	-2	0	1	-1	.987	5	O-62	0.0
1951	Phi-A	70	136	17	26	6	0	0	9	25	8	.191	.320	.235	46	-10	2	2	0	.984	2	O-27	-0.9
Total	17	2012	7356	1124	2138	435	110	89	679	821	457	.291	.364	.416	109	97	174	81	-4	.973	51	*O-1792	6.4

■ DOC MOSKIMAN
Moskiman, William Bankhead b: 12/20/1879, Oakland, Cal. d: 1/11/53, San Leandro, Cal. BR/TR, 6', 170 lbs. Deb: 8/23/10

YEAR	TM/L	G	AB	R	H	2B	3B	HR	RBI	BB	SO	AVG	OBP	SLG	PRO+	BR/A	SB	CS	SBR	FA	FR	G/POS	TPR
1910	Bos-A	5	9	1	1	0	0	0	1	0	0	.111	.273	.111	20	-1	0			1.000	0	/1-2,O-1	0.0

■ JIM MOSOLF
Mosolf, James Frederick b: 8/21/05, Puyallup, Wash. d: 12/28/79, Dallas, Ore. BL/TR, 5'10", 186 lbs. Deb: 9/9/29

YEAR	TM/L	G	AB	R	H	2B	3B	HR	RBI	BB	SO	AVG	OBP	SLG	PRO+	BR/A	SB	CS	SBR	FA	FR	G/POS	TPR
1929	Pit-N	8	13	3	6	1	1	0	2	1	1	.462	.500	.692	188	2	0			1.000	0	/O-3	0.2
1930	Pit-N	40	51	16	17	2	1	0	9	8	7	.333	.424	.412	103	1	0			.765	-3	O-12/P-1	-0.3
1931	Pit-N	39	44	7	11	1	0	1	8	4	5	.250	.365	.341	92	-0	0			1.000	0	O-4	-0.1
1933	Chi-N	31	82	13	22	5	1	1	9	5	8	.268	.326	.390	104	0	0			.964	1	O-22	-0.0
Total	4	118	190	39	56	9	3	2	28	22	21	.295	.374	.405	107	3	0			.929	-4	/O-41,P-1	-0.2

YEAR	TM/L	G	AB	R	H	2B	3B	HR	RBI	BB	SO	AVG	OBP	SLG	PRO+	BR/A	SB	CS	SBR	FA	FR	G/POS	TPR

■ **CHARLIE MOSS** Moss, Charles Crosby b: 3/20/11, Meridian, Miss. BR/TR, 5'10", 160 lbs. Deb: 5/19/34

YEAR	TM/L	G	AB	R	H	2B	3B	HR	RBI	BB	SO	AVG	OBP	SLG	PRO+	BR/A	SB	CS	SBR	FA	FR	G/POS	TPR
1934	Phi-A	10	10	3	2	0	0	0	1	0	1	.200	.200	.200	4	-1	0	0	0	1.000	-1	/C-6	-0.2
1935	Phi-A	4	3	1	1	0	0	0	1	1	0	.333	.500	.333	120	0	0	0	0	.000	0	/C-1	0.0
1936	Phi-A	33	44	2	11	1	1	0	10	6	5	.250	.340	.318	65	-2	1	0	0	.929	-2	C-19	-0.3
Total	3	47	57	6	14	1	1	0	12	7	5	.246	.328	.298	58	-4	1	0	0	.935	-2	/C-26	-0.5

■ **HOWIE MOSS** Moss, Howard Glenn b: 10/17/19, Gastonia, N.C. d: 5/7/89, Baltimore, Md. BR/TR, 5'11.5", 185 lbs. Deb: 4/14/42

YEAR	TM/L	G	AB	R	H	2B	3B	HR	RBI	BB	SO	AVG	OBP	SLG	PRO+	BR/A	SB	CS	SBR	FA	FR	G/POS	TPR
1942	NY-N	7	14	0	0	0	0	0	0	0	4	.000	.000	.000	-99	-3	0			1.000	0	/O-3	-0.4
1946	Cin-N	7	26	1	5	0	0	0	1	0	4	.192	.222	.192	19	-3	0			1.000	0	/O-6	-0.3
	Cle-A	8	32	2	2	0	0	0	0	3	9	.063	.143	.063	-44	-6	0	1	-1	.857	0	/3-8	-0.7
Total	2	22	72	3	7	0	0	0	1	3	17	.097	.145	.097	-32	-12	0	1		1.000	0	/O-9,3-8	-1.4

■ **LES MOSS** Moss, John Lester b: 5/14/25, Tulsa, Okla. BR/TR, 5'11", 205 lbs. Deb: 9/10/46 MC

YEAR	TM/L	G	AB	R	H	2B	3B	HR	RBI	BB	SO	AVG	OBP	SLG	PRO+	BR/A	SB	CS	SBR	FA	FR	G/POS	TPR
1946	StL-A	12	35	4	13	3	0	0	5	3	5	.371	.436	.457	142	2	1	0	0	.968	1	C-12	0.4
1947	StL-A	96	274	17	43	5	2	6	27	35	48	.157	.255	.255	41	-22	0	0	0	.983	-5	C-96	-2.3
1948	StL-A	107	335	35	86	12	1	14	46	39	50	.257	.334	.424	98	-2	0	0	0	.988	-9	*C-103	-0.4
1949	StL-A	97	278	28	81	11	0	10	39	49	32	.291	.399	.439	117	8	0	1	-1	.970	-5	C-83	0.7
1950	StL-A	84	222	24	59	6	0	8	34	26	32	.266	.343	.401	87	-5	0	1	-1	.957	-1	C-60	-0.4
1951	StL-A	16	47	5	8	2	0	1	7	6	8	.170	.264	.277	45	-4	0	0	0	.967	-0	C-12	-0.3
	Bos-A	71	202	18	40	6	0	3	26	25	34	.198	.289	.272	48	-15	0	0	0	.984	-1	C-69	-1.3
	Yr	87	249	23	48	8	0	4	33	31	42	.193	.285	.273	47	-19	0	0	0	.981	-1	C-81	-1.6
1952	StL-A	52	118	11	29	3	0	3	12	15	13	.246	.331	.347	86	-2	0	1	-1	.957	-3	C-39	-0.5
1953	StL-A	78	239	21	66	14	1	2	28	18	31	.276	.329	.368	86	-5	0	0	0	.978	-6	C-71	-0.8
1954	Bal-A	50	126	7	31	3	0	0	5	14	16	.246	.321	.270	68	-5	0	0	0	.972	-2	C-38	-0.6
1955	Bal-A	29	56	5	19	1	0	2	6	7	4	.339	.413	.464	146	4	0	1	-1	1.000	2	C-17	0.5
	Chi-A	32	59	5	15	2	0	2	7	6	10	.254	.333	.390	91	-1	0	0	0	.990	-0	C-32	0.0
	Yr	61	115	10	34	3	0	4	13	13	14	.296	.372	.426	116	3	0	1	-1	.994	2	C-49	0.5
1956	Chi-A	56	127	20	31	4	0	10	22	18	15	.244	.338	.512	120	3	0	0	0	.994	-6	C-49	-0.2
1957	Chi-A	42	115	10	31	3	0	2	12	20	18	.270	.378	.348	99	1	0	0	0	.980	-7	C-39	-0.5
1958	Chi-A	2	1	0	0	0	0	0	0	0	1	.000	.000	.000	51	0	0	0	0	.000	0	H	0.0
Total	13	824	2234	210	552	75	4	63	276	282	316	.247	.333	.369	86	-44	1	5	-3	.978	-42	C-720	-5.7

■ **JOHNNY MOSTIL** Mostil, John Anthony "Bananas" b: 6/1/1896, Chicago, Ill. d: 12/10/70, Midlothian, Ill. BR/TR, 5'8.5", 168 lbs. Deb: 6/20/18

YEAR	TM/L	G	AB	R	H	2B	3B	HR	RBI	BB	SO	AVG	OBP	SLG	PRO+	BR/A	SB	CS	SBR	FA	FR	G/POS	TPR
1918	Chi-A	10	33	4	9	2	2	0	4	1	6	.273	.294	.455	125	1	1			.923	-2	/2-9	-0.1
1921	Chi-A	100	326	43	98	21	7	3	42	28	35	.301	.379	.436	109	5	10	12	-4	.946	0	O-91/2-1	-0.5
1922	Chi-A	132	458	74	139	28	14	7	70	38	39	.303	.375	.472	120	13	14	10	-2	.966	5	*O-123	0.7
1923	Chi-A	153	546	91	159	37	15	3	64	62	51	.291	.376	.430	113	11	41	16	3	.974	22	*O-143/3-5,S	2.6
1924	Chi-A	118	385	75	125	22	5	4	49	45	41	.325	.401	.439	120	12	7	11	-5	.974	7	*O-102	0.8
1925	Chi-A	153	605	**135**	181	36	16	2	50	**90**	52	.299	.400	.421	115	16	**43**	20	1	**.985**	7	*O-153	1.3
1926	Chi-A	148	600	120	197	41	15	4	42	79	55	.328	.415	.467	134	32	35	14	2	.968	17	*O-147	4.0
1927	Chi-A	13	16	3	2	0	0	0	1	0	1	.125	.176	.125	-21	-3	1	0	0	.857	-2	/O-6	-0.4
1928	Chi-A	133	503	69	136	19	8	0	51	66	54	.270	.360	.340	86	-8	23	21	-6	.976	18	*O-131	-0.5
1929	Chi-A	12	35	4	8	3	0	0	3	6	2	.229	.341	.314	71	-1	1	1	-0	.963	-1	O-11	-0.3
Total	10	972	3507	618	1054	209	82	23	376	415	336	.301	.386	.427	113	78	176	105		.971	72	O-907/2-10,3S	7.6

■ **ANDY MOTA** Mota, Andres Alberto (Matos) b: 3/4/66, Santo Domingo, D.R. BR/TR, 5'10", 180 lbs. Deb: 8/31/91 F

YEAR	TM/L	G	AB	R	H	2B	3B	HR	RBI	BB	SO	AVG	OBP	SLG	PRO+	BR/A	SB	CS	SBR	FA	FR	G/POS	TPR
1991	Hou-N	27	90	4	17	2	0	1	6	1	17	.189	.198	.244	25	-9	2	0	1	.970	-3	2-27	-1.2

■ **JOSE MOTA** Mota, Jose Manuel (Matos) b: 3/16/65, Santo Domingo, D.R. BB/TR, 5'9", 155 lbs. Deb: 5/25/91 F

YEAR	TM/L	G	AB	R	H	2B	3B	HR	RBI	BB	SO	AVG	OBP	SLG	PRO+	BR/A	SB	CS	SBR	FA	FR	G/POS	TPR
1991	SD-N	17	36	4	8	0	0	0	2	7	5	.222	.282	.222	42	-3	0	0	0	.962	0	2-13/S-3	-0.2

■ **MANNY MOTA** Mota, Manuel Rafael (Geronimo) b: 2/18/38, Santo Domingo, D.R. BR/TR, 5'11", 168 lbs. Deb: 4/16/62 FC

YEAR	TM/L	G	AB	R	H	2B	3B	HR	RBI	BB	SO	AVG	OBP	SLG	PRO+	BR/A	SB	CS	SBR	FA	FR	G/POS	TPR
1962	SF-N	47	74	9	13	1	0	0	9	7	8	.176	.256	.189	22	-8	3	2	-0	1.000	-2	O-27/3-7,2	-1.0
1963	Pit-N	59	126	20	34	2	3	0	7	9	18	.270	.313	.333	86	-2	0	2	-1	.953	-5	O-37/2-1	-1.1
1964	Pit-N	115	271	43	75	8	3	5	32	10	31	.277	.310	.384	94	-2	4	1	1	.961	-16	O-93/C-1,2	-2.2
1965	Pit-N	121	294	47	82	7	6	4	29	22	32	.279	.333	.384	101	0	2	2	-1	.985	-14	O-95	-1.9
1966	Pit-N	116	322	54	107	16	7	5	46	25	28	.332	.387	.472	137	17	7	7	-2	.994	-11	O-96/3-4	-0.1
1967	Pit-N	120	349	53	112	14	8	4	56	14	46	.321	.351	.441	125	10	3	2	-0	.988	-6	O-99/3-2	0.0
1968	Pit-N	111	331	35	93	10	2	1	33	20	19	.281	.324	.332	99	-1	4	2	0	.981	-7	O-92/2-1,3	-1.4
1969	Mon-N	31	89	6	28	1	1	0	0	6	11	.315	.358	.348	98	-0	1	3	-2	.907	-2	O-22	-0.6
	LA-N	85	294	35	95	6	4	3	30	26	25	.323	.380	.401	128	11	5	4	-1	.969	-0	O-80	0.6
	Yr	116	383	41	123	7	5	3	30	32	36	.321	.375	.389	120	11	6	7	-2	.954	-2	*O-102	0.0
1970	LA-N	124	417	63	127	12	6	3	37	47	37	.305	.379	.384	110	7	11	6	-0	.973	-3	*O-111/3-1	0.2
1971	LA-N	91	269	24	84	13	5	0	34	20	20	.312	.362	.398	122	8	4	3	-1	.965	-9	O-80	-0.6
1972	LA-N	118	371	57	120	16	5	5	48	27	15	.323	.377	.434	133	16	4	4	-1	.993	-8	O-99	0.2
1973	LA-N★	89	293	33	92	11	2	0	23	25	12	.314	.370	.365	109	4	1	3	-2	1.000	-6	O-74	-0.7
1974	*LA-N	66	57	5	16	2	0	0	16	5	4	.281	.349	.316	91	-1	0	0	0	1.000	-0	/O-5	-0.1
1975	LA-N	52	49	3	13	1	0	0	10	5	1	.265	.357	.286	84	-1	0	0	0	1.000	-0	/O-6	-0.1
1976	LA-N	50	52	1	15	3	0	0	13	7	6	.288	.373	.346	107	1	0	0	0	1.000	-0	/O-6	0.1
1977	*LA-N	49	38	5	15	1	0	1	4	10	0	.395	.521	.500	176	5	1	1	-0	1.000	0	/H	0.5
1978	*LA-N	37	33	2	10	1	0	0	6	3	4	.303	.361	.333	95	-0	0	0	0	1.000	0	H	-0.1
1979	LA-N	47	42	1	15	0	0	0	3	3	4	.357	.400	.357	110	1	0	0	0	.000	-0	/O-1	0.0
1980	LA-N	7	7	0	3	0	0	0	0	0	2	.429	.429	.429	143	-0	0	0	0	.000	0	/H	0.0
1982	LA-N	1	1	0	0	0	0	0	0	0	0	.000	.000	.000	-99	-0	0	0	0	.000	-0	/H	0.0
Total	20	1536	3779	496	1149	125	52	31	438	289	320	.304	.358	.389	112	65	50	42	-10	.979	-87	*O-1021/3-15,2C	-8.4

■ **DARRYL MOTLEY** Motley, Darryl De Wayne b: 1/21/60, Muskogee, Okla. BR/TR, 5'9", 196 lbs. Deb: 8/10/81

YEAR	TM/L	G	AB	R	H	2B	3B	HR	RBI	BB	SO	AVG	OBP	SLG	PRO+	BR/A	SB	CS	SBR	FA	FR	G/POS	TPR
1981	KC-A	42	125	15	29	4	0	2	7	15	.232	.278	.312	70	-5	1	3	-2	.968	3	O-39	-0.5
1983	KC-A	19	68	9	16	1	2	3	11	2	4	.235	.268	.441	91	-1	2	1	0	.978	1	O-18/D-1	-0.1
1984	*KC-A	146	522	64	148	25	6	15	70	28	73	.284	.321	.441	108	4	10	12	-4	.984	-2	*O-138	-0.6
1985	*KC-A	123	383	45	85	20	1	17	49	18	57	.222	.261	.413	81	-12	6	4	0	.967	-8	*O-114/D-7	-2.4
1986	KC-A	72	217	22	44	9	1	7	20	11	31	.203	.241	.350	57	-13	0	0	0	.979	-8	O-66/D-2	-2.4
	Atl-N	5	10	1	2	1	0	0	0	1	1	.200	.273	.300	55	-1	0	0	0	1.000	-0	/O-3	-0.1
1987	Atl-N	6	8	0	0	0	0	0	1	0	1	.000	.000	.000	-95	-2	0	0	0	1.000	-0	/O-2	-0.3
Total	6	413	1333	156	324	60	10	44	159	67	186	.243	.282	.402	86	-30	19	22	-8	.976	-15	O-380/D-10	-6.4

■ **BITSY MOTT** Mott, Elisha Matthew b: 6/12/18, Arcadia, Fla. BR/TR, 5'8", 155 lbs. Deb: 4/17/45

YEAR	TM/L	G	AB	R	H	2B	3B	HR	RBI	BB	SO	AVG	OBP	SLG	PRO+	BR/A	SB	CS	SBR	FA	FR	G/POS	TPR
1945	Phi-N	90	289	21	64	8	0	0	22	27	25	.221	.290	.249	52	-18	2			.944	13	S-63,2-27/3	0.0

■ **CURT MOTTON** Motton, Curtell Howard b: 9/24/40, Darnell, La. BR/TR, 5'7.5", 175 lbs. Deb: 7/5/67 C

YEAR	TM/L	G	AB	R	H	2B	3B	HR	RBI	BB	SO	AVG	OBP	SLG	PRO+	BR/A	SB	CS	SBR	FA	FR	G/POS	TPR
1967	Bal-A	27	65	5	13	2	0	2	9	5	14	.200	.278	.323	78	-2	0	1	-1	.973	1	O-18	-0.3
1968	Bal-A	83	217	27	43	7	0	8	25	31	43	.198	.301	.341	94	-1	1	3	-2	.989	2	O-54	-0.4
1969	*Bal-A	56	89	15	27	6	0	6	21	13	19	.303	.398	.573	167	8	3	1	0	1.000	0	O-20	0.5
1970	Bal-A	52	84	16	19	3	1	2	19	18	20	.226	.369	.393	109	2	1	2	-1	1.000	-1	O-21	-0.1
1971	*Bal-A	38	53	13	10	1	0	4	8	10	12	.189	.317	.434	112	1	0	0	0	1.000	-2	O-16	-0.2

YEAR	TM/L	G	AB	R	H	2B	3B	HR	RBI	BB	SO	AVG	OBP	SLG	PRO+	BR/A	SB	CS	SBR	FA	FR	G/POS	TPR
1972	Mil-A	6	6	1	1	0	0	0	2	1	2	.167	.286	.667	181	1	0	0	0	.000	-1	/O-3	-0.1
	Cal-A	42	39	6	6	1	0	0	1	5	12	.154	.250	.179	31	-3	0	0	0	1.000	-0	/O-9	-0.4
	Yr	48	45	7	7	1	0	1	3	6	14	.156	.255	.244	52	-3	0	0	0	1.000	-1	O-12	-0.5
1973	Bal-A	5	6	2	2	0	0	1	4	1	1	.333	.429	.833	250	1	0	0	0	.000	-0	/O-1,D-1	0.1
1974	*Bal-A	7	8	0	0	0	0	0	0	2	2	.000	.200	.000	-40	-1	0	0	0	1.000	-0	/O-2,D-1	-0.2
Total	8	316	567	85	121	20	1	25	89	86	116	.213	.322	.384	105	4	5	7	-3	.991	-5	O-144/D-2	-1.1

■ FRANK MOTZ
Motz, Frank H.   b: 10/1/1868, Freeburg, Pa.   d: 3/18/44, Akron, Ohio   6′, 160 lbs.   Deb: 8/27/1890

YEAR	TM/L	G	AB	R	H	2B	3B	HR	RBI	BB	SO	AVG	OBP	SLG	PRO+	BR/A	SB	CS	SBR	FA	FR	G/POS	TPR
1890	Phi-N	1	2	1	0	0	0	0	3	1	1	.000	.333	.000	-1	-0	1			1.000	0	/1-1	0.0
1893	Cin-N	43	156	16	40	7	1	2	25	19	10	.256	.352	.353	85	-3	3			.981	6	1-43	0.1
1894	Cin-N	18	69	8	14	4	0	0	12	9	1	.203	.304	.261	36	-7	2			.995	4	1-18	-0.3
Total	3	62	227	25	54	11	1	2	40	29	12	.238	.337	.322	68	-11	6			.985	10	/1-62	-0.2

■ ALLIE MOULTON
Moulton, Albert Theodore   b: 1/16/1886, Medway, Mass.   d: 7/10/68, Peabody, Mass.   BR/TR, 5′6″, 155 lbs.   Deb: 9/25/11

YEAR	TM/L	G	AB	R	H	2B	3B	HR	RBI	BB	SO	AVG	OBP	SLG	PRO+	BR/A	SB	CS	SBR	FA	FR	G/POS	TPR
1911	StL-A	4	15	4	1	0	0	0	1	4		.067	.263	.067	-6	-2	0			.938	1	/2-4	-0.3

■ FRANK MOUNTAIN
Mountain, Frank Henry   b: 5/17/1860, Ft.Edward, N.Y.   d: 11/19/39, Schenectady, N.Y.   BR/TR, 5′11″, 185 lbs.   Deb: 7/19/1880

YEAR	TM/L	G	AB	R	H	2B	3B	HR	RBI	BB	SO	AVG	OBP	SLG	PRO+	BR/A	SB	CS	SBR	FA	FR	G/POS	TPR
1880	Tro-N	2	9	1	2	0	0	0	0	0	4	.222	.222	.222	49	-0				1.000	0	/P-2	0.0
1881	Det-N	7	25	0	4	1	1	0	4	2	8	.160	.222	.280	55	-1				.923	-1	/P-7	0.0
1882	Wor-N	5	16	1	1	0	0	0	1	0	5	.063	.063	.063	-58	-3				.889	-1	/P-5	0.0
	Phi-a	9	36	5	12	3	0	0		2		.333	.368	.417	147	2				.917	1	/P-8,O-1	0.0
	Wor-N	20	70	8	19	2	2	2	5	3	18	.271	.301	.443	132	2				.870	-3	P-13/O-6,1S	-0.2
1883	Col-a	70	276	36	60	14	5	3		9		.217	.242	.337	92	-2				.848	2	P-59,O-12	0.0
1884	Col-a	58	210	26	50	7	3	4		9		.238	.283	.357	117	4				.919	2	P-42,O-17	0.0
1885	Pit-a	5	20	1	2	0	1	0		1		.100	.143	.200	8	-2				.846	0	/P-5	0.0
1886	Pit-a	18	55	6	8	1	1	0		13		.145	.319	.200	64	-2	3			.959	-0	1-16/P-2	-0.3
Total	7	194	717	84	158	28	13	9	10	39	35	.220	.265	.333	96	-2	3			.880	2	P-143/O-36,1S	-0.5

■ JAMES MOUTON
Mouton, James Raleigh   b: 12/19/68, Denver, Colo.   BR/TR, 5′9″, 175 lbs.   Deb: 4/4/94

YEAR	TM/L	G	AB	R	H	2B	3B	HR	RBI	BB	SO	AVG	OBP	SLG	PRO+	BR/A	SB	CS	SBR	FA	FR	G/POS	TPR
1994	Hou-N	99	310	43	76	11	0	2	16	27	69	.245	.316	.300	63	-16	24	5	4	.982	-5	O-96	-1.9

■ RAY MOWE
Mowe, Raymond Benjamin   b: 7/12/1889, Rochester, Ind.   d: 8/14/68, Sarasota, Fla.   BL/TR, 5′7.5″, 160 lbs.   Deb: 9/25/13

YEAR	TM/L	G	AB	R	H	2B	3B	HR	RBI	BB	SO	AVG	OBP	SLG	PRO+	BR/A	SB	CS	SBR	FA	FR	G/POS	TPR
1913	Bro-N	5	9	0	1	0	0	0	0	0	1	.111	.200	.111	-10	-1	0			.941	1	/S-2	0.0

■ MIKE MOWREY
Mowrey, Harry Harlan   b: 4/20/1884, Browns Mill, Pa.   d: 3/20/47, Chambersburg, Pa.   BR/TR, 5′10″, 180 lbs.   Deb: 9/24/05

YEAR	TM/L	G	AB	R	H	2B	3B	HR	RBI	BB	SO	AVG	OBP	SLG	PRO+	BR/A	SB	CS	SBR	FA	FR	G/POS	TPR
1905	Cin-N	7	30	4	8	1	0	0	6	1		.267	.290	.300	69	-1	0			.759	-0	/3-7	-0.1
1906	Cin-N	21	53	3	17	3	0	0	6	5		.321	.379	.377	130	2	2			.930	4	3-15/2-1,S	0.6
1907	Cin-N	138	448	43	113	16	6	1	44	35		.252	.308	.321	93	-4	10			.929	-19	*3-127,S-11	-2.1
1908	Cin-N	77	227	17	50	9	1	0	23	12		.220	.266	.269	73	-7	5			.936	-7	3-56/S-3,O2	-1.4
1909	Cin-N	38	115	10	22	5	0	0	5	20		.191	.311	.235	70	-3	2			.947	1	3-22,S-13	-0.2
	StL-N	12	29	3	7	1	0	0	4	4		.241	.333	.276	95	-0	1			.921	-1	/2-7,3-2	-0.1
	Yr	50	144	13	29	6	0	0	9	24		.201	.315	.243	75	-3	3			.948	-1	3-24,S-13/2	-0.3
1910	StL-N	143	489	69	138	24	6	2	70	67	38	.282	.375	.368	121	15	21			.927	12	*3-141	3.2
1911	StL-N	137	471	59	126	29	7	0	61	59	46	.268	.355	.359	103	3	15			.944	7	*3-134/S-1	1.1
1912	StL-N	114	408	59	104	13	8	2	50	46	29	.255	.341	.341	87	-7	19			.931	3	*3-108	-0.3
1913	StL-N	132	450	40	117	18	4	0	33	53	40	.260	.342	.318	90	-4	21			.953	16	*3-131	1.4
1914	Pit-N	79	284	24	72	7	5	1	25	22	20	.254	.316	.324	94	-2	8			.960	-2	3-78	-0.2
1915	Pit-F	151	521	56	146	26	6	1	49	66	39	.280	.362	.359	95	-2	40			**.959**	-19	*3-151	-1.6
1916	*Bro-N	144	495	57	121	22	6	0	60	50	60	.244	.320	.313	92	-3	16			**.965**	0	*3-144	0.2
1917	Bro-N	83	271	20	58	9	5	0	25	29	25	.214	.292	.284	75	-7	7			.952	-3	3-80/2-2	-1.0
Total	13	1276	4291	485	1099	183	54	7	461	469	297	.256	.334	.329	94	-21	167			.944	-10	*3-1196/S-29,2O	-0.5

■ JOE MOWRY
Mowry, Joseph Aloysius   b: 4/6/08, St.Louis, Mo.   d: 2/9/94, St.Louis, Mo.   BB/TR, 6′, 198 lbs.   Deb: 5/13/33

YEAR	TM/L	G	AB	R	H	2B	3B	HR	RBI	BB	SO	AVG	OBP	SLG	PRO+	BR/A	SB	CS	SBR	FA	FR	G/POS	TPR
1933	Bos-N	86	249	25	55	8	5	0	20	15	22	.221	.273	.293	67	-11	1			.994	1	O-64	-1.5
1934	Bos-N	25	79	9	17	3	0	1	4	3	13	.215	.244	.291	46	-6	0			.976	0	O-20/2-1	-0.7
1935	Bos-N	81	136	17	36	8	1	1	13	11	13	.265	.324	.360	91	-2	0			.970	-7	O-45	-1.0
Total	3	192	464	51	108	19	6	2	37	29	48	.233	.284	.313	71	-19	1			.985	-7	O-129/2-1	-3.2

■ MIKE MOYNAHAN
Moynahan, Michael   b: 1856, Chicago, Ill.   d: 4/9/1899, Chicago, Ill.   BL/TR,   Deb: 8/20/1880

YEAR	TM/L	G	AB	R	H	2B	3B	HR	RBI	BB	SO	AVG	OBP	SLG	PRO+	BR/A	SB	CS	SBR	FA	FR	G/POS	TPR
1880	Buf-N	27	100	12	33	5	1	0	14	6	9	.330	.368	.400	157	6				.862	-6	S-27	0.1
1881	Cle-N	33	135	12	31	5	1	0	8	3	14	.230	.246	.281	69	-5				.883	-2	O-32/3-1	-0.7
	Det-N	1	4	1	1	0	0	0	0	0	1	.250	.250	.250	55	-0				.857	1	/3-1	0.0
	Yr	34	139	13	32	5	1	0	8	3	15	.230	.246	.281	69	-5				.883	-2	O-32/3-2	-0.7
1883	Phi-a	95	400	90	124	18	10	1		31		.310	.360	.412	137	15				.833	0	*S-95	1.5
1884	Phi-a	1	4	0	0	0	0	0	0			.000	.000	.000	-94	-1				.000	-0	/O-1	-0.1
	Cle-N	12	45	9	13	2	1	0	6	7	11	.289	.385	.378	136	2				.852	-0	/2-6,S-3,O	0.2
Total	4	169	688	124	202	30	13	1	28	47	35	.294	.339	.379	126	17				.837	-9	S-125/O-36,23	1.0

■ HEINIE MUELLER
Mueller, Clarence Francis   b: 9/16/1899, Creve Coeur, Mo.   d: 1/23/75, DeSoto, Mo.   BL/TL, 5′8″, 158 lbs.   Deb: 9/25/20

YEAR	TM/L	G	AB	R	H	2B	3B	HR	RBI	BB	SO	AVG	OBP	SLG	PRO+	BR/A	SB	CS	SBR	FA	FR	G/POS	TPR
1920	StL-N	4	22	0	7	1	0	0	1	2	4	.318	.375	.364	117	1	1	0	0	1.000	0	/O-4	0.1
1921	StL-N	55	176	25	62	10	6	1	34	11	22	.352	.397	.494	137	9	2	4	-2	.976	-3	O-54	0.1
1922	StL-N	61	159	20	43	7	2	3	26	14	18	.270	.329	.396	91	-3	2	1	0	.947	-3	O-44	-0.8
1923	StL-N	78	265	39	91	16	9	5	41	18	16	.343	.392	.528	144	16	4	3	-1	.963	2	O-74	1.2
1924	StL-N	92	296	39	78	12	6	2	37	19	16	.264	.312	.365	82	-8	8	7	-2	.962	-2	O-53,1-27	-1.7
1925	StL-N	78	243	33	76	16	4	1	26	17	11	.313	.365	.424	99	-0	3	3	-2	.955	-3	O-72	-0.9
1926	StL-N	52	191	36	51	7	5	3	28	11	6	.267	.330	.403	93	-2	8			.950	-1	O-51	-0.6
	NY-N	85	305	36	76	6	2	4	29	21	17	.249	.300	.321	68	-14	7			.950	5	O-82	-1.5
	Yr	137	496	72	127	13	7	7	57	32	23	.256	.312	.353	78	-16	15			.950	4	*O-133	-2.1
1927	NY-N	84	190	33	55	6	1	3	19	25	12	.289	.384	.379	105	2	2			.944	-7	O-56/1-1	-0.7
1928	Bos-N	42	151	25	34	3	1	0	19	17	9	.225	.316	.258	54	-10	1			.985	6	O-41	-0.6
1929	Bos-N	46	93	10	19	2	1	0	11	12	12	.204	.302	.247	39	-9	2			1.000	-4	O-24	-1.3
1935	StL-A	16	27	0	5	1	0	0	1	1	4	.185	.214	.222	12	-4	0	0	0	.955	-1	/1-3,O-2	-0.4
Total	11	693	2118	296	597	87	37	22	272	168	147	.282	.342	.389	94	-20	37	18		.960	-11	O-557/1-31	-7.1

■ DON MUELLER
Mueller, Donald Frederick "Mandrake The Magician"   b: 4/14/27, St.Louis, Mo.   BL/TR, 6′, 185 lbs.   Deb: 8/2/48   F

YEAR	TM/L	G	AB	R	H	2B	3B	HR	RBI	BB	SO	AVG	OBP	SLG	PRO+	BR/A	SB	CS	SBR	FA	FR	G/POS	TPR
1948	NY-N	36	81	12	29	4	1	2	9	0	3	.358	.358	.469	121	0	2			.973	-1	O-22	0.0
1949	NY-N	51	56	5	13	4	0	0	1	5	6	.232	.295	.304	61	-3	0			1.000	-1	/O-6	-0.4
1950	NY-N	132	525	60	153	15	6	9	84	10	26	.291	.309	.383	80	-16	1			.986	-5	*O-125	-2.5
1951	NY-N	122	469	58	130	10	7	16	69	19	13	.277	.307	.431	95	-5	1	1	-0	.983	-2	*O-115	-1.1
1952	NY-N	126	456	61	128	14	7	12	49	34	24	.281	.333	.421	107	4	2	1	0	.987	-2	*O-120	-0.2
1953	NY-N	131	480	56	160	12	4	6	60	19	13	.333	.360	.404	97	-2	2	0	1	.972	-4	*O-122	-1.0
1954	*NY-N★	153	619	90	**212**	35	8	4	71	22	17	.342	.367	.444	110	8	2	3	-1	.979	-0	*O-153	-0.4
1955	NY-N★	147	605	67	185	21	4	8	83	19	12	.306	.330	.393	91	-8	1	2	-1	.976	-11	*O-146	-2.7
1956	NY-N	138	453	38	122	12	5	8	41	15	7	.269	.293	.333	68	-20	2	0	-1	.989	-9	*O-117	-3.7
1957	NY-N	135	450	45	116	7	1	6	37	13	16	.258	.280	.318	60	-25	2	0	1	.989	-1	*O-115	-3.3

YEAR	TM/L	G	AB	R	H	2B	3B	HR	RBI	BB	SO	AVG	OBP	SLG	PRO+	BR/A	SB	CS	SBR	FA	FR	G/POS	TPR
1958	Chi-A	70	166	7	42	5	0	6	16	11	9	.253	.299	.283	62	-8	0	0	0	.968	-5	O-43	-1.6
1959	Chi-A	4	4	0	2	0	0	0	0	0	0	.500	.500	.500	178	0	0	0	0	.000	0	H	0.0
Total	12	1245	4364	499	1292	139	37	65	520	167	146	.296	.324	.390	89	-74	11	8		.982	-38	*O-1084	-16.5

■ HEINIE MUELLER
Mueller, Emmett Jerome   b: 7/20/12, St.Louis, Mo.   d: 10/3/86, Orlando, Fla.   BB/TR, 5'6", 167 lbs.   Deb: 4/19/38

YEAR	TM/L	G	AB	R	H	2B	3B	HR	RBI	BB	SO	AVG	OBP	SLG	PRO+	BR/A	SB	CS	SBR	FA	FR	G/POS	TPR
1938	Phi-N	136	444	53	111	12	4	4	34	64	43	.250	.346	.322	87	-6	2			.967	-27	*2-111,3-21	-2.7
1939	Phi-N	115	341	46	95	19	4	9	43	33	34	.279	.342	.437	111	5	4			.964	-14	2-51,3-17,O/S	-0.6
1940	Phi-N	97	263	24	65	13	2	3	28	37	23	.247	.344	.346	95	-1	2			.966	-9	2-34,O-31,3/1	-0.9
1941	Phi-N	93	233	21	53	11	1	1	22	22	24	.227	.302	.296	72	-9	2			.980	-4	2-29,O-21,3	-1.2
Total	4	441	1281	144	324	55	11	17	127	156	124	.253	.337	.353	93	-11	10			.968	-54	2-225/3-70,01S	-5.4

■ RAY MUELLER
Mueller, Ray Coleman "Iron Man"   b: 3/8/12, Pittsburg, Kan.   BR/TR, 5'9", 175 lbs.   Deb: 5/11/35   C

YEAR	TM/L	G	AB	R	H	2B	3B	HR	RBI	BB	SO	AVG	OBP	SLG	PRO+	BR/A	SB	CS	SBR	FA	FR	G/POS	TPR
1935	Bos-N	42	97	10	22	5	0	3	11	3	11	.227	.250	.371	70	-5	0			.978	-2	C-40	-0.5
1936	Bos-N	24	71	5	14	4	0	0	5	5	17	.197	.250	.254	38	-6	0			.986	-4	C-23	-0.9
1937	Bos-N	64	187	21	47	9	2	2	26	18	36	.251	.317	.353	90	-3	1			.995	2	C-57	0.2
1938	Bos-N	83	274	23	65	8	6	4	35	16	28	.237	.282	.354	82	-8	3			.993	-2	C-75	-0.7
1939	Pit-N	86	180	14	42	8	1	2	18	14	22	.233	.289	.322	65	-9	0			.971	-3	C-81	-0.9
1940	Pit-N	4	3	1	1	0	0	0	1	2	0	.333	.600	.333	165	1	0			1.000	1	/C-4	0.1
1943	Cin-N	141	427	50	111	19	4	8	52	56	42	.260	.347	.379	111	7	1			.988	20	*C-140	3.8
1944	Cin-N★	155	555	54	159	24	4	10	73	53	47	.286	.353	.398	115	11	4			.983	-5	*C-155	1.6
1946	Cin-N	114	378	35	96	18	4	8	48	27	37	.254	.309	.386	100	-2	0			.994	10	*C-100	1.4
1947	Cin-N	71	192	17	48	11	0	6	33	16	25	.250	.311	.401	88	-4	1			.984	-1	C-55	-0.2
1948	Cin-N	14	34	2	7	1	0	0	2	4	3	.206	.289	.235	45	-3	0			.982	1	C-10	-0.1
1949	Cin-N	32	106	7	29	4	0	1	13	5	13	.274	.319	.340	76	-4	1			1.000	-3	C-31	-0.4
	NY-N	56	170	17	38	2	2	5	23	13	14	.224	.279	.347	67	-8	1			.982	1	C-56	-0.5
	Yr	88	276	24	67	6	2	6	36	18	27	.243	.294	.344	70	-12	2			.988	-2	C-87	-0.9
1950	NY-N	4	11	0	1	1	0	0	0	0	2	.091	.091	.182	-30	-2	0			1.000	2	/C-4	0.0
	Pit-N	67	156	17	42	7	0	6	24	11	14	.269	.321	.429	92	-2	2			.996	2	C-63	0.2
	Yr	71	167	17	43	8	0	6	24	11	16	.257	.307	.413	85	-4	2			.996	4	C-67	0.2
1951	Bos-N	28	70	8	11	2	0	1	9	7	11	.157	.234	.229	27	-7	0	0	0	1.000	3	C-23	-0.4
Total	14	985	2911	281	733	123	23	56	373	250	322	.252	.314	.368	91	-44	14	0		.988	21	C-917	2.7

■ WALTER MUELLER
Mueller, Walter John   b: 12/6/1894, Central, Mo.   d: 8/16/71, St.Louis, Mo.   BR/TR, 5'8", 160 lbs.   Deb: 5/7/22   F

YEAR	TM/L	G	AB	R	H	2B	3B	HR	RBI	BB	SO	AVG	OBP	SLG	PRO+	BR/A	SB	CS	SBR	FA	FR	G/POS	TPR
1922	Pit-N	32	122	21	33	5	1	2	18	5	7	.270	.305	.377	74	-5	1	0		.976	7	O-31	0.0
1923	Pit-N	40	111	11	34	4	4	0	20	4	6	.306	.336	.414	95	-1	2	2	-1	.941	1	O-26	-0.2
1924	Pit-N	30	50	6	13	1	1	0	8	4	4	.260	.327	.320	73	-2	1	0	0	1.000	0	O-15	-0.3
1926	Pit-N	19	62	8	15	0	1	0	3	0	2	.242	.242	.274	37	-5	0			.969	0	O-15	-0.6
Total	4	121	345	46	95	10	7	2	49	13	19	.275	.307	.362	74	-13	4	2		.966	8	/O-87	-1.1

■ BILL MUELLER
Mueller, William Lawrence "Hawk"   b: 11/9/20, Bay City, Mich.   BR/TR, 6'1.5", 180 lbs.   Deb: 8/29/42

YEAR	TM/L	G	AB	R	H	2B	3B	HR	RBI	BB	SO	AVG	OBP	SLG	PRO+	BR/A	SB	CS	SBR	FA	FR	G/POS	TPR
1942	Chi-A	26	85	5	14	1	0	0	5	12	9	.165	.276	.176	29	-8	1	2	0	.978	7	O-26	-0.2
1945	Chi-A	13	9	3	0	0	0	0	0	2	1	.000	.182	.000	-47	-2	0	0	0	.778	-3	/O-7	-0.4
Total	2	39	94	8	14	1	0	0	5	14	10	.149	.266	.160	22	-9	1	0		.960	4	/O-33	-0.6

■ MIKE MULDOON
Muldoon, Michael D.   b: 1858, Ireland   5'8", 165 lbs.   Deb: 5/1/1882

YEAR	TM/L	G	AB	R	H	2B	3B	HR	RBI	BB	SO	AVG	OBP	SLG	PRO+	BR/A	SB	CS	SBR	FA	FR	G/POS	TPR
1882	Cle-N	84	341	50	84	17	5	6	45	10	28	.246	.268	.378	108	3				.880	3	*3-61,O-23	0.7
1883	Cle-N	98	378	54	86	22	3	0	29	10	39	.228	.247	.302	67	-15				.825	-9	*3-98/O-2	-2.2
1884	Cle-N	110	422	46	101	16	6	2	38	18	67	.239	.270	.320	82	-9				.833	-7	*3-109/O-1,2	-1.4
1885	Bal-a	102	410	47	103	20	6	2		20		.251	.264	.344	102	1				.870	-3	*3-101/2-1	0.0
1886	Bal-a	101	381	57	76	13	8	0	34			.199	.269	.276	72	-12	12			.912	-5	2-57,3-44	-0.5
Total	5	495	1932	254	450	88	28	10	112	92	134	.233	.270	.323	86	-31	12			.846	-14	3-413/2-59,O	-3.4

■ TONY MULLANE
Mullane, Anthony John "Count" or "The Apollo Of The Box"   b: 1/20/1859, Cork, Ireland   d: 4/25/44, Chicago, Ill.   BB/TB, 5'10.5", 165 lbs.   Deb: 8/27/1881

YEAR	TM/L	G	AB	R	H	2B	3B	HR	RBI	BB	SO	AVG	OBP	SLG	PRO+	BR/A	SB	CS	SBR	FA	FR	G/POS	TPR
1881	Det-N	5	19	0	5	0	0	0	1	0	0	.263	.263	.263	63	-1				.882	0	/P-5	0.0
1882	Lou-a	77	303	46	78	13	1	0		13		.257	.288	.307	107	3				.959	10	*P-55,1-13,O/2	-0.1
1883	StL-a	83	307	38	69	11	6	0		13		.225	.256	.300	74	-9				.851	2	P-53,O-30/21	-0.3
1884	Tol-a	95	352	49	97	19	3	3		33		.276	.339	.372	127	11				.885	7	P-67,O-19/13S2	0.0
1886	Cin-a	91	324	59	73	12	5	0		25		.225	.283	.293	78	-9	20			.899	-0	P-63,O-27/13S2	-0.6
1887	Cin-a	56	199	35	44	6	3	3		16		.221	.292	.327	71	-8	20			.944	-2	P-48/O-9	-0.2
1888	Cin-a	51	175	27	44	4	4	1	16			.251	.296	.337	97	-1	12			.888	-2	P-44/1-4,O2	-0.2
1889	Cin-a	63	196	53	58	16	4	0	29	27	21	.296	.387	.418	125	7	24			.920	-1	P-33,3-18,O/1	0.3
1890	Cin-N	81	286	41	79	9	8	0	34	39	30	.276	.375	.364	116	7	19			.941	-2	O-28,P-25,3S/1	0.3
1891	Cin-N	64	209	16	31	1	2	0	10	18	33	.148	.229	.172	17	-22	4			.958	-3	P-51,O-12/3	-0.6
1892	Cin-N	39	118	14	20	3	1	0	6	5		.169	.246	.212	39	-9	4			.926	5	P-37/1-2	0.0
1893	Cin-N	16	52	11	15	0	0	1	6	5	3	.288	.383	.346	92	-0	1			.939	0	P-15/3-1	0.0
	Bal-N	38	114	15	26	2	1	0	14	5	14	.228	.261	.263	39	-10	5			.943	2	P-34/O-2,1	-0.1
	Yr	54	166	26	41	2	1	1	20	10	17	.247	.302	.289	56	-11	6			.942	2	P-49/O-2,31	-0.1
1894	Bal-N	21	53	3	21	3	0	0	9	6	3	.396	.475	.453	120	2	2			.889	-1	P-21	0.0
	Cle-N	4	13	0	1	0	0	0	0	4	2	.077	.294	.077	-6	-2	1			.944	2	/P-4	0.0
	Yr	25	66	3	22	3	0	0	9	10	5	.333	.436	.379	94	-0	3			.911	1	P-25	0.0
Total	13	784	2720	407	661	99	38	8	128	221	114	.243	.307	.316	87	-42	112			.918	18	P-555,O-154/31S2	-1.5

■ GREG MULLEAVY
Mulleavy, Gregory Thomas "Moe"   b: 9/25/05, Detroit, Mich.   d: 2/1/80, Arcadia, Cal.   BR/TR, 5'9", 167 lbs.   Deb: 7/4/30   C

YEAR	TM/L	G	AB	R	H	2B	3B	HR	RBI	BB	SO	AVG	OBP	SLG	PRO+	BR/A	SB	CS	SBR	FA	FR	G/POS	TPR
1930	Chi-A	77	289	27	76	14	5	0	28	20	23	.263	.311	.346	69	-14	5	2	0	.918	-5	S-73	-0.9
1932	Chi-A	1	3	0	0	0	0	0	0	0	0	.000	.000	.000	-99	-1	0	0	0	1.000	0	/2-1	0.0
1933	Bos-A	1	0	1	0	0	0	0	0	0	0	—	—	—		0	0	0	0	.000	0	/R	0.0
Total	3	79	292	28	76	14	5	0	28	20	23	.260	.308	.342	67	-15	5	2	0	.918	-5	/S-73,2-1	-1.0

■ MULLEN
Mullen   Deb: 8/17/1872

YEAR	TM/L	G	AB	R	H	2B	3B	HR	RBI	BB	SO	AVG	OBP	SLG	PRO+	BR/A	SB	CS	SBR	FA	FR	G/POS	TPR
1872	Cle-n	1	4	1	0	0	0	0	0	0	0	.000	.000	.000	-99	-1						/O-1	-0.1

■ CHARLIE MULLEN
Mullen, Charles George   b: 3/15/1889, Seattle, Wash.   d: 6/6/63, Seattle, Wash.   BR/TR, 5'10.5", 155 lbs.   Deb: 5/18/10

YEAR	TM/L	G	AB	R	H	2B	3B	HR	RBI	BB	SO	AVG	OBP	SLG	PRO+	BR/A	SB	CS	SBR	FA	FR	G/POS	TPR
1910	Chi-A	41	123	15	24	2	1	0	13	4		.195	.220	.228	42	-8	4			.982	1	1-37/O-2	-0.9
1911	Chi-A	20	59	7	12	2	1	0	5	5		.203	.266	.271	51	-4	1			.969	0	1-20	-0.4
1914	NY-A	93	323	33	84	8	0	0	44	33	55	.260	.332	.285	86	-5	11	17	-7	.994	3	1-93	-1.2
1915	NY-A	40	90	11	24	1	0	0	7	10	12	.267	.340	.278	85	-1	5	2	0	.982	1	1-27	-0.1
1916	NY-A	59	146	11	39	9	1	0	18	9	13	.267	.310	.342	94	-2	7			.943	-4	2-20,1-17/O	-0.6
Total	5	253	741	77	183	22	3	0	87	61	80	.247	.306	.285	78	-20	28	19		.988	0	1-194/2-20,O	-3.2

■ MOON MULLEN
Mullen, Ford Parker   b: 2/9/17, Olympia, Wash.   BL/TR, 5'9", 165 lbs.   Deb: 4/18/44

YEAR	TM/L	G	AB	R	H	2B	3B	HR	RBI	BB	SO	AVG	OBP	SLG	PRO+	BR/A	SB	CS	SBR	FA	FR	G/POS	TPR
1944	Phi-N	118	464	51	124	9	4	0	31	28	32	.267	.315	.304	77	-14	4			.963	-7	*2-114/3-1	-1.5

■ JOHN MULLEN
Mullen, John   b: Philadelphia, Pa.   BL/TL,   Deb: 9/9/1876

YEAR	TM/L	G	AB	R	H	2B	3B	HR	RBI	BB	SO	AVG	OBP	SLG	PRO+	BR/A	SB	CS	SBR	FA	FR	G/POS	TPR
1876	Phi-N	1	3	0	0	0	0	0	0	0	0	.000	.000	.000	-99	-1				.714	0	/C-1	0.0

YEAR	TM/L	G	AB	R	H	2B	3B	HR	RBI	BB	SO	AVG	OBP	SLG	PRO+	BR/A	SB	CS	SBR	FA	FR	G/POS	TPR

■ BILLY MULLEN
Mullen, William John   b: 1/23/1896, St.Louis, Mo.   d: 5/4/71, St.Louis, Mo.   BR/TR, 5'8", 160 lbs.   Deb: 10/2/20

1920	StL-A	2	4	0	0	0	0	0	0	0	0	.000	.000	.000	-97	-1	0	0	0	1.000	-1	/2-1	-0.2
1921	StL-A	4	4	0	0	0	0	0	0	2	1	.000	.333	.000	-8	-1	0	0	0	1.000	0	/3-2	-0.1
1923	Bro-N	4	11	1	3	0	0	0	0	0	0	.273	.273	.273	46	-1	0	0	0	.875	-0	/3-4	-0.1
1926	Det-A	11	13	2	1	0	0	0	0	5	1	.077	.333	.077	11	-1	1	0	0	.875	-0	/3-9	-0.1
1928	StL-A	15	18	2	7	1	0	0	2	3	4	.389	.476	.444	139	1	0	0	0	.867	1	/3-6	0.2
Total	5	36	50	5	11	1	0	0	2	10	6	.220	.350	.240	56	-3	1	0	0	.884	-1	/3-21,2-1	-0.2

■ FREDDIE MULLER
Muller, Frederick William   b: 12/21/07, Newark, Cal.   d: 10/20/76, Davis, Cal.   BR/TR, 5'10", 170 lbs.   Deb: 7/8/33

1933	Bos-A	15	48	6	9	1	1	0	3	5	5	.188	.264	.250	37	-4	1	0	0	.923	-4	2-14	-0.7
1934	Bos-A	2	1	1	0	0	0	0	0	1	0	.000	.500	.000	36	-0	0	0	0	.800	-0	/2-1,3-1	0.0
Total	2	17	49	7	9	1	1	0	3	6	5	.184	.273	.245	38	-4	1	0	0	.914	-5	/2-15,3-1	-0.7

■ MULLIGAN
Mulligan   Deb: 6/14/1884

1884	Was-U	1	4	2	1	0	0	0		0		.250	.250	.250	38	-0				1.000	1	/3-1	0.1

■ EDDIE MULLIGAN
Mulligan, Edward Joseph   b: 8/27/1894, St.Louis, Mo.   d: 3/15/82, San Rafael, Cal.   BR/TR, 5'9", 152 lbs.   Deb: 9/23/15

1915	Chi-N	11	22	5	8	1	0	0	2	5	1	.364	.481	.409	170	2	2		-1	.907	3	S-10/3-1	0.5
1916	Chi-N	58	189	13	29	3	4	0	9	8	30	.153	.200	.212	24	-17	1			.888	3	S-58	-1.2
1921	Chi-A	151	609	82	153	21	12	1	45	32	53	.251	.293	.330	59	-38	13	18	-7	.955	-13	*3-151/S-1	-4.6
1922	Chi-A	103	372	39	87	14	8	0	31	22	32	.234	.278	.315	55	-26	7	7	-2	.971	4	3-84/S-7	-1.6
1928	Pit-N	27	43	4	10	2	0	0	1	3	4	.233	.283	.279	45	-3	0			.929	0	/3-6,2-4	-0.3
Total	5	350	1235	143	287	41	24	1	88	70	120	.232	.278	.307	54	-82	23	27		.961	-3	3-242/S-76,2	-7.2

■ GEORGE MULLIN
Mullin, George Joseph "Wabash George"   b: 7/4/1880, Toledo, Ohio   d: 1/7/44, Wabash, Ind.   BR/TR, 5'11", 188 lbs.   Deb: 5/4/02

1902	Det-A	40	120	20	39	4	3	0	11	8		.325	.367	.408	113	2	1			.921	1	P-35/O-4	-0.1
1903	Det-A	46	126	11	35	9	1	1	12	2		.278	.295	.389	107	1	1			.936	5	P-41/O-1	0.0
1904	Det-A	53	155	14	45	10	2	0	8	10		.290	.337	.381	131	5	1			.936	7	P-45/O-2	-0.1
1905	Det-A	47	135	15	35	4	0	0	12	12		.259	.320	.289	93	-1	4			.962	7	P-44/O-1	0.0
1906	Det-A	50	142	13	32	6	4	0	6	4		.225	.247	.324	76	-4	2			.957	2	P-40/2-1,O	-0.1
1907	*Det-A	70	157	16	34	5	3	0	13	12		.217	.276	.287	77	-4	2			.961	4	P-46/1-1	0.0
1908	*Det-A	55	125	13	32	2	2	1	8	7		.256	.306	.328	102	0	2			.961	3	P-39	0.0
1909	*Det-A	53	126	13	27	7	0	0	17	13		.214	.288	.270	73	-4	2			.973	0	P-40/O-2	-0.1
1910	Det-A	50	129	15	33	6	2	1	11	8		.256	.299	.357	99	-1	1			.944	-0	P-38/O-2	-0.1
1911	Det-A	40	98	4	28	7	2	0	5	10		.286	.352	.398	104	0	1			.941	-2	P-30	0.0
1912	Det-A	38	90	13	25	5	1	0	12	17		.278	.393	.356	118	3	0			.929	0	P-30	0.0
1913	Det-A	12	20	1	7	0	0	0	1	4	1	.350	.458	.350	139	1	0			.952	1	/P-7	0.0
	Was-A	11	21	4	4	0	0	0	0	2	5	.190	.292	.190	41	-1	1			.958	1	P-11	0.0
	Yr	23	41	5	11	0	0	0	1	6	6	.268	.375	.268	89	-0	1			.956	1	P-18	0.0
1914	Ind-F	43	77	11	24	5	3	0	21	11	15	.312	.404	.455	110	1	0			.915	-4	P-36	0.0
1915	New-F	6	10	0	1	0	0	0	2	0		.100	.250	.100	-5	-1	0			1.000	-1	/P-5	0.0
Total	14	614	1531	163	401	70	23	3	137	122	21	.262	.319	.344	98	-3	18			.947	24	P-487/O-13,12	-0.5

■ HENRY MULLIN
Mullin, Henry J.   b: 4/1862, St.John, N.B., Canada   d: 11/8/27, Beverly, Mass.   BR,   Deb: 6/4/1884

1884	Was-a	34	120	13	17	3	1	0		8		.142	.195	.183	27	-9				.869	-1	O-34/3-1	-0.9
	Bos-U	2	8	1	0	0	0	0		0		.000	.000	.000	-99	-2				1.000	3	/O-2	0.0
Total	1	36	128	14	17	3	1	0		8		.133	.184	.172	17	-11				.882	2	/O-36,3-1	-0.9

■ JIM MULLIN
Mullin, James Henry   b: 10/16/1883, New York, N.Y.   d: 1/24/25, Philadelphia, Pa.   BR/TR, 5'10", 173 lbs.   Deb: 6/1/04

1904	Phi-A	22	52	5	14	1	0	1	5	3		.269	.321	.346	106	0	2			.985	-5	/1-7,2-5,SO	-0.6
	Was-A	27	102	10	19	2	2	0	4	4		.186	.224	.245	49	-6	3			.981	6	2-27	0.1
	Phi-A	19	58	4	10	0	0	0	4	2		.172	.238	.172	29	-4	2			.984	-1	1-19	-0.6
	Yr	68	212	19	43	3	2	1	13	9		.203	.252	.250	58	-10	7			.965	-0	2-32,1-26/SO	-1.1
1905	Was-A	50	163	18	31	7	6	0	13	5		.190	.214	.307	67	-7	5			.928	-4	2-40/1-6	-1.1
Total	2	118	375	37	74	10	8	1	26	14		.197	.236	.275	62	-17	12			.946	-4	/2-72,1-32,SO	-2.2

■ PAT MULLIN
Mullin, Patrick Joseph   b: 11/1/17, Trotter, Pa.   BL/TR, 6'2", 190 lbs.   Deb: 9/18/40   C

1940	Det-A	4	4	0	0	0	0	0	0	0	0	.000	.000	.000	-91	-1	0	0	0	.000	-1	/O-1	-0.2
1941	Det-A	54	220	42	76	11	5	5	23	18	18	.345	.400	.509	126	8	5	1	1	.944	-4	O-51	0.1
1946	Det-A	93	276	34	68	13	4	3	35	25	36	.246	.311	.355	81	-7	3	5	-2	.949	-3	O-75	-1.6
1947	Det-A☆	116	398	62	102	28	6	15	62	63	66	.256	.359	.470	126	13	3	8	-4	.988	8	*O-106	1.2
1948	Det-A★	138	496	91	143	16	11	23	80	77	57	.288	.385	.504	132	22	1	2	-1	.972	0	*O-131	1.3
1949	Det-A	104	310	55	83	8	6	12	59	42	29	.268	.357	.448	112	4	1	2	-1	.989	-4	O-79	-0.4
1950	Det-A	69	142	16	31	0	6	2	23	20	23	.218	.315	.380	75	-6	1	4	-2	1.000	1	O-32	-0.9
1951	Det-A	110	295	41	83	11	6	12	51	40	38	.281	.367	.481	128	11	2	2	-1	.939	-9	O-83	-0.2
1952	Det-A	97	255	29	64	13	5	7	35	31	30	.251	.332	.424	108	2	4	2	0	.979	2	O-65	0.2
1953	Det-A	79	97	11	26	1	0	4	17	14	15	.268	.360	.402	107	1	0	1	-1	.944	-2	O-14	-0.2
Total	10	864	2493	381	676	106	43	87	385	330	312	.271	.358	.453	115	47	20	27	-10	.970	-14	O-637	-0.7

■ RANCE MULLINIKS
Mulliniks, Steven Rance   b: 1/15/56, Tulare, Cal.   BL/TR, 6', 170 lbs.   Deb: 6/18/77

1977	Cal-A	78	271	36	73	13	2	3	21	23	36	.269	.329	.365	93	-3	1	1	-0	.963	2	S-77	0.7
1978	Cal-A	50	119	6	22	3	1	1	6	8	23	.185	.242	.252	41	-9	2	0	1	.953	2	S-47/D-2	-0.3
1979	Cal-A	22	68	7	10	0	0	1	8	4	14	.147	.205	.191	8	-7	0	0	0	.957	-7	S-22	-1.4
1980	KC-A	36	54	8	14	3	0	0	6	7	10	.259	.344	.315	81	-1	0	0	0	.981	2	S-18,2-14	0.3
1981	KC-A	24	44	6	10	3	0	0	5	2	7	.227	.261	.295	61	-2	0	1	-1	.900	3	2-10/S-7,3	0.1
1982	Tor-A	112	311	32	76	25	0	4	35	37	49	.244	.327	.363	82	-8	3	2	-0	.938	-16	*3-102,S-16	-2.5
1983	Tor-A	129	364	54	100	34	3	10	49	57	43	.275	.374	.467	122	12	0	2	-1	.971	-18	*3-116,S-15/2	-0.8
1984	Tor-A	125	343	41	111	21	5	3	42	33	44	.324	.385	.440	123	11	2	3	-1	.968	-13	*3-119/S-3,2	-0.4
1985	*Tor-A	129	366	55	108	26	1	10	57	55	54	.295	.387	.454	126	15	2	0	1	.971	-16	*3-119	-0.3
1986	Tor-A	117	348	50	90	22	0	11	45	43	60	.259	.342	.417	103	2	1	1	-0	.975	-1	*3-110/2-1,D	-0.2
1987	Tor-A	124	332	37	103	28	1	11	44	34	55	.310	.374	.500	127	13	1	1	-0	.927	-6	3-96,D-22/S	0.4
1988	Tor-A	119	337	49	101	21	1	12	48	56	57	.300	.399	.475	143	21	1	0	0	1.000	-0	*D-108/3-7	1.9
1989	*Tor-A	103	273	25	65	11	2	3	29	34	40	.238	.322	.326	85	-5	0	0	0	.985	1	D-73,3-29	-0.5
1990	Tor-A	57	97	11	28	4	0	2	16	22	19	.289	.420	.392	126	5	2	1	0	.949	-0	D-22,D-10/1	0.4
1991	*Tor-A	97	240	27	60	12	1	2	24	44	44	.250	.366	.333	92	-1	0	0	0	1.000	0	D-81/3-5	-0.4
1992	Tor-A	3	2	1	1	0	0	0	0	1	0	.500	.667	.500	221	0	0	0	0	.000	0	/D-2	0.0
Total	16	1325	3569	445	972	226	17	73	435	460	555	.272	.357	.407	107	40	15	12	-3	.961	-68	3-730,D-303,S/21	-3.0

■ FRAN MULLINS
Mullins, Francis Joseph   b: 5/14/57, Oakland, Cal.   BR/TR, 6', 180 lbs.   Deb: 9/1/80

1980	Chi-A	21	62	9	12	4	0	0	3	9	8	.194	.296	.258	53	-4	0	1	-1	.981	-2	3-21	-0.7
1984	SF-N	57	110	8	24	8	0	2	10	9	29	.218	.277	.345	77	-4	3	1	0	.969	9	S-28,3-28/2	0.8
1986	Cle-A	28	40	3	7	4	0	0	5	2	11	.175	.214	.275	33	-4	0	0	0	.953	8	2-13,S-11/1D	0.4
Total	3	106	212	20	43	16	0	2	18	20	48	.203	.272	.307	61	-11	3	2	-0	.968	15	/3-49,S-39,2D1	0.5

YEAR	TM/L	G	AB	R	H	2B	3B	HR	RBI	BB	SO	AVG	OBP	SLG	PRO+	BR/A	SB	CS	SBR	FA	FR	G/POS	TPR

■ **JOE MULVEY**   Mulvey, Joseph H. b: 10/27/1858, Providence, R.I. d: 8/21/28, Philadelphia, Pa. BR/TR, 5'11.5", 178 lbs. Deb: 5/31/1883

1883	Pro-N	4	16	1	2	1	0	0	2	0	1	.125	.125	.188	-6	-2				.692	-3	/S-4	-0.4
	Phi-N	3	12	2	6	1	0	0	3	0	1	.500	.500	.583	250	2				.750	-1	/3-3	0.1
	Yr	7	28	3	8	2	0	0	5	0	2	.286	.286	.357	96	-0				.692	-3	/S-4,3-3	-0.3
1884	Phi-N	100	401	47	92	11	2	2	32	4	49	.229	.237	.282	66	-15				.834	11	*3-100	-0.3
1885	Phi-N	107	443	74	119	25	6	6	64	3	18	.269	.274	.393	116	6				.848	-7	*3-107	0.1
1886	Phi-N	107	430	71	115	16	10	2	53	15	31	.267	.292	.365	98	-2	27			.879	-19	*3-107/O-1	-1.6
1887	Phi-N	111	474	93	136	21	6	2	78	21	14	.287	.321	.369	86	-10	43			.865	-15	*3-111	-2.0
1888	Phi-N	100	398	37	86	12	3	0	39	9	33	.216	.235	.261	55	-20	18			.891	-14	*3-100	-3.2
1889	Phi-N	129	544	77	157	21	9	6	77	23	25	.289	.319	.393	91	-11	23			.893	1	*3-129	-0.4
1890	Phi-P	120	519	96	149	26	15	6	87	27	36	.287	.326	.430	99	-5	20			.857	-16	*3-120	-1.3
1891	Phi-a	113	453	62	115	9	13	5	66	17	32	.254	.287	.364	84	-13	11			.894	2	*3-113	-0.5
1892	Phi-N	25	98	9	14	1	1	0	4	6	9	.143	.200	.173	13	-10	2			.883	3	3-25	-0.6
1893	Was-N	55	226	21	53	9	4	0	19	7	8	.235	.264	.310	54	-16	2			.874	5	3-55	-0.8
1895	Bro-N	13	49	8	15	4	1	0	8	2	0	.306	.333	.429	104	0	1			.917	2	3-13	0.2
Total	12	987	4063	598	1059	157	70	29	532	134	257	.261	.287	.355	84	-96	147			.871	-48	3-983/S-4,O	-10.7

■ **JERRY MUMPHREY**   Mumphrey, Jerry Wayne b: 9/9/52, Tyler, Tex. BB/TR, 6'2", 185 lbs. Deb: 9/10/74

1974	StL-N	5	2	2	0	0	0	0	0	0	0	.000	.000	.000	-99	-1	0	0	0	.000	-0	/O-1	-0.1
1975	StL-N	11	16	2	6	2	0	0	1	4	3	.375	.500	.500	172	2	0	0	0	1.000	1	/O-3	0.2
1976	StL-N	112	384	51	99	15	5	1	26	37	53	.258	.325	.331	86	-7	22	6	3	.993	6	O-94	-0.2
1977	StL-N	145	463	73	133	20	10	2	38	47	70	.287	.354	.387	100	1	22	15	-2	.971	-2	*O-133	-0.8
1978	StL-N	125	367	41	96	13	4	2	37	30	40	.262	.319	.335	84	-8	14	10	-2	.995	-8	*O-116	-2.3
1979	StL-N	124	339	53	100	10	3	3	32	26	39	.295	.345	.369	94	-2	8	11	-4	.984	-13	*O-114	-2.4
1980	SD-N	160	564	61	168	24	3	4	59	49	90	.298	.354	.372	109	7	52	5	13	.974	8	*O-153	2.3
1981	*NY-A	80	319	44	98	11	5	6	32	24	27	.307	.356	.429	127	11	14	9	-1	.966	7	O-79	1.5
1982	NY-A	123	477	76	143	24	10	9	68	50	66	.300	.366	.449	124	16	11	3	2	.986	9	*O-123	2.3
1983	NY-A	83	267	41	70	11	4	7	36	28	33	.262	.332	.412	107	3	2	3	-1	.983	7	O-83	0.6
	Hou-N	44	134	17	48	10	2	1	17	22	23	.336	.428	.455	154	11	5	0	2	.990	0	O-43	1.2
1984	Hou-N★	151	524	66	152	20	3	9	83	56	79	.290	.359	.391	119	13	15	7	0	.988	0	*O-137	1.0
1985	Hou-N	130	444	52	123	25	2	8	61	37	57	.277	.333	.396	106	3	6	7	-2	.969	-0	*O-126	-0.3
1986	Chi-N	111	309	37	94	11	2	5	32	26	45	.304	.358	.401	101	1	2	3	-1	.982	-16	O-92	-1.9
1987	Chi-N	118	309	41	103	19	2	13	44	35	47	.333	.401	.534	140	18	1	1	-0	.992	-2	O-85	1.3
1988	Chi-N	63	66	3	9	2	0	0	9	7	16	.136	.219	.167	12	-7	0	0	0	1.000	-1	/O-4	-0.9
Total	15	1585	4993	660	1442	217	55	70	575	478	688	.289	.351	.396	109	61	174	80	4	.981	-3	*O-1386	1.5

■ **JOHN MUNCE**   Munce, John Lewis "Big John" b: 11/18/1857, Philadelphia, Pa. d: 3/15/17, Philadelphia, Pa. 6', Deb: 8/19/1884

| 1884 | Wil-U | 7 | 21 | 1 | 4 | 0 | 0 | 0 | | 0 | 1 | .190 | .227 | .190 | 14 | -2 | | | | .667 | -1 | /O-7 | -0.3 |

■ **JAKE MUNCH**   Munch, Jacob Ferdinand b: 11/16/1890, Morton, Pa. d: 6/8/66, Lansdowne, Pa. BL/TL, 6'2.5", 170 lbs. Deb: 5/27/18

| 1918 | Phi-A | 22 | 30 | 3 | 8 | 0 | 1 | 0 | 0 | 0 | 5 | .267 | .267 | .333 | 80 | -1 | 0 | | | .667 | -2 | /O-3,1-2 | -0.3 |

■ **GEORGE MUNDINGER**   Mundinger, George b: 11/20/1854, New Orleans, La. d: 10/12/10, Covington, La. BR/TR, 6'2", 200 lbs. Deb: 5/9/1884

| 1884 | Ind-a | 3 | 8 | 1 | 2 | 0 | 0 | 0 | | 0 | | .250 | .250 | .250 | 65 | -0 | | | | .750 | -3 | /C-3 | -0.3 |

■ **BILL MUNDY**   Mundy, William Edward b: 6/28/1889, Salineville, Ohio d: 9/23/58, Kalamazoo, Mich. BL/TL, 5'10", 154 lbs. Deb: 8/17/13

| 1913 | Bos-A | 16 | 47 | 4 | 12 | 0 | 0 | 0 | 4 | 4 | 12 | .255 | .314 | .255 | 65 | -2 | 0 | | | .952 | -2 | 1-14 | -0.5 |

■ **HORATIO MUNN**   Munn, Horatio B. Deb: 9/6/1875

| 1875 | Atl-n | 1 | 4 | 0 | 0 | 0 | 0 | 0 | | | | .000 | .000 | .000 | -99 | -1 | | | | | | /2-1 | -0.1 |

■ **PEDRO MUNOZ**   Munoz, Pedro Javier (Gonzalez) b: 9/19/68, Ponce, P.R. BR/TR, 5'11", 170 lbs. Deb: 9/1/90

1990	Min-A	22	85	13	23	4	1	0	5	2	16	.271	.287	.341	70	-3	3	0	1	.972	-1	O-21/D-1	-0.5
1991	Min-A	51	138	15	39	7	1	7	26	9	31	.283	.331	.500	121	3	3	0	1	.989	0	O-44/D-2	0.4
1992	Min-A	127	418	44	113	16	3	12	71	17	90	.270	.300	.409	94	-5	4	5	-2	.987	-1	*O-122/D-3	-1.0
1993	Min-A	104	326	34	76	11	1	13	38	25	97	.233	.294	.393	82	-9	1	2	-1	.983	-6	*O-102	-1.7
1994	Min-A	75	244	35	72	15	2	11	36	19	67	.295	.351	.508	118	6	0	0	0	.965	-4	O-58,D-12	0.0
Total	5	379	1211	141	323	53	8	43	176	72	301	.267	.312	.430	97	-8	11	7	-1	.982	-12	O-347/D-18	-2.8

■ **RED MUNSON**   Munson, Clarence Hanford b: 7/31/1883, Cincinnati, Ohio d: 2/19/57, Mishawaka, Ind. TR , Deb: 8/28/05

| 1905 | Phi-N | 9 | 26 | 1 | 3 | 1 | 0 | 0 | 2 | 0 | | .115 | .115 | .154 | -21 | -4 | 0 | | | .857 | -1 | /C-8 | -0.4 |

■ **JOE MUNSON**   Munson, Joseph Martin Napoleon (b: Joseph Martin Napoleon Carlson)
b: 11/6/1899, Renovo, Pa. d: 2/24/91, Drexel Hill, Pa. BL/TR, 5'9", 184 lbs. Deb: 9/18/25

1925	Chi-N	9	35	5	13	3	1	0	3	3	1	.371	.436	.514	140	2	1	1	-0	1.000	-0	/O-9	0.1
1926	Chi-N	33	101	17	26	2	2	3	15	8	4	.257	.318	.406	93	-1	0			.898	-2	O-28	-0.5
Total	2	42	136	22	39	5	3	3	18	11	5	.287	.349	.434	105	1	1	1	_1_	.922	-2	/O-37	-0.4

■ **THURMAN MUNSON**   Munson, Thurman Lee b: 6/7/47, Akron, Ohio d: 8/2/79, Canton, Ohio BR/TR, 5'11", 191 lbs. Deb: 8/8/69

1969	NY-A	26	86	6	22	1	2	1	9	10	10	.256	.333	.349	94	-1	0	1	-1	.986	-1	C-25	-0.1
1970	NY-A	132	453	59	137	25	4	6	53	57	56	.302	.389	.415	128	19	5	7	-3	.989	6	*C-125	3.0
1971	NY-A★	125	451	71	113	15	4	10	42	52	65	.251	.335	.368	106	4	6	5	-1	**.998**	-1	*C-117/O-1	0.6
1972	NY-A	140	511	54	143	16	3	7	46	47	58	.280	.344	.364	115	9	6	4	-2	.977	-5	*C-132	0.9
1973	NY-A★	147	519	80	156	29	4	20	74	48	64	.301	.364	.487	143	28	4	6	-2	.984	6	*C-142/D-1	3.8
1974	NY-A★	144	517	64	135	19	2	13	60	44	66	.261	.320	.381	104	2	2	0	1	.974	2	*C-137/D-4	1.1
1975	NY-A★	157	597	83	190	24	3	12	102	45	52	.318	.372	.429	129	23	3	2	-0	.972	9	*C-130,D-22/103	3.6
1976	*NY-A★	152	616	79	186	27	1	17	105	29	38	.302	.343	.432	127	19	14	11	-2	.981	-6	*C-121,D-21,O	1.4
1977	*NY-A★	149	595	85	183	28	5	18	100	39	55	.308	.352	.462	121	16	5	6	-2	.984	-5	*C-136,D-10	1.3
1978	*NY-A†	154	617	73	183	27	1	6	71	35	70	.297	.337	.373	102	1	2	3	-1	.986	-0	*C-125,D-14,O	0.2
1979	NY-A	97	382	42	110	18	3	3	39	32	37	.288	.343	.374	95	-2	1	2	-1	.978	-6	C-88/1-3,D	-0.5
Total	11	1423	5344	696	1558	229	32	113	701	438	571	.292	.350	.410	117	119	48	50	-16	.982	-2	*C-1278/D-77,O13	15.3

■ **JOHN MUNYAN**   Munyan, John B. b: 11/14/1860, Chester, Pa. d: 2/18/45, Endicott, N.Y. Deb: 7/12/1887

1887	Cle-a	16	58	9	14	1	1	0		3		.241	.279	.293	61	-3	4			.762	-2	O-12/C-3,3	-0.4
1890	Col-a	2	7	1	1	0	0	0		0		.143	.143	.143	17	-1	0			.667	-1	/O-2	-0.1
	StL-a	96	342	61	91	15	7	4		32		.266	.341	.386	100	-3	11			.939	-3	C-83/O-7,23S	0.1
	Yr	98	349	62	92	15	7	4		32		.264	.339	.381	99	-4	11			.939	-3	C-83/O-9,23S	0.0
1891	StL-a	62	182	44	42	4	3	0	20	43	39	.231	.389	.286	81	-4	13			.943	-6	C-45,O-12/S3	-0.6
Total	3	176	589	115	148	20	11	4	_20_	78	_39_	.251	.351	.343	90	-11	28			.937	-10	C-131/O-33,3S2	-1.0

■ **BOBBY MURCER**   Murcer, Bobby Ray b: 5/20/46, Oklahoma City, Okla BL/TR, 5'11", 180 lbs. Deb: 9/8/65

1965	NY-A	11	37	2	9	0	1	1	4	5	12	.243	.333	.378	102	0	0	0	0	.932	7	S-11	0.8
1966	NY-A	21	69	3	12	1	1	0	5	4	5	.174	.219	.217	27	-7	2	2	-1	.931	-4	S-18	-1.0
1969	NY-A	152	564	82	146	24	4	26	82	50	103	.259	.323	.454	120	12	7	5	-1	.964	-5	*O-118,3-31	-0.1
1970	NY-A	159	581	95	146	23	3	23	78	87	100	.251	.351	.420	118	14	15	10	-2	.992	10	*O-155	1.5

YEAR	TM/L	G	AB	R	H	2B	3B	HR	RBI	BB	SO	AVG	OBP	SLG	PRO+	BR/A	SB	CS	SBR	FA	FR	G/POS	TPR
1971	NY-A★	146	529	94	175	25	6	25	94	91	60	.331	**.429**	.543	**185**	61	14	8	-1	.985	-1	*O-143	**5.5**
1972	NY-A★	153	585	**102**	171	30	7	33	96	63	67	.292	.363	.537	171	49	11	9	-2	.992	10	*O-151	**5.5**
1973	NY-A★	160	616	83	187	29	2	22	95	50	67	.304	.359	.464	135	27	6	7	-2	.985	2	*O-160	1.9
1974	NY-A★	156	606	69	166	25	4	10	88	57	59	.274	.338	.378	109	7	14	5	1	.978	0	*O-156	0.2
1975	SF-N★	147	526	80	157	29	4	11	91	91	45	.298	.404	.432	127	22	9	5	-0	.981	-8	*O-144	0.9
1976	SF-N	147	533	73	138	20	2	23	90	84	78	.259	.364	.433	122	17	12	7	-1	.961	-0	*O-146	1.0
1977	Chi-N	154	554	90	147	18	3	27	89	80	77	.265	.361	.455	106	5	16	7	1	.980	-4	*O-150/2-1,S	-0.5
1978	Chi-N	146	499	66	140	22	6	9	64	80	57	.281	.380	.403	106	6	14	5	1	.979	-17	*O-138	-1.6
1979	Chi-N	58	190	22	49	4	1	7	22	36	20	.258	.379	.400	103	2	2	3	-1	1.000	3	O-54	0.1
	NY-A	74	264	42	72	12	0	8	33	25	32	.273	.340	.409	103	1	1	1	-0	.983	-4	O-70	-0.6
1980	*NY-A	100	297	41	80	9	1	13	57	34	28	.269	.348	.438	116	7	2	0	1	.955	-9	O-59,D-33	-0.5
1981	*NY-A	50	117	14	31	6	0	6	24	12	15	.265	.333	.470	131	4	0	0	0	.000	0	D-33	0.3
1982	NY-A	65	141	12	32	6	0	7	30	12	15	.227	.292	.418	94	-2	2	1	0	.000	0	D-47	0.2
1983	NY-A	9	22	2	4	2	0	1	1	1	1	.182	.217	.409	71	-1	0	0	0	.000	0	/D-5	-0.1
Total	17	1908	6730	972	1862	285	45	252	1043	862	841	.277	.361	.445	124	224	127	75	-7	.981	-19	*O-1644,D-118/3S2	13.0

■ SIMMY MURCH
Murch, Simeon Augustus   b: 11/21/1880, Castine, Me.   d: 6/6/39, Exeter, N.H.   BR/TR, 6'4", 220 lbs.   Deb: 9/20/04

YEAR	TM/L	G	AB	R	H	2B	3B	HR	RBI	BB	SO	AVG	OBP	SLG	PRO+	BR/A	SB	CS	SBR	FA	FR	G/POS	TPR
1904	StL-N	13	51	3	7	1	0	0	1			.137	.154	.157	-4	-6	0			.905	-3	/2-6,3-6,S	-0.9
1905	StL-N	4	9	0	1	0	0	0	0			.111	.111	.111	-35	-1	0			.750	-3	/2-2,S-1	-0.5
1908	Bro-N	6	11	1	2	1	0	0	1			.182	.250	.273	70	-0	0			.964	-1	/1-2	-0.1
Total	3	23	71	4	10	2	0	0	1	2		.141	.164	.169	3	-8	0			.880	-6	/2-8,3-6,1S	-1.5

■ WILBUR MURDOCH
Murdoch, Wilbur Edwin   b: 3/14/1875, Avon, N.Y.   d: 10/29/41, Los Angeles, Cal.   Deb: 8/29/08

YEAR	TM/L	G	AB	R	H	2B	3B	HR	RBI	BB	SO	AVG	OBP	SLG	PRO+	BR/A	SB	CS	SBR	FA	FR	G/POS	TPR
1908	StL-N	27	62	5	16	3	0	0	5	3		.258	.292	.306	96	-0	4			.913	-5	O-16	-0.6

■ TIM MURNANE
Murnane, Timothy Hayes   b: 6/4/1852, Naugatuck, Conn.   d: 2/7/17, Boston, Mass.   BL/TR, 5'9.5", 172 lbs.   Deb: 4/26/1872   M

YEAR	TM/L	G	AB	R	H	2B	3B	HR	RBI	BB	SO	AVG	OBP	SLG	PRO+	BR/A	SB	CS	SBR	FA	FR	G/POS	TPR
1872	Man-n	24	115	29	39	3	0	0	13	0	1	.339	.339	.365	124	4						1-24	0.4
1873	Ath-n	41	176	53	39	3	1	0	10	8	13	.222	.255	.267	50	-12						O-31/1-9,2	-0.7
1874	Ath-n	21	81	11	18	2	0	0			2	.222	.241	.247	51	-5						O-12/2-6,1	-0.4
1875	Phi-n	69	311	70	85	4	0	1			8	.273	.292	.296	100	-1						1-31,O-26,2	-0.1
1876	Bos-N	69	308	60	87	4	3	2	34	8	12	.282	.301	.334	109	3				.927	-4	*1-65/O-3,2	-0.2
1877	Bos-N	35	140	23	39	7	1	1	15	6	7	.279	.308	.364	107	1				.815	-1	O-30/1-5	-0.1
1878	Pro-N	49	188	35	45	6	1	0	14	8	12	.239	.270	.282	82	-3				.940	1	*1-48/O-1	-0.4
1884	Bos-U	76	311	55	73	5	2	0	22			.235	.285	.264	51	-20				.950	-5	1-63,O-16M	-2.9
Total	4 n	155	683	163	181	12	1	2	<u>23</u>	18	<u>14</u>	.265	.284	.294	83	-14						/O-69,1-65,2	-0.8
Total	4	229	947	173	244	22	7	3	<u>63</u>	44	<u>31</u>	.258	.291	.305	82	-20				.938	-8	1-181/O-50,2	-3.6

■ MURPHY
Murphy   Deb: 8/16/1884

YEAR	TM/L	G	AB	R	H	2B	3B	HR	RBI	BB	SO	AVG	OBP	SLG	PRO+	BR/A	SB	CS	SBR	FA	FR	G/POS	TPR
1884	Bos-U	1	3	0	0	0	0	0	1			.000	.250	.000	-27	-1				.333	-3	/C-1,O-1	-0.3

■ CLARENCE MURPHY
Murphy, Clarence   Deb: 6/17/1886

YEAR	TM/L	G	AB	R	H	2B	3B	HR	RBI	BB	SO	AVG	OBP	SLG	PRO+	BR/A	SB	CS	SBR	FA	FR	G/POS	TPR
1886	Lou-a	1	3	0	0	0	0	0	0			.000	.000	.000	-95	-1	0			1.000	0	/O-1	-0.1

■ CONNIE MURPHY
Murphy, Cornelius David "Stone Face"   b: 11/1/1870, Northfield, Mass.   d: 12/14/45, New Bedford, Mass.   BL/TR, 5'8", 155 lbs.   Deb: 9/17/1893

YEAR	TM/L	G	AB	R	H	2B	3B	HR	RBI	BB	SO	AVG	OBP	SLG	PRO+	BR/A	SB	CS	SBR	FA	FR	G/POS	TPR
1893	Cin-N	6	17	3	3	1	0	0	2	1	2	.176	.222	.235	21	-2	0			.917	-2	/C-4	-0.3
1894	Cin-N	1	4	0	0	0	0	0	0	1	1	.000	.200	.000	-46	-1	0			.500	-1	/C-1	-0.2
Total	2	7	21	3	3	1	0	0	2	2	3	.143	.217	.190	6	-3	0			.857	-3	/C-5	-0.5

■ DALE MURPHY
Murphy, Dale Bryan   b: 3/12/56, Portland, Ore.   BR/TR, 6'5", 215 lbs.   Deb: 9/13/76

YEAR	TM/L	G	AB	R	H	2B	3B	HR	RBI	BB	SO	AVG	OBP	SLG	PRO+	BR/A	SB	CS	SBR	FA	FR	G/POS	TPR
1976	Atl-N	19	65	3	17	6	0	0	9	7	9	.262	.333	.354	89	-1	0	0	0	.974	-0	C-19	0.0
1977	Atl-N	18	76	5	24	8	1	2	14	0	8	.316	.316	.526	108	1	0	1	-1	.954	-2	C-18	-0.1
1978	Atl-N	151	530	66	120	14	3	23	79	42	145	.226	.287	.394	80	-16	11	7	-1	.984	4	*1-129,C-21	-2.1
1979	Atl-N	104	384	53	106	7	2	21	57	38	67	.276	.344	.469	111	5	6	1	1	.980	-9	1-76,C-27	-0.6
1980	Atl-N★	156	569	98	160	27	2	33	89	59	133	.281	.350	.510	133	23	9	6	-1	.985	11	*O-154/1-1	2.8
1981	Atl-N	104	369	43	91	12	1	13	50	44	72	.247	.327	.390	100	0	14	5	1	.981	4	*O-103/1-3	0.2
1982	*Atl-N★	162	598	113	168	23	2	36	**109**	93	134	.281	.380	.507	140	33	23	11	4	.979	-1	*O-162	2.9
1983	Atl-N★	162	589	131	178	24	4	36	**121**	90	110	.302	.396	**.540**	146	38	30	4	7	.985	-5	*O-160	4.6
1984	Atl-N★	162	607	94	176	32	8	36	100	79	134	.290	.374	**.547**	145	36	19	7	2	.987	-1	*O-160	3.4
1985	Atl-N★	162	616	**118**	185	32	2	**37**	111	**90**	141	.300	.390	.539	148	40	10	3	1	.980	-5	*O-161	3.3
1986	Atl-N★	160	614	89	163	29	7	29	83	75	141	.265	.347	.477	118	15	7	7	-2	.981	-4	*O-159	0.4
1987	Atl-N★	159	566	115	167	27	1	44	105	115	136	.295	.420	.580	154	47	16	6	1	.977	12	*O-159	5.4
1988	Atl-N	156	592	77	134	35	4	24	77	74	125	.226	.314	.421	104	3	3	5	-2	.992	18	*O-156	1.4
1989	Atl-N	154	574	60	131	16	0	20	84	65	142	.228	.309	.361	88	-8	3	2	-0	.985	4	*O-151	-0.9
1990	Atl-N	97	349	38	81	14	0	17	55	41	84	.232	.315	.418	94	-3	9	2	2	.981	4	O-97	0.0
	Phi-N	57	214	22	57	9	1	7	28	20	46	.266	.329	.416	104	1	0	1	-1	.992	3	O-55	0.2
	Yr	154	563	60	138	23	1	24	83	61	130	.245	.320	.417	98	-2	9	3	1	.985	7	O-152	0.2
1991	Phi-N	153	544	66	137	33	1	18	81	48	93	.252	.313	.415	104	2	1	0	0	.983	4	*O-147	0.2
1992	Phi-N	18	62	5	10	1	0	2	7	1	13	.161	.175	.274	25	-6	0	0	0	.950	-3	O-16	-1.1
1993	Col-N	26	42	1	6	1	0	0	7	5	15	.143	.234	.167	8	-6	0	0	0	1.000	1	O-13	-0.7
Total	18	2180	7960	1197	2111	350	39	398	1266	986	1748	.265	.348	.469	119	203	161	68	8	.983	45	*O-1853,1-209/C	19.3

■ DANNY MURPHY
Murphy, Daniel Francis   b: 8/11/1876, Philadelphia, Pa.   d: 11/22/55, Jersey City, N.J.   BR/TR, 5'9", 175 lbs.   Deb: 9/17/00   C

YEAR	TM/L	G	AB	R	H	2B	3B	HR	RBI	BB	SO	AVG	OBP	SLG	PRO+	BR/A	SB	CS	SBR	FA	FR	G/POS	TPR
1900	NY-N	22	74	11	20	1	0	0	6	8		.270	.341	.284	77	-2	4			.888	-6	2-22	-0.6
1901	NY-N	5	20	0	4	0	0	0	0	1		.200	.238	.200	29	-2	0			.895	-3	/2-5	-0.4
1902	Phi-A	76	291	48	91	11	8	1	48	13		.313	.351	.416	107	2	12			.963	-12	2-76	-0.6
1903	Phi-A	133	513	66	140	31	11	1	60	13		.273	.295	.382	97	-3	17			.949	-13	*2-133	-1.1
1904	Phi-A	150	557	78	160	30	17	7	77	22		.287	.320	.440	132	18	22			.941	13	*2-150	3.9
1905	*Phi-A	151	537	71	149	34	4	6	71	42		.277	.339	.389	129	17	23			.955	-9	*2-151	1.0
1906	Phi-A	119	448	48	135	28	6	2	60	21		.301	.341	.404	129	14	17			.955	-11	*2-119	0.4
1907	Phi-A	124	469	51	127	23	3	2	57	30		.271	.317	.345	109	4	11			.965	13	*2-122	1.7
1908	Phi-A	142	525	51	139	28	7	4	66	32		.265	.309	.368	112	5	16			.963	10	O-84,2-56/1	1.3
1909	Phi-A	149	541	61	152	28	14	5	69	35		.281	.332	.412	132	18	19			**.977**	-2	*O-149	1.2
1910	*Phi-A	151	560	70	168	28	18	4	64	31		.300	.338	.436	143	24	18			.974	-2	*O-151	1.7
1911	*Phi-A	141	508	104	167	27	11	6	66	50		.329	.398	.461	142	28	22			.961	6	*O-136/2-4	2.6
1912	Phi-A	36	130	27	42	6	2	2	20	16		.323	.401	.446	147	8	6			.891	-9	O-36	0.0
1913	Phi-A	40	59	3	19	5	1	0	6	4	8	.322	.365	.441	139	3	0			1.000	-2	/O-9	0.0
1914	Bro-F	52	161	16	49	9	4	2	32	17	16	.304	.374	.435	110	2	4			.986	1	O-46	0.1
1915	Bro-F	5	6	0	1	0	0	0	0	0	0	.167	.167	.167	-11	-1	0			1.000	-1	/2-1,O-1	-0.2
Total	16	1496	5399	705	1563	289	102	44	702	335	<u>24</u>	.289	.336	.405	123	137	193			.953	-24	2-839,O-612/1	11.0

■ DANNY MURPHY
Murphy, Daniel Francis   b: 8/23/42, Beverly, Mass.   BL/TR, 5'11", 185 lbs.   Deb: 6/18/60

YEAR	TM/L	G	AB	R	H	2B	3B	HR	RBI	BB	SO	AVG	OBP	SLG	PRO+	BR/A	SB	CS	SBR	FA	FR	G/POS	TPR
1960	Chi-N	31	75	7	9	2	0	1	6	4	13	.120	.175	.187	-1	-11	0	0	0	.976	-1	O-21	-1.3
1961	Chi-N	4	13	3	5	0	0	2	3	1	5	.385	.429	.846	225	2	0	0	0	1.000	0	/O-4	0.2
1962	Chi-N	14	35	5	7	1	0	1	3	1	9	.200	.243	.343	53	-2	0	0	0	1.000	-3	/O-5	-0.5
1969	Chi-A	17	1	0	0	0	0	0	0	2	0	.000	.667	.000	95	0	0	0	0	1.000	-0	P-17	0.0

YEAR	TM/L	G	AB	R	H	2B	3B	HR	RBI	BB	SO	AVG	OBP	SLG	PRO+	BR/A	SB	CS	SBR	FA	FR	G/POS	TPR
1970	Chi-A	51	6	3	2	0	0	0	1	2	2	.333	.500	.833	252	1	0	0	0	.933	-1	P-51	0.0
Total	5	117	130	18	23	5	1	4	13	11	29	.177	.246	.323	53	-9	0	0	0	.947	-4	/P-68,O-30	-1.6

■ **DANNY MURPHY**   Murphy, Daniel Joseph "Handsome Dan" b: 9/10/1864, Brooklyn, N.Y. d: 12/14/15, Brooklyn, N.Y. 156 lbs. Deb: 4/26/1892

YEAR	TM/L	G	AB	R	H	2B	3B	HR	RBI	BB	SO	AVG	OBP	SLG	PRO+	BR/A	SB	CS	SBR	FA	FR	G/POS	TPR
1892	NY-N	8	26	2	3	0	0	0	0	5	4	.115	.258	.115	14	-2	0			.900	-2	/C-8	-0.4

■ **DAVE MURPHY**   Murphy, David Francis "Dirty Dave" b: 5/4/1876, Adams, Mass. d: 4/8/40, Adams, Mass. TR, Deb: 8/28/05

YEAR	TM/L	G	AB	R	H	2B	3B	HR	RBI	BB	SO	AVG	OBP	SLG	PRO+	BR/A	SB	CS	SBR	FA	FR	G/POS	TPR
1905	Bos-N	3	11	0	2	0	0	0	1	0		.182	.182	.182	9	-1	0			1.000	-2	/S-2,3-1	-0.4

■ **DWAYNE MURPHY**   Murphy, Dwayne Keith b: 3/18/55, Merced, Cal. BL/TR, 6'1", 185 lbs. Deb: 4/8/78

YEAR	TM/L	G	AB	R	H	2B	3B	HR	RBI	BB	SO	AVG	OBP	SLG	PRO+	BR/A	SB	CS	SBR	FA	FR	G/POS	TPR
1978	Oak-A	60	52	15	10	2	0	0	5	7	14	.192	.288	.231	50	-3	0	1	-1	1.000	-10	O-45/D-5	-1.5
1979	Oak-A	121	388	57	99	10	4	11	40	84	80	.255	.389	.387	116	13	15	11	-2	.988	8	*O-118	1.3
1980	Oak-A	159	573	86	157	18	2	13	68	102	96	.274	.386	.380	119	19	26	15	-1	.990	24	*O-158	3.5
1981	*Oak-A	107	390	58	98	10	3	15	60	73	91	.251	.372	.408	131	18	10	4	1	.985	12	*O-106/D-1	2.8
1982	Oak-A	151	543	84	129	15	1	27	94	94	122	.238	.353	.418	116	14	26	8	3	.983	22	*O-147/S-1,D	3.4
1983	Oak-A	130	471	55	107	17	2	17	75	62	105	.227	.317	.380	97	-2	7	5	-1	.979	10	*O-124/D-7	0.3
1984	Oak-A	153	559	93	143	18	2	33	88	74	111	.256	.346	.472	133	24	4	5	-2	.988	21	*O-153	3.8
1985	Oak-A	152	523	77	122	21	3	20	59	84	123	.233	.343	.400	111	9	4	5	-2	.989	9	*O-150	1.1
1986	Oak-A	98	329	50	83	11	3	9	39	56	80	.252	.368	.386	114	8	3	1	0	.993	11	O-97/D-1	1.6
1987	Oak-A	82	219	39	51	7	0	8	35	58	61	.233	.394	.374	113	7	4	4	-1	.984	0	O-79/1-1,2	0.3
1988	Det-A	49	144	14	36	5	0	4	19	24	31	.250	.361	.368	109	2	1	1	-0	1.000	1	O-43/D-3	0.2
1989	Phi-N	98	156	20	34	5	0	9	27	29	44	.218	.341	.423	117	4	0	1	-1	.986	-6	O-52	-0.4
Total	12	1360	4347	648	1069	139	20	166	609	747	953	.246	.359	.402	116	113	100	61	-7	.987	102	*O-1272/D-18,21S	16.4

■ **ED MURPHY**   Murphy, Edward Joseph b: 8/23/18, Joliet, Ill. d: 12/10/91, Joliet, Ill. BR/TR, 5'11", 190 lbs. Deb: 9/10/42

YEAR	TM/L	G	AB	R	H	2B	3B	HR	RBI	BB	SO	AVG	OBP	SLG	PRO+	BR/A	SB	CS	SBR	FA	FR	G/POS	TPR
1942	Phi-N	13	28	2	7	2	0	0	4	2	4	.250	.300	.321	86	-1	0			1.000	-0	/1-8	-0.1

■ **FRANK MURPHY**   Murphy, Francis Patrick b: 4/16/1875, N.Tarrytown, N.Y. d: 11/2/12, Islip, N.Y. Deb: 7/2/01

YEAR	TM/L	G	AB	R	H	2B	3B	HR	RBI	BB	SO	AVG	OBP	SLG	PRO+	BR/A	SB	CS	SBR	FA	FR	G/POS	TPR
1901	Bos-N	45	176	13	46	5	3	1	18	4		.261	.282	.341	73	-7	6			.939	4	O-45	-0.6
	NY-N	35	130	10	21	3	0	0	8	6		.162	.199	.185	12	-15	2			.847	-10	2-23,O-12	-2.5
	Yr	80	306	23	67	8	3	1	26	10		.219	.246	.275	49	-20	8			.940	-6	O-57,2-23	-3.1

■ **TONY MURPHY**   Murphy, Frank J. b: Brooklyn, N.Y. Deb: 10/15/1884

YEAR	TM/L	G	AB	R	H	2B	3B	HR	RBI	BB	SO	AVG	OBP	SLG	PRO+	BR/A	SB	CS	SBR	FA	FR	G/POS	TPR
1884	NY-a	1	3	1	1	0	0	0		0		.333	.333	.333	121	0				1.000	-1	/C-1	-0.1

■ **DUMMY MURPHY**   Murphy, Herbert Courtland b: 12/18/1886, Olney, Ill. d: 8/10/62, Tallahassee, Fla. BR/TR, 5'10", 165 lbs. Deb: 4/14/14

YEAR	TM/L	G	AB	R	H	2B	3B	HR	RBI	BB	SO	AVG	OBP	SLG	PRO+	BR/A	SB	CS	SBR	FA	FR	G/POS	TPR
1914	Phi-N	9	26	1	4	1	0	0	3	0	4	.154	.185	.192	12	-3	0			.864	3	/S-9	0.1

■ **HOWARD MURPHY**   Murphy, Howard b: 1/1/1882, Birmingham, Ala. d: 10/5/26, Fort Worth, Tex. BL/TR, 5'8.5", 150 lbs. Deb: 8/4/09

YEAR	TM/L	G	AB	R	H	2B	3B	HR	RBI	BB	SO	AVG	OBP	SLG	PRO+	BR/A	SB	CS	SBR	FA	FR	G/POS	TPR
1909	StL-N	25	60	3	12	0	0	0	3	4		.200	.250	.200	42	-4	1			.925	-2	O-19	-0.7

■ **EDDIE MURPHY**   Murphy, John Edward b: 10/2/1891, Hancock, N.Y. d: 2/21/69, Dunmore, Pa. BL/TR, 5'9", 155 lbs. Deb: 8/26/12

YEAR	TM/L	G	AB	R	H	2B	3B	HR	RBI	BB	SO	AVG	OBP	SLG	PRO+	BR/A	SB	CS	SBR	FA	FR	G/POS	TPR
1912	Phi-A	33	142	24	45	4	1	0	6	11		.317	.370	.359	113	3	7			.947	0	O-33	0.1
1913	*Phi-A	137	508	105	150	14	7	1	30	70	44	.295	.391	.356	122	17	21			.942	-12	*O-135	-0.1
1914	*Phi-A	148	573	101	156	12	9	3	43	87	46	.272	.379	.340	121	19	36	32	-8	.941	-5	*O-148	-0.1
1915	Phi-A	68	260	37	60	3	4	0	17	29	15	.231	.315	.273	79	-6	13	3	2	.899	-3	O-58/3-6	-1.3
	Chi-A	70	273	51	86	11	5	0	26	39	12	.315	.410	.392	136	14	20	12	-1	.952	-1	O-70	0.9
	Yr	138	533	88	146	14	9	0	43	68	27	.274	.365	.334	109	8	33	15	1	.933	-6	*O-128/3-6	-0.4
1916	Chi-A	51	105	14	22	5	1	0	4	9	5	.210	.284	.276	68	-4	3			1.000	-3	O-24/3-1	-0.9
1917	Chi-A	53	51	9	16	2	1	0	16	5	1	.314	.386	.392	135	2	4			1.000	-4	/O-9	-0.2
1918	Chi-A	91	286	36	85	9	3	0	23	22	18	.297	.350	.350	110	3	6			.958	-10	O-63/2-8	-1.1
1919	*Chi-A	30	35	8	17	4	0	0	5	7	0	.486	.571	.600	228	7	0			.917	-0	/O-6	0.6
1920	Chi-A	58	118	22	40	2	1	0	19	12	4	.339	.405	.373	107	2	1	3	-2	.886	1	O-19/3-3	0.0
1921	Chi-A	6	5	1	1	0	0	0	0	0	0	.200	.200	.200	2	-1	0	0	0	.000	0	H	-0.1
1926	Pit-N	16	17	3	2	0	0	0	6	3	0	.118	.250	.118	2	-2	0			1.000	-0	/O-3	-0.3
Total	11	761	2373	411	680	66	32	4	195	294	145	.287	.374	.346	114	53	111	50		.942	-39	O-568/3-10,2	-2.5

■ **JOHN MURPHY**   Murphy, John Patrick b: 1879, New Haven, Conn. d: 4/20/49, Andover, Mass. 5'7.5", 160 lbs. Deb: 9/10/02

YEAR	TM/L	G	AB	R	H	2B	3B	HR	RBI	BB	SO	AVG	OBP	SLG	PRO+	BR/A	SB	CS	SBR	FA	FR	G/POS	TPR
1902	StL-N	1	3	1	2	1	0	0	1	1		.667	.750	1.000	458	1	0			1.000	-1	/3-1	0.1
1903	Det-A	5	22	1	4	1	0	0	1	0		.182	.182	.227	23	-2	0			.852	-1	/S-5	-0.3
Total	2	6	25	2	6	2	0	0	2	1		.240	.269	.320	79	-1	0			.852	-2	/S-5,3-1	-0.2

■ **LARRY MURPHY**   Murphy, Lawrence Patrick BL, Deb: 5/30/1891

YEAR	TM/L	G	AB	R	H	2B	3B	HR	RBI	BB	SO	AVG	OBP	SLG	PRO+	BR/A	SB	CS	SBR	FA	FR	G/POS	TPR
1891	Was-a	101	400	73	106	15	3	1	35	63	27	.265	.372	.325	104	6	29			.874	-5	*O-101	-0.3

■ **LEO MURPHY**   Murphy, Leo Joseph "Red" b: 1/7/1889, Terre Haute, Ind. d: 8/12/60, Racine, Wis. BR/TR, 6'1", 179 lbs. Deb: 5/2/15

YEAR	TM/L	G	AB	R	H	2B	3B	HR	RBI	BB	SO	AVG	OBP	SLG	PRO+	BR/A	SB	CS	SBR	FA	FR	G/POS	TPR
1915	Pit-N	31	41	4	4	0	0	0	4	4	12	.098	.178	.098	-16	-5	0			.932	-3	C-20	-0.9

■ **MIKE MURPHY**   Murphy, Michael Jerome b: 8/19/1888, Forestville, Pa. d: 10/26/52, Johnson City, N.Y. BR/TR, 5'9", 170 lbs. Deb: 5/17/12

YEAR	TM/L	G	AB	R	H	2B	3B	HR	RBI	BB	SO	AVG	OBP	SLG	PRO+	BR/A	SB	CS	SBR	FA	FR	G/POS	TPR
1912	StL-N	1	1	0	0	0	0	0	1	0	0	.000	.000	.000	-99	-0	0			.000	0	/C-1	0.0
1916	Phi-A	14	27	0	3	0	0	0	1	1	3	.111	.143	.111	-25	-4	0			.973	-3	/C-12	-0.8
Total	2	15	28	0	3	0	0	0	2	1	3	.107	.138	.107	-28	-4	0			.973	-3	/C-13	-0.8

■ **MORGAN MURPHY**   Murphy, Morgan Edward b: 2/14/1867, E.Providence, R.I. d: 10/3/38, Providence, R.I. BR/TR, 5'8", 160 lbs. Deb: 4/22/1890

YEAR	TM/L	G	AB	R	H	2B	3B	HR	RBI	BB	SO	AVG	OBP	SLG	PRO+	BR/A	SB	CS	SBR	FA	FR	G/POS	TPR
1890	Bos-P	68	246	38	56	10	2	2	32	24	31	.228	.301	.309	59	-15	16			.903	4	C-67/S-2,O3	-0.5
1891	Bos-a	106	402	60	87	11	4	4	54	36	58	.216	.289	.294	68	-18	17			**.954**	11	*C-104/O-4	0.2
1892	Cin-N	74	234	29	46	8	2	2	24	25	57	.197	.277	.274	68	-9	4			.955	0	C-74	-0.4
1893	Cin-N	57	200	25	47	5	1	1	19	14	35	.235	.295	.285	53	-14	1			.932	-5	C-56/1-1	-1.2
1894	Cin-N	75	255	42	70	9	0	1	37	26	34	.275	.344	.322	59	-17	0			.901	-4	C-74/S-1,3	-1.2
1895	Cin-N	25	82	15	22	2	0	0	16	11	8	.268	.355	.293	65	-4	6			.907	-3	C-25	-0.4
1896	StL-N	49	175	12	45	5	2	0	11	8	14	.257	.290	.309	60	-10	1			.926	-3	C-48	-0.6
1897	StL-N	62	207	13	35	2	0	0	12	6		.169	.196	.179	-1	-30	1			.950	-3	C-53/1-8	-2.4
1898	Pit-N	5	16	0	2	0	0	0	2	1		.125	.176	.125	-14	-2	0			.957	1	/C-5	-0.1
	Phi-N	25	86	6	17	3	0	0	11	6		.198	.258	.233	43	-6	0			.964	0	C-25	-0.4
	Yr	30	102	6	19	3	0	0	13	7		.186	.245	.216	34	-9	0			.963	2	C-30	-0.5
1900	Phi-N	11	36	2	10	0	1	0	3	3		.278	.278	.333	69	-2	0			.980	2	C-11	0.1
1901	Phi-A	9	28	5	6	1	0	0	6	0		.214	.214	.250	27	-3	1			.929	0	/C-8,1-1	-0.2
Total	11	566	1967	247	443	56	12	10	227	157	237	.225	.287	.281	54	-131	53			.936	2	C-550/1-10,OS3	-7.1

■ **PAT MURPHY**   Murphy, Patrick J. b: 1/2/1857, Auburn, Mass. d: 5/16/27, Worcester, Mass. TR, 5'10", 160 lbs. Deb: 9/2/1887

YEAR	TM/L	G	AB	R	H	2B	3B	HR	RBI	BB	SO	AVG	OBP	SLG	PRO+	BR/A	SB	CS	SBR	FA	FR	G/POS	TPR
1887	NY-N	17	56	4	12	2	0	0	4	2	4	.214	.241	.250	38	-5	1			.847	2	C-17	-0.1
1888	*NY-N	28	106	11	18	1	0	0	4	6	11	.170	.214	.179	27	-8	3			.913	3	C-28	-0.3
1889	NY-N	9	28	5	10	1	1	2	4	2	0	.357	.400	.571	170	2	0			.872	-2	/C-9	0.1
1890	NY-N	32	119	14	28	5	1	0	9	14	13	.235	.321	.294	79	-3	3			.905	-5	C-29/O-3,S	-0.5
Total	4	86	309	34	68	9	2	2	21	24	28	.220	.278	.272	64	-13	7			.895	-3	/C-83,O-3,S	-0.8

YEAR	TM/L	G	AB	R	H	2B	3B	HR	RBI	BB	SO	AVG	OBP	SLG	PRO+	BR/A	SB	CS	SBR	FA	FR	G/POS	TPR
■ **DICK MURPHY**						Murphy, Richard Lee		b: 10/25/31, Cincinnati, Ohio				BL/TL, 5'11", 170 lbs.		Deb: 6/13/54									
1954	Cin-N	6	1	1	0	0	0	0	0	0	1	.000	.000	.000	-97	-0	0	0	0	.000	0	H	0.0
■ **BUZZ MURPHY**						Murphy, Robert R.		b: 4/26/1895, Denver, Colo.		d: 5/11/38, Denver, Colo.		BL/TL, 5'8.5", 155 lbs.		Deb: 7/14/18									
1918	Bos-N	9	32	6	12	2	3	1	9	3	5	.375	.429	.719	259	6	0			1.000	-2	/O-9	0.4
1919	Was-A	79	252	19	66	7	4	0	28	19	32	.262	.326	.321	83	-5	5			.959	2	O-73	-0.9
Total	2	88	284	25	78	9	7	1	37	22	37	.275	.338	.366	101	0	5			.961	0	/O-82	-0.5
■ **BILLY MURPHY**						Murphy, William Eugene		b: 5/7/44, Pineville, La.		BR/TR, 6'1", 190 lbs.		Deb: 4/15/66										
1966	NY-N	84	135	15	31	4	1	3	13	7	34	.230	.273	.341	71	-5	1	2	-1	.955	-9	O-57	-1.8
■ **YALE MURPHY**						Murphy, William Henry "Tot" or "Midget"		b: 11/11/1869, Southville, Mass.		d: 2/14/06, Southville, Mass.		BL/TR, 5'3", 125 lbs.		Deb: 4/19/1894							
1894	*NY-N	74	280	64	76	6	2	0	28	51	23	.271	.384	.307	69	-12	28			.898	-1	S-49,O-20/321	-1.7
1895	NY-N	51	184	35	37	6	2	0	16	27	13	.201	.303	.255	46	-14	7			.944	-4	O-33/S-8,32	-1.7
1897	NY-N	5	8	1	0	0	0	0	1	2		.000	.200	.000	-46	-2	0			.800	-2	/S-3,2-2	-0.3
Total	3	130	472	100	113	12	4	0	45	80	36	.239	.350	.282	59	-28	35			.890	-17	/S-60,O-53,321	-3.7
■ **WILLIE MURPHY**						Murphy, William N. "Gentle Willie"		b: 1865, Boston, Mass.		BL, 5'11", 198 lbs.		Deb: 5/1/1884									
1884	Cle-N	42	168	18	38	3	3	1	9	1	23	.226	.231	.298	63	-7				.720	-5	O-42	-1.2
	Was-a	5	21	3	10	0	0	0		1		.476	.542	.476	266	4				.700	-0	/O-4,2-1	0.3
Total	1	47	189	21	48	3	3	1	9	2	23	.254	.269	.317	83	-3				.718	-5	/O-46,2-1	-0.9
■ **TONY MURRAY**						Murray, Anthony Joseph		b: 4/30/04, Chicago, Ill.		d: 3/19/74, Chicago, Ill.		BR/TR, 5'10.5", 154 lbs.		Deb: 10/6/23							
1923	Chi-N	2	4	0	1	0	0	0	0	0	0	.250	.400	.250	75	-0	0	0	0	1.000	-2	/O-2	-0.2
■ **EDDIE MURRAY**						Murray, Eddie Clarence		b: 2/24/56, Los Angeles, Cal.		BB/TR, 6'2", 200 lbs.		Deb: 4/7/77 F								
1977	Bal-A	160	611	81	173	29	2	27	88	48	104	.283	.336	.470	125	19	0	1	-1	.992	-4	*D-111,1-42/O	0.8
1978	Bal-A☆	161	610	85	174	32	3	27	95	70	97	.285	.360	.480	143	34	6	5	-1	.997	1	*1-157/3-3,D	2.4
1979	*Bal-A	159	606	90	179	30	2	25	99	72	78	.295	.372	.475	132	27	10	2	2	.994	-1	*1-157	1.7
1980	Bal-A	158	621	100	186	36	2	32	116	54	71	.300	.357	.519	138	31	7	2	1	.994	-9	*1-154/D-1	1.3
1981	Bal-A★	99	378	57	111	21	2	**22**	**78**	40	43	.294	.363	.534	156	26	2	3	-1	**.999**	10	1-99	3.0
1982	Bal-A★	151	550	87	174	30	1	32	110	70	82	.316	.395	.549	157	43	7	2	1	**.997**	1	*1-149/D-2	3.6
1983	*Bal-A★	156	582	115	178	30	3	33	111	86	90	.306	.398	.538	**158**	**47**	5	1	1	.993	4	*1-153/D-2	4.2
1984	Bal-A★	162	588	97	180	26	3	29	110	**107**	87	.306	**.415**	.509	157	**50**	10	2	2	.992	8	*1-159/D-3	4.9
1985	Bal-A★	156	583	111	173	37	1	31	124	84	68	.297	.387	.523	151	42	5	2	0	.987	13	*1-154/D-2	4.4
1986	Bal-A☆	137	495	61	151	25	1	17	84	78	49	.305	.400	.463	136	27	3	0	1	.989	-3	*1-119,D-16	1.6
1987	Bal-A	160	618	89	171	28	3	30	91	73	80	.277	.353	.477	121	18	1	2	-1	.993	12	*1-156/D-4	1.6
1988	Bal-A	161	603	75	171	27	2	28	84	75	78	.284	.363	.474	136	29	5	2	0	.989	10	*1-103,D-58	2.9
1989	LA-N	160	594	66	147	29	1	20	88	87	85	.247	.346	.401	115	13	7	2	1	**.996**	13	*1-159/3-2	1.5
1990	LA-N	155	558	96	184	22	3	26	95	82	64	.330	.417	.520	160	48	8	5	-1	.992	4	*1-150	4.1
1991	LA-N★	153	576	69	150	23	1	19	96	55	74	.260	.325	.403	106	4	10	3	1	.995	9	*1-149/3-1	0.4
1992	NY-N	156	551	64	144	37	2	16	93	66	74	.261	.340	.423	117	12	4	2	0	.991	-4	*1-154	-0.3
1993	NY-N	154	610	77	174	28	1	27	100	40	61	.285	.329	.467	112	8	2	2	-1	.988	-1	*1-154	-0.6
1994	Cle-A	108	433	57	110	21	1	17	76	31	53	.254	.304	.425	82	-13	8	4	0	.988	-2	D-82,1-26	-1.9
Total	18	2706	10167	1477	2930	511	34	458	1738	1218	1338	.288	.365	.480	133	463	100	42	5	.993	60	*1-2394,D-282/30	35.6
■ **ED MURRAY**						Murray, Edward Francis		b: 5/8/1895, Mystic, Conn.		d: 11/8/70, Cheyenne, Wyoming		BR/TR, 5'6", 145 lbs.		Deb: 6/24/17						
1917	StL-A	1	1	0	0	0	0	0	0	0	1	.000	.000	.000	-99	-0				.000	0	/S-1	0.0
■ **JIM MURRAY**						Murray, James Oscar		b: 1/16/1878, Galveston, Tex.		d: 4/25/45, Galveston, Tex.		BR/TL, 5'10", 180 lbs.		Deb: 9/2/02						
1902	Chi-N	12	47	3	8	0	0	0	1	2		.170	.204	.170	16	-5	0			1.000	-1	O-12	-0.6
1911	StL-A	31	102	8	19	5	0	3	11	5		.186	.224	.324	54	-7	0			.935	-0	O-25	-0.8
1914	Bos-N	39	112	10	26	4	2	0	12	6	24	.232	.277	.304	73	-4	2			.941	-8	O-32	-1.4
Total	3	82	261	21	53	9	2	3	24	13	24	.203	.244	.287	56	-16	2			.949	-9	/O-69	-2.8
■ **MIAH MURRAY**						Murray, Jeremiah J.		b: 1/1/1865, Boston, Mass.		d: 1/11/22, Boston, Mass.		BR/TR, 5'11.5", 170 lbs.		Deb: 5/17/1884 U					
1884	Pro-N	8	27	1	5	0	0	0	1	1	8	.185	.214	.185	28	-2				.836	-4	/C-7,O-1,1	-0.6
1885	Lou-a	12	43	4	8	0	0	0		2		.186	.239	.186	36	-3				.863	1	C-12/1-2	-0.1
1888	Was-N	12	42	1	4	1	0	0	3	1	7	.095	.116	.119	-26	-6	0			.912	-0	C-10/1-2	-0.5
1891	Was-a	2	8	0	0	0	0	0		0	1	.000	.000	.000	-99	-2	0			1.000	3	/C-2	0.1
Total	4	34	120	6	17	1	0	0	4	4	16	.142	.176	.150	3	-13	0			.884	-1	/C-31,1-5,O	-1.1
■ **RED MURRAY**						Murray, John Joseph		b: 3/4/1884, Arnot, Pa.		d: 12/4/58, Sayre, Pa.		BR/TR, 5'10.5", 190 lbs.		Deb: 6/16/06						
1906	StL-N	46	144	18	37	9	7	1	16	9		.257	.305	.438	137	5	5			.962	-3	O-34/C-7	0.2
1907	StL-N	132	485	46	127	10	10	7	46	24		.262	.301	.367	113	5	23			.935	5	*O-131	0.5
1908	StL-N	154	593	64	167	19	15	7	62	37		.282	.332	.400	140	24	48			.914	-4	*O-154	1.6
1909	NY-N	149	570	74	150	15	12	**7**	91	45		.263	.319	.368	112	6	48			.947	3	*O-149	0.4
1910	NY-N	149	553	78	153	27	8	4	87	52	51	.277	.345	.376	110	7	57			.948	4	*O-148	0.4
1911	*NY-N	140	488	70	142	27	15	3	78	43	37	.291	.354	.426	114	8	48			.954	-11	*O-131	-0.9
1912	*NY-N	143	549	83	152	26	20	3	92	27	45	.277	.320	.413	97	-5	38			**.968**	2	*O-143	-1.0
1913	*NY-N	147	520	70	139	21	3	2	59	34	21	.267	.320	.331	85	-10	35			.965	10	*O-147	-0.7
1914	NY-N	86	139	19	31	6	3	0	23	9	7	.223	.270	.309	75	-5	11			1.000	-14	O-49	-1.7
1915	NY-N	45	127	12	28	1	2	3	11	7	15	.220	.261	.331	83	-3	2	3	-1	.959	-1	O-34	-0.7
	Chi-N	51	144	20	43	6	1	0	11	8	8	.299	.340	.354	110	2	6	5	-1	.966	1	O-40/2-1	0.0
	Yr	96	271	32	71	7	3	3	22	15	23	.262	.303	.343	98	-1	8	8	-2	.963	1	O-74/2-1	-0.7
1917	NY-N	22	22	1	1	1	0	0	3	4	3	.045	.192	.091	-12	-3	0			1.000	-3	O-11/C-1	-0.7
Total	11	1264	4334	555	1170	168	96	37	579	299	194	.270	.323	.379	108	30	321	8		.950	-6	*O-1171/C-8,2	-2.6
■ **LARRY MURRAY**						Murray, Larry		b: 4/1/53, Chicago, Ill.		BB/TR, 5'11", 179 lbs.		Deb: 9/7/74							
1974	NY-A	6	1	1	0	0	0	0	0	0	0	.000	.000	.000	-99	-0	0	1	-1	1.000	-2	/O-3	-0.3
1975	NY-A	6	1	1	0	0	0	0	0	0	0	.000	.000	.000	-99	-0	0	0	0	1.000	-2	/O-4	-0.2
1976	NY-A	8	10	2	1	0	0	0	2	1	2	.100	.182	.100	-16	-1	2	0	1	1.000	-1	/O-7	-0.2
1977	Oak-A	90	162	19	29	5	2	1	9	17	36	.179	.257	.253	40	-13	12	3	2	.992	-13	O-78/S-1,D	-2.6
1978	Oak-A	11	12	1	1	0	0	0	0	3	2	.083	.267	.083	3	-1	0	0	0	1.000	-1	/O-6	-0.3
1979	Oak-A	105	226	25	42	11	2	2	20	28	34	.186	.276	.279	53	-15	6	6	-2	.963	4	O-90/2-3	-2.0
Total	6	226	412	49	73	16	4	3	31	49	74	.177	.265	.257	44	-32	20	10	0	.975	-20	O-188/2-3,DS	-5.6
■ **RAY MURRAY**						Murray, Raymond Lee "Deacon"		b: 10/12/17, Spring Hope, N.C.		BR/TR, 6'3", 204 lbs.		Deb: 4/25/48						
1948	Cle-A	4	4	0	0	0	0	0	0	0	0	.000	.000	.000	-99	-1	0	0	0	.000	0	H	-0.1
1950	Cle-A	55	139	16	38	8	2	1	13	12	13	.273	.331	.381	85	-4	1	0	0	.972	-5	C-45	-0.6
1951	Cle-A	1	1	0	1	0	0	0	1	0	0	1.000	1.000	1.000	468	1	0	0	0	1.000	1	/C-1	0.1
	Phi-A	40	122	10	26	6	0	0	13	14	14	.213	.294	.262	50	-8	0	0	0	.985	-3	C-39	-0.9
	Yr	41	123	10	27	6	0	0	14	14	14	.220	.299	.268	53	-8	0	0	0	.986	-2	C-40	-0.8
1952	Phi-A	44	136	14	28	5	0	4	14	9	13	.206	.255	.265	42	-11	0	0	0	.995	7	C-42	-0.1
1953	Phi-A	84	268	25	76	14	3	6	41	18	25	.284	.331	.425	99	-1	0	0	0	.989	4	C-78	0.6

YEAR	TM/L	G	AB	R	H	2B	3B	HR	RBI	BB	SO	AVG	OBP	SLG	PRO+	BR/A	SB	CS	SBR	FA	FR	G/POS	TPR
1954	Bal-A	22	61	4	15	4	1	2	2	2	5	.246	.270	.344	73	-3	0	0	0	.989	1	C-21	-0.1
Total	6	250	731	69	184	37	6	8	80	55	67	.252	.305	.352	75	-27	1	0	0	.987	6	C-226	-1.1

■ RICH MURRAY
Murray, Richard Dale   b: 7/6/57, Los Angeles, Cal.   BR/TR, 6'4", 195 lbs.   Deb: 6/7/80   F

YEAR	TM/L	G	AB	R	H	2B	3B	HR	RBI	BB	SO	AVG	OBP	SLG	PRO+	BR/A	SB	CS	SBR	FA	FR	G/POS	TPR
1980	SF-N	53	194	19	42	8	2	4	24	11	48	.216	.259	.340	67	-9	2	1	0	.987	0	1-53	-1.3
1983	SF-N	4	10	0	2	0	0	0	1	0	3	.200	.200	.200	11	-1	0	0	0	1.000	-0	/1-3	-0.2
Total	2	57	204	19	44	8	2	4	25	11	51	.216	.256	.333	65	-10	2	1	0	.988	0	/1-56	-1.5

■ BOBBY MURRAY
Murray, Robert Hayes   b: 7/4/1894, St.Albans, Vt.   d: 1/4/79, Nashua, N.H.   BL/TR, 5'7", 155 lbs.   Deb: 9/24/23

YEAR	TM/L	G	AB	R	H	2B	3B	HR	RBI	BB	SO	AVG	OBP	SLG	PRO+	BR/A	SB	CS	SBR	FA	FR	G/POS	TPR
1923	Was-A	10	37	2	7	1	0	0	2	1	4	.189	.211	.216	13	-5	1	0	0	1.000	2	3-10	-0.1

■ TOM MURRAY
Murray, Thomas W.   b: 1866, Savannah, Ga.   Deb: 6/20/1894

YEAR	TM/L	G	AB	R	H	2B	3B	HR	RBI	BB	SO	AVG	OBP	SLG	PRO+	BR/A	SB	CS	SBR	FA	FR	G/POS	TPR
1894	Phi-N	1	2	0	0	0	0	0	0	0	2	.000	.000	.000	-99	-1	0			.833	0	/S-1	0.0

■ BILL MURRAY
Murray, William Allenwood "Dasher"   b: 9/6/1893, Vinalhaven, Me.   d: 9/14/43, Boston, Mass.   BB/TR, 5'11", 165 lbs.   Deb: 6/27/17

YEAR	TM/L	G	AB	R	H	2B	3B	HR	RBI	BB	SO	AVG	OBP	SLG	PRO+	BR/A	SB	CS	SBR	FA	FR	G/POS	TPR
1917	Was-A	8	21	2	3	0	1	0	4	2	2	.143	.217	.238	39	-2	1			.889	-2	/2-6,S-1	-0.3

■ IVAN MURRELL
Murrell, Ivan Augustus (Peters)   b: 4/24/45, Almirante, Panama   BR/TR, 6'2", 196 lbs.   Deb: 9/28/63

YEAR	TM/L	G	AB	R	H	2B	3B	HR	RBI	BB	SO	AVG	OBP	SLG	PRO+	BR/A	SB	CS	SBR	FA	FR	G/POS	TPR
1963	Hou-N	2	5	1	1	0	0	0	0	0	2	.200	.200	.200	17	-1	0	0	0	1.000	-0	/O-2	-0.1
1964	Hou-N	10	14	1	2	1	0	0	1	0	6	.143	.143	.214	-1	-2	0	0	0	1.000	-1	/O-6	-0.3
1967	Hou-N	10	29	2	9	0	0	0	1	1	9	.310	.333	.310	88	-0	1	0	0	.846	-0	/O-6	-0.1
1968	Hou-N	32	59	3	6	1	1	0	3	1	17	.102	.117	.153	-20	-9	0	0	0	.931	2	O-15	-0.9
1969	SD-N	111	247	19	63	10	6	3	25	11	65	.255	.292	.381	91	-4	3	4	-2	.959	-3	O-72/1-2	-1.2
1970	SD-N	125	347	43	85	9	3	12	35	17	93	.245	.288	.392	84	-10	9	7	-2	.970	3	*O-101/1-1	-1.2
1971	SD-N	103	255	23	60	6	3	7	24	7	60	.235	.264	.365	82	-8	5	2	0	.978	0	O-72	-1.1
1972	SD-N	5	7	0	1	0	0	0	1	0	3	.143	.143	.143	-20	-1	0	0	0	1.000	-0	/O-1	-0.1
1973	SD-N	93	210	23	48	13	1	9	21	2	52	.229	.236	.429	87	-6	2	0	1	.959	-1	O-37,1-24	-0.9
1974	Atl-N	73	133	11	33	1	1	2	12	5	35	.248	.275	.316	62	-7	0	0	0	.983	-1	O-32,1-13	-1.0
Total	10	564	1306	126	308	41	15	33	123	44	342	.236	.266	.366	77	-46	20	13	-2	.965	-2	O-343/1-40	-6.9

■ DANNY MURTAUGH
Murtaugh, Daniel Edward   b: 10/8/17, Chester, Pa.   d: 12/2/76, Chester, Pa.   BR/TR, 5'9", 165 lbs.   Deb: 7/6/41   MC

YEAR	TM/L	G	AB	R	H	2B	3B	HR	RBI	BB	SO	AVG	OBP	SLG	PRO+	BR/A	SB	CS	SBR	FA	FR	G/POS	TPR
1941	Phi-N	85	347	34	76	8	1	0	11	26	31	.219	.275	.248	50	-23	**18**			.978	2	2-85/S-1	-1.5
1942	Phi-N	144	506	48	122	16	4	0	27	49	39	.241	.311	.289	80	-12	13			.939	6	S-60,3-53,2	0.0
1943	Phi-N	113	451	65	123	17	4	1	35	57	23	.273	.357	.335	104	4	4			.974	0	*2-113	1.2
1946	Phi-N	6	19	1	4	1	0	1	3	2	2	.211	.286	.421	102	-0	0			.958	-4	/2-6	-0.4
1947	Bos-N	3	8	0	1	0	0	0	0	1	2	.125	.222	.125	-6	-1	0			1.000	-0	/2-2,3-2	-0.1
1948	Pit-N	146	514	56	149	21	5	1	71	60	40	.290	.365	.356	94	-2	10			.979	1	*2-146	0.7
1949	Pit-N	75	236	16	48	7	2	2	24	29	17	.203	.291	.275	51	-16	2			.975	3	2-74	-1.0
1950	Pit-N	118	367	34	108	20	5	2	37	47	42	.294	.376	.392	99	1	2			.976	3	*2-108	0.8
1951	Pit-N	77	151	9	30	7	0	1	11	16	19	.199	.284	.265	47	-11	0	0	0	.970	-2	2-65/3-3	-1.2
Total	9	767	2599	263	661	97	21	8	219	287	215	.254	.331	.317	81	-61	49	<u>0</u>		.975	10	2-631/S-61,3	-1.5

■ TONY MUSER
Muser, Anthony Joseph   b: 8/1/47, Van Nuys, Cal.   BL/TL, 6'2", 190 lbs.   Deb: 9/14/69   C

YEAR	TM/L	G	AB	R	H	2B	3B	HR	RBI	BB	SO	AVG	OBP	SLG	PRO+	BR/A	SB	CS	SBR	FA	FR	G/POS	TPR
1969	Bos-A	2	9	0	1	0	0	0	1	1	1	.111	.200	.111	-10	-1	0	0	0	1.000	1	/1-2	-0.1
1971	Chi-A	11	16	2	5	0	1	0	0	1	1	.313	.353	.438	119	0	0	0	0	.963	0	/1-4	-0.1
1972	Chi-A	44	61	6	17	2	2	1	9	2	6	.279	.302	.426	113	1	1	1	-0	.986	-1	1-29/O-1	-0.1
1973	Chi-A	109	309	38	88	14	3	4	30	33	36	.285	.354	.388	105	3	8	4	0	.992	-3	1-89/D-15,O	-0.6
1974	Chi-A	103	206	16	60	5	1	1	18	6	22	.291	.315	.340	86	-4	1	4	-2	.998	-4	1-80,D-13	-1.3
1975	Chi-A	43	111	11	27	3	0	0	6	7	8	.243	.288	.270	58	-6	2	1	0	.993	2	1-41	-0.6
	Bal-A	80	82	11	26	3	0	0	11	8	9	.317	.378	.354	115	2	0	0	0	.996	1	1-62	0.2
	Yr	123	193	22	53	6	0	0	17	15	17	.275	.327	.306	83	-4	2	1	0	.994	3	*1-103	-0.4
1976	Bal-A	136	326	25	74	7	1	1	30	21	34	.227	.274	.264	62	-16	1	1	-0	.991	1	*1-109,O-12,D	-2.2
1977	Bal-A	120	118	14	27	6	0	0	7	13	16	.229	.305	.280	65	-6	1	2	-1	.992	1	1-77,O-11/D	-0.6
1978	Mil-A	15	30	0	4	1	1	0	5	3	5	.133	.212	.233	25	-3	0	0	0	.988	-0	1-12	-0.4
Total	9	663	1268	123	329	41	9	7	117	95	138	.259	.312	.323	82	-30	14	13	-4	.992	-1	1-505/D-37,O	-5.6

■ STAN MUSIAL
Musial, Stanley Frank "Stan The Man"   b: 11/21/20, Donora, Pa.   BL/TL, 6', 175 lbs.   Deb: 9/17/41   H

YEAR	TM/L	G	AB	R	H	2B	3B	HR	RBI	BB	SO	AVG	OBP	SLG	PRO+	BR/A	SB	CS	SBR	FA	FR	G/POS	TPR
1941	StL-N	12	47	8	20	4	0	1	7	2	1	.426	.449	.574	175	4	1			1.000	0	O-11	0.4
1942	*StL-N	140	467	87	147	32	10	10	72	62	25	.315	.397	.490	148	28	6			.984	1	*O-135	2.5
1943	*StL-N★	157	617	108	**220**	48	**20**	13	81	72	18	**.357**	**.425**	**.562**	176	60	9			.982	11	*O-155	**6.4**
1944	*StL-N★	146	568	112	**197**	51	14	12	94	90	28	.347	.440	.549	174	59	7			.987	3	*O-146	5.4
1946	*StL-N★	156	624	**124**	**228**	50	**20**	16	103	73	31	.365	.434	.587	180	65	7			.989	-1	*1-114,O-42	5.7
1947	StL-N★	149	587	113	183	30	13	19	95	80	24	.312	.398	.504	132	28	4			.994	-7	*1-149	1.5
1948	StL-N★	155	611	**135**	**230**	46	18	39	**131**	79	34	**.376**	**.450**	**.702**	196	81	7			.981	-8	*O-155/1-2	6.3
1949	StL-N★	157	612	128	**207**	41	**13**	36	123	107	38	.338	**.438**	.624	174	65	3			**.991**	-19	*O-156/1-1	3.8
1950	StL-N★	146	555	105	192	41	7	28	109	87	36	.346	.437	.596	161	51	5			.964	-13	O-77,1-69	3.2
1951	StL-N★	152	578	**124**	205	30	**12**	32	108	98	40	**.355**	.449	.614	182	69	4	5	-2	.974	4	O-91,1-60	6.4
1952	StL-N★	154	578	**105**	**194**	42	6	21	91	96	29	**.336**	.432	.538	167	56	7	7	-2	.987	-7	*O-129,1-25/P	4.2
1953	StL-N★	157	593	127	200	**53**	9	30	113	**105**	32	.337	**.437**	.609	169	63	3	4	-2	.984	-9	*O-157	4.4
1954	StL-N★	153	591	**120**	195	41	9	35	126	103	39	.330	.433	.607	166	60	1	7	-4	**.990**	-2	*O-152,1-10	4.6
1955	StL-N★	154	562	97	179	30	5	33	108	80	39	.319	.411	.566	156	47	5	4	-1	.992	1	*1-110,O-51	3.8
1956	StL-N★	156	594	87	184	33	6	27	**109**	75	39	.310	.390	.522	142	36	2	0	1	.993	1	*1-103,O-53	3.3
1957	StL-N★	134	502	82	176	38	3	29	102	66	34	**.351**	**.428**	.612	172	52	1	1	-0	.992	2	*1-130	4.5
1958	StL-N★	135	472	64	159	35	2	17	62	72	26	.337	.426	.528	145	33	0	0	0	.989	8	*1-124	3.4
1959	StL-N★	115	341	37	87	13	2	14	44	60	34	.255	.367	.428	104	3	0	2	-1	.990	-1	1-90/O-3	-0.1
1960	StL-N★	116	331	49	91	17	1	17	63	41	34	.275	.358	.486	118	8	1	1	0	.990	-1	O-59,1-29	0.3
1961	StL-N★	123	372	46	107	22	4	15	70	52	35	.288	.376	.489	116	9	0	0	0	**.994**	0	*O-103	0.3
1962	StL-N★	135	433	57	143	18	1	19	82	64	46	.330	.420	.508	135	23	3	0	1	.977	-3	*O-119	1.4
1963	StL-N★	124	337	34	86	10	2	12	58	35	43	.255	.329	.404	100	7	2	0	-1	.968	-7	O-96	-1.1
Total	22	3026	10972	1949	3630	725	177	475	1951	1599	696	.331	.418	.559	157	899	78	<u>31</u>		.984	-38	*O-1890,1-1016/P	70.5

■ DANNY MUSSER
Musser, William Daniel   b: 9/5/05, Zion, Pa.   BL/TR, 5'9.5", 160 lbs.   Deb: 9/18/32

YEAR	TM/L	G	AB	R	H	2B	3B	HR	RBI	BB	SO	AVG	OBP	SLG	PRO+	BR/A	SB	CS	SBR	FA	FR	G/POS	TPR
1932	Was-A	1	2	0	1	0	0	0	0	0	0	.500	.500	.500	162	0	0	0	0	.000	0	/3-1	0.0

■ GEORGE MYATT
Myatt, George Edward "Mercury', "Stud" or "Foghorn"   b: 6/14/14, Denver, Colo.   BL/TR, 5'11", 167 lbs.   Deb: 8/16/38   MC

YEAR	TM/L	G	AB	R	H	2B	3B	HR	RBI	BB	SO	AVG	OBP	SLG	PRO+	BR/A	SB	CS	SBR	FA	FR	G/POS	TPR
1938	NY-N	43	170	27	52	2	1	3	10	14	13	.306	.362	.382	104	1	10			.919	7	S-24,3-19	1.1
1939	NY-N	22	53	7	10	2	0	0	3	6	6	.189	.271	.226	35	-5	2			.907	1	3-14	-0.4
1943	Was-A	42	53	11	13	3	0	0	3	13	7	.245	.394	.302	109	1	3	0	1	.930	-1	2-11/S-2,3	0.2
1944	Was-A	140	538	86	153	19	6	0	40	54	44	.284	.357	.342	105	5	26	10	2	.957	-22	*2-121,S-15/O	-0.8
1945	Was-A	133	490	81	145	17	7	1	39	63	43	.296	.378	.365	127	18	30	11	2	.972	-19	2-94,O-32/3S	0.6
1946	Was-A	15	34	7	8	1	0	0	4	2	3	.235	.297	.265	61	-2	1	1	-0	.900	-2	/3-7,2-2	-0.4
1947	Was-A	12	7	1	0	0	0	0	0	4	4	.000	.364	.000	61	-1	0	0	0	1.000	0	/2-1	-0.1
Total	7	407	1345	220	381	44	14	4	99	156	120	.283	.362	.346	108	19	72	<u>22</u>		.962	-35	2-229/3-48,SO	0.2

GLENN MYATT — Myatt, Glenn Calvin b: 7/9/1897, Argenta, Ark. d: 8/9/69, Houston, Tex. BL/TR, 5'11", 165 lbs. Deb: 4/15/20

YEAR	TM/L	G	AB	R	H	2B	3B	HR	RBI	BB	SO	AVG	OBP	SLG	PRO+	BR/A	SB	CS	SBR	FA	FR	G/POS	TPR
1920	Phi-A	70	196	14	49	8	3	0	18	12	22	.250	.293	.321	62	-11	1	3	-2	.900	-5	O-37,C-22	-1.9
1921	Phi-A	44	69	6	14	2	0	0	5	6	7	.203	.267	.232	28	-7	1	0	0	.939	2	C-27	-0.4
1923	Cle-A	92	220	36	63	7	6	3	40	16	18	.286	.338	.414	97	-2	0	2	-1	.934	-8	C-69	-0.8
1924	Cle-A	105	342	55	117	22	7	8	73	33	12	.342	.402	.518	134	16	6	1	1	.978	-15	C-95	0.8
1925	Cle-A	106	358	51	97	15	9	11	54	29	24	.271	.329	.455	97	-4	3	1	0	.973	-18	C-98/O-1	-1.5
1926	Cle-A	56	117	14	29	5	2	0	13	13	13	.248	.323	.325	69	-5	1	0	0	1.000	-1	C-35	-0.4
1927	Cle-A	55	94	15	23	6	0	2	8	12	7	.245	.336	.372	83	-2	1	1	-0	.978	2	C-26	0.0
1928	Cle-A	58	125	9	36	7	2	1	15	13	13	.288	.355	.400	97	-0	0	2	-1	.967	-9	C-30	-0.8
1929	Cle-A	59	129	14	30	4	1	1	17	7	5	.233	.277	.302	47	-10	0	1	-1	.976	-1	C-41	-0.9
1930	Cle-A	86	265	30	78	23	2	2	37	18	17	.294	.342	.419	88	-5	2	3	-1	.977	-7	C-53	-0.6
1931	Cle-A	65	195	21	48	14	2	1	29	21	13	.246	.319	.354	73	-8	2	1	0	.991	-4	C-65	-0.8
1932	Cle-A	82	252	45	62	12	1	8	46	27	21	.246	.326	.397	81	-8	2	2	-1	.988	-8	C-65	-1.2
1933	Cle-A	40	77	10	18	4	0	0	7	15	8	.234	.372	.286	73	-2	0	1	-1	.965	-1	C-27	-0.2
1934	Cle-A	36	107	18	34	6	1	0	12	13	5	.318	.392	.393	101	1	1	0	0	.980	-1	C-34	0.2
1935	Cle-A	10	36	1	3	1	0	0	2	4	3	.083	.175	.111	-24	-7	0	0	0	1.000	-1	C-10	-0.7
	NY-N	13	18	2	4	0	1	1	6	0	3	.222	.222	.500	90	-0	0			1.000	-1	/C-4	-0.1
1936	Det-A	27	78	5	17	1	0	0	6	3	3	.218	.299	.231	32	-8	0	0		1.000	-2	C-27	-0.8
Total	16	1004	2678	346	722	137	37	38	387	248	195	.270	.334	.391	85	-63	20	18		.974	-78	C-734/O-38	-10.1

BUDDY MYER — Myer, Charles Solomon b: 3/16/04, Ellisville, Miss. d: 10/31/74, Baton Rouge, La. BL/TR, 5'10.5", 163 lbs. Deb: 9/26/25

YEAR	TM/L	G	AB	R	H	2B	3B	HR	RBI	BB	SO	AVG	OBP	SLG	PRO+	BR/A	SB	CS	SBR	FA	FR	G/POS	TPR
1925	*Was-A	4	8	1	2	0	0	0	0	0	1	.250	.250	.250	28	-1	0	0		1.000	-2	/S-4	-0.3
1926	Was-A	132	434	66	132	18	6	1	62	45	19	.304	.370	.380	98	-0	10	11	-4	.928	-18	*S-118/3-8	-1.0
1927	Was-A	15	51	7	11	1	0	0	7	8	3	.216	.322	.235	47	-4	3	1	0	.933	-3	S-15	-0.4
	Bos-A	133	469	59	135	22	11	2	47	48	15	.288	.359	.394	97	-2	9	5	-0	.940	7	*S-101,3-14,O/2	1.0
	Yr	148	520	66	146	23	11	2	54	56	18	.281	.355	.379	92	-5	12	6	0	.939	4	*S-116,3-14,O/2	1.0
1928	Bos-A	147	536	78	168	26	6	1	44	53	28	.313	.379	.390	104	5	**30**	16	-1	.967	4	*3-144	1.5
1929	Was-A	141	563	80	169	29	10	3	82	63	33	.300	.373	.403	99	-0	18	7	1	.958	-15	2-88,3-53	-0.7
1930	Was-A	138	541	97	164	18	8	2	61	58	31	.303	.373	.377	90	-6	14	11	-2	.965	-19	*2-134/O-2	-1.8
1931	Was-A	139	591	114	173	33	11	4	56	58	42	.293	.360	.406	100	1	11	14	-5	**.984**	-17	*2-137	-1.1
1932	Was-A	143	577	120	161	38	16	5	52	69	33	.279	.360	.426	104	4	12	7	-1	.975	-18	*2-139	-0.7
1933	*Was-A	131	530	95	160	29	15	4	61	60	29	.302	.374	.436	115	12	6	8	-3	.978	-1	*2-129	1.4
1934	Was-A	139	524	103	160	33	8	3	57	102	31	.305	.419	.416	121	21	6	6	-2	.975	-13	*2-135	1.4
1935	Was-A☆	151	616	115	215	36	11	5	100	96	40	**.349**	.440	.468	139	41	7	6	-2	.979	-13	*2-151	5.4
1936	Was-A	51	156	31	42	5	2	0	15	42	11	.269	.427	.327	94	1	7	2	1	.985	3	*2-43	0.8
1937	Was-A☆	125	430	54	126	16	10	1	65	78	41	.293	.407	.384	105	7	2	6	-3	.966	-17	*2-119/O-1	-0.4
1938	Was-A	127	437	79	147	22	8	6	71	93	32	.336	.454	.465	140	33	9	5	-0	**.982**	2	*2-121	3.7
1939	Was-A	83	258	33	78	10	3	1	32	40	18	.302	.396	.376	106	4	4	1	1	.968	-1	2-65	0.7
1940	Was-A	71	210	28	61	14	4	0	29	34	10	.290	.389	.395	111	5	6	3	0	.967	4	2-54	1.1
1941	Was-A	53	107	14	27	3	1	0	9	18	10	.252	.360	.299	80	-2	2	0	1	.982	-8	2-24	-0.8
Total	17	1923	7038	1174	2131	353	130	38	850	965	428	.303	.389	.406	108	120	156	109	-19	.974	-103	*2-1340,S-238,3/O	10.2

GEORGE MYERS — Myers, George D. b: 11/13/1860, Buffalo, N.Y. d: 12/14/26, Buffalo, N.Y. BR/TR, 5'8", 170 lbs. Deb: 5/2/1884

YEAR	TM/L	G	AB	R	H	2B	3B	HR	RBI	BB	SO	AVG	OBP	SLG	PRO+	BR/A	SB	CS	SBR	FA	FR	G/POS	TPR
1884	Buf-N	78	325	34	59	9	2	2	32	13	33	.182	.213	.240	41	-22				.837	-10	C-49,O-34	-2.6
1885	Buf-N	89	326	40	67	7	2	0	19	23	40	.206	.258	.239	60	-14				.899	-6	C-69,O-23	-1.4
1886	StL-N	79	295	26	56	7	3	0	27	18	42	.190	.236	.234	46	-18	6			.928	-13	C-72/O-6,3	-2.1
1887	Ind-N	69	235	25	51	8	1	1	20	22	7	.217	.298	.272	62	-11	26			.929	-13	C-50,O-15/13	-1.7
1888	Ind-N	66	248	36	59	9	0	2	16	16	14	.238	.292	.298	87	-3	28			.929	-8	C-47,3-14,O/1	-0.7
1889	Ind-N	43	149	22	29	3	0	0	12	11	13	.195	.294	.215	42	-11	12			.909	4	O-23,C-18/1	-0.3
Total	6	424	1578	183	321	43	8	5	126	109	149	.203	.260	.250	56	-80	72			.901	-46	C-305,O-111/31	-9.0

GREG MYERS — Myers, Gregory Richard b: 4/14/66, Riverside, Cal. BL/TR, 6'1", 200 lbs. Deb: 9/12/87

YEAR	TM/L	G	AB	R	H	2B	3B	HR	RBI	BB	SO	AVG	OBP	SLG	PRO+	BR/A	SB	CS	SBR	FA	FR	G/POS	TPR
1987	Tor-A	7	9	1	1	0	0	0	0	0	3	.111	.111	.111	-40	-2	0	0	0	1.000	2	/C-7	0.0
1989	Tor-A	17	44	0	5	2	0	0	1	2	9	.114	.152	.159	-12	-7	0	1	-1	1.000	4	C-11/D-6	-0.5
1990	Tor-A	87	250	33	59	7	1	5	22	22	33	.236	.298	.332	75	-9	0	1	-1	.993	-0	C-87	-0.5
1991	Tor-A	107	309	25	81	22	0	8	36	21	45	.262	.309	.411	94	-3	0	0	0	.979	-4	*C-104	-0.3
1992	Tor-A	22	61	4	14	6	0	1	13	5	5	.230	.288	.377	81	-2	0	0	0	.991	0	C-18/D-1	0.0
	Cal-A	8	17	0	4	1	0	0	0	3	6	.235	.235	.294	47	-1	0	0	0	1.000	2	/C-8	0.1
	Yr	30	78	4	18	7	0	1	13	5	11	.231	.277	.359	74	-3	0	0	0	.993	2	C-26/D-1	0.1
1993	Cal-A	108	290	27	74	10	0	7	40	17	47	.255	.301	.362	75	-11	3	3	-2	.986	-8	C-97/D-2	-1.5
1994	Cal-A	45	126	10	31	6	0	2	8	10	27	.246	.301	.341	63	-7	0	2	-1	.991	-1	C-41/D-1	-0.7
Total	7	401	1106	100	269	54	1	23	120	77	175	.243	.294	.356	75	-41	3	7	-3	.987	-8	C-373/D-10	-3.4

HENRY MYERS — Myers, Henry C. b: 5/1858, Philadelphia, Pa. d: 4/18/1895, Philadelphia, Pa. BR/TR, 5'9", 159 lbs. Deb: 8/20/1881 M

YEAR	TM/L	G	AB	R	H	2B	3B	HR	RBI	BB	SO	AVG	OBP	SLG	PRO+	BR/A	SB	CS	SBR	FA	FR	G/POS	TPR
1881	Pro-N	1	4	0	0	0	0	0	0	0	0	.000	.000	.000	-99	-1				1.000	-0	/S-1	-0.1
1882	Bal-a	69	294	43	53	3	0	0	0	0	12	.180	.212	.190	40	-17				.822	-7	*S-68/P-6M	-1.8
1884	Wil-U	6	24	3	3	0	0	0	0	0	0	.125	.125	.125	-31	-4				.875	4	/S-5,2-1	0.0
Total	3	76	322	46	56	3	0	0	0	12	2	.174	.204	.183	31	-22				.826	-3	/S-74,P-6,2	-1.9

HY MYERS — Myers, Henry Harrison b: 4/27/1889, E.Liverpool, Ohio d: 5/1/65, Minerva, Ohio BR/TR, 5'9.5", 175 lbs. Deb: 8/30/09

YEAR	TM/L	G	AB	R	H	2B	3B	HR	RBI	BB	SO	AVG	OBP	SLG	PRO+	BR/A	SB	CS	SBR	FA	FR	G/POS	TPR
1909	Bro-N	6	22	1	5	1	0	0		6	2	.227	.292	.273	78	-1	1			1.000	-1	/O-6	-0.2
1911	Bro-N	13	43	2	7	1	0	0	0	2	3	.163	.200	.186	9	-5	1			.889	-2	O-13	-0.8
1914	Bro-N	70	227	35	65	3	9	0	17	7	24	.286	.316	.379	104	0	2			.964	-6	O-60	-0.9
1915	Bro-N	153	605	69	150	21	7	2	46	17	51	.248	.275	.316	77	-18	19	22	-8	.964	7	*O-153	-2.9
1916	*Bro-N	113	412	54	108	12	14	3	36	21	35	.262	.308	.381	108	3	17			.969	1	*O-106	-0.2
1917	Bro-N	120	471	37	126	15	10	1	41	18	25	.268	.294	.348	94	-4	5			.982	-3	O-66,1-22,23	-1.2
1918	Bro-N	107	407	36	104	9	8	4	40	20	26	.256	.292	.346	95	-4	17			.975	13	*O-107	0.3
1919	Bro-N	133	512	62	157	23	**14**	5	**73**	23	34	.307	.339	.436	129	16	13			.979	9	*O-131	1.8
1920	*Bro-N	154	582	83	177	36	**22**	4	80	35	54	.304	.345	.462	126	18	9	13	-5	.978	4	*O-152/3-2	0.6
1921	Bro-N	144	549	51	158	14	4	6	68	22	51	.288	.318	.350	74	-20	8	6	-1	.968	6	*O-124,2-21/3	-2.4
1922	Bro-N	153	618	82	196	20	9	6	89	13	26	.317	.331	.408	90	-10	9	10	-3	.974	5	*O-152/1	-1.8
1923	StL-N	96	330	29	99	18	2	2	48	12	19	.300	.330	.385	90	-5	5	3	-0	.977	6	O-87	-1.6
1924	StL-N	43	124	12	26	5	1	1	15	3	10	.210	.228	.290	39	-11	1	2	-1	.945	-3	O-22,3-12/2	-1.6
1925	StL-N	1	1	0	0	0	0	0	0	0	0	.000	.000	.000	-98	-0	0	0	0	.000	0	H	0.0
	Cin-N	3	6	1	1	1	0	0	0	0	0	.167	.167	.333	25	-1	0	0	0	1.000	-1	/O-3	-0.1
	StL-N	1	1	1	1	1	0	0	0	0	0	1.000	1.000	1.000	403	-0	0	0	0	1.000	-1	H	0.0
	Yr	5	8	2	2	1	0	0	0	0	0	.250	.250	.375	58	-1	0	0	0	1.000	-1	/O-3	-0.1
Total	14	1310	4910	555	1380	179	100	32	559	195	358	.281	.312	.378	95	-42	107	56		.972	38	*O-1182/2-44,31	-9.8

BERT MYERS — Myers, James Albert b: 4/8/1874, Frederick, Md. d: 10/12/15, Washington, D.C. BR/TR, 5'10", Deb: 4/25/1896

YEAR	TM/L	G	AB	R	H	2B	3B	HR	RBI	BB	SO	AVG	OBP	SLG	PRO+	BR/A	SB	CS	SBR	FA	FR	G/POS	TPR
1896	StL-N	122	454	47	116	12	8	0	37	40	32	.256	.320	.317	71	-19	8			.867	-9	*3-121/S-1	-2.1
1898	Was-N	31	110	14	29	1	4	0	13	13		.264	.341	.345	97	-0	2			.835	-3	3-31	-0.3
1900	Phi-N	7	28	5	5	1	0	0	2	3		.179	.258	.214	31	-3	1			.909	2	/3-7	-0.1
Total	3	160	592	66	150	14	12	0	52	56	32	.253	.321	.318	74	-21	11			.863	-10	3-159/S-1	-2.5

YEAR	TM/L	G	AB	R	H	2B	3B	HR	RBI	BB	SO	AVG	OBP	SLG	PRO+	BR/A	SB	CS	SBR	FA	FR	G/POS	TPR

■ AL MYERS
Myers, James Albert "Cod" b: 10/22/1863, Danville, Ill. d: 12/24/27, Marshall, Ill. BR/TR, 5'8.5", 165 lbs. Deb: 9/27/1884

YEAR	TM/L	G	AB	R	H	2B	3B	HR	RBI	BB	SO	AVG	OBP	SLG	PRO+	BR/A	SB	CS	SBR	FA	FR	G/POS	TPR
1884	Mil-U	12	46	6	15	6	0	0	0	0		.326	.326	.457	204	4				.848	2	2-12	0.6
1885	Phi-N	93	357	25	73	13	2	1	28	11	41	.204	.228	.261	59	-16				.884	-17	*2-93	-2.9
1886	KC-N	118	473	69	131	22	9	4	51	22	42	.277	.309	.387	104	0	3			.913	2	*2-118	0.6
1887	Was-N	105	362	45	84	9	5	2	36	40	26	.232	.312	.301	75	-11	18			.909	-5	2-78,S-27	-1.1
1888	Was-N	132	502	46	104	12	7	2	46	37	46	.207	.270	.271	77	-12	20			.918	-25	*2-132	-3.1
1889	Was-N	46	176	24	46	3	0	0	20	22	7	.261	.347	.278	81	-3	10			.942	3	2-46	0.2
	Phi-N	75	305	52	82	14	2	0	28	36	9	.269	.354	.328	84	-7	8			.853	-8	2-75	-0.9
	Yr	121	481	76	128	17	2	0	48	58	16	.266	.351	.310	83	-10	18			.886	-4	*2-121	-0.7
1890	Phi-N	117	487	95	135	29	7	2	81	57	46	.277	.365	.378	114	9	44			.948	14	*2-117	2.6
1891	Phi-N	135	514	67	118	27	2	2	69	69	46	.230	.331	.302	83	-10	8			.937	-10	*2-135	-1.2
Total	8	833	3222	429	788	135	34	13	359	294	263	.245	.314	.320	88	-45	111			.914	-42	2-806/S-27	-5.2

■ LYNN MYERS
Myers, Lynnwood Lincoln b: 2/23/14, Enola, Pa. BR/TR, 5'6.5", 145 lbs. Deb: 7/13/38 F

YEAR	TM/L	G	AB	R	H	2B	3B	HR	RBI	BB	SO	AVG	OBP	SLG	PRO+	BR/A	SB	CS	SBR	FA	FR	G/POS	TPR
1938	StL-N	70	227	18	55	10	2	1	19	9	25	.242	.277	.317	58	-13	9			.944	-1	S-69	-0.9
1939	StL-N	74	117	24	28	6	1	0	10	12	23	.239	.310	.308	63	-6	1			.897	5	S-36,3-13/2	0.1
Total	2	144	344	42	83	16	3	1	29	21	48	.241	.285	.314	60	-19	10			.930	4	S-105/3-13,2	-0.8

■ HAP MYERS
Myers, Ralph Edward b: 4/8/1888, San Francisco, Cal. d: 6/30/67, San Francisco, Cal. BR/TR, 6'3", 175 lbs. Deb: 4/16/10

YEAR	TM/L	G	AB	R	H	2B	3B	HR	RBI	BB	SO	AVG	OBP	SLG	PRO+	BR/A	SB	CS	SBR	FA	FR	G/POS	TPR
1910	Bos-A	3	6	0	2	0	0	0	0	0		.333	.333	.333	106	0	0			1.000	0	/O-2	0.0
1911	StL-A	11	37	4	11	1	0	0	1	1		.297	.316	.324	82	-1	0			.976	-2	1-11	-0.3
	Bos-A	13	38	3	14	2	0	0	0	4		.368	.429	.421	139	2	4			.947	-1	1-12	0.1
	Yr	24	75	7	25	3	0	0	1	5		.333	.375	.373	111	1	4			.963	-3	1-23	-0.2
1913	Bos-N	140	524	74	143	20	1	2	50	38	48	.273	.343	.326	87	-8	57			.987	5	*1-135	-0.5
1914	Bro-F	92	305	61	67	10	5	1	29	44	43	.220	.322	.295	61	-17	43			.989	1	1-88	-1.9
1915	Bro-F	118	341	61	98	9	1	1	36	32	39	.287	.352	.328	83	-7	28			.990	1	*1-107	-0.9
Total	5	377	1251	203	335	42	7	4	116	119	130	.268	.338	.322	81	-31	132			.987	4	1-353/O-2	-3.5

■ RICHIE MYERS
Myers, Richard b: 4/7/30, Sacramento, Cal. BR/TR, 5'6", 150 lbs. Deb: 4/21/56

YEAR	TM/L	G	AB	R	H	2B	3B	HR	RBI	BB	SO	AVG	OBP	SLG	PRO+	BR/A	SB	CS	SBR	FA	FR	G/POS	TPR
1956	Chi-N	4	1	1	0	0	0	0	0	0	0	.000	.000	.000	-99	-0	0	0	0	.000	0	H	0.0

■ BILLY MYERS
Myers, William Harrison b: 8/14/10, Enola, Pa. BR/TR, 5'8", 168 lbs. Deb: 4/16/35 F

YEAR	TM/L	G	AB	R	H	2B	3B	HR	RBI	BB	SO	AVG	OBP	SLG	PRO+	BR/A	SB	CS	SBR	FA	FR	G/POS	TPR
1935	Cin-N	117	445	60	119	15	10	5	36	29	81	.267	.315	.380	89	-8	10			.939	3	*S-112	0.1
1936	Cin-N	98	323	45	87	9	6	2	27	28	56	.269	.328	.390	99	-1	6			.938	8	S-98	1.2
1937	Cin-N	124	335	35	84	13	3	4	43	44	57	.251	.339	.370	97	-1	0			.948	4	*S-121/2-6	1.1
1938	Cin-N	134	442	57	112	18	6	12	47	41	80	.253	.317	.403	99	-1	2			.939	2	*S-123,2-11	1.1
1939	*Cin-N	151	509	79	143	18	6	9	56	71	90	.281	.369	.393	104	5	4			.951	6	*S-151	2.4
1940	*Cin-N	90	282	33	57	14	2	5	30	30	56	.202	.283	.319	65	-14	0			.961	-5	S-88	-1.1
1941	Chi-N	24	63	10	14	1	0	1	4	7	25	.222	.310	.286	71	-2	1			.939	4	S-19/2-1	0.3
Total	7	738	2399	319	616	88	33	45	243	250	445	.257	.328	.377	93	-22	23			.946	23	S-712/2-18	5.1

■ TIM NAEHRING
Naehring, Timothy James b: 2/1/67, Cincinnati, Ohio BR/TR, 6'2", 190 lbs. Deb: 7/15/90

YEAR	TM/L	G	AB	R	H	2B	3B	HR	RBI	BB	SO	AVG	OBP	SLG	PRO+	BR/A	SB	CS	SBR	FA	FR	G/POS	TPR
1990	Bos-A	24	85	10	23	6	0	2	12	8	15	.271	.333	.412	102	0	0	0	0	.918	-1	S-19/3-5,2	0.1
1991	Bos-A	20	55	1	6	1	0	0	3	6	15	.109	.197	.127	-8	-8	0	0	0	.956	-1	S-17/3-2,2	-0.8
1992	Bos-A	72	186	12	43	8	0	3	14	18	31	.231	.309	.323	72	-7	0	0	0	.992	16	S-30,2-23,3/OD	1.1
1993	Bos-A	39	127	14	42	10	0	1	17	10	26	.331	.380	.433	111	2	1	0	0	.973	-4	2-15,D-10/3S	-0.1
1994	Bos-A	80	297	41	82	18	1	7	42	30	56	.276	.350	.414	90	-4	1	3	-2	.981	-1	2-49,3-11/1SD	-0.5
Total	5	235	750	78	196	43	1	13	88	72	143	.261	.332	.373	84	-17	2	3	-1	.982	9	/2-89,S-78,3D10	-0.2

■ BILL NAGEL
Nagel, William Taylor b: 8/19/15, Memphis, Tenn. d: 10/8/81, Freehold, N.J. BR/TR, 6'1", 190 lbs. Deb: 4/20/39

YEAR	TM/L	G	AB	R	H	2B	3B	HR	RBI	BB	SO	AVG	OBP	SLG	PRO+	BR/A	SB	CS	SBR	FA	FR	G/POS	TPR
1939	Phi-A	105	341	39	86	19	4	12	39	25	86	.252	.307	.437	90	-7	2	1	0	.944	-15	2-56,3-43/P	-1.7
1941	Phi-N	17	56	2	8	1	1	0	6	3	14	.143	.186	.196	8	-7	0			.935	3	2-12/O-2,3	-0.3
1945	Chi-A	67	220	21	46	10	3	3	27	15	41	.209	.263	.323	71	-9	3	1	0	.984	-3	1-57/3-1	-1.7
Total	3	189	617	62	140	30	8	15	72	43	141	.227	.281	.374	77	-23	5	2		.942	-15	/2-68,1-57,3OP	-3.7

■ LOU NAGELSEN
Nagelsen, Louis Marcellus (b: Louis Marcellus Nageleisen) b: 6/29/1887, Piqua, Ohio d: 10/21/65, Fort Wayne, Ind. BR/TR, 6'2", 180 lbs. Deb: 9/10/12

YEAR	TM/L	G	AB	R	H	2B	3B	HR	RBI	BB	SO	AVG	OBP	SLG	PRO+	BR/A	SB	CS	SBR	FA	FR	G/POS	TPR
1912	Cle-A	2	3	0	0	0	0	0	0	0	0	.000	.000	.000	-97	-1	0			1.000	-1	/C-2	-0.2

■ RUSS NAGELSON
Nagelson, Russell Charles b: 9/19/44, Cincinnati, Ohio BL/TR, 6', 205 lbs. Deb: 9/11/68

YEAR	TM/L	G	AB	R	H	2B	3B	HR	RBI	BB	SO	AVG	OBP	SLG	PRO+	BR/A	SB	CS	SBR	FA	FR	G/POS	TPR
1968	Cle-A	5	3	0	1	0	0	0	0	0	2	.333	.600	.333	192	1	0	0	0	.000	0	H	0.1
1969	Cle-A	12	17	1	6	0	0	0	3	3	3	.353	.450	.353	123	1	0	0	0	1.000	-1	/O-3,1-1	0.0
1970	Cle-A	17	24	3	3	1	0	1	2	3	9	.125	.222	.292	39	-2	0	0	0	1.000	-0	/O-4	-0.3
	Det-A	28	32	5	6	0	0	0	2	5	6	.188	.297	.188	36	-3	0	0	0	1.000	-1	/O-4,1-1	-0.4
	Yr	45	56	8	9	1	0	1	4	8	15	.161	.266	.232	38	-5	0	0	0	1.000	-1	/O-8,1-1	-0.7
Total	3	62	76	9	16	1	0	1	4	13	20	.211	.326	.263	64	-3	0	0	0	1.000	-2	/O-11,1-2	-0.6

■ TOM NAGLE
Nagle, Thomas Edward b: 10/30/1865, Milwaukee, Wis. d: 3/9/46, Milwaukee, Wis. BR/TR, 5'10", 150 lbs. Deb: 4/22/1890

YEAR	TM/L	G	AB	R	H	2B	3B	HR	RBI	BB	SO	AVG	OBP	SLG	PRO+	BR/A	SB	CS	SBR	FA	FR	G/POS	TPR
1890	Chi-N	38	144	21	39	5	1	1	11	7	24	.271	.318	.340	88	-3	4			.939	-7	C-33/O-6	-0.6
1891	Chi-N	8	25	3	3	0	0	0	1	1	3	.120	.154	.120	-20	-4	0			.906	-4	/C-7,O-1	-0.6
Total	2	46	169	24	42	5	1	1	12	8	27	.249	.294	.308	73	-6	4			.935	-11	/C-40,O-7	-1.2

■ BILL NAHORODNY
Nahorodny, William Gerard b: 8/31/53, Hamtramck, Mich. BR/TR, 6'2", 200 lbs. Deb: 9/27/76

YEAR	TM/L	G	AB	R	H	2B	3B	HR	RBI	BB	SO	AVG	OBP	SLG	PRO+	BR/A	SB	CS	SBR	FA	FR	G/POS	TPR
1976	Phi-N	3	5	0	1	1	0	0	0	0	0	.200	.200	.400	65	-0	0	0	0	1.000	0	/C-2	0.0
1977	Chi-A	7	23	3	6	1	0	1	4	2	3	.261	.320	.435	104	0	0	0	0	1.000	-1	/C-7	-0.1
1978	Chi-A	107	347	29	82	11	2	8	35	23	52	.236	.288	.349	77	-11	1	0	0	.980	-3	*C-104/1-4,D	-1.2
1979	Chi-A	65	179	20	46	10	0	6	29	18	23	.257	.325	.413	98	-1	0	1	-1	.973	-0	C-60/D-3	-1.0
1980	Atl-N	59	157	14	38	12	0	5	18	8	21	.242	.287	.414	91	-2	0	2	-1	.990	-7	C-54/1-1	-1.0
1981	Atl-N	14	13	0	3	1	0	0	2	1	3	.231	.286	.308	67	-1	0	0	0	1.000	0	/C-3,1-1	-0.1
1982	Cle-A	39	94	6	21	5	1	4	18	2	9	.223	.240	.426	79	-3	0	0	0	1.000	-3	C-35	-0.6
1983	Det-A	2	1	0	0	0	0	0	0	0	0	.000	.500	.000	53	0	0	0	0	.000	0	/H	0.0
1984	Sea-A	12	25	2	6	0	0	1	3	4	7	.240	.321	.360	89	-0	0	1	-1	.976	-3	C-10/1-1	-0.3
Total	9	308	844	74	203	41	3	25	109	56	118	.241	.292	.385	85	-18	1	4	-2	.983	-17	C-275/1-7,D	-3.3

■ FRANK NALEWAY
Naleway, Frank "Chick" b: 7/5/02, Chicago, Ill. d: 1/28/49, Chicago, Ill. BR/TR, 5'9.5", 165 lbs. Deb: 9/16/24

YEAR	TM/L	G	AB	R	H	2B	3B	HR	RBI	BB	SO	AVG	OBP	SLG	PRO+	BR/A	SB	CS	SBR	FA	FR	G/POS	TPR
1924	Chi-A	1	2	0	0	0	0	0	0	0	1	.000	.333	.000	-10	0	0	0	0	.750	-1	/S-1	-0.1

■ DOC NANCE
Nance, William G. "Kid" (b: Willie G. Cooper) b: 8/2/1876, Ft. Worth, Tex. d: 5/28/58, Fort Worth, Tex. BR/TR, 5'7", 165 lbs. Deb: 8/19/1897

YEAR	TM/L	G	AB	R	H	2B	3B	HR	RBI	BB	SO	AVG	OBP	SLG	PRO+	BR/A	SB	CS	SBR	FA	FR	G/POS	TPR
1897	Lou-N	35	120	25	29	3	3	17	20			.242	.355	.408	105	1	3			.986	4	O-35	0.2
1898	Lou-N	22	76	13	24	5	0	1	16	12		.316	.416	.421	142	5	2			.946	2	O-22	0.5
1901	Det-A	132	461	72	129	24	5	3	66	51		.280	.335	.373	98	-1	9			.932	1	*O-132	-0.9
Total	3	189	657	110	182	34	8	7	99	83		.277	.362	.385	104	5	14			.943	6	O-189	-0.2

■ AL NAPLES
Naples, Aloysius Francis b: 8/29/27, St.George, N.Y. BR/TR, 5'9", 168 lbs. Deb: 6/25/49

YEAR	TM/L	G	AB	R	H	2B	3B	HR	RBI	BB	SO	AVG	OBP	SLG	PRO+	BR/A	SB	CS	SBR	FA	FR	G/POS	TPR
1949	StL-A	2	7	0	1	1	0	0	0	0	1	.143	.143	.286	12	-1	0	0	0	.875	-1	/S-2	-0.2

YEAR	TM/L	G	AB	R	H	2B	3B	HR	RBI	BB	SO	AVG	OBP	SLG	PRO+	BR/A	SB	CS	SBR	FA	FR	G/POS	TPR

■ DANNY NAPOLEON
Napoleon, Daniel b: 1/11/42, Claysburg, Pa.   BR/TR, 5'11", 190 lbs.   Deb: 4/14/65

1965	NY-N	68	97	5	14	1	1	0	7	8	23	.144	.224	.175	15	-11	0	0	0	.941	1	O-15/3-7	-1.1
1966	NY-N	12	33	2	7	2	0	0	0	1	10	.212	.235	.273	42	-3	0	1	-1	.929	-0	O-10	-0.4
Total	2	80	130	7	21	3	1	0	7	9	33	.162	.227	.200	22	-14	0	1	-1	.938	1	/O-25,3-7	-1.5

■ HAL NARAGON
Naragon, Harold Richard b: 10/1/28, Zanesville, Ohio   BL/TR, 6', 175 lbs.   Deb: 9/23/51 C

1951	Cle-A	3	8	0	2	0	0	0	0	1	0	.250	.400	.250	83	-0	0	0	0	.929	0	/C-2	0.0
1954	*Cle-A	46	101	10	24	2	2	0	12	9	12	.238	.300	.297	63	-5	0	0	0	1.000	-2	C-45	-0.5
1955	Cle-A	57	127	12	41	9	2	1	14	15	8	.323	.394	.449	122	4	1	0	0	.991	-4	C-52	0.2
1956	Cle-A	53	122	11	35	3	1	3	18	13	9	.287	.360	.402	99	-0	0	0	0	.988	-12	C-48	-1.0
1957	Cle-A	57	121	12	31	1	1	0	8	12	9	.256	.328	.281	69	-5	0	0	0	.990	-2	C-39	-0.6
1958	Cle-A	9	9	2	3	0	1	0	0	0	3	.333	.333	.556	144	0	0	0	0	.000	0	H	0.0
1959	Cle-A	14	36	6	10	4	1	0	5	3	2	.278	.350	.444	121	1	0	0	0	1.000	-1	C-10	0.0
	Was-A	71	195	12	47	3	2	0	11	8	9	.241	.275	.277	52	-13	0	1	-1	.993	-2	C-54	-1.2
	Yr	85	231	18	57	7	3	0	16	11	11	.247	.287	.303	63	-12	0	1	-1	.994	-3	C-64	-1.2
1960	Was-A	33	92	7	19	2	0	0	5	8	4	.207	.277	.228	39	-8	0	0	0	.978	-2	C-29	-0.9
1961	Min-A	57	139	10	42	2	1	2	11	4	8	.302	.326	.374	82	-4	0	0	0	.994	-5	C-36	-0.7
1962	Min-A	24	35	1	8	0	1	0	3	3	1	.229	.289	.257	47	-3	0	0	0	1.000	0	/C-9	-0.2
Total	10	424	985	83	262	27	11	6	87	76	62	.266	.323	.334	77	-31	1	1	-0	.991	-29	C-324	-4.9

■ BILL NARLESKI
Narleski, William Edward "Cap" b: 6/9/1899, Perth Amboy, N.J. d: 7/22/64, Laurel Springs, N.J.   BR/TR, 5'9", 160 lbs.   Deb: 4/18/29 F

1929	Bos-A	96	260	30	72	16	1	0	25	21	22	.277	.333	.346	77	-9	4	4	-1	.957	-17	S-51,2-29/3	-1.9
1930	Bos-A	39	98	11	23	9	0	0	7	7	5	.235	.306	.327	63	-6	0	0	0	.915	-8	S-19,3-14/2	-1.1
Total	2	135	358	41	95	25	1	0	32	28	27	.265	.326	.341	73	-14	4	4	-1	.949	-25	/S-70,2-34,3	-3.0

■ JERRY NARRON
Narron, Jerry Austin b: 1/15/56, Goldsboro, N.C.   BL/TR, 6'3", 205 lbs.   Deb: 4/13/79 C

1979	NY-A	61	123	17	21	3	1	4	18	9	26	.171	.227	.309	44	-10	0	0	0	.973	-5	C-56	-1.3
1980	Sea-A	48	107	7	21	0	0	4	18	13	18	.196	.283	.336	68	-5	0	0	0	.992	-10	C-39/D-1	-1.3
1981	Sea-A	76	203	13	45	5	0	3	17	16	35	.222	.285	.291	64	-9	0	0	0	.996	-14	C-65	-2.3
1983	Cal-A	10	22	1	3	0	0	1	4	1	3	.136	.174	.273	21	-2	0	0	0	.895	-1	/C-6,D-1	-0.3
1984	Cal-A	69	150	9	37	5	0	3	17	8	12	.247	.289	.340	74	-5	0	0	0	.994	-8	C-46/1-7	-1.2
1985	Cal-A	67	132	12	29	4	0	5	14	11	17	.220	.280	.364	75	-5	0	0	0	1.000	2	C-45/1-1,D	-0.1
1986	*Cal-A	57	95	5	21	3	1	1	8	9	14	.221	.295	.305	65	-5	0	0	0	.988	1	C-51/D-2	-0.1
1987	Sea-A	4	8	0	0	0	0	0	0	0	2	.000	.000	.000	-95	-2	0	0	0	1.000	-0	/C-3	-0.2
Total	8	392	840	64	177	23	2	21	96	67	127	.211	.272	.318	62	-44	0	0	0	.989	-34	C-311/D-11,1	-6.8

■ SAM NARRON
Narron, Samuel b: 8/25/13, Middlesex, N.C.   BR/TR, 5'10", 180 lbs.   Deb: 9/15/35 C

1935	StL-N	4	7	0	3	0	0	0	0	0	0	.429	.429	.429	126	0	0	0	0	1.000	-0	/C-1	0.0
1942	StL-N	10	10	0	4	0	0	0	1	0	0	.400	.400	.400	125	0	0	0	0	1.000	-0	/C-2	0.0
1943	*StL-N	10	11	0	1	0	0	0	0	1	2	.091	.167	.091	-24	-2	0	0	0	1.000	1	/C-3	-0.1
Total	3	24	28	0	8	0	0	0	1	1	2	.286	.310	.286	67	-1	0	0	0	1.000	0	/C-6	-0.1

■ COTTON NASH
Nash, Charles Francis b: 7/24/42, Jersey City, N.J.   BR/TR, 6'6", 220 lbs.   Deb: 9/1/67

1967	Chi-A	3	3	1	0	0	0	0	0	0	0	.000	.250	.000	-21	-0	0	0	0	.833	-1	/1-3	-0.1
1969	Min-A	6	9	0	2	0	0	0	0	1	2	.222	.300	.222	47	-1	0	0	0	1.000	1	/1-6,O-1	0.0
1970	Min-A	4	4	1	1	0	0	0	2	1	1	.250	.400	.250	82	-0	0	1	-1	1.000	-0	/1-2	-0.1
Total	3	13	16	2	3	0	0	0	2	3	3	.188	.316	.188	45	-1	0	1	-1	.965	0	/1-11,O-1	-0.2

■ KEN NASH
Nash, Kenneth Leland (Played One Game In 1912 under name of Costello)
b: 7/14/1888, Weymouth, Mass. d: 2/16/77, Epsom, N.H.   BB/TR, 5'8", 140 lbs.   Deb: 7/4/12

1912	Cle-A	11	23	2	4	0	0	0	0	3		.174	.269	.174	27	-2	0			.826	-3	/S-8	-0.5
1914	StL-N	24	51	4	14	3	1	0	6	6	10	.275	.351	.373	116	1	0			.875	-6	3-10/2-6,S	-0.6
Total	2	35	74	6	18	3	1	0	6	9	10	.243	.325	.311	87	-1	0			.760	-10	/S-11,3-10,2	-1.1

■ BILLY NASH
Nash, William Mitchell b: 6/24/1865, Richmond, Va. d: 11/15/29, E.Orange, N.J.   BR/TR, 5'8.5", 167 lbs.   Deb: 8/5/1884 MU

1884	Ric-a	45	166	31	33	8	8	1		12		.199	.281	.361	109	2				.828	8	3-45	0.9
1885	Bos-N	26	94	9	24	4	0	0	11	2	9	.255	.271	.298	87	-1				.864	-4	3-19/2-8	-0.4
1886	Bos-N	109	417	61	117	11	8	1	45	24	28	.281	.320	.353	108	4	16			.863	-5	*3-90,S-17/O	0.2
1887	Bos-N	121	475	100	140	24	12	6	94	60	30	.295	.376	.434	124	17	43			.884	9	*3-117/O-5	2.3
1888	Bos-N	135	526	71	149	18	15	4	75	50	46	.283	.350	.397	136	22	20			.913	26	*3-105,2-31	4.9
1889	Bos-N	128	481	84	132	20	2	3	76	79	44	.274	.379	.343	97	-0	26			.905	12	*3-128/P-1	1.4
1890	Bos-P	129	488	103	130	28	6	5	90	88	43	.266	.383	.379	97	-2	26			.866	18	*3-129/P-1	1.7
1891	Bos-N	140	537	92	148	24	9	5	95	74	50	.276	.369	.382	106	2	28			.900	-12	*3-140	-0.3
1892	*Bos-N	135	526	94	137	25	5	4	95	59	41	.260	.338	.350	99	-2	31			.898	24	*3-135/O-1	2.5
1893	Bos-N	128	485	115	141	27	6	10	123	85	29	.291	.399	.433	112	8	30			.923	3	*3-128	1.0
1894	Bos-N	132	512	132	148	23	6	8	87	91	23	.289	.394	.404	87	-11	20			.933	6	*3-132	-0.4
1895	Bos-N	132	508	97	147	23	6	10	108	74	19	.289	.383	.417	99	-2	18			.882	-8	*3-132	-0.7
1896	Phi-N	65	227	29	56	9	1	3	30	34	21	.247	.355	.335	83	-4	3			.911	7	3-65,M	0.3
1897	Phi-N	104	337	45	87	20	2	0	39	60		.258	.373	.329	89	-3	4			.919	-7	3-79,S-19/2	-0.6
1898	Phi-N	20	70	9	17	2	1	0	9	11		.243	.346	.300	89	-1	0			.958	-1	3-20	-0.1
Total	15	1549	5849	1072	1606	266	87	60	977	803	383	.275	.366	.381	103	29	265			.897	76	*3-1464/2-43,SOP	12.7

■ ROB NATAL
Natal, Robert Marcel b: 11/13/65, Long Beach, Cal.   BR/TR, 5'11", 190 lbs.   Deb: 7/18/92

1992	Mon-N	5	6	0	0	0	0	0	0	1	1	.000	.143	.000	-57	-1	0	0	0	.909	-0	/C-4	-0.2
1993	Fla-N	41	117	3	25	4	1	1	6	6	22	.214	.276	.291	49	-8	1	0	0	1.000	2	C-38	-0.4
1994	Fla-N	10	29	2	8	2	0	0	2	5	5	.276	.382	.345	87	-0	1	0	0	.983	3	/C-8	0.3
Total	3	56	152	5	33	6	1	1	8	12	28	.217	.292	.289	53	-10	2	0	1	.993	4	/C-50	-0.3

■ PETE NATON
Naton, Peter Alphonsus b: 9/9/31, Flushing, N.Y.   BR/TR, 6'1", 200 lbs.   Deb: 6/16/53

1953	Pit-N	6	12	2	2	0	0	0	1	2	1	.167	.286	.167	22	-1	0	0	0	1.000	-1	/C-4	-0.2

■ SANDY NAVA
Nava, Vincent P. (b: Irwin Sandy) b: 4/12/1850, San Francisco, Cal d: 6/15/06, Baltimore, Md.   5'6", 155 lbs.   Deb: 5/5/1882

1882	Pro-N	28	97	15	20	1	0	0		1	13	.206	.214	.227	42	-6				.867	-7	C-27/O-1	-1.1
1883	Pro-N	29	100	18	24	4	2	0	16	3	17	.240	.262	.320	74	-3				.813	-4	C-27/O-2	-0.5
1884	Pro-N	34	116	10	11	0	0	0	6	11	35	.095	.173	.095	-14	-15				.887	1	C-27/S-6,2	-0.6
1885	Bal-a	8	27	2	5	1	0	0		1		.185	.214	.222	39	-2				.825	-5	C-8	-0.6
1886	Bal-a	2	5	0	1	0	0	0		0		.200	.200	.200	26	-0	1			.500	-1	/S-1,C-1	-0.1
Total	5	101	345	45	61	7	2	0	29	16	65	.177	.213	.209	33	-26	1			.857	-16	/C-90,S-7,O2	-3.3

■ TITO NAVARRO
Navarro, Norberto (Rodriguez) b: 9/12/70, Rio Piedras, P.R.   BB/TR, 5'10", 165 lbs.   Deb: 9/6/93

1993	NY-N	12	17	1	1	0	0	0	1	0	4	.059	.059	.059	-69	-4	0	0	0	1.000	1	/S-2	-0.3

■ EARL NAYLOR
Naylor, Earl Eugene b: 5/19/19, Kansas City, Mo. d: 1/16/90, Winter Haven, Fla.   BR/TR, 6', 190 lbs.   Deb: 4/15/42

1942	Phi-N	76	168	9	33	4	1	0	14	11	18	.196	.246	.232	42	-12	1			.984	-5	O-34,P-20	-1.8
1943	Phi-N	33	120	12	21	2	0	3	14	12	16	.175	.256	.267	53	-7	1			.964	6	O-33	-0.3

YEAR	TM/L	G	AB	R	H	2B	3B	HR	RBI	BB	SO	AVG	OBP	SLG	PRO+	BR/A	SB	CS	SBR	FA	FR	G/POS	TPR
1946	Bro-N	3	2	1	0	0	0	0	0	0	1	.000	.000	.000	-99	-1	0			.000	0	H	-0.1
Total	3	112	290	22	54	6	1	3	28	23	35	.186	.248	.245	46	-20	2			.971	1	/O-67,P-20	-2.2

■ JACK NEAGLE
Neagle, John Henry b: 1/2/1858, Syracuse, N.Y. d: 9/20/04, Syracuse, N.Y. BR/TR, 5'6", 155 lbs. Deb: 7/8/1879

YEAR	TM/L	G	AB	R	H	2B	3B	HR	RBI	BB	SO	AVG	OBP	SLG	PRO+	BR/A	SB	CS	SBR	FA	FR	G/POS	TPR
1879	Cin-N	3	12	1	2	0	0	0	2	0	0	.167	.167	.167	11	-1				.000	-1	/O-2,P-2	-0.1
1883	Phi-N	18	73	6	12	1	0	0	4	1	9	.164	.176	.178	9	-8				.840	-2	O-12/P-8	-0.5
	Bal-a	9	35	3	10	4	0	0		2		.286	.324	.400	128	1				.769	-3	/P-6,O-5	-0.2
	Pit-a	27	101	14	19	0	1	0		5		.188	.226	.208	43	-6				.839	-3	P-16,O-15	-0.5
	Yr	36	136	17	29	4	1	0		7		.213	.252	.257	66	-5				.818	-6	P-22,O-20	-0.7
1884	Pit-a	43	148	13	22	6	0	0		6		.149	.187	.189	23	-12				.760	-5	P-38/O-6	-0.4
Total	3	100	369	37	65	11	1	0	6	14	9	.176	.208	.211	35	-26				.785	-14	/P-70,O-40	-1.7

■ CHARLIE NEAL
Neal, Charles Lenard b: 1/30/31, Longview, Tex. BR/TR, 5'10", 165 lbs. Deb: 4/17/56

YEAR	TM/L	G	AB	R	H	2B	3B	HR	RBI	BB	SO	AVG	OBP	SLG	PRO+	BR/A	SB	CS	SBR	FA	FR	G/POS	TPR
1956	*Bro-N	62	136	22	39	5	1	2	14	14	19	.287	.353	.382	91	-1	2	2	-1	.972	2	2-51/S-1	0.2
1957	Bro-N	128	448	62	121	13	7	12	62	53	83	.270	.358	.411	96	-1	11	4	1	.949	-3	*S-100,3-23/2	0.7
1958	LA-N	140	473	87	120	9	6	22	65	61	91	.254	.345	.438	102	2	7	6	-2	.976	12	*2-132/S-9	2.2
1959	*LA-N★	151	616	103	177	30	11	19	83	43	86	.287	.338	.464	103	2	17	6	2	.989	20	*2-151/S-1	3.5
1960	LA-N★	139	477	60	122	23	2	8	40	48	75	.256	.325	.363	83	-11	5	5	-2	.977	-16	*2-136/S-3	-1.6
1961	LA-N	108	341	40	80	6	1	10	48	30	49	.235	.298	.346	65	-17	3	2	-0	.976	2	*2-104	-0.6
1962	NY-N	136	508	59	132	14	9	11	58	56	90	.260	.333	.388	91	-6	2	8	-4	.970	-8	2-85,S-39,3	-0.6
1963	NY-N	72	253	26	57	12	1	3	18	27	49	.225	.302	.316	77	-7	1	2	-1	.961	5	3-66/S-8	-0.8
	Cin-N	34	64	2	10	1	0	0	3	5	15	.156	.217	.172	13	-7	0	1	-1	.927	-2	3-19/2-1,S	-1.1
	Yr	106	317	28	67	13	1	3	21	32	64	.211	.286	.287	64	-14	1	3	-2	.955	3	3-85/S-9,2	-1.9
Total	8	970	3316	461	858	113	38	87	391	337	557	.259	.331	.394	90	-47	48	36	-7	.978	7	2-663,S-162,3	1.9

■ OFFA NEAL
Neal, Theophilus Fountain b: 6/5/1876, Logan, Ill. d: 4/12/50, Mt.Vernon, Ill. BL/TR, 6', 185 lbs. Deb: 9/30/05

YEAR	TM/L	G	AB	R	H	2B	3B	HR	RBI	BB	SO	AVG	OBP	SLG	PRO+	BR/A	SB	CS	SBR	FA	FR	G/POS	TPR
1905	NY-N	4	13	0	0	0	0	0	0			.000	.000	.000	-98	-3	0			1.000	-1	/3-3,2-1	-0.4

■ GREASY NEALE
Neale, Alfred Earle b: 11/5/1891, Parkersburg, W.Va. d: 11/2/73, Lake Worth, Fla. BL/TR, 6', 170 lbs. Deb: 4/12/16 C

YEAR	TM/L	G	AB	R	H	2B	3B	HR	RBI	BB	SO	AVG	OBP	SLG	PRO+	BR/A	SB	CS	SBR	FA	FR	G/POS	TPR
1916	Cin-N	138	530	53	139	13	5	0	20	19	79	.262	.295	.306	87	-9	17			.973	11	*O-133	-0.5
1917	Cin-N	121	385	40	113	14	9	3	33	24	36	.294	.343	.400	133	14	25			.979	-5	*O-119	0.4
1918	Cin-N	107	371	57	100	11	11	1	32	24	38	.270	.324	.367	112	5	23			.981	10	*O-102	1.0
1919	*Cin-N	139	500	57	121	10	12	1	54	47	51	.242	.316	.316	93	-3	28			.959	2	*O-138	-1.2
1920	Cin-N	150	530	55	135	10	7	3	46	45	48	.255	.322	.317	85	-9	29	12	2	.987	14	*O-150	-0.4
1921	Phi-N	22	57	7	12	1	0	0	1	14	9	.211	.366	.228	56	-3	3	4	-2	.842	-5	O-16	-1.1
	Cin-N	63	241	39	58	10	5	0	12	22	16	.241	.307	.324	70	-10	9	6	-1	.964	1	O-60	-1.5
	Yr	85	298	46	70	11	5	0	13	36	25	.235	.319	.305	67	-13	12	10	-3	.950	-4	O-76	-2.6
1922	Cin-N	25	43	11	10	2	1	0	2	6	3	.233	.353	.326	77	-1	5	2	0	.864	-4	O-16	-0.5
1924	Cin-N	3	4	0	0	0	0	0	0	0	0	.000	.000	.000	-99	-1	0			1.000	-0	/O-2	-0.2
Total	8	768	2661	319	688	71	50	8	200	201	281	.259	.319	.332	94	-18	139	24		.972	24	O-736	-4.0

■ JOE NEALE
Neale, Joseph Hunt b: 5/7/1866, Wadsworth, Ohio d: 12/30/13, Akron, Ohio BR/TR, 5'8", 153 lbs. Deb: 6/21/1886

YEAR	TM/L	G	AB	R	H	2B	3B	HR	RBI	BB	SO	AVG	OBP	SLG	PRO+	BR/A	SB	CS	SBR	FA	FR	G/POS	TPR
1886	Lou-a	2	5	0	0	0	0	0		0		.000	.000	.000	-95	-1	0			1.000	0	/O-2,P-1	-0.1
1887	Lou-a	5	19	3	1	0	0	0		3		.053	.182	.053	-32	-3	1			.833	0	/P-5	0.0
1890	StL-a	11	30	4	2	0	0	0		3		.067	.152	.067	-31	-5	0			1.000	-2	P-10/O-1	0.0
1891	StL-a	15	51	6	6	0	1	1	8	3	11	.118	.167	.216	8	-7	1			.933	2	P-15	0.0
Total	4	33	105	13	9	0	1	1	8	9	11	.086	.158	.133	-14	-16	2			.930	0	/P-31,O-3	-0.1

■ JIM NEALON
Nealon, James Joseph b: 12/15/1884, Sacramento, Cal. d: 4/2/10, San Francisco, Cal. BR/TR, 6'1.5", Deb: 4/12/06

YEAR	TM/L	G	AB	R	H	2B	3B	HR	RBI	BB	SO	AVG	OBP	SLG	PRO+	BR/A	SB	CS	SBR	FA	FR	G/POS	TPR
1906	Pit-N	154	556	82	142	21	12	3	83	53		.255	.327	.353	107	4	15			.987	1	*1-154	0.0
1907	Pit-N	105	381	29	98	10	8	0	47	23		.257	.301	.325	95	-3	11			.978	0	*1-104	-0.7
Total	2	259	937	111	240	31	20	3	130	76		.256	.317	.342	102	1	26			.983	1	1-258	-0.7

■ TOM NEEDHAM
Needham, Thomas J. "Deerfoot" b: 4/7/1879, Ireland d: 12/13/26, Steubenville, Ohio BR/TR, 5'10", 180 lbs. Deb: 5/12/04

YEAR	TM/L	G	AB	R	H	2B	3B	HR	RBI	BB	SO	AVG	OBP	SLG	PRO+	BR/A	SB	CS	SBR	FA	FR	G/POS	TPR
1904	Bos-N	84	269	18	70	12	3	4	19	11		.260	.292	.372	108	1	3			.945	4	C-77/O-1	1.4
1905	Bos-N	83	271	21	59	6	1	2	17	24		.218	.293	.269	70	-10	3			.949	-8	C-77/O-3,1	-1.1
1906	Bos-N	83	285	11	54	8	2	1	12	13		.189	.230	.242	49	-18	3			.959	-2	C-76/2-5,130	-1.3
1907	Bos-N	86	260	19	51	6	2	1	19	18		.196	.264	.246	60	-12	4			.967	-11	C-78/1-1	-1.8
1908	NY-N	54	91	8	19	3	0	0	11	12		.209	.339	.242	82	-1	0			.975	7	C-47	1.0
1909	Chi-N	13	28	3	4	0	0	0	0	0		.143	.143	.143	-11	-4	0			.980	1	/C-7	-0.2
1910	*Chi-N	31	76	9	14	3	1	0	10	10	10	.184	.287	.250	57	-4	1			.982	3	C-27/1-1	0.2
1911	Chi-N	27	62	4	12	2	0	0	5	9	14	.194	.315	.226	52	-4	2			.984	6	C-23	0.4
1912	Chi-N	33	90	12	16	5	0	0	10	7	13	.178	.260	.233	36	-8	3			.994	-1	C-32	-0.6
1913	Chi-N	20	42	5	10	4	1	0	11	4	8	.238	.304	.381	95	-0	0			.962	4	C-14/1-1	0.5
1914	Chi-N	9	17	3	2	1	0	0	3	1	4	.118	.167	.176	2	-2	1			.943	1	/C-7	0.0
Total	11	523	1491	113	311	50	10	8	117	109	49	.209	.274	.272	66	-60	20			.962	5	C-465/1-7,203	-1.5

■ TROY NEEL
Neel, Troy Lee b: 9/14/65, Freeport, Tex. BL/TR, 6'4", 210 lbs. Deb: 5/30/92

YEAR	TM/L	G	AB	R	H	2B	3B	HR	RBI	BB	SO	AVG	OBP	SLG	PRO+	BR/A	SB	CS	SBR	FA	FR	G/POS	TPR
1992	Oak-A	24	53	8	14	3	0	3	9	5	15	.264	.339	.491	137	2	0	1	-1	.846	-2	/O-9,1-2,D	0.0
1993	Oak-A	123	427	59	124	21	0	19	63	49	101	.290	.369	.473	132	19	3	5	-2	.981	-0	D-85,1-34	1.1
1994	Oak-A	83	278	43	74	13	0	15	48	38	61	.266	.358	.475	122	9	2	3	-1	.994	-0	1-45,D-35	0.3
Total	3	230	758	110	212	37	0	37	120	92	177	.280	.363	.475	129	31	5	9	-4	.986	-3	D-129/1-81,O	1.4

■ CAL NEEMAN
Neeman, Calvin Amandus b: 2/18/29, Valmeyer, Ill. BR/TR, 6'1", 192 lbs. Deb: 4/16/57

YEAR	TM/L	G	AB	R	H	2B	3B	HR	RBI	BB	SO	AVG	OBP	SLG	PRO+	BR/A	SB	CS	SBR	FA	FR	G/POS	TPR
1957	Chi-N	122	415	37	107	17	1	10	39	22	87	.258	.300	.376	81	-11	0	0	0	.990	1	*C-118	-0.6
1958	Chi-N	76	201	30	52	7	0	5	29	21	41	.259	.338	.473	113	3	0	0	0	.992	1	C-71	0.8
1959	Chi-N	44	105	7	17	2	0	3	9	11	23	.162	.241	.267	36	-10	0	0	0	.994	-1	C-38	-1.0
1960	Chi-N	9	13	0	2	1	0	0	0	0	5	.154	.154	.231	4	-2	0	0	0	1.000	4	/C-9	0.2
	Phi-N	59	160	13	29	6	2	4	13	16	42	.181	.264	.319	59	-9	0	0	0	.979	5	C-52	-0.2
	Yr	68	173	13	31	7	2	4	13	16	47	.179	.257	.312	55	-11	0	0	0	.982	9	C-61	0.0
1961	Phi-N	19	31	0	7	1	0	0	2	4	8	.226	.314	.258	55	-2	0	0	0	.986	2	C-19	0.1
1962	Pit-N	24	50	5	9	1	1	1	5	3	10	.180	.226	.300	40	-4	0	0	0	.983	2	C-24	0.4
1963	Cle-A	9	9	0	0	0	0	0	0	0	1	.000	.100	.000	-70	-2	0	0	0	1.000	3	/C-9	0.1
	Was-A	14	18	1	1	0	0	0	0	1	0	.056	.105	.056	-54	-4	0	0	0	.970	2	C-12	-0.2
	Yr	23	27	1	1	0	0	0	0	1	1	.037	.103	.037	-59	-6	0	0	0	.985	5	C-21	-0.1
Total	7	376	1002	93	224	35	4	30	97	79	221	.224	.286	.356	72	-41	1	0		.988	24	C-352	-0.4

■ DOUG NEFF
Neff, Douglas Williams b: 10/8/1891, Harrisonburg, Va. d: 5/23/32, Cape Charles, Va. BR/TR, 5'9", 141 lbs. Deb: 6/26/14

YEAR	TM/L	G	AB	R	H	2B	3B	HR	RBI	BB	SO	AVG	OBP	SLG	PRO+	BR/A	SB	CS	SBR	FA	FR	G/POS	TPR
1914	Was-A	3	2	0	0	0	0	0	0	0	0	.000	.000	.000	-96	-0	0			.889	2	/S-3	0.1
1915	Was-A	30	60	1	10	1	0	0	4	4	6	.167	.219	.183	20	-6	1	2	-1	.867	-4	3-12,2-10/S	-1.1
Total	2	33	62	1	10	1	0	0	4	4	6	.161	.212	.177	16	-6	1	2		.900	-2	/3-12,2-10,S	-1.0

■ CY NEIGHBORS
Neighbors, Flemon Cecil b: 9/23/1880, Fayetteville, Mo. d: 5/20/64, Tacoma, Wash. BR, Deb: 4/29/08

YEAR	TM/L	G	AB	R	H	2B	3B	HR	RBI	BB	SO	AVG	OBP	SLG	PRO+	BR/A	SB	CS	SBR	FA	FR	G/POS	TPR
1908	Pit-N	1	0	0	0	0	0	0	0	0	0	—	—	—	—	—	0			.000	-1	/O-1	-0.1

YEAR	TM/L	G	AB	R	H	2B	3B	HR	RBI	BB	SO	AVG	OBP	SLG	PRO+	BR/A	SB	CS	SBR	FA	FR	G/POS	TPR

◼ BOB NEIGHBORS   Neighbors, Robert Otis   b: 11/9/17, Talihina, Okla.   d: 8/8/52, North Korea (Mia)   BR/TR, 5′11″, 165 lbs.   Deb: 9/16/39

1939	StL-A	7	11	3	2	0	0	1	1	0	1	.182	.182	.455	56	-1	0	0	0	.917	-0	/S-5	-0.1

◼ TOMMY NEILL   Neill, Thomas White   b: 11/7/19, Hartselle, Ala.   d: 9/22/80, Houston, Tex.   BL/TR, 6′2″, 200 lbs.   Deb: 9/10/46

1946	Bos-N	13	45	8	12	2	0	0	7	2	1	.267	.298	.311	72	-2	0			1.000	-1	O-13	-0.4
1947	Bos-N	7	10	1	2	0	1	0	0	1	2	.200	.333	.400	96	-0	0			1.000	-1	/O-2	-0.1
Total	2	20	55	9	14	2	1	0	7	3	3	.255	.305	.327	77	-2	0			1.000	-2	/O-15	-0.5

◼ BERNIE NEIS   Neis, Bernard Edmund   b: 9/26/1895, Bloomington, Ill.   d: 11/29/72, Inverness, Fla.   BB/TR, 5′7″, 160 lbs.   Deb: 4/14/20

1920	*Bro-N	95	249	38	63	11	2	2	22	26	35	.253	.329	.337	89	-3	9	9	-3	.957	-2	O-83	-1.3
1921	Bro-N	102	230	34	59	5	4	4	34	25	41	.257	.332	.365	81	-6	9	7	-2	.946	-6	O-77/2-1	-0.7
1922	Bro-N	61	70	15	16	4	1	1	9	13	8	.229	.349	.357	83	-2	3	2	-0	.897	-5	O-27	-0.7
1923	Bro-N	126	445	78	122	17	4	5	37	36	38	.274	.330	.364	85	-10	8	8	-2	.941	6	*O-111	-1.2
1924	Bro-N	80	211	43	64	8	3	4	26	27	17	.303	.385	.427	121	7	4	2	0	.937	-4	O-62	-0.1
1925	Bos-N	106	355	47	101	20	2	5	45	38	19	.285	.354	.394	100	-0	8	10	-4	.970	11	O-87	0.1
1926	Bos-N	30	93	16	20	5	2	0	8	8	10	.215	.277	.312	64	-5	4			.925	2	O-23	-0.5
1927	Cle-A	32	96	17	29	9	0	4	18	18	9	.302	.412	.521	140	6	0	1	-1	.978	5	O-29	0.8
	Chi-A	45	76	9	22	5	0	0	11	10	9	.289	.372	.355	92	-1	1	0		.927	-3	O-21	-0.4
	Yr	77	172	26	51	14	0	4	29	28	18	.297	.395	.448	120	6	1	1	-0	.962	2	O-50	0.4
Total	8	677	1825	297	496	84	18	25	210	201	186	.272	.346	.379	94	-13	46	39		.950	3	O-520/2-1	-5.0

◼ ERNIE NEITZKE   Neitzke, Ernest Fredrich   b: 11/13/1894, Toledo, Ohio   d: 4/27/77, Sylvania, Ohio   BR/TR, 5′10″, 180 lbs.   Deb: 6/2/21

1921	Bos-A	11	25	3	6	0	0	0	2	4	4	.240	.345	.240	53	-2	0	0	0	.875	-1	/O-8,P-2	-0.3

◼ DAVE NELSON   Nelson, David Earl   b: 6/20/44, Fort Sill, Okla.   BR/TR, 5′10″, 160 lbs.   Deb: 4/11/68   C

1968	Cle-A	88	189	26	44	4	5	0	19	17	35	.233	.300	.307	85	-3	23	7	3	.987	-2	2-59,S-14	0.1
1969	Cle-A	52	123	11	25	0	0	0	6	9	26	.203	.263	.203	31	-11	4	3	-1	.966	4	2-33/O-2	-0.5
1970	Was-A	47	107	5	17	1	0	0	4	7	24	.159	.211	.168	6	-14	2	1	0	.986	4	2-33	-1.1
1971	Was-A	85	329	47	92	11	3	5	33	23	29	.280	.329	.377	105	1	17	8	0	.938	-13	3-84/2-1	-1.3
1972	Tex-A	145	499	60	113	16	3	2	28	67	81	.226	.324	.283	85	-7	51	17	5	.945	-12	*3-119,O-15	-1.8
1973	Tex-A★	142	576	71	165	24	4	7	48	34	78	.286	.326	.378	102	0	43	16	3	.984	-12	*2-140	0.0
1974	Tex-A	121	474	71	112	13	1	3	42	34	72	.236	.293	.287	69	-19	25	13	-0	.969	1	*2-120/D-1	-1.3
1975	Tex-A	28	80	9	17	1	0	2	10	8	10	.213	.292	.300	68	-3	6	0	0	.959	1	2-23/D-1	0.1
1976	*KC-A	78	153	24	36	4	2	1	17	14	26	.235	.299	.307	77	-4	15	5	2	.975	-2	2-46,D-22/1	0.0
1977	KC-A	27	48	8	9	3	1	0	4	7	11	.188	.291	.292	59	-3	1	3	-2	.926	-2	2-11/D-7	-0.6
Total	10	813	2578	340	630	77	19	20	211	220	392	.244	.307	.312	81	-62	187	73	12	.976	-31	2-466,3-203/DOS1	-6.4

◼ ROCKY NELSON   Nelson, Glenn Richard   b: 11/18/24, Portsmouth, Ohio   BL/TL, 5′11″, 178 lbs.   Deb: 4/27/49

1949	StL-N	82	244	28	54	8	4	4	32	11	12	.221	.258	.336	55	-16	1			1.000	-4	1-70	-2.0
1950	StL-N	76	235	27	58	10	4	1	20	26	9	.247	.324	.336	71	-10	4			.992	3	1-70	-0.8
1951	StL-N	9	18	3	4	1	0	0	1	1	0	.222	.263	.278	45	-1	0	0	0	1.000	-0	/1-4,O-1	-0.3
	Pit-N	71	195	29	52	7	4	1	14	10	7	.267	.302	.359	75	-7	1	1	-0	.990	1	1-32,O-12	-0.9
	Yr	80	213	32	56	8	4	1	15	11	7	.263	.299	.352	73	-8	1	1	-0	.991	-0	1-36,O-13	-1.2
	Chi-A	6	5	0	0	0	0	0	1	0	1	.000	.167	.000	-53	-1	0	0	0	.000	0	H	-0.1
1952	*Bro-N	37	39	6	10	1	0	0	3	7	4	.256	.370	.282	82	-1	0	0	0	1.000	-1	/1-5	-0.2
1954	Cle-A	4	4	0	0	0	0	0	0	0	1	.000	.000	.000	-98	-1	0	0	0	1.000	-0	/1-2	-0.1
1956	Bro-N	31	96	7	20	2	0	4	15	4	10	.208	.240	.354	53	-7	0	0	0	.991	2	1-25	-0.7
	StL-N	38	56	6	13	5	0	3	8	6	6	.232	.306	.482	108	1	0	0	0	1.000	1	1-14/O-8	0.0
	Yr	69	152	13	33	7	0	7	23	10	16	.217	.265	.401	73	-6	0	0	0	.993	2	1-39/O-8	-0.7
1959	Pit-N	98	175	31	51	11	0	6	32	23	19	.291	.383	.457	124	6	0	0	0	.994	-4	1-56/O-2	0.0
1960	*Pit-N	93	200	34	60	11	1	7	35	24	15	.300	.389	.470	133	10	1	2	-1	.996	1	1-73	0.6
1961	Pit-N	75	127	15	25	5	1	5	13	17	11	.197	.301	.370	77	-4	0	0	0	.996	1	1-35	-0.7
Total	9	620	1394	186	347	61	14	31	173	130	94	.249	.318	.379	84	-31	7	3		.995	-3	1-386/O-23	-5.2

◼ JAMIE NELSON   Nelson, James Victor   b: 9/5/59, Clinton, Okla.   BR/TR, 5′11″, 180 lbs.   Deb: 7/21/83

1983	Sea-A	40	96	9	21	3	0	1	5	13	12	.219	.312	.281	62	-5	4	2	0	.978	3	C-39	0.0

◼ CANDY NELSON   Nelson, John W   b: 3/12/1854, Portland, Maine   d: 9/4/10, Brooklyn, N.Y.   BL/TR, 5′6″, 145 lbs.   Deb: 6/11/1872

1872	Tro-n	4	17	1	6	0	0	0	4	0	2	.353	.353	.353	116	0						/O-3,S-1	0.0
	Eck-n	18	76	12	19	2	0	0	7	2	2	.250	.269	.276	80	-1						/2-8,O-8,3	-0.1
	Yr	22	93	13	25	2	0	0	11	2	4	.269	.284	.290	88	-0						O-11/2-8,3S	-0.1
1873	Mut-n	36	168	28	55	6	1	0	22	1	2	.327	.331	.375	108	2						2-27/O-6,3C1	0.0
1874	Mut-n	65	295	55	71	8	5	0	9			.241	.263	.302	77	-8						*2-51,S-14	-0.8
1875	Mut-n	70	276	29	56	8	0	0	10			.203	.231	.232	57	-12						2-47,3-22/O	-1.1
1878	Ind-N	19	84	12	11	1	0	0	5	5	11	.131	.180	.143	8	-8				.841	-6	S-19	-1.3
1879	Tro-N	28	106	17	28	7	1	0	10	8	4	.264	.316	.349	127	4				.834	4	S-24/O-4	0.8
1881	Wor-N	24	103	13	29	1	0	1	15	5	6	.282	.315	.320	95	-1				.898	3	S-24	0.3
1883	NY-a	97	417	75	127	19	6	0		31		.305	.353	.379	130	13				.875	-6	*S-97	0.9
1884	*NY-a	111	432	114	110	15	3	1	**74**			.255	.375	.310	129	19				.879	-17	*S-110/2-1	0.3
1885	NY-a	107	420	98	107	12	4	1	**61**			.255	.353	.310	120	15				.892	13	*S-107/3-1	2.6
1886	NY-a	109	413	89	93	7	2	0	64			.225	.332	.252	88	-2	14			.855	-8	S-73,O-36	-0.9
1887	NY-a	68	257	61	63	5	1	0	48			.245	.380	.272	87	0	29			.895	10	O-37,S-32/2	0.8
	NY-N	1	2	0	0	0	0	0			1	.000	.000	.000	-99	-1	0			.000	0	/3-1	0.0
1890	Bro-a	60	223	44	56	3	2	0	35			.251	.365	.283	94	1	12			.866	5	S-57/O-4	-0.3
Total	4 n	193	832	125	207	24	6	0	33	22	6	.249	.268	.292	78	-19	3					2-133/3-29,OS1C	-2.0
Total	9	624	2457	523	624	70	19	3	30	331	22	.254	.349	.302	108	41	55			.875	-16	S-543/O-81,32	3.2

◼ LYNN NELSON   Nelson, Lynn Bernard "Line Drive"   b: 2/24/05, Sheldon, N.Dak.   d: 2/15/55, Kansas City, Mo.   BL/TR, 5′10.5″, 170 lbs.   Deb: 4/18/30

1930	Chi-N	37	18	0	4	1	1	0	2	0	1	.222	.222	.389	44	-2	0			.966	1	P-37	0.0
1933	Chi-N	29	21	5	5	1	1	0	1	1	3	.238	.273	.381	85	-0	0			1.000	1	P-24	0.0
1934	Chi-N	2	0	0	0	0	0	0	0	0	0	—	—	—	—	0	0			.000	-0	/P-2	0.0
1937	Phi-A	74	113	18	40	6	2	4	29	6	13	.354	.387	.549	135	6	1	0	0	1.000	-0	P-30/O-6	0.3
1938	Phi-A	67	112	12	31	0	0	15	7	12	.277	.319	.277	52	-8	0	0	0	.952	1	P-32	0.0
1939	Phi-A	40	80	3	15	2	0	0	5	2	13	.188	.217	.213	10	-11	0	0	-1	.950	-1	P-35	0.0
1940	Det-A	19	23	4	8	0	0	1	3	0	6	.348	.348	.478	102	0	0	0	0	1.000	0	/P-6	0.0
Total	7	268	367	42	103	10	4	5	55	16	48	.281	.313	.371	74	-16	1	1		.967	1	P-166/O-6	0.3

◼ RAY NELSON   Nelson, Raymond "Kell" (b: Raymond Nelson Kellogg)   b: 8/4/1875, Holyoke, Mass.   d: 1/8/61, Mt.Vernon, N.Y.   BR/TR, 5′9″, 150 lbs.   Deb: 5/6/01

1901	NY-N	39	130	12	26	2	0	0	7	10		.200	.262	.215	41	-9	3			.885	-3	2-39	-1.1

◼ RICKY NELSON   Nelson, Ricky Lee   b: 5/8/59, Eloy, Ariz.   BL/TR, 6′, 200 lbs.   Deb: 5/17/83

1983	Sea-A	98	291	32	74	13	3	5	36	17	50	.254	.295	.371	79	-9	7	4	0	.971	-8	O-91/D-1	-1.9
1984	Sea-A	9	15	2	3	0	0	0	2	1	4	.200	.250	.400	91	-0	0	0	0	1.000	-0	/O-2,D-3	-0.1
1985	Sea-A	6	2	2	0	0	0	0	0	0	1	.000	.000	.000	-99	-1	0	0	0	1.000	-1	/O-3	-0.2

YEAR	TM/L	G	AB	R	H	2B	3B	HR	RBI	BB	SO	AVG	OBP	SLG	PRO+	BR/A	SB	CS	SBR	FA	FR	G/POS	TPR
1986	Sea-A	10	12	2	2	0	0	0	1	0	4	.167	.167	.167	-9	-2	1	0	0	.667	-0	/O-1,D-5	-0.2
Total	4	123	320	38	79	13	3	6	39	19	59	.247	.289	.363	75	-11	8	4	0	.965	-9	/O-97,D-9	-2.4

■ ROB NELSON
Nelson, Robert Augustus b: 5/17/64, Pasadena, Cal. BL/TL, 6'4", 215 lbs. Deb: 9/9/86

YEAR	TM/L	G	AB	R	H	2B	3B	HR	RBI	BB	SO	AVG	OBP	SLG	PRO+	BR/A	SB	CS	SBR	FA	FR	G/POS	TPR
1986	Oak-A	5	9	1	2	1	0	0	1	1	4	.222	.300	.333	78	-0	0	0	0	.800	0	/1-2,D-1	0.0
1987	Oak-A	7	24	1	4	1	0	0	0	0	12	.167	.167	.208	-2	-3	0	0	0	.968	3	/1-7	-0.1
	SD-N	10	11	0	1	0	0	0	1	1	8	.091	.167	.091	-31	-2	0	0	0	1.000	0	/1-2	-0.2
1988	SD-N	7	21	4	4	0	0	1	3	2	9	.190	.261	.333	71	-1	0	0	0	.981	1	/1-5	-0.1
1989	SD-N	42	82	6	16	0	1	3	7	20	29	.195	.353	.329	96	0	1	3	-2	.991	3	1-31	0.1
1990	SD-N	5	5	0	0	0	0	0	0	0	4	.000	.000	.000	-99	-1	0	0	0	.000	0	/H	-0.2
Total	5	76	152	12	27	2	1	4	11	24	66	.178	.290	.283	62	-8	1	3	-2	.983	6	/1-47,D-1	-0.5

■ TEX NELSON
Nelson, Robert Sidney "Babe" b: 8/7/36, Dallas, Tex. BL/TR, 6'3", 205 lbs. Deb: 6/22/55

YEAR	TM/L	G	AB	R	H	2B	3B	HR	RBI	BB	SO	AVG	OBP	SLG	PRO+	BR/A	SB	CS	SBR	FA	FR	G/POS	TPR
1955	Bal-A	25	31	4	6	0	0	0	1	7	13	.194	.342	.194	50	-1	0	0	0	.889	0	/O-6,1-2	-0.2
1956	Bal-A	39	68	5	14	2	0	0	5	7	22	.206	.280	.235	40	-6	0	0	0	.939	-3	O-24	-0.9
1957	Bal-A	15	23	2	5	0	2	0	5	1	5	.217	.280	.391	87	-1	0	0	0	1.000	-2	/O-8	-0.3
Total	3	79	122	11	25	2	2	0	11	15	40	.205	.297	.254	52	-8	0	0	0	.938	-5	/O-38,1-2	-1.4

■ TOMMY NELSON
Nelson, Tom Cousineau b: 5/1/17, Chicago, Ill. d: 9/24/73, San Diego, Cal. BR/TR, 5'11.5", 180 lbs. Deb: 4/17/45

YEAR	TM/L	G	AB	R	H	2B	3B	HR	RBI	BB	SO	AVG	OBP	SLG	PRO+	BR/A	SB	CS	SBR	FA	FR	G/POS	TPR
1945	Bos-N	40	121	6	20	2	0	0	6	3	16	.165	.192	.182	4	-16	1			.910	-3	3-20,2-12	-1.8

■ DICK NEN
Nen, Richard Le Roy b: 9/24/39, South Gate, Cal. BL/TL, 6'2", 205 lbs. Deb: 9/18/63 F

YEAR	TM/L	G	AB	R	H	2B	3B	HR	RBI	BB	SO	AVG	OBP	SLG	PRO+	BR/A	SB	CS	SBR	FA	FR	G/POS	TPR
1963	LA-N	7	8	2	1	0	0	1	3	3	3	.125	.364	.500	157	1	0	0	0	1.000	-1	/1-5	0.0
1965	Was-A	69	246	18	64	7	1	6	31	19	47	.260	.316	.370	96	-2	1	2	-1	.993	8	1-65	0.2
1966	Was-A	94	235	20	50	8	0	6	30	28	46	.213	.297	.323	79	-6	0	2	-1	.990	-2	1-76	-1.5
1967	Was-A	110	238	21	52	7	1	6	29	21	39	.218	.282	.332	84	-5	0	1	-1	.995	1	1-65/O-1	-0.9
1968	Chi-N	81	94	8	17	1	1	2	16	6	17	.181	.230	.277	48	-6	0	1	0	.987	-1	1-52	-0.9
1970	Was-A	6	5	1	1	0	0	0	0	0	0	.200	.200	.200	11	-1	0	0	0	1.000	0	/1-1	0.0
Total	6	367	826	70	185	23	3	21	107	77	152	.224	.291	.335	82	-19	1	5	-3	.992	7	1-264/O-1	-3.1

■ JACK NESS
Ness, John Charles b: 11/11/1885, Chicago, Ill. d: 12/3/57, DeLand, Fla. BR/TR, 6'2", 165 lbs. Deb: 5/9/11

YEAR	TM/L	G	AB	R	H	2B	3B	HR	RBI	BB	SO	AVG	OBP	SLG	PRO+	BR/A	SB	CS	SBR	FA	FR	G/POS	TPR
1911	Det-A	12	39	6	6	0	0	0	2	2		.154	.195	.154	-2	-5	0			.977	1	1-12	-0.5
1916	Chi-A	75	258	32	69	7	5	1	34	9	32	.267	.310	.345	96	-2	4			.979	-5	1-69	-1.1
Total	2	87	297	38	75	7	5	1	36	11	32	.253	.295	.320	82	-8	4			.978	-4	/1-81	-1.6

■ GRAIG NETTLES
Nettles, Graig b: 8/20/44, San Diego, Cal. BL/TR, 6', 186 lbs. Deb: 9/6/67 FC

YEAR	TM/L	G	AB	R	H	2B	3B	HR	RBI	BB	SO	AVG	OBP	SLG	PRO+	BR/A	SB	CS	SBR	FA	FR	G/POS	TPR
1967	Min-A	3	3	0	1	1	0	0	0	0	0	.333	.333	.667	175	0	0	0	0	.000	0	H	0.0
1968	Min-A	22	76	13	17	2	1	5	8	7	20	.224	.298	.474	125	0	0	0	0	.968	1	O-16/3-5,1	0.2
1969	*Min-A	96	225	27	50	9	2	7	26	32	47	.222	.322	.373	92	-2	1	2	-1	.987	-5	O-54,3-21	-1.1
1970	Cle-A	157	549	81	129	13	1	26	62	81	77	.235	.336	.404	99	-1	3	1	0	.967	28	*3-154/O-3	2.7
1971	Cle-A	158	598	78	156	18	1	28	86	82	56	.261	.353	.435	112	10	7	4	-0	.973	42	*3-158	5.3
1972	Cle-A	150	557	65	141	28	0	17	70	57	50	.253	.328	.395	110	7	2	3	-1	.956	5	*3-150	1.0
1973	NY-A	160	552	65	129	18	0	22	81	78	74	.234	.336	.386	107	6	0	0	0	.953	26	*3-157/D-2	3.1
1974	NY-A	155	566	74	139	21	1	22	75	59	75	.246	.320	.403	110	6	1	0	0	.961	16	*3-154/S-1	2.2
1975	NY-A★	157	581	71	155	24	4	21	91	51	88	.267	.328	.430	116	11	1	3	-2	.964	11	*3-157	2.0
1976	*NY-A	158	583	88	148	29	2	32	93	62	94	.254	.330	.475	135	24	11	6	-0	.965	17	*3-158/S-1	4.1
1977	*NY-A	158	589	99	150	23	4	37	107	68	79	.255	.335	.496	124	18	2	5	-2	.974	-3	*3-156/D-1	1.1
1978	*NY-A★	159	587	81	162	23	2	27	93	59	60	.276	.348	.460	128	21	1	1	-0	.975	-6	*3-159/S-2	1.3
1979	NY-A★	145	521	71	132	15	1	20	73	59	53	.253	.329	.401	98	-3	1	2	-1	.966	9	*3-144	0.5
1980	*NY-A★	89	324	52	79	14	0	16	45	42	42	.244	.332	.435	110	4	0	0	0	.960	-3	3-88/S-1	0.0
1981	*NY-A	103	349	46	85	7	1	15	46	47	49	.244	.335	.398	112	6	0	2	-1	.972	8	3-97/D-4	1.2
1982	NY-A	122	405	47	94	11	2	18	55	51	49	.232	.319	.402	98	-1	1	5	-3	.934	-3	*3-113/D-3	0.1
1983	NY-A	129	462	56	123	17	3	20	75	51	65	.266	.343	.446	120	12	0	1	-1	.956	1	*3-126/D-1	1.0
1984	*SD-N	124	395	56	90	11	1	20	65	58	55	.228	.334	.413	109	5	0	0	0	.936	-10	*3-119	-0.7
1985	SD-N★	137	440	66	115	23	1	15	61	72	59	.261	.365	.420	121	14	0	0	0	.959	-9	*3-130	0.4
1986	SD-N	126	354	36	77	9	0	16	55	41	62	.218	.302	.379	88	-6	0	1	-1	.941	-2	*3-114	-1.1
1987	Atl-N	112	177	16	37	8	1	5	33	22	25	.209	.296	.350	67	-8	1	0	0	.951	1	3-40/1-6	-0.9
1988	Mon-N	80	93	5	16	4	1	1	14	9	19	.172	.245	.247	40	-7	0	2	-2	.818	-2	3-12/1-5	-1.0
Total	22	2700	8986	1193	2225	328	28	390	1314	1088	1209	.248	.332	.421	110	119	32	36	-12	.961	132	*3-2412/O-73,1DS	21.4

■ JIM NETTLES
Nettles, James William b: 3/2/47, San Diego, Cal. BL/TL, 6', 186 lbs. Deb: 9/7/70 F

YEAR	TM/L	G	AB	R	H	2B	3B	HR	RBI	BB	SO	AVG	OBP	SLG	PRO+	BR/A	SB	CS	SBR	FA	FR	G/POS	TPR
1970	Min-A	13	20	3	5	0	0	0	1	1	5	.250	.286	.250	48	-1	0	1	-1	1.000	-2	O-11	-0.5
1971	Min-A	70	168	17	42	5	1	6	24	19	24	.250	.326	.399	101	0	3	2	-0	.986	2	O-62	-0.1
1972	Min-A	102	235	28	48	5	2	4	15	32	52	.204	.302	.294	74	-0	4	3	-1	.982	-1	O-78/1-1	-1.3
1974	Det-A	43	141	20	32	5	1	6	17	15	26	.227	.306	.404	99	-0	3	4	-2	1.000	-1	O-41	-0.5
1979	KC-A	11	23	0	2	0	0	0	1	3	2	.087	.192	.087	-21	-4	0	0	0	1.000	-0	/O-8,1-1	-0.4
1981	Oak-A	1	0	0	0	0	0	0	0	0	0	—	—	—	—		0	0	0	.000	-0	/O-1	0.0
Total	6	240	587	68	129	15	4	16	57	70	109	.220	.305	.341	83	-12	10	10	-3	.988	-3	O-201/1-2	-2.8

■ MORRIS NETTLES
Nettles, Morris b: 1/26/52, Los Angeles, Cal. BL/TL, 6'1", 170 lbs. Deb: 4/26/74

YEAR	TM/L	G	AB	R	H	2B	3B	HR	RBI	BB	SO	AVG	OBP	SLG	PRO+	BR/A	SB	CS	SBR	FA	FR	G/POS	TPR
1974	Cal-A	56	175	27	48	4	0	0	8	16	38	.274	.335	.297	88	-2	20	11	-1	.990	-6	O-54	-1.2
1975	Cal-A	112	294	50	68	11	0	0	23	26	57	.231	.296	.269	65	-13	22	15	-2	.974	-2	O-90/D-9	-2.1
Total	2	168	469	77	116	15	0	0	31	42	95	.247	.311	.279	74	-16	42	26	-3	.980	-8	O-144/D-9	-3.3

■ MILO NETZEL
Netzel, Miles A. b: 5/12/1886, Eldred, Pa. d: 3/18/38, Oxnard, Cal. TL, Deb: 9/16/09

YEAR	TM/L	G	AB	R	H	2B	3B	HR	RBI	BB	SO	AVG	OBP	SLG	PRO+	BR/A	SB	CS	SBR	FA	FR	G/POS	TPR
1909	Cle-A	10	37	2	7	1	0	0	3			.189	.250	.216	49	-2	1			.800	-3	/3-6,O-2	-0.6

■ OTTO NEU
Neu, Otto Adam b: 9/24/1894, Springfield, Ohio d: 9/19/32, Kenton, Ohio BR/TR, 5'11", 170 lbs. Deb: 7/10/17

YEAR	TM/L	G	AB	R	H	2B	3B	HR	RBI	BB	SO	AVG	OBP	SLG	PRO+	BR/A	SB	CS	SBR	FA	FR	G/POS	TPR
1917	StL-A	1	0	0	0	0	0	0	0	0	0	—	—	—			0			.000	0	/S-1	0.0

■ JOHNNY NEUN
Neun, John Henry b: 10/28/1900, Baltimore, Md. d: 3/28/90, Baltimore, Md. BB/TL, 5'10.5", 175 lbs. Deb: 4/14/25 MC

YEAR	TM/L	G	AB	R	H	2B	3B	HR	RBI	BB	SO	AVG	OBP	SLG	PRO+	BR/A	SB	CS	SBR	FA	FR	G/POS	TPR
1925	Det-A	60	75	15	20	3	3	0	4	9	12	.267	.345	.387	87	-2	2	3	-1	.990	4	1-13	-0.4
1926	Det-A	97	242	47	72	14	4	0	15	27	26	.298	.370	.388	97	-1	4	7	-3	.993	-3	1-49	-0.9
1927	Det-A	79	204	38	66	9	4	0	27	35	13	.324	.427	.407	116	7	22	7	2	.980	-3	1-53	0.3
1928	Det-A	36	108	15	23	3	1	0	5	7	10	.213	.261	.259	36	-10	2	2	-1	.975	-0	1-25	-1.2
1930	Bos-N	81	212	39	69	12	2	2	23	21	18	.325	.389	.429	101	1	9			.991	6	1-55	-0.4
1931	Bos-N	79	104	17	23	1	3	0	11	11	14	.221	.302	.288	62	-5	2			.994	-0	1-36	-0.7
Total	6	432	945	171	273	42	17	2	85	110	93	.289	.366	.376	91	-10	41	19		.987	-7	1-231	-3.3

■ ALEXANDER NEVIN
Nevin, Alexander Brown b: 10/3/1850, Alegheny City, Pa. d: 10/10/21, Pensacola, Fla. Deb: 6/17/1873

YEAR	TM/L	G	AB	R	H	2B	3B	HR	RBI	BB	SO	AVG	OBP	SLG	PRO+	BR/A	SB	CS	SBR	FA	FR	G/POS	TPR
1873	Res-n	13	54	7	11	0	2	0	3			.204	.204	.278	44	-3						3-12/O-1	-0.3

■ DON NEWCOMBE
Newcombe, Donald "Newk" b: 6/14/26, Madison, N.J. BL/TR, 6'4", 225 lbs. Deb: 5/20/49

YEAR	TM/L	G	AB	R	H	2B	3B	HR	RBI	BB	SO	AVG	OBP	SLG	PRO+	BR/A	SB	CS	SBR	FA	FR	G/POS	TPR
1949	*Bro-N★	39	96	8	22	4	0	0	10	5	16	.229	.267	.271	43	-8	0			1.000	1	P-38	0.0
1950	Bro-N★	40	97	8	24	3	1	1	8	10	19	.247	.318	.330	69	-4	0			.969	-0	P-40	0.0
1951	Bro-N★	40	103	11	23	3	1	0	8	9	9	.223	.286	.272	50	-7	0	0	0	.958	1	P-40	0.0

YEAR	TM/L	G	AB	R	H	2B	3B	HR	RBI	BB	SO	AVG	OBP	SLG	PRO+	BR/A	SB	CS	SBR	FA	FR	G/POS	TPR
1954	Bro-N	31	47	6	15	1	0	0	4	4	6	.319	.373	.340	85	-1	0	0	0	.931	-1	P-29	0.0
1955	*Bro-N★	57	117	18	42	9	1	7	23	6	18	.359	.395	.632	163	10	1	0	0	.907	-2	P-34	0.0
1956	*Bro-N	52	111	13	26	6	0	2	16	12	18	.234	.315	.342	71	-4	1	0	0	.985	0	P-38	0.0
1957	Bro-N	34	74	8	17	2	0	1	7	11	11	.230	.329	.297	64	-4	0	1	-1	.964	1	P-28	0.0
1958	LA-N	11	12	2	5	0	0	0	0	2	2	.417	.500	.417	141	1	0	0	0	1.000	0	P-11	0.0
	Cin-N	39	60	9	21	1	0	1	9	8	10	.350	.426	.417	118	2	0	0	0	1.000	-2	P-20	0.0
	Yr	50	72	11	26	1	0	1	9	10	12	.361	.439	.417	122	3	0	0	0	**1.000**	-2	P-31	0.0
1959	Cin-N	61	105	10	32	2	0	3	21	17	23	.305	.402	.410	113	3	0	0	0	.978	-1	P-30	0.0
1960	Cin-N	24	36	0	5	1	0	0	1	3	8	.139	.205	.167	3	-5	0	0	0	.895	-1	P-16	0.0
	Cle-A	24	20	1	6	1	0	0	1	1	7	.300	.333	.350	88	-0	0	0	0	.889	-1	P-20	0.0
Total	10	452	878	94	238	33	3	15	108	87	147	.271	.339	.367	85	-17	2	1		.963	-6	P-344	0.0

■ JOHN NEWELL
Newell, John A. b: 1/14/1868, Wilmington, Del. d: 1/28/19, Wilmington, Del. BR/TL, Deb: 7/22/1891

YEAR	TM/L	G	AB	R	H	2B	3B	HR	RBI	BB	SO	AVG	OBP	SLG	PRO+	BR/A	SB	CS	SBR	FA	FR	G/POS	TPR
1891	Pit-N	5	18	1	2	0	0	0	2	0	0	.111	.158	.111	-22	-3	0			.846	-2	/3-5	-0.4

■ T. E. NEWELL
Newell, T. E. b: St.Louis, Mo. Deb: 8/8/1877

YEAR	TM/L	G	AB	R	H	2B	3B	HR	RBI	BB	SO	AVG	OBP	SLG	PRO+	BR/A	SB	CS	SBR	FA	FR	G/POS	TPR
1877	StL-N	1	3	0	0	0	0	0	0	0	0	.000	.000	.000	-99	-1				.833	0	/S-1	0.0

■ MARC NEWFIELD
Newfield, Marc Alexander b: 10/19/72, Sacramento, Cal. BR/TR, 6'4", 205 lbs. Deb: 7/6/93

YEAR	TM/L	G	AB	R	H	2B	3B	HR	RBI	BB	SO	AVG	OBP	SLG	PRO+	BR/A	SB	CS	SBR	FA	FR	G/POS	TPR
1993	Sea-A	22	66	5	15	3	0	1	7	2	8	.227	.261	.318	54	-4	0	1	-1	1.000	-2	D-15/O-5	-0.7
1994	Sea-A	12	38	3	7	1	0	1	4	2	4	.184	.225	.289	31	-4	0	0	0	1.000	-1	/O-3,D-9	-0.5
Total	2	34	104	8	22	4	0	2	11	4	12	.212	.248	.308	45	-8	0	1	-1	1.000	-3	/D-24,O-8	-1.2

■ AL NEWMAN
Newman, Albert Dwayne b: 6/30/60, Kansas City, Mo. BB/TR, 5'9", 183 lbs. Deb: 6/14/85

YEAR	TM/L	G	AB	R	H	2B	3B	HR	RBI	BB	SO	AVG	OBP	SLG	PRO+	BR/A	SB	CS	SBR	FA	FR	G/POS	TPR
1985	Mon-N	25	29	7	5	1	0	0	1	3	4	.172	.250	.207	31	-3	2	1	0	1.000	10	2-15/S-2	0.7
1986	Mon-N	95	185	23	37	3	0	1	8	21	20	.200	.282	.232	44	-14	11	11	-3	.967	9	2-59,S-22	-0.6
1987	*Min-A	110	307	44	68	15	5	0	29	34	27	.221	.299	.303	58	-18	15	11	-2	.982	-11	S-55,2-47,3/OD	-2.5
1988	Min-A	105	260	35	58	7	0	0	19	29	34	.223	.301	.250	54	-15	12	3	2	.966	-4	3-60,S-28,2/D	-1.6
1989	Min-A	141	446	62	113	18	2	0	38	59	46	.253	.343	.303	78	-11	25	12	0	.980	-22	2-84,3-37,S/OD	-2.9
1990	Min-A	144	388	43	94	14	0	0	30	33	34	.242	.305	.278	60	-20	13	6	0	.993	-6	2-89,S-48,3/O	-1.8
1991	*Min-A	118	246	25	47	5	0	0	19	23	21	.191	.263	.211	31	-22	4	5	-2	.987	-1	S-55,2-35,3/10D	-2.2
1992	Tex-A	116	246	25	54	5	0	0	12	34	26	.220	.317	.240	60	-12	9	6	-1	.983	12	2-72,3-28,S/OD	0.1
Total	8	854	2107	264	476	68	7	1	156	236	212	.226	.306	.266	58	-115	91	55	-6	.984	-10	2-424,S-261,3/DO1	-10.8

■ CHARLIE NEWMAN
Newman, Charles "Decker" b: 11/5/1868, Juda, Wis. d: 11/23/47, San Diego, Cal. BR/TR, Deb: 9/11/1892

YEAR	TM/L	G	AB	R	H	2B	3B	HR	RBI	BB	SO	AVG	OBP	SLG	PRO+	BR/A	SB	CS	SBR	FA	FR	G/POS	TPR
1892	NY-N	3	12	1	4	0	0	0	1	2	0	.333	.429	.333	133	1	3			.750	-0	/O-3	0.0
	Chi-N	16	61	4	10	0	0	0	2	1	6	.164	.177	.164	3	-7	2			.950	-3	O-16	-1.0
	Yr	19	73	5	14	0	0	0	3	3	6	.192	.224	.192	26	-7	5			.917	-3	O-19	-1.0

■ JEFF NEWMAN
Newman, Jeffrey Lynn b: 9/11/48, Fort Worth, Tex. BR/TR, 6'2", 218 lbs. Deb: 6/30/76 MC

YEAR	TM/L	G	AB	R	H	2B	3B	HR	RBI	BB	SO	AVG	OBP	SLG	PRO+	BR/A	SB	CS	SBR	FA	FR	G/POS	TPR
1976	Oak-A	43	77	5	15	4	0	0	4	4	12	.195	.235	.247	43	-6	0	0	0	.981	6	C-43	0.1
1977	Oak-A	94	162	17	36	9	0	4	15	4	24	.222	.246	.352	61	-9	2	0	1	.970	10	C-94/P-1	0.3
1978	Oak-A	105	268	25	64	7	1	9	32	18	40	.239	.289	.373	90	-5	0	3	-2	.969	-5	C-61,1-36/D	-1.2
1979	Oak-A☆	143	516	53	119	17	2	22	71	27	88	.231	.270	.399	82	-15	2	1	0	.977	-1	C-81,1-46/3D	-1.6
1980	Oak-A	127	438	37	102	19	1	15	56	25	81	.233	.276	.384	85	-11	3	4	-2	.982	-9	1-60,C-55/32D	-2.3
1981	*Oak-A	68	216	17	50	12	0	3	15	9	22	.231	.262	.329	73	-8	0	2	-1	.995	2	C-37,1-30	-0.8
1982	Oak-A	72	251	19	50	11	0	6	30	14	49	.199	.242	.315	54	-17	0	1	-1	.989	-1	C-67/1-3,3D	-1.6
1983	Bos-A	59	132	11	25	4	0	3	7	10	31	.189	.257	.288	46	-10	0	1		.990	2	C-51/D-6	-0.7
1984	Bos-A	24	63	5	14	2	0	1	3	5	16	.222	.279	.302	58	-4	0	0	0	.992	2	C-24	-0.1
Total	9	735	2123	189	475	85	4	63	233	116	369	.224	.266	.357	73	-84	7	12	-5	.981	7	C-513,1-175/D32P	-7.9

■ PATRICK NEWNAM
Newnam, Patrick Henry b: 12/10/1880, Hempstead, Tex. d: 6/20/38, San Antonio, Tex. BL/TR, 6', 180 lbs. Deb: 5/29/10

YEAR	TM/L	G	AB	R	H	2B	3B	HR	RBI	BB	SO	AVG	OBP	SLG	PRO+	BR/A	SB	CS	SBR	FA	FR	G/POS	TPR
1910	StL-A	103	384	45	83	3	8	2	26	29		.216	.275	.281	79	-10	16			.972	-4	*1-103	-1.6
1911	StL-A	20	62	11	12	4	0	0	5	12		.194	.351	.258	74	-1	4			.986	1	1-20	-0.1
Total	2	123	446	56	95	7	8	2	31	41		.213	.287	.278	78	-11	20			.974	-3	1-123	-1.7

■ SKEETER NEWSOME
Newsome, Lamar Ashby b: 10/18/10, Phenix City, Ala. d: 8/31/89, Columbus, Ga. BR/TR, 5'9", 155 lbs. Deb: 4/19/35

YEAR	TM/L	G	AB	R	H	2B	3B	HR	RBI	BB	SO	AVG	OBP	SLG	PRO+	BR/A	SB	CS	SBR	FA	FR	G/POS	TPR
1935	Phi-A	59	145	18	30	7	1	1	10	5	9	.207	.233	.290	35	-14	2			.956	5	S-24,2-13/3O	-0.5
1936	Phi-A	127	471	41	106	15	2	0	46	25	27	.225	.266	.265	32	-51	13	4	2	.957	7	*S-123/2-2,3O	-3.1
1937	Phi-A	122	438	53	111	22	1	1	30	37	22	.253	.312	.315	59	-27	11	5	0	.954	7	*S-122	-1.1
1938	Phi-A	17	48	7	13	4	0	0	7	1	4	.271	.286	.354	61	-3	1	1	-0	.971	1	S-15	-0.1
1939	Phi-A	99	248	22	55	9	1	0	17	19	12	.222	.277	.266	40	-22	5	7	-3	.950	1	S-93/2-2	-1.6
1941	Bos-A	93	227	28	51	6	0	2	17	22	11	.225	.296	.278	51	-16	10	4	1	.958	15	S-69,2-23	0.4
1942	Bos-A	29	95	7	26	6	0	0	9	9	5	.274	.337	.337	87	-2	2	1	0	.925	3	3-12,2-10/S	0.2
1943	Bos-A	114	449	48	119	21	2	1	22	21	21	.265	.301	.327	82	-11	5	6	-2	.962	14	S-98,3-15	0.9
1944	Bos-A	136	472	41	114	26	3	0	41	33	21	.242	.291	.309	72	-17	4	3	-1	.963	11	*S-126/2-8,3	0.3
1945	Bos-A	125	438	45	127	30	1	1	48	20	15	.290	.322	.370	98	-2	6	3	0	.963	22	2-82,S-33,3	2.9
1946	Phi-N	112	375	35	87	10	2	1	23	30	23	.232	.289	.277	63	-18	4			.955	-12	*S-107/2-3,3	-2.6
1947	Phi-N	95	310	36	71	8	2	2	22	24	24	.229	.284	.287	54	-21	4			.969	2	S-85/2-6,3	-1.5
Total	12	1128	3716	381	910	164	15	9	292	246	194	.245	.293	.304	62	-205	67	35		.959	78	S-902,2-149/3O	-5.8

■ WARREN NEWSON
Newson, Warren Dale b: 7/3/64, Newnan, Ga. BL/TL, 5'7", 190 lbs. Deb: 5/29/91

YEAR	TM/L	G	AB	R	H	2B	3B	HR	RBI	BB	SO	AVG	OBP	SLG	PRO+	BR/A	SB	CS	SBR	FA	FR	G/POS	TPR
1991	Chi-A	71	132	20	39	5	0	4	25	28	34	.295	.419	.424	137	8	2	2	-1	.962	-10	O-50/D-3	-0.3
1992	Chi-A	63	136	19	30	3	0	1	11	37	38	.221	.385	.265	87	-0	3	0	1	1.000	-4	O-50/D-4	-0.4
1993	*Chi-A	26	40	9	12	0	0	2	6	9	12	.300	.429	.450	139	3	0	0	0	1.000	-1	D-10/O-5	0.1
1994	Chi-A	63	102	16	26	5	0	2	7	14	23	.255	.345	.363	83	-2	1	0	0	.979	-4	O-34/D-3	-0.6
Total	4	223	410	64	107	13	0	9	49	88	107	.261	.392	.359	107	8	6	2	1	.983	-19	O-139/D-20	-1.2

■ GUS NIARHOS
Niarhos, Constantine Gregory b: 12/6/20, Birmingham, Ala. BR/TR, 6', 165 lbs. Deb: 6/9/46 C

YEAR	TM/L	G	AB	R	H	2B	3B	HR	RBI	BB	SO	AVG	OBP	SLG	PRO+	BR/A	SB	CS	SBR	FA	FR	G/POS	TPR
1946	NY-A	37	40	11	9	1	1	0	2	11	2	.225	.392	.300	94	0	1	0	0	.989	6	C-29	0.8
1948	NY-A	83	228	41	61	12	2	0	19	52	15	.268	.404	.338	99	3	1	3	-2	.990	11	C-82	1.6
1949	*NY-A	32	43	7	12	2	1	0	6	13	8	.279	.456	.372	120	2	0	0	0	1.000	4	C-30	0.7
1950	NY-A	1	0	0	0	0	0	0	0	0	0	—	—	—			0	0	0	.000	0	R	0.0
	Chi-A	41	105	17	34	4	0	0	16	14	6	.324	.408	.362	101	1	0	0	0	.978	8	C-36	1.0
	Yr	42	105	17	34	4	0	0	16	14	6	.324	.408	.362	101	1	0	0	0	.978	8	C-36	1.0
1951	Chi-A	66	168	27	43	6	1	0	10	47	9	.256	.419	.310	101	4	4	3	-1	.985	4	C-59	0.9
1952	Bos-A	29	58	4	6	0	0	0	4	12	9	.103	.268	.103	6	-7	0	0	0	.992	6	C-25	0.1
1953	Bos-A	16	35	6	7	1	0	0	2	9	2	.200	.300	.286	56	-2	0	1	-1	.985	4	C-16	0.1
1954	Phi-N	3	5	0	1	0	0	0	0	0	1	.200	.200	.200	5	-1	0	0	0	1.000	0	/C-3	0.0
1955	Phi-N	7	9	1	1	0	0	0	0	2	1	.111	.111	.111	-42	-2	0	0	0	1.000	0	/C-7	-0.1
Total	9	315	691	114	174	26	5	1	59	153	56	.252	.390	.308	89	-2	6	7	-2	.988	45	C-287	5.0

■ SAM NICHOL
Nichol, Samuel Anderson b: 4/20/1869, Ireland d: 4/19/37, Steubenville, Ohio BR/TR, 5'10", 178 lbs. Deb: 10/5/1888

YEAR	TM/L	G	AB	R	H	2B	3B	HR	RBI	BB	SO	AVG	OBP	SLG	PRO+	BR/A	SB	CS	SBR	FA	FR	G/POS	TPR
1888	Pit-N	8	22	3	1	0	0	0	0	2	2	.045	.125	.045	-47	-4	0			.952	0	/O-8	-0.3

YEAR	TM/L	G	AB	R	H	2B	3B	HR	RBI	BB	SO	AVG	OBP	SLG	PRO+	BR/A	SB	CS	SBR	FA	FR	G/POS	TPR
1890	Col-a	14	56	7	9	0	0	0		2		.161	.190	.161	4	-7	3			.903	3	O-14	-0.4
Total	2	22	78	10	10	0	0	0	0	4	2	.128	.171	.128	-10	-10	3			.923	3	/O-22	-0.7

■ DON NICHOLAS
Nicholas, Donald Leigh b: 10/30/30, Phoenix, Ariz.   BL/TR, 5'7", 150 lbs.   Deb: 4/16/52

YEAR	TM/L	G	AB	R	H	2B	3B	HR	RBI	BB	SO	AVG	OBP	SLG	PRO+	BR/A	SB	CS	SBR	FA	FR	G/POS	TPR
1952	Chi-A	3	2	0	0	0	0	0	0	0	0	.000	.000	.000	-99	-1	0	0	0	.000	0	H	-0.1
1954	Chi-A	7	0	3	0	0	0	0	0	1	0	—	1.000	—	185	0	0	1	-1	.000	0	H	0.0
Total	2	10	2	3	0	0	0	0	0	1	0	.000	.333	.000	-2	-0	0	1	-1		0	-0,-0	-0.1

■ SIMON NICHOLLS
Nicholls, Simon Burdette b: 7/18/1882, Germantown, Md.   d: 3/12/11, Baltimore, Md.   BL/TR, 5'11.5", 165 lbs.   Deb: 9/18/03

YEAR	TM/L	G	AB	R	H	2B	3B	HR	RBI	BB	SO	AVG	OBP	SLG	PRO+	BR/A	SB	CS	SBR	FA	FR	G/POS	TPR
1903	Det-A	2	8	0	3	0	0	0		0		.375	.375	.375	129	0	0			.600	-2	/S-2	-0.2
1906	Phi-A	12	44	1	8	1	0	0		1	3	.182	.234	.205	36	-3	0			.965	-2	S-12	-0.6
1907	Phi-A	124	460	75	139	12	2	0	23	24		.302	.338	.337	113	6	13			.930	-20	S-82,2-28,3	-1.3
1908	Phi-A	150	550	58	119	17	3	6	31	35		.216	.265	.280	72	-18	14			.913	-21	*S-120,2-23/3	-4.1
1909	Phi-A	21	71	10	15	2	1	0	3	3		.211	.243	.268	60	-3	0			.889	1	S-14/3-5,1	-0.1
1910	Cle-A	3	0	0	0	0	0	0	0	0		—	—	—		0	0			.000	-1	/S-3	
Total	6	312	1133	144	284	32	6	6	58	65		.251	.292	.300	86	-18	27			.917	-45	S-233/2-51,31	-6.6

■ AL NICHOLS
Nichols, Albert H. b: Brooklyn, N.Y.   5'11", 180 lbs.   Deb: 4/24/1875

YEAR	TM/L	G	AB	R	H	2B	3B	HR	RBI	BB	SO	AVG	OBP	SLG	PRO+	BR/A	SB	CS	SBR	FA	FR	G/POS	TPR
1875	Atl-n	32	129	4	20	3	0	0				.155	.155	.178	17	-10						3-32	-0.8
1876	NY-N	57	212	20	38	4	0	0	9	2	3	.179	.187	.198	33	-14				.779	5	*3-57	-0.6
1877	Lou-N	6	19	1	4	0	1	0	0	0	2	.211	.211	.316	54	-1				.706	4	/2-3,S-1,31	0.3
Total	2	63	231	21	42	4	1	0	9	2	5	.182	.189	.208	35	-15				.785	9	/3-58,2-3,1S	-0.3

■ ART NICHOLS
Nichols, Arthur Francis (b: Arthur Francis Meikle)
b: 7/14/1871, Manchester, N.H.   d: 8/9/45, Willimantic, Conn.   BR/TR, 5'10", 175 lbs.   Deb: 9/16/1898

YEAR	TM/L	G	AB	R	H	2B	3B	HR	RBI	BB	SO	AVG	OBP	SLG	PRO+	BR/A	SB	CS	SBR	FA	FR	G/POS	TPR
1898	Chi-N	14	42	7	12	1	0	0	6	4		.286	.388	.310	101	0	6			.968	1	C-14	0.2
1899	Chi-N	17	47	5	12	2	0	1	11	0		.255	.286	.362	79	-2	3			.931	-1	C-15	-0.2
1900	Chi-N	8	25	1	5	0	0	0	0	3		.200	.286	.200	36	-2	1			.938	-1	/C-7	-0.2
1901	StL-N	93	308	50	75	11	3	1	33	10		.244	.290	.308	77	-9	14			.960	-4	C-47,O-40	-1.0
1902	StL-N	73	251	36	67	12	0	1	31	21		.267	.333	.327	108	3	18			.984	-7	1-56,C-11/O	-0.4
1903	StL-N	36	120	13	23	2	0	0	9	12		.192	.281	.208	42	-9	9			.972	-5	1-25/O-7,C	-1.4
Total	6	241	793	112	194	28	3	3	90	50		.245	.308	.299	81	-18	51			.952	-17	/C-96,1-81,O	-3.0

■ CARL NICHOLS
Nichols, Carl Edward b: 10/14/62, Los Angeles, Cal.   BR/TR, 6', 208 lbs.   Deb: 9/14/86

YEAR	TM/L	G	AB	R	H	2B	3B	HR	RBI	BB	SO	AVG	OBP	SLG	PRO+	BR/A	SB	CS	SBR	FA	FR	G/POS	TPR
1986	Bal-A	5	5	0	0	0	0	0	0	1	4	.000	.167	.000	-51	-1	0	0	0	1.000	-0	/C-5	-0.1
1987	Bal-A	13	21	4	8	1	0	0	3	1	4	.381	.409	.429	126	1	0	0	0	1.000	1	C-13	0.2
1988	Bal-A	18	47	2	9	1	0	0	1	3	10	.191	.240	.213	29	-4	0	0	0	.987	6	C-13/O-3	0.2
1989	Hou-N	8	13	0	1	0	0	0	2	0	3	.077	.077	.077	-58	-4	0	0	0	1.000	-0	/C-6	-0.3
1990	Hou-N	32	49	7	10	3	0	0	11	8	11	.204	.328	.265	67	-2	0	0	0	.986	3	C-15/1-3,O	0.1
1991	Hou-N	20	51	3	10	3	0	0	1	5	17	.196	.268	.255	51	-3	0	0	0	.971	3	C-17	0.1
Total	6	96	186	16	38	9	0	0	18	18	49	.204	.278	.247	49	-13	0	0	0	.985	12	/C-69,O-4,1	0.2

■ ROY NICHOLS
Nichols, Roy b: 3/3/21, Little Rock, Ark.   BR/TR, 5'11", 155 lbs.   Deb: 5/6/44

YEAR	TM/L	G	AB	R	H	2B	3B	HR	RBI	BB	SO	AVG	OBP	SLG	PRO+	BR/A	SB	CS	SBR	FA	FR	G/POS	TPR
1944	NY-N	11	9	3	2	1	0	0		2	2	.222	.364	.333	97	0				1.000	2	/2-1,3-1	0.2

■ REID NICHOLS
Nichols, Thomas Reid b: 8/5/58, Ocala, Fla.   BR/TR, 5'11", 165 lbs.   Deb: 9/16/80

YEAR	TM/L	G	AB	R	H	2B	3B	HR	RBI	BB	SO	AVG	OBP	SLG	PRO+	BR/A	SB	CS	SBR	FA	FR	G/POS	TPR
1980	Bos-A	12	36	5	8	0	1	0	3	3	8	.222	.282	.278	51	-2	0	1	-1	.962	0	/O-9,D-1	-0.3
1981	Bos-A	39	48	13	9	0	1	0	3	2	6	.188	.220	.229	28	-4	0	1	-1	1.000	-4	O-27/3-1,D	-1.0
1982	Bos-A	92	245	35	74	16	1	7	33	14	28	.302	.342	.461	112	3	5	3	-0	.989	-2	O-82/D-4	0.0
1983	Bos-A	100	274	35	78	22	1	6	22	26	36	.285	.353	.438	108	3	7	5	-1	.994	2	O-72,D-18/S	0.2
1984	Bos-A	74	124	14	28	5	1	1	14	12	18	.226	.309	.306	68	-5	2	1	0	.988	-4	O-48/D-1	-1.0
1985	Bos-A	21	32	3	6	1	0	1	3	2	4	.188	.257	.313	53	-2	1	0	0	.933	-2	O-10/2-3,D	-0.4
	Chi-A	51	118	20	35	7	1	1	15	15	13	.297	.376	.398	108	2	5	5	-2	1.000	-12	O-48/D-1	-1.2
	Yr	72	150	23	41	8	1	2	18	17	17	.273	.351	.380	96	-0	6	5	-1	.988	-14	O-58/D-5,2	-1.6
1986	Chi-A	74	136	9	31	4	0	2	18	11	23	.228	.286	.301	58	-8	5	4	-1	.989	-4	O-53/2-2,D	-1.4
1987	Mon-N	77	147	22	39	8	2	4	20	14	13	.265	.333	.429	97	-1	2	1	0	.990	-4	O-59/3-3	-0.5
Total	8	540	1160	156	308	63	8	22	131	99	149	.266	.328	.391	91	-14	27	21	-5	.990	-29	O-408/D-39,23S	-5.6

■ DAVE NICHOLSON
Nicholson, David Lawrence b: 8/29/39, St.Louis, Mo.   BR/TR, 6'2", 215 lbs.   Deb: 5/24/60

YEAR	TM/L	G	AB	R	H	2B	3B	HR	RBI	BB	SO	AVG	OBP	SLG	PRO+	BR/A	SB	CS	SBR	FA	FR	G/POS	TPR
1960	Bal-A	54	113	17	21	1	1	5	11	20	55	.186	.308	.345	77	-4	0	2	-1	.982	-5	O-44	-1.1
1962	Bal-A	97	173	25	30	4	1	9	15	27	76	.173	.289	.364	79	-6	3	4	-2	.983	-7	O-80	-1.7
1963	Chi-A	126	449	53	103	11	4	22	70	63	175	.229	.324	.419	108	5	2	1	0	.970	-2	*O-123	0.1
1964	Chi-A	97	294	40	60	6	1	13	39	52	126	.204	.330	.364	95	-1	2	2	-1	.972	-2	O-92	-0.9
1965	Chi-A	54	85	11	13	2	1	2	12	9	40	.153	.234	.271	46	-6	0	0	0	1.000	-9	O-36	-1.7
1966	Hou-N	100	280	36	69	8	4	10	31	46	92	.246	.359	.411	122	9	1	1	-0	.968	-2	O-90	0.7
1967	Atl-N	10	25	2	5	0	0	0	1	2	9	.200	.259	.200	34	-2	0	0	0	1.000	-0	/O-7	-0.3
Total	7	538	1419	184	301	32	12	61	179	219	573	.212	.320	.381	97	-4	6	10	-4	.974	-19	O-472	-4.9

■ FRED NICHOLSON
Nicholson, Fred "Shoemaker" b: 9/1/1894, Honey Grove, Tex.   d: 1/23/72, Kilgore, Tex.   BR/TR, 5'10.5", 173 lbs.   Deb: 4/11/17

YEAR	TM/L	G	AB	R	H	2B	3B	HR	RBI	BB	SO	AVG	OBP	SLG	PRO+	BR/A	SB	CS	SBR	FA	FR	G/POS	TPR
1917	Det-A	13	14	4	4	1	0	0	1	1	2	.286	.333	.357	111	0	0			1.000	-1	/O-3	-0.1
1919	Pit-N	30	66	8	18	2	2	1	6	6	11	.273	.333	.409	118	1	2			.939	-1	O-17/1-1	-0.1
1920	Pit-N	99	247	33	89	16	7	4	30	18	31	.360	.404	.530	162	19	9	6	-1	.957	2	O-58	1.7
1921	Bos-N	83	245	36	80	11	7	5	41	17	29	.327	.370	.490	133	11	5	4	-1	.983	-7	O-59/1-4,2	0.0
1922	Bos-N	78	222	31	56	4	5	2	29	23	24	.252	.336	.342	79	-7	5	7	-3	.915	-4	O-63	-1.7
Total	5	303	794	112	247	34	21	12	107	65	97	.311	.367	.452	124	25	21	17		.950	-11	O-200/1-5,2	-0.2

■ OVID NICHOLSON
Nicholson, Ovid Edward b: 12/30/1888, Salem, Ind.   d: 3/24/68, Salem, Ind.   BL/TR, 5'9.5", 155 lbs.   Deb: 9/17/12

YEAR	TM/L	G	AB	R	H	2B	3B	HR	RBI	BB	SO	AVG	OBP	SLG	PRO+	BR/A	SB	CS	SBR	FA	FR	G/POS	TPR
1912	Pit-N	6	11	2	5	0	0	0		3	2	.455	.500	.455	165	1	0			1.000	1	/O-4	0.0

■ PARSON NICHOLSON
Nicholson, Thomas C. "Deacon" b: 4/14/1863, Blaine, Ohio   d: 2/28/17, Bellaire, Ohio   6'6", 190 lbs.   Deb: 9/14/1888

YEAR	TM/L	G	AB	R	H	2B	3B	HR	RBI	BB	SO	AVG	OBP	SLG	PRO+	BR/A	SB	CS	SBR	FA	FR	G/POS	TPR
1888	Det-N	24	85	11	22	2	3	1	9	2	7	.259	.284	.388	113	1	6			.935	-2	2-24	0.0
1890	Tol-a	134	523	78	140	16	11	4		42		.268	.333	.363	102	-0	46			.929	-8	*2-134/C-1	0.0
1895	Was-N	10	38	7	7	2	1	0	5	7	4	.184	.311	.289	56	-2	6			.797	-2	S-10	-0.3
Total	3	168	646	96	169	20	15	5	14	51	11	.262	.325	.362	100	-2	58			.930	-12	2-158/S-10,C	-0.3

■ BILL NICHOLSON
Nicholson, William Beck "Swish" b: 12/11/14, Chestertown, Md.   BL/TR, 6', 205 lbs.   Deb: 6/13/36

YEAR	TM/L	G	AB	R	H	2B	3B	HR	RBI	BB	SO	AVG	OBP	SLG	PRO+	BR/A	SB	CS	SBR	FA	FR	G/POS	TPR
1936	Phi-A	11	12	2	0	0	0	0	0	0	5	.000	.000	.000	-99	-4	0	0	0	1.000	-0	/O-1	-0.4
1939	Chi-N	58	220	37	65	12	5	5	38	20	29	.295	.354	.464	116	5	0			.955	1	O-58	0.4
1940	Chi-N★	135	491	78	146	27	7	25	98	50	97	.297	.366	.534	148	31	2			.950	-2	*O-123	2.2
1941	Chi-N★	147	532	74	135	26	1	26	98	82	91	.254	.357	.453	132	22	11			.971	6	*O-143	2.0
1942	Chi-N	152	588	83	173	22	11	21	78	76	80	.294	.382	.476	156	42	8			.986	11	*O-151	4.8
1943	Chi-N★	154	608	95	188	30	9	29	128	71	86	.309	.386	.531	166	50	4			.978	6	*O-154	4.9
1944	Chi-N★	156	582	116	167	35	8	33	122	93	71	.287	.391	.545	162	48	3			.979	2	*O-156	4.2
1945	*Chi-N†	151	559	82	136	28	4	13	88	92	73	.243	.356	.377	106	7	4			.990	1	*O-151	-0.1
1946	Chi-N	105	296	36	65	13	6	8	41	44	44	.220	.325	.358	95	-2	0			.973	2	O-80	-0.3
1947	Chi-N	148	487	69	119	28	1	26	75	87	83	.244	.364	.466	124	17	1			.990	-1	*O-140	0.9

YEAR	TM/L	G	AB	R	H	2B	3B	HR	RBI	BB	SO	AVG	OBP	SLG	PRO+	BR/A	SB	CS	SBR	FA	FR	G/POS	TPR
1948	Chi-N	143	494	68	129	24	5	19	67	81	60	.261	.371	.445	125	18	2			.980	-3	*O-136	0.8
1949	Phi-N	98	299	42	70	8	3	11	40	45	53	.234	.344	.391	99	0	1			.995	3	O-91	-0.1
1950	Phi-N	41	58	3	13	2	1	3	10	8	16	.224	.318	.448	101	-0	0			.952	-2	O-15	-0.1
1951	Phi-N	85	170	23	41	9	2	8	30	25	24	.241	.342	.459	115	3	0	1	-1	.987	-3	O-41	-0.1
1952	Phi-N	55	88	17	24	3	0	6	19	14	26	.273	.390	.511	150	6	0	0	0	1.000	-2	O-19	0.4
1953	Phi-N	38	62	12	13	5	1	2	16	12	20	.210	.338	.419	97	-0	0	0	0	1.000	-2	O-12	-0.1
Total	16	1677	5546	837	1484	272	60	235	948	800	828	.268	.365	.465	133	243	27	1		.979	17	*O-1471	19.0

■ GEORGE NICOL   Nicol, George Edward b: 10/17/1870, Barry, Ill. d: 8/10/24, Milwaukee, Wis. TL , 5'7″, 155 lbs. Deb: 9/23/1890

YEAR	TM/L	G	AB	R	H	2B	3B	HR	RBI	BB	SO	AVG	OBP	SLG	PRO+	BR/A	SB	CS	SBR	FA	FR	G/POS	TPR
1890	StL-a	3	7	4	2	1	0	0		4		.286	.545	.429	164	1	0			1.000	-0	/P-3	0.0
1891	Chi-N	3	6	0	2	0	1	0	3	0	1	.333	.333	.667	189	1	0			.000	-1	/P-3	0.0
1894	Pit-N	8	20	8	9	1	0	0	3	0	1	.450	.450	.500	130	1	0			.800	-1	/P-8	0.0
	Lou-N	27	108	12	38	6	4	0	19	2	3	.352	.375	.481	113	2	4			.791	-5	O-26/P-1	-0.4
	Yr	35	128	20	47	7	4	0	22	2	4	.367	.386	.484	115	3	4			.791	-6	O-26/P-9	-0.4
Total	3	41	141	24	51	8	5	0	25	6	5	.362	.396	.489	121	4	4			.692	-7	/O-26,P-15	-0.4

■ HUGH NICOL   Nicol, Hugh b: 1/1/1858, Campsie, Scotland d: 6/27/21, Lafayette, Ind. BR/TR, 5'4″, 145 lbs. Deb: 5/3/1881 M

YEAR	TM/L	G	AB	R	H	2B	3B	HR	RBI	BB	SO	AVG	OBP	SLG	PRO+	BR/A	SB	CS	SBR	FA	FR	G/POS	TPR
1881	Chi-N	26	108	13	22	2	0	0	7	4	12	.204	.232	.222	42	-7				.932	3	O-26/S-1	-0.4
1882	Chi-N	47	186	19	37	9	1	1	16	7	29	.199	.228	.274	58	-9				.887	10	O-47/S-8	0.1
1883	StL-a	94	368	73	105	13	3	0			18	.285	.319	.337	105	1				.916	12	*O-84,2-11	1.1
1884	StL-a	110	442	79	115	14	5	0			22	.260	.300	.314	97	-2				.873	23	*O-87,2-23/S3	1.8
1885	*StL-a	112	425	59	88	11	1	0			34	.207	.271	.238	59	-20				.888	13	*O-111/3-1	-0.9
1886	StL-a	67	253	44	52	6	3	0			26	.206	.280	.253	64	-11	38			.942	-4	O-57/S-8,2	-1.4
1887	Cin-a	125	475	122	102	18	2	1			86	.215	.341	.267	69	-17	138			.918	-3	*O-125	-1.7
1888	Cin-a	135	548	112	131	10	2	1	35	67		.239	.330	.270	88	-6	103			.957	-3	*O-125,2-12/S	-1.1
1889	Cin-a	122	474	82	121	7	8	2	58	54	35	.255	.338	.316	84	-9	80			.918	-6	*O-115/2-7,3	-0.9
1890	Cin-N	50	186	28	39	1	4	0	19	19	12	.210	.283	.258	58	-10	24			.921	-6	O-46/S-3,2	-1.5
Total	10	888	3465	631	812	91	29	5	135	337	88	.234	.306	.282	78	-88	383			.912	49	O-823/2-58,S3	-4.9

■ STEVE NICOSIA   Nicosia, Steven Richard b: 8/6/55, Paterson, N.J. BR/TR, 5'10″, 185 lbs. Deb: 7/8/78

YEAR	TM/L	G	AB	R	H	2B	3B	HR	RBI	BB	SO	AVG	OBP	SLG	PRO+	BR/A	SB	CS	SBR	FA	FR	G/POS	TPR
1978	Pit-N	3	5	0	0	0	0	0	1	0		.000	.167	.000	-48	-1	0	0	0	1.000	1	/C-1	0.0
1979	*Pit-N	70	191	22	55	16	0	4	13	23	17	.288	.364	.435	112	3	0	2	-1	.991	4	C-65	0.8
1980	Pit-N	60	176	16	38	8	0	1	22	19	16	.216	.296	.278	60	-9	0	1	-1	.984	-1	C-58	-0.9
1981	Pit-N	54	169	21	39	10	1	2	18	13	10	.231	.286	.337	74	-6	3	1	0	.982	1	C-52	-0.4
1982	Pit-N	39	100	6	28	3	0	1	7	11	13	.280	.351	.340	91	-1	0	1	-1	.990	3	C-35/O-3	0.3
1983	Pit-N	21	46	4	6	2	0	1	3	1	7	.130	.149	.239	6	-6	0	0	0	.988	-1	C-15	-0.7
	SF-N	15	33	4	11	0	0	0	6	3	2	.333	.389	.333	105	4	0	0	0	.984	2	/C-9	0.3
	Yr	36	79	8	17	2	0	1	9	4	9	.215	.253	.278	47	-6	0	0	0	.986	1	C-24	-0.4
1984	SF-N	48	132	9	40	11	2	2	19	8	14	.303	.343	.462	129	4	1	1	-0	.985	-5	C-41	0.0
1985	Mon-N	42	71	4	12	2	0	0	1	7	11	.169	.244	.197	26	-7	1	0	0	.988	-5	C-23/1-2	-1.2
	Tor-A	6	15	0	4	0	0	0	1	0	0	.267	.267	.267	46	-1	0	0	0	1.000	1	/C-6	0.0
Total	8	358	938	86	233	52	3	11	88	86	90	.248	.312	.345	82	-23	5	6	-2	.987	-1	C-305/O-3,1	-1.8

■ CHARLIE NIEBERGALL   Niebergall, Charles Arthur "Nig" b: 5/23/1899, New York, N.Y. d: 8/29/82, Holiday, Fla. BR/TR, 5'10″, 160 lbs. Deb: 6/17/21

YEAR	TM/L	G	AB	R	H	2B	3B	HR	RBI	BB	SO	AVG	OBP	SLG	PRO+	BR/A	SB	CS	SBR	FA	FR	G/POS	TPR
1921	StL-N	5	6	1	1	0	0	0	0	0	0	.167	.167	.167	-12	-1	0	0	0	1.000	-1	/C-3	-0.1
1923	StL-N	9	28	2	3	1	0	0	1	2	2	.107	.167	.143	-18	-5	0	0	0	1.000	-0	/C-7	-0.5
1924	StL-N	40	58	6	17	6	0	0	7	3	9	.293	.339	.397	98	-0	0	0	0	.951	1	C-34	0.2
Total	3	54	92	9	21	7	0	0	8	5	11	.228	.276	.304	55	-6	0	0	0	.966	1	/C-44	-0.4

■ AL NIEHAUS   Niehaus, Albert Bernard b: 6/1/1899, Cincinnati, Ohio d: 10/14/31, Cincinnati, Ohio BR/TR, 5'11″, 175 lbs. Deb: 4/22/25

YEAR	TM/L	G	AB	R	H	2B	3B	HR	RBI	BB	SO	AVG	OBP	SLG	PRO+	BR/A	SB	CS	SBR	FA	FR	G/POS	TPR
1925	Pit-N	17	64	7	14	8	0	0	7	1	5	.219	.242	.344	45	-6	0	0	0	.962	-1	1-15	-0.7
	Cin-N	51	147	16	44	10	2	0	14	13	10	.299	.360	.395	95	-1	1	4	-2	.988	2	1-45	-0.3
	Yr	68	211	23	58	18	2	0	21	14	15	.275	.326	.379	80	-7	1	4	-2	.981	1	1-60	-1.0

■ BERT NIEHOFF   Niehoff, John Albert b: 5/13/1884, Louisville, Colo. d: 12/8/74, Inglewood, Cal. BR/TR, 5'10.5″, 170 lbs. Deb: 10/4/13 C

YEAR	TM/L	G	AB	R	H	2B	3B	HR	RBI	BB	SO	AVG	OBP	SLG	PRO+	BR/A	SB	CS	SBR	FA	FR	G/POS	TPR
1913	Cin-N	2	8	0	0	0	0	0	0	0	2	.000	.000	.000	-99	-2	0			.917	2	/3-2	0.0
1914	Cin-N	142	484	46	117	16	9	4	49	38	77	.242	.298	.337	86	-9	20			.924	7	*3-134/2-3	0.3
1915	*Phi-N	148	529	61	126	27	2	4	49	30	63	.238	.280	.308	77	-15	21	11	-0	.946	-7	*2-148	-2.3
1916	Phi-N	146	548	65	133	42	4	4	61	37	57	.243	.292	.356	95	-4	20	14	-2	.936	-2	*2-144/3-2	-0.4
1917	Phi-N	114	361	30	92	17	4	2	42	23	29	.255	.303	.341	93	-3	8			.945	18	2-96/1-7,3	2.2
1918	StL-N	22	84	5	15	2	0	0	5	3	10	.179	.207	.202	26	-7	2			.975	2	2-22	-0.5
	NY-N	7	23	3	6	0	0	0	1	0	4	.261	.261	.261	60	-1	0			.871	-2	/2-7	-0.4
	Yr	29	107	8	21	2	0	0	6	3	14	.196	.218	.215	33	-9	2			.954	-1	2-29	-0.9
Total	6	581	2037	210	489	104	19	12	207	131	242	.240	.288	.327	84	-42	71	25		.943	18	2-420,3-144/1	-1.1

■ MILT NIELSEN   Nielsen, Milton Robert b: 2/8/25, Tyler, Minn. BL/TL, 5'11″, 190 lbs. Deb: 9/27/49

YEAR	TM/L	G	AB	R	H	2B	3B	HR	RBI	BB	SO	AVG	OBP	SLG	PRO+	BR/A	SB	CS	SBR	FA	FR	G/POS	TPR
1949	Cle-A	3	9	1	1	0	0	0	0	2	4	.111	.273	.111	4	-1	0	0	0	1.000	-0	/O-3	-0.2
1951	Cle-A	16	6	1	0	0	0	0	0	1	5	.000	.143	.000	-63	-1	0	0	0	.000	0	H	-0.1
Total	2	19	15	2	1	0	0	0	0	3	9	.067	.222	.067	-22	-3	0	0	0	1.000	-0	/O-3	-0.3

■ BUTCH NIEMAN   Nieman, Elmer Le Roy b: 2/8/18, Herkimer, Kan. d: 11/2/93, Topeka, Kan. BL/TL, 6'2″, 195 lbs. Deb: 5/2/43

YEAR	TM/L	G	AB	R	H	2B	3B	HR	RBI	BB	SO	AVG	OBP	SLG	PRO+	BR/A	SB	CS	SBR	FA	FR	G/POS	TPR
1943	Bos-N	101	335	39	84	15	8	7	46	39	39	.251	.331	.406	114	5	4			.963	1	O-93	0.2
1944	Bos-N	134	468	65	124	16	6	16	65	47	47	.265	.332	.427	108	4	5			.975	-2	*O-126	-0.4
1945	Bos-N	97	247	43	61	15	0	14	56	43	33	.247	.361	.478	131	10	11			.932	0	O-57	0.7
Total	3	332	1050	147	269	46	14	37	167	129	119	.256	.339	.432	116	20	20			.961	-0	O-276	0.5

■ BOB NIEMAN   Nieman, Robert Charles b: 1/26/27, Cincinnati, Ohio d: 3/10/85, Corona, Cal. BR/TR, 5'11″, 195 lbs. Deb: 9/14/51

YEAR	TM/L	G	AB	R	H	2B	3B	HR	RBI	BB	SO	AVG	OBP	SLG	PRO+	BR/A	SB	CS	SBR	FA	FR	G/POS	TPR
1951	StL-A	12	43	6	16	3	1	2	8	3	5	.372	.413	.628	174	4	0	0	0	.962	0	O-11	0.4
1952	StL-A	131	478	66	138	22	2	18	74	46	73	.289	.352	.456	120	12	0	4	-2	.976	1	*O-125	0.5
1953	Det-A	142	508	72	143	32	5	15	69	57	57	.281	.354	.453	118	10	3	-2		.979	3	*O-135	0.8
1954	Det-A	91	251	24	66	14	1	8	35	22	32	.263	.322	.422	105	1	0	1	-1	.984	-2	O-62	-0.5
1955	Chi-A	99	272	36	77	11	2	11	53	36	37	.283	.371	.460	119	7	1	0	-1	.976	-7	O-78	-0.2
1956	Chi-A	14	40	3	12	1	0	2	4	4	4	.300	.364	.475	118	1	0	0	0	1.000	1	O-10	0.0
	Bal-A	114	388	60	125	20	6	12	64	86	59	.322	.445	.497	161	38	0	5	-3	.980	7	*O-114	3.5
	Yr	128	428	63	137	21	6	14	68	90	63	.320	.438	.495	156	39	0	5	-3	.982	7	*O-124	3.5
1957	Bal-A	129	445	61	123	17	6	13	70	63	86	.276	.369	.429	125	16	4	4	-1	.980	5	*O-120	1.3
1958	Bal-A	105	366	56	119	20	2	16	60	44	57	.325	.398	.522	159	29	2	8	-4	.961	-2	*O-100	1.3
1959	Bal-A	118	360	49	105	13	2	21	60	42	55	.292	.369	.528	146	22	1	2	-1	.973	-0	O-97	1.6
1960	StL-N	81	188	19	54	13	5	4	31	24	31	.287	.374	.473	120	5	0	1	-1	.940	-8	O-55	-0.6
1961	StL-N	6	17	0	8	1	0	1	3	1	1	.471	.471	.529	150	1	0	0	0	1.000	-1	/O-4	0.0
	Cle-A	39	65	2	23	6	0	2	10	7	4	.354	.417	.538	157	5	0	0	0	.960	0	O-12	0.5
1962	Cle-A	4	1	0	0	0	0	0	0	0	0	.000	.000	.000	-99	-0	0	0	0	.000	0	H	0.0
	*SF-N	30	30	1	9	2	0	1	9	3	1	.300	.323	.467	111	0	0	0	0	1.000	-1	/O-3	0.0
Total	12	1113	3452	455	1018	180	32	125	544	435	512	.295	.375	.474	132	154	10	30	-15	.975	-8	O-926	8.6

YEAR	TM/L	G	AB	R	H	2B	3B	HR	RBI	BB	SO	AVG	OBP	SLG	PRO+	BR/A	SB	CS	SBR	FA	FR	G/POS	TPR

■ AL NIEMIEC　Niemiec, Alfred Joseph　b: 5/18/11, Meriden, Conn.　BR/TR, 5'11", 158 lbs.　Deb: 9/19/34

1934	Bos-A	9	32	2	7	0	0	0	3	3	4	.219	.286	.219	30	-3	0	0	0	1.000	4	/2-9	0.1
1936	Phi-A	69	203	22	40	3	2	1	20	26	16	.197	.291	.246	35	-21	2	2	-1	.972	10	2-52/S-5	-0.6
Total	2	78	235	24	47	3	2	1	23	29	20	.200	.291	.243	34	-24	2	2	-1	.976	15	/2-61,S-5	-0.5

■ TOM NIETO　Nieto, Thomas Andrew　b: 10/27/60, Downey, Cal.　BR/TR, 6'1", 205 lbs.　Deb: 5/10/84

1984	StL-N	33	86	7	24	4	0	3	12	5	18	.279	.319	.430	112	1	0	0	0	.994	4	C-32	0.6
1985	*StL-N	95	253	15	57	10	2	0	34	26	37	.225	.305	.281	65	-11	0	2	-1	.990	-4	C-95	-1.3
1986	Mon-N	30	65	5	13	3	1	1	7	6	21	.200	.278	.323	66	-3	0	1	-1	.978	-3	C-30	-0.5
1987	Min-A	41	105	7	21	7	1	1	12	8	24	.200	.276	.314	54	-7	0	0	0	.996	2	C-40/D-1	-0.3
1988	Min-A	24	60	1	4	0	0	0	0	1	17	.067	.097	.067	-52	-12	0	0	0	.991	3	C-24	-0.8
1989	Phi-N	11	20	1	3	0	0	0	0	6	7	.150	.370	.150	54	-1	0	0	0	1.000	3	C-11	0.3
1990	Phi-N	17	30	1	5	0	0	0	4	3	11	.167	.265	.167	21	-3	0	0	0	.984	2	C-17	0.0
Total	7	251	619	37	127	24	4	5	69	55	135	.205	.281	.281	56	-36	0	3	-2	.991	7	C-249/D-1	-2.0

■ MELVIN NIEVES　Nieves, Melvin Ramos　b: 12/28/71, San Juan, P.R.　BB/TR, 6'2", 186 lbs.　Deb: 9/1/92

1992	Atl-N	12	19	0	4	1	0	0	1	2	7	.211	.286	.263	53	-1	0	0	0	.727	-1	/O-6	-0.3
1993	SD-N	19	47	4	9	0	0	2	3	3	21	.191	.255	.319	52	-3	0	0	0	.931	-1	O-15	-0.5
1994	SD-N	10	19	2	5	1	0	1	4	3	10	.263	.364	.474	117	0	0	0	0	1.000	1	/O-6	0.1
Total	3	41	85	6	18	2	0	3	8	8	38	.212	.287	.341	67	-4	0	0	0	.904	-2	/O-27	-0.7

■ TOM NILAND　Niland, Thomas James "Honest Tom"　b: 4/14/1870, Brookfield, Mass.　d: 4/30/50, Lynn, Mass.　BR/TR, 5'11", 160 lbs.　Deb: 4/19/1896

| 1896 | StL-N | 18 | 68 | 3 | 12 | 0 | 1 | 0 | 3 | 5 | 4 | .176 | .243 | .206 | 20 | -8 | 0 | | | .913 | -4 | O-13/S-5 | -1.1 |

■ HARRY NILES　Niles, Herbert Clyde　b: 9/10/1880, Buchanan, Mich.　d: 4/18/53, Sturgis, Mich.　BR/TR, 5'8", 175 lbs.　Deb: 4/24/06

1906	StL-A	142	541	71	124	14	4	2	31	46		.229	.297	.281	85	-9	30			.967	6	*O-108,3-34	-0.8
1907	StL-A	120	492	65	142	9	5	2	35	46		.289	.331	.339	114	7	19			.949	-6	*2-116/O-1	0.0
1908	NY-A	96	362	43	90	14	6	4	24	25		.249	.304	.354	112	4	18			.928	-24	2-85/O-7	-2.4
	Bos-A	17	32	4	8	0	0	1	3	6		.250	.385	.344	133	2	3			1.000	-1	/2-8,S-2	0.1
	Yr	113	394	47	98	14	6	5	27	31		.249	.312	.353	114	6	21			.934	-24	2-93/O-7,S	-2.3
1909	Bos-A	145	546	64	134	12	5	1	38	39		.245	.311	.291	88	-6	27			.952	-0	*O-117,3-13/S2	-1.2
1910	Bos-A	18	57	6	12	3	0	1	3	4		.211	.262	.316	79	-2	1			.920	-0	O-15	-0.3
	Cle-A	70	240	25	51	6	4	1	18	15		.213	.267	.283	72	-8	9			.975	-4	O-50/S-7,3	-1.6
	Yr	88	297	31	63	9	4	2	21	19		.212	.266	.290	73	-10	10			.962	-4	O-65/S-7,3	-1.9
Total	5	608	2270	278	561	58	24	12	152	163		.247	.306	.310	95	-12	107			.960	-29	O-298,2-214/3S	-6.2

■ BILL NILES　Niles, William E.　b: 1/11/1867, Covington, Ky.　d: 7/3/36, Springfield, Ohio　160 lbs.　Deb: 5/13/1895

| 1895 | Pit-N | 11 | 37 | 2 | 8 | 0 | 0 | 0 | 0 | 5 | 2 | .216 | .310 | .216 | 39 | -3 | 2 | | | .930 | 1 | 3-10/2-1 | -0.2 |

■ RABBIT NILL　Nill, George Charles　b: 7/14/1881, Ft.Wayne, Ind.　d: 5/24/62, Fort Wayne, Ind.　BR/TR, 5'7", 160 lbs.　Deb: 9/27/04

1904	Was-A	15	48	4	8	0	1	0	3	5		.167	.273	.208	54	-2	0			.878	-4	2-15	-0.6
1905	Was-A	103	319	46	58	7	3	3	31	33		.182	.269	.251	68	-11	12			.897	-3	3-52,2-33/S	-1.3
1906	Was-A	89	315	37	74	8	2	0	15	47		.235	.340	.273	97	2	16			.882	4	S-31,2-25,3O	0.7
1907	Was-A	66	215	21	47	7	3	0	25	15		.219	.282	.279	86	-3	6			.962	-2	2-39,O-18/3	-0.7
	Cle-A	12	43	5	12	1	0	0	2	3		.279	.326	.302	100	0	2			.815	-4	/3-7,S-4	-0.4
	Yr	78	258	26	59	8	3	0	27	18		.229	.289	.283	88	-3	8			.962	-5	2-39,O-18/3S	-1.1
1908	Cle-A	11	23	3	5	0	0	0	1	0		.217	.217	.217	41	-2	0			.833	0	/S-6,O-3,2	-0.1
Total	5	296	963	116	204	23	9	3	77	103		.212	.297	.264	82	-17	36			.943	-7	2-113/3-75,SO	-2.4

■ DAVE NILSSON　Nilsson, David Wayne　b: 12/14/69, Brisbane, Queensland, Australia　BL/TR, 6'3", 185 lbs.　Deb: 5/18/92

1992	Mil-A	51	164	15	38	8	0	4	25	17	18	.232	.304	.354	85	-3	2	2	-1	.992	0	C-46/1-3,D	-0.1
1993	Mil-A	100	296	35	76	10	2	7	40	37	36	.257	.339	.375	93	-2	3	6	-3	.981	-10	C-91/1-4,D	-1.1
1994	Mil-A	109	397	51	109	28	3	12	69	34	61	.275	.332	.451	97	-2	1	0	0	.994	-6	C-60,D-43/1	-0.6
Total	3	260	857	101	223	46	5	23	134	88	115	.260	.329	.406	94	-8	6	8	-3	.987	-16	C-197/D-49,1	-1.8

■ AL NIXON　Nixon, Albert Richard "Humpty Dumpty"　b: 4/11/1886, Atlantic City, N.J　d: 11/9/60, Opelousas, La.　BR/TL, 5'7.5", 164 lbs.　Deb: 9/4/15

1915	Bro-N	14	26	3	6	1	0	0	2	2	4	.231	.286	.269	67	-1	1	1	-0	1.000	-2	O-14	-0.4
1916	Bro-N	1	2	0	2	0	0	0	0	0	0	1.000	1.000	1.000	501	1	0			.000	-0	/O-1	0.1
1918	Bro-N	6	11	1	5	0	0	0	0	0	0	.455	.455	.455	178	1	0			1.000	-0	/O-4	0.1
1921	Bos-N	55	138	25	33	6	3	1	9	7	11	.239	.281	.348	69	-7	3	2	-0	.980	-4	O-43	-1.1
1922	Bos-N	86	318	35	84	14	4	2	22	9	19	.264	.284	.352	66	-17	6	6	-2	.975	1	O-79	-2.2
1923	Bos-N	88	321	53	88	12	4	0	19	24	14	.274	.334	.336	81	-9	2	3	-1	.987	9	O-80	-0.6
1926	Phi-N	93	311	38	91	18	2	4	41	13	20	.293	.323	.402	90	-5	5			.977	-2	O-88	-1.3
1927	Phi-N	54	154	18	48	7	0	0	18	5	5	.312	.333	.357	84	-4	1			.969	-1	O-44	-0.6
1928	Phi-N	25	64	7	15	2	0	0	7	6	4	.234	.300	.266	47	-5	1			1.000	-0	O-20	-0.6
Total	9	422	1345	180	372	60	13	7	118	66	77	.277	.314	.356	78	-45	19	12		.980	2	O-373	-6.6

■ OTIS NIXON　Nixon, Otis Junior　b: 1/9/59, Columbus Co., N.C.　BB/TR, 6'2", 180 lbs.　Deb: 9/9/83　F

1983	NY-A	13	14	2	2	0	0	0	1	5		.143	.200	.143		2	0	1	.938	-1	/O-9	-0.2
1984	Cle-A	49	91	16	14	0	0	0	1	8	11	.154	.222	.154	6	-11	12	6	0	1.000	-2	O-46	-1.5
1985	Cle-A	104	162	34	38	4	0	3	9	8	27	.235	.271	.315	60	-9	20	11	-1	.971	-7	O-80,D-11	-1.8
1986	Cle-A	105	95	33	25	4	1	0	8	13	12	.263	.352	.326	88	-1	23	6	3	.969	-23	O-95/D-5	-2.2
1987	Cle-A	19	17	2	1	0	0	0	1	3	4	.059	.200	.059	-26	-3	2	3	-1	1.000	-4	O-17/D-2	-0.8
1988	Mon-N	90	271	47	66	8	2	0	15	28	42	.244	.314	.288	71	-9	46	13	6	.994	-2	O-82	-0.8
1989	Mon-N	126	258	41	56	7	2	0	21	33	36	.217	.306	.260	62	-12	37	12	4	.988	-15	O-98	-2.6
1990	Mon-N	119	231	46	58	6	2	1	20	28	33	.251	.332	.307	80	-6	50	13	6	.994	-9	O-88/S-1	-0.9
1991	Atl-N	124	401	81	119	10	1	0	26	47	40	.297	.373	.327	93	-2	72	21	9	.987	1	*O-115	0.6
1992	*Atl-N	120	456	79	134	14	2	2	22	39	54	.294	.349	.346	92	-4	41	18	2	.991	13	*O-111	0.9
1993	*Atl-N	134	461	77	124	12	3	1	24	61	63	.269	.354	.315	80	-11	47	13	6	.990	8	*O-116	0.1
1994	Bos-A	103	398	60	109	15	1	0	25	55	65	.274	.362	.317	72	-15	42	10	7	.989	-7	*O-103	-0.8
Total	12	1106	2855	518	746	80	14	7	172	324	392	.261	.337	.306	76	-84	394	126	43	.988	-39	O-960/D-18,S	-10.0

■ DONELL NIXON　Nixon, Robert Donell　b: 12/31/61, Evergreen, N.C.　BR/TR, 6'1", 185 lbs.　Deb: 4/7/87　F

1987	Sea-A	46	132	17	33	4	0	3	12	9	28	.250	.327	.348	75	-5	21	7	2	1.000	0	O-32/D-6	-0.3
1988	SF-N	59	78	15	27	3	0	0	6	10	12	.346	.420	.385	138	4	11	8	-0	.983	-8	O-46	-0.7
1989	*SF-N	95	166	23	44	2	0	1	15	11	30	.265	.311	.295	76	-5	10	3	1	.967	-14	O-64	-2.0
1990	Bal-A	8	20	1	5	2	0	0	2	1	7	.250	.286	.350	79	-1	5	0	2	1.000	-1	/O-4,D-3	0.0
Total	4	208	396	56	109	11	0	4	35	35	77	.275	.337	.333	88	-6	47	18	3	.983	-23	O-146/D-9	-3.0

■ RUSS NIXON　Nixon, Russell Eugene　b: 2/19/35, Cleves, Ohio　BL/TR, 6'1", 200 lbs.　Deb: 4/20/57　MC

1957	Cle-A	62	185	15	52	7	2	18	12	12		.281	.325	.362	88	-3	0	1	-1	.984	-6	C-57	-0.8
1958	Cle-A	113	376	42	113	17	4	9	46	13	38	.301	.324	.439	111	4	0	3	-2	.991	-10	*C-101	-0.2
1959	Cle-A	82	258	23	62	10	3	1	29	15	28	.240	.282	.314	66	-12	0	0	0	.985	-7	C-74	-1.5
1960	Cle-A	25	82	6	20	5	0	1	6	6	6	.244	.311	.341	79	-2	0	1	-1	.993	-0	C-25	-0.2
	Bos-A	80	272	24	81	17	3	6	35	13	23	.298	.330	.438	102	0	0	1	-1	.987	-17	C-74	-1.3

YEAR	TM/L	G	AB	R	H	2B	3B	HR	RBI	BB	SO	AVG	OBP	SLG	PRO+	BR/A	SB	CS	SBR	FA	FR	G/POS	TPR
	Yr	105	354	30	101	22	3	6	39	19	29	.285	.325	.415	97	-2	0	2	-1	.989	-17	C-99	-1.5
1961	Bos-A	87	242	24	70	12	2	1	19	13	19	.289	.331	.368	84	-5	0	1	-1	.975	-3	C-66	-0.6
1962	Bos-A	65	151	11	42	7	2	1	19	8	14	.278	.314	.371	81	-4	0	0	0	1.000	-2	C-38	-0.5
1963	Bos-A	98	287	27	77	18	1	5	30	22	32	.268	.329	.390	98	-1	0	0	0	.992	-10	C-76	-0.8
1964	Bos-A	81	163	10	38	7	0	1	20	14	29	.233	.302	.294	64	-8	0	0	0	.990	-4	C-45	-1.0
1965	Bos-A	59	137	11	37	5	1	0	11	6	23	.270	.301	.321	72	-5	0	0	0	.981	-6	C-38	-1.0
1966	Min-A	51	96	5	25	2	1	0	7	7	13	.260	.317	.302	74	-3	0	0	0	.986	-4	C-32	-0.6
1967	Min-A	74	170	16	40	6	1	1	22	18	29	.235	.309	.300	74	-5	0	0	0	.994	-12	C-69	-1.5
1968	Bos-A	29	85	1	13	0	0	0	6	7	13	.153	.217	.176	19	-8	0	0	0	.994	-5	C-27	-1.3
Total	12	906	2504	215	670	115	19	27	266	154	279	.268	.313	.361	84	-53	0	7	-4	.988	-85	C-722	-11.3

■ RAY NOBLE Noble, Rafael Miguel (Magee) b: 3/15/19, Central Hatillo, Cuba BR/TR, 5'11", 210 lbs. Deb: 4/18/51

YEAR	TM/L	G	AB	R	H	2B	3B	HR	RBI	BB	SO	AVG	OBP	SLG	PRO+	BR/A	SB	CS	SBR	FA	FR	G/POS	TPR
1951	*NY-N	55	141	16	33	6	0	5	26	6	26	.234	.265	.383	72	-6	0	0	0	.974	-5	C-41	-0.9
1952	NY-N	6	5	0	0	0	0	0	0	0	1	.000	.000	.000	-99	-1	0	0	0	1.000	0	/C-5	-0.1
1953	NY-N	46	97	15	20	0	1	4	14	19	14	.206	.353	.351	83	-2	1	0	0	.982	-1	C-41	-0.1
Total	3	107	243	31	53	6	1	9	40	25	41	.218	.299	.362	74	-9	1	0	0	.979	-5	/C-87	-1.1

■ JUNIOR NOBOA Noboa, Milciades Arturo (Diaz) b: 11/10/64, Azua, D.R. BR/TR, 5'10", 160 lbs. Deb: 8/22/84

YEAR	TM/L	G	AB	R	H	2B	3B	HR	RBI	BB	SO	AVG	OBP	SLG	PRO+	BR/A	SB	CS	SBR	FA	FR	G/POS	TPR
1984	Cle-A	23	11	3	4	0	0	0	0	0	2	.364	.364	.364	100	0	1	0	0	1.000	4	2-19/D-1	0.4
1987	Cle-A	39	80	7	18	2	1	0	7	3	6	.225	.253	.275	40	-7	1	0	0	.983	4	2-21/S-8,3D	-0.2
1988	Cal-A	21	16	4	1	0	0	0	0	0	1	.063	.063	.063	-67	-4	0	0	0	.967	9	/2-9,S-3,3	0.5
1989	Mon-N	21	44	3	10	0	0	0	1	1	3	.227	.244	.227	35	-4	0	0	0	1.000	7	2-13/S-4,3	0.4
1990	Mon-N	81	158	15	42	7	2	0	14	7	14	.266	.301	.335	78	-5	4	1	1	1.000	-17	2-31/O-9,3SP	-2.2
1991	Mon-N	67	95	5	23	3	0	1	2	1	8	.242	.250	.305	56	-6	2	3	-1	1.000	-3	/O-7,2-6,3S1	-1.0
1992	NY-N	46	47	7	7	0	0	0	3	3	8	.149	.216	.149	5	-6	0	0	0	.977	6	2-16/3-3,S	0.0
1994	Oak-A	17	40	3	13	1	1	0	6	2	5	.325	.357	.400	103	0	1	0	0	.943	1	2-14/S-1	0.1
	Pit-N	2	2	0	0	0	0	0	0	0	0	.000	.000	.000	-99	-1	0	0	0	1.000	0	/S-1	-0.1
Total	8	317	493	47	118	13	4	1	33	17	47	.239	.268	.288	54	-31	9	4	0	.981	10	2-129/S-28,30D1P	-2.1

■ PAUL NOCE Noce, Paul David b: 12/16/59, San Francisco, Cal. BR/TR, 5'10", 175 lbs. Deb: 6/1/87

YEAR	TM/L	G	AB	R	H	2B	3B	HR	RBI	BB	SO	AVG	OBP	SLG	PRO+	BR/A	SB	CS	SBR	FA	FR	G/POS	TPR
1987	Chi-N	70	180	17	41	9	2	3	14	6	49	.228	.261	.350	58	-11	5	3	-0	.983	19	2-36,S-35/3	1.0
1990	Cin-N	1	1	0	1	0	0	0	0	0	0	1.000	1.000	1.000	434	0	0	0	0	.000	0	/H	0.0
Total	2	71	181	17	42	9	2	3	14	6	49	.232	.265	.354	60	-11	5	3	-0	.983	19	/2-36,S-35,3	1.0

■ GEORGE NOFTSKER Noftsker, George Washington b: 8/24/1859, Shippensburg, Pa. d: 5/8/31, Shippensburg, Pa. BR/TR, 5'8", 135 lbs. Deb: 4/17/1884

YEAR	TM/L	G	AB	R	H	2B	3B	HR	RBI	BB	SO	AVG	OBP	SLG	PRO+	BR/A	SB	CS	SBR	FA	FR	G/POS	TPR
1884	Alt-U	7	25	0	1	0	0	0		0		.040	.040	.040	-77	-6				.818	1	/O-5,C-3	-0.4

■ MATT NOKES Nokes, Matthew Dodge b: 10/31/63, San Diego, Cal. BL/TR, 6'1", 185 lbs. Deb: 9/3/85

YEAR	TM/L	G	AB	R	H	2B	3B	HR	RBI	BB	SO	AVG	OBP	SLG	PRO+	BR/A	SB	CS	SBR	FA	FR	G/POS	TPR
1985	SF-N	19	53	3	11	2	0	2	5	1	9	.208	.236	.358	67	-3	0	0	0	.977	-1	C-14	-0.3
1986	Det-A	7	24	2	8	1	0	1	2	1	1	.333	.360	.500	132	1	0	0	0	1.000	2	/C-7	0.3
1987	*Det-A★	135	461	69	133	14	2	32	87	35	70	.289	.347	.536	135	22	2	1	0	.992	-9	*C-109,D-19/O3	1.8
1988	Det-A	122	382	53	96	18	0	16	53	34	58	.251	.314	.424	109	4	0	1	-1	.989	4	*C-110/D-4	0.8
1989	Det-A	87	268	15	67	10	0	9	39	17	37	.250	.300	.388	95	-3	1	0	0	.978	-6	C-51,D-33	-0.7
1990	Det-A	44	111	12	30	5	1	3	8	4	14	.270	.308	.414	99	-0	0	0	0	.984	-3	D-24,C-19	-0.3
	NY-A	92	240	21	57	4	0	8	32	20	33	.237	.307	.354	84	-5	2	2	-1	.995	-7	C-46,D-30/O	-1.2
	Yr	136	351	33	87	9	1	11	40	24	47	.248	.307	.373	89	-6	2	2	-1	.993	-10	C-65,D-54/O	-1.5
1991	NY-A	135	456	52	122	20	0	24	77	25	49	.268	.313	.469	113	6	3	2	-0	.992	-14	*C-130/D-3	-0.1
1992	NY-A	121	384	42	86	9	1	22	59	37	62	.224	.297	.424	101	-1	0	1	-1	.993	-11	*C-111	-0.6
1993	NY-A	76	217	25	54	8	0	10	35	16	31	.249	.306	.424	97	-2	0	0	0	.992	-5	C-56,D-11	-0.4
1994	NY-A	28	79	11	23	3	0	7	19	5	16	.291	.333	.595	142	4	0	0	0	.975	0	C-17/1-4,D	0.5
Total	10	866	2675	305	687	94	4	134	416	195	380	.257	.314	.445	108	23	8	7	-2	.990	-56	C-670,D-129/O13	-0.2

■ JOE NOLAN Nolan, Joseph William b: 5/12/51, St.Louis, Mo. BL/TR, 6', 190 lbs. Deb: 9/21/72

YEAR	TM/L	G	AB	R	H	2B	3B	HR	RBI	BB	SO	AVG	OBP	SLG	PRO+	BR/A	SB	CS	SBR	FA	FR	G/POS	TPR
1972	NY-N	4	10	0	0	0	0	0	0	1	3	.000	.091	.000	-74	-2	0	0	0	.938	-1	/C-3	-0.3
1975	Atl-N	4	4	0	1	0	0	0	0	1	0	.250	.400	.250	80	-0	0	0	0	1.000	-0	/C-1	0.0
1977	Atl-N	62	82	13	23	3	0	3	9	13	12	.280	.379	.427	103	1	1	0	0	1.000	-1	C-19	0.1
1978	Atl-N	95	213	22	49	7	3	4	22	34	28	.230	.339	.347	83	-4	3	2	0	.979	-4	C-61	-1.0
1979	Atl-N	89	230	28	57	9	3	4	21	27	28	.248	.335	.365	85	-4	1	3	-2	.983	-7	C-74	-1.1
1980	Atl-N	17	22	2	6	1	0	0	2	2	4	.273	.333	.318	80	-1	0	0	0	1.000	1	/C-6	0.1
	Cin-N	53	154	14	48	7	0	3	24	13	8	.312	.365	.416	117	4	0	0	0	.982	1	C-51	0.7
	Yr	70	176	16	54	8	0	3	26	15	12	.307	.361	.403	112	3	0	0	0	.983	2	C-57	0.8
1981	Cin-N	81	236	25	73	18	1	1	26	24	19	.309	.375	.407	120	7	1	2	-1	.995	-11	C-81	-0.3
1982	Bal-A	77	219	24	51	7	1	6	35	16	35	.233	.285	.356	75	-8	1	1	-0	.978	-3	C-72	-0.9
1983	*Bal-A	73	184	25	51	11	1	5	24	16	31	.277	.342	.429	113	3	0	0	0	.980	-10	C-65	-0.5
1984	Bal-A	35	62	2	18	1	1	1	9	12	10	.290	.405	.387	123	3	0	0	0	.962	-1	D-11/C-6	0.2
1985	Bal-A	31	38	1	5	2	0	0	6	5	5	.132	.233	.184	16	-5	0	0	0	1.000	1	/C-5,D-4	-0.4
Total	11	621	1454	156	382	66	10	27	178	164	183	.263	.340	.378	95	-7	7	8	-3	.984	-37	C-444/D-15	-3.4

■ RED NONNENKAMP Nonnenkamp, Leo William b: 7/7/11, St.Louis, Mo. BL/TL, 5'11", 165 lbs. Deb: 9/6/33

YEAR	TM/L	G	AB	R	H	2B	3B	HR	RBI	BB	SO	AVG	OBP	SLG	PRO+	BR/A	SB	CS	SBR	FA	FR	G/POS	TPR
1933	Pit-N	1	1	0	0	0	0	0	0	0	1	.000	.000	.000	-99	-0	0			.000	0	H	0.0
1938	Bos-A	87	180	37	51	4	1	0	18	21	13	.283	.358	.317	67	-8	6	1	1	.968	2	O-39/1-5	-0.6
1939	Bos-A	58	75	12	18	2	1	0	5	12	6	.240	.345	.293	62	-4	0	1	-1	.962	-3	O-15	-0.7
1940	Bos-A	9	7	0	0	0	0	0	1	0	4	.000	.125	.000	-62	-2	0	0	0	.000	0	H	-0.2
Total	4	155	263	49	69	6	2	0	24	33	24	.262	.347	.300	62	-14	6	2		.966	-1	/O-54,1-5	-1.5

■ PETE NOONAN Noonan, Peter John b: 11/24/1881, W.Stockbridge, Mass. d: 2/11/65, Great Barrington, Mass. BR/TR, 6', 180 lbs. Deb: 6/20/04

YEAR	TM/L	G	AB	R	H	2B	3B	HR	RBI	BB	SO	AVG	OBP	SLG	PRO+	BR/A	SB	CS	SBR	FA	FR	G/POS	TPR
1904	Phi-A	39	114	13	23	3	1	2	13	1		.202	.209	.298	56	-6	1			.969	-4	C-22,1-10	-0.9
1906	Chi-N	5	3	0	1	0	0	0	0	0		.333	.333	.333	102	0	0			1.000	0	/1-1	0.0
	StL-N	44	125	8	21	1	3	1	9	11		.168	.235	.248	53	-7	1			.957	-4	C-23,1-16	-0.2
	Yr	49	128	8	22	1	3	1	9	11		.172	.237	.250	54	-7	1			.957	-4	C-23,1-17	-0.2
1907	StL-N	74	237	19	53	7	3	1	16	9		.224	.252	.291	73	-9	3			.951	3	C-70	0.1
Total	3	162	479	40	98	11	7	4	38	21		.205	.238	.282	64	-22	5			.955	-5	C-115/1-27	-0.9

■ TIM NORDBROOK Nordbrook, Timothy Charles b: 7/7/49, Baltimore, Md. BR/TR, 6'1", 180 lbs. Deb: 9/13/74

YEAR	TM/L	G	AB	R	H	2B	3B	HR	RBI	BB	SO	AVG	OBP	SLG	PRO+	BR/A	SB	CS	SBR	FA	FR	G/POS	TPR
1974	Bal-A	6	15	4	4	0	0	0	1	2	2	.267	.353	.267	83	-0	1	0	0	1.000	1	/S-5,2-1	0.2
1975	Bal-A	40	34	6	4	1	0	0	0	7	7	.118	.268	.147	21	-3	0	0	0	.970	5	S-37/2-3	0.3
1976	Bal-A	27	22	4	5	0	0	0	0	3	5	.227	.320	.227	66	-1	0	0	0	1.000	3	2-14,S-12	0.3
	Cal-A	5	8	1	0	0	0	0	0	1	3	.000	.111	.000	-70	-2	0	0	0	.941	0	/S-4,2-1,D	0.1
	Yr	32	30	5	5	0	0	0	0	4	8	.167	.265	.167	30	-3	0	0	0	.978	5	S-16,2-15/D	0.4
1977	Chi-A	15	20	2	5	1	0	0	1	7	4	.250	.444	.250	95	0	0	0	0	.850	-2	S-11/3-1,D	0.0
	Tor-A	24	63	9	11	0	1	0	1	4	7	.175	.224	.206	18	-7	2	0	1	.989	1	S-24	-0.4
	Yr	39	83	11	16	1	1	0	2	11	11	.193	.287	.217	39	-7	2	0	1	.947	-1	S-35/D-2,3	-0.4
1978	Tor-A	7	0	0	0	0	0	0	0	0	0	—	1.000	—	200	0	0	0	0	1.000	0	/S-7	0.2
	Mil-A	2	5	1	0	0	0	0	0	1	1	.000	.167	.000	-49	-1	0	0	0	.909	0	/S-2	0.0
	Yr	9	5	1	0	0	0	0	0	1	1	.000	.286	.000	-13	-1	0	0	0	.941	0	/S-9	0.2

YEAR	TM/L	G	AB	R	H	2B	3B	HR	RBI	BB	SO	AVG	OBP	SLG	PRO+	BR/A	SB	CS	SBR	FA	FR	G/POS	TPR
1979	Mil-A	2	2	0	1	0	0	0	0	0	0	.500	.500	.500	171	0	0	0	0	1.000	-1	/S-2	0.0
Total	6	128	169	27	30	1	1	0	3	25	33	.178	.287	.195	38	-13	4	0	1	.961	12	S-104/2-19,D3	0.7

■ WAYNE NORDHAGEN
Nordhagen, Wayne Oren b: 7/4/48, Thief River Falls, Minn. BR/TR, 6'2", 205 lbs. Deb: 7/16/76

YEAR	TM/L	G	AB	R	H	2B	3B	HR	RBI	BB	SO	AVG	OBP	SLG	PRO+	BR/A	SB	CS	SBR	FA	FR	G/POS	TPR
1976	Chi-A	22	53	6	10	2	0	0	5	4	12	.189	.246	.226	39	-4	0	0	0	1.000	0	O-10/C-5,D	-0.4
1977	Chi-A	52	124	16	39	7	3	4	22	2	12	.315	.325	.516	125	4	1	0	0	.944	-10	O-46/C-3,D	-0.7
1978	Chi-A	68	206	28	62	16	0	5	35	5	18	.301	.318	.451	113	3	0	1	-1	.941	-8	O-36,D-16,C	-0.8
1979	Chi-A	78	193	20	54	15	0	7	25	13	22	.280	.325	.466	111	2	0	0	-1	1.000	0	D-47,O-12/CP	0.1
1980	Chi-A	123	415	45	115	22	4	15	59	10	45	.277	.296	.458	104	0	0	1	-1	.969	-5	O-74,D-32	-0.9
1981	Chi-A	65	208	19	64	8	1	6	33	10	25	.308	.342	.442	127	7	0	1	-1	.947	-7	O-60	-0.2
1982	Tor-A	44	115	8	32	3	0	1	14	9	13	.278	.331	.330	75	-4	0	2	-1	1.000	-1	D-32,O-10	-0.7
	Pit-N	1	4	0	2	0	0	0	2	0	1	.500	.500	.500	175	0	0	0	0	1.000	0	/O-1	0.0
	Tor-A	28	70	4	18	3	0	1	6	1	9	.257	.268	.300	51	-5	0	0	0	.000	0	D-28	-0.6
1983	Chi-N	21	35	1	5	1	0	1	4	0	5	.143	.167	.257	15	-4	0	0	0	1.000	-1	/O-7	-0.6
Total	8	502	1423	147	401	77	8	39	205	54	162	.282	.309	.429	101	-1	1	5	-3	.962	-30	O-256,D-163/CP	-4.8

■ LOU NORDYKE
Nordyke, Louis Ellis b: 8/7/1876, Brighton, Iowa d: 9/27/45, Los Angeles, Cal. BR/TR, 6', 185 lbs. Deb: 4/18/06

YEAR	TM/L	G	AB	R	H	2B	3B	HR	RBI	BB	SO	AVG	OBP	SLG	PRO+	BR/A	SB	CS	SBR	FA	FR	G/POS	TPR
1906	StL-A	25	53	4	13	1	0	0	7		10	.245	.365	.264	102	1	3			.942	-3	1-12	-0.2

■ IRV NOREN
Noren, Irving Arnold b: 11/29/24, Jamestown, N.Y. BL/TL, 6', 190 lbs. Deb: 4/18/50 C

YEAR	TM/L	G	AB	R	H	2B	3B	HR	RBI	BB	SO	AVG	OBP	SLG	PRO+	BR/A	SB	CS	SBR	FA	FR	G/POS	TPR
1950	Was-A	138	542	80	160	27	10	14	98	67	77	.295	.373	.459	118	14	5	2	0	.984	16	*O-121,1-17	2.3
1951	Was-A	129	509	82	142	33	5	8	86	51	35	.279	.345	.411	105	3	10	7	-1	.978	21	*O-126	1.8
1952	Was-A	12	49	4	12	3	1	0	2	6	3	.245	.327	.347	91	-1	1	0	0	1.000	3	O-12	0.2
	*NY-A	93	272	36	64	13	2	5	21	26	34	.235	.316	.353	91	-4	4	2	0	1.000	-7	O-60,1-19	-1.4
	Yr	105	321	40	76	16	3	5	23	32	37	.237	.318	.352	91	-4	5	2	0	1.000	-4	O-72,1-19	-1.2
1953	*NY-A	109	345	55	92	12	6	6	46	42	39	.267	.350	.388	103	1	3	3	-1	.991	-1	O-96	-0.4
1954	NY-A★	125	426	70	136	21	6	12	66	43	38	.319	.383	.481	140	23	4	6	-2	.980	-1	*O-116/1-1	1.5
1955	*NY-A	132	371	49	94	19	1	8	59	43	31	.253	.336	.375	92	-4	5	2	0	.980	-0	*O-126	-0.9
1956	NY-A	29	37	4	8	1	0	0	6	12	7	.216	.408	.243	78	-0	0	0	0	.875	-2	O-10/1-1	-0.3
1957	KC-A	81	160	8	34	8	0	2	16	11	19	.213	.267	.300	54	-10	0	1	0	.990	-2	1-25/O-6	-1.4
	StL-N	17	30	3	11	4	1	0	10	4	6	.367	.441	.667	189	4	0	1	-1	1.000	-2	/O-8	0.1
1958	StL-N	117	178	24	47	9	1	4	22	13	21	.264	.328	.393	87	-3	0	1	-1	.974	-17	O-77	-2.3
1959	StL-N	8	8	0	1	1	0	0	0	0	2	.125	.125	.250	-3	-1	0	0	0	.000	-1	/O-2,1-1	-0.2
	Chi-N	65	156	27	50	6	2	4	19	13	24	.321	.384	.462	125	6	2	0	1	1.000	3	O-40/1-1	0.8
	Yr	73	164	27	51	7	2	4	19	13	26	.311	.372	.451	118	6	2	0	1	1.000	3	O-42/1-2	0.6
1960	Chi-N	12	11	0	1	0	0	0	1	3	4	.091	.286	.091	9	-1	0	0	0	.833	-1	/1-1,O-1	-0.2
	LA-N	26	25	1	5	0	0	1	1	1	8	.200	.231	.320	46	-2	0	0	0	.000	-1	H	-0.2
	Yr	38	36	1	6	0	0	1	2	4	12	.167	.250	.250	36	-3	0	0	0	1.000	-1	/1-1,O-1	-0.4
Total	11	1093	3119	443	857	157	35	65	453	335	350	.275	.349	.410	106	23	34	24	-4	.984	10	O-801/1-66	-0.6

■ DAN NORMAN
Norman, Daniel Edmund b: 1/11/55, Los Angeles, Cal. BR/TR, 6'2", 195 lbs. Deb: 9/27/77

YEAR	TM/L	G	AB	R	H	2B	3B	HR	RBI	BB	SO	AVG	OBP	SLG	PRO+	BR/A	SB	CS	SBR	FA	FR	G/POS	TPR
1977	NY-N	7	16	2	4	1	0	0	0	4	2	.250	.400	.313	99	-1	0	0	0	1.000	-1	/O-6	-0.1
1978	NY-N	19	64	7	17	0	1	4	10	2	14	.266	.288	.484	116	1	1	0	0	1.000	-1	O-18	0.0
1979	NY-N	44	110	9	27	3	1	3	11	10	26	.245	.314	.373	90	-2	2	0	1	.967	-0	O-33	-0.3
1980	NY-N	69	92	5	17	1	1	2	9	6	14	.185	.235	.283	45	-7	5	0	2	1.000	-3	O-19	-0.9
1982	Mon-N	53	66	6	14	3	0	2	7	7	20	.212	.288	.348	76	-2	0	1	-1	.969	-6	O-31	-0.9
Total	5	192	348	29	79	8	3	11	37	29	76	.227	.288	.362	81	-10	8	1	2	.981	-11	O-107	-2.2

■ BILL NORMAN
Norman, Henry Willis Patrick b: 7/16/10, St.Louis, Mo. d: 4/21/62, Milwaukee, Wis. BR/TR, 6'2", 190 lbs. Deb: 8/8/31 MC

YEAR	TM/L	G	AB	R	H	2B	3B	HR	RBI	BB	SO	AVG	OBP	SLG	PRO+	BR/A	SB	CS	SBR	FA	FR	G/POS	TPR
1931	Chi-A	24	55	7	10	2	0	0	6	4	10	.182	.237	.218	22	-6	0	1	-1	.933	-1	O-17	-0.8
1932	Chi-A	13	48	6	11	3	1	0	2	2	3	.229	.260	.333	56	-3	0	0	0	.917	-2	O-13	-0.6
Total	2	37	103	13	21	5	1	0	8	6	13	.204	.248	.272	38	-10	0	1	-1	.928	-3	/O-30	-1.4

■ NELSON NORMAN
Norman, Nelson Augusto b: 5/23/58, San Pedro De Macoris, D.R. BB/TR, 6'2", 160 lbs. Deb: 5/20/78

YEAR	TM/L	G	AB	R	H	2B	3B	HR	RBI	BB	SO	AVG	OBP	SLG	PRO+	BR/A	SB	CS	SBR	FA	FR	G/POS	TPR
1978	Tex-A	23	34	1	9	1	0	0	1	0	5	.265	.265	.324	64	-2	0	0	0	.984	10	S-18/3-6	0.9
1979	Tex-A	147	343	36	76	9	3	0	21	19	41	.222	.262	.265	43	-27	4	1	1	.952	-15	*S-142/2-1	-2.9
1980	Tex-A	17	32	4	7	0	0	0	1	1	1	.219	.242	.219	28	-3	0	1	-1	.943	7	S-17	0.4
1981	Tex-A	7	13	1	3	1	0	0	2	1	2	.231	.286	.308	75	-0	0	0	0	.963	3	/S-5	0.3
1982	Pit-N	3	3	0	0	0	0	0	0	0	0	.000	.000	.000	-97	-1	0	0	0	.000	-1	/2-2,S-1	-0.2
1987	Mon-N	1	4	0	0	0	0	0	0	0	1	.000	.000	.000	-97	-1	0	0	0	.667	-1	/S-1	-0.2
Total	6	198	429	42	95	12	3	0	25	21	50	.221	.258	.263	42	-34	4	2	0	.954	3	S-184/3-6,2	-1.7

■ JIM NORRIS
Norris, James Francis b: 12/20/48, Brooklyn, N.Y. BL/TL, 5'10", 175 lbs. Deb: 4/7/77

YEAR	TM/L	G	AB	R	H	2B	3B	HR	RBI	BB	SO	AVG	OBP	SLG	PRO+	BR/A	SB	CS	SBR	FA	FR	G/POS	TPR
1977	Cle-A	133	440	59	119	23	6	2	37	64	57	.270	.363	.364	102	3	26	17	-2	.982	12	*O-124/1-3	0.8
1978	Cle-A	113	315	41	89	14	5	2	27	42	20	.283	.367	.378	111	6	12	7	-1	.988	0	O-78,D-15/1	0.2
1979	Cle-A	124	353	50	87	15	6	3	30	44	35	.246	.330	.348	83	-8	15	10	-2	.982	0	O-93,D-13	-1.3
1980	Tex-A	119	174	23	43	5	0	0	16	23	16	.247	.335	.276	72	-6	6	3	0	1.000	-18	O-82,1-10/D	-2.6
Total	4	489	1282	173	338	57	17	7	110	173	128	.264	.351	.351	95	-6	59	37	-5	.985	-5	O-377/D-29,1	-2.9

■ LEO NORRIS
Norris, Leo John b: 5/17/08, Bay St.Louis, Miss d: 2/13/87, Zachary, La. BR/TR, 5'11", 165 lbs. Deb: 4/14/36

YEAR	TM/L	G	AB	R	H	2B	3B	HR	RBI	BB	SO	AVG	OBP	SLG	PRO+	BR/A	SB	CS	SBR	FA	FR	G/POS	TPR
1936	Phi-N	154	581	64	154	27	4	11	76	39	79	.265	.315	.382	79	-18	4			.936	-8	*S-121,2-38	-1.6
1937	Phi-N	116	381	45	98	24	3	9	36	21	53	.257	.296	.407	82	-11	3			.949	-11	2-74,3-24,S	-1.6
Total	2	270	962	109	252	51	7	20	112	60	132	.262	.307	.392	80	-29	7			.940	-20	S-141,2-112/3	-3.2

■ BILLY NORTH
North, William Alex b: 5/15/48, Seattle, Wash. BB/TR, 5'11", 185 lbs. Deb: 9/3/71

YEAR	TM/L	G	AB	R	H	2B	3B	HR	RBI	BB	SO	AVG	OBP	SLG	PRO+	BR/A	SB	CS	SBR	FA	FR	G/POS	TPR
1971	Chi-N	8	16	3	6	0	0	0	0	4	6	.375	.524	.375	138	1	1	1	-0	1.000	-2	/O-6	-0.1
1972	Chi-N	66	127	22	23	2	3	0	4	13	33	.181	.262	.244	40	-10	6	0	2	.955	-8	O-48	-1.9
1973	Oak-A	146	554	98	158	10	5	5	34	78	89	.285	.376	.348	111	11	53	20	24	.980	24	*O-138/D-6	3.3
1974	*Oak-A	149	543	79	141	20	5	4	33	69	86	.260	.348	.337	105	5	54	26	1	.991	18	*O-138/D-8	1.9
1975	*Oak-A	140	524	74	143	17	5	1	43	81	80	.273	.374	.330	103	6	30	12	2	.975	20	*O-138/D-1	2.2
1976	Oak-A	154	590	91	163	20	5	2	31	73	95	.276	.358	.337	109	9	75	29	5	.978	6	*O-144/D-8	1.5
1977	Oak-A	56	184	32	48	3	3	1	9	32	25	.261	.376	.326	95	-1	17	13	-3	.983	-4	O-52/D-1	-0.8
1978	Oak-A	24	52	5	11	4	0	0	5	9	13	.212	.349	.288	86	-1	3	2	-0	1.000	-2	O-17	-0.4
	*LA-N	110	304	54	71	10	0	0	10	66	48	.234	.372	.266	81	-4	27	8	3	.975	-2	*O-103	-0.7
1979	SF-N	142	460	87	119	15	4	5	30	96	84	.259	.388	.341	108	10	58	24	3	.987	-3	*O-130	1.0
1980	SF-N	128	415	73	104	12	1	1	19	81	78	.251	.374	.292	90	-1	45	19	2	.982	10	*O-115	0.7
1981	SF-N	44	131	12	29	7	0	1	12	26	28	.221	.354	.298	88	-1	26	8	3	.966	-2	O-37	-0.2
Total	11	1169	3900	640	1016	120	31	20	230	627	665	.261	.366	.323	99	26	395	162	21	.981	61	*O-1066/D-24	6.5

■ HUB NORTHEN
Northen, Hubbard Elwin b: 8/16/1885, Atlanta, Tex. d: 10/1/47, Shreveport, La. BL/TL, 5'8", 175 lbs. Deb: 9/10/10

YEAR	TM/L	G	AB	R	H	2B	3B	HR	RBI	BB	SO	AVG	OBP	SLG	PRO+	BR/A	SB	CS	SBR	FA	FR	G/POS	TPR
1910	StL-A	26	96	6	19	1	0	0	16		5	.198	.238	.208	42	-6	2			.926	-2	O-26	-1.1
1911	Cin-N	1	0	0	0	0	0	0	0		0	—	—	—	0		0			.000	0	H	
	Bro-N	19	76	16	24	2	2	0	1	14	9	.316	.429	.395	137	5	4			.911	2	O-19	0.5
	Yr	20	76	16	24	2	2	0	1	14	9	.316	.429	.395	137	5	4			.911	2	O-19	0.5

YEAR	TM/L	G	AB	R	H	2B	3B	HR	RBI	BB	SO	AVG	OBP	SLG	PRO+	BR/A	SB	CS	SBR	FA	FR	G/POS	TPR
1912	Bro-N	118	412	54	116	26	6	3	46	41	46	.282	.352	.396	109	5	8			.950	-7	*O-102	-0.8
Total	3	164	584	76	159	29	8	3	63	60	55	.272	.345	.365	103	3	14			.939	-7	O-147	-1.4

■ RON NORTHEY
Northey, Ronald James b: 4/26/20, Mahanoy City, Pa. d: 4/16/71, Pittsburgh, Pa. BL/TR, 5'10", 195 lbs. Deb: 4/14/42 FC

YEAR	TM/L	G	AB	R	H	2B	3B	HR	RBI	BB	SO	AVG	OBP	SLG	PRO+	BR/A	SB	CS	SBR	FA	FR	G/POS	TPR
1942	Phi-N	127	402	31	101	13	2	5	31	28	33	.251	.300	.331	89	-7	2			.952	1	*O-109	-1.2
1943	Phi-N	147	586	72	163	31	5	16	68	51	52	.278	.339	.430	127	17	2			.978	9	*O-145	1.4
1944	Phi-N	152	570	72	164	35	9	22	104	67	51	.288	.367	.496	146	33	1			.981	4	*O-151	3.0
1946	Phi-N	128	438	55	109	24	6	16	62	39	59	.249	.313	.441	116	6	1			.971	-6	*O-111	-0.6
1947	Phi-N	13	47	7	12	3	0	0	3	6	3	.255	.340	.319	79	-1	1			1.000	-1	O-13	-0.3
	StL-N	110	311	52	91	19	3	15	63	48	29	.293	.391	.518	133	15	0			.949	-12	O-94/3-2	0.0
	Yr	123	358	59	103	22	3	15	66	54	32	.288	.384	.492	127	14	1			.955	-13	*O-107/3-2	-0.3
1948	StL-N	96	246	40	79	10	1	13	64	38	25	.321	.420	.528	147	17	0			.989	-10	O-67	-1.5
1949	StL-N	90	265	28	69	18	2	7	50	31	15	.260	.338	.423	98	-1	0			.980	-11	O-73	-0.2
1950	Cin-N	27	77	11	20	5	0	5	9	15	6	.260	.380	.519	134	4	0			.955	-5	O-24	-0.2
	Chi-N	53	114	11	32	9	0	4	20	10	9	.281	.339	.465	110	1	0			.976	-1	O-27	0.0
	Yr	80	191	22	52	14	0	9	29	25	15	.272	.356	.487	120	5	0			.969	-6	O-51	-0.2
1952	Chi-N	1	1	0	0	0	0	0	0	0	0	.000	.000	.000	-99	-0	0	0	0	.000	0	H	0.0
1955	Chi-A	14	14	1	5	2	0	1	4	3	3	.357	.471	.714	209	2	0	0	0	1.000	-1	/O-2	0.2
1956	Chi-A	53	48	4	17	2	0	3	23	8	1	.354	.446	.583	168	5	0	0	0	1.000	-1	/O-4	0.4
1957	Chi-A	40	27	0	5	1	0	0	7	11	5	.185	.421	.222	80	0	0	0	0	.000	0	H	0.0
	Phi-N	33	26	1	7	0	0	1	5	6	6	.269	.406	.385	118	1	0	0	0	.000	0	H	0.1
Total	12	1084	3172	385	874	172	28	108	513	361	297	.276	.352	.450	124	93	7	0		.972	-38	O-820/3-2	1.7

■ SCOTT NORTHEY
Northey, Scott Richard b: 10/15/46, Philadelphia, Pa. BR/TR, 6', 175 lbs. Deb: 9/2/69 F

YEAR	TM/L	G	AB	R	H	2B	3B	HR	RBI	BB	SO	AVG	OBP	SLG	PRO+	BR/A	SB	CS	SBR	FA	FR	G/POS	TPR
1969	KC-A	20	61	11	16	2	2	1	7	7	19	.262	.338	.410	108	1	6	3	0	.973	-0	O-18	-0.1

■ JIM NORTHRUP
Northrup, James Thomas b: 11/24/39, Breckenridge, Mich. BL/TR, 6'3", 190 lbs. Deb: 9/30/64

YEAR	TM/L	G	AB	R	H	2B	3B	HR	RBI	BB	SO	AVG	OBP	SLG	PRO+	BR/A	SB	CS	SBR	FA	FR	G/POS	TPR
1964	Det-A	5	12	1	1	1	0	0	0	0	3	.083	.083	.167	-32	-2	1	0		1.000	-1	/O-2	-0.3
1965	Det-A	80	219	20	45	12	3	2	16	12	50	.205	.253	.315	60	-12	1	1	-0	.976	-4	O-54	-1.9
1966	Det-A	123	419	53	111	24	6	16	58	33	52	.265	.325	.465	121	11	4	7	-3	.980	10	*O-113	1.3
1967	Det-A	144	495	63	134	18	6	10	61	43	83	.271	.333	.392	110	6	7	1	2	.972	-20	*O-143	-2.0
1968	*Det-A	154	580	76	153	29	7	21	90	50	87	.264	.326	.447	129	19	4	5	-2	.979	8	*O-143	1.9
1969	Det-A	148	543	79	160	31	5	25	66	52	83	.295	.360	.508	135	23	4	2	0	.985	4	*O-143	2.0
1970	Det-A	139	504	71	132	21	3	24	80	58	47	.262	.346	.458	119	13	3	6	-3	.993	3	*O-136	0.6
1971	Det-A	136	459	72	124	27	2	16	71	60	43	.270	.357	.442	121	13	7	4	-0	.981	-20	*O-108,1-32	-1.6
1972	*Det-A	134	426	40	111	15	2	8	42	38	47	.261	.324	.362	101	0	4	7	-3	.978	-16	*O-127/1-2	-2.8
1973	Det-A	119	404	55	124	14	7	12	44	38	41	.307	.368	.465	125	13	4	4	-1	.982	-9	O-97	-0.2
1974	Det-A	97	376	41	89	12	1	11	42	36	46	.237	.303	.362	88	-6	0	0	0	.973	3	O-13	-0.8
	Mon-N	21	54	3	13	1	0	2	8	5	9	.241	.305	.370	84	-1	0	0	0	1.000	-2	/O-13	0.2
	Bal-A	8	7	2	4	0	0	1	3	2	1	.571	.667	1.000	386	3	0	0	0	1.000	-1	/O-6,D-1	0.2
1975	Bal-A	84	194	27	53	13	0	5	29	22	22	.273	.353	.418	125	6	0	1	-1	.979	-12	O-58/D-3	-0.8
Total	12	1392	4692	603	1254	218	42	153	610	449	635	.267	.335	.429	115	86	39	38	-11	.981	-57	*O-1267/1-34,D	-4.8

■ FRANK NORTON
Norton, Frank Prescott Deb: 5/5/1871

YEAR	TM/L	G	AB	R	H	2B	3B	HR	RBI	BB	SO	AVG	OBP	SLG	PRO+	BR/A	SB	CS	SBR	FA	FR	G/POS	TPR
1871	Oly-n	1	1	0	0	0	0	0	0	0	1	.000	.000	.000	-99	-0	0					/O-1	0.0

■ WILLIE NORWOOD
Norwood, Willie b: 11/7/50, Greene County, Ala. BR/TR, 6', 185 lbs. Deb: 4/21/77

YEAR	TM/L	G	AB	R	H	2B	3B	HR	RBI	BB	SO	AVG	OBP	SLG	PRO+	BR/A	SB	CS	SBR	FA	FR	G/POS	TPR
1977	Min-A	39	83	15	19	3	0	3	9	6	17	.229	.281	.373	78	-3	6	1	1	.952	-4	O-28/D-5	-0.6
1978	Min-A	125	428	56	109	22	3	6	46	28	64	.255	.305	.376	89	-7	25	10	2	.944	-2	*O-115/D-6	-1.3
1979	Min-A	96	270	32	67	13	3	6	30	20	51	.248	.300	.385	80	-8	9	5	-0	.974	-4	O-71,D-14	-1.5
1980	Min-A	34	73	6	12	2	0	1	8	3	13	.164	.197	.233	16	-8	1	1	-0	1.000	-1	O-17/D-9	-1.1
Total	4	294	854	109	207	40	6	18	93	57	145	.242	.292	.367	79	-26	41	17	2	.959	-12	O-231/D-34	-4.5

■ JOE NOSSEK
Nossek, Joseph Rudolph b: 11/8/40, Cleveland, Ohio BR/TR, 6', 178 lbs. Deb: 4/18/64 C

YEAR	TM/L	G	AB	R	H	2B	3B	HR	RBI	BB	SO	AVG	OBP	SLG	PRO+	BR/A	SB	CS	SBR	FA	FR	G/POS	TPR
1964	Min-A	7	1	1	0	0	0	0	0	0	0	.000	.000	.000	-99		0	0	0	.000	-1	/O-2	-0.1
1965	*Min-A	87	170	19	37	9	0	2	16	7	22	.218	.253	.306	55	-10	2	0	-1	.970	-6	O-48/3-9	-1.8
1966	Min-A	4	0	0	0	0	0	0	0	0	0	—	—	—	—		0	0	0	.000	-1	/O-2	-0.1
	KC-A	87	230	13	60	10	3	1	27	8	21	.261	.286	.343	83	-6	4	2	0	.983	3	O-78/3-1	-0.6
	Yr	91	230	13	60	10	3	1	27	8	21	.261	.286	.343	82	-6	4	2	0	.983	3	O-80/3-1	-0.7
1967	KC-A	87	166	12	34	6	1	0	10	4	26	.205	.224	.253	42	-12	2	0	1	.982	-3	O-63	-1.9
1969	Oak-A	13	6	0	0	0	0	0	0	0	0	.000	.000	.000	-99	-2	0	0	0	1.000	-4	/O-1	-0.6
	StL-N	9	5	2	1	0	0	0	0	0	3	.200	.200	.200	12	-1	0	0	0	1.000	0	H	-0.1
1970	StL-N	1	1	0	0	0	0	0	0	0	0	.000	.000	.000	-98	-0	0	0	0	.000	0	H	0.0
Total	6	295	579	47	132	25	4	3	53	19	72	.228	.254	.301	60	-31	8	2	1	.980	-11	O-206/3-10	-5.2

■ LOU NOVIKOFF
Novikoff, Louis Alexander "The Mad Russian" b: 10/12/15, Glendale, Ariz. d: 9/30/70, South Gate, Cal. BR/TR, 5'10", 185 lbs. Deb: 4/15/41

YEAR	TM/L	G	AB	R	H	2B	3B	HR	RBI	BB	SO	AVG	OBP	SLG	PRO+	BR/A	SB	CS	SBR	FA	FR	G/POS	TPR
1941	Chi-N	62	203	22	49	8	0	5	24	11	15	.241	.284	.355	82	-6	0			1.000	-4	O-54	-1.3
1942	Chi-N	128	483	48	145	25	5	7	64	24	28	.300	.337	.416	125	12	3			.964	-2	*O-120	0.4
1943	Chi-N	78	233	22	65	7	3	0	28	18	15	.279	.333	.335	95	-2	0			.980	-8	O-61	-1.4
1944	Chi-N	71	139	15	39	4	2	3	19	10	11	.281	.329	.403	106	-0	0			.976	-5	O-29	-0.6
1946	Phi-N	17	23	0	7	1	0	0	3	1	2	.304	.333	.348	96	-0	1			1.000	0	/O-3	0.0
Total	5	356	1081	107	305	45	10	15	138	64	71	.282	.325	.384	107	6	4			.976	-19	O-267	-2.9

■ RUBE NOVOTNEY
Novotney, Ralph Joseph b: 8/5/24, Streator, Ill. d: 7/16/87, Redondo Beach, Cal. BR/TR, 6', 187 lbs. Deb: 4/29/49

YEAR	TM/L	G	AB	R	H	2B	3B	HR	RBI	BB	SO	AVG	OBP	SLG	PRO+	BR/A	SB	CS	SBR	FA	FR	G/POS	TPR
1949	Chi-N	22	67	4	18	2	1	0	6	3	11	.269	.300	.328	70	-3	0			.958	0	C-20	-0.1

■ LES NUNAMAKER
Nunamaker, Leslie Grant b: 1/25/1889, Malcolm, Neb. d: 11/14/38, Hastings, Neb. BR/TR, 6'2", 190 lbs. Deb: 4/28/11

YEAR	TM/L	G	AB	R	H	2B	3B	HR	RBI	BB	SO	AVG	OBP	SLG	PRO+	BR/A	SB	CS	SBR	FA	FR	G/POS	TPR
1911	Bos-A	62	183	18	47	4	3	0	19	12		.257	.303	.311	72	-7	1			.972	4	C-59	0.4
1912	Bos-A	35	103	15	26	5	2	0	6	6		.252	.313	.340	82	-3	2			.971	-3	C-35	-0.3
1913	Bos-A	29	65	9	14	2	0	0	9	8	8	.215	.311	.354	92	-1	2			.977	3	C-27	0.5
1914	Bos-A	5	5	0	1	0	0	0	0	1	0	.200	.333	.200	61	-0	0			1.000	0	/C-3,1-1	0.0
	NY-A	87	257	19	68	10	3	2	29	22	34	.265	.327	.350	104	1	11	9	-2	.971	4	C-70/1-5	1.0
	Yr	92	262	19	69	10	3	2	29	23	34	.263	.328	.347	103	1	11	9	-2	.971	4	C-73/1-6	1.0
1915	NY-A	87	249	24	56	6	3	0	17	23	24	.225	.293	.273	70	-9	3	2	-0	.983	-6	C-79	-0.8
1916	NY-A	91	260	25	77	14	7	0	28	34	21	.296	.380	.404	133	11	4			.976	-4	C-91	1.1
1917	NY-A	104	310	22	81	9	4	0	33	21	25	.261	.310	.303	86	-5	6			.979	-7	C-81/1-1,O	0.7
1918	StL-A	85	274	22	71	9	2	0	22	28	16	.259	.330	.307	98	-0	6			.927	-4	C-16	-0.7
1919	Cle-A	26	56	6	14	1	1	0	7	6	6	.250	.276	.304	59	-3	2			.963	1	C-17/1-6	0.4
1920	*Cle-A	34	54	10	18	3	0	0	14	4	5	.333	.379	.500	128	2	1	0	0	.970	4	C-46	0.8
1921	Cle-A	46	131	16	47	7	2	0	25	11	8	.359	.408	.443	115	3	1	1	0	.936	-2	C-13	-0.3
1922	Cle-A	25	43	8	13	2	0	0	5	8	6	.302	.392	.349	95	-1	0	0	0	.972	-5	C-13	-0.3
Total	12	716	1990	194	533	75	30	2	216	176	150	.268	.332	.339	95	-12	36	12		.972	-5	C-614/1-15,O	2.5

■ EMORY NUSZ
Nusz, Emory Moberly b: 4/2/1866, Frederick, Md. d: 8/3/1893, Point Of Rocks, Md. Deb: 4/26/1884

YEAR	TM/L	G	AB	R	H	2B	3B	HR	RBI	BB	SO	AVG	OBP	SLG	PRO+	BR/A	SB	CS	SBR	FA	FR	G/POS	TPR
1884	Was-U	1	4	1	0	1	0	0	0	0	0	.000	.000	.000	-99	-1	1			.500	-0	/O-1	-0.1

YEAR	TM/L	G	AB	R	H	2B	3B	HR	RBI	BB	SO	AVG	OBP	SLG	PRO+	BR/A	SB	CS	SBR	FA	FR	G/POS	TPR

■ DIZZY NUTTER
Nutter, Everett Clarence b: 8/27/1893, Roseville, Ohio d: 7/25/58, Battle Creek, Mich. BL/TR, 5'9", 160 lbs. Deb: 9/7/19

YEAR	TM/L	G	AB	R	H	2B	3B	HR	RBI	BB	SO	AVG	OBP	SLG	PRO+	BR/A	SB	CS	SBR	FA	FR	G/POS	TPR
1919	Bos-N	18	52	4	11	0	0	0	3	4	5	.212	.268	.212	47	-3	1			1.000	2	O-12	-0.3

■ CHARLIE NYCE
Nyce, Charles Reiff (b: Charles Reiff Nice) b: 7/1/1870, Philadelphia, Pa. d: 5/9/08, Philadelphia, Pa. 5'8", 160 lbs. Deb: 5/28/1895

YEAR	TM/L	G	AB	R	H	2B	3B	HR	RBI	BB	SO	AVG	OBP	SLG	PRO+	BR/A	SB	CS	SBR	FA	FR	G/POS	TPR
1895	Bos-N	9	35	7	8	5	0	2	9	4	2	.229	.325	.543	113	0	0			.889	-1	/S-9	0.0

■ CHRIS NYMAN
Nyman, Christopher Curtis b: 6/6/55, Pomona, Cal. BR/TR, 6'4", 200 lbs. Deb: 7/28/82 F

YEAR	TM/L	G	AB	R	H	2B	3B	HR	RBI	BB	SO	AVG	OBP	SLG	PRO+	BR/A	SB	CS	SBR	FA	FR	G/POS	TPR
1982	Chi-A	28	65	6	16	1	0	0	2	3	9	.246	.279	.262	50	-4	3	2	-0	.994	0	1-24/O-2	-0.6
1983	Chi-A	21	28	12	8	0	0	2	4	4	7	.286	.394	.500	139	2	2	2	-1	1.000	1	1-10,D-10	0.1
Total	2	49	93	18	24	1	0	2	6	7	16	.258	.317	.333	78	-3	5	4	-1	.996	1	/1-34,D-10,O	-0.5

■ NYLS NYMAN
Nyman, Nyls Wallace Rex b: 3/7/54, Detroit, Mich. BL/TR, 6', 170 lbs. Deb: 9/6/74 F

YEAR	TM/L	G	AB	R	H	2B	3B	HR	RBI	BB	SO	AVG	OBP	SLG	PRO+	BR/A	SB	CS	SBR	FA	FR	G/POS	TPR
1974	Chi-A	5	14	5	9	2	1	0	4	0	1	.643	.667	.929	347	4	1	0	0	1.000	1	/O-3	0.5
1975	Chi-A	106	327	36	74	6	3	2	28	11	34	.226	.256	.281	51	-21	10	4	1	.958	-4	O-94/D-4	-2.9
1976	Chi-A	8	15	2	2	1	0	0	1	0	3	.133	.133	.200	-3	-2	1	0	0	1.000	-1	/O-7	-0.3
1977	Chi-A	1	1	0	0	0	0	0	0	0	0	.000	.000	.000	-99	-0	0	0	0	.000	0	H	0.0
Total	4	120	357	43	85	9	4	2	33	11	38	.238	.267	.303	60	-19	12	4	1	.962	-4	O-104/D-4	-2.7

■ REBEL OAKES
Oakes, Ennis Telfair b: 12/17/1886, Homer, La. d: 2/29/48, Rocky Springs, Lisbon, La. BL/TR, 5'8", 170 lbs. Deb: 4/14/09 M

YEAR	TM/L	G	AB	R	H	2B	3B	HR	RBI	BB	SO	AVG	OBP	SLG	PRO+	BR/A	SB	CS	SBR	FA	FR	G/POS	TPR
1909	Cin-N	120	415	55	112	10	5	3	31	40		.270	.341	.340	112	6	23			.979	-2	*O-113	0.0
1910	StL-N	131	468	50	118	14	6	0	43	38	38	.252	.320	.308	85	-9	18			.939	-7	*O-127	-2.3
1911	StL-N	154	551	69	145	13	6	2	59	41	35	.263	.320	.319	81	-14	25			.961	11	*O-151	-1.1
1912	StL-N	136	495	57	139	19	5	3	58	31	24	.281	.328	.358	90	-8	26			.947	-2	*O-136	-1.6
1913	StL-N	147	539	60	158	14	5	0	49	43	32	.293	.350	.338	98	-0	22			.968	-2	*O-145	-1.0
1914	Pit-F	145	571	82	178	18	10	7	75	35	22	.312	.359	.415	101	-0	28			.960	6	*O-145,M	0.0
1915	Pit-F	153	580	55	161	24	5	0	82	37	19	.278	.323	.336	77	-19	21			.973	-3	*O-153,M	-3.3
Total	7	986	3619	428	1011	112	42	15	397	265	170	.279	.334	.346	91	-44	163			.961	1	O-970	-9.3

■ PRINCE OANA
Oana, Henry Kauhane b: 1/22/08, Waipahu, Hawaii d: 6/19/76, Austin, Tex. BR/TR, 6'2", 193 lbs. Deb: 4/22/34

YEAR	TM/L	G	AB	R	H	2B	3B	HR	RBI	BB	SO	AVG	OBP	SLG	PRO+	BR/A	SB	CS	SBR	FA	FR	G/POS	TPR
1934	Phi-N	6	21	3	5	1	0	0	3	0	1	.238	.238	.286	35	-2	0			1.000	1	/O-4	-0.1
1943	Det-A	20	26	5	10	2	1	1	7	1	2	.385	.407	.654	193	3	0	0	0	1.000	1	/O-4	0.0
1945	Det-A	4	5	0	1	0	0	0	0	0	0	.200	.200	.200	15	-1	0	0	0	.750	-0	P-10	0.0
Total	3	30	52	8	16	3	1	1	10	1	3	.308	.321	.462	108	-1	0	0	0	.778	0	/P-13,O-4	-0.1

■ JOHNNY OATES
Oates, Johnny Lane b: 1/21/46, Sylva, N.C. BL/TR, 5'11", 188 lbs. Deb: 9/17/70 MC

YEAR	TM/L	G	AB	R	H	2B	3B	HR	RBI	BB	SO	AVG	OBP	SLG	PRO+	BR/A	SB	CS	SBR	FA	FR	G/POS	TPR
1970	Bal-A	5	18	2	5	0	1	0	2	2	0	.278	.350	.389	102	0	0	0	0	.939	1	/C-4	0.1
1972	Bal-A	85	253	20	66	12	1	4	21	28	31	.261	.335	.364	105	2	5	7	-3	.995	-3	C-82	-0.1
1973	Atl-N	93	322	27	80	6	0	4	27	22	31	.248	.299	.304	63	-16	1	4	-2	.981	-6	C-86	-2.1
1974	Atl-N	100	291	22	65	10	0	1	21	23	24	.223	.280	.268	52	-19	2	3	-1	.992	12	C-91	-0.5
1975	Atl-N	8	18	0	4	1	0	0	0	1	4	.222	.263	.278	48	-1	0	0	0	1.000	-0	/C-6	-0.2
	Phi-N	90	269	28	77	14	0	1	25	33	29	.286	.364	.349	95	-1	1	0	0	.990	2	C-82	0.5
	Yr	98	287	28	81	15	0	1	25	34	33	.282	.358	.345	92	-2	1	0	0	.990	1	C-88	0.3
1976	*Phi-N	37	99	10	25	2	0	1	8	8	12	.253	.308	.273	64	-4	0	1	-1	.994	-0	C-33	-0.3
1977	*LA-N	60	156	18	42	4	0	3	11	11	11	.269	.317	.353	80	-4	0	1	-1	.987	5	C-56	0.2
1978	*LA-N	40	75	2	23	1	0	0	6	5	3	.307	.350	.320	89	-1	0	1	-1	.956	-2	C-24	-0.3
1979	LA-N	26	46	4	6	2	0	0	2	4	1	.130	.200	.174	3	-6	0	1	-1	.975	3	C-20	-0.4
1980	NY-A	39	64	6	12	3	0	1	3	2	3	.188	.224	.281	38	-6	1	2	-1	.991	3	C-39	-0.4
1981	NY-A	10	26	4	5	1	0	0	0	2	0	.192	.250	.231	40	-2	0	0	0	.963	1	C-10	-0.3
Total	11	593	1637	146	410	56	2	14	126	141	149	.250	.311	.313	73	-58	11	19	-8	.987	16	C-533	-3.5

■ SHERMAN OBANDO
Obando, Sherman Omar (Gainor) b: 1/23/70, Bocas Del Toro, Pan. BR/TR, 6'4", 215 lbs. Deb: 4/10/93

YEAR	TM/L	G	AB	R	H	2B	3B	HR	RBI	BB	SO	AVG	OBP	SLG	PRO+	BR/A	SB	CS	SBR	FA	FR	G/POS	TPR
1993	Bal-A	31	92	8	25	2	0	3	15	4	26	.272	.309	.391	83	0	0	0	0	.929	-1	D-21/O-8	-0.4

■ HENRY OBERBECK
Oberbeck, Henry A. b: 5/17/1858, Missouri d: 8/26/21, St.Louis, Mo. Deb: 5/7/1883

YEAR	TM/L	G	AB	R	H	2B	3B	HR	RBI	BB	SO	AVG	OBP	SLG	PRO+	BR/A	SB	CS	SBR	FA	FR	G/POS	TPR
1883	Pit-a	2	9	1	2	1	0	0		0		.222	.222	.333	80	-0				1.000	0	/1-2	0.0
	StL-a	4	14	0	0	0	0	0		0		.000	.000	.000	-95	-3				.833	1	/O-4	-0.2
	Yr	6	23	1	2	1	0	0		0		.087	.087	.130	-30	-3				.833	1	/O-4,1-2	-0.2
1884	Bal-U	33	125	19	23	4	0	0		3		.184	.203	.216	13	-15				.878	2	O-28/3-8,P	-1.2
	KC-U	27	90	7	17	0	0	0		7		.189	.247	.222	33	-8				.823	7	3-15/O-7,P1	0.0
	Yr	60	215	26	40	7	0	0		10		.186	.222	.219	20	-23				.908	9	O-35,3-23/P1	-1.2
Total	2	66	238	27	42	8	0	0		10		.176	.210	.210	16	-27				.901	9	/O-39,3-23,P1	-1.4

■ KEN OBERKFELL
Oberkfell, Kenneth Ray b: 5/4/56, Highland, Ill. BL/TR, 6', 210 lbs. Deb: 8/22/77

YEAR	TM/L	G	AB	R	H	2B	3B	HR	RBI	BB	SO	AVG	OBP	SLG	PRO+	BR/A	SB	CS	SBR	FA	FR	G/POS	TPR
1977	StL-N	9	9	0	1	1	0	0	0	0	1	.111	.111	.111	-41	-2	0	0	0	1.000	-1	/2-6	-0.2
1978	StL-N	24	50	7	6	1	0	0	0	3	1	.120	.170	.140	-13	-8	0	0	0	.987	3	2-17/3-4	-0.5
1979	StL-N	135	369	53	111	19	5	1	35	57	35	.301	.400	.388	115	10	4	1	1	.985	-4	*2-117,3-17/S	1.4
1980	StL-N	116	422	58	128	27	6	3	46	51	23	.303	.380	.417	118	12	4	4	-1	.989	-8	*2-101,3-16	0.9
1981	StL-N	102	376	43	110	12	6	2	45	37	28	.293	.356	.372	104	7	13	5	1	.956	11	*3-102/S-1	1.3
1982	*StL-N	137	470	55	136	22	5	2	34	40	31	.289	.346	.370	99	0	11	9	-2	.972	11	*3-135/2-1	0.6
1983	StL-N	151	488	62	143	26	5	3	38	61	27	.293	.373	.385	110	9	12	6	0	.960	3	*3-127,2-32/S	1.2
1984	StL-N	50	152	17	47	11	1	0	11	16	10	.309	.379	.395	121	3	1	2	-1	.967	4	3-46/2-2,S	0.8
	Atl-N	50	172	21	40	8	1	0	10	15	17	.233	.294	.308	65	-8	1	3	-2	.964	-5	3-45/2-4	-1.6
	Yr	100	324	38	87	19	2	0	21	31	27	.269	.334	.349	90	-4	2	5	-2	.966	-1	3-91/2-6,S	-0.8
1985	Atl-N	134	412	30	112	19	4	3	35	51	38	.272	.360	.359	96	-0	1	2	-1	.963	-1	*3-117,2-16	-0.4
1986	Atl-N	151	503	62	136	24	3	5	48	83	40	.270	.376	.360	98	2	7	4	-0	.976	3	*3-130,2-41	1.0
1987	Atl-N	135	508	59	142	29	2	3	48	48	29	.280	.344	.362	83	-11	3	3	-1	.979	-4	*3-126,2-11	-1.8
1988	Atl-N	120	422	42	117	20	4	3	40	32	28	.277	.331	.365	95	-3	4	5	-2	.951	-7	*3-113/2-1	-1.3
	Pit-N	20	54	7	12	2	0	0	2	5	6	.222	.288	.259	59	-3	0	0	0	1.000	0	2-11/S-3,31	-0.6
	Yr	140	476	49	129	22	4	3	42	37	34	.271	.326	.353	91	-5	4	5	-2	.952	-10	*3-115,2-12/S1	-1.9
1989	Pit-N	14	40	2	5	1	0	0	2	2	2	.125	.167	.150	-9	-6	0	1	-1	.988	-1	/1-9,2-3	-0.7
	*SF-N	83	116	17	37	5	1	2	15	8	8	.319	.373	.431	133	5	0	1	-1	.971	-4	3-38/1-7,2	0.0
	Yr	97	156	19	42	6	1	2	17	10	10	.269	.321	.359	97	-1	0	1	-1	.971	-5	3-38,1-16,2	-0.7
1990	Hou-N	77	150	10	31	4	0	1	12	15	17	.207	.283	.280	57	-9	1	1	-0	.935	-2	3-24,1-11,2	-1.2
1991	Hou-N	53	70	7	16	4	0	0	14	14	8	.229	.357	.286	88	-0	0	0	0	1.000	0	1-13/3-4	-0.1
1992	Cal-A	41	91	6	24	1	0	0	10	8	5	.264	.323	.275	69	-1	0	0	0	.986	-7	2-21/1-2,D	-1.1
Total	16	1602	4874	558	1354	237	44	29	446	546	356	.278	.353	.362	97	-7	62	47	-10	.965	-5	*3-1046,2-402/1SD	-2.2

■ MIKE O'BERRY
O'Berry, Preston Michael b: 4/20/54, Birmingham, Ala. BR/TR, 6'2", 195 lbs. Deb: 4/8/79

YEAR	TM/L	G	AB	R	H	2B	3B	HR	RBI	BB	SO	AVG	OBP	SLG	PRO+	BR/A	SB	CS	SBR	FA	FR	G/POS	TPR
1979	Bos-A	43	59	8	10	1	0	1	5	8	16	.169	.246	.237	29	-6	0	0	0	.957	0	C-43	-0.5
1980	Chi-N	19	48	7	10	1	0	0	5	5	13	.208	.283	.229	41	-4	0	0	0	.982	4	C-19	0.1
1981	Cin-N	55	111	6	20	5	1	0	5	14	19	.180	.272	.252	49	-7	0	0	0	.983	3	C-55	-0.3
1982	Cin-N	21	45	5	10	2	0	0	3	10	13	.222	.364	.267	77	-1	0	0	0	.990	-1	C-21	-0.3
1983	Cal-A	26	60	7	10	1	0	1	5	6	13	.167	.206	.233	21	-7	0	0	0	1.000	-1	C-26	-0.6
1984	NY-A	13	32	3	8	2	0	0	5	2	2	.250	.294	.313	71	-1	0	0	0	1.000	1	C-12/3-1	0.0

YEAR	TM/L	G	AB	R	H	2B	3B	HR	RBI	BB	SO	AVG	OBP	SLG	PRO+	BR/A	SB	CS	SBR	FA	FR	G/POS	TPR
1985	Mon-N	20	21	2	4	0	0	0	0	4	3	.190	.320	.190	49	-1	1	0	0	1.000	3	C-20	0.3
Total	7	197	376	38	72	10	1	3	27	43	77	.191	.276	.247	46	-27	1	0	0	.984	10	C-196/3-1	-1.1

■ JIM OBRADOVICH
Obradovich, James Thomas b: 9/13/49, Fort Campbell, Ky. BL/TL, 6'2", 200 lbs. Deb: 9/12/78

YEAR	TM/L	G	AB	R	H	2B	3B	HR	RBI	BB	SO	AVG	OBP	SLG	PRO+	BR/A	SB	CS	SBR	FA	FR	G/POS	TPR
1978	Hou-N	10	17	3	3	0	1	0	2	1	3	.176	.222	.294	47	-1	0	0	0	1.000	-0	/1-3	-0.2

■ CHARLIE O'BRIEN
O'Brien, Charles Hugh b: 5/1/60, Tulsa, Okla. BR/TR, 6'2", 195 lbs. Deb: 6/2/85

YEAR	TM/L	G	AB	R	H	2B	3B	HR	RBI	BB	SO	AVG	OBP	SLG	PRO+	BR/A	SB	CS	SBR	FA	FR	G/POS	TPR
1985	Oak-A	16	11	3	3	1	0	0	1	3	3	.273	.429	.364	129	1	0	0	0	.958	-0	C-16	0.1
1987	Mil-A	10	35	2	7	3	1	0	0	4	4	.200	.282	.343	63	-2	0	1	-1	1.000	6	C-10	0.4
1988	Mil-A	40	118	12	26	6	0	2	9	5	16	.220	.252	.322	59	-7	0	1	-1	.991	12	C-40	0.8
1989	Mil-A	62	188	22	44	10	0	6	35	21	11	.234	.339	.383	104	2	0	0	0	.986	7	C-62	1.1
1990	Mil-A	46	145	11	27	7	2	0	11	11	25	.186	.253	.262	45	-11	0	0	0	.992	5	C-46	-0.3
	NY-N	28	68	6	11	3	0	0	9	10	8	.162	.278	.206	36	-6	0	0	0	.986	9	C-28	0.5
1991	NY-N	69	168	16	31	6	0	2	14	17	25	.185	.275	.256	51	-11	0	2	-1	.991	-19	C-67	1.0
1992	NY-N	68	156	15	33	12	0	2	13	16	18	.212	.289	.327	75	-5	0	1	-1	.979	5	C-64	0.2
1993	NY-N	67	188	15	48	11	0	4	23	14	14	.255	.314	.378	85	-4	1	1	0	.986	11	C-65	0.9
1994	Atl-N	51	152	24	37	11	0	8	28	15	24	.243	.324	.474	104	1	0	0	0	.991	2	C-48	0.5
Total	9	457	1229	126	267	70	3	24	143	116	149	.217	.296	.338	75	-42	1	6	-3	.988	75	C-446	5.2

■ EDDIE O'BRIEN
O'Brien, Edward Joseph b: 12/11/30, S.Amboy, N.J. BR/TR, 5'9", 165 lbs. Deb: 4/25/53 FC

YEAR	TM/L	G	AB	R	H	2B	3B	HR	RBI	BB	SO	AVG	OBP	SLG	PRO+	BR/A	SB	CS	SBR	FA	FR	G/POS	TPR
1953	Pit-N	89	261	21	62	5	3	0	14	17	30	.238	.289	.280	50	-19	6	1	-1	.935	-14	S-81	-2.6
1955	Pit-N	75	236	26	55	3	1	0	8	18	13	.233	.290	.254	47	-18	4	5	-2	.993	1	O-56/3-7,S	-2.1
1956	Pit-N	63	53	17	14	2	0	0	3	2	8	.264	.291	.302	61	-3	1	1	-0	.978	9	S-23/O-6,32P	0.7
1957	Pit-N	3	4	0	0	0	0	0	0	0	0	.000	.000	.000	-99	-1	0	0	0	1.000	-0	/P-3	0.0
1958	Pit-N	1	0	0	0	0	0	0	0	0	0	—	—	—	—	0	0	0	0	.000	-0	/P-1	0.0
Total	5	231	554	64	131	10	4	0	25	37	45	.236	.288	.269	48	-41	11	7	-1	.942	-4	S-108/O-62,3P2	-4.0

■ MICKEY O'BRIEN
O'Brien, Frank Aloysius b: 9/13/1894, San Francisco, Cal. d: 11/4/71, Monterey Park, Cal. BR/TR, 5'8", 160 lbs. Deb: 4/26/23

YEAR	TM/L	G	AB	R	H	2B	3B	HR	RBI	BB	SO	AVG	OBP	SLG	PRO+	BR/A	SB	CS	SBR	FA	FR	G/POS	TPR
1923	Phi-N	15	21	3	7	2	0	0	2	1		.333	.391	.429	104	0	0	0		.909	0	/C-9	0.1

■ GEORGE O'BRIEN
O'Brien, George Joseph b: 11/4/1889, Cleveland, Ohio d: 3/24/66, Columbus, Ohio BR/TR, 6', 185 lbs. Deb: 8/16/15

YEAR	TM/L	G	AB	R	H	2B	3B	HR	RBI	BB	SO	AVG	OBP	SLG	PRO+	BR/A	SB	CS	SBR	FA	FR	G/POS	TPR
1915	StL-A	3	9	1	2	0	0	0	1	2		.222	.300	.222	59	-0	0			.933	-1	/C-3	-0.1

■ JERRY O'BRIEN
O'Brien, Jeremiah b: 2/2/1864, New York d: 7/4/11, Binghamton, N.Y. Deb: 7/30/1887

YEAR	TM/L	G	AB	R	H	2B	3B	HR	RBI	BB	SO	AVG	OBP	SLG	PRO+	BR/A	SB	CS	SBR	FA	FR	G/POS	TPR
1887	Was-N	1	4	0	0	0	0	0	0	0	2	.000	.000	.000	-99	-1	0			.714	-0	/2-1	-0.1

■ JOHN O'BRIEN
O'Brien, John E. b: 10/22/1851, Columbus, Ohio d: 12/31/14, Fall River, Mass. TR, 5'11.5", 187 lbs. Deb: 4/19/1884

YEAR	TM/L	G	AB	R	H	2B	3B	HR	RBI	BB	SO	AVG	OBP	SLG	PRO+	BR/A	SB	CS	SBR	FA	FR	G/POS	TPR
1884	Bal-U	18	77	7	19	1	1	0		2		.247	.266	.286	45	-6				.865	0	O-18	-0.5

■ JOHN O'BRIEN
O'Brien, John J. "Chewing Gum" b: 7/14/1870, St.John, N.B., Can d: 5/13/13, Lewiston, Maine BL/TR, 175 lbs. Deb: 4/22/1891

YEAR	TM/L	G	AB	R	H	2B	3B	HR	RBI	BB	SO	AVG	OBP	SLG	PRO+	BR/A	SB	CS	SBR	FA	FR	G/POS	TPR
1891	Bro-N	43	167	22	41	4	2	0	26	12	17	.246	.308	.293	76	-5	4			.854	-22	2-43	-2.3
1893	Chi-N	4	14	3	5	0	1	0	1	2	2	.357	.471	.500	160	1	0			.900	-2	/2-4	0.0
1895	Lou-N	128	539	82	138	10	4	1	50	45	20	.256	.325	.295	65	-26	15			.938	3	*2-125/1-3	-1.4
1896	Lou-N	49	186	24	63	9	1	2	24	13	7	.339	.385	.430	119	5	4			.919	3	2-49	0.6
	Was-N	73	270	38	72	6	3	4	33	27	12	.267	.344	.356	85	-6	4			.952	3	2-73	0.1
	Yr	122	456	62	135	15	4	6	57	40	19	.296	.361	.386	98	-1	8			.938	2	*2-122	0.7
1897	Was-N	86	320	37	78	12	2	3	45	19		.244	.309	.322	67	-16	6			.942	4	2-86	-0.6
1899	Bal-N	39	135	14	26	4	0	1	17	15		.193	.283	.244	43	-11	4			.966	7	2-39	-0.1
	Pit-N	79	279	26	63	2	4	1	33	21		.226	.285	.272	53	-18	8			.946	3	2-79	-1.0
	Yr	118	414	40	89	6	4	2	50	36		.215	.284	.263	50	-28	12			.953	10	*2-118	-1.1
Total	6	501	1910	246	486	47	17	12	229	154	58	.254	.322	.316	72	-75	45			.936	-6	2-498/1-3	-4.7

■ JACK O'BRIEN
O'Brien, John Joseph b: 2/5/1873, Watervliet, N.Y. d: 6/10/33, Watervliet, N.Y. BL/TR, 6'1", 165 lbs. Deb: 4/14/1899

YEAR	TM/L	G	AB	R	H	2B	3B	HR	RBI	BB	SO	AVG	OBP	SLG	PRO+	BR/A	SB	CS	SBR	FA	FR	G/POS	TPR
1899	Was-N	127	468	68	132	11	5	6	51	31		.282	.331	.365	92	-6	17			.926	4	*O-121/3-4	-1.0
1901	Was-A	11	45	5	8	0	0	0	5	3		.178	.245	.178	19	-5	2			.929	-0	O-11	-0.5
	Cle-A	92	375	54	106	14	5	0	39	22		.283	.329	.347	91	-4	13			.941	-3	O-92/3-1	-1.3
	Yr	103	420	59	114	14	5	0	44	25		.271	.320	.329	83	-9	15			.939	-3	*O-103/3-1	-1.8
1903	*Bos-A	96	338	44	71	14	4	3	38	21		.210	.262	.302	65	-14	10			.958	-6	O-71,3-11/2S	-2.6
Total	3	326	1226	171	317	39	14	9	133	77		.259	.308	.335	82	-29	42			.937	-5	O-295/3-16,2S	-5.4

■ JACK O'BRIEN
O'Brien, John K. (b: John K. Bryne) b: 6/12/1860, Philadelphia, Pa. d: 11/20/10, Philadelphia, Pa. BR/TR, 5'10", 184 lbs. Deb: 5/2/1882

YEAR	TM/L	G	AB	R	H	2B	3B	HR	RBI	BB	SO	AVG	OBP	SLG	PRO+	BR/A	SB	CS	SBR	FA	FR	G/POS	TPR
1882	Phi-a	62	241	44	73	13	3	3		13		.303	.339	.419	138	8				.925	11	C-45,O-18/31	1.9
1883	Phi-a	94	390	74	113	14	10	0		25		.290	.333	.377	118	7				.876	-4	C-58,O-25,3/S	0.7
1884	Phi-a	36	138	25	39	6	1	1		9		.283	.340	.362	121	3				.930	-0	C-30/O-5,1	0.4
1885	Phi-a	62	225	35	60	9	1	2		20		.267	.340	.342	109	2				.903	-8	C-43/S-9,103	-0.3
1886	Phi-a	105	423	65	107	25	7	0		38		.253	.325	.345	109	4	23			.918	-15	C-36,3-27,1S/20	-0.7
1887	Bro-a	30	123	18	28	4	1	1		6		.228	.264	.301	56	-8	8			.839	-8	C-25/O-4,2	-1.0
1888	Bal-a	57	196	25	44	11	5	0	18	17		.224	.300	.332	105	1	14			.925	-15	C-37,O-13/1	-1.0
1890	Phi-a	109	433	80	113	24	14	4		52		.261	.356	.369	128	15	31			.976	4	*1-109/O-1,C	1.2
Total	8	555	2169	366	577	106	42	11	18	180		.266	.331	.369	115	33	76			.903	-31	C-275,1-149/O3S2	1.2

■ JOHNNY O'BRIEN
O'Brien, John Thomas b: 12/11/30, S.Amboy, N.J. BR/TR, 5'9", 170 lbs. Deb: 4/19/53 F

YEAR	TM/L	G	AB	R	H	2B	3B	HR	RBI	BB	SO	AVG	OBP	SLG	PRO+	BR/A	SB	CS	SBR	FA	FR	G/POS	TPR
1953	Pit-N	89	279	28	69	13	2	2	22	21	36	.247	.309	.330	67	-13	1	1	-0	.982	-5	2-77/S-1	-1.4
1955	Pit-N	84	278	22	83	15	2	1	25	20	19	.299	.348	.378	94	-2	1	1	-0	.969	5	2-78	0.8
1956	Pit-N	73	104	13	18	1	0	0	3	5	7	.173	.211	.183	7	-13	0	0	0	.959	5	2-53/P-8,S	-0.5
1957	Pit-N	34	35	7	11	2	1	0	1	1	4	.314	.368	.429	117	1	0	0	0	.857	-2	P-16/S-8,2	-0.1
1958	Pit-N	3	1	1	0	0	0	0	0	0	1	.000	.000	.000	-99	-0	0	0	0	.000	0	H	0.0
	StL-N	12	2	3	0	0	0	0	0	1		.000	.333	.000	-2	-0	0	0	0	1.000	0	/S-5,P-1,2	0.0
	Yr	15	3	4	0	0	0	0	0	1	1	.000	.250	.000	-26	-1	0	0	0	1.000	0	/S-5,P-1,2	0.0
1959	Mil-N	44	116	16	23	4	0	1	8	11	15	.198	.273	.259	47	-9	0	0	0	.987	-3	2-37	-0.9
Total	6	339	815	90	204	35	5	4	59	59	82	.250	.307	.320	68	-38	2	2	-1	.974	0	2-248/P-25,S	-2.1

■ PETE O'BRIEN
O'Brien, Peter J. b: 6/17/1877, Binghamton, N.Y. d: 1/31/17, Jersey City, N.J. BL/TR, 5'7", 170 lbs. Deb: 9/21/01

YEAR	TM/L	G	AB	R	H	2B	3B	HR	RBI	BB	SO	AVG	OBP	SLG	PRO+	BR/A	SB	CS	SBR	FA	FR	G/POS	TPR
1901	Cin-N	16	54	1	11	1	0	1	3	2		.204	.232	.278	51	-4	0			.889	-2	2-15	-0.5
1906	StL-N	151	524	44	122	9	4	2	57	42		.233	.293	.277	82	-10	25			.933	-41	*2-120,3-20,S	-5.5
1907	Cle-A	43	145	9	33	5	2	0	6	7		.228	.263	.290	76	-4	1			.943	-11	2-17,3-12,S	-1.7
	Was-A	39	134	6	25	3	1	0	12	12		.187	.259	.224	59	-6	4			.912	4	3-26,S-13/2	-0.1
	Yr	82	279	15	58	8	3	0	18	19		.208	.261	.258	68	-10	5			.905	-7	3-38,S-24,2	-1.8
Total	3	249	857	60	191	18	7	3	78	63		.223	.279	.271	76	-24	30			.929	-50	2-153/3-58,S	-7.8

■ PETE O'BRIEN
O'Brien, Peter James b: 6/16/1867, Chicago, Ill. d: 6/30/37, York Township, Du Page County, Ill. BR/TR, 5'9.5", 165 lbs. Deb: 4/29/1890

YEAR	TM/L	G	AB	R	H	2B	3B	HR	RBI	BB	SO	AVG	OBP	SLG	PRO+	BR/A	SB	CS	SBR	FA	FR	G/POS	TPR
1890	Chi-N	27	106	15	30	7	0	3	16	7		.283	.315	.434	113	1	4			.929	-2	2-27	0.1

■ PETE O'BRIEN
O'Brien, Peter Michael b: 2/9/58, Santa Monica, Cal. BL/TL, 6'1", 198 lbs. Deb: 9/3/82

YEAR	TM/L	G	AB	R	H	2B	3B	HR	RBI	BB	SO	AVG	OBP	SLG	PRO+	BR/A	SB	CS	SBR	FA	FR	G/POS	TPR
1982	Tex-A	20	67	13	16	4	1	4	13	6	6	.239	.301	.507	124	2	1	0	0	1.000	-0	O-11/1-3,D	0.1
1983	Tex-A	154	524	53	124	24	5	8	53	58	62	.237	.314	.347	83	-11	5	4	-1	.993	13	*1-133,O-27/D	-0.7

YEAR	TM/L	G	AB	R	H	2B	3B	HR	RBI	BB	SO	AVG	OBP	SLG	PRO+	BR/A	SB	CS	SBR	FA	FR	G/POS	TPR
1984	Tex-A	142	520	57	149	26	2	18	80	53	50	.287	.353	.448	116	11	3	5	-2	.992	1	*1-141/O-1	0.1
1985	Tex-A	159	573	69	153	34	3	22	92	69	53	.267	.347	.452	115	12	5	10	-5	.995	-6	*1-159	-0.8
1986	Tex-A	156	551	86	160	23	3	23	90	87	66	.290	.387	.468	128	24	4	4	-1	.992	2	*1-155	1.3
1987	Tex-A	159	569	84	163	26	1	23	88	59	61	.286	.354	.457	113	10	4	4	-2	.992	16	*1-158/O-2,D	1.2
1988	Tex-A	156	547	57	149	24	1	16	71	72	73	.272	.357	.408	111	9	1	4	-2	.995	13	*1-155/D-1	0.7
1989	Cle-A	155	554	75	144	24	1	12	55	83	48	.260	.358	.372	104	6	3	1	0	.994	3	*1-154/D-1	-0.4
1990	Sea-A	108	366	32	82	18	0	5	27	44	33	.224	.311	.314	74	-12	0	0	0	.995	4	1-97/O-6,D	-1.5
1991	Sea-A	152	560	58	139	29	3	17	88	44	61	.248	.304	.402	93	-6	0	1	-1	**.997**	1	*1-132,D-18,O	-1.5
1992	Sea-A	134	396	40	88	15	1	14	52	40	27	.222	.294	.371	85	-9	2	1	0	.996	2	1-81,D-36	-1.4
1993	Sea-A	72	210	30	54	7	0	7	27	26	21	.257	.330	.390	94	-2	0	0	0	.988	0	D-52/1-9,O	-0.4
Total	12	1567	5437	654	1421	254	21	169	736	641	563	.261	.340	.409	104	34	24	34	-13	.994	49	*1-1377,D-120/O	-3.3

■ RAY O'BRIEN
O'Brien, Raymond Joseph b: 10/31/1892, St.Louis, Mo. d: 3/31/42, St.Louis, Mo. BL/TL, 5'9", 175 lbs. Deb: 6/27/16

YEAR	TM/L	G	AB	R	H	2B	3B	HR	RBI	BB	SO	AVG	OBP	SLG	PRO+	BR/A	SB	CS	SBR	FA	FR	G/POS	TPR
1916	Pit-N	16	57	5	12	3	2	0	3	1	14	.211	.224	.333	69	-2	0			.864	-1	O-14	-0.4

■ SYD O'BRIEN
O'Brien, Sydney Lloyd b: 12/18/44, Compton, Cal. BR/TR, 6'1", 185 lbs. Deb: 4/15/69

YEAR	TM/L	G	AB	R	H	2B	3B	HR	RBI	BB	SO	AVG	OBP	SLG	PRO+	BR/A	SB	CS	SBR	FA	FR	G/POS	TPR
1969	Bos-A	100	263	47	64	10	5	9	29	15	37	.243	.287	.422	91	-4	2	3	-1	.939	-1	3-53,S-15,2	-0.5
1970	Chi-A	121	441	48	109	13	2	8	44	22	62	.247	.286	.340	69	-19	3	3	-1	.938	-6	3-68,2-43/S	-2.4
1971	Cal-A	90	251	25	50	8	1	5	21	15	33	.199	.247	.299	58	-15	0	2	-1	.961	-1	S-52/3-7,310	-1.2
1972	Cal-A	36	39	10	7	2	0	1	1	6	10	.179	.289	.308	82	-1	0	0	0	.889	1	/3-8,S-4,21	0.0
	Mil-A	31	58	5	12	2	0	1	5	2	13	.207	.233	.293	57	-3	0	1	-1	.852	-1	/3-9,2-7	-0.5
	Yr	67	97	15	19	4	0	2	6	8	23	.196	.257	.299	68	-4	0	1	-1	.861	0	3-17,2-10/S1	-0.5
Total	4	378	1052	135	242	35	8	24	100	60	155	.230	.274	.347	72	-42	5	9	-4	.934	-8	3-144/S-76,210	-4.6

■ TOMMY O'BRIEN
O'Brien, Thomas Edward "Obie" b: 12/19/18, Anniston, Ala. d: 11/5/78, Anniston, Ala. BR/TR, 5'11", 195 lbs. Deb: 4/24/43

YEAR	TM/L	G	AB	R	H	2B	3B	HR	RBI	BB	SO	AVG	OBP	SLG	PRO+	BR/A	SB	CS	SBR	FA	FR	G/POS	TPR
1943	Pit-N	89	232	35	72	12	7	2	26	15	24	.310	.352	.448	126	7	0			.964	-6	O-48/3-9	-0.1
1944	Pit-N	85	156	27	39	6	2	3	20	21	12	.250	.343	.372	97	-0	1			.965	-9	O-48/3-1	-1.2
1945	Pit-N	58	161	23	54	6	5	0	18	9	13	.335	.374	.435	120	4	0			.961	-6	O-45	-0.4
1949	Bos-A	49	125	24	28	5	0	3	10	21	12	.224	.336	.336	73	-5	1	0	0	.984	-2	O-32	-0.8
1950	Bos-A	9	31	0	4	1	0	0	3	3	5	.129	.206	.161	-5	-5	0	0	0	1.000	-1	/O-9	-0.6
	Was-A	3	9	1	1	0	0	0	1	1	0	.111	.200	.111	-20	-2	0	0	0	1.000	1	/O-3	-0.1
	Yr	12	40	1	5	1	0	0	4	4	5	.125	.205	.150	-8	-7	0	0	0	1.000	-0	O-12	-0.7
Total	5	293	714	110	198	30	14	8	78	70	66	.277	.344	.392	100	-1	2	0		.970	-23	O-185/3-10	-3.2

■ TOM O'BRIEN
O'Brien, Thomas H. b: 6/22/1860, Salem, Mass. d: 4/21/21, Worcester, Mass. BR/TR, 6'1", 185 lbs. Deb: 6/14/1882

YEAR	TM/L	G	AB	R	H	2B	3B	HR	RBI	BB	SO	AVG	OBP	SLG	PRO+	BR/A	SB	CS	SBR	FA	FR	G/POS	TPR
1882	Wor-N	22	89	9	18	1	1	0	7	1	10	.202	.211	.236	42	-6				.789	-2	O-20/2-2,3	-0.7
1883	Bal-a	33	138	16	37	6	4	0		5		.268	.294	.370	109	1				.825	-4	2-29/O-4	-0.2
1884	Bos-U	103	449	80	118	31	8	4		12		.263	.282	.394	83	-11				.853	1	*2-99/O-3,1C	-0.7
1885	Bal-a	8	33	4	7	3	0	0		2		.212	.257	.303	78	-1				.932	1	/1-6,2-2	0.0
1887	NY-a	31	129	13	25	3	2	0		2		.194	.212	.248	29	-12	10			.963	2	1-20/O-8,32P	-1.3
1890	Roc-a	73	273	36	52	6	5	0		30		.190	.273	.249	58	-14	6			.971	-4	1-68/2-8	-1.9
Total	6	270	1111	158	257	50	20	4	7	52	10	.231	.267	.323	71	-43	16			.846	-10	2-142/1-96,03PC	-4.8

■ TOM O'BRIEN
O'Brien, Thomas J. b: 2/20/1873, Verona, Pa. d: 2/4/01, Phoenix, Ariz. Deb: 5/10/1897

YEAR	TM/L	G	AB	R	H	2B	3B	HR	RBI	BB	SO	AVG	OBP	SLG	PRO+	BR/A	SB	CS	SBR	FA	FR	G/POS	TPR
1897	*Bal-N	50	147	25	37	6	0	0	32	20		.252	.349	.293	70	-6	7			.968	0	1-25,O-24	-0.6
1898	Bal-N	18	60	9	13	0	0	0	14	10		.217	.338	.217	59	-3	0			.833	0	O-16	-0.3
	Pit-N	107	413	53	107	10	8	1	45	25		.259	.318	.329	87	-7	13			.924	-3	O-69,1-21/32S	-1.4
	Yr	125	473	62	120	10	8	1	59	35		.254	.321	.315	84	-10	13			.911	-3	O-85,1-21/32S	-1.7
1899	NY-N	150	573	100	170	21	10	6	77	44		.297	.351	.400	109	7	23			.933	-2	*O-127,3-21/S1	-0.4
1900	*Pit-N	102	376	61	109	22	6	3	61	21		.290	.349	.404	107	3	12			.961	-11	1-65,O-25/2S	-0.9
Total	4	427	1569	248	436	59	24	10	229	120		.278	.341	.365	97	-6	55			.928	-15	O-261,1-112/32S	-3.6

■ DARBY O'BRIEN
O'Brien, William D. b: 9/1/1863, Peoria, Ill. d: 6/15/1893, Peoria, Ill. BR/TR, 6'1", 186 lbs. Deb: 4/16/1887

YEAR	TM/L	G	AB	R	H	2B	3B	HR	RBI	BB	SO	AVG	OBP	SLG	PRO+	BR/A	SB	CS	SBR	FA	FR	G/POS	TPR
1887	NY-a	127	522	97	157	30	13	5		40		.301	.355	.437	126	18	49			.913	6	*O-121,1-10/S3P	1.7
1888	Bro-a	136	532	105	149	27	6	2	65	30		.280	.327	.365	122	12	55			.932	2	*O-136	0.9
1889	*Bro-a	136	567	146	170	30	11	5	80	61	76	.300	.384	.418	128	22	91			.906	-7	*O-136	1.0
1890	*Bro-N	85	350	78	110	28	6	2	63	32	43	.314	.378	.446	139	17	38			.960	4	O-85	1.5
1891	Bro-N	103	395	79	100	18	6	5	57	39	53	.253	.331	.367	104	2	31			.951	2	*O-103	0.0
1892	Bro-N	122	490	72	119	14	5	1	56	29	52	.243	.289	.298	81	-12	57			.956	4	*O-122	-1.3
Total	6	709	2856	577	805	147	47	20	321	231	224	.282	.344	.387	117	58	321			.934	11	O-703/1-10,SP3	3.8

■ BILLY O'BRIEN
O'Brien, William Smith b: 3/14/1860, Albany, N.Y. d: 5/26/11, Kansas City, Mo. BR, 6', 185 lbs. Deb: 9/27/1884

YEAR	TM/L	G	AB	R	H	2B	3B	HR	RBI	BB	SO	AVG	OBP	SLG	PRO+	BR/A	SB	CS	SBR	FA	FR	G/POS	TPR
1884	StP-U	8	30	1	7	3	0	0		0		.233	.233	.333	96	-2				.840	1	/3-8,P-2	0.0
	KC-U	4	17	2	4	0	0	0		0		.235	.235	.235	32	-2				.714	-1	/3-3,1-1	-0.1
	Yr	12	47	3	11	3	0	0		0		.234	.234	.298	67	-3				.795	2	3-11/P-2,1	-0.1
1887	Was-N	113	453	71	126	16	12	**19**	73	21	17	.278	.317	.492	128	15	11			.974	-3	*1-104/O-4,32	0.1
1888	Was-N	133	528	42	119	15	2	9	66	9	70	.225	.238	.313	79	-13	10			.975	-4	*1-132/3-1	-3.0
1889	Was-N	2	8	1	0	0	0	0	0	1	1	.000	.111	.000	-72	-2	0			1.000	-0	/1-2	-0.2
1890	Bro-a	96	388	47	108	25	8	4		28		.278	.332	.415	124	10	5			.973	-2	*1-96	0.2
Total	5	356	1424	164	364	59	22	32	139	59	88	.256	.289	.395	107	7	26			.974	-8	1-335/3-16,02P	-3.0

■ WHITEY OCK
Ock, Harold David b: 3/17/12, Brooklyn, N.Y. d: 3/18/75, Mt.Kisco, N.Y. BR/TR, 5'11", 180 lbs. Deb: 9/29/35

YEAR	TM/L	G	AB	R	H	2B	3B	HR	RBI	BB	SO	AVG	OBP	SLG	PRO+	BR/A	SB	CS	SBR	FA	FR	G/POS	TPR
1935	Bro-N	1	3	0	0	0	0	0	0	1	2	.000	.250	.000	-27	-1	0			1.000	-0	/C-1	-0.1

■ DANNY O'CONNELL
O'Connell, Daniel Francis b: 1/21/27, Paterson, N.J. d: 10/2/69, Clifton, N.J. BR/TR, 6', 180 lbs. Deb: 7/14/50 C

YEAR	TM/L	G	AB	R	H	2B	3B	HR	RBI	BB	SO	AVG	OBP	SLG	PRO+	BR/A	SB	CS	SBR	FA	FR	G/POS	TPR
1950	Pit-N	79	315	39	92	16	1	8	32	24	33	.292	.342	.425	97	-2	7			.977	17	S-65,3-12	2.0
1953	Pit-N	149	588	88	173	26	8	7	55	57	42	.294	.354	.401	99	0	3	4	-2	.958	8	*3-104,2-47	0.6
1954	Mil-N	146	541	61	151	28	4	2	37	38	46	.279	.329	.357	84	-13	2	2	-1	.979	9	*2-103,3-35/1S	0.1
1955	Mil-N	124	453	47	102	15	4	6	40	28	43	.225	.278	.316	60	-27	2	2	-1	.981	16	*2-114/3-7,S	-0.3
1956	Mil-N	139	498	71	119	17	9	4	42	76	42	.239	.344	.321	86	-8	3	3	-1	.985	-6	*2-138/3-4,S	-0.4
1957	Mil-N	48	183	29	43	9	1	1	8	19	20	.235	.314	.311	74	-7	1	0	0	.982	7	2-48	0.4
	NY-N	95	364	57	97	18	3	7	28	33	30	.266	.331	.390	93	-3	8	3	1	.980	4	2-68,3-30	0.9
	Yr	143	547	86	140	27	4	8	36	52	50	.256	.325	.364	87	-10	9	3	1	.981	12	*2-116,3-30	1.3
1958	SF-N	107	306	44	71	12	2	3	23	51	35	.232	.342	.314	77	-9	2	1	0	.986	3	*2-104/3-3	0.1
1959	SF-N	34	58	6	11	3	0	0	5	9	15	.190	.254	.241	34	-5	1	0	-1	.927	7	3-26/2-8	0.1
1961	Was-A	138	493	61	128	30	1	1	37	77	62	.260	.363	.331	88	-5	15	5	2	.939	1	3-73,2-61	0.5
1962	Was-A	84	236	24	62	7	2	2	18	23	28	.263	.328	.335	80	-6	5	1	1	.961	-1	3-41,2-22	-0.5
Total	10	1143	4035	527	1049	181	35	39	320	431	396	.260	.335	.351	84	-86	48	22		.980	67	2-713,3-335/S1	3.5

■ JIMMY O'CONNELL
O'Connell, James Joseph b: 2/11/01, Sacramento, Cal. d: 11/11/76, Bakersfield, Cal. BL/TR, 5'10.5", 175 lbs. Deb: 4/17/23

YEAR	TM/L	G	AB	R	H	2B	3B	HR	RBI	BB	SO	AVG	OBP	SLG	PRO+	BR/A	SB	CS	SBR	FA	FR	G/POS	TPR
1923	*NY-N	87	252	42	63	9	2	6	39	34	32	.250	.351	.373	92	-2	7	3	0	.980	-8	O-64/1-8	-1.4
1924	NY-N	52	104	24	33	4	2	2	18	11	16	.317	.388	.452	128	4	2	1	0	.952	-7	O-29/2-1	-0.4
Total	2	139	356	66	96	13	4	8	57	45	48	.270	.361	.396	102	2	9	4	0	.974	-15	/O-93,1-8,2	-1.8

YEAR	TM/L	G	AB	R	H	2B	3B	HR	RBI	BB	SO	AVG	OBP	SLG	PRO+	BR/A	SB	CS	SBR	FA	FR	G/POS	TPR

■ JOHN O'CONNELL   O'Connell, John Charles b: 6/13/04, Berona, Pa.   d: 10/17/92, Canton, Ohio   BR/TR, 6', 170 lbs.   Deb: 8/16/28

1928	Pit-N	1	1	0	0	0	0	0	0	0	0	.000	.000	.000	-96	-0	0			1.000	1	/C-1	0.0
1929	Pit-N	2	7	1	1	1	0	0	0	1	1	.143	.250	.286	32	-1	0			1.000	-0	/C-2	-0.1
Total	2	3	8	1	1	1	0	0	0	1	1	.125	.222	.250	17	-1	0			1.000	0	/C-3	-0.1

■ JOHN O'CONNELL   O'Connell, John Joseph d: 5/14/08, Derry, N.H.   Deb: 8/22/1891

1891	Bal-a	8	29	2	5	1	0	0	7	3	6	.172	.250	.207	31	-3	2			.938	-3	/S-3,2-3,O	-0.5
1902	Det-A	8	22	1	4	0	0	0	0	3		.182	.280	.182	29	-2	0			.919	1	/2-6,1-2	-0.1
Total	2	16	51	3	9	1	0	0	7	6	6	.176	.263	.196	30	-5	2			.885	-2	/2-9,S-3,1O	-0.6

■ PAT O'CONNELL   O'Connell, Patrick H. b: 6/10/1861, Bangor, Me.   d: 1/24/43, Lewiston, Maine   BR/TR, 5'10", 175 lbs.   Deb: 7/22/1886

1886	Bal-a	42	166	20	30	3	2	0	11			.181	.236	.223	45	-10	10			.782	-4	O-41/1-1,P	-1.4
1890	Bro-n	11	40	7	9	2	1	0	7			.225	.340	.325	100	0	3			.830	-1	3-10/1-1	0.0
Total	2	53	206	27	39	5	3	0	18			.189	.258	.243	57	-10	13			1.000	-5	O-41,3-10,1P	-1.4

■ DAN O'CONNOR   O'Connor, Daniel Cornelius b: 8/1868, Guelph, Ont., Canada   d: 3/3/42, Guelph, Ont., Canada   BL/TR, 6'2", 185 lbs.   Deb: 6/3/1890

| 1890 | Lou-a | 6 | 26 | 3 | 12 | 1 | 1 | 0 | 1 | | | .462 | .481 | .577 | 217 | 4 | 5 | | | 1.000 | -1 | /1-6 | 0.2 |

■ JOHNNY O'CONNOR   O'Connor, John Charles "Bucky" b: 12/1/1891, Cahersiveen, Ire.   d: 5/30/82, Bonner Springs, Kan.   BR/TR, 5'9", Deb: 9/16/16

| 1916 | Chi-N | 1 | 0 | 0 | 0 | 0 | 0 | 0 | 0 | 0 | 0 | — | — | — | | | 0 | | | .000 | 0 | /C-1 | 0.0 |

■ JACK O'CONNOR   O'Connor, John Joseph "Rowdy Jack" or "Peach Pie"
b: 6/2/1869, St.Louis, Mo.   d: 11/14/37, St.Louis, Mo.   BR/TR, 5'10", 170 lbs.   Deb: 4/20/1887   M

1887	Cin-a	12	40	4	4	0	0	0			2	.100	.143	.100	-31	-7	3			.947	3	/O-7,C-5	-0.3
1888	Cin-a	36	137	14	28	3	1	1	17	6		.204	.243	.263	59	-7	12			.795	-0	O-34/C-2	-0.7
1889	Col-a	107	398	69	107	17	7	4	60	33	37	.269	.331	.377	107	3	26			.955	-1	C-84,O-19/21	0.8
1890	Col-a	121	457	89	148	14	10	2		38		.324	.377	.411	142	24	29			.962	10	*C-106/O-9,S23	3.7
1891	Col-a	56	229	28	61	12	3	0	37	11	14	.266	.300	.345	90	-4	10			.878	3	O-40,C-21	-0.1
1892	*Cle-N	140	572	71	142	22	5	1	58	25	48	.248	.282	.309	76	-19	17			.935	9	*O-106,C-34	-1.1
1893	Cle-N	96	384	72	110	23	1	4	75	29	12	.286	.341	.383	87	-9	29			.949	-2	C-56,O-44	-0.7
1894	Cle-N	86	330	67	104	23	7	2	51	15	7	.315	.345	.445	86	-9	15			.942	7	C-45,O-33/1	-0.1
1895	Cle-N	89	340	51	99	14	10	0	58	30	22	.291	.354	.391	87	-8	11			.923	-6	C-47,1-41/3	-0.7
1896	*Cle-N	68	256	41	76	11	1	0	43	15	12	.297	.343	.359	81	-8	15			.966	-7	C-37,1-17,O	-0.9
1897	Cle-N	103	397	49	115	21	4	2	69	26		.290	.338	.378	84	-10	20			.941	-12	O-52,1-36,C	-2.1
1898	Cle-N	131	478	50	119	17	4	1	56	26		.249	.291	.308	72	-18	8			.983	3	1-69,C-48,O	-1.1
1899	StL-N	84	289	33	73	5	6	0	43	15		.253	.299	.311	66	-14	7			.943	-2	C-57,1-26	-0.7
1900	StL-N	10	32	4	7	0	0	0	6	2		.219	.306	.219	46	-2	0			.957	-1	C-10	-0.2
	*Pit-N	43	147	15	35	4	1	0	19	3		.238	.263	.279	49	-10	5			.944	-9	C-40/1-2	-1.5
	Yr	53	179	19	42	4	1	0	25	5		.235	.271	.268	49	-13	5			.947	-10	C-50/1-2	-1.7
1901	Pit-N	61	202	16	39	7	3	0	22	10		.193	.238	.257	42	-15	2			.978	-1	C-59	-1.0
1902	Pit-N	49	170	13	50	1	2	1	28	3		.294	.306	.341	96	-1	2			.979	-3	C-42/1-6,O	0.0
1903	NY-A	64	212	13	43	4	1	0	12	8		.203	.235	.231	38	-16	4			.988	1	C-63/1-1	-0.9
1904	StL-A	14	47	4	10	1	0	0	2	2		.213	.245	.234	55	-2	0			.943	-4	C-14	-0.6
1906	StL-A	55	174	8	33	0	0	0	11	2		.190	.199	.190	23	-16	4			.990	10	C-51	-0.1
1907	StL-A	25	89	2	14	2	0	0	4	0		.157	.176	.180	13	-9	0			.991	-0	C-25	-1.0
1910	StL-A	1	0	0	0							—	—	—		—	0			1.000	-0	/C-1,M	0.0
Total	21	1451	5380	713	1417	201	66	19	671	301	152	.263	.307	.336	79	-157	219			.961	-2	C-860,O-372,1/S23	-9.3

■ PADDY O'CONNOR   O'Connor, Patrick Francis b: 8/4/1879, County Kerry, Ireland   d: 8/17/50, Springfield, Mass.   BR/TR, 5'8", 168 lbs.   Deb: 4/17/08   C

1908	Pit-N	12	16	1	3	0	0	0	2	0		.188	.188	.188	20	-1	0			.889	-2	/C-4	-0.3
1909	*Pit-N	9	16	1	5	1	0	0	3	0		.313	.313	.375	104	-0	0			.700	-2	/C-3,3-1	-0.2
1910	Pit-N	6	4	0	1	0	0	0	0	1	1	.250	.400	.250	85	-0	0			1.000	-0	/C-1	0.0
1914	StL-N	10	9	0	0	0	0	0	0	2	2	.000	.250	.000	-24	-1	0			1.000	-0	/C-7	-0.2
1915	Pit-F	70	219	15	50	10	1	0	16	14	30	.228	.278	.283	51	-16	4			.987	4	C-66	-0.7
1918	NY-A	1	3	0	1	0	0	0	0	0		.333	.333	.333	99	-0	0			1.000	-0	/C-1	0.0
Total	6	108	267	17	60	11	1	0	21	17	34	.225	.276	.273	51	-18	4			.979	-0	/C-82,3-1	-1.4

■ KEN O'DEA   O'Dea, James Kenneth b: 3/16/13, Lima, N.Y.   d: 12/17/85, Lima, N.Y.   BL/TR, 6', 180 lbs.   Deb: 4/21/35

1935	*Chi-N	76	202	30	52	13	2	6	38	26	18	.257	.345	.431	106	2	0			.964	-2	C-63	0.3
1936	Chi-N	80	189	36	58	10	3	2	38	38	18	.307	.423	.423	126	9	0			.979	-3	C-55	0.8
1937	Chi-N	83	219	31	66	7	5	4	32	24	26	.301	.370	.434	113	4	1			.985	-6	C-64	0.1
1938	*Chi-N	86	247	22	65	12	1	3	33	12	18	.263	.297	.356	77	-8	1			.970	4	C-71	-0.1
1939	NY-N	52	97	7	17	1	0	3	11	10	16	.175	.252	.278	42	-8	0			.947	-2	C-30	-0.9
1940	NY-N	48	96	9	23	4	1	0	12	16	15	.240	.348	.302	80	-2	0			.992	2	C-31	0.2
1941	NY-N	59	89	13	19	5	1	3	17	8	20	.213	.278	.393	86	-2	0			1.000	1	C-14	0.0
1942	*StL-N	58	192	22	45	7	1	5	32	17	23	.234	.297	.359	85	-4	0			.979	10	C-49	1.1
1943	*StL-N	71	203	15	57	11	2	3	25	19	25	.281	.345	.399	110	2	0			.989	6	C-56	1.2
1944	*StL-N	85	265	35	66	11	2	6	37	29	29	.249	.343	.374	100	0	1			.994	7	C-69	1.2
1945	StL-N†	100	307	36	78	18	2	4	43	50	31	.254	.359	.365	99	1	0			.995	9	C-91	0.9
1946	StL-N	22	57	2	7	2	0	1	3	8	4	.123	.231	.211	25	-6	0			.991	5	C-22	-0.1
	Bos-N	12	32	4	7	0	0	0	2	8	4	.219	.375	.219	70	-1	0			1.000	-1	C-12	-0.1
	Yr	34	89	6	14	2	0	1	5	16	12	.157	.286	.213	41	-7	0			.994	4	C-34	-0.1
Total	12	832	2195	262	560	101	20	40	323	273	251	.255	.338	.374	95	-12	3			.983	26	C-627	4.7

■ PAUL O'DEA   O'Dea, Paul "Lefty" b: 7/3/20, Cleveland, Ohio   d: 12/11/78, Cleveland, Ohio   BL/TL, 6', 200 lbs.   Deb: 4/19/44

1944	Cle-A	76	173	25	55	9	0	0	13	23	21	.318	.401	.370	126	7	2	2	-1	.949	-5	O-41/P-3,1	0.0
1945	Cle-A	87	221	21	52	2	2	1	21	20	26	.235	.299	.276	70	-8	3	0	1	.992	2	O-53/P-1	-0.9
Total	2	163	394	46	107	11	2	1	34	43	47	.272	.345	.317	95	-1	5	2	0	.975	-2	/O-94,P-4,1	-0.9

■ HEINIE ODOM   Odom, Herman Boyd b: 10/13/1900, Rusk, Tex.   d: 8/31/70, Rusk, Tex.   BB/TR, 6', 170 lbs.   Deb: 4/22/25

| 1925 | NY-A | 1 | 1 | 0 | 1 | 0 | 0 | 0 | 0 | 0 | 0 | 1.000 | 1.000 | 1.000 | 416 | 0 | 0 | 0 | 0 | 1.000 | 0 | /3-1 | 0.1 |

■ BLUE MOON ODOM   Odom, Johnny Lee b: 5/29/45, Macon, Ga.   BR/TR, 6', 185 lbs.   Deb: 9/5/64

1964	KC-A	5	5	1	0	0	0	0	0	0	4	.000	.167	.000	-47	-1	0	0	0	.800	0	/P-5	0.0
1965	KC-A	1	0	0	0	0	0	0	0	0	0	—	—	—			0	0	0	1.000	0	/P-1	0.0
1966	KC-A	17	31	1	3	0	0	0	2	3	16	.097	.176	.097	-20	-5	0	0	0	.970	2	P-14	0.0
1967	KC-A	33	28	4	8	1	0	0	4	1	14	.286	.310	.321	90	-0	0	1	-1	.897	0	P-29	0.0
1968	Oak-A★	42	78	14	17	2	0	1	6	2	29	.218	.282	.282	75	-2	0	0	0	.964	1	P-32	0.0
1969	Oak-A★	43	79	15	21	2	1	5	16	2	24	.266	.293	.506	125	2	0	0	0	.937	5	P-32	0.0
1970	Oak-A	37	54	8	13	2	0	3	9	3	18	.241	.281	.444	100	-0	2	0	0	.929	2	P-29	0.0
1971	Oak-A	37	50	8	8	0	1	1	2	3	24	.160	.192	.260	28	-5	0	0	0	.850	-1	P-25	0.0
1972	*Oak-A	59	66	16	8	1	1	0	2	1	29	.121	.134	.152	7	-8	4	2	0	.873	5	P-31	0.0
1973	*Oak-A	51	5	1	0	0	0	0	0	1	0	.000	.000	.000	-99	-0	1	1	0	.875	-1	P-30	0.0
1974	*Oak-A	43	0	3	0	0	0	0	0	0	0						1	0	0	.821	0	P-34	0.0
1975	Oak-A	8	0	0	0	0	0	0	0	0	0									.750	0	/P-7	0.0

YEAR	TM/L	G	AB	R	H	2B	3B	HR	RBI	BB	SO	AVG	OBP	SLG	PRO+	BR/A	SB	CS	SBR	FA	FR	G/POS	TPR
	Cle-A	3	0	0	0	0	0	0	0	0	0	—	—	—	—	0	0	0	0	1.000	-0	/P-3	0.0
	Yr	11	0	1	0	0	0	0	0	0	0	—	—	—	—	0	0	0	0	.800	-0	P-10	0.0
	Atl-N	15	13	0	1	1	0	0	1	0	5	.077	.077	.154	-36	-2	0	0	0	.944	-0	P-15	0.0
1976	Chi-A	8	0	0	0	0	0	0	0	0	0	—	—	—	—	0	0	0	0	.600	-1	/P-8	0.0
Total	13	402	405	76	79	9	2	12	31	19	163	.195	.235	.316	60	-22	6	5	-1	.904	5	P-295	0.0

■ O'DONNELL   O'Donnell b: Littlestown, Pa.   Deb: 7/16/1884

YEAR	TM/L	G	AB	R	H	2B	3B	HR	RBI	BB	SO	AVG	OBP	SLG	PRO+	BR/A	SB	CS	SBR	FA	FR	G/POS	TPR
1884	Phi-U	1	4	0	1	0	0	0		0	0	.250	.250	.250	39	-0				.545	-2	/C-1	-0.2

■ HARRY O'DONNELL   O'Donnell, Harry Herman "Butch" b: 4/2/1894, Philadelphia, Pa. d: 1/31/58, Philadelphia, Pa. BR/TR, 5'8", 175 lbs. Deb: 4/30/27

YEAR	TM/L	G	AB	R	H	2B	3B	HR	RBI	BB	SO	AVG	OBP	SLG	PRO+	BR/A	SB	CS	SBR	FA	FR	G/POS	TPR
1927	Phi-N	16	16	1	1	0	0	0	2	2	2	.063	.167	.063	-36	-3	0			1.000	1	C-12	-0.2

■ LEFTY O'DOUL   O'Doul, Francis Joseph b: 3/4/1897, San Francisco, Cal. d: 12/7/69, San Francisco, Cal. BL/TL, 6', 180 lbs. Deb: 4/29/19

YEAR	TM/L	G	AB	R	H	2B	3B	HR	RBI	BB	SO	AVG	OBP	SLG	PRO+	BR/A	SB	CS	SBR	FA	FR	G/POS	TPR
1919	NY-A	19	16	2	4	0	0	0	1	1	2	.250	.294	.250	53	-1	1			.500	-1	/P-3,O-1	-0.1
1920	NY-A	13	12	2	2	1	0	0	1	1	1	.167	.231	.250	26	-1	0	0	0	.000	-1	/P-2,O-1	-0.1
1922	NY-A	8	9	0	3	1	0	0	4	0	1	.333	.333	.444	99	-0	0	0	0	1.000	-1	/P-6	0.0
1923	Bos-A	36	35	2	5	0	0	0	4	2	3	.143	.189	.143	-12	-6	0	0	0	.958	1	P-23/O-1	-0.1
1928	NY-N	114	354	67	113	19	4	8	46	30	8	.319	.372	.463	117	8	9			.962	-12	O-94	-0.9
1929	Phi-N	154	638	152	**254**	35	6	32	122	76	19	**.398**	**.465**	.622	157	58	2			.971	-5	*O-154	4.7
1930	Phi-N	140	528	122	202	37	7	22	97	63	21	.383	.453	.604	142	38	3			.953	-5	*O-131	2.0
1931	Bro-N	134	512	85	172	32	11	7	75	48	16	.336	.396	.482	136	26	5			.954	-1	*O-132	1.6
1932	Bro-N	148	595	120	219	32	8	21	90	50	20	**.368**	.423	.555	164	54	11			.979	-5	*O-148	3.9
1933	Bro-N	43	159	14	40	5	1	5	21	15	6	.252	.320	.390	106	1	2			.947	-3	O-41	-0.4
	*NY-N★	78	229	31	70	9	1	9	35	29	17	.306	.388	.472	147	15	1			.974	-6	O-63	0.6
	Yr	121	388	45	110	14	2	14	56	44	23	.284	.361	.438	130	16	3			.962	-8	*O-104	0.2
1934	NY-N	83	177	27	56	4	3	9	46	18	7	.316	.383	.525	144	11	2			.968	-5	O-38	0.4
Total	11	970	3264	624	1140	175	41	113	542	333	122	.349	.413	.532	142	202	36	0		.964	-33	O-804/P-34	11.6

■ FRED ODWELL   Odwell, Frederick William "Fritz" b: 9/25/1872, Downsville, N.Y. d: 8/19/48, Downsville, N.Y. BL/TR, 5'9.5", 160 lbs. Deb: 4/16/04

YEAR	TM/L	G	AB	R	H	2B	3B	HR	RBI	BB	SO	AVG	OBP	SLG	PRO+	BR/A	SB	CS	SBR	FA	FR	G/POS	TPR
1904	Cin-N	129	468	75	133	22	10	1	58	26		.284	.333	.380	110	4	30			.956	14	*O-126/2-1	1.2
1905	Cin-N	130	468	79	113	10	9	**9**	65	26		.241	.293	.359	85	-11	21			.967	4	O-126	-1.4
1906	Cin-N	58	202	20	45	5	4	0	21	15		.223	.286	.287	76	-6	11			.963	3	O-57	-0.6
1907	Cin-N	94	274	24	74	5	7	0	24	22		.270	.336	.339	107	2	10			.975	5	O-84/2-1	0.5
Total	4	411	1412	198	365	42	30	10	168	89		.258	.313	.352	96	-10	72			.964	26	O-393/2-2	-0.3

■ CHUCK OERTEL   Oertel, Charles Frank "Ducky" or "Snuffy" b: 3/12/31, Coffeyville, Kan. BL/TL, 5'8", 165 lbs. Deb: 9/1/58

YEAR	TM/L	G	AB	R	H	2B	3B	HR	RBI	BB	SO	AVG	OBP	SLG	PRO+	BR/A	SB	CS	SBR	FA	FR	G/POS	TPR
1958	Bal-A	14	12	4	2	0	0	1	1	1	1	.167	.231	.417	78	-0	0	0	0	1.000	-1	/O-2	-0.1

■ RON OESTER   Oester, Ronald John b: 5/5/56, Cincinnati, Ohio BB/TR, 6'2", 190 lbs. Deb: 9/10/78 C

YEAR	TM/L	G	AB	R	H	2B	3B	HR	RBI	BB	SO	AVG	OBP	SLG	PRO+	BR/A	SB	CS	SBR	FA	FR	G/POS	TPR
1978	Cin-N	6	8	1	3	0	0	0	1	0	2	.375	.375	.375	110	0	0	0	0	1.000	1	/S-6	0.1
1979	Cin-N	6	3	0	0	0	0	0	0	0	1	.000	.000	.000	-99	-1	0	0	0	1.000	1	/S-2	0.0
1980	Cin-N	100	303	40	84	16	2	2	20	26	44	.277	.336	.363	95	-2	6	2	1	.980	-14	2-79,S-17/3	-1.0
1981	Cin-N	105	354	45	96	16	7	5	42	42	49	.271	.348	.398	110	5	2	5	-2	.980	5	*2-103/S-9	1.5
1982	Cin-N	151	549	63	143	19	4	9	47	35	82	.260	.305	.359	83	-13	5	6	-2	.972	4	*2-118,S-29,3	-0.4
1983	Cin-N	157	549	63	145	23	5	11	58	49	106	.264	.326	.384	93	-6	2	2	-1	.977	-25	*2-154	-2.5
1984	Cin-N	150	553	54	134	26	3	3	38	41	97	.242	.296	.316	69	-23	7	2	1	.980	-16	*2-147/S-1	-3.4
1985	Cin-N	152	526	59	155	26	3	1	34	51	65	.295	.357	.361	97	-1	5	0	2	.989	5	*2-149	1.1
1986	Cin-N	153	523	52	135	23	2	8	44	52	84	.258	.326	.356	84	-11	9	2	2	.978	18	*2-151	1.5
1987	Cin-N	69	237	28	60	9	6	2	23	22	51	.253	.317	.367	77	-8	2	3	-1	.974	-6	2-69	0.0
1988	Cin-N	54	150	20	42	7	0	0	10	9	24	.280	.321	.327	83	-3	0	2	-1	.995	2	2-49/S-5	0.0
1989	Cin-N	109	305	23	75	15	0	1	14	32	47	.246	.308	.305	76	-9	1	0	0	.985	-8	*2-102/S-2	0.2
1990	*Cin-N	64	154	10	46	10	1	0	13	10	29	.299	.341	.377	93	-1	1	2	-1	.982	-8	2-50/3-3	-1.0
Total	13	1276	4214	458	1118	190	33	42	344	369	681	.265	.325	.356	87	-71	40	26	-4	.980	-14	*2-1171/S-71,3	-3.9

■ BOB O'FARRELL   O'Farrell, Robert Arthur b: 10/19/1896, Waukegan, Ill. d: 2/20/88, Waukegan, Ill. BR/TR, 5'9.5", 180 lbs. Deb: 9/5/15 M

YEAR	TM/L	G	AB	R	H	2B	3B	HR	RBI	BB	SO	AVG	OBP	SLG	PRO+	BR/A	SB	CS	SBR	FA	FR	G/POS	TPR
1915	Chi-N	2	3	0	1	0	0	0	0	0	0	.333	.333	.333	102	-0				.667	-1	/C-2	-0.1
1916	Chi-N	1	0	0	0	0	0	0	0	0	0					0				.000	0	/C-1	0.0
1917	Chi-N	3	8	1	3	2	0	0	1	1	0	.375	.444	.625	210	1	1			1.000	-1	/C-3	0.0
1918	*Chi-N	52	113	9	32	7	3	1	14	10	15	.283	.347	.425	132	4	0			.974	-6	C-45	0.1
1919	Chi-N	49	125	11	27	4	2	0	9	7	10	.216	.258	.280	61	-6	2			.965	-4	C-38	-0.7
1920	Chi-N	94	270	29	67	11	4	3	19	34	23	.248	.332	.352	95	-1	1	0		.956	-5	C-86	-0.1
1921	Chi-N	96	260	32	65	12	7	4	32	18	14	.250	.299	.396	82	-7	2	0	1	.967	-5	C-90	-0.7
1922	Chi-N	128	392	68	127	18	8	4	60	79	34	.324	.439	.441	125	19	5	3	-0	.977	16	*C-125	3.8
1923	Chi-N	131	452	73	144	25	4	12	84	67	38	.319	.408	.471	131	22	10	3	1	.976	1	*C-124	2.9
1924	Chi-N	71	183	25	44	6	2	3	28	30	13	.240	.347	.344	85	-3	2	0	1	.984	-2	C-57	-0.1
1925	Chi-N	17	22	2	4	0	1	0	3	2	5	.182	.250	.273	33	-2	0	0	0	1.000	-1	/C-3	-0.3
	StL-N	94	317	37	88	13	2	3	32	46	26	.278	.373	.360	86	-5	0	1	-1	.975	-5	C-92	-0.5
	Yr	111	339	39	92	13	3	3	35	48	31	.271	.363	.354	83	-7	0	1	-1	.975	-6	C-95	-0.8
1926	*StL-N	147	492	63	144	30	9	7	68	61	44	.293	.371	.433	111	8	1			.983	10	*C-146	2.7
1927	StL-N	61	178	19	47	10	1	0	18	23	22	.264	.348	.331	80	-4	3			.979	-0	C-53,M	-0.1
1928	StL-N	16	52	6	11	1	0	0	4	13	9	.212	.369	.231	59	-2	2			.985	0	C-14	-0.1
	NY-N	75	133	23	26	6	0	2	20	34	16	.195	.359	.286	70	-5	2			.988	-1	C-63	-0.2
	Yr	91	185	29	37	7	0	2	24	47	25	.200	.362	.270	67	-7	4			.987	-1	C-77	-0.3
1929	NY-N	91	248	35	76	14	3	4	42	28	30	.306	.384	.435	103	2	3			.979	-5	C-84	0.3
1930	NY-N	94	249	37	75	16	4	4	54	31	21	.301	.381	.446	101	1	1			.973	0	C-69	0.6
1931	NY-N	85	174	11	39	8	3	1	19	21	23	.224	.311	.322	72	-7	0			.980	1	C-80	-0.2
1932	NY-N	50	67	7	16	3	0	0	8	11	10	.239	.354	.284	76	-2	0			.969	2	C-41	0.1
1933	StL-N	55	163	16	39	4	2	2	20	15	25	.239	.303	.325	76	-5	0			.970	-5	C-50	-0.8
1934	Cin-N	44	123	10	30	8	3	1	9	11	19	.244	.306	.382	85	-3	0			.993	1	C-42,M	-0.1
	Chi-N	22	67	3	15	3	0	0	5	3	11	.224	.257	.269	42	-3	0			1.000	0	C-22	-0.3
	Yr	66	190	13	45	11	3	1	14	14	30	.237	.289	.342	70	-8	0			.996	2	C-64	-0.4
1935	StL-N	14	10	0	0	0	0	0	0	1	0	.000	.167	.000	-49	-2	0			1.000	1	/C-8	-0.1
Total	21	1492	4101	517	1120	201	58	51	549	547	408	.273	.360	.388	97	-3	35	7		.976	-10	*C-1338	6.1

■ JOSE OFFERMAN   Offerman, Jose Antonio (Dono) b: 11/8/68, San Pedro De Macoris, D.R. BB/TR, 6', 150 lbs. Deb: 8/19/90

YEAR	TM/L	G	AB	R	H	2B	3B	HR	RBI	BB	SO	AVG	OBP	SLG	PRO+	BR/A	SB	CS	SBR	FA	FR	G/POS	TPR
1990	LA-N	29	58	7	9	0	0	1	7	4	14	.155	.210	.207	15	-7	1	0	0	.946	-2	S-27	-0.7
1991	LA-N	52	113	10	22	2	0	0	3	25	32	.195	.345	.212	62	-4	3	2	-0	.945	2	S-50	0.0
1992	LA-N	149	534	67	139	20	8	1	30	57	98	.260	.332	.333	90	-6	23	16	-3	.935	-18	*S-149	-1.7
1993	LA-N	158	590	77	159	21	6	1	62	71	75	.269	.350	.331	88	-8	30	13	1	.950	-7	*S-158	-0.1
1994	LA-N	72	243	27	51	8	4	1	25	38	38	.210	.317	.288	63	-13	2	1	0	.967	-4	S-72	-1.1
Total	5	460	1538	188	380	51	18	4	127	195	257	.247	.333	.311	80	-37	59	32	-2	.947	-29	S-456	-3.6

■ ROWLAND OFFICE   Office, Rowland Johnie b: 10/25/52, Sacramento, Cal. BL/TL, 6', 170 lbs. Deb: 8/5/72

YEAR	TM/L	G	AB	R	H	2B	3B	HR	RBI	BB	SO	AVG	OBP	SLG	PRO+	BR/A	SB	CS	SBR	FA	FR	G/POS	TPR
1972	Atl-N	2	5	1	2	0	0	0	0	1	2	.400	.500	.400	145	0	0	0	0	1.000	0	/O-1	0.0
1974	Atl-N	131	248	20	61	16	1	3	31	16	30	.246	.292	.355	77	-8	5	3	-0	.994	-25	*O-119	-3.8

YEAR	TM/L	G	AB	R	H	2B	3B	HR	RBI	BB	SO	AVG	OBP	SLG	PRO+	BR/A	SB	CS	SBR	FA	FR	G/POS	TPR
1975	Atl-N	126	355	30	103	14	1	3	30	23	41	.290	.339	.361	91	-4	2	2	-1	.967	-6	*O-107	-1.6
1976	Atl-N	99	359	51	101	17	1	4	34	37	49	.281	.352	.368	98	-0	2	8	-4	.986	-3	O-92	-1.2
1977	Atl-N	124	428	42	103	13	1	5	39	23	58	.241	.284	.311	53	-28	2	4	-2	.988	7	*O-104/1-1	-2.7
1978	Atl-N	146	404	40	101	13	1	9	40	22	52	.250	.299	.354	73	-15	8	6	-1	.990	-3	*O-136	-2.5
1979	Atl-N	124	277	35	69	14	2	2	37	27	33	.249	.320	.336	74	-10	5	4	-1	.988	-13	O-97	-2.7
1980	Mon-N	116	292	36	78	13	4	6	30	36	39	.267	.348	.401	108	4	3	3	-1	.987	-11	O-97	-1.2
1981	Mon-N	26	40	4	7	0	0	0	0	4	6	.175	.250	.175	22	-4	0	0	0	.938	-3	O-15	-0.8
1982	Mon-N	3	3	0	1	1	0	0	0	0	1	.333	.333	.667	170	0	0	0	0	1.000	0	/O-1	0.0
1983	NY-A	2	2	0	0	0	0	0	1	0	0	.000	.000	.000	-99	-1	0	0	0	1.000	-1	/O-2	-0.1
Total	11	899	2413	259	626	101	11	32	242	189	311	.259	.317	.350	79	-66	27	30	-10	.985	-57	O-771/1-1	-16.6

■ JIM OGLESBY   Oglesby, James Dorn   b: 8/10/05, Schofield, Mo.   d: 9/1/55, Tulsa, Okla.   BL/L, 6', 190 lbs.   Deb: 4/14/36

YEAR	TM/L	G	AB	R	H	2B	3B	HR	RBI	BB	SO	AVG	OBP	SLG	PRO+	BR/A	SB	CS	SBR	FA	FR	G/POS	TPR
1936	Phi-A	3	11	0	2	0	0	0	2	2	0	.182	.308	.182	24	-1	0	0	0	1.000	0	/1-3	-0.1

■ BEN OGLIVIE   Oglivie, Benjamin Ambrosio (Palmer)   b: 2/11/49, Colon, Panama   BL/TL, 6'2", 170 lbs.   Deb: 9/4/71

YEAR	TM/L	G	AB	R	H	2B	3B	HR	RBI	BB	SO	AVG	OBP	SLG	PRO+	BR/A	SB	CS	SBR	FA	FR	G/POS	TPR
1971	Bos-A	14	38	2	10	3	0	0	4	0	5	.263	.263	.342	66	-2	0	0	0	.958	1	O-11	-0.1
1972	Bos-A	94	253	27	61	10	2	8	30	18	61	.241	.294	.391	97	-1	1	1	-0	.981	-1	O-65	-0.6
1973	Bos-A	58	147	16	32	9	1	2	9	9	32	.218	.272	.333	66	-7	1	1	-0	.983	0	O-32,D-13	-0.9
1974	Det-A	92	252	28	68	11	3	4	29	34	38	.270	.357	.385	109	4	12	3	2	.947	-5	O-63,1-10/D	-0.3
1975	Det-A	100	332	45	95	14	1	9	36	16	62	.286	.323	.416	103	0	11	8	-2	.975	6	O-86/1-5,D	0.1
1976	Det-A	115	305	36	87	12	3	15	47	11	44	.285	.317	.492	129	9	9	4	0	.986	1	O-64/1-9,D	0.8
1977	Det-A	132	450	63	118	24	2	21	61	40	80	.262	.327	.464	107	3	9	9	-3	.976	7	*O-118/D-2	0.3
1978	Mil-A	128	469	71	142	29	4	18	72	52	69	.303	.372	.497	142	26	11	7	-1	.980	1	O-89,D-27,1	2.1
1979	Mil-A	139	514	88	145	30	4	29	81	48	56	.282	.346	.525	131	21	12	5	1	.985	-0	*O-120,D-13/1	1.5
1980	Mil-A★	156	592	94	180	26	2	**41**	118	54	71	.304	.367	.563	156	43	11	9	-2	.978	21	*O-152/D-4	5.4
1981	*Mil-A	107	400	53	97	15	2	14	72	37	49	.243	.316	.395	109	4	2	2	-1	.982	-3	*O-101/D-6	-0.3
1982	*Mil-A★	159	602	92	147	22	1	34	102	70	81	.244	.327	.453	119	14	3	5	-2	.982	13	*O-159	2.0
1983	Mil-A★	125	411	49	115	19	3	13	66	60	64	.280	.377	.436	133	20	4	6	-2	.985	6	*O-113/D-8	2.0
1984	Mil-A	131	461	49	121	16	2	12	60	44	56	.262	.328	.384	100	0	0	6	-4	.970	-4	*O-125/D-1	-1.1
1985	Mil-A	101	341	40	99	17	2	10	61	37	51	.290	.363	.440	119	9	0	2	-1	.965	-3	O-91/D-4	0.2
1986	Mil-A	103	346	31	98	20	1	5	53	30	33	.283	.340	.390	95	-2	1	2	-1	.991	4	O-50,D-42	-0.2
Total	16	1754	5913	784	1615	277	33	235	901	560	852	.273	.340	.450	119	142	87	70	-16	.978	44	*O-1439,D-127/1	10.9

■ BRUCE OGRODOWSKI   Ogrodowski, Ambrose Francis "Brusie"   b: 2/17/12, Hoytville, Pa.   d: 3/5/56, San Francisco, Cal.   BR/TR, 5'11", 175 lbs.   Deb: 4/14/36

YEAR	TM/L	G	AB	R	H	2B	3B	HR	RBI	BB	SO	AVG	OBP	SLG	PRO+	BR/A	SB	CS	SBR	FA	FR	G/POS	TPR
1936	StL-N	94	237	28	54	15	1	1	20	10	20	.228	.259	.312	53	-16	0			.989	4	C-85	-0.8
1937	StL-N	90	279	37	65	10	3	3	31	11	17	.233	.267	.323	58	-17	2			.984	2	C-87	-1.0
Total	2	184	516	65	119	25	4	4	51	21	37	.231	.263	.318	56	-32	2			.986	6	C-172	-1.8

■ HAL O'HAGEN   O'Hagen, Harry P.   b: 9/30/1873, Washington, D.C.   d: 1/14/13, Newark, N.J.   6', 173 lbs.   Deb: 9/24/1892

YEAR	TM/L	G	AB	R	H	2B	3B	HR	RBI	BB	SO	AVG	OBP	SLG	PRO+	BR/A	SB	CS	SBR	FA	FR	G/POS	TPR
1892	Was-N	1	4	1	1	0	0	0	0	0	2	.250	.250	.250	53	-0	0			1.000	1	/C-1	0.0
1902	Chi-N	31	108	10	21	1	3	0	10	11		.194	.269	.259	65	-4	8			.982	3	1-31	-0.2
	NY-N	4	11	0	1	0	0	0	0	0		.091	.091	.091	-44	-2	0			1.000	-1	/O-4	-0.3
	Cle-A	3	13	2	5	2	0	0	1	0		.385	.385	.538	160	1	2			1.000	1	/1-3	0.1
	NY-N	22	73	5	11	2	1	0	8	2		.151	.195	.205	24	-7	3			.973	-0	1-18/O-4	-0.8
	Yr	57	192	15	33	2	4	0	18	13		.172	.232	.224	45	-13	11			.979	2	1-49/O-8	-1.3
Total	2	61	209	18	39	5	4	0	19	13	2	.187	.241	.249	51	-12	13			.981	3	/1-52,O-8,C	-1.2

■ GREG O'HALLORAN   O'Halloran, Gregory Joseph   b: 5/21/68, Toronto, Ont., Can.   BL/TR, 6'2", 205 lbs.   Deb: 5/16/94

YEAR	TM/L	G	AB	R	H	2B	3B	HR	RBI	BB	SO	AVG	OBP	SLG	PRO+	BR/A	SB	CS	SBR	FA	FR	G/POS	TPR
1994	Fla-N	12	11	1	2	0	0	0	1	0	1	.182	.182	.182	-5	-2	0	0	0	1.000	0	/C-1	-0.1

■ KID O'HARA   O'Hara, James Francis   b: 12/19/1875, Wilkes-Barre, Pa.   d: 12/1/54, Canton, Ohio   BB/TR, 5'7.5", 152 lbs.   Deb: 9/15/04

YEAR	TM/L	G	AB	R	H	2B	3B	HR	RBI	BB	SO	AVG	OBP	SLG	PRO+	BR/A	SB	CS	SBR	FA	FR	G/POS	TPR
1904	Bos-N	8	29	3	6	0	0	0		0	4	.207	.303	.207	60	-1	1			.923	0	/O-8	-0.2

■ TOM O'HARA   O'Hara, Thomas F.   b: 7/13/1885, Waverly, N.Y.   d: 6/8/54, Denver, Colo.   Deb: 9/19/06

YEAR	TM/L	G	AB	R	H	2B	3B	HR	RBI	BB	SO	AVG	OBP	SLG	PRO+	BR/A	SB	CS	SBR	FA	FR	G/POS	TPR
1906	StL-N	14	53	8	16	1	0	0	3			.302	.339	.321	110	1	3			.889	-2	O-14	-0.2
1907	StL-N	48	173	11	41	2	1	0	5	12		.237	.286	.260	74	-5	1			.943	-1	O-47	-0.9
Total	2	62	226	19	57	3	1	0	5	15		.252	.299	.274	82	-5	4			.930	-3	/O-61	-1.1

■ BILL O'HARA   O'Hara, William Alexander   b: 8/14/1883, Toronto, Ont., Can.   d: 6/15/31, Jersey City, N.J.   BL/TR, 5'10",   Deb: 4/15/09

YEAR	TM/L	G	AB	R	H	2B	3B	HR	RBI	BB	SO	AVG	OBP	SLG	PRO+	BR/A	SB	CS	SBR	FA	FR	G/POS	TPR
1909	NY-N	115	360	48	85	9	3	1	30	41		.236	.318	.286	86	-5	31			.978	2	*O-111	-0.8
1910	StL-N	9	20	1	3	0	0	0	2	1	3	.150	.190	.150	20	-3	0			1.000	-0	/O-4,P-1,1	-0.3
Total	2	124	380	49	88	9	3	1	32	42	3	.232	.311	.279	82	-7	31			.979	2	O-115/1-1,P	-1.1

■ LEN OKRIE   Okrie, Leonard Joseph   b: 7/16/23, Detroit, Mich.   BR/TR, 6', 185 lbs.   Deb: 6/16/48   FC

YEAR	TM/L	G	AB	R	H	2B	3B	HR	RBI	BB	SO	AVG	OBP	SLG	PRO+	BR/A	SB	CS	SBR	FA	FR	G/POS	TPR
1948	Was-A	19	42	1	10	0	1	0	1	7		.238	.256	.286	45	-3	0	0	0	.981	2	C-17	-0.1
1950	Was-A	17	27	1	6	0	0	0	2	6	7	.222	.382	.222	61	-1	0	0	0	1.000	1	C-17	0.0
1951	Was-A	5	8	1	1	1	0	0	0	2	1	.125	.300	.250	51	-1	0	0	0	.850	1	/C-5	0.0
1952	Bos-A	1	1	0	0	0	0	0	0	0	1	.000	.000	.000	-93	-0	0	0	0	1.000	-0	/C-1	0.0
Total	4	42	78	3	17	1	1	0	3	9	16	.218	.307	.256	51	-5	0	0	0	.965	2	/C-40	-0.1

■ JIM OLANDER   Olander, James Bentley   b: 2/21/63, Tucson, Ariz.   BR/TR, 6'1", 185 lbs.   Deb: 9/20/91

YEAR	TM/L	G	AB	R	H	2B	3B	HR	RBI	BB	SO	AVG	OBP	SLG	PRO+	BR/A	SB	CS	SBR	FA	FR	G/POS	TPR
1991	Mil-A	12	9	2	0	0	0	0	0	2	5	.000	.182	.000	-46	-2	0	0	0	1.000	-2	/O-9,D-2	-0.4

■ DAVE OLDFIELD   Oldfield, David   b: 12/18/1864, Philadelphia, Pa.   d: 8/28/39, Philadelphia, Pa.   BB/TL, 5'7", 175 lbs.   Deb: 6/28/1883

YEAR	TM/L	G	AB	R	H	2B	3B	HR	RBI	BB	SO	AVG	OBP	SLG	PRO+	BR/A	SB	CS	SBR	FA	FR	G/POS	TPR
1883	Bal-a	1	4	0	0	0	0	0		0		.000	.000	.000	-97	-1				.667	-1	/C-1	-0.2
1885	Bro-a	10	25	2	8	1	0	0		3		.320	.414	.360	145	2				.873	1	/C-9,O-2	0.3
1886	Bro-a	14	55	7	13	1	0	0		2		.236	.263	.255	62	-2	1			.833	-3	C-13/S-1,O	-0.3
	Was-N	21	71	2	10	2	0	0		5	15	.141	.197	.169	13	-7	0			.899	-3	C-12/O-9	-0.9
Total	3	46	155	11	31	4	0	0	2	10	15	.200	.253	.226	50	-9	1			.857	-7	/C-35,O-12,S	-1.1

■ JOHN OLDHAM   Oldham, John Hardin   b: 11/6/32, Salinas, Cal.   BR/TL, 6'3", 198 lbs.   Deb: 9/2/56

YEAR	TM/L	G	AB	R	H	2B	3B	HR	RBI	BB	SO	AVG	OBP	SLG	PRO+	BR/A	SB	CS	SBR	FA	FR	G/POS	TPR
1956	Cin-N	1	0	0	0	0	0	0	0	0	0	—	—	—			0	0	0	.000	0	R	0.0

■ BOB OLDIS   Oldis, Robert Carl   b: 1/5/28, Preston, Iowa   BR/TR, 6'1", 185 lbs.   Deb: 4/28/53   C

YEAR	TM/L	G	AB	R	H	2B	3B	HR	RBI	BB	SO	AVG	OBP	SLG	PRO+	BR/A	SB	CS	SBR	FA	FR	G/POS	TPR
1953	Was-A	7	16	0	4	0	0	0	3	1	2	.250	.294	.250	49	-1	0	0	0	1.000	2	/C-7	0.1
1954	Was-A	11	24	1	8	0	0	0	5	1	3	.333	.360	.375	107	1	0	0	0	.941	-1	/C-8,3-2	0.0
1955	Was-A	6	6	1	0	0	0	0	0	1	0	.000	.143	.000	-62	-1	0	0	0	1.000	1	/C-6	-0.1
1960	*Pit-N	22	20	1	4	1	0	0	1	1	2	.200	.238	.250	34	-2	0	0	0	1.000	3	C-22	0.1
1961	Pit-N	4	5	0	0	0	0	0	0	0	0	.000	.000	.000	-99	-1	0	0	0	1.000	3	/C-4	0.1
1962	Phi-N	38	80	9	21	1	0	1	10	13	10	.262	.366	.313	87	-1	0	0	0	.987	1	C-30	0.0
1963	Phi-N	47	85	8	19	4	0	0	3	3	5	.224	.250	.259	47	-6	1	0	0	.979	5	C-43	0.0
Total	7	135	236	20	56	6	0	1	22	20	22	.237	.297	.275	60	-12	1	0	0	.983	12	C-120/3-2	0.2

■ RUBE OLDRING   Oldring, Reuben Henry   b: 5/30/1884, New York, N.Y.   d: 9/9/61, Bridgeton, N.J.   BR/TR, 5'10", 186 lbs.   Deb: 10/2/05

YEAR	TM/L	G	AB	R	H	2B	3B	HR	RBI	BB	SO	AVG	OBP	SLG	PRO+	BR/A	SB	CS	SBR	FA	FR	G/POS	TPR
1905	NY-A	8	30	2	9	0	1	1	6	2		.300	.344	.467	140	1	4			.967	5	/S-8	0.7
1906	Phi-A	59	174	15	42	10	1	0	19	2		.241	.263	.310	77	-5	7			.897	2	3-49/S-3,21	-0.2

YEAR	TM/L	G	AB	R	H	2B	3B	HR	RBI	BB	SO	AVG	OBP	SLG	PRO+	BR/A	SB	CS	SBR	FA	FR	G/POS	TPR
1907	Phi-A	117	441	48	126	27	8	1	40	7		.286	.305	.390	118	7	29			.974	-10	*O-117	-0.8
1908	Phi-A	116	434	38	96	14	2	1	39	18		.221	.267	.270	70	-15	13			.941	3	*O-116	-2.0
1909	Phi-A	90	326	39	75	13	8	1	28	20		.230	.287	.328	92	-4	17			.963	-1	O-89/1-1	-0.9
1910	Phi-A	134	546	79	168	27	14	4	57	23		.308	.340	.430	143	23	17			.978	-1	*O-134	1.7
1911	*Phi-A	121	495	84	147	11	14	3	59	21		.297	.332	.394	104	1	21			.979	-9	*O-119	-1.4
1912	Phi-A	99	395	61	119	14	5	1	24	10		.301	.324	.370	102	-1	17			.974	-3	O-98	-0.9
1913	*Phi-A	137	538	101	152	27	9	5	71	34	37	.283	.328	.394	113	6	40			.968	-7	*O-131/S-5	-0.6
1914	*Phi-A	119	466	68	129	21	7	3	49	18	35	.277	.308	.371	108	2	14	16	-5	.965	-6	*O-117	-1.6
1915	Phi-A	107	408	49	101	23	3	6	42	22	21	.248	.293	.363	100	-3	11	6	-0	.982	5	O-96/3-8	-0.2
1916	Phi-A	40	146	10	36	8	3	0	14	9	9	.247	.290	.363	95	-2	1			.897	-2	O-40	-0.7
	NY-A	43	158	17	37	8	0	1	12	12	13	.234	.288	.304	76	-5	6			.957	-3	O-43	-1.2
	Yr	83	304	27	73	16	3	1	26	21	22	.240	.289	.322	85	-7	7			.926	-5	O-83	-1.9
1918	Phi-A	49	133	5	31	2	1	0	11	8	10	.233	.282	.263	64	-6	0			.949	-8	O-30/2-2,3	-1.8
Total	13	1239	4690	616	1268	205	76	27	471	206	125	.270	.307	.364	103	0	197	22		.966	-35	*O-1130/3-59,S21	-9.9

■ CHARLEY O'LEARY

O'Leary, Charles Timothy b: 10/15/1882, Chicago, Ill. d: 1/6/41, Chicago, Ill. BR/TR, 5'7", 165 lbs. Deb: 4/14/04 C

YEAR	TM/L	G	AB	R	H	2B	3B	HR	RBI	BB	SO	AVG	OBP	SLG	PRO+	BR/A	SB	CS	SBR	FA	FR	G/POS	TPR
1904	Det-A	135	456	39	97	10	3	1	16	21		.213	.254	.254	63	-19	9			.933	6	*S-135	-1.1
1905	Det-A	148	512	47	109	13	1	0	33	29		.213	.259	.242	59	-24	13			.933	-8	*S-148	-3.2
1906	Det-A	128	443	34	97	13	2	2	34	17		.219	.253	.271	62	-20	8			.926	-8	*S-127	-2.6
1907	*Det-A	139	465	61	112	19	1	0	34	32		.241	.298	.286	83	-8	11			.943	-4	*S-138	-0.9
1908	*Det-A	65	211	21	53	9	3	0	17	9		.251	.295	.322	96	-1	11			.920	-13	S-64/2-1	-1.4
1909	*Det-A	76	261	29	53	10	0	0	13	6		.203	.224	.241	45	-17	9			.922	-4	3-54,2-15/SO	-2.2
1910	Det-A	65	211	23	51	7	1	0	9	9		.242	.276	.284	71	-8	7			.935	1	2-38,S-18/3	-0.7
1911	Det-A	74	256	29	68	8	2	0	25	21		.266	.336	.313	77	-7	10			.966	4	2-67/3-6	-0.5
1912	Det-A	3	10	1	2	0	0	0	1	0		.200	.200	.200	15	-1				1.000	2	/2-3	0.0
1913	StL-N	121	406	32	88	15	5	0	31	20	34	.217	.260	.278	55	-24	3			.951	-8	*S-103,2-15	-2.5
1934	StL-A	1	1	1	1	0	0	0	0	0	0	1.000	1.000	1.000	385	0	0	0	0	.000	0	H	0.0
Total	11	955	3232	317	731	104	18	3	213	164	34	.226	.270	.272	67	-129	74	0		.935	-32	S-737,2-139/3O	-15.1

■ DAN O'LEARY

O'Leary, Daniel "Hustling Dan" b: 10/22/1856, Detroit, Mich. d: 6/24/22, Chicago, Ill. BL, 5'10", 165 lbs. Deb: 9/3/1879 M

YEAR	TM/L	G	AB	R	H	2B	3B	HR	RBI	BB	SO	AVG	OBP	SLG	PRO+	BR/A	SB	CS	SBR	FA	FR	G/POS	TPR
1879	Pro-N	2	7	1	3	0	0	0		1	0	.429	.429	.429	187	1				.000	-1	/O-2	0.0
1880	Bos-N	3	12	1	3	2	0	0	1	0	3	.250	.250	.417	126	0				1.000	-1	/O-3	-0.1
1881	Det-N	2	8	0	0	0	0	0		0	2	.000	.000	.000	-96	-2				.714	-1	/O-2	-0.2
1882	Wor-N	6	22	2	4	1	0	0	2	5		.182	.333	.227	82	-0				.800	-2	/O-6	-0.2
1884	Cin-U	32	132	14	34	0	2	1		5		.258	.285	.311	57	-8				.862	2	O-32,M	-0.6
Total	5	45	181	18	44	3	2	1	5	10	10	.243	.283	.298	62	-9				.843	-2	/O-45	-1.1

■ TROY O'LEARY

O'Leary, Troy Franklin b: 8/4/69, Compton, Cal. BL/TL, 6', 175 lbs. Deb: 5/9/93

YEAR	TM/L	G	AB	R	H	2B	3B	HR	RBI	BB	SO	AVG	OBP	SLG	PRO+	BR/A	SB	CS	SBR	FA	FR	G/POS	TPR
1993	Mil-A	19	41	3	12	3	0	0	3	5	9	.293	.370	.366	100	0	0	0	0	1.000	-1	O-19	-0.1
1994	Mil-A	27	66	9	18	1	1	2	7	5	12	.273	.333	.409	88	-1	0	0	0	1.000	-1	O-21/D-1	-0.3
Total	2	46	107	12	30	4	1	2	10	10	21	.280	.347	.393	93	-1	1	1	-0	1.000	-2	/O-40,D-1	-0.4

■ JOHN OLERUD

Olerud, John Garrett b: 8/5/68, Seattle, Wash. BL/TL, 6'5", 205 lbs. Deb: 9/3/89

YEAR	TM/L	G	AB	R	H	2B	3B	HR	RBI	BB	SO	AVG	OBP	SLG	PRO+	BR/A	SB	CS	SBR	FA	FR	G/POS	TPR
1989	Tor-A	6	8	2	3	0	0	0	0	0	1	.375	.375	.375	114	0	0	0	0	1.000	0	/1-5,D-1	0.0
1990	Tor-A	111	358	43	95	15	1	14	48	57	75	.265	.368	.430	120	11	0	2	-1	.986	-4	D-90,1-18	0.5
1991	*Tor-A	139	454	64	116	30	1	17	68	68	84	.256	.360	.438	115	10	0	2	-1	.996	-4	*1-135/D-1	-0.4
1992	Tor-A	138	458	68	130	28	0	16	66	70	61	.284	.380	.450	126	17	1	0	0	.994	-2	*1-133/D-1	0.6
1993	*Tor-A★	158	551	109	200	54	2	24	107	114	65	.363	.478	.599	186	74	0	2	-1	.992	1	*1-137,D-20	5.9
1994	Tor-A	108	384	47	114	29	2	12	67	61	53	.297	.397	.477	123	15	1	2	-1	.993	2	*1-104/D-3	0.6
Total	6	660	2213	333	658	156	6	83	356	370	339	.297	.402	.486	137	127	2	8	-4	.994	-4	1-532,D-116	7.2

■ FRANK OLIN

Olin, Franklin Walter b: 1/9/1860, Woodford, Vt. d: 5/21/51, St.Louis, Mo. BL, Deb: 7/4/1884

YEAR	TM/L	G	AB	R	H	2B	3B	HR	RBI	BB	SO	AVG	OBP	SLG	PRO+	BR/A	SB	CS	SBR	FA	FR	G/POS	TPR
1884	Was-a	21	83	12	32	4	1	0		8		.386	.440	.458	218	11				.775	-7	2-12,O-11	0.4
	Was-U	1	4	0	0	0	0	0		0		.000	.000	.000	-99	-1				.000	-0	/O-1	-0.1
	Tol-a	26	86	16	22	0	1	1		5		.256	.304	.314	99	-0				.875	0	O-26	0.0
1885	Det-N	4	1	1	2	0	0	0	0	0	0	.500	.500	.500	224	1				.667	-0	/3-1	0.0
Total	2	49	177	29	56	4	2	1	0	13	0	.316	.366	.379	148	11				.849	-2	/O-38,2-12,3	0.3

■ JOSE OLIVA

Oliva, Jose (Galvez) b: 3/3/71, San Pedro De Macoris, D.R. BR/TR, 6'1", 150 lbs. Deb: 7/1/94

YEAR	TM/L	G	AB	R	H	2B	3B	HR	RBI	BB	SO	AVG	OBP	SLG	PRO+	BR/A	SB	CS	SBR	FA	FR	G/POS	TPR
1994	Atl-N	19	59	9	17	5	0	6	11	7	10	.288	.364	.678	163	5	0	1	-1	.932	5	3-16	0.6

■ TONY OLIVA

Oliva, Pedro (Lopez) b: 7/20/40, Pinar Del Rio, Cuba BL/TR, 6'2", 190 lbs. Deb: 9/9/62 C

YEAR	TM/L	G	AB	R	H	2B	3B	HR	RBI	BB	SO	AVG	OBP	SLG	PRO+	BR/A	SB	CS	SBR	FA	FR	G/POS	TPR
1962	Min-A	9	9	3	4	1	0	0	3	3	2	.444	.583	.556	201	2	0	0	0	1.000	-0	/O-2	0.1
1963	Min-A	7	7	0	3	0	0	0	1	0	2	.429	.429	.429	138	0	0	0	0	.000	0	H	0.0
1964	Min-A★	161	672	109	217	43	9	32	94	34	68	.323	.361	.557	150	42	12	6	0	.981	5	*O-159	4.1
1965	*Min-A★	149	576	107	185	40	5	16	98	55	64	.321	.384	.491	141	31	19	9	0	.964	7	*O-147	3.3
1966	Min-A★	159	622	99	191	32	7	25	87	42	72	.307	.356	.502	135	27	13	7	-0	.972	14	*O-159	3.5
1967	Min-A★	146	557	76	161	34	6	17	83	44	61	.289	.340	.463	128	19	11	3	2	.987	12	*O-146	2.7
1968	Min-A★	128	470	54	136	24	5	18	68	45	61	.289	.360	.477	145	25	10	9	-2	.983	8	*O-126	2.7
1969	*Min-A†	153	637	97	197	39	4	24	101	45	66	.309	.358	.496	134	26	10	13	-5	.982	13	*O-152	2.7
1970	*Min-A★	157	628	96	204	36	7	23	107	38	67	.325	.366	.514	138	30	5	4	-1	.968	21	*O-157	4.3
1971	*Min-A†	126	487	73	164	30	3	22	81	25	44	.337	.372	.546	152	31	4	1	1	.969	-1	*O-121	2.6
1972	Min-A	10	28	1	9	1	0	0	1	2	5	.321	.367	.357	111	0	0	0	0	.857	-3	/O-9	-0.3
1973	Min-A	146	571	63	166	20	0	16	92	45	44	.291	.347	.410	108	6	2	1	0	.000	-0	*D-142	0.2
1974	Min-A	127	459	43	131	16	2	13	57	27	31	.285	.328	.414	108	4	0	1	-1	.000	0	*D-112	0.0
1975	Min-A	131	455	46	123	10	0	13	58	41	45	.270	.348	.378	103	2	0	0	0	.000	0	*D-120	-0.1
1976	Min-A	67	123	3	26	3	0	1	16	2	13	.211	.236	.260	44	-9	0	0	0	.000	0	D-32	-1.0
Total	15	1676	6301	870	1917	329	48	220	947	448	645	.304	.356	.476	130	237	86	55	-7	.975	76	*O-1178,D-406	24.8

■ ED OLIVARES

Olivares, Edward (Balzac) b: 11/5/38, Mayaguez, P.R. BR/TR, 5'11", 180 lbs. Deb: 9/16/60 F

YEAR	TM/L	G	AB	R	H	2B	3B	HR	RBI	BB	SO	AVG	OBP	SLG	PRO+	BR/A	SB	CS	SBR	FA	FR	G/POS	TPR
1960	StL-N	3	5	0	0	0	0	0	0	0	3	.000	.000	.000	-92	-1	0	0	0	.500	-0	/3-1	-0.2
1961	StL-N	21	30	2	5	0	0	1	1	1	4	.167	.167	.167	-10	-5	1	0	0	1.000	-2	O-10	-0.7
Total	2	24	35	2	5	0	0	1	1	1	7	.143	.143	.143	-21	-6	1	0	0	1.000	-3	/O-10,3-1	-0.9

■ AL OLIVER

Oliver, Albert b: 10/14/46, Portsmouth, Ohio BL/TL, 6', 195 lbs. Deb: 9/23/68

YEAR	TM/L	G	AB	R	H	2B	3B	HR	RBI	BB	SO	AVG	OBP	SLG	PRO+	BR/A	SB	CS	SBR	FA	FR	G/POS	TPR
1968	Pit-N	4	8	1	1	0	0	0	0	0	0	.125	.125	.125	-25	-1	0	0	0	1.000	0	/O-1	-0.1
1969	Pit-N	129	463	55	132	19	2	17	70	21	38	.285	.334	.445	119	10	8	5	-1	.991	-1	*1-106,O-21	-0.1
1970	*Pit-N	151	551	63	149	33	5	12	83	35	35	.270	.330	.414	100	-1	1	1	-0	.986	1	O-80,1-77	-1.0
1971	*Pit-N	143	529	69	149	31	7	14	64	27	72	.282	.323	.446	116	9	4	3	-1	.981	8	*O-116,1-25	1.0
1972	*Pit-N★	140	565	88	176	27	4	12	89	34	44	.312	.356	.437	127	19	2	4	-2	.985	1	*O-138/1-3	1.1
1973	Pit-N	158	654	90	191	38	7	20	99	22	52	.292	.320	.463	118	12	6	6	-2	.964	-2	*O-109,1-50	0.3
1974	*Pit-N	147	617	96	198	38	12	11	85	33	58	.321	.360	.475	131	27	10	1	2	.986	7	O-98,1-49	3.0
1975	*Pit-N★	155	628	90	176	39	8	18	84	25	73	.280	.313	.454	112	6	4	2	0	.987	0	*O-153/1-4	0.1
1976	*Pit-N★	121	443	62	143	22	5	12	61	26	29	.323	.367	.476	137	20	5	2	1	.984	7	*O-106/1-3	2.4
1977	Pit-N	154	568	75	175	29	6	19	82	40	38	.308	.358	.481	119	15	13	16	-6	.981	0	*O-148	0.3

YEAR	TM/L	G	AB	R	H	2B	3B	HR	RBI	BB	SO	AVG	OBP	SLG	PRO+	BR/A	SB	CS	SBR	FA	FR	G/POS	TPR
1978	Tex-A	133	525	65	170	35	5	14	89	31	41	.324	.364	.490	138	24	8	9	-3	.987	6	*O-107,D-26	2.2
1979	Tex-A	136	492	69	159	28	4	12	76	34	34	.323	.372	.470	127	18	4	5	-2	.975	0	*O-119,D-10	1.1
1980	Tex-A★	163	656	96	209	43	3	19	117	39	47	.319	.349	.480	132	27	5	7	-3	.973	4	*O-157/1-1,D	2.2
1981	Tex-A★	102	421	53	130	29	1	4	55	24	28	.309	.349	.411	125	12	3	0	1	1.000	4	*D-101/1-1	1.0
1982	Mon-N★	160	617	90	**204**	**43**	2	22	**109**	61	59	**.331**	.394	.514	149	41	5	2	0	.986	-9	*1-159	2.5
1983	Mon-N★	157	614	70	184	**38**	3	8	84	44	44	.300	.348	.410	110	8	1	3	-2	.990	-0	*1-153/O-1	0.0
1984	SF-N	91	339	27	101	19	2	0	34	20	27	.298	.339	.366	101	0	2	2	-1	.985	-1	1-82	-0.7
	Phi-N	28	93	9	29	7	0	0	14	7	9	.312	.360	.387	108	1	1	2	-1	.987	-3	1-19/O-5	-0.5
	Yr	119	432	36	130	26	2	0	48	27	36	.301	.343	.370	103	1	3	4	-2	.985	-4	*1-101/O-5	-1.2
1985	LA-N	35	79	1	20	5	0	0	8	5	11	.253	.298	.316	74	-3	1	0	0	.882	-2	O-17	-0.6
	*Tor-A	61	187	20	47	6	1	5	23	7	13	.251	.282	.374	76	-6	0	0	0	1.000	0	D-59/1-1	-0.8
Total	18	2368	9049	1189	2743	529	77	219	1326	535	756	.303	.348	.451	122	238	84	64	-13	.980	19	*O-1376,1-733,D	13.4

■ DAVE OLIVER Oliver, David Jacob b: 4/7/51, Stockton, Cal. BL/TR, 5'11", 175 lbs. Deb: 9/25/77 C

YEAR	TM/L	G	AB	R	H	2B	3B	HR	RBI	BB	SO	AVG	OBP	SLG	PRO+	BR/A	SB	CS	SBR	FA	FR	G/POS	TPR
1977	Cle-A	7	22	2	7	0	1	0	3	4	0	.318	.444	.409	139	2	0	0	0	.949	1	/2-7	0.2

■ GENE OLIVER Oliver, Eugene George b: 3/22/35, Moline, Ill. BR/TR, 6'2", 225 lbs. Deb: 6/6/59

YEAR	TM/L	G	AB	R	H	2B	3B	HR	RBI	BB	SO	AVG	OBP	SLG	PRO+	BR/A	SB	CS	SBR	FA	FR	G/POS	TPR
1959	StL-N	68	172	14	42	9	0	6	28	7	41	.244	.274	.401	72	-7	3	2	-0	.955	-5	O-42/C-9,1	-1.5
1961	StL-N	22	52	8	14	2	0	4	9	6	10	.269	.367	.538	124	2	0	0	0	1.000	4	C-15/O-1	0.4
1962	StL-N	122	345	42	89	19	1	14	45	50	59	.258	.354	.441	102	1	5	2	0	.991	-4	C-98/O-8,1	0.0
1963	StL-N	39	102	10	23	4	0	6	18	13	19	.225	.313	.441	105	1	0	0	0	.981	1	C-35	0.3
	Mil-N	95	296	34	74	12	2	11	47	27	59	.250	.323	.416	112	5	4	4	-1	.985	-14	1-55,O-35/C	-1.5
	Yr	134	398	44	97	16	2	17	65	40	78	.244	.321	.422	110	5	4	4	-1	.985	-13	1-55,C-37,O	-1.2
1964	Mil-N	93	279	45	77	15	1	13	49	17	41	.276	.320	.477	120	7	3	7	-3	.982	-6	1-76/C-1	-0.6
1965	Mil-N	122	392	56	106	20	0	21	58	36	61	.270	.336	.482	127	13	5	4	-1	.976	1	C-64,1-52/O	1.5
1966	Atl-N	76	191	19	37	9	1	8	24	16	43	.194	.256	.377	72	-8	2	0	1	.990	11	C-48/1-5,O	0.7
1967	Atl-N	17	51	8	10	2	0	3	6	6	8	.196	.281	.412	97	-0	0	0	0	.968	2	C-14	0.3
	Phi-N	85	263	29	59	16	0	7	34	29	56	.224	.304	.365	90	-4	2	2	0	.987	-12	C-79/1-2	-1.3
	Yr	102	314	37	69	18	0	10	40	35	64	.220	.300	.373	91	-4	2	2	-1	.984	-10	C-93/1-2	-1.0
1968	Bos-A	16	35	2	5	0	0	1	3	4	12	.143	.250	.143	20	-3	0	0	0	.984	-2	C-10/O-1	-0.5
	Chi-N	8	11	1	4	0	0	0	1	3	2	.364	.500	.364	152	1	0	0	0	1.000	0	/1-2,C-1,O	0.1
1969	Chi-N	23	27	0	6	3	0	0	0	1	9	.222	.276	.333	62	-1	0	0	0	1.000	0	/C-6	0.1
Total	10	786	2216	268	546	111	5	93	320	215	420	.246	.317	.427	103	5	24	21	-5	.985	-24	C-382,1-200/O	-2.0

■ JOE OLIVER Oliver, Joseph Melton b: 7/24/65, Memphis, Tenn. BR/TR, 6'3", 215 lbs. Deb: 7/15/89

YEAR	TM/L	G	AB	R	H	2B	3B	HR	RBI	BB	SO	AVG	OBP	SLG	PRO+	BR/A	SB	CS	SBR	FA	FR	G/POS	TPR
1989	Cin-N	49	151	13	41	8	0	3	23	6	28	.272	.304	.384	92	-2	0	0	0	.986	-1	C-47	0.0
1990	*Cin-N	121	364	34	84	23	0	8	52	37	75	.231	.305	.360	79	-11	1	1	-0	**.992**	2	*C-118	-0.2
1991	Cin-N	94	269	21	58	11	0	11	41	18	53	.216	.265	.379	76	-9	0	0	0	.980	-1	C-90	-0.6
1992	Cin-N	143	485	42	131	25	1	10	57	35	75	.270	.321	.388	97	-2	2	3	-1	.992	-1	*C-141/1-1	0.4
1993	Cin-N	139	482	40	115	28	0	14	75	27	91	.239	.280	.384	76	-18	0	0	0	.992	-9	*C-133,1-12/O	-2.0
1994	Cin-N	6	19	1	4	0	0	1	5	2	3	.211	.286	.368	69	-1	0	0	0	.980	2	/C-6	0.1
Total	6	552	1770	151	433	95	1	47	253	125	325	.245	.296	.379	83	-43	3	4	-2	.989	-9	C-535/1-13,O	-2.3

■ NATE OLIVER Oliver, Nathaniel "Peewee" b: 12/13/40, St.Petersburg, Fla. BR/TR, 5'10", 160 lbs. Deb: 4/9/63

YEAR	TM/L	G	AB	R	H	2B	3B	HR	RBI	BB	SO	AVG	OBP	SLG	PRO+	BR/A	SB	CS	SBR	FA	FR	G/POS	TPR
1963	LA-N	65	163	23	39	2	3	1	9	13	25	.239	.299	.307	80	-4	3	4	-2	.961	5	2-57/S-2	0.4
1964	LA-N	99	321	28	78	9	0	0	21	31	57	.243	.310	.271	70	-12	7	4	-0	.967	-10	2-98/S-1	-1.6
1965	LA-N	8	1	3	1	0	0	0	0	0	0	1.000	1.000	1.000	498	1	1	0	0	1.000	1	/2-2	0.2
1966	*LA-N	80	119	17	23	2	0	0	3	13	13	.193	.278	.210	41	-9	3	3	-1	.977	11	2-68/S-2,3	0.4
1967	LA-N	77	232	18	55	6	2	0	7	13	50	.237	.283	.280	67	-10	3	2	0	.973	-8	2-39,S-32/O	-1.5
1968	SF-N	36	73	3	13	4	1	0	1	1	13	.178	.198	.205	18	-7	0	1	-1	.950	1	2-14,S-13/3	-0.7
1969	NY-A	1	1	0	0	0	0	0	0	0	0	.000	.000	.000	-99	-0	0	0	0	.000	0	H	0.0
	Chi-N	44	44	15	7	0	0	1	4	1	10	.159	.196	.295	32	-4	0	1	-1	1.000	11	2-13	0.7
Total	7	410	954	107	216	24	5	2	45	72	172	.226	.284	.268	62	-47	17	15	-4	.969	10	2-291/S-50,3O	-2.1

■ BOB OLIVER Oliver, Robert Lee b: 2/8/43, Shreveport, La. BR/TR, 6'2", 215 lbs. Deb: 9/10/65 F

YEAR	TM/L	G	AB	R	H	2B	3B	HR	RBI	BB	SO	AVG	OBP	SLG	PRO+	BR/A	SB	CS	SBR	FA	FR	G/POS	TPR
1965	Pit-N	3	2	1	0	0	0	0	0	0	0	.000	.000	.000	-99	-1	0	0	0	1.000	-0	/O-3	-0.1
1969	KC-A	118	394	43	100	8	4	13	43	21	74	.254	.295	.393	91	-6	5	5	-2	.977	5	O-98,1-12/3	-0.9
1970	KC-A	160	612	83	159	24	6	27	99	42	126	.260	.311	.451	108	4	3	3	-1	.993	-8	*1-115,3-46	-1.6
1971	KC-A	128	373	35	91	12	2	8	52	14	88	.244	.281	.351	79	-12	0	0	0	.988	-0	1-68,O-48/3	-2.0
1972	KC-A	16	63	7	17	2	1	1	6	2	12	.270	.292	.381	100	-0	1	0	0	.979	3	O-16	0.3
	Cal-A	134	509	47	137	20	4	19	70	27	97	.269	.310	.436	127	14	4	3	-1	.994	-0	*1-127/O-8	-0.4
	Yr	150	572	54	154	22	5	20	76	29	109	.269	.308	.430	124	13	5	3	-0	.994	-3	*1-127,O-24	-0.1
1973	Cal-A	151	544	51	144	24	1	18	89	33	100	.265	.313	.412	111	5	1	1	-0	.952	-3	3-49,O-47,1D	-1.0
1974	Cal-A	110	359	22	89	9	1	8	55	16	51	.248	.282	.345	84	-8	2	1	0	.985	-12	1-57,3-46/OD	-2.6
	Bal-A	9	20	1	3	2	0	0	4	0	5	.150	.150	.250	14	-2	1	1	0	.974	-1	/1-4,D-1	-0.2
	Yr	119	379	23	92	11	1	8	59	16	56	.243	.275	.340	81	-11	3	2	-0	.984	-11	1-61,3-46/OD	-2.8
1975	NY-A	18	38	3	5	1	0	0	1	0	5	.132	.154	.158	-12	-6	0	0	0	1.000	-0	/1-8,3-1,D	-0.7
Total	8	847	2914	293	745	102	19	94	419	156	562	.256	.298	.400	100	-13	17	14	-3	.991	-19	1-423,O-224,3/D	-8.3

■ TOM OLIVER Oliver, Thomas Noble "Rebel" b: 1/15/03, Montgomery, Ala. d: 2/26/88, Montgomery, Ala. BR/TR, 6', 168 lbs. Deb: 4/14/30 C

YEAR	TM/L	G	AB	R	H	2B	3B	HR	RBI	BB	SO	AVG	OBP	SLG	PRO+	BR/A	SB	CS	SBR	FA	FR	G/POS	TPR
1930	Bos-A	154	646	86	189	34	2	0	46	42	25	.293	.339	.351	78	-21	6	6	-2	.982	15	*O-154	-1.7
1931	Bos-A	148	586	52	162	35	5	0	70	25	17	.276	.307	.353	77	-21	4	6	-2	**.993**	13	*O-148	-1.9
1932	Bos-A	122	455	39	120	23	3	0	37	25	12	.264	.305	.327	66	-23	1	6	-3	.983	8	*O-116	-2.4
1933	Bos-A	90	244	25	63	9	1	0	23	13	7	.258	.296	.303	60	-14	1	1	0	.985	-1	O-86	-1.8
Total	4	514	1931	202	534	101	11	0	176	105	61	.277	.316	.340	73	-79	12	19	-8	.986	35	O-504	-7.8

■ LUIS OLMO Olmo, Luis Francisco (Rodriguez) (b: Luis Francisco Rodriquez (Olmo)) b: 8/11/19, Arecibo, P.R. BR/TR, 5'11.5", 190 lbs. Deb: 7/23/43

YEAR	TM/L	G	AB	R	H	2B	3B	HR	RBI	BB	SO	AVG	OBP	SLG	PRO+	BR/A	SB	CS	SBR	FA	FR	G/POS	TPR
1943	Bro-N	57	238	39	72	6	4	4	37	8	20	.303	.325	.412	112		3			.957	-2	O-57	-0.2
1944	Bro-N	136	520	65	134	20	5	9	85	17	37	.258	.284	.367	84	-13	10			.971	-8	O-64,2-42,3	-2.3
1945	Bro-N	141	556	62	174	27	**13**	10	110	36	33	.313	.356	.462	127	18	15			.971	-9	*O-106,3-31/2	0.4
1949	*Bro-N	38	105	15	32	4	1	1	14	5	11	.305	.336	.390	91	-1	2			.950	-7	O-34	-0.7
1950	Bos-N	69	154	23	35	7	1	5	22	18	23	.227	.308	.383	86	-4	3			.974	-3	O-55/3-1	-1.4
1951	Bos-N	21	56	4	11	1	1	0	4	4	4	.196	.250	.250	38	-5	0	1		1.000	0	O-16	-0.9
Total	6	462	1629	208	458	65	25	29	272	88	128	.281	.319	.405	102	-3	33	1		.968	-34	O-332/3-63,2	-5.1

■ BARNEY OLSEN Olsen, Bernard Charles b: 9/11/19, Everett, Mass. d: 3/30/77, Everett, Mass. BR/TR, 5'11", 179 lbs. Deb: 4/17/41

YEAR	TM/L	G	AB	R	H	2B	3B	HR	RBI	BB	SO	AVG	OBP	SLG	PRO+	BR/A	SB	CS	SBR	FA	FR	G/POS	TPR
1941	Chi-N	24	73	13	21	6	1	1	4	4	11	.288	.325	.438	118	1	0			.947	1	O-23	0.1

■ GREG OLSON Olson, Gregory William b: 9/6/60, Marshall, Minn. BR/TR, 6', 200 lbs. Deb: 6/27/89

YEAR	TM/L	G	AB	R	H	2B	3B	HR	RBI	BB	SO	AVG	OBP	SLG	PRO+	BR/A	SB	CS	SBR	FA	FR	G/POS	TPR
1989	Min-A	3	2	0	1	0	0	0	0	0	0	.500	.500	.500	171	0	0	0	0	1.000	0	/C-3	0.0
1990	Atl-N★	100	298	36	78	12	1	7	36	30	51	.262	.333	.379	90	-4	1	1	-0	.987	-7	C-97/3-1	-0.5
1991	*Atl-N	133	411	46	99	25	0	6	44	44	48	.241	.319	.345	82	-9	1	1	-0	.995	3	*C-127	-0.3
1992	Atl-N	95	302	27	72	14	2	3	27	34	31	.238	.318	.328	78	-8	2	1	0	.998	9	*C-94	0.5
1993	*Atl-N	83	262	23	59	10	0	4	24	29	27	.225	.305	.309	64	-13	1	0	0	.988	-1	C-81	-1.0
Total	5	414	1275	132	309	61	3	20	131	137	157	.242	.319	.342	79	-34	5	3	-0	.992	3	C-402/3-1	-1.0

YEAR	TM/L	G	AB	R	H	2B	3B	HR	RBI	BB	SO	AVG	OBP	SLG	PRO+	BR/A	SB	CS	SBR	FA	FR	G/POS	TPR

■ IVY OLSON Olson, Ivan Massie b: 10/14/1885, Kansas City, Mo. d: 9/1/65, Inglewood, Cal. BR/TR, 5'10.5", 175 lbs. Deb: 4/12/11 C

YEAR	TM/L	G	AB	R	H	2B	3B	HR	RBI	BB	SO	AVG	OBP	SLG	PRO+	BR/A	SB	CS	SBR	FA	FR	G/POS	TPR
1911	Cle-A	140	545	89	142	20	8	1	50	34		.261	.311	.332	79	-17	20			.909	-16	*S-139/3-1	-2.3
1912	Cle-A	125	467	68	118	13	1	0	33	21		.253	.291	.285	63	-23	16			.917	6	S-56,3-36,2/O	-1.2
1913	Cle-A	104	370	47	92	13	3	0	32	22	28	.249	.296	.300	72	-13	7			.953	4	3-73,1-21/2	-1.0
1914	Cle-A	89	310	22	75	6	2	1	20	13	24	.242	.275	.284	65	-14	15	9	-1	.942	12	S-31,2-23,3/O1	0.0
1915	Cin-N	63	207	18	48	5	4	0	14	12	13	.232	.274	.295	71	-7	10	6	-1	.938	13	2-39,3-15/1	0.6
	Bro-N	18	26	2	2	0	1	0	3	1	0	.077	.111	.154	-20	-4	0			.909	-1	/S-7,2-1,3O	-0.5
	Yr	81	233	20	50	5	5	0	17	13	13	.215	.256	.279	61	-11	10	6	-1	.938	12	2-40,3-16/1SO	0.1
1916	*Bro-N	108	351	29	89	13	4	1	38	21	27	.254	.298	.322	88	-5	14			.920	-12	*S-103/2-3,1	-1.3
1917	Bro-N	139	580	64	156	18	5	2	38	14	34	.269	.291	.328	87	-10	6			.941	-6	*S-133/3-6	-1.1
1918	Bro-N	126	506	63	121	16	4	1	17	27	18	.239	.286	.292	77	-14	21			.918	-25	*S-126	-3.9
1919	Bro-N	140	590	73	**164**	14	9	1	38	30	12	.278	.316	.337	94	-4	26			.947	-2	*S-140	0.3
1920	*Bro-N	143	637	71	162	13	11	1	46	20	19	.254	.278	.314	68	-27	4	7	-3	.935	-7	*S-125,2-21	-2.8
1921	Bro-N	151	652	88	174	22	10	3	35	28	26	.267	.301	.345	68	-30	4	9	-4	.943	5	*S-133,2-20	-1.6
1922	Bro-N	136	551	63	150	26	6	1	47	25	10	.272	.306	.347	69	-26	8	5	-1	.960	-6	2-85,S-51	-2.4
1923	Bro-N	82	292	33	76	11	1	0	35	14	10	.260	.296	.315	63	-16	5	0	2	.974	5	2-72/3-4,1S	-0.8
1924	Bro-N	10	27	0	6	1	0	0	0	3	1	.222	.300	.259	53	-2	0	0	0	.941	-2	/S-8,2-2	-0.3
Total	14	1574	6111	730	1575	191	69	13	446	285	222	.258	.295	.318	74	-212	156	36		.932	-34	*S-1054,2-288,3/10	-18.3

■ KARL OLSON Olson, Karl Arthur "Ole" b: 7/6/30, Kentfield, Cal. BR/TR, 6'3", 205 lbs. Deb: 6/30/51

YEAR	TM/L	G	AB	R	H	2B	3B	HR	RBI	BB	SO	AVG	OBP	SLG	PRO+	BR/A	SB	CS	SBR	FA	FR	G/POS	TPR
1951	Bos-A	5	10	0	1	0	0	0	0	0	3	.100	.100	.100	-42	-2	0	0	0	1.000	-1	/O-5	-0.3
1953	Bos-A	25	57	5	7	2	0	1	6	1	9	.123	.138	.211	-7	-9	0	0	0	.970	-4	O-24	-1.3
1954	Bos-A	101	227	25	59	12	2	1	20	12	23	.260	.297	.344	68	-10	2	1	0	.957	-8	O-78	-2.1
1955	Bos-A	26	48	7	12	1	2	0	1	1	10	.250	.265	.354	60	-3	0	0	0	1.000	-5	O-21	-0.8
1956	Was-A	106	313	34	77	10	2	4	22	28	41	.246	.310	.329	69	-14	1	1	-0	.990	-10	*O-101	-2.8
1957	Was-A	8	12	2	2	0	0	0	0	1	2	.167	.231	.167	10	-1	0	0	0	1.000	-1	/O-6	-0.3
	Det-A	8	14	1	2	0	0	0	1	0	6	.143	.143	.143	-21	-2	0	0	0	1.000	-1	/O-5	-0.4
	Yr	16	26	3	4	0	0	0	1	1	8	.154	.181	.154	-6	-4	0	0	0	1.000	-2	O-11	-0.7
Total	6	279	681	74	160	25	6	6	50	43	94	.235	.281	.316	57	-42	3	2	-0	.979	-28	O-240	-8.0

■ MARV OLSON Olson, Marvin Clement "Sparky" b: 5/28/07, Gayville, S.Dak. BR/TR, 5'7", 160 lbs. Deb: 9/13/31

YEAR	TM/L	G	AB	R	H	2B	3B	HR	RBI	BB	SO	AVG	OBP	SLG	PRO+	BR/A	SB	CS	SBR	FA	FR	G/POS	TPR
1931	Bos-A	15	53	8	10	1	0	0	5	3		.189	.306	.208	40	-4	0	0	0	.963	3	2-15	0.0
1932	Bos-A	115	403	58	100	14	6	0	25	61	26	.248	.347	.313	74	-14	1	5	-3	.955	-15	*2-106/3-1	-2.4
1933	Bos-A	3	1	1	0	0	0	0	0	0	0	.000	.000	.000	-99	-0	0	0	0	.000	0	/2-1	0.0
Total	3	133	457	67	110	15	6	0	30	70	30	.241	.342	.300	70	-18	1	5	-3	.956	-12	2-122/3-1	-2.4

■ TOM O'MALLEY O'Malley, Thomas Patrick b: 12/25/60, Orange, N.J. BL/TR, 6', 190 lbs. Deb: 5/8/82

YEAR	TM/L	G	AB	R	H	2B	3B	HR	RBI	BB	SO	AVG	OBP	SLG	PRO+	BR/A	SB	CS	SBR	FA	FR	G/POS	TPR
1982	SF-N	92	291	26	80	12	4	2	27	32	39	.275	.351	.364	100	1	0	3	-2	.965	0	3-83/2-1,S	-0.3
1983	SF-N	135	410	40	106	16	1	5	45	52	47	.259	.348	.339	94	-2	2	4	-2	.940	1	*3-117	-0.5
1984	SF-N	13	25	2	3	0	0	0	0	2	9	.120	.185	.120	-13	-4	0	0	0	1.000	-0	/3-7	-0.5
	Chi-A	12	16	0	2	0	0	0	3	0	5	.125	.125	.125	-29	-3	0	0	0	1.000	-2	/3-6	-0.5
1985	Bal-A	8	14	1	1	0	0	1	2	0	2	.071	.071	.286	-8	-2	0	0	0	.833	-1	/3-3	-0.3
1986	Bal-A	56	181	19	46	9	0	1	18	17	21	.254	.318	.320	76	-6	0	1	-1	.938	-1	3-55	-0.9
1987	Tex-A	45	117	10	32	8	0	1	12	15	9	.274	.356	.368	92	-1	0	0	0	.962	-4	3-40/2-1	-0.6
1988	Mon-N	14	27	3	7	2	0	0	2	3	4	.259	.333	.259	69	-1	0	0	0	.905	1	/3-7	0.0
1989	NY-N	9	11	2	6	2	0	0	8	0	2	.545	.545	.727	274	2	0	0	0	1.000	-0	/3-3	0.2
1990	NY-N	82	121	14	27	7	0	3	14	11	20	.223	.288	.355	76	-4	0	0	0	.983	2	3-38/1-3	-0.2
Total	9	466	1213	117	310	54	5	13	131	133	151	.256	.332	.340	87	-19	2	8	-4	.951	-5	3-359/1-3,2S	-3.6

■ OLLIE O'MARA O'Mara, Oliver Edward b: 3/8/1891, St.Louis, Mo. d: 10/24/89, Reno, Nev. BR/TR, 5'9", 155 lbs. Deb: 9/8/12

YEAR	TM/L	G	AB	R	H	2B	3B	HR	RBI	BB	SO	AVG	OBP	SLG	PRO+	BR/A	SB	CS	SBR	FA	FR	G/POS	TPR
1912	Det-A	1	4	0	0	0	0	0	0	0		.000	.000	.000	-99	-1	0			.857	0	/S-1	-0.1
1914	Bro-N	67	247	41	65	10	2	1	7	16	26	.263	.316	.332	91	-3	14			.918	-12	S-63	-1.1
1915	*Bro-N	149	577	77	141	26	3	0	31	51	40	.244	.308	.300	83	-11	11	12	-4	.906	-34	*S-149	-4.2
1916	*Bro-N	72	193	18	39	5	2	0	15	12	20	.202	.249	.249	52	-11	10			.898	-5	S-51	-1.5
1918	Bro-N	121	450	29	96	8	1	1	24	7	16	.213	.242	.242	48	-28	11			.951	-2	*3-121	-3.1
1919	Bro-N	2	7	1	0	0	0	0	0	0	2	.000	.000	.000	-98	-2	0			.875	-0	/3-2	-0.2
Total	6	412	1478	166	341	49	8	3	77	86	104	.231	.280	.279	69	-56	46	12		.907	-53	S-264,3-123	-10.2

■ TOM O'MEARA O'Meara, Thomas Edward b: 12/12/1872, Chicago, Ill. d: 2/16/02, Fort Wayne, Ind. Deb: 9/29/1895

YEAR	TM/L	G	AB	R	H	2B	3B	HR	RBI	BB	SO	AVG	OBP	SLG	PRO+	BR/A	SB	CS	SBR	FA	FR	G/POS	TPR
1895	Cle-N	1	1	1	0	0	0	0	0	1	0	.000	.500	.000	34	-0	0			.500	-0	/C-1	0.0
1896	Cle-N	12	33	5	5	0	0	0	6	5	7	.152	.263	.152	10	-4	0			.914	-1	/C-9,1-1	-0.4
Total	2	13	34	6	5	0	0	0	6	7		.147	.275	.147	12	-4	0			.892	-2	/C-10,1-1	-0.4

■ O'NEAL O'Neal Deb: 10/23/1874

YEAR	TM/L	G	AB	R	H	2B	3B	HR	RBI	BB	SO	AVG	OBP	SLG	PRO+	BR/A	SB	CS	SBR	FA	FR	G/POS	TPR
1874	Har-n	1	3	0	0	0	0	0		0		.000	.000	.000	-95	-1						/O-1	0.0

■ DENNY O'NEIL O'Neil, Dennis b: 11/22/1866, Holyoke, Mass. d: 11/15/22, Rushville, Ind. BL/TL, 6'2.5", 200 lbs. Deb: 6/18/1893

YEAR	TM/L	G	AB	R	H	2B	3B	HR	RBI	BB	SO	AVG	OBP	SLG	PRO+	BR/A	SB	CS	SBR	FA	FR	G/POS	TPR
1893	StL-N	7	25	3	3	0	0	0	2	4	0	.120	.241	.120	-3	-4	3			.986	-1	/1-7	-0.4

■ MICKEY O'NEIL O'Neil, George Michael b: 4/12/1900, St.Louis, Mo. d: 4/8/64, St.Louis, Mo. BR/TR, 5'10", 185 lbs. Deb: 9/12/19 C

YEAR	TM/L	G	AB	R	H	2B	3B	HR	RBI	BB	SO	AVG	OBP	SLG	PRO+	BR/A	SB	CS	SBR	FA	FR	G/POS	TPR
1919	Bos-N	11	28	3	6	0	0	0	1	1	7	.214	.241	.214	39	-2				.981	3	C-11	0.2
1920	Bos-N	112	304	19	86	5	4	0	28	21	20	.283	.339	.326	96	-1	4	4	-1	.962	8	*C-105/2-1	1.3
1921	Bos-N	98	277	26	69	9	4	2	29	23	21	.249	.307	.332	73	-11	2	2	-1	.968	8	C-95	0.1
1922	Bos-N	83	251	18	56	5	2	0	26	14	11	.223	.267	.259	38	-23	1	0	0	.978	0	C-79	-1.8
1923	Bos-N	96	306	29	65	7	4	0	20	17	14	.212	.258	.261	39	-27	3	2	-0	.973	14	C-95	-0.9
1924	Bos-N	106	362	32	89	4	1	0	22	14	27	.246	.276	.262	47	-27	4	3	-1	.985	1	*C-106	-2.0
1925	Bos-N	70	222	29	57	6	5	2	30	21	16	.257	.327	.356	81	-6	7	1	2	.972	-8	C-69	-1.1
1926	Bro-N	75	201	19	42	5	3	0	20	23	8	.209	.293	.264	52	-13	3			.965	-3	C-74	-1.2
1927	Was-A	5	6	0	0	0	0	0	0	0	0	.000	.000	.000	-99	-2	0	0	0	1.000	-0	/C-4	-0.2
	NY-N	16	38	2	5	0	0	0	3	5	2	.132	.233	.132	-0	-5	0			.969	3	C-16	-0.1
Total	9	672	1995	177	475	41	23	4	179	139	127	.238	.292	.288	58	-118	18	13		.972	26	C-654/2-1	-5.7

■ JOHN O'NEIL O'Neil, John Francis b: 4/19/20, Shelbiana, Ky. BR/TR, 5'9", 155 lbs. Deb: 4/16/46

YEAR	TM/L	G	AB	R	H	2B	3B	HR	RBI	BB	SO	AVG	OBP	SLG	PRO+	BR/A	SB	CS	SBR	FA	FR	G/POS	TPR
1946	Phi-N	46	94	12	25	3	0	0	9	5	12	.266	.303	.298	73	-3	0			.940	4	S-32	0.2

■ FRED O'NEILL O'Neill, Frederick James "Tip" b: 1865, London, Ontario, Canada d: 3/7/1892, London, Ont., Can. 5'7", 142 lbs. Deb: 5/3/1887

YEAR	TM/L	G	AB	R	H	2B	3B	HR	RBI	BB	SO	AVG	OBP	SLG	PRO+	BR/A	SB	CS	SBR	FA	FR	G/POS	TPR
1887	NY-a	6	26	4	8	1	1	0		1		.308	.357	.423	122	1	3			.800	-1	/O-6	-0.1

■ HARRY O'NEILL O'Neill, Harry Mink b: 5/8/17, Philadelphia, Pa. d: 3/6/45, Iwo Jima, Marianas Islands BR/TR, 6'3", 205 lbs. Deb: 7/23/39

YEAR	TM/L	G	AB	R	H	2B	3B	HR	RBI	BB	SO	AVG	OBP	SLG	PRO+	BR/A	SB	CS	SBR	FA	FR	G/POS	TPR
1939	Phi-A	1	0	0	0	0	0	0	0	0	0	—	—	—	—		0			.000	0	/C-1	0.0

■ TIP O'NEILL O'Neill, James Edward b: 5/25/1858, Woodstock, Ont., Canada d: 12/31/15, Montreal, Que., Can BR/TR, 6'1.5", 167 lbs. Deb: 5/5/1883

YEAR	TM/L	G	AB	R	H	2B	3B	HR	RBI	BB	SO	AVG	OBP	SLG	PRO+	BR/A	SB	CS	SBR	FA	FR	G/POS	TPR
1883	NY-N	23	76	8	15	3	0	0	5	3	15	.197	.228	.237	42	-5				.917	-2	P-19/O-7	-0.2
1884	StL-a	78	297	49	82	13	11	3		12		.276	.309	.424	132	9				.811	-6	O-64,P-17/1	0.0
1885	*StL-a	52	206	44	72	7	4	3		13		.350	.399	.466	165	15				.881	-1	O-52	1.1

YEAR	TM/L	G	AB	R	H	2B	3B	HR	RBI	BB	SO	AVG	OBP	SLG	PRO+	BR/A	SB	CS	SBR	FA	FR	G/POS	TPR
1886	*StL-a	138	579	106	190	28	14	3		47		.328	.385	.440	151	32	9			.927	8	*O-138	3.2
1887	*StL-a	124	517	**167**	**225**	**52**	**19**	**14**		50		**.435**	**.490**	**.691**	205	**68**	30			.895	-6	*O-124	**4.7**
1888	*StL-a	130	529	96	**177**	24	10	5	98	44		**.335**	.390	.446	151	27	26			.937	-1	*O-130	2.1
1889	StL-a	134	534	123	179	33	8	9	110	72	37	.335	.419	.478	137	23	28			.936	-2	*O-134	1.5
1890	Chi-P	137	577	112	174	20	16	3	75	65	36	.302	.377	.407	105	3	29			.926	-12	*O-137	-1.1
1891	StL-a	129	521	112	167	28	4	10	95	62	33	.321	.402	.447	124	12	25			.935	-13	*O-129	-0.4
1892	Cin-N	109	419	63	105	14	6	2	52	53	25	.251	.339	.327	103	3	14			.922	-3	*O-109	-0.5
Total	10	1054	4255	880	1386	222	92	52	435	421	146	.326	.392	.458	140	188	161			.917	-38	*O-1024/P-36,1	10.4

■ JIM O'NEILL
O'Neill, James Leo b: 2/23/1893, Minooka, Pa. d: 9/5/76, Chambersburg, Pa. BR/TR, 5'10.5", 165 lbs. Deb: 4/15/20 F

YEAR	TM/L	G	AB	R	H	2B	3B	HR	RBI	BB	SO	AVG	OBP	SLG	PRO+	BR/A	SB	CS	SBR	FA	FR	G/POS	TPR
1920	Was-A	86	294	27	85	17	7	1	40	13	30	.289	.324	.405	95	-3	7	3	0	.943	-5	S-80/2-2	-0.2
1923	Was-A	23	33	6	9	1	0	0	3	1	3	.273	.294	.303	60	-2	0	0	0	.946	3	/2-8,3-4,SO	0.1
Total	2	109	327	33	94	18	7	1	43	14	33	.287	.321	.394	91	-5	7	3	0	.943	-3	/S-81,2-10,3O	-0.1

■ JOHN O'NEILL
O'Neill, John J. b: New York, N.Y. TR, Deb: 9/6/1899

YEAR	TM/L	G	AB	R	H	2B	3B	HR	RBI	BB	SO	AVG	OBP	SLG	PRO+	BR/A	SB	CS	SBR	FA	FR	G/POS	TPR
1899	NY-N	2	7	0	0	0	0	0	0	0	0	.000	.000	.000	-99	-2	0			.929	1	/C-2	-0.1
1902	NY-N	2	8	0	0	0	0	0	0	0	0	.000	.000	.000	-99	-2	0			.933	1	/C-2	-0.1
Total	2	4	15	0	0	0	0	0	0	0	0	.000	.000	.000	-99	-4	0			.931	2	/C-4	-0.2

■ JACK O'NEILL
O'Neill, John Joseph b: 1/10/1873, Galway, Ireland d: 6/29/35, Scranton, Pa. BR/TR, 5'10", 165 lbs. Deb: 4/21/02 F

YEAR	TM/L	G	AB	R	H	2B	3B	HR	RBI	BB	SO	AVG	OBP	SLG	PRO+	BR/A	SB	CS	SBR	FA	FR	G/POS	TPR
1902	StL-N	63	192	13	27	1	1	0	12	13		.141	.214	.156	15	-19	2			.973	1	C-59	-1.3
1903	StL-N	75	246	23	58	9	1	0	27	13		.236	.288	.280	64	-11	11			.972	16	C-74	1.1
1904	Chi-N	51	168	8	36	5	0	1	19	6		.214	.258	.262	61	-8	1			.981	5	C-49	0.2
1905	Chi-N	53	172	16	34	4	2	0	12	8		.198	.244	.244	54	-10	6			.974	7	C-50	0.3
1906	Bos-N	61	167	14	30	5	1	0	4	12		.180	.243	.222	46	-10				.971	12	C-48/1-2,O	0.6
Total	5	303	945	74	185	24	5	1	74	52		.196	.258	.235	49	-58	20			.974	40	C-280/1-2,O	0.9

■ MIKE O'NEILL
O'Neill, Michael Joyce (a.k.a. Michael Joyce In 1901) b: 9/7/1877, Galway, Ireland d: 8/12/59, Scranton, Pa. BR/TR, 5'11", 185 lbs. Deb: 9/20/01 F

YEAR	TM/L	G	AB	R	H	2B	3B	HR	RBI	BB	SO	AVG	OBP	SLG	PRO+	BR/A	SB	CS	SBR	FA	FR	G/POS	TPR
1901	StL-N	6	15	3	6	0	0	0	2		3	.400	.526	.400	179	2	0			.875	-1	/P-5	0.0
1902	StL-N	51	135	21	43	5	3	2	15		2	.319	.333	.444	145	6	0			.920	-0	P-36/O-3	0.0
1903	StL-N	41	110	12	25	2	2	0	6		8	.227	.303	.282	69	-4	3			.882	-1	P-19,O-13	-0.3
1904	StL-N	30	91	9	21	7	2	0	16		5	.231	.286	.352	101	-0	0			.910	1	P-25/O-3	0.0
1907	Cin-N	9	29	5	2	0	2	0	2		2	.069	.129	.207	5	-3	1			.864	-0	/O-9	-0.5
Total	5	137	380	50	97	14	9	2	41		20	.255	.306	.355	102	0	4			.907	-1	/P-85,O-28	-0.8

■ PAUL O'NEILL
O'Neill, Paul Andrew b: 2/25/63, Columbus, Ohio BL/TL, 6'4", 205 lbs. Deb: 9/3/85

YEAR	TM/L	G	AB	R	H	2B	3B	HR	RBI	BB	SO	AVG	OBP	SLG	PRO+	BR/A	SB	CS	SBR	FA	FR	G/POS	TPR
1985	Cin-N	5	12	1	4	1	0	0	1	0	2	.333	.333	.417	103	0	0	0	0	1.000	1	/O-2	0.1
1986	Cin-N	3	2	0	0	0	0	0	0	0	1	.000	.000	.000	-0	-0	0	0	0	.000	0	/H	0.0
1987	Cin-N	84	160	24	41	14	1	7	28	18	29	.256	.331	.488	109	2	2	1	0	.949	-3	O-42/1-2,P	-0.3
1988	Cin-N	145	485	58	122	25	3	16	73	38	65	.252	.309	.414	102	0	8	6	-1	.984	1	*O-118,1-21	-0.6
1989	Cin-N	117	428	49	118	24	2	15	74	46	64	.276	.349	.446	122	12	20	5	3	.983	4	*O-115	1.7
1990	*Cin-N	145	503	59	136	28	0	16	78	53	103	.270	.342	.421	104	3	13	11	-3	.993	6	*O-141	0.4
1991	Cin-N★	152	532	71	136	36	0	28	91	73	107	.256	.347	.481	126	18	12	7	-1	.994	13	*O-150	2.8
1992	Cin-N	148	496	59	122	19	1	14	66	77	85	.246	.350	.373	102	3	6	3	0	**.997**	15	*O-143	1.7
1993	NY-A	141	498	71	155	34	1	20	75	44	69	.311	.369	.504	137	25	2	4	-2	.992	-11	*O-138/D-2	0.8
1994	NY-A★	103	368	68	132	25	1	21	83	72	56	**.359**	.464	.603	185	50	5	4	-1	.995	2	O-99/D-4	4.4
Total	10	1043	3484	460	966	206	9	137	569	422	581	.277	.357	.460	122	112	68	41	-4	.990	27	O-948/1-23,DP	11.0

■ PEACHES O'NEILL
O'Neill, Philip Bernard b: 8/30/1879, Anderson, Ind. d: 8/2/55, Anderson, Ind. BR/TR, 5'11", 165 lbs. Deb: 4/16/04

YEAR	TM/L	G	AB	R	H	2B	3B	HR	RBI	BB	SO	AVG	OBP	SLG	PRO+	BR/A	SB	CS	SBR	FA	FR	G/POS	TPR
1904	Cin-N	8	15	0	4	0	0	0		0	1	.267	.313	.267	73	-0	0			.900	-3	/C-5,1-1	-0.4

■ STEVE O'NEILL
O'Neill, Stephen Francis b: 7/6/1891, Minooka, Pa. d: 1/26/62, Cleveland, Ohio BR/TR, 5'10", 165 lbs. Deb: 9/18/11 FMC

YEAR	TM/L	G	AB	R	H	2B	3B	HR	RBI	BB	SO	AVG	OBP	SLG	PRO+	BR/A	SB	CS	SBR	FA	FR	G/POS	TPR
1911	Cle-A	9	27	1	4	1	0	0	1		4	.148	.281	.185	31	-2	2			.986	4	/C-9	0.2
1912	Cle-A	69	215	17	49	4	0	0	14		12	.228	.272	.247	47	-15	2			.961	9	C-68	0.1
1913	Cle-A	80	234	19	69	13	3	0	29	10	24	.295	.329	.376	103	0	5			.973	3	C-80	1.1
1914	Cle-A	87	269	28	68	12	0	0	20	15	35	.253	.292	.312	79	-8	1	3	-2	.956	0	C-82/1-1	-0.2
1915	Cle-A	121	386	32	91	14	2	2	34	26	41	.236	.293	.298	75	-13	2	3	-1	.968	5	*C-115	0.1
1916	Cle-A	130	378	30	89	23	0	0	29	24	33	.235	.288	.296	71	-14	2			.971	5	*C-128	0.2
1917	Cle-A	129	370	21	68	10	2	0	29	41	55	.184	.272	.222	47	-23	1			.980	1	*C-127	-1.3
1918	Cle-A	114	359	34	87	8	7	1	35	48	22	.242	.343	.312	89	-4	5			**.983**	1	*C-113	0.8
1919	Cle-A	125	398	46	115	35	7	2	47	48	21	.289	.373	.427	117	9	4			.977	-7	*C-123	1.3
1920	*Cle-A	149	489	63	157	39	5	3	55	69	39	.321	.408	.440	121	17	3	5	-2	.976	-5	*C-148	2.0
1921	Cle-A	106	335	39	108	22	1	0	50	57	22	.322	.424	.403	110	8	0	1	-1	.982	3	*C-105	1.6
1922	Cle-A	133	392	33	122	27	4	2	65	73	22	.311	.423	.416	118	15	2	2	-1	.974	-14	*C-130	0.6
1923	Cle-A	113	330	31	82	12	0	0	50	64	34	.248	.384	.285	75	-9	0	4	-2	.968	-12	*C-111	-1.7
1924	Bos-A	106	307	29	73	15	1	0	38	63	23	.238	.371	.293	73	-10	2	2	-1	.970	4	O-92	-0.5
1925	NY-A	35	91	7	26	5	1	0	13	10	3	.286	.363	.374	89	-1	0	0	0	.946	3	C-31	0.3
1927	StL-A	74	191	14	44	7	0	1	22	20	6	.230	.303	.283	51	-14	0	3	-2	.983	-1	C-60	-1.0
1928	StL-A	10	24	4	7	1	0	0	6	8	0	.292	.485	.333	115	1	0	0	0	.958	-4	C-10	-0.2
Total	17	1590	4795	448	1259	248	34	13	537	592	383	.263	.349	.337	88	-61	30	23		.972	-6	*C-1532/1-1	3.2

■ BILL O'NEILL
O'Neill, William John b: 1/22/1880, St.John, N.B., Can. d: 7/20/20, Woodhaven, N.Y. BB/TR, 5'11", 175 lbs. Deb: 5/7/04

YEAR	TM/L	G	AB	R	H	2B	3B	HR	RBI	BB	SO	AVG	OBP	SLG	PRO+	BR/A	SB	CS	SBR	FA	FR	G/POS	TPR
1904	Bos-A	17	51	7	10	1	0	0	5	2		.196	.226	.216	38	-4	0			.933	-2	/O-9,S-2	-0.7
	Was-A	95	365	33	89	10	1	1	16	22		.244	.294	.285	85	-6	22			.899	-10	O-93/2-3	-2.4
	Yr	112	416	40	99	11	1	1	21	24		.238	.286	.276	79	-10	22			.902	-12	*O-102/2-3,S	-3.1
1906	*Chi-A	94	330	37	82	4	1	1	21	22		.248	.301	.276	83	-6	19			.949	-6	O-93	-1.8
Total	2	206	746	77	181	15	2	2	42	46		.243	.293	.276	81	-15	41			.921	-18	O-195/2-3,S	-4.9

■ RALPH ONIS
Onis, Manuel Dominguez "Curly" b: 10/24/08, Tampa, Fla. BR/TR, 5'9", 180 lbs. Deb: 4/27/35

YEAR	TM/L	G	AB	R	H	2B	3B	HR	RBI	BB	SO	AVG	OBP	SLG	PRO+	BR/A	SB	CS	SBR	FA	FR	G/POS	TPR
1935	Bro-N	1	1	0	0	0	0	0	0	0	0	1.000	1.000	1.000	449	0	0			.500	-0	/C-1	0.0

■ EDDIE ONSLOW
Onslow, Edward Joseph b: 2/17/1893, Meadville, Pa. d: 5/8/81, Dennison, Ohio BL/TL, 6', 170 lbs. Deb: 8/7/12 F

YEAR	TM/L	G	AB	R	H	2B	3B	HR	RBI	BB	SO	AVG	OBP	SLG	PRO+	BR/A	SB	CS	SBR	FA	FR	G/POS	TPR
1912	Det-A	36	128	11	29	1	2	1	13	3		.227	.250	.289	56	-8	3			.972	-3	1-35	-1.2
1913	Det-A	17	55	7	14	1	0	0	8	5	9	.255	.328	.273	77	-1	1			.990	-1	1-17	-0.3
1918	Cle-A	2	6	0	1	0	0	0	0	1		.167	.167	.167	1	-1	0			.000	0	/O-1	-0.2
1927	Was-A	9	18	1	4	1	0	0	1	0	1	.222	.263	.278	41	-2	0	0	0	1.000	0	/1-5	-0.2
Total	4	64	207	19	48	3	2	1	22	9	10	.232	.271	.280	59	-12	4	0		.979	-5	/1-57,O-1	-1.9

■ JACK ONSLOW
Onslow, John James b: 10/13/1888, Scottdale, Pa. d: 12/22/60, Concord, Mass. BR/TR, 5'11", 180 lbs. Deb: 5/2/12 FMC

YEAR	TM/L	G	AB	R	H	2B	3B	HR	RBI	BB	SO	AVG	OBP	SLG	PRO+	BR/A	SB	CS	SBR	FA	FR	G/POS	TPR
1912	Det-A	36	69	7	11	1	0	0	4	10		.159	.284	.174	33	-6	1			.948	1	C-35/O-1	-0.2
1917	NY-N	9	8	1	2	1	0	0	0	0		.250	.333	.375	121	0	0			.929	-0	/C-9	0.0
Total	2	45	77	8	13	2	0	0	4	10	1	.169	.289	.195	41	-5	1			.947	0	/C-44,O-1	-0.2

■ STEVE ONTIVEROS
Ontiveros, Steven Robert b: 10/26/51, Bakersfield, Cal. BB/TR, 6', 185 lbs. Deb: 8/5/73

YEAR	TM/L	G	AB	R	H	2B	3B	HR	RBI	BB	SO	AVG	OBP	SLG	PRO+	BR/A	SB	CS	SBR	FA	FR	G/POS	TPR
1973	SF-N	24	33	3	8	0	0	1	5	4	7	.242	.324	.333	79	-1	0	0	0	1.000	1	/1-5,O-1	0.0

YEAR	TM/L	G	AB	R	H	2B	3B	HR	RBI	BB	SO	AVG	OBP	SLG	PRO+	BR/A	SB	CS	SBR	FA	FR	G/POS	TPR
1974	SF-N	120	343	45	91	15	1	4	33	57	41	.265	.375	.350	99	2	0	0	0	.929	-6	3-75,1-19/O	-0.6
1975	SF-N	108	325	21	94	16	0	3	31	55	44	.289	.395	.366	108	6	2	0	1	.923	-2	3-89/O-8,1	0.5
1976	SF-N	59	74	8	13	3	0	0	5	6	11	.176	.247	.216	31	-7	0	0	0	1.000	-5	/3-7,O-7,1	-1.3
1977	Chi-N	156	546	54	163	32	3	10	68	81	69	.299	.392	.423	107	7	3	3	-1	.955	-2	*3-155	0.3
1978	Chi-N	82	276	34	67	14	4	1	22	34	33	.243	.326	.333	75	-9	0	2	-1	.965	10	3-77/1-1	-0.1
1979	Chi-N	152	519	58	148	28	2	4	57	58	68	.285	.365	.370	92	-4	0	1	-1	.941	-4	*3-142/1-1	-1.1
1980	Chi-N	31	77	7	16	3	0	1	3	14	17	.208	.330	.286	68	-3	0	0	0	.929	-1	3-24	-0.4
Total	8	732	2193	230	600	111	10	24	224	309	290	.274	.367	.366	94	-8	5	6	-2	.944	-9	3-569/1-34,O	-2.7

■ JOSE OQUENDO
Oquendo, Jose Manuel (Contreras)   b: 7/4/63, Rio Piedras, P.R.   BB/TR, 5'10", 160 lbs.   Deb: 5/2/83

YEAR	TM/L	G	AB	R	H	2B	3B	HR	RBI	BB	SO	AVG	OBP	SLG	PRO+	BR/A	SB	CS	SBR	FA	FR	G/POS	TPR
1983	NY-N	120	328	29	70	7	0	1	17	19	60	.213	.261	.244	41	-26	8	9	-3	.960	6	*S-116	-1.4
1984	NY-N	81	189	23	42	5	0	0	10	15	26	.222	.286	.249	52	-12	10	1	2	.972	2	S-67	-0.3
1986	StL-N	76	138	20	41	4	1	0	13	15	20	.297	.366	.341	97	-0	2	3	-1	.956	-6	S-29,2-21/3O	-0.5
1987	*StL-N	116	248	43	71	9	0	1	24	54	29	.286	.414	.335	99	3	4	4	-1	1.000	3	O-46,2-32,S/3P	0.5
1988	StL-N	148	451	36	125	10	4	7	46	52	40	.277	.352	.350	101	2	4	6	-2	.997	8	2-69,3-47,S10/PC	1.1
1989	StL-N	163	556	59	162	28	7	1	48	79	59	.291	.380	.372	112	12	3	5	-2	**.994**	20	*2-156/S-7,1	3.8
1990	StL-N	156	469	38	118	17	5	1	37	74	46	.252	.354	.316	85	-7	1	1	-0	**.996**	-1	*2-150/S-4	-0.5
1991	StL-N	127	366	37	88	11	4	1	26	67	48	.240	.350	.301	87	-3	1	2	-1	.988	15	*2-118,S-22/1P	1.5
1992	StL-N	14	35	3	9	3	1	0	3	5	3	.257	.350	.400	115	1	0	0	-1	1.000	1	/2-9,S-5	0.1
1993	StL-N	46	73	7	15	0	0	0	4	12	8	.205	.318	.205	44	-5	0	0	0	.988	14	S-22,2-16	1.0
1994	StL-N	55	129	13	34	2	2	0	9	21	16	.264	.367	.310	82	-3	1	1	-0	.945	-5	S-28,2-16	-0.6
Total	11	1102	2982	308	775	96	21	12	237	413	355	.260	.351	.318	87	-38	34	32	-9	.993	57	2-587,S-340/O31PC	4.7

■ TOM ORAN
Oran, Thomas   b: 1845,   d: 9/22/1886, St.Louis, Mo.   Deb: 5/4/1875

YEAR	TM/L	G	AB	R	H	2B	3B	HR	RBI	BB	SO	AVG	OBP	SLG	PRO+	BR/A	SB	CS	SBR	FA	FR	G/POS	TPR
1875	RS-n	19	81	7	16	5	1	0		1		.198	.207	.284	75	-1						O-18	-0.1

■ ERNIE ORAVETZ
Oravetz, Ernest Eugene   b: 1/24/32, Johnstown, Pa.   BB/TL, 5'4", 145 lbs.   Deb: 4/11/55

YEAR	TM/L	G	AB	R	H	2B	3B	HR	RBI	BB	SO	AVG	OBP	SLG	PRO+	BR/A	SB	CS	SBR	FA	FR	G/POS	TPR
1955	Was-A	100	263	24	71	5	1	0	25	26	19	.270	.338	.297	76	-8	1	2	-1	.967	-3	O-57	-1.5
1956	Was-A	88	137	20	34	3	2	0	11	27	20	.248	.372	.299	79	-3	1	0	0	.946	-2	O-31	-0.6
Total	2	188	400	44	105	8	3	0	36	53	39	.262	.350	.298	77	-11	2	2	-1	.961	-5	/O-88	-2.1

■ TONY ORDENANA
Ordenana, Antonio (Rodriguez) "Mosquito"   b: 10/30/18, Guanabacoa, Havana, Cuba   d: 9/29/88, Miami, Fla.   BR/TR, 5'9", 158 lbs.   Deb: 10/3/43

YEAR	TM/L	G	AB	R	H	2B	3B	HR	RBI	BB	SO	AVG	OBP	SLG	PRO+	BR/A	SB	CS	SBR	FA	FR	G/POS	TPR
1943	Pit-N	1	4	0	2	0	0	0	3	0	0	.500	.500	.500	183	0	0			1.000	1	/S-1	0.1

■ JOE ORENGO
Orengo, Joseph Charles   b: 11/29/14, San Francisco, Cal   d: 7/24/88, San Francisco, Cal.   BR/TR, 6', 185 lbs.   Deb: 4/18/39

YEAR	TM/L	G	AB	R	H	2B	3B	HR	RBI	BB	SO	AVG	OBP	SLG	PRO+	BR/A	SB	CS	SBR	FA	FR	G/POS	TPR
1939	StL-N	7	3	0	0	0	0	0	0	0	1	.000	.000	.000	-94	-1	0			.667	-0	/S-7	-0.1
1940	StL-N	129	415	58	119	23	4	7	56	65	90	.287	.383	.412	113	9	9			.952	5	2-77,3-34,S	2.1
1941	NY-N	77	252	23	54	11	2	4	25	28	49	.214	.298	.321	73	-9	1			.958	18	3-59/S-9,2	1.2
1943	NY-N	83	266	28	58	8	2	6	29	36	46	.218	.311	.331	85	-5	1			.992	4	1-82	-0.5
	Bro-N	7	15	1	3	2	0	0	1	4	2	.200	.368	.333	103	0	0			1.000	-0	/3-6	0.0
	Yr	90	281	29	61	10	2	6	30	40	48	.217	.315	.331	86	-5	1			.992	4	1-82/3-6	-0.5
1944	Det-A	46	154	14	31	10	0	0	10	20	29	.201	.297	.266	58	-8	1	1	-0	.903	6	S-29,3-11/12	0.0
1945	Chi-A	17	15	5	1	0	0	0	1	3	2	.067	.222	.067	-15	-2	0	0	0	.923	1	/3-7,2-1	-0.1
Total	6	366	1120	129	266	54	8	17	122	156	219	.237	.320	.346	88	-16	12	1		.957	34	3-117/1-87,2S	2.6

■ GEORGE ORME
Orme, George William   b: 9/16/1891, Lebanon, Ind.   d: 3/16/62, Indianapolis, Ind.   BR/TR, 5'10", 160 lbs.   Deb: 9/14/20

YEAR	TM/L	G	AB	R	H	2B	3B	HR	RBI	BB	SO	AVG	OBP	SLG	PRO+	BR/A	SB	CS	SBR	FA	FR	G/POS	TPR
1920	Bos-A	4	6	4	2	0	0	0	1	3	0	.333	.556	.333	146	1	0	0	0	1.000	-0	/O-3	0.1

■ JESS ORNDORFF
Orndorff, Jesse Walworth Thayer   b: 1/15/1881, Chicago, Ill.   d: 9/28/60, Cardiff-By-The-Sea, Cal.   BB/TR, 6', 168 lbs.   Deb: 4/18/07

YEAR	TM/L	G	AB	R	H	2B	3B	HR	RBI	BB	SO	AVG	OBP	SLG	PRO+	BR/A	SB	CS	SBR	FA	FR	G/POS	TPR
1907	Bos-N	5	17	0	2	0	0	0	0	0		.118	.118	.118	-26	-2	0			.900	-2	/C-5	-0.5

■ FRANK O'ROURKE
O'Rourke, James Francis "Blackie"   b: 11/28/1894, Hamilton, Ont., Can   d: 5/14/86, Chatham, N.J.   BR/TR, 5'10.5", 165 lbs.   Deb: 6/12/12

YEAR	TM/L	G	AB	R	H	2B	3B	HR	RBI	BB	SO	AVG	OBP	SLG	PRO+	BR/A	SB	CS	SBR	FA	FR	G/POS	TPR
1912	Bos-N	61	196	11	24	3	1	0	16	11	50	.122	.177	.148	-10	-30	1			.915	-7	S-59/3-1	-3.3
1917	Bro-N	64	198	18	47	7	1	0	15	14	25	.237	.294	.283	75	-6	11			.954	7	3-58	0.3
1918	Bro-N	4	12	0	2	0	0	0	2	1	3	.167	.231	.167	22	-1	0			.857	1	/2-2,O-1	0.0
1920	Was-A	14	54	8	16	1	0	0	5	2	5	.296	.321	.315	71	-2	2	1	0	.952	4	S-13/3-1	0.3
1921	Was-A	123	444	51	104	17	8	3	54	26	56	.234	.287	.329	60	-29	6	7	-2	.922	-7	*S-122	-2.5
1922	Bos-A	67	216	28	57	14	1	0	17	20	28	.264	.335	.370	84	-5	6	6	-0	.909	-12	S-49,3-20	-1.2
1924	Det-A	47	181	28	50	11	2	0	19	12	19	.276	.332	.359	79	-6	7	4	-0	.970	11	2-40/S-7	0.6
1925	Det-A	124	482	88	141	40	7	5	57	32	37	.293	.350	.436	100	-2	5	8	-3	**.971**	15	*2-118/3-6	1.1
1926	Det-A	111	363	43	88	16	1	1	41	35	33	.242	.321	.300	62	-20	8	6	-1	.936	10	3-60,2-41,S	-0.6
1927	StL-A	140	538	85	144	25	3	1	39	64	43	.268	.338	.331	77	-16	18	9	1	.955	11	*3-121,2-16/1	0.2
1928	StL-A	99	391	54	103	24	3	1	62	21	19	.263	.303	.348	68	-18	10	2	0	.954	-9	3-96/S-2	-2.0
1929	StL-A	154	585	81	147	23	9	2	62	41	28	.251	.306	.332	62	-34	14	7	0	.943	-18	*3-151/2-3,S	-4.3
1930	StL-A	115	400	52	107	15	4	1	41	35	30	.268	.326	.333	65	-21	11	9	-2	.950	10	*3-84,S-23/1	-0.5
1931	StL-A	8	9	0	2	0	0	0	0	0	2	.222	.222	.222	17	-1	1	0		1.000	1	/S-2,1-1	0.0
Total	14	1131	4069	547	1032	196	42	15	430	314	377	.254	.315	.333	68	-189	100	59		.949	16	3-598,S-289,2/1O	-12.0

■ JIM O'ROURKE
O'Rourke, James Henry "Orator Jim"   b: 9/1/1850, Bridgeport, Conn.   d: 1/8/19, Bridgeport, Conn.   BR/TR, 5'8", 185 lbs.   Deb: 4/26/1872   FMUH

YEAR	TM/L	G	AB	R	H	2B	3B	HR	RBI	BB	SO	AVG	OBP	SLG	PRO+	BR/A	SB	CS	SBR	FA	FR	G/POS	TPR
1872	Man-n	23	100	27	33	3	0	0	15	2	0	.330	.343	.360	124	3						S-16/C-5,3	0.2
1873	Bos-n	57	280	79	98	22	3	1	46	14	1	.350	.381	.461	135	10						1-32,O-22/C	0.9
1874	Bos-n	70	332	82	105	12	6	**5**			2	.316	.320	.434	130	9						*1-70	0.7
1875	Bos-n	75	364	98	106	16	8	**6**			10	.291	.310	.429	147	16						O-45,3-27/1	1.4
1876	Bos-N	70	312	61	102	17	3	2	43	15	17	.327	.358	.420	156	18				.856	-3	*O-68/1-2,C	1.3
1877	Bos-N	61	265	**68**	96	14	4	0	23	**20**	9	.362	**.407**	.445	162	19				.846	-0	*O-60/1-1	1.4
1878	Bos-N	60	255	44	71	17	1	7	29	5	21	.278	.292	.412	120	4				.860	4	*O-57/1-2,C	0.4
1879	Pro-N	81	362	69	126	19	9	1	46	13	10	.348	**.371**	.459	174	28				.785	-9	*O-56,1-20/C3	1.5
1880	Bos-N	86	363	71	100	20	11	**6**	45	21	6	.275	.315	.441	158	22				.907	-3	O-37,1-19,S3/C	1.8
1881	Buf-N	83	348	71	105	27	7	0	30	27	18	.302	.352	.402	139	16				.821	-20	*3-56,O-18/CS1M	-0.2
1882	Buf-N	84	370	62	104	28	2	2	37	13	13	.281	.305	.370	114	5				.866	-0	*O-81/S-2,C3M	0.4
1883	Buf-N	94	436	102	143	29	8	1	38	15	13	.328	.350	.438	135	17				.866	-12	O-61,C-33/3SPM	0.6
1884	Buf-N	108	467	119	**162**	33	7	5	63	35	17	**.347**	.392	.480	167	35				.894	-11	*O-86,1-18,C/P3M	2.0
1885	NY-N	112	477	119	143	21	**16**	5	42	40	21	.300	.354	.442	158	31				.940	-16	*O-112/C-8	1.2
1886	NY-N	105	440	106	136	26	6	1	34	39	21	.309	.365	.402	132	17	14			.926	8	O-63,C-47/1	2.6
1887	NY-N	103	397	73	113	15	13	3	88	36	11	.285	.352	.411	116	10	46			.890	-9	C-40,3-38,O/2	0.4
1888	*NY-N	107	409	50	112	16	6	4	50	24	30	.274	.319	.372	121	10	25			.960	-1	*O-87,C-15/13	0.7
1889	*NY-N	128	502	89	161	36	4	3	81	40	34	.321	.372	.438	126	16	33			.893	-8	*O-128/C-1	0.5
1890	NY-P	111	478	112	172	37	4	9	115	33	23	.360	.410	.515	134	20	23			.930	5	*O-111	1.6
1891	NY-N	136	555	92	164	28	7	5	95	33	21	.295	.334	.398	118	10	19			.906	-1	*O-126,C-14	0.6
1892	NY-N	115	448	62	136	28	5	0	56	30	15	.304	.354	.388	127	14	16			.913	-10	*O-111/C-4,1	0.1
1893	Was-N	129	547	75	157	22	5	2	95	49	26	.287	.354	.356	91	-6	15			.927	-3	O-87,1-33/CM	-0.4
1904	NY-N	1	4	1	1	0	0	0	1	0	0	.250	.250	.250	52	-0	0			.800	-1	/C-1	-0.1
Total	4 n	225	1076	286	342	53	17	12	61	28	1	.318	.335	.432	137	39						1-105/O-67,3SC	3.2
Total	19	1774	7435	1446	2304	414	132	50	1010	481	348	.310	.355	.421	133	286	191			.898	-80	*O-1377,C-209,31/SP2	16.1

YEAR	TM/L	G	AB	R	H	2B	3B	HR	RBI	BB	SO	AVG	OBP	SLG	PRO+	BR/A	SB	CS	SBR	FA	FR	G/POS	TPR
■ **CHARLIE O'ROURKE**					O'Rourke, James Patrick	b: 6/22/37, Walla Walla, Wash.				BR/TR, 6'2", 195 lbs.	Deb: 6/16/59												
1959	StL-N	2	2	0	0	0	0	0	0	0	0	.000	.000	.000	-94	-1	0	0	0	.000	0	H	-0.1
■ **QUEENIE O'ROURKE**					O'Rourke, James Stephen	b: 12/26/1883, Bridgeport, Conn.				d: 12/22/55, Sparrows Point, Md	BR/TR, 5'7", 150 lbs.	Deb: 8/15/08	F										
1908	NY-A	34	108	5	25	1	0	0	3	4		.231	.259	.241	62	-5	4			1.000	-6	O-14,S-11/23	-1.3
■ **JOHN O'ROURKE**					O'Rourke, John	b: 8/23/1849, Bridgeport, Conn.				d: 6/23/11, Boston, Mass.	BL/TL, 6', 190 lbs.	Deb: 5/1/1879	F										
1879	Bos-N	72	317	69	108	17	11	6	**62**	8	32	.341	.357	**.521**	181	26				.882	2	*O-71	2.3
1880	Bos-N	81	313	30	86	22	8	3	36	18	32	.275	.314	.425	153	17				.871	5	*O-81	1.9
1883	NY-a	77	315	49	85	19	5	2		21		.270	.315	.381	118	6				.856	-3	*O-76/1-1	0.1
Total	3	230	945	148	279	58	24	11	98	47	64	.295	.329	.442	150	49				.871	4	O-228/1-1	4.3
■ **JOE O'ROURKE**					O'Rourke, Joseph Leo Jr.	b: 10/28/04, Philadelphia, Pa.				d: 6/27/90, Philadelphia, Pa.	BL/TR, 5'7", 145 lbs.	Deb: 4/19/29	F										
1929	Phi-N	3	3	0	0	0	0	0	0	0	0	.000	.000	.000	-94	-1	0			.000	0	H	-0.1
■ **PATSY O'ROURKE**					O'Rourke, Joseph Leo Sr.	b: 4/13/1881, Philadelphia, Pa.				d: 4/18/56, Philadelphia, Pa.	BR/TR, 5'7", 160 lbs.	Deb: 4/16/08	F										
1908	StL-N	53	164	8	32	4	2	0	16	14		.195	.263	.244	65	-6	2			.860	-7	S-53	-1.5
■ **TOM O'ROURKE**					O'Rourke, Thomas Joseph	b: 10/1865, New York, N.Y.				d: 7/19/29, New York, N.Y.	TR, 5'9", 158 lbs.	Deb: 5/11/1887											
1887	Bos-N	22	78	12	12	3	0	0	10	7	6	.154	.233	.192	19	-8	4			.777	-5	C-21/O-1,3	-1.0
1888	Bos-N	20	74	3	13	0	0	0	4	1	9	.176	.187	.176	16	-7	2			.881	1	C-20/O-1	-0.4
1890	NY-a	2	7	1	0	0	0	0	0	1	0	.000	.125	.000	-63	-1	0			.864	1	/C-2	0.0
	Syr-a	41	153	16	33	8	0	0		12		.216	.277	.268	68	-6	2			.907	-12	C-40/1-1	-1.3
Total	3	85	312	32	58	11	0	0	14	21	15	.186	.242	.221	39	-23	8			.867	-15	/C-83,O-2,13	-2.7
■ **TIM O'ROURKE**					O'Rourke, Timothy Patrick "Voiceless Tim"	b: 5/18/1864, Chicago, Ill.				d: 4/20/38, Seattle, Wash.	BL/TR, 5'10", 170 lbs.	Deb: 5/27/1890											
1890	Syr-a	87	332	48	94	13	6	1		36		.283	.360	.367	128	13	22			.866	-11	3-87	0.4
1891	Col-a	34	136	22	38	1	3	0	12	15	7	.279	.359	.331	104	1	9			.879	0	3-34	0.3
1892	Bal-N	63	239	40	74	8	4	0	35	24	19	.310	.383	.377	123	7	12			.869	-14	S-58/O-4,3	-0.4
1893	Bal-N	31	135	22	49	4	1	0	19	12	4	.363	.423	.407	119	4	5			.980	-4	O-25/3-5,S	-0.1
	Lou-N	92	352	80	99	8	4	0	53	77	15	.281	.421	.327	108	11	22			.865	-21	S-60,O-26/3	-0.6
	Yr	123	487	102	148	12	5	0	72	89	19	.304	.422	.349	112	16	27			.861	-25	S-61,O-51,3	-0.7
1894	Lou-N	55	220	46	61	3	3	0	27	23	9	.277	.351	.318	67	-11	9			.977	-1	1-30,O-18/S32	-1.0
	StL-N	18	71	10	20	4	1	0	10	8	3	.282	.354	.366	74	-3	2			.861	-2	3-18	-0.4
	Was-N	7	25	4	5	2	1	0	2	2	1	.200	.259	.360	50	-2	0			.909	1	/2-4,S-3	-0.1
	Yr	80	316	60	86	9	5	0	39	33	13	.272	.345	.332	67	-16	11			.977	-2	1-30,3-21,O/S2	-1.5
Total	5	387	1510	272	440	43	23	1	158	197	58	.291	.380	.352	105	20	81			.861	-51	3-154,S-125/O12	-1.9
■ **DAVE ORR**					Orr, David L.	b: 9/29/1859, New York, N.Y.				d: 6/3/15, Brooklyn, N.Y.	BR/TR, 5'11", 250 lbs.	Deb: 5/17/1883	M										
1883	NY-a	1	4	1	1	1	0	0		0		.250	.250	.500	130	0				1.000	0	/1-1	0.0
	NY-N	1	3	0	0	0	0	0	0	0	1	.000	.000	.000	-99	-1				1.000	0	/O-1	-0.1
	NY-a	12	46	5	15	3	3	2		0		.326	.326	.652	198	5				.938	-2	1-12	0.2
1884	*NY-a	110	458	82	**162**	32	13	9		5		.354	.362	.539	195	45				.960	-5	*1-110/O-3	2.4
1885	NY-a	107	444	76	152	29	**21**	6		8		.342	.358	**.543**	197	47				.966	-3	*1-107/P-3	2.7
1886	NY-a	136	571	93	**193**	25	**31**	7	17			**.338**	.363	**.527**	186	52	16			**.981**	-0	*1-136	3.1
1887	NY-a	84	345	63	127	25	10	2	22			.368	.368	.516	164	29	17			.969	-1	1-81/O-3M	1.6
1888	Bro-a	99	394	57	120	20	5	1	59	7		.305	.330	.388	130	12	11			.979	4	*1-99	0.6
1889	Col-a	134	560	70	183	31	12	4	87	9	38	.327	.340	.446	129	18	12			.983	9	*1-134	1.5
1890	Bro-P	107	464	89	173	32	13	6	124	30	11	.373	.411	.537	145	26	10			.972	-5	*1-107	1.2
Total	8	791	3289	536	1126	198	108	37	270	98	50	.342	.366	.502	163	232	66			.973	-3	1-787/O-7,P	13.2
■ **BILLY ORR**					Orr, William John	b: 4/22/1891, San Francisco, Cal				d: 3/10/67, Santarium, Cal.	BR/TR, 5'11", 168 lbs.	Deb: 5/3/13											
1913	Phi-A	30	67	6	13	1	1	0	7	4	10	.194	.239	.239	41	-5	1			.967	-2	S-16/1-3,32	-0.6
1914	Phi-A	10	24	3	4	1	1	0	1	2	5	.167	.231	.292	59	-1	1	1	-0	.810	-4	/S-6,3-1	-0.6
Total	2	40	91	9	17	2	2	0	8	6	15	.187	.237	.253	46	-6	2	1		.927	-6	/S-22,3-4,12	-1.2
■ **ERNIE ORSATTI**					Orsatti, Ernest Ralph	b: 9/8/02, Los Angeles, Cal.				d: 9/4/68, Canoga Park, Cal.	BL/TL, 5'7.5", 154 lbs.	Deb: 9/4/27											
1927	StL-N	27	92	15	29	7	3	0	12	11	12	.315	.388	.457	122	3	2			.922	-1	O-26	0.1
1928	*StL-N	27	69	10	21	6	0	3	15	10	11	.304	.400	.522	137	4	0			1.000	4	O-17/1-5	0.1
1929	StL-N	113	346	64	115	21	7	3	39	33	43	.332	.394	.460	110	6	7			.974	4	O-77,1-10	0.4
1930	*StL-N	48	131	24	42	8	4	1	15	12	18	.321	.382	.466	100	0	1			.985	4	1-22,O-11	0.1
1931	*StL-N	70	158	27	46	16	6	0	19	14	16	.291	.349	.468	113	3	1			.988	-5	O-45/1-1	-0.5
1932	StL-N	101	375	44	126	27	6	2	44	18	29	.336	.368	.456	117	9	5			.976	-9	O-96/1-1	-0.6
1933	StL-N	120	436	55	130	21	6	0	38	33	33	.298	.348	.374	101	-1	14			.986	2	*O-107/1-3	-0.4
1934	*StL-N	105	337	39	101	14	4	0	31	27	31	.300	.353	.365	87	-5	6			.986	-2	O-90	-1.1
1935	StL-N	90	221	28	53	9	3	1	24	18	25	.240	.297	.321	64	-11	10			.975	-5	O-60	-1.8
Total	9	701	2165	306	663	129	39	10	237	176	218	.306	.360	.416	102	8	46			.979	-14	O-529/1-42	-3.7
■ **JOHN ORSINO**					Orsino, John Joseph "Horse"	b: 4/22/38, Teaneck, N.J.				BR/TR, 6'3", 215 lbs.	Deb: 7/14/61												
1961	SF-N	25	83	5	23	4	2	4	12	3	13	.277	.310	.506	116	1	0	0	0	.959	-3	C-25	0.0
1962	*SF-N	18	48	4	13	2	0	0	4	5	11	.271	.340	.313	78	-1	0	0	0	.963	-2	C-16	-0.2
1963	Bal-A	116	379	53	103	18	1	19	56	38	53	.272	.352	.475	134	17	2	3	-1	.990	-6	*C-109/1-3	1.4
1964	Bal-A	81	248	21	55	10	0	8	23	23	55	.222	.293	.359	81	-7	0	0	0	.976	1	C-66/1-5	-0.4
1965	Bal-A	77	232	30	54	10	2	9	28	23	51	.233	.315	.409	102	1	1	0	0	.987	-8	C-62/1-5	-0.4
1966	Was-A	14	23	1	4	1	0	0	0	0	7	.174	.174	.217	12	-3	0	0	0	1.000	-0	/1-5,C-2	-0.3
1967	Was-A	1	1	0	0	0	0	0	0	0	1	.000	.000	.000	-99	-0	0	0	0	.000	0	H	-0.0
Total	7	332	1014	114	252	44	5	40	123	92	191	.249	.321	.420	106	8	3	3	-1	.982	-18	C-280/1-18	0.1
■ **JOE ORSULAK**					Orsulak, Joseph Michael	b: 5/31/62, Glen Ridge, N.J.				BL/TL, 6'1", 186 lbs.	Deb: 9/1/83												
1983	Pit-N	7	11	0	2	0	0	0	0	0	1	.182	.182	.182	1	0	1	1	-1	1.000	0	/O-4	-0.2
1984	Pit-N	32	67	12	17	1	2	0	3	1	7	.254	.275	.328	69	-3	3	1	0	1.000	-1	O-25	-0.5
1985	Pit-N	121	397	54	119	14	6	0	21	26	27	.300	.344	.365	100	-0	24	11	1	.976	-0	*O-115	-0.3
1986	Pit-N	138	401	60	100	19	6	2	19	28	38	.249	.300	.342	75	-14	24	11	2	.981	-5	*O-120	-2.2
1988	Bal-A	125	379	48	109	21	3	8	27	23	30	.288	.333	.422	113	6	9	6	0	.979	-6	*O-117	-0.5
1989	Bal-A	123	390	59	111	22	5	7	55	41	35	.285	.354	.421	122	11	5	3	-0	.985	7	*O-109/D-5	-0.5
1990	Bal-A	124	413	49	111	14	3	11	57	46	48	.269	.343	.397	110	6	6	2	0	.989	11	*O-109/D-5	1.1
1991	Bal-A	143	486	57	135	22	5	5	43	28	45	.278	.322	.358	92	-6	6	2	1	.997	10	*O-132/D-2	0.2
1992	Bal-A	117	391	45	113	18	3	4	39	28	34	.289	.343	.381	100	0	5	4	-1	.983	4	*O-110/D-1	0.1
1993	NY-N	134	409	59	116	15	4	8	35	28	25	.284	.333	.399	96	-3	5	4	-1	.978	-6	*O-114/1-4	-1.2
1994	NY-N	96	292	39	76	3	4	8	42	16	21	.260	.305	.353	70	-13	4	2	0	.979	-8	O-90/1-6	-2.3
Total	11	1160	3636	482	1009	149	33	53	342	265	312	.278	.330	.380	97	-17	91	55	-6	.984	5	*O-1045/D-13,1	-4.3
■ **JORGE ORTA**					Orta, Jorge (Nunez)	b: 11/26/50, Mazatlan, Mexico				BL/TR, 5'10", 175 lbs.	Deb: 4/15/72												
1972	Chi-A	51	124	20	25	3	3	1	11	6	37	.202	.244	.315	64	-6	3	3	-1	.958	-0	S-18,2-14/3	-0.5
1973	Chi-A	128	425	46	113	9	10	6	40	37	87	.266	.326	.376	94	-3	8	8	-2	.969	-27	*2-122/S-1	-2.6

YEAR	TM/L	G	AB	R	H	2B	3B	HR	RBI	BB	SO	AVG	OBP	SLG	PRO+	BR/A	SB	CS	SBR	FA	FR	G/POS	TPR
1974	Chi-A	139	525	73	166	31	2	10	67	40	88	.316	.368	.440	128	19	9	5	-0	.971	-13	*2-123,D-10/S	1.2
1975	Chi-A†	140	542	64	165	26	10	11	83	48	67	.304	.365	.450	128	19	16	9	-1	.978	-12	*2-135/D-2	1.4
1976	Chi-A	158	636	74	174	29	8	14	72	38	77	.274	.320	.410	112	8	24	8	2	.971	2	O-77,3-49,D	0.8
1977	Chi-A	144	564	71	159	27	8	11	84	46	49	.282	.338	.417	105	3	4	4	-1	.970	-47	*2-139	-3.5
1978	Chi-A	117	420	45	115	19	2	13	53	42	39	.274	.345	.421	114	8	1	2	-1	.984	-22	*2-114/D-2	-0.7
1979	Chi-A	113	325	49	85	18	3	11	46	44	33	.262	.351	.437	111	5	1	5	-3	.978	-10	D-62,2-41	-0.7
1980	Cle-A☆	129	481	78	140	18	3	10	64	71	44	.291	.384	.403	116	13	6	5	-1	.982	13	*O-120/D-7	2.0
1981	Cle-A	88	338	50	92	14	3	5	34	21	43	.272	.317	.376	100	-0	4	3	-1	.994	4	O-86	0.0
1982	LA-N	86	115	13	25	5	0	2	8	12	13	.217	.297	.313	73	-4	0	1	-1	.947	1	O-17	-0.4
1983	Tor-A	103	245	30	58	6	3	10	38	19	29	.237	.292	.408	85	-6	1	2	-1	1.000	-3	D-70,O-17	-1.2
1984	*KC-A	122	403	50	120	23	7	9	50	28	39	.298	.346	.457	119	10	0	1	-1	.980	-3	D-83,O-26/2	0.4
1985	*KC-A	110	300	32	80	21	1	4	45	22	28	.267	.321	.383	92	-4	2	1	-0	.000	0	D-85	-0.5
1986	KC-A	106	336	35	93	14	2	9	46	23	34	.277	.323	.411	96	-2	0	3	-2	.000	0	D-87	-0.6
1987	KC-A	21	50	3	9	4	0	2	4	3	8	.180	.226	.380	55	-3	0	0	-0	.000	0	D-12	-0.4
Total	16	1755	5829	733	1619	267	63	130	745	500	715	.278	.338	.412	108	56	79	60	-12	.974	-117	2-689,D-451,O/3S	-5.3

■ FRANK ORTENZIO

Ortenzio, Frank Joseph b: 2/24/51, Fresno, Cal. BR/TR, 6'2", 215 lbs. Deb: 9/9/73

YEAR	TM/L	G	AB	R	H	2B	3B	HR	RBI	BB	SO	AVG	OBP	SLG	PRO+	BR/A	SB	CS	SBR	FA	FR	G/POS	TPR
1973	KC-A	9	25	1	7	2	0	1	6	2	3	.280	.333	.480	118	0	0	0		.983	1	/1-7,D-1	0.1

■ AL ORTH

Orth, Albert Lewis "Smiling Al" or "The Curveless Wonder" b: 9/5/1872, Tipton, Ind. d: 10/8/48, Lynchburg, Va. BL/TR, 6', 200 lbs. Deb: 8/15/1895 U

YEAR	TM/L	G	AB	R	H	2B	3B	HR	RBI	BB	SO	AVG	OBP	SLG	PRO+	BR/A	SB	CS	SBR	FA	FR	G/POS	TPR
1895	Phi-N	11	45	8	16	4	0	1	13	1	6	.356	.370	.511	125	1	0			.842	-2	P-11	0.0
1896	Phi-N	25	82	12	21	3	3	1	13	3	11	.256	.282	.402	80	-3	2			.901	1	P-25	0.0
1897	Phi-N	53	152	26	50	7	4	1	17	3		.329	.342	.447	110	1	5			.929	0	P-36/O-6	0.0
1898	Phi-N	39	123	17	36	6	4	1	14	3		.293	.310	.431	117	2	1			.959	1	P-32/O-1	0.1
1899	Phi-N	22	62	5	13	3	1	1	5	1		.210	.222	.339	55	-4	2			.793	-4	P-21/O-1	-0.1
1900	Phi-N	39	129	6	40	4	1	1	21	2		.310	.326	.380	95	-1	2			.943	1	P-33/O-3	0.0
1901	Phi-N	41	128	14	36	6	0	1	15	3		.281	.301	.352	88	-2	3			.945	1	P-35/O-4	-0.1
1902	Was-A	56	175	20	38	3	2	2	10	9		.217	.255	.291	51	-12	2			.923	-0	P-38,O-13/1S	-0.4
1903	Was-A	55	162	19	49	9	7	0	11	4		.302	.323	.444	126	4	3			.920	-2	P-36/S-7,O1	-0.1
1904	Was-A	31	102	7	22	3	1	0	11	1		.216	.238	.265	60	-5	2			.816	-2	O-18,P-10	-0.8
	NY-A	24	64	6	19	1	1	0	7	0		.297	.308	.344	101	-0	2			.968	1	P-20/O-2	-0.0
	Yr	55	166	13	41	4	2	0	18	1		.247	.265	.295	76	-5	4			.969	-2	P-30,O-20	-0.8
1905	NY-A	55	131	13	24	3	1	1	8	4		.183	.213	.244	40	-9	2			.940	-0	P-40/1-1,O	-0.1
1906	NY-A	47	135	12	37	2	2	1	17	6		.274	.305	.341	93	-1	2			.934	0	P-45/O-1	0.0
1907	NY-A	44	105	11	34	6	0	1	13	4		.324	.355	.410	133	3	1			.920	2	P-36/O-1	0.0
1908	NY-A	38	69	4	20	1	2	0	4	2		.290	.310	.362	117	1	0			.980	-1	P-21	0.0
1909	NY-A	22	34	3	9	0	1	0	5	5		.265	.359	.324	115	1	1			1.000	-2	/2-6,P-1	-0.1
Total	15	602	1698	183	464	61	30	12	184	51	17	.273	.298	.366	91	-24	30			.932	-5	P-440/O-55,S21	-1.4

■ JUNIOR ORTIZ

Ortiz, Adalberto Colon b: 10/24/59, Humacao, P.R. BR/TR, 5'11", 176 lbs. Deb: 9/20/82

YEAR	TM/L	G	AB	R	H	2B	3B	HR	RBI	BB	SO	AVG	OBP	SLG	PRO+	BR/A	SB	CS	SBR	FA	FR	G/POS	TPR
1982	Pit-N	7	15	1	3	1	0	0	0	1	3	.200	.250	.267	43	-1	0	0	0	1.000	1	/C-7	0.0
1983	Pit-N	5	8	1	1	0	0	0	0	1	0	.125	.222	.125	-1	-1	0	0	0	1.000	0	/C-4	-0.1
	NY-N	68	185	10	47	5	0	0	12	3	34	.254	.270	.281	53	-12	1	0	0	.965	1	C-67	-0.9
	Yr	73	193	11	48	5	0	0	12	4	34	.249	.268	.275	51	-13	1	0	0	.967	1	C-71	-1.0
1984	NY-N	40	91	6	18	3	0	0	11	5	15	.198	.240	.231	33	-8	1	0	0	.980	-4	C-32	-1.1
1985	Pit-N	23	72	4	21	2	0	1	5	3	17	.292	.320	.361	91	-1	1	0	0	.985	1	C-23	0.1
1986	Pit-N	49	110	12	37	6	0	0	14	9	13	.336	.387	.391	112	2	0	1	-1	.983	-1	C-36	0.3
1987	Pit-N	75	192	16	52	8	1	1	22	15	23	.271	.324	.339	75	-7	0	2	-1	.975	-0	C-72	-0.4
1988	Pit-N	49	118	8	33	6	0	2	18	9	9	.280	.341	.381	109	1	1	4	-2	.983	-2	C-40	0.0
1989	Pit-N	91	230	16	50	6	1	1	22	20	20	.217	.286	.265	61	-12	2	2	-1	.995	-10	C-84	-2.0
1990	Min-N	71	170	18	57	7	1	0	18	12	16	.335	.386	.388	110	3	0	4	-2	1.000	1	C-68/D-3	0.5
1991	*Min-A	61	134	9	28	5	1	0	11	15	12	.209	.293	.261	52	-8	0	1	-0	.995	-0	C-60	-0.7
1992	Cle-A	86	244	20	61	7	0	0	24	12	23	.250	.296	.279	63	-12	1	3	-2	.989	-1	C-86	-1.1
1993	Cle-A	95	249	19	55	13	0	0	20	11	24	.221	.268	.273	46	-19	1	0	0	.990	11	C-95	-0.3
1994	Tex-A	29	76	3	21	2	0	0	9	5	11	.276	.320	.303	69	-3	0	1	-1	.992	-2	C-28	-0.4
Total	13	749	1894	142	484	71	4	5	186	121	222	.256	.306	.305	70	-78	8	18	-8	.986	-4	C-702/D-3	-6.1

■ JAVIER ORTIZ

Ortiz, Javier Victor b: 1/22/63, Boston, Mass. BR/TR, 6'4", 220 lbs. Deb: 6/15/90

YEAR	TM/L	G	AB	R	H	2B	3B	HR	RBI	BB	SO	AVG	OBP	SLG	PRO+	BR/A	SB	CS	SBR	FA	FR	G/POS	TPR
1990	Hou-N	30	77	7	21	5	1	1	10	12	11	.273	.371	.403	116	2	1	1	-0	.978	-3	O-25	-0.2
1991	Hou-N	47	83	7	23	4	1	1	5	14	14	.277	.381	.386	123	3	0	0	-0	1.000	-3	O-24	0.0
Total	2	77	160	14	44	9	2	2	15	26	25	.275	.376	.394	120	5	1	1	-0	.987	-6	/O-49	-0.2

■ JOSE ORTIZ

Ortiz, Jose Luis (Irizarry) b: 6/25/47, Ponce, P.R. BR/TR, 5'9.5", 155 lbs. Deb: 9/4/69

YEAR	TM/L	G	AB	R	H	2B	3B	HR	RBI	BB	SO	AVG	OBP	SLG	PRO+	BR/A	SB	CS	SBR	FA	FR	G/POS	TPR
1969	Chi-A	16	11	0	3	1	0	0	2	1	0	.273	.333	.364	90	-0	0	0	0	1.000	0	/O-8	-0.3
1970	Chi-A	15	24	4	8	1	0	1	2	2	2	.333	.407	.375	113	1	1	0	0	1.000	1	/O-8	0.2
1971	Chi-N	36	88	10	26	7	1	0	3	4	10	.295	.347	.398	96	-0	2	2	-1	1.000	-2	O-30	-0.5
Total	3	67	123	14	37	9	1	0	6	7	12	.301	.358	.390	99	0	3	2	-0	1.000	-3	/O-46	-0.6

■ LUIS ORTIZ

Ortiz, Luis Alberto (Galarza) b: 5/25/70, Santo Domingo, D.R. BR/TR, 6', 190 lbs. Deb: 8/31/93

YEAR	TM/L	G	AB	R	H	2B	3B	HR	RBI	BB	SO	AVG	OBP	SLG	PRO+	BR/A	SB	CS	SBR	FA	FR	G/POS	TPR
1993	Bos-A	9	12	0	3	0	0	0	1	0	2	.250	.250	.250	33	-1	0	0	0	1.000	1	/3-5,D-3	-0.1
1994	Bos-A	7	18	3	3	2	0	0	6	1	5	.167	.211	.278	23	-2	0	0	0	.000	0	/D-6	-0.2
Total	2	16	30	3	6	2	0	0	7	1	7	.200	.226	.267	27	-3	0	0	0	1.000	1	/D-9,3-5	-0.3

■ ROBERTO ORTIZ

Ortiz, Roberto Gonzalo (Nunez) b: 6/30/15, Camaguey, Cuba d: 9/15/71, Miami, Fla. BR/TR, 6'4", 200 lbs. Deb: 9/6/41 F

YEAR	TM/L	G	AB	R	H	2B	3B	HR	RBI	BB	SO	AVG	OBP	SLG	PRO+	BR/A	SB	CS	SBR	FA	FR	G/POS	TPR
1941	Was-A	22	79	10	26	1	2	1	17	3	10	.329	.354	.430	112	1	0	1	-1	.860	-2	O-21	-0.2
1942	Was-A	20	42	4	7	1	3	1	4	5	11	.167	.271	.405	89	-1	0	0	-0	.941	-1	/O-9	-0.2
1943	Was-A	4	4	0	1	0	0	0	0	0	0	.250	.250	.250	48	-0	0	1	-1	1.000	0	/O-1	-0.1
1944	Was-A	85	316	36	80	11	4	5	35	19	47	.253	.312	.361	96	-2	4	1	1	.949	-3	O-80	-1.0
1949	Was-A	40	129	12	36	3	0	1	11	9	12	.279	.326	.326	74	-5	0	0	-0	.946	-1	O-32	-0.8
1950	Was-A	39	75	4	17	2	0	0	8	7	12	.227	.301	.280	52	-5	0	0	-0	1.000	0	O-19	-0.8
	Phi-A	6	14	1	1	0	0	0	3	0	3	.071	.071	.071	-65	-3	0	0	-0	1.000	-1	/O-3	-0.4
	Yr	45	89	5	18	2	0	0	11	7	15	.202	.268	.247	34	-9	0	0	-0	1.000	-3	O-22	-1.2
Total	6	213	659	67	168	18	10	8	78	43	95	.255	.310	.349	84	-16	4	3	-1	.942	-10	O-165	-3.5

■ JOHN ORTON

Orton, John Andrew b: 12/8/65, Santa Cruz, Cal. BR/TR, 6'1", 195 lbs. Deb: 8/20/89

YEAR	TM/L	G	AB	R	H	2B	3B	HR	RBI	BB	SO	AVG	OBP	SLG	PRO+	BR/A	SB	CS	SBR	FA	FR	G/POS	TPR
1989	Cal-A	16	39	4	7	1	0	0	4	2	17	.179	.220	.205	21	-4	0	0	0	.988	5	C-16	0.1
1990	Cal-A	31	84	8	16	5	0	1	6	5	31	.190	.244	.286	49	-6	0	1	-1	.987	1	C-31	0.6
1991	Cal-A	29	69	7	14	4	0	0	3	10	17	.203	.313	.261	60	-3	0	1	-1	.994	9	C-28/D-1	0.6
1992	Cal-A	43	114	11	25	3	0	2	12	7	32	.219	.276	.298	61	-6	1	1	-0	.981	8	C-43	0.4
1993	Cal-A	37	95	5	18	5	0	1	4	7	24	.189	.252	.274	40	-9	1	2	-0	.980	5	C-35/O-1	-0.2
Total	5	156	401	35	80	18	0	4	29	31	121	.200	.265	.274	49	-28	2	5	-2	.985	28	C-153/O-1,D	0.5

■ OSSIE ORWOLL

Orwoll, Oswald Christian b: 11/17/1900, Portland, Ore. d: 5/8/67, Decorah, Iowa BL/TL, 6', 174 lbs. Deb: 4/13/28

YEAR	TM/L	G	AB	R	H	2B	3B	HR	RBI	BB	SO	AVG	OBP	SLG	PRO+	BR/A	SB	CS	SBR	FA	FR	G/POS	TPR
1928	Phi-A	64	170	28	52	13	2	0	22	16	24	.306	.366	.406	100	0	3	1	0	.983	-1	1-34,P-27	-0.3

YEAR	TM/L	G	AB	R	H	2B	3B	HR	RBI	BB	SO	AVG	OBP	SLG	PRO+	BR/A	SB	CS	SBR	FA	FR	G/POS	TPR
1929	Phi-A	30	51	6	13	2	1	0	6	2	11	.255	.283	.333	56	-3	0	0	0	1.000	-2	P-12/O-9	-0.4
Total	2	94	221	34	65	15	3	0	28	18	35	.294	.347	.389	90	-3	3	1	0	.970	-3	/P-39,1-34,O	-0.7

■ FRED OSBORN
Osborn, Wilfred Pearl "Ossie" b: 11/28/1883, Nevada, Ohio d: 9/2/54, Upper Sandusky, O. BL/TR, 5'9", 178 lbs. Deb: 6/8/07

YEAR	TM/L	G	AB	R	H	2B	3B	HR	RBI	BB	SO	AVG	OBP	SLG	PRO+	BR/A	SB	CS	SBR	FA	FR	G/POS	TPR
1907	Phi-N	56	163	22	45	2	3	0	9	3		.276	.298	.325	97	-1	4			1.000	-4	O-36/1-1	-0.8
1908	Phi-N	152	555	62	148	19	12	2	44	30		.267	.305	.355	107	3	16			.969	2	*O-152	-0.2
1909	Phi-N	58	189	14	35	4	1	0	19	12		.185	.238	.217	41	-13	6			.979	10	O-54	-0.6
Total	3	266	907	98	228	25	16	2	72	45		.251	.290	.321	91	-12	26			.975	8	O-242/1-1	-1.6

■ FRED OSBORNE
Osborne, Frederick W. b: Hampton, Iowa TL , Deb: 7/14/1890

YEAR	TM/L	G	AB	R	H	2B	3B	HR	RBI	BB	SO	AVG	OBP	SLG	PRO+	BR/A	SB	CS	SBR	FA	FR	G/POS	TPR
1890	Pit-N	41	168	24	40	8	3	1	14	6	18	.238	.269	.339	87	-4	0			.828	1	O-35/P-8	-0.3

■ BOBO OSBORNE
Osborne, Lawrence Sidney b: 10/12/35, Chattahoochee, Ga. BL/TR, 6'1", 205 lbs. Deb: 6/27/57 F

YEAR	TM/L	G	AB	R	H	2B	3B	HR	RBI	BB	SO	AVG	OBP	SLG	PRO+	BR/A	SB	CS	SBR	FA	FR	G/POS	TPR
1957	Det-A	11	27	4	4	1	0	0	1	3	7	.148	.233	.185	15	-3	0	0	0	1.000	-1	/O-5,1-4	-0.4
1958	Det-A	2	2	0	0	0	0	0	0	0	0	.000	.000	.000	-93	-1	0	0	0	.000	0	H	-0.1
1959	Det-A	86	209	27	40	7	1	3	21	16	41	.191	.256	.278	44	-16	1	0	0	.983	-1	1-56/O-1	-2.1
1961	Det-A	71	93	8	20	7	0	2	13	20	15	.215	.354	.355	88	-1	1	0	0	.957	-2	/3-8,1-11	-0.4
1962	Det-A	64	74	12	17	1	0	0	7	16	25	.230	.374	.243	68	-3	0	0	0	.857	-2	3-13/1-7,C	-0.4
1963	Was-A	125	358	42	76	14	1	12	44	49	83	.212	.312	.358	87	-6	0	0	0	.988	-3	1-81,3-16	-1.3
Total	6	359	763	93	157	30	2	17	86	104	171	.206	.306	.317	71	-29	2	0	0	.987	-9	1-159/3-37,OC	-4.7

■ HARRY OSTDIEK
Ostdiek, Henry Girard b: 4/12/1881, Ottumwa, Iowa d: 5/6/56, Minneapolis, Minn. BR/TR, 5'11", 185 lbs. Deb: 9/10/04

YEAR	TM/L	G	AB	R	H	2B	3B	HR	RBI	BB	SO	AVG	OBP	SLG	PRO+	BR/A	SB	CS	SBR	FA	FR	G/POS	TPR
1904	Cle-A	7	18	1	3	0	1	0	3	3	3	.167	.318	.278	90	-0	1			.946	-0	/C-7	0.0
1908	Bos-A	1	3	0	0	0	0	0	0	0	0	.000	.000	.000	-97	-1	0			.889	1	/C-1	0.0
Total	2	8	21	1	3	0	1	0	3	3	3	.143	.280	.238	65	-1	1			.935	0	/C-8	0.0

■ CHAMP OSTEEN
Osteen, James Champlin b: 2/24/1877, Hendersonville, N.C. d: 12/14/62, Greenville, S.C. BL/TR, 5'8", 150 lbs. Deb: 9/18/03

YEAR	TM/L	G	AB	R	H	2B	3B	HR	RBI	BB	SO	AVG	OBP	SLG	PRO+	BR/A	SB	CS	SBR	FA	FR	G/POS	TPR
1903	Was-A	10	40	4	8	0	2	0	4	2		.200	.256	.300	65	-2	0			.938	1	S-10	0.0
1904	NY-A	28	107	15	21	1	4	2	9	1		.196	.218	.336	71	-4	0			.930	-2	3-17/S-8,1	-0.6
1908	StL-N	29	112	2	22	4	0	0	11	0		.196	.204	.232	41	-8	0			.847	-6	S-17,3-12	-1.6
1909	StL-N	16	45	6	9	1	0	0	7	7		.200	.308	.222	69	-1	1			.879	-6	S-16	-0.8
Total	4	83	304	27	60	6	6	2	31	10		.197	.233	.276	60	-15	1			.890	-13	/S-51,3-29,1	-3.0

■ RED OSTERGARD
Ostergard, Roy Lund b: 5/16/1896, Denmark, Wis. d: 1/13/77, Hemet, Cal. BR/TR, 5'10.5", 175 lbs. Deb: 6/14/21

YEAR	TM/L	G	AB	R	H	2B	3B	HR	RBI	BB	SO	AVG	OBP	SLG	PRO+	BR/A	SB	CS	SBR	FA	FR	G/POS	TPR
1921	Chi-A	12	11	2	4	0	0	0	0	0	2	.364	.364	.364	87	-0	0	0	0	.000	-0	H	0.0

■ CHARLIE OSTERHOUT
Osterhout, Charles H. b: 1856, Syracuse, N.Y. d: 5/21/33, Syracuse, N.Y. TR , Deb: 6/23/1879

YEAR	TM/L	G	AB	R	H	2B	3B	HR	RBI	BB	SO	AVG	OBP	SLG	PRO+	BR/A	SB	CS	SBR	FA	FR	G/POS	TPR
1879	Syr-N	2	8	0	0	0	0	0	0	0	0	.000	.000	.000	-99	-2				1.000	-0	/O-1,C-1	-0.2

■ BRIAN OSTROSSER
Ostrosser, Brian Leonard b: 6/17/49, Hamilton, Ont., Can BL/TR, 6', 175 lbs. Deb: 8/5/73

YEAR	TM/L	G	AB	R	H	2B	3B	HR	RBI	BB	SO	AVG	OBP	SLG	PRO+	BR/A	SB	CS	SBR	FA	FR	G/POS	TPR
1973	NY-N	4	5	0	0	0	0	0	0	0	2	.000	.000	.000	-99	-1	0	0	0	1.000	-0	/S-4	-0.2

■ JOHNNY OSTROWSKI
Ostrowski, John Thaddeus b: 10/17/17, Chicago, Ill. d: 11/13/92, Chicago, Ill. BR/TR, 5'10.5", 170 lbs. Deb: 9/24/43

YEAR	TM/L	G	AB	R	H	2B	3B	HR	RBI	BB	SO	AVG	OBP	SLG	PRO+	BR/A	SB	CS	SBR	FA	FR	G/POS	TPR
1943	Chi-N	10	29	2	6	0	1	0	3	3	8	.207	.303	.276	69	-1	0			1.000	-2	/O-5,3-4	-0.4
1944	Chi-N	8	13	2	2	1	0	0	2	1	4	.154	.214	.231	25	-1	0			.500	-1	/O-2	-0.2
1945	Chi-N	7	10	4	3	2	0	0	1	0		.300	.300	.500	123	-1	0			.750	-1	/3-4	-0.1
1946	Chi-N	64	160	20	34	4	2	3	12	20	31	.213	.300	.319	77	-5	1			.934	1	3-50/2-1	-0.3
1948	Bos-N	1	1	0	0	0	0	0	0	0	1	.000	.000	.000	-95	-0	0			.000	0	H	0.0
1949	Chi-A	49	158	19	42	9	4	5	31	15	41	.266	.333	.468	115	0	2	4	3	-1	.944	-4	O-41/3-8	-0.4
1950	Chi-A	21	45	9	10	1	1	2	2	9	8	.222	.364	.422	104	0	0	0	0	1.000	-1	O-14	-0.1
	Was-A	55	141	16	32	2	1	4	23	20	31	.227	.327	.340	75	-6	2	0	1	.947	-0	O-45	-0.6
	Chi-A	1	4	1	2	1	0	0	0	0	1	.500	.500	.750	223	1	0	0	0	1.000	-0	/O-1	0.0
	Yr	77	190	26	44	4	2	6	25	29	40	.232	.339	.368	85	-4	2	0	1	.958	-2	O-60	-0.7
Total	7	216	561	73	131	20	9	14	74	68	125	.234	.321	.376	89	-10	7	3		.950	-9	O-108/3-66,2	-2.1

■ REGGIE OTERO
Otero, Regino Jose (Gomez) b: 9/7/15, Havana, Cuba d: 10/21/88, Hialeah, Fla. BL/TR, 6', 165 lbs. Deb: 9/2/45 C

YEAR	TM/L	G	AB	R	H	2B	3B	HR	RBI	BB	SO	AVG	OBP	SLG	PRO+	BR/A	SB	CS	SBR	FA	FR	G/POS	TPR
1945	Chi-N	14	23	1	9	0	0	0	5	2	2	.391	.440	.391	135	1	0			.967	0	/1-8	0.1

■ AMOS OTIS
Otis, Amos Joseph b: 4/26/47, Mobile, Ala. BR/TR, 5'11", 166 lbs. Deb: 9/6/67 C

YEAR	TM/L	G	AB	R	H	2B	3B	HR	RBI	BB	SO	AVG	OBP	SLG	PRO+	BR/A	SB	CS	SBR	FA	FR	G/POS	TPR
1967	NY-N	19	59	6	13	2	0	1	5	5	13	.220	.292	.254	59	-3	0	4	-2	1.000	-2	O-16/3-1	-0.9
1969	NY-N	48	93	6	14	3	1	0	4	6	27	.151	.202	.204	14	-11	1	0	0	1.000	-2	O-35/3-3	-1.5
1970	KC-A★	159	620	91	176	**36**	9	11	58	68	67	.284	.356	.424	114	12	33	2	**9**	.990	14	*O-159	2.7
1971	KC-A★	147	555	80	167	26	4	15	79	40	74	.301	.350	.443	125	16	**52**	8	**11**	.990	20	*O-144	4.2
1972	KC-A†	143	540	75	158	28	2	11	54	50	59	.293	.356	.413	129	19	28	12	1	.992	10	*O-137	2.6
1973	KC-A	148	583	89	175	21	4	26	93	63	47	.300	.369	.484	129	21	13	9	-2	.986	3	*O-135,D-14	1.6
1974	KC-A	146	552	87	157	31	9	12	73	58	67	.284	.355	.438	120	14	18	5	2	.986	10	*O-143/D-2	2.1
1975	KC-A	132	470	87	116	26	6	9	46	66	48	.247	.344	.385	103	3	39	11	5	.988	3	*O-130	0.5
1976	*KC-A★	153	592	93	165	**40**	2	18	86	55	100	.279	.345	.444	129	21	26	7	4	.992	-5	*O-152	1.4
1977	*KC-A	142	478	85	120	20	8	17	78	71	88	.251	.348	.433	110	8	23	7	5	.991	10	*O-140	0.6
1978	*KC-A	141	486	74	145	30	7	22	96	66	54	.298	.387	.525	150	33	32	8	5	**.995**	10	*O-136/D-1	4.2
1979	*KC-A	151	577	100	170	28	2	18	90	68	92	.295	.372	.444	117	14	30	5	5	**.992**	5	*O-146/D-4	1.9
1980	*KC-A	107	394	56	99	16	3	10	53	39	70	.251	.323	.383	92	-4	16	1	4	.988	7	*O-105	0.2
1981	*KC-A	99	372	49	100	23	3	9	57	31	59	.269	.328	.417	114	6	16	7	1	.993	11	O-97/D-1	1.4
1982	KC-A	125	475	73	136	25	3	11	88	37	65	.286	.340	.421	108	5	9	5	-0	.997	-1	*O-125	0.0
1983	KC-A	98	356	35	93	16	3	4	41	27	63	.261	.313	.357	84	-8	5	2	0	.996	3	O-96/D-1	-0.7
1984	Pit-N	40	97	6	16	4	0	0	10	7	15	.165	.221	.206	21	-10	5	0	0	.964	0	O-32	-1.0
Total	17	1998	7299	1092	2020	374	66	193	1007	757	1008	.277	.347	.425	114	136	341	93	47	.991	87	*O-1928/D-23,3	19.3

■ BILL OTIS
Otis, Paul Franklin b: 12/24/1889, Scituate, Mass. d: 12/15/90, Duluth, Minn. BL/TR, 5'10.5", 150 lbs. Deb: 7/4/12

YEAR	TM/L	G	AB	R	H	2B	3B	HR	RBI	BB	SO	AVG	OBP	SLG	PRO+	BR/A	SB	CS	SBR	FA	FR	G/POS	TPR
1912	NY-A	4	17	1	1	0	0	0	2	3		.059	.200	.059	-24	-3	0			.917	1	/O-4	-0.2

■ MEL OTT
Ott, Melvin Thomas "Master Melvin" b: 3/2/09, Gretna, La. d: 11/21/58, New Orleans, La. BL/TR, 5'9", 170 lbs. Deb: 4/27/26 MH

YEAR	TM/L	G	AB	R	H	2B	3B	HR	RBI	BB	SO	AVG	OBP	SLG	PRO+	BR/A	SB	CS	SBR	FA	FR	G/POS	TPR
1926	NY-N	35	60	7	23	2	0	0	4	1	9	.383	.393	.417	120	2	1			.913	1	O-10	0.2
1927	NY-N	82	163	23	46	7	3	1	19	13	9	.282	.335	.380	91	-2	2			.982	-7	O-32	-1.1
1928	NY-N	124	435	69	140	26	4	18	77	52	36	.322	.397	.524	138	24	3			.970	-3	*O-115/2-5,3	1.4
1929	NY-N	150	545	138	179	37	2	42	151	**113**	38	.328	.449	.635	166	59	6			.973	9	*O-149/2-1	5.2
1930	NY-N	148	521	122	182	34	5	25	119	103	35	.349	**.458**	.578	152	48	9			.969	6	*O-146	3.8
1931	NY-N	138	497	104	145	23	8	29	115	**80**	44	.292	.392	.545	**153**	38	10			.981	8	*O-137	3.6
1932	NY-N	154	566	119	180	30	8	**38**	123	**100**	39	.318	**.424**	.601	175	63	6			.984	2	*O-154	**5.3**
1933	*NY-N	152	580	98	164	36	1	23	103	**75**	48	.283	.367	.467	139	30	1			.983	-14	*O-152	0.9
1934	NY-N★	153	582	119	190	29	10	**35**	**135**	85	43	.326	.415	.591	147	-9	5			.981	3	*O-153	4.1
1935	NY-N★	152	593	113	191	33	6	31	114	82	58	.322	.407	.555	159	50	7			**.990**	6	*O-137,3-15	4.9
1936	*NY-N★	150	534	120	175	28	6	**33**	135	111	41	.328	.448	**.588**	179	63	6			.985	-0	*O-148	5.2
1937	NY-N★	151	545	99	160	28	2	31	95	**102**	69	.294	.408	.523	149	42	7			.939	-5	3-60,O-91	3.7
1938	NY-N★	150	527	**116**	164	23	6	36	116	118	47	.311	**.442**	.583	178	61	2			.957	1	*3-113,O-37	6.1
1939	NY-N★	125	396	85	122	23	2	27	80	100	50	.308	**.449**	.581	173	45	2			.973	-5	O-96,3-20	3.6

YEAR	TM/L	G	AB	R	H	2B	3B	HR	RBI	BB	SO	AVG	OBP	SLG	PRO+	BR/A	SB	CS	SBR	FA	FR	G/POS	TPR
1940	NY-N★	151	536	89	155	27	3	19	79	100	50	.289	.407	.457	137	31	6			.982	2	*O-111,3-42	2.8
1941	NY-N★	148	525	89	150	29	0	27	90	100	68	.286	.403	.495	149	37	5			.968	5	*O-145	3.3
1942	NY-N★	152	549	**118**	162	21	0	**30**	93	**109**	61	.295	.415	.497	**165**	**49**	6			.990	-1	*O-152,M	4.2
1943	NY-N★	125	380	65	89	12	2	18	47	95	48	.234	.391	.418	133	20	7			.975	1	*O-111/3-1M	1.5
1944	NY-N★	120	399	91	115	16	4	26	82	90	47	.288	.423	.544	171	41	2			.986	-4	*O-103/3-4M	3.2
1945	NY-N†	135	451	73	139	23	0	21	79	71	41	.308	.411	.499	150	32	1			.983	-4	*O-118,M	2.2
1946	NY-N	31	68	2	5	1	0	1	4	8	15	.074	.171	.132	-13	-10	0			1.000	-1	O-16,M	-1.3
1947	NY-N	4	4	0	0	0	0	0	0	0	0	.000	.000	.000	-99	-1	0			.000	0	HM	-0.1
Total	22	2730	9456	1859	2876	488	72	511	1860	1708	896	.304	.414	.533	155	776	89			.980	-10	*O-2313,3-256/2	62.7

■ ED OTT
Ott, Nathan Edward b: 7/11/51, Muncy, Pa. BL/TR, 5'10", 198 lbs. Deb: 6/10/74 C

YEAR	TM/L	G	AB	R	H	2B	3B	HR	RBI	BB	SO	AVG	OBP	SLG	PRO+	BR/A	SB	CS	SBR	FA	FR	G/POS	TPR
1974	Pit-N	7	5	1	0	0	0	0	0	0	1	.000	.000	.000	-99	-1	0	0	0	1.000	-1	/O-2	-0.2
1975	Pit-N	5	5	0	1	0	0	0	0	0	0	.200	.200	.200	11	-1	0	0	0	1.000	-0	/C-2	-0.1
1976	Pit-N	27	39	2	12	2	0	0	5	3	5	.308	.357	.359	103	0	0	0	0	1.000	-1	/C-8	0.0
1977	Pit-N	104	311	40	82	14	3	7	38	32	41	.264	.336	.395	93	-3	7	7	-2	.982	-5	C-90	-0.8
1978	Pit-N	112	379	49	102	18	4	9	38	27	56	.269	.318	.409	97	-2	4	1	1	.975	-9	C-97/O-4	-0.8
1979	*Pit-N	117	403	49	110	20	2	7	51	26	62	.273	.317	.385	86	-8	0	1	-1	.994	-3	*C-116	-0.7
1980	Pit-N	120	392	35	102	14	0	8	41	33	47	.260	.318	.357	87	-7	1	6	-3	.983	-4	*C-117/O-3	-1.0
1981	Cal-A	75	258	20	56	8	1	2	22	17	42	.217	.268	.279	58	-14	2	1	0	.979	1	C-72	-1.1
Total	8	567	1792	196	465	76	10	33	195	138	254	.259	.314	.368	86	-36	14	16	-5	.983	-21	C-502/O-9	-4.7

■ BILLY OTT
Ott, William Joseph b: 11/23/40, New York, N.Y. BB/TR, 6'1", 180 lbs. Deb: 9/4/62

YEAR	TM/L	G	AB	R	H	2B	3B	HR	RBI	BB	SO	AVG	OBP	SLG	PRO+	BR/A	SB	CS	SBR	FA	FR	G/POS	TPR
1962	Chi-N	12	28	3	4	0	0	0	2	2	10	.143	.200	.250	19	-3	0	0	0	1.000	-0	/O-7	-0.4
1964	Chi-N	20	39	4	7	3	0	0	1	3	10	.179	.244	.256	38	-3	0	1	-1	1.000	-2	O-10	-0.6
Total	2	32	67	7	11	3	0	1	3	5	20	.164	.222	.254	30	-6	0	1	-1	1.000	-2	/O-17	-1.0

■ JOE OTTEN
Otten, Joseph G. b: Murphysboro, Ill. TR, Deb: 7/5/1895

YEAR	TM/L	G	AB	R	H	2B	3B	HR	RBI	BB	SO	AVG	OBP	SLG	PRO+	BR/A	SB	CS	SBR	FA	FR	G/POS	TPR
1895	StL-N	26	87	8	21	0	0	0	8	5	8	.241	.283	.241	36	-8	2			.947	-4	C-24/O-2	-0.8

■ BILLY OTTERSON
Otterson, William John b: 5/4/1862, Pittsburgh, Pa. d: 9/21/40, Pittsburgh, Pa. BR/TR, 5'7", 124 lbs. Deb: 9/4/1887

YEAR	TM/L	G	AB	R	H	2B	3B	HR	RBI	BB	SO	AVG	OBP	SLG	PRO+	BR/A	SB	CS	SBR	FA	FR	G/POS	TPR
1887	Bro-a	30	100	16	20	4	1	2		8		.200	.259	.320	60	-6	8			.859	1	S-30	-0.4

■ PHIL OUELLETTE
Ouellette, Philip Roland b: 11/10/61, Salem, Ore. BB/TR, 6', 190 lbs. Deb: 9/10/86

YEAR	TM/L	G	AB	R	H	2B	3B	HR	RBI	BB	SO	AVG	OBP	SLG	PRO+	BR/A	SB	CS	SBR	FA	FR	G/POS	TPR
1986	SF-N	10	23	1	4	0	0	0	0	3	3	.174	.269	.174	26	-2	0	0	0	1.000	0	/C-9	-0.2

■ JOHNNY OULLIBER
Oulliber, John Andrew b: 2/24/11, New Orleans, La. d: 12/26/80, New Orleans, La. BR/TR, 5'11", 165 lbs. Deb: 7/25/33

YEAR	TM/L	G	AB	R	H	2B	3B	HR	RBI	BB	SO	AVG	OBP	SLG	PRO+	BR/A	SB	CS	SBR	FA	FR	G/POS	TPR
1933	Cle-A	22	75	9	20	1	0	0	3	4	5	.267	.313	.280	55	-5	0	0	0	1.000	-3	O-18	-0.9

■ CHINK OUTEN
Outen, William Austin b: 6/17/05, Mt.Holly, N.C. d: 9/11/61, Durham, N.C. BL/TR, 6', 200 lbs. Deb: 4/16/33

YEAR	TM/L	G	AB	R	H	2B	3B	HR	RBI	BB	SO	AVG	OBP	SLG	PRO+	BR/A	SB	CS	SBR	FA	FR	G/POS	TPR
1933	Bro-N	93	153	20	38	10	0	4	17	20	15	.248	.335	.392	112	3	1			.982	-13	C-56	-0.9

■ JIMMY OUTLAW
Outlaw, James Paulus b: 1/20/13, Orme, Tenn. BR/TR, 5'8", 168 lbs. Deb: 4/20/37

YEAR	TM/L	G	AB	R	H	2B	3B	HR	RBI	BB	SO	AVG	OBP	SLG	PRO+	BR/A	SB	CS	SBR	FA	FR	G/POS	TPR
1937	Cin-N	49	165	18	45	7	3	0	11	3	31	.273	.290	.352	77	-6	2			.914	4	3-41	-0.1
1938	Cin-N	4	0	1	0	0	0	0	0	0	0	—	—	—	—	0	0			.000	0	R	0.0
1939	Bos-N	65	133	15	35	2	0	0	5	10	14	.263	.315	.278	65	-6	1			.964	-3	O-39/3-2	-1.1
1943	Det-A	20	67	8	18	1	0	0	6	8	4	.269	.347	.328	91	-1	0	0	0	1.000	0	O-16	-0.1
1944	Det-A	139	535	69	146	20	6	3	57	41	40	.273	.327	.350	88	-8	7	8	-3	.964	-3	*O-137	-2.2
1945	*Det-A	132	446	56	121	16	5	0	34	45	33	.271	.338	.330	88	-6	6	7	-2	.967	-4	*O-105,3-21	-1.8
1946	Det-A	92	299	36	78	14	2	2	31	29	24	.261	.328	.341	82	-7	5	4	-1	1.000	-8	O-43,3-38	-1.8
1947	Det-A	70	127	20	29	7	1	0	15	21	14	.228	.338	.299	76	-4	3	1	0	.983	-7	O-37/3-9	-1.2
1948	Det-A	74	198	33	56	12	0	0	25	31	15	.283	.383	.343	91	-1	0	1	-1	.920	1	3-47,O-13	-0.2
1949	Det-A	5	4	1	1	0	0	0	0	0	0	.250	.250	.250	32	-0	0	0	0	.000	0	H	0.0
Total	10	650	1974	257	529	79	17	6	184	188	176	.268	.333	.334	85	-39	24	21		.972	-19	O-390,3-158	-8.5

■ MICKEY OWEN
Owen, Arnold Malcolm b: 4/4/16, Nixa, Mo. BR/TR, 5'10", 190 lbs. Deb: 5/2/37 C

YEAR	TM/L	G	AB	R	H	2B	3B	HR	RBI	BB	SO	AVG	OBP	SLG	PRO+	BR/A	SB	CS	SBR	FA	FR	G/POS	TPR
1937	StL-N	80	234	17	54	4	2	0	20	15	13	.231	.277	.265	47	-17	1			.974	-3	C-78	-1.6
1938	StL-N	122	397	45	106	25	2	4	36	32	13	.267	.325	.370	86	-8	2			.980	1	*C-116	-0.1
1939	StL-N	131	344	32	89	18	2	3	35	43	28	.259	.344	.349	82	-8	6			.982	4	*C-126	0.2
1940	StL-N	117	307	27	81	16	2	0	27	34	13	.264	.341	.329	81	-7	4			.980	3	*C-113	0.2
1941	*Bro-N★	128	386	32	89	15	2	1	44	34	14	.231	.296	.288	62	-19	1			.995	6	*O-128	-0.3
1942	Bro-N★	133	421	53	109	16	3	0	44	44	21	.259	.330	.311	87	-6	10			.987	5	*C-133	0.9
1943	Bro-N☆	106	365	31	95	11	2	0	54	25	15	.260	.309	.301	77	-11	4			.987	-6	*C-100/3-3,S	-1.0
1944	Bro-N☆	130	461	43	126	20	3	1	42	36	17	.273	.326	.336	88	-7	4			.979	-11	*C-125/2-1	-1.1
1945	Bro-N	24	84	5	24	9	0	0	11	10	2	.286	.368	.393	113	2	0			.963	-3	C-24	0.0
1949	Chi-N	62	198	15	54	9	3	2	18	12	13	.273	.348	.379	88	-4	1			.969	-1	C-59	-0.1
1950	Chi-N	86	259	22	63	11	0	2	21	13	16	.243	.282	.309	56	-17	2			.978	3	C-86	-1.0
1951	Chi-N	58	125	10	23	6	0	0	15	19	13	.184	.292	.232	42	-10	1	0	0	.969	8	C-57	0.0
1954	Bos-A	32	68	6	16	3	0	1	11	9	6	.235	.325	.324	70	-3	0	1	-1	.989	-2	C-30	-0.5
Total	13	1209	3649	338	929	163	21	14	378	326	181	.255	.318	.322	76	-114	36	1		.982	3	*C-1175/3-3,2S	-4.4

■ DAVE OWEN
Owen, Dave b: 4/25/58, Cleburne, Tex. BB/TR, 6'2", 170 lbs. Deb: 9/6/83 F

YEAR	TM/L	G	AB	R	H	2B	3B	HR	RBI	BB	SO	AVG	OBP	SLG	PRO+	BR/A	SB	CS	SBR	FA	FR	G/POS	TPR
1983	Chi-N	16	22	1	2	0	1	0	2	2	7	.091	.167	.182	-3	-3	1	0	0	1.000	4	S-14/3-3	0.1
1984	Chi-N	47	93	8	18	2	2	0	10	2	15	.194	.272	.290	53	-6	1	2	-1	.969	1	S-35/3-6,2	-0.4
1985	Chi-N	22	19	6	7	0	0	0	4	1	5	.368	.400	.368	105	0	1	1	-0	.917	2	/S-7,3-7,2	0.2
1988	KC-A	7	5	0	0	0	0	0	0	0	3	.000	.000	.000	-99	-1	0	0	0	.941	3	/S-7	0.3
Total	4	92	139	15	27	2	3	1	16	11	30	.194	.263	.273	47	-10	3	3	-1	.969	10	/S-63,3-16,2	0.2

■ LARRY OWEN
Owen, Lawrence Thomas b: 5/31/55, Cleveland, Ohio BR/TR, 5'11", 185 lbs. Deb: 8/14/81

YEAR	TM/L	G	AB	R	H	2B	3B	HR	RBI	BB	SO	AVG	OBP	SLG	PRO+	BR/A	SB	CS	SBR	FA	FR	G/POS	TPR
1981	Atl-N	13	16	0	0	0	0	0	0	0	4	.000	.059	.000	-80	-4	0	0	0	.964	2	C-10	-0.2
1982	Atl-N	2	3	1	1	1	0	0	0	0	0	.333	.333	.667	167	0	0	0	0	1.000	-0	/C-2	0.0
1983	Atl-N	17	17	0	2	0	0	0	1	0	2	.118	.118	.118	-32	-3	0	1	-1	.970	1	C-16	-0.3
1985	Atl-N	26	71	7	17	3	0	2	12	8	17	.239	.316	.366	85	-1	0	0	0	.966	3	C-25	0.2
1987	KC-A	76	164	17	31	6	0	5	14	16	51	.189	.261	.317	51	-12	0	1	-1	.983	19	C-75	1.0
1988	KC-A	37	81	5	17	1	0	1	9	9	23	.210	.304	.259	59	-4	0	0	0	.989	5	C-37	0.3
Total	6	171	352	30	68	11	0	8	30	34	98	.193	.268	.293	51	-24	0	2	-2	.980	29	C-165	1.0

■ MARV OWEN
Owen, Marvin James "Freck" b: 3/22/06, Agnew, Cal. d: 6/22/91, Mountain View, Cal. BR/TR, 6'1", 175 lbs. Deb: 4/16/31

YEAR	TM/L	G	AB	R	H	2B	3B	HR	RBI	BB	SO	AVG	OBP	SLG	PRO+	BR/A	SB	CS	SBR	FA	FR	G/POS	TPR
1931	Det-A	105	377	35	84	11	6	3	39	29	38	.223	.282	.308	53	-26	2	2	-1	.937	1	S-37,3-37,1/2	-2.0
1933	Det-A	138	550	77	144	24	6	2	65	44	56	.262	.321	.349	76	-19	2	2	-1	.944	-11	*3-136	-2.1
1934	*Det-A	154	565	79	179	34	9	8	96	59	37	.317	.385	.451	115	13	3	3	-1	.956	-7	3-154	1.0
1935	*Det-A	134	483	52	127	24	5	2	71	43	37	.263	.326	.346	76	-17	1	4	-2	.958	-19	3-131	-2.3
1936	Det-A	154	583	72	172	20	4	9	105	53	41	.295	.361	.389	85	-13	9	6	-1	.952	-4	*3-153/1-2	-1.1
1937	Det-A	107	396	48	114	22	5	1	45	44	24	.288	.358	.376	83	-10	2	1	-1	**.970**	0	3-106	-0.8
1938	Chi-A	141	577	84	162	23	4	6	55	46	31	.281	.337	.373	76	-22	5	6	-1	.948	0	3-140	-1.8
1939	Chi-A	58	194	22	46	9	0	0	15	16	15	.237	.302	.284	49	-15	2	4	-2	.953	-2	3-55	-1.7

YEAR	TM/L	G	AB	R	H	2B	3B	HR	RBI	BB	SO	AVG	OBP	SLG	PRO+	BR/A	SB	CS	SBR	FA	FR	G/POS	TPR
1940	Bos-A	20	57	4	12	0	0	0	6	8	4	.211	.308	.211	36	-5	0	0	0	.962	2	/3-9,1-8	-0.4
Total	9	1011	3782	473	1040	167	44	31	497	338	283	.275	.339	.367	80	-114	30	30	-9	.953	-30	3-921/1-37,S2	-11.2

■ SPIKE OWEN   Owen, Spike Dee   b: 4/19/61, Cleburne, Tex.   BB/TR, 5'10", 170 lbs.   Deb: 6/25/83   F

YEAR	TM/L	G	AB	R	H	2B	3B	HR	RBI	BB	SO	AVG	OBP	SLG	PRO+	BR/A	SB	CS	SBR	FA	FR	G/POS	TPR
1983	Sea-A	80	306	36	60	11	3	2	21	24	44	.196	.259	.271	44	-23	10	6	-1	.970	-0	S-80	-1.6
1984	Sea-A	152	530	67	130	18	8	3	43	46	63	.245	.309	.326	77	-16	16	8	0	.977	16	*S-151	1.5
1985	Sea-A	118	352	41	91	10	6	6	37	34	72	.259	.324	.372	89	-5	11	5	0	.975	**30**	*S-117	3.5
1986	Sea-A	112	402	46	99	22	6	0	35	34	42	.246	.307	.331	73	-15	1	3	-2	.972	34	*S-112	2.7
	*Bos-A	42	126	21	23	2	1	1	10	17	9	.183	.285	.238	44	-10	3	1	0	.976	-2	S-42	-0.7
	Yr	154	528	67	122	24	7	1	45	51	51	.231	.301	.309	66	-24	4	4	-1	.973	**32**	*S-154	2.0
1987	Bos-A	132	437	50	113	17	7	2	48	53	43	.259	.340	.343	80	-12	11	8	-2	.975	-14	*S-130	-1.5
1988	*Bos-A	89	257	40	64	14	1	5	18	27	27	.249	.325	.370	90	-3	0	1	-1	.967	-1	S-76/D-7	0.1
1989	Mon-N	142	437	52	102	17	4	6	41	76	44	.233	.351	.332	95	-0	3	2	-0	**.979**	11	*S-142	2.2
1990	Mon-N	149	453	55	106	24	5	5	35	70	60	.234	.337	.342	91	-4	8	6	-1	**.989**	-12	*S-148	-0.8
1991	Mon-N	139	424	39	108	22	8	3	26	42	61	.255	.323	.366	95	-3	2	6	-3	.986	8	*S-133	1.1
1992	Mon-N	122	386	52	104	16	3	7	40	50	30	.269	.353	.381	109	5	9	4	0	.982	-10	*S-116	0.4
1993	NY-A	103	334	41	78	16	2	2	20	29	30	.234	.295	.311	65	-16	3	2	-0	.968	10	S-96/D-2	0.0
1994	Cal-A	82	268	30	83	17	2	3	37	49	17	.310	.418	.422	114	8	2	8	-4	.956	0	3-70/S-5,12D	0.4
Total	12	1462	4712	570	1161	206	56	45	411	551	497	.246	.327	.343	84	-94	79	60	-12	.977	69	*S-1348/3-70,D12	7.3

■ J OWENS   Owens, Claude Jayhawk   b: 2/10/69, Cincinnati, Ohio   BR/TR, 6'1", 200 lbs.   Deb: 6/6/93

YEAR	TM/L	G	AB	R	H	2B	3B	HR	RBI	BB	SO	AVG	OBP	SLG	PRO+	BR/A	SB	CS	SBR	FA	FR	G/POS	TPR
1993	Col-N	33	86	12	18	5	0	3	6	6	30	.209	.277	.372	62	-5	1	0	0	.957	1	C-32	-0.2
1994	Col-N	6	12	4	3	0	1	0	1	3	3	.250	.400	.417	97	0	0	0	0	1.000	1	/C-6	0.1
Total	2	39	98	16	21	5	1	3	7	9	33	.214	.294	.378	67	-5	1	0	0	.964	2	/C-38	-0.1

■ FRANK OWENS   Owens, Frank Walter "Yip"   b: 1/26/1886, Toronto, Ont., Can.   d: 7/2/58, Minneapolis, Minn.   BR/TR, 6', 170 lbs.   Deb: 9/11/05

YEAR	TM/L	G	AB	R	H	2B	3B	HR	RBI	BB	SO	AVG	OBP	SLG	PRO+	BR/A	SB	CS	SBR	FA	FR	G/POS	TPR
1905	Bos-A	1	2	0	0	0	0	0	0	0	0	.000	.000	.000	-99	-0	0			1.000	-0	/C-1	-0.1
1909	Chi-A	64	174	12	35	4	1	0	17	8		.201	.245	.236	54	-9	3			.959	-6	C-57	-1.2
1914	Bro-F	58	184	15	51	7	3	2	20	9	16	.277	.314	.380	80	-6	2			.967	-14	C-58	-1.7
1915	Bal-F	99	334	32	84	14	7	3	28	17	34	.251	.290	.362	72	-15	4			.976	2	C-99	-0.5
Total	4	222	694	59	170	25	11	5	65	34	50	.245	.284	.334	70	-30	9			.969	-19	C-215	-3.5

■ JACK OWENS   Owens, Furman Lee   b: 5/6/08, Converse, S.C.   d: 11/14/58, Greenville, S.C.   BR/TR, 6'1", 186 lbs.   Deb: 9/21/35

YEAR	TM/L	G	AB	R	H	2B	3B	HR	RBI	BB	SO	AVG	OBP	SLG	PRO+	BR/A	SB	CS	SBR	FA	FR	G/POS	TPR
1935	Phi-A	2	8	0	2	0	0	0	1	0	1	.250	.250	.250	30	-1	0	0	0	.900	-0	/C-2	-0.1

■ RED OWENS   Owens, Thomas Llewellyn   b: 11/1/1874, Pottsville, Pa.   d: 8/20/52, Harrisburg, Pa.   BR/TR,   Deb: 7/28/1899

YEAR	TM/L	G	AB	R	H	2B	3B	HR	RBI	BB	SO	AVG	OBP	SLG	PRO+	BR/A	SB	CS	SBR	FA	FR	G/POS	TPR
1899	Phi-N	8	21	0	1	0	0	0	1	2		.048	.130	.048	-52	-4	0			.914	-1	/2-8	-0.4
1905	Bro-N	43	168	14	36	6	2	1	20	6		.214	.241	.292	63	-8	1			.929	4	2-43	-0.4
Total	2	51	189	14	37	6	2	1	21	8		.196	.228	.265	49	-13	1			.927	3	/2-51	-0.8

■ HENRY OXLEY   Oxley, Henry Havelock   b: 1/4/1858, Covehead, P.E.I., Canada.   d: 10/12/45, Somerville, Mass.   Deb: 7/30/1884

YEAR	TM/L	G	AB	R	H	2B	3B	HR	RBI	BB	SO	AVG	OBP	SLG	PRO+	BR/A	SB	CS	SBR	FA	FR	G/POS	TPR
1884	NY-N	3	4	0	0	0	0	0	0	1	2	.000	.200	.000	-31	-1				.900	1	/C-2	0.0
	NY-a	1	3	0	0	0	0	0	0	0		.000	.000	.000	-99	-1				.889	0	/C-1	0.0
Total	1	4	7	0	0	0	0	0	0	1	2	.000	.125	.000	-56	-1				.895	1	/C-3	0.0

■ ANDY OYLER   Oyler, Andrew Paul "Pepper"   b: 5/5/1880, Newville, Pa.   d: 10/24/70, E.Pennsboro, Pa.   BR/TR, 5'6.5", 138 lbs.   Deb: 5/8/02

YEAR	TM/L	G	AB	R	H	2B	3B	HR	RBI	BB	SO	AVG	OBP	SLG	PRO+	BR/A	SB	CS	SBR	FA	FR	G/POS	TPR
1902	Bal-A	27	77	9	17	1	0	1	6	8		.221	.318	.273	62	-4	3			.947	-8	3-20/O-3,S2	-1.1

■ RAY OYLER   Oyler, Raymond Francis   b: 8/4/38, Indianapolis, Ind.   d: 1/26/81, Seattle, Wash.   BR/TR, 5'11", 165 lbs.   Deb: 4/18/65

YEAR	TM/L	G	AB	R	H	2B	3B	HR	RBI	BB	SO	AVG	OBP	SLG	PRO+	BR/A	SB	CS	SBR	FA	FR	G/POS	TPR
1965	Det-A	82	194	22	36	6	0	5	13	21	61	.186	.265	.294	58	-11	1	0	0	.955	6	S-57,2-11/13	-0.1
1966	Det-A	71	210	16	36	8	3	1	9	23	62	.171	.263	.252	48	-14	0	0	0	.965	15	S-69	0.6
1967	Det-A	148	367	33	76	14	2	1	29	37	91	.207	.283	.264	61	-17	0	2	-1	.964	15	*S-146	0.9
1968	*Det-A	111	215	13	29	6	1	1	12	20	59	.135	.215	.186	22	-20	0	2	-1	.977	9	*S-111	-0.5
1969	Sea-A	106	255	24	42	5	0	7	22	31	80	.165	.260	.267	48	-18	1	2	-1	.965	9	*S-106	-0.1
1970	Cal-A	24	24	2	2	0	0	0	1	3	6	.083	.185	.083	-24	-4	0	0	0	1.000	-5	S-13/3-2	-0.5
Total	6	542	1265	110	221	39	6	15	86	135	359	.175	.259	.251	48	-84	2	6	-3	.966	52	S-502/2-11,31	0.3

■ CHARLIE PABOR   Pabor, Charles Henry   b: 9/24/1846, New York, N.Y.   d: 4/22/13, New Haven, Conn.   BL/TL, 5'8", 155 lbs.   Deb: 5/4/1871   M

YEAR	TM/L	G	AB	R	H	2B	3B	HR	RBI	BB	SO	AVG	OBP	SLG	PRO+	BR/A	SB	CS	SBR	FA	FR	G/POS	TPR
1871	Cle-n	29	142	24	42	2	4	0	18	1	3	.296	.301	.366	96	-0	1					*O-28/P-7M	0.1
1872	Cle-n	21	90	12	19	0	0	0	7	0	0	.211	.211	.211	32	-6						O-19/P-2	-0.3
1873	Atl-n	55	228	36	82	7	4	0	41	6	3	.360	.376	.425	151	16						*O-55	1.3
1874	Phi-n	17	77	11	18	0	0	1		0		.234	.234	.273	59	-4						/O-17	-0.3
1875	Atl-n	42	153	15	36	1	3	0		1		.235	.240	.281	91	-0						O-41/P-1M	0.0
	NH-n	6	23	4	8	0	2	0		0		.348	.348	.522	225	3						O-6,M	0.2
	Yr	48	176	19	44	1	5	0		1		.250	.254	.313	109	3						O-47/P-1	0.2
Total	5 n	170	713	102	205	10	13	1		8		.288	.295	.342	104	9						O-166/P-10	1.0

■ ED PABST   Pabst, Edward D. A.   b: 1868, St.Louis, Mo.   d: 6/19/40, St.Louis, Mo.   5'11", 170 lbs.   Deb: 9/26/1890

YEAR	TM/L	G	AB	R	H	2B	3B	HR	RBI	BB	SO	AVG	OBP	SLG	PRO+	BR/A	SB	CS	SBR	FA	FR	G/POS	TPR
1890	Phi-a	8	25	7	10	2	0	0		5		.400	.500	.480	193	3	3			.963	4	/O-8	0.6
	StL-a	4	14	1	2	0	1	0		0		.143	.143	.286	23	-2	0			1.000	1	/O-4	0.0
	Yr	12	39	8	12	2	1	0		5		.308	.386	.410	131	1	3			.972	5	O-12	0.6

■ JIM PACIOREK   Paciorek, James Joseph   b: 6/7/60, Detroit, Mich.   BR/TR, 6'3", 203 lbs.   Deb: 4/9/87   F

YEAR	TM/L	G	AB	R	H	2B	3B	HR	RBI	BB	SO	AVG	OBP	SLG	PRO+	BR/A	SB	CS	SBR	FA	FR	G/POS	TPR
1987	Mil-A	48	101	16	23	5	0	2	10	12	20	.228	.310	.337	69	-4	1	0	0	.980	-4	1-21,3-15/OD	-0.9

■ JOHN PACIOREK   Paciorek, John Francis   b: 2/11/45, Detroit, Mich.   BR/TR, 6'2", 200 lbs.   Deb: 9/29/63   F

YEAR	TM/L	G	AB	R	H	2B	3B	HR	RBI	BB	SO	AVG	OBP	SLG	PRO+	BR/A	SB	CS	SBR	FA	FR	G/POS	TPR
1963	Hou-N	1	3	4	3	0	0	0	3	2	0	1.000	1.000	1.000	509	2	0	0	0	1.000	0	/O-1	0.2

■ TOM PACIOREK   Paciorek, Thomas Marian   b: 11/2/46, Detroit, Mich.   BR/TR, 6'4", 215 lbs.   Deb: 9/12/70   F

YEAR	TM/L	G	AB	R	H	2B	3B	HR	RBI	BB	SO	AVG	OBP	SLG	PRO+	BR/A	SB	CS	SBR	FA	FR	G/POS	TPR
1970	LA-N	8	9	2	2	1	0	0	1	0	3	.222	.300	.333	73	-0	0	0	0	1.000	-1	/O-3	-0.1
1971	LA-N	2	2	0	1	0	0	0	0	1	0	.500	.500	.500	196	0	0	0	0	1.000	-0	/O-1	0.0
1972	LA-N	11	47	4	12	4	0	1	6	1	7	.255	.271	.404	92	-1	1	0	0	.979	1	/1-6,O-6	0.0
1973	LA-N	96	195	26	51	8	0	5	18	11	35	.262	.304	.379	92	-3	3	3	-1	.979	-15	O-77/1-4	-2.2
1974	*LA-N	85	175	23	42	8	1	4	24	10	32	.240	.285	.371	86	-4	1	3	-2	.944	-16	O-77/1-1	-2.5
1975	LA-N	62	145	14	28	8	0	1	5	11	29	.193	.250	.269	46	-11	4	3	-1	.972	-9	O-54	-2.4
1976	Atl-N	111	324	39	94	10	4	6	36	19	57	.290	.335	.383	97	-1	2	3	-1	.983	-12	O-84,1-12/3	-2.0
1977	Atl-N	72	155	20	37	8	0	3	15	6	46	.239	.267	.348	57	-10	1	0	0	.984	-2	1-32/O-9,3	-1.3
1978	Atl-N	5	9	2	3	0	0	0	0	0	1	.333	.333	.333	78	-0	0	0	0	1.000	-0	/1-2	-0.1
	Sea-A	70	251	32	75	20	3	4	30	15	39	.299	.338	.450	121	6	2	2	-1	.980	-3	O-54,D-12/1	0.0
1979	Sea-A	103	310	38	89	23	4	6	42	28	62	.287	.356	.445	113	5	6	4	-1	1.000	-2	O-75,1-15	-0.1
1980	Sea-A	126	418	44	114	19	1	15	59	17	67	.273	.303	.431	98	-3	2	4	-2	1.000	-3	O-60,1-36,D	-1.0
1981	Sea-A★	104	405	50	132	28	2	14	66	35	50	.326	.385	.509	150	25	13	10	-2	.974	6	*O-103	2.7
1982	Chi-A	104	382	49	119	27	4	11	55	24	53	.312	.366	.490	133	17	3	3	-3	.993	-1	*1-102/O-6	0.9
1983	*Chi-A	115	420	65	129	32	3	9	63	25	58	.307	.350	.462	117	9	0	0	-0	1.000	-0	1-67,O-55/D	-0.5
1984	Chi-A	111	363	35	93	18	2	6	58	25	69	.256	.311	.358	81	-9	5	6	0	.993	-13	1-67,O-41	-2.5
1985	Chi-A	46	122	14	30	2	0	0	9	8	22	.246	.298	.262	53	-8	2	0	1	.970	-2	O-23,D-12/1	-1.0

YEAR	TM/L	G	AB	R	H	2B	3B	HR	RBI	BB	SO	AVG	OBP	SLG	PRO+	BR/A	SB	CS	SBR	FA	FR	G/POS	TPR
	NY-N	46	116	14	33	3	1	1	11	6	14	.284	.325	.353	92	-1	1	0	0	1.000	-5	O-29/1-8	-0.7
1986	Tex-A	88	213	17	61	7	0	4	22	3	41	.286	.306	.376	82	-5	1	3	-2	.967	-1	O-25,1-23,3/SD	-1.0
1987	Tex-A	27	60	6	17	3	0	3	12	1	19	.283	.306	.483	105	0	0	1	-1	1.000	-0	1-12,O-12/D	-0.1
Total	18	1392	4121	494	1162	232	30	86	503	245	704	.282	.328	.415	102	6	55	38	-6	.979	-89	O-794,1-396/D3S	-13.9

■ FRANKIE PACK
Pack, Frank b: 4/10/28, Morristown, Tenn. BL/TR, 6', 190 lbs. Deb: 6/5/49

YEAR	TM/L	G	AB	R	H	2B	3B	HR	RBI	BB	SO	AVG	OBP	SLG	PRO+	BR/A	SB	CS	SBR	FA	FR	G/POS	TPR
1949	StL-A	1	1	0	0	0	0	0	0	0	1	.000	.000	.000	-96	-0	0	0	0	.000	0	H	0.0

■ DICK PADDEN
Padden, Richard Joseph "Brains" b: 9/17/1870, Martins Ferry, O. d: 10/31/22, Martins Ferry, O. BR/TR, 5'10", 165 lbs. Deb: 7/15/1896

YEAR	TM/L	G	AB	R	H	2B	3B	HR	RBI	BB	SO	AVG	OBP	SLG	PRO+	BR/A	SB	CS	SBR	FA	FR	G/POS	TPR
1896	Pit-N	61	219	33	53	4	8	2	24	14	9	.242	.294	.361	75	-9	8			.931	-12	2-61	-1.5
1897	Pit-N	134	517	84	146	16	10	2	58	38		.282	.350	.364	92	-5	18			.941	2	*2-134	0.3
1898	Pit-N	128	463	61	119	7	6	2	43	35		.257	.335	.311	87	-7	11			.947	-2	*2-128	0.0
1899	Was-N	134	451	66	125	20	7	2	61	24		.277	.337	.366	94	-4	27			.913	8	S-85,2-48	1.2
1901	StL-N	123	489	71	125	17	7	2	62	31		.256	.315	.331	92	-5	26			.950	1	*2-115/S-8	0.1
1902	StL-A	117	413	54	109	26	3	1	40	30		.264	.327	.349	89	-6	11			**.967**	18	*2-117	1.6
1903	StL-A	29	94	7	19	3	0	0	6	9		.202	.306	.234	65	-3	5			.955	6	2-29	0.4
1904	StL-A	132	453	42	108	19	4	0	36	40		.238	.325	.298	104	4	23			.959	-9	*2-132	-0.2
1905	StL-A	16	58	5	10	1	1	0	4	3		.172	.213	.224	41	-4	3			.950	-0	2-16	-0.4
Total	9	874	3157	423	814	113	46	11	334	224	9	.258	.326	.333	90	-39	132			.950	11	2-780/S-93	1.5

■ TOM PADDEN
Padden, Thomas Francis b: 10/6/08, Manchester, N.H. d: 6/10/73, Manchester, N.H. BR/TR, 5'11.5", 170 lbs. Deb: 5/29/32

YEAR	TM/L	G	AB	R	H	2B	3B	HR	RBI	BB	SO	AVG	OBP	SLG	PRO+	BR/A	SB	CS	SBR	FA	FR	G/POS	TPR
1932	Pit-N	47	118	13	31	6	1	0	10	9	7	.263	.315	.331	75	-4	0			.985	-1	C-43	-0.3
1933	Pit-N	30	90	5	19	2	0	0	8	2	6	.211	.237	.233	35	-8	0			.984	6	C-27	0.0
1934	Pit-N	82	237	27	76	12	2	0	22	20	23	.321	.399	.388	109	5	3			.978	-5	C-76	0.3
1935	Pit-N	97	302	35	82	9	1	1	30	48	26	.272	.371	.318	84	-4	1			.966	14	C-94	1.4
1936	Pit-N	88	281	22	70	9	2	1	31	22	41	.249	.346	.306	63	-14	0			.976	2	C-87	-0.8
1937	Pit-N	35	98	14	28	2	0	0	8	13	11	.286	.369	.306	85	-1	1			.983	6	C-34	0.6
1943	Phi-N	17	41	5	12	0	0	0	1	2	6	.293	.341	.293	87	-1	0			1.000	4	C-16	0.4
	Was-A	3	3	1	0	0	0	0	0	1	1	.000	.250	.000	-25	-0	0	0	0	1.000		/C-2	0.0
Total	7	399	1170	122	318	40	6	2	110	127	121	.272	.345	.321	80	-28	5			.977	27	C-379	1.6

■ DEL PADDOCK
Paddock, Delmar Harold b: 6/8/1887, Volga, S.Dak. d: 2/6/52, Remer, Minn BL/TR, 5'9", 165 lbs. Deb: 4/14/12

YEAR	TM/L	G	AB	R	H	2B	3B	HR	RBI	BB	SO	AVG	OBP	SLG	PRO+	BR/A	SB	CS	SBR	FA	FR	G/POS	TPR
1912	Chi-A	1	1	0	0	0	0	0	0	0	0	.000	.000	.000	-99	-0	0			.000	0	H	0.0
	NY-A	46	156	26	45	5	3	1	14	23		.288	.393	.378	114	4	9			.894	-7	3-41/2-2,O	-0.3
	Yr	47	157	26	45	5	3	1	14	23		.287	.391	.376	113	3	9			.894	-7	3-41/2-2,O	-0.3

■ DON PADGETT
Padgett, Don Wilson b: 12/5/11, Caroleen, N.C. d: 12/9/80, High Point, N.C. BL/TR, 6', 190 lbs. Deb: 4/23/37

YEAR	TM/L	G	AB	R	H	2B	3B	HR	RBI	BB	SO	AVG	OBP	SLG	PRO+	BR/A	SB	CS	SBR	FA	FR	G/POS	TPR
1937	StL-N	123	446	62	140	22	6	10	74	30	43	.314	.357	.457	117	10	4			.955	3	*O-109	0.8
1938	StL-N	110	388	59	105	26	5	8	65	18	28	.271	.303	.455	93	-5	0			.962	5	O-71,1-16/C	-0.4
1939	StL-N	92	233	38	93	15	3	5	53	18	11	**.399**	.444	.554	157	19	1			.978	-3	C-61/1-6	1.8
1940	StL-N	93	240	24	58	15	1	6	41	26	14	.242	.321	.387	89	-4	1			.962	-8	C-72/1-2	-0.7
1941	StL-N	107	324	39	80	18	0	5	44	21	16	.247	.293	.349	75	-11	1			.959	-9	O-62,C-18/1	-2.4
1946	Bro-N	19	30	2	5	1	0	1	9	4	4	.167	.265	.300	59	-2	0			1.000	-1	C-10	-0.3
	Bos-N	44	98	6	25	3	0	2	21	5	7	.255	.291	.347	80	-3	0			.939	-6	C-26	-0.8
	Yr	63	128	8	30	4	0	3	30	9	11	.234	.285	.336	75	-5	0			.954	-7	C-36	-1.1
1947	Phi-N	75	158	14	50	8	1	0	24	16	5	.316	.383	.380	107	2	0			.962	-7	C-39	-0.3
1948	Phi-N	36	74	3	17	3	0	0	7	3	2	.230	.260	.270	44	-6	0			.957	-4	C-19	-0.9
Total	8	699	1991	247	573	111	16	37	338	141	130	.288	.336	.415	101	1	6			.962	-32	C-251,O-242/1	-3.2

■ ERNIE PADGETT
Padgett, Ernest Kitchen "Red" b: 3/1/1899, Philadelphia, Pa. d: 4/15/57, E.Orange, N.J. BR/TR, 5'8", 155 lbs. Deb: 10/3/23

YEAR	TM/L	G	AB	R	H	2B	3B	HR	RBI	BB	SO	AVG	OBP	SLG	PRO+	BR/A	SB	CS	SBR	FA	FR	G/POS	TPR
1923	Bos-N	4	11	3	2	0	0	0	2	0		.182	.308	.182	33	-1	0	0	0	.947	2	/S-2,2-1	0.1
1924	Bos-N	138	502	42	128	25	9	1	46	37	56	.255	.310	.347	79	-15	4	9	-4	.967	-10	*3-113,2-29	-2.1
1925	Bos-N	86	256	31	78	9	7	0	29	14	14	.305	.341	.395	96	-2	3	5	-2	.964	-20	2-47,S-18/3	-2.1
1926	Cle-A	36	62	7	13	0	1	0	6	8	3	.210	.300	.242	42	-5	0	0	0	.930	-1	3-29/S-2	-0.2
1927	Cle-A	7	7	1	2	0	0	0	0	0	0	.286	.286	.286	48	-1	0	0	0	1.000	-0	/2-4	-0.1
Total	5	271	838	84	223	34	17	1	81	61	75	.266	.318	.351	80	-24	8	14	-6	.957	-26	3-149/2-81,S	-4.4

■ DENNIS PAEPKE
Paepke, Dennis Ray b: 4/17/45, Long Beach, Cal. BR/TR, 6', 202 lbs. Deb: 6/2/69

YEAR	TM/L	G	AB	R	H	2B	3B	HR	RBI	BB	SO	AVG	OBP	SLG	PRO+	BR/A	SB	CS	SBR	FA	FR	G/POS	TPR
1969	KC-A	12	27	2	3	1	0	0	0	2	3	.111	.172	.148	-10	-4	0	0	0	1.000	3	/C-8	-0.1
1971	KC-A	60	152	11	31	6	0	2	14	8	29	.204	.244	.283	49	-10	0	0	0	.994	-3	C-32,O-17	-1.5
1972	KC-A	2	6	0	0	0	0	0	0	0	2	.000	.143	.000	-55	-1	0	0	0	.842	1	/C-2	0.0
1974	KC-A	6	12	0	2	0	0	0	0	1	2	.167	.231	.167	15	-1	0	1	-1	1.000	-1	/C-4,O-1	-0.3
Total	4	80	197	13	36	7	0	2	14	12	36	.183	.230	.249	36	-17	0	1	-1	.984	-1	/C-46,O-18	-1.9

■ ANDY PAFKO
Pafko, Andrew "Handy Andy" or "Pruschka" b: 2/25/21, Boyceville, Wis. BR/TR, 6', 190 lbs. Deb: 9/24/43 C

YEAR	TM/L	G	AB	R	H	2B	3B	HR	RBI	BB	SO	AVG	OBP	SLG	PRO+	BR/A	SB	CS	SBR	FA	FR	G/POS	TPR
1943	Chi-N	13	58	7	22	3	0	0	10	2	5	.379	.400	.431	142	3	1			1.000	-2	O-13	0.0
1944	Chi-N	128	469	47	126	16	2	6	62	28	23	.269	.315	.350	87	-8	2			.983	15	*O-123	0.0
1945	*Chi-N†	144	534	64	159	24	12	12	110	45	36	.298	.361	.455	129	19	5			**.995**	3	*O-140	1.5
1946	Chi-N	65	234	18	66	6	4	3	39	27	15	.282	.366	.380	114	5	4			.978	11	O-64	1.3
1947	Chi-N★	129	513	68	155	25	7	13	66	31	39	.302	.346	.454	115	9	4			.985	7	*O-127	0.9
1948	Chi-N★	142	548	82	171	30	2	26	101	50	50	.312	.375	.516	145	32	3			.938	13	*3-139	4.3
1949	Chi-N★	144	519	79	146	29	2	18	69	63	33	.281	.369	.449	121	16	4			.987	-7	O-98,3-49	0.4
1950	Chi-N★	146	514	95	156	24	8	36	92	69	32	.304	.397	.591	158	43	4			.978	-1	*O-144	3.5
1951	Chi-N	49	178	26	47	5	3	12	35	17	10	.264	.342	.528	128	6	1	1	-0	.992	2	O-48	0.6
	Bro-N	84	277	42	69	11	0	18	58	35	27	.249	.350	.484	120	7	1	4	-2	.993	-2	O-76	0.1
	Yr	133	455	68	116	16	3	30	93	52	37	.255	.347	.501	123	14	2	5	-2	.993	0	O-124	0.7
1952	*Bro-N	150	551	76	158	17	5	19	85	64	48	.287	.366	.439	121	16	4	3	-1	.988	-7	O-139,3-13	0.1
1953	Mil-N	140	516	70	153	23	4	17	72	37	33	.297	.347	.455	114	9	2	1	0	.976	-4	O-139	0.1
1954	Mil-N	138	510	61	146	22	4	14	69	37	36	.286	.339	.427	105	2	1	2	-1	.969	-4	O-138	-0.8
1955	Mil-N	86	252	29	67	3	5	5	34	7	23	.266	.297	.377	81	-7	1	2	-1	.980	-8	O-58,3-12	-1.9
1956	Mil-N	45	93	15	24	5	0	2	9	10	13	.258	.330	.376	95	-1	0			.978	-5	O-37	-0.7
1957	*Mil-N	83	220	31	61	6	1	8	27	10	22	.277	.312	.423	102	-0	0			.982	-6	O-69	-0.9
1958	*Mil-N	95	164	17	39	7	1	3	23	15	17	.238	.309	.348	80	-5	0			1.000	-14	O-93	-2.2
1959	Mil-N	71	142	17	31	8	2	5	15	14	15	.218	.293	.324	70	-6	0			.978	-12	O-64	-2.0
Total	17	1852	6292	844	1796	264	62	213	976	561	477	.285	.351	.449	118	141	38	13		.984	-21	*O-1570,3-213	4.5

■ JOSE PAGAN
Pagan, Jose Antonio (Rodriguez) b: 5/5/35, Barceloneta, P.R. BR/TR, 5'9", 165 lbs. Deb: 8/4/59 C

YEAR	TM/L	G	AB	R	H	2B	3B	HR	RBI	BB	SO	AVG	OBP	SLG	PRO+	BR/A	SB	CS	SBR	FA	FR	G/POS	TPR
1959	SF-N	31	46	7	8	1	0	0	1	2	8	.174	.208	.196	9	-6	1	0	0	.900	3	3-18/S-5,2	-0.2
1960	SF-N	18	49	8	14	2	0	2		1	6	.286	.340	.408	97	-0	2	2	-1	.917	-8	S-11/3-1	-0.9
1961	SF-N	134	434	38	110	15	2	5	46	31	45	.253	.306	.332	72	-18	8	5	-1	.964	-19	*S-132/O-4	-2.6
1962	*SF-N	164	580	73	150	25	6	7	57	47	77	.259	.315	.359	82	-15	13	9	-2	**.973**	-25	*S-164	-2.7
1963	SF-N	148	483	46	113	12	1	6	39	26	67	.234	.279	.300	67	-20	10	7	-1	.970	-18	*S-143/2-1,O	-3.2
1964	SF-N	134	367	33	82	10	1	6	28	35	56	.223	.293	.264	55	-20	5	4	-1	.958	-18	*S-132/O-8	-3.3
1965	SF-N	26	83	10	17	4	0	0	5	8	9	.205	.275	.253	48	-6	1	0	0	.941	-5	S-26	-1.0
	Pit-N	42	38	6	9	1	0	0	1	1	7	.237	.275	.263	52	-2	1	0	0	.923	8	3-15/S-7	0.6

YEAR	TM/L	G	AB	R	H	2B	3B	HR	RBI	BB	SO	AVG	OBP	SLG	PRO+	BR/A	SB	CS	SBR	FA	FR	G/POS	TPR
	Yr	68	121	16	26	5	0	0	6	9	16	.215	.275	.256	50	-8	2	0	1	.923	3	S-33,3-15	-0.4
1966	Pit-N	109	368	44	97	15	6	4	54	13	38	.264	.296	.370	84	-8	0	2	-1	.949	3	3-83,S-18/2O	-0.8
1967	Pit-N	81	211	17	61	6	2	1	19	10	28	.289	.330	.351	95	-1	1	1	-0	.938	10	3-25,O-23,S/2C	0.9
1968	Pit-N	80	163	24	36	7	1	4	21	11	32	.221	.282	.350	90	-2	2	3	-1	.924	-5	3-30,O-19/S21	-0.9
1969	Pit-N	108	274	29	78	11	4	9	42	17	46	.285	.329	.453	119	6	1	0	-0	.954	-4	3-44,O-23/2	0.2
1970	*Pit-N	95	230	21	61	14	1	7	29	20	24	.265	.324	.426	101	-0	1	1	-0	.957	-3	3-53/O-4,12	-0.4
1971	*Pit-N	57	158	16	38	1	0	5	15	16	25	.241	.314	.342	86	-3	0	0	0	.980	-2	3-41/O-3,1	-0.6
1972	Pit-N	53	127	11	32	9	0	3	8	5	17	.252	.286	.394	93	-2	0	0	0	.899	-8	3-32/O-2	-1.1
1973	Phi-N	46	78	4	16	5	0	0	5	1	15	.205	.215	.269	33	-7	0	1	-1	.958	-1	3-16/1-5,O2	-1.0
Total	15	1326	3689	387	922	138	26	52	372	244	510	.250	.300	.344	79	-105	46	35	-7	.963	-91	S-662,3-358/O21C	-17.0

■ **MIKE PAGE**   Page, Michael Randy b: 7/12/40, Woodruff, S.C. BL/TR, 6'2.5", 210 lbs. Deb: 6/30/68

YEAR	TM/L	G	AB	R	H	2B	3B	HR	RBI	BB	SO	AVG	OBP	SLG	PRO+	BR/A	SB	CS	SBR	FA	FR	G/POS	TPR
1968	Atl-N	20	28	1	5	0	0	0	1	1	9	.179	.207	.179	16	-3	0	0	0	1.000	-1	/O-6	-0.5

■ **MITCHELL PAGE**   Page, Mitchell Otis b: 10/15/51, Los Angeles, Cal. BL/TR, 6'2", 205 lbs. Deb: 4/9/77

YEAR	TM/L	G	AB	R	H	2B	3B	HR	RBI	BB	SO	AVG	OBP	SLG	PRO+	BR/A	SB	CS	SBR	FA	FR	G/POS	TPR
1977	Oak-A	145	501	85	154	28	8	21	75	78	95	.307	.407	.521	153	39	42	5	**10**	.954	7	*O-133/D-8	4.9
1978	Oak-A	147	516	62	147	25	7	17	70	53	95	.285	.356	.459	135	23	23	19	-5	.973	-1	*O-114,D-33	1.2
1979	Oak-A	133	478	51	118	11	2	9	42	52	93	.247	.325	.335	83	-11	17	16	-5	1.000	-0	*D-126/O-4	-2.0
1980	Oak-A	110	348	58	85	10	4	17	51	35	87	.244	.315	.443	113	5	14	7	0	.000	0	*D-101	0.1
1981	Oak-A	34	92	9	13	1	0	4	13	7	29	.141	.202	.283	40	-7	2	1	0	.000	0	D-29	-0.9
1982	Oak-A	31	78	14	20	5	0	4	7	7	24	.256	.333	.474	124	2	3	4	-2	.000	0	D-24	-0.0
1983	Oak-A	57	79	16	19	3	0	0	1	10	22	.241	.341	.278	77	-2	3	3	-1	1.000	-2	D-34,O-10	-0.6
1984	Pit-N	16	12	2	4	1	0	0	0	3	4	.333	.467	.417	150	1	0	0	0	.000	0	H	0.1
Total	8	673	2104	297	560	84	21	72	259	245	449	.266	.348	.429	118	50	104	55	-2	.963	3	D-355,O-261	2.8

■ **KARL PAGEL**   Pagel, Karl Douglas b: 3/29/55, Madison, Wis. BL/TL, 6'2", 190 lbs. Deb: 9/21/78

YEAR	TM/L	G	AB	R	H	2B	3B	HR	RBI	BB	SO	AVG	OBP	SLG	PRO+	BR/A	SB	CS	SBR	FA	FR	G/POS	TPR
1978	Chi-N	2	2	0	0	0	0	0	0	0	2	.000	.000	.000	-89	-0	0	0	0	.000	0	H	-0.1
1979	Chi-N	1	1	0	0	0	0	0	0	0	1	.000	.000	.000	-91	-0	0	0	0	.000	0	/H	0.0
1981	Cle-A	14	15	3	4	0	2	1	4	4	1	.267	.421	.733	230	3	0	0	0	1.000	2	/1-6,D-1	0.4
1982	Cle-A	23	18	3	3	0	0	0	2	7	11	.167	.400	.167	63	-0	0	0	0	.970	1	1-10/D-1	-0.1
1983	Cle-A	8	20	1	6	0	0	0	1	0	5	.300	.300	.300	63	-1	0	0	0	.000	-1	/O-1,D-5	-0.2
Total	5	48	56	7	13	0	2	1	7	11	20	.232	.358	.357	99	0	0	0	0	.985	1	/1-16,D-7,O	0.0

■ **JIM PAGLIARONI**   Pagliaroni, James Vincent "Pag" b: 12/8/37, Dearborn, Mich. BR/TR, 6'4", 210 lbs. Deb: 8/13/55

YEAR	TM/L	G	AB	R	H	2B	3B	HR	RBI	BB	SO	AVG	OBP	SLG	PRO+	BR/A	SB	CS	SBR	FA	FR	G/POS	TPR
1955	Bos-A	1	0	0	0	0	0	0	1	0	0	—	—	—	—	-0	0	0	0	.000	0	/C-1	0.0
1960	Bos-A	28	62	7	19	5	2	2	9	13	11	.306	.434	.548	158	6	0	0	0	.990	-3	C-18	0.4
1961	Bos-A	120	376	50	91	17	0	16	58	55	74	.242	.345	.415	100	0	1	1	-0	.984	-4	*C-108	0.2
1962	Bos-A	90	260	39	67	14	0	11	37	36	55	.258	.359	.438	110	4	2	1	0	.987	-3	C-73	0.4
1963	Pit-N	92	252	27	58	5	0	11	26	36	57	.230	.331	.381	104	2	0	0	0	.988	4	C-85	1.0
1964	Pit-N	97	302	33	89	12	3	6	36	41	56	.295	.383	.454	135	15	1	0	0	.992	1	C-96	2.1
1965	Pit-N	134	403	42	108	15	3	17	65	41	84	.268	.340	.432	115	8	0	0	0	.994	-4	*C-131	1.1
1966	Pit-N	123	374	37	88	20	0	11	49	50	71	.235	.332	.377	96	-1	0	5	-3	.997	-14	*C-118	-1.1
1967	Pit-N	44	100	4	20	1	1	0	9	16	26	.200	.316	.230	59	-5	0	0	0	.984	-0	C-38	-0.3
1968	Oak-A	66	199	19	49	4	0	6	20	24	42	.246	.333	.357	115	4	0	0	0	.997	-9	C-63	-0.1
1969	Oak-A	14	27	1	4	1	0	1	2	5	2	.148	.303	.296	71	-1	0	0	0	.981	2	/C-7	0.1
	Sea-A	40	110	10	29	4	1	5	14	13	16	.264	.341	.455	123	3	0	0	0	.988	-6	C-29/1-2,O	-0.2
	Yr	54	137	11	33	5	1	6	16	18	18	.241	.333	.423	113	2	0	0	0	.987	-4	C-36/1-2,O	-0.1
Total	11	849	2465	269	622	98	7	90	326	330	494	.252	.346	.407	109	35	4	7	-3	.991	-36	C-767/1-2,O	3.6

■ **MIKE PAGLIARULO**   Pagliarulo, Michael Timothy b: 3/15/60, Medford, Mass. BL/TR, 6'1", 205 lbs. Deb: 7/7/84

YEAR	TM/L	G	AB	R	H	2B	3B	HR	RBI	BB	SO	AVG	OBP	SLG	PRO+	BR/A	SB	CS	SBR	FA	FR	G/POS	TPR
1984	NY-A	67	201	24	48	15	3	7	34	15	46	.239	.292	.448	105	1	0	0	0	.955	6	3-67	0.6
1985	NY-A	138	380	55	91	16	2	19	62	45	86	.239	.324	.442	111	5	0	0	0	.951	-17	*3-134	-1.3
1986	NY-A	149	504	71	120	24	3	28	71	54	120	.238	.317	.464	111	6	4	1	1	.953	6	*3-143/S-2	1.0
1987	NY-A	150	522	76	122	26	3	32	87	53	111	.234	.307	.479	105	2	1	3	-2	.959	4	*3-147/1-1	0.3
1988	NY-A	125	444	46	96	20	1	15	67	37	104	.216	.280	.367	80	-13	1	0	0	.943	-0	*3-124	-1.4
1989	NY-A	74	223	19	44	10	0	4	16	19	43	.197	.266	.296	59	-12	1	1	-0	.936	-4	3-69/D-1	-1.7
	SD-N	50	148	12	29	7	3	3	14	18	39	.196	.287	.304	69	-6	2	0	1	.936	0	3-49	-0.5
1990	SD-N	128	398	29	101	23	2	7	38	39	66	.254	.325	.374	91	-5	1	3	-2	.955	2	*3-116	-0.4
1991	*Min-A	121	365	38	102	20	6	6	36	21	55	.279	.324	.384	91	-5	1	2	-1	.965	12	*3-118/2-1	0.7
1992	Min-A	42	105	10	21	4	0	0	9	1	17	.200	.215	.238	26	-10	1	0	0	.962	3	3-37/D-1	-0.8
1993	Min-A	83	253	31	74	16	4	3	23	18	34	.292	.351	.423	107	2	6	6	-2	.984	0	3-79	0.1
	Bal-A	33	117	24	38	9	0	6	21	8	15	.325	.373	.556	140	6	0	0	0	.937	-1	3-28/1-4	0.5
	Yr	116	370	55	112	25	4	9	44	26	49	.303	.358	.465	118	9	6	6	-2	.969	-1	*3-107/1-4	0.6
Total	10	1160	3660	435	886	190	18	130	478	328	736	.242	.309	.410	96	-28	18	16	-4	.954	11	*3-1111/1-5,DS2	-2.9

■ **TOM PAGNOZZI**   Pagnozzi, Thomas Alan b: 7/30/62, Tucson, Ariz. BR/TR, 6', 190 lbs. Deb: 4/12/87

YEAR	TM/L	G	AB	R	H	2B	3B	HR	RBI	BB	SO	AVG	OBP	SLG	PRO+	BR/A	SB	CS	SBR	FA	FR	G/POS	TPR
1987	*StL-N	27	48	8	9	1	0	2	9	4	13	.188	.250	.333	52	-3	1	0	0	1.000	-4	C-25/1-1	-0.6
1988	StL-N	81	195	17	55	9	0	0	15	11	32	.282	.320	.328	86	-4	0	0	0	.971	-2	C-28,1-28/3	-0.6
1989	StL-N	52	80	3	12	2	0	0	3	6	19	.150	.218	.175	13	-9	0	0	0	.982	-3	C-38/1-2,3	-1.2
1990	StL-N	69	220	20	61	15	0	2	23	14	37	.277	.323	.373	91	-3	1	1	-0	.989	10	C-63/1-2	1.0
1991	StL-N	140	459	38	121	24	5	2	57	36	63	.264	.323	.351	89	-7	9	13	-5	.991	-7	*C-139/1-3	-1.1
1992	StL-N★	139	485	33	121	26	3	7	44	28	64	.249	.292	.359	86	-10	2	5	-2	.999	-16	*C-138	-2.3
1993	StL-N	92	330	31	85	15	1	7	41	19	30	.258	.300	.373	80	-10	1	0	0	.991	-13	C-92	-1.7
1994	StL-N	70	243	21	66	12	1	7	40	21	39	.272	.330	.416	96	-2	0	0	0	.998	-8	C-70/1-1	-0.5
Total	8	670	2060	171	530	104	10	27	232	139	297	.257	.307	.357	84	-47	14	19	-7	.992	-43	C-593/1-37,3	-7.0

■ **REY PALACIOS**   Palacios, Robert Rey b: 11/8/62, Brooklyn, N.Y. BR/TR, 5'10", 190 lbs. Deb: 9/8/88

YEAR	TM/L	G	AB	R	H	2B	3B	HR	RBI	BB	SO	AVG	OBP	SLG	PRO+	BR/A	SB	CS	SBR	FA	FR	G/POS	TPR
1988	KC-A	5	11	2	1	0	0	0	0	0	4	.091	.091	.091	-48	-2	0	0	0	1.000	1	/C-3,3-1,D	-0.1
1989	KC-A	55	47	12	8	2	0	1	8	2	14	.170	.220	.277	39	-4	0	1	-1	.958	4	3-21,1-18,C/OD	-0.1
1990	KC-A	41	56	8	13	3	0	2	9	5	24	.232	.295	.393	92	-1	2	1	-0	.992	4	C-27/1-7,3O	0.4
Total	3	101	114	22	22	5	0	3	17	7	42	.193	.246	.316	57	-7	2	3	-1	.994	9	/C-43,1-25,3DO	0.2

■ **ERV PALICA**   Palica, Ervin Martin (b: Ervin Martin Pavliecivich)
b: 2/9/28, Lomita, Cal. d: 5/29/82, Huntington Beach, Cal. BR/TR, 6'1.5", 180 lbs. Deb: 4/21/45

YEAR	TM/L	G	AB	R	H	2B	3B	HR	RBI	BB	SO	AVG	OBP	SLG	PRO+	BR/A	SB	CS	SBR	FA	FR	G/POS	TPR
1945	Bro-N	2	0	0	0	0	0	0	0	0	0	—	—	—	—	0	0			.000	0	R	0.0
1947	Bro-N	3	0	0	0	0	0	0	0	0	0	—	—	—	—	0	0			.000	-0	/P-3	0.0
1948	Bro-N	45	39	6	5	1	1	0	3	4	12	.128	.209	.205	12	-5	0			1.000	-1	P-41	0.0
1949	*Bro-N	49	19	2	3	1	0	0	2	2	6	.158	.238	.211	20	-2	0			.875	-0	P-49	0.0
1950	Bro-N	48	68	4	15	4	0	0	8	2	8	.221	.221	.324	40	-6	2			.889	-4	P-43	0.0
1951	Bro-N	20	13	1	2	0	0	0	0	2	5	.154	.267	.154	16	-1	0			1.000	0	P-19	0.0
1953	Bro-N	4	1	0	1	0	0	0	1	0	0	1.000	1.000	1.000	414	0	0			1.000	-0	/P-4	0.0
1954	Bro-N	28	16	2	4	1	0	0	1	1	4	.250	.294	.313	56	-1	0			1.000	-0	P-25	0.0
1955	Bal-A	33	55	3	13	1	0	1	4	2	18	.236	.288	.255	50	-4	0			.905	-1	P-33	0.0
1956	Bal-A	30	32	4	5	0	0	0	1	0	10	.156	.156	.156	-19	-6	0			.917	-0	P-29	0.0
Total	10	262	243	22	48	8	1	1	17	13	63	.198	.238	.251	31	-24	2		0	.921	-7	P-246	0.0

YEAR	TM/L	G	AB	R	H	2B	3B	HR	RBI	BB	SO	AVG	OBP	SLG	PRO+	BR/A	SB	CS	SBR	FA	FR	G/POS	TPR

■ RAFAEL PALMEIRO — Palmeiro, Rafael (Corrales) b: 9/24/64, Havana, Cuba BL/TL, 6', 180 lbs. Deb: 9/8/86

YEAR	TM/L	G	AB	R	H	2B	3B	HR	RBI	BB	SO	AVG	OBP	SLG	PRO+	BR/A	SB	CS	SBR	FA	FR	G/POS	TPR
1986	Chi-N	22	73	9	18	4	0	3	12	4	6	.247	.295	.425	89	-1	1	1	-0	.900	-0	O-20	-0.2
1987	Chi-N	84	221	32	61	15	1	14	30	20	26	.276	.339	.543	124	7	2	2	-1	1.000	-4	O-45,1-18	0.0
1988	Chi-N★	152	580	75	178	41	5	8	53	38	34	.307	.353	.436	120	14	2	2	2	.983	4	*O-147/1-5	1.7
1989	Tex-A	156	559	76	154	23	4	8	64	63	48	.275	.355	.374	104	4	4	3	-1	.991	10	*1-147/D-6	0.2
1990	Tex-A	154	598	72	191	35	6	14	89	40	59	.319	.365	.468	131	24	3	3	-1	.995	-1	*1-146/D-6	1.1
1991	Tex-A★	159	631	115	203	49	3	26	88	68	72	.322	.389	.532	156	48	4	3	-1	.992	-4	*1-157/D-2	3.3
1992	Tex-A	159	608	84	163	27	4	22	85	72	83	.268	.355	.434	124	20	2	3	-1	.995	14	*1-156/D-2	2.2
1993	Tex-A	160	597	124	176	40	2	37	105	73	85	.295	.376	.554	153	43	22	3	5	.997	15	*1-160	4.7
1994	Bal-A	111	436	82	139	32	0	23	76	54	63	.319	.392	.550	132	21	7	3	0	.996	-2	*1-111	0.9
Total	9	1157	4303	669	1283	266	25	155	602	432	476	.298	.367	.480	131	180	57	23	3	.994	32	1-900,O-212/D	13.9

■ DEAN PALMER — Palmer, Dean William b: 12/27/68, Tallahassee, Fla. BR/TR, 6'1", 175 lbs. Deb: 9/1/89

YEAR	TM/L	G	AB	R	H	2B	3B	HR	RBI	BB	SO	AVG	OBP	SLG	PRO+	BR/A	SB	CS	SBR	FA	FR	G/POS	TPR
1989	Tex-A	16	19	0	2	2	0	0	1	0	12	.105	.105	.211	-13	-3	0	0	0	.667	-0	/3-6,S-1,OD	-0.3
1991	Tex-A	81	268	38	50	9	2	15	37	32	98	.187	.281	.403	88	-5	0	2	-1	.944	-10	3-50,O-29/D	-1.7
1992	Tex-A	152	541	74	124	25	0	26	72	62	154	.229	.313	.420	107	4	10	4	1	.945	-10	*3-150	-0.6
1993	Tex-A	148	519	88	127	31	2	33	96	53	154	.245	.324	.503	123	15	11	10	-3	.922	-12	*3-148/S-1	0.0
1994	Tex-A	93	342	50	84	14	2	19	59	26	89	.246	.303	.465	101	-1	3	4	-2	.912	-2	3-91	-0.4
Total	5	490	1689	250	387	81	6	93	265	173	507	.229	.307	.449	107	9	24	20	-5	.929	-34	3-445/O-30,DS	-3.0

■ EDDIE PALMER — Palmer, Edwin Henry "Baldy" b: 6/1/1893, Petty, Tex. d: 1/9/83, Marlow, Okla. BR/TR, 5'9.5", 175 lbs. Deb: 9/6/17

YEAR	TM/L	G	AB	R	H	2B	3B	HR	RBI	BB	SO	AVG	OBP	SLG	PRO+	BR/A	SB	CS	SBR	FA	FR	G/POS	TPR
1917	Phi-A	16	52	7	11	1	0	0	5	7	7	.212	.305	.231	65	-2	1			.898	0	3-13/S-1	-0.2

■ JOE PALMISANO — Palmisano, Joseph b: 11/19/02, West Point, Ga. d: 11/5/71, Albuquerque, N.Mex. BR/TR, 5'8", 160 lbs. Deb: 5/31/31

YEAR	TM/L	G	AB	R	H	2B	3B	HR	RBI	BB	SO	AVG	OBP	SLG	PRO+	BR/A	SB	CS	SBR	FA	FR	G/POS	TPR
1931	Phi-A	19	44	5	10	2	0	0	4	6	3	.227	.320	.273	54	-3	0	0	0	.960	-2	C-16/2-1	-0.3

■ STAN PALYS — Palys, Stanley Francis b: 5/1/30, Blakely, Pa. BR/TR, 6'2", 190 lbs. Deb: 9/20/53

YEAR	TM/L	G	AB	R	H	2B	3B	HR	RBI	BB	SO	AVG	OBP	SLG	PRO+	BR/A	SB	CS	SBR	FA	FR	G/POS	TPR
1953	Phi-N	2	2	0	0	0	0	0	0	1	0	.000	.333	.000	-4	-0	0	0	0	.000	-0	/O-1	-0.1
1954	Phi-N	2	4	0	1	0	0	0	0	1	1	.250	.400	.250	74	-0	0	0	0	1.000	-0	/O-1	0.0
1955	Phi-N	15	52	8	15	3	0	1	8	6	5	.288	.362	.404	105	0	1	0	0	1.000	-0	O-15	0.0
	Cin-N	79	222	29	51	14	0	7	30	12	35	.230	.272	.387	69	-11	1	1	-0	.992	2	O-55/1-1	-1.1
	Yr	94	274	37	66	17	0	8	38	18	40	.241	.290	.391	75	-10	2	1	0	.993	2	O-70/1-1	-1.1
1956	Cin-N	40	53	5	12	0	0	2	5	6	13	.226	.305	.340	69	-2	0	0	0	.929	-2	O-10	-0.5
Total	4	138	333	42	79	17	0	10	43	26	54	.237	.294	.378	74	-13	2	1	0	.988	-1	/O-82,1-1	-1.7

■ JIM PANKOVITS — Pankovits, James Franklin b: 8/6/55, Pennington Gap, Va. BR/TR, 5'10", 195 lbs. Deb: 5/27/84

YEAR	TM/L	G	AB	R	H	2B	3B	HR	RBI	BB	SO	AVG	OBP	SLG	PRO+	BR/A	SB	CS	SBR	FA	FR	G/POS	TPR
1984	Hou-N	53	81	6	23	7	0	1	14	2	20	.284	.301	.407	105	-0	1	0	0	.925	-5	2-15/S-4/O	-0.5
1985	Hou-N	75	172	24	42	3	0	4	14	17	29	.244	.316	.331	84	-4	1	0	0	.983	-5	O-33,2-21/S3	-0.4
1986	*Hou-N	70	113	12	32	6	1	1	7	11	25	.283	.347	.381	103	1	1	1	-0	.969	3	2-26/O-5,C	0.4
1987	Hou-N	50	61	7	14	2	0	1	8	6	13	.230	.299	.311	64	-3	2	0	1	1.000	5	/2-9,O-6,3	0.2
1988	Hou-N	68	140	13	31	7	1	2	12	8	28	.221	.273	.329	75	-5	2	1	0	.939	-2	2-31,3-11/1	-0.7
1990	Bos-A	2	0	0	0	0	0	0	0	0	0	—	—	—	—		0	0	0	.000	0	/2-2	0.0
Total	6	318	567	62	142	25	2	9	55	44	115	.250	.308	.349	86	-11	8	3	1	.961	-4	2-104/O-47,3S1C	-1.0

■ KEN PAPE — Pape, Kenneth Wayne b: 10/1/51, San Antonio, Tex. BR/TR, 5'11", 195 lbs. Deb: 5/17/76

YEAR	TM/L	G	AB	R	H	2B	3B	HR	RBI	BB	SO	AVG	OBP	SLG	PRO+	BR/A	SB	CS	SBR	FA	FR	G/POS	TPR
1976	Tex-A	21	23	7	5	1	0	0	4	3	2	.217	.357	.391	117	1	0	1	-1	.968	4	/S-6,3-4,2D	0.5

■ STAN PAPI — Papi, Stanley Gerard b: 2/4/51, Fresno, Cal. BR/TR, 6', 178 lbs. Deb: 4/11/74

YEAR	TM/L	G	AB	R	H	2B	3B	HR	RBI	BB	SO	AVG	OBP	SLG	PRO+	BR/A	SB	CS	SBR	FA	FR	G/POS	TPR
1974	StL-N	8	4	0	1	0	0	0	1	0	0	.250	.250	.250	40	-0	0	0	0	1.000	1	/S-7,2-1	0.0
1977	Mon-N	13	43	5	10	2	1	0	4	1	9	.233	.250	.326	55	-3	1	0	0	.952	-5	3-10/S-2,2	-0.7
1978	Mon-N	67	152	15	35	11	0	0	11	10	28	.230	.287	.303	65	-7	0	0	0	.976	-3	S-22,3-15/2	-0.8
1979	Bos-A	50	117	9	22	8	0	1	6	5	20	.188	.221	.282	33	-11	0	0	0	.982	12	2-26,S-21	0.3
1980	Bos-A	1	0	0	0	0	0	0	0	0	0	—	—	—	—		0	0	0	.000	0	/3-1	0.0
	Det-A	46	114	12	27	3	4	3	17	5	24	.237	.269	.412	82	-3	0	0	0	.973	-2	2-31,3-11/S1	-0.4
	Yr	47	114	12	27	3	4	3	17	5	24	.237	.269	.412	82	-3	0	0	0	.973	-2	2-31,3-12/S1	-0.4
1981	Det-A	40	93	8	19	2	1	3	12	3	18	.204	.229	.344	61	-5	1	0	0	.941	-1	3-32/1-1,2OD	-0.7
Total	6	225	523	49	114	26	6	7	51	24	99	.218	.255	.331	60	-30	2	0	1	.931	2	/3-69,2-65,SD10	-2.3

■ ERIK PAPPAS — Pappas, Erik Daniel b: 4/25/66, Chicago, Ill. BR/TR, 6', 190 lbs. Deb: 4/19/91

YEAR	TM/L	G	AB	R	H	2B	3B	HR	RBI	BB	SO	AVG	OBP	SLG	PRO+	BR/A	SB	CS	SBR	FA	FR	G/POS	TPR
1991	Chi-N	7	17	1	3	0	0	0	2	1	5	.176	.222	.176	13	-2	0	0	0	1.000	1	/C-6	0.0
1993	StL-N	82	228	25	63	12	0	1	28	35	35	.276	.373	.342	95	-0	1	3	-2	.982	5	C-63,O-16/1	0.6
1994	StL-N	15	44	8	4	1	0	0	5	10	13	.091	.273	.114	6	-6	0	0	0	.955	-5	C-15	-1.0
Total	3	104	289	34	70	13	0	1	35	46	53	.242	.348	.298	76	-8	1	3	-2	.978	1	/C-84,O-16,1	-0.4

■ CRAIG PAQUETTE — Paquette, Craig Harold b: 3/28/69, Long Beach, Cal. BR/TR, 6', 190 lbs. Deb: 6/1/93

YEAR	TM/L	G	AB	R	H	2B	3B	HR	RBI	BB	SO	AVG	OBP	SLG	PRO+	BR/A	SB	CS	SBR	FA	FR	G/POS	TPR
1993	Oak-A	105	393	35	86	20	4	12	46	14	108	.219	.246	.382	70	-19	4	2	0	.950	-9	*3-104/O-1,D	-2.8
1994	Oak-A	14	49	0	7	2	0	0	0	0	14	.143	.143	.184	-18	-9	1	0	0	1.000	1	3-14	-0.7
Total	2	119	442	35	93	22	4	12	46	14	122	.210	.235	.360	60	-28	5	2	0	.956	-8	3-118/D-1,O	-3.5

■ AL PARDO — Pardo, Alberto Judas b: 9/8/62, Oviedo, Spain BB/TR, 6'2", 187 lbs. Deb: 7/3/85

YEAR	TM/L	G	AB	R	H	2B	3B	HR	RBI	BB	SO	AVG	OBP	SLG	PRO+	BR/A	SB	CS	SBR	FA	FR	G/POS	TPR
1985	Bal-A	34	75	3	10	1	0	0	1	3	15	.133	.167	.147	-14	-12	0	0	0	.979	3	C-29	-0.7
1986	Bal-A	16	51	3	7	1	0	1	3	0	14	.137	.137	.216	-6	-7	0	0	0	.987	-2	C-14/D-1	-0.9
1988	Phi-N	2	2	0	0	0	0	0	0	0	2	.000	.000	.000	-98	-0	0	0	0	1.000	-0	/C-2	-0.1
1989	Phi-N	1	1	0	0	0	0	0	0	0	0	.000	.000	.000	-99	-0	0	0	0	1.000	-0	/C-1	-0.0
Total	4	53	129	6	17	2	0	1	4	3	31	.132	.152	.171	-12	-20	0	0	0	.982	1	/C-46,D-1	-1.7

■ JOHNNY PAREDES — Paredes, Johnny Alfonso (Isambert) b: 9/2/62, Maracaibo, Venez. BR/TR, 5'11", 165 lbs. Deb: 4/29/88

YEAR	TM/L	G	AB	R	H	2B	3B	HR	RBI	BB	SO	AVG	OBP	SLG	PRO+	BR/A	SB	CS	SBR	FA	FR	G/POS	TPR
1988	Mon-N	35	91	6	17	2	0	1	10	9	17	.187	.282	.242	49	-6	5	2	0	.976	0	2-28/O-1	-0.5
1990	Det-A	6	8	2	1	0	0	0	0	1	0	.125	.222	.125	-0	-1	0	0	0	.917	1	/2-4	0.0
	Mon-N	3	6	1	2	1	0	0	1	1	0	.333	.429	.500	161	1	0	0	0	.889	1	/2-2	0.1
1991	Det-A	16	18	4	6	0	0	0	0	1	1	.333	.333	.333	84	-0	1	1	-0	.958	4	/2-7,3-1,SD	0.3
Total	3	60	123	12	26	3	0	1	11	11	18	.211	.292	.260	56	-7	6	3	0	.965	6	/2-41,D-2,S3O	-0.1

■ FREDDY PARENT — Parent, Frederick Alfred b: 11/25/1875, Biddeford, Me. d: 11/2/72, Sanford, Maine BR/TR, 5'7", 154 lbs. Deb: 7/14/1899

YEAR	TM/L	G	AB	R	H	2B	3B	HR	RBI	BB	SO	AVG	OBP	SLG	PRO+	BR/A	SB	CS	SBR	FA	FR	G/POS	TPR
1899	StL-N	2	8	0	1	0	0	0	1	0		.125	.125	.125	-31	-1	0			.889	-1	/2-2	-0.2
1901	Bos-A	138	517	87	158	23	9	4	59	41		.306	.367	.408	117	12	16			.918	-0	*S-138	2.1
1902	Bos-A	138	567	91	156	31	8	3	62	24		.275	.309	.374	86	-12	16			.932	4	*S-138	0.0
1903	*Bos-A	139	560	83	170	31	17	4	80	13		.304	.326	.441	122	13	24			.930	9	*S-139	2.9
1904	Bos-A	155	591	85	172	22	9	6	77	28		.291	.330	.389	120	12	20			.929	-8	*S-155	1.0
1905	Bos-A	153	602	55	141	16	5	0	33	47		.234	.296	.277	81	-12	25			.920	-7	*S-153	-1.8
1906	Bos-A	149	600	67	141	14	10	1	49	31		.235	.277	.297	80	-15	16			.933	-7	*S-143/2-6	-0.9
1907	Bos-A	114	409	51	113	19	5	1	26	22		.276	.321	.355	116	7	12			.978	-0	O-47,S-43/32	0.7
1908	Chi-A	119	391	28	81	7	5	0	35	50		.207	.300	.251	81	-6	9			.930	5	*S-118	0.1
1909	Chi-A	136	472	61	123	10	5	0	30	46		.261	.335	.303	106	5	32			.929	17	S-98,O-38/2	2.4
1910	Chi-A	81	258	23	46	6	1	1	16	29		.178	.266	.221	55	-13	14			.970	-3	O-62,2-11/S3	-2.0

YEAR	TM/L	G	AB	R	H	2B	3B	HR	RBI	BB	SO	AVG	OBP	SLG	PRO+	BR/A	SB	CS	SBR	FA	FR	G/POS	TPR
1911	Chi-A	3	9	2	4	1	0	0	3	2		.444	.545	.556	214	2	0			1.000	1	/2-3	0.2
Total	12	1327	4984	633	1306	180	74	20	471	333		.262	.315	.340	99	-8	184			.927	9	*S-1129,O-147/23	3.5

■ MARK PARENT
Parent, Mark Alan b: 9/16/61, Ashland, Ore. BR/TR, 6'5", 224 lbs. Deb: 9/20/86

YEAR	TM/L	G	AB	R	H	2B	3B	HR	RBI	BB	SO	AVG	OBP	SLG	PRO+	BR/A	SB	CS	SBR	FA	FR	G/POS	TPR
1986	SD-N	8	14	1	2	0	0	0	0	1	3	.143	.200	.143	-4	-2	0	0	0	.889	-1	/C-3	-0.3
1987	SD-N	12	25	0	2	0	0	0	2	0	9	.080	.080	.080	-60	-6	0	0	0	1.000	-0	C-10	-0.5
1988	SD-N	41	118	9	23	3	0	6	15	6	23	.195	.234	.373	73	-5	0	0	0	.986	5	C-36	0.3
1989	SD-N	52	141	12	27	4	0	7	21	8	34	.191	.235	.369	70	-6	1	0	0	1.000	6	C-41/1-1	0.2
1990	SD-N	65	189	13	42	11	0	3	16	16	29	.222	.283	.328	67	-9	1	0	0	.992	8	C-60	0.3
1991	Tex-A	3	1	0	0	0	0	0	0	0	1	.000	.000	.000	-99	-0	0	0	0	1.000	1	/C-3	0.0
1992	Bal-A	17	34	4	8	1	0	2	4	3	7	.235	.316	.441	107	-0	0	0	0	.988	4	C-16	0.5
1993	Bal-A	22	54	7	14	2	0	4	12	3	14	.259	.298	.519	110	-0	0	0	0	.989	-1	C-21/D-1	0.0
1994	Chi-N	44	99	8	26	4	0	3	16	13	24	.263	.354	.361	97	-0	0	1	-1	.976	4	C-37	0.4
Total	9	264	675	54	144	25	0	25	86	50	144	.213	.270	.361	73	-27	2	1	0	.988	26	C-227/D-1,1	0.9

■ KELLY PARIS
Paris, Kelly Jay b: 10/17/57, Encino, Cal. BR/TR, 6', 180 lbs. Deb: 9/1/82

YEAR	TM/L	G	AB	R	H	2B	3B	HR	RBI	BB	SO	AVG	OBP	SLG	PRO+	BR/A	SB	CS	SBR	FA	FR	G/POS	TPR
1982	StL-N	12	29	1	3	0	0	0	1	0	7	.103	.103	.103	-42	-5	0	0	0	.867	2	/3-5,S-4	-0.3
1983	Cin-N	56	120	13	30	6	0	0	7	15	22	.250	.338	.300	75	-3	8	2	1	1.000	-2	3-16,2-10/S1	-0.4
1985	Bal-A	5	9	0	0	0	0	0	0	0	1	.000	.000	.000	-99	-2	0	0	0	.857	-0	/2-2,D-2	-0.3
1986	Bal-A	5	10	0	2	0	0	0	0	0	0	.200	.200	.200	9	-1	0	1	-1	.857	1	/3-3,D-2	-0.1
1988	Chi-A	14	44	6	11	0	0	3	6	0	9	.250	.250	.455	93	-1	0	0	0	1.000	-0	/1-9,3-4,D	-0.1
Total	5	92	212	20	46	6	0	3	14	15	39	.217	.272	.288	54	-13	8	3	1	.944	1	/3-28,1-12,2SD	-1.2

■ TONY PARISSE
Parisse, Louis Peter b: 6/25/11, Philadelphia, Pa. d: 6/2/56, Philadelphia, Pa. BR/TR, 5'10", 165 lbs. Deb: 9/22/43

YEAR	TM/L	G	AB	R	H	2B	3B	HR	RBI	BB	SO	AVG	OBP	SLG	PRO+	BR/A	SB	CS	SBR	FA	FR	G/POS	TPR
1943	Phi-A	6	17	0	3	0	0	0	1	2	2	.176	.263	.176	30	-1	0	0	0	1.000	0	/C-5	-0.1
1944	Phi-A	4	4	0	0	0	0	0	0	0	1	.000	.000	.000	-99	-1	0	0	0	.500	-1	/C-2	-0.2
Total	2	10	21	0	3	0	0	0	1	2	3	.143	.217	.143	6	-2	0	0	0	.960	-1	/C-7	-0.3

■ ACE PARKER
Parker, Clarence McKay b: 5/17/12, Portsmouth, Va. BR/TR, 6', 180 lbs. Deb: 4/24/37

YEAR	TM/L	G	AB	R	H	2B	3B	HR	RBI	BB	SO	AVG	OBP	SLG	PRO+	BR/A	SB	CS	SBR	FA	FR	G/POS	TPR
1937	Phi-A	38	94	8	11	0	1	2	13	4	17	.117	.153	.202	-11	-17	0	0	0	.905	-5	S-19/2-9,O	-1.9
1938	Phi-A	56	113	12	26	5	0	0	12	10	16	.230	.293	.274	44	-10	1	2	-1	.972	-5	S-26/2-9,3	-1.3
Total	2	94	207	20	37	5	1	2	25	14	33	.179	.231	.242	19	-26	1	2	-1	.934	-10	/S-45,2-18,3O	-3.2

■ PAT PARKER
Parker, Clarence Perkins b: 5/22/1893, Somerville, Mass. d: 3/21/67, Claremont, N.H. BR/TR, 5'7", 160 lbs. Deb: 8/10/15

YEAR	TM/L	G	AB	R	H	2B	3B	HR	RBI	BB	SO	AVG	OBP	SLG	PRO+	BR/A	SB	CS	SBR	FA	FR	G/POS	TPR
1915	StL-A	3	6	0	1	0	0	0	1	0	3	.167	.167	.167	-0	-1	0	1	-1	1.000	-0	/O-2	-0.2

■ DAVE PARKER
Parker, David Gene b: 6/9/51, Calhoun, Miss. BL/TR, 6'5", 230 lbs. Deb: 7/12/73

YEAR	TM/L	G	AB	R	H	2B	3B	HR	RBI	BB	SO	AVG	OBP	SLG	PRO+	BR/A	SB	CS	SBR	FA	FR	G/POS	TPR
1973	Pit-N	54	139	17	40	9	1	4	14	2	27	.288	.308	.453	111	1	1	1	-0	.964	0	O-39	
1974	*Pit-N	73	220	27	62	10	3	4	29	10	53	.282	.322	.409	107	1	3	3	-1	.964	1	O-49/1-6	-0.1
1975	*Pit-N	148	558	75	172	35	10	25	101	38	89	.308	.358	.541	148	33	8	6	-1	.972	11	*O-141	3.7
1976	Pit-N	138	537	82	168	28	10	13	90	30	80	.313	.351	.475	132	20	19	7	2	.956	7	*O-134	2.5
1977	Pit-N★	159	637	107	215	44	8	21	88	58	107	.338	.399	.531	143	39	17	19	-6	.965	33	*O-158/2-1	5.8
1978	Pit-N	148	581	102	194	32	12	30	117	57	92	.334	.395	.585	163	48	20	7	2	.960	8	*O-147	5.3
1979	*Pit-N★	158	622	109	193	45	7	25	94	67	101	.310	.385	.526	140	34	20	4	4	.960	9	*O-158	4.0
1980	Pit-N★	139	518	71	153	31	1	17	79	25	69	.295	.330	.458	116	9	10	7	-1	.965	4	*O-130	0.7
1981	Pit-N★	67	240	29	62	14	3	9	48	9	25	.258	.291	.454	106	0	6	2	1	.941	-2	O-60	-0.4
1982	Pit-N	73	244	41	66	19	3	6	29	22	45	.270	.333	.447	113	4	7	5	-1	.957	-1	O-63	0.0
1983	Pit-N	144	552	68	154	29	4	12	69	28	89	.279	.311	.411	97	-4	12	9	-2	.973	7	*O-142	-0.3
1984	Cin-N	156	607	73	173	28	0	16	94	41	89	.285	.331	.410	103	1	11	10	-3	.974	5	*O-151	-0.1
1985	Cin-N★	160	635	88	198	42	4	34	125	52	80	.312	.367	.551	146	37	5	13	-6	.972	13	*O-159	3.9
1986	Cin-N★	162	637	89	174	31	3	31	116	56	126	.273	.333	.477	116	12	1	6	-3	.970	-2	*O-159	0.1
1987	Cin-N	153	589	77	149	28	0	26	97	44	104	.253	.314	.433	91	-9	7	3	0	.967	8	*O-142/1-9	-0.5
1988	*Oak-A	101	377	43	97	18	1	12	55	32	70	.257	.315	.406	104	1	0	1	-1	.953	-0	D-61,O-34/1-1	-0.2
1989	*Oak-A	144	553	56	146	27	0	22	97	38	91	.264	.313	.432	112	6	0	0	0	1.000	-0	*D-140/O-1	0.3
1990	Mil-A☆	157	610	71	176	30	3	21	92	41	102	.289	.337	.451	119	14	4	7	-3	.960	-1	*D-153/1-3	0.5
1991	Cal-A	119	466	45	108	22	2	11	56	29	91	.232	.281	.358	76	-16	3	3	-1	*D-119			-2.2
	Tor-A	13	36	2	12	4	0	0	3	4	7	.333	.400	.444	128	1	0	1	-1	1.000	-0	D-11	0.0
	Yr	132	502	47	120	26	2	11	59	33	98	.239	.290	.365	80	-15	3	3	-1	.000	-0	*D-130	-2.2
Total	19	2466	9358	1272	2712	526	75	339	1493	683	1537	.290	.342	.471	121	233	154	116	-22	.965	98	*O-1867,D-484/12	23.0

■ DIXIE PARKER
Parker, Douglas Woolley b: 4/24/1895, Forest Home, Ala. d: 5/15/72, Tuscaloosa, Ala. BL/TR, 5'11", 160 lbs. Deb: 7/28/23

YEAR	TM/L	G	AB	R	H	2B	3B	HR	RBI	BB	SO	AVG	OBP	SLG	PRO+	BR/A	SB	CS	SBR	FA	FR	G/POS	TPR
1923	Phi-N	4	5	0	1	0	0	0	1	0	1	.200	.200	.200	5	-1	0	0	0	.500	-1	/C-2	-0.1

■ SALTY PARKER
Parker, Francis James b: 7/8/13, E.St.Louis, Ill. d: 7/27/92, Houston, Tex. BR/TR, 6', 173 lbs. Deb: 8/13/36 MC

YEAR	TM/L	G	AB	R	H	2B	3B	HR	RBI	BB	SO	AVG	OBP	SLG	PRO+	BR/A	SB	CS	SBR	FA	FR	G/POS	TPR
1936	Det-A	11	25	6	7	2	0	0	4	0	1	.280	.333	.360	71	-1	0	2	-1	.906	3	/S-7,1-2	0.1

■ WES PARKER
Parker, Maurice Wesley b: 11/13/39, Evanston, Ill. BB/TL, 6'1", 180 lbs. Deb: 4/19/64

YEAR	TM/L	G	AB	R	H	2B	3B	HR	RBI	BB	SO	AVG	OBP	SLG	PRO+	BR/A	SB	CS	SBR	FA	FR	G/POS	TPR
1964	LA-N	124	214	29	55	7	1	3	10	14	45	.257	.306	.341	88	-4	5	4	-1	.971	-10	O-69,1-31	-1.8
1965	*LA-N	154	542	80	129	24	7	8	51	75	95	.238	.336	.352	101	2	13	7	-0	.997	-1	*1-154/O-1	-0.8
1966	*LA-N	156	475	67	120	17	5	12	51	69	83	.253	.353	.385	114	11	7	3	0	.992	6	*1-140,O-14	0.3
1967	LA-N	139	413	56	102	16	5	5	31	65	83	.247	.359	.346	112	9	10	5	0	.996	5	*1-112,O-18	0.7
1968	LA-N	135	468	42	112	22	3	3	27	49	87	.239	.314	.314	96	-2	4	6	-2	.999	9	*1-114,O-28	-1.5
1969	LA-N	132	471	76	131	23	4	13	68	56	46	.278	.357	.427	128	17	4	1	1	.995	0	*1-128/O-2	0.8
1970	LA-N	161	614	84	196	47	4	10	111	79	70	.319	.392	.458	134	31	8	2	1	.996	4	*1-161	2.2
1971	LA-N	157	533	69	146	24	1	6	62	63	63	.274	.352	.356	107	6	6	1	1	.996	3	*1-148,O-18	-0.3
1972	LA-N	130	427	45	119	14	3	4	59	62	43	.279	.371	.354	110	8	3	5	-2	.997	1	*1-120/O-5	-0.3
Total	9	1288	4157	548	1110	194	32	64	470	532	615	.267	.353	.375	112	78	60	34	-2	.996	5	*1-1108,O-155	-0.7

■ RICK PARKER
Parker, Richard Alan b: 3/20/63, Kansas City, Mo. BR/TR, 6', 185 lbs. Deb: 5/4/90

YEAR	TM/L	G	AB	R	H	2B	3B	HR	RBI	BB	SO	AVG	OBP	SLG	PRO+	BR/A	SB	CS	SBR	FA	FR	G/POS	TPR
1990	SF-N	54	107	19	26	5	0	2	14	10	15	.243	.314	.346	84	-2	6	1	1	.978	-10	O-35/2-2,3S	-1.2
1991	SF-N	13	14	0	1	0	0	0	1	1	5	.071	.133	.071	-42	-3	0	0	0	1.000	-1	/O-4	-0.4
1993	Hou-N	45	45	11	15	3	0	0	4	3	8	.333	.375	.400	112	1	1	2	0	1.000	-5	O-16/2-1,S	-0.5
1994	NY-N	8	16	1	1	0	0	0	0	0	2	.063	.063	.063	-67	-4	0	0	0	1.000	-0	/O-6	-0.4
Total	4	120	182	31	43	8	0	2	19	14	30	.236	.294	.313	68	-8	7	3	0	.988	-15	/O-61,2-3,S3	-2.5

■ BILLY PARKER
Parker, William David b: 1/14/47, Hayneville, Ala. BR/TR, 5'8", 168 lbs. Deb: 9/9/71

YEAR	TM/L	G	AB	R	H	2B	3B	HR	RBI	BB	SO	AVG	OBP	SLG	PRO+	BR/A	SB	CS	SBR	FA	FR	G/POS	TPR
1971	Cal-A	20	70	4	16	0	1	2	6	2	20	.229	.250	.300	59	-4	1	1	-0	.958	-1	2-20	-0.4
1972	Cal-A	36	80	11	17	2	0	2	9	8	17	.213	.292	.313	85	-2	0	2	-1	.951	-0	3-21/2-9,OS	-0.4
1973	Cal-A	38	102	14	23	2	1	0	7	8	23	.225	.288	.265	61	-5	0	1	-1	.959	-3	2-32/S-3,D	-0.7
Total	3	94	252	29	56	4	2	4	21	19	60	.222	.279	.290	68	-11	1	4	-2	.963	-5	/2-61,3-21,OSD	-1.5

■ FRANK PARKINSON
Parkinson, Frank Joseph "Parky" b: 3/23/1895, Dickson City, Pa. d: 7/4/60, Trenton, N.J. BR/TR, 5'11", 175 lbs. Deb: 4/13/21

YEAR	TM/L	G	AB	R	H	2B	3B	HR	RBI	BB	SO	AVG	OBP	SLG	PRO+	BR/A	SB	CS	SBR	FA	FR	G/POS	TPR
1921	Phi-N	108	391	36	99	20	2	5	32	13	81	.253	.277	.353	61	-23	3	4	-2	.931	9	*S-105/3-1	-0.5
1922	Phi-N	141	545	86	150	18	6	15	70	55	93	.275	.344	.413	86	-12	3	4	-2	.963	31	*2-139	2.0
1923	Phi-N	67	219	21	53	12	0	3	28	13	31	.242	.288	.338	58	-14	0	4	-2	.950	3	2-37,S-15,3	-1.1

YEAR	TM/L	G	AB	R	H	2B	3B	HR	RBI	BB	SO	AVG	OBP	SLG	PRO+	BR/A	SB	CS	SBR	FA	FR	G/POS	TPR
1924	Phi-N	62	156	14	33	7	0	1	19	14	28	.212	.281	.276	44	-12	3	1	0	.952	7	3-28,S-21,2	-0.2
Total	4	378	1311	157	335	57	8	24	149	95	233	.256	.308	.366	69	-61	9	13	-5	.962	50	2-186,S-141/3	0.2

■ ART PARKS Parks, Artie William b:11/1/11, Paris, Ark. d:12/6/89, Little Rock, Ark. BL/TR, 5'9", 170 lbs. Deb: 9/25/37

YEAR	TM/L	G	AB	R	H	2B	3B	HR	RBI	BB	SO	AVG	OBP	SLG	PRO+	BR/A	SB	CS	SBR	FA	FR	G/POS	TPR
1937	Bro-N	7	16	2	5	2	0	0	0	2	2	.313	.389	.438	122	1	0			1.000	0	/O-4	0.0
1939	Bro-N	71	239	27	65	13	2	1	19	28	14	.272	.348	.356	86	-4	2			.977	-4	O-65	-1.0
Total	2	78	255	29	70	15	2	1	19	30	16	.275	.351	.361	89	-3	2			.978	-4	/O-69	-1.0

■ DEREK PARKS Parks, Derek Gavin b:9/29/68, Covina, Cal. BR/TR, 6', 205 lbs. Deb: 9/11/92

YEAR	TM/L	G	AB	R	H	2B	3B	HR	RBI	BB	SO	AVG	OBP	SLG	PRO+	BR/A	SB	CS	SBR	FA	FR	G/POS	TPR
1992	Min-A	7	6	1	2	0	0	0	0	1	1	.333	.500	.333	133	0	0	0	0	1.000	1	/C-7	0.2
1993	Min-A	7	20	3	4	0	0	0	1	1	2	.200	.238	.200	19	-2	0	0	0	.970	-0	/C-7	-0.2
1994	Min-A	31	89	6	17	6	0	1	9	4	20	.191	.242	.292	37	-9	0	1	-1	.993	-3	C-31	-1.0
Total	3	45	115	10	23	6	0	1	10	6	23	.200	.258	.278	40	-10	0	1	-1	.989	-2	/C-45	-1.0

■ BILL PARKS Parks, William Robert b:6/4/1849, Easton, Pa. d:10/10/11, Easton, Pa. BR/TR, 5'8", 150 lbs. Deb: 4/26/1875 M

YEAR	TM/L	G	AB	R	H	2B	3B	HR	RBI	BB	SO	AVG	OBP	SLG	PRO+	BR/A	SB	CS	SBR	FA	FR	G/POS	TPR
1875	Was-n	26	112	13	20	1	0	0		0			.179	.179	.188	28	-8						O-15,P-14M	-0.2
	Phi-n	2	6	0	1	0	0	0		0			.167	.167	.167	15	-1						/P-2,O-2	0.0
	Yr	28	118	13	21	1	0	0		0			.178	.178	.186	27	-8						O-17,P-16	-0.2
1876	Bos-N	1	4	0	0	0	0	0	0	0	0	.000	.000	.000	-98	-1				.750	0	/O-1	-0.1

■ SAM PARRILLA Parrilla, Samuel (Monge) b:6/12/43, Santurce, P.R. d:2/9/94, Brooklyn, N.Y. BR/TR, 5'11", 185 lbs. Deb: 4/11/70

YEAR	TM/L	G	AB	R	H	2B	3B	HR	RBI	BB	SO	AVG	OBP	SLG	PRO+	BR/A	SB	CS	SBR	FA	FR	G/POS	TPR
1970	Phi-N	11	16	0	2	1	0	0	0	1	4	.125	.176	.188	-3	-2	0	0	0	1.000	0	/O-3	-0.2

■ LANCE PARRISH Parrish, Lance Michael b:6/15/56, Clairton, Pa. BR/TR, 6'3", 220 lbs. Deb: 9/5/77

YEAR	TM/L	G	AB	R	H	2B	3B	HR	RBI	BB	SO	AVG	OBP	SLG	PRO+	BR/A	SB	CS	SBR	FA	FR	G/POS	TPR
1977	Det-A	12	46	10	9	2	0	3	7	5	12	.196	.275	.435	85	-1	0	0	0	1.000	2	C-12	0.1
1978	Det-A	85	288	37	63	11	3	14	41	11	71	.219	.255	.424	85	-7	0	0	0	.987	5	C-79	-0.1
1979	Det-A	143	493	65	136	26	3	19	65	49	105	.276	.344	.456	110	6	6	7	-2	.989	4	*C-142	1.3
1980	Det-A★	144	553	79	158	34	6	24	82	31	109	.286	.327	.499	120	13	6	4	-1	.990	-5	C-121,D-16/1O	1.1
1981	Det-A	96	348	39	85	18	2	10	46	34	52	.244	.312	.394	98	-1	2	3	-1	.993	-2	C-90/D-5	-0.1
1982	Det-A★	133	486	75	138	19	2	32	87	40	99	.284	.340	.529	134	21	3	4	-2	.989	9	*C-132/O-1	3.3
1983	Det-A	155	605	80	163	42	3	27	114	44	106	.269	.320	.483	120	15	1	3	-2	.995	0	*C-131/D-27	1.8
1984	*Det-A	147	578	75	137	16	2	33	98	41	120	.237	.290	.443	100	-2	2	3	-1	.991	1	*C-127/D-22	0.4
1985	Det-A†	140	549	64	150	27	1	28	98	41	90	.273	.326	.479	118	12	2	6	-3	.993	-6	*C-120/D-22	0.9
1986	Det-A★	91	327	53	84	6	1	22	62	38	83	.257	.343	.483	122	10	0	0	0	.989	2	C-85/D-6	1.7
1987	Phi-N	130	466	42	114	21	0	17	67	47	104	.245	.315	.399	85	-5	0	0	0	.989	-3	*C-127	-0.5
1988	Phi-N★	123	424	44	91	17	2	15	60	47	93	.215	.296	.370	88	-7	0	0	0	.988	-4	*C-117/1-1	-0.2
1989	Cal-A	124	433	48	103	12	1	17	50	42	104	.238	.308	.388	97	-3	1	1	-0	.993	-2	*C-122/D-2	0.2
1990	Cal-A★	133	470	54	126	14	0	24	70	46	107	.268	.340	.451	122	13	2	2	-1	.993	10	*C-131/1-4,D	3.1
1991	Cal-A	119	402	38	87	12	0	19	51	35	117	.216	.287	.388	85	-9	1	1	-1	.997	-5	*C-111/1-3,D	-0.3
1992	Cal-A	24	83	7	19	2	0	4	11	5	22	.229	.273	.398	85	-2	0	0	0	.975	-5	C-22/D-2	-0.6
	Sea-A	69	192	19	45	11	1	8	21	19	48	.234	.307	.427	103	-0	1	1	-0	.995	-4	C-34,1-16,D	-0.4
	Yr	93	275	26	64	13	1	12	32	24	70	.233	.297	.418	98	-2	1	1	-0	.987	-9	C-56,D-16,1	-1.0
1993	Cle-A	10	20	2	4	1	0	1	2	4	5	.200	.333	.400	97	-0	1	0	0	.950	4	C-10	0.4
1994	Pit-N	40	126	10	34	5	0	3	16	18	28	.270	.366	.381	95	-0	1	1	-0	.988	-2	C-38/1-1	-0.1
Total	18	1918	6889	841	1746	296	27	320	1048	597	1475	.253	.316	.444	107	47	28	37	-14	.991	5	*C-1751,D-122/1O	12.0

■ LARRY PARRISH Parrish, Larry Alton b:11/10/53, Winter Haven, Fla. BR/TR, 6'3", 215 lbs. Deb: 9/6/74

YEAR	TM/L	G	AB	R	H	2B	3B	HR	RBI	BB	SO	AVG	OBP	SLG	PRO+	BR/A	SB	CS	SBR	FA	FR	G/POS	TPR
1974	Mon-N	25	69	9	14	5	0	0	4	6	19	.203	.286	.275	54	-4	0	0	0	.986	8	3-24	0.3
1975	Mon-N	145	532	50	146	32	5	10	65	28	74	.274	.316	.410	96	-5	4	5	-2	.919	-3	*3-143/2-1,S	-1.0
1976	Mon-N	154	543	65	126	28	5	11	61	41	91	.232	.288	.363	81	-15	2	6	-3	.945	5	*3-153	-1.6
1977	Mon-N	123	402	50	99	19	2	11	46	37	71	.246	.316	.390	90	-6	2	4	-2	.936	-9	*3-115	-1.9
1978	Mon-N	144	520	68	144	39	4	15	70	32	103	.277	.321	.454	116	9	2	3	-1	.947	-3	*3-139	0.4
1979	Mon-N★	153	544	83	167	39	2	30	82	41	101	.307	.358	.551	146	32	5	1	1	.947	-9	*3-153	2.2
1980	Mon-N	126	452	55	115	27	3	15	72	36	80	.254	.315	.427	105	2	2	6	-3	.949	-8	*3-124	-1.1
1981	*Mon-N	97	349	41	85	19	3	8	44	28	73	.244	.300	.384	92	-5	0	0	0	.935	-17	3-95	-2.6
1982	Tex-A	128	440	59	116	15	0	17	62	30	84	.264	.316	.414	104	1	5	2	0	.962	-7	*O-124/3-3,D	-0.9
1983	Tex-A	145	555	76	151	26	4	26	88	46	91	.272	.331	.474	121	14	2	1	0	.962	-5	*O-132,D-13	0.5
1984	Tex-A	156	613	72	175	42	1	22	101	42	116	.285	.337	.465	116	12	4	4	-2	.982	4	O-81,D-63,3	1.0
1985	Tex-A	94	346	44	86	11	1	17	51	33	77	.249	.316	.434	101	0	2	0	-1	.991	-5	O-69,D-22/3	-0.6
1986	Tex-A	129	464	67	128	22	1	28	94	52	114	.276	.351	.509	127	17	3	1	0	.935	-5	D-98,3-30	0.9
1987	Tex-A★	152	557	79	149	22	1	32	100	49	154	.268	.330	.483	112	8	3	1	0	.918	-9	*D-122,3-28/O	-0.4
1988	Tex-A	68	248	22	47	9	1	7	26	20	79	.190	.256	.319	58	-14	0	0	0	.000	0	D-67	-1.6
	*Bos-A	52	158	10	41	5	0	7	26	8	32	.259	.299	.424	96	-1	0	1	-1	.988	3	1-36,D-14	-0.2
	Yr	120	406	32	88	14	1	14	52	28	111	.217	.272	.360	73	-15	0	1	-1	.988	3	D-81,1-36	-1.8
Total	15	1891	6792	850	1789	360	33	256	992	529	1359	.263	.321	.439	106	45	30	36	-13	.941	-62	*3-1021,O-407/D/1S2	-7.0

■ TOM PARROTT Parrott, Thomas William "Tacky Tom" b:4/10/1868, Portland, Ore. d:1/1/32, Dundee, Ore. BR/TR, 5'10.5", 170 lbs. Deb: 6/18/1893 F

YEAR	TM/L	G	AB	R	H	2B	3B	HR	RBI	BB	SO	AVG	OBP	SLG	PRO+	BR/A	SB	CS	SBR	FA	FR	G/POS	TPR
1893	Chi-N	7	27	4	7	1	0	0	3	1	2	.259	.286	.296	56	-2	0			.800	-1	/P-4,3-2,2	-0.1
	Cin-N	24	68	5	13	1	1	1	9	1	8	.191	.203	.279	27	-8	0			.915	7	P-22/O-1	-0.1
	Yr	31	95	9	20	2	1	1	12	2	10	.211	.227	.284	35	-9	0			.906	-0	P-26/3-2,2O	-0.2
1894	Cin-N	68	229	51	74	12	6	4	40	17	10	.323	.372	.480	101	-1	4			.929	5	P-41,O-13,1/S32	0.1
1895	Cin-N	64	201	35	69	13	7	3	41	11	6	.343	.377	.522	125	6	10			.922	1	P-41,1-14/O	0.0
1896	StL-N	118	474	62	138	13	12	7	70	11	24	.291	.307	.414	93	-8	12			.951	13	*O-108/P-7,1	-0.2
Total	4	281	999	157	301	40	26	15	163	41	53	.301	.329	.438	96	-12	26			.940	19	O-131,P-115/132S	-0.3

■ JIGGS PARROTT Parrott, Walter Edward b:7/14/1871, Portland, Ore. d:4/16/1898, Phoenix, Ariz. 5'11", 160 lbs. Deb: 7/11/1892 F

YEAR	TM/L	G	AB	R	H	2B	3B	HR	RBI	BB	SO	AVG	OBP	SLG	PRO+	BR/A	SB	CS	SBR	FA	FR	G/POS	TPR
1892	Chi-N	78	333	38	67	8	5	2	22	8	30	.201	.222	.273	49	-22	7			.891	-2	3-78	-2.0
1893	Chi-N	110	455	54	111	10	9	1	65	13	25	.244	.267	.312	54	-32	25			.904	9	*3-99/2-7,O	-1.7
1894	Chi-N	124	517	82	128	17	9	3	64	16	35	.248	.274	.333	43	-51	30			.931	-4	*2-123/3-1	-4.0
1895	Chi-N	3	4	0	1	0	0	0	0	0	0	.250	.250	.250	27	-0	0			.000	-2	/O-1,S-1,1	-0.2
Total	4	315	1309	174	307	35	23	6	151	37	90	.235	.258	.310	48	-105	62			.899	-1	3-178,2-130/O1S	-7.9

■ CASEY PARSONS Parsons, Casey Robert b:4/14/54, Wenatchee, Wash. BL/TR, 6'1", 180 lbs. Deb: 5/31/81

YEAR	TM/L	G	AB	R	H	2B	3B	HR	RBI	BB	SO	AVG	OBP	SLG	PRO+	BR/A	SB	CS	SBR	FA	FR	G/POS	TPR
1981	Sea-A	36	22	6	5	1	0	1	5	1	4	.227	.320	.409	105	0	0	0	0	1.000	-5	O-24/1-1	-0.5
1983	Chi-A	8	5	1	1	0	0	0	0	2	1	.200	.429	.200	77	-0	0	0	0	1.000	0	/O-3,D-2	-0.1
1984	Chi-A	1	1	0	0	0	0	0	0	0	1	.000	.000	.000	-96	-0	0	0	0	.000	0	/H	0.0
1987	Cle-A	18	25	2	4	0	0	1	5	0	5	.160	.160	.280	13	-3	0	0	0	1.000	-1	/O-2,1-1,D	-0.4
Total	4	63	53	9	10	1	0	2	10	3	11	.189	.259	.321	57	-3	0	0	0	1.000	-6	/O-29,D-7,1	-1.0

■ DIXIE PARSONS Parsons, Edward Dixon b:5/12/16, Talladega, Ala. d:10/31/91, Longview, Tex. BR/TR, 6'2", 180 lbs. Deb: 8/16/39

YEAR	TM/L	G	AB	R	H	2B	3B	HR	RBI	BB	SO	AVG	OBP	SLG	PRO+	BR/A	SB	CS	SBR	FA	FR	G/POS	TPR
1939	Det-A	5	1	0	0	0	0	0	0	0	0	.000	.500	.000	36	-0				1.000	0	/C-4	0.0
1942	Det-A	63	188	8	37	4	0	2	11	13	22	.197	.249	.250	37	-16	1	0	0	.981	10	C-62	-0.2
1943	Det-A	40	106	2	15	3	0	0	4	6	17	.142	.188	.170	4	-13	0	0	0	.975	5	C-40	-0.6
Total	3	108	295	10	52	7	0	2	15	20	39	.176	.229	.220	26	-29	1	0	0	.979	15	C-106	-0.8

YEAR	TM/L	G	AB	R	H	2B	3B	HR	RBI	BB	SO	AVG	OBP	SLG	PRO+	BR/A	SB	CS	SBR	FA	FR	G/POS	TPR

■ **JOHN PARSONS**   Parsons, John S. b: Napoleon, Ohio 5'6", 138 lbs. Deb: 10/15/1884

| 1884 | Cin-a | 1 | 3 | 0 | 0 | 0 | 0 | 0 | 0 | | | .000 | .000 | .000 | -95 | -1 | | | | 1.000 | -1 | /O-1 | -0.1 |

■ **ROY PARTEE**   Partee, Roy Robert b: 9/7/17, Los Angeles, Cal. BR/TR, 5'10", 180 lbs. Deb: 4/23/43

1943	Bos-A	96	299	30	84	14	2	0	31	39	33	.281	.368	.341	106	4	0	0	0	.983	-6	C-91	0.4
1944	Bos-A	89	280	18	68	12	0	2	41	37	29	.243	.333	.307	85	-5	0	1	-1	.989	-6	C-85	-0.7
1946	*Bos-A	40	111	13	35	5	2	0	9	13	14	.315	.387	.396	113	2	0	0	0	.974	-6	C-38	-0.2
1947	Bos-A	60	169	14	39	2	0	0	16	18	23	.231	.305	.243	50	-11	0	0	0	.975	-1	C-54	-0.9
1948	StL-A	82	231	14	47	8	1	0	17	25	21	.203	.284	.247	41	-19	2	2	-1	.982	1	C-76	-1.5
Total	5	367	1090	89	273	41	5	2	114	132	120	.250	.334	.303	78	-29	2	3	-1	.982	-18	C-344	-2.9

■ **STEVE PARTENHEIMER**   Partenheimer, Harold Philip b: 8/30/1891, Greenfield, Mass. d: 6/16/71, Mansfield, Ohio BR/TR, 5'8.5", 145 lbs. Deb: 6/18/13 F

| 1913 | Det-A | 1 | 2 | 0 | 0 | 0 | 0 | 0 | 0 | 0 | 0 | .000 | .333 | .000 | -1 | -0 | 0 | | | .750 | 0 | /3-1 | 0.0 |

■ **JAY PARTRIDGE**   Partridge, James Bugg b: 11/15/02, Mountville, Ga. d: 1/14/74, Nashville, Tenn. BL/TR, 5'11", 160 lbs. Deb: 4/12/27

1927	Bro-N	146	572	72	149	17	6	7	40	20	36	.260	.289	.348	70	-26	9			.938	-16	*2-140	-3.6
1928	Bro-N	37	73	18	18	0	1	0	12	13	6	.247	.368	.274	71	-2	2			.908	-5	2-18/3-2	-0.7
Total	2	183	645	90	167	17	7	7	52	33	42	.259	.299	.340	70	-28	11			.935	-20	2-158/3-2	-4.3

■ **BEN PASCHAL**   Paschal, Benjamin Edwin b: 10/13/1895, Enterprise, Ala. d: 11/10/74, Charlotte, N.C. BR/TR, 5'11", 185 lbs. Deb: 8/16/15

1915	Cle-A	9	9	0	1	0	0	0	0	0	3	.111	.111	.111	-33	-1	0			.000	-0	H	-0.2
1920	Bos-A	9	28	5	10	0	0	0	5	5	2	.357	.455	.357	122	1	1	0	0	1.000	-0	/O-7	0.1
1924	NY-A	4	12	2	3	1	0	0	3	1	0	.250	.308	.333	65	-1	0	0	0	1.000	-0	/O-4	-0.1
1925	NY-A	89	247	49	89	16	5	12	56	22	29	.360	.417	.611	161	22	14	9	-1	.953	-4	O-66	1.2
1926	*NY-A	96	258	46	74	12	3	7	32	26	35	.287	.354	.438	107	2	7	6	-2	.935	-3	O-74	-0.7
1927	NY-A	50	82	16	26	9	2	2	16	4	10	.317	.349	.549	134	3	0	2	-1	.976	-5	O-27	-0.3
1928	*NY-A	65	79	12	25	6	1	1	15	8	11	.316	.379	.456	122	3	1	0	0	1.000	-6	O-25	-0.3
1929	NY-A	42	72	13	15	3	0	2	11	6	3	.208	.269	.333	58	-5	1	1	-0	.951	-1	O-20	-0.7
Total	8	364	787	143	243	47	11	24	138	72	93	.309	.369	.488	123	24	24	18		.953	-19	O-223	-1.0

■ **JOHNNY PASEK**   Pasek, John Paul b: 6/25/05, Niagara Falls, N.Y. d: 3/13/76, Niagara Falls, N.Y BR/TR, 5'10", 175 lbs. Deb: 7/28/33

1933	Det-A	28	61	6	15	4	0	0	4	7	7	.246	.324	.311	68	-3	2	0	1	.989	-1	C-28	-0.1
1934	Chi-A	4	9	1	3	0	0	0	1	1	1	.333	.400	.333	88	-0	0	0	0	1.000	0	/C-4	0.0
Total	2	32	70	7	18	4	0	0	4	8	8	.257	.333	.314	70	-3	2	0	1	.990	-1	/C-32	-0.1

■ **DODE PASKERT**   Paskert, George Henry b: 8/28/1881, Cleveland, Ohio d: 2/12/59, Cleveland, Ohio BR/TR, 5'11", 165 lbs. Deb: 9/21/07

1907	Cin-N	16	50	10	14	4	0	1	8	2		.280	.333	.420	130	2	2			.973	1	O-16	0.2
1908	Cin-N	118	395	40	96	14	4	1	36	27		.243	.298	.306	96	-2	25			.953	5	*O-116	-0.2
1909	Cin-N	104	322	49	81	7	4	0	33	34		.252	.327	.298	95	-1	23			.968	0	O-82/1-6	-0.5
1910	Cin-N	144	506	63	152	21	5	2	46	70	60	.300	.389	.374	128	20	51			.957	14	*O-139/1-2	2.9
1911	Phi-N	153	560	96	153	18	5	4	47	70	70	.273	.358	.345	96	-2	28			.979	8	*O-153	-0.2
1912	Phi-N	145	540	102	170	37	5	2	43	91	67	.315	.420	.413	120	19	36			.967	5	*O-141/2-2,3	1.6
1913	Phi-N	124	454	83	119	21	9	4	29	65	69	.262	.358	.374	105	4	12			.972	18	*O-120	1.7
1914	Phi-N	132	451	59	119	25	6	3	44	56	68	.264	.349	.366	106	4	23			.958	12	*O-128/S-4	1.1
1915	*Phi-N	109	328	51	80	17	4	3	39	35	38	.244	.319	.348	100	0	9	6	-1	.970	-2	O-92/1-5	-0.8
1916	Phi-N	149	555	82	155	30	7	8	46	54	76	.279	.346	.402	125	17	22	21	-6	.983	-1	*O-146/S-1	0.5
1917	Phi-N	141	546	78	137	27	11	4	43	62	63	.251	.331	.363	108	6	19			.984	-2	*O-138	-0.4
1918	*Chi-N	127	461	69	132	24	3	3	59	52	49	.286	.362	.371	121	13	20			.980	-3	*O-121/3-6	0.4
1919	Chi-N	88	270	21	53	11	3	2	29	28	33	.196	.274	.281	67	-11	7			.969	-6	O-80	-2.4
1920	Chi-N	139	487	57	136	22	10	5	71	64	58	.279	.366	.396	117	12	16	14	-4	.956	1	*O-137	0.0
1921	Cin-N	27	92	8	16	1	1	0	4	4	8	.174	.208	.207	11	-12	0	2	-1	.984	1	O-24	-1.4
Total	15	1716	6017	868	1613	279	77	42	577	715	659	.268	.350	.361	108	70	293	43		.969	52	*O-1633/1-13,3S2	2.5

■ **KEVIN PASLEY**   Pasley, Kevin Patrick b: 7/22/53, Bronx, N.Y. BR/TR, 6', 185 lbs. Deb: 10/2/74

1974	LA-N	1	0	0	0	0	0	0	0	0	0	—	—	—	—	0	0	0	0	1.000	-0	/C-1	0.0
1976	LA-N	23	52	4	12	2	0	0	2	3	7	.231	.273	.269	55	-3	0	0	0	.971	5	C-23	0.2
1977	LA-N	2	3	0	1	0	0	0	0	0	0	.333	.333	.333	80	-0	0	0	0	1.000	-0	/C-2	0.0
	Sea-A	4	13	1	5	0	0	0	1	0	2	.385	.429	.385	125	1	0	0	0	1.000	-2	/C-4	-0.1
1978	Sea-A	25	54	3	13	5	0	1	6	3	4	.241	.268	.389	83	-1	0	0	0	1.000	-3	/C-25	-0.1
Total	4	55	122	8	31	7	0	1	9	6	13	.254	.289	.336	76	-4	0	0	0	.986	-3	/C-55	0.0

■ **DAN PASQUA**   Pasqua, Daniel Anthony b: 10/17/61, Yonkers, N.Y. BL/TL, 6', 203 lbs. Deb: 5/30/85

1985	NY-A	60	148	17	31	3	1	9	25	16	38	.209	.291	.426	96	-1	0	0	0	1.000	1	O-37,D-14	-0.1
1986	NY-A	102	280	44	82	17	0	16	45	47	78	.293	.400	.525	151	21	2	0	1	.987	-2	O-81/1-5,D	1.7
1987	NY-A	113	318	42	74	7	1	17	42	40	99	.233	.320	.421	96	-2	0	2	-1	.985	-2	O-74,D-20,1	-0.8
1988	Chi-A	129	422	48	96	16	2	20	50	46	100	.227	.308	.417	101	0	1	0	0	.996	7	*O-112/1-7,D	0.4
1989	Chi-A	73	246	26	61	9	1	11	47	25	58	.248	.320	.427	111	3	1	2	0	.993	2	O-66/D-5	0.2
1990	Chi-A	112	325	43	89	27	3	13	58	37	66	.274	.352	.495	137	16	1	1	-0	.962	0	D-57,O-43	1.3
1991	Chi-A	134	417	71	108	22	5	18	66	62	86	.259	.359	.465	129	17	0	2	-1	.991	-8	1-83,O-59/D	0.3
1992	Chi-A	93	265	26	56	16	1	6	33	36	57	.211	.308	.347	84	-5	0	1	-1	.963	-2	O-81/1-5,D	-1.0
1993	*Chi-A	78	176	22	36	10	1	5	20	26	51	.205	.307	.358	80	-5	2	2	0	.984	-3	O-37,1-32/D	-1.0
1994	Chi-A	11	23	2	5	2	0	2	2	0	4	.217	.217	.565	94	-1	0	0	0	.867	-1	/O-5,1-3	-0.1
Total	10	905	2620	341	638	129	15	117	390	335	642	.244	.334	.438	112	42	7	10	-4	.984	-8	O-595,1-147,D	0.9

■ **MIKE PASQUELLA**   Pasquella, Michael John "Toney" (b: Michael John Pasquariello) b: 11/7/1898, Philadelphia, Pa. d: 4/5/65, Bridgeport, Conn. BR/TR, 5'11", 167 lbs. Deb: 7/9/19

1919	Phi-N	1	1	1	1	0	0	0	0	0	0	1.000	1.000	1.000	469	0	0			.000	0	/1-1	0.0
	StL-N	1	1	0	0	0	0	0	0	0	0	.000	.000	.000	-99	-0	0			.000	0	H	0.0
	Yr	2	2	1	1	0	0	0	0	0	0	.500	.500	.500	200	0	0			.000	0	/1-1	0.0

■ **CLIFF PASTORNICKY**   Pastornicky, Clifford Scott b: 11/18/58, Seattle, Was. BR/TR, 5'10", 170 lbs. Deb: 6/14/83

| 1983 | KC-A | 10 | 32 | 4 | 4 | 0 | 0 | 0 | 1 | 3 | 4 | .125 | .125 | .313 | 16 | -4 | 0 | 0 | 0 | .929 | -0 | 3-10 | -0.4 |

■ **BOB PATE**   Pate, Robert Wayne b: 12/3/53, Los Angeles, Cal. BR/TR, 6'3.5", 200 lbs. Deb: 6/2/80

1980	Mon-N	23	39	3	10	2	0	0	5	3	6	.256	.310	.308	73	-1	0	1	0	1.000	-4	O-18	-0.6
1981	Mon-N	8	6	0	2	0	0	0	0	1	0	.333	.429	.333	117	0	0	0	0	1.000	-2	/O-5	-0.2
Total	2	31	45	3	12	2	0	0	5	4	6	.267	.327	.311	79	-1	0	1	-1	1.000	-5	/O-23	-0.8

■ **FREDDIE PATEK**   Patek, Frederick Joseph "The Flea" b: 10/9/44, Seguin, Tex. BR/TR, 5'5", 148 lbs. Deb: 6/3/68

1968	Pit-N	61	208	31	53	4	2	2	18	12	37	.255	.302	.322	89	-3	18	7	1	.976	-1	S-52/O-5,3	0.2
1969	Pit-N	147	460	48	110	9	4	3	32	53	86	.239	.319	.296	75	-14	15	8	-0	.954	-2	*S-146	-0.2
1970	*Pit-N	84	237	42	58	10	5	1	19	29	46	.245	.327	.342	81	-6	8	2	1	.971	11	S-65	1.3
1971	KC-A	147	591	86	158	21	**11**	6	36	44	86	.267	.323	.371	97	-3	49	14	6	.968	10	*S-147	3.4
1972	KC-A†	136	518	59	110	25	4	0	32	47	64	.212	.282	.276	67	-21	33	7	6	.971	**30**	*S-136	3.8
1973	KC-A	135	501	82	117	19	5	5	45	54	63	.234	.312	.321	73	-18	36	14	2	.966	**35**	*S-135	3.8

YEAR	TM/L	G	AB	R	H	2B	3B	HR	RBI	BB	SO	AVG	OBP	SLG	PRO+	BR/A	SB	CS	SBR	FA	FR	G/POS	TPR
1974	KC-A	149	537	72	121	18	6	3	38	77	69	.225	.326	.298	76	-15	33	15	1	.967	4	*S-149	1.0
1975	KC-A	136	483	58	110	14	5	5	45	42	65	.228	.292	.308	68	-20	32	7	5	.959	-7	*S-136/D-1	-0.7
1976	*KC-A★	144	432	58	104	19	3	1	43	50	63	.241	.322	.306	84	-8	51	15	6	.962	-6	*S-143/D-1	1.0
1977	*KC-A	154	497	72	130	26	6	5	60	41	84	.262	.324	.368	88	-8	**53**	13	8	.958	-19	*S-154	-0.2
1978	*KC-A★	138	440	54	109	23	1	2	46	42	56	.248	.315	.318	76	-13	38	11	5	.949	-25	*S-137	-1.7
1979	KC-A	106	306	30	77	17	0	1	37	16	42	.252	.295	.317	64	-15	11	12	-4	.955	-28	*S-104	-3.6
1980	Cal-A	86	273	41	72	10	5	5	34	15	26	.264	.304	.392	92	-4	7	6	-2	.953	-18	S-81	-1.5
1981	Cal-A	27	47	3	11	1	1	0	5	1	6	.234	.250	.298	57	-3	1	0	0	.983	2	2-16/3-7,S	0.0
Total	14	1650	5530	736	1340	216	55	41	490	523	787	.242	.311	.324	79	-151	385	131	37	.962	-15	*S-1588/2-16,30D	6.6

■ **BOB PATRICK**   Patrick, Robert Lee b: 10/27/17, Ft.Smith, Ark. BR/TR, 6'2", 190 lbs. Deb: 9/20/41

YEAR	TM/L	G	AB	R	H	2B	3B	HR	RBI	BB	SO	AVG	OBP	SLG	PRO+	BR/A	SB	CS	SBR	FA	FR	G/POS	TPR
1941	Det-A	5	7	2	2	0	0	0	0	0	1	.286	.286	.286	47	-1	0	0	0	.750	-1	/O-3	-0.2
1942	Det-A	4	8	1	2	1	0	1	3	1	0	.250	.333	.750	185	1	0	0	0	1.000	-0	/O-3	0.0
Total	2	9	15	3	4	1	0	1	3	1	1	.267	.313	.533	118	0	0	0	0	.889	-1	/O-6	-0.2

■ **HARRY PATTEE**   Pattee, Harry Ernest b: 1/17/1882, Charlestown, Mass. d: 7/17/71, Lynchburg, Va. BL/TR, 5'8", 149 lbs. Deb: 4/14/08

YEAR	TM/L	G	AB	R	H	2B	3B	HR	RBI	BB	SO	AVG	OBP	SLG	PRO+	BR/A	SB	CS	SBR	FA	FR	G/POS	TPR
1908	Bro-N	80	264	19	57	5	2	0	9	25		.216	.286	.250	74	-7	24			.964	12	2-74	0.5

■ **DAN PATTERSON**   Patterson, Daniel Thomas b: 1846, New York, N.Y. TL, 5'9", 143 lbs. Deb: 5/18/1871

YEAR	TM/L	G	AB	R	H	2B	3B	HR	RBI	BB	SO	AVG	OBP	SLG	PRO+	BR/A	SB	CS	SBR	FA	FR	G/POS	TPR
1871	Mut-n	32	151	31	31	2	0	0	13	1	0	.205	.211	.219	26	-13	2					*O-31/2-1	-0.8
1872	Eck-n	12	47	6	8	1	0	0	3	0	1	.170	.170	.191	13	-4						O-11/1-1	-0.2
1874	Mut-n	1	5	1	2	0	0	0				.400	.400	.400	151	0						/1-1,O-1	0.0
1875	Atl-n	11	41	3	8	0	0	0				.195	.195	.195	41	-2						/2-5,O-5	-0.2
Total	4 n	56	244	41	49	3	0	0			1	.201	.204	.213	28	-19						/O-48,2-6,1	-1.2

■ **HAM PATTERSON**   Patterson, Hamilton b: 10/13/1877, Belleville, Ill. d: 11/25/45, E.St.Louis, Ill. BR/TR, 6'2", 185 lbs. Deb: 5/18/09 F

YEAR	TM/L	G	AB	R	H	2B	3B	HR	RBI	BB	SO	AVG	OBP	SLG	PRO+	BR/A	SB	CS	SBR	FA	FR	G/POS	TPR
1909	StL-A	17	49	2	10	1	0	0	5		0	.204	.204	.224	38	-4	1			1.000	-1	/1-6,O-6	-0.6
	Chi-A	1	3	2	0	0	0	0	0	1		.000	.250	.000	-21	-0				1.000	1	/1-1	0.0
	Yr	18	52	4	10	1	0	0	5	1		.192	.208	.212	35	-4	1			1.000	-1	/1-7,O-6	-0.6

■ **HANK PATTERSON**   Patterson, Henry Joseph Colquit b: 7/17/07, San Francisco, Cal. d: 9/30/70, Panorama City, Cal. BR/TR, 5'11.5", 170 lbs. Deb: 9/5/32

YEAR	TM/L	G	AB	R	H	2B	3B	HR	RBI	BB	SO	AVG	OBP	SLG	PRO+	BR/A	SB	CS	SBR	FA	FR	G/POS	TPR
1932	Bos-A	1	1	0	0	0	0	0	0	0	0	.000	.000	.000	-99	-0	0	0	0	.000	-0	/C-1	0.0

■ **JOHN PATTERSON**   Patterson, John Allen b: 2/11/67, Key West, Fla. BB/TR, 5'9", 160 lbs. Deb: 4/6/92

YEAR	TM/L	G	AB	R	H	2B	3B	HR	RBI	BB	SO	AVG	OBP	SLG	PRO+	BR/A	SB	CS	SBR	FA	FR	G/POS	TPR
1992	SF-N	32	103	10	19	1	1	0	4	5	24	.184	.229	.214	28	-10	5	1	1	.960	6	2-22/O-5	-0.3
1993	SF-N	16	16	1	3	0	0	1	2	0	5	.188	.188	.375	48	-1	0	1	-1	.000	0	H	-0.3
1994	SF-N	85	240	36	57	10	1	3	32	16	43	.237	.315	.325	70	-11	13	3	2	.979	-9	2-63	-1.6
Total	3	133	359	47	79	11	2	4	38	21	72	.220	.286	.295	58	-22	18	5	2	.974	-3	/2-85,O-5	-2.2

■ **CLAIRE PATTERSON**   Patterson, Lorenzo Claire b: 10/5/1887, Arkansas City, Kan. d: 3/28/13, Mojave, Cal. BL/TR, 6' ", 180 lbs. Deb: 9/5/09

YEAR	TM/L	G	AB	R	H	2B	3B	HR	RBI	BB	SO	AVG	OBP	SLG	PRO+	BR/A	SB	CS	SBR	FA	FR	G/POS	TPR
1909	Cin-N	4	8	0	1	0	0	0		0		.125	.125	.125	-23	-0				1.000	-0	/O-2	-0.2

■ **MIKE PATTERSON**   Patterson, Michael Lee b: 1/26/58, Santa Monica, Cal. BL/TR, 5'10", 170 lbs. Deb: 4/15/81

YEAR	TM/L	G	AB	R	H	2B	3B	HR	RBI	BB	SO	AVG	OBP	SLG	PRO+	BR/A	SB	CS	SBR	FA	FR	G/POS	TPR
1981	Oak-A	12	23	4	8	1	1	0	1	2	5	.348	.400	.478	160	2	0	1	-1	1.000	-1	/O-5,D-2	0.0
	NY-A	4	9	2	2	0	2	0	0	0	0	.222	.222	.667	150	0	0	0	0	1.000	-1	/O-4	0.0
	Yr	16	32	6	10	1	3	0	1	2	5	.313	.353	.531	158	2	0	1	-1	1.000	-1	/O-9,D-2	0.0
1982	NY-A	11	16	3	3	1	0	1		2	6	.188	.278	.438	94	-0	1	0	0	1.000	-1	/O-9,D-1	-0.3
Total	2	27	48	9	13	2	3	1	2	4	11	.271	.327	.500	135	2	1	1	-0	1.000	-5	/O-18,D-3	-0.3

■ **PAT PATTERSON**   Patterson, William Jennings Bryan b: 1/29/01, Belleville, Ill. d: 10/1/77, St.Louis, Mo. BR/TR, 6', 175 lbs. Deb: 4/14/21 F

YEAR	TM/L	G	AB	R	H	2B	3B	HR	RBI	BB	SO	AVG	OBP	SLG	PRO+	BR/A	SB	CS	SBR	FA	FR	G/POS	TPR
1921	NY-N	23	35	5	14	0	0	1	5	2	5	.400	.432	.486	142	2	0	1	-1	.970	4	3-14/S-7	0.6

■ **GEORGE PATTISON**   Pattison, George Deb: 4/24/1884

YEAR	TM/L	G	AB	R	H	2B	3B	HR	RBI	BB	SO	AVG	OBP	SLG	PRO+	BR/A	SB	CS	SBR	FA	FR	G/POS	TPR
1884	Phi-U	2	7	0	1	0	0	0		0		.143	.143	.143	-24	-1				.500	-0	/O-2	-0.1

■ **GENE PATTON**   Patton, Gene Tunney b: 7/8/26, Coatesville, Pa. BL/TR, 5'10", 165 lbs. Deb: 6/17/44

YEAR	TM/L	G	AB	R	H	2B	3B	HR	RBI	BB	SO	AVG	OBP	SLG	PRO+	BR/A	SB	CS	SBR	FA	FR	G/POS	TPR
1944	Bos-N	1	0	0	0	0	0	0	0	0	0	—	—	—		0	0			.000	0	R	0.0

■ **BILL PATTON**   Patton, George William b: 10/7/12, Cornwall, Pa. d: 3/15/86, Philadelphia, Pa. BR/TR, 6'2", 180 lbs. Deb: 6/29/35

YEAR	TM/L	G	AB	R	H	2B	3B	HR	RBI	BB	SO	AVG	OBP	SLG	PRO+	BR/A	SB	CS	SBR	FA	FR	G/POS	TPR
1935	Phi-A	9	10	1	3	1	0	0	2	2	3	.300	.417	.400	113	0	0	0	0	1.000	0	/C-3	0.1

■ **TOM PATTON**   Patton, Thomas Allen b: 9/5/35, Honey Brook, Pa. BR/TR, 5'9.5", 185 lbs. Deb: 4/30/57

YEAR	TM/L	G	AB	R	H	2B	3B	HR	RBI	BB	SO	AVG	OBP	SLG	PRO+	BR/A	SB	CS	SBR	FA	FR	G/POS	TPR
1957	Bal-A	1	2	0	0	0	0	0	0	0	2	.000	.000	.000	-99	-1	0	0	0	1.000	1	/C-1	0.1

■ **LOU PAUL**   Paul, Louis BR/TR, Deb: 9/5/1876

YEAR	TM/L	G	AB	R	H	2B	3B	HR	RBI	BB	SO	AVG	OBP	SLG	PRO+	BR/A	SB	CS	SBR	FA	FR	G/POS	TPR
1876	Phi-N	3	12	2	2	1	0	0	0	0	0	.167	.167	.250	37	-1				.643	-2	/C-3	-0.3

■ **CARLOS PAULA**   Paula, Carlos (Conill) b: 11/28/27, Havana, Cuba d: 4/25/83, Miami, Fla. BR/TR, 6'3", 195 lbs. Deb: 9/6/54

YEAR	TM/L	G	AB	R	H	2B	3B	HR	RBI	BB	SO	AVG	OBP	SLG	PRO+	BR/A	SB	CS	SBR	FA	FR	G/POS	TPR
1954	Was-A	9	24	2	4	0	0	2		2	4	.167	.231	.208	22	-3	0	0	0	1.000	1	/O-6	-0.2
1955	Was-A	115	351	34	105	20	7	6	45	17	43	.299	.335	.447	115	5	2	3	-1	.941	-2	O-85	-0.2
1956	Was-A	33	82	8	15	2	1	3	13	8	15	.183	.256	.341	56	-6	0	2	-1	.974	-2	O-20	-0.9
Total	3	157	457	44	124	23	8	9	60	27	62	.271	.315	.416	99	-3	2	5	-2	.950	-2	O-111	-1.3

■ **GENE PAULETTE**   Paulette, Eugene Edward b: 5/26/1891, Centralia, Ill. d: 2/8/66, Little Rock, Ark. BR/TR, 6', 150 lbs. Deb: 6/16/11

YEAR	TM/L	G	AB	R	H	2B	3B	HR	RBI	BB	SO	AVG	OBP	SLG	PRO+	BR/A	SB	CS	SBR	FA	FR	G/POS	TPR
1911	NY-N	10	12	1	2	0	0	0	1	0	1	.167	.167	.167	-6	-2				.938	-1	/1-7,S-1,3	-0.3
1916	StL-A	5	4	1	2	0	0	0	0	0	0	.500	.600	.500	242	1	0			.000	0	H	0.1
1917	StL-A	12	22	3	4	0	0	0	0	3	3	.182	.280	.182	43	-1	0			.982	0	/1-5,2-3,3	-0.1
	StL-N	95	332	32	88	21	7	0	34	16	16	.265	.303	.370	109	2	9			.993	-1	1-93	-0.3
1918	StL-N	125	461	33	126	15	3	0	52	27	16	.273	.316	.319	97	-2	11			.983	5	1-97,S-12/203P	0.0
1919	StL-N	43	144	11	31	6	0	0	11	9	6	.215	.261	.257	60	-7	4			.990	2	1-35/S-3	-0.7
	Phi-N	67	243	20	63	8	3	1	31	19	10	.259	.316	.329	88	-3	10			.957	0	2-58,O-10/1	-0.1
	Yr	110	387	31	94	14	3	1	42	28	16	.243	.296	.302	78	-10	14			.957	2	2-58,1-36,O/S	-0.8
1920	Phi-N	143	562	59	162	16	6	1	36	33	16	.288	.332	.343	90	-7	9	8	-2	.988	6	*1-139/S-2	-0.6
Total	6	500	1780	160	478	66	19	2	165	108	69	.269	.314	.330	92	-19	43	_8_		.988	11	1-377/2-68,S03P	-2.0

■ **SI PAUXTIS**   Pauxtis, Simon Francis b: 7/20/1885, Pittston, Pa. d: 3/13/61, Philadelphia, Pa. BR/TR, 6' ", 175 lbs. Deb: 9/18/09

YEAR	TM/L	G	AB	R	H	2B	3B	HR	RBI	BB	SO	AVG	OBP	SLG	PRO+	BR/A	SB	CS	SBR	FA	FR	G/POS	TPR
1909	Cin-N	4	8	2	1	0	0	0		0		.125	.222	.125	8	-1				1.000	-1	/C-4	-0.2

■ **DON PAVLETICH**   Pavletich, Donald Stephen b: 7/13/38, Milwaukee, Wis. BR/TR, 5'11", 209 lbs. Deb: 4/20/57

YEAR	TM/L	G	AB	R	H	2B	3B	HR	RBI	BB	SO	AVG	OBP	SLG	PRO+	BR/A	SB	CS	SBR	FA	FR	G/POS	TPR
1957	Cin-N	1	1	0	0	0	0	0	0	0	0	.000	.000	.000	-93	-0	0	0	0	.000	0	H	0.0
1959	Cin-N	1	0	1	0	0	0	0	0	0	0	—	—	—		0	0	0	0	.000	0	R	0.0
1962	Cin-N	34	63	7	14	3	0	1	7	8	18	.222	.310	.317	67	-3	0	0	0	1.000	1	1-25/C-2	-0.3
1963	Cin-N	71	183	18	38	11	0	5	18	17	12	.208	.275	.350	76	-6	0	0	0	.991	-3	1-57,C-13	-1.1
1964	Cin-N	34	91	12	22	4	0	5	11	10	17	.242	.317	.451	109	1	0	0	0	.983	-3	C-27/1-1	-0.1
1965	Cin-N	68	191	25	61	11	1	8	32	23	27	.319	.395	.513	144	11	1	1	-0	.986	-6	C-54/1-9	1.1
1966	Cin-N	83	235	29	69	13	2	12	38	18	37	.294	.346	.519	126	8	0	0	0	.975	-10	C-55,1-10	0.1
1967	Cin-N	74	231	25	55	14	3	6	34	21	38	.238	.313	.403	93	-2	2	1	0	.986	-5	C-66/1-6,3	-0.4

YEAR	TM/L	G	AB	R	H	2B	3B	HR	RBI	BB	SO	AVG	OBP	SLG	PRO+	BR/A	SB	CS	SBR	FA	FR	G/POS	TPR
1968	Cin-N	46	98	11	28	3	1	2	11	8	23	.286	.352	.398	117	2	0	0	0	1.000	-0	1-22/C-5	0.1
1969	Chi-A	78	188	26	46	12	0	6	33	28	45	.245	.343	.404	103	1	0	0	0	.974	-6	C-51,1-13	-0.4
1970	Bos-A	32	65	4	9	1	1	0	6	10	15	.138	.253	.185	21	-7	1	0	0	1.000	1	1-16,C-10	-0.7
1971	Bos-A	14	27	5	7	1	0	1	3	5	5	.259	.375	.407	113	1	0	0	0	.973	-2	/C-8	-0.4
Total	12	536	1373	163	349	73	8	46	193	148	237	.254	.330	.420	103	6	5	2	0	.983	-31	C-291,1-159/3	-1.8

■ TED PAWELEK
Pawelek, Theodore John "Porky" b: 8/15/19, Chicago Heights, Ill. d: 2/12/64, Chicago Heights, Ill. BL/TR, 5'10.5", 202 lbs. Deb: 9/13/46

YEAR	TM/L	G	AB	R	H	2B	3B	HR	RBI	BB	SO	AVG	OBP	SLG	PRO+	BR/A	SB	CS	SBR	FA	FR	G/POS	TPR
1946	Chi-N	4	4	0	1	1	0	0	0	0	2	.250	.250	.500	112	0	0			.000	-0	/C-1	0.0

■ STAN PAWLOSKI
Pawloski, Stanley Walter b: 9/6/31, Wanamie, Pa. BR/TR, 6'1", 175 lbs. Deb: 9/24/55

YEAR	TM/L	G	AB	R	H	2B	3B	HR	RBI	BB	SO	AVG	OBP	SLG	PRO+	BR/A	SB	CS	SBR	FA	FR	G/POS	TPR
1955	Cle-A	2	8	0	1	0	0	0	0	0	2	.125	.125	.125	-31	-1	0	0	0	1.000	1	/2-2	0.0

■ FRED PAYNE
Payne, Frederick Thomas b: 9/2/1880, Camden, N.Y. d: 1/16/54, Camden, N.Y. BR/TR, 5'10", 162 lbs. Deb: 4/21/06

YEAR	TM/L	G	AB	R	H	2B	3B	HR	RBI	BB	SO	AVG	OBP	SLG	PRO+	BR/A	SB	CS	SBR	FA	FR	G/POS	TPR
1906	Det-A	72	222	23	60	5	5	0	20	13		.270	.316	.338	102	0	4			.966	-1	C-47,O-17	0.4
1907	*Det-A	53	169	17	28	2	2	0	14	7		.166	.221	.201	34	-13	4			.981	3	C-46/O-5	-0.6
1908	Det-A	20	45	3	3	0	0	0	2	3		.067	.176	.067	-20	-6	1			.954	-3	C-17/O-1	-0.9
1909	Chi-A	32	82	8	20	2	0	0	12	5		.244	.295	.268	82	-2	0			.987	-2	C-27/O-3	-0.1
1910	Chi-A	91	252	17	56	5	4	0	19	11		.222	.260	.274	70	-9	6			.974	-5	C-78/O-2	-0.7
1911	Chi-A	66	133	14	27	2	1	1	19	8		.203	.259	.256	45	-10	6			.963	-4	C-56	-1.0
Total	6	334	903	82	194	16	12	1	86	47		.215	.265	.262	64	-39	21			.972	-11	C-271/O-28	-2.9

■ GEORGE PAYNTER
Paynter, George Washington (b: George Washington Paner) b: 7/6/1871, Cincinnati, Ohio d: 10/1/50, Cincinnati, Ohio BR/TR, 5'9", 125 lbs. Deb: 8/12/1894

YEAR	TM/L	G	AB	R	H	2B	3B	HR	RBI	BB	SO	AVG	OBP	SLG	PRO+	BR/A	SB	CS	SBR	FA	FR	G/POS	TPR
1894	StL-N	1	4	0	0	0	0	0	0	1		.000	.200	.000	-48	-1	1			1.000	1	/O-1	0.0

■ JOHNNY PEACOCK
Peacock, John Gaston b: 1/10/10, Fremont, N.C. d: 10/17/81, Wilson, N.C. BL/TR, 5'11", 165 lbs. Deb: 9/23/37

YEAR	TM/L	G	AB	R	H	2B	3B	HR	RBI	BB	SO	AVG	OBP	SLG	PRO+	BR/A	SB	CS	SBR	FA	FR	G/POS	TPR
1937	Bos-A	9	32	3	10	2	1	0	6	1	0	.313	.333	.438	89	-1	0	0		.980	1	/C-9	0.1
1938	Bos-A	72	195	29	59	7	1	1	39	17	4	.303	.358	.364	78	-6	4	1	1	.984	-9	C-57/1-1,O	-1.1
1939	Bos-A	92	274	33	76	11	4	0	36	29	11	.277	.347	.347	75	-10	1	1	-0	.972	-8	C-84	-1.2
1940	Bos-A	63	131	20	37	4	1	0	13	23	10	.282	.390	.328	85	-2	1	1	-0	.994	-6	C-48	-0.6
1941	Bos-A	79	261	28	74	20	1	0	27	21	3	.284	.339	.368	85	-6	2	1	-0	.988	-4	C-70	-0.3
1942	Bos-A	88	286	17	76	7	3	0	25	21	11	.266	.316	.311	74	-10	1	1	-0	.988	-6	C-82	-1.0
1943	Bos-A	48	114	7	23	3	1	0	7	10	9	.202	.266	.246	49	-7	1	1	-0	.972	-1	C-32	-0.7
1944	Bos-A	4	4	0	0	0	0	0	0	0	0	.000	.000	.000	-99	-1	0	0		1.000	-0	/C-2	-0.1
	Phi-N	83	253	21	57	9	3	0	21	31	15	.225	.310	.285	70	-9	1			.990	1	C-73/2-1	-0.4
1945	Phi-N	33	74	6	15	6	0	0	6	6	0	.203	.262	.284	53	-5	1			.969	-5	C-23	-0.9
	Bro-N	48	110	11	28	5	1	0	14	24	10	.255	.388	.318	98	1	2			.975	-1	C-38	0.3
	Yr	81	184	17	43	11	1	0	20	30	10	.234	.341	.304	82	-4	3			.973	-5	C-61	-0.6
Total	9	619	1734	175	455	74	16	1	194	183	73	.262	.333	.325	76	-56	14	6		.983	-37	C-518/2-1,O1	-5.9

■ ELIAS PEAK
Peak, Elias b: 5/23/1859, Philadelphia, Pa. d: 12/17/16, Philadelphia, Pa. Deb: 4/19/1884

YEAR	TM/L	G	AB	R	H	2B	3B	HR	RBI	BB	SO	AVG	OBP	SLG	PRO+	BR/A	SB	CS	SBR	FA	FR	G/POS	TPR
1884	Bos-U	1	3	2	2	0	0	0		1		.667	.750	.667	293	1				1.000	-0	/O-1	0.1
	Phi-U	54	215	35	42	6	4	0		7		.195	.221	.260	33	-20				.825	-6	2-47/O-5,S	-2.2
	Yr	55	218	37	44	6	4	0		8		.202	.230	.266	37	-19				.825	-6	2-47/O-6,S	-2.1

■ HARRY PEARCE
Pearce, Harry James b: 7/12/1889, Philadelphia, Pa. d: 1/8/42, Philadelphia, Pa. BR/TR, 5'9", 158 lbs. Deb: 10/2/17

YEAR	TM/L	G	AB	R	H	2B	3B	HR	RBI	BB	SO	AVG	OBP	SLG	PRO+	BR/A	SB	CS	SBR	FA	FR	G/POS	TPR
1917	Phi-N	7	16	2	4	3	0	0	2	0	4	.250	.294	.438	118	0	0			.967	5	/S-4	0.5
1918	Phi-N	60	164	16	40	3	2	0	18	9	31	.244	.295	.287	73	-5	5			.944	5	2-46/S-2,13	0.3
1919	Phi-N	68	244	24	44	3	3	0	9	8	27	.180	.209	.217	26	-22	6			.948	-1	2-43,S-23/3	-2.2
Total	3	135	424	42	88	9	5	0	29	17	62	.208	.247	.252	48	-27	11			.946	9	/2-89,S-29,31	-1.4

■ DICKEY PEARCE
Pearce, Richard J. b: 2/29/1836, Brooklyn, N.Y. d: 10/12/08, Wareham, Mass. BR/TR, 5'3.5", 161 lbs. Deb: 5/18/1871 MU

YEAR	TM/L	G	AB	R	H	2B	3B	HR	RBI	BB	SO	AVG	OBP	SLG	PRO+	BR/A	SB	CS	SBR	FA	FR	G/POS	TPR
1871	Mut-n	33	163	31	44	5	0	0	20	4	1	.270	.287	.301	76	-3						*S-33	-0.2
1872	Mut-n	44	206	32	40	1	1	1	24	4	1	.194	.210	.223	36	-14						*S-42/O-1M	-1.0
1873	Atl-n	55	262	42	72	6	0	1	25	8	2	.275	.296	.309	88	-1						*S-55/1-1,2	-0.2
1874	Atl-n	56	254	48	75	4	0	0		7		.295	.314	.311	113	6						*S-56/3-2	0.3
1875	StL-n	70	312	51	77	5	3	0		7		.247	.263	.282	98	1						*S-70/P-2M	-0.1
1876	StL-N	25	102	12	21	1	0	0	10	3	5	.206	.229	.216	51	-5				.902	5	S-23/O-1,2	0.0
1877	StL-N	8	29	1	5	0	0	0	4	1	4	.172	.200	.172	19	-3				.950	1	/S-8	0.0
Total	5 n	258	1197	204	308	21	4	2	69	30	4	.257	.275	.287	84	-12						S-256/P-2,3210	-1.2
Total	2	33	131	13	26	1	0	0	14	4	9	.198	.222	.206	44	-7				.914	7	/S-31,2-1,O	0.0

■ DUCKY PEARCE
Pearce, William C. b: 3/17/1885, Corning, Ohio d: 5/22/33, Brownstown, Ind. BR/TR, 6'1", 185 lbs. Deb: 7/1/08

YEAR	TM/L	G	AB	R	H	2B	3B	HR	RBI	BB	SO	AVG	OBP	SLG	PRO+	BR/A	SB	CS	SBR	FA	FR	G/POS	TPR
1908	Cin-N	2	2	0	0	0	0	0	0	0		.000	.000	.000	-99	-0	0			1.000	1	/C-2	0.1
1909	Cin-N	2	2	0	0	0	0	0	0	0		.000	.000	.000	-99	-0	0			1.000	1	/C-2	-0.1
Total	2	4	4	0	0	0	0	0	0	0		.000	.000	.000	-99	-1	0			1.000	1	/C-4	0.0

■ ALBIE PEARSON
Pearson, Albert Gregory b: 9/12/34, Alhambra, Cal. BL/TL, 5'5", 141 lbs. Deb: 4/14/58

YEAR	TM/L	G	AB	R	H	2B	3B	HR	RBI	BB	SO	AVG	OBP	SLG	PRO+	BR/A	SB	CS	SBR	FA	FR	G/POS	TPR
1958	Was-A	146	530	63	146	25	5	3	33	64	31	.275	.356	.358	99	1	7	8	-3	.980	6	*O-141	-0.4
1959	Was-A	25	80	9	15	1	0	0	2	14	9	.188	.309	.200	43	-6	1	1	-0	.974	-2	O-21	-1.0
	Bal-A	80	138	22	32	4	2	0	6	13	5	.232	.296	.290	64	-7	4	0	1	.987	-7	O-50	-1.4
	Yr	105	218	31	47	5	2	0	8	27	8	.216	.302	.257	56	-13	5	1	1	.983	-9	O-71	-2.4
1960	Bal-A	48	82	17	20	2	0	1	6	17	3	.244	.374	.305	87	-1	4	0	1	.975	-5	O-32	-0.6
1961	LA-A	144	427	92	123	21	3	7	41	96	40	.288	.420	.400	109	9	11	3	2	.956	-1	*O-113	0.3
1962	LA-A	160	614	**115**	160	29	6	5	42	95	36	.261	.361	.352	96	-1	15	6	1	.989	9	*O-160	-0.1
1963	LA-A★	154	578	92	176	26	5	6	47	92	37	.304	.403	.398	133	30	17	10	-1	.983	7	*O-148	2.9
1964	LA-A	107	265	34	59	5	1	2	16	35	22	.223	.316	.272	72	-9	6	4	-1	.978	-3	O-66	-1.7
1965	Cal-A	122	360	41	100	17	2	4	21	51	17	.278	.370	.369	114	8	12	1	3	.988	-4	*O-101	0.4
1966	Cal-A	2	3	0	0	0	0	0	0	0	0	.000	.000	.000	-99	-1	0	0		.000	-0	/O-1	-0.1
Total	9	988	3077	485	831	130	24	28	214	477	195	.270	.370	.355	102	24	77	33	3	.980	1	O-833	-1.7

■ CHARLIE PECHOUS
Pechous, Charles Edward b: 10/5/1896, Chicago, Ill. d: 9/13/80, Kenosha, Wis. BR/TR, 6', 170 lbs. Deb: 9/14/15

YEAR	TM/L	G	AB	R	H	2B	3B	HR	RBI	BB	SO	AVG	OBP	SLG	PRO+	BR/A	SB	CS	SBR	FA	FR	G/POS	TPR
1915	Chi-F	18	51	4	9	3	0	0	4	4	15	.176	.236	.235	28	-5	1			.938	-1	3-18	-0.6
1916	Chi-N	22	69	5	10	1	1	0	3	4	21	.145	.181	.188	12	-7	1			.940	8	3-22	0.2
1917	Chi-N	13	41	2	10	0	0	0	2	1	9	.244	.295	.244	61	-2	1			1.000	-2	/3-7,S-5	-0.4
Total	3	53	161	11	29	4	1	0	9	9	45	.180	.228	.217	30	-14	3			.947	6	/3-47,S-5	-0.8

■ HAL PECK
Peck, Harold Arthur b: 4/20/17, Big Bend, Wis. BL/TL, 5'11", 175 lbs. Deb: 5/13/43

YEAR	TM/L	G	AB	R	H	2B	3B	HR	RBI	BB	SO	AVG	OBP	SLG	PRO+	BR/A	SB	CS	SBR	FA	FR	G/POS	TPR
1943	Bro-N	1	1	0	0	0	0	0	0	0	0	.000	.000	.000	-99	-0	0			.000	0	H	0.0
1944	Phi-A	2	8	0	2	0	0	0	2	0	0	.250	.250	.250	44	-1	0	2	-1	1.000	0	/O-2	-0.2
1945	Phi-A	112	449	51	124	22	9	5	39	37	28	.276	.331	.399	112	5	5	4	-1	.943	-9	*O-110	-1.1
1946	Phi-A	48	150	14	37	8	2	0	11	16	14	.247	.319	.367	92	-2	1	2	-1	.981	-3	O-35	-0.8
1947	Cle-A	114	392	58	115	18	2	8	44	27	31	.293	.342	.411	112	5	3	3	1	.983	-6	O-97	-0.8
1948	*Cle-A	45	63	12	18	3	0	0	8	6	9	.286	.328	.333	78	-2	1	0	1	1.000	4	/O-6	-0.4
1949	Cle-A	33	29	1	9	1	0	2	8	1	5	.310	.375	.345	93	-0	0			1.000	-1	/O-2	-0.1
Total	7	355	1092	136	305	52	13	15	112	87	86	.279	.334	.392	106	5	10	10		.965	-21	O-255	-3.4

YEAR	TM/L	G	AB	R	H	2B	3B	HR	RBI	BB	SO	AVG	OBP	SLG	PRO+	BR/A	SB	CS	SBR	FA	FR	G/POS	TPR

◼ ROGER PECKINPAUGH
Peckinpaugh, Roger Thorpe b: 2/5/1891, Wooster, Ohio d: 11/17/77, Cleveland, Ohio BR/TR, 5'10.5", 165 lbs. Deb: 9/15/10 M

YEAR	TM/L	G	AB	R	H	2B	3B	HR	RBI	BB	SO	AVG	OBP	SLG	PRO+	BR/A	SB	CS	SBR	FA	FR	G/POS	TPR
1910	Cle-A	15	45	1	9	0	0	0	6	1		.200	.234	.200	36	-3	3			.906	-6	S-14	-1.0
1912	Cle-A	70	236	18	50	4	1	1	22	16		.212	.262	.250	45	-17	11			.924	-2	S-68	-1.4
1913	Cle-A	1	0	1	0	0	0	0	0	0	0	—	—	—	—	0	0			.000	0	H	0.0
	NY-A	95	340	35	91	10	7	1	32	24	47	.268	.316	.347	94	-4	19			.931	-6	S-93	-0.1
	Yr	96	340	36	91	10	7	1	32	24	47	.268	.316	.347	94	-4	19			.931	-6	S-93	-0.1
1914	NY-A	157	570	55	127	14	6	3	51	51	73	.223	.288	.284	72	-20	38	17	1	.956	3	*S-157,M	-0.2
1915	NY-A	142	540	67	119	18	7	5	44	49	72	.220	.288	.307	79	-16	19	12	-2	.942	11	*S-142	0.5
1916	NY-A	145	552	65	141	22	8	4	58	62	50	.255	.332	.346	101	1	18			.946	1	*S-145	1.1
1917	NY-A	148	543	63	141	24	7	0	41	64	46	.260	.340	.330	103	3	17			.934	10	*S-148	2.2
1918	NY-A	122	446	59	103	15	3	0	43	43	41	.231	.300	.278	74	-14	12			.961	25	*S-122	1.8
1919	NY-A	122	453	89	138	20	2	7	33	59	37	.305	.390	.404	122	15	10			.943	28	*S-121	5.1
1920	NY-A	139	534	109	144	26	6	8	54	72	47	.270	.356	.386	93	-5	8	12	-5	.962	3	*S-137	0.6
1921	*NY-A	149	577	128	166	25	7	8	71	84	44	.288	.380	.397	96	-1	2	2	-1	.948	-5	*S-149	0.7
1922	Was-A	147	520	62	132	14	4	2	48	55	36	.254	.329	.308	70	-22	11	6	-0	.951	20	*S-147	1.3
1923	Was-A	154	568	73	150	18	4	2	62	64	30	.264	.340	.320	78	-17	10	8	-2	.948	23	*S-154	1.9
1924	*Was-A	155	523	72	142	20	5	2	73	72	45	.272	.360	.340	84	-11	9	6	-1	.963	9	*S-155	1.3
1925	*Was-A	126	422	67	124	16	4	4	64	49	23	.294	.367	.379	91	-5	13	4	2	.952	-16	*S-124/1-1	-0.5
1926	Was-A	57	147	19	35	4	1	0	14	28	12	.238	.360	.299	75	-4	2	2		.960	-1	S-46/1-1	0.0
1927	Chi-A	68	217	23	64	6	3	0	23	21	6	.295	.360	.350	87	-4	2	3	-1	.964	-1	S-60	0.0
Total	17	2012	7233	1006	1876	256	75	48	739	814	609	.259	.336	.335	87	-122	205	70		.949	97	*S-1982/1-2	13.3

◼ BILL PECOTA
Pecota, William Joseph b: 2/16/60, Redwood City, Cal. BR/TR, 6'2", 195 lbs. Deb: 9/19/86

YEAR	TM/L	G	AB	R	H	2B	3B	HR	RBI	BB	SO	AVG	OBP	SLG	PRO+	BR/A	SB	CS	SBR	FA	FR	G/POS	TPR
1986	KC-A	12	29	3	6	2	0	0	2	3	3	.207	.303	.276	58	-2	0	2	-1	.974	6	3-12/S-2,D	0.3
1987	KC-A	66	156	22	43	5	1	3	14	15	25	.276	.343	.378	89	-2	5	0	2	.977	7	S-36,3-17,2/D	0.9
1988	KC-A	90	178	25	37	3	1	1	15	18	34	.208	.288	.275	58	-10	7	2	1	.976	11	S-41,3-21,1/OD2C	0.4
1989	KC-A	65	83	21	17	4	2	3	5	7	9	.205	.275	.410	91	-1	5	0	2	.988	4	S-29,O-15,2/31D	0.5
1990	KC-A	87	240	43	58	15	2	5	20	33	39	.242	.336	.383	102	1	8	5	-1	.986	6	2-50,S-21,3/01D	0.9
1991	KC-A	125	398	53	114	23	2	6	45	41	45	.286	.356	.399	108	5	16	7	1	.983	-13	*3-102,2-34/S1DOP	-0.6
1992	NY-N	117	269	28	61	13	0	2	26	25	40	.227	.295	.297	69	-11	9	3	1	.926	10	3-48,S-39,2/P1	0.2
1993	*Atl-N	72	62	17	20	2	1	0	5	2	5	.323	.344	.387	94	-1	1	1	-0	1.000	1	3-23/2-4,O	0.1
1994	Atl-N	64	112	11	24	5	0	2	16	16	16	.214	.313	.313	64	-6	1	0	0	.974	7	3-31/2-1,O	0.2
Total	9	698	1527	223	380	72	11	22	148	160	216	.249	.324	.354	87	-26	52	20	4	.968	39	3-272,S-177,2/01DPO	2.9

◼ LES PEDEN
Peden, Leslie Earl "Gooch" b: 9/17/23, Azle, Tex. BR/TR, 6'1.5", 212 lbs. Deb: 4/17/53

YEAR	TM/L	G	AB	R	H	2B	3B	HR	RBI	BB	SO	AVG	OBP	SLG	PRO+	BR/A	SB	CS	SBR	FA	FR	G/POS	TPR
1953	Was-A	9	28	4	7	1	0	1	4	3	.250	.344	.393	101	0	0	0	0	1.000	-1	/C-8	0.0

◼ STU PEDERSON
Pederson, Stuart Russell b: 1/28/60, Palo Alto, Cal. BL/TL, 6', 185 lbs. Deb: 9/8/85

YEAR	TM/L	G	AB	R	H	2B	3B	HR	RBI	BB	SO	AVG	OBP	SLG	PRO+	BR/A	SB	CS	SBR	FA	FR	G/POS	TPR
1985	LA-N	8	4	1	0	0	0	0	1	0	2	.000	.000	.000	-99	-1	0	0	0	1.000	-1	/O-5	-0.3

◼ JORGE PEDRE
Pedre, Jorge Enrique b: 10/12/66, Culver City, Cal. BR/TR, 5'11", 210 lbs. Deb: 9/7/91

YEAR	TM/L	G	AB	R	H	2B	3B	HR	RBI	BB	SO	AVG	OBP	SLG	PRO+	BR/A	SB	CS	SBR	FA	FR	G/POS	TPR
1991	KC-A	10	19	2	5	1	1	0	3	3	5	.263	.364	.421	116	0	0	0	0	.971	-0	/C-9,1-1	0.1
1992	Chi-N	4	4	0	0	0	0	0	0	0	1	.000	.000	.000	-98	-1	0	0	0	1.000	-1	/C-4	-0.2
Total	2	14	23	2	5	1	1	0	3	3	6	.217	.308	.348	81	-1	0	0	0	.973	-1	/C-13,1-1	-0.1

◼ AL PEDRIQUE
Pedrique, Alfredo Jose (Garcia) b: 8/11/60, Aragua, Venez. BR/TR, 6' ", 155 lbs. Deb: 4/14/87

YEAR	TM/L	G	AB	R	H	2B	3B	HR	RBI	BB	SO	AVG	OBP	SLG	PRO+	BR/A	SB	CS	SBR	FA	FR	G/POS	TPR
1987	NY-N	5	6	1	0	0	0	0	1	2	.000	.143	.000	-61	-1	0	0	0	1.000	1	/S-4,2-1	0.0
	Pit-N	88	246	23	74	10	1	1	27	18	27	.301	.356	.362	90	-3	5	4	-1	.968	-12	S-76/3-3,2	-0.9
	Yr	93	252	24	74	10	1	1	27	19	29	.294	.350	.353	87	-4	5	4	-1	.969	-10	S-80/2-3,3	-0.9
1988	Pit-N	50	128	7	23	5	0	0	4	8	17	.180	.234	.219	31	-11	0	0	0	.974	2	S-46/3-5	-0.7
1989	Det-N	31	69	1	14	3	0	0	5	2	15	.203	.225	.246	34	-6	0	0	0	.960	1	3-12,S-12/2	0.2
Total	3	174	449	32	111	18	1	1	36	29	61	.247	.299	.298	64	-22	5	4	-1	.971	-1	S-138/3-20,2	-1.4

◼ CHICK PEDROES
Pedroes, Charles P. b: 10/27/1869, Chicago, Ill. d: 8/6/27, Chicago, Ill. Deb: 8/21/02

YEAR	TM/L	G	AB	R	H	2B	3B	HR	RBI	BB	SO	AVG	OBP	SLG	PRO+	BR/A	SB	CS	SBR	FA	FR	G/POS	TPR
1902	Chi-N	2	6	0	0	0	0	0	0	0		.000	.000	.000	-99	-1	0			1.000	-0	/O-2	-0.2

◼ HOMER PEEL
Peel, Homer Hefner b: 10/10/02, Port Sullivan, Tex BR/TR, 5'9.5", 170 lbs. Deb: 9/13/27

YEAR	TM/L	G	AB	R	H	2B	3B	HR	RBI	BB	SO	AVG	OBP	SLG	PRO+	BR/A	SB	CS	SBR	FA	FR	G/POS	TPR
1927	StL-N	2	2	0	0	0	0	0	0	0	1	.000	.000	.000	-97	-1	0			.000	-1	/O-1	-0.1
1929	Phi-N	53	156	16	42	12	1	0	19	12	7	.269	.329	.359	66	-8	1			.990	-4	O-39/1-1	-1.2
1930	StL-N	26	73	9	12	2	0	0	10	3	4	.164	.197	.192	-5	-12	0			.968	-4	O-21	-1.6
1933	*NY-N	84	148	16	38	1	1	1	12	14	10	.257	.325	.297	80	-3	0			.962	-12	O-45	-1.8
1934	NY-N	21	41	7	8	0	0	1	3	1	2	.195	.214	.268	29	-4	0			.929	-3	O-10	-0.7
Total	5	186	420	48	100	15	2	2	44	30	24	.238	.294	.298	53	-29	1			.974	-22	O-116/1-1	-5.4

◼ JACK PEERSON
Peerson, Jack Chiles b: 8/28/10, Brunswick, Ga. d: 10/23/66, Ft.Walton Beach, Fla. BR/TR, 5'11", 175 lbs. Deb: 9/7/35

YEAR	TM/L	G	AB	R	H	2B	3B	HR	RBI	BB	SO	AVG	OBP	SLG	PRO+	BR/A	SB	CS	SBR	FA	FR	G/POS	TPR
1935	Phi-A	10	19	3	6	1	0	0	1	1	1	.316	.350	.368	87	-0	0	0	0	.952	3	/S-4	0.0
1936	Phi-A	8	34	7	11	1	1	0	5	0	3	.324	.324	.412	82	-1	0	1	-1	.942	4	/S-7,2-1	0.2
Total	2	18	53	10	17	2	1	0	6	1	4	.321	.333	.396	84	-1	0	1	-1	.945	4	/S-11,2-1	0.2

◼ CHARLIE PEETE
Peete, Charles "Mule" b: 2/22/29, Franklin, Va. d: 11/27/56, Caracas, Venez. BL/TR, 5'9.5", 190 lbs. Deb: 7/17/56

YEAR	TM/L	G	AB	R	H	2B	3B	HR	RBI	BB	SO	AVG	OBP	SLG	PRO+	BR/A	SB	CS	SBR	FA	FR	G/POS	TPR
1956	StL-N	23	52	3	10	2	2	0	6	6	10	.192	.288	.308	60	-3	0	2	-1	1.000	-1	O-21	-0.7

◼ MONTE PEFFER
Peffer, Monte (b: Montague Pfeiffer) b: 10/8/1891, New York, N.Y. d: 9/27/41, New York, N.Y. BR/TR, 5'4.5", 147 lbs. Deb: 9/29/13

YEAR	TM/L	G	AB	R	H	2B	3B	HR	RBI	BB	SO	AVG	OBP	SLG	PRO+	BR/A	SB	CS	SBR	FA	FR	G/POS	TPR
1913	Phi-A	1	3	0	0	0	0	0	0	0	1	.000	.250	.000	-26	-0	0			.800	-0	/S-1	-0.1

◼ JULIO PEGUERO
Peguero, Julio Cesar b: 9/7/68, San Isidro, D.R. BB/TR, 6', 160 lbs. Deb: 4/8/92

YEAR	TM/L	G	AB	R	H	2B	3B	HR	RBI	BB	SO	AVG	OBP	SLG	PRO+	BR/A	SB	CS	SBR	FA	FR	G/POS	TPR
1992	Phi-N	14	9	3	2	0	0	0	0	3	3	.222	.417	.222	86	0	0	0	0	1.000	-5	O-14	-0.5

◼ STEVE PEGUES
Pegues, Steven Antone b: 5/21/68, Pontotoc, Miss. BR/TR, 6'2", 190 lbs. Deb: 7/6/94

YEAR	TM/L	G	AB	R	H	2B	3B	HR	RBI	BB	SO	AVG	OBP	SLG	PRO+	BR/A	SB	CS	SBR	FA	FR	G/POS	TPR
1994	Cin-N	11	10	1	3	0	0	0	0	1	3	.300	.364	.300	76	-0	0	0	0	.833	-1	/O-4	-0.1
	Pit-N	7	26	1	10	2	0	1	2	1	2	.385	.407	.462	127	1	1	0	0	1.000	-1	/O-7	0.0
	Yr	18	36	2	13	2	0	1	2	2	5	.361	.395	.417	113	1	1	0	0	.929	-2	/O-11	-0.1

◼ HEINIE PEITZ
Peitz, Henry Clement b: 11/28/1870, St.Louis, Mo. d: 10/23/43, Cincinnati, Ohio BR/TR, 5'11", 165 lbs. Deb: 10/15/1892 FC

YEAR	TM/L	G	AB	R	H	2B	3B	HR	RBI	BB	SO	AVG	OBP	SLG	PRO+	BR/A	SB	CS	SBR	FA	FR	G/POS	TPR
1892	StL-N	1	3	0	0	0	0	0	0	0	0	.000	.000	.000	-99	-1	0			1.000	-0	/C-1	-0.1
1893	StL-N	96	362	53	92	12	9	1	45	54	20	.254	.353	.345	85	-7	12			.948	9	C-74,S-11,O/1	0.6
1894	StL-N	99	338	52	89	19	9	3	49	43	21	.263	.348	.399	80	-12	14			.897	4	3-47,C-39,1/P	-0.3
1895	StL-N	90	334	44	95	14	12	1	65	29	20	.284	.345	.416	97	-2	7			.937	1	C-71,1-11,3	0.9
1896	Cin-N	68	211	33	63	12	5	0	34	30	15	.299	.386	.431	108	2	7			.968	1	C-67	0.9
1897	Cin-N	77	266	35	78	11	7	1	44	18		.293	.340	.398	89	-5	3			.979	7	C-71/P-2	0.8
1898	Cin-N	105	330	49	90	15	5	1	43	35		.273	.348	.358	96	-2	9			.945	-3	*C-101	0.5
1899	Cin-N	93	290	45	79	13	5	1	43	45		.272	.374	.341	95	-0	11			.977	-1	C-91/P-1	0.5
1900	Cin-N	91	294	30	75	14	3	1	34	20		.255	.318	.330	81	-8	5			.958	6	C-80/1-8	0.5
1901	Cin-N	82	269	24	82	13	5	1	24	23		.305	.361	.401	130	11	3			.982	2	C-49,2-21/31	1.8
1902	Cin-N	112	387	54	122	22	5	1	60	24		.315	.369	.406	127	12	7			.919	-2	2-48,C-47/13	1.7

YEAR	TM/L	G	AB	R	H	2B	3B	HR	RBI	BB	SO	AVG	OBP	SLG	PRO+	BR/A	SB	CS	SBR	FA	FR	G/POS	TPR
1903	Cin-N	105	358	45	93	15	3	0	42	37		.260	.331	.318	77	-11	7			.970	-2	C-78,1-11/32	-0.5
1904	Cin-N	84	272	32	66	13	2	1	30	14		.243	.282	.316	78	-8	1			.975	4	C-64,1-18/3	0.3
1905	Pit-N	88	278	18	62	10	0	0	27	24		.223	.289	.259	62	-13	2			.965	-11	C-87/2-1	-1.5
1906	Pit-N	40	125	13	30	8	0	0	20	13		.240	.321	.304	91	-1	1			.979	-0	C-38	0.3
1913	StL-N	3	4	1	1	0	1	0	0	0	0	.250	.250	.750	182	0	0			.625	-2	/C-2,O-1	-0.1
Total	16	1234	4121	532	1117	191	66	16	560	409	76	.271	.342	.361	92	-45	91			.963	14	C-960/3-79,120SP	5.9

■ **JOE PEITZ** Peitz, Joseph b: 11/8/1869, St.Louis, Mo. d: 12/4/19, St.Louis, Mo. Deb: 7/5/1894 F

1894	StL-N	7	26	10	11	2	3	0	3	6	1	.423	.531	.731	202	5	2			.818	1	/O-7	0.3

■ **EDDIE PELLAGRINI** Pellagrini, Edward Charles b: 3/13/18, Boston, Mass. BR/TR, 5'9", 165 lbs. Deb: 4/22/46

1946	Bos-A	22	71	7	15	3	1	2	4	3	18	.211	.253	.366	68	-3	1	0	0	.891	-0	3-14/S-9	-0.3
1947	Bos-A	74	231	29	47	8	1	4	19	23	35	.203	.289	.299	57	-14	2	2	-1	.926	-6	3-42,S-26	-2.0
1948	StL-A	105	290	31	69	8	3	2	27	34	40	.238	.320	.307	65	-14	1	2	-1	.964	24	S-98	1.3
1949	StL-A	79	235	26	56	8	1	2	15	14	24	.238	.284	.306	54	-16	2	1	0	.961	7	S-76	-0.4
1951	Phi-N	86	197	31	46	4	5	3	30	23	25	.234	.326	.381	91	-3	5	1	1	.990	-17	2-53/S-8,3	-1.6
1952	Cin-N	46	100	15	17	2	0	1	3	8	18	.170	.231	.220	26	-10	1	0	0	.983	10	2-22/1-8,S3	0.1
1953	Pit-N	78	174	16	44	3	2	4	19	14	20	.253	.309	.362	75	-7	1	1	-0	.972	-4	2-31,3-12/S	-0.9
1954	Pit-N	73	125	12	27	6	0	0	16	9	21	.216	.290	.264	46	-10	0	0	0	.968	2	3-31/2-7,S	-0.8
Total	8	563	1423	167	321	42	13	20	133	128	201	.226	.295	.316	62	-76	13	7	-1	.956	15	S-222,2-113,3/1	-4.6

■ **LOUIS PELOUZE** Pelouze, Louis H. BR/TR, 5'8", 170 lbs. Deb: 7/24/1886

1886	StL-N	1	3	0	0	0	0	0	0	0	2	.000	.000	.000	-99	-1	0			1.000	0	/O-1	0.0

■ **DAN PELTIER** Peltier, Daniel Edward b: 6/30/68, Clifton Park, N.Y. BL/TL, 6'1", 200 lbs. Deb: 6/26/92

1992	Tex-A	12	24	1	4	0	0	0	2	0	3	.167	.167	.167	-7	-3	0	0	0	.857	-3	O-10	-0.7
1993	Tex-A	65	160	23	43	7	1	1	17	20	27	.269	.354	.344	92	-1	0	4	-2	.950	-7	O-55/1-5	-1.1
Total	2	77	184	24	47	7	1	1	19	20	30	.255	.332	.321	80	-5	0	4	-2	.943	-10	/O-65,1-5	-1.8

■ **JOHN PELTZ** Peltz, John b: 4/23/1861, New Orleans, La. d: 2/27/06, New Orleans, La. BR/TR, Deb: 5/1/1884

1884	Ind-a	106	393	40	86	13	17	3		7		.219	.236	.361	95	-3				.818	4	*O-106	-0.1
1888	Bal-a	1	4	1	1	0	0	0	0	0		.250	.250	.250	62	-0	1			.500	-0	/O-1	-0.1
1890	Bro-a	98	384	55	87	9	6	1			32	.227	.289	.289	73	-13	10			.904	3	*O-98	-1.2
	Syr-a	5	17	2	3	1	1	0			3	.176	.300	.353	103	0	0			.857	0	/O-5	0.0
	Tol-a	20	73	8	18	2	2	0			3	.247	.286	.329	79	-2	7			.886	-2	O-20	-0.4
	Yr	123	474	65	108	12	9	1			38	.228	.289	.297	75	-16	17			.900	1	*O-123	-1.6
Total	3	230	871	106	195	25	26	4	0		45	.224	.266	.326	84	-18	18			.865	5	O-230	-1.8

■ **BROCK PEMBERTON** Pemberton, Brock b: 11/5/53, Tulsa, Okla. BB/TL, 6'3", 190 lbs. Deb: 9/10/74

1974	NY-N	11	22	0	4	0	0	0	1	0	3	.182	.182	.182	2	-3	0	1	-1	1.000	1	/1-4	-0.3
1975	NY-N	2	2	0	0	0	0	0	0	0	1	.000	.000	.000	-99	-1	0	0	0	.000	0	H	-0.1
Total	2	13	24	0	4	0	0	0	1	0	4	.167	.167	.167	-7	-3	0	1	-1	1.000	1	/1-4	-0.4

■ **BERT PENA** Pena, Adalberto (Rivera) b: 7/11/59, Santurce, P.R. BR/TR, 5'11", 165 lbs. Deb: 9/14/81

1981	Hou-N	4	2	0	1	0	0	0	0	0	0	.500	.500	.500	194	0	0	0	0	1.000	0	/S-3	0.0
1983	Hou-N	4	8	0	1	0	0	0	0	2	2	.125	.300	.125	23	-1	0	0	0	1.000	-1	/S-4	-0.2
1984	Hou-N	24	39	3	8	1	0	1	4	3	8	.205	.262	.308	64	-2	0	0	0	.956	6	S-21	0.5
1985	Hou-N	20	29	4	8	2	0	0	1	1	4	.276	.300	.345	82	-1	0	0	0	1.000	-1	/3-7,S-6,2	-0.1
1986	Hou-N	15	29	3	6	1	0	0	2	5	5	.207	.324	.241	60	-1	0	0	0	.907	-1	S-10/3-2,2	0.1
1987	Hou-N	21	46	5	7	0	0	0	2	2	7	.152	.204	.152	-4	-7	1	0	0	.982	-1	S-19/3-1	-0.7
Total	6	88	153	18	31	4	0	1	10	13	28	.203	.269	.248	45	-12	1	0	0	.953	3	/S-63,3-10,2	-0.4

■ **TONY PENA** Pena, Antonio Francisco (Padilla) b: 6/4/57, Monte Cristi, D.R. BR/TR, 6', 181 lbs. Deb: 9/1/80 F

1980	Pit-N	8	21	1	9	1	1	0	1	0	4	.429	.429	.571	174	2	0	1	-1	.952	2	/C-6	0.3
1981	Pit-N	66	210	16	63	9	1	2	17	8	23	.300	.329	.381	98	-1	1	2	-1	.985	2	C-64	0.2
1982	Pit-N★	138	497	53	147	28	4	11	63	17	57	.296	.324	.435	107	3	2	5	-2	.982	-7	*C-137	0.0
1983	Pit-N	151	542	51	163	22	3	15	70	31	73	.301	.339	.435	110	6	6	7	-2	.992	-0	*C-149	1.1
1984	Pit-N★	147	546	77	156	27	2	15	78	36	79	.286	.334	.425	112	8	12	8	-1	.991	13	*C-146	2.8
1985	Pit-N★	147	546	53	136	27	2	10	59	29	67	.249	.287	.361	81	-15	12	8	-1	.988	9	*C-146/1-1	0.0
1986	Pit-N★	144	510	56	147	26	2	10	52	53	69	.288	.356	.406	107	6	9	10	-3	.981	5	*C-139/1-4	1.7
1987	*StL-N	116	384	40	82	13	4	5	44	36	54	.214	.283	.307	55	-25	6	1	1	.988	-1	*C-112/1-4,O	-1.7
1988	StL-N	149	505	55	133	23	1	10	51	33	60	.263	.310	.372	94	-4	6	2	1	**.994**	6	*C-142/1-3	1.3
1989	StL-N★	141	424	36	110	17	2	4	37	35	33	.259	.319	.337	85	-8	5	3	-0	**.997**	11	*C-134/O-1	1.0
1990	*Bos-A	143	491	62	129	19	1	7	56	43	71	.263	.323	.348	84	-10	8	6	-1	.995	11	*C-142/1-1	0.8
1991	Bos-A	141	464	45	107	23	2	5	48	37	53	.231	.293	.321	66	-21	8	3	1	.995	9	*C-140	-0.4
1992	Bos-A	133	410	39	99	21	1	1	38	24	61	.241	.285	.305	61	-21	3	2	-0	.993	11	*C-132	-0.3
1993	Bos-A	126	304	20	55	11	0	4	19	25	46	.181	.248	.257	34	-29	1	3	-2	.995	22	*C-125/D-1	-0.2
1994	Cle-A	40	112	18	33	8	1	2	10	9	11	.295	.347	.438	96	-1	0	1	-1	.996	5	C-40	0.5
Total	15	1790	5966	622	1569	275	27	101	643	416	761	.263	.313	.369	87	-111	79	62	-14	.990	98	*C-1754/1-13,OD	7.1

■ **GERONIMO PENA** Pena, Geronimo (Martinez) b: 3/29/67, Distrito Nacional, D.R. BB/TR, 6'1", 170 lbs. Deb: 9/5/90

1990	StL-N	18	45	5	11	2	0	0	2	4	14	.244	.320	.289	69	-2	1	1	-0	.982	-1	2-11	-0.3
1991	StL-N	104	185	38	45	8	3	5	17	18	45	.243	.327	.400	103	1	15	5	2	.976	-3	2-83/O-4	0.0
1992	StL-N	62	203	31	62	12	1	7	31	24	37	.305	.392	.478	150	14	13	8	-1	.984	8	2-57	2.3
1993	StL-N	74	254	34	65	19	2	5	30	25	71	.256	.332	.406	98	-1	13	5	1	.966	-1	2-64	0.1
1994	StL-N	83	213	33	54	13	1	11	34	24	54	.254	.346	.479	117	5	9	1	2	.990	6	2-59/3-1	1.3
Total	5	341	900	141	237	54	7	28	114	95	221	.263	.347	.432	113	17	51	20	3	.979	9	2-274/O-4,3	3.4

■ **ROBERTO PENA** Pena, Roberto Cesar "Baby" (b: Roberto Cesar Zapata (Pena)) b: 4/17/37, Santo Domingo, D.R. d: 7/23/82, Santiago, D.R. BR/TR, 5'8", 175 lbs. Deb: 4/12/65

1965	Chi-N	51	170	17	37	5	1	2	12	16	19	.218	.293	.294	64	-8	1	2	-1	.930	-10	S-50	-1.6
1966	Chi-N	6	17	0	3	2	0	0	1	0	4	.176	.176	.294	28	-2	0	0	0	.957	0	/S-5	-0.1
1968	Phi-N	138	500	56	130	13	2	1	38	34	63	.260	.310	.300	84	-9	3	5	-2	.954	6	*S-133	1.0
1969	SD-N	139	472	44	118	16	3	4	30	21	63	.250	.286	.322	73	-18	0	3	-2	.977	-23	S-65,2-33,31	-3.7
1970	Oak-A	19	58	4	15	1	0	0	3	3	4	.259	.295	.276	61	-3	1	1	-0	.961	-1	S-12/3-5	-0.4
	Mil-A	121	416	36	99	19	1	3	42	25	45	.238	.284	.310	63	-21	3	5	-2	.981	-16	S-99,2-15/1	-2.8
	Yr	140	474	40	114	20	1	3	45	28	49	.241	.286	.306	63	-24	4	6	-2	**.979**	-17	*S-111,2-15/13	-3.2
1971	Mil-A	113	274	17	65	9	3	3	28	15	37	.237	.279	.325	71	-11	2	1	-0	.996	-3	1-50,3-37,S/2	-1.8
Total	6	587	1907	174	467	65	10	13	154	114	235	.245	.291	.310	72	-72	10	17	-7	.962	-49	*S-387/1-69,32	-9.4

■ **ELMER PENCE** Pence, Elmer Clair b: 8/17/1900, Valley Springs, Cal. d: 9/17/68, San Francisco, Cal. BR/TR, 6', 185 lbs. Deb: 8/23/22

1922	Chi-A	1	0	0	0	0	0	0	0	0	0	—	—	—	—		0	0	0	1.000	-0	/O-1	0.0

■ **JIM PENDLETON** Pendleton, James Edward b: 1/7/24, St.Charles, Mo. BR/TR, 6', 185 lbs. Deb: 4/17/53

1953	Mil-N	120	251	48	75	12	4	7	27	7	36	.299	.323	.462	108	2	6	5	-1	.961	-13	*O-105/S-7	-1.4
1954	Mil-N	71	173	20	38	3	1	1	16	4	21	.220	.237	.266	33	-17	2	1	0	.950	-4	O-50	-2.3

YEAR	TM/L	G	AB	R	H	2B	3B	HR	RBI	BB	SO	AVG	OBP	SLG	PRO+	BR/A	SB	CS	SBR	FA	FR	G/POS	TPR
1955	Mil-N	8	10	0	0	0	0	0	0	0	2	.000	.000	.000	-99	-3	0	0	0	1.000	-0	/S-1,3-1,O	-0.3
1956	Mil-N	14	11	0	0	0	0	0	0	1	3	.000	.083	.000	-80	-3	0	0	0	1.000	-0	/S-3,3-2,12	-0.3
1957	Pit-N	46	59	9	18	1	1	0	9	9	14	.305	.406	.356	110	1	0	0	0	.917	-3	/O-9,3-2,S	-0.2
1958	Pit-N	3	3	0	1	0	0	0	0	0	0	.333	.333	.333	79	-0	0	0	0	.000	0	H	0.0
1959	Cin-N	65	113	13	29	2	0	3	9	8	18	.257	.311	.354	75	-4	3	0	1	.971	0	O-24,3-16/S	-0.4
1962	Hou-N	117	321	30	79	12	2	8	36	14	57	.246	.282	.371	79	-11	0	0	0	.963	-6	O-90/1-8,3S	-2.1
Total 8		444	941	120	240	30	8	19	97	43	151	.255	.292	.365	76	-35	11	6	-0	.959	-26	O-279/3-24,S12	-7.0

■ TERRY PENDLETON

Pendleton, Terry Lee b: 7/16/60, Los Angeles, Cal. BB/TR, 5'9", 180 lbs. Deb: 7/18/84

YEAR	TM/L	G	AB	R	H	2B	3B	HR	RBI	BB	SO	AVG	OBP	SLG	PRO+	BR/A	SB	CS	SBR	FA	FR	G/POS	TPR
1984	StL-N	67	262	37	85	16	3	1	33	16	32	.324	.363	.420	123	7	20	5	3	.943	0	3-66	1.9
1985	*StL-N	149	559	56	134	16	3	5	69	37	75	.240	.287	.306	66	-25	17	12	-2	.965	23	*3-149	-0.7
1986	StL-N	159	578	56	138	26	5	1	59	34	59	.239	.282	.306	63	-30	24	6	4	.962	24	*3-156/O-1	-0.5
1987	*StL-N	159	583	82	167	29	4	12	96	70	74	.286	.365	.412	103	4	19	12	-2	.949	16	*3-158	1.6
1988	StL-N	110	391	44	99	20	2	6	53	21	51	.253	.295	.361	86	-7	3	3	-1	.963	11	*3-101	0.2
1989	StL-N	162	613	83	162	28	5	13	74	44	81	.264	.314	.390	97	-3	9	5	-0	.971	30	*3-161	2.9
1990	StL-N	121	447	46	103	20	2	6	58	30	58	.230	.280	.324	66	-21	7	5	-1	.947	7	*3-117	-1.5
1991	*Atl-N	153	586	94	187	34	8	22	86	43	70	.319	.363	.517	138	28	10	2	2	.950	28	*3-148	5.9
1992	*Atl-N★	160	640	98	199	39	1	21	105	37	67	.311	.349	.473	123	18	5	2	0	.960	13	*3-158	3.3
1993	*Atl-N	161	633	81	172	33	1	17	84	36	97	.272	.314	.408	91	-10	5	1	1	.959	12	*3-161	0.4
1994	Atl-N	77	309	25	78	18	3	7	30	12	57	.252	.280	.398	74	-13	2	0	1	.950	6	3-77	-0.6
Total 11		1478	5601	702	1524	279	37	111	747	380	721	.272	.319	.395	95	-52	121	53	5	.958	178	*3-1452/O-1	12.9

■ WILL PENNYFEATHER

Pennyfeather, William Nathaniel b: 5/25/68, Perth Amboy, N.J. BR/TR, 6'2", 195 lbs. Deb: 6/27/92

YEAR	TM/L	G	AB	R	H	2B	3B	HR	RBI	BB	SO	AVG	OBP	SLG	PRO+	BR/A	SB	CS	SBR	FA	FR	G/POS	TPR
1992	Pit-N	15	9	2	2	0	0	0	0	0	0	.222	.222	.222	26	-1	0	0	0	1.000	-4	O-10	-0.5
1993	Pit-N	21	34	4	7	1	0	0	2	0	6	.206	.206	.235	18	-4	0	1	-1	1.000	-5	O-17	-1.0
1994	Pit-N	4	3	0	0	0	0	0	0	0	0	.000	.000	.000	-99	-1	0	0	0	.000	-0	/O-1	-0.1
Total 3		40	46	6	9	1	0	0	2	0	6	.196	.196	.217	11	-6	0	1	-1	1.000	-9	/O-28	-1.6

■ JIMMY PEOPLES

Peoples, James Elsworth b: 10/8/1863, Big Beaver, Mich. d: 8/29/20, Detroit, Mich. TR, 5'8", 200 lbs. Deb: 5/29/1884 U

YEAR	TM/L	G	AB	R	H	2B	3B	HR	RBI	BB	SO	AVG	OBP	SLG	PRO+	BR/A	SB	CS	SBR	FA	FR	G/POS	TPR
1884	Cin-a	69	267	28	45	2	2	1		6		.169	.187	.202	26	-22				.829	0	S-47,C-14,O/31	-1.9
1885	Cin-a	7	22	1	4	0	0	0		1		.182	.217	.182	27	-2				.826	0	/C-5,P-2,O	-0.2
	Bro-a	41	151	21	30	4	1	1		5		.199	.229	.258	53	-8				.895	-2	C-37/S-2,130	-0.6
	Yr	48	173	22	34	4	1	1		6		.197	.228	.249	50	-10				.889	-4	C-42/P-2,OS13	-0.8
1886	Bro-a	93	340	43	74	7	3	3		20		.218	.261	.282	70	-12	20			.879	19	C-76,S-14/O3	1.2
1887	Bro-a	73	268	36	68	14	2	1		16		.254	.306	.332	77	-9	22			.853	-6	C-57/O-8,S12	-0.8
1888	Bro-a	32	103	15	20	5	3	0	17	8		.194	.259	.301	79	-2	10			.904	10	C-25/S-5,O	0.9
1889	Col-a	29	100	13	23	6	2	1	16	6	8	.230	.274	.360	84	-3	3			.922	-4	C-22/O-5,2S	-0.4
Total 6		344	1251	157	264	38	13	7	33	62	8	.211	.252	.279	62	-58	55			.886	15	C-236/S-73,O123P	-1.8

■ JOE PEPITONE

Pepitone, Joseph Anthony "Pepi" b: 10/9/40, Brooklyn, N.Y. BL/TL, 6'2", 200 lbs. Deb: 4/10/62 C

YEAR	TM/L	G	AB	R	H	2B	3B	HR	RBI	BB	SO	AVG	OBP	SLG	PRO+	BR/A	SB	CS	SBR	FA	FR	G/POS	TPR
1962	NY-A	63	138	14	33	3	2	7	17	3	21	.239	.255	.442	86	-4	1	1	-0	1.000	-9	O-32,1-16	-1.5
1963	*NY-A★	157	580	79	157	16	3	27	89	23	63	.271	.307	.448	109	5	3	5	-2	.995	4	*1-143,O-16	0.0
1964	*NY-A★	160	613	71	154	12	3	28	100	24	63	.251	.281	.418	90	-10	2	1	0	.988	-6	*1-155,O-30	-2.4
1965	NY-A	143	531	51	131	18	3	18	62	43	59	.247	.306	.394	98	-2	4	2	0	.997	-3	*1-115,O-41	-1.4
1966	NY-A	152	585	85	149	21	4	31	83	29	58	.255	.292	.463	118	10	4	3	-1	.995	1	*1-119,O-55	0.1
1967	NY-A	133	501	45	126	18	3	13	64	34	62	.251	.303	.377	104	1	1	3	-2	.976	6	*O-123/1-6	-0.2
1968	NY-A	108	380	41	93	9	3	15	56	37	45	.245	.313	.403	119	8	8	2	1	.980	-6	O-92,1-12	-0.3
1969	NY-A	135	513	49	124	16	4	27	70	30	42	.242	.285	.442	105	-1	8	6	-1	.995	-6	*1-132	-1.9
1970	Hou-N	75	279	44	70	9	5	14	35	18	28	.251	.299	.470	107	1	5	2	0	.995	-1	1-50,O-28	-0.5
	Chi-N	56	213	38	57	9	2	12	44	15	15	.268	.316	.498	102	-1	0	2	-1	.992	0	O-56,1-13	-0.3
	Yr	131	492	82	127	18	7	26	79	33	43	.258	.306	.482	105	1	5	4	-1	.989	1	O-84,1-63	-0.8
1971	Chi-N	115	427	50	131	19	4	16	61	24	41	.307	.349	.482	117	8	1	2	-1	.990	-3	1-95,O-23	-0.6
1972	Chi-N	66	214	23	56	5	0	8	21	13	22	.262	.313	.397	91	-3	1	2	0	.997	-0	1-66	-0.9
1973	Chi-N	31	112	16	30	3	0	3	18	8	6	.268	.322	.375	86	-2	3	1	0	.985	0	1-28	-0.4
	Atl-N	3	11	0	4	0	0	0	1	1	1	.364	.417	.364	110	-0	0	0	0	.963	-1	/1-3	-0.1
	Yr	34	123	16	34	3	0	3	19	9	7	.276	.331	.374	88	-2	3	1	0	.983	-1	1-31	-0.5
Total 12		1397	5097	606	1315	158	35	219	721	302	526	.258	.303	.432	105	12	41	32	-7	.993	-21	1-953,O-496	-10.4

■ HENRY PEPLOSKI

Peploski, Henry Stephen "Pep" b: 9/15/05, Garlin, Poland d: 1/28/82, Dover, N.J. BL/TR, 5'9", 155 lbs. Deb: 9/19/29 F

YEAR	TM/L	G	AB	R	H	2B	3B	HR	RBI	BB	SO	AVG	OBP	SLG	PRO+	BR/A	SB	CS	SBR	FA	FR	G/POS	TPR
1929	Bos-N	6	10	1	2	0	0	0	1	1	3	.200	.273	.200	20	-1	0			1.000	-0	/3-2	-0.1

■ PEPPER PEPLOSKI

Peploski, Joseph Aloysius b: 9/12/1891, Brooklyn, N.Y. d: 7/13/72, New York, N.Y. BR/TR, 5'8", 155 lbs. Deb: 6/24/13 F

YEAR	TM/L	G	AB	R	H	2B	3B	HR	RBI	BB	SO	AVG	OBP	SLG	PRO+	BR/A	SB	CS	SBR	FA	FR	G/POS	TPR
1913	Det-A	2	4	1	2	0	0	0	0	0	0	.500	.500	.500	196	0	0			1.000	-1	/3-2	0.0

■ DON PEPPER

Pepper, Donald Hoyte b: 10/8/43, Saratoga Sprgs., N.Y BL/TR, 6'4.5", 215 lbs. Deb: 9/10/66

YEAR	TM/L	G	AB	R	H	2B	3B	HR	RBI	BB	SO	AVG	OBP	SLG	PRO+	BR/A	SB	CS	SBR	FA	FR	G/POS	TPR
1966	Det-A	4	3	0	0	0	0	0	0	0	1	.000	.000	.000	-98	-1	0	0	0	1.000	-0	/1-1	-0.1

■ RAY PEPPER

Pepper, Raymond Watson b: 8/5/05, Decatur, Ala. BR/TR, 6'2", 195 lbs. Deb: 4/15/32

YEAR	TM/L	G	AB	R	H	2B	3B	HR	RBI	BB	SO	AVG	OBP	SLG	PRO+	BR/A	SB	CS	SBR	FA	FR	G/POS	TPR
1932	StL-N	21	57	3	14	2	1	0	7	5	13	.246	.306	.316	66	-3	1			.971	-0	O-17	-0.4
1933	StL-N	3	9	2	2	0	0	1	2	0	1	.222	.222	.556	110	0	0			1.000	-0	/O-2	0.0
1934	StL-A	148	564	71	168	24	6	7	101	29	67	.298	.333	.399	81	-17	1	4	-2	.963	5	*O-136	-1.9
1935	StL-A	92	261	20	66	15	3	4	37	20	32	.253	.306	.379	73	-11	0	2	-1	.982	-3	O-57	-1.6
1936	StL-A	75	124	13	35	5	0	2	23	5	23	.282	.310	.371	66	-7	0	2	-1	.941	-2	O-18	-1.0
Total 5		339	1015	109	285	46	10	14	170	59	136	.281	.321	.387	77	-38	2	8		.967	-1	O-230	-4.9

■ JACK PERCONTE

Perconte, John Patrick b: 8/31/54, Joliet, Ill. BL/TR, 5'10", 160 lbs. Deb: 9/13/80

YEAR	TM/L	G	AB	R	H	2B	3B	HR	RBI	BB	SO	AVG	OBP	SLG	PRO+	BR/A	SB	CS	SBR	FA	FR	G/POS	TPR
1980	LA-N	14	17	2	4	0	0	0	0	1	1	.235	.316	.235	57	-1	3	0	1	1.000	3	/2-9	0.4
1981	LA-N	8	9	2	2	0	1	0	1	2	2	.222	.364	.444	133	0	1	1	-0	1.000	5	/2-2	0.5
1982	Cle-A	93	219	27	52	4	4	0	15	22	25	.237	.307	.292	66	-10	9	3	1	.976	8	2-82/D-2	0.2
1983	Cle-A	14	26	1	7	1	0	0	0	5	2	.269	.387	.308	91	-0	3	1	0	.950	8	2-13	0.8
1984	Sea-A	155	612	93	180	24	4	0	31	57	47	.294	.359	.346	97	-0	29	6	5	.981	0	*2-150	1.1
1985	Sea-A	125	485	60	128	17	7	2	23	50	36	.264	.336	.340	85	-9	31	2	8	.986	0	*2-125	0.4
1986	Chi-A	24	73	6	16	1	0	0	4	11	10	.219	.321	.233	52	-1	2	0	1	.990	0	2-24	-1.0
Total 7		433	1441	191	389	47	16	2	76	149	123	.270	.342	.329	86	-23	78	13	16	.982	18	2-405/D-2	2.4

■ TONY PEREZ

Perez, Atanasio (Rigal) b: 5/14/42, Camaguey, Cuba BR/TR, 6'2", 205 lbs. Deb: 7/26/64 FCM

YEAR	TM/L	G	AB	R	H	2B	3B	HR	RBI	BB	SO	AVG	OBP	SLG	PRO+	BR/A	SB	CS	SBR	FA	FR	G/POS	TPR
1964	Cin-N	12	25	1	2	1	0	0	1	3	9	.080	.179	.120	-14	-4	0	0	0	.981	-1	/1-6	-0.6
1965	Cin-N	104	281	40	73	14	4	12	47	21	67	.260	.316	.466	110	3	0	2	-1	.989	-2	1-93	-0.5
1966	Cin-N	99	257	25	68	10	4	4	39	14	44	.265	.308	.381	86	-6	1	0	0	.989	-5	1-75	-1.6
1967	Cin-N★	156	600	78	174	28	7	26	102	33	102	.290	.331	.490	119	13	0	3	-2	.963	-22	*3-139,1-18/2	-1.5
1968	Cin-N★	160	625	93	176	25	7	18	92	51	92	.282	.342	.430	123	17	3	2	-0	.952	5	*3-160	2.6
1969	Cin-N	160	629	103	185	31	2	37	122	63	131	.294	.363	.526	138	30	4	2	0	.937	1	*3-160	3.3
1970	*Cin-N★	158	587	107	186	28	6	40	129	83	134	.317	.405	.589	162	52	8	3	1	.923	-7	*3-153/1-8	4.3
1971	Cin-N	158	609	72	164	22	3	25	91	51	120	.269	.327	.438	117	12	4	1	1	.959	7	*3-148,1-44	1.8
1972	*Cin-N	136	515	64	146	33	7	21	90	55	121	.283	.353	.497	148	30	4	2	0	.993	-5	*1-136	1.4

YEAR	TM/L	G	AB	R	H	2B	3B	HR	RBI	BB	SO	AVG	OBP	SLG	PRO+	BR/A	SB	CS	SBR	FA	FR	G/POS	TPR
1973	*Cin-N	151	564	73	177	33	3	27	101	74	117	.314	.396	.527	162	47	3	1	0	.991	-4	*1-151	3.3
1974	Cin-N★	158	596	81	158	28	2	28	101	61	112	.265	.335	.460	123	16	1	3	-2	**.996**	-6	*1-157	-0.1
1975	*Cin-N★	137	511	74	144	28	3	20	109	54	101	.282	.354	.466	124	15	1	2	-1	.993	-5	*1-132	0.1
1976	*Cin-N★	139	527	77	137	32	6	19	91	50	88	.260	.330	.452	117	10	10	5	0	.996	-4	*1-136	-0.2
1977	Mon-N	154	559	71	158	32	6	19	91	63	111	.283	.357	.463	122	17	4	3	-1	.992	9	*1-148	1.6
1978	Mon-N	148	544	63	158	38	3	14	78	38	104	.290	.339	.449	120	13	2	0	1	.991	-1	*1-145	0.4
1979	Mon-N	132	489	58	132	29	4	13	73	38	82	.270	.326	.425	104	2	2	1	0	.991	-6	*1-129	-1.3
1980	Bos-A	151	585	73	161	31	3	25	105	41	93	.275	.324	.467	108	5	1	0	0	.993	-1	*1-137,D-13	-0.4
1981	Bos-A	84	306	35	77	11	3	9	39	27	66	.252	.312	.395	97	-2	0	0	0	.993	0	1-56,D-23	-0.6
1982	Bos-A	69	196	18	51	14	2	6	31	19	48	.260	.326	.444	103	1	0	1	-1	.857	0	D-46/1-2	-0.2
1983	*Phi-N	91	253	18	61	11	2	6	43	28	57	.241	.319	.372	92	-3	1	0	0	.998	1	1-69	-0.5
1984	Cin-N	71	137	9	33	6	1	2	15	11	21	.241	.297	.343	76	-4	0	0	0	.990	-2	1-31	-0.8
1985	Cin-N	72	183	25	60	8	0	6	33	22	22	.328	.400	.470	136	9	0	2	-1	.995	-2	1-50	0.4
1986	Cin-N	77	200	14	51	12	1	2	29	25	25	.255	.338	.355	87	-3	0	0	0	.984	-3	1-55	-1.0
Total	23	2777	9778	1272	2732	505	79	379	1652	925	1867	.279	.344	.463	122	270	49	33	-5	.992	-54	*1-1778,3-760/D2	9.9

■ EDUARDO PEREZ
Perez, Eduardo Atanasio   b: 9/11/69, Cincinnati, Ohio   BR/TR, 6'4", 215 lbs.   Deb: 7/27/93   F

YEAR	TM/L	G	AB	R	H	2B	3B	HR	RBI	BB	SO	AVG	OBP	SLG	PRO+	BR/A	SB	CS	SBR	FA	FR	G/POS	TPR
1993	Cal-A	52	180	16	45	6	2	4	30	9	39	.250	.293	.372	75	-7	5	4	-1	.962	10	3-45/D-3	0.3
1994	Cal-A	38	129	10	27	7	0	5	16	12	29	.209	.277	.380	65	-7	3	0	1	.997	-3	1-38	-1.1
Total	2	90	309	26	72	13	2	9	46	21	68	.233	.286	.375	71	-14	8	4	0	.962	7	/3-45,1-38,D	-0.8

■ MARTY PEREZ
Perez, Martin Roman   b: 2/28/47, Visalia, Cal.   BR/TR, 5'11", 160 lbs.   Deb: 9/9/69

YEAR	TM/L	G	AB	R	H	2B	3B	HR	RBI	BB	SO	AVG	OBP	SLG	PRO+	BR/A	SB	CS	SBR	FA	FR	G/POS	TPR
1969	Cal-A	13	13	3	3	0	0	0	0	2	1	.231	.333	.231	63	-1	0	0	0	1.000	6	/S-7,2-2,3	0.6
1970	Cal-A	3	3	0	0	0	0	0	1	0	0	.000	.000	.000	-99	-1	0	0	0	.833	1	/S-2	0.0
1971	Atl-N	130	410	28	93	15	3	4	32	25	44	.227	.273	.307	60	-22	1	2	-1	.955	-14	*S-126/2-1	-2.3
1972	Atl-N	141	479	33	109	13	1	1	28	30	55	.228	.277	.265	50	-31	0	3	-2	.957	-34	*S-141	-5.2
1973	Atl-N	141	501	66	125	15	5	8	57	49	66	.250	.319	.347	79	-14	2	3	-1	.962	-9	*S-139	-0.8
1974	Atl-N	127	447	51	116	20	5	2	34	35	51	.260	.315	.340	80	-12	2	0	1	.985	-9	*2-102,S-14/3	-1.5
1975	Atl-N	120	461	50	127	14	2	2	34	37	44	.275	.329	.328	80	-12	2	0	-1	.985	-8	*2-116/S-7	-1.5
1976	Atl-N	31	96	12	24	4	0	1	6	8	9	.250	.308	.323	74	-3	0	0	0	.976	-2	2-18,S-17/3	-0.3
	SF-N	93	332	37	86	13	1	2	26	30	28	.259	.322	.322	80	-8	3	4	-2	.979	7	2-89/S-5	0.3
	Yr	124	428	49	110	17	1	3	32	38	37	.257	.318	.322	79	-11	3	4	-2	.978	5	*2-107,S-22/3	0.0
1977	NY-A	1	4	0	2	0	0	0	0	0	1	.500	.500	.500	175	0	0	0	0	1.000	1	/3-1	0.1
	Oak-A	115	373	32	86	14	5	2	23	29	65	.231	.291	.311	65	-18	1	3	-2	.974	0	*2-105,3-12/S	-1.3
	Yr	116	377	32	88	14	5	2	23	29	66	.233	.292	.313	66	-17	1	3	-2	.974	1	*2-105,3-13/S	-1.2
1978	Oak-A	16	12	1	0	0	0	0	0	0	5	.000	.000	.000	-99	-3	0	0	0	1.000	2	3-11/S-3,2	-0.1
Total	10	931	3131	313	771	108	22	22	241	245	369	.246	.303	.316	70	-124	11	17	-7	.958	-59	S-465,2-434/3	-12.0

■ ROBERT PEREZ
Perez, Robert Alexander (Jimenez)   b: 6/4/69, Bolivar, Venez.   BR/TR, 6'3", 205 lbs.   Deb: 7/20/94

YEAR	TM/L	G	AB	R	H	2B	3B	HR	RBI	BB	SO	AVG	OBP	SLG	PRO+	BR/A	SB	CS	SBR	FA	FR	G/POS	TPR
1994	Tor-A	4	8	0	1	0	0	0	0	0	1	.125	.125	.125	-35	-2	0	0	0	1.000	-0	/O-4	-0.2

■ TONY PEREZCHICA
Perezchica, Antonio Llamas (Gonzales)   b: 4/20/66, Mexicali, Mex.   BR/TR, 5'11", 165 lbs.   Deb: 9/7/88

YEAR	TM/L	G	AB	R	H	2B	3B	HR	RBI	BB	SO	AVG	OBP	SLG	PRO+	BR/A	SB	CS	SBR	FA	FR	G/POS	TPR
1988	SF-N	7	8	1	1	0	0	0	1	2	1	.125	.300	.125	27	-1	0	0	0	1.000	-1	/2-6	-0.2
1990	SF-N	4	3	1	1	0	0	0	0	1	2	.333	.500	.333	139	0	0	0	0	1.000	-2	/2-2,S-2	-0.1
1991	SF-N	23	48	2	11	4	1	0	3	2	12	.229	.260	.354	73	-2	0	1	-1	.947	-3	S-13/2-6	-0.5
	Cle-A	17	22	4	8	2	0	0	3	0	5	.364	.440	.455	147	2	0	0	0	1.000	-1	/S-6,3-3,2D	0.1
1992	Cle-A	18	20	2	2	1	0	0	1	5	6	.100	.182	.150	-6	-3	0	0	0	.875	-1	/3-9,2-4,SD	-0.4
Total	4	69	101	10	23	7	1	0	5	10	26	.228	.297	.317	74	-4	0	1	-1	.944	-8	/S-25,2-20,3D	-1.1

■ BRODERICK PERKINS
Perkins, Broderick Phillip   b: 11/23/54, Pittsburg, Cal.   BL/TL, 5'10", 180 lbs.   Deb: 7/7/78

YEAR	TM/L	G	AB	R	H	2B	3B	HR	RBI	BB	SO	AVG	OBP	SLG	PRO+	BR/A	SB	CS	SBR	FA	FR	G/POS	TPR
1978	SD-N	62	217	14	52	14	1	2	33	5	29	.240	.257	.341	71	-10	4	0	1	.993	3	1-59	-0.9
1979	SD-N	57	87	8	23	0	0	0	8	8	12	.264	.326	.264	67	-4	0	0	0	.982	-1	1-28	-0.5
1980	SD-N	43	100	18	37	9	0	2	14	11	10	.370	.432	.520	175	10	2	1	0	.988	-4	1-20,O-10	0.5
1981	SD-N	92	254	27	71	18	3	2	40	14	16	.280	.317	.398	110	2	0	4	-2	.997	-3	1-80/O-3	-0.7
1982	SD-N	125	347	32	94	10	4	2	34	26	20	.271	.327	.340	92	-4	2	1	0	.994	-1	1-98/O-11	-1.0
1983	Cle-A	79	184	23	50	10	0	0	24	9	19	.272	.306	.326	71	-7	1	5	-3	.991	0	1-19,O-17,D	-1.1
1984	Cle-A	58	66	5	13	1	0	0	4	7	10	.197	.284	.212	39	-5	0	0	0	1.000	-0	D-10/1-2	-0.6
Total	7	516	1255	127	340	62	8	8	157	80	116	.271	.317	.352	90	-18	9	11	-4	.993	-4	1-306/O-41,D	-4.3

■ CY PERKINS
Perkins, Ralph Foster   b: 2/27/1896, Gloucester, Mass.   d: 10/2/63, Philadelphia, Pa.   BR/TR, 5'10.5", 158 lbs.   Deb: 9/25/15   MC

YEAR	TM/L	G	AB	R	H	2B	3B	HR	RBI	BB	SO	AVG	OBP	SLG	PRO+	BR/A	SB	CS	SBR	FA	FR	G/POS	TPR
1915	Phi-A	7	20	2	4	0	0	0	3	3	3	.200	.304	.250	68	-1	0			.920	1	/C-6	0.0
1917	Phi-A	6	18	1	3	0	0	0	2	2	1	.167	.250	.167	28	-1	0			.978	4	/C-6	0.3
1918	Phi-A	68	218	9	41	4	1	1	14	8	15	.188	.217	.229	34	-18	1			.990	12	C-60	-0.1
1919	Phi-A	101	305	22	77	12	7	2	29	27	22	.252	.313	.357	87	-6	2			.971	7	C-87/S-8	1.0
1920	Phi-A	148	492	40	128	24	6	5	52	28	35	.260	.303	.364	75	-19	5	6	-2	.979	**23**	*C-146/2-1	1.1
1921	Phi-A	141	538	58	155	31	4	12	73	32	32	.288	.329	.428	91	-9	5	9	-4	.971	5	*C-141	0.0
1922	Phi-A	148	505	58	135	20	6	6	69	40	30	.267	.322	.366	77	-17	1	7	-4	.984	-4	*C-141	-1.7
1923	Phi-A	143	500	53	135	34	5	2	66	65	30	.270	.356	.370	90	-6	1	3	-2	.971	-7	*C-137	-0.8
1924	Phi-A	128	392	31	95	19	4	0	32	31	20	.242	.304	.311	58	-25	3	4	-2	.983	-0	*C-128	-1.8
1925	Phi-A	65	140	21	43	10	1	1	18	26	6	.307	.426	.400	104	2	3	1	0	.980	11	C-58/3-1	1.4
1926	Phi-A	63	148	14	43	9	0	1	19	18	7	.291	.371	.331	80	-4	0	2	-1	.984	9	C-55	0.6
1927	Phi-A	59	137	11	35	7	2	1	15	12	8	.255	.315	.358	70	-6	0	2	-1	.979	1	C-54/1-1	-0.4
1928	Phi-A	19	29	1	5	0	0	0	1	1	1	.172	.200	.172	-1	-4	0	0	0	.982	4	C-19	-0.1
1929	Phi-A	38	76	4	16	4	0	0	9	5	4	.211	.259	.263	34	-8	0	0	0	.990	2	C-38	-0.4
1930	Phi-A	20	38	1	6	2	0	0	3	4	3	.158	.200	.211	4	-6	0	0	0	.964	0	C-19/1-1	-0.4
1931	NY-A	16	47	3	12	1	0	0	7	1	4	.255	.286	.277	51	-3	0	0	0	1.000	-5	C-16	-0.7
1934	Det-A	1	1	0	0	0	0	0	0	0	0	.000	.000	.000	-99	-0	0	0	0	.000	0	H	0.0
Total	17	1171	3604	329	933	175	35	30	409	301	221	.259	.319	.352	75	-131	18	<u>34</u>		.978	62	*C-1111/S-8,132	-2.0

■ SAM PERLOZZO
Perlozzo, Samuel Benedict   b: 3/4/51, Cumberland, Md.   BR/TR, 5'9", 170 lbs.   Deb: 9/13/77   C

YEAR	TM/L	G	AB	R	H	2B	3B	HR	RBI	BB	SO	AVG	OBP	SLG	PRO+	BR/A	SB	CS	SBR	FA	FR	G/POS	TPR
1977	Min-A	10	24	6	7	0	2	0	0	2	3	.292	.346	.458	119	1	0	0	0	1.000	-3	2-10/3-1	-0.2
1979	SD-N	2	2	0	0	0	0	0	0	1	0	.000	.333	.000	-1	-0	0	0	0	.500	-1	/2-2	-0.2
Total	2	12	26	6	7	0	2	0	0	3	3	.269	.345	.423	110	0	0	0	0	.967	-5	/2-12,3-1	-0.4

■ JOHN PERRIN
Perrin, John Stephenson   b: 2/4/1898, Escanaba, Mich.   d: 6/24/69, Detroit, Mich.   BL/TR, 5'9", 160 lbs.   Deb: 7/11/21

YEAR	TM/L	G	AB	R	H	2B	3B	HR	RBI	BB	SO	AVG	OBP	SLG	PRO+	BR/A	SB	CS	SBR	FA	FR	G/POS	TPR
1921	Bos-A	4	13	3	3	0	0	0	1	0	3	.231	.231	.231	19	-2	0	0	0	1.000	-2	/O-4	-0.3

■ NIG PERRINE
Perrine, John Grover   b: 1/14/1885, Clinton, Wis.   d: 8/13/48, Kansas City, Mo.   BR/TR, 5'9", 160 lbs.   Deb: 4/11/07

YEAR	TM/L	G	AB	R	H	2B	3B	HR	RBI	BB	SO	AVG	OBP	SLG	PRO+	BR/A	SB	CS	SBR	FA	FR	G/POS	TPR
1907	Was-A	44	146	13	25	4	1	0	15	13		.171	.253	.212	53	-7	10			.946	-3	2-24,S-18/3	-1.2

■ GEORGE PERRING
Perring, George Wilson   b: 8/13/1884, Sharon, Wis.   d: 8/20/60, Beloit, Wis.   BR/TR, 6', 190 lbs.   Deb: 4/25/08

YEAR	TM/L	G	AB	R	H	2B	3B	HR	RBI	BB	SO	AVG	OBP	SLG	PRO+	BR/A	SB	CS	SBR	FA	FR	G/POS	TPR
1908	Cle-A	89	310	23	67	8	5	0	19	16		.216	.255	.274	72	-10	8			.928	-6	S-48,3-41	-1.6
1909	Cle-A	88	283	26	63	10	9	0	20	19		.223	.283	.322	87	-5	6			.932	6	3-67,S-11/2	0.5
1910	Cle-A	39	122	14	27	6	3	0	8	3		.221	.240	.320	74	-4	3			.931	2	3-33/1-4	-0.2
1914	KC-F	144	496	68	138	28	10	2	69	59	39	.278	.355	.387	96	-3	7			.934	9	*3-101,1-41/PS	0.9

YEAR	TM/L	G	AB	R	H	2B	3B	HR	RBI	BB	SO	AVG	OBP	SLG	PRO+	BR/A	SB	CS	SBR	FA	FR	G/POS	TPR
1915	KC-F	153	553	67	143	23	7	7	67	57	30	.259	.329	.363	89	-10	10			.958	15	*3-102,1-31,2/S	1.0
Total	5	513	1764	198	438	75	34	9	183	154	69	.248	.311	.345	87	-32	34			.939	26	3-344/1-76,S2P	0.6

■ BOYD PERRY
Perry, Boyd Glenn   b: 3/21/14, Snow Camp, N.C.   d: 6/29/90, Burlington, N.C.   BR/TR, 5'10", 158 lbs.   Deb: 5/23/41

YEAR	TM/L	G	AB	R	H	2B	3B	HR	RBI	BB	SO	AVG	OBP	SLG	PRO+	BR/A	SB	CS	SBR	FA	FR	G/POS	TPR
1941	Det-A	36	83	9	15	5	0	0	11	10	9	.181	.269	.241	32	-8	1	0	0	.974	-0	S-25,2-11	-0.6

■ CLAY PERRY
Perry, Clayton Shields   b: 12/18/1881, Rice Lake, Wis.   d: 1/16/54, Rice Lake, Wis.   BR/TR, 5'10.5", 175 lbs.   Deb: 9/2/08

YEAR	TM/L	G	AB	R	H	2B	3B	HR	RBI	BB	SO	AVG	OBP	SLG	PRO+	BR/A	SB	CS	SBR	FA	FR	G/POS	TPR
1908	Det-A	7	17	0	2	0	0	0	0	0	0	.118	.167	.118	-7	-2	0			.917	-1	/3-7	-0.3

■ GERALD PERRY
Perry, Gerald June   b: 10/30/60, Savannah, Ga.   BL/TR, 6', 190 lbs.   Deb: 8/11/83

YEAR	TM/L	G	AB	R	H	2B	3B	HR	RBI	BB	SO	AVG	OBP	SLG	PRO+	BR/A	SB	CS	SBR	FA	FR	G/POS	TPR
1983	Atl-N	27	39	5	14	2	1	6	6	5	4	.359	.432	.487	144	2	0	1	-1	.982	-2	/1-7,O-1	-0.1
1984	Atl-N	122	347	52	92	12	2	7	47	61	38	.265	.378	.372	104	4	15	12	-3	.988	-8	1-64,O-53	-1.2
1985	Atl-N	110	238	22	51	5	0	3	13	23	28	.214	.284	.273	53	-15	9	5	-0	.985	-0	1-55/O-1	-1.9
1986	Atl-N	29	70	6	19	2	0	2	11	8	4	.271	.346	.386	96	-0	1	1	-1	.889	-5	O-21/1-1	-0.7
1987	Atl-N	142	533	77	144	35	2	12	74	48	63	.270	.332	.411	91	-7	42	16	3	.990	-10	*1-136/O-7	-2.4
1988	Atl-N★	141	547	61	164	29	1	8	74	36	49	.300	.344	.400	108	5	29	14	0	.988	1	*1-141	-0.6
1989	Atl-N	72	266	24	67	11	0	4	21	32	28	.252	.339	.338	92	-2	10	6	-1	.987	1	1-72	-0.7
1990	KC-A	133	465	57	118	22	2	8	57	39	56	.254	.316	.361	90	-6	17	4	3	.986	2	D-68,1-51	-0.7
1991	StL-N	109	242	29	58	8	4	6	36	22	34	.240	.303	.380	90	-3	15	8	-0	.989	-4	1-61/O-5	-1.1
1992	StL-N	87	143	13	34	8	0	1	18	15	23	.238	.314	.315	81	-3	3	6	-3	.987	-4	1-29	-1.2
1993	StL-N	96	98	21	33	5	0	4	16	18	23	.337	.440	.510	157	9	1	1	-0	.976	-1	1-15/O-1	0.6
1994	StL-N	60	77	12	25	7	0	3	18	15	12	.325	.435	.532	156	7	1	1	-0	.990	-2	1-13	0.4
Total	12	1128	3065	379	819	146	11	59	391	322	362	.267	.339	.380	97	-10	142	75	-2	.988	-32	1-645/O-89,D	-9.6

■ HERB PERRY
Perry, Herbert Edward   b: 9/15/69, Live Oak, Fla.   BR/TR, 6'2", 210 lbs.   Deb: 5/3/94

YEAR	TM/L	G	AB	R	H	2B	3B	HR	RBI	BB	SO	AVG	OBP	SLG	PRO+	BR/A	SB	CS	SBR	FA	FR	G/POS	TPR
1994	Cle-A	4	9	1	1	0	0	0	1	3	1	.111	.385	.111	35	-1	0	0	0	1.000	1	/1-2,3-2	0.0

■ BOB PERRY
Perry, Melvin Gray   b: 9/14/34, New Bern, N.C.   BR/TR, 6'2", 180 lbs.   Deb: 5/17/63

YEAR	TM/L	G	AB	R	H	2B	3B	HR	RBI	BB	SO	AVG	OBP	SLG	PRO+	BR/A	SB	CS	SBR	FA	FR	G/POS	TPR
1963	LA-A	61	166	16	42	9	0	3	14	9	31	.253	.303	.361	91	-2	1	1	-0	.946	-7	O-55	-1.3
1964	LA-A	70	221	19	61	8	1	3	16	14	52	.276	.319	.362	99	-1	1	1	-0	.975	-4	O-62	-0.9
Total	2	131	387	35	103	17	1	6	30	23	83	.266	.312	.362	95	-4	2	2	-1	.962	-11	O-117	-2.2

■ HANK PERRY
Perry, William Henry "Socks"   b: 7/28/1886, Howell, Mich.   d: 7/18/56, Pontiac, Mich.   BL/TR, 5'11", 190 lbs.   Deb: 4/12/12

YEAR	TM/L	G	AB	R	H	2B	3B	HR	RBI	BB	SO	AVG	OBP	SLG	PRO+	BR/A	SB	CS	SBR	FA	FR	G/POS	TPR
1912	Det-A	13	36	3	6	1	0	0	3			.167	.231	.194	23	-4	0			1.000	2	/O-7	-0.2

■ JOHNNY PESKY
Pesky, John Michael (b: John Michael Paveskovich)   b: 9/27/19, Portland, Ore.   BL/TR, 5'9", 168 lbs.   Deb: 4/14/42   MC

YEAR	TM/L	G	AB	R	H	2B	3B	HR	RBI	BB	SO	AVG	OBP	SLG	PRO+	BR/A	SB	CS	SBR	FA	FR	G/POS	TPR
1942	Bos-A	147	620	105	**205**	29	9	2	51	42	36	.331	.375	.416	118	14	12	7	-1	.955	18	*S-147	4.1
1946	*Bos-A★	153	621	115	**208**	43	4	2	55	65	29	.335	.401	.427	124	22	9	8	-2	.969	12	*S-153	4.2
1947	Bos-A	155	638	106	**207**	27	8	0	39	72	22	.324	.393	.392	110	11	12	9	-2	.976	-11	*S-133,3-22	0.5
1948	Bos-A	143	565	124	159	26	6	3	55	99	32	.281	.394	.365	98	2	3	5	-2	.951	6	*3-141	0.4
1949	Bos-A	148	604	111	185	27	7	2	69	100	19	.306	.408	.384	103	6	8	4	0	.970	21	*3-148	2.4
1950	Bos-A	127	490	112	153	22	6	1	49	104	31	.312	.437	.388	103	7	2	1	-0	.974	22	*3-116/S-8	2.5
1951	Bos-A	131	480	93	150	20	6	3	41	84	15	.313	.417	.398	110	10	2	2	-1	.961	9	*S-106,3-11/2	2.5
1952	Bos-A	25	67	10	10	2	0	0	2	15	5	.149	.313	.179	36	-5	0	3	-2	.917	-6	3-19/S-2	-1.4
	Det-A	69	177	26	45	4	0	1	9	41	11	.254	.394	.294	93	1	1	2	-1	.952	-6	S-41,2-22/3	-0.2
	Yr	94	244	36	55	6	0	1	11	56	16	.225	.372	.262	77	-5	1	5	-3	.953	-11	S-43,3-22,2	-1.6
1953	Det-A	103	308	43	90	22	1	2	24	27	10	.292	.353	.390	102	1	3	7	-3	.991	-14	2-73	-1.2
1954	Det-A	20	17	5	3	0	0	0	1	3	1	.176	.300	.353	80	-1	0	0	0	.000	0	H	-0.1
	Was-A	49	158	17	40	4	3	0	9	10	7	.253	.298	.316	72	-6	1	1	-0	.979	-8	2-37/S-1	-1.3
	Yr	69	175	22	43	4	3	0	10	13	8	.246	.298	.320	72	-7	1	1	-0	.979	-8	2-37/S-1	-1.4
Total	10	1270	4745	867	1455	226	50	17	404	662	218	.307	.394	.386	106	62	53	49	-14	.964	43	S-591,3-460,2	12.4

■ ROBERTO PETAGINE
Petagine, Roberto Antonio (Guerra)   b: 6/7/71, Nueva Esparita, Venez.   BL/TL, 6'1", 170 lbs.   Deb: 4/4/94

YEAR	TM/L	G	AB	R	H	2B	3B	HR	RBI	BB	SO	AVG	OBP	SLG	PRO+	BR/A	SB	CS	SBR	FA	FR	G/POS	TPR
1994	Hou-N	8	7	0	0	0	0	0	0	1	3	.000	.125	.000	-65	-2	0	0	0	1.000	-0	/1-2	-0.2

■ BILL PETERMAN
Peterman, William David   b: 3/20/21, Philadelphia, Pa.   BR/TR, 6'2", 185 lbs.   Deb: 4/26/42

YEAR	TM/L	G	AB	R	H	2B	3B	HR	RBI	BB	SO	AVG	OBP	SLG	PRO+	BR/A	SB	CS	SBR	FA	FR	G/POS	TPR
1942	Phi-N	1	1	0	1	0	0	0	0	0	0	1.000	1.000	1.000	512	0	0			.000	0	/C-1	0.1

■ JOHN PETERS
Peters, John Paul   b: 4/8/1850, Louisiana, Mo.   d: 1/4/24, St.Louis, Mo.   BR/TR, 5'7", 180 lbs.   Deb: 5/23/1874

YEAR	TM/L	G	AB	R	H	2B	3B	HR	RBI	BB	SO	AVG	OBP	SLG	PRO+	BR/A	SB	CS	SBR	FA	FR	G/POS	TPR
1874	Chi-n	55	240	39	69	10	0	1		2		.287	.293	.342	101	-0						S-32,2-21/3	-0.2
1875	Chi-n	69	298	40	86	18	0	0		0		.289	.289	.349	118	5						*S-66/2-4	0.2
1876	Chi-N	66	316	70	111	14	2	1	47	3	2	.351	.357	.418	141	11				.932	-1	*S-66/P-1	0.8
1877	Chi-N	60	265	45	84	10	3	0	41	1	7	.317	.320	.377	106	0				.883	19	*S-60	1.8
1878	Mil-N	55	246	33	76	6	1	0	22	5	8	.309	.323	.341	111	2				.853	5	2-34,S-22	0.9
1879	Chi-N	83	379	45	93	13	2	1	31	1	19	.245	.247	.298	74	-11				.837	-8	*S-83	-1.4
1880	Pro-N	86	359	30	82	5	0	0	24	5	15	.228	.239	.242	66	-12				.900	-1	*S-86	-0.7
1881	Buf-N	54	229	21	49	8	1	0	3	3	12	.214	.224	.258	52	-12				.869	7	S-53/O-1	-0.2
1882	Pit-a	78	333	46	96	10	1	0		4		.288	.297	.324	115	5				.883	6	*S-77/2-1	1.3
1883	Pit-a	8	28	3	3	0	0	0		0		.107	.107	.107	-32	-4				.818	3	/S-8	-0.1
1884	Pit-a	1	4	0	0	0	0	0		0		.000	.000	.000	-98	-1				.667	-1	/S-1	-0.2
Total	2 n	124	538	79	155	28	0	1		2		.288	.291	.346	110	5						/S-98,2-25,3	
Total	9	491	2159	293	594	66	10	2	190	22	63	.275	.282	.318	94	-23				.881	28	S-456/2-35,OP	2.2

■ JOHN PETERS
Peters, John William "Big Pete" or "Shotgun"   b: 7/14/1893, Kansas City, Kan.   d: 2/21/32, Kansas City, Mo.   BR/TR, 6', 192 lbs.   Deb: 5/1/15

YEAR	TM/L	G	AB	R	H	2B	3B	HR	RBI	BB	SO	AVG	OBP	SLG	PRO+	BR/A	SB	CS	SBR	FA	FR	G/POS	TPR
1915	Det-A	1	3	0	0	0	0	0	0	0	0	.000	.000	.000	-95	-1	0			1.000	1	/C-1	0.1
1918	Cle-A	1	1	0	0	0	0	0	0	0	1	.000	.500	.000	46	0	0			.500	1	/C-1	-0.1
1921	Phi-N	55	155	7	45	4	0	3	23	6	13	.290	.329	.374	79	-5	1	0	0	.933	-13	C-44	-1.5
1922	Phi-N	55	143	15	35	9	1	4	24	9	18	.245	.308	.420	76	-6	0	1	-1	.953	-5	C-39	-0.9
Total	4	112	302	22	80	13	1	7	47	16	33	.265	.317	.384	76	-11	1	1		.934	-18	/C-85	-2.4

■ RICK PETERS
Peters, Richard Devin   b: 11/21/55, Lynwood, Cal.   BB/TR, 5'9", 170 lbs.   Deb: 9/8/79

YEAR	TM/L	G	AB	R	H	2B	3B	HR	RBI	BB	SO	AVG	OBP	SLG	PRO+	BR/A	SB	CS	SBR	FA	FR	G/POS	TPR
1979	Det-A	12	19	3	5	0	0	0	2	5	3	.263	.417	.263	85	-0	0	0	0	.000	-1	/3-3,2-2,OD	-0.1
1980	Det-A	133	477	79	139	19	7	2	42	54	48	.291	.371	.373	102	3	13	7	-0	.977	0	*O-109,D-11	-0.2
1981	Det-A	63	207	26	53	7	3	0	15	29	28	.256	.353	.319	91	-1	6	3	-3	.991	3	O-38,D-19	-0.3
1983	Oak-A	55	178	20	51	7	0	0	20	12	21	.287	.335	.326	88	-3	4	9	-4	.986	5	O-47/D-8	-0.4
1986	Oak-A	44	38	7	7	1	0	0	1	7	7	.184	.311	.211	49	-2	2	2	-1	1.000	-5	O-27/2-1	-0.9
Total	5	307	919	135	255	34	10	2	80	107	107	.277	.358	.343	95	-3	20	24	-8	.983	1	O-222/D-41,23	-1.9

■ RUSTY PETERS
Peters, Russell Dixon   b: 12/14/14, Roanoke, Va.   BR/TR, 5'11", 170 lbs.   Deb: 4/14/36

YEAR	TM/L	G	AB	R	H	2B	3B	HR	RBI	BB	SO	AVG	OBP	SLG	PRO+	BR/A	SB	CS	SBR	FA	FR	G/POS	TPR
1936	Phi-A	45	119	12	26	3	2	3	16	4	28	.218	.244	.353	47	-11	1			.898	-8	S-25,3-10/O2	-0.8
1937	Phi-A	116	339	39	88	17	6	3	43	41	59	.260	.339	.372	80	-10	4	4	-1	.966	-13	2-70,3-31,S	-1.8
1938	Phi-A	2	7	0	0	0	0	0	0	0	1	.000	.000	.000	-99	-2	0	0	0	.714	3	/S-2	-0.4
1940	Cle-A	30	71	5	17	3	2	0	7	4	14	.239	.280	.338	61	-4	0	1	-0	.922	-0	/2-9,S-6,31	-0.3
1941	Cle-A	29	63	6	13	2	0	2	7	7	7	.206	.286	.238	42	-5	1			.891	2	S-11/3-9,2	-0.3
1942	Cle-A	34	58	7	13	1	1	0	2	2	14	.224	.250	.345	70	-3	0	1	-0	.944	2	S-24/2-1,3	-0.3
1943	Cle-A	79	215	22	47	6	2	1	19	18	29	.219	.282	.279	69	-9	1	1	-0	.913	-6	3-46,S-14/2O	-1.5

YEAR	TM/L	G	AB	R	H	2B	3B	HR	RBI	BB	SO	AVG	OBP	SLG	PRO+	BR/A	SB	CS	SBR	FA	FR	G/POS	TPR
1944	Cle-A	88	282	23	63	13	3	1	24	15	35	.223	.268	.301	65	-14	2	1	0	.976	-3	2-63,S-13/3	-1.4
1946	Cle-A	9	21	0	6	0	0	0	2	1	1	.286	.318	.286	74	-1	0	1	-1	1.000	0	/S-7	-0.1
1947	StL-A	39	47	10	16	4	0	0	2	6	8	.340	.415	.426	131	2	0	0	0	.955	7	2-13/S-2	1.0
Total	10	471	1222	123	289	53	16	8	117	98	199	.236	.295	.326	69	-57	9	9	-3	.966	-13	2-166,S-117,3/01	-5.6

■ BUDDY PETERSON
Peterson, Carl Francis   b: 4/23/25, Portland, Ore.   BR/TR, 5'9.5", 170 lbs.   Deb: 9/14/55

YEAR	TM/L	G	AB	R	H	2B	3B	HR	RBI	BB	SO	AVG	OBP	SLG	PRO+	BR/A	SB	CS	SBR	FA	FR	G/POS	TPR
1955	Chi-A	6	21	7	6	1	0	0	2	3	1	.286	.400	.333	96	0	0	0	0	.962	-1	/S-6	0.0
1957	Bal-A	7	17	1	3	2	0	0	0	2	2	.176	.263	.294	55	-1	0	0	0	.963	-1	/S-7	-0.2
Total	2	13	38	8	9	3	0	0	2	5	3	.237	.341	.316	80	-1	0	0	0	.962	-2	/S-13	-0.2

■ CAP PETERSON
Peterson, Charles Andrew   b: 8/15/42, Tacoma, Wash.   d: 5/16/80, Tacoma, Wash.   BR/TR, 6'2", 195 lbs.   Deb: 9/12/62

YEAR	TM/L	G	AB	R	H	2B	3B	HR	RBI	BB	SO	AVG	OBP	SLG	PRO+	BR/A	SB	CS	SBR	FA	FR	G/POS	TPR
1962	SF-N	4	6	1	1	0	0	0	0	1	4	.167	.286	.167	25	-1	0	0	0	1.000	-1	/S-2	-0.1
1963	SF-N	22	54	7	14	2	0	1	2	2	13	.259	.286	.352	83	-1	0	0	0	.917	-7	/2-8,3-5,OS	-0.8
1964	SF-N	66	74	8	15	1	1	1	8	3	20	.203	.234	.284	44	-5	0	0	0	1.000	-3	O-10/1-2,23	-0.9
1965	SF-N	63	105	14	26	7	0	3	15	10	16	.248	.313	.400	97	-1	0	0	0	1.000	-4	O-27	-0.5
1966	SF-N	89	190	13	45	6	1	2	19	11	32	.237	.282	.311	63	-9	2	0	1	1.000	-3	O-51/1-2	-1.4
1967	Was-A	122	405	35	97	17	2	8	46	32	61	.240	.300	.351	95	-3	0	3	-2	.970	1	*O-101	-1.0
1968	Was-A	94	226	20	46	8	1	3	18	18	31	.204	.265	.288	70	-9	2	1	0	1.000	-1	O-53	-1.4
1969	Cle-A	76	110	8	25	3	0	1	14	24	18	.227	.370	.282	82	-1	0	0	0	.977	-2	O-30/3-4	-0.5
Total	8	536	1170	106	269	44	5	19	122	101	195	.230	.294	.325	80	-30	4	4	-1	.983	-18	O-275/3-10,21S	-6.6

■ HARDY PETERSON
Peterson, Harding William   b: 10/17/29, Perth Amboy, N.J.   BR/TR, 6', 205 lbs.   Deb: 5/5/55

YEAR	TM/L	G	AB	R	H	2B	3B	HR	RBI	BB	SO	AVG	OBP	SLG	PRO+	BR/A	SB	CS	SBR	FA	FR	G/POS	TPR
1955	Pit-N	32	81	7	20	6	0	1	10	7	7	.247	.315	.358	79	-2	0	0	0	.965	6	C-31	0.4
1957	Pit-N	30	73	10	22	2	1	2	11	9	10	.301	.378	.438	122	2	0	1	-1	.985	2	C-30	0.4
1958	Pit-N	2	6	0	2	0	0	0	0	1	0	.333	.429	.333	108	0	0	0	0	1.000	-0	/C-2	0.0
1959	Pit-N	2	1	0	0	0	0	0	0	0	0	.000	.000	.000	-99	0	0	0	0	1.000	1	/C-2	0.0
Total	4	66	161	17	44	8	1	3	21	17	17	.273	.346	.391	99	-0	0	1	-1	.976	7	/C-65	0.8

■ BOB PETERSON
Peterson, Robert A.   b: 7/16/1884, Philadelphia, Pa.   d: 11/27/62, Evesham, N.J.   BR/TR, 6'1", 160 lbs.   Deb: 4/18/06

YEAR	TM/L	G	AB	R	H	2B	3B	HR	RBI	BB	SO	AVG	OBP	SLG	PRO+	BR/A	SB	CS	SBR	FA	FR	G/POS	TPR
1906	Bos-A	39	118	10	24	1	1	1	9	11		.203	.277	.254	67	-4	1			.899	-7	C-30/2-3,1O	-0.9
1907	Bos-A	4	13	1	1	0	0	0	0	0		.077	.077	.077	-51	-2	0			1.000	0	/C-4	-0.2
Total	2	43	131	11	25	1	1	1	9	11		.191	.259	.237	56	-6	1			.910	-7	/C-34,2-3,1O	-1.1

■ TED PETOSKEY
Petoskey, Frederick Lee   b: 1/5/11, St.Charles, Mich.   BR/TR, 5'11.5", 183 lbs.   Deb: 9/9/34

YEAR	TM/L	G	AB	R	H	2B	3B	HR	RBI	BB	SO	AVG	OBP	SLG	PRO+	BR/A	SB	CS	SBR	FA	FR	G/POS	TPR
1934	Cin-N	6	7	0	0	0	0	0	1	0	5	.000	.000	.000	-99	-2	0			1.000	1	/O-2	-0.1
1935	Cin-N	4	5	0	2	0	0	0	0	0	1	.400	.400	.400	119	0	1			1.000	-1	/O-2	-0.1
Total	2	10	12	0	2	0	0	0	1	0	6	.167	.167	.167	-11	-2	1			1.000	0	/O-4	-0.2

■ GENO PETRALLI
Petralli, Eugene James   b: 9/25/59, Sacramento, Cal.   BL/TR, 6'2", 185 lbs.   Deb: 9/4/82

YEAR	TM/L	G	AB	R	H	2B	3B	HR	RBI	BB	SO	AVG	OBP	SLG	PRO+	BR/A	SB	CS	SBR	FA	FR	G/POS	TPR
1982	Tor-A	16	44	3	16	2	0	0	1	4	6	.364	.417	.409	117	1	0	0	0	.981	-2	C-12/3-3	-0.1
1983	Tor-A	6	4	0	0	0	0	0	0	1	1	.000	.200	.000	-37	-1	0	0	0	1.000	0	/C-5,D-1	0.0
1984	Tor-A	3	3	0	0	0	0	0	0	0	0	.000	.000	.000	-97	-1	0	0	0	1.000	0	/C-1,D-1	0.0
1985	Tex-A	42	100	7	27	2	0	0	11	8	12	.270	.330	.290	71	-4	0	0	0	.990	2	C-41	-0.2
1986	Tex-A	69	137	17	35	9	3	2	18	5	14	.255	.282	.409	83	-4	3	0	1	.988	-8	C-41,3-15/2D	-0.9
1987	Tex-A	101	202	28	61	11	2	7	31	27	29	.302	.390	.480	129	9	0	2	-1	.995	0	C-63,3-17/120D	1.0
1988	Tex-A	129	351	35	99	14	2	7	36	41	52	.282	.360	.393	108	5	0	1	-1	.981	-1	C-85,D-23/312	0.9
1989	Tex-A	70	184	18	56	7	0	4	23	17	24	.304	.369	.408	117	4	0	0	0	.989	-12	C-49,D-16	-0.6
1990	Tex-A	133	325	28	83	13	1	0	21	50	49	.255	.360	.302	87	-4	0	2	-1	.991	-4	*C-118/3-7,2	-0.2
1991	Tex-A	87	199	21	54	8	1	2	20	21	25	.271	.341	.352	94	-1	2	1	0	.972	-10	C-66/3-7,D	-0.8
1992	Tex-A	94	192	11	38	12	0	1	18	20	34	.198	.274	.276	56	-11	0	0	0	.990	3	C-54,D-14/32	-0.6
1993	Tex-A	59	133	16	32	5	0	1	13	22	17	.241	.348	.301	79	-3	2	0	1	.990	-7	C-39/2-1,3D	-0.7
Total	12	809	1874	184	501	83	9	24	192	216	263	.267	.346	.360	95	-9	8	6	-1	.987	-37	C-574/D-66,3210	-2.0

■ RICO PETROCELLI
Petrocelli, Americo Peter   b: 6/27/43, Brooklyn, N.Y.   BR/TR, 6', 185 lbs.   Deb: 9/21/63

YEAR	TM/L	G	AB	R	H	2B	3B	HR	RBI	BB	SO	AVG	OBP	SLG	PRO+	BR/A	SB	CS	SBR	FA	FR	G/POS	TPR
1963	Bos-A	1	4	0	1	1	0	0	1	0	1	.250	.250	.500	101	-0	0	0	0	.833	-0	/S-1	0.0
1965	Bos-A	103	323	38	75	15	2	13	33	36	71	.232	.311	.412	98	-1	0	2	-1	.958	10	S-93	1.5
1966	Bos-A	139	522	58	124	20	1	18	59	41	99	.238	.297	.383	85	-11	1	1	-0	.954	1	*S-127/3-5	0.1
1967	*Bos-A★	142	491	53	127	24	2	17	66	49	93	.259	.332	.420	112	7	2	4	-2	.970	3	*S-141	2.3
1968	Bos-A	123	406	41	95	17	2	12	46	31	73	.234	.295	.374	95	-3	0	1	-1	**.978**	11	*S-117/1-1	2.2
1969	Bos-A★	154	535	92	159	32	2	40	97	98	68	.297	.407	.589	167	48	3	5	-2	**.981**	5	*S-153/3-1	**6.9**
1970	Bos-A	157	583	82	152	31	3	29	103	67	82	.261	.339	.473	114	10	1	1	-0	.970	-10	*S-141,3-18	1.7
1971	Bos-A	158	553	82	139	24	4	28	89	91	108	.251	.359	.461	122	17	2	0	1	**.976**	1	*3-156	1.7
1972	Bos-A	147	521	62	125	15	2	15	75	78	91	.240	.341	.363	104	4	0	1	-1	.970	-1	*3-146	0.1
1973	Bos-A	100	356	44	87	13	1	13	45	47	64	.244	.334	.396	99	-0	0	1	-1	.980	5	3-99	0.4
1974	Bos-A	129	454	53	121	23	1	15	76	48	74	.267	.339	.421	110	5	1	0	0	.962	-19	*3-116/D-9	-1.4
1975	*Bos-A	115	402	31	96	15	1	7	59	41	66	.239	.314	.333	76	-12	0	2	-1	.960	-18	*3-113/D-1	-3.4
1976	Bos-A	85	240	17	51	7	1	3	24	34	36	.213	.310	.287	67	-9	0	5	-3	.967	-4	3-73/2-5,1SD	-1.8
Total	13	1553	5390	653	1352	237	22	210	773	661	926	.251	.336	.420	108	55	10	22	-10	.969	-18	S-774,3-727/D21	10.3

■ PAT PETTEE
Pettee, Patrick E.   b: 1/10/1863, Natick, Mass.   d: 10/9/34, Natick, Mass.   BR/TR, 5'10", 170 lbs.   Deb: 4/8/1891

YEAR	TM/L	G	AB	R	H	2B	3B	HR	RBI	BB	SO	AVG	OBP	SLG	PRO+	BR/A	SB	CS	SBR	FA	FR	G/POS	TPR
1891	Lou-a	2	5	1	0	0	0	0	0	3	1	.000	.375	.000	9	-0	1			.818	-1	/2-2	-0.1

■ NED PETTIGREW
Pettigrew, Jim Ned   b: 8/25/1881, Honey Grove, Tex.   d: 8/20/52, Duncan, Okla.   BR/TR, 5'11", 175 lbs.   Deb: 4/23/14

YEAR	TM/L	G	AB	R	H	2B	3B	HR	RBI	BB	SO	AVG	OBP	SLG	PRO+	BR/A	SB	CS	SBR	FA	FR	G/POS	TPR
1914	Buf-F	2	2	0	0	0	0	0	0	0	0	.000	.000	.000	-98	-1	0			.000	0	H	-0.1

■ JOE PETTINI
Pettini, Joseph Paul   b: 1/26/55, Wheeling, W.Va.   BR/TR, 5'9", 165 lbs.   Deb: 7/10/80

YEAR	TM/L	G	AB	R	H	2B	3B	HR	RBI	BB	SO	AVG	OBP	SLG	PRO+	BR/A	SB	CS	SBR	FA	FR	G/POS	TPR
1980	SF-N	63	190	19	44	3	1	1	9	17	33	.232	.295	.274	61	-10	5	2	0	.955	-13	S-42,3-18/2	-1.9
1981	SF-N	35	29	3	2	1	0	0	2	4	5	.069	.182	.103	-18	-4	1	0	0	.920	4	2-12,S-12/3	0.0
1982	SF-N	29	39	5	8	1	0	0	7	6	9	.205	.262	.231	39	-3	0	1	-1	.934	-1	S-26/3-1	-0.3
1983	SF-N	61	86	11	16	0	1	0	7	6	11	.186	.263	.209	33	-8	4	1	1	.949	11	S-26,2-14,3	0.5
Total	4	188	344	38	70	5	2	1	20	33	53	.203	.273	.238	45	-25	10	4	1	.943	2	S-106/3-40,2	-1.7

■ GARY PETTIS
Pettis, Gary George   b: 4/3/58, Oakland, Cal.   BB/TR, 6'1", 165 lbs.   Deb: 9/13/82

YEAR	TM/L	G	AB	R	H	2B	3B	HR	RBI	BB	SO	AVG	OBP	SLG	PRO+	BR/A	SB	CS	SBR	FA	FR	G/POS	TPR
1982	Cal-A	10	5	5	1	0	0	1	1	0	2	.200	.200	.800	159	0	0	0	0	1.000	-2	/O-8	-0.2
1983	Cal-A	22	85	19	25	2	3	3	6	7	15	.294	.348	.494	130	3	8	3	1	.982	2	O-21	0.5
1984	Cal-A	140	397	63	90	11	6	2	29	60	115	.227	.333	.300	77	-10	48	17	4	.983	1	*O-134	-0.9
1985	Cal-A	125	443	67	114	10	4	1	32	62	125	.257	.349	.323	86	-7	56	9	11	.990	17	*O-122	1.7
1986	*Cal-A	154	539	93	139	23	4	5	58	69	132	.258	.342	.343	88	-7	50	13	7	.985	21	*O-153/D-1	1.6
1987	Cal-A	133	394	49	82	13	2	1	17	52	124	.208	.302	.259	53	-26	24	5	4	.980	6	*O-131	-1.9
1988	Det-A	129	458	65	96	14	4	3	36	47	85	.210	.285	.277	60	-24	44	10	7	.987	10	*O-126/D-2	-1.0
1989	Det-A	119	444	77	114	8	6	1	18	84	116	.257	.375	.309	97	2	43	15	4	.988	5	*O-119	0.5
1990	Tex-A	136	423	66	101	16	8	3	31	57	118	.239	.335	.336	88	-6	38	15	2	.993	4	*O-128/D-2	-0.2
1991	Tex-A	137	282	37	61	7	5	0	19	54	91	.216	.342	.277	75	-8	29	13	1	.977	-11	*O-126/D-3	-1.9
1992	SD-N	30	30	0	6	2	0	0	0	2	11	.200	.250	.233	37	-2	1	0	0	.952	-3	O-14	-0.6

YEAR	TM/L	G	AB	R	H	2B	3B	HR	RBI	BB	SO	AVG	OBP	SLG	PRO+	BR/A	SB	CS	SBR	FA	FR	G/POS	TPR
	Det-A	48	129	27	26	4	3	1	12	27	34	.202	.340	.302	81	-2	13	4	2	.993	5	O-46	0.3
Total	11	1183	3629	568	855	109	49	21	259	521	958	.236	.333	.310	80	-86	354	104	44	.986	54	*O-1128/D-8	-1.8

■ BOB PETTIT
Pettit, Robert Henry   b: 7/19/1861, Williamstown, Mass.   d: 11/1/10, Derby, Conn.   BL/TR, 5'9", 160 lbs.   Deb: 9/3/1887

YEAR	TM/L	G	AB	R	H	2B	3B	HR	RBI	BB	SO	AVG	OBP	SLG	PRO+	BR/A	SB	CS	SBR	FA	FR	G/POS	TPR
1887	Chi-N	32	138	29	36	3	3	2	12	8	15	.261	.301	.370	76	-6	16			.894	-1	O-32/C-1,P	-0.6
1888	Chi-N	43	169	23	43	1	4	4	23	7	9	.254	.288	.379	104	0	7			.931	-4	O-43	-0.5
1891	Mil-a	21	80	10	14	4	0	1	5	7	7	.175	.267	.262	43	-7	2			.932	-7	/2-9,O-7,3	-1.2
Total	3	96	387	62	93	8	7	7	40	22	31	.240	.288	.351	79	-13	25			.919	-11	/O-82,2-9,3PC	-2.3

■ MARTY PEVEY
Pevey, Marty Ashley   b: 12/25/62, Savannah, Ga.   BL/TR, 6'1", 185 lbs.   Deb: 5/16/89

YEAR	TM/L	G	AB	R	H	2B	3B	HR	RBI	BB	SO	AVG	OBP	SLG	PRO+	BR/A	SB	CS	SBR	FA	FR	G/POS	TPR
1989	Mon-N	13	41	2	9	1	1	0	3	0	8	.220	.220	.293	45	-3	0	0	0	.985	-2	C-11/O-1	-0.5

■ LARRY PEZOLD
Pezold, Lorenz Johannes   b: 6/22/1893, New Orleans, La.   d: 10/22/57, Baton Rouge, La.   BR/TR, 5'9.5", 175 lbs.   Deb: 7/27/14

YEAR	TM/L	G	AB	R	H	2B	3B	HR	RBI	BB	SO	AVG	OBP	SLG	PRO+	BR/A	SB	CS	SBR	FA	FR	G/POS	TPR
1914	Cle-A	23	71	4	16	0	1	0	5	9	6	.225	.313	.254	68	-3	2	3	-1	.827	-1	3-20/O-1	-0.5

■ FRED PFEFFER
Pfeffer, Nathaniel Frederick "Fritz" or "Dandelion"
b: 3/17/1860, Louisville, Ky.   d: 4/10/32, Chicago, Ill.   BR/TR, 5'10.5", 184 lbs.   Deb: 5/1/1882   M

YEAR	TM/L	G	AB	R	H	2B	3B	HR	RBI	BB	SO	AVG	OBP	SLG	PRO+	BR/A	SB	CS	SBR	FA	FR	G/POS	TPR
1882	Tro-N	85	330	26	72	7	4	1	43	1	24	.218	.221	.273	60	-14				.857	11	*S-83/2-2	0.1
1883	Chi-N	96	371	41	87	22	7	1	45	8	50	.235	.251	.340	73	-13				.887	17	*2-79,S-18/31	0.5
1884	Chi-N	112	467	105	135	10	10	25	101	25	47	.289	.325	.514	147	22				.903	**46**	*2-112/P-1	**6.1**
1885	*Chi-N	112	469	90	113	12	7	5	73	26	47	.241	.281	.328	84	-12				.893	25	*2-109/P-5,O	1.7
1886	*Chi-N	118	474	88	125	17	8	7	95	36	46	.264	.316	.378	96	-6	30			.903	7	*2-118/1-1	0.5
1887	Chi-N	123	479	95	133	21	6	16	89	34	20	.278	.327	.447	100	-4	57			.917	25	*2-123/O-2	2.0
1888	Chi-N	135	517	90	129	22	10	8	57	32	38	.250	.297	.377	106	2	64			.931	**38**	*2-135	4.4
1889	Chi-N	134	531	85	121	15	7	7	77	53	51	.228	.302	.322	71	-22	45			.943	19	*2-134	0.4
1890	Chi-P	124	499	86	128	21	8	5	80	44	23	.257	.319	.361	78	-18	27			.916	24	*2-124	1.1
1891	Chi-N	137	498	93	123	12	9	7	77	79	60	.247	.353	.349	105	5	40			.921	25	*2-137	3.2
1892	Lou-N	124	470	78	121	14	9	2	76	67	36	.257	.353	.338	119	13	27			.933	12	*2-116,1-10/PM	2.5
1893	Lou-N	125	508	85	129	29	12	3	75	51	18	.254	.322	.376	92	-7	32			.939	6	*2-125	0.2
1894	Lou-N	104	409	68	126	12	14	5	59	30	14	.308	.357	.443	99	-2	31			.937	12	*2-90,S-15/P	1.1
1895	Lou-N	11	45	8	13	1	0	0	5	5	3	.289	.360	.311	79	-1	2			.742	-3	/S-5,2-3,1	-0.3
1896	NY-N	4	14	1	2	0	0	0	4	1	1	.143	.250	.143	5	-2	0			.760	-1	/2-4	-0.3
	Chi-N	94	360	45	88	16	7	2	52	23	20	.244	.294	.344	65	-20	22			.947	9	*2-94	-0.4
	Yr	98	374	46	90	16	7	2	56	24	21	.241	.292	.337	63	-21	22			.939	8	2-98	-0.7
1897	Chi-N	32	114	10	26	0	1	0	11	12		.228	.318	.246	48	-8	5			.883	-6	2-32	-1.1
Total	16	1670	6555	1094	1671	231	119	94	1019	527	498	.255	.312	.369	92	-86	382			.920	266	*2-1537,S-121/1PO3	21.7

■ BOBBY PFEIL
Pfeil, Robert Raymond   b: 11/13/43, Passaic, N.J.   BR/TR, 6'1", 180 lbs.   Deb: 6/26/69

YEAR	TM/L	G	AB	R	H	2B	3B	HR	RBI	BB	SO	AVG	OBP	SLG	PRO+	BR/A	SB	CS	SBR	FA	FR	G/POS	TPR
1969	NY-N	62	211	20	49	9	0	0	10	7	27	.232	.260	.275	49	-14	0	1	-1	.976	-4	3-49,2-11/O	-1.9
1971	Phi-N	44	70	5	19	3	0	2	9	6	9	.271	.329	.400	106	0	1	1	-0	1.000	-2	3-15/C-4,012S	-0.1
Total	2	106	281	25	68	12	0	2	19	13	36	.242	.278	.306	63	-14	1	2	-1	.980	-6	/3-64,2-12,0CS1	-2.1

■ GEORGE PFISTER
Pfister, George Edward   b: 9/4/18, Bound Brook, N.J.   BR/TR, 6', 200 lbs.   Deb: 9/27/41   C

YEAR	TM/L	G	AB	R	H	2B	3B	HR	RBI	BB	SO	AVG	OBP	SLG	PRO+	BR/A	SB	CS	SBR	FA	FR	G/POS	TPR
1941	Bro-N	1	2	0	0	0	0	0	0	0	0	.000	.000	.000	-96	-1	0			.000	0	/C-1	-0.1

■ MONTE PFYL
Pfyl, Meinhard Charles   b: 5/11/1884, St.Louis, Mo.   d: 10/18/45, San Francisco, Cal   BL/TL, 6'3", 190 lbs.   Deb: 7/30/07

YEAR	TM/L	G	AB	R	H	2B	3B	HR	RBI	BB	SO	AVG	OBP	SLG	PRO+	BR/A	SB	CS	SBR	FA	FR	G/POS	TPR
1907	NY-N	1	0	0	0	0	0	0	0	0		—	—	—	—	-0				.000	0	/1-1	0.0

■ ART PHELAN
Phelan, Arthur Thomas "Dugan"   b: 8/14/1887, Niantic, Ill.   d: 12/27/64, Ft.Worth, Tex.   BR/TR, 5'8", 160 lbs.   Deb: 6/25/10

YEAR	TM/L	G	AB	R	H	2B	3B	HR	RBI	BB	SO	AVG	OBP	SLG	PRO+	BR/A	SB	CS	SBR	FA	FR	G/POS	TPR
1910	Cin-N	23	42	7	9	0	0	0	4	7	6	.214	.327	.214	61	-2	5			1.000	-2	/3-8,2-5,OS	-0.4
1912	Cin-N	130	461	56	112	9	11	3	54	46	37	.243	.314	.330	97	-14	25			.924	-2	*3-127/2-3	-1.4
1913	Chi-N	91	261	41	65	11	6	2	35	29	26	.249	.331	.360	99	-1	8			.931	-8	2-46,3-38/S	-0.9
1914	Chi-N	25	46	5	13	2	1	0	3	4	3	.283	.340	.370	111	1	0			.905	-2	/3-7,2-3,S	0.1
1915	Chi-N	133	448	41	98	16	7	3	35	55	42	.219	.307	.306	86	-7	12	9	-2	.939	-2	*3-110,2-24	-0.6
Total	5	402	1258	150	297	38	25	8	131	141	114	.236	.317	.325	85	-23	50	9		.931	-14	3-290/2-81,SO	-3.2

■ DAN PHELAN
Phelan, Daniel T.   b: 7/23/1864, Thomaston, Conn.   d: 12/7/45, West Haven, Conn.   Deb: 4/18/1890

YEAR	TM/L	G	AB	R	H	2B	3B	HR	RBI	BB	SO	AVG	OBP	SLG	PRO+	BR/A	SB	CS	SBR	FA	FR	G/POS	TPR
1890	Lou-a	8	32	4	8	1	1	0	0			.250	.250	.344	77	-1	1			.975	0	/1-8	-0.1

■ DICK PHELAN
Phelan, James Dickson   b: 12/10/1854, Towanda, Pa.   d: 2/13/31, San Antonio, Tex.   BR,   Deb: 4/17/1884

YEAR	TM/L	G	AB	R	H	2B	3B	HR	RBI	BB	SO	AVG	OBP	SLG	PRO+	BR/A	SB	CS	SBR	FA	FR	G/POS	TPR
1884	Bal-U	101	402	63	99	13	3	3		12		.246	.268	.316	53	-28				.872	-9	*2-100/3-5,O	-3.0
1885	Buf-N	4	16	2	2	0	0	1	3	0	3	.125	.125	.313	37	-1				.808	-1	/2-4	-0.2
	StL-N	2	4	1	1	1	0	0	1	0	2	.250	.250	.500	147	0				1.000	-1	/3-2	0.0
	Yr	6	20	3	3	1	0	1	4	0	5	.150	.150	.350	58	-1				.808	-2	/2-4,3-2	-0.2
Total	2	107	422	66	102	14	3	4	4	12	5	.242	.263	.318	53	-29				.869	-10	2-104/3-7,O	-3.2

■ NEALY PHELPS
Phelps, Cornelius Carman   b: 11/19/1840, New York, N.Y.   d: 2/12/1885, New York, N.Y.   Deb: 7/1/1871

YEAR	TM/L	G	AB	R	H	2B	3B	HR	RBI	BB	SO	AVG	OBP	SLG	PRO+	BR/A	SB	CS	SBR	FA	FR	G/POS	TPR
1871	Kek-n	1	3	0	0	0	0	0	1	0	0	.000	.250	.000	-20	-0	0					/1-1	0.0
1873	Mut-n	1	6	0	0	0	0	0	0	0	0	.000	.000	.000	-99	-1						/O-1	-0.1
1874	Mut-n	6	24	5	3	0	0	0	0	0	0	.125	.125	.125	-20	-3						/O-6	-0.2
1875	Mut-n	2	6	1	2	0	0	0	0	0	0	.333	.333	.333	125	0						/O-2	0.0
1876	NY-N	1	3	0	0	0	0	0	0	0	1	.000	.000	.000	-99	-1				.667	-0	/O-1	-0.1
	Phi-N	1	4	0	0	0	0	0	0	0	0	.000	.000	.000	-99	-1				.571	-1	/C-1	-0.2
	Yr	2	7	0	0	0	0	0	0	0	1	.000	.000	.000	-99	-1				.667	-2	/O-1,C-1	-0.3
Total	4 n	10	39	6	5	0	0	0		0	1	.128	.150	.128	-11	-5						/O-9,1-1	-0.3

■ ED PHELPS
Phelps, Edward Jaykill "Yaller"   b: 3/3/1879, Albany, N.Y.   d: 1/31/42, E.Greenbush, N.Y.   BR/TR, 5'11", 185 lbs.   Deb: 9/3/02

YEAR	TM/L	G	AB	R	H	2B	3B	HR	RBI	BB	SO	AVG	OBP	SLG	PRO+	BR/A	SB	CS	SBR	FA	FR	G/POS	TPR
1902	Pit-N	18	61	5	13	6	0	0	6	4		.213	.284	.230	57	-3	2			.968	-6	C-13/1-5	-0.8
1903	*Pit-N	81	273	32	77	7	3	2	31	17		.282	.338	.352	94	-2	2			.980	-8	C-76/1-3	-0.3
1904	Pit-N	94	302	29	73	5	3	0	28	15		.242	.289	.278	79	-9	2			.964	-10	C-91/1-1	-1.1
1905	Cin-N	44	156	18	36	5	3	0	18	12		.231	.306	.301	73	-5	4			.949	-6	C-44	-0.7
1906	Cin-N	12	40	3	11	0	2	1	9	5		.275	.326	.450	136	1	2			.987	-1	C-12	-0.1
	Pit-N	43	118	9	28	3	1	0	12	9		.237	.302	.280	78	-3	1			.971	-4	C-40	-0.3
	Yr	55	158	12	39	3	3	1	17	12		.247	.308	.323	93	-2	3			.975	-4	C-52	-0.1
1907	Pit-N	43	113	11	24	1	0	0	12	9		.212	.282	.221	57	-5	1			.979	-5	C-35/1-1	-0.6
1908	Pit-N	34	64	3	15	2	0	0	2	2		.234	.269	.328	90	-1	0			.977	-0	C-20	0.0
1909	StL-N	104	306	43	76	13	1	0	22	39		.248	.350	.297	108	5	7			.954	-9	C-83	0.3
1910	StL-N	93	270	25	71	4	2	0	37	36	29	.263	.356	.293	93	-1	9			.976	-15	C-80	-0.9
1912	Bro-N	52	111	8	32	7	0	0	23	16	15	.288	.388	.378	114	3	0			.976	-4	C-32	0.1
1913	Bro-N	15	9	0	2	0	0	0	1	1		.222	.263	.222	82	-0	0			.875	-2	/C-4	-0.3
Total	11	633	1832	186	460	45	20	3	205	163	46	.251	.325	.302	88	-22	31			.968	-69	C-530/1-10	-4.4

■ BABE PHELPS
Phelps, Ernest Gordon "Blimp"   b: 4/19/08, Odenton, Md.   d: 12/10/92, Odenton, Md.   BL/TR, 6'2", 225 lbs.   Deb: 9/17/31

YEAR	TM/L	G	AB	R	H	2B	3B	HR	RBI	BB	SO	AVG	OBP	SLG	PRO+	BR/A	SB	CS	SBR	FA	FR	G/POS	TPR
1931	Was-A	3	3	0	1	0	0	0	0	0	1	.333	.333	.333	75	-0	0					H	0.0
1933	Chi-N	3	7	0	2	0	0	0	2	0	1	.286	.286	.286	64	-0	0			1.000	1	/C-2	0.0
1934	Chi-N	44	70	7	20	5	2	2	12	1	8	.286	.296	.500	111	1	0			.981	-2	C-18	-0.1

YEAR	TM/L	G	AB	R	H	2B	3B	HR	RBI	BB	SO	AVG	OBP	SLG	PRO+	BR/A	SB	CS	SBR	FA	FR	G/POS	TPR
1935	Bro-N	47	121	17	44	7	2	5	22	9	10	.364	.408	.579	165	11	0			.957	-2	C-34	1.0
1936	Bro-N	115	319	36	117	23	2	5	57	27	18	.367	.421	.498	145	21	1			.977	-16	C-98/O-1	0.9
1937	Bro-N	121	409	42	128	37	3	7	58	25	28	.313	.357	.469	121	11	2			.971	-7	*C-111	1.0
1938	Bro-N†	66	208	33	64	12	2	5	46	23	15	.308	.379	.457	126	8	2			.980	-4	C-55	0.6
1939	Bro-N★	98	323	33	92	21	2	6	42	24	24	.285	.336	.418	98	-1	0			.980	2	C-92	0.5
1940	Bro-N★	118	370	47	109	24	5	13	61	30	27	.295	.349	.492	122	10	2			.977	-9	C-99/1-1	0.8
1941	Bro-N	16	30	3	7	3	0	2	4	1	2	.233	.258	.533	114	0	0			.971	-1	C-11	0.0
1942	Pit-N	95	257	21	73	11	1	9	41	20	24	.284	.345	.440	126	8	2			.959	-3	C-72	1.1
Total	11	726	2117	239	657	143	19	54	345	160	157	.310	.362	.472	124	67	9	0		.974	-41	C-592/1-1,O	5.8

■ KEN PHELPS
Phelps, Kenneth Allen b: 8/6/54, Seattle, Wash. BL/TL, 6'1", 209 lbs. Deb: 9/20/80

YEAR	TM/L	G	AB	R	H	2B	3B	HR	RBI	BB	SO	AVG	OBP	SLG	PRO+	BR/A	SB	CS	SBR	FA	FR	G/POS	TPR
1980	KC-A	3	4	0	0	0	0	0	0	0	2	.000	.000	.000	-99	-1	0	0	0	1.000	-0	/1-2	-0.1
1981	KC-A	21	22	1	3	0	1	0	1	1	13	.136	.174	.227	15	-2	0	0	0	1.000	0	/1-2,D-4	-0.2
1982	Mon-N	10	8	0	2	0	0	0	0	0	3	.250	.333	.250	64	-0	0	0	0	.000	0	H	-0.1
1983	Sea-A	50	127	10	30	4	1	7	16	13	25	.236	.307	.449	101	-0	0	0	0	1.000	2	1-22,D-19	0.0
1984	Sea-A	101	290	52	70	9	0	24	51	61	73	.241	.382	.521	149	21	3	3	-1	.987	-1	D-84/1-9	1.6
1985	Sea-A	61	116	18	24	3	0	9	24	24	33	.207	.343	.466	118	3	2	0	1	1.000	-0	D-25/1-8	0.3
1986	Sea-A	125	344	69	85	16	4	24	64	88	96	.247	.409	.526	151	28	2	3	-1	.983	-4	1-55,D-52	1.8
1987	Sea-A	120	332	68	86	13	1	27	68	80	75	.259	.414	.548	145	24	1	1	-0	1.000	-0	*D-114/1-1	1.9
1988	Sea-A	72	190	37	54	8	0	14	32	51	35	.284	.438	.547	167	19	1	0	0	.952	0	D-68/1-3	1.8
	NY-A	45	107	17	24	5	0	10	22	19	26	.224	.341	.551	147	6	0	0	0	.000	-0	D-24/1-1	0.6
	Yr	117	297	54	78	13	0	24	54	70	61	.263	.405	.549	160	26	1	0	0	.952	-0	D-92/1-4	2.4
1989	NY-A	86	185	26	46	3	0	7	29	27	47	.249	.344	.378	105	2	0	0	0	.980	-1	D-55/1-8	-0.1
	*Oak-A	11	9	0	1	1	0	0	0	4	0	.111	.385	.222	78	-0	0	0	0	.000	0	/1-1,D-1	0.0
	Yr	97	194	26	47	4	0	7	29	31	47	.242	.347	.371	104	2	0	0	0	.980	-1	D-56/1-9	-0.1
1990	Oak-A	32	59	6	11	2	0	1	6	12	10	.186	.324	.271	71	-2	0	0	0	.964	0	D-15/1-5	-0.2
	Cle-A	24	61	4	7	0	0	0	0	10	11	.115	.239	.115	2	-8	1	0	0	1.000	0	1-14/D-6	-0.9
	Yr	56	120	10	18	2	0	1	6	22	21	.150	.282	.192	36	-10	1	0	0	.992	0	D-21,1-19	-1.1
Total	11	761	1854	308	443	64	7	123	313	390	449	.239	.377	.480	132	89	10	7	-1	.987	-4	D-467,1-131	6.4

■ DAVE PHILLEY
Philley, David Earl b: 5/16/20, Paris, Tex. BB/TR, 6', 188 lbs. Deb: 9/6/41

YEAR	TM/L	G	AB	R	H	2B	3B	HR	RBI	BB	SO	AVG	OBP	SLG	PRO+	BR/A	SB	CS	SBR	FA	FR	G/POS	TPR
1941	Chi-A	7	9	4	2	0	0	0	0	3	3	.222	.417	.333	102	0	0	0	0	.000	-1	/O-2	-0.1
1946	Chi-A	17	68	10	24	2	3	0	17	4	4	.353	.389	.471	145	4	5	0	2	.983	5	O-17	1.0
1947	Chi-A	143	551	55	142	25	11	2	45	35	39	.258	.303	.354	85	-13	21	16	-3	.986	2	*O-133/3-4	-2.2
1948	Chi-A	137	488	51	140	28	3	5	42	50	33	.287	.353	.387	100	-0	8	10	-1	.978	15	*O-128	0.4
1949	Chi-A	146	598	84	171	20	8	0	44	54	51	.286	.347	.346	86	-12	13	4	2	.977	2	*O-145	-1.6
1950	Chi-A	156	619	60	150	21	5	14	80	52	57	.242	.302	.360	71	-30	6	3	0	.980	1	*O-154	-3.3
1951	Chi-A	7	25	0	6	2	0	0	2	2	3	.240	.296	.320	68	-1	0	0	0	.938	-0	/O-6	-0.2
	Phi-A	125	468	71	123	18	7	7	59	63	38	.263	.354	.376	95	-2	9	6	-1	.978	2	*O-120/3-2	-0.6
	Yr	132	493	71	129	20	7	7	61	65	41	.262	.351	.373	94	-3	9	6	-1	.976	2	*O-126/3-2	-0.8
1952	Phi-A	151	586	80	154	25	4	7	71	59	35	.263	.334	.355	86	-10	11	4	1	.991	2	*O-149/3-2	-0.3
1953	Phi-A	157	620	80	188	30	9	9	59	51	35	.303	.358	.424	106	5	13	5	1	.981	-4	*O-157/3-1	-0.4
1954	*Cle-A	133	452	48	102	13	3	12	60	57	48	.226	.312	.347	79	-13	2	4	-2	.984	-4	*O-129	-2.5
1955	Cle-A	43	104	15	31	4	2	2	9	12	10	.298	.371	.433	111	2	0	2	-1	1.000	-3	O-34	-0.3
	Bal-A	83	311	50	93	13	3	6	41	34	38	.299	.368	.418	119	8	1	2	-1	.970	-7	O-82/3-2	-0.3
	Yr	126	415	65	124	17	5	8	50	46	48	.299	.369	.422	116	9	1	4	-2	.976	-9	*O-116/3-2	-0.6
1956	Bal-A	32	117	13	24	4	2	1	17	18	13	.205	.311	.299	67	-6	3	1	0	.935	-4	O-31/3-5	-1.1
	Chi-A	86	279	44	74	14	2	4	47	28	27	.265	.334	.373	85	-6	1	3	-2	.978	-9	1-51,O-30	-2.0
	Yr	118	396	57	98	18	4	5	64	46	40	.247	.327	.351	80	-11	4	4	-1	.965	-13	O-61,1-51/3	-3.1
1957	Chi-A	22	71	9	23	4	0	0	9	4	10	.324	.360	.380	102	0	1	1	-0	.975	1	O-17/1-2	-0.1
	Det-A	65	173	15	49	8	1	2	16	7	16	.283	.311	.376	85	-4	3	1	0	.996	1	1-27,O-12/3	-0.5
	Yr	87	244	24	72	12	1	2	25	11	26	.295	.325	.377	90	-4	4	2	0	.965	2	O-29,1-29/3	-0.6
1958	Phi-N	91	207	30	64	11	4	3	31	15	20	.309	.359	.444	113	4	1	1	-0	1.000	-4	O-24/1-18	-0.2
1959	Phi-N	99	254	32	74	18	2	7	37	18	27	.291	.341	.461	109	3	0	0	0	1.000	1	O-34,1-24	0.1
1960	Phi-N	14	15	2	5	2	0	0	4	3	2	.333	.444	.467	149	1	0	0	0	.000	-0	/O-3,1-2	-0.1
	SF-N	39	61	5	10	0	0	1	7	6	14	.164	.239	.213	26	-6	0	0	0	.941	-1	O-10/3-3	-0.8
	Yr	53	76	7	15	2	0	1	11	9	16	.197	.282	.263	53	-5	0	0	0	.941	-3	O-13/3-3,1	-0.9
	Bal-A	14	34	6	9	2	1	1	5	4	5	.265	.342	.471	119	1	1	0	0	1.000	-0	/O-8,3-1	0.0
1961	Bal-A	99	144	13	36	9	2	1	23	10	20	.250	.299	.361	78	-5	2	0	1	1.000	-6	O-25/1-1	-1.1
1962	Bos-A	38	42	3	6	2	0	0	4	5	3	.143	.250	.190	20	-5	0	0	0	1.000	-0	/O-4	-0.5
Total	18	1904	6296	789	1700	276	72	84	729	594	551	.270	.335	.377	91	-86	101	63	-8	.981	-0	*O-1454,1-125/3	-16.7

■ ADOLFO PHILLIPS
Phillips, Adolfo Emilio (Lopez) b: 12/16/41, Bethania, Panama BR/TR, 6', 177 lbs. Deb: 9/2/64

YEAR	TM/L	G	AB	R	H	2B	3B	HR	RBI	BB	SO	AVG	OBP	SLG	PRO+	BR/A	SB	CS	SBR	FA	FR	G/POS	TPR
1964	Phi-N	13	13	4	3	0	0	0	0	3	3	.231	.375	.231	76	-0	0	0	0	1.000	-0	/O-4	-0.1
1965	Phi-N	41	87	14	20	4	0	3	5	5	34	.230	.272	.379	83	-2	3	3	-1	1.000	-4	O-32	-0.8
1966	Phi-N	2	3	1	0	0	0	0	0	0	0	.000	.000	.000	-99	-1	0	0	0	1.000	-0	/O-1	-0.1
	Chi-N	116	416	68	109	29	1	16	36	43	135	.262	.348	.452	119	11	32	15	1	.978	12	*O-111	1.9
	Yr	118	419	69	109	29	1	16	36	43	135	.260	.346	.449	118	10	32	15	1	.979	12	*O-112	1.8
1967	Chi-N	144	448	66	120	20	7	17	70	80	93	.268	.386	.458	134	23	24	10	1	.981	15	*O-141	3.4
1968	Chi-N	143	439	49	106	20	5	13	33	47	90	.241	.322	.399	108	5	9	7	-2	.979	6	*O-141	0.3
1969	Chi-N	28	49	5	11	3	1	0	1	16	15	.224	.424	.327	140	1	1	3	-2	.956	-3	O-25	-0.4
	Mon-N	58	199	25	43	4	4	4	7	19	62	.216	.288	.337	74	-7	6	5	-1	.981	-0	O-53	-1.3
	Yr	86	248	30	54	7	5	4	8	35	77	.218	.319	.335	80	-6	7	8	-3	.973	-3	O-78	-1.7
1970	Mon-N	92	214	36	51	6	3	6	21	36	51	.238	.353	.379	96	-0	7	1	2	.985	-6	O-75	-0.8
1972	Cle-A	12	2	0	0	0	0	0	0	0	2	.000	.222	.000	-29	-1	0	0	0	1.000	-0	O-10	-0.4
Total	8	649	1875	270	463	86	21	59	173	251	485	.247	.344	.410	110	27	82	44	-2	.980	17	O-593	1.7

■ J. R. PHILLIPS
Phillips, Charles Gene b: 4/29/70, West Covina, Cal. BL/TL, 6'1", 185 lbs. Deb: 9/3/93

YEAR	TM/L	G	AB	R	H	2B	3B	HR	RBI	BB	SO	AVG	OBP	SLG	PRO+	BR/A	SB	CS	SBR	FA	FR	G/POS	TPR
1993	SF-N	11	16	1	5	1	0	1	4	0	5	.313	.313	.688	164	1	0	0	0	.971	0	/1-5	0.1
1994	SF-N	15	38	1	5	0	0	1	3	1	13	.132	.154	.211	-7	-6	1	0	0	.989	1	1-10	-0.5
Total	2	26	54	2	10	1	1	2	7	1	18	.185	.200	.352	43	-5	1	0	0	.984	1	/1-15	-0.4

■ DAMON PHILLIPS
Phillips, Damon Roswell "Dee" b: 6/8/19, Corsicana, Tex. BR/TR, 6', 176 lbs. Deb: 7/19/42

YEAR	TM/L	G	AB	R	H	2B	3B	HR	RBI	BB	SO	AVG	OBP	SLG	PRO+	BR/A	SB	CS	SBR	FA	FR	G/POS	TPR
1942	Cin-N	28	84	4	17	2	0	0	6	7	5	.202	.264	.226	44	-6	0			.964	0	S-27	0.3
1944	Bos-N	140	489	35	126	30	1	1	53	28	34	.258	.301	.329	74	-17	1			.932	-4	3-90,S-60	-1.6
1946	Bos-N	2	2	0	1	0	0	0	0	0	0	.500	.500	.500	182	0	0			.000	0	H	0.0
Total	3	170	575	39	144	32	1	1	59	35	39	.250	.296	.315	70	-23	1			.956	3	/3-90,S-87	-1.3

■ EDDIE PHILLIPS
Phillips, Edward David b: 2/17/01, Worcester, Mass. d: 1/26/68, Buffalo, N.Y. BR/TR, 6', 178 lbs. Deb: 5/4/24

YEAR	TM/L	G	AB	R	H	2B	3B	HR	RBI	BB	SO	AVG	OBP	SLG	PRO+	BR/A	SB	CS	SBR	FA	FR	G/POS	TPR
1924	Bos-N	3	3	0	0	0	0	0	0	0	2	.000	.000	.000	-99	-1	0			1.000	0	/C-1	-0.1
1929	Det-A	68	221	24	52	13	1	2	21	20	16	.235	.302	.330	62	-13	0	1	-1	.967	-5	C-63	-1.2
1931	Pit-N	106	353	30	82	18	3	7	44	41	49	.232	.317	.360	82	-9	1			.986	-7	*C-103	-0.8
1932	NY-A	9	31	4	9	1	0	2	8	2	3	.290	.333	.516	123	1	0			1.000	1	/C-9	0.2
1934	Was-A	56	169	6	33	6	1	2	16	26	24	.195	.306	.278	54	-12	1	0	-1	.984	-7	C-53	-1.5

YEAR	TM/L	G	AB	R	H	2B	3B	HR	RBI	BB	SO	AVG	OBP	SLG	PRO+	BR/A	SB	CS	SBR	FA	FR	G/POS	TPR
1935	Cle-A	70	220	18	60	16	1	1	41	15	21	.273	.319	.368	76	-8	0	0	0	.980	-8	C-69	-1.3
Total	6	312	997	82	236	54	6	14	126	104	115	.237	.312	.345	72	-41	3	1		.980	-27	C-298	-4.7

■ EDDIE PHILLIPS
Phillips, Howard Edward   b: 7/8/31, St.Louis, Mo.   BB/TR, 6'1", 180 lbs.   Deb: 9/10/53

YEAR	TM/L	G	AB	R	H	2B	3B	HR	RBI	BB	SO	AVG	OBP	SLG	PRO+	BR/A	SB	CS	SBR	FA	FR	G/POS	TPR
1953	StL-N	9	0	4	0	0	0	0	0	0	0	—	—	—		0	0	0	0	.000	0	R	0.0

■ JACK PHILLIPS
Phillips, Jack Dorn "Stretch"   b: 9/6/21, Clarence, N.Y.   BR/TR, 6'4", 193 lbs.   Deb: 8/22/47

YEAR	TM/L	G	AB	R	H	2B	3B	HR	RBI	BB	SO	AVG	OBP	SLG	PRO+	BR/A	SB	CS	SBR	FA	FR	G/POS	TPR
1947	*NY-A	16	36	5	10	1	1	1	2	3	5	.278	.333	.417	109	0	0	0	0	.986	-2	1-10	-0.2
1948	NY-A	1	2	0	0	0	0	0	0	0	1	.000	.000	.000	-99	-1	0	0	0	.889	-0	/1-1	-0.1
1949	NY-A	45	91	16	28	4	1	1	10	12	9	.308	.388	.407	110	2	1	0	0	.977	-2	1-38	0.0
	Pit-N	18	56	6	13	3	1	0	3	4	6	.232	.283	.321	60	-3	1			1.000	0	1-16/3-1	-0.3
1950	Pit-N	69	208	25	61	7	6	5	34	20	17	.293	.355	.457	108	2	1			.986	2	1-54/3-3,P	0.3
1951	Pit-N	70	156	12	37	7	3	0	12	15	17	.237	.304	.321	66	-7	1	2	-1	.991	-1	1-53/3-4	-1.1
1952	Pit-N	1	1	0	0	0	0	0	0	0	0	.000	.000	.000	-97	-0	0	0	0	1.000	-0	/1-1	0.0
1955	Det-A	55	117	15	37	8	2	1	20	10	12	.316	.370	.444	121	3	0	0	0	.992	-1	1-35/3-3	0.0
1956	Det-A	67	224	31	66	13	2	1	20	21	19	.295	.355	.384	95	-2	1	1	-0	.981	-1	1-56/2-1,O	-0.7
1957	Det-A	1	1	1	0	0	0	0	0	0	0	.000	.000	.000	-97	-0	0	0	0	.000	0	H	0.0
Total	9	343	892	111	252	42	16	9	101	85	86	.283	.345	.396	95	-6	5	3		.986	-6	1-264/3-11,02P	-2.1

■ BUBBA PHILLIPS
Phillips, John Melvin   b: 2/24/28, West Point, Miss.   d: 6/22/93, Hattiesburg, Miss.   BR/TR, 5'9", 180 lbs.   Deb: 4/30/55

YEAR	TM/L	G	AB	R	H	2B	3B	HR	RBI	BB	SO	AVG	OBP	SLG	PRO+	BR/A	SB	CS	SBR	FA	FR	G/POS	TPR
1955	Det-A	95	184	18	43	4	0	3	23	14	20	.234	.295	.304	63	-10	1	1	0	.992	-1	O-65/3-4	-1.3
1956	Chi-A	67	99	16	27	6	0	2	11	6	12	.273	.321	.394	87	-2	1	2	-1	1.000	-1	O-35/3-2	-0.5
1957	Chi-A	121	393	38	106	13	3	7	42	28	32	.270	.323	.372	89	-6	5	3	-0	.958	16	3-97,O-20	1.0
1958	Chi-A	84	260	26	71	10	6	5	30	15	14	.273	.315	.369	89	-4	3	0	1	.954	7	3-47,O-37	0.2
1959	*Chi-A	117	379	43	100	27	1	5	40	27	28	.264	.320	.380	92	-4	1	1	-0	.951	3	*3-100,O-23	-0.3
1960	Cle-A	113	304	34	63	14	1	4	33	14	37	.207	.252	.299	50	-22	1	0	0	.953	-8	3-85,O-25/S	-3.2
1961	Cle-A	143	546	64	144	23	1	18	72	29	61	.264	.307	.408	92	-8	1	0	0	.958	-18	*3-143	-2.5
1962	Cle-A	148	562	53	145	26	0	10	54	20	55	.258	.292	.358	76	-20	4	0	1	.977	-15	*3-145/O-3,2	-3.3
1963	Det-A	128	464	42	114	11	2	5	45	19	42	.246	.281	.310	63	-22	6	2	1	.961	1	*3-117/O-5	-2.2
1964	Det-A	46	87	14	22	1	0	3	6	10	13	.253	.330	.368	92	-1	2	1	-1	.983	2	3-22/O-1	0.0
Total	10	1062	3278	348	835	135	8	62	356	182	314	.255	.300	.358	79	-100	25	11	1	.960	-16	3-762,O-214/2S	-12.1

■ JACK PHILLIPS
Phillips, John Stephen   b: 5/24/19, St.Louis, Mo.   d: 6/16/58, St.Louis, Mo.   BR/TR, 6'1", 185 lbs.   Deb: 7/13/45

YEAR	TM/L	G	AB	R	H	2B	3B	HR	RBI	BB	SO	AVG	OBP	SLG	PRO+	BR/A	SB	CS	SBR	FA	FR	G/POS	TPR
1945	NY-N	2	2	1	1	0	0	0	0	0	0	.500	.500	.500	176	0				1.000	-0	/P-1	0.0

■ TONY PHILLIPS
Phillips, Keith Anthony   b: 4/25/59, Atlanta, Ga.   BB/TR, 5'10", 160 lbs.   Deb: 5/10/82

YEAR	TM/L	G	AB	R	H	2B	3B	HR	RBI	BB	SO	AVG	OBP	SLG	PRO+	BR/A	SB	CS	SBR	FA	FR	G/POS	TPR
1982	Oak-A	40	81	11	17	2	2	0	8	12	26	.210	.326	.284	73	-3	2	3	-1	.953	-5	S-39	-0.5
1983	Oak-A	148	412	54	102	12	3	4	35	48	70	.248	.329	.320	85	-8	16	5	2	.941	1	*S-101,2-63/3D	0.5
1984	Oak-A	154	451	62	120	24	3	4	37	42	86	.266	.329	.359	97	-2	10	6	-1	.941	-11	S-91,2-90/O	-0.4
1985	Oak-A	42	161	23	45	12	4	4	17	13	34	.280	.333	.453	122	4	3	2	-0	.980	-0	3-31,2-24	0.4
1986	Oak-A	118	441	76	113	14	5	5	52	76	82	.256	.369	.345	103	5	15	10	-2	.976	1	2-88,S-30/OSD	0.7
1987	Oak-A	111	379	48	91	20	0	10	46	57	76	.240	.339	.372	95	-2	7	6	-2	.974	-3	2-87,3-11/SOD	-0.1
1988	*Oak-A	79	212	32	43	8	4	2	17	36	50	.203	.321	.307	80	-5	0	2	-1	.913	-20	3-32,O-31,2S/1D	-2.6
1989	*Oak-A	143	451	48	118	15	6	4	47	58	66	.262	.350	.348	101	2	3	8	-4	.985	-24	2-84,3-49,SO/1	-2.6
1990	Det-A	152	573	97	144	23	5	8	55	99	85	.251	.365	.351	100	4	19	9	0	.931	6	*3-104,2-47,S/OD	1.3
1991	Det-A	146	564	87	160	28	4	17	72	79	95	.284	.371	.438	122	19	10	5	0	.992	6	O-56,3-46,2DS	2.5
1992	Det-A	159	606	**114**	167	32	3	10	64	114	93	.276	.391	.388	118	20	12	10	-2	.968	4	O-69,2-57,D3/S	2.9
1993	Det-A	151	566	113	177	27	0	7	57	**132**	102	.313	.446	.398	130	33	16	11	-2	.969	-1	*O-108,2-51/3D	2.9
1994	Det-A	114	438	91	123	19	3	19	61	95	105	.281	.411	.468	127	21	13	5	1	.980	7	*O-104,2-12/D	2.5
Total	13	1557	5335	856	1420	236	40	94	568	861	970	.266	.371	.378	108	89	126	82	-11	.982	-39	2-666,O-399,3S/D1	6.9

■ MARR PHILLIPS
Phillips, Marr B.   b: 6/16/1857, Pittsburgh, Pa.   d: 4/1/28, Pittsburgh, Pa.   BR , 5'6.5", 164 lbs.   Deb: 5/1/1884

YEAR	TM/L	G	AB	R	H	2B	3B	HR	RBI	BB	SO	AVG	OBP	SLG	PRO+	BR/A	SB	CS	SBR	FA	FR	G/POS	TPR
1884	Ind-a	97	413	41	111	18	8	0		5		.269	.279	.351	107	3				.862	14	*S-97	1.6
1885	Det-N	33	139	13	29	5	0	0	17	0	13	.209	.209	.245	46	-8				.881	2	S-33	-0.5
	Pit-a	4	15	1	4	0	0	0		2		.267	.353	.267	99	0				.875	-1	/S-4	-0.1
1890	Roc-a	64	257	18	53	8	0	0		16		.206	.261	.237	51	-16	10			.918	6	S-64	-0.6
Total	3	198	824	73	197	31	8	0	17	23	13	.239	.263	.296	79	-21	10			.884	21	S-198	0.4

■ MIKE PHILLIPS
Phillips, Michael Dwaine   b: 8/19/50, Beaumont, Tex.   BL/TR, 6'1", 185 lbs.   Deb: 4/15/73

YEAR	TM/L	G	AB	R	H	2B	3B	HR	RBI	BB	SO	AVG	OBP	SLG	PRO+	BR/A	SB	CS	SBR	FA	FR	G/POS	TPR
1973	SF-N	63	104	18	25	3	4	1	9	6	17	.240	.288	.375	79	-3	0	3	-2	.931	-0	3-28,S-20/2	-0.4
1974	SF-N	100	283	19	62	6	1	2	20	14	37	.219	.258	.269	45	-21	4	5	-2	.909	4	3-34,2-30,S	-1.6
1975	SF-N	10	31	3	6	0	0	0	1	6	4	.194	.324	.194	44	-2	1	0	0	.969	4	/2-6,3-6	0.2
	NY-N	116	383	31	98	10	7	1	28	25	47	.256	.303	.326	78	-12	3	0	1	.944	1	*S-115/2-1	0.1
	Yr	126	414	34	104	10	7	1	29	31	51	.251	.305	.316	76	-14	4	0	1	.944	4	*S-115/2-7,3	0.3
1976	NY-N	87	262	30	67	4	6	4	29	25	29	.256	.321	.363	99	-1	2	2	-1	.955	-9	S-53,2-19,3	-0.4
1977	NY-N	38	86	5	18	2	1	1	3	2	15	.209	.244	.291	45	-7	0	1	-1	1.000	-5	S-24/3-9,2	-1.1
	StL-N	48	87	17	21	3	2	0	9	9	13	.241	.320	.322	74	-3	1	0	0	.971	5	2-31/S-5,3	0.4
	Yr	86	173	22	39	5	3	1	12	11	28	.225	.283	.306	60	-10	1	1	-0	.973	0	2-35,S-29,3	-0.7
1978	StL-N	76	164	14	44	9	4	1	28	13	25	.268	.330	.348	91	-2	0	0	0	.971	0	2-55,S-10/3	0.1
1979	StL-N	44	97	10	22	3	1	1	6	10	9	.227	.306	.309	68	-4	0	0	0	.973	13	S-25,2-16/3	1.1
1980	StL-N	63	128	13	30	5	0	0	7	9	17	.234	.285	.273	55	-8	0	0	0	.971	13	S-37/2-9,3	0.9
1981	SD-N	14	29	1	6	0	1	0	0	0	3	.207	.207	.276	39	-2	1	0	0	.979	4	/2-9,S-1	0.2
	*Mon-N	34	55	5	12	2	0	1	4	5	15	.218	.283	.255	53	-3	0	1	-1	.974	0	S-26/2-6	-0.2
	Yr	48	84	6	18	2	1	1	4	5	18	.214	.258	.262	49	-6	1	1	-0	.974	4	S-27,2-15	0.0
1982	Mon-N	14	8	0	1	0	0	0	1	0	3	.125	.125	.125	-29	-1	0	0	0	1.000	3	2-10/S-2	0.1
1983	Mon-N	1	0	0	0	0	0	0	0	0	0	.000	.000	.000	-99	-1	0	0	0	.000	-1	/S-3,3-2	-0.2
Total	11	712	1719	166	412	46	24	11	145	124	234	.240	.294	.314	70	-70	12	12	-4	.956	29	S-344,2-203,3	-0.8

■ DICK PHILLIPS
Phillips, Richard Eugene   b: 11/24/31, Racine, Wis.   BL/TR, 6', 180 lbs.   Deb: 4/15/62   C

YEAR	TM/L	G	AB	R	H	2B	3B	HR	RBI	BB	SO	AVG	OBP	SLG	PRO+	BR/A	SB	CS	SBR	FA	FR	G/POS	TPR
1962	SF-N	5	3	1	0	0	0	0	0	0	1	.000	.250	.000	-27	-1	0	0	0	1.000	-0	/1-1	-0.1
1963	Was-A	124	321	33	76	8	0	10	32	29	35	.237	.304	.355	84	-7	1	0	0	.994	4	1-68/2-5,3	-0.6
1964	Was-A	109	234	17	54	6	1	2	23	27	22	.231	.313	.291	70	-9	1	2	-1	.994	2	1-61/3-4	-1.1
1966	Was-A	25	37	3	6	0	0	0	4	2	5	.162	.225	.162	13	-4	0	0	0	1.000	-1	/1-5	-0.5
Total	4	263	595	54	136	14	1	12	60	59	63	.229	.302	.316	74	-20	2	2	-1	.995	4	1-135/3-8,2	-2.3

■ BILL PHILLIPS
Phillips, William B.   b: 1857, St.John, N.B., Canada   d: 10/7/1900, Chicago, Ill.   BR/TR, 202 lbs.   Deb: 5/1/1879

YEAR	TM/L	G	AB	R	H	2B	3B	HR	RBI	BB	SO	AVG	OBP	SLG	PRO+	BR/A	SB	CS	SBR	FA	FR	G/POS	TPR
1879	Cle-N	81	365	58	99	15	4	0	29	2	20	.271	.275	.334	101	5				.954	-5	*1-75,C-11/O	-0.6
1880	Cle-N	85	334	41	85	14	10	1	36	6	29	.254	.268	.365	115	5				.963	2	*1-85	-0.1
1881	Cle-N	85	357	51	97	18	1	1	44	5	19	.272	.282	.387	114	5				.966	-1	*1-85	-0.3
1882	Cle-N	78	335	40	87	17	7	4	47	7	18	.260	.275	.388	114	5				.971	3	*1-78/C-1	-0.1
1883	Cle-N	97	382	42	94	29	8	2	40	8	49	.246	.262	.380	93	-3				.967	-2	*1-97	-1.4
1884	Cle-N	111	464	58	128	25	12	3	46	18	80	.276	.303	.401	115	7				.959	-2	*1-111	-0.7
1885	Bro-a	99	391	65	118	16	11	3		27		.302	.364	.422	147	21				**.973**	0	*1-99	0.8
1886	Bro-a	141	585	68	160	26	15	0		33		.274	.313	.369	113	6	13			.978	-2	*1-141	-1.1
1887	Bro-a	132	533	82	142	34	11	2		45		.266	.330	.383	97	-3	16			**.982**	4	*1-132	-1.0

YEAR	TM/L	G	AB	R	H	2B	3B	HR	RBI	BB	SO	AVG	OBP	SLG	PRO+	BR/A	SB	CS	SBR	FA	FR	G/POS	TPR
1888	KC-a	129	509	57	120	20	10	1	56	27		.236	.284	.320	88	-9	10			.980	3	*1-129	-1.7
Total	10	1038	4255	562	1130	214	98	17	298	178	215	.266	.299	.374	109	35	39			.971	1	*1-1032/C-12,O	-6.2

■ BILL PHYLE
Phyle, William Joseph b: 6/25/1875, Duluth, Minn. d: 8/6/53, Los Angeles, Cal. TR , Deb: 9/17/1898

YEAR	TM/L	G	AB	R	H	2B	3B	HR	RBI	BB	SO	AVG	OBP	SLG	PRO+	BR/A	SB	CS	SBR	FA	FR	G/POS	TPR
1898	Chi-N	4	9	1	1	0	0	0	0	0	2	.111	.273	.111	11	-1	0			.800	-1	/P-3	0.0
1899	Chi-N	10	34	2	6	0	0	0	1	0		.176	.176	.176	-3	-5	0			.935	1	P-10	0.0
1901	NY-N	25	66	8	12	2	0	0	3	2		.182	.206	.212	22	-7	0			.903	1	P-24/S-1	0.0
1906	StL-N	22	73	6	13	3	1	0	4	5		.178	.231	.247	51	-4	2			.935	2	3-21	-0.2
Total	4	61	182	17	32	5	1	0	8	9		.176	.215	.214	28	-17	2			.907	3	/P-37,3-21,S	-0.2

■ MIKE PIAZZA
Piazza, Michael Joseph b: 9/4/68, Norristown, Pa. BR/TR, 6'3", 200 lbs. Deb: 9/1/92

YEAR	TM/L	G	AB	R	H	2B	3B	HR	RBI	BB	SO	AVG	OBP	SLG	PRO+	BR/A	SB	CS	SBR	FA	FR	G/POS	TPR
1992	LA-N	21	69	5	16	3	0	1	7	4	12	.232	.284	.319	71	-3	0	0	0	.990	-2	C-16	-0.4
1993	LA-N★	149	547	81	174	24	2	35	112	46	86	.318	.374	.561	155	41	3	4	-2	.989	11	*C-146/1-1	5.2
1994	LA-N★	107	405	64	129	18	0	24	92	33	65	.319	.371	.541	142	24	1	3	-2	.985	-11	*C-104	1.6
Total	3	277	1021	150	319	45	2	60	211	83	163	.312	.367	.537	145	61	4	7	-3	.988	-7	C-266/1-1	6.4

■ ROB PICCIOLO
Picciolo, Robert Michael b: 2/4/53, Santa Monica, Cal. BR/TR, 6'2", 185 lbs. Deb: 4/9/77 C

YEAR	TM/L	G	AB	R	H	2B	3B	HR	RBI	BB	SO	AVG	OBP	SLG	PRO+	BR/A	SB	CS	SBR	FA	FR	G/POS	TPR
1977	Oak-A	148	419	35	84	12	3	2	22	9	55	.200	.219	.258	30	-41	1	4	-2	.966	7	*S-148	-2.3
1978	Oak-A	78	93	16	21	1	0	2	7	2	13	.226	.242	.301	55	-6	1	1	-0	.958	12	S-41,2-19,3	0.9
1979	Oak-A	115	348	37	88	16	2	2	27	3	45	.253	.261	.328	61	-20	2	1	0	.964	-3	*S-105/2-6,3O	-1.2
1980	Oak-A	95	271	32	65	9	2	5	18	2	63	.240	.245	.343	64	-15	1	1	-0	.977	-23	S-49,2-47/O	-3.1
1981	*Oak-A	82	179	23	48	5	3	4	13	5	22	.268	.292	.397	102	-0	0	1	-1	.981	-15	S-82	-1.0
1982	Oak-A	18	49	3	11	1	0	0	1	0	10	.224	.240	.245	35	-4	1	0		.979	3	S-18	0.1
	Mil-A	22	21	7	6	1	0	0	1	1	4	.286	.318	.333	84	-0	0	0		1.000	3	2-11/S-6,D	0.1
	Yr	40	70	10	17	2	0	0	4	2	14	.243	.264	.271	50	-5	1	0		.973	5	S-24,2-11/D	0.2
1983	Mil-A	14	27	2	6	3	0	0	1	0	4	.222	.222	.333	55	-2	0	0		1.000	4	/S-7,2-3,31D	0.1
1984	Cal-A	87	119	18	24	6	0	1	9	0	21	.202	.202	.277	31	-11	0	1	-1	.974	13	S-66,3-13/2O	0.4
1985	Oak-A	71	102	19	28	2	0	1	8	2	17	.275	.288	.324	73	-4	3	2	-0	.889	7	3-19,2-17,1D/S	0.3
Total	9	730	1628	192	381	56	10	17	109	25	254	.234	.247	.312	55	-103	9	11	-4	.970	6	S-531,2-111/31DO	-5.7

■ NICK PICCIUTO
Picciuto, Nicholas Thomas b: 8/27/21, Newark, N.J. BR/TR, 5'8.5", 165 lbs. Deb: 5/11/45

YEAR	TM/L	G	AB	R	H	2B	3B	HR	RBI	BB	SO	AVG	OBP	SLG	PRO+	BR/A	SB	CS	SBR	FA	FR	G/POS	TPR
1945	Phi-N	36	89	7	12	6	0	0	6	6	17	.135	.189	.202	9	-11	0			.839	-6	3-30/2-4	-1.6

■ VAL PICINICH
Picinich, Valentine John b: 9/8/1896, New York, N.Y. d: 12/5/42, Nobleboro, Maine BR/TR, 5'9", 165 lbs. Deb: 7/25/16 C

YEAR	TM/L	G	AB	R	H	2B	3B	HR	RBI	BB	SO	AVG	OBP	SLG	PRO+	BR/A	SB	CS	SBR	FA	FR	G/POS	TPR
1916	Phi-A	40	118	8	23	3	1	0	5	6	33	.195	.234	.237	44	-9	1			.967	-0	C-37	-0.7
1917	Phi-A	2	6	0	2	0	0	0	1	0	2	.333	.429	.333	135	0	0			.786	-1	/C-2	-0.1
1918	Was-A	47	148	13	34	3	3	0	12	9	25	.230	.274	.291	72	-6	0			.960	-2	C-46	-0.4
1919	Was-A	80	212	18	58	12	3	3	22	17	43	.274	.330	.401	106	1	6			.978	15	C-69	2.1
1920	Was-A	48	133	14	27	6	2	3	14	9	33	.203	.259	.346	61	-8	0	0	0	.978	9	C-45	0.4
1921	Was-A	45	141	10	39	9	0	0	12	16	21	.277	.354	.340	82	-3	0	3	-2	.966	3	C-45	0.0
1922	Was-A	76	210	16	48	12	2	0	19	23	33	.229	.311	.305	64	-11	1	0	0	.976	7	C-76	0.3
1923	Bos-A	87	268	33	74	21	1	2	31	46	32	.276	.386	.384	103	3	3	5	-2	.957	-2	C-81	0.3
1924	Bos-A	69	161	25	44	6	3	1	24	29	19	.273	.394	.366	97	0	5	1	1	.951	-4	C-52	0.0
1925	Bos-A	90	251	31	64	21	0	1	25	33	21	.255	.344	.351	77	-9	2	0	1	.968	-8	C-74/1-2	-1.1
1926	Cin-N	89	240	33	63	16	1	2	31	29	22	.262	.342	.363	92	-2	4			.967	-0	C-86	0.2
1927	Cin-N	65	173	16	44	8	3	0	12	24	15	.254	.345	.363	85	-3	3			.980	5	C-61	0.6
1928	Cin-N	96	324	29	98	15	1	7	35	20	25	.302	.354	.420	100	-1	1			.983	-3	C-93	0.4
1929	Bro-N	93	273	28	71	16	6	4	31	34	24	.260	.342	.407	86	-6	3			.979	-4	C-85	-0.2
1930	Bro-N	23	46	4	10	3	0	0	3	5	6	.217	.294	.283	41	-4	1			.944	-2	C-22	-0.4
1931	Bro-N	24	45	5	12	4	0	1	4	4	9	.267	.327	.422	100	-0	1			.967	1	C-15	0.1
1932	Bro-N	41	70	8	18	6	0	1	11	4	9	.257	.297	.386	84	-2	0			.985	-2	C-24	-0.3
1933	Bro-N	6	6	1	1	1	0	0	0	0	1	.167	.167	.333	42	-0	0			.889	0	/C-6	0.0
	Pit-N	16	52	6	13	4	0	1	7	5	10	.250	.316	.385	99	-0	0			.982	-3	C-16	-0.2
	Yr	22	58	7	14	5	0	1	7	5	11	.241	.302	.379	95	-0	0			.969	-3	C-22	-0.2
Total	18	1037	2877	298	743	166	26	26	298	314	382	.258	.334	.361	86	-60	31	9		.970	11	C-935/1-2	0.7

■ CHARLIE PICK
Pick, Charles Thomas b: 4/10/1888, Brookneal, Va. d: 6/26/54, Lynchburg, Va. BL/TR, 5'10", 160 lbs. Deb: 9/20/14

YEAR	TM/L	G	AB	R	H	2B	3B	HR	RBI	BB	SO	AVG	OBP	SLG	PRO+	BR/A	SB	CS	SBR	FA	FR	G/POS	TPR
1914	Was-A	10	23	0	9	0	0	0	1	4	4	.391	.481	.391	157	2	1	2	-1	.833	-0	/O-7	0.1
1915	Was-A	3	2	0	0	0	0	0	0	0	0	.000	.000	.000	-98	-0	0			.000	0	H	-0.1
1916	Phi-A	121	398	29	96	10	3	0	20	40	24	.241	.315	.281	83	-8	25	16	-2	.899	4	*3-108/O-8	-0.3
1918	*Chi-N	29	89	13	29	4	1	0	12	14	4	.326	.417	.393	144	5	7			.964	5	2-20/3-8	0.7
1919	Chi-N	75	269	27	65	8	6	1	18	14	12	.242	.292	.316	82	-6	17			.946	12	2-71/3-3	1.0
	Bos-N	34	114	12	29	1	1	1	7	7	5	.254	.325	.307	94	-0	4			.924	-2	2-21/3-5,O1	-0.2
	Yr	109	383	39	94	9	7	1	25	21	17	.245	.302	.313	86	-6	21			.942	10	2-92/3-8,O1	0.8
1920	Bos-N	95	383	34	105	16	6	2	28	23	11	.274	.320	.363	100	-0	10	16	-7	.952	0	2-94	-0.4
Total	6	367	1278	115	333	39	17	3	86	102	60	.261	.323	.325	95	-8	64	34		.949	14	2-206,3-124/O1	0.8

■ EDDIE PICK
Pick, Edgar Everett b: 5/7/1899, Attleboro, Mass. d: 5/13/67, Santa Monica, Cal. BB/TR, 6', 185 lbs. Deb: 9/13/23

YEAR	TM/L	G	AB	R	H	2B	3B	HR	RBI	BB	SO	AVG	OBP	SLG	PRO+	BR/A	SB	CS	SBR	FA	FR	G/POS	TPR
1923	Cin-N	9	8	2	3	0	0	0	2	3	3	.375	.545	.375	150	1	0	0	0	1.000	-1	/O-4	-0.1
1924	Cin-N	3	2	0	0	0	0	0	0	0	1	.000	.000	.000	-99	-1	0	0	0	1.000	-0	/O-1	-0.1
1927	Chi-N	54	181	23	31	5	2	2	15	20	26	.171	.254	.254	36	-16	0			.910	-6	3-49/2-1,O	-2.0
Total	3	66	191	25	34	5	2	2	17	23	30	.178	.266	.257	40	-16	0	0		1.000	-8	/3-49,O-6,2	-2.2

■ OLLIE PICKERING
Pickering, Oliver Daniel b: 4/9/1870, Olney, Ill. d: 1/20/52, Vincennes, Ind. BL/TR, 5'11", 170 lbs. Deb: 8/9/1896

YEAR	TM/L	G	AB	R	H	2B	3B	HR	RBI	BB	SO	AVG	OBP	SLG	PRO+	BR/A	SB	CS	SBR	FA	FR	G/POS	TPR
1896	Lou-N	45	165	28	50	6	4	1	22	12	11	.303	.350	.406	103	0	13			.901	3	O-45	0.0
1897	Lou-N	63	246	34	62	5	2	1	20	25		.252	.326	.301	68	-11	20			.937	5	O-62	-0.9
	Cle-N	46	182	33	64	5	2	1	22	11		.352	.392	.418	108	2	18			.950	-0	O-46/2-1	-0.1
	Yr	109	428	67	126	10	4	2	42	36		.294	.353	.350	86	-8	38			.943	4	*O-108/2-1	-1.0
1901	Cle-A	137	547	102	169	25	6	0	40	58		.309	.383	.377	116	15	36			.949	15	*O-137	1.7
1902	Cle-A	69	293	46	75	5	2	3	26	19		.256	.306	.317	76	-9	22			.979	-2	O-64/1-2	-1.6
1903	Phi-A	137	512	93	144	18	6	1	36	53		.281	.353	.346	105	5	40			.970	4	*O-135	0.0
1904	Phi-A	124	455	56	103	10	3	0	30	45		.226	.299	.262	74	-12	17			.939	-1	*O-121	-2.2
1907	StL-A	151	576	63	159	15	10	0	60	35		.276	.321	.337	110	6	15			.949	-11	*O-151	-1.2
1908	Was-A	113	373	45	84	7	4	2	30	28		.225	.285	.282	92	-4	13			.940	-8	*O-98	-1.7
Total	8	885	3349	500	910	96	39	9	286	286	11	.272	.334	.332	97	-8	194			.949	5	O-859/1-2,2	-6.0

■ URBANE PICKERING
Pickering, Urbane Henry "Pick" b: 6/3/1899, Hoxie, Kan. d: 5/13/70, Modesto, Cal. BR/TR, 5'10", 180 lbs. Deb: 4/18/31

YEAR	TM/L	G	AB	R	H	2B	3B	HR	RBI	BB	SO	AVG	OBP	SLG	PRO+	BR/A	SB	CS	SBR	FA	FR	G/POS	TPR
1931	Bos-A	103	341	48	86	13	4	9	52	33	53	.252	.318	.393	91	-5	3	4	-2	.967	-2	3-74,2-16	-0.3
1932	Bos-A	132	457	47	119	28	5	2	40	39	71	.260	.320	.357	77	-16	3	4	-0	.941	-7	*3-126/C-1	-1.5
Total	2	235	798	95	205	41	9	11	92	72	124	.257	.319	.372	83	-21	6	8	-3	.951	-9	3-200/2-16,C	-1.8

■ DAVE PICKETT
Pickett, David T. b: 5/26/1874, Brookline, Mass. d: 4/22/50, Easton, Mass. 5'7.5", 170 lbs. Deb: 7/21/1898

YEAR	TM/L	G	AB	R	H	2B	3B	HR	RBI	BB	SO	AVG	OBP	SLG	PRO+	BR/A	SB	CS	SBR	FA	FR	G/POS	TPR
1898	Bos-N	14	43	3	12	1	0	0	3	6		.279	.380	.302	91	-0	2			.955	-2	O-14	-0.3

YEAR	TM/L	G	AB	R	H	2B	3B	HR	RBI	BB	SO	AVG	OBP	SLG	PRO+	BR/A	SB	CS	SBR	FA	FR	G/POS	TPR

■ JOHN PICKETT   Pickett, John Thomas b: 2/20/1866, Chicago, Ill. d: 7/4/22, Chicago, Ill.   BR/TR, Deb: 6/6/1889

1889	KC-a	53	201	20	45	7	0	0	12	11	21	.224	.271	.259	48	-14	7			.900	-16	O-28,3-14,2	-2.6
1890	Phi-P	100	407	82	114	7	9	4	64	40	17	.280	.347	.371	90	-7	12			.893	-22	*2-100	-1.8
1892	Bal-N	36	141	13	30	2	3	1	12	7	10	.213	.260	.291	65	-6	2			.915	-5	2-36	-1.0
Total	3	189	749	115	189	16	12	5	88	58	48	.252	.311	.326	74	-27	21			.900	-42	2-147/O-28,3	-5.4

■ TY PICKUP   Pickup, Clarence William b: 10/29/1897, Philadelphia, Pa. d: 8/2/74, Philadelphia, Pa. BR/TR, 6', 180 lbs. Deb: 4/30/18

| 1918 | Phi-N | 1 | 1 | 0 | 1 | 0 | 0 | 0 | 0 | 0 | 0 | 1.000 | 1.000 | 1.000 | 478 | 0 | 0 | | | 1.000 | -0 | /O-1 | 0.0 |

■ GRACIE PIERCE   Pierce, Grayson S. b: New York, N.Y. d: 8/28/1894, New York, N.Y. BR/TR, Deb: 5/2/1882 U

1882	Lou-a	9	33	3	10	1	0	0			1	.303	.324	.333	129	1				.864	1	/2-9	0.2
	Bal-a	41	151	8	30	2	1	0			3	.199	.214	.225	52	-7				.796	-10	2-38/O-3,S	-1.5
	Yr	50	184	11	40	3	1	0			4	.217	.234	.245	66	-6				.808	-9	2-47/O-3,S	-1.3
1883	Col-a	11	41	5	7	0	0	0			0	.171	.171	.171	11	-4				.744	-1	/2-6,O-5	-0.4
	NY-N	18	62	3	5	0	1	0	2	1	9	.081	.095	.113	-37	-10				.850	-2	O-18/2-1	-1.1
1884	NY-a	5	20	2	5	1	0	0			0	.250	.250	.300	81	-0				1.000	-5	/O-3,2-3	-0.5
Total	3	84	307	21	57	4	2	0	2	5	9	.186	.199	.212	36	-20				.795	-17	/2-57,O-29,S	-3.3

■ JACK PIERCE   Pierce, Lavern Jack b: 6/2/48, Laurel, Miss. BL/TR, 6', 210 lbs. Deb: 4/27/73

1973	Atl-N	11	20	0	1	0	0	0	0	1	8	.050	.095	.050	-55	-4	0	0	0	1.000	1	/1-6	-0.4
1974	Atl-N	6	9	1	1	0	0	0	0	1	0	.111	.111	.111	-11	-1	0	0	0	.958	0	/1-2	-0.1
1975	Det-A	53	170	19	40	6	1	8	22	20	40	.235	.323	.424	105	1	0	0	0	.971	-4	1-49	-0.7
Total	3	70	199	20	42	6	1	8	22	22	48	.211	.296	.372	83	-5	0	0	0	.973	-3	/1-57	-1.2

■ MAURY PIERCE   Pierce, Maurice b: Baltimore, Md. Deb: 4/23/1884

| 1884 | Was-U | 2 | 7 | 0 | 1 | 0 | 0 | 0 | | | 0 | .143 | .143 | .143 | -23 | -1 | | | | .778 | 0 | /3-2 | -0.1 |

■ ANDY PIERCY   Piercy, Andrew J. b: 8/1856, San Jose, Cal. d: 12/27/32, San Jose, Cal. TR, Deb: 5/12/1881

| 1881 | Chi-N | 2 | 8 | 1 | 2 | 0 | 0 | 0 | 0 | 0 | 1 | .250 | .250 | .250 | 55 | -0 | | | | .750 | -1 | /3-1,2-1 | -0.2 |

■ JIM PIERSALL   Piersall, James Anthony b: 11/14/29, Waterbury, Conn. BR/TR, 6', 175 lbs. Deb: 9/7/50 C

1950	Bos-A	6	7	4	2	0	0	0	0	4	0	.286	.545	.286	107	0	0	0	0	1.000	1	/O-2	0.1
1952	Bos-A	56	161	28	43	8	0	1	16	28	26	.267	.379	.335	93	-1	3	3	-1	.928	-6	S-30,O-22/3	-0.7
1953	Bos-A	151	585	76	159	21	9	3	52	41	52	.272	.329	.354	80	-16	11	10	-3	.987	16	*O-151	-0.9
1954	Bos-A★	133	474	77	135	24	2	8	38	36	42	.285	.339	.395	90	-7	5	1	1	.985	0	*O-126	-1.1
1955	Bos-A	149	515	68	146	25	5	13	62	67	52	.283	.366	.427	104	3	6	1	1	.993	13	*O-147	1.1
1956	Bos-A★	155	601	91	176	40	6	14	87	58	48	.293	.356	.449	99	-2	7	7	-2	.991	18	*O-155	0.5
1957	Bos-A	151	609	103	159	27	5	19	63	62	54	.261	.333	.415	98	-2	14	6	1	.990	13	*O-151	0.2
1958	Bos-A	130	417	55	99	13	5	8	48	42	43	.237	.307	.350	75	-14	12	2	2	.985	9	*O-125	-0.9
1959	Cle-A	100	317	42	78	13	2	4	30	25	31	.246	.305	.338	79	-9	6	3	0	.982	0	O-91/3-1	-1.3
1960	Cle-A	138	486	70	137	12	4	18	66	24	38	.282	.316	.434	104	0	18	5	2	.992	10	*O-134	0.7
1961	Cle-A	121	484	81	156	26	7	6	40	43	46	.322	.380	.442	122	15	8	2	1	.991	16	*O-120	2.5
1962	Was-A	135	471	38	115	20	4	4	31	39	53	.244	.302	.329	70	-20	12	7	-1	.997	7	*O-132	-2.1
1963	Was-A	29	94	9	23	1	0	1	5	6	11	.245	.290	.287	63	-5	4	0	1	1.000	1	O-25	-0.4
	NY-N	40	124	13	24	4	1	1	10	10	14	.194	.254	.266	49	-8	1	2	-1	1.000	-2	O-38	-1.4
	LA-A	20	52	4	16	1	0	0	4	5	6	.308	.368	.327	103	0	0	1	-1	1.000	-2	O-18	-0.4
1964	LA-A	87	255	28	80	11	0	2	13	16	32	.314	.354	.380	116	5	5	3	-0	1.000	-6	O-72	-0.5
1965	Cal-A	53	112	10	30	5	2	2	12	5	15	.268	.305	.402	101	-0	2	2	-1	.984	-4	O-41	-0.6
1966	Cal-A	75	123	14	26	5	0	0	14	13	19	.211	.287	.252	58	-6	1	2	-1	.973	-10	O-63	-2.1
1967	Cal-A	5	3	0	0	0	0	0	0	0	0	.000	.000	.000	-99	-1	0	0	0	1.000	-0	/O-1	-0.1
Total	17	1734	5890	811	1604	256	52	104	591	524	583	.272	.334	.386	92	-66	115	57	0	.990	73	*O-1614/S-30,3	-7.4

■ DAVE PIERSON   Pierson, David P. b: 8/20/1855, Wilkes-Barre, Pa. d: 11/11/22, Trenton, N.J. BR/TR, 5'7", 142 lbs. Deb: 4/25/1876 F

| 1876 | Cin-N | 57 | 233 | 33 | 55 | 4 | 1 | 0 | 13 | 1 | 9 | .236 | .239 | .262 | 78 | -4 | | | | .760 | -2 | C-31,0-30/S32P | -0.5 |

■ DICK PIERSON   Pierson, Edmund Dana b: 10/24/1857, Wilkes-Barre, Pa. d: 7/20/22, Newark, N.J. TR, Deb: 6/23/1885 F

| 1885 | NY-a | 3 | 9 | 1 | 1 | 0 | 0 | 0 | | | 2 | .111 | .273 | .111 | 27 | -1 | | | | .682 | -2 | /2-3 | -0.2 |

■ TONY PIET   Piet, Anthony Francis (b: Anthony Francis Pietruszka) b: 12/7/06, Berwick, Pa. d: 12/1/81, Hinsdale, Ill. BR/TR, 6', 175 lbs. Deb: 8/15/31

1931	Pit-N	44	167	22	50	12	4	0	24	13	24	.299	.354	.419	108	2	10			.987	-4	2-44/S-1	0.0
1932	Pit-N	154	574	66	162	25	8	7	85	46	56	.282	.343	.390	98	-1	19			.970	-28	*2-154	-2.0
1933	Pit-N	107	362	45	117	21	5	1	42	19	28	.323	.367	.417	124	11	12			.955	-5	2-97	1.2
1934	Cin-N	106	421	58	109	20	5	1	38	23	44	.259	.307	.337	74	-15	6			.934	-10	3-51,2-49	-2.0
1935	Cin-N	6	5	2	1	1	0	0	2	0	0	.200	.200	.400	59	-0	0			1.000	-0	/O-1	-0.1
	Chi-A	77	292	47	87	17	5	3	27	33	27	.298	.375	.421	103	2	2	1	0	.975	4	2-59,3-17	1.0
1936	Chi-A	109	352	69	96	15	2	7	42	66	48	.273	.400	.386	92	-2	15	5	2	.966	2	2-68,3-32	0.9
1937	Chi-A	100	332	34	78	15	1	4	38	32	36	.235	.314	.322	61	-20	14	6	1	.939	2	3-86,2-13	-1.4
1938	Det-A	41	80	9	17	6	0	0	14	15	11	.213	.351	.287	58	-5	2	4	-2	.919	2	3-18/2-1	-0.6
Total	8	744	2585	352	717	132	30	23	312	247	274	.277	.350	.378	91	-29	80	16		.967	-37	2-485,3-204/OS	-3.0

■ SANDY PIEZ   Piez, Charles William b: 10/13/1892, New York, N.Y. d: 12/29/30, Atlantic City, N.J BR/TR, 5'10", 170 lbs. Deb: 4/17/14

| 1914 | NY-N | 37 | 8 | 9 | 3 | 0 | 1 | 0 | 3 | 0 | 1 | .375 | .375 | .625 | 202 | 1 | 4 | | | 1.000 | -1 | /O-5 | 0.0 |

■ JOE PIGNATANO   Pignatano, Joseph Benjamin b: 8/4/29, Brooklyn, N.Y. BR/TR, 5'10", 180 lbs. Deb: 4/28/57 C

1957	Bro-N	8	14	0	3	1	0	0	1	0	5	.214	.214	.286	30	-1	0	0	0	1.000	3	/C-6	0.2
1958	LA-N	63	142	18	31	4	0	9	17	16	26	.218	.306	.437	91	-2	0	1	1	1.000	10	C-57	1.0
1959	*LA-N	52	139	17	33	4	1	1	11	21	15	.237	.346	.302	69	-5	1	0	0	.997	7	C-49	0.4
1960	LA-N	58	90	11	21	4	0	2	9	15	17	.233	.343	.344	83	-2	1	1	-0	.984	15	C-40	1.5
1961	KC-A	92	243	31	59	10	3	4	22	36	42	.243	.350	.358	88	-2	2	2	-1	.979	1	C-83/3-2	0.1
1962	SF-N	7	5	2	1	0	0	0	0	0	0	.200	.556	.200	114	1	0	0	0	1.000	-1	/C-7	0.0
	NY-N	27	56	2	13	2	0	0	2	11	11	.232	.259	.268	41	-5	0	0	0	.991	4	C-25	0.0
	Yr	34	61	4	14	2	0	0	2	11	11	.230	.299	.262	51	-4	0	0	0	.992	4	C-32	0.0
Total	6	307	689	81	161	25	4	16	62	94	116	.234	.332	.351	80	-18	4	4	0	.990	39	C-267/3-2	3.2

■ JAY PIKE   Pike, Jacob Emanuel b: Brooklyn, N.Y. BL/TL, Deb: 8/27/1877 F

| 1877 | Har-N | 1 | 4 | 0 | 1 | 0 | 0 | 0 | 0 | 0 | 0 | .250 | .250 | .250 | 65 | -0 | | | | .000 | -1 | /O-1 | -0.1 |

■ JESS PIKE   Pike, Jess Willard b: 7/31/15, Dustin, Okla. d: 3/28/84, San Diego, Cal. BL/TR, 6'3", 175 lbs. Deb: 4/18/46

| 1946 | NY-N | 16 | 41 | 4 | 7 | 1 | 1 | 1 | 6 | 6 | 9 | .171 | .277 | .317 | 68 | -2 | 0 | | | .929 | -2 | O-10 | -0.5 |

■ LIP PIKE   Pike, Lipman Emanuel b: 5/25/1845, New York, N.Y. d: 10/10/1893, Brooklyn, N.Y. BL/TL, 5'8", 158 lbs. Deb: 5/9/1871 FM

1871	Tro-n	28	130	43	49	10	7	4	39	5	7	.377	.400	.654	194	15	3				O-18/2-6,1M	1.0
1872	Bal-n	56	285	68	84	10	4	6	62	3	5	.295	.302	.421	115	3					O-24,2-21/3	0.3
1873	Bal-n	56	287	71	90	18	4	4	48	6	4	.314	.328	.474	133	11					*O-56/2-2	1.0
1874	Har-n	52	238	58	81	24	5	1				.340	.340	.496	155	13					O-27,S-18/2M	1.0
1875	StL-n	70	312	61	107	21	10	0			3	.343	.349	.474	200	32					*O-62/2-8	2.7

YEAR	TM/L	G	AB	R	H	2B	3B	HR	RBI	BB	SO	AVG	OBP	SLG	PRO+	BR/A	SB	CS	SBR	FA	FR	G/POS	TPR
1876	StL-N	63	282	55	91	19	10	1	50	8	9	.323	.341	.472	178	23				.896	-4	*O-62/2-2	1.6
1877	Cin-N	58	262	45	78	12	4	4	23	9	7	.298	.321	.420	148	15				.802	-3	O-38,2-22/SM	1.0
1878	Cin-N	31	145	28	47	5	1	0	11	4	9	.324	.342	.372	149	8				.824	-4	O-31	0.2
	Pro-N	5	22	4	5	0	1	0	4	1	1	.227	.261	.318	90	-0				.788	-3	/2-5	-0.3
	Yr	36	167	32	52	5	2	0	15	5	10	.311	.331	.365	140	7				.824	-7	O-31/2-5	-0.1
1881	Wor-N	5	18	1	2	0	0	0	0	4	3	.111	.273	.111	24	-1				.647	-1	/O-5	-0.2
1887	NY-a	1	4	0	0	0	0	0	0	0		.000	.000	.000	-99	-1	0			1.000	-0	/O-1	-0.1
Total	5 n	262	1252	301	411	83	34	15	149	17	16	.328	.337	.485	154	74	18					O-187/2-44,S31	6.0
Total	5	163	733	133	223	36	16	5	88	26	29	.304	.328	.417	152	43	0			.833	-15	O-137/2-29,S	2.2

■ AL PILARCIK
Pilarcik, Alfred James   b: 7/3/30, Whiting, Ind.   BL/TL, 5'10", 180 lbs.   Deb: 7/13/56

YEAR	TM/L	G	AB	R	H	2B	3B	HR	RBI	BB	SO	AVG	OBP	SLG	PRO+	BR/A	SB	CS	SBR	FA	FR	G/POS	TPR
1956	KC-A	69	239	28	60	10	1	4	22	30	32	.251	.335	.351	81	-6	9	2	2	.976	3	O-67	-0.5
1957	Bal-A	142	407	52	113	16	3	9	49	53	28	.278	.366	.398	116	10	14	7	0	.996	0	*O-126	0.4
1958	Bal-A	141	379	40	92	21	0	1	24	42	37	.243	.322	.306	78	-11	7	3	0	.986	-14	*O-119	-3.1
1959	Bal-A	130	273	37	77	12	1	3	16	30	25	.282	.355	.366	101	1	9	3	1	.978	-16	*O-106	-1.7
1960	Bal-A	104	194	30	48	5	1	4	17	15	16	.247	.315	.345	79	-6	0	2	-1	1.000	-11	O-75	-2.0
1961	KC-A	35	60	9	12	1	1	0	9	6	7	.200	.273	.250	40	-5	1	0	0	1.000	-1	O-21	-0.7
	Chi-A	47	62	9	11	1	0	1	6	9	5	.177	.282	.242	42	-5	1	1	0	.944	-0	O-17	-0.6
	Yr	82	122	18	23	2	1	1	15	15	12	.189	.277	.246	41	-10	2	1	0	.971	-1	O-38	-1.3
Total	6	668	1614	205	413	66	7	22	143	185	150	.256	.336	.346	89	-22	41	18	2	.986	-39	O-531	-8.2

■ ANDY PILNEY
Pilney, Antone James   b: 1/19/13, Frontenac, Kan.   BR/TR, 5'11", 174 lbs.   Deb: 6/12/36

YEAR	TM/L	G	AB	R	H	2B	3B	HR	RBI	BB	SO	AVG	OBP	SLG	PRO+	BR/A	SB	CS	SBR	FA	FR	G/POS	TPR
1936	Bos-N	3	2	0	0	0	0	0	0	0	1	.000	.000	.000	-99	-1	0			.000	0	H	-0.1

■ BABE PINELLI
Pinelli, Ralph Arthur (b: Rinaldo Angelo Paolinelli)   b: 10/18/1895, San Francisco, Cal   d: 10/22/84, Daly City, Cal.   BR/TR, 5'9", 165 lbs.   Deb: 8/3/18   U

YEAR	TM/L	G	AB	R	H	2B	3B	HR	RBI	BB	SO	AVG	OBP	SLG	PRO+	BR/A	SB	CS	SBR	FA	FR	G/POS	TPR
1918	Chi-A	24	78	7	18	1	1	1	7	5	7	.231	.302	.308	83	-2	3			.847	-7	3-24	-0.9
1920	Det-A	102	284	33	65	9	3	0	21	25	16	.229	.296	.282	55	-18	6	8	-3	.954	20	3-74,S-18/2	0.3
1922	Cin-N	156	547	77	167	19	7	1	72	48	37	.305	.368	.331	93	-4	17	22	-8	.945	21	*3-156	1.9
1923	Cin-N	117	423	44	117	14	5	0	51	27	29	.277	.320	.333	74	-16	10	14	-5	.938	9	*3-116	-0.2
1924	Cin-N	144	510	61	156	16	7	0	70	32	32	.306	.353	.365	94	-4	23	17	3	.956	27	*3-143	3.1
1925	Cin-N	130	492	68	139	33	6	2	49	22	28	.283	.316	.386	80	-15	8	19	-9	.945	21	*3-109,S-17	0.6
1926	Cin-N	71	207	26	46	7	4	0	24	15	5	.222	.284	.295	58	-12	2			.978	5	3-40,S-27/2	-0.7
1927	Cin-N	30	76	11	15	2	0	1	4	6	7	.197	.265	.263	43	-6	2			.968	-2	3-15/S-9,2	-0.6
Total	8	774	2617	327	723	101	33	5	298	182	162	.276	.328	.346	79	-77	71	80		.947	91	3-677/S-71,2	3.5

■ LOU PINIELLA
Piniella, Louis Victor   b: 8/28/43, Tampa, Fla.   BR/TR, 6'2", 198 lbs.   Deb: 9/4/64   MC

YEAR	TM/L	G	AB	R	H	2B	3B	HR	RBI	BB	SO	AVG	OBP	SLG	PRO+	BR/A	SB	CS	SBR	FA	FR	G/POS	TPR
1964	Bal-A	4	1	0	0	0	0	0	0	0	0	.000	.000	.000	-99	-0	0	0	0	.000	0	H	0.0
1968	Cle-A	6	5	1	0	0	0	0	1	0	0	.000	.000	.000	-99	-1	0	0	0	1.000	0	/O-2	-0.2
1969	KC-A	135	493	43	139	21	6	11	68	33	56	.282	.331	.416	107	3	2	4	-2	.977	15	*O-129	1.0
1970	KC-A	144	542	54	163	24	5	11	88	35	42	.301	.345	.424	111	7	3	6	-3	.984	4	*O-139/1-1	0.2
1971	KC-A	126	448	43	125	21	5	3	51	21	43	.279	.314	.368	94	-5	5	3	-0	.986	1	*O-115	-1.1
1972	KC-A★	151	574	65	179	33	4	11	72	34	59	.312	.359	.441	138	25	7	2	1	.976	3	*O-150	2.5
1973	KC-A	144	513	53	128	28	1	9	69	30	65	.250	.294	.361	77	-16	5	7	-3	.986	-5	*O-128/D-9	-3.1
1974	NY-A	140	518	71	158	26	0	9	70	32	58	.305	.348	.407	120	12	1	8	-5	.989	11	*O-130/1-1,D	1.4
1975	NY-A	74	199	7	39	4	1	0	22	16	22	.196	.266	.226	41	-15	0	0	0	.986	-3	O-46,D-12	-2.0
1976	*NY-A	100	327	36	92	16	6	3	38	18	34	.281	.323	.394	110	3	0	1	-1	.982	2	O-49,D-38	0.1
1977	*NY-A	103	339	47	112	19	3	12	45	20	31	.330	.369	.510	138	17	2	2	-1	.975	-4	O-51,D-43/1	0.9
1978	*NY-A	130	472	67	148	34	5	6	69	34	36	.314	.362	.445	129	17	3	1	0	.969	2	*O-103,D-23	1.5
1979	NY-A	130	461	49	137	22	2	11	69	17	31	.297	.325	.425	103	1	3	2	-0	.982	3	*O-112,D-16	-0.1
1980	*NY-A	116	321	39	92	18	0	2	27	29	20	.287	.346	.361	96	-1	0	2	-1	.971	-7	O-104/D-7	-1.3
1981	*NY-A	60	159	16	44	9	0	5	18	13	9	.277	.331	.428	119	4	0	1	-1	.986	1	O-36,D-19	0.2
1982	NY-A	102	261	33	80	17	1	6	37	18	18	.307	.354	.448	120	7	0	1	-1	1.000	-1	D-55,O-40	0.2
1983	NY-A	53	148	19	43	9	1	2	16	11	12	.291	.344	.405	109	2	1	1	-0	.959	-2	O-43/D-1	-0.1
1984	NY-A	29	86	8	26	4	1	1	6	7	5	.302	.355	.407	115	2	0	0	0	1.000	1	O-24/D-2	0.2
Total	18	1747	5867	651	1705	305	41	102	766	368	541	.291	.336	.409	109	61	32	41	-15	.981	21	*O-1401,D-231/1	0.3

■ ED PINKHAM
Pinkham, Edward   b: 1849, Brooklyn, N.Y.   TL, 5'7", 142 lbs.   Deb: 5/8/1871

YEAR	TM/L	G	AB	R	H	2B	3B	HR	RBI	BB	SO	AVG	OBP	SLG	PRO+	BR/A	SB	CS	SBR	FA	FR	G/POS	TPR
1871	Chi-n	24	95	27	25	5	5	1	17	18	3	.263	.381	.453	125	2	5					3-16/O-7,P	0.1

■ GEORGE PINKNEY
Pinkney, George Burton   b: 1/11/1862, Orange Prairie, Ill.   d: 11/10/26, Peoria, Ill.   BR/TR, 5'7", 160 lbs.   Deb: 8/16/1884

YEAR	TM/L	G	AB	R	H	2B	3B	HR	RBI	BB	SO	AVG	OBP	SLG	PRO+	BR/A	SB	CS	SBR	FA	FR	G/POS	TPR
1884	Cle-N	36	144	18	45	9	0	0	16	10	7	.313	.357	.375	126	4				.848	-8	2-25,S-11	-0.3
1885	Bro-a	110	447	77	124	16	5	0		27		.277	.328	.336	109	5				.904	-1	2-57,3-51/S	-0.2
1886	Bro-a	141	597	119	156	22	7	0	70			.261	.339	.322	106	6	32			.858	-16	*3-141/P-1	-0.6
1887	Bro-a	138	580	133	155	26	6	3	61			.267	.343	.348	92	-6	59			.890	13	*3-136/S-2	0.8
1888	Bro-a	143	575	134	156	18	8	4	52	66		.271	.358	.351	128	21	51			.898	-26	*3-143	-0.2
1889	*Bro-a	138	545	103	134	25	7	4	82	59	43	.246	.327	.339	90	-7	47			.897	-8	*3-138	-0.9
1890	*Bro-N	126	485	115	150	20	9	7	83	80	19	.309	.411	.431	145	30	47			.933	-15	*3-126	1.8
1891	Bro-N	135	501	80	137	19	6	2	71	66	32	.273	.366	.347	109	8	44			.904	-20	*3-130/S-5	-0.5
1892	StL-N	78	290	31	50	7	3	0	25	36	26	.172	.268	.197	43	-19	4			.888	-8	3-78	-2.2
1893	Lou-N	118	446	64	105	12	6	1	62	50	8	.235	.323	.296	70	-17	12			.923	-2	*3-118	-1.4
Total	10	1163	4610	874	1212	170	56	21	391	525	135	.263	.345	.338	103	26	296			.897	-99	*3-1061/2-82,SP	-3.7

■ VADA PINSON
Pinson, Vada Edward   b: 8/11/36, Memphis, Tenn.   BL/TL, 5'11", 181 lbs.   Deb: 4/15/58   C

YEAR	TM/L	G	AB	R	H	2B	3B	HR	RBI	BB	SO	AVG	OBP	SLG	PRO+	BR/A	SB	CS	SBR	FA	FR	G/POS	TPR
1958	Cin-N	27	96	20	26	7	0	1	8	11	18	.271	.352	.375	88	-1	2	1	0	1.000	2	O-27	-0.1
1959	Cin-N★	154	648	131	205	47	9	20	84	55	98	.316	.371	.509	128	25	21	6	3	.984	20	*O-154	3.9
1960	Cin-N★	154	652	107	187	37	12	20	61	47	96	.287	.339	.472	117	14	32	12	2	.981	9	*O-154	1.9
1961	*Cin-N	154	607	101	208	34	8	16	87	39	63	.343	.383	.504	131	27	23	10	1	.976	19	*O-153	3.7
1962	Cin-N	155	619	107	181	31	7	23	100	45	68	.292	.344	.477	114	11	26	8	3	.989	7	*O-152	1.2
1963	Cin-N	162	652	96	204	37	14	22	106	36	80	.313	.350	.514	141	32	27	8	1	.979	9	*O-162	3.8
1964	Cin-N	156	625	99	166	23	11	23	84	42	99	.266	.317	.448	109	6	8	3	1	.972	4	*O-156	0.4
1965	Cin-N	159	669	97	204	34	10	22	94	43	81	.305	.353	.484	125	21	21	8	2	.992	15	*O-159	3.1
1966	Cin-N	156	618	70	178	35	6	16	76	33	83	.288	.329	.442	103	2	18	10	-1	.964	5	*O-154	-0.1
1967	Cin-N	158	650	90	187	28	13	18	66	26	86	.288	.318	.454	106	4	26	8	3	.986	5	*O-157	0.4
1968	Cin-N	130	499	60	135	29	6	5	48	32	59	.271	.315	.383	102	1	17	11	-2	.978	-1	*O-123	-0.9
1969	StL-N	132	495	58	126	22	6	10	70	35	63	.255	.308	.384	92	-4	4	4	-1	.996	1	*O-124	-1.4
1970	Cle-A	148	574	74	164	28	6	24	82	36	69	.286	.322	.481	113	8	7	6	1	.982	5	*O-141/1-7	0.4
1971	Cle-A	146	566	60	149	23	4	11	35	21	58	.263	.297	.376	82	-14	25	6	4	.978	4	*O-141/1-3	-1.5
1972	Cal-A	136	484	56	133	24	2	7	49	30	54	.275	.324	.376	114	7	17	6	2	.991	-5	*O-134/1-1	-0.3
1973	Cal-A	124	466	56	121	14	4	8	57	20	55	.260	.290	.367	91	-8	5	4	1	.965	-4	*O-120	-0.7
1974	KC-A	115	406	46	112	18	2	6	41	21	45	.276	.315	.374	92	-5	21	5	3	.980	-5	*O-110/1-1,D	-1.2
1975	KC-A	103	319	38	71	14	5	4	22	10	21	.223	.251	.335	63	-17	5	6	-2	.993	-3	O-82/1-4,D	-2.6
Total	18	2469	9645	1366	2757	485	127	256	1170	574	1196	.286	.330	.442	110	106	305	122	18	.981	87	*O-2403/1-16,D	8.8

YEAR	TM/L	G	AB	R	H	2B	3B	HR	RBI	BB	SO	AVG	OBP	SLG	PRO+	BR/A	SB	CS	SBR	FA	FR	G/POS	TPR

■ WALLY PIPP Pipp, Walter Clement b: 2/17/1893, Chicago, Ill. d: 1/11/65, Grand Rapids, Mich BL/TL, 6'1", 180 lbs. Deb: 6/29/13

1913	Det-A	12	31	3	5	0	3	0	5	2	6	.161	.235	.355	73	-1	0			.977	-1	1-10	-0.2
1915	NY-A	136	479	59	118	20	13	4	60	66	81	.246	.339	.367	112	7	18	7	1	.992	3	*1-134	0.8
1916	NY-A	151	545	70	143	20	14	**12**	93	54	82	.262	.331	.417	122	12	16			.992	6	*1-148	1.3
1917	NY-A	155	587	82	143	29	12	**9**	70	60	66	.244	.320	.380	112	7	11			.990	4	*1-155	0.7
1918	NY-A	91	349	48	106	15	9	2	44	22	34	.304	.345	.415	127	9	11			.988	0	1-91	0.7
1919	NY-A	138	523	74	144	23	10	7	50	39	42	.275	.330	.398	103	1	9			.991	1	*1-138	-0.3
1920	NY-A	153	610	109	171	30	14	11	76	48	54	.280	.339	.430	99	-3	4	10	-5	.991	0	*1-153	-1.1
1921	*NY-A	153	588	96	174	35	9	8	97	45	28	.296	.347	.427	94	-6	17	10	-1	.991	-4	*1-153	-1.4
1922	*NY-A	152	577	96	190	32	10	9	90	56	32	.329	.392	.466	120	18	7	12	-5	.993	-5	*1-152	0.1
1923	*NY-A	144	569	79	173	19	8	6	108	26	28	.304	.352	.397	95	-5	6	13	-6	.992	-4	*1-144	-2.1
1924	NY-A	153	589	88	174	30	**19**	9	114	51	36	.295	.352	.457	108	4	12	5	1	**.994**	2	*1-153	-0.3
1925	NY-A	62	178	19	41	8	3	3	24	13	12	.230	.286	.348	61	-11	3	3	-1	.991	4	1-47	-1.0
1926	Cin-N	155	574	72	167	22	6	6	99	49	26	.291	.352	.413	108	6	8			.992	2	*1-155	-0.1
1927	Cin-N	122	449	49	115	19	6	2	41	32	11	.260	.309	.343	77	-15	2			**.996**	0	*1-114	-2.2
1928	Cin-N	95	272	30	77	11	3	2	26	23	13	.283	.341	.368	87	-5	1			.989	1	1-72	-1.0
Total	15	1872	6914	974	1941	311	148	90	997	596	551	.281	.341	.408	104	18	125	<u>60</u>		.992	9	*1-1819	-6.1

■ JIM PIRIE Pirie, James Moir b: 3/31/1853, Ontario, Canada d: 6/2/34, Dundas, Ont., Can. 5'8", 169 lbs. Deb: 9/25/1883

| 1883 | Phi-N | 5 | 19 | 1 | 3 | 0 | 0 | 0 | 0 | 0 | 2 | .158 | .158 | .158 | -4 | -2 | | | | .577 | -4 | /S-5 | -0.6 |

■ GREG PIRKL Pirkl, Gregory Daniel b: 8/7/70, Long Beach, Cal. BR/TR, 6'5", 225 lbs. Deb: 8/13/93

1993	Sea-A	7	23	1	4	0	0	1	4	0	4	.174	.174	.304	25	-2	0	0	0	1.000	1	/1-5,D-2	-0.2
1994	Sea-A	19	53	7	14	3	0	6	11	1	12	.264	.291	.660	133	2	0	0	0	.983	-1	D-10/1-7	0.0
Total	2	26	76	8	18	3	0	7	15	1	16	.237	.256	.553	102	-0	0	0	0	.990	-0	/D-12,1-12	-0.2

■ JIM PISONI Pisoni, James Pete b: 8/14/29, St.Louis, Mo. BR/TR, 5'10", 169 lbs. Deb: 9/25/53

1953	StL-A	3	12	1	1	0	0	1	1	0	5	.083	.083	.333	8	-2	0	0	0	1.000	-0	/O-3	-0.2
1956	KC-A	10	30	4	8	0	0	2	5	2	8	.267	.313	.467	103	-0	0	0	0	.966	4	/O-9	0.4
1957	KC-A	44	97	14	23	2	2	3	12	10	17	.237	.321	.392	92	-1	0	0	0	.989	-3	O-44	-0.6
1959	Mil-N	9	24	4	4	1	0	0	2	6	7	.167	.231	.208	20	-3	0	0	0	.941	-1	/O-9	-0.4
	NY-A	17	17	2	3	0	1	0	1	1	9	.176	.222	.294	42	-1	0	0	0	1.000	-3	O-15	-0.4
1960	NY-A	20	9	1	1	0	0	1	0	1	2	.111	.200	.111	-14	-1	0	0	0	.938	-5	O-18	-0.7
Total	5	103	189	26	40	3	3	6	20	16	47	.212	.280	.354	71	-8	0	0	0	.978	-7	/O-98	-1.9

■ ALEX PITKO Pitko, Alexander "Spunk" b: 11/22/14, Burlington, N.J. BR/TR, 5'10", 180 lbs. Deb: 9/11/38

1938	Phi-N	7	19	2	6	1	0	0	2	3	3	.316	.409	.368	118	1	1			.889	-2	/O-7	-0.1
1939	Was-A	4	8	0	1	0	0	0	1	1	3	.125	.222	.125	-10	-1	0	0	0	1.000	-1	/O-3	-0.2
Total	2	11	27	2	7	1	0	0	3	4	6	.259	.355	.296	80	-1	1	<u>0</u>		.917	-3	/O-10	-0.3

■ JAKE PITLER Pitler, Jacob Albert b: 4/22/1894, New York, N.Y. d: 2/3/68, Binghamton, N.Y. BR/TR, 5'8", 150 lbs. Deb: 5/30/17 C

1917	Pit-N	109	382	39	89	8	5	0	23	30	24	.233	.297	.280	75	-11	6			**.966**	-12	*2-106/O-3	-1.9
1918	Pit-N	2	1	1	0	0	0	0	0	1	0	.000	.500	.000	55	-0	2			.667	0	/2-1	0.1
Total	2	111	383	40	89	8	5	0	23	31	24	.232	.298	.279	75	-11	8			.962	-11	2-107/O-3	-1.8

■ CHRIS PITTARO Pittaro, Christopher Francis b: 9/16/61, Trenton, N.J. BB/TR, 5'11", 170 lbs. Deb: 4/8/85

1985	Det-A	28	62	10	15	3	1	0	7	5	13	.242	.299	.323	71	-2	1	1	-0	.881	-1	3-22/2-4,D	-0.3
1986	Min-A	11	21	0	2	0	0	0	0	0	8	.095	.095	.095	-47	-4	0	0	0	.969	2	/2-8,S-4	-0.2
1987	Min-A	14	12	6	4	0	0	0	0	1	0	.333	.385	.333	90	-0	1	0	0	1.000	2	/2-8,D-2	0.2
Total	3	53	95	16	21	3	1	0	7	6	21	.221	.267	.274	48	-7	2	1	0	.968	4	/3-22,2-20,SD	-0.3

■ PINKY PITTINGER Pittinger, Clarke Alonzo b: 2/24/1899, Hudson, Mich. d: 11/4/77, Ft.Lauderdale, Fla. BR/TR, 5'10", 160 lbs. Deb: 4/15/21

1921	Bos-A	40	91	6	18	1	0	0	5	4	13	.198	.232	.209	13	-12	3	2	-0	.985	3	O-27/3-3,S2	-1.0
1922	Bos-A	66	186	16	48	3	0	0	7	9	10	.258	.299	.274	51	-13	2	5	-2	.920	-3	3-33,S-29	-0.6
1923	Bos-A	60	177	15	38	5	0	0	15	5	10	.215	.236	.243	26	-19	3	1	0	.959	-11	2-42,S-10/3	-2.8
1925	Chi-N	59	173	21	54	7	2	0	15	12	7	.312	.364	.376	88	-3	5	4	-1	.940	4	S-24,3-24	0.4
1927	Cin-N	31	84	17	23	5	0	1	10	2	5	.274	.291	.369	78	-3	4			.963	3	2-20/S-9,3	0.1
1928	Cin-N	40	38	12	9	1	0	0	4	0	1	.237	.237	.289	37	-4	2			.892	8	S-12/2-4,3	0.5
1929	Cin-N	77	210	31	62	11	0	0	27	5	4	.295	.318	.348	68	-11	8			.956	2	S-50/3-8,2	-0.2
Total	7	373	959	118	252	32	3	1	83	37	50	.263	.294	.306	55	-64	27	<u>12</u>		.938	13	S-136/3-77,2O	-3.6

■ JOE PITTMAN Pittman, Joseph Wayne b: 1/1/54, Houston, Tex. BR/TR, 6'1", 180 lbs. Deb: 4/25/81

1981	*Hou-N	52	135	11	38	4	2	0	7	11	16	.281	.336	.341	97	-1	4	4	-1	.980	-9	2-35/3-4	-1.0
1982	Hou-N	15	10	0	2	1	0	0	0	0	2	.200	.200	.300	41	-1	0	0	0	1.000	0	/3-3,O-1	-0.1
	SD-N	55	118	16	30	2	0	0	7	9	13	.254	.307	.271	66	-5	8	3	1	.964	-3	2-30,S-13	-0.6
	Yr	70	128	16	32	3	0	0	7	9	15	.250	.299	.273	65	-6	8	3	1	.964	-2	2-30,S-13/3O	-0.7
1984	SF-N	17	22	2	5	0	0	0	2	0	6	.227	.227	.227	29	-2	1	1	-0	.900	-3	/S-6,2-5,3	-0.5
Total	3	139	285	29	75	7	2	0	16	20	37	.263	.311	.302	77	-9	13	8	-1	.974	-14	/2-70,S-19,3O	-2.2

■ GAYLEN PITTS Pitts, Gaylen Richard b: 6/6/46, Wichita, Kan. BR/TR, 6'1", 175 lbs. Deb: 5/12/74 C

1974	Oak-A	18	41	4	10	3	0	0	3	5	4	.244	.326	.317	92	-0	0	0	0	.909	0	3-11/2-6,1	0.0
1975	Oak-A	10	3	1	1	1	0	0	1	0	0	.333	.333	.667	181	-0	0	0	0	.800	2	/3-6,S-2,2	0.2
Total	2	28	44	5	11	4	0	0	4	5	4	.250	.327	.341	98	-0	0	0	0	.895	2	/3-17,2-7,S1	0.2

■ HERMAN PITZ Pitz, Herman b: 7/18/1865, Brooklyn, N.Y. d: 9/3/24, Far Rockaway, N.Y. 5'6", 140 lbs. Deb: 4/18/1890

1890	Bro-a	61	189	26	26	0	0	0		45		.138	.312	.138	34	-13	25			.885	-7	C-34,3-16/OS2	-1.4
	Syr-a	29	95	17	21	0	0	0		13		.221	.321	.221	67	-3	14			.929	-5	C-27/S-1,O	-0.5
	Yr	90	284	43	47	0	0	0		58		.165	.315	.165	44	-16	39			.906	-12	C-61,3-16,O/S2	-1.9

■ PHIL PLANTIER Plantier, Phillip Alan b: 1/27/69, Manchester, N.H. BL/TR, 6', 175 lbs. Deb: 8/21/90

1990	Bos-A	14	15	1	2	1	0	0	3	4	6	.133	.350	.200	55	-1	0	0	0	.000	-0	/O-1,D-4	-0.1
1991	Bos-A	53	148	27	49	7	1	11	35	23	38	.331	.424	.615	175	15	1	0	0	.976	-0	O-40/D-5	1.4
1992	Bos-A	108	349	46	86	19	0	7	30	44	83	.246	.334	.361	89	-5	2	3	-1	.975	-2	O-76,D-23	-0.6
1993	SD-N	138	462	67	111	20	1	34	100	61	124	.240	.338	.509	121	13	4	5	-2	.990	14	*O-134	2.2
1994	SD-N	96	341	44	75	21	0	18	41	36	91	.220	.304	.440	92	-5	3	1	0	.988	6	O-91	-0.1
Total	5	409	1315	185	323	68	2	70	209	168	342	.246	.338	.460	110	17	10	9	-2	.984	21	O-342/D-32	2.8

■ DON PLARSKI Plarski, Donald Joseph b: 11/9/29, Chicago, Ill. d: 12/29/81, St.Louis, Mo. BR/TR, 5'6", 160 lbs. Deb: 7/20/55

| 1955 | KC-A | 8 | 11 | 0 | 1 | 0 | 0 | 0 | 0 | 0 | 1 | .091 | .091 | .091 | -50 | -2 | 1 | 0 | 0 | 1.000 | -2 | /O-6 | -0.4 |

■ ELMO PLASKETT Plaskett, Elmo Alexander b: 6/27/38, Frederiksted, V.I. BR/TR, 5'10", 195 lbs. Deb: 9/8/62

1962	Pit-N	7	14	2	4	0	0	1	3	1	3	.286	.333	.500	120	0	0	0	0	1.000	-1	/C-4	-0.1
1963	Pit-N	10	21	1	3	0	0	0	2	0	5	.143	.143	.143	-17	-3	0	0	0	1.000	-2	/C-5,3-1	-0.5
Total	2	17	35	3	7	0	0	1	5	1	8	.200	.222	.286	41	-3	0	0	0	1.000	-3	/C-9,3-1	-0.6

YEAR	TM/L	G	AB	R	H	2B	3B	HR	RBI	BB	SO	AVG	OBP	SLG	PRO+	BR/A	SB	CS	SBR	FA	FR	G/POS	TPR

■ WHITEY PLATT
Platt, Mizell George   b: 8/21/20, W.Palm Beach, Fla.   d: 7/27/70, W.Palm Beach, Fla   BR/TR, 6'2", 195 lbs.   Deb: 9/16/42

YEAR	TM/L	G	AB	R	H	2B	3B	HR	RBI	BB	SO	AVG	OBP	SLG	PRO+	BR/A	SB	CS	SBR	FA	FR	G/POS	TPR
1942	Chi-N	4	16	1	1	0	0	0	2	0	3	.063	.063	.063	-66	-3	0			1.000	0	/O-4	-0.4
1943	Chi-N	20	41	2	7	3	0	0	2	1	9	.171	.190	.244	25	-4	0			.952	-3	O-14	-0.9
1946	Chi-A	84	247	28	62	8	5	3	32	17	34	.251	.307	.360	89	-4	1	7	-4	.971	-3	O-61	-1.5
1948	StL-A	123	454	57	123	22	10	7	82	39	51	.271	.331	.410	94	-6	1	4	-2	.948	-6	*O-114	-2.0
1949	StL-A	102	244	29	63	8	3	3	29	24	27	.258	.325	.344	74	-10	0	1	-1	.986	0	O-59/1-2	-1.2
Total	5	333	1002	117	256	41	17	13	147	81	122	.255	.314	.369	83	-27	2	<u>12</u>		.964	-12	O-252/1-2	-6.0

■ AL PLATTE
Platte, Alfred Frederick Joseph   b: 4/13/1890, Grand Rapids, Mich   d: 8/29/76, Grand Rapids, Mich   BL/TL, 5'7", 160 lbs.   Deb: 9/1/13

YEAR	TM/L	G	AB	R	H	2B	3B	HR	RBI	BB	SO	AVG	OBP	SLG	PRO+	BR/A	SB	CS	SBR	FA	FR	G/POS	TPR
1913	Det-A	9	18	1	2	1	0	0	1	0	1	.111	.158	.167	-5	-2	0			.800	-1	/O-5	-0.4

■ RANCE PLESS
Pless, Rance   b: 12/6/25, Greeneville, Tenn.   BR/TR, 6', 145 lbs.   Deb: 4/21/56

YEAR	TM/L	G	AB	R	H	2B	3B	HR	RBI	BB	SO	AVG	OBP	SLG	PRO+	BR/A	SB	CS	SBR	FA	FR	G/POS	TPR
1956	KC-A	48	85	4	23	3	1	0	9	10	13	.271	.354	.329	81	-2	0	1	-1	1.000	2	1-15/3-5	-0.1

■ HERB PLEWS
Plews, Herbert Eugene   b: 6/14/28, Helena, Mont.   BL/TR, 5'11", 160 lbs.   Deb: 4/18/56

YEAR	TM/L	G	AB	R	H	2B	3B	HR	RBI	BB	SO	AVG	OBP	SLG	PRO+	BR/A	SB	CS	SBR	FA	FR	G/POS	TPR
1956	Was-A	91	256	24	69	10	7	1	25	26	40	.270	.339	.375	88	-4	1	2	-1	.947	-3	2-66/S-5,3	-0.4
1957	Was-A	104	329	51	89	19	4	1	26	28	39	.271	.331	.362	90	-4	0	3	-2	.979	-15	2-79,3-11/S	-1.5
1958	Was-A	111	380	46	98	12	6	2	29	17	45	.258	.291	.337	74	-14	2	3	-1	.976	-21	2-64,3-36	-3.3
1959	Was-A	27	40	4	9	0	0	0	2	3	5	.225	.279	.225	40	-3	0	1	-1	.971	1	/2-6	-0.2
	Bos-A	13	12	0	1	1	0	0	0	0	4	.083	.083	.167	-32	-2	0	0	0	.833	1	/2-2	-0.1
	Yr	40	52	4	10	1	0	0	2	3	9	.192	.236	.212	24	-5	0	1	-1	.951	2	/2-8	-0.3
Total	4	346	1017	125	266	42	17	4	82	74	133	.262	.314	.348	80	-28	3	9	-5	.967	-36	2-217/3-49,S	-5.5

■ WALTER PLOCK
Plock, Walter S.   b: 7/2/1869, Philadelphia, Pa.   d: 4/28/1900, Richmond, Va.   6'3",   Deb: 8/21/1891

YEAR	TM/L	G	AB	R	H	2B	3B	HR	RBI	BB	SO	AVG	OBP	SLG	PRO+	BR/A	SB	CS	SBR	FA	FR	G/POS	TPR
1891	Phi-N	2	5	2	2	0	0	0	0	0	1	.400	.500	.400	159	0	0			.000	-1	/O-2	-0.1

■ BILL PLUMMER
Plummer, William Francis   b: 3/21/47, Oakland, Cal.   BR/TR, 6'1", 200 lbs.   Deb: 4/19/68   MC

YEAR	TM/L	G	AB	R	H	2B	3B	HR	RBI	BB	SO	AVG	OBP	SLG	PRO+	BR/A	SB	CS	SBR	FA	FR	G/POS	TPR
1968	Chi-N	2	2	0	0	0	0	0	0	0	1	.000	.000	.000	-94	-0	0	0	0	1.000	0	/C-1	0.0
1970	Cin-N	4	8	0	1	0	0	0	0	0	2	.125	.222	.125	-4	-1	0	0	0	.857	-2	/C-4	-0.3
1971	Cin-N	10	19	0	0	0	0	0	0	0	4	.000	.000	.000	-99	-5	0	0	0	1.000	0	/C-4,3-2	-0.5
1972	Cin-N	38	102	8	19	4	0	2	9	4	20	.186	.217	.284	44	-8	0	0	0	.994	0	C-36/1-1,3	-0.7
1973	Cin-N	50	119	8	18	3	0	2	11	18	26	.151	.268	.227	41	-9	1	0	0	.994	-1	C-42/3-5	-0.9
1974	Cin-N	50	120	7	27	7	0	2	10	6	21	.225	.262	.333	67	-6	0	0	0	.974	-5	C-49/3-1	0.1
1975	Cin-N	65	159	17	29	7	0	1	19	24	28	.182	.297	.245	51	-10	1	0	0	.990	-3	C-63	-1.1
1976	Cin-N	56	153	16	38	6	1	4	19	14	36	.248	.311	.379	93	-2	0	2	-1	.977	6	C-54	0.5
1977	Cin-N	51	117	10	16	5	0	1	7	17	34	.137	.246	.205	22	-13	1	1	-0	.986	-1	C-50	-1.3
1978	Sea-A	41	93	6	20	5	0	2	7	12	19	.215	.305	.333	80	-2	0	0	0	.978	-5	C-40	-0.7
Total	10	367	892	72	168	37	1	14	82	95	191	.188	.269	.279	53	-57	4	3	-1	.984	0	C-343/3-9,1	-4.9

■ BIFF POCOROBA
Pocoroba, Biff   b: 7/25/53, Burbank, Cal.   BB/TR, 5'10", 180 lbs.   Deb: 4/25/75

YEAR	TM/L	G	AB	R	H	2B	3B	HR	RBI	BB	SO	AVG	OBP	SLG	PRO+	BR/A	SB	CS	SBR	FA	FR	G/POS	TPR
1975	Atl-N	67	188	15	48	7	1	1	22	20	11	.255	.327	.319	77	-5	0	0	0	.970	-4	C-62	-0.8
1976	Atl-N	54	174	16	42	7	0	0	14	19	12	.241	.316	.282	66	-7	1	0	0	.978	4	C-54	-0.1
1977	Atl-N	113	321	46	93	24	1	8	44	57	27	.290	.398	.445	113	7	3	4	-2	.989	2	*C-100	1.1
1978	Atl-N★	92	289	21	70	8	0	6	34	29	14	.242	.316	.332	73	-10	0	3	-2	.990	1	C-79	-1.0
1979	Atl-N	28	38	6	12	4	0	0	4	7	0	.316	.422	.421	122	1	1	1	-0	.933	-2	/C-7	0.2
1980	Atl-N	70	83	4	22	4	0	2	8	11	11	.265	.351	.386	102	0	0	1	-0	.934	-1	C-10	0.1
1981	Atl-N	57	122	4	22	4	0	0	8	12	15	.180	.265	.213	36	-10	0	0	0	.938	-5	3-21/C-9	-1.6
1982	*Atl-N	56	120	5	33	7	0	2	22	13	12	.275	.351	.383	101	0	0	0	0	.988	-1	C-36/3-2	-0.3
1983	Atl-N	55	120	11	32	6	0	2	16	12	7	.267	.333	.367	87	-2	0	0	0	.983	-3	C-34	-0.3
1984	Atl-N	4	2	1	0	0	0	0	0	0	0	.000	.000	.000	48	0	0	0	0	.000	0	/H	0.0
Total	10	596	1457	132	374	71	2	21	172	182	109	.257	.342	.351	86	-25	6	8	-3	.982	-9	C-391/3-23	-2.7

■ MIKE POEPPING
Poepping, Michael Harold   b: 8/7/50, Little Falls, Minn.   BR/TR, 6'6", 230 lbs.   Deb: 9/6/75

YEAR	TM/L	G	AB	R	H	2B	3B	HR	RBI	BB	SO	AVG	OBP	SLG	PRO+	BR/A	SB	CS	SBR	FA	FR	G/POS	TPR
1975	Min-A	14	37	5	5	1	0	1	5	1	7	.135	.238	.162	15	-4	0	0	0	.950	-2	O-13	-0.7

■ JIMMY POFAHL
Pofahl, James Willard   b: 6/18/17, Faribault, Minn.   d: 9/14/84, Owatonna, Minn.   BR/TR, 5'11", 185 lbs.   Deb: 4/16/40

YEAR	TM/L	G	AB	R	H	2B	3B	HR	RBI	BB	SO	AVG	OBP	SLG	PRO+	BR/A	SB	CS	SBR	FA	FR	G/POS	TPR
1940	Was-A	119	406	34	95	23	5	2	36	37	55	.234	.298	.330	67	-21	5	0	1	.952	-5	*S-112/2-4	-1.5
1941	Was-A	22	75	9	14	3	2	0	6	10	11	.187	.282	.280	52	-5	1	0	0	.934	-4	S-21	-0.7
1942	Was-A	84	283	22	59	7	2	0	28	29	30	.208	.282	.247	50	-18	4	3	-1	.956	1	S-49,2-15,3	-1.5
Total	3	225	764	65	168	33	9	2	70	76	96	.220	.290	.295	59	-44	7	3	0	.951	-8	S-182/2-19,3	-3.7

■ JOHN POFF
Poff, John William   b: 10/23/52, Chillicothe, Ohio   BL/TL, 6'2", 190 lbs.   Deb: 9/8/79

YEAR	TM/L	G	AB	R	H	2B	3B	HR	RBI	BB	SO	AVG	OBP	SLG	PRO+	BR/A	SB	CS	SBR	FA	FR	G/POS	TPR
1979	Phi-N	12	19	2	2	1	0	0	1	1	4	.105	.150	.158	-15	-3	0	0	0	.875	-0	/O-4,1-1	-0.4
1980	Mil-A	19	68	7	17	1	2	1	7	3	7	.250	.282	.368	79	-2	0	0	0	1.000	-1	/O-7,1-3,D	-0.3
Total	2	31	87	9	19	2	2	1	8	4	11	.218	.253	.322	57	-5	0	0	0	.957	-1	/O-11,D-7,1	-0.7

■ AARON POINTER
Pointer, Aaron Elton "Hawk"   b: 4/19/42, Little Rock, Ark.   BR/TR, 6'2", 185 lbs.   Deb: 9/22/63

YEAR	TM/L	G	AB	R	H	2B	3B	HR	RBI	BB	SO	AVG	OBP	SLG	PRO+	BR/A	SB	CS	SBR	FA	FR	G/POS	TPR
1963	Hou-N	2	5	0	1	0	0	0	0	0	1	.200	.200	.200	17	-1	0	0	0	1.000	-0	/O-1	-0.1
1966	Hou-N	11	26	5	9	1	0	1	5	5	6	.346	.469	.500	182	3	1	1	-0	1.000	2	O-11	0.4
1967	Hou-N	27	70	6	11	4	0	1	10	13	26	.157	.298	.257	62	-3	1	0	0	.951	1	O-22	-0.3
Total	3	40	101	11	21	5	0	2	15	18	33	.208	.339	.317	91	-0	2	1	0	.966	3	/O-34	0.0

■ HUGH POLAND
Poland, Hugh Reid   b: 1/19/13, Tompkinsville, Ky.   d: 3/30/84, Guthrie, Ky.   BL/TR, 5'11.5", 185 lbs.   Deb: 4/22/43

YEAR	TM/L	G	AB	R	H	2B	3B	HR	RBI	BB	SO	AVG	OBP	SLG	PRO+	BR/A	SB	CS	SBR	FA	FR	G/POS	TPR
1943	NY-N	4	12	1	1	0	0	0	2	1	0	.083	.154	.250	16	-1	0			.889	-2	/C-4	-0.3
	Bos-N	44	141	5	27	7	0	0	13	4	11	.191	.214	.241	32	-13	0			.973	-2	C-38	-1.3
	Yr	48	153	6	28	7	1	0	15	5	11	.183	.209	.242	30	-14	0			.969	-4	C-42	-1.6
1944	Bos-N	8	23	1	3	1	0	0	2	0	1	.130	.130	.174	-14	-3	0			.939	1	/C-6	-0.2
1946	Bos-N	4	6	0	1	0	0	0	1	0	0	.167	.167	.333	40	-1	0			1.000	-1	/C-2	0.0
1947	Phi-N	4	8	0	0	0	0	0	0	0	0	.000	.000	.000	-99	-2	0			1.000	1	/C-2	-0.2
	Cin-N	16	18	1	6	1	0	0	2	1	4	.333	.368	.389	102	1	0			.667	-1	/C-3	-0.1
	Yr	20	26	1	6	1	0	0	2	1	4	.231	.259	.269	41	-2	0			.867	-1	/C-5	-0.3
1948	Cin-N	3	3	0	1	0	0	0	0	0	0	.333	.333	.333	84	-0	0			.000	0	/H	0.0
Total	5	83	211	8	39	10	1	0	19	6	16	.185	.207	.242	28	-20	0			.958	-4	C-55	-2.1

■ MARK POLHEMUS
Polhemus, Mark S. "Humpty Dumpty"   b: 10/4/1862, Brooklyn, N.Y.   d: 11/12/23, Lynn, Mass.   5'6.5", 185 lbs.   Deb: 7/13/1887

YEAR	TM/L	G	AB	R	H	2B	3B	HR	RBI	BB	SO	AVG	OBP	SLG	PRO+	BR/A	SB	CS	SBR	FA	FR	G/POS	TPR
1887	Ind-N	20	75	6	18	1	0	0	8	2	9	.240	.260	.253	45	-5	4			.744	0	O-20	-0.5

■ GUS POLIDOR
Polidor, Gustavo Adolfo (Gonzalez)   b: 10/26/61, Caracas, Venezuela   BR/TR, 6', 170 lbs.   Deb: 9/7/85

YEAR	TM/L	G	AB	R	H	2B	3B	HR	RBI	BB	SO	AVG	OBP	SLG	PRO+	BR/A	SB	CS	SBR	FA	FR	G/POS	TPR
1985	Cal-A	2	1	1	1	0	0	0	0	0	0	1.000	1.000	1.000	452	0	0	0	0	1.000	0	/S-1,O-1	0.0
1986	Cal-A	6	19	1	5	1	0	0	1	1	0	.263	.300	.316	69	-1	0	0	0	1.000	0	/2-4,S-1,3	-0.1
1987	Cal-A	63	137	12	36	3	0	2	15	2	15	.263	.279	.328	62	-8	0	0	0	.983	-6	S-46,3-11/2	-1.0
1988	Cal-A	54	81	4	12	3	0	0	4	3	11	.148	.179	.185	2	-11	0	0	0	1.000	3	S-25,3-22/2D	-1.0
1989	Mil-A	79	175	15	34	7	0	0	14	6	18	.194	.230	.234	31	-16	3	0	1	.923	3	3-30,2-29,S/D	-1.1
1990	Mil-A	18	15	0	1	0	0	0	1	0	1	.067	.067	.067	-63	-3	0	0	0	1.000	2	3-14/2-2,S	-0.2

YEAR	TM/L	G	AB	R	H	2B	3B	HR	RBI	BB	SO	AVG	OBP	SLG	PRO+	BR/A	SB	CS	SBR	FA	FR	G/POS	TPR
1993	Fla-N	7	6	0	1	1	0	0	0	0	2	.167	.167	.333	28	-1	0	0	0	.000	-0	/2-1,3-1	-0.1
Total	7	229	434	33	90	15	0	2	35	12	47	.207	.234	.256	35	-38	3	0	1	.970	-1	/S-96,3-79,2DO	-3.5

■ NICK POLLY
Polly, Nicholas (b: Nicholas Joseph Polachanin) b: 4/18/17, Chicago, Ill. d: 1/17/93, Chicago, Ill. BR/TR, 5'11", 190 lbs. Deb: 9/11/37

YEAR	TM/L	G	AB	R	H	2B	3B	HR	RBI	BB	SO	AVG	OBP	SLG	PRO+	BR/A	SB	CS	SBR	FA	FR	G/POS	TPR
1937	Bro-N	10	18	2	4	0	0	0	2	0	1	.222	.222	.222	21	-2	0			.850	2	/3-7	0.0
1945	Bos-A	4	7	0	1	0	0	0	1	0	0	.143	.143	.143	-17	-1	0	0	0	1.000	-0	/3-2	-0.1
Total	2	14	25	2	5	0	0	0	3	0	1	.200	.200	.200	11	-3	0	0		.870	2	/3-9	-0.1

■ LUIS POLONIA
Polonia, Luis Andrew (Almonte) b: 10/12/64, Santiago, D.R. BL/TL, 5'8", 155 lbs. Deb: 4/24/87

YEAR	TM/L	G	AB	R	H	2B	3B	HR	RBI	BB	SO	AVG	OBP	SLG	PRO+	BR/A	SB	CS	SBR	FA	FR	G/POS	TPR
1987	Oak-A	125	435	78	125	16	10	4	49	32	64	.287	.336	.398	100	-0	29	7	5	.979	-1	*O-104,D-18	-0.1
1988	*Oak-A	84	288	51	84	11	4	2	27	21	40	.292	.340	.378	104	2	24	9	2	.988	1	O-76/D-2	0.2
1989	Oak-A	59	206	31	59	6	4	1	17	9	15	.286	.316	.369	96	-2	13	4	2	.985	5	O-55	0.3
	NY-A	66	227	39	71	11	2	2	29	16	29	.313	.363	.405	118	5	9	4	0	.982	4	O-53/D-9	0.8
	Yr	125	433	70	130	17	6	3	46	25	44	.300	.341	.388	108	4	22	8	2	.984	8	*O-108/D-9	1.1
1990	NY-A	11	22	2	7	0	0	0	3	0	1	.318	.318	.318	78	-1	1	0	0	.000	-0	/D-4	0.0
	Cal-A	109	381	50	128	7	9	2	32	25	42	.336	.378	.417	125	13	20	14	-2	.980	-5	O-85,D-11	0.3
	Yr	120	403	52	135	7	9	2	35	25	43	.335	.375	.412	122	12	21	14	-2	.980	-5	O-85,D-11/H	0.3
1991	Cal-A	150	604	92	179	28	8	2	50	52	74	.296	.353	.379	103	3	48	23	1	.981	1	*O-143/D-4	0.1
1992	Cal-A	149	577	83	165	17	4	0	35	45	64	.286	.339	.329	87	-9	51	21	3	.980	2	O-99,D-47	-0.8
1993	Cal-A	152	576	75	156	17	6	1	32	48	53	.271	.329	.326	74	-20	55	24	2	.984	9	*O-141/D-4	-1.2
1994	NY-A	95	350	62	109	21	6	1	36	37	36	.311	.384	.414	113	8	20	12	-1	.976	2	O-84/D-2	0.7
Total	8	1000	3666	563	1083	134	53	15	310	285	418	.295	.348	.373	99	-2	270	118	10	.982	17	O-840,D-101	0.3

■ CARLOS PONCE
Ponce, Carlos Antonio (Diaz) b: 2/7/59, Rio Piedras, P.R. BR/TR, 5'10", 170 lbs. Deb: 8/14/85

YEAR	TM/L	G	AB	R	H	2B	3B	HR	RBI	BB	SO	AVG	OBP	SLG	PRO+	BR/A	SB	CS	SBR	FA	FR	G/POS	TPR
1985	Mil-A	21	62	4	10	2	0	1	5	1	9	.161	.175	.242	13	-7	0	0	0	1.000	-0	1-10/O-6,D	-0.9

■ RALPH POND
Pond, Ralph Benjamin b: 5/4/1888, Eau Claire, Wis. d: 9/8/47, Cleveland, Ohio Deb: 6/8/10

YEAR	TM/L	G	AB	R	H	2B	3B	HR	RBI	BB	SO	AVG	OBP	SLG	PRO+	BR/A	SB	CS	SBR	FA	FR	G/POS	TPR
1910	Bos-A	1	4	0	1	0	0	0	0	0		.250	.250	.250	55	-0	1			.000	-1	/O-1	-0.1

■ HARLIN POOL
Pool, Harold G "Samson" b: 3/12/08, Lakeport, Cal. d: 2/15/63, Rodeo, Cal. BL/TR, 5'10", 195 lbs. Deb: 5/30/34

YEAR	TM/L	G	AB	R	H	2B	3B	HR	RBI	BB	SO	AVG	OBP	SLG	PRO+	BR/A	SB	CS	SBR	FA	FR	G/POS	TPR
1934	Cin-N	99	358	38	117	22	5	2	50	17	18	.327	.369	.433	117	8	3			.953	-0	O-94	0.4
1935	Cin-N	28	68	8	12	6	2	0	11	2	2	.176	.200	.324	39	-6	0			.962	-3	O-18	-1.0
Total	2	127	426	46	129	28	7	2	61	19	20	.303	.343	.415	105	2	3			.954	-3	O-112	-0.6

■ ED POOLE
Poole, Edward I. b: 9/7/1874, Canton, Ohio d: 3/11/19, Malvern, Ohio BR/TR, 5'10", 175 lbs. Deb: 10/6/00

YEAR	TM/L	G	AB	R	H	2B	3B	HR	RBI	BB	SO	AVG	OBP	SLG	PRO+	BR/A	SB	CS	SBR	FA	FR	G/POS	TPR
1900	Pit-N	2	4	1	2	0	1	1	3	0		.500	.500	1.750	504	2	0			.500	-0	/O-1,P-1	0.0
1901	Pit-N	26	78	6	16	4	0	1	4	4		.205	.244	.295	54	-5	1			.933	-2	P-12,O-12/23	-0.5
1902	Pit-N	1	4	0	1	0	0	0	0	0		.250	.250	.250	52	-0	0			.667	-0	/P-1	0.0
	Cin-N	17	61	7	7	2	0	0	1	0		.115	.115	.148	-17	-8	0			1.000	-1	P-16/O-1	-0.1
	Yr	18	65	7	8	2	0	0	1	0		.123	.123	.154	-13	-9	0			.976	-1	P-17/O-1	-0.1
1903	Cin-N	25	70	7	17	1	0	0	7	2		.243	.264	.257	44	-5	0			.929	2	P-25	0.0
1904	Bro-N	25	62	3	8	1	0	0	0	0		.129	.129	.145	-16	-8	0			.973	3	P-25	0.0
Total	5	96	279	24	51	8	1	2	15	6		.183	.200	.240	29	-25	1			.954	3	/P-80,O-14,32	-0.6

■ JIM POOLE
Poole, James Robert "Easy" b: 5/12/1895, Taylorsville, N.C. d: 1/2/75, Hickory, N.C. BL/TR, 6', 175 lbs. Deb: 4/14/25

YEAR	TM/L	G	AB	R	H	2B	3B	HR	RBI	BB	SO	AVG	OBP	SLG	PRO+	BR/A	SB	CS	SBR	FA	FR	G/POS	TPR
1925	Phi-A	133	480	65	143	29	8	5	67	27	37	.298	.338	.423	86	-12	5	4	-1	.992	-7	*1-123	-2.5
1926	Phi-A	112	361	49	106	23	5	8	63	23	25	.294	.339	.452	99	-2	4	3	-1	.992	0	*1-101/O-1	-0.8
1927	Phi-A	38	99	4	22	2	0	0	10	9	6	.222	.287	.242	36	-9	0	0		.993	0	1-31	-1.0
Total	3	283	940	118	271	54	13	13	140	59	68	.288	.333	.415	86	-23	9	7	-2	.987	-7	1-255/O-1	-4.3

■ RAY POOLE
Poole, Raymond Herman b: 1/16/20, Salisbury, N.C. BL/TR, 6', 180 lbs. Deb: 9/9/41

YEAR	TM/L	G	AB	R	H	2B	3B	HR	RBI	BB	SO	AVG	OBP	SLG	PRO+	BR/A	SB	CS	SBR	FA	FR	G/POS	TPR
1941	Phi-A	2	2	0	0	0	0	0	0	0	1	.000	.000	.000	-99	-1	0	0	0	.000	0	H	-0.1
1947	Phi-A	13	13	1	3	0	0	0	1	1	4	.231	.286	.231	44	-1	0	0	0	.000	0	H	-0.1
Total	2	15	15	1	3	0	0	0	1	1	5	.200	.250	.200	25	-2	0	0	0		0	-0,-0	-0.2

■ TOM POORMAN
Poorman, Thomas Iverson b: 10/14/1857, Lock Haven, Pa. d: 2/18/05, Lock Haven, Pa. BL/TR, 5'7", 135 lbs. Deb: 5/5/1880

YEAR	TM/L	G	AB	R	H	2B	3B	HR	RBI	BB	SO	AVG	OBP	SLG	PRO+	BR/A	SB	CS	SBR	FA	FR	G/POS	TPR
1880	Buf-N	19	70	5	11	1	0	0	1	0	13	.157	.157	.171	11	-6				.879	-2	P-11,O-10	-0.6
	Chi-N	7	25	3	5	1	2	0	0	0	2	.200	.200	.400	92	-0				.778	-2	/O-7,P-2	-0.1
	Yr	26	95	8	16	2	2	0	1	0	15	.168	.168	.232	33	-6				.750	-4	O-17,P-13	-0.7
1884	Tol-a	94	382	56	89	8	7	0		10		.233	.254	.291	75	-11				.845	4	*O-93/P-1	-0.8
1885	Bos-N	56	227	44	54	5	3	3	25	7	32	.238	.261	.326	92	-2				.867	-2	O-56	-0.6
1886	Bos-N	88	371	72	97	16	6	3	41	19	52	.261	.297	.361	103	1	31			.902	6	*O-88	0.4
1887	Phi-a	135	585	140	155	18	**19**	4		35		.265	.317	.381	94	-6	88			.911	-6	*O-135/2-2,P	-0.5
1888	Phi-a	97	383	76	87	16	6	2	44	31		.227	.294	.316	96	-1	46			.898	-10	*O-97	-1.3
Total	6	496	2043	396	498	65	43	12	111	102	99	.244	.285	.335	90	-26	165			.885	-4	O-486/P-15,2	-3.5

■ DAVE POPE
Pope, David b: 6/17/25, Talladega, Ala. BL/TR, 5'10.5", 170 lbs. Deb: 7/1/52

YEAR	TM/L	G	AB	R	H	2B	3B	HR	RBI	BB	SO	AVG	OBP	SLG	PRO+	BR/A	SB	CS	SBR	FA	FR	G/POS	TPR
1952	Cle-A	12	34	9	10	1	1	1	4	1	7	.294	.314	.471	124	1	0	0	0	1.000	-1	O-10	-0.1
1954	*Cle-A	60	102	21	30	2	1	4	13	10	22	.294	.357	.451	118	2	2	1	0	1.000	-4	O-29	-0.2
1955	Cle-A	35	104	17	31	5	0	6	22	12	31	.298	.376	.519	134	5	0	0	0	.954	-3	O-31	0.1
	Bal-A	86	222	21	55	8	4	1	30	16	34	.248	.304	.333	77	-8	5	2	0	1.000	-8	O-73	-1.9
	Yr	121	326	38	86	13	4	7	52	28	65	.264	.329	.393	97	-2	5	2	0	.986	-11	*O-104	-1.8
1956	Bal-A	12	19	1	3	0	0	0	1	0	7	.158	.200	.158	-5	-3	0	0	0	1.000	0	/O-4	-0.4
	Cle-A	25	70	6	17	3	1	0	3	1	12	.243	.254	.314	48	-5	0	0	0	1.000	-1	O-18	-0.7
	Yr	37	89	7	20	3	1	0	4	1	19	.225	.242	.281	38	-8	0	0	0	1.000	-2	O-22	-1.1
Total	4	230	551	75	146	19	7	12	73	40	113	.265	.319	.390	92	-9	7	3	0	.990	-18	O-165	-3.2

■ PAUL POPOVICH
Popovich, Paul Edward b: 8/18/40, Flemington, W.Va. BB/TR, 6', 175 lbs. Deb: 4/19/64

YEAR	TM/L	G	AB	R	H	2B	3B	HR	RBI	BB	SO	AVG	OBP	SLG	PRO+	BR/A	SB	CS	SBR	FA	FR	G/POS	TPR
1964	Chi-N	1	1	0	1	0	0	0	0	0	0	1.000	1.000	1.000	447	0	0	0	0	.000	0	H	0.0
1966	Chi-N	2	6	0	0	0	0	0	0	0	2	.000	.000	.000	-99	-2	0	0	0	.889	-1	/2-2	-0.3
1967	Chi-N	49	159	18	34	0	2	0	9	12	.214	.265	.239	43	-11	0	1	-1	.967	-4	S-31,2-17/3	-1.3
1968	LA-N	134	418	35	97	8	1	2	25	29	37	.232	.283	.270	72	-15	1	3	-2	.983	3	2-89,S-45/3	-0.5
1969	LA-N	28	50	5	10	0	0	0	4	1	4	.200	.216	.200	18	-5	0	0	0	.985	0	2-23/S-3	-0.4
	Chi-N	60	154	26	48	6	0	1	14	18	14	.312	.387	.370	100	1	0	0	-1	.974	-6	2-25/S-7,3O	-0.4
	Yr	88	204	31	58	6	0	1	18	19	18	.284	.344	.328	85	-4	0	0	-1	.978	-6	2-48,S-10/3O	-0.8
1970	Chi-N	78	186	22	47	5	1	4	20	18	18	.253	.325	.355	73	-7	0	0	-1	.990	-6	2-22,S-17,3	-1.0
1971	Chi-N	89	226	24	49	7	1	4	28	14	17	.217	.262	.310	54	-14	0	0	-1	.985	4	2-40,3-16/S	-0.9
1972	Chi-N	58	129	8	25	3	2	1	11	12	8	.194	.262	.271	47	-9	0	0	-1	.981	19	2-36/S-8,3	1.2
1973	Chi-N	99	280	24	66	3	3	2	24	18	27	.236	.284	.300	58	-16	0	0	-1	.981	26	2-84/S-9,3	1.5
1974	*Pit-N	59	83	9	18	2	0	0	5	5	10	.217	.261	.265	49	-6	0	0	0	.962	-1	2-12,S-10	-0.6
1975	Pit-N	25	40	5	8	1	0	0	1	3	2	.200	.273	.225	40	-3	0	0	0	1.000	-3	/2-8,S-8	-0.6
Total	11	682	1732	176	403	42	9	14	134	127	151	.233	.288	.292	62	-87	4	10	-5	.982	31	2-358,S-139/3O	-3.3

■ GEORGE POPPLEIN
Popplein, George J. b: Baltimore, Md. Deb: 7/11/1873

YEAR	TM/L	G	AB	R	H	2B	3B	HR	RBI	BB	SO	AVG	OBP	SLG	PRO+	BR/A	SB	CS	SBR	FA	FR	G/POS	TPR
1873	Mar-n	1	4	0	0	0	0	0	0	0	0	.000	.000	.000	-99	-1						/3-1,O-1	-0.1

YEAR	TM/L	G	AB	R	H	2B	3B	HR	RBI	BB	SO	AVG	OBP	SLG	PRO+	BR/A	SB	CS	SBR	FA	FR	G/POS	TPR
■ TOM POQUETTE	Poquette, Thomas Arthur b: 10/30/51, Eau Claire, Wis. BL/TR, 5'10", 175 lbs. Deb: 9/1/73																						
1973	KC-A	21	28	4	6	1	0	0	3	1	4	.214	.267	.250	43	-2	1	1	-0	.870	-4	O-20	-0.7
1976	*KC-A	104	344	43	104	18	10	2	34	29	31	.302	.363	.430	131	13	6	5	-1	.979	-8	O-98/D-2	0.1
1977	*KC-A	106	342	43	100	23	6	2	33	19	21	.292	.339	.412	103	1	1	4	-2	1.000	-2	O-96	-0.6
1978	*KC-A	80	204	16	44	9	2	4	30	14	9	.216	.266	.338	67	-9	2	0	1	.955	4	O-63/D-1	-0.7
1979	KC-A	21	26	1	5	0	0	0	3	1	4	.192	.222	.192	13	-3	0	0	0	1.000	-0	O-10	-0.5
	Bos-A	63	154	14	51	9	0	2	23	8	7	.331	.376	.429	110	2	2	2	-1	.949	-7	O-43/D-4	-0.6
	Yr	84	180	15	56	9	0	2	26	9	11	.311	.354	.394	97	-1	2	2	-1	.954	-9	O-53/D-4	-1.1
1981	Bos-A	3	2	0	0	0	0	0	0	0	0	.000	.000	.000	-94	-0	0	0	0	.000	-1	/O-2	-0.2
	Tex-A	30	64	2	10	1	0	0	7	5	1	.156	.229	.172	18	-7	0	1	-1	.963	-3	O-18	-1.2
	Yr	33	66	2	10	1	0	0	7	5	1	.152	.222	.167	14	-7	0	1	-1	.963	-4	O-20	-1.4
1982	KC-A	24	62	4	9	1	0	0	3	4	5	.145	.209	.161	3	-8	1	0	0	.957	-1	O-23	-0.9
Total	7	452	1226	127	329	62	18	10	136	81	82	.268	.321	.373	92	-13	13	13	-4	.971	-24	O-373/D-7	-5.3
■ DAN PORTER	Porter, Daniel Edward b: 10/17/31, Decatur, Ill. BL/TL, 6', 164 lbs. Deb: 8/16/51																						
1951	Was-A	13	19	2	4	0	0	0	0	2	4	.211	.286	.211	36	-2	0	0	0	1.000	-0	/O-3	-0.2
■ DARRELL PORTER	Porter, Darrell Ray b: 1/17/52, Joplin, Mo. BL/TR, 6', 193 lbs. Deb: 9/2/71																						
1971	Mil-A	22	70	4	15	2	0	2	9	9	20	.214	.304	.329	80	-2	2	2	-1	.977	2	C-22	0.1
1972	Mil-A	18	56	2	7	1	0	1	2	5	21	.125	.210	.196	22	-5	0	0	0	.976	5	C-18	0.0
1973	Mil-A	117	350	50	89	19	2	16	67	57	85	.254	.365	.457	133	16	5	2	0	.977	-4	C-90,D-19	1.7
1974	Mil-A☆	131	432	59	104	15	4	12	56	50	88	.241	.326	.377	103	2	8	7	-2	.978	-3	C-117/D-9	0.2
1975	Mil-A	130	409	66	95	12	5	18	60	89	77	.232	.376	.418	123	16	2	5	-2	.979	-2	*C-124/D-2	1.7
1976	Mil-A	119	389	43	81	14	1	5	32	51	61	.208	.302	.288	75	-12	2	0	1	.975	-5	*C-111/D-2	-1.4
1977	*KC-A	130	425	61	117	21	3	16	60	53	70	.275	.357	.452	118	11	1	0	0	.982	1	*C-125/D-1	1.5
1978	*KC-A★	150	520	77	138	27	6	18	78	75	75	.265	.360	.444	122	16	0	5	-3	.988	-6	*C-145/D-4	1.1
1979	KC-A★	157	533	101	155	23	10	20	112	**121**	65	.291	**.429**	.484	143	38	3	4	-2	.982	-2	*C-141,D-15	3.8
1980	*KC-A★	118	418	51	104	14	2	7	51	69	52	.249	.358	.342	92	-2	1	1	-0	.978	-2	C-81,D-34	0.1
1981	StL-N	61	174	22	39	10	2	6	31	39	32	.224	.369	.408	117	5	1	2	-1	.979	-3	C-52	0.4
1982	*StL-N	120	373	46	86	18	5	12	48	66	66	.231	.349	.402	109	6	1	1	-0	.983	-5	*C-111	0.4
1983	StL-N	145	443	57	116	24	3	15	66	68	94	.262	.365	.431	120	13	1	3	-2	.989	-7	*C-133	1.0
1984	StL-N	127	422	56	98	16	3	11	68	60	79	.232	.335	.363	98	0	5	3	-0	.984	-12	*C-122	-0.6
1985	*StL-N	84	240	30	53	12	2	10	36	41	48	.221	.337	.412	109	3	6	1	1	.990	-8	C-82	0.7
1986	Tex-A	68	155	21	41	6	0	12	29	22	51	.265	.360	.535	136	8	1	1	-0	.994	2	C-25,D-19	1.1
1987	Tex-A	85	130	19	31	3	0	7	21	30	43	.238	.389	.423	115	4	0	0	0	1.000	-0	D-35/C-7,1	0.3
Total	17	1782	5539	765	1369	237	48	188	826	905	1025	.247	.357	.409	113	116	39	37	-11	.982	-38	*C-1506,D-140/1	12.1
■ IRV PORTER	Porter, Irving Marble b: 5/17/1888, Lynn, Mass. d: 2/20/71, Lynn, Mass. BB/TR, 5'9", 155 lbs. Deb: 8/20/14																						
1914	Chi-A	1	4	1	1	0	0	0	0	1	.250	.250	.250	51	-0	0			1.000	-0	/O-1	-0.1
■ JAY PORTER	Porter, J W "J W" b: 1/17/33, Shawnee, Okla. BR/TR, 6'2", 180 lbs. Deb: 7/30/52																						
1952	StL-A	33	104	12	26	4	1	0	7	10	10	.250	.316	.308	72	-4	4	0	1	.973	-1	O-29/3-2	-0.5
1955	Det-A	24	55	6	13	2	0	1	3	8	15	.236	.333	.273	66	-2	0	0	0	1.000	-3	/1-6,C-4,O	-0.6
1956	Det-A	14	21	0	2	0	0	0	3	0	8	.095	.095	.095	-49	-4	0	0	0	1.000	-1	/C-2,O-2	-0.5
1957	Det-A	58	140	14	35	8	0	2	18	14	20	.250	.323	.350	82	-3	0	0	0	.953	-3	O-27,C-12/1	-0.8
1958	Cle-A	40	85	13	17	1	0	4	19	9	23	.200	.284	.353	76	-3	0	0	0	1.000	-3	O-20/1-4,3	-0.5
1959	Was-A	37	106	8	24	4	0	1	10	11	16	.226	.305	.292	65	-5	0	0	0	.993	-1	C-34/1-2	-0.5
	StL-N	23	33	5	7	3	0	1	2	1	4	.212	.257	.394	66	-2	0	0	0	1.000	-0	C-19/1-1	-0.1
Total	6	229	544	58	124	22	1	8	62	53	96	.228	.301	.316	68	-24	4	0	1	.990	-12	/C-91,O-62,13	-3.5
■ MATTHEW PORTER	Porter, Matthew Sheldon b: Kansas City, Mo. Deb: 6/27/1884 M																						
1884	KC-U	3	12	1	1	1	0	0	0	0	.083	.083	.167	-39	-2				.750	1	/O-3,M	-0.1
■ DICK PORTER	Porter, Richard Twilley "Wiggles" or "Twitches"																						
		b: 12/30/01, Princess Anne, Md. d: 9/24/74, Philadelphia, Pa. BL/TR, 5'10", 170 lbs. Deb: 4/16/29																						
1929	Cle-A	71	192	26	63	16	5	1	24	17	14	.328	.386	.479	117	5	3	5	-2	.941	-5	O-28,2-20	-0.3
1930	Cle-A	119	480	100	168	43	8	4	57	55	31	.350	.420	.498	127	21	3	3	-1	.962	-4	*O-118	0.7
1931	Cle-A	114	414	82	129	24	3	1	38	56	36	.312	.395	.391	102	3	6	9	-4	.970	-6	*O-109/2-1	-1.3
1932	Cle-A	146	621	106	191	42	8	4	60	64	43	.308	.373	.420	99	-1	2	4	-2	.982	-11	*O-145	-2.1
1933	Cle-A	132	499	73	133	19	6	0	41	51	42	.267	.335	.329	73	-19	4	4	-1	**.996**	-1	*O-124	-2.6
1934	Cle-A	13	44	9	10	2	1	1	6	4	5	.227	.292	.386	73	-2	0	0	0	1.000	-1	O-10	-0.4
	Bos-A	80	265	30	80	13	6	0	56	21	15	.302	.355	.396	87	-5	5	2	0	.940	-6	O-65	-1.2
	Yr	93	309	39	90	15	7	1	62	25	20	.291	.346	.395	85	-7	5	2	0	.947	-7	O-75	-1.6
Total	6	675	2515	426	774	159	37	11	282	268	186	.308	.376	.414	99	2	23	27	-9	.973	-35	O-599/2-21	-7.2
■ BOB PORTER	Porter, Robert Lee b: 7/22/59, Yuma, Ariz. BL/TL, 5'10", 180 lbs. Deb: 5/13/81																						
1981	Atl-N	17	14	2	4	1	0	0	4	2	1	.286	.375	.357	106	0	0	0	0	.000	0	/H	0.0
1982	Atl-N	24	27	1	3	0	0	0	0	1	9	.111	.143	.111	-27	-5	0	0	0	1.000	-1	/O-4,1-1	-0.6
Total	2	41	41	3	7	1	0	0	4	3	10	.171	.227	.195	19	-4	0	0	0	1.000	-1	/O-4,1-1	-0.6
■ LEO POSADA	Posada, Leopoldo Jesus (Hernandez) b: 4/15/36, Havana, Cuba BR/TR, 5'11", 175 lbs. Deb: 9/21/60																						
1960	KC-A	10	36	8	13	0	2	1	2	3	7	.361	.410	.556	158	3	1	0	0	1.000	-2	/O-9	0.1
1961	KC-A	116	344	37	87	10	4	7	53	36	84	.253	.331	.366	85	-7	0	0	0	.973	-3	*O-102	-1.5
1962	KC-A	29	46	6	9	1	1	0	3	7	14	.196	.302	.261	51	-3	0	0	0	1.000	-0	O-11	-0.4
Total	3	155	426	51	109	11	7	8	58	46	105	.256	.334	.371	87	-8	1	0	0	.976	-5	O-122	-1.8
■ SCOTT POSE	Pose, Scott Vernon b: 2/11/67, Davenport, Iowa BL/TR, 5'11", 165 lbs. Deb: 4/5/93																						
1993	Fla-N	15	41	0	8	2	0	0	3	2	4	.195	.233	.244	26	-4	0	2	-1	1.000	-3	O-10	-0.9
■ LEW POST	Post, Lewis G. b: 4/12/1875, Hastings, Mich. d: 8/21/44, Chicago, Ill. Deb: 9/21/02																						
1902	Det-A	3	12	2	1	0	0	0	2	0	.083	.083	.083	-53	-2	0			.800	-1	/O-3	-0.3
■ SAM POST	Post, Samuel Gilbert b: 11/17/1896, Richmond, Va. d: 3/31/71, Portsmouth, Va. BL/TL, 6'1.5", 170 lbs. Deb: 4/22/22																						
1922	Bro-N	9	25	3	7	0	0	0	4	1	4	.280	.308	.280	53	-2	1	0	0	.982	-1	/1-8	-0.3
■ WALLY POST	Post, Walter Charles b: 7/9/29, St.Wendelin, Ohio d: 1/6/82, St.Henry, Ohio BR/TR, 6'1", 203 lbs. Deb: 9/18/49																						
1949	Cin-N	6	8	1	2	0	0	0	1	0	3	.250	.250	.250	34	-1	0			.750	-1	/O-3	-0.2
1951	Cin-N	15	41	6	9	3	0	1	7	3	4	.220	.273	.366	69	-2	0	0	0	.963	1	/O-9	-0.2
1952	Cin-N	19	58	5	9	1	0	2	7	4	20	.155	.222	.276	37	-5	0	0	0	1.000	2	O-16	-0.4
1953	Cin-N	11	33	3	8	1	0	1	4	4	6	.242	.324	.364	78	-1	0	0	0	.960	1	O-11	-0.1
1954	Cin-N	130	451	46	115	21	3	18	83	26	70	.255	.300	.435	86	-11	2	2	-1	.957	5	*O-116	-1.1
1955	Cin-N	154	601	116	186	30	3	40	109	60	102	.309	.374	.574	139	32	7	4	-0	.978	-2	*O-154	2.6
1956	Cin-N	143	539	94	134	25	3	36	83	37	124	.249	.302	.506	105	2	6	0	2	.969	12	*O-136	0.9
1957	Cin-N	134	467	68	114	26	2	20	74	33	84	.244	.294	.437	87	-10	2	2	-1	.985	10	*O-124	-0.7
1958	Phi-N	110	379	51	107	21	3	12	62	32	74	.282	.343	.449	109	4	0	3	-1	.952	8	O-91	0.6

YEAR	TM/L	G	AB	R	H	2B	3B	HR	RBI	BB	SO	AVG	OBP	SLG	PRO+	BR/A	SB	CS	SBR	FA	FR	G/POS	TPR
1959	Phi-N	132	468	62	119	17	6	22	94	36	101	.254	.312	.457	100	-1	0	0	0	.992	9	*O-120	0.1
1960	Phi-N	34	84	11	24	6	1	2	12	9	24	.286	.355	.452	119	2	0	0	0	1.000	1	O-22	0.2
	Cin-N	77	249	36	70	14	0	17	38	28	51	.281	.354	.542	139	13	0	2	-1	.985	4	O-67	1.3
	Yr	111	333	47	94	20	1	19	50	37	75	.282	.354	.520	134	15	0	2	-1	.989	5	O-89	1.5
1961	*Cin-N	99	282	44	83	16	3	20	57	22	61	.294	.348	.585	140	15	0	1	-1	.959	1	O-81	1.1
1962	Cin-N	109	285	43	75	10	3	17	62	32	67	.263	.342	.498	118	7	1	0	0	.935	-4	O-90	-0.1
1963	Cin-N	5	7	1	0	0	0	0	0	0	1	.000	.125	.000	-59	-1	0	0	0	1.000	0	/O-1	-0.1
	Min-A	21	47	6	9	0	1	2	6	2	17	.191	.224	.362	60	-3	0	0	0	1.000	-2	/O-12	-0.5
1964	Cle-A	5	8	1	0	0	0	0	0	3	4	.000	.273	.000	-16	-1	0	0	0	.667	-1	/O-2	-0.2
Total	15	1204	4007	594	1064	194	28	210	699	331	813	.266	.325	.485	109	39	19	13		.970	46	*O-1055	3.2

■ MIKE POTTER
Potter, Michael Gary b: 5/16/51, Montebello, Cal. BR/TR, 6'1", 195 lbs. Deb: 9/6/76

YEAR	TM/L	G	AB	R	H	2B	3B	HR	RBI	BB	SO	AVG	OBP	SLG	PRO+	BR/A	SB	CS	SBR	FA	FR	G/POS	TPR
1976	StL-N	9	16	0	0	0	0	0	0	1	6	.000	.059	.000	-82	-4	0	0	0	1.000	0	/O-4	-0.4
1977	StL-N	5	7	0	0	0	0	0	0	0	2	.000	.000	.000	-99	-2	0	0	0	.000	-0	/O-1	-0.2
Total	2	14	23	0	0	0	0	0	0	1	8	.000	.042	.000	-87	-6	0	0	0	1.000	-0	/O-5	-0.6

■ DAN POTTS
Potts, Vivian b: 1/1869, Bristol, Pa. Deb: 10/3/1892

YEAR	TM/L	G	AB	R	H	2B	3B	HR	RBI	BB	SO	AVG	OBP	SLG	PRO+	BR/A	SB	CS	SBR	FA	FR	G/POS	TPR
1892	Was-N	1	4	0	1	0	0	0	0	0	1	.250	.250	.250	53	-0	0			1.000	1	/C-1	0.0

■ JOHN POTTS
Potts, John Frederick "Fred" b: 2/6/1887, Tipp City, Ohio d: 9/5/62, Cleveland, Ohio BL/TR, 5'7", 165 lbs. Deb: 4/18/14

YEAR	TM/L	G	AB	R	H	2B	3B	HR	RBI	BB	SO	AVG	OBP	SLG	PRO+	BR/A	SB	CS	SBR	FA	FR	G/POS	TPR
1914	KC-F	41	102	14	27	4	0	1	9	25	13	.265	.414	.333	99	-1	7			.933	-4	O-31	-0.4

■ KEN POULSEN
Poulsen, Ken Sterling b: 8/4/47, Van Nuys, Cal. BL/TR, 6'1", 190 lbs. Deb: 7/3/67

YEAR	TM/L	G	AB	R	H	2B	3B	HR	RBI	BB	SO	AVG	OBP	SLG	PRO+	BR/A	SB	CS	SBR	FA	FR	G/POS	TPR
1967	Bos-A	5	5	0	1	1	0	0	0	0	2	.200	.200	.400	68	-0	0	0	0	.667	-1	/3-2,S-1	-0.1

■ ALONZO POWELL
Powell, Alonzo Sidney b: 12/12/64, San Francisco, Cal. BR/TR, 6'2", 190 lbs. Deb: 4/6/87

YEAR	TM/L	G	AB	R	H	2B	3B	HR	RBI	BB	SO	AVG	OBP	SLG	PRO+	BR/A	SB	CS	SBR	FA	FR	G/POS	TPR
1987	Mon-N	14	41	3	8	3	0	0	4	5	17	.195	.283	.268	46	-3	0	0	0	1.000	-1	O-11	-0.5
1991	Sea-A	57	111	16	24	6	1	3	12	11	24	.216	.293	.369	82	-3	0	2	-1	.960	-9	O-40/1-7,D	-1.4
Total	2	71	152	19	32	9	1	3	16	16	41	.211	.290	.342	71	-6	0	2	-1	.968	-10	/O-51,D-7,1	-1.9

■ JAKE POWELL
Powell, Alvin Jacob b: 7/15/08, Silver Spring, Md d: 11/4/48, Washington, D.C. BR/TR, 5'11.5", 180 lbs. Deb: 8/3/30

YEAR	TM/L	G	AB	R	H	2B	3B	HR	RBI	BB	SO	AVG	OBP	SLG	PRO+	BR/A	SB	CS	SBR	FA	FR	G/POS	TPR
1930	Was-A	3	4	1	0	0	0	0	0	0	1	.000	.000	.000	-99	-1	0	0	0	1.000	-0	/O-2	-0.1
1934	Was-A	9	35	6	10	2	0	0	1	4	2	.286	.359	.343	85	-1	1	1	-0	.955	1	/O-9	0.0
1935	Was-A	139	551	88	172	26	10	6	98	37	37	.312	.360	.428	107	4	15	7	0	.976	0	*O-136/2-2	0.0
1936	Was-A	53	210	40	62	11	5	1	30	18	21	.295	.357	.410	94	-2	10	4	1	.951	-7	O-53	-1.0
	*NY-A	87	328	62	99	13	3	7	48	33	30	.302	.364	.424	98	-1	16	7	1	.976	1	O-84	-0.3
	Yr	140	538	102	161	24	8	8	78	51	51	.299	.362	.418	96	-1	26	11	1	.967	-7	*O-137	-1.3
1937	*NY-A	97	365	54	96	22	3	3	45	25	36	.263	.314	.364	70	-17	7	5	-1	.981	1	O-94	-1.9
1938	*NY-A	45	164	27	42	12	1	2	20	15	20	.256	.326	.378	76	-6	3	1	0	.978	-3	O-43	-0.9
1939	NY-A	31	86	12	21	4	1	1	9	3	8	.244	.270	.349	58	-6	1	2	-1	.983	1	O-23	-0.7
1940	NY-A	12	27	3	5	0	0	0	2	1	4	.185	.214	.185	5	-4	0	0	0	1.000	0	/O-7	-0.4
1943	Was-A	37	132	14	35	10	2	0	20	5	13	.265	.297	.371	99	-1	3	5	-2	.978	2	O-33	-0.3
1944	Was-A	96	367	29	88	9	1	1	37	16	26	.240	.272	.278	60	-20	7	2	1	.980	0	O-90/3-1	-2.5
1945	Was-A	31	98	4	19	2	0	0	3	8	13	.194	.255	.214	40	-8	1	1	0	.950	-1	O-27	-1.2
	Phi-N	48	173	13	40	5	0	1	14	8	13	.231	.265	.277	52	-11	1			.986	-4	O-44	-1.8
Total	11	688	2540	353	689	116	26	22	327	173	219	.271	.320	.363	81	-75	65	35		.975	-9	O-645/2-2,3	-11.1

■ ABNER POWELL
Powell, Charles Abner "Ab" b: 12/15/1860, Shenandoah, Pa. d: 8/7/53, New Orleans, La. BL/TR, 5'7", 160 lbs. Deb: 8/4/1884

YEAR	TM/L	G	AB	R	H	2B	3B	HR	RBI	BB	SO	AVG	OBP	SLG	PRO+	BR/A	SB	CS	SBR	FA	FR	G/POS	TPR
1884	Was-U	48	191	36	54	10	5	0		3		.283	.294	.387	86	-4				.875	-2	O-30,P-18/3S2	-0.6
1886	Bal-a	11	39	4	7	2	1	0		1		.179	.200	.282	52	-2	4			.917	1	/P-7,O-4	-0.2
	Cin-a	19	74	13	17	1	1	0		4		.230	.269	.270	67	-3	0			.760	2	O-13/S-6,P	-0.2
	Yr	30	113	17	24	3	2	0		5		.212	.246	.274	62	-5	4			.735	3	O-17,P-11/S	-0.4
Total	2	78	304	53	78	13	7	0		8		.257	.276	.345	78	-9	4			.817	-1	/O-47,P-29,S32	-1.0

■ HOSKEN POWELL
Powell, Hosken b: 5/14/55, Selma, Ala. BL/TL, 6'1", 185 lbs. Deb: 4/5/78

YEAR	TM/L	G	AB	R	H	2B	3B	HR	RBI	BB	SO	AVG	OBP	SLG	PRO+	BR/A	SB	CS	SBR	FA	FR	G/POS	TPR
1978	Min-A	121	381	55	94	20	2	3	31	45	31	.247	.326	.333	84	-7	11	5	0	.983	-1	*O-117	-1.3
1979	Min-A	104	338	49	99	17	3	2	36	33	25	.293	.361	.379	96	-1	5	1	1	.977	-2	O-93/D-5	-0.6
1980	Min-A	137	485	58	127	17	5	6	35	32	46	.262	.312	.355	76	-16	14	3	2	.968	7	*O-129	-1.1
1981	Min-A	80	264	30	63	11	3	2	25	17	31	.239	.287	.326	71	-10	7	4	-0	.970	2	O-64/D-8	-1.1
1982	Tor-A	112	265	43	73	13	4	3	26	12	23	.275	.307	.389	82	-7	4	4	-1	.974	-4	O-75,D-19	-2.0
1983	Tor-A	40	83	6	14	0	0	1	7	5	8	.169	.216	.205	16	-10	2	0	1	.981	-4	O-33/1-1,D	-1.3
Total	6	594	1816	241	470	78	17	17	160	144	164	.259	.316	.349	79	-50	43	17	3	.975	-8	O-511/D-33,1	-7.4

■ JIM POWELL
Powell, James Edwin b: 8/30/1859, Richmond, Va. d: 11/20/29, Butte, Mont. 5'10", 170 lbs. Deb: 8/5/1884

YEAR	TM/L	G	AB	R	H	2B	3B	HR	RBI	BB	SO	AVG	OBP	SLG	PRO+	BR/A	SB	CS	SBR	FA	FR	G/POS	TPR
1884	Ric-a	41	151	23	37	8	4	0		7		.245	.296	.351	112	2				.943	1	1-41	-0.2

■ BOOG POWELL
Powell, John Wesley b: 8/17/41, Lakeland, Fla. BL/TR, 6'4", 240 lbs. Deb: 9/26/61

YEAR	TM/L	G	AB	R	H	2B	3B	HR	RBI	BB	SO	AVG	OBP	SLG	PRO+	BR/A	SB	CS	SBR	FA	FR	G/POS	TPR
1961	Bal-A	4	13	0	1	0	0	0	1	0	2	.077	.077	.077	-61	-3	0	0	0	1.000	-1	/O-3	-0.4
1962	Bal-A	124	400	44	97	13	2	15	53	38	79	.243	.311	.398	95	-4	1	1	-0	.969	-7	*O-112/1-1	-1.8
1963	Bal-A	140	491	67	130	22	2	25	82	49	87	.265	.331	.470	126	16	1	2	-1	.969	-8	*O-121,1-23	0.1
1964	Bal-A	134	424	74	123	17	0	39	99	76	91	.290	.400	.606	176	44	0	0	0	.974	4	*O-124/1-5	4.4
1965	Bal-A	144	472	54	117	20	2	17	72	71	93	.248	.351	.407	112	9	1	1	-0	.992	3	1-78,O-71	0.6
1966	*Bal-A	140	491	78	141	18	0	34	109	67	125	.287	.374	.532	159	38	0	4	-3	.989	-7	*1-136	2.1
1967	Bal-A	125	415	53	97	14	1	13	55	55	94	.234	.326	.366	105	3	1	3	-2	.986	-4	*1-114	-1.0
1968	Bal-A★	154	550	60	137	21	1	22	85	73	97	.249	.340	.411	127	18	7	1	2	.990	-5	*1-149	0.4
1969	*Bal-A★	152	533	83	162	25	0	37	121	72	76	.304	.388	.559	161	42	1	1	0	.995	-2	*1-144	3.0
1970	*Bal-A★	154	526	82	156	28	0	35	114	104	80	.297	.417	.549	163	48	1	1	-0	.992	-3	*1-145	3.3
1971	*Bal-A†	128	418	59	107	19	2	22	92	82	64	.256	.383	.459	139	24	1	0	0	.995	-3	*1-124	1.1
1972	Bal-A	140	465	53	117	20	1	21	81	65	92	.252	.348	.434	129	17	4	0	1	.988	-3	*1-133	0.5
1973	*Bal-A	114	370	52	98	13	1	11	54	65	64	.265	.402	.395	126	17	0	2	-1	.989	2	*1-111	0.9
1974	*Bal-A	110	344	37	91	11	1	12	45	52	58	.265	.361	.413	126	13	0	1	-1	.996	1	*1-102/D-1	0.7
1975	Cle-A	134	435	64	129	18	0	27	86	59	72	.297	.382	.524	154	31	3	3	-2	.997	-2	*1-121/D-5	2.0
1976	Cle-A	95	293	29	63	9	0	9	33	41	43	.215	.311	.338	91	-3	1	1	0	.987	1	1-89	-0.9
1977	LA-N	50	41	0	10	0	0	0	5	12	9	.244	.415	.244	82	-0	0	0	0	.938	-1	/1-4	-0.1
Total	17	2042	6681	889	1776	270	11	339	1187	1001	1226	.266	.364	.462	134	310	20	21	-7	.991	-33	*1-1479,O-431/D	14.9

■ MARTIN POWELL
Powell, Martin J. b: 3/25/1856, Fitchburg, Mass. d: 2/5/1888, Fitchburg, Mass. BL/TL, 6', 170 lbs. Deb: 6/18/1881

YEAR	TM/L	G	AB	R	H	2B	3B	HR	RBI	BB	SO	AVG	OBP	SLG	PRO+	BR/A	SB	CS	SBR	FA	FR	G/POS	TPR
1881	Det-N	55	219	47	74	9	4	1	38	15	9	.338	.380	.429	148	12				.947	-3	1-55/C-1	0.4
1882	Det-N	80	338	44	81	13	0	0	29	19	27	.240	.280	.278	80	-7				.940	-5	1-80	-1.9
1883	Det-N	101	421	76	115	17	5	1	48	28	23	.273	.318	.344	106	5				.950	3	*1-101	-0.7
1884	Cin-U	43	185	46	59	4	2	1		13		.319	.364	.378	94	-1				.940	-2	1-43	-0.8
1885	Phi-a	19	75	5	12	0	3	0		1		.160	.192	.240	34	-6				.973	-0	1-19	-0.8
Total	5	298	1238	218	341	43	14	3	115	76	59	.275	.318	.340	101	2				.947	-13	1-298/C-1	-3.8

■ PAUL POWELL
Powell, Paul Ray b: 3/19/48, San Angelo, Tex. BR/TR, 5'11", 185 lbs. Deb: 4/7/71

YEAR	TM/L	G	AB	R	H	2B	3B	HR	RBI	BB	SO	AVG	OBP	SLG	PRO+	BR/A	SB	CS	SBR	FA	FR	G/POS	TPR
1971	Min-A	20	31	7	5	0	0	1	2	3	12	.161	.235	.258	38	-3	0	0	0	1.000	-2	O-15	-0.6

YEAR	TM/L	G	AB	R	H	2B	3B	HR	RBI	BB	SO	AVG	OBP	SLG	PRO+	BR/A	SB	CS	SBR	FA	FR	G/POS	TPR
1973	LA-N	2	1	0	0	0	0	0	0	0	1	.000	.000	.000	-99	-0	0	0	0	.000	-0	/O-1	-0.1
1975	LA-N	8	10	2	2	1	0	0	0	1	2	.200	.273	.300	61	-1	0	0	0	.955	1	/C-7,O-1	0.0
Total	3	30	42	9	7	1	0	1	2	4	15	.167	.239	.262	41	-3	0	0	0	1.000	-2	/O-17,C-7	-0.7

■ RAY POWELL
Powell, Raymond Reath "Rabbit"   b: 11/20/1888, Siloam Springs, Ark.   d: 10/16/62, Chillicothe, Mo.   BL/TR, 5'9", 160 lbs.   Deb: 4/16/13

YEAR	TM/L	G	AB	R	H	2B	3B	HR	RBI	BB	SO	AVG	OBP	SLG	PRO+	BR/A	SB	CS	SBR	FA	FR	G/POS	TPR
1913	Det-A	2	0	0	0	0	0	0	0	0	0	—	—	—	—	0		0		.000	0	/O-1	0.0
1917	Bos-N	88	357	42	97	10	4	4	30	24	54	.272	.318	.356	113	5	12			.976	9	O-88	0.9
1918	Bos-N	53	188	31	40	7	5	0	20	29	30	.213	.321	.303	95	-0	2			.949	-0	O-53	-0.4
1919	Bos-N	123	470	51	111	12	12	2	33	41	79	.236	.303	.326	93	-4	16			.951	1	*O-122	-1.3
1920	Bos-N	147	609	69	137	12	12	6	29	44	83	.225	.282	.314	74	-21	10	18	-8	.956	5	*O-147	-3.8
1921	Bos-N	149	624	114	191	25	**18**	12	74	58	85	.306	.369	.462	125	22	6	17	-8	.954	3	*O-149	0.5
1922	Bos-N	142	550	82	163	22	11	6	37	59	66	.296	.369	.409	105	5	3	12	-6	.980	12	*O-136	-0.3
1923	Bos-N	97	338	57	102	20	4	4	38	45	36	.302	.385	.420	117	10	1	6	-3	.941	-4	O-84	-0.3
1924	Bos-N	74	188	21	49	9	1	1	15	21	28	.261	.338	.335	85	-4	1	3	-2	.947	4	O-46	-0.4
Total	9	875	3324	467	890	117	67	35	276	321	461	.268	.336	.375	102	11	51	56		.959	29	O-826	-4.8

■ LEROY POWELL
Powell, Robert Leroy   b: 10/17/33, Flint, Mich.   BR/TR, 6'1", 190 lbs.   Deb: 9/16/55

YEAR	TM/L	G	AB	R	H	2B	3B	HR	RBI	BB	SO	AVG	OBP	SLG	PRO+	BR/A	SB	CS	SBR	FA	FR	G/POS	TPR
1955	Chi-A	1	0	0	0	0	0	0	0	0	0	—	—	—	—	0	0	0	0	.000	0	R	0.0
1957	Chi-A	1	0	1	0	0	0	0	0	0	0	—	—	—	—	0	0	0	0	.000	0	R	0.0
Total	2	2	0	1	0	0	0	0	0	0	0	—	—	—	—	0	0	0	0		0	-0,-0	0.0

■ TOM POWER
Power, Thomas E.   b: San Francisco, Cal.   d: 2/25/1898, San Francisco, Cal   5'11", 164 lbs.   Deb: 8/27/1890

YEAR	TM/L	G	AB	R	H	2B	3B	HR	RBI	BB	SO	AVG	OBP	SLG	PRO+	BR/A	SB	CS	SBR	FA	FR	G/POS	TPR
1890	Bal-a	38	125	11	26	3	1	0	13			.208	.293	.248	57	-7	6			.960	-4	1-26,2-12	-1.0

■ VIC POWER
Power, Victor Pellot (b: Victor Felipe Pellot (Pove)   b: 11/1/27, Arecibo, P.R.   BR/TR, 5'11", 195 lbs.   Deb: 4/13/54

YEAR	TM/L	G	AB	R	H	2B	3B	HR	RBI	BB	SO	AVG	OBP	SLG	PRO+	BR/A	SB	CS	SBR	FA	FR	G/POS	TPR
1954	Phi-A	127	462	36	118	17	5	8	38	19	19	.255	.288	.366	78	-16	2	1	0	.985	10	*O-101,1-21/S3	-1.1
1955	KC-A★	147	596	91	190	34	10	19	76	35	27	.319	.357	.505	128	20	0	2	-1	.993	14	*1-144	2.4
1956	KC-A★	127	530	77	164	21	5	14	63	24	16	.309	.341	.447	106	3	2	2	-1	.993	8	1-76,2-47/O	0.8
1957	KC-A	129	467	48	121	15	1	14	42	19	21	.259	.292	.385	82	-13	3	2	-0	**.998**	12	*1-113/O-6,2	-0.8
1958	KC-A	52	205	35	62	13	4	4	27	7	3	.302	.335	.463	112	3	1	1	-0	.992	6	1-50/2-1	0.5
	Cle-A	93	385	63	122	24	6	12	53	13	11	.317	.341	.504	133	15	2	1	-0	.977	6	3-42,1-41,2/SO	2.1
	Yr	145	590	98	184	37	**10**	16	80	20	14	.312	.336	.490	125	17	3	2	-0	.992	11	1-91,3-42,2/SO	2.6
1959	Cle-A★	147	595	102	170	31	6	10	60	40	22	.289	.330	.412	108	5	9	13	-5	**.995**	10	*1-121,2-21/3	0.4
1960	Cle-A★	147	580	69	167	26	3	10	84	24	20	.288	.316	.395	94	-7	9	5	-0	**.996**	21	*1-147/S-5,3	0.3
1961	Cle-A	147	563	64	151	34	4	5	63	38	16	.268	.316	.369	85	-13	4	3	-1	.994	18	*1-141/2-7	-0.7
1962	Min-A	144	611	80	177	28	2	16	63	22	35	.290	.318	.421	93	-7	7	1	2	.993	9	*1-142/2-2	-0.6
1963	Min-A	138	541	65	146	28	2	10	52	22	24	.270	.298	.384	88	-9	3	1	-0	.992	-1	*1-124,2-18/3	-1.4
1964	Min-A	19	45	6	10	2	0	0	1	1	3	.222	.239	.267	40	-4	0	0	0	.990	1	1-12/2-1	-0.3
	LA-A	68	221	17	55	6	0	3	13	8	14	.249	.278	.317	72	-9	1	1	-0	1.000	2	1-48,3-28/2	-0.9
	Yr	87	266	23	65	8	0	3	14	9	17	.244	.272	.308	66	-13	1	1	-0	.998	1	1-60,3-28/2	-1.2
	Phi-N	18	48	1	10	4	0	0	3	2	3	.208	.240	.292	50	-3	0	0	0	.993	1	1-17	-0.3
1965	Cal-A	124	197	11	51	7	1	1	20	5	13	.259	.281	.320	72	-8	2	2	-1	.996	6	*1-107/2-6,3	-0.5
Total	12	1627	6046	765	1716	290	49	126	658	279	247	.284	.317	.411	97	-43	45	35	-7	.994	123	*1-1304,2-139,O/3S	-0.1

■ MIKE POWERS
Powers, Ellis Foree   b: 3/2/06, Toddspoint, Ky.   d: 12/2/83, Louisville, Ky.   BL/TL, 6'1", 185 lbs.   Deb: 8/19/32

YEAR	TM/L	G	AB	R	H	2B	3B	HR	RBI	BB	SO	AVG	OBP	SLG	PRO+	BR/A	SB	CS	SBR	FA	FR	G/POS	TPR
1932	Cle-A	14	33	4	6	4	0	0	5	2	2	.182	.229	.303	34	-3	0	0	0	.917	-2	/O-8	-0.5
1933	Cle-A	24	47	6	13	2	1	0	2	6	6	.277	.358	.362	87	-1	2	1	0	.952	-2	O-11	-0.3
Total	2	38	80	10	19	6	1	0	7	8	8	.237	.307	.338	65	-4	2	1	0	.939	-3	/O-19	-0.8

■ JOHN POWERS
Powers, John Calvin   b: 7/8/29, Birmingham, Ala.   BL/TR, 6', 190 lbs.   Deb: 9/24/55

YEAR	TM/L	G	AB	R	H	2B	3B	HR	RBI	BB	SO	AVG	OBP	SLG	PRO+	BR/A	SB	CS	SBR	FA	FR	G/POS	TPR
1955	Pit-N	2	4	0	1	0	0	0	0	0	0	.250	.250	.250	34	-0	0	0	0	1.000	-0	/O-2	0.0
1956	Pit-N	11	21	0	1	0	0	0	0	1	4	.048	.091	.048	-63	-5	0	0	0	1.000	-0	/O-5	-0.5
1957	Pit-N	20	35	7	10	3	0	2	8	5	9	.286	.419	.543	161	3	0	0	0	1.000	0	/O-9	0.3
1958	Pit-N	57	82	6	15	1	0	2	8	2	19	.183	.256	.268	40	-7	0	0	0	1.000	0	O-14	-0.8
1959	Cin-N	43	43	8	11	2	1	2	4	3	13	.256	.319	.488	108	0	0	0	0	1.000	-1	/O-5	-0.1
1960	Bal-N	10	18	3	2	0	0	0	0	3	1	.111	.238	.111	-2	-3	0	0	0	.833	-1	/O-4	-0.1
	Cle-A	8	12	2	2	1	1	0	0	2	2	.167	.286	.417	90	-0	0	0	0	1.000	-0	/O-5	-0.1
	Yr	18	30	5	4	1	1	0	0	5	3	.133	.257	.233	34	-3	0	0	0	.929	-1	/O-9	-0.5
Total	6	151	215	26	42	7	2	6	14	22	48	.195	.282	.330	64	-11	0	0	0	.986	-2	/O-44	-1.6

■ LES POWERS
Powers, Leslie Edwin   b: 11/5/09, Ballard, Wash.   d: 11/13/78, Santa Monica, Cal.   BL/TL, 6', 175 lbs.   Deb: 9/17/38

YEAR	TM/L	G	AB	R	H	2B	3B	HR	RBI	BB	SO	AVG	OBP	SLG	PRO+	BR/A	SB	CS	SBR	FA	FR	G/POS	TPR
1938	NY-N	2	3	0	0	0	0	0	0	0	1	.000	.000	.000	-99	-1		0		.000	0	H	-0.1
1939	Phi-N	19	52	7	18	1	1	0	2	4	6	.346	.393	.404	118	1		0		.983	-2	1-13	-0.2
Total	2	21	55	7	18	1	1	0	2	4	7	.327	.373	.382	106	1		0		.983	-2	/1-13	-0.3

■ DOC POWERS
Powers, Michael Riley   b: 9/22/1870, Pittsfield, Mass.   d: 4/26/09, Philadelphia, Pa.   BR/TR,   Deb: 6/12/1898

YEAR	TM/L	G	AB	R	H	2B	3B	HR	RBI	BB	SO	AVG	OBP	SLG	PRO+	BR/A	SB	CS	SBR	FA	FR	G/POS	TPR
1898	Lou-N	34	99	13	27	4	3	1	19	5		.273	.308	.404	105	0	1			.962	-3	C-22/1-6,O	-0.1
1899	Lou-N	49	169	15	35	8	2	0	22	6		.207	.239	.278	42	-14	1			.942	-8	C-38/1-7	-1.7
	Was-N	14	38	3	10	2	0	0	3	1		.263	.282	.316	65	-2	0			.942	-0	C-12/1-1	-0.1
	Yr	63	207	18	45	10	2	0	25	7		.217	.247	.285	46	-16	1			.942	-8	C-50/1-8	-1.8
1901	Phi-A	116	431	53	108	26	5	1	47	18		.251	.292	.341	72	-17	3			.952	-5	*C-111/1-3	-1.0
1902	Phi-A	71	246	35	65	7	1	2	39	14		.264	.312	.325	74	-9	3			.950	5	C-68/1-3	0.3
1903	Phi-A	75	247	19	56	11	1	0	23	5		.227	.242	.279	54	-14	1			.982	-2	C-66/1-7	-1.0
1904	Phi-A	57	184	11	35	3	0	0	11	6		.190	.220	.207	33	-14	3			.965	-5	C-56/O-1	-1.4
1905	*Phi-A	21	60	6	10	1	0	0	5	0		.167	.180	.167	10	-6	2			.928	3	C-21	-0.1
	NY-A	11	33	3	6	1	0	0	2	1		.182	.206	.212	29	-3	0			.975	-0	/1-7,C-4	-0.3
	*Phi-A	19	61	2	8	0	0	0	5	3		.131	.172	.131	-3	-7	2			.991	-5	C-19	-1.2
	Yr	51	154	11	24	1	0	0	12	4		.156	.182	.162	9	-16	4			.957	-2	C-44/1-7	-1.6
1906	Phi-A	58	185	5	29	1	0	0	7	1		.157	.170	.162	4	-20	2			.974	9	C-57/1-1	-0.6
1907	Phi-A	59	159	9	29	3	0	0	9	3		.182	.217	.201	33	-12	1			.983	14	C-59	0.7
1908	Phi-A	62	172	8	31	6	1	0	7	5		.180	.217	.227	41	-11	7			.967	7	C-60/1-2	0.1
1909	Phi-A	1	4	1	1	0	0	0	0	0		.250	.250	.250	57	-0	0			1.000	0	/C-1	0.0
Total	11	647	2088	183	450	72	13	4	199	72		.216	.248	.268	51	-129	27			.965	12	C-594/1-37,O	-6.4

■ PHIL POWERS
Powers, Phillip B. "Grandmother"   b: 7/26/1854, New York, N.Y.   d: 12/22/14, New York, N.Y.   BR/TR, 5'7", 166 lbs.   Deb: 8/31/1878   U

YEAR	TM/L	G	AB	R	H	2B	3B	HR	RBI	BB	SO	AVG	OBP	SLG	PRO+	BR/A	SB	CS	SBR	FA	FR	G/POS	TPR
1878	Chi-N	8	31	2	5	1	1	0		2	1	.161	.188	.258	42	-2				.930	5	/C-8	0.3
1880	Bos-N	37	126	11	18	5	0	0	10	5	15	.143	.176	.183	22	-10				.851	-5	C-37/O-2	-1.4
1881	Cle-N	5	15	1	1	0	0	0	0	1	2	.067	.125	.067	-40	-2				.955	-1	/C-4,3-1	-0.3
1882	Cin-a	6	60	4	13	1	1	0			3	.217	.254	.267	72	-2				.921	3	C-10/1-5,O	0.1
1883	Cin-a	30	114	16	28	1	4	0			3	.246	.265	.325	84	-2				.893	-2	C-17,O-13	-0.3
1884	Cin-a	34	130	10	18	1	0	0			5	.138	.170	.146	4	-14				.891	5	C-31/O-2,1	-0.6
1885	Cin-a	15	60	6	16	2	0	0				.267	.267	.300	77	-2				.833	-3	C-15	-0.3
	Bal-a	9	34	6	4	0	0	0		1		.118	.143	.147	-8	-4				.844	-4	/C-8,O-1	-0.7
	Yr	24	94	12	20	3	0	0		1		.213	.221	.245	47	-6				.837	-7	C-23/O-1	-1.0
Total	7	154	570	56	103	12	6	0	12	19	22	.181	.207	.223	40	-37				.877	-2	C-130/O-19,13	-3.2

YEAR	TM/L	G	AB	R	H	2B	3B	HR	RBI	BB	SO	AVG	OBP	SLG	PRO+	BR/A	SB	CS	SBR	FA	FR	G/POS	TPR

■ CARL POWIS   Powis, Carl Edgar "Jug"   b: 1/11/28, Philadelphia, Pa.   BR/TR, 6', 185 lbs.   Deb: 4/15/57

| 1957 | Bal-A | 15 | 41 | 4 | 8 | 3 | 1 | 0 | 2 | 7 | 9 | .195 | .327 | .317 | 82 | -1 | 2 | 0 | 1 | .909 | -1 | O-13 | -0.2 |

■ JOHNNY PRAMESA   Pramesa, John Steven   b: 8/28/25, Barton, Ohio   BR/TR, 6'2", 210 lbs.   Deb: 4/24/49

1949	Cin-N	17	25	2	6	1	0	1	2	3	5	.240	.321	.400	91	-0	0			.966	-1	C-13	-0.1
1950	Cin-N	74	228	14	70	10	1	5	30	19	15	.307	.363	.425	106	2	0			.981	0	C-73	0.5
1951	Cin-N	72	227	12	52	5	2	6	22	5	17	.229	.246	.348	57	-14	0	0	0	.968	-7	C-63	-1.9
1952	Chi-N	22	46	1	13	1	0	1	5	4	4	.283	.340	.370	96	-0	0	0	0	.958	2	C-17	0.2
Total	4	185	526	29	141	17	3	13	59	31	41	.268	.310	.386	84	-13	0	0		.973	-6	C-166	-1.3

■ DEL PRATT   Pratt, Derrill Burnham   b: 1/10/1888, Walhalla, S.C.   d: 9/30/77, Texas City, Tex.   BR/TR, 5'11", 175 lbs.   Deb: 4/11/12

1912	StL-A	152	570	76	172	26	15	5	69	36		.302	.348	.426	125	16	24			.943	14	*2-122,S-21/O3	2.8
1913	StL-A	155	592	60	175	31	13	2	87	40	57	.296	.341	.402	121	13	37			.951	5	*2-146/1-9	1.6
1914	StL-A	158	584	85	165	34	13	5	65	50	45	.283	.341	.411	131	19	37	28	-6	.944	-2	*2-152/O-5,S	1.2
1915	StL-A	159	602	61	175	31	11	3	78	26	43	.291	.323	.394	119	10	32	23	-4	.965	12	*2-158	2.0
1916	StL-A	158	596	64	159	35	12	5	**103**	54	56	.267	.331	.391	123	14	26	17	-2	.966	22	*2-158	4.2
1917	StL-A	123	450	40	111	22	8	1	53	33	36	.247	.301	.338	98	-2	18			.959	15	*2-119/1-2	2.0
1918	NY-A	126	477	65	131	19	7	2	55	35	26	.275	.327	.356	104	1	12			.969	12	*2-126	2.3
1919	NY-A	140	527	69	154	27	7	4	56	36	24	.292	.342	.393	105	3	22			.969	**28**	*2-140	3.8
1920	NY-A	154	574	84	180	37	8	4	97	50	24	.314	.372	.427	107	6	12	10	-2	.971	12	*2-154	2.0
1921	Bos-A	135	521	80	169	36	10	5	102	44	10	.324	.378	.461	116	12	8	10	-4	.961	-1	*2-134	1.0
1922	Bos-A	154	607	73	183	44	7	6	86	53	20	.301	.361	.427	106	5	7	10	-4	.966	-13	*2-154	-0.8
1923	Det-A	101	297	43	92	18	3	0	40	25	9	.310	.375	.391	104	2	6	1	1	.947	-10	2-60,1-17,3	-0.6
1924	Det-A	121	429	56	130	32	3	1	77	31	10	.303	.353	.399	95	-4	6	9	-4	.948	-2	2-65,1-51/3O	-1.1
Total	13	1836	6826	856	1996	392	117	43	968	513	360	.292	.345	.403	112	93	247	108		.960	91	*2-1688/1-79,S30	20.4

■ FRANK PRATT   Pratt, Francis Bruce "Truckhorse"   b: 8/24/1897, Blocton, Ala.   d: 3/8/74, Centreville, Ala.   BL/TR, 5'9.5", 155 lbs.   Deb: 5/13/21

| 1921 | Chi-A | 1 | 1 | 0 | 0 | 0 | 0 | 0 | 0 | 0 | 0 | .000 | .000 | .000 | -99 | -0 | 0 | 0 | 0 | .000 | 0 | H | 0.0 |

■ LARRY PRATT   Pratt, Lester John   b: 10/8/1886, Gibson City, Ill.   d: 1/8/69, Peoria, Ill.   BR/TR, 6' ", 183 lbs.   Deb: 9/19/14

1914	Bos-A	5	4	0	0	0	0	0	0	0	4	.000	.000	.000	-99	-1	0			.923	2	/C-5	0.1
1915	Bro-F	20	49	5	9	1	0	1	2	2	18	.184	.216	.265	29	-5	2			.949	-1	C-17	-0.5
	New-F	5	4	2	2	2	0	0	0	3	1	.500	.714	1.000	378	2	2			1.000	-1	/C-3	0.2
	Yr	25	53	7	11	3	0	1	2	5	19	.208	.276	.321	60	-3	4			.953	-1	C-20	-0.3
Total	2	30	57	7	11	3	0	1	2	5	23	.193	.258	.298	50	-4	4			.949	0	/C-25	-0.2

■ TOM PRATT   Pratt, Thomas J.   b: 1/26/1844, Chelsea, Mass.   d: 9/28/08, Philadelphia, Pa.   TL, 5'7.5", 150 lbs.   Deb: 10/18/1871   U

| 1871 | Ath-n | 1 | 6 | 2 | 2 | 0 | 0 | 0 | 1 | 0 | 0 | .333 | .333 | .333 | 93 | -0 | 0 | | | | | /1-1 | 0.0 |

■ TODD PRATT   Pratt, Todd Alan   b: 2/9/67, Bellevue, Neb.   BR/TR, 6'3", 195 lbs.   Deb: 7/29/92

1992	Phi-N	16	46	6	13	2	0	2	10	4	12	.283	.340	.435	118	1	0	0	0	.972	-1	C-11	0.1
1993	*Phi-N	33	87	8	25	6	0	5	13	5	19	.287	.333	.529	128	3	0	0	0	.989	5	C-26	0.9
1994	Phi-N	28	102	10	20	6	1	2	9	12	29	.196	.281	.333	60	-6	0	1	-1	1.000	-1	C-28	-0.6
Total	3	77	235	24	58	13	1	9	32	21	60	.247	.311	.426	96	-2	0	1		.991	3	/C-65	0.4

■ MEL PREIBISCH   Preibisch, Melvin Adolphus "Primo"   b: 11/23/14, Sealy, Tex.   d: 4/12/80, Sealy, Tex.   BR/TR, 5'11", 185 lbs.   Deb: 9/17/40

1940	Bos-N	11	40	3	9	2	0	0	5	2	4	.225	.262	.275	51	-3	0			1.000	1	O-11	-0.3
1941	Bos-N	5	4	0	0	0	0	0	0	1	2	.000	.200	.000	-42	-1	0			1.000	-1	/O-2	-0.2
Total	2	16	44	3	9	2	0	0	5	3	6	.205	.255	.250	42	-3	0			1.000	-0	/O-13	-0.5

■ BOBBY PRESCOTT   Prescott, George Bertrand   b: 3/27/31, Colon, Panama   BR/TR, 5'11", 180 lbs.   Deb: 6/17/61

| 1961 | KC-A | 10 | 12 | 0 | 1 | 0 | 0 | 0 | 0 | 2 | 5 | .083 | .214 | .083 | -17 | -2 | 0 | 0 | 0 | .000 | -1 | /O-2 | -0.3 |

■ JIM PRESLEY   Presley, James Arthur   b: 10/23/61, Pensacola, Fla.   BR/TR, 6'1", 200 lbs.   Deb: 6/24/84

1984	Sea-A	70	251	27	57	12	1	10	36	6	63	.227	.248	.402	78	-9	1	1	-0	.958	-3	3-69/D-1	-1.3
1985	Sea-A	155	570	71	157	33	1	28	84	44	100	.275	.328	.484	118	13	2	2	-1	.961	7	*3-154	1.7
1986	Sea-A☆	155	616	83	163	33	4	27	107	32	172	.265	.305	.463	105	2	0	4	-2	.965	6	*3-155	0.2
1987	Sea-A	152	575	78	142	23	6	24	88	38	157	.247	.298	.433	86	-13	2	0	1	.953	11	3-148/S-4,D	-0.3
1988	Sea-A	150	544	50	125	26	0	14	62	36	114	.230	.283	.355	74	-20	3	5	-2	.940	-13	*3-146/D-4	-3.6
1989	Sea-A	117	390	42	92	20	1	12	41	21	107	.236	.277	.385	82	-11	0	0	-0	.924	-4	3-90,1-30/D	-1.6
1990	Atl-N	140	541	59	131	34	1	19	72	29	130	.242	.284	.414	85	-13	1	1	-0	.930	-3	*3-133,1-17	-1.7
1991	SD-N	20	59	3	8	0	1	1	5	4	16	.136	.203	.186	10	-7	0	1	-1	.923	-3	3-16	-1.2
Total	8	959	3546	413	875	181	14	135	495	210	859	.247	.292	.420	90	-57	9	14	-6	.949	-2	3-911/1-47,DS	-7.8

■ WALT PRESTON   Preston, Walter B.   b: 1870, Richmond, Va.   BL/TR, 6', 175 lbs.   Deb: 4/18/1895

| 1895 | Lou-N | 50 | 197 | 42 | 55 | 6 | 4 | 1 | 24 | 17 | 17 | .279 | .366 | .365 | 95 | -1 | 11 | | | .893 | -7 | O-26,3-25 | -0.7 |

■ JIM PRICE   Price, Jimmie William   b: 10/13/41, Harrisburg, Pa.   BR/TR, 6', 195 lbs.   Deb: 4/11/67

1967	Det-A	44	92	9	24	4	0	4	8	4	10	.261	.292	.304	74	-3	0	0	0	.974	0	C-24	-0.2
1968	*Det-A	64	132	12	23	4	0	3	13	13	14	.174	.253	.273	58	-7	0	0	0	.996	2	C-42	-0.3
1969	Det-A	72	192	21	45	8	0	9	28	18	20	.234	.300	.417	95	-2	0	0	0	.989	4	C-51	0.4
1970	Det-A	52	132	12	24	4	0	5	15	21	23	.182	.294	.326	70	-5	0	0	0	.979	-1	C-38	-0.5
1971	Det-A	29	54	4	13	2	0	1	7	6	3	.241	.328	.333	84	-1	0	0	0	.981	1	C-25	0.1
Total	5	261	602	58	129	22	0	18	71	62	70	.214	.290	.341	78	-18	0	0	0	.985	5	C-180	-0.5

■ JACKIE PRICE   Price, John Thomas Reid "Johnny"   b: 11/13/12, Windborn, Miss.   d: 10/2/67, San Francisco, Cal.   BL/TR, 5'10.5", 150 lbs.   Deb: 8/18/46

| 1946 | Cle-A | 7 | 13 | 1 | 3 | 0 | 0 | 0 | 0 | 0 | 0 | .231 | .231 | .231 | 31 | -1 | 0 | 0 | 0 | .947 | 2 | /S-4 | 0.0 |

■ JOE PRICE   Price, Joseph Preston "Lumber"   b: 4/10/1897, Milligan College, Tenn.   d: 1/15/61, Washington, D.C.   BR/TR, 6'1.5", 187 lbs.   Deb: 9/5/28

| 1928 | NY-N | 1 | 1 | 0 | 0 | 0 | 0 | 0 | 0 | 0 | 1 | .000 | .000 | .000 | -99 | -0 | 0 | | | .000 | -1 | /O-1 | -0.1 |

■ BOB PRICHARD   Prichard, Robert Alexander   b: 10/21/17, Paris, Tex.   d: 9/25/91, Abilene, Tex.   BL/TL, 6'1", 195 lbs.   Deb: 6/14/39

| 1939 | Was-A | 26 | 85 | 8 | 20 | 5 | 0 | 0 | 8 | 19 | 16 | .235 | .375 | .294 | 79 | -2 | 0 | 2 | -1 | .992 | -1 | 1-26 | -0.6 |

■ JERRY PRIDDY   Priddy, Gerald Edward   b: 11/9/19, Los Angeles, Cal.   d: 3/3/80, N.Hollywood, Cal.   BR/TR, 5'11.5", 180 lbs.   Deb: 4/17/41

1941	NY-A	56	174	18	37	7	0	1	26	18	16	.213	.290	.270	50	-13	4	2	0	.968	9	2-31,3-14,1	-0.2
1942	*NY-A	59	189	23	53	9	2	2	28	31	27	.280	.385	.381	118	6	0	1	-1	.944	5	3-35,1-11/2S	1.1
1943	Was-A	149	560	68	152	31	3	4	62	67	76	.271	.350	.359	112	9	5	5	-2	.971	4	*2-134,S-15/3	2.2
1946	Was-A	138	511	54	130	22	8	6	58	57	73	.254	.332	.364	100	-0	9	3	1	.962	2	*2-138	1.2
1947	Was-A	147	505	42	108	20	3	3	49	62	79	.214	.301	.283	65	-24	7	6	-2	.980	-2	*2-146	-1.8
1948	StL-A	151	560	96	166	40	4	8	79	86	71	.296	.391	.443	118	16	6	5	-1	.968	24	*2-146	4.4
1949	StL-A	145	544	83	158	26	4	11	63	80	81	.290	.382	.414	106	5	5	5	-0	.968	-3	*2-145	0.8
1950	Det-A	157	618	104	171	26	6	13	75	95	95	.277	.376	.401	96	-3	2	7	-4	.981	**31**	*2-157	3.0
1951	Det-A	154	584	73	152	22	9	8	57	69	73	.260	.338	.360	88	-9	4	3	-1	.980	10	*2-154/S-1	0.7
1952	Det-A	75	279	37	79	23	3	4	20	42	29	.283	.379	.430	124	10	3	1	-1	.968	2	2-75	0.8

YEAR	TM/L	G	AB	R	H	2B	3B	HR	RBI	BB	SO	AVG	OBP	SLG	PRO+	BR/A	SB	CS	SBR	FA	FR	G/POS	TPR
1953	Det-A	65	196	14	46	6	2	1	24	17	19	.235	.299	.301	63	-10	1	1	-0	.977	4	2-45,1-11/3	-0.5
Total	11	1296	4720	612	1252	232	46	61	541	624	639	.265	.353	.373	97	-13	44	44	-13	.973	82	*2-1179/3-52,1S	11.7

■ CURTIS PRIDE   Pride, Curtis John   b: 12/17/68, Washington, D.C.   BL/TR, 6', 205 lbs.   Deb: 9/14/93

YEAR	TM/L	G	AB	R	H	2B	3B	HR	RBI	BB	SO	AVG	OBP	SLG	PRO+	BR/A	SB	CS	SBR	FA	FR	G/POS	TPR
1993	Mon-N	10	9	3	4	1	1	1	5	0	3	.444	.444	1.111	288	2	1	0	0	1.000	-0	/O-2	0.2

■ JOHNNY PRIEST   Priest, John Gooding   b: 6/23/1886, St.Joseph, Mo.   d: 11/4/79, Washington, D.C.   BR/TR, 5'11", 170 lbs.   Deb: 5/30/11

YEAR	TM/L	G	AB	R	H	2B	3B	HR	RBI	BB	SO	AVG	OBP	SLG	PRO+	BR/A	SB	CS	SBR	FA	FR	G/POS	TPR
1911	NY-A	8	21	2	3	0	0	0	2	2		.143	.250	.143	10	-2	3			.824	-3	/2-5,3-2	-0.6
1912	NY-A	2	2	1	1	0	0	0	1	0		.500	.500	.500	176	0	0			.000	0	H	0.0
Total	2	10	23	3	4	0	0	0	3	2		.174	.269	.174	23	-2	3			.824	-3	/2-5,3-2	-0.6

■ TOM PRINCE   Prince, Thomas Albert   b: 8/13/64, Kankakee, Ill.   BR/TR, 5'11", 185 lbs.   Deb: 9/22/87

YEAR	TM/L	G	AB	R	H	2B	3B	HR	RBI	BB	SO	AVG	OBP	SLG	PRO+	BR/A	SB	CS	SBR	FA	FR	G/POS	TPR
1987	Pit-N	4	9	1	2	1	0	0	2	0	2	.222	.222	.667	123	0	0	0	0	1.000	1	/C-4	0.1
1988	Pit-N	29	74	3	13	2	0	0	6	4	15	.176	.218	.203	22	-7	0	0	0	.983	-2	C-28	-0.9
1989	Pit-N	21	52	1	7	4	0	0	5	6	12	.135	.224	.212	26	-5	1	1	-0	.960	-0	C-21	-0.5
1990	Pit-N	4	10	1	1	0	0	0	0	1	2	.100	.182	.100	-21	-2	0	0	0	1.000	-0	/C-3	-0.2
1991	Pit-N	26	34	4	9	3	0	1	2	7	3	.265	.405	.441	140	2	0	0	-1	.984	1	C-19/1-1	0.4
1992	Pit-N	27	44	1	4	2	0	0	5	6	9	.091	.200	.136	-3	-6	1	1	-0	.977	3	C-19/3-1	-0.3
1993	Pit-N	66	179	14	35	14	0	2	24	13	38	.196	.276	.307	56	-11	1	1	-0	.984	-1	C-59	-0.9
1994	LA-N	3	6	2	2	0	0	0	1	1	3	.333	.429	.333	109	0	0	0	0	1.000	0	/C-3	0.0
Total	8	180	408	27	73	26	0	4	45	38	84	.179	.262	.272	48	-29	3	4	-2	.981	3	C-156/3-1,1	-2.3

■ WALTER PRINCE   Prince, Walter Farr   b: 5/9/1861, Amherst, N.H.   d: 3/2/38, Bristol, N.H.   BL/TR, 5'9", 150 lbs.   Deb: 8/7/1883

YEAR	TM/L	G	AB	R	H	2B	3B	HR	RBI	BB	SO	AVG	OBP	SLG	PRO+	BR/A	SB	CS	SBR	FA	FR	G/POS	TPR
1883	Lou-a	4	11	1	2	0	0	0		0		.182	.182	.182	19	-1				.500	-2	/O-2,1-,S	-0.3
1884	Det-N	7	21	0	3	0	0	0		3	4	.143	.250	.143	29	-2				.375	-3	/O-7	-0.5
	Was-a	43	166	22	36	3	2	1		13		.217	.286	.277	95	-0				.940	-6	1-43	-0.9
	Was-U	1	4	0	1	0	0	0		0		.250	.250	.250	38	-0				.818	-0	/1-1	-0.1
Total	2	55	202	23	42	3	2	1	1	16	4	.208	.276	.257	82	-2				.935	-11	/1-46,O-9,S	-1.8

■ BUDDY PRITCHARD   Pritchard, Harold William   b: 1/25/36, South Gate, Cal.   BR/TR, 6'1", 195 lbs.   Deb: 4/21/57

YEAR	TM/L	G	AB	R	H	2B	3B	HR	RBI	BB	SO	AVG	OBP	SLG	PRO+	BR/A	SB	CS	SBR	FA	FR	G/POS	TPR
1957	Pit-N	23	11	1	1	0	0	0	0	0	4	.091	.091	.091	-53	-2	0	0	0	.947	5	S-10/2-3	0.2

■ GEORGE PROESER   Proeser, George "Yatz"   b: 5/30/1864, Cincinnati, Ohio   d: 10/13/41, New Burlington, O.   BL/TL, 5'10", 190 lbs.   Deb: 9/15/1888

YEAR	TM/L	G	AB	R	H	2B	3B	HR	RBI	BB	SO	AVG	OBP	SLG	PRO+	BR/A	SB	CS	SBR	FA	FR	G/POS	TPR
1888	Cle-a	7	23	5	7	2	0	0		1	1	.304	.333	.304	136	1	0			.846	-1	/P-7	0.0
1890	Syr-a	13	53	11	13	1	1	0		10		.245	.365	.358	126	2	1			.895	-2	O-13	0.0
Total	2	20	76	16	20	3	1	0	1	11		.263	.356	.368	129	3	1			.895	-3	/O-13,P-7	0.0

■ JAKE PROPST   Propst, William Jacob   b: 3/10/1895, Kennedy, Ala.   d: 2/24/67, Columbus, Miss.   BL/TR, 5'10", 165 lbs.   Deb: 8/7/23

YEAR	TM/L	G	AB	R	H	2B	3B	HR	RBI	BB	SO	AVG	OBP	SLG	PRO+	BR/A	SB	CS	SBR	FA	FR	G/POS	TPR
1923	Was-A	1	1	0	0	0	0	0	0	0	0	.000	.000	.000	-99	0	0	0	0	.000	0	H	0.0

■ DOC PROTHRO   Prothro, James Thompson   b: 7/16/1893, Memphis, Tenn.   d: 10/14/71, Memphis, Tenn.   BR/TR, 5'10.5", 170 lbs.   Deb: 9/26/20   M

YEAR	TM/L	G	AB	R	H	2B	3B	HR	RBI	BB	SO	AVG	OBP	SLG	PRO+	BR/A	SB	CS	SBR	FA	FR	G/POS	TPR
1920	Was-A	6	13	2	5	0	0	0	2	0	4	.385	.385	.385	107	0	0	0	0	1.000	-1	/S-2,3-2	0.0
1923	Was-A	6	8	2	2	0	0	1	3	1	3	.250	.333	.500	124	0	0	0	0	1.000	3	/3-6	0.3
1924	Was-A	46	159	17	53	11	5	0	24	15	11	.333	.394	.465	125	6	4	4	-1	.915	-11	3-45	-0.3
1925	Bos-A	119	415	44	130	23	3	0	51	52	21	.313	.390	.383	97	-0	9	11	-4	.945	-6	*3-108/S-3	-0.2
1926	Cin-N	3	5	1	1	0	0	0	1	1	1	.200	.333	.600	151	0	0	0	0	1.000	-0	/3-2	0.0
Total	5	180	600	66	191	34	10	0	81	69	40	.318	.390	.408	105	6	13	15		.940	-14	3-163/S-5	-0.2

■ EARL PRUESS   Pruess, Earl Henry "Gibby"   b: 4/2/1895, Chicago, Ill.   d: 8/28/79, Branson, Mo.   BR/TR, 5'10.5", 170 lbs.   Deb: 9/15/20

YEAR	TM/L	G	AB	R	H	2B	3B	HR	RBI	BB	SO	AVG	OBP	SLG	PRO+	BR/A	SB	CS	SBR	FA	FR	G/POS	TPR
1920	StL-A	1	0	1	0	0	0	0	0	0	0	—	1.000	—	176	0	1	0	0	1.000	0	/O-1	0.1

■ JIM PRUETT   Pruett, James Calvin   b: 12/16/17, Nashville, Tenn.   BR/TR, 5'10", 178 lbs.   Deb: 9/26/44

YEAR	TM/L	G	AB	R	H	2B	3B	HR	RBI	BB	SO	AVG	OBP	SLG	PRO+	BR/A	SB	CS	SBR	FA	FR	G/POS	TPR
1944	Phi-A	3	4	1	1	0	0	0	0	1	0	.250	.500	.250	119	0	0	0	0	1.000	1	/C-2	0.1
1945	Phi-A	6	9	1	2	0	0	0	0	1	2	.222	.300	.222	53	-1	0	1	-1	1.000	1	/C-4	-0.1
Total	2	9	13	2	3	0	0	0	0	2	2	.231	.375	.231	77	-0	0	1	-1	1.000	1	/C-6	0.0

■ RON PRUITT   Pruitt, Ronald Ralph   b: 10/21/51, Flint, Mich.   BR/TR, 6', 185 lbs.   Deb: 6/25/75

YEAR	TM/L	G	AB	R	H	2B	3B	HR	RBI	BB	SO	AVG	OBP	SLG	PRO+	BR/A	SB	CS	SBR	FA	FR	G/POS	TPR
1975	Tex-A	14	17	2	3	0	0	0	0	1	3	.176	.222	.176	14	-2	0	0	0	1.000	-1	C-13/O-1	-0.3
1976	Cle-A	47	86	7	23	1	1	0	5	16	8	.267	.382	.302	103	1	2	3	-1	1.000	2	O-26/C-6,31D	0.2
1977	Cle-A	78	219	29	63	10	2	2	32	28	22	.288	.373	.379	109	4	2	3	-1	.972	-8	O-69/C-4,3D	-0.7
1978	Cle-A	71	187	17	44	6	1	6	17	16	20	.235	.296	.374	88	-3	2	1	0	.984	-6	C-48,O-16/3D	-0.6
1979	Cle-A	64	166	23	47	7	0	2	21	19	21	.283	.357	.361	94	-1	2	0	1	.957	-5	O-29,D-14,C/3	-0.6
1980	Cle-A	23	36	1	11	1	0	0	4	4	6	.306	.375	.333	95	-0	0	0	0	1.000	1	/O-6,3-2,D	0.0
	Chi-A	33	70	8	21	2	0	2	11	8	7	.300	.372	.414	116	2	0	0	0	1.000	-1	O-11/C-5,31D	0.0
	Yr	56	106	9	32	3	0	2	15	12	13	.302	.373	.387	109	2	0	0	0	1.000	-1	O-17/D-9,3C1	0.0
1981	Cle-A	5	9	0	0	0	0	0	0	1	2	.000	.100	.000	-70	-2	0	0	0	1.000	-1	/O-3,C-1,D	-0.3
1982	SF-N	5	4	1	2	1	0	0	2	1	1	.500	.600	.750	276	1	0	0	0	1.000	1	/C-1,O-1	0.1
1983	SF-N	1	1	0	0	0	0	0	0	0	0	.000	.000	.000	-99	-0	0	0	0	.000	0	/H	0.0
Total	9	341	795	88	214	28	4	12	92	94	90	.269	.348	.360	97	-1	8	7	-2	.977	-19	O-162/C-89,D31	-2.6

■ GREG PRYOR   Pryor, Gregory Russell   b: 10/2/49, Marietta, Ohio   BR/TR, 6', 186 lbs.   Deb: 6/4/76

YEAR	TM/L	G	AB	R	H	2B	3B	HR	RBI	BB	SO	AVG	OBP	SLG	PRO+	BR/A	SB	CS	SBR	FA	FR	G/POS	TPR
1976	Tex-A	5	8	2	3	0	0	0	0	1	0	.375	.375	.375	118	0	0	0	0	1.000	1	/2-3,S-1,3	0.1
1978	Chi-A	82	222	27	58	11	0	2	15	11	18	.261	.299	.338	78	-7	3	1	0	.966	6	2-35,S-28,3	-0.4
1979	Chi-A	143	476	60	131	23	3	3	34	35	41	.275	.327	.355	84	-10	3	4	-2	.961	-5	*S-119,2-25,3	-0.4
1980	Chi-A	122	338	32	81	18	4	1	29	12	35	.240	.270	.325	63	-18	2	5	-1	.975	22	S-76,3-41/2D	1.1
1981	Chi-A	47	76	4	17	1	0	1	7	3	8	.224	.298	.237	57	-4	0	0	0	.931	4	3-27,S-13/2	0.0
1982	KC-A	73	152	23	41	10	1	2	12	10	20	.270	.315	.388	92	-2	2	1	0	.951	3	3-40,2-15,1/S	0.6
1983	KC-A	68	115	9	25	4	0	1	14	7	8	.217	.262	.278	49	-8	0	0	0	.958	11	3-60/1-6,2	0.2
1984	*KC-A	123	270	32	71	11	4	2	25	12	28	.263	.302	.356	80	-7	0	3	-2	.970	17	*3-105,2-22/S1D	0.8
1985	*KC-A	63	114	8	25	3	0	1	8	3	12	.219	.237	.272	49	-8	1	0	0	.946	2	3-26,2-20,S/1D	-0.5
1986	KC-A	63	112	7	19	4	0	0	7	3	14	.170	.191	.205	8	-14	1	0	0	.935	6	3-35,S-17,2/1	-0.9
Total	10	789	1883	204	471	85	9	14	146	104	185	.250	.293	.327	70	-78	11	12	-4	.952	70	3-377,S-276,2/1D	1.4

■ GEORGE PUCCINELLI   Puccinelli, George Lawrence "Pooch" or "Count"   b: 6/22/07, San Francisco, Cal.   d: 4/16/56, San Francisco, Cal   BR/TR, 6'0.5", 190 lbs.   Deb: 7/17/30

YEAR	TM/L	G	AB	R	H	2B	3B	HR	RBI	BB	SO	AVG	OBP	SLG	PRO+	BR/A	SB	CS	SBR	FA	FR	G/POS	TPR
1930	*StL-N	11	16	5	9	1	0	3	8	0	1	.563	.563	1.188	298	5	0			1.000	-1	/O-3	0.3
1932	StL-N	31	108	17	30	8	3	2	11	12	13	.278	.350	.435	107	2	0			.942	2	O-30	0.0
1934	StL-A	10	26	4	6	1	0	0	2	5	9	.231	.286	.500	92	-1	0	0	0	.941	1	/O-6	0.0
1936	Phi-A	135	457	83	127	30	3	11	78	65	70	.278	.369	.429	98	-1	2	3	-1	.948	0	*O-117	-0.6
Total	4	187	607	109	172	40	6	19	102	78	92	.283	.367	.453	105	4	2	3		.947	2	O-156	-0.1

■ KIRBY PUCKETT   Puckett, Kirby   b: 3/14/61, Chicago, Ill.   BR/TR, 5'8", 210 lbs.   Deb: 5/8/84

YEAR	TM/L	G	AB	R	H	2B	3B	HR	RBI	BB	SO	AVG	OBP	SLG	PRO+	BR/A	SB	CS	SBR	FA	FR	G/POS	TPR
1984	Min-A	128	557	63	165	12	5	0	31	16	69	.296	.321	.336	78	-16	14	7	0	.993	30	*O-128	1.0
1985	Min-A	161	691	80	199	29	13	4	74	41	87	.288	.332	.385	90	-9	21	12	-1	.984	21	*O-161	0.6
1986	Min-A★	161	680	119	223	37	6	31	96	34	99	.328	.366	.537	138	34	20	12	-1	.986	11	*O-160	3.8
1987	*Min-A★	157	624	96	**207**	32	5	28	99	32	91	.332	.370	.534	131	26	12	7	-1	.986	5	*O-147/D-8	2.5

YEAR	TM/L	G	AB	R	H	2B	3B	HR	RBI	BB	SO	AVG	OBP	SLG	PRO+	BR/A	SB	CS	SBR	FA	FR	G/POS	TPR
1988	Min-A★	158	657	109	**234**	42	5	24	121	23	83	.356	.380	.545	151	42	6	7	-2	.994	20	*O-158	5.4
1989	Min-A★	159	635	75	**215**	45	4	9	85	41	59	**.339**	.381	.465	129	23	11	4	1	.991	18	*O-157/D-2	3.9
1990	Min-A★	146	551	82	164	40	3	12	80	57	73	.298	.367	.460	119	14	5	4	-1	.989	8	*O-141/2-1,3SD	1.7
1991	*Min-A★	152	611	92	195	29	6	15	89	31	78	.319	.356	.460	118	14	11	5	0	.985	4	*O-152	1.5
1992	Min-A★	160	639	104	**210**	38	4	19	110	44	97	.329	.377	.490	137	30	17	7	1	.993	6	*O-149/2-2,3SD	3.4
1993	Min-A★	156	622	89	184	39	3	22	89	47	93	.296	.352	.474	119	16	8	6	-1	.994	4	*O-139,D-17	1.4
1994	Min-A★	108	439	79	139	32	3	20	**112**	28	47	.317	.362	.540	130	18	6	3	0	.986	8	O-95,D-13	2.2
Total	11	1646	6706	988	2135	375	57	184	986	394	876	.318	.361	.474	122	192	131	74	-5	.989	135	*O-1587/D-53,32S	27.4

■ JOHN PUHL   Puhl, John G.   b: 1/10/1876, Brooklyn, N.Y.   d: 8/24/1900, Bayonne, N.J.   Deb: 10/13/1898

YEAR	TM/L	G	AB	R	H	2B	3B	HR	RBI	BB	SO	AVG	OBP	SLG	PRO+	BR/A	SB	CS	SBR	FA	FR	G/POS	TPR
1898	NY-N	2	9	1	2	0	0	0	1	0		.222	.222	.222	28	-1	0			.667	-1	/3-2	-0.1
1899	NY-N	1	2	0	0	0	0	0	0	0		.000	.333	.000	-6	-0	0			.667	-0	/3-1	0.0
Total	2	3	11	1	2	0	0	0	1	0		.182	.250	.182	24	-1	0			.667	-1	/3-3	-0.1

■ TERRY PUHL   Puhl, Terry Stephen   b: 7/8/56, Melville, Sask., Can   BL/TR, 6'2", 200 lbs.   Deb: 7/12/77

YEAR	TM/L	G	AB	R	H	2B	3B	HR	RBI	BB	SO	AVG	OBP	SLG	PRO+	BR/A	SB	CS	SBR	FA	FR	G/POS	TPR
1977	Hou-N	60	229	40	69	13	5	0	10	30	31	.301	.385	.402	122	8	10	1	2	.992	3	O-59	1.1
1978	Hou-N☆	149	585	87	169	25	6	3	35	48	46	.289	.347	.368	108	6	32	14	1	.992	15	*O-148	1.6
1979	Hou-N	157	600	87	172	22	4	8	49	58	46	.287	.353	.377	105	5	30	22	-4	**1.000**	3	*O-152	-0.3
1980	*Hou-N	141	535	75	151	24	5	13	55	60	52	.282	.359	.419	126	19	27	11	2	.991	14	*O-135	3.0
1981	*Hou-N	96	350	43	88	19	4	3	28	31	49	.251	.319	.354	96	-2	22	4	4	**1.000**	5	O-88	0.3
1982	Hou-N	145	507	64	133	17	9	8	50	51	49	.262	.332	.379	106	4	17	9	-0	.989	-6	*O-138	-0.7
1983	Hou-N	137	465	66	136	25	7	8	44	36	48	.292	.346	.428	121	12	24	11	1	.991	-4	*O-124	0.5
1984	Hou-N	132	449	66	135	19	7	9	55	59	45	.301	.383	.434	129	24	13	8	-1	.986	-2	*O-126	1.9
1985	Hou-N	57	194	34	55	14	3	2	23	18	23	.284	.347	.418	116	4	6	2	1	1.000	0	O-53	0.3
1986	*Hou-N	81	172	17	42	10	0	3	14	15	24	.244	.305	.355	84	-4	3	2	-0	1.000	-4	O-47	-1.0
1987	Hou-N	90	122	9	28	5	0	2	15	11	16	.230	.293	.320	65	-7	6	1	-0	.980	-6	O-40	-1.3
1988	Hou-N	113	234	42	71	7	2	3	19	35	30	.303	.396	.389	131	11	22	4	4	.983	-7	O-78	0.7
1989	Hou-N	121	354	41	96	25	4	0	27	45	39	.271	.355	.364	110	6	9	8	-2	1.000	-2	*O-103/1-3	-0.1
1990	Hou-N	37	41	5	12	1	0	0	8	5	7	.293	.383	.317	98	0	1	2	-1	1.000	-2	/O-8,1-1	-0.3
1991	KC-A	15	18	0	4	1	0	0	3	3	2	.222	.333	.222	57	-1	0	1	0	.000	-0	/O-1,D-2	-0.3
Total	15	1531	4855	676	1361	226	56	62	435	505	507	.280	.351	.388	113	84	217	99	6	.993	8	*O-1300/1-4,D	5.6

■ RICH PUIG   Puig, Richard Gerald   b: 3/16/53, Tampa, Fla.   BL/TR, 5'10", 165 lbs.   Deb: 9/13/74

YEAR	TM/L	G	AB	R	H	2B	3B	HR	RBI	BB	SO	AVG	OBP	SLG	PRO+	BR/A	SB	CS	SBR	FA	FR	G/POS	TPR
1974	NY-N	4	10	0	0	0	0	0	1	2		.000	.091	.000	-74	-2	0	0	0	.923	-0	/2-3,3-1	-0.3

■ LUIS PUJOLS   Pujols, Luis Bienvenido (Toribio)   b: 11/18/55, Santiago, D.R.   BR/TR, 6'1", 195 lbs.   Deb: 9/22/77   C

YEAR	TM/L	G	AB	R	H	2B	3B	HR	RBI	BB	SO	AVG	OBP	SLG	PRO+	BR/A	SB	CS	SBR	FA	FR	G/POS	TPR
1977	Hou-N	6	15	0	1	0	0	0	0	0	5	.067	.067	.067	-70	-7	0	0	0	1.000	0	/C-6	-0.4
1978	Hou-N	56	153	11	20	8	1	1	11	12	45	.131	.199	.216	17	-18	0	0	0	.981	0	C-55/1-1	-1.8
1979	Hou-N	26	75	7	17	2	1	0	8	2	14	.227	.247	.280	46	-8	0	0	0	.993	1	C-26	-0.4
1980	*Hou-N	78	221	15	44	6	1	0	20	13	29	.199	.247	.235	38	-19	0	0	0	.990	-3	C-75/3-1	-2.1
1981	*Hou-N	40	117	5	28	3	1	1	14	10	17	.239	.299	.308	76	-4	1	0	0	.995	-1	C-39	-0.3
1982	Hou-N	65	176	8	35	6	2	4	15	10	40	.199	.242	.324	62	-10	0	3	-2	.991	5	C-64	-0.5
1983	Hou-N	40	87	4	17	2	1	0	12	5	14	.195	.239	.218	29	-8	0	0	0	.971	5	C-39	-0.3
1984	KC-A	4	5	0	1	0	0	0	1	0		.200	.200	.200	11	-1	0	0	0	1.000	0	/C-4	0.0
1985	Tex-A	1	1	0	1	0	0	0	0	0		1.000	1.000	1.000	444	0	0	0	0	1.000	-0	/C-1	0.0
Total	9	316	850	50	164	27	6	6	81	52	164	.193	.241	.260	43	-68	1	3	-2	.987	7	C-309/3-1,1	-5.8

■ HARVEY PULLIAM   Pulliam, Harvey Jerome   b: 10/20/67, San Francisco, Cal.   BR/TR, 6', 210 lbs.   Deb: 8/10/91

YEAR	TM/L	G	AB	R	H	2B	3B	HR	RBI	BB	SO	AVG	OBP	SLG	PRO+	BR/A	SB	CS	SBR	FA	FR	G/POS	TPR
1991	KC-A	18	33	4	9	1	0	3	4	3	9	.273	.333	.576	146	2	0	0	0	.917	-2	O-15	0.0
1992	KC-A	4	5	2	1	1	0	0	1	0	3	.200	.333	.400	102	0	0	0	0	1.000	0	/O-1,D-2	0.0
1993	KC-A	27	62	7	16	5	0	1	6	2	14	.258	.292	.387	76	-2	0	0	0	.971	-5	O-26	-0.8
Total	3	49	100	13	26	7	0	4	10	6	26	.260	.308	.450	100	-0	0	0	0	.951	-7	/O-42,D-2	-0.8

■ BLONDIE PURCELL   Purcell, William Aloysius   b: Paterson, N.J.   BR/TR, 5'9.5", 159 lbs.   Deb: 5/1/1879   M

YEAR	TM/L	G	AB	R	H	2B	3B	HR	RBI	BB	SO	AVG	OBP	SLG	PRO+	BR/A	SB	CS	SBR	FA	FR	G/POS	TPR
1879	Syr-N	63	277	32	72	6	3	0	25	3	13	.260	.268	.303	99	0				.773	-13	O-47,P-22/C	-1.2
	Cin-N	12	50	10	11	0	0	0	4	0	3	.220	.220	.220	48	-3				.750	1	O-10/P-2	-0.2
	Yr	75	327	42	83	6	3	0	29	3	16	.254	.261	.291	91	-3				.767	-13	O-57,P-24/C	-1.4
1880	Cin-N	77	325	48	95	13	6	1	24	5	13	.292	.303	.378	131	10				.814	-2	O-55,P-25/S	0.4
1881	Cle-N	20	80	3	14	2	1	0	4	5	8	.175	.224	.225	44	-5				.786	-2	O-20	-0.7
	Buf-N	30	113	15	33	7	2	0	17	8	8	.292	.339	.389	130	4				.706	-6	O-25/P-9	-0.3
	Yr	50	193	18	47	9	3	0	21	13	16	.244	.291	.321	95	-1				.748	-8	O-45/P-9	-1.0
1882	Buf-N	84	380	79	105	18	6	2	40	14	27	.276	.302	.371	113	5				.820	-5	*O-82/P-6	-0.1
1883	Phi-N	97	425	70	114	20	5	1	32	13	26	.268	.290	.346	101	2				.777	5	3-46,O-44,PM	0.4
1884	Phi-N	103	428	67	108	11	7	1	31	29	30	.252	.300	.318	99	1				.874	-0	*O-103/P-1	-0.1
1885	Phi-a	66	304	71	90	15	5	0		16		.296	.337	.378	119	5				.858	-1	O-66/P-1	0.2
	Bos-N	21	87	9	19	1	0	0	3	3	15	.218	.244	.253	63	-3				.840	-3	O-21	-0.7
1886	Bal-a	26	85	17	19	0	1	0		17		.224	.365	.247	96	1	13			.867	-1	O-26/S-1,P	0.0
1887	Bal-a	140	567	101	142	25	8	4		46		.250	.318	.344	90	-7	88			.925	-4	*O-140/P-1	-1.0
1888	Bal-a	101	406	53	96	9	4	2	39	27		.236	.289	.293	89	-5	16			.906	-6	*O-100/S-2,1	-1.2
	Phi-a	18	66	10	11	3	1	0	6	5		.167	.236	.242	54	-3	10			.903	0	O-17/3-1	-0.3
	Yr	119	472	63	107	12	5	2	45	32		.227	.281	.286	84	-8	26			.905	-6	*O-117/S-2,13	-1.5
1889	Phi-a	129	507	72	160	19	7	0	85	50	27	.316	.383	.381	119	14	22			.903	-10	*O-129	0.1
1890	Phi-a	110	463	110	128	28	3	2	46	48		.276	.343	.363	111	6	48			.949	-1	*O-110	0.1
Total	12	1097	4563	767	1217	177	60	13	310	284	170	.267	.314	.340	103	22	197			.869	-49	O-995/P-79,3S1C	-4.6

■ PID PURDY   Purdy, Everett Virgil   b: 6/15/04, Beatrice, Neb.   d: 1/16/51, Beatrice, Neb.   BL/TR, 5'6", 150 lbs.   Deb: 9/7/26

YEAR	TM/L	G	AB	R	H	2B	3B	HR	RBI	BB	SO	AVG	OBP	SLG	PRO+	BR/A	SB	CS	SBR	FA	FR	G/POS	TPR
1926	Chi-A	11	33	5	6	2	0	0	6	2	1	.182	.229	.303	39	-3	0	1	-1	1.000	0	/O-9	-0.4
1927	Cin-N	18	62	15	22	2	4	1	12	4	3	.355	.412	.565	164	5	0			.946	-3	O-16	0.1
1928	Cin-N	70	223	32	69	11	1	0	25	23	13	.309	.368	.368	97	-0	1			.966	0	O-61	-0.4
1929	Cin-N	82	181	22	49	7	5	1	16	19	8	.271	.350	.381	85	-4	2			.978	-1	O-42	-0.7
Total	4	181	499	74	146	22	11	2	59	48	25	.293	.362	.393	97	-2	3	1		.969	-4	O-128	-1.4

■ JESSE PURNELL   Purnell, Jesse Rhoades   b: 5/11/1881, Glenside, Pa.   d: 7/4/66, Philadelphia, Pa.   BL/TR, 5'5.5", 140 lbs.   Deb: 10/1/04

YEAR	TM/L	G	AB	R	H	2B	3B	HR	RBI	BB	SO	AVG	OBP	SLG	PRO+	BR/A	SB	CS	SBR	FA	FR	G/POS	TPR
1904	Phi-N	7	19	2	2	0	0	0	1	4		.105	.292	.105	25	-1	1			.864	-1	/3-7	-0.2

■ BILLY PURTELL   Purtell, William Patrick   b: 1/6/1886, Columbus, Ohio   d: 3/17/62, Bradenton, Fla.   BR/TR, 5'9", 170 lbs.   Deb: 4/16/08

YEAR	TM/L	G	AB	R	H	2B	3B	HR	RBI	BB	SO	AVG	OBP	SLG	PRO+	BR/A	SB	CS	SBR	FA	FR	G/POS	TPR
1908	Chi-A	26	69	3	9	2	0	0	3	2		.130	.155	.159	2	-7	2			.940	6	3-25	0.0
1909	Chi-A	103	361	34	93	9	3	0	40	19		.258	.302	.299	94	-3	14			.929	5	3-71,2-32	0.4
1910	Chi-A	102	368	21	82	5	1	1	36	21		.223	.272	.261	70	-13	5			.907	4	*3-102	-0.7
	Bos-A	49	168	15	35	1	2	1	15	18		.208	.289	.256	69	-6	2			.908	-5	3-41/S-8	-1.0
	Yr	151	536	36	117	6	3	2	51	39		.218	.278	.259	70	-19	7			.907	-1	*3-143/S-8	-1.7
1911	Bos-A	27	82	5	23	5	0	0	7	1		.280	.298	.415	99	-1	1			.867	-1	3-15/2-3,SO	-0.1
1914	Det-A	28	76	4	13	4	0	0	3	2		.171	.203	.224	27	-7	0	2	-1	.946	-1	3-16/S-2,2	-0.9
Total	5	335	1124	82	255	26	11	2	104	63	7	.227	.275	.275	73	-37	24	2		.915	9	3-270/2-36,SO	-2.3

YEAR	TM/L	G	AB	R	H	2B	3B	HR	RBI	BB	SO	AVG	OBP	SLG	PRO+	BR/A	SB	CS	SBR	FA	FR	G/POS	TPR

■ ED PUTMAN   Putman, Eddy William   b: 9/25/53, Los Angeles, Cal.   BR/TR, 6'1", 190 lbs.   Deb: 9/7/76

1976	Chi-N	5	7	0	3	0	0	0	0	0	0	.429	.429	.429	132	0	0	0	0	1.000	0	/C-3,1-1	0.0
1978	Chi-N	17	25	2	5	0	0	0	3	4	6	.200	.310	.200	40	-2	0	0	0	.950	-0	/3-8,1-3,C	-0.2
1979	Det-A	21	39	4	9	3	0	2	4	4	12	.231	.302	.462	99	-0	0	1	-1	1.000	1	C-16/1-5	0.0
Total	3	43	71	6	17	3	0	2	7	8	18	.239	.316	.366	81	-2	0	1	-1	1.000	1	/C-21,1-9,3	-0.2

■ PAT PUTNAM   Putnam, Patrick Edward   b: 12/3/53, Bethel, Vt.   BL/TR, 6'1", 214 lbs.   Deb: 9/2/77

1977	Tex-A	11	26	3	8	4	0	0	3	1	4	.308	.333	.462	113	0	0	1	-1	1.000	-1	/1-7,D-3	-0.1
1978	Tex-A	20	46	4	7	1	0	1	2	2	5	.152	.188	.239	19	-5	0	0	0	1.000	0	D-12/1-4	-0.6
1979	Tex-A	139	426	57	118	19	2	18	64	23	50	.277	.323	.458	109	4	1	6	-3	.994	-1	1-96,D-32	-0.5
1980	Tex-A	147	410	42	108	16	2	13	55	36	49	.263	.323	.407	102	0	0	2	-1	.992	5	*1-137/3-1,D	-0.3
1981	Tex-A	95	297	33	79	17	2	8	35	17	38	.266	.306	.418	113	3	4	2	0	.993	3	1-94/O-3	0.2
1982	Tex-A	43	122	14	28	8	0	2	9	10	18	.230	.293	.344	78	-4	0	2	-1	.990	1	1-39/3-1,O	-0.6
1983	Sea-A	144	469	58	126	23	2	19	67	39	57	.269	.329	.448	107	4	2	1	0	.994	4	*1-125,D-11	0.0
1984	Sea-A	64	155	11	31	6	0	2	16	12	27	.200	.257	.277	49	-11	3	0	1	1.000	-1	D-30,O-13/1	-1.3
	Min-A	14	38	1	3	1	0	0	4	4	12	.079	.167	.105	-22	-6	0	0	0	.000	0	D-11	-0.7
	Yr	78	193	12	34	7	0	2	20	16	39	.176	.239	.244	34	-17	3	0	1	1.000	-1	D-41,O-13/1	-2.0
Total	8	677	1989	223	508	95	8	63	255	144	260	.255	.309	.406	96	-14	10	14	-5	.993	10	1-508,D-100/O3	-3.9

■ JIM PYBURN   Pyburn, James Edward   b: 11/1/32, Fairfield, Ala.   BR/TR, 6', 190 lbs.   Deb: 4/17/55

1955	Bal-A	39	98	5	20	2	0	0	7	8	24	.204	.271	.265	48	-7	1	1	-0	1.000	-5	3-33/O-1	-1.3
1956	Bal-A	84	156	23	27	3	3	2	11	17	26	.173	.254	.269	41	-14	4	1	1	.975	-11	O-77	-2.6
1957	Bal-A	35	40	8	9	0	0	1	2	9	6	.225	.367	.300	90	-0	1	0	0	1.000	-2	O-28/C-1	-0.3
Total	3	158	294	36	56	5	3	3	20	34	56	.190	.277	.272	51	-21	6	2	1	.982	-18	O-106/3-33,C	-4.2

■ EDDIE PYE   Pye, Robert Edward   b: 2/13/67, Columbia, Tenn.   BR/TR, 5'10", 175 lbs.   Deb: 6/3/94

1994	LA-N	7	10	2	1	0	0	0	0	1	4	.100	.182	.100	-25	-2	0	0	0	1.000	2	/2-3,S-3	0.1

■ FRANKIE PYTLAK   Pytlak, Frank Anthony   b: 7/30/08, Buffalo, N.Y.   d: 5/8/77, Buffalo, N.Y.   BR/TR, 5'7.5", 160 lbs.   Deb: 4/22/32

1932	Cle-A	12	29	5	7	1	1	0	4	3	2	.241	.333	.345	71	-1	0	0	0	1.000	3	C-12	0.2
1933	Cle-A	80	248	36	77	10	6	2	33	17	10	.310	.355	.423	101	-0	3	4	-2	1.000	11	C-69	1.2
1934	Cle-A	91	289	46	75	12	4	0	35	36	11	.260	.352	.329	75	-10	11	2	2	.989	-10	C-88	-1.3
1935	Cle-A	55	149	14	44	6	1	1	12	11	4	.295	.348	.369	84	-3	3	2	-0	.984	-1	C-48	-0.2
1936	Cle-A	75	224	35	72	15	4	0	31	24	11	.321	.394	.424	101	1	5	2	0	.996	-6	C-58	-0.1
1937	Cle-A	125	397	60	125	15	5	1	44	52	15	.315	.404	.390	100	3	16	5	2	.986	10	*C-115	1.9
1938	Cle-A	113	364	46	112	14	7	1	43	36	15	.308	.381	.393	95	-2	9	5	-0	.987	-8	C-99	-0.4
1939	Cle-A	63	183	20	49	2	5	0	14	20	5	.268	.343	.333	76	-6	4	1	1	1.000	3	C-51	0.0
1940	Cle-A	62	149	16	21	2	1	0	16	17	5	.141	.234	.168	6	-21	0	1	-1	.996	7	C-58/O-1	-1.0
1941	Bos-A	106	336	36	91	23	1	6	39	28	19	.271	.329	.363	81	-9	5	7	-3	.991	1	C-91	-0.4
1945	Bos-A	9	17	1	2	0	0	0	1	0	0	.118	.250	.118	8	-2	0	0	0	1.000	1	/C-6	-0.1
1946	Bos-A	4	14	1	2	0	0	0	1	0	0	.143	.143	.143	-19	-2	0	0	0	1.000	2	/C-4	0.0
Total	12	795	2399	316	677	100	36	7	272	247	97	.282	.355	.363	84	-53	56	29	-1	.991	12	C-699/O-1	-0.2

■ TIM PYZNARSKI   Pyznarski, Timothy Matthew   b: 2/4/60, Chicago, Ill.   BR/TR, 6'2", 195 lbs.   Deb: 9/14/86

1986	SD-N	15	42	3	10	1	0	0	0	4	11	.238	.319	.262	63	-2	2	0	1	.977	-0	1-13	-0.3

■ JIM QUALLS   Qualls, James Robert   b: 10/9/46, Exeter, Cal.   BB/TR, 5'10", 158 lbs.   Deb: 4/10/69

1969	Chi-N	43	120	12	30	5	3	0	9	2	14	.250	.268	.342	62	-6	2	1	0	1.000	-3	O-35/2-4	-1.2
1970	Mon-N	9	9	1	1	0	0	0	1	0	0	.111	.111	.111	-40	-2	0	0	0	1.000	-1	/2-2,O-2	-0.3
1972	Chi-A	11	10	0	0	0	0	0	0	0	2	.000	.000	.000	-98	-2	0	0	0	1.000	0	/O-1	-0.3
Total	3	63	139	13	31	5	3	0	10	2	16	.223	.239	.302	46	-10	2	1	0	1.000	-4	/O-38,2-6	-1.8

■ MEL QUEEN   Queen, Melvin Douglas   b: 3/26/42, Johnson City, N.Y.   BL/TR, 6'1", 197 lbs.   Deb: 4/13/64 FC

1964	Cin-N	48	95	7	19	2	0	2	12	4	19	.200	.232	.284	43	-7	0	1	-1	.977	1	O-20	-0.8
1965	Cin-N	5	3	0	0	0	0	0	0	0	1	.000	.000	.000	-94	-1	0	0	0	1.000	-0	/O-1	-0.1
1966	Cin-N	56	55	4	7	1	0	0	5	10	12	.127	.262	.145	16	-6	0	0	0	1.000	-4	O-32/P-7	-1.1
1967	Cin-N	49	81	6	17	4	0	0	5	4	10	.210	.247	.259	40	-6	2	0	1	.941	-2	P-31	0.0
1968	Cin-N	10	8	2	1	0	0	0	1	0	3	.125	.222	.125	-6	-1	0	0	0	1.000	-0	/P-5	0.0
1969	Cin-N	2	6	0	1	0	0	0	0	0	0	.167	.167	.167	-6	-1	0	0	0	1.000	-0	/P-2	0.0
1970	Cal-A	37	16	1	4	0	0	0	1	0	2	.250	.250	.250	40	-1	0	0	0	1.000	-1	P-34	0.0
1971	Cal-A	45	8	0	0	0	0	0	1	1	0	.000	.111	.000	-71	-2	0	0	0	.900	-1	P-44	0.0
1972	Cal-A	17	2	0	0	0	0	0	0	1	1	.000	.333	.000	5	-0	0	0	0	1.000	-0	P-17	0.0
Total	9	269	274	20	49	7	0	2	25	21	50	.179	.237	.226	30	-25	2	1	0	.951	-7	P-140/O-53	-2.0

■ BILLY QUEEN   Queen, William Eddleman "Doc"   b: 11/28/28, Gastonia, N.C.   BR/TR, 6'1", 185 lbs.   Deb: 4/13/54

1954	Mil-N	3	2	0	0	0	0	0	0	0	2	.000	.000	.000	-99	-0	0	0	0	1.000	-0	/O-1	-0.1

■ GEORGE QUELLICH   Quellich, George William   b: 2/10/06, Johnsville, Cal.   d: 8/31/58, Johnsville, Cal.   BR/TR, 6'1", 180 lbs.   Deb: 8/1/31

1931	Det-A	13	54	6	12	5	0	1	11	3	4	.222	.263	.370	63	-3	0	0	0	1.000	1	O-13	-0.2

■ JOE QUEST   Quest, Joseph L.   b: 11/16/1852, New Castle, Pa.   d: 11/14/24, San Diego, Cal.   BR/TR, 5'6", 150 lbs.   Deb: 8/30/1871 U

1871	Cle-n	3	13	1	3	0	0	0	2	1	0	.231	.286	.308	75	-0	0					/2-2,S-1	0.0
1878	Ind-N	62	278	45	57	3	2	0	13	12	24	.205	.238	.230	63	-10				.876	2	*2-62	-0.4
1879	Chi-N	83	334	38	69	16	1	0	22	9	33	.207	.227	.260	57	-16				.925	14	*2-83	0.4
1880	Chi-N	82	300	37	71	12	1	0	27	8	16	.237	.256	.283	78	-7				.895	4	*2-80/S-2,3	0.1
1881	Chi-N	78	293	35	72	6	0	1	26	2	29	.246	.251	.276	63	-13				.929	6	*2-77/S-1	-0.4
1882	Chi-N	42	159	24	32	5	2	0	15	8	16	.201	.240	.258	57	-8				.879	-5	2-41/S-1	-1.1
1883	Det-N	37	137	22	32	8	2	0	25	10	18	.234	.286	.321	88	-1				.897	0	2-37	-0.1
	StL-a	19	78	12	20	3	1	0		4		.256	.266	.321	83	-2				.890	-6	2-19	-0.7
1884	StL-a	81	310	46	64	9	5	0		19		.206	.257	.268	69	-11				.894	-9	*2-81	-1.7
	Pit-a	12	43	2	9	3	0	0		0		.209	.227	.279	63	-2				.938	0	/2-7,S-5	-0.1
	Yr	93	353	48	73	12	5	0		19		.207	.253	.269	68	-12				.898	-9	2-88/S-5	-1.8
1885	Det-N	55	200	24	39	8	2	0	21	14	25	.195	.248	.255	63	-8				.898	-2	2-39,S-15/O	-0.8
1886	Phi-a	42	150	14	31	4	1	0		20		.207	.300	.247	71	-4	5			.847	-5	S-41/2-2	-0.2
Total	9	593	2282	299	496	77	17	1	149	103	161	.217	.252	.267	67	-81	5			.902	5	2-528/S-65,O3	-5.0

■ HAL QUICK   Quick, James Harold "Blondie"   b: 10/4/17, Rome, Ga.   d: 3/9/74, Swansea, Ill.   BR/TR, 5'10.5", 163 lbs.   Deb: 9/7/39

1939	Was-A	12	41	3	10	0	0	0	2	1	1	.244	.279	.268	44	-4	1	0	0	.927	1	S-10	-0.1

■ FRANK QUILICI   Quilici, Francis Ralph "Guido"   b: 5/11/39, Chicago, Ill.   BR/TR, 6', 175 lbs.   Deb: 7/18/65 MC

1965	*Min-A	56	149	16	31	5	1	0	7	15	33	.208	.280	.255	51	-9	1	1	-0	.990	1	2-52/S-4	-0.3
1967	Min-A	23	19	2	2	1	0	0	5	0	6	.105	.227	.158	14	-2	0	0	0	1.000	1	2-13/3-8,S	-0.1
1968	Min-A	97	229	22	56	11	4	1	22	21	45	.245	.311	.341	93	-2	0	0	0	1.000	17	2-48,3-40/S1	2.0
1969	Min-A	118	144	19	25	3	1	2	12	12	22	.174	.237	.250	36	-13	2	0	1	.935	24	3-84,2-36/S	1.5

YEAR	TM/L	G	AB	R	H	2B	3B	HR	RBI	BB	SO	AVG	OBP	SLG	PRO+	BR/A	SB	CS	SBR	FA	FR	G/POS	TPR
1970	*Min-A	111	141	19	32	3	0	2	12	15	16	.227	.301	.291	63	-7	0	2	-1	.987	15	2-73,3-27/S	1.0
Total	5	405	682	78	146	23	6	5	53	66	120	.214	.284	.287	63	-33	3	3	-1	.993	60	2-222,3-159/S1	4.1

■ LEE QUILLEN
Quillen, Leon Abner   b: 5/5/1882, North Branch, Minn.   d: 5/14/65, St.Paul, Minn.   BR/TR, 5'10", 165 lbs.   Deb: 9/30/06

YEAR	TM/L	G	AB	R	H	2B	3B	HR	RBI	BB	SO	AVG	OBP	SLG	PRO+	BR/A	SB	CS	SBR	FA	FR	G/POS	TPR
1906	Chi-A	4	9	1	3	0	0	0	0	0		.333	.333	.333	112	0	1			.600	-2	/S-3	-0.2
1907	Chi-A	49	151	17	29	5	0	0	14	10		.192	.256	.225	56	-7	8			.871	-0	3-48	-0.7
Total	2	53	160	18	32	5	0	0	14	10		.200	.260	.231	59	-7	9			.871	-2	/3-48,S-3	-0.9

■ QUINLAN
Quinlan   Deb: 9/7/1874

YEAR	TM/L	G	AB	R	H	2B	3B	HR	RBI	BB	SO	AVG	OBP	SLG	PRO+	BR/A	SB	CS	SBR	FA	FR	G/POS	TPR
1874	Phi-n	1	4	0	1	0	0	0		0		.250	.250	.250	58	-0						S-1	0.0

■ FRANK QUINLAN
Quinlan, Francis Patrick   b: 3/9/1869, Marlborough, Mass.   d: 5/4/04, Brockton, Mass.   Deb: 10/5/1891

YEAR	TM/L	G	AB	R	H	2B	3B	HR	RBI	BB	SO	AVG	OBP	SLG	PRO+	BR/A	SB	CS	SBR	FA	FR	G/POS	TPR
1891	Bos-a	2	5	0	0	0	0	0	0	0	2	.000	.000	.000	-99	-1				1.000	-1	/C-1,O-1	-0.2

■ FINNERS QUINLAN
Quinlan, Thomas Finners   b: 10/21/1887, Scranton, Pa.   d: 2/17/66, Scranton, Pa.   BL/TL, 5'8", 154 lbs.   Deb: 9/6/13

YEAR	TM/L	G	AB	R	H	2B	3B	HR	RBI	BB	SO	AVG	OBP	SLG	PRO+	BR/A	SB	CS	SBR	FA	FR	G/POS	TPR
1913	StL-N	13	50	1	8	0	0	0	1	1	9	.160	.176	.160	-4	-7	0			.897	2	O-12	-0.6
1915	Chi-A	42	114	11	22	3	0	0	7	4	11	.193	.270	.219	45	-8	3	4	-2	1.000	-2	O-32	-1.3
Total	2	55	164	12	30	3	0	0	8	5	20	.183	.243	.201	31	-14	3	4		.961	0	/O-44	-1.9

■ TOM QUINLAN
Quinlan, Thomas Raymond   b: 3/27/68, St.Paul, Minn.   BR/TR, 6'3", 200 lbs.   Deb: 9/4/90

YEAR	TM/L	G	AB	R	H	2B	3B	HR	RBI	BB	SO	AVG	OBP	SLG	PRO+	BR/A	SB	CS	SBR	FA	FR	G/POS	TPR
1990	Tor-A	1	2	0	1	0	0	0	0	0	1	.500	.667	.500	227	1	0	0		1.000	-0	/3-1	0.0
1992	Tor-A	13	15	2	1	1	0	0	2	2	9	.067	.176	.133	-12	-2	0	0		.909	-1	3-13	-0.3
1994	Phi-N	24	35	6	7	2	0	1	3	3	13	.200	.263	.343	57	-2	0	0		.966	2	3-20	0.0
Total	3	38	52	8	9	3	0	1	5	5	23	.173	.259	.288	45	-4	0	0		.951	1	/3-34	-0.3

■ QUINN
Quinn   Deb: 6/21/1877

YEAR	TM/L	G	AB	R	H	2B	3B	HR	RBI	BB	SO	AVG	OBP	SLG	PRO+	BR/A	SB	CS	SBR	FA	FR	G/POS	TPR
1877	Chi-N	4	14	1	1	0	0	0	0	1	0	.071	.133	.071	-30	-2				.667	0	/O-4	-0.2

■ QUINN
Quinn   Deb: 9/7/1881

YEAR	TM/L	G	AB	R	H	2B	3B	HR	RBI	BB	SO	AVG	OBP	SLG	PRO+	BR/A	SB	CS	SBR	FA	FR	G/POS	TPR
1881	Bos-N	1	4	0	0	0	0	0	0	0	0	.000	.000	.000	-99	-1				1.000	-0	/1-1	-0.1
	Wor-N	2	7	0	1	0	0	0	1	1	2	.143	.250	.143	25	-1				.714	-3	/C-2	-0.3
	Yr	3	11	0	1	0	0	0	1	1	2	.091	.167	.091	-16	-1				.714	-3	/C-2,1-1	-0.4

■ FRANK QUINN
Quinn, Frank J.   b: 1876, Grand Rapids, Mich.   d: 2/17/20, Camden, Ind.   5'8",   Deb: 8/9/1899

YEAR	TM/L	G	AB	R	H	2B	3B	HR	RBI	BB	SO	AVG	OBP	SLG	PRO+	BR/A	SB	CS	SBR	FA	FR	G/POS	TPR
1899	Chi-N	12	34	6	6	0	1	0	1	6		.176	.300	.235	49	-2	1			.909	-4	O-10/2-1	-0.6

■ JOHN QUINN
Quinn, John Edward "Pick"   b: 9/12/1885, Framingham, Mass.   d: 4/9/56, Marlboro, Mass.   BR/TR, 5'11", 150 lbs.   Deb: 10/9/11

YEAR	TM/L	G	AB	R	H	2B	3B	HR	RBI	BB	SO	AVG	OBP	SLG	PRO+	BR/A	SB	CS	SBR	FA	FR	G/POS	TPR
1911	Phi-N	1	2	0	0	0	0	0	0	0	0	.000	.000	.000	-99	-1	0			1.000	-0	/C-1	-0.1

■ JOE QUINN
Quinn, Joseph C.   b: 8/1849, Chicago, Ill.   d: 1/2/09, Chicago, Ill.   5'8.5", 148 lbs.   Deb: 7/26/1871

YEAR	TM/L	G	AB	R	H	2B	3B	HR	RBI	BB	SO	AVG	OBP	SLG	PRO+	BR/A	SB	CS	SBR	FA	FR	G/POS	TPR
1871	Kek-n	5	17	8	4	0	0	0	2	4	0	.235	.381	.235	81	-0	3					/C-5	0.0
1875	Wes-n	11	43	4	14	2	0	0		0		.326	.326	.372	133	1						/C-7,O-4	0.1
	Har-n	5	13	1	3	0	0	0		1		.231	.286	.231	77	-0						/C-2,O-1	0.0
	Chi-n	17	59	12	14	0	0	0		1		.237	.237	.237	64	-2						C-10/O-8	-0.1
	Yr	33	115	17	31	2	0	0		1		.270	.276	.287	92	-1						C-19,O-13	0.0
Total	2 n	38	132	25	35	2	0	0		5		.265	.292	.280	91	-1						/C-24,O-13	0.0

■ JOE QUINN
Quinn, Joseph J.   b: 12/25/1864, Sydney, Australia   d: 11/12/40, St.Louis, Mo.   BR/TR, 5'7", 158 lbs.   Deb: 4/26/1884   M

YEAR	TM/L	G	AB	R	H	2B	3B	HR	RBI	BB	SO	AVG	OBP	SLG	PRO+	BR/A	SB	CS	SBR	FA	FR	G/POS	TPR
1884	StL-U	103	429	74	116	21	1	0		9		.270	.285	.324	63	-22				.945	-1	*1-100/O-3,S	-3.1
1885	StL-N	97	343	27	73	8	2	0	15	9	38	.213	.233	.248	59	-15				.875	-6	O-57,3-31,1	-2.2
1886	StL-N	75	271	33	63	11	3	1	21	8	31	.232	.254	.306	75	-8	12			.895	-1	0-48,2-15/13S	-0.9
1888	Bos-N	38	156	19	47	8	3	4	29	2	5	.301	.310	.468	143	7	12			.914	-7	2-38	0.1
1889	Bos-N	112	444	57	116	13	5	2	69	25	21	.261	.308	.327	73	-17	24			.860	-29	S-63,2-47/3	-3.5
1890	Bos-P	130	509	87	153	19	8	7	82	44	24	.301	.359	.411	99	-4	29			.942	15	*2-130	1.5
1891	Bos-N	124	508	70	122	8	10	3	63	28	28	.240	.288	.313	67	-25	24			.938	-23	*2-124	-3.8
1892	*Bos-N	143	532	63	116	14	1	1	59	35	40	.218	.275	.254	55	-30	17			.951	2	*2-143	-2.4
1893	StL-N	135	547	68	126	18	6	0	71	33	7	.230	.279	.285	50	-41	24			.942	-30	*2-135	-5.6
1894	StL-N	106	405	59	116	18	1	4	61	24	8	.286	.328	.365	67	-22	25			.952	21	*2-106	0.3
1895	StL-N	134	543	84	169	19	9	2	74	36	6	.311	.356	.390	74	-5	22			.946	-2	*2-134,M	0.0
1896	StL-N	48	191	19	40	6	1	1	17	9	5	.209	.242	.267	39	-17	8			.956	2	2-48	-1.1
	*Bal-N	24	82	22	27	1	1	0	5	6	1	.329	.375	.366	94	-1	6			.951	-3	/2-8,O-8,3S	-0.3
	Yr	72	273	41	67	7	2	1	22	15	6	.245	.290	.297	56	-18	14			.955	-1	2-56/O-8,3S	-1.4
1897	Bal-N	75	285	33	74	11	4	1	45	13		.260	.299	.337	68	-14	12			.946	9	3-37,S-21,2/01	-0.3
1898	Bal-N	12	32	5	8	1	0	0	5	1		.250	.273	.281	58	-2	0			.893	0	/3-8,2-1,O	-0.1
	StL-N	103	375	35	94	10	5	0	36	24		.251	.301	.304	72	-14	13			.962	-1	2-62,S-41/O	-0.9
	Yr	115	407	40	102	11	5	0	41	25		.251	.299	.302	71	-16	13			.960	-0	2-63,S-41/3O	-1.0
1899	Cle-N	147	615	73	176	24	6	0	72	21		.286	.312	.345	86	-13	22			.962	3	*2-147,M	-0.2
1900	StL-N	22	80	12	21	2	0	1	11	10		.262	.344	.325	86	-1	4			.933	-8	2-14/S-6,3	-0.8
	Cin-N	74	266	18	73	5	2	0	25	16		.274	.316	.308	74	-9	7			.950	-18	2-74	-2.2
	Yr	96	346	30	94	7	2	1	36	26		.272	.323	.312	77	-10	11			.947	-26	2-88/S-6,3	-3.0
1901	Was-A	66	266	33	67	11	2	2	34	11		.252	.287	.331	72	-10	7			.954	-14	2-66	-2.0
Total	17	1768	6879	891	1797	228	70	29	794	364	214	.261	.302	.327	73	-265	268			.946	-91	*2-1303,S-135,01/3	-27.5

■ PATRICK QUINN
Quinn, Patrick   5'8", 162 lbs.   Deb: 9/9/1875

YEAR	TM/L	G	AB	R	H	2B	3B	HR	RBI	BB	SO	AVG	OBP	SLG	PRO+	BR/A	SB	CS	SBR	FA	FR	G/POS	TPR
1875	Atl-n	2	7	2	1	0	0	0		0		.143	.143	.143	-1	-1						/O-2	-0.1

■ TOM QUINN
Quinn, Thomas Oscar   b: 4/25/1864, Annapolis, Md.   d: 7/24/32, Pittsburgh, Pa.   BR/TR, 5'8", 180 lbs.   Deb: 9/2/1886

YEAR	TM/L	G	AB	R	H	2B	3B	HR	RBI	BB	SO	AVG	OBP	SLG	PRO+	BR/A	SB	CS	SBR	FA	FR	G/POS	TPR
1886	Pit-a	3	11	1	0	0	0	0	0	0		.000	.000	.000	-99	-2	1			.929	-2	/C-3	-0.3
1889	Bal-a	55	194	18	34	2	1	2	15	19	22	.175	.252	.211	32	-17	6			.925	8	C-55	-0.4
1890	Pit-P	55	207	23	44	4	3	1	15	17	8	.213	.282	.275	54	-13	1			.888	-4	C-55	-1.1
Total	3	113	412	42	78	6	4	2	30	36	30	.189	.261	.238	40	-33	8			.910	2	C-113	-1.8

■ LUIS QUINONES
Quinones, Luis Raul   b: 4/28/62, Ponce, P.R.   BB/TR, 5'11", 175 lbs.   Deb: 5/27/83

YEAR	TM/L	G	AB	R	H	2B	3B	HR	RBI	BB	SO	AVG	OBP	SLG	PRO+	BR/A	SB	CS	SBR	FA	FR	G/POS	TPR
1983	Oak-A	19	42	5	8	0	0	1	4	1	4	.190	.209	.286	37	-4	1	1	-0	1.000	1	/2-6,3-4,0SD	-0.3
1986	SF-N	71	106	13	19	1	3	0	11	3	17	.179	.209	.245	26	-11	3	1	0	.922	-7	S-33,3-31/2	-1.7
1987	Chi-N	49	101	12	22	6	0	0	8	10	16	.218	.288	.277	49	-7	0	0	0	.965	-7	S-28/2-4,3	-1.2
1988	Cin-N	23	52	4	12	3	0	1	11	2	11	.231	.259	.346	70	-2	1	1	0	.974	1	S-10/2-4,3	-0.1
1989	Cin-N	97	340	43	83	13	4	12	34	25	46	.244	.302	.412	99	-1	2	4	-2	.979	-5	2-53,3-50/S	-0.7
1990	*Cin-N	83	145	10	35	7	0	2	17	13	29	.241	.308	.331	73	-5	1	0	0	.981	9	3-22,2-13/S1	0.5
1991	Cin-N	97	212	15	47	4	3	4	20	21	31	.222	.298	.325	72	-8	1	2	-1	.975	-2	2-33,3-19/S	-1.2
1992	Min-A	3	5	0	1	0	0	0	1	0		.200	.200	.200	12	-1	0	0		.714	-0	/3-1,S-1,D	-0.1
Total	8	442	1003	102	227	36	11	19	106	75	154	.226	.285	.341	72	-39	9	9	-3	.937	-11	3-132,2-121/SDO1	-4.8

■ REY QUINONES
Quinones, Rey Francisco (Santiago)   b: 11/11/63, Rio Piedras, P.R.   BR/TR, 5'11", 160 lbs.   Deb: 5/17/86

YEAR	TM/L	G	AB	R	H	2B	3B	HR	RBI	BB	SO	AVG	OBP	SLG	PRO+	BR/A	SB	CS	SBR	FA	FR	G/POS	TPR
1986	Bos-A	62	190	26	45	12	1	2	15	19	26	.237	.316	.342	79	-5	3	2	-0	.940	-8	S-62	-0.8
	Sea-A	36	122	6	23	4	0	0	7	5	31	.189	.220	.221	21	-13	1	1	-0	.945	1	S-36	-1.0

YEAR	TM/L	G	AB	R	H	2B	3B	HR	RBI	BB	SO	AVG	OBP	SLG	PRO+	BR/A	SB	CS	SBR	FA	FR	G/POS	TPR
	Yr	98	312	32	68	16	1	2	22	24	57	.218	.280	.295	56	-19	4	3	-1	.942	-7	S-98	-1.8
1987	Sea-A	135	478	55	132	18	2	12	56	26	71	.276	.319	.397	84	-11	1	3	-2	.959	-10	*S-135	-1.0
1988	Sea-A	140	499	63	124	30	3	12	52	23	71	.248	.286	.393	84	-12	0	3	-2	.963	3	*S-135/D-4	0.0
1989	Sea-A	7	19	2	2	0	0	0	0	1	1	.105	.150	.105	-26	-3	0	0	0	.889	-2	/S-7	-0.5
	Pit-N	71	225	21	47	11	0	3	29	15	40	.209	.261	.298	62	-12	0	2	-1	.934	-11	S-69	-2.0
Total	4	451	1533	173	373	75	6	29	159	89	240	.243	.290	.357	74	-56	5	11	-5	.952	-27	S-444/D-4	-5.3

■ CARLOS QUINTANA

Quintana, Carlos Narcis (Hernandez) b: 8/26/65, Estado Miranda, Venez. BR/TR, 6′, 175 lbs. Deb: 9/16/88

YEAR	TM/L	G	AB	R	H	2B	3B	HR	RBI	BB	SO	AVG	OBP	SLG	PRO+	BR/A	SB	CS	SBR	FA	FR	G/POS	TPR
1988	Bos-A	5	6	1	2	0	0	0	2	2	3	.333	.500	.333	133	0	0	0	0	1.000	-0	/O-3,D-1	0.0
1989	Bos-A	34	77	6	16	5	0	0	6	7	12	.208	.274	.273	51	-5	0	0	0	.926	-5	O-21/1-1,D	-1.0
1990	*Bos-A	149	512	56	147	28	0	7	67	52	74	.287	.355	.383	102	2	1	2	-1	.987	15	*1-148/O-3	0.5
1991	Bos-A	149	478	69	141	21	1	11	71	61	66	.295	.377	.412	113	10	1	0	0	.993	7	*1-138,O-13/D	0.9
1993	Bos-A	101	303	31	74	5	0	1	19	31	52	.244	.318	.271	57	-18	1	0	0	.991	-1	1-53,O-51	-2.2
Total	5	438	1376	163	380	59	1	19	165	153	207	.276	.351	.362	93	-11	3	2	0	.990	15	1-340/O-91,D	-1.8

■ MARSHALL QUINTON

Quinton, Marshall J. b: Philadelphia, Pa. 5′11″, 190 lbs. Deb: 8/7/1884

YEAR	TM/L	G	AB	R	H	2B	3B	HR	RBI	BB	SO	AVG	OBP	SLG	PRO+	BR/A	SB	CS	SBR	FA	FR	G/POS	TPR
1884	Ric-a	26	94	12	22	5	0	0		0		.234	.242	.287	73	-3				.878	-9	C-14,O-10/S	-1.0
1885	Phi-a	7	29	6	6	1	0	0		1		.207	.258	.241	55	-2				.869	-2	/C-7	-0.3
Total		33	123	18	28	6	0	0		1		.228	.246	.276	68	-4				.874	-11	/C-21,O-10,S	-1.3

■ JAMIE QUIRK

Quirk, James Patrick b: 10/22/54, Whittier, Cal. BL/TR, 6′4″, 200 lbs. Deb: 9/4/75 C

YEAR	TM/L	G	AB	R	H	2B	3B	HR	RBI	BB	SO	AVG	OBP	SLG	PRO+	BR/A	SB	CS	SBR	FA	FR	G/POS	TPR
1975	KC-A	14	39	2	10	0	0	1	5	2	7	.256	.293	.333	75	-1	0	0	0	.909	0	O-10/3-2,D	-0.1
1976	*KC-A	64	114	11	28	6	0	1	15	5	22	.246	.259	.325	70	-5	0	0	0	1.000	-1	D-19,S-12,3/1	-0.6
1977	Mil-A	93	221	16	48	14	1	3	13	8	47	.217	.251	.330	57	-14	0	1	-1	.950	0	D-53,O-10/3	-1.6
1978	KC-A	17	29	3	6	2	0	0	2	5	4	.207	.324	.276	68	-1	0	0	0	.926	2	3-10/S-2,D	0.1
1979	KC-A	51	79	8	24	6	1	1	11	5	13	.304	.353	.443	111	1	0	0	0	.944	-1	/C-9,S-5,3D	0.1
1980	KC-A	62	163	13	45	5	0	5	21	7	24	.276	.310	.399	92	-2	3	2	-0	.929	-1	3-28,C-15/O1D	-0.3
1981	KC-A	46	100	8	25	7	0	0	10	6	17	.250	.299	.320	79	-3	0	2	-1	.985	-3	C-22/3-8,2O	-0.7
1982	KC-A	36	78	8	18	3	0	1	5	3	15	.231	.259	.308	55	-5	0	0	0	1.000	2	C-29/1-6,3O	-0.3
1983	StL-N	48	86	3	18	2	1	2	11	6	27	.209	.269	.326	64	-4	0	0	0	.929	-3	C-22/3-7,S	-0.9
1984	Chi-A	3	2	0	0	0	0	0	0	0	0	.000	.000	.000	-96	-1	0	0	0	1.000	0	/3-1	-0.1
	Cle-A	1	1	1	1	0	0	1	1	0	0	1.000	1.000	4.000	1189	1	0	0	0	1.000	0	/C-1	0.1
	Yr	4	3	1	1	0	0	1	2	0	1	.333	.333	1.333	324	1	0	0	0	1.000	0	/3-1,C-1	0.0
1985	*KC-A	19	57	3	16	3	1	0	4	2	9	.281	.305	.368	83	-1	0	0	0	.986	-3	C-17/1-1	-0.3
1986	KC-A	80	219	24	47	10	0	8	26	17	41	.215	.274	.370	72	-9	0	1	-1	.989	11	C-41,3-24/1O	0.3
1987	KC-A	109	296	24	70	8	0	5	33	28	56	.236	.311	.345	72	-12	1	0	0	.986	-4	*C-108/S-1	-0.8
1988	KC-A	84	196	22	47	7	1	8	25	28	41	.240	.338	.408	107	2	1	5	-3	.982	14	C-79/1-1,3	1.8
1989	NY-A	13	24	0	2	0	0	0	0	3	5	.083	.185	.083	-22	-4	0	0	-1	1.000	1	/C-6,S-1,D	-0.3
	Oak-A	9	10	1	2	0	0	1	1	0	4	.200	.200	.500	95	0	0	1	-0	.500	0	/3-3,C-2,1O	-0.1
	Bal-A	25	51	5	11	2	0	0	9	9	11	.216	.333	.255	70	-2	0	1	-1	1.000	5	C-24	0.4
	Yr	47	85	6	15	2	0	1	10	12	20	.176	.278	.235	47	-6	0	2	-1	1.000	6	C-32/3-3,SD10	0.0
1990	*Oak-A	56	121	12	34	5	1	3	26	14	34	.281	.360	.413	121	4	0	0	0	.977	-2	C-37/1-8,3OD	0.4
1991	Oak-A	76	203	16	53	4	0	1	17	16	28	.261	.321	.296	76	-6	0	3	-2	.982	6	C-54/1-8,3D	0.0
1992	*Oak-A	78	177	13	39	7	1	2	11	16	28	.220	.296	.305	72	-7	0	0	0	.973	5	C-59/1-9,3D	0.1
Total	18	984	2266	193	544	100	7	43	247	177	435	.240	.300	.347	78	-68	5	16	-8	.982	28	C-525,3-118/D10S2	-2.8

■ JOHN RABB

Rabb, John Andrew b: 6/23/60, Los Angeles, Cal. BR/TR, 6′1″, 180 lbs. Deb: 9/4/82

YEAR	TM/L	G	AB	R	H	2B	3B	HR	RBI	BB	SO	AVG	OBP	SLG	PRO+	BR/A	SB	CS	SBR	FA	FR	G/POS	TPR
1982	SF-N	2	2	0	1	0	1	0	0	0	1	.500	.500	1.500	441	1	0	0	0	1.000	-0	/O-1	0.1
1983	SF-N	40	104	10	24	9	0	1	14	9	17	.231	.292	.346	79	-3	1	0	0	.973	4	C-31/O-2	0.3
1984	SF-N	54	82	10	16	1	0	3	9	10	33	.195	.283	.317	71	-3	1	1	-0	.988	-1	1-13/O-8,C	-0.6
1985	Atl-N	3	3	0	0	0	0	0	0	0	1	.000	.000	.000	-94	-1	0	0	0	.000	-0	/O-1	-0.1
1988	Sea-A	9	14	2	5	2	0	0	4	0	1	.357	.357	.500	131	1	0	0	0	1.000	0	/O-2,1-1,D	0.1
Total	5	108	204	22	46	12	1	4	27	19	53	.225	.291	.353	81	-6	2	1	0	.966	2	/C-37,1-14,OD	-0.2

■ JOE RABBITT

Rabbitt, Joseph Patrick b: 1/16/1900, Frontenac, Kan. d: 12/5/69, Norwalk, Conn. BL/TR, 5′10″, 165 lbs. Deb: 9/15/22

YEAR	TM/L	G	AB	R	H	2B	3B	HR	RBI	BB	SO	AVG	OBP	SLG	PRO+	BR/A	SB	CS	SBR	FA	FR	G/POS	TPR
1922	Cle-A	2	3	1	1	0	0	0	0	0	0	.333	.333	.333	74	-0	0	0	0	.000	-1	/O-1	-0.1

■ MARV RACKLEY

Rackley, Marvin Eugene b: 7/25/21, Seneca, S.C. BL/TL, 5′10″, 170 lbs. Deb: 4/15/47

YEAR	TM/L	G	AB	R	H	2B	3B	HR	RBI	BB	SO	AVG	OBP	SLG	PRO+	BR/A	SB	CS	SBR	FA	FR	G/POS	TPR
1947	Bro-N	18	9	2	2	0	0	0	2	1	0	.222	.300	.222	39	-1	0			1.000	0	/O-2	0.0
1948	Bro-N	88	281	55	92	13	5	0	15	19	25	.327	.370	.409	107	3	8			.949	-5	O-74	-0.6
1949	*Bro-N	9	9	2	4	1	0	0	1	0	0	.444	.500	.556	175	1	0			1.000	-0	/O-3	0.1
	Pit-N	11	35	5	11	2	0	0	2	2	3	.314	.351	.371	92	-0	1			1.000	0	/O-8	-0.1
	*Bro-N	54	141	23	41	4	1	1	14	13	8	.291	.351	.355	86	-2	1			.986	-8	O-44	-1.2
	Yr	74	185	30	56	7	1	1	17	16	11	.303	.358	.368	91	-2	2			.990	-8	O-55	-1.2
1950	Cin-N	5	2	0	1	0	0	0	1	0	0	.500	.500	.500	163	0	0			.000	0	H	0.0
Total	4	185	477	87	151	20	6	1	35	36	36	.317	.365	.390	100	0	10			.966	-13	O-131	-1.8

■ CHARLEY RADBOURN

Radbourn, Charles Gardner "Old Hoss" b: 12/11/1854, Rochester, N.Y. d: 2/5/1897, Bloomington, Ill. BR/TR, 5′9″, 168 lbs. Deb: 5/5/1880 H

YEAR	TM/L	G	AB	R	H	2B	3B	HR	RBI	BB	SO	AVG	OBP	SLG	PRO+	BR/A	SB	CS	SBR	FA	FR	G/POS	TPR
1880	Buf-N	6	21	1	3	0	0	0	1	0	1	.143	.143	.143	-3	-2				.900	4	/O-3,2-3	0.2
1881	Pro-N	72	270	27	59	9	0	0	28	10	15	.219	.246	.252	58	-12				.906	-2	P-41,O-25,S	-0.9
1882	Pro-N	83	326	30	78	11	0	1	32	12	22	.239	.266	.282	76	-8				.912	1	P-55,O-31/S	-0.2
1883	Pro-N	89	381	59	108	11	3	3	48	14	16	.283	.309	.352	98	-1				.920	2	*P-76,O-20/1	-0.3
1884	*Pro-N	87	361	48	83	7	1	1	37	26	42	.230	.282	.263	74	-10				.892	-6	*P-75/O-7,1S2	-0.3
1885	Pro-N	66	249	34	58	9	2	0	22	36	27	.233	.330	.285	104	3				.937	0	P-49,O-16/2	-0.3
1886	Bos-N	66	253	30	60	5	1	2	22	17	36	.237	.285	.289	78	-6	5			.924	1	P-58/O-6	-0.2
1887	Bos-N	51	175	25	40	2	1	1	24	18	21	.229	.308	.280	64	-8	6			.848	-4	P-50/O-2	-0.1
1888	Bos-N	24	79	6	17	1	0	0	6	3	14	.215	.262	.228	56	-4	4			.895	-1	P-24	0.0
1889	Bos-N	35	122	17	23	1	0	1	13	9	19	.189	.256	.221	32	-11	3			.975	1	P-33/O-2,3	-0.2
1890	Bos-P	45	154	20	39	6	0	0	16	9	20	.253	.299	.292	54	-11	7			.935	0	P-41/O-4,1	-0.2
1891	Cin-N	29	96	11	17	2	2	0	10	4	5	.177	.225	.240	35	-5	1			.880	-3	P-26/O-2,3	-0.1
Total	12	653	2487	308	585	64	11	9	259	158	244	.235	.283	.281	72	-78	26			.913	-6	P-528,O-118/S123	-2.5

■ JOHN RADCLIFF

Radcliff, John Y. b: 6/29/1848, Philadelphia, Pa. d: 7/26/11, Ocean City, N.J. 5′6″, 140 lbs. Deb: 5/20/1871

YEAR	TM/L	G	AB	R	H	2B	3B	HR	RBI	BB	SO	AVG	OBP	SLG	PRO+	BR/A	SB	CS	SBR	FA	FR	G/POS	TPR
1871	Ath-n	28	145	47	44	7	5	0	22	6	1	.303	.331	.421	115	3	5					*S-28	0.2
1872	Bal-n	56	298	70	87	10	4	1	46	0	2	.292	.292	.362	96	-3						*S-48/3-5,2	-0.3
1873	Bal-n	45	245	59	70	10	1	0	33	3	2	.286	.294	.335	85	-4						3-24,S-23/2	-0.4
1874	Phi-n	23	102	20	26	6	0	1		2		.255	.269	.343	90	-1						O-16/2-3,S13	-0.1
1875	Cen-n	5	24	2	4	0	0	0	0	0		.167	.167	.167	17	-2						/S-5	-0.1
Total	5 n	157	814	198	231	33	10	2		11		.284	.293	.356	94	-7						S-106/3-30,O21	-0.8

■ RIP RADCLIFF

Radcliff, Raymond Allen b: 1/19/06, Kiowa, Okla. d: 5/23/62, Enid, Okla. BL/TL, 5′10″, 170 lbs. Deb: 9/17/34

YEAR	TM/L	G	AB	R	H	2B	3B	HR	RBI	BB	SO	AVG	OBP	SLG	PRO+	BR/A	SB	CS	SBR	FA	FR	G/POS	TPR
1934	Chi-A	14	56	7	15	2	1	0	5	0	2	.268	.268	.339	54	-4	1	0	0	.946	1	O-14	-0.3
1935	Chi-A	146	623	95	178	28	8	10	68	53	21	.286	.346	.404	91	-9	4	4	-1	.968	-18	*O-142	-3.1
1936	Chi-A★	138	618	120	207	31	7	8	82	44	12	.335	.381	.447	100	-0	6	3	0	.936	-17	*O-132	-2.0

YEAR	TM/L	G	AB	R	H	2B	3B	HR	RBI	BB	SO	AVG	OBP	SLG	PRO+	BR/A	SB	CS	SBR	FA	FR	G/POS	TPR
1937	Chi-A	144	584	105	190	38	10	4	79	53	25	.325	.383	.445	108	8	6	1	1	.966	-4	*O-139	0.0
1938	Chi-A	129	503	64	166	23	6	5	81	36	17	.330	.376	.429	99	-1	5	7	-3	.979	-1	O-99,1-23	-0.9
1939	Chi-A	113	397	49	105	25	2	2	53	26	21	.264	.313	.353	68	-20	6	4	-1	.970	-10	O-78,1-20	-3.3
1940	StL-A	150	584	83	**200**	33	9	7	81	47	20	.342	.392	.466	119	17	1	1	-1	.973	-6	*O-139/1-4	0.2
1941	StL-A	19	71	12	20	2	2	5	14	10	1	.282	.370	.451	112	1	1	1	-0	1.000	-2	O-14/1-3	-0.2
	Det-A	96	379	47	120	14	5	3	40	19	13	.317	.351	.404	90	-6	4	4	-1	.970	-5	O-87	-1.7
	Yr	115	450	59	140	16	7	5	54	29	14	.311	.354	.411	94	-5	5	5	-2	.974	-8	*O-101/1-3	-1.9
1942	Det-A	62	144	13	36	5	0	1	20	9	6	.250	.294	.306	64	-7	0	1	-1	.978	-4	O-24/1-4	-1.0
1943	Det-A	70	115	3	30	4	0	0	10	13	3	.261	.341	.296	81	-2	1	1	-0	1.000	0	O-19/1-1	-0.4
Total	10	1081	4074	598	1267	205	50	42	533	310	141	.311	.362	.417	96	-23	40	30	-6	.967	-62	O-887/1-55	-12.7

■ DAVE RADER
Rader, David Martin b: 12/26/48, Claremore, Okla. BL/TR, 5'11", 165 lbs. Deb: 9/5/71

YEAR	TM/L	G	AB	R	H	2B	3B	HR	RBI	BB	SO	AVG	OBP	SLG	PRO+	BR/A	SB	CS	SBR	FA	FR	G/POS	TPR
1971	SF-N	3	4	0	0	0	0	0	0	0	0	.000	.000	.000	-99	-1	0	0	0	1.000	-0	/C-1	-0.1
1972	SF-N	133	459	44	119	14	1	6	41	29	31	.259	.308	.333	81	-12	1	2	-1	.985	-13	*C-127	-2.2
1973	SF-N	148	462	59	106	15	4	9	41	63	22	.229	.330	.338	82	-10	0	0	0	.991	-12	*C-148	-1.7
1974	SF-N	113	323	26	94	16	2	1	26	31	21	.291	.353	.362	96	-1	1	0	0	.984	-9	*C-109	-0.6
1975	SF-N	98	292	39	85	15	0	5	31	32	30	.291	.368	.394	106	3	1	0	0	.984	-3	C-94	0.4
1976	SF-N	88	255	25	67	15	1	1	22	27	21	.263	.333	.333	87	-4	2	0	1	.984	-9	C-81	-1.0
1977	StL-N	66	114	15	30	7	1	1	16	9	10	.263	.317	.368	85	-3	1	0	0	.976	4	C-38	0.2
1978	Chi-N	116	305	29	62	13	3	3	36	34	26	.203	.285	.295	56	-18	1	1	-0	.977	-13	*C-114	-3.1
1979	Phi-N	31	54	3	11	1	1	1	5	6	7	.204	.283	.315	61	-3	0	0	0	.932	-4	C-25	-0.6
1980	Bos-A	50	137	14	45	11	0	3	17	14	12	.328	.391	.474	129	6	1	1	-0	.981	3	C-34/D-9	0.9
Total	10	846	2405	254	619	107	12	30	235	245	180	.257	.329	.349	86	-43	8	4	0	.983	-56	C-771/D-9	-7.8

■ DON RADER
Rader, Donald Russell b: 9/5/1893, Wolcott, Ind. d: 6/26/83, Walla Walla, Wash BL/TR, 5'10", 164 lbs. Deb: 7/25/13

YEAR	TM/L	G	AB	R	H	2B	3B	HR	RBI	BB	SO	AVG	OBP	SLG	PRO+	BR/A	SB	CS	SBR	FA	FR	G/POS	TPR
1913	Chi-A	4	3	1	1	1	0	0	0	0	0	.333	.333	.667	193	0	0			.000	-1	/3-1,O-1	0.0
1921	Phi-N	9	32	4	9	2	0	0	3	3	5	.281	.343	.344	76	-1	0	0	0	1.000	-6	/S-9	-0.6
Total	2	13	35	5	10	3	0	0	3	3	5	.286	.342	.371	84	-1	0	0		1.000	-6	/S-9,O-1,3	-0.6

■ DOUG RADER
Rader, Douglas Lee "Rojo" or "The Red Rooster" b: 7/30/44, Chicago, Ill. BR/TR, 6'3", 215 lbs. Deb: 7/31/67 MC

YEAR	TM/L	G	AB	R	H	2B	3B	HR	RBI	BB	SO	AVG	OBP	SLG	PRO+	BR/A	SB	CS	SBR	FA	FR	G/POS	TPR
1967	Hou-N	47	162	24	54	10	4	2	26	7	31	.333	.368	.481	146	9	0	3	-2	.972	-1	1-36/3-7	0.5
1968	Hou-N	98	333	42	89	16	4	6	43	31	51	.267	.332	.393	119	8	2	2	-1	.930	1	3-86/1-5	0.9
1969	Hou-N	155	569	62	140	25	3	11	83	62	103	.246	.327	.359	94	-5	1	5	-3	.945	14	*3-154/1-4	0.8
1970	Hou-N	156	576	90	145	25	3	25	87	57	102	.252	.323	.436	106	3	3	2	-0	**.966**	24	*3-154/1-1	2.5
1971	Hou-N	135	484	51	118	21	4	12	56	40	112	.244	.306	.378	95	-4	5	1	1	.946	2	3-135	-0.3
1972	Hou-N	152	553	70	131	24	7	22	90	57	120	.237	.314	.425	110	6	5	5	-2	.958	18	*3-152	2.2
1973	Hou-N	154	574	79	146	26	0	21	89	46	97	.254	.313	.409	99	-2	4	3	-1	.945	-5	*3-152	-0.9
1974	Hou-N	152	533	61	137	27	3	17	78	60	131	.257	.337	.415	114	9	7	2	-1	.965	5	*3-152	1.4
1975	Hou-N	129	448	41	100	23	2	12	48	42	101	.223	.297	.364	89	-9	5	4	-1	**.971**	8	*3-124/S-2	-0.2
1976	SD-N	139	471	45	121	22	4	9	55	55	102	.257	.338	.378	112	7	3	4	-2	.955	14	*3-137	1.9
1977	SD-N	52	170	19	46	8	3	5	27	33	40	.271	.392	.441	137	10	0	1	-1	.961	4	3-51	1.0
	Tor-A	96	313	47	75	18	2	13	40	38	65	.240	.328	.435	104	2	2	1	0	.966	1	3-45,D-34/1O	0.0
Total	11	1465	5186	631	1302	245	39	155	722	528	1055	.251	.325	.403	106	34	37	33	-9	.956	82	*3-1349/1-53,DSO	9.8

■ PAUL RADFORD
Radford, Paul Revere "Shorty" b: 10/14/1861, Roxbury, Mass. d: 2/21/45, Boston, Mass. BR/TR, 5'6", 148 lbs. Deb: 5/1/1883

YEAR	TM/L	G	AB	R	H	2B	3B	HR	RBI	BB	SO	AVG	OBP	SLG	PRO+	BR/A	SB	CS	SBR	FA	FR	G/POS	TPR
1883	Bos-N	72	258	46	53	6	3	0	14	9	26	.205	.232	.252	46	-16				.836	-5	*O-72	-1.9
1884	*Pro-N	97	355	56	70	11	2	1	29	25	43	.197	.250	.248	59	-16				.882	5	*O-96/P-2	-1.1
1885	Pro-N	105	371	55	90	12	5	0	32	33	43	.243	.304	.302	101	2				.852	1	*O-88,S-16/P2	0.0
1886	KC-N	122	493	78	113	17	5	0	20	58	48	.229	.310	.284	77	-13	39			.890	10	*O-92,S-30/2	-0.5
1887	NY-a	128	486	127	129	15	5	4		106		.265	.403	.342	114	17	73			.833	-2	S-76,O-37,2/P	1.3
1888	Bro-a	90	308	48	67	9	3	2	29		35	.218	.305	.286	90	-2	33			.944	9	O-88/2-2	0.4
1889	Cle-N	136	487	94	116	21	5	1	46	91	37	.238	.365	.308	91	-1	30			.942	-0	*O-136/3-1	-0.4
1890	Cle-P	122	466	98	136	24	12	2	62	82	28	.292	.404	.408	128	24	25			.895	9	0-80,S-36/32P	2.5
1891	Bos-N	133	456	102	118	11	5	0	65	96	36	.259	.393	.305	102	7	55			.906	20	*S-131/O-4,P	2.9
1892	Was-N	137	510	93	130	19	4	1	37	86	47	.255	.366	.314	109	10	35			.933	-7	O-62,3-54,S/2	0.3
1893	Was-N	124	464	87	106	18	3	2	34	105	42	.228	.380	.293	82	-6	32			.901	7	*O-123/2-1,P	-0.4
1894	Was-N	95	325	61	78	13	5	0	49	65	23	.240	.378	.311	70	-13	24			.852	-5	S-47,2-25,O	-0.8
Total	12	1361	4979	945	1206	176	57	13	417	791	373	.242	.351	.308	92	-8	346			.901	46	O-902,S-356/32P	2.3

■ JACK RADTKE
Radtke, Jack William b: 4/14/13, Denver, Colo. BB/TR, 5'7", 160 lbs. Deb: 8/1/36

YEAR	TM/L	G	AB	R	H	2B	3B	HR	RBI	BB	SO	AVG	OBP	SLG	PRO+	BR/A	SB	CS	SBR	FA	FR	G/POS	TPR
1936	Bro-N	33	31	8	3	0	0	0	2	4	9	.097	.200	.097	-18	-5	3			1.000	5	2-14/3-5,S	0.0

■ JACK RAFTER
Rafter, John Cornelius b: 2/20/1875, Troy, N.Y. d: 1/5/43, Troy, N.Y. BR/TR, 5'8", 165 lbs. Deb: 9/24/04

YEAR	TM/L	G	AB	R	H	2B	3B	HR	RBI	BB	SO	AVG	OBP	SLG	PRO+	BR/A	SB	CS	SBR	FA	FR	G/POS	TPR
1904	Pit-N	1	3	0	0	0	0	0	0	0	0	.000	.000	.000	-97	-1	0			1.000	0	/C-1	-0.1

■ TOM RAFTERY
Raftery, Thomas Francis b: 10/5/1881, Boston, Mass. d: 12/31/54, Boston, Mass. BR/TR, 5'10.5", 175 lbs. Deb: 4/18/09

YEAR	TM/L	G	AB	R	H	2B	3B	HR	RBI	BB	SO	AVG	OBP	SLG	PRO+	BR/A	SB	CS	SBR	FA	FR	G/POS	TPR
1909	Cle-A	8	32	6	7	2	1	0		0	4	.219	.306	.344	101	0	1			1.000	-1	/O-8	-0.1

■ TOM RAGLAND
Ragland, Thomas b: 6/16/46, Talladega, Ala. BR/TR, 5'10", 155 lbs. Deb: 4/5/71

YEAR	TM/L	G	AB	R	H	2B	3B	HR	RBI	BB	SO	AVG	OBP	SLG	PRO+	BR/A	SB	CS	SBR	FA	FR	G/POS	TPR
1971	Was-A	10	23	1	4	0	0	0	0	0	5	.174	.208	.174	10	-3	0	0	0	1.000	-1	2-10	-0.3
1972	Tex-A	25	58	3	10	2	0	0	2	5	11	.172	.238	.207	35	-5	0	1	-1	.982	-3	2-13/3-5,S	-0.9
1973	Cle-A	67	183	16	47	7	1	0	12	8	31	.257	.292	.306	67	-8	2	3	-1	.984	13	2-65/S-2	0.7
Total	3	102	264	20	61	9	1	0	14	13	47	.231	.272	.273	56	-15	2	4	-2	.985	10	/2-88,S-5,3	-0.5

■ LARRY RAINES
Raines, Lawrence Glenn Hope b: 3/9/30, St.Albans, W.Va. d: 1/28/78, Lansing, Mich. BR/TR, 5'10", 165 lbs. Deb: 4/16/57

YEAR	TM/L	G	AB	R	H	2B	3B	HR	RBI	BB	SO	AVG	OBP	SLG	PRO+	BR/A	SB	CS	SBR	FA	FR	G/POS	TPR
1957	Cle-A	96	244	39	64	14	0	2	16	19	40	.262	.318	.344	82	-6	5	2	0	.922	-5	3-27,S-25,2/O	-0.9
1958	Cle-A	7	9	1	0	0	0	0	0	0	5	.000	.000	.000	-99	-2	0	1	-1	.933	4	/2-2	0.0
Total	2	103	253	40	64	14	0	2	16	19	45	.253	.308	.332	76	-9	5	3	-0	.963	-2	/3-27,S-25,2O	-0.9

■ TIM RAINES
Raines, Timothy "Rock" b: 9/16/59, Sanford, Fla. BB/TR, 5'8", 178 lbs. Deb: 9/11/79

YEAR	TM/L	G	AB	R	H	2B	3B	HR	RBI	BB	SO	AVG	OBP	SLG	PRO+	BR/A	SB	CS	SBR	FA	FR	G/POS	TPR
1979	Mon-N	6	0	3	0	0	0	0	0	0	0	—	—	—	—	0	2	0	1	.000	0	/R	0.0
1980	Mon-N	15	20	5	1	0	0	0	0	6	3	.050	.269	.050	-6	-3	5	0	2	1.000	2	/2-7,O-1	0.1
1981	*Mon-N★	88	313	61	95	13	7	5	37	45	31	.304	.394	.438	134	15	**71**	11	**15**	.976	2	O-81/2-1	3.1
1982	Mon-N★	156	647	90	179	32	8	4	43	75	83	.277	.354	.369	101	2	**78**	16	**14**	.992	3	*O-120,2-36	1.8
1983	Mon-N★	156	615	**133**	183	32	8	11	71	97	70	.298	.393	.429	129	27	**90**	14	**19**	.988	16	*O-154/2-7	5.8
1984	Mon-N★	160	622	106	192	**38**	9	8	60	87	69	.309	.395	.437	140	35	**75**	10	**17**	.988	16	*O-160/2-2	5.8
1985	Mon-N★	150	575	115	184	30	13	11	41	81	60	.320	.407	.475	155	44	70	9	16	.993	10	*O-146	**6.6**
1986	Mon-N★	151	580	91	194	35	10	9	62	78	60	**.334**	**.415**	.476	146	39	70	9	16	.979	11	*O-147	**6.2**
1987	Mon-N★	139	530	**123**	175	34	8	18	68	90	52	.330	.431	.526	148	40	50	5	12	.987	16	*O-139	6.1
1988	Mon-N★	109	429	66	116	19	7	12	48	53	44	.270	.353	.431	119	11	33	7	6	.988	7	*O-108	2.2
1989	Mon-N★	145	517	76	148	29	6	9	60	93	48	.286	.398	.418	132	25	41	9	7	.996	3	*O-139	3.3
1990	Mon-N	130	457	65	131	11	5	9	62	70	43	.287	.379	.392	119	14	49	16	7	.976	-1	*O-123	0.8
1991	Chi-A	155	609	102	163	20	6	5	50	83	52	.268	.360	.345	98	2	51	15	6	.990	10	*O-133,D-19	1.4
1992	Chi-A	144	551	102	162	22	9	7	54	81	48	.294	.384	.405	123	19	45	6	10	.994	14	*O-129,D-14	4.0
1993	*Chi-A	115	415	75	127	16	4	16	54	64	35	.306	.402	.480	139	25	21	7	2	**1.000**	-1	*O-112	2.3

YEAR	TM/L	G	AB	R	H	2B	3B	HR	RBI	BB	SO	AVG	OBP	SLG	PRO+	BR/A	SB	CS	SBR	FA	FR	G/POS	TPR
1994	Chi-A	101	384	80	102	15	5	10	52	61	43	.266	.368	.409	101	2	13	0	4	.981	4	O-96	0.7
Total	16	1920	7264	1293	2152	346	105	134	762	1064	757	.296	.389	.428	127	299	764	134	149	.988	106	*O-1788/2-53,D	51.0

■ JOHN RAINEY
Rainey, John Paul b: 7/26/1864, Birmingham, Mich. d: 11/11/12, Detroit, Mich. BL/TR, 6'1.5", 164 lbs. Deb: 8/25/1887

YEAR	TM/L	G	AB	R	H	2B	3B	HR	RBI	BB	SO	AVG	OBP	SLG	PRO+	BR/A	SB	CS	SBR	FA	FR	G/POS	TPR
1887	NY-N	17	58	6	17	3	0	0	12	5	6	.293	.349	.345	98	0	0			.818	-3	3-17	-0.2
1890	Buf-P	42	166	29	39	5	1	1	20	24	15	.235	.349	.295	79	-3	12			.870	0	O-28/S-7,32	-0.3
Total	2	59	224	35	56	8	1	1	32	29	21	.250	.349	.308	84	-3	12			.827	-3	/O-28,3-23,S2	-0.5

■ GARY RAJSICH
Rajsich, Gary Louis b: 10/28/54, Youngstown, Ohio BL/TL, 6'2", 210 lbs. Deb: 4/9/82 F

YEAR	TM/L	G	AB	R	H	2B	3B	HR	RBI	BB	SO	AVG	OBP	SLG	PRO+	BR/A	SB	CS	SBR	FA	FR	G/POS	TPR
1982	NY-N	80	162	17	42	8	3	2	12	17	40	.259	.333	.383	100	0	1	3	-2	1.000	-2	O-35/1-2	-0.5
1983	NY-N	11	36	5	12	3	0	1	3	3	1	.333	.400	.500	149	2	0	0	0	1.000	-0	1-10	0.2
1984	StL-N	7	7	1	1	0	0	0	2	2	1	.143	.333	.143	39	-0	0	0	0	1.000	-0	/1-3	-0.1
1985	SF-N	51	91	5	15	6	0	0	10	17	22	.165	.296	.231	52	-5	0	1	-1	.990	-1	1-23	-0.9
Total	4	149	296	28	70	17	3	3	27	39	64	.236	.329	.345	90	-3	1	4	-2	.994	-4	/1-38,O-35	-1.3

■ DOC RALSTON
Ralston, Samuel Beryl b: 8/3/1885, Pierpont, Ohio d: 8/29/50, Lancaster, Pa. BR/TR, 6', 185 lbs. Deb: 9/8/10

YEAR	TM/L	G	AB	R	H	2B	3B	HR	RBI	BB	SO	AVG	OBP	SLG	PRO+	BR/A	SB	CS	SBR	FA	FR	G/POS	TPR
1910	Was-A	21	73	4	15	1	0	0	3	3		.205	.256	.219	52	-4	2			.976	2	O-21	-0.4

■ BOB RAMAZZOTTI
Ramazzotti, Robert Louis b: 1/16/17, Elanora, Pa. BR/TR, 5'8.5", 175 lbs. Deb: 4/20/46

YEAR	TM/L	G	AB	R	H	2B	3B	HR	RBI	BB	SO	AVG	OBP	SLG	PRO+	BR/A	SB	CS	SBR	FA	FR	G/POS	TPR
1946	Bro-N	62	120	10	25	4	0	1	7	16	13	.208	.264	.242	43	-9	0			.939	5	3-30,2-16	-0.3
1948	Bro-N	4	3	0	0	0	0	0	0	0	1	.000	.000	.000	-97	-1	0			1.000	0	/3-2,2-1	-0.1
1949	Bro-N	5	13	1	2	0	0	1	3	0	3	.154	.154	.385	38	-1	0			.833	-1	/3-3	-0.1
	Chi-N	65	190	14	34	3	1	0	6	5	33	.179	.200	.205	9	-24	9			.972	6	3-36,S-12/2	-1.8
	Yr	70	203	15	36	3	1	1	9	5	36	.177	.197	.217	11	-26	9			.965	5	3-39,S-12/2	-2.0
1950	Chi-N	61	145	19	38	3	3	1	6	4	16	.262	.287	.345	66	-7	3			.961	-2	2-31,3-10/S	-0.8
1951	Chi-N	73	158	13	39	5	2	1	15	10	23	.247	.292	.323	64	-8	0	0	0	.950	13	S-51/2-6,3	0.7
1952	Chi-N	50	183	26	52	5	3	1	12	14	14	.284	.338	.361	93	-2	3	1	0	.979	-2	2-50	-0.1
1953	Chi-N	26	39	3	6	2	0	0	4	3	4	.154	.214	.205	10	-5	0	0	0	.911	-0	2-18	-0.5
Total	7	346	851	86	196	22	9	4	53	45	107	.230	.271	.291	52	-58	15	1		.966	18	2-126/3-82,S	-3.1

■ MANNY RAMIREZ
Ramirez, Manuel Aristides (Onelcida) b: 5/30/72, Brooklyn, N.Y. BR/TR, 6', 190 lbs. Deb: 9/2/93

YEAR	TM/L	G	AB	R	H	2B	3B	HR	RBI	BB	SO	AVG	OBP	SLG	PRO+	BR/A	SB	CS	SBR	FA	FR	G/POS	TPR
1993	Cle-A	22	53	5	9	1	0	2	5	2	8	.170	.200	.302	33	-5	0	0	0	1.000	0	D-20/O-1	-0.6
1994	Cle-A	91	290	51	78	22	0	17	60	42	72	.269	.361	.521	119	8	4	2	0	.994	-1	O-84/D-5	0.5
Total	2	113	343	56	87	23	0	19	65	44	80	.254	.339	.487	107	2	4	2	0	.994	-0	/O-85,D-25	-0.1

■ MARIO RAMIREZ
Ramirez, Mario (Torres) b: 9/12/57, Yauco, P.R. BR/TR, 5'9", 159 lbs. Deb: 4/25/80

YEAR	TM/L	G	AB	R	H	2B	3B	HR	RBI	BB	SO	AVG	OBP	SLG	PRO+	BR/A	SB	CS	SBR	FA	FR	G/POS	TPR
1980	NY-N	18	24	2	5	0	0	0	0	1	7	.208	.240	.208	27	-2	0	0		1.000	3	/S-7/2-4,3	0.1
1981	SD-N	13	13	1	1	0	0	0	1	2	5	.077	.190	.077	-21	-2	0	0		1.000	4	/S-2,3-2	0.2
1982	SD-N	13	23	1	4	1	0	0	1	2	4	.174	.240	.217	30	-2	0	0		.963	-2	/S-8,2-1,3	-0.2
1983	SD-N	55	107	11	21	6	3	0	12	20	23	.196	.328	.308	80	-2	0	0		.985	-2	S-38/3-1	0.0
1984	*SD-N	48	59	12	7	1	0	2	9	13	14	.119	.278	.237	46	-4	0	0	0	.971	-1	S-33/3-6,2	-0.3
1985	SD-N	37	60	6	17	0	0	2	5	3	11	.283	.317	.383	97	-0	0	0	0	.918	-5	S-27/2-7	-0.4
Total	6	184	286	33	55	8	3	4	28	41	64	.192	.296	.283	64	-13	0	0		.970	1	S-115/2-14,3	-0.6

■ MILT RAMIREZ
Ramirez, Milton (Barboza) b: 4/2/50, Mayaguez, P.R. BR/TR, 5'9", 150 lbs. Deb: 4/11/70

YEAR	TM/L	G	AB	R	H	2B	3B	HR	RBI	BB	SO	AVG	OBP	SLG	PRO+	BR/A	SB	CS	SBR	FA	FR	G/POS	TPR
1970	StL-N	62	79	8	15	2	1	0	3	8	9	.190	.264	.241	36	-7	0	1	-1	.923	10	S-59/3-1	0.5
1971	StL-N	4	11	2	3	0	0	0	0	2	1	.273	.385	.273	86	-0	0	0	0	.947	-1	/S-4	-0.1
1979	Oak-A	28	62	4	10	1	1	0	3	3	8	.161	.200	.210	11	-8	0	0	0	.923	-5	3-12,2-11/S	-1.2
Total	3	94	152	14	28	3	2	0	6	13	18	.184	.248	.230	30	-15	0	1	-1	.920	4	/S-71,3-13,2	-0.8

■ ORLANDO RAMIREZ
Ramirez, Orlando (Leal) b: 12/18/51, Cartagena, Colombia BR/TR, 5'10", 175 lbs. Deb: 7/6/74

YEAR	TM/L	G	AB	R	H	2B	3B	HR	RBI	BB	SO	AVG	OBP	SLG	PRO+	BR/A	SB	CS	SBR	FA	FR	G/POS	TPR
1974	Cal-A	31	86	4	14	0	0	0	7	6	23	.163	.217	.163	11	-10	2	1	0	.956	5	S-31	-0.1
1975	Cal-A	44	100	10	24	4	1	0	4	11	22	.240	.315	.300	80	-2	9	6	-1	.905	0	S-40	0.0
1976	Cal-A	30	70	3	14	1	0	0	5	6	11	.200	.263	.214	44	-5	3	2	0	.966	4	S-30	0.1
1977	Cal-A	25	13	6	1	0	0	0	0	0	3	.077	.077	.077	-60	-3	1	0	0	1.000	8	/2-5,S-3,D	0.6
1979	Cal-A	13	12	1	0	0	0	0	0	1	6	.000	.143	.000	-60	-3	1	0	0	.844	4	S-10	0.1
Total	5	143	281	24	53	5	1	0	16	24	65	.189	.255	.214	37	-23	16	9	-1	.931	21	S-114/2-5,D	0.7

■ RAFAEL RAMIREZ
Ramirez, Rafael Emilio (Peguero) b: 2/18/58, San Pedro De Macoris, D.R. BR/TR, 6', 185 lbs. Deb: 8/4/80

YEAR	TM/L	G	AB	R	H	2B	3B	HR	RBI	BB	SO	AVG	OBP	SLG	PRO+	BR/A	SB	CS	SBR	FA	FR	G/POS	TPR
1980	Atl-N	50	165	17	44	6	1	2	11	2	33	.267	.292	.352	76	-5	2	1	0	.949	-10	S-46	-1.1
1981	Atl-N	95	307	30	67	16	2	2	20	24	47	.218	.277	.303	63	-15	7	3	0	.942	-2	S-95	-0.8
1982	*Atl-N	157	609	74	169	24	4	10	52	36	49	.278	.321	.379	91	-7	27	14	-0	.956	17	*S-157	2.4
1983	Atl-N	152	622	82	185	13	5	7	58	36	48	.297	.338	.368	89	-9	16	12	-2	.949	8	*S-152	1.2
1984	Atl-N☆	145	591	51	157	22	4	2	48	26	70	.266	.298	.327	70	-23	14	17	-6	.959	-3	*S-145	-2.0
1985	Atl-N	138	568	54	141	25	4	5	58	20	63	.248	.274	.333	65	-27	6	3	-3	.954	9	*S-133	-0.9
1986	Atl-N	134	496	57	119	21	1	8	33	21	60	.240	.275	.335	64	-25	19	8	1	.952	13	S-86,3-57/O	-0.4
1987	Atl-N	56	179	22	47	12	0	1	8	16	22	.263	.302	.346	68	-8	6	3	0	.946	-6	S-38,3-12	-1.1
1988	Hou-N	155	566	51	156	30	6	6	58	18	61	.276	.302	.378	98	-4	3	2	-0	.965	-10	*S-154	-0.2
1989	Hou-N	151	537	46	132	20	2	6	54	29	64	.246	.284	.324	76	-18	3	1	0	.945	-41	*S-149	-5.1
1990	Hou-N	132	445	44	116	19	3	2	37	24	40	.261	.300	.330	75	-15	10	5	0	.953	-18	*S-129	-2.5
1991	Hou-N	101	233	17	55	10	0	1	20	13	40	.236	.276	.292	64	-12	3	3	-1	.953	-14	S-45,2-27/3	-2.5
1992	Hou-N	73	176	17	44	6	0	1	13	7	24	.250	.283	.301	68	-8	0	1	0	.961	-6	S-57/3-1	-1.1
Total	13	1539	5494	562	1432	224	31	53	484	264	621	.261	.297	.342	77	-177	112	75	-11	.953	-64	*S-1386/3-72,2O	-14.1

■ DOMINGO RAMOS
Ramos, Domingo Antonio (De Ramos) b: 3/29/58, Santiago, D.R. BR/TR, 5'10", 155 lbs. Deb: 9/8/78

YEAR	TM/L	G	AB	R	H	2B	3B	HR	RBI	BB	SO	AVG	OBP	SLG	PRO+	BR/A	SB	CS	SBR	FA	FR	G/POS	TPR
1978	NY-A	1	0	0	0	0	0	0	0	0	0					0	0	0	0	.000	0	/S-1	0.0
1980	Tor-A	5	16	0	2	0	0	0	0	2	5	.125	.222	.125	-2	-2	0	0	0	1.000	-0	/2-2,S-2,D	-0.2
1982	Sea-A	8	26	3	4	2	0	0	1	3	2	.154	.241	.231	30	-3	0	0	0	.920	-5	/S-8	-0.8
1983	Sea-A	53	127	14	36	4	0	2	10	7	12	.283	.326	.362	86	-2	3	1	0	.948	8	S-28/2-8,3D	0.8
1984	Sea-A	59	81	6	15	2	0	0	2	5	12	.185	.233	.210	24	-8	2	2	0	.911	-8	3-38,S-13/12	-1.8
1985	Sea-A	75	168	19	33	6	0	1	15	17	23	.196	.270	.250	43	-13	0	1	-1	.951	-8	S-36,2-20,1/3	-1.8
1986	Sea-A	49	99	8	18	2	0	0	5	8	13	.182	.250	.202	25	-10	0	1	-1	.966	13	S-21,2-16/3D	0.3
1987	Sea-A	42	103	9	32	6	0	2	11	3	12	.311	.336	.427	96	-1	0	1	-1	.953	7	S-25/3-7,2D	0.7
1988	Cle-A	22	46	7	12	1	0	0	5	3	7	.261	.320	.283	68	-2	0	0	0	1.000	0	2-11/1-5,S3	0.0
	Cal-A	10	15	3	2	0	0	0	0	1	1	.133	.133	.133	-26	-2	0	0	0	1.000	-0	/3-8,O-1	-0.3
	Yr	32	61	10	14	1	0	0	5	4	8	.230	.277	.246	47	-4	0	0	0	1.000	0	2-11,3-10/1SO	-0.3
1989	*Chi-N	85	179	18	47	6	2	1	19	17	23	.263	.333	.335	85	-3	1	1	-0	.959	3	S-42,3-30	0.2
1990	Chi-N	98	226	22	60	5	0	2	17	22	29	.265	.346	.314	77	-6	0	0	0	.932	-15	S-66,S-21/2	-2.1
Total	11	507	1086	109	261	34	2	8	85	92	138	.240	.304	.297	64	-53	6	9	-4	.955	7	S-201,3-174/21DO	-3.7

■ CHUCHO RAMOS
Ramos, Jesus Manuel (Garcia) b: 4/12/18, Maturin, Venez. d: 9/2/77, Caracas, Venez. BR/TL, 5'10.5", 167 lbs. Deb: 5/7/44

YEAR	TM/L	G	AB	R	H	2B	3B	HR	RBI	BB	SO	AVG	OBP	SLG	PRO+	BR/A	SB	CS	SBR	FA	FR	G/POS	TPR
1944	Cin-N	4	10	1	5	1	0	0	1	0	0	.500	.500	.600	217	1	0			1.000	-1	/O-3	0.0

■ JOHN RAMOS
Ramos, John Joseph b: 8/6/65, Tampa, Fla. BR/TR, 6', 190 lbs. Deb: 9/18/91

YEAR	TM/L	G	AB	R	H	2B	3B	HR	RBI	BB	SO	AVG	OBP	SLG	PRO+	BR/A	SB	CS	SBR	FA	FR	G/POS	TPR
1991	NY-A	10	26	4	8	1	0	0	3	1	3	.308	.333	.346	88	-0	0	0	0	1.000	0	/C-5,D-4	0.0

YEAR	TM/L	G	AB	R	H	2B	3B	HR	RBI	BB	SO	AVG	OBP	SLG	PRO+	BR/A	SB	CS	SBR	FA	FR	G/POS	TPR

■ PEDRO RAMOS
Ramos, Pedro (Guerra) "Pete" b: 4/28/35, Pinar Del Rio, Cuba BB/TR, 6', 185 lbs. Deb: 4/11/55

YEAR	TM/L	G	AB	R	H	2B	3B	HR	RBI	BB	SO	AVG	OBP	SLG	PRO+	BR/A	SB	CS	SBR	FA	FR	G/POS	TPR
1955	Was-A	59	38	6	3	0	0	0	0	2	18	.079	.125	.079	-47	-8	0	1	-1	.964	-1	P-45	0.0
1956	Was-A	56	44	9	9	0	2	0	2	2	16	.205	.239	.295	40	-4	0	1	-1	1.000	-0	P-37	0.0
1957	Was-A	56	76	6	13	0	0	1	10	2	27	.171	.192	.211	10	-9	0	0	0	1.000	-0	P-43	0.0
1958	Was-A	53	88	9	21	1	0	0	10	0	33	.239	.239	.250	35	-8	0	0	0	.982	-1	P-43	0.0
1959	Was-A☆	45	75	7	11	1	1	1	2	4	38	.147	.190	.227	14	-9	1	0	0	1.000	-1	P-37	0.0
1960	Was-A	53	86	6	10	3	0	2	4	1	36	.116	.126	.221	-8	-13	0	0	0	1.000	0	P-43	0.0
1961	Min-A	53	93	8	16	1	0	3	11	3	42	.172	.206	.280	27	-10	0	0	0	.955	-3	P-42	0.0
1962	Cle-A	39	68	6	10	3	0	3	8	1	29	.147	.171	.324	31	-7	0	0	0	.962	-2	P-37	0.0
1963	Cle-A	54	55	13	6	0	0	3	7	3	32	.109	.155	.273	17	-6	0	0	0	.963	-2	P-36	0.0
1964	Cle-A	44	39	6	7	0	0	2	2	2	22	.179	.220	.333	52	-3	0	0	0	.960	-1	P-36	0.0
	NY-A	13	5	0	0	0	0	0	0	0	2	.000	.000	.000	-98	-1	0	0	0	.000	-1	P-13	
	Yr	57	44	6	7	0	0	2	2	2	24	.159	.196	.295	34	-4	0	0	0	.960	-2	P-49	
1965	NY-A	65	12	0	1	0	0	0	0	0	6	.083	.083	.083	-53	-2	1	0	0	.895	-1	P-65	0.0
1966	NY-A	52	13	0	2	0	0	0	0	0	5	.154	.154	.154	-12	-2	0	0	0	.952	0	P-52	0.0
1967	Phi-N	6	1	0	0	0	0	0	0	0	0	.000	.000	.000	-99	-0	0	0	0	1.000	1	/P-6	0.0
1969	Pit-N	5	1	0	0	0	0	0	0	0	1	.000	.000	.000	-99	-0	0	0	0	1.000	0	/P-5	0.0
	Cin-N	38	8	0	0	0	0	0	0	1	4	.000	.111	.000	-63	-2	0	0	0	1.000	-0	P-38	
	Yr	43	9	0	0	0	0	0	0	1	5	.000	.100	.000	-67	-2	0	0	0	1.000	-0	P-43	
1970	Was-A	5	0	0	0	0	0	0	0	1	0	.000	.500	.000	52	0	0	0	0	1.000	0	/P-4	0.0
Total	15	696	703	76	109	9	3	15	56	22	316	.155	.183	.240	14	-85	2	2	-1	.977	-9	P-582	0.0

■ BOBBY RAMOS
Ramos, Roberto b: 11/5/55, Havana, Cuba BR/TR, 5'11", 208 lbs. Deb: 9/26/78

YEAR	TM/L	G	AB	R	H	2B	3B	HR	RBI	BB	SO	AVG	OBP	SLG	PRO+	BR/A	SB	CS	SBR	FA	FR	G/POS	TPR
1978	Mon-N	2	4	0	0	0	0	0	0	0	1	.000	.000	.000	-99	-1	0	0	0	1.000	0	/C-1	-0.1
1980	Mon-N	13	32	5	5	2	0	0	2	5	5	.156	.270	.219	38	-3	0	0	0	.964	0	C-12	-0.2
1981	Mon-N	26	41	4	8	1	0	1	3	3	5	.195	.250	.293	53	-3	0	0	0	.974	4	C-23	0.1
1982	NY-A	4	11	1	1	0	0	1	2	0	3	.091	.091	.364	18	-1	0	0	0	1.000	1	/C-4	0.0
1983	Mon-N	27	61	2	14	3	1	0	5	8	11	.230	.329	.311	79	-2	0	0	0	.984	4	C-25	0.4
1984	Mon-N	31	83	8	16	1	0	2	5	6	13	.193	.247	.277	49	-6	0	0	0	.982	7	C-31	0.2
Total	6	103	232	20	44	7	1	4	17	22	38	.190	.263	.280	53	-15	0	0	0	.980	15	/C-96	0.4

■ FERNANDO RAMSEY
Ramsey, Fernando David (Ramsey) b: 12/20/65, Rainbow, Panama BR/TR, 6'1", 175 lbs. Deb: 9/7/92

YEAR	TM/L	G	AB	R	H	2B	3B	HR	RBI	BB	SO	AVG	OBP	SLG	PRO+	BR/A	SB	CS	SBR	FA	FR	G/POS	TPR
1992	Chi-N	18	25	0	3	0	0	0	2	0	6	.120	.120	.120	-31	-4	0	0	0	1.000	-4	O-15	-1.0

■ MIKE RAMSEY
Ramsey, Michael James b: 7/8/60, Thomson, Ga. BB/TL, 6', 170 lbs. Deb: 4/6/87

YEAR	TM/L	G	AB	R	H	2B	3B	HR	RBI	BB	SO	AVG	OBP	SLG	PRO+	BR/A	SB	CS	SBR	FA	FR	G/POS	TPR
1987	LA-N	48	125	18	29	4	2	0	12	10	32	.232	.289	.296	57	-8	2	4	-2	.973	-3	O-43	-1.4

■ MIKE RAMSEY
Ramsey, Michael Jeffrey b: 3/29/54, Roanoke, Va. BB/TR, 6'1", 170 lbs. Deb: 9/4/78

YEAR	TM/L	G	AB	R	H	2B	3B	HR	RBI	BB	SO	AVG	OBP	SLG	PRO+	BR/A	SB	CS	SBR	FA	FR	G/POS	TPR
1978	StL-N	12	5	4	1	0	0	0	0	0	1	.200	.200	.200	12	-1	0	0	0	.909	4	/S-4	0.3
1980	StL-N	59	126	11	33	8	1	0	8	3	17	.262	.279	.341	70	-5	0	0	0	.960	-3	2-24,S-20/3	-0.3
1981	StL-N	47	124	19	32	3	0	0	9	8	13	.258	.303	.282	65	-5	4	0	1	.966	13	S-35/3-5,2O	1.1
1982	*StL-N	112	256	18	59	8	2	1	21	22	34	.230	.294	.289	63	-12	6	5	-1	.963	8	2-43,3-28,S/O	-0.2
1983	StL-N	97	175	25	46	4	3	1	16	12	23	.263	.314	.337	80	-5	4	2	0	.968	3	2-66,S-20/3O	0.2
1984	StL-N	21	15	1	1	1	0	0	0	1	3	.067	.125	.133	-28	-3	0	0	0	1.000	4	/2-7,S-7,3	0.2
	Mon-N	37	70	2	15	1	0	0	3	0	13	.214	.214	.229	26	-7	0	0	0	.975	1	S-26,2-12	-0.4
	Yr	58	85	3	16	2	0	0	3	1	16	.188	.198	.212	16	-10	0	0	0	.978	5	S-33,2-19/3	-0.2
1985	LA-N	9	15	1	2	1	0	0	2	4	2	.133	.235	.200	24	-2	0	0	0	.923	-0	/S-4,2-2	-0.1
Total	7	394	786	81	189	26	6	2	57	48	111	.240	.286	.296	63	-39	14	7	0	.964	33	2-155,S-138/3O	0.6

■ BILL RAMSEY
Ramsey, William Thrace "Square Jaw" b: 10/20/20, Osceola, Ark. BR/TR, 6', 175 lbs. Deb: 4/19/45

YEAR	TM/L	G	AB	R	H	2B	3B	HR	RBI	BB	SO	AVG	OBP	SLG	PRO+	BR/A	SB	CS	SBR	FA	FR	G/POS	TPR
1945	Bos-N	78	137	16	40	8	0	1	12	4	12	.292	.326	.372	93	-2	1			.963	-7	O-43	-1.0

■ DICK RAND
Rand, Richard Hilton b: 3/7/31, South Gate, Cal. BR/TR, 6'2", 185 lbs. Deb: 9/16/53

YEAR	TM/L	G	AB	R	H	2B	3B	HR	RBI	BB	SO	AVG	OBP	SLG	PRO+	BR/A	SB	CS	SBR	FA	FR	G/POS	TPR
1953	StL-N	9	31	3	9	1	0	0	1	2	6	.290	.333	.323	72	-1	0	0	0	.984	3	/C-9	0.2
1955	StL-N	3	10	1	3	0	0	1	3	1	1	.300	.364	.600	150	1	0	1	-1	1.000	-2	/C-3	-0.1
1957	Pit-N	60	105	7	23	2	1	1	9	11	24	.219	.293	.286	58	-6	0	0	0	.973	0	C-57	-0.5
Total	3	72	146	11	35	3	1	2	13	14	31	.240	.306	.315	68	-7	0	1	-1	.977	2	/C-69	-0.4

■ SAP RANDALL
Randall, James Odell b: 8/19/60, Mobile, Ala. BB/TR, 5'11", 195 lbs. Deb: 8/2/88

YEAR	TM/L	G	AB	R	H	2B	3B	HR	RBI	BB	SO	AVG	OBP	SLG	PRO+	BR/A	SB	CS	SBR	FA	FR	G/POS	TPR
1988	Chi-A	4	12	1	0	0	0	0	1	2	3	.000	.143	.000	-57	-3	0	0	0	1.000	0	/1-2,O-1,D	-0.3

■ NEWT RANDALL
Randall, Newton J. b: 2/3/1880, New Lowell, Ont., Canada d: 5/3/55, Duluth, Minn. BR/TR, 5'10", Deb: 4/18/07

YEAR	TM/L	G	AB	R	H	2B	3B	HR	RBI	BB	SO	AVG	OBP	SLG	PRO+	BR/A	SB	CS	SBR	FA	FR	G/POS	TPR
1907	Chi-N	22	78	6	16	4	2	0	4	8		.205	.279	.308	79	-2	2			.904	1	O-21	-0.2
	Bos-N	75	258	16	55	6	3	0	15	19		.213	.285	.260	71	-8	4			.920	-8	O-73	-2.1
	Yr	97	336	22	71	10	5	0	19	27		.211	.284	.271	73	-10	6			.915	-7	O-94	-2.3

■ BOB RANDALL
Randall, Robert Lee b: 6/10/48, Norton, Kan. BR/TR, 6'3", 180 lbs. Deb: 4/13/76 C

YEAR	TM/L	G	AB	R	H	2B	3B	HR	RBI	BB	SO	AVG	OBP	SLG	PRO+	BR/A	SB	CS	SBR	FA	FR	G/POS	TPR
1976	Min-A	153	475	55	127	18	4	1	34	28	38	.267	.319	.328	87	-7	3	5	-2	.969	-4	*2-153	-0.5
1977	Min-A	103	306	36	73	13	2	0	22	15	25	.239	.290	.294	60	-17	1	4	-2	.985	10	*2-101/1-1,3D	-0.2
1978	Min-A	119	330	36	89	11	3	0	21	24	22	.270	.331	.321	82	-7	5	3	-0	.983	10	*2-116/3-2,D	1.0
1979	Min-A	80	199	25	49	7	0	0	14	15	17	.246	.299	.281	55	-12	2	2	-1	.983	7	2-71/3-7,SO	-0.3
1980	Min-A	5	15	2	3	1	0	0	0	1	0	.200	.250	.267	39	-1	0	0	0	.909	0	/3-4,2-1	0.0
Total	5	460	1325	154	341	50	9	1	91	83	102	.257	.311	.311	74	-44	11	14	-5	.979	22	2-442/3-14,DOS1	-0.1

■ LEN RANDLE
Randle, Leonard Shenoff b: 2/12/49, Long Beach, Cal. BB/TR, 5'10", 169 lbs. Deb: 6/16/71

YEAR	TM/L	G	AB	R	H	2B	3B	HR	RBI	BB	SO	AVG	OBP	SLG	PRO+	BR/A	SB	CS	SBR	FA	FR	G/POS	TPR
1971	Was-A	75	215	27	47	11	0	2	13	24	56	.219	.300	.298	74	-7	1	1	-0	.967	5	2-66	0.3
1972	Tex-A	74	249	23	48	13	1	2	21	13	51	.193	.236	.269	52	-15	4	5	-2	.952	1	2-65/S-4,O	-1.5
1973	Tex-A	10	29	3	6	1	1	1	2	1	2	.207	.237	.414	74	-1	0	2	-1	.964	-2	/2-5,O-2	-0.5
1974	Tex-A	151	520	65	157	17	4	1	49	29	43	.302	.341	.356	103	2	26	17	-2	.935	1	3-89,2-40,O/SD	0.1
1975	Tex-A	156	601	85	166	24	7	4	57	57	80	.276	.343	.359	99	0	16	19	-7	.973	15	2-79,O-66,3/CSD	1.0
1976	Tex-A	142	539	53	121	11	6	1	51	46	63	.224	.288	.273	63	-24	30	15	-0	.971	-4	*2-113,O-30/3D	-2.3
1977	NY-N	136	513	78	156	22	7	5	27	65	70	.304	.384	.404	117	14	33	21	-3	.961	-7	*3-110,2-20/OS	0.9
1978	NY-N	132	437	53	102	16	8	2	35	64	57	.233	.333	.320	86	-7	14	11	-2	.967	-7	*3-124/2-5	-1.8
1979	NY-A	20	39	2	7	0	0	0	3	3	2	.179	.238	.179	15	-5	0	0	0	1.000	-0	O-11	-0.5
1980	Chi-N	130	489	67	135	19	6	5	39	50	55	.276	.344	.370	93	-4	19	13	-2	.929	-7	*3-111,2-17/O	-0.4
1981	Sea-A	82	273	22	63	9	1	4	25	17	22	.231	.278	.315	68	-11	11	6	-0	.986	9	3-59,2-21/OS	-0.4
1982	Sea-A	30	46	10	8	2	0	1	4	4	4	.174	.240	.217	26	-5	2	1	-1	.964	2	D-13/3-9,2	0.0
Total	12	1138	3950	488	1016	145	40	27	322	372	505	.257	.323	.335	87	-63	156	112	-20	.953	9	3-521,2-437,O/DSC	-6.5

■ WILLIE RANDOLPH
Randolph, Willie Larry b: 7/6/54, Holly Hill, S.C. BR/TR, 5'11", 166 lbs. Deb: 7/29/75 C

YEAR	TM/L	G	AB	R	H	2B	3B	HR	RBI	BB	SO	AVG	OBP	SLG	PRO+	BR/A	SB	CS	SBR	FA	FR	G/POS	TPR
1975	*Pit-N	30	61	9	10	1	0	0	3	7	6	.164	.250	.180	21	-6	1	0	0	.962	4	2-14/3-1	-0.2
1976	*NY-A†	125	430	59	115	15	4	1	40	58	39	.267	.358	.328	103	3	37	12	4	.974	15	*2-124	3.2
1977	*NY-A★	147	551	91	151	28	11	4	40	64	53	.274	.351	.387	102	3	13	6	0	.980	6	*2-147	1.9
1978	NY-A	134	499	87	139	18	6	3	42	82	51	.279	.385	.357	112	12	36	7	7	.978	-8	*2-134	2.1
1979	NY-A	153	574	98	155	15	13	5	61	95	39	.270	.376	.368	104	7	33	12	3	.985	9	*2-153	2.9

YEAR	TM/L	G	AB	R	H	2B	3B	HR	RBI	BB	SO	AVG	OBP	SLG	PRO+	BR/A	SB	CS	SBR	FA	FR	G/POS	TPR
1980	*NY-A★	138	513	99	151	23	7	7	46	**119**	45	.294	.429	.407	133	31	30	5	6	.976	-7	*2-138	3.8
1981	*NY-A★	93	357	59	83	14	3	2	24	57	24	.232	.338	.305	88	-4	14	5	1	.977	-2	2-93	0.1
1982	NY-A	144	553	85	155	21	4	3	36	75	35	.280	.369	.349	100	3	16	9	-1	.981	-3	*2-142/D-1	0.7
1983	NY-A	104	420	73	117	21	1	2	38	53	32	.279	.361	.348	100	2	12	4	1	.979	3	*2-104	1.1
1984	NY-A	142	564	86	162	24	2	2	31	86	42	.287	.382	.348	108	10	10	6	-1	.983	11	*2-142	2.5
1985	NY-A	143	497	75	137	21	2	5	40	85	39	.276	.386	.356	107	9	16	9	-1	.985	-3	*2-143	1.1
1986	NY-A	141	492	76	136	15	2	5	50	94	49	.276	.396	.346	105	9	15	2	3	.972	-12	*2-139/D-1	0.5
1987	NY-A★	120	449	96	137	24	2	7	67	82	25	.305	.415	.414	122	19	11	1	3	.981	-2	*2-119/D-1	2.4
1988	NY-A	110	404	43	93	20	1	2	34	55	39	.230	.325	.300	77	-11	8	4	0	.988	8	*2-110	0.1
1989	LA-N★	145	549	62	155	18	0	2	36	71	51	.282	.369	.326	102	4	7	6	-2	.987	-1	*2-140	0.7
1990	LA-N	26	96	15	26	4	0	1	9	13	6	.271	.364	.344	98	0	1	0	0	.969	-2	2-26	-0.1
	*Oak-A	93	292	37	75	9	3	1	21	32	25	.257	.332	.318	86	-5	6	1	1	.982	-12	2-84/D-6	-1.4
1991	Mil-A	124	431	60	141	14	3	0	54	75	38	.327	.427	.374	127	20	4	2	0	.969	10	*2-121/D-2	3.3
1992	NY-N	90	286	29	72	11	1	2	15	40	34	.252	.352	.318	92	-1	1	3	-2	.977	-14	2-79	-1.6
Total	18	2202	8018	1239	2210	316	65	54	687	1243	675	.276	.375	.351	105	105	271	94	25	.980	0	*2-2152/D-11,3	23.1

■ MERRITT RANEW
Ranew, Merritt Thomas b: 5/10/38, Albany, Ga.   BL/TR, 5'10", 180 lbs. Deb: 4/13/62

YEAR	TM/L	G	AB	R	H	2B	3B	HR	RBI	BB	SO	AVG	OBP	SLG	PRO+	BR/A	SB	CS	SBR	FA	FR	G/POS	TPR
1962	Hou-N	71	218	26	51	6	8	4	24	14	43	.234	.289	.390	87	-5	2	2	-1	.980	-6	C-58	-0.9
1963	Chi-N	78	154	18	52	8	1	3	15	9	32	.338	.382	.461	134	7	1	0	0	.980	-5	C-37/1-9	0.3
1964	Chi-N	16	33	0	3	0	0	0	1	2	6	.091	.167	.091	-24	-5	0	0	0	1.000	2	/C-9	-0.3
	Mil-N	9	17	1	2	0	0	0	0	0	3	.118	.118	.118	-33	-3	0	1	-1	1.000	-1	/C-3	-0.5
	Yr	25	50	1	5	0	0	0	1	2	9	.100	.150	.100	-27	-8	0	1	-1	1.000	1	C-12	-0.8
1965	Cal-A	41	91	12	19	4	0	1	10	7	22	.209	.265	.286	58	-5	0	0	0	.988	-10	C-24	-1.5
1969	Sea-A	54	81	11	20	2	0	0	4	10	14	.247	.330	.272	71	-3	0	0	0	.969	-6	C-13/O-3,3	-0.9
Total	5	269	594	68	147	20	9	8	54	42	120	.247	.304	.352	83	-14	3	3	-1	.982	-25	C-144/1-9,O3	-3.8

■ JEFF RANSOM
Ransom, Jeffrey Dean b: 11/11/60, Fresno, Cal.   BR/TR, 5'11", 185 lbs. Deb: 9/5/81

YEAR	TM/L	G	AB	R	H	2B	3B	HR	RBI	BB	SO	AVG	OBP	SLG	PRO+	BR/A	SB	CS	SBR	FA	FR	G/POS	TPR
1981	SF-N	5	15	2	4	1	0	0	0	1	1	.267	.313	.333	85	-0	0	0	0	1.000	2	/C-5	0.2
1982	SF-N	15	44	5	7	0	0	0	3	6	7	.159	.260	.159	20	-5	0	0	0	.988	2	C-14	-0.3
1983	SF-N	6	20	3	4	0	0	1	3	4	7	.200	.333	.350	92	-0	0	0	0	.946	-2	/C-6	-0.1
Total	3	26	79	10	15	1	0	1	6	11	15	.190	.289	.241	50	-5	0	0	0	.980	2	/C-25	-0.2

■ EARL RAPP
Rapp, Earl Wellington b: 5/20/21, Corunna, Mich. d: 2/13/92, Swedesboro, N.J. BL/TR, 6'2", 185 lbs. Deb: 4/28/49

YEAR	TM/L	G	AB	R	H	2B	3B	HR	RBI	BB	SO	AVG	OBP	SLG	PRO+	BR/A	SB	CS	SBR	FA	FR	G/POS	TPR
1949	Det-A	1	0	0	0	0	0	0	0	1	0	—	1.000	—	175	0	0	0	0	.000	0	H	0.0
	Chi-A	19	54	3	14	1	1	0	11	5	6	.259	.322	.315	71	-2	1	1	-0	.974	2	O-13	-0.1
	Yr	20	54	3	14	1	1	0	11	6	6	.259	.333	.315	74	-2	1	1	-0	.974	2	O-13	-0.1
1951	NY-N	13	11	0	1	0	0	0	1	2	3	.091	.231	.091	-10	-2	0	0	0	.000	0	H	-0.2
	StL-A	26	98	14	32	5	3	2	14	11	11	.327	.394	.500	137	5	1	0	0	.979	0	O-25	0.4
1952	StL-A	30	49	3	7	4	0	0	4	0	8	.143	.143	.224	1	-7	0	0	0	1.000	-1	/O-7	-0.8
	Was-A	46	67	7	19	6	0	0	9	6	13	.284	.351	.373	105	0	0	0	0	.917	-2	O-10	-0.2
	Yr	76	116	10	26	10	0	0	13	6	21	.224	.268	.310	61	-6	0	0	0	.958	-3	O-17	-1.0
Total	3	135	279	27	73	16	4	2	39	25	41	.262	.325	.369	89	-5	2	1	0	.973	-1	/O-55	-0.9

■ GOLDIE RAPP
Rapp, Joseph Aloysius b: 2/6/1892, Cincinnati, Ohio d: 7/1/66, LaMesa, Cal. BB/TR, 5'10", 165 lbs. Deb: 4/13/21

YEAR	TM/L	G	AB	R	H	2B	3B	HR	RBI	BB	SO	AVG	OBP	SLG	PRO+	BR/A	SB	CS	SBR	FA	FR	G/POS	TPR
1921	NY-N	58	181	21	39	9	1	0	15	15	13	.215	.276	.276	46	-14	3	11	-6	.941	13	3-56	-0.3
	Phi-N	52	202	28	56	7	1	0	10	14	8	.277	.324	.337	70	-9	6	7	-2	.950	-2	3-50/2-1	-1.0
	Yr	110	383	49	95	16	2	0	25	29	21	.248	.301	.308	59	-22	9	18	-8	.945	10	*3-106/2-1	-1.3
1922	Phi-N	119	502	58	127	26	3	0	38	32	29	.253	.299	.317	54	-35	6	12	-5	.948	1	*3-117/S-2	-2.5
1923	Phi-N	47	179	27	47	5	0	1	10	14	14	.263	.320	.307	59	-10	1	1	0	.947	-1	3-45	-0.7
Total	3	276	1064	134	269	47	5	2	73	75	64	.253	.303	.312	57	-68	16	31	-14	.947	14	3-268/S-2,2	-4.5

■ BILL RARIDEN
Rariden, William Angel "Bedford Bill" b: 2/4/1888, Bedford, Ind. d: 8/28/42, Bedford, Ind. BR/TR, 5'10", 168 lbs. Deb: 8/12/09

YEAR	TM/L	G	AB	R	H	2B	3B	HR	RBI	BB	SO	AVG	OBP	SLG	PRO+	BR/A	SB	CS	SBR	FA	FR	G/POS	TPR
1909	Bos-N	13	42	1	6	1	0	0	1	4		.143	.217	.167	18	-4	1			.912	-3	C-13	-0.7
1910	Bos-N	49	137	15	31	5	1	1	14	12	22	.226	.293	.299	70	-5	1			.962	3	C-49	0.2
1911	Bos-N	70	246	22	56	9	0	0	21	21	18	.228	.288	.264	51	-16	3			.952	1	C-65/3-3,2	-0.8
1912	Bos-N	79	247	27	55	3	1	1	14	18	35	.223	.281	.255	46	-18	3			.964	-5	C-73	-1.6
1913	Bos-N	95	246	31	58	9	2	3	30	30	21	.236	.324	.325	84	-5	5			.976	-4	C-87	0.2
1914	Ind-F	131	396	44	93	15	5	0	47	61	43	.235	.337	.298	59	-23	12			.981	20	*C-130	1.0
1915	New-F	142	444	49	120	30	7	0	40	60	29	.270	.361	.369	101	1	8			.978	23	*C-142	3.8
1916	NY-N	120	351	23	78	9	3	1	29	55	32	.222	.333	.274	92	-1	4			.972	-9	*C-119	0.0
1917	*NY-N	101	266	20	72	10	1	0	25	42	17	.271	.372	.316	116	7	3			.971	-17	*C-100	-0.3
1918	NY-N	69	183	15	41	5	1	0	17	15	15	.224	.283	.262	68	-7	1			**.984**	-9	C-63	-1.3
1919	*Cin-N	74	218	16	47	6	3	1	24	17	19	.216	.275	.284	70	-8	4			.983	3	C-70	0.1
1920	Cin-N	39	101	9	25	8	0	0	10	5	0	.248	.283	.277	62	-5	2	0	1	.972	0	C-37	-0.3
Total	12	982	2877	272	682	105	24	7	272	340	251	.237	.320	.298	76	-83	47	0		.973	8	C-948/3-3,2	0.3

■ MORRIE RATH
Rath, Morris Charles b: 12/25/1886, Mobeetie, Tex. d: 11/18/45, Upper Darby, Pa. BL/TR, 5'8.5", 160 lbs. Deb: 9/28/09

YEAR	TM/L	G	AB	R	H	2B	3B	HR	RBI	BB	SO	AVG	OBP	SLG	PRO+	BR/A	SB	CS	SBR	FA	FR	G/POS	TPR
1909	Phi-A	7	26	4	7	1	0	0	3	2		.269	.387	.308	117	1	1			.846	2	/S-4,3-2	0.3
1910	Phi-A	18	26	3	4	1	0	0	1	5		.154	.290	.154	40	-2	0			.950	-2	3-11/2-3	-0.4
	Cle-A	24	67	5	13	3	0	0	0	10		.194	.299	.239	68	-2	2			.950	2	3-22/S-1	0.1
	Yr	42	93	8	17	3	0	0	1	15		.183	.299	.215	60	-4	2			.950	0	3-33/2-3,S	-0.3
1912	Chi-A	157	591	104	161	10	2	1	19	95		.272	.380	.301	98	5	30			**.963**	18	*2-157	1.9
1913	Chi-A	92	295	37	59	2	0	0	12	46	22	.200	.310	.207	52	-16	22			.962	-2	2-86	-2.0
1919	*Cin-N	138	537	77	142	13	1	1	29	64	24	.264	.343	.298	96	0	17			.977	-7	*2-138	2.2
1920	Cin-N	129	506	61	135	7	2	0	28	36	24	.267	.319	.308	82	-11	10	11	-4	**.977**	-7	*2-126/3-1,O	-1.9
Total	6	565	2048	291	521	36	7	4	92	258	70	.254	.342	.285	86	-25	82	11		.970	25	2-510/3-36,SO	0.2

■ GENE RATLIFF
Ratliff, Kelly Eugene b: 9/28/45, Macon, Ga.   BR/TR, 6'5", 185 lbs. Deb: 5/15/65

YEAR	TM/L	G	AB	R	H	2B	3B	HR	RBI	BB	SO	AVG	OBP	SLG	PRO+	BR/A	SB	CS	SBR	FA	FR	G/POS	TPR
1965	Hou-N	4	4	0	0	0	0	0	0	0	4	.000	.000	.000	-99	-1	0	0	0	.000	0	H	-0.1

■ PAUL RATLIFF
Ratliff, Paul Hawthorne b: 1/23/44, San Diego, Cal.   BL/TR, 6'2", 190 lbs. Deb: 4/14/63

YEAR	TM/L	G	AB	R	H	2B	3B	HR	RBI	BB	SO	AVG	OBP	SLG	PRO+	BR/A	SB	CS	SBR	FA	FR	G/POS	TPR
1963	Min-A	10	21	2	4	1	0	1	3	2	7	.190	.292	.381	85	-0	0	0	0	.976	2	/C-7	0.2
1970	*Min-A	69	149	19	40	7	2	5	22	15	51	.268	.363	.443	119	4	0	0	0	.980	-15	C-53	-1.0
1971	Min-A	21	44	3	7	1	0	2	6	4	17	.159	.229	.318	52	-3	0	0	0	1.000	1	C-15	-0.2
	Mil-A	23	41	3	7	1	0	3	7	5	21	.171	.277	.415	95	-0	0	0	0	.966	-1	C-13	-0.1
	Yr	44	85	6	14	2	0	5	13	9	38	.165	.253	.365	72	-3	0	0	0	.985	0	C-28	-0.3
1972	Mil-A	22	42	1	3	0	0	0	4	2	23	.071	.114	.143	-25	-6	0	0	0	1.000	0	C-13	-1.0
Total	4	145	297	28	61	10	2	12	42	28	119	.205	.293	.374	86	-6	0	0	0	.983	-16	C-101	-2.1

■ TOMMY RAUB
Raub, Thomas Jefferson b: 12/1/1870, Raubsville, Pa. d: 2/16/49, Phillipsburg, N.J. BR/TR, 5'10", 155 lbs. Deb: 5/3/03

YEAR	TM/L	G	AB	R	H	2B	3B	HR	RBI	BB	SO	AVG	OBP	SLG	PRO+	BR/A	SB	CS	SBR	FA	FR	G/POS	TPR
1903	Chi-N	36	84	6	19	3	0	0	7	5		.226	.278	.310	69	-4	3			.900	-4	C-12/1-6,O3	-0.7
1906	StL-N	24	78	9	22	2	4	0	2	4		.282	.325	.410	135	3	2			.957	-4	C-22	0.1
Total	2	60	162	15	41	5	6	0	9	9		.253	.301	.358	99	-1	5			.940	-8	/C-34,1-6,O3	-0.6

YEAR	TM/L	G	AB	R	H	2B	3B	HR	RBI	BB	SO	AVG	OBP	SLG	PRO+	BR/A	SB	CS	SBR	FA	FR	G/POS	TPR

■ BOB RAUDMAN Raudman, Robert Joyce "Shorty" b: 3/14/42, Erie, Pa. BL/TL, 5'9.5", 185 lbs. Deb: 9/13/66

YEAR	TM/L	G	AB	R	H	2B	3B	HR	RBI	BB	SO	AVG	OBP	SLG	PRO+	BR/A	SB	CS	SBR	FA	FR	G/POS	TPR
1966	Chi-N	8	29	1	7	2	0	0	2	1	4	.241	.267	.310	59	-2	0	0	0	.909	0	/O-8	-0.2
1967	Chi-N	8	26	0	4	0	0	0	1	1	4	.154	.185	.154	-2	-3	0	0	0	.875	0	/O-8	-0.4
Total	2	16	55	1	11	2	0	0	3	2	8	.200	.228	.236	30	-5	0	0	0	.889	0	/O-16	-0.6

■ JOHNNY RAWLINGS Rawlings, John William "Red" b: 8/17/1892, Bloomfield, Iowa d: 10/16/72, Inglewood, Cal. BR/TR, 5'8", 158 lbs. Deb: 4/14/14

YEAR	TM/L	G	AB	R	H	2B	3B	HR	RBI	BB	SO	AVG	OBP	SLG	PRO+	BR/A	SB	CS	SBR	FA	FR	G/POS	TPR
1914	Cin-N	33	60	9	13	1	0	0	8	6	8	.217	.288	.233	54	-3	1			.885	0	3-10/2-7,S	-0.3
	KC-F	61	193	19	41	3	0	0	15	22	25	.212	.296	.228	39	-17	6			.937	17	S-61	0.5
1915	KC-F	120	399	40	86	9	2	2	24	27	40	.216	.269	.263	44	-32	17			.926	-4	*S-120	-3.0
1917	Bos-N	122	371	37	95	9	4	2	31	38	32	.256	.337	.318	107	4	12			.977	11	2-96,S-17/3O	2.3
1918	Bos-N	111	410	32	85	7	3	0	21	30	31	.207	.265	.239	56	-21	10			.956	2	S-71,2-20,O	-1.8
1919	Bos-N	77	275	30	70	8	2	1	16	16	20	.255	.298	.309	86	-5	10			.961	-12	2-58,O-10/S	-1.7
1920	Bos-N	5	3	0	0	0	0	0	2	0	1	.000	.000	.000	-99	-1	0	0	0	1.000	-1	/2-1	-0.1
	Phi-N	98	384	39	90	19	2	3	30	22	25	.234	.278	.318	67	-16	9	6	-1	.970	-2	2-97	-1.7
	Yr	103	387	39	90	19	2	3	32	22	26	.233	.276	.315	67	-17	9	6	-1	.970	-2	2-98	-1.8
1921	Phi-N	60	254	20	74	14	2	1	16	8	12	.291	.318	.374	76	-9	4	5	-2	.954	5	2-60	-0.4
	*NY-N	86	307	40	82	8	1	1	30	18	19	.267	.316	.309	66	-14	4	4	-1	.970	-1	2-86/S-1	-1.5
	Yr	146	561	60	156	22	3	2	46	26	31	.278	.317	.339	71	-23	8	9	-3	.963	3	*2-146/S-1	-1.9
1922	NY-N	88	308	46	87	13	8	1	30	23	15	.282	.342	.386	87	-6	7	6	-2	.984	-8	2-77/3-5	-0.9
1923	Pit-N	119	461	53	131	18	4	1	45	25	29	.284	.322	.347	75	-17	9	0	3	.958	-8	*2-119	-2.0
1924	Pit-N	3	3	0	1	0	0	0	2	0	0	.333	.333	.333	78	-0	0	0	0	.000	0	H	0.0
1925	Pit-N	36	110	17	31	7	0	2	13	8	8	.282	.336	.400	82	-3	0	1	-1	.981	3	2-29	0.0
1926	Pit-N	61	181	27	42	6	0	0	20	14	10	.232	.287	.265	47	-13	3			.970	-3	2-59	-1.5
Total	12	1080	3719	409	928	122	28	14	303	257	275	.250	.303	.309	70	-153	92	22		.968	3	2-709,S-280/O3	-12.1

■ IRV RAY Ray, Irving Burton "Stubby" b: 1/22/1864, Harrington, Me. d: 2/21/48, Harrington, Me. BL/TR, 5'6", 165 lbs. Deb: 7/7/1888

YEAR	TM/L	G	AB	R	H	2B	3B	HR	RBI	BB	SO	AVG	OBP	SLG	PRO+	BR/A	SB	CS	SBR	FA	FR	G/POS	TPR
1888	Bos-N	50	206	26	51	2	3	2	26	6	11	.248	.272	.316	85	-4	7			.879	-11	S-48/2-3	-1.4
1889	Bos-N	9	33	8	10	1	0	0	2	4	0	.303	.378	.333	94	-0	1			.875	-4	/S-5,3-4	-0.4
	Bal-a	26	106	20	36	4	1	0	17	7	6	.340	.397	.396	124	3	12			.784	-7	S-20/O-6	-0.3
1890	Bal-a	38	139	28	50	6	2	1		15		.360	.433	.453	154	9	11			.894	-10	S-38	0.2
1891	Bal-a	103	418	72	116	17	5	0	58	54	18	.278	.366	.342	102	2	28			.885	-14	O-64,S-40	-1.0
Total	4	226	902	154	263	30	11	3	103	86	35	.292	.360	.359	109	11	59			.863	-46	S-151/O-70,32	-2.9

■ JOHNNY RAY Ray, John Cornelius b: 3/1/57, Chouteau, Okla. BB/TR, 5'11", 185 lbs. Deb: 9/2/81

YEAR	TM/L	G	AB	R	H	2B	3B	HR	RBI	BB	SO	AVG	OBP	SLG	PRO+	BR/A	SB	CS	SBR	FA	FR	G/POS	TPR
1981	Pit-N	31	102	10	25	11	0	0	6	6	9	.245	.287	.353	78	-3	0	0	0	.987	2	2-31	0.0
1982	Pit-N	162	647	79	182	30	7	7	63	36	34	.281	.320	.382	93	-7	16	7	1	.977	8	*2-162	1.1
1983	Pit-N	151	576	68	163	**38**	7	5	53	35	26	.283	.324	.399	97	-3	18	9	0	.983	17	*2-151	2.2
1984	Pit-N	155	555	75	173	**38**	6	6	67	37	31	.312	.358	.434	122	15	11	6	-0	.984	-7	*2-149	1.1
1985	Pit-N	154	594	67	163	33	7	7	70	46	24	.274	.328	.375	97	-3	13	9	-2	.976	-15	*2-151	-1.4
1986	Pit-N	155	579	67	174	33	0	7	78	58	47	.301	.367	.394	107	7	6	9	-4	.993	5	*2-151	1.5
1987	Pit-N	123	472	48	129	19	3	5	54	41	36	.273	.331	.358	82	-12	4	2	0	.981	4	*2-119	-0.2
	Cal-A	30	127	16	44	11	0	0	15	3	10	.346	.362	.433	113	2	0	0		.986	-1	2-29/D-1	0.3
1988	Cal-A★	153	602	75	184	42	7	6	83	36	38	.306	.349	.429	120	15	4	1	1	.972	-7	*2-104,O-40/D	1.1
1989	Cal-A	134	530	52	153	16	3	5	62	36	30	.289	.334	.358	97	-2	6	3	0	.984	4	*2-130	0.6
1990	Cal-A	105	404	47	112	23	0	5	43	19	44	.277	.310	.371	91	-6	2	3	-1	.987	12	*2-100/D-1	0.3
Total	10	1353	5188	604	1502	294	36	53	594	353	329	.290	.336	.391	101	4	80	49	-5	.982	20	*2-1277/O-40,D	7.0

■ LARRY RAY Ray, Larry Dale b: 3/11/58, Madison, Ind. BL/TR, 6'1", 195 lbs. Deb: 9/10/82

YEAR	TM/L	G	AB	R	H	2B	3B	HR	RBI	BB	SO	AVG	OBP	SLG	PRO+	BR/A	SB	CS	SBR	FA	FR	G/POS	TPR
1982	Hou-N	5	6	0	1	0	0	0	1	0	4	.167	.167	.167	-7	-1	0	0	0	1.000	-0	/O-1	-0.1

■ FLOYD RAYFORD Rayford, Floyd Kinnard b: 7/27/57, Memphis, Tenn. BR/TR, 5'10", 195 lbs. Deb: 4/17/80

YEAR	TM/L	G	AB	R	H	2B	3B	HR	RBI	BB	SO	AVG	OBP	SLG	PRO+	BR/A	SB	CS	SBR	FA	FR	G/POS	TPR
1980	Bal-A	8	18	1	4	0	0	0	1	0	5	.222	.222	.222	22	-2	0	0	0	.900	0	/3-4,2-1,D	-0.2
1982	Bal-A	34	53	7	7	0	0	3	5	6	14	.132	.220	.302	42	-4	0	1	-1	.898	5	3-27/C-2,D	-0.1
1983	StL-N	56	104	5	22	4	0	3	14	10	27	.212	.281	.337	70	-4	1	0	0	.883	-4	3-33	-0.9
1984	Bal-A	86	250	24	64	14	0	4	27	12	51	.256	.298	.360	83	-6	0	3	-2	.991	11	C-66,3-22/1	0.5
1985	Bal-A	105	359	55	110	21	1	18	48	10	69	.306	.325	.521	131	13	3	1	0	.972	-2	3-78,C-29/D	1.2
1986	Bal-A	81	210	15	37	4	0	8	19	15	50	.176	.231	.310	46	-16	0	0	0	.912	4	3-72,C-10/D	-1.3
1987	Bal-A	20	50	5	11	0	0	2	3	2	9	.220	.250	.340	56	-3	0	0	0	.980	5	C-17/3-1,D	-0.3
Total	7	390	1044	112	255	43	1	38	117	55	225	.244	.284	.397	86	-23	4	5	-2	.931	21	3-237,C-124/D12	-0.4

■ FRED RAYMER Raymer, Frederick Charles b: 11/12/1875, Leavenworth, Kan. d: 6/11/57, Los Angeles, Cal. BR/TR, 5'11", 185 lbs. Deb: 4/24/01

YEAR	TM/L	G	AB	R	H	2B	3B	HR	RBI	BB	SO	AVG	OBP	SLG	PRO+	BR/A	SB	CS	SBR	FA	FR	G/POS	TPR
1901	Chi-N	120	463	41	108	14	2	0	43	11		.233	.257	.272	56	-27	18			.881	-17	3-82,S-29/12	-4.1
1904	Bos-N	114	419	28	88	12	3	1	27	13		.210	.236	.260	55	-23	17			**.958**	7	*2-114	-1.4
1905	Bos-N	137	498	26	105	14	2	0	31	8		.211	.232	.247	44	-35	15			.949	-18	*2-134/1-1,O	-5.5
Total	3	371	1380	95	301	40	7	1	101	32		.218	.242	.259	51	-85	50			.954	-28	2-251/3-82,S10	-11.0

■ HARRY RAYMOND Raymond, Harry H. "Jack" b: 2/20/1862, Utica, N.Y. d: 3/21/25, San Diego, Cal. 5'9", 179 lbs. Deb: 9/9/1888

YEAR	TM/L	G	AB	R	H	2B	3B	HR	RBI	BB	SO	AVG	OBP	SLG	PRO+	BR/A	SB	CS	SBR	FA	FR	G/POS	TPR
1888	Lou-a	32	123	8	26	2	0	0	13	1		.211	.218	.228	44	-8	7			.884	-1	3-31/O-1	-0.8
1889	Lou-a	130	515	58	123	12	9	0	47	19	45	.239	.270	.297	63	-26	19			.886	-1	*3-129/O-1,P	-1.9
1890	*Lou-a	123	521	91	135	7	4	2		22		.259	.293	.299	76	-17	18			.874	-2	*3-119/S-4	-1.3
1891	Lou-a	14	59	4	12	0	2	0	2	5	6	.203	.288	.237	51	-4	3			.898	5	S-14	0.2
1892	Pit-N	12	49	4	4	0	1	0	2	4	8	.082	.151	.122	-17	-7	1			.867	-2	3-12	-0.8
	Was-N	4	15	2	1	0	0	0	0	3	2	.067	.222	.067	-12	-2	1			.783	1	/3-4	-0.1
	Yr	16	64	6	5	0	1	0	2	7	10	.078	.169	.109	-15	-9	2			.838	-1	3-16	-0.8
Total	5	315	1282	167	301	23	14	2	64	54	61	.235	.270	.279	62	-63	49			.878	1	3-295/S-18,OP	-4.7

■ LOU RAYMOND Raymond, Louis Anthony (b: Louis Anthony Raymondjack) b: 12/11/1894, Buffalo, N.Y. d: 5/2/79, Rochester, N.Y. BR/TR, 5'10.5", 187 lbs. Deb: 5/2/19

YEAR	TM/L	G	AB	R	H	2B	3B	HR	RBI	BB	SO	AVG	OBP	SLG	PRO+	BR/A	SB	CS	SBR	FA	FR	G/POS	TPR
1919	Phi-N	1	2	0	1	0	0	0	0	0	0	.500	.500	.500	188	0	0			.000	0	/2-1	0.0

■ AL REACH Reach, Alfred James b: 5/25/1840, London, England d: 1/14/28, Atlantic City, N.J BL/TL, 5'6", 155 lbs. Deb: 5/20/1871 FM

YEAR	TM/L	G	AB	R	H	2B	3B	HR	RBI	BB	SO	AVG	OBP	SLG	PRO+	BR/A	SB	CS	SBR	FA	FR	G/POS	TPR
1871	Ath-n	26	133	43	47	7	6	0	34	5	6	.353	.377	.496	150	9	2					*2-26	0.4
1872	Ath-n	24	118	21	23	0	0	0	11	4	0	.195	.221	.195	29	-9						O-19/1-4	-0.6
1873	Ath-n	13	73	13	16	5	1	0	9	0		.219	.219	.315	51	-5						/O-9,2-7	-0.3
1874	Ath-n	14	55	8	7	2	0	0		0		.127	.127	.164	-7	-7						O-14	-0.5
1875	Ath-n	3	14	4	4	1	0	0		0		.286	.286	.357	109	0						/O-5,2-0	0.0
Total	5 n	80	393	89	97	15	7	0		9		.247	.264	.321	73	-13						/O-47,2-33,1	-1.0

■ BOB REACH Reach, Robert b: 8/28/1843, Williamsburg, N.Y. d: 5/19/22, Springfield, Mass. 5'5", 155 lbs. Deb: 4/23/1872 F

YEAR	TM/L	G	AB	R	H	2B	3B	HR	RBI	BB	SO	AVG	OBP	SLG	PRO+	BR/A	SB	CS	SBR	FA	FR	G/POS	TPR
1872	Oly-n	2	8	1	2	0	0	0	0	0	0	.250	.250	.250	57	-0						/S-1	0.0
1873	Was-n	1	5	1	1	0	0	0	0	0	0	.200	.200	.200	19	-0						/S-1	0.0
Total	2 n	3	13	2	3	0	0	0	0	0	0	.231	.231	.231	42	-1						/S-2	0.0

■ RANDY READY Ready, Randy Max b: 1/8/60, Fremont, Cal. BR/TR, 5'11", 180 lbs. Deb: 9/4/83

YEAR	TM/L	G	AB	R	H	2B	3B	HR	RBI	BB	SO	AVG	OBP	SLG	PRO+	BR/A	SB	CS	SBR	FA	FR	G/POS	TPR
1983	Mil-A	12	37	8	15	3	2	1	6	6	3	.405	.488	.676	234	7	0	1	-1	1.000	0	/3-4,D-6	0.6

YEAR	TM/L	G	AB	R	H	2B	3B	HR	RBI	BB	SO	AVG	OBP	SLG	PRO+	BR/A	SB	CS	SBR	FA	FR	G/POS	TPR
1984	Mil-A	37	123	13	23	6	1	3	13	14	18	.187	.270	.325	66	-6	0	0	0	.946	3	3-36	-0.3
1985	Mil-A	48	181	29	48	9	5	1	21	14	23	.265	.321	.387	93	-2	0	0	0	.989	4	O-37/3-7,2D	0.1
1986	Mil-A	23	79	8	15	4	0	1	4	9	9	.190	.273	.278	49	-6	2	0	1	.950	-4	O-11/2-7,3D	-0.9
	SD-N	1	3	0	0	0	0	0	0	0	1	.000	.000	.000	-99	-1	0	0	0	.667	-0	/3-1	-0.1
1987	SD-N	124	350	69	108	26	6	12	54	67	44	.309	.424	.520	154	30	7	3	0	.912	2	3-52,2-51,O	3.2
1988	SD-N	114	331	43	88	16	2	7	39	39	38	.266	.349	.390	114	6	6	2	1	.952	-10	3-57,2-26,O	-0.3
1989	SD-N	28	67	4	17	2	1	0	5	11	6	.254	.359	.313	94	-0	0	0	0	.963	1	3-18/2-2,O	0.2
	Phi-N	72	187	33	50	11	1	8	21	31	31	.267	.377	.465	140	10	4	3	-1	.962	-6	O-36,3-14/2	0.4
	Yr	100	254	37	67	13	2	8	26	42	37	.264	.372	.425	127	10	4	3	-1	.962	-4	O-37,3-32/2	0.6
1990	Phi-N	101	217	26	53	9	1	1	26	29	35	.244	.336	.309	79	-5	3	2	-0	1.000	-6	O-30,2-28	-1.2
1991	Phi-N	76	205	32	51	10	1	1	20	47	25	.249	.391	.322	104	4	2	1	0	.989	-7	2-66	-0.2
1992	*Oak-A	61	125	17	25	2	0	3	17	25	21	.200	.333	.288	80	-3	1	0	0	1.000	-3	O-24,D-24/312	-0.7
1993	Mon-N	40	134	22	34	8	1	1	10	23	8	.254	.367	.351	89	-1	2	1	0	.968	3	2-28,1-13/3	0.2
1994	Phi-N	17	42	5	16	1	0	1	3	8	6	.381	.458	.476	152	4	0	1	-1	1.000	-3	2-11/3-1	0.0
Total	12	754	2081	309	543	107	21	40	239	323	270	.261	.363	.390	110	38	27	14	-0	.979	-26	2-233,3-203,O/D1	1.0

■ LEROY REAMS

Reams, Leroy b: 8/11/43, Pine Bluff, Ark. BL/TR, 6'2", 175 lbs. Deb: 5/7/69

YEAR	TM/L	G	AB	R	H	2B	3B	HR	RBI	BB	SO	AVG	OBP	SLG	PRO+	BR/A	SB	CS	SBR	FA	FR	G/POS	TPR
1969	Phi-N	1	1	0	0	0	0	0	0	0	1	.000	.000	.000	-99	-0	0	0	0	.000		H	0.0

■ PHIL REARDON

Reardon, Philip Michael b: 10/3/1883, Brooklyn, N.Y. d: 9/28/20, Brooklyn, N.Y. BR/TR, Deb: 9/19/06

YEAR	TM/L	G	AB	R	H	2B	3B	HR	RBI	BB	SO	AVG	OBP	SLG	PRO+	BR/A	SB	CS	SBR	FA	FR	G/POS	TPR
1906	Bro-N	5	14	0	1	0	0	0	0	0	0	.071	.133	.071	-39	-2	0			.917	1	/O-4	-0.2

■ ART REBEL

Rebel, Arthur Anthony b: 3/4/15, Cincinnati, Ohio BL/TL, 5'8", 180 lbs. Deb: 4/19/38

YEAR	TM/L	G	AB	R	H	2B	3B	HR	RBI	BB	SO	AVG	OBP	SLG	PRO+	BR/A	SB	CS	SBR	FA	FR	G/POS	TPR
1938	Phi-N	7	9	2	2	0	0	0	1	1	1	.222	.300	.222	47	-1	0			1.000	-1	/O-3	-0.1
1945	StL-N	26	72	12	25	4	0	0	5	6	4	.347	.397	.403	120	2	1			.976	2	O-18	0.3
Total	2	33	81	14	27	4	0	0	6	7	5	.333	.386	.383	112	1	1			.978	1	/O-21	0.2

■ JEFF REBOULET

Reboulet, Jeffrey Allen b: 4/30/64, Dayton, Ohio BR/TR, 6', 167 lbs. Deb: 5/12/92

YEAR	TM/L	G	AB	R	H	2B	3B	HR	RBI	BB	SO	AVG	OBP	SLG	PRO+	BR/A	SB	CS	SBR	FA	FR	G/POS	TPR
1992	Min-A	73	137	15	26	7	1	1	16	23	26	.190	.341	.277	64	-6	3	4	-0	.971	21	S-36,3-22,2/OD	1.6
1993	Min-A	109	240	33	62	8	0	1	15	35	37	.258	.357	.304	79	-5	5	5	-2	.982	13	S-62,3-35,2/OD	0.9
1994	Min-A	74	189	28	49	11	1	3	23	18	23	.259	.327	.376	81	-5	0	0	0	.963	-7	S-42,2-14,1/30D	-1.0
Total	3	256	566	76	137	26	2	5	54	76	86	.242	.336	.322	76	-17	8	7	-2	.973	26	S-140/3-63,201D	1.5

■ JOHN RECCIUS

Reccius, John b: 10/29/1859, Louisville, Ky. d: 9/1/30, Louisville, Ky. 5'6.5", Deb: 5/2/1882 F

YEAR	TM/L	G	AB	R	H	2B	3B	HR	RBI	BB	SO	AVG	OBP	SLG	PRO+	BR/A	SB	CS	SBR	FA	FR	G/POS	TPR
1882	Lou-a	74	266	46	63	12	3	1	23			.237	.298	.316	113	5				.857	-3	*O-65,P-13	0.2
1883	Lou-a	18	63	10	9	2	0	0	7			.143	.229	.175	34	-4				.833	-1	O-18/P-1	-0.5
Total	2	92	329	56	72	14	3	1	30			.219	.284	.289	98	1				.851	-4	/O-83,P-14	-0.3

■ PHIL RECCIUS

Reccius, Phillip b: 6/7/1862, Louisville, Ky. d: 2/15/03, Louisville, Ky. 5'9", 163 lbs. Deb: 9/25/1882 F

YEAR	TM/L	G	AB	R	H	2B	3B	HR	RBI	BB	SO	AVG	OBP	SLG	PRO+	BR/A	SB	CS	SBR	FA	FR	G/POS	TPR
1882	Lou-a	4	15	0	2	0	0	0			0	.133	.133	.133	-10	-2				.778	-0	/O-4	-0.2
1883	Lou-a	1	3	1	1	1	0	0			0	.333	.333	.667	231	0				1.000	-0	/O-1	0.0
1884	Lou-a	73	263	23	63	9	2	3			5	.240	.267	.323	96	-1				.845	-2	3-51/P-18,S	-0.2
1885	Lou-a	102	402	57	97	8	10	1			13	.241	.267	.318	84	-8				.829	-8	*3-97/P-7	-0.7
1886	Lou-a	5	13	4	4	1	1	0			3	.308	.471	.538	204	2	0			.889	1	/O-5,P-1	0.2
1887	Lou-a	11	37	9	9	2	0	0			8	.243	.391	.297	92	0	3			.926	2	O-10/S-1	0.1
	Cle-a	62	229	23	47	6	3	0			24	.205	.295	.258	56	-12	9			.877	8	3-62/P-1	-0.3
	Yr	73	266	32	56	8	3	0			32	.211	.309	.263	62	-12	12			.877	10	3-62,O-10/SP	-0.2
1888	Lou-a	2	9	0	2	1	0	0	4	1		.222	.300	.333	105	0	0			.750	-2	/3-2	-0.1
1890	Roc-a	1	4	0	0	0	0	0			0	.000	.000	.000	-99	-1	0			.000	-0	/O-1	-0.1
Total	8	261	975	117	225	28	16	4	4	54		.231	.280	.305	81	-21	12			.848	5	3-212/P-27,OS	-1.3

■ JOHNNY REDER

Reder, John Anthony b: 9/24/09, Lublin, Poland d: 4/12/90, Fall River, Mass. BR/TR, 6', 184 lbs. Deb: 4/16/32

YEAR	TM/L	G	AB	R	H	2B	3B	HR	RBI	BB	SO	AVG	OBP	SLG	PRO+	BR/A	SB	CS	SBR	FA	FR	G/POS	TPR
1932	Bos-A	17	37	4	5	1	0	0	3	6	6	.135	.256	.162	11	-5	0	0	0	.990	0	1-10/3-1	-0.5

■ BUCK REDFERN

Redfern, George Howard b: 4/7/02, Asheville, N.C. d: 9/8/64, Asheville, N.C. BR/TR, 5'11", 165 lbs. Deb: 4/11/28

YEAR	TM/L	G	AB	R	H	2B	3B	HR	RBI	BB	SO	AVG	OBP	SLG	PRO+	BR/A	SB	CS	SBR	FA	FR	G/POS	TPR
1928	Chi-A	86	261	22	61	6	3	0	35	12	19	.234	.267	.280	44	-21	8	2	1	.953	6	2-45,S-33/3	-0.9
1929	Chi-A	21	46	0	6	0	0	0	3	3	3	.130	.184	.130	-18	-8	1	1	-0	.967	-5	2-11/3-5,S	-1.2
Total	2	107	307	22	67	6	3	0	38	15	22	.218	.255	.257	35	-29	9	3	1	.955	1	/2-56,S-37,3	-2.1

■ JOE REDFIELD

Redfield, Joseph Randall b: 1/14/61, Doylestown, Pa. BR/TR, 6'2", 190 lbs. Deb: 6/4/88

YEAR	TM/L	G	AB	R	H	2B	3B	HR	RBI	BB	SO	AVG	OBP	SLG	PRO+	BR/A	SB	CS	SBR	FA	FR	G/POS	TPR
1988	Cal-A	1	2	0	0	0	0	0	0	0	0	.000	.000	.000	-99	-1	0	0	0	1.000	0	/3-1	0.0
1991	Pit-N	11	18	1	2	0	0	0	0	4	1	.111	.273	.111	12	-2	0	1	-1	.917	-1	/3-9	-0.3
Total	2	12	20	1	2	0	0	0	0	4	1	.100	.250	.100	2	-3	0	1	-1	.923	-0	/3-10	-0.3

■ GLENN REDMON

Redmon, Glenn Vincent b: 1/11/48, Detroit, Mich. BR/TR, 5'11", 180 lbs. Deb: 9/8/74

YEAR	TM/L	G	AB	R	H	2B	3B	HR	RBI	BB	SO	AVG	OBP	SLG	PRO+	BR/A	SB	CS	SBR	FA	FR	G/POS	TPR
1974	SF-N	7	17	0	4	3	0	0	4	1	3	.235	.278	.412	87	-1	0	0	0	.955	-1	/2-4	-0.1

■ HARRY REDMOND

Redmond, Harry John b: 9/13/1887, Cleveland, Ohio d: 7/10/60, Cleveland, Ohio TR , Deb: 9/7/09

YEAR	TM/L	G	AB	R	H	2B	3B	HR	RBI	BB	SO	AVG	OBP	SLG	PRO+	BR/A	SB	CS	SBR	FA	FR	G/POS	TPR
1909	Bro-N	6	19	3	0	0	0	0	1		0	.000	.000	.000	-99	-4	0			.892	4	/2-5	-0.1

■ WAYNE REDMOND

Redmond, Howard Wayne b: 11/25/45, Athens, Ala. BR/TR, 5'10", 165 lbs. Deb: 9/7/65

YEAR	TM/L	G	AB	R	H	2B	3B	HR	RBI	BB	SO	AVG	OBP	SLG	PRO+	BR/A	SB	CS	SBR	FA	FR	G/POS	TPR
1965	Det-A	4	4	1	0	0	0	0	0	1	1	.000	.200	.000	-38	-1	0	0	0	1.000	0	/O-2	-0.1
1969	Det-A	5	3	0	0	0	0	0	0	1	3	.000	.000	.000	-96	-1	0	0	0	.000	0	H	-0.1
Total	2	9	7	1	0	0	0	0	0	2	4	.000	.125	.000	-60	-1	0	0	0	1.000	0	/O-2	-0.2

■ JACK REDMOND

Redmond, John McKittrick "Red" b: 9/3/10, Florence, Ariz. d: 7/27/68, Garland, Tex. BL/TR, 5'11", 185 lbs. Deb: 4/22/35

YEAR	TM/L	G	AB	R	H	2B	3B	HR	RBI	BB	SO	AVG	OBP	SLG	PRO+	BR/A	SB	CS	SBR	FA	FR	G/POS	TPR
1935	Was-A	22	34	8	6	1	0	1	7	3	1	.176	.243	.294	40	-3	0	0	0	.978	2	C-15	-0.1

■ BILLY REDMON

Redmon, William T. b: Brooklyn, N.Y. BL/TL, Deb: 5/4/1875

YEAR	TM/L	G	AB	R	H	2B	3B	HR	RBI	BB	SO	AVG	OBP	SLG	PRO+	BR/A	SB	CS	SBR	FA	FR	G/POS	TPR
1875	RS-n	19	82	12	16	2	0	0	2			.195	.214	.220	56	-3						S-17/3-1	-0.3
1877	Cin-N	3	12	1	3	1	0	0	3			.250	.308	.333	115	0				.833	2	/S-3	0.2
1878	Mil-N	48	187	16	43	8	0	0	21	8	13	.230	.262	.273	71	-6				.785	-17	S-39/O-7,3C	-2.1
Total	2	51	199	17	46	9	0	0	24	9	14	.231	.264	.276	73	-6				.791	-16	/S-42,O-7,3C	-1.9

■ GARY REDUS

Redus, Gary Eugene b: 11/1/56, Athens, Ala. BR/TR, 6'1", 185 lbs. Deb: 9/7/82

YEAR	TM/L	G	AB	R	H	2B	3B	HR	RBI	BB	SO	AVG	OBP	SLG	PRO+	BR/A	SB	CS	SBR	FA	FR	G/POS	TPR
1982	Cin-N	20	83	12	18	3	2	1	7	5	21	.217	.261	.337	65	-4	11	2	2	.970	1	O-20	-0.2
1983	Cin-N	125	453	90	112	20	9	17	51	71	111	.247	.353	.444	115	10	39	14	3	.972	9	*O-120	1.9
1984	Cin-N	123	394	69	100	21	3	7	22	52	71	.254	.342	.376	97	-1	48	11	8	.967	-2	*O-114	0.3
1985	Cin-N	101	246	51	62	14	4	6	28	44	52	.252	.368	.415	113	5	48	12	7	.986	-10	O-85	0.1
1986	Phi-N	90	340	62	84	22	4	11	33	47	78	.247	.344	.432	109	4	25	7	3	.980	10	O-89	1.5
1987	Chi-A	130	475	78	112	26	6	12	48	69	90	.236	.333	.392	89	-7	52	11	4	.979	4	*O-123/D-4	0.1
1988	Chi-A	77	262	42	69	10	6	6	34	33	52	.263	.350	.401	110	4	26	2	7	.987	1	O-68/D-2	0.9
	Pit-N	30	71	12	14	2	2	2	9	12	14	.197	.345	.310	90	-0	5	2	0	.957	2	O-19	0.1
1989	Pit-N	98	279	42	79	18	7	6	33	40	51	.283	.375	.462	143	16	25	6	4	.987	6	1-72/O-16	1.5
1990	*Pit-N	96	227	32	56	7	6	2	23	33	38	.247	.347	.419	114	5	25	5	0	.988	-2	1-72/O-7	-0.1
1991	*Pit-N	98	252	45	62	12	2	7	24	28	39	.246	.329	.393	104	1	17	3	3	.990	-11	1-47,O-33	-1.1

YEAR	TM/L	G	AB	R	H	2B	3B	HR	RBI	BB	SO	AVG	OBP	SLG	PRO+	BR/A	SB	CS	SBR	FA	FR	G/POS	TPR
1992	*Pit-N	76	176	26	45	7	3	3	12	17	25	.256	.321	.381	99	-0	11	4	1	1.000	-4	1-36,O-15	-0.6
1993	Tex-A	77	222	28	64	12	4	6	31	23	35	.288	.355	.459	122	7	4	4	-1	.981	-8	O-61/1-5,2D	-0.4
1994	Tex-A	18	33	2	9	1	0	0	2	4	6	.273	.351	.303	76	-1	0	0	0	1.000	-2	/O-7,1-5	-0.3
Total	13	1159	3513	591	886	183	51	90	352	481	688	.252	.345	.410	107	39	322	83	47	.974	-12	O-777,1-237/D2	3.7

■ BOB REECE
Reece, Robert Scott b: 1/5/51, Sacramento, Cal. BR/TR, 6'1", 190 lbs. Deb: 4/22/78

YEAR	TM/L	G	AB	R	H	2B	3B	HR	RBI	BB	SO	AVG	OBP	SLG	PRO+	BR/A	SB	CS	SBR	FA	FR	G/POS	TPR
1978	Mon-N	9	11	2	2	1	0	0	3	0	4	.182	.182	.273	26	-1	0	0	0	.947	1	/C-9	0.0

■ DARREN REED
Reed, Darren A. Douglass b: 10/16/65, Ojai, Cal. BR/TR, 6'1", 190 lbs. Deb: 5/1/90

YEAR	TM/L	G	AB	R	H	2B	3B	HR	RBI	BB	SO	AVG	OBP	SLG	PRO+	BR/A	SB	CS	SBR	FA	FR	G/POS	TPR
1990	NY-N	26	39	5	8	4	1	1	2	3	11	.205	.262	.436	89	-1	1	0	0	.955	-1	O-14	-0.2
1992	Mon-N	42	81	10	14	2	0	5	10	6	23	.173	.239	.383	74	-3	0	0	0	1.000	-3	O-29	-0.7
	Min-A	14	33	2	6	2	0	0	4	2	11	.182	.229	.242	31	-3	0	0	0	1.000	-2	O-13/D-1	-0.6
Total	2	82	153	17	28	8	1	6	16	11	45	.183	.242	.366	68	-7	1	0	0	.987	-6	/O-56,D-1	-1.5

■ HUGH REED
Reed, Hugh b: 1837, Chicago, Ill. d: 11/3/1883, Chicago, Ill. Deb: 8/26/1874

YEAR	TM/L	G	AB	R	H	2B	3B	HR	RBI	BB	SO	AVG	OBP	SLG	PRO+	BR/A	SB	CS	SBR	FA	FR	G/POS	TPR
1874	Bal-n	1	4	0	0	0	0	0		0	0	.000	.000	.000	-99	-1						/O-1	-0.1

■ JEFF REED
Reed, Jeffrey Scott b: 11/12/62, Joliet, Ill. BL/TR, 6'2", 190 lbs. Deb: 4/5/84

YEAR	TM/L	G	AB	R	H	2B	3B	HR	RBI	BB	SO	AVG	OBP	SLG	PRO+	BR/A	SB	CS	SBR	FA	FR	G/POS	TPR
1984	Min-A	18	21	3	3	3	0	0	1	2	6	.143	.217	.286	36	-2	0	0	0	.977	2	C-18	0.1
1985	Min-A	7	10	2	2	0	0	0	0	0	3	.200	.200	.200	9	-1	0	0	0	1.000	-0	/C-7	-0.1
1986	Min-A	68	165	13	39	6	1	2	9	16	19	.236	.308	.321	70	-7	1	0	0	.994	8	C-64	0.5
1987	Mon-N	75	207	15	44	11	0	1	21	12	20	.213	.259	.280	42	-17	0	1	-1	.970	-4	C-74	-1.8
1988	Mon-N	43	123	10	27	3	2	0	9	13	22	.220	.294	.276	62	-6	1	0	0	.995	2	C-39	-0.1
	Cin-N	49	142	10	33	6	0	1	7	15	19	.232	.306	.296	71	-5	0	0	0	.993	5	C-49	0.4
	Yr	92	265	20	60	9	2	1	16	28	41	.226	.300	.287	66	-11	1	0	0	.994	8	C-88	0.3
1989	Cin-N	102	287	16	64	11	0	3	23	34	46	.223	.310	.293	71	-10	0	0	0	.988	-5	C-99	-1.1
1990	*Cin-N	72	175	12	44	8	1	3	16	24	26	.251	.342	.360	89	-2	0	0	0	.987	-2	C-70	0.3
1991	Cin-N	91	270	20	72	15	2	3	31	23	38	.267	.327	.370	92	-3	0	1	-1	.991	-2	C-89	0.0
1992	Cin-N	15	25	2	4	0	0	0	2	1	4	.160	.192	.160	1	-3	0	0	0	1.000	-0	/C-6	-0.3
1993	SF-N	66	119	10	31	3	0	6	12	16	22	.261	.348	.437	112	2	0	1	-1	1.000	3	C-37	0.6
1994	SF-N	50	103	11	18	3	0	1	7	11	21	.175	.254	.233	29	-11	0	0	0	.993	-4	C-33	-1.3
Total	11	656	1647	124	381	69	6	20	138	167	246	.231	.304	.317	70	-65	2	3	-1	.989	9	C-585	-2.8

■ JODY REED
Reed, Jody Eric b: 7/26/62, Tampa, Fla. BR/TR, 5'9", 170 lbs. Deb: 9/12/87

YEAR	TM/L	G	AB	R	H	2B	3B	HR	RBI	BB	SO	AVG	OBP	SLG	PRO+	BR/A	SB	CS	SBR	FA	FR	G/POS	TPR
1987	Bos-A	9	30	4	9	1	1	0	8	4	0	.300	.382	.400	105	0	1	1	-0	1.000	5	/S-4,2-2,3	0.5
1988	*Bos-A	109	338	60	99	23	1	1	28	45	21	.293	.382	.376	109	6	1	3	-2	.971	3	S-94,2-11/3D	1.5
1989	Bos-A	146	524	76	151	42	2	3	40	73	44	.288	.379	.393	111	10	4	5	-2	.967	1	S-77,2-70/30D	1.7
1990	*Bos-A	155	598	70	173	45	0	5	51	75	65	.289	.372	.390	108	9	4	4	-1	.990	-6	*2-119,S-50/D	0.8
1991	Bos-A	153	618	87	175	42	2	5	60	60	53	.283	.350	.382	98	-1	6	5	0	.982	1	*2-152/S-6	0.2
1992	Bos-A	143	550	64	136	27	1	3	40	62	44	.247	.324	.316	75	-17	7	8	-3	.982	24	*2-142/D-1	0.7
1993	LA-N	132	445	48	123	21	2	2	31	38	40	.276	.335	.346	88	-7	1	3	-2	.993	19	*2-132	1.4
1994	Mil-A	108	399	48	108	22	0	2	37	57	34	.271	.365	.341	82	-9	5	4	-1	.995	11	*2-106	0.4
Total	8	955	3502	457	974	223	9	21	295	414	301	.278	.358	.365	96	-10	29	33	-11	.987	59	2-734,S-231/3DO	7.2

■ JACK REED
Reed, John Burwell b: 2/2/33, Silver City, Miss. BR/TR, 6', 185 lbs. Deb: 4/23/61

YEAR	TM/L	G	AB	R	H	2B	3B	HR	RBI	BB	SO	AVG	OBP	SLG	PRO+	BR/A	SB	CS	SBR	FA	FR	G/POS	TPR
1961	*NY-A	28	13	4	2	0	0	1	1	1	1	.154	.214	.154	0	-2	0	0	0	.933	-9	O-27	-1.1
1962	NY-A	88	43	17	13	2	1	1	4	4	7	.302	.362	.465	125	1	2	1	0	.941	-23	O-75	-2.2
1963	NY-A	106	73	18	15	3	1	0	1	9	14	.205	.293	.274	60	-4	5	1	1	1.000	-21	O-89	-2.6
Total	3	222	129	39	30	5	2	1	6	14	22	.233	.308	.326	76	-4	7	2	1	.972	-53	O-191	-5.9

■ MILT REED
Reed, Milton D. b: 7/4/1890, Atlanta, Ga. d: 7/27/38, Atlanta, Ga. BL/TR, 5'9.5", 150 lbs. Deb: 9/9/11

YEAR	TM/L	G	AB	R	H	2B	3B	HR	RBI	BB	SO	AVG	OBP	SLG	PRO+	BR/A	SB	CS	SBR	FA	FR	G/POS	TPR
1911	StL-N	1	1	0	0	0	0	0	0	0	0	.000	.000	.000	-99	-0	0			.000	0	H	0.0
1913	Phi-N	13	24	4	6	1	0	0	0	1	5	.250	.280	.292	61	-1	1			.900	-4	/S-9,2-3	-0.5
1914	Phi-N	44	107	10	22	2	1	0	2	10	13	.206	.280	.243	52	-6	4			.887	-17	S-22,2-11/3	-2.4
1915	Bro-F	10	31	2	9	1	1	0	8	2	0	.290	.353	.387	99	-0	2			.864	-5	S-10	-0.5
Total	4	68	163	16	37	4	2	0	10	13	18	.227	.292	.276	62	-8	7			.880	-26	/S-41,2-14,3	-3.4

■ TED REED
Reed, Ralph Edwin b: 10/18/1890, Beaver, Pa. d: 2/16/59, Beaver, Pa. BR/TR, 5'11", 190 lbs. Deb: 9/10/15

YEAR	TM/L	G	AB	R	H	2B	3B	HR	RBI	BB	SO	AVG	OBP	SLG	PRO+	BR/A	SB	CS	SBR	FA	FR	G/POS	TPR
1915	New-F	20	77	5	20	1	2	0	4	2	7	.260	.287	.325	67	-4	1			.863	-3	3-20	-0.6

■ BILLY REED
Reed, William Joseph b: 11/12/22, Shawano, Wis. BL/TR, 5'10.5", 175 lbs. Deb: 4/15/52

YEAR	TM/L	G	AB	R	H	2B	3B	HR	RBI	BB	SO	AVG	OBP	SLG	PRO+	BR/A	SB	CS	SBR	FA	FR	G/POS	TPR
1952	Bos-N	15	52	4	13	0	0	0	0	0	5	.250	.264	.250	45	-4	0	0	0	.931	-7	2-14	-1.0

■ ICICLE REEDER
Reeder, James Edward b: 1865, Cincinnati, Ohio BR , Deb: 6/24/1884

YEAR	TM/L	G	AB	R	H	2B	3B	HR	RBI	BB	SO	AVG	OBP	SLG	PRO+	BR/A	SB	CS	SBR	FA	FR	G/POS	TPR
1884	Cin-a	3	14	0	2	0	0	0	0	0	0	.143	.143	.143	-6	-2	1			1.000	-0	/O-3	-0.2
	Was-U	3	12	0	2	0	0	0	0			.167	.167	.167	-9	-2	0			.500	-1	/O-3	-0.3
Total	1	6	26	0	4	0	0	0	0			.154	.154	.154	-8	-3				.714	-1	/O-6	-0.5

■ NICK REEDER
Reeder, Nicholas (b: Nicholas Herchenroeder) b: 3/22/1867, Louisville, Ky. d: 9/26/1894, Louisville, Ky. BR/TR, 5'9", 189 lbs. Deb: 4/11/1891

YEAR	TM/L	G	AB	R	H	2B	3B	HR	RBI	BB	SO	AVG	OBP	SLG	PRO+	BR/A	SB	CS	SBR	FA	FR	G/POS	TPR
1891	Lou-a	1	2	0	0	0	0	0	0	0	1	.000	.000	.000	-99	-1	0			1.000	-0	/3-1	-0.1

■ RANDY REESE
Reese, Andrew Jackson b: 2/7/04, Tupelo, Miss. d: 1/10/66, Tupelo, Miss. BR/TR, 5'11", 180 lbs. Deb: 4/15/27

YEAR	TM/L	G	AB	R	H	2B	3B	HR	RBI	BB	SO	AVG	OBP	SLG	PRO+	BR/A	SB	CS	SBR	FA	FR	G/POS	TPR
1927	NY-N	97	355	43	94	14	2	4	21	13	52	.265	.298	.349	73	-14	5			.912	-1	3-64,O-16/1	-1.3
1928	NY-N	109	406	61	125	18	4	6	44	13	24	.308	.331	.416	94	-5	7			.941	-10	0-64,2-26/1S3	-1.7
1929	NY-N	58	209	36	55	11	3	0	21	15	19	.263	.316	.344	64	-12	8			.960	-3	2-44/O-8,3	-0.9
1930	NY-N	67	172	26	47	4	2	4	25	10	12	.273	.313	.390	70	-9	1			.957	-3	O-32,3-10/1	-1.2
Total	4	331	1142	166	321	47	11	14	111	51	107	.281	.315	.378	78	-39	21			.954	-14	0-120/3-84,21S	-5.1

■ PEE WEE REESE
Reese, Harold Henry b: 7/23/18, Ekron, Ky. BR/TR, 5'9", 175 lbs. Deb: 4/23/40 CH

YEAR	TM/L	G	AB	R	H	2B	3B	HR	RBI	BB	SO	AVG	OBP	SLG	PRO+	BR/A	SB	CS	SBR	FA	FR	G/POS	TPR
1940	Bro-N	84	312	58	85	8	4	5	28	45	42	.272	.366	.372	98	0	15			.960	-6	S-83	-0.7
1941	*Bro-N	152	595	76	136	23	5	2	46	68	56	.229	.311	.294	68	-24	10			.946	8	*S-151	-0.5
1942	Bro-N★	151	564	87	144	24	5	3	53	82	55	.255	.350	.332	98	1	15			.959	17	*S-151	2.9
1946	Bro-N†	152	542	79	154	16	10	5	60	87	71	.284	.384	.378	116	14	10			.966	-4	*S-152	2.1
1947	*Bro-N★	142	476	81	135	24	4	12	73	104	67	.284	.414	.426	119	17	7			.966	-2	*S-142	2.2
1948	Bro-N★	151	566	96	155	31	4	9	75	79	63	.274	.363	.390	100	2	25			.962	10	*S-149	2.1
1949	*Bro-N★	155	617	132	172	27	3	16	73	116	63	.279	.396	.410	112	15	26			.977	2	*S-155	2.7
1950	Bro-N★	141	531	97	138	21	5	11	52	91	62	.260	.369	.380	96	-1	17			.963	2	*S-134/3-7	1.1
1951	Bro-N★	154	616	94	176	20	8	10	84	81	57	.286	.371	.393	103	5	20	14	-2	.953	-8	*S-154	0.6
1952	Bro-N★	149	559	94	152	18	8	6	58	86	59	.272	.369	.365	103	5	30	5	6	.969	-11	*S-145	1.1
1953	Bro-N★	140	524	108	142	25	7	13	61	82	61	.271	.374	.420	104	5	22	6	3	.966	-1	*S-135	1.7
1954	Bro-N☆	141	554	98	171	35	4	10	69	90	62	.309	.408	.455	121	20	8	5	1	.965	-4	*S-140	2.7
1955	*Bro-N	145	553	99	156	29	4	10	61	78	60	.282	.374	.403	103	5	8	7	-2	.965	-13	*S-142	0.2
1956	Bro-N	147	572	85	147	19	2	9	46	56	69	.257	.324	.344	74	-20	13	4	2	.965	-9	*S-136,3-12	-1.7
1957	Bro-N	103	330	33	74	3	1	1	29	39	32	.224	.308	.248	47	-23	3	6	1	.943	10	S-75,S-23	-1.0
1958	LA-N	59	147	21	33	7	2	4	17	26	15	.224	.341	.381	88	-2	1	2	-1	.929	-8	S-22,3-21	-0.9
Total	16	2166	8058	1338	2170	330	80	126	885	1210	890	.269	.366	.377	98	19	232	45		.962	-25	*S-2014,3-115	14.6

YEAR	TM/L	G	AB	R	H	2B	3B	HR	RBI	BB	SO	AVG	OBP	SLG	PRO+	BR/A	SB	CS	SBR	FA	FR	G/POS	TPR

■ JIMMIE REESE Reese, James Herman (b: James Herman Soloman) b: 10/1/01, New York, N.Y. d: 7/13/94, Santa Ana, Cal. BL/TR, 5'11.5", 165 lbs. Deb: 4/19/30 C

1930	NY-A	77	188	44	65	14	2	3	18	11	8	.346	.382	.489	125	7	1	1	-0	.974	-9	2-48/3-5	-0.1
1931	NY-A	65	245	41	59	10	2	3	26	17	10	.241	.293	.335	68	-12	2	3	-1	.972	5	2-61	-0.4
1932	StL-N	90	309	38	82	15	0	2	26	20	19	.265	.314	.333	72	-12	4			.979	9	2-77	0.1
Total	3	232	742	123	206	39	4	8	70	48	37	.278	.324	.373	84	-17	7	4		.975	4	2-186/3-5	-0.4

■ RICH REESE Reese, Richard Benjamin b: 9/29/41, Leipsic, Ohio BL/TL, 6'3", 200 lbs. Deb: 9/4/64

1964	Min-A	10	7	0	0	0	0	0	0	0	1	.000	.000	.000	-99	-2	0	0	0	1.000	0	/1-1	-0.2
1965	Min-A	14	7	0	2	1	0	0	0	2	2	.286	.444	.429	143	1	0	0	0	1.000	-0	/1-6,O-1	0.0
1966	Min-A	3	2	0	0	0	0	0	0	1	2	.000	.333	.000	5	-0	0	0	0	.000	0	H	0.0
1967	Min-A	95	101	13	25	5	0	4	20	8	17	.248	.303	.416	102	0	0	0	0	.990	-1	1-36,O-10	-0.2
1968	Min-A	126	332	40	86	15	2	4	28	18	36	.259	.303	.352	93	-3	3	1	0	.991	-2	1-87,O-15	-1.2
1969	*Min-A	132	419	52	135	24	4	16	69	23	57	.322	.365	.513	140	21	1	5	-3	.993	-4	*1-117/O-5	0.6
1970	*Min-A	153	501	63	131	15	5	10	56	48	70	.261	.335	.371	93	-4	5	4	-1	.992	-2	*1-146	-1.9
1971	Min-A	120	329	40	72	8	3	10	39	20	35	.219	.274	.353	74	-12	7	4	0	.994	-5	1-95/O-9	-2.4
1972	Min-A	132	197	23	43	3	2	5	26	25	27	.218	.306	.330	85	-3	0	1	-1	.988	3	1-98,O-13	-0.5
1973	Det-A	59	102	10	14	1	0	2	4	7	17	.137	.193	.206	11	-12	0	0	0	1.000	-3	1-37,O-21	-1.8
	Min-A	22	23	7	4	1	1	1	3	6	6	.174	.345	.435	114	1	0	0	0	1.000	1	1-17	0.1
	Yr	81	125	17	18	2	1	3	7	13	23	.144	.225	.248	31	-12	0	0	0	1.000	-2	1-54/O-21	-1.7
Total	10	866	2020	248	512	73	17	52	245	158	270	.253	.314	.384	95	-15	16	15	-4	.992	-10	1-640/O-74	-7.5

■ BOBBY REEVES Reeves, Robert Edwin "Gunner" b: 6/24/04, Hill City, Tenn. d: 6/4/93, Chattanooga, Tenn. BR/TR, 5'11", 170 lbs. Deb: 6/9/26

1926	Was-A	20	49	4	11	0	1	0	7	6	9	.224	.321	.265	56	-3	1	1	-0	.940	1	3-16/2-1,S	-0.1
1927	Was-A	112	380	37	97	11	5	1	39	21	53	.255	.296	.318	60	-23	3	1	0	.923	-7	S-96,3-12/2	-1.8
1928	Was-A	102	353	44	107	16	8	3	42	24	47	.303	.351	.419	102	1	4	8	-4	.908	-4	S-66,2-22/3O	0.2
1929	Bos-A	140	460	66	114	19	2	2	28	60	57	.248	.343	.311	71	-18	7	8	-3	.912	1	*3-131/2-2,S1	-1.4
1930	Bos-A	92	272	41	59	7	4	2	18	50	36	.217	.345	.294	66	-12	6	2	1	.895	5	2-29/3-15,2	-0.2
1931	Bos-A	36	84	11	14	2	2	0	1	14	16	.167	.293	.238	43	-7	0	1	-1	.912	-8	2-29/P-1	-1.3
Total	6	502	1598	203	402	55	22	8	135	175	218	.252	.331	.329	73	-62	21	21	-6	.906	-11	3-229,S-180/2P1O	-4.6

■ RUDY REGALADO Regalado, Rudolph Valentino b: 5/21/30, Los Angeles, Cal. BR/TR, 6'1", 185 lbs. Deb: 4/13/54

1954	*Cle-A	65	180	21	45	5	0	2	24	19	16	.250	.335	.311	76	-5	0	2	-1	.967	-5	3-50/2-2	-1.3
1955	Cle-A	10	26	2	7	2	0	0	5	2	4	.269	.321	.346	77	-1	0	0	0	.955	2	/3-8,2-1	0.1
1956	Cle-A	16	47	4	11	1	0	0	2	4	1	.234	.308	.255	49	-3	0	0	0	.783	-7	3-14/1-1	-1.0
Total	3	91	253	27	63	8	0	2	31	25	21	.249	.329	.304	71	-10	0	2	-1	.944	-9	/3-72,2-3,1	-2.2

■ JOE REGAN Regan, Joseph Charles b: 7/12/1872, Seymour, Conn. d: 11/18/48, Hartford, Conn. BR/TR, 6'1", Deb: 9/21/1898

1898	NY-N	2	5	1	1	0	0	0	2	0		.200	.200	.200	15	-1	0			1.000	-1	/O-2	-0.1

■ BILL REGAN Regan, William Wright b: 1/23/1899, Pittsburgh, Pa. d: 6/11/68, Pittsburgh, Pa. BR/TR, 5'10", 155 lbs. Deb: 6/2/26

1926	Bos-A	108	403	40	106	21	3	4	34	23	37	.263	.309	.360	76	-15	6	3	0	.965	17	*2-106	0.5
1927	Bos-A	129	468	43	128	37	10	2	66	26	51	.274	.315	.408	88	-10	10	10	-3	.960	3	*2-121	-0.6
1928	Bos-A	138	511	53	135	30	6	7	75	21	40	.264	.296	.387	80	-17	9	6	-1	.963	15	*2-137/O-1	0.0
1929	Bos-A	104	371	38	107	27	7	1	54	22	38	.288	.328	.407	90	-6	7	5	-1	.962	-16	2-91,3-10/1	-1.8
1930	Bos-A	134	507	54	135	35	10	3	53	25	60	.266	.303	.393	78	-19	4	2	0	.963	-10	*2-127/3-2	-2.0
1931	Pit-N	28	104	8	21	8	0	1	10	5	19	.202	.239	.308	46	-8	2			.944	-2	2-28	-0.7
Total	6	641	2364	236	632	158	36	18	292	122	245	.267	.306	.387	81	-75	38	26		.962	8	2-610/3-12,1O	-4.6

■ TONY REGO Rego, Antone (b: Antone Do Rego) b: 10/31/1897, Wailuku, Hawaii d: 1/6/78, Tulsa, Okla. BR/TR, 5'4", 165 lbs. Deb: 6/21/24

1924	StL-A	24	59	5	13	1	0	0	5	1	3	.220	.233	.237	20	-7	0	0	0	.972	0	C-23	-0.6
1925	StL-A	20	32	5	13	2	1	0	3	3	2	.406	.472	.531	147	2	0	0	0	.979	2	C-19	0.5
Total	2	44	91	10	26	3	1	0	8	4	5	.286	.323	.341	66	-5	0	0	0	.975	2	/C-42	-0.1

■ WALLY REHG Rehg, Walter Phillip b: 8/31/1888, Summerfield, Ill. d: 4/5/46, Burbank, Cal. BR/TR, 5'8", 160 lbs. Deb: 4/14/12

1912	Pit-N	8	9	1	0	0	0	0	0	0	1	.000	.000	.000	-99	-2	0			1.000	-1	/O-2	-0.3
1913	Bos-A	30	101	13	28	3	2	0	9	2	7	.277	.291	.347	84	-2	4			.943	-3	O-26	-0.7
1914	Bos-A	88	151	14	33	4	2	0	11	18	11	.219	.306	.272	74	-5	5	8	-3	.980	-5	O-43	-1.6
1915	Bos-A	5	5	2	1	0	0	0	0	0	1	.200	.200	.200	20	-1	1			1.000	-0	/O-1	0.0
1917	Bos-N	87	341	48	92	12	6	1	31	24	32	.270	.320	.349	111	4	13			.956	-5	O-86	-0.6
1918	Bos-N	40	133	6	32	5	1	1	12	5	14	.241	.268	.316	81	-3	3			.988	2	O-38	-0.1
1919	Cin-N	5	12	1	2	0	0	0	3	1	0	.167	.231	.167	21	-1	0			.875	0	/O-5	-0.1
Total	7	263	752	85	188	24	11	2	66	50	66	.250	.299	.319	90	-11	26	8		.965	-12	O-201	-3.7

■ FRANK REIBER Reiber, Frank Bernard "Tubby" b: 9/19/09, Huntington, W.Va. BR/TR, 5'8.5", 169 lbs. Deb: 4/13/33

1933	Det-A	13	18	3	5	0	1	1	3	2	3	.278	.350	.556	134	1	0	0	0	.929	-2	/C-6	-0.1
1934	Det-A	3	1	0	0	0	0	0	0	2	0	.000	.667	.000	84	0	0	0	0	.000	0	H	0.0
1935	Det-A	8	11	3	3	0	0	0	1	3	3	.273	.429	.273	88	0	0	0	0	1.000	-1	C-5	0.0
1936	Det-A	20	55	7	15	2	0	1	5	5	7	.273	.333	.364	72	-2	0	1	-1	.982	-4	C-17/O-1	-0.5
Total	4	44	85	13	23	2	1	2	9	12	13	.271	.361	.388	89	-1	0	1	-1	.975	-6	/C-28,O-1	-0.6

■ HERMAN REICH Reich, Herman Charles b: 11/23/17, Bell, Cal. BR/TL, 6'2", 200 lbs. Deb: 5/3/49

1949	Was-A	2	2	0	0	0	0	0	0	0	1	.000	.000	.000	-99	-1	0	0	0	.000	0	H	-0.1
	Cle-A	1	2	0	1	0	0	0	0	1	0	.500	.667	.500	215	1	0	0	0	.000	-0	/O-1	0.1
	Yr	3	4	0	1	0	0	0	0	1	1	.250	.400	.250	75	-0	0	0	0	.000	-0	/O-1	-0.1
	Chi-N	108	386	43	108	18	2	3	34	13	32	.280	.305	.360	80	-12	4			.989	14	1-85,O-16	0.1
Total	1	111	390	43	109	18	2	3	34	14	33	.279	.306	.359	80	-12	4	0		.969	14	/1-85,O-17	0.0

■ RICK REICHARDT Reichardt, Frederic Carl b: 3/16/43, Madison, Wis. BR/TR, 6'3", 215 lbs. Deb: 9/1/64

1964	LA-A	11	37	0	6	0	0	0	1	1	12	.162	.184	.162	-3	-5	0			1.000	0	O-11	-0.6
1965	Cal-A	20	75	8	20	4	0	1	6	5	12	.267	.321	.360	95	0	4	1	1	.975	1	O-20	0.0
1966	Cal-A	89	319	48	92	5	4	16	44	27	61	.288	.368	.480	145	19	8	4	0	.976	-1	O-87	1.4
1967	Cal-A	146	498	56	132	14	2	17	69	35	90	.265	.322	.404	118	10	5	3	-0	.974	10	*O-138	1.4
1968	Cal-A	151	534	62	136	20	3	21	73	42	118	.255	.330	.421	131	19	8	7	-2	.989	9	*O-148	2.2
1969	Cal-A	137	493	60	125	11	4	13	68	43	100	.254	.324	.371	99	-2	3	6	-3	.981	-4	*O-136/1-3	-0.4
1970	Cal-A	9	6	1	1	0	0	0	1	0	1	.167	.444	.167	78	0	0	0	0	1.000	-0	/O-1	0.0
	Was-A	107	277	42	70	14	2	15	46	23	69	.253	.330	.480	127	9	2	4	-2	.985	-8	O-79/3-1	-0.5
	Yr	116	283	43	71	14	2	15	47	26	69	.251	.333	.473	126	9	2	4	-2	.985	-8	O-80/3-1	-0.5
1971	Chi-A	138	496	53	138	14	2	19	62	37	90	.278	.336	.429	112	7	5	10	-5	.981	-7	*O-128/1-9	-1.3
1972	Chi-A	101	291	31	73	14	0	4	43	28	63	.251	.323	.409	114	5	2	2	-1	.987	-10	O-90	-1.1
1973	Chi-A	46	153	15	42	8	1	3	16	8	29	.275	.315	.399	96	-1	2	3	-1	1.000	-2	O-37/D-6	-0.6
	KC-A	41	127	15	28	5	2	3	17	11	28	.220	.283	.362	75	-5	0	1	-1	1.000	-1	D-31/O-7	-0.7
	Yr	87	280	30	70	13	3	6	33	19	57	.250	.300	.382	86	-6	2	4	-1	1.000	-3	O-44,D-37	-1.3
1974	KC-A	1	1	0	1	0	0	0	1	0	0	1.000	1.000	1.000	451	0	0	0	0				0.0
Total	11	997	3307	391	864	109	24	116	445	263	672	.261	.328	.414	115	56	40	41	-13	.982	-2	O-882/D-37,13	-0.2

YEAR	TM/L	G	AB	R	H	2B	3B	HR	RBI	BB	SO	AVG	OBP	SLG	PRO+	BR/A	SB	CS	SBR	FA	FR	G/POS	TPR

■ DICK REICHLE Reichle, Richard Wendell b: 11/23/1896, Lincoln, Ill. d: 6/13/67, St.Louis, Mo. BL/TR, 6', 185 lbs. Deb: 9/19/22

1922	Bos-A	6	24	3	6	1	0	0	0	0	2	.250	.280	.292	50	-2	0	0	0	1.000	-0	/O-6	-0.3
1923	Bos-A	122	361	40	93	17	3	1	39	22	34	.258	.315	.330	69	-16	3	6	-3	.976	-7	O-93/1-2	-3.1
Total	2	128	385	43	99	18	3	1	39	22	36	.257	.313	.327	68	-18	3	6	-3	.977	-7	/O-99,1-2	-3.4

■ JESSIE REID Reid, Jessie Thomas b: 6/1/62, Honolulu, Hawaii BL/TL, 6'1", 200 lbs. Deb: 9/9/87

1987	SF-N	6	8	1	1	0	0	1	1	1	5	.125	.222	.500	89	-0	0	0	0	1.000	-1	/O-3	-0.1
1988	SF-N	2	2	0	0	0	0	0	0	0	1	.000	.000	.000	-99	-1	0	0	0	.000	0	H	-0.1
Total	2	8	10	1	1	0	0	1	1	1	6	.100	.182	.400	54	-1	0	0	0	1.000	-1	/O-3	-0.2

■ SCOTT REID Reid, Scott Donald b: 1/7/47, Chicago, Ill. BL/TR, 6'1", 195 lbs. Deb: 9/10/69

1969	Phi-N	13	19	5	4	0	0	0	7	5	.211	.423	.211	85	0	0	1	-1	1.000	-1	/O-5	-0.2
1970	Phi-N	25	49	5	6	1	0	0	1	11	22	.122	.283	.143	18	-5	0	0	0	1.000	3	O-18	-0.3
Total	2	38	68	10	10	1	0	0	1	18	27	.147	.326	.162	37	-5	0	1	-1	1.000	2	/O-23	-0.5

■ BILLY REID Reid, William Alexander b: 5/17/1857, London, Ont., Can. d: 6/26/40, London, Ont., Can. BL/TR, 6', 170 lbs. Deb: 5/1/1883

1883	Bal-a	24	97	14	27	3	0	0	4			.278	.307	.309	96	-1				.842	-8	2-23/S-1	-0.7
1884	Pit-a	19	70	11	17	2	0	0	4			.243	.293	.271	84	-1				.724	-4	O-17/3-1,2	-0.5
Total	2	43	167	25	44	5	0	0	8			.263	.301	.293	91	-2				.839	-12	/2-24,O-17,3S	-1.2

■ DUKE REILLEY Reilley, Alexander Aloysius "Midget" b: 8/25/1884, Chicago, Ill. d: 3/4/68, Indianapolis, Ind. BB/TR, 5'4.5", 148 lbs. Deb: 8/28/09

| 1909 | Cle-A | 20 | 62 | 10 | 13 | 0 | 0 | 0 | 0 | 4 | .210 | .258 | .210 | 46 | -4 | 5 | | | .979 | 2 | O-18 | -0.3 |

■ CHARLIE REILLEY Reilley, Charles E. b: 1856, Hartford, Conn. BR/TR, 5'10", 165 lbs. Deb: 5/1/1879

1879	Tro-N	62	236	17	54	5	1	0	19	1	20	.229	.232	.258	66	-8				.867	-16	C-49,1-11/O	-2.2
1880	Cin-N	30	103	8	21	1	0	0	9	0	5	.204	.204	.214	42	-6				.759	-5	O-16,C-13/3	-1.1
1881	Det-N	19	70	8	12	2	0	0	3	0	10	.171	.171	.200	16	-7				.889	-4	C-10/O-4,S31	-0.9
	Wor-N	2	8	2	3	0	0	0	1	0	1	.375	.375	.375	129	0				1.000	-2	/C-2	-0.2
	Yr	21	78	10	15	2	0	0	4	0	11	.192	.192	.218	28	-6				.897	-6	C-12/O-4,S31	-1.1
1882	Pro-N	3	11	0	2	0	0	0	2	1	2	.182	.250	.182	41	-1				.714	-2	/C-3	-0.3
1884	Bos-U	3	11	1	0	0	0	0	1			.000	.083	.000	-77	-3				1.000	-1	/O-2,3-1	-0.3
Total	5	119	439	36	92	8	1	0	34	3	38	.210	.215	.232	48	-24				.867	-30	/C-77,O-24,13S	-5.0

■ ARCH REILLY Reilly, Archer Edwin b: 8/17/1891, Alton, Ill. d: 11/29/63, Columbus, Ohio BR/TR, 5'10", 163 lbs. Deb: 6/1/17

| 1917 | Pit-N | 1 | 0 | 0 | 0 | 0 | 0 | 0 | 0 | 0 | 0 | — | — | — | — | 0 | 0 | | | 1.000 | 0 | /3-1 | 0.0 |

■ BARNEY REILLY Reilly, Bernard Eugene b: 2/7/1885, Brockton, Mass. d: 11/15/34, St.Joseph, Mo. BR/TR, 6' ", 175 lbs. Deb: 7/2/09

| 1909 | Chi-A | 12 | 25 | 3 | 5 | 0 | 0 | 0 | 3 | 3 | | .200 | .286 | .200 | 56 | -1 | 2 | | | .962 | 4 | 2-11/O-1 | 0.2 |

■ JOSH REILLY Reilly, Charles b: 1868, San Francisco, Cal. d: 6/13/38, San Francisco, Cal. Deb: 5/2/1896

| 1896 | Chi-N | 9 | 42 | 6 | 9 | 1 | 0 | 0 | 2 | 1 | 1 | .214 | .233 | .238 | 23 | -5 | 2 | | | .857 | -1 | /2-8,S-1 | -0.4 |

■ CHARLIE REILLY Reilly, Charles Thomas "Princeton Charlie" (b: Charles Thomas O'Reilly) b: 2/15/1867, Princeton, N.J. d: 12/16/37, Los Angeles, Cal. BB/TR, 5'11", 190 lbs. Deb: 10/9/1889

1889	Col-a	6	23	5	11	1	0	3	6	2	2	.478	.538	.913	326	7	9			.923	-3	/3-6	0.7
1890	Col-a	137	530	75	141	23	3	4		35		.266	.319	.343	102	1	43			.893	28	*3-137	2.9
1891	Pit-N	114	415	43	91	8	5	3	44	29	58	.219	.277	.284	65	-19	20			.857	2	*3-99,S-11/O	-1.1
1892	Phi-N	91	331	42	65	7	3	1	24	18	43	.196	.242	.245	47	-21	13			.905	10	3-70,O-15/2	-0.9
1893	Phi-N	104	416	64	102	16	7	4	56	33	36	.245	.314	.346	76	-16	13			.895	-1	*3-104	-1.2
1894	Phi-N	39	135	21	40	1	2	0	19	16	10	.296	.383	.333	76	-4	9			.874	2	3-28/O-5,2S1	-0.2
1895	Phi-N	49	179	28	48	6	1	0	25	13	12	.268	.335	.313	67	-8	7			.900	-3	S-34,3-11/2O	-0.8
1897	Was-N	101	351	64	97	18	3	2	60	34		.276	.359	.362	91	-4	18			.905	18	*3-101	1.4
Total	8	641	2380	342	595	80	24	17	234	180	161	.250	.314	.325	80	-65	132			.890	59	3-556/S-46,021	0.8

■ HAL REILLY Reilly, Harold John b: 4/1/1894, Oshkosh, Wis. d: 12/24/57, Chicago, Ill. BR/TR, 6', 180 lbs. Deb: 6/19/19

| 1919 | Chi-N | 1 | 3 | 0 | 0 | 0 | 0 | 0 | 0 | 0 | 1 | .000 | .000 | .000 | -99 | -1 | 0 | | | .000 | -1 | /O-1 | -0.1 |

■ JOHN REILLY Reilly, John Good "Long Jong" b: 10/5/1858, Cincinnati, Ohio d: 5/31/37, Cincinnati, Ohio BR/TR, 6'3", 178 lbs. Deb: 5/18/1880

1880	Cin-N	73	272	21	56	8	4	0	16	3	36	.206	.215	.265	62	-10				.947	-4	*1-72/O-3	-2.0
1883	Cin-a	98	437	103	136	21	14	9		9		.311	.325	.485	149	21				.961	-1	*1-98/O-1	0.9
1884	Cin-a	105	448	114	152	24	19	11		5		.339	.366	.551	186	39				.971	0	*1-103/O-3,S	2.3
1885	Cin-a	111	482	92	143	18	11	5		11		.297	.322	.411	128	13				.963	-5	*1-107/O-7	-0.4
1886	Cin-a	115	441	92	117	12	11	6		31		.265	.321	.383	116	7	19			.967	-1	*1-110/O-6	-0.7
1887	Cin-a	134	551	106	170	35	14	10		22		.309	.352	.477	127	17	50			.980	-0	*1-127/O-9	0.2
1888	Cin-a	127	527	112	169	28	14	13	103	17		.321	.363	.501	167	36	82			.977	-0	*1-117,O-10	2.2
1889	Cin-a	111	427	84	111	24	13	5	66	34	37	.260	.340	.412	110	4	43			.984	-2	*1-109/O-2	-0.4
1890	Cin-N	133	553	114	166	25	26	6	86	16	41	.300	.328	.472	133	18	29			.977	-3	*1-132/O-1	0.7
1891	Cin-N	135	546	60	132	20	13	4	64	9	42	.242	.267	.348	78	-18	22			.982	-7	*1-100,O-36	-2.8
Total	10	1142	4684	898	1352	215	139	69	335	157	156	.289	.325	.438	128	127	245			.972	-25	*1-1075/O-78,S	0.8

■ JOE REILLY Reilly, Joseph J. b: 1861, New York, N.Y. 5'10", 140 lbs. Deb: 6/8/1885

| 1885 | NY-a | 10 | 40 | 6 | 7 | 3 | 0 | 0 | 2 | | | .175 | .214 | .250 | 50 | -2 | | | | .848 | 1 | /2-8,3-2 | 0.0 |

■ TOM REILLY Reilly, Thomas Henry b: 8/3/1884, St.Louis, Mo. d: 10/18/18, New Orleans, La. BR/TR, 5'10", Deb: 7/27/08

1908	StL-N	29	81	5	14	1	0	1	3	2	.173	.193	.222	34	-6	4			.866	-6	S-29	-1.4
1909	StL-N	5	7	0	2	0	1	0	2	0	.286	.286	.571	176	0	0			1.000	0	/S-5	0.1
1914	Cle-A	1	1	0	0	0	0	0	0	0	.000	.000	.000	-96	-0	0			.000	0	H	0.0
Total	3	35	89	5	16	1	1	1	5	2	0	.180	.198	.247	44	-6	4			.875	-6	/S-34	-1.3

■ KEVIN REIMER Reimer, Kevin Michael b: 6/28/64, Macon, Ga. BL/TR, 6'2", 215 lbs. Deb: 9/13/88

1988	Tex-A	12	25	2	3	0	0	0	2	0	6	.120	.120	.240	-2	-3	0	0	0	.000	-0	/O-1,D-7	-0.4
1989	Tex-A	3	5	0	0	0	0	0	0	0	1	.000	.000	.000	-98	-1	0	0	0	.000	0	/D-1	-0.1
1990	Tex-A	64	100	5	26	9	1	2	15	10	22	.260	.333	.430	112	1	0	1	-1	.857	-2	D-21/O-9	-0.2
1991	Tex-A	136	394	46	106	22	0	20	69	33	93	.269	.336	.477	125	12	0	3	-2	.948	-5	O-66,D-56	0.1
1992	Tex-A	148	494	56	132	32	2	16	58	42	103	.267	.337	.437	120	12	2	4	-2	.949	-3	*O-110,D-32	0.5
1993	Mil-A	125	437	53	109	22	1	13	60	30	72	.249	.305	.394	88	-9	5	4	-1	.962	1	D-83,O-37	-1.4
Total	6	488	1455	162	376	85	4	52	204	115	297	.258	.323	.430	108	12	7	12	-5	.948	-11	O-223,D-200	-1.5

■ MIKE REINBACH Reinbach, Michael Wayne b: 8/6/49, San Diego, Cal. BL/TR, 6'2", 195 lbs. Deb: 4/7/74

| 1974 | Bal-A | 12 | 20 | 2 | 5 | 1 | 0 | 0 | 2 | 5 | 0 | .250 | .318 | .300 | 81 | 0 | 0 | 0 | 0 | 1.000 | -1 | /O-3,D-3 | -0.1 |

■ ART REINHOLZ Reinholz, Arthur August b: 1/27/03, Detroit, Mich. d: 12/29/80, New Port Richey, Fla. BR/TR, 5'10.5", 175 lbs. Deb: 9/27/28

| 1928 | Cle-A | 2 | 3 | 0 | 1 | 0 | 0 | 0 | 0 | 0 | 0 | .333 | .500 | .333 | 122 | 0 | 0 | 0 | 0 | .833 | 1 | /3-2 | 0.1 |

■ WALLY REINECKER Reinecker, Walter (b: Walter Joseph Smith) b: 4/21/1890, Pittsburgh, Pa. d: 4/18/57, Pittsburgh, Pa. BR/TR, 5'6", 150 lbs. Deb: 9/17/15

| 1915 | Bal-F | 3 | 8 | 0 | 1 | 0 | 0 | 0 | 0 | 1 | .125 | .222 | .125 | -6 | -1 | 0 | | | .571 | -2 | /3-3 | -0.3 |

YEAR	TM/L	G	AB	R	H	2B	3B	HR	RBI	BB	SO	AVG	OBP	SLG	PRO+	BR/A	SB	CS	SBR	FA	FR	G/POS	TPR

■ CHARLIE REIPSCHLAGER
Reipschlager, Charles W. BR/TR, 5'6.5", 160 lbs. Deb: 5/2/1883

YEAR	TM/L	G	AB	R	H	2B	3B	HR	RBI	BB	SO	AVG	OBP	SLG	PRO+	BR/A	SB	CS	SBR	FA	FR	G/POS	TPR
1883	NY-a	37	145	8	27	4	2	0	4			.186	.208	.241	42	-9				.936	5	C-29/O-8	-0.2
1884	*NY-a	59	233	21	56	13	2	0	1			.240	.250	.313	85	-4				.925	19	C-51/O-8	1.7
1885	NY-a	72	268	29	65	11	1	0		9		.243	.270	.291	84	-4				.879	-8	C-59/O-6,3S2	-0.6
1886	NY-a	65	232	21	49	4	6	0		9		.211	.244	.280	67	-9	2			.880	-6	C-57/O-9	-0.8
1887	Cle-a	63	231	20	49	8	3	0		11		.212	.251	.273	47	-16	7			.888	3	C-48,1-16	-0.8
Total	5	296	1109	99	246	40	14	0	34			.222	.248	.283	66	-43	9			.900	12	C-244/O-31,132S	-0.7

■ BOBBY REIS
Reis, Robert Joseph Thomas b: 1/2/09, Woodside, N.Y. d: 5/1/73, St.Paul, Minn. BR/TR, 6'1", 175 lbs. Deb: 9/19/31

YEAR	TM/L	G	AB	R	H	2B	3B	HR	RBI	BB	SO	AVG	OBP	SLG	PRO+	BR/A	SB	CS	SBR	FA	FR	G/POS	TPR
1931	Bro-N	6	17	3	5	0	0	0	2	2	0	.294	.368	.294	81	-0	0			.933	-1	/3-6	-0.1
1932	Bro-N	1	4	0	1	0	0	0	0	0	1	.250	.250	.250	36	-0	0			.500	1	/3-1	-0.1
1935	Bro-N	52	85	10	21	3	2	0	4	6	13	.247	.297	.329	70	-4	2			.950	2	O-21,P-14/213	-0.2
1936	Bos-N	37	60	3	13	2	0	0	5	3	6	.217	.254	.250	39	-5	0			1.000	3	P-35/O-2	-0.1
1937	Bos-N	45	86	10	21	5	0	0	6	13	12	.244	.343	.302	84	-2	2			1.000	-4	O-18/P-4,1	-0.6
1938	Bos-N	34	49	6	9	0	0	0	4	1	3	.184	.200	.184	7	-6	1			1.000	-2	P-16,O-10/SC2	-0.7
Total	6	175	301	32	70	10	2	0	21	25	35	.233	.291	.279	59	-17	5			1.000	-2	/P-69,O-51,312SCD	-1.8

■ PETE REISER
Reiser, Harold Patrick b: 3/17/19, St.Louis, Mo. d: 10/25/81, Palm Springs, Cal. BL/TR, 5'11", 185 lbs. Deb: 7/23/40 C

YEAR	TM/L	G	AB	R	H	2B	3B	HR	RBI	BB	SO	AVG	OBP	SLG	PRO+	BR/A	SB	CS	SBR	FA	FR	G/POS	TPR
1940	Bro-N	58	225	34	66	11	4	3	20	15	33	.293	.338	.418	101	0	2			.960	-4	3-30,O-17/S	-0.3
1941	*Bro-N★	137	536	**117**	184	**39**	**17**	14	76	46	71	**.343**	.406	**.558**	163	43	4			.981	12	*O-133	**4.7**
1942	Bro-N★	125	480	89	149	33	5	10	64	48	45	.310	.375	.463	142	25	**20**			.969	-2	*O-125	1.8
1946	Bro-N☆	122	423	75	117	21	5	11	73	55	58	.277	.361	.428	122	12	**34**			.978	7	O-97,3-15	1.6
1947	*Bro-N	110	388	68	120	23	2	5	46	68	41	.309	.415	.418	117	13	14			.988	-5	*O-108	0.2
1948	Bro-N	64	127	17	30	8	2	1	19	29	21	.236	.382	.354	97	1	4			.981	-5	O-30/3-4	-0.6
1949	Bos-N	84	221	32	60	8	3	8	40	33	42	.271	.369	.443	123	8	3			.980	-1	O-63/3-4	0.4
1950	Bos-N	53	78	12	16	2	0	1	10	18	22	.205	.367	.269	75	-2	1			.979	-2	O-24/3-1	-0.4
1951	Pit-N	74	140	22	38	9	3	2	13	27	20	.271	.389	.421	115	4	2	2	0	.982	-2	O-27/3-5	0.1
1952	Cle-A	34	44	7	6	1	0	3	7	4	16	.136	.208	.364	61	-3	1	-1	0	1.000	-1	O-10	-0.5
Total	10	861	2662	473	786	155	41	58	368	343	369	.295	.380	.450	127	100	87	3		.979	-4	O-634/3-59,S	7.0

■ CHARLIE REISING
Reising, Charles "Pop" b: 8/28/1861, Lanesville, Ind. d: 7/26/15, Louisville, Ky. Deb: 7/19/1884

YEAR	TM/L	G	AB	R	H	2B	3B	HR	RBI	BB	SO	AVG	OBP	SLG	PRO+	BR/A	SB	CS	SBR	FA	FR	G/POS	TPR
1884	Ind-a	2	8	0	0	0	0	0	1			.000	.111	.000	-62	-1				.400	-1	/O-2	-0.3

■ AL REISS
Reiss, Albert Allen b: 1/8/09, Elizabeth, N.J. d: 5/13/89, Red Bank, N.J. BB/TR, 5'10.5", 165 lbs. Deb: 6/22/32

YEAR	TM/L	G	AB	R	H	2B	3B	HR	RBI	BB	SO	AVG	OBP	SLG	PRO+	BR/A	SB	CS	SBR	FA	FR	G/POS	TPR
1932	Phi-A	9	5	0	1	0	0	0	1	1	1	.200	.333	.200	40	-0	0			1.000	0	/S-6	0.0

■ HEINIE REITZ
Reitz, Henry P. b: 6/29/1867, Chicago, Ill. d: 11/10/14, Sacramento, Cal BL/TR, 5'7", 158 lbs. Deb: 4/27/1893

YEAR	TM/L	G	AB	R	H	2B	3B	HR	RBI	BB	SO	AVG	OBP	SLG	PRO+	BR/A	SB	CS	SBR	FA	FR	G/POS	TPR
1893	Bal-N	130	490	90	140	17	13	1	76	65	32	.286	.377	.380	100	1	24			.939	-1	*2-130	0.3
1894	*Bal-N	108	446	86	135	22	**31**	2	105	42	24	.303	.372	.504	105	0	18			**.968**	27	*2-97,3-12	2.4
1895	Bal-N	71	245	45	72	15	5	0	29	18	11	.294	.350	.396	90	-4	15			.938	-5	2-48,3-18/S	-0.5
1896	*Bal-N	120	464	76	133	15	6	4	106	49	32	.287	.357	.371	91	-6	28			.952	-18	*2-118/S-3	-1.4
1897	*Bal-N	128	477	76	138	15	6	2	84	50		.289	.370	.358	93	-3	23			**.962**	22	*2-128	2.1
1898	Was-N	132	489	62	148	20	2	2	47	32		.303	.354	.364	107	4	11			**.959**	6	*2-132	1.8
1899	Pit-N	34	130	11	34	4	2	0	15	10		.262	.314	.323	75	-4	3			.975	1	2-34	-0.1
Total	7	723	2741	446	800	108	65	11	462	266	99	.292	.363	.391	97	-13	122			.955	33	2-687/3-30,S	4.6

■ KEN REITZ
Reitz, Kenneth John b: 6/24/51, San Francisco, Cal BR/TR, 6', 185 lbs. Deb: 9/5/72

YEAR	TM/L	G	AB	R	H	2B	3B	HR	RBI	BB	SO	AVG	OBP	SLG	PRO+	BR/A	SB	CS	SBR	FA	FR	G/POS	TPR
1972	StL-N	21	78	5	28	4	0	0	10	2	4	.359	.375	.410	125	2	0	1	-1	.956	-4	3-20	-0.2
1973	StL-N	147	426	40	100	20	2	6	42	9	25	.235	.257	.333	63	-23	0	1	-1	**.974**	-6	*3-135/S-1	-3.2
1974	StL-N	154	579	48	157	28	2	7	54	23	63	.271	.301	.363	86	-13	0	0	0	**.974**	-17	*3-151/S-2,2	-3.3
1975	StL-N	161	592	43	159	25	1	5	63	22	54	.269	.300	.340	75	-21	1	1	-0	.946	-21	*3-160	-4.5
1976	SF-N	155	577	40	154	21	1	5	66	24	48	.267	.297	.333	76	-19	5	4	-1	.959	2	*3-155/S-1	-2.0
1977	StL-N	157	587	58	153	36	1	17	79	19	74	.261	.292	.412	88	-12	2	6	-3	**.980**	-2	*3-157	-1.9
1978	StL-N	150	540	41	133	26	2	10	75	20	61	.246	.283	.357	79	-17	1	0	0	**.973**	1	*3-150	-1.9
1979	StL-N	159	605	42	162	41	2	8	73	25	85	.268	.301	.382	84	-14	1	0	-1	.972	-13	*3-158	-2.9
1980	StL-N★	151	523	39	141	33	0	8	58	22	44	.270	.303	.379	86	-10	0	1	-1	**.979**	-4	*3-150	-1.9
1981	Chi-N	82	260	10	56	9	2	2	28	15	56	.215	.266	.281	53	-16	0	0	0	**.977**	4	3-81	-1.3
1982	Pit-N	7	10	0	0	0	0	0	0	1	4	.000	.091	.000	-70	-2	0	0	0	1.000	1	/3-4	-0.2
Total	11	1344	4777	366	1243	243	12	68	548	184	518	.260	.293	.359	79	-144	10	14	-5	.970	-58	*3-1321/S-4,2	-23.3

■ BUTCH REMENTER
Rementer, Willis J. H. b: 3/14/1878, Philadelphia, Pa. d: 9/23/22, Philadelphia, Pa. TR, Deb: 10/8/04

YEAR	TM/L	G	AB	R	H	2B	3B	HR	RBI	BB	SO	AVG	OBP	SLG	PRO+	BR/A	SB	CS	SBR	FA	FR	G/POS	TPR
1904	Phi-N	1	2	0	0	0	0	0	0	0		.000	.000	.000	-99	-0	0			1.000	-0	/C-1	-0.1

■ JACK REMSEN
Remsen, John Jay b: 4/1850, Brooklyn, N.Y. BR/TR, 5'11", 189 lbs. Deb: 5/2/1872

YEAR	TM/L	G	AB	R	H	2B	3B	HR	RBI	BB	SO	AVG	OBP	SLG	PRO+	BR/A	SB	CS	SBR	FA	FR	G/POS	TPR
1872	Atl-n	37	164	26	40	6	5	0	13	2	5	.244	.253	.341	69	-9						*O-35	-0.6
1873	Atl-n	50	207	29	61	7	6	1	29	2	2	.295	.301	.401	117	6						*O-50	0.5
1874	Mut-n	64	285	52	65	11	4	2	0			.228	.228	.316	90	-10						*O-63/1-1	-0.7
1875	Har-n	86	354	69	96	10	4	0	5			.271	.281	.322	103	-0						*O-85	0.0
1876	Har-n	69	324	62	89	12	5	1	30	1	15	.275	.277	.352	100	-2				.887	8	*O-69	0.5
1877	StL-N	33	123	14	32	3	4	0	13	4	3	.260	.283	.350	104	1				.906	2	O-33	0.1
1878	Chi-N	56	224	32	52	11	1	1	19	**17**	33	.232	.286	.304	88	-3				**.944**	6	*O-56	0.0
1879	Chi-N	42	152	14	33	4	2	0	8	2	23	.217	.227	.270	60	-7				.862	-2	O-31,1-11	-1.0
1881	Cle-N	48	172	14	30	4	1	0	9	3	31	.174	.215	.233	43	-11				.873	-1	O-48	-1.2
1884	Phi-N	12	43	9	9	2	0	0	3	6	9	.209	.306	.256	83	-1				.952	0	O-12	-0.1
	Bro-a	81	301	45	67	6	6	3		23		.223	.278	.312	92	-2				.914	4	*O-81	0.0
Total	4 n	237	1010	176	262	34	19	3	42	9	7	.259	.266	.340	90	-14						O-233/1-1	-0.8
Total	6	341	1339	190	312	42	21	5	86	62	114	.233	.267	.307	84	-24				.900	17	O-330/1-11	-1.7

■ JERRY REMY
Remy, Gerald Peter b: 11/8/52, Fall River, Mass. BL/TR, 5'9", 165 lbs. Deb: 4/7/75

YEAR	TM/L	G	AB	R	H	2B	3B	HR	RBI	BB	SO	AVG	OBP	SLG	PRO+	BR/A	SB	CS	SBR	FA	FR	G/POS	TPR
1975	Cal-A	147	569	82	147	17	5	1	46	45	55	.258	.313	.311	82	-13	34	21	-2	.982	10	*2-147	0.2
1976	Cal-A	143	502	64	132	14	3	0	28	38	43	.263	.315	.303	87	-8	35	16	1	.977	15	*2-133/D-5	1.7
1977	Cal-A	154	575	74	145	19	10	4	44	59	53	.252	.324	.341	85	-11	41	17	2	.975	-12	*2-152/3-1	-1.0
1978	Bos-A☆	148	583	87	162	24	6	2	44	40	55	.278	.324	.350	81	-15	30	13	1	.983	2	*2-140/S-1,D	-0.1
1979	Bos-A	80	306	49	91	11	2	0	29	26	25	.297	.352	.346	85	-6	14	9	-1	.970	-21	2-76	-2.3
1980	Bos-A	63	230	24	72	7	2	0	9	10	14	.313	.342	.361	88	-4	14	6	1	.977	-3	2-60/O-1	-0.3
1981	Bos-A	88	358	55	110	9	1	0	31	36	30	.307	.371	.338	99	-1	16	8	0	.984	-7	2-87	0.0
1982	Bos-A	155	636	89	178	22	3	0	47	55	77	.280	.339	.324	79	-17	16	9	-1	.982	-16	*2-154	-2.6
1983	Bos-A	146	592	73	163	16	5	0	43	40	35	.275	.321	.319	72	-22	11	3	2	.990	-31	*2-144	-4.5
1984	Bos-A	30	104	8	26	1	0	0	7	6	17	.250	.297	.279	58	-6	6	3	1	.973	-3	2-24	-0.9
Total	10	1154	4455	605	1226	140	38	7	329	356	404	.275	.329	.328	82	-101	208	99	3	.981	-67	*2-1117/D-9,OS3	-9.8

■ RICK RENICK
Renick, Warren Richard b: 3/16/44, London, Ohio BR/TR, 6', 190 lbs. Deb: 7/11/68 C

YEAR	TM/L	G	AB	R	H	2B	3B	HR	RBI	BB	SO	AVG	OBP	SLG	PRO+	BR/A	SB	CS	SBR	FA	FR	G/POS	TPR
1968	Min-A	42	97	16	21	5	2	3	19	3	42	.216	.283	.402	101	0	0	0	0	.946	-0	S-40	0.3
1969	*Min-A	71	139	21	34	3	0	5	17	12	32	.245	.309	.374	88	-2	0	1	-1	.913	-8	3-30,O-10/S	-1.1
1970	*Min-A	81	179	20	41	8	0	7	25	22	29	.229	.317	.391	93	-2	0	2	-1	.987	-3	3-30,O-25/S	-0.8

YEAR	TM/L	G	AB	R	H	2B	3B	HR	RBI	BB	SO	AVG	OBP	SLG	PRO+	BR/A	SB	CS	SBR	FA	FR	G/POS	TPR
1971	Min-A	27	45	4	10	2	0	1	8	5	14	.222	.314	.333	81	-1	0	0	0	.846	-3	/3-7,O-7	-0.5
1972	Min-A	55	93	10	16	2	0	4	8	15	25	.172	.287	.323	77	-2	0	1	-1	1.000	-4	O-21/1-6,3S	-0.9
Total	5	276	553	71	122	20	2	20	71	63	142	.221	.304	.373	89	-8	0	4	-2	.940	-18	/3-71,O-63,S1	-3.0

■ BILL RENNA
Renna, William Beneditto "Big Bill" b: 10/14/24, Hanford, Cal. BR/TR, 6'3", 218 lbs. Deb: 4/14/53

YEAR	TM/L	G	AB	R	H	2B	3B	HR	RBI	BB	SO	AVG	OBP	SLG	PRO+	BR/A	SB	CS	SBR	FA	FR	G/POS	TPR
1953	NY-A	61	121	19	38	6	3	2	13	13	31	.314	.385	.463	133	6	0	1	-1	.983	-6	O-40	-0.2
1954	Phi-A	123	422	52	98	15	4	13	53	41	60	.232	.305	.379	86	-9	1	3	-2	.972	6	*O-115	-1.0
1955	KC-A	100	249	33	53	7	3	7	28	31	42	.213	.305	.349	75	-9	0	3	-2	.992	-6	O-79	-2.1
1956	KC-A	33	48	12	13	3	0	2	5	3	10	.271	.314	.458	101	-0	1	0	0	.950	-6	O-25	-0.6
1958	Bos-A	39	56	5	15	5	0	4	18	6	14	.268	.339	.571	136	3	0	0	0	1.000	-1	O-11	0.1
1959	Bos-A	14	22	2	2	0	0	0	2	5	9	.091	.259	.091	0	-3	0	0	0	1.000	-2	/O-7	-0.5
Total	6	370	918	123	219	36	10	28	119	99	166	.239	.317	.391	91	-14	2	7	-4	.979	-15	O-277	-4.3

■ TONY RENSA
Rensa, George Anthony "Pug" b: 9/29/01, Parsons, Pa. d: 1/4/87, Wilkes-Barre, Pa. BR/TR, 5'10", 180 lbs. Deb: 5/5/30

YEAR	TM/L	G	AB	R	H	2B	3B	HR	RBI	BB	SO	AVG	OBP	SLG	PRO+	BR/A	SB	CS	SBR	FA	FR	G/POS	TPR
1930	Det-A	20	37	6	10	2	1	1	3	6	7	.270	.386	.459	111	1	1	0	0	.964	-1	C-18	0.1
	Phi-N	54	172	31	49	11	2	3	31	10	18	.285	.328	.424	75	-7	0			.932	-11	C-49	-1.3
1931	Phi-N	19	29	2	3	1	0	0	2	6	2	.103	.257	.138	8	-4	0			.958	2	C-17	-0.1
1933	NY-A	8	29	4	9	2	1	0	3	1	3	.310	.333	.448	112	0	0	1	-1	.977	-1	/C-8	-0.1
1937	Chi-A	26	57	10	17	5	1	0	5	8	6	.298	.385	.421	103	0	3	0	1	.975	1	C-23	0.3
1938	Chi-A	59	165	15	41	5	0	3	19	25	16	.248	.351	.333	71	-7	1	1	-0	.982	6	C-57	0.1
1939	Chi-A	14	25	3	5	0	0	0	2	1	2	.200	.231	.200	11	-3	0	0	0	.972	1	C-13	-0.2
Total	6	200	514	71	134	26	5	7	65	57	54	.261	.338	.372	74	-20	5	2		.965	-4	C-185	-1.2

■ RICH RENTERIA
Renteria, Richard Avina b: 12/25/61, Harbor City, Cal. BR/TR, 5'9", 172 lbs. Deb: 9/14/86

YEAR	TM/L	G	AB	R	H	2B	3B	HR	RBI	BB	SO	AVG	OBP	SLG	PRO+	BR/A	SB	CS	SBR	FA	FR	G/POS	TPR
1986	Pit-N	10	12	2	3	1	0	0	1	0	4	.250	.250	.333	58	-1	0	0	0	.600	0	/3-1	-0.1
1987	Sea-A	12	10	2	1	0	0	0	0	1	2	.100	.182	.200	1	-1	1	0	0	.833	1	/2-4,S-1,D	-0.1
1988	Sea-A	31	88	6	18	9	0	0	6	2	8	.205	.222	.307	45	-7	1	3	-2	.958	-4	D-12,S-11/32	-0.3
1993	Fla-N	103	263	27	67	9	2	2	30	21	31	.255	.315	.327	68	-11	0	2	-1	.989	-4	2-45,3-25/O	-1.6
1994	Fla-N	28	49	5	11	0	2	4	1	4	4	.224	.269	.347	56	-3	0	1	-1	.929	-1	3-14/2-6,O	-0.4
Total	5	184	422	42	100	20	2	4	41	25	49	.237	.286	.322	60	-23	2	6	-3	.986	1	/2-59,3-45,DSO	-2.4

■ BOB REPASS
Repass, Robert Willis b: 11/6/17, W.Pittston, Pa. BR/TR, 6'1", 185 lbs. Deb: 9/18/39

YEAR	TM/L	G	AB	R	H	2B	3B	HR	RBI	BB	SO	AVG	OBP	SLG	PRO+	BR/A	SB	CS	SBR	FA	FR	G/POS	TPR
1939	StL-N	3	6	0	2	1	0	0	1	0	2	.333	.333	.500	114	0	0			1.000	0	/2-2	0.1
1942	Was-A	81	259	30	62	11	1	2	23	33	30	.239	.328	.313	81	-6	6	1	1	.973	-3	2-33,3-29,S	-0.4
Total	2	84	265	30	64	12	1	2	24	33	32	.242	.328	.317	82	-6	6	1		.973	-2	/2-35,3-29,S	-0.3

■ ROGER REPOZ
Repoz, Roger Allen b: 8/3/40, Bellingham, Wash. BL/TL, 6'3", 195 lbs. Deb: 9/11/64

YEAR	TM/L	G	AB	R	H	2B	3B	HR	RBI	BB	SO	AVG	OBP	SLG	PRO+	BR/A	SB	CS	SBR	FA	FR	G/POS	TPR
1964	NY-A	11	1	1	0	0	0	0	0	1	1	.000	.500	.000	52		0	0	0	1.000	-3	/O-9	-0.3
1965	NY-A	79	218	34	48	7	4	12	28	25	57	.220	.300	.454	112	3	1	1	-0	.993	-2	O-69	-0.2
1966	NY-A	37	43	4	15	4	0	0	9	4	8	.349	.404	.488	161	3	0	0	0	1.000	-10	O-30	-0.8
	KC-A	101	319	40	69	10	3	11	34	44	80	.216	.315	.370	99	0	3	3	-1	.991	-3	O-52,1-45	-1.0
	Yr	138	362	44	84	14	4	11	43	48	88	.232	.325	.384	106	3	3	3	-1	.992	-13	O-82,1-45	-1.8
1967	KC-A	40	87	6	21	6	1	2	8	12	20	.241	.340	.402	122	3	4	2	0	1.000	1	O-31	0.3
	Cal-A	74	176	25	44	9	1	5	20	19	37	.250	.323	.398	116	3	2	2	-1	.959	-3	O-63	-0.3
	Yr	114	263	34	65	15	2	7	28	31	57	.247	.329	.399	118	6	6	4	-1	.972	-1	O-94	0.0
1968	Cal-A	133	375	30	90	8	1	13	54	38	83	.240	.315	.371	111	5	8	7	-2	.987	-5	*O-114	-0.8
1969	Cal-A	103	219	25	36	1	1	8	19	32	52	.164	.271	.288	59	-12	1	3	-2	.985	-1	O-48,1-31	-2.4
1970	Cal-A	137	407	50	97	17	6	18	47	45	94	.238	.319	.442	112	5	4	2	0	.995	-4	*O-110,1-18	-0.6
1971	Cal-A	113	297	39	59	11	1	13	41	60	69	.199	.335	.374	108	4	3	5	-2	1.000	-4	O-97,1-13	-0.8
1972	Cal-A	3	3	0	1	0	0	0	0	0	2	.333	.333	.333	105		0	0	0	.000	0	H	0.0
Total	9	831	2145	257	480	73	19	82	260	280	499	.224	.316	.390	106	14	26	25	-7	.989	-39	O-623,1-107	-6.9

■ RIP REPULSKI
Repulski, Eldon John b: 10/4/27, Sauk Rapids, Minn. d: 2/10/93, Waite Park, Minn. BR/TR, 6', 195 lbs. Deb: 4/14/53

YEAR	TM/L	G	AB	R	H	2B	3B	HR	RBI	BB	SO	AVG	OBP	SLG	PRO+	BR/A	SB	CS	SBR	FA	FR	G/POS	TPR
1953	StL-N	153	567	75	156	25	4	15	66	33	71	.275	.325	.413	91	-8	3	6	-3	.987	-7	*O-153	-2.3
1954	StL-N	152	619	99	175	39	5	19	79	43	75	.283	.333	.454	102	0	8	10	-4	.975	-5	*O-152	-1.5
1955	StL-N	147	512	64	138	28	2	23	73	49	66	.270	.338	.467	111	7	5	7	-3	.974	-5	*O-141	-0.7
1956	StL-N★	112	376	44	104	18	3	11	55	24	46	.277	.332	.428	102	1	2	2	-1	.974	-4	*O-100	-0.5
1957	Phi-N	134	516	65	134	23	4	20	68	19	74	.260	.293	.436	95	-5	1	2	0	.968	3	*O-130	-0.9
1958	Phi-N	85	238	33	58	9	4	13	40	15	47	.244	.300	.479	103	-0	0	0	0	.949	-2	O-56	0.1
1959	*LA-N	53	94	11	24	4	0	2	14	13	23	.255	.346	.362	83	-2	0	1	-1	1.000	-5	O-31	-0.9
1960	LA-N	4	5	0	1	0	0	0	0	0	1	.200	.200	.200	9	-1	0	0	0	1.000	-1	/O-2	-0.1
	Bos-A	73	136	14	33	6	1	3	20	10	25	.243	.295	.368	75	-5	0	0	0	1.000	-2	O-33	-0.8
1961	Bos-A	15	25	2	7	1	0	1	1	1	5	.280	.308	.320	66	-1	0	2	-1	1.000	-1	/O-4	-0.3
Total	9	928	3088	407	830	153	23	106	416	207	433	.269	.322	.436	98	-14	25	29	-10	.976	-24	O-802	-8.5

■ LARRY RESSLER
Ressler, Lawrence P. b: 8/10/1848, France d: 6/12/18, Reading, Pa. Deb: 4/26/1875

YEAR	TM/L	G	AB	R	H	2B	3B	HR	RBI	BB	SO	AVG	OBP	SLG	PRO+	BR/A	SB	CS	SBR	FA	FR	G/POS	TPR
1875	Was-n	27	106	17	21	1	0	0		1		.198	.206	.208	45	-5						O-19/2-7	-0.5

■ DINO RESTELLI
Restelli, Dino Paul "Dingo" b: 9/23/24, St.Louis, Mo. BR/TR, 6'1.5", 191 lbs. Deb: 6/14/49

YEAR	TM/L	G	AB	R	H	2B	3B	HR	RBI	BB	SO	AVG	OBP	SLG	PRO+	BR/A	SB	CS	SBR	FA	FR	G/POS	TPR
1949	Pit-N	72	232	41	58	11	0	12	40	35	26	.250	.358	.453	113	4	3			.961	5	O-61/1-1	0.6
1951	Pit-N	21	38	1	7	1	0	1	3	2	4	.184	.225	.289	36	-3	0	0	0	.920	-1	O-11	-0.5
Total	2	93	270	42	65	12	0	13	43	37	30	.241	.341	.430	103	1	3	0		.956	4	/O-72,1-1	0.1

■ MERV RETTENMUND
Rettenmund, Mervin Weldon b: 6/6/43, Flint, Mich. BR/TR, 5'10", 195 lbs. Deb: 4/14/68 C

YEAR	TM/L	G	AB	R	H	2B	3B	HR	RBI	BB	SO	AVG	OBP	SLG	PRO+	BR/A	SB	CS	SBR	FA	FR	G/POS	TPR
1968	Bal-A	31	64	10	19	5	0	2	7	18	20	.297	.458	.469	181	8	1	1	-0	1.000	-5	O-23	0.1
1969	*Bal-A	95	190	27	47	10	3	4	25	28	28	.247	.344	.395	105	2	6	1	1	.991	-10	O-78	-1.1
1970	*Bal-A	106	338	60	109	17	2	18	58	38	59	.322	.396	.544	155	25	13	7	-0	.976	-1	O-93	2.0
1971	*Bal-A	141	491	81	156	23	4	11	75	87	60	.318	.424	.448	149	36	15	6	1	.977	-3	*O-134	2.8
1972	Bal-A	102	301	40	70	10	2	6	21	41	37	.233	.325	.339	95	-1	6	4	1	.989	-6	O-98	-1.3
1973	*Bal-A	95	321	59	84	17	2	9	44	57	38	.262	.380	.411	124	12	11	2	2	.985	3	O-90	1.4
1974	Cin-N	80	208	30	45	6	0	6	28	37	39	.216	.340	.332	90	-2	5	1	1	1.000	-5	O-69	-0.9
1975	*Cin-N	93	188	24	45	6	1	2	19	35	22	.239	.359	.314	86	-2	5	0	2	1.000	-5	O-61/3-1	-0.8
1976	SD-N	86	140	16	32	7	0	2	11	29	23	.229	.361	.321	103	2	4	1	1	.977	2	O-43	0.3
1977	SD-N	107	126	23	36	6	1	4	17	33	28	.286	.438	.444	153	12	1	2	-1	1.000	-4	O-27/3-1	0.6
1978	Cal-A	50	108	16	29	5	1	1	14	30	13	.269	.436	.361	131	7	0	3	-2	.968	-3	O-22,D-18	0.1
1979	*Cal-A	35	76	7	20	2	0	1	10	11	14	.263	.364	.329	91	-0	1	0	0	1.000	-9	D-17/O-9	-0.3
1980	Cal-A	2	4	0	1	0	0	0	0	1	0	.250	.400	.250	84	-0	0	0	0	.000	0	/D-1	0.0
Total	13	1023	2555	393	693	114	16	66	329	445	382	.271	.383	.406	124	97	68	28	4	.985	-41	O-747/D-36,3	2.9

■ KEN RETZER
Retzer, Kenneth Leo b: 4/30/34, Wood River, Ill. BL/TR, 6', 185 lbs. Deb: 9/9/61

YEAR	TM/L	G	AB	R	H	2B	3B	HR	RBI	BB	SO	AVG	OBP	SLG	PRO+	BR/A	SB	CS	SBR	FA	FR	G/POS	TPR
1961	Was-A	16	53	7	18	4	0	1	3	4	5	.340	.386	.472	130	2	1	0	0	.988	1	C-16	0.4
1962	Was-A	109	340	36	97	11	2	8	37	26	21	.285	.336	.400	98	-1	2	0	1	.985	0	C-99	0.3
1963	Was-A	95	265	21	64	10	0	5	31	17	20	.242	.292	.336	76	-9	2	0	1	.981	-11	C-81	-1.7
1964	Was-A	17	32	1	3	1	0	0	1	5	4	.094	.237	.094	-4	-4	0	0	0	.971	4	C-13	0.0
Total	4	237	690	65	182	25	2	14	72	52	50	.264	.318	.367	87	-12	5	0	2	.983	-6	C-209	-1.0

YEAR	TM/L	G	AB	R	H	2B	3B	HR	RBI	BB	SO	AVG	OBP	SLG	PRO+	BR/A	SB	CS	SBR	FA	FR	G/POS	TPR

■ DAVE REVERING   Revering, David Alvin   b: 2/12/53, Roseville, Cal.   BL/TR, 6'4", 210 lbs.   Deb: 4/8/78

YEAR	TM/L	G	AB	R	H	2B	3B	HR	RBI	BB	SO	AVG	OBP	SLG	PRO+	BR/A	SB	CS	SBR	FA	FR	G/POS	TPR
1978	Oak-A	152	521	49	141	21	3	16	46	26	55	.271	.305	.415	106	2	0	1	-1	.989	9	*1-138/D-3	0.3
1979	Oak-A	125	472	63	136	25	5	19	77	34	65	.288	.337	.483	125	15	1	4	-2	.986	2	*1-104,D-18	0.7
1980	Oak-A	106	376	48	109	21	5	15	62	32	37	.290	.346	.492	136	17	1	0	0	.989	3	1-95/D-5	1.5
1981	Oak-A	31	87	12	20	1	1	2	10	11	12	.230	.323	.333	94	-0	0	1	-1	.995	-1	1-29/D-2	-0.4
	*NY-A	45	119	8	28	4	1	2	7	11	20	.235	.300	.336	84	-2	0	1	-1	.994	3	1-44	-0.2
	Yr	76	206	20	48	5	2	4	17	22	32	.233	.310	.335	88	-3	0	2	-2	.994	2	1-73/D-2	-0.6
1982	NY-A	14	40	2	6	2	0	0	2	3	4	.150	.209	.200	13	-5	0	0	0	1.000	-2	1-13/D-1	-0.7
	Tor-A	55	135	15	29	6	0	5	18	22	30	.215	.325	.370	83	-3	0	3	-2	1.000	-0	D-49/1-4	-0.7
	Sea-A	29	82	8	17	3	1	3	12	9	17	.207	.286	.378	78	-3	0	0	0	.986	-1	1-27	-0.5
	Yr	98	257	25	52	11	1	8	32	34	51	.202	.296	.346	71	-10	0	3	-2	.992	-3	D-50,1-44	-1.9
Total	5	557	1832	205	486	83	16	62	234	148	240	.265	.321	.430	110	20	2	10	-5	.989	13	1-454/D-78	-0.0

■ HENRY REVILLE   Reville, Henry   b: Baltimore, Md.   Deb: 10/14/1874

YEAR	TM/L	G	AB	R	H	2B	3B	HR	RBI	BB	SO	AVG	OBP	SLG	PRO+	BR/A	SB	CS	SBR	FA	FR	G/POS	TPR
1874	Bal-n	1	4	0	0	0	0	0		0		.000	.000	.000	-99	-1						/O-1	-0.1

■ WILLIAM REXTER   Rexter, William H.   b: Brooklyn, N.Y.   Deb: 9/25/1875

YEAR	TM/L	G	AB	R	H	2B	3B	HR	RBI	BB	SO	AVG	OBP	SLG	PRO+	BR/A	SB	CS	SBR	FA	FR	G/POS	TPR
1875	Atl-n	1	4	0	0	0	0	0		0		.000	.000	.000	-99	-1						/O-1	-0.1

■ GILBERTO REYES   Reyes, Gilberto Rolando (Polanco)   b: 12/10/63, Santo Domingo, D.R.   BR/TR, 6'2", 203 lbs.   Deb: 6/11/83

YEAR	TM/L	G	AB	R	H	2B	3B	HR	RBI	BB	SO	AVG	OBP	SLG	PRO+	BR/A	SB	CS	SBR	FA	FR	G/POS	TPR
1983	LA-N	19	31	1	5	2	0	0	0	0	5	.161	.188	.226	14	-4	0	0	0	.944	2	C-19	-0.1
1984	LA-N	4	5	0	0	0	0	0	0	0	3	.000	.000	.000	-99	-1	0	0	0	1.000	-0	/C-2	-0.2
1985	LA-N	6	1	0	0	0	0	0	0	1	1	.000	.667	.000	105	0	0	0	0	1.000	0	/C-6	0.2
1987	LA-N	1	0	0	0	0	0	0	0	0	0	—	—	—	—	0	0	0	0	.000	-0	/C-1	0.0
1988	LA-N	4	9	1	1	0	0	0	0	0	3	.111	.111	.111	-37	-2	0	0	0	1.000	0	/C-5	-0.1
1989	Mon-N	4	5	0	1	0	0	0	1	0	1	.200	.200	.200	14	-1	0	0	0	1.000	1	/C-4	0.0
1991	Mon-N	83	207	11	45	9	0	0	13	19	51	.217	.286	.261	56	-12	2	4	-2	.975	14	C-80	0.4
Total	7	122	258	13	52	11	0	0	14	20	64	.202	.267	.244	45	-19	2	4	-2	.973	17	C-117	0.2

■ NAP REYES   Reyes, Napoleon Aguilera   b: 11/24/19, Santiago De Cuba, Cuba   BR/TR, 6'1", 205 lbs.   Deb: 5/19/43

YEAR	TM/L	G	AB	R	H	2B	3B	HR	RBI	BB	SO	AVG	OBP	SLG	PRO+	BR/A	SB	CS	SBR	FA	FR	G/POS	TPR
1943	NY-N	40	125	13	32	4	2	0	13	4	12	.256	.290	.320	76	-4	2			.994	-5	1-38/3-1	-1.2
1944	NY-N	116	374	38	108	16	5	8	53	15	24	.289	.325	.422	109	3	2			.990	2	1-63,3-37/O	0.3
1945	NY-N	122	431	39	124	15	4	5	44	25	26	.288	.338	.376	97	-2	1			.961	-4	*3-115/1-5	-0.3
1950	NY-N	1	1	0	0	0	0	0	0	0	0	.000	.000	.000	-99	-0	0			.667	-0	/1-1	-0.1
Total	4	279	931	90	264	35	11	13	110	44	62	.284	.326	.387	99	-3	5			.960	-7	3-153,1-107/O	-1.3

■ CARL REYNOLDS   Reynolds, Carl Nettles   b: 2/1/03, LaRue, Tex.   d: 5/29/78, Houston, Tex.   BR/TR, 6', 194 lbs.   Deb: 9/1/27

YEAR	TM/L	G	AB	R	H	2B	3B	HR	RBI	BB	SO	AVG	OBP	SLG	PRO+	BR/A	SB	CS	SBR	FA	FR	G/POS	TPR
1927	Chi-A	14	42	5	9	3	0	1	7	5	7	.214	.313	.357	75	-2	1	2	-1	1.000	2	O-13	-0.1
1928	Chi-A	84	291	51	94	21	11	2	36	17	13	.323	.371	.491	126	10	15	3	3	.979	-2	O-74	0.6
1929	Chi-A	131	517	81	164	24	12	11	67	20	37	.317	.348	.474	111	6	19	9	0	.949	-2	*O-130	-0.4
1930	Chi-A	138	563	103	202	25	18	22	104	20	39	.359	.388	.584	148	38	16	4	2	.975	10	*O-132	3.6
1931	Chi-A	118	462	71	134	24	14	6	77	24	26	.290	.333	.442	108	4	17	6	2	.949	-4	*O-109	-0.6
1932	Was-A	102	406	53	124	28	7	9	63	13	19	.305	.332	.475	108	3	8	4	0	.983	5	O-95	0.1
1933	StL-A	135	475	81	136	26	14	8	71	49	25	.286	.357	.451	106	3	5	4	-1	.965	-2	*O-124	-0.5
1934	Bos-A	113	413	61	125	26	9	4	86	27	28	.303	.350	.438	95	-4	5	3	-0	.977	3	*O-100	-0.5
1935	Bos-A	78	244	33	66	13	4	6	35	24	20	.270	.336	.430	91	-4	4	1	1	.975	6	O-64	0.0
1936	Was-A	89	293	41	81	18	2	4	41	21	22	.276	.329	.392	82	-9	8	4	0	.968	-0	O-72	-1.1
1937	Chi-N	7	11	0	3	1	0	0	1	2	2	.273	.385	.364	100	0	0			.800	-0	/O-2	0.0
1938	*Chi-N	125	497	59	150	28	10	3	67	22	32	.302	.335	.416	103	1	9			.983	-3	*O-125	-0.5
1939	Chi-N	88	281	33	69	10	6	4	44	16	38	.246	.298	.367	76	-10	5			.972	2	O-72	-1.1
Total	13	1222	4495	672	1357	247	107	80	699	260	308	.302	.346	.458	107	36	112	40		.970	15	*O-1112	-0.5

■ CHARLIE REYNOLDS   Reynolds, Charles Lawrence   b: 5/1/1865, Williamsburg, Ind.   d: 7/3/44, Denver, Colo.   5'9", 175 lbs.   Deb: 5/8/1889

YEAR	TM/L	G	AB	R	H	2B	3B	HR	RBI	BB	SO	AVG	OBP	SLG	PRO+	BR/A	SB	CS	SBR	FA	FR	G/POS	TPR
1889	KC-a	1	4	1	1	0	0	0	1	0	1	.250	.250	.250	40	-0	0			1.000	-1	/C-1	-0.1
	Bro-a	12	42	5	9	1	1	0	3	1	6	.214	.233	.286	47	-3	2			.892	1	C-12	-0.1
	Yr	13	46	6	10	1	1	0	4	1	7	.217	.234	.283	46	-3	2			.893	-1	C-13	-0.2

■ DANNY REYNOLDS   Reynolds, Daniel Vance "Squirrel"   b: 11/27/19, Stony Point, N.C.   BR/TR, 5'11", 158 lbs.   Deb: 5/26/45

YEAR	TM/L	G	AB	R	H	2B	3B	HR	RBI	BB	SO	AVG	OBP	SLG	PRO+	BR/A	SB	CS	SBR	FA	FR	G/POS	TPR
1945	Chi-A	29	72	6	12	2	1	0	4	3	8	.167	.200	.222	23	-7	1	2	-1	.947	2	S-14,2-11	-0.5

■ DON REYNOLDS   Reynolds, Donald Edward   b: 4/16/53, Arkadelphia, Ark.   BR/TR, 5'8", 178 lbs.   Deb: 4/7/78   F

YEAR	TM/L	G	AB	R	H	2B	3B	HR	RBI	BB	SO	AVG	OBP	SLG	PRO+	BR/A	SB	CS	SBR	FA	FR	G/POS	TPR
1978	SD-N	57	87	8	22	2	0	0	15	14	14	.253	.363	.276	87	-1	1	0	0	.923	-4	O-25	-0.6
1979	SD-N	30	45	6	10	1	2	0	6	7	6	.222	.327	.333	86	-1	0	1	-1	.950	-1	O-14	-0.3
Total	2	87	132	14	32	3	2	0	16	22	20	.242	.351	.295	87	-2	1	1	-0	.935	-5	/O-39	-0.9

■ CRAIG REYNOLDS   Reynolds, Gordon Craig   b: 12/27/52, Houston, Tex.   BL/TR, 6'1", 175 lbs.   Deb: 8/1/75

YEAR	TM/L	G	AB	R	H	2B	3B	HR	RBI	BB	SO	AVG	OBP	SLG	PRO+	BR/A	SB	CS	SBR	FA	FR	G/POS	TPR
1975	*Pit-N	31	76	8	17	3	0	0	4	3	5	.224	.253	.263	44	-6	0	1	-1	.969	4	S-30	0.0
1976	Pit-N	7	4	1	1	0	0	1	1	0	0	.250	.250	1.000	241	1	0	0	0	.889	2	/S-4,2-1	0.2
1977	Sea-A	135	420	41	104	12	3	4	28	15	23	.248	.279	.319	63	-22	6	6	-2	.955	8	*S-134	-0.2
1978	Sea-A☆	148	548	57	160	16	7	5	44	36	41	.292	.339	.374	101	1	9	6	-1	.960	4	*S-146	2.2
1979	Hou-N★	146	555	63	147	20	9	0	39	21	49	.265	.294	.333	75	-20	12	6	0	.965	-15	*S-143	-2.0
1980	*Hou-N	137	381	34	86	9	6	3	28	20	39	.226	.264	.304	63	-20	2	1	0	.969	12	*S-135	0.4
1981	*Hou-N	87	323	43	84	10	**12**	4	31	12	31	.260	.287	.402	99	-3	3	3	-1	.973	-5	S-85	0.1
1982	Hou-N	54	118	16	30	2	3	1	7	11	9	.254	.323	.347	95	-1	3	1	0	.958	2	S-35/3-7	0.4
1983	Hou-N	65	98	10	21	3	0	1	6	6	10	.214	.260	.276	52	-7	0	1	-1	.956	-4	2-26,3-15/SO	-1.1
1984	Hou-N	146	527	61	137	15	11	6	60	22	53	.260	.290	.364	89	-10	7	4	2	.965	18	*S-143/3-1	2.3
1985	Hou-N	107	379	43	103	18	8	4	32	12	30	.272	.294	.393	94	-5	4	4	0	.977	10	*S-102/2-1	1.4
1986	*Hou-N	114	313	32	78	7	3	6	41	12	31	.249	.277	.348	73	-12	3	1	0	.978	-12	S-98/1-5,3OP	-1.7
1987	Hou-N	135	374	35	95	17	3	4	28	30	44	.254	.309	.348	77	-13	5	1	1	.970	-12	*S-129/3-2	-1.4
1988	Hou-N	78	161	20	41	7	0	1	14	8	23	.255	.290	.317	77	-5	0	1	0	.970	-5	S-22,3-19,21	-0.8
1989	Hou-N	101	189	16	38	4	0	2	14	19	18	.201	.274	.254	54	-11	1	0	0	.979	3	2-29,S-26,3/1PO	-0.1
Total	15	1491	4466	480	1142	143	65	42	377	227	406	.256	.293	.345	80	-133	58	32	-2	.966	17	*S-1240/2-68,310P	-0.3

■ HAROLD REYNOLDS   Reynolds, Harold Craig   b: 11/26/60, Eugene, Ore.   BB/TR, 5'11", 165 lbs.   Deb: 9/2/83   F

YEAR	TM/L	G	AB	R	H	2B	3B	HR	RBI	BB	SO	AVG	OBP	SLG	PRO+	BR/A	SB	CS	SBR	FA	FR	G/POS	TPR
1983	Sea-A	20	59	8	12	4	1	0	1	2	9	.203	.230	.305	44	-5	2	2	-1	.975	-1	2-18	-0.6
1984	Sea-A	10	10	3	3	0	0	0	0	1	1	.300	.364	.300	87	-0	1	1	-0	1.000	4	/2-6	0.4
1985	Sea-A	67	104	15	15	3	1	0	6	17	14	.144	.264	.192	27	-10	3	2	0	.960	19	2-61	1.0
1986	Sea-A	126	445	46	99	19	4	1	24	29	42	.222	.275	.290	53	-29	30	12	2	.977	29	*2-126	0.7
1987	Sea-A★	160	530	73	146	31	8	1	35	39	34	.275	.327	.370	80	-15	**60**	20	6	.977	19	*2-160	1.7
1988	Sea-A★	158	598	61	169	26	**11**	4	41	51	51	.283	.341	.383	98	-1	35	29	-7	.977	16	*2-158	0.5
1989	Sea-A	153	613	87	184	24	9	0	43	55	45	.300	.361	.369	103	3	25	18	-3	.980	**27**	*2-151/D-1	3.2
1990	Sea-A	160	642	100	162	36	5	5	55	81	52	.252	.339	.347	91	-6	31	16	0	.978	15	*2-160	1.3
1991	Sea-A	161	631	95	160	34	6	3	57	72	63	.254	.335	.341	87	-9	28	8	4	.978	5	*2-159/D-1	0.3
1992	Sea-A	140	458	55	113	23	3	3	33	45	41	.247	.318	.330	81	-11	15	12	-3	.982	2	*2-134/O-1,D	-0.9
1993	Bal-A	145	485	64	122	20	4	4	47	46	47	.252	.346	.334	80	-12	12	11	-3	.986	3	*2-141/D-1	-0.8

YEAR	TM/L	G	AB	R	H	2B	3B	HR	RBI	BB	SO	AVG	OBP	SLG	PRO+	BR/A	SB	CS	SBR	FA	FR	G/POS	TPR
1994	Cal-A	74	207	33	48	10	1	0	11	23	18	.232	.312	.290	55	-14	10	7	-1	.996	-13	2-65/D-3	-2.4
Total	12	1374	4782	640	1233	230	53	21	353	480	417	.258	.329	.341	83	-107	250	138	-8	.979	116	*2-1339/D-7,O	4.4

■ R. J. REYNOLDS
Reynolds, Robert James b: 4/19/59, Sacramento, Cal. BB/TR, 6', 190 lbs. Deb: 9/1/83

YEAR	TM/L	G	AB	R	H	2B	3B	HR	RBI	BB	SO	AVG	OBP	SLG	PRO+	BR/A	SB	CS	SBR	FA	FR	G/POS	TPR
1983	LA-N	24	55	5	13	0	0	2	11	3	11	.236	.276	.345	72	-2	5	0	2	.931	-2	O-18	-0.3
1984	LA-N	73	240	24	62	12	2	2	24	14	38	.258	.302	.350	84	-6	7	5	-1	.973	-7	O-63	-1.6
1985	LA-N	73	207	22	55	10	4	0	25	13	31	.266	.312	.353	88	-4	6	3	0	.970	-2	O-54	-0.7
	Pit-N	31	130	22	40	5	3	3	17	9	18	.308	.357	.462	129	5	12	2	2	.958	1	O-31	0.7
	Yr	104	337	44	95	15	7	3	42	22	49	.282	.330	.395	104	1	18	5	2	.965	-1	O-85	0.0
1986	Pit-N	118	402	63	108	30	2	9	48	40	78	.269	.336	.420	105	-2	16	9	-1	.955	-15	*O-112	-1.7
1987	Pit-N	117	335	47	87	24	1	7	51	34	80	.260	.328	.400	91	-4	14	1	4	.993	-6	O-99	-1.0
1988	Pit-N	130	323	35	80	14	2	6	51	20	62	.248	.292	.359	87	-6	15	2	3	.974	-6	O-95	-1.2
1989	Pit-N	125	363	45	98	16	2	6	48	34	66	.270	.334	.375	106	-3	22	5	4	.990	-1	O-98	0.4
1990	*Pit-N	95	215	25	62	10	1	0	19	23	35	.288	.357	.344	98	-0	12	2	-2	.972	-6	O-59	-0.5
Total	8	786	2270	288	605	121	17	35	294	190	419	.267	.325	.381	97	-12	109	29	15	.973	-44	O-629	-5.9

■ RONN REYNOLDS
Reynolds, Ronn Dwayne b: 9/28/58, Wichita, Kan. BR/TR, 6', 200 lbs. Deb: 9/29/82

YEAR	TM/L	G	AB	R	H	2B	3B	HR	RBI	BB	SO	AVG	OBP	SLG	PRO+	BR/A	SB	CS	SBR	FA	FR	G/POS	TPR
1982	NY-N	2	4	0	0	0	0	0	0	1	1	.000	.200	.000	-40	-1	0	0	0	1.000	-1	/C-2	-0.2
1983	NY-N	24	66	4	13	1	0	0	2	8	12	.197	.284	.212	40	-5	0	0	0	.942	-1	C-24	-0.5
1985	NY-N	28	43	4	9	2	0	0	1	0	18	.209	.227	.256	36	-4	0	0	0	.990	6	C-25	0.3
1986	Phi-N	43	126	8	27	4	0	3	10	5	30	.214	.244	.317	52	-8	0	0	0	.991	1	C-42	-0.5
1987	Hou-N	38	102	5	17	4	0	1	7	3	29	.167	.190	.235	12	-13	0	1	-1	.975	4	C-38	-0.8
1990	SD-N	8	15	1	1	1	0	0	1	1	6	.067	.125	.133	-29	-3	0	0	0	1.000	1	/C-8	-0.2
Total	6	143	356	22	67	12	0	4	21	18	96	.188	.229	.256	32	-34	0	1	-1	.977	10	C-139	-1.9

■ TOMMIE REYNOLDS
Reynolds, Tommie D b: 8/15/41, Arizona, La. BR/TR, 6'2", 190 lbs. Deb: 9/5/63 C

YEAR	TM/L	G	AB	R	H	2B	3B	HR	RBI	BB	SO	AVG	OBP	SLG	PRO+	BR/A	SB	CS	SBR	FA	FR	G/POS	TPR
1963	KC-A	8	19	1	1	0	0	0	1	0	7	.053	.143	.105	-28	-3	0	0	0	.800	-1	/O-5	-0.5
1964	KC-A	31	94	11	19	1	0	2	9	10	22	.202	.292	.277	58	-5	0	0	0	.976	-0	O-25/3-3	-0.7
1965	KC-A	90	270	34	64	11	3	1	22	36	41	.237	.327	.311	83	-5	9	2	2	.982	7	O-83/3-1	0.0
1967	NY-N	101	136	16	28	1	0	2	9	11	26	.206	.280	.257	56	-8	1	1	-0	.971	-13	O-72/3-5,C	-2.5
1969	Oak-A	107	315	51	81	10	0	2	20	34	29	.257	.345	.308	87	-4	1	3	-2	.979	6	O-89	-0.5
1970	Cal-A	59	120	11	30	3	1	1	6	6	10	.250	.291	.317	70	-5	1	1	-0	.969	0	O-32/3-1	-0.7
1971	Cal-A	45	86	4	16	3	0	2	8	9	6	.186	.286	.291	68	-4	0	1	-1	.978	-2	O-26/3-1	-0.7
1972	Mil-A	72	130	13	26	5	1	2	13	10	25	.200	.262	.300	68	-5	0	0	0	.961	-1	O-41/1-1,3	-0.9
Total	8	513	1170	141	265	35	5	12	87	117	166	.226	.307	.296	73	-39	12	8	-1	.973	-4	O-373/3-12,1C	-6.5

■ BILL REYNOLDS
Reynolds, William Dee b: 8/14/1884, Eastland, Tex. d: 6/5/24, Carnegie, Okla. BR/TR, 6', 185 lbs. Deb: 9/15/13

YEAR	TM/L	G	AB	R	H	2B	3B	HR	RBI	BB	SO	AVG	OBP	SLG	PRO+	BR/A	SB	CS	SBR	FA	FR	G/POS	TPR
1913	NY-A	5	5	0	0	0	0	0	0	0	1	.000	.000	.000	-99	-1	0			.917	0	/C-5	-0.1
1914	NY-A	4	5	0	2	0	0	0	0	0	3	.400	.400	.400	141	-0	0			1.000	0	/C-1	0.1
Total	2	9	10	0	2	0	0	0	0	0	4	.200	.200	.200	19	-1	0			.941	0	/C-6	0.0

■ ROCKY RHAWN
Rhawn, Robert John b: 2/13/19, Catawissa, Pa. d: 6/9/84, Danville, Pa. BR/TR, 5'8", 180 lbs. Deb: 9/17/47

YEAR	TM/L	G	AB	R	H	2B	3B	HR	RBI	BB	SO	AVG	OBP	SLG	PRO+	BR/A	SB	CS	SBR	FA	FR	G/POS	TPR
1947	NY-N	13	45	7	14	3	1	0	3	8	1	.311	.415	.444	128	2	0			.913	0	/2-8,3-5	0.3
1948	NY-N	36	44	11	12	2	1	1	8	8	6	.273	.385	.432	120	1	3			.872	1	S-14/3-7	0.2
1949	NY-N	14	29	8	5	0	0	0	2	7	2	.172	.333	.172	40	-2	1			.959	4	/2-8	0.2
	Pit-N	3	7	0	1	0	0	0	0	0	0	.143	.143	.143	-23	-1	0			.889	1	/3-2	0.0
	Yr	17	36	8	6	0	0	0	2	7	2	.167	.302	.167	29	-3	1			.959	4	/2-8,3-2	0.2
	Chi-A	24	73	12	15	4	1	0	5	12	8	.205	.318	.288	63	-4	0	1	-1	.959	3	3-19/S-3	-0.2
Total	3	90	198	38	47	9	2	2	18	35	17	.237	.352	.333	84	-4	4	1		.963	7	/3-33,S-17,2	0.5

■ CY RHEAM
Rheam, Kenneth Johnston b: 9/28/1893, Pittsburgh, Pa. d: 10/23/47, Pittsburgh, Pa. BR/TR, 6' ", 175 lbs. Deb: 5/20/14

YEAR	TM/L	G	AB	R	H	2B	3B	HR	RBI	BB	SO	AVG	OBP	SLG	PRO+	BR/A	SB	CS	SBR	FA	FR	G/POS	TPR
1914	Pit-F	73	214	15	45	5	3	0	20	9	33	.210	.242	.262	31	-22	6			.976	-5	1-43,3-13,2/O	-2.9
1915	Pit-F	34	69	10	12	0	0	1	5	1	7	.174	.186	.217	8	-9	4			.959	0	O-22/1-1	-1.1
Total	2	107	283	25	57	5	3	1	25	10	40	.201	.229	.251	25	-32	10			.976	-5	/1-44,O-23,32	-4.0

■ BILLY RHIEL
Rhiel, William Joseph b: 8/16/1900, Youngstown, Ohio d: 8/16/46, Youngstown, Ohio BR/TR, 5'11", 175 lbs. Deb: 4/20/29

YEAR	TM/L	G	AB	R	H	2B	3B	HR	RBI	BB	SO	AVG	OBP	SLG	PRO+	BR/A	SB	CS	SBR	FA	FR	G/POS	TPR
1929	Bro-N	76	205	27	57	9	4	4	25	19	25	.278	.339	.420	89	-4	0			.979	1	2-47/3-7,S	-0.1
1930	Bos-N	20	47	3	8	4	0	0	4	2	5	.170	.204	.255	11	-7	0			.947	-4	3-13/2-2	-0.9
1932	Det-A	85	250	30	70	13	3	3	38	17	23	.280	.328	.392	82	-7	2	0		.956	-5	3-37,1-12/O2	-1.0
1933	Det-A	19	17	1	3	0	1	0	1	5	4	.176	.364	.294	75	-0	0	0	0	1.000	0	/O-1	0.0
Total	4	200	519	61	138	26	8	7	68	43	57	.266	.323	.387	78	-18	2	0		.949	-8	/3-57,2-50,10S	-2.0

■ DUSTY RHODES
Rhodes, James Lamar b: 5/13/27, Mathews, Ala. BL/TR, 6', 180 lbs. Deb: 7/15/52

YEAR	TM/L	G	AB	R	H	2B	3B	HR	RBI	BB	SO	AVG	OBP	SLG	PRO+	BR/A	SB	CS	SBR	FA	FR	G/POS	TPR
1952	NY-N	67	176	34	44	8	1	10	36	23	33	.250	.340	.477	123	5	1	0		.917	-4	O-56	0.0
1953	NY-N	76	163	18	38	7	0	11	30	10	28	.233	.277	.479	91	-3	0	1	-1	.965	1	O-47	-0.4
1954	*NY-N	82	164	31	56	7	3	15	50	18	25	.341	.410	.695	181	19	1	0	0	.984	-3	O-37	1.5
1955	NY-N	94	187	22	57	5	2	6	32	27	26	.305	.393	.449	122	7	1	1	-0	.986	-4	O-45	0.1
1956	NY-N	111	244	20	53	10	3	8	33	30	41	.217	.303	.381	83	-6	0	0	0	.963	-5	O-68	-1.4
1957	NY-N	92	190	20	39	5	1	4	19	18	34	.205	.278	.305	57	-12	0	0	0	1.000	-6	O-44	-2.0
1959	SF-N	54	48	1	9	2	0	0	7	5	9	.188	.264	.229	34	-5	0	0	0	.000	0	H	-0.5
Total	7	576	1172	146	296	44	10	54	207	131	196	.253	.329	.445	104	5	3	3		.963	-20	O-297	-2.7

■ KARL RHODES
Rhodes, Karl Derrick "Tuffy" b: 8/21/68, Cincinnati, Ohio BL/TL, 6', 175 lbs. Deb: 8/7/90

YEAR	TM/L	G	AB	R	H	2B	3B	HR	RBI	BB	SO	AVG	OBP	SLG	PRO+	BR/A	SB	CS	SBR	FA	FR	G/POS	TPR
1990	Hou-N	38	86	12	21	6	1	1	3	13	12	.244	.343	.372	100	0	4	1	0	.955	-1	O-30	-0.1
1991	Hou-N	44	136	7	29	3	1	1	12	14	26	.213	.291	.272	63	-7	2	2	-1	.958	3	O-44	-0.5
1992	Hou-N	5	4	0	0	0	0	0	0	0	2	.000	.000	.000	-99	-1	0	0	0	.000	-1	/O-1	-0.2
1993	Hou-N	5	2	0	0	0	0	0	0	0	0	.000	.000	.000	-99	-1	0	0	0	1.000	-1	/O-4	-0.2
	Chi-N	15	52	12	15	2	1	3	7	11	9	.288	.413	.538	155	4	2	0	1	.970	-3	O-14	0.2
	Yr	20	54	12	15	2	1	3	7	11	9	.278	.400	.519	147	4	2	0	1	.971	-4	O-18	0.0
1994	Chi-N	95	269	39	63	17	6	8	19	33	64	.234	.320	.387	85	-6	4	4	-1	.967	-8	O-76	-1.6
Total	5	202	549	70	128	28	3	13	41	71	113	.233	.323	.366	88	-10	14	7	0	.963	-11	O-169	-2.4

■ KEVIN RHOMBERG
Rhomberg, Kevin Jay b: 11/22/55, Dubuque, Iowa BR/TR, 6', 175 lbs. Deb: 9/1/82

YEAR	TM/L	G	AB	R	H	2B	3B	HR	RBI	BB	SO	AVG	OBP	SLG	PRO+	BR/A	SB	CS	SBR	FA	FR	G/POS	TPR
1982	Cle-A	16	18	3	6	0	0	1	1	2	4	.333	.400	.500	146	1	0	2	-1	.900	-0	/O-7,3-1,D	0.0
1983	Cle-A	12	21	2	10	0	0	0	2	2	4	.476	.522	.476	170	2	1	1	-0	1.000	-2	/O-9,D-1	0.0
1984	Cle-A	13	8	0	2	0	0	0	0	3	3	.250	.250	.250	38	-1	0	0	0	1.000	-2	/O-7,1-1,2D	-0.2
Total	3	41	47	5	18	0	0	1	3	4	11	.383	.431	.447	140	3	1	3	-2	.963	-4	/O-23,D-6,213	-0.2

■ HAL RHYNE
Rhyne, Harold J. b: 3/30/1899, Paso Robles, Cal. d: 1/7/71, Orangevale, Cal. BR/TR, 5'8.5", 163 lbs. Deb: 4/18/26

YEAR	TM/L	G	AB	R	H	2B	3B	HR	RBI	BB	SO	AVG	OBP	SLG	PRO+	BR/A	SB	CS	SBR	FA	FR	G/POS	TPR
1926	Pit-N	109	366	46	92	14	3	2	39	35	21	.251	.327	.352	71	-14	1			.967	8	2-66,S-44/3	0.0
1927	*Pit-N	62	168	21	46	5	0	0	17	14	9	.274	.330	.304	66	-8	0			.963	-7	2-45,3-10/S	-1.2
1929	Bos-A	120	346	41	87	24	5	0	38	25	14	.251	.309	.350	71	-15	4	1	1	.935	-3	*S-113/3-1,O	-0.5
1930	Bos-A	107	296	34	60	8	5	0	25	25	19	.203	.269	.264	37	-28	1	4	-2	.944	4	*S-107	-1.5
1931	Bos-A	147	565	75	154	34	3	0	51	57	41	.273	.341	.343	85	-11	3	3	-1	**.963**	17	*S-147	1.7
1932	Bos-A	71	207	26	47	12	5	0	14	23	14	.227	.310	.333	69	-10	3	2	-0	.966	-2	S-55/3-4,2	-0.6

YEAR	TM/L	G	AB	R	H	2B	3B	HR	RBI	BB	SO	AVG	OBP	SLG	PRO+	BR/A	SB	CS	SBR	FA	FR	G/POS	TPR
1933	Chi-A	39	83	9	22	1	1	0	10	5	9	.265	.315	.301	67	-4	1	1	-0	.955	5	2-19,3-13/S	0.2
Total	7	655	2031	252	508	98	22	2	192	184	127	.250	.318	.323	69	-91	13	11		.950	23	S-475,2-131/3O	-1.9

■ DEL RICE
Rice, Delbert b: 10/27/22, Portsmouth, Ohio d: 1/26/83, Buena Park, Cal. BR/TR, 6'2", 190 lbs. Deb: 5/2/45 MC

YEAR	TM/L	G	AB	R	H	2B	3B	HR	RBI	BB	SO	AVG	OBP	SLG	PRO+	BR/A	SB	CS	SBR	FA	FR	G/POS	TPR
1945	StL-N	83	253	27	66	17	3	1	28	16	33	.261	.313	.364	86	-5	0			.994	9	C-77	0.7
1946	*StL-N	55	139	10	38	8	1	1	12	8	16	.273	.313	.367	89	-2	0			.977	-0	C-53	0.0
1947	StL-N	97	261	28	57	7	3	12	44	36	40	.218	.315	.406	87	-6	1			.981	4	C-94	0.3
1948	StL-N	100	290	24	57	10	1	4	34	37	46	.197	.298	.279	54	-18	1			**.996**	8	C-99	-0.4
1949	StL-N	92	284	25	67	16	1	4	29	30	40	.236	.320	.342	74	-10	0			.992	-3	C-92	-0.8
1950	StL-N	130	414	39	101	20	3	9	54	43	65	.244	.323	.372	78	-13	0			.984	6	*C-130	-0.1
1951	StL-N	122	374	34	94	13	1	9	47	34	26	.251	.319	.364	83	-9	0	0	0	.985	2	*C-120	-0.2
1952	StL-N	147	495	43	128	27	2	11	65	33	38	.259	.313	.388	93	-6	0	1	-1	.992	-4	*C-147	-0.4
1953	StL-N†	135	419	32	99	22	1	6	37	48	49	.236	.323	.337	72	-16	0	0	0	.988	-5	*C-135	-1.5
1954	StL-N	56	147	13	37	10	1	2	16	16	21	.252	.325	.374	81	-4	0	1	-1	.985	6	C-52	0.3
1955	StL-N	20	59	6	12	3	0	1	7	7	6	.203	.288	.305	58	-4	0	0	0	.964	-5	C-18	-0.8
	Mil-N	27	71	5	14	0	1	2	7	6	12	.197	.260	.310	53	-5	0	0	0	.981	1	C-22	-0.4
	Yr	47	130	11	26	3	1	3	14	13	18	.200	.273	.308	55	-9	0	0	0	.973	-5	C-40	-1.2
1956	Mil-N	71	188	15	40	9	1	3	17	18	34	.213	.282	.319	65	-10	0	0	0	.983	2	C-65	-0.5
1957	*Mil-N	54	144	15	33	1	1	9	20	17	37	.229	.311	.438	106	1	0	0	0	.992	6	C-48	0.9
1958	Mil-N	43	121	10	27	7	0	1	8	8	30	.223	.271	.306	57	-8	0	0	0	.995	-0	C-38	-0.6
1959	Mil-N	13	29	3	6	0	0	0	1	2	3	.207	.258	.207	28	-3	0	0	0	.956	-0	/C-9	-0.3
1960	Chi-N	18	52	2	12	3	0	0	4	2	7	.231	.259	.288	50	-4	0	0	0	.968	-2	/C-18	-0.5
	StL-N	1	2	0	0	0	0	0	0	1	0	.000	.333	.000	1	-0	0	0	0	1.000	0	/C-1	-0.1
	Yr	19	54	2	12	3	0	0	4	3	7	.222	.263	.278	49	-4	0	0	0	.970	-2	/C-19	-0.6
	Bal-A	1	1	0	0	0	0	0	0	0	0	.000	.000	.000	-99	-0	0	0	0	1.000	-0	/C-1	0.0
1961	LA-A	44	83	11	20	4	0	4	11	20	19	.241	.388	.434	107	1	0	1	-1	.994	2	C-30	0.3
Total	17	1309	3826	342	908	177	20	79	441	382	522	.237	.312	.356	78	-122	2	3		.987	25	*C-1249	-4.1

■ SAM RICE
Rice, Edgar Charles b: 2/20/1890, Morocco, Ind. d: 10/13/74, Rossmoor, Md. BL/TR, 5'9", 150 lbs. Deb: 8/7/15 H

YEAR	TM/L	G	AB	R	H	2B	3B	HR	RBI	BB	SO	AVG	OBP	SLG	PRO+	BR/A	SB	CS	SBR	FA	FR	G/POS	TPR
1915	Was-A	4	8	0	3	0	0	0	0	0	1	.375	.375	.375	122	0	0			.889	0	/P-4	0.0
1916	Was-A	58	197	26	59	8	3	1	17	15	13	.299	.352	.386	123	5	4			.957	2	O-46/P-5	0.5
1917	Was-A	155	586	77	177	25	7	0	69	50	41	.302	.360	.369	124	16	35			.960	8	*O-155	1.8
1918	Was-A	7	23	3	8	1	0	0	3	2	0	.348	.400	.391	141	1	1			1.000	3	/O-6	0.4
1919	Was-A	141	557	80	179	23	9	3	71	42	26	.321	.376	.411	122	16	26			.962	8	*O-141	1.5
1920	Was-A	153	624	83	211	29	9	3	80	39	23	.338	.381	.428	117	15	**63**	30	1	.960	21	*O-153	2.5
1921	Was-A	143	561	83	185	39	13	4	79	38	10	.330	.382	.467	121	17	26	12	1	.964	11	*O-141	1.6
1922	Was-A	154	633	91	187	37	13	6	69	48	13	.295	.347	.423	105	3	20	9	1	.951	9	*O-154	0.1
1923	Was-A	148	595	117	188	35	**18**	3	75	57	12	.316	.381	.450	125	20	20	8	1	.970	8	*O-147	1.9
1924	*Was-A	154	646	106	**216**	39	14	1	76	46	24	.334	.382	.443	116	14	24	13	-1	.967	4	*O-154	0.6
1925	*Was-A	152	649	111	227	31	13	1	87	37	10	.350	.388	.442	113	12	26	11	-1	.968	5	*O-152	1.1
1926	Was-A	152	641	98	**216**	32	14	3	76	42	20	.337	.380	.445	117	15	24	23	-7	.961	7	*O-152	0.5
1927	Was-A	142	603	98	179	33	14	2	65	36	11	.297	.336	.408	93	-7	19	6	2	.975	-0	*O-139	-1.4
1928	Was-A	148	616	95	202	32	15	2	55	49	15	.328	.379	.438	115	14	16	3	**3**	.973	-8	*O-147	-0.2
1929	Was-A	150	616	119	199	39	10	1	62	55	9	.323	.382	.424	106	7	16	8	0	.970	7	*O-147	0.0
1930	Was-A	147	593	121	207	35	13	1	73	55	14	.349	.407	.457	118	18	13	8	-1	.963	4	*O-145	1.0
1931	Was-A	120	413	81	128	21	8	0	42	35	11	.310	.365	.400	100	1	6	5	-1	.970	1	*O-105	-0.6
1932	Was-A	106	288	58	93	16	7	1	34	32	6	.323	.391	.438	116	7	7	4	-0	.972	-3	O-69	0.0
1933	*Was-A	73	85	19	25	4	3	1	12	2	7	.294	.326	.447	104	0	0	2	-1	1.000	-8	O-39	-0.9
1934	Cle-A	97	335	48	98	19	1	1	33	26	9	.293	.351	.364	83	-8	7	7	-1	.963	-7	O-78	-1.6
Total	20	2404	9269	1514	2987	498	184	34	1078	708	275	.322	.374	.427	113	166	351	143		.965	76	*O-2270/P-9	9.1

■ HAL RICE
Rice, Harold Housten "Hoot" b: 2/11/24, Morganette, W.Va. BL/TR, 6'1", 195 lbs. Deb: 4/29/48

YEAR	TM/L	G	AB	R	H	2B	3B	HR	RBI	BB	SO	AVG	OBP	SLG	PRO+	BR/A	SB	CS	SBR	FA	FR	G/POS	TPR
1948	StL-N	8	31	3	10	1	2	0	3	2	4	.323	.364	.484	121	1	0			1.000	-1	/O-8	0.0
1949	StL-N	40	46	3	9	2	1	1	9	3	7	.196	.245	.348	55	-3	0			1.000	-2	O-10	-0.6
1950	StL-N	44	128	12	27	3	1	2	11	10	10	.211	.268	.297	46	-10	0			.972	-1	O-37	-1.3
1951	StL-N	69	236	20	60	12	1	4	38	24	22	.254	.323	.364	84	-5	0	1	-1	.953	-3	O-63	-1.1
1952	StL-N	98	295	37	85	14	5	7	45	16	26	.288	.325	.441	110	3	1	3	-2	.972	-5	O-81	-0.7
1953	StL-N	8	8	0	2	0	0	0	0	0	3	.250	.250	.250	31	-1	0	0	0	.000	0	H	-0.1
	Pit-N	78	286	39	89	16	1	4	42	17	22	.311	.350	.416	99	-0	0	1	-1	.973	14	O-70	1.0
	Yr	86	294	39	91	16	1	4	42	17	25	.310	.347	.412	97	-1	0	1	-1	.973	14	O-70	0.9
1954	Pit-N	28	81	10	14	4	1	1	9	14	24	.173	.295	.284	52	-6	0	0	-1	1.000	3	O-24	-0.5
	Chi-N	51	72	5	11	0	0	0	5	8	15	.153	.237	.153	4	-10	0	0	0	.897	-4	O-24	-1.5
	Yr	79	153	15	25	4	1	1	14	22	39	.163	.269	.222	29	-16	0	0	-1	.966	-2	O-48	-2.0
Total	7	424	1183	129	307	52	12	19	162	94	133	.260	.314	.372	82	-32	1	7		.969	0	O-317	-4.8

■ HARRY RICE
Rice, Harry Francis b: 11/22/01, Ware Station, Ill. d: 1/1/71, Portland, Ore. BL/TR, 5'9", 185 lbs. Deb: 4/18/23

YEAR	TM/L	G	AB	R	H	2B	3B	HR	RBI	BB	SO	AVG	OBP	SLG	PRO+	BR/A	SB	CS	SBR	FA	FR	G/POS	TPR
1923	StL-A	4	3	0	0	0	0	0	0	0	0	.000	.000	.000	-95	-1	0	0	0	.000	0	H	-0.1
1924	StL-A	54	93	19	26	7	0	0	15	7	5	.280	.350	.355	77	-3	1	3	-2	.917	-0	3-15/2-4,1SO	-0.4
1925	StL-A	103	354	87	127	25	8	11	47	54	15	.359	.450	.568	149	28	8	7	-2	.984	6	O-85/1-3,C23	2.4
1926	StL-A	148	578	86	181	27	10	9	59	63	40	.313	.384	.441	110	9	10	11	-4	.970	7	*O-133/3-8,2S	0.3
1927	StL-A	137	520	90	149	26	9	7	68	50	21	.287	.351	.412	94	-5	5	4	-1	.938	12	*O-130/3-7	-0.2
1928	Det-A	131	510	87	154	21	12	6	81	44	27	.302	.360	.425	104	3	20	13	-1	.962	1	*O-129/3-2	-0.7
1929	Det-A	130	536	97	163	33	7	6	69	61	23	.304	.379	.425	106	6	6	10	-4	.960	4	*O-127/3-3	-0.1
1930	Det-A	37	128	16	39	6	0	2	24	19	8	.305	.403	.398	102	1	0	3	-2	.944	-0	O-35	-0.3
	NY-A	100	346	62	103	17	5	7	74	31	21	.298	.361	.436	106	3	3	3	-1	.969	8	O-87/1-6,3	0.4
	Yr	137	474	78	142	23	5	9	98	50	29	.300	.372	.426	105	4	3	6	-3	.964	7	*O-122/1-6,3	0.1
1931	Was-A	47	162	32	43	5	6	0	15	12	10	.265	.320	.370	81	-5	2	1	0	.968	-1	O-42	-0.8
1933	Cin-N	143	510	44	133	19	6	0	54	35	24	.261	.316	.322	84	-10	4			**.991**	3	*O-141/3-1	-1.6
Total	10	1034	3740	620	1118	186	63	48	506	376	194	.299	.368	.421	104	25	59	55		.966	39	O-911/3-38,12SC	-1.1

■ JIM RICE
Rice, James Edward b: 3/8/53, Anderson, S.C. BR/TR, 6'2", 205 lbs. Deb: 8/19/74 C

YEAR	TM/L	G	AB	R	H	2B	3B	HR	RBI	BB	SO	AVG	OBP	SLG	PRO+	BR/A	SB	CS	SBR	FA	FR	G/POS	TPR
1974	Bos-A	24	67	6	18	2	1	1	13	4	12	.269	.319	.373	92	-1	0	0	0	.800	-1	D-16/O-3	-0.2
1975	Bos-A	144	564	92	174	29	4	22	102	36	122	.309	.354	.491	126	17	10	5	0	1.000	-1	O-90,D-54	1.2
1976	Bos-A	153	581	75	164	25	8	25	85	28	123	.282	.320	.482	118	10	8	5	-1	.967	0	O-98,D-54	0.4
1977	Bos-A★	160	644	104	206	29	15	**39**	114	53	120	.320	.379	**.593**	143	36	5	4	-1	.956	1	*D-114,O-44	3.0
1978	Bos-A★	163	677	121	**213**	25	**15**	**46**	**139**	58	126	.315	.370	**.600**	153	44	7	5	-1	.989	10	*O-114,D-49	4.8
1979	Bos-A★	158	619	117	201	39	6	39	130	57	97	.325	.385	.596	152	43	9	4	0	.984	-3	*O-125,D-33	3.7
1980	Bos-A†	124	504	81	148	22	6	24	86	30	87	.294	.338	.504	121	13	8	3	1	.988	7	*O-109,D-15	1.5
1981	Bos-A	108	451	51	128	18	1	17	62	34	76	.284	.338	.441	114	8	2	5	-1	.988	5	*O-108	0.9
1982	Bos-A	145	573	86	177	24	5	24	97	55	98	.309	.376	.494	129	23	0	1	-1	.969	-1	*O-145	1.8
1983	Bos-A★	155	626	90	191	34	1	**39**	126	52	102	.305	.364	.550	137	30	0	2	-1	.984	-0	*O-151/D-4	4.1
1984	Bos-A★	159	657	98	184	25	7	28	122	44	102	.280	.326	.467	111	9	4	5	-1	.989	12	*O-157/D-2	1.7
1985	Bos-A★	140	546	85	159	20	3	27	103	51	75	.291	.354	.487	122	16	2	0	1	.964	0	*O-130/D-7	1.2
1986	*Bos-A★	157	618	98	200	39	2	20	110	62	78	.324	.389	.490	137	32	0	1	-1	.977	17	*O-156/D-1	4.2

YEAR	TM/L	G	AB	R	H	2B	3B	HR	RBI	BB	SO	AVG	OBP	SLG	PRO+	BR/A	SB	CS	SBR	FA	FR	G/POS	TPR
1987	Bos-A	108	404	66	112	14	0	13	62	45	77	.277	.360	.408	100	1	1	1	-0	.977	4	O-94,D-12	0.1
1988	*Bos-A	135	485	57	128	18	3	15	72	48	89	.264	.334	.406	102	1	1	1	-0	.968	-2	*D-112,O-19	-0.4
1989	Bos-A	56	209	22	49	10	2	3	28	13	39	.234	.283	.344	71	-8	1	0	0	.000	0	D-55	-1.0
Total	16	2089	8225	1249	2452	373	79	382	1451	670	1423	.298	.356	.502	127	275	58	34	-3	.980	71	*O-1543,D-530	27.0

■ LEN RICE   Rice, Leonard Oliver b: 9/2/18, Lead, S.Dak. d: 6/13/92, Sonora, Cal. BR/TR, 6', 175 lbs. Deb: 4/26/44

YEAR	TM/L	G	AB	R	H	2B	3B	HR	RBI	BB	SO	AVG	OBP	SLG	PRO+	BR/A	SB	CS	SBR	FA	FR	G/POS	TPR
1944	Cin-N	10	4	1	0	0	0	0	0	0	0	.000	.000	.000	-99	-1				1.000	1	/C-5	0.0
1945	Chi-N	32	99	10	23	3	0	0	7	5	8	.232	.269	.263	49	-7	2			.976	-1	C-29	-0.6
Total	2	42	103	11	23	3	0	0	7	5	8	.223	.259	.252	44	-8	2			.977	0	/C-34	-0.6

■ BOB RICE   Rice, Robert Turnbull b: 5/28/1899, Philadelphia, Pa. d: 2/20/86, Elizabethtown, Pa BR/TR, 5'10", 170 lbs. Deb: 9/1/26

YEAR	TM/L	G	AB	R	H	2B	3B	HR	RBI	BB	SO	AVG	OBP	SLG	PRO+	BR/A	SB	CS	SBR	FA	FR	G/POS	TPR
1926	Phi-N	19	54	3	8	0	1	0	10	3	4	.148	.193	.185	2	-7	0			.864	1	3-15/2-2,S	-0.6

■ LEE RICHARD   Richard, Lee Edward "Bee Bee" b: 9/18/48, Lafayette, La. BR/TR, 5'11", 165 lbs. Deb: 4/7/71

YEAR	TM/L	G	AB	R	H	2B	3B	HR	RBI	BB	SO	AVG	OBP	SLG	PRO+	BR/A	SB	CS	SBR	FA	FR	G/POS	TPR
1971	Chi-A	87	260	38	60	7	3	2	17	20	46	.231	.288	.304	66	-12	8	9	-3	.920	-0	S-68,O-16	-0.8
1972	Chi-A	11	29	5	7	0	0	0	1	0	7	.241	.241	.241	43	-2	1	0	0	1.000	-0	/O-6,S-1	-0.2
1974	Chi-A	32	67	5	11	1	0	0	1	5	8	.164	.222	.179	16	-7	0	0	0	.821	3	3-12/S-6,2OD	-0.4
1975	Chi-A	43	45	11	9	0	1	0	5	4	7	.200	.265	.244	44	-3	2	3	-1	1.000	6	3-12/S-9,2D	0.2
1976	StL-N	66	91	12	16	4	2	0	5	4	9	.176	.211	.264	34	-8	1	0	0	.975	12	2-26,S-12/3	0.5
Total	5	239	492	71	103	12	6	2	29	33	77	.209	.260	.270	50	-32	12	12	-4	.923	20	/S-96,2-34,30D	-0.7

■ GENE RICHARDS   Richards, Eugene b: 9/29/53, Monticello, S.C. BL/TL, 6', 175 lbs. Deb: 4/6/77

YEAR	TM/L	G	AB	R	H	2B	3B	HR	RBI	BB	SO	AVG	OBP	SLG	PRO+	BR/A	SB	CS	SBR	FA	FR	G/POS	TPR
1977	SD-N	146	525	79	152	16	11	5	32	60	80	.290	.365	.390	114	11	56	12	10	.963	1	*O-109,1-32	1.6
1978	SD-N	154	555	90	171	26	12	4	45	64	80	.308	.384	.420	135	26	37	17	1	.965	-12	*O-124,1-26	0.9
1979	SD-N	150	545	77	152	17	9	4	41	47	62	.279	.345	.365	100	0	24	8	2	.973	4	*O-132	0.1
1980	SD-N	158	642	91	193	26	8	4	41	61	73	.301	.363	.385	116	14	61	16	9	.979	15	*O-156	3.3
1981	SD-N	104	393	47	113	14	12	3	42	53	44	.288	.374	.407	131	17	20	8	1	.975	3	*O-102	1.8
1982	SD-N	132	521	63	149	13	8	3	28	36	52	.286	.335	.359	99	-1	30	20	-3	.977	0	*O-103/1-25	-0.8
1983	SD-N	95	233	37	64	11	3	3	22	17	17	.275	.327	.386	100	-0	14	5	1	.980	-1	O-54	-0.2
1984	SF-N	87	135	18	34	4	0	0	4	18	28	.252	.340	.281	79	-3	5	3	-0	.940	-1	O-26	-0.5
Total	8	1026	3549	502	1028	127	63	26	255	356	436	.290	.358	.383	113	63	247	89	21	.972	10	O-806/1-83	6.2

■ FRED RICHARDS   Richards, Fred Charles "Fuzzy" b: 11/3/27, Warren, Ohio BL/TL, 6'1.5", 185 lbs. Deb: 9/15/51

YEAR	TM/L	G	AB	R	H	2B	3B	HR	RBI	BB	SO	AVG	OBP	SLG	PRO+	BR/A	SB	CS	SBR	FA	FR	G/POS	TPR
1951	Chi-N	10	27	1	8	2	0	0	4	2	3	.296	.345	.370	91	-0	0	0	0	1.000	1	/1-9	0.1

■ PAUL RICHARDS   Richards, Paul Rapier b: 11/21/08, Waxahachie, Tex. d: 5/4/86, Waxahachie, Tex. BR/TR, 6'1.5", 180 lbs. Deb: 4/17/32 M

YEAR	TM/L	G	AB	R	H	2B	3B	HR	RBI	BB	SO	AVG	OBP	SLG	PRO+	BR/A	SB	CS	SBR	FA	FR	G/POS	TPR
1932	Bro-N	3	8	0	0	0	0	0	0	0	2	.000	.000	.000	-99	-2	0			1.000	4	/C-3	0.1
1933	NY-N	51	87	4	17	3	0	0	10	3	12	.195	.222	.230	30	-8	0			.989	-1	/C-36	-0.6
1934	NY-N	42	75	10	12	1	0	0	3	13	8	.160	.284	.173	26	-7	0			1.000	2	C-37	-0.4
1935	NY-N	7	4	0	1	0	0	0	0	2	1	.250	.500	.250	110	-0	0			1.000	1	/C-4	0.2
	Phi-A	85	257	31	63	10	1	4	29	24	12	.245	.310	.339	68	-12	0	0	0	.977	-3	C-79	-1.1
1943	Det-A	100	313	32	69	7	1	5	33	38	35	.220	.307	.297	71	-11	1	0	0	.986	21	*C-100	1.8
1944	Det-A	95	300	24	71	13	0	3	37	35	30	.237	.318	.310	76	-9	8	3	1	.979	16	C-90	1.3
1945	*Det-A	83	234	26	60	12	1	3	32	19	31	.256	.315	.355	88	-4	0	1	1	.995	12	C-83	1.4
1946	Det-A	57	139	13	28	5	2	0	11	23	18	.201	.315	.266	60	-7	2	0	1	.997	15	C-54	1.2
Total	8	523	1417	140	321	51	5	15	155	157	149	.227	.305	.301	68	-60	15	3		.987	69	C-486	3.9

■ RICHARDSON   Richardson b: Boston, Mass. 5'4", 136 lbs. Deb: 7/10/1884

YEAR	TM/L	G	AB	R	H	2B	3B	HR	RBI	BB	SO	AVG	OBP	SLG	PRO+	BR/A	SB	CS	SBR	FA	FR	G/POS	TPR
1884	CP-U	1	4	0	0	0	0	0		0		.000	.000	.000	-99	-1				.667	-1	/2-1	-0.2

■ HARDY RICHARDSON   Richardson, Abram Harding "Old True Blue" b: 4/21/1855, Clarksboro, N.J. d: 1/14/31, Utica, N.Y. BR/TR, 5'9.5", 170 lbs. Deb: 5/1/1879

YEAR	TM/L	G	AB	R	H	2B	3B	HR	RBI	BB	SO	AVG	OBP	SLG	PRO+	BR/A	SB	CS	SBR	FA	FR	G/POS	TPR
1879	Buf-N	79	336	54	95	18	10	0	37	16	30	.283	.315	.396	130	10				.843	-6	*3-78/C-1	0.6
1880	Buf-N	83	343	48	89	18	8	0	17	14	37	.259	.289	.359	116	5				.848	-7	*3-81/C-5	0.1
1881	Buf-N	83	344	62	100	18	9	2	53	12	27	.291	.315	.413	129	11				.914	25	*O-79/2-5,S3	3.1
1882	Buf-N	83	354	61	96	20	8	2	57	11	33	.271	.293	.390	115	5				.898	16	*2-83	2.1
1883	Buf-N	92	399	73	124	34	7	1	56	22	27	.311	.347	.439	134	16				.903	19	*2-92	3.1
1884	Buf-N	102	439	85	132	27	9	6	60	22	41	.301	.334	.444	138	18				.897	8	2-71,O-24/31	2.3
1885	Buf-N	96	426	90	136	19	11	6	44	20	22	.319	.350	.458	154	24				.905	13	2-50,O-48/SP	3.4
1886	Det-N	125	538	125	189	27	11	11	61	46	21	.351	.402	.504	169	44	42			.899	10	O-80,2-42/PS3	4.8
1887	*Det-N	120	543	131	178	25	18	8	94	31	40	.328	.366	.484	130	20	29			.941	17	2-64,O-59	3.2
1888	Det-N	58	266	60	77	18	2	6	32	17	23	.289	.335	.440	145	13	13			.925	4	2-58	1.9
1889	Bos-N	132	536	122	163	33	10	6	79	48	44	.304	.367	.437	117	10	47			.924	13	2-86,O-46	2.3
1890	Bos-P	130	555	126	181	26	14	13	146	42	46	.326	.384	.494	125	16	42			.950	2	*O-124/S-6,1	1.1
1891	Bos-a	74	278	45	71	9	4	7	52	40	26	.255	.351	.392	114	5	16			.955	-0	O-60/3-9,S1	0.3
1892	Was-N	10	37	2	4	0	0	0	0	5	3	.108	.214	.108	-2	-4	2			.941	-0	/O-7,3-2,2	-0.4
	NY-N	64	248	36	53	11	5	2	34	21	26	.214	.278	.323	83	-6	14			.931	-1	2-33,O-17/1S	-0.6
	Yr	74	285	38	57	11	5	2	34	26	29	.200	.269	.295	72	-10	16			.933	-1	2-34,0-24/1S3	-1.0
Total	14	1331	5642	1120	1688	303	126	70	822	377	445	.299	.344	.435	130	186	205			.915	113	2-585,O-544,3/S1CP	27.3

■ NOLEN RICHARDSON   Richardson, Clifford Nolen b: 1/18/03, Chattanooga, Tenn. d: 9/25/51, Athens, Ga. BR/TR, 6'1.5", 170 lbs. Deb: 4/16/29

YEAR	TM/L	G	AB	R	H	2B	3B	HR	RBI	BB	SO	AVG	OBP	SLG	PRO+	BR/A	SB	CS	SBR	FA	FR	G/POS	TPR
1929	Det-A	13	21	2	4	0	0	0	2	2	1	.190	.261	.190	18	-3	1	1	-0	.839	-4	S-13	-0.6
1931	Det-A	38	148	13	40	9	2	0	16	6	3	.270	.299	.358	70	-7	2	1	0	.946	-2	3-38	-0.6
1932	Det-A	69	155	30	34	5	2	0	12	9	13	.219	.262	.277	38	-14	5	2	0	.986	11	3-65/S-4	-0.9
1935	NY-A	12	46	3	10	1	1	0	5	3	1	.217	.265	.283	44	-4	0	0	0	.922	-6	S-12	-0.9
1938	Cin-N	35	100	8	29	4	0	0	10	3	4	.290	.311	.330	78	-3	0			.966	-1	S-35	-0.2
1939	Cin-N	1	3	0	0	0	0	0	0	0	0	.000	.000	.000	-99	-1				1.000	1	/S-1	0.0
Total	6	168	473	39	117	19	5	0	45	23	22	.247	.282	.309	55	-31	8	4		.969	-0	3-103/S-65	-2.3

■ DANNY RICHARDSON   Richardson, Daniel b: 1/25/1863, Elmira, N.Y. d: 9/12/26, New York, N.Y. BR/TR, 5'8", 165 lbs. Deb: 5/22/1884 M

YEAR	TM/L	G	AB	R	H	2B	3B	HR	RBI	BB	SO	AVG	OBP	SLG	PRO+	BR/A	SB	CS	SBR	FA	FR	G/POS	TPR
1884	NY-N	74	277	36	70	8	1	1	27	16	17	.253	.294	.300	85	-5				.907	2	O-55,S-19	-0.4
1885	NY-N	49	198	26	52	9	3	0	25	10	14	.263	.298	.338	107	1				.950	-1	O-22,3-21/P	0.1
1886	NY-N	68	237	43	55	9	1	1	27	17	21	.232	.283	.291	74	-7	12			.953	-0	O-64/P-5,S32	0.1
1887	NY-N	122	450	79	125	19	10	3	62	36	25	.278	.337	.384	105	4	41			.928	15	*2-108,3-14/P	1.8
1888	*NY-N	135	561	82	127	16	7	8	61	15	35	.226	.248	.323	82	-12	35			.942	9	*2-135	0.2
1889	*NY-N	125	497	80	139	12	4	7	100	46	37	.280	.342	.398	105	3	32			.934	13	*2-125	2.0
1890	NY-P	123	528	102	135	12	9	4	80	37	19	.256	.307	.335	66	-29	37			.900	25	S-68,2-56	0.0
1891	NY-N	123	516	85	139	18	5	4	51	33	27	.269	.313	.347	96	-4	28			.952	49	*2-114/S-9	4.5
1892	Was-N	142	551	48	132	13	4	3	58	25	45	.240	.274	.294	74	-19	25			.931	58	S-93,2-49/3M	4.0
1893	Bro-N	54	206	36	46	6	0	2	27	13	18	.223	.279	.272	49	-15	7			.949	-17	2-46/3-5,S	-2.6
1894	Lou-N	116	430	51	109	17	4	0	40	35	31	.253	.317	.309	55	-31	8			.916	3	*S-107,2-10	-1.7
Total	11	1131	4451	676	1129	149	52	32	558	283	289	.254	.301	.332	82	-113	225			.940	156	2-644,S-300,O/3P	7.2

■ JEFF RICHARDSON   Richardson, Jeffrey Scott b: 8/26/65, Grand Island, Neb. BR/TR, 6'2", 175 lbs. Deb: 7/14/89

YEAR	TM/L	G	AB	R	H	2B	3B	HR	RBI	BB	SO	AVG	OBP	SLG	PRO+	BR/A	SB	CS	SBR	FA	FR	G/POS	TPR
1989	Cin-N	53	125	10	21	4	0	2	11	10	23	.168	.235	.248	37	-10	1	0	0	.969	-2	S-39/3-8	-1.0

YEAR	TM/L	G	AB	R	H	2B	3B	HR	RBI	BB	SO	AVG	OBP	SLG	PRO+	BR/A	SB	CS	SBR	FA	FR	G/POS	TPR
1991	Pit-N	6	4	0	1	0	0	0	0	0	3	.250	.250	.250	42	-0	0	0	0	.000	-1	/3-3,S-2	-0.1
1993	Bos-A	15	24	3	5	2	0	0	2	1	3	.208	.240	.292	40	-2	0	0	0	1.000	6	/2-8,S-5,3D	0.4
Total	3	74	153	13	27	6	0	2	13	11	29	.176	.236	.255	38	-13	1	0	0	.971	3	/S-46,3-12,2D	-0.7

■ KEN RICHARDSON
Richardson, Kenneth Franklin b: 5/2/15, Orleans, Ind. d: 12/7/87, Woodland Hills, Cal   BR/TR, 5'10.5", 187 lbs. Deb: 4/14/42

YEAR	TM/L	G	AB	R	H	2B	3B	HR	RBI	BB	SO	AVG	OBP	SLG	PRO+	BR/A	SB	CS	SBR	FA	FR	G/POS	TPR
1942	Phi-A	6	15	1	1	0	0	0	0	2	0	.067	.176	.067	-30	-3	0			1.000	0	/O-3,1-1,3	-0.3
1946	Phi-N	6	20	1	3	1	0	0	2	0	2	.150	.150	.200	-1	-3	0			.939	-0	/2-6	-0.3
Total	2	12	35	2	4	1	0	0	2	2	2	.114	.162	.143	-14	-5	0	0		.939	-0	/2-6,O-3,31	-0.6

■ BOBBY RICHARDSON
Richardson, Robert Clinton b: 8/19/35, Sumter, S.C. BR/TR, 5'9", 170 lbs. Deb: 8/5/55

YEAR	TM/L	G	AB	R	H	2B	3B	HR	RBI	BB	SO	AVG	OBP	SLG	PRO+	BR/A	SB	CS	SBR	FA	FR	G/POS	TPR
1955	NY-A	11	26	2	4	0	0	0	3	2	0	.154	.214	.154	0	-4	1	1	-0	.864	-5	/2-6,S-4	-0.9
1956	NY-A	5	7	1	1	0	0	0	0	0	1	.143	.143	.143	-25	-1	0	0	0	1.000	0	/2-5	0.1
1957	*NY-A☆	97	305	36	78	11	1	0	19	6	26	.256	.277	.298	58	-18	1	3	-2	.979	5	2-93	-0.8
1958	*NY-A	73	182	18	45	6	2	0	14	8	5	.247	.279	.302	62	-10	1	3	-2	.973	8	2-51,3-13/S	0.0
1959	*NY-A☆	134	469	53	141	18	6	2	33	26	20	.301	.337	.377	99	-1	5	5	-2	.970	2	*2-109,S-14,3	0.9
1960	*NY-A	150	460	45	116	12	3	1	26	35	19	.252	.305	.298	68	-21	6	6	-2	.973	-4	*2-141,3-11	-1.5
1961	*NY-A	162	662	80	173	17	5	3	49	30	23	.261	.295	.316	67	-32	9	7	-2	.978	-9	*2-161	-2.6
1962	*NY-A★	161	692	99	**209**	38	5	8	59	37	24	.302	.338	.406	103	1	11	9	-2	.982	-3	*2-161	1.3
1963	*NY-A★	151	630	72	167	20	6	3	48	25	22	.265	.295	.330	76	-21	15	4	1	.984	7	*2-150	0.5
1964	*NY-A★	159	679	90	181	25	4	4	50	26	36	.267	.296	.333	73	-25	11	2	2	.982	-14	*2-157/S-1	-2.4
1965	NY-A★	160	664	76	164	28	2	6	47	37	39	.247	.288	.322	74	-24	7	5	-1	.981	-3	*2-158	-1.4
1966	NY-A★	149	610	71	153	21	3	7	42	25	28	.251	.281	.330	78	-19	6	6	-2	.980	3	*2-147/3-2	-0.8
Total	12	1412	5386	643	1432	196	37	34	390	262	243	.266	.301	.335	77	-173	73	48	-7	.979	-11	*2-1339/3-38,S	-7.6

■ TOM RICHARDSON
Richardson, Thomas Mitchell b: 8/7/1883, Louisville, Ill. d: 11/15/39, Onawa, Iowa BR/TR, 6', 190 lbs. Deb: 8/2/17

YEAR	TM/L	G	AB	R	H	2B	3B	HR	RBI	BB	SO	AVG	OBP	SLG	PRO+	BR/A	SB	CS	SBR	FA	FR	G/POS	TPR
1917	StL-A	1	1	0	0	0	0	0	0	0	0	.000	.000	.000	-99	-0	0			.000	0	H	0.0

■ BILL RICHARDSON
Richardson, William Henry b: 9/24/1878, Salem, Ind. d: 11/6/49, Sullivan, Ind. BR/TR, 5'11", 200 lbs. Deb: 9/20/01

YEAR	TM/L	G	AB	R	H	2B	3B	HR	RBI	BB	SO	AVG	OBP	SLG	PRO+	BR/A	SB	CS	SBR	FA	FR	G/POS	TPR
1901	StL-N	15	52	7	11	2	0	2	7	6		.212	.293	.365	95	-0	1			.981	-1	1-15	-0.2

■ MIKE RICHARDT
Richardt, Michael Anthony b: 5/24/58, Los Angeles, Cal. BR/TR, 6', 170 lbs. Deb: 8/30/80

YEAR	TM/L	G	AB	R	H	2B	3B	HR	RBI	BB	SO	AVG	OBP	SLG	PRO+	BR/A	SB	CS	SBR	FA	FR	G/POS	TPR
1980	Tex-A	22	71	2	16	2	0	0	8	1	7	.225	.236	.254	35	-6	0	0	0	.978	-1	2-20/D-1	-0.6
1982	Tex-A	119	402	34	97	10	0	3	43	23	42	.241	.284	.289	61	-22	9	1	2	.988	4	2-98,D-15/O	-1.1
1983	Tex-A	22	83	9	13	2	1	1	7	2	11	.157	.176	.241	14	-10	2	1	0	.992	2	2-20	-0.7
1984	Tex-A	6	9	0	1	0	0	0	0	0	1	.111	.200	.111	-11	-1	0	1	-1	1.000	1	/2-4	-0.1
	Hou-N	16	15	1	4	1	0	0	2	0	1	.267	.267	.333	73	-1	0			.000	0	H	-0.1
Total	4	185	580	46	131	15	1	4	60	27	62	.226	.262	.276	50	-40	11	3	2	.988	6	2-142/D-16,O	-2.6

■ LANCE RICHBOURG
Richbourg, Lance Clayton b: 12/18/1897, DeFuniak Springs, Fla. d: 9/10/75, Crestview, Fla. BL/TR, 5'10.5", 160 lbs. Deb: 7/4/21

YEAR	TM/L	G	AB	R	H	2B	3B	HR	RBI	BB	SO	AVG	OBP	SLG	PRO+	BR/A	SB	CS	SBR	FA	FR	G/POS	TPR
1921	Phi-N	10	5	2	1	1	0	0	0	0	3	.200	.200	.400	51	-0	1	1	-0	1.000	2	/2-4	0.1
1924	Was-A	15	32	3	9	2	1	0	1	2	0	.281	.324	.406	90	-1	0	0	0	1.000	1	/O-7	-1.0
1927	Bos-N	115	450	57	139	12	9	2	34	22	30	.309	.342	.389	104	1	24			.953	-4	*O-110	-1.0
1928	Bos-N	148	612	105	206	26	12	2	52	62	39	.337	.399	.428	123	22	11			.972	7	*O-148	1.8
1929	Bos-N	139	557	76	170	24	13	3	56	42	26	.305	.355	.411	93	-6	7			.971	5	*O-134	-1.0
1930	Bos-N	130	529	81	161	23	8	3	54	19	31	.304	.331	.395	77	-20	13			.971	-3	*O-128	-2.8
1931	Bos-N	97	286	32	82	11	6	2	29	19	14	.287	.331	.388	96	-2	9			.981	-3	O-71	-1.0
1932	Chi-N	44	148	22	38	2	2	1	21	8	4	.257	.295	.318	65	-7	0			.986	-1	O-33	-1.0
Total	8	698	2619	378	806	101	51	13	247	174	147	.308	.352	.400	97	-14	65	1		.970	4	O-631/2-4	-4.9

■ ROB RICHIE
Richie, Robert Eugene b: 9/5/65, Reno, Nev. BL/TR, 6'2", 190 lbs. Deb: 8/19/89

YEAR	TM/L	G	AB	R	H	2B	3B	HR	RBI	BB	SO	AVG	OBP	SLG	PRO+	BR/A	SB	CS	SBR	FA	FR	G/POS	TPR
1989	Det-A	19	49	6	13	4	2	1	5	10	10	.265	.333	.490	132	2	0	1	-1	.917	-1	O-13/D-4	0.0

■ DON RICHMOND
Richmond, Donald Lester b: 10/27/19, Gillett, Pa. d: 5/24/81, Elmira, N.Y. BL/TR, 6'1", 175 lbs. Deb: 9/16/41

YEAR	TM/L	G	AB	R	H	2B	3B	HR	RBI	BB	SO	AVG	OBP	SLG	PRO+	BR/A	SB	CS	SBR	FA	FR	G/POS	TPR
1941	Phi-A	9	35	3	7	1	1	0	5	0	1	.200	.200	.286	28	-4	0	2	-1	.957	-2	/3-9	-0.7
1946	Phi-A	16	62	3	18	3	0	1	9	0	10	.290	.290	.387	89	-1	0	0	0	.940	-3	3-16	-0.4
1947	Phi-A	19	21	2	4	1	1	0	4	3	1	.190	.292	.333	72	-0	0	0	0	.500	-3	/3-4,2-1	-0.4
1951	StL-N	12	34	3	3	1	0	1	4	3	3	.088	.162	.206	-2	-5	0	1	-1	1.000	1	3-11	-0.1
Total	4	56	152	11	32	6	2	2	22	6	17	.211	.241	.316	51	-11	1	3	-2	.957	-4	/3-40,2-1	-1.6

■ JOHN RICHMOND
Richmond, John H. b: 1854, Pennsylvania TR , Deb: 4/22/1875

YEAR	TM/L	G	AB	R	H	2B	3B	HR	RBI	BB	SO	AVG	OBP	SLG	PRO+	BR/A	SB	CS	SBR	FA	FR	G/POS	TPR
1875	Ath-n	29	126	29	25	1	0	0		0		.198	.198	.206	36	-9						2-16,O-11/C	-0.8
1879	Syr-N	62	254	31	54	8	4	1	23	4	24	.213	.225	.287	76	-6				.874	-7	O-35,S-28/C	-1.2
1880	Bos-N	32	129	12	32	3	1	0	9	2	18	.248	.260	.287	88	-2				.844	-12	S-31/O-1	-1.1
1881	Bos-N	32	98	13	27	2	2	1	12	6	7	.276	.317	.367	120	2				.969	-0	O-25/S-2	0.2
1882	Cle-N	41	140	12	24	6	2	0	11	11	27	.171	.232	.243	54	-7				.917	3	O-41	-0.4
	Phi-a	18	65	8	12	2	2	0		11		.185	.303	.277	87	-1				.892	0	O-18	-0.1
1883	Col-a	92	385	63	109	7	8	0		25		.283	.327	.343	126	13				.877	26	*S-91/O-2	3.5
1884	Col-a	105	398	57	100	13	7	3		35		.251	.317	.342	125	13				.866	-9	*S-105	0.4
1885	Pit-a	34	131	14	27	2	2	0		8		.206	.262	.252	64	-5				.849	-10	S-23,O-11	-1.3
Total	7	411	1600	210	385	43	28	5	55	102	76	.241	.288	.312	101	8				.866	-10	S-280,O-133/C	

■ LEE RICHMOND
Richmond, J. Lee b: 5/5/1857, Sheffield, Ohio d: 10/1/29, Toledo, Ohio TL , 5'10", 142 lbs. Deb: 9/27/1879

YEAR	TM/L	G	AB	R	H	2B	3B	HR	RBI	BB	SO	AVG	OBP	SLG	PRO+	BR/A	SB	CS	SBR	FA	FR	G/POS	TPR
1879	Bos-N	1	6	0	2	0	0	0	1	0	1	.333	.333	.333	118	0				1.000	0	/P-1	0.0
1880	Wor-N	77	309	44	70	8	4	0	34	9	32	.227	.248	.278	72	-10				.827	-13	*P-74,O-20	-0.7
1881	Wor-N	61	252	31	63	5	1	0	28	10	10	.250	.279	.278	71	-8				.937	-1	P-53,O-11	-0.4
1882	Wor-N	55	228	50	64	8	9	2	28	9	11	.281	.308	.421	128	7				.889	2	P-48,O-11	0.0
1883	Pro-N	49	194	41	55	8	6	1	19	15	19	.284	.335	.402	120	5				.714	-10	O-41,P-12	-0.6
1886	Cin-a	8	29	3	8	0	0	0		3		.276	.344	.276	92	-0	0			.400	-4	/O-7,P-3	-0.3
Total	6	251	1018	169	262	29	20	3	110	46	73	.257	.289	.334	94	-7				.886	-26	P-191/O-90	-2.0

■ AL RICHTER
Richter, Allen Gordon b: 2/7/27, Norfolk, Va. BR/TR, 5'11", 165 lbs. Deb: 9/23/51

YEAR	TM/L	G	AB	R	H	2B	3B	HR	RBI	BB	SO	AVG	OBP	SLG	PRO+	BR/A	SB	CS	SBR	FA	FR	G/POS	TPR
1951	Bos-A	5	11	1	1	0	0	0	0	3	0	.091	.286	.091	5	-1	0	0	0	1.000	2	/S-3	0.1
1953	Bos-A	1	0	0	0	0	0	0	0	0	0	—	—	—		0	0	0	0	1.000	0	/S-1	0.0
Total	2	6	11	1	1	0	0	0	0	3	0	.091	.286	.091	5	-1	0	0	0	1.000	3	/S-4	0.1

■ JOHN RICHTER
Richter, John M. b: 2/8/1873, Louisville, Ky. d: 10/4/27, Louisville, Ky. 6', 178 lbs. Deb: 10/6/1898

YEAR	TM/L	G	AB	R	H	2B	3B	HR	RBI	BB	SO	AVG	OBP	SLG	PRO+	BR/A	SB	CS	SBR	FA	FR	G/POS	TPR
1898	Lou-N	3	13	1	2	0	0	0		0		.154	.154	.154	-12	-2	0			.929	0	/3-3	-0.1

■ JOE RICKERT
Rickert, Joseph Francis "Diamond Joe" b: 12/12/1876, London, Ohio d: 10/15/43, Springfield, Ohio BR/TR, 5'10.5", 165 lbs. Deb: 10/12/1898

YEAR	TM/L	G	AB	R	H	2B	3B	HR	RBI	BB	SO	AVG	OBP	SLG	PRO+	BR/A	SB	CS	SBR	FA	FR	G/POS	TPR
1898	Pit-N	2	6	0	1	0	0	0		0		.167	.167	.167	-5	-1	0			1.000	1	/O-2	0.0
1901	Bos-N	13	60	6	10	1	2	0	1	3		.167	.206	.250	29	-6	1			.974	2	O-13	-0.4
Total	2	15	66	6	11	1	2	0	1	3		.167	.203	.242	27	-6	1			.979	3	/O-15	-0.4

■ MARV RICKERT
Rickert, Marvin August "Twitch" b: 1/8/21, Longbranch, Wash. d: 6/3/78, Oakville, Wash. BL/TR, 6'2", 195 lbs. Deb: 9/10/42

YEAR	TM/L	G	AB	R	H	2B	3B	HR	RBI	BB	SO	AVG	OBP	SLG	PRO+	BR/A	SB	CS	SBR	FA	FR	G/POS	TPR
1942	Chi-N	8	26	5	7	0	0	0	1	1	5	.269	.296	.269	69	-1	0			1.000	1	/O-6	0.0
1946	Chi-N	111	392	44	103	18	3	7	47	28	54	.263	.314	.378	98	-3	3			.972	-6	*O-104	-1.4

YEAR	TM/L	G	AB	R	H	2B	3B	HR	RBI	BB	SO	AVG	OBP	SLG	PRO+	BR/A	SB	CS	SBR	FA	FR	G/POS	TPR
1947	Chi-N	71	137	7	20	0	0	2	15	15	17	.146	.230	.190	13	-17	0			.982	-1	O-30/1-7	-2.0
1948	Cin-N	8	6	0	1	0	0	0	0	0	0	.167	.167	.167	-10	-1	0			.000	0	H	-0.1
	*Bos-N	3	13	1	3	0	1	0	2	0	1	.231	.286	.385	81	-0	0			1.000	1	/O-3	0.1
	Yr	11	19	1	4	0	1	0	2	0	1	.211	.250	.316	54	-1	0			1.000	1	/O-3	0.0
1949	Bos-N	100	277	44	81	18	3	6	49	23	38	.292	.347	.444	117	6	1			.981	-0	O-75,1-12	0.2
1950	Pit-N	17	20	0	3	0	0	0	4	0	4	.150	.150	.150	-20	-3	0			.000	-0	H	-0.5
	Chi-A	84	278	38	66	9	2	4	27	21	42	.237	.291	.327	60	-18	0	1	-1	.968	-6	O-78/1-1	-2.6
Total	6	402	1149	139	284	45	9	19	145	88	161	.247	.302	.352	79	-38	4	1		.976	-12	O-299/1-20	-6.3

■ DAVE RICKETTS
Ricketts, David William b: 7/12/35, Pottstown, Pa.   BB/TR, 6'2", 195 lbs.   Deb: 9/25/63 FC

YEAR	TM/L	G	AB	R	H	2B	3B	HR	RBI	BB	SO	AVG	OBP	SLG	PRO+	BR/A	SB	CS	SBR	FA	FR	G/POS	TPR
1963	StL-N	3	8	0	2	0	0	0	0	0	2	.250	.250	.250	41	-1	0	0	0	1.000	-0	/C-3	-0.1
1965	StL-N	11	29	1	7	0	0	0	0	1	3	.241	.267	.241	40	-2	0	0	0	.977	-2	C-11	-0.4
1967	*StL-N	52	99	11	27	8	0	1	14	4	7	.273	.301	.384	96	-1	0	0	0	1.000	-0	C-21	0.0
1968	*StL-N	20	22	1	3	0	0	0	1	0	3	.136	.136	.136	-18	-3	0	0	0	1.000	-0	/C-1	-0.4
1969	StL-N	30	44	2	12	1	0	0	5	4	5	.273	.333	.295	77	-1	0	0	0	.983	1	/C-8	0.0
1970	Pit-N	14	11	0	2	0	0	0	0	1	3	.182	.250	.182	18	-1	0	0	0	.909	1	/C-7	-0.1
Total	6	130	213	15	53	9	0	1	20	10	23	.249	.283	.305	67	-9	0	0	0	.988	-1	/C-51	-1.0

■ BRANCH RICKEY
Rickey, Wesley Branch "The Mahatma" b: 12/20/1881, Lucasville, Ohio   d: 12/9/65, Columbia, Mo.   BL/TR, 5'9", 175 lbs.   Deb: 6/16/05 MH

YEAR	TM/L	G	AB	R	H	2B	3B	HR	RBI	BB	SO	AVG	OBP	SLG	PRO+	BR/A	SB	CS	SBR	FA	FR	G/POS	TPR
1905	StL-A	1	3	0	0	0	0	0	0	0		.000	.000	.000	-99	-0	0			1.000	-0	/C-1	-0.1
1906	StL-A	65	201	22	57	7	3	3	24	16		.284	.345	.393	137	8	4			.954	-8	C-55/O-1	0.7
1907	NY-A	52	137	16	25	1	3	0	15	11		.182	.253	.234	51	-7	4			.846	-5	O-22,C-11/1	-1.4
1914	StL-A	2	2	0	0	0	0	0	0	0	1	.000	.000	.000	-99	-0	0			.000	0	HM	-0.1
Total	4	120	343	38	82	8	6	3	39	27	1	.239	.304	.324	97	-0	8			.940	-13	/C-67,O-23,1	-0.9

■ CHRIS RICKLEY
Rickley, Christian b: 10/7/1859, Philadelphia, Pa.   d: 10/25/11, Philadelphia, Pa.   5'8", 160 lbs.   Deb: 6/9/1884

YEAR	TM/L	G	AB	R	H	2B	3B	HR	RBI	BB	SO	AVG	OBP	SLG	PRO+	BR/A	SB	CS	SBR	FA	FR	G/POS	TPR
1884	Phi-U	6	25	5	5	2	0	0		2		.200	.259	.280	50	-2				.757	0	/S-6	-0.1

■ JOHN RICKS
Ricks, John   Deb: 9/21/1891

YEAR	TM/L	G	AB	R	H	2B	3B	HR	RBI	BB	SO	AVG	OBP	SLG	PRO+	BR/A	SB	CS	SBR	FA	FR	G/POS	TPR
1891	StL-a	5	18	3	3	0	0	0	0	0	2	.167	.167	.167	-4	-3	0			.810	-1	/3-5	-0.3
1894	StL-N	1	1	0	0	0	0	0	0	0	0	.000	.000	.000	-99	-0	0			.250	-1	/3-1	-0.1
Total	2	6	19	3	3	0	0	0	0	0	2	.158	.158	.158	-9	-3	0			.720	-2	/3-6	-0.4

■ FRED RICO
Rico, Alfredo (Cruz) b: 7/4/44, Jerome, Ariz.   BR/TR, 5'10", 180 lbs.   Deb: 9/1/69

YEAR	TM/L	G	AB	R	H	2B	3B	HR	RBI	BB	SO	AVG	OBP	SLG	PRO+	BR/A	SB	CS	SBR	FA	FR	G/POS	TPR
1969	KC-A	12	26	2	6	2	0	0	2	9	10	.231	.429	.308	108	1	0	1	-1	1.000	4	/O-9,3-1	0.4

■ ART RICO
Rico, Arthur Raymond b: 7/23/1896, Roxbury, Mass.   d: 1/3/19, Boston, Mass.   BR/TR, 5'9.5", 185 lbs.   Deb: 7/31/16

YEAR	TM/L	G	AB	R	H	2B	3B	HR	RBI	BB	SO	AVG	OBP	SLG	PRO+	BR/A	SB	CS	SBR	FA	FR	G/POS	TPR
1916	Bos-N	4	4	0	0	0	0	0	0	0	0	.000	.000	.000	-99	-1	0			1.000	-0	/C-4	-0.1
1917	Bos-N	13	14	1	4	1	0	0	2	0	2	.286	.286	.357	102	-0	0			.950	-2	C-11/O-2	-0.1
Total	2	17	18	1	4	1	0	0	2	0	2	.222	.222	.278	56	-1	0			.962	-2	/C-15,O-2	-0.2

■ HARRY RICONDA
Riconda, Henry Paul b: 3/17/1897, New York, N.Y.   d: 11/15/58, Mahopac, N.Y.   BR/TR, 5'10", 175 lbs.   Deb: 4/19/23

YEAR	TM/L	G	AB	R	H	2B	3B	HR	RBI	BB	SO	AVG	OBP	SLG	PRO+	BR/A	SB	CS	SBR	FA	FR	G/POS	TPR
1923	Phi-A	55	175	23	46	11	4	0	12	12	18	.263	.317	.371	80	-6	4	2	0	.911	4	3-47/S-2	0.2
1924	Phi-A	83	281	34	71	16	3	1	21	27	43	.253	.323	.342	71	-13	3	4	-2	.927	1	3-73/S-2	-0.7
1926	Bos-N	4	12	1	2	0	0	0	0	2	2	.167	.286	.167	27	-1	0			.818	-1	/3-4	-0.2
1928	Bro-N	92	281	22	63	15	4	3	35	20	28	.224	.285	.338	63	-16	6			.957	3	2-53,3-21,S	-0.9
1929	Pit-N	8	15	3	7	2	0	0	2	0	0	.467	.467	.600	158	1	0			.840	-0	/S-4	0.1
1930	Cin-N	1	1	0	0	0	0	0	0	0	0	.000	.000	.000	-99	-0	0			.000	0	H	0.0
Total	6	243	765	83	189	44	11	4	70	61	91	.247	.309	.349	71	-34	13	6		.922	6	3-145/2-53,S	-1.5

■ JOHN RIDDLE
Riddle, John H. b: 2/1864, Pennsylvania   BR/TR,   Deb: 9/18/1889

YEAR	TM/L	G	AB	R	H	2B	3B	HR	RBI	BB	SO	AVG	OBP	SLG	PRO+	BR/A	SB	CS	SBR	FA	FR	G/POS	TPR
1889	Was-N	11	37	3	8	3	0	0	3	2	8	.216	.256	.297	58	-2	0			.841	1	/C-9,O-2	-0.1
1890	Phi-a	27	85	7	7	0	1	0		17		.082	.243	.106	3	-10	4			.914	-2	C-13,O-12/23	-1.0
Total	2	38	122	10	15	3	1	0	3	19	8	.123	.246	.164	20	-12	4			.880	-2	/C-22,O-14,23	-1.1

■ JOHNNY RIDDLE
Riddle, John Ludy "Mutt" b: 10/3/05, Clinton, S.C.   BR/TR, 5'11", 190 lbs.   Deb: 4/17/30 FC

YEAR	TM/L	G	AB	R	H	2B	3B	HR	RBI	BB	SO	AVG	OBP	SLG	PRO+	BR/A	SB	CS	SBR	FA	FR	G/POS	TPR
1930	Chi-A	25	58	7	14	3	1	0	4	3	6	.241	.290	.328	58	-4	0	0	0	1.000	-3	C-25	-0.4
1937	Was-A	8	26	2	7	0	0	0	3	0	2	.269	.296	.269	46	-2	0	0	0	.971	0	/C-8	-0.1
	Bos-N	2	3	0	0	0	0	0	0	1	0	.000	.250	.000	-29	-1	0			1.000	1	/C-2	0.0
1938	Bos-N	19	57	6	16	1	0	0	2	4	2	.281	.328	.298	81	-1	0			.951	4	C-19	0.3
1941	Cin-N	10	10	2	3	0	0	0	1	0	0	.300	.300	.300	69	-0	0			1.000	1	C-10	0.1
1944	Cin-N	1										—	—	—	—		0			.000	0	/C-1	0.0
1945	Cin-N	23	45	0	8	0	0	0	2	4	6	.178	.245	.178	19	-5	0			1.000	6	C-23	-0.1
1948	Pit-N	10	15	1	3	0	0	0	1	1	2	.200	.250	.200	23	-2	0			1.000	0	C-10	-0.1
Total	7	98	214	18	51	4	1	0	11	13	19	.238	.288	.266	51	-15	0	0		.983	7	/C-98	-0.3

■ HANK RIEBE
Riebe, Harvey Donald b: 10/10/21, Cleveland, Ohio   BR/TR, 5'9.5", 175 lbs.   Deb: 8/26/42

YEAR	TM/L	G	AB	R	H	2B	3B	HR	RBI	BB	SO	AVG	OBP	SLG	PRO+	BR/A	SB	CS	SBR	FA	FR	G/POS	TPR
1942	Det-A	11	35	1	11	2	0	0	6	0	6	.314	.314	.371	85	-1	0	0	0	1.000	-1	C-11	-0.1
1947	Det-A	8	7	0	0	0	0	0	2	0	2	.000	.000	.000	-97	-2	0	0	0	1.000	-0	/C-3	-0.2
1948	Det-A	25	62	0	12	0	0	0	5	3	5	.194	.231	.194	13	-8	0	1	-1	1.000	0	C-24	-0.7
1949	Det-A	17	33	1	6	2	0	0	2	0	5	.182	.182	.242	12	-4	1	0	-0	.960	-2	C-11	-0.5
Total	4	61	137	2	29	4	0	0	11	3	18	.212	.229	.241	26	-15	1	1	-0	.994	-3	/C-49	-1.5

■ NIKCO RIESGO
Riesgo, Damon Nikco b: 1/11/67, Long Beach, Cal.   BR/TR, 6'2", 185 lbs.   Deb: 4/20/91

YEAR	TM/L	G	AB	R	H	2B	3B	HR	RBI	BB	SO	AVG	OBP	SLG	PRO+	BR/A	SB	CS	SBR	FA	FR	G/POS	TPR
1991	Mon-N	4	7	1	1	0	0	0	0	3	1	.143	.400	.143	60	-0	0	0	0	.500	-0	/O-2	0.0

■ JOE RIGGERT
Riggert, Joseph Aloysius b: 12/11/1886, Janesville, Wis.   d: 12/10/73, Kansas City, Mo.   BR/TR, 5'9.5", 170 lbs.   Deb: 5/12/11

YEAR	TM/L	G	AB	R	H	2B	3B	HR	RBI	BB	SO	AVG	OBP	SLG	PRO+	BR/A	SB	CS	SBR	FA	FR	G/POS	TPR
1911	Bos-A	50	146	19	31	4	4	2	13	12		.212	.290	.336	75	-5	5			.929	-4	O-39	-1.1
1914	Bro-N	27	83	6	16	1	3	2	6	4	20	.193	.230	.349	70	-4	2			.972	-1	O-20	-0.5
	StL-N	34	89	9	19	5	2	0	8	5	14	.213	.255	.315	70	-4	4			.961	-3	O-30	-0.9
	Yr	61	172	15	35	6	5	2	14	9	34	.203	.243	.331	70	-7	6			.966	-4	O-50	-1.4
1919	Bos-N	63	240	34	68	8	5	4	17	25	30	.283	.356	.458	135	10	9			.950	2	O-61	0.9
Total	3	174	558	68	134	18	14	8	44	46	64	.240	.305	.366	98	-2	20			.950	-6	O-150	-1.6

■ LEW RIGGS
Riggs, Lewis Sidney b: 4/22/10, Mebane, N.C.   d: 8/12/75, Durham, N.C.   BL/TR, 6', 175 lbs.   Deb: 4/28/34

YEAR	TM/L	G	AB	R	H	2B	3B	HR	RBI	BB	SO	AVG	OBP	SLG	PRO+	BR/A	SB	CS	SBR	FA	FR	G/POS	TPR
1934	StL-N	2	1	0	0	0	0	0	0	0	1	.000	.000	.000	-94	-0	0			.000	0	H	0.0
1935	Cin-N	142	532	73	148	26	8	5	46	43	32	.278	.334	.385	96	-3	8			.928	8	*3-135	1.0
1936	Cin-N★	141	538	69	138	20	12	6	57	38	33	.257	.314	.372	90	-9	5			.968	12	*3-140	0.8
1937	Cin-N	122	384	43	93	17	5	6	45	24	17	.242	.289	.359	79	-13	4			.941	20	*3-100/2-4,S	1.0
1938	Cin-N	142	531	53	134	21	13	2	55	40	28	.252	.311	.352	84	-12	3			.947	-1	*3-140	-1.1
1939	Cin-N	22	38	5	6	1	0	0	1	5	4	.158	.256	.184	20	-4	1			.957	-1	3-11	-0.5
1940	*Cin-N	41	72	8	21	7	1	1	9	2	4	.292	.311	.458	109	0	0			.943	2	3-11	0.2
1941	*Bro-N	77	197	27	60	13	4	5	36	16	12	.305	.357	.487	131	7	1			.932	-7	3-43/1-1,2	0.1
1942	Bro-N	70	180	20	50	5	2	3	22	13	9	.278	.333	.356	100	-0	0			.944	-6	3-46/1-1	-0.6
1946	Bro-N	1	4	0	0	0	0	0	0	0	0	.000	.000	.000	-99	-1	0			1.000	0	/3-1	-0.1
Total	10	760	2477	298	650	110	43	28	271	181	140	.262	.317	.375	91	-35	22			.945	27	3-627/2-5,1S	0.8

YEAR	TM/L	G	AB	R	H	2B	3B	HR	RBI	BB	SO	AVG	OBP	SLG	PRO+	BR/A	SB	CS	SBR	FA	FR	G/POS	TPR

■ **TOPPER RIGNEY**   Rigney, Emory Elmo   b: 1/7/1897, Groveton, Tex.   d: 6/6/72, San Antonio, Tex.   BR/TR, 5'9", 150 lbs.   Deb: 4/12/22

1922	Det-A	155	536	68	161	17	7	2	63	68	44	.300	.380	.369	99	2	17	8	0	.938	-13	*S-155	0.5
1923	Det-A	129	470	63	148	24	11	1	74	55	35	.315	.389	.419	115	11	7	5	-1	.944	-16	*S-129	0.7
1924	Det-A	147	499	81	144	29	9	4	94	102	39	.289	.410	.407	113	14	11	11	-3	.967	10	*S-146	3.4
1925	Det-A	62	146	21	36	5	2	2	18	21	15	.247	.341	.349	77	-5	2	2	-1	.934	-14	S-51/3-4	-1.5
1926	Bos-A	148	525	71	142	32	6	4	53	108	31	.270	.395	.377	105	9	6	8	-3	.969	20	*S-146	3.9
1927	Bos-A	8	18	0	2	1	0	0	0	1	2	.111	.158	.167	-16	-3	0	0	0	1.000	-1	/3-4,S-1	-0.4
	Was-A	45	132	20	36	5	4	0	13	22	10	.273	.381	.371	97	0	1	2	-1	.929	-3	S-32/3-6	0.0
	Yr	53	150	20	38	6	4	0	13	23	12	.253	.356	.347	84	-3	1	2	-1	.932	-4	S-33,3-10	-0.4
Total	6	694	2326	324	669	113	39	13	315	377	176	.288	.388	.387	104	28	44	36	-8	.953	-18	S-660/3-14	6.6

■ **BILL RIGNEY**   Rigney, William Joseph "Specs" or "The Cricket"   b: 1/29/18, Alameda, Cal.   BR/TR, 6'1", 178 lbs.   Deb: 4/16/46   MC

1946	NY-N	110	360	38	85	9	1	3	31	36	29	.236	.307	.292	70	-14	9			.965	3	3-73,S-33	-0.9
1947	NY-N	130	531	84	142	24	3	17	59	51	54	.267	.337	.420	99	-1	7			.974	1	2-72,3-41,S	0.5
1948	NY-N★	113	424	72	112	17	3	10	43	47	54	.264	.342	.389	97	-2	4			.967	-11	*2-105/S-7	-0.7
1949	NY-N	122	389	53	108	19	6	6	47	47	38	.278	.356	.404	103	2	3			.928	-17	S-81,2-26,3	-0.8
1950	NY-N	56	83	8	15	2	0	0	8	8	13	.181	.253	.205	22	-9	0			.966	6	2-23,3-11	-0.3
1951	*NY-N	44	69	9	16	3	0	4	9	8	7	.232	.321	.435	100	-0	0	1	-1	.953	5	3-12/2-9	0.5
1952	NY-N	60	90	15	27	5	1	1	14	11	6	.300	.388	.411	121	3	2	3	-1	.889	-1	3-10/2-9,S1	0.1
1953	NY-N	19	20	2	5	0	0	0	1	0	5	.250	.250	.250	30	-2	0	0	0	1.000	0	/3-2,2-1	-0.2
Total	8	654	1966	281	510	78	14	41	212	208	206	.259	.334	.376	91	-23	25	4		.971	-13	2-245,3-163,S/1	-1.8

■ **CULLEY RIKARD**   Rikard, Culley   b: 5/9/14, Oxford, Miss.   BL/TR, 5'11", 183 lbs.   Deb: 9/20/41

1941	Pit-N	6	20	1	4	1	0	0	1	1	1	.200	.238	.250	38	-2	0			1.000	1	/O-5	-0.1
1942	Pit-N	38	52	6	10	2	1	0	5	7	8	.192	.288	.269	62	-2	0			.958	-4	O-16	-0.7
1947	Pit-N	109	324	57	93	16	4	4	32	50	39	.287	.384	.398	105	4	1			.978	-1	O-79	-0.1
Total	3	153	396	64	107	19	5	4	37	58	48	.270	.365	.374	97	-0	1			.978	-4	O-100	-0.9

■ **ERNEST RILES**   Riles, Ernest   b: 10/2/60, Cairo, Ga.   BL/TR, 6'1", 180 lbs.   Deb: 5/14/85

1985	Mil-A	116	448	54	128	12	7	5	45	36	54	.286	.342	.377	97	-1	2	2	-1	.957	-19	*S-115/D-1	-0.9
1986	Mil-A	145	524	69	132	24	2	9	47	54	80	.252	.323	.357	82	-12	7	7	-2	.964	-30	*S-142	-3.1
1987	Mil-A	83	276	38	72	11	1	4	38	30	47	.261	.336	.351	80	-7	3	4	-2	.935	-6	3-65,S-21	-1.3
1988	Mil-A	41	127	7	32	6	1	1	9	7	26	.252	.291	.339	75	-4	2	2	-1	.958	1	3-28/S-9,D	-0.3
	SF-N	79	187	26	55	7	2	3	28	10	33	.294	.330	.401	114	3	1	2	-1	.975	8	3-30,2-17,S	1.2
1989	*SF-N	122	302	43	84	13	2	7	40	28	50	.278	.343	.404	116	6	0	6	-4	.962	-10	3-83,2-18/SO	-0.7
1990	SF-N	92	155	22	31	2	1	8	21	26	26	.200	.315	.381	94	-1	0	0	0	.986	-4	3-26,2-24,3	-0.4
1991	Oak-A	108	281	30	60	8	4	5	32	31	42	.214	.294	.324	75	-10	3	2	-0	.939	-10	3-69,S-20/21	-1.9
1992	Hou-N	39	61	5	16	1	0	1	4	2	11	.262	.286	.328	77	-2	1	0	0	1.000	-2	/S-6,3-5,12	-0.4
1993	Bos-A	94	143	15	27	8	0	5	20	20	40	.189	.297	.350	69	-7	1	3	-2	1.000	5	2-20,D-15,3/1	-0.4
Total	9	919	2504	309	637	92	20	48	284	244	409	.254	.323	.365	89	-36	20	28	-11	.964	-67	S-362,3-301/2D10	-8.2

■ **JIM RILEY**   Riley, James Joseph   b: 11/10/1886, Buffalo, N.Y.   d: 3/25/49, Buffalo, N.Y.   BR/TR, 6', 165 lbs.   Deb: 8/2/10

1910	Bos-N	1	1	0	0	0	0	0	0	1	1	.000	.500	.000	46	0	0			.600	-0	/O-1	0.0

■ **JIM RILEY**   Riley, James Norman   b: 5/25/1895, Bayfield, N.B., Can   d: 5/25/69, Seguin, Tex.   BL/TR, 5'10.5", 185 lbs.   Deb: 7/3/21

1921	StL-A	4	11	0	0	0	0	0	0	1	3	.000	.083	.000	-73	-3	0	0	0	.818	-3	/2-4	-0.6
1923	Was-A	2	3	1	0	0	0	0	0	2	0	.000	.400	.000	12	-0	0	0	0	.882	-1	/1-2	-0.1
Total	2	6	14	1	0	0	0	0	0	3	3	.000	.176	.000	-50	-3	0	0	0	.818	-4	/2-4,1-2	-0.7

■ **LEE RILEY**   Riley, Leon Francis   b: 8/20/06, Princeton, Neb.   d: 9/13/70, Schenectady, N.Y.   BL/TR, 6'1", 185 lbs.   Deb: 4/19/44

1944	Phi-N	4	12	1	1	1	0	0	1	0	0	.083	.083	.167	-32	-2	0			1.000	-1	/O-3	-0.4

■ **BILLY RILEY**   Riley, William James "Pigtail Billy"   b: 1855, Cincinnati, Ohio   d: 11/9/1887, Cincinnati, Ohio   BR/TR, 5'10", 160 lbs.   Deb: 5/5/1875

1875	Wes-n	8	33	4	5	1	0	0		1		.152	.176	.182	23	-3						/O-8	-0.2
1879	Cle-N	44	165	14	24	2	0	0	9	2	26	.145	.156	.158	4	-16				.850	4	O-43/1-1,C	-1.4

■ **FRANK RINGO**   Ringo, Frank C.   b: 10/12/1860, Parkville, Mo.   d: 4/12/1889, Kansas City, Mo.   BR , 5'11", 175 lbs.   Deb: 5/1/1883

1883	Phi-N	60	221	24	42	10	1	0	12	6	34	.190	.211	.244	42	-14				.847	-9	C-39,O-11/S32	-1.8
1884	Phi-N	26	91	4	12	2	0	0	6	3	19	.132	.160	.154	-1	-10				.783	-16	C-26	-2.2
	Phi-a	2	6	0	0	0	0	0		0	0	.000	.000	.000	-94	-1				.762	1	/C-2	0.0
1885	Det-N	17	65	12	16	3	0	0	0	0	0	.246	.246	.292	73	-2				.852	2	/C-8,3-8,O	0.1
	Pit-a	3	11	0	2	0	0	0		0	0	.182	.182	.182	15	-1				.941	0	/C-3	0.2
1886	Pit-a	15	56	3	12	2	0	0		1		.214	.228	.321	72	-2	0			.934	-0	/1-9,C-6	-0.2
	KC-N	16	56	6	13	7	0	0	7	5	10	.232	.295	.357	92	-1	0			.904	-6	C-13/O-2,3	-0.4
Total	4	139	506	49	97	24	3	0	27	15	70	.192	.215	.251	46	-32	0			.844	-24	/C-97,3-14,01S2	-4.3

■ **BOB RINKER**   Rinker, Robert John   b: 4/21/21, Audenried, Pa.   BR/TR, 6', 190 lbs.   Deb: 9/6/50

1950	Phi-A	3	3	0	1	0	0	0	0	0	0	.333	.333	.333	72	-0	0	0	0	.000	0	/C-1	0.0

■ **JUAN RIOS**   Rios, Juan Onofre Velez (b: Juan Onofre Velez (Rios))   b: 6/14/42, Mayaguez, P.R.   BR/TR, 6'3", 185 lbs.   Deb: 4/9/69

1969	KC-A	87	196	20	44	5	1	5	17	9	25	.224	.262	.276	50	-13	1	3	-2	.967	-16	2-46,S-32/3	-2.8

■ **CAL RIPKEN**   Ripken, Calvin Edwin Jr.   b: 8/24/60, Havre De Grace, Md.   BR/TR, 6'4", 215 lbs.   Deb: 8/10/81   F

1981	Bal-A	23	39	1	5	0	0	0	0	1	8	.128	.150	.128	-19	-6	0	0	0	.946	0	S-12/3-6	-0.6
1982	Bal-A	160	598	90	158	32	5	28	93	46	95	.264	.320	.475	115	11	3	3	-1	.972	-7	S-94,3-71	1.0
1983	*Bal-A★	162	663	**121**	**211**	**47**	2	27	102	58	97	.318	.373	.517	145	39	0	4	-2	.970	16	*S-162	**6.7**
1984	Bal-A	162	641	103	195	37	7	27	86	71	89	.304	.375	.510	146	39	2	1	0	.971	**39**	*S-162	**9.1**
1985	Bal-A★	161	642	116	181	32	5	26	110	67	68	.282	.351	.469	125	22	2	3	-1	.967	7	*S-161	4.3
1986	Bal-A★	162	627	98	177	35	1	25	81	70	60	.282	.358	.461	123	20	4	2	0	.982	10	*S-162	4.4
1987	Bal-A★	162	624	97	157	28	3	27	98	81	77	.252	.339	.436	106	6	3	5	-2	.973	-4	*S-161	1.3
1988	Bal-A★	161	575	87	152	25	1	23	81	102	69	.264	.377	.431	129	26	2	2	-1	.973	-2	*S-161	3.7
1989	Bal-A★	162	646	80	166	30	0	21	93	57	72	.257	.320	.401	105	3	3	2	-0	.990	4	*S-162	2.0
1990	Bal-A★	161	600	78	150	28	4	21	84	82	66	.250	.345	.415	115	13	3	1	-0	**.996**	-29	*S-161	-0.3
1991	Bal-A★	162	650	99	210	46	5	34	114	53	46	.323	.379	.566	164	54	6	1	1	**.986**	18	*S-162	**8.3**
1992	Bal-A★	162	637	73	160	29	1	14	72	64	50	.251	.323	.366	91	-7	4	3	-1	.984	-13	*S-162	-0.9
1993	Bal-A★	162	641	87	165	26	3	24	90	65	58	.257	.331	.420	96	-4	1	4	-2	.977	-5	*S-162	0.2
1994	Bal-A★	112	444	71	140	19	3	13	75	32	41	.315	.360	.459	105	3	1	0	0	**.985**	14	*S-112	1.0
Total	14	2074	8027	1201	2227	414	40	310	1179	849	896	.277	.350	.455	120	219	34	31	-8	.979	21	*S-1997/3-77	39.2

■ **BILLY RIPKEN**   Ripken, William Oliver   b: 12/16/64, Havre De Grace, Md.   BR/TR, 6'1", 183 lbs.   Deb: 7/11/87   F

1987	Bal-A	58	234	27	72	9	0	2	20	21	23	.308	.365	.372	99	4	4	1	1	.990	-3	2-58	0.0
1988	Bal-A	150	512	52	106	18	1	2	34	33	63	.207	.262	.258	47	-36	8	2	1	.984	2	*2-149/3-2,D	-2.7
1989	Bal-A	115	318	31	76	11	2	2	26	22	53	.239	.288	.305	69	-13	1	2	-1	.985	13	*2-114/D-1	0.2
1990	Bal-A	129	406	48	118	28	1	3	38	28	43	.291	.342	.382	107	9	5	2	0	.987	-9	*2-127	-0.2
1991	Bal-A	104	287	24	62	11	1	0	14	15	31	.216	.255	.261	45	-22	0	1	-1	.986	6	*2-103	-1.6

YEAR	TM/L	G	AB	R	H	2B	3B	HR	RBI	BB	SO	AVG	OBP	SLG	PRO+	BR/A	SB	CS	SBR	FA	FR	G/POS	TPR
1992	Bal-A	111	330	35	76	15	0	4	36	18	26	.230	.276	.312	63	-17	2	3	-1	**.993**	0	*2-108/D-2	-1.6
1993	Tex-A	50	132	12	25	4	0	0	11	11	19	.189	.272	.220	35	-12	0	2	-1	.992	4	2-34,S-18/3	-0.7
1994	Tex-A	32	81	9	25	5	0	0	6	3	11	.309	.333	.370	87	-2	2	0	1	.970	2	3-18,2-12/S1	0.1
Total	8	749	2300	238	560	101	5	13	185	151	269	.243	.295	.309	69	-97	22	13	-1	.987	13	2-705/3-21,SD1	-6.5

■ JIMMY RIPPLE
Ripple, James Albert b: 10/14/09, Export, Pa. d: 7/16/59, Greensburg, Pa. BL/TR, 5'10″, 170 lbs. Deb: 4/20/36

YEAR	TM/L	G	AB	R	H	2B	3B	HR	RBI	BB	SO	AVG	OBP	SLG	PRO+	BR/A	SB	CS	SBR	FA	FR	G/POS	TPR
1936	*NY-N	96	311	42	95	17	2	7	47	28	15	.305	.365	.441	117	7	1			.980	-0	O-76	0.4
1937	*NY-N	121	426	70	135	23	3	5	66	29	20	.317	.362	.420	110	6	3			.980	-9	*O-111	-0.7
1938	NY-N	134	501	68	131	21	3	10	60	49	21	.261	.333	.375	94	-4	2			.976	-3	*O-131	-1.1
1939	NY-N	66	123	10	28	4	0	1	12	8	7	.228	.286	.285	53	-8	0			1.000	-2	O-23	-1.0
	Bro-N	28	106	18	35	8	4	0	22	11	8	.330	.398	.481	131	5	0			1.000	-2	O-28	0.2
	Yr	94	229	28	63	12	4	1	34	19	15	.275	.339	.376	90	-3	0			1.000	-3	O-51	-0.8
1940	Bro-N	7	13	0	3	0	0	0	0	2	2	.231	.333	.231	55	-1	0			1.000	1	/O-3	0.0
	*Cin-N	32	101	15	31	10	0	4	20	13	5	.307	.397	.525	151	7	1			1.000	-5	O-30	0.1
	Yr	39	114	15	34	10	0	4	20	15	7	.298	.389	.491	139	6	1			1.000	-4	O-33	0.1
1941	Cin-N	38	102	10	22	6	1	1	9	9	4	.216	.279	.324	69	-4	0			1.000	-2	O-25	-0.9
1943	Phi-N	32	126	8	30	3	1	0	15	7	7	.238	.284	.278	65	-6	0	0	0	1.000	-4	O-31	-1.3
Total	7	554	1809	241	510	92	14	28	251	156	89	.282	.343	.395	101	2	7	0		.984	-27	O-458	-4.3

■ SWEDE RISBERG
Risberg, Charles August b: 10/13/1894, San Francisco, Cal d: 10/13/75, Red Bluff, Cal. BR/TR, 6', 175 lbs. Deb: 4/11/17

YEAR	TM/L	G	AB	R	H	2B	3B	HR	RBI	BB	SO	AVG	OBP	SLG	PRO+	BR/A	SB	CS	SBR	FA	FR	G/POS	TPR
1917	*Chi-A	149	474	59	96	20	8	1	45	59	65	.203	.297	.285	76	-13	16			.913	-39	*S-146	-5.1
1918	Chi-A	82	273	36	70	12	3	1	27	23	32	.256	.321	.333	97	-1	5			.944	-8	S-30,3-24,2/10	-0.8
1919	Chi-A	119	414	48	106	19	6	2	38	35	38	.256	.317	.345	86	-8	19			.934	-13	S-97,1-22	-1.7
1920	Chi-A	126	458	53	122	21	10	2	65	31	45	.266	.316	.369	81	-14	12	10	-2	.934	-4	*S-124	-0.9
Total	4	476	1619	196	394	72	27	6	175	148	180	.243	.311	.332	83	-36	52	10		.928	-64	S-397/1-29,320	-8.5

■ POP RISING
Rising, Percival Sumner b: 1/2/1872, Industry, Pa. d: 1/28/38, Rochester, Pa. Deb: 8/10/05

YEAR	TM/L	G	AB	R	H	2B	3B	HR	RBI	BB	SO	AVG	OBP	SLG	PRO+	BR/A	SB	CS	SBR	FA	FR	G/POS	TPR
1905	Bos-A	11	29	2	3	1	1	0	2	2		.103	.161	.207	16	-3	0			1.000	0	/O-6,3-1	-0.3

■ CLAUDE RITCHEY
Ritchey, Claude Cassius "Little All Right" b: 10/5/1873, Emlenton, Pa. d: 11/8/51, Emlenton, Pa. BB/TR, 5'6.5″, 167 lbs. Deb: 4/22/1897

YEAR	TM/L	G	AB	R	H	2B	3B	HR	RBI	BB	SO	AVG	OBP	SLG	PRO+	BR/A	SB	CS	SBR	FA	FR	G/POS	TPR
1897	Cin-N	101	337	58	95	12	4	0	41	42		.282	.370	.341	83	-8	11			.897	-16	S-70,O-22/2	-2.0
1898	Lou-N	151	551	65	140	10	4	5	51	46		.254	.322	.314	84	-11	19			.919	-16	S-80,2-71	-1.8
1899	Lou-N	147	536	65	161	15	7	4	71	49		.300	.370	.377	105	5	21			.938	-6	*2-137,S-11	0.6
1900	*Pit-N	123	476	62	139	17	8	1	67	29		.292	.339	.368	94	-4	18			.952	7	*2-123	0.8
1901	Pit-N	140	540	66	160	20	4	1	74	47		.296	.358	.354	104	4	15			.941	-2	*2-139/S-1	1.1
1902	Pit-N	115	405	54	112	13	1	2	55	53		.277	.370	.328	112	8	10			**.966**	6	*2-114/O-1	1.9
1903	*Pit-N	138	506	66	145	28	10	0	59	55		.287	.360	.381	108	6	15			**.961**	19	*2-137	2.8
1904	Pit-N	156	544	79	143	22	12	0	51	59		.263	.338	.347	109	7	12			.958	-2	*2-156/S-2	0.9
1905	Pit-N	153	533	54	136	29	6	0	52	51		.255	.324	.332	93	-4	12			**.961**	-5	*2-153/S-2	-0.8
1906	Pit-N	152	484	46	130	21	5	1	62	68		.269	.369	.339	116	11	6			**.966**	1	*2-151	1.5
1907	Bos-N	144	499	45	127	17	4	2	51	50		.255	.329	.317	103	2	8			**.971**	14	*2-144	1.7
1908	Bos-N	121	421	44	115	10	3	2	36	50		.273	.361	.325	121	12	7			.967	16	*2-120	3.1
1909	Bos-N	30	87	4	15	1	0	0	3	8		.172	.242	.184	31	-7	1			.959	2	2-25	-0.1
Total	13	1671	5919	708	1618	215	68	18	673	607		.273	.348	.342	101	21	155			.957	19	*2-1478,S-166/O	9.0

■ CHARLIE RITTER
Ritter, Charles J. Deb: 9/21/1885

YEAR	TM/L	G	AB	R	H	2B	3B	HR	RBI	BB	SO	AVG	OBP	SLG	PRO+	BR/A	SB	CS	SBR	FA	FR	G/POS	TPR
1885	Buf-N	2	6	0	1	0	0	0	0	0	2	.167	.167	.167	8	-1				.813	0	/2-2	0.0

■ FLOYD RITTER
Ritter, Floyd Alexander b: 6/1/1870, Dorset, Ohio d: 2/7/43, Stevenson, Wash. BR/TR, 5'8″, 155 lbs. Deb: 6/4/1890

YEAR	TM/L	G	AB	R	H	2B	3B	HR	RBI	BB	SO	AVG	OBP	SLG	PRO+	BR/A	SB	CS	SBR	FA	FR	G/POS	TPR
1890	Tol-a	1	3	0	0	0	0	0		0		.000	.000	.000	-97	-1	0			.778	0	/C-1	-0.1

■ LEW RITTER
Ritter, Lewis Elmer "Old Dog" b: 9/7/1875, Liverpool, Pa. d: 5/27/52, Harrisburg, Pa. BR/TR, 5'9″, 150 lbs. Deb: 9/10/02

YEAR	TM/L	G	AB	R	H	2B	3B	HR	RBI	BB	SO	AVG	OBP	SLG	PRO+	BR/A	SB	CS	SBR	FA	FR	G/POS	TPR
1902	Bro-N	16	57	5	12	1	0	0	2	1		.211	.237	.228	43	-4	2			.973	3	C-16	0.1
1903	Bro-N	78	259	26	61	9	6	0	37	19		.236	.290	.317	75	-9	9			.940	-17	C-74/O-2	-1.8
1904	Bro-N	72	214	23	53	4	1	0	19	20		.248	.318	.276	86	-3	17			.966	6	C-57/2-5,3	1.0
1905	Bro-N	92	311	32	68	10	5	1	28	15		.219	.255	.293	68	-13	16			.951	-14	C-84/O-4,3	-2.0
1906	Bro-N	73	226	22	47	1	3	0	15	16		.208	.263	.239	61	-10	6			.978	-8	C-53/O-9,13	-1.6
1907	Bro-N	93	271	15	55	6	1	0	17	18		.203	.255	.232	57	-14	5			.969	-1	C-89	-0.8
1908	Bro-N	38	99	6	19	2	1	0	2	7		.192	.245	.232	55	-5	0			.961	-3	C-37	-0.7
Total	7	462	1437	129	315	33	17	1	120	96		.219	.271	.268	67	-58	55			.960	-35	C-410/O-15,321	-5.8

■ WHITEY RITTERSON
Ritterson, Edward West b: 4/26/1855, Philadelphia, Pa. d: 7/28/17, Sellersville, Pa. BR/TR, 5'8″, Deb: 5/3/1876

YEAR	TM/L	G	AB	R	H	2B	3B	HR	RBI	BB	SO	AVG	OBP	SLG	PRO+	BR/A	SB	CS	SBR	FA	FR	G/POS	TPR
1876	Phi-N	16	52	8	13	3	0	0	4	0	2	.250	.250	.308	86	-1				.671	-8	C-14/O-4,3	-0.7

■ JIM RITZ
Ritz, James L. b: 1874, Pittsburgh, Pa. d: 11/10/1896, Pittsburgh, Pa. Deb: 7/20/1894

YEAR	TM/L	G	AB	R	H	2B	3B	HR	RBI	BB	SO	AVG	OBP	SLG	PRO+	BR/A	SB	CS	SBR	FA	FR	G/POS	TPR
1894	Pit-N	1	4	1	0	0	0	0	0	0	0	.000	.200	.000	-49	-1	1			.750	-0	/3-1	-0.1

■ GERMAN RIVERA
Rivera, German (Diaz) b: 7/6/60, Santurce, P.R. BR/TR, 6'2″, 195 lbs. Deb: 9/2/83

YEAR	TM/L	G	AB	R	H	2B	3B	HR	RBI	BB	SO	AVG	OBP	SLG	PRO+	BR/A	SB	CS	SBR	FA	FR	G/POS	TPR
1983	LA-N	13	17	1	6	1	0	0	0	2	2	.353	.421	.412	132	1	0	1	-1	.929	2	/3-8	0.2
1984	LA-N	94	227	20	59	12	2	2	17	21	30	.260	.325	.357	92	-2	1	0	0	.937	16	3-90	1.4
1985	Hou-N	13	36	3	7	2	1	0	2	4	8	.194	.275	.306	64	-2	0	0	0	.941	3	3-11	0.1
Total	3	120	280	24	72	15	3	2	19	27	40	.257	.325	.354	91	-3	1	1	-0	.937	20	3-109	1.7

■ BOMBO RIVERA
Rivera, Jesus Manuel (Torres) b: 8/2/52, Ponce, P.R. BR/TR, 5'10″, 187 lbs. Deb: 4/17/75

YEAR	TM/L	G	AB	R	H	2B	3B	HR	RBI	BB	SO	AVG	OBP	SLG	PRO+	BR/A	SB	CS	SBR	FA	FR	G/POS	TPR
1975	Mon-N	5	9	1	1	0	0	0	0	2	3	.111	.273	.111	9	-1	0	0	0	.889	-1	/O-5	-0.2
1976	Mon-N	68	185	22	51	11	4	2	19	13	32	.276	.323	.411	103	0	1	0	0	.950	-0	O-56	-0.1
1978	Min-A	101	251	35	68	8	2	3	23	35	47	.271	.365	.355	101	2	5	3	-0	.982	9	O-94/D-1	-1.1
1979	Min-A	112	263	37	74	13	5	2	31	17	40	.281	.325	.392	89	-4	5	5	-2	.989	-4	*O-105	-1.3
1980	Min-A	44	113	13	25	7	0	3	10	4	20	.221	.248	.363	61	-6	0	0	0	.922	-4	O-37/D-1	-1.2
1982	KC-A	5	10	1	1	0	0	0	0	0	2	.100	.100	.100	-45	-2	0	0	0	1.000	-1	/O-3	-0.3
Total	6	335	831	109	220	39	11	10	83	71	144	.265	.324	.374	90	-12	11	8	-2	.970	-19	O-300/D-2	-4.2

■ LUIS RIVERA
Rivera, Luis Antonio (Pedraza) b: 1/3/64, Cidra, P.R. BR/TR, 5'9″, 170 lbs. Deb: 8/3/86

YEAR	TM/L	G	AB	R	H	2B	3B	HR	RBI	BB	SO	AVG	OBP	SLG	PRO+	BR/A	SB	CS	SBR	FA	FR	G/POS	TPR
1986	Mon-N	55	166	20	34	11	1	0	13	17	33	.205	.286	.283	58	-9	1	1	-0	.953	-9	S-55	-1.5
1987	Mon-N	18	32	0	5	2	0	0	1	1	8	.156	.182	.219	5	-4	0	0	0	.923	2	S-15	-0.2
1988	Mon-N	123	371	35	83	17	3	4	30	24	69	.224	.273	.318	66	-16	3	4	-2	.962	-6	*S-116	-1.6
1989	Bos-A	93	323	35	83	17	1	5	29	20	60	.257	.302	.362	81	-4	2	1	-0	.958	-3	S-90/2-1,D	-0.6
1990	*Bos-A	118	346	38	78	20	0	7	45	25	58	.225	.280	.344	70	-14	4	4	-1	.965	11	*S-112/2-3,3	0.4
1991	Bos-A	129	414	64	107	22	3	8	40	35	86	.258	.321	.384	90	-6	4	4	-1	.959	3	*S-129	0.6
1992	Bos-A	102	288	17	62	11	0	0	29	26	56	.215	.287	.260	51	-18	4	3	-1	.966	14	S-93/2-1,30D	0.4
1993	Bos-A	62	130	13	27	8	1	1	7	11	36	.208	.275	.308	53	-9	2	1	-1	.969	12	S-27,S-27/3D	0.4
1994	NY-N	32	43	11	12	2	1	3	5	4	14	.279	.367	.581	141	3	0	1	-1	.971	5	S-11/2-5	0.7
Total	9	732	2113	233	491	110	11	28	199	163	420	.232	.292	.335	71	-84	19	21	-7	.961	29	S-648/2-37,D30	-1.7

■ JIM RIVERA
Rivera, Manuel Joseph "Jungle Jim" b: 7/22/22, New York, N.Y. BL/TL, 6', 196 lbs. Deb: 4/15/52

YEAR	TM/L	G	AB	R	H	2B	3B	HR	RBI	BB	SO	AVG	OBP	SLG	PRO+	BR/A	SB	CS	SBR	FA	FR	G/POS	TPR
1952	StL-A	97	336	45	86	13	6	4	30	29	59	.256	.319	.366	88	-6	8	7	-2	.976	9	O-88	-0.3

YEAR	TM/L	G	AB	R	H	2B	3B	HR	RBI	BB	SO	AVG	OBP	SLG	PRO+	BR/A	SB	CS	SBR	FA	FR	G/POS	TPR
	Chi-A	53	201	27	50	7	3	3	18	21	27	.249	.320	.358	88	-4	13	2	3	.988	4	O-53	0.1
	Yr	150	537	72	136	20	9	7	48	50	86	.253	.319	.363	88	-10	21	9	1	.980	12	*O-141	-0.2
1953	Chi-A	156	567	79	147	26	**16**	11	78	53	70	.259	.329	.420	98	-3	22	15	-2	.976	-1	*O-156	-1.2
1954	Chi-A	145	490	62	140	16	8	13	61	49	68	.286	.358	.431	111	7	18	10	-1	.959	-17	*O-143	-1.6
1955	Chi-A	147	454	71	120	24	4	10	52	62	59	.264	.354	.401	100	0	**25**	16	-2	.981	2	*O-143	-0.6
1956	Chi-A	139	491	76	125	23	5	12	66	49	75	.255	.326	.395	88	-9	20	9	1	.976	1	*O-134	-1.4
1957	Chi-A	125	402	51	103	21	6	14	52	40	80	.256	.328	.443	108	4	18	2	**4**	.974	-7	O-86,1-31	-0.6
1958	Chi-A	116	276	37	62	8	4	9	35	24	49	.225	.289	.380	84	-7	21	3	5	.994	-3	O-99	-1.0
1959	*Chi-A	80	177	18	39	9	4	4	19	11	19	.220	.270	.384	78	-6	5	3	-0	.976	-8	O-69	-1.6
1960	Chi-A	48	17	17	5	0	0	1	1	3	3	.294	.400	.471	136	1	4	0	1	1.000	-6	O-24	-0.4
1961	Chi-A	1	0	0	0	0	0	0	0	0	0	—	—	—	—	0	0	1	-1	.000	0	H	-0.1
	KC-A	64	141	20	34	8	0	2	10	24	14	.241	.352	.340	84	-3	6	2	1	.981	-9	O-43	-1.3
	Yr	65	141	20	34	8	0	2	10	24	14	.241	.352	.340	84	-3	6	3	0	.981	-9	O-43	-1.4
Total	10	1171	3552	503	911	155	56	83	422	365	523	.256	.330	.402	96	-25	160	70	6	.977	-36	*O-1038/1-31	-10.0

■ MICKEY RIVERS

Rivers, John Milton b: 10/31/48, Miami, Fla.   BL/TL, 5'10", 165 lbs.   Deb: 8/4/70

YEAR	TM/L	G	AB	R	H	2B	3B	HR	RBI	BB	SO	AVG	OBP	SLG	PRO+	BR/A	SB	CS	SBR	FA	FR	G/POS	TPR
1970	Cal-A	17	25	6	8	2	0	0	3	3	5	.320	.414	.400	130	1	1	0	0	1.000	0	/O-5	0.1
1971	Cal-A	79	268	31	71	12	2	1	12	19	38	.265	.316	.336	91	-4	13	1	3	.976	-3	O-76	-0.7
1972	Cal-A	58	159	18	34	6	2	0	7	8	26	.214	.256	.277	62	-8	4	3	-1	.981	-1	O-48	-1.3
1973	Cal-A	30	129	26	45	6	4	0	16	8	11	.349	.391	.457	150	8	8	3	1	.909	-4	O-29	0.4
1974	Cal-A	118	466	69	133	19	**11**	3	31	39	47	.285	.342	.393	118	10	30	13	1	.994	10	*O-116	1.7
1975	Cal-A	155	616	70	175	17	**13**	1	53	43	42	.284	.333	.359	103	1	**70**	14	**13**	.977	11	*O-152/D-1	1.9
1976	*NY-A★	137	590	95	184	31	8	8	67	13	51	.312	.330	.432	123	14	43	7	9	.986	9	*O-136	2.8
1977	*NY-A	138	565	79	184	18	5	12	69	18	45	.326	.351	.439	115	11	22	14	-2	.982	13	*O-136/D-1	1.6
1978	*NY-A	141	559	78	148	25	8	11	48	29	51	.265	.305	.397	98	-3	25	5	5	.980	10	*O-138	0.5
1979	NY-A	74	286	37	82	18	5	3	25	13	21	.287	.320	.416	99	-1	3	7	-3	.974	-6	O-69	-1.3
	Tex-A	58	247	35	74	9	3	6	25	9	18	.300	.327	.433	104	1	7	2	1	.981	3	O-57	0.2
	Yr	132	533	72	156	27	8	9	50	22	39	.293	.323	.424	101	-0	10	9	-2	.978	-3	*O-126	-1.1
1980	Tex-A	147	630	96	210	32	6	7	60	20	34	.333	.355	.437	119	15	18	7	1	.978	10	*O-141/D-4	2.0
1981	Tex-A	99	399	62	114	21	2	3	26	24	31	.286	.328	.371	107	3	9	5	-0	.996	4	O-97	0.3
1982	Tex-A	19	68	6	16	1	1	1	4	0	7	.235	.235	.324	54	-4	0	0	0	.000	0	D-16	-0.5
1983	Tex-A	96	309	37	88	17	0	1	20	11	21	.285	.312	.350	83	-7	9	4	0	.980	-3	D-53,O-23	-0.9
1984	Tex-A	102	313	40	94	13	1	4	33	9	23	.300	.320	.387	91	-4	5	5	-2	1.000	0	D-48,O-30	-0.8
Total	15	1468	5629	785	1660	247	71	61	499	266	471	.295	.329	.397	106	32	267	90	26	.982	57	*O-1253,D-123	6.0

■ JOHNNY RIZZO

Rizzo, John Costa b: 7/30/12, Houston, Tex.   d: 12/4/77, Houston, Tex.   BR/TR, 6', 190 lbs.   Deb: 4/19/38

YEAR	TM/L	G	AB	R	H	2B	3B	HR	RBI	BB	SO	AVG	OBP	SLG	PRO+	BR/A	SB	CS	SBR	FA	FR	G/POS	TPR
1938	Pit-N	143	555	97	167	31	9	23	111	54	61	.301	.368	.514	139	28	1			.951	-8	*O-140	1.6
1939	Pit-N	94	330	49	86	23	3	6	55	42	27	.261	.349	.403	103	2	0			.974	-0	O-86	-0.2
1940	Pit-N	9	28	1	5	1	0	0	2	5	5	.179	.324	.214	51	-2	0			.818	-2	/O-7	-0.4
	Cin-N	31	110	17	31	6	0	4	17	14	14	.282	.363	.445	121	3	1			.974	5	O-30	0.6
	Phi-N	103	367	53	107	12	2	20	53	37	31	.292	.358	.499	139	19	2			.968	6	O-91/3-7	2.0
	Yr	143	505	71	143	19	2	24	72	56	50	.283	.357	.471	130	20	3			.964	9	*O-128/3-7	2.2
1941	Phi-N	99	235	20	51	9	2	4	24	24	34	.217	.295	.323	77	-7	1			.968	-0	O-62/3-2	-1.1
1942	Bro-N	78	217	31	50	8	0	4	27	24	25	.230	.307	.323	83	-5	2			.977	-2	O-70	-1.0
Total	5	557	1842	268	497	90	16	61	289	200	197	.270	.345	.435	116	38	7			.964	-1	O-486/3-9	1.5

■ PHIL RIZZUTO

Rizzuto, Philip Francis "Scooter" (b: Fiero Francis Rizzuto) b: 9/25/17, Brooklyn, N.Y.   BR/TR, 5'6", 160 lbs.   Deb: 4/15/41   H

YEAR	TM/L	G	AB	R	H	2B	3B	HR	RBI	BB	SO	AVG	OBP	SLG	PRO+	BR/A	SB	CS	SBR	FA	FR	G/POS	TPR
1941	*NY-A	133	515	65	158	20	9	3	46	27	36	.307	.343	.398	97	-3	14	5	1	.957	16	*S-128	2.2
1942	*NY-A☆	144	553	79	157	24	7	4	68	44	40	.284	.343	.374	104	2	22	6	3	.962	19	*S-144	4.0
1946	NY-A	126	471	53	121	17	1	2	38	34	39	.257	.315	.310	74	-16	14	7	0	.961	13	*S-125	0.5
1947	*NY-A	153	549	78	150	26	9	2	60	57	31	.273	.350	.364	100	0	11	6	-0	.969	16	*S-151	2.5
1948	NY-A	128	464	65	117	13	2	6	50	60	24	.252	.340	.328	79	-13	6	5	-1	.973	-11	*S-128	-1.8
1949	*NY-A	153	614	110	169	22	7	5	65	72	34	.275	.352	.358	88	-10	18	6	2	**.971**	3	*S-152	0.5
1950	*NY-A★	155	617	125	200	36	7	7	66	92	39	.324	.418	.439	123	25	12	8	-1	**.982**	9	*S-155	**4.1**
1951	*NY-A	144	540	87	148	21	6	2	43	58	27	.274	.350	.346	92	-5	18	3	**4**	.968	5	*S-154	1.5
1952	*NY-A★	152	578	89	147	24	10	2	43	67	42	.254	.337	.341	95	-4	17	6	2	.976	19	*S-152	2.8
1953	*NY-A★	134	413	54	112	21	3	2	54	71	39	.271	.383	.351	103	5	4	3	-1	.963	-3	*S-133	1.1
1954	NY-A	127	307	47	60	11	0	2	15	41	23	.195	.292	.251	51	-20	3	2	-0	.968	-1	*S-126/2-1	-1.3
1955	*NY-A	81	143	19	37	4	1	1	9	22	18	.259	.369	.322	88	-1	7	1	2	.957	-9	S-79/2-1	-0.5
1956	NY-A	31	52	6	12	0	0	0	6	6	6	.231	.310	.231	46	-4	3	0	1	.934	5	S-30	0.2
Total	13	1661	5816	877	1588	239	62	38	563	651	398	.273	.351	.355	93	-44	149	58	10	.968	86	*S-1647/2-2	15.8

■ MEL ROACH

Roach, Melvin Earl b: 1/25/33, Richmond, Va.   BR/TR, 6'1", 190 lbs.   Deb: 7/31/53

YEAR	TM/L	G	AB	R	H	2B	3B	HR	RBI	BB	SO	AVG	OBP	SLG	PRO+	BR/A	SB	CS	SBR	FA	FR	G/POS	TPR
1953	Mil-N	5	2	1	0	0	0	0	0	0	1	.000	.000	.000	-99	-1	0	0	0	.000	0	/2-1	-0.1
1954	Mil-N	3	4	0	0	0	0	0	0	0	1	.000	.000	.000	-99	-1	0	0	0	1.000	-0	/1-1	-0.1
1957	Mil-N	7	6	1	1	0	0	0	0	0	3	.167	.167	.167	-11	-1	0	0	0	1.000	0	/2-5	-0.1
1958	Mil-N	44	136	14	42	7	0	3	10	6	15	.309	.338	.426	110	1	0	0	0	.993	-2	2-27/O-7,1	0.2
1959	Mil-N	19	31	1	3	0	0	0	0	2	4	.097	.152	.097	-35	-6	0	0	0	.880	1	/2-8,O-4,3	-0.5
1960	Mil-N	48	140	12	42	12	0	3	18	6	19	.300	.333	.450	121	3	0	0	0	.975	-8	O-21,2-20/13	-0.4
1961	Mil-N	13	36	3	6	0	0	1	6	2	4	.167	.250	.250	35	-3	0	0	0	1.000	-0	/O-9,1-2	-0.6
	Chi-N	23	39	1	5	2	0	0	1	3	9	.128	.190	.179	-1	-6	0	0	0	.981	-1	/1-7,2-7	-0.7
	Yr	36	75	4	11	2	0	1	7	5	13	.147	.220	.213	16	-9	1	0	0	1.000	-3	/O-9,1-9,2	-1.3
1962	Phi-N	65	105	9	20	4	0	0	8	5	19	.190	.227	.229	23	-11	1	0	0	.951	-1	3-26/2-9,1O	-1.2
Total	8	227	499	42	119	25	0	7	43	24	75	.238	.278	.331	66	-24	1	0	0	.969	-12	/2-77,O-44,31	-3.5

■ MIKE ROACH

Roach, Michael Stephen b: 12/23/1873, New York, N.Y.   d: 11/12/16, New York, N.Y.   Deb: 8/10/1899

YEAR	TM/L	G	AB	R	H	2B	3B	HR	RBI	BB	SO	AVG	OBP	SLG	PRO+	BR/A	SB	CS	SBR	FA	FR	G/POS	TPR
1899	Was-N	24	78	7	17	1	0	0	7	3		.218	.265	.231	37	-7	3			.964	-5	C-20/1-3	-0.9

■ ROXEY ROACH

Roach, Wilbur Charles b: 11/28/1882, Anita, Pa.   d: 12/26/47, Bay City, Mich.   BR/TR, 5'11", 160 lbs.   Deb: 5/2/10

YEAR	TM/L	G	AB	R	H	2B	3B	HR	RBI	BB	SO	AVG	OBP	SLG	PRO+	BR/A	SB	CS	SBR	FA	FR	G/POS	TPR
1910	NY-A	70	220	27	47	9	2	0	20	29		.214	.313	.273	79	-5	15			.913	-7	S-58/O-9	-1.1
1911	NY-A	13	40	4	10	2	1	0	2	6		.250	.348	.350	89	-1	0			.891	-1	/S-8,2-5	-0.1
1912	Was-A	2	2	1	1	0	0	1	1	0		.500	.500	2.000	600	1	0			.500	-1	/S-2	0.0
1915	Buf-F	92	346	35	93	20	3	2	31	17	34	.269	.303	.361	76	-13	11			.959	15	S-92	1.0
Total	4	177	608	67	151	31	6	3	54	52	34	.248	.311	.334	80	-17	26			.938	7	S-160/O-9,2	-0.2

■ MIKE ROARKE

Roarke, Michael Thomas b: 11/8/30, West Warwick, R.I.   BR/TR, 6'2", 195 lbs.   Deb: 4/19/61   C

YEAR	TM/L	G	AB	R	H	2B	3B	HR	RBI	BB	SO	AVG	OBP	SLG	PRO+	BR/A	SB	CS	SBR	FA	FR	G/POS	TPR
1961	Det-A	86	229	21	51	6	1	2	22	20	31	.223	.285	.284	51	-16	0	0	0	.988	4	C-85	-0.9
1962	Det-A	56	136	11	29	4	1	4	14	13	17	.213	.287	.346	67	-6	0	0	0	.982	6	C-53	0.1
1963	Det-A	23	44	5	14	0	0	0	1	2	3	.318	.362	.318	89	-0	0	0	0	.986	1	C-16	0.1
1964	Det-A	29	82	4	19	1	0	2	7	10	10	.232	.315	.244	57	-4	0	0	0	.994	3	C-27	0.0
Total	4	194	491	41	113	11	2	6	44	45	61	.230	.297	.297	60	-27	0	0	0	.987	14	C-181	-0.7

■ FRED ROAT

Roat, Frederick R. b: 11/10/1867, Oregon, Ill.   d: 9/24/13, Oregon, Ill.   TR,   Deb: 5/10/1890

YEAR	TM/L	G	AB	R	H	2B	3B	HR	RBI	BB	SO	AVG	OBP	SLG	PRO+	BR/A	SB	CS	SBR	FA	FR	G/POS	TPR
1890	Pit-N	57	215	18	48	2	0	2	17	16	22	.223	.286	.260	67	-8	7			.847	2	3-44/1-9,O	-0.5

YEAR	TM/L	G	AB	R	H	2B	3B	HR	RBI	BB	SO	AVG	OBP	SLG	PRO+	BR/A	SB	CS	SBR	FA	FR	G/POS	TPR
1892	Chi-N	8	31	4	6	0	1	0	2	2	3	.194	.242	.258	51	-2	2			.897	-3	/2-8	-0.5
Total	2	65	246	22	54	2	1	2	19	18	25	.220	.281	.260	65	-10	9			.847	-1	/3-44,1-9,2O	-1.0

■ TOMMY ROBELLO
Robello, Thomas Vardasco "Tony" b: 2/9/13, San Leandro, Cal. BR/TR, 5'10.5", 175 lbs. Deb: 8/13/33

YEAR	TM/L	G	AB	R	H	2B	3B	HR	RBI	BB	SO	AVG	OBP	SLG	PRO+	BR/A	SB	CS	SBR	FA	FR	G/POS	TPR
1933	Cin-N	14	30	1	7	3	0	0	3	1	5	.233	.258	.333	69	-1	0			1.000	2	2-11/3-2	0.1
1934	Cin-N	2	2	0	0	0	0	0	0	0	1	.000	.000	.000	-99	-1	0			.000	0	H	-0.1
Total	2	16	32	1	7	3	0	0	3	1	6	.219	.242	.313	58	-2	0			1.000	2	/2-11,3-2	0.0

■ SKIPPY ROBERGE
Roberge, Joseph Albert Armand b: 5/19/17, Lowell, Mass. d: 6/7/93, Lowell, Mass. BR/TR, 5'11", 185 lbs. Deb: 7/18/41

YEAR	TM/L	G	AB	R	H	2B	3B	HR	RBI	BB	SO	AVG	OBP	SLG	PRO+	BR/A	SB	CS	SBR	FA	FR	G/POS	TPR
1941	Bos-N	55	167	12	36	6	0	0	15	9	18	.216	.256	.251	45	-12	0			.978	5	2-46/3-5,S	-0.5
1942	Bos-N	74	172	10	37	7	0	1	12	9	19	.215	.258	.273	57	-10	1			.977	8	2-29,3-27/S	0.0
1946	Bos-N	48	169	13	39	6	2	2	20	7	12	.231	.270	.325	68	-8	1			.973	2	3-48	-0.5
Total	3	177	508	35	112	19	2	3	47	25	49	.220	.261	.283	57	-30	2			.967	15	/3-80,2-75,S	-1.0

■ KEVIN ROBERSON
Roberson, Kevin Lynn b: 1/29/68, Decatur, Ill. BB/TR, 6'4", 210 lbs. Deb: 7/15/93

YEAR	TM/L	G	AB	R	H	2B	3B	HR	RBI	BB	SO	AVG	OBP	SLG	PRO+	BR/A	SB	CS	SBR	FA	FR	G/POS	TPR
1993	Chi-N	62	180	23	34	4	1	9	27	12	48	.189	.251	.372	65	-10	0	1	-1	.963	-6	O-51	-1.8
1994	Chi-N	44	55	8	12	4	0	4	9	2	14	.218	.271	.509	100	-0	0	0	0	.800	-2	/O-9	-0.2
Total	2	106	235	31	46	8	1	13	36	14	62	.196	.256	.404	74	-10	0	1	-1	.946	-8	/O-60	-2.0

■ RED ROBERTS
Roberts, Charles Emory b: 8/8/18, Carrollton, Ga. BR/TR, 6', 170 lbs. Deb: 9/3/43

YEAR	TM/L	G	AB	R	H	2B	3B	HR	RBI	BB	SO	AVG	OBP	SLG	PRO+	BR/A	SB	CS	SBR	FA	FR	G/POS	TPR
1943	Was-A	9	23	1	6	1	0	1	3	4	2	.261	.370	.435	140	1	0	0	0	.778	-5	/S-6,3-1	-0.3

■ SKIPPER ROBERTS
Roberts, Clarence Ashley b: 1/11/1888, Wardner, Idaho d: 12/24/63, Long Beach, Cal. BL/TR, 5'10.5", 175 lbs. Deb: 6/12/13

YEAR	TM/L	G	AB	R	H	2B	3B	HR	RBI	BB	SO	AVG	OBP	SLG	PRO+	BR/A	SB	CS	SBR	FA	FR	G/POS	TPR
1913	StL-N	26	41	4	6	2	0	0	3	3	13	.146	.205	.195	15	-5	1			.859	-2	C-16	-0.6
1914	Pit-F	33	55	7	12	2	1	0	4	1	11	.218	.246	.291	39	-5	2			.941	-1	C-14	-0.6
	Chi-F	4	3	0	1	0	0	0	1	1	1	.333	.500	.333	126	0	0			.000	0	H	0.0
	Pit-F	19	39	5	10	2	1	1	4	1	8	.256	.293	.436	88	-1	1			.923	-4	C-9,O-1	-0.4
	Yr	56	97	12	23	4	2	1	9	3	20	.237	.275	.351	62	-6	3			.935	-5	C-23/O-1	-1.0
Total	2	82	138	16	29	6	2	1	12	6	33	.210	.253	.304	49	-11	4			.906	-7	/C-39,O-1	-1.6

■ CURT ROBERTS
Roberts, Curtis Benjamin b: 8/16/29, Pineland, Tex. d: 11/14/69, Oakland, Cal. BR/TR, 5'8", 165 lbs. Deb: 4/13/54

YEAR	TM/L	G	AB	R	H	2B	3B	HR	RBI	BB	SO	AVG	OBP	SLG	PRO+	BR/A	SB	CS	SBR	FA	FR	G/POS	TPR
1954	Pit-N	134	496	47	115	18	7	1	36	55	49	.232	.311	.302	62	-27	6	3	0	.969	2	*2-131	-1.6
1955	Pit-N	6	17	1	2	1	0	0	0	2	1	.118	.211	.176	4	-2	0	0	0	.913	-1	/2-6	-0.3
1956	Pit-N	31	62	6	11	5	2	0	4	5	12	.177	.239	.323	50	-5	1	0	0	.988	-2	2-27	-0.4
Total	3	171	575	54	128	24	9	1	40	62	62	.223	.300	.301	59	-34	7	3	0	.969	2	2-164	-2.3

■ DAVE ROBERTS
Roberts, David Leonard b: 6/30/33, Panama City, Pan. BL/TL, 6', 172 lbs. Deb: 9/5/62

YEAR	TM/L	G	AB	R	H	2B	3B	HR	RBI	BB	SO	AVG	OBP	SLG	PRO+	BR/A	SB	CS	SBR	FA	FR	G/POS	TPR
1962	Hou-N	16	53	3	13	3	0	1	10	8	12	.245	.355	.358	99	0	0	0	0	1.000	-1	O-12/1-6	-0.2
1964	Hou-N	61	125	9	23	4	1	1	7	14	28	.184	.271	.256	52	-8	0	1	-1	.983	4	1-34/O-4	-0.6
1966	Pit-N	14	16	3	2	1	0	0	0	0	7	.125	.125	.188	-15	-2	0	0	0	.950	0	/1-2	-0.2
Total	3	91	194	15	38	8	1	2	17	22	43	.196	.284	.278	60	-10	0	1	-1	.983	3	/1-42,O-16	-1.0

■ DAVE ROBERTS
Roberts, David Wayne b: 2/17/51, Lebanon, Ore. BR/TR, 6'3", 215 lbs. Deb: 6/7/72 C

YEAR	TM/L	G	AB	R	H	2B	3B	HR	RBI	BB	SO	AVG	OBP	SLG	PRO+	BR/A	SB	CS	SBR	FA	FR	G/POS	TPR
1972	SD-N	100	418	38	102	17	0	5	33	18	64	.244	.275	.321	74	-16	7	2	1	.931	-6	3-84,2-20/SC	-2.3
1973	SD-N	127	479	56	137	20	3	21	64	17	83	.286	.312	.472	124	12	11	2	2	.942	3	*3-111,2-12	1.7
1974	SD-N	113	318	26	53	10	1	5	18	32	69	.167	.247	.252	41	-26	2	0	1	.955	-4	*3-103/S-3,O	-3.1
1975	SD-N	33	113	7	32	2	0	2	12	19	19	.283	.367	.354	107	3	3	1	0	.925	-4	3-30/2-5	-0.2
1977	SD-N	82	186	15	41	14	1	1	23	11	32	.220	.268	.323	64	-10	2	4	0	.982	-4	C-63/2-2,3S	-1.3
1978	SD-N	54	97	7	21	4	1	1	7	12	25	.216	.309	.309	79	-3	0	0	0	.980	-1	C-41/1-8,O	-0.4
1979	Tex-A	44	84	12	22	2	1	3	14	7	17	.262	.319	.417	98	-0	1	0	0	.980	1	C-14,O-11/213	0.1
1980	Tex-A	101	235	27	56	4	0	10	30	13	38	.238	.281	.383	83	-6	0	1	-1	.930	-21	3-37,S-33,C/O12	-2.6
1981	*Hou-N	27	54	4	13	3	0	1	5	3	6	.241	.281	.352	83	-1	1	0	0	.958	0	1-10/3-7,2C	-0.2
1982	Phi-N	28	33	2	6	1	0	0	2	2	8	.182	.229	.212	23	-3	0	1	-1	.818	1	3-11,C-10/2	-0.3
Total	10	709	2017	194	483	77	7	49	208	128	361	.239	.288	.357	83	-53	27	8	3	.939	-36	3-386,C-152/2S10	-8.6

■ BIP ROBERTS
Roberts, Leon Joseph b: 10/27/63, Berkeley, Cal. BB/TR, 5'7", 160 lbs. Deb: 4/7/86

YEAR	TM/L	G	AB	R	H	2B	3B	HR	RBI	BB	SO	AVG	OBP	SLG	PRO+	BR/A	SB	CS	SBR	FA	FR	G/POS	TPR
1986	SD-N	101	241	34	61	5	2	1	12	14	29	.253	.294	.303	66	-11	14	12	-3	.971	4	2-87	-0.8
1988	SD-N	5	9	1	3	0	0	0	0	1	2	.333	.400	.333	115	0	0	2	-1	.500	-1	/3-2,2-1	-0.2
1989	SD-N	117	329	81	99	15	8	3	25	49	45	.301	.393	.422	133	16	21	11	-0	.976	-8	O-54,3-37,S/2	0.8
1990	SD-N	149	556	104	172	36	3	9	44	55	65	.309	.378	.433	122	17	46	12	7	.982	-1	O-75,3-56,S/2	2.4
1991	SD-N	117	424	66	119	13	3	3	32	37	71	.281	.344	.347	92	-4	26	11	1	.978	-7	2-68,O-46	-0.9
1992	Cin-N★	147	532	92	172	34	6	4	45	62	54	.323	.396	.432	131	24	44	16	4	.993	-14	O-79,2-42,3	1.4
1993	Cin-N	83	292	46	70	13	0	1	18	38	46	.240	.333	.295	70	-11	26	6	4	.984	-9	2-64,O-11/3S	-1.5
1994	SD-N	105	403	52	129	15	5	2	31	39	57	.320	.384	.397	105	5	21	7	2	.976	-15	2-90,O-20	-0.6
Total	8	824	2786	476	825	131	27	23	207	295	369	.296	.367	.387	107	35	198	77	13	.977	-51	2-369,O-285,3/S	0.6

■ LEON ROBERTS
Roberts, Leon Kauffman b: 1/22/51, Vicksburg, Mich. BR/TR, 6'3", 200 lbs. Deb: 9/3/74

YEAR	TM/L	G	AB	R	H	2B	3B	HR	RBI	BB	SO	AVG	OBP	SLG	PRO+	BR/A	SB	CS	SBR	FA	FR	G/POS	TPR
1974	Det-A	17	63	5	17	3	2	0	7	3	10	.270	.303	.381	92	-1	0	2	-1	.926	-3	O-17	-0.6
1975	Det-A	129	447	51	115	17	5	10	38	36	94	.257	.318	.385	94	-4	3	7	-3	.982	8	*O-127/D-1	-0.5
1976	Hou-N	87	235	31	68	11	2	7	33	19	43	.289	.350	.443	136	10	1	0	0	.980	-4	O-60	0.5
1977	Hou-N	19	27	1	2	0	0	0	2	1	8	.074	.107	.074	-55	-6	0	0	0	1.000	-2	/O-9	-0.8
1978	Sea-A	134	472	78	142	21	7	22	92	41	52	.301	.367	.515	146	28	3	6	0	.975	10	*O-128/D-2	3.3
1979	Sea-A	140	450	61	122	24	6	15	54	56	64	.271	.354	.451	114	9	3	3	-1	.983	4	*O-136	0.7
1980	Sea-A	119	374	48	94	18	3	10	33	43	59	.251	.330	.396	97	-1	8	4	0	.984	4	*O-104/D-4	-0.2
1981	Tex-A	72	233	26	65	17	2	4	31	25	38	.279	.351	.421	128	8	3	4	-2	.992	-4	O-71	0.0
1982	Tex-A	31	73	7	17	3	0	1	6	4	16	.233	.282	.315	67	-2	0	0	0	1.000	-5	O-28/D-1	-0.9
	Tor-A	40	105	6	24	4	0	1	5	7	16	.229	.277	.295	52	-7	1	1	0	1.000	-2	D-21,O-16	-1.0
	Yr	71	178	13	41	7	0	2	11	11	30	.230	.279	.303	58	-10	1	1	-0	1.000	-7	O-44,D-22	-1.9
1983	KC-A	84	213	24	55	7	0	8	24	17	27	.258	.316	.404	96	-1	1	1	-0	.979	-6	O-76/D-1	-1.0
1984	KC-A	29	45	4	10	1	1	0	6	4	10	.222	.300	.289	63	-2	0	0	0	1.000	-3	O-16/P-1,D	-0.5
Total	11	901	2737	342	731	126	28	78	328	256	428	.267	.335	.419	108	29	26	25	-7	.982	-3	O-788/D-33,P	-1.0

■ JIM ROBERTSON
Robertson, Alfred James b: 1/29/28, Chicago, Ill. BR/TR, 5'9", 183 lbs. Deb: 4/15/54

YEAR	TM/L	G	AB	R	H	2B	3B	HR	RBI	BB	SO	AVG	OBP	SLG	PRO+	BR/A	SB	CS	SBR	FA	FR	G/POS	TPR
1954	Phi-A	63	147	9	27	8	0	0	8	23	25	.184	.298	.238	48	-10	0	0	0	.974	-2	C-50	-1.0
1955	KC-A	6	8	1	2	0	0	0	0	1	2	.250	.333	.250	58	-0	0	0	0	1.000	0	/C-4	0.0
Total	2	69	155	10	29	8	0	0	8	24	27	.187	.300	.239	49	-10	0	0	0	.975	-2	/C-54	-1.0

■ ANDRE ROBERTSON
Robertson, Andre Levett b: 10/2/57, Orange, Tex. BR/TR, 5'10", 160 lbs. Deb: 9/3/81

YEAR	TM/L	G	AB	R	H	2B	3B	HR	RBI	BB	SO	AVG	OBP	SLG	PRO+	BR/A	SB	CS	SBR	FA	FR	G/POS	TPR
1981	*NY-A	10	19	1	5	1	0	0	0	3	3	.263	.263	.316	67	-1	1	1	-0	1.000	4	/S-8,2-3	0.3
1982	NY-A	44	118	16	26	5	0	2	9	8	19	.220	.270	.314	61	-6	2	3	0	.966	8	S-27,2-15/3	0.4
1983	NY-A	98	322	37	80	16	3	1	22	8	54	.248	.273	.326	67	-15	2	4	-2	.960	22	S-78,2-29	1.2
1984	NY-A	52	140	10	30	5	1	0	6	4	20	.214	.236	.264	40	-12	1	1	-1	.930	11	S-49/2-6	0.2
1985	NY-A	50	125	16	41	5	0	2	17	6	24	.328	.364	.416	116	3	1	2	-1	.867	-6	3-33,S-14/2	-0.4
Total	5	254	724	80	182	32	4	5	54	26	120	.251	.281	.327	69	-31	4	8	-4	.953	38	S-176/2-55,3	1.7

YEAR	TM/L	G	AB	R	H	2B	3B	HR	RBI	BB	SO	AVG	OBP	SLG	PRO+	BR/A	SB	CS	SBR	FA	FR	G/POS	TPR

■ DARYL ROBERTSON
Robertson, Daryl Berdene b: 1/5/36, Cripple Creek, Colo BR/TR, 6', 184 lbs. Deb: 5/4/62

| 1962 | Chi-N | 9 | 19 | 0 | 2 | 0 | 0 | 0 | 2 | 2 | 10 | .105 | .190 | .105 | -18 | -3 | 0 | 0 | 0 | 1.000 | -1 | /S-6,3-1 | -0.4 |

■ DAVE ROBERTSON
Robertson, Davis Aydelotte b: 9/25/1889, Portsmouth, Va. d: 11/5/70, Virginia Beach, Va. BL/TL, 6', 186 lbs. Deb: 6/5/12

1912	NY-N	3	2	0	1	0	0	0	1	0	1	.500	.500	.500	169	0	1			1.000	-1	/1-1,O-1	0.0
1914	NY-N	82	256	25	68	12	3	2	32	10	26	.266	.299	.359	99	-2	9			.950	-2	O-71	-0.7
1915	NY-N	141	544	72	160	17	10	3	58	22	52	.294	.326	.379	120	11	22	10	1	.956	-1	*O-138	0.4
1916	NY-N	150	587	88	180	18	8	12	69	14	56	.307	.326	.426	137	22	21	17	-4	.960	5	*O-144	1.7
1917	*NY-N	142	532	64	138	16	9	12	54	10	47	.259	.276	.391	107	1	17			.942	1	*O-140	-0.7
1919	NY-N	1	0	0	0	0	0	0	0	0	0	—	—	—	—	0	0			.000	0	R	0.0
	Chi-N	27	96	8	20	2	0	1	10	1	10	.208	.224	.260	45	-6	3			.932	-2	O-25	-1.2
	Yr	28	96	8	20	2	0	1	10	1	10	.208	.224	.260	45	-6	3			.932	-2	O-25	-1.2
1920	Chi-N	134	500	68	150	29	11	10	75	40	44	.300	.353	.462	130	18	17	23	-9	.968	-9	*O-134	-0.9
1921	Chi-N	22	36	7	8	3	0	0	14	1	3	.222	.243	.306	44	-3	0	2	-1	1.000	-1	/O-7	-0.7
	Pit-N	60	230	29	74	18	3	6	48	12	16	.322	.361	.504	123	7	4	5	-2	.960	-4	O-58	-0.3
	Yr	82	266	36	82	21	3	6	62	13	19	.308	.345	.477	113	4	4	7	-3	.962	-6	O-65	-1.0
1922	NY-N	42	47	5	13	2	0	1	3	3	7	.277	.320	.383	80	-1	0	0		.909	-2	/O-8	-0.3
Total	9	804	2830	366	812	117	44	47	364	113	262	.287	.318	.409	117	46	94	57		.955	-16	O-726/1-1	-2.7

■ DON ROBERTSON
Robertson, Donald Alexander b: 10/15/30, Harvey, Ill. BL/TL, 5'10", 180 lbs. Deb: 4/13/54

| 1954 | Chi-N | 14 | 6 | 2 | 0 | 0 | 0 | 0 | 0 | 0 | 2 | .000 | .000 | .000 | -99 | -2 | 0 | 0 | 0 | 1.000 | -2 | /O-6 | -0.4 |

■ GENE ROBERTSON
Robertson, Eugene Edward b: 12/25/1898, St.Louis, Mo. d: 10/21/81, Fallon, Nev. BL/TR, 5'7", 152 lbs. Deb: 7/4/19

1919	StL-A	5	7	1	1	0	0	0	0	0	0	.143	.250	.143	11	-1	0			.750	-2	/S-2	-0.2
1922	StL-A	18	27	2	8	2	1	0	1	1	1	.296	.321	.444	95	-0	1	0	0	.875	1	/3-7,S-6,2	0.1
1923	StL-A	78	251	36	62	10	1	0	17	21	7	.247	.310	.295	57	-16	4	2	0	.935	-15	3-74/2-1	-2.4
1924	StL-A	121	439	70	140	25	4	4	52	36	14	.319	.373	.421	99	-1	3	5	-2	.958	-11	*3-111/2-2	-0.5
1925	StL-A	154	582	97	158	26	5	14	76	81	30	.271	.364	.405	90	-8	10	7	-1	.939	-2	*3-154/S-1	-0.1
1926	StL-A	78	247	23	62	12	6	1	19	17	10	.251	.302	.360	69	-12	5	1	1	.924	-5	3-55,S-10/2	-1.1
1928	*NY-A	83	251	29	73	9	0	1	36	14	6	.291	.328	.339	78	-8	2	4	-2	.926	-2	3-70/2-3	-1.4
1929	NY-A	90	309	45	92	15	6	0	35	28	6	.298	.358	.385	98	-1	3	3	-1	.966	-11	3-77	-1.0
	Bos-N	8	28	1	8	0	0	0	6	1	0	.286	.310	.286	51	-2	1			.875	-2	/3-6,S-1	-0.3
1930	Bos-N	21	59	7	11	1	0	0	7	5	3	.186	.250	.203	12	-8	0			.949	-2	3-17	-0.9
Total	9	656	2200	311	615	100	23	20	249	205	79	.280	.344	.373	83	-58	29	22		.941	-56	3-571/S-20,2	-7.8

■ BOB ROBERTSON
Robertson, Robert Eugene b: 10/2/46, Frostburg, Md. BR/TR, 6'1", 210 lbs. Deb: 9/18/67

1967	Pit-N	9	35	4	6	0	0	3	2	3	12	.171	.237	.343	64	-2	0	0	0	.990	-0	/1-9	-0.3
1969	Pit-N	32	96	7	20	4	1	1	9	8	30	.208	.269	.302	61	-5	1	0	0	.996	1	1-26	-0.6
1970	*Pit-N	117	390	69	112	19	4	27	82	51	98	.287	.372	.564	150	27	4	1	1	.995	3	1-99/3-5,O	2.1
1971	*Pit-N	131	469	65	127	18	2	26	72	60	101	.271	.358	.484	137	23	1	2	-1	.993	15	*1-126	2.6
1972	*Pit-N	115	306	25	59	11	0	12	41	41	84	.193	.294	.346	83	-7	1	1	-0	.993	9	1-89,O-23,3	-0.4
1973	Pit-N	119	397	43	95	16	0	14	40	55	77	.239	.333	.385	101	1	0	4	-2	.995	5	*1-107	-0.5
1974	*Pit-N	91	236	25	54	11	0	16	48	33	48	.229	.323	.479	127	7	0	0	0	.991	-1	1-63	0.3
1975	*Pit-N	75	124	17	34	4	0	6	18	23	25	.274	.396	.452	136	7	0	0	0	.996	1	1-27	0.7
1976	Pit-N	61	129	10	28	5	1	2	25	16	23	.217	.303	.318	76	-4	0	1	-1	.996	-0	1-29	-0.7
1978	Sea-A	64	174	17	40	5	2	8	28	24	39	.230	.327	.420	109	2	0	0	0	1.000	-1	D-29,1-18	-0.1
1979	Tor-A	15	29	1	3	0	0	0	1	3	9	.103	.188	.207	6	-4	0	0	0	1.000	-1	/1-9	-0.3
Total	11	829	2385	283	578	93	10	115	368	317	546	.242	.334	.434	115	45	7	9	-3	.994	33	1-602/D-29,O3	2.8

■ SHERRY ROBERTSON
Robertson, Sherrard Alexander b: 1/1/19, Montreal, Que., Can. d: 10/23/70, Houghton, S.Dak. BL/TR, 6', 180 lbs. Deb: 9/8/40 C

1940	Was-A	10	33	4	7	0	1	0	0	5	6	.212	.316	.273	58	-2	0	0	0	.940	1	S-10	0.0
1941	Was-A	1	3	0	0	0	0	0	0	0	3	.000	.000	.000	-99	-1	0	0	0	.750	0	/3-1	-0.1
1943	Was-A	59	120	22	26	4	1	3	14	17	19	.217	.319	.342	97	-0	0	2	-1	.897	-4	3-27/S-1	-0.6
1946	Was-A	74	230	30	46	6	3	6	19	30	42	.200	.292	.330	78	-7	6	2	1	.902	-6	3-38,2-14,S/O	-1.1
1947	Was-A	95	266	25	62	9	3	1	23	32	52	.233	.318	.301	74	-9	4	5	-2	.949	0	O-55,3-10/2	-1.4
1948	Was-A	71	187	19	46	11	3	2	22	24	26	.246	.335	.369	90	-3	8	0	2	.939	-1	O-51	-0.4
1949	Was-A	110	374	59	94	17	3	11	42	42	35	.251	.329	.401	95	-5	10	3	1	.947	-0	2-71,3-19,O	-0.9
1950	Was-A	71	123	19	32	3	3	2	16	22	18	.260	.372	.382	98	0	1	1	-0	.952	-9	O-14,2-12/3	-0.8
1951	Was-A	62	111	14	21	2	1	1	10	9	22	.189	.256	.252	38	-10	2	1	0	.949	3	O-22	-0.7
1952	Was-A	1	0	0	0	0	0	0	0	0	0	—	—	—	—	0	0	0	0	.000	0	R	0.0
	Phi-A	43	60	8	12	3	0	0	5	21	15	.200	.407	.250	81	-0	1	2	-1	.958	-3	/2-8,O-7,3	-0.5
	Yr	44	60	8	12	3	0	0	5	21	15	.200	.407	.250	81	-0	1	2	-1	.958	-3	/2-8,O-7,3	-0.5
Total	10	597	1507	200	346	55	18	26	151	202	238	.230	.323	.342	83	-37	32	16	0	.946	-27	O-163,2-109/3S	-6.5

■ BILLY JO ROBIDOUX
Robidoux, William Joseph b: 1/13/64, Ware, Mass. BL/TR, 6'1", 200 lbs. Deb: 9/11/85

1985	Mil-A	18	51	5	9	2	0	3	8	12	16	.176	.333	.392	98	0	0	0	0	1.000	-1	O-11/1-6,D	-0.1
1986	Mil-A	56	181	15	41	8	0	1	21	33	36	.227	.346	.287	72	-6	0	0	0	.986	-2	1-43,D-10	-1.1
1987	Mil-A	23	62	9	12	0	0	0	4	8	17	.194	.286	.194	30	-6	0	1	-1	.983	-0	1-10,D-10	-0.7
1988	Mil-A	33	91	9	23	5	0	0	5	8	14	.253	.313	.308	74	-1	0	2	-1	.983	2	1-30/D-1	-0.3
1989	Chi-A	16	39	2	5	2	0	0	1	4	9	.128	.209	.179	11	-5	0	0	0	.990	-1	1-15/O-1	-0.6
1990	Bos-A	27	44	3	8	4	0	1	4	6	14	.182	.294	.341	74	-2	0	0	0	.981	-0	1-11/D-4	-0.2
Total	6	173	468	43	98	21	0	5	43	71	106	.209	.315	.286	65	-21	1	2	-1	.986	-1	1-115/D-26,O	-3.0

■ AARON ROBINSON
Robinson, Aaron Andrew b: 6/23/15, Lancaster, S.C. d: 3/9/66, Lancaster, S.C. BL/TR, 6'2", 205 lbs. Deb: 5/6/43

1943	NY-A	1	1	0	0	0	0	0	0	0	1	.000	.000	.000	-99	-0	0	0	0	.000	0	H	0.0
1945	NY-A	50	160	19	45	6	1	8	24	21	23	.281	.368	.481	139	8	0	0	0	1.000	0	C-45	0.8
1946	NY-A	100	330	32	98	17	2	16	64	48	39	.297	.388	.506	146	21	0	1	-1	.983	-11	C-95	1.5
1947	*NY-A☆	82	252	23	68	11	5	5	36	40	26	.270	.370	.413	119	7	0	1	-1	.997	-0	C-74	1.1
1948	Chi-A	98	326	47	82	14	2	8	39	46	30	.252	.344	.380	96	-2	0	1	-1	.989	-5	C-92	-0.1
1949	Det-A	110	331	38	89	12	0	13	56	73	21	.269	.402	.423	118	11	0	2	-1	.986	-1	*C-108	1.4
1950	Det-A	107	283	37	64	7	0	7	37	75	35	.226	.388	.346	86	-3	0	1	-1	.993	-3	*C-103	-0.2
1951	Det-A	36	82	3	17	6	0	0	9	17	9	.207	.343	.280	70	-3	0	0	0	1.000	0	C-35	-0.4
	Bos-A	26	74	9	15	1	1	2	7	17	10	.203	.352	.324	79	-2	0	0	0	.983	-1	C-25	-0.2
	Yr	62	156	12	32	7	1	2	16	34	19	.205	.347	.301	73	-5	0	0	0	.991	-3	C-60	-0.6
Total	8	610	1839	208	478	74	11	61	272	337	194	.260	.375	.412	112	35	0	6	-4	.990	-26	C-577	3.9

■ VAL ROBINSON
Robinson, Alfred Valentine Deb: 5/1/1872

| 1872 | Oly-n | 7 | 32 | 6 | 6 | 0 | 0 | 0 | 4 | 1 | 1 | .188 | .212 | .188 | 25 | -3 | | | | | | /O-7 | -0.2 |

■ BROOKS ROBINSON
Robinson, Brooks Calbert b: 5/18/37, Little Rock, Ark. BR/TR, 6'1", 190 lbs. Deb: 9/17/55 CH

1955	Bal-A	6	22	0	2	0	0	0	1	0	10	.091	.091	.091	-55	-5	0	0	0	.833	-2	/3-6	-0.7
1956	Bal-A	15	44	5	10	4	0	1	1	5	12	.227	.244	.386	70	-2	0	0	0	.944	3	3-14/2-1	-0.1
1957	Bal-A	50	117	13	28	6	1	2	14	7	10	.239	.288	.359	81	-4	0	1	0	.971	4	3-47	0.1
1958	Bal-A	145	463	31	110	16	3	3	32	31	51	.238	.293	.305	68	-21	1	2	-1	.953	10	*3-140,2-16	-1.0
1959	Bal-A	88	313	29	89	15	2	4	24	17	37	.284	.325	.383	96	-2	2	2	-1	.955	7	3-87/2-1	0.4

YEAR	TM/L	G	AB	R	H	2B	3B	HR	RBI	BB	SO	AVG	OBP	SLG	PRO+	BR/A	SB	CS	SBR	FA	FR	G/POS	TPR
1960	Bal-A★	152	595	74	175	27	9	14	88	35	49	.294	.333	.440	109	5	2	2	-1	**.977**	12	*3-152/2-3	1.6
1961	Bal-A★	163	668	89	192	38	7	7	61	47	57	.287	.338	.397	99	-2	1	3	-2	**.972**	-6	*3-163/2-2,S	-0.7
1962	Bal-A★	162	634	77	192	29	9	23	86	42	70	.303	.347	.486	129	23	3	1	0	**.979**	7	*3-162/S-3,2	3.2
1963	Bal-A★	161	589	67	148	26	4	11	67	46	84	.251	.307	.365	91	-8	2	3	-1	**.976**	9	*3-160/S-1	0.0
1964	Bal-A★	163	612	82	194	35	3	28	**118**	51	64	.317	.373	.521	146	37	1	0	0	**.972**	-2	*3-163	3.5
1965	Bal-A★	144	559	81	166	25	2	18	80	47	47	.297	.354	.445	123	16	3	0	1	.967	-6	*3-143	0.9
1966	*Bal-A★	157	620	91	167	35	2	23	100	56	36	.269	.335	.444	123	18	2	3	-1	**.976**	4	*3-157	1.9
1967	Bal-A★	158	610	88	164	25	5	22	77	54	54	.269	.332	.434	126	19	1	3	-2	**.980**	31	*3-158	5.0
1968	Bal-A★	162	608	65	154	36	6	17	75	44	55	.253	.308	.416	118	11	1	1	-0	.970	17	*3-162	3.2
1969	*Bal-A★	156	598	73	140	21	3	23	84	56	55	.234	.303	.395	93	-7	2	1	0	**.976**	19	*3-156	1.3
1970	*Bal-A★	158	608	84	168	31	4	18	94	53	53	.276	.338	.429	109	7	1	1	-0	.966	-1	*3-156	0.4
1971	*Bal-A★	156	589	67	160	21	1	20	92	63	50	.272	.345	.413	115	11	0	0	0	.968	7	*3-156	1.8
1972	Bal-A★	153	556	48	139	23	2	8	64	43	45	.250	.306	.342	90	-7	1	0	0	**.977**	6	*3-152	-0.3
1973	*Bal-A★	155	549	53	141	17	2	9	72	55	50	.257	.328	.344	90	-7	2	0	1	.970	9	*3-154	0.2
1974	*Bal-A★	153	553	46	159	27	0	7	59	56	47	.288	.356	.374	114	11	2	0	1	.967	21	*3-153	3.2
1975	Bal-A	144	482	50	97	15	1	6	53	44	33	.201	.269	.274	57	-28	0	0	0	**.979**	4	*3-143	-2.5
1976	Bal-A	71	218	16	46	8	2	3	11	8	24	.211	.242	.307	64	-11	0	0	0	.969	0	3-71	-1.2
1977	Bal-A	24	47	3	7	2	0	1	4	4	4	.149	.216	.255	30	-5	0	0	0	1.000	6	3-15	-0.3
Total	23	2896	10654	1232	2848	482	68	268	1357	860	990	.267	.325	.401	105	52	28	22	-5	.971	151	*3-2870/2-25,S	19.8

■ BRUCE ROBINSON
Robinson, Bruce Philip b: 4/16/54, LaJolla, Cal. BL/TR, 6'1", 185 lbs. Deb: 8/19/78 F

YEAR	TM/L	G	AB	R	H	2B	3B	HR	RBI	BB	SO	AVG	OBP	SLG	PRO+	BR/A	SB	CS	SBR	FA	FR	G/POS	TPR
1978	Oak-A	28	84	5	21	3	1	0	8	3	8	.250	.276	.310	68	-4	0	0	0	.965	7	C-28	0.4
1979	NY-A	6	12	0	2	0	0	0	2	1	0	.167	.231	.167	9	-2	0	0	0	.943	2	/C-6	0.1
1980	NY-A	4	5	0	0	0	0	0	0	0	4	.000	.000	.000	-99	-1	0	0	0	1.000	-0	/C-3	-0.2
Total	3	38	101	5	23	3	1	0	10	4	12	.228	.257	.277	52	-7	0	0	0	.962	9	/C-37	0.3

■ CHARLIE ROBINSON
Robinson, Charles Henry b: 7/27/1856, Westerly, R.I. d: 5/18/13, BL/TR, Deb: 8/2/1884

YEAR	TM/L	G	AB	R	H	2B	3B	HR	RBI	BB	SO	AVG	OBP	SLG	PRO+	BR/A	SB	CS	SBR	FA	FR	G/POS	TPR
1884	Ind-a	20	80	11	23	2	0	0			3	.287	.313	.313	108	1				.967	-1	C-17/S-3,O	0.1
1885	Bro-a	11	40	5	6	2	1	0			3	.150	.209	.250	44	-3				.840	-4	C-11	-0.5
Total	2	31	120	16	29	4	1	0			6	.242	.278	.292	85	-2				.919	-5	/C-28,S-3,O	-0.4

■ RABBIT ROBINSON
Robinson, Clyde b: 3/5/1882, Wellsburg, W.Va. d: 4/9/15, Waterbury, Conn. BR/TR, 5'6", 148 lbs. Deb: 4/22/03

YEAR	TM/L	G	AB	R	H	2B	3B	HR	RBI	BB	SO	AVG	OBP	SLG	PRO+	BR/A	SB	CS	SBR	FA	FR	G/POS	TPR
1903	Was-A	103	373	41	79	10	8	1	20	33		.212	.279	.290	69	-13	16			.917	2	2-45,O-30,S/3	-1.1
1904	Det-A	101	320	30	77	13	6	0	37	29		.241	.314	.319	103	2	14			.925	1	S-30,3-26,O2	0.5
1910	Cin-N	2	7	0	0	0	0	0	1	1	0	.000	.125	.000	-66	-1	0			1.000	-1	/3-2	-0.3
Total	3	206	700	71	156	23	14	1	58	63	0	.223	.294	.300	83	-13	30			.940	3	/2-64,S-54,O3	-0.9

■ CRAIG ROBINSON
Robinson, Craig George b: 8/21/48, Abington, Pa. BR/TR, 5'10", 165 lbs. Deb: 9/9/72

YEAR	TM/L	G	AB	R	H	2B	3B	HR	RBI	BB	SO	AVG	OBP	SLG	PRO+	BR/A	SB	CS	SBR	FA	FR	G/POS	TPR
1972	Phi-N	5	15	0	3	1	0	0	0	1	2	.200	.250	.267	46	-1	0	0	0	1.000	2	/S-4	0.2
1973	Phi-N	46	146	11	33	7	0	0	7	0	25	.226	.226	.274	37	-12	1	1	-0	.945	1	S-42/2-4	-0.8
1974	Atl-N	145	452	52	104	4	6	0	29	30	57	.230	.282	.265	52	-29	11	2	2	.956	-17	*S-142	-2.8
1975	Atl-N	10	17	1	1	0	0	0	0	0	5	.059	.059	.059	-65	-4	0	0	0	1.000	1	/S-7	-0.2
	SF-N	29	29	4	2	1	0	0	0	2	6	.069	.129	.103	-34	-5	0	0	0	.941	5	S-12/2-9	0.0
	Yr	39	46	5	3	1	0	0	0	2	11	.065	.104	.087	-45	-9	0	0	0	.967	6	S-19/2-9	-0.2
1976	SF-N	15	13	4	4	1	0	0	2	3	4	.308	.438	.385	131	1	0	1	-1	.952	4	/2-7,3-2,S	0.4
	Atl-N	15	17	4	4	0	0	0	3	5	2	.235	.409	.235	81	-0	0	0	0	.952	2	/2-5,S-2,3	0.2
	Yr	30	30	8	8	1	0	0	5	8	6	.267	.421	.300	102	1	0	1	-1	.952	6	2-12/3-3,S	0.6
1977	Atl-N	27	29	4	6	1	0	0	1	1	6	.207	.233	.241	25	-3	0	0	0	1.000	6	S-23	0.3
Total	6	292	718	80	157	15	6	0	42	42	107	.219	.265	.256	44	-54	12	4	1	.956	3	S-233/2-25,3	-2.7

■ DAVE ROBINSON
Robinson, David Tanner b: 5/22/46, Minneapolis, Minn. BB/TL, 6'1", 186 lbs. Deb: 9/10/70 F

YEAR	TM/L	G	AB	R	H	2B	3B	HR	RBI	BB	SO	AVG	OBP	SLG	PRO+	BR/A	SB	CS	SBR	FA	FR	G/POS	TPR
1970	SD-N	15	38	5	12	2	0	2	6	5	4	.316	.395	.526	151	3	2	0	1	1.000	0	O-13	0.4
1971	SD-N	7	6	0	0	0	0	0	0	1	3	.000	.143	.000	-61	-1	0	0	0	.000	0	H	-0.1
Total	2	22	44	5	12	2	0	2	6	6	7	.273	.360	.455	124	1	2	0	1	1.000	1	/O-13	0.3

■ EARL ROBINSON
Robinson, Earl John b: 11/3/36, New Orleans, La. BR/TR, 6'1", 190 lbs. Deb: 9/10/58

YEAR	TM/L	G	AB	R	H	2B	3B	HR	RBI	BB	SO	AVG	OBP	SLG	PRO+	BR/A	SB	CS	SBR	FA	FR	G/POS	TPR
1958	LA-N	8	15	3	3	0	0	0	0	0	4	.200	.250	.200	20	-2	0	0	0	1.000	1	/3-6	0.0
1961	Bal-A	96	222	37	59	12	3	8	30	31	54	.266	.356	.455	119	6	4	3	-1	.973	-3	O-82	-0.1
1962	Bal-A	29	63	12	18	3	1	1	4	8	10	.286	.366	.413	116	2	2	0	1	1.000	0	O-17	0.2
1964	Bal-A	37	121	11	33	5	1	3	10	7	24	.273	.313	.405	98	-1	1	2	0	.986	1	O-34	-0.2
Total	4	170	421	63	113	20	5	12	44	47	92	.268	.342	.425	109	5	7	5	-1	.980	-1	O-133/3-6	-0.1

■ FLOYD ROBINSON
Robinson, Floyd Andrew b: 5/9/36, Prescott, Ark. BL/TR, 5'9", 175 lbs. Deb: 8/10/60

YEAR	TM/L	G	AB	R	H	2B	3B	HR	RBI	BB	SO	AVG	OBP	SLG	PRO+	BR/A	SB	CS	SBR	FA	FR	G/POS	TPR
1960	Chi-A	22	46	7	13	0	0	0	1	11	8	.283	.431	.283	98	1	2	3	-1	.960	-2	O-17	-0.4
1961	Chi-A	132	432	69	134	20	7	11	59	52	32	.310	.389	.465	129	19	7	4	-0	.991	4	O-106	1.6
1962	Chi-A	156	600	89	187	**45**	10	11	109	72	47	.312	.387	.475	131	27	4	2	0	.973	-10	*O-155	0.8
1963	Chi-A	146	527	71	149	21	6	13	71	62	43	.283	.363	.419	120	15	4	3	-1	.984	-7	*O-137	0.1
1964	Chi-A	141	525	83	158	17	3	11	59	70	41	.301	.384	.408	125	20	9	5	-0	.987	-12	*O-138	0.1
1965	Chi-A	156	577	70	153	15	6	14	66	76	51	.265	.356	.385	117	15	4	1	1	.985	-4	*O-153	0.4
1966	Chi-A	127	342	44	81	11	2	5	35	44	32	.237	.332	.325	96	-1	8	2	1	.962	-14	*O-113	-1.9
1967	Cin-N	55	130	19	31	6	2	1	10	14	14	.238	.313	.338	77	-4	3	1	0	.981	-4	O-39	-1.0
1968	Oak-A	53	81	5	20	5	0	1	14	4	10	.247	.282	.346	94	-1	1	0	0	1.000	1	O-18	-0.3
	Bos-A	23	24	1	3	0	0	0	2	3	4	.125	.250	.125	15	-2	1	0	0	.833	-3	O-10	-0.6
	Yr	76	105	6	23	5	0	1	16	7	14	.219	.274	.295	74	-3	1	0	0	.963	-4	O-28	-0.9
Total	9	1011	3284	458	929	140	36	67	426	408	282	.283	.367	.409	118	90	42	21	0	.981	-53	O-886	-1.2

■ FRANK ROBINSON
Robinson, Frank b: 8/31/35, Beaumont, Tex. BR/TR, 6'1", 195 lbs. Deb: 4/17/56 MCH

YEAR	TM/L	G	AB	R	H	2B	3B	HR	RBI	BB	SO	AVG	OBP	SLG	PRO+	BR/A	SB	CS	SBR	FA	FR	G/POS	TPR
1956	Cin-N★	152	572	**122**	166	27	6	38	83	64	95	.290	.379	.558	139	32	8	4	0	.976	6	*O-152	3.0
1957	Cin-N★	150	611	97	197	29	5	29	75	44	92	.322	.379	.529	131	27	10	2	2	.989	19	O-136,1-24	3.8
1958	Cin-N	148	554	90	149	25	6	31	83	62	80	.269	.350	.504	116	12	10	1	2	.991	9	*O-138,3-11	1.7
1959	Cin-N★	146	540	106	168	31	4	36	125	69	93	.311	.397	.583	152	41	18	8	1	.984	-9	*1-125,O-40	2.3
1960	Cin-N	139	464	86	138	33	6	31	83	82	67	.297	.443	**.595**	169	46	13	6	0	.993	7	1-78,O-51/3	4.5
1961	*Cin-N★	153	545	117	176	32	7	37	124	71	64	.323	.411	**.611**	164	51	22	3	5	.990	10	*O-150/3-1	5.5
1962	Cin-N★	162	609	**134**	208	**51**	2	39	136	76	62	.342	**.424**	**.624**	172	62	18	9	0	.994	9	*O-161	6.0
1963	Cin-N	140	482	79	125	19	3	21	91	81	69	.259	.381	.442	132	23	26	10	2	.984	0	*O-139/1-1	2.9
1964	Cin-N	156	568	103	174	38	6	29	96	79	67	.306	.399	.548	158	43	23	5	4	.986	-2	*O-156	4.6
1965	Cin-N★	156	582	109	172	33	5	33	113	70	100	.296	.388	.540	148	38	13	9	-2	.990	2	*O-155	3.3
1966	*Bal-A★	155	576	**122**	182	34	2	**49**	**122**	87	90	.316	.415	**.637**	200	76	8	5	-1	.985	-4	*O-151/1-3	**6.7**
1967	Bal-A†	129	479	83	149	23	7	30	94	71	84	.311	.408	.576	189	54	2	3	-1	.990	-2	*O-126/1-2	4.8
1968	Bal-A	130	421	69	113	27	1	15	52	73	84	.268	.391	.444	153	30	11	2	-2	.962	-8	*O-117/1-3	2.0
1969	*Bal-A★	148	539	111	166	19	5	32	100	88	62	.308	.417	.540	164	49	9	3	1	.987	-1	*O-134,1-19	4.2
1970	*Bal-A★	132	471	88	144	24	1	25	78	69	70	.306	.402	.520	151	34	2	3	-1	.987	6	*O-120/1-7	3.4
1971	*Bal-A★	133	455	82	128	16	2	28	99	72	62	.281	.390	.510	154	34	3	0	1	.973	-4	O-92,1-37	2.4
1972	LA-N	103	342	41	86	6	1	19	59	55	76	.251	.358	.442	129	14	2	3	-1	.967	-1	O-95	0.8
1973	Cal-A	147	534	85	142	29	0	30	97	82	93	.266	.374	.489	153	38	1	1	-0	.976	4	*D-127,O-17	3.8

YEAR	TM/L	G	AB	R	H	2B	3B	HR	RBI	BB	SO	AVG	OBP	SLG	PRO+	BR/A	SB	CS	SBR	FA	FR	G/POS	TPR
1974	Cal-A★	129	427	75	107	26	2	20	63	75	85	.251	.375	.461	148	28	5	1	1	.000	-0	*D-123/O-1	2.7
	Cle-A	15	50	6	10	1	1	2	5	10	10	.200	.333	.380	106	1	0	1	-1	.958	-1	D-11/1-4	-0.1
	Yr	144	477	81	117	27	3	22	68	85	95	.245	.371	.453	143	29	5	2	0	.958	-1	*D-134/1-4,O	2.6
1975	Cle-A	49	118	19	28	5	0	9	24	29	15	.237	.388	.508	152	9	0	0	0	.000	0	D-42,M	0.8
1976	Cle-A	36	67	5	15	0	0	3	10	11	12	.224	.333	.358	104	9	0	0	0	1.000	-1	D-18/1-2,OM	-0.1
Total	21	2808	10006	1829	2943	528	72	586	1812	1420	1532	.294	.392	.537	154	744	204	77	15	.984	52	*O-2132,D-321,1/3	69.0

■ FRED ROBINSON
Robinson, Frederic Henry b: 7/6/1856, South Acton, Mass. d: 12/18/33, Hudson, Mass. BR/TR, Deb: 4/17/1884 F

YEAR	TM/L	G	AB	R	H	2B	3B	HR	RBI	BB	SO	AVG	OBP	SLG	PRO+	BR/A	SB	CS	SBR	FA	FR	G/POS	TPR
1884	Cin-U	3	13	1	3	0	0	0		0		.231	.231	.231	24	-1				.727	-3	/2-3	-0.4

■ JACKIE ROBINSON
Robinson, John Roosevelt b: 1/31/19, Cairo, Ga. d: 10/24/72, Stamford, Conn. BR/TR, 5'11", 204 lbs. Deb: 4/15/47 H

YEAR	TM/L	G	AB	R	H	2B	3B	HR	RBI	BB	SO	AVG	OBP	SLG	PRO+	BR/A	SB	CS	SBR	FA	FR	G/POS	TPR
1947	*Bro-N	151	590	125	175	31	5	12	48	74	36	.297	.383	.427	111	11	**29**			.989	-3	*1-151	0.2
1948	Bro-N	147	574	108	170	38	8	12	85	57	37	.296	.367	.453	117	13	22			.980	1	*2-116,1-30/3	2.0
1949	*Bro-N★	156	593	122	203	38	12	16	124	86	27	**.342**	.432	.528	150	45	**37**			.981	-1	*2-156	4.9
1950	Bro-N★	144	518	99	170	39	4	14	81	80	24	.328	.423	.500	139	32	12			**.986**	11	*2-144	**4.7**
1951	Bro-N★	153	548	106	185	33	7	19	88	79	27	.338	.429	.527	153	43	25	8	3	**.992**	17	*2-150	**6.8**
1952	*Bro-N★	149	510	104	157	17	3	19	75	106	40	.308	**.440**	.465	149	41	24	7	3	.974	4	*2-146	**5.6**
1953	Bro-N★	136	484	109	159	34	7	12	95	74	30	.329	.425	.502	137	30	17	4	3	.981	8	O-76,3-44/21S	3.5
1954	Bro-N★	124	386	62	120	22	4	15	59	63	20	.311	.417	.505	135	22	7	3	0	1.000	-9	O-74,3-50/2	1.0
1955	Bro-N	105	317	51	81	6	2	8	36	61	18	.256	.378	.363	96	1	12	3	2	.966	7	3-84,O-10/12	0.9
1956	Bro-N	117	357	61	98	15	2	10	43	60	32	.275	.383	.412	106	5	12	5	1	.967	15	3-72,2-22/1O	2.2
Total	10	1382	4877	947	1518	273	54	137	734	740	291	.311	.410	.474	131	241	197	30		.983	49	2-748,3-256,10/S	31.8

■ JACK ROBINSON
Robinson, John W. "Bridgeport" b: 7/15/1880, Portland, Maine d: 7/22/21, Macon, Ga. TR, Deb: 9/6/02

YEAR	TM/L	G	AB	R	H	2B	3B	HR	RBI	BB	SO	AVG	OBP	SLG	PRO+	BR/A	SB	CS	SBR	FA	FR	G/POS	TPR
1902	NY-N	4	9	0	0	0	0	0		0		.000	.000	.000	-99	-2	0			1.000	1	/C-3	-0.1

■ WILBERT ROBINSON
Robinson, Wilbert "Uncle Robby" b: 6/29/1863, Bolton, Mass. d: 8/8/34, Atlanta, Ga. BR/TR, 5'8.5", 215 lbs. Deb: 4/19/1886 FMCH

YEAR	TM/L	G	AB	R	H	2B	3B	HR	RBI	BB	SO	AVG	OBP	SLG	PRO+	BR/A	SB	CS	SBR	FA	FR	G/POS	TPR
1886	Phi-a	87	342	57	69	11	3	1	21			.202	.254	.260	61	-16	33			.893	-10	C-61,1-22/O	-1.9
1887	Phi-a	68	264	28	60	6	2	1	14			.227	.269	.277	52	-17	15			.901	1	C-67/1-3,O	-0.8
1888	Phi-a	66	254	32	62	7	2	1	31	9		.244	.270	.299	83	-5	11			.938	25	C-65/1-1	2.4
1889	Phi-a	69	264	31	61	13	2	0	28	6	34	.231	.251	.295	56	-16	9			.943	4	C-69	-0.5
1890	Phi-a	82	329	32	78	13	4	4	16			.237	.279	.337	83	-9	20			.930	-9	C-82	-0.9
	Bal-a	14	48	7	13	1	0	0	3			.271	.314	.292	75	-2	1			.989	6	C-11/1-3	0.5
	Yr	96	377	39	91	14	4	4	19			.241	.283	.332	82	-10	21			.938	-3	C-93/1-3	-0.4
1891	Bal-a	93	334	25	72	8	5	2	46	16	37	.216	.251	.287	54	-22	18			.954	3	C-92/O-1	-0.9
1892	Bal-N	90	330	36	88	14	4	2	57	15	35	.267	.303	.352	95	-3	5			.921	-18	C-87/1-2,O	-1.4
1893	Bal-N	95	359	49	120	21	3	3	57	26	22	.334	.382	.435	115	7	17			.942	-8	*C-93/1-1	0.6
1894	*Bal-N	109	414	69	146	21	4	1	98	46	18	.353	.421	.430	101	2	12			.944	-5	*C-109	0.5
1895	*Bal-N	77	282	38	74	19	1	0	48	12	19	.262	.295	.337	61	-17	11			**.979**	14	C-75	0.3
1896	Bal-N	67	245	43	85	9	6	2	38	14	13	.347	.385	.457	120	6	9			.948	3	C-67	1.4
1897	Bal-N	48	181	25	57	9	0	0	23	8		.315	.347	.365	88	-3	0			.965	-2	C-48	0.0
1898	Bal-N	79	289	29	80	12	2	0	38	16		.277	.317	.332	84	-6	3			.965	-5	C-77	-0.4
1899	Bal-N	108	356	40	101	15	2	0	47	31		.284	.344	.337	83	-8	5			.949	-18	*C-105	-1.7
1900	StL-N	60	210	26	52	5	1	0	28	11		.248	.291	.281	59	-12	7			.974	-1	C-54	-0.7
1901	Bal-A	68	239	32	72	12	3	0	26	10		.301	.335	.377	93	-3	9			.949	-2	C-67	0.2
1902	Bal-A	91	335	38	98	16	7	1	57	12		.293	.321	.391	93	-4	11			.949	-15	C-87,M	-1.0
Total	17	1371	5075	637	1388	212	51	18	622	286	178	.273	.316	.346	83	-129	196			.941	-36	*C-1316/1-32,O	-4.3

■ EDDIE ROBINSON
Robinson, William Edward b: 12/15/20, Paris, Tex. BL/TR, 6'2.5", 210 lbs. Deb: 9/9/42 C

YEAR	TM/L	G	AB	R	H	2B	3B	HR	RBI	BB	SO	AVG	OBP	SLG	PRO+	BR/A	SB	CS	SBR	FA	FR	G/POS	TPR
1942	Cle-A	8	8	1	1	0	0	0	2	1	0	.125	.222	.125	-1	-1	0	0	0	1.000	-0	/1-1	-0.1
1946	Cle-A	8	30	6	12	1	0	3	4	2	4	.400	.438	.733	238	5	0	0	0	.988	-2	/1-8	0.3
1947	Cle-A	95	318	52	78	10	1	14	52	30	18	.245	.314	.415	105	0	1	0	0	.994	-2	1-87	-0.4
1948	*Cle-A	134	493	53	125	18	5	16	83	36	42	.254	.307	.408	91	-9	1	0	0	**.995**	-1	*1-131	-1.0
1949	Was-A★	143	527	66	155	27	3	18	78	67	30	.294	.381	.459	125	18	3	4	-2	.987	-2	*1-143	1.3
1950	Was-A	36	129	21	30	4	2	1	13	25	4	.233	.365	.318	80	0	0	0	0	1.000	0	1-36	-0.4
	Chi-A	119	424	62	133	11	2	20	73	60	28	.314	.405	.491	132	21	0	0	0	.987	-7	*1-119	1.1
	Yr	155	553	83	163	15	4	21	86	85	32	.295	.395	.450	120	18	0	0	0	.990	-7	*1-155	0.7
1951	Chi-A★	151	564	85	159	23	5	29	117	77	54	.282	.371	.495	135	27	2	5	-2	.988	-6	*1-147	1.1
1952	Chi-A★	155	594	79	176	33	1	22	104	70	49	.296	.382	.466	134	27	2	0	1	.990	-8	*1-155	1.5
1953	Phi-A★	156	615	64	152	28	4	22	102	63	56	.247	.322	.413	94	-7	1	2	-1	.988	-14	*1-155	-2.8
1954	NY-A	85	142	11	37	9	0	3	27	19	21	.261	.348	.387	105	1	0	0	0	.980	1	1-29	0.0
1955	*NY-A	88	173	25	36	1	0	16	42	36	26	.208	.360	.491	129	7	0	0	0	.995	-2	1-46	0.3
1956	NY-A	26	54	7	12	1	0	5	11	5	2	.222	.323	.519	123	1	0	0	-1	1.000	-0	1-14	0.0
	KC-A	75	172	13	34	5	1	2	12	26	20	.198	.310	.273	55	-11	0	0	0	.977	-4	1-47	-1.7
	Yr	101	226	20	46	6	1	7	23	31	23	.204	.313	.332	71	-10	0	0	-1	.983	-4	1-61	-1.7
1957	Det-A	13	9	0	0	0	0	0	0	3	0	.000	.308	.000	-9	-1	0	0	0	1.000	-0	/1-1	-0.1
	Cle-A	19	27	1	6	1	0	1	3	0	3	.222	.250	.370	68	-1	0	0	0	1.000	-0	/1-7	-0.1
	Bal-A	4	3	0	0	0	0	0	0	1	1	.000	.250	.000	-28	-1	0	0	0	.000	-0	H	-0.1
	Yr	36	39	1	6	1	0	1	3	4	4	.154	.267	.256	44	-3	0	0	0	1.000	-0	/1-8	-0.3
Total	13	1315	4282	546	1146	172	24	172	723	521	359	.268	.354	.440	113	73	10	12	-4	.990	-45	*1-1126	-1.1

■ YANK ROBINSON
Robinson, William H. b: 9/19/1859, Philadelphia, Pa. d: 8/25/1894, St.Louis, Mo. BR/TR, 5'6.5", 170 lbs. Deb: 8/24/1882

YEAR	TM/L	G	AB	R	H	2B	3B	HR	RBI	BB	SO	AVG	OBP	SLG	PRO+	BR/A	SB	CS	SBR	FA	FR	G/POS	TPR
1882	Det-N	11	39	1	7	1	0	0	2	1	13	.179	.200	.205	30	-3				.800	-4	S-10/O-1,P	-0.6
1884	Bal-U	102	415	101	111	24	4	2	**37**			.267	.327	.359	78	-14				.831	16	3-71,S-14,CP/2	0.7
1885	*StL-a	78	287	63	75	8	8	0	29			.261	.344	.345	113	5				.862	-6	O-52,2-19/C31	-0.1
1886	*StL-a	133	481	89	132	26	9	3	64			.274	.377	.385	132	19	51			.888	-4	*2-125/3-6,OSP	1.8
1887	*StL-a	125	430	102	131	32	4	1	92			.305	.445	.405	125	17	75			.899	-13	*2-117/3-6,OSCP	0.6
1888	*StL-a	134	455	111	105	17	6	3	53	**116**		.231	**.400**	.314	117	-3	56			.895	-44	*2-102,S-34	-2.4
1889	StL-a	132	452	97	94	17	3	5	70	**118**	55	.208	.378	.292	81	-10	39			.887	-35	*2-132	-3.3
1890	Pit-P	98	306	59	70	10	3	0	38	101	33	.229	.434	.281	101	12	17			.887	-19	*2-98	-0.1
1891	Cin-a	97	342	48	61	9	4	1	37	68	51	.178	.328	.237	57	-19	23			.867	-11	*2-97	-2.2
	StL-a	1	3	0	0	0	0	0	0	0	0	.000	.000	.000	-87	-1	0			.750	-1	/2-1	-0.1
	Yr	98	345	48	61	9	4	1	37	68	51	.177	.325	.235	56	-19	23			.866	-12	2-98	-2.3
1892	Was-N	67	218	26	39	4	3	1	19	38	24	.179	.301	.225	61	-9	11			.852	-4	3-58/S-5,2	-1.1
Total	10	978	3428	697	825	148	44	15	219	664	180	.241	.375	.323	98	11	272			.887	-124	2-698,3-143/SOCP1	-6.7

■ BILL ROBINSON
Robinson, William Henry b: 6/26/43, McKeesport, Pa. BR/TR, 6'3", 205 lbs. Deb: 9/20/66 C

YEAR	TM/L	G	AB	R	H	2B	3B	HR	RBI	BB	SO	AVG	OBP	SLG	PRO+	BR/A	SB	CS	SBR	FA	FR	G/POS	TPR
1966	Atl-N	6	11	1	3	0	0	0	3	0	1	.273	.273	.455	96	-0	0	0	0	.800	-1	/O-5	-0.2
1967	NY-A	116	342	31	67	6	1	7	29	28	56	.196	.261	.281	62	-16	2	2	-1	.968	-2	*O-102	-2.6
1968	NY-A	107	342	34	82	16	7	6	40	26	54	.240	.297	.380	107	2	7	6	-2	.985	-3	O-98	-0.8
1969	NY-A	87	222	23	38	11	2	3	21	16	39	.171	.227	.279	42	-18	3	1	0	.963	-3	O-62/1-1	-2.6
1972	Phi-N	82	188	19	45	9	1	8	21	5	30	.239	.259	.426	89	-4	2	3	0	.982	-5	O-72	-1.6
1973	Phi-N	124	452	62	130	32	6	25	65	27	91	.288	.329	.529	131	16	5	5	0	.979	-7	*O-113,3-14	0.4
1974	Phi-N	100	280	32	66	14	1	5	29	17	61	.236	.282	.346	72	-11	5	3	0	.971	-3	O-87	-1.9

YEAR	TM/L	G	AB	R	H	2B	3B	HR	RBI	BB	SO	AVG	OBP	SLG	PRO+	BR/A	SB	CS	SBR	FA	FR	G/POS	TPR
1975	*Pit-N	92	200	26	56	12	2	6	33	11	36	.280	.318	.450	112	2	3	1	0	.991	-2	O-57	-0.1
1976	Pit-N	122	393	55	119	22	3	21	64	16	73	.303	.332	.534	142	18	2	4	-2	.993	-12	O-78,3-37/1	0.2
1977	Pit-N	137	507	74	154	32	1	26	104	25	92	.304	.340	.525	125	16	12	6	0	.992	-14	1-86,O-43,3	-0.5
1978	Pit-N	136	499	70	123	36	2	14	80	35	105	.246	.302	.411	93	-6	14	11	-2	.988	-4	*O-127,3-29/1	-1.8
1979	*Pit-N	148	421	59	111	17	6	24	75	24	81	.264	.305	.504	111	4	13	2	3	.982	-13	*O-125,1-28/3	-1.1
1980	Pit-N	100	272	28	78	10	1	12	36	15	46	.287	.324	.463	116	5	1	4	-2	.985	-10	1-49,O-41	-1.2
1981	Pit-N	39	88	8	19	3	0	2	8	5	18	.216	.258	.318	61	-5	1	0	0	1.000	-0	1-23/O-7,3	-0.6
1982	Pit-N	31	71	8	17	3	0	4	12	5	19	.239	.289	.451	101	-0	0	1	-1	1.000	-1	O-22	-0.2
	Phi-N	35	69	6	18	6	0	3	19	7	15	.261	.329	.478	121	2	1	1	0	.960	-1	O-19/1-5	0.0
	Yr	66	140	14	35	9	0	7	31	12	34	.250	.309	.464	111	1	1	2	-1	.984	-1	O-41/1-5	-0.2
1983	Phi-N	10	7	0	1	0	0	0	2	1	4	.143	.250	.143	12	-1	0	0	0	1.000	-1	/1-3,3-2,O	-0.2
Total	16	1472	4364	536	1127	229	29	166	641	263	820	.258	.303	.438	104	4	71	49	-8	.979	-84	*O-1059,1-201,3	-14.8

■ RAFAEL ROBLES
Robles, Rafael Orlando (Natera) b: 10/20/47, San Pedro De Macoris, D.R. Deb: 4/8/69

YEAR	TM/L	G	AB	R	H	2B	3B	HR	RBI	BB	SO	AVG	OBP	SLG	PRO+	BR/A	SB	CS	SBR	FA	FR	G/POS	TPR
1969	SD-N	6	20	1	2	0	0	0	0	1	3	.100	.143	.100	-32	-4	1	1	-0	.895	-4	/S-6	-0.8
1970	SD-N	23	89	5	19	1	0	0	3	5	11	.213	.263	.225	33	-8	3	0	1	.968	2	S-23	-0.3
1972	SD-N	18	24	1	4	0	0	0	0	0	3	.167	.167	.167	-5	-3	0	0	0	.952	-2	S-15/3-1	-0.5
Total	3	47	133	7	25	1	0	0	3	6	17	.188	.229	.195	17	-15	4	1	1	.958	-4	/S-44,3-1	-1.6

■ SERGIO ROBLES
Robles, Sergio (Valenzuela) b: 4/16/46, Magdalena, Mexico BR/TR, 6'2", 190 lbs. Deb: 8/27/72

YEAR	TM/L	G	AB	R	H	2B	3B	HR	RBI	BB	SO	AVG	OBP	SLG	PRO+	BR/A	SB	CS	SBR	FA	FR	G/POS	TPR
1972	Bal-A	2	5	0	1	0	0	0	0	0	0	.200	.200	.200	19	-0	0	0	0	1.000	-1	/C-1	-0.2
1973	Bal-A	8	13	0	1	0	0	0	0	0	3	.077	.250	.077	-4	-2	0	0	0	1.000	3	/C-8	0.1
1976	LA-N	6	3	0	0	0	0	0	0	0	2	.000	.000	.000	-99	-1	0	0	0	1.000	1	/C-6	0.0
Total	3	16	21	0	2	0	0	0	0	0	5	.095	.208	.095	-11	-3	0	0	0	1.000	3	/C-15	-0.1

■ TOM ROBSON
Robson, Thomas James b: 1/15/46, Rochester, N.Y. BR/TR, 6'3", 215 lbs. Deb: 9/14/74 C

YEAR	TM/L	G	AB	R	H	2B	3B	HR	RBI	BB	SO	AVG	OBP	SLG	PRO+	BR/A	SB	CS	SBR	FA	FR	G/POS	TPR
1974	Tex-A	6	13	2	3	1	0	0	2	4	3	.231	.412	.308	112	0	0	0	0	1.000	-0	/1-1,D-5	0.0
1975	Tex-A	17	35	3	7	0	0	0	2	1	3	.200	.222	.200	20	-4	0	0	0	1.000	-0	/1-5,D-4	-0.4
Total	2	23	48	5	10	1	0	0	4	5	6	.208	.283	.229	48	-3	0	0	0	1.000	-0	/D-9,1-6	-0.4

■ ADAM ROCAP
Rocap, Adam b: 1854, Philadelphia, Pa. d: 3/29/1892, Philadelphia, Pa. 5'9", 170 lbs. Deb: 5/5/1875

YEAR	TM/L	G	AB	R	H	2B	3B	HR	RBI	BB	SO	AVG	OBP	SLG	PRO+	BR/A	SB	CS	SBR	FA	FR	G/POS	TPR
1875	Ath-n	16	70	13	12	0	0	0		0		.171	.171	.171	17	-6						O-11/2-3	-0.5

■ MIKE ROCCO
Rocco, Michael Dominick b: 3/2/16, St.Paul, Minn. BL/TL, 5'11", 188 lbs. Deb: 6/5/43

YEAR	TM/L	G	AB	R	H	2B	3B	HR	RBI	BB	SO	AVG	OBP	SLG	PRO+	BR/A	SB	CS	SBR	FA	FR	G/POS	TPR
1943	Cle-A	108	405	43	97	14	4	5	46	51	40	.240	.328	.331	99	-0	1	2	-1	**.995**	-5	*1-108	-1.4
1944	Cle-A	155	653	87	174	29	7	13	70	56	51	.266	.325	.392	108	5	4	8	-4	.993	17	*1-155	1.1
1945	Cle-A	143	565	81	149	28	6	10	56	52	40	.264	.326	.388	111	6	0	4	-2	**.992**	4	*1-141	-0.2
1946	Cle-A	34	98	8	24	2	0	2	14	15	15	.245	.345	.327	94	-0	1	1	0	.996	5	1-27	0.3
Total	4	440	1721	219	444	73	17	30	186	174	146	.258	.327	.372	106	11	6	15	-7	.994	21	1-431	-0.2

■ JACK ROCHE
Roche, John Joseph "Red" b: 11/22/1890, Los Angeles, Cal. d: 3/30/83, Peoria, Ariz. BR/TR, 6'1", 178 lbs. Deb: 5/24/14

YEAR	TM/L	G	AB	R	H	2B	3B	HR	RBI	BB	SO	AVG	OBP	SLG	PRO+	BR/A	SB	CS	SBR	FA	FR	G/POS	TPR
1914	StL-N	12	9	1	6	2	1	0	3	0	1	.667	.700	1.111	441	4	1			.667	-2	/C-9	0.2
1915	StL-N	46	39	2	8	0	1	0	6	4	8	.205	.295	.256	68	-1	1			1.000	0	/C-4	-0.1
1917	StL-N	1	1	0	0	0	0	0	0	0	0	.000	.000	.000	-99	0	0			.000	-1	/C-1	-0.1
Total	3	59	49	3	14	2	2	0	9	4	9	.286	.364	.408	133	2	2			.750	-2	/C-14	0.0

■ BEN ROCHEFORT
Rochefort, Bennett Harold (b: Bennett Harold Rochefort Gilbert) b: 8/15/1896, Camden, N.J. d: 4/2/81, Red Bank, N.J. BL/TR, 6'2", 185 lbs. Deb: 10/3/14

YEAR	TM/L	G	AB	R	H	2B	3B	HR	RBI	BB	SO	AVG	OBP	SLG	PRO+	BR/A	SB	CS	SBR	FA	FR	G/POS	TPR
1914	Phi-A	1	2	0	1	0	0	0	0	0	1	.500	.500	.500	209	1				1.000	-0	/1-1	0.1

■ LOU ROCHELLI
Rochelli, Louis Joseph b: 1/11/19, Staunton, Ill. d: 10/23/92, Victoria, Tex. BR/TR, 6'1", 175 lbs. Deb: 8/25/44

YEAR	TM/L	G	AB	R	H	2B	3B	HR	RBI	BB	SO	AVG	OBP	SLG	PRO+	BR/A	SB	CS	SBR	FA	FR	G/POS	TPR
1944	Bro-N	5	17	0	3	0	1	0	2	2	6	.176	.263	.294	58	-1	0			.964	-0	/2-5	-0.1

■ LES ROCK
Rock, Lester Henry (b: Lester Henry Schwarzrock) b: 8/19/12, Springfield, Minn. d: 9/9/91, Davis, Cal. BL/TR, 6'2", 184 lbs. Deb: 9/11/36

YEAR	TM/L	G	AB	R	H	2B	3B	HR	RBI	BB	SO	AVG	OBP	SLG	PRO+	BR/A	SB	CS	SBR	FA	FR	G/POS	TPR
1936	Chi-A	2	1	0	0	0	0	0	0	0	0	.000	.000	.000	-97	-0	0	0	0	.000	0	/1-2	0.0

■ IKE ROCKENFIELD
Rockenfield, Isaac Broc b: 11/3/1876, Omaha, Neb. d: 2/21/27, San Diego, Cal. BR/TR, 5'7", 150 lbs. Deb: 5/5/05

YEAR	TM/L	G	AB	R	H	2B	3B	HR	RBI	BB	SO	AVG	OBP	SLG	PRO+	BR/A	SB	CS	SBR	FA	FR	G/POS	TPR
1905	StL-A	95	322	40	70	12	0	0	16	46		.217	.340	.255	95	-2	11			.926	-9	2-95	-0.7
1906	StL-A	27	89	3	21	4	0	0	8	1		.236	.277	.281	78	-0				.956	-5	2-26	-0.8
Total	2	122	411	43	91	16	0	0	24	47		.221	.328	.260	91	-1	11			.933	-14	2-121	-1.5

■ PAT ROCKETT
Rockett, Patrick Edward b: 1/9/55, San Antonio, Tex. BR/TR, 5'11", 170 lbs. Deb: 9/17/76

YEAR	TM/L	G	AB	R	H	2B	3B	HR	RBI	BB	SO	AVG	OBP	SLG	PRO+	BR/A	SB	CS	SBR	FA	FR	G/POS	TPR
1976	Atl-N	4	5	0	1	0	0	0	0	0	0	.200	.200	.200	13	-1	0	0	0	1.000	-1	/S-2	-0.2
1977	Atl-N	93	264	27	67	10	1	1	24	27	32	.254	.330	.303	64	-13	1	2	-1	.940	-11	S-84	-1.6
1978	Atl-N	55	142	6	20	2	0	0	4	13	12	.141	.213	.155	13	-18	1	2	-1	.970	-10	S-51	-2.6
Total	3	152	411	33	88	12	1	1	28	40	45	.214	.289	.251	43	-32	2	4	-2	.949	-21	S-137	-4.4

■ ANDRE RODGERS
Rodgers, Kenneth Andre Ian "Andy" b: 12/2/34, Nassau, Bahamas BR/TR, 6'3", 200 lbs. Deb: 4/16/57

YEAR	TM/L	G	AB	R	H	2B	3B	HR	RBI	BB	SO	AVG	OBP	SLG	PRO+	BR/A	SB	CS	SBR	FA	FR	G/POS	TPR
1957	NY-N	32	86	8	21	2	1	3	9	9	21	.244	.323	.395	92	-1	0	0	0	.950	5	S-20/3-8	0.6
1958	SF-N	22	63	7	13	3	1	2	11	4	14	.206	.254	.381	67	-3	0	0	0	.972	-3	S-18	-0.5
1959	SF-N	71	228	32	57	12	1	6	24	32	50	.250	.345	.390	98	-0	2	1	0	.933	-9	S-66	-0.4
1960	SF-N	81	217	22	53	8	5	2	22	24	44	.244	.328	.355	92	-2	1	1	-0	.953	-4	S-41,3-21/1O	-0.4
1961	Chi-N	73	214	27	57	17	3	6	23	25	54	.266	.346	.430	103	0	1	1	0	.983	-4	1-42,S-24/O2	0.0
1962	Chi-N	138	461	40	128	20	8	5	44	44	93	.278	.344	.388	93	-0	4	5	-2	.960	7	*S-133/1-1	1.3
1963	Chi-N	150	516	51	118	17	4	5	33	65	93	.229	.325	.306	79	-12	5	7	-3	.954	-3	*S-150	-0.7
1964	Chi-N	129	448	50	107	17	3	12	46	53	88	.239	.319	.371	90	-5	5	1	1	.965	19	*S-126	2.4
1965	Pit-N	75	178	17	51	12	0	2	25	18	28	.287	.352	.388	108	2	2	1	0	.950	-6	S-33,3-15/12	-0.2
1966	Pit-N	36	49	6	9	1	0	0	4	8	12	.184	.298	.204	43	-4	0	1	-1	.913	-1	/S-5,3-3,O1	-0.5
1967	Pit-N	47	61	8	14	3	0	2	4	8	10	.230	.319	.377	98	-0	1	1	-0	1.000	2	/1-9,3-5,S2	0.2
Total	11	854	2521	268	628	112	23	45	245	290	507	.249	.331	.365	90	-29	22	20	-5	.956	9	S-619/1-66,3O2	1.8

■ BUCK RODGERS
Rodgers, Robert Leroy b: 8/16/38, Delaware, Ohio BB/TR, 6'2", 195 lbs. Deb: 9/8/61 MC

YEAR	TM/L	G	AB	R	H	2B	3B	HR	RBI	BB	SO	AVG	OBP	SLG	PRO+	BR/A	SB	CS	SBR	FA	FR	G/POS	TPR
1961	LA-A	16	56	8	18	2	0	2	13	1	6	.321	.333	.464	99	-0	0	0	0	.965	-1	C-14	0.0
1962	LA-A	155	565	65	146	34	6	6	61	45	68	.258	.313	.372	86	-12	1	8	-5	.989	1	*C-150	-1.0
1963	LA-A	100	300	24	70	6	0	4	23	29	35	.233	.305	.293	73	-11	2	2	-1	.979	-14	C-85	-2.4
1964	LA-A	148	514	38	125	18	3	4	54	40	71	.243	.303	.313	80	-15	4	3	-1	.987	14	*C-146	0.5
1965	Cal-A	132	411	33	86	14	3	1	32	35	61	.209	.276	.265	56	-23	4	1	-2	.991	6	*C-128	-1.4
1966	Cal-A	133	454	45	107	20	3	7	48	29	57	.236	.285	.339	81	-12	3	4	-2	.992	-4	*C-133	-1.1
1967	Cal-A	139	429	29	94	13	3	6	41	34	55	.219	.280	.305	76	-13	1	4	-2	.991	2	*C-134/O-1	-0.7
1968	Cal-A	91	258	13	49	7	0	1	16	16	48	.190	.245	.225	45	-17	2	1	0	.985	0	C-87	-1.4
1969	Cal-A	18	46	4	9	1	0	0	8	6	18	.196	.288	.217	46	-3	0	0	0	1.000	-0	C-18	-0.3
Total	9	932	3033	259	704	114	18	31	288	234	409	.232	.291	.312	74	-107	17	27	-11	.988	3	C-895/O-1	-7.8

■ BILL RODGERS
Rodgers, Wilbur Kincaid "Rawmeat Bill" b: 4/18/1887, Pleasant Ridge, O. d: 12/24/78, Goliad, Tex. BL/TR, 5'9.5", 170 lbs. Deb: 4/15/15

YEAR	TM/L	G	AB	R	H	2B	3B	HR	RBI	BB	SO	AVG	OBP	SLG	PRO+	BR/A	SB	CS	SBR	FA	FR	G/POS	TPR
1915	Cle-A	16	45	8	14	2	0	0	7	8	7	.311	.415	.356	128	2	3	3	-1	.945	-4	2-13	-0.3
	Bos-A	11	6	2	0	0	0	0	0	3	2	.000	.333	.000	-0	-1	0			.900	1	/2-6	0.1

YEAR	TM/L	G	AB	R	H	2B	3B	HR	RBI	BB	SO	AVG	OBP	SLG	PRO+	BR/A	SB	CS	SBR	FA	FR	G/POS	TPR
	Yr	27	51	10	14	2	0	0	7	11	9	.275	.403	.314	115	2	3	3	-1	.938	-3	2-19	-0.2
	Cin-N	72	213	20	51	13	4	0	12	11	29	.239	.299	.338	91	-3	8	5	-1	.947	5	2-56/S-6,3O	0.3
1916	Cin-N	3	4	0	0	0	0	0	0	0	0	.000	.000	.000	-99	-1	0			1.000	-0	/S-1	-0.2
Total	2	102	268	30	65	15	4	0	19	22	40	.243	.316	.328	93	-2	11	8		.945	2	/2-75,S-7,O3	-0.1

■ BILL RODGERS
Rodgers, William Sherman   b: 12/5/22, Harrisburg, Pa.   BL/TL, 6', 162 lbs.   Deb: 9/27/44

YEAR	TM/L	G	AB	R	H	2B	3B	HR	RBI	BB	SO	AVG	OBP	SLG	PRO+	BR/A	SB	CS	SBR	FA	FR	G/POS	TPR
1944	Pit-N	2	4	1	1	0	0	0	0	0	1	.250	.250	.250	39	-0	0			.000	-1	/O-1	-0.1
1945	Pit-N	1	1	0	1	0	0	0	0	0	0	1.000	1.000	1.000	440	0	0			.000	0	H	0.0
Total	2	3	5	1	2	0	0	0	0	0	1	.400	.400	.400	120	0	0			—	-1	/O-1	-0.1

■ ERIC RODIN
Rodin, Eric Chapman   b: 2/5/30, Orange, N.J.   d: 1/4/91, Somerville, N.J.   BR/TR, 6'2", 215 lbs.   Deb: 9/7/54

YEAR	TM/L	G	AB	R	H	2B	3B	HR	RBI	BB	SO	AVG	OBP	SLG	PRO+	BR/A	SB	CS	SBR	FA	FR	G/POS	TPR
1954	NY-N	5	6	0	0	0	0	0	0	0	2	.000	.000	.000	-99	-2	0	0	0	1.000	-1	/O-3	-0.3

■ ALEX RODRIGUEZ
Rodriguez, Alexander Emmanuel   b: 7/27/75, New York, N.Y.   BR/TR, 6'3", 190 lbs.   Deb: 7/8/94

YEAR	TM/L	G	AB	R	H	2B	3B	HR	RBI	BB	SO	AVG	OBP	SLG	PRO+	BR/A	SB	CS	SBR	FA	FR	G/POS	TPR
1994	Sea-A	17	54	4	11	0	0	0	2	3	20	.204	.246	.204	17	-7	3	0	1	.915	1	S-17	-0.3

■ AURELIO RODRIGUEZ
Rodriguez, Aurelio (Ituarte)   b: 12/28/47, Cananea, Mexico   BR/TR, 5'10", 180 lbs.   Deb: 9/1/67

YEAR	TM/L	G	AB	R	H	2B	3B	HR	RBI	BB	SO	AVG	OBP	SLG	PRO+	BR/A	SB	CS	SBR	FA	FR	G/POS	TPR
1967	Cal-A	29	130	14	31	3	1	1	8	2	21	.238	.250	.300	64	-6	1	0	0	.989	5	3-29	-0.2
1968	Cal-A	76	223	14	54	10	1	1	16	17	36	.242	.299	.309	88	-3	0	2	-1	.921	-7	3-70/2-2	-1.3
1969	Cal-A	159	561	47	130	17	2	7	49	32	88	.232	.276	.307	66	-27	5	3	-0	.954	8	*3-159	-2.0
1970	Cal-A	17	63	6	17	2	2	0	7	3	6	.270	.313	.365	90	-1	0	1	-1	1.000	4	3-17	0.2
	Was-A	142	547	64	135	31	5	19	76	37	81	.247	.303	.426	104	0	15	5	2	.961	13	*3-136/S-7	1.4
	Yr	159	610	70	152	33	7	19	83	40	87	.249	.304	.420	102	-1	15	6	1	.965	17	*3-153/S-7	1.6
1971	Det-A	154	604	68	153	30	7	15	39	27	93	.253	.289	.401	90	-10	4	6	-2	.953	15	*3-153/S-1	0.1
1972	*Det-A	153	601	65	142	23	5	13	56	28	104	.236	.273	.356	83	-14	2	3	-1	.969	24	*3-153/S-2	0.9
1973	Det-A	160	555	46	123	27	3	9	58	31	85	.222	.267	.330	63	-28	3	1	0	.971	10	*3-160/S-1	-1.9
1974	Det-A	159	571	54	127	23	5	5	49	26	70	.222	.258	.306	60	-30	2	0	1	.961	22	*3-159	-1.0
1975	Det-A	151	507	47	124	20	6	13	60	30	63	.245	.287	.385	85	-12	1	1	0	.953	21	*3-151	0.8
1976	Det-A	128	480	40	115	23	2	8	50	19	61	.240	.270	.325	71	-19	0	4	-2	**.978**	13	*3-128	-0.9
1977	Det-A	96	306	30	67	14	1	10	32	16	36	.219	.258	.369	65	-15	0	1	0	.972	16	3-95/S-1	-0.1
1978	Det-A	134	385	40	102	25	2	7	43	19	37	.265	.305	.395	93	-5	0	1	-1	**.987**	2	*3-131	-0.5
1979	Det-A	106	343	27	87	18	0	5	36	11	40	.254	.279	.350	66	-17	0	2	-1	.956	9	*3-106/1-1	-1.3
1980	SD-N	89	175	7	35	7	2	2	13	6	26	.200	.227	.297	48	-13	1	0	0	.965	10	3-88/S-2	-0.4
	*NY-A	52	164	14	36	6	1	3	14	7	35	.220	.251	.323	57	-10	0	0	0	.954	-5	3-49/2-6	-1.6
1981	*NY-A	27	52	4	18	2	0	2	8	2	10	.346	.370	.500	151	3	0	0	0	.951	4	3-20/2-3,1D	0.7
1982	Chi-A	118	257	24	62	15	1	3	31	11	35	.241	.275	.342	68	-11	0	0	0	.969	19	*3-112/2-3,S	0.6
1983	Bal-A	45	67	0	8	0	0	0	2	0	13	.119	.132	.119	-31	-12	0	0	0	.969	3	3-45	-1.1
	*Chi-A	22	20	1	4	1	0	1	1	0	3	.200	.200	.400	58	-1	0	0	0	1.000	4	3-22	0.3
	Yr	67	87	1	12	1	0	1	3	0	16	.138	.148	.184	-9	-13	0	0	0	.978	6	3-67	-0.8
Total	17	2017	6611	612	1570	287	46	124	648	324	943	.237	.276	.351	75	-232	35	31	-8	.964	184	*3-1983/S-16,2D1	-7.3

■ CARLOS RODRIGUEZ
Rodriguez, Carlos (Marquez)   b: 11/1/67, Mexico City, Mexico   BB/TR, 5'9", 160 lbs.   Deb: 6/16/91

YEAR	TM/L	G	AB	R	H	2B	3B	HR	RBI	BB	SO	AVG	OBP	SLG	PRO+	BR/A	SB	CS	SBR	FA	FR	G/POS	TPR
1991	NY-A	15	37	1	7	0	0	0	1	1	1	.189	.211	.189	11	-4	0	0	0	.957	1	S-11/2-3	-0.3
1994	Bos-A	57	174	15	50	14	1	1	13	11	13	.287	.330	.397	81	-5	1	0	0	.973	2	S-32,2-20/3	0.0
Total	2	72	211	16	57	14	1	1	15	12	15	.270	.309	.360	70	-9	1	0	0	.969	3	/S-43,2-23,3	-0.3

■ EDWIN RODRIGUEZ
Rodriguez, Edwin (Morales)   b: 8/14/60, Ponce, P.R.   BR/TR, 5'11", 175 lbs.   Deb: 9/28/82

YEAR	TM/L	G	AB	R	H	2B	3B	HR	RBI	BB	SO	AVG	OBP	SLG	PRO+	BR/A	SB	CS	SBR	FA	FR	G/POS	TPR
1982	NY-A	3	9	2	3	0	0	0	1	1	1	.333	.400	.333	106	0	0	0	0	.875	1	/2-3	0.1
1983	SD-N	7	12	1	2	0	0	0	1	0	3	.167	.231	.250	34	-1	0	0	0	1.000	-1	/2-5,S-2,3	-0.2
1985	SD-N	1	1	0	0	0	0	0	0	0	0	.000	.000	.000	-99	-0	0	0	0	.000	0	/H	-0.2
Total	3	11	22	3	5	1	0	0	1	2	4	.227	.292	.273	58	-1	0	0	0	.935	0	/2-8,S-2,3	-0.1

■ ELLIE RODRIGUEZ
Rodriguez, Eliseo (Delgado)   b: 5/24/46, Fajardo, P.R.   BR/TR, 5'11", 185 lbs.   Deb: 5/26/68

YEAR	TM/L	G	AB	R	H	2B	3B	HR	RBI	BB	SO	AVG	OBP	SLG	PRO+	BR/A	SB	CS	SBR	FA	FR	G/POS	TPR
1968	NY-A	9	24	1	5	0	0	0	1	3	3	.208	.296	.208	57	-1	0	0	0	1.000	0	/C-9	0.0
1969	KC-A☆	95	267	27	63	10	0	2	20	31	26	.236	.333	.296	77	-7	3	2	-0	.990	-8	C-90	-1.2
1970	KC-A	80	231	25	52	8	2	1	15	27	35	.225	.317	.290	68	-9	2	1	0	.988	12	C-75	0.6
1971	Mil-A	115	319	28	67	10	1	1	30	41	51	.210	.315	.257	64	-13	1	1	0	.992	6	*C-114	-0.4
1972	Mil-A☆	116	355	31	101	14	2	2	35	52	43	.285	.386	.352	123	13	1	4	-2	.983	-11	*C-114	0.5
1973	Mil-A	94	290	30	78	8	1	0	30	41	28	.269	.378	.303	96	1	4	3	-1	.986	7	C-75,D-14	0.7
1974	Cal-A	140	395	48	100	20	1	6	36	69	56	.253	.376	.357	119	13	4	5	-2	.992	-10	*C-137/D-1	0.8
1975	Cal-A	90	226	20	53	6	0	3	27	49	37	.235	.384	.301	103	4	2	2	-1	.991	-7	C-90	0.0
1976	LA-N	36	66	10	14	0	0	0	9	19	12	.212	.409	.212	82	0	0	0	0	.986	4	C-33	0.6
Total	9	775	2173	220	533	76	6	16	203	332	291	.245	.359	.308	94	0	17	18	-6	.989	-10	C-737/D-15	1.6

■ HECTOR RODRIGUEZ
Rodriguez, Hector Antonio (Ordenana)   b: 6/13/20, Alquizar, Cuba   BR/TR, 5'8", 165 lbs.   Deb: 4/15/52

YEAR	TM/L	G	AB	R	H	2B	3B	HR	RBI	BB	SO	AVG	OBP	SLG	PRO+	BR/A	SB	CS	SBR	FA	FR	G/POS	TPR
1952	Chi-A	124	407	55	108	14	0	1	40	47	22	.265	.346	.307	82	-8	7	6	-3	.959	2	*3-113	-1.0

■ HENRY RODRIGUEZ
Rodriguez, Henry Anderson (Lorenzo)   b: 11/8/67, Santo Domingo, D.R.   BL/TL, 6'1", 180 lbs.   Deb: 7/5/92

YEAR	TM/L	G	AB	R	H	2B	3B	HR	RBI	BB	SO	AVG	OBP	SLG	PRO+	BR/A	SB	CS	SBR	FA	FR	G/POS	TPR
1992	LA-N	53	146	11	32	7	0	3	14	8	30	.219	.260	.329	67	-7	0	0	0	.960	1	O-48/1-1	-0.7
1993	LA-N	76	176	20	39	10	0	8	23	11	39	.222	.267	.415	84	-5	0	1	0	.984	-6	O-48,1-13	-1.2
1994	LA-N	104	306	33	82	14	2	8	49	17	58	.268	.311	.405	90	-5	0	1	-1	.986	0	O-86,1-17	-0.8
Total	3	233	628	64	153	31	2	19	86	36	127	.244	.287	.390	83	-17	1	1	-1	.979	-4	O-182/1-31	-2.7

■ IVAN RODRIGUEZ
Rodriguez, Ivan (Torres) "Pudge"   b: 11/27/71, Manati, P.R.   BR/TR, 5'9", 165 lbs.   Deb: 6/20/91

YEAR	TM/L	G	AB	R	H	2B	3B	HR	RBI	BB	SO	AVG	OBP	SLG	PRO+	BR/A	SB	CS	SBR	FA	FR	G/POS	TPR
1991	Tex-A	88	280	24	74	16	0	3	27	5	42	.264	.277	.354	75	-10	0	1	-1	.983	14	C-88	0.7
1992	Tex-A★	123	420	39	109	16	1	8	37	24	73	.260	.301	.360	87	-8	0	0	0	.983	8	*C-116/D-2	0.7
1993	Tex-A★	137	473	56	129	28	4	10	66	29	70	.273	.320	.412	99	-2	8	7	-2	.991	6	*C-134/D-1	0.9
1994	Tex-A★	99	363	56	108	19	1	16	57	31	42	.298	.364	.488	125	13	6	3	0	.992	-7	C-99	1.1
Total	4	447	1536	175	420	79	6	37	187	89	227	.273	.318	.405	98	-7	14	11	-2	.987	21	C-437/D-3	3.4

■ JOSE RODRIGUEZ
Rodriguez, Jose "El Hombre Goma"   b: 2/23/1894, Havana, Cuba   d: 1/21/53, Havana, Cuba   BR/TR, 5'8", 150 lbs.   Deb: 10/5/16

YEAR	TM/L	G	AB	R	H	2B	3B	HR	RBI	BB	SO	AVG	OBP	SLG	PRO+	BR/A	SB	CS	SBR	FA	FR	G/POS	TPR
1916	NY-N	1	0	0	0	0	0	0	0	0	0	—	—	—			0	0		.000	0	R	0.0
1917	NY-N	7	20	2	4	0	1	0	2	2	1	.200	.273	.300	78	-1	2			1.000	-1	/1-7	-0.2
1918	NY-N	50	125	15	20	0	2	0	15	12	3	.160	.239	.192	33	-10	6			.978	4	/2-40/1-8,3	-0.4
Total	3	58	145	17	24	0	3	0	17	14	4	.166	.244	.207	39	-10	8			.989	3	/2-40,1-15,3	-0.6

■ RUBEN RODRIGUEZ
Rodriguez, Ruben Dario (Martinez)   b: 8/4/64, Cabrera, D.R.   BR/TR, 6'3", 190 lbs.   Deb: 9/17/86

YEAR	TM/L	G	AB	R	H	2B	3B	HR	RBI	BB	SO	AVG	OBP	SLG	PRO+	BR/A	SB	CS	SBR	FA	FR	G/POS	TPR
1986	Pit-N	2	3	0	0	0	0	0	0	0	0	.000	.000	.000	-98	-1	0	0	0	1.000	1	/C-2	0.0
1988	Pit-N	2	5	1	1	0	0	0	1	0	3	.200	.200	.600	123	0	0	0	0	1.000	0	/C-2	0.0
Total	2	4	8	1	1	0	0	0	1	0	3	.125	.125	.375	36	-1	0	0	0	1.000	1	/C-4	0.0

■ VIC RODRIGUEZ
Rodriguez, Victor Manuel (Rivera)   b: 7/14/61, New York, N.Y.   BR/TR, 5'11", 173 lbs.   Deb: 9/5/84

YEAR	TM/L	G	AB	R	H	2B	3B	HR	RBI	BB	SO	AVG	OBP	SLG	PRO+	BR/A	SB	CS	SBR	FA	FR	G/POS	TPR
1984	Bal-A	11	17	4	7	3	0	0	2	0	2	.412	.412	.588	177	2	0	0	0	.958	2	/2-7,D-1	0.3
1989	Min-A	6	11	2	5	2	0	0	0	0	1	.455	.455	.636	191	1	0	0	0	.900	1	/3-5,D-1	0.2
Total	2	17	28	6	12	5	0	0	2	0	3	.429	.429	.607	183	3	0	0	0	.958	3	/2-7,3-5,D	0.5

YEAR	TM/L	G	AB	R	H	2B	3B	HR	RBI	BB	SO	AVG	OBP	SLG	PRO+	BR/A	SB	CS	SBR	FA	FR	G/POS	TPR

■ GARY ROENICKE Roenicke, Gary Steven b: 12/5/54, Covina, Cal. BR/TR, 6'3", 205 lbs. Deb: 6/8/76 F

YEAR	TM/L	G	AB	R	H	2B	3B	HR	RBI	BB	SO	AVG	OBP	SLG	PRO+	BR/A	SB	CS	SBR	FA	FR	G/POS	TPR
1976	Mon-N	29	90	9	20	3	1	2	5	4	18	.222	.263	.344	69	-4	0	0	0	.955	-1	O-25	-0.6
1978	Bal-A	27	58	5	15	3	0	3	15	8	3	.259	.358	.466	138	3	0	1	-1	1.000	-3	O-20	-0.1
1979	*Bal-A	133	376	60	98	16	1	25	64	61	74	.261	.381	.508	143	24	1	3	-2	.981	-8	*O-130	0.9
1980	Bal-A	118	297	40	71	13	0	10	28	41	49	.239	.343	.384	100	1	2	0	1	**1.000**	-13	*O-113	-1.5
1981	Bal-A	85	219	31	59	16	0	3	20	23	29	.269	.344	.384	110	3	1	2	-1	.983	-13	O-83	-1.4
1982	Bal-A	137	393	58	106	25	1	21	74	70	73	.270	.392	.499	143	25	6	7	-2	.990	-9	*O-125,1-10	1.1
1983	*Bal-A	115	323	45	84	13	0	19	64	30	55	.260	.331	.477	121	9	2	2	-1	.982	-14	*O-100/1-7,3D	-0.8
1984	Bal-A	121	326	36	73	19	1	10	44	58	43	.224	.348	.380	104	3	1	2	-1	.995	-10	*O-117	-1.1
1985	Bal-A	114	225	36	49	9	0	15	43	44	36	.218	.346	.458	121	7	1	2	-1	.993	-8	O-89,D-17	-0.4
1986	NY-A	69	136	11	36	5	0	3	18	27	30	.265	.390	.368	109	3	1	1	-0	1.000	-6	O-37,D-15/31	-0.4
1987	Atl-N	67	151	25	33	8	0	9	28	32	23	.219	.359	.450	107	2	0	0	0	.968	-3	O-44/1-9	-0.3
1988	Atl-N	49	114	11	26	5	0	1	7	8	15	.228	.279	.298	63	-5	0	0	0	1.000	-4	O-35/1-1	-1.1
Total	12	1064	2708	367	670	135	4	121	410	406	428	.247	.354	.434	117	70	16	20	-7	.988	-92	O-918/D-34,13	-5.7

■ RON ROENICKE Roenicke, Ronald Jon b: 8/19/56, Covina, Cal. BB/TL, 6', 180 lbs. Deb: 9/2/81 F

YEAR	TM/L	G	AB	R	H	2B	3B	HR	RBI	BB	SO	AVG	OBP	SLG	PRO+	BR/A	SB	CS	SBR	FA	FR	G/POS	TPR
1981	LA-N	22	47	6	11	0	0	0	6	6	8	.234	.321	.234	62	-2	1	1	-0	1.000	-19	O-20	-0.3
1982	LA-N	109	143	18	37	8	0	1	12	21	32	.259	.361	.336	99	1	5	0	2	.984	-19	O-72	-1.9
1983	LA-N	81	145	12	32	4	0	2	12	14	26	.221	.289	.290	61	-8	3	2	-0	.987	-12	O-62	-2.2
	Sea-A	59	198	23	50	12	0	4	23	33	22	.253	.365	.374	100	1	6	1	1	.993	7	O-54/1-8,D	0.6
1984	*SD-N	12	20	4	6	1	0	1	2	2	5	.300	.364	.500	141	1	0	0	0	1.000	-2	O-10	-0.2
1985	SF-N	65	133	23	34	9	1	3	13	35	27	.256	.411	.406	136	8	6	2	1	.984	-2	O-35	0.7
1986	Phi-N	102	275	42	68	13	1	5	42	61	52	.247	.384	.356	102	3	2	2	-1	.989	-2	O-83	-0.2
1987	Phi-N	63	78	9	13	3	1	1	4	14	15	.167	.293	.269	49	-6	1	0	0	.964	-6	O-26	-1.2
1988	Cin-N	14	37	4	5	1	0	0	5	4	8	.135	.238	.162	16	-4	0	0	0	1.000	-2	O-14	-0.7
Total	8	527	1076	141	256	51	3	17	113	190	195	.238	.355	.338	92	-5	24	9	2	.989	-37	O-376/1-8,D	-5.4

■ OSCAR ROETTGER Roettger, Oscar Frederick Louis "Okkie" b: 2/19/1900, St.Louis, Mo. d: 7/4/86, St.Louis, Mo. BR/TR, 6', 170 lbs. Deb: 7/7/23 F

YEAR	TM/L	G	AB	R	H	2B	3B	HR	RBI	BB	SO	AVG	OBP	SLG	PRO+	BR/A	SB	CS	SBR	FA	FR	G/POS	TPR
1923	NY-A	5	2	0	0	0	0	0	0	0	0	.000	.000	.000	-98	0	0	0	0	.000	0	/P-5	0.0
1924	NY-A	1	0	0	0	0	0	0	0	0	0	—	—	—	—	0	0	0	0	.000	0	/P-1	0.0
1927	Bro-N	5	4	0	0	0	0	0	0	1	1	.000	.333	.000	-4	-0	0			.000	-1	/O-1	-0.1
1932	Phi-A	26	60	7	14	1	0	0	6	5	4	.233	.292	.250	40	-5	0	0	0	.978	-2	1-15	-0.7
Total	4	37	66	7	14	1	0	0	6	6	5	.212	.288	.227	34	-6	0	0	0	1.000	-2	/1-15,P-6,O	-0.8

■ WALLY ROETTGER Roettger, Walter Henry b: 8/28/02, St.Louis, Mo. d: 9/14/51, Champaign, Ill. BR/TR, 6'1.5", 190 lbs. Deb: 5/1/27 F

YEAR	TM/L	G	AB	R	H	2B	3B	HR	RBI	BB	SO	AVG	OBP	SLG	PRO+	BR/A	SB	CS	SBR	FA	FR	G/POS	TPR
1927	StL-N	5	1	0	0	0	0	1	0	0	0	.000	.500	.000	42	0				.500	-1	/O-3	-0.1
1928	StL-N	68	261	29	89	17	4	6	44	10	22	.341	.372	.506	125	9	2			.981	-1	O-66	0.4
1929	StL-N	79	269	27	68	11	3	3	42	13	27	.253	.287	.349	56	-19	0			.993	-4	O-69	-2.5
1930	NY-N	121	420	51	119	15	5	5	51	25	29	.283	.330	.379	72	-19	1			**.992**	-6	*O-114	-2.9
1931	Cin-N	44	185	25	65	11	4	1	20	7	9	.351	.378	.470	135	8	1			.990	-1	O-44	0.4
	*StL-N	45	151	16	43	12	2	0	17	9	14	.285	.337	.391	92	-2	0			.974	-6	O-42	-1.1
	Yr	89	336	41	108	23	6	1	37	16	23	.321	.360	.435	114	6	1			.983	-7	O-86	-0.7
1932	Cin-N	106	347	26	96	18	3	3	43	23	24	.277	.323	.372	89	-5	0			.991	-1	O-94	-1.2
1933	Cin-N	84	209	13	50	7	1	1	17	8	10	.239	.267	.297	62	-11	0			.977	0	O-55	-1.4
1934	Pit-N	47	106	7	26	5	0	0	11	3	8	.245	.266	.311	53	-7	0			1.000	1	O-23	-0.7
Total	8	599	1949	192	556	96	23	19	245	99	143	.285	.324	.387	85	-46	4			.986	-19	O-510	-9.1

■ ED ROETZ Roetz, Edward Bernard b: 8/6/05, Philadelphia, Pa. d: 3/16/65, Philadelphia, Pa. BR/TR, 5'10", 160 lbs. Deb: 5/26/29

YEAR	TM/L	G	AB	R	H	2B	3B	HR	RBI	BB	SO	AVG	OBP	SLG	PRO+	BR/A	SB	CS	SBR	FA	FR	G/POS	TPR
1929	StL-A	16	45	7	11	4	1	0	5	4	6	.244	.306	.378	72	-2	0	0	0	.909	-1	/S-8,1-5,23	-0.2

■ BILLY ROGELL Rogell, William George b: 11/24/04, Springfield, Ill. BB/TR, 5'10.5", 163 lbs. Deb: 4/14/25

YEAR	TM/L	G	AB	R	H	2B	3B	HR	RBI	BB	SO	AVG	OBP	SLG	PRO+	BR/A	SB	CS	SBR	FA	FR	G/POS	TPR
1925	Bos-A	58	169	12	33	5	1	0	17	11	17	.195	.244	.237	22	-20	0	3	-2	.935	6	2-49/S-6	-1.4
1927	Bos-A	82	207	35	55	14	6	2	28	24	28	.266	.342	.420	99	-1	3	1	0	.966	6	3-53/2-2,O	0.7
1928	Bos-A	102	296	33	69	10	4	0	29	22	47	.233	.295	.294	56	-19	2	6	-3	.935	-13	S-67,2-22/O3	-2.7
1930	Det-A	54	144	20	24	4	2	0	9	15	23	.167	.250	.222	20	-18	1	2	-1	.938	4	S-33,3-13/O	-1.0
1931	Det-A	48	185	21	56	12	3	2	24	17	17	.303	.383	.432	110	3	8	8	-2	.958	11	S-48	1.5
1932	Det-A	144	552	88	150	29	6	9	61	50	38	.271	.332	.394	84	-14	14	6	1	.944	9	*S-139/3-4	0.6
1933	Det-A	155	587	67	173	42	11	0	57	79	33	.295	.381	.404	106	7	6	9	-4	.944	20	*S-155	3.2
1934	*Det-A	154	592	114	175	32	8	3	100	74	36	.296	.374	.392	97	-1	13	3	2	.962	9	*S-154	1.8
1935	*Det-A	150	560	88	154	23	11	6	71	80	29	.275	.367	.387	99	0	3	6	-3	**.971**	12	*S-150	1.7
1936	Det-A	146	585	85	160	27	6	6	68	73	41	.274	.357	.368	79	-19	14	10	-2	**.965**	-1	*S-146/3-1	-1.1
1937	Det-A	146	536	85	148	30	7	8	64	83	48	.276	.376	.403	94	-3	5	5	-2	**.967**	2	*S-146	0.7
1938	Det-A	136	501	76	130	22	8	3	55	86	37	.259	.373	.353	78	-15	9	2	0	.959	8	*S-134	0.4
1939	Det-A	74	174	24	40	6	3	2	23	26	14	.230	.330	.333	65	-9	3	1	0	.931	2	S-43,3-21/2	-0.3
1940	Chi-N	33	59	7	8	0	0	1	3	2	8	.136	.164	.186	-4	-8	1			.900	-5	S-14/3-9,2	-1.3
Total	14	1482	5149	755	1375	256	75	42	609	649	416	.267	.351	.370	84	-115	82	62		.956	68	*S-1235,3-104/20	2.8

■ EMMETT ROGERS Rogers, Emmett b: 1865, Rome, N.Y. BB, 5'10", 165 lbs. Deb: 4/19/1890

YEAR	TM/L	G	AB	R	H	2B	3B	HR	RBI	BB	SO	AVG	OBP	SLG	PRO+	BR/A	SB	CS	SBR	FA	FR	G/POS	TPR
1890	Tol-a	35	110	18	19	3	3	0		14		.173	.266	.255	52	-7	2			.924	5	C-34/O-1	0.1

■ FRALEY ROGERS Rogers, Fraley W. b: 1850, Brooklyn, N.Y. d: 5/10/1881, New York, N.Y. 5'8", 184 lbs. Deb: 4/30/1872

YEAR	TM/L	G	AB	R	H	2B	3B	HR	RBI	BB	SO	AVG	OBP	SLG	PRO+	BR/A	SB	CS	SBR	FA	FR	G/POS	TPR
1872	Bos-n	45	204	39	58	10	1	1	28	1	4	.284	.288	.358	93	-3						O-42/1-6	0.0
1873	Bos-n	1	6	1	2	2	0	0	2	0	1	.333	.333	.667	172	0						/1-1	0.0
Total	2 n	46	210	40	60	12	1	1	30	1	5	.286	.289	.367	95	-3						/O-42,1-7	0.0

■ JIM ROGERS Rogers, James F. b: 4/9/1872, Hartford, Conn. 5'7.5", 180 lbs. Deb: 4/17/1896 M

YEAR	TM/L	G	AB	R	H	2B	3B	HR	RBI	BB	SO	AVG	OBP	SLG	PRO+	BR/A	SB	CS	SBR	FA	FR	G/POS	TPR
1896	Was-N	38	154	21	43	6	4	1	30	10	9	.279	.323	.390	87	-3	3			.882	-6	3-32/2-6,O	-0.7
	Lou-N	72	290	39	75	8	6	0	38	15	14	.259	.297	.328	67	-14	13			.971	-2	1-60,S-12	-1.3
	Yr	110	444	60	118	14	10	1	68	25	23	.266	.306	.349	74	-17	16			.971	-8	1-60,3-32,S/2O	-2.0
1897	Lou-N	41	150	22	22	3	2	2	22	22		.147	.260	.233	32	-15	4			.933	-4	2-39/1-3M	-1.5
Total	2	151	594	82	140	17	12	3	90	47	23	.236	.294	.320	64	-32	20			.970	-12	/1-63,2-45,3SO	-3.5

■ JAY ROGERS Rogers, Jay Lewis b: 8/3/1888, Sandusky, N.Y. d: 7/1/64, Carlisle, N.Y. BR/TR, 5'11.5", 178 lbs. Deb: 5/22/14

YEAR	TM/L	G	AB	R	H	2B	3B	HR	RBI	BB	SO	AVG	OBP	SLG	PRO+	BR/A	SB	CS	SBR	FA	FR	G/POS	TPR
1914	NY-A	5	8	0	0	0	0	0	0	0	4	.000	.000	.000	-99	-2	0			.923	-0	/C-4	-0.2

■ PACKY ROGERS Rogers, Stanley Frank (b: Stanley Frank Hazinski) b: 4/26/13, Swoyersville, Pa. BR/TR, 5'8", 175 lbs. Deb: 7/12/38

YEAR	TM/L	G	AB	R	H	2B	3B	HR	RBI	BB	SO	AVG	OBP	SLG	PRO+	BR/A	SB	CS	SBR	FA	FR	G/POS	TPR
1938	Bro-N	23	37	3	7	1	1	0	5	6	6	.189	.302	.270	57	-2	0			1.000	-1	/S-9,3-8,2O	-0.2

■ MIKE ROGODZINSKI Rogodzinski, Michael George b: 2/22/48, Evanston, Ill. BL/TR, 6', 185 lbs. Deb: 5/4/73

YEAR	TM/L	G	AB	R	H	2B	3B	HR	RBI	BB	SO	AVG	OBP	SLG	PRO+	BR/A	SB	CS	SBR	FA	FR	G/POS	TPR
1973	Phi-N	66	80	13	19	3	0	2	7	12	19	.237	.337	.350	88	-1	0	0	0	.947	-3	O-16	-0.4
1974	Phi-N	17	15	1	1	0	0	0	1	2	3	.067	.176	.067	-29	-3	0	0	0	.000	-0	/O-1	-0.3
1975	Phi-N	16	19	3	5	1	0	0	4	2	2	.263	.364	.316	86	-0	1	1	-1	.667	-1	/O-2	-0.2
Total	3	99	114	17	25	4	0	2	12	17	24	.219	.321	.307	73	-4	1	1	-1	.909	-4	/O-19	-0.9

YEAR	TM/L	G	AB	R	H	2B	3B	HR	RBI	BB	SO	AVG	OBP	SLG	PRO+	BR/A	SB	CS	SBR	FA	FR	G/POS	TPR

■ DAVE ROHDE Rohde, David Grant b: 5/8/64, Los Altos, Cal. BB/TR, 6'2", 180 lbs. Deb: 4/9/90

1990	Hou-N	59	98	8	18	4	0	0	5	9	20	.184	.286	.224	44	-7	0	0	0	1.000	-0	2-32/3-4,S	-0.7
1991	Hou-N	29	41	3	5	0	0	0	0	5	8	.122	.217	.122	-2	-6	0	0	0	1.000	1	/2-4,3-3,S1	-0.5
1992	Cle-A	5	7	0	0	0	0	0	0	2	3	.000	.222	.000	-34	-1	0	0	0	.900	0	/3-5	-0.1
Total	3	93	146	11	23	4	0	0	5	16	31	.158	.263	.185	27	-14	0	0	0	1.000	2	2-36,3-12,S1	-1.3

■ GEORGE ROHE Rohe, George Anthony "Whitey" b: 9/15/1875, Cincinnati, Ohio d: 6/10/57, Cincinnati, Ohio BR/TR, 5'9", 165 lbs. Deb: 5/7/01

1901	Bal-A	14	36	7	10	2	0	0	4	5		.278	.381	.333	95	-0	1			.912	-3	/1-8,3-6	-0.2
1905	Chi-A	34	113	14	24	1	0	1	12	12		.212	.310	.248	81	-2	2			.934	-4	2-17,3-17	-0.6
1906	*Chi-A	77	225	14	58	5	1	0	25	16		.258	.316	.289	92	-2	8			.926	2	3-57/2-5,O	0.2
1907	Chi-A	144	494	46	105	11	2	2	51	39		.213	.274	.255	71	-15	16			.898	-5	3-76,2-39,S	-2.0
Total	4	269	868	81	197	19	3	3	92	72		.227	.294	.266	79	-19	27			.917	-10	3-156/2-61,S10	-2.6

■ DAN ROHN Rohn, Daniel Jay b: 1/10/56, Alpena, Mich. BL/TR, 5'7", 165 lbs. Deb: 9/2/83

1983	Chi-N	23	31	3	12	3	0	0	6	2	2	.387	.424	.613	176	3	1	0	0	.923	-0	/2-6,S-1	0.3
1984	Chi-N	25	31	1	4	0	0	1	3	1	6	.129	.156	.226	6	-4	0	0	0	1.000	0	/3-7,2-5,S	-0.4
1986	Cle-A	6	10	1	2	0	0	0	2	1	1	.200	.273	.200	32	-1	0	0	0	.900	1	/2-2,3-2,S	0.0
Total	3	54	72	5	18	3	2	1	11	4	9	.250	.289	.389	82	-2	1	0	0	.930	1	/2-13,3-9,S	-0.1

■ RAY ROHWER Rohwer, Ray b: 6/5/1895, Dixon, Cal. d: 1/24/88, Davis, Cal. BL/TL, 5'10", 155 lbs. Deb: 4/13/21

1921	Pit-N	30	40	6	10	3	2	0	6	4	8	.250	.318	.425	93	-1	0	-1		.842	-1	O-10	-0.3
1922	Pit-N	53	129	19	38	6	3	3	22	10	17	.295	.350	.457	105	1	1	0		.938	0	O-30	-0.1
Total	2	83	169	25	48	9	5	3	28	14	25	.284	.342	.450	102	0	1	1	-0	.917	-1	/O-40	-0.4

■ TONY ROIG Roig, Anton Ambrose b: 12/23/27, New Orleans, La. BR/TR, 6'1", 180 lbs. Deb: 9/13/53

1953	Was-A	3	8	0	1	1	0	0	0	0	1	.125	.125	.250	-1	-1	0	0	0	1.000	2	/2-2	0.0
1955	Was-A	29	57	3	13	1	1	0	4	2	15	.228	.254	.281	46	-5	0	0	0	.932	1	S-21/3-8,2	-0.3
1956	Was-A	44	119	11	25	5	2	0	7	20	29	.210	.324	.286	62	-6	2	0	1	.973	6	2-27,S-19	0.4
Total	3	76	184	14	39	7	3	0	11	22	45	.212	.296	.283	55	-12	2	0	1	.927	9	/S-40,2-30,3	0.1

■ COOKIE ROJAS Rojas, Octavio Victor (Rivas) b: 3/6/39, Havana, Cuba BR/TR, 5'10", 170 lbs. Deb: 4/10/62 MC

1962	Cin-N	39	86	9	19	2	0	0	6	9	4	.221	.302	.244	47	-6	1	1	-0	.949	-2	2-30/3-1	-0.6
1963	Phi-N	64	77	18	17	0	1	1	2	3	8	.221	.259	.286	57	-4	1	1	1	.991	16	2-25/O-1	1.5
1964	Phi-N	109	340	58	99	19	5	2	31	22	17	.291	.338	.394	107	3	1	3	-1	.967	-11	O-70,2-20,S/C3	-1.1
1965	Phi-N★	142	521	78	158	25	3	3	42	42	33	.303	.359	.380	110	8	5	5	-2	.986	-3	2-84,O-55,S/C1	0.9
1966	Phi-N	156	626	77	168	18	1	6	55	35	46	.268	.311	.329	78	-18	4	6	-2	.983	-9	*2-106,O-56/S	-2.6
1967	Phi-N	147	528	60	137	21	2	4	45	30	58	.259	.299	.330	79	-14	8	4	-0	.977	-4	*2-137/O-9,CSP3	-1.1
1968	Phi-N	152	621	53	144	19	0	9	48	16	55	.232	.251	.306	67	-26	4	8	-4	**.987**	11	*2-150/C-1	-1.2
1969	Phi-N	110	391	35	89	11	4	1	30	23	23	.228	.272	.292	60	-22	1	6	-3	.980	-3	2-95/O-2	-2.2
1970	StL-N	23	47	2	5	0	0	0	2	3	4	.106	.176	.106	-22	-9	0	0	0	1.000	0	2-10/O-3,S	-0.7
	KC-A	98	384	36	100	13	3	2	28	20	29	.260	.297	.326	72	-15	3	7	-5	.982	-1	2-97	-1.1
1971	KC-A★	115	414	56	124	22	2	6	59	39	35	.300	.363	.406	118	10	8	3	1	**.991**	-12	*2-111/S-2,O	0.9
1972	KC-A★	137	487	49	127	25	0	3	53	41	35	.261	.319	.331	94	-3	2	8	-4	.986	-2	*2-131/3-6,S	-0.2
1973	KC-A★	139	551	78	152	29	3	6	69	37	38	.276	.323	.372	88	-9	18	4	3	.982	9	*2-137	1.1
1974	KC-A☆	144	542	52	147	17	1	6	60	30	43	.271	.313	.339	83	-12	8	4	0	**.987**	-24	*2-141	-3.1
1975	KC-A	120	406	34	103	18	2	2	37	30	24	.254	.305	.323	75	-13	4	5	-2	.980	-15	*2-117/D-1	-2.5
1976	*KC-A	63	132	11	32	6	0	0	16	8	15	.242	.286	.288	68	-5	2	0	1	1.000	-13	2-40/3-6,1D	-1.7
1977	*KC-A	64	156	8	39	9	1	0	10	8	7	.250	.287	.321	65	-8	1	3	-0	.944	3	3-31,2-16/D	-0.5
Total	16	1822	6309	714	1660	254	25	54	593	396	489	.263	.309	.337	83	-144	74	68	-19	.984	-60	*2-1447,O-197/3SDC1P	-14.2

■ STAN ROJEK Rojek, Stanley Andrew b: 4/21/19, N.Tonawanda, N.Y. BR/TR, 5'10", 170 lbs. Deb: 9/22/42

1942	Bro-N	1	0	1	0	0	0	0	0	0	0	—	—	—			0			.000	0	R	0.0
1946	Bro-N	45	47	11	13	2	1	0	2	4	1	.277	.340	.362	96	-0	1			.974	5	S-15/2-6,3	0.6
1947	Bro-N	32	80	7	21	0	1	0	7	7	3	.262	.322	.287	61	-4	1			.971	9	S-17/3-9,2	0.4
1948	Pit-N	156	641	85	186	27	5	4	51	61	41	.290	.355	.367	94	-4	24			.962	-9	*S-156	-0.4
1949	Pit-N	144	557	72	136	19	2	0	31	50	31	.244	.309	.285	59	-31	4			.966	1	*S-144	-2.0
1950	Pit-N	76	230	28	59	12	1	0	17	18	13	.257	.313	.317	64	-12	2			.967	-15	S-68/2-3	-2.2
1951	Pit-N	8	16	0	3	0	0	0	0	0	1	.188	.188	.188	1	-2	0	0	0	.900	-1	/S-8	-0.3
	StL-N	51	186	21	51	7	3	0	14	10	10	.274	.318	.344	78	-6	0	3	-2	.974	1	S-51	-0.4
	Yr	59	202	21	54	7	3	0	14	10	11	.267	.308	.332	72	-8	0	3	-2	.968	-1	S-59	-0.7
1952	StL-A	9	7	0	1	0	0	0	0	2	0	.143	.333	.143	35	-1	0	0	0	1.000	2	/S-4,2-1	0.1
Total	8	522	1764	225	470	67	13	4	122	152	100	.266	.327	.326	74	-61	32	3		.965	-9	S-463/2-17,3	-4.2

■ RED ROLFE Rolfe, Robert Abial b: 10/17/08, Penacook, N.H. d: 7/8/69, Gilford, N.H. BL/TR, 5'11.5", 170 lbs. Deb: 6/29/31 MC

1931	NY-A	1	0	0	0	0	0	0	0	0	0	—	—	—			0			1.000	-0	/S-1	0.0
1934	NY-A	89	279	54	80	13	2	0	18	26	16	.287	.348	.348	86	-6	2	3	-1	.944	4	S-46,3-26	0.0
1935	NY-A	149	639	108	192	33	9	5	67	57	39	.300	.361	.404	103	3	7	3	0	**.964**	-7	*3-136,S-17	0.2
1936	*NY-A	135	568	116	181	39	**15**	10	70	68	38	.319	.392	.493	121	18	3	0	1	**.957**	3	*3-133	2.4
1937	*NY-A★	154	648	143	179	34	10	4	62	90	53	.276	.365	.378	87	-11	4	2	0	.962	1	*3-154	-0.2
1938	*NY-A☆	151	631	132	196	36	8	10	80	74	44	.311	.386	.441	107	8	13	1	3	.959	-7	*3-151	0.6
1939	*NY-A★	152	648	**139**	**213**	**46**	10	14	80	81	41	.329	.404	.495	131	31	7	6	-2	.958	-15	*3-152	1.5
1940	NY-A†	139	588	102	147	26	6	10	53	50	48	.250	.311	.366	78	-20	4	2	0	.949	-1	*3-138	-1.7
1941	*NY-A	136	561	106	148	22	5	8	42	57	38	.264	.332	.364	85	-12	3	2	-0	.946	-10	*3-134	-1.9
1942	*NY-A	69	265	42	58	8	2	8	25	23	18	.219	.281	.355	80	-8	1	1	0	.959	5	3-60	-0.3
Total	10	1175	4827	942	1394	257	67	69	497	526	335	.289	.360	.413	100	2	44	20	1	.956	-22	*3-1084/S-64	0.6

■ RAY ROLLING Rolling, Raymond Copeland b: 9/8/1886, Martinsburg, Mo. d: 8/25/66, St.Paul, Minn. BR/TR, 5'10.5", 160 lbs. Deb: 9/6/12

| 1912 | StL-N | 5 | 15 | 0 | 3 | 0 | 0 | 0 | 0 | 0 | 5 | .200 | .200 | .200 | 10 | -2 | 0 | | | .947 | -0 | /2-4 | -0.2 |

■ RED ROLLINGS Rollings, William Russell b: 3/21/04, Mobile, Ala. d: 12/31/64, Mobile, Ala. BL/TR, 5'11", 167 lbs. Deb: 4/17/27

1927	Bos-A	82	184	19	49	4	1	0	9	12	10	.266	.325	.299	64	-9	3	1	0	.938	-5	3-44,1-10/2	-1.2
1928	Bos-A	50	48	7	11	3	1	0	9	6	8	.229	.315	.333	72	-2	0	0	0	1.000	-2	/1-5,2-4,O3	-0.4
1930	Bos-N	52	123	10	29	6	0	0	10	9	5	.236	.288	.285	40	-12	2			.973	3	3-28,2-10	-0.7
Total	3	184	355	36	89	13	2	0	28	27	23	.251	.311	.299	57	-23	5	1		.947	-5	/3-73,2-16,1O	-2.3

■ RICH ROLLINS Rollins, Richard John "Red" b: 4/16/38, Mount Pleasant, Pa. BR/TR, 5'10", 185 lbs. Deb: 6/16/61

1961	Min-A	13	17	3	5	0	0	0	0	0	0	.294	.400	.353	98	0	0	0	0	1.000	1	/2-5,3-4	0.1
1962	Min-A★	159	624	96	186	23	5	16	96	75	61	.298	.379	.428	112	13	3	1	0	.943	-5	*3-159/S-1	1.0
1963	Min-A	136	531	75	163	23	1	16	61	36	59	.307	.360	.444	122	15	2	0	1	.935	-7	*3-132/2-1	1.0
1964	Min-A	148	596	87	161	25	**10**	12	68	58	80	.270	.335	.406	104	3	2	5	-2	.947	-2	*3-146	-0.3
1965	*Min-A	140	469	59	117	22	5	5	32	37	54	.249	.310	.333	79	-12	4	0	1	.958	-4	*3-112,2-16	-1.7
1966	Min-A	90	269	30	66	7	1	10	40	19	26	.245	.290	.390	88	-5	0	4		.953	-4	3-65/2-2,O	-1.2
1967	Min-A	109	339	31	83	11	2	6	39	27	58	.245	.306	.342	84	-6	1	1	-0	.963	-10	3-97	-1.9
1968	Min-A	93	203	14	49	6	0	3	30	10	34	.241	.287	.355	89	B-3	1	1	0	.931	-2	3-56	-0.5
1969	Sea-A	58	187	15	42	7	0	4	21	7	19	.225	.271	.326	68	-9	2	0	1	.948	3	3-47/S-1	-0.5

YEAR	TM/L	G	AB	R	H	2B	3B	HR	RBI	BB	SO	AVG	OBP	SLG	PRO+	BR/A	SB	CS	SBR	FA	FR	G/POS	TPR
1970	Mil-A	14	25	3	5	1	0	0	5	3	4	.200	.286	.240	46	-2	0	0	0	1.000	1	/3-7	-0.1
	Cle-A	42	43	6	10	0	0	2	4	3	5	.233	.283	.372	75	-2	0	0	0	.600	-1	/3-5	-0.3
	Yr	56	68	9	15	1	0	2	9	6	9	.221	.284	.324	65	-3	0	0	0	.900	-0	3-12	-0.4
Total	10	1002	3303	419	887	125	20	77	399	266	410	.269	.330	.388	98	-7	17	10	-1	.947	-30	3-830/2-24,SO	-4.4

■ ROLLINSON Rollinson Deb: 6/17/1884

YEAR	TM/L	G	AB	R	H	2B	3B	HR	RBI	BB	SO	AVG	OBP	SLG	PRO+	BR/A	SB	CS	SBR	FA	FR	G/POS	TPR
1884	Was-U	1	3	0	0	0	0	0	0	0	0	.000	.000	.000	-99	-1				.714	0	/C-1	0.0

■ BILL ROMAN Roman, William Anthony b: 10/11/38, Detroit, Mich. BL/TL, 6'4", 190 lbs. Deb: 9/30/64

YEAR	TM/L	G	AB	R	H	2B	3B	HR	RBI	BB	SO	AVG	OBP	SLG	PRO+	BR/A	SB	CS	SBR	FA	FR	G/POS	TPR
1964	Det-A	3	8	2	3	0	0	1	1	0	2	.375	.375	.750	201	1	0	0	0	1.000	0	/1-2	0.1
1965	Det-A	21	27	0	2	0	0	0	0	2	7	.074	.138	.074	-38	-5	0	0	0	1.000	-0	/1-6	-0.6
Total	2	24	35	2	5	0	0	1	1	2	9	.143	.189	.229	17	-4	0	0	0	1.000	-0	/1-8	-0.5

■ JOHNNY ROMANO Romano, John Anthony "Honey" b: 8/23/34, Hoboken, N.J. BR/TR, 5'11", 205 lbs. Deb: 9/12/58

YEAR	TM/L	G	AB	R	H	2B	3B	HR	RBI	BB	SO	AVG	OBP	SLG	PRO+	BR/A	SB	CS	SBR	FA	FR	G/POS	TPR
1958	Chi-A	4	7	1	2	0	0	0	1	1	0	.286	.375	.286	86	-0	0	0	0	1.000	1	/C-2	0.1
1959	*Chi-A	53	126	20	37	5	1	5	25	23	18	.294	.407	.468	141	8	0	1	-1	.979	1	C-38	1.0
1960	Cle-A	108	316	40	86	12	2	16	52	37	50	.272	.354	.475	126	11	0	0	0	.988	-11	C-99	0.6
1961	Cle-A★	142	509	76	152	29	1	21	80	61	60	.299	.379	.483	132	24	0	0	0	.989	-9	*C-141	2.2
1962	Cle-A★	135	459	71	120	19	3	25	81	73	64	.261	.369	.479	130	20	0	1	-1	.990	-9	*C-130	1.6
1963	Cle-A	89	255	28	55	5	2	10	34	38	49	.216	.322	.369	94	-2	4	3	-1	.993	-11	C-71/O-4	-1.1
1964	Cle-A	106	352	46	85	18	1	19	47	51	83	.241	.349	.460	124	12	2	2	-1	.991	-5	C-96/1-1	1.2
1965	Chi-A	122	356	39	86	11	0	18	48	59	74	.242	.357	.424	129	15	0	2	-1	.992	4	*C-111/O-4,1	2.4
1966	Chi-A	122	329	33	76	12	0	15	47	58	72	.231	.348	.404	124	11	0	0	0	.993	3	*C-102	2.2
1967	StL-N	24	58	1	7	1	0	0	2	13	13	.121	.282	.138	24	-5	1	0	0	.983	-1	C-20	-0.5
Total	10	905	2767	355	706	112	10	129	417	414	485	.255	.358	.443	123	93	7	9	-3	.990	-36	C-810/O-8,1	9.7

■ TOM ROMANO Romano, Thomas Michael b: 10/25/58, Syracuse, N.Y. BR/TR, 5'10", 170 lbs. Deb: 9/1/87

YEAR	TM/L	G	AB	R	H	2B	3B	HR	RBI	BB	SO	AVG	OBP	SLG	PRO+	BR/A	SB	CS	SBR	FA	FR	G/POS	TPR
1987	Mon-N	7	3	1	0	0	0	0	0	0	1	.000	.000	.000	-97	-1	0	0	0	.000	-1	/O-3	-0.2

■ ED ROMERO Romero, Edgardo Ralph (Rivera) b: 12/9/57, Santurce, P.R. BR/TR, 5'11", 175 lbs. Deb: 7/16/77

YEAR	TM/L	G	AB	R	H	2B	3B	HR	RBI	BB	SO	AVG	OBP	SLG	PRO+	BR/A	SB	CS	SBR	FA	FR	G/POS	TPR
1977	Mil-A	10	25	4	7	1	0	0	2	4	3	.280	.379	.320	93	-0	0	0	0	.971	0	S-10	0.1
1980	Mil-A	42	104	20	27	7	0	1	10	9	11	.260	.319	.356	87	-2	2	0	1	.894	4	S-22,2-15/3	0.6
1981	*Mil-A	44	91	6	18	3	0	1	10	4	9	.198	.232	.264	45	-7	0	2	-1	.949	10	S-22,2-18/3	0.5
1982	Mil-A	52	144	18	36	8	0	1	7	8	16	.250	.289	.326	73	-5	0	0	-1	.975	-1	2-39,S-10/3O	-0.5
1983	Mil-A	59	145	17	46	7	0	1	18	8	8	.317	.353	.386	112	2	0	0	-1	.962	-10	S-22,0-15/32D	-0.6
1984	Mil-A	116	357	36	90	12	0	1	31	29	25	.252	.310	.294	71	-13	3	3	-1	.943	2	3-59,S-39,2/10D	-1.0
1985	Mil-A	88	251	24	63	11	1	0	21	26	20	.251	.321	.303	72	-9	1	1	0	.977	8	S-43,2-31,O/3	0.4
1986	*Bos-A	100	233	41	49	11	0	2	23	18	16	.210	.273	.283	51	-16	2	0	1	.959	-8	S-75,3-18/2O	-1.7
1987	Bos-A	88	235	23	64	5	0	0	14	18	22	.272	.324	.294	64	-12	0	2	-1	.973	2	2-29,S-24,3/1	-0.8
1988	*Bos-A	31	75	3	18	3	0	0	5	3	8	.240	.278	.280	55	-5	0	0	0	1.000	-1	3-15/S-8/21D	-0.4
1989	Bos-A	46	113	14	24	4	0	0	6	7	7	.212	.264	.248	42	-9	0	2	-1	.983	13	2-22,3-14,S	0.4
	Atl-N	7	19	1	5	1	0	1	1	0	0	.263	.263	.474	104	1	0	0	0	.947	5	/2-4,S-2,3	0.5
	Mil	15	50	3	10	3	0	0	3	0	10	.200	.200	.260	29	-5	0	0	0	1.000	6	2-11/3-4,SD	-0.4
1990	Det-A	32	70	8	16	3	0	0	4	6	4	.229	.289	.271	57	-4	0	0	0	.982	6	3-27/D-3	0.2
Total	12	730	1912	218	473	79	1	8	155	140	159	.247	.300	.302	67	-83	9	10	-3	.958	30	S-288,2-192,3/01D	-2.7

■ KEVIN ROMINE Romine, Kevin Andrew b: 5/23/61, Exeter, N.H. BR/TR, 5'11", 185 lbs. Deb: 9/5/85

YEAR	TM/L	G	AB	R	H	2B	3B	HR	RBI	BB	SO	AVG	OBP	SLG	PRO+	BR/A	SB	CS	SBR	FA	FR	G/POS	TPR
1985	Bos-A	24	28	3	6	2	0	0	1	1	4	.214	.241	.286	42	-2	1	0	0	1.000	-5	O-23/D-1	-0.8
1986	Bos-A	35	35	6	9	2	0	0	2	3	9	.257	.316	.314	72	-1	2	0	1	1.000	-6	O-33	-0.7
1987	Bos-A	9	24	5	7	2	0	0	2	2	6	.292	.346	.375	89	-0	0	0	0	1.000	-0	/O-7,D-2	-0.1
1988	*Bos-A	57	78	17	15	2	1	1	6	7	15	.192	.259	.282	49	-5	2	0	1	.957	-13	O-45/D-5	-1.8
1989	Bos-A	92	274	30	75	13	0	1	23	21	53	.274	.330	.332	82	-6	1	1	-0	.982	-2	O-89/D-2	-1.0
1990	Bos-A	70	136	21	37	7	0	2	14	12	27	.272	.336	.368	92	-1	4	0	1	.976	-11	O-64/D-1	-1.2
1991	Bos-A	44	55	7	9	2	0	1	7	3	10	.164	.207	.255	26	-6	1	1	-0	.964	-4	O-23,D-14	-1.1
Total	7	331	630	89	158	30	1	5	55	49	124	.251	.308	.325	73	-22	11	2	2	.980	-41	O-284/D-25	-6.7

■ MARC RONAN Ronan, Edward Marcus b: 9/19/69, Ozark, Ala. BL/TR, 6'2", 190 lbs. Deb: 9/21/93

YEAR	TM/L	G	AB	R	H	2B	3B	HR	RBI	BB	SO	AVG	OBP	SLG	PRO+	BR/A	SB	CS	SBR	FA	FR	G/POS	TPR
1993	StL-N	6	12	0	1	0	0	0	0	0	5	.083	.083	.083	-56	-3	0	0	0	1.000	2	/C-6	-0.1

■ HENRI RONDEAU Rondeau, Henri Joseph b: 5/5/1887, Danielson, Conn. d: 5/28/43, Woonsocket, R.I. BR/TR, 5'10.5", 175 lbs. Deb: 4/11/13

YEAR	TM/L	G	AB	R	H	2B	3B	HR	RBI	BB	SO	AVG	OBP	SLG	PRO+	BR/A	SB	CS	SBR	FA	FR	G/POS	TPR
1913	Det-A	35	70	5	13	2	0	0	5	14	16	.186	.321	.214	58	-3	1			1.000	-2	C-16/1-6	-0.4
1915	Was-A	14	40	3	7	0	0	0	4	4	3	.175	.250	.175	27	-4	1	2	-1	1.000	3	O-11	-0.3
1916	Was-A	50	162	20	36	5	3	1	28	18	18	.222	.311	.309	87	-2	7			.958	3	O-48	-0.1
Total	3	99	272	28	56	7	3	1	37	36	37	.206	.305	.265	71	-9	9	2		.967	4	/O-59,C-16,1	-0.8

■ GENE ROOF Roof, Eugene Lawrence b: 1/13/58, Paducah, Ky. BB/TR, 6'2", 180 lbs. Deb: 9/3/81 F

YEAR	TM/L	G	AB	R	H	2B	3B	HR	RBI	BB	SO	AVG	OBP	SLG	PRO+	BR/A	SB	CS	SBR	FA	FR	G/POS	TPR
1981	StL-N	23	60	11	18	6	0	0	3	12	16	.300	.417	.400	129	3	5	1	1	.950	-2	O-20	0.2
1982	StL-N	11	15	3	4	0	0	0	2	1	4	.267	.313	.267	63	-1	2	0	1	1.000	-1	/O-5	-0.2
1983	StL-N	6	3	1	0	0	0	0	0	0	0	.000	.000	.000	-99	-1	0	0	0	.000	-1	/O-1	-0.1
	Mon-N	8	12	2	2	2	0	0	1	1	3	.167	.231	.333	55	-1	0	0	0	1.000	-1	/O-5	-0.2
	Yr	14	15	3	2	2	0	0	1	1	3	.133	.188	.267	25	-2	0	0	0	1.000	-2	/O-6	-0.3
Total	3	48	90	17	24	8	0	0	6	14	23	.267	.365	.356	102	1	7	1	2	.958	-5	/O-31	-0.3

■ PHIL ROOF Roof, Phillip Anthony b: 3/5/41, Paducah, Ky. BR/TR, 6'3", 210 lbs. Deb: 4/29/61 FC

YEAR	TM/L	G	AB	R	H	2B	3B	HR	RBI	BB	SO	AVG	OBP	SLG	PRO+	BR/A	SB	CS	SBR	FA	FR	G/POS	TPR
1961	Mil-N	1	0	0	0	0	0	0	0	0	0	—	—	—	0	0	0	0	0	1.000	0	/C-1	0.0
1964	Mil-N	1	2	0	0	0	0	0	0	0	1	.000	.000	.000	-99	-1	0	0	0	1.000	1	/C-1	0.1
1965	Cal-A	9	22	1	3	0	0	0	0	0	6	.136	.136	.136	-23	-3	0	0	0	.983	6	/C-9	0.2
	Cle-A	43	52	3	9	1	0	0	3	5	13	.173	.259	.192	30	-5	0	0	0	.994	13	C-41	1.0
	Yr	52	74	4	12	1	0	0	3	5	19	.162	.225	.176	15	-8	0	0	0	.992	19	C-50	1.2
1966	KC-A	127	369	33	77	14	3	7	44	37	95	.209	.286	.320	76	-11	2	5	-2	.985	-1	*C-123/1-2	-0.7
1967	KC-A	114	327	23	67	14	5	6	24	23	85	.205	.268	.333	79	-9	4	1	1	.991	-1	*C-113	-0.5
1968	Oak-A	34	64	5	12	0	0	1	2	2	15	.188	.212	.234	37	-5	1	0	0	.968	-1	C-32	-0.5
1969	Oak-A	106	247	19	58	6	0	2	19	33	55	.235	.337	.291	81	-5	1	0	0	.983	-1	*C-106	-0.2
1970	Mil-A	110	321	39	73	7	1	13	37	32	58	.227	.307	.377	87	-6	3	2	-0	.988	8	*C-107/1-1	0.6
1971	Mil-A	41	114	6	22	3	0	1	10	8	28	.193	.252	.254	44	-8	0	0	0	.975	3	C-39	-0.4
	Min-A	31	87	6	21	4	0	0	6	8	18	.241	.305	.287	67	-4	0	0	0	.985	8	C-29	0.5
	Yr	72	201	12	43	6	1	1	16	16	46	.214	.275	.269	54	-12	0	0	0	.980	11	C-68	0.1
1972	Min-A	61	146	16	30	11	1	3	12	6	27	.205	.237	.356	71	-6	0	0	0	.978	-2	C-61	-0.8
1973	Min-A	44	117	10	23	3	0	1	13	6	27	.197	.277	.274	53	-7	0	0	0	.992	6	C-47	0.5
1974	Min-A	44	97	10	19	1	0	2	13	6	24	.196	.257	.268	49	-6	0	0	0	1.000	8	C-44	0.3
1975	Min-A	63	126	18	38	6	0	7	21	9	28	.302	.353	.484	132	5	0	0	0	.989	7	C-63	1.3
1976	Min-A	18	46	5	10	3	0	0	4	2	6	.217	.250	.283	54	-3	0	0	0	.962	5	C-12/D-1	0.3
	Chi-A	4	9	0	1	0	0	0	0	0	3	.111	.111	.111	-35	-2	0	0	0	1.000	-0	/C-4	-0.2
	Yr	22	55	1	11	3	0	0	4	2	9	.200	.228	.255	40	-4	0	0	0	.967	5	C-16/D-1	0.1

YEAR	TM/L	G	AB	R	H	2B	3B	HR	RBI	BB	SO	AVG	OBP	SLG	PRO+	BR/A	SB	CS	SBR	FA	FR	G/POS	TPR
1977	Tor-A	3	5	0	0	0	0	0	0	0	0	.000	.000	.000	-99	-1	0	0	0	1.000	1	/C-3	0.0
Total	15	857	2151	190	463	69	13	43	210	184	504	.215	.284	.319	73	-78	11	10	-3	.986	58	C-835/1-3,D	1.1

■ GEORGE ROOKS
Rooks, George Brinton McClellan (b: George Brinton Mc Clellan Ruckser)
b: 10/21/1863, Chicago, Ill.   d: 3/11/35, Chicago, Ill.   BR/TR, 5'11", 170 lbs.   Deb: 5/12/1891   F

YEAR	TM/L	G	AB	R	H	2B	3B	HR	RBI	BB	SO	AVG	OBP	SLG	PRO+	BR/A	SB	CS	SBR	FA	FR	G/POS	TPR
1891	Bos-N	5	16	1	2	0	0	0	4	1		.125	.300	.125	23	-2	0			1.000	1	/O-5	-0.1

■ ROLANDO ROOMES
Roomes, Rolando Audley   b: 2/15/62, Kingston, Jamaica   BR/TR, 6'3", 180 lbs.   Deb: 4/12/88

YEAR	TM/L	G	AB	R	H	2B	3B	HR	RBI	BB	SO	AVG	OBP	SLG	PRO+	BR/A	SB	CS	SBR	FA	FR	G/POS	TPR
1988	Chi-N	17	16	3	3	0	0	0	0	0	4	.188	.188	.188	8	-2	0	1	-1	.833	-1	/O-5	-0.4
1989	Cin-N	107	315	36	83	18	5	7	34	13	100	.263	.299	.419	100	-1	12	8	-1	.981	-3	*O-100	-0.7
1990	Cin-N	30	61	5	13	0	0	2	7	0	20	.213	.213	.311	41	-5	0	0	0	1.000	-0	/O-19	-0.6
	Mon-N	16	14	1	4	0	1	0	1	1	6	.286	.333	.429	112	0	0	2	-1	1.000	-1	/O-6	-0.3
	Yr	46	75	6	17	0	1	2	8	1	26	.227	.237	.333	54	-5	0	2	-1	1.000	-2	O-25	-0.9
Total	3	170	406	45	103	18	6	9	42	14	130	.254	.284	.394	88	-8	12	11	-3	.980	-5	O-130	-2.0

■ FRANK ROONEY
Rooney, Frank (b: Frank Rovny)   b: 10/12/1884, Podebrady, Bohemia (Austria-Hungary)   d: 4/6/77, Bessemer, Mich.   Deb: 4/18/14

YEAR	TM/L	G	AB	R	H	2B	3B	HR	RBI	BB	SO	AVG	OBP	SLG	PRO+	BR/A	SB	CS	SBR	FA	FR	G/POS	TPR
1914	Ind-F	12	35	1	7	0	1	1	8	1	0	.200	.222	.343	41	-3	2			.980	-1	/1-9	-0.5

■ PAT ROONEY
Rooney, Patrick Eugene   b: 11/28/57, Chicago, Ill.   BR/TR, 6'1", 190 lbs.   Deb: 9/9/81

YEAR	TM/L	G	AB	R	H	2B	3B	HR	RBI	BB	SO	AVG	OBP	SLG	PRO+	BR/A	SB	CS	SBR	FA	FR	G/POS	TPR
1981	Mon-N	4	5	0	0	0	0	0	0	0	3	.000	.000	.000	-99	-1	0	0	0	1.000	-1	/O-2	-0.2

■ JORGE ROQUE
Roque, Jorge (Vargas)   b: 4/28/50, Ponce, P.R.   BR/TR, 5'10", 158 lbs.   Deb: 9/4/70

YEAR	TM/L	G	AB	R	H	2B	3B	HR	RBI	BB	SO	AVG	OBP	SLG	PRO+	BR/A	SB	CS	SBR	FA	FR	G/POS	TPR
1970	StL-N	5	1	2	0	0	0	0	0	0	1	.000	.500	.000	45	0	0	0	0	.000	-0	/O-1	0.0
1971	StL-N	3	10	2	3	0	0	0	1	0	3	.300	.300	.300	68	-0	1	0	0	1.000	-0	/O-3	0.0
1972	StL-N	32	67	3	7	2	1	1	5	6	19	.104	.178	.209	10	-8	1	1	-0	.980	-1	O-24	-1.1
1973	Mon-N	25	61	7	9	2	0	1	6	4	17	.148	.212	.230	22	-7	2	2	-1	.878	-3	O-24	-1.1
Total	4	65	139	14	19	4	1	2	12	10	40	.137	.205	.223	20	-15	4	3	-1	.934	-4	/O-52	-2.2

■ LUIS ROSADO
Rosado, Luis (Robles)   b: 12/6/55, Santurce, P.R.   BR/TR, 6', 180 lbs.   Deb: 9/8/77

YEAR	TM/L	G	AB	R	H	2B	3B	HR	RBI	BB	SO	AVG	OBP	SLG	PRO+	BR/A	SB	CS	SBR	FA	FR	G/POS	TPR
1977	NY-N	9	24	1	5	1	0	0	3	1	3	.208	.269	.250	42	-2	0	0	0	.980	-0	/1-7,C-1	-0.3
1980	NY-N	2	4	0	0	0	0	0	0	0	1	.000	.000	.000	-99	-1	0	0	0	1.000	-0	/1-1	-0.1
Total	2	11	28	1	5	1	0	0	3	1	4	.179	.233	.214	23	-3	0	0	0	.983	-0	/1-8,C-1	-0.4

■ BUDDY ROSAR
Rosar, Warren Vincent   b: 7/3/14, Buffalo, N.Y.   d: 3/13/94, Rochester, N.Y.   BR/TR, 5'9", 190 lbs.   Deb: 4/29/39

YEAR	TM/L	G	AB	R	H	2B	3B	HR	RBI	BB	SO	AVG	OBP	SLG	PRO+	BR/A	SB	CS	SBR	FA	FR	G/POS	TPR
1939	NY-A	43	105	18	29	5	1	0	12	13	10	.276	.356	.343	81	-3	4	0	1	.980	4	C-35	0.4
1940	NY-A	73	228	34	68	11	3	4	37	19	10	.298	.357	.425	106	2	7	1	2	.983	8	C-63	0.8
1941	*NY-A	67	209	25	60	17	2	1	36	22	10	.287	.355	.402	101	0	0	0	0	.996	0	C-60	0.5
1942	*NY-A☆	69	209	18	48	10	0	2	34	17	20	.230	.288	.306	68	-9	1	2	-1	.996	4	C-58	-0.2
1943	Cle-A☆	115	382	53	108	17	1	1	41	33	12	.283	.340	.340	106	2	0	4	-2	.983	7	*C-114	1.5
1944	Cle-A	99	331	29	87	9	3	0	30	34	17	.263	.339	.308	89	-4	1	2	-1	**.989**	4	*C-98	0.5
1945	Phi-A	92	300	23	63	12	1	1	25	20	16	.210	.262	.267	54	-18	2	1	0	.987	-0	C-85	-1.5
1946	Phi-A★	121	424	34	120	22	2	2	47	36	17	.283	.339	.358	96	-3	1	3	-2	**1.000**	7	*C-117	1.0
1947	Phi-A★	102	359	40	93	20	2	1	33	40	13	.259	.335	.334	85	-7	1	3	-2	.996	13	*C-102	1.2
1948	Phi-A★	90	302	30	77	13	0	4	41	39	12	.255	.344	.338	82	-7	0	2	-1	**.997**	-3	C-90	-0.5
1949	Phi-A	32	95	7	19	2	0	0	6	16	5	.200	.315	.221	45	-7	0	0	0	.992	-2	C-31	-0.8
1950	Bos-A	27	84	13	25	2	0	1	12	7	4	.298	.352	.357	75	-3	0	0	0	.991	-1	C-25	-0.3
1951	Bos-A	58	170	11	39	7	1	0	13	19	14	.229	.307	.288	56	-10	0	0	0	.996	0	C-56	-0.8
Total	13	988	3198	335	836	147	15	18	367	315	161	.261	.330	.334	84	-67	17	18	-6	.992	33	C-934	1.8

■ JIMMY ROSARIO
Rosario, Angel Ramon (Ferrer)   b: 5/5/45, Bayamon, P.R.   BB/TR, 5'10", 155 lbs.   Deb: 4/8/71

YEAR	TM/L	G	AB	R	H	2B	3B	HR	RBI	BB	SO	AVG	OBP	SLG	PRO+	BR/A	SB	CS	SBR	FA	FR	G/POS	TPR
1971	*SF-N	92	192	26	43	6	1	0	13	33	35	.224	.341	.266	75	-5	7	4	-0	1.000	1	O-67	-0.9
1972	SF-N	7	1	1	0	0	0	0	0	0	0	.000	.000	.000	-99	-1	0	1	-1	1.000	-1	/O-1	-0.2
1976	Mil-A	15	37	4	7	0	0	1	5	3	8	.189	.250	.270	53	-2	1	3	-2	1.000	-2	O-12/D-2	-0.7
Total	3	114	231	31	50	6	1	1	18	36	43	.216	.325	.264	70	-8	8	8	-2	1.000	-4	/O-80,D-2	-1.8

■ SANTIAGO ROSARIO
Rosario, Santiago   b: 7/25/39, Guayanilla, P.R.   BL/TL, 5'11", 165 lbs.   Deb: 6/23/65

YEAR	TM/L	G	AB	R	H	2B	3B	HR	RBI	BB	SO	AVG	OBP	SLG	PRO+	BR/A	SB	CS	SBR	FA	FR	G/POS	TPR
1965	KC-A	81	85	8	20	3	0	2	8	6	16	.235	.293	.341	81	-1	0	0	0	.991	-1	1-31/O-3	-0.4

■ VICTOR ROSARIO
Rosario, Victor Manuel (Rivera)   b: 8/26/66, Hato Mayor Del Rey, D.R.   BR/TR, 5'11", 155 lbs.   Deb: 9/6/90

YEAR	TM/L	G	AB	R	H	2B	3B	HR	RBI	BB	SO	AVG	OBP	SLG	PRO+	BR/A	SB	CS	SBR	FA	FR	G/POS	TPR
1990	Atl-N	9	7	3	1	0	0	0	0	1	1	.143	.250	.143	10	-1	0	0	0	1.000	-1	/S-3,2-1	0.0

■ PETE ROSE
Rose, Peter Edward "Charlie Hustle"   b: 4/14/41, Cincinnati, Ohio   BB/TR, 5'11", 200 lbs.   Deb: 4/8/63   M

YEAR	TM/L	G	AB	R	H	2B	3B	HR	RBI	BB	SO	AVG	OBP	SLG	PRO+	BR/A	SB	CS	SBR	FA	FR	G/POS	TPR
1963	Cin-N	157	623	101	170	25	9	6	41	55	72	.273	.337	.371	101	1	13	15	-5	.971	-23	*2-157/O-1	-1.3
1964	Cin-N	136	516	64	139	13	2	4	34	36	51	.269	.319	.326	79	-13	4	10	-5	.979	-14	*2-128	-2.3
1965	Cin-N★	162	670	117	**209**	35	11	11	81	69	76	.312	.383	.446	124	23	8	3	1	.975	-18	*2-162	2.1
1966	Cin-N	156	654	97	205	38	5	16	70	37	61	.313	.351	.460	113	11	4	9	-4	.981	-8	*2-140,3-16	1.0
1967	Cin-N★	148	585	86	176	32	8	12	76	56	66	.301	.365	.444	117	13	11	6	-0	.982	-4	*O-123,2-35	0.6
1968	Cin-N†	149	626	94	**210**	42	6	10	49	56	76	**.335**	**.394**	.470	149	38	3	7	-3	.990	7	*O-148/2-3,1	3.8
1969	Cin-N★	156	627	**120**	218	33	11	16	82	88	65	.348	.432	.512	155	49	7	10	-4	.988	5	*O-156/2-2	4.3
1970	*Cin-N★	159	649	120	**205**	37	9	15	52	73	64	.316	.387	.470	128	26	12	7	-1	**.997**	5	*O-159	2.2
1971	Cin-N	160	632	86	192	27	4	13	44	68	50	.304	.374	.421	127	24	13	9	-2	.994	4	*O-158	1.9
1972	*Cin-N	154	645	107	**198**	31	11	6	57	73	46	.307	.383	.417	135	31	10	3	1	.994	16	*O-154	4.3
1973	*Cin-N★	160	680	115	**230**	36	8	5	64	65	42	**.338**	.401	.437	139	37	10	7	-1	.992	17	*O-159	4.6
1974	Cin-N★	163	652	**110**	185	**45**	7	3	51	106	54	.284	.388	.388	119	21	2	4	-2	**.997**	18	*O-163	3.0
1975	*Cin-N★	162	662	**112**	210	**47**	4	7	74	89	50	.317	.407	.432	130	31	0	1	-1	.963	-36	*3-137,O-35	-0.7
1976	*Cin-N★	162	665	**130**	215	**42**	6	10	63	86	54	.323	.406	.450	139	37	9	5	-0	**.969**	-12	*3-159/O-1	2.5
1977	Cin-N★	162	655	95	204	38	7	9	64	66	42	.311	.379	.432	115	15	16	4	2	.958	-24	*3-161	-0.8
1978	Cin-N★	159	655	103	198	**51**	3	7	52	62	30	.302	.362	.421	119	17	13	9	-2	.961	-28	*3-156/O-7,1	-1.3
1979	Phi-N★	163	628	90	208	40	5	4	59	95	32	.331	.421	.430	128	29	20	11	-1	.995	-5	*1-159/3-5,2	1.4
1980	*Phi-N★	162	655	95	185	**42**	1	1	64	66	33	.282	.354	.354	93	-4	12	8	-1	**.997**	9	*1-162	-0.6
1981	*Phi-N★	107	431	73	**140**	18	5	0	33	46	26	.325	.394	.390	118	12	4	4	-1	.996	9	*1-107	1.4
1982	Phi-N★	162	634	80	172	25	4	3	54	66	32	.271	.347	.338	90	-6	8	8	-2	.995	6	*1-162	-1.3
1983	*Phi-N★	151	493	52	121	14	3	0	45	52	28	.245	.320	.286	70	-19	7	7	-2	.990	-2	*1-112,O-35	-3.0
1984	Mon-N	95	278	34	72	6	2	0	23	31	22	.259	.335	.295	82	-6	1	1	0	.988	8	1-40,O-28	-0.2
	Cin-N	26	96	9	35	9	1	0	11	9	7	.365	.430	.458	143	6	0	0	0	.990	-3	1-23/M	0.2
	Yr	121	374	43	107	15	2	0	34	40	27	.286	.360	.337	99	1	1	1	0	.989	5	1-63,O-28	0.0
1985	Cin-N★	119	405	60	107	12	2	2	46	86	35	.264	.398	.319	98	4	8	1	2	.995	-1	*1-110/M	-0.1
1986	Cin-N	72	237	15	52	8	2	0	25	30	31	.219	.317	.270	61	-12	3	0	0	.990	-1	1-61/M	-1.7
Total	24	3562	14053	2165	4256	746	135	160	1314	1566	1143	.303	.375	.409	117	366	198	149	-30	.991	-71	*O-1327,1-939,32	20.0

■ BOBBY ROSE
Rose, Robert Richard   b: 3/15/67, Covina, Cal.   BR/TR, 5'11", 170 lbs.   Deb: 8/12/89

YEAR	TM/L	G	AB	R	H	2B	3B	HR	RBI	BB	SO	AVG	OBP	SLG	PRO+	BR/A	SB	CS	SBR	FA	FR	G/POS	TPR
1989	Cal-A	14	38	4	8	1	2	1	3	2	10	.211	.268	.421	93	-1	0	0	0	.920	-1	3-10/2-3	-0.1
1990	Cal-A	7	13	5	5	0	0	1	2	2	1	.385	.467	.615	204	2	0	0	0	1.000	-1	/2-4,3-3	0.1
1991	Cal-A	22	65	9	18	5	1	1	8	3	11	.277	.309	.431	102	-0	0	0	0	1.000	-1	/2-8,O-7,31	-0.1
1992	Cal-A	30	84	10	18	5	0	2	10	8	9	.214	.298	.345	79	-2	1	1	-0	.953	8	2-28/1-2	0.6
Total	4	73	200	24	49	11	3	5	23	15	33	.245	.307	.405	98	-1	1	1	-0	.965	6	/2-43,3-17,O1	0.5

YEAR	TM/L	G	AB	R	H	2B	3B	HR	RBI	BB	SO	AVG	OBP	SLG	PRO+	BR/A	SB	CS	SBR	FA	FR	G/POS	TPR

■ JOHNNY ROSEBORO   Roseboro, John Junior   b: 5/13/33, Ashland, Ohio   BL/TR, 5'11.5", 190 lbs.   Deb: 6/14/57 C

1957	Bro-N	35	69	6	10	2	0	2	6	10	20	.145	.253	.261	35	-6	0	0	0	.972	3	C-19/1-5	-0.3
1958	LA-N☆	114	384	52	104	11	9	14	43	36	56	.271	.336	.456	104	2	11	8	-2	.987	-16	*C-104/O-5	-1.0
1959	*LA-N	118	397	39	92	14	7	10	38	52	69	.232	.325	.378	81	-11	7	5	-1	.991	6	*C-117	0.2
1960	LA-N	103	287	22	61	15	3	8	42	44	53	.213	.325	.369	84	-6	7	6	-2	.993	7	*C-87/1-1,3	0.1
1961	LA-N★	128	394	59	99	16	6	18	59	56	62	.251	.350	.459	104	2	6	4	-1	.986	7	*C-125	1.4
1962	LA-N★	128	389	45	97	16	7	7	55	50	60	.249	.345	.380	101	1	12	3	2	.985	-2	*C-128	0.6
1963	*LA-N	135	470	50	111	13	7	9	49	36	50	.236	.295	.351	91	-6	7	6	-2	.992	-10	*C-134	-1.4
1964	LA-N	134	414	42	119	24	1	3	45	44	61	.287	.361	.372	115	9	3	3	-1	.993	1	*C-128	1.6
1965	*LA-N	136	437	42	102	10	0	8	57	34	51	.233	.292	.311	75	-15	1	6	-3	.994	-2	*C-131/3-1	-1.5
1966	*LA-N	142	445	47	123	23	2	9	53	44	51	.276	.346	.398	115	9	3	2	-0	.993	6	*C-138	2.4
1967	LA-N	116	334	37	91	18	2	4	38	38	33	.272	.350	.374	117	8	2	4	-2	.984	-11	*C-107	0.0
1968	Min-A	135	380	31	82	12	0	8	39	46	57	.216	.304	.311	82	-7	2	3	-1	.991	-5	*C-117	-0.6
1969	*Min-A★	115	361	33	95	12	0	3	32	39	44	.263	.335	.321	83	-8	5	5	-2	.980	0	*C-111	-0.4
1970	Was-A	46	86	7	20	4	0	1	6	18	10	.233	.365	.314	94	-0	1	1	-0	1.000	-3	C-30	-0.2
Total	14	1585	4847	512	1206	190	44	104	548	547	677	.249	.329	.371	95	-28	67	56	-14	.989	-22	*C-1476/1-6,O3	0.9

■ BOB ROSELLI   Roselli, Robert Edward   b: 12/10/31, San Francisco, Cal.   BR/TR, 5'11", 185 lbs.   Deb: 8/16/55

1955	Mil-N	6	9	1	2	1	0	0	0	1	4	.222	.364	.333	91	-0	0	0	0	.917	0	/C-6	0.0
1956	Mil-N	4	2	1	1	0	0	1	0	1	0	.500	.500	2.000	564	1	0	0	0	1.000	2	/C-3	0.3
1958	Mil-N	1	1	0	0	0	0	0	0	0	0	.000	.000	.000	-99	-0	0	0	0	.000	0	H	0.0
1961	Chi-A	22	38	2	10	3	0	0	4	0	11	.263	.263	.342	61	-2	0	0	0	1.000	-1	C-10	-0.3
1962	Chi-A	35	64	4	12	3	1	1	5	11	15	.188	.316	.313	70	-3	1	0	0	.988	-1	C-20	-0.3
Total	5	68	114	8	25	7	1	2	10	12	31	.219	.305	.351	76	-4	1	0	0	.986	-1	/C-35	-0.3

■ DAVE ROSELLO   Rosello, David (Rodriguez)   b: 6/26/50, Mayaguez, P.R.   BR/TR, 5'11", 160 lbs.   Deb: 9/10/72

1972	Chi-N	5	12	2	3	0	0	0	3	3	2	.250	.400	.500	139	1	0	0	0	.846	1	/S-5	0.2
1973	Chi-N	16	38	4	10	2	0	0	2	2	4	.263	.300	.316	66	-2	2	2	-1	.964	3	2-13/S-1	0.1
1974	Chi-N	62	148	9	30	7	0	0	10	10	28	.203	.253	.250	39	-12	1	1	-0	.972	3	2-49,S-12	-0.7
1975	Chi-N	19	58	7	15	2	0	1	8	9	8	.259	.358	.345	92	-0	0	1	-1	.952	1	S-19	0.2
1976	Chi-N	91	227	27	55	5	1	1	11	41	33	.242	.361	.286	78	-5	1	2	-1	.966	-7	S-86/2-1	-0.4
1977	Chi-N	56	82	18	18	2	1	1	9	12	12	.220	.319	.305	62	-4	0	0	0	.938	-3	3-21,S-10/2	-0.7
1979	Cle-A	59	107	20	26	6	1	3	14	15	27	.243	.336	.402	98	-0	0	0	0	.976	-5	2-33,3-14,S	-0.3
1980	Cle-A	71	117	16	29	3	0	2	12	9	19	.248	.302	.325	71	-5	0	0	0	.980	3	2-43,3-22/SD	0.0
1981	Cle-A	43	84	11	20	4	0	1	7	7	12	.238	.297	.321	79	-2	0	1	-1	.979	3	2-26/3-8,SD	0.1
Total	9	422	873	114	206	31	3	10	76	108	145	.236	.321	.313	73	-29	5	7	-3	.975	-1	2-168,S-151/3D	-1.5

■ CHIEF ROSEMAN   Roseman, James John   b: 1856, New York, N.Y.   d: 7/4/38, Brooklyn, N.Y.   BR/TR, 5'7", 167 lbs.   Deb: 5/1/1882 M

1882	Tro-N	82	331	41	78	21	6	1	29	3	41	.236	.243	.344	90	-3				.853	-3	*O-82	-0.6
1883	NY-a	93	398	48	100	13	6	0	11			.251	.271	.314	84	-8				.855	-3	*O-91/1-2	-1.1
1884	*NY-a	107	436	97	130	16	11	4	21			.298	.339	.413	148	23				.885	-2	*O-107	1.7
1885	NY-a	101	410	72	114	13	14	4	25			.278	.331	.407	145	22				.865	-7	*O-101/P-1	1.1
1886	NY-a	134	559	90	127	19	10	5	24			.227	.269	.324	89	-8	6			.891	-3	*O-134/P-1	-1.2
1887	Phi-a	21	73	16	16	2	1	0	10			.219	.352	.274	76	-2	3			.821	-0	O-21	-0.2
	NY-a	60	241	30	55	10	1	1	9			.228	.265	.290	57	-14	3			.868	-3	O-59/1-3,P	-1.8
	Bro-a	1	3	2	1	0	0	0	0			.333	.500	.333	133	0				1.000	-3	/O-1	-0.3
	Yr	82	317	48	72	12	2	1	19			.227	.290	.287	63	-15	6			.856	-11	O-81/1-3,P	-2.3
1890	StL-a	80	302	47	103	26	0	2	30			.341	.449	.447	144	16	7			.819	-8	O-58,1-22M	0.4
	Lou-a	2	8	0	2	0	0	0	0			.250	.250	.250	48	-1	0			.864	-1	/1-2	-0.1
	Yr	82	310	47	105	26	0	2	30			.339	.444	.442	142	16	7			.819	-9	O-58/1-24	0.3
Total	7	681	2761	443	726	120	49	17	29	133	41	.263	.312	.360	109	27	19			.866	-38	O-654/1-29,P	-2.1

■ AL ROSEN   Rosen, Albert Leonard "Flip"   b: 2/29/24, Spartanburg, S.C.   BR/TR, 5'10.5", 180 lbs.   Deb: 9/10/47

1947	Cle-A	7	9	1	1	0	0	0	0	0	3	.111	.111	.111	-39	-2	0	0	0	.000	1	/3-2,O-1	-0.1
1948	*Cle-A	5	5	0	1	0	0	0	0	0	2	.200	.200	.200	7	-1	0	0	0	1.000	0	/3-2	-0.1
1949	Cle-A	23	44	3	7	2	0	0	5	7	4	.159	.275	.205	28	-5	0	1	-1	1.000	-1	3-10	-0.6
1950	Cle-A	155	554	100	159	23	4	37	116	100	72	.287	.405	.543	146	38	5	7	-3	.969	1	*3-154	3.1
1951	Cle-A	154	573	82	152	30	1	24	102	85	71	.265	.342	.447	125	19	7	5	-1	.958	-15	*3-154	0.1
1952	Cle-A★	148	567	101	171	32	5	28	105	75	54	.302	.387	.524	162	46	8	6	-1	.958	-20	*3-147/1-4,S	2.3
1953	Cle-A★	155	599	115	201	27	5	43	145	85	48	.336	.422	.613	181	67	8	7	-2	.964	1	*3-154/1-1,S	6.2
1954	*Cle-A★	137	466	76	140	20	2	24	102	85	43	.300	.412	.506	148	33	6	2	1	.959	-14	3-87,1-46/2S	1.6
1955	Cle-A	139	492	61	120	13	1	21	81	92	44	.244	.367	.402	103	4	4	2	0	.963	3	*3-106,1-41	0.4
1956	Cle-A	121	416	64	111	18	2	15	61	58	44	.267	.357	.428	104	2	1	3	-2	.945	-8	*3-116	-0.5
Total	10	1044	3725	603	1063	165	20	192	717	587	385	.285	.386	.495	138	202	39	33	-8	.961	-52	3-932/1-92,S2O	12.4

■ GOODY ROSEN   Rosen, Goodwin George   b: 8/28/12, Toronto, Ont., Can.   d: 4/6/94, Toronto, Ont., Can.   BL/TL, 5'10", 155 lbs.   Deb: 9/14/37

1937	Bro-N	22	77	10	24	5	1	0	6	6	6	.312	.361	.403	106	1	2			.981	1	O-21	0.1
1938	Bro-N	138	473	75	133	17	11	4	51	65	43	.281	.368	.389	106	5	0			.989	13	*O-113	1.5
1939	Bro-N	54	183	22	46	6	4	1	12	23	21	.251	.335	.344	80	-5	4			1.000	-3	O-47	-1.0
1944	Bro-N	89	264	38	69	8	3	0	23	26	27	.261	.330	.314	83	-5	0			.991	12	O-65	0.4
1945	Bro-N†	145	606	126	197	24	11	12	75	59	36	.325	.379	.460	134	26	4			.993	2	*O-141	2.1
1946	Bro-N	3	3	0	1	0	0	0	0	0	1	.333	.333	.333	89	-0	0			.000	-1	/O-1	-0.1
	NY-N	100	310	39	87	11	4	5	30	48	32	.281	.377	.390	117	8	2			.976	4	O-84	0.8
	Yr	103	313	39	88	11	4	5	30	48	33	.281	.377	.390	117	8	2			.976	3	O-85	0.7
Total	6	551	1916	310	557	71	34	22	197	218	166	.291	.364	.398	111	31	12			.989	28	O-472	3.8

■ HARRY ROSENBERG   Rosenberg, Harry   b: 6/22/09, San Francisco, Cal.   BR/TR, 5'9.5", 160 lbs.   Deb: 7/15/30 F

| 1930 | NY-N | 9 | 5 | 1 | 0 | 0 | 0 | 0 | 0 | 0 | 0 | .000 | .167 | .000 | -56 | -1 | 0 | | | 1.000 | -1 | /O-3 | -0.2 |

■ LOU ROSENBERG   Rosenberg, Louis   b: 3/5/04, San Francisco, Cal.   d: 9/8/91, Daly City, Cal.   BR/TR, 5'7", 155 lbs.   Deb: 5/22/23 F

| 1923 | Chi-A | 3 | 4 | 0 | 1 | 0 | 0 | 0 | 0 | 0 | 1 | .250 | .250 | .250 | 32 | -0 | 0 | 1 | -1 | 1.000 | -1 | /2-2 | -0.2 |

■ MAX ROSENFELD   Rosenfeld, Max   b: 12/23/02, New York, N.Y.   d: 3/10/69, Miami, Fla.   BR/TR, 5'8", 175 lbs.   Deb: 4/21/31

1931	Bro-N	3	9	0	2	1	0	0	0	1	1	.222	.300	.333	70	-0	0			1.000	-1	/O-3	-0.1
1932	Bro-N	34	39	8	14	3	0	2	7	1	10	.359	.359	.590	153	3	0			.970	-9	O-30	-0.7
1933	Bro-N	5	9	0	1	0	0	0	0	1	1	.111	.200	.111	-10	-1	0			1.000	0	/O-2	-0.1
Total	3	42	57	8	17	4	0	2	7	2	12	.298	.322	.474	115	1	2			.978	-9	/O-35	-0.9

■ LARRY ROSENTHAL   Rosenthal, Lawrence John   b: 5/21/10, St.Paul, Minn.   d: 3/4/92, Woodbury, Minn.   BL/TL, 6'0.5", 190 lbs.   Deb: 6/20/36

1936	Chi-A	85	317	71	89	15	8	3	46	59	37	.281	.394	.407	95	-1	2	0	1	.977	6	O-80	0.2
1937	Chi-A	58	97	20	28	5	1	2	9	9	20	.289	.355	.402	90	-1	1	0	0	.980	-3	O-25	-0.4
1938	Chi-A	61	105	14	30	5	1	1	12	12	13	.286	.359	.381	83	-3	0	1	-1	.959	-3	O-22	-0.6
1939	Chi-A	107	324	50	86	21	5	10	51	53	46	.265	.369	.454	106	3	6	4	-1	.990	-3	O-93	-0.3
1940	Chi-A	107	276	46	83	14	5	6	42	64	32	.301	.432	.453	128	15	2	3	1	.977	-3	O-92	0.6
1941	Chi-A	20	59	9	14	4	0	1	6	12	5	.237	.366	.305	80	-1	0	0	0	.938	-1	O-18	-0.3

YEAR	TM/L	G	AB	R	H	2B	3B	HR	RBI	BB	SO	AVG	OBP	SLG	PRO+	BR/A	SB	CS	SBR	FA	FR	G/POS	TPR
	Cle-A	45	75	10	14	3	1	1	8	9	10	.187	.274	.293	53	-5	1	0	0	1.000	0	O-14/1-1	-0.5
	Yr	65	134	19	28	7	1	1	9	21	15	.209	.316	.299	66	-6	1	0	0	.971	-1	O-32/1-1	-0.8
1944	NY-A	36	101	9	20	3	0	0	9	19	15	.198	.325	.228	57	-5	1	0	0	.986	3	O-26	-0.3
	Phi-A	32	54	5	11	2	0	1	6	5	9	.204	.271	.296	63	-3	0	0	0	.960	-4	O-19	-0.8
	Yr	68	155	14	31	5	0	1	15	24	24	.200	.307	.252	60	-7	1	0	0	.979	-2	O-45	-1.1
1945	Phi-A	28	75	6	15	3	2	0	5	9	8	.200	.286	.293	68	-3	0	1	-1	1.000	0	O-21	-0.8
Total	8	579	1483	240	390	75	25	22	189	251	195	.263	.370	.392	96	-5	13	9	-2	.979	-11	O-410/1-1	-3.2

■ SI ROSENTHAL Rosenthal, Simon b: 11/13/03, Boston, Mass. d: 4/7/69, Boston, Mass. BL/TL, 5'9", 165 lbs. Deb: 9/8/25

YEAR	TM/L	G	AB	R	H	2B	3B	HR	RBI	BB	SO	AVG	OBP	SLG	PRO+	BR/A	SB	CS	SBR	FA	FR	G/POS	TPR
1925	Bos-A	19	72	6	19	5	2	0	8	7	3	.264	.329	.389	82	-2	1	0	0	.919	0	O-17	-0.3
1926	Bos-A	104	285	34	76	12	3	4	34	19	18	.267	.317	.372	82	-9	4	1	1	.962	-13	O-67	-2.5
Total	2	123	357	40	95	17	5	4	42	26	21	.266	.319	.375	82	-11	5	1	1	.950	-13	/O-84	-2.8

■ BUNNY ROSER Roser, John William Joseph "Jack" b: 11/15/01, St.Louis, Mo. d: 5/6/79, Rocky Hill, Conn. BL/TL, 5'11", 175 lbs. Deb: 8/24/22

YEAR	TM/L	G	AB	R	H	2B	3B	HR	RBI	BB	SO	AVG	OBP	SLG	PRO+	BR/A	SB	CS	SBR	FA	FR	G/POS	TPR
1922	Bos-N	32	113	13	27	3	4	0	16	10	19	.239	.306	.336	69	-5	2	1	0	.915	-2	O-32	-1.0

■ CHET ROSS Ross, Chester James b: 4/1/17, Buffalo, N.Y. d: 2/21/89, Buffalo, N.Y. BR/TR, 6'1", 195 lbs. Deb: 9/15/39

YEAR	TM/L	G	AB	R	H	2B	3B	HR	RBI	BB	SO	AVG	OBP	SLG	PRO+	BR/A	SB	CS	SBR	FA	FR	G/POS	TPR
1939	Bos-N	11	31	4	10	1	1	0		2	10	.323	.364	.419	118	1				1.000	1	/O-8	0.1
1940	Bos-N	149	569	84	160	23	14	17	89	59	127	.281	.352	.460	130	22	4			.962	7	*O-149	2.1
1941	Bos-N	29	50	1	6	1	0	0	4	9	12	.120	.254	.140	14	-6	0			1.000	1	O-12	-0.7
1942	Bos-N	76	220	20	43	7	2	5	19	16	37	.195	.250	.314	66	-10	0			.992	-1	O-57	-1.5
1943	Bos-N	94	285	27	62	12	2	7	32	26	67	.218	.285	.347	84	-7	1			.977	3	O-73	-0.8
1944	Bos-N	54	154	20	35	9	2	5	26	12	23	.227	.287	.409	91	-3	1			1.000	3	O-38	-0.2
Total	6	413	1309	156	316	53	21	34	170	124	281	.241	.309	.392	100	-3	6			.976	11	O-337	-1.0

■ DON ROSS Ross, Donald Raymond b: 7/16/14, Pasadena, Cal. BR/TR, 6'1", 185 lbs. Deb: 4/19/38

YEAR	TM/L	G	AB	R	H	2B	3B	HR	RBI	BB	SO	AVG	OBP	SLG	PRO+	BR/A	SB	CS	SBR	FA	FR	G/POS	TPR
1938	Det-A	77	265	22	69	7	1	0	30	29	11	.260	.333	.306	58	-17	1	0	0	.946	4	3-75	-1.0
1940	Bro-N	10	38	4	11	2	0	1	8	3	3	.289	.341	.421	103	0	1			.879	-0	3-10	0.0
1942	Det-A	87	226	29	62	10	2	3	30	36	16	.274	.379	.376	104	2	2	1	0	.964	-3	O-38,3-20	-0.3
1943	Det-A	89	247	19	66	13	0	0	18	20	3	.267	.325	.320	82	-5	2	0	1	.985	-1	O-38,S-18/23	-1.4
1944	Det-A	66	167	14	35	5	0	2	15	14	9	.210	.275	.275	54	-10	2	1	0	.958	-1	O-37/S-2,1	-1.4
1945	Det-A	8	29	3	11	4	0	0	4	5	1	.379	.471	.517	175	3	2	0	1	.960	-0	/3-8	0.4
	Cle-A	106	363	26	95	15	1	2	43	42	15	.262	.340	.325	97	-1	0	4	-2	.958	-13	*3-106	-1.5
	Yr	114	392	29	106	19	1	2	47	47	16	.270	.350	.339	104	3	2	4	-2	.958	-14	*3-114	-1.1
1946	Cle-A	55	153	12	41	7	0	3	14	17	12	.268	.341	.373	106	1	0	0	0	.944	-12	3-41/O-2	-1.1
Total	7	498	1488	129	390	63	4	12	162	166	70	.262	.338	.334	86	-26	10	6		.946	-33	3-261,O-115/S21	-6.3

■ JOE ROSSI Rossi, Joseph Anthony b: 3/13/23, Oakland, Cal. BR/TR, 6'1", 205 lbs. Deb: 4/20/52

YEAR	TM/L	G	AB	R	H	2B	3B	HR	RBI	BB	SO	AVG	OBP	SLG	PRO+	BR/A	SB	CS	SBR	FA	FR	G/POS	TPR
1952	Cin-N	55	145	14	32	0	1	1	6	20	20	.221	.319	.255	61	-7	1	0	0	.982	2	C-46	-0.3

■ CLAUDE ROSSMAN Rossman, Claude R. b: 6/17/1881, Philmont, N.Y. d: 1/16/28, Poughkeepsie, N.Y. BL/TL, 6', 188 lbs. Deb: 9/16/04

YEAR	TM/L	G	AB	R	H	2B	3B	HR	RBI	BB	SO	AVG	OBP	SLG	PRO+	BR/A	SB	CS	SBR	FA	FR	G/POS	TPR
1904	Cle-A	18	62	5	13	5	0	0	6	0		.210	.210	.290	58	-3	0			.933	-4	O-17	-0.9
1906	Cle-A	118	396	49	122	13	2	0	53	17		.308	.338	.359	120	8	11			.984	-8	*1-105/O-1	-0.3
1907	*Det-A	153	571	60	158	21	4	0	69	33		.277	.318	.342	107	3	20			.981	-14	*1-153	-1.6
1908	*Det-A	138	524	45	154	33	13	2	71	27		.294	.330	.418	137	19	8			.981	6	*1-138	2.4
1909	Det-A	82	287	16	75	8	0	0	39	13		.261	.293	.310	87	-5	10			.981	-6	1-75	-1.3
	StL-A	2	8	0	1	0	0	0	0	0		.125	.125	.125	-23	-1	0			1.000	-0	/O-2	-0.2
	Yr	84	295	16	76	8	0	0	39	13		.258	.289	.305	84	-6	10			.981	-6	1-75/O-2	-1.5
Total	5	511	1848	175	523	80	26	3	238	90		.283	.318	.359	113	21	49			.982	-26	1-471/O-20	-1.9

■ RICO ROSSY Rossy, Elam Jose (Ramos) b: 2/16/64, San Juan, P.R. BR/TR, 5'10", 175 lbs. Deb: 9/11/91

YEAR	TM/L	G	AB	R	H	2B	3B	HR	RBI	BB	SO	AVG	OBP	SLG	PRO+	BR/A	SB	CS	SBR	FA	FR	G/POS	TPR
1991	Atl-N	5	1	0	0	0	0	0	0	0	1	.000	.000	.000	-94	-0	0	0	0	.000	0	/S-1	0.0
1992	KC-A	59	149	21	32	8	1	1	12	20	20	.215	.312	.302	71	-5	0	3	-2	.961	5	S-51/3-9,2	0.1
1993	KC-A	46	86	10	19	4	0	2	12	9	11	.221	.302	.337	68	-4	0	0	0	.987	1	2-24,3-16,S	-0.2
Total	3	110	236	31	51	12	1	3	24	29	32	.216	.307	.314	69	-10	0	3	-2	.966	6	/S-63,2-27,3	-0.1

■ FRANK ROTH Roth, Francis Charles b: 10/11/1878, Chicago, Ill. d: 3/27/55, Burlington, Wis. BR/TR, 5'10", 160 lbs. Deb: 4/18/03 FC

YEAR	TM/L	G	AB	R	H	2B	3B	HR	RBI	BB	SO	AVG	OBP	SLG	PRO+	BR/A	SB	CS	SBR	FA	FR	G/POS	TPR
1903	Phi-N	68	220	27	60	11	4	0	22	9		.273	.304	.359	92	-3	3			.935	-7	C-60/3-1	-0.3
1904	Phi-N	81	229	28	59	8	1	1	20	12		.258	.298	.314	92	-2	1			.958	-11	C-67/1-1,2	-0.7
1905	StL-A	35	107	9	25	3	0	0	7	6		.234	.274	.262	74	-3	1			.962	-7	C-29	-0.7
1906	Chi-A	16	51	4	10	1	1	0	7	6		.196	.241	.255	57	-3	1			.990	3	C-15	0.2
1909	Cin-N	56	147	12	35	7	2	0	16	6		.238	.287	.313	87	-3	5			.967	-3	C-54	-0.2
1910	Cin-N	26	29	3	7	2	0	0	3	0	2	.241	.267	.310	71	-1	1			.938	-0	/C-4,O-1	-0.1
Total	6	282	783	83	196	32	8	1	75	36	2	.250	.289	.315	86	-15	19			.956	-24	C-229/O-1,2,1,3	-1.8

■ BRAGGO ROTH Roth, Robert Frank b: 8/28/1892, Burlington, Wis. d: 9/11/36, Chicago, Ill. BR/TR, 5'7.5", 170 lbs. Deb: 9/1/14 F

YEAR	TM/L	G	AB	R	H	2B	3B	HR	RBI	BB	SO	AVG	OBP	SLG	PRO+	BR/A	SB	CS	SBR	FA	FR	G/POS	TPR
1914	Chi-A	34	126	14	37	4	6	1	10	8	25	.294	.355	.444	142	6	3	3	-1	.924	2	O-34	0.5
1915	Chi-A	70	240	44	60	6	10	3	35	29	50	.250	.338	.396	116	4	12	6	0	.837	-15	3-35,O-30	-1.2
	Cle-A	39	144	23	43	4	7	4	20	22	22	.299	.399	.507	168	12	14	4	2	.878	-6	O-39	0.6
	Yr	109	384	67	103	10	17	7	55	51	72	.268	.361	.438	135	16	26	10	2	.906	-21	O-69,3-35	-0.6
1916	Cle-A	125	409	50	117	19	7	4	72	38	48	.286	.350	.396	117	8	29	14	0	.954	-0	*O-112	0.6
1917	Cle-A	145	495	69	141	30	9	1	72	52	73	.285	.358	.388	118	10	51			.957	-0	*O-135	0.3
1918	Cle-A	106	375	53	106	21	12	1	59	53	41	.283	.383	.411	127	13	35			.936	-3	*O-106	0.4
1919	Phi-A	48	195	33	63	13	8	5	29	15	21	.323	.377	.549	156	13	11			.975	-5	O-48	0.6
	Bos-A	63	227	32	58	9	4	0	23	24	32	.256	.337	.330	93	-2	9			.943	-4	O-58	-1.0
	Yr	111	422	65	121	22	12	5	52	39	53	.287	.355	.431	124	12	20			.955	-9	*O-106	-0.4
1920	Was-A	138	468	80	136	23	8	9	92	75	57	.291	.395	.432	122	17	24	12	0	.952	-10	*O-128	-0.2
1921	NY-A	43	152	29	43	9	2	2	10	19	20	.283	.370	.408	96	-1	1	2		.923	-7	O-37	-0.7
Total	8	811	2831	427	804	138	73	30	422	335	389	.284	.367	.416	122	81	189	41		.944	-42	O-727/3-35	-0.1

■ BOB ROTHEL Rothel, Robert Burton b: 9/17/23, Columbia Station, Ohio d: 3/21/84, Huron, Ohio BR/TR, 5'10.5", 170 lbs. Deb: 4/22/45

YEAR	TM/L	G	AB	R	H	2B	3B	HR	RBI	BB	SO	AVG	OBP	SLG	PRO+	BR/A	SB	CS	SBR	FA	FR	G/POS	TPR
1945	Cle-A	4	10	0	2	0	0	0	0	3	1	.200	.385	.200	75	-0	0	0	0	.875	-1	/3-4	-0.1

■ BOBBY ROTHERMEL Rothermel, Edward Hill b: 12/18/1870, Fleetwood, Pa. d: 2/11/27, Detroit, Mich. Deb: 6/18/1899

YEAR	TM/L	G	AB	R	H	2B	3B	HR	RBI	BB	SO	AVG	OBP	SLG	PRO+	BR/A	SB	CS	SBR	FA	FR	G/POS	TPR
1899	Bal-N	10	21	1	2	0	0	0	3	1		.095	.136	.095	-34	-4	0			.867	-2	/2-5,3-2,S	-0.6

■ JACK ROTHFUSS Rothfuss, John Albert b: 4/18/1872, Newark, N.J. d: 4/20/47, Basking Ridge, N.J BR/TR, 5'11.5", 195 lbs. Deb: 8/2/1897

YEAR	TM/L	G	AB	R	H	2B	3B	HR	RBI	BB	SO	AVG	OBP	SLG	PRO+	BR/A	SB	CS	SBR	FA	FR	G/POS	TPR
1897	Pit-N	35	115	20	36	3	1	2	18	5		.313	.352	.409	104	1	3			.984	-1	1-32	0.0

■ CLAUDE ROTHGEB Rothgeb, Claude James b: 1/1/1880, Milford, Ill. d: 7/6/44, Manitowoc, Wis. BB, 6'0.5", 200 lbs. Deb: 6/17/05

YEAR	TM/L	G	AB	R	H	2B	3B	HR	RBI	BB	SO	AVG	OBP	SLG	PRO+	BR/A	SB	CS	SBR	FA	FR	G/POS	TPR
1905	Was-A	7	16	2	2	0	0	0	0			.125	.125	.125	-22	-2	0			1.000	0	/O-4	-0.2

■ JACK ROTHROCK Rothrock, John Houston b: 3/14/05, Long Beach, Cal. d: 2/2/80, San Bernardino, Cal BB/TR, 5'11.5", 165 lbs. Deb: 7/28/25

YEAR	TM/L	G	AB	R	H	2B	3B	HR	RBI	BB	SO	AVG	OBP	SLG	PRO+	BR/A	SB	CS	SBR	FA	FR	G/POS	TPR
1925	Bos-A	22	55	6	19	3	3	0	7	3	7	.345	.379	.509	124	2	0	0	0	.893	-4	S-22	0.0
1926	Bos-A	15	17	3	5	1	0	0	2	3	1	.294	.400	.353	101	0	0	0	0	.692	-2	/S-2	-0.1
1927	Bos-A	117	428	61	111	24	8	1	36	24	46	.259	.302	.360	73	-19	5	5	-2	.953	4	S-40,2-36,31	-1.1

YEAR	TM/L	G	AB	R	H	2B	3B	HR	RBI	BB	SO	AVG	OBP	SLG	PRO+	BR/A	SB	CS	SBR	FA	FR	G/POS	TPR
1928	Bos-A	117	344	52	92	9	4	3	22	33	40	.267	.333	.343	79	-10	12	6	0	.979	-17	O-53,3-17,1S/2PC	-2.9
1929	Bos-A	143	473	70	142	19	7	6	59	43	47	.300	.361	.408	100	0	23	13	-1	.970	2	*O-128	-0.7
1930	Bos-A	45	65	4	18	3	1	0	4	2	9	.277	.299	.354	67	-3	0	2	-1	.947	1	/O-9,3-1	-0.4
1931	Bos-A	133	475	81	132	32	3	4	42	47	48	.278	.343	.383	96	-3	13	7	-0	.982	-1	O-79,2-23/13S	-0.8
1932	Bos-A	12	48	3	10	1	0	0	0	5	5	.208	.283	.229	35	-5	3	0	1	.973	2	O-12	-0.2
	Chi-A	39	64	8	12	2	1	0	6	5	9	.188	.246	.250	31	-7	1	0	0	.929	-9	O-19/3-8,1	-1.4
	Yr	51	112	11	22	3	1	0	6	10	14	.196	.262	.241	33	-11	4	0	1	.961	-7	O-31/3-8,1	-1.6
1934	*StL-N	154	647	106	184	35	3	11	72	49	56	.284	.336	.399	90	-9	10			.975	5	*O-154/2-1	-1.1
1935	StL-N	129	502	76	137	18	5	3	56	57	29	.273	.347	.347	84	-10	7			.980	1	*O-127	-1.4
1937	Phi-A	88	232	28	62	15	0	0	21	28	15	.267	.346	.332	73	-9	1	0	0	.992	-6	O-58/2-1	-1.5
Total	11	1014	3350	498	924	162	35	28	327	299	312	.276	.336	.370	85	-73	75	33		.976	-24	O-639/S-78,231CP	-11.6

■ EDD ROUSH
Roush, Edd J b: 5/8/1893, Oakland City, Ind. d: 3/21/88, Bradenton, Fla. BL/TL, 5'11", 170 lbs. Deb: 8/20/13 CH

YEAR	TM/L	G	AB	R	H	2B	3B	HR	RBI	BB	SO	AVG	OBP	SLG	PRO+	BR/A	SB	CS	SBR	FA	FR	G/POS	TPR
1913	Chi-A	9	10	2	1	0	0	0	0	0	2	.100	.100	.100	-42	-2	0			1.000	-0	/O-2	-0.2
1914	Ind-F	74	166	26	54	8	4	1	30	6	20	.325	.353	.440	94	-2	12			.989	2	O-43/1-2	-0.2
1915	New-F	145	551	73	164	20	11	3	60	38	25	.298	.350	.390	104	1	28			.972	4	*O-144	-0.2
1916	NY-N	39	69	4	13	0	1	0	5	1	4	.188	.200	.217	30	-6	4			.952	-1	O-15	-0.9
	Cin-N	69	272	34	78	7	14	0	15	13	19	.287	.336	.415	133	10	15			.971	6	O-69	1.4
	Yr	108	341	38	91	7	15	0	20	14	23	.267	.309	.375	114	4	19			.969	5	O-84	0.5
1917	Cin-N	136	522	82	178	19	14	4	67	27	24	.341	.353	.454	162	36	21			.962	2	*O-134	3.4
1918	Cin-N	113	435	61	145	18	10	5	62	22	10	.333	.368	.455	153	26	24			.960	8	*O-113	3.0
1919	*Cin-N	133	504	73	162	19	12	4	71	42	19	.321	.380	.431	147	29	20			.989	10	*O-133	3.3
1920	Cin-N	149	579	81	196	22	16	4	90	42	22	.339	.386	.453	142	31	36	24	-4	.975	16	*O-139,1-11/2	3.4
1921	Cin-N	112	418	68	147	27	12	4	71	31	8	.352	.403	.502	145	27	19	17	-5	.980	2	*O-108	1.6
1922	Cin-N	49	165	29	58	7	4	1	24	19	5	.352	.428	.461	132	9	5	3	-0	.990	1	O-43	0.6
1923	Cin-N	138	527	88	185	41	18	6	88	46	16	.351	.406	.531	149	36	10	15	-6	.970	-4	*O-137	1.7
1924	Cin-N	121	483	67	168	23	21	4	72	22	11	.348	.386	.501	135	22	17	13	-3	.959	-5	*O-119	0.7
1925	Cin-N	134	540	91	183	28	16	8	83	35	14	.339	.383	.494	125	20	22	20	-5	.978	1	*O-134	0.6
1926	Cin-N	144	563	95	182	37	10	7	79	38	17	.323	.366	.462	125	18	8			.955	-12	*O-143/1-1	-0.4
1927	NY-N	140	570	83	173	27	4	7	58	26	15	.304	.335	.402	97	-4	18			.975	-4	*O-138	-1.6
1928	NY-N	46	163	20	41	5	3	2	13	14	8	.252	.315	.356	75	-6	1			.955	2	O-39	-0.7
1929	NY-N	115	450	76	146	19	7	8	52	45	16	.324	.390	.451	108	6	6			.982	-1	*O-107	-0.2
1931	Cin-N	101	376	46	102	12	5	1	41	17	5	.271	.308	.338	78	-12	2			.981	-4	O-88	-2.2
Total	18	1967	7363	1099	2376	339	182	68	981	484	260	.323	.369	.446	125	240	268	92		.972	23	*O-1848/1-14,2	13.1

■ PHIL ROUTCLIFFE
Routcliffe, Philip John "Chicken" b: 10/24/1870, Oswego, N.Y. d: 10/4/18, Oswego, N.Y. BR/TR, 6', 175 lbs. Deb: 4/21/1890

YEAR	TM/L	G	AB	R	H	2B	3B	HR	RBI	BB	SO	AVG	OBP	SLG	PRO+	BR/A	SB	CS	SBR	FA	FR	G/POS	TPR
1890	Pit-N	1	4	1	1	0	0	0	1	0	0	.250	.400	.250	102	-0	1			1.000	0	/O-1	0.0

■ DAVE ROWAN
Rowan, David (b: David Drohan) b: 12/6/1882, Elora, Ont., Canada d: 7/30/55, Toronto, Ont., Can BL/TL, 5'11", 175 lbs. Deb: 5/27/11

YEAR	TM/L	G	AB	R	H	2B	3B	HR	RBI	BB	SO	AVG	OBP	SLG	PRO+	BR/A	SB	CS	SBR	FA	FR	G/POS	TPR
1911	StL-A	18	65	7	25	1	1	0	11	4		.385	.420	.431	143	4	0			.945	-2	1-18	0.2

■ WADE ROWDON
Rowdon, Wade Lee b: 9/7/60, Riverhead, N.Y. BR/TR, 6'2", 180 lbs. Deb: 9/8/84

YEAR	TM/L	G	AB	R	H	2B	3B	HR	RBI	BB	SO	AVG	OBP	SLG	PRO+	BR/A	SB	CS	SBR	FA	FR	G/POS	TPR
1984	Cin-N	4	7	0	2	0	0	0	0	0	1	.286	.286	.286	58	-0	0	0	0	1.000	1	/S-1,3-1	0.1
1985	Cin-N	5	9	2	2	0	0	0	2	2	1	.222	.364	.222	64	-0	0	0	0	.667	-1	/3-4	-0.2
1986	Cin-N	38	80	9	20	5	1	0	10	9	17	.250	.333	.338	82	-2	2	0	1	.889	-7	/3-7,S-6,O2	-0.8
1987	Chi-N	11	31	2	7	1	1	1	4	3	10	.226	.294	.419	83	-1	0	2	-1	.818	-1	/3-9	-0.4
1988	Bal-A	20	30	1	3	0	0	0	0	0	6	.100	.100	.100	-45	-6	1	1	-0	.947	1	/3-8,O-5,D	-0.2
Total	5	78	157	14	34	6	2	1	16	14	35	.217	.285	.299	59	-9	3	3	-1	.866	-7	/3-29,O-10,SD2	-1.8

■ DAVE ROWE
Rowe, David Elwood b: 10/9/1854, Harrisburg, Pa. d: 12/9/30, Glendale, Cal. BR/TR, 5'9", 180 lbs. Deb: 5/30/1877 FM

YEAR	TM/L	G	AB	R	H	2B	3B	HR	RBI	BB	SO	AVG	OBP	SLG	PRO+	BR/A	SB	CS	SBR	FA	FR	G/POS	TPR
1877	Chi-N	2	7	0	2	0	0	0	0	0	3	.286	.286	.286	72	-1				.667	-1	/O-2,P-1	-0.1
1882	Cle-N	24	97	13	25	4	3	1	17	4	9	.258	.287	.392	119	2				.837	-3	O-23/P-1	-0.1
1883	Bal-a	59	256	40	80	11	6	0			2	.313	.318	.402	126	6				.798	-9	O-50/S-7,1P	-0.3
1884	StL-U	109	485	95	142	32	11	4			10	.293	.307	.429	95	-5				.947	-2	*O-92,S-14/21P	-0.8
1885	StL-N	16	62	8	10	3	0	0	3	5	8	.161	.224	.210	44	-4				.906	-2	O-16	-0.5
1886	KC-N	105	429	53	103	24	8	3	57	15	43	.240	.266	.354	82	-11	2			.851	-5	*O-90,S-11/2M	-1.6
1888	KC-a	32	122	14	21	3	4	0	13	6		.172	.217	.262	50	-7	2			.914	2	O-32,M	-0.5
Total	7	347	1458	223	383	77	32	8	90	42	63	.263	.284	.376	92	-19	4			.878	-19	O-305/S-32,21P	-4.0

■ HARLAND ROWE
Rowe, Harland Stimson "Hypie" b: 4/20/1896, Springvale, Me. d: 5/26/69, Springvale, Maine BL/TR, 6'1", 170 lbs. Deb: 6/23/16

YEAR	TM/L	G	AB	R	H	2B	3B	HR	RBI	BB	SO	AVG	OBP	SLG	PRO+	BR/A	SB	CS	SBR	FA	FR	G/POS	TPR
1916	Phi-A	17	36	2	5	1	0	0	3	2	8	.139	.184	.167	6	-4	0			.842	-3	/3-8,O-1	-0.7

■ JACK ROWE
Rowe, John Charles b: 12/8/1856, Harrisburg, Pa. d: 4/25/11, St.Louis, Mo. BL/TR, 5'8", 170 lbs. Deb: 9/6/1879 FM

YEAR	TM/L	G	AB	R	H	2B	3B	HR	RBI	BB	SO	AVG	OBP	SLG	PRO+	BR/A	SB	CS	SBR	FA	FR	G/POS	TPR
1879	Buf-N	8	34	8	12	1	0	0	8	0	1	.353	.353	.382	139	1				.905	2	/C-6,O-2	0.3
1880	Buf-N	79	326	43	82	10	6	1	36	6	17	.252	.265	.328	98	-1				.897	-19	*C-60,O-25/3	-2.0
1881	Buf-N	64	246	30	82	11	11	1	43	1	12	.333	.336	.480	156	15				.900	-7	C-46/S-7,3O	0.9
1882	Buf-N	75	308	43	82	14	5	1	42	12	0	.266	.294	.354	105	1				.950	-13	C-46,S-22/3O	-0.9
1883	Buf-N	87	374	65	104	18	7	1	38	15	14	.278	.306	.372	102	1				.899	-17	C-49,O-28,S/3	-1.2
1884	Buf-N	93	400	85	126	14	14	4	61	23	14	.315	.342	.450	146	20				.943	-10	C-65,O-30/S	1.3
1885	Buf-N	98	421	62	122	28	8	2	51	13	19	.290	.311	.409	127	11				.834	-14	S-65,C-23,O	-0.1
1886	Det-N	111	468	97	142	21	9	6	87	26	27	.303	.340	.425	128	14	12			.880	-21	*S-110/C-3	-0.5
1887	*Det-N	124	537	135	171	30	10	6	96	39	11	.318	.368	.445	121	14	22			.907	-27	*S-124	-1.0
1888	Det-N	105	451	62	125	19	8	2	74	19	28	.277	.311	.368	116	7	10			.861	-9	*S-105	0.1
1889	Pit-N	75	317	57	82	14	3	2	32	12	16	.259	.313	.341	91	-4	5			.896	-10	S-75	-0.8
1890	Buf-P	125	504	77	126	22	7	2	76	48	18	.250	.324	.333	83	-12	10			.901	-2	*S-125,M	-0.4
Total	12	1044	4386	764	1256	202	88	28	644	224	177	.286	.323	.392	115	68	59			.882	-147	S-657,C-298,O/3	-4.3

■ SCHOOLBOY ROWE
Rowe, Lynwood Thomas b: 1/11/10, Waco, Tex. d: 1/8/61, ElDorado, Ark. BR/TR, 6'4.5", 210 lbs. Deb: 4/15/33 C

YEAR	TM/L	G	AB	R	H	2B	3B	HR	RBI	BB	SO	AVG	OBP	SLG	PRO+	BR/A	SB	CS	SBR	FA	FR	G/POS	TPR
1933	Det-A	21	50	6	11	1	0	0	6	1	4	.220	.235	.240	26	-5	0	0	0	1.000	1	P-19	0.0
1934	*Det-A	51	109	15	33	8	1	2	22	6	20	.303	.339	.450	102	2	0	0	0	1.000	-0	P-45	0.0
1935	*Det-A☆	45	109	19	34	3	2	3	28	12	12	.312	.380	.459	120	3	0	0	0	.981	-2	P-42	0.0
1936	Det-A★	45	90	16	23	2	1	1	12	13	15	.256	.346	.333	71	-4	0	0	0	.984	2	P-41	0.0
1937	Det-A	10	10	2	2	0	0	0	1	1	4	.200	.273	.200	21	-1	0	0	0	1.000	0	P-10	0.0
1938	Det-A	4	6	1	1	1	0	0	0	1	1	.167	.167	.333	21	-1	0	0	0	.889	1	/P-4	0.0
1939	Det-A	31	61	9	15	0	1	0	12	5	7	.246	.303	.328	57	-4	1	1	-0	.947	0	P-28	0.0
1940	*Det-A	27	67	7	18	6	1	1	18	5	13	.269	.319	.433	85	-2	1	1	-0	1.000	-0	P-27	0.0
1941	Det-A	32	55	10	15	0	3	1	12	5	8	.273	.333	.436	93	-1	0	0	0	.927	1	P-27	0.0
1942	Det-A	2	4	0	0	0	0	0	0	0	0	.000	.000	.000	-93	-1	0	0	0	1.000	0	/P-2	0.0
	Bro-N	14	19	2	4	0	0	0	2	0	2	.211	.250	.211	35	-2	0	0	0	1.000	0	/P-9	0.0
1943	Phi-N	82	120	14	36	5	0	4	18	15	21	.300	.382	.458	148	7				.981	0	P-17	0.0
1946	Phi-N	30	61	4	11	5	0	1	6	3	16	.180	.219	.311	51	-4				1.000	-2	P-17	0.0
1947	Phi-N★	43	79	10	22	2	0	2	13	6	7	.278	.380	.380	106	1				.974	-1	P-31	0.0
1948	Phi-N	30	47	3	10	0	0	0	6	3	6	.192	.250	.255	38	-5	1			.976	1	P-30	0.0
1949	Phi-N	23	17	1	4	1	0	0	1	2	4	.235	.316	.471	111	0				.870	1	P-23	0.0
Total	15	491	909	116	239	36	9	18	153	86	157	.263	.328	.382	87	-17	3	2		.974	2	P-382	0.0

YEAR	TM/L	G	AB	R	H	2B	3B	HR	RBI	BB	SO	AVG	OBP	SLG	PRO+	BR/A	SB	CS	SBR	FA	FR	G/POS	TPR

■ BAMA ROWELL   Rowell, Carvel William   b: 1/13/16, Citronelle, Ala.   d: 8/16/93, Citronelle, Ala.   BL/TR, 5'11", 185 lbs.   Deb: 9/4/39

YEAR	TM/L	G	AB	R	H	2B	3B	HR	RBI	BB	SO	AVG	OBP	SLG	PRO+	BR/A	SB	CS	SBR	FA	FR	G/POS	TPR
1939	Bos-N	21	59	5	11	2	2	0	6	1	4	.186	.200	.288	32	-6	0			.853	-2	O-16	-0.9
1940	Bos-N	130	486	46	148	19	8	3	58	18	22	.305	.331	.395	105	2	12			.953	-3	*2-115/O-7	0.6
1941	Bos-N	138	483	49	129	23	6	7	60	39	36	.267	.322	.383	102	0	11			.935	-10	*2-112,O-14/3	-0.3
1946	Bos-N	95	293	37	82	12	6	3	31	29	15	.280	.345	.392	108	3	5			.978	-0	O-85	-0.1
1947	Bos-N	113	384	48	106	23	2	5	40	18	14	.276	.310	.385	86	-9	7			.945	-8	*O-100/2-7,3	-2.1
1948	Phi-N	77	196	15	47	16	2	1	22	8	14	.240	.270	.357	70	-9	2			.821	-12	3-18,O-17,2	-2.1
Total	6	574	1901	200	523	95	26	19	217	113	105	.275	.316	.382	95	-20	37			.945	-35	2-246,O-239/3	-4.9

■ ED ROWEN   Rowen, W. Edward   b: 10/22/1857, Bridgeport, Conn.   d: 2/22/1892, Bridgeport, Conn.   5'6", 155 lbs.   Deb: 5/1/1882

YEAR	TM/L	G	AB	R	H	2B	3B	HR	RBI	BB	SO	AVG	OBP	SLG	PRO+	BR/A	SB	CS	SBR	FA	FR	G/POS	TPR
1882	Bos-N	83	327	36	81	7	4	1	43	19	18	.248	.289	.303	90	-3				.885	-12	O-48,C-34/S3	-1.3
1883	Phi-a	49	196	28	43	10	1	0		11		.219	.261	.281	69	-7				.855	-2	C-44/O-8,32	-0.6
1884	Phi-a	4	15	4	6	1	0	0		1		.400	.471	.467	194	2				.806	-3	/C-4	-0.1
Total	3	136	538	68	130	18	5	1	43	31	18	.242	.284	.299	85	-9				.866	-17	/C-82,O-56,S32	-2.0

■ CHUCK ROWLAND   Rowland, Charlie Leland   b: 7/23/1899, Warrenton, N.C.   d: 1/21/92, Raleigh, N.C.   BR/TR, 6'1", 185 lbs.   Deb: 5/11/23

YEAR	TM/L	G	AB	R	H	2B	3B	HR	RBI	BB	SO	AVG	OBP	SLG	PRO+	BR/A	SB	CS	SBR	FA	FR	G/POS	TPR
1923	Phi-A	5	6	0	0	0	0	0	0	0	2	.000	.000	.000	-99	-2	0	0	0	1.000	0	/C-4	-0.1

■ RICH ROWLAND   Rowland, Richard Garnet   b: 2/25/64, Cloverdale, Cal.   BR/TR, 6'1", 210 lbs.   Deb: 9/7/90

YEAR	TM/L	G	AB	R	H	2B	3B	HR	RBI	BB	SO	AVG	OBP	SLG	PRO+	BR/A	SB	CS	SBR	FA	FR	G/POS	TPR
1990	Det-A	7	19	3	3	1	0	0	0	2	4	.158	.238	.211	26	-2	0	0	0	.967	-0	/C-5,D-2	-0.2
1991	Det-A	4	4	0	1	0	0	0	1	1	2	.250	.400	.250	83	-0	0	0	0	1.000	0	/C-2,D-1	0.0
1992	Det-A	6	14	2	3	0	0	0	0	3	3	.214	.353	.214	62	-1	0	0	0	1.000	0	/C-3,1-1,3D	-0.1
1993	Det-A	21	46	2	10	3	0	0	4	5	16	.217	.294	.283	56	-3	0	0	0	.988	5	C-17/D-3	0.2
1994	Bos-A	46	118	14	27	3	0	9	20	11	35	.229	.295	.483	90	-2	0	0	0	.972	-1	C-39/1-1,D	-0.1
Total	5	84	201	21	44	7	0	9	25	22	60	.219	.296	.388	76	-8	0	0	0	.976	4	/C-66,D-12,13	-0.2

■ JIM ROXBURGH   Roxburgh, James A.   b: 1/17/1858, San Francisco, Cal   d: 2/21/34, San Francisco, Cal   BR/TR, 5'10", 170 lbs.   Deb: 5/30/1884

YEAR	TM/L	G	AB	R	H	2B	3B	HR	RBI	BB	SO	AVG	OBP	SLG	PRO+	BR/A	SB	CS	SBR	FA	FR	G/POS	TPR
1884	Bal-a	2	4	1	2	0	0	0		1		.500	.667	.500	275	1				.824	-0	/C-2	0.1
1887	Phi-a	2	8	0	1	0	0	0		0		.125	.125	.125	-30	-1	0			.875	-2	/C-2,2-1	-0.2
Total	2	4	12	1	3	0	0	0		1		.250	.357	.250	81	-0	0			.840	-2	/C-4,2-1	-0.1

■ STAN ROYER   Royer, Stanley Dean   b: 8/31/67, Olney, Ill.   BR/TR, 6'3", 195 lbs.   Deb: 9/11/91

YEAR	TM/L	G	AB	R	H	2B	3B	HR	RBI	BB	SO	AVG	OBP	SLG	PRO+	BR/A	SB	CS	SBR	FA	FR	G/POS	TPR
1991	StL-N	9	21	1	6	1	0	0	1	1	2	.286	.318	.333	83	-0	0	0	0	1.000	-2	/3-5	-0.2
1992	StL-N	13	31	6	10	2	0	2	9	1	4	.323	.344	.581	162	2	0	0	0	.900	-3	/3-5,1-4	0.2
1993	StL-N	24	46	4	14	2	0	1	8	2	14	.304	.333	.413	100	-0	0	1	-1	.857	-0	3-10/1-2	-0.1
1994	StL-N	39	57	3	10	5	0	1	2	0	18	.175	.175	.316	26	-6	0	0	0	.972	-1	1-11/3-5	-0.7
	Bos-A	4	9	0	1	0	0	0	1	0	3	.111	.111	.111	-40	-2	0	0	0	.833	-0	/3-3,1-1	-0.2
Total	4	89	164	14	41	10	0	4	21	4	41	.250	.268	.384	75	-7	0	1	-1	.895	-3	/3-28,1-18	-1.0

■ JERRY ROYSTER   Royster, Jeron Kennis   b: 10/18/52, Sacramento, Cal.   BR/TR, 6', 165 lbs.   Deb: 8/14/73   C

YEAR	TM/L	G	AB	R	H	2B	3B	HR	RBI	BB	SO	AVG	OBP	SLG	PRO+	BR/A	SB	CS	SBR	FA	FR	G/POS	TPR
1973	LA-N	10	19	1	4	0	0	0	0	0	5	.211	.211	.211	18	-2	1	0	0	.842	2	/3-6,2-1	0.0
1974	LA-N	6	0	2	0	0	0	0	0	0	0	—	—	—	—	0	0	0	0	1.000	1	/2-1,3-1,O	0.1
1975	LA-N	13	36	2	9	2	1	0	1	1	3	.250	.270	.361	77	-1	1	0	0	1.000	-3	/O-7,2-4,3S	-0.4
1976	Atl-N	149	533	65	132	13	1	5	45	52	53	.248	.316	.304	72	-19	24	13	-1	.962	17	*3-148/S-2	-0.4
1977	Atl-N	140	445	64	96	10	2	6	28	38	67	.216	.279	.288	47	-33	28	10	2	.953	-29	3-56,S-51,2/O	-5.5
1978	Atl-N	140	529	67	137	17	8	2	35	56	49	.259	.333	.333	78	-15	27	17	-2	.974	-13	2-75,S-60/3	-1.7
1979	Atl-N	154	601	103	164	25	6	3	51	62	59	.273	.341	.349	83	-13	35	8	6	.948	13	3-80,2-77	1.0
1980	Atl-N	123	392	42	95	17	5	1	20	37	48	.242	.309	.319	73	-14	22	13	-1	.948	-11	2-49,3-48,O	-2.6
1981	Atl-N	64	93	13	19	4	1	0	9	7	14	.204	.260	.269	49	-6	7	5	-1	.950	3	3-24,2-13	-0.4
1982	*Atl-N	108	261	43	77	13	2	2	25	22	36	.295	.354	.383	102	1	14	6	1	.943	-2	3-62,O-25,2S	-0.1
1983	Atl-N	91	268	32	63	10	3	3	30	28	35	.235	.307	.328	71	-10	11	7	-1	.940	7	3-47,2-26,OS	-0.4
1984	Atl-N	81	227	22	47	13	2	1	21	15	41	.207	.259	.295	52	-15	6	4	-1	.973	5	2-29,3-17,SO	-0.9
1985	SD-N	90	249	31	70	13	2	5	31	32	31	.281	.365	.410	118	7	6	5	-1	.975	2	2-58,3-29/SO	1.0
1986	SD-N	118	257	31	66	12	0	5	26	32	45	.257	.339	.362	95	-1	3	5	-2	.931	-4	3-59,S-24,2/O	-0.6
1987	Chi-A	55	154	25	37	11	0	7	23	19	26	.240	.328	.448	101	-0	2	1	0	.969	-5	3-30,O-13/2D	-0.8
	NY-A	18	42	1	15	2	0	0	4	4	4	.357	.413	.405	120	1	2	1	0	.909	1	3-13/2-1,SO	0.3
	Yr	73	196	26	52	13	0	7	27	23	32	.265	.345	.439	104	1	4	2	0	.954	-5	3-43,O-14/2DS	-0.5
1988	Atl-N	68	102	8	18	3	0	1	6	16	.176	.222	.206	22	-10	0	0	0	1.000	-0	O-26,3-10/2S	-1.3
Total	16	1428	4208	552	1049	165	33	40	352	411	534	.249	.318	.333	76	-130	189	95	-0	.951	-19	3-634,2-416,SO/D	-12.7

■ WILLIE ROYSTER   Royster, Willie Arthur   b: 4/11/54, Clarksville, Va.   BR/TR, 5'11", 180 lbs.   Deb: 9/3/81

YEAR	TM/L	G	AB	R	H	2B	3B	HR	RBI	BB	SO	AVG	OBP	SLG	PRO+	BR/A	SB	CS	SBR	FA	FR	G/POS	TPR
1981	Bal-A	4	4	0	0	0	0	0	0	0	2	.000	.000	.000	-99	-1	0	0	0	1.000	-0	/C-4	-0.1

■ VIC ROZNOVSKY   Roznovsky, Victor Joseph   b: 10/19/38, Shiner, Tex.   BL/TR, 6'1", 180 lbs.   Deb: 6/28/64

YEAR	TM/L	G	AB	R	H	2B	3B	HR	RBI	BB	SO	AVG	OBP	SLG	PRO+	BR/A	SB	CS	SBR	FA	FR	G/POS	TPR
1964	Chi-N	35	76	2	15	1	0	0	2	5	18	.197	.247	.211	29	-7	0	1	-1	.976	-6	C-26	-1.3
1965	Chi-N	71	172	9	38	4	1	3	15	16	30	.221	.298	.308	70	-7	1	0	0	.984	2	C-63	-0.2
1966	Bal-A	41	97	4	23	5	0	1	10	9	11	.237	.308	.320	82	-2	0	0	0	.995	-3	C-34	-0.3
1967	Bal-A	45	97	7	20	5	0	0	10	1	20	.206	.214	.258	39	-7	0	0	0	.993	-2	C-23	-0.9
1969	Phi-N	13	13	0	3	0	0	0	1	1	4	.231	.286	.231	47	-1	0	0	0	1.000	0	/C-2	-0.1
Total	5	205	455	22	99	15	1	4	38	32	83	.218	.275	.281	59	-24	1	1	-0	.988	-9	C-148	-2.8

■ AL RUBELING   Rubeling, Albert William   b: 5/10/13, Baltimore, Md.   d: 1/28/88, Baltimore, Md.   BR/TR, 6', 185 lbs.   Deb: 4/16/40

YEAR	TM/L	G	AB	R	H	2B	3B	HR	RBI	BB	SO	AVG	OBP	SLG	PRO+	BR/A	SB	CS	SBR	FA	FR	G/POS	TPR
1940	Phi-A	108	376	49	92	16	6	4	38	48	58	.245	.330	.351	78	-12	4	5	-2	.933	-7	3-98,2-10	-1.7
1941	Phi-A	6	19	0	5	0	0	0	2	2	1	.263	.333	.263	61	-1	0			.833	-2	/3-6	-0.2
1943	Pit-N	47	168	23	44	8	4	0	9	8	17	.262	.295	.357	85	-4	0			.974	-0	2-44/3-1	-0.2
1944	Pit-N	92	184	22	45	7	2	4	30	19	19	.245	.322	.370	90	-2	4			1.000	-1	O-18,2-17,3	-0.3
Total	4	253	747	94	186	31	12	8	79	77	95	.249	.321	.355	82	-19	8	5		.939	-10	3-121/2-71,O	-2.4

■ SONNY RUBERTO   Ruberto, John Edward   b: 1/2/46, Staten Island, N.Y.   BR/TR, 5'11", 175 lbs.   Deb: 5/25/69   C

YEAR	TM/L	G	AB	R	H	2B	3B	HR	RBI	BB	SO	AVG	OBP	SLG	PRO+	BR/A	SB	CS	SBR	FA	FR	G/POS	TPR
1969	SD-N	19	21	3	3	0	0	0	0	0	7	.143	.182	.143	-8	-3	0	0	0	1.000	4	C-15	0.1
1972	Cin-N	2	3	0	0	0	0	0	0	1	.000	.250	.000	-25	-0	0	0	0	1.000	-0	/C-2	-0.1
Total	2	21	24	3	3	0	0	0	0	0	8	.125	.192	.125	-10	-3	0	0	0	1.000	4	/C-17	0.0

■ ART RUBLE   Ruble, William Arthur "Speedy"   b: 3/11/03, Knoxville, Tenn.   d: 11/1/83, Maryville, Tenn.   BL/TR, 5'10.5", 168 lbs.   Deb: 4/18/27

YEAR	TM/L	G	AB	R	H	2B	3B	HR	RBI	BB	SO	AVG	OBP	SLG	PRO+	BR/A	SB	CS	SBR	FA	FR	G/POS	TPR
1927	Det-A	56	91	16	15	4	2	0	11	14	15	.165	.283	.253	39	-8	2	1	-1	.970	-7	O-43	-1.7
1934	Phi-N	19	54	7	15	4	0	0	8	7	3	.278	.361	.352	81	-1	0			.839	-2	O-14	-0.3
Total	2	75	145	23	30	8	2	0	19	21	18	.207	.311	.290	55	-10	2	2		.929	-9	/O-57	-2.0

■ JOHNNY RUCKER   Rucker, John Joel   b: 1/15/17, Crabapple, Ga.   d: 8/7/85, Moultrie, Ga.   BL/TR, 6'2", 175 lbs.   Deb: 4/16/40

YEAR	TM/L	G	AB	R	H	2B	3B	HR	RBI	BB	SO	AVG	OBP	SLG	PRO+	BR/A	SB	CS	SBR	FA	FR	G/POS	TPR
1940	NY-N	86	277	38	82	7	5	4	23	7	32	.296	.313	.401	95	-3	4			.954	-3	O-57	-0.9
1941	NY-N	143	622	95	179	38	9	1	42	29	61	.288	.320	.383	95	-6	8			.967	5	*O-142	-0.9
1943	NY-N	132	505	56	138	19	4	2	46	22	44	.273	.304	.339	85	-11	4			.969	-0	*O-117	-1.6
1944	NY-N	144	587	79	143	14	8	6	39	24	48	.244	.275	.325	69	-26	8			.985	-6	*O-139	-4.1
1945	NY-N	105	429	58	117	19	11	7	51	20	36	.273	.305	.417	98	-3	8			.978	-1	O-98	-1.0

YEAR	TM/L	G	AB	R	H	2B	3B	HR	RBI	BB	SO	AVG	OBP	SLG	PRO+	BR/A	SB	CS	SBR	FA	FR	G/POS	TPR
1946	NY-N	95	197	28	52	8	2	1	13	7	27	.264	.300	.340	81	-5	4			.948	-10	O-54	-1.8
Total	6	705	2617	354	711	105	39	21	214	109	248	.272	.302	.366	87	-54	35			.971	-13	O-607	-10.3

■ JOHN RUDDERHAM
Rudderham, John Edmund b: 8/30/1863, Quincy, Mass. d: 4/3/42, Randolph, Mass. BR/TR, 5'8", 170 lbs. Deb: 9/18/1884

YEAR	TM/L	G	AB	R	H	2B	3B	HR	RBI	BB	SO	AVG	OBP	SLG	PRO+	BR/A	SB	CS	SBR	FA	FR	G/POS	TPR
1884	Bos-U	1	4	0	1	0	0	0		0		.250	.250	.250	37	-0				.000	-1	/O-1	-0.1

■ JOE RUDI
Rudi, Joseph Oden b: 9/7/46, Modesto, Cal. BR/TR, 6'2", 200 lbs. Deb: 4/11/67 C

YEAR	TM/L	G	AB	R	H	2B	3B	HR	RBI	BB	SO	AVG	OBP	SLG	PRO+	BR/A	SB	CS	SBR	FA	FR	G/POS	TPR
1967	KC-A	19	43	4	8	2	0	0	1	3	7	.186	.239	.233	41	-3	0	0	0	.984	-2	/1-9,O-6	-0.6
1968	Oak-A	68	181	10	32	5	1	1	12	12	32	.177	.236	.232	44	-12	1	1	-0	.987	-3	O-56	-2.2
1969	Oak-A	35	122	10	23	3	1	2	6	5	16	.189	.220	.279	41	-10	1	1	-0	1.000	2	O-18,1-11	-1.1
1970	Oak-A	106	350	40	108	23	2	11	42	16	61	.309	.342	.480	129	12	3	1	0	.982	-2	O-63,1-28	0.4
1971	*Oak-A	127	513	62	137	23	4	10	52	28	62	.267	.306	.386	97	-4	3	2	-0	.996	7	*O-121/1-5	-0.4
1972	*Oak-A★	147	593	94	181	32	9	19	75	37	62	.305	.348	.486	154	36	3	4	-2	.992	-1	*O-147/3-1	3.0
1973	*Oak-A	120	437	53	118	25	1	12	66	30	72	.270	.320	.414	111	9	5	0	0	.992	4	*O-117/1-1,D	0.3
1974	*Oak-A★	158	593	73	174	39	4	22	99	34	92	.293	.337	.484	143	29	2	3	-1	.984	-7	*O-140,1-27/D	1.5
1975	*Oak-A★	126	468	66	130	26	6	21	75	40	56	.278	.339	.494	136	20	2	1	0	.991	-12	1-91,O-44/D	0.0
1976	Oak-A	130	500	54	135	32	3	13	94	41	71	.270	.329	.424	124	14	6	1	1	.989	-1	*O-126/1-2,D	0.9
1977	Cal-A	64	242	48	64	13	2	13	53	22	48	.264	.336	.496	128	9	1	0	0	1.000	6	O-61/D-3	1.2
1978	Cal-A	133	497	58	127	21	1	17	79	28	82	.256	.298	.416	103	-0	2	1	0	.992	7	*O-111,D-11,1	0.1
1979	Cal-A	90	330	35	80	11	3	11	61	24	61	.242	.296	.394	87	-7	0	0	0	.989	6	O-80/1-5,D	-0.5
1980	Cal-A	104	372	42	88	17	1	16	53	17	84	.237	.279	.417	90	-7	1	0	0	.991	8	O-90/1-6,D	-0.2
1981	Bos-A	49	122	14	22	3	0	6	24	8	29	.180	.242	.352	66	-6	0	0	0	1.000	-1	D-21/1-5,O	-0.9
1982	Oak-A	71	193	21	41	6	1	5	18	24	35	.212	.304	.332	77	-6	0	0	0	.991	-7	1-49,O-14/D	-1.5
Total	16	1547	5556	684	1468	287	39	179	810	369	870	.264	.314	.427	112	69	25	15	-1	.991	3	*O-1195,1-249/D3	-0.0

■ DUTCH RUDOLPH
Rudolph, John Herman b: 7/10/1882, Natrona, Pa. d: 4/17/67, Natrona, Pa. BL/TL, 5'10", 160 lbs. Deb: 7/3/03

YEAR	TM/L	G	AB	R	H	2B	3B	HR	RBI	BB	SO	AVG	OBP	SLG	PRO+	BR/A	SB	CS	SBR	FA	FR	G/POS	TPR
1903	Phi-N	1	1	0	0	0	0	0	0	0		.000	.000	.000	-99	-0	0			.000		H	0.0
1904	Chi-N	2	3	0	1	0	0	0	0	0		.333	.333	.333	106	-0	0			1.000	-1	/O-2	-0.1
Total	2	3	4	0	1	0	0	0	0	0		.250	.250	.250	52	-0	0			1.000	-1	/O-2	-0.1

■ KEN RUDOLPH
Rudolph, Kenneth Victor b: 12/29/46, Rockford, Ill. BR/TR, 6'1", 185 lbs. Deb: 4/20/69

YEAR	TM/L	G	AB	R	H	2B	3B	HR	RBI	BB	SO	AVG	OBP	SLG	PRO+	BR/A	SB	CS	SBR	FA	FR	G/POS	TPR
1969	Chi-N	27	34	7	7	1	0	1	6	6	11	.206	.325	.324	73	-1	0	0	0	.977	0	C-11/O-3	-0.1
1970	Chi-N	20	40	1	4	1	0	0	2	1	12	.100	.122	.125	-30	-7	0	0	0	1.000	1	C-16	-0.5
1971	Chi-N	25	76	5	15	3	0	0	7	6	20	.197	.265	.237	38	-6	0	0	0	1.000	7	C-25	0.2
1972	Chi-N	42	106	10	25	1	1	2	9	6	14	.236	.283	.321	64	-5	1	2	-1	.966	5	C-41	0.1
1973	Chi-N	64	170	12	35	8	1	2	17	7	25	.206	.242	.300	46	-13	1	4	-2	.970	-3	C-64	-1.6
1974	SF-N	57	158	11	41	3	0	0	10	21	15	.259	.350	.278	74	-5	0	0	0	.996	3	C-56	-0.1
1975	StL-N	44	80	5	16	2	0	1	6	3	10	.200	.229	.262	35	-7	0	0	0	.972	2	C-31	-0.5
1976	StL-N	27	50	1	8	3	0	0	5	1	7	.160	.176	.220	12	-6	0	0	0	.940	2	C-11	-0.4
1977	SF-N	11	15	1	3	0	0	0	0	1	3	.200	.250	.200	22	-2	0	0	0	.946	3	C-11	0.1
	Bal-N	11	14	2	4	1	0	0	2	0	4	.286	.286	.357	79	-0	0	0	0	1.000	5	C-11	0.4
Total	9	328	743	55	158	23	2	6	64	52	121	.213	.268	.273	48	-52	2	6	-3	.980	24	C-280/O-3	-2.3

■ MUDDY RUEL
Ruel, Herold Dominic b: 2/20/1896, St. Louis, Mo. d: 11/13/63, Palo Alto, Cal. BR/TR, 5'9", 150 lbs. Deb: 5/29/15 MC

YEAR	TM/L	G	AB	R	H	2B	3B	HR	RBI	BB	SO	AVG	OBP	SLG	PRO+	BR/A	SB	CS	SBR	FA	FR	G/POS	TPR
1915	StL-A	10	14	0	0	0	0	0	1	5	5	.000	.263	.000	-22	-2	0			.958	-1	/C-6	-0.3
1917	NY-A	6	17	1	2	0	0	0	1	2	2	.118	.211	.118	0	-2	1			1.000	-1	/C-6	-0.3
1918	NY-A	3	6	0	2	0	0	0	0	2	1	.333	.500	.333	148	1	1			1.000	0	/C-2	0.1
1919	NY-A	79	233	18	56	6	0	0	31	34	26	.240	.340	.266	71	-8	4			.975	2	C-79	0.1
1920	NY-A	82	261	30	70	14	1	1	15	15	18	.268	.310	.341	70	-12	4	2	0	.984	0	C-80	-0.6
1921	Bos-A	113	358	41	99	21	1	1	45	41	15	.277	.352	.349	82	-9	2	7	-4	.977	-10	*C-109	-1.6
1922	Bos-A	116	361	34	92	15	1	0	28	41	26	.255	.333	.302	67	-17	4	2	0	.978	-2	*C-112	-1.2
1923	Was-A	136	449	63	142	24	3	0	54	55	21	.316	.394	.383	111	9	4	6	-2	.980	19	*C-133	3.0
1924	*Was-A	149	501	50	142	20	2	0	57	62	20	.283	.370	.331	84	-9	7	11	-5	.980	14	*C-147	0.9
1925	*Was-A	127	393	55	122	9	2	0	54	63	16	.310	.411	.344	95	1	4	5	-2	.982	12	*C-126/1-1	1.6
1926	Was-A	117	368	42	110	22	4	1	53	61	14	.299	.401	.389	109	8	7	6	-2	.989	2	*C-117	1.4
1927	Was-A	131	428	61	132	16	5	1	52	63	18	.308	.403	.376	104	6	9	6	-1	.988	-3	*C-128	1.1
1928	Was-A	108	350	31	90	18	2	0	55	44	14	.257	.342	.320	75	-11	12	10	-2	.989	7	*C-101/1-2	0.1
1929	Was-A	69	188	16	46	4	2	0	20	31	7	.245	.352	.287	66	-8	0	4	-2	.990	9	C-62	0.3
1930	Was-A	66	198	18	50	8	3	0	26	24	13	.253	.342	.308	66	-9	1	0	0	.986	0	C-60	0.0
1931	Bos-A	33	83	6	25	5	0	0	6	9	6	.301	.370	.361	98	0	0	0	0	.945	1	C-30	0.3
	Det-A	14	50	1	6	1	0	0	3	5	1	.120	.200	.140	-9	-8	0	0	0	.975	3	C-14	-0.4
	Yr	47	133	7	31	6	0	0	9	14	7	.233	.306	.278	56	-8	0	0	0	.958	4	C-44	-0.1
1932	Det-A	51	136	10	32	4	2	0	18	17	6	.235	.320	.294	58	-8	1	0	0	.989	-2	C-49	-0.7
1933	StL-A	38	63	13	12	2	0	0	8	24	4	.190	.414	.222	68	-1	0	0	0	1.000	3	C-28	0.2
1934	Chi-A	22	57	4	12	3	0	0	7	8	5	.211	.308	.263	47	-4	0	0	0	.976	-2	C-21	-0.5
Total	19	1468	4514	494	1242	187	29	4	534	606	238	.275	.365	.332	83	-84	61	59		.982	53	*C-1410/1-3	3.5

■ DUTCH RUETHER
Ruether, Walter Henry b: 9/13/1893, Alameda, Cal. d: 5/16/70, Phoenix, Ariz. BL/TL, 6'1.5", 180 lbs. Deb: 4/13/17

YEAR	TM/L	G	AB	R	H	2B	3B	HR	RBI	BB	SO	AVG	OBP	SLG	PRO+	BR/A	SB	CS	SBR	FA	FR	G/POS	TPR
1917	Chi-N	31	44	3	12	1	3	0	11	8	11	.273	.385	.432	139	2				1.000	0	P-10/1-5	0.1
	Cin-N	19	24	1	5	2	0	0	1	3	6	.208	.296	.292	84	-0	1			.833	-0	/P-7	0.0
	Yr	50	68	4	17	3	3	0	12	11	17	.250	.354	.382	122	2	1			.920	0	P-17/1-5	0.1
1918	Cin-N	2	3	0	0	0	0	0	0	0	2	.000	.000	.000	-99	-1	0			1.000	-0	/P-2	0.0
1919	*Cin-N	42	92	8	24	2	3	0	6	4	18	.261	.292	.348	94	-1	1			.971	-3	P-33	0.0
1920	Cin-N	45	104	3	20	0	0	0	10	6	24	.192	.229	.231	33	-9	0	0	0	.952	0	P-37/1-1	0.0
1921	Bro-N	49	97	12	34	5	2	2	13	4	9	.351	.376	.505	127	3	1	0	0	.966	-1	P-36	0.0
1922	Bro-N	67	125	12	26	6	1	2	20	12	11	.208	.283	.320	56	-9	0	0	0	1.000	0	P-35	0.0
1923	Bro-N	49	117	6	32	1	0	0	12	10	12	.274	.341	.282	68	-5	0	0	0	.968	-2	P-34/1-1	0.0
1924	Bro-N	34	62	5	15	1	1	0	4	5	2	.242	.299	.290	60	-3	0	1		.981	1	P-30	0.0
1925	*Was-A	55	108	18	36	3	2	1	15	10	8	.333	.390	.426	109	1	0	1	-1	.962	-3	P-30/1-1	0.0
1926	Was-A	47	92	6	23	2	1	1	11	6	10	.250	.296	.304	58	-6	0	0	0	.974	-2	P-23	0.0
	*NY-A	13	21	2	2	0	0	0	0	5	1	.095	.136	.095	-39	-4	0	0	0	.875	-1	/P-5	0.0
	Yr	60	113	8	25	2	1	1	11	11	11	.221	.267	.265	40	-10	0	0	0	.957	-3	P-28	0.0
1927	NY-A	35	80	7	21	3	1	0	8	8	15	.262	.330	.338	76	-3	0	0	0	1.000	0	P-27	0.0
Total	11	488	969	83	250	30	12	7	111	77	129	.258	.314	.335	79	-33	3	1		.970	-9	P-309/1-8	0.1

■ RUDY RUFER
Rufer, Rudolph Joseph b: 10/28/26, Ridgewood, N.Y. BR/TR, 6'0.5", 165 lbs. Deb: 9/22/49

YEAR	TM/L	G	AB	R	H	2B	3B	HR	RBI	BB	SO	AVG	OBP	SLG	PRO+	BR/A	SB	CS	SBR	FA	FR	G/POS	TPR
1949	NY-N	7	15	1	1	0	0	0	2	2	0	.067	.176	.067	-32	-3	0			.957	-1	/S-7	-0.3
1950	NY-N	15	11	1	1	0	0	0	0	0	1	.091	.091	.091	-52	-2	1			.889	1	/S-8	-0.1
Total	2	22	26	2	2	0	0	0	2	2	1	.077	.143	.077	-40	-5	1			.938	1	/S-15	-0.4

■ RED RUFFING
Ruffing, Charles Herbert b: 5/3/04, Granville, Ill. d: 2/17/86, Mayfield Hts., O. BR/TR, 6'1.5", 205 lbs. Deb: 5/31/24 CH

YEAR	TM/L	G	AB	R	H	2B	3B	HR	RBI	BB	SO	AVG	OBP	SLG	PRO+	BR/A	SB	CS	SBR	FA	FR	G/POS	TPR
1924	Bos-A	8	7	0	1	0	0	0	0	0	1	.143	.143	.429	44	-1	0	0	0	1.000	-1	/P-8	0.0
1925	Bos-A	37	79	6	17	4	2	0	11	1	22	.215	.235	.316	39	-8	0	0	0	.983	-1	P-37	0.0
1926	Bos-A	37	51	8	10	3	0	1	5	2	12	.196	.226	.275	31	-5	0	1	-1	.978	-1	P-37	0.0
1927	Bos-A	29	55	5	14	3	1	0	4	0	6	.255	.268	.345	59	-4	0	0	0	.978	0	P-26	0.0

YEAR	TM/L	G	AB	R	H	2B	3B	HR	RBI	BB	SO	AVG	OBP	SLG	PRO+	BR/A	SB	CS	SBR	FA	FR	G/POS	TPR
1928	Bos-A	60	121	12	38	13	1	2	19	3	12	.314	.331	.488	115	2	0	0	0	.951	-3	P-42	0.0
1929	Bos-A	60	114	9	35	9	0	2	17	2	13	.307	.325	.439	97	-1	0	0	0	.946	-2	P-35/O-2	-0.1
1930	Bos-A	6	11	2	3	2	0	0	1	0	1	.273	.273	.455	84	-0	0	0	0	.667	-1	/P-4	0.0
	NY-A	52	99	15	37	6	2	4	21	7	7	.374	.415	.596	160	9	0	0	0	.938	-2	P-34	0.0
	Yr	58	110	17	40	8	2	4	22	7	8	.364	.382	.582	153	8	0	0	0	.914	-3	P-38	0.0
1931	NY-A	48	109	14	36	8	1	3	12	1	13	.330	.336	.505	125	3	0	0	0	**1.000**	-3	P-37/O-1	0.0
1932	*NY-A	55	124	20	38	6	1	3	19	6	10	.306	.338	.444	106	1	0	0	0	.955	-2	P-35	0.0
1933	NY-A	55	115	10	29	3	1	2	13	7	15	.252	.295	.348	74	-5	0	0	0	.964	-0	P-35	0.0
1934	NY-A★	45	113	11	28	3	0	2	13	3	17	.248	.274	.327	58	-8	0	0	0	.933	-3	P-36	0.0
1935	NY-A	50	109	13	37	10	0	2	18	3	9	.339	.363	.486	125	3	0	0	0	**1.000**	-2	P-30	0.0
1936	*NY-A	53	127	14	37	5	0	5	22	11	12	.291	.348	.449	99	-1	0	0	0	.986	-2	P-33	0.0
1937	*NY-A	54	129	11	26	3	0	1	10	13	24	.202	.275	.248	32	-13	0	0	0	.974	-4	P-31	0.0
1938	*NY-A☆	45	107	12	24	4	1	3	17	17	21	.224	.331	.364	74	-4	0	0	0	**1.000**	-2	P-31	0.0
1939	*NY-A★	44	114	12	35	1	0	1	20	7	18	.307	.347	.342	78	-4	1	0	0	.952	-2	P-28	0.0
1940	NY-A★	33	89	8	11	4	0	1	7	3	9	.124	.152	.202	-9	-15	0	0	0	.947	-3	P-30	0.0
1941	*NY-A☆	38	89	10	27	8	1	2	22	4	12	.303	.333	.483	115	1	0	0	0	**1.000**	-3	P-23	0.0
1942	*NY-A☆	30	80	8	20	4	0	1	13	5	13	.250	.302	.338	81	-2	0	0	0	.974	-2	P-24	0.0
1945	NY-A	21	46	4	10	0	1	1	5	0	8	.217	.217	.326	54	-3	0	0	0	.929	-2	P-11	0.0
1946	NY-A	8	25	1	3	1	0	0	1	1	8	.120	.154	.160	-12	-4	0	0	0	1.000	-1	/P-8	0.0
1947	Chi-A	14	24	2	5	0	0	0	3	1	3	.208	.240	.208	26	-2	0	0	0	1.000	-0	/P-9	0.0
Total	22	882	1937	207	521	98	13	36	273	97	266	.269	.306	.389	81	-60	1	1	-0	.968	-35	P-624/O-3	-0.1

■ **CHICO RUIZ**   Ruiz, Hiraldo (Sablon) b: 12/5/38, Santo Domingo, Cuba d: 2/9/72, San Diego, Cal. BR/TR, 6', 173 lbs. Deb: 4/13/64

YEAR	TM/L	G	AB	R	H	2B	3B	HR	RBI	BB	SO	AVG	OBP	SLG	PRO+	BR/A	SB	CS	SBR	FA	FR	G/POS	TPR
1964	Cin-N	77	311	33	76	13	2	2	16	7	41	.244	.270	.318	63	-15	11	3	2	.942	-10	3-49,2-30	-2.4
1965	Cin-N	29	18	7	2	1	0	0	1	0	5	.111	.111	.167	-21	-3	1	2	-1	.875	2	/3-4,S-3	-0.2
1966	Cin-N	82	110	13	28	2	1	0	5	5	14	.255	.287	.291	56	-6	1	2	-1	.927	-1	3-27/O-8,S	-0.9
1967	Cin-N	105	250	32	55	12	4	0	13	11	35	.220	.259	.300	53	-15	9	4	0	.969	0	2-56,3-13,S/O	-1.2
1968	Cin-N	85	139	15	36	2	1	0	9	12	14	.259	.318	.288	78	-3	4	3	-1	.979	8	2-34,1-16/3S	0.6
1969	Cin-N	88	196	19	48	4	1	0	13	14	28	.245	.295	.276	58	-11	4	2	0	.949	-7	2-39,S-29/310	-1.3
1970	Cal-A	68	107	10	26	3	1	0	12	7	16	.243	.296	.290	64	-5	3	0	1	.985	-0	3-27/2-3,S1C	-0.4
1971	Cal-A	31	19	4	5	0	0	0	0	2	7	.263	.333	.263	76	-1	1	0	0	1.000	2	/3-3,2-2	0.2
Total	8	565	1150	133	276	37	10	2	69	58	164	.240	.281	.295	60	-59	34	16	1	.966	-6	2-164,3-135/S10C	-5.6

■ **CHICO RUIZ**   Ruiz, Manuel (Cruz) b: 11/1/51, Santurce, P.R. BR/TR, 5'11.5", 170 lbs. Deb: 7/29/78

YEAR	TM/L	G	AB	R	H	2B	3B	HR	RBI	BB	SO	AVG	OBP	SLG	PRO+	BR/A	SB	CS	SBR	FA	FR	G/POS	TPR
1978	Atl-N	18	46	3	13	3	0	0	2	2	4	.283	.313	.348	76	-1	0	0	0	.984	1	2-14/3-1	0.1
1980	Atl-N	25	26	3	8	2	1	0	2	3	7	.308	.379	.462	129	1	0	1	-1	.875	2	3-16/S-4,2	0.2
Total	2	43	72	6	21	5	1	0	4	5	11	.292	.338	.389	95	-0	0	1	-1	.880	3	/3-17,2-16,S	0.3

■ **JOE RULLO**   Rullo, Joseph Vincent b: 6/16/16, New York, N.Y. d: 10/28/69, Philadelphia, Pa. BR/TR, 5'11", 168 lbs. Deb: 9/22/43

YEAR	TM/L	G	AB	R	H	2B	3B	HR	RBI	BB	SO	AVG	OBP	SLG	PRO+	BR/A	SB	CS	SBR	FA	FR	G/POS	TPR
1943	Phi-A	16	55	2	16	0	0	0	6	8	7	.291	.381	.345	114	1	0	0	0	.963	-1	2-16	0.2
1944	Phi-A	35	96	5	16	0	0	0	5	6	19	.167	.223	.167	12	-11	1	0	0	.954	3	2-33/1-1,O	-0.6
Total	2	51	151	7	32	0	0	0	11	14	26	.212	.283	.232	50	-10	1	0	0	.957	2	/2-49,O-1,1	-0.4

■ **WILLIAM RUMLER**   Rumler, William George b: 3/27/1891, Milford, Neb. d: 5/26/66, Lincoln, Neb. BR/TR, 6'1", 190 lbs. Deb: 5/4/14

YEAR	TM/L	G	AB	R	H	2B	3B	HR	RBI	BB	SO	AVG	OBP	SLG	PRO+	BR/A	SB	CS	SBR	FA	FR	G/POS	TPR
1914	StL-A	34	46	2	8	1	0	0	6	3	12	.174	.240	.196	32	-4	2	2	-1	1.000	-3	C-10/O-6	-0.8
1916	StL-A	27	37	6	12	3	0	0	10	3	7	.324	.375	.405	141	2				.971	-3	/C-9	0.3
1917	StL-A	78	88	7	23	3	4	1	16	8	9	.261	.323	.420	132	3	2			.938	-0	/O-9	0.3
Total	3	139	171	15	43	7	4	1	32	14	28	.251	.312	.357	107	1	4	2		.986	-3	/C-19,O-15	-0.2

■ **PAUL RUNGE**   Runge, Paul William b: 5/21/58, Kingston, N.Y. BR/TR, 6', 175 lbs. Deb: 9/25/81

YEAR	TM/L	G	AB	R	H	2B	3B	HR	RBI	BB	SO	AVG	OBP	SLG	PRO+	BR/A	SB	CS	SBR	FA	FR	G/POS	TPR
1981	Atl-N	10	27	2	7	1	0	0	2	4	4	.259	.355	.296	84	-0	0	0	0	.911	-1	S-10	-0.1
1982	Atl-N	4	2	0	0	0	0	0	0	0	0	.000	.000	.000	-96	-1	0	0	0	.000	0	/H	-0.1
1983	Atl-N	5	8	0	2	0	0	0	1	1	4	.250	.333	.250	59	-0	0	0	0	1.000	-1	/2-2	-0.1
1984	Atl-N	28	90	5	24	3	1	0	3	10	14	.267	.340	.322	81	-2	5	3	-0	.970	10	2-22/S-7,3	0.9
1985	Atl-N	50	87	15	19	3	0	1	5	18	18	.218	.352	.287	76	-2	0	1	-1	.929	4	3-28/S-5,2	0.1
1986	Atl-N	7	8	1	2	0	0	0	0	2	4	.250	.400	.250	79	-0	0	0	0	1.000	2	/2-5	0.2
1987	Atl-N	27	47	9	10	1	0	3	8	5	10	.213	.288	.426	82	-0	0	1	-1	.923	-1	3-10/S-9,2	-0.1
1988	Atl-N	52	76	11	16	5	0	0	7	14	21	.211	.333	.276	73	-2	0	0	0	1.000	-1	3-19/2-7,S	-0.4
Total	8	183	345	43	80	13	1	4	26	54	75	.232	.336	.310	77	-9	5	5	-2	.941	13	/3-60,2-40,S	0.4

■ **TOM RUNNELLS**   Runnells, Thomas William b: 4/17/55, Greeley, Colo. BB/TR, 6', 175 lbs. Deb: 8/9/85 MC

YEAR	TM/L	G	AB	R	H	2B	3B	HR	RBI	BB	SO	AVG	OBP	SLG	PRO+	BR/A	SB	CS	SBR	FA	FR	G/POS	TPR
1985	Cin-N	28	35	3	7	1	0	0	4	4	4	.200	.263	.229	37	-3	0	0	0	1.000	1	S-11/2-1	-0.2
1986	Cin-N	12	11	1	1	1	0	0	0	0	2	.091	.091	.182	-26	-2	0	0	0	1.000	1	/2-4,3-3	-0.1
Total	2	40	46	4	8	2	0	0	4	4	6	.174	.224	.217	23	-5	0	0	0	1.000	2	/S-11,2-5,3	-0.3

■ **PETE RUNNELS**   Runnels, James Edward (b: James Edward Runnells) b: 1/28/28, Lufkin, Tex. d: 5/20/91, Pasadena, Tex. BL/TR, 6', 170 lbs. Deb: 7/1/51 MC

YEAR	TM/L	G	AB	R	H	2B	3B	HR	RBI	BB	SO	AVG	OBP	SLG	PRO+	BR/A	SB	CS	SBR	FA	FR	G/POS	TPR
1951	Was-A	78	273	31	76	12	2	0	25	31	24	.278	.354	.337	89	-3	0	3	-2	.949	-21	S-73	-2.1
1952	Was-A	152	555	70	158	18	3	1	64	72	55	.285	.368	.333	99	2	0	10	-6	.966	-15	*S-147/2-1	-0.8
1953	Was-A	137	486	64	125	15	5	2	50	64	36	.257	.347	.321	83	-10	3	4	-2	.958	-33	*S-121,2-11	-3.5
1954	Was-A	139	488	75	131	17	15	3	56	78	60	.268	.369	.383	112	10	2	3	-1	.953	-19	*S-107,2-27/O	0.0
1955	Was-A	134	503	66	143	16	4	2	49	55	51	.284	.356	.344	94	-3	3	9	-5	.976	-3	*2-132/S-2	0.0
1956	Was-A	147	578	72	179	29	9	8	76	58	64	.310	.375	.433	113	11	5	5	-2	.995	0	1-81,2-69/S	1.0
1957	Was-A	134	473	53	109	18	4	2	35	55	51	.230	.313	.298	69	-20	2	3	-1	.995	1	1-72,3-32,2	-2.2
1958	Bos-A	147	568	103	183	32	5	8	59	87	49	.322	.414	.438	127	25	1	2	-1	.985	8	*2-106,1-42	3.8
1959	Bos-A★	147	560	95	176	33	6	6	57	95	48	.314	.415	.427	126	24	6	5	-1	.982	6	*2-101,1-44/S	3.3
1960	Bos-A★	143	528	80	169	29	2	2	35	71	51	**.320**	.403	.394	112	12	5	2	0	**.986**	9	*2-129,1-57/3	3.2
1961	Bos-A	143	360	49	114	20	3	3	38	46	32	.317	.399	.414	115	9	5	1	1	**.995**	1	*1-113,3-11/2S	0.5
1962	Bos-A★	152	562	80	183	33	5	10	60	79	57	**.326**	.411	.456	129	26	2	2	-1	.993	-1	*1-151	1.3
1963	Hou-N	124	388	35	98	9	1	2	23	46	42	.253	.335	.296	89	-4	2	0	1	.993	-10	1-70,2-36/3	-1.5
1964	Hou-N	22	51	3	10	1	0	0	3	8	7	.196	.305	.216	53	-3	0	0	0	.986	-2	1-14	-0.6
Total	14	1799	6373	876	1854	282	64	49	630	844	627	.291	.376	.378	106	76	37	51	-20	.994	-78	1-644,2-642,S/30	2.4

■ **JOHN RUSS**   Russ, John b: 4/1/1858, Cannelton, Ind. d: 1/18/12, Louisville, Ky. Deb: 7/4/1882

YEAR	TM/L	G	AB	R	H	2B	3B	HR	RBI	BB	SO	AVG	OBP	SLG	PRO+	BR/A	SB	CS	SBR	FA	FR	G/POS	TPR
1882	Bal-a	1	3	0	1	0	0	0		0		.333	.333	.333	136	0				.000	-1	/O-1,P-1	0.0

■ **REB RUSSELL**   Russell, Ewell Albert b: 4/12/1889, Jackson, Miss. d: 9/30/73, Indianapolis, Ind BL/TL, 5'11", 185 lbs. Deb: 4/18/13

YEAR	TM/L	G	AB	R	H	2B	3B	HR	RBI	BB	SO	AVG	OBP	SLG	PRO+	BR/A	SB	CS	SBR	FA	FR	G/POS	TPR
1913	Chi-A	52	106	9	20	5	3	1	7	1	29	.189	.204	.321	54	-7	0			.952	-5	P-52	0.0
1914	Chi-A	46	64	6	17	1	1	0	7	1	14	.266	.277	.313	78	-2	0			.946	-2	P-38	0.0
1915	Chi-A	45	86	11	21	2	3	0	7	4	14	.244	.293	.337	86	-2	1			.971	-2	P-41	0.0
1916	Chi-A	56	91	9	13	2	0	0	6	0	18	.143	.152	.165	-5	-12	1			.974	-2	P-56	0.0
1917	*Chi-A	39	68	5	19	3	3	0	7	3	10	.279	.300	.412	115	1	0			.984	-1	P-35/O-1	0.0
1918	Chi-A	27	50	2	7	3	0	0	3	0	6	.140	.157	.200	8	-6	0			1.000	-2	P-19/O-1	0.0
1919	Chi-A	1	0	0	0	0	0	0	0			—	—	—			0			.000	-0	/P-1	0.0
1922	Pit-N	60	220	51	81	14	8	12	75	14	18	.368	.423	.668	175	23	4	2	0	.968	-2	O-60	1.6

YEAR	TM/L	G	AB	R	H	2B	3B	HR	RBI	BB	SO	AVG	OBP	SLG	PRO+	BR/A	SB	CS	SBR	FA	FR	G/POS	TPR
1923	Pit-N	94	291	49	84	18	7	9	58	20	21	.289	.341	.491	115	5	3	1	0	.970	-2	O-76	-0.2
Total	9	420	976	142	262	48	25	22	172	42	130	.268	.309	.436	104	0	9	3		.968	-15	P-242,O-138	1.4

■ RIP RUSSELL
Russell, Glen David   b: 1/26/15, Los Angeles, Cal.   d: 9/26/76, Los Alamitos, Cal   BR/TR, 6'1", 180 lbs.   Deb: 5/5/39

YEAR	TM/L	G	AB	R	H	2B	3B	HR	RBI	BB	SO	AVG	OBP	SLG	PRO+	BR/A	SB	CS	SBR	FA	FR	G/POS	TPR
1939	Chi-N	143	542	55	148	24	5	9	79	36	56	.273	.318	.386	87	-11	2			.988	-5	*1-143	-3.1
1940	Chi-N	68	215	15	53	7	2	5	33	8	23	.247	.277	.367	78	-7	1			.982	-6	1-51/3-3	-1.8
1941	Chi-N	6	17	1	5	1	0	0	1	1	5	.294	.333	.353	97	-0	0			.975	0	/1-5	0.0
1942	Chi-N	102	302	32	73	9	0	8	41	17	21	.242	.282	.351	88	-6	0			.974	-12	1-35,2-24,3/O	-2.0
1946	*Bos-A	80	274	22	57	10	1	6	35	13	30	.208	.247	.318	54	-18	1	1	-0	.942	-1	3-70/2-3	-1.9
1947	Bos-A	26	52	8	8	1	0	1	3	8	7	.154	.267	.231	36	-4	0	0	0	.923	1	3-13	-0.3
Total	6	425	1402	133	344	52	8	29	192	83	142	.245	.289	.356	77	-46	4	1		.984	-22	1-234/3-96,2O	-9.1

■ HARVEY RUSSELL
Russell, Harvey Holmes   b: 1/10/1887, Marshall, Va.   d: 1/8/80, Alexandria, Va.   BL/TR, 5'9.5", 163 lbs.   Deb: 4/17/14

YEAR	TM/L	G	AB	R	H	2B	3B	HR	RBI	BB	SO	AVG	OBP	SLG	PRO+	BR/A	SB	CS	SBR	FA	FR	G/POS	TPR
1914	Bal-F	81	168	18	39	3	2	0	13	18	17	.232	.310	.274	50	-12	2			.956	-17	C-47/S-1,O	-2.7
1915	Bal-F	53	73	5	19	1	2	0	11	14	5	.260	.407	.329	95	1	1			.989	-4	C-21	-0.2
Total	2	134	241	23	58	4	4	0	24	32	22	.241	.342	.290	64	-11	3			.965	-22	/C-68,O-1,S	-2.9

■ JIM RUSSELL
Russell, James William   b: 10/1/18, Fayette City, Pa.   d: 11/24/87, Pittsburgh, Pa.   BB/TR, 6'1", 181 lbs.   Deb: 9/12/42

YEAR	TM/L	G	AB	R	H	2B	3B	HR	RBI	BB	SO	AVG	OBP	SLG	PRO+	BR/A	SB	CS	SBR	FA	FR	G/POS	TPR
1942	Pit-N	5	14	2	1	0	0	0	0	1	4	.071	.133	.071	-38	-2	0			1.000	1	/O-3	-0.2
1943	Pit-N	146	533	79	138	19	11	4	44	77	67	.259	.354	.358	102	3	12			.990	3	*O-134/1-6	-0.2
1944	Pit-N	152	580	109	181	34	14	8	66	79	63	.312	.399	.460	136	29	6			.986	13	*O-149	3.5
1945	Pit-N	146	510	88	145	24	8	12	77	71	40	.284	.377	.433	120	15	15			.973	3	*O-140	1.1
1946	Pit-N	146	516	68	143	29	6	8	50	67	54	.277	.362	.403	114	10	11			.966	-2	*O-134/1-5	0.1
1947	Pit-N	128	478	68	121	21	8	8	51	63	58	.253	.343	.381	89	-7	7			.980	11	*O-119	-0.2
1948	Bos-N	89	322	44	85	18	1	9	54	46	31	.264	.361	.410	110	5	4			.992	6	O-84	0.6
1949	Bos-N	130	415	57	96	22	1	8	54	64	68	.231	.337	.347	88	-6	3			.975	-9	*O-120	-2.1
1950	Bro-N	77	214	37	49	8	2	10	32	31	36	.229	.329	.425	95	-2	1			.993	4	O-55	0.0
1951	Bro-N	16	13	2	0	0	0	0	0	4	6	.000	.278	.000	-18	-2	0	0	0	1.000	-1	/O-4	-0.3
Total	10	1035	3595	554	959	175	51	67	428	503	427	.267	.360	.400	108	44	59	0		.981	27	O-942/1-11	2.3

■ JOHN RUSSELL
Russell, John William   b: 1/5/61, Oklahoma City, Okla.   BR/TR, 6', 200 lbs.   Deb: 6/22/84

YEAR	TM/L	G	AB	R	H	2B	3B	HR	RBI	BB	SO	AVG	OBP	SLG	PRO+	BR/A	SB	CS	SBR	FA	FR	G/POS	TPR
1984	Phi-N	39	99	11	28	8	1	2	11	12	33	.283	.360	.444	123	3	0	1	-1	1.000	-1	O-29/C-2	0.1
1985	Phi-N	81	216	22	47	12	0	9	23	18	72	.218	.278	.398	85	-5	2	0	1	1.000	-6	O-49,1-18	-1.4
1986	Phi-N	93	315	35	76	21	2	13	60	25	103	.241	.303	.444	100	-1	0	1	-1	.976	-5	C-89	-0.1
1987	Phi-N	24	62	5	9	1	0	3	8	3	17	.145	.185	.306	26	-7	0	1	-1	.955	0	O-10/C-7	-0.7
1988	Phi-N	22	49	5	12	1	0	2	4	3	15	.245	.302	.388	95	-0	0	0	0	.945	3	C-15	0.3
1989	Atl-N	74	159	14	29	2	0	2	9	8	53	.182	.236	.233	31	-14	0	0	0	.990	-7	C-45,O-14/13P	-2.1
1990	Tex-A	68	128	16	35	4	0	2	8	11	41	.273	.331	.352	91	-1	1	0	0	.980	2	C-31,D-19/O13	0.1
1991	Tex-A	22	27	3	3	0	0	0	1	1	7	.111	.143	.111	-29	-5	0	0	0	1.000	-0	/O-8,C-5,D	-0.5
1992	Tex-A	7	10	1	1	0	0	0	2	1	4	.100	.250	.100	2	-1	0	0	0	1.000	1	/C-4,O-2,D	0.0
1993	Tex-A	18	22	1	5	1	0	1	3	2	10	.227	.292	.409	90	-0	0	0	0	1.000	-2	C-11/1-1,3O	-0.2
Total	10	448	1087	113	245	50	3	34	129	84	355	.225	.285	.371	79	-32	3	3	-1	.979	-16	C-209,O-119/D13P	-4.5

■ LLOYD RUSSELL
Russell, Lloyd Opal   b: 4/10/13, Atoka, Okla.   d: 5/24/68, Waco, Tex.   BR/TR, 5'11", 166 lbs.   Deb: 4/26/38

YEAR	TM/L	G	AB	R	H	2B	3B	HR	RBI	BB	SO	AVG	OBP	SLG	PRO+	BR/A	SB	CS	SBR	FA	FR	G/POS	TPR
1938	Cle-A	2	0	0	0	0	0	0	0	0	0	—	—	—		0	0	0	0	.000	0	R	0.0

■ PAUL RUSSELL
Russell, Paul A.   b: 1870, Reading, Pa.   d: Pottstown, Pa.   Deb: 7/29/1894

YEAR	TM/L	G	AB	R	H	2B	3B	HR	RBI	BB	SO	AVG	OBP	SLG	PRO+	BR/A	SB	CS	SBR	FA	FR	G/POS	TPR
1894	StL-N	3	10	1	1	0	0	0	0	0	2	.100	.100	.100	-52	-2	0			1.000	0	/O-1,3-1,2	-0.2

■ BILL RUSSELL
Russell, William Ellis   b: 10/21/48, Pittsburg, Kan.   BR/TR, 6', 175 lbs.   Deb: 4/7/69   C

YEAR	TM/L	G	AB	R	H	2B	3B	HR	RBI	BB	SO	AVG	OBP	SLG	PRO+	BR/A	SB	CS	SBR	FA	FR	G/POS	TPR
1969	LA-N	98	212	35	48	6	2	5	15	22	45	.226	.302	.344	87	-4	4	1	1	.978	-7	O-86	-1.4
1970	LA-N	81	278	30	72	11	9	0	28	16	28	.259	.306	.363	82	-8	9	1	2	.983	6	O-79/S-1	-0.3
1971	LA-N	91	211	29	48	7	4	2	15	11	39	.227	.266	.327	71	-9	6	3	0	.964	-6	2-41,O-40/S	-1.4
1972	LA-N	129	434	47	118	19	5	4	34	34	64	.272	.328	.366	99	-1	14	7	0	.949	15	*S-121/O-6	3.3
1973	LA-N★	162	615	55	163	26	3	4	56	34	63	.265	.305	.337	81	-17	15	7	0	.963	9	*S-162	1.4
1974	*LA-N	160	553	61	149	18	6	5	65	53	53	.269	.338	.351	97	-2	14	5	1	.946	-19	*S-160/O-1	0.1
1975	LA-N	84	252	24	52	9	2	0	14	23	28	.206	.278	.258	52	-17	5	0	2	.967	-21	S-83	-3.0
1976	LA-N★	149	554	53	152	17	3	5	65	21	46	.274	.304	.343	85	-12	15	5	2	.963	-14	*S-149	-0.7
1977	*LA-N	153	634	84	176	28	6	4	51	24	43	.278	.306	.360	78	-20	16	7	1	.963	10	*S-153	0.8
1978	*LA-N	155	625	72	179	32	4	3	46	30	34	.286	.321	.365	92	-8	10	6	-1	.962	12	*S-155	2.5
1979	LA-N	153	627	72	170	26	4	7	56	24	43	.271	.299	.359	80	-19	6	9	-4	.957	-26	*S-150	-3.3
1980	LA-N★	130	466	38	123	23	2	3	34	18	44	.264	.296	.341	79	-14	13	2	3	.968	-22	*S-129	-1.9
1981	*LA-N	82	262	20	61	9	2	0	22	19	20	.233	.287	.282	64	-12	2	1	0	.965	10	S-80	0.5
1982	LA-N	153	497	64	136	20	2	3	46	63	30	.274	.360	.340	99	2	10	2	2	.961	-4	*S-150	1.4
1983	*LA-N	131	451	47	111	13	1	1	30	33	31	.246	.303	.286	64	-21	13	9	-2	.964	1	*S-127	-1.0
1984	LA-N	89	262	25	70	12	1	0	19	25	24	.267	.331	.321	85	-5	4	4	-1	.965	-4	S-65,O-18/2	-0.6
1985	LA-N	76	169	19	44	6	1	0	18	19	9	.260	.335	.308	83	-3	4	0	1	.919	-7	S-23,O-21/23	-0.7
1986	LA-N	105	216	21	54	11	0	0	18	15	23	.250	.305	.301	73	-8	7	0	2	1.000	-7	O-48,S-32/23	-1.2
Total	18	2181	7318	796	1926	293	57	46	627	483	667	.263	.312	.338	83	-177	167	69	9	.960	-74	*S-1746,O-299/23	-5.5

■ HANK RUSZKOWSKI
Ruszkowski, Henry Alexander   b: 11/10/25, Cleveland, Ohio   BR/TR, 6', 190 lbs.   Deb: 9/26/44

YEAR	TM/L	G	AB	R	H	2B	3B	HR	RBI	BB	SO	AVG	OBP	SLG	PRO+	BR/A	SB	CS	SBR	FA	FR	G/POS	TPR
1944	Cle-A	3	8	1	3	0	0	0	1	0	1	.375	.375	.375	119	0	0	0	0	1.000	-0	/C-2	0.0
1945	Cle-A	14	49	2	10	0	0	0	5	4	9	.204	.264	.204	38	-4	0	0	0	.975	3	C-14	0.0
1947	Cle-A	23	27	5	7	2	0	3	4	2	6	.259	.310	.667	172	2	0	0	0	1.000	0	C-16	0.1
Total	3	40	84	8	20	2	0	3	10	6	16	.238	.289	.369	91	-2	0	0	0	.981	1	/C-32	0.1

■ BABE RUTH
Ruth, George Herman "The Bambino" or "The Sultan Of Swat"
b: 2/6/1895, Baltimore, Md.   d: 8/16/48, New York, N.Y.   BL/TL, 6'2", 215 lbs.   Deb: 7/11/14   CH

YEAR	TM/L	G	AB	R	H	2B	3B	HR	RBI	BB	SO	AVG	OBP	SLG	PRO+	BR/A	SB	CS	SBR	FA	FR	G/POS	TPR
1914	Bos-A	5	10	1	2	1	0	0	2	0	4	.200	.200	.300	50	-1	0			1.000	-0	/P-4	0.0
1915	*Bos-A	42	92	16	29	10	1	4	21	9	23	.315	.376	.576	191	9	0			.976	1	P-32	0.0
1916	*Bos-A	67	136	18	37	5	3	3	15	10	23	.272	.322	.419	122	3	0			.973	0	P-44	0.0
1917	Bos-A	52	123	14	40	6	3	2	12	12	18	.325	.385	.472	163	9	0			.984	2	P-41	0.0
1918	*Bos-A	95	317	50	95	26	11	11	66	57	58	.300	.410	.555	194	36	6			.949	3	O-59,P-20,1	2.6
1919	Bos-A	130	432	**103**	139	34	12	**29**	114	101	58	.322	**.456**	**.657**	224	74	7			**.996**	5	*O-111,P-17/1	6.3
1920	NY-A	142	458	**158**	172	36	9	**54**	137	148	80	.376	**.530**	**.847**	252	107	14	14	-4	.936	0	*O-141/1-2,P	8.6
1921	*NY-A	152	540	**177**	204	44	16	**59**	171	144	81	.378	**.512**	**.846**	236	115	17	13	-3	.966	4	*O-152/P-2,1	9.4
1922	*NY-A	110	406	94	128	24	8	35	99	84	80	.315	.434	**.672**	181	48	2	5	-2	.964	1	*O-110/1-1	3.7
1923	*NY-A	152	522	**151**	205	45	13	41	131	170	93	**.393**	**.545**	**.764**	238	116	17	21	-8	.973	16	*O-148/1-4	10.6
1924	NY-A	153	529	**143**	200	39	7	46	121	142	81	**.378**	**.513**	**.739**	221	101	9	13	-5	.962	7	*O-152	8.5
1925	NY-A	98	359	61	104	12	2	25	66	59	68	.290	.393	.543	138	20	2	4	-2	.974	9	*O-98	1.9
1926	*NY-A	152	495	**139**	184	30	5	**47**	146	144	76	.372	**.516**	**.737**	228	100	11	9	-2	.979	1	*O-149/1-2	8.4
1927	*NY-A	151	540	**158**	192	29	8	**60**	164	**138**	89	.356	**.487**	**.772**	229	106	7	6	-2	.963	5	*O-151	9.2
1928	*NY-A	154	536	**163**	173	29	8	**54**	142	135	87	.323	**.461**	**.709**	210	89	4	5	-2	.975	-3	*O-154	7.0
1929	NY-A	135	499	121	172	26	6	46	154	72	60	.345	.430	**.697**	199	71	5	3	-0	.984	-9	*O-133	4.9
1930	NY-A	145	518	150	186	28	9	49	153	**136**	61	.359	**.493**	**.732**	216	98	10	10	-3	.965	-0	*O-144/P-1	7.3

YEAR	TM/L	G	AB	R	H	2B	3B	HR	RBI	BB	SO	AVG	OBP	SLG	PRO+	BR/A	SB	CS	SBR	FA	FR	G/POS	TPR
1931	NY-A	145	534	149	199	31	3	**46**	163	**128**	51	.373	**.495**	**.700**	**223**	102	5	4	-1	.972	-12	*O-142/1-1	**7.3**
1932	*NY-A	133	457	120	156	13	5	41	137	**130**	62	.341	**.489**	.661	**206**	79	2	2	-1	.961	-7	*O-128/1-1	5.8
1933	NY-A★	137	459	97	138	21	3	34	103	**114**	90	.301	.442	.582	180	57	4	5	-2	.970	-7	*O-132/P-1,1	3.8
1934	NY-A★	125	365	78	105	17	4	22	84	103	63	.288	.447	.537	164	40	1	3	-2	.962	-6	*O-111	2.5
1935	Bos-N	28	72	13	13	0	0	6	12	20	24	.181	.359	.431	121	3	0			.952	-4	O-26	-0.2
Total	22	2503	8399	2174	2873	506	136	714	2213	2056	1330	.342	.474	.690	209	1382	123	117		.968	5	*O-2241,P-163/1	107.6

■ JIM RUTHERFORD
Rutherford, James Hollis b: 9/26/1886, Stillwater, Minn. d: 9/18/56, Cleveland, Ohio BL/TR, 6'1", 180 lbs. Deb: 7/12/10

YEAR	TM/L	G	AB	R	H	2B	3B	HR	RBI	BB	SO	AVG	OBP	SLG	PRO+	BR/A	SB	CS	SBR	FA	FR	G/POS	TPR
1910	Cle-A	1	2	0	1	0	0	0	0			.500	.500	.500	210	0	0			1.000	-0	/O-1	0.0

■ MICKEY RUTNER
Rutner, Milton b: 3/18/20, Hempstead, N.Y. BR/TR, 5'11", 190 lbs. Deb: 9/11/47

YEAR	TM/L	G	AB	R	H	2B	3B	HR	RBI	BB	SO	AVG	OBP	SLG	PRO+	BR/A	SB	CS	SBR	FA	FR	G/POS	TPR
1947	Phi-A	12	48	4	12	1	0	1	4	3	2	.250	.294	.333	73	-2	0	0	0	.885	-3	3-11	-0.5

■ MARK RYAL
Ryal, Mark Dwayne b: 4/28/60, Henryetta, Okla. BL/TL, 6'1", 185 lbs. Deb: 9/7/82

YEAR	TM/L	G	AB	R	H	2B	3B	HR	RBI	BB	SO	AVG	OBP	SLG	PRO+	BR/A	SB	CS	SBR	FA	FR	G/POS	TPR
1982	KC-A	6	13	0	1	0	0	0	0	1	3	.077	.143	.077	-38	-2	0	0	0	.900	-1	/O-5	-0.3
1985	Chi-A	12	33	4	5	3	0	0	3	3	3	.152	.222	.242	26	-3	0	0	0	1.000	-1	O-12	-0.5
1986	Cal-A	13	32	6	12	0	0	2	5	2	4	.375	.412	.563	164	-3	1	0	0	.900	-1	/O-6,1-4,D	0.2
1987	Cal-A	58	100	7	20	6	0	5	18	3	15	.200	.223	.410	65	-5	0	0	0	.955	-6	O-21/1-4,D	-1.1
1989	Phi-N	29	33	2	8	2	0	0	5	1	6	.242	.265	.303	62	-2	0	0	0	1.000	-1	/1-4,O-4	-0.3
1990	Pit-N	9	12	0	1	0	0	0	0	0	3	.083	.083	.083	-56	-3	0	0	0	1.000	-1	/O-4	-0.4
Total	6	127	223	19	47	11	0	7	31	10	34	.211	.245	.354	61	-13	1	0	0	.957	-11	/O-52,1-12,D	-2.4

■ CONNIE RYAN
Ryan, Cornelius Joseph b: 2/27/20, New Orleans, La. BR/TR, 5'11", 175 lbs. Deb: 4/14/42 MC

YEAR	TM/L	G	AB	R	H	2B	3B	HR	RBI	BB	SO	AVG	OBP	SLG	PRO+	BR/A	SB	CS	SBR	FA	FR	G/POS	TPR
1942	NY-N	11	27	4	5	0	0	0	2	4	3	.185	.290	.185	40	-2	1			.944	7	2-11	0.5
1943	Bos-N	132	457	52	97	10	2	1	24	58	56	.212	.301	.249	61	-22	7			.962	-20	*2-100,3-30	-3.8
1944	Bos-N★	88	332	56	98	18	5	4	25	36	40	.295	.364	.416	114	7	13			.974	13	2-80,3-14	2.4
1946	Bos-N	143	502	55	121	28	8	1	48	55	63	.241	.317	.335	84	-11	7			.968	-2	*2-120,3-24	-0.5
1947	Bos-N	150	544	60	144	33	5	5	69	71	60	.265	.351	.371	94	-4	5			.973	-7	*2-150/S-1	0.0
1948	*Bos-N	51	122	14	26	3	0	0	10	21	16	.213	.333	.238	58	-6	0			.966	4	2-40/3-4	0.0
1949	Bos-N	85	208	28	52	13	1	6	20	21	30	.250	.319	.409	99	-1	1			.973	5	3-25,S-18,2/1	0.6
1950	Bos-N	20	72	12	14	2	0	3	6	12	9	.194	.326	.347	82	-2	0			1.000	1	2-20	0.0
	Cin-N	106	367	45	95	18	5	3	43	52	46	.259	.352	.360	87	-5	4			.973	11	*2-103	0.9
	Yr	126	439	57	109	20	5	6	49	64	55	.248	.348	.358	87	-7	4			.978	12	*2-123	0.9
1951	Cin-N	136	473	75	112	17	4	16	53	79	72	.237	.350	.391	97	-0	11	6	-0	.970	-3	*2-121/3-3,1O	0.2
1952	Phi-N	154	577	81	139	24	6	12	49	69	72	.241	.327	.366	93	-5	13	5	1	.972	-5	*2-154	-0.1
1953	Phi-N	90	247	47	73	14	6	5	26	30	35	.296	.372	.462	116	6	5	1	1	.958	-5	2-65/1-2	0.5
	Chi-A	17	54	6	12	1	0	0	6	9	12	.222	.333	.241	55	-3	2	0	1	.927	-1	3-16	-0.4
1954	Cin-N	1	0	0	0	0	0	0	0	1	0	—	1.000	—	182	0	0	0	0	.000	0	H	0.0
Total	12	1184	3982	535	988	181	42	56	381	518	514	.248	.337	.357	90	-48	69	12		.970	-1	2-980,3-116/S1O	0.3

■ CYCLONE RYAN
Ryan, Daniel R. b: 1866, Cappagh White, Ireland d: 1/30/17, Medfield, Mass. TR, 6', Deb: 8/8/1887

YEAR	TM/L	G	AB	R	H	2B	3B	HR	RBI	BB	SO	AVG	OBP	SLG	PRO+	BR/A	SB	CS	SBR	FA	FR	G/POS	TPR
1887	NY-a	8	32	4	7	1	0	0			3	.219	.286	.250	52	-2	1			.938	-0	/1-8,P-2	-0.2
1891	Bos-N	1	1	0	0	0	0	0	0	0	0	.000	.000	.000	-89	-0	0			1.000	0	/P-1	0.0
Total	2	9	33	4	7	1	0	0	0	3	0	.212	.278	.242	48	-2	1			1.000	0	/1-8,P-3	-0.2

■ MIKE RYAN
Ryan, J. b: St.Louis, Mo. Deb: 7/25/1895

YEAR	TM/L	G	AB	R	H	2B	3B	HR	RBI	BB	SO	AVG	OBP	SLG	PRO+	BR/A	SB	CS	SBR	FA	FR	G/POS	TPR
1895	StL-N	2	2	0	0	0	0	0	0	0	0	.000	.000	.000	-99	-1	0			.000	-1	/3-2	-0.1

■ JIMMY RYAN
Ryan, James Edward "Pony" b: 2/11/1863, Clinton, Mass. d: 10/26/23, Chicago, Ill. BR/TL, 5'9", 162 lbs. Deb: 10/8/1885

YEAR	TM/L	G	AB	R	H	2B	3B	HR	RBI	BB	SO	AVG	OBP	SLG	PRO+	BR/A	SB	CS	SBR	FA	FR	G/POS	TPR
1885	Chi-N	3	13	2	6	1	1	1		1	1	.462	.500	.538	205	2				.737	1	/S-2,O-1	0.2
1886	*Chi-N	84	327	58	100	17	6	4	53	12	28	.306	.330	.431	113	2	10			.828	1	O-70/S-6,32P	0.1
1887	Chi-N	126	508	117	145	23	10	1	74	53	19	.285	.360	.435	106	1	50			.857	-2	*O-122/P-8,2	-0.5
1888	Chi-N	129	549	115	**182**	**33**	10	**16**	64	35	50	.332	.377	**.515**	170	41	60			.878	4	*O-128/P-8	3.8
1889	Chi-N	135	576	140	177	31	14	17	72	70	62	.307	.388	.498	140	29	45			.926	6	*O-106,S-29	2.9
1890	Chi-P	118	486	99	165	32	5	6	89	60	36	.340	.416	.463	129	20	30			.919	2	*O-118	1.5
1891	Chi-N	118	505	110	140	22	15	9	66	53	38	.277	.355	.434	129	18	27			.905	5	*O-117/S-2,P	1.7
1892	Chi-N	128	505	105	148	25	11	10	65	61	41	.293	.375	.438	144	27	27			.921	5	*O-120/S-9	2.5
1893	Chi-N	83	341	82	102	21	7	3	30	59	25	.299	.407	.428	124	14	8			.908	-1	O-73,S-10/P	0.7
1894	Chi-N	108	474	132	171	37	7	3	62	50	23	.361	.425	.487	113	10	11			.910	9	*O-108	0.9
1895	Chi-N	108	438	83	139	22	8	6	49	48	22	.317	.392	.445	109	5	18			.937	2	*O-108	-0.1
1896	Chi-N	128	489	83	149	24	10	3	86	46	16	.305	.369	.413	102	1	29			.912	-0	*O-128	-0.9
1897	Chi-N	136	520	103	156	33	5	5	85	50		.300	.369	.458	113	8	27			.945	-7	*O-136	0.4
1898	Chi-N	144	572	122	185	32	13	4	79	73		.323	.405	.446	144	34	29			.914	-7	*O-144	1.6
1899	Chi-N	125	525	91	158	20	10	6	68	43		.301	.357	.394	109	6	19			.956	-1	*O-125	-0.4
1900	Chi-N	105	415	66	115	25	4	5	59	29		.277	.329	.393	102	0	19			.913	-11	*O-105	-1.7
1902	Was-A	120	484	92	155	32	6	6	44	43		.320	.384	.448	129	19	10			.949	3	*O-120	1.3
1903	Was-A	114	437	42	109	25	4	7	46	17		.249	.290	.373	96	-3	9			.970	-1	*O-114	-0.7
Total	18	2012	8164	1642	2502	451	157	118	1093	803	**361**	.306	.374	.444	123	232	418			.918	26	*O-1943/S-58,P23	13.3

■ JACK RYAN
Ryan, John Bernard b: 11/12/1868, Haverhill, Mass. d: 8/21/52, Boston, Mass. BR/TR, 5'10.5", 165 lbs. Deb: 9/2/1889 C

YEAR	TM/L	G	AB	R	H	2B	3B	HR	RBI	BB	SO	AVG	OBP	SLG	PRO+	BR/A	SB	CS	SBR	FA	FR	G/POS	TPR
1889	Lou-a	21	79	8	14	1	0	0	2	3	17	.177	.207	.190	14	-9	2			.864	-6	C-15/O-4,3	-1.2
1890	*Lou-a	93	337	43	73	16	4	0		12		.217	.244	.288	58	-19	6			.932	5	C-89/O-3,S1	-0.6
1891	Lou-a	75	253	24	57	5	4	2	25	15	40	.225	.271	.300	64	-13	3			.930	-1	C-56,1-11/3O2	-0.8
1894	Bos-N	53	201	39	54	12	7	1	29	13	16	.269	.316	.413	69	-12	3			.911	-3	C-51/1-2	-0.5
1895	Bos-N	49	189	22	55	7	0	0	18	6	6	.291	.313	.328	61	-12	3			.951	1	C-43/2-5,O	-0.5
1896	Bos-N	8	32	2	3	1	0	0	0	0	1	.094	.094	.125	-40	-7	0			.911	2	/C-8	-0.3
1898	Bro-N	87	301	39	57	11	4	0	24	15		.189	.233	.252	39	-24	5			.960	3	C-84/3-4,1	-1.3
1899	Bal-N	2	4	0	2	1	0	0	1	0		.500	.500	.750	229	1	1			1.000	1	/C-2	0.2
1901	StL-N	83	300	27	59	6	5	0	31	7		.197	.218	.250	37	-24	5			.982	5	C-65/2-9,1O	-1.3
1902	StL-N	76	267	23	48	4	4	0	14	4		.180	.195	.225	31	-22	2			.966	-7	C-66/1-4,32S	-2.4
1903	StL-N	67	227	18	54	5	1	1	10	10		.238	.273	.282	60	-12	7			.971	-9	C-47,1-18/S	-1.6
1912	Was-A	1	1	0	0	0	0	0	0	0		.000	.000	.000	-99	-0	0			1.000	0	/3-1	0.0
1913	Was-A	1	1	0	0	0	0	0	1	0		.000	.000	.000	-98	-0	0			1.000	0	/C-1	0.0
Total	13	616	2192	245	476	69	29	4	**154**	85	80	.217	.249	.281	50	-154	32			.947	-6	C-527/1-42,23OS	-10.3

■ BUDDY RYAN
Ryan, John Budd b: 10/6/1885, Denver, Colo. d: 7/9/56, Sacramento, Cal. BL/TR, 5'9.5", 172 lbs. Deb: 4/11/12

YEAR	TM/L	G	AB	R	H	2B	3B	HR	RBI	BB	SO	AVG	OBP	SLG	PRO+	BR/A	SB	CS	SBR	FA	FR	G/POS	TPR
1912	Cle-A	93	328	53	89	12	6	1	31	30		.271	.343	.372	101	0	12			.963	5	O-90	0.0
1913	Cle-A	73	243	26	72	6	4	0	32	11	13	.296	.332	.329	91	-3	9			.986	-2	O-68/1-1	-0.8
Total	2	166	571	79	161	18	10	1	63	41	13	.282	.339	.354	97	-3	21			.973	3	O-158/1-1	-0.8

■ BLONDY RYAN
Ryan, John Collins b: 1/4/06, Lynn, Mass. d: 11/28/59, Swampscott, Mass. BR/TR, 6'1", 178 lbs. Deb: 7/13/30

YEAR	TM/L	G	AB	R	H	2B	3B	HR	RBI	BB	SO	AVG	OBP	SLG	PRO+	BR/A	SB	CS	SBR	FA	FR	G/POS	TPR
1930	Chi-A	28	87	9	18	4	1	0	10	6	13	.207	.258	.333	50	-7	2	0	1	.875	-1	3-23/S-2,2	-0.6
1933	*NY-N	146	525	47	125	10	5	3	48	15	62	.238	.259	.293	58	-29	0			.950	17	*S-146	-0.2
1934	NY-N	110	385	35	93	19	0	2	41	19	68	.242	.277	.306	57	-23	3			.953	12	3-65,S-30,2	-0.6
1935	Phi-N	39	129	13	34	3	0	1	10	7	20	.264	.312	.310	61	-7	1			.912	2	S-35/2-1,3	-0.3

YEAR	TM/L	G	AB	R	H	2B	3B	HR	RBI	BB	SO	AVG	OBP	SLG	PRO+	BR/A	SB	CS	SBR	FA	FR	G/POS	TPR
	NY-A	30	105	12	25	1	3	0	11	3	10	.238	.259	.305	48	-8	0	0	0	.908	-4	S-30	-1.1
1937	*NY-N	21	75	10	18	3	1	1	13	6	8	.240	.296	.347	73	-3	0			.941	1	S-19/2-1,3	-0.1
1938	NY-N	12	24	1	5	0	0	0	0	1	3	.208	.240	.208	24	-2	0			1.000	-1	/2-5,3-3,S	-0.3
Total	6	386	1330	127	318	36	13	8	133	57	184	.239	.271	.304	57	-80	6	0		.936	26	S-264/3-93,2	-3.2

■ JACK RYAN Ryan, John Francis b: 5/5/05, Mineral, Kan. d: 9/2/67, Rochester, Minn. BR/TR, 6', 185 lbs. Deb: 6/18/29

YEAR	TM/L	G	AB	R	H	2B	3B	HR	RBI	BB	SO	AVG	OBP	SLG	PRO+	BR/A	SB	CS	SBR	FA	FR	G/POS	TPR
1929	Bos-A	2	3	0	0	0	0	0	0	0	0	.000	.000	.000	-99	-1	0	0	0	1.000	-1	/O-2	-0.2

■ JOHNNY RYAN Ryan, John Joseph b: 10/1853, Philadelphia, Pa. d: 3/22/02, Philadelphia, Pa. 5'7.5", 150 lbs. Deb: 8/19/1873

YEAR	TM/L	G	AB	R	H	2B	3B	HR	RBI	BB	SO	AVG	OBP	SLG	PRO+	BR/A	SB	CS	SBR	FA	FR	G/POS	TPR
1873	Phi-n	2	8	1	2	0	0	0	1	0	0	.250	.250	.250	46	-1						/1-1,O-1	0.0
1874	Bal-n	47	184	29	33	7	1	0			5	.179	.201	.228	37	-12						*O-47/P-1	-0.9
1875	NH-n	37	146	17	23	2	1	0			3	.158	.174	.185	28	-9						O-29/P-10,S3	-0.5
1876	Lou-N	64	241	32	61	5	1	1	18	6	23	.253	.271	.295	75	-9				.886	-7	*O-64/P-1	-1.5
1877	Cin-N	6	26	2	4	0	1	0	2	1	5	.154	.185	.231	34	-2				.769	-1	/O-6	-0.3
Total	3 n	86	338	47	58	9	2	0		1	8	.172	.191	.210	34	-22						/O-77,P-11,3S1	-1.4
Total	2	70	267	34	65	5	2	1	20	7	28	.243	.263	.288	72	-11				.877	-9	/O-70,P-1	-1.8

■ JOHN RYAN Ryan, John M. b: Washington, D.C. Deb: 6/11/1884

YEAR	TM/L	G	AB	R	H	2B	3B	HR	RBI	BB	SO	AVG	OBP	SLG	PRO+	BR/A	SB	CS	SBR	FA	FR	G/POS	TPR
1884	Was-U	7	28	2	4	0	1	0		1		.143	.172	.214	5	-4				.667	-1	/O-7,3-1	-0.5
	Wil-U	2	6	0	1	0	0	0		1		.167	.286	.167	25	-1				.800	-0	/O-2	-0.1
	Yr	9	34	2	5	0	1	0		2		.147	.194	.206	9	-4				.706	-1	/O-9,3-1	-0.6

■ MIKE RYAN Ryan, Michael James b: 11/25/41, Haverhill, Mass. BR/TR, 6'2", 205 lbs. Deb: 10/3/64 C

YEAR	TM/L	G	AB	R	H	2B	3B	HR	RBI	BB	SO	AVG	OBP	SLG	PRO+	BR/A	SB	CS	SBR	FA	FR	G/POS	TPR
1964	Bos-A	1	3	0	1	0	0	0	2	1	0	.333	.500	.333	131	-1	0	0	0	1.000	-1	/C-1	0.0
1965	Bos-A	33	107	7	17	0	1	3	9	5	19	.159	.196	.262	27	-10	0	0	0	.981	0	C-33	-0.9
1966	Bos-A	116	369	27	79	15	3	2	32	29	68	.214	.271	.287	55	-21	1	0	0	.992	1	*C-114	-1.4
1967	*Bos-A	79	226	21	45	4	2	2	27	26	42	.199	.285	.261	58	-11	2	0	1	.988	1	C-79	-0.6
1968	Phi-N	96	296	12	53	6	1	1	15	15	59	.179	.219	.216	31	-25	0	3	-2	.991	-4	C-96	-2.8
1969	Phi-N	133	446	41	91	17	2	12	44	30	66	.204	.257	.332	66	-22	1	1	-0	.991	2	*C-132	-1.4
1970	Phi-N	46	134	14	24	8	0	2	11	16	24	.179	.267	.284	49	-10	0	0	0	.992	-12	C-46	-2.1
1971	Phi-N	43	134	9	22	5	1	3	16	10	32	.164	.222	.284	42	-10	0	0	0	1.000	12	C-43	0.3
1972	Phi-N	46	106	6	19	4	0	2	10	10	25	.179	.256	.274	49	-7	0	0	0	.992	6	C-46	0.0
1973	Phi-N	28	69	7	16	1	2	1	6	6	19	.232	.293	.348	75	-2	0	0	0	.992	1	C-27	-0.1
1974	Pit-N	15	30	2	3	0	0	0	1	2	6	.100	.206	.100	-13	-5	0	0	0	1.000	3	C-15	-0.1
Total	11	636	1920	146	370	60	12	28	161	152	370	.193	.253	.280	51	-124	4	4	-1	.991	10	C-632	-9.1

■ TOM RYDER Ryder, Thomas BL, Deb: 7/22/1884

YEAR	TM/L	G	AB	R	H	2B	3B	HR	RBI	BB	SO	AVG	OBP	SLG	PRO+	BR/A	SB	CS	SBR	FA	FR	G/POS	TPR
1884	StL-U	8	28	4	7	1	0	0		2		.250	.300	.286	58	-2				.650	-0	/O-8	-0.2

■ GENE RYE Rye, Eugene Rudolph "Half-Pint" (b: Eugene Rudolph Mercantelli) b: 11/15/06, Chicago, Ill. d: 1/21/80, Park Ridge, Ill. BL/TR, 5'6", 165 lbs. Deb: 4/22/31

YEAR	TM/L	G	AB	R	H	2B	3B	HR	RBI	BB	SO	AVG	OBP	SLG	PRO+	BR/A	SB	CS	SBR	FA	FR	G/POS	TPR
1931	Bos-A	17	39	3	7	0	0	0	1	2	5	.179	.220	.179	6	-5	0	0	0	.944	-1	O-10	-0.7

■ ALEX SABO Sabo, Alexander "Giz" (b: Alexander Szabo) b: 2/14/10, New Brunswick, N.J BR/TR, 6', 192 lbs. Deb: 8/1/36

YEAR	TM/L	G	AB	R	H	2B	3B	HR	RBI	BB	SO	AVG	OBP	SLG	PRO+	BR/A	SB	CS	SBR	FA	FR	G/POS	TPR
1936	Was-A	4	8	1	3	0	0	0	1	0	2	.375	.375	.375	91	-0	0	0	0	.923	1	/C-4	0.1
1937	Was-A	1	0	0	0	0	0	0	0	0	0	—	—	—			0	0	0	1.000	-0	/C-1	0.0
Total	2	5	8	1	3	0	0	0	1	0	2	.375	.375	.375	91	-0	0	0	0	.929	1	/C-5	0.1

■ CHRIS SABO Sabo, Christopher Andrew b: 1/19/62, Detroit, Mich. BR/TR, 5'11", 185 lbs. Deb: 4/4/88

YEAR	TM/L	G	AB	R	H	2B	3B	HR	RBI	BB	SO	AVG	OBP	SLG	PRO+	BR/A	SB	CS	SBR	FA	FR	G/POS	TPR
1988	Cin-N★	137	538	74	146	40	2	11	44	29	52	.271	.316	.414	104	2	46	14	5	**.966**	19	*3-135/S-2	2.7
1989	Cin-N	82	304	40	79	21	1	6	29	25	33	.260	.318	.395	99	-1	14	9	-1	.943	-3	3-76	-0.5
1990	*Cin-N★	148	567	95	153	38	2	25	71	61	58	.270	.345	.476	118	14	25	10	2	**.966**	-6	*3-146	1.1
1991	Cin-N★	153	582	91	175	35	5	26	88	44	79	.301	.356	.505	134	25	19	6	2	.966	-15	*3-151	1.3
1992	Cin-N	96	344	42	84	19	3	12	43	30	54	.244	.307	.422	102	-0	4	5	-2	.961	-1	3-93	-0.3
1993	Cin-N	148	552	86	143	33	2	21	82	43	105	.259	.319	.440	101	-1	6	4	-1	.967	-15	*3-148	-1.6
1994	Bal-A	68	258	41	66	15	3	11	42	20	38	.256	.322	.465	94	-3	1	1	-0	.958	-11	3-37,O-22,D	-1.4
Total	7	832	3145	469	846	201	16	112	399	252	419	.269	.329	.450	110	35	115	49	5	.963	-32	3-786/O-22,DS	1.3

■ FRANK SACKA Sacka, Frank b: 8/30/24, Romulus, Mich. BR/TR, 6', 195 lbs. Deb: 4/29/51

YEAR	TM/L	G	AB	R	H	2B	3B	HR	RBI	BB	SO	AVG	OBP	SLG	PRO+	BR/A	SB	CS	SBR	FA	FR	G/POS	TPR
1951	Was-A	7	16	1	4	0	0	0	3	0	5	.250	.250	.250	36	-1	0	0	0	.962	2	/C-6	0.0
1953	Was-A	7	18	2	5	0	0	0	3	3	1	.278	.381	.278	82	-0	0	0	0	1.000	1	/C-6	0.2
Total	2	14	34	3	9	0	0	0	6	3	6	.265	.324	.265	62	-2	0	0	0	.982	3	/C-12	0.2

■ MIKE SADEK Sadek, Michael George b: 5/30/46, Minneapolis, Minn. BR/TR, 5'9", 165 lbs. Deb: 4/13/73

YEAR	TM/L	G	AB	R	H	2B	3B	HR	RBI	BB	SO	AVG	OBP	SLG	PRO+	BR/A	SB	CS	SBR	FA	FR	G/POS	TPR
1973	SF-N	39	66	6	11	1	1	0	4	11	8	.167	.286	.212	38	-5	1	0	0	.981	7	C-35	0.3
1975	SF-N	42	106	14	25	5	1	0	9	14	14	.236	.325	.321	76	-3	1	0	0	.995	7	C-38	0.5
1976	SF-N	55	93	8	19	2	0	0	7	11	10	.204	.295	.226	48	-6	1	0	0	.985	8	C-51	0.3
1977	SF-N	61	126	12	29	7	0	1	15	12	5	.230	.297	.310	63	-6	2	1	0	.992	10	C-57	0.4
1978	SF-N	40	109	15	26	3	0	2	9	10	11	.239	.303	.321	77	-3	1	0	0	.975	2	C-37	-0.1
1979	SF-N	63	126	14	30	5	0	1	11	15	9	.238	.324	.302	77	-4	1	0	0	.993	1	C-60/O-1	-0.1
1980	SF-N	64	151	14	38	4	1	1	16	27	18	.252	.365	.311	93	-0	0	0	0	.974	4	C-59	0.6
1981	SF-N	19	36	5	6	3	0	0	3	8	7	.167	.318	.250	64	-1	0	0	0	.979	7	C-19	0.6
Total	8	383	813	88	184	30	4	5	74	108	97	.226	.319	.292	70	-30	6	1	1	.985	45	C-356/O-1	2.5

■ ED SADOWSKI Sadowski, Edward Roman b: 1/19/31, Pittsburgh, Pa. d: 11/6/93, Garden Grove, Cal. BR/TR, 5'11", 175 lbs. Deb: 4/20/60 F

YEAR	TM/L	G	AB	R	H	2B	3B	HR	RBI	BB	SO	AVG	OBP	SLG	PRO+	BR/A	SB	CS	SBR	FA	FR	G/POS	TPR
1960	Bos-A	38	93	10	20	2	0	3	8	8	13	.215	.284	.333	64	-5	0	0	0	.995	6	C-36	0.2
1961	LA-A	69	164	16	38	13	0	4	12	11	33	.232	.280	.384	68	-8	2	3	-1	.987	8	C-56	0.1
1962	LA-A	27	55	4	11	4	0	1	3	2	14	.200	.228	.327	49	-4	1	0	0	.968	3	C-18	-0.1
1963	LA-A	80	174	24	30	1	1	4	15	17	34	.172	.246	.259	44	-13	2	1	0	.997	20	C-68	0.9
1966	Atl-N	3	9	1	1	0	0	0	1	1	1	.111	.200	.111	-10	-1	0	0	0	1.000	1	/C-3	-0.1
Total	5	217	495	55	100	20	2	12	39	39	94	.202	.262	.319	56	-31	5	4	-1	.991	37	C-181	1.0

■ BOB SADOWSKI Sadowski, Robert Frank "Sid" b: 1/15/37, St.Louis, Mo. BL/TR, 6', 175 lbs. Deb: 9/16/60

YEAR	TM/L	G	AB	R	H	2B	3B	HR	RBI	BB	SO	AVG	OBP	SLG	PRO+	BR/A	SB	CS	SBR	FA	FR	G/POS	TPR
1960	StL-N	1	1	0	0	0	0	0	0	1	0	.000	.000	.000	47	0	0	0	0	.000	-1	/2-1	-0.1
1961	Phi-N	16	54	4	7	0	0	0	0	4	7	.130	.203	.130	-9	-8	1	0	0	.971	-1	3-14	-0.9
1962	Chi-A	79	130	22	30	3	3	6	24	13	22	.231	.301	.438	97	-1	0	0	0	.955	5	3-16,2-12	0.5
1963	LA-A	88	144	12	36	6	0	1	22	15	34	.250	.321	.313	83	-3	2	1	0	1.000	-3	O-25/3-6,2	-0.7
Total	4	184	329	38	73	9	3	7	46	33	63	.222	.295	.331	73	-13	3	1	0	.953	-0	/3-36,O-25,2	-1.2

■ OLMEDO SAENZ Saenz, Olmedo (Sanchez) b: 10/8/70, Chitre Herrera, Pan. BR/TR, 6'2", 185 lbs. Deb: 5/28/94

YEAR	TM/L	G	AB	R	H	2B	3B	HR	RBI	BB	SO	AVG	OBP	SLG	PRO+	BR/A	SB	CS	SBR	FA	FR	G/POS	TPR
1994	Chi-A	5	14	2	2	0	0	0	1	0	3	.143	.143	.286	7	-2	0	0	0	1.000	-0	/3-5	-0.2

■ TOM SAFFELL Saffell, Thomas Judson b: 7/26/21, Etowah, Tenn. BL/TR, 5'11", 170 lbs. Deb: 7/2/49

YEAR	TM/L	G	AB	R	H	2B	3B	HR	RBI	BB	SO	AVG	OBP	SLG	PRO+	BR/A	SB	CS	SBR	FA	FR	G/POS	TPR
1949	Pit-N	73	205	36	66	7	1	2	25	21	27	.322	.385	.395	107	3	5			.992	-3	O-53	-0.3
1950	Pit-N	67	182	18	37	7	0	2	6	14	34	.203	.264	.275	41	-16	1			.993	6	O-43	-1.1
1951	Pit-N	49	65	11	13	0	0	0	5	5	18	.200	.257	.246	35	-6	1	1	-0	.929	-4	O-17	-1.0

YEAR	TM/L	G	AB	R	H	2B	3B	HR	RBI	BB	SO	AVG	OBP	SLG	PRO+	BR/A	SB	CS	SBR	FA	FR	G/POS	TPR
1955	Pit-N	73	113	21	19	1	0	1	3	15	22	.168	.266	.204	27	-12	1	0	0	.964	-7	O-47	-2.0
	KC-A	9	37	5	8	0	0	0	1	4	7	.216	.293	.216	38	-3	1	0	0	.962	-0	/O-9	-0.3
Total	4	271	602	91	143	15	1	6	40	59	108	.238	.307	.296	60	-34	9	1		.980	-8	O-169	-4.7

■ HARRY SAGE
Sage, Harry "Doc" b: 3/16/1864, Rock Island, Ill. d: 5/27/47, Rock Island, Ill. BR/TR, 5'10", 185 lbs. Deb: 4/17/1890

YEAR	TM/L	G	AB	R	H	2B	3B	HR	RBI	BB	SO	AVG	OBP	SLG	PRO+	BR/A	SB	CS	SBR	FA	FR	G/POS	TPR
1890	Tol-a	81	275	40	41	8	4	2	29			.149	.235	.229	36	-23	10			.948	8	C-80/O-1	-0.7

■ PONY SAGER
Sager, Samuel B. b: 1847, Marshalltown, Iowa 140 lbs. Deb: 5/6/1871

YEAR	TM/L	G	AB	R	H	2B	3B	HR	RBI	BB	SO	AVG	OBP	SLG	PRO+	BR/A	SB	CS	SBR	FA	FR	G/POS	TPR
1871	Rok-n	8	39	9	11	0	0	0	5	2	2	.282	.317	.282	77	-1	5					/S-4,O-4	0.0

■ VIC SAIER
Saier, Victor Sylvester b: 5/4/1891, Lansing, Mich. d: 5/14/67, E.Lansing, Mich. BL/TR, 5'11", 185 lbs. Deb: 5/3/11

YEAR	TM/L	G	AB	R	H	2B	3B	HR	RBI	BB	SO	AVG	OBP	SLG	PRO+	BR/A	SB	CS	SBR	FA	FR	G/POS	TPR
1911	Chi-N	86	259	42	67	15	1	1	37	25	37	.259	.340	.336	89	-3	11			.980	-4	1-73	-0.8
1912	Chi-N	122	451	74	130	25	14	2	61	34	65	.288	.340	.419	107	3	11			.992	-5	*1-120	-0.4
1913	Chi-N	149	519	94	150	15	21	14	92	62	62	.289	.370	.480	141	27	26			.983	-5	*1-149	2.1
1914	Chi-N	153	537	87	129	24	8	18	72	94	61	.240	.357	.415	130	21	19			.986	-11	*1-153	0.8
1915	Chi-N	144	497	74	131	35	11	11	64	64	62	.264	.350	.445	140	23	29	9	3	.985	-5	*1-139	2.0
1916	Chi-N	147	498	60	126	25	3	7	50	79	68	.253	.356	.357	108	7	20	17	-4	.984	-0	*1-147	-0.3
1917	Chi-N	6	21	5	5	1	0	0	2	2	1	.238	.304	.286	75	-1	0			1.000	2	/1-6	0.1
1919	Pit-N	58	166	19	37	3	3	2	17	18	13	.223	.306	.313	83	-3	5			.985	-5	1-51	-1.0
Total	8	865	2948	455	775	143	61	55	395	378	369	.263	.351	.409	119	75	121	26		.986	-33	1-838	2.5

■ EBBA ST.CLAIRE
St.Claire, Edward Joseph b: 8/5/21, Whitehall, N.Y. d: 8/22/82, Whitehall, N.Y. BR/TR, 6'1", 219 lbs. Deb: 4/17/51 F

YEAR	TM/L	G	AB	R	H	2B	3B	HR	RBI	BB	SO	AVG	OBP	SLG	PRO+	BR/A	SB	CS	SBR	FA	FR	G/POS	TPR
1951	Bos-N	72	220	22	62	17	2	1	25	12	24	.282	.322	.391	98	-2	2	0	1	.977	3	C-62	0.4
1952	Bos-N	39	108	5	23	2	0	2	4	8	12	.213	.267	.287	56	-7	0	1	-1	.972	4	C-34	-0.2
1953	Mil-N	33	80	7	16	3	0	2	5	3	9	.200	.229	.313	42	-7	0	0	0	.992	3	C-27	-0.3
1954	NY-N	20	42	5	11	1	0	2	6	12	7	.262	.408	.429	126	2	0	0	0	.975	2	C-16	0.5
Total	4	164	450	39	112	23	2	7	40	35	52	.249	.306	.356	81	-13	2	1	0	.978	12	C-139	0.4

■ LENN SAKATA
Sakata, Lenn Haruki b: 6/8/54, Honolulu, Hawaii BR/TR, 5'9", 160 lbs. Deb: 7/21/77

YEAR	TM/L	G	AB	R	H	2B	3B	HR	RBI	BB	SO	AVG	OBP	SLG	PRO+	BR/A	SB	CS	SBR	FA	FR	G/POS	TPR
1977	Mil-A	53	154	13	25	2	0	2	12	9	22	.162	.209	.214	14	-18	1	3	-2	.985	17	2-53	0.1
1978	Mil-A	30	78	8	15	4	0	3	3	8	11	.192	.267	.244	44	-6	1	0	0	.975	0	2-29	-0.4
1979	Mil-A	4	14	1	7	2	0	0	1	0	1	.500	.500	.643	206	2	0	0	0	1.000	0	/2-4	0.4
1980	Bal-A	43	83	12	16	3	2	1	9	6	10	.193	.247	.313	53	-6	2	1	0	.984	6	2-34/S-4,D	0.2
1981	Bal-A	61	150	19	34	4	0	5	15	11	18	.227	.284	.353	83	-4	4	0	1	.963	2	S-42,2-20	0.2
1982	Bal-A	136	343	40	89	18	1	6	31	30	39	.259	.326	.370	91	-4	7	4	-0	.977	-6	2-83,S-56	-0.3
1983	*Bal-A	66	134	23	34	7	0	3	12	16	17	.254	.338	.373	97	-0	8	4	0	.990	4	2-60/C-1,D	0.6
1984	Bal-A	81	157	23	30	1	0	3	11	6	15	.191	.221	.255	32	-15	4	1	1	.988	5	2-76/O-1	-0.7
1985	Bal-A	55	97	15	22	3	0	3	6	6	15	.227	.279	.351	73	-4	3	2	-0	.960	-1	2-50/D-1	-0.4
1986	Oak-A	17	34	4	12	2	0	0	5	3	6	.353	.405	.412	133	2	0	1	-1	.984	5	2-16/D-1	0.6
1987	NY-A	19	45	5	12	0	1	2	4	2	4	.267	.313	.444	99	-0	0	1	-1	.929	1	3-12/2-6	0.0
Total	11	565	1289	163	296	46	4	25	109	97	158	.230	.288	.330	71	-52	30	17	-1	.982	36	2-431,S-102/3DOC	0.5

■ MARK SALAS
Salas, Mark Bruce b: 3/8/61, Montebello, Cal. BL/TR, 6', 205 lbs. Deb: 6/19/84

YEAR	TM/L	G	AB	R	H	2B	3B	HR	RBI	BB	SO	AVG	OBP	SLG	PRO+	BR/A	SB	CS	SBR	FA	FR	G/POS	TPR
1984	StL-N	14	20	1	2	1	0	0	1	0	3	.100	.100	.150	-31	-3	0	0	0	1.000	-1	/C-4,O-3	-0.5
1985	Min-A	120	360	51	108	20	5	9	41	18	37	.300	.335	.458	108	3	0	1	-1	.991	2	*C-115/D-3	1.0
1986	Min-A	91	258	28	60	7	4	8	33	18	32	.233	.285	.384	78	-8	3	1	0	.980	-6	C-69/D-8	-1.0
1987	Min-A	22	45	8	17	2	0	3	9	5	6	.378	.440	.622	171	5	0	1	-1	.989	1	C-14	0.5
	NY-A	50	115	13	23	4	0	3	12	10	17	.200	.281	.313	58	-7	0	0	0	1.000	-3	C-41/O-1,D	-0.7
	Yr	72	160	21	40	6	0	6	21	15	23	.250	.326	.400	91	-2	0	1	-1	.996	-2	C-55/D-4,O	-0.2
1988	Chi-A	75	196	17	49	7	0	3	9	12	17	.250	.303	.332	78	-6	0	0	0	.979	0	C-69/D-1	-0.2
1989	Cle-A	30	77	4	17	4	1	2	7	5	13	.221	.277	.377	81	-2	0	0	0	1.000	-0	D-20/C-5	-0.3
1990	Det-A	74	164	18	38	3	0	9	24	21	28	.232	.323	.415	104	1	0	0	0	.988	-4	C-57/3-1,D	-0.1
1991	Det-A	33	57	2	5	1	0	1	7	0	10	.088	.119	.158	-24	-10	0	0	0	1.000	0	C-11/1-5,D	-1.0
Total	8	509	1292	142	319	49	10	38	143	89	163	.247	.302	.389	86	-27	3	3	-1	.987	-11	C-385/D-47,1O3	-2.3

■ ANGEL SALAZAR
Salazar, Argenis Antonio (Yepez) b: 11/4/61, ElTigre, Venez. BR/TR, 6', 173 lbs. Deb: 8/10/83

YEAR	TM/L	G	AB	R	H	2B	3B	HR	RBI	BB	SO	AVG	OBP	SLG	PRO+	BR/A	SB	CS	SBR	FA	FR	G/POS	TPR
1983	Mon-N	36	37	5	8	1	1	0	1	1	8	.216	.237	.297	47	-3	0	0	0	.966	-2	S-34	0.1
1984	Mon-N	80	174	12	27	4	2	0	12	4	38	.155	.179	.201	7	-22	1	1	-0	.960	-3	S-80	-2.1
1986	KC-A	117	298	24	73	20	2	0	24	7	47	.245	.267	.326	59	-17	1	1	-0	.978	-5	*S-115/2-1	-1.3
1987	KC-A	116	317	24	65	7	0	2	21	6	46	.205	.220	.246	23	-35	4	4	-1	.981	22	*S-116	-0.6
1988	Chi-N	34	60	4	15	1	1	0	1	1	11	.250	.262	.300	58	-3	0	0	0	.966	7	S-29/2-2,3	0.5
Total	5	383	886	69	188	33	6	2	59	19	150	.212	.231	.270	36	-80	6	6	-2	.974	23	S-374/2-3,3	-3.4

■ LUIS SALAZAR
Salazar, Luis Ernesto (Garcia) b: 5/19/56, Barcelona, Venez. BR/TR, 5'9", 180 lbs. Deb: 8/15/80

YEAR	TM/L	G	AB	R	H	2B	3B	HR	RBI	BB	SO	AVG	OBP	SLG	PRO+	BR/A	SB	CS	SBR	FA	FR	G/POS	TPR
1980	SD-N	44	169	28	57	4	7	1	25	9	25	.337	.374	.462	140	8	11	2	2	.944	-2	3-42/O-4	0.8
1981	SD-N	109	400	37	121	19	6	3	38	16	72	.303	.331	.403	116	6	11	8	-2	.955	-1	3-94,O-23	0.2
1982	SD-N	145	524	55	127	15	5	8	62	23	80	.242	.277	.336	75	-20	32	9	4	.938	16	*3-129,S-18/O	-0.1
1983	SD-N	134	481	52	124	16	2	14	45	17	80	.258	.286	.387	88	-10	24	9	2	.949	10	*3-118,S-19	0.2
1984	*SD-N	93	228	20	55	7	2	3	17	6	38	.241	.261	.333	65	-11	11	7	-1	.970	5	3-58,O-24/S	-0.9
1985	Chi-A	122	327	39	80	18	2	10	45	12	60	.245	.271	.404	79	-10	14	4	2	.968	-19	O-84,3-39/1D	-3.0
1986	Chi-A	4	7	1	1	0	0	0	0	1	3	.143	.250	.143	10	-1	0	0	0	.000	0	/D-2	-0.1
1987	SD-N	84	189	13	48	6	1	4	17	14	30	.254	.305	.328	70	-8	3	3	-1	.957	-9	3-38,S-22,O/P1	-1.7
1988	Det-A	130	452	61	122	14	1	12	62	21	70	.270	.307	.385	96	-4	6	0	2	.992	-10	O-68,S-37,3/21	-1.1
1989	SD-N	95	246	27	66	7	2	4	22	11	44	.268	.302	.411	102	-0	1	3	-2	.968	7	3-72,O-14/S1	0.6
	*Chi-N	26	80	7	26	5	0	1	12	4	13	.325	.357	.425	114	1	0	1	-1	.921	-6	3-25/O-2	-0.5
	Yr	121	326	34	92	12	2	9	34	15	57	.282	.316	.414	105	1	1	4	-2	.959	1	3-97,O-16/S1	0.1
1990	Chi-N	115	410	44	104	13	3	12	47	19	59	.254	.293	.388	80	-12	3	1	0	.950	-20	3-91,O-28	-3.3
1991	Chi-N	103	333	34	86	14	1	14	38	15	45	.258	.292	.432	97	-3	0	3	-2	.956	-9	3-86/1-7,O	-1.2
1992	Chi-N	98	255	20	53	8	2	5	25	11	34	.208	.241	.310	53	-16	1	1	-0	.935	3	3-40,O-34,S/1	-1.5
Total	13	1302	4101	438	1070	144	33	94	455	179	653	.261	.294	.381	88	-79	117	51	5	.950	-33	3-863,O-293,S/1D2P	-11.6

■ ED SALES
Sales, Edward A. b: 1861, Harrisburg, Pa. d: 8/10/12, New Haven, Conn. BL/TR, Deb: 7/15/1890

YEAR	TM/L	G	AB	R	H	2B	3B	HR	RBI	BB	SO	AVG	OBP	SLG	PRO+	BR/A	SB	CS	SBR	FA	FR	G/POS	TPR
1890	Pit-N	51	189	19	43	7	3	1	23	16	15	.228	.298	.312	88	-3	3			.871	-14	S-51	-1.2

■ BILL SALKELD
Salkeld, William Franklin b: 3/8/17, Pocatello, Idaho d: 4/22/67, Los Angeles, Cal. BL/TR, 5'10", 190 lbs. Deb: 4/18/45 F

YEAR	TM/L	G	AB	R	H	2B	3B	HR	RBI	BB	SO	AVG	OBP	SLG	PRO+	BR/A	SB	CS	SBR	FA	FR	G/POS	TPR
1945	Pit-N	95	267	45	83	16	1	15	52	50	16	.311	.420	.547	161	23	2			.973	-9	C-86	1.9
1946	Pit-N	69	160	18	47	8	0	3	19	39	16	.294	.432	.400	133	9	2			.972	-1	C-51	1.2
1947	Pit-N	47	61	5	13	2	0	0	6	8	6	.213	.284	.246	41	-5	0			.971	-3	C-15	-0.7
1948	*Bos-N	78	198	26	48	8	1	8	28	42	37	.242	.378	.414	116	6	1			.990	5	C-59	1.5
1949	Bos-N	66	161	17	41	5	0	5	25	44	24	.255	.417	.379	121	8	1			.980	-4	C-63	0.7
1950	Chi-A	1	3	0	0	0	0	0	0	1	0	.000	.250	.000	-33	-1	0	0	0	1.000	-0	/C-1	-0.1
Total	6	356	850	111	232	39	2	31	132	182	101	.273	.402	.433	129	40	6	0		.979	-11	C-275	4.5

■ CHICO SALMON
Salmon, Ruthford Eduardo b: 12/3/40, Colon, Panama BR/TR, 5'10", 170 lbs. Deb: 6/28/64

YEAR	TM/L	G	AB	R	H	2B	3B	HR	RBI	BB	SO	AVG	OBP	SLG	PRO+	BR/A	SB	CS	SBR	FA	FR	G/POS	TPR
1964	Cle-A	86	283	43	87	17	2	4	25	13	37	.307	.342	.424	113	4	10	6	-1	1.000	-8	O-53,2-32,1	-0.4

YEAR	TM/L	G	AB	R	H	2B	3B	HR	RBI	BB	SO	AVG	OBP	SLG	PRO+	BR/A	SB	CS	SBR	FA	FR	G/POS	TPR
1965	Cle-A	79	120	20	29	8	0	3	12	5	19	.242	.283	.383	87	-2	7	4	-0	.985	-6	1-28,O-17/23	-1.0
1966	Cle-A	126	422	46	108	13	2	7	40	21	41	.256	.291	.346	82	-10	10	1	2	.958	-18	S-61,2-28,10/3	-2.2
1967	Cle-A	90	203	19	46	13	1	2	19	17	29	.227	.290	.330	82	-5	10	4	1	1.000	1	O-28,1-24,2S/3	-0.2
1968	Cle-A	103	276	24	59	8	1	3	12	12	30	.214	.254	.283	63	-13	7	7	-2	.971	-15	2-45,3-18,SO1	-3.1
1969	*Bal-A	52	91	18	27	5	0	3	12	10	22	.297	.379	.451	130	4	0	0	0	1.000	-5	1-17/2-9,S30	-0.1
1970	*Bal-A	63	172	19	43	4	0	7	22	8	30	.250	.287	.395	85	-4	2	2	-1	.946	-20	S-33,2-12,3/1	-2.2
1971	Bal-A	42	84	11	15	1	0	2	7	3	21	.179	.207	.262	32	-8	0	0	0	1.000	-3	/1-9,2-9,3S	-1.1
1972	Bal-A	17	16	2	1	1	0	0	0	0	4	.063	.063	.125	-44	-3	0	0	0	1.000	0	/1-2,3-1	-0.8
Total	9	658	1667	202	415	70	6	31	149	89	233	.249	.291	.354	84	-36	46	24	-1	.959	-75	2-164,S-137,10/3	-10.6

■ TIM SALMON
Salmon, Timothy James　b: 8/24/68, Long Beach, Cal.　BR/TR, 6'3", 200 lbs.　Deb: 8/21/92

YEAR	TM/L	G	AB	R	H	2B	3B	HR	RBI	BB	SO	AVG	OBP	SLG	PRO+	BR/A	SB	CS	SBR	FA	FR	G/POS	TPR
1992	Cal-A	23	79	8	14	1	0	2	6	11	23	.177	.286	.266	55	-5	1	1	-0	.953	-0	O-21	-0.6
1993	Cal-A	142	515	93	146	35	1	31	95	82	135	.283	.387	.536	141	30	5	6	-2	.980	15	*O-140/D-1	3.8
1994	Cal-A	100	373	67	107	18	2	23	70	54	102	.287	.384	.531	129	16	1	3	-2	.966	8	O-99	1.9
Total	3	265	967	168	267	54	3	56	171	147	260	.276	.378	.512	130	42	7	10	-4	.973	23	O-260/D-1	5.1

■ JACK SALTZGAVER
Saltzgaver, Otto Hamlin　b: 1/23/03, Croton, Iowa　d: 2/1/78, Keokuk, Iowa　BL/TR, 5'11", 165 lbs.　Deb: 4/12/32

YEAR	TM/L	G	AB	R	H	2B	3B	HR	RBI	BB	SO	AVG	OBP	SLG	PRO+	BR/A	SB	CS	SBR	FA	FR	G/POS	TPR
1932	NY-A	20	47	10	6	2	1	0	5	10	10	.128	.281	.213	31	-5	1	1	-0	.958	-3	2-16	-0.7
1934	NY-A	94	350	64	95	8	1	6	36	48	28	.271	.359	.351	90	-4	8	1	2	.953	-16	3-84/1-4	-1.4
1935	NY-A	61	149	17	39	6	0	3	18	23	12	.262	.368	.362	95	-1	0	2	-1	.937	-13	2-25,3-18/1	-1.2
1936	NY-A	34	90	14	19	5	0	1	13	13	18	.211	.311	.300	53	-7	0	0	0	.972	-5	3-16/2-6,1	-0.9
1937	NY-A	17	11	6	2	0	0	0	0	3	4	.182	.357	.182	40	-1	0	0	0	1.000	0	/1-4	-0.1
1945	Pit-N	52	117	20	38	5	3	0	10	8	8	.325	.368	.419	114	2	0	0	0	.963	-4	2-31/3-1	0.0
Total	6	278	764	131	199	26	5	10	82	105	80	.260	.351	.347	85	-15	9	4		.957	-40	3-119/2-78,1	-4.3

■ ED SAMCOFF
Samcoff, Edward William　b: 9/1/24, Sacramento, Cal.　BR/TR, 5'10", 165 lbs.　Deb: 4/21/51

YEAR	TM/L	G	AB	R	H	2B	3B	HR	RBI	BB	SO	AVG	OBP	SLG	PRO+	BR/A	SB	CS	SBR	FA	FR	G/POS	TPR
1951	Phi-A	4	11	0	0	0	0	0	1	2	0	.000	.083	.000	-75	-2	0	0	0	1.000	-2	/2-3	-0.4

■ RON SAMFORD
Samford, Ronald Edward　b: 2/28/30, Dallas, Tex.　BR/TR, 5'11", 156 lbs.　Deb: 4/15/54

YEAR	TM/L	G	AB	R	H	2B	3B	HR	RBI	BB	SO	AVG	OBP	SLG	PRO+	BR/A	SB	CS	SBR	FA	FR	G/POS	TPR
1954	NY-N	12	5	2	0	0	0	0	0	0	1	.000	.000	.000	-99	-1	0	1	-1	1.000	1	/2-3	-0.1
1955	Det-A	1	1	0	0	0	0	0	0	0	1	.000	.000	.000	-99	-0	0	0	0	1.000	0	/S-1	0.0
1957	Det-A	54	91	6	20	1	2	0	5	6	15	.220	.276	.275	49	-6	1	0	0	.964	13	S-35,2-11/3	0.9
1959	Was-A	91	237	23	53	13	0	5	22	11	29	.224	.264	.342	65	-12	1	0	0	.947	3	S-64,2-23	-0.6
Total	4	158	334	31	73	14	2	5	27	17	46	.219	.263	.317	58	-20	2	1	0	.952	15	S-100/2-37,3	0.2

■ BILL SAMPLE
Sample, William Amos　b: 4/2/55, Roanoke, Va.　BR/TR, 5'9", 175 lbs.　Deb: 9/2/78

YEAR	TM/L	G	AB	R	H	2B	3B	HR	RBI	BB	SO	AVG	OBP	SLG	PRO+	BR/A	SB	CS	SBR	FA	FR	G/POS	TPR
1978	Tex-A	8	15	2	7	2	0	0	3	0	3	.467	.467	.600	197	2	0	0	0	.000	-1	/O-2,D-3	0.1
1979	Tex-A	128	325	60	95	21	2	5	35	37	28	.292	.368	.415	112	6	8	6	-1	1.000	-4	*O-103/D-9	-0.2
1980	Tex-A	99	204	29	53	10	0	4	19	18	15	.260	.338	.368	96	-1	8	5	-1	.973	-9	O-72/D-4	-1.3
1981	Tex-A	66	230	36	65	16	0	3	25	17	21	.283	.350	.391	120	6	4	1	1	.993	-1	O-64	0.4
1982	Tex-A	97	360	56	94	14	2	10	29	27	35	.261	.318	.394	99	-1	10	2	2	.981	-2	O-91/D-1	0.4
1983	Tex-A	147	554	80	152	28	3	12	57	44	46	.274	.333	.401	103	2	44	8	8	.988	6	*O-146	1.2
1984	Tex-A	130	489	67	121	20	2	5	33	29	46	.247	.290	.327	68	-21	18	6	2	.986	0	*O-122/D-2	-2.3
1985	NY-A	59	139	18	40	5	0	1	15	9	10	.288	.340	.345	90	-2	2	1	0	.989	-4	O-55	-0.7
1986	Atl-N	92	200	23	57	11	0	6	14	14	26	.285	.341	.430	105	1	4	2	0	.986	-8	O-56/2-1	-0.8
Total	9	826	2516	371	684	127	9	46	230	195	230	.272	.331	.384	98	-7	98	31	11	.987	-19	O-711/D-19,2	-3.6

■ AMADO SAMUEL
Samuel, Amado Ruperto　b: 12/6/38, San Pedro De Macoris, D.R.　BR/TR, 6'1", 170 lbs.　Deb: 4/10/62

YEAR	TM/L	G	AB	R	H	2B	3B	HR	RBI	BB	SO	AVG	OBP	SLG	PRO+	BR/A	SB	CS	SBR	FA	FR	G/POS	TPR
1962	Mil-N	76	209	16	43	10	0	3	20	12	54	.206	.249	.297	47	-16	0	2	-1	.958	-4	S-36,2-28/3	-1.7
1963	Mil-N	15	17	0	3	1	0	0	0	0	4	.176	.176	.235	18	-2	0	1	-1	.786	2	/S-7,2-4	-0.0
1964	NY-N	53	142	7	33	7	0	0	5	4	24	.232	.264	.282	55	-9	0	1	-1	.945	6	S-34,3-17/2	-0.2
Total	3	144	368	23	79	18	0	3	25	16	82	.215	.251	.288	49	-26	0	4	-2	.942	4	/S-77,2-35,3	-1.9

■ JUAN SAMUEL
Samuel, Juan Milton　b: 12/9/60, San Pedro De Macoris, , D.R.　BR/TR, 5'11", 170 lbs.　Deb: 8/24/83

YEAR	TM/L	G	AB	R	H	2B	3B	HR	RBI	BB	SO	AVG	OBP	SLG	PRO+	BR/A	SB	CS	SBR	FA	FR	G/POS	TPR
1983	*Phi-N	18	65	14	18	1	2	2	5	4	16	.277	.329	.446	114	1	3	2	-0	.916	3	2-18	0.5
1984	Phi-N☆	160	701	105	191	36	19	15	69	28	168	.272	.307	.442	107	1	72	15	13	.962	-22	*2-160	-0.1
1985	Phi-N	161	663	101	175	31	13	19	74	33	141	.264	.305	.436	102	-0	53	19	5	.983	-2	*2-159	0.8
1986	Phi-N	145	591	90	157	36	12	16	78	26	142	.266	.306	.448	102	-1	42	14	4	.967	-9	*2-143	0.0
1987	Phi-N★	160	655	113	178	37	15	28	100	60	162	.272	.338	.502	115	12	35	15	2	.978	-19	*2-160	0.3
1988	Phi-N	157	629	68	153	32	9	12	67	39	151	.243	.300	.380	92	-7	33	10	4	.978	-26	*2-152/O-3,3	-2.5
1989	Phi-N	51	199	32	49	3	1	8	20	18	45	.246	.312	.392	100	-0	11	3	2	.993	5	O-50	0.5
	NY-N	86	333	37	76	13	1	3	28	24	75	.228	.300	.300	76	-10	31	9	4	.986	7	O-84	-0.2
	Yr	137	532	69	125	16	2	11	48	42	120	.235	.304	.335	85	-10	42	12	5	.989	11	*O-134	0.3
1990	LA-N	143	492	62	119	24	3	13	52	51	126	.242	.319	.382	95	-4	38	20	-1	.972	-5	*2-108,O-31	-0.9
1991	LA-N★	153	594	74	161	22	6	12	58	49	133	.271	.330	.389	104	2	23	8	2	.978	4	*2-152	1.2
1992	LA-N	47	122	7	32	3	1	0	15	7	22	.262	.308	.303	75	-2	2	2	-1	.974	-2	2-38/O-1	-0.6
	KC-A	29	102	15	29	5	3	0	8	7	27	.284	.336	.392	101	0	6	1	1	.903	-3	O-18,2-10	-0.2
1993	Cin-N	103	261	31	60	10	4	4	26	23	53	.230	.300	.345	72	-11	9	7	-2	.971	3	2-70/1-6,3O	-0.7
1994	Det-A	59	136	32	42	9	5	5	21	10	26	.309	.369	.559	136	7	5	2	0	1.000	3	O-27,D-10/21	0.9
Total	12	1472	5543	781	1440	262	94	137	621	379	1287	.260	.315	.415	100	-12	363	127	33	.973	-64	*2-1178,O-217/D13	-1.0

■ IKE SAMULS
Samuls, Samuel Earl　b: 2/20/1876, Chicago, Ill.　d: 1/1/42, Los Angeles, Cal.　BR/TR,　Deb: 8/3/1895

YEAR	TM/L	G	AB	R	H	2B	3B	HR	RBI	BB	SO	AVG	OBP	SLG	PRO+	BR/A	SB	CS	SBR	FA	FR	G/POS	TPR
1895	StL-N	24	74	5	17	2	0	0	5	5	7	.230	.278	.257	39	-7	5			.750	-3	3-21/S-3	-0.8

■ GUS SANBERG
Sanberg, Gustave E.　b: 2/23/1896, Long Island City, N.Y.　d: 2/3/30, Los Angeles, Cal.　BR/TR, 6'1", 189 lbs.　Deb: 5/11/23

YEAR	TM/L	G	AB	R	H	2B	3B	HR	RBI	BB	SO	AVG	OBP	SLG	PRO+	BR/A	SB	CS	SBR	FA	FR	G/POS	TPR
1923	Cin-N	7	17	1	3	1	0	0	1	1	0	.176	.222	.235	21	-2	0	0	0	1.000	-1	/C-5	-0.3
1924	Cin-N	24	52	1	9	0	0	0	3	2	7	.173	.204	.173	2	-7	0	0	0	1.000	0	C-24	-0.6
Total	2	31	69	2	12	1	0	0	4	3	8	.174	.208	.188	7	-9	0	0	0	1.000	-1	/C-29	-0.9

■ ALEJANDRO SANCHEZ
Sanchez, Alejandro (Pimentel)　b: 2/14/59, San Pedro De Macoris, D.R.　BR/TR, 6', 185 lbs.　Deb: 9/6/82

YEAR	TM/L	G	AB	R	H	2B	3B	HR	RBI	BB	SO	AVG	OBP	SLG	PRO+	BR/A	SB	CS	SBR	FA	FR	G/POS	TPR
1982	Phi-N	7	14	3	4	1	0	2	4	0	4	.286	.286	.786	186	1	0	0	0	1.000	-0	/O-4	0.1
1983	Phi-N	8	7	2	2	0	0	0	2	0	2	.286	.286	.286	59	-0	0	0	0	.500	1	/O-2	-0.1
1984	SF-N	13	41	3	8	0	1	0	2	0	12	.195	.195	.244	23	-4	2	3	-1	.952	0	O-11	-0.6
1985	Det-A	71	133	19	33	6	2	6	12	0	39	.248	.248	.459	89	-3	2	2	-1	.923	-6	O-31,D-28	-1.0
1986	Min-A	8	16	1	2	0	0	0	1	1	8	.125	.176	.125	-16	-3	0	0	0	.000	-0	/O-1,D-3	-0.3
1987	Oak-A	2	3	0	0	0	0	0	0	1	1	.000	.000	.000	-99	-0	0	0	0	1.000	-0	/O-1,D-1	-0.1
Total	6	109	214	28	49	7	3	8	21	1	66	.229	.233	.402	71	-9	4	5	-2	.929	-7	/O-50,D-32	-2.0

■ CELERINO SANCHEZ
Sanchez, Celerino (Perez)　b: 2/3/44, Veracruz, Mexico　d: 5/1/92, Leon, Mexico　BR/TR, 5'11", 160 lbs.　Deb: 6/13/72

YEAR	TM/L	G	AB	R	H	2B	3B	HR	RBI	BB	SO	AVG	OBP	SLG	PRO+	BR/A	SB	CS	SBR	FA	FR	G/POS	TPR
1972	NY-A	71	250	18	62	8	3	0	22	12	30	.248	.293	.304	81	-6	0	0	0	.939	4	3-68	-0.4
1973	NY-A	34	64	12	14	3	1	1	9	2	12	.219	.242	.313	57	-4	1	1	-0	1.000	1	3-11,D-11/SO	-0.3
Total	2	105	314	30	76	11	3	1	31	14	42	.242	.283	.306	76	-10	1	1	-0	.943	5	/3-79,D-11,OS	-0.7

■ ORLANDO SANCHEZ
Sanchez, Orlando (Marquez)　b: 9/7/56, Canovanas, P.R.　BL/TR, 6'1", 195 lbs.　Deb: 5/6/81

YEAR	TM/L	G	AB	R	H	2B	3B	HR	RBI	BB	SO	AVG	OBP	SLG	PRO+	BR/A	SB	CS	SBR	FA	FR	G/POS	TPR
1981	StL-N	27	49	5	14	2	1	0	6	2	6	.286	.314	.367	90	-1	0	0	0	.926	-2	C-18	-0.2
1982	StL-N	26	37	6	7	0	1	0	3	5	5	.189	.286	.243	49	-2	0	0	0	1.000	-1	C-15	-0.3

YEAR	TM/L	G	AB	R	H	2B	3B	HR	RBI	BB	SO	AVG	OBP	SLG	PRO+	BR/A	SB	CS	SBR	FA	FR	G/POS	TPR
1983	StL-N	6	6	0	0	0	0	0	0	0	4	.000	.000	.000	-99	-2	0	0	0	1.000	-0	/C-1	-0.2
1984	KC-A	10	10	0	1	1	0	0	2	0	2	.100	.100	.200	-19	-2	0	0	0	1.000	-0	/C-1	-0.2
	Bal-A	4	8	0	2	0	0	0	1	0	2	.250	.250	.250	40	-1	0	0	0	1.000	-0	/C-4	-0.1
	Yr	14	18	0	3	1	0	0	3	0	4	.167	.167	.222	7	-2	0	0	0	1.000	-0	/C-5	-0.3
Total	4	73	110	11	24	3	2	0	12	7	19	.218	.265	.282	53	-7	1	0	0	.962	-3	/C-39	-1.0

■ REY SANCHEZ   Sanchez, Rey Francisco (Guadalupe)   b: 10/5/67, Rio Piedras, P.R.   BR/TR, 5'10", 180 lbs.   Deb: 9/8/91

YEAR	TM/L	G	AB	R	H	2B	3B	HR	RBI	BB	SO	AVG	OBP	SLG	PRO+	BR/A	SB	CS	SBR	FA	FR	G/POS	TPR
1991	Chi-N	13	23	1	6	0	0	0	2	4	3	.261	.370	.261	77	-0	0	1	0	1.000	2	S-10/2-2	0.2
1992	Chi-N	74	255	24	64	14	3	1	19	10	17	.251	.287	.341	75	-9	2	1	0	.974	14	S-68/2-4	1.1
1993	Chi-N	105	344	35	97	11	2	0	28	15	22	.282	.318	.326	74	-13	1	1	-0	.969	27	S-98	2.1
1994	Chi-N	96	291	26	83	13	1	0	24	20	29	.285	.346	.337	81	-7	2	5	-2	.993	29	2-50,S-30,3	2.1
Total	4	288	913	86	250	38	6	1	73	49	71	.274	.320	.332	77	-29	5	7	-3	.971	72	S-206/2-56,3	5.5

■ HEINIE SAND   Sand, John Henry   b: 7/3/1897, San Francisco, Cal   d: 11/3/58, San Francisco, Cal.   BR/TR, 5'8", 160 lbs.   Deb: 4/17/23

YEAR	TM/L	G	AB	R	H	2B	3B	HR	RBI	BB	SO	AVG	OBP	SLG	PRO+	BR/A	SB	CS	SBR	FA	FR	G/POS	TPR
1923	Phi-N	132	470	85	107	16	5	4	32	82	56	.228	.347	.309	67	-21	7	3	0	.934	-2	*S-120,3-11	-1.0
1924	Phi-N	137	539	79	132	21	6	6	40	52	57	.245	.316	.340	67	-25	5	4	-1	**.959**	2	*S-137	-0.9
1925	Phi-N	148	496	69	138	30	7	3	55	64	65	.278	.364	.385	84	-11	1	1	-0	.928	-6	*S-143	-0.2
1926	Phi-N	149	567	99	154	30	5	4	37	66	56	.272	.350	.363	88	-9	2			.939	-3	*S-149	0.3
1927	Phi-N	141	535	87	160	22	8	1	49	58	59	.299	.369	.376	98	0	5			.949	-15	S-86,3-58	-0.3
1928	Phi-N	141	426	38	90	26	1	0	38	60	47	.211	.310	.277	53	-29	1			.951	-1	*S-137	-1.4
Total	6	848	3033	457	781	145	32	18	251	382	340	.258	.343	.344	77	-94	21	8		.943	-25	S-772/3-69	-3.5

■ RYNE SANDBERG   Sandberg, Ryne Dee   b: 9/18/59, Spokane, Wash.   BR/TR, 6'2", 180 lbs.   Deb: 9/2/81

YEAR	TM/L	G	AB	R	H	2B	3B	HR	RBI	BB	SO	AVG	OBP	SLG	PRO+	BR/A	SB	CS	SBR	FA	FR	G/POS	TPR
1981	Phi-N	13	6	2	1	0	0	0	0	0	1	.167	.167	.167	-5	-7	0	0	0	1.000	4	/S-5,2-1	0.3
1982	Chi-N	156	635	103	172	33	5	7	54	36	90	.271	.314	.372	89	-10	32	12	2	.970	5	*3-133,2-24	-0.5
1983	Chi-N	158	633	94	165	25	4	8	48	51	79	.261	.319	.351	81	-16	37	11	5	**.986**	41	*2-157/S-1	3.8
1984	*Chi-N★	156	636	**114**	200	36	**19**	19	84	52	101	.314	.369	.520	135	28	32	7	5	**.993**	23	*2-156	6.4
1985	Chi-N★	153	609	113	186	31	6	26	83	57	97	.305	.366	.504	127	21	54	11	10	.986	9	*2-153/S-1	4.6
1986	Chi-N★	154	627	68	178	28	5	14	76	46	79	.284	.333	.411	97	-4	34	11	4	**.994**	5	*2-153	1.2
1987	Chi-N★	132	523	81	154	25	2	16	59	59	79	.294	.368	.442	109	8	21	2	5	.985	1	*2-131	2.0
1988	Chi-N★	155	618	77	163	23	8	19	69	54	91	.264	.324	.419	107	5	25	10	2	.987	11	*2-153	2.5
1989	*Chi-N★	157	606	**104**	176	25	5	30	76	59	85	.290	.357	.497	132	24	15	5	2	.992	1	*2-155	3.3
1990	Chi-N★	155	615	**116**	188	30	3	**40**	100	50	84	.306	.359	.559	138	30	25	7	3	.989	7	*2-154	4.3
1991	Chi-N★	158	585	104	170	32	2	26	100	87	89	.291	.384	.485	137	30	22	8	2	**.995**	11	*2-157	4.7
1992	Chi-N★	158	612	100	186	32	8	26	87	68	73	.304	.374	.510	145	35	17	6	2	.990	14	*2-157	5.7
1993	Chi-N★	117	456	67	141	20	0	9	45	37	62	.309	.364	.412	109	6	9	2	2	.988	-4	*2-115	0.7
1994	Chi-N	57	223	36	53	9	5	5	24	23	40	.238	.312	.390	84	-6	2	3	-1	.987	3	2-57	-0.2
Total	14	1879	7384	1179	2133	349	72	245	905	679	1050	.289	.351	.455	116	151	325	95	41	.990	130	*2-1723,3-133/S	38.8

■ BEN SANDERS   Sanders, Alexander Bennett   b: 2/16/1865, Catharpin, Va.   d: 8/29/30, Memphis, Tenn.   BR/TR, 6', 210 lbs.   Deb: 6/6/1888

YEAR	TM/L	G	AB	R	H	2B	3B	HR	RBI	BB	SO	AVG	OBP	SLG	PRO+	BR/A	SB	CS	SBR	FA	FR	G/POS	TPR
1888	Phi-N	57	236	26	58	11	4	1	25	8	12	.246	.276	.322	86	-4	13			.929	3	P-31,O-25/3	-0.3
1889	Phi-N	44	169	21	47	8	2	0	21	6	11	.278	.307	.349	76	-6	4			.879	-3	P-44/O-3	-0.1
1890	Phi-P	52	189	31	59	6	6	0	30	10	10	.312	.347	.407	99	-1	2			.924	1	P-43,O-10	-0.1
1891	Phi-a	40	156	24	39	6	4	1	19	7	12	.250	.291	.359	83	-5	2			.839	-6	O-22,P-19	-0.7
1892	Lou-N	54	198	30	54	12	2	3	18	16	17	.273	.330	.399	131	7	6			.930	-3	P-31,1-15/O	0.0
Total	5	247	948	132	257	43	16	5	113	47	62	.271	.310	.366	95	-9	27			.916	-8	P-168/O-69,13	-1.2

■ DEION SANDERS   Sanders, Deion Luwynn   b: 8/9/67, Ft.Myers, Fla.   BL/TL, 6'1", 195 lbs.   Deb: 5/31/89

YEAR	TM/L	G	AB	R	H	2B	3B	HR	RBI	BB	SO	AVG	OBP	SLG	PRO+	BR/A	SB	CS	SBR	FA	FR	G/POS	TPR
1989	NY-A	14	47	7	11	2	0	2	7	3	8	.234	.280	.404	92	-1	1	0	0	.969	-0	O-14	-0.1
1990	NY-A	57	133	24	21	2	2	3	9	13	27	.158	.238	.271	42	-11	8	2	1	.973	-4	O-42/D-4	-1.5
1991	Atl-N	54	110	16	21	1	2	4	13	12	23	.191	.270	.345	68	-5	11	3	2	.952	-5	O-44	-0.9
1992	*Atl-N	97	303	54	92	6	**14**	8	28	18	52	.304	.347	.495	128	10	26	9	2	.983	-1	O-75	1.1
1993	*Atl-N	95	272	42	75	18	6	6	28	16	42	.276	.323	.452	104	1	19	7	2	.986	-0	O-60	0.1
1994	Atl-N	46	191	32	55	10	4	4	21	16	28	.288	.346	.403	94	-1	19	7	2	.980	-4	O-46	-0.3
	Cin-N	46	184	26	51	7	4	0	7	16	35	.277	.342	.359	83	-4	19	9	0	1.000	2	O-45	-0.3
	Yr	92	375	58	106	17	8	4	28	32	63	.283	.344	.381	89	-6	38	16	2	.991	0	O-91	-0.6
Total	6	409	1240	201	326	46	28	27	113	94	215	.263	.319	.410	95	-11	103	37	9	.981	-10	O-326/D-4	-1.9

■ JOHN SANDERS   Sanders, John Frank   b: 11/20/45, Grand Island, Neb.   BR/TR, 6'2", 200 lbs.   Deb: 4/13/65

YEAR	TM/L	G	AB	R	H	2B	3B	HR	RBI	BB	SO	AVG	OBP	SLG	PRO+	BR/A	SB	CS	SBR	FA	FR	G/POS	TPR
1965	KC-A	1	0	0	0	0	0	0	0	0	0	—	—	—	—	0	0	0	0	.000	0	R	0.0

■ RAY SANDERS   Sanders, Raymond Floyd   b: 12/4/16, Bonne Terre, Mo.   d: 10/28/83, Washington, Mo.   BL/TR, 6'2", 185 lbs.   Deb: 4/14/42

YEAR	TM/L	G	AB	R	H	2B	3B	HR	RBI	BB	SO	AVG	OBP	SLG	PRO+	BR/A	SB	CS	SBR	FA	FR	G/POS	TPR
1942	*StL-N	95	282	37	71	17	2	5	39	42	31	.252	.351	.379	106	3	2			.991	-4	1-77	-0.6
1943	*StL-N	144	478	69	134	21	5	11	73	77	33	.280	.381	.414	124	17	1			.995	-7	*1-141	0.2
1944	*StL-N	154	601	87	177	34	9	12	102	71	50	.295	.371	.441	126	21	2			**.994**	-13	*1-152	0.0
1945	StL-N	143	537	85	148	29	3	8	78	83	55	.276	.375	.385	109	9	3			.986	-5	*1-142	-0.5
1946	Bos-N	80	259	43	63	12	6	6	35	50	38	.243	.368	.359	105	3	0			.988	4	1-77	0.3
1948	*Bos-N	5	4	0	1	0	0	0	2	1	0	.250	.400	.250	81	-0	0			.000	0	H	0.0
1949	Bos-N	9	21	0	3	1	0	0	0	4	9	.143	.280	.190	30	-2	0			.984	2	/1-7	0.0
Total	7	630	2182	321	597	114	19	42	329	328	216	.274	.370	.401	115	50	8			.991	-22	1-596	-0.6

■ REGGIE SANDERS   Sanders, Reginald Jerome   b: 9/9/49, Birmingham, Ala.   BR/TR, 6'2", 205 lbs.   Deb: 9/1/74

YEAR	TM/L	G	AB	R	H	2B	3B	HR	RBI	BB	SO	AVG	OBP	SLG	PRO+	BR/A	SB	CS	SBR	FA	FR	G/POS	TPR
1974	Det-A	26	99	12	27	7	0	3	10	5	20	.273	.308	.434	108	1	1	0	0	.987	1	1-25/D-1	0.0

■ REGGIE SANDERS   Sanders, Reginald Laverne   b: 12/1/67, Florence, S.C.   BR/TR, 6'1", 180 lbs.   Deb: 8/22/91

YEAR	TM/L	G	AB	R	H	2B	3B	HR	RBI	BB	SO	AVG	OBP	SLG	PRO+	BR/A	SB	CS	SBR	FA	FR	G/POS	TPR
1991	Cin-N	9	40	6	8	0	0	1	3	0	9	.200	.200	.275	31	-4	1	1	-0	1.000	1	/O-9	-0.4
1992	Cin-N	116	385	62	104	26	6	12	36	48	98	.270	.357	.462	127	14	16	7	1	.978	5	*O-110	1.9
1993	Cin-N	138	496	90	136	16	4	20	83	51	118	.274	.348	.444	110	7	27	10	2	.975	8	*O-137	1.4
1994	Cin-N	107	400	66	105	20	8	17	62	41	114	.262	.334	.480	110	5	21	9	1	.975	12	*O-104	1.5
Total	4	370	1321	224	353	62	18	50	184	140	339	.267	.342	.455	112	22	65	27	3	.977	25	O-360	4.4

■ MIKE SANDLOCK   Sandlock, Michael Joseph   b: 10/17/15, Old Greenwich, Conn.   BB/TR, 6'1", 185 lbs.   Deb: 9/19/42

YEAR	TM/L	G	AB	R	H	2B	3B	HR	RBI	BB	SO	AVG	OBP	SLG	PRO+	BR/A	SB	CS	SBR	FA	FR	G/POS	TPR
1942	Bos-N	2	1	1	1	0	0	0	0	0	0	1.000	1.000	1.000	496	0	0			.000	0	/S-2	0.1
1944	Bos-N	30	30	1	3	0	0	0	2	5	3	.100	.250	.100	1	-4	0			.956	7	3-22/S-7	0.3
1945	Bro-N	80	195	21	55	14	2	2	17	18	19	.282	.346	.405	109	2	2			.991	1	C-47,S-22/23	0.6
1946	Bro-N	19	34	1	5	0	0	0	0	3	4	.147	.216	.147	4	-4	0			.973	6	C-17/3-1	0.3
1953	Pit-N	64	186	10	43	5	0	0	12	12	19	.231	.281	.258	42	-16	0	0	0	.991	16	C-64	0.3
Total	5	195	446	34	107	19	2	2	31	38	45	.240	.304	.305	66	-21	2	0		.989	30	C-128/S-31,32	1.6

■ CHARLIE SANDS   Sands, Charles Duane   b: 12/17/47, Newport News, Va.   BL/TR, 6'2", 215 lbs.   Deb: 6/21/67

YEAR	TM/L	G	AB	R	H	2B	3B	HR	RBI	BB	SO	AVG	OBP	SLG	PRO+	BR/A	SB	CS	SBR	FA	FR	G/POS	TPR
1967	NY-A	1	1	0	0	0	0	0	0	0	1	.000	.000	.000	-99	-0	0	0	0	.000	0	H	0.0
1971	*Pit-N	28	25	4	5	2	0	1	5	7	6	.200	.375	.400	120	1	0	0	0	1.000	0	/C-3	0.1
1972	Pit-N	1	1	0	0	0	0	0	0	0	0	.000	.000	.000	-99	-0	0	0	0	.000	0	H	0.0
1973	Cal-A	17	33	5	9	2	1	1	5	5	10	.273	.368	.485	150	3	0	0	0	.917	-8	C-10	-0.5
1974	Cal-A	43	83	6	16	2	0	4	13	23	17	.193	.374	.361	119	3	0	0	0	1.000	-1	D-21/C-5	0.2

YEAR	TM/L	G	AB	R	H	2B	3B	HR	RBI	BB	SO	AVG	OBP	SLG	PRO+	BR/A	SB	CS	SBR	FA	FR	G/POS	TPR
1975	Oak-A	3	2	0	1	0	0	0	0	1	1	.500	.667	.500	239	1	0	0	0	.000	0	/D-1	0.1
Total	6	93	145	15	31	6	1	6	23	36	35	.214	.374	.393	125	6	0	0	0	.955	-8	/D-22,C-18	-0.1

■ TOMMY SANDT
Sandt, Thomas James b: 12/22/50, Brooklyn, N.Y. BR/TR, 5′11″, 175 lbs. Deb: 6/29/75 C

YEAR	TM/L	G	AB	R	H	2B	3B	HR	RBI	BB	SO	AVG	OBP	SLG	PRO+	BR/A	SB	CS	SBR	FA	FR	G/POS	TPR
1975	Oak-A	1	0	0	0	0	0	0	0	0	0	—	—	—		0	0	0	0	.000	0	/2-1	0.0
1976	Oak-A	41	67	6	14	1	0	0	3	7	9	.209	.284	.224	52	-4	0	0	0	.966	3	S-29/2-9,3	0.1
Total	2	42	67	6	14	1	0	0	3	7	9	.209	.284	.224	52	-4	0	0	0	1.000	3	/S-29,2-10,3	0.1

■ JACK SANFORD
Sanford, John Doward b: 6/23/17, Chatham, Va. BR/TR, 6′3″, 195 lbs. Deb: 8/24/40

YEAR	TM/L	G	AB	R	H	2B	3B	HR	RBI	BB	SO	AVG	OBP	SLG	PRO+	BR/A	SB	CS	SBR	FA	FR	G/POS	TPR
1940	Was-A	34	122	5	24	4	2	0	10	6	17	.197	.234	.262	30	-13	0	0	0	.993	-2	1-34	-1.7
1941	Was-A	3	5	1	2	0	1	0	0	1	1	.400	.500	.600	251	1	0	0	0	1.000	-0	/1-1	0.1
1946	Was-A	10	26	7	6	0	1	0	1	2	6	.231	.286	.308	70	-1	0	0	0	.971	-1	/1-6	-0.3
Total	3	47	153	13	32	4	4	0	11	9	24	.209	.253	.288	44	-13	0	0	0	.989	-4	/1-41	-1.9

■ MANNY SANGUILLEN
Sanguillen, Manuel De Jesus (Magan) b: 3/21/44, Colon, Panama BR/TR, 6′, 193 lbs. Deb: 7/23/67

YEAR	TM/L	G	AB	R	H	2B	3B	HR	RBI	BB	SO	AVG	OBP	SLG	PRO+	BR/A	SB	CS	SBR	FA	FR	G/POS	TPR
1967	Pit-N	30	96	6	26	4	0	0	8	4	12	.271	.300	.313	75	-3	0	1	-1	.986	-5	C-28	-0.8
1969	Pit-N	129	459	62	139	21	6	5	57	12	48	.303	.325	.407	106	-2	8	4	0	.981	8	*C-113	1.3
1970	*Pit-N	128	486	63	158	19	9	5	61	17	45	.325	.348	.444	113	7	2	3	-1	.988	1	*C-125	1.3
1971	*Pit-N☆	138	533	60	170	26	5	7	81	19	32	.319	.346	.426	118	11	6	4	-1	.994	5	*C-135	2.2
1972	*Pit-N★	136	520	55	155	18	8	7	71	21	38	.298	.325	.404	108	4	1	2	-1	.988	-3	*C-127/O-2	0.6
1973	Pit-N	149	589	64	166	26	7	12	65	17	29	.282	.305	.411	99	-3	2	5	-2	.983	-6	C-89,O-59	-0.1
1974	*Pit-N	151	596	77	171	21	4	7	68	21	27	.287	.317	.371	95	-6	2	2	-1	.985	-6	*C-151	-0.7
1975	*Pit-N☆	133	481	60	158	24	4	9	58	48	31	.328	.393	.451	135	23	5	4	-1	.987	-5	*C-132	2.4
1976	Pit-N	114	389	52	113	16	6	2	36	28	18	.290	.341	.378	103	1	2	4	-2	.978	-7	*C-111	-0.4
1977	Oak-A	152	571	42	157	17	5	6	58	22	35	.275	.304	.354	80	-16	2	5	-2	.985	-8	C-77,D-58/O1	-2.7
1978	Pit-N	85	220	15	58	5	1	3	16	9	10	.264	.299	.336	74	-8	2	2	-1	1.000	-2	1-40,C-18	-1.3
1979	*Pit-N	56	74	8	17	5	2	0	4	2	5	.230	.250	.351	59	-4	0	0	0	.947	0	/C-8,1-5	-0.4
1980	Pit-N	47	48	2	12	3	0	0	2	3	1	.250	.294	.313	68	-2	3	2	-0	.956	0	/1-5	-0.2
Total	13	1448	5062	566	1500	205	57	65	585	223	331	.296	.329	.398	103	6	35	38	-12	.986	-23	*C-1114/O-70,D1	1.2

■ ED SANICKI
Sanicki, Edward Robert "Butch" b: 7/7/23, Wallington, N.J. BR/TR, 5′9″, 175 lbs. Deb: 9/14/49

YEAR	TM/L	G	AB	R	H	2B	3B	HR	RBI	BB	SO	AVG	OBP	SLG	PRO+	BR/A	SB	CS	SBR	FA	FR	G/POS	TPR
1949	Phi-N	7	13	4	3	0	0	3	7	1	4	.231	.286	.923	217	2	0			1.000	-1	/O-6	0.1
1951	Phi-N	13	4	1	2	1	0	1	1	1	1	.500	.600	.750	265	1	0	0	0	1.000	-4	O-10	-0.3
Total	2	20	17	5	5	1	0	4	8	2	5	.294	.368	.882	231	3	0	0		1.000	-5	/O-16	-0.2

■ BEN SANKEY
Sankey, Benjamin Turner b: 9/2/07, Nauvoo, Ala. BR/TR, 5′10″, 155 lbs. Deb: 10/5/29

YEAR	TM/L	G	AB	R	H	2B	3B	HR	RBI	BB	SO	AVG	OBP	SLG	PRO+	BR/A	SB	CS	SBR	FA	FR	G/POS	TPR
1929	Pit-N	2	7	1	1	0	0	0	0	1	1	.143	.143	.143	-28	-1	0			.909	-0	/S-2	-0.1
1930	Pit-N	13	30	6	5	0	0	0	2	3		.167	.219	.167	-5	-5	0			.871	-0	/S-6,2-4	-0.4
1931	Pit-N	57	132	14	30	2	5	0	14	14	10	.227	.301	.318	67	-6	0			.920	-9	S-49/2-2,3	-1.1
Total	3	72	169	21	36	2	5	0	14	16	14	.213	.281	.284	49	-13	0			.914	-10	/S-57,2-6,3	-1.6

■ ANDRES SANTANA
Santana, Andres Confesor (Belonis) b: 2/5/68, San Pedro De Macoris, D.R. BB/TR, 5′11″, 160 lbs. Deb: 9/16/90

YEAR	TM/L	G	AB	R	H	2B	3B	HR	RBI	BB	SO	AVG	OBP	SLG	PRO+	BR/A	SB	CS	SBR	FA	FR	G/POS	TPR
1990	SF-N	6	2	0	0	0	0	0	0	1	0	.000	.000	.000	-99	-1	0	0	0	1.000	1	/S-3	0.0

■ RAFAEL SANTANA
Santana, Rafael Francisco (De La Cruz) b: 1/31/58, LaRomana, D.R. BR/TR, 6′1″, 165 lbs. Deb: 4/5/83

YEAR	TM/L	G	AB	R	H	2B	3B	HR	RBI	BB	SO	AVG	OBP	SLG	PRO+	BR/A	SB	CS	SBR	FA	FR	G/POS	TPR
1983	StL-N	30	14	1	3	0	0	0	2	2	2	.214	.353	.214	61	-1	0	1	-1	.857	2	/2-9,S-6,3	0.1
1984	NY-N	51	152	14	42	11	1	1	12	9	17	.276	.317	.382	97	-1	0	3	-2	.970	-3	S-50	-0.1
1985	NY-N	154	529	41	136	19	1	1	29	29	54	.257	.296	.302	69	-22	1	0	0	.965	-11	*S-153	-1.9
1986	*NY-N	139	394	38	86	11	0	1	28	36	43	.218	.287	.254	52	-25	0	0	0	.973	17	*S-137/2-1	0.2
1987	NY-N	139	439	41	112	21	2	5	44	29	57	.255	.303	.346	75	-16	1	1	-0	.973	15	*S-138	0.9
1988	NY-A	148	480	50	115	12	1	4	38	33	61	.240	.290	.294	64	-23	1	2	-1	.966	-9	*S-148	-2.1
1990	Cle-A	7	13	3	3	0	0	1	3	0	0	.231	.231	.462	89	-0	0	0	0	1.000	-2	/S-7	-0.2
Total	7	668	2021	188	497	74	5	13	156	138	234	.246	.296	.307	68	-88	3	7	-3	.969	9	S-639/2-10,3	-3.1

■ BENITO SANTIAGO
Santiago, Benito (Rivera) b: 3/9/65, Ponce, P.R. BR/TR, 6′1″, 185 lbs. Deb: 9/14/86

YEAR	TM/L	G	AB	R	H	2B	3B	HR	RBI	BB	SO	AVG	OBP	SLG	PRO+	BR/A	SB	CS	SBR	FA	FR	G/POS	TPR
1986	SD-N	17	62	10	18	2	0	3	6	2	12	.290	.313	.468	115	1	0	1	-1	.946	-6	C-17	-0.5
1987	SD-N	146	546	64	164	33	2	18	79	16	112	.300	.326	.467	111	6	21	12	-1	.976	-7	*C-146	0.8
1988	SD-N	139	492	49	122	22	2	10	46	24	82	.248	.284	.362	86	-10	15	7	0	.985	-5	*C-136	-0.5
1989	SD-N★	129	462	50	109	16	3	16	62	26	89	.236	.278	.387	88	-9	11	6	-0	.975	-6	*C-127	-0.8
1990	SD-N†	100	344	42	93	8	5	11	53	27	55	.270	.329	.419	103	3	5	5	-2	.980	5	C-98	0.1
1991	SD-N★	152	580	60	155	22	3	17	87	23	114	.267	.300	.403	93	-7	8	10	-4	.985	-1	*C-151/O-1	-0.2
1992	SD-N★	106	386	37	97	21	0	10	42	21	52	.251	.290	.383	88	-7	2	5	-2	.982	-11	*C-103	-1.6
1993	Fla-N	139	469	49	108	19	6	13	50	37	88	.230	.294	.380	74	-18	10	7	-1	.987	-8	*C-136/O-1	-1.9
1994	Fla-N	101	337	35	92	14	2	11	41	25	57	.273	.325	.424	88	-6	1	2	-1	.991	5	C-97	0.3
Total	9	1029	3678	396	958	157	23	109	466	201	661	.260	.302	.405	92	-48	73	55	-11	.982	-42	*C-1011/O-2	-4.3

■ RON SANTO
Santo, Ronald Edward b: 2/25/40, Seattle, Wash. BR/TR, 6′, 190 lbs. Deb: 6/26/60

YEAR	TM/L	G	AB	R	H	2B	3B	HR	RBI	BB	SO	AVG	OBP	SLG	PRO+	BR/A	SB	CS	SBR	FA	FR	G/POS	TPR
1960	Chi-N	95	347	44	87	24	2	9	44	31	44	.251	.312	.409	97	-2	0	3	-2	.945	-19	3-94	-2.4
1961	Chi-N	154	578	84	164	32	6	23	83	73	77	.284	.364	.479	120	17	2	3	-1	.937	5	*3-153	2.2
1962	Chi-N	162	604	44	137	20	4	17	83	65	94	.227	.304	.358	74	-22	4	1	1	.955	11	3-157/S-8	-0.8
1963	Chi-N★	162	630	79	187	29	6	25	99	42	92	.297	.345	.481	128	22	6	4	-1	.951	13	*3-162	3.6
1964	Chi-N☆	161	592	94	185	33	13	30	114	86	96	.313	.401	.564	162	50	3	4	-2	.963	17	*3-161	6.5
1965	Chi-N★	164	608	88	173	30	4	33	101	88	109	.285	.379	.510	144	37	3	1	0	.957	19	*3-164	5.4
1966	Chi-N★	155	561	93	175	21	8	30	94	95	78	.312	.417	.538	161	50	4	5	-2	.956	29	*3-152/S-8	7.5
1967	Chi-N	161	586	107	176	23	4	31	98	96	103	.300	.401	.512	153	43	1	5	-3	.957	31	*3-161	7.3
1968	Chi-N★	162	577	86	142	17	3	26	98	96	106	.246	.357	.421	124	20	3	4	-2	.971	17	*3-162	4.0
1969	Chi-N★	160	575	97	166	18	4	29	123	96	97	.289	.392	.485	128	23	1	3	-2	.947	6	*3-160	2.9
1970	Chi-N	154	555	83	148	30	4	26	114	92	108	.267	.372	.476	112	9	2	0	1	.945	13	*3-152/O-1	2.1
1971	Chi-N★	154	555	77	148	22	1	21	88	79	95	.267	.358	.423	105	4	4	0	1	.958	-3	*3-149/O-6	0.2
1972	Chi-N★	133	464	68	140	25	5	17	74	69	75	.302	.397	.487	135	23	1	4	-2	.948	6	*3-129/2-3,SO	2.7
1973	Chi-N★	149	536	65	143	29	2	20	77	63	97	.267	.348	.440	109	7	1	2	-1	.950	-12	*3-146	-0.7
1974	Chi-A	117	375	29	83	12	1	5	41	37	72	.221	.295	.299	69	-14	0	2	-1	.970	6	D-47,2-39,3/1S	-1.0
Total	15	2243	8143	1138	2254	365	67	342	1331	1108	1343	.277	.366	.464	123	264	35	41	-14	.954	138	*3-2130/D-47,2SO1	39.5

■ RAFAEL SANTO DOMINGO
Santo Domingo, Rafael (Molina) b: 11/24/55, Orocovis, P.R. BB/TR, 6′, 160 lbs. Deb: 9/7/79

YEAR	TM/L	G	AB	R	H	2B	3B	HR	RBI	BB	SO	AVG	OBP	SLG	PRO+	BR/A	SB	CS	SBR	FA	FR	G/POS	TPR
1979	Cin-N	7	6	0	1	0	0	0	1	0	3	.167	.286	.167	26	-1	0	0	0	.000	0	/H	-0.1

■ NELSON SANTOVENIA
Santovenia, Nelson Gil (Mayol) b: 7/27/61, Pinar Del Rio, Cuba BR/TR, 6′3″, 215 lbs. Deb: 9/16/87

YEAR	TM/L	G	AB	R	H	2B	3B	HR	RBI	BB	SO	AVG	OBP	SLG	PRO+	BR/A	SB	CS	SBR	FA	FR	G/POS	TPR
1987	Mon-N	2	1	0	0	0	0	0	0	0	0	.000	.000	.000	-97	-0	0	0	0	1.000	-0	/C-1	0.0
1988	Mon-N	92	309	26	73	20	2	8	41	24	77	.236	.298	.392	92	-4	2	3	-1	.983	2	C-86/1-1	0.4
1989	Mon-N	97	304	30	76	14	1	5	31	24	37	.250	.311	.352	88	-5	2	1	0	.981	12	C-89/1-1	1.3
1990	Mon-N	59	163	13	31	3	1	6	28	8	31	.190	.228	.331	54	-11	0	3	-2	.980	-4	C-51	-0.9
1991	Mon-N	41	96	7	24	5	0	2	14	2	18	.250	.265	.365	76	-3	0	0	0	.976	-4	C-30/1-7	-0.6
1992	Chi-A	2	3	1	1	0	0	1	2	0	1	.333	.333	1.333	352	1	0	0	0	1.000	-0	/C-2	0.1

YEAR	TM/L	G	AB	R	H	2B	3B	HR	RBI	BB	SO	AVG	OBP	SLG	PRO+	BR/A	SB	CS	SBR	FA	FR	G/POS	TPR
1993	KC-A	4	8	0	1	0	0	0	0	1	2	.125	.222	.125	-4	-1	0	0	0	1.000	0	/C-4	-0.1
Total	7	297	884	77	206	42	4	22	116	59	165	.233	.286	.364	82	-23	4	7	-3	.981	12	C-263/1-9	0.2

■ EDWARD SANTRY
Santry, Edward   b: Chicago, Ill.   d: 3/6/1899, Chicago, Ill.   Deb: 8/7/1884

YEAR	TM/L	G	AB	R	H	2B	3B	HR	RBI	BB	SO	AVG	OBP	SLG	PRO+	BR/A	SB	CS	SBR	FA	FR	G/POS	TPR
1884	Det-N	6	22	1	4	0	0	0	0	1	2	.182	.217	.182	29	-2				.821	-0	/S-5,2-1	-0.2

■ JOE SARGENT
Sargent, Joseph Alexander "Horse Belly"   b: 9/24/1893, Rochester, N.Y.   d: 7/5/50, Rochester, N.Y.   BR/TR, 5'10", 165 lbs.   Deb: 4/27/21

YEAR	TM/L	G	AB	R	H	2B	3B	HR	RBI	BB	SO	AVG	OBP	SLG	PRO+	BR/A	SB	CS	SBR	FA	FR	G/POS	TPR
1921	Det-A	66	178	21	45	8	5	2	22	24	26	.253	.342	.388	87	-4	2	3	-1	.927	3	2-24,3-23,S	0.1

■ BILL SARNI
Sarni, William Florine   b: 9/19/27, Los Angeles, Cal.   d: 4/15/83, Creve Coeur, Mo.   BR/TR, 5'11", 187 lbs.   Deb: 5/9/51   C

YEAR	TM/L	G	AB	R	H	2B	3B	HR	RBI	BB	SO	AVG	OBP	SLG	PRO+	BR/A	SB	CS	SBR	FA	FR	G/POS	TPR
1951	StL-N	36	86	7	15	1	0	0	2	9	13	.174	.253	.186	20	-10	1	0	0	.984	0	C-35	-0.8
1952	StL-N	3	5	0	1	0	0	0	0	0	1	.200	.200	.200	11	-1	0	0	0	1.000	2	/C-3	0.2
1954	StL-N	123	380	40	114	18	4	9	70	25	42	.300	.343	.439	101	0	3	3	-1	.996	-13	*C-118	-0.8
1955	StL-N	107	325	32	83	15	2	3	34	27	33	.255	.314	.342	74	-12	1	1	-0	.987	-6	C-99	-1.5
1956	StL-N	43	148	12	43	7	2	5	22	8	15	.291	.331	.466	111	2	1	0	0	.992	3	C-41	0.7
	NY-N	78	238	16	55	9	3	5	23	20	31	.231	.293	.357	74	-9	0	1	-1	.993	-6	C-78	-1.3
	Yr	121	386	28	98	16	5	10	45	28	46	.254	.308	.399	88	-7	1	1	-0	.992	-3	*C-119	-0.6
Total	5	390	1182	107	311	50	11	22	151	89	135	.263	.316	.380	84	-29	6	5	-1	.991	-19	C-374	-3.5

■ MACKEY SASSER
Sasser, Mack Daniel   b: 8/3/62, Fort Gaines, Ga.   BL/TR, 6'1", 210 lbs.   Deb: 7/17/87

YEAR	TM/L	G	AB	R	H	2B	3B	HR	RBI	BB	SO	AVG	OBP	SLG	PRO+	BR/A	SB	CS	SBR	FA	FR	G/POS	TPR
1987	SF-N	2	4	0	0	0	0	0	0	0	0	.000	.000	.000	-99	-1	0	0	0	1.000	0	/C-1	-0.1
	Pit-N	12	23	2	5	0	0	0	2	0	2	.217	.217	.217	16	-3	0	0	0	1.000	-1	/C-5	-0.4
	Yr	14	27	2	5	0	0	0	2	0	2	.185	.185	.185	-2	-4	0	0	0	1.000	-1	/C-6	-0.5
1988	*NY-N	60	123	9	35	10	1	1	17	6	9	.285	.318	.407	112	1	0	0	0	.977	9	C-42/3-1,O	1.3
1989	NY-N	72	182	17	53	14	2	1	22	7	15	.291	.317	.407	111	2	0	1	-1	.992	0	C-62/3-1	0.4
1990	NY-N	100	270	31	83	14	0	6	41	15	19	.307	.346	.426	111	4	0	0	0	.975	-9	C-87/1-1	0.0
1991	NY-N	96	228	18	62	14	2	5	35	9	19	.272	.303	.417	101	-1	0	2	-1	.994	-9	C-43,O-21,1	-1.0
1992	NY-N	92	141	7	34	6	0	2	18	3	10	.241	.257	.326	65	-7	0	0	0	.989	-11	C-27,1-12/O	-1.9
1993	Sea-A	83	188	18	41	10	2	1	21	15	30	.218	.279	.309	57	-12	1	0	0	.946	-3	O-37,D-19/C1	-1.5
1994	Sea-A	3	4	0	0	0	0	0	0	0	0	.000	.000	.000	-98	-1	0	0	0	.000	0	/C-1,O-1	-0.1
Total	8	520	1163	102	313	68	7	16	156	55	104	.269	.304	.381	91	-17	1	3	-2	.983	-24	C-272/O-69,1D3	-3.3

■ TOM SATRIANO
Satriano, Thomas Victor Nicholas   b: 8/28/40, Pittsburgh, Pa.   BL/TR, 6'1", 190 lbs.   Deb: 7/23/61

YEAR	TM/L	G	AB	R	H	2B	3B	HR	RBI	BB	SO	AVG	OBP	SLG	PRO+	BR/A	SB	CS	SBR	FA	FR	G/POS	TPR
1961	LA-A	35	96	15	19	5	1	1	8	12	16	.198	.294	.302	53	-6	2	0	1	.915	0	3-23,2-10/S	-0.5
1962	LA-A	10	19	4	8	2	0	2	6	0	1	.421	.421	.842	238	3	0	0	0	.833	0	/3-5	0.3
1963	LA-A	23	50	1	9	1	0	0	2	9	10	.180	.305	.200	48	-3	0	0	0	.952	3	3-13/C-2,1	0.0
1964	LA-A	108	255	18	51	9	0	1	17	30	37	.200	.284	.247	55	-16	0	2	-1	.917	-2	3-38,1-32,C/S2	-2.0
1965	Cal-A	47	79	8	13	2	0	1	4	10	10	.165	.258	.228	40	-6	1	1	-0	1.000	6	3-15,C-12,2/1	-0.6
1966	Cal-A	103	226	16	54	5	3	0	24	27	32	.239	.320	.288	78	-6	3	3	-1	.991	-9	C-43,1-36,3/2	-1.5
1967	Cal-A	90	201	13	45	7	0	4	21	28	25	.224	.319	.318	92	-1	1	0	0	.962	-7	3-38,C-23,2/1	-0.8
1968	Cal-A	111	297	20	75	9	0	8	35	37	44	.253	.337	.364	117	6	0	0	0	.989	-9	C-85,2-14,3/1	0.3
1969	Cal-A	41	108	5	28	2	0	1	16	18	15	.259	.370	.306	95	0	0	2	-1	1.000	-1	C-36/1-5,2	0.0
	Bos-A	47	127	9	24	2	0	0	11	22	12	.189	.318	.205	46	-8	0	0	0	.978	-2	C-44	-0.8
	Yr	88	235	14	52	4	0	1	27	40	27	.221	.342	.251	68	-8	0	2	-1	.987	-2	C-80/1-5,2	-0.8
1970	Bos-A	59	165	21	39	9	1	3	13	21	25	.236	.326	.358	83	-4	0	0	0	.985	0	C-51	-0.1
Total	10	674	1623	130	365	53	5	21	157	214	225	.225	.317	.303	79	-41	7	8	-3	.987	-26	C-321,3-168/12S	-5.7

■ FRANK SAUCIER
Saucier, Francis Field   b: 5/28/26, Leslie, Mo.   BL/TR, 6'1", 180 lbs.   Deb: 7/21/51

YEAR	TM/L	G	AB	R	H	2B	3B	HR	RBI	BB	SO	AVG	OBP	SLG	PRO+	BR/A	SB	CS	SBR	FA	FR	G/POS	TPR
1951	StL-A	18	14	4	1	1	0	0	1	3	4	.071	.278	.143	16	-2	0	0	0	.714	-1	/O-3	-0.2

■ ED SAUER
Sauer, Edward "Horn"   b: 1/3/20, Pittsburgh, Pa.   d: 7/1/88, Thousand Oaks, Cal   BR/TR, 6'1", 188 lbs.   Deb: 9/17/43   F

YEAR	TM/L	G	AB	R	H	2B	3B	HR	RBI	BB	SO	AVG	OBP	SLG	PRO+	BR/A	SB	CS	SBR	FA	FR	G/POS	TPR
1943	Chi-N	14	55	3	15	3	0	0	9	3	6	.273	.322	.327	89	-1	1			1.000	2	O-13	0.1
1944	Chi-N	23	50	3	11	4	0	0	5	2	6	.220	.250	.300	55	-3	0			.960	-0	O-12	-0.4
1945	*Chi-N	49	93	8	24	4	1	2	11	8	23	.258	.317	.387	97	-1	2			1.000	-2	O-26	-0.4
1949	StL-N	24	45	5	10	2	1	0	1	3	8	.222	.271	.311	53	-3	0			1.000	-2	O-10	-0.5
	Bos-N	79	214	26	57	12	0	3	31	17	34	.266	.323	.364	89	-4	0			.972	-7	O-71	-1.4
	Yr	103	259	31	67	14	1	3	32	20	42	.259	.314	.355	82	-7	0			.974	-9	O-81	-1.9
Total	4	189	457	45	117	25	2	5	57	33	77	.256	.309	.352	83	-11	3			.981	-10	O-132	-2.6

■ HANK SAUER
Sauer, Henry John   b: 3/17/17, Pittsburgh, Pa.   BR/TR, 6'4", 199 lbs.   Deb: 9/9/41   FC

YEAR	TM/L	G	AB	R	H	2B	3B	HR	RBI	BB	SO	AVG	OBP	SLG	PRO+	BR/A	SB	CS	SBR	FA	FR	G/POS	TPR
1941	Cin-N	9	33	4	10	4	0	0	5	1	4	.303	.324	.424	109	0	0			.957	1	/O-8	0.1
1942	Cin-N	7	20	4	5	0	0	2	4	2	2	.250	.318	.550	152	1	0			.976	0	/1-4	0.1
1945	Cin-N	31	116	18	34	1	0	5	20	6	16	.293	.328	.431	112	1	2			.972	1	O-28/1-3	0.1
1948	Cin-N	145	530	78	138	22	1	35	97	60	85	.260	.340	.504	130	20	2			.973	4	*O-132,1-12	1.6
1949	Cin-N	42	152	22	36	6	0	4	16	18	19	.237	.318	.355	79	-4	0			.956	9	O-39/1-1	-0.1
	Chi-N	96	357	59	104	17	1	27	83	37	47	.291	.363	.571	151	24	0			.981	2	O-96	2.0
	Yr	138	509	81	140	23	1	31	99	55	66	.275	.349	.507	129	19	0			.972	7	*O-135/1-1	1.9
1950	Chi-N★	145	540	85	148	32	2	32	103	60	97	.274	.350	.519	127	19	1			.965	-1	*O-125,1-18	1.2
1951	Chi-N	141	525	77	138	19	4	30	89	45	77	.263	.325	.486	113	7	2	1	0	.981	10	*O-132	1.3
1952	Chi-N★	151	567	89	153	31	**3**	**37**	**121**	77	92	.270	.361	.531	143	32	1	2	-1	.983	17	*O-151	4.2
1953	Chi-N	108	378	61	104	16	5	19	60	50	56	.275	.364	.473	109	5	0	0	0	.970	3	*O-105	0.4
1954	Chi-N	142	520	98	150	8	1	41	103	70	68	.288	.379	.563	140	30	2	1	0	.963	-2	*O-141	2.2
1955	Chi-N	79	261	29	55	8	1	12	28	26	47	.211	.287	.387	77	-9	0	0	0	.984	-1	O-68	-1.4
1956	StL-N	75	151	11	45	4	0	5	24	25	31	.298	.408	.424	124	6	0	0	0	1.000	-1	O-37	0.3
1957	NY-N	127	378	46	98	14	1	26	76	49	59	.259	.344	.508	126	13	1	0	0	.992	-12	O-98	-0.4
1958	SF-N	88	236	27	59	8	0	12	46	35	37	.250	.356	.436	111	4	0	0	0	.950	-2	O-67	-0.3
1959	SF-N	13	15	1	1	0	0	1	1	0	7	.067	.067	.267	-17	-3	0	0	0	.000	-0	/O-1	-0.3
Total	15	1399	4796	709	1278	200	19	288	876	561	714	.266	.347	.496	123	146	11	<u>4</u>		.974	22	*O-1228/1-38	11.0

■ DOUG SAUNDERS
Saunders, Douglas Long   b: 12/13/69, Yorba Linda, Cal.   BR/TR, 6', 172 lbs.   Deb: 6/13/93

YEAR	TM/L	G	AB	R	H	2B	3B	HR	RBI	BB	SO	AVG	OBP	SLG	PRO+	BR/A	SB	CS	SBR	FA	FR	G/POS	TPR
1993	NY-N	28	67	8	14	2	0	0	3	3	4	.209	.243	.239	30	-7	0	0	0	.955	1	2-22/3-4,S	-0.5

■ RUSTY SAUNDERS
Saunders, Russell Collier   b: 3/12/06, Trenton, N.J.   d: 11/24/67, Trenton, N.J.   BR/TR, 6'2", 205 lbs.   Deb: 9/24/27

YEAR	TM/L	G	AB	R	H	2B	3B	HR	RBI	BB	SO	AVG	OBP	SLG	PRO+	BR/A	SB	CS	SBR	FA	FR	G/POS	TPR
1927	Phi-A	5	15	2	2	1	0	0	2	3	2	.133	.278	.200	24	-2	0	0	0	.818	0	/O-4	-0.2

■ AL SAUTERS
Sauters, Al   b: Philadelphia, Pa.   Deb: 9/8/1890

YEAR	TM/L	G	AB	R	H	2B	3B	HR	RBI	BB	SO	AVG	OBP	SLG	PRO+	BR/A	SB	CS	SBR	FA	FR	G/POS	TPR
1890	Phi-a	14	41	1	4	0	0	0		1	1	.098	.288	.098	14	-4	0			.850	-4	3-11/O-2,2	-0.7

■ DON SAVAGE
Savage, Donald Anthony   b: 3/5/19, Bloomfield, N.J.   d: 12/25/61, Montclair, N.J.   BR/TR, 6', 180 lbs.   Deb: 4/18/44

YEAR	TM/L	G	AB	R	H	2B	3B	HR	RBI	BB	SO	AVG	OBP	SLG	PRO+	BR/A	SB	CS	SBR	FA	FR	G/POS	TPR
1944	NY-A	71	239	31	63	7	5	4	24	20	41	.264	.323	.385	98	-1	1	1	-0	.946	-10	3-60	-1.2
1945	NY-A	34	58	5	13	1	0	0	3	3	14	.224	.262	.241	44	-4	1	0	0	.891	1	3-14/O-2	-0.3
Total	2	105	297	36	76	8	5	4	27	23	55	.256	.312	.357	88	-5	2	1	0	.935	-10	/3-74,O-2	-1.5

■ JIMMIE SAVAGE
Savage, James Harold   b: 8/29/1883, Southington, Conn.   d: 6/26/40, New Castle, Pa.   BB/TR, 5'5", 150 lbs.   Deb: 9/3/12

YEAR	TM/L	G	AB	R	H	2B	3B	HR	RBI	BB	SO	AVG	OBP	SLG	PRO+	BR/A	SB	CS	SBR	FA	FR	G/POS	TPR
1912	Phi-N	2	3	1	0	0	0	0	0	1	0	.000	.250	.000	-27	-1	0			.750	-0	/2-1	-0.1
1914	Pit-F	132	479	81	136	9	9	1	26	67	32	.284	.372	.347	88	-7	17			.963	-9	O-93,3-29,S/2	-1.8

YEAR	TM/L	G	AB	R	H	2B	3B	HR	RBI	BB	SO	AVG	OBP	SLG	PRO+	BR/A	SB	CS	SBR	FA	FR	G/POS	TPR
1915	Pit-F	14	21	0	3	0	0	0	0	1	0	.143	.182	.143	-13	-3	0			1.000	-1	/O-3,3-1	-0.5
Total	3	148	503	82	139	9	9	1	26	69	32	.276	.364	.336	83	-10	17			.964	-10	/O-96,3-30,S2	-2.4

■ TED SAVAGE
Savage, Theodore Edmund (b: Ephesian Savage) b: 2/21/36, Venice, Ill. BR/TR, 6'1", 185 lbs. Deb: 4/9/62

YEAR	TM/L	G	AB	R	H	2B	3B	HR	RBI	BB	SO	AVG	OBP	SLG	PRO+	BR/A	SB	CS	SBR	FA	FR	G/POS	TPR
1962	Phi-N	127	335	54	89	11	2	7	39	40	66	.266	.347	.373	96	-1	16	5	2	.974	1	*O-109	-0.4
1963	Pit-N	85	149	22	29	2	1	5	14	14	31	.195	.268	.322	69	-6	4	3	-1	.943	-5	O-47	-1.5
1965	StL-N	30	63	7	10	3	0	1	4	6	9	.159	.232	.254	34	-6	1	1	-0	.938	-2	O-20	-0.9
1966	StL-N	16	29	4	5	2	1	0	3	4	7	.172	.273	.310	61	-2	4	0	1	1.000	-1	/O-7	-0.2
1967	StL-N	9	8	1	1	0	0	0	0	1	3	.125	.222	.125	2	-1	0	0		.000	0	H	-0.1
	Chi-N	96	225	40	49	10	1	5	33	40	54	.218	.348	.338	93	-1	7	6	-2	.979	-5	O-86/3-1	-1.2
	Yr	105	233	41	50	10	1	5	33	41	57	.215	.344	.330	90	-1	7	6	-2	.979	-5	O-86/3-1	-1.3
1968	Chi-N	3	8	0	2	0	0	0	0	0	1	.250	.250	.250	47	-1	0	1	-1	1.000	-1	/O-2	-0.2
	LA-N	61	126	7	26	6	1	2	7	10	20	.206	.270	.317	82	-3	1	2	-1	.985	0	O-39	-0.6
	Yr	64	134	7	28	6	1	2	7	10	21	.209	.269	.313	80	-4	1	3	-2	.986	-1	O-41	-0.8
1969	Cin-N	68	110	20	25	7	0	2	11	20	27	.227	.346	.345	90	-1	3	0	1	.983	-6	O-42/2-1	-0.7
1970	Mil-A	114	276	43	77	10	5	12	50	57	44	.279	.406	.482	143	18	10	6	1	.953	-10	O-82/1-1	0.4
1971	Mil-A	14	17	2	3	0	0	0	1	5	4	.176	.364	.176	58	-1	1	0	0	1.000	-2	/O-6	-0.3
	KC-A	19	29	2	5	0	0	0	1	3	6	.172	.250	.172	22	-3	2	0	1	1.000	-1	O-9	-0.5
	Yr	33	46	4	8	0	0	0	2	8	10	.174	.296	.174	36	-4	3	0	1	1.000	-3	O-15	-0.8
Total	9	642	1375	202	321	51	11	34	163	200	272	.233	.335	.361	94	-6	49	24	0	.970	-32	O-449/1-1,23	-6.2

■ BOB SAVERINE
Saverine, Robert Paul "Rabbit" b: 6/2/41, Norwalk, Conn. BB/TR, 5'9", 165 lbs. Deb: 9/12/59

YEAR	TM/L	G	AB	R	H	2B	3B	HR	RBI	BB	SO	AVG	OBP	SLG	PRO+	BR/A	SB	CS	SBR	FA	FR	G/POS	TPR
1959	Bal-A	1	0	1	0	0	0	0	0	0	0	—	—	—			0	0		.000	0	R	0.0
1962	Bal-A	8	21	2	5	2	0	0	3	1	3	.238	.273	.333	66	-1	0	2	-1	1.000	2	/2-7	0.0
1963	Bal-A	115	167	21	39	1	2	1	12	25	44	.234	.333	.281	77	-4	8	3	1	.976	-9	O-59,2-19,S	-1.2
1964	Bal-A	46	34	14	5	1	0	0	0	3	6	.147	.216	.176	11	-4	3	1	0	1.000	5	S-15/O-2	0.1
1966	Was-A	120	406	54	102	10	4	5	24	27	62	.251	.301	.333	83	-9	4	3	-1	.972	-19	2-70,3-26,S/O	-2.5
1967	Was-A	89	233	22	55	13	0	0	8	17	34	.236	.288	.292	75	-7	8	0	2	.957	-20	2-48,S-10/3O	-2.4
Total	6	379	861	114	206	27	6	6	47	73	149	.239	.300	.305	76	-26	23	9	2	.971	-40	2-144/O-72,S3	-6.0

■ CARL SAWATSKI
Sawatski, Carl Ernest "Swats" b: 11/4/27, Shickshinny, Pa. d: 11/24/91, Little Rock, Ark. BL/TR, 5'10", 210 lbs. Deb: 9/29/48

YEAR	TM/L	G	AB	R	H	2B	3B	HR	RBI	BB	SO	AVG	OBP	SLG	PRO+	BR/A	SB	CS	SBR	FA	FR	G/POS	TPR
1948	Chi-N	2	2	0	0	0	0	0	0	0	0	.000	.000	.000	-99	-1	0			.000	0	H	-0.1
1950	Chi-N	38	103	4	18	1	0	1	7	11	19	.175	.254	.214	25	-11	0			.983	-1	C-32	-1.1
1953	Chi-N	43	59	5	13	3	0	1	5	7	7	.220	.303	.322	62	-3	0	0	0	.943	-3	C-15	-0.3
1954	Chi-A	43	109	6	20	3	3	1	12	15	20	.183	.282	.294	56	-7	0	0	0	.987	-1	C-33	-0.5
1957	*Mil-N	58	105	13	25	4	0	6	17	10	15	.238	.316	.448	110	1	0	0	0	.986	6	C-28	0.8
1958	Mil-N	10	10	1	1	0	0	0	1	2	5	.100	.250	.100	-3	-3	0	0	0	1.000	1	/C-3	-0.1
	Phi-N	60	183	12	42	4	1	5	12	16	42	.230	.302	.344	72	-8	0	0	0	.986	-3	C-53	-0.8
	Yr	70	193	13	43	4	1	5	13	18	47	.223	.299	.332	68	-9	0	0	0	.987	-3	C-56	-0.9
1959	Phi-N	74	198	15	58	10	0	6	43	32	36	.293	.394	.480	129	9	0	0	0	.979	-14	C-69	-0.1
1960	StL-N	78	179	16	41	4	0	6	27	22	24	.229	.313	.352	75	-6	0	0	0	.993	-7	C-67	-1.0
1961	StL-N	86	174	23	52	8	0	10	33	25	17	.299	.387	.517	125	6	0	0	0	.996	-7	C-60/O-1	0.2
1962	StL-N	85	222	26	56	9	1	13	42	36	38	.252	.357	.477	111	3	0	0	0	.997	-1	C-70	0.5
1963	StL-N	56	105	12	25	0	0	6	14	15	22	.238	.333	.410	103	1	2	0	1	.986	-5	C-27	-0.3
Total	11	633	1449	133	351	46	5	58	213	191	251	.242	.333	.401	92	-16	2	0		.988	-32	C-457/O-1	-2.8

■ CARL SAWYER
Sawyer, Carl Everett "Huck" b: 10/19/1890, Seattle, Wash. d: 1/17/57, Los Angeles, Cal. BR/TR, 5'11", 160 lbs. Deb: 9/11/15

YEAR	TM/L	G	AB	R	H	2B	3B	HR	RBI	BB	SO	AVG	OBP	SLG	PRO+	BR/A	SB	CS	SBR	FA	FR	G/POS	TPR
1915	Was-A	10	32	8	8	1	0	0	3	4	5	.250	.351	.281	88	-0	2			.964	-2	/2-6,S-4	-0.2
1916	Was-A	16	31	3	6	1	0	0	2	4	4	.194	.306	.226	60	-1	3			.963	2	/2-6,S-5,3	0.1
Total	2	26	63	11	14	2	0	0	5	8	9	.222	.329	.254	74	-2	5			.964	-1	/2-12,S-9,3	-0.1

■ DAVE SAX
Sax, David John b: 9/22/58, Sacramento, Cal. BR/TR, 6', 185 lbs. Deb: 9/1/82 F

YEAR	TM/L	G	AB	R	H	2B	3B	HR	RBI	BB	SO	AVG	OBP	SLG	PRO+	BR/A	SB	CS	SBR	FA	FR	G/POS	TPR
1982	LA-N	2	2	0	0	0	0	0	0	0	0	.000	.000	.000	-99	-1	0	0	0	1.000	-0	/O-1	-0.1
1983	LA-N	7	8	0	0	0	0	0	1	0	0	.000	.000	.000	-99	-2	0	0	0	.917	-0	/C-4	-0.2
1985	Bos-A	22	36	2	11	3	0	0	6	3	3	.306	.359	.389	101	0	0	1	-1	.985	-2	C-16/O-4	-0.2
1986	Bos-A	4	11	1	5	1	0	1	1	0	1	.455	.455	.818	237	2	0	0	0	1.000	-1	/C-2,1-1	0.1
1987	Bos-A	2	3	0	0	0	0	0	0	0	1	.000	.000	.000	-97	-0	0	0	0	1.000	1	/C-2	0.0
Total	5	37	60	3	16	4	0	1	8	3	5	.267	.302	.383	84	-1	0	1	-1	.980	-2	/C-24,O-5,1	-0.4

■ OLLIE SAX
Sax, Erik Oliver b: 11/5/04, Branford, Conn. d: 3/21/82, Newark, N.J. BR/TR, 5'8", 164 lbs. Deb: 4/13/28

YEAR	TM/L	G	AB	R	H	2B	3B	HR	RBI	BB	SO	AVG	OBP	SLG	PRO+	BR/A	SB	CS	SBR	FA	FR	G/POS	TPR
1928	StL-A	16	17	4	3	0	0	0	0	5	3	.176	.364	.176	45	-1	0	0	0	.955	3	/3-9	0.2

■ STEVE SAX
Sax, Stephen Louis b: 1/29/60, Sacramento, Cal. BR/TR, 5'11", 185 lbs. Deb: 8/18/81 F

YEAR	TM/L	G	AB	R	H	2B	3B	HR	RBI	BB	SO	AVG	OBP	SLG	PRO+	BR/A	SB	CS	SBR	FA	FR	G/POS	TPR
1981	*LA-N	31	119	15	33	2	0	2	9	7	14	.277	.317	.345	91	-2	5	7	-3	.975	2	2-29	-0.1
1982	LA-N★	150	638	88	180	23	7	4	47	49	53	.282	.335	.359	97	-3	49	19	3	.977	-9	*2-149	0.0
1983	*LA-N★	155	623	94	175	18	5	5	41	58	73	.281	.343	.350	93	-5	56	30	-1	.961	-30	*2-152	-3.0
1984	LA-N	145	569	70	138	24	4	1	35	47	53	.243	.301	.304	71	-21	34	19	-1	.973	12	*2-141	-0.6
1985	*LA-N	136	488	62	136	8	4	1	42	54	43	.279	.354	.318	92	-3	27	11	2	.969	-9	*2-135/3-1	-0.6
1986	LA-N★	157	633	91	210	43	4	6	56	59	58	.332	.391	.441	139	33	40	17	2	.980	-5	*2-154	3.7
1987	LA-N	157	610	84	171	22	7	6	46	44	61	.280	.332	.369	88	-11	37	11	5	.982	1	*2-152/3-1,O	0.3
1988	*LA-N	160	632	70	175	19	4	5	57	45	51	.277	.326	.343	95	-4	42	12	5	.981	-19	*2-158	-1.2
1989	NY-A★	158	651	88	205	26	3	5	63	52	44	.315	.366	.387	114	13	43	17	3	**.987**	-10	*2-158	1.1
1990	NY-A★	155	615	70	160	24	2	4	42	49	46	.260	.319	.325	80	-16	43	9	8	.987	-13	*2-154	-1.9
1991	NY-A	158	652	85	198	38	2	10	56	41	38	.304	.348	.414	110	8	31	11	3	.990	-7	*2-149/3-5,D	0.7
1992	Chi-A	143	567	74	134	26	4	4	47	43	42	.236	.292	.317	72	-22	30	12	2	.972	-28	*2-141/D-1	-4.6
1993	Chi-A	57	119	20	28	5	0	1	8	8	6	.235	.283	.303	59	-7	7	3	0	1.000	-5	O-32,D-21/2	-1.2
1994	Oak-A	7	24	2	6	0	1	0	1	0	2	.250	.250	.333	53	-2	0	0	0	1.000	4	/2-6	0.1
Total	14	1769	6940	913	1949	278	47	54	550	556	584	.281	.336	.358	95	-41	444	178	26	.978	-117	*2-1679/O-33,D3	-7.3

■ JIMMY SAY
Say, James I. b: 1862, Baltimore, Md. d: 6/23/1894, Baltimore, Md. Deb: 7/22/1882 F

YEAR	TM/L	G	AB	R	H	2B	3B	HR	RBI	BB	SO	AVG	OBP	SLG	PRO+	BR/A	SB	CS	SBR	FA	FR	G/POS	TPR
1882	Lou-a	1	4	1	1	0	0	0		0		.250	.250	.250	73	-0				.333	-1	/3-1	-0.1
	Phi-a	22	82	12	17	2	0	1		1		.207	.217	.268	56	-4				.884	1	S-22	-0.2
	Yr	23	86	13	18	2	0	1		1		.209	.218	.267	57	-4				.884	0	S-22/3-1	-0.3
1884	Wil-U	16	59	3	13	1	2	0		1		.220	.233	.305	44	-5				.733	-3	3-16	-0.7
	KC-U	2	8	0	2	0	0	0		0		.250	.250	.250	42	-1				.200	-2	/3-2	-0.3
	Yr	18	67	3	15	1	2	0		1		.224	.235	.299	44	-5				.680	-5	3-18	-1.0
1887	Cle-a	16	64	9	24	5	3	0		1		.375	.385	.547	163	5	0			.714	-4	3-16	0.1
Total	3	57	217	25	57	8	5	1		3		.263	.273	.359	83	-5	0			.690	-9	/3-35,S-22	-1.2

■ LOU SAY
Say, Louis I. b: 2/4/1854, Baltimore, Md. d: 6/5/30, Fallston, Md. BR/TR, 5'7", 145 lbs. Deb: 4/14/1873 F

YEAR	TM/L	G	AB	R	H	2B	3B	HR	RBI	BB	SO	AVG	OBP	SLG	PRO+	BR/A	SB	CS	SBR	FA	FR	G/POS	TPR
1873	Mar-n	3	12	1	2	0	0	0		2	0	0	.167	.167	.167	-2	-1						/S-2,O-1	-0.1
1874	Bal-n	18	67	4	14	3	0	0				.209	.209	.254	47	-1						S-18	-0.4
1875	Was-n	11	39	4	10	0	0	0				.256	.256	.256	81	-1						/S-8,2-1,O	-0.1
1880	Cin-N	48	191	14	38	8	1	0	15	6	4	31	.199	.215	.251	58	-8				.832	1	S-48	-0.4
1882	Phi-a	49	199	35	45	4	3	1		8		.226	.256	.291	75	-6				.867	6	S-49	0.2

YEAR	TM/L	G	AB	R	H	2B	3B	HR	RBI	BB	SO	AVG	OBP	SLG	PRO+	BR/A	SB	CS	SBR	FA	FR	G/POS	TPR
1883	Bal-a	74	324	52	83	13	2	1		10		.256	.278	.318	89	-5				.794	7	*S-74	0.4
1884	Bal-U	78	339	65	81	14	2	2		11		.239	.263	.310	50	-25				.795	2	*S-78	-2.0
	KC-U	17	70	6	14	2	0	1		2		.200	.222	.271	38	-6				.860	9	S-16/2-1	0.2
	Yr	95	409	71	95	16	2	3		13		.232	.256	.303	48	-30				.808	10	S-94/2-1	-1.8
Total	3 n	32	118	9	26	3	0	0	2	0		.220	.220	.246	53	-6						/S-28,O-2,2	-0.6
Total	4	266	1123	172	261	41	8	5	15	35	31	.232	.256	.297	65	-49				.820	24	S-265/2-1	-1.6

■ JERRY SCALA
Scala, Gerard Daniel b: 9/27/26, Bayonne, N.J. BL/TR, 5'11", 178 lbs. Deb: 4/22/48

YEAR	TM/L	G	AB	R	H	2B	3B	HR	RBI	BB	SO	AVG	OBP	SLG	PRO+	BR/A	SB	CS	SBR	FA	FR	G/POS	TPR
1948	Chi-A	3	6	1	0	0	0	0	0	0	3	.000	.000	.000	-99	-2	0	0	0	1.000	-0	/O-2	-0.2
1949	Chi-A	37	120	17	30	7	1	1	13	17	19	.250	.348	.350	88	-2	3	3	-1	.988	-3	O-37	-0.8
1950	Chi-A	40	67	8	13	2	1	0	6	10	10	.194	.299	.254	44	-6	0	0	0	1.000	-4	O-23	-1.0
Total	3	80	193	26	43	9	2	1	19	27	32	.223	.321	.306	67	-9	3	3	-1	.993	-7	/O-62	-2.0

■ SKEETER SCALZI
Scalzi, Frank John b: 6/16/13, Lafferty, Ohio d: 8/25/84, Pittsburgh, Pa. BR/TR, 5'6", 160 lbs. Deb: 7/21/39

YEAR	TM/L	G	AB	R	H	2B	3B	HR	RBI	BB	SO	AVG	OBP	SLG	PRO+	BR/A	SB	CS	SBR	FA	FR	G/POS	TPR
1939	NY-N	11	18	3	6	0	0	0	0	3	2	.333	.429	.333	106	0	1			.875	2	/S-5,3-1	0.3

■ JOHNNY SCALZI
Scalzi, John Anthony b: 3/22/07, Stamford, Conn. d: 9/27/62, Port Chester, N.Y BR/TR, 5'7", 170 lbs. Deb: 6/19/31

YEAR	TM/L	G	AB	R	H	2B	3B	HR	RBI	BB	SO	AVG	OBP	SLG	PRO+	BR/A	SB	CS	SBR	FA	FR	G/POS	TPR
1931	Bos-N	2	1	0	0	0	0	0	0	0	1	.000	.000	.000	-99	-0	0			.000	0	H	0.0

■ MORT SCANLAN
Scanlan, Mortimer J. b: 3/18/1861, Chicago, Ill. d: 12/29/28, Chicago, Ill. 6'1", 186 lbs. Deb: 4/21/1890

YEAR	TM/L	G	AB	R	H	2B	3B	HR	RBI	BB	SO	AVG	OBP	SLG	PRO+	BR/A	SB	CS	SBR	FA	FR	G/POS	TPR
1890	NY-N	3	10	0	0	0	0	0	0	2	5	.000	.167	.000	-50	-2	1			1.000	-0	/1-3	-0.2

■ PATRICK SCANLAN
Scanlan, Patrick J. b: 3/25/1861, Novs Scotia d: 7/17/13, Springfield, Mass. Deb: 7/4/1884

YEAR	TM/L	G	AB	R	H	2B	3B	HR	RBI	BB	SO	AVG	OBP	SLG	PRO+	BR/A	SB	CS	SBR	FA	FR	G/POS	TPR
1884	Bos-U	6	24	2	7	1	0	0		0		.292	.292	.333	71	-1				.800	0	/O-6	-0.1

■ PAT SCANLON
Scanlon, James Patrick b: 9/23/52, Minneapolis, Minn. BL/TR, 6', 180 lbs. Deb: 9/27/74

YEAR	TM/L	G	AB	R	H	2B	3B	HR	RBI	BB	SO	AVG	OBP	SLG	PRO+	BR/A	SB	CS	SBR	FA	FR	G/POS	TPR
1974	Mon-N	2	4	1	1	0	0	0	0	0	1	.250	.250	.250	38	-0	0	0	0	1.000	1	/3-1	0.0
1975	Mon-N	60	109	5	20	3	1	2	15	17	25	.183	.294	.284	58	-6	0	1	-1	.957	2	3-28/1-1	-0.5
1976	Mon-N	11	27	2	5	1	0	1	2	2	5	.185	.241	.333	59	-2	0	0	0	.842	-1	/3-7,1-1	-0.3
1977	SD-N	47	79	9	15	3	0	1	11	12	20	.190	.297	.266	58	-5	0	0	0	.957	-5	2-15,3-11/O	-0.9
Total	4	120	219	17	41	7	1	4	28	31	51	.187	.288	.283	58	-13	0	1	-1	.938	-3	/3-47,2-15,1O	-1.7

■ RUSS SCARRITT
Scarritt, Russell Mallory b: 1/14/03, Pensacola, Fla. BL/TR, 5'10.5", 165 lbs. Deb: 4/18/29

YEAR	TM/L	G	AB	R	H	2B	3B	HR	RBI	BB	SO	AVG	OBP	SLG	PRO+	BR/A	SB	CS	SBR	FA	FR	G/POS	TPR
1929	Bos-A	151	540	69	159	26	17	1	71	34	38	.294	.337	.411	94	-6	13	11	-3	.944	1	*O-145	-1.7
1930	Bos-A	113	447	48	129	17	8	2	48	12	49	.289	.312	.376	76	-17	4	7	-3	.967	4	*O-110	-2.1
1931	Bos-A	10	39	2	6	1	0	0	1	2	2	.154	.195	.179	-1	-6	0	0	0	1.000	1	/O-9	-0.5
1932	Phi-N	11	11	0	2	0	0	0	0	1	2	.182	.250	.182	16	-1	0			1.000	-0	/O-1	-0.1
Total	4	285	1037	119	296	44	25	3	120	49	91	.285	.320	.385	82	-30	17	18		.956	6	O-265	-4.4

■ LES SCARSELLA
Scarsella, Leslie George b: 11/23/13, Santa Cruz, Cal. d: 12/17/58, San Francisco, Cal BL/TL, 5'11", 185 lbs. Deb: 9/15/35

YEAR	TM/L	G	AB	R	H	2B	3B	HR	RBI	BB	SO	AVG	OBP	SLG	PRO+	BR/A	SB	CS	SBR	FA	FR	G/POS	TPR
1935	Cin-N	6	10	4	2	1	0	0	3	1		.200	.385	.300	89	0	0			1.000	1	/1-2	0.0
1936	Cin-N	115	485	63	152	21	9	3	65	14	36	.313	.335	.412	107	3	6			.989	2	*1-115	-0.7
1937	Cin-N	110	329	35	81	11	4	3	34	17	26	.246	.285	.331	70	-14	5			.984	-5	1-65,O-14	-2.7
1939	Cin-N	16	14	0	2	0	0	0	0	0	1	.143	.143	.143	-23	-2	0			.000	0	H	-0.2
1940	Bos-N	18	60	7	18	4	3	0	8	3	5	.300	.344	.417	115	1	2			.986	-1	1-15	-0.1
Total	5	265	898	109	255	34	16	6	109	37	70	.284	.315	.378	92	-13	13			.988	-4	1-197/O-14	-3.7

■ STEVE SCARSONE
Scarsone, Steven Wayne b: 4/11/66, Anaheim, Cal. BR/TR, 6'2", 170 lbs. Deb: 5/15/92

YEAR	TM/L	G	AB	R	H	2B	3B	HR	RBI	BB	SO	AVG	OBP	SLG	PRO+	BR/A	SB	CS	SBR	FA	FR	G/POS	TPR
1992	Phi-N	7	13	1	2	0	0	0	0	1	6	.154	.214	.154	6	-2	0	0	0	1.000	-2	/2-3	-0.4
	Bal-A	11	17	2	3	0	0	0	1	1	6	.176	.222	.176	13	-2	0	0	0	.889	-1	/2-5,3-2,S	-0.3
1993	SF-N	44	103	16	26	9	0	2	15	4	32	.252	.280	.398	82	-3	0	1	-1	1.000	-5	2-20/3-8,1	-0.8
1994	SF-N	52	103	21	28	8	0	2	13	10	20	.272	.336	.408	96	-1	0	2	-1	.990	9	2-22/3-8,1S	0.8
Total	3	114	236	40	59	17	0	4	28	16	64	.250	.298	.373	79	-7	0	3	-2	.990	1	/2-50,3-18,1S	-0.7

■ PAUL SCHAAL
Schaal, Paul b: 3/3/43, Pittsburgh, Pa. BR/TR, 5'11", 180 lbs. Deb: 9/3/64

YEAR	TM/L	G	AB	R	H	2B	3B	HR	RBI	BB	SO	AVG	OBP	SLG	PRO+	BR/A	SB	CS	SBR	FA	FR	G/POS	TPR
1964	LA-A	17	32	3	4	0	0	0	2	5	.125	.176	.125	-16	-5	0	1	-1	1.000	-1	/2-9,3-9	-0.7
1965	Cal-A	155	483	48	108	12	2	9	45	61	88	.224	.312	.313	80	-12	6	3	0	.970	-10	*3-153/2-1	-2.8
1966	Cal-A	138	386	59	94	15	7	6	24	68	56	.244	.364	.365	113	9	6	4	-1	.948	-2	*3-131	0.4
1967	Cal-A	99	272	31	51	9	1	6	20	38	39	.188	.289	.294	76	-8	2	2	-1	.970	-2	3-88/S-2,2	-1.2
1968	Cal-A	60	219	22	46	7	1	2	16	29	25	.210	.308	.279	82	-4	5	7	-3	.958	9	3-58	0.3
1969	KC-A	61	205	22	54	6	0	1	13	25	27	.263	.349	.307	84	-3	2	1	0	.897	-19	3-49/2-6,S	-2.2
1970	KC-A	124	380	50	102	12	3	5	35	43	39	.268	.344	.355	93	-3	7	4	-0	.938	-16	3-97,S-10/2	-2.0
1971	KC-A	161	548	80	150	31	6	11	63	103	51	.274	.391	.412	129	25	7	5	-1	.940	-12	*3-161	1.1
1972	KC-A	127	435	47	99	19	3	6	41	61	59	.228	.325	.326	95	-1	1	3	-2	.947	-16	3-123/S-1	-2.3
1973	KC-A	121	396	61	114	14	3	8	42	63	45	.288	.392	.399	114	10	5	6	-2	.913	-12	*3-121	-0.5
1974	KC-A	12	34	3	6	2	0	1	4	5	5	.176	.300	.324	75	-1	0	0	0	.949	1	3-12	-0.1
	Cal-A	53	165	10	41	5	0	2	20	18	27	.248	.322	.315	89	-2	2	2	-1	.903	-10	3-51	-1.4
	Yr	65	199	13	47	7	0	3	24	23	32	.236	.318	.317	86	-3	2	2	-1	.914	-9	3-63	-1.5
Total	11	1128	3555	436	869	132	26	57	323	516	466	.244	.344	.344	98	4	43	38	-10	.943	-91	*3-1053/2-23,S	-11.4

■ GERMANY SCHAEFER
Schaefer, Herman A. b: 2/4/1877, Chicago, Ill. d: 5/16/19, Saranac Lake, N.Y. BR/TR, 5'9", 175 lbs. Deb: 10/5/01

YEAR	TM/L	G	AB	R	H	2B	3B	HR	RBI	BB	SO	AVG	OBP	SLG	PRO+	BR/A	SB	CS	SBR	FA	FR	G/POS	TPR
1901	Chi-N	2	5	0	3	1	0	0	2		.600	.714	.800	352	2	0			1.000	1	/2-1,3-1	0.3
1902	Chi-N	81	291	32	57	2	3	0	14	19		.196	.250	.223	48	-18	12			.864	-9	3-75/1-3,OS	-2.8
1905	Det-A	153	554	64	135	17	9	2	47	45		.244	.302	.318	96	-3	19			.955	7	*2-151/S-3	0.6
1906	Det-A	124	446	48	106	14	3	2	42	32		.238	.290	.296	81	-10	31			.948	9	*2-114/S-7	0.0
1907	*Det-A	109	372	45	96	12	3	1	32	30		.258	.313	.315	97	-1	21			.961	-6	2-74,S-18,3/O	-0.7
1908	*Det-A	153	584	96	151	20	10	3	52	37		.259	.304	.342	106	2	40			.918	4	S-68,2-58,3	0.9
1909	Det-A	87	280	26	70	12	0	0	22	14		.250	.286	.293	79	-7	12			.966	14	2-86/O-1	0.6
	Was-A	37	128	13	31	5	1	0	4	6		.242	.281	.320	94	-1	2			.941	0	2-32/3-1	-0.2
	Yr	124	408	39	101	17	1	0	26	20		.248	.284	.301	84	-8	14			.960	14	*2-118/O-1,3	0.4
1910	Was-A	74	229	27	63	6	0	0	14	25		.275	.352	.345	124	7	17			.953	-1	2-35,O-26/3	0.5
1911	Was-A	125	440	74	147	14	7	0	45	57		.334	.412	.398	129	19	22			.980	-1	*1-108/O-7	1.8
1912	Was-A	60	166	21	41	7	3	0	19	23		.247	.342	.325	90	-2	11			.900	-11	O-19,1-15,2/P	-1.4
1913	Was-A	54	100	17	32	1	1	0	7	15	12	.320	.419	.350	123	4	6			.926	-2	2-16/1-6,3PO	0.1
1914	Was-A	30	29	6	7	1	0	0	2	3	5	.241	.313	.276	74	-1	4	1	1	1.000	0	/2-3,O-3	0.0
1915	New-F	59	154	26	33	5	3	0	8	25	11	.214	.328	.286	69	-6	3			.952	1	/O-17,1-13/32	-0.9
1916	NY-A	1	1	0	0	0	0	0	0	0		.000	.000	.000	-98	-0				.000	0	/O-1	0.0
1918	Cle-A	1	5	2	0	0	0	0	0	0	0	.000	.000	.000	-91	-1	1			1.000	-0	/2-1	-0.2
Total	15	1150	3784	497	972	117	48	9	308	333	28	.257	.319	.320	96	-15	201	1		.954	4	2-588,1-145,3/SOP	-1.4

■ JEFF SCHAEFER
Schaefer, Jeffrey Scott b: 5/31/60, Patchogue, N.Y. BR/TR, 5'10", 170 lbs. Deb: 4/7/89

YEAR	TM/L	G	AB	R	H	2B	3B	HR	RBI	BB	SO	AVG	OBP	SLG	PRO+	BR/A	SB	CS	SBR	FA	FR	G/POS	TPR
1989	Chi-A	15	10	2	1	0	0	0	0	2	1	.100	.100	.100	-45	-2	1	1	-0	.900	1	/S-5,2-4,3D	-0.1
1990	Sea-A	55	107	11	22	3	0	0	6	3	11	.206	.241	.234	33	-10	4	1	1	.933	11	3-26,S-24/2	0.4
1991	Sea-A	84	164	19	41	7	1	1	11	5	25	.250	.272	.323	64	-8	3	1	0	.968	2	S-46,3-30,2/D	-0.3
1992	Sea-A	65	70	5	8	2	0	1	3	2	10	.114	.139	.186	-10	-10	0	1	-1	.922	14	S-33,3-21/2D	0.5

YEAR	TM/L	G	AB	R	H	2B	3B	HR	RBI	BB	SO	AVG	OBP	SLG	PRO+	BR/A	SB	CS	SBR	FA	FR	G/POS	TPR
1994	Oak-A	6	8	0	1	0	0	0	0	0	1	.125	.125	.125	-38	-2	0	0	0	.800	-1	/3-3,S-2,1	-0.2
Total	5	225	359	37	73	12	1	2	20	10	49	.203	.229	.259	35	-32	8	4	0	.957	28	S-110/3-84,2D1	0.3

■ HARRY SCHAFER   Schafer, Harry C. "Silk Stocking" b: 8/14/1846, Philadelphia, Pa.   d: 2/28/35, Philadelphia, Pa.   BR/TR, 5'9.5", 143 lbs.   Deb: 5/5/1871

YEAR	TM/L	G	AB	R	H	2B	3B	HR	RBI	BB	SO	AVG	OBP	SLG	PRO+	BR/A	SB	CS	SBR	FA	FR	G/POS	TPR
1871	Bos-n	31	149	38	42	7	5	0	28	3	1	.282	.296	.396	94	-2	13					*3-31/2-1	-0.3
1872	Bos-n	48	226	50	66	12	5	1	37	0	8	.292	.292	.403	106	-0						*3-43/O-5	-0.2
1873	Bos-n	60	295	65	79	8	3	2	43	3	1	.268	.275	.336	73	-12						*3-47,O-13	-1.1
1874	Bos-n	71	325	69	84	13	3	1		0		.258	.258	.326	80	-8						*3-71	-0.7
1875	Bos-n	51	216	47	62	9	0	0		0		.287	.287	.329	108	1						*3-50/O-1	0.1
1876	Bos-N	70	286	47	72	11	0	0	35	4	11	.252	.262	.290	82	-5				.810	3	*3-70	0.0
1877	Bos-N	33	141	20	39	5	2	0	13	0	7	.277	.277	.340	90	-2				.621	-12	O-23/3-9,S	-1.3
1878	Bos-N	2	8	0	1	0	0	0		0		.125	.125	.125	-16	-1				1.000	-1	/O-2	-0.2
Total	5 n	261	1211	269	333	49	16	4	108	6	10	.275	.279	.352	89	-21						3-242/O-19,2	-2.2
Total	3	105	435	67	112	16	2	0	48	4	19	.257	.264	.303	83	-8				.810	-9	/3-79,O-25,S	-1.5

■ JIMMIE SCHAFFER   Schaffer, Jimmie Ronald b: 4/5/36, Limeport, Pa.   BR/TR, 5'9", 185 lbs.   Deb: 5/20/61   C

YEAR	TM/L	G	AB	R	H	2B	3B	HR	RBI	BB	SO	AVG	OBP	SLG	PRO+	BR/A	SB	CS	SBR	FA	FR	G/POS	TPR
1961	StL-N	68	153	15	39	7	0	1	16	9	29	.255	.301	.320	59	-9	0	0	0	.996	4	C-68	-0.3
1962	StL-N	70	66	7	16	2	1	0	6	6	16	.242	.306	.303	58	-4	1	0	0	.993	7	C-69	0.4
1963	Chi-N	57	142	17	34	7	0	7	19	11	35	.239	.294	.437	102	-0	0	0	0	.996	1	C-54	0.3
1964	Chi-N	54	122	9	25	6	1	2	9	17	17	.205	.307	.320	74	-4	2	4	-2	.970	-8	C-43	-1.2
1965	Chi-A	17	31	2	6	3	1	0	1	3	4	.194	.265	.355	79	-1	0	0	0	1.000	3	C-14	0.2
	NY-N	24	37	0	5	2	0	0	0	1	15	.135	.158	.189	-3	-5	0	0	0	.968	-1	C-21	-0.5
1966	Phi-N	8	15	2	2	1	0	1	4	1	7	.133	.188	.400	58	-1	0	0	0	.952	-1	/C-6	-0.1
1967	Phi-N	2	2	1	0	0	0	0	0	1	1	.000	.333	.000	3	-0	0	0	0	1.000	0	/C-1	0.0
1968	Cin-N	4	6	0	1	0	0	0	1	0	3	.167	.167	.167	0	-1	0	0	0	1.000	-1	/C-2	-0.2
Total	8	304	574	53	128	28	3	11	56	49	127	.223	.286	.340	69	-24	3	4	-2	.989	5	C-278	-1.4

■ JOHNNY SCHAIVE   Schaive, John Edward b: 2/25/34, Springfield, Ill.   BR/TR, 5'8", 175 lbs.   Deb: 9/19/58

YEAR	TM/L	G	AB	R	H	2B	3B	HR	RBI	BB	SO	AVG	OBP	SLG	PRO+	BR/A	SB	CS	SBR	FA	FR	G/POS	TPR
1958	Was-A	7	24	1	6	0	0	0	1	1	4	.250	.280	.250	48	-2	0	0	0	1.000	-1	/2-6	-0.2
1959	Was-A	16	59	3	9	2	0	0	2	0	7	.153	.167	.186	-3	-8	0	0	0	.977	4	2-16	-0.3
1960	Was-A	6	12	1	3	1	0	0	0	0	3	.250	.250	.333	57	-1	0	0	0	.917	-0	/2-4	-0.1
1962	Was-A	82	225	20	57	15	1	6	29	6	25	.253	.273	.409	81	-7	0	1	-1	.967	4	3-49/2-6	-0.3
1963	Was-A	3	3	0	0	0	0	0	0	0	1	.000	.000	.000	-99	-1	0	0	0	.000	0	H	-0.1
Total	5	114	323	25	75	18	1	6	32	7	40	.232	.251	.350	61	-18	0	1	-1	.980	7	/3-49,2-32	-1.0

■ ROY SCHALK   Schalk, Le Roy John b: 11/9/08, Chicago, Ill.   d: 3/11/90, Gainesville, Tex.   BR/TR, 5'10", 168 lbs.   Deb: 9/17/32

YEAR	TM/L	G	AB	R	H	2B	3B	HR	RBI	BB	SO	AVG	OBP	SLG	PRO+	BR/A	SB	CS	SBR	FA	FR	G/POS	TPR
1932	NY-A	3	12	3	3	1	0	0	2	2	2	.250	.357	.333	84	-0	0	0	0	.867	-2	/2-3	-0.1
1944	Chi-A	146	587	47	129	14	4	1	44	45	52	.220	.276	.262	55	-34	5	4	-1	.964	-14	*2-142/S-5	-4.4
1945	Chi-A	133	513	50	127	23	1	1	65	32	41	.248	.293	.302	75	-17	3	6	-3	.977	6	*2-133	-0.6
Total	3	282	1112	100	259	38	5	2	109	79	95	.233	.285	.281	64	-52	8	10	-4	.970	-9	2-278/S-5	-5.1

■ RAY SCHALK   Schalk, Raymond William "Cracker" b: 8/12/1892, Harvey, Ill.   d: 5/19/70, Chicago, Ill.   BR/TR, 5'9", 165 lbs.   Deb: 8/11/12   MCH

YEAR	TM/L	G	AB	R	H	2B	3B	HR	RBI	BB	SO	AVG	OBP	SLG	PRO+	BR/A	SB	CS	SBR	FA	FR	G/POS	TPR
1912	Chi-A	23	63	7	18	2	0	0	8	3		.286	.357	.317	96	-0	2			.917	4	C-23	0.6
1913	Chi-A	129	401	38	98	15	5	1	38	27	36	.244	.297	.314	80	-11	14			.980	-0	*C-125	-0.1
1914	Chi-A	136	392	30	106	13	2	0	36	38	24	.270	.347	.314	100	1	24	11	1	.974	6	*C-125	2.0
1915	Chi-A	135	413	46	110	14	4	1	54	62	21	.266	.366	.327	104	4	15	18	-6	.984	-3	*C-134	0.6
1916	Chi-A	129	410	36	95	12	9	0	41	41	31	.232	.311	.305	84	-8	30	13	1	.988	9	*C-124	1.3
1917	*Chi-A	140	424	48	96	12	5	2	51	59	27	.226	.331	.292	88	-4	19			.981	5	*C-139	1.4
1918	Chi-A	108	333	35	73	6	3	0	22	36	22	.219	.301	.255	67	-12	12			.978	-4	*C-106	-0.9
1919	*Chi-A	131	394	57	111	9	3	0	34	51	25	.282	.367	.320	93	-1	11			.981	1	*C-129	1.0
1920	Chi-A	151	485	64	131	25	5	1	61	68	19	.270	.362	.348	89	-6	10	4	1	.986	-1	*C-151	0.4
1921	Chi-A	128	416	32	105	24	4	0	47	40	36	.252	.328	.329	69	-19	3	4	-2	.985	8	*C-126	-0.6
1922	Chi-A	142	442	57	124	22	3	4	60	67	36	.281	.379	.371	97	0	12	4	1	.989	20	*C-142	2.8
1923	Chi-A	123	382	42	87	12	2	1	44	39	28	.228	.306	.277	55	-25	7	4	-0	.983	5	*C-121	-1.3
1924	Chi-A	57	153	15	30	4	2	1	11	21	10	.196	.301	.268	49	-12	1	5	-3	.959	6	C-56	-0.5
1925	Chi-A	125	343	44	94	18	1	0	52	57	27	.274	.382	.332	87	-4	11	5	0	.983	3	*C-125	0.5
1926	Chi-A	82	226	26	60	9	1	0	32	27	11	.265	.349	.314	77	-7	5	1	1	.977	-6	C-80	-0.8
1927	Chi-A	16	26	2	6	2	0	0	2	2	1	.231	.286	.308	55	-2	0	1	0	1.000	5	C-15,M	0.1
1928	Chi-A	2	1	0	1	0	0	0	0	0	0	1.000	1.000	1.000	433	-0	1	0	0	1.000	1	/C-1,M	0.1
1929	NY-N	5	2	0	0	0	0	0	0	0	1	.000	.000	.000	-99	-1	0			1.000	1	/C-5	0.0
Total	18	1762	5306	579	1345	199	49	11	594	638	355	.253	.340	.316	83	-105	177	69		.981	55	*C-1727	6.5

■ BIFF SCHALLER   Schaller, Walter b: 9/23/1889, Chicago, Ill.   d: 10/9/39, Emeryville, Cal.   BL/TR, 5'11", 168 lbs.   Deb: 4/30/11

YEAR	TM/L	G	AB	R	H	2B	3B	HR	RBI	BB	SO	AVG	OBP	SLG	PRO+	BR/A	SB	CS	SBR	FA	FR	G/POS	TPR
1911	Det-A	40	60	8	8	0	1	1	7	4		.133	.200	.217	15	-7	1			1.000	-1	O-16/1-1	-0.8
1913	Chi-A	36	96	12	21	3	0	0	4	20	16	.219	.353	.250	78	-2	5			.918	-6	O-32	-1.0
Total	2	76	156	20	29	3	1	1	11	24	16	.186	.298	.237	54	-9	6			.949	-7	/O-48,1-1	-1.8

■ BOBBY SCHANG   Schang, Robert Martin b: 12/7/1886, Wales Center, N.Y.   d: 8/29/66, Sacramento, Cal.   BR/TR, 5'7", 165 lbs.   Deb: 9/23/14   F

YEAR	TM/L	G	AB	R	H	2B	3B	HR	RBI	BB	SO	AVG	OBP	SLG	PRO+	BR/A	SB	CS	SBR	FA	FR	G/POS	TPR
1914	Pit-N	11	35	0	8	1	1	0	1	0	10	.229	.229	.314	64	-2	0			.964	-2	C-10	-0.3
1915	Pit-N	56	125	13	23	6	3	0	4	14	32	.184	.271	.280	68	-5	2	2	-1	.974	-7	C-45	-1.0
	NY-N	12	21	1	3	0	0	0	1	4	5	.143	.280	.143	31	-2	1			.875	-3	/C-6	-0.4
	Yr	68	146	14	26	6	3	0	5	18	37	.178	.273	.260	63	-6	3	2	-0	.960	-9	C-51	-1.4
1927	StL-N	3	5	0	1	0	0	0	0	0	0	.200	.200	.200	7	-1	0			1.000	-0	/C-3	-0.1
Total	3	82	186	14	35	7	4	0	6	18	47	.188	.263	.269	62	-9	3	2		.962	-11	/C-64	-1.8

■ WALLY SCHANG   Schang, Walter Henry b: 8/22/1889, S.Wales, N.Y.   d: 3/6/65, St.Louis, Mo.   BB/TR, 5'10", 180 lbs.   Deb: 5/9/13   FC

YEAR	TM/L	G	AB	R	H	2B	3B	HR	RBI	BB	SO	AVG	OBP	SLG	PRO+	BR/A	SB	CS	SBR	FA	FR	G/POS	TPR
1913	*Phi-A	79	207	32	55	16	3	3	30	34	44	.266	.392	.415	139	12	4			.967	-5	C-72	1.4
1914	*Phi-A	107	307	44	88	11	8	3	45	32	33	.287	.371	.404	138	15	7	7	-2	.956	1	*C-100	2.4
1915	Phi-A	116	359	64	89	9	11	1	44	66	47	.248	.385	.343	122	14	18	3	4	.890	1	3-43,O-41,C	1.9
1916	Phi-A	110	338	41	90	15	8	7	38	38	44	.266	.358	.420	140	16	14			.966	5	O-61,C-36	2.3
1917	Phi-A	118	316	41	90	14	9	3	36	29	24	.285	.362	.415	139	14	6			.956	-10	C-80,3-12/O	-0.7
1918	*Bos-A	88	225	36	55	7	1	0	20	46	35	.244	.377	.284	101	3	4			.962	-13	C-57,O-16/3S	-0.7
1919	Bos-A	113	330	43	101	16	3	0	55	71	42	.306	.436	.373	136	21	15			.972	-4	*C-103	2.7
1920	Bos-A	122	387	58	118	30	7	4	51	64	37	.305	.413	.450	134	22	7	7	-2	.958	-3	C-73,O-40	1.8
1921	*NY-A	134	424	77	134	30	5	6	55	78	35	.316	.428	.453	122	18	7	4	-0	.969	-6	*C-132	1.8
1922	*NY-A	124	408	46	130	21	7	1	53	53	36	.319	.405	.412	111	9	12	6	0	.976	3	*C-119	1.5
1923	*NY-A	84	272	39	75	8	2	2	29	27	17	.276	.360	.342	84	-5	5	2	0	.970	-8	*C-81	-0.9
1924	NY-A	114	356	46	104	19	7	5	52	48	43	.292	.382	.427	109	5	6	6	-3	.972	-2	*C-108	0.7
1925	NY-A	73	167	17	40	8	1	2	24	17	9	.240	.310	.335	65	-9	2	1	0	.974	2	C-58	-0.4
1926	StL-A	103	285	36	94	19	5	4	50	32	20	.330	.405	.516	133	13	5	5	-1	.968	-1	C-82/O-3	1.5
1927	StL-A	97	264	40	88	15	2	5	42	41	33	.333	.418	.447	119	7	3	2	-0	.976	-9	C-75	0.5
1928	StL-A	91	245	41	70	10	5	3	39	68	26	.286	.448	.404	121	12	8	2	1	.984	-12	C-82	0.8
1929	StL-A	94	249	43	59	10	5	0	36	74	22	.237	.424	.378	104	6	1	4	-2	.988	-6	C-85	0.5
1930	Phi-A	45	92	16	16	4	1	0	9	17	15	.174	.309	.272	47	-7	0	0	0	.973	2	C-36	-0.3

YEAR	TM/L	G	AB	R	H	2B	3B	HR	RBI	BB	SO	AVG	OBP	SLG	PRO+	BR/A	SB	CS	SBR	FA	FR	G/POS	TPR
1931	Det-A	30	76	9	14	2	0	0	2	14	11	.184	.311	.211	38	-6	1	0	0	.965	-0	C-30	-0.4
Total	19	1842	5307	769	1506	264	90	59	710	849	573	.284	.393	.401	117	160	121	49		.967	-69	*C-1435,O-167/3S	18.3

■ ART SCHAREIN

Scharein, Arthur Otto "Scoop"   b: 6/30/05, Decatur, Ill.   d: 7/2/69, San Antonio, Tex.   BR/TR, 5'11", 155 lbs.   Deb: 7/6/32   F

YEAR	TM/L	G	AB	R	H	2B	3B	HR	RBI	BB	SO	AVG	OBP	SLG	PRO+	BR/A	SB	CS	SBR	FA	FR	G/POS	TPR
1932	StL-A	81	303	43	92	19	2	0	42	25	10	.304	.363	.380	87	-5	4	8	-4	.965	14	3-77/S-3,2	1.4
1933	StL-A	123	471	49	96	13	3	0	26	41	21	.204	.269	.244	35	-44	7	9	-3	.949	14	3-95,S-24/2	-2.5
1934	StL-A	1	2	0	1	0	0	0	2	0	0	.500	.500	.500	146	0	0	0	0	.000	0	H	0.0
Total	3	205	776	92	189	32	5	0	70	66	31	.244	.306	.298	56	-49	11	17	-7	.956	32	3-172/S-27,2	-1.1

■ GEORGE SCHAREIN

Scharein, George Albert "Tom"   b: 11/21/14, Decatur, Ill.   d: 12/23/81, Decatur, Ill.   BR/TR, 6'1", 174 lbs.   Deb: 4/19/37   F

YEAR	TM/L	G	AB	R	H	2B	3B	HR	RBI	BB	SO	AVG	OBP	SLG	PRO+	BR/A	SB	CS	SBR	FA	FR	G/POS	TPR
1937	Phi-N	146	511	44	123	20	1	0	57	36	47	.241	.293	.284	53	-33	13			.947	10	*S-146	-1.2
1938	Phi-N	117	390	47	93	16	4	1	29	16	33	.238	.268	.308	60	-22	11			.921	-2	S-77,2-39/3	-1.7
1939	Phi-N	118	399	35	95	17	1	1	33	13	40	.238	.262	.293	50	-28	4			.958	-9	*S-117	-2.9
1940	Phi-N	7	17	0	5	0	0	0	0	0	3	.294	.294	.294	65	-1	0			.839	-1	/S-7	-0.1
Total	4	388	1317	126	316	53	6	2	119	65	123	.240	.277	.294	54	-84	28			.943	-2	S-347/2-39,3	-5.9

■ NICK SCHARF

Scharf, Edward T.   b: 7/1858, Baltimore, Md.   d: 5/12/37, Baltimore, Md.   TR,   Deb: 5/18/1882

YEAR	TM/L	G	AB	R	H	2B	3B	HR	RBI	BB	SO	AVG	OBP	SLG	PRO+	BR/A	SB	CS	SBR	FA	FR	G/POS	TPR
1882	Bal-a	10	39	4	8	1	1	1		0		.205	.205	.359	94	-0				.727	-2	/O-9,3-1	-0.2
1883	Bal-a	3	13	1	2	1	0	0		1		.154	.214	.231	42	-1				.643	-3	/S-3	-0.3
Total	2	13	52	5	10	2	1	1		1		.192	.208	.327	79	-1				.727	-4	/O-9,S-3,3	-0.5

■ AL SCHEER

Scheer, Allan G.   b: 10/21/1888, Dayton, Ohio   d: 5/6/59, Logansport, Ind.   BL/TR, 5'9", 165 lbs.   Deb: 8/2/13

YEAR	TM/L	G	AB	R	H	2B	3B	HR	RBI	BB	SO	AVG	OBP	SLG	PRO+	BR/A	SB	CS	SBR	FA	FR	G/POS	TPR
1913	Bro-N	6	22	3	5							.227	.292	.227	48	-1	1			.800	-1	/O-6	-0.3
1914	Ind-F	120	363	63	111	23	6	3	45	49	39	.306	.396	.427	102	2	9			.926	-5	*O-102/2-4,S	-0.7
1915	New-F	155	546	75	146	25	14	2	60	65	38	.267	.353	.375	101	0	31			.971	-2	*O-155	-1.0
Total	3	281	931	141	262	48	20	5	105	116	81	.281	.368	.392	100	1	41			.953	-9	O-263/2-4,S	-2.0

■ HEINIE SCHEER

Scheer, Henry   b: 7/31/1900, New York, N.Y.   d: 3/21/76, New Haven, Conn.   BR/TR, 5'8", 146 lbs.   Deb: 4/20/22

YEAR	TM/L	G	AB	R	H	2B	3B	HR	RBI	BB	SO	AVG	OBP	SLG	PRO+	BR/A	SB	CS	SBR	FA	FR	G/POS	TPR
1922	Phi-A	51	135	10	23	3	0	4	12	3	25	.170	.188	.281	21	-16	1	0	0	.976	9	2-30,3-10	-0.6
1923	Phi-A	69	210	26	50	8	1	2	21	17	41	.238	.301	.314	61	-12	3	4	-2	.971	-8	2-61	-2.1
Total	2	120	345	36	73	11	1	6	33	20	66	.212	.259	.301	46	-28	4	4	-1	.973	0	/2-91,3-10	-2.7

■ FRITZ SCHEEREN

Scheeren, Frederick "Dutch"   b: 9/8/1891, Kokomo, Ind.   d: 6/17/73, Oil City, Pa.   BR/TR, 6', 180 lbs.   Deb: 9/14/14

YEAR	TM/L	G	AB	R	H	2B	3B	HR	RBI	BB	SO	AVG	OBP	SLG	PRO+	BR/A	SB	CS	SBR	FA	FR	G/POS	TPR
1914	Pit-N	11	31	4	9	0	1	1	2	1	6	.290	.313	.452	132	1	1			.824	-3	O-10	-0.3
1915	Pit-N	4	3	0	0	0	0	0	0	0	0	.000	.000	.000	-99	-1	0			.000	-1	/O-1	-0.1
Total	2	15	34	4	9	0	1	1	2	1	6	.265	.286	.412	111	0	1			.824	-4	/O-11	-0.4

■ BOB SCHEFFING

Scheffing, Robert Boden   b: 8/11/13, Overland, Mo.   d: 10/26/85, Phoenix, Ariz.   BR/TR, 6'2", 189 lbs.   Deb: 4/27/41   MC

YEAR	TM/L	G	AB	R	H	2B	3B	HR	RBI	BB	SO	AVG	OBP	SLG	PRO+	BR/A	SB	CS	SBR	FA	FR	G/POS	TPR
1941	Chi-N	51	132	9	32	8	0	1	20	5	19	.242	.270	.326	70	-6	2			.966	-3	C-34	-0.7
1942	Chi-N	44	102	7	20	3	0	2	12	7	11	.196	.248	.284	58	-6	2			.986	4	C-32	0.0
1946	Chi-N	63	115	8	32	4	1	0	18	12	18	.278	.346	.330	94	-1	0			1.000	-7	C-40	-0.6
1947	Chi-N	110	363	33	96	11	5	5	50	25	25	.264	.312	.364	82	-10	2			.984	-6	C-97	-1.0
1948	Chi-N	102	293	23	88	18	2	5	45	22	27	.300	.351	.427	114	5	0			.989	-5	C-78	0.6
1949	Chi-N	55	149	12	40	6	1	3	19	9	2	.268	.314	.383	88	-3	0			.977	-3	C-40	-0.4
1950	Chi-N	12	16	0	3	1	0	0	1	0	2	.188	.188	.250	14	-2	0			.917	0	/C-3	-0.2
	Cin-N	21	47	4	13	0	0	2	6	4	2	.277	.333	.404	93	-1	0			1.000	-4	C-11	-0.4
	Yr	33	63	4	16	1	0	2	7	4	4	.254	.299	.365	74	-3	0			.982	-3	C-14	-0.6
1951	Cin-N	47	122	9	31	2	0	2	14	16	9	.254	.345	.320	79	-3	0	0	0	.976	-4	C-41	-0.5
	StL-N	12	18	0	2	0	0	0	2	3	5	.111	.238	.111	-3	-3	0	0	0	1.000	1	C-11	-0.1
	Yr	59	140	9	33	2	0	2	16	19	14	.236	.331	.293	68	-6	0	0	0	.980	-2	C-52	-0.6
Total	8	517	1357	105	357	53	9	20	187	103	127	.263	.316	.360	86	-28	6	0		.984	-25	C-387	-3.3

■ TED SCHEFFLER

Scheffler, Theodore J.   b: 4/5/1864, New York, N.Y.   d: 2/24/49, Jamaica, N.Y.   BR/TR, 5'10", 160 lbs.   Deb: 8/7/1888

YEAR	TM/L	G	AB	R	H	2B	3B	HR	RBI	BB	SO	AVG	OBP	SLG	PRO+	BR/A	SB	CS	SBR	FA	FR	G/POS	TPR
1888	Det-N	27	94	17	19	3	1	0	4	9	9	.202	.286	.255	74	-2	4			.847	-4	O-27	-0.7
1890	Roc-a	119	445	111	109	12	6	3		78		.245	.374	.319	113	13	77			.911	9	*O-119/C-1	1.6
Total	2	146	539	128	128	15	7	3	4	87	9	.237	.360	.308	106	11	81			.899	5	O-146/C-1	0.9

■ FRANK SCHEIBECK

Scheibeck, Frank S.   b: 6/28/1865, Detroit, Mich.   d: 10/22/56, Detroit, Mich.   BR/TR, 5'7", 145 lbs.   Deb: 5/9/1887

YEAR	TM/L	G	AB	R	H	2B	3B	HR	RBI	BB	SO	AVG	OBP	SLG	PRO+	BR/A	SB	CS	SBR	FA	FR	G/POS	TPR
1887	Cle-a	3	9	2	2	0	0	0		2		.222	.364	.222	67	-0	0			.500	-2	/S-1,3-1,P	-0.1
1888	Det-N	1	4	0	0	0	0	0	0	0	0	.000	.000	.000	-99	-1	0			.500	-1	/S-1	-0.3
1890	Tol-a	134	485	72	117	13	5	1		76		.241	.350	.295	88	-5	57			.883	1	*S-134	0.3
1894	Pit-N	28	102	20	36	2	3	1	10	11	9	.353	.416	.461	112	2	7			.891	-8	S-11/O-9,32	-0.4
	Was-N	52	196	49	45	2	4	0	17	45	24	.230	.384	.281	64	-9	11			.876	5	S-52	-0.1
	Yr	80	298	69	81	4	7	1	27	56	33	.272	.394	.342	81	-7	18			.878	-3	S-63/O-9,32	-0.5
1895	Was-N	48	167	17	31	5	2	0	25	17	21	.186	.265	.240	31	-17	5			.877	-1	S-27	-0.8
1899	Was-N	27	94	19	27	4	1	0	9	11		.287	.368	.351	99	-0	3			.897	-14	S-92	-2.7
1901	Cle-A	93	329	33	70	11	3	0	38	18		.213	.258	.264	47	-24	3			.897	-14	S-92	-2.7
1906	Det-A	3	10	1	1	1	0	0	0	2		.100	.250	.100	11	-1	0			.889	-1	/2-3	-0.2
Total	8	389	1396	213	329	37	18	2	99	182	54	.236	.329	.292	70	-55	88			.884	-33	S-362/O-9,23P	-5.7

■ RICHIE SCHEINBLUM

Scheinblum, Richard Alan   b: 11/5/42, New York, N.Y.   BB/TR, 6'1", 180 lbs.   Deb: 9/1/65

YEAR	TM/L	G	AB	R	H	2B	3B	HR	RBI	BB	SO	AVG	OBP	SLG	PRO+	BR/A	SB	CS	SBR	FA	FR	G/POS	TPR
1965	Cle-A	4	1	0	0	0	0	0	0	0	0	.000	.000	.000	-99	-0	0	0	0	.000	0	H	0.0
1967	Cle-A	18	66	8	21	4	2	0	6	5	10	.318	.366	.439	136	3	0	2	-1	.943	-0	O-18	0.1
1968	Cle-A	19	55	3	12	5	0	0	5	5	8	.218	.295	.309	84	-1	0	0	0	1.000	1	O-16	-0.1
1969	Cle-A	102	199	13	37	5	1	1	13	19	30	.186	.257	.236	37	-17	0	2	-1	.974	-1	O-50	-2.3
1971	Was-A	27	49	5	7	3	0	0	4	8	5	.143	.263	.204	36	-4	0	0	0	.933	3	O-13	-0.2
1972	KC-A★	134	450	60	135	21	4	8	66	58	40	.300	.385	.418	139	23	0	1	-1	.965	-3	*O-119	1.7
1973	Cin-N	29	54	5	12	2	0	1	8	10	4	.222	.344	.315	88	-1	0	0	0	.960	-2	O-19	-0.4
	Cal-A	77	229	28	75	10	2	3	21	35	27	.328	.419	.428	150	17	0	0	0	.969	-0	O-54/D-7	1.4
1974	Cal-A	10	26	1	4	2	0	0	0	3	5	.154	.185	.154	-2	-3	0	0	-1	.929	-1	D-17/O-2	-0.5
	KC-A	36	83	7	15	2	0	2	9	6	5	.181	.253	.205	31	-7	0	1	-1	.000	-1	D-18,O-10	-1.0
	Yr	46	109	8	19	4	0	2	9	9	10	.174	.237	.193	24	-10	0	1	-1	.929	-2	D-18,O-10	-1.5
	StL-N	6	6	0	2	0	0	0	0	0	1	.333	.333	.333	88	0	0	0	0	.000	0	H	0.0
Total	8	462	1218	131	320	52	9	13	127	149	135	.263	.346	.352	104	10	0	6	-4	.965	-4	O-299/D-25	-1.3

■ DANNY SCHELL

Schell, Clyde Daniel   b: 12/26/27, Fostoria, Mich.   d: 5/11/72, Mayville, Mich.   BR/TR, 6'1", 195 lbs.   Deb: 4/13/54

YEAR	TM/L	G	AB	R	H	2B	3B	HR	RBI	BB	SO	AVG	OBP	SLG	PRO+	BR/A	SB	CS	SBR	FA	FR	G/POS	TPR
1954	Phi-N	92	272	25	77	14	3	7	33	17	31	.283	.330	.434	97	-2	0	3	-2	.974	1	O-69	-0.6
1955	Phi-N	2	2	0	0	0	0	0	0	0	1	.000	.000	.000	-99	-1	0	0	0	.000	0	H	-0.1
Total	2	94	274	25	77	14	3	7	33	17	32	.281	.328	.431	96	-2	0	3	-2	.974	1	/O-69	-0.7

■ AL SCHELLHASE

Schellhase, Albert Herman "Schelley"   b: 9/13/1864, Evansville, Ind.   d: 1/3/19, Evansville, Ind.   BR/TR, 5'8", 148 lbs.   Deb: 5/7/1890

YEAR	TM/L	G	AB	R	H	2B	3B	HR	RBI	BB	SO	AVG	OBP	SLG	PRO+	BR/A	SB	CS	SBR	FA	FR	G/POS	TPR
1890	Bos-N	9	29	1	4	0	0	0	1	1	10	.138	.167	.138	-10	-4	0			.778	-1	/O-5,C-2,S3	-0.4
1891	Lou-a	7	20	4	3	0	0	0	1	2		.150	.190	.150	-2	-3	3			.943	0	/C-7	-0.2
Total	2	16	49	5	7	0	0	0	2	3	12	.143	.176	.143	-7	-7	3			.922	-1	/C-9,O-5,3S	-0.6

YEAR	TM/L	G	AB	R	H	2B	3B	HR	RBI	BB	SO	AVG	OBP	SLG	PRO+	BR/A	SB	CS	SBR	FA	FR	G/POS	TPR

■ FRED SCHEMANSKE Schemanske, Frederick George "Buck" b: 4/28/03, Detroit, Mich. d: 2/18/60, Detroit, Mich. BR/TR, 6'2", 190 lbs. Deb: 9/15/23

| 1923 | Was-A | 2 | 2 | 0 | 2 | 0 | 0 | 0 | 2 | 1 | 0 | 1.000 | 1.000 | 1.000 | 450 | 1 | 0 | 0 | | .000 | -0 | /P-1 | 0.0 |

■ MIKE SCHEMER Schemer, Michael "Lefty" b: 11/20/17, Baltimore, Md. d: 4/22/83, Miami, Fla. BL/TL, 6', 180 lbs. Deb: 8/8/45

1945	NY-N	31	108	10	36	3	1	1	10	6	1	.333	.368	.407	114	2	2			.993	4	1-27	0.4
1946	NY-N	1	1	0	0	0	0	0	0	0	0	.000	.000	.000	-99	-0	0			.000	0	H	0.0
Total	2	32	109	10	36	3	1	1	10	6	1	.330	.365	.404	112	2	2			.993	4	/1-27	0.4

■ BILL SCHENCK Schenck, William G. b: Brooklyn, N.Y. 5'7", 171 lbs. Deb: 5/29/1882

1882	Lou-a	60	231	37	60	11	3	0		8		.260	.285	.333	114	4				.814	-7	*3-58/S-2,P	-0.1
1884	Ric-a	42	151	14	31	4	0	3		1		.205	.216	.291	65	-6				.836	-5	S-40/2-2	-1.0
1885	Bro-a	1	4	0	0	0	0	0		0		.000	.000	.000	-99	-1				1.000	0	/3-1	-0.1
Total	3	103	386	51	91	15	3	3		9		.236	.255	.313	92	-3				.817	-12	/3-59,S-42,2P	-1.2

■ HANK SCHENZ Schenz, Henry Leonard b: 4/11/19, New Richmond, Ohio d: 5/12/88, Cincinnati, Ohio BR/TR, 5'9.5", 175 lbs. Deb: 9/18/46

1946	Chi-N	6	11	0	2	0	0	0	1	0	1	.182	.182	.182	3	-1	1			1.000	0	/3-5	-0.1
1947	Chi-N	7	14	2	1	0	0	0	0	2	1	.071	.235	.071	-16	-2	0			.917	0	/3-5	-0.2
1948	Chi-N	96	337	43	88	17	1	1	14	18	15	.261	.306	.326	74	-12	3			.974	-5	2-78/3-5	-1.4
1949	Chi-N	7	14	2	6	0	0	0	1	1	0	.429	.467	.429	146	1	2			1.000	1	/3-5	0.2
1950	Pit-N	58	101	17	23	4	2	1	5	6	7	.228	.271	.337	57	-6	0			.987	3	2-21,3-12/S	-0.3
1951	Pit-N	25	61	5	13	1	0	0	3	0	2	.213	.226	.230	22	-7	0	2	-1	.961	-3	2-19/3-2	-1.0
*NY-N	8	0	1	0	0	0	0	0	0	0	—	—	—			0	0	0	.000	0	R	0.0
Yr	33	61	6	13	1	0	0	3	0	2	.213	.226	.230	22	-7	0	2	-1	.961	-3	2-19/3-2	-1.0
Total	6	207	538	70	133	22	3	2	24	27	25	.247	.291	.310	63	-28	6	2		.974	-5	2-118/3-34,S	-2.8

■ JOE SCHEPNER Schepner, Joseph Maurice "Gentleman Joe" b: 8/10/1895, Aliquippa, Pa. d: 7/25/59, Mobile, Ala. BR/TR, 5'10", 160 lbs. Deb: 9/11/19

| 1919 | StL-A | 14 | 48 | 2 | 10 | 4 | 0 | 0 | | 6 | 5 | .208 | .224 | .292 | 43 | -4 | 0 | | | .947 | -1 | 3-13 | -0.5 |

■ BOB SCHERBARTH Scherbarth, Robert Elmer b: 1/18/26, Milwaukee, Wis. BR/TR, 6', 180 lbs. Deb: 4/23/50

| 1950 | Bos-A | 1 | 0 | 0 | 0 | 0 | 0 | 0 | 0 | 0 | 0 | — | — | — | | 0 | 0 | 0 | 0 | .000 | 0 | /C-1 | 0.0 |

■ HARRY SCHERER Scherer, Harry Deb: 7/24/1889

| 1889 | Lou-a | 1 | 3 | 0 | 1 | 0 | 0 | 0 | 0 | 0 | 0 | .333 | .333 | .333 | 92 | -0 | 0 | | | .500 | -1 | /O-1 | -0.1 |

■ LOU SCHIAPPACASSE Schiappacasse, Louis Joseph b: 3/29/1881, Ann Arbor, Mich. d: 9/20/10, Ann Arbor, Mich. BR/TR, Deb: 9/7/02

| 1902 | Det-A | 2 | 5 | 0 | 0 | 0 | 0 | 0 | 1 | 1 | | .000 | .167 | .000 | -50 | -1 | 0 | | | .000 | -1 | /O-2 | -0.2 |

■ MORRIE SCHICK Schick, Maurice Francis b: 4/17/1892, Chicago, Ill. d: 10/25/79, Hazel Crest, Ill. BR/TR, 5'11", 170 lbs. Deb: 4/15/17

| 1917 | Chi-N | 14 | 34 | 3 | 5 | 0 | 0 | 0 | 3 | 3 | 10 | .147 | .216 | .147 | 11 | -3 | 0 | | | .960 | 0 | O-12 | -0.4 |

■ CHUCK SCHILLING Schilling, Charles Thomas b: 10/25/37, Brooklyn, N.Y. BR/TR, 5'11", 170 lbs. Deb: 4/11/61

1961	Bos-A	158	646	87	167	25	2	5	62	78	77	.259	.340	.327	77	-19	7	6	-2	**.991**	15	*2-158	1.2
1962	Bos-A	119	413	48	95	17	1	7	35	29	48	.230	.287	.327	63	-22	1	0	-0	.985	13	*2-118	0.4
1963	Bos-A	146	576	63	135	25	0	8	33	41	72	.234	.291	.319	69	-24	3	2	-0	.985	-14	*2-143	-2.6
1964	Bos-A	47	163	18	32	6	0	0	7	15	22	.196	.264	.233	38	-13	0	1	-1	.974	-0	2-42	-1.2
1965	Bos-A	71	171	14	41	3	2	3	9	13	17	.240	.293	.333	73	-6	0	1	-1	.976	10	2-41	0.7
Total	5	541	1969	230	470	76	5	23	146	176	236	.239	.305	.317	68	-84	11	10	-3	.985	24	2-502	-1.5

■ BILL SCHINDLER Schindler, William Gibbons b: 7/10/1896, Perryville, Mo. d: 2/6/79, Perryville, Mo. BR/TR, 5'11", 160 lbs. Deb: 9/3/20

| 1920 | StL-N | 1 | 2 | 0 | 0 | 0 | 0 | 0 | 0 | 0 | 1 | .000 | .000 | .000 | -99 | -1 | 0 | | | 1.000 | -0 | /C-1 | -0.1 |

■ DUTCH SCHIRICK Schirick, Harry Ernest b: 6/15/1890, Ruby, N.Y. d: 11/12/68, Kingston, N.Y. BR/TR, 5'8", 160 lbs. Deb: 9/17/14

| 1914 | StL-A | 1 | 0 | 0 | 0 | 0 | 0 | 0 | 0 | 1 | 0 | — | 1.000 | — | 211 | 0 | 2 | | | .000 | 0 | H | 0.1 |

■ LARRY SCHLAFLY Schlafly, Harry Linton b: 9/20/1878, Port Washington, Ohio d: 6/27/19, Canton, Ohio BR/TR, 5'11", 182 lbs. Deb: 9/18/02 M

1902	Chi-N	10	31	5	10	0	3	0	5	6		.323	.432	.516	198	4	2			1.000	-4	/O-5,2-4,3	0.0
1906	Was-A	123	426	60	105	13	8	2	30	50		.246	.345	.329	117	11	29			.961	14	*2-123	2.8
1907	Was-A	24	74	10	10	0	0	1	4	22		.135	.354	.176	75	0	7			.928	-9	2-24	-1.1
1914	Buf-F	51	127	16	33	7	1	2	19	12	22	.260	.338	.378	83	-3	3			.951	2	2-23/1-7,C3OM	-0.2
Total	4	208	658	91	158	20	12	5	58	90	22	.240	.349	.330	109	11	41			.954	3	2-174/1-7,O3C	1.5

■ ADMIRAL SCHLEI Schlei, George Henry b: 1/12/1878, Cincinnati, Ohio d: 1/24/58, Huntington, W.Va. BR/TR, 5'8.5", 179 lbs. Deb: 4/24/04

1904	Cin-N	97	291	25	69	8	3	0	32	17		.237	.297	.285	74	-9	7			.977	10	C-88	1.1
1905	Cin-N	99	314	32	71	8	3	1	36	22		.226	.285	.280	62	-15	9			.962	16	C-89/1-6	1.0
1906	Cin-N	116	388	44	95	13	8	4	54	29		.245	.304	.351	100	-1	7			.961	9	C-91,1-21	1.8
1907	Cin-N	84	246	28	67	3	2	0	27	28		.272	.347	.301	99	1	5			.980	7	C-67/1-3,O	1.5
1908	Cin-N	92	300	31	66	6	4	1	22	22		.220	.278	.277	79	-7	2			.962	-8	C-88	-0.8
1909	NY-N	92	279	25	68	12	0	0	30	40		.244	.343	.287	94	-0	4			.963	3	C-89	1.2
1910	NY-N	55	99	10	19	2	1	0	8	14	10	.192	.304	.232	57	-5	4			.986	0	C-49	-0.2
1911	NY-N	1	1	0	0	0	0	0	0	0	1	.000	.000	.000	-97	-0	0			.000	0	H	0.0
Total	8	636	1918	195	455	52	21	6	209	172	11	.237	.307	.296	83	-37	38			.968	37	C-561/1-30,O	5.6

■ RUDY SCHLESINGER Schlesinger, William Cordes b: 11/5/41, Cincinnati, Ohio BR/TR, 6'2", 175 lbs. Deb: 5/4/65

| 1965 | Bos-A | 1 | 1 | 0 | 0 | 0 | 0 | 0 | 0 | 0 | 0 | .000 | .000 | .000 | -94 | -0 | 0 | 0 | 0 | .000 | 0 | H | 0.0 |

■ DUTCH SCHLIEBNER Schliebner, Frederick Paul b: 5/19/1891, Charlottenburg, Germany d: 4/15/75, Toledo, Ohio BR/TR, 5'10", 180 lbs. Deb: 4/17/23

1923	Bro-N	19	76	11	19	4	0	0	4	5	7	.250	.296	.303	60	-4	1	0	0	.981	3	1-19	-0.3
	StL-A	127	444	50	122	19	6	4	52	39	60	.275	.339	.372	82	-12	3	2	-0	.989	-0	*1-127	-1.9
Total	1	146	520	61	141	23	6	4	56	44	67	.271	.333	.362	79	-16	4	2	-0	.988	2	1-146	-2.2

■ JAY SCHLUETER Schlueter, Jay D b: 7/31/49, Phoenix, Ariz. BR/TR, 6', 182 lbs. Deb: 6/18/71

| 1971 | Hou-N | 7 | 3 | 1 | 1 | 0 | 0 | 0 | 0 | 0 | 1 | .333 | .333 | .333 | 92 | -0 | 0 | 0 | 0 | 1.000 | -0 | /O-2 | 0.0 |

■ NORM SCHLUETER Schlueter, Norman John "Duke" b: 9/25/16, Belleville, Ill. BR/TR, 5'10", 175 lbs. Deb: 5/28/38

1938	Chi-A	35	118	11	27	5	1	0	4	4	15	.229	.254	.288	35	-12	1	0		.952	-3	C-34	-1.2
1939	Chi-A	34	56	5	13	2	0	1	8	1	11	.232	.246	.304	39	-5	2	0	1	.988	1	C-32	-0.3
1944	Cle-A	49	122	2	15	4	0	0	11	12	22	.123	.201	.156	3	-15	0	2	-1	.985	-8	C-43	-2.4
Total	3	118	296	18	55	11	2	0	26	17	48	.186	.230	.236	24	-33	3	2	-0	.974	-10	C-109	-3.9

■ RAY SCHMANDT Schmandt, Raymond Henry b: 1/25/1896, St.Louis, Mo. d: 2/2/69, St.Louis, Mo. BR/TR, 6'1", 175 lbs. Deb: 6/24/15

1915	StL-A	3	4	0	0	0	0	0	0	0	0	.000	.000	.000	-99	-1	0			1.000	-0	/1-1	-0.1
1918	Bro-N	34	114	11	35	5	4	0	18	7	7	.307	.347	.421	134	4	1			.934	-4	2-34	0.3
1919	Bro-N	47	127	8	21	0	0	0	10	4	13	.165	.191	.197	16	-13	0			.911	0	2-18,1-12/3	-1.3
1920	*Bro-N	28	63	7	15	2	1	0	7	3		.238	.273	.302	63	-3	1	1	-0	.995	3	1-20	-0.3
1921	Bro-N	95	350	42	107	8	5	1	43	11	22	.306	.329	.366	81	-10	3	4	-2	.989	0	1-92	-1.3
1922	Bro-N	110	396	54	106	17	3	2	44	21	28	.268	.306	.341	67	-20	6	2	-2	.989	5	*1-110	-2.0
Total	6	317	1054	122	284	36	13	3	122	46	75	.269	.301	.337	72	-42	11	11		.990	5	1-235/2-52,3	-4.4

YEAR	TM/L	G	AB	R	H	2B	3B	HR	RBI	BB	SO	AVG	OBP	SLG	PRO+	BR/A	SB	CS	SBR	FA	FR	G/POS	TPR

■ GEORGE SCHMEES   Schmees, George Edward "Rocky" b: 9/6/24, Cincinnati, Ohio   BL/TL, 6′, 190 lbs.   Deb: 4/15/52

1952	StL-A	34	61	9	8	1	1	0	3	2	18	.131	.159	.180	-6	-9	0	0	0	.932	-1	O-19/1-2	-1.0
	Bos-A	42	64	8	13	3	0	0	3	10	11	.203	.311	.250	53	-4	0	1	-1	1.000	-7	O-29/P-2,1	-1.4
	Yr	76	125	17	21	4	1	0	6	12	29	.168	.241	.216	26	-12	0	1	-1	.960	-8	O-48/1-4,P	-2.4

■ BOSS SCHMIDT   Schmidt, Charles b: 9/12/1880, Coal Hill, Ark. d: 11/14/32, Clarksville, Ark.   BB/TR, 5′11″, 200 lbs.   Deb: 4/30/06 F

1906	Det-A	68	216	13	47	4	3	0	10	6		.218	.242	.264	57	-11	1			.958	7	C-67	0.3
1907	*Det-A	104	349	32	85	6	6	0	23	5		.244	.269	.295	77	-10	8			.944	3	*C-103	0.3
1908	*Det-A	122	419	45	111	14	3	1	38	16		.265	.297	.320	96	-3	5			.951	8	*C-121	1.9
1909	*Det-A	84	253	21	53	8	2	1	28	7		.209	.240	.269	58	-13	7			.955	-6	C-66	-1.4
1910	Det-A	71	197	22	51	7	7	1	23	2		.259	.277	.381	99	-2	2			1.000	-2	/C-9,O-1	-0.3
1911	Det-A	28	46	4	13	2	1	0	2	0		.283	.298	.370	82	-1	0			.955	3	C-447/O-2	-0.1
Total	6	477	1480	137	360	41	22	3	124	36		.243	.270	.307	79	-39	23			.955	3	C-447/O-2	

(Note: Total G/POS reads C-447/O-2; TPR column values: individual years 0.3, 0.3, 1.9, -1.4, -0.3, -0.1)

■ BUTCH SCHMIDT   Schmidt, Charles John "Butcher Boy" b: 7/19/1886, Baltimore, Md. d: 9/4/52, Baltimore, Md.   BL/TL, 6′1.5″, 200 lbs.   Deb: 5/11/09

1909	NY-A	1	2	0	0	0	0	0	0	0		.000	.000	.000	-99	-0	0			.500	-1	/P-1	0.0
1913	Bos-N	22	78	6	24	2	2	1	14	2	5	.308	.333	.423	113	1	1			.983	1	1-22	0.2
1914	*Bos-N	147	537	67	153	17	9	1	71	43	55	.285	.350	.356	111	8	14			.990	3	*1-147	0.7
1915	Bos-N	127	458	46	115	26	7	2	60	36	59	.251	.318	.352	107	4	3	10	-5	.987	-4	*1-127	-1.0
Total	4	297	1075	119	292	45	18	4	145	81	119	.272	.335	.358	109	12	18	10		.988	-1	1-296/P-1	-0.1

■ DAVE SCHMIDT   Schmidt, David Frederick b: 12/22/56, Mesa, Ariz.   BR/TR, 6′1″, 190 lbs.   Deb: 4/28/81

| 1981 | Bos-A | 15 | 42 | 6 | 10 | 1 | 0 | 2 | 3 | 7 | 17 | .238 | .347 | .405 | 109 | 1 | 0 | 0 | 0 | 1.000 | -4 | C-15 | -0.3 |

■ MIKE SCHMIDT   Schmidt, Michael Jack b: 9/27/49, Dayton, Ohio   BR/TR, 6′2″, 203 lbs.   Deb: 9/12/72 H

1972	Phi-N	13	34	2	7	0	0	1	3	5	15	.206	.325	.294	75	-1	0	0	0	.964	2	3-11/2-1	0.1
1973	Phi-N	132	367	43	72	11	0	18	52	62	136	.196	.326	.373	91	-4	8	2	1	.954	21	*3-125/2-4,1S	1.9
1974	Phi-N★	162	568	108	160	28	7	36	116	106	138	.282	.398	.546	156	43	23	12	0	.954	26	*3-162	6.9
1975	Phi-N★	158	562	93	140	34	3	38	95	101	180	.249	.367	.523	139	29	29	12	2	.954	24	*3-151,S-10	5.7
1976	*Phi-N★	160	584	112	153	31	4	38	107	100	149	.262	.380	.524	150	39	14	9	-1	.961	25	*3-160	6.4
1977	*Phi-N★	154	544	114	149	27	11	38	101	104	122	.274	.399	.574	151	40	15	8	-0	.964	29	*3-149/S-2,2	6.7
1978	*Phi-N	145	513	93	129	27	2	21	78	91	103	.251	.368	.435	122	17	19	6	2	.963	10	*3-139/S-1	2.9
1979	*Phi-N★	160	541	109	137	25	4	45	114	120	115	.253	.392	.564	153	41	9	5	-0	.954	18	*3-157/S-2	5.8
1980	*Phi-N†	150	548	104	157	25	8	48	121	89	119	.286	.388	.624	169	50	12	4	1	.946	23	*3-149	7.3
1981	*Phi-N★	102	354	78	112	19	2	31	91	73	71	.316	.439	.644	195	46	12	4	1	.956	23	*3-101	7.0
1982	*Phi-N★	148	514	108	144	26	3	35	87	107	131	.280	.407	.547	161	45	14	7	0	.950	19	*3-148	6.1
1983	*Phi-N★	154	534	104	136	16	4	40	109	128	148	.255	.402	.524	156	45	7	8	-3	.959	23	*3-153/S-2	6.4
1984	Phi-N★	151	528	93	146	23	3	36	106	92	116	.277	.388	.536	155	39	5	7	-3	.941	12	*1-106,3-54/S	4.8
1985	Phi-N	158	549	89	152	31	5	33	93	87	117	.277	.379	.532	148	36	1	3	-2	.993	-7	*3-124,1-35	3.3
1986	Phi-N★	160	552	97	160	29	1	37	119	89	84	.290	.395	.547	152	40	1	2	-1	.980	-7	*3-138/1-9,S	2.8
1987	Phi-N★	147	522	88	153	28	0	35	113	83	80	.293	.392	.548	141	32	2	1	0	.971	13	*3-138/1-9,S	4.1
1988	Phi-N	108	390	52	97	21	2	12	62	49	42	.249	.342	.405	111	6	3	0	1	.939	3	3-104/1-3	1.0
1989	Phi-N†	42	148	19	30	7	0	6	28	21	17	.203	.302	.372	91	-2	0	1	-1	.918	-5	3-42	-0.8
Total	18	2404	8352	1506	2234	408	59	548	1595	1507	1883	.267	.384	.527	147	543	174	92	-3	.955	265	*3-2212,1-157/S2	78.4

■ BOB SCHMIDT   Schmidt, Robert Benjamin b: 4/22/33, St.Louis, Mo.   BR/TR, 6′2″, 205 lbs.   Deb: 4/16/58

1958	SF-N☆	127	393	46	96	20	2	14	54	33	59	.244	.308	.412	90	-6	0	1	-1	.982	-3	*C-123	-0.3
1959	SF-N	71	181	17	44	7	1	5	20	13	24	.243	.297	.376	80	-6	0	2	-1	1.000	-0	C-70	-0.4
1960	SF-N	110	344	31	92	12	1	8	37	26	51	.267	.319	.378	96	-3	0	3	-2	.981	-3	*C-108	-0.2
1961	SF-N	2	6	0	1	0	0	0	1	0	1	.167	.167	.167	-12	-1	0	0	0	1.000	1	/C-2	0.0
	Cin-N	27	70	4	9	0	0	1	4	8	14	.129	.218	.171	5	-10	0	0	0	.993	1	C-27	-0.7
	Yr	29	76	4	10	0	0	1	5	8	15	.132	.214	.171	4	-10	0	0	0	.994	3	C-29	-0.7
1962	Was-A	88	256	28	62	14	0	10	31	14	37	.242	.284	.414	86	-6	0	0	0	.997	-2	C-88	-0.5
1963	Was-A	9	15	3	3	1	0	0	0	3	5	.200	.333	.267	71	-0	0	0	0	1.000	-1	/C-6	-0.2
1965	NY-A	20	40	4	10	1	0	1	3	3	8	.250	.302	.350	85	-1	0	0	0	.990	2	C-20	0.2
Total	7	454	1305	133	317	55	4	39	150	100	199	.243	.299	.381	84	-33	0	6	-4	.988	-5	C-444	-2.1

■ WALTER SCHMIDT   Schmidt, Walter Joseph b: 3/20/1887, Coal Hill, Ark. d: 7/4/73, Modesto, Cal.   BR/TR, 5′9″, 159 lbs.   Deb: 4/13/16 F

1916	Pit-N	64	184	16	35	1	2	2	15	10	13	.190	.236	.250	49	-11	3			.976	0	C-57	-0.8
1917	Pit-N	72	183	9	45	7	0	0	17	11	11	.246	.296	.284	76	-5	4			.978	8	C-61	0.8
1918	Pit-N	105	323	31	77	6	3	0	27	17	19	.238	.281	.276	67	-12	7			.981	16	*C-104	1.3
1919	Pit-N	85	267	23	67	9	2	0	29	23	9	.251	.310	.300	81	-6	5			.982	1	C-85	0.3
1920	Pit-N	94	310	22	86	8	4	0	20	24	15	.277	.337	.329	89	-4	9	3	1	.971	-5	C-92	-0.1
1921	Pit-N	114	393	30	111	9	3	0	38	12	13	.282	.307	.321	65	-20	10	6	-1	.986	7	*C-111	-0.7
1922	Pit-N	40	152	21	50	11	2	0	22	1	5	.329	.333	.414	91	-2	2	1	0	.995	-5	C-40	-0.5
1923	Pit-N	97	335	39	83	7	2	0	37	22	12	.248	.300	.281	59	-22	10	5	0	.981	-9	C-96	-2.6
1924	Pit-N	58	177	16	43	7	3	1	20	13	5	.243	.295	.299	59	-10	6	1	1	.986	2	C-57	-0.4
1925	StL-N	37	87	9	22	2	1	0	9	4	3	.253	.293	.299	51	-6	1	0	0	.967	6	C-31	0.1
Total	10	766	2411	216	619	63	20	3	234	137	105	.257	.302	.303	69	-99	57	16		.980	21	C-734	-2.6

■ HANK SCHMULBACH   Schmulbach, Henry Alrives b: 1/17/25, E.St.Louis, Ill.   BL/TR, 5′11″, 165 lbs.   Deb: 9/27/43

| 1943 | StL-A | 1 | 0 | 1 | 0 | 0 | 0 | 0 | 0 | 0 | 0 | — | — | — | | | 0 | 0 | 0 | .000 | 0 | R | 0.0 |

■ DAVE SCHNECK   Schneck, David Lee b: 6/18/49, Allentown, Pa.   BL/TL, 5′10″, 200 lbs.   Deb: 7/14/72

1972	NY-N	37	123	7	23	3	2	3	10	10	26	.187	.254	.317	63	-6	0	1	-1	.985	-1	O-33	-1.0
1973	NY-N	13	36	2	7	0	1	0	0	1	4	.194	.216	.250	29	-3	0	0	0	1.000	0	O-12	-0.4
1974	NY-N	93	254	23	52	11	1	5	25	16	43	.205	.255	.315	60	-15	4	1	1	.974	0	O-84	-1.7
Total	3	143	413	32	82	14	4	8	35	27	73	.199	.251	.310	58	-24	4	2	0	.979	0	O-129	-3.1

■ RED SCHOENDIENST   Schoendienst, Albert Fred b: 2/2/23, Germantown, Ill.   BB/TR, 6′, 170 lbs.   Deb: 4/17/45 MCH

1945	StL-N	137	565	89	157	22	6	1	47	21	17	.278	.305	.343	78	-18	26			.983	3	*O-118,S-10/2	-2.1
1946	*StL-N★	142	606	94	170	28	5	0	34	37	27	.281	.322	.343	85	-12	12			.984	-1	*2-128,3-12/S	-0.4
1947	StL-N	151	659	91	167	25	9	3	48	48	27	.253	.304	.332	66	-32	6			.976	-2	*2-142/3-5,O	-2.4
1948	StL-N★	119	408	64	111	21	4	4	36	28	16	.272	.319	.373	82	-11	1			.980	1	2-96	-0.5
1949	StL-N★	151	640	102	190	25	2	3	54	51	18	.297	.351	.356	86	-11	8			.987	24	*2-138,S-14/3O	1.9
1950	StL-N★	153	642	81	177	43	9	7	63	33	32	.276	.313	.403	83	-17	3			.985	8	*2-124/S-8	-0.2
1951	StL-N★	135	553	88	160	32	7	6	54	35	23	.289	.335	.405	98	-3	1	1	-1	.990	16	*2-124/S-8	1.9
1952	StL-N☆	152	620	91	188	40	7	7	67	42	30	.303	.347	.424	113	10	9	6	-1	.977	33	*2-142,3-11/S	4.9
1953	StL-N★	146	564	107	193	35	5	15	79	60	23	.342	.405	.502	135	30	3	3	-1	.983	25	*2-140	5.8
1954	StL-N★	148	610	98	192	38	8	5	79	54	22	.315	.371	.428	107	7	4	2	0	.980	33	*2-144	4.8
1955	StL-N★	145	553	68	148	21	3	11	51	54	28	.268	.337	.376	89	-8	7	7	-2	.985	-15	*2-142	-1.4
1956	StL-N	40	153	22	48	9	0	0	15	13	5	.314	.367	.373	100	0	1	0	0	.995	-5	2-36	0.1
	NY-N	92	334	39	99	12	3	2	14	28	10	.296	.354	.368	95	-1	2	1	-1	.993	-11	2-85	-0.6
	Yr	132	487	61	147	21	3	2	29	41	15	.302	.358	.370	97	-1	3	1	-2	.993	-12	*2-121	-0.5
1957	NY-N	57	254	35	78	8	4	9	33	10	8	.307	.338	.476	116	5	2			.984	-2	2-57	0.8

YEAR	TM/L	G	AB	R	H	2B	3B	HR	RBI	BB	SO	AVG	OBP	SLG	PRO+	BR/A	SB	CS	SBR	FA	FR	G/POS	TPR
	*Mil-N★	93	394	56	122	23	4	6	32	23	7	.310	.349	.434	117	8	2	3	-1	.987	4	2-92/O-2	1.9
	Yr	150	648	91	**200**	31	8	15	65	33	15	.309	.345	.451	117	14	4	4	-1	.986	3	*2-149/O-2	2.7
1958	*Mil-N	106	427	47	112	23	1	1	24	31	21	.262	.314	.328	77	-15	3	1	0	**.987**	1	*2-105	-0.7
1959	Mil-N	5	3	0	0	0	0	0	0	0	0	.000	.000	.000	-99	-1	0	0	0	.667	-0	/2-4	-0.1
1960	Mil-N	68	226	21	58	9	1	1	19	17	13	.257	.311	.319	79	-7	1	0	0	.964	-17	2-62	-1.9
1961	StL-N	72	120	9	36	9	0	1	12	12	6	.300	.364	.400	93	-1	1	0	0	.955	-11	2-32	-0.9
1962	StL-N	98	143	21	43	4	0	2	12	9	12	.301	.346	.371	84	-3	0	0	0	.986	-0	2-21/3-4	-0.2
1963	StL-N	6	5	0	0	0	0	0	0	0	1	.000	.000	.000	-91	-1	0	0	0	.000	0	H	-0.1
Total	19	2216	8479	1223	2449	427	78	84	773	606	346	.289	.338	.387	93	-82	89	27		.983	88	*2-1834,0-123/S3	10.6

■ JUMBO SCHOENECK
Schoeneck, Louis N. b: 3/3/1862, Chicago, Ill. d: 1/20/30, Chicago, Ill. BR/TR, 6'3", 223 lbs. Deb: 4/20/1884

YEAR	TM/L	G	AB	R	H	2B	3B	HR	RBI	BB	SO	AVG	OBP	SLG	PRO+	BR/A	SB	CS	SBR	FA	FR	G/POS	TPR
1884	CP-U	90	366	56	116	22	2	2			8	.317	.332	.404	100	-1				.956	0	*1-90	-1.0
	Bal-U	16	60	5	15	2	0	0			0	.250	.250	.283	40	-5				.962	2	1-16	-0.5
	Yr	106	426	61	131	24	2	2			8	.308	.320	.387	90	-6				**.957**	2	*1-106	-1.5
1888	Ind-N	48	169	15	40	4	0	0	20	9	24	.237	.283	.260	73	-5	11			.974	-1	1-48/P-2	-1.0
1889	Ind-N	16	62	3	15	2	2	0	8	3	3	.242	.299	.339	76	-2	1			.978	2	1-16	-0.1
Total	3	170	657	79	186	30	4	2	28	20	27	.283	.308	.350	85	-13	12			.964	3	1-170/P-2	-2.6

■ DICK SCHOFIELD
Schofield, John Richard "Ducky" b: 1/7/35, Springfield, Ill. BB/TR, 5'9", 165 lbs. Deb: 7/3/53 F

YEAR	TM/L	G	AB	R	H	2B	3B	HR	RBI	BB	SO	AVG	OBP	SLG	PRO+	BR/A	SB	CS	SBR	FA	FR	G/POS	TPR
1953	StL-N	33	39	9	7	0	0	2	4	2	11	.179	.220	.333	42	-3	0	0	0	.917	10	S-15	0.6
1954	StL-N	43	7	17	1	0	1	0	1	0	3	.143	.143	.429	42	-1	1	1	-0	1.000	2	S-11	0.1
1955	StL-N	12	4	3	0	0	0	0	0	0	1	.000	.000	.000	-99	-1	0	0	0	1.000	1	/S-3	-0.1
1956	StL-N	16	30	3	3	2	0	0	1	0	6	.100	.100	.167	-30	-5	0	0	0	.923	-1	/S-9	-0.6
1957	StL-N	65	56	10	9	0	0	0	1	7	13	.161	.254	.161	14	-7	1	3	-2	.948	10	S-23	0.2
1958	StL-N	39	108	16	23	4	0	1	8	23	15	.213	.351	.278	67	-4	0	2	-1	.932	-5	S-27	-0.8
	Pit-N	26	27	4	4	0	1	0	2	3	6	.148	.233	.222	22	-3	0	1	-1	1.000	0	/S-5,3-2	-0.3
	Yr	65	135	20	27	4	1	1	10	26	21	.200	.329	.267	59	-7	0	3	-2	.943	-5	S-32/3-2	-1.1
1959	Pit-N	81	145	21	34	10	1	1	9	16	22	.234	.311	.338	73	-5	1	1	-0	.980	10	S-28/S-8,O	0.7
1960	*Pit-N	65	102	9	34	4	1	0	10	16	20	.333	.429	.392	126	5	0	1	-1	.947	8	S-23,2-10/3	1.4
1961	Pit-N	60	78	16	15	2	1	0	2	10	19	.192	.284	.244	42	-6	0	1	-1	.923	9	3-11/S-9,2O	-0.3
1962	Pit-N	54	104	19	30	3	0	2	10	17	22	.288	.388	.375	106	2	0	1	-1	.933	-6	3-20/2-2,S	-0.4
1963	Pit-N	138	541	54	133	18	2	3	32	69	83	.246	.334	.303	84	-8	2	4	-2	.966	10	*S-117,2-20/3	1.1
1964	Pit-N	121	398	50	98	22	5	3	36	54	60	.246	.346	.349	97	-2	1	2	-1	.950	2	*S-111	0.9
1965	Pit-N	31	109	13	25	5	0	0	6	15	19	.229	.323	.275	70	-4	1	0	0	.974	4	S-28	0.3
	SF-N	101	379	39	77	10	1	2	19	33	50	.203	.272	.251	47	-26	2	4	-2	.984	-6	S-93	-2.9
	Yr	132	488	52	102	15	1	2	25	48	69	.209	.284	.256	52	-30	3	4	-2	**.981**	-2	*S-121	-2.6
1966	SF-N	11	16	4	1	0	0	0	0	2	2	.063	.167	.063	-32	-3	0	0	0	1.000	2	/S-8	-0.1
	NY-A	25	58	5	9	0	0	0	2	9	8	.155	.269	.190	36	-5	0	0	0	.909	5	S-19	-0.5
	LA-N	20	70	10	18	0	0	0	4	8	8	.257	.350	.257	78	-2	1	1	-0	.923	-3	3-19/S-3	-0.5
1967	LA-N	84	232	23	50	10	1	2	15	31	40	.216	.308	.293	79	-6	1	2	-1	.976	-0	S-69/2-4,3	-0.1
1968	*StL-N	69	127	14	28	7	1	1	8	13	31	.220	.303	.315	87	-2	1	2	-1	.973	9	S-43,2-23	1.0
1969	Bos-A	94	226	30	58	9	3	2	20	29	44	.257	.351	.350	92	-2	0	2	-1	.981	2	2-37,S-11/3O	0.3
1970	Bos-A	76	139	16	26	1	2	1	14	21	26	.187	.298	.245	48	-9	0	1	-1	.969	-4	2-15,3-15/S	-1.4
1971	Mil-A	23	28	2	3	2	0	0	1	2	8	.107	.194	.179	6	-4	0	0	0	1.000	-2	3-12/S-4,2	-0.5
	StL-N	34	60	7	13	2	1	0	6	10	9	.217	.347	.300	82	-1	0	0	0	.935	0	S-17,2-13/3	0.3
Total	19	1321	3083	394	699	113	20	21	211	390	526	.227	.319	.297	73	-101	12	29	-14	.961	58	S-660,2-159/3O	-0.3

■ DICK SCHOFIELD
Schofield, Richard Craig b: 11/21/62, Springfield, Ill. BR/TR, 5'10", 176 lbs. Deb: 9/8/83 F

YEAR	TM/L	G	AB	R	H	2B	3B	HR	RBI	BB	SO	AVG	OBP	SLG	PRO+	BR/A	SB	CS	SBR	FA	FR	G/POS	TPR
1983	Cal-A	21	54	4	11	2	0	3	4	6	8	.204	.295	.407	92	-1	0	0	0	.929	5	S-21	0.5
1984	Cal-A	140	400	39	77	10	3	4	21	33	79	.192	.264	.262	47	-29	5	2	0	**.982**	3	*S-140	-1.2
1985	Cal-A	147	438	50	96	19	3	8	41	35	70	.219	.289	.331	70	-18	11	4	1	.963	1	*S-147	-0.3
1986	*Cal-A	139	458	67	114	17	6	13	57	48	55	.249	.327	.397	97	-2	23	5	4	.972	15	*S-137	2.9
1987	Cal-A	134	479	52	120	17	3	9	46	37	63	.251	.307	.355	78	-16	19	3	4	**.984**	-18	*S-131/2-2,D	-1.8
1988	Cal-A	155	527	61	126	11	6	6	34	40	57	.239	.304	.371	76	-16	20	5	3	**.983**	23	*S-155	2.3
1989	Cal-A	91	302	42	69	11	2	4	26	28	47	.228	.300	.318	76	-10	9	3	1	.983	-8	S-90	-0.9
1990	Cal-A	99	310	41	79	8	1	1	18	52	61	.255	.365	.297	89	-2	3	4	-2	.966	12	S-99	1.6
1991	Cal-A	134	427	44	96	9	3	0	31	50	69	.225	.310	.260	60	-22	8	4	0	.975	12	*S-133	0.5
1992	Cal-A	1	3	0	1	0	0	0	0	1	0	.333	.500	.333	137	0	0	0	0	1.000	-1	/S-1	-0.1
	NY-N	142	420	52	86	18	2	4	36	60	82	.205	.311	.286	71	-14	11	4	1	**.988**	13	*S-141	1.0
1993	*Tor-A	36	110	11	21	1	2	0	5	16	25	.191	.294	.236	44	-8	3	0	1	.976	2	S-36	-0.2
1994	Tor-A	95	325	38	83	14	1	4	32	34	62	.255	.333	.342	74	-12	7	7	-2	.972	-9	S-95	-1.5
Total	12	1334	4253	501	979	137	32	56	351	440	678	.230	.309	.317	73	-150	119	41	11	.976	50	*S-1326/2-2,D	2.3

■ OTTO SCHOMBERG
Schomberg, Otto H. (b: Otto H. Shambrick) b: 11/14/1864, Milwaukee, Wis. d: 5/3/27, Ottawa, Kan. BL/TL, Deb: 7/7/1886

YEAR	TM/L	G	AB	R	H	2B	3B	HR	RBI	BB	SO	AVG	OBP	SLG	PRO+	BR/A	SB	CS	SBR	FA	FR	G/POS	TPR
1886	Pit-a	72	246	53	67	6	6	5		57		.272	.417	.358	144	17	7			.966	-7	1-72	0.1
1887	Ind-N	112	419	91	129	18	16	5	83	56	32	.308	.397	.463	143	27	21			.958	-10	*1-112/O-1	0.4
1888	Ind-N	30	112	11	24	5	1	0	10	10	12	.214	.290	.304	88	-1	6			.857	-5	O-15,1-15	-0.8
Total	3	214	777	155	220	29	23	7	93	123	44	.283	.389	.407	136	43	34			.961	-22	1-199/O-16	-0.3

■ JERRY SCHOONMAKER
Schoonmaker, Jerald Lee b: 12/14/33, Seymour, Mo. BR/TR, 5'11", 190 lbs. Deb: 6/11/55

YEAR	TM/L	G	AB	R	H	2B	3B	HR	RBI	BB	SO	AVG	OBP	SLG	PRO+	BR/A	SB	CS	SBR	FA	FR	G/POS	TPR
1955	Was-A	20	46	5	7	0	1	1	4	5	11	.152	.235	.261	35	-4	1	0	0	.960	-1	O-15	-0.6
1957	Was-A	30	23	5	2	1	0	0	0	2	11	.087	.160	.130	-20	-4	0	0	0	1.000	-3	O-13	-0.7
Total	2	50	69	10	9	1	1	1	4	7	22	.130	.211	.217	16	-8	1	0	0	.975	-4	/O-28	-1.3

■ GENE SCHOTT
Schott, Arthur Eugene b: 7/14/13, Batavia, Ohio d: 11/16/92, Sun City Center, Fla. BR/TR, 6'2", 185 lbs. Deb: 4/16/35

YEAR	TM/L	G	AB	R	H	2B	3B	HR	RBI	BB	SO	AVG	OBP	SLG	PRO+	BR/A	SB	CS	SBR	FA	FR	G/POS	TPR
1935	Cin-N	36	60	6	12	2	0	0	2	3	13	.200	.238	.233	28	-6	0			.965	3	P-33	0.0
1936	Cin-N	39	60	10	18	3	1	1	8	5	18	.300	.354	.433	118	1	0			.947	1	P-31	0.0
1937	Cin-N	50	49	5	7	2	0	0	4	1	14	.143	.160	.184	-7	-7	0			.961	1	P-37	0.0
1938	Cin-N	31	24	3	3	0	0	0	0	1	4	.125	.160	.125	-21	-4	0			1.000	1	P-31	0.0
1939	Phi-N	8	6	3	2	0	1	0	0	0	0	.333	.333	.667	168	0	0			.500	-1	/P-4	0.0
	Bro-N	1	0	0	0	0	0	0	0	0	0					0	0			.000	0	R	0.0
	Yr	9	6	3	2	0	1	0	0	0	0	.333	.333	.667	166	0	0			.500	-1	/P-4	0.0
Total	5	165	199	27	42	7	2	1	14	10	49	.211	.249	.281	45	-15	0			.959	6	P-136	0.0

■ PAUL SCHRAMKA
Schramka, Paul Edward b: 3/22/28, Milwaukee, Wis. BL/TL, 6', 185 lbs. Deb: 4/14/53

YEAR	TM/L	G	AB	R	H	2B	3B	HR	RBI	BB	SO	AVG	OBP	SLG	PRO+	BR/A	SB	CS	SBR	FA	FR	G/POS	TPR
1953	Chi-N	2	0	0	0	0	0	0	0	0	0	—	—	—	—	0	0	0	0	.000	-0	/O-1	0.0

■ OSSEE SCHRECKENGOST
Schreckengost, Ossee Freeman (a.k.a. Ossee Schreck)
b: 4/11/1875, New Bethlehem, Pa. d: 7/9/14, Philadelphia, Pa. BR/TR, 5'10", 180 lbs. Deb: 9/8/1897

YEAR	TM/L	G	AB	R	H	2B	3B	HR	RBI	BB	SO	AVG	OBP	SLG	PRO+	BR/A	SB	CS	SBR	FA	FR	G/POS	TPR
1897	Lou-N	1	3	0	0	0	0	0	0	0		.000	.000	.000	-99	-1	0			1.000	-0	/C-1	-0.1
1898	Cle-N	10	35	5	11	2	3	0	10	0		.314	.314	.543	146	2	0			.860	0	/C-9	0.2
1899	StL-N	6	8	0	0	0	0	0	0	1		.000	.111	.000	-67	-2	0			1.000	-1	/1-1,O-1	-0.2
	Cle-N	43	150	15	47	8	3	0	10	6		.313	.348	.407	115	3	4			.911	-5	C-39/1-1,SO	-0.6
	StL-N	66	269	42	77	12	2	2	37	14		.286	.324	.368	88	-5	14			.963	-8	1-41,C-25/2	-0.6
	Yr	115	427	57	124	20	5	2	47	21		.290	.328	.375	94	-5	18			.927	-9	C-64,1-43/OS2	-0.8

YEAR	TM/L	G	AB	R	H	2B	3B	HR	RBI	BB	SO	AVG	OBP	SLG	PRO+	BR/A	SB	CS	SBR	FA	FR	G/POS	TPR
1901	Bos-A	86	280	37	85	13	5	0	38	19		.304	.356	.386	108	3	6			.926	2	C-72/1-4	1.1
1902	Cle-A	18	74	5	25	0	0	0	9	0		.338	.338	.338	91	-1	2			.967	-1	1-17	-0.3
	Phi-A	79	284	45	92	17	2	2	43	9		.324	.347	.419	107	2	3			.960	22	C-71/1-7,O	2.9
	Yr	97	358	50	117	17	2	2	52	9		.327	.345	.402	104	1	5			.960	20	C-71,1-24/O	2.6
1903	Phi-A	92	306	26	78	13	4	3	30	11		.255	.285	.353	87	-5	0			.975	18	C-77,1-10	2.1
1904	Phi-A	95	311	23	58	9	1	1	21	5		.186	.199	.232	34	-23	3			.979	5	C-84/1-9	-1.0
1905	*Phi-A	123	420	30	114	19	6	0	45	3		.271	.278	.345	96	-4	9			.984	12	*C-114/1-2	2.1
1906	Phi-A	98	338	29	96	20	1	1	41	10		.284	.305	.358	104	0	5			.971	8	C-89/1-4	1.8
1907	Phi-A	101	356	30	97	16	3	0	38	17		.272	.306	.334	102	-0	4			.985	16	C-99/1-2	2.8
1908	Phi-A	71	207	16	46	7	1	0	16	6		.222	.248	.266	63	-9	1			.978	9	C-65/1-1	0.6
	Chi-A	6	16	1	3	0	0	0	0	1		.188	.235	.188	38	-1	0			.982	4	/C-6	0.4
	Yr	77	223	17	49	7	1	0	16	7		.220	.247	.260	61	-10	1			.978	13	C-71/1-1	1.0
Total	11	895	3057	304	829	136	31	9	338	102		.271	.297	.345	90	-42	52			.970	86	C-751/1-99,02S	11.8

■ HANK SCHREIBER

Schreiber, Henry Walter b: 7/12/1891, Cleveland, Ohio d: 2/23/68, Indianapolis, Ind. BR/TR, 5'11", 165 lbs. Deb: 4/14/14

YEAR	TM/L	G	AB	R	H	2B	3B	HR	RBI	BB	SO	AVG	OBP	SLG	PRO+	BR/A	SB	CS	SBR	FA	FR	G/POS	TPR
1914	Chi-A	1	2	0	0	0	0	0	0	0	1	.000	.000	.000	-99	-0	0			.000	-1	/O-1	-0.1
1917	Bos-N	2	7	1	2	0	0	0	0	0	1	.286	.286	.286	80	-0	0			1.000	-1	/S-1,3-1	-0.1
1919	Cin-N	19	58	5	13	4	0	0	4	0	12	.224	.224	.293	56	-3	0			.984	7	3-17/S-2	0.4
1921	NY-N	4	6	2	2	0	0	0	2	1	1	.333	.429	.333	104	0	0	0	0	.500	-0	/2-2,S-2,3	0.0
1926	Chi-N	10	18	2	1	1	0	0	0	0	1	.056	.056	.111	-55	-4	0			1.000	1	/S-3,3-3,2	-0.3
Total	5	36	91	10	18	5	0	0	6	1	16	.198	.207	.253	34	-8	0		0	.986	6	/3-22,S-8,2O	-0.1

■ TED SCHREIBER

Schreiber, Theodore Henry b: 7/11/38, Brooklyn, N.Y. BR/TR, 5'11", 175 lbs. Deb: 4/14/63

YEAR	TM/L	G	AB	R	H	2B	3B	HR	RBI	BB	SO	AVG	OBP	SLG	PRO+	BR/A	SB	CS	SBR	FA	FR	G/POS	TPR
1963	NY-N	39	50	1	8	0	0	0	2	4	14	.160	.236	.160	16	-5	0	1	-1	.977	8	3-17/S-9,2	0.2

■ POP SCHRIVER

Schriver, William Frederick b: 7/11/1865, Brooklyn, N.Y. d: 12/27/32, Brooklyn, N.Y. BR/TR, 5'9.5", 172 lbs. Deb: 4/29/1886

YEAR	TM/L	G	AB	R	H	2B	3B	HR	RBI	BB	SO	AVG	OBP	SLG	PRO+	BR/A	SB	CS	SBR	FA	FR	G/POS	TPR
1886	Bro-a	8	21	2	1	0	0	0			2	.048	.130	.048	-43	-3	0			.667	0	/O-5,C-3	-0.3
1888	Phi-N	40	134	15	26	5	2	1	23	7	21	.194	.250	.284	66	-5	2			.870	-3	C-27/S-6,3O	-0.6
1889	Phi-N	55	211	24	56	10	0	1	19	16	8	.265	.323	.327	75	-8	5			.920	3	C-48/2-6,3	0.0
1890	Phi-N	57	223	37	61	9	6	0	35	22	15	.274	.339	.368	103	0	9			.916	-3	C-34,1-10/32O	0.1
1891	Chi-N	27	90	15	30	1	4	1	21	10	9	.333	.412	.467	156	7	1			.964	2	C-27/1-2	0.9
1892	Chi-N	92	326	40	73	10	6	1	34	27	25	.224	.297	.301	80	-8	4			.929	-9	C-82,O-10	-1.1
1893	Chi-N	64	229	49	65	8	3	4	34	14	9	.284	.336	.397	96	-2	4			.926	2	C-56/O-5	0.4
1894	Chi-N	96	349	55	96	12	3	3	47	29	21	.275	.341	.352	64	-21	9			.923	-3	*C-88/S-3,31	-1.0
1895	NY-N	24	92	16	29	2	1	1	16	9	10	.315	.382	.391	102	1	3			.898	-3	C-18/1-6	0.0
1897	Cin-N	61	178	29	54	12	4	1	30	19		.303	.374	.433	105	1	3			.959	-4	C-53	0.2
1898	Pit-N	95	315	25	72	15	3	0	32	23		.229	.287	.295	68	-13	0			.957	-5	C-92/1-1	-0.8
1899	Pit-N	91	301	31	85	19	5	1	49	23		.282	.343	.389	101	0	4			.958	5	C-78/1-8	1.0
1900	*Pit-N	37	92	12	27	7	0	1	12	10		.293	.381	.402	115	2	0			.959	-4	C-24/1-1	0.0
1901	StL-N	53	166	17	45	7	3	1	23	12		.271	.335	.367	109	2	2			.971	4	C-24,1-19	0.8
Total	14	800	2727	367	720	117	40	16	375	223	118	.264	.329	.354	88	-48	46			.934	-15	C-654/1-49,032S	-0.4

■ BOB SCHRODER

Schroder, Robert James b: 12/30/44, Ridgefield, N.J. BL/TR, 6', 175 lbs. Deb: 4/20/65

YEAR	TM/L	G	AB	R	H	2B	3B	HR	RBI	BB	SO	AVG	OBP	SLG	PRO+	BR/A	SB	CS	SBR	FA	FR	G/POS	TPR
1965	SF-N	31	9	4	2	0	0	0	1	1	1	.222	.300	.222	48	-1	0	0	0	1.000	3	/2-4,3-1	0.3
1966	SF-N	10	33	0	8	0	0	0	2	0	2	.242	.242	.242	34	-3	0	0	0	.963	-5	/S-9	-0.8
1967	SF-N	62	135	20	31	4	0	0	7	15	15	.230	.307	.259	64	-6	1	0	0	.993	4	2-45/3-4	-1.5
1968	SF-N	35	44	5	7	1	1	0	2	7	3	.159	.288	.227	56	-2	0	0	0	.960	-3	2-12/S-4,3	-0.6
Total	4	138	221	29	48	5	1	0	12	23	21	.217	.294	.249	58	-11	1	0	0	.989	-15	/2-61,S-13,3	-2.6

■ BILL SCHROEDER

Schroeder, Alfred William b: 9/7/58, Baltimore, Md. BR/TR, 6'2", 200 lbs. Deb: 7/13/83

YEAR	TM/L	G	AB	R	H	2B	3B	HR	RBI	BB	SO	AVG	OBP	SLG	PRO+	BR/A	SB	CS	SBR	FA	FR	G/POS	TPR
1983	Mil-A	23	73	7	13	2	1	3	7	3	23	.178	.221	.356	60	-4	0	1	-1	.980	-3	C-23	-0.7
1984	Mil-A	61	210	29	54	6	0	14	25	8	54	.257	.291	.486	115	3	0	1	-1	.987	-5	C-58/1-1,D	-0.3
1985	Mil-A	53	194	18	47	8	0	8	25	12	61	.242	.293	.407	90	-3	0	1	-1	.987	-7	C-48/1-1,D	-0.9
1986	Mil-A	64	217	32	46	14	0	7	19	9	59	.212	.263	.373	69	-10	1	0	0	.995	-4	C-35,1-19,D	-1.2
1987	Mil-A	75	250	35	83	12	0	14	42	16	56	.332	.379	.548	138	13	5	2	0	.995	-6	C-67/1-4,D	1.1
1988	Mil-A	41	122	9	19	2	0	5	10	6	36	.156	.208	.295	44	-10	0	0	0	1.000	5	C-30,1-10/D	-0.4
1989	Cal-A	41	138	16	28	2	0	6	15	3	44	.203	.220	.348	59	-9	0	0	0	.991	10	C-33/1-8	0.3
1990	Cal-A	18	58	7	13	3	0	4	9	1	10	.224	.237	.483	98	-1	0	0	0	1.000	2	C-15/1-3	0.0
Total	8	376	1262	153	303	49	1	61	152	58	343	.240	.282	.426	91	-20	6	5	-3	.992	-8	C-309/1-46,D	-1.6

■ RICK SCHU

Schu, Richard Spencer b: 1/26/62, Philadelphia, Pa. BR/TR, 6', 170 lbs. Deb: 9/1/84

YEAR	TM/L	G	AB	R	H	2B	3B	HR	RBI	BB	SO	AVG	OBP	SLG	PRO+	BR/A	SB	CS	SBR	FA	FR	G/POS	TPR
1984	Phi-N	17	29	12	8	2	1	2	5	6	6	.276	.400	.621	180	3	0	0	0	.952	-0	3-15	0.3
1985	Phi-N	112	416	54	105	21	4	7	24	38	78	.252	.318	.373	90	-6	8	6	-1	.933	-10	*3-111	-2.0
1986	Phi-N	92	208	32	57	10	1	8	25	18	44	.274	.338	.447	111	3	2	2	-1	.913	1	3-58	0.3
1987	Phi-N	92	196	24	46	6	3	7	23	20	36	.235	.312	.403	85	-4	0	2	-1	.905	-3	3-45,1-28	-0.9
1988	Bal-A	89	270	22	69	9	4	4	20	21	49	.256	.316	.363	92	-3	6	4	-1	.937	-12	3-72/1-4,D	-1.6
1989	Bal-A	1	0	0	0	0	0	0	0	0	0	—	—	—	—	0	0	0	0	1.000	-0	/2-1	0.0
	Det-A	98	266	25	57	11	0	7	21	24	37	.214	.279	.335	74	-10	1	2	-1	.934	-2	3-83/2-5,1SD	-1.2
	Yr	99	266	25	57	11	0	7	21	24	37	.214	.279	.335	74	-10	1	2	-1	.934	-2	3-83/D-9,21S	-1.2
1990	Cal-A	61	157	19	42	8	0	6	14	11	28	.268	.315	.433	110	0	1	2	-1	.918	-3	3-38,1-15/O2	0.1
1991	Phi-N	17	22	1	2	0	0	0	2	3	4	.091	.190	.091	-37	-4	0	0	0	.667	-1	/3-3,1-1	-0.5
Total	8	579	1564	189	386	67	13	41	134	139	282	.247	.312	.385	92	-19	17	16	-5	.927	-3	3-425/1-51,D2OS	-5.5

■ HEINIE SCHUBLE

Schuble, Henry George b: 11/1/06, Houston, Tex. d: 10/2/90, Baytown, Tex. BR/TR, 5'9", 152 lbs. Deb: 7/8/27

YEAR	TM/L	G	AB	R	H	2B	3B	HR	RBI	BB	SO	AVG	OBP	SLG	PRO+	BR/A	SB	CS	SBR	FA	FR	G/POS	TPR
1927	StL-N	65	218	29	56	6	2	4	28	7	27	.257	.283	.358	69	-10	0			.915	-7	S-65	-1.0
1929	Det-A	92	258	35	60	11	7	2	28	19	23	.233	.288	.353	64	-15	3	2	-0	.886	-10	S-86/3-2	-1.5
1932	Det-A	102	340	58	92	20	6	5	52	24	37	.271	.319	.409	84	-9	14	5	1	.941	8	3-76,S-16	0.6
1933	Det-A	49	96	12	21	4	1	0	6	5	17	.219	.257	.281	42	-8	2	0	1	.951	1	3-23/S-2,2	-0.5
1934	Det-A	11	15	2	4	2	0	0	2	1	4	.267	.313	.400	83	-0	0			1.000	1	/S-3,3-2,2	0.1
1935	Det-A	11	8	3	2	0	0	0	0	1	0	.250	.333	.250	55	-0	0			.714	0	/3-2,2-1	0.1
1936	StL-N	2	0	0	0	0	0	0	0	0	0	—	—	—			0			.000	0	/3-1	0.0
Total	7	332	935	139	235	43	16	11	116	57	108	.251	.296	.367	70	-43	19	7		.906	-6	S-172,3-106/2	-2.3

■ WES SCHULMERICH

Schulmerich, Edward Wesley b: 8/21/01, Hillsboro, Ore. d: 6/26/85, Corvallis, Ore. BR/TR, 5'11", 210 lbs. Deb: 5/1/31

YEAR	TM/L	G	AB	R	H	2B	3B	HR	RBI	BB	SO	AVG	OBP	SLG	PRO+	BR/A	SB	CS	SBR	FA	FR	G/POS	TPR
1931	Bos-N	95	327	36	101	17	7	2	43	28	30	.309	.363	.422	115	7	0			.966	-4	O-87	-0.3
1932	Bos-N	119	404	47	105	22	5	11	57	27	61	.260	.314	.421	99	-1	5			.968	3	*O-101	-0.5
1933	Bos-N	29	85	10	21	6	1	1	13	5	10	.247	.289	.376	97	-1	0			.980	1	O-21	-0.1
	Phi-N	97	365	53	122	19	4	8	59	32	45	.334	.394	.474	130	15	1			.977	-2	O-97	0.8
	Yr	126	450	63	143	25	5	9	72	37	55	.318	.375	.456	126	15	1			.978	-1	*O-118	0.7
1934	Phi-N	15	52	2	13	1	0	1	4	8		.250	.316	.269	51	-3	0			.963	-1	O-13	-0.4
	Cin-N	74	209	21	55	8	3	5	19	22	43	.263	.333	.402	98	-1	1			.976	-2	O-56	-0.5
	Yr	89	261	23	68	9	3	5	20	26	51	.261	.330	.375	88	-4	1			.974	-3	O-69	-0.9
Total	4	429	1442	169	417	73	20	27	192	118	197	.289	.347	.424	109	15	7			.971	-6	O-375	-1.0

YEAR	TM/L	G	AB	R	H	2B	3B	HR	RBI	BB	SO	AVG	OBP	SLG	PRO+	BR/A	SB	CS	SBR	FA	FR	G/POS	TPR

■ ART SCHULT
Schult, Arthur William "Dutch" b: 6/20/28, Brooklyn, N.Y. BR/TR, 6'4", 220 lbs. Deb: 5/17/53

YEAR	TM/L	G	AB	R	H	2B	3B	HR	RBI	BB	SO	AVG	OBP	SLG	PRO+	BR/A	SB	CS	SBR	FA	FR	G/POS	TPR
1953	NY-A	7	0	3	0	0	0	0	0	0	0	—	—	—	—	0	0	0	0	.000	0	R	0.0
1956	Cin-N	5	7	3	3	0	0	0	2	1	1	.429	.500	.429	144	1	0	0	0	.000	-0	/O-1	0.0
1957	Cin-N	21	34	4	9	2	0	0	4	0	2	.265	.286	.324	59	-2	0	0	0	1.000	1	/O-5	-0.2
	Was-A	77	247	30	65	14	0	4	35	14	30	.263	.305	.368	84	-6	0	1	-1	.987	-1	1-35,O-31	-1.1
1959	Chi-N	42	118	17	32	7	0	2	14	7	14	.271	.323	.381	88	-2	0	0	0	.985	-4	1-23,O-15	-0.8
1960	Chi-N	12	15	1	2	1	0	0	1	1	3	.133	.188	.200	6	-2	0	0	0	1.000	0	/O-4,1-1	-0.3
Total	5	164	421	58	111	24	0	6	56	23	50	.264	.308	.363	81	-11	0	1	-1	.987	-5	/1-59,O-56	-2.4

■ FRANK SCHULTE
Schulte, Frank M. "Wildfire" b: 9/17/1882, Cohocton, N.Y. d: 10/2/49, Oakland, Cal. BL/TR, 5'11", 170 lbs. Deb: 9/21/04

YEAR	TM/L	G	AB	R	H	2B	3B	HR	RBI	BB	SO	AVG	OBP	SLG	PRO+	BR/A	SB	CS	SBR	FA	FR	G/POS	TPR
1904	Chi-N	20	84	16	24	4	3	2	13	2		.286	.310	.476	141	3	1			.949	0	O-20	0.3
1905	Chi-N	123	493	67	135	15	14	1	47	32		.274	.326	.367	102	0	16			.981	-7	*O-123	-1.3
1906	*Chi-N	146	563	77	158	18	**13**	7	60	31		.281	.324	.396	118	9	25			.975	0	*O-146	0.2
1907	*Chi-N	97	342	44	98	14	7	2	32	22		.287	.339	.386	120	7	7			.973	-3	O-92	0.0
1908	*Chi-N	102	386	42	91	20	2	1	43	29		.236	.294	.306	88	-5	15			.994	-6	*O-102	-1.8
1909	Chi-N	140	538	57	142	16	11	4	60	24		.264	.298	.357	101	-2	23			.968	-13	*O-140	-2.4
1910	*Chi-N	151	559	93	168	29	15	**10**	68	39	57	.301	.349	.460	137	22	22			.968	-6	*O-150	0.9
1911	Chi-N	154	577	105	173	30	21	**21**	**107**	76	71	.300	.384	**.534**	155	40	23			.971	-5	*O-154	2.7
1912	Chi-N	139	553	90	146	27	11	12	64	53	70	.264	.336	.418	106	3	17			.952	-4	*O-139	-0.8
1913	Chi-N	132	497	85	138	28	6	9	68	39	68	.278	.336	.412	113	7	21			.956	-8	*O-130	-0.7
1914	Chi-N	137	465	54	112	22	7	5	61	39	55	.241	.306	.351	95	-3	16			.954	-10	*O-134	-2.0
1915	Chi-N	151	550	66	137	20	6	12	62	49	68	.249	.313	.373	107	4	19	17	-5	.962	4	*O-147	-0.4
1916	Chi-N	72	230	31	68	11	1	5	27	20	35	.296	.352	.417	123	6	9			.951	-3	O-67	0.0
	Pit-N	55	177	12	45	5	3	0	14	17	19	.254	.323	.316	96	-0	5			.968	-2	O-48	-0.5
	Yr	127	407	43	113	16	4	5	41	37	54	.278	.339	.373	111	6	14			.958	-5	*O-115	-0.5
1917	Pit-N	30	103	11	22	5	1	0	7	10	14	.214	.283	.282	71	-3	5			.963	-0	O-28	-0.6
	Phi-N	64	149	21	32	10	0	1	15	16	22	.215	.299	.302	81	-3	4			.923	-10	O-42	-1.7
	Yr	94	252	32	54	15	1	1	22	26	36	.214	.293	.294	77	-6	9			.943	-10	O-70	-2.3
1918	Was-A	93	267	35	77	14	3	0	44	47	36	.288	.406	.363	135	14	5			.969	1	O-75	1.2
Total	15	1806	6533	906	1766	288	124	92	792	545	**515**	.270	.332	.395	114	98	233	17		.966	-70	*O-1737	-6.9

■ FRED SCHULTE
Schulte, Fred William "Fritz" (b: Fred William Schult) b: 1/13/01, Belvidere, Ill. d: 5/20/83, Belvidere, Ill. BR/TR, 6'1", 183 lbs. Deb: 4/15/27

YEAR	TM/L	G	AB	R	H	2B	3B	HR	RBI	BB	SO	AVG	OBP	SLG	PRO+	BR/A	SB	CS	SBR	FA	FR	G/POS	TPR
1927	StL-A	60	189	32	60	16	5	3	34	20	14	.317	.383	.503	124	6	5	3	-0	.916	-3	O-49	0.5
1928	StL-A	146	556	90	159	44	6	7	85	51	60	.286	.347	.424	99	-2	6	5	-1	.973	17	*O-143	0.5
1929	StL-A	121	446	63	137	24	5	3	71	59	44	.307	.389	.404	101	2	8	3	1	**.989**	13	*O-116	0.7
1930	StL-A	113	392	59	109	23	5	5	62	41	44	.278	.348	.401	86	-8	12	8	-1	.966	-2	O-98/1-5	-1.7
1931	StL-A	134	553	100	168	32	7	9	65	56	49	.304	.369	.436	107	6	6	8	-3	.971	6	*O-134	-0.1
1932	StL-A	146	565	106	166	35	6	9	73	71	44	.294	.373	.425	100	1	5	9	-4	.986	0	*O-129/1-5	-1.1
1933	*Was-A	144	550	98	162	30	7	5	87	61	27	.295	.366	.402	104	4	10	12	-4	.980	16	*O-142	0.8
1934	Was-A	136	524	72	156	32	6	3	73	53	34	.298	.363	.399	100	1	3	7	-3	.986	-1	O-134	-1.1
1935	Was-A	76	226	33	60	6	4	2	23	26	22	.265	.344	.354	83	-5	0	3	-2	.980	-8	O-56	-1.6
1936	Pit-N	74	238	28	62	7	3	1	17	20	20	.261	.320	.328	73	-9	1			.977	-3	O-55	-1.4
1937	Pit-N	29	20	5	2	0	0	0	3	4	3	.100	.280	.100	7	-2	0			.800	-1	/O-4	-0.4
Total	11	1179	4259	686	1241	249	54	47	593	462	361	.291	.362	.408	98	-7	56	58		.976	35	*O-1060/1-10	-5.1

■ HAM SCHULTE
Schulte, Herman Joseph (b: Herman Joseph Schultehenrich) b: 9/1/12, St.Louis, Mo. d: 12/21/92, St.Charles, Mo. BR/TR, 5'8.5", 158 lbs. Deb: 4/16/40 F

YEAR	TM/L	G	AB	R	H	2B	3B	HR	RBI	BB	SO	AVG	OBP	SLG	PRO+	BR/A	SB	CS	SBR	FA	FR	G/POS	TPR
1940	Phi-N	120	436	44	103	18	2	1	21	32	30	.236	.288	.294	63	-22	3			**.980**	-10	*2-119/S-1	-2.5

■ JOHNNY SCHULTE
Schulte, John Clement b: 9/8/1896, Fredericktown, Mo. d: 6/28/78, St.Louis, Mo. BL/TR, 5'11", 190 lbs. Deb: 4/18/23 C

YEAR	TM/L	G	AB	R	H	2B	3B	HR	RBI	BB	SO	AVG	OBP	SLG	PRO+	BR/A	SB	CS	SBR	FA	FR	G/POS	TPR
1923	StL-A	7	3	1	0	0	0	0	1	4	0	.000	.571	.000	56	0	0	0	0	1.000	1	/C-1,1-1	0.1
1927	StL-N	64	156	35	45	8	2	9	32	47	19	.288	.456	.538	160	16	1			.956	3	C-59	2.1
1928	Phi-N	65	113	14	28	2	2	4	17	15	12	.248	.336	.407	90	-2	0			.949	-0	C-34	-0.5
1929	Chi-N	31	69	6	18	3	0	0	9	7	11	.261	.329	.304	58	-4	0			.978	-0	C-30	-0.2
1932	StL-A	15	24	2	5	2	0	0	3	1	6	.208	.240	.292	35	-2	0			.864	-1	/C-6	-0.2
	Bos-N	10	9	1	2	0	0	1	2	2	1	.222	.364	.556	149	1	0			1.000	1	C-10	0.2
Total	5	192	374	59	98	15	4	14	64	76	49	.262	.388	.436	112	8	1	0		.957	-2	C-140/1-1	1.5

■ JACK SCHULTE
Schulte, John Herman Frank b: 11/15/1881, Cincinnati, Ohio d: 8/17/75, Roseville, Mich. BR/TR, 5'9", 180 lbs. Deb: 8/19/06

YEAR	TM/L	G	AB	R	H	2B	3B	HR	RBI	BB	SO	AVG	OBP	SLG	PRO+	BR/A	SB	CS	SBR	FA	FR	G/POS	TPR
1906	Bos-N	2	7	0	0	0	0	0	0	0		.000	.000	.000	-99	-2	0			1.000	-1	/S-2	-0.3

■ LEN SCHULTE
Schulte, Leonard Bernard (b: Leonard Bernard Schultehenrich) b: 12/5/16, St.Charles, Mo. d: 5/6/86, Orlando, Fla. BR/TR, 5'10", 160 lbs. Deb: 9/27/44 F

YEAR	TM/L	G	AB	R	H	2B	3B	HR	RBI	BB	SO	AVG	OBP	SLG	PRO+	BR/A	SB	CS	SBR	FA	FR	G/POS	TPR
1944	StL-A	1	0	0	0	0	0	0	0	0	0	—	1.000	—	188	0	0	0	0	.000	0	H	0.0
1945	StL-A	119	430	37	106	16	1	0	36	24	35	.247	.286	.288	64	-20	0	3	-2	.961	-8	3-71,2-37,S	-2.8
1946	StL-A	4	5	1	2	0	0	0	2	0	0	.400	.400	.400	118	0	0	0	0	1.000	1	/2-1,3-1	0.1
Total	3	124	435	38	108	16	1	0	38	25	35	.248	.289	.290	65	-20	0	3	-2	.962	-7	/3-72,2-38,S	-2.7

■ HOWIE SCHULTZ
Schultz, Howard Henry "Stretch" or "Steeple" b: 7/3/22, St.Paul, Minn. BR/TR, 6'6", 200 lbs. Deb: 8/16/43

YEAR	TM/L	G	AB	R	H	2B	3B	HR	RBI	BB	SO	AVG	OBP	SLG	PRO+	BR/A	SB	CS	SBR	FA	FR	G/POS	TPR
1943	Bro-N	45	182	20	49	12	0	1	34	6	24	.269	.300	.352	88	-3	3			.986	2	1-45	-0.5
1944	Bro-N	138	526	59	134	32	3	11	83	24	67	.255	.290	.390	92	-8	6			.988	0	*1-136	-1.6
1945	Bro-N	39	142	18	34	8	2	1	19	10	14	.239	.294	.345	78	-5	2			.984	3	1-38	-0.4
1946	Bro-N	90	249	27	63	14	1	3	27	16	34	.253	.298	.353	84	-6	2			.989	5	1-87	-0.5
1947	Bro-N	2	1	0	0	0	0	0	0	0	0	.000	.000	.000	-96	-0	0			1.000	-0	/1-1	0.0
	Phi-N	114	403	30	90	19	1	6	35	21	70	.223	.264	.320	56	-27	0			.993	-1	*1-114	-3.1
	Yr	116	404	30	90	19	1	6	35	21	70	.223	.263	.319	56	-27	0			.993	-1	*1-115	-3.1
1948	Phi-N	6	13	0	1	0	0	0	1	1	2	.077	.143	.077	-40	-3	0			1.000	-0	/1-3	-0.2
	Cin-N	36	72	9	12	0	0	2	9	4	7	.167	.211	.250	25	-8	2			.982	-3	1-26	-1.1
	Yr	42	85	9	13	0	0	2	10	5	9	.153	.200	.224	15	-10	2			.984	-3	1-29	-1.3
Total	6	470	1588	163	383	85	7	24	208	82	218	.241	.281	.349	75	-60	15			.989	6	1-450	-7.4

■ JOHN SCHULTZ
Schultz, John b: St.Louis, Mo. Deb: 8/7/1891

YEAR	TM/L	G	AB	R	H	2B	3B	HR	RBI	BB	SO	AVG	OBP	SLG	PRO+	BR/A	SB	CS	SBR	FA	FR	G/POS	TPR
1891	StL-a	1	2	0	0	0	0	0	0	0	0	.000	.000	.000	-87	-0	0			1.000	0	/C-1	0.0

■ JOE SCHULTZ
Schultz, Joseph Charles Jr. "Dode" b: 8/29/18, Chicago, Ill. BL/TR, 5'11", 184 lbs. Deb: 9/27/39 FMC

YEAR	TM/L	G	AB	R	H	2B	3B	HR	RBI	BB	SO	AVG	OBP	SLG	PRO+	BR/A	SB	CS	SBR	FA	FR	G/POS	TPR
1939	Pit-N	4	14	3	4	2	0	0	2	2	0	.286	.375	.429	117	0	0			1.000	1	/C-4	0.1
1940	Pit-N	16	36	2	7	0	1	0	4	2	1	.194	.237	.250	35	-3	0			.917	-3	C-13	-0.6
1941	Pit-N	2	2	1	1	0	0	0	0	0	0	.500	.500	.500	183	0	0			.000	0	/C-2	0.0
1943	StL-A	46	92	6	22	0	0	0	8	9	8	.239	.307	.293	74	-3	0	1	-1	.979	-5	C-26	-0.8
1944	StL-A	3	8	1	2	0	0	0	0	1	0	.250	.250	.250	41	-1	0			.818	-1	/C-3	-0.1
1945	StL-A	41	44	1	13	2	0	0	8	3	1	.295	.340	.341	93	-0	0			.941	5	/C-4	0.0
1946	StL-A	42	57	3	22	4	0	0	14	11	2	.386	.485	.456	156	5	0			1.000	-5	C-17	0.1
1947	StL-A	43	38	3	7	0	0	0	8	4	5	.184	.262	.263	45	-3	0			.000	0	H	-0.3

YEAR	TM/L	G	AB	R	H	2B	3B	HR	RBI	BB	SO	AVG	OBP	SLG	PRO+	BR/A	SB	CS	SBR	FA	FR	G/POS	TPR
1948	StL-A	43	37	0	7	0	0	0	9	6	3	.189	.302	.189	32	-3	0	0	0	.000	0	H	-0.3
Total	9	240	328	18	85	13	1	1	46	37	21	.259	.334	.314	81	-8	0	1		.964	-12	/C-69	-1.9

■ JOE SCHULTZ
Schultz, Joseph Charles Sr. "Germany" b: 7/24/1893, Pittsburgh, Pa. d: 4/13/41, Columbia, S.C. BR/TR, 5'11.5", 172 lbs. Deb: 9/28/12 F

YEAR	TM/L	G	AB	R	H	2B	3B	HR	RBI	BB	SO	AVG	OBP	SLG	PRO+	BR/A	SB	CS	SBR	FA	FR	G/POS	TPR
1912	Bos-N	4	12	1	3	1	0	0	4	0	2	.250	.250	.333	58	-1	0			.824	-0	/2-4	-0.1
1913	Bos-N	9	18	2	4	0	0	0	1	2	7	.222	.333	.222	59	-1	0			1.000	0	/O-5,2-1	-0.1
1915	Bro-N	56	120	13	35	3	2	0	4	10	18	.292	.346	.350	109	1	3	4	-2	.894	-4	3-27/S-1	-0.3
	Chi-N	7	8	1	2	0	0	0	3	0	2	.250	.250	.250	51	-0	0			.857	0	/2-2	0.0
	Yr	63	128	14	37	3	2	0	7	10	20	.289	.341	.344	106	1	3	4	-2	.894	-3	3-27/2-2,S	-0.3
1916	Pit-N	77	204	18	53	8	2	0	22	7	14	.260	.298	.319	88	-3	6			.840	-15	2-24,3-24/OS	-1.9
1919	StL-N	88	229	24	58	9	1	2	21	11	7	.253	.287	.328	90	-3	4			1.000	-7	O-49/2-6,3	-1.4
1920	StL-N	99	320	38	84	5	5	0	32	21	11	.262	.308	.309	81	-8	5	4	-1	.945	-4	O-80	-2.0
1921	StL-N	92	275	37	85	20	3	6	45	15	11	.309	.347	.469	116	6	4	3	-1	.977	-2	O-67/3-1,3,1	-0.1
1922	StL-N	112	344	50	108	13	4	2	64	19	10	.314	.350	.392	96	-3	3	1	0	.976	2	O-89	-0.6
1923	StL-N	2	7	0	2	0	0	0	1	1	0	.286	.375	.286	78	-0	0	0	0	1.000	0	/O-2	0.0
1924	StL-N	12	12	0	2	0	0	0	2	3	0	.167	.333	.167	39	-1	0	0	0	1.000	-1	/O-2	-0.2
	Phi-N	88	284	35	80	15	1	5	29	20	18	.282	.329	.394	83	-7	6	2	1	.960	-6	O-76	-1.8
	Yr	100	296	35	82	15	1	5	31	23	18	.277	.329	.385	82	-8	6	2	1	.960	-7	O-78	-2.0
1925	Phi-N	24	64	10	22	6	0	0	8	4	1	.344	.382	.438	100	0	1	1	-0	.923	-2	O-20	-0.3
	Cin-N	33	62	6	20	3	1	0	13	3	1	.323	.354	.403	95	-0	3	1	0	.950	-4	O-15/2-1	-0.5
	Yr	57	126	16	42	9	1	0	21	7	2	.333	.368	.421	99	-0	4	2	0	.932	-6	O-35/2-1	-0.8
Total	11	703	1959	235	558	83	19	15	249	116	102	.285	.327	.370	93	-21	35	16		.966	-43	O-411/3-55,21S	-9.3

■ JEFF SCHULZ
Schulz, Jeffrey Alan b: 6/2/61, Evansville, Ind. BL/TR, 6'1", 190 lbs. Deb: 9/2/89

YEAR	TM/L	G	AB	R	H	2B	3B	HR	RBI	BB	SO	AVG	OBP	SLG	PRO+	BR/A	SB	CS	SBR	FA	FR	G/POS	TPR
1989	KC-A	7	9	0	2	0	0	0	0	2	.222	.222	.222	26	-1	0	0	0	1.000	-0	/O-5	-0.1
1990	KC-A	30	66	5	17	5	1	0	6	6	13	.258	.319	.364	92	-1	0	0	0	.943	-3	O-22/D-1	-0.4
1991	Pit-N	3	3	0	0	0	0	0	0	0	2	.000	.000	.000	-99	-1	0	0	0	.000	0	/H	-0.1
Total	3	40	78	5	19	5	1	0	7	6	17	.244	.298	.333	77	-2	0	0	0	.951	-4	/O-27,D-1	-0.6

■ BILL SCHUSTER
Schuster, William Charles "Broadway Bill" b: 8/4/12, Buffalo, N.Y. d: 6/28/87, ElMonte, Cal. BR/TR, 5'9", 164 lbs. Deb: 9/29/37

YEAR	TM/L	G	AB	R	H	2B	3B	HR	RBI	BB	SO	AVG	OBP	SLG	PRO+	BR/A	SB	CS	SBR	FA	FR	G/POS	TPR
1937	Pit-N	3	6	2	3	0	0	0	1	1	0	.500	.571	.500	193		0			1.000	1	/S-2	0.2
1939	Bos-N	2	3	0	0	0	0	0	0	0	1	.000	.000	.000	-99	-1	0			.833	-0	/S-1,3-1	-0.1
1943	Chi-N	13	51	3	15	2	1	0	0	3	2	.294	.333	.373	105	0	0			.977	7	S-13	0.8
1944	Chi-N	60	154	14	34	7	1	1	14	12	16	.221	.277	.299	62	-8	3			.946	-8	S-38/2-6	-1.0
1945	*Chi-N	45	47	8	9	2	1	0	2	7	4	.191	.296	.277	61	-2	2			.949	8	S-22/2-3,3,3	0.7
Total	5	123	261	27	61	11	3	1	17	23	23	.234	.296	.310	72	-10	6			.954	11	/S-76,2-9,3	0.6

■ RANDY SCHWARTZ
Schwartz, Douglas Randall b: 2/9/44, Los Angeles, Cal. BL/TL, 6'3", 230 lbs. Deb: 9/8/65

YEAR	TM/L	G	AB	R	H	2B	3B	HR	RBI	BB	SO	AVG	OBP	SLG	PRO+	BR/A	SB	CS	SBR	FA	FR	G/POS	TPR
1965	KC-A	6	7	0	2	0	0	0	1	0	4	.286	.286	.286	64	-0	0	0	0	1.000	1	/1-2	0.0
1966	KC-A	10	11	0	1	0	0	0	1	1	3	.091	.167	.091	-24	-2	0	0	0	1.000	-0	/1-2	-0.2
Total	2	16	18	0	3	0	0	0	2	1	7	.167	.211	.167	10	-2	0	0	0	1.000	0	/1-4	-0.2

■ BILL SCHWARTZ
Schwartz, William August "Pop" or "Scooper Bill" b: 4/3/1864, Jamestown, Ky. d: 12/22/40, Newport, Ky. BR/TR, 6'1", 195 lbs. Deb: 5/3/1883

YEAR	TM/L	G	AB	R	H	2B	3B	HR	RBI	BB	SO	AVG	OBP	SLG	PRO+	BR/A	SB	CS	SBR	FA	FR	G/POS	TPR
1883	Col-a	2	4	0	1	0	0	0		0		.250	.250	.250	67	-0				.600	-1	/1-1,C-1	-0.1
1884	Cin-U	29	106	14	25	4	0	1		3		.236	.257	.302	48	-8				.837	-4	C-25/O-3,3	-0.9
Total	2	31	110	14	26	4	0	1		3		.236	.257	.300	48	-8				.828	-6	/C-26,O-3,31	-1.0

■ BILL SCHWARTZ
Schwartz, William Charles "Blab" b: 4/22/1884, Cleveland, Ohio d: 8/29/61, Nashville, Tenn. BR/TR, 6'2", 185 lbs. Deb: 5/2/04

YEAR	TM/L	G	AB	R	H	2B	3B	HR	RBI	BB	SO	AVG	OBP	SLG	PRO+	BR/A	SB	CS	SBR	FA	FR	G/POS	TPR
1904	Cle-A	24	86	5	13	2	0	0	6		3	.151	.151	.174	3	-9	4			.980	-4	1-22/3-1	-1.6

■ BILL SCHWARZ
Schwarz, William De Witt b: 1/30/1891, Birmingham, Ala. d: 6/24/49, Jacksonville, Fla TR , Deb: 8/20/14

YEAR	TM/L	G	AB	R	H	2B	3B	HR	RBI	BB	SO	AVG	OBP	SLG	PRO+	BR/A	SB	CS	SBR	FA	FR	G/POS	TPR
1914	NY-A	1	1	0	0	0	0	0	0	0	0	.000	.000	.000	-99	-0	0			1.000	0	/C-1	0.0

■ AL SCHWEITZER
Schweitzer, Albert Caspar "Cheese" b: 12/23/1882, Cleveland, Ohio d: 1/27/69, Newark, Ohio BR/TR, 5'6", 170 lbs. Deb: 4/30/08

YEAR	TM/L	G	AB	R	H	2B	3B	HR	RBI	BB	SO	AVG	OBP	SLG	PRO+	BR/A	SB	CS	SBR	FA	FR	G/POS	TPR
1908	StL-A	64	182	22	53	4	2	1	14	20		.291	.374	.352	135	8	6			.952	5	O-55	1.2
1909	StL-A	27	76	7	17	2	0	0	2	5		.224	.298	.250	79	-2	3			.933	-3	O-22	-0.6
1910	StL-A	113	379	37	87	11	2	2	37	36		.230	.303	.285	90	-4	26			.937	-4	*O-109	-1.5
1911	StL-A	76	237	31	51	11	4	0	34	43		.215	.338	.295	80	-5	12			.934	-1	O-68	-0.9
Total	4	280	874	97	208	28	8	3	87	104		.238	.327	.299	95	-3	47			.940	-3	O-254	-1.8

■ PI SCHWERT
Schwert, Pius Louis b: 11/22/1892, Angola, N.Y. d: 3/11/41, Washington, D.C. BR/TR, 5'10.5", 160 lbs. Deb: 10/6/14

YEAR	TM/L	G	AB	R	H	2B	3B	HR	RBI	BB	SO	AVG	OBP	SLG	PRO+	BR/A	SB	CS	SBR	FA	FR	G/POS	TPR
1914	NY-A	2	5	0	0	0	0	0	0	2	2	.000	.286	.000	-13	-1	0			.909	1	/C-2	0.0
1915	NY-A	9	18	6	5	3	0	0	6	1	6	.278	.316	.444	128	0	0			.972	0	/C-9	0.1
Total	2	11	23	6	5	3	0	0	6	3	8	.217	.308	.348	97	-0	0			.957	1	/C-11	0.1

■ ART SCHWIND
Schwind, Arthur Edwin b: 11/4/1889, Ft.Wayne, Ind. d: 1/13/68, Sullivan, Ill. BB/TR, 5'8", 150 lbs. Deb: 10/3/12

YEAR	TM/L	G	AB	R	H	2B	3B	HR	RBI	BB	SO	AVG	OBP	SLG	PRO+	BR/A	SB	CS	SBR	FA	FR	G/POS	TPR
1912	Bos-N	1	2	0	1	0	0	0	0	0	0	.500	.500	.500	171	0	0			.000	0	/3-1	0.0

■ JERRY SCHYPINSKI
Schypinski, Gerald Albert b: 9/16/31, Detroit, Mich. BL/TR, 5'10", 170 lbs. Deb: 8/31/55

YEAR	TM/L	G	AB	R	H	2B	3B	HR	RBI	BB	SO	AVG	OBP	SLG	PRO+	BR/A	SB	CS	SBR	FA	FR	G/POS	TPR
1955	KC-A	22	69	7	15	2	0	0	5	1	6	.217	.229	.246	27	-7	0	0	0	.932	-2	S-21/2-2	-0.8

■ MIKE SCIOSCIA
Scioscia, Michael Lorri b: 11/27/58, Upper Darby, Pa. BL/TR, 6'2", 220 lbs. Deb: 4/20/80

YEAR	TM/L	G	AB	R	H	2B	3B	HR	RBI	BB	SO	AVG	OBP	SLG	PRO+	BR/A	SB	CS	SBR	FA	FR	G/POS	TPR
1980	LA-N	54	134	8	34	5	1	1	8	12	9	.254	.315	.328	81	-3	1	0	0	.992	3	C-54	0.2
1981	*LA-N	93	290	27	80	10	2	2	29	36	18	.276	.358	.331	100	1	0	2	-1	.987	-3	C-91	0.0
1982	LA-N	129	365	31	80	11	1	5	38	44	31	.219	.305	.296	70	-14	2	0	1	.986	-7	*C-123	-1.7
1983	LA-N	12	35	3	11	3	0	1	7	5	2	.314	.400	.486	145	2	0	0	0	1.000	-0	C-11	0.0
1984	LA-N	114	341	29	93	18	0	5	38	52	26	.273	.371	.370	110	6	2	0	0	.985	14	*C-112	2.6
1985	*LA-N	141	429	47	127	26	3	7	53	77	21	.296	.409	.420	136	25	3	3	-1	.986	3	*C-139	3.4
1986	LA-N	122	374	36	94	18	1	5	26	62	25	.251	.362	.345	103	4	3	3	-1	.982	-1	*C-119	1.0
1987	LA-N	142	461	44	122	26	1	6	38	55	23	.265	.344	.364	90	-6	7	4	-0	.989	11	*C-138	1.4
1988	*LA-N	130	408	29	105	18	0	3	35	38	31	.257	.321	.324	88	-6	0	3	-2	.991	9	*C-123	1.0
1989	LA-N★	133	408	40	102	16	0	10	44	52	29	.250	.339	.363	102	2	0	2	-1	.988	18	*C-130	2.7
1990	LA-N★	135	435	46	115	25	0	12	66	55	31	.264	.351	.405	110	7	4	1	1	.989	5	*C-132	2.1
1991	LA-N	119	345	39	91	16	2	8	40	47	32	.264	.357	.391	113	7	3	6	-3	.990	9	*C-115	2.1
1992	LA-N	117	348	19	77	6	3	3	24	32	31	.221	.289	.282	63	-17	3	2	0	.988	-8	*C-108	0.0
Total	13	1441	4373	398	1131	198	12	68	446	567	307	.259	.347	.356	99	9	29	24	-6	.988	67	*C-1395	14.8

■ LOU SCOFFIC
Scoffic, Louis "Weaser" b: 5/20/13, Herrin, Ill. BR/TR, 5'10", 182 lbs. Deb: 4/16/36

YEAR	TM/L	G	AB	R	H	2B	3B	HR	RBI	BB	SO	AVG	OBP	SLG	PRO+	BR/A	SB	CS	SBR	FA	FR	G/POS	TPR
1936	StL-N	4	7	2	3	0	0	0	2	1	2	.429	.500	.429	153	1	0			.875	-0	/O-3	0.0

■ DARYL SCONIERS
Sconiers, Daryl Anthony b: 10/3/58, San Bernardino, Cal. BL/TL, 6'2", 195 lbs. Deb: 9/13/81

YEAR	TM/L	G	AB	R	H	2B	3B	HR	RBI	BB	SO	AVG	OBP	SLG	PRO+	BR/A	SB	CS	SBR	FA	FR	G/POS	TPR
1981	Cal-A	15	52	6	14	1	1	1	7	1	10	.269	.283	.385	91	-1	0	0	0	1.000	1	1-12/D-3	-0.1
1982	Cal-A	12	13	0	2	0	0	0	0	2	3	.154	.267	.154	19	-1	0	0	0	1.000	0	/1-3,D-1	-0.1
1983	Cal-A	106	314	49	86	19	3	8	46	24	41	.274	.311	.430	102	0	4	2	0	.986	-5	1-57,D-27/O	-0.8
1984	Cal-A	57	160	14	39	8	0	4	17	13	17	.244	.301	.344	78	-5	1	2	-1	.990	-1	1-41/D-1	-0.9

YEAR	TM/L	G	AB	R	H	2B	3B	HR	RBI	BB	SO	AVG	OBP	SLG	PRO+	BR/A	SB	CS	SBR	FA	FR	G/POS	TPR
1985	Cal-A	44	98	14	28	6	1	2	12	15	18	.286	.381	.429	122	3	2	1	0	.973	-1	D-20/1-6	0.2
Total	5	234	637	83	169	30	5	15	84	48	87	.265	.317	.399	97	-3	7	5	-1	.989	-6	1-119/D-52,O	-1.7

■ SCOTT   Scott,   Deb: 7/16/1884

YEAR	TM/L	G	AB	R	H	2B	3B	HR	RBI	BB	SO	AVG	OBP	SLG	PRO+	BR/A	SB	CS	SBR	FA	FR	G/POS	TPR
1884	Bal-U	13	53	10	12	1	1	1		2		.226	.255	.340	54	-4				.909	-2	O-13/3-1	-0.5

■ TONY SCOTT   Scott, Anthony b: 9/18/51, Cincinnati, Ohio BB/TR, 6', 175 lbs. Deb: 9/1/73

YEAR	TM/L	G	AB	R	H	2B	3B	HR	RBI	BB	SO	AVG	OBP	SLG	PRO+	BR/A	SB	CS	SBR	FA	FR	G/POS	TPR
1973	Mon-N	11	1	2	0	0	0	0	0	0	1	.000	.000	.000	-97	-0	0	0	0	.000	-2	/O-3	-0.2
1974	Mon-N	19	7	2	2	0	0	0	1	1	3	.286	.375	.286	82	-0	1	1	-0	1.000	-5	O-16	-0.6
1975	Mon-N	92	143	19	26	4	2	0	11	12	38	.182	.259	.238	37	-12	5	6	-2	.962	-9	O-71	-2.6
1977	StL-N	95	292	38	85	16	3	3	41	33	48	.291	.369	.397	107	4	13	10	-2	.996	5	O-89	0.3
1978	StL-N	96	219	28	50	5	2	1	14	14	41	.228	.281	.283	59	-12	5	6	-2	.946	-9	O-77	-2.7
1979	StL-N	153	587	69	152	22	10	6	68	34	92	.259	.305	.361	80	-16	37	17	1	.984	17	*O-151	-0.5
1980	StL-N	143	415	51	104	19	3	0	28	35	68	.251	.310	.311	72	-15	22	10	1	.997	1	*O-134	-2.0
1981	StL-N	45	176	21	40	5	2	2	17	5	22	.227	.253	.313	58	-10	10	7	-1	1.000	1	O-44	-1.3
	*Hou-N	55	225	28	66	13	2	2	22	15	32	.293	.338	.396	113	3	8	3	1	.985	1	O-55	0.3
	Yr	100	401	49	106	18	4	4	39	20	54	.264	.301	.359	88	-7	18	10	-1	.992	2	O-99	-1.0
1982	Hou-N	132	460	43	110	16	3	1	29	15	56	.239	.265	.293	61	-26	18	4	3	.982	-3	*O-129	-3.1
1983	Hou-N	80	186	20	42	6	1	2	17	11	39	.226	.269	.301	62	-10	5	4	-1	1.000	-12	O-61	-2.6
1984	Hou-N	25	21	2	4	1	0	0	0	4	3	.190	.320	.238	63	-1	0	0	0	1.000	-1	/O-6	-0.2
	Mon-N	45	71	8	18	4	0	0	5	7	21	.254	.321	.310	81	-2	1	1	-0	1.000	-1	O-17	-0.4
	Yr	70	92	10	22	5	0	0	5	11	24	.239	.320	.293	78	-3	1	1	-0	1.000	-3	O-23	-0.6
Total	11	991	2803	331	699	111	28	17	253	186	464	.249	.300	.327	75	-97	125	69	-4	.986	-18	O-853	-15.6

■ DONNIE SCOTT   Scott, Donald Malcolm b: 8/16/61, Dunedin, Fla. BB/TR, 5'11", 185 lbs. Deb: 9/30/83

YEAR	TM/L	G	AB	R	H	2B	3B	HR	RBI	BB	SO	AVG	OBP	SLG	PRO+	BR/A	SB	CS	SBR	FA	FR	G/POS	TPR
1983	Tex-A	2	4	0	0	0	0	0	0	0	0	.000	.000	.000	-99	-1	0	0	0	1.000	1	/C-2	0.0
1984	Tex-A	81	235	16	52	9	0	3	20	20	44	.221	.282	.298	59	-13	0	1	-1	.974	4	C-80	-0.6
1985	Sea-A	80	185	18	41	13	0	4	23	15	41	.222	.280	.357	72	-7	1	1	-0	.981	-7	C-74	-1.2
1991	Cin-N	10	19	0	3	0	0	0	0	0	2	.158	.158	.158	-11	-3	0	0	0	1.000	-3	/C-8	-0.6
Total	4	173	443	34	96	22	0	7	43	35	87	.217	.274	.314	60	-24	1	2	-1	.977	-5	C-164	-2.4

■ PETE SCOTT   Scott, Floyd John b: 12/21/1898, Woodland, Cal. d: 5/3/53, Daly City, Cal. BR/TR, 5'11.5", 175 lbs. Deb: 4/13/26

YEAR	TM/L	G	AB	R	H	2B	3B	HR	RBI	BB	SO	AVG	OBP	SLG	PRO+	BR/A	SB	CS	SBR	FA	FR	G/POS	TPR
1926	Chi-N	77	189	34	54	13	1	3	34	22	31	.286	.363	.413	107	2	3			.968	-1	O-59/3-1	-0.2
1927	Chi-N	71	156	28	49	18	1	0	21	19	18	.314	.392	.442	123	5	1			.986	-2	O-36	0.1
1928	Pit-N	60	177	33	55	10	4	5	33	18	14	.311	.378	.497	122	5	1			.979	2	O-42/1-8	0.4
Total	3	208	522	95	158	41	6	8	88	59	63	.303	.377	.450	117	13	5			.976	-1	O-137/1-8,3	0.3

■ GARY SCOTT   Scott, Gary Thomas b: 8/22/68, New Rochelle, N.Y. BR/TR, 6', 175 lbs. Deb: 4/9/91

YEAR	TM/L	G	AB	R	H	2B	3B	HR	RBI	BB	SO	AVG	OBP	SLG	PRO+	BR/A	SB	CS	SBR	FA	FR	G/POS	TPR
1991	Chi-N	31	79	8	13	3	0	1	5	13	14	.165	.305	.241	53	-5	0	1	-1	.969	-3	3-31	-0.4
1992	Chi-N	36	96	8	15	2	0	2	11	5	14	.156	.198	.240	23	-10	0	1	-1	.922	-2	3-29/S-2	-1.4
Total	2	67	175	16	28	5	0	3	16	18	28	.160	.250	.240	38	-14	0	2	-1	.946	-0	/3-60,S-2	-1.8

■ GEORGE SCOTT   Scott, George Charles "Boomer" b: 3/23/44, Greenville, Miss. BR/TR, 6'2", 215 lbs. Deb: 4/12/66

YEAR	TM/L	G	AB	R	H	2B	3B	HR	RBI	BB	SO	AVG	OBP	SLG	PRO+	BR/A	SB	CS	SBR	FA	FR	G/POS	TPR
1966	Bos-A★	162	601	73	147	18	7	27	90	65	152	.245	.326	.433	105	4	4	0	1	.991	3	*1-158/3-5	-0.3
1967	*Bos-A	159	565	74	171	21	7	19	82	63	119	.303	.377	.465	136	26	10	8	-2	.987	-5	*1-152/3-2	1.1
1968	Bos-A	124	350	23	60	14	0	3	25	26	88	.171	.239	.237	42	-24	3	5	-2	.987	1	*1-112/3-6	-3.7
1969	Bos-A	152	549	63	139	14	5	16	52	61	74	.253	.332	.384	95	-4	4	3	-1	.954	-6	*3-109,1-53	-1.4
1970	Bos-A	127	480	50	142	24	5	16	63	44	95	.296	.357	.467	117	11	4	11	-5	.934	-8	3-68,1-59	-0.9
1971	Bos-A	146	537	72	141	16	4	24	78	41	102	.263	.321	.441	106	3	0	3	-2	.992	-7	*1-143	-2.1
1972	Mil-A	152	578	71	154	24	4	20	88	43	130	.266	.322	.426	123	15	16	4	2	.992	-5	*1-139,3-23	0.0
1973	Mil-A	158	604	98	185	30	4	24	107	61	94	.306	.372	.488	144	34	9	5	-0	.994	7	*1-157/D-1	2.8
1974	Mil-A	158	604	74	170	36	2	17	82	59	90	.281	.348	.432	124	18	9	9	-3	.992	8	*1-148/D-9	1.3
1975	Mil-A★	158	617	86	176	26	4	36	109	51	97	.285	.343	.515	139	29	6	5	-1	.989	5	*1-144,D-12/3	2.1
1976	Mil-A	156	606	73	166	21	5	18	77	53	118	.274	.337	.414	122	15	0	1	-1	.991	-2	*1-155	0.2
1977	Bos-A★	157	584	103	157	26	5	33	95	57	112	.269	.340	.500	112	8	1	1	-0	.985	-1	*1-157	-0.1
1978	Bos-A	120	412	51	96	16	4	12	54	44	86	.233	.307	.379	83	-10	1	1	-0	.991	-8	*1-113/D-7	-2.6
1979	Bos-A	45	156	18	35	9	1	4	23	17	22	.224	.301	.372	76	-5	0	0	-0	.986	-2	1-41	-1.0
	KC-A	44	146	19	39	8	2	1	20	12	32	.267	.331	.370	89	-3	1	1	-0	.989	-3	1-41/3-1,D	-0.8
	NY-A	16	44	9	14	3	1	1	6	2	7	.318	.340	.500	128	2	1	0	0	1.000	0	D-15/1-1	0.1
	Yr	105	346	46	88	20	4	6	49	31	61	.254	.319	.387	87	-6	2	1	-0	.987	-5	1-83,D-17/3	-1.7
Total	14	2034	7433	957	1992	306	60	271	1051	699	1418	.268	.335	.435	113	119	69	57	-14	.990	-25	*1-1773,3-219/D	-5.3

■ JIM SCOTT   Scott, James Walter b: 9/22/1888, Shenandoah, Pa. d: 5/12/72, S.Pasadena, Fla. BR/TR, 5'9.5", 165 lbs. Deb: 4/22/14

YEAR	TM/L	G	AB	R	H	2B	3B	HR	RBI	BB	SO	AVG	OBP	SLG	PRO+	BR/A	SB	CS	SBR	FA	FR	G/POS	TPR
1914	Pit-F	8	24	2	6	1	0	0	1	5	0	.250	.379	.292	76	-1	1			.800	-3	/S-8	-0.3

■ JOHN SCOTT   Scott, John Henry b: 1/24/52, Jackson, Miss. BR/TR, 6'2", 165 lbs. Deb: 9/7/74

YEAR	TM/L	G	AB	R	H	2B	3B	HR	RBI	BB	SO	AVG	OBP	SLG	PRO+	BR/A	SB	CS	SBR	FA	FR	G/POS	TPR
1974	SD-N	14	15	3	1	0	0	0	0	0	4	.067	.067	.067	-65	-3	1	0	-0	1.000	-1	/O-8	-0.4
1975	SD-N	25	9	6	0	0	0	0	0	0	2	.000	.000	.000	-99	-2	2	0	1	1.000	-1	/O-1	-0.3
1977	Tor-A	79	233	26	56	9	0	2	15	8	39	.240	.266	.305	54	-15	10	8	-2	.963	-5	O-67/D-2	-2.4
Total	3	118	257	35	57	9	0	2	15	8	45	.222	.245	.280	43	-21	13	8	-1	.965	-6	/O-76,D-2	-3.1

■ LE GRANT SCOTT   Scott, Le Grant Edward b: 7/25/10, Cleveland, Ohio d: 11/12/93, Birmingham, Ala. BL/TL, 5'8.5", 170 lbs. Deb: 4/19/39

YEAR	TM/L	G	AB	R	H	2B	3B	HR	RBI	BB	SO	AVG	OBP	SLG	PRO+	BR/A	SB	CS	SBR	FA	FR	G/POS	TPR
1939	Phi-N	76	232	31	65	15	1	1	26	22	14	.280	.343	.366	93	-2	1			.959	1	O-55	-0.3

■ EVERETT SCOTT   Scott, Lewis Everett "Deacon" b: 11/19/1892, Bluffton, Ind. d: 11/2/60, Fort Wayne, Ind. BR/TR, 5'8", 148 lbs. Deb: 4/14/14

YEAR	TM/L	G	AB	R	H	2B	3B	HR	RBI	BB	SO	AVG	OBP	SLG	PRO+	BR/A	SB	CS	SBR	FA	FR	G/POS	TPR
1914	Bos-A	144	539	66	129	15	6	0	37	32	43	.239	.286	.301	76	-17	9	14	-6	.949	-11	*S-143	-2.4
1915	*Bos-A	100	359	25	72	11	0	0	28	17	21	.201	.237	.231	41	-27	4	7	-3	.961	4	*S-100	-2.0
1916	*Bos-A	123	366	37	85	19	2	0	27	23	24	.232	.283	.295	73	-13	8			.967	7	*S-121/2-1,3	-0.1
1917	Bos-A	157	528	40	127	24	7	0	50	20	46	.241	.268	.313	78	-16	12			.953	8	*S-157	-0.1
1918	*Bos-A	126	443	40	98	11	5	0	43	12	16	.221	.242	.269	55	-26	11			.976	18	*S-126	-0.3
1919	Bos-A	138	507	41	141	19	0	0	38	19	26	.278	.306	.316	79	-15	8			.976	7	*S-138	0.0
1920	Bos-A	154	569	41	153	21	12	4	61	21	15	.269	.300	.369	80	-19	4	11	-5	.973	17	*S-154	0.6
1921	Bos-A	154	576	65	151	21	9	4	62	27	21	.262	.295	.335	62	-34	5	9	-4	.972	38	*S-154	1.4
1922	*NY-A	154	557	64	150	23	5	3	45	23	22	.269	.304	.345	67	-27	2	3	-1	.966	17	*S-154	0.5
1923	*NY-A	152	533	48	131	16	4	6	60	13	19	.246	.266	.325	54	-37	1	3	-2	.961	-11	*S-152	-3.5
1924	NY-A	153	548	56	137	12	6	4	64	21	15	.250	.278	.316	53	-40	3	7	-3	.966	10	*S-153	-1.6
1925	NY-A	22	60	3	13	0	0	0	4	2	2	.217	.242	.217	17	-8	0	1	-1	.988	3	S-18	-0.3
	Was-A	33	103	10	28	6	1	0	18	4	4	.272	.299	.350	65	-6	1	2	-1	.932	3	S-30/3-2	-0.1
	Yr	55	163	13	41	6	1	0	22	6	6	.252	.278	.301	48	-13	1	3	-2	.952	6	S-48/3-2	-0.4
1926	Chi-A	40	143	15	36	10	1	0	13	9	8	.252	.296	.336	67	-7	1	3	-2	.955	-5	S-39	0.0
	Cin-N	4	6	1	4	0	0	0	0	0	0	.667	.667	.667	267	1	0			.875	0	/S-4	0.2
Total	13	1654	5837	552	1455	208	58	20	551	243	282	.249	.281	.315	65	-291	69	60		.965	115	*S-1643/3-3,2	-7.6

■ MILT SCOTT   Scott, Milton Parker "Mikado Milt" b: 1/17/1866, Chicago, Ill. d: 11/3/38, Baltimore, Md. BR, 5'9", 160 lbs. Deb: 9/30/1882

YEAR	TM/L	G	AB	R	H	2B	3B	HR	RBI	BB	SO	AVG	OBP	SLG	PRO+	BR/A	SB	CS	SBR	FA	FR	G/POS	TPR
1882	Chi-N	1	5	1	2	0	0	0	0	0	0	.400	.400	.400	151	0				1.000	0	/1-1	0.0

YEAR	TM/L	G	AB	R	H	2B	3B	HR	RBI	BB	SO	AVG	OBP	SLG	PRO+	BR/A	SB	CS	SBR	FA	FR	G/POS	TPR
1884	Det-N	110	438	29	108	17	5	3	50	9	62	.247	.262	.329	90	-5				.968	-1	*1-110	-1.7
1885	Det-N	38	148	14	39	7	0	0	12	4	16	.264	.283	.311	92	-2				.967	2	1-38	-0.4
	Pit-a	55	210	15	52	7	1	0			5	.248	.272	.290	79	-5				.986	3	1-55	-0.8
1886	Bal-a	137	484	48	92	11	4	2		22		.190	.239	.242	52	-26	11			.974	8	*1-137/P-1	-3.0
Total	4	341	1285	107	293	42	10	5	62	40	78	.228	.257	.288	74	-38	11			.973	12	1-341/P-1	-5.9

■ DICK SCOTT
Scott, Richard Edward b: 7/19/62, Ellsworth, Maine BR/TR, 6'1", 170 lbs. Deb: 5/19/89

YEAR	TM/L	G	AB	R	H	2B	3B	HR	RBI	BB	SO	AVG	OBP	SLG	PRO+	BR/A	SB	CS	SBR	FA	FR	G/POS	TPR
1989	Oak-A	3	2	0	0	0	0	0	1	0	0	.000	.000	.000	-99	-1	0	0	0	.000	0	/S-3	-0.1

■ RODNEY SCOTT
Scott, Rodney Darrell b: 10/16/53, Indianapolis, Ind. BB/TR, 6', 160 lbs. Deb: 4/11/75

YEAR	TM/L	G	AB	R	H	2B	3B	HR	RBI	BB	SO	AVG	OBP	SLG	PRO+	BR/A	SB	CS	SBR	FA	FR	G/POS	TPR
1975	KC-A	48	15	13	1	0	0	0	0	1	3	.067	.125	.067	-43	-3	4	2	0	1.000	6	D-22/2-9,SR	0.2
1976	Mon-N	7	10	3	4	0	0	0	0	1	1	.400	.455	.400	138	1	2	0	1	1.000	-0	/2-6,S-3	0.1
1977	Oak-A	133	364	56	95	4	4	0	20	43	50	.261	.344	.294	77	-10	33	18	-1	.963	-30	2-71,S-70/30D	-3.2
1978	Chi-N	78	227	41	64	5	1	0	15	43	41	.282	.403	.313	91	-0	27	10	2	.929	-9	3-59,O-10/2S	-0.8
1979	Mon-N	151	562	69	134	12	5	3	42	66	82	.238	.321	.294	69	-22	39	12	5	.980	-15	*2-113,S-39	-2.1
1980	Mon-N	154	567	84	127	13	**13**	0	46	70	75	.224	.310	.293	69	-22	63	13	11	.982	-16	*2-129,S-21	-1.7
1981	*Mon-N	95	336	43	69	9	3	0	26	50	35	.205	.310	.250	60	-16	30	7	5	.983	-15	2-93	-2.2
1982	Mon-N	14	25	2	5	0	0	0	1	3	2	.200	.286	.200	37	-2	5	0	2	.971	-1	2-12	-0.1
	NY-A	10	26	5	5	0	0	0	0	4	2	.192	.300	.192	39	-2	2	0	1	.963	1	/S-6,2-4	0.0
Total	8	690	2132	316	504	43	26	3	150	281	291	.236	.328	.285	71	-77	205	62	24	.979	-81	2-443,S-153/3DO	-9.8

■ JIM SCRANTON
Scranton, James Dean b: 4/5/60, Torrance, Cal. BR/TR, 6', 175 lbs. Deb: 9/5/84

YEAR	TM/L	G	AB	R	H	2B	3B	HR	RBI	BB	SO	AVG	OBP	SLG	PRO+	BR/A	SB	CS	SBR	FA	FR	G/POS	TPR
1984	KC-A	2	2	0	0	0	0	0	0	0	0	.000	.000	.000	-99	-1	0	0	0	1.000	-1	/S-1,3-1	-0.1
1985	KC-A	6	4	1	0	0	0	0	0	0	0	.000	.000	.000	-99	-1	0	0	0	1.000	2	/S-5	0.1
Total	2	8	6	1	0	0	0	0	0	0	0	.000	.000	.000	-99	-2	0	0	0	1.000	2	/S-6,3-1	0.0

■ CHUCK SCRIVENER
Scrivener, Wayne Allison b: 10/3/47, Alexandria, Va. BR/TR, 5'9", 170 lbs. Deb: 9/18/75

YEAR	TM/L	G	AB	R	H	2B	3B	HR	RBI	BB	SO	AVG	OBP	SLG	PRO+	BR/A	SB	CS	SBR	FA	FR	G/POS	TPR
1975	Det-A	4	16	0	4	1	0	0		0	1	.250	.250	.313	56					1.000	-2	/3-3,S-2	-0.3
1976	Det-A	80	222	28	49	7	1	2	16	19	34	.221	.282	.288	65	-10	1	0	0	.976	7	2-43,S-37/3	0.4
1977	Det-A	61	72	10	6	0			2	5	9	.083	.143	.083	-35	-13	0	0	0	.981	10	S-50/2-8,3	-0.1
Total	3	145	310	38	59	8	1	2	18	24	44	.190	.249	.242	40	-24	2	0	1	.970	15	/S-89,2-51,3	-0.0

■ TONY SCRUGGS
Scruggs, Anthony Raymond b: 3/19/66, Riverside, Cal. BR/TR, 6'1", 210 lbs. Deb: 4/8/91

YEAR	TM/L	G	AB	R	H	2B	3B	HR	RBI	BB	SO	AVG	OBP	SLG	PRO+	BR/A	SB	CS	SBR	FA	FR	G/POS	TPR
1991	Tex-A	5	6	1	0	0	0	0	0	0	1	.000	.000	.000	-99	-2	0	0	0	1.000	-1	/O-5	-0.3

■ KEN SEARS
Sears, Kenneth Eugene "Ziggy" b: 7/6/17, Streator, Ill. d: 7/17/68, Bridgeport, Tex. BL/TR, 6'1", 200 lbs. Deb: 5/2/43

YEAR	TM/L	G	AB	R	H	2B	3B	HR	RBI	BB	SO	AVG	OBP	SLG	PRO+	BR/A	SB	CS	SBR	FA	FR	G/POS	TPR
1943	NY-A	60	187	22	52	7	0	2	22	11	18	.278	.328	.348	97	-1	1	3	-2	.974	1	C-50	0.2
1946	StL-A	7	15	1	5	0	0	0	1	3	0	.333	.444	.333	114	1	0	0	0	1.000	-3	/C-4	-0.2
Total	2	67	202	23	57	7	0	2	23	14	18	.282	.338	.347	99	-0	1	3	-2	.975	-2	/C-54	0.0

■ JIMMY SEBRING
Sebring, James Dennison b: 3/22/1882, Liberty, Pa. d: 12/22/09, Williamsport, Pa. BL/TR, 6', 180 lbs. Deb: 9/8/02

YEAR	TM/L	G	AB	R	H	2B	3B	HR	RBI	BB	SO	AVG	OBP	SLG	PRO+	BR/A	SB	CS	SBR	FA	FR	G/POS	TPR
1902	Pit-N	19	80	15	26	4	4	0	15		5	.325	.365	.475	153	5	2			.974	4	O-19	0.7
1903	*Pit-N	124	506	71	140	16	13	4	64		32	.277	.325	.383	98	-3	20			.927	7	*O-124	-0.3
1904	Pit-N	80	305	28	82	11	7	0	32		17	.269	.307	.351	100	-1	8			.959	9	O-80	0.3
	Cin-N	56	222	22	50	9	2	0	24		14	.225	.271	.284	65	-9	8			1.000	4	O-56	-1.0
	Yr	136	527	50	132	20	9	0	56		31	.250	.292	.323	85	-10	16			.974	12	*O-136	-0.7
1905	Cin-N	58	217	31	62	10	5	2	28		14	.286	.329	.406	107	1	11			.885	-6	O-56	-0.9
1909	Bro-N	25	81	11	8	1	1	0	5		11	.099	.207	.136	7	-9	3			.951	-2	O-25	-1.3
	Was-A	1	0	0	0	0	0	0	0		0	—	—	—	—	0	0			.000	-1	/O-1	-0.1
Total	5	363	1411	178	368	51	32	6	168		93	.261	.308	.355	93	-16	52			.945	14	O-361	-2.6

■ FRANK SECORY
Secory, Frank Edward b: 8/24/12, Mason City, Iowa BR/TR, 6'1", 200 lbs. Deb: 4/28/40 U

YEAR	TM/L	G	AB	R	H	2B	3B	HR	RBI	BB	SO	AVG	OBP	SLG	PRO+	BR/A	SB	CS	SBR	FA	FR	G/POS	TPR
1940	Det-A	1	1	0	0	0	0	0	0	0	0	.000	.000	.000	-91	-0	0	0	0	.000	0	H	0.0
1942	Cin-N	2	5	1	0	0	0	0	1	3	2	.000	.375	.000	14	-0	0			.857	0	/O-2	0.0
1944	Cin-N	22	56	10	18	1	0	4	17	6	8	.321	.387	.554	163	5	1			1.000	0	O-17	0.4
1945	*Chi-N	35	57	4	9	1	0	0	6	2	7	.158	.186	.175	1	-8	0			1.000	-1	O-12	-1.0
1946	Chi-N	33	43	6	10	3	0	3	12	6	7	.233	.327	.512	139	2	0			.833	-3	/O-9	-0.1
Total	5	93	162	21	37	5	0	7	36	17	24	.228	.302	.389	95	-2	1	0		.964	-4	/O-40	-0.7

■ CHARLIE SEE
See, Charles Henry "Chad" b: 10/13/1896, Pleasantville, N.Y. d: 7/19/48, Bridgeport, Conn. BL/TR, 5'10.5", 175 lbs. Deb: 8/6/19

YEAR	TM/L	G	AB	R	H	2B	3B	HR	RBI	BB	SO	AVG	OBP	SLG	PRO+	BR/A	SB	CS	SBR	FA	FR	G/POS	TPR
1919	Cin-N	8	14	1	4	0	0	0	1	1	0	.286	.333	.286	89	-0	0			.833	-1	/O-4	-0.2
1920	Cin-N	47	82	9	25	4	0	0	15	1	7	.305	.329	.354	97	-0	2	4	-2	1.000	5	O-17/P-1	-0.1
1921	Cin-N	37	106	11	26	5	1	1	7	7	5	.245	.298	.340	72	-4	3	2	0	.954	-0	O-30	-0.7
Total	3	92	202	21	55	9	1	1	23	9	12	.272	.313	.342	83	-5	5	6		.967	4	/O-51,P-1	-1.0

■ LARRY SEE
See, Ralph Laurence b: 6/20/60, Norwalk, Cal. BR/TR, 6'1", 195 lbs. Deb: 9/3/86

YEAR	TM/L	G	AB	R	H	2B	3B	HR	RBI	BB	SO	AVG	OBP	SLG	PRO+	BR/A	SB	CS	SBR	FA	FR	G/POS	TPR
1986	LA-N	13	20	1	5	2	0	0	2	2	7	.250	.318	.350	90	-0	0	0	0	.979	1	/1-9	0.0
1988	Tex-A	13	23	0	3	0	0	0	0	1	8	.130	.167	.130	-15	-3	0	0	0	1.000	-0	/C-2,1-2/3D	-0.4
Total	2	26	43	1	8	2	0	0	2	3	15	.186	.239	.233	32	-4	0	0	0	.967	1	/1-11,D-7,C3	-0.4

■ BOB SEEDS
Seeds, Ira Robert "Suitcase Bob" b: 2/24/07, Ringgold, Tex. d: 10/28/93, Erick, Okla. BR/TR, 6', 180 lbs. Deb: 4/19/30

YEAR	TM/L	G	AB	R	H	2B	3B	HR	RBI	BB	SO	AVG	OBP	SLG	PRO+	BR/A	SB	CS	SBR	FA	FR	G/POS	TPR
1930	Cle-A	85	277	37	79	11	3	3	32	12	22	.285	.315	.379	72	-12	1	3	-2	.953	2	O-70	-1.5
1931	Cle-A	48	134	26	41	4	1	1	10	11	11	.306	.359	.373	88	-2	1	0	0	.966	-2	O-33/1-2	-0.6
1932	Cle-A	2	4	0	0	0	0	0	0	0	0	.000	.000	.000	-94	-1	0	0	0	.000	-0	/O-1	-0.2
	Chi-A	116	434	53	126	18	6	2	45	31	37	.290	.342	.373	91	-6	5	7	-3	.964	-9	*O-112	-2.2
	Yr	118	438	53	126	18	6	2	45	31	37	.288	.339	.370	89	-7	5	7	-3	.964	-9	*O-113	-2.4
1933	Bos-A	82	230	26	56	13	4	0	23	21	20	.243	.310	.335	71	-10	1	3	-2	.985	-5	1-41,O-32	-2.0
1934	Bos-A	8	6	0	1	0	0	0	0	0	1	.167	.167	.167	-13	-1	0	0	0	.000	-0	/O-1	-0.1
	Cle-A	61	186	28	46	8	1	0	18	20	13	.247	.327	.301	62	-10	2	1	0	.977	-4	O-48	-1.5
	Yr	69	192	28	47	8	1	0	19	21	14	.245	.322	.297	59	-11	2	1	0	.977	-4	O-49	-1.6
1936	*NY-A	13	42	12	11	1	0	4	10	5	3	.262	.340	.571	126	1	3	1	0	1.000	1	/O-9,3-3	0.2
1938	NY-N	81	296	35	86	12	3	9	52	20	33	.291	.338	.443	112	4	0			.987	6	O-76	-0.3
1939	NY-N	63	173	33	46	5	1	5	26	22	31	.266	.352	.393	99	0	1			.975	-8	O-50	-0.9
1940	NY-N	56	155	18	45	5	2	4	21	17	19	.290	.371	.426	118	4	0			.985	-4	O-44	-0.2
Total	9	615	1937	268	537	77	21	28	233	160	190	.277	.336	.382	89	-32	14	15		.970	-35	O-472/1-43,3	-9.3

■ PAT SEEREY
Seerey, James Patrick b: 3/17/23, Wilburton, Okla. d: 4/28/86, Jennings, Mo. BR/TR, 5'10", 200 lbs. Deb: 6/9/43

YEAR	TM/L	G	AB	R	H	2B	3B	HR	RBI	BB	SO	AVG	OBP	SLG	PRO+	BR/A	SB	CS	SBR	FA	FR	G/POS	TPR
1943	Cle-A	26	72	8	16	3	0	1	5	4	19	.222	.263	.306	70	0	0	0	0	.974	1	O-16	-0.3
1944	Cle-A	101	342	39	80	16	0	15	39	19	99	.234	.276	.412	99	-3	0	2	-1	.986	1	O-86	-0.8
1945	Cle-A	126	414	56	98	22	2	14	56	66	97	.237	.342	.401	120	11	1	2	-1	.975	-15	*O-117	-1.2
1946	Cle-A	117	404	57	91	17	2	26	62	65	101	.225	.334	.470	131	15	2	3	-1	.981	-5	*O-115	0.4
1947	Cle-A	82	216	24	37	4	1	11	29	34	66	.171	.284	.352	78	-7	0	1	-1	.957	-8	O-68	-1.9
1948	Cle-A	10	23	7	6	0	0	1	6	7	8	.261	.433	.391	123	1	0	0	0	1.000	-0	/O-7	-0.1
	Chi-A	95	340	44	78	11	0	19	64	61	94	.229	.347	.421	107	3	0	0	0	.981	-0	O-93	-0.2
	Yr	105	363	51	84	11	0	19	70	68	102	.231	.353	.419	108	4	0	0	0	.982	-2	*O-100	-0.3

YEAR	TM/L	G	AB	R	H	2B	3B	HR	RBI	BB	SO	AVG	OBP	SLG	PRO+	BR/A	SB	CS	SBR	FA	FR	G/POS	TPR
1949	Chi-A	4	4	1	0	0	0	0	0	3	1	.000	.429	.000	19	-0	0	0	0	1.000	-1	/O-2	-0.1
Total	7	561	1815	236	406	73	5	86	261	259	485	.224	.321	.412	109	16	3	8	-4	.978	-27	O-504	-4.2

■ EMMETT SEERY   Seery, John Emmett b: 2/13/1861, Princeville, Ill.   d: 8/8/30, Saranac Lake, N.Y.   BL/TR   Deb: 4/17/1884

YEAR	TM/L	G	AB	R	H	2B	3B	HR	RBI	BB	SO	AVG	OBP	SLG	PRO+	BR/A	SB	CS	SBR	FA	FR	G/POS	TPR
1884	Bal-U	105	463	113	144	25	7	2		20		.311	.340	.408	93	-7				.828	7	*O-103/C-3,3	-0.1
	KC-U	1	4	2	2	1	0	0		1		.500	.600	.750	304	1				.000	-0	/O-1	0.1
	Yr	106	467	115	146	26	7	2		21		.313	.342	.411	94	-6				.828	6	*O-104/C-3,3	0.0
1885	StL-N	59	216	20	35	7	0	1	14	16	37	.162	.220	.208	42	-13				.874	5	O-59/3-1	-0.9
1886	StL-N	126	453	73	108	22	6	2	48	57	82	.238	.324	.327	105	5	24			.883	-5	*O-126/P-2	-0.2
1887	Ind-N	122	465	104	104	18	15	4	28	71	68	.224	.331	.353	93	-2	48			.891	7	*O-122/S-1	0.2
1888	Ind-N	133	500	87	110	20	10	5	50	64	73	.220	.316	.330	104	4	80			.939	9	*O-133/S-1	0.9
1889	Ind-N	127	526	123	165	26	12	6	59	67	59	.314	.401	.454	136	27	19			.909	1	*O-127	2.1
1890	Bro-P	104	394	78	88	12	7	1	50	70	36	.223	.348	.297	69	-17	44			.894	7	*O-104	-1.1
1891	Cin-a	97	372	77	106	15	10	4	36	81	52	.285	.423	.411	128	15	19			.898	3	O-97	1.3
1892	Lou-N	42	154	18	31	6	1	0	15	24	19	.201	.309	.253	77	-3	6			.961	3	O-42	-0.2
Total	9	916	3547	695	893	152	68	27	300	471	426	.252	.345	.356	101	11	240			.896	36	O-914/3-3,CSP	2.1

■ KAL SEGRIST   Segrist, Kal Hill b: 4/14/31, Greenville, Tex.   BR/TR, 6', 180 lbs.   Deb: 7/16/52

YEAR	TM/L	G	AB	R	H	2B	3B	HR	RBI	BB	SO	AVG	OBP	SLG	PRO+	BR/A	SB	CS	SBR	FA	FR	G/POS	TPR
1952	NY-A	13	23	3	1	0	0	0	1	3	1	.043	.154	.043	-46	-5	0	0	0	.971	0	2-11/3-1	-0.4
1955	Bal-A	7	9	1	3	0	0	0	0	2	0	.333	.455	.333	123	0	0	0	0	1.000	0	/3-3,1-1,2	0.1
Total	2	20	32	4	4	0	0	0	1	5	1	.125	.243	.125	4	-4	0	0	0	.971	1	/2-12,3-4,1	-0.3

■ DAVID SEGUI   Segui, David Vincent b: 7/19/66, Kansas City, Kan.   BB/TL, 6'1", 170 lbs.   Deb: 5/8/90   F

YEAR	TM/L	G	AB	R	H	2B	3B	HR	RBI	BB	SO	AVG	OBP	SLG	PRO+	BR/A	SB	CS	SBR	FA	FR	G/POS	TPR
1990	Bal-A	40	123	14	30	7	0	2	15	11	15	.244	.311	.350	87	-2	0	0	0	.990	1	1-36/D-4	-0.3
1991	Bal-A	86	212	15	59	7	0	2	22	12	19	.278	.317	.340	85	-4	1	1	-0	.996	1	1-42,O-33/D	-0.6
1992	Bal-A	115	189	21	44	9	0	1	17	20	23	.233	.306	.296	68	-8	1	0	0	.998	2	1-95,O-18	-0.8
1993	Bal-A	146	450	54	123	27	0	10	60	58	53	.273	.346	.400	99	-0	2	1	0	.996	4	*1-144/D-1	-0.7
1994	NY-N	92	336	46	81	17	1	10	43	33	43	.241	.311	.387	80	-10	0	0	0	.996	-3	1-78,O-21	-1.9
Total	5	479	1310	150	337	67	1	25	157	134	153	.257	.327	.367	86	-25	4	2	0	.996	6	1-395/O-72,D	-4.3

■ KURT SEIBERT   Seibert, Kurt Elliott b: 10/16/55, Cheverly, Md.   BB/TR, 6', 165 lbs.   Deb: 9/3/79

YEAR	TM/L	G	AB	R	H	2B	3B	HR	RBI	BB	SO	AVG	OBP	SLG	PRO+	BR/A	SB	CS	SBR	FA	FR	G/POS	TPR
1979	Chi-N	7	2	2	0	0	0	0	0	0	1	.000	.000	.000	-91	-1	0	0	0	1.000	0	/2-1	0.0

■ SOCKS SEIBOLD   Seibold, Harry b: 4/3/1896, Philadelphia, Pa.   d: 9/21/65, Philadelphia, Pa.   BR/TR, 5'8.5", 162 lbs.   Deb: 9/18/15

YEAR	TM/L	G	AB	R	H	2B	3B	HR	RBI	BB	SO	AVG	OBP	SLG	PRO+	BR/A	SB	CS	SBR	FA	FR	G/POS	TPR
1915	Phi-A	10	26	3	3	1	0	0	2	4	4	.115	.233	.154	16	-3	0			.714	-4	/S-7	-0.7
1916	Phi-A	5	12	0	2	1	0	0	1	0	4	.167	.167	.250	26	-1	0			1.000	2	/P-3,O-1	0.0
1917	Phi-A	36	59	6	13	1	1	0	5	4	8	.220	.281	.271	70	-2	1			.978	-2	P-33/O-2	-0.1
1919	Phi-A	15	13	1	2	0	0	0	1	0	1	.154	.154	.154	-13	-2	0			.941	0	P-14	0.0
1929	Bos-N	33	70	6	20	2	0	0	9	6	6	.286	.342	.314	67	-3	0			1.000	-1	P-33	0.0
1930	Bos-N	36	90	6	19	2	0	1	5	6	6	.211	.260	.267	29	-11	0			.941	-3	P-36	0.0
1931	Bos-N	33	70	3	9	0	0	0	2	1	9	.129	.141	.129	-28	-13	0			1.000	2	P-33	0.0
1932	Bos-N	28	46	2	7	0	0	0	2	2	0	.152	.188	.152	-8	-7	0			1.000	2	P-28	0.0
1933	Bos-N	11	9	0	1	0	0	0	0	2	2	.111	.273	.111	14	-1	0			1.000	0	P-11	0.0
Total	9	207	395	27	76	7	1	1	27	25	43	.192	.242	.223	25	-42	1			.982	-5	P-191/S-7,O	-0.8

■ RICKY SEILHEIMER   Seilheimer, Ricky Allen b: 8/30/60, Brenham, Tex.   BL/TR, 5'11", 185 lbs.   Deb: 7/5/80

YEAR	TM/L	G	AB	R	H	2B	3B	HR	RBI	BB	SO	AVG	OBP	SLG	PRO+	BR/A	SB	CS	SBR	FA	FR	G/POS	TPR
1980	Chi-A	21	52	4	11	3	1	1	3	4	15	.212	.268	.365	72	-2	1	0	0	.946	-3	C-21	-0.4

■ KEVIN SEITZER   Seitzer, Kevin Lee b: 3/26/62, Springfield, Ill.   BR/TR, 5'11", 180 lbs.   Deb: 9/3/86

YEAR	TM/L	G	AB	R	H	2B	3B	HR	RBI	BB	SO	AVG	OBP	SLG	PRO+	BR/A	SB	CS	SBR	FA	FR	G/POS	TPR
1986	KC-A	28	96	16	31	4	1	2	11	19	14	.323	.440	.448	140	6	0	0	0	.987	1	1-22/O-5,3	0.6
1987	KC-A★	161	641	105	207	33	8	15	83	80	85	.323	.400	.470	126	26	12	7	-1	.947	8	*3-141,1-25/OD	2.9
1988	KC-A	149	559	90	170	32	5	5	60	72	64	.304	.389	.406	122	19	10	8	-2	.938	3	*3-147/O-1,D	1.9
1989	KC-A	160	597	78	168	17	2	4	48	102	76	.281	.391	.337	107	11	17	8	0	.950	-11	*3-159/S-6,O1	0.3
1990	KC-A	158	622	91	171	31	5	6	38	67	66	.275	.347	.370	102	3	7	5	-4	.953	-9	*3-152,2-10	-0.6
1991	KC-A	85	234	28	62	11	3	1	25	29	21	.265	.351	.350	94	-1	4	1	1	.940	0	3-68/D-3	0.0
1992	Mil-A	148	540	74	146	35	1	5	71	57	44	.270	.342	.367	101	1	13	11	-3	.969	-13	*3-146/2-2,1	-1.5
1993	Oak-A	73	255	24	65	10	2	4	27	27	33	.255	.329	.357	90	-4	4	7	-3	.933	-9	3-46,1-24/O2PDS	-1.7
	Mil-A	47	162	21	47	6	0	7	30	17	15	.290	.361	.457	120	5	3	0	1	.942	-2	3-33/1-7,20D	0.3
	Yr	120	417	45	112	16	2	11	57	44	48	.269	.341	.396	102	1	7	7	-2	.937	-11	3-79,1-31/DO2PS	-1.4
1994	Mil-A	80	309	44	97	24	2	5	49	30	38	.314	.378	.453	111	5	2	1	0	.924	-4	3-43,1-35/D	-0.1
Total	9	1089	4015	571	1164	203	29	54	442	500	456	.290	.372	.395	111	73	72	48	-7	.948	-36	3-938,1-116/O2DSP	2.1

■ KIP SELBACH   Selbach, Albert Karl b: 3/24/1872, Columbus, Ohio   d: 2/17/56, Columbus, Ohio   BR/TR, 5'7", 190 lbs.   Deb: 4/24/1894

YEAR	TM/L	G	AB	R	H	2B	3B	HR	RBI	BB	SO	AVG	OBP	SLG	PRO+	BR/A	SB	CS	SBR	FA	FR	G/POS	TPR
1894	Was-N	97	372	69	114	21	17	7	71	51	20	.306	.390	.511	120	11	21			.915	-9	O-80,S-19	-0.2
1895	Was-N	129	516	115	166	21	22	6	55	69	28	.322	.403	.483	129	23	31			.912	16	*O-118/S-6,2	2.4
1896	Was-N	127	487	100	148	17	13	5	100	76	28	.304	.405	.423	119	16	49			.946	7	*O-126	1.1
1897	Was-N	124	486	113	152	25	16	5	59	80		.313	.414	.461	131	24	46			.955	13	*O-124	2.4
1898	Was-N	132	515	88	156	28	11	3	60	64		.303	.383	.417	130	21	25			.948	20	*O-131/S-1	2.9
1899	Cin-N	140	521	104	154	27	11	3	87	70		.296	.384	.407	115	12	38			.953	17	*O-140	1.6
1900	NY-N	141	523	98	176	29	12	4	68	72		.337	.420	.461	151	40	36			.951	10	*O-141	3.5
1901	NY-N	125	502	89	145	29	6	1	56	45		.289	.350	.376	115	10	8			.942	-10	*O-125	-0.9
1902	Bal-A	128	503	86	161	27	9	3	60	58		.320	.393	.427	122	16	22			.941	9	*O-127	1.6
1903	Was-A	140	533	68	134	23	12	3	49	41		.251	.305	.356	96	-3	20			.956	-3	*O-140/3-1	-1.5
1904	Was-A	48	178	15	49	8	4	0	14	24		.275	.361	.365	132	7	9			.931	3	O-48	0.8
	Bos-A	98	376	50	97	19	8	0	30	48		.258	.347	.351	114	8	10			.961	1	O-98	0.3
	Yr	146	554	65	146	27	12	0	44	72		.264	.351	.356	120	15	19			.950	4	*O-146	1.1
1905	Bos-A	121	418	54	103	16	6	4	47	67		.246	.355	.342	120	12	12			.928	-1	*O-112	0.6
1906	Bos-A	60	228	15	48	9	2	0	23	18		.211	.277	.268	71	-7	7			.966	1	O-58	-1.1
Total	13	1610	6158	1064	1803	299	149	44	779	783	76	.293	.376	.411	121	190	334			.944	74	*O-1568/S-26,23	13.5

■ GEORGE SELKIRK   Selkirk, George Alexander "Twinkletoes" b: 1/4/08, Huntsville, Ont., Canada   d: 1/19/87, Ft.Lauderdale, Fla   BL/TR, 6'1", 182 lbs.   Deb: 8/12/34

YEAR	TM/L	G	AB	R	H	2B	3B	HR	RBI	BB	SO	AVG	OBP	SLG	PRO+	BR/A	SB	CS	SBR	FA	FR	G/POS	TPR
1934	NY-A	46	176	23	55	7	1	5	38	15	17	.313	.370	.449	118	4	1	1	-0	.989	-2	O-46	0.1
1935	NY-A	128	491	64	153	29	12	11	94	44	36	.312	.372	.487	128	18	2	7	-4	.975	6	*O-127	1.5
1936	*NY-A★	137	493	93	152	28	9	18	107	94	60	.308	.420	.511	133	28	13	7	-0	.974	3	*O-135	2.2
1937	*NY-A	78	256	49	84	13	5	18	68	34	24	.328	.411	.629	157	22	8	2	1	.987	5	O-69	2.3
1938	*NY-A	99	335	58	85	12	5	10	62	68	52	.254	.384	.409	99	1	9	4	0	.973	-1	O-95	-0.4
1939	*NY-A★	128	418	103	128	17	4	21	101	103	49	.306	.452	.517	149	37	12	5	1	.989	-4	*O-124	2.6
1940	*NY-A	118	379	68	102	17	5	19	71	84	43	.269	.406	.491	137	23	3	6	-3	.962	-3	*O-111	1.2
1941	*NY-A	70	164	30	36	5	0	6	25	28	30	.220	.340	.360	86	-3	1	0	0	.967	-2	O-47	-0.7
1942	*NY-A	42	78	15	15	3	0	1	9	16	8	.192	.330	.231	60	-3	0	0	0	1.000	-1	O-19	-0.6
Total	9	846	2790	503	810	131	41	108	576	486	319	.290	.400	.483	128	127	49	32	-5	.977	-1	O-773	8.2

■ RUBE SELLERS   Sellers, Oliver b: 3/7/1881, Duquesne, Pa.   d: 1/14/52, Pittsburgh, Pa.   BR/TR, 5'10", 180 lbs.   Deb: 8/12/10

YEAR	TM/L	G	AB	R	H	2B	3B	HR	RBI	BB	SO	AVG	OBP	SLG	PRO+	BR/A	SB	CS	SBR	FA	FR	G/POS	TPR
1910	Bos-N	12	32	3	5	0	0	0	2	6	5	.156	.289	.156	29	-3	1			1.000	-2	/O-9	-0.6

YEAR	TM/L	G	AB	R	H	2B	3B	HR	RBI	BB	SO	AVG	OBP	SLG	PRO+	BR/A	SB	CS	SBR	FA	FR	G/POS	TPR
■ **FRANK SELMAN**			Selman, Frank C. (a.k.a. Frank C. Williams 1871-75)				b: Baltimore, Md.				Deb: 5/4/1871											
1871	Kek-n	14	65	14	15	3	0	1	10	4	0	.231	.275	.323	70	-3	1					3-13/C-2,S	-0.2
1872	Oly-n	9	41	3	10	3	0	0	1	0	0	.244	.244	.317	75	-1						/C-6,3-2	-0.2
1873	Mar-n	1	3	1	1	0	0	0	0	0	0	.333	.333	.333	126	0						/P-1	0.0
1874	Bal-n	12	54	9	16	4	1	0		0	0	.296	.296	.407	122	1						/S-7,C-6,O	0.1
1875	Was-n	1	3	0	1	0	0	0		0	0	.333	.333	.333	136	0						/1-1	0.0
Total	5 n	37	166	27	43	10	1	1		4	0	.259	.276	.349	89	-2						/3-15,C-14,S10P	-0.3
■ **CAREY SELPH**			Selph, Carey Isom b: 12/5/01, Donaldson, Ark. d: 2/24/76, Houston, Tex. BR/TR, 5'9.5", 175 lbs. Deb: 5/25/29																				
1929	StL-N	25	51	8	12	1	1	0	7	6	4	.235	.316	.294	52	-4	1			.981	-5	2-16	-0.7
1932	Chi-A	116	396	50	112	19	8	0	51	31	9	.283	.341	.371	90	-6	7	6	-2	.910	-6	3-71,2-26	-0.7
Total	2	141	447	58	124	20	9	0	58	37	13	.277	.338	.362	85	-10	8	6		.955	-11	/3-71,2-42	-1.4
■ **MIKE SEMBER**			Sember, Michael David b: 2/24/53, Hammond, Ind. BR/TR, 6', 185 lbs. Deb: 8/18/77																				
1977	Chi-N	3	4	0	1	0	0	0	0	0	2	.250	.250	.250	31	-0	0	0	0	1.000	1	/2-1	0.0
1978	Chi-N	9	3	2	1	0	0	0	0	1	1	.333	.500	.333	122	-0	0	0	0	.667	1	/3-7,S-1	0.1
Total	2	12	7	2	2	0	0	0	0	1	3	.286	.375	.286	74	-0	0	0	0	.667	1	/3-7,S-1,2	0.1
■ **ANDY SEMINICK**			Seminick, Andrew Wasil b: 9/12/20, Pierce, W.Va. BR/TR, 5'11", 187 lbs. Deb: 9/14/43 C																				
1943	Phi-N	22	72	9	13	2	0	2	5	7	22	.181	.253	.292	60	-4	0			.930	1	C-22/O-1	-0.2
1944	Phi-N	22	63	9	14	2	1	0	4	6	17	.222	.300	.286	68	-3	2			.963	1	C-11/O-7	-0.2
1945	Phi-N	80	188	18	45	7	2	6	26	18	38	.239	.313	.394	98	-1	3			.979	-0	C-70/3-4,O	0.2
1946	Phi-N	124	406	55	107	15	5	12	52	39	86	.264	.334	.414	115	7	2			.974	-6	*C-118	0.8
1947	Phi-N	111	337	48	85	16	2	13	50	58	69	.252	.370	.427	115	8	4			.978	7	*C-107	2.1
1948	Phi-N	125	391	49	88	11	3	13	44	58	68	.225	.328	.368	90	-5	4			.965	6	*C-124	0.9
1949	Phi-N★	109	334	52	81	11	2	24	68	69	74	.243	.380	.503	138	19	0			.975	7	*C-98	3.1
1950	*Phi-N	130	393	55	113	15	3	24	68	68	50	.288	.400	.524	143	26	0			.976	4	*C-124	3.5
1951	Phi-N	101	291	42	66	8	1	11	37	63	67	.227	.370	.375	102	3	1	0	0	.979	-3	C-91	0.4
1952	Cin-N	108	336	38	86	16	1	14	50	35	65	.256	.330	.435	111	4	1	3	-2	.973	-4	C-99	0.4
1953	Cin-N	119	387	46	91	12	0	19	64	49	82	.235	.323	.413	90	-6	2	2	-1	.982	-5	*C-112	-0.6
1954	Cin-N	86	247	25	58	9	4	7	30	48	39	.235	.364	.389	93	-1	0	0	0	.989	3	C-82	0.6
1955	Cin-N	6	15	1	2	0	0	1	1	0	3	.133	.133	.333	18	-2	0	0	0	1.000	2	/C-5	0.0
	Phi-N	93	289	32	71	12	1	11	34	32	59	.246	.330	.408	97	-1	1	2	-1	.994	10	C-88	1.1
	Yr	99	304	33	73	12	1	12	35	32	62	.240	.325	.405	93	-3	1	2	-1	.994	12	C-93	1.1
1956	Phi-N	60	161	16	32	3	1	7	23	31	38	.199	.332	.360	88	-2	3	0	1	.976	-8	C-54	-0.7
1957	Phi-N	8	11	0	1	0	0	0	0	1	3	.091	.167	.091	-29	-2	0	0	0	1.000	1	/C-8	-0.1
Total	15	1304	3921	495	953	139	26	164	556	582	780	.243	.347	.417	107	40	23	7		.977	15	*C-1213/O-9,3	11.3
■ **SONNY SENERCHIA**			Senerchia, Emanuel Robert b: 4/6/31, Newark, N.J. BR/TR, 6'1", 195 lbs. Deb: 8/22/52																				
1952	Pit-N	29	100	5	22	5	0	3	11	4	21	.220	.250	.360	66	-5	0	3	-2	.953	-8	3-28	-1.7
■ **COUNT SENSENDERFER**			Sensenderfer, John Phillips Jenkins b: 12/28/1847, Philadelphia, Pa. d: 5/3/03, Philadelphia, Pa. 5'9", 170 lbs. Deb: 5/20/1871																				
1871	Ath-n	25	127	38	41	5	2	0	23	0	1	.323	.323	.394	106	1	5					*O-25	0.1
1872	Ath-n	1	5	2	2	0	0	0	1	0	0	.400	.400	.400	146	0						/O-1	0.0
1873	Ath-n	20	86	12	24	1	0	0	8	0	2	.279	.279	.291	63	-4						O-19/1-1	-0.4
1874	Ath-n	5	16	3	3	0	0	0		0	0	.188	.188	.188	18	-2						/O-4	-0.1
Total	4 n	51	234	55	70	6	2	0		0	5	.299	.299	.342	84	-5						/O-49,1-1	-0.4
■ **PAUL SENTELL**			Sentell, Leopold Theodore b: 8/27/1879, New Orleans, La. d: 4/27/23, Cincinnati, Ohio BR/TR, 5'9", 176 lbs. Deb: 4/12/06 U																				
1906	Phi-N	63	192	19	44	5	1	1	14	14		.229	.292	.281	79	-5	15			.887	-9	3-33,2-19/OS	-1.4
1907	Phi-N	3	3	0	0	0	0	0	0	1		.000	.250	.000	-22	-0	0			1.000	-2	/S-2,O-1	-0.3
Total	2	66	195	19	44	5	1	1	14	15		.226	.291	.277	77	-5	15			1.000	-11	/3-33,2-19,SO	-1.7
■ **TED SEPKOWSKI**			Sepkowski, Theodore Walter (b: Theodore Walter Sczepkowski) b: 11/9/23, Baltimore, Md. BL/TR, 5'11", 190 lbs. Deb: 9/9/42																				
1942	Cle-A	5	10	0	1	0	0	0	0	0	3	.100	.100	.100	-46	-2	0	0	0	.824	-1	/2-2	-0.1
1946	Cle-A	2	8	2	4	1	0	0	1	0	0	.500	.500	.625	228	1	0	0	0	.833	-1	/3-2	-0.1
1947	Cle-A	10	8	0	1	1	0	0	0	1	1	.125	.222	.250	32	-1	0	0	0	.000	-0	/O-1	-0.1
	NY-A	2	0	1	0							—	—	—		-0	0	1	-1	1.000	0	R	-0.1
	Yr	12	8	1	1	1	0	0	0	1	1	.125	.222	.250	32	-1	0	1	-1	.000	-0	/O-1	-0.2
Total	3	19	26	3	6	2	0	0	1	1	4	.231	.259	.308	61	-1	0	1	-1	.833	-1	/3-2,2-2,O	-0.2
■ **BILL SERENA**			Serena, William Robert b: 10/2/24, Alameda, Cal. BR/TR, 5'9.5", 175 lbs. Deb: 9/16/49																				
1949	Chi-N	12	37	3	8	3	0	1	7	7	9	.216	.341	.378	95	-0	0			.923	-4	3-11	-0.5
1950	Chi-N	127	435	56	104	20	4	17	61	65	75	.239	.339	.421	100	-0	1			.945	-2	*3-125	-0.4
1951	Chi-N	13	39	8	13	3	1	1	4	11	4	.333	.490	.538	173	5	0	2	-1	.941	-4	3-12	0.0
1952	Chi-N	122	390	49	107	21	5	15	61	39	83	.274	.345	.469	122	11	0	0	0	.971	-1	3-58,2-49	1.1
1953	Chi-N	93	275	30	69	10	5	10	52	41	46	.251	.350	.433	100	0	0	0	0	.983	-15	2-49,3-28	-1.2
1954	Chi-N	41	63	8	10	0	1	4	13	14	18	.159	.321	.381	81	-2	0	0	0	.933	-3	3-12/2-2	-0.5
Total	6	408	1239	154	311	57	16	48	198	177	235	.251	.348	.439	108	14	2	2		.951	-30	3-246,2-100	-1.5
■ **PAUL SERNA**			Serna, Paul David b: 11/16/58, ElCentro, Cal. BR/TR, 5'8", 170 lbs. Deb: 9/1/81																				
1981	Sea-A	30	94	11	24	2	0	4	9	3	11	.255	.293	.404	95	-1	2	3	-1	.954	-3	S-23/2-7	-0.2
1982	Sea-A	65	169	15	38	3	0	3	8	4	13	.225	.247	.296	47	-12	0	5	-3	.936	3	S-31,2-18,3/D	-1.0
Total	2	95	263	26	62	5	0	7	17	7	24	.236	.264	.335	64	-13	2	8	-4	.945	0	/S-54,2-25,3D	-1.2
■ **SCOTT SERVAIS**			Servais, Scott Daniel b: 6/4/67, LaCrosse, Wis. BR/TR, 6'2", 195 lbs. Deb: 7/12/91																				
1991	Hou-N	16	37	0	6	3	0	0	6	4	8	.162	.244	.243	40	-3	0	0	0	.988	2	C-14	0.0
1992	Hou-N	77	205	12	49	9	0	0	15	11	25	.239	.294	.283	67	-9	0	0	0	.995	-2	C-73	-0.8
1993	Hou-N	85	258	24	63	11	0	11	32	22	45	.244	.316	.415	97	-2	0	0	0	.996	3	C-82	0.4
1994	Hou-N	78	251	27	49	15	1	9	41	10	44	.195	.238	.371	57	-17	0	0	0	.996	1	C-78	-1.2
Total	4	256	751	63	167	38	1	20	94	47	122	.222	.281	.356	73	-31	0	0	0	.995	3	C-247	-1.6
■ **WALTER SESSI**			Sessi, Walter Anthony "Watsie" b: 7/23/18, Finleyville, Pa. BL/TL, 6'3", 225 lbs. Deb: 9/18/41																				
1941	StL-N	5	13	2	0	0	0	0	0	1	2	.000	.071	.000	-74	-3	0			.750	-1	/O-3	-0.4
1946	StL-N	15	14	2	2	0	0	1	2	1	4	.143	.200	.357	54	-1	0			.000	0	H	-0.1
Total	2	20	27	4	2	0	0	1	2	2	6	.074	.138	.185	-9	-4	0			.750	-1	/O-3	-0.5
■ **JOHN SEVCIK**			Sevcik, John Joseph b: 7/11/42, Oak Park, Ill. BR/TR, 6'2", 205 lbs. Deb: 4/24/65																				
1965	Min-A	12	16	1	1	1	0	0	0	1	5	.063	.118	.125	-30	-3	0	0	0	1.000	3	C-11	0.0
■ **HANK SEVEREID**			Severeid, Henry Levai b: 6/1/1891, Story City, Iowa d: 12/17/68, San Antonio, Tex. BR/TR, 6', 175 lbs. Deb: 5/15/11																				
1911	Cin-N	37	56	5	17	6	1	0	10	3	6	.304	.350	.446	127	2	0			.913	-3	C-22	0.0
1912	Cin-N	50	114	10	27	0	3	0	13	8	11	.237	.287	.289	60	-6	0			.943	10	C-20/1-7,O	-1.4
1913	Cin-N	6	6	0	0	0	0	0	0	1	1	.000	.143	.000	-58	-1	0			1.000	-1	/C-2,O-1	-0.2
1915	StL-A	80	203	12	45	6	1	1	22	16	25	.222	.279	.276	68	-8	2	1	0	.966	-10	C-64	-1.5

YEAR	TM/L	G	AB	R	H	2B	3B	HR	RBI	BB	SO	AVG	OBP	SLG	PRO+	BR/A	SB	CS	SBR	FA	FR	G/POS	TPR
1916	StL-A	100	293	23	80	8	2	0	34	26	17	.273	.341	.314	102	1	3			.976	-16	C-89/1-1,3	-1.0
1917	StL-A	143	501	45	133	23	4	1	57	28	20	.265	.306	.333	99	-3	6			.966	-19	*C-139/1-1	-1.2
1918	StL-A	51	133	8	34	4	0	0	11	18	4	.256	.357	.286	97	0	4			.946	-5	C-42	-0.2
1919	StL-A	112	351	16	87	12	2	0	36	21	13	.248	.298	.293	65	-16	2			.983	-5	*C-103	-1.3
1920	StL-A	123	422	46	117	14	5	2	49	33	11	.277	.336	.348	79	-13	5	3	-0	.983	3	*C-117	-0.2
1921	StL-A	143	472	66	153	23	7	2	78	42	9	.324	.379	.415	97	-2	7	2	1	.972	-3	*C-126	0.3
1922	StL-A	137	517	49	166	32	7	3	78	28	12	.321	.356	.427	100	-1	1	4	-2	.984	7	*C-133	1.1
1923	StL-A	122	432	50	133	27	6	3	51	31	11	.308	.356	.419	98	-2	3	0	1	.993	9	*C-116	1.3
1924	StL-A	137	432	37	133	23	2	4	48	36	15	.308	.362	.398	90	-7	1	6	-3	.989	-2	*C-130	-0.4
1925	StL-A	34	109	15	40	9	0	1	21	11	2	.367	.425	.477	122	4	0	2	-1	.993	-0	C-31	0.4
	*Was-A	50	110	11	39	8	1	0	14	13	6	.355	.423	.445	123	4	0	0	0	.986	2	C-35	0.7
	Yr	84	219	26	79	17	1	1	35	24	8	.361	.424	.461	123	9	0	2	-1	.990	1	C-66	1.1
1926	Was-A	22	34	2	7	1	0	0	4	3	2	.206	.270	.235	33	-3	0	0	0	.977	0	C-16	-0.2
	*NY-A	41	127	13	34	8	1	0	13	13	4	.268	.336	.346	79	-4	1	1	-0	.988	-3	C-40	-0.5
	Yr	63	161	15	41	9	1	0	17	16	6	.255	.322	.323	70	-7	1	1	-0	.985	-3	C-56	-0.7
Total	15	1390	4312	408	1245	204	42	17	539	331	169	.289	.342	.367	91	-55	35	19		.978	-56	*C-1225/1-9,O3	-4.3

■ RICH SEVERSON
Severson, Richard Allen b: 1/18/45, Artesia, Cal.   BR/TR, 6', 174 lbs.   Deb: 4/10/70

YEAR	TM/L	G	AB	R	H	2B	3B	HR	RBI	BB	SO	AVG	OBP	SLG	PRO+	BR/A	SB	CS	SBR	FA	FR	G/POS	TPR
1970	KC-A	77	240	22	60	11	1	1	22	16	33	.250	.300	.317	70	-10	0	0	0	.962	1	S-50,2-25	-0.2
1971	KC-A	16	30	4	9	0	2	0	1	3	5	.300	.364	.433	126	1	0	0	0	1.000	6	/2-6,S-6,3	0.8
Total	2	93	270	26	69	11	3	1	23	19	38	.256	.307	.330	76	-9	0	0	0	.958	7	/S-56,2-31,3	0.6

■ ED SEWARD
Seward, Edward William (b: Edward William Sourhardt) b: 6/29/1867, Cleveland, Ohio   d: 7/30/47, Cleveland, Ohio   TR , 5'7", 175 lbs.   Deb: 9/30/1885   U

YEAR	TM/L	G	AB	R	H	2B	3B	HR	RBI	BB	SO	AVG	OBP	SLG	PRO+	BR/A	SB	CS	SBR	FA	FR	G/POS	TPR
1885	Pro-N	1	3	0	0	0	0	0	0	0	2	.000	.000	.000	-99	-1				1.000	1	/P-1	0.0
1887	Phi-a	74	266	31	50	10	0	5		0	16	.188	.239	.282	45	-20	14			.901	-3	P-55,O-21	-0.5
1888	Phi-a	64	225	27	32	3	3	2	14	18		.142	.215	.209	36	-16	12			.887	4	P-57/O-7	-0.1
1889	Phi-a	46	143	22	31	5	3	2	17	22	19	.217	.333	.336	92	-1	6			.885	-4	P-39/O-8,2	-0.2
1890	Phi-a	26	72	7	10	4	0	0		8		.139	.244	.194	30	-6	3			.811	-2	P-21/O-6	-0.2
1891	Cle-N	7	19	2	4	2	0	0	1	3	4	.211	.318	.316	81	-0	0			1.000	-2	/O-3,P-3,1	-0.2
Total	6	218	728	89	127	24	6	9	32	67	25	.174	.253	.261	52	-44	35			.882	-7	P-176/O-45,12	-1.2

■ GEORGE SEWARD
Seward, George E. b: St.Louis, Mo.   5'7.5", 145 lbs.   Deb: 5/19/1875

YEAR	TM/L	G	AB	R	H	2B	3B	HR	RBI	BB	SO	AVG	OBP	SLG	PRO+	BR/A	SB	CS	SBR	FA	FR	G/POS	TPR
1875	StL-n	25	97	13	24	2	0	0		1		.247	.255	.268	89	-1						C-17/O-5,2	0.0
1876	NY-N	1	3	0	0	0	0	0		0	0	.000	.000	.000	-99	-1				1.000	1	/2-1	0.0
1882	StL-a	38	144	23	31	1	1	0		12		.215	.276	.236	71	-4				.776	-0	O-35/C-5	-0.4
Total	2	39	147	23	31	1	1	0	0	12	0	.211	.270	.231	68	-5				.776	0	/O-35,C-5,2	-0.4

■ LUKE SEWELL
Sewell, James Luther b: 1/5/01, Titus, Ala.   d: 5/14/87, Akron, Ohio   BR/TR, 5'9", 160 lbs.   Deb: 6/30/21   FMC

YEAR	TM/L	G	AB	R	H	2B	3B	HR	RBI	BB	SO	AVG	OBP	SLG	PRO+	BR/A	SB	CS	SBR	FA	FR	G/POS	TPR
1921	Cle-A	3	6	0	0	0	0	0	1	0	3	.000	.000	.000	-99	-2	0	0	0	1.000	1	/C-3	-0.1
1922	Cle-A	41	87	14	23	5	0	0	10	5	8	.264	.312	.322	65	-4	1	1	-0	.963	0	C-39	-0.3
1923	Cle-A	10	10	2	2	0	1	0	1	1	0	.200	.273	.400	76	-0	0	0	0	.833	1	/C-7	0.0
1924	Cle-A	63	165	27	48	9	1	0	17	22	13	.291	.387	.358	92	-1	1	0	0	.959	5	C-57	0.7
1925	Cle-A	74	220	30	51	10	2	0	18	33	18	.232	.337	.295	61	-12	6	2	1	.971	7	C-66/O-2	-0.2
1926	Cle-A	126	433	41	103	16	4	0	46	36	27	.238	.302	.293	55	-28	9	3	1	.983	5	*C-125	-1.7
1927	Cle-A	128	470	52	138	27	6	0	53	20	23	.294	.328	.377	82	-13	4	8	-4	.963	-2	*C-126	-0.9
1928	Cle-A	122	411	52	111	16	9	3	52	26	27	.270	.318	.375	81	-12	3	4	-2	.972	13	*C-118	0.9
1929	Cle-A	124	406	41	96	16	3	1	39	29	26	.236	.287	.298	49	-31	6	6	-2	.966	4	*C-124	-1.6
1930	Cle-A	76	292	40	75	21	2	1	43	14	9	.257	.293	.353	61	-18	5	2	0	.974	-1	C-76	-1.1
1931	Cle-A	108	375	45	103	30	4	1	53	36	17	.275	.341	.384	86	-8	1	1	-0	.980	-8	*C-104	-0.8
1932	Cle-A	87	300	36	76	20	2	2	52	38	24	.253	.337	.353	74	-11	4	5	-2	.978	4	C-84	-0.4
1933	*Was-A	141	474	65	125	30	4	2	61	48	24	.264	.335	.357	84	-10	7	2	1	.990	-6	*C-141	-0.7
1934	Was-A	72	207	21	49	7	3	2	21	22	10	.237	.313	.329	68	-10	0	1	-1	.994	-1	C-50/O-7,123	-0.9
1935	Chi-A	118	421	52	120	19	3	2	67	32	18	.285	.336	.359	78	-14	3	2	-0	.988	6	*C-112	-0.2
1936	Chi-A	128	451	59	113	20	5	5	73	54	16	.251	.332	.350	66	-24	11	2	2	.984	12	*C-126	-0.4
1937	Chi-A☆	122	412	51	111	21	6	1	61	46	18	.269	.343	.357	77	-14	4	5	-2	.985	6	*C-118	-0.3
1938	Chi-A	65	211	23	45	4	1	0	27	20	20	.213	.284	.242	32	-22	0	0	0	.985	6	C-65	-1.1
1939	Cle-A	16	20	1	3	0	0	0	1	3	1	.150	.261	.200	20	-2	0	0	0	.966	-1	C-15/1-1	-0.2
1942	StL-A	6	12	1	1	0	0	0	0	1	5	.083	.154	.083	-32	-2	0	0	0	.944	1	/C-6,M	-0.1
Total	20	1630	5383	653	1393	272	56	20	696	486	307	.259	.323	.341	70	-242	65	44	-7	.978	48	*C-1562/O-9,132	-9.4

■ JOE SEWELL
Sewell, Joseph Wheeler b: 10/9/1898, Titus, Ala.   d: 3/6/90, Mobile, Ala.   BL/TR, 5'6.5", 155 lbs.   Deb: 9/10/20   FCH

YEAR	TM/L	G	AB	R	H	2B	3B	HR	RBI	BB	SO	AVG	OBP	SLG	PRO+	BR/A	SB	CS	SBR	FA	FR	G/POS	TPR
1920	*Cle-A	22	70	14	23	4	1	0	12	9	4	.329	.412	.414	116	2	1	0	0	.884	3	S-22	0.6
1921	Cle-A	154	572	101	182	36	12	4	93	80	17	.318	.412	.444	117	17	7	6	-2	.944	-3	*S-154	2.5
1922	Cle-A	153	558	80	167	28	7	2	83	73	20	.299	.386	.385	101	3	10	12	-4	.939	12	*S-139,2-12	2.5
1923	Cle-A	153	553	98	195	41	10	3	109	98	12	.353	.456	.479	147	43	9	6	-1	.930	5	*S-151	5.9
1924	Cle-A	153	594	99	188	45	5	4	106	67	13	.316	.388	.429	109	9	3	3	-1	.960	21	*S-153	4.3
1925	Cle-A	155	608	78	204	37	7	1	98	64	4	.336	.402	.424	109	10	7	6	-2	.967	16	*S-153/2-3	3.8
1926	Cle-A	154	578	91	187	41	4	4	85	65	6	.324	.399	.433	116	15	17	7	1	.955	3	*S-154	3.3
1927	Cle-A	153	569	83	180	48	5	1	92	51	7	.316	.382	.424	108	7	3	16	-9	.962	6	*S-153	1.9
1928	Cle-A	155	588	79	190	40	2	4	70	58	9	.323	.391	.418	111	11	7	1	2	.963	27	*S-137,3-19	5.4
1929	Cle-A	152	578	90	182	38	3	7	73	48	4	.315	.372	.427	102	2	6	6	-2	.975	15	*3-152	2.0
1930	Cle-A	109	353	44	102	17	6	0	48	41	3	.289	.374	.371	86	-6	1	4	-2	.950	3	3-97	-0.2
1931	NY-A	130	484	102	146	22	1	6	64	61	8	.302	.390	.388	111	11	1	1	-0	.952	-2	*3-121/2-1	1.5
1932	*NY-A	125	503	95	137	21	3	11	68	56	3	.272	.349	.392	96	-2	0	2	-1	.974	2	*3-123	0.6
1933	NY-A	135	524	87	143	18	1	2	54	71	4	.273	.361	.323	90	-7	2	2	1	.964	3	*3-131	0.3
Total	14	1903	7132	1141	2226	436	68	49	1055	842	114	.312	.391	.413	109	116	74	72	-21	.951	106	*S-1216,3-643/2	34.4

■ TOMMY SEWELL
Sewell, Thomas Wesley b: 4/16/06, Titus, Ala.   d: 7/30/56, Montgomery, Ala.   BL/TR, 5'7.5", 155 lbs.   Deb: 6/21/27   F

YEAR	TM/L	G	AB	R	H	2B	3B	HR	RBI	BB	SO	AVG	OBP	SLG	PRO+	BR/A	SB	CS	SBR	FA	FR	G/POS	TPR
1927	Chi-N	1	1	0	0	0	0	0	0	0	0	.000	.000	.000	-99	-0	0			.000	0	H	0.0

■ JIMMY SEXTON
Sexton, Jimmy Dale b: 12/15/51, Mobile, Ala.   BR/TR, 5'10", 175 lbs.   Deb: 9/2/77

YEAR	TM/L	G	AB	R	H	2B	3B	HR	RBI	BB	SO	AVG	OBP	SLG	PRO+	BR/A	SB	CS	SBR	FA	FR	G/POS	TPR
1977	Sea-A	14	37	5	8	1	1	1	2	4	6	.216	.256	.378	71	-2	1	1	-0	.929	3	S-12	0.2
1978	Hou-N	88	141	17	29	3	2	2	6	13	28	.206	.274	.298	64	-7	16	2	4	.981	-3	S-58/3-8,2	-0.2
1979	Hou-N	52	43	8	9	0	0	0	1	7	7	.209	.320	.209	50	-3	1	4	-2	.943	7	S-11/3-4,2	0.3
1981	Oak-A	7	3	0	0	0	0	0	0	0	2	.000	.000	.000	-99	-1	2	0	1	1.000	1	/3-1,D-1	0.1
1982	Oak-A	69	139	19	34	4	0	2	14	9	24	.245	.295	.317	71	-6	16	0	5	.957	-3	S-47/3-8,D	-0.1
1983	StL-N	6	9	1	1	1	0	0	1	0	4	.111	.200	.222	17	-1	0	0	0	1.000	1	/S-4,3-2	0.0
Total	6	236	372	53	81	9	3	5	24	32	71	.218	.281	.298	64	-19	36	6	7	.962	5	S-132/3-23,D2	0.3

■ TOM SEXTON
Sexton, Thomas William b: 3/14/1865, Rock Island, Ill.   d: 2/8/34, Rock Island, Ill.   Deb: 9/27/1884

YEAR	TM/L	G	AB	R	H	2B	3B	HR	RBI	BB	SO	AVG	OBP	SLG	PRO+	BR/A	SB	CS	SBR	FA	FR	G/POS	TPR
1884	Mil-U	12	47	9	11	2	0	0		4		.234	.294	.277	103	-1				.853	-1	S-12	-0.2

■ SOCKS SEYBOLD
Seybold, Ralph Orlando b: 11/23/1870, Washingtonville, O   d: 12/22/21, Greensburg, Pa.   BR/TR, 5'11", 175 lbs.   Deb: 8/20/1899

YEAR	TM/L	G	AB	R	H	2B	3B	HR	RBI	BB	SO	AVG	OBP	SLG	PRO+	BR/A	SB	CS	SBR	FA	FR	G/POS	TPR
1899	Cin-N	22	85	13	19	5	1	0	8	6		.224	.283	.306	60	-5	2			.917	1	O-22	-0.5
1901	Phi-A	114	449	74	150	24	14	8	90	40		.334	.397	.503	142	25	15			.954	-5	*O-100,1-14	1.0

YEAR	TM/L	G	AB	R	H	2B	3B	HR	RBI	BB	SO	AVG	OBP	SLG	PRO+	BR/A	SB	CS	SBR	FA	FR	G/POS	TPR
1902	Phi-A	137	522	91	165	27	12	**16**	97	43		.316	.375	.506	137	24	6			.963	2	*O-136	1.6
1903	Phi-A	137	522	76	156	**45**	8	8	84	38		.299	.353	.462	137	23	5			.964	-2	*O-120,1-18	1.4
1904	Phi-A	143	510	56	149	26	9	3	64	42		.292	.351	.396	129	17	12			.975	1	*O-129,1-13	1.2
1905	*Phi-A	133	492	64	135	37	4	6	59	42		.274	.341	.402	133	18	5			.983	9	*O-133	2.2
1906	Phi-A	116	411	41	130	23	2	5	59	30		.316	.367	.418	141	19	9			.925	-5	*O-114	0.9
1907	Phi-A	147	564	58	153	29	4	5	92	40		.271	.324	.363	116	10	10			.973	1	*O-147	0.5
1908	Phi-A	48	130	5	28	2	0	0	3	12		.215	.287	.231	64	-5	2			.921	-4	O-34	-1.1
Total	9	997	3685	478	1085	218	54	51	556	293		.294	.353	.424	129	126	66			.961	-4	O-935/1-45	7.2

■ CY SEYMOUR
Seymour, James Bentley   b: 12/9/1872, Albany, N.Y.   d: 9/20/19, New York, N.Y.   BL/TL, 6', 200 lbs.   Deb: 4/22/1896

YEAR	TM/L	G	AB	R	H	2B	3B	HR	RBI	BB	SO	AVG	OBP	SLG	PRO+	BR/A	SB	CS	SBR	FA	FR	G/POS	TPR
1896	NY-N	12	32	2	7	0	0	0	0	0	7	.219	.219	.219	16	-4	0			.857	0	P-11/O-1	-0.1
1897	NY-N	44	137	13	33	5	1	2	14	4		.241	.262	.336	59	-9	3			.850	7	P-38/O-6	-0.2
1898	NY-N	80	297	41	82	5	2	4	23	9		.276	.300	.347	88	-6	8			.887	7	P-45,O-35/2	-0.7
1899	NY-N	50	159	25	52	3	2	2	27	4		.327	.344	.409	110	1	2			.839	3	P-32/O-8,13	-0.2
1900	NY-N	23	40	9	12	0	0	0	2	3		.300	.349	.300	84	-1	0			.828	4	P-13/O-3,1	-0.2
1901	Bal-A	134	547	84	166	19	8	1	77	28		.303	.337	.373	93	-6	38			.945	14	*O-133/1-1	-0.2
1902	Bal-A	72	280	38	75	8	8	3	41	18		.268	.317	.386	90	-4	12			.956	1	O-72	-0.8
	Cin-N	62	244	27	83	8	2	2	37	12		.340	.378	.414	132	8	8			.920	2	O-61/P-1,3	0.9
1903	Cin-N	135	558	85	191	25	15	7	72	33		.342	.382	.478	130	18	25			.902	5	*O-135	1.4
1904	Cin-N	131	531	71	166	26	13	6	58	29		.313	.352	.439	132	17	11			.951	13	*O-130	2.4
1905	Cin-N	149	581	95	**219**	40	21	8	**121**	51		**.377**	.429	**.559**	175	51	21			.947	12	*O-149	5.7
1906	Cin-N	79	307	35	79	7	2	4	38	24		.257	.317	.332	98	-1	9			.968	10	O-79	0.6
	NY-N	72	269	35	86	12	3	4	42	18		.320	.365	.431	145	13	20			.978	-2	O-72	0.8
	Yr	151	576	70	165	19	5	8	80	42		.286	.339	.378	120	12	29			.972	8	*O-151	1.4
1907	NY-N	131	473	46	139	25	8	3	75	36		.294	.350	.440	131	16	21			.975	3	*O-126	1.6
1908	NY-N	156	587	60	157	23	2	5	92	30		.267	.306	.339	101	-1	18			.949	11	*O-155	0.5
1909	NY-N	80	280	37	87	12	5	1	30	25		.311	.369	.400	137	12	14			.968	0	O-74	1.0
1910	NY-N	79	287	32	76	9	4	1	40	23	18	.265	.324	.334	92	-3	10			.936	-6	O-76	-1.4
1913	Bos-N	39	73	2	13	2	0	0	10	7	7	.178	.259	.205	33	-6	2			.950	0	O-18	-0.7
Total	16	1528	5682	737	1723	229	96	52	799	354	32	.303	.347	.405	117	95	222			.945	81	*O-1333,P-140/132	10.4

■ TILLIE SHAFER
Shafer, Arthur Joseph   b: 3/22/1889, Los Angeles, Cal.   d: 1/10/62, Los Angeles, Cal.   BB/TR, 5'10", 165 lbs.   Deb: 4/24/09

YEAR	TM/L	G	AB	R	H	2B	3B	HR	RBI	BB	SO	AVG	OBP	SLG	PRO+	BR/A	SB	CS	SBR	FA	FR	G/POS	TPR
1909	NY-N	38	84	11	15	2	1	0	7	14		.179	.296	.226	61	-3	6			.750	-0	3-16,2-13/O	-0.4
1910	NY-N	29	21	5	4	1	0	0	1	6		.190	.190	.238	25	-2	0			.889	5	/3-8,2-2,S	0.3
1912	*NY-N	78	163	48	47	4	1	0	23	30	19	.288	.408	.325	99	2	22			.879	-7	S-31,3-16,2	-0.3
1913	*NY-N	138	508	74	146	17	12	5	52	61	55	.287	.369	.398	118	13	32			.923	-9	3-79,2-25,SO	0.6
Total	4	283	776	138	212	24	14	5	83	105	80	.273	.366	.360	106	10	60			.903	-12	3-119/2-55,SO	0.2

■ RALPH SHAFER
Shafer, Ralph Newton   b: 3/17/1894, Cincinnati, Ohio   d: 2/5/50, Akron, Ohio   5'11",   Deb: 7/25/14

YEAR	TM/L	G	AB	R	H	2B	3B	HR	RBI	BB	SO	AVG	OBP	SLG	PRO+	BR/A	SB	CS	SBR	FA	FR	G/POS	TPR
1914	Pit-N	1	0	0	0	0	0	0	0	0	0	—	—	—	—		0	0		.000	0	H	0.0

■ SHAFFER
Shaffer   Deb: 9/15/1875

YEAR	TM/L	G	AB	R	H	2B	3B	HR	RBI	BB	SO	AVG	OBP	SLG	PRO+	BR/A	SB	CS	SBR	FA	FR	G/POS	TPR
1875	Atl-n	1	4	0	0	0	0	0		0		.000	.000	.000	-99	-1						/O-1	-0.1

■ FRANK SHAFFER
Shaffer, Frank   Deb: 4/24/1884

YEAR	TM/L	G	AB	R	H	2B	3B	HR	RBI	BB	SO	AVG	OBP	SLG	PRO+	BR/A	SB	CS	SBR	FA	FR	G/POS	TPR
1884	Alt-U	19	74	11	21	2	0	0			3	.284	.312	.311	69	-3				.889	-3	O-17/C-2,3	-0.6
	KC-U	44	164	18	28	3	2	0			15	.171	.240	.213	28	-16				.768	-3	O-41/C-2,2S3	-1.7
	Bal-U	3	13	1	1	0	0	0			0	.077	.077	.077	-53	-3				.750	-1	O-3	-0.3
	Yr	66	251	30	50	5	2	0			18	.199	.253	.235	36	-21				.796	-6	O-61/C-4,32S	-2.6

■ ORATOR SHAFFER
Shaffer, George   b: 1852, Philadelphia, Pa.   BL/TR, 5'9", 165 lbs.   Deb: 5/23/1874   F

YEAR	TM/L	G	AB	R	H	2B	3B	HR	RBI	BB	SO	AVG	OBP	SLG	PRO+	BR/A	SB	CS	SBR	FA	FR	G/POS	TPR
1874	Har-n	9	34	6	8	0	0	1			0	.235	.235	.324	72	-1						/O-9	-0.1
	Mut-n	1	5	1	1	0	0	0			0	.200	.200	.200	27	-0						/O-1	0.0
	Yr	10	39	7	9	0	0	1			0	.231	.231	.308	67	-2						O-10	-0.1
1875	Phi-n	19	70	10	17	2	1	0			0	.243	.243	.300	83	-1						O-10/3-6,1	-0.1
1877	Lou-n	61	260	38	74	9	5	3	34	9	17	.285	.309	.392	101	-2				.835	14	*O-60/1-1	0.8
1878	Ind-N	63	266	48	90	19	6	0	30	13	20	.338	.369	.455	**196**	**28**				.842	8	*O-63	**2.9**
1879	Chi-N	73	316	53	96	13	0	0	35	6	28	.304	.317	.345	111	3				.801	20	*O-72/3-1	1.8
1880	Cle-N	83	338	62	90	14	9	0	21	17	36	.266	.301	.361	126	9				.901	17	*O-83	2.3
1881	Cle-N	85	343	48	88	13	6	1	34	23	20	.257	.303	.338	107	4				.880	2	*O-85	0.4
1882	Cle-N	84	313	37	67	14	2	3	28	27	27	.214	.276	.300	88	-3				.805	-9	*O-84	-1.2
1883	Buf-N	95	401	67	117	11	3	0	41	27	39	.292	.336	.334	103	2				.861	20	*O-95	1.8
1884	StL-U	106	467	130	168	**40**	10	2		30		.360	.398	.501	138	24				.870	-3	*O-100/2-7,1	1.7
1885	StL-N	69	257	30	50	11	2	0	18	19	31	.195	.253	.253	67	-8				.918	11	O-69	0.1
	Phi-a	2	9	1	2	0	1	0	1			.222	.300	.444	125	0				1.000	-1	/O-2	0.0
1886	Phi-a	21	82	15	22	3	3	0		8		.268	.333	.378	121	2	3			.815	0	O-21	0.2
1890	Phi-a	100	390	55	110	15	5	1		47		.282	.367	.354	115	9	29			**.958**	2	*O-98/1-3	0.6
Total	2 n	29	109	17	26	2	1	1		0		.239	.239	.303	77	-3	0					/O-20,3-6,1	-0.2
Total	11	842	3442	584	974	162	52	10	241	227	218	.283	.328	.369	116	66	32			.865	82	O-832/2-7,13	11.4

■ TAYLOR SHAFFER
Shaffer, Taylor   b: 7/1870, Philadelphia, Pa.   Deb: 4/17/1890   F

YEAR	TM/L	G	AB	R	H	2B	3B	HR	RBI	BB	SO	AVG	OBP	SLG	PRO+	BR/A	SB	CS	SBR	FA	FR	G/POS	TPR
1890	Phi-a	69	261	28	45	3	4	0		28		.172	.258	.215	40	-19	19			.921	4	2-69	-1.0

■ ART SHAMSKY
Shamsky, Arthur Louis   b: 10/14/41, St.Louis, Mo.   BL/TL, 6'1", 175 lbs.   Deb: 4/17/65

YEAR	TM/L	G	AB	R	H	2B	3B	HR	RBI	BB	SO	AVG	OBP	SLG	PRO+	BR/A	SB	CS	SBR	FA	FR	G/POS	TPR
1965	Cin-N	64	96	13	25	4	3	2	10	10	29	.260	.330	.427	104	1	1	0	0	.966	0	O-18/1-1	0.0
1966	Cin-N	96	234	41	54	5	0	21	47	32	45	.231	.330	.521	120	6	0	2	-1	.973	-3	O-74	-0.1
1967	Cin-N	76	147	6	29	3	1	3	13	15	34	.197	.276	.293	56	-8	0	1	-1	.984	-2	O-40	-1.4
1968	NY-N	116	345	30	82	14	4	12	48	21	58	.238	.295	.406	108	3	1	0	0	.993	1	O-82,1-17	-0.2
1969	*NY-N	100	303	42	91	9	3	14	47	36	32	.300	.380	.488	139	16	1	2	-1	.992	-6	O-78/1-9	0.4
1970	NY-N	122	403	48	118	19	2	11	49	49	33	.293	.374	.432	115	9	1	1	-0	1.000	1	O-58,1-56	0.2
1971	NY-N	68	135	13	25	6	2	5	18	21	18	.185	.299	.370	90	-2	0	1	-0	.984	2	O-38/1-1	-0.2
1972	Chi-N	15	16	1	2	0	0	0	1	3	3	.125	.263	.125	12	-2	0	0	0	1.000	0	/1-4	-0.2
	Oak-A	8	7	0	0	0	0	0	0	1	2	.000	.125	.000	-64	-1	0	0	0	.000	0	H	-0.2
Total	8	665	1686	194	426	60	15	68	233	188	254	.253	.333	.427	109	21	4	7	-8	.987	-8	O-388/1-88	-1.7

■ JIM SHANDLEY
Shandley, James H.   b: New York   d: 11/4/04, Brooklyn, N.Y.   Deb: 5/3/1876

YEAR	TM/L	G	AB	R	H	2B	3B	HR	RBI	BB	SO	AVG	OBP	SLG	PRO+	BR/A	SB	CS	SBR	FA	FR	G/POS	TPR
1876	NY-N	2	8	0	1	0	0	0	0	0	0	.125	.125	.125	-19	-1				.600	-1	/O-2	-0.1

■ WALLY SHANER
Shaner, Walter Dedaker "Skinny"   b: 5/24/1900, Lynchburg, Va.   d: 11/13/92, Las Vegas, Nev.   BR/TR, 6'2", 195 lbs.   Deb: 5/4/23

YEAR	TM/L	G	AB	R	H	2B	3B	HR	RBI	BB	SO	AVG	OBP	SLG	PRO+	BR/A	SB	CS	SBR	FA	FR	G/POS	TPR
1923	Cle-A	3	4	1	1	0	0	0	0	1		.250	.400	.250	74	-0	0	0	0	1.000	-1	/O-2,3-1	-0.1
1926	Bos-A	69	191	20	54	12	2	0	21	17	13	.283	.348	.366	89	-3	1	0	0	.965	0	O-48	-0.6
1927	Bos-A	122	406	54	111	33	6	3	49	21	35	.273	.311	.406	87	-10	11	4	1	.955	-8	O-108/1-1	-2.2
1929	Cin-N	13	28	5	9	0	0	1	4	4	5	.321	.406	.429	112	1	1			1.000	-1	/1-8,O-2	-0.1
Total	4	207	629	80	175	45	6	4	74	43	54	.278	.327	.394	89	-12	13	4		.959	-9	O-160/1-9,3	-3.0

YEAR	TM/L	G	AB	R	H	2B	3B	HR	RBI	BB	SO	AVG	OBP	SLG	PRO+	BR/A	SB	CS	SBR	FA	FR	G/POS	TPR

■ HOWIE SHANKS Shanks, Howard Samuel "Hank" b: 7/21/1890, Chicago, Ill. d: 7/30/41, Monaca, Pa. BR/TR, 5'11", 170 lbs. Deb: 5/9/12 C

1912	Was-A	116	399	52	92	14	7	1	48	40		.231	.305	.308	75	-13	21			.962	-2	*O-114	-2.1
1913	Was-A	109	390	38	99	11	5	1	37	15	40	.254	.287	.315	75	-14	24			.978	3	*O-109	-1.6
1914	Was-A	143	500	44	112	22	10	4	64	29	51	.224	.269	.332	78	-16	18	16	-4	.954	-0	*O-139	-3.0
1915	Was-A	141	492	52	123	19	8	0	47	30	42	.250	.297	.321	83	-12	12	14	-5	.982	7	O-80,3-49,2	-1.2
1916	Was-A	140	471	51	119	15	7	1	48	41	34	.253	.317	.321	92	-5	23	12	-0	.987	10	O-88,3-31/S1	0.2
1917	Was-A	126	430	45	87	15	5	0	28	33	37	.202	.269	.260	62	-20	15			.929	13	S-90,O-26/1	-0.5
1918	Was-A	120	436	42	112	19	4	1	56	31	21	.257	.312	.326	94	-4	23			.957	1	O-64,2-48/3	-0.4
1919	Was-A	135	491	33	122	8	7	1	54	25	48	.248	.289	.299	66	-23	13			.922	-11	S-94,2-34/O	-2.9
1920	Was-A	128	444	56	119	16	7	4	37	29	43	.268	.316	.363	82	-13	11	6	-0	.951	-6	3-63,O-35,1/2S	-1.8
1921	Was-A	154	562	81	170	24	**18**	7	69	57	38	.302	.370	.447	113	10	11	10	-3	**.960**	5	*3-154/2-1	2.2
1922	Was-A	84	272	35	77	10	9	1	32	25	25	.283	.352	.397	100	-0	6	0	2	.920	7	3-54,O-27	1.0
1923	Bos-A	131	464	38	118	19	5	3	57	19	37	.254	.285	.336	63	-26	6	6	-2	.939	-19	3-83,2-38/OS	-3.9
1924	Bos-A	72	193	22	50	16	3	0	25	21	12	.259	.332	.373	81	-6	1	0	0	.972	7	S-41,3-22/O12	0.6
1925	NY-A	66	155	15	40	3	1	1	18	20	15	.258	.343	.310	68	-7	1	0	0	.938	-6	3-26,2-21/O	-1.0
Total	14	1665	5699	604	1440	211	96	25	620	415	443	.253	.308	.337	82	-148	185	64		.971	10	O-702,3-485,S2/1	-14.4

■ DOC SHANLEY Shanley, Harry Root b: 1890, Granbury, Tex. d: 12/13/34, St.Petersburg, Fla BR/TR, 6', 174 lbs. Deb: 9/15/12

| 1912 | StL-A | 5 | 8 | 1 | 0 | 0 | 0 | 0 | | 1 | 2 | .000 | .200 | .000 | -43 | -1 | 0 | | | .833 | -2 | /S-4 | -0.3 |

■ WARREN SHANNABROOK Shannabrook, Warren H. b: 11/30/1880, Massillon, Ohio d: 3/10/64, N.Canton, Ohio BR/TR, 6', 170 lbs. Deb: 8/13/06

| 1906 | Was-A | 1 | 2 | 0 | 0 | 0 | 0 | 0 | | 0 | 0 | .000 | .000 | .000 | -99 | -0 | 0 | | | 1.000 | -1 | /3-1 | -0.1 |

■ DAN SHANNON Shannon, Daniel Webster b: 3/23/1865, Bridgeport, Conn. d: 10/25/13, Bridgeport, Conn. 5'9", 175 lbs. Deb: 4/17/1889 M

1889	Lou-a	121	498	90	128	22	12	4	48	42	52	.257	.315	.373	97	-3	26			.910	7	*2-121,M	0.9
1890	Phi-P	19	75	15	18	5	1	5	16	4	12	.240	.278	.373	72	-4	4			.926	-4	2-19	-0.6
	NY-P	83	324	59	70	7	8	3	44	25	34	.216	.274	.315	53	-25	21			.908	1	2-77/S-6	-1.5
	Yr	102	399	74	88	12	9	4	60	29	46	.221	.275	.326	56	-28	25			.911	-3	2-96/S-6	-2.1
1891	Was-a	19	67	7	9	2	0	0	3	6	9	.134	.205	.164	6	-8	3			.878	1	S-14/2-5M	-0.6
Total	3	242	964	171	225	36	21	8	111	77	107	.233	.291	.339	73	-39	54			.911	5	2-222/S-20	-1.8

■ FRANK SHANNON Shannon, John Francis b: 12/3/1873, San Francisco, Cal. d: 2/27/34, Boston, Mass. 5'3", 155 lbs. Deb: 10/1/1892

1892	Was-N	1	4	0	1	0	0	0		0		.250	.250	.250	53	-0				.625	-1	/S-1	-0.1
1896	Lou-N	31	115	14	18	1	1	1	15	13	15	.157	.248	.209	22	-13	3			.830	-13	S-28/3-3	-2.2
Total	2	32	119	14	19	1	1	1	17	13	17	.160	.248	.210	23	-13	3			.820	-14	/S-29,3-3	-2.3

■ JOE SHANNON Shannon, Joseph Aloysius b: 2/11/1897, Jersey City, N.J. d: 7/28/55, Jersey City, N.J. BR/TR, 5'11", 170 lbs. Deb: 7/7/15 F

| 1915 | Bos-N | 5 | 10 | 3 | 2 | 0 | 0 | 0 | | 1 | 0 | .200 | .200 | .200 | 22 | -1 | 0 | | | .750 | -0 | /O-4,2-1 | -0.1 |

■ RED SHANNON Shannon, Maurice Joseph b: 2/11/1897, Jersey City, N.J. d: 4/12/70, Jersey City, N.J. BB/TR, 5'11", 170 lbs. Deb: 10/7/15 F

1915	Bos-N	1	3	0	0	0	0	0	0	0	0	.000	.000	.000	-99	-1	0			.857	1	/2-1	0.0
1917	Phi-A	11	35	8	10	0	0	0	7	6	9	.286	.390	.286	108	1	2			.875	-0	S-10	0.1
1918	Phi-A	72	225	23	54	6	5	0	16	42	52	.240	.367	.311	103	3	5			.898	-4	S-45,2-26	0.3
1919	Phi-A	39	155	14	42	7	2	0	14	12	28	.271	.331	.342	88	-2	4			.948	-5	2-37	-0.6
	Bos-A	80	290	36	75	11	7	0	17	17	42	.259	.313	.345	90	-5	7			.973	-4	2-79	-0.6
	Yr	119	445	50	117	18	9	0	31	29	70	.263	.320	.344	89	-7	11			.965	-9	*2-116	-1.2
1920	Was-A	63	222	30	64	8	7	0	30	22	32	.288	.352	.387	99	-0	2	5	-2	.919	-19	S-31,2-16,3	-1.8
	Phi-A	24	88	4	15	1	1	0	3	4	12	.170	.207	.205	9	-12	1	1	-0	.945	-1	S-24	-1.1
	Yr	87	310	34	79	9	8	0	33	26	44	.255	.313	.335	73	-12	3	6	-3	.931	-21	S-55,2-16,3	-2.9
1921	Phi-A	1	1	0	0	0	0	0	0	0	0	.000	.000	.000	-99	-0	0	0	0	.000	-0	H	0.0
1926	Chi-N	19	51	9	17	5	0	0	4	6	3	.333	.414	.431	126	2	0	0	0	.957	-2	S-13	0.0
Total	7	310	1070	124	277	38	22	0	91	109	178	.259	.334	.336	89	-14	21	6		.957	-35	2-159,S-123/3	-3.6

■ MIKE SHANNON Shannon, Thomas Michael "Moonman" b: 7/5/39, St.Louis, Mo. BR/TR, 6'3", 195 lbs. Deb: 9/11/62

1962	StL-N	10	15	3	2	0	0	0		1	3	.133	.188	.133	-11	-2	0	0	0	1.000	-0	/O-7	-0.3
1963	StL-N	32	26	3	8	0	0	1	2	0	6	.308	.333	.423	106	0	0	1	-1	.944	-5	O-26	-0.6
1964	*StL-N	88	253	30	66	8	2	9	43	19	54	.261	.313	.415	95	-2	4	0	1	.983	-6	O-88	-1.1
1965	StL-N	124	244	32	54	17	3	6	25	28	46	.221	.307	.352	78	-7	2	1	0	.994	-1	*O-101/C-4	-1.1
1966	StL-N	137	459	61	132	20	6	16	64	37	106	.288	.341	.462	120	12	8	4	0	.985	6	*O-129/C-1	1.3
1967	*StL-N	130	482	53	118	18	3	12	77	37	89	.245	.304	.369	93	-5	2	4	-2	.919	-11	*3-122/O-6	-2.1
1968	*StL-N	156	576	62	153	29	2	15	79	37	114	.266	.312	.401	114	9	1	2	-1	.952	-7	*3-156	0.1
1969	StL-N	150	551	51	140	15	5	12	55	49	87	.254	.316	.365	90	-8	1	4	-2	.945	-19	*3-149	-3.0
1970	StL-N	55	174	18	37	9	2	0	22	16	20	.213	.279	.287	51	-12	1	1	-0	.919	-13	3-51	-2.7
Total	9	882	2780	313	710	116	23	68	367	224	525	.255	.313	.387	96	-16	19	17	-5	.938	-57	3-478,O-357/C	-9.5

■ OWEN SHANNON Shannon, Owen Dennis Ignatius b: 12/22/1879, Omaha, Neb. d: 4/10/18, Omaha, Neb. BR/TR, Deb: 9/6/03

1903	StL-A	9	28	1	6	2	0	0	3	1		.214	.241	.286	59	-1	0			.957	-0	/C-8,1-1	-0.1
1907	Was-A	4	7	0	1	0	0	0	0	0		.143	.143	.143	-10	-1	0			1.000	3	/C-4	0.2
Total	2	13	35	1	7	2	0	0	3	1		.200	.222	.257	47	-2	0			.970	2	/C-12,1-1	0.1

■ WALLY SHANNON Shannon, Walter Charles b: 1/23/33, Cleveland, Ohio d: 2/8/92, Creve Coeur, Mo. BL/TR, 6', 178 lbs. Deb: 7/9/59

1959	StL-N	47	95	5	27	5	0	0	5	0	12	.284	.292	.337	63	-5	0	0	0	1.000	-11	S-21,2-10	-1.4
1960	StL-N	18	23	2	4	0	0	0	1	3	6	.174	.296	.174	30	-2	0	0	0	1.000	2	2-15/S-1	0.1
Total	2	65	118	7	31	5	0	0	6	3	18	.263	.293	.305	56	-7	0	0	0	.955	-9	/2-25,S-22	-1.3

■ SPIKE SHANNON Shannon, William Porter b: 2/7/1878, Pittsburg, Pa. d: 5/16/40, Minneapolis, Minn. BB/TR, 5'11", 180 lbs. Deb: 4/15/04 U

1904	StL-N	134	500	84	140	10	3	1	26	50		.280	.349	.318	111	9	34			**.978**	9	*O-133	1.0
1905	StL-N	140	544	73	146	16	3	0	41	47		.268	.327	.309	92	-4	27			**.984**	0	*O-140	-1.1
1906	StL-N	80	302	36	78	4	0	0	25	36		.258	.337	.272	94	-1	15			.972	6	O-80	0.1
	NY-N	76	287	42	73	5	0	0	25	34		.254	.342	.279	91	-1	18			.958	-7	O-76	-1.3
	Yr	156	589	78	151	9	0	0	50	70		.256	.339	.275	93	-2	33			.966	-1	*O-156	-1.2
1907	NY-N	155	585	**104**	155	12	5	1	33	82		.265	.363	.308	107	9	33			.977	2	*O-155	0.5
1908	NY-N	77	268	34	60	2	1	1	21	28		.224	.314	.250	77	-6	13			.976	-3	O-74	-1.4
	Pit-N	32	127	10	25	0	2	0	12	9		.197	.250	.228	53	-7	5			.947	1	O-32	-0.8
	Yr	109	395	44	85	2	3	1	33	37		.215	.294	.243	69	-12	18			.964	-2	*O-106	-2.2
Total	5	694	2613	383	677	49	15	3	183	286		.259	.337	.293	96	-1	145			.974	8	O-690	-3.0

■ BILLY SHANTZ Shantz, Wilmer Ebert b: 7/31/27, Pottstown, Pa. d: 12/13/93, Lauderhill, Fla. BR/TR, 6'1", 160 lbs. Deb: 4/13/54 F

1954	Phi-A	51	164	13	42	9	3	1	17	17	23	.256	.326	.366	89	-3	0	0	0	.975	-13	C-51	-1.4
1955	KC-A	79	217	18	56	4	1	1	12	11	14	.258	.294	.300	59	-13	0	0	0	.990	-10	C-78	-2.1
1960	NY-A	1	0	0	0	0	0	0	0	0	0	—	—	—		0	0	0	0	1.000	-0	/C-1	0.0
Total	3	131	381	31	98	13	4	2	29	28	37	.257	.308	.328	72	-15	0	0	0	.984	-23	C-130	-3.5

■ RALPH SHARMAN Sharman, Ralph Edward "Bally" b: 4/11/1895, Cleveland, Ohio d: 5/24/18, Camp Sheridan, Ala BR/TR, 5'11", 176 lbs. Deb: 9/10/17

| 1917 | Phi-A | 13 | 37 | 2 | 11 | 2 | 1 | 0 | 2 | 3 | 2 | .297 | .366 | .405 | 137 | 2 | 1 | | | .941 | -1 | O-10 | 0.0 |

YEAR	TM/L	G	AB	R	H	2B	3B	HR	RBI	BB	SO	AVG	OBP	SLG	PRO+	BR/A	SB	CS	SBR	FA	FR	G/POS	TPR
■ **DICK SHARON**			Sharon, Richard Louis		b: 4/15/50, San Mateo, Cal.					BR/TR, 6'2", 195 lbs.		Deb: 5/13/73											
1973	Det-A	91	178	20	43	9	0	7	16	10	31	.242	.282	.410	87	-4	2	0	1	.970	-10	O-91	-1.5
1974	Det-A	60	129	12	28	4	0	2	10	14	29	.217	.294	.295	67	-5	4	4	-1	.989	-5	O-56	-1.4
1975	SD-N	91	160	14	31	7	0	4	20	26	35	.194	.306	.313	77	-5	0	2	-1	.948	-7	O-57	-1.6
Total	3	242	467	46	102	20	0	13	46	50	95	.218	.294	.345	79	-14	6	6	-2	.969	-22	O-204	-4.5
■ **BILL SHARP**			Sharp, William Howard		b: 1/18/50, Lima, Ohio					BL/TL, 5'10", 178 lbs.		Deb: 5/26/73											
1973	Chi-A	77	196	23	54	8	3	4	22	19	28	.276	.349	.408	109	2	2	3	-1	.981	2	O-70/D-1	0.1
1974	Chi-A	100	320	45	81	13	2	4	24	25	37	.253	.311	.344	86	-6	0	3	-2	.986	-1	O-99	-1.3
1975	Chi-A	18	35	1	7	0	0	0	4	2	3	.200	.243	.200	26	-3	0	0	0	.941	-3	O-14	-0.7
	Mil-A	125	373	37	95	27	3	1	34	19	26	.255	.293	.351	81	-10	0	3	-2	.994	-3	*O-124	-2.0
	Yr	143	408	38	102	27	3	1	38	21	29	.250	.288	.338	76	-14	0	3	-2	.991	-6	*O-138	-2.7
1976	Mil-A	78	180	16	44	4	0	0	11	10	15	.244	.288	.267	64	-8	1	3	-2	.975	0	O-56/D-7	-1.2
Total	4	398	1104	122	281	52	8	9	95	75	109	.255	.306	.341	83	-25	3	12	-6	.985	-5	O-363/D-8	-5.1
■ **BUD SHARPE**			Sharpe, Bayard Heston		b: 8/6/1881, West Chester, Pa.		d: 5/31/16, Haddock, Ga.			BL/TR,		Deb: 4/14/05											
1905	Bos-N	46	170	8	31	3	2	0	11	7		.182	.215	.224	31	-15	0			.904	2	O-42/C-3,1	-1.5
1910	Bos-N	115	439	30	105	14	3	0	29	14	31	.239	.264	.285	58	-25	4			.987	7	*1-113	-1.9
	Pit-N	4	16	2	3	0	1	0	1	0	2	.188	.188	.313	43	-1	0			1.000	0	/1-4	-0.1
	Yr	119	455	32	108	14	4	0	30	14	33	.237	.262	.286	57	-26	4			.987	8	*1-117	-2.0
Total	2	165	625	40	139	17	6	0	41	21	33	.222	.249	.269	50	-41	4			.987	9	1-118/O-42,C	-3.5
■ **MIKE SHARPERSON**			Sharperson, Michael Tyrone		b: 10/4/61, Orangeburg, S.C.			BR/TR, 6'3", 190 lbs.			Deb: 4/6/87												
1987	Tor-A	32	96	4	20	4	1	0	9	7	15	.208	.269	.271	43	-8	2	1	0	.971	-5	2-32	-1.1
	LA-N	10	33	7	9	2	0	0	1	4	5	.273	.351	.333	85	-1	0	0	0	1.000	2	/3-7,2-6	0.1
1988	*LA-N	46	59	8	16	1	0	0	4	1	12	.271	.295	.288	70	-2	0	1	-1	.949	-3	/2-20/3-6,S	-0.3
1989	LA-N	27	28	2	7	3	0	0	5	4	7	.250	.344	.357	102	0	0	1	-1	1.000	-0	/2-4,1-2,3S	0.0
1990	LA-N	129	357	42	106	14	2	3	36	46	39	.297	.379	.373	111	7	15	6	1	.949	6	*3-106,S-15/21	1.4
1991	LA-N	105	216	24	60	11	2	2	20	25	24	.278	.355	.375	108	3	1	3	-2	.981	-5	3-68,S-16,1/2	-0.3
1992	LA-N★	128	317	48	95	21	0	3	36	47	33	.300	.390	.394	125	12	2	2	-1	.979	1	2-63,3-60/S	1.4
1993	LA-N	73	90	13	23	4	0	2	10	5	17	.256	.302	.367	83	-2	0	0	1	.945	1	2-17/3-6,S10	0.0
Total	7	550	1196	148	336	60	5	10	121	139	152	.281	.358	.365	103	9	22	14	-2	.952	-0	3-255,2-156/S10	1.2
■ **JACK SHARROTT**			Sharrott, John Henry		b: 8/13/1869, Bangor, Me.		d: 12/31/27, Los Angeles, Cal.			BR/TR, 5'9", 165 lbs.		Deb: 4/22/1890											
1890	NY-N	32	109	16	22	3	2	0	14	0	14	.202	.202	.266	36	-9	6			.932	-2	P-25/O-9	-0.6
1891	NY-N	10	30	5	10	2	0	1	7	1	2	.333	.355	.500	154	2	3			.950	1	P-10	0.1
1892	NY-N	4	8	1	1	0	0	0	0	0	1	.125	.125	.125	-25	-1	0			.333	-1	/O-3,P-1	-0.2
1893	Phi-N	50	152	25	38	4	3	1	22	8	14	.250	.287	.336	65	-8	6			.824	-8	O-33,P-12	-1.3
Total	4	96	299	47	71	9	5	2	43	9	31	.237	.260	.321	61	-17	15			.927	-10	/P-48,O-45	-2.1
■ **SHAG SHAUGHNESSY**			Shaughnessy, Francis Joseph		b: 4/8/1883, Amboy, Ill.		d: 5/15/69, Montreal, Que., Can			BR/TR, 6'1.5", 185 lbs.		Deb: 4/17/05 C											
1905	Was-A	1	3	0	0	0	0	0	0	0		.000	.250	.000	-19	-0	0			.667	-0	/O-1	-0.1
1908	Phi-A	8	29	2	9	0	0	0	1	2		.310	.355	.310	109	0	3			1.000	-1	/O-8	-0.1
Total	2	9	32	2	9	0	0	0	1	2		.281	.343	.281	97	-0	3			.938	-1	/O-9	-0.2
■ **JON SHAVE**			Shave, Jonathan Taylor		b: 11/4/67, Waycross, Ga.			BR/TR, 6', 185 lbs.		Deb: 5/15/93													
1993	Tex-A	17	47	3	15	2	0	0	7	0	8	.319	.319	.362	86	-1	1	3	-2	.917	-2	/S-9,2-8	-0.4
■ **AL SHAW**			Shaw, Albert Simpson		b: 3/1/1881, Toledo, Ill.		d: 12/30/74, Danville, Ill.			BL/TR, 5'8.5", 165 lbs.		Deb: 9/28/07											
1907	StL-N	9	25	2	7	0	0	0	1	3		.280	.379	.280	110	1	1			.947	-1	/O-9	0.0
1908	StL-N	107	367	40	97	13	4	1	19	25		.264	.311	.330	110	3	9			.931	7	O-91/S-4,3	0.7
1909	StL-N	114	331	45	82	12	7	2	34	55		.248	.355	.344	125	11	15			.940	-1	O-92	0.7
1914	Bro-F	112	376	81	122	27	7	5	49	44	59	.324	.395	.473	125	14	24			.955	1	*O-102	1.1
1915	KC-F	132	448	67	126	22	10	6	67	46	45	.281	.348	.415	108	4	15			.942	-14	*O-124	-1.7
Total	5	474	1547	235	434	74	28	14	170	173	104	.281	.353	.392	117	33	64			.942	-8	O-418/S-4,3	0.8
■ **AL SHAW**			Shaw, Alfred "Shoddy"		b: 10/3/1874, Burslem, England		d: 3/25/58, Uhrichsville, Ohio			BR/TR, 5'8", 170 lbs.		Deb: 6/8/01											
1901	Det-A	55	171	20	46	1	0	0	23	10		.269	.321	.327	76	-6	2			.938	-0	C-42/1-9,3S	-0.2
1907	Bos-A	76	198	10	38	1	3	0	7	18		.192	.269	.227	59	-9	4			.971	15	C-73/1-1	1.4
1908	Chi-A	32	49	0	4	1	0	0	2	2		.082	.118	.102	-29	-7	0			.953	2	C-29	-0.4
1909	Bos-N	18	41	1	4	0	0	0	0	5		.098	.213	.098	-3	-5	0			.975	4	C-14	0.0
Total	4	181	459	31	92	9	3	1	32	35		.200	.267	.240	53	-26	6			.961	21	C-158/1-10,3S	0.8
■ **BEN SHAW**			Shaw, Benajmin Nathaniel		b: 6/18/1893, LaCenter, Ky.		d: 3/16/59, Cleveland, Ohio			BR/TR, 5'11.5", 190 lbs.		Deb: 4/11/17											
1917	Pit-N	2	2	0	0	0	0	0	0	0	0	.000	.000	.000	-97	-0	0			.000	0	H	-0.1
1918	Pit-N	21	36	5	7	1	0	0	2	2	2	.194	.275	.222	50	-2	0			.981	-2	/1-9,C-5	-0.4
Total	2	23	38	5	7	1	0	0	2	2	2	.184	.262	.211	43	-2	0			.981	-2	/1-9,C-5	-0.5
■ **HUNKY SHAW**			Shaw, Royal N		b: 9/29/1884, Yakima, Wash.		d: 7/3/69, Yakima, Wash.			BB/TR, 5'8", 165 lbs.		Deb: 5/16/08											
1908	Pit-N	1	1	0	0	0	0	0	0	0		.000	.000	.000	-99	-0	0			.000	0	H	0.0
■ **MARTY SHAY**			Shay, Arthur Joseph		b: 4/25/1896, Boston, Mass.		d: 2/20/51, Worcester, Mass.			BR/TR, 5'7.5", 148 lbs.		Deb: 9/16/16											
1916	Chi-N	2	7	0	2	0	0	0	0	0	1	.286	.286	.286	68	-0	0			.917	0	/S-2	0.0
1924	Bos-N	19	68	4	16	3	1	0	2	5	5	.235	.297	.309	65	-3	2	1	0	.950	-12	2-19/S-1	-1.5
Total	2	21	75	4	18	3	1	0	2	5	6	.240	.296	.307	66	-4	2	1		.929	-12	/2-19,S-3	-1.5
■ **DANNY SHAY**			Shay, Daniel C.		b: 11/8/1876, Springfield, Ohio		d: 12/1/27, Kansas City, Mo.			TR, 5'10",		Deb: 4/30/01											
1901	Cle-A	19	75	4	17	2	2	0	10	2		.227	.266	.307	61	-4	0			.901	-4	S-19	-0.6
1904	StL-N	99	340	45	87	11	1	1	18	39		.256	.338	.303	103	3	36			.911	-7	S-97/2-2	-0.2
1905	StL-N	78	281	30	67	12	1	0	28	35		.238	.331	.288	88	-3	11			.953	-13	2-39,S-39	-1.6
1907	NY-N	35	79	10	15	1	1	0	6	12		.190	.304	.266	76	-2	5			.931	-7	2-13/S-9,O	-1.1
Total	4	231	775	89	186	26	5	2	62	88		.240	.325	.294	90	-6	52			.902	-31	S-164/2-54,O	-3.5
■ **GERRY SHEA**			Shea, Gerald J.		b: 7/26/1881, St.Louis, Mo.		d: 5/3/64, Berkeley, Mo.			TR, 5'7", 160 lbs.		Deb: 10/1/05											
1905	StL-N	2	6	0	2	0	0	0	0	0		.333	.333	.333	102	-0	0			.917	1	/C-2	0.1
■ **NAP SHEA**			Shea, John Edward "Napoleon"		b: 5/23/1874, Ware, Mass.		d: 7/8/68, Bloomfield Hills, Mich.			BR/TR, 5'5", 155 lbs.		Deb: 9/11/02											
1902	Phi-N	3	8	1	1	0	0	0	0	1		.125	.300	.125	32	-1	0			1.000	-0	/C-3	-0.1
■ **MERV SHEA**			Shea, Mervyn David John		b: 9/5/1900, San Francisco, Cal		d: 1/27/53, Sacramento, Cal.			BR/TR, 5'11", 175 lbs.		Deb: 4/23/27 C											
1927	Det-A	34	85	5	15	6	3	0	9	7	15	.176	.239	.318	43	-8	0	0	0	.949	-4	C-31	-0.6
1928	Det-A	39	85	8	20	2	3	0	9	9	11	.235	.316	.329	69	-4	2	2	-1	.951	4	C-30	0.1
1929	Det-A	50	162	23	47	6	0	3	24	19	18	.290	.365	.383	92	-1	2	1	0	.964	-6	C-46	-0.3
1933	Bos-A	16	56	1	8	0	0	0	8	4	7	.143	.200	.196	5	-8	0	0	0	1.000	0	C-16	-0.8
	StL-A	94	279	26	73	11	1	1	27	43	26	.262	.360	.319	76	-8	2	0	1	.995	9	C-85	0.6
	Yr	110	335	27	81	14	1	1	35	47	33	.242	.335	.299	65	-16	2	0	1	**.996**	7	*C-101	-0.2

YEAR	TM/L	G	AB	R	H	2B	3B	HR	RBI	BB	SO	AVG	OBP	SLG	PRO+	BR/A	SB	CS	SBR	FA	FR	G/POS	TPR
1934	Chi-A	62	176	8	28	3	0	0	5	24	19	.159	.260	.176	14	-22	0	1	-1	.972	1	C-60	-1.8
1935	Chi-A	46	122	8	28	2	0	0	13	30	9	.230	.382	.246	64	-5	0	0	0	.990	8	C-43	0.5
1936	Chi-A	14	24	3	3	0	0	0	2	6	5	.125	.300	.125	8	-3	0	0	0	1.000	1	C-14	-0.2
1937	Chi-A	25	71	7	15	1	0	0	5	15	10	.211	.349	.225	48	-5	1	0	0	.966	3	C-25	-0.1
1938	Bro-N	48	120	14	22	5	0	0	12	28	20	.183	.338	.225	56	-6	1			.977	-1	C-47	-0.5
1939	Det-A	4	2	0	0	0	0	0	0	0	1	.000	.000	.000	-93	-1	0	0	0	.500	-1	/C-4	-0.1
1944	Phi-N	7	15	2	4	0	0	1	1	4	4	.267	.421	.467	155	1	0			.952	-0	/C-6	0.1
Total	11	439	1197	105	263	39	7	5	115	189	145	.220	.327	.277	58	-70	8	4		.976	16	C-407	-3.1

■ DANNY SHEAFFER   Sheaffer, Danny Todd   b: 8/2/61, Jacksonville, Fla.   BR/TR, 6' ", 185 lbs.   Deb: 4/9/87

YEAR	TM/L	G	AB	R	H	2B	3B	HR	RBI	BB	SO	AVG	OBP	SLG	PRO+	BR/A	SB	CS	SBR	FA	FR	G/POS	TPR
1987	Bos-A	25	66	5	8	1	0	1	5	0	14	.121	.121	.182	-21	-11	0	0	0	.977	-3	C-25	-1.2
1989	Cle-N	7	16	1	1	0	0	0	0	2	2	.063	.167	.063	-32	-3	0	0	0	.000	-0	/3-2,O-1,D	-0.3
1993	Col-N	82	216	26	60	9	1	4	32	8	15	.278	.307	.384	72	-9	2	3	-1	.994	-1	C-65/1-7,O3	-0.8
1994	Col-N	44	110	11	24	4	0	1	12	10	11	.218	.283	.282	41	-10	0	2	-1	.995	4	C-30/1-2,O	-0.6
Total	4	158	408	43	93	14	1	6	49	20	42	.228	.266	.311	46	-33	2	5	-2	.991	1	C-120/1-9,0D3	-2.9

■ DAVE SHEAN   Shean, David William   b: 7/9/1883, Arlington, Mass.   d: 5/22/63, Boston, Mass.   BR/TR, 5'11", 175 lbs.   Deb: 9/10/06

YEAR	TM/L	G	AB	R	H	2B	3B	HR	RBI	BB	SO	AVG	OBP	SLG	PRO+	BR/A	SB	CS	SBR	FA	FR	G/POS	TPR
1906	Phi-A	22	75	7	16	3	2	0	3	5		.213	.280	.307	81	-2	6			.980	-2	2-22	-0.4
1908	Phi-N	14	48	4	7	2	0	0	2	1		.146	.180	.188	17	-5	1			.871	-6	S-14	-1.3
1909	Phi-N	36	112	14	26	2	2	0	4	14		.232	.323	.286	88	-1	3			.982	-2	2-14,1-11/OS	-0.4
	Bos-N	75	267	32	66	11	4	1	29	17		.247	.297	.330	90	-4	14			.956	8	2-72	0.3
	Yr	111	379	46	92	13	6	1	33	31		.243	.305	.317	90	-5	17			.960	6	2-86,1-11/OS	-0.1
1910	Bos-N	150	543	52	130	12	7	3	36	42	45	.239	.294	.304	71	-21	16			.953	43	*2-148	2.0
1911	Chi-N	54	145	17	28	4	0	0	15	8	15	.193	.240	.221	29	-14	4			.947	1	2-23,S-19/3	-1.2
1912	Bos-N	4	10	1	3	0	0	0	0	1	2	.300	.417	.300	96	-0	0			.917	-1	/S-4	-0.1
1917	Cin-N	131	442	36	93	9	5	2	35	22	39	.210	.249	.267	61	-21	10			.961	19	*2-131	0.4
1918	*Bos-A	115	425	58	112	16	3	0	34	40	25	.264	.331	.315	97	-1	11			.967	-9	*2-115	-0.3
1919	Bos-A	29	100	4	14	0	0	0	8	5	7	.140	.189	.140	-7	-14	1			.981	4	2-29	-0.9
Total	9	630	2167	225	495	59	23	6	166	155	133	.228	.284	.285	70	-82	66			.961	55	2-554/S-38,103	-1.9

■ RAY SHEARER   Shearer, Ray Solomon   b: 9/19/29, Jacobus, Pa.   d: 2/21/82, York, Pa.   BR/TR, 6', 200 lbs.   Deb: 9/18/57

YEAR	TM/L	G	AB	R	H	2B	3B	HR	RBI	BB	SO	AVG	OBP	SLG	PRO+	BR/A	SB	CS	SBR	FA	FR	G/POS	TPR
1957	Mil-N	2	2	1	1	0	0	0	0	1	1	.500	.667	.500	237	1	0	0	0	.000	-0	/O-1	0.0

■ JOHN SHEARON   Shearon, John M.   b: 1870, Pittsburgh, Pa.   d: 2/1/23, Bradford, Pa.   Deb: 7/28/1891

YEAR	TM/L	G	AB	R	H	2B	3B	HR	RBI	BB	SO	AVG	OBP	SLG	PRO+	BR/A	SB	CS	SBR	FA	FR	G/POS	TPR
1891	Cle-N	30	124	10	30	1	1	0	13	1	15	.242	.248	.266	48	-9	6			.814	-4	O-25/P-6	-1.1
1896	Cle-N	16	64	6	11	0	1	0	3	4	6	.172	.221	.203	11	-8	3			.818	-4	O-16	-1.2
Total	2	46	188	16	41	1	2	0	16	5	21	.218	.238	.245	34	-17	9			.815	-9	/O-41,P-6	-2.3

■ JIMMY SHECKARD   Sheckard, Samuel James Tilden   b: 11/23/1878, Upper Chanceford, Pa.   d: 1/15/47, Lancaster, Pa.   BL/TR, 5'9", 175 lbs.   Deb: 9/14/1897

YEAR	TM/L	G	AB	R	H	2B	3B	HR	RBI	BB	SO	AVG	OBP	SLG	PRO+	BR/A	SB	CS	SBR	FA	FR	G/POS	TPR
1897	Bro-N	13	49	12	14	3	2	3	14	6		.286	.364	.612	164	4	5			.753	-5	S-11/O-2	0.0
1898	Bro-N	105	408	51	113	17	9	4	64	37		.277	.349	.392	113	6	8			.926	-4	*O-105/3-1	-0.5
1899	Bal-N	147	536	104	158	18	10	3	75	56		.295	.380	.382	104	4	**77**			.943	21	*O-146/1-1	1.3
1900	Bro-N	85	273	74	82	19	10	1	39	42		.300	.416	.454	132	13	30			.925	2	O-78	0.9
1901	Bro-N	133	554	116	196	29	**19**	11	104	47		.354	.409	**.534**	168	46	35			.944	7	*O-121,3-12	4.3
1902	Bal-A	4	15	3	4	0	0	0	0	1		.267	.313	.333	76	-0	2			1.000	-1	/O-4	-0.2
	Bro-N	123	486	86	129	20	10	4	37	57		.265	.349	.372	122	13	23			.964	8	*O-123	1.4
1903	Bro-N	139	515	99	171	29	9	**9**	75	75		.332	.423	.476	161	**43**	**67**			.951	23	*O-139	5.4
1904	Bro-N	143	507	70	121	23	6	1	46	56		.239	.317	.314	97	-0	21			.956	7	*O-141/2-2	-0.1
1905	Bro-N	130	480	58	140	20	11	3	41	61		.292	.380	.398	142	27	23			.967	15	*O-129	3.6
1906	*Chi-N	149	549	90	144	27	10	1	45	67		.262	.349	.353	112	9	30			.986	0	*O-149	0.2
1907	*Chi-N	143	484	76	129	23	1	1	36	76		.267	.373	.324	112	10	31			.975	-10	*O-142	-0.7
1908	*Chi-N	115	403	54	93	18	3	2	22	62		.231	.336	.305	101	3	18			.955	-2	*O-115	-0.5
1909	Chi-N	148	525	81	134	29	5	1	43	72		.255	.346	.335	109	7	15			.967	-3	*O-148	-0.2
1910	*Chi-N	144	507	82	130	27	6	5	51	83	53	.256	.366	.363	114	11	22			.976	7	*O-143	1.2
1911	Chi-N	156	539	**121**	149	26	11	4	50	**147**	58	.276	**.434**	.388	130	32	32			.963	15	*O-156	3.8
1912	Chi-N	146	523	85	128	22	10	3	47	**122**	81	.245	.392	.342	102	8	15			.962	8	*O-146	0.8
1913	StL-N	52	136	18	27	2	1	0	17	41	25	.199	.388	.228	79	-1	5			.953	-3	O-46	-0.6
	Cin-N	47	116	16	22	1	3	0	7	27	16	.190	.343	.250	71	-3	6			.969	-3	O-38	-0.8
	Yr	99	252	34	49	3	4	0	24	68	41	.194	.368	.238	76	-4	11			.960	-6	O-84	-1.4
Total	17	2122	7605	1296	2084	354	136	56	813	1135	233	.274	.375	.378	120	232	465			.958	82	*O-2071/3-13,S21	19.3

■ JIM SHEEHAN   Sheehan, James Thomas "Big Jim"   b: 6/3/13, New Haven, Conn.   BR/TR, 6'2", 196 lbs.   Deb: 9/26/36

YEAR	TM/L	G	AB	R	H	2B	3B	HR	RBI	BB	SO	AVG	OBP	SLG	PRO+	BR/A	SB	CS	SBR	FA	FR	G/POS	TPR
1936	NY-N	1	4	0	0	0	0	0	0	0	2	.000	.000	.000	-99	-1	0			.833	-0	/C-1	-0.1

■ JACK SHEEHAN   Sheehan, John Thomas   b: 4/15/1893, Chicago, Ill.   d: 5/29/87, W.Palm Beach, Fla.   BB/TR, 5'8.5", 165 lbs.   Deb: 9/11/20

YEAR	TM/L	G	AB	R	H	2B	3B	HR	RBI	BB	SO	AVG	OBP	SLG	PRO+	BR/A	SB	CS	SBR	FA	FR	G/POS	TPR
1920	*Bro-N	3	5	0	2	1	0	0	0	1	0	.400	.500	.600	208	1	0	0	0	.875	0	/S-2,3-1	0.1
1921	Bro-N	5	12	2	0	0	0	0	0	0	1	.000	.000	.000	-97	-3	0	0	0	.900	-0	/2-2,S-1,3	-0.3
Total	2	8	17	2	2	1	0	0	0	1	1	.118	.167	.176	-7	-3	0	0	0	.909	0	/S-3,2-2,3	-0.2

■ TOMMY SHEEHAN   Sheehan, Thomas H.   b: 11/6/1877, Sacramento, Cal.   d: 5/22/59, Panama City, Pan.   BR/TR, 5'8", 160 lbs.   Deb: 8/2/00

YEAR	TM/L	G	AB	R	H	2B	3B	HR	RBI	BB	SO	AVG	OBP	SLG	PRO+	BR/A	SB	CS	SBR	FA	FR	G/POS	TPR
1900	NY-N	1	2	0	0	0	0	0	0	0	0	.000	.000	.000	-99	-1	0			.000	0	/S-1	-0.1
1906	Pit-N	95	315	28	76	6	3	1	34	18		.241	.284	.289	75	-9	13			.947	-5	3-90	-1.3
1907	Pit-N	75	226	23	62	2	3	0	25	23		.274	.341	.310	103	1	10			.941	-1	3-57,S-10	0.3
1908	Bro-N	146	468	45	100	18	2	0	29	53		.214	.302	.261	83	-7	9			.930	-6	*3-145	-0.9
Total	4	317	1011	96	238	26	8	1	88	94		.235	.305	.280	85	-16	32			.938	-12	3-292/S-11	-2.0

■ BIFF SHEEHAN   Sheehan, Timothy James   b: 2/13/1868, Hartford, Conn.   d: 10/21/23, Hartford, Conn.   TR, 5'9", 165 lbs.   Deb: 7/22/1895

YEAR	TM/L	G	AB	R	H	2B	3B	HR	RBI	BB	SO	AVG	OBP	SLG	PRO+	BR/A	SB	CS	SBR	FA	FR	G/POS	TPR
1895	StL-N	52	180	24	57	3	6	1	18	20	6	.317	.394	.417	111	3	7			.940	-2	O-41,1-11	-0.1
1896	StL-N	6	19	0	3	0	0	0	1	4	0	.158	.304	.158	25	-2	0			1.000	-1	/O-6	-0.3
Total	2	58	199	24	60	3	6	1	19	24	6	.302	.385	.392	103	2	7			.948	-3	/O-47,1-11	-0.4

■ EARL SHEELY   Sheely, Earl Homer "Whitey"   b: 2/12/1893, Bushnell, Ill.   d: 9/16/52, Seattle, Wash.   BR/TR, 6'3.5", 195 lbs.   Deb: 4/14/21   F

YEAR	TM/L	G	AB	R	H	2B	3B	HR	RBI	BB	SO	AVG	OBP	SLG	PRO+	BR/A	SB	CS	SBR	FA	FR	G/POS	TPR
1921	Chi-A	154	563	68	171	25	6	11	95	57	34	.304	.375	.428	106	5	4	9	-4	.988	5	*1-154	0.2
1922	Chi-A	149	526	72	167	37	4	6	80	60	27	.317	.393	.437	117	14	4	6	-2	.993	-1	*1-149	0.7
1923	Chi-A	156	570	74	169	25	3	4	88	79	30	.296	.387	.372	102	4	5	5	-2	.992	-1	*1-156	-0.6
1924	Chi-A	146	535	84	171	34	3	3	103	95	28	.320	.426	.411	120	21	7	4	-0	.991	-10	*1-146	-0.1
1925	Chi-A	153	600	93	189	43	3	9	111	68	23	.315	.389	.442	117	16	3	3	-1	.988	-5	*1-153	0.1
1926	Chi-A	145	525	77	157	40	2	6	89	75	13	.299	.394	.417	116	14	3	1	0	**.995**	0	*1-144	0.6
1927	Chi-A	45	129	11	27	3	0	2	16	20	5	.209	.320	.279	58	-8	1	3	-2	.982	-4	1-36	-1.5
1929	Pit-N	139	485	63	142	22	4	6	88	75	24	.293	.392	.392	93	-5	0			**.996**	-0	*1-139	-1.6
1931	Bos-N	147	538	30	147	15	2	1	77	34	21	.273	.319	.314	73	-20	0			.992	-3	*1-143	-3.6
Total	9	1234	4471	572	1340	244	27	48	747	563	205	.300	.383	.399	104	45	33	31		.991	-14	*1-1220	-5.5

■ BUD SHEELY   Sheely, Hollis Kimball   b: 11/26/20, Spokane, Wash.   d: 10/17/85, Sacramento, Cal.   BL/TR, 6'1", 200 lbs.   Deb: 7/26/51   F

YEAR	TM/L	G	AB	R	H	2B	3B	HR	RBI	BB	SO	AVG	OBP	SLG	PRO+	BR/A	SB	CS	SBR	FA	FR	G/POS	TPR
1951	Chi-A	34	89	2	16	2	0	0	7	6	7	.180	.240	.202	21	-10	0	0	0	.986	3	C-33	-0.5

YEAR	TM/L	G	AB	R	H	2B	3B	HR	RBI	BB	SO	AVG	OBP	SLG	PRO+	BR/A	SB	CS	SBR	FA	FR	G/POS	TPR
1952	Chi-A	36	75	1	18	2	0	0	3	12	7	.240	.352	.267	73	-2	0	1	-1	.992	-2	C-31	-0.3
1953	Chi-A	31	46	4	10	1	0	0	2	9	8	.217	.345	.239	58	-2	0	0	0	1.000	0	C-17	-0.1
Total	3	101	210	7	44	5	0	0	12	27	22	.210	.305	.233	49	-14	0	1	-1	.991	2	/C-81	-0.9

■ CHUCK SHEERIN
Sheerin, Charles Joseph   b: 4/17/09, Brooklyn, N.Y.   d: 9/27/86, Valley Stream, N.Y.   BR/TR, 5'11.5", 198 lbs.   Deb: 4/21/36

YEAR	TM/L	G	AB	R	H	2B	3B	HR	RBI	BB	SO	AVG	OBP	SLG	PRO+	BR/A	SB	CS	SBR	FA	FR	G/POS	TPR
1936	Phi-N	39	72	4	19	4	0	0	4	7	18	.264	.329	.319	68	-3	0			.942	-3	2-17,3-13/S	-0.5

■ LARRY SHEETS
Sheets, Larry Kent   b: 12/6/59, Staunton, Va.   BL/TR, 6'3", 225 lbs.   Deb: 9/18/84

YEAR	TM/L	G	AB	R	H	2B	3B	HR	RBI	BB	SO	AVG	OBP	SLG	PRO+	BR/A	SB	CS	SBR	FA	FR	G/POS	TPR
1984	Bal-A	8	16	3	7	1	0	1	2	1	3	.438	.471	.688	221	3	0	0	0	1.000	0	/O-7	0.3
1985	Bal-A	113	328	43	86	8	0	17	50	28	52	.262	.324	.442	110	4	0	1	-1	.875	-2	D-93/O-9,1	-0.1
1986	Bal-A	112	338	42	92	17	1	18	60	21	56	.272	.319	.488	117	7	2	0	1	.984	-0	D-58,0-32/C13	0.5
1987	Bal-A	135	469	74	148	23	0	31	94	31	67	.316	.362	.563	144	28	1	1	-0	.975	-4	*O-124/1-3,D	1.8
1988	Bal-A	136	452	38	104	19	1	10	47	42	72	.230	.304	.343	83	-10	1	6	-3	.974	1	O-76,D-50/1	-1.6
1989	Bal-A	102	304	33	74	12	1	7	33	26	58	.243	.309	.359	90	-4	1	1	-0	.000	0	D-88	-0.7
1990	Det-A	131	360	40	94	17	2	10	52	24	42	.261	.311	.403	97	-2	1	3	-2	.981	-7	O-79,D-44	-1.4
1993	Sea-A	11	17	0	2	1	0	0	1	2	1	.118	.250	.176	17	-2	0	0	0	1.000	-0	/O-1,D-5	-0.2
Total	8	748	2284	273	607	98	5	94	339	175	351	.266	.323	.437	109	23	6	12	-5	.976	-12	D-345,0-328/1C3	-1.4

■ GARY SHEFFIELD
Sheffield, Gary Antonian   b: 11/18/68, Tampa, Fla.   BR/TR, 5'11", 190 lbs.   Deb: 9/3/88

YEAR	TM/L	G	AB	R	H	2B	3B	HR	RBI	BB	SO	AVG	OBP	SLG	PRO+	BR/A	SB	CS	SBR	FA	FR	G/POS	TPR
1988	Mil-A	24	80	12	19	1	0	4	12	7	7	.237	.299	.400	93	-1	3	1	0	.967	-10	S-24	-0.9
1989	Mil-A	95	368	34	91	18	0	5	32	27	33	.247	.306	.337	82	-9	10	6	-1	.959	-17	S-70,3-21/D	-2.2
1990	Mil-A	125	487	67	143	30	1	10	67	44	41	.294	.356	.421	117	11	25	10	2	.934	-4	*3-125	0.9
1991	Mil-A	50	175	25	34	12	2	2	22	19	15	.194	.284	.320	69	-8	5	5	-2	.922	-12	3-43/D-5	-2.1
1992	SD-N★	146	557	87	184	34	3	33	100	48	40	**.330**	.390	.580	168	48	5	6	-2	.961	10	*3-144	5.8
1993	SD-N	68	258	34	76	12	2	10	36	18	30	.295	.348	.473	115	5	5	1	1	.905	-11	3-67	-0.5
	Fla-N★	72	236	33	69	8	3	10	37	29	34	.292	.384	.479	122	8	12	4	1	.894	-4	3-66	0.5
	Yr	140	494	67	145	20	5	20	73	47	64	.294	.365	.476	119	13	17	5	2	.899	-16	*3-133	0.0
1994	Fla-N	87	322	61	89	16	1	27	78	51	50	.276	.385	.584	140	19	12	6	0	.970	0	O-87	1.7
Total	7	667	2483	353	705	131	12	101	384	243	250	.284	.355	.468	123	74	77	39	-0	.933	-49	3-466/S-94,OD	3.2

■ JOHN SHELBY
Shelby, John T.   b: 2/23/58, Lexington, Ky.   BB/TR, 6'1", 175 lbs.   Deb: 9/15/81

YEAR	TM/L	G	AB	R	H	2B	3B	HR	RBI	BB	SO	AVG	OBP	SLG	PRO+	BR/A	SB	CS	SBR	FA	FR	G/POS	TPR
1981	Bal-A	7	2	2	0	0	0	0	0	0	1	.000	.000	.000	-99	-1	2	0	1	1.000	-2	/O-4	-0.2
1982	Bal-A	26	35	8	11	3	0	1	2	0	5	.314	.314	.486	116	1	0	1	-1	1.000	-8	O-24	-0.8
1983	*Bal-A	126	325	52	84	15	2	5	27	18	64	.258	.297	.363	82	-8	15	2	3	.981	-14	*O-115/D-1	-2.2
1984	Bal-A	128	383	44	80	12	5	6	30	20	71	.209	.248	.313	55	-24	12	4	1	.993	-10	*O-124	-3.6
1985	Bal-A	69	205	28	58	6	2	7	27	7	44	.283	.307	.434	103	0	5	1	1	.981	0	O-59/2-1,D	0.0
1986	Bal-A	135	404	54	92	14	4	11	49	18	75	.228	.264	.364	70	-18	18	6	2	.978	-12	*O-121/D-2	-3.1
1987	Bal-A	21	32	4	6	0	0	1	3	1	13	.188	.212	.281	30	-3	0	1	-1	1.000	-3	O-19/D-1	-0.7
	LA-N	120	476	61	132	26	0	21	69	31	97	.277	.323	.464	108	4	16	6	1	.972	11	*O-117	1.2
1988	*LA-N	140	494	65	130	23	6	10	64	44	128	.263	.323	.395	109	5	16	5	2	.982	7	*O-140	1.0
1989	LA-N	108	345	28	63	11	1	1	12	25	92	.183	.238	.229	35	-29	10	7	-1	.991	0	O-98	-3.5
1990	LA-N	25	24	2	6	1	0	0	2	0	7	.250	.250	.292	50	-2	1	0	0	1.000	-3	O-12	-0.5
	Det-A	78	222	22	55	9	3	4	20	10	51	.248	.280	.369	80	-7	3	5	-2	.973	-1	O-68/D-5	-1.1
1991	Det-A	53	143	19	22	8	1	3	8	8	23	.154	.204	.287	34	-13	0	2	-1	.982	-1	O-47/D-4	-1.6
Total	11	1036	3090	389	739	128	24	70	313	182	671	.239	.282	.364	79	-96	98	40	5	.982	-36	O-948/D-16,2	-15.1

■ BOB SHELDON
Sheldon, Bob Mitchell   b: 11/27/50, Montebello, Cal.   BL/TR, 6', 170 lbs.   Deb: 4/10/74

YEAR	TM/L	G	AB	R	H	2B	3B	HR	RBI	BB	SO	AVG	OBP	SLG	PRO+	BR/A	SB	CS	SBR	FA	FR	G/POS	TPR
1974	Mil-A	10	17	4	2	1	1	0	0	4	2	.118	.286	.294	67	-1	0	1	-1	1.000	-1	/2-3,D-4	-0.2
1975	Mil-A	53	181	17	52	3	3	0	14	13	14	.287	.342	.337	92	-2	0	3	-2	.977	-8	2-44/D-6	-1.0
1977	Mil-A	31	64	9	13	4	1	0	3	6	9	.203	.271	.297	55	-4	0	0	0	1.000	1	D-17/2-5	-0.4
Total	3	94	262	30	67	8	5	0	17	23	25	.256	.321	.324	81	-6	0	4	-2	.979	-9	/2-52,D-27	-1.6

■ HUGH SHELLEY
Shelley, Hubert Leneirre   b: 10/26/10, Rogers, Tex.   d: 6/16/78, Beaumont, Tex.   BR/TR, 6', 170 lbs.   Deb: 6/25/35

YEAR	TM/L	G	AB	R	H	2B	3B	HR	RBI	BB	SO	AVG	OBP	SLG	PRO+	BR/A	SB	CS	SBR	FA	FR	G/POS	TPR
1935	Det-A	7	8	1	2	0	0	0	1	2	1	.250	.400	.250	74	-0	0	0	0	1.000	-1	/O-5	-0.2

■ SKEETER SHELTON
Shelton, Andrew Kemper   b: 6/29/1888, Huntington, W.Va.   d: 1/9/54, Huntington, W.Va.   BR/TR, 5'11", 175 lbs.   Deb: 8/25/15

YEAR	TM/L	G	AB	R	H	2B	3B	HR	RBI	BB	SO	AVG	OBP	SLG	PRO+	BR/A	SB	CS	SBR	FA	FR	G/POS	TPR
1915	NY-A	10	40	1	1	0	0	0	0	2	10	.025	.071	.025	-71	-8	0	0	0	1.000	0	O-10	-1.0

■ BEN SHELTON
Shelton, Benjamin Davis   b: 9/21/69, Chicago, Ill.   BR/TL, 6'3", 210 lbs.   Deb: 6/16/93

YEAR	TM/L	G	AB	R	H	2B	3B	HR	RBI	BB	SO	AVG	OBP	SLG	PRO+	BR/A	SB	CS	SBR	FA	FR	G/POS	TPR
1993	Pit-N	15	24	3	6	1	0	2	3	3	3	.250	.333	.542	130	1	0	0	0	.889	-0	/O-6,1-2	0.0

■ STEVE SHEMO
Shemo, Stephen Michael   b: 4/9/15, Swoyersville, Pa.   d: 4/13/92, Eden, N.C.   BR/TR, 5'11", 175 lbs.   Deb: 4/18/44

YEAR	TM/L	G	AB	R	H	2B	3B	HR	RBI	BB	SO	AVG	OBP	SLG	PRO+	BR/A	SB	CS	SBR	FA	FR	G/POS	TPR
1944	Bos-N	18	31	3	9	2	0	0	1	3	3	.290	.313	.355	84	-1	0			.966	3	2-16/3-2	0.3
1945	Bos-N	17	46	4	11	1	0	0	7	1	3	.239	.255	.261	43	-4	0			.921	-6	2-12/3-3,S	-0.9
Total	2	35	77	7	20	3	0	0	8	2	6	.260	.278	.299	60	-4	0			.948	-3	/2-28,3-5,S	-0.6

■ JACK SHEPARD
Shepard, Jack Leroy   b: 5/13/32, Clovis, Cal.   d: 12/31/94, Atherton, Cal.   BR/TR, 6'2", 195 lbs.   Deb: 6/19/53

YEAR	TM/L	G	AB	R	H	2B	3B	HR	RBI	BB	SO	AVG	OBP	SLG	PRO+	BR/A	SB	CS	SBR	FA	FR	G/POS	TPR
1953	Pit-N	2	4	0	1	0	0	0	0	0	2	.250	.250	.250	31	-0	0	0	0	.750	-0	/C-2	-0.1
1954	Pit-N	82	227	24	69	8	2	3	22	26	33	.304	.375	.396	103	2	0	0	0	.977	2	C-67	0.6
1955	Pit-N	94	264	24	63	10	2	2	23	33	25	.239	.323	.314	71	-10	1	0	0	.982	-10	C-77	-1.8
1956	Pit-N	100	256	24	62	11	2	7	30	25	37	.242	.310	.383	87	-5	1	1	-0	.990	1	C-86/1-2	-0.1
Total	4	278	751	72	195	29	6	12	75	84	97	.260	.334	.362	86	-14	2	1	0	.982	-8	C-232/1-2	-1.4

■ RAY SHEPARDSON
Shepardson, Raymond Francis   b: 5/3/1897, Little Falls, N.Y.   d: 11/8/75, Little Falls, N.Y.   BR/TR, 5'11.5", 170 lbs.   Deb: 9/19/24

YEAR	TM/L	G	AB	R	H	2B	3B	HR	RBI	BB	SO	AVG	OBP	SLG	PRO+	BR/A	SB	CS	SBR	FA	FR	G/POS	TPR
1924	StL-N	3	6	1	0	0	0	0	0	0	3	.000	.000	.000	-99	-2	0	0	0	1.000	0	/C-3	-0.2

■ RON SHEPHERD
Shepherd, Ronald Wayne   b: 10/27/60, Longview, Tex.   BR/TR, 6'4", 175 lbs.   Deb: 9/5/84

YEAR	TM/L	G	AB	R	H	2B	3B	HR	RBI	BB	SO	AVG	OBP	SLG	PRO+	BR/A	SB	CS	SBR	FA	FR	G/POS	TPR
1984	Tor-A	12	4	3	0	0	0	0	0	0	3	.000	.000	.000	-97	-1	0	1	-1	1.000	-1	/O-5,D-4	-0.3
1985	Tor-A	38	35	7	4	2	0	0	1	2	12	.114	.162	.171	-8	-5	3	0	1	1.000	-4	O-16,D-15	-0.9
1986	Tor-A	65	69	16	14	4	0	2	4	3	22	.203	.236	.348	55	-4	0	0	0	1.000	-8	O-32,D-16	-1.3
Total	3	115	108	23	18	6	0	2	5	5	37	.167	.204	.278	29	-11	3	1	0	1.000	-13	/O-53,D-35	-2.5

■ JOHN SHEPPARD
Sheppard, John   b: Baltimore, Md.   Deb: 6/27/1873

YEAR	TM/L	G	AB	R	H	2B	3B	HR	RBI	BB	SO	AVG	OBP	SLG	PRO+	BR/A	SB	CS	SBR	FA	FR	G/POS	TPR
1873	Mar-n	3	11	1	0	0	0	0	0	0	0	.000	.000	.000	-99	-3						/O-2,C-1	-0.2

■ SHERIDAN
Sheridan   Deb: 10/9/1875

YEAR	TM/L	G	AB	R	H	2B	3B	HR	RBI	BB	SO	AVG	OBP	SLG	PRO+	BR/A	SB	CS	SBR	FA	FR	G/POS	TPR
1875	Atl-n	1	4	0	0	0	0	0	0			.000	.000	.000	-99	-1						/O-1	-0.1

■ RED SHERIDAN
Sheridan, Eugene Anthony   b: 11/14/1896, Brooklyn, N.Y.   d: 11/25/75, Queens Village, N.Y.   BR/TR, 5'10.5", 160 lbs.   Deb: 7/3/18

YEAR	TM/L	G	AB	R	H	2B	3B	HR	RBI	BB	SO	AVG	OBP	SLG	PRO+	BR/A	SB	CS	SBR	FA	FR	G/POS	TPR
1918	Bro-N	2	4	0	1	0	0	0	0	0	0	.250	.400	.250	100	0	1			1.000	-1	/2-2	-0.1
1920	Bro-N	3	2	0	0	0	0	0	0	0	1	.000	.000	.000	-97	-0	0	0	0	1.000	0	/S-3	0.1
Total	2	5	6	0	1	0	0	0	0	0	1	.167	.286	.167	37	-0	1	0		1.000	1	/S-3,2-2	0.0

■ NEILL SHERIDAN
Sheridan, Neill Rawlins "Wild Horse"   b: 11/20/21, Sacramento, Cal.   BR/TR, 6'1.5", 195 lbs.   Deb: 9/19/48

YEAR	TM/L	G	AB	R	H	2B	3B	HR	RBI	BB	SO	AVG	OBP	SLG	PRO+	BR/A	SB	CS	SBR	FA	FR	G/POS	TPR
1948	Bos-A	2	1	0	0	0	0	0	0	0	1	.000	.000	.000	-95	-0	0	0	0	.000	0	H	0.0

YEAR	TM/L	G	AB	R	H	2B	3B	HR	RBI	BB	SO	AVG	OBP	SLG	PRO+	BR/A	SB	CS	SBR	FA	FR	G/POS	TPR

■ PAT SHERIDAN   Sheridan, Patrick Arthur b: 12/4/57, Ann Arbor, Mich.   BL/TR, 6'3", 175 lbs.   Deb: 9/16/81

1981	KC-A	3	1	0	0	0	0	0	0	0	1	.000	.000	.000	-99	-0	0	0	0	1.000	-1	/O-3	-0.1
1983	KC-A	109	333	43	90	12	2	7	36	20	64	.270	.312	.381	89	-5	12	3	2	.988	-2	*O-100	-0.8
1984	*KC-A	138	481	64	136	24	4	8	53	41	91	.283	.340	.399	103	2	19	6	2	.986	-3	*O-134	-0.3
1985	*KC-A	78	206	18	47	9	2	3	17	23	38	.228	.309	.335	76	-7	11	3	2	.983	-4	O-69/D-1	-1.1
1986	Det-A	98	236	41	56	9	1	6	19	21	57	.237	.302	.360	80	-7	9	2	2	.977	-10	O-90/D-5	-1.7
1987	*Det-A	141	421	57	109	19	3	6	49	44	90	.259	.330	.361	87	-7	18	13	-2	.976	-12	*O-137	-2.4
1988	Det-A	127	347	47	88	9	5	11	47	44	64	.254	.340	.403	112	6	8	6	-1	.981	-6	*O-111/D-3	-0.4
1989	Det-A	50	120	16	29	3	0	3	15	17	21	.242	.336	.342	93	-1	4	0	1	.982	-3	O-35/D-8	-0.4
	*SF-N	70	161	20	33	3	4	3	14	13	45	.205	.264	.329	71	-7	4	1	1	.983	-4	O-66	-1.2
1991	NY-A	62	113	13	23	3	0	2	7	13	30	.204	.286	.336	71	-5	1	1	-0	1.000	-3	O-34/D-2	-0.8
Total	9	876	2419	319	611	91	21	51	257	236	501	.253	.321	.371	91	-30	86	35	5	.983	-48	O-779/D-19	-9.2

■ ED SHERLING   Sherling, Edward Creech "Shine" b: 7/17/1897, Coalburg, Ala. d: 11/16/65, Enterprise, Cal. BR/TR, 6'1", 185 lbs. Deb: 8/13/24

| 1924 | Phi-A | 4 | 2 | 2 | 1 | 1 | 0 | 0 | 0 | 0 | 0 | .500 | .500 | 1.000 | 278 | 0 | 0 | 0 | 0 | .000 | 0 | H | 0.0 |

■ MONK SHERLOCK   Sherlock, John Clinton b: 10/26/04, Buffalo, N.Y. d: 11/26/85, Buffalo, N.Y. BR/TR, 5'10", 175 lbs. Deb: 4/20/30 F

| 1930 | Phi-N | 92 | 299 | 51 | 97 | 18 | 2 | 0 | 38 | 27 | 28 | .324 | .380 | .398 | 83 | -8 | 0 | | | .990 | 4 | 1-70/2-5,O | -0.9 |

■ VINCE SHERLOCK   Sherlock, Vincent Thomas "Baldy" b: 3/27/09, Buffalo, N.Y. BR/TR, 6', 180 lbs. Deb: 9/18/35 F

| 1935 | Bro-N | 9 | 26 | 4 | 12 | 1 | 0 | 0 | 6 | 1 | 2 | .462 | .481 | .500 | 168 | 3 | 1 | | | .907 | -1 | /2-8 | 0.2 |

■ DARRELL SHERMAN   Sherman, Darrell Edward b: 12/4/67, Los Angeles, Cal. BL/TL, 5'9", 160 lbs. Deb: 4/8/93

| 1993 | SD-N | 37 | 63 | 8 | 14 | 1 | 0 | 0 | 2 | 6 | 8 | .222 | .319 | .238 | 51 | -4 | 2 | 1 | 0 | 1.000 | -3 | O-26 | -0.8 |

■ DENNIS SHERRILL   Sherrill, Dennis Lee b: 3/3/56, Miami, Fla. BR/TR, 6', 165 lbs. Deb: 9/4/78

1978	NY-A	2	1	1	0	0	0	0	0	0	1	.000	.000	.000	-99	-0	0	0	0	.000	-0	/3-1,D-1	-0.1
1980	NY-A	3	4	0	1	0	0	0	0	0	1	.250	.250	.250	38	-0	0	0	0	1.000	-0	/S-2,2-1	-0.1
Total	2	5	5	1	1	0	0	0	0	0	2	.200	.200	.200	11	-1	0	0	0	1.000	-1	/S-2,2-1,D3	-0.2

■ NORM SHERRY   Sherry, Norman Burt b: 7/16/31, New York, N.Y. BR/TR, 5'11", 181 lbs. Deb: 4/12/59 FMC

1959	LA-N	2	3	0	1	0	0	0	2	0	0	.333	.500	.333	119	0	0	0	0	1.000	-1	/C-2	-0.1
1960	LA-N	47	138	22	39	4	1	8	19	12	29	.283	.353	.500	122	4	0	0	0	.993	-4	C-44	0.2
1961	LA-N	47	121	10	31	2	0	5	21	9	30	.256	.308	.397	78	-4	0	0	0	.993	-4	C-45	0.1
1962	LA-N	35	88	7	16	2	0	3	16	6	17	.182	.242	.307	49	-7	0	0	0	.992	9	C-34	0.3
1963	NY-N	63	147	6	20	1	0	2	11	10	26	.136	.206	.184	13	-16	1	0	0	.980	3	C-61	-1.2
Total	5	194	497	45	107	9	1	18	69	37	102	.215	.280	.346	69	-23	1	0	0	.989	11	C-186	-0.7

■ BARRY SHETRONE   Shetrone, Barry Stevan b: 7/6/38, Baltimore, Md. BL/TR, 6'2", 190 lbs. Deb: 7/27/59

1959	Bal-A	33	79	8	16	1	1	0	5	5	9	.203	.250	.241	36	-7	3	0	1	.947	-4	O-23	-1.2
1960	Bal-A	1	0	1	0	0	0	0	0	0	0	—	—	—	—	0	0	0	0	.000	0	R	0.0
1961	Bal-A	3	7	0	1	0	0	0	1	0	2	.143	.143	.143	-24	-1	0	0	0	1.000	-0	/O-2	-0.2
1962	Bal-A	21	24	3	6	1	0	1	1	0	5	.250	.250	.417	81	-1	0	0	0	1.000	-0	/O-6	-0.1
1963	Was-A	2	2	0	0	0	0	0	0	0	0	.000	.000	.000	-99	-1	0	0	0	.000	0	H	-0.1
Total	5	60	112	12	23	2	1	1	7	5	16	.205	.239	.268	39	-9	3	0	1	.962	-5	/O-31	-1.6

■ JOHN SHETZLINE   Shetzline, John Henry b: 1850, Philadelphia, Pa. d: 12/15/1892, Philadelphia, Pa. 5'11.5", 190 lbs. Deb: 5/2/1882

| 1882 | Bal-a | 73 | 282 | 23 | 62 | 8 | 3 | 0 | | 5 | | .220 | .233 | .270 | 75 | -7 | | | | .800 | 3 | 3-52,2-20/OS | -0.2 |

■ JIMMY SHEVLIN   Shevlin, James Cornelius b: 7/9/09, Cincinnati, Ohio d: 10/30/74, Ft.Lauderdale, Fla BL/TL, 5'10.5", 155 lbs. Deb: 6/29/30

1930	Det-A	28	14	4	2	0	0	0	2	2	3	.143	.250	.143	2	-2	0	0	0	1.000	1	1-25	-0.2
1932	Cin-N	7	24	3	5	2	0	0	4	4	0	.208	.345	.292	76	-1	4			.985	-0	/1-7	-0.2
1934	Cin-N	18	39	6	12	2	0	0	6	6	5	.308	.400	.359	107	1	0			1.000	1	/1-10	0.0
Total	3	53	77	13	19	4	0	0	12	12	8	.247	.356	.299	77	-2	4	0		.995	1	/1-42	-0.4

■ PETE SHIELDS   Shields, Francis Leroy b: 9/21/1891, Swiftwater, Miss. d: 2/11/61, Jackson, Miss. BR/TR, 6', 175 lbs. Deb: 4/14/15

| 1915 | Cle-A | 23 | 72 | 4 | 15 | 6 | 0 | 0 | 6 | 4 | 14 | .208 | .250 | .292 | 61 | -4 | 3 | 3 | -1 | .974 | 0 | 1-23 | -0.6 |

■ TOMMY SHIELDS   Shields, Thomas Charles b: 8/14/64, Fairfax, Va. BL/TR, 6', 180 lbs. Deb: 7/25/92

1992	Bal-A	2	0	0	0	0	0	0	0	0	0	—	—	—	—	0	0	0	0	.000	0	/R	0.0
1993	Chi-N	20	34	4	6	1	0	0	1	2	10	.176	.222	.206	16	-4	0	0	0	1.000	2	/2-7,3-7,1O	-0.2
Total	2	22	34	4	6	1	0	0	1	2	10	.176	.222	.206	16	-4	0	0	0	1.000	2	/3-7,2-7,O1	-0.2

■ JIM SHILLING   Shilling, James Robert b: 5/14/14, Tulsa, Okla. d: 9/12/86, Tulsa, Okla. BR/TR, 5'11", 175 lbs. Deb: 4/21/39

1939	Cle-A	31	98	8	27	7	2	0	12	7	9	.276	.324	.388	84	-3	1	0	0	.935	4	2-27/S-3	0.2
	Phi-N	11	33	3	10	1	3	0	4	1	4	.303	.324	.515	126	1	0			.944	-2	/2-5,S-3,3O	0.0
Total	1	42	131	11	37	8	5	0	16	8	13	.282	.324	.420	94	-2	1	0		.936	2	/2-32,S-6,3O	0.2

■ GINGER SHINAULT   Shinault, Enoch Erskine b: 9/7/1892, Benton, Ark. d: 12/29/30, Denver, Colo. BR/TR, 5'11", 170 lbs. Deb: 7/4/21

1921	Cle-A	22	29	5	11	1	0	0	4	6	5	.379	.486	.414	129	2	1	0	0	.917	2	C-20	0.4
1922	Cle-A	13	15	1	2	1	0	0	0	0	2	.133	.133	.200	-14	-3	0	0	0	.400	-4	C-11	-0.6
Total	2	35	44	6	13	2	0	0	4	6	7	.295	.380	.341	85	-1	1	0	0	.868	-2	/C-31	-0.2

■ BILLY SHINDLE   Shindle, William b: 12/5/1860, Gloucester, N.J. d: 6/3/36, Lakeland, N.J. BR/TR, 5'8.5", 155 lbs. Deb: 10/5/1886

1886	Det-N	7	26	4	7	0	0	0	4	0	5	.269	.269	.269	62	-1	2			.900	1	/S-7	0.0
1887	Det-N	22	84	17	24	3	2	0	12	7	10	.286	.341	.369	94	-1	13			.818	-5	3-21/O-1	-0.4
1888	Bal-a	135	514	61	107	14	8	1	53	20		.208	.249	.272	69	-18	52			.922	37	*3-135	1.9
1889	Bal-a	138	567	122	178	24	7	3	64	42	37	.314	.369	.397	116	11	56			.862	20	*3-138	3.0
1890	Phi-P	132	584	127	188	21	21	10	90	40	30	.322	.369	.481	123	16	51			.856	8	*S-130/3-2	2.5
1891	Phi-N	103	415	68	87	13	1	0	38	33	39	.210	.278	.246	51	-26	17			.874	6	*3-100/S-3	-1.3
1892	Bal-N	143	619	100	156	20	18	3	50	35	34	.252	.301	.357	96	-6	24			.882	36	*3-134/S-9	3.2
1893	Bal-N	125	521	100	136	22	11	1	75	66	17	.261	.353	.351	86	-10	17			.885	8	*3-125	-0.8
1894	Bro-N	116	476	94	141	22	9	4	96	29	20	.296	.344	.405	86	-11	19			.897	1	*3-116	-0.8
1895	Bro-N	116	477	91	133	21	2	3	69	47	28	.279	.357	.350	90	-5	17			.897	0	*3-116	-0.2
1896	Bro-N	131	516	75	144	24	9	1	61	24	20	.279	.316	.366	84	-13	24			.912	-12	*3-131	-1.9
1897	Bro-N	134	542	83	154	32	6	4	105	35		.284	.336	.387	96	-4	23			.904	-12	*3-134	-1.1
1898	Bro-N	125	466	50	105	10	3	1	41	10		.225	.249	.266	48	-32	3			.911	7	*3-120	-2.3
Total	13	1422	5807	992	1560	226	97	31	758	388	240	.269	.323	.357	88	-100	318			.892	96	*3-1272,S-149/O	2.6

■ RAZOR SHINES   Shines, Anthony Raymond "Ray" b: 7/18/56, Durham, N.C. BB/TR, 6'1", 210 lbs. Deb: 9/9/83

1983	Mon-N	3	2	0	1	0	0	0	0	0	0	.500	.500	.500	179	-0	0	0	0	.000	-0	/O-1	0.0
1984	Mon-N	12	20	0	6	1	0	0	2	0	3	.300	.300	.350	86	-0	0	0	0	1.000	-1	/1-3,3-1	-0.2
1985	Mon-N	47	50	0	6	0	0	0	3	4	9	.120	.185	.120	-14	-8	0	1	-1	.950	0	/1-5,P-1	-0.8
1987	Mon-N	6	9	0	2	0	0	0	0	1	0	.222	.364	.222	58	-0	1	0	0	1.000	-0	/1-2	0.0
Total	4	68	81	0	15	1	0	0	5	5	12	.185	.241	.198	24	-8	1	1	-0	.975	-1	/1-10,P-1,3O	-1.0

YEAR	TM/L	G	AB	R	H	2B	3B	HR	RBI	BB	SO	AVG	OBP	SLG	PRO+	BR/A	SB	CS	SBR	FA	FR	G/POS	TPR

■ RALPH SHINNERS   Shinners, Ralph Peter b: 10/4/1895, Monches, Wis. d: 7/23/62, Milwaukee, Wis. BR/TR, 6', 180 lbs. Deb: 4/12/22

YEAR	TM/L	G	AB	R	H	2B	3B	HR	RBI	BB	SO	AVG	OBP	SLG	PRO+	BR/A	SB	CS	SBR	FA	FR	G/POS	TPR
1922	NY-N	56	135	16	34	4	2	0	15	5	22	.252	.308	.311	60	-8	3	5	-2	.915	-4	O-37	-1.5
1923	NY-N	33	13	5	2	1	0	0	0	2	1	.154	.267	.231	33	-1	0	0	0	1.000	-1	/O-6	-0.2
1925	StL-N	74	251	39	74	9	2	7	36	12	19	.295	.330	.430	90	-4	8	5	-1	.982	-3	O-66	-1.1
Total	3	163	399	60	110	14	4	7	51	19	42	.276	.320	.383	78	-13	11	10	-3	.959	-8	O-109	-2.8

■ TIM SHINNICK   Shinnick, Timothy James "Dandy" or "Good Eye" b: 11/6/1867, Exeter, N.H. d: 5/18/44, Exeter, N.H. BB/TR, 5'9", 150 lbs. Deb: 4/19/1890

YEAR	TM/L	G	AB	R	H	2B	3B	HR	RBI	BB	SO	AVG	OBP	SLG	PRO+	BR/A	SB	CS	SBR	FA	FR	G/POS	TPR
1890	*Lou-a	133	493	87	126	16	11	1		62		.256	.348	.339	105	4	62			.925	-25	*2-130/3-3	-1.1
1891	Lou-a	128	443	79	98	10	11	1	54	54	47	.221	.314	.300	77	-13	36			.915	-21	*2-120/3-7,S	-2.5
Total	2	261	936	166	224	26	22	2	54	116	47	.239	.332	.321	91	-9	98			.920	-45	2-250/3-10,S	-3.6

■ BILL SHIPKE   Shipke, William Martin "Skipper Bill" or "Muskrat Bill" (b: William Martin Shipkrethaver) b: 11/18/1882, St.Louis, Mo. d: 9/10/40, Omaha, Neb. BR/TR, 5'7", 145 lbs. Deb: 4/23/06

YEAR	TM/L	G	AB	R	H	2B	3B	HR	RBI	BB	SO	AVG	OBP	SLG	PRO+	BR/A	SB	CS	SBR	FA	FR	G/POS	TPR
1906	Cle-A	2	6	0	0	0	0	0	0	0	0	.000	.000	.000	-99	-1	0			.933	2	/2-2	0.0
1907	Was-A	64	189	17	37	3	2	1	9	15		.196	.262	.249	68	-7	6			.944	7	3-63	0.3
1908	Was-A	111	341	40	71	7	8	0	20	38		.208	.297	.276	94	-1	15			.932	-6	*3-110/2-1	-0.4
1909	Was-A	9	16	2	2	1	0	0	0	2		.125	.222	.188	31	-1	0			.905	2	/3-6,S-2	0.1
Total	4	186	552	59	110	11	10	1	29	55		.199	.280	.261	81	-10	21			.935	5	3-179/2-3,S	0.0

■ CRAIG SHIPLEY   Shipley, Craig Barry b: 1/7/63, Parramatta, Australia BR/TR, 6'1", 175 lbs. Deb: 6/22/86

YEAR	TM/L	G	AB	R	H	2B	3B	HR	RBI	BB	SO	AVG	OBP	SLG	PRO+	BR/A	SB	CS	SBR	FA	FR	G/POS	TPR
1986	LA-N	12	27	3	3	1	0	0	4	2	5	.111	.200	.148	-3	-4	0	0	0	.914	-1	S-10/2-1,3	-0.4
1987	LA-N	26	35	3	9	1	0	0	2	0	6	.257	.257	.286	45	-3	0	0	0	.949	3	S-18/3-6	0.0
1989	NY-N	4	7	3	1	0	0	0	0	0	1	.143	.143	.143	-19	-1	0	0	0	1.000	-0	/S-3,3-2	-0.1
1991	SD-N	37	91	6	25	3	0	1	6	2	14	.275	.298	.341	77	-3	0	1	-1	.902	-3	S-19,2-14	-0.3
1992	SD-N	52	105	7	26	6	0	0	7	2	21	.248	.262	.305	59	-6	1	1	-0	.986	10	S-23,2-11/3	0.5
1993	SD-N	105	230	25	54	9	0	4	22	10	31	.235	.276	.326	59	-13	12	3	2	.964	-9	S-38,3-37,2/O	-1.8
1994	SD-N	81	240	32	80	14	4	4	30	9	28	.333	.365	.475	118	6	6	6	-2	.936	-8	3-53,S-14,2/01	-0.2
Total	7	317	735	79	198	34	4	9	71	25	106	.269	.301	.363	78	-24	19	11	-1	.951	-6	S-125,3-107/201	-2.3

■ ART SHIRES   Shires, Charles Arthur "Art The Great" b: 8/13/07, Italy, Tex. d: 7/13/67, Italy, Tex. BL/TR, 6'1", 195 lbs. Deb: 8/20/28

YEAR	TM/L	G	AB	R	H	2B	3B	HR	RBI	BB	SO	AVG	OBP	SLG	PRO+	BR/A	SB	CS	SBR	FA	FR	G/POS	TPR
1928	Chi-A	33	123	20	42	6	1	1	11	13	10	.341	.409	.431	122	5	0	3	-2	.990	3	1-32	0.3
1929	Chi-A	100	353	41	110	20	7	3	41	32	20	.312	.370	.433	108	4	4	5	-2	.991	0	1-90/2-3	-0.6
1930	Chi-A	37	128	14	33	5	1	1	18	6	6	.258	.291	.336	61	-8	2	0	1	.979	-2	1-33	-1.2
	Was-A	38	84	11	31	5	0	1	19	5	5	.369	.404	.464	119	3	1	3	-2	.982	0	1-21	0.0
	Yr	75	212	25	64	10	1	2	37	11	11	.302	.336	.387	84	-5	3	3	-1	.980	-2	1-54	-1.2
1932	Bos-N	82	298	32	71	9	3	5	30	25	21	.238	.299	.339	74	-11	1			.988	-2	1-80	-2.0
Total	4	290	986	118	287	45	12	11	119	81	62	.291	.347	.395	95	-8	8	11		.988	-1	1-256/2-3	-3.5

■ BART SHIRLEY   Shirley, Barton Arvin b: 1/4/40, Corpus Christi, Tex. BR/TR, 5'10", 183 lbs. Deb: 9/14/64

YEAR	TM/L	G	AB	R	H	2B	3B	HR	RBI	BB	SO	AVG	OBP	SLG	PRO+	BR/A	SB	CS	SBR	FA	FR	G/POS	TPR
1964	LA-N	18	62	6	17	1	1	0	7	4	8	.274	.318	.323	87	-1	0	0	0	.900	1	3-10/S-8	0.0
1966	LA-N	12	5	2	1	0	0	0	0	0	2	.200	.200	.200	13	-1	0	0	0	1.000	1	/S-5	0.1
1967	NY-N	6	12	1	0	0	0	0	0	0	5	.000	.000	.000	-99	-3	0	0	0	.917	0	/2-3	-0.3
1968	LA-N	39	83	6	15	3	0	0	4	10	13	.181	.269	.217	51	-5	0	1	-1	.903	3	S-21,2-18	-0.1
Total	4	75	162	15	33	4	1	0	11	14	28	.204	.267	.241	53	-10	0	1	-1	.936	5	/S-34,2-21,3	-0.3

■ MULE SHIRLEY   Shirley, Ernest Raeford b: 5/24/01, Snow Hill, N.C. d: 8/4/55, Goldsboro, N.C. BL/TL, 5'11", 180 lbs. Deb: 5/6/24

YEAR	TM/L	G	AB	R	H	2B	3B	HR	RBI	BB	SO	AVG	OBP	SLG	PRO+	BR/A	SB	CS	SBR	FA	FR	G/POS	TPR
1924	*Was-A	30	77	12	18	2	0	0	16	3	7	.234	.262	.312	49	-6	0	0	0	.984	0	1-25	-0.7
1925	Was-A	14	23	2	3	1	0	0	2	1	7	.130	.167	.174	-14	-4	0	0	0	1.000	0	/1-9	-0.4
Total	2	44	100	14	21	3	0	0	18	4	14	.210	.240	.280	34	-10	0	0	0	.988	0	/1-34	-1.1

■ IVEY SHIVER   Shiver, Ivey Merwin "Chick" b: 1/22/07, Sylvester, Ga. d: 8/31/72, Savannah, Ga. BR/TR, 6'1.5", 190 lbs. Deb: 4/14/31

YEAR	TM/L	G	AB	R	H	2B	3B	HR	RBI	BB	SO	AVG	OBP	SLG	PRO+	BR/A	SB	CS	SBR	FA	FR	G/POS	TPR
1931	Det-A	2	9	2	1	0	0	0	0	0	3	.111	.111	.111	-40	-2	0	0		1.000	-1	/O-2	-0.2
1934	Cin-N	19	59	6	12	1	0	2	6	3	15	.203	.242	.322	51	-4	1			1.000	-2	O-15	-0.7
Total	2	21	68	8	13	1	0	2	6	3	18	.191	.225	.294	38	-6	1	0		1.000	-3	/O-17	-0.9

■ GEORGE SHOCH   Shoch, George Quintus b: 1/6/1859, Philadelphia, Pa. d: 9/30/37, Philadelphia, Pa. BR/TR, 5'6", 158 lbs. Deb: 9/10/1886

YEAR	TM/L	G	AB	R	H	2B	3B	HR	RBI	BB	SO	AVG	OBP	SLG	PRO+	BR/A	SB	CS	SBR	FA	FR	G/POS	TPR
1886	Was-N	26	95	11	28	2	1	0	18	2	13	.295	.309	.368	112	1	2			.882	-5	O-25/S-1	-0.4
1887	Was-N	70	264	47	63	9	1	1	28	21	16	.239	.344	.292	70	-10	29			.897	7	O-63/S-6,2	-0.3
1888	Was-N	90	317	46	58	6	3	2	24	25	22	.183	.262	.240	64	-11	23			.900	3	S-52,O-35/2P	-0.7
1889	Was-N	30	109	12	26	2	0	0	11	20	5	.239	.385	.257	86	0	9			.905	3	O-29/S-1	0.2
1891	Mil-a	34	127	29	40	7	1	1	16	18	5	.315	.435	.409	118	2	12			.932	3	S-25/3-9	0.6
1892	Bal-N	76	308	42	85	15	3	1	50	24	19	.276	.340	.354	107	2	14			.872	0	S-57,O-12/3	0.4
1893	Bro-N	94	327	53	86	17	1	2	54	48	13	.263	.366	.339	92	-2	9			.892	-3	O-46,3-37,S/2	-0.5
1894	Bro-N	64	239	47	77	6	5	1	37	26	6	.322	.400	.402	101	2	16			.926	-1	O-35,S-14/2S	-0.1
1895	Bro-N	61	216	49	56	9	7	0	29	32	8	.259	.368	.366	97	1	7			.952	-6	2-39,2-13/S3	-0.6
1896	Bro-N	76	250	29	73	7	4	1	28	33	10	.292	.381	.364	103	3	11			.941	-13	2-62,O-10/3S	-0.6
1897	Bro-N	85	284	42	79	9	2	0	38	49		.278	.393	.324	96	1	6			.941	5	2-68,S-13/O	0.9
Total	11	706	2536	414	671	89	28	10	323	298	115	.265	.355	.334	93	-10	138			.912	-6	O-298,S-179,2/3P	-1.1

■ COSTEN SHOCKLEY   Shockley, John Costen b: 2/8/42, Georgetown, Del. BL/TL, 6'2", 200 lbs. Deb: 7/17/64

YEAR	TM/L	G	AB	R	H	2B	3B	HR	RBI	BB	SO	AVG	OBP	SLG	PRO+	BR/A	SB	CS	SBR	FA	FR	G/POS	TPR
1964	Phi-N	11	35	4	8	0	0	1	2	2	8	.229	.270	.314	65	-2	0	0	0	.968	-1	/1-9	-0.3
1965	Cal-A	40	107	5	20	2	0	2	17	9	16	.187	.256	.262	49	-7	0	0	0	.996	0	1-31/O-1	-0.9
Total	2	51	142	9	28	2	0	3	19	11	24	.197	.260	.275	53	-9	0	0	0	.991	-1	/1-40,O-1	-1.2

■ CHARLIE SHOEMAKER   Shoemaker, Charles Landis b: 8/10/39, Los Angeles, Cal. d: 5/31/90, Mount Penn, Pa. BL/TR, 5'10", 155 lbs. Deb: 9/9/61

YEAR	TM/L	G	AB	R	H	2B	3B	HR	RBI	BB	SO	AVG	OBP	SLG	PRO+	BR/A	SB	CS	SBR	FA	FR	G/POS	TPR
1961	KC-A	7	26	5	10	2	0	0	1	2	2	.385	.429	.462	135	1	0	0	0	1.000	0	/2-6	0.2
1962	KC-A	5	11	1	2	0	0	0	0	0	2	.182	.182	.182	-2	-2	0	0	0	1.000	1	/2-4	0.0
1964	KC-A	16	52	6	11	2	2	0	4	2	13	.212	.212	.327	46	-4	0	0	0	.964	-5	2-14	-0.8
Total	3	28	89	12	23	4	2	0	4	2	13	.258	.275	.348	67	-4	0	0	0	.981	-3	/2-24	-0.6

■ STRICK SHOFNER   Shofner, Frank Strickland b: 7/23/19, Crawford, Tex. BL/TR, 5'10.5", 187 lbs. Deb: 4/19/47

YEAR	TM/L	G	AB	R	H	2B	3B	HR	RBI	BB	SO	AVG	OBP	SLG	PRO+	BR/A	SB	CS	SBR	FA	FR	G/POS	TPR
1947	Bos-A	5	13	1	2	0	1	0	0	0	3	.154	.154	.308	25	-1	0	0	0	1.000	1	/3-4	-0.1

■ EDDIE SHOKES   Shokes, Edward Christopher b: 1/27/20, Charleston, S.C. BL/TL, 6', 170 lbs. Deb: 6/9/41

YEAR	TM/L	G	AB	R	H	2B	3B	HR	RBI	BB	SO	AVG	OBP	SLG	PRO+	BR/A	SB	CS	SBR	FA	FR	G/POS	TPR
1941	Cin-N	1	1	0	0	0	0	0	0	0	1	.000	.000	.000	-99	-0	0			.000	0	H	0.0
1946	Cin-N	31	83	3	10	0	0	0	5	18	21	.120	.277	.133	19	-8	1			.996	-1	1-29	-1.2
Total	2	32	84	3	10	0	0	0	5	18	22	.119	.275	.131	18	-9	1			.996	-1	/1-29	-1.2

■ RAY SHOOK   Shook, Raymond Curtis b: 11/18/1889, Perry, Ohio d: 9/16/70, South Bend, Ind. BR/TR, 5'7.5", 155 lbs. Deb: 4/16/16

YEAR	TM/L	G	AB	R	H	2B	3B	HR	RBI	BB	SO	AVG	OBP	SLG	PRO+	BR/A	SB	CS	SBR	FA	FR	G/POS	TPR
1916	Chi-A	1	0	0	0	0	0	0	0	0	0	—	—	—	—	0	0			.000	0	R	0.0

■ RON SHOOP   Shoop, Ronald Lee b: 9/19/31, Rural Valley, Pa. BR/TR, 5'11", 180 lbs. Deb: 8/22/59

YEAR	TM/L	G	AB	R	H	2B	3B	HR	RBI	BB	SO	AVG	OBP	SLG	PRO+	BR/A	SB	CS	SBR	FA	FR	G/POS	TPR
1959	Det-A	3	7	1	1	0	0	0	1	0	1	.143	.143	.143	-20	-1	0			1.000	0	/C-3	-0.2

■ TOM SHOPAY   Shopay, Thomas Michael b: 2/21/45, Bristol, Conn. BL/TR, 5'9.5", 160 lbs. Deb: 9/17/67

YEAR	TM/L	G	AB	R	H	2B	3B	HR	RBI	BB	SO	AVG	OBP	SLG	PRO+	BR/A	SB	CS	SBR	FA	FR	G/POS	TPR
1967	NY-A	8	27	2	8	1	0	2	6	1	5	.296	.321	.556	161	2	2	0	1	.917	1	/O-7	0.3

YEAR	TM/L	G	AB	R	H	2B	3B	HR	RBI	BB	SO	AVG	OBP	SLG	PRO+	BR/A	SB	CS	SBR	FA	FR	G/POS	TPR
1969	NY-A	28	48	2	4	0	1	0	0	2	10	.083	.120	.125	-33	-9	0	1	-1	1.000	1	O-11	-1.0
1971	*Bal-A	47	74	10	19	2	0	0	5	3	7	.257	.286	.284	62	-4	2	1	0	1.000	-1	O-13	-0.5
1972	Bal-A	49	40	3	9	0	0	0	2	5	12	.225	.311	.225	60	-2	0	0	0	1.000	-0	/O-3	-0.2
1975	Bal-A	40	31	4	5	1	0	0	2	4	7	.161	.257	.194	31	-3	3	0	1	1.000	-3	O-13/C-1,D	-0.5
1976	Bal-A	14	20	4	4	0	0	0	1	3	3	.200	.304	.200	53	-1	1	0	0	1.000	-4	O-11/C-1	-0.5
1977	Bal-A	67	69	15	13	3	0	1	4	8	7	.188	.273	.275	53	-4	3	3	-1	1.000	-18	O-52/D-2	-2.5
Total	7	253	309	40	62	7	1	3	20	26	51	.201	.263	.259	50	-21	11	5	0	.993	-24	O-110/D-5,C	-4.9

■ DAVE SHORT
Short, David Orvis b: 5/11/17, Magnolia, Ark. d: 11/22/83, Shreveport, La. BL/TR, 5'11.5", 162 lbs. Deb: 9/16/40

YEAR	TM/L	G	AB	R	H	2B	3B	HR	RBI	BB	SO	AVG	OBP	SLG	PRO+	BR/A	SB	CS	SBR	FA	FR	G/POS	TPR
1940	Chi-A	4	3	1	1	0	0	0	0	1	2	.333	.500	.333	119	0	0	0	0	.000	0	H	0.0
1941	Chi-A	3	8	0	0	0	0	0	0	2	1	.000	.200	.000	-44	-2	0	0	0	.800	-0	/O-2	-0.2
Total	2	7	11	1	1	0	0	0	0	3	3	.091	.286	.091	3	-1	0	0	0	.800	-0	/O-2	-0.2

■ CHICK SHORTEN
Shorten, Charles Henry b: 4/19/1892, Scranton, Pa. d: 10/23/65, Scranton, Pa. BL/TL, 6', 175 lbs. Deb: 9/22/15

YEAR	TM/L	G	AB	R	H	2B	3B	HR	RBI	BB	SO	AVG	OBP	SLG	PRO+	BR/A	SB	CS	SBR	FA	FR	G/POS	TPR
1915	Bos-A	6	14	1	3	1	0	0	0	0	2	.214	.214	.286	51	-1	0			1.000	-1	/O-5	-0.2
1916	*Bos-A	53	112	14	33	2	1	0	11	10	8	.295	.352	.330	105	1	1			1.000	-8	O-33	-0.9
1917	Bos-A	69	168	12	30	4	2	0	16	10	10	.179	.229	.226	39	-12	2			.977	-5	O-43	-2.2
1919	Det-A	95	270	37	85	9	3	0	22	22	13	.315	.366	.370	110	4	5			.973	-6	O-75	-0.8
1920	Det-A	116	364	35	105	9	6	1	40	28	14	.288	.339	.354	86	-7	2	4	-2	.989	-7	O-99	-1.7
1921	Det-A	92	217	33	59	11	3	0	23	20	11	.272	.333	.350	75	-8	2	3	-1	.981	-4	O-51	-1.6
1922	StL-A	55	131	22	36	12	5	2	16	16	8	.275	.354	.489	114	2	0	1	-1	1.000	-2	O-31	-0.3
1924	Cin-N	41	69	7	19	3	0	0	6	4	2	.275	.315	.319	71	-3	0	0	0	1.000	-4	O-15	-0.7
Total	8	527	1345	161	370	51	20	3	134	110	68	.275	.330	.349	87	-25	12	8		.985	-31	O-352	-8.4

■ BURT SHOTTON
Shotton, Burton Edwin "Barney" b: 10/18/1884, Brownhelm, Ohio d: 7/29/62, Lake Wales, Fla. BL/TR, 5'11", 175 lbs. Deb: 9/13/09 MC

YEAR	TM/L	G	AB	R	H	2B	3B	HR	RBI	BB	SO	AVG	OBP	SLG	PRO+	BR/A	SB	CS	SBR	FA	FR	G/POS	TPR
1909	StL-A	17	61	5	16	0	1	0	0	5		.262	.328	.295	104	0	3			.915	1	O-17	0.1
1911	StL-A	139	572	84	146	11	8	0	36	51		.255	.317	.302	76	-18	26			.950	7	*O-139	-1.8
1912	StL-A	154	580	87	168	15	8	2	40	86		.290	.390	.353	117	18	35			.941	7	*O-154	1.6
1913	StL-A	147	549	105	163	23	8	1	28	99	63	.297	.405	.373	132	27	43			.951	13	*O-146	3.5
1914	StL-A	154	579	82	156	19	9	0	38	64	66	.269	.344	.333	108	6	40	29	-5	.940	2	*O-152	-0.5
1915	StL-A	156	559	93	158	18	11	1	30	118	62	.283	.409	.360	135	31	43	32	-6	.931	-3	*O-154	1.6
1916	StL-A	157	618	97	174	23	6	1	36	111	67	.282	.391	.343	127	26	41	28	-5	.950	10	*O-157	2.5
1917	StL-A	118	398	47	89	9	1	1	20	62	47	.224	.330	.259	83	-6	16			.923	-12	*O-107	-2.6
1918	Was-A	126	505	68	132	16	7	0	21	67	40	.261	.349	.321	104	4	25			.942	6	*O-122	0.3
1919	StL-N	85	270	35	77	13	5	1	20	22	25	.285	.341	.381	125	8	16			.927	-5	O-67	-0.1
1920	StL-N	62	180	28	41	5	0	1	12	18	14	.228	.305	.272	69	-7	5	1	1	.959	1	O-51	-0.9
1921	StL-N	38	48	9	12	1	1	1	7	7	4	.250	.357	.375	96	-0	0	2	-1	.958	-0	O-11	-0.2
1922	StL-N	34	30	5	6	1	0	0	2	4	6	.200	.294	.233	39	-3	0	1	-1	1.000	-1	/O-3	-0.4
1923	StL-N	1	0	1	0	0	0	0	0	0	0	—	—	—	—		0	0	0	.000	0	R	0.0
Total	14	1388	4949	746	1338	154	65	9	290	714	382	.270	.365	.333	110	87	293	93		.942	25	*O-1280	3.1

■ JOHN SHOUPE
Shoupe, John F. b: 9/30/1851, Cincinnati, Ohio d: 2/13/20, Cincinnati, Ohio BL/TL, 5'7", 140 lbs. Deb: 5/3/1879

YEAR	TM/L	G	AB	R	H	2B	3B	HR	RBI	BB	SO	AVG	OBP	SLG	PRO+	BR/A	SB	CS	SBR	FA	FR	G/POS	TPR
1879	Tro-N	11	44	5	4	0	0	0		1	3	.091	.091	.091	-43	-6				.820	-3	S-10/2-1	-0.8
1882	StL-a	2	7	1	0	0	0	0				.000	.000	.000	-96	-1				1.000	1	/2-2	0.0
1884	Was-U	1	4	1	3	0	0	0		0		.750	.750	.750	319	1				.857	2	/O-1	0.2
Total	3	14	55	7	7	0	0	0		1	3	.127	.127	.127	-18	-7				.857	-0	/S-10,2-3,O	-0.6

■ BRIAN SHOUSE
Shouse, Brian Douglas b: 9/26/68, Effingham, Ill. BL/TL, 5'11", 180 lbs. Deb: 7/31/93

YEAR	TM/L	G	AB	R	H	2B	3B	HR	RBI	BB	SO	AVG	OBP	SLG	PRO+	BR/A	SB	CS	SBR	FA	FR	G/POS	TPR
1993	Pit-N	16	0	0	0	0	0	0	0	0	0	—	—	—	—		0	0	0	1.000	0	/P-6	0.0

■ JOHN SHOVLIN
Shovlin, John Joseph "Brode" b: 1/14/1891, Drifton, Pa. d: 2/16/76, Bethesda, Md. BR/TR, 5'7", 163 lbs. Deb: 6/21/11

YEAR	TM/L	G	AB	R	H	2B	3B	HR	RBI	BB	SO	AVG	OBP	SLG	PRO+	BR/A	SB	CS	SBR	FA	FR	G/POS	TPR
1911	Pit-N	2	1	1	0	0	0	0	0	0	1	.000	.000	.000	-96	-0	0			.000	0	H	0.0
1919	StL-A	9	35	4	7	0	0	0	1	5	2	.200	.300	.200	41	-3	0			.936	-2	/2-9	-0.4
1920	StL-A	7	7	2	2	0	0	0	2	0	0	.286	.286	.286	50	-0	0	0	0	1.000	1	/S-5	0.0
Total	3	18	43	7	9	0	0	0	3	5	3	.209	.292	.209	39	-3	0			.936	-1	/2-9,S-5	-0.4

■ GEORGE SHUBA
Shuba, George Thomas "Shotgun" b: 12/13/24, Youngstown, Ohio BL/TR, 5'11", 180 lbs. Deb: 7/2/48

YEAR	TM/L	G	AB	R	H	2B	3B	HR	RBI	BB	SO	AVG	OBP	SLG	PRO+	BR/A	SB	CS	SBR	FA	FR	G/POS	TPR
1948	Bro-N	63	161	21	43	6	0	4	32	34	31	.267	.395	.379	107	3	1			.936	-10	O-56	-0.9
1949	Bro-N	1	0	0	0	0	0	0	0	0	0	.000	.000	.000	-96	-0	0			.000	0	H	0.0
1950	Bro-N	34	111	15	23	8	2	3	12	13	12	.207	.302	.396	80	-3	2			.984	3	O-27	-0.2
1952	*Bro-N	94	256	40	78	12	1	9	40	38	29	.305	.395	.465	136	13	1	3	-2	.992	-2	O-67	0.7
1953	*Bro-N	74	169	19	43	12	1	5	23	17	20	.254	.326	.426	92	-2	1	2	-1	.984	-5	O-44	-1.0
1954	*Bro-N	45	65	3	10	5	0	2	10	7	10	.154	.247	.323	46	-5	0	0	0	.913	-1	O-13	-0.7
1955	*Bro-N	44	51	8	14	2	0	1	8	11	10	.275	.422	.373	110	1	0	0	0	.909	-2	/O-9	-0.1
Total	7	355	814	106	211	45	4	24	125	120	122	.259	.359	.413	104	6	5	5		.967	-18	O-216	-2.2

■ FRANK SHUGART
Shugart, Frank Harry (b: Frank Harry Shugarts)
b: 12/10/1866, Luthersburg, Pa. d: 9/9/44, Clearfield, Pa. BL/TR, 5'8", 170 lbs. Deb: 8/23/1890

YEAR	TM/L	G	AB	R	H	2B	3B	HR	RBI	BB	SO	AVG	OBP	SLG	PRO+	BR/A	SB	CS	SBR	FA	FR	G/POS	TPR
1890	Chi-P	29	106	8	20	5	5	0	15	5	13	.189	.232	.330	47	-9	5			.881	-5	S-25/O-5	-1.0
1891	Pit-N	75	320	57	88	19	8	3	33	20	26	.275	.324	.412	117	5	21			.902	4	S-75	1.2
1892	Pit-N	137	554	94	148	19	14	0	62	47	48	.267	.329	.352	106	3	28			.886	9	*S-134/C-2,O	1.6
1893	Pit-N	52	210	37	55	7	3	1	32	19	15	.262	.332	.338	80	-6	12			.882	-3	S-51	-0.5
	StL-N	59	246	41	69	10	4	0	28	22	10	.280	.354	.354	88	-4	13			.907	-3	O-28,S-23/3	-0.6
	Yr	111	456	78	124	17	7	1	60	41	25	.272	.344	.346	84	-10	25			.868	-6	S-74,O-28/3	-1.1
1894	StL-N	133	527	103	154	19	18	7	72	38	37	.292	.349	.436	88	-12	21			.912	-3	*O-122/S-7,3	-1.8
1895	Lou-N	113	473	61	125	14	13	4	70	31	25	.264	.315	.374	82	-13	14			.874	-17	*S-88,O-27	-2.4
1897	Phi-N	40	163	20	41	8	2	5	25	8		.252	.287	.417	87	-4	5			.872	-4	S-40	-0.6
1901	Chi-A	107	415	62	104	9	12	2	47	28		.251	.301	.345	81	-11	12			.885	-8	*S-107	-0.9
Total	8	745	3014	483	804	110	79	22	384	218	174	.267	.323	.378	90	-52	131			.883	-30	S-550,O-183/3C	-5.0

■ TERRY SHUMPERT
Shumpert, Terrance Darnell b: 8/16/66, Paducah, Ky. BR/TR, 5'11", 190 lbs. Deb: 5/1/90

YEAR	TM/L	G	AB	R	H	2B	3B	HR	RBI	BB	SO	AVG	OBP	SLG	PRO+	BR/A	SB	CS	SBR	FA	FR	G/POS	TPR
1990	KC-A	32	91	7	25	6	1	0	8	2	17	.275	.298	.363	85	-2	3	3	-1	.977	2	2-27/D-3	0.0
1991	KC-A	144	369	45	80	16	4	5	34	30	75	.217	.285	.322	67	-17	17	11	-2	.975	3	*2-144	-1.3
1992	KC-A	36	94	6	14	5	1	1	11	3	17	.149	.175	.255	19	-10	2	2	-1	.969	1	2-33/S-1,D	-1.0
1993	KC-A	8	10	0	1	0	0	0	0	2	2	.100	.250	.100	-2	-1	1	0	0	1.000	2	/2-8	0.1
1994	KC-A	64	183	28	44	6	2	8	24	13	39	.240	.291	.426	76	-7	18	3	4	.964	-8	2-38,3-24/SD	-1.0
Total	5	284	747	86	164	33	8	14	77	50	150	.220	.274	.341	65	-38	41	19		.973	-1	2-250/3-24,DS	-3.2

■ VINCE SHUPE
Shupe, Vincent William b: 9/5/21, E.Canton, Ohio d: 4/5/62, Canton, Ohio BL/TL, 5'11", 180 lbs. Deb: 7/7/45

YEAR	TM/L	G	AB	R	H	2B	3B	HR	RBI	BB	SO	AVG	OBP	SLG	PRO+	BR/A	SB	CS	SBR	FA	FR	G/POS	TPR
1945	Bos-N	78	283	22	76	8	0	0	15	17	16	.269	.312	.297	69	-11	3			.989	1	1-77	-1.5

■ ED SICKING
Sicking, Edward Joseph b: 3/30/1897, St.Bernard, Ohio d: 8/30/78, Madeira, Ohio BR/TR, 5'9.5", 165 lbs. Deb: 8/26/16

YEAR	TM/L	G	AB	R	H	2B	3B	HR	RBI	BB	SO	AVG	OBP	SLG	PRO+	BR/A	SB	CS	SBR	FA	FR	G/POS	TPR
1916	Chi-N	1	1	0	0	0	0	0	0	0	0	.000	.000	.000	-90	-0	0			.000	0	H	0.0
1918	NY-N	46	132	9	33	4	0	0	12	6	11	.250	.283	.280	73	-4	2			.917	-8	3-24,2-18/S	-1.3
1919	NY-N	6	15	2	5	0	0	0	3	1	0	.333	.412	.333	127	1	0			.971	3	/S-6	0.4

YEAR	TM/L	G	AB	R	H	2B	3B	HR	RBI	BB	SO	AVG	OBP	SLG	PRO+	BR/A	SB	CS	SBR	FA	FR	G/POS	TPR
	Phi-N	61	185	16	40	2	1	0	15	8	17	.216	.253	.238	45	-12	4			.925	5	S-35,2-22	-0.5
	Yr	67	200	18	45	2	1	0	18	9	17	.225	.265	.245	51	-12	4			.933	8	S-41,2-22	-0.1
1920	NY-N	46	134	11	23	3	1	0	9	10	10	.172	.234	.209	28	-12	6	2	1	.915	4	3-28,2-15/S	-0.7
	Cin-N	37	123	12	33	3	0	0	17	13	5	.268	.338	.293	83	-2	2	3	-1	.955	7	2-25/S-9,3	-0.1
	Yr	83	257	23	56	6	1	0	26	23	15	.218	.285	.249	55	-14	8	5	-1	.952	4	2-40,3-30,S	-0.8
1927	Pit-N	6	7	1	1	1	0	0	3	1	0	.143	.250	.286	40	-1	0			1.000	2	/2-5	0.1
Total	5	203	597	51	135	13	2	0	59	39	43	.226	.277	.255	57	-31	14	5		.965	5	/2-85,S-56,3	-2.1

■ JOE SIDDALL
Siddall, Joseph Todd b: 10/25/67, Windsor, Ont., Can. BL/TR, 6'1", 197 lbs. Deb: 7/28/93

YEAR	TM/L	G	AB	R	H	2B	3B	HR	RBI	BB	SO	AVG	OBP	SLG	PRO+	BR/A	SB	CS	SBR	FA	FR	G/POS	TPR
1993	Mon-N	19	20	0	2	1	0	0	1	1	5	.100	.143	.150	-21	-3	0	0	0	1.000	2	C-15/1-1,O	-0.1

■ NORM SIEBERN
Siebern, Norman Leroy b: 7/26/33, St.Louis, Mo. BL/TR, 6'3", 205 lbs. Deb: 6/15/56

YEAR	TM/L	G	AB	R	H	2B	3B	HR	RBI	BB	SO	AVG	OBP	SLG	PRO+	BR/A	SB	CS	SBR	FA	FR	G/POS	TPR
1956	*NY-A	54	162	27	33	1	4	4	21	19	38	.204	.287	.333	66	-9	1	1	-0	.971	0	O-51	-1.1
1958	*NY-A	134	460	79	138	19	5	14	55	66	87	.300	.389	.454	136	24	5	8	-3	.982	5	*O-133	2.0
1959	NY-A	120	380	52	103	17	0	11	53	41	71	.271	.345	.403	108	4	3	1	0	.989	-2	O-93/1-2	-0.2
1960	KC-A	144	520	69	145	31	6	19	69	72	68	.279	.369	.471	125	18	0	0	0	.987	-1	O-75,1-69	0.9
1961	KC-A	153	560	68	166	36	5	18	98	82	91	.296	.387	.475	127	23	2	4	-2	.989	-1	*1-109,O-47	0.9
1962	KC-A★	162	600	114	185	25	6	25	117	110	88	.308	.416	.495	138	35	3	1	0	.994	5	*1-162	2.9
1963	KC-A☆	152	556	80	151	25	2	16	83	79	82	.272	.362	.410	110	9	1	4	-2	.991	4	*1-131,O-16	0.4
1964	Bal-A★	150	478	92	117	24	2	12	56	106	87	.245	.384	.379	114	13	2	3	-1	.995	4	*1-149	1.0
1965	Bal-A	106	297	44	76	13	4	8	42	50	49	.256	.365	.407	117	8	1	2	-1	.991	1	1-76	0.4
1966	Cal-A	125	336	29	83	14	1	5	41	63	61	.247	.366	.339	107	6	0	1	-1	.992	1	1-99	0.0
1967	SF-N	46	58	6	9	1	1	0	4	14	13	.155	.319	.207	54	-3	0	0	0	1.000	-0	1-15/O-2	-0.4
	*Bos-A	33	44	2	9	0	2	0	7	6	8	.205	.300	.295	71	-1	0	0	0	.981	1	1-13/O-1	-0.2
1968	Bos-A	27	30	0	2	0	0	0	0	0	5	.067	.067	.067	-56	-5	0	0	0	1.000	-1	/1-2,O-2	-0.7
Total	12	1406	4481	662	1217	206	38	132	636	708	748	.272	.372	.423	117	122	18	25	-10	.992	17	1-827,O-420	5.9

■ DICK SIEBERT
Siebert, Richard Walther b: 2/19/12, Fall River, Mass. d: 12/9/78, Minneapolis, Minn. BL/TL, 6', 170 lbs. Deb: 9/7/32 F

YEAR	TM/L	G	AB	R	H	2B	3B	HR	RBI	BB	SO	AVG	OBP	SLG	PRO+	BR/A	SB	CS	SBR	FA	FR	G/POS	TPR
1932	Bro-N	6	7	1	2	0	0	0	0	2	2	.286	.444	.286	104	0	0			1.000	-0	/1-2	0.0
1936	Bro-N	2	2	0	0	0	0	0	0	0	0	.000	.000	.000	-99	-1	0			1.000	0	/O-1	0.0
1937	StL-N	22	38	3	7	2	0	0	2	4	8	.184	.279	.237	41	-3	1			.979	-1	/1-7	-0.4
1938	StL-N	1	1	0	1	0	0	0	0	0	0	1.000	1.000	1.000	427	0	0			.000	0	H	0.0
	Phi-A	48	194	24	55	8	3	0	28	10	9	.284	.329	.356	73	-8	2	3	-1	1.000	5	1-46	-0.9
1939	Phi-A	101	402	58	118	28	3	6	47	21	22	.294	.329	.423	93	-6	4	1	1	.991	5	1-99	-1.0
1940	Phi-A	154	595	69	170	31	4	5	77	33	34	.286	.325	.383	85	-14	8	6	-1	.985	8	*1-154	-2.1
1941	Phi-A	123	467	63	156	28	8	5	79	37	22	.334	.385	.460	126	17	1	3	-2	.990	6	*1-123	1.2
1942	Phi-A	153	612	57	159	25	7	2	74	24	17	.260	.291	.333	76	-21	4	5	-2	.989	-2	*1-152	-3.6
1943	Phi-A★	146	558	50	140	26	7	1	72	33	21	.251	.295	.328	83	-14	6	7	-2	.990	4	*1-145	-2.2
1944	Phi-A	132	468	52	143	27	5	6	52	62	17	.306	.387	.423	133	21	2	0	1	.993	-4	1-74,O-58	1.2
1945	Phi-A	147	573	62	153	29	1	7	51	50	33	.267	.328	.358	99	-1	2	7	-4	.991	10	*1-147	-0.5
Total	11	1035	3917	439	1104	204	40	32	482	276	185	.282	.332	.379	96	-29	30	32		.990	31	1-949/O-59	-8.3

■ FRED SIEFKE
Siefke, Frederick Edwin b: 3/27/1870, New York, N.Y. d: 4/18/1893, New York, N.Y. 5'11", 168 lbs. Deb: 5/2/1890

YEAR	TM/L	G	AB	R	H	2B	3B	HR	RBI	BB	SO	AVG	OBP	SLG	PRO+	BR/A	SB	CS	SBR	FA	FR	G/POS	TPR
1890	Bro-a	16	58	1	8	2	0	0		5		.138	.206	.172	12	-6	2			.811	0	3-16	-0.5

■ JOHN SIEGEL
Siegel, John b: York, Pa. Deb: 6/9/1884

YEAR	TM/L	G	AB	R	H	2B	3B	HR	RBI	BB	SO	AVG	OBP	SLG	PRO+	BR/A	SB	CS	SBR	FA	FR	G/POS	TPR
1884	Phi-U	8	31	4	7	2	0	0		1		.226	.250	.290	50	-2				.533	-5	/3-8	-0.6

■ JOHNNY SIEGLE
Siegle, John Herbert b: 7/8/1874, Urbana, Ohio d: 2/12/68, Urbana, Ohio BR/TR, 5'10", 165 lbs. Deb: 9/15/05

YEAR	TM/L	G	AB	R	H	2B	3B	HR	RBI	BB	SO	AVG	OBP	SLG	PRO+	BR/A	SB	CS	SBR	FA	FR	G/POS	TPR
1905	Cin-N	17	56	9	17	1	2	1	8	7		.304	.391	.446	135	2	0			.960	-1	O-16	0.0
1906	Cin-N	22	68	4	8	2	2	0	7	3		.118	.178	.206	19	-7	0			.959	0	O-21	-0.8
Total	2	39	124	13	25	3	4	1	15	10		.202	.277	.315	75	-4	0			.959	-1	/O-37	-0.8

■ OSCAR SIEMER
Siemer, Oscar Sylvester "Cotton" b: 8/14/01, St.Louis, Mo. d: 12/5/59, St.Louis, Mo. BR/TR, 5'9", 162 lbs. Deb: 5/20/25

YEAR	TM/L	G	AB	R	H	2B	3B	HR	RBI	BB	SO	AVG	OBP	SLG	PRO+	BR/A	SB	CS	SBR	FA	FR	G/POS	TPR
1925	Bos-N	16	46	5	14	0	1	1	6	1	0	.304	.319	.413	94	-1	0	0	0	.900	-2	C-16	-0.2
1926	Bos-N	31	73	3	15	1	0	0	5	2	7	.205	.227	.219	22	-8	0			.920	-2	C-30	-0.9
Total	2	47	119	8	29	1	1	1	11	3	7	.244	.262	.294	51	-9	0	0		.913	-4	/C-46	-1.1

■ RUBEN SIERRA
Sierra, Ruben Angel (Garcia) b: 10/6/65, Rio Piedras, P.R. BB/TR, 6'1", 175 lbs. Deb: 6/1/86

YEAR	TM/L	G	AB	R	H	2B	3B	HR	RBI	BB	SO	AVG	OBP	SLG	PRO+	BR/A	SB	CS	SBR	FA	FR	G/POS	TPR
1986	Tex-A	113	382	50	101	13	10	16	55	22	65	.264	.306	.476	106	2	7	8	-3	.972	-10	*O-107/D-3	-1.4
1987	Tex-A	158	643	97	169	35	4	30	109	39	114	.263	.307	.470	102	-0	16	11	-2	.963	5	*O-157	-0.2
1988	Tex-A	156	615	77	156	32	2	23	91	44	91	.254	.305	.424	99	-2	18	4	3	.979	5	*O-153/D-1	0.2
1989	Tex-A★	162	634	101	194	35	14	29	119	43	82	.306	.352	.543	146	36	8	2	1	.973	6	*O-162	3.9
1990	Tex-A	159	608	70	170	37	2	16	96	49	86	.280	.334	.426	111	8	9	9	0	.967	5	*O-151/D-7	0.7
1991	Tex-A★	161	661	110	203	44	5	25	116	56	91	.307	.357	.502	139	33	16	4	2	.979	5	*O-161	3.6
1992	Tex-A★	124	500	66	139	30	6	14	70	31	59	.278	.320	.446	117	9	12	4	1	.970	7	*O-119/D-4	0.8
	*Oak-A	27	101	17	28	4	1	3	17	14	9	.277	.365	.426	128	4	2	0	1	1.000	1	O-25/D-2	0.5
	Yr	151	601	83	167	34	7	17	87	45	68	.278	.328	.443	119	13	14	4	2	.976	7	O-144/D-6	1.3
1993	Oak-A	158	630	77	147	23	5	22	101	52	97	.233	.292	.390	87	-14	25	5	5	.977	7	*O-133,D-25	-0.7
1994	Oak-A★	110	426	71	114	21	1	23	92	23	64	.268	.305	.484	108	2	8	5	-1	.948	-4	O-98,D-10	-0.4
Total	9	1328	5200	736	1421	274	50	201	866	373	758	.273	.323	.461	114	76	121	43	11	.972	17	*O-1266/D-52	7.0

■ ROY SIEVERS
Sievers, Roy Edward "Squirrel" b: 11/18/26, St.Louis, Mo. BR/TR, 6'1", 195 lbs. Deb: 4/21/49 C

YEAR	TM/L	G	AB	R	H	2B	3B	HR	RBI	BB	SO	AVG	OBP	SLG	PRO+	BR/A	SB	CS	SBR	FA	FR	G/POS	TPR
1949	StL-A	140	471	84	144	28	1	16	91	70	75	.306	.398	.471	124	16	1	5	-3	.973	6	*O-125/3-7	1.3
1950	StL-A	113	370	46	88	20	4	10	57	34	42	.238	.305	.395	75	-16	1	3	-2	.983	6	O-78,3-21	-1.4
1951	StL-A	31	89	10	20	2	1	1	11	9	21	.225	.303	.303	62	-5	0	0	0	.985	-2	O-25	-0.7
1952	StL-A	11	30	3	6	3	0	0	5	1	4	.200	.226	.300	44	-2	0	0	0	.968	-1	/1-7	-0.4
1953	StL-A	92	285	37	77	15	0	8	35	32	47	.270	.344	.407	100	-0	0	1	-1	.992	-6	1-76	-1.0
1954	Was-A	145	514	75	119	26	6	24	102	80	77	.232	.337	.446	120	12	2	1	0	.971	9	*O-133/1-8	1.6
1955	Was-A	144	509	74	138	20	8	25	106	73	66	.271	.367	.489	136	24	1	2	0	.988	-1	O-129,1-17/3	1.0
1956	Was-A★	152	550	92	139	27	2	29	95	100	88	.253	.373	.467	121	17	0	3	-2	.987	2	O-78,1-76	1.0
1957	Was-A☆	152	572	99	172	23	5	42	114	76	55	.301	.388	.579	163	49	1	0	0	.985	4	*O-130,1-7	4.4
1958	Was-A	148	550	85	162	18	1	39	108	53	63	.295	.361	.544	148	34	3	1	0	.991	5	*O-114,1-33	3.1
1959	Was-A★	115	385	55	93	19	0	21	49	53	56	.242	.336	.455	116	8	1	1	0	.989	5	1-93,O-13	0.5
1960	Chi-A	127	444	87	131	22	0	28	93	74	69	.295	.399	.534	152	33	1	1	0	.993	-7	*1-114/O-6	1.7
1961	Chi-A★	141	492	76	145	26	6	27	92	61	62	.295	.379	.537	144	30	1	0	0	.993	0	*1-132	1.9
1962	Phi-N	144	477	61	125	19	5	21	80	56	80	.262	.348	.455	117	11	2	1	0	.991	1	*1-130/O-7	0.4
1963	Phi-N	138	450	46	108	19	2	19	82	43	72	.240	.313	.418	110	5	0	2	-1	.989	1	*1-126	-0.2
1964	Phi-N	49	120	7	22	3	1	4	16	13	20	.183	.269	.325	67	-5	0	0	0	.992	-1	1-33	0.0
	Was-A	33	58	5	10	1	0	2	11	9	14	.172	.284	.397	87	-1	0	0	0	1.000	1	1-15	0.0
1965	Was-A	12	21	3	4	1	0	0	4	3	3	.190	.320	.238	62	-1	0	0	0	1.000	-1	/1-7	-0.2
Total	17	1887	6387	945	1703	292	42	318	1147	841	920	.267	.357	.475	124	210	14	19	-7	.991	19	1-888,O-838/3	12.7

■ FRANK SIFFELL
Siffell, Frank b: 1860, Germany d: 10/26/09, Philadelphia, Pa. Deb: 6/14/1884

YEAR	TM/L	G	AB	R	H	2B	3B	HR	RBI	BB	SO	AVG	OBP	SLG	PRO+	BR/A	SB	CS	SBR	FA	FR	G/POS	TPR
1884	Phi-a	7	17	3	3	1	0	0		0		.176	.222	.235	46	-1				.875	-3	/C-7	-0.3

YEAR	TM/L	G	AB	R	H	2B	3B	HR	RBI	BB	SO	AVG	OBP	SLG	PRO+	BR/A	SB	CS	SBR	FA	FR	G/POS	TPR
1885	Phi-a	3	10	0	1	0	0	0		0		.100	.100	.100	-35	-2				.750	-3	/C-2,O-1	-0.4
Total	2	10	27	3	4	1	0	0		0		.148	.179	.185	16	-3				.841	-6	/C-9,O-1	-0.7

■ FRANK SIGAFOOS
Sigafoos, Francis Leonard b: 3/21/04, Easton, Pa.   d: 4/12/68, Indianapolis, Ind.   BR/TR, 5'9", 170 lbs.   Deb: 9/3/26

YEAR	TM/L	G	AB	R	H	2B	3B	HR	RBI	BB	SO	AVG	OBP	SLG	PRO+	BR/A	SB	CS	SBR	FA	FR	G/POS	TPR
1926	Phi-A	13	43	4	11	0	0	0	2	0	3	.256	.256	.256	32	-4	0	0	0	.915	-3	S-12	-0.6
1929	Det-A	14	23	3	4	1	0	0	2	5	4	.174	.321	.217	41	-2	0	2	-1	.909	-2	/3-6,S-5	-0.4
	Chi-A	7	3	1	1	0	0	0	1	2	1	.333	.600	.333	148	1	0	0	0	1.000	1	/2-6	0.2
	Yr	21	26	4	5	1	0	0	3	7	5	.192	.364	.231	56	-1	0	2	-1	.909	-1	/3-6,2-6,S	-0.2
1931	Cin-N	21	65	6	11	2	0	0	8	0	6	.169	.182	.200	3	-9	0			.881	-3	3-15/S-2	-1.1
Total	3	55	134	14	27	3	0	0	13	7	14	.201	.246	.224	25	-15	0	2		.887	-7	/3-21,S-19,2	-1.9

■ PADDY SIGLIN
Siglin, Wesley Peter b: 9/24/1891, Aurelia, Iowa   d: 8/5/56, Oakland, Cal.   BR/TR, 5'10", 160 lbs.   Deb: 9/12/14

YEAR	TM/L	G	AB	R	H	2B	3B	HR	RBI	BB	SO	AVG	OBP	SLG	PRO+	BR/A	SB	CS	SBR	FA	FR	G/POS	TPR
1914	Pit-N	14	39	4	6	0	0	0	2	4	6	.154	.233	.154	16	-4	1			.911	-6	2-11	-1.1
1915	Pit-N	6	7	1	2	0	0	0	0	1	2	.286	.375	.286	103	0	1			.800	-0	/2-1	0.0
1916	Pit-N	3	4	0	1	0	0	0	0	0	2	.250	.250	.250	53	-0	0			.857	0	/2-3	0.0
Total	3	23	50	5	9	0	0	0	2	5	10	.180	.255	.180	32	-4	2			.895	-5	2-15	-1.1

■ TRIPP SIGMAN
Sigman, Wesley Triplett b: 1/17/1899, Mooresville, N.C.   d: 3/8/71, Augusta, Ga.   BL/TR, 6', 180 lbs.   Deb: 9/18/29

YEAR	TM/L	G	AB	R	H	2B	3B	HR	RBI	BB	SO	AVG	OBP	SLG	PRO+	BR/A	SB	CS	SBR	FA	FR	G/POS	TPR
1929	Phi-N	10	29	8	15	1	0	2	9	3	1	.517	.563	.759	210	5	0			.944	-2	O-10	0.2
1930	Phi-N	52	100	15	27	4	1	4	6	6	9	.270	.324	.450	79	-4	1			.932	-1	O-19	-0.6
Total	2	62	129	23	42	5	1	6	15	9	10	.326	.379	.519	108	1	1			.935	-3	/O-29	-0.4

■ EDDIE SILBER
Silber, Edward James b: 6/6/14, Philadelphia, Pa.   d: 10/26/76, Dunedin, Fla.   BR/TR, 5'11", 170 lbs.   Deb: 9/3/37

YEAR	TM/L	G	AB	R	H	2B	3B	HR	RBI	BB	SO	AVG	OBP	SLG	PRO+	BR/A	SB	CS	SBR	FA	FR	G/POS	TPR
1937	StL-A	22	83	10	26	2	0	0	4	5	13	.313	.352	.337	74	-3	0	2	-1	.871	-7	O-21	-1.1
1939	StL-A	1	1	0	0	0	0	0	0	0	0	.000	.000	.000	-98	-0	0	0	0	.000	0	H	0.0
Total	2	23	84	10	26	2	0	0	4	5	14	.310	.348	.333	72	-3	0	2	-1	.871	-7	/O-21	-1.1

■ ED SILCH
Silch, Edward "Baldy" b: 2/22/1865, St.Louis, Mo.   d: 1/15/1895, St.Louis, Mo.   TR,   Deb: 4/29/1888

YEAR	TM/L	G	AB	R	H	2B	3B	HR	RBI	BB	SO	AVG	OBP	SLG	PRO+	BR/A	SB	CS	SBR	FA	FR	G/POS	TPR
1888	Bro-a	14	48	5	13	4	0	0	3	4		.271	.327	.354	118	1	4			.870	-2	O-14	-0.1

■ DANNY SILVA
Silva, Daniel James b: 10/5/1896, Everett, Mass.   d: 4/4/74, Hyannis, Mass.   BR/TR, 6', 170 lbs.   Deb: 8/11/19

YEAR	TM/L	G	AB	R	H	2B	3B	HR	RBI	BB	SO	AVG	OBP	SLG	PRO+	BR/A	SB	CS	SBR	FA	FR	G/POS	TPR
1919	Was-A	1	4	0	1	0	0	0	0	0	0	.250	.250	.250	41	-0	0			1.000	1	/3-1	0.0

■ AL SILVERA
Silvera, Aaron Albert b: 8/26/35, San Diego, Cal.   BR/TR, 6', 180 lbs.   Deb: 6/12/55

YEAR	TM/L	G	AB	R	H	2B	3B	HR	RBI	BB	SO	AVG	OBP	SLG	PRO+	BR/A	SB	CS	SBR	FA	FR	G/POS	TPR
1955	Cin-N	13	7	3	1	0	0	0	2	0	1	.143	.143	.143	-23	-1	0	0	0	.000	-0	/O-1	-0.2
1956	Cin-N	1	0	0	0	0	0	0	0	0	0	—	—	—		0	0	0	0	.000	0	R	0.0
Total	2	14	7	3	1	0	0	0	2	0	1	.143	.143	.143	-23	-1	0	0	0	—	-0	/O-1	-0.2

■ CHARLIE SILVERA
Silvera, Charles Anthony Ryan "Swede" b: 10/13/24, San Francisco, Cal   BR/TR, 5'10", 175 lbs.   Deb: 9/29/48   C

YEAR	TM/L	G	AB	R	H	2B	3B	HR	RBI	BB	SO	AVG	OBP	SLG	PRO+	BR/A	SB	CS	SBR	FA	FR	G/POS	TPR
1948	NY-A	4	14	1	8	0	1	0	1	0	1	.571	.571	.714	243	3	0	0	0	1.000	0	/C-4	0.3
1949	*NY-A	58	130	8	41	2	0	0	13	18	5	.315	.403	.331	95	0	2	1	0	.985	4	C-51	0.6
1950	NY-A	18	25	2	4	0	0	0	1	1	2	.160	.192	.160	-9	-4	0	0	0	.959	3	C-15	-0.1
1951	NY-A	18	51	5	14	3	0	0	7	5	3	.275	.339	.392	101	-0	0	0	0	1.000	0	C-18	0.1
1952	NY-A	20	55	4	18	3	0	0	11	5	2	.327	.383	.382	121	2	0	3	-2	1.000	-3	C-20	-0.2
1953	NY-A	42	82	11	23	3	1	0	12	9	5	.280	.352	.341	91	-1	0	1	-1	.992	6	C-39/3-1	0.6
1954	NY-A	20	37	1	10	1	0	0	4	3	2	.270	.341	.297	79	-1	0	1	-1	.962	5	C-18	0.4
1955	NY-A	14	26	1	5	0	0	0	1	6	4	.192	.344	.192	48	-2	0	0	0	1.000	3	C-11	0.2
1956	NY-A	7	9	0	2	0	0	0	0	2	3	.222	.364	.222	60	-0	0	0	0	.909	-1	/C-7	-0.1
1957	Chi-N	26	53	1	11	3	0	0	2	4	5	.208	.263	.264	43	-4	0	0	0	.982	3	C-26	-0.1
Total	10	227	482	34	136	15	2	0	52	53	32	.282	.356	.328	86	-8	2	6	-3	.985	21	C-209/3-1	1.7

■ LUIS SILVERIO
Silverio, Luis Pascual (Delmonte) b: 10/23/56, Villa Gonzalez, D.R   BR/TR, 5'11", 165 lbs.   Deb: 9/9/78

YEAR	TM/L	G	AB	R	H	2B	3B	HR	RBI	BB	SO	AVG	OBP	SLG	PRO+	BR/A	SB	CS	SBR	FA	FR	G/POS	TPR
1978	KC-A	8	11	7	6	2	1	0	3	2	3	.545	.615	.909	315	3	1	1	-0	.833	-2	/O-6,D-2	0.1

■ TOM SILVERIO
Silverio, Tomas Roberto (Veloz) b: 10/14/45, Santiago, D.R.   BL/TL, 5'10", 170 lbs.   Deb: 4/30/70

YEAR	TM/L	G	AB	R	H	2B	3B	HR	RBI	BB	SO	AVG	OBP	SLG	PRO+	BR/A	SB	CS	SBR	FA	FR	G/POS	TPR
1970	Cal-A	15	15	1	0	0	0	0	0	2	4	.000	.118	.000	-67	-3	0	1	-1	1.000	-2	/O-5,1-1	-0.7
1971	Cal-A	3	3	0	1	0	0	0	0	0	0	.333	.333	.333	96	-0	0	0	0	.000	-1	/O-1	-0.1
1972	Cal-A	13	12	1	2	0	0	0	0	0	5	.167	.167	.167	-1	-1	0	0	0	1.000	-1	/O-4	-0.3
Total	3	31	30	2	3	0	0	0	0	2	9	.100	.156	.100	-27	-5	0	1	-1	1.000	-4	/O-10,1-1	-1.1

■ DAVE SILVESTRI
Silvestri, David Joseph b: 9/29/67, St.Louis, Mo.   BR/TR, 6', 180 lbs.   Deb: 4/27/92

YEAR	TM/L	G	AB	R	H	2B	3B	HR	RBI	BB	SO	AVG	OBP	SLG	PRO+	BR/A	SB	CS	SBR	FA	FR	G/POS	TPR
1992	NY-A	7	13	3	4	0	2	0	1	0	3	.308	.308	.615	154	1	0	0	0	.889	1	/S-6	0.2
1993	NY-A	7	21	4	6	1	0	1	4	5	3	.286	.423	.476	146	2	0	0	0	.955	2	/S-4,3-3	0.3
1994	NY-A	12	18	3	2	0	1	1	2	4	9	.111	.273	.389	73	-1	0	1	-1	1.000	1	/2-9,3-2,S	-0.1
Total	3	26	52	10	12	1	3	2	7	9	15	.231	.344	.481	123	2	0	1	-1	.915	4	/S-11,2-9,3	0.4

■ KEN SILVESTRI
Silvestri, Kenneth Joseph "Hawk" b: 5/3/16, Chicago, Ill.   d: 3/31/92, Tallahassee, Fla.   BB/TR, 6'1", 200 lbs.   Deb: 4/18/39   MC

YEAR	TM/L	G	AB	R	H	2B	3B	HR	RBI	BB	SO	AVG	OBP	SLG	PRO+	BR/A	SB	CS	SBR	FA	FR	G/POS	TPR
1939	Chi-A	22	75	6	13	3	0	2	5	6	13	.173	.244	.293	36	-8	0	1	-1	.947	-0	C-20	-0.7
1940	Chi-A	28	24	5	6	2	0	2	10	4	7	.250	.357	.583	138	1	0	0	0	1.000	-0	/C-1	0.1
1941	NY-A	17	40	6	10	5	0	1	4	7	8	.250	.362	.450	115	1	0	0	0	1.000	0	C-13	0.2
1946	NY-A	13	21	4	6	0	0	0	1	3	7	.286	.375	.333	98	0	0	0	0	.977	2	C-12	0.3
1947	NY-A	3	10	0	2	0	0	0	0	2	2	.200	.333	.200	51	-1	0	0	0	1.000	-2	/C-3	-0.2
1949	Phi-N	4	4	1	0	0	0	0	0	2	1	.000	.333	.000	-3	-0	0	0	0	1.000	0	/C-1,2-1,S	0.0
1950	*Phi-N	11	20	2	5	0	1	0	4	4	3	.250	.400	.350	101	0	0	0	0	1.000	-1	/C-9	-0.1
1951	Phi-N	4	9	2	2	0	0	0	1	3	2	.222	.417	.222	78	-0	0	0	0	1.000	-3	/C-3,2-1	-0.3
Total	8	102	203	26	44	11	1	5	25	31	41	.217	.326	.355	78	-6	0	1		.974	-3	/C-62,2-2,S	-0.7

■ AL SIMMONS
Simmons, Aloysius Harry "Bucketfoot Al" (b: Aloys Szymanski)
b: 5/22/02, Milwaukee, Wis.   d: 5/26/56, Milwaukee, Wis.   BR/TR, 5'11", 190 lbs.   Deb: 4/15/24   CH

YEAR	TM/L	G	AB	R	H	2B	3B	HR	RBI	BB	SO	AVG	OBP	SLG	PRO+	BR/A	SB	CS	SBR	FA	FR	G/POS	TPR
1924	Phi-A	152	594	69	183	31	9	8	102	30	60	.308	.343	.431	98	-4	16	15	-4	.976	7	*O-152	-1.1
1925	Phi-A	153	654	122	**253**	43	12	24	129	35	41	.387	.419	.599	146	42	7	14	-6	.966	5	*O-153	2.8
1926	Phi-A	147	583	90	199	53	10	19	109	48	49	.341	.392	.564	139	31	11	3	2	.975	-4	*O-147	1.7
1927	Phi-A	106	406	86	159	36	11	15	108	31	30	.392	.436	.645	168	39	10	2	2	.985	3	*O-105	3.4
1928	Phi-A	119	464	78	163	33	9	15	107	31	30	.351	.396	.558	144	28	4	1	-2	.988	2	*O-114	1.9
1929	*Phi-A	143	581	114	212	41	9	34	157	31	38	.365	.398	.642	158	46	4	2	0	.989	17	*O-142	4.9
1930	*Phi-A	138	554	**152**	211	41	16	36	165	39	34	**.381**	.423	.708	173	58	9	2	2	**.990**	6	*O-136	4.6
1931	*Phi-A	128	513	105	200	37	13	22	128	47	45	**.390**	.444	.641	172	52	3	3	-1	.987	8	*O-128	4.6
1932	Phi-A	154	670	144	**216**	28	9	35	151	47	76	.322	.368	.548	129	26	4	2	0	.980	-5	*O-154	1.0
1933	Chi-A★	146	605	85	200	29	10	14	119	39	49	.331	.373	.481	130	24	5	1	0	.990	14	*O-145	3.0
1934	Chi-A★	138	558	102	192	36	7	18	104	53	58	.344	.403	.530	135	28	3	2	-0	.987	5	*O-138	2.5
1935	Chi-A★	128	525	68	140	22	7	16	79	33	43	.267	.313	.427	87	-12	4	6	-2	.981	1	*O-126	-1.8
1936	Det-A	143	568	96	186	38	6	13	112	49	35	.327	.383	.484	112	10	6	4	-1	**.986**	-4	*O-138/1-1	0.0
1937	Was-A	103	419	60	117	21	10	8	84	29	35	.279	.329	.434	95	-5	3	2	-0	.984	5	*O-102	-0.4
1938	Was-A	125	470	79	142	23	6	21	95	38	40	.302	.357	.511	123	14	2	1	0	.983	-8	*O-117	0.2
1939	Bos-N	93	330	39	93	17	5	7	43	22	40	.282	.331	.427	110	3	0			.982	-0	O-82	0.0
	*Cin-N	9	21	0	3	0	0	0	1	2	3	.143	.217	.143	-1	-3	0			.938	1	/O-5	-0.2

YEAR	TM/L	G	AB	R	H	2B	3B	HR	RBI	BB	SO	AVG	OBP	SLG	PRO+	BR/A	SB	CS	SBR	FA	FR	G/POS	TPR
	Yr	102	351	39	96	17	5	7	44	24	43	.274	.324	.410	103	-0	0			.978	1	O-87	-0.2
1940	Phi-A	37	81	7	25	4	0	1	19	4	8	.309	.341	.395	92	-1	0	0	0	.963	2	O-18	0.0
1941	Phi-A	9	24	1	3	1	0	0	1	1	2	.125	.160	.167	-14	-4	0	0	0	1.000	1	/O-5	-0.4
1943	Bos-A	40	133	9	27	5	0	1	12	8	21	.203	.248	.263	49	-9	0	1	-1	.986	-2	/O-33	-1.4
1944	Phi-A	4	6	1	3	0	0	0	2	0	0	.500	.500	.500	189	1	0	0	0	1.000	-0	/O-2	0.0
Total	20	2215	8759	1507	2927	539	149	307	1827	615	737	.334	.380	.535	132	361	88	64		.982	53	*O-2142/1-1	25.6

■ HACK SIMMONS   Simmons, George Washington   b: 1/29/1885, Brooklyn, N.Y.   d: 4/26/42, Arverne, N.Y.   BR/TR, 5'8", 179 lbs.   Deb: 4/15/10

YEAR	TM/L	G	AB	R	H	2B	3B	HR	RBI	BB	SO	AVG	OBP	SLG	PRO+	BR/A	SB	CS	SBR	FA	FR	G/POS	TPR
1910	Det-A	42	110	12	25	3	1	0	9	10		.227	.303	.273	75	-3	1			.984	-0	1-22/3-7,O	-0.3
1912	NY-A	110	401	45	96	17	2	0	41	33		.239	.308	.292	68	-17	19			.946	-21	2-88,1-13/S	-4.0
1914	Bal-F	114	352	50	95	16	5	1	38	32	26	.270	.341	.352	77	-11	7			.894	-8	O-73,2-26/1S3	-2.4
1915	Bal-F	39	88	8	18	7	1	0	14	10	9	.205	.293	.341	67	-4	1			1.000	-3	2-13,O-13	-0.9
Total	4	305	951	115	234	43	9	2	102	85	35	.246	.318	.317	72	-36	28			.953	-32	2-127/O-88,13S	-7.6

■ JOHN SIMMONS   Simmons, John Earl   b: 7/7/24, Birmingham, Ala.   BR/TR, 6'1.5", 192 lbs.   Deb: 4/22/49

YEAR	TM/L	G	AB	R	H	2B	3B	HR	RBI	BB	SO	AVG	OBP	SLG	PRO+	BR/A	SB	CS	SBR	FA	FR	G/POS	TPR
1949	Was-A	62	93	12	20	0	0	0	5	11	6	.215	.298	.215	38	-8	0	0	0	1.000	-5	O-26	-1.4

■ JOE SIMMONS   Simmons, Joseph S.   b: 6/13/1845, New York, N.Y.   5'9", 166 lbs.   Deb: 5/8/1871   M

YEAR	TM/L	G	AB	R	H	2B	3B	HR	RBI	BB	SO	AVG	OBP	SLG	PRO+	BR/A	SB	CS	SBR	FA	FR	G/POS	TPR
1871	Chi-n	27	129	29	28	6	1	0	17	1	0	.217	.223	.279	39	-12	4					*O-25/1-2	-0.7
1872	Cle-n	18	89	11	23	5	1	0	9	1	2	.258	.267	.337	90	-1						1-14/O-3	0.0
1875	Wes-n	13	53	5	9	1	0	0	0			.170	.170	.189	23	-4						O-10/1-3M	-0.4
Total	3 n	58	271	45	60	12	2	0			2	.221	.227	.280	51	-16						/O-38,1-19	-1.1

■ NELSON SIMMONS   Simmons, Nelson Bernard   b: 6/27/63, Washington, D.C.   BB/TR, 6'1", 185 lbs.   Deb: 9/4/84

YEAR	TM/L	G	AB	R	H	2B	3B	HR	RBI	BB	SO	AVG	OBP	SLG	PRO+	BR/A	SB	CS	SBR	FA	FR	G/POS	TPR
1984	Det-A	9	30	4	13	2	0	0	3	2	5	.433	.469	.500	169	3	1	0	0	1.000	-1	/O-5,D-4	0.2
1985	Det-A	75	251	31	60	11	0	10	33	26	41	.239	.310	.402	94	-2	1	0	0	.945	-1	O-38,D-31	-0.5
1987	Bal-A	16	49	3	13	1	1	1	4	3	8	.265	.308	.388	85	-1	0	1	-1	1.000	-1	O-13/D-1	-0.1
Total	3	100	330	38	86	14	1	11	40	31	54	.261	.324	.409	99	-1	2	1	0	.963	-1	/O-56,D-36	-0.4

■ TED SIMMONS   Simmons, Ted Lyle   b: 8/9/49, Highland Park, Mich.   BB/TR, 6', 200 lbs.   Deb: 9/21/68

YEAR	TM/L	G	AB	R	H	2B	3B	HR	RBI	BB	SO	AVG	OBP	SLG	PRO+	BR/A	SB	CS	SBR	FA	FR	G/POS	TPR
1968	StL-N	2	3	0	1	0	0	0	1	1	1	.333	.500	.333	156	0	0	0	0	1.000	-1	/C-2	0.0
1969	StL-N	5	14	0	3	0	1	0	3	1	1	.214	.267	.357	73	-1	0	0	0	.957	-1	/C-4	-0.2
1970	StL-N	82	284	29	69	8	3	2	24	37	37	.243	.334	.317	74	-10	2	2	-1	.990	-3	C-79	-0.0
1971	StL-N	133	510	64	155	32	4	7	77	36	50	.304	.353	.424	115	10	1	3	-2	.989	-13	*C-130	0.9
1972	StL-N☆	152	594	70	180	36	6	16	96	29	57	.303	.338	.465	127	19	1	3	-2	.991	6	*C-135,1-15	3.0
1973	StL-N★	161	619	62	192	36	2	13	91	61	47	.310	.374	.438	124	21	2	2	-1	.987	10	*C-153/1-6,O	3.7
1974	StL-N☆	152	599	66	163	33	6	20	103	47	35	.272	.331	.447	117	11	0	0	0	.986	-4	*C-141,1-12	1.3
1975	StL-N	157	581	80	193	32	3	18	100	63	35	.332	.398	.491	141	32	1	3	-2	.983	-6	*C-154/1-2,O	3.2
1976	StL-N	150	546	60	159	35	3	5	75	73	35	.291	.375	.394	117	14	0	7	-4	.993	-9	*C-113,1-30/O3	0.2
1977	StL-N★	150	516	82	164	25	3	21	95	79	37	.318	.410	.500	145	35	2	6	-3	.987	-14	*C-143/O-1	2.2
1978	StL-N★	152	516	71	148	40	5	22	80	77	39	.287	.383	.512	150	35	1	1	-0	.988	-6	*C-134,O-23	3.3
1979	StL-N†	123	448	68	127	22	0	26	87	61	34	.283	.374	.507	137	23	0	1	-1	.985	-5	*C-122	2.2
1980	StL-N	145	495	84	150	33	2	21	98	59	45	.303	.379	.505	140	27	1	0	0	.985	-9	*C-129/O-5	2.4
1981	*Mil-A★	100	380	45	82	13	3	14	61	23	32	.216	.266	.376	88	-8	0	1	-1	.980	-9	C-75,D-22/1	-1.6
1982	*Mil-A	137	539	73	145	29	0	23	97	32	40	.269	.312	.451	114	8	0	0	0	**.995**	-1	*C-121,D-15	1.1
1983	Mil-A★	153	600	76	185	39	3	13	108	41	51	.308	.355	.448	129	22	4	2	0	.975	-4	C-86,D-66	2.0
1984	Mil-A	132	497	44	110	23	2	4	52	30	40	.221	.267	.300	60	-28	3	0	1	.995	-1	D-77,1-37,3	-3.3
1985	Mil-A	143	528	60	144	28	2	12	76	57	32	.273	.345	.402	104	4	1	1	-0	.992	-3	D-99,1-28,C/3	-0.3
1986	Atl-N	76	127	14	32	5	0	4	25	12	14	.252	.321	.386	89	-2	1	1	0	.964	-3	1-14,C-10/3	-0.5
1987	Atl-N	73	177	20	49	8	0	4	30	21	23	.277	.354	.390	92	-2	1	1	-0	.984	-1	1-28,C-15/3	-0.4
1988	Atl-N	78	107	6	21	6	0	2	11	15	9	.196	.295	.308	70	-4	0	0	0	.993	-1	1-19,C-10	-0.6
Total	21	2456	8680	1074	2472	483	47	248	1389	855	694	.285	.352	.437	118	208	21	33	-14	.987	-79	*C-1771,D-279,1/O3	16.8

■ MIKE SIMMS   Simms, Michael Howard   b: 1/12/67, Orange, Cal.   BR/TR, 6'4", 185 lbs.   Deb: 9/5/90

YEAR	TM/L	G	AB	R	H	2B	3B	HR	RBI	BB	SO	AVG	OBP	SLG	PRO+	BR/A	SB	CS	SBR	FA	FR	G/POS	TPR
1990	Hou-N	12	13	3	4	1	0	1	2	0	4	.308	.308	.615	152	1	0	0	0	1.000	-0	/1-6	0.1
1991	Hou-N	49	123	18	25	5	0	3	16	18	38	.203	.305	.317	80	-3	0	0	0	.889	-5	O-41	-0.9
1992	Hou-N	15	24	1	6	1	0	1	3	2	9	.250	.333	.417	116	0	0	0	0	1.000	-1	/O-9,1-1	-0.1
1994	Hou-N	6	12	1	1	1	0	0	1	0	5	.083	.083	.167	-38	-2	1	0	0	.857	-0	/O-3	-0.2
Total	4	82	172	23	36	8	0	5	21	20	56	.209	.295	.343	82	-4	2	0	0	.899	-6	/O-53,1-7	-1.1

■ HANK SIMON   Simon, Henry Joseph   b: 8/25/1862, Hawkinsville, N.Y.   d: 1/1/25, Albany, N.Y.   BR/TR,   Deb: 10/7/1887

YEAR	TM/L	G	AB	R	H	2B	3B	HR	RBI	BB	SO	AVG	OBP	SLG	PRO+	BR/A	SB	CS	SBR	FA	FR	G/POS	TPR
1887	Cle-a	3	10	1	1	0	0	0	0			.100	.100	.100	-45	-2	0			1.000	-1	/O-3	-0.2
1890	Bro-a	89	373	66	96	17	11	0		34		.257	.337	.362	105	2	23			.951	6	O-89	0.4
	Syr-a	38	156	33	47	5	3	2		17		.301	.370	.410	145	9	12			.941	-3	O-38	0.4
	Yr	127	529	99	143	22	14	2		51		.270	.337	.376	116	10	35			.948	3	*O-127	0.8
Total	2	130	539	100	144	22	14	2		51		.267	.333	.371	113	9	35			.949	3	O-130	0.6

■ MIKE SIMON   Simon, Michael Edward   b: 4/13/1883, Hayden, Ind.   d: 6/10/63, Los Angeles, Cal.   BR/TR, 5'11", 188 lbs.   Deb: 6/27/09

YEAR	TM/L	G	AB	R	H	2B	3B	HR	RBI	BB	SO	AVG	OBP	SLG	PRO+	BR/A	SB	CS	SBR	FA	FR	G/POS	TPR
1909	Pit-N	12	18	2	3	0	0	0	2	1		.167	.211	.167	16	-2	0			.917	-1	/C-9	-0.1
1910	Pit-N	22	50	3	10	0	0	0	5	1	2	.200	.216	.240	31	-4	1			1.000	-4	C-14	-0.8
1911	Pit-N	71	215	19	49	4	3	0	22	10	14	.228	.275	.274	52	-14	1			.968	0	C-68	-0.8
1912	Pit-N	42	113	10	34	2	1	0	11	5	9	.301	.331	.336	84	-3	1			.991	3	C-40	0.4
1913	Pit-N	92	255	23	63	6	2	1	17	10	15	.247	.281	.298	68	-11	3			.975	19	C-92	1.5
1914	StL-F	93	276	21	57	11	2	0	21	18	21	.207	.263	.261	34	-27	2			.984	12	C-78	-0.9
1915	Bro-F	47	142	7	25	5	1	0	12	9	12	.176	.225	.225	21	-16	1			.992	-0	C-45	-1.4
Total	7	379	1069	85	241	28	10	1	90	54	73	.225	.269	.273	48	-77	9			.979	30	C-346	-2.1

■ SYL SIMON   Simon, Sylvester Adam "Sammy"   b: 12/14/1897, Evansville, Ind.   d: 2/28/73, Chandler, Ind.   BR/TR, 5'10.5", 170 lbs.   Deb: 10/1/23

YEAR	TM/L	G	AB	R	H	2B	3B	HR	RBI	BB	SO	AVG	OBP	SLG	PRO+	BR/A	SB	CS	SBR	FA	FR	G/POS	TPR
1923	StL-A	1	1	0	0	0	0	0	0			.000	.000	.000	-95	-0	0	0	0	.000	0	H	0.0
1924	StL-A	23	32	5	8	1	1	0	6	3	5	.250	.314	.344	66	-2	0	0	0	.889	-2	/3-6,S-5	-0.1
Total	2	24	33	5	8	1	1	0	6	3	5	.242	.306	.333	61	-2	0	0	0	.889	-0	/3-6,S-5	-0.1

■ MEL SIMONS   Simons, Melbern Ellis "Butch"   b: 7/1/1900, Carlyle, Ill.   d: 11/10/74, Paducah, Ky.   BL/TR, 5'10", 175 lbs.   Deb: 4/14/31

YEAR	TM/L	G	AB	R	H	2B	3B	HR	RBI	BB	SO	AVG	OBP	SLG	PRO+	BR/A	SB	CS	SBR	FA	FR	G/POS	TPR
1931	Chi-A	68	189	24	52	9	0	0	12	12	17	.275	.318	.323	73	-7	1	1	-0	.950	-9	O-59	-1.8
1932	Chi-A	7	5	0	0	0	0	0	0	0	1	.000	.000	.000	-99	-2	0	0	0	1.000	-0	/O-6	-0.4
Total	2	75	194	24	52	9	0	0	12	12	18	.268	.311	.314	69	-9	1	1	-0	.951	-12	/O-65	-2.2

■ HARRY SIMPSON   Simpson, Harry Leon "Suitcase" or "Goody"   b: 12/3/25, Atlanta, Ga.   d: 4/3/79, Akron, Ohio   BL/TR, 6'1", 180 lbs.   Deb: 4/21/51

YEAR	TM/L	G	AB	R	H	2B	3B	HR	RBI	BB	SO	AVG	OBP	SLG	PRO+	BR/A	SB	CS	SBR	FA	FR	G/POS	TPR
1951	Cle-A	122	332	51	76	7	0	7	24	45	48	.229	.325	.313	77	-10	6	4	-1	.971	-4	O-68,1-50	-1.8
1952	Cle-A	146	545	66	145	21	10	10	65	56	82	.266	.337	.396	111	6	5	3	-0	.988	-4	*O-127,1-28	-0.4
1953	Cle-A	82	242	25	55	3	1	7	22	18	27	.227	.284	.335	68	-11	0	0	0	.968	-6	O-69/1-2	-2.0
1955	Cle-A	3	1	1	0	0	0	0	0	0	0	.000	.667	.000	88	0	0	0	0			H	0.0
	KC-A	112	396	42	119	16	7	5	52	34	61	.301	.359	.414	106	3	3	5	0	.978	1	*O-100/1-3	-0.2
	Yr	115	397	43	119	16	7	5	52	34	61	.300	.361	.413	106	3	3	5	0	.978	1	*O-100/1-3	-0.2
1956	KC-A★	141	543	76	159	22	11	21	105	47	82	.293	.350	.490	119	13	2	3	-1	.965	-15	*O-111,1-32	-1.1

YEAR	TM/L	G	AB	R	H	2B	3B	HR	RBI	BB	SO	AVG	OBP	SLG	PRO+	BR/A	SB	CS	SBR	FA	FR	G/POS	TPR
1957	KC-A	50	179	24	53	9	6	6	24	12	28	.296	.340	.514	128	6	0	1	-1	.996	1	1-27,O-21	0.3
	*NY-A	75	224	27	56	7	3	7	39	19	36	.250	.309	.402	94	-2	1	0	0	.952	-2	O-42,1-21	-0.8
	Yr	125	403	51	109	16	**9**	13	63	31	64	.270	.323	.452	110	4	1	1	-0	.957	-2	O-63,1-48	-0.5
1958	NY-A	24	51	1	11	2	1	0	6	6	12	.216	.310	.294	70	-2	0	0	0	1.000	-5	O-15	-0.5
	KC-A	78	212	21	56	7	1	7	27	26	33	.264	.345	.406	104	1	0	2	-1	.990	-3	1-43,O-11	-0.6
	Yr	102	263	22	67	9	2	7	33	32	45	.255	.338	.384	98	-0	0	2	-1	.990	-5	1-43,O-26	-1.1
1959	KC-A	8	14	1	4	0	0	1	2	2	4	.286	.412	.500	146	1	0	0	0	1.000	0	/1-4	0.1
	Chi-A	38	75	5	14	5	1	2	13	4	14	.187	.228	.360	59	-5	0	0	0	.947	-2	O-12/1-1	-0.7
	Yr	46	89	6	18	5	1	3	15	6	18	.202	.260	.382	75	-3	0	0	0	.947	-2	O-12/1-5	-0.6
	Pit-N	9	15	3	4	2	0	0	2	0	2	.267	.267	.400	75	-1	0	0	0	1.000	-0	/O-3	-0.1
Total	8	888	2829	343	752	101	41	73	381	271	429	.266	.332	.408	102	-1	17	18	-6	.974	-37	O-579,1-211	-7.8

■ JOE SIMPSON
Simpson, Joe Allen b: 12/31/51, Purcell, Okla. BL/TL, 6'3", 175 lbs. Deb: 9/2/75

YEAR	TM/L	G	AB	R	H	2B	3B	HR	RBI	BB	SO	AVG	OBP	SLG	PRO+	BR/A	SB	CS	SBR	FA	FR	G/POS	TPR
1975	LA-N	9	6	3	2	0	0	0	0	0	2	.333	.333	.333	89	-0	0	0	0	1.000	-2	/O-6	-0.2
1976	LA-N	23	30	2	4	1	0	0	0	1	6	.133	.161	.167	-7	-4	0	1	-1	1.000	-4	O-20	-1.0
1977	LA-N	29	23	2	4	0	0	0	1	2	6	.174	.240	.174	13	-3	1	1	-0	.957	-6	O-28/1-1	-1.0
1978	LA-N	10	5	1	2	0	0	0	1	0	2	.400	.400	.400	125	0	0	0	0	1.000	-3	O-10	-0.3
1979	Sea-A	120	265	29	75	11	0	2	27	11	21	.283	.314	.347	77	-9	6	3	0	.966	-5	*O-105	-1.6
1980	Sea-A	129	365	42	91	15	3	3	34	28	43	.249	.305	.332	74	-13	17	4	3	.977	-8	*O-119/1-3	-2.3
1981	Sea-A	91	288	32	64	11	3	2	30	15	41	.222	.263	.302	60	-15	12	3	2	.978	-0	O-88	-1.7
1982	Sea-A	105	296	39	76	14	4	2	23	22	48	.257	.313	.351	80	-8	8	14	-6	.984	-7	O-97	-2.3
1983	KC-A	91	119	16	20	2	0	0	8	11	21	.168	.250	.218	30	-11	1	1	-0	.995	-0	1-54,O-38/PD	-1.3
Total	9	607	1397	166	338	54	12	9	124	90	190	.242	.291	.317	67	-63	45	27	-3	.978	-35	O-511/1-58,PD	-11.7

■ MARTY SIMPSON
Simpson, Martin b: Baltimore, Md. Deb: 5/14/1873

YEAR	TM/L	G	AB	R	H	2B	3B	HR	RBI	BB	SO	AVG	OBP	SLG	PRO+	BR/A	SB	CS	SBR	FA	FR	G/POS	TPR
1873	Mar-n	4	15	4	2	0	0	0	1	0	0	.133	.133	.133	-28	-2						/2-3,C-1	-0.2

■ DICK SIMPSON
Simpson, Richard Charles b: 7/28/43, Washington, D.C. BR/TR, 6'4", 176 lbs. Deb: 9/21/62

YEAR	TM/L	G	AB	R	H	2B	3B	HR	RBI	BB	SO	AVG	OBP	SLG	PRO+	BR/A	SB	CS	SBR	FA	FR	G/POS	TPR
1962	LA-A	6	8	1	2	1	0	0	1	2	3	.250	.400	.375	114	0	0	0	0	1.000	-1	/O-4	0.0
1964	LA-A	21	50	11	7	1	0	2	4	8	15	.140	.259	.280	55	-3	2	2	-1	1.000	-2	O-16	-0.7
1965	Cal-A	8	27	2	6	1	0	0	3	2	8	.222	.276	.259	54	-2	1	0	0	.875	-1	O-8	-0.3
1966	Cin-N	92	84	26	20	2	0	4	14	10	32	.238	.333	.405	96	-0	0	1	-1	.921	-18	O-64	-2.1
1967	Cin-N	44	54	8	14	3	0	1	6	7	11	.259	.344	.370	94	-0	0	1	-1	.973	-2	O-26	-0.3
1968	StL-N	26	56	11	13	0	0	3	8	8	21	.232	.328	.393	117	1	0	1	-1	1.000	-0	O-22	-0.4
	Hou-N	59	177	25	33	7	2	3	11	20	61	.186	.284	.299	77	-5	4	4	-1	.970	-6	O-49	-1.7
	Yr	85	233	36	46	7	2	6	19	28	82	.197	.294	.322	86	-4	4	5	-2	.979	-9	O-71	-2.1
1969	NY-A	6	11	2	3	2	0	0	4	3	6	.273	.429	.455	153	1	0	0	0	1.000	-1	/O-5	0.0
	Sea-A	26	51	8	9	2	0	2	5	4	17	.176	.236	.333	59	-3	3	1	0	1.000	-3	O-17	-0.7
	Yr	32	62	10	12	4	0	2	9	7	23	.194	.275	.355	77	-2	3	1	0	1.000	-4	O-22	-0.7
Total	7	288	518	94	107	19	2	15	56	64	174	.207	.301	.338	84	-11	10	10	-3	.967	-35	O-211	-6.2

■ DUKE SIMS
Sims, Duane B b: 6/5/41, Salt Lake City, Ut. BL/TR, 6'2", 205 lbs. Deb: 9/22/64

YEAR	TM/L	G	AB	R	H	2B	3B	HR	RBI	BB	SO	AVG	OBP	SLG	PRO+	BR/A	SB	CS	SBR	FA	FR	G/POS	TPR
1964	Cle-A	2	6	0	0	0	0	0	0	0	2	.000	.000	.000	-99	-2	0	0	0	1.000	-1	/C-1	-0.1
1965	Cle-A	48	118	9	21	0	0	6	15	15	33	.178	.271	.331	69	-5	0	0	0	.980	-2	C-40	-0.5
1966	Cle-A	52	133	12	35	2	2	6	19	11	31	.263	.338	.444	122	4	0	1	-1	.975	-5	C-48	0.1
1967	Cle-A	88	272	25	55	8	2	12	37	30	64	.202	.295	.379	97	-1	3	3	-1	.989	-3	C-85	0.0
1968	Cle-A	122	361	48	90	21	0	11	44	62	68	.249	.367	.399	134	17	1	3	-2	.983	-1	C-84,1-31/O	2.0
1969	Cle-A	114	326	40	77	8	0	18	45	66	80	.236	.374	.426	120	10	2	2	-1	.991	-4	*C-102/O-3,1	1.2
1970	Cle-A	110	345	46	91	12	0	23	56	46	59	.264	.360	.499	128	13	0	4	-2	.993	-2	C-39,O-36,1	0.8
1971	LA-N	90	230	23	63	7	2	6	25	30	39	.274	.360	.400	122	7	0	1	-1	.992	0	C-74	1.0
1972	LA-N	51	151	7	29	7	0	2	11	17	23	.192	.278	.278	60	-8	0	0	0	.989	-1	C-48	-0.8
	*Det-A	38	98	11	31	4	0	4	19	19	18	.316	.432	.480	166	9	0	0	0	.994	-3	C-25/O-4	0.8
1973	Det-A	80	252	31	61	10	0	8	30	30	36	.242	.327	.377	92	-3	1	2	-1	.979	2	C-68/O-6	0.1
	NY-A	4	9	3	3	0	0	1	3	1	3	.333	.500	.667	234	2	0	0	0	1.000	1	/C-1,D-2	0.2
	Yr	84	261	34	64	10	0	9	31	33	37	.245	.334	.387	97	-1	1	2	-1	.979	2	C-69/O-6,D	0.3
1974	NY-A	5	15	1	2	1	0	0	2	1	2	.133	.188	.200	12	-2	0	0	0	1.000	-0	/C-1,D-3	-0.2
	Tex-A	39	106	7	22	0	0	3	6	8	24	.208	.282	.292	67	-4	0	0	0	.970	-3	C-30/O-1,D	-0.7
	Yr	44	121	8	24	1	0	3	8	9	29	.198	.271	.281	60	-6	0	0	0	.971	-3	C-31/D-5,O	-0.9
Total	11	843	2422	263	580	80	6	100	310	338	483	.239	.341	.401	111	38	6	16	-8	.986	-20	C-646/1-61,OD	3.9

■ GREG SIMS
Sims, Gregory Emmett b: 6/28/46, San Francisco, Cal BB/TR, 6', 190 lbs. Deb: 4/15/66

YEAR	TM/L	G	AB	R	H	2B	3B	HR	RBI	BB	SO	AVG	OBP	SLG	PRO+	BR/A	SB	CS	SBR	FA	FR	G/POS	TPR
1966	Hou-N	7	6	1	1	0	0	0	0	1	3	.167	.286	.167	32	-1	0	0	0	.500	-0	/O-1	-0.1

■ MATT SINATRO
Sinatro, Matthew Stephen b: 3/22/60, Hartford, Conn. BR/TR, 5'9", 175 lbs. Deb: 9/22/81

YEAR	TM/L	G	AB	R	H	2B	3B	HR	RBI	BB	SO	AVG	OBP	SLG	PRO+	BR/A	SB	CS	SBR	FA	FR	G/POS	TPR
1981	Atl-N	12	32	4	9	1	1	0	4	5	4	.281	.378	.375	111	1	1	0	0	1.000	4	C-12	0.6
1982	Atl-N	37	81	10	11	2	0	1	4	4	9	.136	.176	.198	4	-10	0	1	-1	1.000	4	C-35	-0.7
1983	Atl-N	7	12	0	2	0	0	0	2	2	1	.167	.286	.167	26	-1	0	0	0	.967	2	/C-7	0.0
1984	Atl-N	2	4	0	0	0	0	0	0	0	0	.000	.000	.000	-93	-1	0	0	0	1.000	-0	/C-2	-0.2
1987	Oak-A	6	3	0	0	0	0	0	0	0	0	.000	.000	.000	-99	-1	0	0	0	1.000	-0	/C-6	-0.1
1988	Oak-A	10	9	1	3	2	0	0	5	0	1	.333	.333	.556	149	1	0	0	0	1.000	2	/C-9	0.3
1989	Det-A	13	25	2	3	0	0	0	1	1	3	.120	.185	.120	-13	-4	0	0	0	1.000	0	C-13	-0.3
1990	Sea-A	30	50	2	15	1	0	0	4	1	10	.300	.352	.320	88	-1	0	0	0	.992	7	C-28	0.7
1991	Sea-A	5	8	1	2	0	0	0	1	1	1	.250	.333	.250	64	-0	0	0	0	1.000	1	/C-5	0.1
1992	Sea-A	18	28	0	3	0	0	0	0	1	5	.107	.107	.107	-40	-5	0	0	0	1.000	1	C-18	-0.5
Total	10	140	252	20	48	6	1	1	21	17	35	.190	.244	.234	34	-22	2	1	0	.996	19	C-135	-0.1

■ HOSEA SINER
Siner, Hosea John b: 3/20/1885, Shelburn, Ind. d: 6/10/48, Sullivan, Ind. BR/TR, 5'10.5", 185 lbs. Deb: 7/28/09

YEAR	TM/L	G	AB	R	H	2B	3B	HR	RBI	BB	SO	AVG	OBP	SLG	PRO+	BR/A	SB	CS	SBR	FA	FR	G/POS	TPR
1909	Bos-N	10	23	1	3	0	0	0	1	0	2	.130	.200	.130		-3	0			.909	-1	/3-5,2-1,S	-0.4

■ DUANE SINGLETON
Singleton, Duane Earl b: 8/6/72, Staten Island, N.Y. BL/TR, 6'1", 170 lbs. Deb: 8/4/94

YEAR	TM/L	G	AB	R	H	2B	3B	HR	RBI	BB	SO	AVG	OBP	SLG	PRO+	BR/A	SB	CS	SBR	FA	FR	G/POS	TPR
1994	Mil-A	2	0	0	0	0	0	0	0	0	0	—	—	—	—		0	0	0	1.000	-1	/O-2	-0.1

■ KEN SINGLETON
Singleton, Kenneth Wayne b: 6/10/47, New York, N.Y. BB/TR, 6'4", 213 lbs. Deb: 6/24/70

YEAR	TM/L	G	AB	R	H	2B	3B	HR	RBI	BB	SO	AVG	OBP	SLG	PRO+	BR/A	SB	CS	SBR	FA	FR	G/POS	TPR
1970	NY-N	69	198	22	52	8	0	5	26	30	48	.263	.362	.379	99		0	1	-0	.968	-0	O-51	-0.3
1971	NY-N	115	298	34	73	5	0	13	46	61	64	.245	.377	.393	120	10	0	1	-1	.974	-5	O-96	0.0
1972	Mon-N	142	507	77	139	23	2	14	50	70	99	.274	.384	.410	118	13	5	10	-5	.972	-0	*O-137	0.2
1973	Mon-N	162	560	100	169	26	2	23	103	123	91	.302	**.429**	.479	146	41	3	8	-4	.983	3	*O-161	3.3
1974	Mon-N	148	511	68	141	20	2	9	74	93	84	.276	.387	.376	108	9	5	2	0	.955	-9	*O-143	-0.6
1975	Bal-A	155	586	88	176	37	4	15	55	118	82	.300	.418	.454	156	49	3	5	-2	.990	-6	*O-155	3.5
1976	Bal-A	154	544	62	151	25	1	13	70	79	76	.278	.369	.403	134	25	2	2	-1	.983	-0	*O-134,D-19	1.6
1977	Bal-A★	152	536	90	176	24	0	24	99	107	101	.328	.442	.507	168	57	0	1	-0	.986	1	*O-150/D-1	4.9
1978	Bal-A	149	502	67	147	21	2	20	81	98	94	.293	.410	.462	**154**	40	0	0	0	.976	-13	*O-140/D-5	2.2
1979	*Bal-A★	159	570	93	168	29	1	35	111	109	118	.295	.409	.533	158	49	3	3	-1	.988	-8	*O-143/D-16	3.6
1980	Bal-A	156	583	85	177	28	2	24	104	92	94	.304	.399	.485	143	37	0	0	-1	.984	-10	*O-151/D-5	1.9
1981	Bal-A★	103	363	48	101	16	1	13	49	61	59	.278	.382	.435	135	18	0	0	0	**1.000**	-3	O-72,D-30	1.2

YEAR	TM/L	G	AB	R	H	2B	3B	HR	RBI	BB	SO	AVG	OBP	SLG	PRO+	BR/A	SB	CS	SBR	FA	FR	G/POS	TPR
1982	Bal-A	156	561	71	141	27	2	14	77	86	93	.251	.353	.381	102	4	0	1	-1	1.000	-0	*D-148/O-5	-0.3
1983	*Bal-A	151	507	52	140	21	3	18	84	99	83	.276	.395	.436	131	25	0	2	-1	.000	0	*D-150	1.9
1984	Bal-A	111	363	28	78	7	1	6	36	37	60	.215	.287	.289	61	-19	0	0	0	.000	0	*D-103	-2.2
Total	15	2082	7189	985	2029	317	25	246	1065	1263	1246	.282	.391	.436	132	359	21	36	-15	.980	-52	*O-1538,D-477	20.9

■ FRED SINGTON
Sington, Frederic William   b: 2/24/10, Birmingham, Ala.   BR/TR, 6'2", 215 lbs.   Deb: 9/23/34

YEAR	TM/L	G	AB	R	H	2B	3B	HR	RBI	BB	SO	AVG	OBP	SLG	PRO+	BR/A	SB	CS	SBR	FA	FR	G/POS	TPR
1934	Was-A	9	35	2	10	2	0	0	6	4	3	.286	.359	.343	85	-1	0	1	-1	.933	-1	/O-9	-0.2
1935	Was-A	20	22	1	4	0	0	0	3	5	1	.182	.333	.182	38	-2	0	0	0	.889	0	/O-4	-0.2
1936	Was-A	25	94	13	30	8	0	1	28	15	9	.319	.413	.436	116	3	0	0	0	.946	-1	O-25	0.1
1937	Was-A	78	228	27	54	15	4	3	36	37	33	.237	.348	.377	87	-4	1	1	-0	.961	-3	O-64	-0.9
1938	Bro-N	17	53	10	19	6	1	2	5	13	5	.358	.493	.623	200	8	1			1.000	-0	O-17	0.6
1939	Bro-N	32	84	13	23	5	0	1	7	15	15	.274	.384	.369	100	1	0			.978	-1	O-22	-0.1
Total	6	181	516	66	140	36	5	7	85	89	66	.271	.382	.401	104	5	2	2		.961	-7	O-141	-0.7

■ DICK SIPEK
Sipek, Richard Francis   b: 1/16/23, Chicago, Ill.   BL/TR, 5'9", 170 lbs.   Deb: 4/28/45

YEAR	TM/L	G	AB	R	H	2B	3B	HR	RBI	BB	SO	AVG	OBP	SLG	PRO+	BR/A	SB	CS	SBR	FA	FR	G/POS	TPR
1945	Cin-N	82	156	14	38	6	2	0	13	9	15	.244	.302	.308	71	-6	0			.972	-0	O-31	-0.8

■ JOHN SIPIN
Sipin, John White   b: 8/29/46, Watsonville, Cal.   BR/TR, 6'1.5", 175 lbs.   Deb: 5/24/69

YEAR	TM/L	G	AB	R	H	2B	3B	HR	RBI	BB	SO	AVG	OBP	SLG	PRO+	BR/A	SB	CS	SBR	FA	FR	G/POS	TPR
1969	SD-N	68	229	22	51	12	2	2	9	8	44	.223	.252	.319	61	-13	2	0	1	.976	-2	2-60	-1.0

■ GEORGE SISLER
Sisler, George Harold "Georgeous George"   b: 3/24/1893, Manchester, Ohio   d: 3/26/73, Richmond Heights, Mo.   BL/TL, 5'11", 170 lbs.   Deb: 6/28/15   FMCH

YEAR	TM/L	G	AB	R	H	2B	3B	HR	RBI	BB	SO	AVG	OBP	SLG	PRO+	BR/A	SB	CS	SBR	FA	FR	G/POS	TPR
1915	StL-A	81	274	28	78	10	2	3	29	7	27	.285	.307	.369	106	0	10	9	-2	.989	-3	1-36,O-29,P	-0.8
1916	StL-A	151	580	83	177	21	11	4	76	40	37	.305	.355	.400	133	21	34	26	-5	.985	-2	*1-141/P-3,O3	0.8
1917	StL-A	135	539	60	190	30	9	2	52	30	19	.353	.390	.453	163	38	37			.985	4	*1-133/2-2	4.0
1918	StL-A	114	452	69	154	21	9	2	41	40	17	.341	.400	.440	159	31	45			.990	9	*1-114/P-2	3.8
1919	StL-A	132	511	96	180	31	15	10	83	27	20	.352	.390	.530	153	33	28			.991	13	*1-131	4.3
1920	StL-A	154	631	137	**257**	49	18	19	122	46	19	**.407**	.449	.632	179	68	42	17	2	.990	15	*1-154/P-1	7.8
1921	StL-A	138	582	125	216	38	**18**	12	104	34	27	.371	.411	.560	137	31	**35**	11	4	.993	8	*1-138	3.6
1922	StL-A	142	586	**134**	**246**	42	**18**	8	105	49	14	**.420**	.467	.594	169	59	**51**	19	4	.988	12	*1-141	**6.6**
1924	StL-A	151	636	94	194	27	10	9	74	31	29	.305	.340	.421	90	-12	19	17	-5	.984	1	*1-151,M	-2.3
1925	StL-A	150	649	100	224	21	15	12	105	27	24	.345	.371	.479	109	6	11	12	-4	.983	11	*1-150/P-1M	0.4
1926	StL-A	150	613	78	178	21	12	7	71	30	30	.290	.327	.398	84	-16	12	8	-1	.987	-4	*1-149/P-1M	-3.0
1927	StL-A	149	614	87	201	32	8	5	97	24	15	.327	.357	.430	100	-1	**27**	7	4	.984	11	*1-149	0.3
1928	Was-A	20	49	1	12	1	0	0	2	1	2	.245	.260	.265	39	-4	0	1	-1	1.000	-2	/1-5,O-5	-0.8
	Bos-N		491	71	167	26	4	4	68	30	15	.340	.380	.434	119	13	11			.988	7	*1-118/P-1	0.9
1929	Bos-N	154	629	67	205	40	8	2	79	33	17	.326	.363	.424	98	-2	6			.982	5	*1-154	-1.3
1930	Bos-N	116	431	54	133	15	7	3	67	23	15	.309	.346	.397	82	-12	7			.987	5	*1-107	-1.6
Total	15	2055	8267	1284	2812	425	164	102	1175	472	327	.340	.379	.468	124	254	375	127		.987	88	*1-1971/O-37,P23	22.7

■ DICK SISLER
Sisler, Richard Allan   b: 11/2/20, St.Louis, Mo.   BL/TR, 6'2", 205 lbs.   Deb: 4/16/46   FMC

YEAR	TM/L	G	AB	R	H	2B	3B	HR	RBI	BB	SO	AVG	OBP	SLG	PRO+	BR/A	SB	CS	SBR	FA	FR	G/POS	TPR
1946	*StL-N	83	235	17	61	11	2	3	42	14	28	.260	.307	.362	86	-5	0			.988	-2	1-37,O-29	-1.1
1947	StL-N	46	74	4	15	2	1	0	9	3	8	.203	.234	.257	29	-8	0			.976	-0	1-10/O-5	-0.8
1948	Phi-N	121	446	60	122	21	3	11	56	47	46	.274	.344	.408	105	3	1			.983	-4	*1-120	-0.2
1949	Phi-N	121	412	42	119	19	6	7	50	25	38	.289	.333	.415	102	0	0			.987	-9	1-96	-0.9
1950	*Phi-N★	141	523	79	155	29	4	13	83	64	50	.296	.373	.442	115	12	1			.987	2	*O-137	0.8
1951	Phi-N	125	428	46	123	20	5	8	52	40	39	.287	.351	.414	107	4	1	0	0	.968	-2	*O-111	0.1
1952	Cin-N	11	27	3	5	1	1	0	4	3	5	.185	.267	.296	56	-2	0	0	0	1.000	-1	/O-7	-0.3
	StL-N	119	418	48	109	14	5	13	60	29	35	.261	.312	.411	99	-2	3	3	-1	.985	2	*1-114	-0.5
	Yr	130	445	51	114	15	6	13	64	32	40	.256	.309	.404	96	-3	3	3	-1	.985	1	*1-114/O-7	-0.8
1953	StL-N	32	43	3	11	1	1	0	4	1	4	.256	.273	.326	55	-3	0	0	0	1.000	1	1-10	-0.2
Total	8	799	2606	302	720	118	28	55	360	226	253	.276	.336	.406	101	-0	6	3		.985	-10	1-387,O-289	-3.1

■ SIBBY SISTI
Sisti, Sebastian Daniel   b: 7/26/20, Buffalo, N.Y.   BR/TR, 5'11", 175 lbs.   Deb: 7/21/39   C

YEAR	TM/L	G	AB	R	H	2B	3B	HR	RBI	BB	SO	AVG	OBP	SLG	PRO+	BR/A	SB	CS	SBR	FA	FR	G/POS	TPR
1939	Bos-N	63	215	19	49	7	1	1	11	12	38	.228	.269	.284	52	-15	4			.994	0	2-34,3-17,S	-1.2
1940	Bos-N	123	459	73	115	19	5	6	34	36	64	.251	.311	.353	87	-9	4			.936	-2	*3-102,2-16	-0.9
1941	Bos-N	140	541	72	140	24	3	1	45	38	76	.259	.309	.320	81	-15	7			.916	-8	*3-137/2-2,S	-2.0
1942	Bos-N	129	407	50	86	11	4	1	35	45	55	.211	.296	.287	73	-14	5			.970	-4	*2-124/O-1	-1.1
1946	Bos-N	1	0	0	0	0	0	0	0	0	0	—	—	—	—		0	0		.000	0	/3-1	—
1947	Bos-N	56	153	22	43	8	0	2	15	20	17	.281	.371	.373	100	1	2			.947	-9	S-51/2-1	-0.6
1948	*Bos-N	83	221	30	54	6	2	0	21	31	34	.244	.340	.290	73	-7	0			.972	-5	2-44,S-26	-0.9
1949	Bos-N	101	268	39	69	12	0	5	22	34	42	.257	.343	.358	93	-2	1			.989	-13	O-48,2-21,S/3	-1.5
1950	Bos-N	69	105	21	18	3	1	2	11	16	19	.171	.287	.276	52	-7	1			.931	9	S-23,2-19,3/10	-0.6
1951	Bos-N	114	362	46	101	20	2	2	38	32	50	.279	.341	.362	96	-2	4	5	-2	.944	-23	S-55,2-52/310	-2.2
1952	Bos-N	90	245	19	52	10	1	4	24	14	43	.212	.255	.310	58	-15	2	0	1	.966	-12	2-33,O-23,S/3	-2.5
1953	Mil-N	38	23	8	5	1	0	0	4	5	2	.217	.357	.261	69	-1	0	0	0	1.000	-2	2-13/S-6,3	0.3
1954	Mil-N	9	0	2	0	0	0	0	0	0	0	—	—	—	—		0	0		.000	0	R	0.0
Total	13	1016	2999	401	732	121	19	27	260	283	440	.244	.313	.324	79	-85	30	5		.973	-72	2-359,3-290,S/O1	-13.1

■ ED SIXSMITH
Sixsmith, Edward   b: 2/26/1863, Philadelphia, Pa.   d: 12/12/26, Philadelphia, Pa.   BR/TR,   Deb: 9/11/1884

YEAR	TM/L	G	AB	R	H	2B	3B	HR	RBI	BB	SO	AVG	OBP	SLG	PRO+	BR/A	SB	CS	SBR	FA	FR	G/POS	TPR
1884	Phi-N	1	2	0	0	0	0	0	0	0	0	.000	.000	.000	-99	-0				1.000	-1	/C-1	-0.1

■ TED SIZEMORE
Sizemore, Theodore Crawford   b: 4/15/45, Gadsden, Ala.   BR/TR, 5'10", 165 lbs.   Deb: 4/7/69

YEAR	TM/L	G	AB	R	H	2B	3B	HR	RBI	BB	SO	AVG	OBP	SLG	PRO+	BR/A	SB	CS	SBR	FA	FR	G/POS	TPR
1969	LA-N	159	590	69	160	20	5	4	46	45	40	.271	.328	.342	95	-5	5	5	-2	.979	-6	*2-118,S-46/O	0.3
1970	LA-N	96	340	40	104	10	1	1	34	34	19	.306	.369	.350	98	0	5	1	1	.984	-7	2-86/O-9,S	0.1
1971	StL-N	135	478	53	126	14	5	3	42	42	26	.264	.324	.333	83	-10	4	6	-2	.976	-3	2-93,S-39,O/3	-0.4
1972	StL-N	120	439	53	116	17	4	2	38	37	36	.264	.327	.335	90	-6	8	3	1	.976	0	*2-111	0.2
1973	StL-N	142	521	69	147	22	1	1	54	68	34	.282	.367	.334	96	-0	6	4	1	.981	9	*2-139/3-3	1.8
1974	StL-N	129	504	68	126	17	4	0	47	70	37	.250	.341	.290	80	-11	8	4	0	.980	13	*2-128/S-1,O	0.9
1975	StL-N	153	562	56	135	23	1	3	49	45	37	.240	.299	.301	64	-27	1	5	-3	.972	-25	*2-153	-4.9
1976	LA-N	84	266	18	64	8	1	0	18	15	22	.241	.281	.278	60	-14	2	3	-1	.986	2	2-71/3-3,C	-1.0
1977	*Phi-N	152	519	64	146	20	3	4	47	52	40	.281	.348	.355	85	-9	8	11	-4	.986	9	*2-152	0.4
1978	*Phi-N	108	351	38	77	12	0	0	25	25	29	.219	.273	.254	48	-24	8	1	2	.978	4	*2-107	-1.1
1979	Chi-N	98	330	36	82	17	0	2	24	32	25	.248	.321	.318	68	-14	3	3	-1	.973	15	2-96	0.8
	Bos-A	26	88	12	23	7	0	1	6	9	6	.261	.301	.375	77	-3	1	0	0	.993	9	2-26/C-2	0.7
1980	Bos-A	9	23	1	5	1	0	0	2	1	0	.217	.217	.261	29	-2	0	0	0	.927	3	/2-8	0.0
Total	12	1411	5011	577	1311	188	21	23	430	469	350	.262	.327	.321	80	-125	59	46	-10	.979	25	*2-1288/S-88,O3C	-1.8

■ FRANK SKAFF
Skaff, Francis Michael   b: 9/30/13, LaCrosse, Wis.   d: 4/12/88, Towson, Md.   BR/TR, 5'10", 185 lbs.   Deb: 9/11/35   MC

YEAR	TM/L	G	AB	R	H	2B	3B	HR	RBI	BB	SO	AVG	OBP	SLG	PRO+	BR/A	SB	CS	SBR	FA	FR	G/POS	TPR
1935	Bro-N	6	11	4	6	1	1	0	3	0	2	.545	.545	.818	267	2	0			.857	-0	/3-3	0.2
1943	Phi-A	32	64	8	18	2	1	1	8	6	11	.281	.343	.391	115	1	0	0	0	.976	1	1-18/3-3,S	0.2
Total	2	38	75	12	24	3	2	1	11	6	13	.320	.370	.453	138	4	0	0		.900	1	/1-18,3-6,S	0.4

■ DAVE SKAGGS
Skaggs, David Lindsey   b: 6/12/51, Santa Monica, Cal.   BR/TR, 6'2", 200 lbs.   Deb: 4/17/77

YEAR	TM/L	G	AB	R	H	2B	3B	HR	RBI	BB	SO	AVG	OBP	SLG	PRO+	BR/A	SB	CS	SBR	FA	FR	G/POS	TPR
1977	Bal-A	80	216	22	62	9	1	1	24	20	34	.287	.347	.352	97	-0	0	0	0	.995	-1	C-80	0.1

YEAR	TM/L	G	AB	R	H	2B	3B	HR	RBI	BB	SO	AVG	OBP	SLG	PRO+	BR/A	SB	CS	SBR	FA	FR	G/POS	TPR
1978	Bal-A	36	86	6	13	1	1	0	2	9	14	.151	.232	.186	20	-9	0	1	-1	.988	5	C-35	-0.5
1979	*Bal-A	63	137	9	34	8	0	1	14	13	14	.248	.313	.328	76	-4	0	0	0	.984	2	C-63	-0.0
1980	Bal-A	2	5	0	1	0	0	0	0	0	1	.200	.200	.200	10	-1	0	0	0	1.000	1	/C-2	0.0
	Cal-A	24	66	7	13	0	0	1	9	9	13	.197	.293	.242	50	-4	0	0	0	.968	-10	C-24	-1.4
	Yr	26	71	7	14	0	0	1	9	9	14	.197	.287	.239	47	-5	0	0	0	.971	-9	C-26	-1.4
Total	4	205	510	44	123	18	2	3	49	51	76	.241	.310	.302	72	-19	0	1	-1	.988	-3	C-204	-1.8

■ BUD SKETCHLEY
Sketchley, Harry Clement b: 3/30/19, Virden, Man., Can. d: 12/19/79, Los Angeles, Cal. BL/TL, 5'10", 180 lbs. Deb: 4/14/42

YEAR	TM/L	G	AB	R	H	2B	3B	HR	RBI	BB	SO	AVG	OBP	SLG	PRO+	BR/A	SB	CS	SBR	FA	FR	G/POS	TPR
1942	Chi-A	13	36	1	7	1	0	0	3	7	4	.194	.326	.222	57	-2	0	1	-1	.952	-1	O-12	-0.4

■ ROE SKIDMORE
Skidmore, Robert Roe b: 10/30/45, Decatur, Ill. BR/TR, 6'3", 188 lbs. Deb: 9/17/70

YEAR	TM/L	G	AB	R	H	2B	3B	HR	RBI	BB	SO	AVG	OBP	SLG	PRO+	BR/A	SB	CS	SBR	FA	FR	G/POS	TPR
1970	Chi-N	1	1	0	1	0	0	0	0	0	0	1.000	1.000	1.000	390	0	0	0	0	.000	0	H	0.0

■ BILL SKIFF
Skiff, William Franklin b: 10/16/1895, New Rochelle, N.Y. d: 12/25/76, Bronxville, N.Y. BR/TR, 5'10", 170 lbs. Deb: 5/17/21

YEAR	TM/L	G	AB	R	H	2B	3B	HR	RBI	BB	SO	AVG	OBP	SLG	PRO+	BR/A	SB	CS	SBR	FA	FR	G/POS	TPR
1921	Pit-N	16	45	7	13	2	0	0	11	0	4	.289	.289	.333	63	-2	1	1	-0	.982	-2	C-13	-0.4
1926	NY-A	6	11	0	1	0	0	0	0	0	1	.091	.091	.091	-53	-2	0	0	0	1.000	-1	/C-6	-0.3
Total	2	22	56	7	14	2	0	0	11	0	5	.250	.250	.286	40	-5	1	1	-0	.984	-3	/C-19	-0.7

■ ALEXANDER SKINNER
Skinner, Alexander b: 8/14/1856, Chicago, Ill. d: 3/5/01, Washington, Mass. Deb: 7/12/1884

YEAR	TM/L	G	AB	R	H	2B	3B	HR	RBI	BB	SO	AVG	OBP	SLG	PRO+	BR/A	SB	CS	SBR	FA	FR	G/POS	TPR
1884	Bal-U	1	3	0	1	0	0	0		0		.333	.333	.333	74	-0				1.000	0	/O-1	0.0
	CP-U	1	3	1	1	0	0	0		0		.333	.333	.333	82	-0				.000	-0	/O-1	0.0
	Yr	2	6	1	2	0	0	0		0		.333	.333	.333	78	-0				1.000	-0	/O-2	0.0

■ CAMP SKINNER
Skinner, Elisha Harrison b: 6/25/1897, Douglasville, Ga. d: 8/4/44, Douglasville, Ga. BL/TR, 5'11", 165 lbs. Deb: 5/2/22

YEAR	TM/L	G	AB	R	H	2B	3B	HR	RBI	BB	SO	AVG	OBP	SLG	PRO+	BR/A	SB	CS	SBR	FA	FR	G/POS	TPR
1922	NY-A	27	33	1	6	0	0	0	2	0	4	.182	.206	.182	2	-5	1	0	0	1.000	-0	O-4	-0.5
1923	Bos-A	7	13	1	3	2	0	0	1	0	0	.231	.231	.385	60	-1	0	0	0	.000	-1	/O-2	-0.2
Total	2	34	46	2	9	2	0	0	3	0	4	.196	.213	.239	18	-6	1	0	0	1.000	-2	/O-6	-0.7

■ JOEL SKINNER
Skinner, Joel Patrick b: 2/21/61, LaJolla, Cal. BR/TR, 6'4", 204 lbs. Deb: 6/12/83 F

YEAR	TM/L	G	AB	R	H	2B	3B	HR	RBI	BB	SO	AVG	OBP	SLG	PRO+	BR/A	SB	CS	SBR	FA	FR	G/POS	TPR
1983	Chi-A	6	11	2	3	0	0	0	1	0	1	.273	.273	.273	49	-1	0	0	0	.960	2	/C-6	0.2
1984	Chi-A	43	80	4	17	2	0	0	3	7	19	.213	.276	.237	42	-6	1	0	0	.989	10	C-43	0.6
1985	Chi-A	22	44	9	15	4	1	1	5	5	13	.341	.408	.545	153	3	0	0	0	.971	4	C-21	0.8
1986	Chi-A	60	149	17	30	5	1	4	20	9	43	.201	.252	.329	55	-10	0	0	0	.988	-7	C-60	-1.3
	NY-A	54	166	6	43	4	0	1	17	7	40	.259	.289	.301	62	-9	0	2	-2	.981	6	C-54	-0.3
	Yr	114	315	23	73	9	1	5	37	16	83	.232	.271	.314	58	-18	1	4	-2	.984	-1	*C-114	-1.6
1987	NY-A	64	139	9	19	4	0	3	14	8	46	.137	.189	.230	11	-18	0	0	0	.984	-3	C-64	-1.7
1988	NY-A	88	251	23	57	15	0	4	23	14	72	.227	.268	.335	68	-11	0	0	0	.990	-7	C-85/O-2,1	-1.3
1989	Cle-A	79	178	10	41	10	0	1	13	9	42	.230	.271	.303	61	-9	1	1	-0	.990	-4	C-79	-1.1
1990	Cle-A	49	139	16	35	4	1	2	16	7	44	.252	.288	.338	75	-5	0	0	0	.996	0	C-49	-0.2
1991	Cle-A	99	284	23	69	14	0	1	24	14	67	.243	.281	.303	61	-15	0	2	-1	.991	1	C-99	-1.0
Total	9	564	1441	119	329	62	3	17	136	80	387	.228	.271	.311	60	-81	3	7	-3	.988	3	C-560/O-2,1	-5.3

■ BOB SKINNER
Skinner, Robert Ralph b: 10/3/31, LaJolla, Cal. BL/TL, 6'4", 190 lbs. Deb: 4/13/54 FMC

YEAR	TM/L	G	AB	R	H	2B	3B	HR	RBI	BB	SO	AVG	OBP	SLG	PRO+	BR/A	SB	CS	SBR	FA	FR	G/POS	TPR
1954	Pit-N	132	470	67	117	15	9	8	46	47	59	.249	.317	.370	80	-15	4	0	1	.986	-3	*1-118/O-2	-2.2
1956	Pit-N	113	233	29	47	8	3	5	29	26	50	.202	.285	.326	65	-12	1	1	-0	.977	-9	O-36,1-23/3	-2.5
1957	Pit-N	126	387	58	118	12	6	13	45	38	50	.305	.370	.468	127	15	10	4	1	.963	3	O-93/1-9,3	1.3
1958	Pit-N★	144	529	93	170	33	9	13	70	58	55	.321	.390	.491	135	27	12	4	1	.977	9	*O-141	3.0
1959	Pit-N	143	547	78	153	18	4	13	61	67	65	.280	.358	.399	102	3	10	7	-1	.964	6	*O-142/1-1	0.1
1960	*Pit-N★	145	571	83	156	33	6	15	86	59	86	.273	.342	.431	109	7	11	8	-2	.981	7	*O-141	0.6
1961	Pit-N	119	381	61	102	20	3	9	42	51	49	.268	.360	.360	91	-3	3	5	-2	.973	3	O-97	-0.8
1962	Pit-N	144	510	87	154	29	7	20	75	76	89	.302	.397	.504	140	30	10	4	1	.960	1	*O-139	2.3
1963	Pit-N	34	122	18	33	5	5	0	8	13	22	.270	.341	.393	110	2	4	1	1	.983	2	O-32	0.2
	Cin-N	72	194	25	49	10	2	3	17	21	42	.253	.332	.371	99	0	1	2	-1	1.000	1	O-51	-0.2
	Yr	106	316	43	82	15	7	3	25	34	64	.259	.335	.380	103	2	5	3	-0	.993	3	O-83	0.0
1964	Cin-N	25	59	6	13	3	0	3	5	4	12	.220	.270	.424	89	-1	0	0	0	.913	1	O-12	-0.1
	*StL-N	55	118	10	32	5	1	1	16	11	20	.271	.333	.339	83	-2	0	0	0	.938	-1	O-31	-0.5
	Yr	80	177	16	45	8	1	4	21	15	32	.254	.313	.367	85	-3	0	0	0	.930	-0	O-43	-0.6
1965	StL-N	80	152	25	47	5	4	5	26	12	30	.309	.360	.493	126	5	1	0	0	.935	-4	O-33	0.0
1966	StL-N	49	45	2	7	0	1	0	5	2	17	.156	.208	.244	25	-5	0	0	0	.000	0	H	-0.5
Total	12	1381	4318	642	1198	197	58	103	531	485	646	.277	.353	.421	108	52	67	36	-2	.969	14	O-950,1-151/3	0.7

■ LOU SKIZAS
Skizas, Louis Peter "The Nervous Greek" b: 6/2/32, Chicago, Ill. BR/TR, 5'11", 175 lbs. Deb: 4/19/56

YEAR	TM/L	G	AB	R	H	2B	3B	HR	RBI	BB	SO	AVG	OBP	SLG	PRO+	BR/A	SB	CS	SBR	FA	FR	G/POS	TPR
1956	NY-A	6	6	0	1	0	0	0	1	0	2	.167	.167	.167	-12	-1	0	0	0	.000	0	H	-0.1
	KC-A	83	297	39	94	11	3	11	39	15	17	.316	.349	.485	118	6	3	1	0	.975	5	O-74	0.8
	Yr	89	303	39	95	11	3	11	40	15	19	.314	.346	.479	116	5	3	1	0	.975	5	O-74	0.7
1957	KC-A	119	376	34	92	14	1	18	44	27	15	.245	.299	.431	95	-4	5	2	0	.976	-9	O-76,3-32	-1.6
1958	Det-A	23	33	4	8	2	0	1	2	5	1	.242	.342	.394	95	-0	0	0	0	.750	-3	/O-5,3-4	-0.3
1959	Chi-A	8	13	3	1	0	0	0	0	3	2	.077	.250	.077	-6	-2	0	0	0	1.000	-0	/O-6	-0.2
Total	4	239	725	80	196	27	4	30	86	50	37	.270	.319	.443	102	-1	8	3	1	.973	-7	O-161/3-36	-1.4

■ BILL SKOWRON
Skowron, William Joseph "Moose" b: 12/18/30, Chicago, Ill. BR/TR, 5'11", 195 lbs. Deb: 4/13/54

YEAR	TM/L	G	AB	R	H	2B	3B	HR	RBI	BB	SO	AVG	OBP	SLG	PRO+	BR/A	SB	CS	SBR	FA	FR	G/POS	TPR
1954	NY-A	87	215	37	73	12	9	7	41	19	18	.340	.396	.577	170	19	2	1	0	.986	-1	1-61/3-5,2	1.7
1955	*NY-A	108	288	46	92	17	3	12	61	21	32	.319	.372	.524	141	15	1	1	-0	.989	-3	1-74/3-3	0.8
1956	*NY-A	134	464	78	143	21	6	23	90	50	60	.308	.383	.528	143	27	4	4	-1	.993	3	*1-120/3-2	2.1
1957	*NY-A★	122	457	54	139	15	5	17	88	31	60	.304	.352	.470	125	14	3	2	-0	.992	6	*1-115	1.3
1958	*NY-A★	126	465	61	127	22	3	14	73	28	69	.273	.320	.424	107	3	1	1	-0	**.993**	-2	*1-118/3-2	-0.8
1959	NY-A★	74	282	39	84	13	5	15	59	20	47	.298	.351	.539	145	16	1	0	0	.991	6	1-72	1.2
1960	*NY-A	146	538	63	166	34	3	26	91	38	60	.309	.356	.528	144	30	2	3	-1	.991	9	*1-142	2.6
1961	*NY-A☆	150	561	76	150	23	4	28	89	35	108	.267	.320	.472	115	8	0	0	0	.993	-1	*1-149	-0.5
1962	*NY-A	140	478	63	129	16	6	23	80	36	99	.270	.328	.473	116	9	0	0	0	.991	-5	*1-135	-0.5
1963	*LA-N	89	237	19	48	8	0	4	19	13	49	.203	.253	.287	59	-13	0	1	-1	.991	-1	1-66/3-1	-1.9
1964	Was-A	73	262	28	71	10	0	13	41	11	56	.271	.308	.458	110	3	0	0	0	.994	3	1-66	-0.2
	Chi-A	73	273	19	80	11	3	4	38	19	36	.293	.341	.399	108	3	0	0	0	.998	-1	1-70	-0.1
	Yr	146	535	47	151	21	3	17	79	30	92	.282	.325	.428	109	3	0	0	0	.996	-3	*1-136	-0.3
1965	Chi-A†	146	559	63	153	24	3	18	78	32	77	.274	.319	.424	116	9	1	3	-2	.994	-6	*1-145	-0.5
1966	Chi-A	120	337	27	84	15	2	6	29	26	45	.249	.309	.359	98	-2	1	1	-0	.991	1	1-98	-0.7
1967	Chi-A	8	8	0	0	0	0	0	1	0	1	.000	.000	.000	-99	-2	0	0	0	.000	0	H	-0.2
	Cal-A	62	123	8	27	2	1	1	10	4	18	.220	.267	.276	63	-6	0	0	0	.988	-1	1-32	-0.9
	Yr	70	131	8	27	2	1	1	11	4	19	.206	.252	.260	53	-8	0	0	0	.988	-1	1-32	-1.1
Total	14	1658	5547	681	1566	243	53	211	888	383	870	.282	.335	.459	121	134	16	18	-6	.992	-3	*1-1463/3-13,2	3.4

■ BOB SKUBE
Skube, Robert Jacob b: 10/8/57, Northridge, Cal. BL/TL, 6', 180 lbs. Deb: 9/17/82

YEAR	TM/L	G	AB	R	H	2B	3B	HR	RBI	BB	SO	AVG	OBP	SLG	PRO+	BR/A	SB	CS	SBR	FA	FR	G/POS	TPR
1982	Mil-A	4	3	0	2	0	0	0	0	0	0	.667	.667	.667	285	1	0	0	0	.000	-1	/O-1,D-1	0.0
1983	Mil-A	12	25	2	5	1	1	0	9	4	7	.200	.310	.320	80	-1	0	0	0	1.000	-1	/O-8,1-1,D	-0.1
Total	2	16	28	2	7	1	1	0	9	4	7	.250	.344	.357	101	0	0	0	0	1.000	-1	/O-9,D-3,1	-0.1

YEAR	TM/L	G	AB	R	H	2B	3B	HR	RBI	BB	SO	AVG	OBP	SLG	PRO+	BR/A	SB	CS	SBR	FA	FR	G/POS	TPR

■ GORDON SLADE　Slade, Gordon Leigh "Oskie"　b: 10/9/04, Salt Lake City, Utah　d: 1/2/74, Long Beach, Cal.　BR/TR, 5'10.5", 160 lbs.　Deb: 4/21/30

1930	Bro-N	25	37	8	8	2	0	1	2	3	5	.216	.275	.351	51	-3	0			.938	10	S-21	0.7
1931	Bro-N	85	272	27	65	13	2	1	29	23	28	.239	.310	.313	68	-12	2			.947	11	S-82/3-2	0.7
1932	Bro-N	79	250	23	60	15	1	1	23	11	26	.240	.280	.320	62	-13	3			.943	11	S-55,3-23	0.2
1933	StL-N	39	62	6	7	1	0	0	3	6	7	.113	.191	.129	-7	-8	1			.941	3	S-31/2-1	-0.5
1934	Cin-N	138	555	61	158	19	8	4	52	25	34	.285	.320	.369	86	-11	6			.952	2	S-97,2-39	-0.1
1935	Cin-N	71	196	22	55	10	0	1	14	16	16	.281	.341	.347	88	-3	0			.927	-12	S-30,2-19/O3	-1.2
Total	6	437	1372	147	353	60	11	8	123	84	116	.257	.307	.335	73	-51	12			.945	25	S-316/2-59,3O	-0.2

■ ART SLADEN　Sladen, Arthur　b: 10/28/1860, Dracut, Mass.　d: 2/28/14, Dracut, Mass.　Deb: 4/22/1884

| 1884 | Bos-U | 2 | 7 | 0 | 0 | 0 | 0 | 0 | | 0 | | .000 | .000 | .000 | -99 | -2 | | | | 1.000 | -1 | /O-2 | -0.2 |

■ JIMMY SLAGLE　Slagle, James Franklin "Rabbit" or "Shorty"　b: 7/11/1873, Worthville, Pa.　d: 5/10/56, Chicago, Ill.　BL/TR, 5'7", 144 lbs.　Deb: 4/17/1899

1899	Was-N	147	599	92	163	15	8	0	41	55		.272	.338	.324	83	-13	22			.953	20	*O-146	-0.3
1900	Phi-N	141	574	115	165	16	9	0	45	60		.287	.358	.347	96	-2	34			.922	1	*O-141	-1.1
1901	Phi-N	48	183	20	37	6	2	1	20	16		.202	.277	.273	59	-10	5			.930	6	O-48	-0.7
	Bos-N	66	255	35	69	7	0	0	7	34		.271	.359	.298	84	-4	14			.935	-2	O-66	-1.1
	Yr	114	438	55	106	13	2	1	27	50		.242	.325	.288	74	-13	19			.932	4	*O-114	-1.8
1902	Chi-N	115	454	64	143	11	4	0	28	53		.315	.387	.357	133	20	40			.965	7	*O-113	2.1
1903	Chi-N	139	543	104	162	20	6	0	44	81		.298	.393	.357	118	17	33			.936	3	*O-139	1.0
1904	Chi-N	120	481	73	125	12	10	1	31	41		.260	.322	.333	102	1	28			.921	-3	*O-120	-0.9
1905	Chi-N	155	568	96	153	19	4	0	37	97		.269	.379	.317	104	8	27			.962	3	*O-155	0.4
1906	Chi-N	127	498	71	119	8	6	0	33	63		.239	.324	.279	83	-8	25			.976	2	*O-127	-1.3
1907	*Chi-N	136	489	71	126	6	6	0	32	76		.258	.359	.294	99	3	28			.962	-10	*O-136	-1.5
1908	Chi-N	104	352	38	78	4	1	0	26	43		.222	.306	.239	71	-10	17			.976	-6	*O-101	-2.3
Total	10	1298	4996	779	1340	124	56	2	344	619		.268	.352	.317	97	3	273			.950	22	*O-1292	-5.7

■ JACK SLATTERY　Slattery, John Terrence　b: 1/6/1878, S.Boston, Mass.　d: 7/17/49, Boston, Mass.　BR/TR, 6'2", 191 lbs.　Deb: 9/28/01　MC

1901	Bos-A	1	3	1	1	0	0	0	1	1		.333	.500	.333	137	0	0			1.000	0	/C-1	0.0
1903	Cle-A	4	11	1	0	0	0	0	0	0		.000	.000	.000	-99	-3	0			.885	-1	/1-2	-0.4
	Chi-A	63	211	8	46	3	2	0	20	2		.218	.233	.251	47	-14	2			.974	-8	C-56/1-5	-1.7
	Yr	67	222	9	46	3	2	0	20	2		.207	.221	.239	40	-16	2			.974	-9	C-56/1-7	-2.1
1906	StL-N	3	7	0	2	0	0	0	0	1		.286	.375	.286	111	0	0			1.000	-1	/C-2	0.0
1909	Was-A	32	56	4	12	2	0	0	6	4		.214	.254	.250	62	-2	1			.953	-1	1-11/C-6	-0.3
Total	4	103	288	14	61	5	2	0	27	6		.212	.236	.243	47	-18	3			.974	-10	/C-65,1-18	-2.4

■ MIKE SLATTERY　Slattery, Michael J.　b: 11/26/1866, Boston, Mass.　d: 10/16/04, Boston, Mass.　BL/TL, 6'2", 210 lbs.　Deb: 4/17/1884

1884	Bos-U	106	413	60	86	6	2	0		4		.208	.216	.232	22	-44				.802	6	*O-96,1-11	-3.6
1888	*NY-N	103	391	50	96	12	6	1	35	13	28	.246	.272	.315	87	-6	26			.919	1	*O-103	-0.8
1889	*NY-N	12	48	7	14	2	0	1	12	4	3	.292	.346	.396	107	0	2			.852	-1	O-12	0.0
1890	NY-P	97	411	80	126	20	11	5	67	27	25	.307	.352	.445	103	-2	18			.905	-14	*O-97	-1.5
1891	Cin-N	41	158	24	33	3	2	1	16	10	10	.209	.256	.272	53	-10	1			.941	-0	O-41	-1.0
	Was-a	15	60	8	17	1	0	0	5	4	5	.283	.358	.300	93	-0	6			.862	-2	O-15	-0.2
Total	5	374	1481	229	372	44	21	8	135	62	71	.251	.284	.325	72	-61	53			.883	-11	O-364/1-11	-7.1

■ DON SLAUGHT　Slaught, Donald Martin　b: 9/11/58, Long Beach, Cal.　BR/TR, 6'1", 190 lbs.　Deb: 7/6/82

1982	KC-A	43	115	14	32	6	0	3	8	9	12	.278	.331	.409	102	0	0	0	0	.994	2	C-43	0.4
1983	KC-A	83	276	21	86	13	4	0	28	11	27	.312	.338	.388	99	-1	3	1	0	.964	-7	C-79/D-1	-0.4
1984	*KC-A	124	409	48	108	27	4	4	42	20	55	.264	.302	.379	86	-8	0	0	0	.982	-10	*C-123/D-1	-1.2
1985	Tex-A	102	343	34	96	17	4	8	35	20	41	.280	.331	.423	103	1	5	4	-1	.990	-1	C-91/D-2	-0.6
1986	Tex-A	95	314	39	83	17	1	13	46	16	59	.264	.310	.449	101	-0	3	2	-0	.993	-6	C-91/D-2	-0.1
1987	Tex-A	95	237	25	53	15	2	8	16	24	51	.224	.298	.405	84	-6	0	3	-2	.985	-0	C-85/D-5	-0.4
1988	NY-A	97	322	33	91	25	1	9	43	24	54	.283	.338	.450	120	8	1	0		.979	-12	C-94/D-1	0.3
1989	NY-A	117	350	34	88	21	3	5	38	30	57	.251	.319	.371	95	-2	1	1	-0	.991	-5	*C-105/D-3	-0.2
1990	*Pit-N	84	230	27	69	18	3	4	29	27	27	.300	.381	.457	134	11	0	1	-1	.993	-3	C-78	1.2
1991	*Pit-N	77	220	19	65	17	1	1	29	21	32	.295	.365	.395	116	5	1	0	-0	.987	-5	C-69/3-1	0.4
1992	*Pit-N	87	255	26	88	17	3	4	37	17	23	.345	.391	.482	147	16	2	2	-1	.988	-5	C-79	1.7
1993	Pit-N	116	377	34	113	19	2	10	55	29	56	.300	.359	.440	113	7	2	1	0	.993	-11	*C-105	0.2
1994	Pit-N	76	240	21	69	7	0	2	21	34	31	.287	.383	.342	91	-1	0	0	0	.994	-1	C-74	0.2
Total	13	1196	3688	375	1041	219	28	71	427	282	525	.282	.340	.415	106	29	18	15	-4	.986	-73	*C-1127/D-13,3	1.5

■ ENOS SLAUGHTER　Slaughter, Enos Bradsher "Country"　b: 4/27/16, Roxboro, N.C.　BL/TR, 5'9", 192 lbs.　Deb: 4/19/38　H

1938	StL-N	112	395	59	109	20	10	8	58	32	38	.276	.330	.438	104	1	1			.970	-2	O-92	-0.4
1939	StL-N	149	604	95	193	**52**	5	12	86	44	53	.320	.371	.482	120	16	2			.968	**16**	*O-149	2.6
1940	StL-N	140	516	96	158	25	13	17	73	50	35	.306	.370	.504	131	21	8			.989	5	*O-132	1.8
1941	StL-N★	113	425	71	132	22	9	13	76	53	28	.311	.390	.496	139	22	4			.947	-8	*O-108	0.7
1942	*StL-N★	152	591	100	**188**	31	**17**	13	98	88	30	.318	.412	.494	153	41	9			.987	6	*O-151	3.9
1946	*StL-N★	156	609	100	183	30	8	18	**130**	69	41	.300	.374	.465	131	24	9			.981	6	*O-156	2.4
1947	StL-N★	147	551	100	162	31	13	10	86	59	27	.294	.366	.452	111	9	4			.982	9	*O-142	1.0
1948	StL-N★	146	549	91	176	27	11	11	90	85	29	.321	.409	.470	130	25	4			.971	6	*O-146	2.2
1949	StL-N★	151	568	92	191	34	**13**	13	96	79	37	.336	.418	.511	141	35	3			.983	1	*O-150	2.8
1950	StL-N★	148	556	82	161	26	7	10	101	66	33	.290	.367	.415	100	1	3			.978	-1	*O-145	-0.6
1951	StL-N★	123	409	48	115	17	8	4	64	67	25	.281	.386	.391	109	8	7	2	1	.995	-0	*O-106	0.5
1952	StL-N★	140	510	73	153	17	12	11	101	70	25	.300	.386	.445	130	22	6	1	1	.989	2	*O-137	2.0
1953	StL-N★	143	492	64	143	34	9	6	89	80	28	.291	.395	.433	116	14	4	4	-1	**.996**	-6	*O-137	0.2
1954	NY-A	69	125	19	31	4	2	1	19	28	8	.248	.386	.336	102	2	0	2	-1	.974	-6	O-30	-0.7
1955	NY-A	10	9	1	1	0	0	0	1	1	1	.111	.200	.111	-15	-1	0	0	0	.000	0	H	-0.1
	KC-A	108	267	49	86	12	5	4	34	40	17	.322	.414	.453	132	13	2	3	-1	.985	-4	O-77	0.5
	Yr	118	276	50	87	12	5	4	35	41	18	.315	.408	.442	127	12	2	3	-1	.985	-4	O-77	0.4
1956	KC-A	91	223	37	62	14	3	2	23	29	20	.278	.364	.395	100	0	1	0	0	.981	-3	O-56	-0.5
	*NY-A	24	83	15	24	4	2	0	4	5	6	.289	.330	.386	91	-1	1	1	0	1.000	0	O-20	-0.4
	Yr	115	306	52	86	18	5	2	27	34	26	.281	.355	.392	97	-1	2	1	0	.985	-5	O-76	-0.9
1957	*NY-A	96	209	24	53	7	1	5	34	40	19	.254	.373	.368	105	3	0	2	-1	1.000	-3	O-64	-0.5
1958	*NY-A	77	138	21	42	4	1	4	19	21	16	.304	.396	.435	133	7	0	0	0	.957	-5	O-35	0.1
1959	NY-A	74	99	10	17	2	0	5	21	13	19	.172	.268	.374	77	-4	1	0	0	.964	-5	O-26	-0.9
	Mil-N	11	18	0	3	0	0	0	1	3	3	.167	.286	.167	27	-2	0	0	0	1.000	-1	/O-5	-0.3
Total	19	2380	7946	1247	2383	413	148	169	1304	1018	538	.300	.382	.453	122	256	71	15		.980	-0	*O-2064	16.3

■ SCOTTIE SLAYBACK　Slayback, Elbert　b: 10/5/01, Paducah, Ky.　d: 11/30/79, Cincinnati, Ohio　BR/TR, 5'8", 165 lbs.　Deb: 9/26/26

| 1926 | NY-N | 2 | 8 | 0 | 0 | 0 | 0 | 0 | 0 | 0 | 0 | .000 | .000 | .000 | -99 | -2 | 0 | | | .889 | -1 | /2-2 | -0.4 |

■ BRUCE SLOAN　Sloan, Bruce Adams "Fatso"　b: 10/4/14, McAlester, Okla.　d: 9/24/73, Oklahoma City, Okla.　BL/TL, 5'9", 195 lbs.　Deb: 4/29/44

| 1944 | NY-N | 59 | 104 | 7 | 28 | 4 | 1 | 1 | 9 | 13 | 8 | .269 | .350 | .356 | 99 | 0 | 0 | | | .935 | -4 | O-21 | -0.5 |

YEAR	TM/L	G	AB	R	H	2B	3B	HR	RBI	BB	SO	AVG	OBP	SLG	PRO+	BR/A	SB	CS	SBR	FA	FR	G/POS	TPR

■ TOD SLOAN
Sloan, Yale Yeastman b: 12/24/1890, Madisonville, Tenn d: 9/12/56, Akron, Ohio BL/TR, 6', 175 lbs. Deb: 9/22/13

YEAR	TM/L	G	AB	R	H	2B	3B	HR	RBI	BB	SO	AVG	OBP	SLG	PRO+	BR/A	SB	CS	SBR	FA	FR	G/POS	TPR
1913	StL-A	7	26	2	7	1	0	0	2	1	9	.269	.321	.308	87	-0	1			.950	2	/O-7	0.1
1917	StL-A	109	313	32	72	6	2	2	25	28	34	.230	.307	.281	83	-6	8			.963	-3	O-77	-1.5
1919	StL-A	27	63	9	15	1	3	0	6	12	3	.238	.368	.349	99	-0	0			.933	-1	O-20	-0.1
Total	3	143	402	43	94	8	5	2	33	41	46	.234	.319	.294	86	-6	9			.957	-1	O-104	-1.5

■ RON SLOCUM
Slocum, Ronald Reece b: 7/2/45, Modesto, Cal. BR/TR, 6'2", 185 lbs. Deb: 9/8/69

YEAR	TM/L	G	AB	R	H	2B	3B	HR	RBI	BB	SO	AVG	OBP	SLG	PRO+	BR/A	SB	CS	SBR	FA	FR	G/POS	TPR
1969	SD-N	13	24	6	7	1	0	1	5	0	5	.292	.292	.458	112	0	0	0	0	.938	-1	/2-4,3-4,S	-0.1
1970	SD-N	60	71	8	10	2	2	1	11	8	24	.141	.237	.268	37	-7	0	1	-1	.978	13	C-19,S-17,3/2	0.6
1971	SD-N	7	18	1	0	0	0	0	0	0	8	.000	.053	.000	-90	-5	0	0	0	.905	1	/3-6	-0.3
Total	3	80	113	15	17	3	2	2	16	8	37	.150	.220	.265	33	-11	0	1	-1	.887	13	/3-21,C-19,S2	0.2

■ CRAIG SMAJSTRLA
Smajstrla, Craig Lee b: 6/19/62, Houston, Tex. BB/TR, 5'9", 165 lbs. Deb: 9/6/88

YEAR	TM/L	G	AB	R	H	2B	3B	HR	RBI	BB	SO	AVG	OBP	SLG	PRO+	BR/A	SB	CS	SBR	FA	FR	G/POS	TPR
1988	Hou-N	8	3	2	0	0	0	0	0	1	0	.000	.000	.000	-99	-1	0	0	0	1.000	0	/2-2	-0.1

■ CHARLIE SMALL
Small, Charles Albert b: 10/24/05, Auburn, Me. d: 1/14/53, Auburn, Me. BL/TR, 5'11", 180 lbs. Deb: 7/7/30

YEAR	TM/L	G	AB	R	H	2B	3B	HR	RBI	BB	SO	AVG	OBP	SLG	PRO+	BR/A	SB	CS	SBR	FA	FR	G/POS	TPR
1930	Bos-A	25	18	1	3	1	0	0	2	5	5	.167	.250	.222	22	-2	1	0	0	1.000	-0	/O-1	-0.2

■ HANK SMALL
Small, George Henry b: 7/31/53, Atlanta, Ga. BR/TR, 6'3", 205 lbs. Deb: 9/27/78

YEAR	TM/L	G	AB	R	H	2B	3B	HR	RBI	BB	SO	AVG	OBP	SLG	PRO+	BR/A	SB	CS	SBR	FA	FR	G/POS	TPR
1978	Atl-N	1	4	0	0	0	0	0	0	0	0	.000	.000	.000	-90	-1	0	0	0	1.000	0	/1-1	-0.1

■ JIM SMALL
Small, James Arthur b: 3/8/37, Portland, Ore. BL/TL, 6'1.5", 180 lbs. Deb: 6/22/55

YEAR	TM/L	G	AB	R	H	2B	3B	HR	RBI	BB	SO	AVG	OBP	SLG	PRO+	BR/A	SB	CS	SBR	FA	FR	G/POS	TPR
1955	Det-A	12	4	2	0	0	0	0	0	1	1	.000	.200	.000	-44	-1	0	0	0	1.000	-1	/O-4	-0.1
1956	Det-A	58	91	13	29	4	2	0	10	6	10	.319	.361	.407	102	0	0	0	0	.940	-3	O-26	-0.3
1957	Det-A	36	42	7	9	2	0	0	0	2	11	.214	.250	.262	39	-4	0	2	-1	1.000	-3	O-14	-0.8
1958	KC-A	2	4	0	0	0	0	0	0	1	0	.000	.200	.000	-39	-1	0	0	0	1.000	0	/O-1	-0.1
Total	4	108	141	22	38	6	2	0	10	10	22	.270	.318	.340	75	-5	0	2	-1	.957	-6	/O-45	-1.3

■ ROY SMALLEY
Smalley, Roy Frederick Jr. b: 10/25/52, Los Angeles, Cal. BB/TR, 6'1", 185 lbs. Deb: 4/30/75 F

YEAR	TM/L	G	AB	R	H	2B	3B	HR	RBI	BB	SO	AVG	OBP	SLG	PRO+	BR/A	SB	CS	SBR	FA	FR	G/POS	TPR
1975	Tex-A	78	250	22	57	8	0	3	33	30	42	.228	.311	.296	73	-8	4	0	1	.941	4	S-59,2-19/C	0.3
1976	Tex-A	41	129	15	29	2	0	1	8	29	27	.225	.367	.264	85	-1	2	0	1	.963	-6	2-38/S-5	-0.3
	Min-A	103	384	46	104	16	3	2	36	47	79	.271	.353	.344	102	2	0	4	-2	.967	5	*S-103	1.8
	Yr	144	513	61	133	18	3	3	44	76	106	.259	.357	.324	98	1	2	4	-2	.966	-1	*S-108,2-38	1.5
1977	Min-A	150	584	93	135	21	5	6	56	74	89	.231	.319	.315	75	-19	5	5	-2	.958	19	*S-150	1.5
1978	Min-A	158	586	80	160	31	3	19	77	85	70	.273	.366	.433	122	18	2	8	-4	.970	18	*S-157	5.3
1979	Min-A★	162	621	94	168	28	3	24	95	80	81	.271	.357	.441	110	9	2	3	-1	.968	33	*S-161/1-1	5.6
1980	Min-A	133	486	64	135	24	1	12	63	65	63	.278	.365	.405	103	3	3	3	-1	.975	21	*S-125/1-3,D	3.7
1981	Min-A	56	167	24	44	7	1	7	22	31	24	.263	.379	.443	128	7	0	0	0	.946	-17	S-37,D-15/1	-0.8
1982	Min-A	4	13	2	2	1	0	0	3	4	1	.154	.313	.231	51	-1	0	0	0	1.000	1	/S-4	-0.1
	NY-A	142	486	55	125	14	2	20	67	68	100	.257	.348	.418	111	8	0	1	-1	.977	-19	S-89,3-53/2D	-0.4
	Yr	146	499	57	127	15	2	20	67	71	104	.255	.347	.413	109	7	0	1	-1	.979	-18	S-93,3-53/D2	-0.4
1983	NY-A	130	451	70	124	24	1	18	62	58	68	.275	.360	.452	127	17	3	3	-1	.959	-16	S-91,3-26,1	0.7
1984	NY-A	67	209	17	50	8	1	7	26	15	35	.239	.290	.388	89	-4	2	1	-0	.905	0	3-35,S-13/1D	-0.4
	Chi-A	47	135	15	23	4	0	4	13	22	30	.170	.287	.289	57	-8	1	1	-0	.947	-8	3-38/S-3,1D	-1.6
	Yr	114	344	32	73	12	1	11	39	37	65	.212	.289	.349	76	-12	3	2	-0	.923	-7	3-73,S-16/D1	-2.0
1985	Min-A	129	388	57	100	20	0	12	45	60	65	.258	.359	.402	102	2	4	0	0	.987	-15	D-56,S-49,3/1	-1.1
1986	Min-A	143	459	59	113	20	4	20	57	68	80	.246	.343	.438	108	6	1	3	-2	.963	-4	*D-114,S-19/3	-0.1
1987	*Min-A	110	309	32	85	16	1	8	34	36	52	.275	.353	.411	98	-0	2	0	1	.850	-3	D-73,3-14/S	-0.5
Total	13	1653	5657	745	1454	244	25	163	694	771	908	.257	.348	.395	103	32	27	34	-12	.966	14	*S-1069,D-272,3/21C	13.7

■ ROY SMALLEY
Smalley, Roy Frederick Sr. b: 6/9/26, Springfield, Mo. BR/TR, 6'3", 190 lbs. Deb: 4/20/48 F

YEAR	TM/L	G	AB	R	H	2B	3B	HR	RBI	BB	SO	AVG	OBP	SLG	PRO+	BR/A	SB	CS	SBR	FA	FR	G/POS	TPR
1948	Chi-N	124	361	25	78	11	4	4	36	23	76	.216	.265	.302	55	-23	0			.941	9	*S-124	-0.8
1949	Chi-N	135	477	57	117	21	10	8	35	36	77	.245	.304	.382	85	-12	2			.947	14	*S-132	1.2
1950	Chi-N	154	557	58	128	21	9	21	85	49	114	.230	.297	.413	85	-14	2			.945	21	*S-154	1.9
1951	Chi-N	79	238	24	55	7	4	3	31	25	53	.231	.304	.395	85	-6	0	0	0	.953	-13	S-74	-1.3
1952	Chi-N	87	261	36	58	14	1	5	30	29	58	.222	.305	.341	78	-8	0	0	0	.952	-11	S-82	-1.4
1953	Chi-N	82	253	20	63	9	0	6	25	28	57	.249	.329	.356	77	-8	0	0	0	.932	-6	S-77	-0.9
1954	Mil-N	25	36	5	8	3	0	1	7	4	9	.222	.317	.306	67	-2	0	0	0	.950	4	/S-9,2-7,1	0.3
1955	Phi-N	92	260	33	51	11	1	7	39	39	58	.196	.306	.327	69	-11	0	0	0	.974	-16	S-87/2-1,3	-2.0
1956	Phi-N	65	168	14	38	9	3	0	16	23	29	.226	.323	.315	74	-6	0	0	0	.949	-1	S-60	-0.3
1957	Phi-N	28	31	5	5	0	1	1	1	1	9	.161	.212	.323	42	-3	0	0	0	.941	1	S-20	-0.1
1958	Phi-N	1	2	0	0	0	0	0	0	0	1	.000	.000	.000	-99	-1	0	0	0	.714	0	/S-1	0.0
Total	11	872	2644	277	601	103	33	61	305	257	541	.227	.300	.360	77	-93	4	0		.947	5	S-820/2-8,13	-3.4

■ WILL SMALLEY
Smalley, William Darwin "Deacon" b: 6/27/1871, Oakland, Cal. d: 10/11/1891, Bay City, Mich. BR/TR, Deb: 4/19/1890

YEAR	TM/L	G	AB	R	H	2B	3B	HR	RBI	BB	SO	AVG	OBP	SLG	PRO+	BR/A	SB	CS	SBR	FA	FR	G/POS	TPR
1890	Cle-N	136	502	62	107	11	1	0	42	60	44	.213	.303	.239	60	-23	10			.895	17	*3-136	-0.2
1891	Was-a	11	38	5	6	0	1	0	3	5	2	.158	.256	.211	35	-3	0			.762	-2	/3-9,2-2	-0.4
Total	2	147	540	67	113	11	2	0	45	65	46	.209	.300	.237	58	-27	10			.887	15	3-145/2-2	-0.6

■ JOE SMAZA
Smaza, Joseph Paul b: 7/7/23, Detroit, Mich. d: 5/30/79, Royal Oak, Mich. BL/TL, 5'11", 175 lbs. Deb: 9/18/46

YEAR	TM/L	G	AB	R	H	2B	3B	HR	RBI	BB	SO	AVG	OBP	SLG	PRO+	BR/A	SB	CS	SBR	FA	FR	G/POS	TPR
1946	Chi-A	2	5	2	1	0	0	0	0	0	0	.200	.200	.200	12	-1	0	0	0	.000	-1	/O-1	-0.1

■ BILL SMILEY
Smiley, William B. b: 1856, Baltimore, Md. d: 7/11/1884, Baltimore, Md. Deb: 10/13/1874

YEAR	TM/L	G	AB	R	H	2B	3B	HR	RBI	BB	SO	AVG	OBP	SLG	PRO+	BR/A	SB	CS	SBR	FA	FR	G/POS	TPR
1874	Bal-n	2	7	0	0	0	0	0		0		.000	.000	.000	-99	-2						/3-2	-0.1
1882	StL-a	59	240	30	51	4	2	0		6		.213	.232	.246	59	-10				.885	-7	*2-57/O-2	-1.5
	Bal-a	16	61	3	9	0	0	0		0		.148	.148	.148	-0	-6				.843	-5	2-16/S-2	-0.4
	Yr	75	301	33	60	4	2	0		6		.199	.215	.226	48	-16				.874	-5	2-73/O-2,S	-1.9

■ EDGAR SMITH
Smith, Albert Edgar b: 10/15/1860, North Haven, Conn. TR, 6', 200 lbs. Deb: 6/20/1883

YEAR	TM/L	G	AB	R	H	2B	3B	HR	RBI	BB	SO	AVG	OBP	SLG	PRO+	BR/A	SB	CS	SBR	FA	FR	G/POS	TPR
1883	Bos-N	30	115	10	25	5	3	0	16	5	11	.217	.250	.313	68	-4				.905	-0	O-30/C-1	-0.4

■ ALECK SMITH
Smith, Alexander Benjamin "Broadway Aleck" b: 1871, New York, N.Y. d: 7/9/19, New York, N.Y. TR , Deb: 4/23/1897

YEAR	TM/L	G	AB	R	H	2B	3B	HR	RBI	BB	SO	AVG	OBP	SLG	PRO+	BR/A	SB	CS	SBR	FA	FR	G/POS	TPR
1897	Bro-N	66	237	36	71	13	1	1	39	4		.300	.317	.376	87	-5	12			.903	-6	C-43,O-18/1	-0.7
1898	Bro-N	52	199	25	52	6	5	0	23	3		.261	.276	.342	77	-7	7			.909	-10	O-26,C-20/321	-1.6
1899	Bro-N	17	61	6	11	0	1	0	6	2		.180	.206	.213	15	-7	0			.917	-3	C-17	-0.8
	Bal-N	41	120	17	46	6	4	0	25	4		.383	.417	.500	144	7	7			.951	-4	C-36/O-2,1	0.5
	Yr	58	181	23	57	6	5	0	31	6		.315	.347	.403	101	-0	7			.939	-7	C-53/O-2,1	-0.3
1900	Bro-N	7	25	2	6	0	0	0	3	1		.240	.269	.240	39	-2	2			.875	-2	/3-6,C-1	-0.4
1901	NY-N	26	78	5	11	0	0	0	6	0		.141	.141	.141	-19	-12	2			.962	-2	C-24	-1.1
1902	Bal-A	41	145	10	34	3	0	0	21	8		.234	.275	.255	45	-11	5			.947	-6	C-27/1-7,023	-1.3
1903	Bos-A	11	33	4	10	1	0	0	4	0		.303	.303	.333	86	-1	0			.932	0	C-10	0.0
1904	Chi-A	10	29	2	6	1	0	0	1	3		.207	.281	.241	62	-1	1			.778	-3	/O-6,C-1,3	-0.3
1906	NY-N	16	28	3	5	0	0	0	2	1		.179	.207	.179	20	-3	1			1.000	-1	/C-8,1-3,O	-0.3
Total	9	287	955	107	252	30	11	1	130	26		.264	.288	.321	69	-41	37			.933	-35	C-187/O-57,132	-6.0

YEAR	TM/L	G	AB	R	H	2B	3B	HR	RBI	BB	SO	AVG	OBP	SLG	PRO+	BR/A	SB	CS	SBR	FA	FR	G/POS	TPR

■ AL SMITH
Smith, Alphonse Eugene "Fuzzy" b: 2/7/28, Kirkwood, Mo.   BR/TR, 6'1", 191 lbs.   Deb: 7/10/53

YEAR	TM/L	G	AB	R	H	2B	3B	HR	RBI	BB	SO	AVG	OBP	SLG	PRO+	BR/A	SB	CS	SBR	FA	FR	G/POS	TPR
1953	Cle-A	47	150	28	36	9	0	3	14	20	25	.240	.341	.360	92	-1	2	0	1	.920	-3	O-39/3-2	-0.6
1954	*Cle-A	131	481	101	135	29	6	11	50	88	65	.281	.399	.435	126	20	2	9	-5	.984	-3	*O-109,3-21/S	0.8
1955	Cle-A★	154	607	**123**	186	27	4	22	77	93	77	.306	.411	.473	132	30	11	6	-0	.977	-17	*O-120,3-45/S2	0.7
1956	Cle-A	141	526	87	144	26	5	16	71	84	72	.274	.382	.433	112	11	6	3	0	.981	-7	*O-122,3-28/2	-0.2
1957	Cle-A	135	507	78	125	23	5	11	49	79	70	.247	.353	.377	100	2	12	6	0	.913	-16	3-84,O-58	-1.6
1958	Chi-A	139	480	61	121	23	5	12	58	48	77	.252	.326	.396	100	-0	3	3	-1	.970	-1	*O-138/3-1	-1.0
1959	*Chi-A	129	472	65	112	16	4	17	55	46	74	.237	.332	.396	94	-5	7	5	-1	.980	10	*O-128/3-1	-0.2
1960	Chi-A★	142	536	80	169	31	3	12	72	50	65	.315	.377	.451	124	18	8	3	1	.966	-5	*O-141	0.7
1961	Chi-A	147	532	88	148	29	4	28	93	56	67	.278	.352	.506	128	20	4	4	-1	.948	-11	3-80,O-71	0.5
1962	Chi-A	142	511	62	149	23	8	16	82	57	60	.292	.366	.462	122	16	3	3	-1	.935	-23	*3-105,O-39	-0.8
1963	Bal-A	120	368	45	100	17	1	10	39	32	74	.272	.335	.405	110	5	9	0	3	.971	-4	O-97	-0.1
1964	Cle-A	61	136	15	22	1	1	4	9	8	32	.162	.214	.272	34	-12	0	1	-1	1.000	-3	O-48/3-1	-1.9
	Bos-A	29	51	10	11	4	0	2	7	13	10	.216	.385	.412	116	2	0	0	0	.917	-2	3-10/O-8	0.0
	Yr	90	187	25	33	5	1	6	16	21	42	.176	.267	.310	59	-10	0	1	-1	.987	-4	O-56,3-11	-1.9
Total	12	1517	5357	843	1458	258	46	164	676	674	768	.272	.360	.429	113	105	67	43	-6	.974	-84	*O-1118,3-378/S2	-3.7

■ TONY SMITH
Smith, Anthony b: 5/14/1884, Chicago, Ill. d: 2/27/64, Galveston, Tex.   BR/TR, 5'9", 150 lbs.   Deb: 8/12/07

YEAR	TM/L	G	AB	R	H	2B	3B	HR	RBI	BB	SO	AVG	OBP	SLG	PRO+	BR/A	SB	CS	SBR	FA	FR	G/POS	TPR
1907	Was-A	51	139	12	26	1	1	0	8	18		.187	.285	.209	63	-5	3			.920	-9	S-51	-1.4
1910	Bro-N	106	321	31	58	10	1	1	16	69	53	.181	.329	.227	65	-11	9			.941	12	*S-101/3-6	0.6
1911	Bro-N	13	40	3	6	1	0	0	2	8	7	.150	.292	.175	33	-3	1			.870	3	S-10/2-3	-0.3
Total	3	170	500	46	90	12	2	1	26	95	60	.180	.314	.218	62	-19	13			.931	4	S-162/3-6,2	-1.1

■ KLONDIKE SMITH
Smith, Armstrong Frederick b: 1/4/1887, London, England d: 11/15/59, Springfield, Mass.   BL/TL, 5'9", 160 lbs.   Deb: 9/28/12

YEAR	TM/L	G	AB	R	H	2B	3B	HR	RBI	BB	SO	AVG	OBP	SLG	PRO+	BR/A	SB	CS	SBR	FA	FR	G/POS	TPR
1912	NY-A	7	27	0	5	1	0	0	0	0	0	.185	.185	.222	15	-3	1			1.000	-1	/O-7	-0.5

■ BILLY SMITH
Smith, Billy Edward b: 7/14/53, Jonesboro, La.   BB/TR, 6'2.5", 185 lbs.   Deb: 4/13/75

YEAR	TM/L	G	AB	R	H	2B	3B	HR	RBI	BB	SO	AVG	OBP	SLG	PRO+	BR/A	SB	CS	SBR	FA	FR	G/POS	TPR
1975	Cal-A	59	143	10	29	5	1	0	14	12	27	.203	.265	.252	50	-10	1	3	-2	.932	-9	S-50/1-6,3D	-1.6
1976	Cal-A	13	8	0	3	0	0	0	0	0	2	.375	.375	.375	128	0	0	0	0	.625	-1	S-10/D-1	0.0
1977	Bal-A	109	367	44	79	12	2	5	29	33	71	.215	.282	.300	62	-19	3	2	-0	.991	4	*2-104/S-5,13	-0.8
1978	Bal-A	85	250	29	65	12	2	5	30	27	40	.260	.335	.384	108	3	3	0	1	.986	-1	2-83/S-2	0.8
1979	*Bal-A	68	189	18	47	9	4	6	33	15	33	.249	.311	.434	102	-0	1	0	0	.980	-8	2-63/S-5	-0.4
1981	SF-N	36	61	6	11	0	0	1	5	9	16	.180	.286	.230	48	-4	0	0	0	.971	-0	S-21/2-5,3	-0.3
Total	6	370	1018	107	234	38	9	17	111	96	189	.230	.299	.335	79	-30	8	5	-1	.987	-15	2-255/S-93,13D	-2.3

■ BOBBY GENE SMITH
Smith, Bobby Gene b: 5/28/34, Hood River, Ore.   BR/TR, 5'11", 185 lbs.   Deb: 4/16/57

YEAR	TM/L	G	AB	R	H	2B	3B	HR	RBI	BB	SO	AVG	OBP	SLG	PRO+	BR/A	SB	CS	SBR	FA	FR	G/POS	TPR
1957	StL-N	93	185	24	39	7	1	3	18	13	35	.211	.263	.308	52	-13	1	1	-0	.973	-8	O-79	-2.5
1958	StL-N	28	88	8	25	3	0	2	5	2	18	.284	.308	.386	79	-3	0	0	0	1.000	-1	O-27	-0.5
1959	StL-N	43	60	11	13	1	1	1	7	1	9	.217	.230	.317	41	-5	0	0	0	.971	-4	O-32	-1.0
1960	Phi-N	98	217	24	62	5	2	4	27	10	28	.286	.317	.382	90	-3	2	3	-1	1.000	1	O-70/3-1	-0.6
1961	Phi-N	79	174	16	44	7	0	2	18	15	32	.253	.316	.328	72	-7	0	1	-1	.971	6	O-47	-0.4
1962	NY-N	8	22	1	3	0	1	0	2	2	3	.136	.240	.227	26	-2	0	1	-1	1.000	-1	/O-6	-0.4
	Chi-N	13	29	3	5	0	0	0	2	2	6	.172	.226	.276	33	-3	0	1	-1	1.000	-1	/O-7	-0.5
	StL-N	91	130	13	30	9	1	2	6	7	14	.231	.270	.300	48	-10	1	1	-0	1.000	-14	O-80	-2.6
	Yr	112	181	17	38	9	2	2	16	12	22	.210	.259	.287	43	-15	1	3	-2	1.000	-15	O-93	-3.5
1965	Cal-A	23	57	1	13	3	0	0	5	2	10	.228	.267	.281	57	-3	0	1	-1	1.000	-0	O-15	-0.5
Total	7	476	962	101	234	35	5	13	96	55	154	.243	.286	.331	64	-48	5	9	-4	.986	-22	O-363/3-1	-9.0

■ BRICK SMITH
Smith, Brick Dudley b: 5/2/59, Charlotte, N.C.   BR/TR, 6'4", 225 lbs.   Deb: 9/13/87

YEAR	TM/L	G	AB	R	H	2B	3B	HR	RBI	BB	SO	AVG	OBP	SLG	PRO+	BR/A	SB	CS	SBR	FA	FR	G/POS	TPR
1987	Sea-A	5	8	1	1	0	0	0	0	2	4	.125	.300	.125	18	-1	0	0	0	.963	0	/1-3,D-1	-0.1
1988	Sea-A	4	10	1	1	0	0	0	1	0	1	.100	.100	.100	-42	-2	0	0	0	1.000	1	/1-4	-0.1
Total	2	9	18	2	2	0	0	0	1	2	5	.111	.200	.111	-12	-3	0	0	0	.983	1	/1-7,D-1	-0.2

■ BERNIE SMITH
Smith, Calvin Bernard b: 9/4/41, Ponchatoula, La.   BR/TR, 5'9", 164 lbs.   Deb: 7/31/70

YEAR	TM/L	G	AB	R	H	2B	3B	HR	RBI	BB	SO	AVG	OBP	SLG	PRO+	BR/A	SB	CS	SBR	FA	FR	G/POS	TPR
1970	Mil-A	44	76	8	21	3	1	1	6	11	12	.276	.382	.382	110	2	1	3	-2	.979	-7	O-39	-0.8
1971	Mil-A	15	36	1	5	1	0	1	3	0	5	.139	.162	.250	15	-4	0	0	0	.923	-3	O-12	-0.8
Total	2	59	112	9	26	4	1	2	9	11	17	.232	.317	.339	83	-3	1	3	-2	.967	-9	/O-51	-1.6

■ REGGIE SMITH
Smith, Carl Reginald b: 4/2/45, Shreveport, La.   BB/TR, 6', 195 lbs.   Deb: 9/18/66   C

YEAR	TM/L	G	AB	R	H	2B	3B	HR	RBI	BB	SO	AVG	OBP	SLG	PRO+	BR/A	SB	CS	SBR	FA	FR	G/POS	TPR
1966	Bos-A	6	26	1	4	1	0	0	0	0	5	.154	.154	.192	-1	-3	0	0	0	.944	1	/O-6	-0.3
1967	*Bos-A	158	565	78	139	24	6	15	61	57	95	.246	.316	.389	99	-1	16	6	1	.983	17	*O-144/2-6	1.2
1968	Bos-A	155	558	78	148	**37**	5	15	69	64	77	.265	.345	.430	125	17	22	18	-4	.985	10	*O-155	1.7
1969	Bos-A★	143	543	87	168	29	7	25	93	54	72	.309	.373	.527	142	29	7	13	-6	.959	6	*O-139	2.2
1970	Bos-A	147	580	109	176	32	7	22	74	51	60	.303	.364	.497	126	20	10	7	-1	.977	16	*O-145	2.7
1971	Bos-A	159	618	85	175	**33**	2	30	96	63	82	.283	.354	.489	128	21	11	3	2	.966	16	*O-159	3.2
1972	Bos-A★	131	467	75	126	25	4	21	74	68	63	.270	.367	.475	142	25	15	4	2	.981	5	*O-104/1-1,D	2.9
1973	Bos-A	115	423	79	128	23	2	21	69	68	49	.303	.400	.515	148	28	3	2	-0	.983	7	*O-132/1-1	2.9
1974	StL-N★	143	517	79	160	26	9	23	100	71	70	.309	.394	.528	158	39	4	3	-1	.976	6	*O-132/1-1	4.0
1975	StL-N★	135	477	67	144	26	3	19	76	63	59	.302	.387	.488	137	24	9	7	-1	.963	-5	O-69,1-66/3	1.1
1976	StL-N	47	170	20	37	7	1	8	23	14	28	.218	.281	.412	94	-1	1	2	-1	.986	7	1-17,O-16,3	0.2
	LA-N	65	225	35	63	8	4	10	26	18	42	.280	.336	.484	133	9	2	0	1	.985	3	O-58/3-1	1.0
	Yr	112	395	55	100	15	5	18	49	32	70	.253	.312	.453	116	6	3	2	-0	.989	10	O-74,1-17,3	1.2
1977	*LA-N★	148	488	104	150	27	4	32	87	104	76	.307	**.432**	.576	**168**	51	7	5	-1	.980	-7	*O-140	3.7
1978	*LA-N★	128	447	82	132	27	2	29	93	70	90	.295	.392	.559	164	38	12	5	1	.950	-4	*O-126	3.1
1979	LA-N	68	234	41	64	13	1	10	32	31	50	.274	.363	.466	126	9	6	5	-1	.988	6	O-62	1.3
1980	LA-N★	92	311	47	100	13	0	15	55	41	63	.322	.402	.508	155	24	5	6	-2	.994	6	O-84	2.6
1981	*LA-N	41	35	5	7	1	0	1	8	7	8	.200	.333	.314	88	-0	0	0	0	1.000	0	/1-2	0.0
1982	SF-N	106	387	51	99	11	0	18	56	46	46	.284	.367	.470	133	15	7	0	2	.982	2	1-99	1.5
Total	17	1987	7033	1123	2020	363	57	314	1092	890	1030	.287	.370	.489	136	342	137	86	-11	.976	93	*O-1668,1-186/3D2	35.0

■ CHARLIE SMITH
Smith, Charles J. b: 12/11/1840, Brooklyn, N.Y. d: 11/15/1897, Great Neck, N.Y.   5'10.5", 150 lbs.   Deb: 5/18/1871

YEAR	TM/L	G	AB	R	H	2B	3B	HR	RBI	BB	SO	AVG	OBP	SLG	PRO+	BR/A	SB	CS	SBR	FA	FR	G/POS	TPR
1871	Mut-n	14	72	15	19	2	1	0	5	1	1	.264	.274	.319	77	-1	6					3-11/2-3	-0.2

■ POP SMITH
Smith, Charles Marvin b: 10/12/1856, Digby, N.S., Canada d: 4/18/27, Boston, Mass.   BR/TR, 5'11", 170 lbs.   Deb: 5/1/1880   U

YEAR	TM/L	G	AB	R	H	2B	3B	HR	RBI	BB	SO	AVG	OBP	SLG	PRO+	BR/A	SB	CS	SBR	FA	FR	G/POS	TPR
1880	Cin-N	83	334	35	69	10	9	0	27	6	36	.207	.221	.290	72	-9				.855	-11	*2-83	-1.6
1881	Cle-N	10	34	1	4	0	0	0	3	0	8	.118	.118	.118	-27	-5				.838	2	3-10	-0.6
	Buf-N	3	11	3	0	0	0	0	1	0	3	.000	.214	.000	-27	-1				.840	-1	/2-3	-0.2
	Wor-N	11	41	1	3	0	0	0	2	3	5	.073	.136	.073	-31	-6				.955	2	/O-8,2-3	-0.4
	Yr	24	86	5	7	0	0	0	6	6	18	.081	.141	.081	-28	-12				.838	-1	3-10/O-8,2	-1.2
1882	Phi-a	20	65	10	6	0	0	0			12	.092	.234	.092	12	-6				.732	2	3-11/S-4,O2	-0.3
	Lou-a	3	11	1	2	0	0	0			0	.182	.182	.182	24	-1				.778	-0	/S-3	-0.1
	Yr	23	76	11	8	0	0	0			12	.105	.227	.105	14	-7				.732	2	3-11/S-7,O2	-0.4
1883	Col-a	97	405	82	106	14	**17**	4			22	.262	.300	.410	137	18				.889	18	*2-73,3-24/P	3.1
1884	Col-a	108	445	78	106	18	10	6			20	.238	.289	.364	122	12				.905	29	*2-108	3.9
1885	Pit-a	106	453	85	113	11	13	0			25	.249	.293	.331	98	-1				.922	33	*2-106	3.2

YEAR	TM/L	G	AB	R	H	2B	3B	HR	RBI	BB	SO	AVG	OBP	SLG	PRO+	BR/A	SB	CS	SBR	FA	FR	G/POS	TPR
1886	Pit-a	126	483	75	105	20	9	2			42	.217	.288	.308	87	-7	38			.895	21	*S-98,2-28/C	1.4
1887	Pit-N	122	456	69	98	12	7	2	54	30	48	.215	.283	.285	62	-22	30			.914	-6	*2-89,S-33	-2.2
1888	Pit-N	131	481	61	99	15	2	4	52	22	78	.206	.248	.270	71	-15	37			.901	-2	S-75,2-56	-1.3
1889	Pit-N	72	258	26	54	10	2	5	27	24	38	.209	.292	.322	79	-7	12			.897	-0	S-58/2-9,3O	-0.3
	Bos-N	59	208	21	54	13	4	0	32	23	30	.260	.345	.361	92	-3	11			.890	-0	S-59	0.1
	Yr	131	466	47	108	23	6	5	59	47	68	.232	.315	.339	85	-9	23			.894	-0	*S-117/2-9,3O	-0.2
1890	Bos-N	134	463	82	106	16	12	1	53	80	81	.229	.353	.322	90	-5	39			.918	-20	*2-134/S-1	-1.5
1891	Was-a	27	90	13	16	2	2	0	13	13	16	.178	.295	.244	57	-5	2			.919	7	2-19/S-5,3	0.3
Total	12	1112	4238	643	941	141	87	24	264	325	345	.222	.287	.313	86	-64	169			.903	70	2-713,S-336/3OPC	3.5

■ CHARLEY SMITH
Smith, Charles William b: 9/15/37, Charleston, S.C. BR/TR, 6', 177 lbs. Deb: 9/8/60

YEAR	TM/L	G	AB	R	H	2B	3B	HR	RBI	BB	SO	AVG	OBP	SLG	PRO+	BR/A	SB	CS	SBR	FA	FR	G/POS	TPR
1960	LA-N	18	60	2	10	1	1	0	5	1	15	.167	.180	.217	8	-8	0	0	0	.953	0	3-18	-0.8
1961	LA-N	9	24	4	6	1	0	2	3	1	6	.250	.280	.542	103	-0	0	0	0	1.000	-0	/3-4,S-3	0.0
	Phi-N	112	411	43	102	13	4	9	47	23	76	.248	.296	.365	75	-15	3	4	-2	.924	-2	3-94,S-14	-1.7
	Yr	121	435	47	108	14	4	11	50	24	82	.248	.295	.375	77	-15	3	4	-2	.926	-3	3-98,S-17	-1.7
1962	Chi-A	65	145	11	30	4	0	2	17	9	32	.207	.258	.276	44	-12	0	1	-1	.944	2	3-54	-1.0
1963	Chi-A	4	7	0	2	0	1	0	1	0	2	.286	.286	.571	136	0	0	0	0	1.000	0	/S-1	0.2
1964	Chi-A	2	7	1	1	0	0	0	0	1	1	.143	.250	.429	87	-0	0	0	0	1.000	3	/3-2	0.3
	NY-N	127	443	44	106	12	0	20	58	19	101	.239	.275	.402	90	-7	2	2	0	.917	-12	3-85,S-36,O	-2.1
1965	NY-N	135	499	49	122	20	3	16	62	17	123	.244	.275	.393	89	-9	2	1	0	.957	10	*3-131/S-6,2	-0.2
1966	StL-N	116	391	34	104	13	4	10	43	22	81	.266	.305	.396	93	-4	0	2	-1	.964	-1	*3-107/S-1	-0.9
1967	NY-A	135	425	38	95	15	3	9	38	32	110	.224	.279	.336	84	-9	0	2	-1	.947	11	*3-115	-0.1
1968	NY-A	46	70	2	16	4	1	1	7	5	18	.229	.280	.357	95	-1	0	0	0	.961	4	3-13	0.3
1969	Chi-N	2	2	0	0	0	0	0	0	0	0	.000	.000	.000	-89	-0	0	0	0	.000	0	H	-0.1
Total	10	771	2484	228	594	83	18	69	281	130	565	.239	.281	.370	82	-65	7	12	-5	.945	16	3-623/S-61,O2	-6.1

■ CHRIS SMITH
Smith, Christopher William b: 7/18/57, Torrance, Cal. BB/TR, 6', 185 lbs. Deb: 5/14/81

YEAR	TM/L	G	AB	R	H	2B	3B	HR	RBI	BB	SO	AVG	OBP	SLG	PRO+	BR/A	SB	CS	SBR	FA	FR	G/POS	TPR
1981	Mon-N	7	7	0	0	0	0	0	0	0	2	.000	.000	.000	-99	-2	0	0	0	1.000	0	/2-1	-0.2
1982	Mon-N	2	2	0	0	0	0	0	0	0	1	.000	.000	.000	-98	-1	0	0	0	.000	0	/H	-0.1
1983	SF-N	22	67	13	22	6	1	1	11	7	12	.328	.408	.493	153	5	0	0	0	.976	-2	1-15/O-4,3	0.2
Total	3	31	76	13	22	6	1	1	11	7	15	.289	.365	.434	124	3	0	0	0	.976	-2	/1-15,O-4,32	-0.1

■ EARL SMITH
Smith, Earl Calvin b: 3/14/28, Sunnyside, Wash. BR/TR, 6', 185 lbs. Deb: 4/14/55

YEAR	TM/L	G	AB	R	H	2B	3B	HR	RBI	BB	SO	AVG	OBP	SLG	PRO+	BR/A	SB	CS	SBR	FA	FR	G/POS	TPR
1955	Pit-N	5	16	1	1	0	0	0	0	4	2	.063	.286	.063	-1	-2	0	0	0	1.000	0	/O-5	-0.3

■ EARL SMITH
Smith, Earl Leonard "Sheriff" b: 1/20/1891, Oak Hill, Ohio d: 3/14/43, Portsmouth, Ohio BB/TR, 5'11", 170 lbs. Deb: 9/12/16

YEAR	TM/L	G	AB	R	H	2B	3B	HR	RBI	BB	SO	AVG	OBP	SLG	PRO+	BR/A	SB	CS	SBR	FA	FR	G/POS	TPR
1916	Chi-N	14	27	2	7	1	1	0	4	2	5	.259	.310	.370	98	-0	1			.800	-3	/O-7	-0.3
1917	StL-A	52	199	31	56	7	7	0	10	15	21	.281	.332	.387	124	5	5			.977	5	O-51	0.8
1918	StL-A	89	286	28	77	10	5	0	32	13	16	.269	.303	.339	97	-3	13			.952	1	O-81	-0.6
1919	StL-A	88	252	21	63	12	5	1	36	18	27	.250	.300	.349	80	-7	1			.971	10	O-68	-0.2
1920	StL-A	103	353	45	108	21	8	3	55	13	18	.306	.336	.436	100	-1	11	4	1	.916	-5	3-70,O-15	-0.3
1921	StL-A	25	78	7	26	4	2	2	14	3	4	.333	.366	.513	115	1	0	0	0	.878	-3	3-13/O-4	-0.1
	Was-A	59	180	20	39	5	2	2	12	10	19	.217	.266	.300	46	-15	1	0	0	.949	4	O-43/3-1	-1.3
	Yr	84	258	27	65	9	4	4	26	13	23	.252	.296	.364	69	-13	1	0	0	.944	0	O-47,3-14	-1.4
1922	Was-A	65	205	22	53	12	2	1	23	8	17	.259	.293	.351	71	-10	4	4	-1	.917	1	O-49/3-2	-1.3
Total	7	495	1580	176	429	72	32	9	186	82	127	.272	.311	.375	90	-30	36	8		.952	10	O-318/3-86	-3.3

■ EARL SMITH
Smith, Earl Sutton "Oil" b: 2/14/1897, Hot Springs, Ark. d: 6/8/63, Little Rock, Ark. BL/TR, 5'10.5", 180 lbs. Deb: 4/24/19

YEAR	TM/L	G	AB	R	H	2B	3B	HR	RBI	BB	SO	AVG	OBP	SLG	PRO+	BR/A	SB	CS	SBR	FA	FR	G/POS	TPR
1919	NY-N	21	36	5	9	2	1	0	8	3	3	.250	.308	.361	102	0				.973	-3	C-14/2-1	-0.2
1920	NY-N	91	262	20	77	7	1	1	30	18	16	.294	.344	.340	98	-0	5	2	0	.976	-5	C-82	0.0
1921	*NY-N	89	229	35	77	8	4	10	51	27	8	.336	.409	.537	148	16	4	3	-1	.965	-10	C-78	0.9
1922	*NY-N	90	234	29	65	11	4	9	39	37	12	.278	.383	.474	119	7	1	1	-0	.978	-2	C-75	0.8
1923	NY-N	24	34	2	7	1	1	1	4	4	1	.206	.289	.382	77	-1	0	0	0	.975	2	C-12	0.1
	Bos-N	72	191	22	55	15	1	3	19	22	10	.288	.364	.424	112	3	0	1	-1	.975	-4	C-54	0.2
	Yr	96	225	24	62	16	2	4	23	26	11	.276	.353	.418	106	2	0	1	-1	.975	-2	C-66	0.3
1924	Bos-N	33	59	1	16	3	0	0	8	6	3	.271	.338	.322	81	-1	0	1	-1	.946	-1	C-13	-0.2
	Pit-N	39	111	12	41	10	1	4	21	13	4	.369	.435	.586	148	12	2	0	1	.974	0	C-35	1.3
	Yr	72	170	13	57	13	1	4	29	19	7	.335	.402	.494	140	10	2	1	0	.967	-1	C-48	1.1
1925	*Pit-N	109	329	34	103	22	3	8	64	31	13	.313	.374	.471	107	3	4	1	1	.968	11	C-96	1.9
1926	Pit-N	105	292	29	101	17	2	2	46	28	7	.346	.407	.438	121	9	1			.964	-4	C-98	1.9
1927	*Pit-N	66	189	16	51	3	1	5	25	21	7	.270	.346	.376	87	-3	0			.986	-4	C-61	-0.4
1928	Pit-N	32	85	8	21	6	0	2	11	11	7	.247	.333	.388	85	-2	0			.967	-4	C-28	-0.3
	*StL-N	24	58	3	13	2	0	0	7	5	4	.224	.286	.259	42	-5	0			1.000	-1	C-18	-0.4
	Yr	56	143	11	34	8	0	2	18	16	11	.238	.314	.336	68	-7	0			.980	-5	C-46	-0.7
1929	StL-N	57	145	9	50	8	0	1	22	18	6	.345	.417	.421	107	3	0			.962	-5	C-50	0.1
1930	StL-N	8	10	0	0	0	0	0	0	3	1	.000	.231	.000	-36	-2	0			.913	1	/C-6	-0.1
Total	12	860	2264	225	686	115	19	46	355	247	106	.303	.374	.432	111	37	18	9		.971	-20	C-720/2-1	5.6

■ EDGAR SMITH
Smith, Edgar Eugene b: 6/12/1862, Providence, R.I. d: 11/3/1892, Providence, R.I. BR/TR, 5'10", 160 lbs. Deb: 5/25/1883

YEAR	TM/L	G	AB	R	H	2B	3B	HR	RBI	BB	SO	AVG	OBP	SLG	PRO+	BR/A	SB	CS	SBR	FA	FR	G/POS	TPR
1883	Pro-N	2	9	2	2	1	0	0	0	0	2	.222	.222	.333	64	-0				1.000	-0	/1-2,O-2	-0.1
	Phi-N	1	4	1	3	0	0	0	1	0	0	.750	.750	.750	393	1				.000	-1	/P-1,O-1	0.0
	Yr	3	13	3	5	1	0	0	2	0	2	.385	.385	.462	158	1				1.000	-1	/O-3,1-2,P	-0.1
1884	Was-a	14	57	5	5	1	0		1	0	1	.088	.103	.123	-30	-8				.794	5	O-12/P-3	-0.2
1885	Pro-N	1	4	0	1	0	0	0	0	0	0	.250	.250	.250	65	-0				.750	0	/P-1	0.0
1890	Cle-N	8	24	2	7	0	1	0	4	4	1	.292	.393	.375	126	1	0			.900	5	/P-6,O-2	0.0
Total	4	26	98	10	18	1	2	0	6	5	3	.184	.223	.235	47	-6	0			.821	5	/O-17,P-11,1	-0.3

■ MAYO SMITH
Smith, Edward Mayo b: 1/17/15, New London, Mo. d: 11/24/77, Boynton Beach, Fla BL/TR, 6', 183 lbs. Deb: 6/24/45 M

YEAR	TM/L	G	AB	R	H	2B	3B	HR	RBI	BB	SO	AVG	OBP	SLG	PRO+	BR/A	SB	CS	SBR	FA	FR	G/POS	TPR
1945	Phi-A	73	203	18	43	5	0	0	11	36	13	.212	.333	.236	67	-7	0	1	-1	.976	-8	O-65	-2.0

■ ELMER SMITH
Smith, Elmer Ellsworth b: 3/23/1868, Pittsburgh, Pa. d: 11/3/45, Pittsburgh, Pa. BL/TL, 5'11", 178 lbs. Deb: 9/10/1886

YEAR	TM/L	G	AB	R	H	2B	3B	HR	RBI	BB	SO	AVG	OBP	SLG	PRO+	BR/A	SB	CS	SBR	FA	FR	G/POS	TPR
1886	Cin-a	9	28	6	8	1	1	0			9	.286	.459	.393	163	3				.600	-0	P-9/O-1	0.0
1887	Cin-a	52	186	26	47	10	6	0			11	.253	.298	.371	84	-5	5			.851	-6	P-52/O-2	-0.1
1888	Cin-a	40	129	15	29	4	1	0		9	20	.225	.329	.271	88	-1	2			.838	-6	P-40/O-2	-0.1
1889	Cin-a	29	83	12	23	3	1	2	17	7	18	.277	.348	.410	112	1	1			.821	-4	P-29	0.0
1892	Pit-N	138	511	86	140	16	14	4	63	82	43	.274	.375	.384	129	20	22			.885	-5	*O-124,P-17	0.8
1893	Pit-N	128	518	121	179	26	23	6	103	77	23	.346	.435	.525	158	44	26			.921	3	*O-128	3.3
1894	Pit-N	125	489	128	174	33	19	6	72	65	33	.356	.436	.538	135	29	33			.933	4	*O-125/P-1	1.9
1895	Pit-N	124	480	88	145	14	12	1	81	55	25	.302	.381	.387	104	5	34			.896	-3	*O-123	-0.6
1896	Pit-N	122	484	121	175	21	14	6	94	74	18	.362	.454	.500	158	45	33			.946	9	*O-122	3.6
1897	Pit-N	123	467	99	145	19	17	6	54	70		.310	.408	.463	135	26	25			.904	3	*O-123	1.6
1898	Cin-N	123	486	79	166	21	10	1	66	69		.342	.425	.432	136	25	20			.949	4	*O-123/P-1	1.8
1899	Cin-N	87	339	65	101	13	6	1	24	47		.298	.385	.381	108	5	7			.922	-1	O-87	-0.2
1900	Cin-N	29	111	14	31	8	4	1	18	18		.279	.389	.414	125	4	5			.930	0	O-27	0.2
	NY-N	85	312	47	81	9	7	2	34	24		.260	.317	.353	89	-5	14			.953	-8	O-83	-1.8

YEAR	TM/L	G	AB	R	H	2B	3B	HR	RBI	BB	SO	AVG	OBP	SLG	PRO+	BR/A	SB	CS	SBR	FA	FR	G/POS	TPR
	Yr	114	423	61	112	13	11	3	52	42		.265	.337	.369	99	-1	19			.944	-8	*O-110	-1.6
1901	Pit-N	4	4	0	0	0	0	0	0	0	2	.000	.333	.000	1	-0	0			1.000	-0	/O-1	-0.1
	Bos-N	16	57	5	10	2	1	0	3	6		.175	.254	.246	41	-4	2			.833	-3	O-15	-0.8
	Yr	20	61	5	10	2	1	0	3	8		.164	.261	.230	40	-5	2			.846	-3	O-16	-0.9
Total	14	1234	4684	912	1454	196	136	37	638	636	139	.310	.398	.434	126	191	232			.921	-15	*O-1086,P-149	9.5

■ ELMER SMITH
Smith, Elmer John b: 9/21/1892, Sandusky, Ohio d: 8/3/84, Columbia, Ky. BL/TR, 5'10", 165 lbs. Deb: 9/20/14

YEAR	TM/L	G	AB	R	H	2B	3B	HR	RBI	BB	SO	AVG	OBP	SLG	PRO+	BR/A	SB	CS	SBR	FA	FR	G/POS	TPR
1914	Cle-A	13	53	5	17	3	0	0	8	2	11	.321	.345	.377	113	1	1	1	-0	1.000	1	O-13	0.1
1915	Cle-A	144	476	37	118	23	12	3	67	36	75	.248	.301	.366	97	-4	10	11	-4	.923	0	*O-123	-1.4
1916	Cle-A	79	213	25	59	15	3	3	40	18	35	.277	.336	.418	119	4	3			.966	-2	O-57	0.0
	Was-A	45	168	12	36	10	3	2	27	18	28	.214	.298	.345	94	-2	4			.988	1	O-45	-0.3
	Yr	124	381	37	95	25	6	5	67	36	63	.249	.319	.386	108	2	7			.976	-1	*O-102	-0.3
1917	Was-A	35	117	8	26	4	3	0	17	5	14	.222	.260	.308	74	-4	1			.901	-0	O-29	-0.7
	Cle-A	64	161	21	42	5	1	3	22	13	18	.261	.316	.360	99	-1	6			.986	-1	O-40	-0.4
	Yr	99	278	29	68	9	4	3	39	18	32	.245	.293	.338	89	-5	7			.943	-1	O-69	-1.1
1919	Cle-A	114	395	60	110	24	6	9	54	41	30	.278	.354	.438	115	7	15			.957	-6	*O-111	-0.7
1920	*Cle-A	129	456	82	144	37	10	12	103	53	35	.316	.391	.520	135	22	5	4	-1	.970	-8	*O-129	0.5
1921	Cle-A	129	431	98	125	28	9	16	85	56	46	.290	.374	.508	121	13	0	2	-1	.971	-8	*O-127	-0.4
1922	Bos-A	73	231	43	66	13	6	6	32	25	21	.286	.358	.472	116	5	0	3	-2	.947	-2	O-58	0.1
	*NY-A	21	27	1	5	0	0	1	5	3	5	.185	.267	.296	46	-2	0	0	0	.933	-2	O-11	-0.4
	Yr	94	258	44	71	13	6	7	37	28	26	.275	.348	.453	108	2	0	3	-2	.945	1	O-69	-0.3
1923	NY-A	70	183	30	56	6	2	7	35	21	21	.306	.377	.475	121	5	3	1	0	.948	-2	O-47	0.1
1925	Cin-N	96	284	47	77	13	7	8	46	28	20	.271	.339	.451	102	0	6	5	-1	.967	-5	O-80	-1.0
Total	10	1012	3195	469	881	181	62	70	541	319	359	.276	.344	.437	112	44	54	27		.957	-29	O-870	-4.5

■ MIKE SMITH
Smith, Elwood Hope b: 11/16/04, Norfolk, Va. d: 5/31/81, Chesapeake, Va. BL/TR, 5'11.5", 170 lbs. Deb: 9/4/26

YEAR	TM/L	G	AB	R	H	2B	3B	HR	RBI	BB	SO	AVG	OBP	SLG	PRO+	BR/A	SB	CS	SBR	FA	FR	G/POS	TPR
1926	NY-N	4	7	0	1	0	0	0	0	0	2	.143	.143	.143	-23	-1	0			1.000	0	/O-1	-0.1

■ CARR SMITH
Smith, Emamuel Carr b: 4/8/01, Kernersville, N.C. d: 4/14/89, Miami, Fla. BR/TR, 6'1", 175 lbs. Deb: 9/23/23

YEAR	TM/L	G	AB	R	H	2B	3B	HR	RBI	BB	SO	AVG	OBP	SLG	PRO+	BR/A	SB	CS	SBR	FA	FR	G/POS	TPR
1923	Was-A	5	9	0	1	1	0	0	1	0	0	.111	.111	.222	-14	-2	0	0	0	1.000	-1	/O-4	-0.3
1924	Was-A	5	10	1	2	0	0	0	0	0	3	.200	.200	.200	3	-1	0	0	0	1.000	-1	/O-4	-0.3
Total	2	10	19	1	3	1	0	0	1	0	3	.158	.158	.211	-5	-3	0	0	0	1.000	-3	/O-8	-0.6

■ ERNIE SMITH
Smith, Ernest Henry "Kansas City Kid" b: 10/11/1899, Totowa, N.J. d: 4/6/73, Brooklyn, N.Y. BR/TR, 5'8", 155 lbs. Deb: 4/17/30

YEAR	TM/L	G	AB	R	H	2B	3B	HR	RBI	BB	SO	AVG	OBP	SLG	PRO+	BR/A	SB	CS	SBR	FA	FR	G/POS	TPR
1930	Chi-A	24	79	5	19	3	0	0	3	5	6	.241	.286	.278	45	-7	2	0	1	.920	0	S-21	-0.3

■ FRANK SMITH
Smith, Frank L. b: 11/24/1857, Canada d: 10/11/28, Canandaigua, N.Y. Deb: 8/6/1884

YEAR	TM/L	G	AB	R	H	2B	3B	HR	RBI	BB	SO	AVG	OBP	SLG	PRO+	BR/A	SB	CS	SBR	FA	FR	G/POS	TPR
1884	Pit-a	10	36	3	9	0	1	0		0		.250	.250	.306	79	-1				.930	-3	/C-7,O-3	-0.3

■ FRED SMITH
Smith, Fred Vincent b: 7/29/1886, Cleveland, Ohio d: 5/28/61, Cleveland, Ohio BR/TR, 5'11.5", 185 lbs. Deb: 4/17/13 F

YEAR	TM/L	G	AB	R	H	2B	3B	HR	RBI	BB	SO	AVG	OBP	SLG	PRO+	BR/A	SB	CS	SBR	FA	FR	G/POS	TPR
1913	Bos-N	92	285	35	65	9	3	0	27	29	55	.228	.302	.281	65	-12	7			.920	-14	3-59,2-14,S/O	-2.7
1914	Buf-F	145	473	48	104	12	10	2	45	49	78	.220	.297	.300	54	-33	24			.930	-0	*3-127,S-19/1	-2.8
1915	Buf-F	35	114	8	27	2	4	0	11	13	15	.237	.320	.325	71	-5	2			.920	3	S-32/3-1	0.1
	Bro-F	110	385	41	95	16	6	5	58	25	49	.247	.298	.358	76	-15	21			.920	1	S-94,3-15	-0.6
	Yr	145	499	49	122	18	10	5	69	38	64	.244	.303	.351	75	-19	23			.920	5	*S-126,3-16	-0.5
1917	StL-N	56	165	11	30	0	2	1	17	17	22	.182	.262	.224	51	-9	4			.950	7	3-51/2-2,S	-0.2
Total	4	438	1422	143	321	39	25	8	158	133	219	.226	.296	.305	63	-73	58			.932	-3	3-253,S-157/201	-6.2

■ GEORGE SMITH
Smith, George Cornelius b: 7/7/37, St.Petersburg, Fla. d: 6/15/87, St.Petersburg, Fla. BR/TR, 5'10", 170 lbs. Deb: 8/4/63

YEAR	TM/L	G	AB	R	H	2B	3B	HR	RBI	BB	SO	AVG	OBP	SLG	PRO+	BR/A	SB	CS	SBR	FA	FR	G/POS	TPR
1963	Det-A	52	171	16	37	8	2	0	17	18	34	.216	.298	.287	63	-8	4	0	1	.982	11	2-52	0.9
1964	Det-A	5	7	1	2	0	0	0	2	1	4	.286	.375	.286	86	-0	1	0	0	1.000	1	/2-3	0.1
1965	Det-A	32	53	6	5	0	0	1	1	3	18	.094	.143	.151	-16	-8	0	0	0	.984	3	2-22/S-3,3	-0.5
1966	Bos-A	128	403	41	86	19	4	8	37	37	86	.213	.284	.340	71	-15	4	0	1	.969	16	*2-109,S-19	1.1
Total	4	217	634	64	130	27	6	9	57	59	142	.205	.278	.309	62	-31	9	0	3	.974	30	2-186/S-22,3	1.6

■ HEINIE SMITH
Smith, George Henry b: 10/24/1871, Pittsburg, Pa. d: 6/25/39, Buffalo, N.Y. BR/TR, 5'9.5", 160 lbs. Deb: 9/8/1897 M

YEAR	TM/L	G	AB	R	H	2B	3B	HR	RBI	BB	SO	AVG	OBP	SLG	PRO+	BR/A	SB	CS	SBR	FA	FR	G/POS	TPR
1897	Lou-N	21	76	7	20	3	0	1	7	3		.263	.300	.342	72	-3	1			.928	-3	2-21	-0.4
1898	Lou-N	35	121	14	23	4	0	0	13	6		.190	.246	.223	35	-10	6			.910	-6	2-33	-1.3
1899	Pit-N	15	53	9	15	3	1	0	12	5		.283	.345	.377	98	-0	2			.851	-3	2-15/S-1	-0.2
1901	NY-N	9	29	5	6	2	1	1	4	1		.207	.233	.448	99	-0	1			.969	-1	/2-7,P-2	-0.1
1902	NY-N	138	511	46	129	19	2	0	33	17		.252	.278	.297	78	-14	32			.953	4	*2-138,M	-0.6
1903	Det-A	93	336	36	75	11	3	1	22	19		.223	.271	.283	68	-13	12			.928	-2	2-93	-1.2
Total	6	311	1126	117	268	42	7	3	91	51		.238	.276	.296	71	-41	54			.934	-11	2-307/P-2,S	-3.8

■ GERMANY SMITH
Smith, George J. b: 4/21/1863, Pittsburg, Pa. d: 12/1/27, Altoona, Pa. BR/TR, 6', 175 lbs. Deb: 4/17/1884

YEAR	TM/L	G	AB	R	H	2B	3B	HR	RBI	BB	SO	AVG	OBP	SLG	PRO+	BR/A	SB	CS	SBR	FA	FR	G/POS	TPR
1884	Alt-U	25	108	9	34	8	1	0		1		.315	.321	.407	95	-1				.871	6	S-25/P-1	0.5
	Cle-N	72	291	31	74	14	4	4	26	2	45	.254	.259	.371	93	-3				.879	9	2-42,S-30	0.6
1885	Bro-a	108	419	63	108	17	11	4		10		.258	.275	.379	105	1				.884	40	*S-108	3.7
1886	Bro-a	105	426	66	105	17	6	2		19		.246	.279	.329	89	-7	22			.860	13	*S-105/O-1,C	0.6
1887	Bro-a	103	435	79	128	19	16	4		13		.294	.316	.439	108	2	26			.886	32	*S-101/3-2	2.8
1888	Bro-a	103	402	47	86	10	7	3	61	22		.214	.254	.296	76	-11	27			.844	5	*S-103/2-1	-0.3
1889	*Bro-a	121	446	89	103	22	3	3	53	40	42	.231	.296	.314	73	-16	35			.899	-4	*S-120/O-1	-1.1
1890	*Bro-N	129	481	76	92	6	5	1	47	42	23	.191	.260	.231	43	-35	24			.904	4	*S-129	-2.1
1891	Cin-N	138	512	50	103	11	5	3	53	38	32	.201	.258	.260	50	-33	16			.909	11	*S-138	-1.2
1892	Cin-N	139	506	58	121	13	6	8	63	42	52	.239	.297	.336	93	-6	19			.920	25	*S-139	2.3
1893	Cin-N	130	500	63	118	18	4	6	56	38	20	.236	.293	.320	61	-30	14			.934	20	*S-130	-0.4
1894	Cin-N	127	482	73	127	33	5	3	76	41	28	.263	.324	.371	65	-30	15			.911	20	*S-127	-0.3
1895	Cin-N	127	503	75	151	23	6	4	74	34	24	.300	.345	.394	87	-12	13			.923	2	*S-120	-0.3
1896	Cin-N	120	456	65	131	21	7	3	71	28	22	.287	.330	.393	84	-13	22			.926	-10	*S-120	-1.6
1897	Bro-N	112	428	47	86	17	3	0	29	14		.201	.233	.255	30	-44	1			.908	-11	*S-112	-4.5
1898	StL-N	51	157	16	25	2	1	1	9	24		.159	.275	.204	4	-12	1			.904	-5	S-51	-1.5
Total	15	1710	6552	907	1592	251	94	47	618	408	288	.243	.289	.332	74	-249	235			.902	157	S-1665/2-43,3OCP	-2.8

■ GREG SMITH
Smith, Gregory Alan b: 4/5/67, Baltimore, Md. BB/TR, 5'11", 170 lbs. Deb: 9/2/89

YEAR	TM/L	G	AB	R	H	2B	3B	HR	RBI	BB	SO	AVG	OBP	SLG	PRO+	BR/A	SB	CS	SBR	FA	FR	G/POS	TPR
1989	Chi-N	4	5	1	2	0	0	0	2	0	0	.400	.500	.400	149	0	0	0	0	.778	0	/2-2	0.1
1990	Chi-N	18	44	4	9	1	0	0	5	2	5	.205	.239	.295	43	-3	1	0	0	1.000	4	/2-7,S-7	0.1
1991	LA-N	5	3	1	0	0	0	0	0	0	2	.000	.000	.000	-99	-1	0	0	0	.000	0	/2-1	-0.1
Total	3	27	52	6	11	2	0	0	7	2	7	.212	.255	.288	47	-4	1	0	0	.944	4	/2-10,S-7	0.1

■ HAL SMITH
Smith, Harold Raymond "Cura" b: 6/1/31, Barling, Ark. BR/TR, 5'11", 189 lbs. Deb: 5/2/56 C

YEAR	TM/L	G	AB	R	H	2B	3B	HR	RBI	BB	SO	AVG	OBP	SLG	PRO+	BR/A	SB	CS	SBR	FA	FR	G/POS	TPR
1956	StL-N	75	227	27	64	12	0	5	23	15	22	.282	.326	.401	94	-2	1	0	0	.982	-2	C-66	-0.1
1957	StL-N☆	100	333	25	93	12	3	2	37	18	18	.279	.316	.351	78	-10	2	2	-1	.990	-1	C-97	-0.8
1958	StL-N	77	220	13	50	4	1	1	24	14	14	.227	.274	.268	42	-18	0	0	0	.989	-1	C-71	-1.6
1959	StL-N★	142	452	35	122	15	3	13	50	15	28	.270	.295	.403	78	-14	2	6	-3	.989	5	*C-141	-0.6
1960	StL-N	127	337	20	77	16	0	2	28	29	33	.228	.292	.294	56	-20	1	0	0	.990	18	*C-124	0.5

YEAR	TM/L	G	AB	R	H	2B	3B	HR	RBI	BB	SO	AVG	OBP	SLG	PRO+	BR/A	SB	CS	SBR	FA	FR	G/POS	TPR
1961	StL-N	45	125	6	31	4	1	0	10	11	12	.248	.314	.296	57	-7	0	0	0	.993	17	C-45	1.2
1965	Pit-N	4	3	0	0	0	0	0	0	0	1	.000	.000	.000	-99	-1	0	0	0	1.000	2	/C-4	0.1
Total	7	570	1697	126	437	63	8	23	172	102	128	.258	.301	.345	69	-73	6	8	-3	.989	38	C-548	-1.3

■ **HAL SMITH**   Smith, Harold Wayne   b: 12/7/30, W.Frankfort, Ill.   BR/TR, 6', 195 lbs.   Deb: 4/11/55

YEAR	TM/L	G	AB	R	H	2B	3B	HR	RBI	BB	SO	AVG	OBP	SLG	PRO+	BR/A	SB	CS	SBR	FA	FR	G/POS	TPR
1955	Bal-A	135	424	41	115	23	4	4	52	30	21	.271	.322	.373	93	-6	1	3	-2	.986	-3	*C-125	-0.6
1956	Bal-A	77	229	16	60	14	0	3	18	17	22	.262	.316	.362	85	-6	1	0	0	.994	3	C-71	0.0
	KC-A	37	142	15	39	9	2	2	24	3	12	.275	.290	.408	82	-4	1	1	-0	.986	1	C-37	-0.2
	Yr	114	371	31	99	23	2	5	42	20	34	.267	.306	.380	85	-10	2	1	0	.991	5	*C-108	-0.2
1957	KC-A	107	360	41	109	26	0	13	41	14	44	.303	.331	.483	118	7	2	2	-1	.983	-1	*C-103	0.9
1958	KC-A	99	315	32	86	19	2	5	46	25	47	.273	.330	.394	97	-2	0	0	0	.949	-1	3-43,C-31,1	-0.1
1959	KC-A	108	292	36	84	12	0	5	31	34	39	.288	.368	.380	104	3	0	3	-2	.953	7	3-77,C-22	0.9
1960	*Pit-N	77	258	37	76	18	2	11	45	22	48	.295	.355	.508	132	11	1	1	-0	.985	-6	C-71	0.9
1961	Pit-N	67	193	12	43	10	0	3	26	11	38	.223	.268	.321	55	-13	0	0	0	.990	-1	C-65	-1.0
1962	Hou-N	109	345	32	81	14	0	12	35	24	55	.235	.288	.380	84	-9	0	0	0	.986	2	C-92/3-6,1	-0.4
1963	Hou-N	31	58	1	14	2	0	0	2	4	15	.241	.290	.276	68	-2	0	0	0	.985	-3	C-11	-0.5
1964	Cin-N	32	66	6	8	1	0	0	3	12	20	.121	.256	.136	14	-7	1	0	0	.983	-3	C-20	-1.0
Total	10	879	2682	269	715	148	10	58	323	196	361	.267	.320	.394	94	-29	7	10	-4	.986	-3	C-648,3-126/1	-1.1

■ **HARRY SMITH**   Smith, Harry Thomas   b: 10/31/1874, Yorkshire, England   d: 2/17/33, Salem, N.J.   BR/TR,   Deb: 7/11/01   M

YEAR	TM/L	G	AB	R	H	2B	3B	HR	RBI	BB	SO	AVG	OBP	SLG	PRO+	BR/A	SB	CS	SBR	FA	FR	G/POS	TPR
1901	Phi-A	11	34	3	11	1	0	0	3	2		.324	.378	.353	99	0	1			.969	-3	/C-9,O-1	-0.2
1902	Pit-N	50	185	14	35	4	1	0	12	4		.189	.211	.222	32	-15	4			.972	-2	C-50	-1.2
1903	*Pit-N	61	212	15	37	3	2	0	19	12		.175	.222	.208	22	-22	2			.974	-4	C-60/O-1	-1.9
1904	Pit-N	47	141	17	35	3	1	0	18	16		.248	.346	.284	92	-0	5			.964	-3	C-44/O-3	0.1
1905	Pit-N	1	3	0	0	0	0	0	1	0		.000	.000	.000	-98	-1	1			1.000	0	/C-1	-0.1
1906	Pit-N	1	1	0	0	0	0	0	0	0		.000	.000	.000	-96	-0				.800	0	/C-1	0.0
1907	Pit-N	18	38	4	10	1	0	0	1	4		.263	.364	.289	103	0				.939	-1	C-18	-0.1
1908	Bos-N	41	130	13	32	2	2	1	16	7		.246	.295	.315	96	-1	2			.975	0	C-38	0.3
1909	Bos-N	43	113	9	19	4	1	0	4	5		.168	.203	.221	30	-9	3			.972	2	C-31,M	-0.5
1910	Bos-N	70	147	8	35	4	0	1	15	5	14	.238	.263	.286	57	-8	5			.949	3	C-38	-0.2
Total	10	343	1004	83	214	22	7	2	89	55	14	.213	.262	.255	54	-56	23			.967	-9	C-290/O-5	-3.8

■ **HARRY SMITH**   Smith, Harry W.   b: 2/5/1856, N.Vernon, Ind.   d: 6/4/1898, N.Vernon, Ind.   BR/TR, 6', 175 lbs.   Deb: 5/8/1877

YEAR	TM/L	G	AB	R	H	2B	3B	HR	RBI	BB	SO	AVG	OBP	SLG	PRO+	BR/A	SB	CS	SBR	FA	FR	G/POS	TPR
1877	Chi-N	24	94	7	19	1	0	0	3	4	6	.202	.235	.213	37	-7				.853	-7	2-14,O-10	-1.3
	Cin-N	10	36	4	9	2	1	0	3	1	5	.250	.270	.361	109	0				.879	1	/C-8,2-3,O	0.1
	Yr	34	130	11	28	3	1	0	6	5	11	.215	.244	.254	54	-7				.837	-7	2-17,O-13/C	-1.2
1889	Lou-a	1	2	0	1	0	0	0	1	0	1	.500	.500	.500	189	0	0			.000	-2	/O-1,C-1	-0.1
Total	2	35	132	11	29	3	1	0	7	5	12	.220	.248	.258	56	-6	0			.720	-8	/2-17,O-14,C	-1.3

■ **HARVEY SMITH**   Smith, Harvey Fetterhoff   b: 7/24/1871, Union Deposit, Pa   d: 11/12/62, Harrisburg, Pa.   BL/TR, 5'8", 160 lbs.   Deb: 8/19/1896

YEAR	TM/L	G	AB	R	H	2B	3B	HR	RBI	BB	SO	AVG	OBP	SLG	PRO+	BR/A	SB	CS	SBR	FA	FR	G/POS	TPR
1896	Was-N	36	131	21	36	7	2	0	17	12	7	.275	.345	.359	86	-3	9			.861	3	3-36	0.1

■ **HAPPY SMITH**   Smith, Henry Joseph   b: 7/14/1883, Coquille, Ore.   d: 2/26/61, San Jose, Cal.   BL/TR, 6', 185 lbs.   Deb: 4/15/10

YEAR	TM/L	G	AB	R	H	2B	3B	HR	RBI	BB	SO	AVG	OBP	SLG	PRO+	BR/A	SB	CS	SBR	FA	FR	G/POS	TPR
1910	Bro-N	35	76	6	18	2	0	0	5	4	14	.237	.275	.263	59	-4	4			.974	2	O-16	-0.3

■ **JACK SMITH**   Smith, Jack   b: 6/23/1895, Chicago, Ill.   d: 5/2/72, Westchester, Ill.   BL/TL, 5'8", 165 lbs.   Deb: 9/30/15

YEAR	TM/L	G	AB	R	H	2B	3B	HR	RBI	BB	SO	AVG	OBP	SLG	PRO+	BR/A	SB	CS	SBR	FA	FR	G/POS	TPR
1915	StL-N	4	16	2	3	0	1	0	1	0	5	.188	.235	.313	65	-1	0			1.000	-1	/O-4	-0.2
1916	StL-N	130	357	43	87	6	5	6	34	20	50	.244	.291	.339	94	-3	24	16	-2	.949	-11	*O-120	-2.5
1917	StL-N	137	462	64	137	16	11	3	34	38	65	.297	.351	.398	133	18	25			.961	-10	*O-128	0.2
1918	StL-N	42	166	24	35	2	1	0	4	7	21	.211	.260	.235	53	-9	5			.941	1	O-42	-1.3
1919	StL-N	119	408	47	91	16	3	0	15	26	29	.223	.271	.277	69	-16	30			.960	-0	*O-111	-2.6
1920	StL-N	91	313	53	104	22	5	1	28	25	23	.332	.385	.444	143	17	14	9	-1	.963	-10	O-83	0.1
1921	StL-N	116	411	86	135	22	9	7	33	21	24	.328	.361	.477	122	12	11	6	-0	.955	-6	*O-103	-0.2
1922	StL-N	143	510	117	158	23	12	8	46	50	30	.310	.375	.449	117	13	18	7	1	.951	-8	*O-136	-0.3
1923	StL-N	124	407	98	126	16	6	5	41	27	20	.310	.356	.415	105	3	32	11	3	.974	4	*O-109	0.3
1924	StL-N	124	459	91	130	18	6	2	33	33	27	.283	.333	.362	88	-8	24	16	0	.968	10	*O-114	-0.8
1925	StL-N	80	243	53	61	11	4	4	31	19	13	.251	.308	.379	73	-10	20	2	5	.958	-3	O-64	-1.2
1926	StL-N	1	1	0	0	0	0	0	0	0	1	.000	.000	.000	-96	-0	0			.000	0	H	0.3
	Bos-N	96	322	46	100	15	2	2	25	28	12	.311	.369	.388	114	7	11			.973	4	O-83	0.3
	Yr	97	323	46	100	15	2	2	25	28	13	.310	.368	.387	113	6	11			.973	2	O-83	0.3
1927	Bos-N	84	183	27	58	6	4	1	24	16	12	.317	.375	.410	119	5	8			.950	-0	O-48	0.2
1928	Bos-N	96	254	30	71	9	2	1	32	21	14	.280	.335	.343	82	-7	6			.988	1	O-65	-1.0
1929	Bos-N	19	20	2	5	0	0	0	2	2	2	.250	.318	.250	45	-2	0			.833	-3	/O-9	-0.5
Total	15	1406	4532	783	1301	182	71	40	382	334	348	.287	.339	.385	103	18	228	67		.961	-36	*O-1219	-9.5

■ **STUB SMITH**   Smith, James A.   b: 11/26/1876, Elmwood, Ill.   BL/TR, 5'6", 145 lbs.   Deb: 9/10/1898

YEAR	TM/L	G	AB	R	H	2B	3B	HR	RBI	BB	SO	AVG	OBP	SLG	PRO+	BR/A	SB	CS	SBR	FA	FR	G/POS	TPR
1898	Bos-N	3	10	1	1	0	0	0	0	0		.100	.100	.100	-41	-2	0			.933	1	/S-3	-0.1

■ **RED SMITH**   Smith, James Carlisle   b: 4/6/1890, Greenville, S.C.   d: 10/11/66, Atlanta, Ga.   BR/TR, 5'11", 165 lbs.   Deb: 9/5/11

YEAR	TM/L	G	AB	R	H	2B	3B	HR	RBI	BB	SO	AVG	OBP	SLG	PRO+	BR/A	SB	CS	SBR	FA	FR	G/POS	TPR
1911	Bro-N	28	111	10	29	6	1	0	19	5	13	.261	.299	.333	80	-3	5			.900	-2	3-28	-0.5
1912	Bro-N	128	486	75	139	28	6	4	57	54	51	.286	.362	.393	111	8	22			.938	5	*3-125	1.3
1913	Bro-N	151	540	70	160	**40**	10	6	76	45	67	.296	.358	.441	124	16	22			.933	-1	*3-151	1.8
1914	Bro-N	90	330	39	81	10	8	4	48	30	26	.245	.310	.361	97	-2	11			.937	12	3-90	1.5
	Bos-N	60	207	30	65	17	1	3	37	28	24	.314	.401	.449	153	14	4			.937	10	3-60	2.8
	Yr	150	537	69	146	27	9	7	85	58	50	.272	.346	.395	119	12	15			.937	23	*3-150	4.3
1915	Bos-N	157	549	66	145	34	4	2	65	67	49	.264	.345	.352	116	12	10	5	0	.947	-6	*3-157	1.4
1916	Bos-N	150	509	48	132	16	10	3	60	53	55	.259	.333	.348	114	9	13			.928	-4	*3-150	1.1
1917	Bos-N	147	505	60	149	31	6	2	62	53	61	.295	.369	.392	142	26	16			.925	-21	*3-147	0.9
1918	Bos-N	119	429	55	128	20	3	2	65	45	47	.298	.373	.373	133	18	8			.922	4	*3-119	2.7
1919	Bos-N	87	241	24	59	6	0	1	25	40	22	.245	.359	.282	98	2	6			.981	-0	O-48,3-23	0.0
Total	9	1117	3907	477	1087	208	49	27	514	420	415	.278	.353	.377	120	100	117	5		.932	-2	*3-1050/O-48	13.0

■ **HARRY SMITH**   Smith, James Harry   b: 5/15/1890, Baltimore, Md.   d: 4/1/22, Charlotte, N.C.   BR/TR, 5'10", 180 lbs.   Deb: 9/21/14

YEAR	TM/L	G	AB	R	H	2B	3B	HR	RBI	BB	SO	AVG	OBP	SLG	PRO+	BR/A	SB	CS	SBR	FA	FR	G/POS	TPR
1914	NY-N	5	7	0	3	0	0	0	2	3	1	.429	.600	.429	215	1	1			1.000	2	/C-4	0.3
1915	NY-N	21	32	1	4	0	1	0	3	6	12	.125	.263	.188	40	-2	0	1	-1	.967	-3	C-18	-0.5
	Bro-F	28	65	5	13	0	0	0	4	7	16	.200	.278	.246	41	-5	2			.967	-5	C-19/O-1	-1.0
1917	Cin-N	8	17	0	2	0	0	0	1	2	7	.118	.211	.118	2	-2	0			.978	4	/C-7	0.3
1918	Cin-N	13	27	4	5	1	0	0	4	3	6	.185	.267	.370	95	-0	1			1.000	-2	/C-6,O-1	-0.2
Total	4	75	148	10	27	1	1	0	14	21	42	.182	.284	.250	55	-8	4	1		.975	-4	/C-54,O-2	-1.1

■ **JIMMY SMITH**   Smith, James Lawrence "Greenfield Jimmy"   b: 5/15/1895, Pittsburgh, Pa.   d: 1/1/74, Pittsburgh, Pa.   BB/TR, 5'9", 152 lbs.   Deb: 9/26/14

YEAR	TM/L	G	AB	R	H	2B	3B	HR	RBI	BB	SO	AVG	OBP	SLG	PRO+	BR/A	SB	CS	SBR	FA	FR	G/POS	TPR
1914	Chi-F	3	6	1	3	1	0	0	1	0	0	.500	.500	.667	213	1	0			1.000	1	/S-3	0.2
1915	Chi-F	95	318	32	69	11	4	4	30	14	65	.217	.250	.314	54	-23	4			.904	-14	S-92/2-1	-3.3
	Bal-F	33	108	9	19	1	1	1	11	11	23	.176	.258	.231	31	-11	3			.883	-4	S-33	-1.3
	Yr	128	426	41	88	12	5	5	41	25	88	.207	.252	.293	47	-34	7			.898	-18	*S-125/2-1	-4.6

YEAR	TM/L	G	AB	R	H	2B	3B	HR	RBI	BB	SO	AVG	OBP	SLG	PRO+	BR/A	SB	CS	SBR	FA	FR	G/POS	TPR
1916	Pit-N	36	96	4	18	1	1	0	5	6	22	.188	.257	.219	46	-6	0			.929	1	S-27/3-6	-0.4
1917	NY-N	36	96	12	22	5	1	0	9	9	18	.229	.295	.302	86	-2	6			.971	-2	2-29/S-7	-0.3
1918	Bos-N	34	102	8	23	3	4	1	14	3	13	.225	.255	.363	91	-2	1			1.000	-1	2-10/S-9,O3	-0.2
1919	*Cin-N	28	40	9	11	1	3	1	10	4	8	.275	.341	.525	163	3	1			1.000	-2	/3-6,S-5,2O	0.2
1921	Phi-N	67	247	31	57	8	1	4	22	11	28	.231	.266	.320	50	-18	2	8	-4	.971	8	2-66	-1.3
1922	Phi-N	38	114	13	25	1	0	1	6	5	9	.219	.258	.254	30	-12	1	3	-2	.952	-3	S-23,2-13/3	-1.4
Total	8	370	1127	119	247	32	15	12	108	63	186	.219	.265	.306	57	-69	18	11		.910	-16	S-199,2-123/3O	-7.8

■ JIM SMITH
Smith, James Lorne   b: 9/8/54, Santa Monica, Cal.   BR/TR, 6'3", 185 lbs.   Deb: 4/12/82

YEAR	TM/L	G	AB	R	H	2B	3B	HR	RBI	BB	SO	AVG	OBP	SLG	PRO+	BR/A	SB	CS	SBR	FA	FR	G/POS	TPR
1982	Pit-N	42	42	5	10	2	1	0	4	5	7	.238	.319	.333	80	-1	0	1	-1	.929	8	S-29/2-3,3	0.8

■ JOHN SMITH
Smith, John   b: Baltimore, Md.   Deb: 4/14/1873

YEAR	TM/L	G	AB	R	H	2B	3B	HR	RBI	BB	SO	AVG	OBP	SLG	PRO+	BR/A	SB	CS	SBR	FA	FR	G/POS	TPR
1873	Mar-n	5	19	2	2	0	0	0	1	0	0	.105	.105	.105	-49	-3						/S-3,O-2	-0.2
1874	Bal-n	6	20	1	3	1	0	0		0	0	.150	.150	.200	10	-2						/S-5,O-1	-0.2
1875	NH-n	1	3	0	0	0	0	0		0	1	.000	.250	.000	-6	-0						/S-1	0.0
Total	3 n	12	42	3	5	1	0	0	1	0	1	.119	.140	.143	-14	-5						/S-9,O-3	-0.4

■ DWIGHT SMITH
Smith, John Dwight   b: 11/8/63, Tallahassee, Fla.   BL/TR, 5'11", 175 lbs.   Deb: 5/1/89

YEAR	TM/L	G	AB	R	H	2B	3B	HR	RBI	BB	SO	AVG	OBP	SLG	PRO+	BR/A	SB	CS	SBR	FA	FR	G/POS	TPR
1989	*Chi-N	109	343	52	111	19	6	9	52	31	51	.324	.383	.493	138	17	9	4	0	.975	1	*O-102	1.7
1990	Chi-N	117	290	34	76	15	0	6	27	28	46	.262	.331	.376	88	-5	11	6	-0	.986	-4	O-81	-1.1
1991	Chi-N	90	167	16	38	7	2	3	21	11	32	.228	.279	.347	72	-6	2	3	-1	.962	-3	O-42	-1.1
1992	Chi-N	109	217	28	60	10	3	3	24	13	40	.276	.320	.392	98	-1	9	8	-2	.979	-10	O-63	-1.5
1993	Chi-N	111	310	51	93	17	5	11	35	25	51	.300	.358	.494	127	11	8	6	-1	.955	-8	O-89	0.1
1994	Cal-A	45	122	19	32	5	1	5	18	7	20	.262	.302	.443	86	-3	2	3	-1	.912	-2	O-31/D-2	-0.6
	Bal-A	28	74	12	23	2	1	3	12	5	17	.311	.363	.486	109	1	0	1	-1	.939	-2	O-22/D-3	-0.4
	Yr	73	196	31	55	7	2	8	30	12	37	.281	.325	.459	95	-2	2	4	-2	.922	-6	O-53/D-5	-1.0
Total	6	609	1523	212	433	75	18	40	189	120	257	.284	.341	.436	108	14	41	31	-6	.966	-29	O-430/D-5	-2.9

■ JOHN SMITH
Smith, John J.   b: San Francisco, Cal.   5'11", 210 lbs.   Deb: 5/1/1882

YEAR	TM/L	G	AB	R	H	2B	3B	HR	RBI	BB	SO	AVG	OBP	SLG	PRO+	BR/A	SB	CS	SBR	FA	FR	G/POS	TPR
1882	Tro-N	35	149	27	36	4	3	0	14	3	24	.242	.257	.309	84	-2				.960	-0	1-35	-0.6
	Wor-N	19	70	10	17	3	2	0	5	5	10	.243	.293	.343	101	0				.939	1	1-19	-0.1
	Yr	54	219	37	53	7	5	0	19	8	34	.242	.269	.320	90	-2				.952	1	1-54	-0.7

■ JACK SMITH
Smith, John Joseph (b: John Joseph Coffey)   b: 8/8/1893, Oswayo, Pa.   d: 12/4/62, New York, N.Y.   BR/TR, 5'9",   Deb: 5/18/12

YEAR	TM/L	G	AB	R	H	2B	3B	HR	RBI	BB	SO	AVG	OBP	SLG	PRO+	BR/A	SB	CS	SBR	FA	FR	G/POS	TPR
1912	Det-A	1	0	0	0	0	0	0	0	0		—	—	—	—	0	0			1.000	1	/3-1	0.1

■ JOHN SMITH
Smith, John Marshall   b: 9/27/06, Washington, D.C.   d: 5/9/82, Silver Spring, Md.   BB/TR, 6'1", 180 lbs.   Deb: 9/17/31

YEAR	TM/L	G	AB	R	H	2B	3B	HR	RBI	BB	SO	AVG	OBP	SLG	PRO+	BR/A	SB	CS	SBR	FA	FR	G/POS	TPR
1931	Bos-A	4	15	2	2	0	0	0	1	2	1	.133	.235	.133	-1	-2	1	0	0	1.000	-1	/1-4	-0.3

■ JUD SMITH
Smith, Judson Grant   b: 1/13/1869, Green Oak, Mich.   d: 12/7/47, Los Angeles, Cal.   BR/TR,   Deb: 5/21/1893

YEAR	TM/L	G	AB	R	H	2B	3B	HR	RBI	BB	SO	AVG	OBP	SLG	PRO+	BR/A	SB	CS	SBR	FA	FR	G/POS	TPR
1893	Cin-N	17	43	7	10	1	0	1	5	9	5	.233	.365	.326	82	-1	1			.750	-2	/O-9,3-6,S	-0.3
	StL-N	4	13	1	1	0	0	0	0	1	2	.077	.200	.077	-25	-2	0			.889	1	/3-4	-0.1
	Yr	21	56	8	11	1	0	1	5	10	7	.196	.328	.268	58	-3	1			.844	-1	3-10/O-9,S	-0.4
1896	Pit-N	10	35	6	12	2	1	0	4	2	2	.343	.395	.457	129	1	3			.909	2	3-10	0.3
1898	Was-N	66	234	33	71	7	5	3	28	22		.303	.378	.415	127	8	11			.903	-10	3-47,S-10/12	0.0
1901	Pit-N	6	21	1	3	1	0	0	0	3		.143	.250	.190	28	-2	0			.947	0	/3-6	-0.2
Total	4	103	346	48	97	11	6	4	37	37	9	.280	.363	.382	109	5	15			.900	-9	/3-73,S-11,012	-0.3

■ KEITH SMITH
Smith, Keith Lavarne   b: 5/3/53, Palmetto, Fla.   BR/TR, 5'9", 178 lbs.   Deb: 8/2/77

YEAR	TM/L	G	AB	R	H	2B	3B	HR	RBI	BB	SO	AVG	OBP	SLG	PRO+	BR/A	SB	CS	SBR	FA	FR	G/POS	TPR
1977	Tex-A	23	67	13	16	4	0	2	6	4	7	.239	.301	.388	85	-1	2	0	1	.975	-1	O-22	-0.2
1979	StL-N	6	13	1	3	0	0	0	0	0	1	.231	.231	.231	26	-1	0	1	-1	1.000	-1	/O-5	0.0
1980	StL-N	24	31	3	4	1	0	0	2	2	2	.129	.182	.161	-3	-4	0	0	0	1.000	-1	/O-7	-0.6
Total	3	53	111	17	23	5	0	2	8	6	10	.207	.261	.306	54	-7	2	1	0	.985	0	/O-34	-0.8

■ KEN SMITH
Smith, Kenneth Earl   b: 2/12/58, Youngstown, Ohio   BL/TR, 6'1", 195 lbs.   Deb: 9/22/81

YEAR	TM/L	G	AB	R	H	2B	3B	HR	RBI	BB	SO	AVG	OBP	SLG	PRO+	BR/A	SB	CS	SBR	FA	FR	G/POS	TPR
1981	Atl-N	5	3	0	1	1	0	0	0	0	1	.333	.333	.667	174	0	0	0	0	1.000	0	/1-4	0.1
1982	Atl-N	48	41	6	12	1	0	3	6	3	13	.293	.383	.317	94	-0	0	0	0	1.000	-1	/1-6,O-3	-0.2
1983	Atl-N	30	12	2	2	0	0	1	2	1	5	.167	.231	.417	71	-1	1	0	0	1.000	2	1-13	0.2
Total	3	83	56	8	15	2	0	4	8	5	19	.268	.349	.357	93	-0	1	0	0	1.000	1	/1-23,O-3	0.1

■ L. SMITH
Smith, L.   Deb: 9/7/1882

YEAR	TM/L	G	AB	R	H	2B	3B	HR	RBI	BB	SO	AVG	OBP	SLG	PRO+	BR/A	SB	CS	SBR	FA	FR	G/POS	TPR
1882	Bal-a	1	3	0	0	0	0	0	0	0	0	.000	.000	.000	-99	-1				1.000	-0	/O-1	-0.1

■ PADDY SMITH
Smith, Lawrence Patrick   b: 5/16/1894, Pelham, N.Y.   d: 12/2/90, New Rochelle, N.Y.   BL/TR, 6', 195 lbs.   Deb: 7/6/20

YEAR	TM/L	G	AB	R	H	2B	3B	HR	RBI	BB	SO	AVG	OBP	SLG	PRO+	BR/A	SB	CS	SBR	FA	FR	G/POS	TPR
1920	Bos-A	2	2	0	0	0	0	0	0	0	1	.000	.000	.000	-99	-1	0	0	0	.000	0	/C-1	-0.1

■ BULL SMITH
Smith, Lewis Oscar   b: 8/20/1880, Plum, W.Va.   d: 5/1/28, Charleston, W.Va.   BR/TR, 6', 180 lbs.   Deb: 8/30/04

YEAR	TM/L	G	AB	R	H	2B	3B	HR	RBI	BB	SO	AVG	OBP	SLG	PRO+	BR/A	SB	CS	SBR	FA	FR	G/POS	TPR
1904	Pit-N	13	42	2	6	0	1	0		0	1	.143	.163	.190	9	-5	0			.857	-0	O-13	-0.6
1906	Chi-N	1	1	0	0	0	0	0	0	0		.000	.000	.000	-95	-0	0			.000	0	H	0.0
1911	Was-A	1	0	0	0	0	0	0	0	0		—	—	—	—	0	0			.000	0	R	0.0
Total	3	15	43	2	6	0	1	0		0	1	.140	.159	.186	6	-5	0			.857	-0	/O-13	-0.6

■ LEO SMITH
Smith, Lionel H.   b: 5/13/1859, Brooklyn, N.Y.   d: 8/30/35, Brooklyn, N.Y.   5'6", 142 lbs.   Deb: 8/28/1890

YEAR	TM/L	G	AB	R	H	2B	3B	HR	RBI	BB	SO	AVG	OBP	SLG	PRO+	BR/A	SB	CS	SBR	FA	FR	G/POS	TPR
1890	Roc-a	35	112	11	21	1	3	0	14			.188	.283	.250	62	-5	1			.948	8	S-35	0.5

■ LONNIE SMITH
Smith, Lonnie   b: 12/22/55, Chicago, Ill.   BR/TR, 5'9", 170 lbs.   Deb: 9/2/78

YEAR	TM/L	G	AB	R	H	2B	3B	HR	RBI	BB	SO	AVG	OBP	SLG	PRO+	BR/A	SB	CS	SBR	FA	FR	G/POS	TPR
1978	Phi-N	17	4	6	0	0	0	0	0	4	3	.000	.500	.000	50	0	4	0	1	1.000	-3	O-11	-0.2
1979	Phi-N	17	30	4	5	2	0	0	3	1	7	.167	.194	.233	15	-4	2	1	0	1.000	-1	O-11	-0.5
1980	*Phi-N	100	298	69	101	14	4	3	20	26	48	.339	.399	.443	128	12	33	13	2	.969	-9	O-82	0.2
1981	*Phi-N	62	176	40	57	14	3	2	11	18	14	.324	.402	.472	141	10	21	10	0	.971	1	O-51	1.1
1982	*StL-N★	156	592	**120**	182	35	8	8	69	64	74	.307	.383	.434	127	23	68	26	5	.970	-1	*O-149	2.3
1983	StL-N	130	492	83	158	31	5	8	45	41	55	.321	.384	.453	131	21	43	18	2	.941	3	*O-126	2.3
1984	StL-N	145	504	77	126	20	4	6	49	70	90	.250	.352	.341	98	1	50	13	7	.948	-1	*O-140	0.1
1985	StL-N	28	96	15	25	2	2	0	7	15	20	.260	.377	.323	98	1	12	6	0	1.000	-1	O-28	-0.2
	*KC-A	120	448	77	115	23	4	6	41	41	69	.257	.325	.366	88	-7	40	7	8	.958	-3	*O-119	-0.6
1986	KC-A	134	508	80	146	25	7	8	44	46	78	.287	.358	.411	107	6	26	9	2	.965	4	*O-118,D-10	0.7
1987	KC-A	48	167	26	42	7	1	3	8	24	31	.251	.359	.359	89	-2	9	4	0	.915	-2	O-32,D-15	-0.4
1988	Atl-N	43	114	14	27	3	0	3	9	10	25	.237	.298	.342	79	-3	4	2	0	.968	-1	O-35	-0.6
1989	Atl-N	134	482	89	152	34	4	21	79	76	95	.315	**.420**	.533	166	44	25	12	0	.993	9	*O-132	5.2
1990	Atl-N	135	466	72	142	27	9	9	42	58	69	.305	.389	.459	125	17	10	10	-3	.956	-5	*O-122	1.7
1991	*Atl-N	122	353	58	97	19	1	7	44	50	64	.275	.379	.394	111	7	9	5	-0	.965	-8	O-99	-0.3
1992	*Atl-N	84	158	23	39	8	2	6	33	17	37	.247	.331	.437	109	2	4	0	1	.994	0	O-35	0.3
1993	Pit-N	94	199	35	57	5	4	6	24	43	42	.286	.425	.442	133	12	9	4	0	.981	-4	O-60	0.7
	Bal-A	9	24	8	5	1	0	2	3	8	10	.208	.406	.500	136	1	0	0	0	1.000	0	/O-4,D-5	0.2
1994	Bal-A	35	59	13	12	3	0	0	2	11	18	.203	.338	.254	52	-4	1	0	0	1.000	0	D-30/O-2	-0.4
Total	17	1613	5170	909	1488	273	58	98	533	623	849	.288	.374	.420	117	138	370	140	27	.964	-12	*O-1356/D-60	11.6

YEAR	TM/L	G	AB	R	H	2B	3B	HR	RBI	BB	SO	AVG	OBP	SLG	PRO+	BR/A	SB	CS	SBR	FA	FR	G/POS	TPR

■ MARK SMITH   Smith, Mark Edward b: 5/7/70, Pasadena, Cal. BR/TR, 6'3", 205 lbs. Deb: 5/14/94

| 1994 | Bal-A | 3 | 7 | 0 | 1 | 0 | 0 | 0 | 2 | 0 | 2 | .143 | .143 | .143 | -24 | -1 | 0 | 0 | 0 | 1.000 | 0 | /O-3 | -0.1 |

■ RED SMITH   Smith, Marvin Harold b: 7/17/1900, Ashley, Ill. d: 2/19/61, Los Angeles, Cal. BL/TR, 5'7", 165 lbs. Deb: 4/14/25

| 1925 | Phi-A | 20 | 14 | 1 | 4 | 0 | 0 | 0 | 1 | 2 | 5 | .286 | .375 | .286 | 65 | -1 | 0 | 0 | 0 | .864 | 1 | S-16/3-2 | 0.1 |

■ MILT SMITH   Smith, Milton b: 3/27/29, Columbus, Ga. BR/TR, 5'10", 165 lbs. Deb: 7/21/55

| 1955 | Cin-N | 36 | 102 | 15 | 20 | 3 | 1 | 3 | 8 | 13 | 24 | .196 | .293 | .333 | 62 | -6 | 2 | 2 | -1 | .915 | -2 | 3-28/2-5 | -0.8 |

■ NATE SMITH   Smith, Nathaniel Beverly b: 4/26/35, Chicago, Ill. BR/TR, 5'11", 170 lbs. Deb: 9/19/62

| 1962 | Bal-A | 5 | 9 | 3 | 2 | 1 | 0 | 0 | 1 | 0 | 4 | .222 | .364 | .333 | 95 | 0 | 0 | 0 | 0 | 1.000 | 1 | /C-3 | 0.1 |

■ OLLIE SMITH   Smith, Oliver H. b: 1868, Mt.Vernon, Ohio BL/TL, Deb: 7/11/1894

| 1894 | Lou-N | 38 | 134 | 26 | 40 | 6 | 1 | 3 | 20 | 27 | 15 | .299 | .427 | .425 | 114 | 5 | 13 | | | .883 | -2 | O-38 | 0.0 |

■ OZZIE SMITH   Smith, Osborne Earl b: 12/26/54, Mobile, Ala. BB/TR, 5'11", 150 lbs. Deb: 4/7/78

1978	SD-N	159	590	69	152	17	6	1	46	47	43	.258	.312	.312	81	-15	40	12	5	.970	26	*S-159	3.6
1979	SD-N	156	587	77	124	18	6	0	27	37	37	.211	.260	.262	46	-45	28	7	4	.976	21	*S-155	-0.3
1980	SD-N	158	609	67	140	18	5	0	35	71	49	.230	.315	.276	70	-23	57	15	8	.974	41	*S-158	4.7
1981	SD-N★	110	450	53	100	11	2	0	21	41	37	.222	.294	.256	62	-22	22	12	-1	.976	26	*S-110	1.5
1982	*StL-N★	140	488	58	121	24	1	2	43	68	32	.248	.342	.314	84	-8	25	5	5	.984	33	*S-139	4.4
1983	StL-N★	159	552	69	134	30	6	3	50	64	36	.243	.323	.335	82	-12	34	7	6	.975	18	*S-158	2.7
1984	StL-N	124	412	53	106	20	5	1	44	56	17	.257	.349	.337	96	-0	35	7	6	.982	26	*S-124	4.5
1985	*StL-N★	158	537	70	148	22	3	6	54	65	27	.276	.356	.361	102	3	31	8	5	.983	16	*S-158	4.0
1986	StL-N★	153	514	67	144	19	4	0	54	79	27	.280	.378	.333	99	3	31	7	5	.978	-9	*S-144	1.3
1987	*StL-N★	158	600	104	182	40	4	0	75	89	36	.303	.394	.383	105	8	43	9	8	.987	19	*S-158	4.7
1988	StL-N★	153	575	80	155	27	1	3	51	74	43	.270	.354	.336	98	1	57	9	**12**	.972	23	*S-150	5.1
1989	StL-N★	155	593	82	162	30	8	2	50	55	37	.273	.337	.361	96	-2	29	7	5	.976	6	*S-153	2.2
1990	StL-N★	143	512	61	130	21	1	1	50	61	33	.254	.336	.305	77	-14	32	6	6	.980	-13	*S-140	-1.0
1991	StL-N★	150	550	96	157	30	3	3	50	83	36	.285	.380	.367	110	11	35	9	5	.987	-21	*S-150	0.6
1992	StL-N★	132	518	73	153	20	2	0	31	59	34	.295	.367	.342	105	6	43	9	8	.985	8	*S-132	3.3
1993	StL-N	141	545	75	157	22	6	1	53	43	18	.288	.341	.356	89	-8	21	8	2	.974	18	*S-134	2.2
1994	StL-N★	98	381	51	100	18	3	3	30	38	26	.262	.329	.349	80	-11	6	3	0	.982	-2	S-96	-0.5
Total	17	2447	9013	1205	2365	387	66	26	764	1030	568	.262	.340	.329	88	-129	569	140	87	.979	236	*S-2418	43.0

■ KEITH SMITH   Smith, Patrick Keith b: 10/20/61, Los Angeles, Cal. BB/TR, 6'1", 175 lbs. Deb: 4/12/84

1984	NY-A	2	4	0	0	0	0	0	0	0	2	.000	.200	.000	-41	-1	0	0	0	.923	2	/S-2	0.2
1985	NY-A	4	0	1	0	0	0	0	0	0	0	—	—	—		0	0	0	0	1.000	0	/S-3	0.0
Total	2	6	4	1	0	0	0	0	0	0	2	.000	.200	.000	-41	-1	0	0	0	.929	3	/S-5	0.2

■ PAUL SMITH   Smith, Paul Leslie b: 3/19/31, New Castle, Pa. BL/TL, 5'8", 165 lbs. Deb: 4/14/53

1953	Pit-N	118	389	41	110	12	7	4	44	24	23	.283	.329	.380	85	-9	3	0	1	.985	-2	1-74,O-19	-1.3
1957	Pit-N	81	150	12	38	4	0	3	11	12	17	.253	.313	.340	78	-5	0	2	-1	1.000	-3	O-33/1-1	-1.1
1958	Pit-N	6	3	0	1	0	0	0	0	3	0	.333	.667	.333	180	1	0	0	0	.000	0	H	0.1
	Chi-N	18	20	1	3	0	0	0	1	3	4	.150	.261	.150	13	-2	0	0	0	.941	0	/1-4	-0.3
	Yr	24	23	1	4	0	0	0	1	6	4	.174	.345	.174	44	-2	0	0	0	.941	0	/1-4	-0.2
Total	3	223	562	54	152	16	7	7	56	42	44	.270	.326	.361	81	-15	3	2	-0	.984	-5	/1-79,O-52	-2.6

■ PAUL SMITH   Smith, Paul Stoner b: 5/7/1888, Mt.Zion, Ill. d: 7/3/58, Decatur, Ill. BL/TR, 6'1", 190 lbs. Deb: 9/19/16

| 1916 | Cin-N | 10 | 44 | 5 | 10 | 0 | 1 | 0 | 1 | 1 | 8 | .227 | .244 | .273 | 60 | -2 | 3 | | | 1.000 | -1 | O-10 | -0.4 |

■ RAY SMITH   Smith, Raymond Edward b: 9/18/55, Glendale, Cal. BR/TR, 6'1", 185 lbs. Deb: 4/9/81

1981	Min-A	15	40	4	8	1	0	1	0	1	3	.200	.200	.300	40	-3	0	0	0	1.000	1	C-15	-0.1
1982	Min-A	9	23	1	5	0	1	0	1	1	3	.217	.250	.304	50	-2	0	0	0	1.000	1	/C-9	0.0
1983	Min-A	59	152	11	34	5	0	0	8	10	12	.224	.276	.257	46	-11	1	0	0	.984	11	C-59	0.2
Total	3	83	215	16	47	6	1	1	10	11	18	.219	.260	.270	45	-16	1	0	0	.988	14	/C-83	0.1

■ DICK SMITH   Smith, Richard Arthur b: 5/17/39, Lebanon, Ore. BR/TR, 6'2", 205 lbs. Deb: 7/20/63

1963	NY-N	20	42	4	10	0	0	0	3	5	10	.238	.319	.286	74	-1	3	2	-0	1.000	-2	O-10/1-2	-0.4
1964	NY-N	46	94	14	21	6	1	0	3	1	29	.223	.247	.309	57	-6	6	2	1	.987	-3	1-18,O-13	-1.0
1965	LA-N	10	6	0	0	0	0	0	1	0	3	.000	.000	.000	-99	-2	0	0	0	1.000	-3	/O-9	-0.6
Total	3	76	142	18	31	6	2	0	7	6	42	.218	.260	.289	56	-8	9	4	0	1.000	-8	/O-32,1-20	-2.0

■ DICK SMITH   Smith, Richard Harrison b: 7/21/27, Blandburg, Pa. BR/TR, 5'8", 160 lbs. Deb: 9/14/51

1951	Pit-N	12	46	2	8	0	0	0	4	8	8	.174	.296	.174	29	-4	0	2	-1	.936	2	3-12	-0.3
1952	Pit-N	29	66	8	7	1	0	0	5	9	3	.106	.213	.121	-5	-9	0	0	0	.958	5	3-16/2-4,S	-0.5
1953	Pit-N	13	43	4	7	0	1	0	2	6	6	.163	.265	.209	26	-5	0	1	-1	.961	5	S-13	0.1
1954	Pit-N	12	31	2	3	1	1	0	0	6	5	.097	.243	.194	16	-4	0	0	0	.933	2	/3-9	-0.2
1955	Pit-N	4	0	1	0	0	0	0	0	1	0	—	1.000	—	198	0	0	0	0	.000	0	/S-1	0.0
Total	5	70	186	17	25	2	2	0	11	30	22	.134	.255	.167	15	-22	0	3	-2	.944	14	/3-37,S-18,2	-0.9

■ DICK SMITH   Smith, Richard Kelly b: 8/25/44, Lincolnton, N.C. BR/TR, 6'5", 200 lbs. Deb: 8/20/69

| 1969 | Was-A | 21 | 28 | 2 | 3 | 0 | 0 | 0 | 0 | 4 | 7 | .107 | .242 | .107 | 1 | -4 | 0 | 0 | 0 | .909 | -2 | /O-9 | -0.6 |

■ RED SMITH   Smith, Richard Paul b: 5/18/04, Brokaw, Wis. d: 3/8/78, Toledo, Ohio BR/TR, 5'10", 185 lbs. Deb: 5/31/27 C

| 1927 | NY-N | 1 | 0 | 0 | 0 | 0 | 0 | 0 | 0 | 0 | 0 | — | — | — | | 0 | 0 | | | 1.000 | -0 | /C-1 | 0.0 |

■ BOB SMITH   Smith, Robert Eldridge b: 4/22/1895, Rogersville, Tenn. d: 7/19/87, Waycross, Ga. BR/TR, 5'10", 175 lbs. Deb: 4/19/23

1923	Bos-N	115	375	30	94	16	3	0	40	17	35	.251	.285	.309	59	-23	4	9	-4	.944	14	*S-101/2-8	-0.3
1924	Bos-N	106	347	32	79	12	3	2	38	15	26	.228	.260	.297	51	-25	5	2	0	.958	8	S-80,3-23	-0.6
1925	Bos-N	58	174	17	49	9	4	0	23	15	6	.282	.302	.379	80	-6	2	2	-1	.906	3	S-21,2-15,P/O	0.0
1926	Bos-N	40	84	10	25	6	2	0	13	2	4	.298	.314	.417	105	-0	0			.972	3	P-33	0.0
1927	Bos-N	54	109	10	27	3	1	1	10	2	4	.248	.261	.321	60	-7	0			.966	2	P-41	0.0
1928	Bos-N	39	92	11	23	2	0	1	8	1	6	.250	.258	.304	49	-7	2			.965	3	P-38	0.0
1929	Bos-N	39	99	12	17	4	2	1	8	2	8	.172	.188	.283	16	-14	1			.986	4	P-34/S-5	0.2
1930	Bos-N	39	81	7	19	2	0	0	6	0	5	.235	.235	.259	20	-10	0			.984	2	P-38	0.0
1931	Chi-N	36	87	7	19	2	0	0	9	3	3	.218	.261	.241	35	-8	0			**1.000**	1	P-36	0.0
1932	*Chi-N	36	42	5	10	4	1	0	4	0	2	.238	.238	.381	64	-2	1			1.000	1	P-34/2-2	0.2
1933	Cin-N	23	25	2	5	1	0	1	1	0	0	.200	.231	.240	35	-2	1			.882	-1	P-16/S-1	0.0
	Bos-N	14	20	1	4	0	1	0	2	0	1	.200	.200	.300	45	-2	0			1.000	1	P-14	0.0
	Yr	37	45	3	9	1	1	1	3	1	1	.200	.217	.267	39	-4	1			.946	0	P-30/S-1	0.0
1934	Bos-N	42	36	5	9	1	0	0	3	0	1	.250	.250	.278	44	-3	0			1.000	1	P-39	0.0
1935	Bos-N	47	63	3	17	0	0	0	4	1	5	.270	.281	.270	53	-4	0			.980	-1	P-46	0.0
1936	Bos-N	35	45	1	10	2	0	0	6	2	4	.222	.222	.267	44	-4	0			1.000	1	P-35	0.0
1937	Bos-N	19	10	1	2	0	0	0	1	1	2	.200	.273	.200	33	-1	0			1.000	-1	P-18	0.0
Total	15	742	1689	154	409	64	17	5	166	52	110	.242	.265	.309	53	-117	16	13		.941	42	P-435,S-208/230	-0.5

YEAR	TM/L	G	AB	R	H	2B	3B	HR	RBI	BB	SO	AVG	OBP	SLG	PRO+	BR/A	SB	CS	SBR	FA	FR	G/POS	TPR

■ JOE SMITH   Smith, Salvatore (b: Salvatore Persico)   b: 12/29/1893, New York, N.Y.   d: 1/12/74, Yonkers, N.Y.   BR/TR, 5'7", 170 lbs.   Deb: 7/7/13

| | 1913 | NY-A | 14 | 32 | 1 | 5 | 0 | 0 | 0 | 2 | 1 | 14 | .156 | .182 | .156 | -1 | -4 | 1 | | | .952 | 0 | C-14 | -0.3 |

■ SKYROCKET SMITH   Smith, Samuel J.   b: 3/19/1868, St.Louis, Mo.   d: 4/26/16, St.Louis, Mo.   BR, 6'2", 170 lbs.   Deb: 4/18/1888

| 1888 | Lou-a | 58 | 206 | 27 | 49 | 9 | 4 | 1 | 31 | 24 | | .238 | .349 | .335 | 122 | 7 | 5 | | | .970 | -0 | 1-58 | 0.1 |

■ SYD SMITH   Smith, Sydney E.   b: 8/31/1883, Smithville, S.C.   d: 6/5/61, Orangeburg, S.C.   BR/TR, 5'10", 190 lbs.   Deb: 4/14/08

1908	Phi-A	46	128	8	26	8	0	1	10	4		.203	.233	.289	65	-5	0			.975	-0	C-31/1-6,O	-0.3
	StL-A	27	76	6	14	4	0	0	5	4		.184	.225	.237	50	-4	2			.977	8	C-24	0.7
	Yr	73	204	14	40	12	0	1	15	8		.196	.230	.270	60	-9	2			.976	8	C-55/1-6,O	0.4
1910	Cle-A	9	27	1	9	1	0	0	3	3		.333	.400	.370	140	1	0			.958	0	/C-9	0.2
1911	Cle-A	58	154	8	46	8	1	1	21	11		.299	.353	.383	104	1	0			.979	9	C-48/1-1,3	1.3
1914	Pit-N	5	11	1	3	0	0	0	1	0	1	.273	.273	.273	65	-0	0			1.000	-0	/C-3	0.0
1915	Pit-N	1	1	0	0	0	0	0	0	0	0	.000	.000	.000	-99	-0	0			.000	H	0.0
Total	5	146	397	24	98	21	1	2	40	22	1	.247	.291	.320	83	-8	2			.977	16	C-115/1-7,3O	1.9

■ TOM SMITH   Smith, Thomas N.   b: 1851, Guelph, Ontario, Canada   d: 3/28/1889, Detroit, Mich.   Deb: 9/15/1875

| 1875 | Atl-n | 3 | 12 | 0 | 1 | | 0 | 0 | 0 | | | .083 | .083 | .083 | -48 | -2 | | | | | | /2-3 | -0.1 |

■ TOMMY SMITH   Smith, Tommy Alexander   b: 8/1/48, Albemarle, N.C.   BL/TR, 6'3", 215 lbs.   Deb: 9/6/73

1973	Cle-A	14	41	6	10	2	0	2	3	1		.244	.262	.439	93	-1	1	0	0	1.000	-1	O-13	-0.2
1974	Cle-A	23	31	4	3	1	0	0	0	2	7	.097	.176	.129	-11	-4	0	0	0	.938	-2	O-17/D-1	-0.7
1975	Cle-A	8	8	0	1	0	0	0	2	0	1	.125	.125	.125	-29	-1	0	0	0	1.000	-1	/O-3,D-3	-0.2
1976	Cle-A	55	164	17	42	3	1	2	12	8	8	.256	.291	.323	80	-4	8	0	0	.979	-0	O-50/D-2	-0.4
1977	Sea-A	21	27	1	7	1	1	0	4	0	6	.259	.259	.370	70	-1	0	1	-1	1.000	-2	O-14	-0.4
Total	5	121	271	28	63	7	2	4	21	11	24	.232	.265	.317	68	-12	9	1	2	.977	-5	/O-97,D-6	-1.9

■ VINNIE SMITH   Smith, Vincent Ambrose   b: 12/7/15, Richmond, Va.   d: 12/14/79, Virginia Beach, Va   BR/TR, 6'1", 176 lbs.   Deb: 9/10/41   U

1941	Pit-N	9	33	3	10	1	0	0	5	1	5	.303	.324	.333	86	-1	0			.941	-2	/C-9	-0.2
1946	Pit-N	7	21	2	4	0	0	0	0	1	5	.190	.227	.190	19	-2	0			.967	1	/C-7	-0.1
Total	2	16	54	5	14	1	0	0	5	2	10	.259	.286	.278	59	-3	0			.953	-1	/C-16	-0.3

■ WALLY SMITH   Smith, Wallace H.   b: 3/13/1889, Philadelphia, Pa.   d: 6/10/30, Florence, Ariz.   BR/TR, 5'11.5", 180 lbs.   Deb: 4/17/11

1911	StL-N	81	194	23	42	6	5	2	19	21	33	.216	.303	.330	79	-6	5			.936	2	3-26,S-25/2O	-0.2
1912	StL-N	75	219	22	56	5	5	0	26	29	27	.256	.351	.324	87	-3	4			.949	1	3-32,S-22/1	-0.2
1914	Was-A	45	97	11	19	4	1	0	8	3	12	.196	.235	.258	46	-7	3	4	-2	.955	-4	2-12/1-7,S30	-1.3
Total	3	201	510	56	117	15	11	2	53	53	72	.229	.312	.314	77	-15	12	4		.947	-3	/3-63,S-54,210	-1.7

■ WIB SMITH   Smith, Wilbur Floyd   b: 8/30/1886, Evart, Mich.   d: 11/18/59, Fargo, N.D.   BL/TR, 5'10.5", 165 lbs.   Deb: 5/31/09

| 1909 | StL-A | 17 | 42 | 3 | 8 | 0 | 0 | 0 | 2 | 0 | | .190 | .190 | .190 | 22 | -4 | 0 | | | .836 | -9 | C-13/1-1 | -1.4 |

■ RED SMITH   Smith, Willard Jehu   b: 4/11/1892, Logansport, Ind.   d: 7/17/72, Noblesville, Ind.   BR/TR, 5'8", 165 lbs.   Deb: 9/17/17

1917	Pit-N	11	21	1	3	1	0	0	2	3		.143	.250	.190	35	-2	1			1.000	2	/C-6	0.0
1918	Pit-N	15	24	1	4	1	0	0	3	3	0	.167	.259	.208	42	-2	0			.939	-1	C-10	-0.2
Total	2	26	45	2	7	2	0	0	5	6	4	.156	.255	.200	38	-3	1			.969	1	/C-16	-0.2

■ BILL SMITH   Smith, William E.   b: Cleveland, Ohio   d: 8/9/1886, Toronto, Ont., Can.   5'11", 178 lbs.   Deb: 9/17/1884

| 1884 | Cle-N | 1 | 3 | 0 | 0 | 0 | 0 | 0 | 0 | 0 | 2 | .000 | .000 | .000 | -97 | -1 | | | | .000 | -0 | /O-1 | -0.1 |

■ BILL SMITH   Smith, William J.   b: Baltimore, Md.   d: 8/9/1886,   Deb: 4/14/1873   M

| 1873 | Mar-n | 6 | 23 | 2 | 4 | 0 | 0 | 0 | 1 | 0 | | .174 | .174 | .174 | 4 | -2 | | | | | | /O-3,C-2,2M | -0.2 |

■ WILLIE SMITH   Smith, Willie   b: 2/11/39, Anniston, Ala.   BL/TL, 6', 190 lbs.   Deb: 6/18/63

1963	Det-A	17	8	2	1	0	0	0	0	0	1	.125	.125	.125	-29	-1	0	0	0	1.000	0	P-11	0.0
1964	LA-A	118	359	46	108	14	6	11	51	8	39	.301	.320	.465	128	11	7	5	-1	.977	-6	O-87,P-15	-0.1
1965	Cal-A	136	459	52	120	14	9	14	57	32	60	.261	.311	.423	109	4	9	8	-2	.980	-0	*O-123/1-2	-0.4
1966	Cal-A	90	195	18	36	3	2	1	20	12	37	.185	.243	.236	39	-15	1	0	0	.974	-3	O-52	-2.2
1967	Cle-A	21	32	0	7	2	0	0	2	1	10	.219	.242	.281	54	-2	0	2	-1	.800	-1	/O-4,1-3	-0.5
1968	Cle-A	33	42	1	6	2	0	0	3	3	14	.143	.217	.190	25	-4	0	0	0	1.000	-0	/1-7,P-2,O	-0.5
	Chi-N	55	142	13	39	8	2	5	25	12	33	.275	.335	.465	129	5	0	0	0	1.000	-3	O-38/1-4,P	-0.1
1969	Chi-N	103	195	21	48	9	1	9	25	25	49	.246	.332	.441	102	0	1	0	0	.929	-7	O-33,1-24	-1.0
1970	Chi-N	87	167	15	36	9	1	5	24	11	32	.216	.268	.371	62	-10	2	1	0	.994	-5	1-43/O-1	-1.8
1971	Cin-N	31	55	3	9	2	0	1	4	3	9	.164	.207	.255	31	-5	0	0	0	1.000	1	1-10	-0.5
Total	9	691	1654	171	410	63	21	46	211	107	284	.248	.297	.395	94	-18	20	16	-4	.975	-24	O-339/1-93,P	-7.1

■ HOMER SMOOT   Smoot, Homer Vernon "Doc"   b: 3/23/1878, Galestown, Md.   d: 3/25/28, Salisbury, Md.   BL/TL, 5'10", 180 lbs.   Deb: 4/17/02

1902	StL-N	129	518	58	161	19	4	3	48	23		.311	.350	.380	130	17	20			.931	-1	*O-129	0.9
1903	StL-N	129	500	67	148	22	8	4	49	32		.296	.342	.396	114	8	17			.942	-7	*O-129	-0.7
1904	StL-N	137	520	58	146	23	6	3	66	37		.281	.331	.365	120	12	23			.966	2	*O-137	0.6
1905	StL-N	139	534	73	166	21	16	4	58	33		.311	.359	.433	140	24	21			.975	1	*O-138	1.9
1906	StL-N	86	343	41	85	9	10	0	31	11		.248	.289	.332	98	-2	3			.953	2	O-86	-0.6
	Cin-N	60	220	11	57	8	1	1	17	13		.259	.315	.318	93	-2	0			.944	1	O-59	-0.5
	Yr	146	563	52	142	17	11	1	48	24		.252	.300	.327	96	-4	3			.950	2	*O-145	-1.1
Total	5	680	2635	308	763	102	45	15	269	149		.290	.336	.380	120	57	84			.953	-2	O-678	1.6

■ HENRY SMOYER   Smoyer, Henry Neitz "Hennie" (b: Henry Neitz Smowery)   b: 4/24/1890, Fredricksburg, Pa.   d: 2/28/58, Dubois, Pa.   BR/TR, 5'6",   Deb: 8/14/12

| 1912 | StL-A | 6 | 14 | 1 | 3 | 0 | 0 | 0 | 0 | 2 | | .214 | .313 | .214 | 53 | -1 | 0 | | | 1.000 | -0 | /S-4,3-2 | -0.1 |

■ FRANK SMYKAL   Smykal, Frank John (b: Frank John Smejkal)   b: 10/13/1889, Chicago, Ill.   d: 8/11/50, Chicago, Ill.   BR/TR, 5'7", 150 lbs.   Deb: 8/30/16

| 1916 | Pit-N | 6 | 10 | 1 | 3 | 0 | 0 | 0 | 2 | 3 | 1 | .300 | .500 | .300 | 147 | 1 | 1 | | | .842 | -1 | /S-5,3-1 | 0.1 |

■ CLANCY SMYRES   Smyres, Clarence Melvin   b: 5/24/22, Culver City, Cal.   BB/TR, 5'11.5", 175 lbs.   Deb: 4/18/44

| 1944 | Bro-N | 5 | 2 | 1 | 0 | 0 | 0 | 0 | 0 | 0 | 0 | .000 | .000 | .000 | -99 | -1 | 0 | | | .000 | 0 | H | -0.1 |

■ RED SMYTH   Smyth, James Daniel   b: 1/30/1893, Holly Springs, Miss.   d: 4/14/58, Inglewood, Cal.   BL/TR, 5'9", 152 lbs.   Deb: 8/11/15

1915	Bro-N	19	22	3	3	1	0	0	3	4	2	.136	.269	.182	37	-2	1	2	-1	1.000	-1	/O-9	-0.4
1916	Bro-N	2	5	0	0	0	0	0	0	0	3	.000	.000	.000	-97	-1	0			1.000	-0	/2-2	-0.2
1917	Bro-N	29	24	5	3	0	1	0	4	6		.125	.250	.125	16	-2	0			.667	-1	/3-4,O-2	-0.3
	StL-N	38	72	5	15	0	2	0	4	4	9	.208	.269	.264	66	-3	3			.889	-5	O-23	-1.0
	Yr	67	96	10	18	0	3	0	8	5	15	.188	.264	.229	52	-5	3			.871	-6	O-25/3-4	-1.3
1918	StL-N	40	113	19	24	1	2	0	4	16	11	.212	.315	.257	78	-2	3			.956	-0	O-25,2-11	-0.4
Total	4	128	236	32	45	2	4	0	12	28	31	.191	.285	.233	60	-10	2			.934	-7	/O-59,2-13,3	-2.3

■ JOHN SNEED   Sneed, Jonathon L.   b: Columbus, Ohio   d: 1/4/1899, Memphis, Tenn.   5'8", 160 lbs.   Deb: 5/1/1884

| 1884 | Ind-a | 27 | 102 | 14 | 22 | 4 | 0 | 1 | | 6 | | .216 | .259 | .284 | 79 | -2 | | | | .817 | -0 | O-27 | -0.3 |
| 1890 | Tol-a | 9 | 30 | 3 | 6 | 0 | 0 | 0 | | 8 | | .200 | .368 | .200 | 66 | -1 | 5 | | | .889 | 2 | /O-9 | 0.1 |

YEAR	TM/L	G	AB	R	H	2B	3B	HR	RBI	BB	SO	AVG	OBP	SLG	PRO+	BR/A	SB	CS	SBR	FA	FR	G/POS	TPR
	Col-a	128	484	114	141	13	15	2		63		.291	.383	.393	138	26	39			.883	-8	*O-126/S-2	1.2
	Yr	137	514	117	147	13	15	2		71		.286	.382	.381	133	25	44			.883	-5	*O-135/S-2	1.3
1891	Col-a	99	366	66	94	9	6	1	61	55	29	.257	.366	.322	103	4	24			.894	-4	*O-99	-0.3
Total	3	263	982	197	263	26	21	4	61	132	29	.268	.364	.349	117	27	68			.879	-10	O-261/S-2	0.7

■ CHARLIE SNELL   Snell, Charles Anthony (b: Charles Anthony Schnell)
b: 11/29/1893, Hampstead, Md.   d: 4/4/88, Reading, Pa.   BR/TR, 5'11", 160 lbs.   Deb: 7/19/12

YEAR	TM/L	G	AB	R	H	2B	3B	HR	RBI	BB	SO	AVG	OBP	SLG	PRO+	BR/A	SB	CS	SBR	FA	FR	G/POS	TPR
1912	StL-A	8	19	0	4	1	0	0		0	3	.211	.348	.263	78	-0	0			.941	2	/C-8	0.2

■ WALLY SNELL   Snell, Walter Henry "Doc"   b: 5/19/1889, W.Bridgewater, Mass.   d: 7/23/80, Providence, R.I.   BR/TR, 5'10", 170 lbs.   Deb: 8/1/13

YEAR	TM/L	G	AB	R	H	2B	3B	HR	RBI	BB	SO	AVG	OBP	SLG	PRO+	BR/A	SB	CS	SBR	FA	FR	G/POS	TPR
1913	Bos-A	5	8	1	3	0	0	0	0	0	0	.375	.375	.375	117	0	1			1.000	0	/C-1	0.1

■ DUKE SNIDER   Snider, Edwin Donald "The Silver Fox"   b: 9/19/26, Los Angeles, Cal.   BL/TR, 6', 190 lbs.   Deb: 4/17/47   H

YEAR	TM/L	G	AB	R	H	2B	3B	HR	RBI	BB	SO	AVG	OBP	SLG	PRO+	BR/A	SB	CS	SBR	FA	FR	G/POS	TPR
1947	Bro-N	40	83	6	20	3	1	0	5	3	24	.241	.276	.301	51	-6	2			.980	-2	O-25	-0.9
1948	Bro-N	53	160	22	39	6	6	5	21	12	27	.244	.297	.450	96	-2	4			.989	-3	O-47	-0.7
1949	*Bro-N	146	552	100	161	28	7	23	92	56	92	.292	.361	.493	122	16	12			.984	5	*O-145	1.2
1950	Bro-N★	152	620	109	**199**	31	10	31	107	58	79	.321	.379	.553	139	33	16			.983	9	*O-151	3.4
1951	Bro-N★	150	606	96	168	26	6	29	101	62	97	.277	.344	.483	118	14	14	10	-2	.987	3	*O-150	0.9
1952	*Bro-N☆	144	534	80	162	25	7	21	92	55	77	.303	.368	.494	136	25	7	4	-0	.992	-1	*O-141	2.1
1953	*Bro-N★	153	590	**132**	198	38	4	42	126	82	90	.336	.419	**.627**	165	56	16	7	1	.987	-3	*O-151	4.6
1954	Bro-N★	149	584	**120**	199	39	10	40	130	84	96	.341	.427	.647	170	60	6	5	-2	.981	-5	*O-148	4.6
1955	*Bro-N★	148	538	**126**	166	34	6	42	**136**	104	87	.309	.421	.628	169	55	9	7	-2	.989	1	*O-146	4.7
1956	*Bro-N★	151	542	112	158	33	2	**43**	101	**99**	101	.292	**.402**	**.598**	152	41	3	3	-1	.984	-0	*O-150	3.2
1957	Bro-N	139	508	91	139	25	7	40	92	77	104	.274	.370	.587	139	27	3	4	-2	.990	-6	*O-136	1.1
1958	LA-N	106	327	45	102	12	3	15	58	32	49	.312	.375	.505	126	12	2	2	-1	.987	-13	O-92	-0.6
1959	*LA-N	126	370	59	114	11	2	23	88	58	71	.308	.402	.535	137	20	1	5	-3	.975	-17	*O-107	-0.4
1960	LA-N	101	235	38	57	13	5	14	36	46	54	.243	.369	.519	131	11	1	0	0	.965	-12	O-75	-0.4
1961	LA-N	85	233	35	69	8	3	16	56	29	43	.296	.376	.562	133	11	1	1	-0	.975	-2	O-66	0.6
1962	LA-N	80	158	28	44	11	3	5	30	36	32	.278	.418	.481	150	13	2	0	1	.967	-1	O-39	1.0
1963	NY-N★	129	354	44	86	8	3	14	45	56	74	.243	.348	.401	113	7	0	1	-1	.986	-10	*O-106	-0.8
1964	SF-N	91	167	16	35	7	0	4	17	22	40	.210	.302	.323	74	-5	0	0	0	.979	-5	O-43	-1.3
Total	18	2143	7161	1259	2116	358	85	407	1333	971	1237	.295	.381	.540	138	388	99	50		.985	-62	*O-1918	22.3

■ VAN SNIDER   Snider, Van Voorhees   b: 8/11/63, Birmingham, Ala.   BL/TR, 6'3", 185 lbs.   Deb: 9/2/88

YEAR	TM/L	G	AB	R	H	2B	3B	HR	RBI	BB	SO	AVG	OBP	SLG	PRO+	BR/A	SB	CS	SBR	FA	FR	G/POS	TPR
1988	Cin-N	11	28	4	6	1	0	1	6	0	13	.214	.214	.357	59	-1	0	1	-1	1.000	-1	/O-8	-0.3
1989	Cin-N	8	7	1	1	0	0	0	0	0	5	.143	.143	.143	-17	-1	0	0	0	1.000	-2	/O-6	-0.3
Total	2	19	35	5	7	1	0	1	6	0	18	.200	.200	.314	44	-3	0	1	-1	1.000	-2	/O-14	-0.6

■ ROXY SNIPES   Snipes, Wyatt Eure "Rock"   b: 10/28/1896, Marion, S.C.   d: 5/1/41, Fayetteville, N.C.   BL/TR, 6', 185 lbs.   Deb: 7/15/23

YEAR	TM/L	G	AB	R	H	2B	3B	HR	RBI	BB	SO	AVG	OBP	SLG	PRO+	BR/A	SB	CS	SBR	FA	FR	G/POS	TPR
1923	Chi-A	1	1	0	0	0	0	0	0	0	0	.000	.000	.000	-99	-0	0	0	0	.000	0	H	0.0

■ CHAPPIE SNODGRASS   Snodgrass, Amzie Beal   b: 3/18/1870, Springfield, Ohio   d: 9/9/51, New York, N.Y.   BR/TR, 5'10", 165 lbs.   Deb: 5/15/01

YEAR	TM/L	G	AB	R	H	2B	3B	HR	RBI	BB	SO	AVG	OBP	SLG	PRO+	BR/A	SB	CS	SBR	FA	FR	G/POS	TPR
1901	Bal-A	3	10	0	1	0	0	0		1	0	.100	.100	.100	-43	-2	0			.500	-1	/O-2	-0.3

■ FRED SNODGRASS   Snodgrass, Frederick Carlisle "Snow"   b: 10/19/1887, Ventura, Cal.   d: 4/5/74, Ventura, Cal.   BR/TR, 5'11.5", 175 lbs.   Deb: 6/4/08

YEAR	TM/L	G	AB	R	H	2B	3B	HR	RBI	BB	SO	AVG	OBP	SLG	PRO+	BR/A	SB	CS	SBR	FA	FR	G/POS	TPR
1908	NY-N	6	4	2	1	0	1	0	1	0		.250	.250	.250	57	-0	1			1.000	1	/C-3	0.1
1909	NY-N	28	70	10	21	5	0	1	6	7		.300	.387	.414	146	4	10			.921	-1	O-20/C-2,1	0.4
1910	NY-N	123	396	69	127	22	8	2	44	71	52	.321	.440	.432	154	32	33			.970	-8	*O-101/1-9,C3	2.0
1911	*NY-N	151	534	83	157	27	10	1	77	72	59	.294	.393	.388	115	13	51			.973	9	*O-149/1-1,3	1.4
1912	*NY-N	146	535	91	144	24	9	3	69	70	65	.269	.362	.364	96	-1	43			.948	-3	*O-116,1-27/2	-1.1
1913	*NY-N	141	457	65	133	21	6	3	49	53	44	.291	.373	.383	115	11	27			.968	5	*O-133/1-3,2	1.1
1914	NY-N	113	392	54	103	20	4	0	44	37	43	.263	.336	.334	103	2	25			.977	5	O-96,1-14/23	0.2
1915	NY-N	80	252	36	49	9	0	0	20	35	33	.194	.307	.230	68	-8	11	12	-4	.935	4	O-75	-1.3
	Bos-N	23	79	10	22	2	0	0	9	7	9	.278	.352	.304	104	1	0	4	-2	.938	-2	O-18/1-5	-0.5
	Yr	103	331	46	71	11	0	0	29	42	42	.215	.318	.248	76	-7	11	16	-6	.935	2	O-93/1-5	-1.8
1916	Bos-N	112	382	33	95	13	5	1	32	34	54	.249	.318	.317	100	0	14			.983	13	*O-110	0.9
Total	9	923	3101	453	852	143	42	11	351	386	359	.275	.367	.359	110	53	215	16		.965	24	O-818/1-60,C23	3.1

■ CHARLIE SNOW   Snow, Charles M.   b: 8/3/1849, Lowell, Mass.   Deb: 10/1/1874

YEAR	TM/L	G	AB	R	H	2B	3B	HR	RBI	BB	SO	AVG	OBP	SLG	PRO+	BR/A	SB	CS	SBR	FA	FR	G/POS	TPR
1874	Atl-n	1	2	0	1	0	0	0		0		.500	.500	.500	248	0						/O-1	0.0

■ J. T. SNOW   Snow, Jack Thomas   b: 2/26/68, Long Beach, Cal.   BB/TL, 6'2", 200 lbs.   Deb: 9/20/92

YEAR	TM/L	G	AB	R	H	2B	3B	HR	RBI	BB	SO	AVG	OBP	SLG	PRO+	BR/A	SB	CS	SBR	FA	FR	G/POS	TPR
1992	NY-A	7	14	1	2	1	0	0	2	5	5	.143	.368	.214	67	-0	0	0	0	1.000	-0	/1-6,D-1	-0.1
1993	Cal-A	129	419	60	101	18	2	16	57	55	88	.241	.332	.408	95	-3	3	0	1	.995	-3	*1-129	-1.5
1994	Cal-A	61	223	22	49	4	0	8	30	19	48	.220	.290	.345	61	-13	0	1	-1	.996	-1	1-61	-1.8
Total	3	197	656	83	152	23	2	24	89	79	141	.232	.319	.383	83	-17	3	1	0	.995	-3	1-196/D-1	-3.4

■ BERNIE SNYDER   Snyder, Bernard Austin   b: 8/25/13, Philadelphia, Pa.   BR/TR, 6', 165 lbs.   Deb: 9/15/35

YEAR	TM/L	G	AB	R	H	2B	3B	HR	RBI	BB	SO	AVG	OBP	SLG	PRO+	BR/A	SB	CS	SBR	FA	FR	G/POS	TPR
1935	Phi-A	10	32	5	11	1	0	0	3	1	2	.344	.364	.375	92	-0	0	0	0	.880	-3	/2-5,S-4	-0.2

■ CHARLES SNYDER   Snyder, Charles   b: Camden, N.J.   d: 3/3/01, Philadelphia, Pa.   BR/TR,   Deb: 9/19/1890

YEAR	TM/L	G	AB	R	H	2B	3B	HR	RBI	BB	SO	AVG	OBP	SLG	PRO+	BR/A	SB	CS	SBR	FA	FR	G/POS	TPR
1890	Phi-a	9	33	5	9	1	0	0		2		.273	.314	.303	84	-1	0			.583	-3	/O-5,C-5	-0.4

■ POP SNYDER   Snyder, Charles N.   b: 10/6/1854, Washington, D.C.   d: 10/29/24, Washington, D.C.   BR/TR, 5'11.5", 184 lbs.   Deb: 6/16/1873   MU

YEAR	TM/L	G	AB	R	H	2B	3B	HR	RBI	BB	SO	AVG	OBP	SLG	PRO+	BR/A	SB	CS	SBR	FA	FR	G/POS	TPR
1873	Was-n	28	108	16	21	2	0	0	3	3	3	.194	.216	.213	28	-9						C-28/O-3	-0.7
1874	Bal-n	39	152	24	33	4	2	1		2		.217	.227	.289	64	-6						C-39	-0.4
1875	Phi-n	66	263	37	64	7	2	1		4		.243	.255	.297	87	-4						*C-65/O-1	-0.1
1876	Lou-N	56	224	21	44	4	1	1	9	2	7	.196	.204	.237	39	-16				.833	11	*C-55/O-4	-0.3
1877	Lou-N	61	248	23	64	7	2	2	28	3	14	.258	.267	.327	73	-10				.910	15	*C-61/O-1,S	0.7
1878	Bos-N	60	226	21	48	5	0	0	14	1	19	.212	.216	.235	44	-14				.912	8	*C-58/O-2	-0.7
1879	Bos-N	81	329	42	78	16	3	2	35	5	31	.237	.249	.322	85	-6				.925	24	*C-80/O-2	1.9
1881	Bos-N	62	219	14	50	8	0	0	16	3	23	.228	.239	.265	61	-9				.897	3	*C-60/O-1,S2	-0.4
1882	Cin-a	72	309	49	90	12	2	1		9		.291	.311	.353	117	4				.916	19	*C-70/1-2,OM	2.3
1883	Cin-a	58	250	38	64	14	6	0		8		.256	.279	.360	99	-1				.919	14	*C-57/S-2M	1.4
1884	Cin-a	67	268	32	69	7	6	0		7		.257	.279	.358	101	-1				.922	27	*C-65/1-2,OM	2.9
1885	Cin-a	39	152	13	36	4	3	1		6		.237	.270	.322	85	-3				.880	3	C-38/1-1	0.3
1886	Cin-a	60	220	33	41	8	5	0		13		.186	.242	.250	52	-13	11			.874	-5	C-41,1-19/O	-1.3
1887	Cle-a	74	282	33	72	12	6	0		9		.255	.281	.340	75	-10	5			.905	19	C-63/1-13	1.1
1888	Cle-a	64	237	22	51	7	3	0	14	6		.215	.238	.270	64	-10	9			.901	8	C-58/1-4,O	0.3
1889	Cle-N	22	83	5	16	0	0	0	12	2	12	.193	.221	.193	26	-8	4			.907	2	C-22	-0.4
1890	Cle-P	13	48	5	9	1	0	0	9	2	9	.188	.220	.208	16	-6	1			.958	3	C-13	-0.1
1891	Was-a	8	27	4	5	0	0	0	3	1	3	.185	.241	.259	45	-2	0			1.000	0	/1-4,C-3,OM	-0.2
Total	3 n	133	523	77	118	13	4	2		9		.226	.239	.277	67	-19	0					C-132/O-4D	-1.2
Total	15	797	3122	355	737	110	39	7	142	75	118	.236	.256	.303	73	-104	30			.904	148	C-744/1-45,OS2	7.5

YEAR	TM/L	G	AB	R	H	2B	3B	HR	RBI	BB	SO	AVG	OBP	SLG	PRO+	BR/A	SB	CS	SBR	FA	FR	G/POS	TPR

■ REDLEG SNYDER
Snyder, Emanuel Sebastian (b: Emanuel Sebastian Schneider)
b: 12/12/1854, Camden, N.J. d: 11/24/32, Camden, N.J. BR/TR, 5'10", 175 lbs. Deb: 4/25/1876

YEAR	TM/L	G	AB	R	H	2B	3B	HR	RBI	BB	SO	AVG	OBP	SLG	PRO+	BR/A	SB	CS	SBR	FA	FR	G/POS	TPR
1876	Cin-N	55	205	10	31	3	1	0	12	1	19	.151	.155	.176	12	-17				.825	5	*O-55	-1.2
1884	Wil-U	17	52	4	10	0	0	0		1		.192	.208	.192	9	-6				.976	1	1-16/O-1	-0.7
Total	2	72	257	14	41	3	1	0	12	2	19	.160	.166	.179	11	-24				.825	5	/O-56,1-16	-1.9

■ COONEY SNYDER
Snyder, Frank C. b: Toronto, Ontario, Canada d: 3/9/17, Toronto, Ont., Can. Deb: 5/19/1898

YEAR	TM/L	G	AB	R	H	2B	3B	HR	RBI	BB	SO	AVG	OBP	SLG	PRO+	BR/A	SB	CS	SBR	FA	FR	G/POS	TPR
1898	Lou-N	17	61	4	10	0	0	0	6	3		.164	.215	.164	9	-7	0			.935	-6	C-17	-1.1

■ FRANK SNYDER
Snyder, Frank Elton "Pancho" b: 5/27/1893, San Antonio, Tex. d: 1/5/62, San Antonio, Tex. BR/TR, 6'2", 185 lbs. Deb: 8/25/12 C

YEAR	TM/L	G	AB	R	H	2B	3B	HR	RBI	BB	SO	AVG	OBP	SLG	PRO+	BR/A	SB	CS	SBR	FA	FR	G/POS	TPR
1912	StL-N	11	18	2	2	0	0	0	2	7		.111	.200	.111	-14	-3	1			.919	0	C-11	-0.2
1913	StL-N	7	21	1	4	0	1	0	2	0	4	.190	.190	.286	35	-2	0			.956	2	/C-7	0.0
1914	StL-N	100	326	19	75	15	4	1	25	13	28	.230	.262	.310	71	-13	1			.979	5	C-98	0.0
1915	StL-N	144	473	41	141	22	7	2	55	39	49	.298	.353	.387	124	13	3	6	-3	.983	7	*C-142	3.1
1916	StL-N	132	406	23	105	12	4	0	39	18	31	.259	.290	.308	84	-8	7			.973	9	C-72,1-46/S	0.5
1917	StL-N	115	313	18	74	9	2	1	33	27	43	.236	.301	.288	83	-6	4			.975	0	C-94/2-1	0.2
1918	StL-N	39	112	5	28	7	1	0	10	6	13	.250	.288	.330	92	-1	4			.959	2	C-27/1-3	0.3
1919	StL-N	50	154	7	28	4	2	0	14	5	13	.182	.213	.234	36	-12	2			.983	5	C-48/1-1	-0.4
	NY-N	32	92	7	21	6	0	0	11	8		.228	.297	.293	79	-2	1			.983	-4	C-31	-0.5
	Yr	82	246	14	49	10	2	0	25	13	22	.199	.245	.256	53	-14	3			.983	1	C-79/1-1	-0.9
1920	NY-N	87	264	26	66	13	4	3	27	17	18	.250	.295	.364	89	-4	2	2	-1	.978	1	C-84	0.2
1921	*NY-N	108	309	36	99	13	2	8	45	27	24	.320	.382	.453	120	9	3	4	-2	.985	5	*C-101	1.7
1922	*NY-N	104	318	34	109	21	5	5	51	23	25	.343	.387	.487	123	11	1	5	-3	.980	-3	*C-97	0.9
1923	*NY-N	120	402	37	103	13	6	5	63	24	29	.256	.298	.356	73	-17	5	3		.990	3	*C-112	-0.9
1924	*NY-N	118	354	37	107	18	3	5	53	30	43	.302	.357	.412	109	4	3	0	-1	.987	-16	*C-110	-0.4
1925	NY-N	107	325	21	78	9	1	11	51	20	49	.240	.286	.375	70	-16	0	0		.985	3	C-96	-0.7
1926	NY-N	55	148	10	32	3	2	5	16	13	13	.216	.280	.365	73	-6	0			.981	-0	C-55	-0.3
1927	StL-N	63	194	7	50	5	0	1	30	9	18	.258	.291	.299	56	-12	0			.981	0	C-62	-0.8
Total	16	1392	4229	331	1122	170	44	47	525	281	416	.265	.313	.360	90	-65	37	20		.981	17	*C-1247/1-50,2S	2.7

■ JERRY SNYDER
Snyder, Gerald George b: 7/21/29, Jenks, Okla. BR/TR, 6', 170 lbs. Deb: 5/8/52

YEAR	TM/L	G	AB	R	H	2B	3B	HR	RBI	BB	SO	AVG	OBP	SLG	PRO+	BR/A	SB	CS	SBR	FA	FR	G/POS	TPR
1952	Was-A	36	57	5	9	2	0	0	2	5	8	.158	.226	.193	18	-6	1	0	0	.965	7	2-19/S-4	0.2
1953	Was-A	29	62	10	21	4	0	0	4	5	8	.339	.388	.403	117	2	1	1	-0	.988	7	S-17/2-4	0.9
1954	Was-A	64	154	17	36	3	1	0	15	15	18	.234	.302	.266	60	-8	3	0	1	.978	9	S-48/2-3	0.5
1955	Was-A	46	107	7	24	5	0	0	5	6	6	.224	.265	.271	47	-8	1	1	-0	.977	1	2-22,S-20	-0.5
1956	Was-A	43	148	14	40	3	1	2	14	10	9	.270	.321	.345	76	-5	1	0	0	.968	-5	S-35/2-7	-0.6
1957	Was-A	42	93	6	14	1	0	1	4	4	9	.151	.186	.194	4	-12	0	1	-1	.966	1	S-15,2-13/3	-1.1
1958	Was-A	6	9	1	1	0	0	0	1	1	1	.111	.200	.111	-12	-1	0	0	0	1.000	-1	/2-2,S-1	-0.2
Total	7	266	630	60	145	18	2	3	47	46	59	.230	.284	.279	54	-41	7	3	0	.971	20	S-140/2-70,3	-0.8

■ JIM SNYDER
Snyder, James C. A. b: 9/15/1847, Brooklyn, N.Y. d: 12/1/22, Rockaway Beach, N.Y 5'7", 130 lbs. Deb: 5/7/1872

YEAR	TM/L	G	AB	R	H	2B	3B	HR	RBI	BB	SO	AVG	OBP	SLG	PRO+	BR/A	SB	CS	SBR	FA	FR	G/POS	TPR
1872	Eck-n	26	106	16	27	2	3	0	10	0	1	.255	.255	.330	93	0						S-22/O-3,C	0.0

■ CORY SNYDER
Snyder, James Cory b: 11/11/62, Inglewood, Cal. BR/TR, 6'3", 185 lbs. Deb: 6/13/86

YEAR	TM/L	G	AB	R	H	2B	3B	HR	RBI	BB	SO	AVG	OBP	SLG	PRO+	BR/A	SB	CS	SBR	FA	FR	G/POS	TPR
1986	Cle-A	103	416	58	113	21	1	24	69	16	123	.272	.299	.500	115	6	2	3	-1	.987	-7	O-74,S-34,3/D	-0.2
1987	Cle-A	157	577	74	136	24	2	33	82	31	166	.236	.276	.456	89	-12	5	1	1	.971	2	*O-139,S-18	-1.2
1988	Cle-A	142	511	71	139	24	3	26	75	42	101	.272	.329	.483	121	13	5	1	0	.985	14	*O-141/D-1	2.3
1989	Cle-A	132	489	49	105	17	0	18	59	23	134	.215	.253	.360	70	-21	6	5	-1	.997	19	*O-120/S-5	-0.7
1990	Cle-A	123	438	46	102	27	3	14	55	21	118	.233	.271	.404	87	-10	1	4	-2	.975	-2	*O-125/S-7,D	-1.3
1991	Chi-A	50	117	10	22	4	0	3	11	6	41	.188	.228	.299	46	-9	0	0	0	.981	-2	O-29,1-18	-1.2
	Tor-A	21	49	4	7	0	1	0	6	3	19	.143	.192	.184	4	-6	0	0	0	1.000	-3	O-14/1-4,3D	-0.9
	Yr	71	166	14	29	4	1	3	17	9	60	.175	.217	.265	33	-15	0	0	0	.985	-5	O-43,1-22/3D	-2.1
1992	SF-N	124	390	48	105	22	2	14	57	23	96	.269	.313	.444	119	7	4	4	-1	.992	-5	O-70,1-27,3/2S	-0.1
1993	LA-N	143	516	61	137	33	1	11	56	47	147	.266	.332	.397	100	-1	4	1	1	.979	-8	*O-115,3-23,1/S	-1.0
1994	LA-N	73	153	18	36	6	0	6	18	14	47	.235	.304	.392	85	-4	1	0	0	.967	-8	O-50/1-9,3S2	-1.2
Total	9	1068	3656	439	902	178	13	149	488	226	992	.247	.293	.425	95	-36	28	19	-3	.983	3	O-877/S-73,132D	-5.5

■ JIM SNYDER
Snyder, James Robert b: 8/15/32, Dearborn, Mich. BR/TR, 6'1", 185 lbs. Deb: 9/15/61 MC

YEAR	TM/L	G	AB	R	H	2B	3B	HR	RBI	BB	SO	AVG	OBP	SLG	PRO+	BR/A	SB	CS	SBR	FA	FR	G/POS	TPR
1961	Min-A	3	5	0	0	0	0	0	0	0	1	.000	.000	.000	-95	-1	0	0	0	1.000	0	/2-3	-0.1
1962	Min-A	12	10	1	1	0	0	0	1	0	0	.100	.100	.100	-44	-2	0	1	-1	.941	-6	/2-5,1-1	-0.8
1964	Min-A	26	71	3	11	2	0	0	9	4	11	.155	.211	.225	21	-8	0	0	0	.990	-4	2-25	-1.0
Total	3	41	86	4	12	2	0	0	10	4	12	.140	.187	.198	6	-11	0	1	-1	.984	-10	/2-33,1-1	-1.9

■ JACK SNYDER
Snyder, John William b: 10/6/1886, Lincoln Township, Pa. d: 12/13/81, Brownsville, Pa. BR/TR, 5'9", 168 lbs. Deb: 6/13/14

YEAR	TM/L	G	AB	R	H	2B	3B	HR	RBI	BB	SO	AVG	OBP	SLG	PRO+	BR/A	SB	CS	SBR	FA	FR	G/POS	TPR
1914	Buf-F	1	0	0	0	0	0	0	0	1	0	—	1.000	—	170	0				.000	0	/C-1	0.0
1917	Bro-N	7	11	1	3	0	0	0	1	0	2	.273	.273	.273	66	-0	0			1.000	0	/C-5	0.0
Total	2	8	11	1	3	0	0	0	1	1	2	.273	.333	.273	83	-0	0			1.000	0	/C-6	0.0

■ JOSH SNYDER
Snyder, Joshua M. b: 3/1844, Brooklyn, N.Y. d: 4/21/1881, Brooklyn, N.Y. Deb: 5/18/1872

YEAR	TM/L	G	AB	R	H	2B	3B	HR	RBI	BB	SO	AVG	OBP	SLG	PRO+	BR/A	SB	CS	SBR	FA	FR	G/POS	TPR
1872	Eck-n	9	42	3	6	2	0	0	1	1	1	.143	.163	.190	10	-4						/O-9	-0.2

■ RUSS SNYDER
Snyder, Russell Henry b: 6/22/34, Oak, Neb. BL/TR, 6'1", 190 lbs. Deb: 4/18/59

YEAR	TM/L	G	AB	R	H	2B	3B	HR	RBI	BB	SO	AVG	OBP	SLG	PRO+	BR/A	SB	CS	SBR	FA	FR	G/POS	TPR
1959	KC-A	73	243	41	76	13	6	2	21	19	29	.313	.367	.420	113	5	6	2	1	.986	3	O-64	0.5
1960	KC-A	125	304	45	79	10	5	4	26	20	28	.260	.308	.365	81	-9	7	3	0	.986	-10	O-91	-2.2
1961	Bal-A	115	312	46	91	13	5	1	13	20	32	.292	.334	.373	92	-4	5	3	-0	.966	-16	*O-108	-2.5
1962	Bal-A	139	416	47	127	19	4	9	40	17	46	.305	.336	.435	113	6	7	4	-0	.974	-3	*O-121	-0.4
1963	Bal-A	148	429	51	110	21	2	7	36	40	48	.256	.323	.364	95	-3	18	5	2	.988	-18	*O-130	-2.5
1964	Bal-A	56	93	11	27	3	0	1	7	10	22	.290	.365	.355	102	1	0	2	-1	.971	-9	O-40	-1.1
1965	Bal-A	132	345	49	93	11	2	4	29	27	38	.270	.324	.322	83	-7	3	4	-2	1.000	-7	O-106	-2.2
1966	*Bal-A	117	373	66	114	21	5	3	41	38	37	.306	.370	.413	127	13	8	4	-1	.986	-13	*O-104	-0.5
1967	Bal-A	108	275	40	65	8	2	4	23	32	48	.236	.318	.324	91	-3	5	2	0	.985	-1	O-69	-0.8
1968	Chi-A	38	82	2	11	2	0	1	5	4	16	.134	.174	.195	12	-9	0	0	0	1.000	-1	O-22	-1.8
	Cle-A	68	217	30	61	8	2	2	23	25	21	.281	.355	.364	120	6	1	1	-0	.991	-4	O-54/1-1	0.7
	Yr	106	299	32	72	10	2	3	28	29	37	.241	.308	.318	90	-3	1	1	-0	.992	-1	O-76/1-1	-1.1
1969	Cle-A	122	266	26	66	10	2	2	24	25	33	.248	.313	.308	72	-10	3	2	-0	.961	-4	O-84	-1.8
1970	Mil-A	124	276	34	64	11	0	4	31	16	40	.232	.274	.315	62	-15	1	3	-2	.966	-16	O-106	-3.7
Total	12	1365	3631	488	984	150	29	42	319	294	438	.271	.327	.363	94	-28	58	32	-2	.981	-96	*O-1099/1-1	-18.3

■ CHIEF SOCKALEXIS
Sockalexis, Louis M. b: 10/24/1871, Old Town, Maine d: 12/24/13, Burlington, Maine BL/TR, 5'11", 185 lbs. Deb: 4/22/1897

YEAR	TM/L	G	AB	R	H	2B	3B	HR	RBI	BB	SO	AVG	OBP	SLG	PRO+	BR/A	SB	CS	SBR	FA	FR	G/POS	TPR
1897	Cle-N	66	278	43	94	9	8	3	42	18		.338	.385	.460	116	5	16			.888	1	O-66	0.1
1898	Cle-N	21	67	11	15	2	0	0	10	1		.224	.246	.254	44	-5	0			.964	2	O-16	-0.4
1899	Cle-N	7	22	0	6	1	0	0	3	1		.273	.304	.318	76	-1	0			.818	1	/O-5	0.0
Total	3	94	367	54	115	12	8	3	55	20		.313	.355	.414	103	-0	16			.896	4	/O-87	-0.3

YEAR	TM/L	G	AB	R	H	2B	3B	HR	RBI	BB	SO	AVG	OBP	SLG	PRO+	BR/A	SB	CS	SBR	FA	FR	G/POS	TPR

■ BILL SODD
Sodd, William b: 9/18/14, Ft.Worth, Tex. BR/TR, 6'2", 210 lbs. Deb: 9/27/37

| 1937 | Cle-A | 1 | 1 | 0 | 0 | 0 | 0 | 0 | 0 | 0 | 1 | .000 | .000 | .000 | -99 | -0 | 0 | 0 | 0 | .000 | 0 | H | 0.0 |

■ ERIC SODERHOLM
Soderholm, Eric Thane b: 9/24/48, Cortland, N.Y. BR/TR, 5'11", 187 lbs. Deb: 9/3/71

1971	Min-A	21	64	9	10	4	0	1	4	10	17	.156	.299	.266	59	-3	0	1	-1	.942	3	3-20	-0.1
1972	Min-A	93	287	28	54	10	0	13	39	19	48	.188	.246	.359	75	-10	3	3	-1	.942	2	3-79	-1.1
1973	Min-A	35	111	22	33	7	2	1	9	21	16	.297	.414	.423	131	6	1	2	-1	.921	0	3-33/S-1	0.5
1974	Min-A	141	464	63	128	18	3	10	51	48	68	.276	.350	.392	109	6	7	3	0	.956	-4	*3-130/S-1	0.2
1975	Min-A	117	419	62	120	17	2	11	58	53	66	.286	.367	.415	118	11	3	5	-2	.969	12	*3-113/D-3	2.0
1977	Chi-A	130	460	77	129	20	3	25	67	47	47	.280	.352	.500	129	18	2	4	-2	.978	0	*3-126/D-3	1.5
1978	Chi-A	143	457	57	118	17	1	20	67	39	44	.258	.322	.431	109	4	2	2	-1	.964	0	*3-128,D-11/2	0.2
1979	Chi-A	56	210	31	53	8	2	6	34	19	19	.252	.314	.395	90	-3	0	1	-1	.986	15	3-56	1.0
	Tex-A	63	147	15	40	6	0	4	19	12	9	.272	.331	.395	96	-1	0	0	-1	.944	1	3-37,D-14/1	-0.1
	Yr	119	357	46	93	14	2	10	53	31	28	.261	.321	.395	93	-4	0	1	-1	.975	16	3-93,D-14/1	0.9
1980	*NY-A	95	275	38	79	13	1	11	35	27	25	.287	.353	.462	123	9	0	0	0	.952	-1	D-51,3-37	0.5
Total	9	894	2894	402	764	120	14	102	383	295	359	.264	.337	.421	109	36	18	21	-7	.962	28	3-759/D-82,1S2	4.6

■ RICK SOFIELD
Sofield, Richard Michael b: 12/16/56, Cheyenne, Wyo. BL/TR, 6'1", 195 lbs. Deb: 4/6/79

1979	Min-A	35	93	8	28	5	0	0	12	12	27	.301	.381	.355	96	-0	2	3	-1	.954	-3	O-35	-0.5
1980	Min-A	131	417	52	103	18	4	9	49	24	92	.247	.291	.374	75	-15	4	5	-2	.979	-5	*O-126/D-2	-2.6
1981	Min-A	41	102	9	18	2	0	0	5	8	22	.176	.236	.196	24	-10	3	2	-0	.983	-1	O-34	-1.2
Total	3	207	612	69	149	25	4	9	66	44	141	.243	.296	.342	71	-25	9	10	-3	.975	-8	O-195/D-2	-4.3

■ LUIS SOJO
Sojo, Luis Beltran (Sojo) b: 1/3/66, Caracas, Venez. BR/TR, 5'11", 170 lbs. Deb: 7/14/90

1990	Tor-A	33	80	14	18	3	1	9	5	5	.225	.271	.300	58	-4	1	1	-0	.969	-3	2-15/S-5,03D	-0.8
1991	Cal-A	113	364	38	94	14	1	3	20	14	26	.258	.295	.327	72	-14	4	2	0	.981	20	*2-107/S-2,30D	0.8
1992	Cal-A	106	368	37	100	12	3	7	43	14	24	.272	.300	.378	88	-7	7	11	-5	.985	2	2-96/3-9,S	-0.7
1993	Tor-A	19	47	5	8	2	0	0	6	4	2	.170	.235	.213	21	-5	0	0	0	1.000	-1	/2-8,S-8,3	-0.3
1994	Sea-A	63	213	32	59	9	2	6	22	8	25	.277	.309	.423	85	-5	2	1	0	.973	18	2-40/S-24/3D	1.4
Total	5	334	1072	126	279	40	6	17	100	45	82	.260	.295	.356	77	-36	14	15	-5	.981	36	2-266/S-44,3DO	0.1

■ TONY SOLAITA
Solaita, Tolia b: 1/15/47, Nuuyli, Amer.Samoa d: 2/10/90, Tafuna, Amer.Samoa BL/TL, 6', 215 lbs. Deb: 9/16/68

1968	NY-A	1	1	0	0	0	0	0	0	0	0	.000	.000	.000	-99	-0	0	0	0	1.000	-0	/1-1	0.0
1974	KC-A	96	239	31	64	12	0	7	30	35	70	.268	.364	.406	115	5	0	3	-2	.991	3	1-65,D-14/O	0.3
1975	KC-A	93	231	35	60	11	0	16	44	39	79	.260	.371	.515	145	14	0	1	-1	.994	0	D-37,1-35	1.4
1976	KC-A	31	68	4	16	4	0	0	9	6	17	.235	.297	.294	73	-2	0	0	0	.974	0	D-14/1-5	-0.3
	Cal-A	63	215	25	58	9	0	9	33	34	44	.270	.369	.437	145	13	1	1	-0	.998	8	1-54/D-7	1.7
	Yr	94	283	29	74	13	0	9	42	40	61	.261	.353	.403	126	10	1	1	-0	.996	8	1-59,D-21	1.4
1977	Cal-A	116	324	40	78	15	0	14	53	56	77	.241	.353	.417	113	7	1	3	-2	.990	1	1-91/D-6	0.2
1978	Cal-A	60	94	10	21	3	0	1	14	16	25	.223	.336	.287	80	-2	0	0	0	1.000	1	D-18,1-11	-0.2
1979	Mon-N	29	42	5	12	4	0	1	7	11	16	.286	.434	.452	143	3	0	0	0	.989	0	1-13	0.3
	Tor-A	36	102	14	27	8	1	2	13	17	16	.265	.370	.422	112	2	0	0	0	1.000	1	D-26/1-6	0.1
Total	7	525	1316	164	336	66	1	50	203	214	345	.255	.361	.421	120	39	2	8	-4	.993	17	1-281,D-122/O	3.5

■ MOSE SOLOMON
Solomon, Mose Hirsch "The Rabbi Of Swat" b: 12/8/1900, New York, N.Y. d: 6/25/66, Miami, Fla. BL/TL, 5'9.5", 180 lbs. Deb: 9/30/23

| 1923 | NY-N | 2 | 8 | 0 | 3 | 1 | 0 | 0 | 1 | 0 | 1 | .375 | .375 | .500 | 131 | 0 | 0 | 0 | 0 | .833 | -0 | /O-2 | 0.0 |

■ MOOSE SOLTERS
Solters, Julius Joseph (b: Julius Joseph Soltesz) b: 3/22/06, Pittsburgh, Pa. d: 9/28/75, Pittsburgh, Pa. BR/TR, 6', 190 lbs. Deb: 4/17/34

1934	Bos-A	101	365	61	109	25	4	7	58	18	50	.299	.333	.447	93	-5	9	4	0	.933	2	O-89	-0.6
1935	Bos-A	24	79	15	19	6	1	0	8	2	7	.241	.268	.342	53	-6	1	1	-0	.966	3	O-21	-0.4
	StL-A	127	552	79	182	39	6	18	104	34	35	.330	.369	.520	122	15	10	1	2	.989	16	*O-127	2.7
	Yr	151	631	94	201	45	7	18	112	36	42	.319	.356	.498	113	9	11	2	2	.985	19	*O-148	2.3
1936	StL-A	152	628	100	183	45	7	17	134	41	76	.291	.336	.467	93	-10	3	0	1	.956	12	*O-147	-0.3
1937	Cle-A	152	589	90	190	42	11	20	109	42	56	.323	.372	.533	125	19	6	9	-4	.953	2	*O-149	1.2
1938	Cle-A	67	199	30	40	6	3	2	22	13	28	.201	.250	.291	36	-21	4	1	0	.969	1	O-46	-1.8
1939	Cle-A	41	102	19	28	7	1	2	19	9	15	.275	.333	.441	100	-0	2	1	0	.915	-3	O-25	-0.4
	StL-A	40	131	14	27	6	1	0	14	10	20	.206	.262	.267	35	-13	1	0	0	.935	0	O-30	-1.2
	Yr	81	233	33	55	13	2	2	33	19	35	.236	.294	.343	63	-14	3	1	0	.927	-3	O-55	-1.6
1940	Chi-A	116	428	65	132	28	3	12	80	27	54	.308	.351	.472	110	5	3	3	-1	.971	5	*O-107	0.4
1941	Chi-A	76	251	24	65	9	4	4	43	18	31	.259	.311	.375	82	-7	3	2	-0	.966	1	O-63	-1.0
1943	Chi-A	42	97	6	15	0	0	1	8	7	5	.155	.212	.186	17	-10	0	1	-1	.941	-3	O-21	-1.7
Total	9	938	3421	503	990	213	42	83	599	221	377	.289	.334	.449	96	-32	42	23	-1	.960	36	O-825	-3.1

■ JOCK SOMERLOTT
Somerlott, John Wesley b: 10/26/1882, Flint, Ind. d: 4/21/65, Butler, Ind. BR/TR, 6', 160 lbs. Deb: 9/19/10

1910	Was-A	16	63	6	14	0	0	0	2	3		.222	.258	.222	53	-3	2			.994	0	1-16	-0.4
1911	Was-A	13	40	2	7	0	0	0	2	0		.175	.195	.175	4	-5	2			.992	2	1-12	-0.4
Total	2	29	103	8	21	0	0	0	4	3		.204	.234	.204	32	-9	4			.993	2	/1-28	-0.8

■ ED SOMERVILLE
Somerville, Edward G. b: 3/1/1853, Philadelphia, Pa. d: 10/1/1877, London, Ont., Canada BR/TR, Deb: 4/30/1875

1875	Cen-n	14	55	6	13	3	0	0		2		.236	.263	.291	100	0						2-14	0.0
	NH-n	33	134	14	29	4	0	0		1		.216	.222	.246	71	-3						2-30/1-1,S3	-0.3
	Yr	47	189	20	42	7	0	0		3		.222	.234	.259	80	-3						2-44/1-1,S3	-0.3
1876	Lou-N	64	256	29	48	5	1	0	14	1	6	.188	.191	.215	30	-21				.870	30	*2-64	0.7

■ JOE SOMMER
Sommer, Joseph John b: 11/20/1858, Covington, Ky. d: 1/16/38, Cincinnati, Ohio BR/TR, Deb: 7/8/1880

1880	Cin-N	24	88	10	16	1	0	0	6	0	2	.182	.182	.193	28	-6				.913	-1	O-22/S-1,3C	-0.7
1882	Cin-a	80	354	82	102	12	6	1		24		.288	.333	.364	128	10				.925	4	*O-80	1.2
1883	Cin-a	97	413	79	115	5	7	3		20		.278	.312	.346	106	2				.854	-1	*O-94/3-3,P	0.0
1884	Bal-a	107	479	96	129	11	10	4		8		.269	.293	.359	107	2				.841	6	*3-97/O-9,2	0.8
1885	Bal-a	110	471	84	118	23	6	1		24		.251	.291	.331	98	-1				.921	12	*O-107/S-2,3P1	0.7
1886	Bal-a	139	560	79	117	18	4	1		24		.209	.245	.261	60	-26	31			.900	13	*O-95,2-32,3/SP	-1.2
1887	Bal-a	131	463	88	123	11	5	0		63		.266	.358	.311	93	0	29			.902	0	*O-110,2-13,3/SP	-0.1
1888	Bal-a	79	297	31	65	10	0	0	35	18		.219	.266	.253	68	-10	13			.871	-4	O-44,S-34/21	-1.3
1889	Bal-a	106	386	51	85	13	2	1	36	42	49	.220	.298	.272	62	-19	18			.929	9	*O-105/S-1	-1.1
1890	Cle-N	9	35	4	8	1	0	0	2	2	2	.229	.270	.257	55	-2	0			.789	-2	/O-9,P-1	-0.4
	Bal-a	38	129	13	33	4	2	0		10		.256	.324	.318	85	-3	10			.892	1	O-38	-0.3
Total	10	920	3675	617	911	109	42	11	77	238	53	.248	.297	.309	89	-54	101			.901	38	O-713,3-124/2SP1C	-2.4

■ PETE SOMMERS
Sommers, Joseph Andrews b: 10/26/1866, Cleveland, Ohio d: 7/22/08, Cleveland, Ohio BR/TR, 5'11.5", 181 lbs. Deb: 4/27/1887

1887	NY-a	33	116	9	21	1	0	0		11		.181	.234	.233	32	-11	6			.830	-8	C-31/O-1,1	-1.3
1888	Bos-N	4	13	1	3	1	0	0	0	0	3	.231	.231	.308	69	-0				.880	-0	/C-4	-0.1
1889	Chi-N	12	45	5	10	5	0	0	8	1	10	.222	.271	.333	65	-2				.836	-5	C-11/O-1	-0.6
	Ind-N	23	84	12	21	2	2	2	14	1	9	.250	.267	.393	82	-3	2			.905	-2	C-21/O-2	-0.3
	Yr	35	129	17	31	7	2	2	22	3	24	.240	.269	.372	76	-5				.882	-7	C-32/O-3	-0.9
1890	NY-N	17	47	4	5	1	1	0	1	4	13	.106	.192	.170	6	-6	0			.837	1	C-11/1-5,O	-0.4

YEAR	TM/L	G	AB	R	H	2B	3B	HR	RBI	BB	SO	AVG	OBP	SLG	PRO+	BR/A	SB	CS	SBR	FA	FR	G/POS	TPR
	Cle-N	9	34	4	7	1	1	0	1	2	3	.206	.250	.294	60	-2	0			.906	1	/C-8,O-1	-0.1
	Yr	26	81	8	12	2	2	0	2	6	16	.148	.216	.222	28	-8	0			.865	1	C-19/1-5,O	-0.5
Total	4	98	339	35	67	13	4	3	24	16	43	.198	.242	.286	50	-24	8			.860	-15	/C-86,O-7,1	-2.8

■ BILL SOMMERS
Sommers, William Dunn b: 2/17/23, Brooklyn, N.Y. BR/TR, 6', 180 lbs. Deb: 4/25/50

YEAR	TM/L	G	AB	R	H	2B	3B	HR	RBI	BB	SO	AVG	OBP	SLG	PRO+	BR/A	SB	CS	SBR	FA	FR	G/POS	TPR
1950	StL-A	65	137	24	35	5	1	0	14	25	14	.255	.370	.307	72	-5	0	1	-1	.917	-9	3-37,2-21	-1.4

■ BILL SORRELL
Sorrell, William b: 10/14/40, Morehead, Ky. BL/TR, 6', 190 lbs. Deb: 9/2/65

YEAR	TM/L	G	AB	R	H	2B	3B	HR	RBI	BB	SO	AVG	OBP	SLG	PRO+	BR/A	SB	CS	SBR	FA	FR	G/POS	TPR
1965	Phi-N	10	13	2	5	0	0	1	2	2	1	.385	.467	.615	206	2	0	0	0	.000	0	/3-1	0.2
1967	SF-N	18	17	1	3	1	0	0	1	3	2	.176	.300	.235	56	-1	0	0	0	1.000	-2	/O-5	-0.3
1970	KC-A	57	135	12	36	2	0	4	14	10	13	.267	.317	.370	89	-2	1	0	0	.873	-6	3-29/O-4,1	-0.9
Total	3	85	165	15	44	3	0	5	17	15	16	.267	.328	.376	95	-1	1	0	0	.873	-8	/3-30,O-9,1	-1.0

■ CHICK SORRELLS
Sorrells, Raymond Edwin b: 7/31/1896, Stringtown, Okla. d: 7/20/83, Terrell, Tex. BR/TR, 5'9", 155 lbs. Deb: 9/18/22

YEAR	TM/L	G	AB	R	H	2B	3B	HR	RBI	BB	SO	AVG	OBP	SLG	PRO+	BR/A	SB	CS	SBR	FA	FR	G/POS	TPR
1922	Cle-A	2	1	0	0	0	0	0	0	0	0	.000	.000	.000	-99	-0	0	0	0	1.000	1	/S-1	0.1

■ PAUL SORRENTO
Sorrento, Paul Anthony b: 11/17/65, Somerville, Mass. BL/TR, 6'2", 195 lbs. Deb: 9/8/89

YEAR	TM/L	G	AB	R	H	2B	3B	HR	RBI	BB	SO	AVG	OBP	SLG	PRO+	BR/A	SB	CS	SBR	FA	FR	G/POS	TPR
1989	Min-A	14	21	2	5	0	0	0	1	5	4	.238	.385	.238	74	-0	0	0	0	1.000	-0	/1-5,D-5	-0.1
1990	Min-A	41	121	11	25	4	1	5	13	12	31	.207	.284	.380	79	-4	1	1	-0	.992	-1	D-23,1-15	-0.7
1991	*Min-A	26	47	6	12	2	0	4	13	4	11	.255	.314	.553	129	2	0	0	0	1.000	1	1-13/D-2	0.2
1992	Cle-A	140	458	52	123	24	1	18	60	51	89	.269	.343	.443	121	12	0	3	-2	.993	-1	*1-121,D-11	0.1
1993	Cle-A	148	463	75	119	26	1	18	65	58	121	.257	.341	.434	108	5	3	1	0	.995	-0	*1-144/O-3,D	-0.5
1994	Cle-A	95	322	43	90	14	0	14	62	34	68	.280	.348	.453	108	-0	0	1	-1	.995	1	1-86/D-8	-0.6
Total	6	464	1432	189	374	70	3	59	214	164	324	.261	.339	.438	108	14	4	6	-2	.994	-1	1-384/D-50,O	-1.6

■ SAMMY SOSA
Sosa, Samuel Peralta b: 11/10/68, San Pedro De Macoris, D.R. BR/TR, 6', 165 lbs. Deb: 6/16/89

YEAR	TM/L	G	AB	R	H	2B	3B	HR	RBI	BB	SO	AVG	OBP	SLG	PRO+	BR/A	SB	CS	SBR	FA	FR	G/POS	TPR
1989	Tex-A	25	84	8	20	3	0	1	3	0	20	.238	.238	.310	52	-5	0	2	-1	.944	-2	O-19	-0.9
	Chi-A	33	99	19	27	5	0	3	10	11	27	.273	.357	.414	120	3	7	3	0	.969	-5	O-33/D-6	-0.2
	Yr	58	183	27	47	8	0	4	13	11	47	.257	.306	.366	89	-3	7	5	-1	.960	-7	O-52/D-6	-1.1
1990	Chi-A	153	532	72	124	26	10	15	70	33	150	.233	.285	.404	93	-7	32	16	0	.962	9	*O-152	-0.2
1991	Chi-A	116	316	39	64	10	1	10	33	14	98	.203	.241	.335	59	-19	13	6	0	.973	-3	O-111/D-2	-2.3
1992	Chi-N	67	262	41	68	7	2	8	25	19	63	.260	.319	.393	98	-1	15	7	0	.961	-3	O-67	-0.6
1993	Chi-N	159	598	92	156	25	5	33	93	38	135	.261	.309	.485	111	6	36	11	4	.976	5	*O-158	0.7
1994	Chi-N	105	426	59	128	17	6	25	70	25	92	.300	.342	.545	130	16	22	13	1	.973	5	*O-105	1.8
Total	6	658	2317	330	587	93	24	95	304	140	585	.253	.302	.437	100	-7	125	58	3	.969	1	O-645/D-8	-1.7

■ DENNY SOTHERN
Sothern, Dennis Elwood b: 1/20/04, Washington, D.C. d: 12/7/77, Durham, N.C. BR/TR, 5'11", 175 lbs. Deb: 9/10/26

YEAR	TM/L	G	AB	R	H	2B	3B	HR	RBI	BB	SO	AVG	OBP	SLG	PRO+	BR/A	SB	CS	SBR	FA	FR	G/POS	TPR
1926	Phi-N	14	53	5	13	1	0	3	10	4	10	.245	.310	.434	94	-1	0			.975	2	O-13	0.0
1928	Phi-N	141	579	82	165	27	5	5	38	34	53	.285	.327	.375	80	-17	17			.964	8	*O-136	-1.8
1929	Phi-N	76	294	52	90	21	3	5	27	16	24	.306	.346	.449	90	-5	13			.967	3	O-71	-0.6
1930	Phi-N	90	347	66	97	26	1	5	36	22	37	.280	.326	.403	70	-17	6			.967	8	O-84	-1.3
	Pit-N	17	51	4	9	4	0	1	4	3	4	.176	.222	.314	28	-6	2			.971	-1	O-13	-0.7
	Yr	107	398	70	106	30	1	6	40	25	41	.266	.313	.392	65	-23	8			.967	8	O-97	-2.0
1931	Bro-N	19	31	10	5	1	0	0	0	4	8	.161	.257	.194	23	-3	0			.958	-1	O-10	-0.5
Total	5	357	1355	219	379	80	9	19	115	83	136	.280	.325	.394	77	-50	38			.966	20	O-327	-4.9

■ BUD SOUCHOCK
Souchock, Stephen b: 3/3/19, Yatesboro, Pa. BR/TR, 6'2.5", 203 lbs. Deb: 5/25/46

YEAR	TM/L	G	AB	R	H	2B	3B	HR	RBI	BB	SO	AVG	OBP	SLG	PRO+	BR/A	SB	CS	SBR	FA	FR	G/POS	TPR
1946	NY-A	47	86	15	26	3	3	2	10	7	13	.302	.362	.477	131	3	0	3	-2	.964	-2	1-20	-0.1
1948	NY-A	44	118	11	24	3	1	3	11	7	13	.203	.248	.322	51	-9	3	0	1	.988	-2	1-32	-1.0
1949	Chi-A	84	252	29	59	13	5	7	37	25	38	.234	.303	.409	90	-6	3	2	0	.951	2	O-39,1-30	-0.6
1951	Det-A	91	188	33	46	10	3	11	28	18	27	.245	.314	.505	118	3	0	2	-1	.941	-6	O-59/3-3,12	-0.6
1952	Det-A	92	265	40	66	16	4	13	45	21	28	.249	.304	.487	117	4	1	0	0	.964	1	O-56,3-13/1	0.2
1953	Det-A	89	278	29	84	13	3	11	46	8	35	.302	.326	.489	119	5	1	1	0	.962	-1	O-80/1-1	0.2
1954	Det-A	25	39	6	7	0	1	3	8	2	10	.179	.220	.462	84	-1	1	1	-0	1.000	-1	/O-9,3-2	-0.3
1955	Det-A	1	1	0	1	0	0	0	1	0	0	1.000	1.000	1.000	449	0	0	0	0	.000	0	H	0.0
Total	8	473	1227	163	313	58	20	50	186	88	164	.255	.307	.457	106	1	9	15		.957	-10	O-243/1-93,32	-2.2

■ CLYDE SOUTHWICK
Southwick, Clyde Aubra b: 11/3/1886, Maxwell, Iowa d: 10/14/61, Freeport, Ill. BL/TR, 6', 180 lbs. Deb: 8/22/11

YEAR	TM/L	G	AB	R	H	2B	3B	HR	RBI	BB	SO	AVG	OBP	SLG	PRO+	BR/A	SB	CS	SBR	FA	FR	G/POS	TPR
1911	StL-A	4	12	3	3	0	0	0	0	0	1	.250	.308	.250	52	-1	0	0	0	.938	-1	/C-4	-0.1

■ BILL SOUTHWORTH
Southworth, William Frederick b: 11/10/45, Madison, Wis. BR/TR, 6'2", 205 lbs. Deb: 10/2/64

YEAR	TM/L	G	AB	R	H	2B	3B	HR	RBI	BB	SO	AVG	OBP	SLG	PRO+	BR/A	SB	CS	SBR	FA	FR	G/POS	TPR
1964	Mil-N	3	7	2	2	0	0	1	2	0	3	.286	.444	.714	219	1	0	0	0	1.000	-1	/3-2	0.0

■ BILLY SOUTHWORTH
Southworth, William Harrison b: 3/9/1893, Harvard, Neb. d: 11/15/69, Columbus, Ohio BL/TR, 5'9", 170 lbs. Deb: 8/4/13 MC

YEAR	TM/L	G	AB	R	H	2B	3B	HR	RBI	BB	SO	AVG	OBP	SLG	PRO+	BR/A	SB	CS	SBR	FA	FR	G/POS	TPR
1913	Cle-A	1	0	0	0	0	0	0	0	0	0	—	—	—	—	—	0	0		.000	0	/O-1	0.0
1915	Cle-A	60	177	25	39	2	5	0	8	36	12	.220	.352	.288	90	-1	2	4	-2	.942	1	O-44	-0.4
1918	Pit-N	64	246	37	84	5	7	2	43	26	9	.341	.409	.443	154	17	19			.980	9	O-64	2.4
1919	Pit-N	121	453	56	127	14	14	4	61	32	22	.280	.329	.400	114	7	23			.968	5	*O-121	0.4
1920	Pit-N	146	546	64	155	17	13	2	53	52	20	.284	.348	.374	104	4	23	25	-8	.991	10	*O-142	-0.5
1921	Bos-N	141	569	86	175	25	15	7	79	36	13	.308	.351	.441	115	11	22	20	-5	.975	5	*O-141	0.9
1922	Bos-N	43	158	27	51	4	4	4	18	18	1	.323	.392	.475	128	7	4	1	1	.955	5	O-41	0.9
1923	Bos-N	153	611	95	195	29	16	6	78	61	23	.319	.383	.448	124	21	14	16	-5	.943	6	*O-151/2-2	1.1
1924	*NY-N	94	281	40	72	13	0	3	36	32	16	.256	.332	.335	81	-7	1	6	-3	.935	-3	O-75	-1.7
1925	NY-N	123	473	79	138	19	5	6	44	51	11	.292	.363	.391	97	-1	6	13	-6	.964	-7	*O-119	-2.1
1926	NY-N	36	116	23	38	6	1	5	30	7	1	.328	.366	.526	139	6	1			.970	-2	O-29	0.2
	*StL-N	99	391	76	124	22	6	11	69	26	9	.317	.364	.488	123	11	13			.971	-3	O-99	0.2
	Yr	135	507	99	162	28	7	16	99	33	10	.320	.365	.497	127	17	14			.971	-5	*O-128	0.4
1927	StL-N	92	306	52	92	15	5	2	39	23	7	.301	.350	.402	98	-1	10			.970	-7	O-83	-1.3
1929	StL-N	19	32	1	6	1	0	0	2	3	2	.188	.235	.250	20	-4	0			1.000	-0	/O-5,M	-0.4
Total	13	1192	4359	661	1296	173	91	52	561	402	148	.297	.359	.415	111	69	138	85		.965	23	*O-1115/2-2	-0.8

■ JOHN SOWDERS
Sowders, John b: 12/10/1866, Louisville, Ky. d: 7/29/39, Indianapolis, Ind BR/TL, 6', Deb: 6/28/1887 F

YEAR	TM/L	G	AB	R	H	2B	3B	HR	RBI	BB	SO	AVG	OBP	SLG	PRO+	BR/A	SB	CS	SBR	FA	FR	G/POS	TPR
1887	Ind-N	1	2	0	0	0	0	0	0	0	1	.000	.000	.000	-99	-1	0			1.000	-1	/O-1,P-1	0.0
1889	KC-a	28	87	11	19	3	0	0	6	4	20	.218	.269	.253	46	-6	1			.842	-3	P-25/O-3	-0.1
1890	Bro-P	40	132	14	25	3	0	1	20	10	12	.189	.246	.235	27	-14	0			.921	-2	P-39/O-3	-0.1
Total	3	69	221	25	44	6	0	1	26	14	33	.199	.253	.240	33	-21	1			.884	-6	/P-65,O-7	-0.2

■ LEN SOWDERS
Sowders, Leonard b: 6/29/1861, Louisville, Ky. d: 11/19/1888, Indianapolis, Ind. 5'11.5", 172 lbs. Deb: 9/10/1886 F

YEAR	TM/L	G	AB	R	H	2B	3B	HR	RBI	BB	SO	AVG	OBP	SLG	PRO+	BR/A	SB	CS	SBR	FA	FR	G/POS	TPR
1886	Bal-a	23	76	10	20	3	1	0	12			.263	.364	.329	121	2	6			.889	-1	O-23/1-1	0.1

■ AL SPALDING
Spalding, Albert Goodwill b: 9/2/1850, Byron, Ill. d: 9/9/15, San Diego, Cal. BR/TR, 6'1", 170 lbs. Deb: 5/5/1871 MH

YEAR	TM/L	G	AB	R	H	2B	3B	HR	RBI	BB	SO	AVG	OBP	SLG	PRO+	BR/A	SB	CS	SBR	FA	FR	G/POS	TPR
1871	Bos-n	31	144	43	39	10	1	2	31	8	1	.271	.309	.375	92	-2	2					*P-31/O-2	0.3
1872	Bos-n	48	244	60	87	13	5	0	48	3	1	.357	.364	.451	142	10						*P-48/O-2	0.6
1873	Bos-n	52	322	83	106	13	5	3	59	3	1	.329	.335	.391	104	-1						*P-60,O-12	0.8
1874	Bos-n	71	359	80	119	15	1	0			3	.331	.337	.379	121	6						*P-71	0.0
1875	Bos-n	74	343	68	107	12	3	0			4	.312	.320	.364	131	10						*P-72,O-10/1	0.8

YEAR	TM/L	G	AB	R	H	2B	3B	HR	RBI	BB	SO	AVG	OBP	SLG	PRO+	BR/A	SB	CS	SBR	FA	FR	G/POS	TPR
1876	Chi-N	66	292	54	91	14	2	0	44	6	3	.312	.326	.373	118	3				.951	1	*P-61,O-10/1M	-0.2
1877	Chi-N	60	254	29	65	7	6	0	35	3	16	.256	.265	.331	77	-8				.959	6	*1-45,2-13/P3M	-0.2
1878	Chi-N	1	4	0	2	0	0	0	0	0	0	.500	.500	.500	215	0				.429	-2	/2-1	-0.1
Total	5 n	284	1412	334	458	63	12	2	138	21	3	.324	.334	.390	120	23						P-282/O-26,1	2.5
Total	3	127	550	83	158	21	8	0	79	9	19	.287	.299	.355	99	-4				.948	5	/P-65,1-48,203	-0.5

■ DICK SPALDING

Spalding, Charles Harry b: 10/13/1893, Philadelphia, Pa. d: 2/3/50, Philadelphia, Pa. BL/TL, 5'11", 185 lbs. Deb: 4/18/27 C

YEAR	TM/L	G	AB	R	H	2B	3B	HR	RBI	BB	SO	AVG	OBP	SLG	PRO+	BR/A	SB	CS	SBR	FA	FR	G/POS	TPR
1927	Phi-N	115	442	68	131	16	3	0	25	38	40	.296	.352	.346	86	-7	5			.992	3	*O-113	-1.1
1928	Was-A	16	23	1	8	0	0	0	0	0	4	.348	.348	.348	84	-1	0	2	-1	1.000	-3	O-11	-0.5
Total	2	131	465	69	139	16	3	0	25	38	44	.299	.352	.346	86	-8	5	2		.993	-0	O-124	-1.6

■ AL SPANGLER

Spangler, Albert Donald b: 7/8/33, Philadelphia, Pa. BL/TL, 6', 175 lbs. Deb: 9/16/59 C

YEAR	TM/L	G	AB	R	H	2B	3B	HR	RBI	BB	SO	AVG	OBP	SLG	PRO+	BR/A	SB	CS	SBR	FA	FR	G/POS	TPR
1959	Mil-N	6	12	3	5	0	1	0	1	1	1	.417	.462	.583	192	2	1	0	0	1.000	-1	/O-4	0.1
1960	Mil-N	101	105	26	28	5	2	0	6	14	17	.267	.358	.352	103	1	6	2	1	.989	-14	O-92	-1.4
1961	Mil-N	68	97	23	26	2	0	0	6	28	9	.268	.432	.289	102	2	4	2	0	1.000	-7	O-44	-0.6
1962	Hou-N	129	418	51	119	10	9	5	35	70	46	.285	.391	.388	119	14	7	6	-2	.960	-0	*O-121	0.5
1963	Hou-N	120	430	52	121	25	4	4	27	50	38	.281	.358	.386	122	13	5	8	-3	.987	3	*O-113	0.6
1964	Hou-N	135	449	51	110	18	5	4	38	41	43	.245	.314	.334	88	-7	7	8	-3	.964	-5	*O-127	-2.3
1965	Hou-N	38	112	18	24	1	1	1	7	14	8	.214	.302	.268	66	-5	1	1	-0	.956	-1	O-33	-0.8
	Cal-A	51	96	17	25	1	0	0	8	9	9	.260	.317	.271	70	-4	4	0	1	.973	-4	O-24	-0.8
1966	Cal-A	6	9	2	6	0	0	0	0	2	2	.667	.727	.667	312	3	0	0	0	1.000	-1	/O-3	0.2
1967	Chi-N	62	130	18	33	7	0	0	13	23	17	.254	.366	.308	91	-1	2	2	-1	.986	-3	O-41	-0.6
1968	Chi-N	88	177	21	48	9	3	2	18	20	24	.271	.348	.390	114	3	0	1	-1	.973	-5	O-48	-0.5
1969	Chi-N	82	213	23	45	8	1	4	23	21	16	.211	.285	.315	60	-11	0	2	-1	.950	-7	O-58	-2.4
1970	Chi-N	21	14	2	2	1	0	1	1	3	3	.143	.294	.429	81	-0	0	0	0	1.000	-1	/O-6	-0.2
1971	Chi-N	5	5	0	2	0	0	0	0	0	1	.400	.400	.400	111	0	0	0	0	.000	0	H	0.0
Total	13	912	2267	307	594	87	26	21	175	295	234	.262	.350	.351	100	10	37	32	-8	.973	-45	O-714	-8.2

■ BOB SPEAKE

Speake, Robert Charles "Spook" b: 8/22/30, Springfield, Mo. BL/TL, 6'1", 178 lbs. Deb: 4/16/55

YEAR	TM/L	G	AB	R	H	2B	3B	HR	RBI	BB	SO	AVG	OBP	SLG	PRO+	BR/A	SB	CS	SBR	FA	FR	G/POS	TPR
1955	Chi-N	95	261	36	57	9	5	12	43	28	71	.218	.301	.429	91	-4	3	4	-2	.959	-3	O-55/1-8	-1.2
1957	Chi-N	129	418	65	97	14	5	16	50	38	68	.232	.301	.404	89	-8	5	6	-2	.974	6	O-60,1-39	-1.0
1958	SF-N	66	71	9	15	3	0	3	10	13	15	.211	.333	.380	90	-1	0	1	-1	.938	0	O-10	-0.1
1959	SF-N	15	11	0	1	0	0	0	1	1	4	.091	.167	.091	-30	-2	0	0	0	.000	0	H	-0.2
Total	4	305	761	110	170	26	10	31	104	80	158	.223	.302	.406	88	-14	8	11	-4	.966	3	O-125/1-47	-2.5

■ TRIS SPEAKER

Speaker, Tristram E "The Grey Eagle" b: 4/4/1888, Hubbard, Tex. d: 12/8/58, Lake Whitney, Tex. BL/TL, 5'11.5", 193 lbs. Deb: 9/14/07 MH

YEAR	TM/L	G	AB	R	H	2B	3B	HR	RBI	BB	SO	AVG	OBP	SLG	PRO+	BR/A	SB	CS	SBR	FA	FR	G/POS	TPR
1907	Bos-A	7	19	0	3	0	0	0	1	1		.158	.200	.158	14	-2	0			1.000	1	/O-4	-0.1
1908	Bos-A	31	116	12	26	2	2	0	9	4		.224	.262	.276	73	-4	3			1.000	5	O-31	0.0
1909	Bos-A	143	544	73	168	26	13	7	77	38		.309	.362	.443	151	30	35			.973	23	*O-142	5.2
1910	Bos-A	141	538	92	183	20	14	7	65	52		.340	.404	.468	169	42	35			.957	15	*O-140	5.5
1911	Bos-A	141	500	88	167	34	13	8	70	59		.334	.418	.502	158	39	25			.956	6	*O-138	3.7
1912	*Bos-A	153	580	136	222	53	12	10	90	82		.383	.464	.567	185	65	52			.958	22	*O-153	7.7
1913	Bos-A	141	520	94	189	35	22	3	71	65	22	.363	.441	.533	180	53	46			.942	24	*O-139	7.3
1914	Bos-A	158	571	101	193	46	18	4	90	77	25	.338	.423	.503	178	55	42	29	-5	.968	28	*O-156/P-1,1	7.6
1915	*Bos-A	150	547	108	176	25	12	0	69	81	14	.322	.416	.411	152	38	29	25	-6	.976	13	*O-150	4.0
1916	Cle-A	151	546	102	211	41	8	2	79	82	20	.386	.470	.502	181	57	35	27	-6	.975	9	*O-151	5.7
1917	Cle-A	142	523	90	184	42	11	2	60	67	14	.352	.432	.486	168	43	30			.980	8	*O-142	4.7
1918	Cle-A	127	471	73	150	33	11	0	61	64	9	.318	.403	.435	140	23	27			.973	11	*O-127	3.0
1919	Cle-A	134	494	83	146	38	12	2	63	73	12	.296	.395	.433	125	18	15			.983	19	*O-134,M	2.9
1920	*Cle-A	150	552	137	214	50	11	8	107	97	13	.388	.483	.562	171	61	10	13	-5	.977	10	*O-148,M	5.2
1921	Cle-A	132	506	107	183	52	14	3	75	68	12	.362	.439	.538	146	37	2	4	-2	.984	10	*O-128,M	3.3
1922	Cle-A	131	426	85	161	48	8	11	71	77	11	.378	.474	.606	178	52	8	3	1	.983	8	*O-109,M	5.0
1923	Cle-A	150	574	133	218	59	11	17	130	93	15	.380	.469	.610	183	71	8	9	-3	.968	10	*O-150,M	6.4
1924	Cle-A	135	486	94	167	36	9	9	65	72	13	.344	.432	.510	141	31	5	7	-3	.963	5	*O-128,M	2.3
1925	Cle-A	117	429	79	167	35	5	12	87	70	12	.389	.479	.578	166	46	5	2	0	.967	10	*O-109,M	4.5
1926	Cle-A	150	539	96	164	52	8	7	86	94	15	.304	.408	.469	127	23	6	1	1	.981	10	*O-149,M	2.4
1927	Was-A	141	523	71	171	43	6	2	73	55	8	.327	.395	.444	119	15	9	8	-2	.967	1	*O-120,1-17	0.6
1928	Phi-A	64	191	28	51	22	2	3	30	10	5	.267	.310	.450	95	-2	5	1	1	.975	1	O-50	-0.4
Total	22	2789	10195	1882	3514	792	222	117	1529	1381	220	.345	.428	.500	156	793	432	129		.970	248	*O-2698/1-18,P	86.5

■ HORACE SPEED

Speed, Horace Arthur b: 10/4/51, Los Angeles, Cal. BR/TR, 6'1", 180 lbs. Deb: 4/10/75

YEAR	TM/L	G	AB	R	H	2B	3B	HR	RBI	BB	SO	AVG	OBP	SLG	PRO+	BR/A	SB	CS	SBR	FA	FR	G/POS	TPR
1975	SF-N	17	15	2	2	1	0	0	1	1	8	.133	.235	.200	21	-2	0	0	0	.900	-2	/O-9	-0.4
1978	Cle-A	70	106	13	24	4	1	0	4	14	31	.226	.322	.283	72	-3	2	4	-2	.977	-12	O-61/D-3	-1.9
1979	Cle-A	26	14	6	2	0	0	0	1	5	7	.143	.368	.143	44	-1	2	1	0	.875	-5	O-16	-0.5
Total	3	113	135	21	28	5	1	0	6	20	46	.207	.318	.259	63	-6	4	5	-2	.956	-19	/O-86,D-3	-2.8

■ TIM SPEHR

Spehr, Timothy Joseph b: 7/2/66, Excelsior Springs, Mo. BR/TR, 6'2", 205 lbs. Deb: 7/18/91

YEAR	TM/L	G	AB	R	H	2B	3B	HR	RBI	BB	SO	AVG	OBP	SLG	PRO+	BR/A	SB	CS	SBR	FA	FR	G/POS	TPR
1991	KC-A	37	74	7	14	5	0	3	14	9	18	.189	.286	.378	82	-2	1	0	0	.986	12	C-37	1.1
1993	Mon-N	53	87	14	20	6	0	2	10	6	20	.230	.287	.368	71	-4	2	0	1	.954	9	C-49	0.7
1994	Mon-N	52	36	8	9	3	1	0	5	4	11	.250	.325	.389	83	-1	2	0	1	1.000	10	C-46/O-2	1.0
Total	3	142	197	29	43	14	1	5	29	19	49	.218	.294	.376	77	-7	5	0	2	.977	30	C-132/O-2	2.8

■ CHRIS SPEIER

Speier, Chris Edward b: 6/28/50, Alameda, Cal. BR/TR, 6'1", 182 lbs. Deb: 4/7/71

YEAR	TM/L	G	AB	R	H	2B	3B	HR	RBI	BB	SO	AVG	OBP	SLG	PRO+	BR/A	SB	CS	SBR	FA	FR	G/POS	TPR
1971	*SF-N	157	601	74	141	17	6	8	46	56	90	.235	.307	.323	80	-16	4	7	-3	.958	-12	*S-156	-1.1
1972	SF-N★	150	562	74	151	25	2	15	71	82	92	.269	.365	.400	116	14	9	4	0	.974	-5	*S-150	3.3
1973	SF-N★	153	542	58	135	17	4	11	71	66	69	.249	.333	.356	87	-8	4	5	0	.956	-10	*S-150/2-1	0.0
1974	SF-N☆	141	501	55	125	19	5	9	53	62	64	.250	.337	.361	91	-5	3	2	-0	.969	3	*S-135/2-4	1.6
1975	SF-N	141	487	60	132	30	5	10	69	70	50	.271	.364	.415	111	8	4	5	-2	.982	1	*S-136/3-1	2.3
1976	SF-N	145	495	51	112	18	4	3	40	60	52	.226	.315	.297	72	-17	2	2	-1	.974	-1	*S-135/2-7,31	-0.2
1977	SF-N	6	17	1	3	0	0	0	0	0	3	.176	.176	.235	9	-2	0	0	0	.920	2	/S-5	0.0
	Mon-N	139	531	58	125	30	6	5	38	67	78	.235	.322	.343	81	-14	1	2	-1	.970	-12	*S-138	-1.1
	Yr	145	548	59	128	31	6	5	38	67	81	.234	.318	.339	79	-16	1	2	-1	.968	-10	*S-143	-1.1
1978	Mon-N	150	501	47	126	18	3	5	51	60	75	.251	.333	.329	87	-8	1	0	0	.975	1	*S-148	1.3
1979	Mon-N	113	344	31	78	13	1	7	26	43	45	.227	.318	.331	78	-10	0	0	0	.970	-4	*S-112	0.9
1980	Mon-N	128	388	35	103	14	4	1	32	52	38	.265	.352	.330	91	-3	0	3	-2	.965	-0	*S-127/3-1	0.9
1981	*Mon-N	96	307	33	69	10	2	2	25	38	29	.225	.310	.290	70	-11	1	2	-1	.964	-11	S-96	-1.4
1982	Mon-N	156	530	41	136	26	4	7	60	47	67	.257	.318	.360	88	-9	1	6	-3	.982	-21	*S-155	-1.9
1983	Mon-N	88	261	31	67	12	2	2	22	29	37	.257	.336	.341	88	-4	2	1	-1	.962	-11	*S-74,3-12/2	-0.8
1984	Mon-N	25	40	1	6	0	0	0	1	1	8	.150	.171	.150	-10	-6	0	0	0	.960	-2	S-13/3-4	-0.7
	StL-N	38	118	9	21	7	1	3	8	9	19	.178	.242	.331	61	-7	0	0	0	.983	10	S-34/3-2	0.6
	Yr	63	158	10	27	7	1	3	9	10	27	.171	.225	.285	44	-12	0	0	0	.980	8	S-47/3-6	-0.1
	Min-A	12	33	2	7	0	0	0	1	3	9	.212	.278	.212	36	-3	0	0	0	.977	-3	S-12	-0.5
1985	Chi-N	106	218	16	53	8	0	6	24	17	34	.243	.298	.349	72	-8	1	3	-1	.964	2	S-58,3-31,2	-0.4
1986	Chi-N	95	155	21	44	8	0	6	23	15	32	.284	.351	.452	111	2	2	2	-1	.984	9	3-53,S-23/2	1.2

YEAR	TM/L	G	AB	R	H	2B	3B	HR	RBI	BB	SO	AVG	OBP	SLG	PRO+	BR/A	SB	CS	SBR	FA	FR	G/POS	TPR
1987	*SF-N	111	317	39	79	13	0	11	39	42	51	.249	.343	.394	99	-0	4	7	-3	.989	2	2-55,3-44,S	0.1
1988	SF-N	82	171	26	37	9	1	3	18	23	39	.216	.313	.333	89	-2	3	3	-1	.985	3	2-45,3-22,S	0.2
1989	SF-N	28	37	7	9	4	0	0	2	5	9	.243	.333	.351	99	0	0	0	0	1.000	-2	/3-9,S-9,21	-0.2
Total	19	2260	7156	770	1759	302	50	112	720	847	988	.246	.329	.349	88	-107	42	54	-20	.970	-52	*S-1900,3-184,2/1	3.8

■ BOB SPENCE
Spence, John Robert b: 2/10/46, San Diego, Cal. BL/TR, 6'4", 215 lbs. Deb: 9/5/69

YEAR	TM/L	G	AB	R	H	2B	3B	HR	RBI	BB	SO	AVG	OBP	SLG	PRO+	BR/A	SB	CS	SBR	FA	FR	G/POS	TPR
1969	Chi-A	12	26	0	4	1	0	0	3	0	9	.154	.154	.192	-4	-4	0	0	0	1.000	-0	/1-6	-0.5
1970	Chi-A	46	130	11	29	4	1	4	15	11	32	.223	.289	.362	75	-5	0	0	0	.994	3	1-37	-0.5
1971	Chi-A	14	27	2	4	0	0	0	1	5	6	.148	.281	.148	24	-3	0	0	0	.986	-1	/1-7	-0.4
Total	3	72	183	13	37	5	1	4	19	16	47	.202	.270	.306	57	-11	0	0	0	.993	2	/1-50	-1.4

■ STAN SPENCE
Spence, Stanley Orville b: 3/20/15, S.Portsmouth, Ky. d: 1/9/83, Kinston, N.C. BL/TL, 5'10.5", 180 lbs. Deb: 6/8/40

YEAR	TM/L	G	AB	R	H	2B	3B	HR	RBI	BB	SO	AVG	OBP	SLG	PRO+	BR/A	SB	CS	SBR	FA	FR	G/POS	TPR
1940	Bos-A	51	68	5	19	2	1	2	13	4	9	.279	.319	.426	88	-1	0	1	-1	1.000	-4	O-15	-0.6
1941	Bos-A	86	203	22	47	10	3	2	28	18	14	.232	.304	.340	68	-10	1	0	0	1.000	-4	O-52/1-1	-1.3
1942	Was-A☆	149	629	94	203	27	**15**	4	79	62	16	.323	.384	.432	131	26	5	2	0	.973	-3	*O-149	1.6
1943	Was-A	149	570	72	152	23	10	12	88	84	39	.267	.366	.405	130	23	8	1	2	.983	3	*O-148	2.1
1944	Was-A★	153	592	83	187	31	8	18	100	69	28	.316	.391	.486	157	43	3	7	-3	.989	19	*O-150/1-3	5.2
1946	Was-A★	152	578	83	169	50	10	16	87	62	31	.292	.365	.497	148	34	1	7	-4	.982	8	*O-150	3.3
1947	Was-A★	147	506	62	141	22	6	16	73	81	41	.279	.378	.441	131	22	2	2	-1	.984	8	*O-142	2.2
1948	Bos-A	114	391	71	92	17	4	12	61	82	31	.235	.368	.391	97	-1	0	2	-1	.977	-1	O-92,1-14	-0.7
1949	Bos-A	7	20	3	3	1	0	0	1	6	1	.150	.346	.200	43	-1	0	0	0	1.000	1	/O-5	-0.1
	StL-A	104	314	46	77	13	3	13	45	52	36	.245	.356	.430	103	1	1	1	0	.995	3	O-87/1-1	-0.1
	Yr	111	334	49	80	14	3	13	46	58	37	.240	.355	.416	99	-1	1	1	-0	.996	4	O-92/1-1	-0.2
Total	9	1112	3871	541	1090	196	60	95	575	520	248	.282	.369	.437	126	135	21	23	-8	.984	34	O-990/1-19	11.6

■ SPENCER
Spencer Deb: 6/3/1872

YEAR	TM/L	G	AB	R	H	2B	3B	HR	RBI	BB	SO	AVG	OBP	SLG	PRO+	BR/A	SB	CS	SBR	FA	FR	G/POS	TPR
1872	Nat-n	1	4	1	0	0	0	0	0	0	0	.000	.000	.000	-86	-1						/S-2	-0.1

■ CHET SPENCER
Spencer, Chester Arthur b: 3/4/1883, S.Webster, Ohio d: 11/10/38, Portsmouth, Ohio BL/TR, 6', 180 lbs. Deb: 8/22/06

YEAR	TM/L	G	AB	R	H	2B	3B	HR	RBI	BB	SO	AVG	OBP	SLG	PRO+	BR/A	SB	CS	SBR	FA	FR	G/POS	TPR
1906	Bos-N	8	27	1	4	1	0	0				.148	.148	.185	4	-3	0			.875	-1	/O-8	-0.5

■ DARYL SPENCER
Spencer, Daryl Dean "Big Dee" b: 7/13/29, Wichita, Kan. BR/TR, 6'2", 190 lbs. Deb: 9/17/52

YEAR	TM/L	G	AB	R	H	2B	3B	HR	RBI	BB	SO	AVG	OBP	SLG	PRO+	BR/A	SB	CS	SBR	FA	FR	G/POS	TPR
1952	NY-N	7	17	0	5	0	1	0	3	1	4	.294	.333	.412	105	0	0	0	0	1.000	1	/S-3,3-3	0.2
1953	NY-N	118	408	55	85	18	5	20	56	42	74	.208	.287	.424	81	-13	0	1	-1	.927	-10	S-53,3-36,2	-1.8
1956	NY-N	146	489	46	108	13	2	14	42	35	65	.221	.277	.342	66	-24	1	3	-2	.974	-2	2-70,S-66,3	-1.8
1957	NY-N	148	534	65	133	31	2	11	50	50	50	.249	.315	.376	85	-11	3	1	0	.950	14	*S-110,2-36/3	1.6
1958	SF-N	148	539	71	138	20	5	17	74	73	60	.256	.348	.406	101	2	1	1	0	.955	-1	*S-134,2-17	1.4
1959	SF-N	152	555	59	147	20	1	12	62	58	67	.265	.334	.369	89	-8	5	0	2	.970	-4	*2-151/S-4	0.1
1960	StL-N	148	507	70	131	20	3	16	58	81	74	.258	.366	.404	102	3	1	1	0	.946	-24	*S-138,2-16	-1.0
1961	StL-N	37	130	19	33	4	0	4	21	23	17	.254	.366	.377	89	-2	1	0	0	.956	-1	S-37	0.1
	LA-N	60	189	27	46	7	0	8	27	20	35	.243	.329	.407	86	-4	0	1	-1	.964	5	3-57/S-3	0.1
	Yr	97	319	46	79	11	0	12	48	43	52	.248	.344	.395	88	-5	1	0	-0	.964	4	3-57,S-40	0.2
1962	LA-N	77	157	24	37	5	1	2	12	32	31	.236	.365	.318	91	-1	0	0	0	.925	7	3-57,S-10	0.7
1963	LA-N	7	9	0	1	0	0	0	0	3	2	.111	.333	.111	37	-1	0	0	0	1.000	-0	/3-3	-0.1
	Cin-N	50	155	21	37	7	0	1	23	31	37	.239	.369	.303	93	0	1	0	0	.979	3	3-48	0.3
	Yr	57	164	21	38	7	0	1	23	34	39	.232	.367	.293	91	-0	1	0	0	.979	2	3-51	0.2
Total	10	1098	3689	457	901	145	20	105	428	449	516	.244	.329	.380	88	-59	13	7	-0	.953	-13	S-558,2-322,3	-0.2

■ TUBBY SPENCER
Spencer, Edward Russell b: 1/26/1884, Oil City, Pa. d: 2/1/45, San Francisco, Cal. BR/TR, 5'10", 215 lbs. Deb: 7/23/05

YEAR	TM/L	G	AB	R	H	2B	3B	HR	RBI	BB	SO	AVG	OBP	SLG	PRO+	BR/A	SB	CS	SBR	FA	FR	G/POS	TPR
1905	StL-A	35	115	6	27	1	2	0	11		7	.235	.285	.278	83	-2	2			.962	-6	C-34	-0.6
1906	StL-A	58	188	15	33	6	1	0	17		7	.176	.205	.218	34	-15	4			.935	-5	C-54	-1.6
1907	StL-A	71	230	27	61	11	1	1	25		7	.265	.299	.335	102	-0	1			.957	-2	C-63	0.5
1908	StL-A	91	286	19	60	6	1	0	28		17	.210	.254	.238	60	-13	1			.983	-1	C-88	-0.7
1909	Bos-A	28	74	6	12	1	0	0	9		6	.162	.225	.176	26	-6	2			.992	-4	C-26	-0.9
1911	Phi-N	11	32	2	5	1	0	1	3	3	7	.156	.229	.281	42	-3	0			.925	-1	C-11	-0.3
1916	Det-A	19	54	7	20	1	1	1	10	6	6	.370	.443	.481	172	5	2			.988	-7	C-19	0.0
1917	Det-A	70	192	13	46	8	3	0	22	15	15	.240	.324	.313	95	-1	0			.978	-2	C-62	0.1
1918	Det-A	66	155	11	34	8	1	0	8	19	18	.219	.313	.284	83	-3	1			.966	-12	C-48/1-1	-1.3
Total	9	449	1326	106	298	43	10	3	133	87	46	.225	.281	.279	76	-37	13			.966	-40	C-405/1-1	-4.8

■ TOM SPENCER
Spencer, Hubert Thomas b: 2/28/51, Gallipolis, Ohio BR/TR, 6', 170 lbs. Deb: 7/17/78 C

YEAR	TM/L	G	AB	R	H	2B	3B	HR	RBI	BB	SO	AVG	OBP	SLG	PRO+	BR/A	SB	CS	SBR	FA	FR	G/POS	TPR
1978	Chi-A	29	65	3	12	1	0	0	4	2	9	.185	.209	.200	15	-7	0	1	-1	1.000	-1	O-27/D-2	-1.0

■ JIM SPENCER
Spencer, James Lloyd b: 7/30/47, Hanover, Pa. BL/TL, 6'2", 195 lbs. Deb: 9/7/68 F

YEAR	TM/L	G	AB	R	H	2B	3B	HR	RBI	BB	SO	AVG	OBP	SLG	PRO+	BR/A	SB	CS	SBR	FA	FR	G/POS	TPR
1968	Cal-A	19	68	2	13	1	0	0	5	3	10	.191	.236	.206	36	-5	0	0	0	.994	3	1-19	-0.4
1969	Cal-A	113	386	39	98	14	3	10	31	26	53	.254	.304	.383	96	-4	1	0	0	.991	-1	*1-107	-1.4
1970	Cal-A	146	511	61	140	20	4	12	68	28	61	.274	.312	.399	98	-3	0	2	-1	**.995**	-1	*1-142	-1.8
1971	Cal-A	148	510	50	121	21	2	18	59	48	63	.237	.307	.392	104	1	0	1	-1	**.996**	2	*1-145	-1.2
1972	Cal-A	82	212	13	47	9	0	1	14	12	52	.222	.263	.259	59	-11	0	1	-1	.990	-2	1-35,O-24	-2.0
1973	Cal-A	29	87	10	21	4	2	2	11	9	9	.241	.320	.402	111	1	0	0	0	1.000	-2	1-26/D-2	-0.3
	Tex-A★	102	352	35	94	12	3	4	43	34	41	.267	.333	.352	97	-1	0	3	-2	.999	5	1-99/D-1	-0.5
	Yr	131	439	45	115	16	5	6	54	43	50	.262	.331	.362	100	-0	0	3	-2	**.999**	3	*1-125/D-3	-0.8
1974	Tex-A	118	352	36	98	11	4	7	44	22	27	.278	.326	.392	109	3	1	2	-1	.998	1	1-60,D-54	-0.1
1975	Tex-A	132	403	50	107	18	1	11	47	35	43	.266	.327	.397	105	2	0	1	-1	.995	5	1-99,D-25	0.1
1976	Chi-A	150	518	53	131	13	2	14	70	49	52	.253	.319	.367	100	-0	6	4	-1	**.998**	8	*1-143/D-2	-0.3
1977	Chi-A	128	470	56	116	16	1	18	69	36	50	.247	.303	.400	90	-7	1	2	-1	.991	2	*1-125	-1.3
1978	*NY-A	71	150	12	34	9	1	7	24	15	32	.227	.297	.440	107	1	0	0	0	1.000	1	D-35,1-15	-0.1
1979	NY-A	106	295	60	85	15	3	23	53	38	25	.288	.369	.593	158	23	0	0	0	.992	1	D-71,1-26	1.8
1980	*NY-A	97	259	38	61	9	0	13	43	30	44	.236	.317	.421	102	0	0	2	-1	.990	2	1-75,D-15	-0.2
1981	NY-A	25	63	6	9	2	0	2	9	7	9	.143	.250	.270	50	-4	0	0	0	1.000	-2	1-25	-0.3
	*Oak-A	54	171	14	35	6	2	0	9	10	20	.205	.249	.275	53	-11	1	0	0	.997	-1	1-48	-1.1
	Yr	79	234	20	44	8	2	2	13	19	27	.188	.249	.274	52	-15	1	0	0	.998	5	1-73	-1.4
1982	Oak-A	33	101	6	17	3	1	2	9	3	16	.168	.192	.277	28	-10	0	0	0	.992	2	1-32	-0.6
Total	15	1553	4908	541	1227	179	27	146	599	407	582	.250	.310	.387	98	-26	11	19	-8	.995	30	*1-1221,D-205/O	-10.1

■ BEN SPENCER
Spencer, Lloyd Benjamin b: 5/15/1890, Patapsco, Md. d: 9/1/70, Finksburg, Md. BL/TL, 5'8", 160 lbs. Deb: 9/8/13 F

YEAR	TM/L	G	AB	R	H	2B	3B	HR	RBI	BB	SO	AVG	OBP	SLG	PRO+	BR/A	SB	CS	SBR	FA	FR	G/POS	TPR
1913	Was-A	8	21	2	6	1	1	0	2	2	4	.286	.348	.429	124	1	0			.917	-1	/O-8	-0.1

■ ROY SPENCER
Spencer, Roy Hampton b: 2/22/1900, Scranton, N.C. d: 2/8/73, Port Charlotte, Fla BR/TR, 5'10", 168 lbs. Deb: 4/19/25

YEAR	TM/L	G	AB	R	H	2B	3B	HR	RBI	BB	SO	AVG	OBP	SLG	PRO+	BR/A	SB	CS	SBR	FA	FR	G/POS	TPR
1925	Pit-N	14	28	1	6	1	0	0	1	0	3	.214	.241	.250	24	-3	1	0	0	.905	-2	C-11	-0.4
1926	Pit-N	28	43	5	17	3	0	0	4	1	0	.395	.409	.465	128	2	0			.970	-1	C-12	0.2
1927	*Pit-N	38	92	9	26	4	1	0	13		3	.283	.305	.322	67	-4	0			.974	-2	C-34	-0.1
1929	Was-A	50	116	18	18	4	0	0	4		4	.155	.222	.216	13	-15	0	0	0	.967	-2	C-41	-1.3
1930	Was-A	93	321	32	82	11	3	0	36	18	27	.255	.303	.315	57	-21	3	0	0	.989	5	C-93	-0.7
1931	Was-A	145	483	48	133	16	3	1	60	35	21	.275	.327	.327	72	-19	0	0	0	.985	7	*C-145	-0.2

YEAR	TM/L	G	AB	R	H	2B	3B	HR	RBI	BB	SO	AVG	OBP	SLG	PRO+	BR/A	SB	CS	SBR	FA	FR	G/POS	TPR
1932	Was-A	102	317	28	78	9	0	1	41	24	17	.246	.301	.284	53	-22	0	0	-1	.978	-10	C-98	-2.5
1933	Cle-A	75	227	26	46	5	2	0	23	23	17	.203	.282	.242	38	-20	0	0	0	.990	5	C-72	-1.0
1934	Cle-A	5	7	0	1	1	0	0	2	0	1	.143	.143	.286	8	-1	0	0	0	1.000	1	/C-4	0.0
1936	NY-N	19	18	3	5	1	0	0	3	2	3	.278	.350	.333	86	-0				1.000	1	C-14	0.1
1937	Bro-N	51	117	5	24	2	2	0	4	8	17	.205	.256	.256	39	-10		0		1.000	9	C-45	0.1
1938	Bro-N	16	45	2	12	1	1	0	6	5	6	.267	.340	.333	84	-1		0		.968	-0	C-16	-0.1
Total	12	636	1814	177	448	57	13	3	203	128	130	.247	.301	.298	56	-115	4	1		.984	16	C-585	-5.9

■ VERN SPENCER
Spencer, Vernon Murray b: 2/23/1896, Wixom, Mich. d: 6/3/71, Wixom, Mich. BL/TR, 5'7", 165 lbs. Deb: 7/4/20

YEAR	TM/L	G	AB	R	H	2B	3B	HR	RBI	BB	SO	AVG	OBP	SLG	PRO+	BR/A	SB	CS	SBR	FA	FR	G/POS	TPR
1920	NY-N	45	140	15	28	2	3	0	19	11	17	.200	.258	.257	49	-9	4	3	-1	.932	-1	O-40	-1.4

■ PAUL SPERAW
Speraw, Paul Bachman "Polly" or "Birdie" b: 10/5/1893, Annville, Pa. d: 2/22/62, Cedar Rapids, Iowa BR/TR, 5'8.5", 145 lbs. Deb: 9/15/20

YEAR	TM/L	G	AB	R	H	2B	3B	HR	RBI	BB	SO	AVG	OBP	SLG	PRO+	BR/A	SB	CS	SBR	FA	FR	G/POS	TPR
1920	StL-A	1	2	0	0	0	0	0	0	0	0	.000	.000	.000	-97	-1	0	0	0	1.000	0	/3-1	0.0

■ ED SPERBER
Sperber, Edwin George b: 1/21/1895, Cincinnati, Ohio d: 1/5/76, Cincinnati, Ohio BL/TL, 5'11", 175 lbs. Deb: 4/16/24

YEAR	TM/L	G	AB	R	H	2B	3B	HR	RBI	BB	SO	AVG	OBP	SLG	PRO+	BR/A	SB	CS	SBR	FA	FR	G/POS	TPR
1924	Bos-N	24	59	8	17	2	0	1	12	10	9	.288	.400	.373	113	2	3	1	0	.897	-3	O-17	-0.2
1925	Bos-N	2	2	0	0	0	0	0	0	0	0	.000	.000	.000	-99	-1	0	0	0	.000	0	H	-0.1
Total	2	26	61	8	17	2	0	1	12	10	9	.279	.389	.361	106	1	3	1	0	.897	-3	/O-17	-0.3

■ ROB SPERRING
Sperring, Robert Walter b: 10/10/49, San Francisco, Cal. BR/TR, 6'1", 185 lbs. Deb: 8/11/74

YEAR	TM/L	G	AB	R	H	2B	3B	HR	RBI	BB	SO	AVG	OBP	SLG	PRO+	BR/A	SB	CS	SBR	FA	FR	G/POS	TPR
1974	Chi-N	42	107	9	22	3	0	1	5	9	28	.206	.267	.262	46	-8	1	2	-1	.952	5	2-35/S-8	-0.2
1975	Chi-N	65	144	25	30	4	1	1	9	16	31	.208	.292	.271	54	-9	0	2	-1	.946	12	3-22,2-17,S/O	0.3
1976	Chi-N	43	93	8	24	3	0	0	7	9	25	.258	.324	.290	69	-4	0	2	-1	.955	-9	3-20,S-15/2O	-1.3
1977	Hou-N	58	129	6	24	3	0	1	9	12	23	.186	.255	.233	35	-12	0	0	0	.940	-2	S-22,2-20,3	-1.2
Total	4	208	473	48	100	13	1	3	30	46	107	.211	.283	.262	51	-32	1	6	-3	.964	6	/2-76,S-61,3O	-2.4

■ STAN SPERRY
Sperry, Stanley Kenneth b: 2/19/14, Evansville, Wis. d: 9/27/62, Evansville, Wis. BL/TR, 5'10.5", 164 lbs. Deb: 7/28/36

YEAR	TM/L	G	AB	R	H	2B	3B	HR	RBI	BB	SO	AVG	OBP	SLG	PRO+	BR/A	SB	CS	SBR	FA	FR	G/POS	TPR
1936	Phi-N	20	37	2	5	3	0	0	4	3	5	.135	.200	.216	11	-5				.900	-4	2-15	-0.8
1938	Phi-A	60	253	28	69	6	3	0	27	15	9	.273	.313	.320	61	-15	1	2	-1	.959	-8	2-60	-1.9
Total	2	80	290	30	74	9	3	0	31	18	14	.255	.299	.307	54	-20	1	2		.951	-12	/2-75	-2.7

■ BILL SPIERS
Spiers, William James b: 6/5/66, Orangeburg, S.C. BL/TR, 6'2", 190 lbs. Deb: 4/7/89

YEAR	TM/L	G	AB	R	H	2B	3B	HR	RBI	BB	SO	AVG	OBP	SLG	PRO+	BR/A	SB	CS	SBR	FA	FR	G/POS	TPR
1989	Mil-A	114	345	44	88	9	3	4	33	21	63	.255	.300	.333	79	-10	10	2	2	.962	14	S-89,3-12/21D	1.2
1990	Mil-A	112	363	44	88	15	3	2	36	16	45	.242	.276	.317	66	-17	11	6	-0	.976	-7	*S-111	-1.6
1991	Mil-A	133	414	71	117	13	6	8	54	34	55	.283	.340	.401	107	4	14	8	-1	.970	-11	*S-128/O-1,D	0.1
1992	Mil-A	12	16	2	5	2	0	0	2	1	4	.313	.353	.438	123	1	0	1	-0	1.000	-0	/S-5,2-4,3D	-0.2
1993	Mil-A	113	340	43	81	8	4	2	36	29	51	.238	.306	.303	65	-16	9	8	-2	.971	-24	*2-104/O-7,SD	-3.9
1994	Mil-A	73	214	27	54	10	1	0	17	19	42	.252	.316	.308	61	-12	7	1	2	.947	-4	3-35,S-35/01D	-1.2
Total	6	557	1692	231	433	57	17	16	178	120	260	.256	.309	.338	78	-51	52	26	0	.970	-34	S-372,2-112/3D01	-5.6

■ HARRY SPIES
Spies, Henry b: 6/12/1866, New Orleans, La. d: 7/8/42, Los Angeles, Cal. BR/TR, 5'11.5", 170 lbs. Deb: 4/20/1895

YEAR	TM/L	G	AB	R	H	2B	3B	HR	RBI	BB	SO	AVG	OBP	SLG	PRO+	BR/A	SB	CS	SBR	FA	FR	G/POS	TPR
1895	Cin-N	14	50	2	11	0	1	0	5	3	2	.220	.264	.260	34	-5	0			.867	2	C-12/1-2	-0.2
	Lou-N	72	276	42	74	14	7	2	35	11	19	.268	.313	.391	86	-7	4			.981	-3	1-47,C-26/S	-0.5
	Yr	86	326	44	85	14	8	2	40	14	21	.261	.305	.371	78	-12	4			.979	-2	1-49,C-38/S	-0.7

■ ED SPIEZIO
Spiezio, Edward Wayne b: 10/31/41, Joliet, Ill. BR/TR, 5'11", 180 lbs. Deb: 7/23/64

YEAR	TM/L	G	AB	R	H	2B	3B	HR	RBI	BB	SO	AVG	OBP	SLG	PRO+	BR/A	SB	CS	SBR	FA	FR	G/POS	TPR
1964	StL-N	12	12	0	4	0	0	0	0	0	1	.333	.333	.333	81	-0	0	0	0	.000	0	H	0.0
1965	StL-N	10	18	0	3	0	0	0	5	1	4	.167	.250	.167	18	-2	0	0	0	1.000	0	3-3	-0.2
1966	StL-N	26	73	4	16	5	1	2	10	5	11	.219	.269	.397	82	-2	1	0	0	.885	-4	3-19	-0.6
1967	*StL-N	55	105	9	22	2	0	3	10	7	18	.210	.265	.314	66	-5	2	1	0	.962	-0	3-19/O-7	-0.6
1968	*StL-N	29	51	1	8	0	0	0	2	5	6	.157	.232	.157	19	-5	1	1	-0	1.000	0	O-11/3-2	-0.6
1969	SD-N	121	355	29	83	9	0	13	43	38	64	.234	.315	.369	95	-3	1	2	-1	.939	1	3-98/O-1	-0.3
1970	SD-N	110	316	45	90	18	1	12	42	43	42	.285	.377	.462	129	13	4	0	1	.953	2	3-93	1.5
1971	SD-N	97	308	16	71	10	1	7	36	22	50	.231	.290	.338	83	-8	6	5	-1	.962	0	3-91/O-1	-1.0
1972	SD-N	20	29	2	4	2	0	0	4	1	6	.138	.167	.207	6	-4	1	0	0	1.000	-2	/3-5	-0.6
	Chi-A	74	277	20	66	10	1	2	22	13	43	.238	.277	.303	71	-10	0	1	-1	.952	7	3-74	-0.5
Total	9	554	1544	126	367	56	4	39	174	135	245	.238	.306	.355	88	-25	16	10	-1	.949	4	3-404/O-20	-2.9

■ CHARLIE SPIKES
Spikes, Leslie Charles b: 1/23/51, Bogalusa, La. BR/TR, 6'3", 220 lbs. Deb: 9/1/72

YEAR	TM/L	G	AB	R	H	2B	3B	HR	RBI	BB	SO	AVG	OBP	SLG	PRO+	BR/A	SB	CS	SBR	FA	FR	G/POS	TPR
1972	NY-A	14	34	2	5	1	0	0	3	1	13	.147	.171	.176	4	-4	0	1	-1	1.000	0	/O-9	-0.6
1973	Cle-A	140	506	68	120	12	3	23	73	45	103	.237	.306	.409	98	-3	5	3	-0	.964	5	*O-111,D-26	-0.4
1974	Cle-A	155	568	63	154	23	1	22	80	34	100	.271	.320	.431	116	9	10	7	-1	.968	0	*O-154	0.2
1975	Cle-A	111	345	41	79	13	3	11	33	30	51	.229	.291	.380	88	-6	7	6	-2	.974	1	*O-103/D-2	-1.1
1976	Cle-A	101	334	34	79	11	5	3	31	23	50	.237	.296	.326	83	-7	5	6	-2	.985	1	O-98/D-2	-1.3
1977	Cle-A	32	95	13	22	2	0	3	11	11	17	.232	.324	.347	86	-2	0	2	-1	.972	-3	O-27/D-2	-0.7
1978	Det-A	10	28	1	7	1	0	0	2	2	6	.250	.344	.286	77	-1	0	0	0	.909	-3	/O-9	-0.3
1979	Atl-N	66	93	12	26	8	0	3	21	5	30	.280	.316	.462	102	-0	1	0	0	.842	-3	O-15	-0.4
1980	Atl-N	41	36	6	10	1	0	0	2	3	18	.278	.350	.306	82	-1	1	0	0	1.000	-2	/O-7	-0.3
Total	9	670	2039	240	502	72	12	65	256	154	388	.246	.306	.389	96	-14	27	25	-7	.969	0	O-533/D-32	-4.9

■ HARRY SPILMAN
Spilman, William Harry b: 7/18/54, Albany, Ga. BL/TR, 6'1", 190 lbs. Deb: 9/11/78

YEAR	TM/L	G	AB	R	H	2B	3B	HR	RBI	BB	SO	AVG	OBP	SLG	PRO+	BR/A	SB	CS	SBR	FA	FR	G/POS	TPR
1978	Cin-N	4	4	1	1	0	0	0	1	0	1	.250	.250	.250	40	-0	0	0	0	.000	0	H	0.0
1979	*Cin-N	43	56	7	12	3	0	0	5	7	5	.214	.323	.268	63	-3	0	0	0	1.000	-0	1-12/3-4	-0.3
1980	Cin-N	65	101	14	27	4	0	4	19	9	19	.267	.333	.426	110	1	0	0	0	.986	0	1-18/O-2,C3	0.0
1981	Cin-N	23	24	4	4	1	0	0	3	3	7	.167	.259	.208	33	-2	0	0	0	1.000	0	/3-3,1-2	-0.2
	*Hou-N	28	34	5	10	1	0	1	1	2	3	.294	.333	.294	83	-1	0	1	-1	1.000	-1	1-13	-0.2
	Yr	51	58	9	14	1	0	1	4	5	10	.241	.302	.259	61	-3	0	1	-1	.984	-0	1-15/3-3	-0.4
1982	Hou-N	38	61	7	17	3	0	2	11	5	10	.279	.333	.459	129	2	0	0	0	.989	-1	1-11	0.1
1983	Hou-N	42	78	7	13	3	0	1	9	5	12	.167	.217	.244	29	-8	0	0	0	1.000	-2	1-19/C-6	-1.1
1984	Hou-N	32	72	14	19	3	0	2	15	12	10	.264	.369	.375	118	2	0	0	0	.978	-3	1-18/C-8	-0.2
1985	Hou-N	44	66	3	9	1	0	0	4	3	7	.136	.174	.197	4	-6	0	0	0	1.000	-1	1-19/C-2	-1.1
1986	Det-A	24	49	6	12	2	0	2	8	3	8	.245	.288	.469	102	-0	0	0	0	1.000	0	D-11/3-2,C1	0.0
	SF-N	58	94	12	27	7	0	2	22	12	13	.287	.368	.426	124	3	0	0	0	.994	-1	1-19/3-5,C2O	0.2
1987	*SF-N	83	90	5	24	5	0	1	14	9	20	.267	.333	.356	87	-2	1	1	-0	.875	-2	3-10/1-9,C	-0.5
1988	SF-N	40	40	4	7	1	1	1	3	4	6	.175	.250	.325	67	-2	0	0	0	1.000	-1	/1-6,C-2,O	-0.2
	Hou-N	7	5	0	0	0	0	0	0	0	0	.000	.000	.000	-99	-1	0	0	0	1.000	0	/1-1	-0.1
	Yr	47	45	4	7	1	1	1	3	4	9	.156	.224	.289	48	-3	0	0	0	1.000	0	/1-7,C-2,O	-0.3
1989	Hou-N	32	36	7	10	3	0	1	8	7	12	.278	.395	.361	122	1	0	0	0	1.000	0	/1-9,C-1	0.1
Total	12	563	810	96	192	34	1	18	117	81	126	.237	.309	.348	85	-17	1	2	-1	.991	-8	1-157/3-25,CD02	-3.5

■ HAL SPINDEL
Spindel, Harold Stewart b: 5/27/13, Chandler, Okla. BR/TR, 6', 185 lbs. Deb: 4/23/39

YEAR	TM/L	G	AB	R	H	2B	3B	HR	RBI	BB	SO	AVG	OBP	SLG	PRO+	BR/A	SB	CS	SBR	FA	FR	G/POS	TPR
1939	StL-N	48	119	13	32	3	1	0	11	8	7	.269	.315	.311	59	-7	0	2	-1	.993	-0	C-32	-0.6
1945	Phi-N	36	87	7	20	3	0	0	8	6	7	.230	.280	.264	53	-6		0		.964	0	C-31	-0.4
1946	Phi-N	1	3	0	1	0	0	0	0	0	0	.333	.333	.333	92	-0		0		1.000	-0	/C-1	0.0
Total	3	85	209	20	53	6	1	0	20	14	14	.254	.300	.292	57	-13	0	2		.980	0	/C-64	-1.0

YEAR	TM/L	G	AB	R	H	2B	3B	HR	RBI	BB	SO	AVG	OBP	SLG	PRO+	BR/A	SB	CS	SBR	FA	FR	G/POS	TPR

■ ANDY SPOGNARDI   Spognardi, Andrea Ettore   b: 10/18/08, Boston, Mass.   BR/TR, 5'9.5", 160 lbs.   Deb: 9/2/32

| 1932 | Bos-A | 17 | 34 | 9 | 10 | 1 | 0 | 0 | 1 | 6 | 6 | .294 | .400 | .324 | 92 | -0 | 0 | 0 | 0 | .979 | 3 | /2-9,S-3,3 | 0.3 |

■ AL SPOHRER   Spohrer, Alfred Ray   b: 12/3/02, Philadelphia, Pa.   d: 7/17/72, Plymouth, N.H.   BR/TR, 5'10.5", 175 lbs.   Deb: 4/13/28

1928	NY-N	2	2	0	0	0	0	0	0	0	0	.000	.000	.000	-99	-1	0			1.000	0	/C-2	-0.1
	Bos-N	51	124	15	27	3	0	0	9	5	11	.218	.254	.242	32	-12	1			.976	-5	C-48	-1.5
	Yr	53	126	15	27	3	0	0	9	5	11	.214	.250	.238	30	-13	1			.977	-5	C-50	-1.6
1929	Bos-N	114	342	42	93	21	8	2	48	26	35	.272	.327	.398	82	-11	1			.954	-10	*C-109	-1.0
1930	Bos-N	112	356	44	113	22	8	2	37	22	24	.317	.361	.441	96	-3	3			.957	-18	*C-108	-1.0
1931	Bos-N	114	350	23	84	17	5	0	27	22	27	.240	.285	.317	64	-18	2			.982	-0	*C-111	-1.1
1932	Bos-N	104	335	31	90	12	2	0	33	15	26	.269	.300	.316	69	-15	2			.991	10	*C-100	0.1
1933	Bos-N	67	184	11	46	6	1	1	12	11	13	.250	.292	.310	78	-6	3			.972	-6	C-65	-0.9
1934	Bos-N	100	265	25	59	15	0	0	17	14	18	.223	.262	.279	49	-20	1			.977	0	C-98	-1.5
1935	Bos-N	92	260	22	63	7	1	1	16	9	12	.242	.273	.288	55	-17	0			.958	-10	C-90	-2.3
Total	8	756	2218	213	575	103	25	6	199	124	166	.259	.301	.336	70	-101	13			.972	-39	C-731	-9.3

■ JIM SPOTTS   Spotts, James Russell   b: 4/10/09, Honey Brook, Pa.   d: 6/15/64, Medford, N.J.   BR/TR, 5'10.5", 175 lbs.   Deb: 4/23/30

| 1930 | Phi-N | 3 | 2 | 1 | 0 | 0 | 0 | 0 | 0 | 0 | 1 | .000 | .000 | .000 | -93 | -1 | 0 | | | 1.000 | 0 | /C-2 | 0.0 |

■ CHARLIE SPRAGUE   Sprague, Charles Wellington   b: 10/10/1864, Cleveland, Ohio   d: 12/31/12, Des Moines, Iowa   BL/TL, 5'11", 150 lbs.   Deb: 9/17/1887

1887	Chi-N	3	13	0	2	0	0	0	0	0		.154	.154	.154	-13	-2	0			.667	-1	/P-3,O-1	-0.1
1889	Cle-N	2	7	2	1	0	0	0	1	1	0	.143	.250	.143	11	-1	1			.857	1	/P-2	0.0
1890	Tol-a	55	199	25	47	5	6	1		16		.236	.303	.337	86	-4	10			.892	-6	O-40,P-19	-0.7
Total	3	60	219	27	50	5	6	1	1	17	2	.228	.293	.320	77	-7	11			.892	-6	/O-41,P-24	-0.8

■ ED SPRAGUE   Sprague, Edward Nelson Jr.   b: 7/25/67, Castro Valley, Cal.   BR/TR, 6'2", 215 lbs.   Deb: 5/8/91   F

1991	Tor-A	61	160	17	44	7	0	4	20	19	43	.275	.363	.394	105	2	0	3	-2	.870	-1	3-35,1-22/CD	-0.2
1992	*Tor-A	22	47	6	11	2	0	1	7	3	7	.234	.280	.340	70	-2	0	0	0	.985	1	C-15/1-4,3D	-0.1
1993	*Tor-A	150	546	50	142	31	1	12	73	32	85	.260	.313	.386	86	-11	1	0	0	.955	-9	*3-150	-1.9
1994	Tor-A	109	405	38	97	19	1	11	44	23	95	.240	.298	.373	71	-18	1	0	0	.946	-12	*3-107/1-3	-2.8
Total	4	342	1158	111	294	59	2	28	144	77	230	.254	.314	.381	83	-30	2	3	-1	.941	-22	3-293/1-29,CD	-5.0

■ HARRY SPRATT   Spratt, Henry Lee   b: 7/10/1887, Broadford, Va.   d: 7/3/69, Washington, D.C.   BL/TR, 5'8.5", 175 lbs.   Deb: 4/13/11

1911	Bos-N	62	154	22	37	4	4	2	13	13	25	.240	.299	.357	77	-5	1			.892	-8	S-26/2-5,3O	-1.2
1912	Bos-N	27	89	6	23	3	2	3	15	7	11	.258	.313	.438	102	-0	2			.842	-13	S-23	-1.2
Total	2	89	243	28	60	7	6	5	28	20	36	.247	.304	.387	86	-6	3			.871	-22	/S-49,2-5,O3	-2.4

■ GEORGE SPRIGGS   Spriggs, George Herman   b: 5/22/41, Newell, Md.   BL/TR, 5'11", 175 lbs.   Deb: 9/15/65

1965	Pit-N	9	2	5	1	0	0	0	0	0	0	.500	.500	.500	182	0	2	0	1	.000	-0	/O-1	0.0
1966	Pit-N	9	7	0	1	0	0	0	0	0	3	.143	.143	.143	-20	-1	0	0	0	.000	-0	H	-0.1
1967	Pit-N	38	57	14	10	1	1	0	5	6	20	.175	.254	.228	39	-4	3	0	1	1.000	-2	O-13	-0.6
1969	KC-A	23	29	4	4	2	1	0	0	3	8	.138	.242	.276	44	-2	0	0	0	1.000	-1	/O-6	-0.4
1970	KC-A	51	130	12	27	2	3	1	7	14	32	.208	.285	.292	59	-7	4	3	-1	.953	1	O-36	-0.9
Total	5	130	225	35	43	5	5	1	12	23	63	.191	.269	.271	51	-15	9	3	1	.965	-3	/O-56	-2.0

■ STEVE SPRINGER   Springer, Steven Michael   b: 2/11/61, Long Beach, Cal.   BR/TR, 6', 190 lbs.   Deb: 5/22/90

1990	Cle-A	4	12	1	2	0	0	0	0	0	6	.167	.167	.167	-7	-2	0	0	0	1.000	-1	/3-3,D-1	-0.2
1992	NY-N	4	5	0	2	1	0	0	0	0	1	.400	.400	.600	182	0	0	0	0	1.000	-0	/2-1,3-1	0.0
Total	2	8	17	1	4	1	0	0	0	0	7	.235	.235	.294	48	-1	0	0	0	1.000	-1	/3-4,2-1,D	-0.2

■ JOE SPRINZ   Sprinz, Joseph Conrad "Mule"   b: 8/3/02, St.Louis, Mo.   d: 1/11/94, Fremont, Cal.   BR/TR, 5'11", 185 lbs.   Deb: 7/16/30

1930	Cle-A	17	45	5	8	1	0	0	2	4	4	.178	.245	.200	14	-6	0	0	0	1.000	6	C-17	0.1
1931	Cle-A	1	3	0	0	0	0	0	0	0	0	.000	.000	.000	-95	-1	0	0	0	1.000	0	/C-1	-0.1
1933	StL-N	3	5	1	1	0	0	0	0	1	1	.200	.333	.200	53	-0	0			1.000	2	/C-3	0.2
Total	3	21	53	6	9	1	0	0	2	5	5	.170	.241	.189	12	-7	0	0	0	1.000	8	/C-21	0.2

■ FREDDY SPURGEON   Spurgeon, Fred   b: 10/9/1900, Wabash, Ind.   d: 11/5/70, Kalamazoo, Mich.   BR/TR, 5'11.5", 160 lbs.   Deb: 9/19/24

1924	Cle-A	3	7	0	1	0	0	0	0	0	0	.143	.250	.286	37	-1	0	0	0	.882	1	/2-3	0.0
1925	Cle-A	107	376	50	108	9	5	0	32	15	21	.287	.315	.327	62	-22	8	5	-1	.927	-4	3-56,2-46/S	-2.0
1926	Cle-A	149	614	101	181	31	3	0	49	27	36	.295	.327	.355	77	-21	7	2	1	.962	-8	*2-149	-2.3
1927	Cle-A	57	179	30	45	6	1	1	19	18	14	.251	.323	.313	65	-9	8	1	2	.938	-8	2-52	-1.3
Total	4	316	1176	181	335	47	7	1	100	60	71	.285	.322	.339	70	-53	23	8	2	.958	-19	2-250/3-56,S	-5.6

■ ED SPURNEY   Spurney, Edward Frederick   b: 1/19/1872, Cleveland, Ohio   d: 10/12/32, Cleveland, Ohio   Deb: 6/26/1891

| 1891 | Pit-N | 3 | 7 | 2 | 2 | 1 | 0 | 0 | 2 | 1 | | .286 | .444 | .429 | 158 | 1 | 0 | | | .889 | -1 | /S-3 | 0.0 |

■ MIKE SQUIRES   Squires, Michael Lynn   b: 3/5/52, Kalamazoo, Mich.   BL/TL, 5'11", 185 lbs.   Deb: 9/1/75   C

1975	Chi-A	20	65	5	15	0	0	0	4	8	5	.231	.315	.231	55	-3	3	0	1	.988	0	1-20	-0.4
1977	Chi-A	3	3	0	0	0	0	0	0	0	1	.000	.000	.000	-99	-1	0	0	0	1.000	0	/1-1	0.0
1978	Chi-A	46	150	25	42	9	2	0	19	16	21	.280	.349	.367	101	0	4	4	-1	.997	-2	1-45	-0.6
1979	Chi-A	122	295	44	78	10	1	2	22	22	9	.264	.320	.325	74	-10	15	5	2	.995	4	*1-110/O-1	-0.9
1980	Chi-A	131	343	38	97	11	3	0	33	33	24	.283	.347	.350	92	-3	8	9	-3	.995	4	*1-114/C-2	-0.7
1981	Chi-A	92	294	35	78	9	0	0	25	22	17	.265	.316	.296	79	-8	7	2	1	.992	2	1-88/O-1	-0.9
1982	Chi-A	116	195	33	52	9	3	1	21	14	13	.267	.316	.359	85	-4	3	3	-1	.995	7	*1-109	-0.1
1983	*Chi-A	143	153	21	34	4	1	0	11	22	11	.222	.328	.281	67	-6	3	3	-1	.996	6	*1-124/3-1,D	-0.4
1984	Chi-A	104	82	9	15	1	0	0	6	6	7	.183	.239	.195	21	-9	2	2	-1	1.000	1	1-77,3-13/OP	-0.6
1985	Chi-A	2	0	0	0	0	0	0	0	0	0	—	—	—	—	-0	0	0	0	.000	0	/R	0.0
Total	10	779	1580	211	411	53	10	6	141	143	108	.260	.323	.318	78	-43	45	28	2	.995	25	1-688/3-14,DOCP	-4.6

■ MARV STAEHLE   Staehle, Marvin Gustave   b: 3/13/42, Oak Park, Ill.   BL/TR, 5'10", 172 lbs.   Deb: 9/15/64

1964	Chi-A	6	5	0	2	0	0	0	2	0	0	.400	.400	.400	127	0	1	0	0	.000	0	H	0.0
1965	Chi-A	7	7	0	3	0	0	0	0	0	0	.429	.429	.429	154	0	1	0	0	.000	0	H	0.0
1966	Chi-A	8	15	2	2	0	0	0	0	4	2	.133	.316	.133	37	-1	0	1	0	1.000	0	/2-6	0.0
1967	Chi-A	32	54	1	6	1	0	0	1	4	8	.111	.172	.130	-10	-7	1	0	0	1.000	1	2-17/S-5	-0.7
1969	Mon-N	6	17	4	7	2	0	1	1	2	0	.412	.474	.706	226	3	0	0	0	.944	-1	/2-4	0.3
1970	Mon-N	104	321	41	70	9	1	0	26	39	21	.218	.309	.252	52	-21	1	3	-2	.963	-13	2-91/S-1	-2.9
1971	Atl-N	22	36	5	4	0	0	0	1	5	4	.111	.238	.111	2	-5	0	0	0	1.000	0	/2-7,3-1	0.0
Total	7	185	455	53	94	12	1	1	33	54	35	.207	.296	.244	50	-30	4	4	-1	.971	-8	2-125/S-6,3	-3.3

■ HEINIE STAFFORD   Stafford, Henry Alexander   b: 11/1/1891, Orleans, Vt.   d: 1/29/72, Lake Worth, Fla.   BR/TR, 5'7", 160 lbs.   Deb: 10/5/16

| 1916 | NY-N | 1 | 1 | 0 | 0 | 0 | 0 | 0 | 0 | 0 | 0 | .000 | .000 | .000 | -99 | -0 | 0 | | | .000 | 0 | H | 0.0 |

■ GENERAL STAFFORD   Stafford, James Joseph "Jamsey"   b: 7/9/1868, Webster, Mass.   d: 9/18/23, Worcester, Mass.   BR/TR, 5'8", 165 lbs.   Deb: 8/27/1890   F

1890	Buf-P	15	49	11	7	1	0	0	3	7	8	.143	.250	.163	13	-6	2			.893	-2	P-12/O-4	-0.2
1893	NY-N	67	281	58	79	7	4	5	27	25	31	.281	.344	.388	94	-3	19			.901	-7	O-67	-1.1
1894	NY-N	14	46	10	10	1	1	0	4	10	7	.217	.368	.283	59	-3	2			.750	-3	/3-6,O-5,21	-0.5

YEAR	TM/L	G	AB	R	H	2B	3B	HR	RBI	BB	SO	AVG	OBP	SLG	PRO+	BR/A	SB	CS	SBR	FA	FR	G/POS	TPR
1895	NY-N	123	463	79	129	12	5	3	73	40	32	.279	.344	.346	80	-13	42			.911	-9	*2-109,O-12/3	-1.4
1896	NY-N	59	230	28	66	9	1	0	40	13	18	.287	.333	.335	79	-7	15			.897	-5	O-53/S-6	-1.3
1897	NY-N	7	23	0	2	0	0	0	3	3		.087	.192	.087	-26	-4	0			1.000	-3	/O-5,S-2	-0.7
	Lou-N	111	432	68	120	16	5	7	53	31		.278	.330	.387	92	-6	14			.887	-12	*S-103/O-7,3	-1.3
	Yr	118	455	68	122	16	5	7	56	34		.268	.323	.371	86	-10	14			.882	-15	*S-105,O-12/3	-2.1
1898	Lou-N	49	181	26	54	3	0	1	25	19		.298	.368	.331	103	1	7			.901	-8	2-28,O-22/3	-0.6
	Bos-N	37	123	21	32	2	0	1	8	4		.260	.289	.301	66	-6	3			.909	-3	O-35/1-1	-1.1
	Yr	86	304	47	86	5	0	2	33	23		.283	.337	.319	87	-5	10			.924	-12	O-57,2-28/31	-1.7
1899	Bos-N	55	182	29	55	4	2	3	40	7		.302	.328	.396	89	-4	9			.956	-9	O-41/2-5,S	-1.4
	Was-N	31	118	11	29	5	1	1	14	5		.246	.276	.331	67	-6	4			.951	-5	2-17,S-13/3	-0.9
	Yr	86	300	40	84	9	3	4	54	12		.280	.308	.370	81	-9	13			.956	-14	O-41,2-22,S/3	-2.3
Total	8	568	2128	341	583	60	19	21	290	164	96	.274	.331	.350	82	-56	117			.911	-66	O-251,2-160,S/3P1	-10.6

■ BOB STAFFORD
Stafford, Robert M. b: 6/26/1872, Oak Ridge, N.C. d: 8/20/16, Moores Springs, N.C. Deb: 10/12/1890

YEAR	TM/L	G	AB	R	H	2B	3B	HR	RBI	BB	SO	AVG	OBP	SLG	PRO+	BR/A	SB	CS	SBR	FA	FR	G/POS	TPR
1890	Phi-a	1	2	0	0	0	0	0	0			.000	.000	.000	-99	-1	0			1.000	1	/O-1	0.0

■ STEVE STAGGS
Staggs, Stephen Robert b: 5/6/51, Anchorage, Alaska BR/TR, 5'9", 150 lbs. Deb: 7/1/77

YEAR	TM/L	G	AB	R	H	2B	3B	HR	RBI	BB	SO	AVG	OBP	SLG	PRO+	BR/A	SB	CS	SBR	FA	FR	G/POS	TPR
1977	Tor-A	72	290	37	75	11	6	2	28	36	38	.259	.340	.359	90	-3	5	9	-4	.965	-14	2-72	-1.6
1978	Oak-A	47	78	10	19	2	2	0	0	19	17	.244	.392	.321	108	2	2	3	-1	.976	-3	2-40/S-2,3D	0.0
Total	2	119	368	47	94	13	8	2	28	55	55	.255	.352	.351	94	-2	7	12	-5	.968	-17	2-112/D-2,3S	-1.6

■ CHICK STAHL
Stahl, Charles Sylvester b: 1/10/1873, Avila, Ind. d: 3/28/07, W.Baden, Ind. BL/TL, 5'10", 160 lbs. Deb: 4/19/1897 M

YEAR	TM/L	G	AB	R	H	2B	3B	HR	RBI	BB	SO	AVG	OBP	SLG	PRO+	BR/A	SB	CS	SBR	FA	FR	G/POS	TPR
1897	*Bos-N	114	469	112	166	30	13	4	97	38		.354	.406	.499	130	19	18			.928	-8	*O-111	0.6
1898	Bos-N	125	467	72	144	21	8	3	52	46		.308	.375	.407	118	10	6			.968	-2	*O-125	0.9
1899	Bos-N	148	576	122	202	23	19	7	52	72		.351	.426	.493	139	30	33			.969	6	*O-148/P-1	2.2
1900	Bos-N	136	553	88	163	23	16	5	82	34		.295	.336	.421	96	-7	27			**.968**	9	*O-135	-0.7
1901	Bos-A	131	515	105	156	20	16	6	72	54		.303	.377	.439	128	20	29			.957	-1	*O-131	0.9
1902	Bos-A	127	508	92	164	22	11	2	58	37		.323	.375	.421	117	12	24			.953	-5	*O-125	-0.1
1903	*Bos-A	77	299	60	82	12	6	2	44	28		.274	.338	.375	108	3	10			.961	-2	O-74	-0.4
1904	Bos-A	157	587	83	170	27	**19**	3	67	64		.290	.366	.416	139	27	11			.961	-15	*O-157	0.4
1905	Bos-A	134	500	61	129	17	4	0	47	50		.258	.332	.308	102	3	18			.977	-5	*O-134	-1.0
1906	Bos-A	155	595	63	170	24	6	4	51	47		.286	.346	.366	123	16	13			.961	10	*O-155,M	2.0
Total	10	1304	5069	858	1546	219	118	36	622	470		.305	.369	.416	121	133	189			.961	-7	*O-1295/P-1	3.9

■ JAKE STAHL
Stahl, Garland b: 4/13/1879, Elkhart, Ill. d: 9/18/22, Monrovia, Cal. BR/TR, 6'2", 195 lbs. Deb: 4/20/03 M

YEAR	TM/L	G	AB	R	H	2B	3B	HR	RBI	BB	SO	AVG	OBP	SLG	PRO+	BR/A	SB	CS	SBR	FA	FR	G/POS	TPR
1903	Bos-A	40	92	14	22	3	5	2	8	4		.239	.286	.446	111	1	1			.956	-2	C-28/O-1	0.1
1904	Was-A	142	520	54	136	29	12	3	50	21		.262	.309	.381	119	10	25			.978	6	*1-119,O-23	1.3
1905	Was-A	141	501	66	125	22	12	5	66	28		.250	.311	.371	121	11	41			.986	2	*1-140,M	0.9
1906	Was-A	137	482	38	107	9	8	0	51	21		.222	.266	.274	73	-16	30			.983	-2	*1-136,M	-2.4
1908	NY-A	75	274	34	70	18	5	2	42	11		.255	.304	.380	120	5	17			.933	4	O-68/1-6	0.7
	Bos-A	78	262	29	64	9	11	0	23	20		.244	.333	.363	123	7	13			.984	-2	1-78	0.4
	Yr	153	536	63	134	27	16	2	65	31		.250	.319	.371	122	12	30			.984	2	1-84,O-68	1.1
1909	Bos-A	127	435	62	128	19	12	6	60	43		.294	.377	.434	153	27	16			.986	-11	*1-126	1.6
1910	Bos-A	144	531	68	144	19	16	**10**	77	42		.271	.334	.424	134	19	22			.985	-7	*1-142	1.3
1912	*Bos-A	95	326	40	98	21	6	3	60	31		.301	.372	.429	123	9	13			.980	-2	1-92,M	0.6
1913	Bos-A	2	2	0	0	0	0	0	0	0	1	.000	.000	.000	-98	-0	0			.000	0	HM	-0.1
Total	9	981	3425	405	894	149	87	31	437	221	1	.261	.323	.382	120	73	178			.983	-14	1-839/O-92,C	4.4

■ LARRY STAHL
Stahl, Larry Floyd b: 6/29/41, Belleville, Ill. BL/TL, 6'1", 185 lbs. Deb: 9/11/64

YEAR	TM/L	G	AB	R	H	2B	3B	HR	RBI	BB	SO	AVG	OBP	SLG	PRO+	BR/A	SB	CS	SBR	FA	FR	G/POS	TPR
1964	KC-A	15	46	7	12	1	0	3	6	1	10	.261	.277	.478	102	-0	0	0	0	.955	1	O-10	0.0
1965	KC-A	28	81	9	16	2	1	4	14	5	16	.198	.253	.395	82	-2	1	0	0	1.000	1	O-21	-0.2
1966	KC-A	119	312	37	78	11	5	5	34	17	63	.250	.291	.365	90	-5	5	3	-0	.980	-4	O-94	-1.3
1967	NY-N	71	155	9	37	5	0	1	18	8	25	.239	.285	.290	66	-7	2	2	-1	.969	3	O-43	-0.7
1968	NY-N	53	183	15	43	7	2	3	10	21	38	.235	.314	.344	97	-0	3	0	1	.983	1	O-47/1-9	-0.2
1969	SD-N	95	162	10	32	6	2	3	10	17	31	.198	.278	.315	68	-7	3	3	-1	.981	1	O-37,1-13	-0.9
1970	SD-N	52	66	5	12	2	0	0	3	12	14	.182	.206	.212	13	-8	2	2	-1	1.000	-3	O-20	-1.3
1971	SD-N	114	308	27	78	13	4	8	36	26	59	.253	.311	.399	107	2	4	3	-1	.987	6	O-75/1-7	0.3
1972	SD-N	107	297	31	67	9	3	7	20	37	67	.226	.299	.347	89	-5	1	3	-2	.986	-5	O-76/1-1	-1.1
1973	*Cin-N	76	111	17	25	2	2	2	12	14	34	.225	.317	.333	85	-2	1	0	0	1.000	-6	O-29/1-2	-0.9
Total	10	730	1721	167	400	58	19	36	163	142	357	.232	.293	.351	86	-35	22	16	-3	.983	-1	O-452/1-32	-6.3

■ SCOTT STAHOVIAK
Stahoviak, Scott Edmund b: 3/6/70, Waukegan, Ill. BL/TR, 6'5", 210 lbs. Deb: 9/10/93

YEAR	TM/L	G	AB	R	H	2B	3B	HR	RBI	BB	SO	AVG	OBP	SLG	PRO+	BR/A	SB	CS	SBR	FA	FR	G/POS	TPR
1993	Min-A	20	57	1	11	4	0	0	1	3	22	.193	.233	.263	33	-5	0	2	-1	.922	3	3-19	-0.4

■ ROY STAIGER
Staiger, Roy Joseph b: 1/6/50, Tulsa, Okla. BR/TR, 6', 195 lbs. Deb: 9/12/75

YEAR	TM/L	G	AB	R	H	2B	3B	HR	RBI	BB	SO	AVG	OBP	SLG	PRO+	BR/A	SB	CS	SBR	FA	FR	G/POS	TPR
1975	NY-N	13	19	2	3	1	0	0	0	0	4	.158	.158	.211	2	-3	0	0	0	1.000	1	3-13	-0.1
1976	NY-N	95	304	23	67	8	1	2	26	26	35	.220	.282	.273	62	-16	3	3	-1	.967	19	3-93/S-1	0.2
1977	NY-N	40	123	16	31	9	0	2	11	4	20	.252	.276	.374	76	-5	1	0	0	.934	6	3-36/S-1	0.1
1979	NY-A	4	11	1	3	1	0	0	1	1	0	.273	.333	.364	90	-0	0	0	0	1.000	0	/3-4	0.0
Total	4	152	457	42	104	19	1	4	38	30	59	.228	.277	.300	64	-23	4	3	-1	.960	26	3-146/S-2	0.2

■ TUCK STAINBACK
Stainback, George Tucker b: 8/4/11, Los Angeles, Cal. d: 11/29/92, Camarillo, Cal. BR/TR, 5'11.5", 175 lbs. Deb: 4/17/34

YEAR	TM/L	G	AB	R	H	2B	3B	HR	RBI	BB	SO	AVG	OBP	SLG	PRO+	BR/A	SB	CS	SBR	FA	FR	G/POS	TPR
1934	Chi-N	104	359	47	110	14	3	2	46	8	42	.306	.327	.379	90	-5	7			.955	-6	O-96/3-1	-1.5
1935	Chi-N	47	94	16	24	4	0	3	11	0	13	.255	.271	.394	76	-4	1			.932	-5	O-28	-0.9
1936	Chi-N	44	75	13	13	3	0	1	5	6	14	.173	.235	.253	31	-7	1			1.000	-4	O-26	-1.2
1937	Chi-N	72	160	18	37	7	1	0	14	7	16	.231	.268	.287	49	-11	3			.981	-2	O-49	-1.4
1938	StL-N	6	10	2	0	0	0	0	0	0	3	.000	.000	.000	-95	-3	0			1.000	1	/O-2	-0.2
	Phi-N	30	81	9	21	3	0	1	11	3		.259	.294	.333	74	-3	1			.980	-2	O-25	-0.6
	Bro-N	35	104	15	34	6	3	0	20	2	4	.327	.346	.442	113	1	1			.981	-1	O-23	0.0
	Yr	71	195	26	55	9	3	1	31	5	10	.282	.307	.374	86	-4	2			.982	-3	O-50	-0.8
1939	Bro-N	68	201	22	54	7	0	3	19	4	23	.269	.290	.348	68	-9	0			.938	-5	O-55	-1.6
1940	Det-A	15	40	4	9	2	0	0	1	1	9	.225	.262	.275	36	-4	0	0	0	.968	4	/O-9	-0.1
1941	Det-A	94	200	19	49	8	1	2	10	3	21	.245	.266	.325	49	-15	6	3	0	.948	-15	O-80	-3.2
1942	*NY-A	15	10	0	2	0	0	0	0	0	2	.200	.200	.200	13	-1	0	0	0	1.000	-1	/O-3	-0.2
1943	*NY-A	71	231	31	60	11	2	0	10	7	16	.260	.285	.325	77	-7	3			.993	-1	O-60	-1.3
1944	NY-A	30	78	13	17	3	0	0	5	2	9	.218	.247	.256	42	-6	1	0	0	.957	-3	O-24	-1.0
1945	NY-A	95	327	40	84	12	2	5	32	13	20	.257	.289	.352	82	-9	4	4	-2	.968	9	O-83	-0.7
1946	Phi-A	91	291	35	71	10	2	0	20	7	20	.244	.264	.292	56	-18	3	2	-0	.963	3	O-66	-2.0
Total	13	817	2261	284	585	90	14	17	204	64	213	.259	.284	.333	68	-101	27	12		.965	-29	O-629/3-1	-15.8

■ MATT STAIRS
Stairs, Matthew Wade b: 2/27/68, St.John, N.B., Canada BL/TR, 5'9", 175 lbs. Deb: 5/29/92

YEAR	TM/L	G	AB	R	H	2B	3B	HR	RBI	BB	SO	AVG	OBP	SLG	PRO+	BR/A	SB	CS	SBR	FA	FR	G/POS	TPR
1992	Mon-N	13	30	2	5	2	0	0	5	7		.167	.324	.233	61	-1	0	0	0	.933	-1	O-10	-0.3
1993	Mon-N	6	8	1	3	1	0	0	2	0	1	.375	.375	.500	126	0	0	0	0	1.000	-0	/O-1	0.0
Total	2	19	38	3	8	3	0	0	7	7	8	.211	.333	.289	76	-1	0	0	0	.938	-1	/O-11	-0.3

YEAR	TM/L	G	AB	R	H	2B	3B	HR	RBI	BB	SO	AVG	OBP	SLG	PRO+	BR/A	SB	CS	SBR	FA	FR	G/POS	TPR

■ **GALE STALEY**   Staley, George Gaylord b: 5/2/1899, DePere, Wis. d: 4/19/89, Walnut Creek, Cal. BL/TR, 5'8.5", 167 lbs. Deb: 9/16/25

| 1925 | Chi-N | 7 | 26 | 2 | 11 | 2 | 0 | 0 | 3 | 2 | 1 | .423 | .464 | .500 | 144 | 2 | 0 | 1 | -1 | .979 | 4 | /2-7 | 0.5 |

■ **VIRGIL STALLCUP**   Stallcup, Thomas Virgil "Red" b: 1/3/22, Ravensford, N.C. d: 5/2/89, Greenville, S.C. BR/TR, 6'3", 185 lbs. Deb: 4/18/47

1947	Cin-N	8	1	0	0	0	0	0	0	0	1	.000	.000	.000	-99	-0				.000	0	/S-1	0.0
1948	Cin-N	149	539	40	123	30	4	3	65	18	52	.228	.253	.315	55	-36	2			.956	-0	*S-148	-2.8
1949	Cin-N	141	575	49	146	28	5	3	45	9	44	.254	.268	.336	60	-33	1			.962	-10	*S-141	-3.3
1950	Cin-N	136	483	44	121	23	2	8	54	17	39	.251	.276	.356	65	-26	4			**.973**	-5	*S-136	-2.1
1951	Cin-N	121	428	33	103	17	2	5	49	8	40	.241	.251	.346	58	-26	2	4	-2	**.969**	-8	*S-117	-2.8
1952	Cin-N	2	1	0	0	0	0	0	0	0	0	.000	.000	.000	-99	-0	0	0	0	.000	0	/S-1	0.0
	StL-N	29	31	4	4	1	0	0	1	1	5	.129	.156	.161	-12	-5	0	0	0	1.000	2	S-12	-0.3
	Yr	31	32	4	4	1	0	0	1	1	5	.125	.152	.156	-15	-5	0	0	0	1.000	2	S-13	-0.3
1953	StL-N	1	1	0	0	0	0	0	0	0	0	.000	.000	.000	-99	-0	0	0	0	.000	0	H	0.0
Total	7	587	2059	171	497	99	13	22	214	51	181	.241	.260	.334	58	-127	9	4		.965	-21	S-556	-11.3

■ **GEORGE STALLER**   Staller, George Walborn "Stopper" b: 4/1/16, Rutherford Heights, Pa. d: 7/3/92, Harrisburg, Pa. BL/TL, 5'11", 190 lbs. Deb: 9/14/43 C

| 1943 | Phi-A | 21 | 85 | 14 | 23 | 1 | 3 | 3 | 12 | 5 | 6 | .271 | .326 | .459 | 129 | 3 | 1 | 0 | 0 | .977 | -1 | O-20 | 0.1 |

■ **GEORGE STALLINGS**   Stallings, George Tweedy "Gentleman George"
b: 11/17/1867, Augusta, Ga. d: 5/13/29, Haddock, Ga. BR/TR, 6'1", 187 lbs. Deb: 5/22/1890 M

1890	Bro-N	4	11	1	0	0	0	0	0	1	3	.000	.154	.000	-54	-2	0			.933	-1	/C-4	-0.3
1897	Phi-N	2	9	1	2	1	0	0	0	0	0	.222	.222	.333	47	-1	0			1.000	1	/O-1,1-1M	0.0
1898	Phi-N	1	0	1	0	0	0	0	0	0	0	.—	.—	.—	—	0	0			.000	0	/HM	0.0
Total	3	7	20	3	2	1	0	0	0	1	3	.100	.182	.150	-7	-3	0			.933	-1	/C-4,1-1,O	-0.3

■ **OSCAR STANAGE**   Stanage, Oscar Harland b: 3/17/1883, Tulare, Cal. d: 11/11/64, Detroit, Mich. BR/TR, 5'11", 190 lbs. Deb: 5/19/06 C

1906	Cin-N	1	1	0	0	0	0	0	0	0	0	.000	.000	.000	-96	-0	0			1.000	-0	/C-1	0.0
1909	*Det-A	77	252	17	66	8	6	0	21	11		.262	.298	.341	98	-1	2			.964	-8	C-77	-0.3
1910	Det-A	88	275	24	57	7	4	2	25	20		.207	.266	.284	68	-11	1			.952	-4	C-84	-0.7
1911	Det-A	141	503	45	133	13	7	3	51	20		.264	.297	.336	73	-20	3			.952	-13	*C-141	-1.8
1912	Det-A	121	394	35	103	9	4	0	41	34		.261	.326	.305	83	-8	3			.950	-28	*C-120	-2.5
1913	Det-A	80	241	19	54	13	2	0	21	21	35	.224	.292	.295	73	-9	5			.960	-8	C-77	-1.1
1914	Det-A	122	400	16	77	8	4	0	25	24	58	.192	.242	.233	41	-29	2	1	0	.960	-6	*C-122	-2.7
1915	Det-A	100	300	27	67	9	2	1	31	20	41	.223	.274	.277	62	-15	5	1	0	.949	-9	*C-100	-1.7
1916	Det-A	94	291	16	69	17	3	0	30	17	48	.237	.286	.316	78	-9	3			.969	-9	C-94	-1.2
1917	Det-A	99	297	19	61	14	1	0	30	20	35	.205	.262	.259	59	-15	3			.977	-4	C-95	-1.3
1918	Det-A	54	186	9	47	4	1	0	14	11	18	.253	.294	.290	80	-5	2			.980	-8	C-47/1-5,S	-1.1
1919	Det-A	38	120	9	29	4	1	1	15	7	12	.242	.295	.317	73	-4	1			.974	1	C-36/1-1	-0.1
1920	Det-A	78	238	12	55	17	0	0	17	14	21	.231	.277	.303	55	-16	0	0	0	.958	-10	C-77	-2.0
1925	Det-A	3	5	0	1	0	0	0	0	0	0	.200	.200	.200	2	-1	0	0	0	1.000	-1	/C-3	-0.2
Total	14	1096	3503	248	819	123	34	8	321	219	268	.234	.284	.295	69	-142	30	2		.961	-107	*C-1074/1-6,S	-16.7

■ **JERRY STANDAERT**   Standaert, Jerome John b: 11/2/01, Chicago, Ill. d: 8/4/64, Chicago, Ill. BR/TR, 5'10", 168 lbs. Deb: 4/16/25

1925	Bro-N	1	1	0	0	0	0	0	0	0	1	.000	.000	.000	-99	-0	0	0	0	.000	0	H	0.0
1926	Bro-N	66	113	13	39	8	2	0	14	5	7	.345	.378	.451	124	4	0	0	0	.918	-11	2-21,3-14/S	-0.6
1929	Bos-A	19	18	1	3	2	0	0	4	3	2	.167	.286	.278	47	-1	0	0	0	.958	-0	1-10	-0.2
Total	3	86	132	14	42	10	2	0	18	8	10	.318	.362	.424	111	2	0	0	0	.918	-11	/2-21,3-14,1S	-0.8

■ **PETE STANICEK**   Stanicek, Peter Louis b: 4/18/63, Harvey, Ill. BB/TR, 5'11", 175 lbs. Deb: 9/1/87 F

1987	Bal-A	30	113	9	31	3	0	0	9	8	19	.274	.333	.301	72	-4	8	1	2	.975	-6	2-19,D-10/3	-0.7
1988	Bal-A	83	261	29	60	7	1	4	17	28	45	.230	.314	.310	78	-7	12	6	0	.985	-5	O-65,2-16/D	-1.3
Total	2	113	374	38	91	10	1	4	26	36	64	.243	.320	.307	76	-11	20	7	2	.967	-10	/O-65,2-35,D3	-2.0

■ **STEVE STANICEK**   Stanicek, Stephen Blair b: 6/19/61, Lake Forest, Ill. BR/TR, 6' ", 190 lbs. Deb: 9/16/87 F

1987	Mil-A	4	7	2	2	0	0	0	0	0	2	.286	.286	.286	51	-0	0	0	0	.000	0	/D-1	0.0
1989	Phi-N	9	9	0	1	0	0	0	1	0	3	.111	.111	.111	-36	-2	0	0	0	.000	0	H	-0.2
Total	2	13	16	2	3	0	0	0	1	0	5	.188	.188	.188	4	-2	0	0	0	.000	0	/D-1	-0.2

■ **TOM STANKARD**   Stankard, Thomas Francis b: 3/20/1882, Waltham, Mass. d: 6/13/58, Waltham, Mass. BR/TR, 6', 190 lbs. Deb: 7/2/04

| 1904 | Pit-N | 2 | 2 | 0 | 0 | 0 | 0 | 0 | 0 | 0 | 0 | .000 | .000 | .000 | -97 | -0 | 0 | | | 1.000 | -1 | /S-1,3-1 | -0.1 |

■ **ANDY STANKIEWICZ**   Stankiewicz, Andrew Neal b: 8/10/64, Inglewood, Cal. BR/TR, 5'9", 165 lbs. Deb: 4/11/92

1992	NY-A	116	400	52	107	22	2	2	25	38	42	.268	.339	.348	93	-3	9	5	-0	.973	6	S-81,2-34/D	0.9
1993	NY-A	16	9	5	0	0	0	0	0	1	1	.000	.100	.000	-73	-2	0	0	0	1.000	6	/2-6,3-4,SD	0.4
1994	Hou-N	37	54	10	14	3	0	1	5	12	12	.259	.403	.370	106	1	1	1	-0	1.000	0	/S-17/2-6,3	0.1
Total	3	169	463	67	121	25	2	3	30	51	55	.261	.342	.343	92	-4	10	6	-1	.976	12	/S-99,2-46,3D	1.4

■ **EDDIE STANKY**   Stanky, Edward Raymond "The Brat" or "Muggsy" b: 9/3/16, Philadelphia, Pa. BR/TR, 5'8", 170 lbs. Deb: 4/21/43 MC

1943	Chi-N	142	510	92	125	15	4	0	47	92	42	.245	.363	.278	88	-3	4			.966	12	*2-131,S-12/3	1.8
1944	Chi-N	13	25	4	6	0	1	0	0	2	1	.240	.296	.320	74	-1	1			.875	2	/2-3,S-3,3	0.1
	Bro-N	89	261	32	72	9	2	0	16	44	13	.276	.382	.326	102	3	3			.961	-18	2-58,S-35/3	-1.0
	Yr	102	286	36	78	9	3	0	16	46	15	.273	.375	.325	100	2	4			.958	-16	2-61,S-38/3	-0.9
1945	Bro-N	153	555	**128**	143	29	5	1	39	**148**	42	.258	.417	.333	111	18	6			.962	9	2-153/S-1	3.6
1946	Bro-N	144	483	98	132	24	7	0	36	**137**	56	.273	**.436**	.352	124	25	8			.977	-5	2-141	3.1
1947	*Bro-N★	146	559	97	141	24	5	3	53	103	39	.252	.373	.329	85	-8	3			**.985**	7	2-146	0.8
1948	*Bos-N†	67	247	49	79	14	2	2	29	61	13	.320	.455	.417	140	18	3			.981	5	2-66	2.6
1949	Bos-N	138	506	90	144	24	5	1	42	113	41	.285	.417	.358	116	19	3			.979	-9	2-135	1.6
1950	NY-N☆	152	527	115	158	25	5	8	51	**144**	50	.300	**.460**	.412	131	35	9			.976	3	2-151	4.1
1951	*NY-N	145	515	88	127	17	2	14	43	127	63	.247	.401	.369	108	12	8	5	-1	.977	-1	*2-140	1.7
1952	StL-N	53	83	13	19	4	0	0	7	19	9	.229	.373	.277	83	-1	0			1.000	-1	2-20,M	-0.1
1953	StL-N	17	30	5	8	0	0	0	1	6	4	.267	.405	.267	80	-0	0			1.000	1	/2-8,M	0.1
Total	11	1259	4301	811	1154	185	35	29	364	996	374	.268	.410	.348	109	116	48	5		.975	4	*2-1152/S-51,3	18.4

■ **FRED STANLEY**   Stanley, Frederick Blair b: 8/13/47, Farnhamville, Iowa BR/TR, 5'10", 167 lbs. Deb: 9/11/69 C

1969	Sea-A	17	43	2	12	2	1	0	4	3	8	.279	.326	.372	96	-0	1	0	0	.962	-4	S-15/2-1	-0.3
1970	Mil-A	6	0	1	0	0	0	0	0	0	0	.—	.—	.—	—	0	0	0	0	1.000	1	/2-2	0.1
1971	Cle-A	60	129	14	29	4	0	2	12	27	25	.225	.363	.302	83	-2	1	0	0	.971	7	S-55/2-3	1.1
1972	Cle-A	6	12	1	2	1	0	0	0	2	3	.167	.286	.250	58	-1	0	0	0	.917	-3	/S-5,2-1	-0.4
	SD-N	39	85	15	17	0	2	0	5	12	19	.200	.306	.224	57	-4	1	0	0	.989	3	2-21,S-17/3	0.1
1973	NY-A	26	66	6	14	0	1	0	5	7	16	.212	.288	.288	65	-3	0	0	0	.981	5	S-21/2-3	0.3
1974	NY-A	33	38	2	7	0	0	0	3	3	2	.184	.244	.184	25	-4	1	2	-1	.973	12	S-19,2-15	0.9
1975	NY-A	117	252	34	56	9	1	0	15	21	27	.222	.285	.250	54	-15	3	1	0	.977	7	S-83,2-33/3	-0.3
1976	*NY-A	110	260	32	62	2	1	0	20	34	29	.238	.329	.273	78	-6	1	0	0	.983	-24	*S-110/2-3	-1.9
1977	*NY-A	48	46	6	12	1	0	0	7	8	6	.261	.370	.326	93	-0	3	1	0	.958	3	S-42/3-3,2	0.4
1978	*NY-A	81	160	14	35	7	0	1	9	25	31	.219	.324	.281	73	-5	0	0	0	.959	-5	S-71,2-11/3	-0.3

YEAR	TM/L	G	AB	R	H	2B	3B	HR	RBI	BB	SO	AVG	OBP	SLG	PRO+	BR/A	SB	CS	SBR	FA	FR	G/POS	TPR
1979	NY-A	57	100	9	20	1	0	2	14	5	17	.200	.238	.270	38	-9	0	1	-1	.978	13	S-31,3-16/2IO	0.5
1980	NY-A	49	86	13	18	3	0	0	5	5	5	.209	.269	.244	42	-7	0	0	0	.923	7	S-19,2-17,3	0.2
1981	*Oak-A	66	145	15	28	4	0	0	7	15	23	.193	.269	.221	44	-10	2	0	1	.986	-17	S-62/2-6	-2.2
1982	Oak-A	101	228	33	44	7	0	2	17	29	32	.193	.287	.250	51	-15	0	1	-1	.963	-20	S-98/2-2	-2.8
Total	14	816	1650	197	356	38	5	10	120	196	243	.216	.302	.263	62	-80	11	6	-0	.971	-19	S-648,2-128/3O1	-4.6

■ JIM STANLEY
Stanley, James F. b: 1889, BB/TR, 5'6", 148 lbs. Deb: 4/19/14

YEAR	TM/L	G	AB	R	H	2B	3B	HR	RBI	BB	SO	AVG	OBP	SLG	PRO+	BR/A	SB	CS	SBR	FA	FR	G/POS	TPR
1914	Chi-F	54	98	13	19	4	1	0	18	14		.194	.347	.224	53	-6	2			.878	-10	S-40/3-3,2O	-1.4

■ JOE STANLEY
Stanley, Joseph b: New Jersey Deb: 4/24/1884

YEAR	TM/L	G	AB	R	H	2B	3B	HR	RBI	BB	SO	AVG	OBP	SLG	PRO+	BR/A	SB	CS	SBR	FA	FR	G/POS	TPR
1884	Bal-U	6	21	3	5	1	0	0	0			.238	.238	.286	38	-2				.444	-2	/O-6	-0.4

■ JOE STANLEY
Stanley, Joseph Bernard b: 4/2/1881, Washington, D.C. d: 9/13/67, Detroit, Mich. BB/TR, 5'9.5", 150 lbs. Deb: 9/11/1897 F

YEAR	TM/L	G	AB	R	H	2B	3B	HR	RBI	BB	SO	AVG	OBP	SLG	PRO+	BR/A	SB	CS	SBR	FA	FR	G/POS	TPR
1897	Was-N	1	1	0	0	0	0	0	0	0	0	.000	.000	.000	-99	-0	0			.000	-0	/P-1	0.0
1902	Was-A	3	12	2	4	0	0	0	1	0		.333	.333	.333	85	-0	0			.833	-1	/O-3	-0.1
1903	Bos-N	86	308	40	77	12	5	1	47	18		.250	.306	.331	85	-6	10			.902	3	O-77/P-1,S	-0.7
1904	Bos-N	3	8	0	0	0	0	0	0	0		.000	.000	.000	-99	-2	0			.800	1	/O-3	-0.2
1905	Was-A	28	92	13	24	2	1	1	17	7		.261	.313	.337	111	1	4			.944	0	O-27	0.0
1906	Was-A	73	221	18	36	0	4	0	9	20		.163	.236	.199	38	-15	6			.934	-5	O-63/P-1	-2.6
1909	Chi-N	22	52	4	7	1	0	0	2	6		.135	.224	.154	17	-5	0			.947	-4	O-16	-1.1
Total	7	216	694	77	148	15	10	2	76	51		.213	.275	.272	66	-28	20			.918	-6	O-189/P-3,S	-4.7

■ MICKEY STANLEY
Stanley, Mitchell Jack b: 7/20/42, Grand Rapids, Mich BR/TR, 6'1", 195 lbs. Deb: 9/13/64

YEAR	TM/L	G	AB	R	H	2B	3B	HR	RBI	BB	SO	AVG	OBP	SLG	PRO+	BR/A	SB	CS	SBR	FA	FR	G/POS	TPR
1964	Det-A	4	11	3	3	0	0	0	1	0	1	.273	.273	.273	52	-1	0	0	0	1.000	-1	/O-4	-0.2
1965	Det-A	30	117	14	28	6	0	3	13	3	12	.239	.258	.368	75	-4	1	0	0	.986	3	O-29	-0.3
1966	Det-A	92	235	28	68	15	4	3	19	17	20	.289	.337	.426	115	4	2	1	0	1.000	0	O-82	0.4
1967	Det-A	145	333	38	70	7	3	7	24	29	46	.210	.273	.312	71	-12	9	2	2	.982	-8	*O-129/1-8	-2.6
1968	*Det-A	153	583	88	151	16	6	11	60	42	57	.259	.313	.364	102	1	4	3	-1	1.000	3	*O-130,1-15/S2	-0.4
1969	Det-A	149	592	73	139	28	1	16	70	52	56	.235	.299	.367	82	-15	8	4	0	.985	-19	*O-101,S-59/1	-3.6
1970	Det-A	142	568	83	143	21	11	13	47	45	56	.252	.307	.396	92	-8	10	1	2	1.000	6	*O-132/1-9	-0.7
1971	Det-A	139	401	43	117	14	5	7	41	24	44	.292	.332	.404	103	1	1	3	-2	.988	6	*O-139	0.1
1972	*Det-A	142	435	45	102	16	6	14	55	29	49	.234	.282	.395	97	-3	1	0	0	.994	6	*O-139	-0.3
1973	Det-A	157	602	81	147	23	5	17	57	48	65	.244	.300	.384	86	-13	0	4	-2	.993	13	*O-157	-1.0
1974	Det-A	99	394	40	87	13	2	8	34	26	63	.221	.271	.325	68	-17	5	3	-0	.992	6	O-91,1-12/2	-1.7
1975	Det-A	52	164	26	42	7	3	3	19	15	27	.256	.322	.390	96	-1	1	1	-0	.983	-1	O-28,1-14/3D	-0.5
1976	Det-A	84	214	34	55	17	1	4	29	14	19	.257	.303	.402	101	-0	2	0	1	.969	-2	O-38,1-17,3/S2D	-0.4
1977	Det-A	75	222	30	51	9	1	8	23	18	30	.230	.287	.387	78	-7	0	0	0	.972	-6	O-57/1-3,SD	-1.5
1978	Det-A	53	151	15	40	9	0	3	8	9	19	.265	.306	.384	90	-2	0	1	-1	.960	-6	O-34,1-12	-1.1
Total	15	1516	5022	641	1243	201	48	117	500	371	564	.248	.300	.377	89	-77	44	23	-1	.991	2	*O-1290/1-94,S3D2	-13.8

■ MIKE STANLEY
Stanley, Robert Michael b: 6/25/63, Ft.Lauderdale, Fla BR/TR, 6'1", 185 lbs. Deb: 6/24/86

YEAR	TM/L	G	AB	R	H	2B	3B	HR	RBI	BB	SO	AVG	OBP	SLG	PRO+	BR/A	SB	CS	SBR	FA	FR	G/POS	TPR
1986	Tex-A	15	30	4	10	3	0	1	1	3	7	.333	.394	.533	146	2	1	0	0	.857	-1	/3-7,C-4,OD	0.1
1987	Tex-A	78	216	34	59	8	1	6	37	31	48	.273	.347	.403	104	2	3	0	1	.980	-11	C-61,1-12/OD	-0.5
1988	Tex-A	94	249	21	57	8	0	3	27	37	62	.229	.329	.297	75	-7	0	0	0	.991	-3	C-64,D-18/13	-0.7
1989	Tex-A	67	122	9	30	3	1	1	11	12	29	.246	.324	.311	78	-3	0	0	0	.978	-4	C-25,D-21/13	-0.7
1990	Tex-A	103	189	21	47	8	1	2	19	30	25	.249	.352	.333	92	-1	1	0	0	.985	-3	C-63,D-14/31	-0.2
1991	Tex-A	95	181	25	45	13	1	3	25	34	44	.249	.373	.381	111	4	0	0	0	.980	-10	C-58,1-12/30D	-0.4
1992	NY-A	68	173	24	43	7	0	8	27	33	45	.249	.372	.428	124	7	0	0	0	.980	5	C-55/1-4,D	1.4
1993	NY-A	130	423	70	129	17	1	26	84	57	85	.305	.394	.534	152	31	1	1	-0	.996	-8	*C-122/D-2	2.9
1994	NY-A	82	290	54	87	20	0	17	57	39	56	.300	.387	.545	147	20	0	0	0	.993	-7	C-72/1-7,D	2.0
Total	9	732	1873	262	507	87	5	67	288	276	401	.271	.368	.430	118	54	7	1	2	.988	-36	C-524/D-79,130	3.9

■ JACK STANSBURY
Stansbury, John James b: 12/6/1885, Phillipsburg, N.J. d: 12/26/70, Easton, Pa. BR/TR, 5'9", 165 lbs. Deb: 6/30/18

YEAR	TM/L	G	AB	R	H	2B	3B	HR	RBI	BB	SO	AVG	OBP	SLG	PRO+	BR/A	SB	CS	SBR	FA	FR	G/POS	TPR
1918	Bos-A	20	47	3	6	1	0	0	2	6	3	.128	.241	.149	18	-5	0			.980	-0	3-18/O-2	-0.2

■ BUCK STANTON
Stanton, George Washington b: 6/19/06, Stantonsburg, N.C. d: 1/1/92, San Antonio, Tex. BL/TL, 5'10", 150 lbs. Deb: 9/5/31

YEAR	TM/L	G	AB	R	H	2B	3B	HR	RBI	BB	SO	AVG	OBP	SLG	PRO+	BR/A	SB	CS	SBR	FA	FR	G/POS	TPR
1931	StL-A	13	15	3	3	2	0	0	0	0	6	.200	.200	.333	37	-1	0			.750	-0	/O-1	-0.1

■ HARRY STANTON
Stanton, Harry Andrew b: St.Louis, Mo. TR, Deb: 10/14/00

YEAR	TM/L	G	AB	R	H	2B	3B	HR	RBI	BB	SO	AVG	OBP	SLG	PRO+	BR/A	SB	CS	SBR	FA	FR	G/POS	TPR
1900	StL-N	1	0	0	0	0	0	0	0	0	0	—	—	—		0	0			.000	0	/C-1	0.0

■ LEROY STANTON
Stanton, Leroy Bobby b: 4/10/46, Latta, S.C. BR/TR, 6'1", 195 lbs. Deb: 9/10/70

YEAR	TM/L	G	AB	R	H	2B	3B	HR	RBI	BB	SO	AVG	OBP	SLG	PRO+	BR/A	SB	CS	SBR	FA	FR	G/POS	TPR
1970	NY-N	4	4	0	1	0	1	0	1	0	0	.250	.250	.750	157	0	0	0	0	1.000	-0	/O-1	0.0
1971	NY-N	5	21	2	4	1	0	0	2	2	4	.190	.261	.238	43	-2	0	0	0	1.000	-0	/O-5	-0.2
1972	Cal-A	127	402	44	101	15	3	12	39	22	100	.251	.297	.393	110	3	2	3	-1	.983	2	*O-124	-0.2
1973	Cal-A	119	306	41	72	9	2	8	34	27	88	.235	.301	.356	92	-4	3	4	-1	.965	-7	*O-107	-1.6
1974	Cal-A	118	415	48	111	21	2	11	62	33	107	.267	.329	.407	117	8	10	8	-2	.975	4	*O-114	0.6
1975	Cal-A	137	440	67	115	20	3	14	82	52	85	.261	.347	.416	124	14	18	6	2	.961	2	*O-131/D-1	1.3
1976	Cal-A	93	231	12	44	13	1	2	25	24	57	.190	.270	.281	66	-10	2	6	-3	.985	-15	O-79/D-4	-3.3
1977	Sea-A	133	454	56	125	24	1	27	90	42	115	.275	.343	.511	131	18	0	1	-1	.953	1	O-91,D-33	1.7
1978	Sea-A	93	302	24	55	11	0	3	24	34	80	.182	.267	.248	46	-21	1	0	0	1.000	-0	D-59,O-30	-2.5
Total	9	829	2575	294	628	114	13	77	358	236	636	.244	.313	.388	103	6	36	27	-5	.972	-9	O-682/D-97	-4.2

■ TOM STANTON
Stanton, Thomas Patrick b: 10/25/1874, St.Louis, Mo. d: 1/17/57, St.Louis, Mo. BB/TR, 5'10", 175 lbs. Deb: 4/19/04

YEAR	TM/L	G	AB	R	H	2B	3B	HR	RBI	BB	SO	AVG	OBP	SLG	PRO+	BR/A	SB	CS	SBR	FA	FR	G/POS	TPR
1904	Chi-N	1	3	0	0	0	0	0	0	0	0	.000	.000	.000	-99	-1	0			1.000	-0	/C-1	-0.1

■ JOE STAPLES
Staples, Joseph F. b: Buffalo, N.Y. Deb: 9/19/1885

YEAR	TM/L	G	AB	R	H	2B	3B	HR	RBI	BB	SO	AVG	OBP	SLG	PRO+	BR/A	SB	CS	SBR	FA	FR	G/POS	TPR
1885	Buf-N	7	22	0	1	0	0	0	0	0	9	.045	.045	.045	-68	-4				.545	-3	/O-6,2-1	-0.7

■ DAVE STAPLETON
Stapleton, David Leslie b: 1/16/54, Fairhope, Ala. BR/TR, 6'1", 178 lbs. Deb: 5/30/80

YEAR	TM/L	G	AB	R	H	2B	3B	HR	RBI	BB	SO	AVG	OBP	SLG	PRO+	BR/A	SB	CS	SBR	FA	FR	G/POS	TPR
1980	Bos-A	106	449	61	144	33	5	7	46	13	32	.321	.341	.463	112	6	3	2	-0	.979	10	2-94/1-8,O3D	2.1
1981	Bos-A	93	355	45	101	17	1	10	42	21	22	.285	.326	.423	108	3	0	4	-2	.948	-7	S-33,3-25,21/D	-0.4
1982	Bos-A	150	538	66	142	28	1	14	65	31	40	.264	.308	.398	87	-10	2	4	-2	.991	2	*1-106,S-27/230D	-1.3
1983	Bos-A	151	542	54	134	31	1	10	66	40	44	.247	.301	.363	76	-18	1	1	-0	.993	-2	*1-145/2-5	-2.9
1984	Bos-A	13	39	4	9	2	0	0	3	3	3	.231	.286	.282	55	-2	0	0	0	1.000	1	1-10/D-1	-0.2
1985	Bos-A	30	66	4	15	6	0	0	2	4	11	.227	.271	.318	58	-4	0	0	0	1.000	1	2-14/1-8,D	-0.2
1986	*Bos-A	39	39	4	5	1	0	0	3	2	10	.128	.171	.154	-11	-6	0	0	0	1.000	3	1-29/2-6,3	-0.4
Total	7	582	2028	238	550	118	8	41	224	114	162	.271	.312	.398	90	-31	6	11	-5	.993	7	1-318,2-151/S3DO	-3.3

■ WILLIE STARGELL
Stargell, Wilver Dornel b: 3/6/40, Earlsboro, Okla. BL/TL, 6'2.5", 225 lbs. Deb: 9/16/62 CH

YEAR	TM/L	G	AB	R	H	2B	3B	HR	RBI	BB	SO	AVG	OBP	SLG	PRO+	BR/A	SB	CS	SBR	FA	FR	G/POS	TPR
1962	Pit-N	10	31	1	9	3	0	0	4	0	1	.290	.353	.452	114	1	1	0	-1	.929	-0	/O-9	-0.1
1963	Pit-N	108	304	34	74	11	6	11	47	19	85	.243	.292	.428	104	1	0	2	-1	.953	-8	O-65,1-16	-1.3
1964	Pit-N★	117	421	53	115	19	7	21	78	17	92	.273	.305	.501	123	11	1	1	0	.900	-7	O-59,1-50	-0.2
1965	Pit-N★	144	533	68	145	25	8	27	107	39	127	.272	.330	.501	130	19	1	1	0	.965	0	O-137/1-7	1.3
1966	Pit-N★	140	485	84	153	30	6	33	102	48	109	.315	.384	.581	164	8/RA	1	3	1	.945	-4	*O-127,1-15	3.0
1967	Pit-N	134	462	54	125	18	6	20	73	67	103	.271	.367	.465	136	23	1	0	1	.938	-2	O-98,1-37	1.5

YEAR	TM/L	G	AB	R	H	2B	3B	HR	RBI	BB	SO	AVG	OBP	SLG	PRO+	BR/A	SB	CS	SBR	FA	FR	G/POS	TPR
1968	Pit-N	128	435	57	103	15	1	24	67	47	105	.237	.320	.441	129	14	5	0	2	.945	-3	*O-113,1-13	0.7
1969	Pit-N	145	522	89	160	31	6	29	92	61	120	.307	.385	.556	164	44	1	0	0	.970	-2	*O-116,1-23	3.4
1970	*Pit-N★	136	474	70	125	18	3	31	85	44	119	.264	.333	.511	125	14	0	1	-1	.976	7	*O-138	1.5
1971	*Pit-N★	141	511	104	151	26	0	**48**	125	83	154	.295	.401	.628	188	**59**	0	0	0	.984	3	*O-138	**5.8**
1972	*Pit-N★	138	495	75	145	28	2	33	112	65	129	.293	.377	.558	166	42	1	1	-0	.984	-13	*1-101,O-32	2.0
1973	Pit-N★	148	522	106	156	**43**	3	**44**	**119**	80	129	.299	.395	**.646**	**189**	**61**	0	0	0	.975	7	*O-142	**6.3**
1974	*Pit-N	140	508	90	153	37	4	25	96	87	106	.301	.409	.537	**169**	49	0	2	-1	.967	2	*O-135/1-1	4.5
1975	*Pit-N	124	461	71	136	32	2	22	90	58	109	.295	.377	.516	147	29	0	0	0	.992	-10	*1-122	1.1
1976	Pit-N	117	428	54	110	20	3	20	65	50	101	.257	.342	.458	124	13	2	0	1	.988	-10	*1-111	-0.5
1977	Pit-N	63	186	29	51	12	0	13	35	31	55	.274	.386	.548	144	12	0	1	-1	.986	-1	1-55	0.7
1978	Pit-N★	122	390	60	115	18	2	28	97	50	93	.295	.385	.567	156	29	3	2	-0	.994	-2	*1-112	2.2
1979	*Pit-N	126	424	60	119	19	0	32	82	47	105	.281	.357	.552	138	21	0	1	-1	**.997**	-6	*1-113	0.8
1980	Pit-N	67	202	28	53	10	1	11	38	26	52	.262	.352	.485	129	8	0	0	0	.992	0	1-54	0.5
1981	Pit-N	38	60	2	17	4	0	5	9	5	9	.283	.338	.350	93	-1	0	0	0	1.000	-2	/1-9	-0.4
1982	Pit-N	74	73	6	17	4	0	3	17	10	24	.233	.325	.411	102	0	0	0	0	1.000	0	/1-8	0.7
Total	21	2360	7927	1195	2232	423	55	475	1540	937	1936	.282	.363	.529	147	488	17	16	-5	.961	-51	*O-1296,1-848	32.8

■ MATT STARK
Stark, Matthew Scott b: 1/21/65, Whittier, Cal. BR/TR, 6'4", 225 lbs. Deb: 4/8/87

YEAR	TM/L	G	AB	R	H	2B	3B	HR	RBI	BB	SO	AVG	OBP	SLG	PRO+	BR/A	SB	CS	SBR	FA	FR	G/POS	TPR
1987	Tor-A	5	12	0	1	0	0	0	0	0	0	.083	.083	.083	-55	-3	0	0	0	1.000	1	/C-5	-0.2
1990	Chi-A	8	16	0	4	1	0	0	3	1	6	.250	.294	.313	71	-1	0	0	0	.000	0	/D-6	-0.1
Total	2	13	28	0	5	1	0	0	3	1	6	.179	.207	.214	15	-3	0	0	0	1.000	1	/D-6,C-5	-0.3

■ DOLLY STARK
Stark, Monroe Randolph b: 1/19/1885, Ripley, Miss. d: 12/1/24, Memphis, Tenn. BR/TR, 5'9", 160 lbs. Deb: 9/12/09

YEAR	TM/L	G	AB	R	H	2B	3B	HR	RBI	BB	SO	AVG	OBP	SLG	PRO+	BR/A	SB	CS	SBR	FA	FR	G/POS	TPR
1909	Cle-A	19	60	4	12	0	0	0	1	6		.200	.273	.200	48	-3	4			.875	-1	S-19	-1.5
1910	Bro-N	30	103	7	17	3	0	0	8	7	19	.165	.225	.194	23	-10	2			.893	-1	S-30	-1.1
1911	Bro-N	70	193	25	57	4	1	0	19	20	24	.295	.370	.326	100	1	6			.910	-3	S-34,2-18/3	-0.1
1912	Bro-N	8	22	2	4	0	0	0	2	1	3	.182	.217	.182	10	-3	2			.892	0	/S-7	-0.2
Total	4	127	378	38	90	7	1	0	30	34	46	.238	.308	.262	66	-15	14			.896	-14	/S-90,2-18,3	-2.9

■ GEORGE STARNAGLE
Starnagle, George Henry (b: George Henry Steuernagel)
b: 10/6/1873, Belleville, Ill. d: 2/15/46, Belleville, Ill. BR/TR, 5'11", 175 lbs. Deb: 9/14/02

YEAR	TM/L	G	AB	R	H	2B	3B	HR	RBI	BB	SO	AVG	OBP	SLG	PRO+	BR/A	SB	CS	SBR	FA	FR	G/POS	TPR
1902	Cle-A	1	3	0	0	0	0	0	0	0		.000	.000	.000	-99	-1	0			.667	-1	/C-1	-0.1

■ CHARLIE STARR
Starr, Charles Watkin b: 8/30/1878, Pike Co., Ohio d: 10/18/37, Pasadena, Cal. TR , Deb: 4/29/05

YEAR	TM/L	G	AB	R	H	2B	3B	HR	RBI	BB	SO	AVG	OBP	SLG	PRO+	BR/A	SB	CS	SBR	FA	FR	G/POS	TPR
1905	StL-A	26	97	9	20	0	0	0	6	7		.206	.260	.206	51	-5	0			.940	-4	2-18/3-6	-1.0
1908	Pit-N	20	59	8	11	2	0	0	8	13		.186	.342	.220	80	-0	6			.926	-5	2-12/S-5,3	-0.7
1909	Bos-N	61	216	16	48	2	3	0	6	31		.222	.333	.259	80	-4	7			.931	-9	2-54/S-6,3	-1.5
	Phi-N	3	3	0	0	0	0	0	0	0		.000	.000	.000	-99	-1	0			.000	0	H	-0.1
	Yr	64	219	16	48	2	3	0	6	31		.219	.329	.256	78	-4	7			.931	-9	2-54/S-6,3	-1.6
Total	3	110	375	33	79	4	3	0	20	51		.211	.315	.237	72	-10	13			.932	-18	/2-84,S-11,3	-3.3

■ CHICK STARR
Starr, William b: 2/26/11, Brooklyn, N.Y. d: 8/12/91, LaJolla, Cal. BR/TR, 6'1", 175 lbs. Deb: 8/23/35

YEAR	TM/L	G	AB	R	H	2B	3B	HR	RBI	BB	SO	AVG	OBP	SLG	PRO+	BR/A	SB	CS	SBR	FA	FR	G/POS	TPR
1935	Was-A	12	24	1	5	0	0	0	1	0	1	.208	.208	.208	8	-3	0	0	0	.971	2	C-12	-0.1
1936	Was-A	1	0	0	0	0	0	0	0	0	0	—	—	—	—	0	0	0	0	.000	0	/C-1	0.0
Total	2	13	24	1	5	0	0	0	1	0	1	.208	.208	.208	8	-3	0	0	0	.971	2	/C-13	-0.1

■ JOE START
Start, Joseph "Old Reliable" or "Rocks" b: 10/14/1842, New York, N.Y. d: 3/27/27, Providence, R.I. BL/TL, 5'9", 165 lbs. Deb: 5/18/1871 M

YEAR	TM/L	G	AB	R	H	2B	3B	HR	RBI	BB	SO	AVG	OBP	SLG	PRO+	BR/A	SB	CS	SBR	FA	FR	G/POS	TPR
1871	Mut-n	33	161	35	58	5	1	1	34	3	0	.360	.372	.422	140	10	4					*1-33	0.7
1872	Mut-n	55	280	62	74	6	0	0	49	0	0	.264	.264	.286	74	-7						*1-55	-0.3
1873	Mut-n	53	251	42	67	11	3	1	28	4	0	.267	.278	.347	83	-5						*1-53/O-2M	-0.1
1874	Mut-n	63	306	67	94	14	4	2		4		.307	.316	.399	122	7						*1-63	0.5
1875	Mut-n	68	309	56	87	9	5	4		3		.282	.288	.382	123	6						*1-69	0.5
1876	NY-N	56	264	40	73	6	0	0	21	1	2	.277	.279	.299	107	3				.964	3	*1-56	0.4
1877	Har-N	60	271	55	90	3	6	1	21	6	2	.332	.347	.399	150	16				.964	-2	*1-60	1.2
1878	Chi-N	61	285	58	**100**	12	5	1	27	2	3	.351	.355	.439	150	14				.957	-2	*1-61	0.9
1879	Pro-N	66	317	70	101	11	5	2	37	7	4	.319	.333	.404	144	15				.973	0	*1-65/O-1	1.2
1880	Pro-N	82	345	53	96	14	6	0	27	13	20	.278	.304	.354	126	10				.971	-3	*1-82	-0.1
1881	Pro-N	79	348	56	114	12	6	0	29	9	7	.328	.345	.397	135	13				.963	-4	*1-79	0.2
1882	Pro-N	82	356	58	117	8	10	0	48	11	7	.329	.349	.407	142	16				.974	2	*1-82	0.8
1883	Pro-N	87	370	63	105	16	7	1	57	22	16	.284	.324	.373	108	4				.957	-1	*1-87	-0.5
1884	*Pro-N	93	381	80	105	10	5	2	32	35	25	.276	.337	.344	117	9				**.980**	1	*1-93	-0.1
1885	Pro-N	101	374	47	103	11	4	0	41	39	10	.275	.344	.326	122	11				.972	1	*1-101	0.0
1886	Was-N	31	122	10	27	4	1	0	17	5	13	.221	.252	.270	63	-5	4			.973	-2	/1-31	-1.0
Total	5 n	272	1307	262	380	45	13	8	111	14		.291	.298	.363	106	10	8					1-273/O-2	1.3
Total	11	798	3433	590	1031	107	55	7	357	150	109	.300	.330	.370	127	104	4			.968	-7	1-797/O-1	3.0

■ DAVE STATON
Staton, David Alan b: 4/12/68, Seattle, Wash. BR/TR, 6'5", 215 lbs. Deb: 9/8/93

YEAR	TM/L	G	AB	R	H	2B	3B	HR	RBI	BB	SO	AVG	OBP	SLG	PRO+	BR/A	SB	CS	SBR	FA	FR	G/POS	TPR
1993	SD-N	17	42	7	11	3	0	5	9	3	12	.262	.326	.690	161	3	0	0	0	1.000	3	1-12	0.5
1994	SD-N	29	66	6	12	2	0	4	6	10	18	.182	.289	.394	77	-2	0	0	0	1.000	4	1-20	0.0
Total	2	46	108	13	23	5	0	9	15	13	30	.213	.303	.509	109	1	0	0	0	1.000	7	/1-32	0.5

■ JOE STATON
Staton, Joseph b: 3/8/48, Seattle, Wash. BL/TL, 6'3", 175 lbs. Deb: 9/5/72

YEAR	TM/L	G	AB	R	H	2B	3B	HR	RBI	BB	SO	AVG	OBP	SLG	PRO+	BR/A	SB	CS	SBR	FA	FR	G/POS	TPR
1972	Det-A	6	2	1	0	0	0	0	0	0	1	.000	.000	.000	-97	-0	0	1	-1	1.000	0	/1-2	-0.1
1973	Det-A	9	17	2	4	0	0	0	3	0	3	.235	.235	.235	31	-2	1	0	0	.969	2	/1-5	0.0
Total	2	15	19	3	4	0	0	0	3	0	4	.211	.211	.211	18	-2	1	1	-0	.973	2	/1-7	-0.1

■ JIGGER STATZ
Statz, Arnold John b: 10/20/1897, Waukegan, Ill. d: 3/16/88, Corona Del Mar, Cal. BR/TR, 5'7.5", 150 lbs. Deb: 7/30/19

YEAR	TM/L	G	AB	R	H	2B	3B	HR	RBI	BB	SO	AVG	OBP	SLG	PRO+	BR/A	SB	CS	SBR	FA	FR	G/POS	TPR
1919	NY-N	21	60	9	18	2	1	0	6	3	8	.300	.333	.367	112	1	2			.977	-1	O-18/2-5	-0.1
1920	NY-N	16	30	0	4	0	1	0	5	2	9	.133	.188	.200	11	-3	0	1	-1	.944	-3	O-12	-0.8
	Bos-A	2	3	0	0	0	0	0	0	0	0	.000	.000	.000	-99	-1	0			1.000	-1	/O-2	-0.2
1922	Chi-N	110	462	77	137	19	5	1	34	41	31	.297	.355	.366	85	-10	16	13	-3	.959	9	*O-110	-1.1
1923	Chi-N	154	655	110	209	33	8	10	70	56	42	.319	.355	.440	114	14	29	23	-5	.975	18	*O-154	1.5
1924	Chi-N	135	549	69	152	22	5	3	49	37	50	.277	.325	.352	80	-15	13	9	-2	.961	15	*O-131/2-1	-1.1
1925	Chi-N	38	148	21	38	6	3	0	14	11	16	.257	.317	.378	76	-6	4	0	0	.943	2	O-37	-0.5
1927	Bro-N	130	507	64	139	24	7	1	21	26	43	.274	.310	.355	77	-17	10			.990	15	*O-122/2-1	-0.9
1928	Bro-N	77	171	28	40	8	1	0	18	21	12	.234	.311	.292	59	-10	3			.965	-6	O-52/2-1	-1.8
Total	8	683	2585	376	737	114	31	17	215	194	211	.285	.337	.373	87	-47	77	<u>46</u>		.969	48	O-638/2-8	-5.0

■ RUSTY STAUB
Staub, Daniel Joseph b: 4/1/44, New Orleans, La. BL/TR, 6'2", 200 lbs. Deb: 4/9/63 C

YEAR	TM/L	G	AB	R	H	2B	3B	HR	RBI	BB	SO	AVG	OBP	SLG	PRO+	BR/A	SB	CS	SBR	FA	FR	G/POS	TPR
1963	Hou-N	150	513	43	115	17	4	6	45	59	58	.224	.310	.308	84	-10	0	0	0	.989	-1	*1-109,O-49	-1.9
1964	Hou-N	89	292	26	63	10	2	8	35	21	31	.216	.275	.346	78	-9	1	1	-0	.992	-1	1-49,O-38	-1.5
1965	Hou-N	131	410	43	105	20	1	14	63	52	57	.256	.343	.412	120	11	3	0	1	.951	-3	*O-112/1-1	1.1
1966	Hou-N	153	554	60	155	28	3	13	81	58	61	.280	.349	.412	119	14	2	1	0	.962	9	*O-148/1-1	1.7
1967	Hou-N★	149	546	71	182	**44**	1	10	74	60	47	.333	.402	.473	155	40	0	4	-2	.962	7	*O-144	3.9
1968	Hou-N★	161	591	54	172	37	1	6	72	73	57	.291	.376	.387	132	26	2	0	1	.992	-1	*1-147,O-15	1.5

YEAR	TM/L	G	AB	R	H	2B	3B	HR	RBI	BB	SO	AVG	OBP	SLG	PRO+	BR/A	SB	CS	SBR	FA	FR	G/POS	TPR
1969	Mon-N☆	158	549	89	166	26	5	29	79	110	61	.302	.427	.526	165	52	3	4	-2	.966	7	*O-156	5.0
1970	Mon-N★	160	569	98	156	23	7	30	94	112	93	.274	.396	.497	138	33	12	11	-3	.985	11	*O-160	3.3
1971	Mon-N☆	162	599	94	186	34	6	19	97	74	42	.311	.394	.482	147	38	9	5	-0	.945	5	*O-162	3.6
1972	NY-N	66	239	32	70	11	0	9	38	31	13	.293	.379	.452	139	13	0	1	-1	.982	0	O-65	1.0
1973	*NY-N	152	585	77	163	36	1	15	76	74	52	.279	.363	.421	118	15	1	1	-0	.978	11	*O-152	1.9
1974	NY-N	151	561	65	145	22	2	19	78	77	39	.258	.351	.406	113	10	2	1	-0	.983	9	*O-147	1.3
1975	NY-N	155	574	93	162	30	4	19	105	77	55	.282	.376	.448	134	27	2	0	1	.986	8	*O-153	3.0
1976	Det-A★	161	589	73	176	28	3	15	96	83	49	.299	.382	.433	136	29	3	1	0	.970	-6	*O-126,D-36	1.8
1977	Det-A	158	623	84	173	34	3	22	101	59	47	.278	.341	.448	107	6	1	1	0	.000	0	*D-156	0.1
1978	Det-A	162	642	75	175	30	1	24	121	76	35	.273	.352	.435	117	15	3	1	0	.000	0	*D-162	1.0
1979	Det-A	68	246	32	58	12	1	9	40	32	18	.236	.336	.402	95	-2	0	0	0	.000	0	D-66	-0.3
	Mon-N	38	86	9	23	3	0	3	14	14	10	.267	.370	.407	113	2	0	0	0	.994	-2	1-22/O-1	-0.2
1980	Tex-A	109	340	42	102	23	2	9	55	39	18	.300	.375	.459	131	15	1	1	0	.977	-2	D-57,1-30,O	0.8
1981	NY-N	70	161	9	51	9	0	5	21	22	12	.317	.402	.466	148	11	1	0	0	.989	-2	1-41	0.7
1982	NY-N	112	219	11	53	9	0	3	27	24	10	.242	.317	.324	80	-5	0	0	0	.959	2	O-27,1-18	-0.5
1983	NY-N	104	115	5	34	6	0	3	28	14	10	.296	.377	.426	123	4	0	0	0	.976	-1	/1-5,O-5	0.3
1984	NY-N	78	72	2	19	4	0	1	18	4	9	.264	.303	.361	87	-1	0	0	0	1.000	-0	/1-3	-0.2
1985	NY-N	54	45	2	12	3	0	1	8	4	6	.267	.400	.400	128	5	0	0	0	1.000	-0	/O-1	0.2
Total	23	2951	9720	1189	2716	499	47	292	1466	1255	888	.279	.366	.431	125	334	47	33	-6	.969	55	*O-1675,D-477,1	27.6

■ ECKY STEARNS
Stearns, Daniel Eckford b: 10/17/1861, Buffalo, N.Y. d: 6/28/44, Glendale, Cal. BL/TR, 6'1", 185 lbs. Deb: 8/17/1880

YEAR	TM/L	G	AB	R	H	2B	3B	HR	RBI	BB	SO	AVG	OBP	SLG	PRO+	BR/A	SB	CS	SBR	FA	FR	G/POS	TPR
1880	Buf-N	28	104	8	19	6	1	0	13	3	23	.183	.206	.260	55	-5				.774	-9	O-20/C-8,3S	-1.4
1881	Det-N	3	11	1	1	1	0	0	0	0	2	.091	.091	.182	-16	-1				.714	-1	/S-3	-0.2
1882	Cin-a	49	214	28	55	10	2	0		6		.257	.277	.322	96	-1				.931	-2	1-35,O-12/2S	-0.7
1883	Bal-a	93	382	54	94	10	9	1	**34**			.246	.268	.327	101	1				.947	3	*1-92/O-1	-0.5
1884	Bal-a	100	396	61	94	12	3	3		28		.237	.298	.306	94	-3				.949	4	*1-100/2-1	-1.0
1885	Bal-a	67	253	40	47	3	8	1		38		.186	.306	.273	85	-2				.973	1	1-63/O-3,C	-0.8
	Buf-N	30	105	7	21	6	1	0	9	8	23	.200	.257	.276	70	-3				.821	-7	S-19,1-12/C	-1.1
1889	KC-a	139	560	96	160	24	12	3	87	56	69	.286	.351	.387	104	1	67			.967	0	*1-135/3-4	0.6
Total	7	509	2025	295	491	72	36	8	109	173	117	.242	.306	.325	94	-14	67			.956	-10	1-437/O-36,SC32	-6.4

■ JOHN STEARNS
Stearns, John Hardin b: 8/21/51, Denver, Col. BR/TR, 6', 185 lbs. Deb: 9/22/74 C

YEAR	TM/L	G	AB	R	H	2B	3B	HR	RBI	BB	SO	AVG	OBP	SLG	PRO+	BR/A	SB	CS	SBR	FA	FR	G/POS	TPR
1974	Phi-N	1	2	0	1	0	0	0	0	0	0	.500	.500	.500	173	0	0	0	0	1.000	-1	/C-1	0.0
1975	NY-N	59	169	25	32	5	1	3	10	17	15	.189	.271	.284	57	-10	4	1	1	.994	6	C-54	-0.1
1976	NY-N	32	103	13	27	6	0	2	10	16	11	.262	.367	.379	119	3	1	2	-1	.987	3	C-30	0.7
1977	NY-N★	139	431	52	108	25	1	12	55	77	76	.251	.373	.397	112	10	9	8	-2	.982	4	*C-127/1-6	1.5
1978	NY-N	143	477	65	126	24	1	15	73	70	57	.264	.368	.413	122	16	25	13	-0	.985	-3	*C-141/3-1	1.7
1979	NY-N☆	155	538	58	131	29	2	9	66	52	57	.243	.315	.355	86	-11	15	15	-5	.983	5	*C-121,1-16,3/O	-0.8
1980	NY-N★	91	319	42	91	25	1	0	45	33	24	.285	.354	.370	105	3	7	3	0	.985	5	C-74,1-16/3	1.0
1981	NY-N	80	273	25	74	12	1	1	24	24	17	.271	.330	.333	90	-3	12	2	2	.983	-2	C-66/1-9,3	-0.2
1982	NY-N★	98	352	46	103	25	3	4	28	30	35	.293	.352	.415	114	7	17	7	1	.987	-7	C-81,3-12	0.4
1983	NY-N	4	0	2	0	0	0	0	0	—	—	—	—	—	—	0	0	0	0	.000	0	/R	—
1984	NY-N	8	17	6	3	1	0	0	1	4	2	.176	.333	.235	63	-1	1	0	0	1.000	-1	/C-4,1-2	-0.1
Total	11	810	2681	334	696	152	10	46	312	323	294	.260	.345	.375	102	13	91	51	-3	.985	10	C-699/1-49,3O	4.1

■ JOHN STEDRONSKY
Stedronsky, John b: Troy, N.Y. Deb: 9/25/1879

YEAR	TM/L	G	AB	R	H	2B	3B	HR	RBI	BB	SO	AVG	OBP	SLG	PRO+	BR/A	SB	CS	SBR	FA	FR	G/POS	TPR
1879	Chi-N	4	12	0	1	0	0	0	0	0	3	.083	.083	.083	-42	-2				.789	1	/3-4	0.0

■ FARMER STEELMAN
Steelman, Morris James b: 6/29/1875, Millville, N.J. d: 9/16/44, Merchantville, N.J. TR , Deb: 9/15/1899

YEAR	TM/L	G	AB	R	H	2B	3B	HR	RBI	BB	SO	AVG	OBP	SLG	PRO+	BR/A	SB	CS	SBR	FA	FR	G/POS	TPR
1899	Lou-N	4	15	2	1	0	1	0	2	2		.067	.176	.200	3	-2	0			.929	-2	/C-4	-0.3
1900	Bro-N	1	4	0	0	0	0	0	0	0		.000	.000	.000	-94	-1	0			1.000	0	/C-1	-0.1
1901	Bro-N	1	3	0	1	0	0	0	0	0		.333	.333	.333	91	-0	0			.875	1	/C-1	0.1
	Phi-A	27	88	5	23	2	0	0	7	10		.261	.350	.284	74	-3	4			1.000	2	C-14,O-12	0.1
1902	Phi-A	10	32	1	6	1	0	0	6	2		.188	.235	.219	25	-3	2			1.000	1	/C-5,O-5	-0.2
Total	4	43	142	8	31	3	1	0	15	14		.218	.297	.254	52	-9	6			.985	2	/C-25,O-17	-0.5

■ JIM STEELS
Steels, James Earl b: 5/30/61, Jackson, Miss. BL/TL, 5'10", 185 lbs. Deb: 4/6/87

YEAR	TM/L	G	AB	R	H	2B	3B	HR	RBI	BB	SO	AVG	OBP	SLG	PRO+	BR/A	SB	CS	SBR	FA	FR	G/POS	TPR
1987	SD-N	62	68	9	13	1	1	0	6	11	14	.191	.304	.235	47	-5	3	2	-0	.960	-6	O-28	-1.2
1988	Tex-A	36	53	4	10	1	0	0	5	0	15	.189	.189	.208	11	-6	2	0	1	1.000	-5	O-17/1-7,D	-1.1
1989	SF-N	13	12	0	1	0	0	0	0	2	4	.083	.214	.083	-12	-2	0	0	0	1.000	-0	/1-3,O-1	-0.2
Total	3	111	133	13	24	2	1	0	11	13	33	.180	.253	.211	28	-13	5	2	0	.973	-11	/O-46,1-10,D	-2.5

■ GENE STEERE
Steere, Frederick Eugene b: 8/16/1872, S.Scituate, R.I. d: 3/13/42, San Francisco, Cal Deb: 8/29/1894

YEAR	TM/L	G	AB	R	H	2B	3B	HR	RBI	BB	SO	AVG	OBP	SLG	PRO+	BR/A	SB	CS	SBR	FA	FR	G/POS	TPR
1894	Pit-N	10	39	3	8	0	0	0	4	2	1	.205	.244	.205	9	-6	2			.896	-2	S-10	-0.6

■ JOHN STEFERO
Stefero, John Robert b: 9/22/59, Sumter, S.C. BL/TR, 5'8", 185 lbs. Deb: 6/24/83

YEAR	TM/L	G	AB	R	H	2B	3B	HR	RBI	BB	SO	AVG	OBP	SLG	PRO+	BR/A	SB	CS	SBR	FA	FR	G/POS	TPR
1983	Bal-A	9	11	2	5	1	0	0	4	3	2	.455	.571	.545	213	2	0	0	0	.920	0	/C-9	0.2
1986	Bal-A	52	120	14	28	2	0	2	13	16	25	.233	.324	.300	72	-4	0	1	-1	.984	-2	C-50/2-1	-0.4
1987	Mon-N	18	56	4	11	0	0	1	3	3	17	.196	.237	.250	28	-6	0	0	0	.981	-0	C-17	-0.5
Total	3	79	187	20	44	3	0	3	20	22	44	.235	.316	.299	67	-8	0	1	-1	.979	-2	/C-76,2-1	-0.7

■ DAVE STEGMAN
Stegman, David William b: 1/30/54, Inglewood, Cal. BR/TR, 5'11", 190 lbs. Deb: 9/4/78

YEAR	TM/L	G	AB	R	H	2B	3B	HR	RBI	BB	SO	AVG	OBP	SLG	PRO+	BR/A	SB	CS	SBR	FA	FR	G/POS	TPR
1978	Det-A	8	14	3	4	2	0	1	3	1	2	.286	.333	.643	164	1	0	0	0	1.000	-2	/O-7	-0.1
1979	Det-A	12	31	6	6	0	0	2	5	2	3	.194	.242	.484	88	-1	1	1	-0	1.000	1	O-12	-0.1
1980	Det-A	65	130	12	23	5	0	2	9	14	23	.177	.257	.262	41	-10	1	1	-0	.988	-13	O-57/D-2	-2.6
1982	NY-A	2	0	0	0	0	0	0	0	0	0	—	—	—	—	0	0	0	0	.000	0	/D-1	0.0
1983	Chi-A	30	53	5	9	2	0	0	4	10	9	.170	.302	.208	42	-4	0	1	-1	1.000	-7	O-29	-1.2
1984	Chi-A	55	92	13	24	1	2	2	11	4	18	.261	.306	.380	85	-2	3	0	1	.985	-9	O-46/D-3	-1.1
Total	6	172	320	39	66	10	2	8	32	31	55	.206	.280	.325	64	-16	5	3	-0	.991	-31	O-151/D-6	-5.1

■ JUSTIN STEIN
Stein, Justin Marion "Ott" b: 8/9/11, St.Louis, Mo. d: 5/1/92, Creve Coeur, Mo. BR/TR, 5'11", 180 lbs. Deb: 5/28/38

YEAR	TM/L	G	AB	R	H	2B	3B	HR	RBI	BB	SO	AVG	OBP	SLG	PRO+	BR/A	SB	CS	SBR	FA	FR	G/POS	TPR
1938	Phi-N	11	39	6	10	0	1	0	2	2	4	.256	.293	.308	67	-2	0			.880	0	/3-7,2-3	-0.2
	Cin-N	11	18	3	6	1	0	0	1	0	1	.333	.333	.389	101	-0	0			.857	1	/S-7,2-2	-0.1
	Yr	22	57	9	16	1	1	0	3	2	5	.281	.305	.333	78	-2	0			.857	1	/3-7,S-7,2	-0.1

■ BILL STEIN
Stein, William Allen b: 1/21/47, Battle Creek, Mich. BR/TR, 5'10", 170 lbs. Deb: 9/6/72

YEAR	TM/L	G	AB	R	H	2B	3B	HR	RBI	BB	SO	AVG	OBP	SLG	PRO+	BR/A	SB	CS	SBR	FA	FR	G/POS	TPR
1972	StL-N	14	35	2	11	2	0	0	3	0	7	.314	.314	.543	141	2	1	0	0	1.000	-3	/3-4,O-4	-0.2
1973	StL-N	32	55	4	12	2	0	0	2	7	18	.218	.306	.255	57	-3	0	0	0	1.000	-2	O-10/1-2,3	-0.5
1974	Chi-A	13	43	5	12	1	0	1	5	7	8	.279	.380	.302	96	-0	0	0	0	.871	-2	3-11/D-2	-0.2
1975	Chi-A	76	226	23	61	7	1	3	21	18	32	.270	.327	.350	90	-3	2	2	-1	.974	3	2-28,3-24,D/O	-0.3
1976	Chi-A	117	392	32	105	15	2	4	36	22	67	.268	.310	.347	92	-5	4	2	0	.960	-11	2-58,3-58/1SOD	-1.3
1977	Sea-A	151	556	53	144	26	5	13	67	29	75	.259	.302	.394	89	-10	3	4	-2	.964	-11	*3-147/S-2,D	-2.4
1978	Sea-A	144	403	41	105	24	4	4	37	37	56	.261	.323	.370	95	-1	1	0	0	.929	-6	3-111/D-1	-1.0
1979	Sea-A	88	250	28	62	9	2	7	27	19	28	.248	.301	.384	82	-7	1	1	-0	.959	11	3-67,2-17/S	0.3
1980	Sea-A	67	198	16	53	5	1	5	27	16	25	.268	.326	.379	92	-2	1	1	-0	.972	5	3-34,2-14/1D	0.3

YEAR	TM/L	G	AB	R	H	2B	3B	HR	RBI	BB	SO	AVG	OBP	SLG	PRO+	BR/A	SB	CS	SBR	FA	FR	G/POS	TPR
1981	Tex-A	53	115	21	38	6	0	2	22	7	15	.330	.369	.435	138	5	1	2	-1	1.000	1	1-20/O-8,32S	0.4
1982	Tex-A	85	184	14	44	8	0	1	16	12	23	.239	.293	.299	66	-8	0	0	0	.957	3	2-34,3-28/S1OD	-0.5
1983	Tex-A	78	232	21	72	15	1	2	33	8	31	.310	.333	.409	105	1	2	3	-1	.975	0	2-32,1-23,3/D	0.0
1984	Tex-A	27	43	3	12	1	0	0	3	5	9	.279	.354	.302	81	-1	0	0	0	.967	-3	2-11/1-3,3D	-0.3
1985	Tex-A	44	79	5	20	3	1	1	12	1	15	.253	.272	.354	69	-3	0	0	0	.952	1	3-11/1-8,2OD	-0.3
Total	14	959	2811	268	751	122	18	44	311	186	413	.267	.316	.370	91	-37	16	16	-5	.950	-13	3-516,2-200/1DOS	-5.6

■ TERRY STEINBACH
Steinbach, Terry Lee   b: 3/2/62, New Ulm, Minn.   BR/TR, 6'1", 195 lbs.   Deb: 9/12/86

YEAR	TM/L	G	AB	R	H	2B	3B	HR	RBI	BB	SO	AVG	OBP	SLG	PRO+	BR/A	SB	CS	SBR	FA	FR	G/POS	TPR
1986	Oak-A	6	15	3	5	0	0	2	4	1	0	.333	.375	.733	208	2	0	0	0	.962	-0	/C-5	0.2
1987	Oak-A	122	391	66	111	16	3	16	56	32	66	.284	.352	.463	122	12	1	2	-1	.986	-12	*C-107,3-10/1D	0.6
1988	*Oak-A★	104	351	42	93	19	1	9	51	33	47	.265	.338	.402	110	5	3	0	1	.983	5	C-84/3-9,10D	1.6
1989	*Oak-A★	130	454	37	124	13	1	7	42	30	66	.273	.321	.352	93	-5	1	2	-1	.985	-7	*C-103,O-14,1/3D	-0.7
1990	*Oak-A	114	379	32	95	15	2	9	57	19	66	.251	.294	.372	89	-7	0	1	-1	.988	-4	C-83,D-25/1	-0.7
1991	Oak-A	129	456	50	125	31	1	6	67	22	70	.274	.318	.386	99	-2	2	3	-1	.980	-24	*C-117/1-9,D	-2.0
1992	*Oak-A	128	438	48	122	20	1	12	53	45	58	.279	.347	.411	118	10	2	3	-1	.985	-4	*C-124/1-5,D	1.2
1993	Oak-A★	104	389	47	111	19	1	10	43	25	65	.285	.333	.416	107	3	3	3	-1	.989	-22	C-86,1-15/D	-1.6
1994	Oak-A	103	369	51	105	21	2	11	57	26	62	.285	.332	.442	106	2	2	1	0	.998	-2	C-93/1-6,D	0.5
Total	9	940	3242	376	891	154	12	82	430	233	500	.275	.330	.406	106	20	14	14	-4	.987	-69	C-802/D-60,130	-0.9

■ HANK STEINBACHER
Steinbacher, Henry John   b: 3/22/13, Sacramento, Cal.   d: 4/3/77, Sacramento, Cal.   BL/TR, 5'11", 180 lbs.   Deb: 4/21/37

YEAR	TM/L	G	AB	R	H	2B	3B	HR	RBI	BB	SO	AVG	OBP	SLG	PRO+	BR/A	SB	CS	SBR	FA	FR	G/POS	TPR
1937	Chi-A	26	73	13	19	4	1	1	9	4	7	.260	.299	.384	71	-4	2	0	1	.960	-2	O-15	-0.5
1938	Chi-A	106	399	59	132	23	8	4	61	41	19	.331	.393	.459	110	7	1	3	-2	.963	-4	*O-101	-0.2
1939	Chi-A	71	111	16	19	2	1	1	15	21	8	.171	.303	.234	38	-10	0	0	0	1.000	-2	O-22	-1.2
Total	3	203	583	88	170	29	10	6	85	66	34	.292	.364	.407	92	-7	3	3	-1	.968	-8	O-138	-1.9

■ GENE STEINBRENNER
Steinbrenner, Eugene Gass   b: 11/17/1892, Pittsburgh, Pa.   d: 4/25/70, Pittsburgh, Pa.   BR/TR, 5'8.5", 155 lbs.   Deb: 4/25/12

YEAR	TM/L	G	AB	R	H	2B	3B	HR	RBI	BB	SO	AVG	OBP	SLG	PRO+	BR/A	SB	CS	SBR	FA	FR	G/POS	TPR
1912	Phi-N	3	9	0	2	1	0	0	1	0	3	.222	.222	.333	48	-1	0			.900	-1	/2-3	-0.1

■ BILL STEINECKE
Steinecke, William Robert   b: 2/7/07, Cincinnati, Ohio   d: 7/20/86, St.Augustine, Fla   BR/TR, 5'8.5", 175 lbs.   Deb: 9/16/31

YEAR	TM/L	G	AB	R	H	2B	3B	HR	RBI	BB	SO	AVG	OBP	SLG	PRO+	BR/A	SB	CS	SBR	FA	FR	G/POS	TPR
1931	Pit-N	4	4	0	0	0	0	0	0	0	0	.000	.000	.000	-99	-1	0	0	0	.000	0	/C-1	-0.1

■ BEN STEINER
Steiner, Benjamin Saunders   b: 7/28/21, Alexandria, Va.   d: 10/27/88, Venice, Fla.   BL/TR, 5'11", 165 lbs.   Deb: 4/17/45

YEAR	TM/L	G	AB	R	H	2B	3B	HR	RBI	BB	SO	AVG	OBP	SLG	PRO+	BR/A	SB	CS	SBR	FA	FR	G/POS	TPR
1945	Bos-A	78	304	39	78	8	3	3	20	31	29	.257	.327	.332	89	-4	10	6	-1	.967	-4	2-77	-0.4
1946	Bos-A	3	4	1	1	0	0	0	0	0	0	.250	.250	.250	38	-0	0	0	0	.750	0	/3-1	0.0
1947	Det-A	1	0	1	0	0	0	0	0	0	0	—	—	—	—	0	0	0	0	.000	0	R	0.0
Total	3	82	308	41	79	8	3	3	20	31	29	.256	.326	.331	89	-4	10	6	-1	.967	-4	/2-77,3-1	-0.4

■ RED STEINER
Steiner, James Harry   b: 1/7/15, Los Angeles, Cal.   BL/TR, 6', 185 lbs.   Deb: 5/11/45

YEAR	TM/L	G	AB	R	H	2B	3B	HR	RBI	BB	SO	AVG	OBP	SLG	PRO+	BR/A	SB	CS	SBR	FA	FR	G/POS	TPR
1945	Cle-A	12	20	0	3	0	0	0	2	1	4	.150	.190	.150	-1	-3	0	0	0	1.000	1	/C-4	-0.2
	Bos-A	26	59	6	12	1	0	0	4	14	2	.203	.356	.220	67	-2	0	0	0	.986	-5	C-24	-0.6
	Yr	38	79	6	15	1	0	0	6	15	6	.190	.319	.203	52	-4	0	0	0	.989	-4	C-28	-0.8

■ HARRY STEINFELDT
Steinfeldt, Harry M.   b: 9/29/1877, St.Louis, Mo.   d: 8/17/14, Bellevue, Ky.   BR/TR, 5'9.5", 180 lbs.   Deb: 4/22/1898

YEAR	TM/L	G	AB	R	H	2B	3B	HR	RBI	BB	SO	AVG	OBP	SLG	PRO+	BR/A	SB	CS	SBR	FA	FR	G/POS	TPR
1898	Cin-N	88	308	47	91	18	6	0	43	27		.295	.354	.393	107	2	9			.917	-1	2-31,0-29,3/S1	0.1
1899	Cin-N	107	386	62	94	16	8	0	43	40		.244	.324	.326	77	-12	19			.885	-6	3-59,2-40/SO	-1.4
1900	Cin-N	134	510	57	125	29	7	2	66	27		.245	.292	.341	76	-18	14			.922	36	3-67,2-64/OS	1.9
1901	Cin-N	105	382	40	95	18	7	6	47	28		.249	.303	.380	104	1	10			.886	10	3-55,2-50	1.3
1902	Cin-N	129	479	53	133	20	7	1	49	24		.278	.316	.355	98	-3	12			.912	22	*3-129/O-1	2.1
1903	Cin-N	118	439	71	137	32	12	6	83	47		.312	.386	.481	132	16	6			.937	7	*3-104,S-14	2.4
1904	Cin-N	99	349	35	85	11	6	1	52	29		.244	.313	.318	87	-5	16			.887	-7	3-98	-1.0
1905	Cin-N	114	384	49	104	16	9	1	39	30		.271	.329	.367	97	-3	15			.919	14	*3-103/1-1,2O	1.6
1906	*Chi-N	151	539	81	176	27	10	3	83	47		.327	.395	.430	149	31	29			.954	-17	*3-150/2-1	2.0
1907	*Chi-N	152	542	52	144	25	5	1	70	47		.266	.323	.336	100	-0	19			.967	-5	*3-151	-0.1
1908	*Chi-N	150	539	63	130	20	6	1	62	36		.241	.294	.306	88	-8	12			.940	-12	*3-150	-1.6
1909	Chi-N	151	528	73	133	27	6	2	59	57		.252	.331	.337	105	3	22			.940	3	*3-151	1.1
1910	*Chi-N	129	448	70	113	21	1	2	58	36	29	.252	.323	.317	88	-7	10			.946	0	*3-128	-0.4
1911	Bos-N	19	63	5	16	4	0	1	8	6	3	.254	.338	.365	89	-1	1			.810	-5	3-19	-0.6
Total	14	1646	5896	758	1576	284	90	27	762	471	32	.267	.330	.360	101	-4	194			.926	38	*3-1386,2-187/OS1	7.4

■ BILL STELLBAUER
Stellbauer, William Jennings   b: 3/20/1894, Bremond, Tex.   d: 2/16/74, New Braunfels, Tex   BR/TR, 5'10", 175 lbs.   Deb: 4/12/16

YEAR	TM/L	G	AB	R	H	2B	3B	HR	RBI	BB	SO	AVG	OBP	SLG	PRO+	BR/A	SB	CS	SBR	FA	FR	G/POS	TPR
1916	Phi-A	25	48	2	13	2	1	0	5	6	7	.271	.352	.354	118	1	2			.857	-4	O-14	-0.3

■ RICK STELMASZEK
Stelmaszek, Richard Francis   b: 10/8/48, Chicago, Ill.   BL/TR, 6'1", 195 lbs.   Deb: 6/25/71   C

YEAR	TM/L	G	AB	R	H	2B	3B	HR	RBI	BB	SO	AVG	OBP	SLG	PRO+	BR/A	SB	CS	SBR	FA	FR	G/POS	TPR
1971	Was-A	6	9	0	0	0	0	0	0	0	3	.000	.000	.000	-99	-2	0	0	0	1.000	-1	/C-3	-0.3
1973	Tex-A	7	9	0	1	0	0	0	0	0	2	.111	.200	.111	-11	-1	0	0	0	1.000	-0	/C-7	-0.1
	Cal-A	22	26	2	4	1	0	0	3	6	7	.154	.313	.192	49	-2	0	0	0	1.000	-2	C-22	-0.3
	Yr	29	35	2	5	1	0	0	3	7	9	.143	.286	.171	34	-3	0	0	0	1.000	-2	C-29	-0.4
1974	Chi-N	25	44	2	10	2	0	1	7	10	6	.227	.370	.341	96	0	0	0	0	.983	-6	C-16	-0.5
Total	3	60	88	4	15	3	0	1	10	17	18	.170	.305	.239	55	-5	0	0	0	.993	-9	/C-48	-1.2

■ FRED STEM
Stem, Frederick Boothe   b: 9/22/1885, Oxford, N.C.   d: 9/5/64, Darlington, S.C.   BL/TR, 6'2", 160 lbs.   Deb: 9/15/08

YEAR	TM/L	G	AB	R	H	2B	3B	HR	RBI	BB	SO	AVG	OBP	SLG	PRO+	BR/A	SB	CS	SBR	FA	FR	G/POS	TPR
1908	Bos-N	20	72	9	20	0	1	0	3	3		.278	.297	.306	94	-1	1			.995	-1	1-19	-0.2
1909	Bos-N	73	245	13	51	2	3	0	11	12		.208	.254	.241	51	-14	5			.989	10	1-68	-0.5
Total	2	93	317	22	71	2	4	0	14	14		.224	.263	.256	60	-15	6			.990	10	/1-87	-0.7

■ CASEY STENGEL
Stengel, Charles Dillon "The Old Professor"
b: 7/30/1890, Kansas City, Mo.   d: 9/29/75, Glendale, Cal.   BL/TL, 5'11", 175 lbs.   Deb: 9/17/12   MCH

YEAR	TM/L	G	AB	R	H	2B	3B	HR	RBI	BB	SO	AVG	OBP	SLG	PRO+	BR/A	SB	CS	SBR	FA	FR	G/POS	TPR
1912	Bro-N	17	57	9	18	1	0	1	13	15	9	.316	.466	.386	140	5	5			.902	-2	O-17	0.2
1913	Bro-N	124	438	60	119	16	8	7	43	56	58	.272	.356	.393	110	7	19			.960	2	*O-119	0.3
1914	Bro-N	126	412	55	130	13	10	4	60	56	55	.316	.404	.425	143	24	19			.964	-8	*O-121	1.2
1915	Bro-N	132	459	52	109	20	12	3	50	34	46	.237	.294	.353	94	-4	5	10	-5	.959	0	*O-129	-1.6
1916	*Bro-N	127	462	66	129	27	8	8	53	33	51	.279	.329	.424	127	13	11			.965	3	*O-121	1.2
1917	Bro-N	150	549	69	141	23	12	6	73	60	62	.257	.336	.375	115	10	18			.969	13	*O-150	1.6
1918	Pit-N	39	122	18	30	4	1	1	12	16	14	.246	.343	.320	99	0	11			.973	2	O-37	0.1
1919	Pit-N	89	321	38	94	10	10	4	43	35	35	.293	.364	.424	131	13	12			.957	3	O-87	1.0
1920	Phi-N	129	445	53	130	25	6	9	50	38	35	.292	.356	.436	121	12	7	13	-6	.954	-3	*O-118	-0.5
1921	Phi-N	24	59	7	18	3	1	0	4	6	7	.305	.369	.390	94	-0	1	1	-0	.969	2	O-15	0.1
	NY-N	18	22	4	5	1	0	0	6	7	4	.227	.261	.273	41	-2	0	1	-1	.875	-3	O-8	-0.6
	Yr	42	81	11	23	4	1	0	6	7	12	.284	.341	.358	81	-2	1	2	-1	.950	-0	O-23	-0.5
1922	*NY-N	84	250	48	92	8	10	7	48	21	17	.368	.436	.564	155	21	4	2	0	.969	-4	O-77	1.1
1923	*NY-N	75	218	39	74	11	5	5	43	20	18	.339	.400	.505	139	12	6	2	1	.960	-0	O-57	0.3
1924	Bos-N	131	461	57	129	20	6	5	39	45	39	.280	.348	.382	100	0	13	13	-6	.978	-7	*O-126	-1.9
1925	Bos-N	12	13	0	1	0	0	0	2	1	2	.077	.143	.077	-46	-3	0	1	-1	1.000	-0	/O-1	-0.4
Total	14	1277	4288	575	1219	182	89	60	535	437	453	.284	.356	.410	119	107	131	43		.964	-9	O-1183	2.1

YEAR	TM/L	G	AB	R	H	2B	3B	HR	RBI	BB	SO	AVG	OBP	SLG	PRO+	BR/A	SB	CS	SBR	FA	FR	G/POS	TPR

■ MIKE STENHOUSE
Stenhouse, Michael Steven b: 5/29/58, Pueblo, Colo.   BL/TR, 6'1", 195 lbs.   Deb: 10/3/82 F

YEAR	TM/L	G	AB	R	H	2B	3B	HR	RBI	BB	SO	AVG	OBP	SLG	PRO+	BR/A	SB	CS	SBR	FA	FR	G/POS	TPR
1982	Mon-N	1	1	0	0	0	0	0	0	0	1	.000	.000	.000	-98	-0	0	0	0	.000	0	/H	0.0
1983	Mon-N	24	40	2	5	1	0	0	2	4	10	.125	.205	.150	-0	-5	0	0	0	1.000	-3	/O-9,1-5	-0.9
1984	Mon-N	80	175	14	32	8	0	4	16	26	32	.183	.292	.297	69	-7	0	0	0	.986	-3	O-48,1-14	-1.2
1985	Min-A	81	179	23	40	5	0	5	21	29	18	.223	.332	.335	79	-5	1	0	0	.929	0	D-27,O-16/1	-0.6
1986	Bos-A	21	21	1	2	1	0	0	1	12	5	.095	.424	.143	63	-0	0	0	0	1.000	-0	/O-4,1-3	-0.1
Total	5	207	416	40	79	15	0	9	40	71	66	.190	.309	.291	67	-18	1	0	0	.973	-5	/O-77,1-30,D	-2.8

■ RENNIE STENNETT
Stennett, Renaldo Antonio (Porte) b: 4/5/51, Colon, Panama   BR/TR, 5'11", 175 lbs.   Deb: 7/10/71

YEAR	TM/L	G	AB	R	H	2B	3B	HR	RBI	BB	SO	AVG	OBP	SLG	PRO+	BR/A	SB	CS	SBR	FA	FR	G/POS	TPR
1971	Pit-N	50	153	24	54	5	4	1	15	7	9	.353	.381	.458	137	7	1	1	-0	.954	2	2-36	1.2
1972	*Pit-N	109	370	43	106	14	5	3	30	9	43	.286	.307	.376	95	-4	4	3	-1	.977	6	2-49,O-41/S	0.4
1973	Pit-N	128	466	45	113	18	3	10	55	16	63	.242	.268	.358	74	-18	2	3	-1	.981	-0	2-84,S-43/O	-1.0
1974	*Pit-N	157	673	84	196	29	3	7	56	32	51	.291	.325	.374	99	-3	8	9	-3	.980	13	*2-154/O-2	1.5
1975	*Pit-N	148	616	89	176	25	7	7	62	33	42	.286	.326	.383	97	-4	5	4	-1	.979	13	*2-144	1.6
1976	Pit-N	157	654	59	168	31	9	2	60	19	32	.257	.279	.341	75	-23	18	6	2	.981	17	*2-157/S-4	0.6
1977	Pit-N	116	453	53	152	20	4	5	51	29	24	.336	.378	.430	113	9	28	16	-2	.982	-7	*2-113	0.8
1978	Pit-N	106	333	30	81	9	2	3	35	13	22	.243	.276	.309	60	-18	2	1	0	.971	-12	2-80/3-6	-2.5
1979	*Pit-N	108	319	31	76	13	2	0	24	24	25	.238	.292	.292	57	-19	1	4	-2	.974	6	*2-102	-0.9
1980	SF-N	120	397	34	97	13	2	3	37	22	31	.244	.287	.302	66	-18	4	4	-1	.973	-13	*2-111	-2.8
1981	SF-N	38	87	8	20	0	0	1	7	3	6	.230	.264	.264	51	-6	2	1	0	1.000	-2	*2-19	-0.7
Total	11	1237	4521	500	1239	177	41	41	432	207	348	.274	.308	.359	85	-96	75	54	-10	.978	23	*2-1049/S-53,O3	-1.8

■ JAKE STENZEL
Stenzel, Jacob Charles (b: Jacob Charles Stelzle) b: 6/24/1867, Cincinnati, Ohio d: 1/6/19, Cincinnati, Ohio   BR/TR, 5'10", 168 lbs.   Deb: 6/16/1890

YEAR	TM/L	G	AB	R	H	2B	3B	HR	RBI	BB	SO	AVG	OBP	SLG	PRO+	BR/A	SB	CS	SBR	FA	FR	G/POS	TPR
1890	Chi-N	11	41	3	11	1	0	0	3	1	0	.268	.286	.293	66	-2	0			.857	-4	/O-6,C-6	-0.4
1892	Pit-N	3	9	0	0	0	0	0	0	0	3	.000	.100	.000	-69	-2	1			1.000	0	/O-2,C-1	-0.1
1893	Pit-N	60	224	57	81	13	4	4	37	24	17	.362	.423	.509	150	16	16			.905	-9	O-45,C-12/S2	0.4
1894	Pit-N	131	522	148	185	39	20	13	121	75	13	.354	.441	.580	146	40	61			.925	-1	*O-131	2.2
1895	Pit-N	129	514	114	192	38	13	7	97	57	25	.374	.447	.539	162	50	53			.912	-5	*O-129	2.8
1896	Pit-N	114	479	104	173	26	14	2	82	32	13	.361	.409	.486	141	28	57			.922	-3	*O-114/1-1	1.3
1897	*Bal-N	131	536	113	189	**43**	7	4	116	36		.353	.404	.481	133	25	69			.932	-11	*O-131	0.4
1898	Bal-N	35	138	33	35	5	2	0	22	12		.254	.340	.319	87	-2	4			.926	-2	O-35	-0.6
	StL-N	108	404	64	114	15	11	1	33	41		.282	.367	.381	112	7	21			.943	0	*O-108	-0.1
	Yr	143	542	97	149	20	13	1	55	53		.275	.360	.365	106	5	25			.940	-2	*O-143	-0.7
1899	StL-N	35	128	21	35	9	0	1	19	16		.273	.367	.367	99	0	8			.949	-1	O-33	-0.3
	Cin-N	9	29	5	9	1	0	0	3	4		.310	.412	.345	106	1	2			1.000	-1	/O-7	-0.1
	Yr	44	157	26	44	10	0	1	22	20		.280	.376	.363	101	1	10			.957	-2	O-40	-0.4
Total	9	766	3024	662	1024	190	71	32	533	299	_71_	.339	.408	.480	135	160	292			.927	-36	O-741/C-19,12S	5.5

■ RAY STEPHENS
Stephens, Carl Ray b: 9/22/62, Houston, Tex.   BR/TR, 6', 190 lbs.   Deb: 9/20/90

YEAR	TM/L	G	AB	R	H	2B	3B	HR	RBI	BB	SO	AVG	OBP	SLG	PRO+	BR/A	SB	CS	SBR	FA	FR	G/POS	TPR
1990	StL-N	5	15	2	2	1	0	1	1	0	3	.133	.133	.400	41	-1	0	0	0	1.000	2	/C-5	0.1
1991	StL-N	6	7	0	2	0	0	0	0	1	3	.286	.375	.286	88	-0	0	0	0	1.000	1	/C-6	0.1
1992	Tex-A	8	13	0	2	0	0	0	0	0	5	.154	.154	.154	-14	-2	0	0	0	1.000	-0	/C-6,D-1	-0.2
Total	3	19	35	2	6	1	0	1	1	1	11	.171	.194	.286	32	-3	0	0	0	1.000	3	/C-17,D-1	0.0

■ GENE STEPHENS
Stephens, Glen Eugene b: 1/20/33, Gravette, Ark.   BL/TR, 6'3.5", 175 lbs.   Deb: 4/16/52

YEAR	TM/L	G	AB	R	H	2B	3B	HR	RBI	BB	SO	AVG	OBP	SLG	PRO+	BR/A	SB	CS	SBR	FA	FR	G/POS	TPR
1952	Bos-A	21	53	10	12	5	0	0	5	3	8	.226	.268	.321	59	-3	4	2	0	.962	0	O-13	-0.4
1953	Bos-A	78	221	30	45	6	2	3	18	29	56	.204	.302	.290	57	-13	3	3	-1	.966	-7	O-72	-2.3
1955	Bos-A	109	157	25	46	9	4	3	18	20	34	.293	.380	.459	114	3	0	0	0	.947	-11	O-75	-0.9
1956	Bos-A	104	63	22	17	2	0	1	7	12	12	.270	.387	.349	85	-1	0	1	-1	.983	-17	O-71	-1.8
1957	Bos-A	120	173	25	46	6	4	3	26	20	26	.266	.362	.399	102	1	0	2	-1	.987	-19	O-90	-2.2
1958	Bos-A	134	270	38	59	10	4	9	25	22	46	.219	.280	.363	71	-11	1	2	-1	.975	-16	*O-110	-3.3
1959	Bos-A	92	270	34	75	13	1	3	39	29	33	.278	.356	.367	95	-1	5	2	0	.981	1	O-85	-0.3
1960	Bos-A	35	109	9	25	4	0	2	11	14	22	.229	.317	.321	71	-4	5	1	1	.951	-1	O-31	-0.6
	Bal-A	84	193	38	46	11	0	5	11	25	25	.238	.329	.373	91	-2	4	2	0	.992	-10	O-77	-1.6
	Yr	119	302	47	71	15	0	7	22	39	47	.235	.325	.354	83	-7	9	3	1	.979	-11	*O-108	-2.2
1961	Bal-A	32	58	4	11	2	0	0	2	14	7	.190	.347	.224	58	-3	1	1	-0	1.000	-6	O-30	-1.0
	KC-A	62	183	22	38	6	1	4	26	16	27	.208	.279	.317	58	-11	3	2	-0	.968	1	O-54	-1.3
	Yr	94	241	26	49	8	1	4	28	30	34	.203	.297	.295	59	-14	4	3	-1	.975	-5	O-84	-2.3
1962	KC-A	5	4	0	0	0	0	0	0	1	1	.000	.200	.000	-39	-1	0	0	0	.000	0	H	-0.1
1963	Chi-A	6	18	5	7	0	0	1	2	1	3	.389	.421	.556	174	2	0	0	0	.909	1	/O-5	0.3
1964	Chi-A	82	141	21	33	4	2	3	17	21	28	.234	.341	.355	97	-0	1	2	-1	.969	-5	O-59	-0.9
Total	12	964	1913	283	460	78	15	37	207	233	322	.240	.327	.355	82	-45	27	20	-4	.973	-87	O-772	-16.4

■ JIM STEPHENS
Stephens, James Walter "Little Nemo" b: 12/10/1883, Salineville, Ohio d: 1/2/65, Oxford, Ala.   BR/TR, 5'6.5", 157 lbs.   Deb: 4/11/07

YEAR	TM/L	G	AB	R	H	2B	3B	HR	RBI	BB	SO	AVG	OBP	SLG	PRO+	BR/A	SB	CS	SBR	FA	FR	G/POS	TPR
1907	StL-A	58	173	15	35	6	1	0	11	15		.202	.270	.272	73	-5	3			.967	-3	C-56	-0.4
1908	StL-A	47	150	14	30	4	1	0	6	9		.200	.255	.240	61	-6	0			.960	-0	C-45	-0.3
1909	StL-A	79	223	18	49	5	0	3	18	13		.220	.278	.283	83	-5	5			.980	3	C-72	0.5
1910	StL-A	99	289	24	62	3	7	0	23	16		.215	.261	.273	72	-10	3			.971	2	C-96	0.1
1911	StL-A	70	212	11	49	5	5	0	17	17		.231	.300	.302	71	-8	1			.949	-2	C-66	-0.4
1912	StL-A	75	205	13	51	7	5	0	22	7		.249	.274	.332	76	-8	3			.954	4	C-66	-0.3
Total	6	428	1252	95	276	30	21	3	97	77		.220	.273	.285	73	-42	14			.965	3	C-401	-0.3

■ VERN STEPHENS
Stephens, Vernon Decatur "Junior" or "Buster" b: 10/23/20, McAlister, N.Mex. d: 11/3/68, Long Beach, Cal.   BR/TR, 5'10", 185 lbs.   Deb: 9/13/41

YEAR	TM/L	G	AB	R	H	2B	3B	HR	RBI	BB	SO	AVG	OBP	SLG	PRO+	BR/A	SB	CS	SBR	FA	FR	G/POS	TPR
1941	StL-A	3	2	0	1	0	0	0	0	0	0	.500	.500	.500	160	0	0	0	0	.500	-0	/S-1	0.0
1942	StL-A	145	574	84	169	26	6	14	92	41	53	.294	.341	.433	115	9	1	3	-2	.944	-10	*S-144	0.7
1943	StL-A★	137	512	75	148	27	3	22	91	54	73	.289	.357	.482	142	25	3	2	-0	.943	-25	*S-123,O-11	0.8
1944	*StL-A★	145	559	91	164	32	1	20	**109**	62	54	.293	.365	.462	128	19	2	2	-1	.954	-4	*S-143	2.7
1945	StL-A†	149	571	90	165	27	3	**24**	89	55	70	.289	.352	.473	132	21	2	1	0	**.961**	-17	*S-144/3-4	1.7
1946	StL-A★	115	450	67	138	19	4	14	64	35	49	.307	.357	.460	121	11	0	1	-1	.950	0	*S-112	1.8
1947	StL-A	150	562	74	157	18	4	15	83	70	61	.279	.359	.406	110	8	8	4	0	.970	12	*S-149	2.9
1948	Bos-A★	155	635	114	171	25	8	29	137	77	56	.269	.350	.471	112	7	1	0	0	.971	10	*S-155	2.6
1949	Bos-A★	155	610	113	177	31	2	39	**159**	101	73	.290	.391	.539	135	28	2	3	-1	.966	4	*S-155	4.1
1950	Bos-A☆	149	628	125	185	34	6	30	**144**	65	43	.295	.361	.511	120	6	1	0	0	.981	-0	*S-146	1.6
1951	Bos-A★	109	377	62	113	21	2	17	78	38	33	.300	.364	.501	120	9	1	2	-1	.978	14	3-89/S-2	2.1
1952	Bos-A	92	295	35	75	13	2	7	44	39	31	.254	.343	.383	95	-2	2	2	0	.957	4	S-53,3-29	0.5
1953	Chi-A	44	129	14	24	6	1	4	14	13	18	.186	.281	.256	39	-11	2	0	0	.990	-3	3-38/S-3	-1.4
	StL-A	46	165	16	53	8	0	4	17	18	24	.321	.388	.442	121	5	0	0	0	.954	-2	3-46	0.2
	Yr	90	294	30	77	14	0	5	31	31	42	.262	.332	.361	85	-6	2	0	0	.968	-5	3-84/S-3	-1.2
1954	Bal-A	101	365	31	104	17	1	8	46	17	36	.285	.317	.403	104	-1	0	3	-3	.966	-6	3-96	-1.1
1955	Bal-A	3	6	1	1	0	0	0	0	0	0	.167	.167	.167	26	-1	0	0	0	1.000	-1	/3-2	-0.1
	Chi-A	22	56	10	14	3	0	3	7	7	11	.250	.333	.464	110	1	0	0	0	1.000	4	3-18	0.5

YEAR	TM/L	G	AB	R	H	2B	3B	HR	RBI	BB	SO	AVG	OBP	SLG	PRO+	BR/A	SB	CS	SBR	FA	FR	G/POS	TPR
	Yr	25	62	10	15	3	0	3	7	7	11	.242	.329	.435	102	0	0	0	0	1.000	4	3-20	0.4
Total	15	1720	6497	1001	1859	307	42	247	1174	692	685	.286	.355	.460	118	137	25	22	-6	.960	-20	*S-1330,3-322/O	19.6

■ RIGGS STEPHENSON

Stephenson, Jackson Riggs "Old Hoss" b: 1/5/1898, Akron, Ala. d: 11/15/85, Tuscaloosa, Ala. BR/TR, 5'10", 185 lbs. Deb: 4/13/21

YEAR	TM/L	G	AB	R	H	2B	3B	HR	RBI	BB	SO	AVG	OBP	SLG	PRO+	BR/A	SB	CS	SBR	FA	FR	G/POS	TPR
1921	Cle-A	65	206	45	68	17	2	2	34	23	15	.330	.408	.461	119	7	4	1	1	.942	-1	2-54/3-2	0.7
1922	Cle-A	86	233	47	79	24	5	2	32	27	18	.339	.421	.511	141	15	3	0	1	.952	-6	3-34,2-25/O	1.2
1923	Cle-A	91	301	48	96	20	6	5	65	15	25	.319	.357	.475	118	6	5	5	-2	.970	9	2-66/O-3,3	1.4
1924	Cle-A	71	240	33	89	20	0	4	44	27	10	.371	.439	.504	141	15	1	2	-1	.961	-13	2-58/O-7	0.1
1925	Cle-A	19	54	8	16	3	1	1	9	7	3	.296	.387	.444	110	1	1	1	-0	.946	1	O-16	0.1
1926	Chi-N	82	281	40	95	18	3	3	44	31	16	.338	.404	.456	129	12	2			.950	-4	O-74	0.4
1927	Chi-N	152	579	101	199	**46**	9	7	82	65	28	.344	.415	.491	142	36	8			.975	4	*O-146/3-6	3.0
1928	Chi-N	137	512	75	166	36	9	8	90	68	29	.324	.407	.477	132	25	8			.982	0	*O-135	1.6
1929	*Chi-N	136	495	91	179	36	6	17	110	67	21	.362	.445	.562	147	39	10			.984	0	*O-130	2.7
1930	Chi-N	109	341	56	125	21	1	5	68	32	20	.367	.421	.478	116	10	2			.958	-5	O-80	0.0
1931	Chi-N	80	263	34	84	14	4	1	52	37	14	.319	.405	.414	119	9	1			.985	-2	O-66	0.2
1932	*Chi-N	147	583	86	189	49	4	4	85	54	27	.324	.383	.443	123	20	3			.984	-5	*O-147	0.5
1933	Chi-N	97	346	45	114	17	4	0	51	34	16	.329	.397	.436	138	18	5			.985	-2	O-91	1.2
1934	Chi-N	38	74	5	16	0	0	0	7	7	5	.216	.293	.216	39	-6	0			1.000	1	O-15	-0.5
Total	14	1310	4508	714	1515	321	54	63	773	494	247	.336	.407	.473	130	206	53	<u>9</u>		.978	-23	O-913,2-203/3	12.6

■ JOHN STEPHENSON

Stephenson, John Herman b: 4/13/41, S.Portsmouth, Ky. BL/TR, 5'11", 180 lbs. Deb: 4/14/64

YEAR	TM/L	G	AB	R	H	2B	3B	HR	RBI	BB	SO	AVG	OBP	SLG	PRO+	BR/A	SB	CS	SBR	FA	FR	G/POS	TPR
1964	NY-N	37	57	2	9	0	0	1	2	4	18	.158	.226	.211	24	-6	0	0	0	.800	-4	3-14/O-8	-1.1
1965	NY-N	62	121	9	26	5	0	4	15	8	19	.215	.264	.355	75	-4	0	1	-1	.981	-9	C-47/O-2	-1.3
1966	NY-N	63	143	17	28	1	1	1	11	8	28	.196	.248	.238	37	-12	0	0	0	.973	-1	C-52/O-1	-1.2
1967	Chi-N	18	49	3	11	3	1	0	5	1	6	.224	.255	.327	62	-2	0	0	0	1.000	1	C-13	-0.1
1968	Chi-N	2	2	0	0	0	0	0	0	0	0	.000	.000	.000	-94	-0	0	0	0	.000	0	H	-0.1
1969	SF-N	22	27	2	6	2	0	0	3	0	4	.222	.222	.296	45	-2	0	0	0	.941	-3	/C-9,3-1	-0.5
1970	SF-N	23	43	3	3	1	0	0	6	2	7	.070	.111	.093	-45	-9	0	0	0	1.000	2	/C-9,O-1	-0.6
1971	Cal-A	98	279	24	61	17	0	3	25	22	21	.219	.283	.312	74	-10	0	0	0	.992	-9	C-88	-1.7
1972	Cal-A	66	146	14	40	3	1	2	17	11	8	.274	.342	.349	112	2	0	0	0	.993	-7	C-56	-0.4
1973	Cal-A	60	122	9	30	5	0	1	9	7	7	.246	.292	.311	76	-4	0	0	0	.980	-8	C-56	-1.1
Total	10	451	989	83	214	37	3	12	93	63	118	.216	.272	.296	64	-48	0	1	-1	.986	-38	C-330/3-15,O	-8.1

■ JOE STEPHENSON

Stephenson, Joseph Chester b: 6/30/21, Detroit, Mich. BR/TR, 6'2", 185 lbs. Deb: 9/19/43 F

YEAR	TM/L	G	AB	R	H	2B	3B	HR	RBI	BB	SO	AVG	OBP	SLG	PRO+	BR/A	SB	CS	SBR	FA	FR	G/POS	TPR
1943	NY-N	9	24	4	6	1	0	0	4	0	5	.250	.250	.292	56	-1	0			.973	2	/C-6	0.1
1944	Chi-N	4	8	1	1	0	0	0	0	1	3	.125	.222	.125	-1	-1	1			1.000	1	/C-3	0.0
1947	Chi-A	16	35	3	5	0	0	0	3	1	7	.143	.211	.143	-1	-5	0	0	0	.959	0	C-13	-0.4
Total	3	29	67	8	12	1	0	0	4	2	15	.179	.225	.194	19	-7	1	<u>0</u>		.970	3	/C-22	-0.3

■ PHIL STEPHENSON

Stephenson, Phillip Raymond b: 9/19/60, Guthrie, Okla. BL/TL, 6'1", 195 lbs. Deb: 4/5/89

YEAR	TM/L	G	AB	R	H	2B	3B	HR	RBI	BB	SO	AVG	OBP	SLG	PRO+	BR/A	SB	CS	SBR	FA	FR	G/POS	TPR
1989	Chi-N	17	21	0	3	0	0	0	2	0	3	.143	.217	.143	5	-3	1	0	0	1.000	-1	/O-3	-0.3
	SD-N	10	17	4	6	0	0	2	2	3	2	.353	.450	.706	225	3	0	0	0	.977	0	/1-8	0.3
	Yr	27	38	4	9	0	0	2	2	5	5	.237	.326	.395	100	0	1	0	0	.977	-0	/1-8,O-3	0.0
1990	SD-N	103	182	26	38	9	1	4	19	30	43	.209	.321	.335	80	-5	2	1	0	.997	3	1-60	-0.5
1991	SD-N	11	7	0	2	0	0	0	0	2	3	.286	.444	.286	106	0	0	0	0	.000	0	/H	0.0
1992	SD-N	53	71	5	11	2	1	0	8	10	11	.155	.259	.211	34	-6	0	0	0	1.000	-3	O-15/1-7	-1.0
Total	4	194	298	35	60	11	2	6	29	47	62	.201	.310	.312	73	-10	3	1	0	.993	-1	/1-75,O-18	-1.5

■ DUMMY STEPHENSON

Stephenson, Reuben Crandol b: 9/22/1869, Petersburg, N.J. d: 12/1/24, Trenton, N.J. BR/TR, 5'11.5", 180 lbs. Deb: 9/9/1892

YEAR	TM/L	G	AB	R	H	2B	3B	HR	RBI	BB	SO	AVG	OBP	SLG	PRO+	BR/A	SB	CS	SBR	FA	FR	G/POS	TPR
1892	Phi-N	8	37	4	10	3	0	0	5	0	2	.270	.289	.351	94	-0				.800	-2	/O-8	-0.2

■ BOB STEPHENSON

Stephenson, Robert Lloyd b: 8/11/28, Blair, Okla. BR/TR, 6', 165 lbs. Deb: 4/14/55

YEAR	TM/L	G	AB	R	H	2B	3B	HR	RBI	BB	SO	AVG	OBP	SLG	PRO+	BR/A	SB	CS	SBR	FA	FR	G/POS	TPR
1955	StL-N	67	111	19	27	3	0	0	6	5	18	.243	.276	.270	46	-9	2	1	0	.938	-1	S-48/2-7,3	-0.7

■ WALTER STEPHENSON

Stephenson, Walter McQueen "Tarzan" b: 3/27/11, Saluda, N.C. d: 7/4/93, Shreveport, La. BR/TR, 6', 180 lbs. Deb: 4/29/35

YEAR	TM/L	G	AB	R	H	2B	3B	HR	RBI	BB	SO	AVG	OBP	SLG	PRO+	BR/A	SB	CS	SBR	FA	FR	G/POS	TPR
1935	*Chi-N	16	26	2	10	1	1	0	2	1	5	.385	.407	.500	142	1	0			1.000	2	/C-6	0.3
1936	Chi-N	6	12	0	1	0	0	0	1	0	5	.083	.083	.083	-54	-3	0			1.000	-0	/C-4	-0.3
1937	Phi-N	10	23	1	6	0	0	0	2	2	3	.261	.320	.261	55	-1	0			.967	0	/C-7	-0.1
Total	3	32	61	3	17	1	1	0	5	3	13	.279	.313	.328	70	-2	0			.984	2	/C-17	-0.1

■ DUTCH STERRETT

Sterrett, Charles Hurlbut b: 10/1/1889, Milroy, Pa. d: 12/9/65, Baltimore, Md. BR/TR, 5'11.5", 165 lbs. Deb: 6/20/12

YEAR	TM/L	G	AB	R	H	2B	3B	HR	RBI	BB	SO	AVG	OBP	SLG	PRO+	BR/A	SB	CS	SBR	FA	FR	G/POS	TPR
1912	NY-A	66	230	30	61	4	7	1	32	11		.265	.310	.357	85	-5	8			.972	-1	O-37,1-17,C/2	-1.3
1913	NY-A	21	35	0	6	0	0	0	3	1	5	.171	.216	.171	14	-4	1			1.000	-1	/1-6,C-1	-0.5
Total	2	87	265	30	67	4	7	1	35	12	<u>5</u>	.253	.298	.332	77	-9	9			.986	-8	/O-37,1-23,C2	-1.8

■ CHUCK STEVENS

Stevens, Charles Augustus b: 7/10/18, Van Houten, N.Mex BB/TL, 6'1", 180 lbs. Deb: 9/16/41

YEAR	TM/L	G	AB	R	H	2B	3B	HR	RBI	BB	SO	AVG	OBP	SLG	PRO+	BR/A	SB	CS	SBR	FA	FR	G/POS	TPR
1941	StL-A	4	13	2	2	0	0	0	2	0	1	.154	.154	.154	-18	-2	0	0	0	.966	-1	/1-4	-0.3
1946	StL-A	122	432	53	107	17	4	3	27	47	62	.248	.324	.326	78	-12	4	6	-2	**.995**	3	*1-120	-1.9
1948	StL-A	85	287	34	75	12	4	1	26	41	26	.261	.354	.341	83	-6	2	2	-1	.991	1	1-85	-0.7
Total	3	211	732	89	184	29	8	4	55	88	89	.251	.333	.329	79	-20	6	8	-3	.993	3	1-209	-2.9

■ STEVENS

Stevens Deb: 5/4/1875

YEAR	TM/L	G	AB	R	H	2B	3B	HR	RBI	BB	SO	AVG	OBP	SLG	PRO+	BR/A	SB	CS	SBR	FA	FR	G/POS	TPR
1875	Was-n	1	4	0	1	0	0	0		0		.250	.250	.250	76	-0						/O-1	0.0

■ LEE STEVENS

Stevens, De Wain Lee b: 7/10/67, Kansas City, Mo. BL/TL, 6'4", 205 lbs. Deb: 7/16/90

YEAR	TM/L	G	AB	R	H	2B	3B	HR	RBI	BB	SO	AVG	OBP	SLG	PRO+	BR/A	SB	CS	SBR	FA	FR	G/POS	TPR
1990	Cal-A	67	248	28	53	10	0	7	32	22	75	.214	.278	.339	73	-9	1	1	-0	.994	-4	1-67	-1.9
1991	Cal-A	18	58	8	17	7	0	0	9	6	12	.293	.359	.414	113	1	1	2	-1	.989	-1	1-11/O-9	-0.1
1992	Cal-A	106	312	25	69	19	0	7	37	29	64	.221	.289	.349	78	-10	1	4	-2	.995	-4	1-91/D-2	-2.2
Total	3	191	618	61	139	36	0	14	78	57	151	.225	.291	.351	79	-18	3	7	-3	.994	-8	1-169/O-9,D	-4.2

■ ED STEVENS

Stevens, Edward Lee "Big Ed" b: 1/12/25, Galveston, Tex. BL/TL, 6'1", 190 lbs. Deb: 8/9/45 C

YEAR	TM/L	G	AB	R	H	2B	3B	HR	RBI	BB	SO	AVG	OBP	SLG	PRO+	BR/A	SB	CS	SBR	FA	FR	G/POS	TPR
1945	Bro-N	55	201	29	55	14	4	4	29	32	20	.274	.376	.433	125	7	0			.987	0	1-55	0.4
1946	Bro-N	103	310	34	75	13	7	10	60	27	44	.242	.303	.426	104	0	2			.986	-4	1-99	-0.9
1947	Bro-N	5	13	0	2	1	0	0	0	1	5	.154	.214	.231	18	-2	0			.971	1	/1-4	-0.1
1948	Pit-N	128	429	47	109	19	6	10	69	35	53	.254	.313	.396	89	-8	4			**.996**	5	*1-117	-0.3
1949	Pit-N	67	221	22	58	10	1	4	32	22	24	.262	.332	.371	86	-4	1			.995	10	1-58	0.5
1950	Pit-N	17	46	2	9	2	0	0	3	4	5	.196	.260	.239	31	-5	0			1.000	1	1-12	-0.4
Total	6	375	1220	134	308	59	17	28	193	121	151	.252	.322	.398	95	-10	7			.992	13	1-345	-0.8

■ R C STEVENS

Stevens, R C b: 7/22/34, Moultrie, Ga. BL/TR, 6'5", 219 lbs. Deb: 4/15/58

YEAR	TM/L	G	AB	R	H	2B	3B	HR	RBI	BB	SO	AVG	OBP	SLG	PRO+	BR/A	SB	CS	SBR	FA	FR	G/POS	TPR
1958	Pit-N	59	90	16	24	3	1	7	18	5	25	.267	.320	.556	129	3	0	0	0	.991	3	1-52	0.4
1959	Pit-N	3	7	2	2	0	0	1	1	0	0	.286	.286	.714	157	0	0	0	0	1.000	0	/1-1	0.0
1960	Pit-N	9	3	0	0	0	0	0	0	0	1	.000	.000	.000	-99	-1	0	0	0	1.000	0	/1-7	-0.0
1961	Was-A	33	62	2	8	1	0	0	2	7	15	.129	.217	.145	-1	-9	1	0	0	1.000	4	/1-25	-0.6
Total	4	104	162	21	34	4	1	8	21	12	41	.210	.273	.395	77	-6	1	0	0	.995	7	/1-85	-0.2

YEAR	TM/L	G	AB	R	H	2B	3B	HR	RBI	BB	SO	AVG	OBP	SLG	PRO+	BR/A	SB	CS	SBR	FA	FR	G/POS	TPR

■ BOBBY STEVENS Stevens, Robert Jordan b: 4/17/07, Chevy Chase, Md. BL/TR, 5'8", 149 lbs. Deb: 7/3/31

| 1931 | Phi-N | 12 | 35 | 3 | 12 | 0 | 0 | 0 | 4 | 2 | 2 | .343 | .410 | .343 | 97 | 0 | 0 | | | .870 | -5 | S-10 | -0.4 |

■ ACE STEWART Stewart, Asa b: 2/14/1869, Terre Haute, Ind. d: 4/17/12, Terre Haute, Ind. BR/TR, 5'10", 176 lbs. Deb: 4/18/1895

| 1895 | Chi-N | 97 | 365 | 52 | 88 | 8 | 10 | 8 | 76 | 39 | 40 | .241 | .314 | .384 | 75 | -16 | 14 | | | .911 | -8 | *2-97 | -1.6 |

■ TUFFY STEWART Stewart, Charles Eugene b: 7/31/1883, Chicago, Ill. d: 11/18/34, Chicago, Ill. BL/TL, 5'10", 167 lbs. Deb: 8/8/13

1913	Chi-N	9	8	1	1	1	0	0	2	2	5	.125	.300	.250	58	-0	1			1.000	0	/O-1	0.0
1914	Chi-N	2	1	0	0	0	0	0	0	0	0	.000	.000	.000	-99	-0	0			.000	0	H	0.0
Total	2	11	9	1	1	1	0	0	2	2	5	.111	.273	.222	43	-1	1			1.000	0	/O-1	0.0

■ BUD STEWART Stewart, Edward Perry b: 6/15/16, Sacramento, Cal. BL/TR, 5'11", 170 lbs. Deb: 4/19/41

1941	Pit-N	73	172	27	46	7	0	0	10	12	17	.267	.315	.308	76	-5	3			.962	-2	O-41	-0.9
1942	Pit-N	82	183	21	40	8	4	0	20	22	16	.219	.302	.306	76	-5	2			1.000	-4	O-34,3-10/2	-1.1
1948	NY-A	6	5	1	1	1	0	0	0	0	0	.200	.200	.400	58	-0	0	0	0	.000	0	H	0.0
	Was-A	118	401	56	112	17	13	7	69	49	27	.279	.361	.439	115	8	8	9	-3	.975	-4	*O-114	-0.5
	Yr	124	406	57	113	18	13	7	69	49	27	.278	.359	.438	115	7	8	9	-3	.975	-4	*O-114	-0.5
1949	Was-A	118	388	58	110	23	4	8	43	49	33	.284	.368	.425	112	6	6	4	-1	.982	-7	*O-105	-0.6
1950	Was-A	118	378	46	101	15	6	4	35	46	33	.267	.348	.370	88	-7	5	4	-1	.991	-3	*O-100	-1.4
1951	Chi-A	95	217	40	60	13	5	6	40	29	9	.276	.367	.465	127	8	1	6	-3	.983	-7	O-63	-0.4
1952	Chi-A	92	225	23	60	10	0	5	30	28	17	.267	.350	.378	102	1	3	0	1	.982	-4	O-60	-0.5
1953	Chi-A	53	59	16	16	2	0	2	13	14	3	.271	.411	.407	118	2	1	0	0	1.000	-4	O-16	-0.2
1954	Chi-A	18	13	0	1	0	0	0	0	3	2	.077	.250	.077	-7	-2	0	0	0	1.000	-0	/O-2	-0.2
Total	9	773	2041	288	547	96	32	32	260	252	157	.268	.351	.393	102	5	29	23		.982	-35	O-535/3-10,2	-5.8

■ GLEN STEWART Stewart, Glen Weldon "Gabby" b: 9/29/12, Tullahoma, Tenn. BR/TR, 6', 175 lbs. Deb: 6/26/40

1940	NY-N	15	29	1	4	1	0	0	1	0	2	.138	.167	.172	-6	-4	0			.875	1	/3-6,S-5	-0.3
1943	Phi-N	110	336	23	71	10	1	2	24	32	41	.211	.284	.265	61	-17	1			.947	-9	S-77,2-18/1C	-2.1
1944	Phi-N	118	377	32	83	11	5	0	29	28	40	.220	.274	.276	57	-22	0			.963	5	3-83,S-32/2	-1.5
Total	3	243	742	56	158	22	6	2	53	61	83	.213	.275	.267	56	-42	1			.953	-4	S-114/3-89,21C	-3.9

■ JIMMY STEWART Stewart, James Franklin b: 6/11/39, Opelika, Ala. BB/TR, 6', 165 lbs. Deb: 9/3/63

1963	Chi-N	13	37	1	11	2	0	0	1	1	7	.297	.316	.351	87	-1	1	1	-0	.973	1	/S-9,2-1	0.0
1964	Chi-N	132	415	59	105	17	0	3	33	49	61	.253	.335	.316	81	-9	10	8	-2	.981	-7	2-61,S-45/O3	-1.0
1965	Chi-N	116	282	26	63	9	4	0	19	30	53	.223	.303	.284	65	-12	13	3	1	.955	-11	O-55,S-48	-2.3
1966	Chi-N	57	90	4	16	4	1	0	4	7	12	.178	.253	.244	38	-7	1	1	-0	1.000	-1	O-15/2-4,S3	-1.0
1967	Chi-N	6	6	1	1	0	0	0	1	0	0	.167	.167	.167	-4	-1	0	0	0	.000	0	H	-0.1
	Chi-A	24	18	5	3	0	0	0	1	1	6	.167	.211	.167	13	-2	1	0	0	1.000	0	/O-6,2-5,S	-0.2
1969	Cin-N	119	221	26	56	3	4	4	24	19	33	.253	.313	.357	83	-5	4	2	0	.973	-9	O-66,2-18/3S	-1.4
1970	*Cin-N	101	105	15	28	3	1	1	8	8	13	.267	.325	.343	79	-3	5	3	-0	1.000	-11	O-48,2-18/3C1	-1.4
1971	Cin-N	80	82	7	19	2	2	0	9	9	12	.232	.308	.305	76	-3	3	1	0	1.000	-10	O-19/3-9,2	-1.3
1972	Hou-N	68	96	14	21	5	2	0	9	6	9	.219	.265	.313	65	-5	0	1	-1	1.000	-5	O-11/1-9,23	-1.2
1973	Hou-N	61	68	6	13	0	0	0	3	9	12	.191	.295	.191	37	-5	0	0	0	1.000	0	/3-8,O-3,2	-0.7
Total	10	777	1420	164	336	45	14	8	112	139	218	.237	.308	.305	71	-53	38	20	-1	.969	-53	O-227,2-122,S/31C	-10.7

■ STUFFY STEWART Stewart, John Franklin b: 1/31/1894, Jasper, Fla. d: 12/30/80, Lake City, Fla. BR/TR, 5'9.5", 160 lbs. Deb: 9/3/16

1916	StL-N	9	17	0	3	0	0	0	1	0	3	.176	.176	.176	9	-2	0			.833	-2	/2-8	-0.4
1917	StL-N	13	9	4	0	0	0	0	0	0	4	.000	.000	.000	-99	-2	0			1.000	-3	/O-7,2-2	-0.5
1922	Pit-N	3	13	3	2	0	0	0	0	0	1	.154	.154	.154	-20	-2	0			.875	-1	/2-3	-0.3
1923	Bro-N	4	11	3	4	1	0	1	1	1	1	.364	.417	.727	202	2	0	0	0	.786	-1	/2-3	0.0
1925	Was-A	7	17	3	6	1	0	0	3	1	2	.353	.389	.412	105	0	1	0	0	.929	1	/3-5,2-1	0.1
1926	Was-A	62	63	27	17	6	1	0	9	6	6	.270	.343	.397	92	-1	8	4	0	.975	7	2-25/3-1	0.6
1927	Was-A	56	129	24	31	6	2	0	4	8	15	.240	.285	.318	57	-8	12	2	2	.939	1	2-37/3-2	-0.4
1929	Was-A	22	6	10	0	0	0	0	0	1	0	.000	.143	.000	-60	-1	0	1	-1	1.000	2	/2-3	-0.4
Total	8	176	265	74	63	14	3	1	18	17	32	.238	.284	.325	61	-15	21	7		.932	4	/2-82,3-8,O	-0.9

■ MARK STEWART Stewart, Mark "Big Slick" b: 10/11/1889, Whitlock, Tenn. d: 1/17/32, Memphis, Tenn. BL/TR, 6'1", 180 lbs. Deb: 10/4/13

| 1913 | Cin-N | 1 | 1 | 0 | 0 | 0 | 0 | 0 | 0 | 0 | 0 | .000 | .000 | .000 | -99 | -0 | 0 | | | .000 | 0 | /C-1 | 0.0 |

■ NEB STEWART Stewart, Walter Nesbitt b: 5/21/18, S.Charleston, Ohio d: 6/8/90, London, Ohio BR/TR, 6'1", 195 lbs. Deb: 9/8/40

| 1940 | Phi-N | 10 | 31 | 3 | 4 | 0 | 0 | 0 | 1 | 1 | 5 | .129 | .156 | .129 | -21 | -5 | 0 | | | .944 | 0 | /O-9 | -0.5 |

■ BILL STEWART Stewart, William Wayne b: 4/15/28, Bay City, Mich. BR/TR, 5'11", 200 lbs. Deb: 4/17/55

| 1955 | KC-A | 11 | 18 | 2 | 2 | 1 | 0 | 0 | 0 | 1 | 6 | .111 | .158 | .167 | -13 | -3 | 0 | 0 | 0 | 1.000 | -0 | /O-6 | -0.3 |

■ ROYLE STILLMAN Stillman, Royle Eldon b: 1/2/51, Santa Monica, Cal. BL/TL, 5'11", 180 lbs. Deb: 6/22/75

1975	Bal-A	13	14	1	6	0	0	0	1	1	3	.429	.467	.429	165	1	0	0	0	1.000	-0	/O-2	0.1
1976	Bal-A	20	22	0	2	0	0	0	1	3	4	.091	.200	.091	-14	-3	0	0	0	1.000	-0	/1-2,D-5	-0.3
1977	Chi-A	56	119	18	25	7	1	3	13	17	21	.210	.309	.361	82	-3	2	1	0	.977	-3	O-26,D-13/1	-0.7
Total	3	89	155	19	33	7	1	3	15	21	28	.213	.307	.329	77	-5	2	1	0	.978	-3	/O-28,D-18,1	-0.9

■ KURT STILLWELL Stillwell, Kurt Andrew b: 6/4/65, Glendale, Cal. BB/TR, 5'11", 175 lbs. Deb: 4/13/86 F

1986	Cin-N	104	279	31	64	6	1	0	26	30	47	.229	.309	.258	56	-16	6	2	1	.951	-2	S-80	-1.2
1987	Cin-N	131	395	54	102	20	7	4	33	32	50	.258	.317	.375	79	-12	4	6	-2	.914	-21	S-51,2-37,3	-3.1
1988	KC-A★	128	459	63	115	28	5	10	53	47	76	.251	.324	.399	100	0	6	5	-0	.976	-18	*S-124	-0.8
1989	KC-A	130	463	52	121	20	7	7	54	42	64	.261	.327	.380	99	-1	9	6	-1	.970	-32	*S-130	-2.4
1990	KC-A	144	506	60	126	35	4	3	51	39	60	.249	.304	.352	85	-10	0	2	-1	.957	-20	*S-141	-2.1
1991	KC-A	122	385	44	102	17	1	6	51	33	56	.265	.325	.361	89	-6	3	4	-1	.959	-25	*S-118	-2.4
1992	SD-N	114	379	35	86	15	3	2	24	26	58	.227	.278	.298	62	-19	4	1	1	.970	-14	*2-111	-3.3
1993	SD-N	57	121	9	26	4	0	1	11	11	22	.215	.286	.273	49	-9	4	3	-1	.921	-5	S-30/3-3	-1.2
	Cal-A	22	61	2	16	2	2	0	3	4	11	.262	.308	.361	76	-2	2	2	0	.952	-4	2-18/S-7	-0.4
Total	8	952	3048	350	758	147	30	33	306	264	444	.249	.312	.349	82	-74	38	29	-6	.958	-142	S-681,2-166/3	-17.0

■ RON STILLWELL Stillwell, Ronald Roy b: 12/3/39, Los Angeles, Cal. BR/TR, 5'11", 165 lbs. Deb: 7/3/61 F

1961	Was-A	8	16	3	2	1	0	0	1	1	4	.125	.176	.188	-3	-1	0	0	0	.929	-1	/S-5	-0.3
1962	Was-A	6	22	5	6	0	0	0	2	2	2	.273	.333	.273	66	-1	0	0	0	1.000	-2	/2-6,S-1	-0.3
Total	2	14	38	8	8	1	0	0	3	3	6	.211	.268	.237	37	-3	0	0	0	.929	-3	/2-6,S-6	-0.6

■ CRAIG STIMAC Stimac, Craig Steven b: 11/18/54, Oak Park, Ill. BR/TR, 6'2", 185 lbs. Deb: 8/12/80

1980	SD-N	20	50	5	11	2	0	0	7	1	6	.220	.235	.260	40	-4	0	0	0	.982	4	C-11/3-2	0.0
1981	SD-N	9	9	0	1	0	0	0	0	0	1	.111	.111	.111	-40	-2	0	0	0	.000	0	/H	-0.2
Total	2	29	59	5	12	2	0	0	7	1	7	.203	.217	.237	29	-6	0	0	0	.982	4	/C-11,3-2	-0.2

■ KELLY STINNETT Stinnett, Kelly Lee b: 2/14/70, Lawton, Okla. BR/TR, 5'11", 195 lbs. Deb: 4/5/94

| 1994 | NY-N | 47 | 150 | 20 | 38 | 6 | 2 | 2 | 14 | 11 | 28 | .253 | .325 | .360 | 78 | -5 | 2 | 0 | 1 | .979 | -4 | C-44 | -0.6 |

YEAR	TM/L	G	AB	R	H	2B	3B	HR	RBI	BB	SO	AVG	OBP	SLG	PRO+	BR/A	SB	CS	SBR	FA	FR	G/POS	TPR

■ BOB STINSON
Stinson, Gorrell Robert b: 10/11/45, Elkin, N.C. BB/TR, 5'11.5", 185 lbs. Deb: 9/23/69

1969	LA-N	4	8	1	3	0	0	0	2	0	2	.375	.375	.375	119	0	0	1	-1	.952	1	/C-4	0.0
1970	LA-N	4	3	1	0	0	0	0	0	0	1	.000	.000	.000	-99	-1	0	0	0	1.000	-0	/C-3	-0.1
1971	StL-N	17	19	3	4	1	0	0	1	1	7	.211	.250	.263	44	-1	0	0	0	.971	2	/C-6,O-3	0.1
1972	Hou-N	27	35	3	6	1	0	0	2	1	6	.171	.216	.200	19	-4	0	0	0	.964	-4	C-12/O-3	-0.9
1973	Mon-N	48	111	12	29	6	1	3	12	17	15	.261	.374	.414	114	3	0	1	-1	.979	-3	C-35/3-1	0.0
1974	Mon-N	38	87	4	15	2	0	1	6	15	16	.172	.294	.230	45	-6	1	1	-0	1.000	1	C-29	-0.5
1975	KC-A	63	147	18	39	9	1	1	19	18	29	.265	.349	.361	98	0	1	0	0	.993	7	C-59/1-1,20D	1.0
1976	*KC-A	79	209	26	55	7	1	2	25	25	29	.263	.345	.335	99	0	3	1	0	.979	-6	C-79	-0.4
1977	Sea-A	105	297	27	80	11	1	8	32	37	50	.269	.362	.394	107	4	0	3	-2	.984	-7	C-99/D-1	-0.2
1978	Sea-A	124	364	46	94	14	3	11	55	45	42	.258	.349	.445	112	6	2	1	0	.987	-18	*C-123/D-1	-0.9
1979	Sea-A	95	247	19	60	8	0	6	28	33	38	.243	.342	.348	85	-4	1	2	-1	.978	-7	C-91	-0.9
1980	Sea-A	48	107	6	23	2	0	1	8	9	19	.215	.282	.262	50	-7	0	0	0	.979	-9	C-45	-1.5
Total	12	652	1634	166	408	61	7	33	180	201	254	.250	.340	.356	93	-10	8	10	-4	.984	-44	C-585/O-7,D213	-4.3

■ GAT STIRES
Stires, Garrett b: 10/13/1849, Hunterdon Co., N.J d: 6/13/33, Byron, Ill. BL/TR, 5'8", 180 lbs. Deb: 5/6/1871

1871	Rok-n	25	110	23	30	4	6	2	24	7	5	.273	.316	.473	129	5	3					*O-25	0.4

■ SNUFFY STIRNWEISS
Stirnweiss, George Henry b: 10/26/18, New York, N.Y. d: 9/15/58, Newark Bay, N.J. BR/TR, 5'8.5", 175 lbs. Deb: 4/22/43

1943	*NY-A	83	274	34	60	8	4	1	25	47	37	.219	.333	.288	82	-5	11	9	-2	.938	-6	S-68/2-4	-0.9
1944	NY-A	154	643	125	205	35	16	8	43	73	87	.319	.389	.460	137	32	55	11	10	.982	19	*2-154	7.1
1945	NY-A†	152	632	107	195	32	22	10	64	78	62	.309	.385	.476	143	34	33	17	-0	.970	26	*2-152	7.2
1946	NY-A★	129	487	75	122	19	7	0	37	66	58	.251	.340	.318	83	-9	18	6	2	.991	-6	3-79,2-46/S	-0.9
1947	*NY-A	148	571	102	146	18	8	5	41	89	47	.256	.358	.342	96	-1	5	3	-0	.983	-11	*2-148	-0.1
1948	*NY-A	141	515	90	130	20	7	3	32	86	62	.252	.360	.336	87	-8	5	4	-1	.993	-11	*2-141	-1.1
1949	*NY-A	70	157	29	41	8	2	0	11	29	20	.261	.380	.338	90	-1	3	2	0	.974	4	2-51/3-4	0.4
1950	NY-A	7	2	0	0	0	0	0	0	0	0	.000	.000	.000	-99	-1	0	0	0	1.000	1	/2-4	0.0
	StL-N	93	326	32	71	16	2	1	24	51	49	.218	.324	.288	56	-21	3	3	-1	.975	-24	2-62,3-31/S	-4.2
	Yr	100	328	32	71	16	2	1	24	51	49	.216	.322	.287	55	-22	3	3	-1	.975	-23	2-66,3-31/S	-4.2
1951	Cle-A	50	88	10	19	1	0	1	4	22	25	.216	.373	.261	78	-2	1	0	0	.992	7	2-25/3-2	0.7
1952	Cle-A	1	0	0	0	0	0	0	0	0	0	—	—	—	—		0	0	0	.000	0	/3-1	0.0
Total	10	1028	3695	604	989	157	68	29	281	541	447	.268	.362	.371	102	19	134	55	7	.980	-1	2-787,3-117/S	8.2

■ JACK STIVETTS
Stivetts, John Elmer "Happy Jack" b: 3/31/1868, Ashland, Pa. d: 4/18/30, Ashland, Pa. BR/TR, 6'2", 185 lbs. Deb: 6/26/1889

1889	StL-a	27	79	12	18	7	3	0		7	13	.228	.265	.304	55	-5	0			.896	-1	P-26/O-1	-0.1
1890	StL-a	67	226	36	65	15	6	7		16		.288	.337	.500	128	4	2			.894	4	P-54,O-10/1	0.1
1891	StL-a	85	302	45	92	10	2	7	54	10	32	.305	.331	.421	100	-4	4			.898	3	P-64,O-24	-0.2
1892	*Bos-N	71	240	40	71	14	2	3	36	27	28	.296	.369	.408	124	6	8			.904	-5	P-54,O-18/1	0.0
1893	Bos-N	50	172	32	51	5	6	3	25	12	14	.297	.342	.448	101	-1	6			.955	-4	P-38/O-8,3	-0.2
1894	Bos-N	68	244	55	80	12	7	8	64	16	21	.328	.369	.533	107	0	3			.943	-4	P-45,O-16/1	-0.1
1895	Bos-N	46	158	20	30	6	4	0	24	6	18	.190	.220	.278	26	-19	1			.961	-1	P-38/1-5,O	-0.3
1896	Bos-N	67	221	42	76	9	6	3	49	12	10	.344	.380	.480	119	5	4			.946	-6	P-42,O-12/13	-0.2
1897	*Bos-N	61	199	41	73	9	2	5	37	15		.367	.417	.533	141	11	2			.926	-3	O-29,P-18/21	0.1
1898	Bos-N	41	111	16	28	1	1	2	16	10		.252	.314	.333	81	-3	1			.909	-3	O-14,1-10/S2P	-0.8
1899	Cle-N	18	39	8	8	1	1	0	2	6		.205	.326	.282	73	-1	0			1.000	1	/O-7,P-7,S3	-0.2
Total	11	601	1991	347	592	84	46	35	314	133	136	.297	.344	.438	104	-7	31			.924	-17	P-388,O-141/1S32	-1.9

■ MILT STOCK
Stock, Milton Joseph b: 7/11/1893, Chicago, Ill. d: 7/16/77, Fairhope, Ala. BR/TR, 5'8", 154 lbs. Deb: 9/29/13 C

1913	NY-N	7	17	2	3	1	0	0	2	1	2	.176	.263	.235	43	-1	2			.838	2	/S-7	0.1
1914	NY-N	115	365	52	96	17	1	3	41	34	21	.263	.333	.340	103	2	11			.939	15	*3-113/S-1	2.2
1915	*Phi-N	69	227	37	59	7	3	1	15	22	26	.260	.325	.330	98	-0	6	2	1	.971	2	3-55/S-4	0.5
1916	Phi-N	132	509	61	143	25	6	1	43	27	33	.281	.320	.360	105	2	21	26	-9	.955	-6	*3-117,S-15	-1.0
1917	Phi-N	150	564	76	149	27	6	3	53	51	34	.264	.326	.349	103	2	25			.942	-9	*3-133,S-19	-0.4
1918	Phi-N	123	481	62	132	14	1	1	42	35	22	.274	.325	.314	89	-6	20			.946	-5	*3-123	-0.9
1919	StL-N	135	492	56	151	16	4	0	52	49	21	.307	.371	.356	127	17	17			.966	17	2-77,3-58	4.3
1920	StL-N	155	639	85	204	28	6	0	76	40	27	.319	.360	.382	117	14	15	17	-6	.939	-8	*3-155	0.9
1921	StL-N	149	587	96	180	27	6	4	84	48	25	.307	.360	.388	100	1	11	3	2	.940	-22	*3-149	-0.9
1922	StL-N	151	581	85	177	33	9	5	79	42	29	.305	.352	.418	103	1	7	12	-5	.950	-9	*3-149/S-1	-0.1
1923	StL-N	151	603	63	174	33	3	2	96	40	21	.289	.334	.363	86	-13	9	6	-1	.955	-14	*3-150/2-1	-1.4
1924	Bro-N	142	561	66	136	14	4	2	52	26	32	.242	.277	.292	54	-36	3	8	-4	.931	-23	*3-142	-5.2
1925	Bro-N	146	615	98	202	28	9	1	62	38	28	.328	.368	.408	101	1	8	1	2	.978	-5	*2-141/3-5	0.6
1926	Bro-N	3	8	0	0	0	0	0	0	0	1	.000	.111	.000	-69	-2	0			.923	-1	/2-3	-0.2
Total	14	1628	6249	839	1806	270	58	22	696	455	321	.289	.339	.361	98	-17	155	75		.945	-59	*3-1349,2-222/S	-1.5

■ KEVIN STOCKER
Stocker, Kevin Douglas b: 2/13/70, Spokane, Wash. BB/TR, 6'1", 175 lbs. Deb: 7/7/93

1993	*Phi-N	70	259	46	84	12	3	2	31	30	43	.324	.411	.417	124	11	5	0	2	.958	-1	S-70	1.7
1994	Phi-N	82	271	38	74	11	2	2	28	44	41	.273	.388	.351	96	1	2	2	-1	.959	-2	S-82	0.5
Total	2	152	530	84	158	23	5	4	59	74	84	.298	.399	.383	109	11	7	2	1	.958	-3	S-152	2.2

■ LEN STOCKWELL
Stockwell, Leonard Clark b: 8/25/1859, Cordova, Ill. d: 1/28/05, Niles, Cal. BR/TR, 5'11", 165 lbs. Deb: 5/17/1879

1879	Cle-N	2	6	0	0	0	0	0	0	0	2	.000	.000	.000	-99	-1				1.000	1	/O-2	-0.2
1884	Lou-a	2	9	0	1	0	0	0		0		.111	.111	.111	-29	-1				.667	-1	/O-2,C-1	-0.2
1890	Cle-N	2	7	2	2	1	0	0	0	0	3	.286	.286	.429	110	0	0			1.000	0	/O-1,1-1	0.0
Total	3	6	22	2	3	1	0	0	0	0	5	.136	.136	.182	-1	-2	0			.900	1	/O-5,1-1,C	-0.2

■ STODDARD
Stoddard Deb: 9/25/1875

1875	Atl-n	2	9	1	1	1	0	0		0		.111	.111	.222	14	-1						/O-2	-0.1

■ AL STOKES
Stokes, Albert John (b: Albert John Stocek) b: 1/1/1900, Chicago, Ill. d: 12/19/86, Grantham, N.H. BR/TR, 5'9", 175 lbs. Deb: 5/10/25

1925	Bos-A	17	52	7	11	0	1	0	1	4	8	.212	.268	.250	32	-5	0	0	0	.969	3	C-17	-0.2
1926	Bos-A	30	86	7	14	3	3	0	6	8	28	.163	.234	.267	32	-9	0	0	0	.931	-4	C-29	-1.1
Total	2	47	138	14	25	3	4	0	7	12	36	.181	.247	.261	32	-15	0	0	0	.946	-1	/C-46	-1.3

■ GENE STONE
Stone, Eugene Daniel b: 1/16/44, Burbank, Cal. BL/TL, 5'11", 190 lbs. Deb: 5/13/69

1969	Phi-N	18	28	4	6	0	0	0	4	4	9	.214	.313	.286	70	-1	0	0	0	1.000	-1	/1-5	-0.2

■ GEORGE STONE
Stone, George Robert b: 9/3/1877, Lost Nation, Iowa d: 1/3/45, Clinton, Iowa BL/TL, 5'9", 175 lbs. Deb: 4/20/03

1903	Bos-A	2	2	0	0	0	0	0	0	0		.000	.000	.000	-95	-0				.000	0	H	0.0
1905	StL-A	154	632	76	187	25	13	7	52	44		.296	.347	.410	147	32	26			.954	1	*O-154	2.8
1906	StL-A	154	581	91	208	25	20	6	71	52		.358	.417	.501	195	63	35			.968	-1	*O-154	5.8
1907	StL-A	155	596	77	191	13	11	4	59	59		.320	.387	.399	151	36	23			.970	-3	*O-155	2.9
1908	StL-A	148	588	89	165	21	8	5	31	55		.281	.345	.369	131	21	20			.947	-0	*O-148	1.6
1909	StL-A	83	310	33	89	5	4	1	15	24		.287	.340	.332	123	8	8			.928	2	O-81	0.7
1910	StL-A	152	562	60	144	17	12	0	40	48		.256	.315	.329	108	5	20			.972	-2	*O-145	-0.5
Total	7	848	3271	426	984	106	68	23	268	282		.301	.360	.396	145	164	132			.958	-4	O-837	13.3

YEAR	TM/L	G	AB	R	H	2B	3B	HR	RBI	BB	SO	AVG	OBP	SLG	PRO+	BR/A	SB	CS	SBR	FA	FR	G/POS	TPR

■ RON STONE
Stone, Harry Ronald   b: 9/9/42, Corning, Cal.   BL/TL, 6'2", 195 lbs.   Deb: 4/13/66

YEAR	TM/L	G	AB	R	H	2B	3B	HR	RBI	BB	SO	AVG	OBP	SLG	PRO+	BR/A	SB	CS	SBR	FA	FR	G/POS	TPR
1966	KC-A	26	22	2	6	0	0	0	2	0	2	.273	.273	.318	71	-1	1	1	-0	1.000	-1	/O-4,1-3	-0.3
1969	Phi-N	103	222	22	53	7	1	1	24	29	28	.239	.335	.293	79	-5	3	1	0	.978	-3	O-69	-1.2
1970	Phi-N	123	321	30	84	12	5	3	39	38	45	.262	.342	.358	90	-4	5	6	-2	.968	-3	O-99/1-6	-1.4
1971	Phi-N	95	185	16	42	8	1	2	23	25	36	.227	.319	.314	80	-4	2	2	-1	.964	-4	O-51/1-3	-1.2
1972	Phi-N	41	54	3	9	0	1	0	3	9	11	.167	.286	.204	40	-4	0	0	0	1.000	1	O-15	-0.4
Total	5	388	804	73	194	28	8	6	89	101	122	.241	.329	.318	81	-18	11	10	-3	.973	-11	O-238/1-12	-4.5

■ JEFF STONE
Stone, Jeffrey Glen   b: 12/26/60, Kennett, Mo.   BL/TR, 6', 175 lbs.   Deb: 9/9/83

YEAR	TM/L	G	AB	R	H	2B	3B	HR	RBI	BB	SO	AVG	OBP	SLG	PRO+	BR/A	SB	CS	SBR	FA	FR	G/POS	TPR
1983	Phi-N	9	4	2	3	0	2	0	3	0	1	.750	.750	1.750	580	2	4	0	1	.000	-0	/O-1	0.3
1984	Phi-N	51	185	27	67	4	6	1	15	9	26	.362	.398	.465	139	10	27	5	5	.916	-2	O-46	1.1
1985	Phi-N	88	264	36	70	4	3	3	11	15	50	.265	.307	.337	78	-8	15	5	2	.966	-6	O-69	-1.5
1986	Phi-N	82	249	32	69	6	4	6	19	20	52	.277	.341	.406	101	0	19	6	2	.982	2	O-58	0.3
1987	Phi-N	66	125	19	32	7	1	1	16	8	38	.256	.316	.352	74	-5	3	1	0	1.000	-1	O-25	-0.6
1988	Bal-A	26	61	4	10	1	0	0	1	4	11	.164	.215	.180	12	-7	4	1	1	.963	-2	O-21/D-1	-0.9
1989	Tex-A	22	36	5	6	1	2	0	5	3	5	.167	.250	.306	55	-2	2	1	0	.000	-1	D-15/O-3	-0.4
	Bos-A	18	15	3	3	0	0	0	1	1	2	.200	.250	.200	27	-1	1	0	0	1.000	-3	O-11/D-3	-0.5
	Yr	40	51	8	9	1	2	0	6	4	7	.176	.250	.275	46	-4	3	1	0	.000	-5	D-18,O-14	-0.9
1990	Bos-A	10	2	1	1	0	0	0	1	0	1	.500	.500	.500	173	0	0	1	-1	.000	0	/D-2	0.0
Total	8	372	941	129	261	23	18	11	72	60	186	.277	.328	.375	92	-10	75	20	11	.963	-14	O-234/D-21	-2.2

■ JOHN STONE
Stone, John Thomas "Rocky"   b: 10/10/05, Lynchburg, Tenn.   d: 11/30/55, Shelbyville, Tenn.   BL/TR, 6'1", 178 lbs.   Deb: 8/31/28

YEAR	TM/L	G	AB	R	H	2B	3B	HR	RBI	BB	SO	AVG	OBP	SLG	PRO+	BR/A	SB	CS	SBR	FA	FR	G/POS	TPR
1928	Det-A	26	113	20	40	10	3	2	21	5	8	.354	.387	.549	141	6	1	0		.962	1	O-26	0.3
1929	Det-A	51	150	23	39	11	2	2	15	11	13	.260	.311	.400	81	-5	1	1	-0	.986	-1	O-36	-0.8
1930	Det-A	127	425	60	132	29	11	3	56	32	49	.311	.360	.452	102	1	6	9	-4	.966	0	*O-109	-0.9
1931	Det-A	147	584	86	191	28	11	10	76	56	48	.327	.388	.464	119	16	13	13	-4	.959	4	*O-147	0.6
1932	Det-A	145	582	106	173	35	12	17	108	58	64	.297	.361	.486	113	10	2	1	0	.961	3	*O-142	0.3
1933	Det-A	148	574	86	161	33	11	11	80	54	37	.280	.344	.434	103	1	1	4	-2	.970	1	*O-141	-0.7
1934	Was-A	113	419	77	132	28	7	7	67	52	26	.315	.395	.465	126	17	1	2	-1	.966	7	*O-112	1.7
1935	Was-A	125	455	78	143	27	18	1	78	39	29	.314	.372	.459	118	11	4	5	-2	.955	0	*O-114	0.5
1936	Was-A	123	437	95	149	22	11	15	90	60	26	.341	.421	.545	145	31	8	0	2	.967	7	*O-114	3.1
1937	Was-A	139	542	84	179	33	15	6	88	66	36	.330	.403	.480	127	23	6	4	-1	.984	5	*O-137	2.2
1938	Was-A	56	213	24	52	12	4	3	28	30	16	.244	.337	.380	85	-5	2	1	0	.974	-2	O-53	-0.8
Total	11	1200	4494	739	1391	268	105	77	707	463	352	.310	.376	.467	116	106	45	40	-10	.967	24	*O-1131	5.5

■ TIGE STONE
Stone, William Arthur   b: 9/18/01, Macon, Ga.   d: 1/1/60, Jacksonville, Fla.   BR/TR, 5'8", 145 lbs.   Deb: 8/23/23

YEAR	TM/L	G	AB	R	H	2B	3B	HR	RBI	BB	SO	AVG	OBP	SLG	PRO+	BR/A	SB	CS	SBR	FA	FR	G/POS	TPR
1923	StL-N	5	1	0	1	0	0	0	0	2	0	1.000	1.000	1.000	438	1	0	0	0	.000	-2	/O-4,P-1	-0.2

■ JOHN STONEHAM
Stoneham, John Andrew   b: 11/8/08, Wood River, Ill.   BL/TR, 5'9.5", 168 lbs.   Deb: 9/18/33

YEAR	TM/L	G	AB	R	H	2B	3B	HR	RBI	BB	SO	AVG	OBP	SLG	PRO+	BR/A	SB	CS	SBR	FA	FR	G/POS	TPR
1933	Chi-A	10	25	4	3	0	0	1	3	2	2	.120	.185	.240	12	-3	0	0		1.000	-2	/O-9	-0.5

■ HOWIE STORIE
Storie, Howard Edward "Sponge"   b: 5/15/11, Pittsfield, Mass.   d: 7/27/68, Pittsfield, Mass.   BR/TR, 5'10", 175 lbs.   Deb: 9/7/31

YEAR	TM/L	G	AB	R	H	2B	3B	HR	RBI	BB	SO	AVG	OBP	SLG	PRO+	BR/A	SB	CS	SBR	FA	FR	G/POS	TPR
1931	Bos-A	6	17	2	2	0	0	0	0	3	2	.118	.250	.118	-1	-2	0	0	0	1.000	0	/C-6	-0.2
1932	Bos-A	6	8	0	3	0	0	0	0	0	0	.375	.375	.375	98	-0	0	0	0	1.000	0	/C-5	0.0
Total	2	12	25	2	5	0	0	0	0	3	2	.200	.286	.200	31	-2	0	0	0	1.000	1	/C-11	-0.2

■ ALAN STORKE
Storke, Alan Marshall   b: 9/27/1884, Auburn, N.Y.   d: 3/18/10, Newton, Mass.   BR/TR, 6'1", Deb: 9/24/06

YEAR	TM/L	G	AB	R	H	2B	3B	HR	RBI	BB	SO	AVG	OBP	SLG	PRO+	BR/A	SB	CS	SBR	FA	FR	G/POS	TPR
1906	Pit-N	5	12	1	3	1	0	0	1	1		.250	.308	.333	96	-0	1			1.000	0	/3-2,S-1	0.0
1907	Pit-N	112	357	24	92	6	6	1	39	16		.258	.295	.317	90	-5	6			.925	-13	3-67,1-23/2S	-1.8
1908	Pit-N	64	202	20	51	5	3	1	12	9		.252	.284	.322	93	-2	4			.988	-6	1-49/3-6,2	-1.0
1909	Pit-N	37	118	12	30	5	2	0	12	7		.254	.302	.331	89	-2	1			.994	-0	1-18,3-14	-0.2
	StL-N	48	174	11	49	5	0	0	10	12		.282	.328	.310	105	1	5			.958	-1	S-44/2-4,1	0.0
	Yr	85	292	23	79	10	2	0	22	19		.271	.317	.318	97	-1	6			.958	-2	S-44,1-19,3/2	-0.2
Total	4	266	863	68	225	22	11	2	74	45		.261	.300	.319	94	-8	17			.990	-20	/1-91,3-89,S2	-3.0

■ LIN STORTI
Storti, Lindo Ivan   b: 12/5/06, Santa Monica, Cal.   d: 7/24/82, Ontario, Cal.   BB/TR, 5'11", 165 lbs.   Deb: 9/18/30

YEAR	TM/L	G	AB	R	H	2B	3B	HR	RBI	BB	SO	AVG	OBP	SLG	PRO+	BR/A	SB	CS	SBR	FA	FR	G/POS	TPR
1930	StL-A	7	28	6	9	1	0	2	2	2	6	.321	.367	.429	98	-0	0	0	0	.975	1	/2-6	0.1
1931	StL-A	86	273	32	60	15	4	3	26	15	50	.220	.263	.337	55	-19	0	2	-1	.926	9	3-67/2-7	-1.0
1932	StL-A	53	193	19	50	11	2	3	26	5	20	.259	.278	.383	66	-10	1	0	0	.956	-4	3-51	-1.0
1933	StL-A	70	210	26	41	7	4	3	21	25	31	.195	.281	.310	53	-15	2	2	-1	.934	-2	3-32,2-24	-1.4
Total	4	216	704	83	160	34	11	9	75	47	107	.227	.277	.345	59	-44	3	4	-2	.936	4	3-150/2-37	-3.0

■ TOM STOUCH
Stouch, Thomas Carl   b: 12/2/1870, Perryville, Ohio   d: 10/7/56, Lancaster, Pa.   BR/TR, 6'2", 165 lbs.   Deb: 7/7/1898

YEAR	TM/L	G	AB	R	H	2B	3B	HR	RBI	BB	SO	AVG	OBP	SLG	PRO+	BR/A	SB	CS	SBR	FA	FR	G/POS	TPR
1898	Lou-N	4	16	4	5	1	0	0	6	1		.313	.353	.375	110	0	0			.850	-2	/2-4	-0.2

■ GEORGE STOVALL
Stovall, George Thomas "Firebrand"   b: 11/23/1878, Independence, Mo.   d: 11/5/51, Burlington, Iowa   BR/TR, 6'2", 180 lbs.   Deb: 7/4/04   FM

YEAR	TM/L	G	AB	R	H	2B	3B	HR	RBI	BB	SO	AVG	OBP	SLG	PRO+	BR/A	SB	CS	SBR	FA	FR	G/POS	TPR
1904	Cle-A	52	181	18	54	10	1	1	31	2		.298	.317	.381	121	4	3			.978	-2	1-38/2-9,O3	0.1
1905	Cle-A	112	423	41	115	31	1	1	47	13		.272	.295	.357	105	1	13			.975	-5	1-60,2-46/O	-0.6
1906	Cle-A	116	443	54	121	19	5	0	37	8		.273	.288	.339	97	-3	13			.985	-5	1-55,3-30,2	-0.9
1907	Cle-A	124	466	38	110	17	6	1	36	18		.236	.267	.305	82	-11	13			.983	-4	*1-122/3-2	-2.0
1908	Cle-A	138	534	71	156	29	6	2	45	17		.292	.316	.380	126	13	14			**.990**	3	*1-132/O-5,S	1.5
1909	Cle-A	145	565	60	139	17	10	2	49	6		.246	.259	.322	80	-15	25			**.988**	10	*1-145	-0.8
1910	Cle-A	142	521	49	136	19	4	0	52	14		.261	.284	.313	86	-10	16			**.988**	7	*1-132/2-2	-0.4
1911	Cle-A	126	458	48	124	17	7	0	79	21		.271	.306	.338	79	-14	11			**.986**	7	*1-118/2-2M	-0.8
1912	StL-A	116	398	35	101	17	5	0	45	14		.254	.286	.322	76	-14	11			.983	5	1-94,M	-1.0
1913	StL-A	89	303	34	87	14	3	1	24	7	23	.287	.305	.363	98	-3	7			.988	8	1-76,M	0.4
1914	KC-F	124	450	51	128	20	5	7	75	23	35	.284	.325	.398	90	-9	6			.989	4	*1-116/3-1M	-0.7
1915	KC-F	130	480	48	111	21	3	0	44	29	36	.231	.283	.287	55	-32	8			.987	5	*1-129,M	-3.3
Total	12	1414	5222	547	1382	231	56	15	564	172	94	.265	.292	.339	89	-93	142			.986	33	*1-1217/2-78,3OS	-8.5

■ HARRY STOVEY
Stovey, Harry Duffield (b: Harry Duffield Stowe)   b: 12/20/1856, Philadelphia, Pa.   d: 9/20/37, New Bedford, Mass.   BR/TR, 5'11.5", 175 lbs.   Deb: 5/1/1880   M

YEAR	TM/L	G	AB	R	H	2B	3B	HR	RBI	BB	SO	AVG	OBP	SLG	PRO+	BR/A	SB	CS	SBR	FA	FR	G/POS	TPR
1880	Wor-N	83	355	76	94	21	**14**	6	28	12	46	.265	.289	.454	136	11				.860	-5	O-46,1-37/P	0.2
1881	Wor-N	75	341	57	92	25	7	2	30	12	23	.270	.295	.402	111	3				.955	-5	*1-57,O-18M	-0.7
1882	Wor-N	84	360	90	104	13	10	5	26	22	34	.289	.330	.422	136	14				.956	4	1-43,O-41	1.2
1883	Phi-a	94	421	**110**	128	**31**	6	**14**		27		.304	.346	**.506**	158	25				.965	0	*1-93/O-3,P	1.3
1884	Phi-a	104	448	**124**	146	22	**23**	10		26		.326	.368	.545	182	38				.960	-1	*1-104	2.3
1885	Phi-a	112	486	**130**	153	27	9	**13**		39		.315	.371	.488	160	31				.967	4	*1-82,O-30M	2.2
1886	Phi-a	123	489	115	144	28	11	7		64		.294	.377	.440	154	31	**68**			.870	3	O-63,1-62/P	2.2
1887	Phi-a	124	497	125	142	31	12	4		56		.286	.366	.421	119	13	74			.902	12	O-80,1-46	1.5
1888	Phi-a	130	530	127	152	25	**20**	9	65	62		.287	.365	.460	165	**39**	87			.943	4	*O-118,1-13	3.5
1889	Phi-a	137	556	**152**	171	38	13	**19**	**119**	77	68	.308	.393	**.525**	162	45	63			.897	18	O-137/1-1	**4.9**
1890	Bos-P	118	481	142	143	25	11	12	85	81	38	.297	.404	.470	125	16	**97**			.921	2	*O-117/1-1	1.1
1891	Bos-N	134	544	118	152	31	**20**	**16**	95	78	69	.279	.372	**.498**	136	21	57			.910	9	*O-134/1-1	2.2
1892	Bos-N	38	146	21	24	8	1	0	12	14	19	.164	.252	.233	43	-11	20			.901	0	O-38	-1.1

YEAR	TM/L	G	AB	R	H	2B	3B	HR	RBI	BB	SO	AVG	OBP	SLG	PRO+	BR/A	SB	CS	SBR	FA	FR	G/POS	TPR
	Bal-N	74	283	58	77	14	11	4	55	40	32	.272	.364	.442	140	13	20			.913	-3	O-64,1-10	0.6
	Yr	112	429	79	101	22	12	4	67	54	51	.235	.326	.371	106	2	40			.908	-3	*O-102,1-10	-0.5
1893	Bal-N	8	26	4	4	2	0	0	5	8	3	.154	.353	.231	55	-1	1			.864	0	/O-7	-0.1
	Bro-N	48	175	43	44	6	6	1	29	44	11	.251	.402	.371	111	5	22			.901	-3	O-48	0.0
	Yr	56	201	47	48	8	6	1	34	52	14	.239	.395	.353	103	4	23			.895	-2	O-55	-0.1
Total	14	1486	6138	1492	1770	347	174	122	549	662	343	.288	.361	.461	141	293	509			.896	40	O-944,1-550/P	21.3

■ RAY STOVIAK
Stoviak, Raymond Thomas   b: 6/6/15, Scottdale, Pa.   BL/TL, 6'1", 195 lbs.   Deb: 6/5/38

YEAR	TM/L	G	AB	R	H	2B	3B	HR	RBI	BB	SO	AVG	OBP	SLG	PRO+	BR/A	SB	CS	SBR	FA	FR	G/POS	TPR
1938	Phi-N	10	10	1	0	0	0	0	0	0	3	.000	.000	.000	-99	-3	0			1.000	-1	/O-4	-0.4

■ JOE STRAIN
Strain, Joseph Allan   b: 4/30/54, Denver, Colo.   BR/TR, 5'10", 169 lbs.   Deb: 6/28/79

YEAR	TM/L	G	AB	R	H	2B	3B	HR	RBI	BB	SO	AVG	OBP	SLG	PRO+	BR/A	SB	CS	SBR	FA	FR	G/POS	TPR
1979	SF-N	67	257	27	62	8	1	1	12	13	21	.241	.286	.292	62	-14	8	4	0	.982	-1	2-67/3-1	-1.1
1980	SF-N	77	189	26	54	6	0	0	16	10	10	.286	.322	.317	81	-5	1	2	-1	.989	-11	2-42/3-6,S	-1.5
1981	Chi-N	25	74	7	14	1	0	0	1	5	7	.189	.250	.203	28	-7	0	0		.975	7	2-20	0.2
Total	3	169	520	60	130	15	1	1	29	28	38	.250	.293	.288	64	-25	9	6	-1	.983	-5	2-129/3-7,S	-2.4

■ PAUL STRAND
Strand, Paul Edward   b: 12/19/1893, Carbonado, Wash.   d: 7/2/74, Salt Lake City, Utah   BR/TL, 6'0.5", 190 lbs.   Deb: 5/15/13

YEAR	TM/L	G	AB	R	H	2B	3B	HR	RBI	BB	SO	AVG	OBP	SLG	PRO+	BR/A	SB	CS	SBR	FA	FR	G/POS	TPR
1913	Bos-N	7	6	0	1	0	0	0	0	0	0	.167	.167	.167	-5	-1	0			.875		/P-7	0.0
1914	Bos-N	18	24	2	8	2	0	0	3	0	2	.333	.333	.417	123	1	0			.813	-0	P-16	0.0
1915	Bos-N	24	22	3	2	0	0	0	2	0	4	.091	.091	.091	-47	-4	0			.750	-1	/P-6,O-5	-0.2
1924	Phi-A	47	167	15	38	9	4	0	13	4	9	.228	.254	.329	49	-13	3	3	-1	.988	-6	O-44	-2.2
Total	4	96	219	20	49	11	4	0	18	4	15	.224	.244	.311	47	-18	3	3		.989	-7	/O-49,P-29	-2.4

■ LARRY STRANDS
Strands, John Lawrence   b: 12/5/1885, Chicago, Ill.   d: 1/19/57, Forest Park, Ill.   BR/TR, 5'10.5", 165 lbs.   Deb: 4/25/15

YEAR	TM/L	G	AB	R	H	2B	3B	HR	RBI	BB	SO	AVG	OBP	SLG	PRO+	BR/A	SB	CS	SBR	FA	FR	G/POS	TPR
1915	New-F	35	75	7	14	3	1	1	11	6	11	.187	.247	.293	47	-6	1			.852	-7	3-12/2-9,O	-1.3

■ SAMMY STRANG
Strang, Samuel Nicklin "The Dixie Thrush" (b: Samuel Strang Nicklin)   b: 12/16/1876, Chattanooga, Tenn.   d: 3/13/32, Chattanooga, Tenn.   BB/TR, 5'8", 160 lbs.   Deb: 7/10/1896

YEAR	TM/L	G	AB	R	H	2B	3B	HR	RBI	BB	SO	AVG	OBP	SLG	PRO+	BR/A	SB	CS	SBR	FA	FR	G/POS	TPR
1896	Lou-N	14	46	6	12	0	0	0	7	6	6	.261	.346	.261	64	-2	4			.803	-8	S-14	-0.8
1900	Chi-N	27	102	15	29	3	0	0	9	8		.284	.348	.314	86	-1	1			.887	-11	3-16/S-9,2	-1.1
1901	NY-N	135	493	55	139	14	6	1	34	59		.282	.364	.341	109	9	40			.877	2	3-91,2-37/OS	1.2
1902	Chi-A	137	536	108	158	18	5	3	46	76		.295	.387	.364	114	14	38			.890	5	*3-137	1.9
	Chi-N	3	11	1	4	0	0	0	0	0		.364	.364	.364	128	0	1			1.000	-1	/2-2,3-2	0.0
1903	Bro-N	135	508	101	138	21	5	0	38	75		.272	.376	.333	106	8	46			.914	-7	*3-124/O-8,2	0.2
1904	Bro-N	77	271	28	52	11	9	1	9	45		.192	.316	.244	75	-6	16			.910	-32	2-63,3-12/S	-3.9
1905	*NY-N	111	294	51	76	9	4	3	29	58		.259	.389	.347	117	10	23			.915	-17	2-47,O-38/S13	-0.9
1906	NY-N	113	313	50	100	16	4	4	49	54		.319	.423	.435	164	25	21			.944	3	2-57,O-39/S31	3.0
1907	NY-N	123	306	56	77	20	4	4	30	60		.252	.388	.382	137	16	21			.947	-1	O-70,2-13/31S	1.4
1908	NY-N	28	53	9	5	0	0	0	2	9		.094	.385	.094	52	-1	5			.863	-3	2-14/O-5,S	-0.5
Total	10	903	2933	479	790	112	28	16	253	464	6	.269	.377	.343	113	72	216			.891	-70	3-393,2-238,O/S1	0.5

■ ALAN STRANGE
Strange, Alan Cochrane "Inky"   b: 11/7/06, Philadelphia, Pa.   d: 6/27/94, Seattle, Wash.   BR/TR, 5'9", 162 lbs.   Deb: 4/17/34

YEAR	TM/L	G	AB	R	H	2B	3B	HR	RBI	BB	SO	AVG	OBP	SLG	PRO+	BR/A	SB	CS	SBR	FA	FR	G/POS	TPR
1934	StL-A	127	430	39	100	17	2	1	45	48	28	.233	.310	.288	51	-31	3	1	0	.955	4	*S-125	-1.9
1935	StL-A	49	147	8	34	6	1	0	17	17	7	.231	.311	.286	53	-10	0	0	0	.960	2	S-49	-0.6
	Was-A	20	54	3	10	2	1	0	5	4	1	.185	.241	.259	30	-6	0	0	0	.974	3	S-16	-0.2
	Yr	69	201	11	44	8	2	0	22	21	8	.219	.293	.279	47	-16	0	0	0	.963	5	S-65	-0.8
1940	StL-A	54	167	26	31	8	3	0	6	22	12	.186	.284	.269	43	-14	2	1	0	.962	3	S-35/2-4	-0.7
1941	StL-A	45	112	14	26	4	0	1	11	15	5	.232	.323	.268	56	-7	1	0	0	.973	5	S-32/1-2,3	-0.3
1942	StL-A	19	37	3	10	2	0	0	5	3	1	.270	.325	.324	82	-1	0	1	-1	.935	1	3-10/S-3,2	0.3
Total	5	314	947	93	211	39	7	1	89	109	54	.223	.304	.282	50	-69	6	3	0	.959	18	S-260/3-11,21	-3.4

■ DOUG STRANGE
Strange, Joseph Douglas   b: 4/13/64, Greenville, S.C.   BB/TR, 6'2", 170 lbs.   Deb: 7/13/89

YEAR	TM/L	G	AB	R	H	2B	3B	HR	RBI	BB	SO	AVG	OBP	SLG	PRO+	BR/A	SB	CS	SBR	FA	FR	G/POS	TPR
1989	Det-A	64	196	16	42	4	1	1	14	17	36	.214	.280	.260	54	-12	3	3	-1	.878	1	3-54/2-9,SD	-1.1
1991	Chi-N	3	9	0	4	1	0	0	1	0	1	.444	.500	.556	188	1	1	0	0	.800	-1	/3-3	0.0
1992	Chi-N	52	94	7	15	1	0	1	5	10	15	.160	.240	.202	26	-9	1	0	0	.900	-0	3-33,2-12	-1.0
1993	Tex-A	145	484	58	124	29	6	7	60	43	69	.256	.321	.360	86	-10	6	4	-1	.980	-10	*2-135/3-9,S	-1.6
1994	Tex-A	73	226	26	48	12	1	5	26	15	38	.212	.270	.341	60	-14	1	3	-2	.970	7	2-53,3-13/O	-0.7
Total	5	337	1009	107	233	47	2	14	106	85	159	.231	.296	.323	69	-43	12	10	-2	.977	-4	2-209,3-112/SOD	-4.4

■ ASA STRATTON
Stratton, Asa Evans   b: 2/10/1853, Grafton, Mass.   d: 8/14/25, Fitchburg, Mass.   Deb: 6/17/1881

YEAR	TM/L	G	AB	R	H	2B	3B	HR	RBI	BB	SO	AVG	OBP	SLG	PRO+	BR/A	SB	CS	SBR	FA	FR	G/POS	TPR
1881	Wor-N	1	4	0	1	0	0	0	0	0	2	.250	.250	.250	55	-0				.333	-1	/S-1	-0.2

■ SCOTT STRATTON
Stratton, C. Scott   b: 10/2/1869, Campbellsburg, Ky.   d: 3/8/39, Louisville, Ky.   BL/TR, 6', 180 lbs.   Deb: 4/21/1888

YEAR	TM/L	G	AB	R	H	2B	3B	HR	RBI	BB	SO	AVG	OBP	SLG	PRO+	BR/A	SB	CS	SBR	FA	FR	G/POS	TPR
1888	Lou-a	67	249	35	64	8	1	1	29	12		.257	.310	.309	101	0	10			.821	-5	O-38,P-33	-0.5
1889	Lou-a	62	229	30	66	7	5	4	34	13	36	.288	.332	.415	114	3	10			.915	5	O-29,P-19,1	0.3
1890	*Lou-a	55	189	29	61	3	5	0		16		.323	.385	.392	132	8	8			.977	5	P-50/O-5	0.0
1891	Pit-N	2	8	1	1	0	0	0	0	0		.125	.125	.125	-28	-1	0			.900	1	/P-2	0.0
	Lou-a	34	115	9	27	2	0	0	8	11	13	.235	.307	.252	61	-6	8			.939	2	P-20/1-8,O	0.3
1892	Lou-N	63	219	22	56	2	5	0	23	17	21	.256	.318	.347	110	2	9			.915	1	P-42,O-17/1	-0.1
1893	Lou-N	60	217	34	49	8	5	0	16	25	15	.226	.309	.309	70	-9	6			.975	1	P-37,O-23/1	-0.4
1894	Lou-N	13	37	9	12	1	1	0	4	4		.324	.390	.459	112	1	1			.929	2	/P-7,O-5	0.1
	Chi-N	23	96	29	36	5	4	3	23	6	1	.375	.417	.604	136	5	3			.933	-1	P-15/O-5,1	0.0
	Yr	36	133	38	48	6	5	3	27	10		.361	.410	.564	131	6	4			.932	1	P-22,O-10/1	0.1
1895	Chi-N	10	24	3	7	1	1	0	2	4	2	.292	.393	.417	102	0	1			.833	-1	/P-5,O-4	-0.1
Total	8	389	1383	201	379	37	32	8	139	108	93	.274	.335	.364	103	4	56			.938	14	P-230,O-132/1	-1.0

■ JOE STRAUB
Straub, Joseph   b: 1/19/1858, Germany   d: 2/13/29, Pueblo, Colo.   BR/TR, 5'10", 160 lbs.   Deb: 6/24/1880

YEAR	TM/L	G	AB	R	H	2B	3B	HR	RBI	BB	SO	AVG	OBP	SLG	PRO+	BR/A	SB	CS	SBR	FA	FR	G/POS	TPR
1880	Tro-N	3	12	1	3	0	0	0	3	1	3	.250	.308	.250	87	-0				.815	0	/C-3	0.0
1882	Phi-a	8	32	2	6	2	0	0	1	0		.188	.212	.250	50	-2				.830	-1	/C-7,O-1	-0.2
1883	Col-a	27	100	4	13	0	0	0		4		.130	.163	.130	-5	-11				.860	-3	C-14,1-12/O	-1.3
Total	3	38	144	7	22	2	0	0	3	6	3	.153	.187	.167	17	-13				.843	-4	/C-24,1-12,O	-1.5

■ JOE STRAUSS
Strauss, Joseph "Dutch" or "The Socker" (b: Joseph Strasser)   b: 11/16/1858, Cincinnati, Ohio   d: 6/24/06, Cincinnati, Ohio   BR/TR,   Deb: 7/27/1884

YEAR	TM/L	G	AB	R	H	2B	3B	HR	RBI	BB	SO	AVG	OBP	SLG	PRO+	BR/A	SB	CS	SBR	FA	FR	G/POS	TPR
1884	KC-U	16	60	4	12	3	0	0	1			.200	.213	.250	29	-6				.833	-1	O-10/C-3,23	-0.6
1885	Lou-a	2	6	0	1	0	0	0	1			.167	.167	.167	6	-1				1.000	-2	/O-1,C-1	-0.2
1886	Lou-a	74	297	36	64	5	6	1	8			.215	.239	.283	60	-15	25			.857	4	O-73/P-2,C	-1.1
	Bro-a	9	36	6	9	1	1	0				.250	.270	.333	88	-1	4			1.000	1	/O-7,C-2	0.0
	Yr	83	333	42	73	6	7	1				.219	.242	.288	63	-16	29			.866	5	O-80/C-3,P	-1.1
Total	3	101	399	46	86	9	7	1		10		.216	.237	.281	57	-22	29			.861	2	/O-91,C-7,P23	-1.9

■ DARRYL STRAWBERRY
Strawberry, Darryl Eugene   b: 3/12/62, Los Angeles, Cal.   BL/TL, 6'6", 190 lbs.   Deb: 5/6/83

YEAR	TM/L	G	AB	R	H	2B	3B	HR	RBI	BB	SO	AVG	OBP	SLG	PRO+	BR/A	SB	CS	SBR	FA	FR	G/POS	TPR
1983	NY-N	122	420	63	108	15	7	26	74	47	128	.257	.338	.512	134	17	19	6	2	.984	6	*O-117	2.3
1984	NY-N★	147	522	75	131	27	4	26	97	75	131	.251	.343	.467	128	19	27	8	3	.980	4	*O-146	2.3
1985	NY-N★	111	393	78	109	15	4	29	79	73	96	.277	.392	.557	167	36	26	11	1	.991	-4	*O-110	3.0
1986	*NY-N★	136	475	76	123	27	5	27	93	72	141	.259	.363	.507	142	27	28	12	1	.975	2	*O-131	2.7

YEAR	TM/L	G	AB	R	H	2B	3B	HR	RBI	BB	SO	AVG	OBP	SLG	PRO+	BR/A	SB	CS	SBR	FA	FR	G/POS	TPR
1987	NY-N★	154	532	108	151	32	5	39	104	97	122	.284	.401	.583	165	51	36	12	4	.972	1	*O-151	5.0
1988	*NY-N★	153	543	101	146	27	3	**39**	101	85	127	.269	.371	**.545**	**168**	47	29	14	0	.971	7	*O-150	**5.2**
1989	NY-N†	134	476	69	107	26	1	29	77	61	105	.225	.314	.466	126	15	11	4	1	.972	9	*O-131	2.2
1990	NY-N★	152	542	92	150	18	1	37	108	70	110	.277	.364	.518	140	29	15	8	-0	.989	6	*O-149	3.2
1991	LA-N†	139	505	86	134	22	4	28	99	75	125	.265	.364	.491	141	28	10	8	-2	.978	-2	*O-136	2.1
1992	LA-N	43	156	20	37	8	0	5	25	19	34	.237	.324	.385	101	0	3	1	0	.986	-1	O-42	-0.1
1993	LA-N	32	100	12	14	2	0	5	12	16	19	.140	.271	.310	59	-6	0	1	0	.905	-4	O-29	-1.1
1994	SF-N	29	92	13	22	3	1	4	17	19	22	.239	.369	.424	110	2	0	3	-2	.969	-2	O-27	0.1
Total	12	1352	4756	793	1232	222	35	294	886	709	1160	.259	.359	.506	142	265	205	87	9	.977	26	*O-1319	26.9

■ GABBY STREET

Street, Charles Evard "Old Sarge"　b: 9/30/1882, Huntsville, Ala.　d: 2/6/51, Joplin, Mo.　BR/TR, 5'11", 180 lbs.　Deb: 9/13/04　MC

YEAR	TM/L	G	AB	R	H	2B	3B	HR	RBI	BB	SO	AVG	OBP	SLG	PRO+	BR/A	SB	CS	SBR	FA	FR	G/POS	TPR
1904	Cin-N	11	33	1	4	1	0	0	0	1		.121	.147	.152	-7	-4	2			.973	4	C-11	0.1
1905	Cin-N	2	2	0	0	0	0	0	0	2		.000	.500	.000	48	0	0			1.000	1	/C-1	0.1
	Bos-N	3	12	0	2	0	0	0	0	0		.167	.167	.167	-1	-1	1			.778	-2	/C-3	-0.4
	Cin-N	29	91	8	23	5	1	0	8	6		.253	.306	.330	81	-2	1			.975	3	C-26	0.4
	Yr	34	105	8	25	5	1	0	8	8		.238	.298	.305	73	-4	2			.957	2	C-30	0.1
1908	Was-A	131	394	31	81	12	7	1	32	40		.206	.289	.279	92	-3	5			.973	-1	*C-128	0.9
1909	Was-A	137	407	25	86	12	1	0	29	26		.211	.262	.246	63	-17	2			.981	11	*C-137	0.7
1910	Was-A	89	257	13	52	6	0	1	16	23		.202	.273	.237	63	-11	1			**.978**	9	C-86	0.7
1911	Was-A	72	216	16	48	7	1	0	14	14		.222	.279	.264	53	-14	4			.973	7	C-71	0.0
1912	NY-A	29	88	4	16	1	1	0	6	7		.182	.258	.216	34	-8	1			.958	0	C-29	-0.5
1931	StL-N	1	1	0	0	0	0	0	0	0	0	.000	.000	.000	-96	-0	0			1.000	0	/C-1,M	-0.0
Total	8	504	1501	98	312	44	11	2	105	119	0	.208	.273	.256	66	-60	17			.974	32	C-493	2.0

■ WALT STREULI

Streuli, Walter Herbert　b: 9/26/35, Memphis, Tenn.　BR/TR, 6'2", 195 lbs.　Deb: 9/25/54

YEAR	TM/L	G	AB	R	H	2B	3B	HR	RBI	BB	SO	AVG	OBP	SLG	PRO+	BR/A	SB	CS	SBR	FA	FR	G/POS	TPR
1954	Det-A	1	0	0	0	0	0	0	0	1	0	—	1.000	—	195	0	0	0	0	1.000	-0	/C-1	0.0
1955	Det-A	2	4	1	1	0	0	0	1	0	0	.250	.250	.500	100	-0	0	0	0	1.000	0	/C-2	0.0
1956	Det-A	3	8	0	2	1	0	0	1	1	2	.250	.333	.375	87	-0	0	0	0	.933	0	/C-3	0.0
Total	3	6	12	1	3	2	0	0	2	2	2	.250	.357	.417	106	0	0	0	0	.957	0	/C-6	0.0

■ JOHN STRICK

Strick, John Quincy Adams　Deb: 5/18/1882

YEAR	TM/L	G	AB	R	H	2B	3B	HR	RBI	BB	SO	AVG	OBP	SLG	PRO+	BR/A	SB	CS	SBR	FA	FR	G/POS	TPR
1882	Lou-a	32	110	17	18	6	1	0		9		.164	.227	.236	60	-4				.898	-0	C-21/O-6,2S1	-0.3

■ CUB STRICKER

Stricker, John A. (b: John A. Streaker)　b: 2/15/1860, Philadelphia, Pa.　d: 11/19/37, Philadelphia, Pa.　BR/TR, 5'3", 138 lbs.　Deb: 5/2/1882　M

YEAR	TM/L	G	AB	R	H	2B	3B	HR	RBI	BB	SO	AVG	OBP	SLG	PRO+	BR/A	SB	CS	SBR	FA	FR	G/POS	TPR
1882	Phi-a	72	272	34	59	6	1	0		15		.217	.258	.246	63	-12				.904	**23**	*2-72/P-2,O	1.2
1883	Phi-a	89	330	67	90	8	0	1		19		.273	.312	.306	92	-4				.837	-20	*2-88/C-2	-2.0
1884	Phi-a	107	399	59	92	16	11	1		19		.231	.267	.333	89	-6				.870	-34	*2-107/O-1,CP	-3.5
1885	Phi-a	106	398	71	93	9	3	1		21		.234	.284	.279	74	-12				.879	-13	*2-106	-2.0
1887	Cle-a	131	534	122	141	19	4	2		53		.264	.346	.326	87	-8	86			.912	10	*2-126/S-6,P	0.5
1888	Cle-a	127	493	80	115	13	6	1	33	50		.233	.311	.290	96	-0	60			.929	23	*2-122/O-6,P	2.5
1889	Cle-N	136	566	83	142	10	4	1	47	58	18	.251	.323	.288	73	-19	32			.932	7	*2-135/S-1	-0.4
1890	Cle-P	127	544	93	133	19	8	2	65	54	16	.244	.318	.320	77	-17	24			.905	5	*2-109,S-20	-0.3
1891	Bos-a	139	514	96	111	15	4	0	46	63	34	.216	.309	.261	64	-23	54			.942	**24**	*2-139	0.7
1892	StL-N	28	98	12	20	1	0	0	11	10	7	.204	.297	.214	58	-4	4			.939	-4	2-27/S-1M	-0.8
	Bal-N	75	269	45	71	5	5	3	37	32	18	.264	.344	.353	108	3	13			.918	3	2-75	0.6
	Yr	103	367	57	91	6	5	3	48	42	25	.248	.332	.316	96	-1	18			.923	-2	*2-102/S-1	-0.2
1893	Was-N	59	218	28	40	7	1	0	20	20	12	.183	.252	.225	28	-23	4			.903	7	2-39,O-12/S3	-1.3
Total	11	1196	4635	790	1107	128	47	12	259	414	105	.239	.306	.294	78	-124	278			.907	30	*2-1145/S-32,OP3C	-4.8

■ GEORGE STRICKLAND

Strickland, George Bevan "Bo"　b: 1/10/26, New Orleans, La.　BR/TR, 6'1", 180 lbs.　Deb: 5/7/50　MC

YEAR	TM/L	G	AB	R	H	2B	3B	HR	RBI	BB	SO	AVG	OBP	SLG	PRO+	BR/A	SB	CS	SBR	FA	FR	G/POS	TPR
1950	Pit-N	23	27	0	3	0	0	0	3	8		.111	.226	.111	-8	-4	0			.978	3	S-19/3-1	-0.1
1951	Pit-N	138	454	59	98	12	7	9	47	65	83	.216	.318	.333	73	-17	4	2	0	.943	12	*S-125,2-13	0.5
1952	Pit-N	76	232	17	41	6	2	5	22	21	45	.177	.284	.284	46	-17	4	2	0	.953	15	2-45,S-28/13	0.2
	Cle-A	31	88	8	19	4	0	1	8	14	15	.216	.324	.295	78	-2	0	0	0	.964	10	S-30/2-1	0.9
1953	Cle-A	123	419	43	119	17	4	5	47	51	52	.284	.362	.379	103	3	0	0	0	.974	16	*S-122/1-1	2.7
1954	*Cle-A	112	361	42	77	13	2	6	37	55	62	.213	.319	.313	72	-13	2	1	0	.961	-12	*S-112	-1.6
1955	Cle-A	130	388	34	81	9	5	2	34	49	60	.209	.302	.273	54	-25	1	0	0	**.976**	8	*S-128	-0.6
1956	Cle-A	85	171	22	36	1	2	3	17	22	27	.211	.301	.292	56	-11	0	1	-1	.986	16	2-28,S-28,3	0.8
1957	Cle-A	89	201	21	47	8	2	1	19	26	29	.234	.325	.308	75	-7	0	3	-2	.980	15	2-48,S-23,3	1.1
1959	Cle-A	132	441	55	105	15	2	3	48	51	64	.238	.317	.302	74	-15	1	1	-0	.971	-9	3-80,S-50/2	-2.0
1960	Cle-A	32	42	4	7	0	0	1	3	4	8	.167	.255	.238	35	-4	0	0	0	.962	1	S-14,3-12/2	-0.3
Total	10	971	2824	305	633	84	27	36	284	361	453	.224	.314	.311	70	-112	12	10		.963	74	S-679,2-141,3/1	1.6

■ GEORGE STRIEF

Strief, George Andrew　b: 10/16/1856, Cincinnati, Ohio　d: 4/1/46, Cleveland, Ohio　BR/TR, 5'7", 172 lbs.　Deb: 5/1/1879　U

YEAR	TM/L	G	AB	R	H	2B	3B	HR	RBI	BB	SO	AVG	OBP	SLG	PRO+	BR/A	SB	CS	SBR	FA	FR	G/POS	TPR
1879	Cle-N	71	264	24	46	7	1	0	15	10	23	.174	.204	.208	37	-17				.918	-9	O-55,2-16	-2.6
1882	Pit-a	79	297	45	58	9	6	2		13		.195	.229	.286	76	-7				.917	0	*2-78/S-1	-0.4
1883	StL-a	82	302	22	68	9	0	1		13		.225	.255	.265	64	-13				.899	6	*2-67,O-15	-0.5
1884	StL-a	48	184	22	37	5	2	2		13		.201	.254	.283	72	-6				.848	-3	O-44/2-3,1	-0.9
	KC-U	15	56	5	6	5	0	0		4		.107	.167	.196	-2	-8				.900	8	2-15	0.1
	CP-U	15	53	6	11	5	0	0		3		.208	.250	.302	50	-4				.905	-2	2-15	-0.5
	Yr	30	109	11	17	10	0	0		7		.156	.207	.248	25	-11				.902	7	2-30	-0.4
1885	Cle-N	8	29	2	7	2	0	0	0	0	5	.241	.241	.310	70	-1				1.000	-0	/O-6,3-2	-0.1
	Phi-a	44	175	19	48	8	5	0		9		.274	.310	.377	110	1				.828	-2	3-19,S-10/O2	-0.1
Total	5	362	1360	145	281	50	14	5	15	64	28	.207	.242	.275	65	-53				.899	-1	2-201,O-128/3S1	-5.0

■ LOU STRINGER

Stringer, Louis Bernard　b: 5/13/17, Grand Rapids, Mich　BR/TR, 5'11", 173 lbs.　Deb: 4/15/41

YEAR	TM/L	G	AB	R	H	2B	3B	HR	RBI	BB	SO	AVG	OBP	SLG	PRO+	BR/A	SB	CS	SBR	FA	FR	G/POS	TPR
1941	Chi-N	145	512	59	126	31	4	5	53	59	86	.246	.324	.352	94	-4	3			.960	20	*2-137/S-7	2.6
1942	Chi-N	121	406	45	96	10	5	9	41	31	55	.236	.292	.352	92	-6	3			.955	7	*2-113/3-1	0.3
1946	Chi-N	80	209	26	51	3	1	3	19	26	34	.244	.328	.311	83	-4	0			.956	-5	2-62/S-1,3	-0.5
1948	Bos-A	4	11	1	1	0	0	1	1	0	3	.091	.091	.364	17	-1	0	0	0	.947	2	/2-2	0.1
1949	Bos-A	35	41	10	11	4	0	1	6	5	10	.268	.348	.439	100	-0	0	0	0	.978	3	/2-9	0.3
1950	Bos-A	24	17	7	5	1	0	0	2	0	4	.294	.294	.353	59	-1	1	0	0	.778	0	/3-3,2-1,S	0.2
Total	6	409	1196	148	290	49	10	19	122	121	192	.242	.313	.348	90	-17	7			.958	25	2-324/S-9,3	3.0

■ JOE STRIPP

Stripp, Joseph Valentine "Jersey Joe"　b: 2/3/03, Harrison, N.J.　d: 6/10/89, Orlando, Fla.　BR/TR, 5'11.5", 175 lbs.　Deb: 7/2/28

YEAR	TM/L	G	AB	R	H	2B	3B	HR	RBI	BB	SO	AVG	OBP	SLG	PRO+	BR/A	SB	CS	SBR	FA	FR	G/POS	TPR
1928	Cin-N	42	139	18	40	7	3	1	17	8	8	.288	.340	.403	95	-1	0			.931	-7	O-21,3-17/S	-0.8
1929	Cin-N	64	187	24	40	3	2	3	20	24	15	.214	.313	.299	55	-13	2			.960	8	3-55/2-2	-0.4
1930	Cin-N	130	464	74	142	37	6	3	64	51	37	.306	.377	.431	100	1	15			.996	0	1-75,3-48	-0.4
1931	Cin-N	105	426	71	138	26	2	3	42	21	31	.324	.359	.415	114	8	5			.957	4	3-96/1-9	1.6
1932	Bro-N	138	534	94	162	36	6	6	64	36	30	.303	.350	.438	113	9	14			.954	16	3-93,1-43	2.7
1933	Bro-N	141	537	69	149	20	7	1	51	26	23	.277	.312	.346	92	-7	5			.967	5	*3-140	0.7
1934	Bro-N	104	384	50	121	19	6	1	40	22	24	.315	.354	.404	108	4	2			.941	-6	3-96/1-7,S	0.1
1935	Bro-N	109	373	44	114	13	5	3	42	22	15	.306	.344	.391	99	-0	2			.962	7	3-88,1-15/O	0.8
1936	Bro-N	110	439	51	139	31	4	1	60	26	12	.317	.351	.399	100	0	2			**.968**	8	*3-106	1.1
1937	Bro-N	90	300	37	73	10	2	1	26	20	18	.243	.291	.300	60	-17	1			.971	-6	3-66,1-14/S	-2.3

YEAR	TM/L	G	AB	R	H	2B	3B	HR	RBI	BB	SO	AVG	OBP	SLG	PRO+	BR/A	SB	CS	SBR	FA	FR	G/POS	TPR
1938	StL-N	54	199	24	57	7	0	0	18	18	10	.286	.349	.322	81	-5	0			.977	-8	3-51	-1.2
	Bos-N	59	229	19	63	10	0	1	19	10	7	.275	.305	.332	84	-6	2			.966	1	3-58	-0.4
	Yr	113	428	43	120	17	0	1	37	28	17	.280	.326	.321	82	-10	2			.971	-7	*3-109	-1.6
Total	11	1146	4211	575	1238	219	43	24	464	280	226	.294	.340	.384	96	-27	50			.961	21	3-914,1-163/OS2	1.7

■ ALLIE STROBEL   Strobel, Albert Irving   b: 6/11/1884, Boston, Mass.   d: 2/10/55, Hollywood, Fla.   BR/TR, 6', 160 lbs.   Deb: 8/29/05

YEAR	TM/L	G	AB	R	H	2B	3B	HR	RBI	BB	SO	AVG	OBP	SLG	PRO+	BR/A	SB	CS	SBR	FA	FR	G/POS	TPR
1905	Bos-N	5	19	1	2	0	0	0	2	0		.105	.105	.105	-38	-3	0			1.000	-0	/3-4,O-1	-0.4
1906	Bos-N	100	317	28	64	10	3	1	24	29		.202	.273	.262	69	-12	2			.946	-6	2-93/S-6,O	-1.8
Total	2	105	336	29	66	10	3	1	26	29		.196	.264	.253	63	-15	2			1.000	-6	/2-93,S-6,3O	-2.2

■ JIM STRONER   Stroner, James M.   b: 9/26/1892, Chicago, Ill.   d: 11/16/71, Chicago, Ill.   BR/TR, 5'10", 175 lbs.   Deb: 5/1/29

YEAR	TM/L	G	AB	R	H	2B	3B	HR	RBI	BB	SO	AVG	OBP	SLG	PRO+	BR/A	SB	CS	SBR	FA	FR	G/POS	TPR
1929	Pit-N	6	8	0	3	1	0	0	0	1	0	.375	.444	.500	130	0	0			.571	-0	/3-2	0.0

■ ED STROUD   Stroud, Edwin Marvin   b: 10/31/39, Lapine, Ala.   BL/TR, 5'11", 180 lbs.   Deb: 9/11/66

YEAR	TM/L	G	AB	R	H	2B	3B	HR	RBI	BB	SO	AVG	OBP	SLG	PRO+	BR/A	SB	CS	SBR	FA	FR	G/POS	TPR
1966	Chi-A	12	36	3	6	2	0	0	1	2	8	.167	.231	.222	33	-3	3	0	1	1.000	-0	O-11	-0.3
1967	Chi-A	20	27	6	8	0	1	0	3	1	5	.296	.345	.370	116	0	7	2	1	1.000	-1	O-12	0.0
	Was-A	87	204	36	41	5	3	1	10	25	29	.201	.291	.270	69	-7	8	6	-1	.983	-13	O-79	-2.7
	Yr	107	231	42	49	5	4	1	13	26	34	.212	.297	.281	75	-7	15	8	-0	.985	-14	O-91	-2.7
1968	Was-A	105	306	41	73	10	10	4	23	20	50	.239	.285	.376	102	-0	9	3	1	.979	-4	O-84	-0.9
1969	Was-A	123	206	35	52	5	6	4	29	30	33	.252	.353	.393	114	4	12	2	2	.982	-11	O-85	-0.8
1970	Was-A	129	433	69	115	11	5	5	32	40	79	.266	.332	.349	92	-5	29	6	4	.993	2	*O-118	-0.4
1971	Chi-A	53	141	19	25	4	3	0	2	11	20	.177	.237	.248	36	-12	5	4	-2	1.000	-11	O-44	-2.9
Total	6	529	1353	209	320	37	28	14	100	129	224	.237	.307	.336	87	-22	72	26	6	.988	-38	O-433	-8.0

■ STEVE STROUGHTER   Stroughter, Stephen Lewis   b: 3/15/52, Visalia, Cal.   BL/TR, 6'2", 190 lbs.   Deb: 4/7/82

YEAR	TM/L	G	AB	R	H	2B	3B	HR	RBI	BB	SO	AVG	OBP	SLG	PRO+	BR/A	SB	CS	SBR	FA	FR	G/POS	TPR
1982	Sea-A	26	47	4	8	1	0	1	3	3	9	.170	.235	.255	34	-4	0	0	0	1.000	1	/O-3,D-9	-0.3

■ AMOS STRUNK   Strunk, Amos Aaron   b: 1/22/1889, Philadelphia, Pa.   d: 7/22/79, Llanerch, Pa.   BL/TL, 5'11.5", 175 lbs.   Deb: 9/24/08

YEAR	TM/L	G	AB	R	H	2B	3B	HR	RBI	BB	SO	AVG	OBP	SLG	PRO+	BR/A	SB	CS	SBR	FA	FR	G/POS	TPR
1908	Phi-A	12	34	4	8	1	0	0			4	.235	.316	.265	83	-1	0			.903	1	O-11	0.0
1909	Phi-A	11	35	1	4	0	0	0	2	1		.114	.139	.114	-20	-5	2			1.000	-1	/O-9	-0.7
1910	*Phi-A	16	48	9	16	0	1	0	2	3		.333	.373	.375	135	2	4			1.000	1	O-14	0.2
1911	*Phi-A	74	215	42	55	7	2	1	21	35		.256	.363	.321	93	-1	13			.958	1	O-62/1-2	-0.2
1912	Phi-A	122	412	58	119	13	12	3	63	47		.289	.366	.400	123	13	29			.990	11	*O-116	1.8
1913	*Phi-A	94	292	30	89	11	12	0	46	29	23	.305	.368	.425	135	12	14			.962	-2	O-81	0.8
1914	*Phi-A	122	404	58	111	15	3	2	45	57	38	.275	.364	.342	117	10	25	22	-6	.987	9	*O-120	0.9
1915	*Phi-A	132	485	76	144	28	16	1	45	56	45	.297	.371	.427	144	25	17	19	-6	.980	12	*O-111,1-19	2.6
1916	Phi-A	150	544	71	172	30	9	3	49	66	59	.316	.393	.421	152	35	21	23	-8	.978	2	*O-143/1-7	2.4
1917	Phi-A	148	540	83	152	26	7	1	45	68	37	.281	.363	.361	123	16	16			.986	-2	*O-146	0.6
1918	*Bos-A	114	413	50	106	18	9	0	35	36	13	.257	.316	.344	101	-1	20			.988	-5	*O-113	-1.3
1919	Bos-A	48	184	27	50	11	3	0	17	13	13	.272	.323	.364	98	-1	3			.968	-1	O-48	-0.6
	Phi-A	60	194	15	41	6	4	0	13	23	15	.211	.298	.284	63	-9	3			.981	1	O-52	-1.3
	Yr	108	378	42	91	17	7	0	30	36	28	.241	.310	.323	79	-11	6			.974	-1	*O-100	-1.9
1920	Phi-A	58	202	23	60	9	3	0	20	21	9	.297	.363	.371	94	-1	0	6	-4	.990	-4	O-54	-1.3
	Chi-A	53	188	33	45	8	1	1	16	28	15	.239	.338	.309	72	-7	1	0	0	.981	-1	O-49	-1.0
	Yr	111	390	56	105	17	4	1	36	49	24	.269	.351	.341	83	-8	1	6	-3	.985	-5	*O-103	-2.3
1921	Chi-A	121	401	68	133	19	10	3	69	38	27	.332	.391	.451	116	10	7	10	-4	.970	-8	*O-111	-0.9
1922	Chi-A	92	311	36	90	11	4	0	33	33	28	.289	.358	.350	85	-6	9	6	-1	.989	2	O-74/1-7	-1.0
1923	Chi-A	54	54	7	17	0	0	0	8	8	5	.315	.403	.315	92	-0	1	0	0	1.000	-0	/O-5,1-2	0.0
1924	Chi-A	1	1	0	0	0	0	0	0	0	0	.000	.000	.000	-99	-0	0	0	0	.000	0	H	0.0
	Phi-A	30	42	5	6	0	0	0	1	7	4	.143	.265	.143	7	-6	0	0	0	1.000	-3	/O-8	-0.8
	Yr	31	43	5	6	0	0	0	1	7	4	.140	.260	.140	5	-6	0	0	0	1.000	-3	/O-8	-0.8
Total	17	1512	4999	696	1418	213	96	15	530	573	331	.284	.359	.374	112	86	185	86		.980	13	*O-1327/1-37	0.2

■ AL STRUVE   Struve, Albert   b: St.Louis, Mo.   Deb: 6/22/1884

YEAR	TM/L	G	AB	R	H	2B	3B	HR	RBI	BB	SO	AVG	OBP	SLG	PRO+	BR/A	SB	CS	SBR	FA	FR	G/POS	TPR
1884	StL-a	2	7	2	2	0	0	0				.286	.286	.286	84	-0				.000	1	/O-1,C-1	0.1

■ LUKE STUART   Stuart, Luther Lane   b: 5/23/1892, Alamance Co., N.C.   d: 6/15/47, Winston-Salem, N.C.   BR/TR, 5'8", 165 lbs.   Deb: 7/28/21

YEAR	TM/L	G	AB	R	H	2B	3B	HR	RBI	BB	SO	AVG	OBP	SLG	PRO+	BR/A	SB	CS	SBR	FA	FR	G/POS	TPR
1921	StL-A	3	3	2	1	0	1	1	2	0	1	.333	.333	1.333	291	1	0	0		1.000	-1	/2-3	0.0

■ DICK STUART   Stuart, Richard Lee "Dr. Strangeglove"   b: 11/7/32, San Francisco, Cal.   BR/TR, 6'4", 212 lbs.   Deb: 7/10/58

YEAR	TM/L	G	AB	R	H	2B	3B	HR	RBI	BB	SO	AVG	OBP	SLG	PRO+	BR/A	SB	CS	SBR	FA	FR	G/POS	TPR
1958	Pit-N	67	254	38	68	12	5	16	48	11	75	.268	.311	.543	124	7	0	0	0	.973	0	1-64	0.3
1959	Pit-N	118	397	64	118	15	2	27	78	24	86	.297	.367	.549	141	22	1	1	-0	.976	1	*1-105/O-1	1.6
1960	*Pit-N	122	438	48	114	17	5	23	83	39	107	.260	.321	.479	115	8	0	0	0	.986	-1	*1-108	-0.3
1961	Pit-N★	138	532	83	160	28	8	35	117	34	121	.301	.347	.581	140	28	0	3	-2	.983	-2	*1-132/O-1	1.3
1962	Pit-N	114	394	52	90	11	4	16	64	32	94	.228	.290	.398	83	-11	0	1	-1	.982	2	*1-101	-1.7
1963	Bos-A	157	612	81	160	25	4	42	**118**	44	144	.261	.312	.521	125	18	0	0	0	.979	8	*1-155	2.0
1964	Bos-A	156	603	73	168	27	1	33	114	37	130	.279	.323	.491	117	12	0	1	-0	.981	1	*1-155	0.7
1965	Phi-N	149	538	53	126	19	1	28	95	39	136	.234	.290	.429	101	-1	1	0	0	.986	3	*1-143/3-1	-0.5
1966	NY-N	31	87	7	19	0	0	4	13	9	26	.218	.292	.356	81	-2	0	1	-1	.974	-1	1-23	-0.6
	*LA-N	38	91	4	24	1	0	3	9	11	17	.264	.356	.374	112	2	0	1	-1	.991	-0	1-25	0.3
	Yr	69	178	11	43	1	0	7	22	20	43	.242	.325	.365	97	-1	0	2	-1	.982	2	1-48	-0.3
1969	Cal-A	22	51	3	8	2	0	1	4	3	21	.157	.204	.255	29	-5	0	0	0	.991	-1	1-13	-0.8
Total	10	1112	3997	506	1055	157	30	228	743	301	957	.264	.319	.489	117	77	2	7	-4	.982	13	*1-1024/O-2,3	2.3

■ BILL STUART   Stuart, William Alexander "Chauncey"   b: 8/28/1873, Boalsburg, Pa.   d: 10/14/28, Fort Worth, Tex.   5'11", 170 lbs.   Deb: 8/15/1895

YEAR	TM/L	G	AB	R	H	2B	3B	HR	RBI	BB	SO	AVG	OBP	SLG	PRO+	BR/A	SB	CS	SBR	FA	FR	G/POS	TPR
1895	Pit-N	19	77	5	19	3	0	0	10	2	6	.247	.275	.286	47	-6	2			.913	-1	S-17/2-2	-0.5
1899	NY-N	1	3	0	0	0	0	0	0	0		.000	.000	.000	-99	-1	0			1.000	-0	/2-1	-0.1
Total	2	20	80	5	19	3	0	0	10	2	6	.237	.265	.275	42	-7	2			.909	-1	/S-17,2-3	-0.6

■ FRANKLIN STUBBS   Stubbs, Franklin Lee   b: 10/21/60, Richlands, N.C.   BL/TL, 6'2", 215 lbs.   Deb: 4/28/84

YEAR	TM/L	G	AB	R	H	2B	3B	HR	RBI	BB	SO	AVG	OBP	SLG	PRO+	BR/A	SB	CS	SBR	FA	FR	G/POS	TPR
1984	LA-N	87	217	22	42	2	3	8	17	24	63	.194	.274	.341	73	-8	2	2	-1	.993	-1	1-51,O-20	-1.3
1985	LA-N	10	9	0	2	0	0	0	2	0	3	.222	.222	.222	25	-1	0	0	0	1.000	-0	/1-4	-0.1
1986	LA-N	132	420	55	95	11	1	23	58	37	107	.226	.292	.421	101	-2	7	1	2	.969	-4	*O-124,1-13	-0.9
1987	LA-N	129	386	48	90	16	1	16	52	31	85	.233	.292	.415	87	-9	8	1	2	**.994**	7	*1-111,O-18	-0.8
1988	*LA-N	115	242	30	54	13	0	8	34	23	61	.223	.293	.376	94	-2	11	3	2	.978	2	1-84,O-13	-0.4
1989	LA-N	69	103	11	30	6	0	4	15	16	27	.291	.387	.466	145	6	3	2	-0	.948	1	O-28/1-7	0.7
1990	Hou-N	146	448	59	117	23	2	23	71	48	114	.261	.335	.475	124	13	19	6	2	.991	-9	1-72,O-71	0.0
1991	Mil-A	103	362	48	77	16	2	11	38	35	71	.213	.286	.359	79	-11	13	4	3	.991	5	1-92/O-4,D	-1.1
1992	Mil-A	92	288	37	66	11	1	9	42	27	68	.229	.297	.368	87	-5	11	8	-2	.987	6	1-68,D-16/O	-0.7
Total	9	883	2475	310	573	98	12	102	329	241	599	.232	.302	.404	97	-19	74	27	6	.990	7	1-502,O-279/D	-4.6

■ MOOSE STUBING   Stubing, Lawrence George   b: 3/31/38, Bronx, N.Y.   BL/TL, 6'3", 220 lbs.   Deb: 4/14/67   MC

YEAR	TM/L	G	AB	R	H	2B	3B	HR	RBI	BB	SO	AVG	OBP	SLG	PRO+	BR/A	SB	CS	SBR	FA	FR	G/POS	TPR
1967	Cal-A	5	5	0	0	0	0	0	0	0	4	.000	.000	.000	-99	-1	0	0	0	.000	0	H	-0.1

■ SEEM STUDLEY   Studley, Seymour L. "Warhorse"   b: Washington, D.C.   d: 1874, Washington, D.C.   Deb: 4/20/1872

YEAR	TM/L	G	AB	R	H	2B	3B	HR	RBI	BB	SO	AVG	OBP	SLG	PRO+	BR/A	SB	CS	SBR	FA	FR	G/POS	TPR
1872	Nat-n	5	21	3	2	0	0	0	2	0	0	.095	.095	.095	-35	-4						/O-5	-0.2

YEAR	TM/L	G	AB	R	H	2B	3B	HR	RBI	BB	SO	AVG	OBP	SLG	PRO+	BR/A	SB	CS	SBR	FA	FR	G/POS	TPR

■ GEORGE STUMPF   Stumpf, George Frederick   b: 12/15/10, New Orleans, La.   d: 3/6/93, Metairie, La.   BL/TL, 5'8", 155 lbs.   Deb: 9/19/31

1931	Bos-A	7	28	2	7	1	1	0	4	1	2	.250	.276	.357	69	-1	0	0	0	1.000	-1	/O-7	-0.3
1932	Bos-A	79	169	18	34	2	2	1	18	18	21	.201	.278	.254	40	-15	1	1	-0	.952	-7	O-51	-2.3
1933	Bos-A	22	41	8	14	3	0	0	5	4	2	.341	.400	.415	117	1	4	0	1	1.000	-3	O-15	-0.1
1936	Chi-A	10	22	3	6	1	0	0	5	2	1	.273	.333	.318	59	-1	0	0	0	1.000	1	/O-4	-0.1
Total	4	118	260	31	61	7	3	1	32	25	26	.235	.302	.296	57	-17	5	1	1	.969	-11	/O-77	-2.8

■ BILL STUMPF   Stumpf, William Frederick   b: 3/21/1892, Baltimore, Md.   d: 2/14/66, Crownsville, Md.   BR/TR, 6'0.5", 175 lbs.   Deb: 5/11/12

1912	NY-A	42	129	8	31	0	0	0	10	6		.240	.279	.240	46	-9	5			.892	-6	S-26/2-8,310	-1.3
1913	NY-A	12	29	5	6	1	0	0	1	3	3	.207	.281	.241	53	-2	0			.818	-3	/S-6,2-4,O	-0.5
Total	2	54	158	13	37	1	0	0	11	9	3	.234	.280	.241	47	-11	5			.877	-9	/S-32,2-12,301	-1.8

■ GUY STURDY   Sturdy, Guy R.   b: 8/7/1899, Sherman, Tex.   d: 5/4/65, Marshall, Tex.   BL/TL, 6'0.5", 180 lbs.   Deb: 9/30/27

1927	StL-A	5	21	5	9	1	0	0	5	1	0	.429	.455	.476	137	1	2	0	1	.974	-1	/1-5	0.1
1928	StL-A	54	45	3	10	1	0	1	8	8	4	.222	.340	.311	70	-2	1	0	0	1.000	-0	/1-1	-0.2
Total	2	59	66	8	19	2	0	1	13	9	4	.288	.373	.364	91	-1	3	0	1	.975	-1	/1-6	-0.1

■ BOBBY STURGEON   Sturgeon, Robert Howard   b: 8/6/19, Clinton, Ind.   BR/TR, 6', 175 lbs.   Deb: 4/16/40

1940	Chi-N	7	21	1	4	1	0	0	2	0	1	.190	.190	.238	18	-2	0			.848	2	/S-7	0.0
1941	Chi-N	129	433	45	106	15	3	0	25	9	30	.245	.260	.293	58	-25	5			.956	-4	*S-126/2-1,3	-2.1
1942	Chi-N	63	162	8	40	7	1	0	7	4	13	.247	.269	.302	70	-7	2			.988	21	2-32,S-29/3	1.7
1946	Chi-N	100	294	26	87	12	2	1	21	10	18	.296	.319	.361	94	-3	0			.934	-13	S-72,2-21	-1.3
1947	Chi-N	87	232	16	59	10	5	0	21	7	12	.254	.276	.341	66	-12	0			.975	13	S-45,2-30/3	0.4
1948	Bos-N	34	78	10	17	3	1	0	4	4	5	.218	.256	.282	46	-6	0			.938	-3	2-18/S-4,3	-0.9
Total	6	420	1220	106	313	48	12	1	80	34	79	.257	.277	.318	68	-56	7			.951	14	S-283,2-102/3	-2.2

■ DEAN STURGIS   Sturgis, Dean Donnell   b: 12/1/1892, Beloit, Kan.   d: 6/4/50, Uniontown, Pa.   BR/TR, 6'1", 180 lbs.   Deb: 5/1/14

| 1914 | Phi-A | 4 | 4 | 1 | 1 | 0 | 0 | 0 | 0 | 1 | 2 | .250 | .400 | .250 | 100 | 0 | 0 | | | 1.000 | 0 | /C-1 | 0.0 |

■ JOHNNY STURM   Sturm, John Peter Joseph   b: 1/23/16, St.Louis, Mo.   BL/TL, 6'1", 185 lbs.   Deb: 4/15/41

| 1941 | *NY-A | 124 | 524 | 58 | 125 | 17 | 3 | 3 | 36 | 37 | 50 | .239 | .293 | .300 | 58 | -32 | 3 | 5 | -2 | .990 | -2 | *1-124 | -4.5 |

■ GEORGE STUTZ   Stutz, George "Kid" or "Satan"   b: 2/12/1893, Philadelphia, Pa.   d: 12/29/30, Philadelphia, Pa.   BL/TR, 5'5", 150 lbs.   Deb: 8/17/26

| 1926 | Phi-N | 6 | 9 | 0 | 0 | 0 | 0 | 0 | 0 | 0 | 2 | .000 | .000 | .000 | -95 | -2 | 0 | | | .938 | 1 | /S-5 | -0.1 |

■ LENA STYLES   Styles, William Graves   b: 11/27/1899, Gurley, Ala.   d: 3/14/56, Hunstville, Ala.   BR/TR, 6'1", 185 lbs.   Deb: 9/10/19

1919	Phi-A	8	22	0	6	1	0	0	5	1	6	.273	.304	.318	74	-1	0			.974	0	/C-8	0.0
1920	Phi-A	24	50	5	13	3	1	0	5	6	7	.260	.339	.360	84	-1	1	0	0	.966	2	/C-9,1-7	0.1
1921	Phi-A	4	5	0	1	0	0	0	0	0	0	.200	.200	.200	2	-1	0	0	0	.333	-1	/C-2	-0.2
1930	Cin-N	7	12	3	3	0	1	0	1	1	2	.250	.357	.417	91	-0	0			.875	-7	/C-5,1-1	0.0
1931	Cin-N	34	87	7	21	3	0	0	5	8	7	.241	.313	.276	63	-4	0			.949	-7	C-31	-0.9
Total	5	77	176	14	44	7	2	0	16	16	24	.250	.320	.313	71	-7	1	0	0	.929	-6	/C-55,1-8	-1.0

■ NEIL STYNES   Stynes, Cornelius William   b: 12/10/1868, Arlington, Mass.   d: 3/26/44, Somerville, Mass.   BR/TR, 6', 165 lbs.   Deb: 9/8/1890

| 1890 | Cle-P | 2 | 8 | 0 | 0 | 0 | 0 | 0 | 0 | 0 | | .000 | .000 | .000 | -99 | -2 | 0 | | | .846 | 0 | /C-2 | -0.2 |

■ KEN SUAREZ   Suarez, Kenneth Raymond   b: 4/12/43, Tampa, Fla.   BR/TR, 5'9", 175 lbs.   Deb: 4/14/66

1966	KC-A	35	69	5	10	0	1	0	2	15	26	.145	.298	.174	41	-5	2	0	1	.954	5	C-34	0.3
1967	KC-A	39	63	7	15	5	0	2	9	16	21	.238	.392	.413	143	4	1	0	0	.979	7	C-36	1.3
1968	Cle-A	17	10	1	1	0	0	0	1	0	3	.100	.182	.100	-13	-1	0	0	0	1.000	1	C-12/2-1,3O	0.0
1969	Cle-A	36	85	7	25	5	0	1	9	15	12	.294	.400	.388	117	3	1	0	0	.991	6	C-36	1.0
1971	Cle-A	50	123	10	25	7	0	1	9	18	15	.203	.315	.285	65	-5	0	1	-1	.993	9	C-48	0.4
1972	Tex-A	25	33	2	5	1	0	0	4	1	4	.152	.176	.182	7	-4	0	0	0	.965	3	C-17	-0.3
1973	Tex-A	93	278	25	69	11	0	1	26	33	16	.248	.339	.299	84	-5	1	2	-1	.989	3	C-90	0.1
Total	7	295	661	57	150	29	1	5	60	99	97	.227	.334	.297	81	-13	5	3	-0	.984	31	C-273/O-1,32	2.8

■ LUIS SUAREZ   Suarez, Luis Abelardo   b: 8/24/16, Alto Songo, Cuba   d: 6/5/91, Havana, Cuba   BR/TR, 5'11", 170 lbs.   Deb: 5/28/44

| 1944 | Was-A | 1 | 2 | 0 | 0 | 0 | 0 | 0 | 0 | 0 | 0 | .000 | .000 | .000 | -99 | -1 | 0 | 0 | 0 | 1.000 | 0 | /3-1 | 0.0 |

■ TONY SUCK   Suck, Anthony (b: Charles Anthony Zuck)   b: 6/11/1858, Chicago, Ill.   d: 1/29/1895, Chicago, Ill.   5'9", 164 lbs.   Deb: 8/9/1883

1883	Buf-N	2	7	1	0	0	0	0	0	1	4	.000	.125	.000	-56	-1				.000	-2	/O-1,C-1	-0.3
1884	CP-U	53	188	18	28	2	0	0		13		.149	.204	.160	0	-26				.904	-5	C-28,S-15,O/3	-2.5
	Bal-U	3	10	2	3	0	0	0		0		.300	.300	.300	58	-1				.882	2	/C-3	0.1
	Yr	56	198	20	31	2	0	0		13		.157	.209	.167	3	-26				.901	-3	C-31,S-15,O/3	-2.4
Total	2	58	205	21	31	2	0	0	0	14	4	.151	.205	.161	1	-27				.894	-5	/C-32,S-15,O3	-2.7

■ BILL SUDAKIS   Sudakis, William Paul "Suds"   b: 3/27/46, Joliet, Ill.   BB/TR, 6'1", 190 lbs.   Deb: 9/3/68

1968	LA-N	24	87	11	24	4	2	3	12	15	14	.276	.382	.471	168	7	1	0	0	.953	4	3-24	1.3
1969	LA-N	132	462	50	108	17	5	14	53	40	94	.234	.296	.383	96	-5	3	2	-0	.946	11	*3-121	0.7
1970	LA-N	94	269	37	71	11	0	14	44	35	46	.264	.355	.461	122	8	4	0	1	.983	-6	C-38,3-37/O1	0.5
1971	LA-N	41	83	10	16	3	0	2	7	12	22	.193	.302	.337	86	-2	0	1	-1	1.000	1	C-19/3-3,1O	-0.1
1972	NY-N	18	49	3	7	0	0	1	7	6	14	.143	.236	.204	27	-5	0	0	0	.967	-1	/1-7,C-5	-0.5
1973	Tex-A	82	235	32	60	11	0	15	43	23	53	.255	.322	.494	132	9	0	1	-1	.962	-4	3-29,1-24/COD	0.3
1974	NY-A	89	259	26	60	8	0	7	39	25	48	.232	.302	.344	88	-4	0	0	0	.990	2	D-39,1-33/3C	-0.6
1975	Cal-A	30	58	4	7	2	0	1	6	12	15	.121	.282	.207	43	-4	1	1	0	.941	-1	D-13/C-5,1	-0.6
	Cle-A	20	46	4	9	0	0	1	3	4	7	.196	.260	.261	48	-3	0	1	-1	1.000	1	1-12/C-6	-0.5
	Yr	50	104	8	16	2	0	2	9	16	22	.154	.273	.231	45	-7	1	2	-1	1.000	-2	1-14,D-13,C	-1.1
Total	8	530	1548	177	362	56	7	59	214	172	313	.234	.313	.393	103	2	9	6	-1	.942	6	3-217/C-83,1DO	0.5

■ PETE SUDER   Suder, Peter "Pecky"   b: 4/16/16, Aliquippa, Pa.   BR/TR, 6', 175 lbs.   Deb: 4/15/41

1941	Phi-A	139	531	45	130	20	9	4	52	19	47	.245	.271	.339	62	-31	1	3	-2	.957	-7	*3-136/S-3	-3.6
1942	Phi-A	128	476	46	122	20	4	4	54	24	39	.256	.293	.340	78	-15	4	4	-1	.954	8	S-69,3-34,2	-0.8
1943	Phi-A	131	475	30	105	14	5	3	41	14	40	.221	.243	.291	56	-28	1	1	-0	.971	-8	2-95,3-32/S	-3.3
1946	Phi-A	128	455	38	128	20	3	2	50	18	37	.281	.309	.352	85	-10	1	1	0	.959	1	S-67,3-33,2/10	-0.5
1947	Phi-A	145	528	45	127	28	4	5	60	35	44	.241	.290	.337	73	-21	0	3	-2	**.986**	-17	*2-140/S-3,3	-3.1
1948	Phi-A	148	519	64	125	21	5	7	60	60	40	.241	.321	.345	77	-18	1	0	1	.988	-1	*2-148	-1.2
1949	Phi-A	118	445	44	119	24	6	10	75	23	35	.267	.306	.416	93	-8	0	1	-1	.975	7	2-89,3-36/S	0.2
1950	Phi-A	77	248	34	61	10	2	8	35	23	31	.246	.310	.383	78	-9	2	0	1	.979	1	2-47,3-11,S/1	-0.7
1951	Phi-A	123	440	46	108	18	1	1	42	30	42	.245	.295	.298	59	-25	5	5	-2	**.987**	10	*2-103,S-18/3	-1.1
1952	Phi-A	74	228	22	55	7	2	0	16	17	24	.241	.291	.303	61	-12	1	1	1	.991	3	2-43,S-17,3	-1.2
1953	Phi-A	115	454	44	130	11	3	1	35	17	35	.286	.312	.350	76	-16	3	3	-1	.974	4	3-72,2-38/S	-1.2
1954	Phi-A	69	205	8	41	11	1	0	16	7	16	.200	.226	.263	34	-19	0	0	0	.961	9	2-35,3-20/S	-1.0
1955	KC-A	26	81	3	17	4	0	0	5	2	13	.210	.229	.284	37	-7	0	1	-1	.990	-3	2-24	-1.0
Total	13	1421	5085	469	1268	210	44	49	541	288	456	.249	.291	.337	71	-220	19	28	-11	.982	16	2-805,3-395,S/10	-18.0

YEAR	TM/L	G	AB	R	H	2B	3B	HR	RBI	BB	SO	AVG	OBP	SLG	PRO+	BR/A	SB	CS	SBR	FA	FR	G/POS	TPR

■ **WILLIAM SUERO**   Suero, Williams Urban   b: 11/7/66, Santo Domingo, D.R.   BR/TR, 5'9", 175 lbs.   Deb: 4/9/92

1992	Mil-A	18	16	4	3	1	0	0	0	2	1	.188	.316	.250	62	-1	1	1	-0	.971	4	2-15/S-1,D	0.3
1993	Mil-A	15	14	0	4	0	0	0	0	1	3	.286	.333	.286	69	-1	0	1	-1	.944	3	/2-8,3-1	0.2
Total	2	33	30	4	7	1	0	0	0	3	4	.233	.324	.267	65	-1	1	2	-1	.962	7	/2-23,D-2,3S	0.5

■ **JOE SUGDEN**   Sugden, Joseph   b: 7/31/1870, Philadelphia, Pa.   d: 6/28/59, Philadelphia, Pa.   BB/TR, 5'10", 180 lbs.   Deb: 7/20/1893   C

1893	Pit-N	27	92	20	24	4	3	0	12	10	11	.261	.340	.370	90	-1	1			.956	-0	C-27	0.0
1894	Pit-N	39	139	23	46	13	2	2	23	14	2	.331	.404	.496	117	4	3			.910	-5	C-31/3-4,SO	0.1
1895	Pit-N	49	155	28	48	4	1	1	17	16	12	.310	.385	.368	100	1	4			.903	3	C-49	0.7
1896	Pit-N	80	301	42	89	5	7	0	36	19	9	.296	.348	.359	90	-4	5			.952	1	C-70/1-7,O	0.4
1897	Pit-N	84	288	31	64	6	4	0	38	18		.222	.275	.271	46	-22	9			.941	-4	C-81/1-3	-1.5
1898	StL-N	89	289	29	73	7	1	0	34	23		.253	.314	.284	70	-11	5			.937	0	C-60,O-15/1	-0.5
1899	Cle-N	76	250	19	69	5	1	0	14	11		.276	.307	.304	73	-9	2			.935	-0	C-66/O-4,13	-0.4
1901	Chi-A	48	153	21	42	7	1	0	19	13		.275	.339	.333	89	-2	4			.970	4	C-42/1-5	0.6
1902	StL-A	68	200	25	50	7	2	0	15	20		.250	.330	.305	78	-5	2			.956	-2	C-61/1-4,P	-0.1
1903	StL-A	79	241	18	51	4	0	0	22	25		.212	.288	.228	58	-11	4			.983	6	C-66/1-8	0.2
1904	StL-A	105	348	25	93	6	3	0	30	28		.267	.331	.302	107	4	6			**.989**	-1	C-79,1-28	1.3
1905	StL-A	90	266	21	46	4	0	0	23	23		.173	.247	.188	41	-17	3			.983	21	C-76/1-9	1.2
1912	Det-A	1	4	1	1	0	0	0	0	0		.250	.250	.250	44	-0				.941	1	/1-1	0.0
Total	13	835	2726	303	696	72	25	3	283	220	34	.255	.319	.303	78	-75	48			.957	25	C-708/1-76,O3SP	2.0

■ **GUS SUHR**   Suhr, August Richard   b: 1/3/06, San Francisco, Cal.   BL/TR, 6', 180 lbs.   Deb: 4/15/30

1930	Pit-N	151	542	93	155	26	14	17	107	80	56	.286	.380	.480	106	5	11			.992	-7	*1-151	-1.5
1931	Pit-N	87	270	26	57	13	4	4	32	38	25	.211	.308	.333	73	-10	4			.993	0	1-76	-1.6
1932	Pit-N	154	581	78	153	31	16	5	81	63	39	.263	.337	.398	99	-1	7			.988	-10	*1-154	-2.3
1933	Pit-N	154	566	72	151	31	11	10	75	72	52	.267	.350	.413	117	14	2			.991	-4	*1-154	-0.5
1934	Pit-N	151	573	67	162	36	13	13	103	66	52	.283	.360	.459	115	12	4			.994	-5	*1-151	-0.6
1935	Pit-N	153	529	68	144	33	12	10	81	70	54	.272	.357	.437	109	7	6			.989	-7	*1-149/O-2	-1.5
1936	Pit-N☆	156	583	111	182	33	12	11	118	95	34	.312	.410	.467	133	30	8			**.993**	-4	*1-156	1.1
1937	Pit-N	151	575	69	160	28	14	9	97	83	42	.278	.369	.402	109	9	2			.993	-4	*1-151	-1.2
1938	Pit-N	145	530	82	156	35	14	3	64	87	37	.294	.394	.430	126	21	4			.993	-8	*1-145	-0.4
1939	Pit-N	63	204	23	59	10	2	1	31	25	23	.289	.367	.373	101	1	4			.993	-4	1-52	-0.9
	Phi-N	60	198	21	63	12	2	3	24	34	14	.318	.421	.444	137	12	1			.995	1	1-60	0.7
	Yr	123	402	44	122	22	4	4	55	59	37	.303	.394	.408	118	13	5			.994	-4	*1-112	-0.2
1940	Phi-N	10	25	4	4	0	0	2	5	4	5	.160	.300	.400	95	-0	0			.967	-2	/1-7	-0.2
Total	11	1435	5176	714	1446	288	114	84	818	718	433	.279	.368	.428	112	101	53			.992	-53	*1-1406/O-2	-8.9

■ **CLYDE SUKEFORTH**   Sukeforth, Clyde Leroy "Sukey"   b: 11/30/01, Washington, Me.   BL/TR, 5'10", 155 lbs.   Deb: 5/23/26   MC

1926	Cin-N	1	1	0	0	0	0	0	0	0	1	.000	.000	.000	-99	-0	0			.000	0	H	0.0
1927	Cin-N	38	58	12	11	2	0	0	2	7	2	.190	.277	.224	37	-5	2			.970	1	C-24	-0.3
1928	Cin-N	33	53	5	7	2	1	0	3	3	5	.132	.179	.208	1	-8	0			.966	1	C-26	-0.6
1929	Cin-N	84	237	31	84	16	2	1	33	17	6	.354	.398	.451	115	6	8			.981	-8	C-76	0.4
1930	Cin-N	94	296	30	84	9	3	1	19	17	12	.284	.325	.345	65	-17	1			.976	-3	C-82	-1.1
1931	Cin-N	112	351	22	90	15	4	0	25	38	13	.256	.334	.322	82	-8	0			.965	-8	*C-106	-0.8
1932	Bro-N	59	111	14	26	4	4	0	12	6	10	.234	.280	.342	68	-5	1			.991	-3	C-36	-0.7
1933	Bro-N	20	36	1	2	0	0	0	0	6	2	.056	.105	.056	-55	-7	0			.983	3	C-18	-0.4
1934	Bro-N	27	43	5	7	1	0	0	1	1	6	.163	.182	.186	-1	-6	0			1.000	-1	C-18	-0.6
1945	Bro-N	18	51	2	15	1	0	0	1	4	1	.294	.345	.314	85	-1	0			.947	-3	C-13	-0.3
Total	10	486	1237	122	326	50	14	2	96	95	57	.264	.319	.331	71	-51	12			.974	-20	C-399	-4.4

■ **GUY SULARZ**   Sularz, Guy Patrick   b: 11/7/55, Minneapolis, Minn.   BR/TR, 5'11", 165 lbs.   Deb: 9/2/80

1980	SF-N	25	65	3	16	1	1	0	3	9	6	.246	.338	.292	79	-2	1	0	0	.975	12	2-21/3-5	1.2
1981	SF-N	10	20	0	4	0	0	0	2	2	4	.200	.304	.200	46	-1	0	1	-1	1.000	4	/2-6,3-1	0.3
1982	SF-N	63	101	15	23	3	0	1	7	9	11	.228	.291	.287	62	-5	3	0	1	.961	10	S-37,3-14/2	0.9
1983	SF-N	10	20	3	2	0	0	0	0	3	2	.100	.217	.100	-10	-3	0	0	0	.917	3	/S-6,3-4	-0.0
Total	4	108	206	21	45	4	1	1	12	23	23	.218	.300	.262	59	-11	4	1	0	.954	29	/S-43,2-36,3	2.4

■ **ERNIE SULIK**   Sulik, Ernest Richard "Dave"   b: 7/7/10, San Francisco, Cal.   d: 5/31/63, Oakland, Cal.   BL/TL, 5'10", 178 lbs.   Deb: 4/15/36

1936	Phi-N	122	404	69	116	14	4	6	36	40	22	.287	.353	.386	90	-6	4			.971	-6	*O-105	-1.5

■ **SULLIVAN**   Sullivan   b: Bristol, R.I.   Deb: 5/14/1875

1875	NH-n	2	8	3	3	0	0	0		0		.375	.375	.375	184	1						/O-2	0.1

■ **ANDY SULLIVAN**   Sullivan, Andrew R.   b: 8/30/1884, Southborough, Mass   d: 2/14/20, Framingham, Mass.   TR ,   Deb: 9/13/04

1904	Bos-N	1	1	0	0	0	0	0	0	1		.000	.500	.000	61	0	0			1.000	-0	/S-1	0.0

■ **JACKIE SULLIVAN**   Sullivan, Carl Mancel   b: 2/22/18, Princeton, Tex.   d: 10/15/92, Dallas, Tex.   BR/TR, 5'11", 172 lbs.   Deb: 7/6/44

1944	Det-A	1	1	0	0	0	0	0	0	0	0	.000	.000	.000	-95	-0	0	0	0	1.000	-0	/2-1	0.0

■ **DAN SULLIVAN**   Sullivan, Daniel C. "Link"   b: 5/9/1857, Providence, R.I.   d: 10/26/1893, Providence, R.I.   TR , 5'11", 194 lbs.   Deb: 5/2/1882

1882	Lou-a	67	286	44	78	8	2	0		9		.273	.295	.315	112	4				.878	7	*C-54,3-10/OS	1.2
1883	Lou-a	37	147	8	31	5	2	0		3		.211	.227	.272	65	-5				.897	-7	C-32/O-2,3S	-0.9
1884	Lou-a	63	247	27	59	8	6	0		9		.239	.268	.320	95	-1				.930	-15	C-63/O-1	-0.9
1885	Lou-a	13	44	3	8	1	0	0		2		.182	.234	.205	40	-3				.948	-3	C-13	-0.4
	StL-a	17	60	4	7	2	0	0		6		.117	.197	.150	10	-6				.956	1	C-13/1-4	-0.4
	Yr	30	104	7	15	3	0	0		8		.144	.212	.173	22	-9				.952	-2	C-26/1-4	-0.8
1886	Pit-a	1	4	0	0	0	0	0	0	0		.000	.000	.000	-99	-1	0			.600	-1	/C-1	-0.2
Total	5	198	788	86	183	24	10	0		29		.232	.261	.288	84	-12	0			.908	-18	C-176/3-12,O1S	-1.6

■ **DENNY SULLIVAN**   Sullivan, Dennis J.   b: 6/26/1858, Boston, Mass.   d: 12/31/25, Boston, Mass.   TR , 5'9", 170 lbs.   Deb: 8/25/1879

1879	Pro-N	5	19	5	5	2	0	0	2	1	1	.263	.300	.368	121	0				.429	-4	/3-4,O-1	-0.3
1880	Bos-N	1	4	1	1	0	0	0	1	0	1	.250	.250	.250	72	-0				.857	-1	/C-1	-0.1
Total	2	6	23	6	6	2	0	0	3	1	2	.261	.292	.348	113	0				.429	-4	/3-4,C-1,O	-0.4

■ **DENNY SULLIVAN**   Sullivan, Dennis William   b: 9/28/1882, Hillsboro, Wis.   d: 6/2/56, W.Los Angeles, Cal   BL/TR, 5'10",   Deb: 4/22/05

1905	Was-A	3	11	0	0	0	0	0	0	0		.000	.083	.000	-76	-2	0			1.000	-1	/O-3	-0.3
1907	Bos-A	144	551	73	135	18	0	1	26	44		.245	.315	.283	92	-4	16			.975	1	*O-143	-0.9
1908	Bos-A	101	355	33	85	7	8	0	25	14		.239	.276	.304	86	-6	14			.981	7	O-97	-0.3
	Cle-A	4	6	0	0	0	0	0	0	0		.000	.000	.000	-99	-1	0			1.000	-0	/O-2	-0.2
	Yr	105	361	33	85	7	8	0	25	14		.235	.272	.299	83	-7	14			.982	7	O-99	-0.5
1909	Cle-A	3	2	0	1	0	0	0	0	0		.500	.500	.500	207	0	0			.000	-1	/O-2	-0.1
Total	4	255	925	106	221	25	8	1	51	59		.239	.296	.286	87	-13	30			.978	6	O-247	-1.8

■ **HAYWOOD SULLIVAN**   Sullivan, Haywood Cooper   b: 12/15/30, Donalsonville, Ga.   BR/TR, 6'4", 215 lbs.   Deb: 9/20/55   FM

1955	Bos-A	2	6	1	0	0	0	0	0	0	1	.000	.000	.000	-92	-2	0	0	0	1.000	1	/C-2	-0.1

YEAR	TM/L	G	AB	R	H	2B	3B	HR	RBI	BB	SO	AVG	OBP	SLG	PRO+	BR/A	SB	CS	SBR	FA	FR	G/POS	TPR
1957	Bos-A	2	1	0	0	0	0	0	0	0	0	.000	.000	.000	-95	-0	0	0	0	1.000	0	/C-1	0.0
1959	Bos-A	4	2	0	0	0	0	0	0	1	1	.000	.333	.000	-0	-0	0	0	0	1.000	1	/C-2	0.0
1960	Bos-A	52	124	9	20	1	0	3	10	16	24	.161	.257	.242	35	-11	0	0	0	.992	6	C-50	-0.4
1961	KC-A	117	331	42	80	16	2	6	40	46	45	.242	.334	.356	83	-7	1	0	0	.984	-6	C-88,1-16/O	-1.0
1962	KC-A	95	274	33	68	7	2	4	29	31	54	.248	.327	.332	74	-9	1	0	0	.980	-9	C-94/1-1	-1.5
1963	KC-A	40	113	9	24	6	1	0	8	15	15	.212	.305	.283	62	-5	0	0	0	.992	7	C-37	0.3
Total	7	312	851	94	192	30	5	13	87	109	140	.226	.314	.318	69	-36	2	0	1	.985	-0	C-274/1-17,O	-2.7

■ JOHN SULLIVAN
Sullivan, John Eugene b: 2/16/1873, Illinois d: 6/5/24, St.Paul, Minn. BR/TR, 5'10", 170 lbs. Deb: 4/19/05

YEAR	TM/L	G	AB	R	H	2B	3B	HR	RBI	BB	SO	AVG	OBP	SLG	PRO+	BR/A	SB	CS	SBR	FA	FR	G/POS	TPR
1905	Det-A	13	32	4	5	0	0	0	4	4		.156	.250	.156	29	-2	0			.964	4	C-12	0.3
1908	Pit-N	1	1	0	0	0	0	0	0	0		.000	.000	.000	-99	-0	0			1.000	0	/C-1	0.0
Total	2	14	33	4	5	0	0	0	4	4		.152	.243	.152	26	-3	0			.965	4	C-13	0.3

■ CHUB SULLIVAN
Sullivan, John Frank b: 1/12/1856, Boston, Mass. d: 9/12/1881, Boston, Mass. BR/TR, 6', 164 lbs. Deb: 9/24/1877

YEAR	TM/L	G	AB	R	H	2B	3B	HR	RBI	BB	SO	AVG	OBP	SLG	PRO+	BR/A	SB	CS	SBR	FA	FR	G/POS	TPR
1877	Cin-N	8	32	4	8	0	0	0	4	1	0	.250	.273	.250	74	-1				.944	-1	/1-8	-0.1
1878	Cin-N	61	244	29	63	4	2	0	20	2	9	.258	.264	.291	91	-2				.975	5	*1-61	0.1
1880	Wor-N	43	166	22	43	6	3	0	0	4	6	.259	.276	.331	97	-1				.983	3	1-43	-0.2
Total	3	112	442	55	114	10	5	0	24	7	15	.258	.269	.303	92	-4				.976	7	1-112	-0.2

■ JOHN SULLIVAN
Sullivan, John Lawrence b: 3/21/1890, Williamsport, Pa. d: 4/1/66, Milton, Pa. BR/TR, 5'11", 180 lbs. Deb: 4/18/20

YEAR	TM/L	G	AB	R	H	2B	3B	HR	RBI	BB	SO	AVG	OBP	SLG	PRO+	BR/A	SB	CS	SBR	FA	FR	G/POS	TPR
1920	Bos-N	81	250	36	74	14	4	1	28	29	29	.296	.374	.396	126	9	3	2	-0	.977	-2	O-66/1-6	0.3
1921	Bos-N	5	5	0	0	0	0	0	0	0	0	.000	.000	.000	-99	-1	0	0	0	.000	0	H	-0.1
	Chi-N	76	240	28	79	14	4	4	41	19	26	.329	.381	.471	124	8	3	5	-2	.962	-7	O-66	-0.5
	Yr	81	245	28	79	14	4	4	41	19	26	.322	.374	.461	120	7	3	5	-2	.962	-7	O-66	-0.6
Total	2	162	495	64	153	28	8	5	69	48	55	.309	.374	.428	123	16	6	7	-2	.969	-9	O-132/1-6	-0.3

■ JOHN SULLIVAN
Sullivan, John Paul b: 11/2/20, Chicago, Ill. BR/TR, 5'10", 170 lbs. Deb: 6/7/42 C

YEAR	TM/L	G	AB	R	H	2B	3B	HR	RBI	BB	SO	AVG	OBP	SLG	PRO+	BR/A	SB	CS	SBR	FA	FR	G/POS	TPR
1942	Was-A	94	357	38	84	16	1	0	42	25	30	.235	.285	.286	61	-19	2	0	1	.936	-11	S-92	-2.4
1943	Was-A	134	456	49	95	12	2	1	55	57	59	.208	.298	.250	63	-20	6	2	1	.946	11	*S-133	0.1
1944	Was-A	138	471	49	118	12	1	0	30	52	43	.251	.325	.280	77	-13	3	3	-1	.934	-14	*S-138	-1.7
1947	Was-A	49	133	13	34	0	1	0	5	22	14	.256	.361	.271	79	-3	0	2	-1	.963	8	S-40/2-1	0.6
1948	Was-A	85	173	25	36	4	1	0	12	22	25	.208	.297	.243	46	-13	2	2	-1	.951	2	S-57/2-4	-0.8
1949	StL-A	105	243	29	55	8	3	0	18	38	35	.226	.331	.284	61	-13	5	2	0	.942	-9	S-71,3-23/2	-1.8
Total	6	605	1833	203	422	52	9	1	162	216	206	.230	.312	.270	66	-80	18	11	-1	.942	-14	S-531/3-23,2	-6.0

■ JOHN SULLIVAN
Sullivan, John Peter b: 1/3/41, Somerville, N.J. BL/TR, 6', 195 lbs. Deb: 9/20/63

YEAR	TM/L	G	AB	R	H	2B	3B	HR	RBI	BB	SO	AVG	OBP	SLG	PRO+	BR/A	SB	CS	SBR	FA	FR	G/POS	TPR
1963	Det-A	3	5	0	0	0	0	0	0	2	1	.000	.286	.000	-11	-1	0	0	0	1.000	0	/C-2	0.0
1964	Det-A	2	3	0	0	0	0	0	0	0	1	.000	.000	.000	-99	-1	0	0	0	1.000	0	/C-2	-0.1
1965	Det-A	34	86	5	23	0	0	2	11	9	13	.267	.344	.337	93	-0	0	0	0	.994	1	C-29	0.2
1967	NY-N	65	147	4	32	5	0	0	6	6	26	.218	.248	.252	44	-11	0	2	-1	.991	-11	C-57	-2.3
1968	Phi-N	12	18	0	4	0	0	0	1	2	4	.222	.300	.222	59	-1	0	0	0	.967	-0	/C-8	-0.1
Total	5	116	259	9	59	5	0	2	18	19	45	.228	.283	.270	59	-13	0	2	-1	.991	-10	/C-98	-2.3

■ JOE SULLIVAN
Sullivan, Joseph Daniel b: 1/6/1870, Charlestown, Mass. d: 11/2/1897, Charlestown, Mass. 5'10", 178 lbs. Deb: 4/27/1893

YEAR	TM/L	G	AB	R	H	2B	3B	HR	RBI	BB	SO	AVG	OBP	SLG	PRO+	BR/A	SB	CS	SBR	FA	FR	G/POS	TPR
1893	Was-N	128	508	72	135	16	13	2	64	36	24	.266	.324	.360	84	-13	7			.860	-29	*S-128	-2.9
1894	Was-N	17	60	7	15	3	0	0	5	6	2	.250	.357	.300	62	-3	3			.900	-3	/2-8,S-6,3O	-0.4
	Phi-N	75	304	63	107	10	8	3	63	23	10	.352	.407	.467	113	7	10			.887	-16	S-75	-0.4
	Yr	92	364	70	122	13	8	3	68	29	12	.335	.398	.440	105	4	13			.884	-19	S-81/2-8,3O	-0.8
1895	Phi-N	94	373	75	126	7	3	2	50	24	20	.338	.395	.389	102	2	15			.879	-16	*S-89/O-6	-0.9
1896	Phi-N	48	191	45	48	5	3	2	24	18	12	.251	.347	.340	83	-4	9			.962	-4	O-45/S-2,3	-1.0
	StL-N	51	212	25	62	4	2	2	21	9	12	.292	.351	.358	91	-3	5			.955	-6	O-45/2-7	-1.0
	Yr	99	403	70	110	9	5	4	45	27	24	.273	.349	.350	87	-7	14			.959	-10	O-90/2-7,S3	-2.0
Total	4	413	1648	287	493	45	29	11	227	116	80	.299	.363	.382	94	-14	49			.872	-73	S-300/O-97,23	-6.6

■ MARC SULLIVAN
Sullivan, Marc Cooper b: 7/25/58, Quincy, Mass. Deb: 10/1/82 F

YEAR	TM/L	G	AB	R	H	2B	3B	HR	RBI	BB	SO	AVG	OBP	SLG	PRO+	BR/A	SB	CS	SBR	FA	FR	G/POS	TPR
1982	Bos-A	2	6	0	2	0	0	0	0	0	2	.333	.333	.333	79	-0	0	0	0	1.000	1	/C-2	0.1
1984	Bos-A	2	6	1	3	0	0	0	1	1	0	.500	.571	.500	191	1	0	0	0	.950	1	/C-2	0.2
1985	Bos-A	32	69	10	12	2	0	2	3	6	15	.174	.240	.290	43	-6	0	0	0	.993	4	C-32	-0.1
1986	Bos-A	41	119	15	23	4	0	1	14	7	32	.193	.262	.252	40	-10	0	0	0	.986	-5	C-41	-1.2
1987	Bos-A	60	160	11	27	5	0	2	10	4	43	.169	.199	.237	15	-20	0	0	0	.994	0	C-60	-1.6
Total	5	137	360	37	67	11	0	5	28	18	92	.186	.237	.258	33	-34	0	0	0	.990	1	C-137	-2.6

■ MARTY SULLIVAN
Sullivan, Martin C. b: 10/20/1862, Lowell, Mass. d: 1/6/1894, Lowell, Mass. BR/TR, Deb: 4/30/1887

YEAR	TM/L	G	AB	R	H	2B	3B	HR	RBI	BB	SO	AVG	OBP	SLG	PRO+	BR/A	SB	CS	SBR	FA	FR	G/POS	TPR
1887	Chi-N	115	472	98	134	13	16	7	77	36	53	.284	.340	.424	98	-5	35			.847	-7	*O-115/P-1	-1.2
1888	Chi-N	75	314	40	74	12	6	7	39	15	32	.236	.273	.379	99	-2	9			.927	3	O-75	-0.1
1889	Ind-N	69	256	45	73	11	3	4	35	50	31	.285	.404	.398	122	10	15			.910	-5	O-64/1-5	0.2
1890	Bos-N	121	505	82	144	19	7	6	61	56	48	.285	.357	.386	108	3	33			.951	4	*O-120/3-1	0.3
1891	Bos-N	17	67	15	15	1	0	2	7	5	3	.224	.288	.328	71	-3	7			.926	-2	O-17	-0.5
	Cle-N	1	4	0	1	0	0	0	1	0	1	.250	.250	.250	44	-0	0			.000	-0	/O-1	-0.1
	Yr	18	71	15	16	1	0	2	8	5	4	.225	.286	.324	69	-3	7			.926	-3	O-18	-0.6
Total	5	398	1618	280	441	56	32	26	220	162	168	.273	.341	.395	104	3	99			.909	-7	O-392/1-5,3P	-1.4

■ MIKE SULLIVAN
Sullivan, Michael Joseph b: 6/10/1860, Webster, Mass. d: 6/16/29, Webster, Mass. BR/TR, 5'8.5", 165 lbs. Deb: 4/26/1888

YEAR	TM/L	G	AB	R	H	2B	3B	HR	RBI	BB	SO	AVG	OBP	SLG	PRO+	BR/A	SB	CS	SBR	FA	FR	G/POS	TPR
1888	Phi-a	28	112	20	31	5	6	1	19	3		.277	.296	.455	140	4	10			.742	-6	O-18,3-10	-0.2

■ PAT SULLIVAN
Sullivan, Patrick J. b: 12/22/1862, Milwaukee, Wis. TR, 5'11", 165 lbs. Deb: 8/30/1884

YEAR	TM/L	G	AB	R	H	2B	3B	HR	RBI	BB	SO	AVG	OBP	SLG	PRO+	BR/A	SB	CS	SBR	FA	FR	G/POS	TPR
1884	KC-U	31	114	15	22	3	1	0		4		.193	.220	.237	28	-11				.767	1	3-21/O-9,CP	-0.9

■ RUSS SULLIVAN
Sullivan, Russell Guy b: 2/19/23, Fredericksburg, Va BL/TR, 6', 196 lbs. Deb: 9/8/51

YEAR	TM/L	G	AB	R	H	2B	3B	HR	RBI	BB	SO	AVG	OBP	SLG	PRO+	BR/A	SB	CS	SBR	FA	FR	G/POS	TPR
1951	Det-A	7	26	2	5	1	0	1	1	2	1	.192	.250	.346	60	-2	0	0	0	.938	0	/O-7	-0.2
1952	Det-A	15	52	7	17	2	1	3	5	3	5	.327	.375	.577	161	4	1	0	0	.826	-2	O-14	0.2
1953	Det-A	23	72	7	18	5	1	1	6	13	5	.250	.379	.389	109	1	0	0	0	.958	3	O-20	0.4
Total	3	45	150	16	40	8	2	5	12	18	11	.267	.357	.447	118	4	1	0	0	.920	1	/O-41	0.4

■ SUTER SULLIVAN
Sullivan, Suter G. b: 10/14/1872, Baltimore, Md. d: 4/19/25, Baltimore, Md. 6', 170 lbs. Deb: 7/24/1898

YEAR	TM/L	G	AB	R	H	2B	3B	HR	RBI	BB	SO	AVG	OBP	SLG	PRO+	BR/A	SB	CS	SBR	FA	FR	G/POS	TPR
1898	StL-N	42	144	10	32	3	0	0	12	13		.222	.300	.243	55	-8	1			.875	-13	S-23,0-10/21P	-1.9
1899	Cle-N	127	473	37	116	16	3	0	55	25		.245	.294	.292	67	-22	16			.938	5	*3-101,O-20/S12	-1.6
Total	2	169	617	47	148	19	3	0	67	38		.240	.298	.280	64	-30	17			.889	-8	3-101/O-30,S21P	-3.5

■ TOM SULLIVAN
Sullivan, Thomas Brandon b: 12/19/06, Nome, Alaska d: 8/16/44, Seattle, Wash. BR/TR, 6', 190 lbs. Deb: 6/14/25

YEAR	TM/L	G	AB	R	H	2B	3B	HR	RBI	BB	SO	AVG	OBP	SLG	PRO+	BR/A	SB	CS	SBR	FA	FR	G/POS	TPR
1925	Cin-N	1	1	0	0	0	0	0	0	0	0	.000	.000	.000	-99	-0	0	0	0	1.000	-0	/C-1	0.0

■ SLEEPER SULLIVAN
Sullivan, Thomas Jefferson "Old Iron Hands" b: St.Louis, Mo. d: 9/25/1899, Camden, N.J. BR/TR, 175 lbs. Deb: 5/3/1881

YEAR	TM/L	G	AB	R	H	2B	3B	HR	RBI	BB	SO	AVG	OBP	SLG	PRO+	BR/A	SB	CS	SBR	FA	FR	G/POS	TPR
1881	Buf-N	35	121	13	23	4	0	0	15	1	21	.190	.197	.223	32	-9				.853	-12	C-31/O-5	-2.0
1882	StL-a	51	188	24	34	3	3	0		3		.181	.194	.229	40	-12				.840	-18	C-51	-2.7
1883	StL-a	8	27	2	6	0	1	0		0		.222	.222	.296	62	-1				.939	5	/C-6,O-2	0.3

YEAR	TM/L	G	AB	R	H	2B	3B	HR	RBI	BB	SO	AVG	OBP	SLG	PRO+	BR/A	SB	CS	SBR	FA	FR	G/POS	TPR
1884	StL-U	2	9	0	1	0	0	0		0		.111	.111	.111	-38	-2				.000	-1	/O-1,C-1,P	-0.2
Total	4	96	345	39	64	7	4	0	15	4	21	.186	.195	.229	37	-24				.852	-27	/C-89,O-8,P	-4.6

■ TED SULLIVAN
Sullivan, Timothy Paul b: 1851, County Clare, Ireland d: 7/5/29, Washington, D.C. Deb: 9/9/1884 MU

YEAR	TM/L	G	AB	R	H	2B	3B	HR	RBI	BB	SO	AVG	OBP	SLG	PRO+	BR/A	SB	CS	SBR	FA	FR	G/POS	TPR
1884	KC-U	3	9	0	3	0	0	0			1	.333	.400	.333	116	0				1.000	-2	/O-2,S-1M	-0.1

■ BILL SULLIVAN
Sullivan, William b: 7/4/1853, Holyoke, Mass. d: 11/13/1884, Holyoke, Mass. Deb: 8/9/1878

YEAR	TM/L	G	AB	R	H	2B	3B	HR	RBI	BB	SO	AVG	OBP	SLG	PRO+	BR/A	SB	CS	SBR	FA	FR	G/POS	TPR
1878	Chi-N	2	6	1	1	0	0	0	0	0	0	.167	.167	.167	9	-1				1.000	-1	/O-2	-0.1

■ BILLY SULLIVAN
Sullivan, William Joseph Jr. b: 10/23/10, Chicago, Ill. d: 1/4/94, Sarasota, Fla. BL/TR, 6', 170 lbs. Deb: 6/9/31 F

YEAR	TM/L	G	AB	R	H	2B	3B	HR	RBI	BB	SO	AVG	OBP	SLG	PRO+	BR/A	SB	CS	SBR	FA	FR	G/POS	TPR
1931	Chi-A	92	363	48	100	16	5	2	33	20	14	.275	.315	.364	83	-10	4	4	-1	.912	-9	3-83/O-2,1	-1.4
1932	Chi-A	93	307	31	97	16	1	1	45	20	9	.316	.358	.384	99	-1	1	3	-2	.990	-3	1-52,3-17/CO	-0.8
1933	Chi-A	54	125	9	24	0	1	0	13	10	5	.192	.252	.208	24	-14	0	0	0	.982	-3	1-22/C-8	-1.7
1935	Cin-N	85	241	29	64	9	4	2	36	19	16	.266	.324	.361	87	-4	4			.992	2	1-40,3-15/2	-0.5
1936	Cle-A	93	319	39	112	32	6	2	48	16	9	.351	.382	.508	117	7	5	2	0	.968	-2	C-72/3-5,1O	0.8
1937	Cle-A	72	168	26	48	12	3	3	22	17	7	.286	.355	.446	100	-0	1	4	-2	.949	-6	C-38/1-5,3	-0.6
1938	StL-A	111	375	35	104	16	1	7	49	20	10	.277	.316	.381	74	-16	8	5	-1	.990	-1	C-99/1-6	-1.2
1939	StL-A	118	332	53	96	17	5	5	50	34	18	.289	.362	.416	96	-2	3	3	-1	.954	4	O-59,C-19/1	0.0
1940	*Det-A	78	220	36	68	14	4	3	41	31	11	.309	.399	.450	109	4	2	0	1	.976	1	C-57/3-6	0.9
1941	Det-A	85	234	29	66	15	1	3	29	35	11	.282	.375	.393	94	-1	0	3	-2	.976	5	C-63	0.7
1942	Bro-N	43	101	11	27	2	1	1	14	12	6	.267	.345	.337	98	0	1			.962	-0	C-41	0.2
1947	Pit-N	38	55	1	14	3	0	0	8	6	3	.255	.328	.309	68	-2	1			1.000	1	C-12	-0.1
Total	12	962	2840	347	820	152	32	29	388	240	119	.289	.346	.395	91	-40	30	24		.972	-11	C-414,1-133,3/O2	-3.7

■ BILLY SULLIVAN
Sullivan, William Joseph Sr. b: 2/1/1875, Oakland, Wis. d: 1/28/65, Newberg, Ore. BR/TR, 5'9", 155 lbs. Deb: 9/13/1899 FM

YEAR	TM/L	G	AB	R	H	2B	3B	HR	RBI	BB	SO	AVG	OBP	SLG	PRO+	BR/A	SB	CS	SBR	FA	FR	G/POS	TPR
1899	Bos-N	22	74	10	20	2	0	2	12	1		.270	.308	.378	80	-2	2			.952	5	C-22	0.4
1900	Bos-N	72	238	36	65	6	0	8	41	9		.273	.302	.399	83	-7	4			.974	-0	C-66/S-1,2	-0.1
1901	Chi-A	98	367	54	90	15	6	4	56	10		.245	.271	.351	74	-14	12			.967	-1	C-97/3-1	-0.5
1902	Chi-A	76	263	36	64	12	3	1	26	6		.243	.268	.323	66	-13	11			.967	-3	C-70/1-2,O	-0.8
1903	Chi-A	32	111	10	21	4	0	1	7	5		.189	.224	.252	45	-8	3			.988	-2	C-31	-0.7
1904	Chi-A	108	371	29	85	18	4	1	44	12		.229	.255	.307	81	-9	11			.964	2	*C-107	0.5
1905	Chi-A	98	323	25	65	10	3	2	26	13		.201	.239	.269	64	-14	14			.974	-4	*C-92/1-2,3	-1.0
1906	*Chi-A	118	387	37	83	18	4	2	33	22		.214	.262	.297	77	-11	10			.974	-4	*C-118	-0.4
1907	Chi-A	112	329	30	59	8	4	0	36	21		.179	.235	.228	49	-19	6			.983	-1	*C-108/2-1	-1.1
1908	Chi-A	137	430	40	82	8	4	0	29	22		.191	.235	.228	51	-23	15			.985	-20	*C-137	-3.6
1909	Chi-A	97	265	11	43	3	0	0	16	17		.162	.226	.174	28	-21	9			.983	5	C-97,M	-1.0
1910	Chi-A	45	142	10	26	4	1	0	6	7		.183	.227	.225	43	-10	0			.976	12	C-45	0.8
1911	Chi-A	89	256	26	55	9	3	0	31	16		.215	.266	.273	52	-17	1			.986	1	C-89	-0.7
1912	Chi-A	41	91	9	19	2	1	0	15	9		.209	.287	.253	57	-5	0			.975	-2	C-41	-0.1
1914	Chi-A	1	0	0	0	0	0	0	0	0	0	—	—	—	—	0	0			1.000	-0	/C-1	0.0
1916	Det-A	1	0	0	0	0	0	0	0	0	0	—	—	—	—	0	0			.000	0	/C-1	0.0
Total	16	1147	3647	363	777	119	33	21	378	170	0	.213	.254	.281	63	-172	98			.976	-8	*C-1122/1-4,032S	-8.3

■ HOMER SUMMA
Summa, Homer Wayne b: 11/3/1898, Gentry, Mo. d: 1/29/66, Los Angeles, Cal. BL/TR, 5'10.5", 170 lbs. Deb: 9/13/20

YEAR	TM/L	G	AB	R	H	2B	3B	HR	RBI	BB	SO	AVG	OBP	SLG	PRO+	BR/A	SB	CS	SBR	FA	FR	G/POS	TPR
1920	Pit-N	10	22	1	7	1	1	0	1	3	1	.318	.400	.455	141	1	1	0	0	.950	1	/O-6	0.2
1922	Cle-A	12	46	9	16	3	3	1	6	1	1	.348	.400	.609	159	4	1	2	-1	1.000	0	/O-12	0.2
1923	Cle-A	137	525	92	172	27	6	3	69	33	20	.328	.374	.419	109	6	9	13	-5	.951	-13	*O-136	-1.9
1924	Cle-A	111	390	55	113	21	6	2	38	11	16	.290	.311	.390	79	-14	4	2	0	.941	-6	O-95	-2.4
1925	Cle-A	75	224	28	74	10	1	0	25	13	6	.330	.375	.384	92	-2	3	2	-0	.966	-9	O-54/3-2	-1.3
1926	Cle-A	154	581	74	179	31	6	4	76	47	9	.308	.368	.403	100	0	15	8	-0	.975	7	*O-154	-0.3
1927	Cle-A	145	574	73	164	41	7	4	74	32	18	.286	.331	.402	89	-11	6	5	-1	.955	-8	*O-145	-2.8
1928	Cle-A	134	504	60	143	26	3	5	57	20	15	.284	.319	.365	78	-16	4	2	-0	.971	-4	*O-132	-2.9
1929	*Phi-A	37	81	12	22	4	0	0	12	2	1	.272	.298	.321	57	-5	1	1	-0	.980	-5	O-24	-1.1
1930	Phi-A	25	54	10	15	2	1	0	5	4	1	.278	.339	.407	85	-1	0	0	0	.938	5	O-15	-0.2
Total	10	840	3001	414	905	166	34	18	361	166	88	.302	.346	.398	92	-38	44	35	-8	.961	-36	O-773/3-2	-12.5

■ CHAMP SUMMERS
Summers, John Junior b: 6/15/46, Bremerton, Wash. BL/TR, 6'2", 205 lbs. Deb: 5/4/74 C

YEAR	TM/L	G	AB	R	H	2B	3B	HR	RBI	BB	SO	AVG	OBP	SLG	PRO+	BR/A	SB	CS	SBR	FA	FR	G/POS	TPR
1974	Oak-A	20	24	2	3	1	0	0	3	1	5	.125	.160	.167	-6	-3	0	0	0	1.000	-4	O-12/D-2	-0.8
1975	Chi-N	76	91	14	21	5	1	1	16	10	13	.231	.341	.341	78	-3	0	0	0	.889	-4	O-18	-0.8
1976	Chi-N	83	126	11	26	2	0	3	16	13	31	.206	.286	.294	59	-7	1	0	0	.964	-5	O-26,1-10/C	-1.4
1977	Cin-N	59	76	11	13	4	0	3	6	6	16	.171	.241	.342	53	-5	0	0	0	1.000	-1	O-16/3-1	-0.6
1978	Cin-N	13	35	4	9	2	0	1	3	7	4	.257	.381	.400	118	1	2	1	0	.933	-2	O-12	-0.2
1979	Cin-N	27	60	10	12	2	1	1	11	13	15	.200	.351	.317	83	-1	0	1	-1	.941	-2	O-13/1-6	-0.2
	Det	90	246	47	77	12	1	20	51	40	33	.313	.415	.614	168	24	7	6	-2	.989	-10	O-69,D-10/1	1.0
1980	Det-A	120	347	61	103	19	1	17	60	52	52	.297	.396	.504	142	21	4	3	-1	.953	-8	D-64,O-47/1	0.9
1981	Det-A	64	165	16	42	8	0	3	21	19	35	.255	.342	.358	98	0	1	1	-0	.964	-2	D-37,O-18	-0.4
1982	SF-N	70	125	15	31	5	0	4	19	16	17	.248	.347	.384	105	1	0	1	-1	.913	-3	O-31/1-3	-0.4
1983	SF-N	29	22	3	3	0	0	0	3	7	8	.136	.345	.136	39	-1	0	0	0	1.000	0	/O-1	-0.1
1984	*SD-N	47	54	5	10	3	0	1	12	4	15	.185	.254	.296	54	-3	0	0	0	1.000	-1	/1-8	-0.5
Total	11	698	1371	199	350	63	4	54	218	188	244	.255	.353	.425	111	24	15	13	-3	.959	-41	O-263,D-113/13C	-3.7

■ KID SUMMERS
Summers, William b: Toronto, Ont., Canada d: 10/16/1895, Toronto, Ont., Can. TR , Deb: 8/5/1893

YEAR	TM/L	G	AB	R	H	2B	3B	HR	RBI	BB	SO	AVG	OBP	SLG	PRO+	BR/A	SB	CS	SBR	FA	FR	G/POS	TPR
1893	StL-N	2	1	1	0	0	0	0		0	0	.000	.500	.000	37	0	0			.500	-0	/O-1,C-1	0.0

■ CARL SUMNER
Sumner, Carl Ringdahl "Lefty" b: 9/28/08, Cambridge, Mass. BL/TL, 5'8", 170 lbs. Deb: 7/28/28

YEAR	TM/L	G	AB	R	H	2B	3B	HR	RBI	BB	SO	AVG	OBP	SLG	PRO+	BR/A	SB	CS	SBR	FA	FR	G/POS	TPR
1928	Bos-A	16	29	6	8	1	1	0	3	5	6	.276	.382	.379	103	0	0	0	0	.923	-3	O-10	-0.3

■ ART SUNDAY
Sunday, Arthur (b: August Wacher) b: 1/21/1862, Springfield, Ohio BL/TL, 5'9", 193 lbs. Deb: 5/5/1890

YEAR	TM/L	G	AB	R	H	2B	3B	HR	RBI	BB	SO	AVG	OBP	SLG	PRO+	BR/A	SB	CS	SBR	FA	FR	G/POS	TPR
1890	Bro-P	24	83	26	22	5	1	3	15	15	9	.265	.419	.349	100	1				.909	-5	O-24	-0.4

■ BILLY SUNDAY
Sunday, William Ashley "Parson" or "The Evangelist" b: 11/19/1862, Ames, Iowa d: 11/6/35, Chicago, Ill. BL/TR, 5'10", 160 lbs. Deb: 5/22/1883

YEAR	TM/L	G	AB	R	H	2B	3B	HR	RBI	BB	SO	AVG	OBP	SLG	PRO+	BR/A	SB	CS	SBR	FA	FR	G/POS	TPR
1883	Chi-N	14	54	6	13	4	0	0	5	1	18	.241	.255	.315	68	-2				.647	-5	O-14	-0.6
1884	Chi-N	43	176	25	39	4	1	4	28	4	36	.222	.239	.324	70	-7				.663	-9	O-43	-1.5
1885	*Chi-N	46	172	36	44	3	3	2	20	12	33	.256	.304	.343	95	-2				.825	-7	O-46	-1.1
1886	Chi-N	28	103	16	25	2	2	0	6	7	26	.243	.291	.301	70	-4	10			.914	-0	O-28	-0.5
1887	Chi-N	50	199	41	58	6	6	3	32	21	20	.291	.362	.427	105	0	34			.766	-8	O-50	-0.7
1888	Pit-N	120	505	69	119	14	3	6	15	12	36	.236	.256	.275	75	-14	71			.939	17	*O-120	-0.1
1889	Pit-N	81	321	62	77	10	6	2	25	27	33	.240	.307	.327	85	-6	47			.946	8	O-81	0.6
1890	Pit-N	86	358	58	92	9	2	1	33	32	20	.257	.327	.302	94	-1	56			.883	11	O-86/P-1	0.6
	Phi-N	31	119	26	31	3	1	0	6	18	7	.261	.367	.303	93	-0	28			.950	3	O-31	0.2
	Yr	117	477	84	123	12	3	1	39	50	27	.258	.337	.302	94	-1	84			.900	15	*O-117/P-1	0.8
Total	8	499	2007	339	498	55	24	12	170	134	229	.248	.307	.324	86	-37	246			.883	6	O-499/P-1	-3.7

■ JIM SUNDBERG
Sundberg, James Howard b: 5/18/51, Galesburg, Ill. BR/TR, 6', 195 lbs. Deb: 4/4/74

YEAR	TM/L	G	AB	R	H	2B	3B	HR	RBI	BB	SO	AVG	OBP	SLG	PRO+	BR/A	SB	CS	SBR	FA	FR	G/POS	TPR
1974	Tex-A☆	132	368	45	91	13	3	3	36	62	61	.247	.356	.323	99	2	2	4	-2	.990	6	*C-132	1.2

YEAR	TM/L	G	AB	R	H	2B	3B	HR	RBI	BB	SO	AVG	OBP	SLG	PRO+	BR/A	SB	CS	SBR	FA	FR	G/POS	TPR
1975	Tex-A	155	472	45	94	9	0	6	36	51	77	.199	.283	.256	54	-28	3	1	0	.981	5	*C-155	-1.6
1976	Tex-A	140	448	33	102	24	2	3	34	37	61	.228	.287	.310	73	-15	0	0	0	**.991**	17	*C-140	0.6
1977	Tex-A	149	453	61	132	20	3	6	65	53	77	.291	.368	.389	105	5	2	3	-1	**.994**	23	*C-149	3.0
1978	Tex-A★	149	518	54	144	23	6	6	58	64	70	.278	.361	.380	108	7	2	5	-2	**.997**	16	*C-148/D-1	2.5
1979	Tex-A	150	495	50	136	23	4	5	64	51	51	.275	.348	.368	94	-3	3	3	-1	**.995**	10	*C-150	1.2
1980	Tex-A	151	505	59	138	24	1	10	63	64	67	.273	.356	.384	106	6	2	2	-1	.993	6	*C-151	1.6
1981	Tex-A	102	339	42	94	17	2	3	28	50	48	.277	.372	.366	120	10	2	5	-2	.996	-3	C-98/O-2	0.9
1982	Tex-A	139	470	37	118	22	5	10	47	49	57	.251	.323	.383	98	-2	2	6	-3	.991	-2	*C-132/O-1	-0.2
1983	Tex-A	131	378	30	76	14	0	2	28	35	64	.201	.272	.254	47	-27	0	4	-2	.993	5	*C-131	-1.9
1984	Mil-A★	110	348	43	91	19	4	7	43	38	63	.261	.334	.399	106	3	1	1	-0	**.995**	7	*C-109	1.4
1985	*KC-A	115	367	38	90	12	4	10	35	33	67	.245	.309	.381	88	-6	0	2	-1	.992	1	*C-112	-0.1
1986	KC-A	140	429	41	91	9	1	12	42	57	91	.212	.305	.322	69	-18	1	1	-0	**.995**	-1	*C-134	-1.1
1987	Chi-N	61	139	9	28	2	0	4	15	19	40	.201	.306	.302	60	-8	0	0	0	.994	9	C-57	0.3
1988	Chi-N	24	54	8	13	1	0	2	9	8	15	.241	.339	.370	99	0	0	0	0	1.000	-1	C-20	0.0
	Tex-A	38	91	13	26	4	0	4	13	5	17	.286	.323	.462	114	1	0	0	0	1.000	0	C-36	0.3
1989	Tex-A	76	147	13	29	7	1	2	8	23	37	.197	.306	.299	70	-5	0	0	0	.992	1	C-73/D-1	-0.1
Total	16	1962	6021	621	1493	243	36	95	624	699	963	.248	.328	.348	89	-78	20	37	-16	.993	97	*C-1927/O-3,D	8.0

■ B.J. SURHOFF

Surhoff, William James b: 8/4/64, Bronx, N.Y. BL/TR, 6'1", 190 lbs. Deb: 4/8/87 F

YEAR	TM/L	G	AB	R	H	2B	3B	HR	RBI	BB	SO	AVG	OBP	SLG	PRO+	BR/A	SB	CS	SBR	FA	FR	G/POS	TPR
1987	Mil-A	115	395	50	118	22	3	7	68	36	30	.299	.357	.423	103	2	11	10	-3	.984	6	C-98,3-10/1D	1.1
1988	Mil-A	139	493	47	121	21	0	5	38	31	49	.245	.294	.318	71	-19	21	6	3	.990	-8	*C-106,3-31/1SO	-1.7
1989	Mil-A	126	436	42	108	17	4	5	55	25	29	.248	.293	.339	79	-13	14	12	-3	.985	-5	*C-106,D-12/3	-1.6
1990	Mil-A	135	474	55	131	21	4	6	59	41	37	.276	.335	.376	99	-0	18	7	1	.985	-6	*C-125,3-11	0.3
1991	Mil-A	143	505	57	146	19	4	5	68	26	33	.289	.324	.372	94	-4	5	8	-3	.995	-4	*C-127/3-5,02D	-0.4
1992	Mil-A	139	480	63	121	19	1	4	62	46	41	.252	.320	.321	82	-11	14	8	-1	.990	6	*C-109,1-17/O3D	-0.1
1993	Mil-A	148	552	66	151	38	3	7	79	36	47	.274	.320	.391	92	-7	12	9	-2	.949	-7	*3-121,O-24/1CD	-1.6
1994	Mil-A	40	134	20	35	11	2	5	22	16	14	.261	.340	.485	107	1	0	1	-1	.923	-4	3-18,C-12/10D	-0.3
Total	8	985	3469	400	931	168	21	44	451	257	280	.268	.321	.367	89	-52	95	61	-8	.988	-21	C-686,3-205/OD12S	-4.3

■ GEORGE SUSCE

Susce, George Cyril Methodius "Good Kid" b: 8/13/08, Pittsburgh, Pa. d: 2/25/86, Sarasota, Fla. BR/TR, 5'11.5", 200 lbs. Deb: 4/23/29 FC

YEAR	TM/L	G	AB	R	H	2B	3B	HR	RBI	BB	SO	AVG	OBP	SLG	PRO+	BR/A	SB	CS	SBR	FA	FR	G/POS	TPR
1929	Phi-N	17	17	5	5	3	0	1	1	1	2	.294	.368	.647	137	1	0			.900	-2	C-11	-0.1
1932	Det-A	2	0	0	0	0	0	0	0	0	0	—	—	—	—	0	0	0	0	1.000	-0	/C-2	0.0
1939	Pit-N	31	75	8	17	3	1	1	4	12	5	.227	.333	.333	81	-2	0			.984	2	C-31	0.2
1940	StL-A	61	113	6	24	4	0	0	13	9	9	.212	.282	.248	38	-10	1	0	0	.984	6	C-61	-0.1
1941	Cle-A	1	0	0	0	0	0	0	0	0	0	—	—	—	—	0	0			1.000	-0	/C-1	0.0
1942	Cle-A	2	1	1	1	0	0	0	0	1	0	1.000	1.000	1.000	492	1	0	0		1.000	-0	/C-2	0.1
1943	Cle-A	3	1	0	0	0	0	0	0	0	0	.000	.000	.000	-99	-0	0	0		1.000	1	/C-3	0.0
1944	Cle-A	29	61	3	14	1	0	0	4	2	5	.230	.254	.246	45	-4	0	0	0	.948	1	C-29	-0.2
Total	8	146	268	23	61	11	1	2	22	25	21	.228	.301	.299	60	-15	1	0		.974	8	C-140	-0.1

■ PETE SUSKO

Susko, Peter Jonathan b: 7/2/04, Laura, Ohio d: 5/22/78, Jacksonville, Fla. BL/TL, 5'11", 172 lbs. Deb: 8/1/34

YEAR	TM/L	G	AB	R	H	2B	3B	HR	RBI	BB	SO	AVG	OBP	SLG	PRO+	BR/A	SB	CS	SBR	FA	FR	G/POS	TPR
1934	Was-A	58	224	25	64	5	3	2	25	18	10	.286	.342	.362	85	-5	3	4	-2	.988	3	1-58	-0.9

■ BUTCH SUTCLIFFE

Sutcliffe, Charles Inigo b: 7/22/15, Fall River, Mass. d: 3/2/94, Fall River, Mass. BR/TR, 5'8.5", 165 lbs. Deb: 8/28/38

YEAR	TM/L	G	AB	R	H	2B	3B	HR	RBI	BB	SO	AVG	OBP	SLG	PRO+	BR/A	SB	CS	SBR	FA	FR	G/POS	TPR
1938	Bos-N	4	4	1	1	0	0	0	2	2	1	.250	.500	.250	124	0	0			.800	0	/C-3	0.1

■ SY SUTCLIFFE

Sutcliffe, Elmer Ellsworth b: 4/15/1862, Wheaton, Ill. d: 2/13/1893, Wheaton, Ill. BL, 6'2", 170 lbs. Deb: 10/2/1884

YEAR	TM/L	G	AB	R	H	2B	3B	HR	RBI	BB	SO	AVG	OBP	SLG	PRO+	BR/A	SB	CS	SBR	FA	FR	G/POS	TPR
1884	Chi-N	4	15	4	3	1	0	0	2	2	4	.200	.294	.267	72	-0				.976	2	/C-4	0.2
1885	Chi-N	11	43	5	8	1	1	0	4	2	5	.186	.222	.256	47	-3				.838	-5	C-11/O-1	-0.6
	StL-N	16	49	2	6	1	0	0	4	5	10	.122	.204	.143	15	-4				.881	-2	C-14/O-2	-0.5
	Yr	27	92	7	14	2	1	0	8	7	15	.152	.212	.196	32	-7				.862	-7	C-25/O-3	-1.1
1888	Det-N	49	191	17	49	5	3	0	23	5	14	.257	.276	.314	88	-3	6			.901	7	S-24,C-14/102	0.6
1889	Cle-N	46	161	17	40	3	2	1	21	14	6	.248	.309	.311	75	-5	5			.892	9	C-37/1-8,O	0.6
1890	Cle-P	99	386	62	127	14	8	2	60	33	16	.329	.382	.422	125	14	10			.883	-5	C-84,O-15/S3	1.3
1891	Was-a	53	201	29	71	8	3	2	33	17	17	.353	.409	.453	153	14	8			.918	-4	O-35,C-22/S3	0.9
1892	Bal-N	66	276	41	77	10	7	1	27	14	15	.279	.316	.377	107	1	12			.958	-7	1-66	-0.9
Total	7	344	1322	177	381	43	24	6	174	92	87	.288	.336	.371	107	13	41			.887	-5	C-186/1-79,OS32	1.6

■ GARY SUTHERLAND

Sutherland, Gary Lynn b: 9/27/44, Glendale, Cal. BR/TR, 6', 185 lbs. Deb: 9/17/66 F

YEAR	TM/L	G	AB	R	H	2B	3B	HR	RBI	BB	SO	AVG	OBP	SLG	PRO+	BR/A	SB	CS	SBR	FA	FR	G/POS	TPR
1966	Phi-N	3	3	0	0	0	0	0	0	0	0	.000	.000	.000	-99	-1	0	0	0	1.000	1	/S-1	0.0
1967	Phi-N	103	231	23	57	12	1	1	19	17	22	.247	.298	.320	76	-7	0	3	-2	.928	-16	S-66,O-25	-2.3
1968	Phi-N	67	138	16	38	7	0	0	15	8	15	.275	.315	.326	93	-1	0	0	0	.968	-3	2-17,S-10,3/O	-0.3
1969	Mon-N	141	544	63	130	26	1	3	35	37	31	.239	.290	.307	67	-24	5	7	-3	.971	10	*2-139,S-15/O	-0.5
1970	Mon-N	116	359	37	74	10	0	3	26	31	22	.206	.273	.259	43	-29	2	2	-1	.975	3	2-97,S-15/3	-1.8
1971	Mon-N	111	304	25	78	7	2	4	26	18	12	.257	.302	.332	79	-8	3	4	-2	.963	-1	2-56,S-46/O3	-0.3
1972	Hou-N	5	8	0	1	0	0	0	1	0	0	.125	.125	.125	-29	-1	0	0	0	.000	0	/2-1,3-1	-0.2
1973	Hou-N	16	54	8	14	5	0	0	3	5	2	.259	.298	.352	80	-2	0	0	0	.971	-4	2-14/S-1	-0.5
1974	Det-A	149	619	60	157	20	1	5	49	26	37	.254	.284	.313	69	-25	1	3	-2	.976	-23	*2-147,S-10/3	-4.4
1975	Det-A	129	503	51	130	12	3	6	39	45	41	.258	.323	.330	81	-12	0	2	-1	.968	-7	*2-128	-1.4
1976	Det-A	42	117	10	24	5	2	0	6	7	12	.205	.250	.282	53	-2	0	0	-1	.984	1	2-42	-0.4
	Mil-A	59	115	9	25	2	0	1	9	8	7	.217	.274	.261	58	-6	0	2	-1	.955	0	2-45/1-2,D	-0.6
	Yr	101	232	19	49	7	2	1	15	15	19	.211	.262	.272	56	-13	0	3	-2	.970	1	2-87/D-8,1	-1.0
1977	SD-N	80	103	5	25	3	0	0	11	7	15	.243	.291	.301	66	-5	0	0	0	.943	-4	2-30,3-21/1	-0.8
1978	StL-N	10	6	1	1	0	0	0	0	0	0	.167	.167	.167	-7	-1	0	0	0	1.000	1	/2-1	-0.2
Total	13	1031	3104	308	754	109	10	24	239	207	219	.243	.292	.308	69	-129	11	24	-11	.971	-42	2-717,S-164/3OD1	-13.5

■ LEO SUTHERLAND

Sutherland, Leonardo (Cantin) b: 4/6/58, Santiago, Cuba BL/TL, 5'10", 165 lbs. Deb: 8/11/80

YEAR	TM/L	G	AB	R	H	2B	3B	HR	RBI	BB	SO	AVG	OBP	SLG	PRO+	BR/A	SB	CS	SBR	FA	FR	G/POS	TPR
1980	Chi-A	34	89	9	23	3	0	0	5	1	11	.258	.267	.292	53	-6	4	1	1	.943	-1	O-23	-0.7
1981	Chi-A	11	12	6	2	0	0	0	0	3	1	.167	.333	.167	49	-1	2	1	0	1.000	-3	/O-7	-0.4
Total	2	45	101	15	25	3	0	0	5	4	12	.248	.276	.277	53	-6	6	2	1	.949	-4	/O-30	-1.1

■ GLENN SUTKO

Sutko, Glenn Edward b: 5/9/68, Atlanta, Ga. BR/TR, 6'3", 225 lbs. Deb: 10/3/90

YEAR	TM/L	G	AB	R	H	2B	3B	HR	RBI	BB	SO	AVG	OBP	SLG	PRO+	BR/A	SB	CS	SBR	FA	FR	G/POS	TPR
1990	Cin-N	1	1	0	0	0	0	0	0	0	1	.000	.000	.000	-96	-1	0	0	0	1.000	0	/C-1	0.0
1991	Cin-N	10	10	0	1	0	0	0	1	2	6	.100	.250	.100	-2	-1	0	0	0	.875	0	/C-9	-0.1
Total	2	11	11	0	1	0	0	0	1	2	7	.091	.231	.091	-6	-2	0	0	0	.889	0	/C-10	-0.1

■ EZRA SUTTON

Sutton, Ezra Ballou b: 9/17/1850, Palmyra, N.Y. d: 6/20/07, Braintree, Mass. BR/TR, 5'8.5", 153 lbs. Deb: 5/4/1871

YEAR	TM/L	G	AB	R	H	2B	3B	HR	RBI	BB	SO	AVG	OBP	SLG	PRO+	BR/A	SB	CS	SBR	FA	FR	G/POS	TPR
1871	Cle-n	29	128	35	45	3	7	3	23	1	0	.352	.357	.555	166	11	3					*3-29	0.6
1872	Cle-n	22	108	30	30	8	1	0	10	1	1	.278	.284	.370	106	1						3-21	0.0
1873	Ath-n	51	242	51	81	7	7	0	32	2	2	.335	.340	.421	114	2						*3-43/S-8,2	-0.1
1874	Ath-n	55	244	54	72	10	2	0		0		.295	.295	.352	97	-3						3-36,S-20	-0.3
1875	Ath-n	75	358	83	116	11	7	2		1		.324	.326	.411	138	10						*3-73/P-2,1O	0.9
1876	Phi-N	54	236	45	70	12	7	1	31	3	2	.297	.305	.419	110	2				.915	-4	1-29,2-15/3O	0.5
1877	Bos-N	58	253	43	74	9	3	0	39	4	10	.292	.304	.379	110	2				.882	-9	S-36,3-22	-0.4
1878	Bos-N	60	239	31	54	9	3	1	29	2	14	.226	.232	.301	69	-9				.888	-1	*3-59/S-1	-0.7

YEAR	TM/L	G	AB	R	H	2B	3B	HR	RBI	BB	SO	AVG	OBP	SLG	PRO+	BR/A	SB	CS	SBR	FA	FR	G/POS	TPR
1879	Bos-N	84	339	54	84	13	4	0	34	2	18	.248	.252	.310	82	-7				.884	-12	S-51,3-33	-1.4
1880	Bos-N	76	288	41	72	9	2	0	25	7	7	.250	.268	.295	94	-2				.896	4	S-39,3-37	0.6
1881	Bos-N	83	333	43	97	12	4	0	31	13	9	.291	.318	.351	116	6				.877	-3	*3-81/S-2	0.4
1882	Bos-N	81	319	44	80	8	1	2	38	24	25	.251	.303	.301	94	-1				.856	-5	*3-77/S-4	-0.3
1883	Bos-N	94	414	101	134	28	15	3	73	17	12	.324	.350	.486	147	22				.866	-1	*3-93/O-1,S	1.8
1884	Bos-N	110	468	102	**162**	28	7	3	61	29	22	.346	.384	.455	164	34				**.908**	-4	3-110	2.7
1885	Bos-N	110	457	78	143	23	8	4	47	17	25	.313	.338	.425	151	24				.875	-0	*3-91,S-16/21	2.4
1886	Bos-N	116	499	83	138	21	6	3	48	26	21	.277	.312	.361	108	5	18			.859	-5	O-43,S-28,32	0.0
1887	Bos-N	77	326	58	99	14	9	3	46	13	6	.304	.342	.429	113	5	17			.875	15	S-37,O-18,23	1.7
1888	Bos-N	28	110	16	24	3	1	1	16	7	3	.218	.277	.291	80	-2	10			.859	-5	3-27/S-1	-0.7
Total	5 n	232	1080	253	344	39	24	5	65	5	3	.319	.322	.413	123	22	5					3-202/S-28,P201	1.1
Total	13	1031	4281	739	1231	190	73	21	518	164	174	.288	.315	.381	118	88	45			.871	-30	3-677,S-216/O21	6.6

■ DALE SVEUM Sveum, Dale Curtis b: 11/23/63, Richmond, Cal. BB/TR, 6'2", 185 lbs. Deb: 5/12/86

YEAR	TM/L	G	AB	R	H	2B	3B	HR	RBI	BB	SO	AVG	OBP	SLG	PRO+	BR/A	SB	CS	SBR	FA	FR	G/POS	TPR
1986	Mil-A	91	317	35	78	13	2	7	35	32	63	.246	.317	.366	83	-8	4	3	-1	.865	-8	3-65,2-13,S	-1.6
1987	Mil-A	153	535	86	135	27	3	25	95	40	133	.252	.306	.454	95	-5	2	6	-3	.965	-13	*S-142,2-13	-0.8
1988	Mil-A	129	467	41	113	14	4	9	51	21	122	.242	.276	.347	73	-18	1	0	0	.955	-6	*S-127/2-1,D	-1.3
1990	Mil-A	48	117	15	23	7	0	1	12	12	30	.197	.282	.282	59	-6	0	1	-1	.918	-6	3-22,2-16/1S	-1.3
1991	Mil-A	90	266	33	64	19	1	4	43	32	78	.241	.324	.365	93	-2	2	4	-2	.968	-7	S-51,3-38/2D	-0.8
1992	Phi-N	54	135	13	24	4	0	2	16	16	39	.178	.265	.252	47	-9	0	0	0	.948	2	S-34/3-5,1	-0.6
	Chi-A	40	114	15	25	9	0	2	12	12	29	.219	.294	.351	81	-3	1	1	-0	.944	-10	S-37/1-2,3	-1.1
1993	Oak-A	30	79	12	14	2	1	2	6	16	21	.177	.316	.304	72	-3	0	0	0	.976	-4	1-14/3-7,2SOD	-0.8
1994	Sea-A	10	27	3	5	0	0	1	2	2	10	.185	.241	.296	37	-3	0	0	0	.909	1	/3-3,D-4	-0.2
Total	8	645	2057	253	481	95	11	53	272	183	525	.234	.298	.368	81	-57	10	15	-6	.958	-51	S-410,3-142/21DO	-8.5

■ HARRY SWACINA Swacina, Harry Joseph "Swats" b: 8/22/1881, St.Louis, Mo. d: 6/21/44, Birmingham, Ala. BR/TR, 6'2", 190 lbs. Deb: 9/13/07

YEAR	TM/L	G	AB	R	H	2B	3B	HR	RBI	BB	SO	AVG	OBP	SLG	PRO+	BR/A	SB	CS	SBR	FA	FR	G/POS	TPR
1907	Pit-N	26	95	9	19	1	1	0	10	4		.200	.240	.232	47	-6	1			.996	-5	1-26	-0.9
1908	Pit-N	53	176	7	38	6	1	0	13	5		.216	.238	.261	59	-8	4			.983	-5	1-50	-1.7
1914	Bal-F	158	617	70	173	26	8	0	90	14	23	.280	.297	.348	65	-33	15			.985	10	*1-158	-2.8
1915	Bal-F	85	301	24	74	13	1	1	38	9	11	.246	.268	.306	52	-21	9			.986	6	1-75/2-1	-1.9
Total	4	322	1189	110	304	46	11	1	151	32	34	.256	.276	.315	60	-69	29			.986	10	1-309/2-1	-7.3

■ ANDY SWAN Swan, Andrew J. Deb: 7/23/1884

YEAR	TM/L	G	AB	R	H	2B	3B	HR	RBI	BB	SO	AVG	OBP	SLG	PRO+	BR/A	SB	CS	SBR	FA	FR	G/POS	TPR
1884	Was-a	5	21	3	3	1	0	0		0		.143	.143	.190	9	-2				.824	-3	/1-3,3-2	-0.5
	Ric-a	3	10	2	5	0	0	0		0		.500	.500	.500	230	1				1.000	-0	/1-3	0.1
	Yr	8	31	5	8	1	0	0		0		.258	.258	.290	85	-0				.902	-3	/1-6,3-2	-0.4

■ MARTY SWANDELL Swandell, John Martin (b: Martin Schwendel) b: 1845, Brooklyn, N.Y. d: 10/25/06, Brooklyn, N.Y. TL, 5'10.5", 146 lbs. Deb: 5/7/1872 U

YEAR	TM/L	G	AB	R	H	2B	3B	HR	RBI	BB	SO	AVG	OBP	SLG	PRO+	BR/A	SB	CS	SBR	FA	FR	G/POS	TPR
1872	Eck-n	14	55	8	11	0	0	0	4	2	1	.200	.228	.200	39	-3						/3-8,O-4,12	-0.2
1873	Res-n	2	9	1	1	0	0	0	1	0	0	.111	.111	.111	-37	-1						/1-2	-0.1
Total	2 n	16	64	9	12	0	0	0	5	2	1	.188	.212	.188	27	-4						/3-8,O-4,12	-0.3

■ PINKY SWANDER Swander, Edward O. b: 7/4/1880, Portsmouth, Ohio d: 10/24/44, Springfield, Mass. BL/TL, 5'9", 180 lbs. Deb: 9/18/03

YEAR	TM/L	G	AB	R	H	2B	3B	HR	RBI	BB	SO	AVG	OBP	SLG	PRO+	BR/A	SB	CS	SBR	FA	FR	G/POS	TPR
1903	StL-A	14	51	9	14	2	2	0	6	10		.275	.413	.392	146	4				.833	-2	O-14	0.1
1904	StL-A	1	1	0	0	0	0	0	0	0		.000	.000	.000	-99	-0	0			.000	0	H	0.0
Total	2	15	52	9	14	2	2	0	6	10		.269	.406	.385	142	3				.833	-2	/O-14	0.1

■ EVAR SWANSON Swanson, Ernest Evar b: 10/15/02, DeKalb, Ill. d: 7/17/73, Galesburg, Ill. BR/TR, 5'9", 170 lbs. Deb: 4/18/29

YEAR	TM/L	G	AB	R	H	2B	3B	HR	RBI	BB	SO	AVG	OBP	SLG	PRO+	BR/A	SB	CS	SBR	FA	FR	G/POS	TPR
1929	Cin-N	148	574	100	172	35	12	4	43	41	47	.300	.353	.423	96	-5	33			.970	-3	*O-142	-1.6
1930	Cin-N	95	301	43	93	15	3	2	22	11	17	.309	.335	.399	81	-10	4			.963	0	O-71	-1.3
1932	Chi-A	14	52	9	16	3	1	0	8	8	3	.308	.400	.404	116	2	3	1	0	.960	-2	O-14	-0.1
1933	Chi-A	144	539	102	165	25	7	1	63	93	35	.306	.411	.384	117	18	19	11	-1	.973	-5	*O-139	0.4
1934	Chi-A	117	426	71	127	9	5	0	34	59	31	.298	.385	.343	86	-6	10	3	1	.980	-1	*O-105	-1.2
Total	5	518	1892	325	573	87	28	7	170	212	133	.303	.376	.390	98	-1	69	15		.971	-14	O-471	-3.8

■ KARL SWANSON Swanson, Karl Edward b: 12/17/03, N.Henderson, Ill. BL/TR, 5'10", 155 lbs. Deb: 8/12/28

YEAR	TM/L	G	AB	R	H	2B	3B	HR	RBI	BB	SO	AVG	OBP	SLG	PRO+	BR/A	SB	CS	SBR	FA	FR	G/POS	TPR
1928	Chi-A	22	64	2	9	1	0	0	6	4	7	.141	.191	.156	-8	-10	3	0		.943	1	2-21	-0.7
1929	Chi-A	2	1	0	0	0	0	0	0	0	0	.000	.000	.000	-99	-0	0	0	0	.000	0	H	0.0
Total	2	24	65	2	9	1	0	0	6	4	7	.138	.188	.154	-9	-10	3	0	1	.943	1	/2-21	-0.7

■ STAN SWANSON Swanson, Stanley Lawrence b: 5/19/44, Yuba City, Cal. BR/TR, 5'11", 168 lbs. Deb: 6/23/71

YEAR	TM/L	G	AB	R	H	2B	3B	HR	RBI	BB	SO	AVG	OBP	SLG	PRO+	BR/A	SB	CS	SBR	FA	FR	G/POS	TPR
1971	Mon-N	49	106	14	26	3	0	2	11	10	13	.245	.310	.330	81	-3	1	3	-2	1.000	-6	O-38	-1.2

■ BILL SWANSON Swanson, William Andrew b: 10/12/1888, New York, N.Y. d: 10/14/54, New York, N.Y. BB/TR, 5'6", 156 lbs. Deb: 9/2/14

YEAR	TM/L	G	AB	R	H	2B	3B	HR	RBI	BB	SO	AVG	OBP	SLG	PRO+	BR/A	SB	CS	SBR	FA	FR	G/POS	TPR
1914	Bos-A	11	20	0	4	2	0	0	0	3	4	.200	.304	.300	82	-0	0	1	-1	.875	-3	/2-6,3-3,S	-0.5

■ ED SWARTWOOD Swartwood, Cyrus Edward b: 1/12/1859, Rockford, Ill. d: 5/15/24, Pittsburgh, Pa. BL/TR, 198 lbs. Deb: 8/11/1881 U

YEAR	TM/L	G	AB	R	H	2B	3B	HR	RBI	BB	SO	AVG	OBP	SLG	PRO+	BR/A	SB	CS	SBR	FA	FR	G/POS	TPR
1881	Buf-N	1	3	0	1	0	0	0	0	1	0	.333	.500	.333	170	0				.500	-1	/O-1	0.0
1882	Pit-a	76	325	**86**	107	**18**	11	4		21		.329	.370	.489	197	33				.788	-8	*O-73/1-4	2.2
1883	Pit-a	94	412	86	**147**	24	8	3		25		**.357**	**.394**	.476	**187**	**40**				.936	2	1-60,O-37/C	3.1
1884	Pit-a	102	399	74	115	19	6	0		33		.288	.365	.366	137	18				.804	-3	*O-79,1-22/3P	0.9
1885	Bro-a	99	399	80	106	8	9	0		36		.266	.334	.331	110	6				.851	-10	*O-95/1-4,SC	-0.7
1886	Bro-a	122	471	95	132	13	10	3		**70**		.280	.377	.369	133	20	37			.884	7	*O-122/C-1	2.2
1887	Bro-a	91	363	72	92	14	8	1		46		.253	.342	.344	91	-4	29			.835	2	O-91	-0.3
1890	Tol-a	126	462	106	151	23	11	3		80		.327	.444	.444	157	37	53			.925	8	*O-126/P-1	3.5
1892	Pit-N	13	42	8	10	1	0	0	4	13	11	.238	.418	.262	106	1	1			.933	4	O-13	0.4
Total	9	724	2876	607	861	120	63	14	4	325	11	.299	.379	.400	142	152	120			.856	0	O-637/1-90,CPS3	11.3

■ CHARLIE SWEASY Sweasy, Charles James (b: Charles James Swasey) b: 11/2/1847, Newark, N.J. d: 3/30/08, Newark, N.J. BR/TR, 5'9", 172 lbs. Deb: 5/19/1871 M

YEAR	TM/L	G	AB	R	H	2B	3B	HR	RBI	BB	SO	AVG	OBP	SLG	PRO+	BR/A	SB	CS	SBR	FA	FR	G/POS	TPR
1871	Oly-n	5	19	5	4	1	0	0	4	1	0	.211	.250	.263	50	-1	0					/2-5	-0.1
1872	Cle-n	12	52	8	16	0	0	0	6	2	1	.308	.333	.308	104	1						2-10/O-1	0.0
1873	Bos-n	1	4	0	1	0	0	0	0	0	0	.250	.250	.250	44	-0						/2-1	0.0
1874	Bal-n	8	33	2	8	0	0	0		0		.242	.286	.242	70	-1						/2-7,O-1	-0.1
	Atl-n	10	44	4	5	1	0	0		0		.114	.114	.136	-24	-6						2-10	-0.5
	Yr	18	77	6	13	1	0	0		2		.169	.190	.182	20	-6						2-17/O-1	-0.6
1875	RS-n	19	76	7	13	0	0	0		4		.171	.213	.171	38	-4						2-18,M	-0.4
1876	Cin-N	56	225	18	46	5	2	0	10	2	5	.204	.211	.244	60	-8				.864	2	*2-55/O-1	-0.5
1878	Pro-N	55	212	23	37	3	0	0	8	7	23	.175	.201	.189	29	-16				.846	-9	2-55	-1.9
Total	5 n	55	228	26	47	3	0	0	10	9	1	.206	.236	.215	49	-11						/2-51,O-2	-1.1
Total	2	111	437	41	83	8	2	0	18	9	28	.190	.206	.217	44	-24				.855	-6	2-110/O-1	-2.4

■ BUCK SWEENEY Sweeney, Charles Francis b: 4/15/1890, Pittsburgh, Pa. d: 3/13/55, Pittsburgh, Pa. Deb: 9/28/14

YEAR	TM/L	G	AB	R	H	2B	3B	HR	RBI	BB	SO	AVG	OBP	SLG	PRO+	BR/A	SB	CS	SBR	FA	FR	G/POS	TPR
1914	Phi-A	1	1	0	0	0	0	0	0	0	1	.000	.000	.000	-99	-0	0			1.000	-0	/O-1	-0.1

■ CHARLIE SWEENEY Sweeney, Charles J. b: 4/13/1863, San Francisco, Cal. d: 4/2/02, San Francisco, Cal. BR/TR, 5'10.5", 181 lbs. Deb: 5/11/1882

YEAR	TM/L	G	AB	R	H	2B	3B	HR	RBI	BB	SO	AVG	OBP	SLG	PRO+	BR/A	SB	CS	SBR	FA	FR	G/POS	TPR
1882	Pro-N	1	4	0	0	0	0	0	0	0	1	.000	.000	.000	-99	-1				.500	0	/O-1	-0.1

YEAR	TM/L	G	AB	R	H	2B	3B	HR	RBI	BB	SO	AVG	OBP	SLG	PRO+	BR/A	SB	CS	SBR	FA	FR	G/POS	TPR
1883	Pro-N	22	87	9	19	3	0	0	15	2	10	.218	.236	.253	47	-5				.863	3	P-20/O-7	0.0
1884	Pro-N	41	168	24	50	9	0	1	19	11	17	.298	.341	.369	126	5				.940	-2	P-27,O-17/1	-0.2
	StL-U	45	171	31	54	14	2	1			10	.316	.354	.439	110	2				**.943**	4	P-33,O-13/1	-0.1
1885	StL-N	71	267	27	55	7	1	0	24	12	33	.206	.240	.240	59	-11				.827	-3	O-39,P-35	-1.0
1886	StL-N	17	64	4	16	2	0	0	7	3	10	.250	.284	.281	77	-2	0			.929	-0	P-11/O-4,S	-0.1
1887	Cle-a	36	133	22	30	4	4	0		21		.226	.331	.316	83	-2	11			.936	-4	1-20,0-10/PS3	-0.7
Total	6	233	894	117	224	39	7	2	65	59	71	.251	.297	.317	86	-14	11			.909	-3	P-129/O-91,1S3	-2.2

■ DAN SWEENEY   Sweeney, Daniel J. b: 1/28/1868, Philadelphia, Pa. d: 7/13/13, Louisville, Ky. 5'5", 160 lbs. Deb: 4/18/1895

YEAR	TM/L	G	AB	R	H	2B	3B	HR	RBI	BB	SO	AVG	OBP	SLG	PRO+	BR/A	SB	CS	SBR	FA	FR	G/POS	TPR
1895	Lou-N	22	90	18	24	5	0	1	16	17	2	.267	.389	.356	99	1	2			.794	-4	O-22	-0.4

■ JEFF SWEENEY   Sweeney, Edward Francis "Ed" b: 7/19/1888, Chicago, Ill. d: 7/4/47, Chicago, Ill. BR/TR, 6'1", 200 lbs. Deb: 5/16/08

YEAR	TM/L	G	AB	R	H	2B	3B	HR	RBI	BB	SO	AVG	OBP	SLG	PRO+	BR/A	SB	CS	SBR	FA	FR	G/POS	TPR
1908	NY-A	32	82	4	12	2	0	0	2	5		.146	.195	.171	19	-7	0			.955	-0	C-25/1-1,O	-0.6
1909	NY-A	67	176	19	47	3	0	0	21	16		.267	.328	.284	93	-1	3			.947	3	C-62/1-3	0.8
1910	NY-A	78	215	25	43	4	4	0	13	17		.200	.271	.256	62	-10	12			.974	5	C-77	0.2
1911	NY-A	83	229	17	53	6	5	0	18	14		.231	.299	.301	63	-12	8			.964	-3	C-83	-0.7
1912	NY-A	110	351	37	94	12	1	0	30	27		.268	.325	.308	77	-11	6			.955	-1	*C-108	-0.1
1913	NY-A	117	351	35	93	10	2	2	40	37	41	.265	.348	.322	96	-1	11			.964	9	*C-112/1-1,O	1.9
1914	NY-A	87	258	25	55	8	1	1	22	35	30	.213	.316	.264	75	-7	19	6	2	.980	2	C-78	0.5
1915	NY-A	53	137	12	26	2	0	0	5	25	12	.190	.319	.204	57	-6	3	3	-1	.975	-6	C-53	-0.9
1919	Pit-N	17	42	0	4	1	0	0	0	5	6	.095	.191	.119	-5	-5	1			.944	-3	C-15	-0.8
Total	9	644	1841	174	427	48	13	3	151	181	89	.232	.310	.277	73	-59	63	9		.964	7	C-613/1-5,O	0.3

■ HANK SWEENEY   Sweeney, Henry Leon b: 12/28/15, Franklin, Tenn. d: 5/6/80, Columbia, Tenn. BL/TL, 6', 185 lbs. Deb: 10/1/44

YEAR	TM/L	G	AB	R	H	2B	3B	HR	RBI	BB	SO	AVG	OBP	SLG	PRO+	BR/A	SB	CS	SBR	FA	FR	G/POS	TPR
1944	Pit-N	1	2	0	0	0	0	0	0	0	1	.000	.000	.000	-96	-1	0			1.000	0	/1-1	0.0

■ JERRY SWEENEY   Sweeney, Jeremiah H. b: 1860, Boston, Mass. d: 8/25/1891, Boston, Mass. 5'9.5", 157 lbs. Deb: 8/22/1884

YEAR	TM/L	G	AB	R	H	2B	3B	HR	RBI	BB	SO	AVG	OBP	SLG	PRO+	BR/A	SB	CS	SBR	FA	FR	G/POS	TPR
1884	KC-U	31	129	16	34	3	0	0		4		.264	.286	.287	64	-6				.958	3	1-31	-0.7

■ ROONEY SWEENEY   Sweeney, John J. b: 1860, New York, N.Y. d: 6/1/1889, New York, N.Y. 5'8", 155 lbs. Deb: 7/25/1883

YEAR	TM/L	G	AB	R	H	2B	3B	HR	RBI	BB	SO	AVG	OBP	SLG	PRO+	BR/A	SB	CS	SBR	FA	FR	G/POS	TPR
1883	Bal-a	25	101	13	21	5	2	0		4		.208	.238	.297	69	-4				.878	-1	C-23/O-3	-0.3
1884	Bal-U	48	186	37	42	7	1	0		15		.226	.284	.274	47	-14				.917	-8	C-33,O-16/3	-1.7
1885	StL-N	3	11	1	1	0	0	0	0	0	4	.091	.091	.091	-44	-2				.750	-1	/O-2,C-1	-0.2
Total	3	76	298	51	64	12	3	0	0	19	4	.215	.262	.275	51	-19				.905	-9	/C-57,O-21,3	-2.2

■ PETE SWEENEY   Sweeney, Peter Jay b: 12/31/1863, California d: 8/22/01, San Francisco, Cal BR/TR, Deb: 9/28/1888

YEAR	TM/L	G	AB	R	H	2B	3B	HR	RBI	BB	SO	AVG	OBP	SLG	PRO+	BR/A	SB	CS	SBR	FA	FR	G/POS	TPR
1888	Was-N	11	44	3	8	0	1	0	0	0	4	.182	.182	.227	32	-3	0			.784	-0	/3-8,O-3	-0.4
1889	Was-N	49	193	13	44	7	3	1	23	11	26	.228	.284	.311	70	-8	8			.802	-10	3-47/2-1,O	-1.5
	StL-a	9	38	8	14	2	0	0	8	1	5	.368	.415	.421	122	1	2			.780	-1	/3-8,O-1	0.0
1890	StL-a	49	190	23	34	3	2	0		17		.179	.271	.216	38	-16	8			.880	-5	2-23,3-21/1O	-1.7
	Lou-a	2	7	1	1	1	0	0		1		.143	.250	.286	59	-0	1			.889	-1	/S-2	-0.2
	Phi-a	14	49	5	8	1	1	0		7		.163	.281	.224	50	-3	0			.915	-6	/2-9,O-4,3	-0.7
	Yr	65	246	29	43	5	3	0		25		.175	.272	.220	41	-19	9			.889	-12	2-32,3-23/O1S	-2.6
Total	3	134	521	53	109	14	7	1	36	37	35	.209	.280	.269	57	-30	19			.799	-24	/3-86,2-33,O1S	-4.5

■ BILL SWEENEY   Sweeney, William John b: 3/6/1886, Covington, Ky. d: 5/26/48, Cambridge, Mass. BR/TR, 5'11", 175 lbs. Deb: 6/14/07

YEAR	TM/L	G	AB	R	H	2B	3B	HR	RBI	BB	SO	AVG	OBP	SLG	PRO+	BR/A	SB	CS	SBR	FA	FR	G/POS	TPR
1907	Chi-N	3	10	1	1	0	0	0	1	1		.100	.182	.100	-11	-1	1			.571	-4	/S-3	-0.7
	Bos-N	58	191	24	50	2	0	0	18	15		.262	.316	.272	85	-3	8			.871	0	3-23,S-15,O/21	-0.3
	Yr	61	201	25	51	2	0	0	19	16		.254	.309	.264	79	-4	9			.871	-4	3-23,S-18,O/21	-1.0
1908	Bos-N	127	418	44	102	15	3	0	40	45		.244	.317	.294	97	-0	17			.930	12	*3-123/S-3,2	1.8
1909	Bos-N	138	493	44	120	19	3	1	36	37		.243	.296	.300	81	-11	25			.903	8	*3-112,S-26	0.1
1910	Bos-N	150	499	43	133	22	4	5	46	61	28	.267	.349	.357	101	1	25			.903	-1	*S-110,3-21,1	0.5
1911	Bos-N	137	523	92	164	33	6	3	63	77	26	.314	.404	.417	120	15	33			.944	11	*2-136	2.4
1912	Bos-N	153	593	84	204	31	13	1	100	68	34	.344	.416	.445	133	29	27			.959	27	*2-153	5.0
1913	Bos-N	139	502	65	129	17	6	0	47	66	50	.257	.347	.315	88	-6	18			.939	1	*2-137	-0.7
1914	Chi-N	134	463	45	101	14	5	1	38	53	15	.218	.298	.276	71	-15	14			.954	15	*2-134	-0.2
Total	8	1039	3692	442	1004	153	40	11	389	423	153	.272	.349	.344	100	8	172			.949	69	2-566,3-279,S/10	7.9

■ BILL SWEENEY   Sweeney, William Joseph b: 12/29/04, Cleveland, Ohio d: 4/18/57, San Diego, Cal. BR/TR, 5'11", 180 lbs. Deb: 4/13/28

YEAR	TM/L	G	AB	R	H	2B	3B	HR	RBI	BB	SO	AVG	OBP	SLG	PRO+	BR/A	SB	CS	SBR	FA	FR	G/POS	TPR
1928	Det-A	89	309	47	78	15	5	0	19	15	28	.252	.287	.333	62	-18	12	9	-2	.993	4	1-75/O-3	-2.1
1930	Bos-A	88	243	32	75	13	0	4	30	9	15	.309	.333	.412	91	-4	5	3	-0	.997	-1	1-56/3-1	-0.9
1931	Bos-A	131	498	48	147	30	3	1	58	20	30	.295	.322	.373	87	-10	5	12	-6	**.993**	10	*1-124	-1.6
Total	3	308	1050	127	300	58	8	5	107	44	73	.286	.314	.370	80	-32	22	24	-8	.994	13	1-255/O-3,3	-4.6

■ RICK SWEET   Sweet, Ricky Joe b: 9/7/52, Longview, Wash. BB/TR, 6'1", 200 lbs. Deb: 4/8/78 C

YEAR	TM/L	G	AB	R	H	2B	3B	HR	RBI	BB	SO	AVG	OBP	SLG	PRO+	BR/A	SB	CS	SBR	FA	FR	G/POS	TPR
1978	SD-N	88	226	15	50	8	0	1	11	27	22	.221	.307	.270	68	-9	1	4	-2	.984	3	C-76	-0.8
1982	NY-N	3	3	0	1	0	0	0	0	0	1	.333	.333	.333	88	-0	0	0	0	.000	0	/H	0.0
	Sea-A	88	258	29	66	6	1	4	24	20	24	.256	.314	.333	76	-8	3	0	1	.993	-6	C-83	-1.1
1983	Sea-A	93	249	18	55	9	0	1	22	13	26	.221	.260	.269	44	-19	2	2	-1	.987	-3	C-85	-1.9
Total	3	272	736	62	172	23	1	6	57	60	73	.234	.294	.292	63	-37	6	6	-2	.988	-7	C-244	-3.8

■ HAM SWEIGERT   Sweigert, Hampton Deb: 10/12/1890

YEAR	TM/L	G	AB	R	H	2B	3B	HR	RBI	BB	SO	AVG	OBP	SLG	PRO+	BR/A	SB	CS	SBR	FA	FR	G/POS	TPR
1890	Phi-a	1	1	0	0	0	0	0		1		.000	.500	.000	49	0	1			.000	-0	/O-1	0.0

■ AUGIE SWENTOR   Swentor, August William b: 11/21/1899, Seymour, Conn. d: 11/10/69, Waterbury, Conn. BR/TR, 6', 185 lbs. Deb: 9/12/22

YEAR	TM/L	G	AB	R	H	2B	3B	HR	RBI	BB	SO	AVG	OBP	SLG	PRO+	BR/A	SB	CS	SBR	FA	FR	G/POS	TPR
1922	Chi-A	1	1	0	0	0	0	0	0	1		.000	.000	.000	-99	-0	0	0	0	.000	0	H	0.0

■ STEVE SWETONIC   Swetonic, Stephen Albert b: 8/13/03, Mt.Pleasant, Pa. d: 4/22/74, Canonsburg, Pa. BR/TR, 5'11", 185 lbs. Deb: 4/17/29

YEAR	TM/L	G	AB	R	H	2B	3B	HR	RBI	BB	SO	AVG	OBP	SLG	PRO+	BR/A	SB	CS	SBR	FA	FR	G/POS	TPR
1929	Pit-N	42	48	11	13	3	1	0	2	2	6	.271	.314	.375	68	-2				.960	2	P-41	0.0
1930	Pit-N	23	36	2	4	2	0	0	2	1	5	.111	.135	.167	-27	-8	0			1.000	-1	P-23	0.0
1931	Pit-N	14	7	0	1	0	0	0	0	1	3	.143	.250	.143	8	-1	0			1.000	-1	P-14	0.0
1932	Pit-N	24	54	1	5	1	0	0	2	2	7	.093	.125	.111	-37	-10	0			**1.000**	-1	P-24	0.0
1933	Pit-N	31	55	3	11	0	2	0	4	1	7	.200	.214	.273	38	-4	0			.950	-1	P-31	0.0
1935	Pit-N	1	0	0	0	0	0	0				—	—	—						.000	0	R	0.0
Total	6	135	200	18	34	6	3	0	10	7	28	.170	.202	.230	13	-26	0			.973	-6	P-133	0.0

■ POP SWETT   Swett, William E. b: 4/16/1870, San Francisco, Cal d: 11/22/34, San Francisco, Cal Deb: 5/3/1890

YEAR	TM/L	G	AB	R	H	2B	3B	HR	RBI	BB	SO	AVG	OBP	SLG	PRO+	BR/A	SB	CS	SBR	FA	FR	G/POS	TPR
1890	Bos-P	37	94	16	18	4	3	1	12	16	26	.191	.321	.330	69	-5	4			.820	-8	C-34/O-3	-0.8

■ BOB SWIFT   Swift, Robert Virgil b: 3/6/15, Salina, Kan. d: 10/17/66, Detroit, Mich. BR/TR, 5'11.5", 180 lbs. Deb: 4/16/40 MC

YEAR	TM/L	G	AB	R	H	2B	3B	HR	RBI	BB	SO	AVG	OBP	SLG	PRO+	BR/A	SB	CS	SBR	FA	FR	G/POS	TPR
1940	StL-A	130	398	37	97	20	6	0	39	28	39	.244	.295	.299	53	-27	4	1	0	.980	-20	*C-128	-3.6
1941	StL-A	63	170	13	44	7	0	0	21	22	11	.259	.344	.300	69	-7	2	0	1	.985	-4	C-58	-0.6
1942	StL-A	29	76	3	15	4	0	1	8	3	5	.197	.228	.289	44	-6	0	2	-1	1.000	-2	C-28	-0.7
	Phi-A	60	192	9	44	3	0	0	15	13	17	.229	.278	.245	48	-13	1	2	-1	.970	2	C-60	-0.8
	Yr	89	268	12	59	7	0	1	23	16	22	.220	.264	.257	47	-19	1	4	-2	.977	1	C-88	-1.5
1943	Phi-A	77	224	16	43	5	1	1	11	35	16	.192	.301	.237	58	-11	0	0	0	.976	-3	C-77	-0.9

YEAR	TM/L	G	AB	R	H	2B	3B	HR	RBI	BB	SO	AVG	OBP	SLG	PRO+	BR/A	SB	CS	SBR	FA	FR	G/POS	TPR
1944	Det-A	80	247	15	63	11	1	1	19	27	27	.255	.331	.320	82	-5	2	0	1	.982	1	C-76	0.1
1945	*Det-A	95	279	19	65	5	0	0	24	26	22	.233	.298	.251	56	-15	1	0	0	.988	1	C-94	-0.9
1946	Det-A	42	107	13	25	2	0	2	10	14	7	.234	.322	.308	72	-4	0	0	0	.980	-4	C-42	-0.7
1947	Det-A	97	279	23	70	11	0	1	21	33	16	.251	.330	.301	74	-9	2	2	-1	.989	0	C-97	-0.4
1948	Det-A	113	292	23	65	6	0	4	33	51	29	.223	.338	.284	65	-14	1	0	0	.991	6	*C-112	-0.1
1949	Det-A	74	189	16	45	6	0	2	18	26	20	.238	.330	.302	68	-9	0	0	0	.989	1	C-69	-0.5
1950	Det-A	67	132	14	30	4	0	2	9	25	6	.227	.350	.303	66	-6	0	0	0	.995	8	C-66	0.3
1951	Det-A	44	104	8	20	0	0	0	5	12	10	.192	.276	.192	28	-10	0	0	0	.982	2	C-43	-0.7
1952	Det-A	28	58	3	8	1	0	0	4	7	7	.138	.242	.155	12	-7	0	0	0	.977	6	C-28	0.0
1953	Det-A	2	3	0	1	1	0	0	1	2	1	.333	.600	.667	245	1	0	0	0	1.000	1	/C-2	0.2
Total	14	1001	2750	212	635	86	3	14	238	324	233	.231	.313	.280	61	-141	10	6	-1	.985	-5	C-980	-9.3

■ JOSH SWINDELL
Swindell, Joshua Ernest b: 7/5/1883, Rose Hill, Kan. d: 3/19/69, Fruita, Colo. BR/TR, 6′, 180 lbs. Deb: 9/16/11

YEAR	TM/L	G	AB	R	H	2B	3B	HR	RBI	BB	SO	AVG	OBP	SLG	PRO+	BR/A	SB	CS	SBR	FA	FR	G/POS	TPR
1911	Cle-A	4	4	0	1	0	0	0	0	0	0	.250	.250	.250	39	-0	0			.800	-0	/P-4	0.0
1913	Cle-A	1	0	0	0	0	0	0	0	0	0	—	—	—			0			.000	0	H	0.0
Total	2	5	4	0	1	0	0	0	0	0	0	.250	.250	.250	39	-0	0			.800	-0	/P-4	0.0

■ CHARLIE SWINDELLS
Swindells, Charles Jay "Swin" b: 10/26/1878, Rockford, Ill. d: 7/22/40, Portland, Ore. BR/TR, 5′11.5″, 180 lbs. Deb: 9/7/04

YEAR	TM/L	G	AB	R	H	2B	3B	HR	RBI	BB	SO	AVG	OBP	SLG	PRO+	BR/A	SB	CS	SBR	FA	FR	G/POS	TPR
1904	StL-N	3	8	0	1	0	0	0	0	0		.125	.125	.125	-24	-1	0			1.000	-0	/C-3	-0.1

■ STEVE SWISHER
Swisher, Steven Eugene b: 8/9/51, Parkersburg, W.Va. BR/TR, 6′2″, 205 lbs. Deb: 6/14/74

YEAR	TM/L	G	AB	R	H	2B	3B	HR	RBI	BB	SO	AVG	OBP	SLG	PRO+	BR/A	SB	CS	SBR	FA	FR	G/POS	TPR
1974	Chi-N	90	280	21	60	5	0	5	27	37	63	.214	.310	.286	65	-12	0	3	-2	.987	-1	C-90	-1.2
1975	Chi-N	93	254	20	54	16	2	1	22	30	57	.213	.306	.303	66	-11	1	0	0	.979	-8	C-93	-1.6
1976	Chi-N☆	109	377	25	89	13	3	5	42	20	82	.236	.278	.326	65	-18	2	1	0	.983	-3	*C-107	-1.9
1977	Chi-N	74	205	21	39	7	0	5	15	9	47	.190	.231	.298	37	-19	0	0	0	.976	-3	C-72	-2.0
1978	StL-N	45	115	11	32	5	1	1	10	8	14	.278	.331	.365	96	-1	1	0	0	.991	6	C-42	0.7
1979	StL-N	38	73	4	11	1	1	1	3	6	17	.151	.215	.233	22	-8	0	0	0	.974	1	C-33	-0.6
1980	StL-N	18	24	2	6	1	0	0	2	1	7	.250	.280	.292	58	-1	0	0	0	.957	0	/C-8	-0.1
1981	SD-N	16	28	2	4	0	0	0	2	11	.143	.290	.143	-2	-4	0	0	0	.971	-0	C-10	-0.4
1982	SD-N	26	58	2	10	1	0	2	3	5	24	.172	.238	.293	50	-4	0	0	0	.981	1	C-26	-0.2
Total	9	509	1414	108	305	49	7	20	124	118	322	.216	.281	.303	60	-78	4	4	-1	.982	-5	C-481	-7.3

■ RON SWOBODA
Swoboda, Ronald Alan "Rocky" b: 6/30/44, Baltimore, Md. BR/TR, 6′2″, 205 lbs. Deb: 4/12/65

YEAR	TM/L	G	AB	R	H	2B	3B	HR	RBI	BB	SO	AVG	OBP	SLG	PRO+	BR/A	SB	CS	SBR	FA	FR	G/POS	TPR
1965	NY-N	135	399	52	91	15	3	19	50	33	102	.228	.292	.424	102	-0	2	3	-1	.947	1	*O-112	-0.5
1966	NY-N	112	342	34	76	9	4	8	50	31	76	.222	.296	.342	79	-10	4	2	0	.987	0	O-97	-1.4
1967	NY-N	134	449	47	126	17	3	13	53	41	96	.281	.342	.419	119	11	3	1	0	.957	3	*O-108,1-20	0.8
1968	NY-N	132	450	46	109	14	6	11	59	52	113	.242	.326	.373	109	6	8	1	2	.975	4	*O-125	0.6
1969	*NY-N	109	327	38	77	10	2	9	52	43	90	.235	.328	.361	91	-3	1	1	-0	.988	0	O-97	-0.9
1970	NY-N	115	245	29	57	8	2	9	40	40	72	.233	.343	.392	96	-1	2	4	-2	.984	-12	*O-100	-1.8
1971	Mon-N	39	75	7	19	4	3	0	6	11	16	.253	.364	.387	112	2	0	1	-1	.977	-3	O-26	-0.3
	NY-A	54	138	17	36	2	1	2	20	27	35	.261	.393	.333	114	4	0	0	0	.965	-3	O-47	-0.1
1972	NY-A	63	113	9	28	8	0	1	12	17	29	.248	.346	.345	110	2	0	1	-1	.983	-5	O-35/1-2	-0.5
1973	NY-A	35	43	6	5	0	0	1	2	4	18	.116	.191	.186	7	-5	0	0	0	1.000	-4	O-20/D-4	-1.0
Total	9	928	2581	285	624	87	24	73	344	299	647	.242	.325	.379	101	4	20	14	-2	.972	-18	O-767/1-22,D	-5.1

■ LOU SYLVESTER
Sylvester, Louis J. b: 2/14/1855, Springfield, Ill. BR/TR, 5′3″, 165 lbs. Deb: 4/18/1884

YEAR	TM/L	G	AB	R	H	2B	3B	HR	RBI	BB	SO	AVG	OBP	SLG	PRO+	BR/A	SB	CS	SBR	FA	FR	G/POS	TPR
1884	Cin-U	82	333	67	89	13	8	2		18		.267	.305	.372	77	-12				.792	0	*O-81/P-6,S	-1.0
1886	Lou-a	45	154	41	35	5	3	0		29		.227	.350	.299	98	0	3			.913	-0	O-45	-0.1
	Cin-a	17	55	10	10	0	0	3		7		.182	.286	.345	94	-0	2			.909	1	O-17	0.0
	Yr	62	209	51	45	5	3	3		36		.215	.333	.311	97	-0	5			.912	1	O-62	-0.1
1887	StL-a	29	112	20	25	4	3	1		13		.223	.310	.339	73	-5	13			.923	2	O-29/2-1	-0.3
Total	3	173	654	138	159	22	14	6		67		.243	.315	.347	83	-17	18			.854	3	O-172/P-6,S2	-1.4

■ JOE SZEKELY
Szekely, Joseph b: 2/2/25, Cleveland, Ohio BR/TR, 5′11″, 180 lbs. Deb: 9/13/53

YEAR	TM/L	G	AB	R	H	2B	3B	HR	RBI	BB	SO	AVG	OBP	SLG	PRO+	BR/A	SB	CS	SBR	FA	FR	G/POS	TPR
1953	Cin-N	5	13	0	1	0	0	0	0	0	3	.077	.077	.077	-59	-3	0	0	0	1.000	1	/O-3	-0.2

■ KEN SZOTKIEWICZ
Szotkiewicz, Kenneth John b: 2/25/47, Wilmington, Del. BL/TR, 6′, 165 lbs. Deb: 4/7/70

YEAR	TM/L	G	AB	R	H	2B	3B	HR	RBI	BB	SO	AVG	OBP	SLG	PRO+	BR/A	SB	CS	SBR	FA	FR	G/POS	TPR
1970	Det-A	47	84	9	9	1	0	3	9	12	29	.107	.219	.226	23	-9	0	0	0	.971	9	S-44	0.4

■ JERRY TABB
Tabb, Jerry Lynn b: 3/17/52, Altus, Okla. BL/TR, 6′2″, 195 lbs. Deb: 9/8/76

YEAR	TM/L	G	AB	R	H	2B	3B	HR	RBI	BB	SO	AVG	OBP	SLG	PRO+	BR/A	SB	CS	SBR	FA	FR	G/POS	TPR
1976	Chi-N	11	24	2	7	0	0	0	3	2		.292	.370	.292	82	-0	0	0		1.000	-1	/1-6	-0.1
1977	Oak-A	51	144	8	32	3	0	6	19	10	26	.222	.273	.368	74	-6	0	1	-1	.993	-2	1-36/D-5	-1.0
1978	Oak-A	12	9	0	1	0	0	0	1	2	5	.111	.273	.111	12	-1	0	0	0	1.000	-0	/1-2,D-2	-0.1
Total	3	74	177	10	40	3	0	6	20	15	33	.226	.286	.345	72	-7	0	1	-1	.994	-3	/1-44,D-7	-1.2

■ PAT TABLER
Tabler, Patrick Sean b: 2/2/58, Hamilton, Ohio BR/TR, 6′2″, 200 lbs. Deb: 8/21/81

YEAR	TM/L	G	AB	R	H	2B	3B	HR	RBI	BB	SO	AVG	OBP	SLG	PRO+	BR/A	SB	CS	SBR	FA	FR	G/POS	TPR
1981	Chi-N	35	101	11	19	3	1	1	5	13	26	.188	.281	.267	54	-6	0	1	-1	.982	1	2-35	-0.4
1982	Chi-N	25	85	9	20	4	2	1	7	6	20	.235	.293	.365	81	-2	0	0	0	.949	-3	3-25	-0.8
1983	Cle-A	124	430	56	125	23	5	6	65	56	63	.291	.374	.409	111	8	2	4	-2	.948	-3	O-88,3-25/2D	0.0
1984	Cle-A	144	473	66	137	21	3	10	68	47	62	.290	.358	.410	110	7	3	1	0	.998	-13	1-67,O-43,3/2D	-1.1
1985	Cle-A	117	404	47	111	18	3	5	59	27	55	.275	.323	.371	90	-5	0	6	-4	.983	1	1-92,D-18/32	-1.4
1986	Cle-A	130	473	61	154	29	2	6	48	29	75	.326	.368	.433	119	13	3	1	0	.990	0	*1-107,D-18	0.6
1987	Cle-A★	151	553	66	170	34	3	11	86	51	84	.307	.372	.439	113	12	5	2	0	.984	5	1-82,D-66	0.9
1988	Cle-A	41	143	16	32	5	1	1	17	23	27	.224	.335	.294	76	-4	1	0	0	1.000	-1	D-29,1-10	-0.6
	KC-A	89	301	37	93	17	2	1	49	23	41	.309	.362	.389	109	4	2	3	-1	.986	-2	D-40,O-37/13	-0.1
	Yr	130	444	53	125	22	3	2	66	46	68	.282	.353	.358	98	0	3	3	-1	.986	-3	D-69,O-37,1/3	-0.7
1989	KC-A	123	390	36	101	11	1	2	42	37	42	.259	.326	.308	80	-9	0	0	0	.970	2	O-55,D-39,1/23	-1.1
1990	KC-A	75	195	12	53	14	0	1	19	20	21	.272	.343	.359	98	-0	0	2	0	.986	-0	O-42,D-15/31	-0.3
	NY-N	17	43	6	12	1	1	1	10	3	8	.279	.340	.419	108	2	0	0	0	1.000	1	O-10	0.1
1991	*Tor-A	82	185	20	40	5	1	1	21	29	21	.216	.326	.270	64	-8	0	0	0	.985	0	D-57,1-20/O	-1.2
1992	*Tor-A	49	135	11	34	5	0	0	16	11	14	.252	.308	.289	65	-6	0	0	0	1.000	-1	1-34/O-8,3D	-1.0
Total	12	1202	3911	454	1101	190	25	47	512	375	559	.282	.348	.379	99	3	16	20	-7	.988	-14	1-444,D-291,O/32	-6.4

■ GREG TABOR
Tabor, Gregory Steven b: 5/21/61, Castro Valley, Cal. BR/TR, 6′ ″, 165 lbs. Deb: 9/10/87

YEAR	TM/L	G	AB	R	H	2B	3B	HR	RBI	BB	SO	AVG	OBP	SLG	PRO+	BR/A	SB	CS	SBR	FA	FR	G/POS	TPR
1987	Tex-A	9	9	4	1	0	0	0	1	0	4	.111	.111	.222	-15	-1	0	0	0	.938	4	/2-4,D-1	0.2

■ JIM TABOR
Tabor, James Reubin "Rawhide" b: 11/5/16, New Hope, Ala. d: 8/22/53, Sacramento, Cal. BR/TR, 6′2″, 175 lbs. Deb: 8/2/38

YEAR	TM/L	G	AB	R	H	2B	3B	HR	RBI	BB	SO	AVG	OBP	SLG	PRO+	BR/A	SB	CS	SBR	FA	FR	G/POS	TPR
1938	Bos-A	19	57	8	18	3	2	1	8	1	6	.316	.328	.491	98	-0	1	-1		.889	4	3-11/S-2	0.0
1939	Bos-A	149	577	76	167	33	8	14	95	40	54	.289	.337	.447	95	-6	16	10	-1	.923	7	*3-148	0.1
1940	Bos-A	120	459	73	131	28	6	21	81	42	58	.285	.345	.510	114	8	14	10	-2	.926	5	*3-120	1.3
1941	Bos-A	126	498	65	139	29	3	16	101	36	48	.279	.328	.440	100	-2	17	9	-0	.930	2	*3-125	0.3
1942	Bos-A	139	508	56	128	18	2	12	75	37	47	.252	.303	.366	85	-12	6	13	-6	.924	-9	*3-138	-2.5
1943	Bos-A	137	537	57	130	26	3	13	85	43	54	.242	.299	.374	95	-5	7	7	-2	.938	-8	*3-133/O-2	-1.5
1944	Bos-A	116	438	58	125	25	3	13	72	31	38	.285	.334	.445	123	8	7	4		.950	5	*3-114	1.5
1946	Phi-N	124	463	53	124	15	2	10	50	36	51	.268	.322	.374	100	-1	3			.954	-3	*3-124	-0.3

YEAR	TM/L	G	AB	R	H	2B	3B	HR	RBI	BB	SO	AVG	OBP	SLG	PRO+	BR/A	SB	CS	SBR	FA	FR	G/POS	TPR
1947	Phi-N	75	251	27	59	14	0	4	31	20	21	.235	.297	.339	71	-11	2			.916	-17	3-67	-2.8
Total	9	1005	3788	473	1021	191	29	104	598	286	377	.270	.322	.418	99	-20	69	54		.933	-19	3-980/O-2,S	-3.9

■ JEFF TACKETT
Tackett, Jeffrey Wilson b: 12/1/65, Fresno, Cal. BR/TR, 6'2", 200 lbs. Deb: 9/11/91

YEAR	TM/L	G	AB	R	H	2B	3B	HR	RBI	BB	SO	AVG	OBP	SLG	PRO+	BR/A	SB	CS	SBR	FA	FR	G/POS	TPR
1991	Bal-A	6	8	1	1	0	0	0	0	2	2	.125	.300	.125	23	-1	0	0	0	1.000	0	/C-6	0.0
1992	Bal-A	65	179	21	43	8	1	5	24	17	28	.240	.313	.380	91	-2	0	0	0	.997	6	C-64/3-1	0.7
1993	Bal-A	39	87	8	15	3	0	0	9	13	28	.172	.280	.207	32	-8	0	0	0	.989	5	C-38/P-1	-0.2
1994	Bal-A	26	53	5	12	3	1	2	9	5	13	.226	.317	.434	86	-1	0	0	0	.980	2	C-26	0.1
Total	4	136	327	35	71	14	2	7	42	37	71	.217	.304	.336	72	-13	0	0	0	.992	13	C-134/P-1,3	0.6

■ DOUG TAITT
Taitt, Douglas John "Poco" b: 8/3/02, Bay City, Mich. d: 12/12/70, Portland, Ore. BL/TR, 6', 176 lbs. Deb: 4/10/28

YEAR	TM/L	G	AB	R	H	2B	3B	HR	RBI	BB	SO	AVG	OBP	SLG	PRO+	BR/A	SB	CS	SBR	FA	FR	G/POS	TPR
1928	Bos-A	143	482	51	144	28	14	3	61	36	32	.299	.350	.434	107	4	13	6	0	.975	5	*O-139/P-1	0.0
1929	Bos-A	26	65	6	18	4	0	0	6	8	5	.277	.365	.338	84	-1	0	1	-1	.955	-0	O-21	-0.3
	Chi-A	47	124	11	21	7	0	0	12	8	13	.169	.220	.226	15	-16	0	0		.966	0	O-30	-1.7
	Yr	73	189	17	39	11	0	0	18	16	18	.206	.272	.265	39	-17	0	1	-1	.961	0	O-51	-2.0
1931	Phi-N	38	151	13	34	4	2	1	15	4	14	.225	.245	.298	42	-12	0			.990	5	O-38	-1.0
1932	Phi-N	4	2	0	0	0	0	0	1	2	0	.000	.500	.000	43	0	0			.000	0	H	0.0
Total	4	258	824	81	217	43	16	4	95	58	64	.263	.314	.369	79	-26	13	7		.975	10	O-228/P-1	-3.0

■ BOB TALBOT
Talbot, Robert Dale b: 6/6/27, Visalia, Cal. BR/TR, 6', 170 lbs. Deb: 9/16/53

YEAR	TM/L	G	AB	R	H	2B	3B	HR	RBI	BB	SO	AVG	OBP	SLG	PRO+	BR/A	SB	CS	SBR	FA	FR	G/POS	TPR
1953	Chi-N	8	30	5	10	0	0	0	0	0	4	.333	.333	.400	88	-1	1	0	0	1.000	3	/O-7	0.2
1954	Chi-N	114	403	45	97	15	4	1	19	16	25	.241	.275	.305	50	-29	3	6	-3	.985	-6	*O-111	-4.3
Total	2	122	433	50	107	15	5	1	19	16	29	.247	.279	.312	53	-30	4	6	-2	.986	-4	O-118	-4.1

■ TIM TALTON
Talton, Marion Lee b: 1/14/39, Pikeville, N.C. BL/TR, 6'3", 200 lbs. Deb: 7/8/66

YEAR	TM/L	G	AB	R	H	2B	3B	HR	RBI	BB	SO	AVG	OBP	SLG	PRO+	BR/A	SB	CS	SBR	FA	FR	G/POS	TPR
1966	KC-A	37	53	8	18	3	1	2	6	1	5	.340	.364	.547	163	4	0	1	-1	1.000	-1	C-14/1-9	0.3
1967	KC-A	46	59	7	15	3	1	0	5	7	13	.254	.333	.339	102	0	0	0	0	.971	-5	C-22/1-1	-0.4
Total	2	83	112	15	33	6	2	2	11	8	18	.295	.347	.438	131	4	0	1	-1	.980	-6	/C-36,1-10	-0.1

■ JOHN TAMARGO
Tamargo, John Felix b: 11/7/51, Tampa, Fla. BB/TR, 5'10", 180 lbs. Deb: 9/3/76

YEAR	TM/L	G	AB	R	H	2B	3B	HR	RBI	BB	SO	AVG	OBP	SLG	PRO+	BR/A	SB	CS	SBR	FA	FR	G/POS	TPR
1976	StL-N	10	10	2	3	0	0	0	1	3	0	.300	.462	.300	118	1	0	0	0	1.000	-1	/C-1	0.0
1977	StL-N	4	4	0	0	0	0	0	0	0	2	.000	.000	.000	-99	-1	0	0	0	1.000	-0	/C-1	-0.1
1978	StL-N	6	6	0	0	0	0	0	0	0	2	.000	.000	.000	-99	-2	0	0	0	.000	0	/C-1	-0.2
	SF-N	36	92	6	22	4	1	0	8	18	7	.239	.364	.337	101	1	1	1	-0	.965	-2	C-31	-0.1
	Yr	42	98	6	22	4	1	0	8	18	9	.224	.345	.316	89	-1	1	1	-0	.965	-2	C-32	-0.3
1979	SF-N	30	60	7	12	3	0	2	6	4	8	.200	.250	.350	66	-3	0	0	0	.985	-6	C-17	-0.9
	Mon-N	12	21	0	8	2	0	0	5	3	3	.381	.458	.476	157	2	0	0	0	1.000	-1	/C-4	0.1
	Yr	42	81	7	20	5	0	2	11	7	11	.247	.307	.383	92	-1	0	0	0	.989	-7	C-21	-0.8
1980	Mon-N	37	51	4	14	3	0	1	13	6	5	.275	.351	.392	107	1	0	0	0	.975	-2	C-12	0.1
Total	5	135	244	19	59	12	1	4	33	34	27	.242	.335	.348	92	-2	1	1	-0	.974	-12	/C-67	-1.3

■ LEO TANKERSLEY
Tankersley, Lawrence William b: 6/8/01, Terrell, Tex. d: 9/18/80, Dallas, Tex. BR/TR, 6', 176 lbs. Deb: 7/2/25

YEAR	TM/L	G	AB	R	H	2B	3B	HR	RBI	BB	SO	AVG	OBP	SLG	PRO+	BR/A	SB	CS	SBR	FA	FR	G/POS	TPR
1925	Chi-A	1	3	0	0	0	0	0	0	0	0	.000	.000	.000	-99	-1	0	0	0	1.000	-1	/C-1	-0.2

■ JESSE TANNEHILL
Tannehill, Jesse Niles "Powder" b: 7/14/1874, Dayton, Ky. d: 9/22/56, Dayton, Ky. BB/TL, 5'8", 150 lbs. Deb: 6/17/1894 FC

YEAR	TM/L	G	AB	R	H	2B	3B	HR	RBI	BB	SO	AVG	OBP	SLG	PRO+	BR/A	SB	CS	SBR	FA	FR	G/POS	TPR
1894	Cin-N	5	11	0	0	0	0	0	1	1	2	.000	.083	.000	-76	-3	0			.600	-1	/P-5	0.0
1897	Pit-N	56	184	22	49	8	2	0	22	18		.266	.338	.332	80	-5	4			.900	7	O-33,P-21	-0.1
1898	Pit-N	60	152	25	44	9	3	1	17	7		.289	.321	.408	111	1	4			.956	4	P-43/O-7	0.0
1899	Pit-N	47	132	17	34	5	3	0	10	8		.258	.310	.341	79	-4	2			.954	3	P-40/O-1	-0.1
1900	Pit-N	34	110	19	37	7	0	0	17	5		.336	.365	.400	110	1	2			.924	1	P-29/O-4	0.0
1901	Pit-N	42	135	19	33	3	3	1	12	6		.244	.277	.333	74	-5	0			.917	-2	P-32/O-10	-0.1
1902	Pit-N	44	148	27	43	6	1	1	17	12		.291	.348	.365	116	3	3			.969	2	P-26,O-16	-0.2
1903	NY-A	40	111	18	26	6	2	1	13	8		.234	.292	.351	87	-2	1			.969	1	P-32/O-5	-0.2
1904	Bos-A	45	122	14	24	2	6	0	6	9		.197	.252	.311	73	-4	1			.991	2	P-33/O-2	-0.1
1905	Bos-A	37	93	11	21	2	0	1	12	16		.226	.339	.280	96	0	1			.946	2	P-37	0.0
1906	Bos-A	31	79	12	22	2	2	0	4	6		.278	.329	.354	114	1	1			.948	1	P-27	0.0
1907	Bos-A	21	51	2	10	3	1	0	6	2		.196	.241	.294	71	-2	0			.981	0	P-18	0.0
1908	Bos-A	1	2	0	1	0	0	0	0	0		.500	.500	.500	219	0	0			1.000	0	/P-1	0.0
	Was-A	26	43	1	11	1	0	0	3	2		.256	.289	.279	92	-0	0			.897	1	P-10	0.0
	Yr	27	45	1	12	1	0	0	3	2		.267	.298	.289	99	-0	0			.907	2	P-11	0.0
1909	Was-A	16	36	2	6	1	0	0	1	5		.167	.286	.194	55	-2	0			1.000	-0	/O-9,P-3	-0.3
1911	Cin-N	1	1	0	0	0	0	0	0	0	1	.000	.000	.000	-99	-0	0			1.000	0	/P-1	0.0
Total	15	506	1410	189	361	55	23	5	141	105	3	.256	.311	.338	90	-20	19			.953	16	P-358/O-87	-1.1

■ LEE TANNEHILL
Tannehill, Lee Ford b: 10/26/1880, Dayton, Ky. d: 2/16/38, Live Oak, Fla. BR/TR, 5'11", 170 lbs. Deb: 4/22/03 F

YEAR	TM/L	G	AB	R	H	2B	3B	HR	RBI	BB	SO	AVG	OBP	SLG	PRO+	BR/A	SB	CS	SBR	FA	FR	G/POS	TPR
1903	Chi-A	138	503	48	113	14	3	2	50	25		.225	.263	.276	65	-22	10			.908	-4	*S-138	-2.1
1904	Chi-A	153	547	50	125	31	5	0	61	20		.229	.260	.303	81	-13	14			.947	28	*3-153	2.2
1905	Chi-A	142	480	38	96	17	2	0	39	45		.200	.274	.244	67	-17	8			.931	28	*3-142	1.8
1906	*Chi-A	116	378	26	69	8	3	0	33	31		.183	.254	.220	50	-21	7			.951	40	3-99,S-17	2.4
1907	Chi-A	33	108	9	26	2	0	0	11	8		.241	.293	.259	79	-2	3			.912	5	3-31/S-2	0.4
1908	Chi-A	141	482	44	104	15	3	0	35	25		.216	.257	.259	69	-17	6			.935	18	*3-136/S-5	0.7
1909	Chi-A	155	531	39	118	21	5	0	47	31		.222	.269	.281	77	-15	12			.941	3	3-91,S-64	-0.4
1910	Chi-A	67	230	17	51	10	0	1	21	11		.222	.263	.278	73	-8	3			.947	3	S-38,1-23/3	-0.4
1911	Chi-A	141	516	60	131	17	6	0	49	32		.254	.300	.310	73	-20	0			.957	43	*S-102,2-27/31	2.8
1912	Chi-A	4	3	0	0	0	0	0	0	1		.000	.400	.000	18	-0	0			.667	-1	/3-3,S-1	-0.1
Total	10	1090	3778	331	833	135	27	3	346	229		.220	.269	.273	70	-134	63			.938	166	3-668,S-367/12	7.3

■ CHUCK TANNER
Tanner, Charles William b: 7/4/29, New Castle, Pa. BL/TL, 6', 185 lbs. Deb: 4/12/55 FM

YEAR	TM/L	G	AB	R	H	2B	3B	HR	RBI	BB	SO	AVG	OBP	SLG	PRO+	BR/A	SB	CS	SBR	FA	FR	G/POS	TPR
1955	Mil-N	97	243	27	60	9	3	6	27	27	32	.247	.322	.383	91	-3	0	0	0	.981	-4	O-62	-1.0
1956	Mil-N	60	63	6	15	2	0	1	4	10	10	.238	.342	.317	84	-1	0	0	0	.800	-3	/O-8	-0.4
1957	Mil-N	22	69	5	17	3	0	2	6	5	4	.246	.297	.377	86	-2	0	0	0	1.000	-0	O-18	-0.3
	Chi-N	95	318	42	91	16	2	7	42	23	20	.286	.338	.415	103	3	1	2	-1	.988	1	O-82	-0.6
	Yr	117	387	47	108	19	2	9	48	28	24	.279	.331	.408	100	-0	1	2	-1	.990	1	*O-100	-0.9
1958	Chi-N	73	103	10	27	6	0	4	17	9	10	.262	.321	.437	100	-0	1	0	0	.955	-2	O-15	-0.3
1959	Cle-A	14	48	6	12	2	0	1	5	2	9	.250	.280	.354	76	-2	0	0	0	1.000	-1	/O-8	-0.3
1960	Cle-A	21	25	2	7	1	0	0	4	4	6	.280	.379	.320	94	-0	1	0	0	1.000	-1	/O-4	0.0
1961	LA-A	7	8	0	1	0	0	0	0	2	2	.125	.300	.125	16	-1	0	0	0	.000	-0	/O-1	-0.1
1962	LA-A	7	8	0	1	0	0	0	0	0	0	.125	.125	.125	-34	-1	0	0	0	.000	-1	/O-2	-0.2
Total	8	396	885	98	231	39	5	21	105	82	93	.261	.325	.388	93	-10	2	2	-1	.983	-13	O-202	-3.2

■ WALTER TAPPAN
Tappan, Walter Van Dorn "Tap" b: 10/8/1890, Carlinville, Ill. d: 12/19/67, Lynwood, Cal. BR/TR, 5'8", 158 lbs. Deb: 4/16/14

YEAR	TM/L	G	AB	R	H	2B	3B	HR	RBI	BB	SO	AVG	OBP	SLG	PRO+	BR/A	SB	CS	SBR	FA	FR	G/POS	TPR
1914	KC-F	18	39	1	8	1	0	1	3	1	0	.205	.225	.308	39	-4	1			.875	-3	/S-8,3-6,2	-0.7

■ EL TAPPE
Tappe, Elvin Walter b: 5/21/27, Quincy, Ill. BR/TR, 5'11", 180 lbs. Deb: 4/24/54 MC

YEAR	TM/L	G	AB	R	H	2B	3B	HR	RBI	BB	SO	AVG	OBP	SLG	PRO+	BR/A	SB	CS	SBR	FA	FR	G/POS	TPR
1954	Chi-N	46	119	5	22	3	0	0	4	10	9	.185	.248	.210	21	-14	0	0	0	.986	6	C-46	-0.6

YEAR	TM/L	G	AB	R	H	2B	3B	HR	RBI	BB	SO	AVG	OBP	SLG	PRO+	BR/A	SB	CS	SBR	FA	FR	G/POS	TPR
1955	Chi-N	2	0	0	0	0	0	0	0	0	0	—	—	—		0	0	0	0	1.000	1	/C-2	0.1
1956	Chi-N	3	1	0	0	0	0	0	0	1	0	.000	.500	.000	51	0	0	0	0	1.000	0	/C-3	0.0
1958	Chi-N	17	28	2	6	0	0	0	4	3	1	.214	.290	.214	37	-2	0	0	0	.962	-1	C-16	-0.3
1960	Chi-N	51	103	11	24	7	0	0	3	11	12	.233	.313	.301	70	-4	0	1	-1	.992	9	C-49	0.6
1962	Chi-N	26	53	3	11	0	0	0	6	4	3	.208	.288	.208	34	-5	0	0	0	1.000	4	C-26,M	0.2
Total	6	145	304	21	63	10	0	0	17	29	25	.207	.283	.240	41	-25	0	1	-1	.989	19	C-142	-0.2

■ TED TAPPE
Tappe, Theodore Nash   b: 2/2/31, Seattle, Wash.   BL/TR, 6'3", 185 lbs.   Deb: 9/14/50

YEAR	TM/L	G	AB	R	H	2B	3B	HR	RBI	BB	SO	AVG	OBP	SLG	PRO+	BR/A	SB	CS	SBR	FA	FR	G/POS	TPR
1950	Cin-N	7	5	1	1	0	0	1	1	1	1	.200	.333	.800	187	1	0			.000	0	H	0.1
1951	Cin-N	4	3	0	1	0	0	0	0	0	0	.333	.333	.333	79	-0	0			.000	0	H	0.0
1955	Chi-N	23	50	12	13	2	0	4	10	11	11	.260	.413	.540	151	4	0	0	0	1.000	-2	O-15	0.1
Total	3	34	58	13	15	2	0	5	11	12	12	.259	.403	.552	151	5	0	0		1.000	-2	/O-15	0.2

■ TONY TARASCO
Tarasco, Anthony Giacinto   b: 12/9/70, New York, N.Y.   BL/TR, 6', 185 lbs.   Deb: 4/30/93

YEAR	TM/L	G	AB	R	H	2B	3B	HR	RBI	BB	SO	AVG	OBP	SLG	PRO+	BR/A	SB	CS	SBR	FA	FR	G/POS	TPR
1993	*Atl-N	24	35	6	8	2	0	0	2	0	5	.229	.250	.286	43	-3	0	1	-1	1.000	-3	O-12	-0.6
1994	Atl-N	87	132	16	36	6	0	5	19	9	17	.273	.319	.432	93	-2	5	0	2	1.000	-8	O-45	-0.8
Total	2	111	167	22	44	8	0	5	21	9	22	.263	.305	.401	83	-4	5	1	1	1.000	-10	/O-57	-1.4

■ ARLIE TARBERT
Tarbert, Wilbur Arlington   b: 9/10/04, Cleveland, Ohio   d: 11/27/46, Cleveland, Ohio   BR/TR, 6', 160 lbs.   Deb: 6/18/27

YEAR	TM/L	G	AB	R	H	2B	3B	HR	RBI	BB	SO	AVG	OBP	SLG	PRO+	BR/A	SB	CS	SBR	FA	FR	G/POS	TPR
1927	Bos-A	33	69	5	13	1	0	0	5	3	12	.188	.253	.203	20	-8	0	0	0	.944	-4	O-27	-1.3
1928	Bos-A	6	17	1	3	1	0	0	2	1	1	.176	.222	.235	21	-2	1	0	0	.900	-0	/O-6	-0.2
Total	2	39	86	6	16	2	0	0	7	4	13	.186	.247	.209	20	-10	1	0	0	.935	-5	/O-33	-1.5

■ DANNY TARTABULL
Tartabull, Danilo (Mora)   b: 10/30/62, San Juan, P.R.   BR/TR, 6'1", 205 lbs.   Deb: 9/7/84   F

YEAR	TM/L	G	AB	R	H	2B	3B	HR	RBI	BB	SO	AVG	OBP	SLG	PRO+	BR/A	SB	CS	SBR	FA	FR	G/POS	TPR
1984	Sea-A	10	20	3	6	1	0	2	7	2	3	.300	.391	.650	185	2	0	0	0	.931	2	/S-8,2-1	0.4
1985	Sea-A	19	61	8	20	7	1	1	7	8	14	.328	.406	.525	152	4	1	0	0	.940	-3	S-16/3-4	0.3
1986	Sea-A	137	511	76	138	25	6	25	96	61	157	.270	.349	.489	124	17	4	8	-4	.953	1	*O-101,2-31/3D	1.2
1987	KC-A	158	582	95	180	27	3	34	101	79	136	.309	.393	.541	141	35	9	4	0	.976	-6	*O-149/D-6	2.2
1988	KC-A	146	507	80	139	38	3	26	102	76	119	.274	.373	.515	145	31	8	5	-1	.963	-4	*O-130,D-13	2.2
1989	KC-A	133	441	54	118	22	0	18	62	69	123	.268	.370	.440	128	18	4	2	0	.982	-7	O-71,D-55	0.8
1990	KC-A	88	313	41	84	19	0	15	60	36	93	.268	.344	.473	128	11	1	1	-0	.965	-4	O-52,D-32	0.5
1991	KC-A★	132	484	78	153	35	3	31	100	65	121	.316	.400	.593	170	46	6	3	0	.965	-10	*O-124/D-6	3.2
1992	NY-A	123	421	72	112	19	0	25	85	103	115	.266	.410	.489	152	33	2	2	-1	.980	1	O-69,D-53	3.1
1993	NY-A	138	513	87	128	33	2	31	102	92	156	.250	.366	.503	135	26	0	0	0	.978	-1	D-88,O-50	1.9
1994	NY-A	104	399	68	102	24	1	19	67	66	111	.256	.363	.464	119	12	1	1	-0	1.000	-2	D-78,O-26	0.5
Total	11	1188	4252	662	1180	250	19	227	789	657	1148	.278	.376	.505	139	235	36	26	-5	.970	-34	O-772,D-334/2S3	16.3

■ JOSE TARTABULL
Tartabull, Jose Milages (Guzman)   b: 11/27/38, Cienfuegos, Cuba   BL/TL, 5'11", 165 lbs.   Deb: 4/10/62   F

YEAR	TM/L	G	AB	R	H	2B	3B	HR	RBI	BB	SO	AVG	OBP	SLG	PRO+	BR/A	SB	CS	SBR	FA	FR	G/POS	TPR
1962	KC-A	107	310	49	86	6	5	0	22	20	19	.277	.323	.329	73	-12	19	5	3	.974	4	O-85	-1.0
1963	KC-A	79	242	27	58	8	5	1	19	17	17	.240	.290	.326	68	-12	16	1	4	.986	-3	O-71	-1.3
1964	KC-A	104	100	9	20	2	0	0	3	5	12	.200	.238	.220	28	-10	4	0	1	.978	-12	O-59	-2.2
1965	KC-A	68	218	28	68	11	4	1	19	18	20	.312	.364	.413	122	6	11	5	0	.986	7	O-54	1.1
1966	KC-A	37	127	13	30	2	3	0	4	11	13	.236	.297	.299	74	-4	8	1	2	1.000	0	O-32	-0.4
	Bos-A	68	195	28	54	7	4	0	11	6	11	.277	.299	.354	79	-6	11	3	2	.989	-2	O-47	-0.9
	Yr	105	322	41	84	9	7	0	15	17	24	.261	.298	.332	77	-10	19	4	3	.994	-2	O-79	-1.3
1967	*Bos-A	115	247	36	55	1	2	0	10	23	26	.223	.289	.243	54	-13	6	6	-2	.989	-12	O-83	-3.4
1968	Bos-A	72	139	24	39	6	0	0	6	6	5	.281	.310	.324	87	-2	2	3	-1	.984	-4	O-43	-1.0
1969	Oak-A	75	266	28	71	11	1	0	11	9	11	.267	.291	.316	73	-10	3	4	-2	.993	1	O-63	-1.5
1970	Oak-A	24	13	5	3	2	0	0	2	0	2	.231	.231	.385	69	-1	1	0	0	1.000	-2	/O-6	-0.2
Total	9	749	1857	247	484	56	24	2	107	115	136	.261	.304	.320	74	-61	81	28	8	.986	-24	O-543	-10.8

■ LA SCHELLE TARVER
Tarver, La Schelle   b: 1/30/59, Modesto, Cal.   BL/TL, 5'11", 165 lbs.   Deb: 7/12/86

YEAR	TM/L	G	AB	R	H	2B	3B	HR	RBI	BB	SO	AVG	OBP	SLG	PRO+	BR/A	SB	CS	SBR	FA	FR	G/POS	TPR
1986	Bos-A	13	25	3	3	0	0	0	1	1	4	.120	.154	.120	-24	-7	1	1	-1	1.000	-1	/O-9	-0.6

■ WILLIE TASBY
Tasby, Willie   b: 1/8/33, Shreveport, La.   BR/TR, 5'11", 175 lbs.   Deb: 9/9/58

YEAR	TM/L	G	AB	R	H	2B	3B	HR	RBI	BB	SO	AVG	OBP	SLG	PRO+	BR/A	SB	CS	SBR	FA	FR	G/POS	TPR
1958	Bal-A	18	50	6	10	3	0	1	1	7	15	.200	.310	.320	78	-1	1	1	-0	1.000	-4	O-16	-0.7
1959	Bal-A	142	505	69	126	16	5	13	48	34	80	.250	.305	.378	88	-9	3	5	-2	.968	3	*O-137	-1.5
1960	Bal-A	39	85	9	18	2	1	0	3	9	12	.212	.295	.259	52	-6	1	0	0	.980	-8	O-36	-1.4
	Bos-A	105	385	68	108	17	1	7	37	51	54	.281	.372	.384	101	2	3	1	0	.979	3	*O-102	0.0
	Yr	144	470	77	126	19	2	7	40	60	66	.268	.358	.362	93	-3	4	1	1	.979	-5	*O-138	-1.4
1961	Was-A	141	494	54	124	13	2	17	63	58	94	.251	.332	.389	93	-5	4	10	-5	.985	2	*O-139	-1.5
1962	Was-A	11	34	4	7	0	0	0	0	2	6	.206	.250	.206	24	-4	0	0	0	.933	-2	O-10	-0.6
	Cle-A	75	199	25	48	7	0	4	17	25	41	.241	.326	.337	81	-5	0	2	-1	1.000	-12	O-66/3-1	-2.2
	Yr	86	233	29	55	7	0	4	17	27	47	.236	.315	.318	73	-9	0	2	-1	.992	-14	O-76/3-1	-2.8
1963	Cle-A	52	116	11	26	3	0	4	5	15	25	.224	.318	.371	93	-1	0	1	-0	.981	-5	O-37/2-1	-0.8
Total	6	583	1868	246	467	61	10	46	174	201	327	.250	.328	.367	89	-28	12	20	-8	.980	-22	O-543/2-1,3	-8.7

■ POP TATE
Tate, Edward Christopher "Dimples"   b: 12/22/1860, Richmond, Va.   d: 6/25/32, Richmond, Va.   BR/TL, 5'10", 178 lbs.   Deb: 9/26/1885

YEAR	TM/L	G	AB	R	H	2B	3B	HR	RBI	BB	SO	AVG	OBP	SLG	PRO+	BR/A	SB	CS	SBR	FA	FR	G/POS	TPR
1885	Bos-N	4	13	1	2	0	0	0	2	1	3	.154	.214	.154	21	-1				.865	1	/C-4	0.0
1886	Bos-N	31	106	13	24	3	1	0	3	7	17	.226	.274	.274	70	-4	0			.885	-4	C-31	-0.3
1887	Bos-N	60	231	34	60	5	3	0	27	8	9	.260	.296	.307	68	-10	7			.924	13	C-53/O-8	0.7
1888	Bos-N	41	148	18	34	7	1	1	6	8	7	.230	.278	.311	86	-2	3			.854	-3	C-41/O-1	-0.1
1889	Bal-A	72	253	28	46	6	3	1	27	13	37	.182	.236	.241	35	-22	4			.938	-3	C-62,1-10	-1.7
1890	Bal-a	19	71	7	13	1	1	0		4		.183	.284	.225	48	-5	3			.923	-2	C-11/1-8	-0.5
Total	6	227	822	101	179	22	9	2	65	41	73	.218	.269	.274	58	-43	17			.905	3	C-202/1-18,O	-1.9

■ BENNIE TATE
Tate, Henry Bennett   b: 12/3/01, Whitwell, Tenn.   d: 10/27/73, W.Frankfort, Ill.   BL/TR, 5'8", 165 lbs.   Deb: 4/29/24

YEAR	TM/L	G	AB	R	H	2B	3B	HR	RBI	BB	SO	AVG	OBP	SLG	PRO+	BR/A	SB	CS	SBR	FA	FR	G/POS	TPR
1924	*Was-A	21	43	2	13	2	0	0	7	1	2	.302	.318	.349	74	-2	0	0	0	.841	-3	C-14	-0.4
1925	Was-A	16	27	0	13	3	0	0	7	2	1	.481	.517	.593	185	4	0	0	0	.955	2	C-14	0.5
1926	Was-A	59	142	17	38	5	2	1	13	15	1	.268	.338	.352	82	-4	0	0	0	.960	-5	C-45	-0.6
1927	Was-A	61	131	12	41	5	1	1	24	8	4	.313	.357	.389	95	-4	1	0	3	.977	4	C-39	-0.4
1928	Was-A	57	122	10	30	6	0	0	15	10	4	.246	.303	.295	58	-7	0	4	-2	.985	2	C-30	-0.5
1929	Was-A	81	265	26	78	12	3	0	30	16	8	.294	.335	.362	79	-8	2	5	-2	.971	-2	C-74	-0.6
1930	Was-A	14	20	1	5	0	0	0	2	1	0	.250	.250	.250	27	-2	0	0	0	.933	-1	/C-9	-0.2
	Chi-A	72	230	26	73	11	2	0	27	18	10	.317	.367	.383	94	-2	2	1	0	.981	-10	C-70	-0.5
	Yr	86	250	27	78	11	2	0	29	18	11	.312	.358	.372	88	-4	2	1	0	.978	-11	C-79	-0.7
1931	Chi-A	89	273	27	73	12	6	0	22	26	10	.267	.331	.333	80	-8	1	1	0	.987	7	C-85	0.4
1932	Chi-A	4	10	1	1	0	0	0	0	1	0	.100	.182	.100	-27	-2	0	0	0	1.000	0	/C-4	-0.1
	Bos-A	81	273	21	67	12	5	0	26	20	6	.245	.297	.348	68	-13	1	1	0	.974	-5	C-76	-1.4
	Yr	85	283	22	68	12	5	0	26	21	6	.240	.293	.339	65	-15	1	1	0	.975	-5	C-80	-1.5
1934	Chi-N	11	24	1	3	0	0	0	0	1	3	.125	.160	.125	-23	-4	0	0	0	1.000	-3	/C-8	-0.7
Total	10	566	1560	144	435	68	16	4	173	118	50	.279	.330	.351	78	-50	5	15		.974	-14	C-468	-3.7

■ HUGHIE TATE
Tate, Hugh Henry   b: 5/19/1880, Everett, Pa.   d: 8/7/56, Greenville, Pa.   BR/TR, 5'11", 190 lbs.   Deb: 9/21/05

YEAR	TM/L	G	AB	R	H	2B	3B	HR	RBI	BB	SO	AVG	OBP	SLG	PRO+	BR/A	SB	CS	SBR	FA	FR	G/POS	TPR
1905	Was-A	4	13	1	4	0	1	0	2	0		.308	.308	.462	149	1	1			1.000	0	/O-3	0.1

YEAR	TM/L	G	AB	R	H	2B	3B	HR	RBI	BB	SO	AVG	OBP	SLG	PRO+	BR/A	SB	CS	SBR	FA	FR	G/POS	TPR

■ LEE TATE
Tate, Lee Willie "Skeeter" b: 3/18/32, Black Rock, Ark. BR/TR, 5'10", 165 lbs. Deb: 9/12/58

1958	StL-N	10	35	4	7	2	0	0	1	4	3	.200	.282	.257	42	-3	0	0	0	.950	-4	/S-9	-0.6
1959	StL-N	41	50	5	7	1	1	1	4	5	7	.140	.232	.260	29	-5	0	0	0	.927	1	S-39/2-2,3	-0.3
Total	2	51	85	9	14	3	1	1	5	9	10	.165	.253	.259	34	-8	0	0	0	.934	-4	/S-48,3-2,2	-0.9

■ JIM TATUM
Tatum, James Ray b: 10/9/67, Grossmont, Cal. BR/TR, 6'2", 200 lbs. Deb: 9/18/92

1992	Mil-A	5	8	0	1	0	0	0	0	1	2	.125	.222	.125	-0	-1	0	0	0	1.000	-0	/3-5	-0.1
1993	Col-N	92	98	7	20	5	0	1	12	5	27	.204	.250	.286	37	-9	0	0	0	.978	-2	1-12/3-6,O	-1.1
Total	2	97	106	7	21	5	0	1	12	6	29	.198	.248	.274	35	-10	0	0	0	.923	-2	/1-12,3-11,O	-1.2

■ JARVIS TATUM
Tatum, Jarvis b: 10/11/46, Fresno, Cal. BR/TR, 6', 185 lbs. Deb: 9/7/68

1968	Cal-A	17	51	7	9	1	0	0	2	0	9	.176	.176	.196	13	-5	0	0	0	1.000	-0	O-11	-0.7
1969	Cal-A	10	22	2	7	0	0	0	0	0	6	.318	.318	.318	83	-1	0	1	-1	.857	-1	/O-5	-0.2
1970	Cal-A	75	181	28	43	7	0	6	17	35	.238	.303	.276	63	-9	1	0	0	.982	-5	O-58	-1.7
Total	3	102	254	37	59	8	0	6	8	17	50	.232	.280	.264	56	-15	1	1	-0	.979	-6	/O-74	-2.6

■ TOMMY TATUM
Tatum, V T b: 7/16/19, Decatur, Tex. d: 11/7/89, Oklahoma City, Okla. BR/TR, 6', 185 lbs. Deb: 8/1/41

1941	Bro-N	8	12	1	2	0	0	0	1	1	3	.167	.231	.250	34	-1				1.000	-1	/O-4	-0.2
1947	Bro-N	4	6	0	0	0	0	0	0	0	1	.000	.000	.000	-96	-2	0			1.000	-1	/O-3	-0.3
	Cin-N	69	176	19	48	5	2	1	16	16	16	.273	.333	.341	80	-5	7			1.000	4	O-49/2-1	-0.3
	Yr	73	182	19	48	5	2	1	16	16	17	.264	.323	.330	74	-7	7			1.000	3	O-52/2-1	-0.6
Total	2	81	194	20	50	6	2	1	17	17	20	.258	.318	.325	72	-8	7			1.000	2	/O-56,2-1	-0.8

■ EDDIE TAUBENSEE
Taubensee, Edward Kenneth b: 10/31/68, Beeville, Tex. BL/TR, 6'3", 205 lbs. Deb: 5/18/91

1991	Cle-A	26	66	5	16	2	1	0	8	5	16	.242	.296	.303	66	-3	0	0	0	.979	-7	C-25	-0.9
1992	Hou-N	104	297	23	66	15	0	5	28	31	78	.222	.300	.323	80	-8	2	1	0	.992	4	*C-103	0.1
1993	Hou-N	94	288	26	72	11	1	9	42	21	44	.250	.301	.389	86	-6	1	0	0	.992	4	C-90	0.3
1994	Hou-N	5	10	0	1	0	0	0	0	0	3	.100	.100	.100	-49	-2	0	0	0	1.000	-1	/C-5	-0.1
	Cin-N	61	177	29	52	8	2	8	21	15	28	.294	.349	.497	118	4	2	0	1	.990	-1	C-61	0.7
	Yr	66	187	29	53	8	2	8	21	15	31	.283	.337	.476	110	2	2	0	1	.990	-0	C-66	0.6
Total	4	290	838	83	207	36	4	22	99	72	169	.247	.308	.378	88	-15	5	1	1	.991	1	C-284	0.1

■ FRED TAUBY
Tauby, Fred Joseph (b: Fred Joseph Taubensee) b: 3/27/06, Canton, Ohio d: 11/23/55, Concordia, Cal. BR/TR, 5'9.5", 168 lbs. Deb: 9/1/35

1935	Chi-A	13	32	5	4	0	0	0	2	2	3	.125	.176	.156	-13	-5	0	0	0	1.000	2	/O-7	-0.4
1937	Phi-N	11	20	2	0	0	0	0	0	3	5	.000	.000	.000	-93	-5	1			1.000	-2	/O-7	-0.7
Total	2	24	52	7	4	0	0	0	5	2	8	.077	.111	.096	-43	-11	1	0		1.000	-0	/O-14	-1.1

■ DON TAUSSIG
Taussig, Donald Franklin b: 2/19/32, New York, N.Y. BR/TR, 6', 180 lbs. Deb: 4/23/58

1958	SF-N	39	50	10	10	0	0	1	4	3	8	.200	.245	.260	35	-5	0	0	0	1.000	-9	O-36	-1.4
1961	StL-N	98	188	27	54	14	5	2	25	16	34	.287	.343	.447	98	-1	2	2	-1	.992	-9	O-87	-1.3
1962	Hou-N	16	25	1	5	0	0	1	1	2	11	.200	.259	.320	59	-2	0	0	0	1.000	1	/O-4	-0.1
Total	3	153	263	38	69	14	5	4	30	21	53	.262	.317	.399	84	-7	2	2	-1	.994	-17	O-127	-2.8

■ JESUS TAVAREZ
Tavarez, Jesus Rafael b: 3/26/71, Santo Domingo, D.R. BB/TR, 6', 170 lbs. Deb: 5/23/94

1994	Fla-N	17	39	4	7	0	0	0	4	1	5	.179	.200	.179	-0	-6	1	1	-0	1.000	2	O-11	-0.4

■ JACKIE TAVENER
Tavener, John Adam "Rabbit" b: 12/27/1897, Celina, Ohio d: 9/14/69, Fort Worth, Tex. BL/TR, 5'5", 138 lbs. Deb: 9/24/21

1921	Det-A	2	4	0	0	0	0	0	0	0	1	.000	.000	.000	-99	-1	0	0	0	1.000	1	/S-2	0.0
1925	Det-A	134	453	45	111	11	11	0	47	39	60	.245	.309	.318	60	-28	5	4	-1	.963	7	*S-134	-0.8
1926	Det-A	156	532	65	141	22	14	1	58	52	53	.265	.332	.365	80	-16	8	7	-2	.952	9	*S-156	0.8
1927	Det-A	116	419	60	115	22	9	5	59	36	38	.274	.333	.406	90	-7	19	8	1	.948	4	*S-114	0.9
1928	Det-A	132	473	59	123	24	15	5	52	33	51	.260	.314	.406	86	-11	13	8	-1	.944	14	*S-131	1.7
1929	Cle-A	92	250	25	53	9	4	2	27	26	28	.212	.289	.304	51	-19	1	4	-2	.945	23	S-89	1.1
Total	6	632	2131	254	543	88	53	13	243	186	231	.255	.318	.364	75	-82	46	31	-5	.951	58	S-626	3.7

■ ALEX TAVERAS
Taveras, Alejandro Antonio (Betances) b: 10/9/55, Santiago, D.R. BR/TR, 5'10", 155 lbs. Deb: 9/9/76

1976	Hou-N	14	46	3	10	0	0	0	2	1	7	.217	.250	.217	37	-4	1	2	-1	.923	1	/2-7,S-7	-0.3
1982	LA-N	11	3	1	1	1	0	0	2	0	1	.333	.333	.667	178	0	0	0	0	1.000	4	/2-4,3-4,S	0.4
1983	LA-N	10	4	0	0	0	0	0	0	1	1	.000	.000	.000	-99	-1	0	0	0	.000	2	/S-3,2-2,3	0.1
Total	3	35	53	4	11	1	0	0	4	2	9	.208	.236	.226	34	-5	1	2	-1	.938	7	/2-13,S-12,3	0.2

■ FRANK TAVERAS
Taveras, Franklin Crisostomo (Fabian) b: 12/24/49, Las Matas De Santa Cruz, D.R. BR/TR, 6', 168 lbs. Deb: 9/25/71

1971	Pit-N	1	0	0	0	0	0	0	0	0	0	—	—	—		0	0	0	0	.000	0	R	0.0
1972	Pit-N	4	3	0	0	0	0	0	0	0	1	.000	.250	.000	-24	-0	0	0	0	1.000	-1	/S-4	-0.1
1974	*Pit-N	126	333	33	82	4	2	0	26	25	41	.246	.303	.270	63	-16	13	4	2	.941	-17	*S-124	-1.9
1975	*Pit-N	134	378	44	80	9	4	0	23	37	42	.212	.285	.257	52	-24	17	6	2	.953	-15	*S-132	-2.5
1976	Pit-N	144	519	76	134	8	6	0	24	44	79	.258	.321	.297	75	-16	58	11	11	.952	-5	*S-141	0.8
1977	Pit-N	147	544	72	137	20	10	1	29	38	71	.252	.300	.331	69	-23	**70**	18	**10**	.962	-22	*S-146	-2.0
1978	Pit-N	157	654	81	182	31	9	0	38	29	60	.278	.314	.353	82	-16	46	25	-1	.946	-29	*S-157	-2.8
1979	Pit-N	11	45	4	11	3	0	0	1	0	2	.244	.244	.311	48	-3	2	1	0	.935	-4	S-11	-0.7
	NY-N	153	635	89	167	26	9	1	33	33	72	.263	.301	.337	77	-21	42	19	1	.966	-21	*S-153	-2.5
	Yr	164	680	93	178	29	9	1	34	33	74	.262	.298	.335	75	-25	44	20	1	.964	-25	*S-164	-3.2
1980	NY-N	141	562	65	157	27	9	0	25	23	64	.279	.309	.327	80	-16	32	18	-1	.959	-39	*S-140	-4.3
1981	NY-N	84	283	30	65	11	3	0	11	12	36	.230	.266	.290	58	-16	16	4	2	.931	-22	S-79	-3.0
1982	Mon-N	48	87	9	14	5	1	0	4	7	6	.161	.223	.241	29	-8	4	0	1	.947	-1	S-26,2-19	-0.7
Total	11	1150	4043	503	1029	144	44	2	214	249	474	.255	.302	.313	71	-159	300	106	26	.953	-175	*S-1113/2-19	-19.7

■ TAYLOR
Taylor Deb: 9/10/1874

1874	Bal-n	13	48	3	13	1	0	0				.271	.271	.292	80	-1						1-13	-0.1

■ TONY TAYLOR
Taylor, Antonio Nemesio (Sanchez) b: 12/19/35, Central Alava, Cuba BR/TR, 5'9", 179 lbs. Deb: 4/15/58 C

1958	Chi-N	140	497	63	117	15	3	6	27	40	93	.235	.301	.314	64	-25	21	6	3	.968	9	*2-137/3-1	-0.4
1959	Chi-N	150	624	96	175	30	8	8	38	45	86	.280	.335	.393	94	-5	23	9	2	.970	10	*2-149/S-2	1.7
1960	Chi-N	19	76	14	20	3	3	1	9	8	12	.263	.341	.421	108	1	2	0	1	.977	-2	2-19	0.1
	Phi-N★	127	505	66	145	22	4	4	35	33	86	.287	.333	.370	92	-5	24	11	1	.968	-6	*2-123/3-4	0.2
	Yr	146	581	80	165	25	7	5	44	41	98	.284	.334	.377	94	-4	26	11	1	.969	-8	*2-142/3-4	0.3
1961	Phi-N	106	400	47	100	17	3	2	26	29	59	.250	.304	.322	67	-19	11	5	0	.980	0	2-91/3-3	-0.8
1962	Phi-N	152	625	87	162	21	5	7	43	68	82	.259	.337	.342	85	-12	20	9	1	.972	-19	*2-150/S-2	-1.1
1963	Phi-N	157	640	102	180	20	10	5	49	42	99	.281	.332	.367	102	2	23	9	2	**.986**	-9	*2-149,3-13	1.0
1964	Phi-N	154	570	62	143	13	6	4	46	46	74	.251	.321	.316	81	-13	13	7	-0	.977	-21	*2-150	-2.3
1965	Phi-N	106	323	41	74	14	3	3	27	22	58	.229	.283	.319	77	-10	5	4	-1	.958	-2	2-86/3-5	-0.6
1966	Phi-N	125	434	47	105	14	5	4	40	31	56	.242	.294	.346	77	-13	10	9	-2	.968	3	2-68,3-52	-0.0
1967	Phi-N	132	462	55	110	16	6	2	34	32	75	.238	.308	.312	77	-13	10	9	-2	.991	-8	1-58,3-44,2/S	-2.7
1968	Phi-N	145	547	59	137	26	8	5	39	39	60	.250	.304	.311	85	-10	22	5	4	.966	16	*3-138/2-5,1	1.2
1969	Phi-N	138	557	69	146	24	5	3	30	42	62	.262	.318	.339	87	-10	19	10	-0	.967	-2	3-71,2-57,1	-0.9

YEAR	TM/L	G	AB	R	H	2B	3B	HR	RBI	BB	SO	AVG	OBP	SLG	PRO+	BR/A	SB	CS	SBR	FA	FR	G/POS	TPR
1970	Phi-N	124	439	74	132	26	9	9	55	50	67	.301	.376	.462	127	17	9	11	-4	.996	0	2-59,3-38,O/S	1.6
1971	Phi-N	36	107	9	25	2	1	1	5	9	10	.234	.293	.299	68	-4	2	2	-1	1.000	5	2-14,3-11/1	0.0
	Det-A	55	181	27	52	10	2	3	19	12	11	.287	.335	.414	107	1	5	1	1	.995	1	2-51/3-3	0.7
1972	*Det-A	78	228	33	69	12	4	1	20	14	34	.303	.348	.404	119	5	5	1	1	.966	-8	2-67/3-8,1	0.1
1973	Det-A	84	275	35	63	9	3	5	24	17	29	.229	.276	.338	68	-12	9	5	-0	.987	-14	2-72/1-6,30D	-2.3
1974	Phi-N	62	64	5	21	4	0	2	13	6	6	.328	.394	.484	139	3	0	0	0	1.000	-1	/1-7,3-5,2	0.2
1975	Phi-N	79	103	13	25	5	1	1	17	17	18	.243	.355	.340	90	-1	3	3	-1	.913	1	3-16/1-4,2	-0.1
1976	Phi-N	26	23	2	6	1	0	0	3	1	7	.261	.320	.304	76	-1	0	0	0	.000	-0	/2-2,3-1	-0.1
Total	19	2195	7680	1005	2007	298	86	75	598	613	1083	.261	.322	.352	88	-123	234	111	4	.976	-41	*2-1498,3-417/1OSD	-5.1

■ BEN TAYLOR   Taylor, Benjamin Eugene b: 9/30/27, Metropolis, Ill. BL/TL, 6', 175 lbs. Deb: 7/29/51

YEAR	TM/L	G	AB	R	H	2B	3B	HR	RBI	BB	SO	AVG	OBP	SLG	PRO+	BR/A	SB	CS	SBR	FA	FR	G/POS	TPR
1951	StL-A	33	93	14	24	2	1	3	6	9	22	.258	.337	.398	95	-1	1	1	-0	.972	-2	1-25	-0.4
1952	Det-A	7	18	0	3	0	0	0	0	0	5	.167	.167	.167	-7	-3	0	0	0	1.000	-0	/1-4	-0.3
1955	Mil-N	12	10	2	1	0	0	0	0	2	4	.100	.250	.100	-3	-1	0	0	0	1.000	-0	/1-1	-0.2
Total	3	52	121	16	28	2	1	3	6	11	31	.231	.306	.339	73	-5	1	1	-0	.976	-2	/1-30	-0.9

■ CHINK TAYLOR   Taylor, C L b: 2/9/1898, Burnet, Tex. d: 7/7/80, Temple, Tex. BR/TR, 5'9", 160 lbs. Deb: 4/18/25

YEAR	TM/L	G	AB	R	H	2B	3B	HR	RBI	BB	SO	AVG	OBP	SLG	PRO+	BR/A	SB	CS	SBR	FA	FR	G/POS	TPR
1925	Chi-N	8	6	2	0	0	0	0	0	0	0	.000	.000	.000	-99	-2	0	0	0	1.000	-1	/O-2	-0.2

■ CARL TAYLOR   Taylor, Carl Means b: 1/20/44, Sarasota, Fla. BR/TR, 6'2", 207 lbs. Deb: 4/11/68

YEAR	TM/L	G	AB	R	H	2B	3B	HR	RBI	BB	SO	AVG	OBP	SLG	PRO+	BR/A	SB	CS	SBR	FA	FR	G/POS	TPR
1968	Pit-N	44	71	5	15	1	0	0	7	10	10	.211	.309	.225	63	-3	1	0	0	.979	-6	C-29/O-2	-0.8
1969	Pit-N	104	221	30	77	10	1	4	33	31	36	.348	.435	.457	153	17	0	1	-1	.914	-1	O-36,1-24	1.3
1970	StL-N	104	245	39	61	12	2	6	45	41	30	.249	.359	.388	98	0	5	2	0	.986	-4	O-46,1-15/3	-0.6
1971	Pit-N	7	12	1	2	0	1	0	0	0	5	.167	.167	.333	39	-1	0	0	0	1.000	0	/O-1	-0.1
	KC-A	20	39	3	7	0	0	0	3	5	13	.179	.273	.179	30	-3	0	1	-1	.964	1	/O-12	-0.4
1972	KC-A	63	113	17	30	2	1	0	11	17	16	.265	.366	.301	101	1	4	1	1	.982	-5	C-21/O-7,13	-0.4
1973	KC-A	69	145	18	33	6	1	0	16	32	20	.228	.367	.283	79	-3	2	2	-1	.980	2	C-63/1-2,D	0.0
Total	6	411	846	113	225	31	6	10	115	136	130	.266	.371	.352	103	9	12	7	-1	.980	-14	C-113,O-104/13D	-1.0

■ DANNY TAYLOR   Taylor, Daniel Turney b: 12/23/1900, Lash, Pa. d: 10/11/72, Latrobe, Pa. BR/TR, 5'10", 190 lbs. Deb: 6/30/26

YEAR	TM/L	G	AB	R	H	2B	3B	HR	RBI	BB	SO	AVG	OBP	SLG	PRO+	BR/A	SB	CS	SBR	FA	FR	G/POS	TPR
1926	Was-A	21	50	10	15	0	1	1	5	5	7	.300	.364	.400	102	0	1	2	-1	1.000	-1	O-12	-0.3
1929	Chi-N	2	3	0	0	0	0	0	0	1	1	.000	.250	.000	-32	-1	0			1.000	-0	/O-1	-0.1
1930	Chi-N	74	219	43	62	14	3	2	37	27	34	.283	.364	.402	84	-5	4			.971	-1	O-52	-0.9
1931	Chi-N	88	270	48	81	13	6	5	41	31	46	.300	.372	.448	117	7	4			.989	4	O-67	0.6
1932	Chi-N	6	22	3	5	0	0	0	3	3	1	.227	.320	.318	73	-1	1			.900	-0	/O-6	-0.1
	Bro-N	105	395	84	128	22	7	11	48	33	41	.324	.378	.499	136	20	13			.989	4	O-96	1.7
	Yr	111	417	87	133	24	7	11	51	36	42	.319	.374	.489	133	19	14			.983	4	*O-102	1.6
1933	Bro-N	103	358	75	102	21	9	9	40	47	45	.285	.368	.469	144	21	11			.977	2	O-91	1.8
1934	Bro-N	120	405	62	121	24	6	7	57	63	47	.299	.396	.484	130	19	12			.975	-8	*O-108	0.7
1935	Bro-N	112	352	51	102	19	5	7	59	46	32	.290	.372	.432	118	10	6			.970	-6	O-99	0.0
1936	Bro-N	43	116	12	34	6	0	2	15	11	14	.293	.359	.397	102	1	2			.981	-3	O-31	-0.3
Total	9	674	2190	388	650	121	37	44	305	267	268	.297	.374	.446	121	71	56		2	.979	-10	O-563	3.1

■ DWIGHT TAYLOR   Taylor, Dwight Bernard b: 3/24/60, Los Angeles, Cal. BL/TL, 5'9", 166 lbs. Deb: 4/14/86

YEAR	TM/L	G	AB	R	H	2B	3B	HR	RBI	BB	SO	AVG	OBP	SLG	PRO+	BR/A	SB	CS	SBR	FA	FR	G/POS	TPR
1986	KC-A	4	2	1	0	0	0	0	0	0	0	.000	.000	.000	-98	-1	0	0	0	.000	-1	/O-1,D-2	-0.1

■ ED TAYLOR   Taylor, Edward James b: 11/17/01, Chicago, Ill. d: 1/30/92, Chula Vista, Cal. BR/TR, 5'6.5", 160 lbs. Deb: 4/14/26

YEAR	TM/L	G	AB	R	H	2B	3B	HR	RBI	BB	SO	AVG	OBP	SLG	PRO+	BR/A	SB	CS	SBR	FA	FR	G/POS	TPR
1926	Bos-N	92	272	37	73	8	2	0	33	38	26	.268	.368	.313	93	-1	4			.945	-1	3-62,S-33	0.4

■ LIVE OAK TAYLOR   Taylor, Edward S. Deb: 8/21/1877

YEAR	TM/L	G	AB	R	H	2B	3B	HR	RBI	BB	SO	AVG	OBP	SLG	PRO+	BR/A	SB	CS	SBR	FA	FR	G/POS	TPR
1877	Har-N	2	8	0	3	0	0	0	0	0	2	.375	.375	.375	153	0				1.000	-1	/O-2	0.0
1884	Pit-a	41	152	22	32	4	1	0		6		.211	.255	.250	64	-6				.798	-1	/O-41	-0.7
Total	2	43	160	22	35	4	1	0	0	6	2	.219	.260	.256	68	-5				.802	-1	/O-43	-0.7

■ FRED TAYLOR   Taylor, Frederick Rankin b: 12/3/24, Zanesville, Ohio BL/TR, 6'3", 201 lbs. Deb: 9/12/50

YEAR	TM/L	G	AB	R	H	2B	3B	HR	RBI	BB	SO	AVG	OBP	SLG	PRO+	BR/A	SB	CS	SBR	FA	FR	G/POS	TPR
1950	Was-A	6	16	1	2	0	0	0	0	1	2	.125	.176	.125	-23	-3	0	0	0	.968	0	/1-3	-0.3
1951	Was-A	6	12	1	2	0	0	0	0	0	4	.167	.167	.250	12	-0	0	0	0	.962	-0	/1-2	-0.2
1952	Was-A	10	19	3	5	1	0	0	4	3	2	.263	.364	.316	93	-0	0	0	0	1.000	1	/1-5	0.1
Total	3	22	47	5	9	2	0	0	4	4	8	.191	.255	.234	33	-5	0	0	0	.979	1	/1-10	-0.4

■ HARRY TAYLOR   Taylor, Harry Leonard b: 4/4/1866, Halsey Valley, N.Y. d: 7/12/55, Buffalo, N.Y. BL, 6', 160 lbs. Deb: 4/18/1890

YEAR	TM/L	G	AB	R	H	2B	3B	HR	RBI	BB	SO	AVG	OBP	SLG	PRO+	BR/A	SB	CS	SBR	FA	FR	G/POS	TPR
1890	*Lou-a	134	553	115	169	7	7	0	68			.306	.383	.344	117	14	45			.982	5	*1-118,S-12/2C	1.2
1891	Lou-a	93	356	81	105	7	4	2	37	55	33	.295	.397	.354	116	10	15			.979	3	1-92/3-1,2C	0.7
1892	Lou-N	125	493	66	128	7	1	0	34	58	23	.260	.342	.278	96	1	24			.923	-8	O-73,1-34,2/3S	-1.0
1893	Bal-N	88	360	50	102	9	1	1	54	32	11	.283	.347	.322	77	-12	24			.976	-3	*1-88	-1.4
Total	4	440	1762	312	504	30	13	3	125	213	67	.286	.367	.323	102	14	108			.979	-2	1-332/O-73,2S3C	-0.5

■ HARRY TAYLOR   Taylor, Harry Warren b: 12/26/07, McKeesport, Pa. d: 4/27/69, Toledo, Ohio BL/TL, 6'1.5", 185 lbs. Deb: 4/14/32

YEAR	TM/L	G	AB	R	H	2B	3B	HR	RBI	BB	SO	AVG	OBP	SLG	PRO+	BR/A	SB	CS	SBR	FA	FR	G/POS	TPR
1932	Chi-N	10	8	1	1	0	0	0	0	1	1	.125	.222	.125	-4	-1	0			1.000	-0	/1-1	-0.1

■ SANDY TAYLOR   Taylor, James B. 5'10.5", 175 lbs. Deb: 8/11/1879

YEAR	TM/L	G	AB	R	H	2B	3B	HR	RBI	BB	SO	AVG	OBP	SLG	PRO+	BR/A	SB	CS	SBR	FA	FR	G/POS	TPR
1879	Tro-N	24	97	10	21	4	0	0	8	1	8	.216	.224	.258	63	-4				.765	-3	O-24	-0.8

■ ZACK TAYLOR   Taylor, James Wren b: 7/27/1898, Yulee, Fla. d: 9/19/74, Orlando, Fla. BR/TR, 5'11.5", 180 lbs. Deb: 6/15/20 MC

YEAR	TM/L	G	AB	R	H	2B	3B	HR	RBI	BB	SO	AVG	OBP	SLG	PRO+	BR/A	SB	CS	SBR	FA	FR	G/POS	TPR
1920	Bro-N	9	13	3	5	2	0	0	5	0	2	.385	.385	.538	158	1	0	1	-1	.882	-1	/C-9	-0.1
1921	Bro-N	30	102	6	20	0	2	0	8	1	8	.196	.212	.235	17	-12	2	0	1	.965	0	C-30	-1.0
1922	Bro-N	7	14	0	3	0	0	0	2	1	1	.214	.267	.214	26	-2	0	0	0	.950	-1	/C-6	-0.2
1923	Bro-N	96	337	29	97	11	6	0	46	9	13	.288	.312	.356	78	-11	2	5	-2	.967	14	C-84	0.4
1924	Bro-N	99	345	36	100	9	4	1	39	14	14	.290	.314	.348	81	-9	0	1	-1	**.988**	-8	C-93	-1.2
1925	Bro-N	109	352	33	109	16	4	3	44	17	19	.310	.343	.403	92	-4	0	0	0	.959	-9	C-96	-0.8
1926	Bos-N	125	432	36	110	22	3	0	42	28	27	.255	.303	.319	74	-17	1			.985	2	*C-123	-0.7
1927	Bos-N	30	96	8	23	2	1	1	14	8	5	.240	.298	.313	69	-4	0			.988	12	C-27	0.9
	NY-N	83	258	18	60	7	3	0	21	17	20	.233	.283	.283	52	-17	2			.972	-4	C-81	-1.6
	Yr	113	354	26	83	9	4	1	35	25	25	.234	.287	.291	56	-22	2			.978	8	*C-108	-0.7
1928	Bos-N	125	399	36	100	15	1	2	30	33	29	.251	.313	.308	66	-20	2			.985	-12	*C-124	-2.1
1929	Bos-N	34	101	8	25	7	0	0	10	7	9	.248	.303	.317	56	-7	0			.965	6	C-31	0.2
	*Chi-N	64	215	29	59	16	3	1	31	19	18	.274	.336	.391	79	-7	0			.979	-1	C-64	-0.2
	Yr	98	316	37	84	23	3	1	41	26	27	.266	.326	.367	72	-14	0			.974	5	C-95	0.0
1930	Chi-N	32	95	12	22	2	1	1	11	2	12	.232	.255	.305	34	-10	0			1.000	-1	C-28	-0.8
1931	Chi-N	8	4	0	1	0	0	0	0	2	1	.250	.500	.250	106	0	0			1.000	1	/C-5	0.1
1932	Chi-N	21	30	2	6	1	0	0	3	1	4	.200	.226	.233	24	-3	0			1.000	-0	C-14	0.0
1933	Chi-N	16	11	0	0	0	0	0	0	2	1	.000	.000	.000	-99	-3	0			1.000	-0	C-12	-0.3
1934	NY-N	4	7	0	1	0	0	0	0	1	2	.143	.143	.143	-28	-0	0			1.000	-0	/C-3	-0.2
1935	Bro-N	26	54	2	7	3	0	0	5	2	6	.130	.175	.185	-3	-8	0			.970	-0	C-26	-0.1
Total	16	918	2865	258	748	113	28	9	311	161	192	.261	.304	.329	68	-135	9	7		.977	1	C-856	-8.3

YEAR	TM/L	G	AB	R	H	2B	3B	HR	RBI	BB	SO	AVG	OBP	SLG	PRO+	BR/A	SB	CS	SBR	FA	FR	G/POS	TPR

■ JOE TAYLOR
Taylor, Joe Cephus b: 3/2/26, Chapman, Ala. BR/TR, 6'1", 185 lbs. Deb: 8/26/54

YEAR	TM/L	G	AB	R	H	2B	3B	HR	RBI	BB	SO	AVG	OBP	SLG	PRO+	BR/A	SB	CS	SBR	FA	FR	G/POS	TPR
1954	Phi-A	18	58	5	13	1	1	2	8	2	9	.224	.250	.328	57	-4	0	1	-1	.943	-0	O-16	-0.6
1957	Cin-N	33	107	14	28	7	0	4	9	6	24	.262	.301	.439	89	-2	0	1	-1	.971	4	O-27	0.0
1958	StL-N	18	23	2	7	3	0	1	3	2	4	.304	.360	.565	135	1	0	0	0	1.000	-0	/O-5	0.1
	Bal-A	36	77	11	21	4	0	2	9	7	19	.273	.333	.403	107	1	0	0	0	.972	-2	O-21	-0.2
1959	Bal-A	14	32	2	5	1	0	1	2	11	5	.156	.372	.281	84	-0	0	0	0	1.000	-3	O-12	-0.3
Total	4	119	297	34	74	16	1	9	31	28	61	.249	.314	.401	92	-4	0	2	-1	.969	-1	/O-81	-1.0

■ LEO TAYLOR
Taylor, Leo Thomas "Chink" b: 5/13/01, Walla Walla, Wash. d: 5/20/82, Seattle, Wash. BR/TR, 5'10.5", 150 lbs. Deb: 5/3/23

YEAR	TM/L	G	AB	R	H	2B	3B	HR	RBI	BB	SO	AVG	OBP	SLG	PRO+	BR/A	SB	CS	SBR	FA	FR	G/POS	TPR
1923	Chi-A	1	0	0	0	0	0	0	0	0	0	—	—	—	—		0	0	0	.000	0	R	0.0

■ HAWK TAYLOR
Taylor, Robert Dale b: 4/3/39, Metropolis, Ill. BR/TR, 6'2", 190 lbs. Deb: 6/9/57

YEAR	TM/L	G	AB	R	H	2B	3B	HR	RBI	BB	SO	AVG	OBP	SLG	PRO+	BR/A	SB	CS	SBR	FA	FR	G/POS	TPR
1957	Mil-N	7	1	2	0	0	0	0	0	0	0	.000	.000	.000	-99	-0	0	0	0	.000	0	/C-1	0.0
1958	Mil-N	4	8	1	1	1	0	0	0	0	0	.125	.125	.250	-4	-1	0	0	0	1.000	-0	/O-4	-0.2
1961	Mil-N	20	26	1	5	0	0	1	1	3	11	.192	.276	.308	58	-2	0	1	-1	1.000	0	/O-5,C-1	-0.2
1962	Mil-N	20	47	3	12	0	0	0	2	2	10	.255	.286	.255	48	-3	0	1	-1	.960	1	O-11	-0.3
1963	Mil-N	16	29	1	2	0	0	0	0	1	12	.069	.100	.069	-51	-6	0	0	0	1.000	-0	/O-8	-0.7
1964	NY-N	92	225	20	54	8	0	4	23	8	33	.240	.272	.329	70	-9	0	0	0	.981	1	C-45,O-16	-0.8
1965	NY-N	25	46	5	7	0	0	4	10	1	8	.152	.170	.413	61	-3	0	0	0	.962	-2	C-15/1-1	-0.5
1966	NY-N	53	109	5	19	2	0	3	12	3	19	.174	.204	.275	32	-10	0	1	-1	1.000	-4	C-29,1-13	-1.5
1967	NY-N	13	37	3	9	3	0	0	4	2	8	.243	.282	.324	74	-1	0	0	0	.955	5	C-12	0.4
	Cal-A	23	52	5	16	3	0	1	3	4	8	.308	.357	.423	135	2	0	0	0	1.000	2	C-19	0.5
1969	KC-A	64	89	7	24	5	0	3	21	6	18	.270	.316	.427	105	0	0	0	0	.909	-4	O-18/C-6	-0.4
1970	KC-A	57	55	3	9	3	0	0	6	6	16	.164	.258	.218	33	-5	0	0	0	1.000	-0	/C-3,1-1	-0.5
Total	11	394	724	56	158	25	0	16	82	36	146	.218	.259	.319	62	-38	0	3	-2	.984	-1	C-131/O-62,1	-4.2

■ BOB TAYLOR
Taylor, Robert Lee b: 3/20/44, Leland, Miss. BL/TR, 5'9", 170 lbs. Deb: 4/9/70

YEAR	TM/L	G	AB	R	H	2B	3B	HR	RBI	BB	SO	AVG	OBP	SLG	PRO+	BR/A	SB	CS	SBR	FA	FR	G/POS	TPR
1970	SF-N	63	84	12	16	3	0	2	10	12	13	.190	.320	.262	58	-5	0	0	0	1.000	-3	O-26/C-1	-0.9

■ SAMMY TAYLOR
Taylor, Samuel Douglas b: 2/27/33, Woodruff, S.C. BL/TR, 6'2", 185 lbs. Deb: 4/27/58

YEAR	TM/L	G	AB	R	H	2B	3B	HR	RBI	BB	SO	AVG	OBP	SLG	PRO+	BR/A	SB	CS	SBR	FA	FR	G/POS	TPR
1958	Chi-N	96	301	30	78	12	2	6	36	27	46	.259	.320	.372	84	-7	2	1	0	.988	-11	C-87	-1.3
1959	Chi-N	110	353	41	95	13	2	13	43	35	47	.269	.337	.428	103	1	1	0	0	.982	-15	*C-109	-0.8
1960	Chi-N	74	150	14	31	9	0	3	17	6	18	.207	.242	.327	55	-10	0	1	-1	.978	-9	C-43	-1.8
1961	Chi-N	89	235	26	56	8	2	8	23	23	39	.238	.317	.391	86	-5	0	0	0	.989	-8	C-75	-1.0
1962	Chi-N	7	15	0	2	1	0	0	1	3	3	.133	.278	.200	30	-1	0	0	0	1.000	-1	/C-6	-0.3
	NY-N	68	158	12	35	4	2	3	20	23	17	.222	.328	.329	76	-5	0	0	0	.991	-9	C-50	-1.2
	Yr	75	173	12	37	5	2	3	21	26	20	.214	.323	.318	72	-6	0	0	0	.992	-10	C-56	-1.5
1963	NY-N	22	35	3	9	0	1	0	6	5	7	.257	.350	.314	91	-0	0	0	0	1.000	0	C-13	0.0
	Cin-N	3	6	0	0	0	0	0	0	0	2	.000	.000	.000	-97	-1	0	0	0	.833	-1	/C-2	-0.3
	Yr	25	41	3	9	0	1	0	6	5	9	.220	.304	.268	65	-2	0	0	0	.984	-1	C-15	-0.3
	Cle-A	4	10	1	3	0	0	0	1	0	2	.300	.300	.300	69	-0	0	0	0	1.000	-1	/C-2	-0.1
Total	6	473	1263	127	309	47	9	33	147	122	181	.245	.315	.375	84	-29	3	2	-0	.986	-55	C-387	-6.8

■ TOMMY TAYLOR
Taylor, Thomas Livingstone Carlton b: 9/17/1892, Mexia, Tex. d: 4/5/56, Greenville, Miss. BR/TR, 5'8.5", 160 lbs. Deb: 7/9/24

YEAR	TM/L	G	AB	R	H	2B	3B	HR	RBI	BB	SO	AVG	OBP	SLG	PRO+	BR/A	SB	CS	SBR	FA	FR	G/POS	TPR
1924	*Was-A	26	73	11	19	3	1	0	10	2	8	.260	.289	.329	61	-4	2	0	1	.923	-5	3-16/2-2,O	-0.8

■ BILLY TAYLOR
Taylor, William H. b: 12/1870, Butler, Ky. d: 9/12/05, Cincinnati, Ohio 5'10", 160 lbs. Deb: 9/19/1898

YEAR	TM/L	G	AB	R	H	2B	3B	HR	RBI	BB	SO	AVG	OBP	SLG	PRO+	BR/A	SB	CS	SBR	FA	FR	G/POS	TPR
1898	Lou-N	9	24	2	6	1	0	0	2	1		.250	.308	.292	73	-1	1			.909	-1	/3-7,2-1	-0.2

■ BILLY TAYLOR
Taylor, William Henry "Bollicky Bill" b: 1855, Washington, D.C. d: 5/14/1900, Jacksonville, Fla. BR/TR, 5'11.5", 204 lbs. Deb: 5/21/1881

YEAR	TM/L	G	AB	R	H	2B	3B	HR	RBI	BB	SO	AVG	OBP	SLG	PRO+	BR/A	SB	CS	SBR	FA	FR	G/POS	TPR
1881	Wor-N	6	28	3	3	1	0	0	2	0	2	.107	.107	.143	-21	-4				.882	1	/O-5,P-1	-0.2
	Det-N	1	4	0	2	2	0	0	1	0	0	.500	.500	1.000	346	1				.750	-0	/3-1	0.1
	Cle-N	24	103	6	25	1	0	0	12	0	8	.243	.243	.252	59	-5				.859	-1	O-23/P-1,3	-0.6
	Yr	31	135	9	30	4	0	0	15	0	10	.222	.222	.252	50	-7				.864	-0	O-28/P-2,3	-0.7
1882	Pit-a	70	299	40	84	16	13	3			7	.281	.297	.452	157	17				.862	-11	C-27,1-23,3/OP	0.5
1883	Pit-a	83	369	43	96	13	7	2			9	.260	.278	.350	105	3				.747	-15	O-37,C-33,P/1	-0.9
1884	StL-U	43	186	44	68	23	1	3			2	.366	.389	.548	147	11				.872	1	P-33,1-10/O	0.4
	Phi-a	30	111	8	28	6	2	0			2	.252	.272	.342	93	-1				.784	2	P-30	0.0
1885	Phi-a	6	21	0	4	0	0	0				.190	.190	.190	19	-2				.556	-1	/P-6	0.0
1886	Bal-a	10	39	4	12	0	1	0			1	.308	.325	.359	117	1	1			.800	-1	/P-8,1-1,C	0.0
1887	Phi-a	1	4	0	1	0	0	0				.250	.250	.250	40	-0	0			1.000	-0	/P-1	0.0
Total	7	274	1164	148	323	62	24	8	15	26	10	.277	.294	.393	117	21	1			.820	-26	P-100/O-77,C13	-0.7

■ BILL TAYLOR
Taylor, William Michael b: 12/30/29, Alhambra, Cal. BL/TR, 6'3", 212 lbs. Deb: 4/14/54

YEAR	TM/L	G	AB	R	H	2B	3B	HR	RBI	BB	SO	AVG	OBP	SLG	PRO+	BR/A	SB	CS	SBR	FA	FR	G/POS	TPR
1954	NY-N	55	65	4	12	1	0	2	10	3	15	.185	.243	.292	38	-6	0	0	0	1.000	-3	/O-9	-0.9
1955	NY-N	65	64	9	17	4	0	4	12	1	16	.266	.277	.516	104	-0	0	0	0	.000	-1	/O-2	-0.1
1956	NY-N	1	4	0	1	1	0	0	0	0	1	.250	.250	.500	96	-0	0	0	0	1.000	-0	/O-1	0.0
1957	NY-N	11	9	0	0	0	0	0	0	1	2	.000	.100	.000	-70	-2	0	0	0	.000	0	H	-0.2
	Det-A	9	23	4	8	2	0	1	3	0	3	.348	.348	.565	142	1	0	0	0	1.000	-1	/O-5	0.0
1958	Det-A	8	8	0	3	0	0	0	1	0	2	.375	.375	.375	100	-0	0	0	0	1.000	-0	/O-1	0.0
Total	5	149	173	17	41	8	0	7	26	5	39	.237	.267	.405	74	-7	0	0	0	1.000	-5	/O-18	-1.2

■ BIRDIE TEBBETTS
Tebbetts, George Robert b: 11/10/12, Burlington, Vt. BR/TR, 5'11.5", 170 lbs. Deb: 9/16/36 M

YEAR	TM/L	G	AB	R	H	2B	3B	HR	RBI	BB	SO	AVG	OBP	SLG	PRO+	BR/A	SB	CS	SBR	FA	FR	G/POS	TPR
1936	Det-A	10	33	7	10	1	2	1	4	5	3	.303	.395	.545	129	1	0	0	0	.982	2	C-10	0.4
1937	Det-A	50	162	15	31	4	3	2	16	10	13	.191	.238	.290	32	-18	0	0	0	.963	-4	C-48	-1.8
1938	Det-A	53	143	16	42	6	2	1	25	12	13	.294	.348	.385	79	-5	1	2	-1	.985	-5	C-53	-0.7
1939	Det-A	106	341	37	89	22	2	4	53	25	20	.261	.315	.372	70	-16	2	1	0	.970	15	*C-100	0.3
1940	*Det-A	111	379	46	112	24	4	4	46	35	14	.296	.357	.412	90	-6	4	5	-2	.975	18	*C-107	1.8
1941	Det-A☆	110	359	28	102	19	4	2	47	38	29	.284	.354	.376	85	-8	1	2	-1	.977	7	C-98	0.6
1942	Det-A★	99	308	24	76	11	0	2	27	39	17	.247	.335	.292	71	-11	4	0	1	.977	7	C-97	0.5
1946	Det-A	87	280	20	68	11	2	1	34	28	23	.243	.312	.307	69	-11	1	3	-2	.982	-1	C-87	-1.0
1947	Det-A	20	53	1	5	1	0	1	2	3	10	.094	.143	.113	-27	-9	0	1	-1	1.000	8	C-20	-0.1
	Bos-A	90	291	22	87	10	0	1	28	21	30	.299	.346	.344	86	-5	2	4	-2	.974	-3	C-89	-0.4
	Yr	110	344	23	92	11	0	1	30	24	33	.267	.315	.308	69	-14	2	5	-2	.980	5	*C-109	-0.5
1948	Bos-A★	128	446	54	125	26	2	5	68	62	32	.280	.371	.381	95	-2	5	2	0	.981	-9	*C-126	-0.2
1949	Bos-A★	122	403	42	109	14	0	5	48	62	22	.270	.369	.342	83	-9	8	1	2	.980	-6	*C-118	-0.5
1950	Bos-A	79	268	33	83	10	1	8	45	29	26	.310	.377	.444	100	0	1	1	-0	.988	-6	C-74	-0.3
1951	Cle-A	55	137	8	36	5	0	2	18	7	7	.263	.308	.350	82	-4	0	0	0	.977	-1	C-44	-0.3
1952	Cle-A	42	101	4	25	4	0	1	14	8	9	.248	.339	.317	73	-4	0	0	0	.986	-4	C-37	-0.4
Total	14	1162	3704	357	1000	169	22	38	469	389	261	.270	.341	.358	81	-103	29	23	-5	.978	19	*C-1108	-2.1

■ PUSSY TEBEAU
Tebeau, Charles Alston b: 2/22/1870, Worcester, Mass. d: 3/25/50, Pittsfield, Mass. BR/TR, 5'10", 175 lbs. Deb: 7/22/1895

YEAR	TM/L	G	AB	R	H	2B	3B	HR	RBI	BB	SO	AVG	OBP	SLG	PRO+	BR/A	SB	CS	SBR	FA	FR	G/POS	TPR
1895	Cle-N	2	6	3	3	0	0	0	1	2	1	.500	.625	.500	182	1	1			1.000	1	/O-2	0.1

YEAR	TM/L	G	AB	R	H	2B	3B	HR	RBI	BB	SO	AVG	OBP	SLG	PRO+	BR/A	SB	CS	SBR	FA	FR	G/POS	TPR

■ GEORGE TEBEAU
Tebeau, George E. "White Wings"   b: 12/26/1861, St.Louis, Mo.   d: 2/4/23, Denver, Colo.   BR/TR, 5'9", 175 lbs.   Deb: 4/16/1887   F

YEAR	TM/L	G	AB	R	H	2B	3B	HR	RBI	BB	SO	AVG	OBP	SLG	PRO+	BR/A	SB	CS	SBR	FA	FR	G/POS	TPR
1887	Cin-a	85	318	57	94	12	5	4		31		.296	.364	.403	111	4	37			.887	4	O-84/P-1	0.5
1888	Cin-a	121	411	72	94	12	12	3	51	61		.229	.338	.338	111	6	37			.911	4	*O-121	0.6
1889	Cin-a	135	496	110	125	21	11	7	70	69	62	.252	.350	.381	105	3	61			.887	-5	*O-134/1-1	-0.5
1890	Tol-a	94	381	71	102	16	10	1		51		.268	.359	.370	112	6	55			.951	3	O-94/P-1	0.4
1894	Was-N	61	222	41	50	10	6	0	28	37	20	.225	.341	.324	63	-13	17			.857	-9	O-61	-2.0
	Cle-N	40	150	32	47	9	4	0	25	25	18	.313	.411	.427	99	0	9			.928	-5	O-27,1-12/3	-0.5
	Yr	101	372	73	97	19	10	0	53	62	38	.261	.369	.366	78	-12	26			.880	-14	O-88,1-12/3	-2.5
1895	Cle-N	91	337	57	110	16	6	0	68	50	28	.326	.415	.409	107	5	12			.873	-9	O-49,1-42	-0.5
Total	6	627	2315	440	622	96	54	15	242	324	128	.269	.364	.376	103	11	228			.900	-19	O-570/1-55,P3	-2.0

■ PATSY TEBEAU
Tebeau, Oliver Wendell   b: 12/5/1864, St.Louis, Mo.   d: 5/15/18, St.Louis, Mo.   BR/TR, 5'8", 163 lbs.   Deb: 9/20/1887   FM

YEAR	TM/L	G	AB	R	H	2B	3B	HR	RBI	BB	SO	AVG	OBP	SLG	PRO+	BR/A	SB	CS	SBR	FA	FR	G/POS	TPR
1887	Chi-N	20	68	8	11	3	0	0	10	4	4	.162	.208	.206	14	-8	8			.855	-3	3-20	-1.0
1889	Cle-N	136	521	72	147	20	6	8	76	37	41	.282	.332	.390	103	1	26			.897	0	*3-136	0.5
1890	Cle-P	110	450	86	135	26	6	5	74	34	20	.300	.353	.418	115	9	14			.872	13	*3-110,M	2.1
1891	Cle-N	61	249	38	65	8	3	1	41	16	13	.261	.313	.329	84	-6	12			.884	6	3-61/O-1M	0.3
1892	*Cle-N	86	340	47	83	13	3	2	49	23	34	.244	.307	.318	86	-7	6			.911	-2	3-74/2-5,1SM	-0.5
1893	Cle-N	116	486	90	160	32	8	2	102	32	11	.329	.375	.440	110	4	19			.980	6	1-57,3-56/2M	0.8
1894	Cle-N	125	523	82	158	23	7	3	89	35	35	.302	.347	.390	75	-23	30			.977	-5	*1-115,2-10/3SM	-2.1
1895	*Cle-N	63	264	50	84	13	2	2	52	16	18	.318	.362	.405	92	-4	8			.992	6	1-49/2-9,3M	0.3
1896	Cle-N	132	543	56	146	22	6	2	94	21	22	.269	.300	.343	65	-29	20			.985	7	*1-122/3-7,2SPM	-1.8
1897	Cle-N	109	412	62	110	15	9	0	59	30		.267	.323	.347	73	-17	11			.994	5	*1-92,2-18/3SM	-1.4
1898	Cle-N	131	477	53	123	11	4	1	63	53		.258	.341	.304	86	-7	5			.984	3	1-91,2-34/S3M	-0.2
1899	StL-N	77	281	27	69	10	3	1	26	18		.246	.303	.313	67	-13	5			.980	-3	1-65,S-11/32M	-1.3
1900	StL-N	1	4	0	0	0	0	0	0	0		.000	.000	.000	-99	-1	0			.700	-1	/S-1,M	-0.1
Total	13	1167	4618	671	1291	196	57	27	735	319	198	.280	.332	.364	86	-101	164			.984	28	1-595,3-478/2SPO	-4.4

■ DICK TEED
Teed, Richard Leroy   b: 3/8/26, Springfield, Mass.   BB/TR, 5'11", 180 lbs.   Deb: 7/24/53

YEAR	TM/L	G	AB	R	H	2B	3B	HR	RBI	BB	SO	AVG	OBP	SLG	PRO+	BR/A	SB	CS	SBR	FA	FR	G/POS	TPR
1953	Bro-N	1	1	0	0	0	0	0	0	0	1	.000	.000	.000	-98	-0	0	0	0	.000	0	H	0.0

■ WILFREDO TEJADA
Tejada, Wilfredo Aristides (Andujar)   b: 11/12/62, Santo Domingo, D.R.   BR/TR, 6', 175 lbs.   Deb: 9/9/86

YEAR	TM/L	G	AB	R	H	2B	3B	HR	RBI	BB	SO	AVG	OBP	SLG	PRO+	BR/A	SB	CS	SBR	FA	FR	G/POS	TPR
1986	Mon-N	10	25	1	6	1	0	0	2	2	8	.240	.296	.280	60	-1	0	0	0	1.000	-1	C-10	-0.1
1988	Mon-N	8	15	1	4	2	0	0	2	0	4	.267	.267	.400	85	-0	0	0	0	1.000	3	/C-7	0.3
Total	2	18	40	2	10	3	0	0	4	2	12	.250	.286	.325	70	-1	0	0	0	1.000	2	/C-17	0.2

■ JOHNNY TEMPLE
Temple, John Ellis   b: 8/8/27, Lexington, N.C.   d: 1/9/94, Anderson, S.C.   BR/TR, 5'11", 175 lbs.   Deb: 4/15/52   C

YEAR	TM/L	G	AB	R	H	2B	3B	HR	RBI	BB	SO	AVG	OBP	SLG	PRO+	BR/A	SB	CS	SBR	FA	FR	G/POS	TPR
1952	Cin-N	30	97	8	19	3	0	1	5	5	1	.196	.235	.258	37	-8	2	1	0	.984	-1	2-22	-0.8
1953	Cin-N	63	110	14	29	4	0	1	9	7	12	.264	.314	.327	67	-5	1	0	0	.964	10	2-44	0.6
1954	Cin-N	146	505	60	155	14	8	0	44	62	24	.307	.385	.366	94	-1	21	7	2	.973	-10	*2-144	0.0
1955	Cin-N	150	588	94	165	20	3	0	50	80	32	.281	.368	.325	81	-13	19	4	3	.971	-3	*2-149/S-1	-0.1
1956	Cin-N★	154	632	88	180	18	3	2	41	58	40	.285	.346	.332	78	-17	14	4	2	.981	-7	*2-154/O-1	-1.0
1957	Cin-N★	145	557	85	158	24	4	0	37	94	34	.284	.391	.341	92	-2	19	5	3	.974	-21	*2-145	-0.8
1958	Cin-N	141	542	82	166	31	6	3	47	91	41	.306	.406	.402	109	11	15	8	-0	.979	-19	*2-141/1-1	0.2
1959	Cin-N★	149	598	102	186	35	6	8	67	72	40	.311	.387	.430	114	14	14	3	2	.974	-26	*2-149	0.2
1960	Cle-A	98	381	50	102	13	1	2	19	32	20	.268	.326	.323	79	-11	11	5	0	.974	-30	2-77,3-17	-3.4
1961	Cle-A★	129	518	73	143	22	3	3	30	61	36	.276	.352	.347	90	-6	9	5	0	.969	-30	*2-129	-2.2
1962	Bal-A	78	270	28	71	8	1	1	17	36	22	.263	.352	.311	85	-4	7	4	-0	.981	-19	2-71	-1.6
	Hou-N	31	95	14	25	4	0	0	12	7	11	.263	.314	.305	72	-4	1	0	0	.941	-8	2-26/3-1	-0.9
1963	Hou-N	100	322	22	85	12	1	1	17	41	24	.264	.347	.317	99	1	7	2	1	.970	-20	2-61,3-29	-1.4
1964	Cin-N	6	3	0	0	0	0	0	0	2	1	.000	.400	.000	23	-0	0	0	0	.000	0	H	0.0
Total	13	1420	5218	720	1484	208	36	22	395	648	338	.284	.365	.351	91	-46	140	48	13	.974	-183	*2-1312/3-47,1OS	-11.2

■ GARRY TEMPLETON
Templeton, Garry Lewis   b: 3/24/56, Lockney, Tex.   BB/TR, 5'11", 190 lbs.   Deb: 8/9/76

YEAR	TM/L	G	AB	R	H	2B	3B	HR	RBI	BB	SO	AVG	OBP	SLG	PRO+	BR/A	SB	CS	SBR	FA	FR	G/POS	TPR
1976	StL-N	53	213	32	62	8	2	1	17	7	33	.291	.317	.362	91	-3	11	7	-1	.922	1	S-53	0.4
1977	StL-N★	153	621	94	200	19	18	8	79	15	70	.322	.339	.449	111	8	28	24	-6	.958	-3	*S-151	1.6
1978	StL-N	155	647	82	181	31	13	2	47	22	87	.280	.304	.377	91	-10	34	11	4	.953	23	*S-155	3.8
1979	StL-N†	154	672	105	211	32	19	9	62	18	91	.314	.333	.458	113	9	26	10	2	.960	18	*S-154	4.7
1980	StL-N	118	504	83	161	19	9	4	43	18	43	.319	.343	.417	108	4	31	15	0	.959	28	*S-115	4.7
1981	StL-N	80	333	47	96	16	8	1	33	14	55	.288	.317	.393	98	-2	8	12	-5	.960	5	S-76	0.7
1982	SD-N	141	563	76	139	25	8	6	64	26	82	.247	.281	.352	80	-17	27	16	-2	.961	-24	*S-136	-3.2
1983	SD-N	126	460	39	121	20	2	3	40	21	57	.263	.295	.335	77	-15	16	6	1	.960	-14	*S-123	-1.7
1984	*SD-N	148	493	40	127	19	3	2	35	39	81	.258	.313	.320	79	-14	8	3	1	.960	-23	*S-146	-2.4
1985	SD-N★	148	546	63	154	30	2	6	55	41	88	.282	.333	.377	100	-0	16	6	1	.968	-7	*S-148	0.9
1986	SD-N	147	510	42	126	21	2	2	44	35	86	.247	.297	.308	68	-22	10	5	0	.966	-28	*S-144	-3.9
1987	SD-N	148	510	42	113	13	5	5	48	42	92	.222	.282	.296	55	-33	14	3	2	.972	5	*S-146	-1.0
1988	SD-N	110	362	35	90	15	7	3	36	20	50	.249	.288	.354	85	-8	8	2	1	.968	15	*S-105/3-2	1.7
1989	SD-N	142	506	43	129	26	3	6	40	23	80	.255	.287	.354	82	-13	1	3	-2	.970	13	*S-140	1.0
1990	SD-N	144	505	45	125	25	3	9	59	24	59	.248	.282	.362	75	-18	1	4	-2	.957	-9	*S-135	-1.9
1991	SD-N	32	57	5	11	1	1	1	6	1	9	.193	.207	.298	39	-5	0	1	-1	.950	2	3-15/S-1	-0.8
	NY-N	80	219	20	50	9	1	2	20	9	29	.228	.259	.306	59	-12	3	1	0	.963	5	S-40,1-25/3O	-0.6
	Yr	112	276	25	61	10	2	3	26	10	38	.221	.248	.304	54	-17	3	2	0	.963	7	S-41,1-25,3/O	-1.4
Total	16	2079	7721	893	2096	329	106	70	728	375	1092	.271	.306	.369	87	-150	242	129	-5	.961	7	*S-1964/1-25,3O	4.0

■ GENE TENACE
Tenace, Fury Gene (b: Fiore Gino Tennaci)   b: 10/10/46, Russellton, Pa.   BR/TR, 6', 190 lbs.   Deb: 5/29/69   MC

YEAR	TM/L	G	AB	R	H	2B	3B	HR	RBI	BB	SO	AVG	OBP	SLG	PRO+	BR/A	SB	CS	SBR	FA	FR	G/POS	TPR
1969	Oak-A	16	38	1	6	0	0	1	2	1	15	.158	.200	.237	23	-4	0	0	0	1.000	-0	C-13	-0.4
1970	Oak-A	38	105	19	32	6	0	7	20	23	30	.305	.430	.562	178	12	0	2	-1	.990	4	C-30	1.6
1971	*Oak-A	65	179	26	49	7	0	7	25	29	34	.274	.381	.430	132	8	2	1	0	.994	-6	C-52/O-1	0.4
1972	*Oak-A	82	227	22	51	5	3	5	32	24	42	.225	.307	.339	97	-1	0	0	0	.979	-8	C-49/O-9,123	-0.9
1973	*Oak-A	160	510	83	132	18	2	24	84	101	94	.259	.391	.443	142	32	2	2	-1	.989	-11	*1-134,C-33/2D	1.2
1974	*Oak-A	158	484	71	102	17	1	26	73	110	105	.211	.367	.411	133	25	2	9	-5	.995	-9	*1-106,C-79/2	0.9
1975	*Oak-A★	158	498	83	127	17	0	29	87	106	127	.255	.398	.464	146	35	7	4	-0	.984	-16	C-125,1-68/D	2.2
1976	Oak-A	128	417	64	104	19	1	22	66	81	91	.249	.376	.458	150	28	5	4	-1	.995	-20	1-70,C-65/D	0.5
1977	SD-N	147	437	66	102	24	4	15	61	125	119	.233	.417	.410	137	31	5	3	-0	.980	-7	C-99,1-36,3	2.5
1978	SD-N	142	401	60	90	18	4	16	61	101	98	.224	.394	.409	135	24	6	5	-1	.993	-3	1-80,C-71/3	1.8
1979	SD-N	151	463	61	122	16	4	20	67	105	106	.263	.407	.445	141	31	2	6	-3	.998	-3	C-94,1-72	2.5
1980	SD-N	133	316	46	70	11	1	17	50	92	63	.222	.403	.424	139	21	4	4	-1	.979	-7	*C-104,1-19	1.7
1981	StL-N	58	129	26	30	7	0	5	22	38	26	.233	.421	.403	131	6	1	0	-0	.980	-6	C-38/1-7	0.3
1982	*StL-N	66	124	18	32	9	0	7	18	36	31	.258	.439	.500	160	12	1	1	0	.994	-5	C-37/1-7	1.5
1983	Pit-N	53	62	7	11	5	0	0	6	12	17	.177	.346	.258	68	-2	0	1	0	.989	-2	1-19/C-3,O	-0.5
Total	15	1555	4390	653	1060	179	20	201	674	984	998	.241	.391	.429	137	261	36	42	-14	.986	-92	C-892,1-625/3OD2	15.3

■ JOHN TENER
Tener, John Kinley   b: 7/25/1863, County Tyrone, Ireland   d: 5/19/46, Pittsburgh, Pa.   BR/TR, 6'4", 180 lbs.   Deb: 6/8/1885

YEAR	TM/L	G	AB	R	H	2B	3B	HR	RBI	BB	SO	AVG	OBP	SLG	PRO+	BR/A	SB	CS	SBR	FA	FR	G/POS	TPR
1885	Bal-a	1	4	0	0	0	0	0		0		.000	.000	.000	-99	-1				.000	-1	/O-1	-0.2
1888	Chi-N	12	46	4	9	1	0	0		1	15	.196	.229	.217	40	-3	1			.892	0	P-12/O-1	0.0

YEAR	TM/L	G	AB	R	H	2B	3B	HR	RBI	BB	SO	AVG	OBP	SLG	PRO+	BR/A	SB	CS	SBR	FA	FR	G/POS	TPR
1889	Chi-N	42	150	18	41	4	2	1	19	7	22	.273	.306	.347	78	-5	2			.929	3	P-35/O-6,1	-0.1
1890	Pit-P	18	63	7	12	0	0	2	5	7	10	.190	.301	.286	62	-3	1			.966	2	P-14/O-2,3	-0.2
Total	4	73	263	29	62	5	2	3	25	15	47	.236	.287	.304	66	-12	4			.933	4	/P-61,O-10,31	-0.5

■ TOM TENNANT
Tennant, Thomas Francis   b: 7/3/1882, Monroe, Wis.   d: 2/15/55, San Carlos, Cal.   BL/TL, 5'11", 165 lbs.   Deb: 4/18/12

YEAR	TM/L	G	AB	R	H	2B	3B	HR	RBI	BB	SO	AVG	OBP	SLG	PRO+	BR/A	SB	CS	SBR	FA	FR	G/POS	TPR
1912	StL-A	2	2	1	0	0	0	0	0	0	0	.000	.000	.000	-99	-1	0			.000	0	H	-0.1

■ FRED TENNEY
Tenney, Fred Clay   b: 7/9/1859, Marlborough, N.H.   d: 6/15/19, Fall River, Mass.   Deb: 4/28/1884

YEAR	TM/L	G	AB	R	H	2B	3B	HR	RBI	BB	SO	AVG	OBP	SLG	PRO+	BR/A	SB	CS	SBR	FA	FR	G/POS	TPR
1884	Was-U	32	119	17	28	3	1	0	6			.235	.272	.277		-8				.867	-1	O-27/1-6	-0.8
	Bos-U	4	17	1	2	0	0	0	0			.118	.118	.118	-36	-3				.750	-1	/P-4	0.0
	Wil-U	1	3	0	0	0	0	0	0			.000	.000	.000	-97	-1				1.000	0	/P-1	0.0
	Yr	37	139	18	30	3	1	0	6			.216	.248	.252	37	-12				.867	-1	O-27/1-6,P	-0.8

■ FRED TENNEY
Tenney, Frederick   b: 11/26/1871, Georgetown, Mass.   d: 7/3/52, Boston, Mass.   BL/TL, 5'9", 155 lbs.   Deb: 6/16/1894   M

YEAR	TM/L	G	AB	R	H	2B	3B	HR	RBI	BB	SO	AVG	OBP	SLG	PRO+	BR/A	SB	CS	SBR	FA	FR	G/POS	TPR
1894	Bos-N	27	86	23	34	7	1	2	21	12	9	.395	.469	.570	139	5	6			.893	-0	C-20/O-6,1	0.5
1895	Bos-N	49	173	35	47	9	1	1	21	24	5	.272	.360	.353	78	-6	6			.885	-4	O-28,C-21	-0.8
1896	Bos-N	88	348	64	117	14	3	2	49	36	12	.336	.400	.411	108	4	18			.957	1	O-60,C-27	0.3
1897	*Bos-N	132	566	125	180	24	3	1	85	49		.318	.376	.376	93	-6	34			.988	5	*1-128/O-4	0.0
1898	Bos-N	117	488	106	160	25	5	0	62	33		.328	.370	.400	114	8	23			.980	5	*1-117/C-1	1.1
1899	Bos-N	150	603	115	209	19	17	1	67	63		.347	.411	.439	122	17	28			.978	10	*1-150	2.5
1900	Bos-N	112	437	77	122	13	5	1	56	39		.279	.346	.339	80	-13	17			.981	9	*1-111	-0.4
1901	Bos-N	115	451	66	127	13	1	1	22	37		.282	.340	.322	85	-9	15			.976	7	*1-113/C-2	-0.3
1902	Bos-N	134	489	88	154	18	3	2	30	73		.315	.409	.376	141	28	21			**.985**	13	*1-134	3.9
1903	Bos-N	122	447	79	140	22	3	3	41	70		.313	.415	.396	137	26	21			.974	8	*1-122	3.1
1904	Bos-N	147	533	76	144	17	9	1	37	57		.270	.351	.341	118	13	17			.986	8	*1-144/O-4	1.9
1905	Bos-N	149	549	84	158	18	3	0	28	67		.288	.368	.332	111	11	17			.982	22	*1-148/P-1M	2.9
1906	Bos-N	143	544	61	154	12	8	1	28	58		.283	.357	.340	121	15	17			.983	10	*1-143,M	2.2
1907	Bos-N	150	554	83	151	18	8	0	26	82		.273	.371	.334	121	17	15			.989	9	*1-149,M	2.5
1908	NY-N	156	583	**101**	149	20	1	2	49	72		.256	.344	.304	102	4	17			.990	10	*1-156	1.4
1909	NY-N	101	375	43	88	8	2	3	30	52		.235	.333	.291	92	-2	8			.986	8	1-98	0.6
1911	Bos-N	102	369	52	97	13	4	1	36	50	17	.263	.352	.328	84	-7	5			.985	2	1-96/O-2M	-0.5
Total	17	1994	7595	1278	2231	270	77	22	688	874	43	.294	.371	.358	109	107	285			.983	124	*1-1810,O-104/CP	20.9

■ FRANK TEPEDINO
Tepedino, Frank Ronald   b: 11/23/47, Brooklyn, N.Y.   BL/TL, 5'11", 192 lbs.   Deb: 5/12/67

YEAR	TM/L	G	AB	R	H	2B	3B	HR	RBI	BB	SO	AVG	OBP	SLG	PRO+	BR/A	SB	CS	SBR	FA	FR	G/POS	TPR
1967	NY-A	9	5	0	2	0	0	0	0	1	1	.400	.500	.400	175	1	0	0	0	1.000	0	/1-1	0.1
1969	NY-A	13	39	6	9	0	0	0	4	4	4	.231	.302	.231	53	-2	1	0	0	.950	-1	O-13	-0.4
1970	NY-A	16	19	2	6	2	0	0	2	1	2	.316	.350	.421	118	0	0	1	-1	1.000	-0	/1-1,O-1	-0.1
1971	NY-A	6	6	0	0	0	0	0	0	0	0	.000	.000	.000	-99	-2	0	0	0	1.000	-0	/O-1	-0.2
	Mil-A	53	106	11	21	1	0	2	7	4	17	.198	.234	.264	41	-8	2	2	-1	.986	3	1-28	-0.8
	Yr	59	112	11	21	1	0	2	7	4	17	.188	.222	.250	34	-10	2	2	-1	.986	3	1-28/O-1	-1.0
1972	NY-A	8	8	0	0	0	0	0	0	0	1	.000	.000	.000	-99	-2	0	0	0	.000	0	H	-0.2
1973	Atl-N	74	148	20	45	5	0	4	29	13	21	.304	.360	.419	107	1	0	0	0	.992	2	1-58	0.1
1974	Atl-N	78	169	11	39	5	1	0	16	9	13	.231	.274	.272	51	-11	1	2	-1	.988	1	1-46	-1.4
1975	Atl-N	8	7	0	0	0	0	0	0	1	2	.000	.125	.000	-61	-2	0	0	0	.000	0	H	-0.2
Total	8	265	507	50	122	13	1	6	58	33	61	.241	.290	.306	65	-24	4	5	-2	.989	4	1-134/O-15	-3.1

■ JOE TEPSIC
Tepsic, Joseph John   b: 9/18/23, Slovan, Pa.   BR/TR, 5'9", 170 lbs.   Deb: 7/12/46

YEAR	TM/L	G	AB	R	H	2B	3B	HR	RBI	BB	SO	AVG	OBP	SLG	PRO+	BR/A	SB	CS	SBR	FA	FR	G/POS	TPR
1946	Bro-N	15	5	2	0	0	0	0	0	1	1	.000	.167	.000	-50	-1	0			1.000	-0	/O-1	-0.1

■ JERRY TERRELL
Terrell, Jerry Wayne   b: 7/13/46, Waseca, Minn.   BR/TR, 6', 170 lbs.   Deb: 4/14/73

YEAR	TM/L	G	AB	R	H	2B	3B	HR	RBI	BB	SO	AVG	OBP	SLG	PRO+	BR/A	SB	CS	SBR	FA	FR	G/POS	TPR
1973	Min-A	124	438	43	116	15	2	1	32	21	56	.265	.300	.315	71	-17	13	7	-0	.962	-14	S-81,3-30,2/OD	-2.2
1974	Min-A	116	229	43	56	4	6	0	19	11	27	.245	.279	.314	68	-10	3	2	-0	.960	23	S-34,2-26,3D/O1	1.7
1975	Min-A	108	385	48	110	16	2	1	36	19	27	.286	.324	.345	87	-6	4	4	-1	.947	-3	S-41,2-39,13/OD	-0.6
1976	Min-A	89	171	29	42	3	1	0	8	9	15	.246	.287	.275	63	-8	11	2	0	.988	7	2-31,3-26,SD/O	0.3
1977	Min-A	93	214	32	48	6	0	1	20	11	21	.224	.265	.266	46	-16	10	4	1	.953	5	3-59,2-14/S10D	-1.0
1978	KC-A	73	133	14	27	1	0	0	8	4	13	.203	.226	.211	23	-13	8	4	0	1.000	6	2-31,3-25,S/1	-0.6
1979	KC-A	31	40	5	12	3	0	1	2	1	1	.300	.317	.450	102	-0	1	0	0	.963	3	3-19/2-7,PS	0.2
1980	KC-A	23	16	4	1	0	0	0	0	0	0	.063	.063	.063	-65	-4	2	0	0	1.000	2	/O-7,1-3,2PD	-0.2
Total	8	657	1626	218	412	48	11	4	125	76	160	.253	.289	.304	66	-74	50	23	1	.961	27	3-192,S-191,2/D10PD	-2.4

■ TOM TERRELL
Terrell, John Thomas   b: 6/19/1867, Louisville, Ky.   d: 7/9/1893, Louisville, Ky.   Deb: 10/5/1886

YEAR	TM/L	G	AB	R	H	2B	3B	HR	RBI	BB	SO	AVG	OBP	SLG	PRO+	BR/A	SB	CS	SBR	FA	FR	G/POS	TPR
1886	Lou-a	1	4	0	1	0	0	0	0			.250	.250	.250	54	-0	0			.000	-2	/O-1,C-1	-0.2

■ TERRY
Terry   b: Attleboro, Pa.   Deb: 4/26/1875

YEAR	TM/L	G	AB	R	H	2B	3B	HR	RBI	BB	SO	AVG	OBP	SLG	PRO+	BR/A	SB	CS	SBR	FA	FR	G/POS	TPR
1875	Was-n	6	22	0	4	0	1	0	0			.182	.182	.273	57	-1						/O-4,1-2	-0.1

■ ADONIS TERRY
Terry, William H   b: 8/7/1864, Westfield, Mass.   d: 2/24/15, Milwaukee, Wis.   BR/TR, 5'11.5", 168 lbs.   Deb: 5/1/1884   U

YEAR	TM/L	G	AB	R	H	2B	3B	HR	RBI	BB	SO	AVG	OBP	SLG	PRO+	BR/A	SB	CS	SBR	FA	FR	G/POS	TPR
1884	Bro-a	67	236	15	55	10	3	0		8		.233	.258	.301	81	-5				.764	-1	P-56,O-13	0.1
1885	Bro-a	71	264	23	45	1	3	0		10		.170	.201	.208	29	-21				.883	-1	O-47,P-25/3	-1.3
1886	Bro-a	75	299	34	71	8	9	2		10		.237	.265	.344	89	-5	17			.934	4	P-34,O-32,S	-0.4
1887	Bro-a	86	352	56	103	6	10	3		16		.293	.323	.392	90	-2	27			.895	3	O-49,P-40/S	-0.4
1888	Bro-a	30	115	13	29	6	0	0	8	5		.252	.283	.304	89	-2	7			.909	1	P-23/O-7,1	0.0
1889	*Bro-a	49	160	29	48	6	6	2	26	14	14	.300	.356	.450	129	5	8			.963	5	P-41,1-10	0.0
1890	*Bro-N	99	363	63	101	17	9	4	59	40	34	.278	.356	.408	122	10	32			.930	-1	O-54,P-46/1	0.2
1891	Bro-N	30	91	10	19	7	1	0	6	9	26	.209	.301	.308	78	-3	4			.957	-2	P-25/O-5	-0.1
1892	Bal-N	1	4	0	0	0	0	0	0	0	0	.000	.000	.000	-97	-1				1.000	0	/P-1	0.0
	Pit-N	31	100	10	16	0	4	2	11	10	11	.160	.236	.300	62	-5	2			.938	-0	P-30/O-1	-0.1
	Yr	32	104	10	16	0	4	2	11	10	12	.154	.228	.288	56	-6	2			.940	-0	P-31/O-1	-0.1
1893	Pit-N	26	71	9	18	4	3	0	11	3	11	.254	.293	.394	84	-2	1			.920	-2	P-26	0.0
1894	Pit-N	1	0	0	0	0	0	0	0	0	0	—	—	—		0				.000	0	/P-1	0.0
	Chi-N	30	95	19	33	4	2	0	17	11	12	.347	.415	.432	99	-0	1			.875	-2	P-23/O-7,1	-0.1
	Yr	31	95	19	33	4	2	0	17	11	12	.347	.415	.432	99	0	3			.875	-2	P-24/O-7,1	-0.1
1895	Chi-N	40	137	18	30	3	2	1	10	2	17	.219	.236	.292	33	-14	1			.895	2	P-38/O-1,S	-0.1
1896	Chi-N	30	99	14	26	4	2	0	15	8	12	.263	.324	.343	73	-4	4			.968	-2	P-30	0.0
1897	Chi-N	1	3	1	0	0	0	0	0	0	0	.000	.000	.000	-96	-1	0			.750	0	/P-1	0.0
Total	14	667	2389	314	594	76	54	15	163	146	138	.249	.295	.344	85	-50	106			.903	10	P-440,O-216/S13	-2.2

■ BILL TERRY
Terry, William Harold "Memphis Bill"   b: 10/30/1898, Atlanta, Ga.   d: 1/9/89, Jacksonville, Fla.   BL/TL, 6'1", 200 lbs.   Deb: 9/24/23   MH

YEAR	TM/L	G	AB	R	H	2B	3B	HR	RBI	BB	SO	AVG	OBP	SLG	PRO+	BR/A	SB	CS	SBR	FA	FR	G/POS	TPR
1923	NY-N	3	7	1	1	0	0	0	0	0	0	.143	.333	.143	30	-1	0	0	0	1.000	0	/1-2	-0.1
1924	*NY-N	77	163	26	39	7	2	5	24	17	18	.239	.311	.399	91	-2	1	1	-0	.988	-2	1-35	-0.6
1925	NY-N	133	489	75	156	31	6	11	70	42	52	.319	.374	.474	120	14	4	5	-2	.990	4	*1-126	0.8
1926	NY-N	98	225	26	65	12	5	5	43	22	17	.289	.352	.453	117	5	3			.979	4	1-38,O-14	0.5
1927	NY-N	150	580	101	189	32	13	20	121	46	53	.326	.377	.529	141	31	1			.993	5	*1-150	2.6
1928	NY-N	149	568	100	185	36	11	17	101	64	36	.326	.394	.518	136	29	-2			.993	-2	*1-149	1.4
1929	NY-N	150	607	103	226	39	5	14	117	48	35	.372	.418	.522	132	31	10			.994	7	*1-149/O-1	2.0

YEAR	TM/L	G	AB	R	H	2B	3B	HR	RBI	BB	SO	AVG	OBP	SLG	PRO+	BR/A	SB	CS	SBR	FA	FR	G/POS	TPR
1930	NY-N	154	633	139	**254**	39	15	23	129	57	33	**.401**	.452	.619	159	61	8			.990	13	*1-154	5.0
1931	NY-N	153	611	**121**	213	43	**20**	9	112	47	36	.349	.397	.529	150	**42**	8			.990	9	*1-153	3.6
1932	NY-N	154	643	124	225	42	11	28	117	32	23	.350	.382	.580	158	49	4			.991	14	*1-154,M	4.9
1933	*NY-N★	123	475	68	153	20	5	6	58	40	23	.322	.375	.423	129	19	3			.992	1	*1-117,M	0.9
1934	NY-N★	153	602	109	213	30	6	8	83	60	47	.354	.414	.463	138	34	0			**.994**	6	*1-153,M	2.6
1935	NY-N★	145	596	91	203	32	8	6	64	41	55	.341	.383	.451	126	22	7			**.996**	6	*1-143,M	1.2
1936	*NY-N	79	229	36	71	10	5	2	39	19	19	.310	.363	.424	112	4	0			.996	3	1-56,M	0.1
Total	14	1721	6428	1120	2193	373	112	154	1078	537	449	.341	.393	.506	137	338	56	6		.992	67	*1-1579/O-15	24.9

■ ZEB TERRY
Terry, Zebulon Alexander b: 6/17/1891, Denison, Tex. d: 3/14/88, Los Angeles, Cal. BR/TR, 5'8", 129 lbs. Deb: 4/12/16

YEAR	TM/L	G	AB	R	H	2B	3B	HR	RBI	BB	SO	AVG	OBP	SLG	PRO+	BR/A	SB	CS	SBR	FA	FR	G/POS	TPR
1916	Chi-A	94	269	20	51	8	4	0	17	33	36	.190	.292	.249	62	-12	4			.935	-10	S-93	-1.9
1917	Chi-A	2	1	0	0	0	0	0	0	2	0	.000	.667	.000	102	0	0			1.000	-1	/S-1	0.0
1918	Bos-N	28	105	17	32	2	2	0	8	8	14	.305	.360	.362	125	3	1			.977	8	S-27	1.4
1919	Pit-N	129	472	46	107	12	6	0	27	31	26	.227	.280	.278	65	-19	12			.960	-31	*S-127	-4.8
1920	Chi-N	133	496	56	139	26	6	0	52	44	22	.280	.341	.369	102	2	12	16	-6	.962	14	S-70,2-63	1.9
1921	Chi-N	123	488	59	134	18	1	2	45	27	19	.275	.318	.328	71	-20	1	13	-8	.972	6	*2-122	-1.9
1922	Chi-N	131	496	56	142	24	0	2	67	34	16	.286	.335	.343	74	-19	2	11	-6	.964	5	*2-125/S-4,3	-1.2
Total	7	640	2327	254	605	90	24	2	216	179	133	.260	.318	.322	78	-64	32	40		.956	-5	S-322,2-310/3	-6.5

■ WAYNE TERWILLIGER
Terwilliger, Willard Wayne "Twig" b: 6/27/25, Clare, Mich. BR/TR, 5'11", 170 lbs. Deb: 8/6/49 C

YEAR	TM/L	G	AB	R	H	2B	3B	HR	RBI	BB	SO	AVG	OBP	SLG	PRO+	BR/A	SB	CS	SBR	FA	FR	G/POS	TPR
1949	Chi-N	36	112	11	25	2	1	2	10	16	22	.223	.326	.313	74	-4	0			.978	4	2-34	0.2
1950	Chi-N	133	480	63	116	22	3	10	32	43	63	.242	.311	.363	77	-16	13			.967	-9	*2-126/1-1,3O	-1.9
1951	Chi-N	50	192	26	41	6	0	0	10	29	21	.214	.317	.245	52	-12	3	1	0	.969	-4	2-49	-1.3
	Bro-N	37	50	11	14	1	0	0	4	8	7	.280	.390	.300	87	-0	1	0	0	.949	6	2-24/3-1	0.7
	Yr	87	242	37	55	7	0	0	14	37	28	.227	.332	.256	59	-12	4	1	1	.964	2	2-73/3-1	-0.6
1953	Was-A	134	464	62	117	24	4	4	46	64	65	.252	.343	.347	89	-6	7	4	-0	.982	5	*2-133	0.6
1954	Was-A	106	337	42	70	10	1	3	24	32	40	.208	.282	.270	55	-21	3	3	-1	.972	13	2-90,3-10/S	-0.4
1955	NY-N	80	257	29	66	16	1	1	18	36	42	.257	.350	.339	84	-5	2	4	-2	.985	26	2-78/S-1,3	2.4
1956	NY-N	14	18	0	4	1	0	0	0	0	5	.222	.222	.278	34	-2	0	0	0	.958	2	/2-6	0.1
1959	KC-A	74	180	27	48	11	0	2	18	19	31	.267	.337	.361	90	-0	2	2	-1	.972	20	2-63/S-2,3	2.0
1960	KC-A	2	1	0	0	0	0	0	0	0	0	.000	.000	.000	-99	-0	0	0	0	1.000	0	/2-2	0.0
Total	9	666	2091	271	501	93	10	22	162	247	296	.240	.323	.325	76	-69	31	14		.974	64	2-605/3-14,SO1	2.4

■ AL TESCH
Tesch, Albert John "Tiny" b: 1/27/1891, Jersey City, N.J. d: 8/3/47, Jersey City, N.J. BB/TR, 5'10", 155 lbs. Deb: 8/21/15

YEAR	TM/L	G	AB	R	H	2B	3B	HR	RBI	BB	SO	AVG	OBP	SLG	PRO+	BR/A	SB	CS	SBR	FA	FR	G/POS	TPR
1915	Bro-F	8	7	2	2	1	0	0	2	0	0	.286	.286	.429	90	-0	0			.867	3	/2-3	0.3

■ NICK TESTA
Testa, Nicholas b: 6/29/28, New York, N.Y. BR/TR, 5'8", 180 lbs. Deb: 4/23/58 C

YEAR	TM/L	G	AB	R	H	2B	3B	HR	RBI	BB	SO	AVG	OBP	SLG	PRO+	BR/A	SB	CS	SBR	FA	FR	G/POS	TPR
1958	SF-N	1	0	0	0	0	0	0	0	0	0	—	—	—			0	0	0	.000	-1	/C-1	0.0

■ DICK TETTELBACH
Tettelbach, Richard Morley "Tut" b: 6/26/29, New Haven, Conn. BR/TR, 6', 195 lbs. Deb: 9/25/55

YEAR	TM/L	G	AB	R	H	2B	3B	HR	RBI	BB	SO	AVG	OBP	SLG	PRO+	BR/A	SB	CS	SBR	FA	FR	G/POS	TPR
1955	NY-A	2	5	0	0	0	0	0	0	0	0	.000	.000	.000	-99	-1	0	0	0	1.000	0	/O-2	-0.2
1956	Was-A	18	64	10	10	1	2	1	9	14	15	.156	.308	.281	56	-4	0	1	-1	1.000	2	O-18	-0.4
1957	Was-A	9	11	2	2	0	0	0	1	4	2	.182	.400	.182	65	-0	0	0	0	.900	-0	/O-3	-0.1
Total	3	29	80	12	12	1	2	1	10	18	17	.150	.306	.250	49	-6	0	1	-1	.980	2	/O-23	-0.7

■ MICKEY TETTLETON
Tettleton, Mickey Lee b: 9/16/60, Oklahoma City, Okla. BB/TR, 6'2", 200 lbs. Deb: 6/30/84

YEAR	TM/L	G	AB	R	H	2B	3B	HR	RBI	BB	SO	AVG	OBP	SLG	PRO+	BR/A	SB	CS	SBR	FA	FR	G/POS	TPR
1984	Oak-A	33	76	10	20	2	1	1	5	11	21	.263	.356	.355	105	1	0	0	0	.992	0	C-32	0.2
1985	Oak-A	78	211	23	53	12	0	3	15	28	59	.251	.344	.351	98	0	2	2	-1	.989	-1	C-76/D-1	0.2
1986	Oak-A	90	211	26	43	9	0	10	35	39	51	.204	.331	.389	103	1	7	1	2	.984	-2	C-89	0.5
1987	Oak-A	82	211	19	41	3	0	8	26	30	65	.194	.295	.322	68	-10	1	1	-0	.987	4	C-80/1-1,D	-0.2
1988	Bal-A	86	283	31	74	11	1	11	37	28	70	.261	.332	.424	113	5	0	1	-1	.992	-10	C-80	0.1
1989	Bal-A★	117	411	72	106	21	2	26	65	73	117	.258	.371	.509	150	28	3	2	-0	.994	-7	C-75,D-43	2.4
1990	Bal-A	135	444	68	99	21	2	15	51	106	160	.223	.378	.381	117	14	2	4	-2	.991	-13	C-90,D-40/1O	0.4
1991	Det-A	154	501	85	132	17	2	31	89	101	131	.263	.389	.491	140	30	3	3	-1	.990	-15	*C-125,D-24/O1	2.0
1992	Det-A	157	525	82	125	25	0	32	83	**122**	137	.238	.383	.469	137	29	0	6	-4	**.996**	-18	*C-113,D-40/1O	1.2
1993	Det-A	152	522	79	128	25	4	32	110	109	139	.245	.376	.492	132	25	3	7	-3	.992	-18	1-59,C-56,O/D	0.3
1994	Det-A★	107	339	57	84	18	2	17	51	97	98	.248	.422	.463	129	19	0	1	-1	.992	-15	C-53,1-24,DO	0.4
Total	11	1191	3734	552	905	164	14	186	567	744	1048	.242	.371	.443	125	143	21	28	-11	.991	-96	C-869,D-175/1O	7.5

■ TIM TEUFEL
Teufel, Timothy Shawn b: 7/7/58, Greenwich, Conn. BR/TR, 6', 175 lbs. Deb: 9/3/83

YEAR	TM/L	G	AB	R	H	2B	3B	HR	RBI	BB	SO	AVG	OBP	SLG	PRO+	BR/A	SB	CS	SBR	FA	FR	G/POS	TPR
1983	Min-A	21	78	11	24	7	1	3	6	2	8	.308	.325	.538	128	3	0	0	0	.990	-1	2-18/S-1,D	0.2
1984	Min-A	157	568	76	149	30	3	14	61	76	73	.262	.351	.400	103	3	1	3	-2	.984	-12	*2-157	-0.4
1985	Min-A	138	434	58	113	24	3	10	50	48	70	.260	.338	.399	95	-2	4	2	0	.980	-33	*2-137/D-1	-3.1
1986	*NY-N	93	279	35	69	20	1	4	31	32	42	.247	.327	.369	94	-2	1	2	-1	.971	-18	2-84/1-3,3	-1.9
1987	NY-N	97	299	55	92	29	0	14	61	44	53	.308	.400	.545	155	24	3	2	-0	.972	-11	2-92/1-1	1.6
1988	*NY-N	90	273	35	64	20	0	4	31	29	41	.234	.310	.352	94	-2	0	1	-1	.981	12	2-84/1-3	1.2
1989	NY-N	83	219	27	56	7	2	2	15	32	50	.256	.353	.333	102	2	1	3	-2	.960	-4	2-40,1-33	-0.2
1990	NY-N	80	175	28	43	11	0	10	24	15	33	.246	.305	.480	113	2	0	1	-0	.991	-4	1-24,2-24,3	-0.3
1991	NY-N	20	34	2	4	0	0	1	2	2	8	.118	.167	.206	-4	-4	1	1	-0	1.000	0	/1-6,3-5,2	0.0
	SD-N	97	307	39	70	16	0	11	42	49	69	.228	.336	.388	100	1	8	2	1	.987	-14	2-65,3-48	-1.2
	Yr	117	341	41	74	16	0	12	44	51	77	.217	.321	.370	91	-3	9	3	1	.987	-14	2-66,3-53/1	-1.7
1992	SD-N	101	246	23	55	10	0	6	25	34	45	.224	.313	.337	83	-5	2	1	0	.987	-3	2-52,3-26/1	-0.8
1993	SD-N	96	200	26	50	11	2	7	31	27	39	.250	.339	.430	102	1	2	2	-1	.990	-3	2-52/3-9,1	-0.1
Total	11	1073	3112	415	789	185	12	86	379	387	531	.254	.338	.404	104	19	23	19	-5	.980	-88	2-806/3-99,1DS	-5.5

■ GEORGE TEXTOR
Textor, George Bernhardt b: 12/27/1888, Newport, Ky. d: 3/10/54, Massillon, Ohio BB/TR, 5'10.5", 174 lbs. Deb: 4/19/14

YEAR	TM/L	G	AB	R	H	2B	3B	HR	RBI	BB	SO	AVG	OBP	SLG	PRO+	BR/A	SB	CS	SBR	FA	FR	G/POS	TPR
1914	Ind-F	22	57	2	10	0	0	0	4	2	9	.175	.230	.175	5	-8	0			.955	9	C-21	-0.5
1915	New-F	3	6	1	2	0	0	0	0	0	0	.333	.333	.333	83	-0	0			1.000	-1	/C-3	-0.1
Total	2	25	63	3	12	0	0	0	4	2	9	.190	.239	.190	11	-8	0			.957	1	/C-24	-0.6

■ MOE THACKER
Thacker, Morris Benton b: 5/21/34, Louisville, Ky. BR/TR, 6'3", 210 lbs. Deb: 4/20/58

YEAR	TM/L	G	AB	R	H	2B	3B	HR	RBI	BB	SO	AVG	OBP	SLG	PRO+	BR/A	SB	CS	SBR	FA	FR	G/POS	TPR
1958	Chi-N	11	24	4	6	1	0	2	3	1	7	.250	.280	.542	113	0	0	0	0	.952	1	/C-9	0.1
1960	Chi-N	54	90	5	14	1	0	0	6	14	20	.156	.269	.167	23	-9	1	1	-0	.980	5	C-50	-0.3
1961	Chi-N	25	35	3	6	0	0	0	2	11	11	.171	.383	.171	53	-2	0	0	0	.973	-1	C-25	-0.2
1962	Chi-N	65	107	8	20	5	0	0	9	14	40	.187	.287	.234	40	-9	0	1	-1	.996	13	C-65	0.5
1963	StL-N	3	4	0	0	0	0	0	0	0	3	.000	.000	.000	-91	-1	0	0	0	1.000	1	/C-3	0.0
Total	5	158	260	20	46	7	0	2	20	40	81	.177	.291	.227	41	-20	1	2	-1	.984	18	C-152	0.1

■ AL THAKE
Thake, Albert b: 9/21/1849, Wymondham, England d: 9/1/1872, Brooklyn, N.Y. 6', Deb: 6/13/1872

YEAR	TM/L	G	AB	R	H	2B	3B	HR	RBI	BB	SO	AVG	OBP	SLG	PRO+	BR/A	SB	CS	SBR	FA	FR	G/POS	TPR
1872	Atl-n	18	80	14	23	2	2	0	16	0	1	.287	.287	.363	84	-3						O-16/2-1	-0.1

■ RON THEOBALD
Theobald, Ronald Merrill b: 7/28/43, Oakland, Cal. BR/TR, 5'8", 165 lbs. Deb: 4/12/71

YEAR	TM/L	G	AB	R	H	2B	3B	HR	RBI	BB	SO	AVG	OBP	SLG	PRO+	BR/A	SB	CS	SBR	FA	FR	G/POS	TPR
1971	Mil-A	126	388	50	107	12	2	1	23	38	39	.276	.345	.325	92	-3	11	8	-2	.973	1	*2-111/S-1,3	0.6
1972	Mil-A	125	391	45	86	11	0	1	19	68	38	.220	.343	.256	81	-5	0	7	-4	.988	-13	*2-113	-1.9
Total	2	251	779	95	193	23	2	2	42	106	77	.248	.344	.290	87	-9	11	15	-6	.980	-12	2-224/3-1,S	-1.3

YEAR	TM/L	G	AB	R	H	2B	3B	HR	RBI	BB	SO	AVG	OBP	SLG	PRO+	BR/A	SB	CS	SBR	FA	FR	G/POS	TPR

■ GEORGE THEODORE
Theodore, George Basil b: 11/13/47, Salt Lake City, Ut. BR/TR, 6'4", 190 lbs. Deb: 4/14/73

1973	*NY-N	45	116	14	30	4	1	1	15	10	13	.259	.323	.319	80	-3	1	0	0	.984	2	O-33/1-4	-0.2
1974	NY-N	60	76	7	12	1	0	1	1	8	14	.158	.247	.211	29	-7	0	0	0	.990	-5	1-14,O-12	-1.4
Total	2	105	192	21	42	5	0	2	16	18	27	.219	.292	.276	60	-10	1	0	0	.958	-3	/O-45,1-18	-1.6

■ TOMMY THEVENOW
Thevenow, Thomas Joseph b: 9/6/03, Madison, Ind. d: 7/29/57, Madison, Ind. BR/TR, 5'10", 155 lbs. Deb: 9/4/24

1924	StL-N	23	89	4	18	4	1	0	7	1	6	.202	.211	.270	28	-9	1	3	-2	.951	8	S-23	0.0
1925	StL-N	50	175	17	47	7	2	0	17	7	12	.269	.301	.331	60	-11	3	0	1	.950	3	S-50	-0.2
1926	*StL-N	156	563	64	144	15	5	2	63	27	26	.256	.291	.311	60	-32	8			.956	18	*S-156	0.3
1927	StL-N	59	191	23	37	6	1	0	4	14	8	.194	.249	.236	29	-19	2			.945	7	S-59	-0.6
1928	*StL-N	69	171	11	35	8	3	0	13	20	12	.205	.288	.287	50	-13	0			.931	-4	S-64/3-3,1	-1.1
1929	Phi-N	90	317	30	72	11	0	0	35	25	25	.227	.288	.262	35	-32	3			.953	3	S-90	-1.7
1930	Phi-N	156	573	57	164	21	1	0	78	23	26	.286	.316	.326	52	-44	1			.941	-2	*S-156	-2.6
1931	Pit-N	120	404	35	86	12	1	0	38	28	22	.213	.266	.248	39	-34	0			.964	9	*S-120	-1.4
1932	Pit-N	59	194	12	46	3	3	0	26	7	12	.237	.264	.284	48	-14	0			.918	-3	S-29,3-22	-1.1
1933	Pit-N	73	253	20	79	5	1	0	34	3	5	.312	.320	.340	89	-4	2			.975	-13	2-61/S-3,3	-1.4
1934	Pit-N	122	446	37	121	16	2	0	54	20	20	.271	.306	.316	65	-21	0			.969	-18	2-75,3-44/S	-3.3
1935	Pit-N	110	408	38	97	9	9	0	47	12	23	.238	.261	.304	50	-29	1			.951	4	3-82,S-13/2	-2.0
1936	Cin-N	106	321	25	75	7	2	0	36	15	23	.234	.268	.268	48	-24	2			.945	-9	S-68,2-33,3	-2.7
1937	Bos-N	21	34	5	4	0	1	0	2	4	2	.118	.211	.176	7	-4	0			.969	1	S-12/3-6,2	-0.3
1938	Pit-N	15	25	2	5	0	0	0	2	4	0	.200	.333	.200	49	-1	0			1.000	3	/2-9,S-4,3	0.2
Total	15	1229	4164	380	1030	124	32	2	456	210	222	.247	.285	.294	52	-292	23	3		.950	5	S-848,2-188,3/1	-17.9

■ HENRY THIELMAN
Thielman, Henry Joseph b: 10/3/1880, St.Cloud, Minn. d: 9/2/42, New York, N.Y. BR/TR, 5'11", 175 lbs. Deb: 4/17/02 F

1902	NY-N	6	9	0	1	0	0	0	0	2		.111	.273	.111	19	-1	1			.800	1	/P-2,O-3	-0.1
	Cin-N	28	91	6	12	0	2	0	4	5		.132	.177	.176	2	-10	0			.910	-2	P-25/O-3	-0.2
	Yr	34	100	6	13	0	2	0	4	7		.130	.187	.170	9	-11	1			.903	-1	P-27/O-6	-0.3
1903	Bro-N	9	23	3	5	1	0	1	2	5		.217	.357	.391	117	1	0			.750	-0	/O-5,P-4	-0.1
Total	2	43	123	9	18	1	2	1	6	12		.146	.222	.211	30	-10	1			.918	-1	/P-31,O-11	-0.4

■ ANDRES THOMAS
Thomas, Andres Perez (b: Andres Perez (Thomas)) b: 11/10/63, Boca Chica, D.R. BR/TR, 6'1", 185 lbs. Deb: 9/3/85

1985	Atl-N	15	18	6	5	0	0	0	3	0	6	.278	.278	.278	53	-1	0	0	0	.920	3	S-10	0.2
1986	Atl-N	102	323	26	81	17	2	6	32	8	49	.251	.269	.372	71	-14	4	6	-2	.958	26	S-97	1.8
1987	Atl-N	82	324	29	75	11	0	5	39	14	50	.231	.268	.312	50	-23	6	5	-1	.953	9	S-81	-0.8
1988	Atl-N	153	606	54	153	22	2	13	68	14	95	.252	.271	.360	76	-20	7	3	0	.959	-8	*S-150	-1.7
1989	Atl-N	141	554	41	118	18	0	13	57	12	62	.213	.230	.316	53	-35	3	3	-1	.956	6	*S-138	-2.0
1990	Atl-N	84	278	26	61	8	0	5	30	11	43	.219	.249	.302	48	-20	2	1	0	.967	3	S-72/3-5	-1.2
Total	6	577	2103	182	493	76	4	42	228	59	301	.234	.256	.334	61	-113	22	18	-4	.958	38	S-548/3-5	-3.7

■ PINCH THOMAS
Thomas, Chester David b: 1/24/1888, Camp Point, Ill. d: 12/24/53, Modesto, Cal. BL/TR, 5'9.5", 173 lbs. Deb: 4/24/12

1912	Bos-A	13	30	0	6	0	0	0	5	2		.200	.250	.200	28	-3	1			.966	2	/C-8	0.0
1913	Bos-A	38	91	6	26	1	2	1	15	2	11	.286	.309	.374	97	-1	1			.983	1	C-31	0.3
1914	Bos-A	66	130	9	25	1	0	0	5	18	17	.192	.291	.200	48	-8	1			.966	-2	C-64/1-1	-0.6
1915	*Bos-A	86	203	21	48	4	4	0	21	13	20	.236	.286	.296	76	-7	3	2	-0	.969	4	C-82	0.3
1916	*Bos-A	99	216	21	57	10	1	1	21	33	13	.264	.364	.333	109	4	4			.981	-8	C-90	0.2
1917	Bos-A	83	202	24	48	7	0	0	24	27	9	.238	.333	.272	86	-2	2			.986	3	C-77	0.7
1918	Cle-A	32	73	2	18	0	1	0	5	6	6	.247	.304	.274	68	-3	0			.948	1	C-24	-0.1
1919	Cle-A	34	46	2	5	0	0	0	2	4	3	.109	.180	.109	-17	-7	0			.980	-2	C-21	-0.8
1920	*Cle-A	9	9	0	3	1	0	0	0	3	1	.333	.500	.444	147	1	0	0	0	1.000	1	/C-7	0.2
1921	Cle-A	21	35	1	9	3	0	0	4	10	2	.257	.422	.343	96	0	0	0	0	.882	-6	C-19	-0.5
Total	10	481	1035	88	245	27	8	2	102	118	82	.237	.318	.284	78	-25	12	2		.973	-5	C-423/1-1	-0.3

■ DAN THOMAS
Thomas, Danny Lee b: 5/9/51, Birmingham, Ala. d: 6/12/80, Mobile, Ala. BR/TR, 6'2", 190 lbs. Deb: 9/2/76

1976	Mil-A	32	105	13	29	5	1	4	15	14	28	.276	.372	.457	145	6	1	2	-1	.955	-0	O-32	0.4
1977	Mil-A	22	70	11	19	3	2	2	11	8	11	.271	.354	.457	119	2	0	2	-1	1.000	1	/O-9,D-9	0.1
Total	2	54	175	24	48	8	3	6	26	22	39	.274	.365	.457	134	8	1	4	-2	.966	0	/O-41,D-9	0.5

■ DERREL THOMAS
Thomas, Derrel Osbon b: 1/14/51, Los Angeles, Cal. BB/TR, 6', 160 lbs. Deb: 9/14/71

1971	Hou-N	5	5	0	0	0	0	0	0	0	2	.000	.000	.000	-99	-1	0	1	-1	1.000	1	/2-1	-0.1
1972	SD-N	130	500	48	115	15	5	5	36	41	73	.230	.291	.310	76	-17	9	9	-3	.967	-18	2-83,S-49/O	-2.8
1973	SD-N	113	404	41	96	7	1	0	22	34	52	.238	.300	.260	61	-21	15	5	2	.914	-14	S-74,2-47	-2.3
1974	SD-N	141	523	48	129	24	6	3	41	51	58	.247	.315	.333	85	-11	7	8	-3	.976	6	*2-104,3-22,O/S	-0.4
1975	SF-N	144	540	99	149	21	9	6	48	57	56	.276	.348	.381	98	-1	28	13	1	.974	-7	*2-141/O-1	0.0
1976	SF-N	81	272	38	63	5	4	2	19	29	26	.232	.315	.301	73	-9	10	11	-4	.964	2	2-69/O-2,S3	-0.7
1977	SF-N	148	506	75	135	13	10	8	44	46	70	.267	.330	.379	90	-7	15	13	-5	.991	10	O-78,2-27,S/31	-1.1
1978	SD-N	128	352	36	80	10	2	3	26	35	37	.227	.303	.293	73	-13	11	6	-0	.991	3	O-77,2-40,31	-1.1
1979	LA-N	141	406	47	104	15	4	5	44	41	49	.256	.332	.350	87	-6	18	5	2	.996	2	*O-119,3-18/2S1	-0.6
1980	LA-N	117	297	32	79	18	3	1	22	26	48	.266	.327	.357	93	-3	7	9	-3	.987	-1	O-52,S-49,2/C3	-0.4
1981	*LA-N	80	218	25	54	4	0	4	24	25	31	.248	.325	.321	87	-3	7	2	1	.986	-10	2-30,S-26,O3	-1.0
1982	LA-N	66	98	13	26	2	1	0	2	10	12	.265	.333	.306	82	-2	2	3	-1	1.000	-7	O-28,2-18,3/S	-1.0
1983	*LA-N	118	192	38	48	6	6	2	8	27	36	.250	.348	.375	101	1	9	3	1	.990	-12	O-82,S-13/23	-1.1
1984	Mon-N	108	243	26	62	12	2	0	20	20	33	.255	.312	.321	82	-6	0	4	-2	.963	-38	S-62,O-48,2/31	-4.4
	Cal-A	14	29	3	4	0	1	0	2	3	4	.138	.219	.207	19	-3	0	0	0	.889	-5	/O-7,S-4,3	-0.8
1985	Phi-N	52	92	16	19	2	0	4	12	11	14	.207	.291	.359	79	-3	2	0	-1	.906	-8	S-21/O-7,C23	-0.9
Total	15	1597	4677	585	1163	154	54	43	370	456	593	.249	.319	.332	83	-105	140	92	-13	.970	-94	2-608,O-542,S3/1C	-17.6

■ FRANK THOMAS
Thomas, Frank Edward "The Big Hurt" b: 5/27/68, Columbus, Ga. BR/TR, 6'5", 240 lbs. Deb: 8/2/90

1990	Chi-A	60	191	39	63	11	3	7	31	44	54	.330	.460	.529	180	23	0	1	-1	.989	-5	1-51/D-8	1.4
1991	Chi-A	158	559	104	178	31	2	32	109	**138**	112	.318	**.454**	.553	**181**	69	1	2	-1	.996	-4	*D-101,1-56	5.5
1992	Chi-A	160	573	108	185	**46**	2	24	115	**122**	88	.323	**.446**	.536	176	64	6	3	0	.992	-10	*1-158/D-2	4.3
1993	*Chi-A★	153	549	106	174	36	0	41	128	112	54	.317	.434	.607	180	66	4	2	0	.989	-9	*1-150/D-4	4.3
1994	Chi-A★	113	399	**106**	141	34	1	38	101	**109**	61	.353	**.494**	**.729**	212	73	2	3	-1	.991	6	1-99/D-13	**5.0**
Total	5	644	2271	463	741	158	8	142	484	525	369	.326	.455	.590	186	295	13	11	-3	.991	-35	1-514,D-128	20.5

■ FRANK THOMAS
Thomas, Frank Joseph b: 6/11/29, Pittsburgh, Pa. BR/TR, 6'3", 205 lbs. Deb: 8/17/51

1951	Pit-N	39	148	21	39	9	2	2	16	9	15	.264	.306	.392	84	-4	0	2	-1	1.000	1	O-37	-0.5
1952	Pit-N	6	21	1	2	0	0	0	0	2	5	.095	.136	.095	-34	-4	0	0		1.000	-0	/O-5	-0.5
1953	Pit-N	128	455	68	116	22	1	30	102	50	93	.255	.331	.505	115	8	1	2	-1	.976	10	*O-118	1.2
1954	Pit-N★	153	577	81	172	32	7	23	94	51	74	.298	.365	.497	124	19	3	2	-0	.989	12	*O-153	2.4
1955	Pit-N★	142	510	72	125	16	2	25	72	60	76	.245	.327	.431	101	-0	2	0	1	.984	-0	*O-139	-0.6
1956	Pit-N	157	588	69	166	24	3	25	80	36	61	.282	.329	.461	112	4	8	0	5	.942	-8	*3-111,O-56/2	-0.3
1957	Pit-N	151	594	72	172	30	1	23	89	44	66	.290	.342	.460	116	12	3	1	0	.977	-1	1-71,O-59,3	0.5
1958	Pit-N★	149	562	89	158	26	4	35	109	42	79	.281	.339	.528	129	21	3	0	-1	.926	-32	*3-139/O-8,1	-1.1
1959	Cin-N	108	374	41	84	18	2	12	47	27	56	.225	.282	.380	72	-16	0	2	-1	.927	-13	3-64,O-33,1	-3.3

YEAR	TM/L	G	AB	R	H	2B	3B	HR	RBI	BB	SO	AVG	OBP	SLG	PRO+	BR/A	SB	CS	SBR	FA	FR	G/POS	TPR
1960	Chi-N	135	479	54	114	12	1	21	64	28	74	.238	.280	.399	84	-12	1	0	0	.983	-10	1-50,O-49,3	-2.8
1961	Chi-N	15	50	7	13	2	0	2	6	2	8	.260	.288	.420	84	-1	0	0	0	1.000	-1	O-10/1-6	-0.3
	Mil-N	124	423	58	120	13	3	25	67	29	70	.284	.338	.506	128	15	2	4	-2	.954	-0	*O-109,1-11	0.7
	Yr	139	473	65	133	15	3	27	73	31	78	.281	.333	.497	123	14	2	4	-2	.956	-1	*O-119,1-17	0.4
1962	NY-N	156	571	69	152	23	3	34	94	48	95	.266	.332	.496	117	12	2	1	0	.962	8	*O-126,1-11,3	1.1
1963	NY-N	126	420	34	109	9	1	15	60	33	48	.260	.318	.393	102	1	0	0	0	.988	5	O-96,1-15/3	0.0
1964	NY-N	60	197	19	50	6	1	3	19	10	29	.254	.297	.340	81	-5	1	1	-0	1.000	4	O-31,1-19/3	-0.4
	Phi-N	39	143	20	42	11	0	7	26	5	12	.294	.318	.517	132	5	0	1	-1	.976	1	1-36	0.4
	Yr	99	340	39	92	17	1	10	45	15	41	.271	.305	.415	103	0	1	2	-1	.982	5	1-55,O-31/3	0.0
1965	Phi-N	35	77	7	20	4	0	1	7	4	10	.260	.296	.351	83	-2	0	0	0	1.000	-3	O-12,1-11/3	-0.6
	Hou-N	23	58	7	10	2	0	3	9	3	15	.172	.213	.362	63	-3	0	0	0	.984	-2	1-16/3-2,O	-0.6
	Mil-N	15	33	3	7	3	0	0	1	2	11	.212	.257	.303	57	-2	0	0	0	.979	-1	/1-6,O-3	-0.3
	Yr	73	168	17	37	9	0	4	17	9	36	.220	.260	.345	71	-7	0	0	0	.985	-6	1-33,O-16/3	-1.5
1966	Chi-N	5	5	0	0	0	0	0	0	0	0	.000	.000	.000	-99	-1	0	0	0	.000	0	H	-0.1
Total	16	1766	6285	792	1671	262	31	286	962	484	894	.266	.323	.454	108	52	15	22	-9	.978	-31	*O-1045,3-394,1/2	-5.1

■ FRED THOMAS
Thomas, Frederick Harvey "Tommy" b: 12/19/1892, Milwaukee, Wis. d: 1/15/86, Rice Lake, Wis. BR/TR, 5'10", 160 lbs. Deb: 4/22/18

YEAR	TM/L	G	AB	R	H	2B	3B	HR	RBI	BB	SO	AVG	OBP	SLG	PRO+	BR/A	SB	CS	SBR	FA	FR	G/POS	TPR
1918	*Bos-A	44	144	19	37	2	1	1	11	15	20	.257	.331	.306	94	-1	4			.968	5	3-41/S-1	0.6
1919	Phi-A	124	453	42	96	11	10	2	23	43	52	.212	.283	.294	61	-24	12			.945	-5	*3-124	-2.5
1920	Phi-A	76	255	27	59	6	3	1	11	26	17	.231	.307	.290	58	-15	8	4	0	.960	1	3-61,S-12	-1.0
	Was-A	3	7	0	1	0	0	0	0	0	1	.143	.143	.143	-25	-1	0	1	-1	1.000	2	/3-2	0.0
	Yr	79	262	27	60	6	3	1	11	26	18	.229	.303	.286	56	-16	8	5	-1	.962	3	3-63,S-12	-1.0
Total	3	247	859	88	193	19	14	4	45	84	90	.225	.297	.293	65	-41	24	5		.954	3	3-228/S-13	-2.9

■ GEORGE THOMAS
Thomas, George Edward b: 11/29/37, Minneapolis, Minn. BR/TR, 6'3.5", 190 lbs. Deb: 9/11/57 C

YEAR	TM/L	G	AB	R	H	2B	3B	HR	RBI	BB	SO	AVG	OBP	SLG	PRO+	BR/A	SB	CS	SBR	FA	FR	G/POS	TPR
1957	Det-A	1	1	0	0	0	0	0	0	0	1	.000	.000	.000	-97	-0	0	0	0	.000	-0	/3-1	-0.1
1958	Det-A	1	1	0	0	0	0	0	0	0	0	—	—	—	—	0	0	0	0	.000	-0	/O-1	0.0
1961	Det-A	17	6	2	0	0	0	0	0	0	4	.000	.000	.000	-97	-2	0	0	0	.000	0	/O-2,S-1	-0.1
	LA-A	79	282	39	79	12	1	13	59	21	66	.280	.337	.468	101	-0	3	6	-3	.986	-11	O-45,3-38	-1.6
	Yr	96	288	41	79	12	1	13	59	21	70	.274	.330	.458	99	-1	3	6	-3	.986	-10	O-47,3-38/S	-1.7
1962	LA-A	56	181	13	43	10	2	4	12	21	37	.238	.320	.381	91	-2	0	0	0	.957	1	O-51	-0.4
1963	LA-A	53	167	14	35	7	1	4	15	9	32	.210	.254	.335	68	-8	0	0	0	.941	-2	O-39,3-10/1	-1.2
	Det-A	49	109	13	26	4	1	1	11	11	22	.239	.314	.321	76	-3	2	1	0	1.000	-0	O-40/2-1	-0.7
	Yr	102	276	27	61	11	2	5	26	20	54	.221	.279	.330	71	-11	2	1	0	.974	-4	O-79,3-10/12	-1.9
1964	Det-A	105	308	39	88	15	2	12	44	18	53	.286	.331	.464	117	6	4	1	1	.988	-2	O-90/3-1	0.1
1965	Det-A	79	169	19	36	5	1	3	10	12	39	.213	.273	.308	64	-8	2	3	-1	.948	-3	O-59/2-1	-1.5
1966	Bos-A	69	173	25	41	4	0	5	20	23	33	.237	.333	.347	87	-2	1	0	0	1.000	-0	O-48/3-6,C1	-1.7
1967	*Bos-A	65	89	10	19	2	0	1	6	3	23	.213	.255	.270	51	-5	0	1	-1	.973	-8	O-43/1-3,C	-1.7
1968	Bos-A	12	10	3	2	0	0	1	1	1	3	.200	.273	.500	122	0	1	0	0	1.000	-2	/O-9	-0.1
1969	Bos-A	29	51	9	18	3	1	0	8	3	10	.353	.400	.451	131	2	0	0	0	1.000	-4	O-12,1-10/C3	-0.2
1970	Bos-A	38	99	13	34	8	0	2	13	11	12	.343	.420	.485	139	6	0	0	0	.972	-5	O-26/3-6	0.0
1971	Bos-A	9	13	0	1	0	0	0	1	1	4	.077	.143	.077	-34	-2	0	0	0	1.000	-2	/O-5	-0.4
	Min-A	23	30	4	8	1	0	0	2	4	3	.267	.353	.300	84	-0	0	0	0	1.000	-4	O-11/1-3	-0.5
	Yr	32	43	4	9	1	0	0	3	5	7	.209	.292	.233	48	-3	0	0	0	1.000	-6	O-16/1-3	-0.9
Total	13	685	1688	203	430	71	9	46	202	138	343	.255	.318	.389	92	-20	13	12	-3	.976	-42	O-481/3-64,1C2S	-8.8

■ HERB THOMAS
Thomas, Herbert Mark b: 5/26/02, Sampson City, Fla. d: 12/4/91, Starke, Fla. BR/TR, 5'4.5", 157 lbs. Deb: 8/28/24

YEAR	TM/L	G	AB	R	H	2B	3B	HR	RBI	BB	SO	AVG	OBP	SLG	PRO+	BR/A	SB	CS	SBR	FA	FR	G/POS	TPR
1924	Bos-N	32	127	12	28	4	1	1	8	9	8	.220	.288	.291	58	-8	5	2	0	.983	8	O-32	-0.1
1925	Bos-N	5	17	2	4	0	1	0	0	2	0	.235	.350	.353	88	-0	0	1	-1	.963	-1	/2-5	-0.2
1927	Bos-N	24	74	11	17	6	1	0	6	3	9	.230	.269	.338	67	-4	2			.972	-11	2-17/S-2	-1.4
	NY-N	13	17	2	3	1	1	0	1	1	1	.176	.263	.353	64	-1	0			.900	0	/O-3,S-1	-0.1
	Yr	37	91	13	20	7	2	0	7	4	10	.220	.268	.341	65	-5	2			.972	-11	2-17/S-3,O	-1.5
Total	3	74	235	27	52	11	4	1	15	15	18	.221	.285	.315	63	-13	7	3		.976	-4	/O-35,2-22,S	-1.8

■ IRA THOMAS
Thomas, Ira Felix b: 1/22/1881, Ballston Spa, N.Y. d: 10/11/58, Philadelphia, Pa. BR/TR, 6'2", 200 lbs. Deb: 5/18/06 C

YEAR	TM/L	G	AB	R	H	2B	3B	HR	RBI	BB	SO	AVG	OBP	SLG	PRO+	BR/A	SB	CS	SBR	FA	FR	G/POS	TPR
1906	NY-A	44	115	12	23	1	2	0	15	8		.200	.258	.243	52	-6	2			.938	-5	C-42	-0.8
1907	NY-A	80	208	20	40	5	4	1	24	10		.192	.240	.269	58	-10	5			.953	-5	C-61/1-2	0.3
1908	*Det-A	40	101	6	31	1	0	0	8	5		.307	.346	.317	111	1	0			.972	-5	C-29	-0.2
1909	Phi-A	84	256	22	57	9	3	0	31	18		.223	.292	.281	79	-6	4			**.985**	12	C-84	1.5
1910	*Phi-A	60	180	14	50	8	2	1	19	6		.278	.301	.361	108	1	2			.967	8	C-60	1.5
1911	*Phi-A	103	297	33	81	14	3	0	39	23		.273	.341	.340	92	-3	4			.974	6	*C-103	1.2
1912	Phi-A	48	139	14	30	4	2	1	13	8		.216	.268	.295	63	-7	3			.971	-1	C-48	-0.4
1913	Phi-A	22	53	3	15	4	1	0	6	4	8	.283	.333	.396	116	1	0			.983	3	C-21	0.5
1914	Phi-A	2	3	0	0	0	0	0	0	0		.000	.000	.000	-99	-1	0			1.000	0	/C-1	0.0
1915	Phi-A	1	0	0	0	0	0	0	0	0		—	—	—	—	0	0			1.000	0	/C-1	0.0
Total	10	484	1352	124	327	46	17	3	155	82	8	.242	.296	.308	82	-30	20			.970	26	C-450/1-2	3.6

■ GORMAN THOMAS
Thomas, James Gorman b: 12/12/50, Charleston, S.C. BR/TR, 6'2", 210 lbs. Deb: 4/6/73

YEAR	TM/L	G	AB	R	H	2B	3B	HR	RBI	BB	SO	AVG	OBP	SLG	PRO+	BR/A	SB	CS	SBR	FA	FR	G/POS	TPR
1973	Mil-A	59	155	16	29	7	1	2	11	14	61	.187	.254	.284	53	-10	5	5	-2	.957	-4	O-50/3-1,D	-1.7
1974	Mil-A	17	46	10	12	4	0	2	11	8	15	.261	.370	.478	143	3	4	0	1	1.000	-0	O-13/D-2	0.3
1975	Mil-A	121	240	34	43	12	2	10	28	31	84	.179	.273	.371	80	-7	4	2	0	.961	-13	*O-113/D-6	-2.4
1976	Mil-A	99	227	27	45	9	2	8	36	31	67	.198	.297	.361	94	-2	2	3	-1	.986	-5	*O-137	-1.2
1978	Mil-A	137	452	70	111	24	1	32	86	73	133	.246	.353	.515	141	24	3	4	-2	.983	-4	*O-137	1.4
1979	Mil-A	156	557	97	136	29	0	**45**	123	98	175	.244	.359	.539	138	30	1	5	-3	.991	4	*O-152/D-4	2.3
1980	Mil-A	162	628	78	150	26	1	38	105	58	170	.239	.305	.471	113	8	8	5	-1	.985	3	*O-160/D-2	0.5
1981	*Mil-A★	103	363	54	94	22	0	21	65	50	85	.259	.352	.493	149	22	4	5	-2	.979	3	O-97/D-6	2.1
1982	*Mil-A	158	567	96	139	29	1	**39**	112	84	143	.245	.347	.506	139	30	3	7	-3	.991	10	*O-157	3.2
1983	Mil-A	46	164	21	30	6	1	5	18	23	50	.183	.287	.323	73	-6	2	1	0	.992	-0	O-46	-0.8
	Cle-A	106	371	51	82	17	0	17	51	57	98	.221	.326	.404	96	-2	8	3	-1	.982	12	*O-106	0.7
	Yr	152	535	72	112	23	1	22	69	80	148	.209	.314	.379	90	-7	10	4	-1	.985	11	*O-152	-0.1
1984	Sea-A	35	108	6	17	3	0	1	13	28	27	.157	.336	.213	56	-5	0	3	-2	1.000	-0	O-34/D-1	-1.1
1985	Sea-A	135	484	76	104	16	1	32	87	84	126	.215	.332	.450	111	8	3	2	-0	.000	0	*D-133	0.5
1986	Sea-A	57	170	24	33	4	0	10	26	27	55	.194	.308	.394	89	-3	0	2	-1	.000	0	D-52	-0.5
	Mil-A	44	145	21	26	4	1	6	10	31	50	.179	.324	.345	80	-4	2	2	-1	.980	-1	D-36/1-6	-0.6
	Yr	101	315	45	59	8	1	16	36	58	105	.187	.316	.371	85	-6	3	4	-2	.980	-1	D-88/1-6	-1.1
Total	13	1435	4677	681	1051	212	13	268	782	697	1339	.225	.328	.448	114	86	50	49	-14	.984	1	*O-1159,D-246/13	2.7

■ LEE THOMAS
Thomas, James Leroy b: 2/5/36, Peoria, Ill. BL/TR, 6'2", 198 lbs. Deb: 4/22/61 C

YEAR	TM/L	G	AB	R	H	2B	3B	HR	RBI	BB	SO	AVG	OBP	SLG	PRO+	BR/A	SB	CS	SBR	FA	FR	G/POS	TPR
1961	NY-A	2	2	0	1	0	0	0	0	0	0	.500	.500	.500	177	0	0	0	0	.000	0	H	0.0
	LA-A	130	450	77	128	11	5	24	70	47	74	.284	.355	.491	111	6	0	5	-3	.966	-3	O-86,1-34	-0.7
	Yr	132	452	77	129	11	5	24	70	47	74	.285	.355	.491	111	6	0	5	-3	.966	-3	O-86,1-34	-0.7
1962	LA-A★	160	583	88	169	21	2	26	104	55	74	.290	.357	.467	124	19	6	1	-1	.982	-10	1-90,O-74	0.0
1963	LA-A	149	528	52	116	11	3	6	55	53	82	.220	.302	.316	78	-15	6	0	2	.996	3	*1-104,O-43	-1.8
1964	LA-A	47	172	14	47	8	1	2	24	18	22	.273	.342	.366	108	2	1	0	0	.949	-1	O-47/1-1	-0.1

YEAR	TM/L	G	AB	R	H	2B	3B	HR	RBI	BB	SO	AVG	OBP	SLG	PRO+	BR/A	SB	CS	SBR	FA	FR	G/POS	TPR
	Bos-A	107	401	44	103	19	2	13	42	34	29	.257	.321	.411	97	-2	2	1	0	.995	3	*O-107/1-1	-0.4
	Yr	154	573	58	150	27	3	15	66	52	51	.262	.328	.398	100	0	3	1	0	.981	3	*O-154/1-2	-0.5
1965	Bos-A	151	521	74	141	27	4	22	75	72	42	.271	.362	.464	126	18	6	2	1	.984	5	*1-127,O-20	1.7
1966	Atl-N	39	126	11	25	1	1	6	15	10	15	.198	.263	.365	71	-5	1	1	-0	.987	2	1-36	-0.6
	Chi-N	75	149	15	36	4	0	1	9	14	15	.242	.319	.289	70	-6	0	0	0	.992	-1	1-20,O-17	-0.9
	Yr	114	275	26	61	5	1	7	24	24	30	.222	.294	.324	71	-11	1	1	-0	.989	1	1-56,O-17	-1.5
1967	Chi-N	77	191	16	42	4	1	2	23	15	22	.220	.287	.283	61	-9	1	0	0	.969	-4	O-43,1-10	-1.7
1968	Hou-N	90	201	14	39	4	1	0	11	11	22	.194	.250	.229	45	-13	2	1	0	.973	-1	O-48/1-2	-1.9
Total	8	1027	3324	405	847	111	22	106	428	332	397	.255	.328	.397	99	-6	25	11	1	.975	-7	O-485,1-425	-6.4

■ BUD THOMAS
Thomas, John Tillman b: 3/10/29, Sedalia, Mo. BR/TR, 6′, 180 lbs. Deb: 9/2/51

YEAR	TM/L	G	AB	R	H	2B	3B	HR	RBI	BB	SO	AVG	OBP	SLG	PRO+	BR/A	SB	CS	SBR	FA	FR	G/POS	TPR
1951	StL-A	14	20	3	7	0	0	1	1	0	3	.350	.350	.500	124	1	2	0	1	1.000	1	S-14	0.3

■ KITE THOMAS
Thomas, Keith Marshall b: 4/27/24, Kansas City, Kan. BR/TR, 6′1.5″, 195 lbs. Deb: 4/19/52

YEAR	TM/L	G	AB	R	H	2B	3B	HR	RBI	BB	SO	AVG	OBP	SLG	PRO+	BR/A	SB	CS	SBR	FA	FR	G/POS	TPR
1952	Phi-A	75	116	24	29	6	1	6	18	20	27	.250	.365	.474	124	4	0	1	-1	.957	-3	O-29	-0.1
1953	Phi-A	24	49	1	6	0	0	0	2	3	6	.122	.173	.122	-18	-8	0	0	0	1.000	-0	O-15	-0.9
	Was-A	38	58	10	17	3	2	1	12	11	7	.293	.414	.466	141	4	0	0	0	1.000	-2	/O-8,C-1	0.2
	Yr	62	107	11	23	3	2	1	14	14	13	.215	.311	.308	68	-5	0	0	0	1.000	-2	O-23/C-1	-0.7
Total	2	137	223	35	52	9	3	7	32	34	40	.233	.340	.395	98	-1	0	1	-1	.978	-5	/O-52,C-1	-0.8

■ LEO THOMAS
Thomas, Leo Raymond "Tommy" b: 7/26/23, Turlock, Cal. BR/TR, 5′11.5″, 178 lbs. Deb: 4/29/50

YEAR	TM/L	G	AB	R	H	2B	3B	HR	RBI	BB	SO	AVG	OBP	SLG	PRO+	BR/A	SB	CS	SBR	FA	FR	G/POS	TPR
1950	StL-A	35	121	19	24	6	0	1	9	20	14	.198	.312	.273	49	-9	0	1	-1	.964	-4	3-35	-1.3
1952	StL-A	41	124	12	29	5	1	0	12	17	7	.234	.336	.290	73	-4	2	0	1	.934	4	3-37/S-3,2	0.0
	Chi-A	19	24	1	4	0	0	0	6	6	4	.167	.333	.167	42	-2	0	0	0	.952	1	/3-9	-0.1
	Yr	60	148	13	33	5	1	0	18	23	11	.223	.335	.270	68	-5	2	0	1	.936	4	3-46/S-3,2	-0.1
Total	2	95	269	32	57	11	1	1	27	43	25	.212	.325	.271	59	-15	2	1	0	.948	1	/3-81,S-3,2	-1.4

■ RAY THOMAS
Thomas, Raymond Joseph b: 7/9/10, Dover, N.H. d: 12/6/93, Wilson, N.C. BR/TR, 5′10.5″, 175 lbs. Deb: 7/21/38

YEAR	TM/L	G	AB	R	H	2B	3B	HR	RBI	BB	SO	AVG	OBP	SLG	PRO+	BR/A	SB	CS	SBR	FA	FR	G/POS	TPR
1938	Bro-N	1	3	1	1	0	0	0	0	0	0	.333	.333	.333	82	-0	0			1.000	0	/C-1	0.0

■ RED THOMAS
Thomas, Robert William b: 4/25/1898, Hargrove, Ala. d: 3/29/62, Fremont, Ohio BR/TR, 5′11″, 165 lbs. Deb: 9/13/21

YEAR	TM/L	G	AB	R	H	2B	3B	HR	RBI	BB	SO	AVG	OBP	SLG	PRO+	BR/A	SB	CS	SBR	FA	FR	G/POS	TPR
1921	Chi-N	8	30	5	8	3	0	1	5	4	5	.267	.371	.467	120	1	0	1	-1	.962	1	/O-8	0.1

■ ROY THOMAS
Thomas, Roy Allen b: 3/24/1874, Norristown, Pa. d: 11/20/59, Norristown, Pa. BL/TL, 5′11″, 150 lbs. Deb: 4/14/1899 FC

YEAR	TM/L	G	AB	R	H	2B	3B	HR	RBI	BB	SO	AVG	OBP	SLG	PRO+	BR/A	SB	CS	SBR	FA	FR	G/POS	TPR
1899	Phi-N	150	547	137	178	12	4	0	47	115		.325	.457	.362	130	35	42			.952	4	*O-135,1-14	2.6
1900	Phi-N	140	531	**132**	168	4	3	0	33	**115**		.316	.451	.335	119	26	37			.958	-2	*O-139/P-1	1.2
1901	Phi-N	129	479	102	148	5	2	1	28	**100**		.309	.437	.334	123	22	27			.967	-2	*O-129	1.0
1902	Phi-N	138	500	89	143	4	7	0	24	**107**		.286	**.414**	.322	127	24	17			.974	5	*O-138	2.2
1903	Phi-N	130	477	88	156	11	2	1	27	**107**		.327	**.453**	.365	139	34	17			.963	14	*O-130	3.8
1904	Phi-N	139	496	92	144	6	6	3	29	**102**		.290	.416	.345	141	32	28			.974	15	*O-139	4.0
1905	Phi-N	147	562	118	178	11	6	0	31	93		.317	.417	.358	137	32	23			.983	19	*O-147	4.5
1906	Phi-N	142	493	81	125	10	7	0	16	**107**		.254	.393	.302	117	17	22			**.986**	10	*O-142	2.2
1907	Phi-N	121	419	70	102	15	3	1	23	**83**		.243	.374	.301	113	11	11			.980	5	*O-121	1.3
1908	Phi-N	6	24	2	4	0	0	0	0	2		.167	.231	.167	26	-2	0			1.000	-1	/O-6	-0.3
	Pit-N	102	386	52	99	11	10	1	24	49		.256	.344	.345	121	11	11			.975	5	*O-101	1.3
	Yr	108	410	54	103	11	10	1	24	51		.251	.341	.334	116	9	11			.976	4	*O-107	1.0
1909	Bos-N	82	281	36	74	9	1	0	11	47		.263	.369	.302	104	3	5			.976	-2	O-76	-0.1
1910	Phi-N	23	71	7	13	0	2	0	4	7	5	.183	.266	.239	46	-5	4			.952	-2	O-20	-0.8
1911	Phi-N	17	30	5	5	2	0	0	2	8	6	.167	.342	.233	61	-1	0			1.000	1	O-11	-0.1
Total	13	1470	5296	1011	1537	100	53	7	299	1042	11	.290	.413	.333	124	240	244			.972	71	*O-1434/1-14,P	22.8

■ VALMY THOMAS
Thomas, Valmy b: 10/21/28, Santurce, P.R. BR/TR, 5′9″, 165 lbs. Deb: 4/16/57

YEAR	TM/L	G	AB	R	H	2B	3B	HR	RBI	BB	SO	AVG	OBP	SLG	PRO+	BR/A	SB	CS	SBR	FA	FR	G/POS	TPR
1957	NY-N	88	241	30	60	10	3	6	31	16	29	.249	.298	.390	83	-6	0	0	0	.991	2	C-88	-0.1
1958	SF-N	63	143	14	37	5	0	3	16	13	24	.259	.325	.357	82	-4	1	0	0	.992	2	C-61	0.1
1959	Phi-N	66	140	5	28	2	0	1	7	9	19	.200	.253	.236	31	-14	1	0	0	.980	15	C-65/3-1	0.4
1960	Bal-N	8	16	0	1	0	0	0	0	1	0	.063	.118	.063	-51	-3	0	1	-1	1.000	1	/C-8	-0.3
1961	Cle-A	27	86	7	18	3	0	2	6	6	7	.209	.261	.314	54	-6	0	0	0	.988	9	C-27	0.4
Total	5	252	626	56	144	20	3	12	60	45	79	.230	.285	.329	64	-33	2	1	0	.988	29	C-249/3-1	0.5

■ BILL THOMAS
Thomas, William Miskey b: 12/8/1877, Norristown, Pa. d: 1/14/50, Evansburg, Pa. BR/TR, 5′10″, 190 lbs. Deb: 5/1/02 F

YEAR	TM/L	G	AB	R	H	2B	3B	HR	RBI	BB	SO	AVG	OBP	SLG	PRO+	BR/A	SB	CS	SBR	FA	FR	G/POS	TPR
1902	Phi-N	6	17	1	2	0	0	0	0	1		.118	.167	.118	-12	-2	0			.500	-1	/O-3,1-1,2	-0.4

■ WALT THOMAS
Thomas, William Walter "Tommy" b: 4/28/1884, Foot Of Ten, Pa. d: 6/6/50, Altoona, Pa. BR/TR, 5′8″, Deb: 9/18/08

YEAR	TM/L	G	AB	R	H	2B	3B	HR	RBI	BB	SO	AVG	OBP	SLG	PRO+	BR/A	SB	CS	SBR	FA	FR	G/POS	TPR
1908	Bos-N	5	13	2	2	0	0	0	1	3		.154	.313	.154	51	-1	2			.864	-1	/S-5	-0.2

■ ART THOMASON
Thomason, Arthur Wilson b: 2/12/1889, Liberty, Mo. d: 5/2/44, Kansas City, Mo. BL/TL, 5′8″, 150 lbs. Deb: 8/10/10

YEAR	TM/L	G	AB	R	H	2B	3B	HR	RBI	BB	SO	AVG	OBP	SLG	PRO+	BR/A	SB	CS	SBR	FA	FR	G/POS	TPR
1910	Cle-A	20	70	4	12	0	1	0	2	5		.171	.227	.200	33	-5	3			.944	2	O-20	-0.5

■ GARY THOMASSON
Thomasson, Gary Leah b: 7/29/51, San Diego, Cal. BL/TL, 6′1″, 180 lbs. Deb: 9/5/72

YEAR	TM/L	G	AB	R	H	2B	3B	HR	RBI	BB	SO	AVG	OBP	SLG	PRO+	BR/A	SB	CS	SBR	FA	FR	G/POS	TPR
1972	SF-N	10	27	5	9	1	1	0	1	1	7	.333	.357	.444	125	1	0	0	0	1.000	-2	/1-7,O-2	-0.1
1973	SF-N	112	235	35	67	10	4	4	30	22	43	.285	.346	.413	105	2	2	0	1	.992	-3	1-47,O-43	-0.4
1974	SF-N	120	315	41	77	14	3	2	29	38	56	.244	.326	.327	79	-8	7	1	2	.981	1	O-76,1-15	-1.0
1975	SF-N	114	326	44	74	12	3	7	32	37	48	.227	.308	.347	78	-10	9	3	1	.978	7	O-74,1-17	-0.5
1976	SF-N	103	328	45	85	20	5	8	38	30	45	.259	.323	.424	107	2	8	3	1	.959	-7	O-54,1-39	-0.9
1977	SF-N	145	446	63	114	24	6	17	71	75	102	.256	.364	.451	118	12	16	4	2	.959	-5	*O-113,1-31	0.5
1978	Oak-A	47	154	17	31	4	1	5	16	15	44	.201	.272	.338	74	-6	4	1	1	.969	-4	O-44/1-5	-0.5
	*NY-A	55	116	20	32	4	1	3	20	13	22	.276	.349	.405	114	2	0	2	-1	.972	0	O-50/D-1	0.0
	Yr	102	270	37	63	8	2	8	36	28	66	.233	.305	.367	92	-3	4	3	0	.971	-4	O-94/1-5,D	-0.5
1979	LA-N	115	315	39	78	11	1	14	45	43	70	.248	.340	.422	108	4	4	2	0	.980	-12	*O-100/1-1	-1.2
1980	LA-N	80	111	6	24	3	0	1	12	17	26	.216	.326	.270	69	-4	0	0	0	.974	-6	O-31/1-1	-1.2
Total	9	901	2373	315	591	103	25	61	294	291	463	.249	.332	.391	98	-5	50	16	5	.970	-24	O-587,1-163/D	-5.3

■ JIM THOME
Thome, James Howard b: 8/27/70, Peoria, Ill. BL/TR, 6′3″, 190 lbs. Deb: 9/4/91

YEAR	TM/L	G	AB	R	H	2B	3B	HR	RBI	BB	SO	AVG	OBP	SLG	PRO+	BR/A	SB	CS	SBR	FA	FR	G/POS	TPR
1991	Cle-A	27	98	7	25	4	2	1	9	5	16	.255	.298	.367	82	-2	1	1	-0	.900	1	3-27	-0.2
1992	Cle-A	40	117	8	24	3	1	2	12	10	34	.205	.279	.299	63	-6	2	0	1	.882	-6	3-40	-1.2
1993	Cle-A	47	154	28	41	11	0	7	22	29	36	.266	.396	.474	133	8	2	1	0	.950	-2	3-47	0.6
1994	Cle-A	98	321	58	86	20	1	20	52	46	84	.268	.360	.523	119	8	3	3	-1	.940	-1	3-94	0.7
Total	4	212	690	101	176	38	4	30	95	90	170	.255	.347	.452	109	8	8	5	-1	.926	-8	3-208	-0.1

■ ANDREW THOMPSON
Thompson, Andrew M. b: 1845, Illinois Deb: 4/26/1875 M

YEAR	TM/L	G	AB	R	H	2B	3B	HR	RBI	BB	SO	AVG	OBP	SLG	PRO+	BR/A	SB	CS	SBR	FA	FR	G/POS	TPR
1875	Was-n	11	41	3	4	0	1	0		0		.098	.098	.146	-17	-5						C-10/O-1	-0.4

■ BOBBY THOMPSON
Thompson, Bobby La Rue b: 11/3/53, Charlotte, N.C. BB/TR, 5′11″, 175 lbs. Deb: 4/16/78

YEAR	TM/L	G	AB	R	H	2B	3B	HR	RBI	BB	SO	AVG	OBP	SLG	PRO+	BR/A	SB	CS	SBR	FA	FR	G/POS	TPR
1978	Tex-A	64	120	23	27	3	3	2	12	9	26	.225	.290	.350	79	-3	7	2	1	.982	-5	O-52/D-3	-0.9

YEAR	TM/L	G	AB	R	H	2B	3B	HR	RBI	BB	SO	AVG	OBP	SLG	PRO+	BR/A	SB	CS	SBR	FA	FR	G/POS	TPR
■ TIM THOMPSON								Thompson, Charles Lemoine b: 3/1/24, Coalport, Pa. BL/TR, 5'11", 190 lbs. Deb: 4/28/54 C														
1954	Bro-N	10	13	2	2	1	0	0	1	1	1	.154	.214	.231	15	-2	0	0	0	.909	-1	/C-2,O-1	-0.2
1956	KC-A	92	268	21	73	13	2	1	27	17	23	.272	.321	.347	76	-9	2	4	-2	.981	2	C-68	-0.6
1957	KC-A	81	230	25	47	10	0	7	19	18	26	.204	.262	.339	62	-13	0	0	0	.993	-3	C-62	-1.3
1958	Det-A	4	6	1	1	0	0	0	0	3	2	.167	.444	.167	70	-0	0	0	0	1.000	-1	/C-4	-0.1
Total	4	187	517	49	123	24	2	8	47	39	52	.238	.294	.338	68	-24	2	4	-2	.986	-3	C-136/O-1	-2.2
■ DANNY THOMPSON								Thompson, Danny Leon b: 2/1/47, Wichita, Kan. d: 12/10/76, Rochester, Minn. BR/TR, 6', 183 lbs. Deb: 6/25/70														
1970	*Min-A	96	302	25	66	9	0	0	22	9	39	.219	.236	.248	33	-27	0	0	0	.986	-12	2-81,3-37/S	-3.5
1971	Min-A	48	57	10	15	2	0	0	7	7	12	.263	.344	.298	81	-1	0	0	0	.897	1	3-17/2-3,S	0.0
1972	Min-A	144	573	54	158	22	6	4	48	34	57	.276	.319	.356	96	-3	3	4	-2	.957	-9	*S-144	0.8
1973	Min-A	99	347	29	78	13	2	1	36	16	41	.225	.263	.282	52	-22	1	0	0	.950	7	S-95/3-1,D	-0.4
1974	Min-A	97	264	25	66	6	1	4	25	22	29	.250	.313	.326	81	-6	1	1	-0	.963	-21	S-88/3-5,D	-1.9
1975	Min-A	112	355	25	96	11	2	5	37	18	30	.270	.306	.355	84	-8	0	3	-2	.941	-17	*S-100/3-7,2D	-1.8
1976	Min-A	34	124	9	29	4	0	0	6	3	8	.234	.258	.266	52	-8	1	1	-0	.988	-1	S-34	-0.5
	Tex-A	64	196	12	42	3	0	1	13	13	19	.214	.267	.245	49	-12	2	2	-1	.976	-7	3-39,2-14,S/D	-2.0
	Yr	98	320	21	71	7	0	1	19	16	27	.222	.263	.253	50	-20	3	3	-1	.981	-9	S-44,3-39,2/D	-2.5
Total	7	694	2218	189	550	70	11	15	194	120	235	.248	.289	.310	70	-88	8	11	-4	.956	-60	S-478,3-106/2D	-9.3
■ DON THOMPSON								Thompson, Donald Newlin b: 12/28/23, Swepsonville, N.C. BL/TL, 6', 185 lbs. Deb: 4/24/49														
1949	Bos-N	7	11	0	2	0	0	0	0	0	2	.182	.182	.182	-2	-2	0			.800	-0	/O-2	-0.2
1951	Bro-N	80	118	25	27	3	0	0	6	12	12	.229	.305	.254	51	-8	2	8	-4	.987	-11	O-61	-2.5
1953	*Bro-N	96	153	25	37	5	0	1	12	14	13	.242	.310	.294	57	-9	2	3	-1	.989	-14	O-81	-2.6
1954	Bro-N	34	25	2	1	0	0	0	1	5	5	.040	.226	.040	-25	-5	0	0	0	1.000	-9	O-29	-1.4
Total	4	217	307	52	67	8	0	1	19	31	32	.218	.296	.254	46	-23	4	11		.984	-35	O-173	-6.7
■ FRANK THOMPSON								Thompson, Frank Deb: 9/11/1875														
1875	Atl-n	1	5	1	2	0	0	0		0		.400	.400	.400	204	1						O-1	0.0
■ FRANK THOMPSON								Thompson, Frank E b: 7/2/1895, Springfield, Mo. d: 6/27/40, Jasper Co., Mo. BR/TR, 5'8", 155 lbs. Deb: 5/6/20														
1920	StL-A	22	53	7	9	0	0	0	5	13	10	.170	.343	.170	38	-4	1	1	-0	.878	-4	3-14/2-2	-0.8
■ HANK THOMPSON								Thompson, Henry Curtis b: 12/8/25, Oklahoma City, Okla d: 9/30/69, Fresno, Cal. BL/TR, 5'9", 174 lbs. Deb: 7/17/47														
1947	StL-A	27	78	10	20	1	1	0	5	10	7	.256	.341	.295	76	-2	2	1	0	.957	-8	2-19	0.0
1949	NY-N	75	275	51	77	10	4	9	34	42	30	.280	.377	.444	120	8	5			.961	-8	2-69/3-1	0.4
1950	NY-N	148	512	82	148	17	6	20	91	83	60	.289	.391	.463	123	19	8			.944	5	*3-138,O-10	2.1
1951	*NY-N	87	264	37	62	8	4	8	33	47	23	.235	.342	.386	95	-1	1	2	-1	.925	-14	3-71	-1.8
1952	NY-N	128	423	67	110	13	9	17	67	50	38	.260	.344	.454	119	10	4	4	-1	.979	9	O-72,3-46/2	1.4
1953	NY-N	114	388	80	117	15	8	24	74	60	39	.302	.400	.567	146	27	6	5	-1	.956	-3	*3-101/O-9,2	1.9
1954	*NY-N	136	448	76	118	18	1	26	86	90	58	.263	.392	.482	126	19	3	0	1	.945	-4	*3-130/2-2,O	1.3
1955	NY-N	135	432	65	106	13	1	17	63	84	56	.245	.373	.398	105	5	2	2	-1	.943	7	*3-124/2-7,S	0.7
1956	NY-N	83	183	24	43	9	0	8	29	31	26	.235	.349	.415	105	2	2	1	0	.908	2	3-44,O-10/S	0.2
Total	9	933	3003	492	801	104	34	129	482	493	337	.267	.374	.453	118	87	33	15		.941	-13	3-655,O-102,2/S	6.2
■ HOMER THOMPSON								Thompson, Homer Thomas b: 6/1/1891, Spring City, Tenn. d: 9/12/57, Atlanta, Ga. BR/TR, 5'9", 160 lbs. Deb: 10/5/12 F														
1912	NY-A	1	0	0	0	0	0	0	0	0		—	—	—	—	0	0			.500	-0	/C-1	0.0
■ SHAG THOMPSON								Thompson, James Alfred b: 4/29/1893, Haw River, N.C. d: 1/7/90, Black Mountain, N.C BL/TR, 5'8.5", 165 lbs. Deb: 6/8/14														
1914	Phi-A	16	29	3	5	0	1	0	2	7	8	.172	.351	.241	82	-0	1			.941	1	/O-8	0.1
1915	Phi-A	17	33	5	11	2	0	0	2	4	6	.333	.405	.394	144	2	0	1	-1	1.000	-1	/O-7	0.1
1916	Phi-A	15	17	4	0	0	0	0	0	7	6	.000	.292	.000	-12	-2	1			1.000	-1	/O-8	-0.3
Total	3	48	79	12	16	2	1	0	4	18	20	.203	.357	.253	87	-0	2	1		.978	1	/O-23	-0.1
■ JASON THOMPSON								Thompson, Jason Dolph b: 7/6/54, Hollywood, Cal. BL/TL, 6'3", 210 lbs. Deb: 4/23/76														
1976	Det-A	123	412	45	90	12	1	17	54	68	72	.218	.331	.376	103	2	2	4	-2	.994	2	*1-117	-0.7
1977	Det-A☆	158	585	87	158	24	5	31	105	73	91	.270	.352	.487	120	15	0	1	-1	.991	-7	*1-158	-0.2
1978	Det-A★	153	589	79	169	25	3	26	96	74	96	.287	.367	.472	130	24	0	0	0	.993	-5	*1-151	1.0
1979	Det-A	145	492	58	121	16	1	20	79	70	96	.246	.341	.404	97	-2	2	0	1	.994	9	*1-140	-0.9
1980	Det-A	36	126	10	27	5	0	4	20	13	26	.214	.293	.349	73	-5	0	1	-1	1.000	4	1-36	-0.4
	Cal-A	102	312	59	99	14	0	17	70	70	60	.317	.442	.526	168	33	2	0	1	1.000	-3	1-47,D-45	2.6
	Yr	138	438	69	126	19	0	21	90	83	86	.288	.402	.475	141	28	2	1	0	1.000	1	1-83,D-45	2.2
1981	Pit-N	86	223	36	54	13	0	15	42	59	49	.242	.401	.502	150	17	0	0	0	.989	-1	1-78	1.3
1982	Pit-N★	156	550	87	156	32	0	31	101	101	107	.284	.397	.511	148	37	1	0	0	.993	-1	*1-155	2.9
1983	Pit-N	152	517	70	134	20	1	18	76	99	128	.259	.379	.406	115	14	1	0	0	.993	-6	*1-151	-0.1
1984	Pit-N	154	543	61	138	22	0	17	74	87	73	.254	.359	.389	110	9	0	0	0	.990	-10	*1-152	-1.1
1985	Pit-N	123	402	42	97	17	1	12	61	84	58	.241	.372	.378	111	9	0	0	0	.992	2	*1-114	0.5
1986	Mon-N	30	51	6	10	4	0	0	4	18	12	.196	.406	.275	92	1	0	1	-1	.962	-3	1-15	-0.4
Total	11	1418	4802	640	1253	204	12	208	782	816	862	.261	.369	.438	121	155	8	7	-2	.992	-29	*1-1314/D-45	4.5
■ TUG THOMPSON								Thompson, John P. b: London, Ontario, Canada BL/TR, 5'8", 160 lbs. Deb: 8/31/1882														
1882	Cin-a	1	5	0	1	0	0	0		0		.200	.200	.200	33	-0				.000	-1	/O-1	-0.1
1884	Ind-a	24	97	10	20	3	0	0		2		.206	.222	.237	51	-5				.429	-11	O-12,C-12	-1.4
Total	2	25	102	10	21	3	0	0		2		.206	.221	.235	50	-5				.409	-11	/O-13,C-12	-1.5
■ FRESCO THOMPSON								Thompson, Lafayette Fresco "Tommy" b: 6/6/02, Centreville, Ala. d: 11/20/68, Fullerton, Cal. BR/TR, 5'8", 150 lbs. Deb: 9/5/25														
1925	Pit-N	14	37	4	9	2	1	0	8	4	1	.243	.317	.351	66	-2	2	1	0	.977	-2	2-12	-0.4
1926	NY-N	2	8	1	5	0	0	0	1	2	0	.625	.700	.625	262	2	1			1.000	-1	/2-2	0.1
1927	Phi-N	153	597	78	181	32	14	1	70	34	36	.303	.343	.409	99	-1	19			.963	-5	*2-153	-0.1
1928	Phi-N	152	634	99	182	34	11	3	50	42	27	.287	.332	.390	85	-14	19			.966	9	*2-152	-0.1
1929	Phi-N	148	623	115	202	41	3	4	53	75	34	.324	.398	.419	96	-1	16			.965	12	*2-148	1.5
1930	Phi-N	122	478	77	135	34	4	4	46	35	29	.282	.331	.395	70	-24	7			.955	1	*2-112	-1.5
1931	Bro-N	74	181	26	48	6	1	1	21	23	16	.265	.351	.326	84	-3	5			.946	-3	2-43,S-10/3	-0.4
1932	Bro-N	3	1	0	0	0	0	0	0	0	0	.000	.000	.000	-99	-0	0			.000	0	H	0.0
1934	NY-N	1	1	0	0	0	0	0	0	0	0	.000	.000	.000	-99	-0	0			.000	0	H	0.0
Total	9	669	2560	400	762	149	34	13	249	215	143	.298	.353	.398	88	-45	69	1		.962	10	2-622/S-10,3	-0.9
■ MILT THOMPSON								Thompson, Milton Bernard b: 1/5/59, Washington, D.C. BL/TR, 5'11", 170 lbs. Deb: 9/4/84														
1984	Atl-N	25	99	16	30	1	0	2	4	11	11	.303	.373	.374	103	1	14	2	3	.956	3	O-25	0.6
1985	Atl-N	73	182	17	55	7	2	0	6	7	36	.302	.339	.363	91	-2	9	4	0	.964	-5	O-49	-0.9
1986	Phi-N	96	299	38	75	7	1	6	23	26	62	.251	.313	.341	78	-9	19	4	3	.991	4	O-89	-0.5
1987	Phi-N	150	527	86	159	26	9	7	43	42	87	.302	.353	.425	102	2	46	10	8	.989	9	*O-146	1.3
1988	Phi-N	122	378	53	109	16	2	2	33	39	59	.288	.350	.357	103	3	17	9	-0	.983	5	*O-112	0.4
1989	StL-N	155	545	60	158	28	8	4	68	39	91	.290	.342	.393	106	4	27	8	3	.978	2	*O-147	0.7
1990	StL-N	135	418	42	91	14	7	6	30	39	60	.218	.292	.328	70	-17	25	5	5	.971	-4	*O-116	-2.0
1991	StL-N	115	326	55	100	16	5	6	34	32	53	.307	.369	.442	126	11	16	9	-1	.991	9	O-91	1.9

YEAR	TM/L	G	AB	R	H	2B	3B	HR	RBI	BB	SO	AVG	OBP	SLG	PRO+	BR/A	SB	CS	SBR	FA	FR	G/POS	TPR
1992	StL-N	109	208	31	61	9	1	4	17	16	39	.293	.350	.404	116	4	18	6	2	.974	-3	O-45	0.2
1993	*Phi-N	129	340	42	89	14	2	4	44	40	57	.262	.343	.350	87	-5	9	4	0	.994	-3	*O-106	-1.0
1994	Phi-N	87	220	29	60	7	0	3	30	23	28	.273	.350	.345	83	-5	7	2	1	1.000	-6	O-79	-1.1
	Hou-N	9	21	5	6	0	0	1	3	1	2	.286	.318	.429	94	-0	2	0	1	1.000	-0	/O-6	0.0
	Yr	96	241	34	66	7	0	4	33	24	30	.274	.347	.353	84	-5	9	2	2	1.000	-6	O-85	-1.1
Total	11	1205	3563	474	993	145	37	45	335	315	585	.279	.341	.378	97	-14	209	63	25	.984	10	*O-1011	-0.4

■ ROBBY THOMPSON
Thompson, Robert Randall b: 5/10/62, W.Palm Beach, Fla. BR/TR, 5'11", 170 lbs. Deb: 4/8/86

YEAR	TM/L	G	AB	R	H	2B	3B	HR	RBI	BB	SO	AVG	OBP	SLG	PRO+	BR/A	SB	CS	SBR	FA	FR	G/POS	TPR
1986	SF-N	149	549	73	149	27	3	7	47	42	112	.271	.329	.370	97	-3	12	15	-5	.976	1	*2-149/S-1	-0.2
1987	*SF-N	132	420	62	110	26	5	10	44	40	91	.262	.338	.419	104	2	16	11	-2	.972	6	*2-126	1.2
1988	SF-N†	138	477	66	126	24	6	7	48	40	111	.264	.326	.384	108	4	14	5	1	.978	-9	*2-134	0.2
1989	*SF-N	148	547	91	132	26	11	13	50	51	133	.241	.321	.400	108	5	12	2	2	.989	5	*2-148	1.8
1990	SF-N	144	498	67	122	22	3	15	56	34	96	.245	.301	.392	92	-7	14	4	2	.989	28	*2-142	2.6
1991	SF-N	144	492	74	129	24	5	19	48	63	95	.262	.353	.447	128	18	14	7	0	.985	10	*2-144	3.2
1992	SF-N	128	443	54	115	25	1	14	49	43	75	.260	.336	.415	118	10	5	9	-4	.978	20	*2-120	3.1
1993	SF-N†	128	494	85	154	30	2	19	65	45	97	.312	.377	.496	136	25	10	4	1	.988	11	*2-128	3.9
1994	SF-N	35	129	13	27	8	2	2	7	15	32	.209	.292	.349	69	-6	3	1	0	.989	4	2-35	-0.1
Total	9	1146	4049	585	1064	212	38	106	414	373	842	.263	.334	.412	110	49	100	58	-5	.983	75	*2-1126/S-1	15.7

■ TOMMY THOMPSON
Thompson, Rupert Lockhart b: 5/19/10, Elkhart, Ill. d: 5/24/71, Auburn, Cal. BL/TR, 5'9.5", 155 lbs. Deb: 9/3/33

YEAR	TM/L	G	AB	R	H	2B	3B	HR	RBI	BB	SO	AVG	OBP	SLG	PRO+	BR/A	SB	CS	SBR	FA	FR	G/POS	TPR
1933	Bos-N	24	97	6	18	1	0	0	6	4	6	.186	.218	.196	21	-10	0			1.000	2	O-24	-1.0
1934	Bos-N	105	343	40	91	12	3	0	37	13	19	.265	.300	.318	71	-15	2			.964	10	O-82	-0.8
1935	Bos-N	112	297	34	81	7	1	4	30	36	17	.273	.353	.343	96	-1	2			.965	1	O-85	-0.2
1936	Bos-N	106	266	37	76	9	0	4	36	31	12	.286	.362	.365	103	2	3			1.000	0	O-39,1-25	-0.2
1938	Chi-A	19	18	2	2	0	0	0	2	1	2	.111	.158	.111	-31	-4	0	0	0	1.000	-0	/1-1	-0.3
1939	Chi-A	1	0	0	0	0	0	0	1	0	0	—	—	—	—	-0	0	0	0	.000	0	H	0.0
	StL-A	30	86	23	26	5	0	1	7	23	7	.302	.455	.395	117	4	0	0	0	.977	-0	O-23	0.3
	Yr	31	86	23	26	5	0	1	8	23	7	.302	.455	.395	117	4	0	0	0	.977	-0	O-23	0.3
Total	6	397	1107	142	294	34	4	9	119	108	63	.266	.335	.328	84	-23	7	0		.975	13	O-253/1-26	-2.2

■ RYAN THOMPSON
Thompson, Ryan Orlando b: 11/4/67, Chestertown, Md. BR/TR, 6'3", 200 lbs. Deb: 9/1/92

YEAR	TM/L	G	AB	R	H	2B	3B	HR	RBI	BB	SO	AVG	OBP	SLG	PRO+	BR/A	SB	CS	SBR	FA	FR	G/POS	TPR
1992	NY-N	30	108	15	24	7	1	3	10	8	24	.222	.276	.389	88	-2	2	1	-1	.988	0	O-29	-0.3
1993	NY-N	80	288	34	72	19	2	11	26	19	81	.250	.300	.444	98	-2	2	7	-4	.987	10	O-76	0.3
1994	NY-N	98	334	39	75	14	1	18	59	28	94	.225	.304	.434	89	-6	1	1	-0	.989	8	O-98	0.0
Total	3	208	730	88	171	40	4	32	95	55	199	.234	.299	.432	92	-10	5	10	-5	.988	19	O-203	0.0

■ SAM THOMPSON
Thompson, Samuel Luther "Big Sam" b: 3/5/1860, Danville, Ind. d: 11/7/22, Detroit, Mich. BL/TL, 6'2", 207 lbs. Deb: 7/2/1885 H

YEAR	TM/L	G	AB	R	H	2B	3B	HR	RBI	BB	SO	AVG	OBP	SLG	PRO+	BR/A	SB	CS	SBR	FA	FR	G/POS	TPR
1885	Det-N	63	254	58	77	11	9	7	44	16	22	.303	.344	.500	170	19				.885	7	O-62/3-1	2.2
1886	Det-N	122	503	101	156	18	13	8	89	35	31	.310	.355	.445	138	22	13			.945	10	*O-122	2.6
1887	*Det-N	127	545	118	203	29	23	11	166	32	19	.372	.416	.571	166	47	22			.909	7	*O-127	4.3
1888	Det-N	56	238	51	67	10	8	6	40	23	10	.282	.352	.466	159	16	5			.882	-7	O-56	0.7
1889	Phi-N	128	533	103	158	36	4	20	111	36	22	.296	.348	.492	123	11	24			.901	-7	*O-128	0.1
1890	Phi-N	132	549	116	172	41	9	4	102	42	29	.313	.371	.443	133	21	25			.939	2	*O-132	1.7
1891	Phi-N	133	554	108	163	23	10	7	90	52	20	.294	.363	.410	122	15	29			.937	19	*O-133	2.6
1892	Phi-N	153	609	109	186	28	11	9	104	59	19	.305	.377	.432	145	33	28			.937	4	*O-153	2.8
1893	Phi-N	131	600	130	222	37	13	11	126	50	17	.370	.424	.530	153	44	18			.931	-11	*O-131/1-1	2.1
1894	Phi-N	99	437	108	178	29	27	13	141	40	13	.407	.458	.686	177	53	24			.977	-4	*O-99	3.2
1895	Phi-N	119	538	131	211	45	21	18	165	31	11	.392	.430	.654	177	56	27			.943	12	*O-118	4.7
1896	Phi-N	119	517	103	154	28	7	12	100	28	13	.298	.341	.449	109	4	12			.974	18	*O-119	1.0
1897	Phi-N	3	13	2	3	0	1	0	3	1		.231	.286	.385	78	-0				.833	1	/O-3	-0.1
1898	Phi-N	14	63	14	22	5	3	1	15	4		.349	.388	.571	182	6	2			1.000	2	O-14	0.7
1906	Det-A	8	31	4	7	0	1	0	3	1		.226	.250	.290	67	-1	0			1.000	-0	/O-8	-0.2
Total	15	1407	5984	1256	1979	340	160	127	1299	450	226	.331	.384	.505	146	344	229			.935	53	*O-1405/1-1,3	28.4

■ SCOT THOMPSON
Thompson, Vernon Scot b: 12/7/55, Grove City, Pa. BL/TL, 6'3", 195 lbs. Deb: 9/3/78

YEAR	TM/L	G	AB	R	H	2B	3B	HR	RBI	BB	SO	AVG	OBP	SLG	PRO+	BR/A	SB	CS	SBR	FA	FR	G/POS	TPR
1978	Chi-N	19	36	7	15	3	0	0	2	2	4	.417	.447	.500	147	2	0	0	0	1.000	-2	/O-5,1-2	0.0
1979	Chi-N	128	346	36	100	13	5	2	29	17	37	.289	.324	.373	82	-9	4	3	-1	.971	-9	*O-100	-2.3
1980	Chi-N	102	226	26	48	10	1	2	13	28	31	.212	.302	.292	62	-11	6	6	-2	.963	-6	O-66,1-12	-2.2
1981	Chi-N	57	115	8	19	5	0	0	8	7	8	.165	.213	.209	19	-12	2	0	1	.980	-5	O-30/1-3	-1.9
1982	Chi-N	49	74	11	27	5	1	0	7	5	4	.365	.405	.459	138	4	0	1	-1	1.000	-1	O-23/1-4	0.2
1983	Chi-N	53	88	4	17	3	1	0	10	3	14	.193	.220	.250	28	-9	0	0	0	1.000	-5	O-29/1-1	-1.5
1984	SF-N	120	245	30	75	7	1	1	31	30	26	.306	.382	.355	112	5	5	3	-0	.998	-1	1-87/O-6	0.0
1985	SF-N	64	111	8	23	5	0	0	6	2	10	.207	.221	.252	34	-10	0	0	0	.995	2	1-24	-1.0
	Mon-N	34	32	2	9	1	0	0	4	3	7	.281	.343	.313	90	-0	0	0	0	1.000	-0	/1-3,O-3	-0.1
	Yr	98	143	10	32	6	0	0	10	5	17	.224	.250	.266	47	-10	0	0	0	.995	2	1-27/O-3	-1.1
Total	8	626	1273	132	333	52	9	5	110	97	141	.262	.315	.328	76	-40	17	13	-3	.973	-27	O-262,1-136	-8.8

■ BOBBY THOMSON
Thomson, Robert Brown "The Staten Island Scot" b: 10/25/23, Glasgow, Scotland BR/TR, 6'2", 185 lbs. Deb: 9/9/46

YEAR	TM/L	G	AB	R	H	2B	3B	HR	RBI	BB	SO	AVG	OBP	SLG	PRO+	BR/A	SB	CS	SBR	FA	FR	G/POS	TPR
1946	NY-N	18	54	8	17	4	1	2	9	4	5	.315	.362	.537	152	3	0			.935	0	3-16	0.4
1947	NY-N	138	545	105	154	26	5	29	85	40	78	.283	.336	.508	121	13	1			.980	9	*O-127/2-9	1.5
1948	NY-N★	138	471	75	117	20	2	16	63	20	77	.248	.296	.401	87	-11	2			.970	6	*O-125	-1.1
1949	NY-N★	156	641	99	198	35	9	27	109	44	45	.309	.355	.518	132	26	10			.982	20	*O-156	3.6
1950	NY-N	149	563	79	142	27	7	25	85	55	45	.252	.324	.449	101	-1	3			.978	10	*O-149	0.3
1951	*NY-N	148	518	89	152	27	8	32	101	73	57	.293	.385	.562	150	36	5	5	-2	.966	-11	O-77,3-69	2.0
1952	NY-N★	153	608	89	164	29	14	24	108	52	74	.270	.331	.482	122	16	5	2	0	.940	-7	3-91,O-63	0.5
1953	NY-N	154	608	80	175	22	6	26	106	43	57	.288	.338	.472	106	4	4	2	0	.983	3	*O-154	0.1
1954	Mil-N	43	99	7	23	8	2	2	15	12	29	.232	.315	.323	71	-4	0	0	0	.980	1	O-26	-0.5
1955	Mil-N	101	343	40	88	12	3	12	56	34	52	.257	.324	.414	99	-1	2	1	0	.969	0	O-91	-0.5
1956	Mil-N	142	451	59	106	10	4	20	74	43	75	.235	.304	.408	95	-5	2	4	-2	.974	-4	*O-136/3-3	-1.7
1957	Mil-N	41	148	15	35	5	3	4	23	8	27	.236	.285	.392	86	-4	2	1	0	.988	-1	O-38	-0.7
	NY-N	81	215	24	52	7	4	8	38	19	39	.242	.303	.423	93	-3	1	2	-1	.992	-4	O-71/3-1	-1.1
	Yr	122	363	39	87	12	7	12	61	27	66	.240	.296	.410	90	-6	3	3	-1	.990	-5	*O-109/3-1	-1.8
1958	Chi-N	152	547	67	155	27	5	21	82	56	76	.283	.354	.466	117	13	0	4	-1	.989	4	*O-148/3-4	0.8
1959	Chi-N	122	374	55	97	15	2	11	52	35	50	.259	.326	.398	93	-4	1	0	0	.987	-7	*O-116	0.0
1960	Bos-A	40	114	12	30	3	1	5	20	11	15	.263	.328	.439	102	2	0	0	0	.971	2	O-27/1-1	0.0
	Bal-A	3	6	0	0	0	0	0	0	0	3	.000	.000	.000	-99	-2	0	0	0	.000	-1	/O-2	-0.3
	Yr	43	120	12	30	3	1	5	20	11	18	.250	.313	.417	93	-0	0	0	0	.971	1	O-29/1-1	-0.3
Total	15	1779	6305	903	1705	267	74	264	1026	559	804	.270	.333	.462	111	77	38	20		.980	20	*O-1506,3-184/21	1.7

■ DICKIE THON
Thon, Richard William b: 6/20/58, South Bend, Ind. BR/TR, 5'11", 175 lbs. Deb: 5/22/79

YEAR	TM/L	G	AB	R	H	2B	3B	HR	RBI	BB	SO	AVG	OBP	SLG	PRO+	BR/A	SB	CS	SBR	FA	FR	G/POS	TPR
1979	*Cal-A	35	56	6	19	3	0	0	5	6	5	.339	.393	.393	117	2	0	0	0	.923	1	2-24/S-8,3	0.4
1980	Cal-A	80	267	32	68	12	2	0	15	10	24	.255	.284	.315	65	-13	7	5	-1	.928	-12	S-22,2-21,D3/1	-2.3
1981	*Hou-N	49	95	13	26	6	0	0	3	9	13	.274	.337	.337	96	-0	6	1	1	.950	-5	2-28,S-13/3	-0.3
1982	Hou-N	136	496	73	137	31	10	3	36	37	48	.276	.328	.397	110	5	37	8	6	.975	5	*S-119/3-8,2	2.9

YEAR	TM/L	G	AB	R	H	2B	3B	HR	RBI	BB	SO	AVG	OBP	SLG	PRO+	BR/A	SB	CS	SBR	FA	FR	G/POS	TPR
1983	Hou-N★	154	619	81	177	28	9	20	79	54	73	.286	.345	.457	128	21	34	16	1	.966	21	*S-154	5.9
1984	Hou-N	5	17	3	6	0	1	0	1	0	4	.353	.389	.471	151	1	0	1	-1	1.000	-0	/S-5	0.1
1985	Hou-N	84	251	26	63	6	1	6	29	18	50	.251	.301	.355	85	-5	8	3	1	.967	7	S-79	0.9
1986	*Hou-N	106	278	24	69	13	1	3	21	29	49	.248	.319	.335	83	-6	6	5	-1	.972	-2	*S-104	-0.3
1987	Hou-N	32	66	6	14	1	0	1	3	16	13	.212	.366	.273	75	-2	3	0	1	.925	-8	S-31	-0.7
1988	SD-N	95	258	36	68	12	2	1	18	33	49	.264	.349	.337	100	1	19	4	3	.954	-20	S-70/2-2,3	-1.1
1989	Phi-N	136	435	45	118	18	4	15	60	33	81	.271	.323	.434	115	7	6	3	0	.972	16	*S-129	3.4
1990	Phi-N	149	552	54	141	20	4	8	48	37	77	.255	.306	.350	80	-15	12	5	1	.964	3	*S-148	0.0
1991	Phi-N	146	539	44	136	18	4	9	44	25	84	.252	.285	.351	79	-16	11	5	0	.969	-8	*S-146	-1.4
1992	Tex-A	95	275	30	68	15	3	4	37	20	40	.247	.298	.367	89	-5	12	2	2	.958	0	S-87	0.3
1993	Mil-N	85	245	23	66	10	1	1	33	22	39	.269	.330	.331	79	-7	6	5	-1	.966	-11	S-28,3-25,2D	-1.7
Total	15	1387	4449	496	1176	193	42	71	435	348	658	.264	.319	.374	95	-33	167	63	12	.965	-14	*S-1143/2-98,3D1	6.1

■ JACK THONEY

Thoney, John "Bullet Jack" (b: John Thoeny) b: 12/8/1879, Ft.Thomas, Ky. d: 10/24/48, Covington, Ky. BR/TR, 5'10", 175 lbs. Deb: 4/26/02

YEAR	TM/L	G	AB	R	H	2B	3B	HR	RBI	BB	SO	AVG	OBP	SLG	PRO+	BR/A	SB	FA	FR	G/POS	TPR
1902	Cle-A	28	105	14	30	7	1	0	11	9		.286	.342	.371	102	0	4	.891	-15	2-14,S-11/O	-1.3
	Bal-A	3	11	1	0	0	0	0	0	1		.000	.083	.000	-72	-3	1	.778	-2	/3-3	-0.4
	Yr	31	116	15	30	7	1	0	11	10		.259	.317	.336	84	-2	5	.891	-17	2-14,S-11/3O	-1.7
1903	Cle-A	32	122	10	25	3	0	1	9	2		.205	.218	.254	42	-9	7	.889	1	O-24/2-5,3	-0.9
1904	Was-A	17	70	6	21	3	0	0	6	1		.300	.310	.343	108	0	2	.860	2	O-17	0.1
	NY-A	36	128	17	24	4	2	0	12	8		.188	.241	.250	53	-7	9	.826	1	3-26,O-10	-0.7
	Yr	53	198	23	45	7	2	0	18	9		.227	.264	.283	71	-7	11	.886	3	O-27,3-26	-0.6
1908	Bos-A	109	416	58	106	5	9	2	30	13		.255	.282	.325	94	-4	16	.948	0	*O-101	0.0
1909	Bos-A	13	40	1	5	1	0	0	3	2		.125	.167	.150	0	-5	2	.960	1	O-10	-0.4
1911	Bos-A	26	20	5	5	0	0	0	2	0		.250	.250	.250	40	-2	1	.000	0	H	-0.3
Total	6	264	912	112	216	23	12	3	73	36		.237	.269	.298	75	-27	42	.929	-4	O-164/3-31,2S	-3.8

■ ANDY THORNTON

Thornton, Andre b: 8/13/49, Tuskegee, Ala. BR/TR, 6'2", 205 lbs. Deb: 7/28/73

YEAR	TM/L	G	AB	R	H	2B	3B	HR	RBI	BB	SO	AVG	OBP	SLG	PRO+	BR/A	SB	CS	SBR	FA	FR	G/POS	TPR
1973	Chi-N	17	35	3	7	3	0	0	2	4	9	.200	.333	.286	68	-1	0	0	0	.989	2	/1-9	0.0
1974	Chi-N	107	303	41	79	16	4	10	46	48	50	.261	.369	.439	120	9	2	1	0	.992	8	1-90/3-1	1.2
1975	Chi-N	120	372	70	109	21	4	18	60	88	63	.293	.433	.516	156	32	3	2	-0	.988	3	*1-113/3-2	2.8
1976	Chi-N	27	85	8	17	6	0	2	14	20	14	.200	.364	.341	93	-0	2	0	1	.987	1	1-25	0.0
	Mon-N	69	183	20	35	5	2	9	24	28	32	.191	.308	.388	93	-2	2	1	0	.994	-0	1-43,O-11	-0.6
	Yr	96	268	28	52	11	2	11	38	48	46	.194	.327	.373	93	-2	4	1	1	.991	0	1-68,O-11	-0.6
1977	Cle-A	131	433	77	114	20	5	28	70	70	82	.263	.379	.527	149	30	3	4	-2	.995	-3	*1-117/D-9	1.9
1978	Cle-A	145	508	97	133	22	4	33	105	93	72	.262	.382	.516	152	37	4	7	-3	.995	5	*1-145	3.0
1979	Cle-A	143	515	89	120	31	1	26	93	90	93	.233	.351	.449	114	11	5	4	-1	.994	-3	*1-130,D-13	-0.1
1981	Cle-A	69	226	22	54	12	0	6	30	23	37	.239	.309	.372	97	-1	3	1	0	.986	-1	D-53,1-11	-0.4
1982	Cle-A★	161	589	90	161	26	1	32	116	109	81	.273	.389	.484	139	34	6	7	-2	1.000	0	*D-152/1-8	2.5
1983	Cle-A	141	508	78	143	27	1	17	77	87	72	.281	.389	.439	123	18	4	2	0	.991	2	*D-114,1-27	1.4
1984	Cle-A★	155	587	91	159	26	0	33	99	91	79	.271	.371	.484	132	27	6	5	-1	.979	-3	*D-144,1-11	2.1
1985	Cle-A	124	461	49	109	13	0	22	88	47	75	.236	.307	.408	94	-4	3	2	-0	.000	0	*D-122	-0.7
1986	Cle-A	120	401	49	92	14	0	17	66	65	67	.229	.338	.392	100	1	4	1	1	.000	0	*D-110	-0.1
1987	Cle-A	36	85	8	10	2	0	0	5	10	25	.118	.211	.141	-4	-13	1	0	0	.000	0	D-21	-1.3
Total	14	1565	5291	792	1342	244	22	253	895	876	851	.254	.364	.452	123	177	48	37	-8	.992	14	D-738,1-729/O3	11.7

■ JOHN THORNTON

Thornton, John b: 1870, Washington, D.C. 5'10.5", 175 lbs. Deb: 8/14/1889

YEAR	TM/L	G	AB	R	H	2B	3B	HR	RBI	BB	SO	AVG	OBP	SLG	PRO+	BR/A	SB	FA	FR	G/POS	TPR
1889	Was-N	1	4	0	0	0	0	0	1	0	1	.000	.000	.000	-99	-1	0	1.000	-0	/P-1	0.0
1891	Phi-N	39	123	7	17	3	0	0	6	2	10	.138	.152	.163	-8	-17	1	.881	-0	P-37/O-3	-0.2
1892	Phi-N	5	13	1	5	0	0	0	2	0	0	.385	.385	.385	133	0	0	.857	-1	/P-3,O-2	-0.1
	StL-N	1	3	0	0	0	0	0	0	0	2	.000	.000	.000	-99	-1	0	.000	-0	/O-1	-0.1
	Yr	6	16	1	5	0	0	0	2	0	2	.313	.313	.313	90	-0	0	.500	-1	/P-3,O-3	-0.2
Total	3	46	143	8	22	3	0	0	9	2	13	.154	.166	.175	-1	-18	1	.881	-1	/P-41,O-6	-0.4

■ LOU THORNTON

Thornton, Louis b: 4/26/63, Montgomery, Ala. BL/TR, 6'2", 185 lbs. Deb: 4/8/85

YEAR	TM/L	G	AB	R	H	2B	3B	HR	RBI	BB	SO	AVG	OBP	SLG	PRO+	BR/A	SB	CS	SBR	FA	FR	G/POS	TPR
1985	*Tor-A	56	72	18	17	1	1	1	8	2	24	.236	.267	.319	58	-4	1	0	0	.957	-7	O-35,D-16	-1.1
1987	Tor-A	12	2	5	1	0	0	0	1	0	0	.500	.667	.500	212	0	0	1	-1	.000	-4	/O-4,D-6	-0.2
1988	Tor-A	11	2	1	0	0	0	0	0	0	0	.000	.000	.000	-99	-1	0	0	0	1.000	-4	O-10/D-1	-0.5
1989	NY-N	13	13	5	4	1	0	0	1	0	1	.308	.308	.385	102	-0	2	0	1	1.000	-1	/O-6	0.0
1990	NY-N	3	0	0	0	0	0	0	0	0	0	—	—	—			0			1.000	-1	/O-2	-0.1
Total	5	95	89	29	22	2	1	1	9	3	25	.247	.280	.326	65	-4	3	1	0	.965	-13	/O-57,D-23	-1.9

■ OTIS THORNTON

Thornton, Otis Benjamin b: 6/30/45, Docena, Ala. BR/TR, 6'1", 186 lbs. Deb: 7/6/73

YEAR	TM/L	G	AB	R	H	2B	3B	HR	RBI	BB	SO	AVG	OBP	SLG	PRO+	BR/A	SB	CS	SBR	FA	FR	G/POS	TPR
1973	Hou-N	2	3	0	0	0	0	0	1	0	2	.000	.000	.000	-99	-1	0	0	0	1.000	0	/C-2	-0.1

■ WALTER THORNTON

Thornton, Walter Miller b: 2/18/1875, Lewiston, Maine d: 7/14/60, Los Angeles, Cal. BL/TL, 6'1", 180 lbs. Deb: 7/1/1895

YEAR	TM/L	G	AB	R	H	2B	3B	HR	RBI	BB	SO	AVG	OBP	SLG	PRO+	BR/A	SB	FA	FR	G/POS	TPR
1895	Chi-N	8	22	4	7	1	0	1	7	3	1	.318	.400	.500	123	1	0	.900	-1	/P-7,1-1	0.0
1896	Chi-N	9	22	6	8	0	1	0	1	5	2	.364	.481	.455	142	2	2	.800	-3	/P-5,O-3	0.0
1897	Chi-N	75	265	39	85	9	6	0	55	30		.321	.402	.400	108	4	13	.781	-11	O-59,P-16	-1.0
1898	Chi-N	62	210	34	62	5	2	0	14	22		.295	.342	.338	101	1	8	.877	-3	O-34,P-28	-0.3
Total	4	154	519	83	162	15	9	1	77	60	3	.312	.390	.382	108	7	23	.821	-15	/O-96,P-56,1	-1.3

■ BOB THORPE

Thorpe, Benjamin Robert b: 11/19/26, Caryville, Fla. BR/TR, 6'1.5", 190 lbs. Deb: 4/19/51

YEAR	TM/L	G	AB	R	H	2B	3B	HR	RBI	BB	SO	AVG	OBP	SLG	PRO+	BR/A	SB	CS	SBR	FA	FR	G/POS	TPR
1951	Bos-N	2	2	1	1	0	1	0	1	0	0	.500	.500	1.500	448	1	0	0	0	.000	0	H	0.1
1952	Bos-N	81	292	20	76	8	2	3	26	5	42	.260	.275	.332	70	-13	3	1	0	.972	0	O-72	-1.6
1953	Mil-N	27	37	1	6	1	0	0	5	1	6	.162	.184	.189	-3	-6	0	1	-1	1.000	-5	O-18	-1.1
Total	3	110	331	22	83	9	3	3	32	6	48	.251	.266	.323	64	-17	3	2	-0	.975	-5	/O-90	-2.6

■ JIM THORPE

Thorpe, James Francis b: 5/28/1887, Prague, Okla. d: 3/28/53, Long Beach, Cal. BR/TR, 6'1", 185 lbs. Deb: 4/14/13

YEAR	TM/L	G	AB	R	H	2B	3B	HR	RBI	BB	SO	AVG	OBP	SLG	PRO+	BR/A	SB	CS	SBR	FA	FR	G/POS	TPR
1913	NY-N	19	35	6	5	0	0	1	2	1	9	.143	.167	.229	12	-4	2			.944	-1	/O-9	-0.5
1914	NY-N	30	31	5	6	1	0	0	2	0	4	.194	.194	.226	25	-3	1			.750	-2	/O-4	-0.5
1915	NY-N	17	52	8	12	3	1	0	1	2	16	.231	.259	.327	82	-1	4	2	0	.933	-2	O-15	-0.5
1917	Cin-N	77	251	29	62	2	8	4	36	6	35	.247	.267	.367	98	-2	11			.962	2	O-69	-0.5
	*NY-N	26	57	12	11	3	2	0	4	8	10	.193	.303	.316	93	-0	1			.939	-3	O-18	-0.5
	Yr	103	308	41	73	5	10	4	40	14	45	.237	.275	.357	97	-2	12			.958	-1	O-87	-1.0
1918	NY-N	58	113	15	28	4	4	1	11	4	18	.248	.286	.381	105	-1	3			.983	-12	O-44	-1.5
1919	NY-N	2	3	0	1	0	0	0	0	0	0	.333	.333	.333	102	-0	0			1.000	-1	/O-2	-0.1
	Bos-N	60	156	16	51	7	3	1	25	6	30	.327	.360	.429	143	7	7			.926	-7	O-38/1-2	-0.2
	Yr	62	159	16	52	7	3	1	26	6	30	.327	.359	.428	142	7	7			.928	-7	O-40/1-2	-0.3
Total	6	289	698	91	176	20	18	7	82	27	122	.252	.286	.362	99	-3	29	2		.951	-25	O-199/1-2	-4.3

■ BUCK THRASHER

Thrasher, Frank Edward b: 8/6/1889, Watkinsville, Ga. d: 6/12/38, Cleveland, Ohio BL/TR, 5'11", 182 lbs. Deb: 9/27/16

YEAR	TM/L	G	AB	R	H	2B	3B	HR	RBI	BB	SO	AVG	OBP	SLG	PRO+	BR/A	SB	FA	FR	G/POS	TPR
1916	Phi-A	7	29	4	9	2	1	0	4	2	1	.310	.355	.448	148	1	0	1.000	-1	O-7	0.0
1917	Phi-A	23	77	5	18	2	1	0	2	3	12	.234	.272	.286	71	-3	0	.938	-3	O-22	-0.8
Total	2	30	106	9	27	4	2	0	6	5	13	.255	.295	.330	92	-1	0	.951	-4	/O-29	-0.8

■ MARV THRONEBERRY

Throneberry, Marvin Eugene "Marvelous Marv" b: 9/2/33, Collierville, Tenn. d: 6/23/94, Fisherville, Tenn. BL/TL, 6', 197 lbs. Deb: 9/25/55 F

YEAR	TM/L	G	AB	R	H	2B	3B	HR	RBI	BB	SO	AVG	OBP	SLG	PRO+	BR/A	SB	CS	SBR	FA	FR	G/POS	TPR
1955	NY-A	1	2	1	2	1	0	0	3	0	0	1.000	1.000	1.500	574	1	1	0	0	1.000	0	/1-1	0.2
1958	*NY-A	60	150	30	34	5	2	7	19	19	40	.227	.318	.427	107	1	1	1	-0	.991	-1	1-40/O-5	-0.3
1959	NY-A	80	192	27	46	5	0	8	22	18	51	.240	.305	.391	93	-2	0	0	0	.989	-1	1-54,O-13	-0.6
1960	KC-A	104	236	29	59	9	2	11	41	23	60	.250	.317	.445	103	0	0	0	0	.991	1	1-71	-0.4
1961	KC-A	40	130	17	31	2	1	6	24	19	30	.238	.336	.408	96	-1	0	0	0	.996	1	1-30,O-10	-0.2
	Bal-A	56	96	9	20	3	0	5	11	12	20	.208	.296	.396	86	-2	0	0	0	.923	-3	O-15,1-11	-0.6
	Yr	96	226	26	51	5	1	11	35	31	50	.226	.319	.403	93	-3	0	0	0	.991	-2	1-41,O-25	-0.8
1962	Bal-A	9	9	1	0	0	0	0	0	4	6	.000	.308	.000	-9	-1	0	0	0	1.000	-0	/O-2	-0.2
	NY-N	116	357	29	87	11	3	16	49	34	83	.244	.309	.426	94	-4	1	3	-2	.981	4	1-97	-0.8
1963	NY-N	14	14	0	2	1	0	0	1	1	5	.143	.200	.214	19	-1	0	0	0	1.000	0	/1-3	-0.2
Total	7	480	1186	143	281	37	8	53	170	130	295	.237	.313	.416	96	-10	3	4	-2	.987	1	1-307/O-45	-3.1

⊙ FAYE THRONEBERRY

Throneberry, Maynard Faye b: 6/22/31, Fisherville, Tenn. BL/TR, 6', 190 lbs. Deb: 4/15/52 F

YEAR	TM/L	G	AB	R	H	2B	3B	HR	RBI	BB	SO	AVG	OBP	SLG	PRO+	BR/A	SB	CS	SBR	FA	FR	G/POS	TPR
1952	Bos-A	98	310	38	80	11	3	5	23	33	67	.258	.331	.361	86	-6	16	7	1	.955	-0	O-86	-0.9
1955	Bos-A	60	144	20	37	7	3	6	27	14	31	.257	.327	.472	104	-0	0	0	0	.960	1	O-34	-0.1
1956	Bos-A	24	50	6	11	2	0	1	3	3	16	.220	.264	.320	48	-4	0	0	0	.909	-2	O-13	-0.6
1957	Bos-A	1	1	0	0	0	0	0	0	0	1	.000	.000	.000	-95	-0	0	0	0	.000	0	H	0.0
	Was-A	68	195	21	36	8	2	2	12	17	37	.185	.254	.277	45	-15	0	1	-1	.983	-6	O-58	-2.6
	Yr	69	196	21	36	8	2	2	12	17	38	.184	.252	.276	45	-15	0	1	-1	.983	-6	O-58	-2.6
1958	Was-A	44	87	12	16	1	1	4	7	4	28	.184	.245	.356	64	-5	0	1	-1	1.000	-3	O-26	-1.0
1959	Was-A	117	327	36	82	11	2	10	42	33	61	.251	.325	.388	95	-2	6	4	-1	.953	-2	O-86	-0.8
1960	Was-A	85	157	18	39	7	1	1	23	18	33	.248	.330	.325	78	-4	1	1	-0	.947	-3	O-34	-1.0
1961	LA-A	24	31	1	6	1	0	0		5	10	.194	.306	.226	40	-3	0	0	0	1.000	1	O-5	-0.2
Total	8	521	1302	152	307	48	12	29	137	127	284	.236	.309	.358	79	-39	23	14	-2	.962	-15	O-342	-7.2

■ GARY THURMAN

Thurman, Gary Montez b: 11/12/64, Indianapolis, Ind. BR/TR, 5'10", 175 lbs. Deb: 8/30/87

YEAR	TM/L	G	AB	R	H	2B	3B	HR	RBI	BB	SO	AVG	OBP	SLG	PRO+	BR/A	SB	CS	SBR	FA	FR	G/POS	TPR
1987	KC-A	27	81	12	24	2	0	0	5	8	20	.296	.360	.321	81	-2	7	2	1	.971	4	O-27	0.3
1988	KC-A	35	66	6	11	1	0	0	2	4	20	.167	.214	.182	12	-8	5	1	1	.949	-7	O-32/D-1	-1.5
1989	KC-A	72	87	24	17	2	1	0	5	15	26	.195	.314	.241	59	-4	16	0	5	.949	-17	O-60/D-4	-1.8
1990	KC-A	23	60	5	14	3	0	0	3	2	12	.233	.258	.283	52	-4	1	1	-0	1.000	-2	O-21	-0.7
1991	KC-A	80	184	24	51	6	2	0	13	11	42	.277	.321	.359	87	-3	15	5	2	.970	-5	O-72	-0.7
1992	KC-A	88	200	25	49	6	3	0	20	9	34	.245	.281	.305	62	-10	9	6	-1	.986	2	O-67/D-9	-1.0
1993	Det-A	75	89	22	19	2	0	0	13	11	30	.213	.300	.281	58	-5	7	0	2	.950	-12	O-53/D-9	-1.5
Total	7	400	767	118	185	25	6	2	61	60	184	.241	.298	.297	64	-36	60	15	9	.970	-36	O-332/D-23	-6.9

■ BOB THURMAN

Thurman, Robert Burns b: 5/14/17, Wichita, Kan. BL/TL, 6'1", 205 lbs. Deb: 4/14/55

YEAR	TM/L	G	AB	R	H	2B	3B	HR	RBI	BB	SO	AVG	OBP	SLG	PRO+	BR/A	SB	CS	SBR	FA	FR	G/POS	TPR
1955	Cin-N	82	152	19	33	2	3	7	22	17	26	.217	.296	.408	80	-5	0	2	-1	.949	-4	O-36	-1.1
1956	Cin-N	80	139	25	41	5	2	8	22	10	14	.295	.342	.532	123	4	0	0	0	.953	-3	O-29	0.0
1957	Cin-N	74	190	38	47	4	2	16	40	15	33	.247	.306	.542	114	3	0	0	0	.987	0	O-44	0.0
1958	Cin-N	94	178	23	41	7	4	4	20	20	38	.230	.322	.382	81	-5	1	2	-1	.976	2	O-41	-0.6
1959	Cin-N	4	4	1	1	0	0	0	0	0	0	.250	.250	.250	33	-0	0	0	0	.000	0	H	0.0
Total	5	334	663	106	163	18	11	35	106	62	112	.246	.315	.465	99	-3	1	4	-2	.970	-5	O-150	-1.7

■ EDDIE TIEMEYER

Tiemeyer, Edward Carl b: 5/9/1885, Cincinnati, Ohio d: 9/27/46, Cincinnati, Ohio BR/TR, 5'11.5", 185 lbs. Deb: 8/19/06

YEAR	TM/L	G	AB	R	H	2B	3B	HR	RBI	BB	SO	AVG	OBP	SLG	PRO+	BR/A	SB	CS	SBR	FA	FR	G/POS	TPR
1906	Cin-N	5	11	3	2	0	0	0	0		1	.182	.250	.182	33	-1	0			1.000	0	/3-3,P-1	0.0
1907	Cin-N	1	0	1	0	0	0	0	0		1	—	1.000	—	206	0	0			.000	0	H	0.0
1909	NY-A	3	8	1	3	1	0	0	0		1	.375	.444	.500	197	1	0			.962	-1	/1-3	0.0
Total	3	9	19	5	5	1	0	0	0		3	.263	.364	.316	110	0	0			.962	-0	/1-3,3-3,P	0.0

■ MIKE TIERNAN

Tiernan, Michael Joseph "Silent Mike" b: 1/21/1867, Trenton, N.J. d: 11/9/18, New York, N.Y. BL/TL, 5'11", 165 lbs. Deb: 4/30/1887

YEAR	TM/L	G	AB	R	H	2B	3B	HR	RBI	BB	SO	AVG	OBP	SLG	PRO+	BR/A	SB	CS	SBR	FA	FR	G/POS	TPR
1887	NY-N	103	407	82	117	13	12	10	62	32	31	.287	.344	.452	125	14	28			.865	-9	*O-103/P-5	0.3
1888	*NY-N	113	443	75	130	16	8	9	52	42	42	.293	.364	.427	153	28	52			**.960**	-0	*O-113	2.3
1889	*NY-N	122	499	**147**	167	23	14	10	73	**96**	32	.335	.447	.497	163	47	33			.896	-3	*O-122	3.5
1890	NY-N	133	553	132	168	25	21	**13**	59	68	53	.304	.385	**.495**	156	**38**	56			.896	-15	*O-133	1.6
1891	NY-N	134	542	111	166	30	12	**16**	73	69	32	.306	.388	.494	**163**	**43**	53			.901	-9	*O-134	2.7
1892	NY-N	116	450	79	129	16	10	5	66	57	46	.287	.369	.400	135	20	20			.899	-3	*O-116	1.0
1893	NY-N	125	511	114	158	19	12	14	102	72	24	.309	.399	.476	131	23	26			.927	-9	*O-125	0.6
1894	*NY-N	112	424	84	117	19	13	5	77	54	21	.276	.359	.417	87	-9	28			.922	-11	*O-111	-2.1
1895	NY-N	120	476	127	165	23	21	7	70	66	19	.347	.427	.527	149	36	36			.946	-5	*O-119	1.7
1896	NY-N	133	521	132	192	24	16	7	89	77	18	.369	.452	.516	159	48	35			.970	-2	*O-133	2.9
1897	NY-N	127	528	123	174	29	10	5	72	61		.330	.400	.451	128	22	40			.931	-11	*O-127	0.2
1898	NY-N	103	415	90	116	15	11	5	49	43		.280	.357	.405	122	12	19			.973	-12	*O-103	-0.7
1899	NY-N	35	137	17	35	4	2	0	7	10		.255	.306	.314	73	-5	2			.938	-4	O-35	-1.1
Total	13	1476	5906	1313	1834	256	162	106	851	747	318	.311	.392	.463	138	314	428			.924	-92	*O-1474/P-5	12.9

■ COTTON TIERNEY

Tierney, James Arthur b: 2/10/1894, Kansas City, Kan. d: 4/18/53, Kansas City, Mo. BR/TR, 5'8", 175 lbs. Deb: 9/23/20

YEAR	TM/L	G	AB	R	H	2B	3B	HR	RBI	BB	SO	AVG	OBP	SLG	PRO+	BR/A	SB	CS	SBR	FA	FR	G/POS	TPR
1920	Pit-N	12	46	4	11	5	0	0	8	3	4	.239	.286	.348	79	-1	1	1	-0	.964	-2	2-10/S-2	-0.3
1921	Pit-N	117	442	49	132	22	8	3	52	24	31	.299	.338	.405	93	-5	4	6	-2	.965	-27	2-72,3-32/OS	-3.0
1922	Pit-N	122	441	58	152	26	14	7	86	22	40	.345	.378	.515	127	16	7	8	-3	.964	-35	*2-105/O-2,S3	-1.8
1923	Pit-N	29	120	22	35	5	2	2	23	2	10	.292	.309	.417	88	-3	2	1	0	.941	-3	2-29	-0.5
	Phi-N	121	480	68	152	31	1	11	65	24	42	.317	.352	.454	100	-2	3	4	-2	.975	18	*2-115/O-7,3	1.5
	Yr	150	600	90	187	36	3	13	88	26	52	.312	.343	.447	97	-4	5	5	-2	.968	15	*2-144/O-7,3	1.0
1924	Bos-N	136	505	38	131	16	1	6	58	22	37	.259	.296	.331	71	-22	11	8	-2	.964	-1	*2-115,3-22	-2.1
1925	Bro-N	93	265	27	68	14	4	2	39	12	23	.257	.294	.362	68	-13	0	3	-2	.963	-1	3-61/1-1,2	-1.1
Total	6	630	2299	266	681	119	30	31	331	109	187	.296	.332	.415	93	-29	28	31	-10	.966	-50	2-447,3-118/OS1	-7.3

■ BILL TIERNEY

Tierney, William J. b: 5/14/1858, Boston, Mass. d: 9/21/1898, Boston, Mass. Deb: 5/2/1882

YEAR	TM/L	G	AB	R	H	2B	3B	HR	RBI	BB	SO	AVG	OBP	SLG	PRO+	BR/A	SB	CS	SBR	FA	FR	G/POS	TPR
1882	Cin-a	1	5	1	0	0	0	0		0		.000	.000	.000	-95	-1				.917	0	/1-1	-0.1
1884	Bal-U	1	3	0	1	0	0	0		1		.333	.500	.333	118	0				1.000	-0	/O-1	0.0
Total	2	2	8	1	1	0	0	0		1		.125	.222	.125	8	-1				1.000	0	/O-1,1-1	-0.1

■ JOHN TILLEY

Tilley, John C. b: New York, N.Y. BR, 5'7", 154 lbs. Deb: 8/23/1882

YEAR	TM/L	G	AB	R	H	2B	3B	HR	RBI	BB	SO	AVG	OBP	SLG	PRO+	BR/A	SB	CS	SBR	FA	FR	G/POS	TPR
1882	Cle-N	15	56	2	5	1	1	0	4	2	11	.089	.121	.143	-16	-7				.857	2	O-15	-0.5
1884	Tol-a	17	56	5	10	2	0	0	4			.179	.246	.214	50	-3				.632	-4	O-17	-0.7
	StP-U	9	26	2	4	1	0	0		3		.154	.241	.192	36	-3				.938	0	/O-9	-0.3
Total	2	41	138	9	19	4	1	0	4	9	11	.138	.196	.181	20	-13				.818	-2	/O-41	-1.5

■ BOB TILLMAN

Tillman, John Robert b: 3/24/37, Nashville, Tenn. BR/TR, 6'4", 205 lbs. Deb: 4/15/62

YEAR	TM/L	G	AB	R	H	2B	3B	HR	RBI	BB	SO	AVG	OBP	SLG	PRO+	BR/A	SB	CS	SBR	FA	FR	G/POS	TPR
1962	Bos-A	81	249	28	57	6	4	14	38	19	65	.229	.286	.454	93	-4	0	0	0	.983	-4	C-66	-0.5
1963	Bos-A	90	307	24	69	10	2	8	32	34	64	.225	.304	.349	80	-8	0	0	0	.992	1	C-95	-0.4
1964	Bos-A	131	425	43	118	18	1	17	61	49	74	.278	.352	.445	114	9	0	0	0	.989	-8	*C-131	0.7
1965	Bos-A	111	368	20	79	10		6	35	40	69	.215	.292	.307	66	-16	0	0	0	.988	-7	C-106	-1.8
1966	Bos-A	78	204	12	47	9	0	3	24	22	35	.230	.305	.314	71	-7	0	0	0	.990	-3	C-72	-0.7

YEAR	TM/L	G	AB	R	H	2B	3B	HR	RBI	BB	SO	AVG	OBP	SLG	PRO+	BR/A	SB	CS	SBR	FA	FR	G/POS	TPR
1967	Bos-A	30	64	4	12	1	0	1	4	3	18	.188	.224	.250	37	-5	0	0	0	.977	2	C-26	-0.3
	NY-A	22	63	5	16	1	0	2	9	7	17	.254	.329	.365	109	1	0	0	0	.970	0	C-15	0.2
	Yr	52	127	9	28	2	0	3	13	10	35	.220	.277	.307	70	-5	0	0	0	.974	2	C-41	-0.1
1968	Atl-N	86	236	16	52	4	0	5	20	16	55	.220	.278	.301	74	-8	1	0	0	.990	-1	C-75	-0.4
1969	*Atl-N	69	190	18	37	5	0	12	29	18	47	.195	.264	.411	86	-4	0	0	0	.988	-10	C-69	-1.2
1970	Atl-N	71	223	19	53	5	0	11	30	20	66	.238	.300	.408	83	-6	0	0	0	.988	-2	C-70	-0.5
Total	9	775	2329	189	540	68	10	79	282	228	510	.232	.302	.371	85	-49	1	0	0	.988	-31	C-725	-4.9

■ RUSTY TILLMAN
Tillman, Kerry Jerome b: 8/29/60, Jacksonville, Fla. BR/TR, 6', 185 lbs. Deb: 6/6/82

YEAR	TM/L	G	AB	R	H	2B	3B	HR	RBI	BB	SO	AVG	OBP	SLG	PRO+	BR/A	SB	CS	SBR	FA	FR	G/POS	TPR
1982	NY-N	12	13	4	2	1	0	0	0	0	4	.154	.154	.231	6	-2	1	0	0	1.000	-1	/O-3	-0.2
1986	Oak-A	22	39	6	10	1	0	1	6	3	11	.256	.310	.359	88	-1	2	0	1	.952	-3	O-17	-0.4
1988	SF-N	4	4	1	1	0	0	1	3	2	1	.250	.500	1.000	335	1	0	0	0	1.000	-0	/O-1	0.1
Total	3	38	56	11	13	2	0	2	9	5	16	.232	.295	.375	88	-1	3	0	1	.958	-4	/O-21	-0.5

■ BEN TINCUP
Tincup, Austin Ben b: 12/14/1890, Adair, Okla. d: 7/5/80, Claremore, Okla. BL/TR, 6'1", 180 lbs. Deb: 5/22/14 C

YEAR	TM/L	G	AB	R	H	2B	3B	HR	RBI	BB	SO	AVG	OBP	SLG	PRO+	BR/A	SB	CS	SBR	FA	FR	G/POS	TPR
1914	Phi-N	31	53	3	9	1	1	0	1	0	18	.170	.170	.226	16	-6	0			.926	1	P-28	0.0
1915	Phi-N	11	9	1	0	0	0	0	0	0	3	.000	.000	.000	-99	-2	0			1.000	0	P-10	0.0
1916	Phi-N	1	1	0	0	0	0	0	0	0	0	.000	.000	.000	-97	-0	0			.000	0	H	0.0
1918	Phi-N	11	8	0	1	1	0	0	0	0	4	.125	.125	.250	13	-1	0			.800	1	/P-8,O-1	0.0
1928	Chi-N	2	3	0	0	0	0	0	0	0	0	.000	.000	.000	-99	-1	0			1.000	0	/P-2	0.0
Total	5	56	74	4	10	2	1	0	1	0	25	.135	.135	.189	-4	-10	0			.917	2	/P-48,O-1	0.0

■ RON TINGLEY
Tingley, Ronald Irvin b: 5/27/59, Presque Isle, Maine BR/TR, 6'2", 180 lbs. Deb: 9/25/82

YEAR	TM/L	G	AB	R	H	2B	3B	HR	RBI	BB	SO	AVG	OBP	SLG	PRO+	BR/A	SB	CS	SBR	FA	FR	G/POS	TPR
1982	SD-N	8	20	0	2	0	0	0	0	0	7	.100	.100	.100	-46	-4	0	0	0	.957	3	/C-8	-0.1
1988	Cle-A	9	24	1	4	0	0	1	2	2	8	.167	.231	.292	44	-2	0	0	0	1.000	3	/C-9	0.2
1989	Cal-A	4	3	0	1	0	0	0	0	1	0	.333	.500	.333	142	-0	0	0	0	.889	2	/C-4	0.1
1990	Cal-A	5	3	0	0	0	0	0	0	1	1	.000	.250	.000	-25	-0	0	0	0	1.000	1	/C-5	0.0
1991	Cal-A	45	115	11	23	7	0	1	13	8	34	.200	.258	.287	51	-8	1	1	-0	.988	10	C-45	0.4
1992	Cal-A	71	127	15	25	2	1	3	8	13	35	.197	.282	.299	62	-6	0	1	-1	.987	11	C-69	0.7
1993	Cal-A	58	90	7	18	7	0	0	12	9	22	.200	.280	.278	49	-6	1	2	-1	.995	10	C-58	0.4
1994	Fla-N	19	52	4	9	3	1	1	2	5	18	.173	.246	.327	45	-4	0	0	0	.990	2	C-18	-0.1
	Chi-A	5	5	0	0	0	0	0	0	0	0	.000	.000	.000	-99	-1	0	0	0	1.000	1	/C-5	0.0
Total	8	224	439	38	82	19	2	6	37	39	127	.187	.259	.280	47	-32	2	4	-2	.988	42	C-221	1.6

■ JOE TINKER
Tinker, Joseph Bert b: 7/27/1880, Muscotah, Kan. d: 7/27/48, Orlando, Fla. BR/TR, 5'9", 175 lbs. Deb: 4/17/02 MH

YEAR	TM/L	G	AB	R	H	2B	3B	HR	RBI	BB	SO	AVG	OBP	SLG	PRO+	BR/A	SB	CS	SBR	FA	FR	G/POS	TPR
1902	Chi-N	131	494	55	129	19	5	2	54	26		.261	.298	.332	97	-3	27			.906	4	*S-124/3-8	0.9
1903	Chi-N	124	460	67	134	21	7	2	70	37		.291	.345	.380	110	5	27			.906	0	*S-107,3-19	1.0
1904	Chi-N	141	488	55	108	12	13	3	41	29		.221	.268	.318	80	-12	41			.925	19	*S-140/O-1	1.1
1905	Chi-N	149	547	70	135	18	8	2	66	34		.247	.292	.320	79	-15	31			.940	17	*S-149	0.5
1906	*Chi-N	148	523	75	122	18	4	1	64	43		.233	.293	.289	77	-14	30			**.944**	4	*S-147/3-1	-0.6
1907	*Chi-N	117	402	36	89	11	3	1	36	25		.221	.269	.271	65	-17	20			.939	16	*S-113	0.2
1908	*Chi-N	157	548	67	146	22	14	6	68	32		.266	.307	.391	117	8	30			**.958**	30	*S-157	4.8
1909	Chi-N	143	516	56	132	26	11	4	57	17		.256	.280	.372	100	-4	23			**.940**	20	*S-143	2.0
1910	*Chi-N	134	473	48	136	25	9	3	69	24	35	.288	.322	.397	110	3	20			.942	16	*S-132	2.5
1911	Chi-N	144	536	61	149	24	12	4	69	39	31	.278	.327	.390	100	-2	30			**.937**	23	*S-143	3.1
1912	Chi-N	142	550	80	155	24	7	0	75	38	21	.282	.331	.351	87	-11	25			.943	25	*S-142	2.6
1913	Cin-N	110	382	47	121	20	13	1	57	20	26	.317	.352	.445	127	12	10			.968	17	*S-101/3-9M	**3.9**
1914	Chi-F	126	438	50	112	21	7	2	46	38	30	.256	.317	.349	77	-16	19			.947	19	*S-125,M	1.3
1915	Chi-F	31	67	7	18	2	1	0	9	13	5	.269	.387	.328	98	-2	3			.914	-2	S-16/2-5,3M	-0.1
1916	Chi-N	7	10	0	1	0	0	0	1	1	1	.100	.182	.100	-11	-1	0			.909	-0	/S-4,3-2M	-0.2
Total	15	1804	6434	774	1687	263	114	31	782	416	149	.262	.308	.353	94	-66	336			.938	208	*S-1743/3-43,2O	23.0

■ LEE TINSLEY
Tinsley, Lee Owen b: 3/4/69, Shelbyville, Ky. BB/TR, 5'10", 185 lbs. Deb: 4/6/93

YEAR	TM/L	G	AB	R	H	2B	3B	HR	RBI	BB	SO	AVG	OBP	SLG	PRO+	BR/A	SB	CS	SBR	FA	FR	G/POS	TPR
1993	Sea-A	11	19	2	3	1	0	1	2	2	9	.158	.238	.368	60	-1	0	0	0	.900	-1	/O-6,D-2	-0.2
1994	Bos-A	78	144	27	32	4	0	2	14	19	36	.222	.317	.292	55	-10	13	0	4	.991	-5	O-60,D-10	-1.1
Total	2	89	163	29	35	5	0	3	16	21	45	.215	.308	.301	55	-11	13	0	4	.984	-7	/O-66,D-12	-1.3

■ JIM TIPPER
Tipper, James b: 6/18/1849, Middletown, Conn. d: 4/21/1895, New Haven, Conn. 5'5.5", 148 lbs. Deb: 4/26/1872

YEAR	TM/L	G	AB	R	H	2B	3B	HR	RBI	BB	SO	AVG	OBP	SLG	PRO+	BR/A	SB	CS	SBR	FA	FR	G/POS	TPR
1872	Man-n	24	113	23	33	2	0	0	21	0	0	.292	.292	.310	91	-1						O-18/3-6	0.0
1874	Har-n	45	197	35	60	10	0	0		0	0	.305	.305	.355	104	0						*O-45	0.1
1875	NH-n	41	158	10	25	12	0	0		0	0	.158	.158	.158	11	-13						O-41	-1.1
Total	3 n	110	468	68	118	12	0	0		0	0	.252	.252	.278	74	-13						O-104/3-6	-1.0

■ ERIC TIPTON
Tipton, Eric Gordon "Dukie" or "Blue Devil" b: 4/20/15, Petersburg, Va. BR/TR, 5'11", 190 lbs. Deb: 6/9/39

YEAR	TM/L	G	AB	R	H	2B	3B	HR	RBI	BB	SO	AVG	OBP	SLG	PRO+	BR/A	SB	CS	SBR	FA	FR	G/POS	TPR
1939	Phi-A	47	104	12	24	4	2	1	14	13	7	.231	.316	.337	68	-5	2	0	1	.942	-5	O-34	-1.0
1940	Phi-A	2	8	2	1	0	1	0	0	1	1	.125	.222	.375	53	-1	0	0	0	1.000	-0	/O-2	-0.1
1941	Phi-A	1	4	0	2	0	0	0	0	0	0	.500	.500	.500	169	0	0	0	0	1.000	-0	/O-1	0.0
1942	Cin-N	63	207	22	46	5	5	4	18	25	14	.222	.309	.353	94	-2	1			.977	-1	O-58	-0.6
1943	Cin-N	140	493	82	142	26	7	9	49	85	36	.288	.395	.424	138	27	1			.984	-1	*O-139	2.0
1944	Cin-N	140	479	62	144	28	3	3	36	59	32	.301	.380	.390	121	15	5			.983	3	*O-139	1.1
1945	Cin-N	108	331	32	80	17	1	5	34	40	37	.242	.327	.344	89	-5	11			.970	-1	O-83	-1.0
Total	7	501	1626	212	439	80	19	22	151	223	127	.270	.360	.383	112	29	20	0		.977	-6	O-456	0.4

■ JOE TIPTON
Tipton, Joe Hicks b: 2/18/22, McCaysville, Ga. d: 3/1/94, Birmingham, Ala. BR/TR, 5'11", 185 lbs. Deb: 5/2/48

YEAR	TM/L	G	AB	R	H	2B	3B	HR	RBI	BB	SO	AVG	OBP	SLG	PRO+	BR/A	SB	CS	SBR	FA	FR	G/POS	TPR
1948	*Cle-A	47	90	11	26	3	0	1	13	4	10	.289	.333	.356	85	-2	0	0	0	.971	0	C-40	0.0
1949	Chi-A	67	191	20	39	5	3	3	19	27	11	.204	.306	.309	65	-10	1	1	-0	.992	2	C-53	-0.5
1950	Phi-A	64	184	15	49	5	1	6	20	19	16	.266	.335	.402	90	-3	0	0	0	.987	-4	C-59	-0.5
1951	Phi-A	72	213	23	51	9	0	3	20	51	25	.239	.389	.324	92	0	1	1	-0	.969	2	C-72	0.5
1952	Phi-A	23	68	6	13	4	0	3	8	15	10	.191	.337	.382	94	-0	0	0	0	.990	-1	C-23	-0.2
	Cle-A	43	105	15	26	2	0	6	22	21	21	.248	.383	.438	137	6	1	0	0	.971	-8	C-35	-0.1
	Yr	66	173	21	39	6	0	9	30	36	31	.225	.365	.416	119	5	1	0	0	.979	-11	C-58	-0.3
1953	Cle-A	47	109	17	25	2	0	6	13	19	13	.229	.359	.413	111	2	0	0	0	1.000	-7	C-46	-0.4
1954	Was-A	54	157	9	35	6	1	1	10	30	30	.223	.354	.293	83	-2	0	1	-1	.992	5	C-52	0.3
Total	7	417	1117	116	264	36	5	29	125	186	142	.236	.351	.355	91	-11	3	3	-1	.984	-14	C-380	-0.9

■ TOM TISCHINSKI
Tischinski, Thomas Arthur b: 7/12/44, Kansas City, Mo. BR/TR, 5'10", 190 lbs. Deb: 4/11/69

YEAR	TM/L	G	AB	R	H	2B	3B	HR	RBI	BB	SO	AVG	OBP	SLG	PRO+	BR/A	SB	CS	SBR	FA	FR	G/POS	TPR
1969	Min-A	37	47	2	9	0	0	0	2	8	8	.191	.309	.191	42	-3	0	0	0	1.000	0	C-32	-0.3
1970	Min-A	24	46	6	9	0	0	0	2	9	6	.196	.327	.261	63	-2	1	0	0	.990	1	C-22	0.0
1971	Min-A	21	23	0	3	2	0	1	2	1	4	.130	.200	.217	18	-3	0	0	0	.982	3	C-21	0.1
Total	3	82	116	8	21	2	0	1	6	18	18	.181	.296	.224	46	-8	0	0	0	.992	4	/C-75	-0.2

■ JOHN TITUS
Titus, John Franklin "Silent John" b: 2/21/1876, St.Clair, Pa. d: 1/8/43, St.Clair, Pa. BL/TL, 5'9", 156 lbs. Deb: 6/8/03

YEAR	TM/L	G	AB	R	H	2B	3B	HR	RBI	BB	SO	AVG	OBP	SLG	PRO+	BR/A	SB	CS	SBR	FA	FR	G/POS	TPR
1903	Phi-N	72	280	38	80	15	6	2	34	19		.286	.340	.404	115	5	5			.952	3	O-72	0.3
1904	Phi-N	146	504	60	148	25	5	4	55	46		.294	.362	.387	136	22	15			.952	8	*O-140	2.3
1905	Phi-N	147	548	99	169	36	14	2	89	69		.308	.397	.436	154	39	11			.962	9	*O-147	4.1

YEAR	TM/L	G	AB	R	H	2B	3B	HR	RBI	BB	SO	AVG	OBP	SLG	PRO+	BR/A	SB	CS	SBR	FA	FR	G/POS	TPR
1906	Phi-N	145	484	67	129	22	5	1	57	78		.267	.378	.339	124	17	12			.974	7	*O-142	1.9
1907	Phi-N	145	523	72	144	23	12	3	63	47		.275	.345	.382	130	18	9			.928	-5	*O-142	0.9
1908	Phi-N	149	539	75	154	24	5	2	48	53		.286	.365	.360	127	18	27			.963	-3	*O-149	1.1
1909	Phi-N	151	540	69	146	22	6	3	46	66		.270	.367	.350	121	16	23			.971	5	*O-149	1.7
1910	Phi-N	143	535	91	129	26	5	3	35	93	44	.241	.358	.325	96	0	20			.976	1	*O-142	-0.6
1911	Phi-N	76	236	35	67	14	1	8	26	32	16	.284	.372	.453	129	9	3			.979	-1	O-60	0.5
1912	Phi-N	45	157	43	43	9	5	3	22	33	14	.274	.403	.452	125	6	6			.917	-7	O-42	-0.3
	Bos-N	96	345	56	112	23	6	2	48	49	20	.325	.422	.443	134	19	5			.965	-5	O-96	0.9
	Yr	141	502	99	155	32	11	5	70	82	34	.309	.416	.446	131	25	11			.952	-12	O-138	0.6
1913	Bos-N	87	269	33	80	14	2	5	38	35	22	.297	.392	.420	129	12	4			.919	-7	O-75	0.2
Total	11	1402	4960	738	1401	253	72	38	561	620	116	.282	.373	.385	127	181	140			.959	7	*O-1356	13.0

■ JIM TOBIN

Tobin, James Anthony "Abba Dabba" b: 12/27/12, Oakland, Cal. d: 5/19/69, Oakland, Cal. BR/TR, 6', 185 lbs. Deb: 4/30/37 F

YEAR	TM/L	G	AB	R	H	2B	3B	HR	RBI	BB	SO	AVG	OBP	SLG	PRO+	BR/A	SB	CS	SBR	FA	FR	G/POS	TPR
1937	Pit-N	21	34	7	15	4	0	0	6	4	3	.441	.500	.559	187	4	0			.938	-2	P-20	0.0
1938	Pit-N	56	103	8	25	6	1	0	11	9	12	.243	.310	.320	73	-4	0			1.000	-2	P-40	0.0
1939	Pit-N	43	74	9	18	3	1	2	11	2	12	.243	.263	.392	75	-3	0			1.000	1	P-25	0.0
1940	Bos-N	20	43	5	12	3	0	0	3	1	10	.279	.295	.349	82	-1	0			.957	-1	P-15	0.0
1941	Bos-N	43	103	6	19	5	0	0	9	10	31	.184	.257	.233	40	-8	1			.966	4	P-33	0.0
1942	Bos-N	47	114	14	28	2	0	6	15	16	23	.246	.344	.421	126	4	0			.947	6	P-37	0.0
1943	Bos-N	46	107	8	30	4	0	2	12	6	14	.280	.319	.374	101	2	0			.927	2	P-33/1-1	0.0
1944	Bos-N★	62	116	13	22	5	1	2	18	16	28	.190	.288	.302	63	-6	0			.972	7	P-43	0.0
1945	Bos-N	41	77	9	11	3	0	3	12	15	22	.143	.290	.299	64	-4	0			1.000	2	P-27	0.0
	*Det-N	17	25	2	3	0	0	2	5	1	7	.120	.154	.360	44	-2	0	0	0	.950	1	P-14	0.0
Total	9	396	796	81	183	35	3	17	102	80	162	.230	.303	.345	82	-20	1	0		.965	17	P-287/1-1	0.0

■ JOHNNY TOBIN

Tobin, John Martin "Tip" b: 9/15/06, Jamaica Plain, Mass. d: 8/6/83, Rhinebeck, N.Y. BR/TR, 6'3", 187 lbs. Deb: 9/22/32

YEAR	TM/L	G	AB	R	H	2B	3B	HR	RBI	BB	SO	AVG	OBP	SLG	PRO+	BR/A	SB	CS	SBR	FA	FR	G/POS	TPR
1932	NY-N	1	1	0	0	0	0	0	0	0	0	.000	.000	.000	-99	-0	0			.000	0	H	0.0

■ JOHNNY TOBIN

Tobin, John Patrick "Jackie" b: 1/8/21, Oakland, Cal. d: 1/18/82, Oakland, Cal. BL/TR, 6', 165 lbs. Deb: 4/20/45 F

YEAR	TM/L	G	AB	R	H	2B	3B	HR	RBI	BB	SO	AVG	OBP	SLG	PRO+	BR/A	SB	CS	SBR	FA	FR	G/POS	TPR
1945	Bos-A	84	278	25	70	6	2	0	21	26	24	.252	.320	.288	75	-8	2	6	-3	.951	9	3-72/2-5,O	0.0

■ JACK TOBIN

Tobin, John Thomas b: 5/4/1892, St.Louis, Mo. d: 12/10/69, St.Louis, Mo. BL/TL, 5'8", 142 lbs. Deb: 4/16/14 C

YEAR	TM/L	G	AB	R	H	2B	3B	HR	RBI	BB	SO	AVG	OBP	SLG	PRO+	BR/A	SB	CS	SBR	FA	FR	G/POS	TPR
1914	StL-F	139	529	81	143	24	10	7	35	51	53	.270	.340	.393	85	-12	20			.952	5	*O-132	-1.3
1915	StL-F	158	625	92	184	26	13	6	51	68	42	.294	.366	.406	101	2	31			.965	3	*O-158	-0.3
1916	StL-A	77	150	16	32	4	1	0	10	12	13	.213	.272	.253	61	-7	7			.842	-9	O-41	-2.0
1918	StL-A	122	480	59	133	19	5	0	36	48	26	.277	.349	.338	111	7	13			.971	-1	*O-122	-0.1
1919	StL-A	127	486	54	159	22	7	6	57	36	24	.327	.376	.438	125	15	8			.953	2	*O-123	0.9
1920	StL-A	147	593	94	202	34	10	4	62	39	23	.341	.383	.452	117	14	21	13	-2	.960	4	*O-147	0.6
1921	StL-A	150	671	132	236	31	18	8	59	45	22	.352	.395	.487	117	16	7	12	-5	.956	8	*O-150	0.8
1922	StL-A	146	625	122	207	34	8	13	66	56	22	.331	.388	.474	119	17	7	9	-3	.940	-8	*O-145	-0.4
1923	StL-A	151	637	91	202	32	15	13	73	42	13	.317	.363	.476	113	10	8	7	-2	.969	-9	*O-151	-1.1
1924	StL-A	136	569	87	170	30	8	2	48	50	12	.299	.357	.390	87	-11	6	10	-4	.957	2	*O-132	-2.1
1925	StL-A	77	193	25	58	11	0	2	27	9	5	.301	.335	.389	79	-6	2	8	1	1.000	-5	O-39/1-3	-1.2
1926	Was-A	27	33	5	7	0	1	0	3	0	0	.212	.212	.273	26	-4	0	0	0	1.000	-2	/O-7	-0.5
	Bos-A	51	209	26	57	9	0	1	14	16	3	.273	.324	.330	73	-8	6	5	-1	.966	-3	O-51	-1.6
	Yr	78	242	31	64	9	1	1	17	16	3	.264	.310	.322	67	-12	6	5	-1	.970	-5	O-58	-2.1
1927	Bos-A	111	374	52	116	18	3	2	40	36	9	.310	.371	.390	100	0	5	4	-1	.947	-5	O-93	-1.1
Total	13	1619	6174	936	1906	294	99	64	581	508	267	.309	.364	.420	105	33	147	62		.957	-16	*O-1491/1-3	-9.4

■ BILL TOBIN

Tobin, William F. b: 10/10/1854, Hartford, Conn. d: 10/10/12, Hartford, Conn. BL, Deb: 7/21/1880

YEAR	TM/L	G	AB	R	H	2B	3B	HR	RBI	BB	SO	AVG	OBP	SLG	PRO+	BR/A	SB	CS	SBR	FA	FR	G/POS	TPR
1880	Wor-N	5	16	1	2	0	0	0	3	0	5	.125	.125	.125	-14	-2				1.000	-0	/1-5	-0.2
	Tro-N	33	136	14	22	1	1	0	8	4	20	.162	.186	.184	24	-11				.950	-1	1-33	-1.4
	Yr	38	152	15	24	1	1	0	11	4	25	.158	.179	.178	20	-12				.958	-1	1-38	-1.6

■ AL TODD

Todd, Alfred Chester b: 1/7/02, Troy, N.Y. d: 3/8/85, Elmira, N.Y. BR/TR, 6'1", 198 lbs. Deb: 4/25/32

YEAR	TM/L	G	AB	R	H	2B	3B	HR	RBI	BB	SO	AVG	OBP	SLG	PRO+	BR/A	SB	CS	SBR	FA	FR	G/POS	TPR
1932	Phi-N	33	70	8	16	5	0	0	9	1	9	.229	.260	.300	45	-5	1			.899	-4	C-25	-0.9
1933	Phi-N	73	136	13	28	4	0	0	10	4	16	.206	.239	.235	32	-12	1			.983	5	C-34/O-2	-0.6
1934	Phi-N	91	302	33	96	22	2	4	41	10	39	.318	.344	.444	96	-2	3			.976	-2	C-82	-0.1
1935	Phi-N	107	328	40	95	18	3	3	42	19	35	.290	.334	.390	85	-7	3			.968	-12	C-87	-1.4
1936	Pit-N	76	267	28	73	10	5	2	28	11	24	.273	.307	.371	80	-8	4			.976	1	C-70	-0.3
1937	Pit-N	133	514	51	158	18	10	8	86	16	31	.307	.330	.428	104	1	2			.972	-2	*C-128	0.7
1938	Pit-N	133	491	52	130	19	7	7	75	18	31	.265	.296	.375	83	-13	2			.985	10	*C-132	0.4
1939	Bro-N	86	245	28	68	10	0	5	32	13	16	.278	.317	.380	83	-6	1			.985	8	C-73	0.5
1940	Chi-N	104	381	31	97	13	2	6	42	11	29	.255	.283	.346	74	-14	1			.984	-6	*C-104	-1.2
1941	Chi-N	6	6	1	1	0	0	0	0	0	1	.167	.167	.167	-6	-1	0			.000	0	H	-0.1
1943	Chi-N	21	45	1	6	0	0	0	1	1	5	.133	.152	.133	-17	-7	0			.986	4	C-17	-0.3
Total	11	863	2785	286	768	119	29	35	366	104	243	.276	.307	.377	82	-74	18			.977	1	C-752/O-2	-3.3

■ PHIL TODT

Todt, Philip Julius "Hook" b: 8/9/01, St.Louis, Mo. d: 11/15/73, St.Louis, Mo. BL/TL, 6', 175 lbs. Deb: 4/25/24

YEAR	TM/L	G	AB	R	H	2B	3B	HR	RBI	BB	SO	AVG	OBP	SLG	PRO+	BR/A	SB	CS	SBR	FA	FR	G/POS	TPR
1924	Bos-A	52	103	17	27	8	2	1	14	6	9	.262	.309	.408	84	-3	0	1	-1	.983	-3	1-18/O-4	-0.7
1925	Bos-A	141	544	62	151	29	13	11	75	44	29	.278	.343	.439	97	-4	3	2	-0	.991	9	*1-140	-0.9
1926	Bos-A	154	599	56	153	19	12	7	69	40	38	.255	.306	.362	76	-23	2	3	-0	.988	10	*1-154	-2.2
1927	Bos-A	140	516	55	122	22	6	6	52	28	23	.236	.280	.337	61	-32	6	2	1	.991	9	*1-139	-3.0
1928	Bos-A	144	539	61	136	31	8	12	73	26	47	.252	.290	.406	83	-16	6	5	-1	.997	3	*1-144	-2.6
1929	Bos-A	153	534	49	140	38	10	4	64	31	28	.262	.305	.393	80	-17	6	7	-2	.991	3	*1-153	-3.0
1930	Bos-A	111	383	49	103	22	5	11	62	24	33	.269	.312	.439	92	-7	4	1	1	.993	3	*1-104	-1.2
1931	*Phi-A	62	197	23	48	14	2	5	44	8	22	.244	.273	.411	73	-9	1	1	-0	.995	-4	1-52	-1.7
Total	8	957	3415	372	880	183	58	57	453	207	229	.258	.305	.395	81	-111	29	21	-4	.992	24	1-904/O-4	-15.3

■ BOBBY TOLAN

Tolan, Robert b: 11/19/45, Los Angeles, Cal. BL/TL, 5'11", 170 lbs. Deb: 9/3/65 C

YEAR	TM/L	G	AB	R	H	2B	3B	HR	RBI	BB	SO	AVG	OBP	SLG	PRO+	BR/A	SB	CS	SBR	FA	FR	G/POS	TPR
1965	StL-N	17	69	8	13	2	0	0	6	0	4	.188	.200	.217	16	-8	2	1	0	.970	-1	O-17	-1.0
1966	StL-N	43	93	10	16	5	1	1	6	6	15	.172	.238	.280	43	-7	1	2	-1	.952	-1	O-26/1-1	-1.1
1967	*StL-N	110	265	35	67	7	3	6	32	19	43	.253	.313	.370	96	-2	12	7	-1	.992	-9	O-80,1-13	-1.6
1968	*StL-N	92	278	28	64	12	1	5	17	19	42	.230	.272	.335	82	-7	9	5	-0	.967	-2	O-67/1-9	-1.4
1969	Cin-N	152	637	104	194	25	10	21	93	27	92	.305	.348	.474	122	17	26	12	1	.974	11	*O-150	2.0
1970	Cin-N	152	589	112	186	34	6	16	80	62	94	.316	.388	.475	130	25	57	20	5	.978	-6	*O-150	3.0
1972	*Cin-N	149	604	88	171	28	5	8	82	44	88	.283	.338	.386	112	8	42	15	4	.990	13	*O-149	1.9
1973	Cin-N	129	457	42	94	14	2	9	51	27	66	.206	.255	.304	57	-28	15	10	-2	.966	-4	*O-120	-4.1
1974	SD-N	95	357	43	95	16	1	8	40	20	41	.266	.321	.384	101	-1	7	9	-3	.971	-2	O-88	-1.0
1975	SD-N	147	506	58	129	19	5	6	43	28	45	.255	.307	.338	84	-12	11	5	-5	.971	-2	*O-120,1-27	-2.6
1976	*Phi-N	110	272	32	71	7	0	5	35	7	39	.261	.290	.342	76	-9	10	5	0	.992	-12	1-50,O-35	-2.6
1977	Phi-N	15	16	1	2	0	0	0	1	1	4	.125	.176	.125	-17	-3	0	0	-0	.944	-0	/1-5	-0.3
	Pit-N	49	74	7	15	4	0	2	9	4	10	.203	.244	.338	53	-5	1	0	-0	1.000	-0	1-20/O-2	-0.6
	Yr	64	90	8	17	4	0	2	10	5	14	.189	.232	.300	40	-8	1	0	-0	.992	-0	1-25/O-2	-0.9

YEAR	TM/L	G	AB	R	H	2B	3B	HR	RBI	BB	SO	AVG	OBP	SLG	PRO+	BR/A	SB	CS	SBR	FA	FR	G/POS	TPR
1979	SD-N	22	21	2	4	0	1	0	2	0	2	.190	.190	.286	30	-2	0	0	0	1.000	-0	/1-5,O-1	-0.2
Total	13	1282	4238	572	1121	173	34	86	497	258	587	.265	.317	.382	96	-32	193	100	-2	.976	-1	*O-1005,1-130	-9.6

■ JOSE TOLENTINO
Tolentino, Jose (Franco) b: 6/3/61, Mexico City, Mexico   BL/TL, 6'1", 195 lbs.   Deb: 7/28/91

YEAR	TM/L	G	AB	R	H	2B	3B	HR	RBI	BB	SO	AVG	OBP	SLG	PRO+	BR/A	SB	CS	SBR	FA	FR	G/POS	TPR
1991	Hou-N	44	54	6	14	4	0	1	6	4	9	.259	.310	.389	101	-0	0	0	0	.982	1	1-10/O-1	0.1

■ WAYNE TOLLESON
Tolleson, Jimmy Wayne b: 11/22/55, Spartanburg, S.C.   BB/TR, 5'9", 160 lbs.   Deb: 9/1/81

YEAR	TM/L	G	AB	R	H	2B	3B	HR	RBI	BB	SO	AVG	OBP	SLG	PRO+	BR/A	SB	CS	SBR	FA	FR	G/POS	TPR
1981	Tex-A	14	24	6	4	0	0	0	1	1	5	.167	.200	.167	7	-3	2	0	1	1.000	-1	/3-6,S-2	-0.3
1982	Tex-A	38	70	6	8	1	0	0	2	5	14	.114	.173	.129	-16	-11	1	1	-0	.958	5	S-26/3-4,2	-0.5
1983	Tex-A	134	470	64	122	13	2	3	20	40	68	.260	.320	.315	77	-14	33	10	4	.972	-10	*2-112,S-26/D	-1.3
1984	Tex-A	118	338	35	72	9	2	0	9	27	47	.213	.277	.251	46	-24	22	4	4	.979	-7	*2-109/S-7,3OD	-2.3
1985	Tex-A	123	323	45	101	9	5	1	18	21	46	.313	.355	.381	100	0	21	12	-1	.972	-4	S-81,2-29,3/D	0.3
1986	Chi-A	81	260	39	65	7	3	3	29	38	43	.250	.346	.335	84	-5	13	6	0	.955	-10	3-65,S-18/OD	-1.5
	NY-A	60	215	22	61	9	2	0	14	14	33	.284	.333	.344	86	-4	4	4	-1	.981	-4	S-56/3-7,2	0.6
	Yr	141	475	61	126	16	5	3	43	52	76	.265	.340	.339	85	-9	17	10	-1	.981	-4	S-74,3-72/2OD	-0.9
1987	NY-A	121	349	48	77	4	0	1	22	43	72	.221	.306	.241	48	-25	5	3	-0	.970	-3	*S-119/3-3	-1.7
1988	NY-A	21	59	8	15	2	0	0	5	8	12	.254	.343	.288	79	-1	1	0	0	.981	6	2-12,3-10/S	0.5
1989	NY-A	80	140	16	23	5	2	1	9	16	23	.164	.255	.250	43	-10	5	1	1	.912	10	3-28,S-28,2D	0.1
1990	NY-A	73	74	12	11	1	1	0	4	6	21	.149	.213	.189	13	-9	1	0	0	.983	15	S-45,2-13/3D	0.8
Total	10	863	2322	301	559	60	17	9	133	219	384	.241	.308	.293	66	-106	108	41	1	.974	7	S-409,2-292,3/DO	-5.3

■ TIM TOLMAN
Tolman, Timothy Lee b: 4/20/56, Santa Monica, Cal.   BR/TR, 6', 195 lbs.   Deb: 9/9/81

YEAR	TM/L	G	AB	R	H	2B	3B	HR	RBI	BB	SO	AVG	OBP	SLG	PRO+	BR/A	SB	CS	SBR	FA	FR	G/POS	TPR
1981	Hou-N	4	8	0	1	0	0	0	0	0	0	.125	.125	.125	-30	-1	0	0	0	1.000	-1	/O-3	-0.3
1982	Hou-N	15	26	4	5	2	0	0	3	4	3	.192	.300	.385	98	-0	0	0	0	1.000	-0	/O-5,1-1	-0.1
1983	Hou-N	43	56	4	11	4	0	2	10	6	9	.196	.274	.375	83	-2	0	1	-1	1.000	-2	/1-7,O-3	-0.4
1984	Hou-N	14	17	2	3	1	0	0	0	0	3	.176	.176	.235	16	-2	0	0	0	1.000	-1	/O-3,1-1	-0.3
1985	Hou-N	31	43	4	6	1	0	2	8	1	10	.140	.178	.302	33	-4	0	1	-0	1.000	-1	/O-9,1-6	-0.6
1986	Det-A	16	34	4	6	1	0	0	2	6	4	.176	.300	.206	41	-3	1	1	-0	1.000	-1	/O-4,1-3,D	-0.4
1987	Det-A	9	12	3	1	1	0	0	1	7	2	.083	.450	.167	77	0	0	0	0	1.000	-1	/O-7,D-2	-0.1
Total	7	132	196	21	33	10	0	5	24	24	31	.168	.266	.296	58	-11	1	3	-2	1.000	-6	/O-34,1-18,D	-2.2

■ CHICK TOLSON
Tolson, Charles Julius "Toby" b: 11/6/1898, Washington, D.C. d: 4/16/65, Washington, D.C.   BR/TR, 6', 185 lbs.   Deb: 7/3/25

YEAR	TM/L	G	AB	R	H	2B	3B	HR	RBI	BB	SO	AVG	OBP	SLG	PRO+	BR/A	SB	CS	SBR	FA	FR	G/POS	TPR
1925	Cle-A	3	12	0	3	0	0	0	2	1	.250	.357	.250		56	-1	0			1.000	0	/1-3	-0.1
1926	Chi-N	57	80	4	25	6	1	1	8	5	8	.313	.353	.450	113	1	0			.991	0	1-13	0.1
1927	Chi-N	39	54	6	16	4	0	2	17	4	9	.296	.345	.481	119	1	0			1.000	0	/1-8	0.1
1929	*Chi-N	32	109	13	28	5	0	1	19	9	16	.257	.325	.330	63	-6	0			.978	-2	1-31	-1.0
1930	Chi-N	13	20	0	6	1	0	0	1	6	5	.300	.462	.350	99	0	1			.978		1-5	0.0
Total	5	144	275	23	78	16	1	4	45	26	39	.284	.350	.393	90	-4	1	0		.985	-1	/1-60	-0.9

■ ANDY TOMBERLIN
Tomberlin, Andy Lee b: 11/7/66, Monroe, N.C.   BL/TL, 5'11", 160 lbs.   Deb: 8/12/93

YEAR	TM/L	G	AB	R	H	2B	3B	HR	RBI	BB	SO	AVG	OBP	SLG	PRO+	BR/A	SB	CS	SBR	FA	FR	G/POS	TPR
1993	Pit-N	27	42	4	12	0	1	1	5	2	14	.286	.333	.405	97	-0	0	0	0	1.000	-0	/O-7	-0.1
1994	Bos-A	18	36	1	7	0	1	1	1	6	12	.194	.310	.333	62	-2	0	0	0	1.000	-0	O-11/P-1,D	-0.2
Total	2	45	78	5	19	0	2	2	6	8	26	.244	.322	.372	79	-2	0	0	0	1.000	-1	/O-18,D-5,P	-0.3

■ GEORGE TOMER
Tomer, George Clarence b: 11/26/1895, Perry, Iowa d: 12/15/84, Perry, Iowa   BL/TR, 6', 180 lbs.   Deb: 9/17/13

YEAR	TM/L	G	AB	R	H	2B	3B	HR	RBI	BB	SO	AVG	OBP	SLG	PRO+	BR/A	SB	CS	SBR	FA	FR	G/POS	TPR
1913	StL-A	1	1	0	0	0	0	0	0	0	1	.000	.000	.000	-99	-0	0			.000	0	H	0.0

■ PHIL TOMNEY
Tomney, Philip Howard "Buster" b: 7/17/1863, Reading, Pa. d: 3/18/1892, Reading, Pa.   BR/TR, 5'7", 155 lbs.   Deb: 9/7/1888

YEAR	TM/L	G	AB	R	H	2B	3B	HR	RBI	BB	SO	AVG	OBP	SLG	PRO+	BR/A	SB	CS	SBR	FA	FR	G/POS	TPR
1888	Lou-a	34	120	15	18	3	0	0		4	7	.150	.197	.175	20	-11	11			.882	6	S-34	-0.3
1889	Lou-a	112	376	61	80	8	5	4	38	46	47	.213	.304	.293	71	-13	26			.857	27	*S-112	1.7
1890	*Lou-a	108	386	72	107	21	7	1		43		.277	.357	.376	119	9	27			.902	18	*S-108	2.9
Total	3	254	882	148	205	32	12	5	42	96	47	.232	.313	.313	86	-15	64			.878	50	S-254	4.3

■ TONY TONNEMAN
Tonneman, Charles Richard b: 9/10/1881, Chicago, Ill. d: 8/7/51, Prescott, Ariz.   BR/TR, 5'10.5", 175 lbs.   Deb: 9/19/11

YEAR	TM/L	G	AB	R	H	2B	3B	HR	RBI	BB	SO	AVG	OBP	SLG	PRO+	BR/A	SB	CS	SBR	FA	FR	G/POS	TPR
1911	Bos-A	2	5	0	1	1	0	0	3	1		.200	.333	.400	105	0	0			.900	1	/C-2	0.1

■ BERT TOOLEY
Tooley, Albert R. b: 8/30/1886, Howell, Mich. d: 8/17/76, Marshall, Mich.   BR/TR, 5'10", 155 lbs.   Deb: 4/12/11

YEAR	TM/L	G	AB	R	H	2B	3B	HR	RBI	BB	SO	AVG	OBP	SLG	PRO+	BR/A	SB	CS	SBR	FA	FR	G/POS	TPR
1911	Bro-N	119	433	55	89	11	3	1	29	53	63	.206	.295	.252	56	-25	18			.925	-8	*S-114	-2.6
1912	Bro-N	77	265	34	62	6	5	2	37	19	21	.234	.285	.317	67	-13	12			.885	-15	S-76	-2.1
Total	2	196	698	89	151	17	8	3	66	72	84	.216	.291	.277	60	-37	30			.909	-24	S-190	-4.7

■ SPECS TOPORCER
Toporcer, George b: 2/9/1899, New York, N.Y. d: 5/17/89, Huntington Station, N.Y.   BL/TR, 5'10.5", 165 lbs.   Deb: 4/13/21

YEAR	TM/L	G	AB	R	H	2B	3B	HR	RBI	BB	SO	AVG	OBP	SLG	PRO+	BR/A	SB	CS	SBR	FA	FR	G/POS	TPR
1921	StL-N	22	53	4	14	1	0	0	2	3	4	.264	.304	.283	57	-3	1	0		.938	0	2-12/S-2	-0.2
1922	StL-N	116	352	56	114	25	6	3	36	24	18	.324	.370	.455	117	8	2	1	0	.939	-23	S-91/3-6,2O	-0.5
1923	StL-N	97	303	45	77	11	3	3	35	41	14	.254	.349	.340	84	-6	4	3	-1	.945	-13	2-52,S-33/13	-1.5
1924	StL-N	70	198	30	62	10	3	1	24	11	14	.313	.362	.409	108	2	2	3	-1	.974	-16	3-33,S-25/2	-1.0
1925	StL-N	83	268	38	76	13	4	2	26	36	15	.284	.373	.384	92	2	7	2	1	.960	-3	S-66/2-7	0.3
1926	*StL-N	64	88	13	22	3	2	0	9	8	5	.250	.327	.330	74	-3	1			.983	-9	2-27/S-5,3	-1.2
1927	StL-N	86	290	37	72	13	4	0	19	27	16	.248	.314	.321	68	-13	5			.980	-11	3-54,S-27/21	-1.9
1928	StL-N	8	14	0	0	0	0	0	0	0	3	.000	.000	.000	-98	-4	0			1.000	0	/1-1,2-1	-0.4
Total	8	546	1566	223	437	76	22	9	151	150	93	.279	.347	.373	89	-20	22	9		.946	-74	S-249,2-105/310	-6.4

■ JEFF TORBORG
Torborg, Jeffrey Allen b: 11/26/41, Plainfield, N.J.   BR/TR, 6'0.5", 195 lbs.   Deb: 5/10/64   MC

YEAR	TM/L	G	AB	R	H	2B	3B	HR	RBI	BB	SO	AVG	OBP	SLG	PRO+	BR/A	SB	CS	SBR	FA	FR	G/POS	TPR
1964	LA-N	28	43	4	10	1	1	0	4	3	8	.233	.298	.302	75	-1	0	0	0	.977	-2	C-27	-0.3
1965	LA-N	56	150	8	36	5	1	3	13	10	26	.240	.292	.347	85	-3	0	0	0	.991	4	C-53	0.3
1966	LA-N	46	120	4	27	3	0	1	13	10	23	.225	.285	.275	61	-6	0	0	0	.986	6	C-45	0.2
1967	LA-N	76	196	11	42	4	1	2	12	13	31	.214	.267	.276	60	-10	1	3	-2	.989	12	C-75	0.3
1968	LA-N	37	93	2	15	2	0	0	4	6	10	.161	.212	.183	21	-9	0	0	0	.991	10	C-37	0.3
1969	LA-N	51	124	9	23	4	0	0	7	9	17	.185	.241	.218	31	-12	1	0	0	.991	10	C-37	0.3
1970	LA-N	64	134	11	31	9	0	0	17	14	15	.231	.304	.313	69	-6	1	0	0	.996	11	C-50	0.1
1971	Cal-A	55	123	6	25	5	0	0	5	3	6	.203	.222	.244	34	-11	0	0	0	.983	6	C-63	0.5
1972	Cal-A	59	153	5	32	5	0	0	8	14	21	.209	.280	.229	56	-8	0	0	0	.987	16	C-58	1.1
1973	Cal-A	102	255	20	56	7	0	1	21	11	32	.220	.279	.259	57	-15	0	2	-1	.991	8	*C-102	-0.4
Total	10	574	1391	78	297	42	3	8	101	103	189	.214	.270	.265	56	-82	0	5		.990	79	C-559	1.5

■ EARL TORGESON
Torgeson, Clifford Earl "The Earl Of Snohomish" b: 1/1/24, Snohomish, Wash. d: 11/8/90, Everett, Wash.   BL/TL, 6'3", 180 lbs.   Deb: 4/15/47   C

YEAR	TM/L	G	AB	R	H	2B	3B	HR	RBI	BB	SO	AVG	OBP	SLG	PRO+	BR/A	SB	CS	SBR	FA	FR	G/POS	TPR
1947	Bos-N	128	399	73	112	20	6	16	78	82	59	.281	.403	.481	137	24	11			.984	-1	*1-117	1.9
1948	*Bos-N	134	438	70	111	23	5	10	67	81	54	.253	.372	.397	110	9	19			.993	1	*1-129	0.9
1949	Bos-N	25	100	17	26	5	1	4	19	13	4	.260	.345	.450	118	2	4			.988	-3	1-25	-0.1
1950	Bos-N	156	576	120	167	30	3	23	87	119	69	.290	.412	.472	141	39	15			.986	-1	1-156	3.4
1951	Bos-N	155	581	99	153	21	4	24	92	102	70	.263	.375	.437	127	24	20	11	-1	.988	-1	*1-155	1.5
1952	Bos-N	122	382	49	88	17	0	5	34	81	38	.230	.366	.314	94	0	11	7	-1	.989	-1	*1-105/O-5	-0.6
1953	Phi-N	111	379	58	104	25	8	11	64	53	57	.274	.366	.470	117	10	7	1	2	.987	-3	*1-105	0.4
1954	Phi-N	135	490	63	133	22	6	15	54	75	52	.271	.368	.371	93	2	7	1	2	.990	-10	*1-133	-1.8
1955	Phi-N	47	150	29	40	5	1	7	17	32	20	.267	.396	.360	104	2	2	1	2	.990	-1	*1-105	-0.3
	Det-A	89	300	58	85	10	1	9	50	61	29	.283	.404	.413	123	12	9	0	3	.992	-0	1-83	1.0

YEAR	TM/L	G	AB	R	H	2B	3B	HR	RBI	BB	SO	AVG	OBP	SLG	PRO+	BR/A	SB	CS	SBR	FA	FR	G/POS	TPR
1956	Det-A	117	318	61	84	9	3	12	42	78	47	.264	.409	.425	120	12	6	4	-1	.992	-7	1-83	0.0
1957	Det-A	30	50	5	12	2	1	1	5	12	10	.240	.387	.380	108	1	0	1	0	1.000	0	1-17	0.0
	Chi-A	86	251	53	74	11	2	7	46	49	44	.295	.410	.438	131	13	7	3	0	.998	-5	1-70/O-1	0.4
	Yr	116	301	58	86	13	3	8	51	61	54	.286	.406	.429	127	14	7	3	0	.999	-5	1-87/O-1	0.4
1958	Chi-A	96	188	37	50	8	0	10	30	48	29	.266	.415	.468	146	14	7	2	1	.978	-2	1-73	1.0
1959	*Chi-A	127	277	40	61	5	3	9	45	62	55	.220	.363	.357	100	2	7	6	-2	.983	-6	*1-103	-1.1
1960	Chi-A	68	57	12	15	2	0	2	9	21	8	.263	.462	.404	137	5	1	0	0	.983	0	1-10	0.5
1961	Chi-A	20	15	1	1	0	0	0	1	3	5	.067	.222	.067	-19	-3	0	0	0	1.000	-0	/1-1	-0.3
	NY-A	22	18	3	2	0	0	0	0	8	3	.111	.385	.111	42	-1	0	1	-1	.969	-0	/1-8	-0.2
	Yr	42	33	4	3	0	0	0	1	11	8	.091	.318	.091	16	-4	0	1	-1	.970	-0	/1-9	-0.5
Total	15	1668	4969	848	1318	215	46	149	740	980	653	.265	.387	.417	118	162	133	39		.989	-39	*1-1416/O-6	6.6

■ RED TORPHY
Torphy, Walter Anthony b: 11/6/1891, Fall River, Mass. d: 2/11/80, Fall River, Mass. BR/TR, 5'11", 169 lbs. Deb: 9/25/20

YEAR	TM/L	G	AB	R	H	2B	3B	HR	RBI	BB	SO	AVG	OBP	SLG	PRO+	BR/A	SB	CS	SBR	FA	FR	G/POS	TPR
1920	Bos-N	3	15	1	3	2	0	0	2	0	1	.200	.200	.333	54	-1	0	0	0	.969	-1	/1-3	-0.2

■ FRANK TORRE
Torre, Frank Joseph b: 12/30/31, Brooklyn, N.Y. BL/TL, 6'3", 205 lbs. Deb: 4/20/56 F

YEAR	TM/L	G	AB	R	H	2B	3B	HR	RBI	BB	SO	AVG	OBP	SLG	PRO+	BR/A	SB	CS	SBR	FA	FR	G/POS	TPR
1956	Mil-N	111	159	17	41	6	0	0	16	11	4	.258	.306	.296	67	-7	1	0	0	.993	6	1-89	-0.3
1957	*Mil-N	129	364	46	99	19	5	5	40	29	19	.272	.341	.393	104	2	0	0	0	**.996**	1	*1-117	-0.3
1958	*Mil-N	138	372	41	115	22	5	6	55	42	14	.309	.390	.444	131	17	2	0	1	**.994**	6	*1-122	1.8
1959	Mil-N	115	263	23	60	15	1	1	33	35	12	.228	.326	.304	75	-9	0	0	0	.994	-0	1-87	-1.4
1960	Mil-N	21	44	2	9	1	0	0	5	3	2	.205	.255	.227	36	-4	0	0	0	1.000	-1	1-17	-0.6
1962	Phi-N	108	168	13	52	8	2	0	20	24	5	.310	.408	.381	117	5	1	1	-0	.980	3	1-76	0.6
1963	Phi-N	92	112	8	28	7	2	1	10	11	7	.250	.333	.375	105	1	0	0	0	.989	5	1-56	0.5
Total	7	714	1482	150	404	78	15	13	179	155	64	.273	.352	.372	101	5	4	1	1	.993	19	1-564	0.2

■ JOE TORRE
Torre, Joseph Paul b: 7/18/40, Brooklyn, N.Y. BR/TR, 6'2", 212 lbs. Deb: 9/25/60 FM

YEAR	TM/L	G	AB	R	H	2B	3B	HR	RBI	BB	SO	AVG	OBP	SLG	PRO+	BR/A	SB	CS	SBR	FA	FR	G/POS	TPR
1960	Mil-N	2	2	0	1	0	0	0	0	0	1	.500	.500	.500	189	0	0	0	0	.000	0	H	0.0
1961	Mil-N	113	406	40	113	21	4	10	42	28	60	.278	.331	.424	105	2	3	5	-2	.982	-8	*C-112	-0.3
1962	Mil-N	80	220	23	62	8	1	5	26	24	24	.282	.358	.395	105	2	1	0	0	.986	6	C-63	1.0
1963	Mil-N☆	142	501	57	147	19	4	14	71	42	79	.293	.354	.431	126	17	1	5	-3	.994	-7	*C-105,1-37/O	1.0
1964	Mil-N★	154	601	87	193	36	5	20	109	36	67	.321	.366	.498	140	31	2	4	-2	**.995**	-8	C-96,1-70	2.4
1965	Mil-N★	148	523	68	152	21	1	27	80	61	79	.291	.373	.489	140	28	0	1	-1	.991	-6	*C-100,1-49	2.6
1966	Atl-N★	148	546	83	172	20	3	36	101	60	61	.315	.385	.560	157	41	0	4	-3	.984	-3	C-114,1-36	4.2
1967	Atl-N★	135	477	67	132	18	1	20	68	49	75	.277	.348	.444	127	16	2	2	-1	.991	-5	*C-114,1-23	1.7
1968	Atl-N	115	424	45	115	11	2	10	55	34	72	.271	.333	.377	112	7	1	0	0	**.996**	-11	C-92,1-29	0.1
1969	StL-N	159	602	72	174	29	6	18	101	66	85	.289	.364	.447	126	21	0	0	0	.996	-3	*1-144,C-17	0.7
1970	StL-N★	161	624	89	203	27	9	21	100	70	91	.325	.399	.498	136	33	2	2	-1	.987	-8	C-90,3-73/1	2.8
1971	StL-N★	161	634	97	**230**	34	8	24	**137**	63	70	**.363**	.424	.555	169	57	4	1	1	.951	-17	*3-161	4.1
1972	StL-N★	149	544	71	157	26	6	11	81	54	64	.289	.361	.419	123	17	3	0	1	.963	-15	*3-117,1-27	-0.1
1973	StL-N★	141	519	67	149	17	2	13	69	65	78	.287	.377	.403	116	14	2	0	1	.993	-12	*1-114,3-58	-0.6
1974	StL-N	147	529	59	149	28	1	11	70	69	88	.282	.371	.401	117	14	1	2	-1	.992	3	*1-139,3-18	0.8
1975	NY-N	114	361	33	89	16	3	6	35	35	55	.247	.317	.357	91	-5	0	0	0	.950	-1	3-83,1-24	-0.7
1976	NY-N	114	310	36	95	10	3	5	31	21	35	.306	.360	.406	124	9	1	3	-2	.989	3	1-78/3-4	0.6
1977	NY-N	26	51	2	9	3	0	1	9	2	10	.176	.208	.294	34	-5	0	0	0	.988	-1	1-16/3-1M	-0.7
Total	18	2209	7874	996	2342	344	59	252	1185	779	1094	.297	.367	.452	129	299	23	29	-11	.990	-93	C-903,1-787,3/O	19.6

■ GIL TORRES
Torres, Don Gilberto (Nunez) b: 8/23/15, Regla, Cuba d: 1/10/83, Regla, Cuba BR/TR, 6', 155 lbs. Deb: 4/25/40 F

YEAR	TM/L	G	AB	R	H	2B	3B	HR	RBI	BB	SO	AVG	OBP	SLG	PRO+	BR/A	SB	CS	SBR	FA	FR	G/POS	TPR
1940	Was-A	2	0	0	0	0	0	0	0	0	0	—	—	—	0	0	0	0	0	1.000	0	/P-2	0.0
1944	Was-A	134	524	42	140	20	6	0	58	21	24	.267	.297	.328	82	-14	10	7	-1	.952	9	*3-123,2-10/1	-0.5
1945	Was-A	147	562	39	133	12	5	0	48	21	29	.237	.264	.276	62	-30	7	4	-0	.953	-21	*S-145/3-2	-4.3
1946	Was-A	63	185	18	47	8	0	0	13	11	12	.254	.296	.297	70	-8	3	2	-0	.939	2	S-31,3-18/2P	-0.4
Total	4	346	1271	99	320	40	11	0	119	53	65	.252	.282	.301	72	-51	20	13	-2	.951	-11	S-176,3-143/2P1	-5.2

■ FELIX TORRES
Torres, Felix (Sanchez) b: 5/1/32, Ponce, P.R. BR/TR, 5'11", 165 lbs. Deb: 4/10/62

YEAR	TM/L	G	AB	R	H	2B	3B	HR	RBI	BB	SO	AVG	OBP	SLG	PRO+	BR/A	SB	CS	SBR	FA	FR	G/POS	TPR
1962	LA-A	127	451	44	117	19	4	11	74	28	73	.259	.308	.392	90	-7	0	0	0	.938	-3	*3-123	-1.0
1963	LA-A	138	463	40	121	32	1	4	51	30	73	.261	.310	.361	93	-5	1	0	0	.939	-4	*3-122/1-2	-1.0
1964	LA-A	100	277	25	64	10	0	12	28	13	56	.231	.268	.397	91	-5	1	3	-2	.970	-0	3-72/1-3	-0.8
Total	3	365	1191	109	302	61	5	27	153	71	202	.254	.300	.381	91	-18	2	3	-1	.945	-8	3-317/1-5	-2.8

■ HECTOR TORRES
Torres, Hector Epitacio (Marroquin) b: 9/16/45, Monterrey, Mexico BR/TR, 6', 175 lbs. Deb: 4/10/68 C

YEAR	TM/L	G	AB	R	H	2B	3B	HR	RBI	BB	SO	AVG	OBP	SLG	PRO+	BR/A	SB	CS	SBR	FA	FR	G/POS	TPR
1968	Hou-N	128	466	44	104	11	1	1	24	18	64	.223	.252	.258	54	-26	2	3	-1	.958	-4	*S-127/2-1	-2.2
1969	Hou-N	34	69	5	11	1	0	1	8	2	12	.159	.183	.217	12	-8	0	0	0	.944	0	S-22	-0.7
1970	Hou-N	31	65	6	16	1	2	0	5	6	8	.246	.310	.323	73	-3	0	0	0	.947	1	S-22/2-6	0.0
1971	Chi-N	31	58	4	13	3	0	0	2	4	10	.224	.274	.276	49	-4	0	0	0	.962	1	S-18/2-4	-0.2
1972	Mon-N	83	181	14	28	4	1	2	7	13	26	.155	.215	.221	24	-18	0	2	-1	.965	14	2-60,S-16/OP3	-0.2
1973	Hou-N	38	66	3	6	1	0	0	2	7	13	.091	.189	.106	-16	-10	0	0	0	.952	7	S-22,2-13	-0.2
1975	SD-N	112	352	31	91	12	0	5	26	22	32	.259	.302	.335	82	-10	2	3	-1	.971	15	S-75,3-42,2	0.8
1976	SD-N	74	215	8	42	6	0	4	15	16	31	.195	.254	.279	56	-13	2	1	-0	.949	-16	S-63/3-4,2	-2.5
1977	Tor-A	91	266	33	64	7	3	5	26	16	33	.241	.286	.346	70	-11	1	1	-0	.980	-2	S-68,2-23/3	-0.6
Total	9	622	1738	148	375	46	7	18	115	104	229	.216	.262	.281	55	-103	7	11	-5	.962	11	S-433,2-126/3OP	-5.8

■ RICARDO TORRES
Torres, Ricardo J. (Martinez) b: 4/16/1891, Regla, Cuba d: 4/17/60, Regla, Cuba BR/TR, 5'11", 160 lbs. Deb: 5/18/20 F

YEAR	TM/L	G	AB	R	H	2B	3B	HR	RBI	BB	SO	AVG	OBP	SLG	PRO+	BR/A	SB	CS	SBR	FA	FR	G/POS	TPR
1920	Was-A	16	30	8	10	1	0	0	3	1	4	.333	.355	.367	94	-0	0	0	0	1.000	-1	/1-7,C-5	-0.1
1921	Was-A	2	3	1	1	0	0	0	0	1	1	.333	.500	.333	122	0	0	0	0	.750	-1	/C-2	-0.1
1922	Was-A	4	4	0	0	0	0	0	0	0	1	.000	.000	.000	-99	-1	0	0	0	1.000	1	/C-3	0.0
Total	3	22	37	9	11	1	0	0	3	2	6	.297	.333	.324	76	-1	0	0	0	.955	-1	/C-10,1-7	-0.2

■ RUSTY TORRES
Torres, Rosendo (Hernandez) b: 9/30/48, Aquadilla, P.R. BB/TR, 5'10", 180 lbs. Deb: 9/20/71

YEAR	TM/L	G	AB	R	H	2B	3B	HR	RBI	BB	SO	AVG	OBP	SLG	PRO+	BR/A	SB	CS	SBR	FA	FR	G/POS	TPR
1971	NY-A	9	26	5	10	3	1	2	3	0	8	.385	.385	.731	223	4	0	1	-1	1.000	0	/O-5	0.3
1972	NY-A	80	199	15	42	7	0	3	13	18	44	.211	.280	.291	73	-7	0	4	-2	.978	-6	O-62	-2.1
1973	Cle-A	122	312	31	64	8	1	9	28	50	62	.205	.321	.304	76	-9	6	5	-1	.976	-5	*O-114	-2.0
1974	Cle-A	108	150	19	28	2	0	3	12	13	24	.187	.252	.260	48	-10	2	1	0	.959	-19	O-94/D-1	-3.3
1976	Cal-A	120	264	37	54	16	3	6	27	36	39	.205	.300	.356	98	-1	4	4	-1	.990	-11	*O-105/3-1,D	-1.7
1977	Cal-A	58	77	9	12	1	1	3	10	10	18	.156	.253	.312	55	-5	0	1	-1	.984	-12	O-54	-1.9
1978	Chi-A	16	44	7	14	3	0	3	6	6	7	.318	.400	.591	174	4	1	0	0	.964	-2	O-14	0.1
1979	Chi-A	90	170	26	43	5	0	8	24	23	37	.253	.349	.424	107	2	0	0	0	.976	-13	O-85	-1.3
1980	KC-A	51	72	10	12	0	0	0	3	8	7	.167	.250	.167	16	-8	0	3	-2	.973	-4	O-40/D-1	-1.4
Total	9	654	1314	159	279	45	5	35	126	164	246	.212	.303	.334	82	-30	13	20	-8	.977	-73	O-573/D-8,3	-13.3

■ KELVIN TORVE
Torve, Kelvin Curtis b: 1/10/60, Rapid City, S.Dak. BL/TR, 6'3", 205 lbs. Deb: 6/25/88

YEAR	TM/L	G	AB	R	H	2B	3B	HR	RBI	BB	SO	AVG	OBP	SLG	PRO+	BR/A	SB	CS	SBR	FA	FR	G/POS	TPR
1988	Min-A	12	16	1	3	0	0	1	2	1	2	.188	.235	.375	66	-1	0	1	-1	1.000	0	/1-4,D-1	-0.1
1990	NY-N	20	38	0	11	4	0	0	2	4	9	.289	.386	.395	116	1	0	0	0	1.000	-2	/1-9,O-1	-0.2
1991	NY-N	10	8	0	0	0	0	0	0	0	1	.000	.000	.000	-99	-2	0	0	0	1.000	1	/1-1	-0.1
Total	3	42	62	1	14	4	0	1	4	5	12	.226	.304	.339	78	-2	0	1	-1	1.000	-2	/1-14,O-1,D	-0.4

YEAR	TM/L	G	AB	R	H	2B	3B	HR	RBI	BB	SO	AVG	OBP	SLG	PRO+	BR/A	SB	CS	SBR	FA	FR	G/POS	TPR

■ CESAR TOVAR   Tovar, Cesar Leonardo "Pepito" (b: Cesar Leonard Perez (Tovar))
 b: 7/3/40, Caracas, Venez.   d: 7/14/94, Caracas, Venez.   BR/TR, 5′9″, 155 lbs.   Deb: 4/12/65

YEAR	TM/L	G	AB	R	H	2B	3B	HR	RBI	BB	SO	AVG	OBP	SLG	PRO+	BR/A	SB	CS	SBR	FA	FR	G/POS	TPR
1965	Min-A	18	25	3	5	1	0	0	2	2	3	.200	.259	.240	41	-2	2	0	1	.800	1	/2-4,3-2,OS	-0.1
1966	Min-A	134	465	57	121	19	5	2	41	44	50	.260	.329	.335	86	-7	16	6	1	.978	-8	2-76,S-31,O	-0.8
1967	Min-A	164	649	98	164	32	7	6	47	46	51	.267	.328	.365	97	-2	19	11	-1	.994	-4	O-74,3-70,2/S	-1.1
1968	Min-A	157	613	89	167	31	6	6	47	34	41	.272	.328	.372	106	5	35	13	3	.966	-2	O-78,3-75,S2/PC1	0.6
1969	*Min-A	158	535	99	154	25	5	11	52	37	37	.288	.344	.415	109	6	45	12	6	.983	9	*O-113,2-41,3	1.9
1970	*Min-A	161	650	120	195	**36**	**13**	10	54	52	47	.300	.359	.442	118	15	30	15	0	.977	0	*O-151/2-8,3	0.8
1971	Min-A	157	657	94	**204**	29	3	1	45	45	39	.311	.357	.368	103	3	18	14	-3	.986	4	*O-154/3-7,2	-0.4
1972	Min-A	141	548	86	145	20	6	2	31	39	39	.265	.329	.334	93	-4	21	10	0	.983	7	*O-139	-0.4
1973	Phi-N	97	328	49	88	18	4	1	21	29	35	.268	.337	.357	90	-4	6	4	-1	.928	-15	3-46,O-24,2	-2.1
1974	Tex-A	138	562	78	164	24	6	4	58	47	33	.292	.354	.377	114	11	13	9	-2	.980	-1	*O-135/D-3	0.3
1975	Tex-A	102	427	53	110	16	3	0	28	27	25	.258	.306	.316	77	-13	16	11	-2	.919	-3	D-66,O-31/2	-2.2
	*Oak-A	19	26	5	6	1	0	0	3	3	3	.231	.310	.269	66	-1	4	0	1	1.000	-0	/2-4,3-3,SD	0.0
	Yr	121	453	58	116	17	3	0	31	30	28	.256	.307	.313	76	-14	20	11	-1	.919	-3	D-73,O-31/23S	-2.2
1976	Oak-A	29	45	1	8	0	0	0	0	4	4	.178	.275	.178	36	-3	1	2	-1	.958	-5	O-20/D-4	-1.0
	NY-A	13	39	2	6	1	0	0	2	4	3	.154	.250	.179	27	-3	0	1	-1	1.000	1	D-10/2-3	-0.4
	Yr	42	84	3	14	1	0	0	2	8	7	.167	.263	.179	32	-7	1	3	-2	.958	-4	O-20,D-14/2	-1.4
Total	12	1488	5569	834	1546	253	55	46	435	413	410	.278	.337	.368	99	-0	226	108		.980	-18	O-945,3-227,2/DS1CP	-4.9

■ BABE TOWNE   Towne, Jay King   b: 3/12/1880, Coon Rapids, Iowa   d: 10/29/38, Des Moines, Iowa   BR/TR, 5′10″, 180 lbs.   Deb: 8/1/06

YEAR	TM/L	G	AB	R	H	2B	3B	HR	RBI	BB	SO	AVG	OBP	SLG	PRO+	BR/A	SB	CS	SBR	FA	FR	G/POS	TPR
1906	*Chi-A	14	36	3	10	0	0	0	6	7		.278	.395	.278	115	1	0			.923	-1	C-13	-0.2

■ GEORGE TOWNSEND   Townsend, George Hodgson "Sleepy"   b: 6/4/1867, Hartsdale, N.Y.   d: 3/15/30, New Haven, Conn.   BR/TR, 5′7.5″, 180 lbs.   Deb: 6/25/1887

YEAR	TM/L	G	AB	R	H	2B	3B	HR	RBI	BB	SO	AVG	OBP	SLG	PRO+	BR/A	SB	CS	SBR	FA	FR	G/POS	TPR
1887	Phi-a	31	109	12	21	3	0	0		3		.193	.214	.220	21	-12	8			.865	-7	C-28/O-3	-1.3
1888	Phi-a	42	161	13	25	6	0	0	12	4		.155	.181	.193	20	-14	2			.912	-2	C-42	-1.1
1890	Bal-a	18	67	6	16	4	1	0		4		.239	.282	.328	76	-2	3			.930	2	C-18	0.1
1891	Bal-a	61	204	29	39	5	4	0	18	20	21	.191	.279	.255	52	-13	3			.909	-11	C-58/O-3	-1.6
Total	4	152	541	60	101	18	5	0	30	31	21	.187	.239	.238	40	-41	16			.905	-17	C-146/O-6	-3.9

■ JIM TOY   Toy, James Madison   b: 2/20/1858, Beaver Falls, Pa.   d: 3/13/19, Beaver Falls, Pa.   5′6″, 160 lbs.   Deb: 4/20/1887

YEAR	TM/L	G	AB	R	H	2B	3B	HR	RBI	BB	SO	AVG	OBP	SLG	PRO+	BR/A	SB	CS	SBR	FA	FR	G/POS	TPR
1887	Cle-a	109	423	56	94	20	5	1		17		.222	.256	.300	56	-25	8			.975	3	1-82,O-11,C/3S	-2.5
1890	Bro-a	44	160	11	29	3	0	0		11		.181	.238	.200	30	-14	2			.867	-1	C-44	-0.9
Total	2	153	583	67	123	23	5	1		28		.211	.251	.273	50	-39	10			.859	3	/1-82,C-54,O3S	-3.4

■ JIM TRABER   Traber, James Joseph   b: 12/26/61, Columbus, Ohio   BL/TL, 6′, 194 lbs.   Deb: 9/21/84

YEAR	TM/L	G	AB	R	H	2B	3B	HR	RBI	BB	SO	AVG	OBP	SLG	PRO+	BR/A	SB	CS	SBR	FA	FR	G/POS	TPR
1984	Bal-A	10	21	3	5	0	0	0	2	2	4	.238	.304	.238	54	-1	0	0	0	.000		/D-9	-0.1
1986	Bal-A	65	212	28	54	7	0	13	44	18	31	.255	.328	.472	116	4	0	0	0	.988	1	1-29,D-21/O	0.3
1988	Bal-A	103	352	25	78	6	0	10	45	19	42	.222	.263	.324	65	-17	1	2	-1	.990	4	1-57,D-30,O	-1.6
1989	Bal-A	86	234	14	49	8	0	4	26	19	41	.209	.269	.295	61	-12	4	3	-1	.998	5	1-69/D-5	-1.3
Total	4	264	819	70	186	21	0	27	117	58	118	.227	.283	.352	77	-26	5	5	-2	.993	15	1-155/D-65,O	-2.7

■ DICK TRACEWSKI   Tracewski, Richard Joseph   b: 2/3/35, Eynon, Pa.   BR/TR, 5′11″, 167 lbs.   Deb: 4/12/62   MC

YEAR	TM/L	G	AB	R	H	2B	3B	HR	RBI	BB	SO	AVG	OBP	SLG	PRO+	BR/A	SB	CS	SBR	FA	FR	G/POS	TPR
1962	LA-N	15	2	3	0	0	0	0	0	2	0	.000	.500	.000	50		0	0	0	1.000	2	/S-4	0.2
1963	*LA-N	104	217	23	49	2	1	1	10	19	39	.226	.288	.258	63	-10	2	3	-1	.957	19	S-81,2-23	1.3
1964	LA-N	106	304	31	75	13	4	1	26	31	61	.247	.316	.326	88	-5	3	3	-1	.970	-0	2-56,3-30,S	-0.1
1965	*LA-N	78	186	17	40	6	0	1	20	25	30	.215	.315	.263	69	-7	2	6	-3	.950	3	3-53,2-14/S	-0.2
1966	Det-A	81	124	15	24	1	1	0	7	10	32	.194	.254	.218	36	-10	1	1	-0	.947	11	2-70/S-3	0.3
1967	Det-A	74	107	19	30	4	2	1	9	8	20	.280	.330	.383	107	1	1	1	-0	.965	9	S-44,2-12,3	1.3
1968	*Det-A	90	212	30	33	3	1	4	15	24	51	.156	.242	.236	44	-14	3	0	1	.982	-5	S-51,3-16,2	-1.6
1969	Det-A	66	79	10	11	2	0	0	4	15	20	.139	.277	.165	25	-8	3	0	1	.957	16	S-41,2-13/3	1.2
Total	8	614	1231	148	262	31	9	8	91	134	253	.213	.291	.272	65	-53	15	14	-4	.958	60	S-250,2-202,3	2.4

■ JIM TRACY   Tracy, James Edwin   b: 12/31/55, Hamilton, Ohio   BL/TR, 6′, 185 lbs.   Deb: 7/20/80

YEAR	TM/L	G	AB	R	H	2B	3B	HR	RBI	BB	SO	AVG	OBP	SLG	PRO+	BR/A	SB	CS	SBR	FA	FR	G/POS	TPR
1980	Chi-N	42	122	12	31	3	3	3	9	13	37	.254	.326	.402	95	-1	2	2	-1	.950	-7	O-31/1-1	-1.0
1981	Chi-N	45	63	6	15	2	1	0	5	12	14	.238	.360	.302	85	-1	1	0	0	1.000	-1	O-11	-0.2
Total	2	87	185	18	46	5	4	3	14	25	51	.249	.338	.368	92	-2	3	2	-0	.964	-8	/O-42,1-1	-1.2

■ JOHN TRAFFLEY   Traffley, John M.   b: 1862, Chicago, Ill.   d: 5/15/1900, Baltimore, Md.   5′9″, 180 lbs.   Deb: 6/15/1889   F

YEAR	TM/L	G	AB	R	H	2B	3B	HR	RBI	BB	SO	AVG	OBP	SLG	PRO+	BR/A	SB	CS	SBR	FA	FR	G/POS	TPR
1889	Lou-a	1	2	0	1	0	0	0	0	0		.500	.500	.500	189	0				.000	-1	/O-1	0.0

■ BILL TRAFFLEY   Traffley, William F.   b: 12/21/1859, Staten Island, N.Y.   d: 6/24/08, Denver, Colo.   BR/TR, 5′11.5″, 185 lbs.   Deb: 7/27/1878   F

YEAR	TM/L	G	AB	R	H	2B	3B	HR	RBI	BB	SO	AVG	OBP	SLG	PRO+	BR/A	SB	CS	SBR	FA	FR	G/POS	TPR
1878	Chi-N	2	9	1	1	0	0	0	1	0	1	.111	.111	.111	-25	-1				1.000	-1	/C-2	-0.2
1883	Cin-a	30	105	17	21	5	0	0		4		.200	.229	.248	51	-6				.851	-2	C-29/S-2	-0.2
1884	Bal-a	53	210	25	37	4	6	0		3		.176	.192	.252	42	-13				.926	-8	C-47/O-6,1	-1.6
1885	Bal-a	69	254	27	39	4	5	1		17		.154	.215	.220	38	-17				**.943**	2	C-61,O-10/2	-0.9
1886	Bal-a	25	85	15	18	0	1	0		10		.212	.295	.235	68	-3	8			.952	-3	C-25	-0.2
Total	5	179	663	85	116	13	12	1	1	34	1	.175	.220	.235	45	-40	8			.927	-8	C-164/O-16,2S1	-3.1

■ WALT TRAGESSER   Tragesser, Walter Joseph   b: 6/14/1887, Lafayette, Ind.   d: 12/14/70, Lafayette, Ind.   BR/TR, 6′, 175 lbs.   Deb: 7/30/13

YEAR	TM/L	G	AB	R	H	2B	3B	HR	RBI	BB	SO	AVG	OBP	SLG	PRO+	BR/A	SB	CS	SBR	FA	FR	G/POS	TPR
1913	Bos-N	2	0	0	0	0	0	0	0	0		—	—	—			0			1.000	-0	/C-2	0.0
1915	Bos-N	7	7	1	0	0	0	0	0	0	2	.000	.000	.000	-99	-2	0			.944	1	C-7	-0.1
1916	Bos-N	41	54	3	11	1	0	0	4	5	10	.204	.283	.222	59	-2	0			.971	4	C-29	0.3
1917	Bos-N	98	297	23	66	10	2	0	25	15	36	.222	.264	.269	68	-12	5			.971	-2	C-94	-0.7
1918	Bos-N	7	1	0	0	0	0	0	0	0	0	.000	.000	.000	-99	-0	0			.833	1	/C-7	0.0
1919	Bos-N	20	40	3	7	2	0	0	3	2	10	.175	.233	.225	39	-3	1			.959	-0	C-14	-0.3
	Phi-N	35	114	7	27	7	0	0	8	9	31	.237	.298	.298	74	-3	4			.953	4	C-34	0.4
	Yr	55	154	10	34	9	0	0	11	11	41	.221	.281	.279	67	-6	5			.954	4	C-48	0.1
1920	Phi-N	62	176	17	37	11	1	6	26	4	36	.210	.236	.386	73	-7	4	0		.944	-13	C-52	-1.6
Total	7	272	689	54	148	31	3	6	66	35	125	.215	.260	.295	67	-29	14	0		.961	-6	C-239	-2.0

■ RED TRAMBACK   Tramback, Stephen Joseph   b: 11/1/15, Iselin, Pa.   d: 12/28/79, Buffalo, N.Y.   BL/TL, 6′, 175 lbs.   Deb: 9/15/40

YEAR	TM/L	G	AB	R	H	2B	3B	HR	RBI	BB	SO	AVG	OBP	SLG	PRO+	BR/A	SB	CS	SBR	FA	FR	G/POS	TPR
1940	NY-N	2	4	0	1	0	0	0	1	1		.250	.400	.250	82	-0	1			.667	-0	/O-1	0.0

■ ALAN TRAMMELL   Trammell, Alan Stuart   b: 2/21/58, Garden Grove, Cal.   BR/TR, 6′, 175 lbs.   Deb: 9/9/77

YEAR	TM/L	G	AB	R	H	2B	3B	HR	RBI	BB	SO	AVG	OBP	SLG	PRO+	BR/A	SB	CS	SBR	FA	FR	G/POS	TPR
1977	Det-A	19	43	6	8	0	0	0	0	4	12	.186	.255	.186	21	-5	0	0	0	.961	-7	S-19	-1.0
1978	Det-A	139	448	49	120	14	6	2	34	45	56	.268	.337	.339	88	-6	3	1	0	.979	6	*S-139	1.7
1979	Det-A	142	460	68	127	11	4	6	50	43	55	.276	.338	.357	85	-9	17	14	-3	.961	-13	*S-142	-1.0
1980	Det-A★	146	560	107	168	21	5	9	65	69	63	.300	.380	.404	112	11	12	12	-4	.980	-27	*S-144	-0.2
1981	Det-A	105	392	52	101	15	3	2	31	49	31	.258	.345	.327	91	-3	10	3	1	.983	6	*S-105	1.5
1982	Det-A	157	489	66	126	34	3	9	57	52	47	.258	.329	.395	97	-2	19	8	1	.978	6	*S-157	0.6
1983	Det-A	142	505	83	161	31	2	14	66	57	64	.319	.388	.471	139	28	30	10	3	.979	-18	*S-140	2.6
1984	*Det-A†	139	555	85	174	34	5	14	69	60	63	.314	.383	.468	135	27	19	13	-2	.980	1	*S-114,D-22	2.4
1985	Det-A★	149	605	79	156	21	7	13	57	50	71	.258	.317	.380	90	-8	14	5	1	.977	-16	*S-149	-0.8
1986	Det-A	151	574	107	159	33	7	21	75	59	57	.277	.350	.469	121	16	25	12	0	.969	6	*S-149/D-2	3.5

YEAR	TM/L	G	AB	R	H	2B	3B	HR	RBI	BB	SO	AVG	OBP	SLG	PRO+	BR/A	SB	CS	SBR	FA	FR	G/POS	TPR
1987	*Det-A★	151	597	109	205	34	3	28	105	60	47	.343	.406	.551	157	49	21	2	5	.971	-10	*S-149	5.4
1988	Det-A†	128	466	73	145	24	1	15	69	46	46	.311	.378	.464	140	25	7	4	-0	.980	-7	*S-125	2.8
1989	Det-A	121	449	54	109	20	3	5	43	45	45	.243	.317	.334	86	-8	10	2	2	.985	12	*S-117/D-2	1.6
1990	Det-A★	146	559	71	170	37	1	14	89	68	55	.304	.381	.449	130	24	12	10	-2	.979	1	*S-142/D-3	3.3
1991	Det-A	101	375	57	93	20	0	9	55	37	39	.248	.320	.373	90	-5	11	2	2	.979	4	S-92/D-6	0.8
1992	Det-A	29	102	11	28	7	1	1	11	15	4	.275	.373	.392	114	2	2	2	-1	.977	-1	S-27/D-1	0.3
1993	Det-A	112	401	72	132	25	3	12	60	38	38	.329	.390	.496	137	21	12	8	-1	.989	-13	S-63,3-35/OD	1.1
1994	Det-A	76	292	38	78	17	1	8	28	16	35	.267	.307	.414	84	-7	3	0	1	.968	-4	S-63,D-11	-0.6
Total	18	2153	7872	1187	2260	398	55	182	964	813	828	.287	.357	.421	113	151	227	108	3	.977	-101	*S-2036/D-53,3O	24.0

■ CECIL TRAVIS
Travis, Cecil Howell   b: 8/8/13, Riverdale, Ga.   BL/TR, 6'1.5", 185 lbs.   Deb: 5/16/33

YEAR	TM/L	G	AB	R	H	2B	3B	HR	RBI	BB	SO	AVG	OBP	SLG	PRO+	BR/A	SB	CS	SBR	FA	FR	G/POS	TPR
1933	Was-A	18	43	7	13	1	0	0	2	2	5	.302	.348	.326	80	-1	0	0	0	.974	4	3-15	0.3
1934	Was-A	109	392	48	125	22	4	1	53	24	37	.319	.361	.403	101	0	1	5	-3	.937	3	3-99	0.4
1935	Was-A	138	534	85	170	27	8	0	61	41	28	.318	.377	.399	104	4	4	2	0	.963	21	*3-114,O-16	2.7
1936	Was-A	138	517	77	164	34	10	2	92	39	21	.317	.366	.433	102	1	4	4	-1	.938	-13	S-71,O-53/23	-0.9
1937	Was-A	135	526	72	181	27	7	3	66	39	34	.344	.395	.439	115	13	3	2	0	.965	-11	*S-129	1.0
1938	Was-A☆	146	567	96	190	30	5	5	67	58	22	.335	.401	.432	117	16	6	5	-1	.950	3	*S-143	2.6
1939	Was-A	130	476	55	139	20	9	5	63	34	25	.292	.342	.403	97	-3	0	3	-2	.958	-4	*S-118	0.1
1940	Was-A★	136	528	60	170	37	11	2	76	48	23	.322	.381	.445	121	16	0	1	-1	.934	16	*3-113,S-23	3.3
1941	Was-A★	152	608	106	**218**	39	19	7	101	52	25	.359	.410	.520	152	44	2	2	-1	.964	2	*S-136,3-16	5.3
1945	Was-A	15	54	4	13	2	1	0	10	4	5	.241	.293	.315	83	-1	0	1	-1	.920	0	3-14	-0.1
1946	Was-A	137	465	45	117	22	3	1	56	45	47	.252	.323	.318	85	-10	2	4	-2	.959	-19	S-75,3-56	-2.7
1947	Was-A	74	204	10	44	4	1	1	10	16	19	.216	.273	.260	50	-14	1	3	-2	.932	-2	3-39,S-15	-1.8
Total	12	1328	4914	665	1544	265	78	27	657	402	291	.314	.370	.416	109	64	23	32	-12	.955	0	S-710,3-468/O2	10.2

■ BRIAN TRAXLER
Traxler, Brian Lee   b: 9/26/67, Waukegan, Ill.   BL/TL, 5'10", 200 lbs.   Deb: 4/24/90

YEAR	TM/L	G	AB	R	H	2B	3B	HR	RBI	BB	SO	AVG	OBP	SLG	PRO+	BR/A	SB	CS	SBR	FA	FR	G/POS	TPR
1990	LA-N	9	11	0	1	1	0	0	0	0	4	.091	.091	.182	-28	-2	0	0	0	1.000	1	/1-3	-0.2

■ JIM TRAY
Tray, James   b: 2/14/1860, Jackson, Mich.   d: 7/28/05, Jackson, Mich.   5'11", 180 lbs.   Deb: 9/6/1884

YEAR	TM/L	G	AB	R	H	2B	3B	HR	RBI	BB	SO	AVG	OBP	SLG	PRO+	BR/A	SB	CS	SBR	FA	FR	G/POS	TPR
1884	Ind-a	6	21	2	6	0	0	0		2		.286	.348	.286	112	0				.857	-2	/C-4,1-2	-0.1

■ PIE TRAYNOR
Traynor, Harold Joseph   b: 11/11/1899, Framingham, Mass.   d: 3/16/72, Pittsburgh, Pa.   BR/TR, 6', 170 lbs.   Deb: 9/15/20   MH

YEAR	TM/L	G	AB	R	H	2B	3B	HR	RBI	BB	SO	AVG	OBP	SLG	PRO+	BR/A	SB	CS	SBR	FA	FR	G/POS	TPR
1920	Pit-N	17	52	6	11	3	1	0	2	3	6	.212	.268	.308	63	-3	1	3	-2	.860	-6	S-17	-0.9
1921	Pit-N	7	19	0	5	0	0	0	2	1	2	.263	.300	.263	49	-1	0	0	0	.917	1	/3-3,S-1	0.0
1922	Pit-N	142	571	89	161	17	12	4	81	27	28	.282	.319	.375	77	-20	17	3	3	.945	-4	*3-124,S-18	-0.9
1923	Pit-N	153	616	108	208	19	**19**	12	101	34	19	.338	.377	.489	124	20	28	13	1	.950	8	*3-152/S-1	4.0
1924	Pit-N	142	545	86	160	26	13	5	82	37	26	.294	.340	.417	100	-1	24	18	-4	.968	9	*3-141	1.5
1925	*Pit-N	150	591	114	189	39	14	6	106	52	19	.320	.377	.464	106	5	15	9	-1	**.957**	23	*3-150/S-1	3.5
1926	Pit-N	152	574	83	182	25	17	3	92	38	14	.317	.361	.436	108	5	8			.952	7	*3-148/S-3	2.1
1927	*Pit-N	149	573	93	196	32	9	5	106	22	11	.342	.370	.455	112	8	11			.962	13	*3-143/S-9	2.8
1928	Pit-N	144	569	91	192	38	12	3	124	28	10	.337	.370	.462	112	9	12			.946	4	*3-144	2.0
1929	Pit-N	130	540	94	192	27	12	4	108	30	7	.356	.393	.472	111	9	13			.951	-1	*3-130	1.2
1930	Pit-N	130	497	90	182	22	11	9	119	48	19	.366	.423	.509	124	21	7			.941	5	*3-130	2.9
1931	Pit-N	155	615	81	183	37	15	2	103	54	28	.298	.354	.416	107	6	6			.925	-9	*3-155	0.7
1932	Pit-N	135	513	74	169	27	10	2	68	32	20	.329	.373	.433	118	13	6			.936	-3	*3-127	1.9
1933	Pit-N★	154	624	85	190	27	6	1	82	35	24	.304	.342	.372	104	3	5			.946	-1	*3-154	1.3
1934	Pit-N★	119	444	62	137	22	10	1	61	21	27	.309	.341	.410	98	-2	3			.954	-10	*3-110,M	-0.7
1935	Pit-N	57	204	24	57	10	3	1	36	10	17	.279	.323	.373	84	-5	2			.888	-3	/3-49/1-1M	-0.6
1937	Pit-N	5	12	3	2	0	0	0	0	0	1	.167	.167	.167	-9	-2	0			1.000	1	/3-3,M	0.0
Total	17	1941	7559	1183	2416	371	164	58	1273	472	278	.320	.362	.435	107	68	158	<u>46</u>		.947	34	*3-1863/S-50,1	20.8

■ FRED TREACEY
Treacey, Frederick S.   b: 1847, Brooklyn, N.Y.   5'9.5", 145 lbs.   Deb: 5/16/1871   F

YEAR	TM/L	G	AB	R	H	2B	3B	HR	RBI	BB	SO	AVG	OBP	SLG	PRO+	BR/A	SB	CS	SBR	FA	FR	G/POS	TPR
1871	Chi-n	25	124	39	42	7	5	**4**	33	2	5	.339	.349	.573	144	5	13					*O-25	0.4
1872	Ath-n	47	236	53	64	7	2	2	29	5	10	.271	.286	.343	93	-2						*O-46	-0.1
1873	Phi-n	51	243	49	62	7	2	1	32	5	6	.255	.270	.313	68	-10						*O-51	-0.7
1874	Chi-n	35	146	18	28	6	0	0		3		.192	.208	.233	40	-10						O-35	-0.7
1875	Cen-n	11	46	9	12	2	0	0		2		.261	.292	.304	116	1						O-11	0.1
	Phi-n	43	179	24	38	3	3	0		1		.212	.217	.263	62	-7						O-42	-0.6
	Yr	54	225	33	50	5	3	0		3		.222	.232	.271	73	-6						O-53	-0.5
1876	NY-N	57	256	47	54	5	1	0	18	1	5	.211	.214	.238	58	-10				.844	12	*O-57	0.1
Total	5 n	212	974	192	246	32	12	7	<u>94</u>	18	<u>21</u>	.253	.266	.332	82	-23						O-210	-1.6

■ PETE TREACEY
Treacey, Peter   b: 1852, Brooklyn, N.Y.   Deb: 8/5/1876   F

YEAR	TM/L	G	AB	R	H	2B	3B	HR	RBI	BB	SO	AVG	OBP	SLG	PRO+	BR/A	SB	CS	SBR	FA	FR	G/POS	TPR
1876	NY-N	2	5	1	0	0	0	0	0	1	0	.000	.167	.000	-46	-1				.750	-1	/S-2	-0.2

■ RAY TREADAWAY
Treadaway, Edgar Raymond   b: 10/31/07, Ragland, Ala.   d: 10/12/35, Chattanooga, Tenn.   BL/TR, 5'7", 150 lbs.   Deb: 9/17/30

YEAR	TM/L	G	AB	R	H	2B	3B	HR	RBI	BB	SO	AVG	OBP	SLG	PRO+	BR/A	SB	CS	SBR	FA	FR	G/POS	TPR
1930	Was-A	6	19	1	4	2	0	0	1	0	3	.211	.211	.316	31	-2	0	0	0	.833	-1	/3-4	-0.3

■ GEORGE TREADWAY
Treadway, George B.   BL , 6', 185 lbs.   Deb: 4/27/1893

YEAR	TM/L	G	AB	R	H	2B	3B	HR	RBI	BB	SO	AVG	OBP	SLG	PRO+	BR/A	SB	CS	SBR	FA	FR	G/POS	TPR
1893	Bal-N	115	458	78	119	16	17	1	67	57	50	.260	.347	.376	90	-7	24			.901	8	*O-115	-0.4
1894	Bro-N	123	479	124	157	27	26	4	102	72	43	.328	.418	.518	134	28	27			.892	1	*O-122/1-1	1.6
1895	Bro-N	86	339	54	87	14	3	7	54	33	22	.257	.326	.378	88	-6	9			.886	-9	O-86	-1.8
1896	Lou-N	2	7	0	1	0	0	0	1	1	0	.143	.250	.143	5	-1	0			.500	-1	/O-1,1-1	-0.2
Total	4	326	1283	256	364	57	46	12	224	163	115	.284	.368	.428	106	14	60			.891	-1	O-324/1-2	-0.8

■ JEFF TREADWAY
Treadway, Hugh Jeffery   b: 1/22/63, Columbus, Ga.   BL/TR, 5'10", 170 lbs.   Deb: 9/4/87

YEAR	TM/L	G	AB	R	H	2B	3B	HR	RBI	BB	SO	AVG	OBP	SLG	PRO+	BR/A	SB	CS	SBR	FA	FR	G/POS	TPR
1987	Cin-N	23	84	9	28	4	0	2	4	2	6	.333	.356	.452	108	1	1	0		.958	-7	2-21	-0.5
1988	Cin-N	103	301	30	76	19	4	2	23	27	30	.252	.320	.362	92	-3	2	0	1	.984	3	2-97/3-2	0.4
1989	Atl-N	134	473	58	131	18	3	8	40	30	38	.277	.320	.378	96	-3	3	2	-0	.981	-4	*2-123/3-6	0.5
1990	Atl-N	128	474	56	134	20	2	11	59	25	42	.283	.323	.403	93	-5	3	4	-2	.976	10	*2-122	0.6
1991	*Atl-N	106	306	41	98	17	2	3	32	23	19	.320	.372	.418	115	6	2	2	-1	.960	-8	2-93	0.0
1992	*Atl-N	61	126	5	28	6	1	0	5	9	16	.222	.274	.286	55	-7	1	2	-1	.993	4	2-45/3-1	-0.8
1993	Cle-A	97	221	25	67	14	1	2	27	14	21	.303	.340	.403	102	1	1	1	-1	.933	1	3-42,2-19/D	0.2
1994	LA-N	52	67	14	20	3	0	0	5	5	8	.299	.356	.343	89	-1	1	1	0	.950	-1	2-24/3-3	-0.1
Total	8	704	2052	238	582	101	13	28	195	135	180	.284	.332	.386	96	-11	14	12	-3	.975	1	2-544/3-54,D	0.3

■ RED TREADWAY
Treadway, Thadford Leon   b: 4/28/20, Athalone, N.C.   BL/TR, 5'10", 175 lbs.   Deb: 7/25/44

YEAR	TM/L	G	AB	R	H	2B	3B	HR	RBI	BB	SO	AVG	OBP	SLG	PRO+	BR/A	SB	CS	SBR	FA	FR	G/POS	TPR
1944	NY-N	50	170	23	51	5	2	0	5	13	11	.300	.350	.353	98	-0	2			.957	1	O-38	-0.1
1945	NY-N	88	224	31	54	4	2	0	23	20	13	.241	.303	.330	75	-8	3			.940	-9	O-60	-2.0
Total	2	138	394	54	105	9	4	0	28	33	24	.266	.323	.340	85	-8	5			.948	-8	/O-98	-2.1

■ FRANK TRECHOCK
Trechock, Frank Adam   b: 12/24/15, Windber, Pa.   d: 1/16/89, Minneapolis, Minn.   BR/TR, 5'10", 175 lbs.   Deb: 9/19/37

YEAR	TM/L	G	AB	R	H	2B	3B	HR	RBI	BB	SO	AVG	OBP	SLG	PRO+	BR/A	SB	CS	SBR	FA	FR	G/POS	TPR
1937	Was-A	1	4	0	2	0	0	0		0		.500	.500	.500	160	0				.750	0	/S-1	0.1

■ NICK TREMARK
Tremark, Nicholas Joseph   b: 10/15/12, Yonkers, N.Y.   BL/TL, 5'5", 150 lbs.   Deb: 8/9/34

YEAR	TM/L	G	AB	R	H	2B	3B	HR	RBI	BB	SO	AVG	OBP	SLG	PRO+	BR/A	SB	CS	SBR	FA	FR	G/POS	TPR
1934	Bro-N	17	28	3	7	1	0	0	6	2	2	.250	.300	.286	61	-2	0			1.000	-1	/O-9	-0.3

YEAR	TM/L	G	AB	R	H	2B	3B	HR	RBI	BB	SO	AVG	OBP	SLG	PRO+	BR/A	SB	CS	SBR	FA	FR	G/POS	TPR
1935	Bro-N	10	13	1	3	1	0	0	3	1	1	.231	.286	.308	61	-1	0			1.000	-1	/O-4	-0.1
1936	Bro-N	8	32	6	8	2	0	0	1	3	2	.250	.333	.313	74	-1	0			1.000	1	/O-8	0.0
Total	3	35	73	10	18	4	0	0	10	6	5	.247	.313	.301	67	-3	0			1.000	-0	/O-21	-0.4

■ OVERTON TREMPER
Tremper, Carlton Overton b: 3/22/06, Brooklyn, N.Y. BR/TR, 5'10", 163 lbs. Deb: 6/16/27

YEAR	TM/L	G	AB	R	H	2B	3B	HR	RBI	BB	SO	AVG	OBP	SLG	PRO+	BR/A	SB	CS	SBR	FA	FR	G/POS	TPR
1927	Bro-N	26	60	4	14	0	0	0	4	0	2	.233	.246	.233	29	-6	0			1.000	-4	O-18	-1.1
1928	Bro-N	10	31	1	6	2	1	0	1	0	1	.194	.194	.323	33	-3	0			1.000	-0	/O-9	-0.4
Total	2	36	91	5	20	2	1	0	5	0	3	.220	.228	.264	30	-9	0			1.000	-4	/O-27	-1.5

■ GEORGE TRENWITH
Trenwith, George b: Ireland d: 2/1/1890, Philadelphia, Pa. Deb: 4/30/1875

YEAR	TM/L	G	AB	R	H	2B	3B	HR	RBI	BB	SO	AVG	OBP	SLG	PRO+	BR/A	SB	CS	SBR	FA	FR	G/POS	TPR
1875	Cen-n	10	45	5	8	0	0	0			1	.178	.196	.178	33	-3						3-10	-0.2
	NH-n	6	25	1	6	2	0	0			0	.240	.240	.320	105	-0						/3-6	0.0
	Yr	16	70	6	14	2	0	0			1	.200	.211	.229	58	-2						3-16	-0.2

■ MIKE TRESH
Tresh, Michael b: 2/23/14, Hazleton, Pa. d: 10/4/66, Detroit, Mich. BR/TR, 5'11", 170 lbs. Deb: 9/4/38 F

YEAR	TM/L	G	AB	R	H	2B	3B	HR	RBI	BB	SO	AVG	OBP	SLG	PRO+	BR/A	SB	CS	SBR	FA	FR	G/POS	TPR
1938	Chi-A	10	29	3	7	1	0	0	2	8	4	.241	.405	.310	80	-1	0	0	0	.978	2	C-10	0.1
1939	Chi-A	119	352	49	91	5	2	0	38	64	30	.259	.377	.284	70	-13	3	2	-0	.985	2	*C-119	-0.5
1940	Chi-A	135	480	62	135	15	5	1	64	49	40	.281	.349	.340	78	-14	3	10	-5	.983	7	*C-135	-0.1
1941	Chi-A	115	390	38	98	10	1	0	33	38	27	.251	.319	.282	61	-21	1	0	0	.981	10	*C-115	-0.1
1942	Chi-A	72	233	21	54	8	1	0	15	28	24	.232	.314	.275	68	-9	2	0	1	.977	-6	C-72	-0.9
1943	Chi-A	86	279	20	60	3	0	0	20	37	20	.215	.307	.226	57	-14	2	1	0	.982	-1	C-85	-0.9
1944	Chi-A	93	312	22	81	8	1	0	25	37	15	.260	.342	.292	83	-5	0	3	-2	.981	-3	C-93	-0.5
1945	Chi-A†	150	458	50	114	12	0	0	47	65	37	.249	.342	.275	82	-8	6	3	0	.984	-2	*C-150	-0.1
1946	Chi-A	80	217	28	47	5	2	0	21	36	24	.217	.336	.258	70	-7	2	2	-1	.995	14	C-79	1.0
1947	Chi-A	90	274	19	66	6	2	0	20	26	26	.241	.311	.277	67	-12	0	0	-1	.975	-7	C-89	-1.3
1948	Chi-A	39	108	10	27	1	0	1	11	9	9	.250	.308	.287	61	-6	0	0	0	.983	-1	C-34	-0.5
1949	Cle-A	38	37	4	8	0	0	0	1	5	7	.216	.310	.216	41	-3	0	0	0	1.000	6	C-38	0.3
Total	12	1027	3169	326	788	75	14	2	297	402	263	.249	.335	.283	71	-113	19	21	-7	.983	22	*C-1019	-3.5

■ TOM TRESH
Tresh, Thomas Michael b: 9/20/37, Detroit, Mich. BB/TR, 6', 191 lbs. Deb: 9/3/61 F

YEAR	TM/L	G	AB	R	H	2B	3B	HR	RBI	BB	SO	AVG	OBP	SLG	PRO+	BR/A	SB	CS	SBR	FA	FR	G/POS	TPR
1961	NY-A	9	8	1	2	0	0	0	0	0	1	.250	.250	.250	36	-1	0	0	0	1.000	3	/S-3	0.2
1962	*NY-A★	157	622	94	178	26	5	20	93	67	74	.286	.363	.441	119	17	4	8	-4	.970	-11	*S-111,O-43	1.0
1963	*NY-A★	145	520	91	140	28	5	25	71	83	79	.269	.374	.487	140	29	3	3	-1	.981	2	*O-144	2.4
1964	*NY-A	153	533	75	131	25	5	16	73	73	110	.246	.344	.402	105	5	13	4	0	.996	-14	*O-146	-1.3
1965	NY-A	156	602	94	168	29	6	26	74	59	92	.279	.348	.477	133	25	5	2	0	.970	-21	*O-154	-0.3
1966	NY-A	151	537	76	125	12	4	27	68	86	89	.233	.345	.421	123	18	5	4	-1	.985	28	O-84,3-64	4.1
1967	NY-A	130	448	45	98	23	3	14	53	50	86	.219	.303	.377	104	2	1	0	0	.972	4	O-118	-0.1
1968	NY-A	152	507	60	99	18	3	11	52	76	97	.195	.305	.308	89	-5	10	5	0	.951	9	*S-119,O-27	1.7
1969	NY-A	45	143	13	26	5	2	1	9	17	23	.182	.269	.266	52	-9	2	1	0	.980	9	S-41	-0.5
	Det-A	94	331	46	74	13	1	13	37	39	47	.224	.309	.387	90	-5	2	2	-1	.965	-18	S-77,O-11/3	-1.7
	Yr	139	474	59	100	18	3	14	46	56	70	.211	.297	.350	79	-14	4	3	-1	.971	-18	*S-118,O-11/3	-2.2
Total	9	1192	4251	595	1041	179	34	153	530	550	698	.245	.337	.411	113	75	45	25	-2	.979	-19	O-727,S-351/3	5.5

■ ALEX TREVINO
Trevino, Alejandro (Castro) b: 8/26/57, Monterrey, Mex. BR/TR, 5'11", 170 lbs. Deb: 9/11/78 F

YEAR	TM/L	G	AB	R	H	2B	3B	HR	RBI	BB	SO	AVG	OBP	SLG	PRO+	BR/A	SB	CS	SBR	FA	FR	G/POS	TPR
1978	NY-N	6	12	3	3	0	0	0	0	1	2	.250	.308	.250	60	-1	0	0	0	1.000	-	/C-5,3-1	-0.1
1979	NY-N	79	207	24	56	11	1	0	20	20	27	.271	.338	.333	87	-3	2	2	-1	.976	10	C-36,3-27/2	0.7
1980	NY-N	106	355	26	91	11	2	0	37	13	41	.256	.285	.299	65	-17	0	3	-2	.977	-5	C-86,3-14/2	-2.2
1981	NY-N	56	149	17	39	2	0	0	10	13	19	.262	.325	.275	73	-5	3	0	1	.963	2	C-45/2-4,O3	0.0
1982	Cin-N	120	355	24	89	10	3	1	33	34	34	.251	.321	.304	74	-11	3	1	0	.979	4	*C-116/3-2	-0.3
1983	Cin-N	74	167	14	36	8	1	1	13	17	20	.216	.288	.293	59	-9	0	0	0	.987	11	C-63/3-4,2	0.4
1984	Cin-N	6	6	0	1	0	0	0	0	0	2	.167	.167	.167	-6	-1	0	0	0	1.000	-0	/C-4	-0.1
	Atl-N	79	266	36	65	16	0	3	28	16	27	.244	.290	.338	71	-10	5	2	0	.989	7	C-79	0.0
	Yr	85	272	36	66	16	0	3	28	16	29	.243	.287	.335	69	-11	5	2	0	.989	6	C-83	-0.1
1985	SF-N	57	157	17	34	10	1	6	19	20	24	.217	.305	.408	103	0	0	0	0	.978	-0	C-55/3-1	0.2
1986	LA-N	89	202	31	53	13	0	4	26	16	26	.262	.332	.386	111	3	0	0	0	.969	-4	C-63/1-1	0.2
1987	LA-N	72	144	16	32	7	1	3	16	6	28	.222	.273	.347	65	-8	1	0	0	.987	-	C-45/O-2,3	-0.8
1988	Hou-N	78	193	19	48	17	0	2	13	24	29	.249	.341	.368	108	2	5	2	0	.977	-9	C-74/O-1	0.0
1989	Hou-N	59	131	15	38	7	1	2	16	7	18	.290	.331	.405	113	2	0	0	0	.989	-3	C-32/1-2,3	0.2
1990	Hou-N	42	69	3	13	3	0	1	10	6	11	.188	.273	.275	53	-4	0	1	-1	.992	6	C-30/1-1	0.2
	NY-N	9	10	0	3	1	0	0	2	0	1	.300	.364	.400	110	0	0	0	0	.929	0	/C-7	0.1
	Cin-N	7	7	0	3	1	0	0	1	0	0	.429	.500	.571	186	1	0	0	0	1.000	1	/C-2	0.2
	Yr	58	86	3	19	5	0	1	13	7	11	.221	.302	.314	71	-3	0	1	-1	.982	7	C-39/1-1	0.5
Total	13	939	2430	245	604	117	10	23	244	205	317	.249	.312	.333	81	-61	19	11	-2	.979	16	C-742/3-53,201	-1.6

■ BOBBY TREVINO
Trevino, Carlos (Castro) b: 8/15/43, Monterrey, Mexico BR/TR, 6'2", 185 lbs. Deb: 5/22/68 F

YEAR	TM/L	G	AB	R	H	2B	3B	HR	RBI	BB	SO	AVG	OBP	SLG	PRO+	BR/A	SB	CS	SBR	FA	FR	G/POS	TPR
1968	Cal-A	17	40	1	9	1	0	0	1	2	9	.225	.262	.250	58	-2	0	1	-1	.962	-0	O-11	-0.4

■ GUS TRIANDOS
Triandos, Gus b: 7/30/30, San Francisco, Cal BR/TR, 6'3", 215 lbs. Deb: 8/13/53

YEAR	TM/L	G	AB	R	H	2B	3B	HR	RBI	BB	SO	AVG	OBP	SLG	PRO+	BR/A	SB	CS	SBR	FA	FR	G/POS	TPR
1953	NY-A	18	51	5	8	1	0	1	6	3	9	.157	.204	.255	24	-6	0	0	0	.991	0	1-12/C-5	-0.6
1954	NY-A	2	1	0	0	0	0	0	0	0	1	.000	.000	.000	-99	-0	0	0	0	.000	0	/C-1	0.0
1955	Bal-A	140	481	47	133	17	3	12	65	40	55	.277	.335	.399	104	1	0	0	0	.989	0	*1-103,C-36/3	-0.4
1956	Bal-A	131	452	47	126	18	1	21	88	48	73	.279	.351	.462	122	12	0	0	0	.989	10	C-89,1-52	2.2
1957	Bal-A☆	129	418	44	106	21	1	19	72	38	73	.254	.320	.445	114	6	0	0	0	.992	-2	*C-120	0.9
1958	Bal-A★	137	474	59	116	10	0	30	79	60	65	.245	.331	.456	120	12	1	0	0	.987	1	*C-132	0.9
1959	Bal-A★	126	393	43	85	7	1	25	73	65	56	.216	.332	.430	110	5	0	0	0	.981	2	*C-125	1.4
1960	Bal-A	109	364	36	98	18	0	12	54	41	62	.269	.345	.418	107	3	0	0	0	.989	-7	*C-105	1.0
1961	Bal-A	115	397	35	97	21	0	17	63	44	60	.244	.321	.426	101	-0	0	0	0	.989	5	*C-114	1.0
1962	Bal-A	66	207	20	33	7	0	2	23	29	43	.159	.263	.280	49	-15	0	0	0	.985	-1	C-63	-1.5
1963	Det-A	106	327	28	78	13	0	14	41	32	67	.239	.318	.407	98	-1	0	0	0	.998	-6	C-90	-0.3
1964	Phi-N	73	188	17	47	9	0	8	33	29	41	.250	.344	.426	117	5	0	0	0	.985	2	C-64/1-1	1.0
1965	Phi-N	30	82	3	14	2	0	0	4	9	17	.171	.253	.195	29	-8	0	0	0	.975	-5	C-28	-1.3
	Hou-N	24	72	5	13	2	0	2	7	5	14	.181	.244	.292	54	-5	0	0	0	.970	-2	C-20	-0.6
	Yr	54	154	8	27	4	0	2	11	14	31	.175	.249	.240	40	-12	0	0	0	.973	-7	C-48	-1.9
Total	13	1206	3907	389	954	147	6	167	608	440	636	.244	.324	.413	103	10	1	0	0	.987	-2	C-992,1-168/3	4.2

■ MANNY TRILLO
Trillo, Jesus Manuel Marcano (b: Jesus Manuel Marcano (Trillo)) b: 12/25/50, Caripito, Ven. BR/TR, 6'1", 164 lbs. Deb: 6/28/73

YEAR	TM/L	G	AB	R	H	2B	3B	HR	RBI	BB	SO	AVG	OBP	SLG	PRO+	BR/A	SB	CS	SBR	FA	FR	G/POS	TPR
1973	Oak-A	17	12	0	3	2	0	0	3	0	4	.250	.250	.417	90	-0	0	0	0	.941	5	2-16	0.5
1974	*Oak-A	21	33	3	5	0	0	0	2	2	8	.152	.222	.152	10	-4	0	0	0	.949	6	2-21	0.2
1975	Chi-N	154	545	55	135	12	2	7	70	45	78	.248	.309	.316	70	-21	1	1	-4	.967	16	2-153/S-1	-0.1
1976	Chi-N	158	582	42	139	24	3	4	59	53	70	.239	.306	.311	69	-23	17	6	2	.971	18	2-156/S-1	0.7
1977	Chi-N★	152	504	51	141	18	5	7	57	44	58	.280	.344	.377	84	-11	3	5	-2	.970	30	2-149	2.7
1978	Chi-N	152	552	53	144	17	5	4	55	50	67	.261	.325	.332	75	-18	0	7	-4	.978	29	2-149	1.8
1979	Phi-N	118	431	40	112	22	1	6	42	20	59	.260	.299	.357	76	-15	4	7	-3	.987	-4	2-118	-0.4
1980	*Phi-N	141	531	68	155	25	9	4	43	32	46	.292	.336	.412	102	1	8	3	1	.987	19	2-140	3.1
1981	*Phi-N★	94	349	37	100	14	3	6	36	26	37	.287	.341	.395	104	2	10	4	1	.987	11	2-94	2.0

YEAR	TM/L	G	AB	R	H	2B	3B	HR	RBI	BB	SO	AVG	OBP	SLG	PRO+	BR/A	SB	CS	SBR	FA	FR	G/POS	TPR
1982	Phi-N★	149	549	52	149	24	1	0	39	33	53	.271	.316	.319	76	-17	8	10	-4	**.994**	5	*2-149	-0.8
1983	Cle-A★	88	320	33	87	13	1	1	29	21	46	.272	.317	.328	75	-11	1	3	-2	.989	3	2-87	-0.5
	Mon-N	31	121	16	32	8	0	2	16	10	18	.264	.331	.380	97	-0	0	0	0	.979	-6	2-31	-0.5
1984	SF-N	98	401	45	102	21	1	4	36	25	55	.254	.303	.342	84	-9	0	0	0	.988	-8	2-96/3-4	-1.5
1985	SF-N	125	451	36	101	16	2	3	25	40	44	.224	.289	.288	65	-21	2	0	1	.981	4	*2-120/3-1	-1.4
1986	Chi-N	81	152	22	45	10	0	1	19	16	21	.296	.363	.382	98	-0	0	2	-1	.949	0	3-53,1-11/2	-0.2
1987	Chi-N	108	214	27	63	8	0	8	26	25	37	.294	.368	.444	110	3	0	3	-2	.994	-4	1-47,3-35,2/S	-0.6
1988	Chi-N	76	164	15	41	5	0	1	14	8	32	.250	.285	.299	65	-7	2	0	1	.994	1	1-24,3-17,2/S	-0.7
1989	Cin-N	17	39	3	8	0	0	0	0	2	9	.205	.262	.205	34	-3	0	0	0	1.000	-4	2-10/1-3,S	-0.8
Total	17	1780	5950	598	1562	239	33	61	571	452	742	.263	.318	.345	80	-155	56	57	-17	.981	129	*2-1518,3-110/1S	3.5

■ COAKER TRIPLETT

Triplett, Herman Coaker b: 12/18/11, Boone, N.C. d: 1/30/92, Boone, N.C. BR/TR, 5'11", 185 lbs. Deb: 4/19/38

YEAR	TM/L	G	AB	R	H	2B	3B	HR	RBI	BB	SO	AVG	OBP	SLG	PRO+	BR/A	SB	CS	SBR	FA	FR	G/POS	TPR
1938	Chi-N	12	36	4	9	2	1	0	2	0	1	.250	.250	.361	65	-2	0			1.000	-1	/O-9	-0.3
1941	StL-N	76	185	29	53	6	3	3	21	18	27	.286	.350	.400	104	1	0			.965	-3	O-46	-0.4
1942	StL-N	64	154	18	42	7	4	1	23	17	15	.273	.345	.390	107	1	1			.966	-3	O-46	-0.4
1943	StL-N	9	25	1	2	0	0	1	4	1	6	.080	.115	.200	-9	-4	0			1.000	-0	/O-6	-0.4
	Phi-N	105	360	45	98	16	4	14	52	28	28	.272	.325	.456	129	11	2			.970	1	O-90	0.8
	Yr	114	385	46	100	16	4	15	56	29	34	.260	.312	.439	120	7	2			.972	1	O-96	0.4
1944	Phi-N	84	184	15	43	5	1	1	25	19	10	.234	.305	.288	70	-7	1			.989	-1	O-44	-1.0
1945	Phi-N	120	363	46	87	11	1	7	46	40	27	.240	.315	.333	83	-9	6			.945	-3	O-92	-1.7
Total	6	470	1307	148	334	47	14	27	173	123	114	.256	.320	.375	97	-8	10			.965	-9	O-333	-3.4

■ HAL TROSKY

Trosky, Harold Arthur Sr. (b: Harold Arthur Troyavesky Sr.)
b: 11/11/12, Norway, Iowa d: 6/18/79, Cedar Rapids, Ia. BL/TR, 6'2", 207 lbs. Deb: 9/11/33 F

YEAR	TM/L	G	AB	R	H	2B	3B	HR	RBI	BB	SO	AVG	OBP	SLG	PRO+	BR/A	SB	CS	SBR	FA	FR	G/POS	TPR
1933	Cle-A	11	44	6	13	1	2	1	8	2	12	.295	.340	.477	110	-1	0	0	0	.990	-1	1-11	-0.1
1934	Cle-A	154	625	117	206	45	9	35	142	58	49	.330	.388	.598	149	42	2	2	-1	.986	0	*1-154	2.5
1935	Cle-A	154	632	84	171	33	7	26	113	46	60	.271	.321	.468	100	-4	1	2	-1	.993	1	*1-153	-1.9
1936	Cle-A	151	629	124	216	45	9	42	**162**	36	58	.343	.382	.644	148	41	6	5	-1	.985	1	*1-151/2-1	2.3
1937	Cle-A	153	601	104	179	36	9	32	128	65	60	.298	.367	.547	127	21	3	1	0	.993	-2	*1-152	0.2
1938	Cle-A	150	554	106	185	40	9	19	110	67	40	.334	.407	.542	138	32	5	1	1	.993	4	*1-148	1.8
1939	Cle-A	122	448	89	150	31	4	25	104	52	28	.335	.405	.589	157	37	2	3	-1	.992	11	*1-118	3.1
1940	Cle-A	140	522	85	154	39	4	25	93	79	45	.295	.392	.529	140	31	1	2	-1	.991	-7	*1-139	1.0
1941	Cle-A	89	310	55	91	17	0	11	51	44	21	.294	.383	.455	127	12	1	2	-1	.989	-3	1-85	0.3
1944	Chi-A	135	497	55	120	32	2	10	70	62	30	.241	.327	.374	101	1	3	1	0	.993	-9	*1-130	-1.7
1946	Chi-A	88	299	22	76	12	3	2	31	34	37	.254	.330	.334	89	-4	4	3	-1	.991	-8	1-80	-1.8
Total	11	1347	5161	835	1561	331	58	228	1012	545	440	.302	.371	.522	130	210	28	23	-5	.991	-12	*1-1321/2-1	5.7

■ MIKE TROST

Trost, Michael J. b: 1866, Philadelphia, Pa. d: 3/24/01, Philadelphia, Pa. TR, 6'0.5", 180 lbs. Deb: 8/21/1890

YEAR	TM/L	G	AB	R	H	2B	3B	HR	RBI	BB	SO	AVG	OBP	SLG	PRO+	BR/A	SB	CS	SBR	FA	FR	G/POS	TPR
1890	StL-a	17	51	10	13	2	0	1		6		.255	.345	.353	93	-1	4			.890	1	C-13/O-4	0.0
1895	Lou-N	3	12	1	1	0	0	0	1	0	1	.083	.083	.083	-61	-3	1			1.000	-1	/1-3	-0.3
Total	2	20	63	11	14	2	0	1	1	6	1	.222	.300	.302	66	-4	5			.890	0	/C-13,O-4,1	-0.3

■ SAM TROTT

Trott, Samuel W. b: 3/1859, Maryland d: 6/5/25, Catonsville, Md. BL/TL, 5'9", 190 lbs. Deb: 5/29/1880 M

YEAR	TM/L	G	AB	R	H	2B	3B	HR	RBI	BB	SO	AVG	OBP	SLG	PRO+	BR/A	SB	CS	SBR	FA	FR	G/POS	TPR
1880	Bos-N	39	125	14	26	4	1	0	9	5	3	.208	.227	.256	65	-4				.893	6	C-36/O-4	0.2
1881	Det-N	6	25	3	5	2	1	0	2	1	3	.200	.231	.360	80	-1				.868	-2	/C-6	-0.3
1882	Det-N	32	129	11	31	7	1	0	12	0	13	.240	.240	.310	75	-4				.890	7	C-23/S-3,2103	0.3
1883	Det-N	75	295	27	72	14	1	0	29	10	23	.244	.269	.298	76	-8				.882	-17	2-42,C-34/O1	-2.0
1884	Bal-a	71	284	36	73	17	9	3		4		.257	.272	.412	116	4				.931	16	C-60/2-6,O	2.3
1885	Bal-a	21	88	12	24	2	2	0		5		.273	.312	.341	108	1				.882	-5	C-17/O-4,2S	-0.2
1887	Bal-a	85	300	44	77	16	3	0		27		.257	.322	.330	87	-4	8			.915	5	C-69,2-11/01S	0.6
1888	Bal-a	31	108	19	30	11	4	0	22	4		.278	.304	.454	145	5	1			.908	-4	C-27/O-3,21	0.3
Total	8	360	1354	166	338	73	22	3	74	54	44	.250	.280	.343	93	-11	9			.906	6	C-272/2-65,01S3	1.2

■ QUINCY TROUPPE

Trouppe, Quincy Thomas b: 12/25/12, Dublin, Ga. d: 8/12/93, Creve Coeur, Mo. BB/TR, 6'2.5", 225 lbs. Deb: 4/30/52

YEAR	TM/L	G	AB	R	H	2B	3B	HR	RBI	BB	SO	AVG	OBP	SLG	PRO+	BR/A	SB	CS	SBR	FA	FR	G/POS	TPR
1952	Cle-A	6	10	1	1	0	0	0	0	1	3	.100	.182	.100	-22	-2	0	0	0	1.000	2	/C-6	0.1

■ DASHER TROY

Troy, John Joseph b: 5/8/1856, New York, N.Y. d: 3/30/38, Ozone Park, N.Y. BR/TR, 5'5", 154 lbs. Deb: 8/23/1881

YEAR	TM/L	G	AB	R	H	2B	3B	HR	RBI	BB	SO	AVG	OBP	SLG	PRO+	BR/A	SB	CS	SBR	FA	FR	G/POS	TPR
1881	Det-N	11	44	2	15	3	0	0	4	3	8	.341	.383	.409	143	2				.792	-4	/3-7,2-4	-0.1
1882	Det-N	40	152	22	37	7	2	0	14	5	10	.243	.268	.316	86	-2				.847	-19	2-31,S-11	-1.9
	Pro-N	4	17	1	4	0	0	0	1	0	1	.235	.235	.235	52	-1				.750	-1	/S-4	-0.2
	Yr	44	169	23	41	7	2	0	15	5	11	.243	.264	.308	83	-3				.847	-21	2-31,S-15	-2.1
1883	NY-N	85	316	37	68	7	5	0	20	9	33	.215	.237	.269	54	-17				.879	-14	*2-73,S-12	-2.6
1884	*NY-a	107	421	80	111	22	10	2		19		.264	.300	.378	123	10				.879	-21	*2-107	-0.7
1885	NY-a	45	177	24	39	3	3	2		5		.220	.258	.305	84	-3				.866	-13	2-42/O-2,S	-1.3
Total	5	292	1127	166	274	42	20	4	39	41	52	.243	.274	.327	92	-10				.873	-72	2-257/S-28,3O	-6.8

■ FRED TRUAX

Truax, Frederick W. b: 1868, d: 12/18/1899, Omaha, Neb. Deb: 8/18/1890

YEAR	TM/L	G	AB	R	H	2B	3B	HR	RBI	BB	SO	AVG	OBP	SLG	PRO+	BR/A	SB	CS	SBR	FA	FR	G/POS	TPR
1890	Pit-N	1	3	0	1	0	0	0	1	1	1	.333	.500	.333	163	0	0			1.000	0	/O-1	0.0

■ HARRY TRUBY

Truby, Harry Garvin "Bird Eye" b: 5/12/1870, Ironton, Ohio d: 3/21/53, Ironton, Ohio TR, 5'11", 185 lbs. Deb: 8/21/1895 U

YEAR	TM/L	G	AB	R	H	2B	3B	HR	RBI	BB	SO	AVG	OBP	SLG	PRO+	BR/A	SB	CS	SBR	FA	FR	G/POS	TPR
1895	Chi-N	33	119	17	40	3	0	6	16	10	7	.336	.402	.361	92	-1	7			.950	0	2-33	0.1
1896	Chi-N	29	109	13	28	2	2	2	31	6	5	.257	.314	.367	76	-4	4			.935	1	2-28	-0.2
	Pit-N	8	32	1	5	0	0	0	3	2	4	.156	.206	.156	-4	-5	1			.949	-4	/2-8	-0.7
	Yr	37	141	14	33	2	2	2	34	8	9	.234	.289	.319	59	-9	5			.938	-3	2-36	-0.9
Total	2	70	260	31	73	5	2	2	50	18	16	.281	.342	.338	75	-10	12			.944	-3	/2-69	-0.8

■ FRANK TRUESDALE

Truesdale, Frank Day b: 3/31/1884, St.Louis, Mo. d: 8/27/43, Albuquerque, N.Mex. BB/TR, 5'8", 145 lbs. Deb: 4/27/10

YEAR	TM/L	G	AB	R	H	2B	3B	HR	RBI	BB	SO	AVG	OBP	SLG	PRO+	BR/A	SB	CS	SBR	FA	FR	G/POS	TPR
1910	StL-A	123	415	39	91	7	2	1	25	48		.219	.303	.253	79	-9	29			.914	-5	*2-122	-1.7
1911	StL-A	1	1	0	0	0	0	0	0	0	0	—	—	—		0	0			.000	0	R	0.0
1914	NY-A	77	217	22	46	4	0	0	13	39	35	.212	.340	.230	72	-5	11	11	-3	.947	-2	2-67/3-4	-1.2
1918	Bos-A	15	36	6	10	1	0	0	2	4	5	.278	.350	.306	100	-1	1			.913	-1	2-10	0.0
Total	4	216	668	68	147	12	2	1	40	91	40	.220	.318	.249	78	-14	41	11		.924	-7	2-199/3-4	-2.9

■ ED TRUMBULL

Trumbull, Edward J. (b: Edward J. Trembly) b: 11/3/1860, Chicopee, Mass. d: 1/14/37, Kingston, Pa. Deb: 5/10/1884

YEAR	TM/L	G	AB	R	H	2B	3B	HR	RBI	BB	SO	AVG	OBP	SLG	PRO+	BR/A	SB	CS	SBR	FA	FR	G/POS	TPR
1884	Was-a	25	86	5	10	2	0	0		2		.116	.136	.140	-11	-10				.828	-0	O-15,P-10	-0.5

■ GREG TUBBS

Tubbs, Gregory Alan b: 8/31/62, Smithville, Tenn. BR/TR, 5'9", 185 lbs. Deb: 8/1/93

YEAR	TM/L	G	AB	R	H	2B	3B	HR	RBI	BB	SO	AVG	OBP	SLG	PRO+	BR/A	SB	CS	SBR	FA	FR	G/POS	TPR
1993	Cin-N	35	59	10	11	2	1	0	2	4	10	.186	.351	.237	61	-3	3	1	0	.975	-4	O-21	-0.6

■ EDDIE TUCKER

Tucker, Eddie Jack "Scooter" b: 11/18/66, Greenville, Miss. BR/TR, 6'2", 205 lbs. Deb: 6/14/92

YEAR	TM/L	G	AB	R	H	2B	3B	HR	RBI	BB	SO	AVG	OBP	SLG	PRO+	BR/A	SB	CS	SBR	FA	FR	G/POS	TPR
1992	Hou-N	20	50	5	6	1	0	0	3	3	13	.120	.200	.140	-2	-7	1	1	-0	.976	-6	C-19	-1.3
1993	Hou-N	9	26	1	5	1	0	1	3	3	2	.192	.250	.231	31	-3	0	0	0	1.000	2	/C-8	0.0
Total	2	29	76	6	11	2	0	1	6	5	15	.145	.217	.171	10	-9	1	1	-0	.986	-4	/C-27	-1.3

■ OLLIE TUCKER

Tucker, Oliver Dinwiddie b: 1/27/02, Radiant, Va. d: 7/13/40, Radiant, Va. BL/TR, 5'11", 180 lbs. Deb: 4/17/27

YEAR	TM/L	G	AB	R	H	2B	3B	HR	RBI	BB	SO	AVG	OBP	SLG	PRO+	BR/A	SB	CS	SBR	FA	FR	G/POS	TPR
1927	Was-A	20	24	1	5	2	0	0	8	4	2	.208	.321	.292	61	-1	0	0	0	1.000	-0	/O-5	-0.2

YEAR	TM/L	G	AB	R	H	2B	3B	HR	RBI	BB	SO	AVG	OBP	SLG	PRO+	BR/A	SB	CS	SBR	FA	FR	G/POS	TPR
1928	Cle-A	14	47	5	6	0	0	1	2	7	3	.128	.255	.191	19	-6	0	2	-1	1.000	-0	O-14	-0.8
Total	2	34	71	6	11	2	0	1	10	11	5	.155	.277	.225	33	-7	0	2	-1	1.000	-1	/O-19	-1.0

■ TOMMY TUCKER
Tucker, Thomas Joseph "Foghorn" b: 10/28/1863, Holyoke, Mass. d: 10/22/35, Montague, Mass. BB/TR, 5'11", 165 lbs. Deb: 4/16/1887

YEAR	TM/L	G	AB	R	H	2B	3B	HR	RBI	BB	SO	AVG	OBP	SLG	PRO+	BR/A	SB	CS	SBR	FA	FR	G/POS	TPR
1887	Bal-a	136	524	114	144	15	9	6		29		.275	.347	.372	107	7	85			.976	4	*1-136	-0.3
1888	Bal-a	136	520	74	149	17	12	6	61	16		.287	.330	.400	137	21	43			.975	4	*1-129/O-7,P	1.1
1889	Bal-a	134	527	103	196	22	11	5	99	42	26	.372	.450	.484	163	46	63			.964	-1	*1-123,O-12	3.0
1890	Bos-N	132	539	104	159	17	8	1	62	56	22	.295	.387	.362	110	7	43			.979	-2	*1-132	-0.1
1891	Bos-N	140	548	103	148	16	5	2	69	37	30	.270	.349	.328	87	-10	26			.976	-3	*1-140/P-1	-1.9
1892	*Bos-N	149	542	85	153	15	7	1	62	45	35	.282	.365	.341	104	3	22			.972	-12	*1-149	-1.5
1893	Bos-N	121	486	83	138	13	2	7	91	27	31	.284	.342	.362	82	-15	8			.980	-11	*1-121	-2.4
1894	Bos-N	123	500	112	165	24	6	3	100	53	21	.330	.412	.420	94	-5	18			.985	2	*1-123/O-1	-0.2
1895	Bos-N	125	462	87	115	19	6	3	73	61	29	.249	.360	.335	74	-18	15			.978	6	*1-125	-0.8
1896	Bos-N	122	474	74	144	27	5	2	72	30	29	.304	.363	.395	94	-5	6			.985	3	*1-122	-0.8
1897	Bos-N	4	14	0	3	2	0	0	4	2		.214	.313	.357	72	-1	0			.957	1	/1-4	0.0
	Was-N	93	352	52	119	18	5	5	61	27		.338	.403	.460	128	14	18			.984	-3	*1-93	1.0
	Yr	97	366	52	122	20	5	5	65	29		.333	.399	.456	126	14	18			.982	-2	1-97	1.0
1898	Bro-N	73	283	35	79	9	4	1	34	12		.279	.325	.350	94	-3	1			.991	7	1-73	0.4
	StL-N	72	252	18	60	7	2	0	20	18		.238	.319	.282	71	-9	1			.973	-0	1-72	-0.9
	Yr	145	535	53	139	16	6	1	54	30		.260	.322	.318	83	-12	2			.982	7	*1-145	-0.5
1899	Cle-N	127	456	40	110	19	3	0	40	24		.241	.297	.296	68	-20	3			.977	-1	*1-127	-1.9
Total	13	1687	6479	1084	1882	240	85	42	848	479	223	.290	.364	.373	101	12	352			.978	-8	*1-1669/O-20,P	-4.5

■ THURMAN TUCKER
Tucker, Thurman Lowell "Joe E." b: 9/26/17, Gordon, Tex. d: 5/7/93, Oklahoma City, Okla. BL/TR, 5'11", 170 lbs. Deb: 4/14/42

YEAR	TM/L	G	AB	R	H	2B	3B	HR	RBI	BB	SO	AVG	OBP	SLG	PRO+	BR/A	SB	CS	SBR	FA	FR	G/POS	TPR
1942	Chi-A	7	24	2	3	0	1	0	1	0	4	.125	.125	.208	-7	-3	0	0	0	.900	-1	/O-5	-0.5
1943	Chi-A	139	528	81	124	15	6	3	39	79	72	.235	.336	.303	87	-6	29	17	-2	.988	15	*O-132	-0.2
1944	Chi-A★	124	446	59	128	15	6	2	46	57	40	.287	.368	.361	110	7	13	12	-3	.991	18	*O-120	1.6
1946	Chi-A	121	438	62	126	20	3	1	36	54	45	.288	.367	.354	106	5	9	10	-3	.990	2	*O-110	-0.2
1947	Chi-A	89	254	28	60	9	4	1	17	38	25	.236	.336	.315	85	-5	10	4	1	.978	-1	O-65	-0.9
1948	*Cle-A	83	242	52	63	13	2	1	19	31	17	.260	.347	.343	86	-5	11	2	2	1.000	-1	O-66	-0.6
1949	Cle-A	80	197	28	48	5	2	0	14	18	19	.244	.307	.289	59	-12	4	2	0	.984	2	O-42	-1.1
1950	Cle-A	57	101	13	18	2	0	1	7	14	14	.178	.284	.228	34	-10	1	0	0	.968	-5	O-34	-1.5
1951	Cle-A	1	1	0	0	0	0	0	0	0	1	.000	.000	.000	-99	-0	0	0	0	.000	0	H	0.0
Total	9	701	2231	325	570	79	24	9	179	291	237	.255	.342	.325	89	-28	77	47	-5	.988	29	O-574	-3.2

■ BRIAN TURANG
Turang, Brian Craig b: 6/14/67, Long Beach, Cal. BR/TR, 5'10", 170 lbs. Deb: 8/13/93

YEAR	TM/L	G	AB	R	H	2B	3B	HR	RBI	BB	SO	AVG	OBP	SLG	PRO+	BR/A	SB	CS	SBR	FA	FR	G/POS	TPR
1993	Sea-A	40	140	22	35	11	1	0	7	17	20	.250	.343	.343	83	-3	6	2	1	.986	-2	O-38/3-2,2D	-0.5
1994	Sea-A	38	112	9	21	5	1	1	8	7	25	.188	.242	.277	33	-11	3	1	0	.978	-4	O-30/2-5,D	-1.5
Total	2	78	252	31	56	16	2	1	15	24	45	.222	.297	.313	60	-14	9	3	1	.983	-6	/O-68,2-6,D3	-2.0

■ JERRY TURBIDY
Turbidy, Jeremiah b: 7/4/1852, Dudley, Mass. d: 9/5/20, Webster, Mass. 5'8", 165 lbs. Deb: 7/27/1884

YEAR	TM/L	G	AB	R	H	2B	3B	HR	RBI	BB	SO	AVG	OBP	SLG	PRO+	BR/A	SB	CS	SBR	FA	FR	G/POS	TPR
1884	KC-U	13	49	5	11	4	0	0		3		.224	.269	.306	64	-2				.830	6	S-13	0.3

■ EDDIE TURCHIN
Turchin, Edward Lawrence "Smiley" b: 2/10/17, New York, N.Y. d: 2/8/82, Brookhaven, N.Y. BR/TR, 5'10", 165 lbs. Deb: 5/9/43

YEAR	TM/L	G	AB	R	H	2B	3B	HR	RBI	BB	SO	AVG	OBP	SLG	PRO+	BR/A	SB	CS	SBR	FA	FR	G/POS	TPR
1943	Cle-A	11	13	4	3	0	0	0	1	3	1	.231	.375	.231	84	-0	0	0	0	1.000	1	/3-4,S-2	0.2

■ PETE TURGEON
Turgeon, Eugene Joseph b: 1/3/1897, Minneapolis, Minn. d: 1/24/77, Wichita Falls, Tex BR/TR, 5'6", 145 lbs. Deb: 9/20/23

YEAR	TM/L	G	AB	R	H	2B	3B	HR	RBI	BB	SO	AVG	OBP	SLG	PRO+	BR/A	SB	CS	SBR	FA	FR	G/POS	TPR
1923	Chi-N	3	6	1	1	0	0	0	0	0	0	.167	.167	.167	-12	-1	0	0	0	.875	0	/S-2	-0.1

■ CHRIS TURNER
Turner, Christopher Wan b: 3/23/69, Bowling Green, Ky. BR/TR, 6'2", 190 lbs. Deb: 8/27/93

YEAR	TM/L	G	AB	R	H	2B	3B	HR	RBI	BB	SO	AVG	OBP	SLG	PRO+	BR/A	SB	CS	SBR	FA	FR	G/POS	TPR
1993	Cal-A	25	75	9	21	5	1	0	13	9	16	.280	.365	.387	99	-2	1	1	-0	.992	-3	C-25	-0.2
1994	Cal-A	58	149	23	36	7	1	2	12	10	29	.242	.294	.322	57	-10	3	0	1	.997	4	C-57	-0.2
Total	2	83	224	32	57	12	1	2	25	19	45	.254	.318	.344	71	-9	4	1	1	.995	1	/C-82	-0.4

■ EARL TURNER
Turner, Earl Edwin b: 5/6/23, Pittsfield, Mass. BR/TR, 5'9", 170 lbs. Deb: 9/25/48

YEAR	TM/L	G	AB	R	H	2B	3B	HR	RBI	BB	SO	AVG	OBP	SLG	PRO+	BR/A	SB	CS	SBR	FA	FR	G/POS	TPR
1948	Pit-N	2	1	0	0	0	0	0	0	0	0	.000	.000	.000	-98	-0	0			.000	0	/C-1	0.0
1950	Pit-N	40	74	10	18	0	0	3	5	4	13	.243	.282	.365	66	-4	1			.974	2	C-34	-0.1
Total	2	42	75	10	18	0	0	3	5	4	13	.240	.278	.360	64	-4	1			.974	2	/C-35	-0.1

■ TUCK TURNER
Turner, George A. b: 2/13/1873, W.New Brighton, N.Y. d: 7/16/45, Staten Island, N.Y. BB/TL, 5'6.5", 155 lbs. Deb: 8/18/1893

YEAR	TM/L	G	AB	R	H	2B	3B	HR	RBI	BB	SO	AVG	OBP	SLG	PRO+	BR/A	SB	CS	SBR	FA	FR	G/POS	TPR
1893	Phi-N	36	155	32	50	4	3	1	13	9	19	.323	.364	.406	105	1	7			.933	-2	O-36	-0.2
1894	Phi-N	80	339	91	141	21	9	1	82	23	15	.416	.456	.540	143	25	11			.916	-9	O-78/P-1	0.8
1895	Phi-N	59	210	51	81	8	6	2	43	25	11	.386	.453	.510	147	16	14			.847	-8	O-55	0.3
1896	Phi-N	13	32	12	7	2	0	0	8	5		.219	.375	.281	75	-1	6			.905	2	/O-8	0.0
	StL-N	51	203	30	50	7	8	1	27	14	21	.246	.298	.374	80	-7	6			.961	-5	O-51	-1.4
	Yr	64	235	42	57	9	8	1	27	22	26	.243	.310	.362	79	-8	12			.948	-4	O-59	-1.4
1897	StL-N	103	416	58	121	17	12	2	41	35		.291	.350	.404	101	-0	8			.945	-7	*O-102	-1.3
1898	StL-N	35	141	20	28	8	0	0	7	14		.199	.280	.255	52	-9	1			.929	-3	O-34	-1.3
Total	6	377	1496	294	478	67	38	7	213	128	69	.320	.377	.429	111	25	53			.920	-32	O-364/P-1	-3.1

■ JERRY TURNER
Turner, John Webber b: 1/17/54, Texarkana, Ark. BL/TL, 5'9", 180 lbs. Deb: 9/2/74

YEAR	TM/L	G	AB	R	H	2B	3B	HR	RBI	BB	SO	AVG	OBP	SLG	PRO+	BR/A	SB	CS	SBR	FA	FR	G/POS	TPR
1974	SD-N	17	48	4	14	1	0	0	2	3	5	.292	.333	.313	85	-1	2	1	0	1.000	-1	O-13	-0.3
1975	SD-N	11	22	1	6	0	0	0	0	2	1	.273	.333	.273	74	-1	0	0	0	.909	0	/O-4	-0.1
1976	SD-N	105	281	41	75	16	5	5	37	32	38	.267	.342	.413	123	8	12	6	0	.960	-2	O-74	0.3
1977	SD-N	118	289	43	71	16	1	10	48	31	42	.246	.319	.412	105	1	12	4	1	.947	3	O-69	0.3
1978	SD-N	106	225	28	63	9	1	8	37	21	32	.280	.349	.436	128	8	6	4	1	.970	-7	O-58	-0.2
1979	SD-N	138	448	55	111	23	2	9	61	34	58	.248	.304	.368	88	-9	4	2	0	.958	-1	*O-115	-1.5
1980	SD-N	85	153	22	44	5	0	3	18	10	18	.288	.339	.379	106	1	3	1	0	1.000	-4	O-34	-0.4
1981	SD-N	33	31	5	7	0	0	2	6	4	1	.226	.314	.419	115	0	0	1	-1	.833	-1	/O-4	-0.1
	Chi-A	10	12	1	2	0	0	0	2	1	2	.167	.231	.167	16	-1	0	0	0	1.000	0	/O-1	-0.1
1982	Det-A	85	210	21	52	3	0	8	27	20	37	.248	.313	.376	88	-4	1	3	-2	.909	-4	D-50,O-13	-1.1
1983	SD-N	25	23	1	3	0	0	0	0	1	1	.130	.167	.130	-17	-4	0	0	0	.000	0	/O-1	-0.4
Total	10	733	1742	222	448	73	9	45	238	159	245	.257	.322	.387	101	-1	45	24	-1	.959	-18	O-386/D-50	-3.6

■ SHANE TURNER
Turner, Shane Lee b: 1/8/63, Los Angeles, Cal. BL/TR, 5'10", 180 lbs. Deb: 8/19/88

YEAR	TM/L	G	AB	R	H	2B	3B	HR	RBI	BB	SO	AVG	OBP	SLG	PRO+	BR/A	SB	CS	SBR	FA	FR	G/POS	TPR
1988	Phi-N	18	35	1	6	1	0	0	1	5	9	.171	.275	.171	30	-3	0	0	0	.941	-2	/3-8,S-5	-0.6
1991	Bal-A	4	1	0	0	0	0	0	0	0	0	.000	.000	.000	-99	-0	0	0	0	1.000	-0	/2-1,D-1	0.0
1992	Sea-A	34	74	8	20	5	0	0	5	9	15	.270	.349	.338	93	-0	2	1	0	.881	-5	3-18,O-15	-0.6
Total	3	56	110	9	26	6	0	0	6	14	24	.236	.323	.282	71	-3	2	1	0	.898	-7	/3-26,O-15,SD2	-1.2

■ TERRY TURNER
Turner, Terrence Lamont "Cotton Top" b: 2/28/1881, Sandy Lake, Pa. d: 7/18/60, Cleveland, Ohio BR/TR, 5'8", 149 lbs. Deb: 8/25/01 C

YEAR	TM/L	G	AB	R	H	2B	3B	HR	RBI	BB	SO	AVG	OBP	SLG	PRO+	BR/A	SB	CS	SBR	FA	FR	G/POS	TPR
1901	Pit-N	2	7	0	3	0	0	0		0		.429	.429	.429	145	0	0			.833	1	/3-2	0.2
1904	Cle-A	111	404	41	95	9	6	1	45	11		.235	.255	.295	74	-13	5			.940	3	*S-111	-0.7
1905	Cle-A	155	586	49	155	16	14	6	72	14		.265	.289	.360	104	0	17			.945	-25	*S-155	-2.4
1906	Cle-A	147	584	85	170	27	7	2	62	35		.291	.338	.372	124	15	27			.960	24	*S-147	4.7
1907	Cle-A	140	524	57	127	20	7	0	46	19		.242	.272	.307	84	-11	27			.950	-3	*S-139	-1.1

YEAR	TM/L	G	AB	R	H	2B	3B	HR	RBI	BB	SO	AVG	OBP	SLG	PRO+	BR/A	SB	CS	SBR	FA	FR	G/POS	TPR
1908	Cle-A	60	201	21	48	11	1	0	19	15		.239	.298	.303	95	-1	18			.952	-4	O-36,S-17	-0.7
1909	Cle-A	53	208	25	52	7	4	0	16	14		.250	.304	.322	94	-2	14			.969	10	2-26,S-26	0.9
1910	Cle-A	150	574	71	132	14	6	0	33	53		.230	.301	.275	79	-13	31			.973	2	S-94,3-46/2	-0.7
1911	Cle-A	117	417	59	105	16	9	0	28	34		.252	.310	.333	78	-13	29			.970	3	3-94,2-14,S	-0.9
1912	Cle-A	103	370	54	114	14	4	0	33	31		.308	.363	.368	106	3	19			**.951**	-3	*3-103	0.1
1913	Cle-A	120	388	60	96	13	4	0	44	55	35	.247	.348	.302	88	-4	13			.954	16	3-71,2-25,S	1.5
1914	Cle-A	121	428	43	105	14	9	1	33	44	36	.245	.319	.327	91	-5	17	13	-3	**.963**	21	*3-104,2-17	1.9
1915	Cle-A	75	262	35	66	14	1	0	14	29	13	.252	.329	.313	90	-7	12	11	-3	.965	-9	2-51,3-20	-1.4
1916	Cle-A	124	428	52	112	15	3	0	38	40	29	.262	.325	.311	86	-7	15			.963	5	3-77,2-42	0.2
1917	Cle-A	69	180	16	37	7	0	0	15	14	19	.206	.263	.244	51	-11	4			.980	-2	3-40,2-23/S	-1.3
1918	Cle-A	74	233	24	58	7	2	0	23	22	15	.249	.316	.296	77	-6	6			.969	-4	3-46,2-26/S	-0.8
1919	Phi-A	38	127	7	24	3	0	0	6	5	9	.189	.220	.213	21	-13	2			.946	1	S-19,2-17/3	-1.1
Total	17	1659	5921	699	1499	207	77	8	528	435	156	.253	.308	.318	89	-83	256	24		.952	37	S-741,3-604,2/O	-1.6

■ TOM TURNER
Turner, Thomas Richard b: 9/8/16, Custer Co., Okla. d: 5/14/86, Kennewick, Wash. BR/TR, 6'2", 195 lbs. Deb: 4/25/40

YEAR	TM/L	G	AB	R	H	2B	3B	HR	RBI	BB	SO	AVG	OBP	SLG	PRO+	BR/A	SB	CS	SBR	FA	FR	G/POS	TPR
1940	Chi-A	37	96	11	20	1	2	0	6	3	12	.208	.240	.260	29	-10	1	0	0	.969	2	C-29	-0.6
1941	Chi-A	38	126	7	30	5	0	0	8	9	15	.238	.289	.278	51	-9	2	0	1	.979	5	C-35	0.0
1942	Chi-A	*56	182	18	44	9	1	3	21	19	15	.242	.313	.352	89	-3	0	1	-1	.971	-1	C-54	0.0
1943	Chi-A	51	154	16	37	7	1	2	11	13	21	.240	.299	.338	86	-3	1	0	0	.978	4	C-49	0.5
1944	Chi-A	36	113	9	26	6	0	2	13	5	16	.230	.263	.336	71	-5	0	1	-1	.958	-2	C-36	-0.6
	*StL-A	15	25	2	8	1	0	0	4	2	5	.320	.370	.360	103	-0	0	0	0	.969	-1	C-11	0.0
	Yr	51	138	11	34	7	0	2	17	7	21	.246	.283	.341	77	-5	0	1	-1	.960	-3	C-47	-0.6
Total	5	233	696	63	165	29	4	7	63	51	84	.237	.290	.320	70	-29	4	2	0	.972	7	C-214	-0.7

■ BILL TUTTLE
Tuttle, William Robert b: 7/4/29, Elwood, Ill. BR/TR, 6', 190 lbs. Deb: 9/10/52

YEAR	TM/L	G	AB	R	H	2B	3B	HR	RBI	BB	SO	AVG	OBP	SLG	PRO+	BR/A	SB	CS	SBR	FA	FR	G/POS	TPR
1952	Det-A	7	25	2	6	0	0	0	2	0	1	.240	.240	.240	34	-2	0	0	0	1.000	1	/O-6	-0.2
1954	Det-A	147	530	64	141	20	11	7	58	62	60	.266	.345	.385	102	1	5	8	-3	.985	4	*O-145	-0.5
1955	Det-A	154	603	102	168	23	4	14	78	76	54	.279	.360	.400	107	6	6	3	0	.985	15	*O-154	1.4
1956	Det-A	140	546	61	138	22	4	9	65	38	48	.253	.303	.357	73	-22	5	4	-1	.976	10	*O-137	-2.0
1957	Det-A	133	451	49	113	12	4	5	47	44	41	.251	.319	.328	75	-15	4	1	0	.982	4	*O-128	-2.1
1958	KC-A	148	511	77	118	14	9	11	51	74	58	.231	.329	.358	88	-8	7	9	-3	.988	4	*O-145	-1.8
1959	KC-A	126	463	74	139	19	6	7	43	48	38	.300	.371	.413	113	9	10	6	-1	.984	12	*O-121	1.4
1960	KC-A	151	559	75	143	21	3	6	40	66	52	.256	.337	.347	85	-11	1	5	-3	.988	17	*O-148	-0.4
1961	KC-A	25	84	15	22	2	2	0	8	9	9	.262	.333	.333	77	-3	0	0	0	.951	-1	O-25	-0.5
	Min-A	113	370	38	91	12	3	5	38	43	41	.246	.324	.335	73	-14	1	3	-2	.943	-13	3-85,O-64/2	-3.0
	Yr	138	454	53	113	14	5	5	46	52	50	.249	.326	.335	73	-16	1	3	-2	.970	-14	O-89,3-85/2	-3.5
1962	Min-A	110	123	21	26	4	1	1	13	19	14	.211	.322	.285	62	-6	1	0	0	.973	-31	*O-104	-3.9
1963	Min-A	16	3	0	0	0	0	0	0	1	0	.000	.250	.000	-22	-0	0	0	0	1.000	-4	O-14	-0.5
Total	11	1270	4268	578	1105	149	47	67	443	480	416	.259	.336	.363	88	-65	38	44	-15	.983	14	*O-1191/3-85,2	-12.1

■ GUY TUTWILER
Tutwiler, Guy Isbell "King Tut" b: 7/17/1889, Coalburg, Ala. d: 8/15/30, Birmingham, Ala. BL/TR, 6', 175 lbs. Deb: 8/29/11

YEAR	TM/L	G	AB	R	H	2B	3B	HR	RBI	BB	SO	AVG	OBP	SLG	PRO+	BR/A	SB	CS	SBR	FA	FR	G/POS	TPR
1911	Det-A	13	32	3	6	2	0	0	3	2		.188	.235	.250	34	-3	0			.778	-4	/2-6,O-3	-0.7
1913	Det-A	14	47	4	10	0	1	0	7	4	12	.213	.275	.255	56	-3	2			.987	1	1-14	-0.2
Total	2	27	79	7	16	2	1	0	10	6	12	.203	.259	.253	47	-6	2			.987	-3	/1-14,2-6,O	-0.9

■ ART TWINEHAM
Twineham, Arthur W. "Old Hoss" b: 11/26/1866, Galesburg, Ill. BL/TL, 6'1.5", 190 lbs. Deb: 9/11/1893

YEAR	TM/L	G	AB	R	H	2B	3B	HR	RBI	BB	SO	AVG	OBP	SLG	PRO+	BR/A	SB	CS	SBR	FA	FR	G/POS	TPR
1893	StL-N	14	48	8	15	2	0	0	11	1	2	.313	.340	.354	84	-1	0			.928	2	C-14	0.2
1894	StL-N	38	127	22	40	4	1	1	16	9	11	.315	.387	.386	87	-2	2			.939	4	C-38	0.4
Total	2	52	175	30	55	6	1	1	27	10	13	.314	.375	.377	86	-3	2			.936	7	/C-52	0.6

■ LARRY TWITCHELL
Twitchell, Lawrence Grant b: 2/18/1864, Cleveland, Ohio d: 8/23/30, Cleveland, Ohio BR/TR, 6', 185 lbs. Deb: 4/30/1886

YEAR	TM/L	G	AB	R	H	2B	3B	HR	RBI	BB	SO	AVG	OBP	SLG	PRO+	BR/A	SB	CS	SBR	FA	FR	G/POS	TPR
1886	Det-N	4	16	0	1	0	0	0	0	0	2	.063	.063	.063	-60	-3	0			1.000	0	/P-4,O-2	-0.1
1887	*Det-N	65	264	44	88	14	6	0	51	8	19	.333	.358	.432	115	4	12			.871	-6	O-53,P-15	-0.2
1888	Det-N	131	524	71	128	19	4	5	67	28	45	.244	.286	.324	95	-3	14			.885	-9	*O-131/P-2	-1.6
1889	Cle-N	134	549	73	151	16	11	4	95	29	37	.275	.315	.366	92	-7	17			.916	-10	*O-134/P-1	-1.8
1890	Cle-P	56	233	52	52	6	3	2	36	17	14	.223	.279	.300	60	-14	4			.821	-9	O-56	-2.0
	Buf-P	44	172	24	38	3	1	2	17	23	12	.221	.316	.285	67	-7	4			.918	-1	O-32,P-13/1	-0.7
	Yr	100	405	57	90	9	4	4	53	40	29	.222	.295	.294	63	-21	8			.857	-10	O-88,P-13/1	-2.7
1891	Col-a	57	224	32	62	9	4	2	35	20	28	.277	.341	.379	113	3	10			.887	-10	O-56/P-6	-0.7
1892	Was-N	51	192	20	42	9	5	0	20	11	31	.219	.275	.318	82	-5	8			.897	-5	O-48/S-3,3	-1.1
1893	Lou-N	45	187	37	58	11	3	2	31	17	20	.310	.377	.433	125	7	7			.874	-2	O-45	0.2
1894	Lou-N	52	210	28	56	16	3	0	32	15	20	.267	.316	.400	77	-9	8			.908	6	O-51/P-1	-0.5
Total	9	639	2571	362	676	103	40	19	384	168	231	.263	.313	.356	91	-34	84			.890	-45	0-608/P-42,S13	-8.5

■ BABE TWOMBLY
Twombly, Clarence Edward b: 1/18/1896, Jamaica Plain, Mass. d: 11/23/74, San Clemente, Cal. BL/TR, 5'10", 165 lbs. Deb: 4/14/20 F

YEAR	TM/L	G	AB	R	H	2B	3B	HR	RBI	BB	SO	AVG	OBP	SLG	PRO+	BR/A	SB	CS	SBR	FA	FR	G/POS	TPR
1920	Chi-N	78	183	25	43	1	1	2	14	17	20	.235	.303	.284	68	-7	5	9	-4	.970	0	O-45/2-2	-1.5
1921	Chi-N	87	175	22	66	8	1	1	18	11	10	.377	.414	.451	129	8	4	6	-2	.968	0	O-45	0.3
Total	2	165	358	47	109	9	2	3	32	28	30	.304	.357	.366	98	0	9	15	-6	.969	1	/O-90,2-2	-1.2

■ GEORGE TWOMBLY
Twombly, George Frederick "Silent George" b: 6/4/1892, Boston, Mass. d: 2/17/75, Lexington, Mass. BR/TR, 5'9", 165 lbs. Deb: 7/9/14 F

YEAR	TM/L	G	AB	R	H	2B	3B	HR	RBI	BB	SO	AVG	OBP	SLG	PRO+	BR/A	SB	CS	SBR	FA	FR	G/POS	TPR
1914	Cin-N	68	240	22	56	0	5	0	19	14	27	.233	.284	.275	64	-11	12			.968	1	O-68	-1.4
1915	Cin-N	46	66	5	13	0	1	0	5	8	8	.197	.293	.227	57	-3	5	3	-0	1.000	-4	O-24	-0.9
1916	Cin-N	3	5	0	0	0	0	0	0	1	1	.000	.167	.000	-48	-1	0			1.000	0	/O-1	-0.1
1917	Bos-N	32	102	8	19	1	1	0	9	18	5	.186	.314	.216	68	-3	4			.943	-5	O-29/1-1	-1.1
1919	Was-A	1	4	0	0	0	0	0	0	0	0	.000	.000	.000	-99	-1	0			.000	-1	/O-1	-0.2
Total	5	150	417	35	88	1	7	0	33	41	41	.211	.289	.247	62	-18	21	3		.967	-9	O-123/1-1	-3.7

■ JIM TYACK
Tyack, James Frederick b: 1/9/11, Florence, Mont. BL/TR, 6'2", 195 lbs. Deb: 4/20/43

YEAR	TM/L	G	AB	R	H	2B	3B	HR	RBI	BB	SO	AVG	OBP	SLG	PRO+	BR/A	SB	CS	SBR	FA	FR	G/POS	TPR
1943	Phi-A	54	155	11	40	8	1	0	23	14	9	.258	.320	.323	88	-2	1	1	-0	.977	1	O-38	-0.4

■ FRED TYLER
Tyler, Frederick Franklin "Clancy" b: 12/16/1891, Derry, N.H. d: 10/14/45, E.Derry, N.H. BR/TR, 5'10.5", 180 lbs. Deb: 4/14/14 F

YEAR	TM/L	G	AB	R	H	2B	3B	HR	RBI	BB	SO	AVG	OBP	SLG	PRO+	BR/A	SB	CS	SBR	FA	FR	G/POS	TPR
1914	Bos-N	6	19	2	2	0	0	0	2	1	5	.105	.150	.105	-24	-3	0			1.000	-1	/C-6	-0.3

■ JOHNNIE TYLER
Tyler, John Anthony "Ty Ty" or "Katz" (b: John Tylka) b: 7/30/06, Mt.Pleasant, Pa. d: 7/11/72, Mt.Pleasant, Pa. BB/TR, 6', 175 lbs. Deb: 9/16/34

YEAR	TM/L	G	AB	R	H	2B	3B	HR	RBI	BB	SO	AVG	OBP	SLG	PRO+	BR/A	SB	CS	SBR	FA	FR	G/POS	TPR
1934	Bos-N	3	6	0	1	0	0	0	1	0	3	.167	.167	.167	-11	-1	0			1.000	1	/O-1	0.0
1935	Bos-N	13	47	7	16	2	1	2	11	0	4	.340	.404	.553	168	4	0			.893	-0	O-11	0.4
Total	2	16	53	7	17	2	1	2	12	0	7	.321	.379	.509	148	3	0			.906	1	/O-12	0.4

■ EARL TYREE
Tyree, Earl Carlton "Ty" b: 3/4/1890, Huntsville, Ill. d: 5/17/54, Rushville, Ill. BR/TR, 5'8", 160 lbs. Deb: 10/5/14

YEAR	TM/L	G	AB	R	H	2B	3B	HR	RBI	BB	SO	AVG	OBP	SLG	PRO+	BR/A	SB	CS	SBR	FA	FR	G/POS	TPR
1914	Chi-N	1	4	1	0	0	0	0	0	0	0	.000	.000	.000	-99	-1	0			1.000	-1	/C-1	-0.2

■ JIM TYRONE
Tyrone, James Vernon b: 1/29/49, Alice, Tex. BR/TR, 6'1", 185 lbs. Deb: 8/27/72 F

YEAR	TM/L	G	AB	R	H	2B	3B	HR	RBI	BB	SO	AVG	OBP	SLG	PRO+	BR/A	SB	CS	SBR	FA	FR	G/POS	TPR
1972	Chi-N	13	14	0	0	0	0	0	0	0	8	.000	.000	.000	-90	-2	1	0	0	1.000	0	/O-4	-0.1
1974	Chi-N	57	81	19	15	0	1	3	3	6	15	.185	.241	.321	54	-5	1	1	-0	.962	-8	O-32/3-1	-1.5
1975	Chi-N	11	22	0	5	0	1	0	3	1	4	.227	.261	.318	58	-1	1	1	-0	1.000	-1	/O-8	-0.3

YEAR	TM/L	G	AB	R	H	2B	3B	HR	RBI	BB	SO	AVG	OBP	SLG	PRO+	BR/A	SB	CS	SBR	FA	FR	G/POS	TPR
1977	Oak-A	96	294	32	72	11	1	5	26	25	62	.245	.304	.340	76	-10	3	1	0	.950	1	O-81/1-1,SD	-1.1
Total	4	177	405	52	92	11	3	8	32	32	77	.227	.284	.328	67	-18	6	3	0	.955	-7	O-125/D-4,S13	-3.0

■ WAYNE TYRONE
Tyrone, Oscar Wayne b: 8/1/50, Alice, Tex. BR/TR, 6'1", 185 lbs. Deb: 7/15/76 F

YEAR	TM/L	G	AB	R	H	2B	3B	HR	RBI	BB	SO	AVG	OBP	SLG	PRO+	BR/A	SB	CS	SBR	FA	FR	G/POS	TPR
1976	Chi-N	30	57	3	13	1	0	1	8	3	21	.228	.267	.298	55	-3	0	0	0	1.000	-3	/O-7,1-5,3	-0.7

■ TY TYSON
Tyson, Albert Thomas b: 6/1/1892, Wilkes-Barre, Pa. d: 8/16/53, Buffalo, N.Y. BR/TR, 5'11", 169 lbs. Deb: 4/13/26

YEAR	TM/L	G	AB	R	H	2B	3B	HR	RBI	BB	SO	AVG	OBP	SLG	PRO+	BR/A	SB	CS	SBR	FA	FR	G/POS	TPR
1926	NY-N	97	335	40	98	16	1	3	35	15	28	.293	.329	.373	90	-5	6			.980	3	O-92	-0.8
1927	NY-N	43	159	24	42	7	2	1	17	10	19	.264	.308	.352	76	-5	5			.929	-3	O-41	-1.1
1928	Bro-N	59	210	25	57	11	1	1	21	10	14	.271	.317	.348	75	-8	3			.965	0	O-55	-1.1
Total	3	199	704	89	197	34	4	5	73	35	61	.280	.320	.361	82	-19	14			.966	0	O-188	-3.0

■ TURKEY TYSON
Tyson, Cecil Washington "Slim" b: 12/6/14, Elm City, N.C. BL/TR, 6'5.5", 225 lbs. Deb: 4/23/44

YEAR	TM/L	G	AB	R	H	2B	3B	HR	RBI	BB	SO	AVG	OBP	SLG	PRO+	BR/A	SB	CS	SBR	FA	FR	G/POS	TPR
1944	Phi-N	1	1	0	0	0	0	0	0	0	0	.000	.000	.000	-99	-0	0			.000	0	H	0.0

■ MIKE TYSON
Tyson, Michael Ray b: 1/13/50, Rocky Mount, N.C. BR/TR, 5'9", 170 lbs. Deb: 9/5/72

YEAR	TM/L	G	AB	R	H	2B	3B	HR	RBI	BB	SO	AVG	OBP	SLG	PRO+	BR/A	SB	CS	SBR	FA	FR	G/POS	TPR
1972	StL-N	13	37	1	7	1	0	0	0	1	9	.189	.211	.216	22	-4	0	1	-1	.981	4	2-11/S-2	0.0
1973	StL-N	144	469	48	114	15	4	0	33	23	66	.243	.281	.299	61	-25	2	5	-2	.944	-19	*S-128,2-16	-3.0
1974	StL-N	151	422	35	94	14	5	1	37	22	70	.223	.266	.287	55	-26	4	2	0	.955	15	*S-143,2-12	0.6
1975	StL-N	122	368	45	98	16	3	2	37	24	39	.266	.316	.342	80	-10	5	2	0	.971	-12	S-95,2-24/3	-1.3
1976	StL-N	76	245	26	70	12	9	3	28	16	34	.286	.344	.445	117	5	3	1	0	.971	8	2-74	1.8
1977	StL-N	138	418	42	103	15	2	9	57	30	48	.246	.300	.342	73	-16	3	4	-2	.979	22	*2-135	1.3
1978	StL-N	125	377	26	88	16	0	4	26	24	41	.233	.279	.300	63	-19	2	0	1	.977	-1	*2-124	-1.1
1979	StL-N	75	190	18	42	8	2	5	20	13	28	.221	.275	.363	72	-8	2	1	0	.975	8	2-71	0.4
1980	Chi-N	123	341	34	81	19	3	3	23	19	61	.238	.274	.337	65	-16	1	2	-1	.968	9	*2-117	-0.1
1981	Chi-N	50	92	6	17	2	0	2	8	7	15	.185	.250	.272	46	-7	1	0	0	.940	-1	2-36/S-1	-0.5
Total	10	1017	2959	281	714	118	28	27	269	175	411	.241	.287	.327	69	-126	23	18	-4	.973	36	2-620,S-369/3	-1.9

■ BOB UECKER
Uecker, Robert George b: 1/26/35, Milwaukee, Wis. BR/TR, 6'1", 190 lbs. Deb: 4/13/62

YEAR	TM/L	G	AB	R	H	2B	3B	HR	RBI	BB	SO	AVG	OBP	SLG	PRO+	BR/A	SB	CS	SBR	FA	FR	G/POS	TPR
1962	Mil-N	33	64	5	16	2	0	1	8	7	15	.250	.324	.328	78	-2	0	0	0	.982	4	C-24	0.3
1963	Mil-N	13	16	3	4	2	0	0	0	2	5	.250	.333	.375	105	0	0	0	0	.958	1	/C-6	0.1
1964	StL-N	40	106	8	21	1	0	1	6	17	24	.198	.315	.236	53	-6	0	1	-1	.987	5	C-40	-0.1
1965	StL-N	53	145	17	33	7	0	2	10	24	27	.228	.345	.317	80	-3	0	1	-1	.985	-1	C-49	-0.3
1966	Phi-N	78	207	15	43	6	0	7	30	22	36	.208	.284	.338	72	-8	0	0	0	.985	1	C-76	-0.3
1967	Phi-N	18	35	3	6	2	0	0	7	5	9	.171	.275	.229	45	-2	0	0	0	.973	0	C-17	-0.2
	Atl-N	62	158	14	23	2	0	3	13	19	51	.146	.237	.215	31	-14	0	1	-1	.972	5	C-59	-0.8
	Yr	80	193	17	29	4	0	3	20	24	60	.150	.244	.218	33	-16	0	1	-1	.972	5	C-76	-1.0
Total	6	297	731	65	146	22	0	14	74	96	167	.200	.295	.287	63	-35	0	3	-2	.981	14	C-271	-1.3

■ FRENCHY UHALT
Uhalt, Bernard Bartholomew b: 4/27/10, Bakersfield, Cal. BL/TR, 5'10", 180 lbs. Deb: 4/17/34

YEAR	TM/L	G	AB	R	H	2B	3B	HR	RBI	BB	SO	AVG	OBP	SLG	PRO+	BR/A	SB	CS	SBR	FA	FR	G/POS	TPR
1934	Chi-A	57	165	28	40	1	0	1	16	29	12	.242	.359	.285	66	-7	6	5	-1	.935	-1	O-40	-1.0

■ TED UHLAENDER
Uhlaender, Theodore Otto b: 10/21/40, Chicago, Heights, Ill. BL/TR, 6'2", 190 lbs. Deb: 9/4/65

YEAR	TM/L	G	AB	R	H	2B	3B	HR	RBI	BB	SO	AVG	OBP	SLG	PRO+	BR/A	SB	CS	SBR	FA	FR	G/POS	TPR
1965	Min-A	13	22	1	4	0	0	0	1	0	2	.182	.182	.182	3	-1	1	0	0	1.000	1	/O-4	-0.2
1966	Min-A	105	367	39	83	12	2	2	22	27	33	.226	.281	.286	60	-19	10	2	2	.985	12	*O-100	-1.0
1967	Min-A	133	415	41	107	19	7	6	49	13	45	.258	.285	.381	88	-7	4	4	-1	.996	7	*O-118	-0.7
1968	Min-A	140	488	52	138	21	5	7	52	28	46	.283	.330	.389	110	5	16	7	1	.986	-2	*O-129	-0.3
1969	*Min-A	152	554	93	151	18	2	8	62	44	52	.273	.331	.356	90	-7	15	9	-1	.997	-6	*O-150	-2.2
1970	Cle-A	141	473	56	127	21	2	11	46	39	44	.268	.326	.391	92	-5	3	6	-3	.991	-14	*O-134	-3.0
1971	Cle-A	141	500	52	144	20	3	2	47	38	44	.288	.338	.352	88	-7	3	6	-3	.992	1	*O-131	-1.7
1972	*Cin-N	73	113	9	18	3	0	0	6	13	11	.159	.246	.186	26	-11	0	1	-1	.976	-2	O-27	-1.6
Total	8	898	2932	343	772	114	21	36	285	202	277	.263	.313	.353	86	-54	52	35	-5	.991	-3	O-793	-10.7

■ GEORGE UHLE
Uhle, George Ernest "The Bull" b: 9/18/1898, Cleveland, Ohio d: 2/26/85, Lakewood, Ohio BR/TR, 6', 190 lbs. Deb: 4/30/19 C

YEAR	TM/L	G	AB	R	H	2B	3B	HR	RBI	BB	SO	AVG	OBP	SLG	PRO+	BR/A	SB	CS	SBR	FA	FR	G/POS	TPR
1919	Cle-A	26	43	7	13	2	1	0	6	1	5	.302	.318	.395	94	-1	0			.915	-2	P-26	0.0
1920	*Cle-A	27	32	4	11	0	0	0	2	2	2	.344	.382	.344	91	-0	1	0	0	1.000	0	P-27	0.0
1921	Cle-A	48	94	21	23	2	3	1	18	6	9	.245	.290	.362	64	-5	0	0	0	.938	-3	P-41	0.0
1922	Cle-A	56	109	21	29	8	2	0	14	13	6	.266	.350	.376	88	-2	1	2	-1	.932	-3	P-50	0.0
1923	Cle-A	58	144	23	52	10	3	0	22	7	10	.361	.391	.472	127	5	2	1	0	.982	4	P-54	0.0
1924	Cle-A	59	107	10	33	6	1	1	19	4	8	.308	.339	.411	92	-2	0	1	-1	1.000	1	P-28	0.0
1925	Cle-A	55	101	10	29	3	0	0	13	7	7	.287	.339	.376	81	-3	0	0	0	.943	-3	P-29	0.0
1926	Cle-A	50	132	16	30	3	0	1	11	10	12	.227	.287	.273	46	-10	2	0	0	.933	-3	P-39	0.0
1927	Cle-A	43	79	4	21	7	1	0	14	5	12	.266	.310	.380	78	-3	0	1	-1	.974	-1	P-25	0.0
1928	Cle-A	55	98	9	28	3	2	1	17	8	4	.286	.340	.388	90	-2	0	0	0	.972	3	P-31	0.0
1929	Det-A	40	108	18	37	1	1	0	13	6	6	.343	.377	.370	93	-1	0	0	0	.929	-3	P-32	0.0
1930	Det-A	59	117	15	36	4	2	2	21	8	13	.308	.352	.427	95	-1	0	0	0	.975	-1	P-33	0.0
1931	Det-A	53	90	8	22	6	0	2	7	8	8	.244	.306	.378	76	-3	0	1	-1	1.000	-1	P-29	0.0
1932	Det-A	38	55	2	10	3	1	0	6	4	6	.182	.262	.273	37	-5	0	0	0	1.000	-1	P-33	0.0
1933	Det-A	1	0	0	0	0	0	0	0	0	0	—	—	—	—	0	0	0	0	.000	0	/P-1	0.0
	NY-N	8	5	1	0	0	0	0	0	0	1	.000	.167	.000	-50	-1	0	0	0	1.000	0	/P-6	0.0
	NY-A	12	20	1	8	1	0	1	4	2	4	.400	.500	.450	163	2	0	0	0	1.000	-1	P-12	0.0
1934	NY-A	10	5	1	3	0	0	0	1	0	0	.600	.600	1.000	329	2	0	0	0	1.000	0	P-10	0.0
1936	Cle-A	24	21	1	8	1	0	1	4	2	0	.381	.435	.571	145	1	0	0	0	.000	-1	/P-7	0.0
Total	17	722	1360	172	393	60	21	9	187	98	112	.289	.339	.384	86	-29	6	8		.960	-15	P-513	0.0

■ MAURY UHLER
Uhler, Maurice William b: 12/14/1886, Pikesville, Md. d: 5/4/18, Baltimore, Md. BR/TR, 5'11", 165 lbs. Deb: 4/14/14

YEAR	TM/L	G	AB	R	H	2B	3B	HR	RBI	BB	SO	AVG	OBP	SLG	PRO+	BR/A	SB	CS	SBR	FA	FR	G/POS	TPR
1914	Cin-N	46	56	12	12	2	0	0	3	5	11	.214	.279	.250	56	-3	4			.932	-8	O-36	-1.3

■ CHARLIE UHLIR
Uhlir, Charles Karel b: 7/30/12, Chicago, Ill. d: 7/9/84, Spirit Lake, Iowa BL/TL, 5'7.5", 150 lbs. Deb: 8/3/34

YEAR	TM/L	G	AB	R	H	2B	3B	HR	RBI	BB	SO	AVG	OBP	SLG	PRO+	BR/A	SB	CS	SBR	FA	FR	G/POS	TPR
1934	Chi-A	14	27	3	4	0	0	0	3	2	6	.148	.207	.148	-7	-4	0	0	0	1.000	-1	/O-6	-0.5

■ MIKE ULISNEY
Ulisney, Michael Edward "Slugs" b: 9/28/17, Greenwald, Pa. BR/TR, 5'9", 165 lbs. Deb: 5/5/45

YEAR	TM/L	G	AB	R	H	2B	3B	HR	RBI	BB	SO	AVG	OBP	SLG	PRO+	BR/A	SB	CS	SBR	FA	FR	G/POS	TPR
1945	Bos-N	11	18	4	7	1	0	1	4	1	0	.389	.421	.611	184	2	0			.714	-2	/C-4	0.0

■ SCOTT ULLGER
Ullger, Scott Matthew b: 6/10/56, New York, N.Y. BR/TR, 6'2", 186 lbs. Deb: 4/17/83

YEAR	TM/L	G	AB	R	H	2B	3B	HR	RBI	BB	SO	AVG	OBP	SLG	PRO+	BR/A	SB	CS	SBR	FA	FR	G/POS	TPR
1983	Min-A	35	79	8	15	4	0	0	5	5	21	.190	.247	.241	34	-7	0	0	0	.990	5	1-30/3-3,D	-1.1

■ GEORGE ULRICH
Ulrich, George T. b: 6/5/1869, Philadelphia, Pa. Deb: 5/1/1892

YEAR	TM/L	G	AB	R	H	2B	3B	HR	RBI	BB	SO	AVG	OBP	SLG	PRO+	BR/A	SB	CS	SBR	FA	FR	G/POS	TPR
1892	Was-N	6	24	1	7	1	0	0	4	4		.292	.292	.333	92	-0	2			.889	-1	/3-3,S-2,C	-0.1
1893	Cin-N	1	3	0	0	0	0	0	0	0		.000	.250	.000	-31	-1	1			1.000	-0	/O-1	-0.1
1896	NY-N	14	45	4	8	1	0	0	1	1	1	.178	.229	.200	14	-6	0			.920	0	O-11/3-3	-0.5
Total	3	21	72	5	15	2	0	0	5	5		.208	.250	.236	35	-7	3			.923	-1	/O-12,3-6,CS	-0.7

■ TOM UMPHLETT
Umphlett, Thomas Mullen b: 5/12/30, Scotland Neck, N.C BR/TR, 6'2", 180 lbs. Deb: 4/16/53

YEAR	TM/L	G	AB	R	H	2B	3B	HR	RBI	BB	SO	AVG	OBP	SLG	PRO+	BR/A	SB	CS	SBR	FA	FR	G/POS	TPR
1953	Bos-A	137	495	53	140	27	5	3	59	34	30	.283	.331	.376	86	-10	4	2	0	.983	6	*O-136	-0.9
1954	Was-A	114	342	21	75	8	3	1	33	17	42	.219	.256	.269	46	-26	1	2	-1	.989	0	*O-101	-3.2

YEAR	TM/L	G	AB	R	H	2B	3B	HR	RBI	BB	SO	AVG	OBP	SLG	PRO+	BR/A	SB	CS	SBR	FA	FR	G/POS	TPR
1955	Was-A	110	323	34	70	10	0	2	19	24	35	.217	.271	.266	47	-25	2	1	0	.988	4	*O-103	-2.5
Total	3	361	1160	108	285	45	8	6	111	75	107	.246	.293	.314	65	-61	7	5	-1	.986	10	O-340	-6.6

■ BOB UNGLAUB
Unglaub, Robert Alexander b: 7/31/1881, Baltimore, Md. d: 11/29/16, Baltimore, Md. BR/TR, 5'11", 178 lbs. Deb: 4/15/04 M

YEAR	TM/L	G	AB	R	H	2B	3B	HR	RBI	BB	SO	AVG	OBP	SLG	PRO+	BR/A	SB	CS	SBR	FA	FR	G/POS	TPR
1904	NY-A	6	19	2	4	0	0	0	2	0		.211	.211	.211	32	-1	0			.786	-1	/3-4,S-1	-0.3
	Bos-A	9	13	1	2	1	0	0	2	1		.154	.214	.231	39	-1	0			.625	-2	/2-3,3-2,S	-0.3
	Yr	15	32	3	6	1	0	0	4	1		.188	.212	.219	35	-2	0			.842	-3	/3-6,2-3,S	-0.6
1905	Bos-A	43	121	18	27	5	1	0	11	6		.223	.260	.281	71	-4	2			.928	1	3-21/2-7,1	-0.3
1907	Bos-A	139	544	49	138	17	13	1	62	23		.254	.284	.338	99	-3	14			.986	-1	*1-139,M	-0.8
1908	Bos-A	72	266	23	70	11	3	1	25	7		.263	.287	.338	100	-1	6			.980	2	1-72	-0.1
	Was-A	72	276	23	85	10	5	0	29	8		.308	.327	.380	142	11	8			.928	11	3-39,2-27/1	2.5
	Yr	144	542	46	155	21	8	1	54	15		.286	.308	.360	120	9	14			.981	13	1-76,3-39,2	2.4
1909	Was-A	130	480	43	127	14	9	3	41	22		.265	.301	.350	111	4	15			.992	1	1-57,O-42,2/3	0.3
1910	Was-A	124	431	29	101	9	4	0	44	21		.234	.270	.274	74	-14	21			.985	6	*1-124	-1.0
Total	6	595	2150	188	554	67	35	5	216	88		.258	.288	.328	99	-10	66			.986	16	1-398/3-70,2OS	-0.0

■ AL UNSER
Unser, Albert Bernard b: 10/12/12, Morrisonville, Ill BR/TR, 6'1", 175 lbs. Deb: 9/14/42 F

YEAR	TM/L	G	AB	R	H	2B	3B	HR	RBI	BB	SO	AVG	OBP	SLG	PRO+	BR/A	SB	CS	SBR	FA	FR	G/POS	TPR
1942	Det-A	4	8	2	3	0	0	0	0	0	2	.375	.375	.375	103	0	0	0	0	1.000	1	/C-4	0.1
1943	Det-A	38	101	14	25	5	0	0	4	15	15	.248	.350	.297	84	-2	0	1	-1	.982	-3	C-37	-0.3
1944	Det-A	11	25	2	3	0	1	1	3	2		.120	.214	.320	49	-2	0	0		.864	-4	/2-5,C-1	-0.6
1945	Cin-N	67	204	23	54	10	3	3	21	14	24	.265	.318	.387	98	-1	0			.956	0	C-61	0.2
Total	4	120	338	41	85	15	4	4	30	32	43	.251	.322	.355	90	-5	0	1		.967	-7	C-103/2-5	-0.6

■ DEL UNSER
Unser, Delbert Bernard b: 12/9/44, Decatur, Ill. BL/TL, 6'1", 180 lbs. Deb: 4/10/68 FC

YEAR	TM/L	G	AB	R	H	2B	3B	HR	RBI	BB	SO	AVG	OBP	SLG	PRO+	BR/A	SB	CS	SBR	FA	FR	G/POS	TPR
1968	Was-A	156	635	66	146	13	7	1	30	46	66	.230	.284	.277	73	-21	11	6	-0	.988	19	*O-156/1-1	-1.2
1969	Was-A	153	581	69	166	19	8	7	57	58	54	.286	.351	.382	111	8	8	10	-4	.972	6	*O-149	0.2
1970	Was-A	119	322	37	83	5	1	5	30	30	29	.258	.321	.326	83	-7	1	1	-0	.984	-3	*O-103	-1.6
1971	Was-A	153	581	63	148	19	6	9	41	59	68	.255	.326	.355	98	-2	11	6	-0	.981	3	*O-151	-0.7
1972	Cle-A	132	383	29	91	12	0	1	17	28	46	.238	.291	.277	67	-15	5	9	-4	.989	2	*O-119	-2.5
1973	Phi-N	136	440	64	127	20	4	11	52	47	55	.289	.359	.427	114	9	5	8	-3	.988	17	*O-132	1.7
1974	Phi-N	142	454	72	120	18	5	11	61	50	62	.264	.339	.399	101	1	6	4	-1	.981	6	*O-135	0.0
1975	NY-N	147	531	65	156	18	2	10	53	37	76	.294	.340	.392	107	4	4	3	-1	.987	12	*O-144	1.1
1976	NY-N	77	276	28	63	13	2	5	25	18	40	.228	.278	.344	80	-8	4	4	-1	.995	4	O-77	-0.9
	Mon-N	69	220	29	50	6	2	7	15	11	44	.227	.264	.368	75	-8	3	3	-1	.983	-6	O-65	-1.9
	Yr	146	496	57	113	19	4	12	40	29	84	.228	.272	.355	78	-16	7	7	-2	.990	-3	O-142	-2.8
1977	Mon-N	113	289	33	79	14	1	12	40	33	41	.273	.348	.453	116	6	2	5	-2	.976	-7	O-72,1-27	-0.6
1978	Mon-N	130	179	16	35	5	0	2	15	24	29	.196	.294	.257	56	-10	2	0	1	.994	1	1-64,O-33	-1.1
1979	Phi-N	95	141	26	42	8	0	6	29	14	33	.298	.361	.482	124	5	2	0	1	.978	-4	O-30,1-22	-0.1
1980	*Phi-N	96	110	15	29	6	4	0	10	10	21	.264	.325	.391	94	-1	0	1	-1	1.000	3	1-31,O-23	0.0
1981	Phi-N	62	59	5	9	0	0	0	6	13	9	.153	.306	.203	45	-4	0	0	0	1.000	-3	1-18,O-16	-0.7
1982	Phi-N	19	14	0	0	0	0	0	0	3	2	.000	.176	.000	-46	-3	0	0	0	1.000	-1	/1-5,O-2	-0.4
Total	15	1799	5215	617	1344	179	42	87	481	481	675	.258	.321	.358	93	-47	64	60	-17	.984	48	*O-1407,1-168	-8.7

■ JOHN UPHAM
Upham, John Leslie b: 12/29/41, Windsor, Ont., Can. BL/TL, 6', 180 lbs. Deb: 4/16/67

YEAR	TM/L	G	AB	R	H	2B	3B	HR	RBI	BB	SO	AVG	OBP	SLG	PRO+	BR/A	SB	CS	SBR	FA	FR	G/POS	TPR
1967	Chi-N	8	3	1	2	0	0	0	0	0	0	.667	.667	.667	270	1	0	0	0	.000	0	/P-5	0.0
1968	Chi-N	13	10	0	2	0	0	0	0	0	3	.200	.200	.200	19	-1	0	0	0	1.000	-1	/P-2,O-2	-0.1
Total	2	21	13	1	4	0	0	0	0	0	3	.308	.308	.308	78	-0	0	0	0	1.000	-1	/P-7,O-2	-0.1

■ DIXIE UPRIGHT
Upright, R T b: 5/30/26, Kannapolis, N.C. d: 11/13/86, Concord, N.C. BL/TL, 6', 175 lbs. Deb: 4/18/53

YEAR	TM/L	G	AB	R	H	2B	3B	HR	RBI	BB	SO	AVG	OBP	SLG	PRO+	BR/A	SB	CS	SBR	FA	FR	G/POS	TPR
1953	StL-A	9	8	3	2	0	0	1	1	1	3	.250	.333	.625	151	0	0	0	0	.000	0	H	0.0

■ WILLIE UPSHAW
Upshaw, Willie Clay b: 4/27/57, Blanco, Tex. BL/TL, 6', 185 lbs. Deb: 4/9/78 C

YEAR	TM/L	G	AB	R	H	2B	3B	HR	RBI	BB	SO	AVG	OBP	SLG	PRO+	BR/A	SB	CS	SBR	FA	FR	G/POS	TPR
1978	Tor-A	95	224	26	53	8	2	1	17	21	35	.237	.302	.304	69	-9	4	6	-2	.943	-6	O-52,D-18,1	-2.1
1980	Tor-A	34	61	10	13	3	1	1	5	6	14	.213	.284	.344	68	-3	1	0	0	.983	1	1-14,D-12/O	-0.2
1981	Tor-A	61	111	15	19	3	1	4	10	11	16	.171	.252	.324	61	-6	2	1	0	1.000	-2	D-15,1-14,O	-0.9
1982	Tor-A	160	580	77	155	25	7	21	75	52	91	.267	.329	.443	100	-1	8	8	-2	.989	-1	*1-155/D-5	-1.3
1983	Tor-A	160	579	99	177	26	7	27	104	61	98	.306	.377	.515	134	27	10	7	-1	.985	3	*1-159/D-1	1.9
1984	Tor-A	152	569	79	158	31	9	19	84	55	86	.278	.347	.464	118	13	10	4	1	.990	-3	*1-151/D-1	-0.1
1985	*Tor-A	148	501	79	138	31	5	15	65	48	71	.275	.344	.447	112	8	8	8	-2	.992	1	*1-147/D-1	-0.1
1986	Tor-A	155	573	85	144	28	6	9	60	78	87	.251	.343	.368	91	-5	23	5	4	.992	5	*1-154/D-1	-0.8
1987	Tor-A	150	512	68	125	22	4	15	58	58	78	.244	.325	.391	87	-10	10	11	-4	.993	12	*1-146	-1.1
1988	Cle-A	149	493	58	121	22	3	11	50	62	66	.245	.332	.369	94	-3	12	9	-2	.991	1	*1-144	-0.6
Total	10	1264	4203	596	1103	199	45	123	528	452	642	.262	.337	.419	102	12	88	59	-9	.990	11	*1-1094/O-67,D	-6.1

■ TOM UPTON
Upton, Thomas Herbert "Muscles" b: 12/29/26, Esther, Mo. BR/TR, 6', 160 lbs. Deb: 4/19/50 F

YEAR	TM/L	G	AB	R	H	2B	3B	HR	RBI	BB	SO	AVG	OBP	SLG	PRO+	BR/A	SB	CS	SBR	FA	FR	G/POS	TPR
1950	StL-A	124	389	50	92	5	6	2	30	52	45	.237	.328	.296	58	-24	7	2	1	.946	-10	*S-115/2-2,3	-2.3
1951	StL-A	52	131	9	26	4	3	0	12	12	22	.198	.271	.275	46	-10	1	1	-0	.949	-4	S-47	-1.2
1952	Was-A	5	5	1	0	0	0	0	0	1	0	.000	.167	.000	-53	-1	0	0	0	1.000	2	/S-3	0.1
Total	3	181	525	60	118	9	9	2	42	65	67	.225	.313	.288	55	-35	8	3	1	.948	-13	S-165/2-2,3	-3.4

■ LUKE URBAN
Urban, Louis John b: 3/22/1898, Fall River, Mass. d: 12/7/80, Somerset, Mass. BR/TR, 5'8", 168 lbs. Deb: 7/19/27

YEAR	TM/L	G	AB	R	H	2B	3B	HR	RBI	BB	SO	AVG	OBP	SLG	PRO+	BR/A	SB	CS	SBR	FA	FR	G/POS	TPR
1927	Bos-N	35	111	11	32	5	0	0	10	3	6	.288	.313	.333	79	-4	1			.947	-8	C-34	-0.9
1928	Bos-N	15	17	0	3	0	0	0	2	0	1	.176	.222	.176	6	-2	0			1.000	1	C-10	-0.1
Total	2	50	128	11	35	5	0	0	12	3	7	.273	.301	.313	69	-6	1			.955	-7	/C-44	-1.0

■ BILLY URBANSKI
Urbanski, William Michael b: 6/5/03, Linoleumville, N.Y d: 7/12/73, Perth Amboy, N.J. BR/TR, 5'8", 165 lbs. Deb: 7/4/31

YEAR	TM/L	G	AB	R	H	2B	3B	HR	RBI	BB	SO	AVG	OBP	SLG	PRO+	BR/A	SB	CS	SBR	FA	FR	G/POS	TPR
1931	Bos-N	82	303	22	72	13	4	0	17	10	32	.238	.274	.307	58	-18	3			.961	11	3-68,S-19	-0.2
1932	Bos-N	136	563	80	153	25	8	8	46	28	60	.272	.307	.387	89	-10	8			.946	1	*S-136	0.3
1933	Bos-N	144	566	65	142	21	4	0	35	33	48	.251	.298	.302	78	-17	4			.953	-4	*S-143	-1.1
1934	Bos-N	146	605	104	177	30	6	7	53	56	37	.293	.357	.397	110	9	4			**.961**	-10	*S-146	0.7
1935	Bos-N	132	514	53	118	17	0	4	30	40	32	.230	.286	.286	59	-30	3			.939	-27	*S-129	-5.0
1936	Bos-N	122	494	55	129	17	5	0	26	31	42	.261	.310	.316	74	-18	2			.937	-18	S-80,3-38	-3.0
1937	Bos-N	1	1	0	0	0	0	0	0	0	1	.000	.000	.000	-99	-0	0			.000	0	H	0.0
Total	7	763	3046	379	791	123	27	19	207	198	252	.260	.309	.337	81	-85	24			.949	-47	S-653,3-106	-8.3

■ JOSE URIBE
Uribe, Jose Altagracia (Played Under Real Name Of Jose Altagracia Gonzalez (Uribe) In 1984)
b: 1/21/59, San Cristobal, D.R. BB/TR, 5'10", 165 lbs. Deb: 9/13/84

YEAR	TM/L	G	AB	R	H	2B	3B	HR	RBI	BB	SO	AVG	OBP	SLG	PRO+	BR/A	SB	CS	SBR	FA	FR	G/POS	TPR
1984	StL-N	8	19	4	4	0	0	0	2	0	2	.211	.211	.211	19	-2	1	0	0	.955	0	/S-5,2-1	-0.1
1985	SF-N	147	476	46	113	20	4	3	26	30	57	.237	.285	.315	71	-19	8	2	1	.961	-2	*S-145/2-1	-0.7
1986	SF-N	157	453	46	101	15	3	6	43	61	76	.223	.315	.280	69	-18	22	11	0	.977	12	*S-156	0.8
1987	*SF-N	95	309	44	90	16	5	5	30	24	35	.291	.344	.424	107	3	12	2	2	.971	11	S-95	2.3
1988	SF-N	141	493	47	124	10	7	3	35	36	69	.252	.302	.318	82	-12	14	10	-2	.970	-3	*S-140	-0.6
1989	*SF-N	151	453	40	100	12	6	1	30	34	74	.221	.275	.280	61	-23	6	6	-2	.973	8	*S-150	-0.6
1990	SF-N	138	415	35	103	8	6	1	24	29	46	.248	.297	.304	68	-18	5	9	-4	.965	16	*S-134	0.3
1991	SF-N	90	231	23	51	8	4	1	12	20	33	.221	.283	.303	67	-10	3	4	-2	.966	6	S-87	-0.1

YEAR	TM/L	G	AB	R	H	2B	3B	HR	RBI	BB	SO	AVG	OBP	SLG	PRO+	BR/A	SB	CS	SBR	FA	FR	G/POS	TPR
1992	SF-N	66	162	24	39	9	1	2	13	14	25	.241	.301	.346	88	-3	2	2	-1	.971	9	S-62	0.9
1993	Hou-N	45	53	4	13	1	0	0	3	8	5	.245	.355	.264	71	-2	1	0	0	.945	7	S-41	0.6
Total	10	1038	3064	307	738	99	34	19	219	256	425	.241	.300	.314	75	-105	74	46	-5	.969	62	*S-1015/2-2	2.8

■ LON URY
Ury, Louis Newton "Old Sleep" b: 1877, Ft.Scott, Kan. d: 3/4/18, Kansas City, Mo. TR , 6′, Deb: 9/9/03

YEAR	TM/L	G	AB	R	H	2B	3B	HR	RBI	BB	SO	AVG	OBP	SLG	PRO+	BR/A	SB	CS	SBR	FA	FR	G/POS	TPR
1903	StL-N	2	7	0	1	0	0	0	0	0		.143	.143	.143	-19	-1	0			1.000	0	/1-2	-0.1

■ BOB USHER
Usher, Robert Royce b: 3/1/25, San Diego, Cal. BR/TR, 6′1.5″, 180 lbs. Deb: 4/16/46

YEAR	TM/L	G	AB	R	H	2B	3B	HR	RBI	BB	SO	AVG	OBP	SLG	PRO+	BR/A	SB	CS	SBR	FA	FR	G/POS	TPR
1946	Cin-N	92	152	16	31	5	1	1	14	13	27	.204	.271	.270	56	-9	2			.982	-12	O-80/3-1	-2.5
1947	Cin-N	9	22	2	4	0	0	1	1	2	2	.182	.250	.318	50	-2	0			1.000	0	/O-8	-0.2
1950	Cin-N	106	321	51	83	17	0	6	35	27	38	.259	.316	.368	79	-10	3			.985	-5	O-93	-1.8
1951	Cin-N	114	303	27	63	12	2	5	25	19	36	.208	.257	.310	51	-21	4	5	-2	.974	-3	O-98	-3.0
1952	Chi-N	1	0	0	0	0	0	0	0	1	0	—	1.000	—	197	0	0	0	0	.000	0	H	0.0
1957	Cle-A	10	8	1	1	0	0	0	0	1	3	.125	.222	.125	-3	-1	0	0	0	1.000	-2	/O-4,3-1	-0.3
	Was-A	96	295	36	77	7	1	5	27	27	30	.261	.327	.342	84	-6	0	0	0	.979	3	O-95	-0.8
	Yr	106	303	37	78	7	1	5	27	28	33	.257	.324	.337	82	-7	0	0	0	.979	2	O-99/3-1	-1.1
Total	6	428	1101	133	259	41	4	18	102	90	136	.235	.295	.329	69	-49	9	5		.980	-19	O-378/3-2	-8.6

■ DUTCH USSAT
Ussat, William August b: 4/11/04, Dayton, Ohio d: 5/29/59, Dayton, Ohio BR/TR, 6′1″, 170 lbs. Deb: 9/13/25

YEAR	TM/L	G	AB	R	H	2B	3B	HR	RBI	BB	SO	AVG	OBP	SLG	PRO+	BR/A	SB	CS	SBR	FA	FR	G/POS	TPR
1925	Cle-A	1	1	0	0	0	0	0	0	0	0	.000	.000	.000	-99	-0	0	0	0	1.000	0	/2-1	0.0
1927	Cle-A	4	16	4	3	0	1	0	0	1	0	.188	.278	.313	53	-1	0	0	0	1.000	-1	/3-4	-0.2
Total	2	5	17	4	3	0	1	0	0	1	0	.176	.263	.294	44	-1	0	0	0	1.000	-1	/3-4,2-1	-0.2

■ TEX VACHE
Vache, Ernest Lewis b: 11/17/1894, Santa Monica, Cal. d: 6/11/53, Los Angeles, Cal. BR/TR, 6′1″, 200 lbs. Deb: 4/16/25

YEAR	TM/L	G	AB	R	H	2B	3B	HR	RBI	BB	SO	AVG	OBP	SLG	PRO+	BR/A	SB	CS	SBR	FA	FR	G/POS	TPR
1925	Bos-A	110	252	40	79	15	7	3	48	21	33	.313	.382	.464	114	5	2	2	-1	.908	-12	O-53	-1.0

■ GENE VADEBONCOEUR
Vadeboncoeur, Onesime Eugene b: 7/15/1858, Louiseville, Que., Can. d: 10/16/35, Haverhill, Mass. BR/TR, 5′6″, 150 lbs. Deb: 7/11/1884

YEAR	TM/L	G	AB	R	H	2B	3B	HR	RBI	BB	SO	AVG	OBP	SLG	PRO+	BR/A	SB	CS	SBR	FA	FR	G/POS	TPR
1884	Phi-N	4	14	1	3	0	0	0	3	1	2	.214	.267	.214	56	-1				.846	-1	/C-4	-0.1

■ HARRY VAHRENHORST
Vahrenhorst, Harry Henry "Van" b: 2/13/1885, St.Louis, Mo. d: 10/10/43, St.Louis, Mo. BR/TR, 6′1″, 175 lbs. Deb: 9/21/04

YEAR	TM/L	G	AB	R	H	2B	3B	HR	RBI	BB	SO	AVG	OBP	SLG	PRO+	BR/A	SB	CS	SBR	FA	FR	G/POS	TPR
1904	StL-A	1	1	0	0	0	0	0	0	0	0	.000	.000	.000	-99	-0	0			.000	0	H	0.0

■ MIKE VAIL
Vail, Michael Lewis b: 11/10/51, San Francisco, Cal. BR/TR, 6′, 185 lbs. Deb: 8/18/75

YEAR	TM/L	G	AB	R	H	2B	3B	HR	RBI	BB	SO	AVG	OBP	SLG	PRO+	BR/A	SB	CS	SBR	FA	FR	G/POS	TPR
1975	NY-N	38	162	17	49	8	1	3	17	9	37	.302	.339	.420	115	3	0	0	0	.971	11	O-36	1.3
1976	NY-N	53	143	8	31	5	1	0	9	6	19	.217	.248	.266	49	-10	0	1	-1	.941	-1	O-35	-1.4
1977	NY-N	108	279	29	73	12	1	8	35	19	58	.262	.313	.398	94	-3	0	7	-4	.965	2	O-85	-0.8
1978	Cle-A	14	34	2	8	2	1	0	2	1	9	.235	.257	.353	71	-1	1	1	-0	1.000	-0	/O-9,D-1	-0.2
	Chi-N	74	180	15	60	6	2	4	33	3	24	.333	.344	.456	109	2	0	1	-1	.981	-9	O-45/3-1	-1.0
1979	Chi-N	87	179	28	60	8	2	7	35	14	27	.335	.383	.520	131	7	0	2	-1	.964	-1	O-39/3-2	0.1
1980	Chi-N	114	312	30	93	17	2	6	47	14	77	.298	.330	.423	101	0	2	5	-2	.963	-4	O-77	-0.9
1981	Cin-N	31	31	1	5	0	0	0	3	0	9	.161	.161	.161	-8	-4	0	0	0	1.000	-1	/O-3	-0.5
1982	Cin-N	78	189	9	48	10	1	4	29	6	33	.254	.277	.381	81	-5	0	0	0	.988	0	O-52	-0.6
1983	SF-N	18	26	1	4	1	0	0	3	0	7	.154	.185	.192	5	-3	0	0	0	1.000	-1	/1-4,O-2	-0.5
	Mon-N	34	53	5	15	2	0	2	4	8	10	.283	.387	.434	128	2	0	0	0	.958	1	O-15/1-1,3	0.3
	Yr	52	79	6	19	3	0	2	7	8	17	.241	.326	.354	90	-1	0	0	0	.960	-0	O-17/1-5,3	-0.2
1984	LA-N	16	16	1	1	0	0	0	2	1	7	.063	.118	.063	-49	-3	0	0	0	.000	-0	/O-1	-0.4
Total	10	665	1604	146	447	71	11	34	219	81	317	.279	.315	.400	95	-17	3	17	-9	.968	-5	O-399/1-5,3D	-4.6

■ ROY VALDES
Valdes, Rogelio Lazaro (Rojas) b: 2/20/20, Havana, Cuba BR/TR, 5′11″, 185 lbs. Deb: 5/3/44

YEAR	TM/L	G	AB	R	H	2B	3B	HR	RBI	BB	SO	AVG	OBP	SLG	PRO+	BR/A	SB	CS	SBR	FA	FR	G/POS	TPR
1944	Was-A	1	1	0	0	0	0	0	0	0	0	.000	.000	.000	-99	-0	0	0	0	.000	0	H	0.0

■ SANDY VALDESPINO
Valdespino, Hilario (Borroto) b: 1/14/39, San Jose De Las Lajas, Cuba BL/TL, 5′8″, 170 lbs. Deb: 4/12/65

YEAR	TM/L	G	AB	R	H	2B	3B	HR	RBI	BB	SO	AVG	OBP	SLG	PRO+	BR/A	SB	CS	SBR	FA	FR	G/POS	TPR
1965	*Min-A	108	245	38	64	8	1	2	22	20	28	.261	.322	.322	80	-6	7	4	-0	.990	0	O-57	-0.9
1966	Min-A	52	108	11	19	1	1	2	9	4	24	.176	.212	.259	33	-9	2	2	-1	1.000	-1	O-23	-1.3
1967	Min-A	99	97	9	16	2	0	1	3	5	22	.165	.206	.216	23	-9	3	1	0	.977	-11	O-65	-2.4
1968	Atl-N	36	86	8	20	4	1	0	4	10	20	.233	.320	.279	81	-2	0	0	0	.976	1	O-20	-0.2
1969	Hou-N	41	119	17	29	4	0	0	12	15	19	.244	.328	.277	73	-4	2	2	-1	.976	1	O-29	-0.5
	Sea-A	20	38	3	8	1	0	0	2	1	7	.211	.250	.237	37	-3	0	1	-0	.889	2	/O-7	-0.2
1970	Mil-A	8	9	0	0	0	0	0	0	0	0	.000	.000	.000	-99	-2	0	0	0	.000	0	/O-1	-0.3
1971	KC-A	18	63	10	20	6	0	2	15	2	5	.317	.338	.508	138	3	0	0	0	.950	-2	O-15	0.0
Total	7	382	765	96	176	23	3	7	67	57	129	.230	.288	.295	66	-33	14	10	-2	.974	-10	O-217	-5.8

■ JULIO VALDEZ
Valdez, Julio Julian (b: Julio Julian Castillo (Valdez)) b: 6/3/56, San Cristobal, D.R. BB/TR, 6′2″, 160 lbs. Deb: 9/2/80

YEAR	TM/L	G	AB	R	H	2B	3B	HR	RBI	BB	SO	AVG	OBP	SLG	PRO+	BR/A	SB	CS	SBR	FA	FR	G/POS	TPR
1980	Bos-A	8	19	4	5	1	0	1	4	0	5	.263	.300	.474	103	-0	2	0	1	.935	7	/S-8	0.8
1981	Bos-A	17	23	1	5	0	0	0	3	0	2	.217	.217	.217	24	-1	0	1	-1	.955	3	S-17	0.1
1982	Bos-A	28	20	3	5	1	0	0	1	0	7	.250	.250	.300	48	-1	1	0	0	.976	7	S-22/D-3	0.6
1983	Bos-A	12	25	3	3	0	0	0	0	1	4	.120	.185	.120	-13	-4	0	0	0	.939	-1	/2-9,S-2,D	-0.5
Total	4	65	87	11	18	2	0	1	8	1	18	.207	.233	.264	36	-8	3	1	0	.955	16	/S-49,2-9,D	1.0

■ JOSE VALDIVIELSO
Valdivielso, Jose (Lopez) (b: Jose Martinez De Valdivielso (Lopez)) b: 5/22/34, Matanzas, Cuba BR/TR, 6′1″, 175 lbs. Deb: 6/21/55

YEAR	TM/L	G	AB	R	H	2B	3B	HR	RBI	BB	SO	AVG	OBP	SLG	PRO+	BR/A	SB	CS	SBR	FA	FR	G/POS	TPR
1955	Was-A	94	294	32	65	12	5	2	28	21	38	.221	.280	.316	63	-16	1	2	-1	.956	9	S-94	0.0
1956	Was-A	90	246	18	58	8	2	4	29	29	36	.236	.319	.333	72	-10	3	1	0	.947	16	S-90	1.3
1959	Was-A	24	14	1	4	0	0	0	0	1	3	.286	.333	.286	72	-0	0	0	0	1.000	5	S-21	0.5
1960	Was-A	117	268	23	57	1	1	2	19	20	36	.213	.277	.246	43	-21	1	2	-1	.954	-2	*S-115/3-1	-0.7
1961	Min-A	76	149	15	29	5	0	1	9	8	19	.195	.236	.248	28	-15	1	1	-0	.971	-2	S-43,2-15,3	-1.4
Total	5	401	971	89	213	26	8	9	85	79	132	.219	.284	.290	55	-63	6	6	-2	.955	37	S-363/2-15,3	-0.3

■ JOHN VALENTIN
Valentin, John William b: 2/18/67, Mineola, N.Y. BR/TR, 6′, 170 lbs. Deb: 7/27/92

YEAR	TM/L	G	AB	R	H	2B	3B	HR	RBI	BB	SO	AVG	OBP	SLG	PRO+	BR/A	SB	CS	SBR	FA	FR	G/POS	TPR
1992	Bos-A	58	185	21	51	13	0	5	25	20	17	.276	.353	.427	110	3	1	0	0	.963	5	S-58	1.1
1993	Bos-A	144	468	50	130	40	3	11	66	49	77	.278	.349	.447	106	3	3	4	-2	.971	5	*S-144	1.7
1994	Bos-A	84	301	53	95	26	2	9	49	42	38	.316	.405	.505	125	12	3	1	0	.979	1	S-83/D-1	1.8
Total	3	286	954	124	276	79	5	25	140	111	132	.289	.368	.461	113	17	7	5	-1	.972	10	S-285/D-1	4.6

■ JOSE VALENTIN
Valentin, Jose Antonio b: 10/12/69, Manati, P.R. BB/TR, 5′10″, 175 lbs. Deb: 9/17/92

YEAR	TM/L	G	AB	R	H	2B	3B	HR	RBI	BB	SO	AVG	OBP	SLG	PRO+	BR/A	SB	CS	SBR	FA	FR	G/POS	TPR
1992	Mil-A	4	3	1	0	0	0	0	1	0	0	.000	.000	.000	-99	-1	0	0	0	.667	-1	/2-1,S-1	-0.2
1993	Mil-A	19	53	10	13	1	2	1	7	7	16	.245	.344	.396	100	0	1	0	0	.922	-0	S-19	0.1
1994	Mil-A	97	285	47	68	19	0	11	46	38	75	.239	.332	.421	91	-4	12	3	2	.954	**28**	S-83,2-18/3	2.9
Total	3	120	341	58	81	20	2	12	54	45	91	.238	.332	.413	91	-5	13	3	2	.949	27	S-103/2-19,3	2.8

■ ELLIS VALENTINE
Valentine, Ellis Clarence b: 7/30/54, Helena, Ark. BR/TR, 6′4″, 207 lbs. Deb: 9/3/75

YEAR	TM/L	G	AB	R	H	2B	3B	HR	RBI	BB	SO	AVG	OBP	SLG	PRO+	BR/A	SB	CS	SBR	FA	FR	G/POS	TPR
1975	Mon-N	12	33	2	12	1	0	1	4	1	6	.364	.400	.576	161	3	0	0	0	.867	-1	O-11	0.1
1976	Mon-N	94	305	36	85	15	4	7	39	30	51	.279	.343	.410	108	3	14	1	4	.972	0	O-88	0.4
1977	Mon-N★	127	508	63	149	28	2	25	76	30	58	.293	.333	.504	124	15	13	5	1	.972	1	*O-126	1.1
1978	Mon-N	151	570	75	165	35	4	25	76	35	88	.289	.333	.489	129	19	13	8	-1	.970	14	*O-146	2.7
1979	Mon-N	146	548	73	151	29	3	21	82	22	74	.276	.305	.454	105	1	11	9	-2	.983	1	*O-144	-0.6

YEAR	TM/L	G	AB	R	H	2B	3B	HR	RBI	BB	SO	AVG	OBP	SLG	PRO+	BR/A	SB	CS	SBR	FA	FR	G/POS	TPR
1980	Mon-N	86	311	40	98	22	2	13	67	25	44	.315	.372	.524	147	19	5	5	-2	.970	1	O-83	1.6
1981	Mon-N	22	76	8	16	3	0	3	15	6	11	.211	.268	.368	78	-2	0	1	-1	1.000	-0	O-21	-0.4
	NY-N	48	169	15	35	8	1	5	21	5	38	.207	.230	.355	65	-9	0	3	-2	.957	3	O-47	-1.0
	Yr	70	245	23	51	11	1	8	36	11	49	.208	.242	.359	69	-11	0	4	-2	.969	3	O-85	-1.4
1982	NY-N	111	337	33	97	14	1	8	48	5	38	.288	.300	.407	97	-3	1	3	-2	.983	1	O-98	-0.6
1983	Cal-A	86	271	30	65	10	2	13	43	18	48	.240	.287	.435	97	-2	2	1	0	.963	-7	O-85	-1.2
1985	Tex-A	11	38	5	8	1	0	2	4	2	8	.211	.250	.395	72	-2	0	1	-1	1.000	-1	/O-7,D-4	-0.4
Total	10	894	3166	380	881	169	15	123	474	180	462	.278	.319	.458	113	42	59	37	-5	.972	10	O-856/D-4	1.7

■ FRED VALENTINE
Valentine, Fred Lee "Squeaky"   b: 1/19/35, Clarksdale, Miss.   BB/TR, 6'1", 190 lbs.   Deb: 9/7/59

YEAR	TM/L	G	AB	R	H	2B	3B	HR	RBI	BB	SO	AVG	OBP	SLG	PRO+	BR/A	SB	CS	SBR	FA	FR	G/POS	TPR
1959	Bal-A	12	19	0	6	0	0	0	1	3	4	.316	.409	.316	104	0	0	1	-1	.889	-2	/O-8	-0.2
1963	Bal-A	26	41	5	11	1	0	0	1	8	5	.268	.388	.293	98	0	0	0	0	1.000	-1	O-10	-0.2
1964	Was-A	102	212	20	48	5	0	4	20	21	44	.226	.305	.307	71	-8	4	2	0	.978	-4	O-57	-1.5
1965	Was-A	12	29	6	7	0	0	0	1	4	5	.241	.353	.241	73	-1	3	0	1	1.000	-1	O-11	0.0
1966	Was-A	146	508	77	140	29	7	16	59	51	63	.276	.353	.455	132	21	22	10	1	.980	-4	*O-138/1-2	1.2
1967	Was-A	151	457	52	107	16	1	11	44	56	76	.234	.331	.346	104	4	17	3	3	.989	-6	*O-136	-0.6
1968	Was-A	37	101	11	24	2	0	3	7	6	11	.238	.294	.347	96	-1	1	0	0	1.000	-1	O-27	-0.3
	Bal-A	47	91	9	17	3	2	2	5	7	20	.187	.253	.330	75	-3	0	0	0	.972	-1	O-26	-0.6
	Yr	84	192	20	41	5	2	5	12	13	31	.214	.274	.339	86	-4	1	0	0	.986	-3	O-53	-0.9
Total	7	533	1458	180	360	56	10	36	138	156	228	.247	.331	.373	106	13	47	16	5	.983	-20	O-413/1-2	-2.2

■ BOB VALENTINE
Valentine, Robert   Deb: 5/20/1876

YEAR	TM/L	G	AB	R	H	2B	3B	HR	RBI	BB	SO	AVG	OBP	SLG	PRO+	BR/A	SB	CS	SBR	FA	FR	G/POS	TPR
1876	NY-N	1	3	0	0	0	0	0	0	0	0	.000	.000	.000	-99	-1				.400	-0	/C-1	-0.1

■ BOBBY VALENTINE
Valentine, Robert John   b: 5/13/50, Stamford, Conn.   BR/TR, 5'10", 189 lbs.   Deb: 9/2/69   MC

YEAR	TM/L	G	AB	R	H	2B	3B	HR	RBI	BB	SO	AVG	OBP	SLG	PRO+	BR/A	SB	CS	SBR	FA	FR	G/POS	TPR
1969	LA-N	5	0	3	0	0	0	0	0	0	0	—	—	—		0	0			.000	0	R	0.0
1971	LA-N	101	281	32	70	10	2	1	25	15	20	.249	.292	.310	75	-10	5	3	-0	.961	-1	S-37,3-23,2O	-0.7
1972	LA-N	119	391	42	107	11	2	3	32	27	33	.274	.324	.335	90	-5	5	5	-2	.976	-0	2-49,3-39,OS	-0.4
1973	Cal-A	32	126	12	38	5	2	1	13	5	9	.302	.338	.397	112	1	6	1	1	.948	0	S-25/O-8	0.6
1974	Cal-A	117	371	39	97	10	3	3	39	25	25	.261	.313	.329	90	-5	8	5	-1	.950	-8	0-62,S-36,3/2D	-1.3
1975	Cal-A	26	57	5	16	2	0	0	5	4	3	.281	.339	.316	92	-0	0	2	-1	.958	-2	D-13/1-3,3O	-0.4
	SD-N	7	15	1	2	0	0	0	1	4	0	.133	.316	.333	86	-0	1	0	0	1.000	-1	/O-4	-0.1
1976	SD-N	15	49	3	18	4	0	0	4	6	2	.367	.436	.449	165	4	0	1	-1	1.000	1	O-10/1-4	0.4
1977	SD-N	44	67	5	12	3	0	1	10	7	10	.179	.257	.269	46	-5	0	0	0	.962	-0	S-10,3-10/1	-0.6
	NY-N	42	83	8	11	1	0	1	3	6	9	.133	.191	.181	0	-12	0	0	0	1.000	-1	1-15,S-14/3	-1.2
	Yr	86	150	13	23	4	0	2	13	13	19	.153	.221	.220	20	-17	0	0	0	.969	-2	S-24,1-16,3	-1.8
1978	NY-N	69	160	17	43	7	0	1	18	19	18	.269	.350	.331	95	-1	1	1	-0	.977	-9	2-45/3-9	-0.8
1979	Sea-A	62	98	9	27	6	0	0	7	22	5	.276	.408	.337	102	2	1	2	-1	.971	-7	S-29,0-15/23C	-0.6
Total	10	639	1698	176	441	59	9	12	157	140	134	.260	.319	.326	86	-31	27	20	-4	.957	-28	S-161,O-128,23/1DC	-5.1

■ BENNY VALENZUELA
Valenzuela, Benjamin Beltran "Papelero"   b: 6/2/33, Los Mochis, Mexico   BR/TR, 5'10", 175 lbs.   Deb: 4/27/58

YEAR	TM/L	G	AB	R	H	2B	3B	HR	RBI	BB	SO	AVG	OBP	SLG	PRO+	BR/A	SB	CS	SBR	FA	FR	G/POS	TPR
1958	StL-N	10	14	0	3	1	0	0	0	1	0	.214	.267	.286	45	-1	0	0	0	.875	0	/3-3	-0.1

■ DAVE VALLE
Valle, David   b: 10/30/60, Bayside, N.Y.   BR/TR, 6'2", 200 lbs.   Deb: 9/7/84

YEAR	TM/L	G	AB	R	H	2B	3B	HR	RBI	BB	SO	AVG	OBP	SLG	PRO+	BR/A	SB	CS	SBR	FA	FR	G/POS	TPR
1984	Sea-A	13	27	4	8	1	0	1	4	1	5	.296	.321	.444	111	0	0	0	0	1.000	2	C-13	0.3
1985	Sea-A	31	70	2	11	1	0	0	4	1	17	.157	.181	.171	-3	-10	0	0	0	.976	-1	C-31	-1.0
1986	Sea-A	22	53	10	18	3	0	5	15	7	7	.340	.417	.679	191	7	0	0	0	.982	-4	C-12/1-4	0.3
1987	Sea-A	95	324	40	83	16	3	12	53	15	46	.256	.295	.435	86	-7	2	0	1	.989	1	C-75,D-14/1O	-0.1
1988	Sea-A	93	290	29	67	15	2	10	50	18	38	.231	.297	.400	89	-5	0	1	-1	.989	6	C-84/1-1,D	0.7
1989	Sea-A	94	316	32	75	10	3	7	34	29	32	.237	.313	.354	85	-6	0	0	0	.993	-3	C-93	-0.3
1990	Sea-A	107	308	37	66	15	0	7	33	45	48	.214	.328	.331	84	-6	1	2	-1	**.997**	-0	*C-104/1-1	-0.1
1991	Sea-A	132	324	38	63	8	1	8	32	34	49	.194	.289	.299	63	-16	0	2	-1	.992	9	*C-129/1-2	-0.2
1992	Sea-A	124	367	39	88	16	1	9	30	27	58	.240	.306	.362	86	-7	0	0	0	.990	-3	*C-122	-0.4
1993	Sea-A	135	423	48	109	19	0	13	63	48	56	.258	.357	.395	100	1	1	0	0	.995	8	*C-135	1.6
1994	Bos-A	30	76	6	12	2	1	1	5	9	14	.158	.256	.250	29	-8	0	1	-1	.982	-1	C-28/1-2	-0.7
	Mil-A	16	36	8	14	6	1	1	5	9	4	.389	.542	.639	193	6	0	1	-1	1.000	-0	C-12/D-2	0.5
	Yr	46	112	14	26	8	1	2	10	18	18	.232	.348	.375	82	-3	0	2	-1	.986	-1	C-40/1-2,D	-0.2
Total	11	892	2614	293	614	112	11	74	328	243	378	.235	.315	.371	86	-51	4	7	-3	.992	14	C-838/D-19,1O	0.6

■ HECTOR VALLE
Valle, Hector Jose   b: 10/27/40, Vega Baja, P.R.   BR/TR, 5'9", 180 lbs.   Deb: 6/6/65

YEAR	TM/L	G	AB	R	H	2B	3B	HR	RBI	BB	SO	AVG	OBP	SLG	PRO+	BR/A	SB	CS	SBR	FA	FR	G/POS	TPR
1965	LA-N	9	13	1	4	0	0	0	2	2	3	.308	.400	.308	110	0	0	0	0	1.000	-0	/C-6	0.0

■ ELMER VALO
Valo, Elmer William   b: 3/5/21, Ribnik, Czech.   BL/TR, 5'11", 190 lbs.   Deb: 9/22/40   C

YEAR	TM/L	G	AB	R	H	2B	3B	HR	RBI	BB	SO	AVG	OBP	SLG	PRO+	BR/A	SB	CS	SBR	FA	FR	G/POS	TPR
1940	Phi-A	6	23	6	8	0	0	0		3	0	.348	.423	.348	104	0	2	0	1	1.000	1	/O-6	0.1
1941	Phi-A	15	50	13	21	0	1	2	6	4	2	.420	.463	.580	179	6	0	0	0	1.000	-0	O-10	0.4
1942	Phi-A	133	459	64	115	13	10	2	40	70	21	.251	.355	.336	95	-1	13	8	-1	.964	1	*O-122	-0.8
1943	Phi-A	77	249	31	55	6	2	3	18	35	13	.221	.319	.297	81	-5	2	6	-3	.986	1	O-63	-1.3
1946	Phi-A	108	348	59	107	21	6	1	31	60	18	.307	.411	.411	131	17	9	8	-2	.974	1	O-90	1.2
1947	Phi-A	112	370	60	111	12	6	5	36	64	21	.300	.406	.405	123	14	11	3	2	.973	-1	*O-104	1.0
1948	Phi-A	113	383	72	117	17	4	3	46	81	15	.305	.432	.394	120	16	10	6	-1	.983	-1	*O-109	0.9
1949	Phi-A	150	547	86	155	27	12	5	85	119	32	.283	.413	.404	121	21	14	11	-2	.981	10	*O-150	2.1
1950	Phi-A	129	446	62	125	16	5	10	46	82	22	.280	.400	.406	109	9	12	7	-1	.982	4	*O-117	0.6
1951	Phi-A	123	444	75	134	27	8	7	55	75	20	.302	.412	.446	129	21	11	6	-0	.981	-4	*O-116	1.6
1952	Phi-A	129	388	69	109	26	4	5	47	101	16	.281	.432	.407	126	19	12	11	-3	.962	-3	*O-121	1.0
1953	Phi-A	50	85	15	19	3	0	0	9	22	7	.224	.383	.259	73	-2	0	1	-1	1.000	-1	O-25	-0.4
1954	Phi-A	95	224	28	48	11	6	1	33	51	18	.214	.360	.330	90	-1	2	1	-1	.965	2	O-62	-0.3
1955	KC-A	112	283	50	103	17	4	3	37	52	18	.364	.463	.484	153	24	5	3	-0	.987	2	O-72	2.2
1956	KC-A	9	9	1	2	0	0	0	2	1	1	.222	.300	.222	40	-1	0	0	0	.000	0	/O-1	-0.1
	Phi-N	98	291	40	84	13	3	5	37	48	21	.289	.395	.405	118	9	7	6	-2	.966	-0	*O-87	0.4
1957	Bro-N	81	161	14	44	10	1	4	26	25	16	.273	.374	.422	104	1	0	1	-1	1.000	-4	O-36	-0.5
1958	LA-N	65	101	9	25	2	1	1	14	12	11	.248	.327	.317	69	-4	0	0	0	1.000	-6	O-26	-1.2
1959	Cle-A	34	24	3	7	0	0	0	5	7	0	.292	.452	.292	113	1	0	0	0	1.000	-1	/O-2	0.1
1960	NY-A	8	5	1	0	0	0	0	0	2	1	.000	.286	.000	-17	-1	0	0	0	1.000	-0	/O-2	-0.2
	Was-A	76	64	6	18	3	0	0	16	17	4	.281	.439	.328	112	2	0	0	0	1.000	1	/O-6	0.2
	Yr	84	69	7	18	3	0	0	16	19	5	.261	.427	.304	103	2	0	0	0	1.000	0	/O-8	0.0
1961	Min-A	33	32	0	5	2	0	0	2	3	3	.156	.250	.219	25	-3	0	0	0	1.000	-0	/O-1	-0.3
	Phi-N	50	43	4	8	2	0	1	8	8	6	.186	.327	.302	69	-2	0	0	0	.000	-0	/O-1	-0.2
Total	20	1806	5029	768	1420	228	73	58	601	942	284	.282	.399	.391	114	142	110	79	-14	.977	1	*O-1329	6.5

■ DEACON Van BUREN
Van Buren, Edward Eugene   b: 12/14/1870, LaSalle Co., Ill.   d: 6/29/57, Portland, Ore.   BL/TR, 5'10", 175 lbs.   Deb: 4/21/04

YEAR	TM/L	G	AB	R	H	2B	3B	HR	RBI	BB	SO	AVG	OBP	SLG	PRO+	BR/A	SB	CS	SBR	FA	FR	G/POS	TPR
1904	Bro-N	1	1	0	1	0	0	0	0		0	1.000	1.000	1.000	531	0	0			.000	0	H	0.0
	Phi-N	12	43	2	10	2	0	0		3	3	.233	.283	.279	76	-1	2			.962	1	O-12	-0.1
	Yr	13	44	2	11	2	0	0		3	3	.250	.298	.295	86	-1	2			.962	1	O-12	-0.1

YEAR	TM/L	G	AB	R	H	2B	3B	HR	RBI	BB	SO	AVG	OBP	SLG	PRO+	BR/A	SB	CS	SBR	FA	FR	G/POS	TPR

■ TY Van BURKLEO
Van Burkleo, Tyler Lee b: 10/7/63, Oakland, Cal.   BL/TL, 6'5", 225 lbs.   Deb: 7/28/93

YEAR	TM/L	G	AB	R	H	2B	3B	HR	RBI	BB	SO	AVG	OBP	SLG	PRO+	BR/A	SB	CS	SBR	FA	FR	G/POS	TPR
1993	Cal-A	12	33	2	5	3	0	1	1	6	9	.152	.282	.333	63	-2	1	0	0	1.000	-2	1-12	-0.4
1994	Col-N	2	5	0	0	0	0	0	0	0	1	.000	.000	.000	-86	-1	0	0	0	1.000	-0	/1-2	-0.1
Total	2	14	38	2	5	3	0	1	1	6	10	.132	.250	.289	42	-3	1	0	0	1.000	-1	/1-14	-0.5

■ AL Van CAMP
Van Camp, Albert Joseph b: 9/7/03, Moline, Ill. d: 2/2/81, Davenport, Iowa   BR/TR, 5'11.5", 175 lbs.   Deb: 9/11/28

YEAR	TM/L	G	AB	R	H	2B	3B	HR	RBI	BB	SO	AVG	OBP	SLG	PRO+	BR/A	SB	CS	SBR	FA	FR	G/POS	TPR
1928	Cle-A	5	17	0	4	1	0	0	2	0	1	.235	.235	.294	38	-2	1	0	0	.980	-1	/1-5	-0.2
1931	Bos-A	101	324	34	89	15	4	0	33	20	24	.275	.319	.346	79	-10	3	2	-0	.973	-5	O-59,1-25	-2.0
1932	Bos-A	34	103	10	23	4	2	0	6	4	17	.223	.252	.301	44	-9	0	0	0	.985	1	1-25	-1.0
Total	3	140	444	44	116	20	6	0	41	24	42	.261	.301	.333	69	-21	4	2	0	.991	-5	/O-59,1-55	-3.2

■ CARL VANDAGRIFT
Vandagrift, Carl William b: 4/22/1883, Cantrall, Ill. d: 10/9/20, Fort Wayne, Ind.   BR/TR, 5'8", 155 lbs.   Deb: 5/19/14

YEAR	TM/L	G	AB	R	H	2B	3B	HR	RBI	BB	SO	AVG	OBP	SLG	PRO+	BR/A	SB	CS	SBR	FA	FR	G/POS	TPR
1914	Ind-F	43	136	25	34	4	0	0	9	9	15	.250	.301	.279	46	-11	7			.925	-6	2-28,3-12/S	-1.8

■ JOHN VANDERWAL
Vanderwal, John Henry b: 4/29/66, Grand Rapids, Mich.   BL/TL, 6'1", 180 lbs.   Deb: 9/6/91

YEAR	TM/L	G	AB	R	H	2B	3B	HR	RBI	BB	SO	AVG	OBP	SLG	PRO+	BR/A	SB	CS	SBR	FA	FR	G/POS	TPR
1991	Mon-N	21	61	4	13	4	1	1	8	1	18	.213	.226	.361	63	-3	0	0	0	1.000	-1	O-17	-0.5
1992	Mon-N	105	213	21	51	8	2	4	20	24	36	.239	.316	.352	90	-3	3	0	1	.981	0	O-57/1-7	-0.3
1993	Mon-N	106	215	34	50	7	4	5	30	27	30	.233	.321	.372	81	-6	6	3	0	.988	-12	1-42,O-38	-2.1
1994	Col-N	91	110	12	27	3	1	5	15	16	31	.245	.341	.427	85	-3	2	1	0	1.000	-2	1-14/O-7	-0.5
Total	4	323	599	71	141	22	8	15	73	68	115	.235	.314	.374	83	-14	11	4	1	.983	-15	O-119/1-63	-3.4

■ FRED Van DUSEN
Van Dusen, Frederick William b: 7/31/37, Jackson Heights, N.Y.   BL/TL, 6'3", 180 lbs.   Deb: 9/11/55

YEAR	TM/L	G	AB	R	H	2B	3B	HR	RBI	BB	SO	AVG	OBP	SLG	PRO+	BR/A	SB	CS	SBR	FA	FR	G/POS	TPR
1955	Phi-N	1	0	0	0	0	0	0	0	0	0	—	1.000	—	199	0	0			.000	0	H	0.0

■ BILL Van DYKE
Van Dyke, William Jennings b: 12/15/1863, Paris, Ill. d: 5/5/33, ElPaso, Tex.   BR/TR, 5'8", 170 lbs.   Deb: 4/17/1890

YEAR	TM/L	G	AB	R	H	2B	3B	HR	RBI	BB	SO	AVG	OBP	SLG	PRO+	BR/A	SB	CS	SBR	FA	FR	G/POS	TPR
1890	Tol-a	129	502	74	129	14	11	0			25	.257	.296	.341	85	-12	73			.924	-7	*O-110,3-18/2C	-1.9
1892	StL-N	4	16	2	2	0	0	0	1	0	1	.125	.125	.125	-26	-2	0			.875	-1	/O-4	-0.3
1893	Bos-N	3	12	2	3	1	0	0	1	0	1	.250	.250	.333	50	-1	1			1.000	-1	/O-3	-0.1
Total	3	136	530	78	134	15	11	2	2	25	2	.253	.290	.334	81	-16	74			.924	-8	O-117/3-18,2C	-2.3

■ DAVE Van GORDER
Van Gorder, David Thomas b: 3/27/57, Los Angeles, Cal.   BR/TR, 6'2", 205 lbs.   Deb: 6/15/82

YEAR	TM/L	G	AB	R	H	2B	3B	HR	RBI	BB	SO	AVG	OBP	SLG	PRO+	BR/A	SB	CS	SBR	FA	FR	G/POS	TPR
1982	Cin-N	51	137	4	25	3	1	0	7	14	19	.182	.263	.219	35	-12	0	0	0	.986	-2	C-51	-1.2
1984	Cin-N	38	101	10	23	2	0	0	6	12	17	.228	.310	.248	56	-6	0	0	0	1.000	2	C-36/1-1	-0.3
1985	Cin-N	73	151	12	36	7	0	2	24	9	19	.238	.286	.325	67	-7	0	0	0	.989	-5	C-70	-0.8
1986	Cin-N	9	10	0	0	0	0	0	0	1	2	.000	.091	.000	-70	-2	0	0	0	1.000	1	/C-7	-0.2
1987	Bal-A	12	21	4	5	0	0	1	1	3	6	.238	.333	.381	91	-0	0	0	0	.978	1	C-12	0.1
Total	5	183	420	30	89	12	1	3	38	39	63	.212	.282	.267	52	-26	0	0	0	.990	-2	C-176/1-1	-2.4

■ GEORGE Van HALTREN
Van Haltren, George Edward Martin "Rip" b: 3/30/1866, St.Louis, Mo. d: 9/29/45, Oakland, Cal.   BL/TL, 5'11", 170 lbs.   Deb: 6/27/1887 M

YEAR	TM/L	G	AB	R	H	2B	3B	HR	RBI	BB	SO	AVG	OBP	SLG	PRO+	BR/A	SB	CS	SBR	FA	FR	G/POS	TPR
1887	Chi-N	45	172	30	35	4	0	3	17	15	15	.203	.271	.279	47	-13	12			.927	-3	O-27,P-20	-0.9
1888	Chi-N	81	318	46	90	9	14	4	34	22	34	.283	.329	.437	133	11	21			.872	-2	O-57,P-30	0.1
1889	Chi-N	134	543	126	168	20	10	9	81	82	41	.309	.405	.433	128	21	28			.898	-3	*O-130/S-3,2	1.3
1890	Bro-P	92	376	84	126	8	9	5	54	41	23	.335	.405	.444	119	10	35			.896	5	O-67,P-28/S	0.5
1891	Bal-a	139	566	136	180	14	15	9	83	71	46	.318	.398	.443	139	29	75			.882	-12	O-81,S-59/P2	1.5
1892	Bal-a	135	556	105	168	20	12	7	57	70	34	.302	.382	.419	139	26	49			.850	0	*O-129/P-4,31SM	1.9
	Pit-N	13	55	10	11	2	2	0	5	6	0	.200	.279	.309	77	-2	6			.905	-2	O-13	-0.4
	Yr	148	611	115	179	22	14	7	62	76	34	.293	.373	.409	133	25	55			.854	-2	*O-142/P-4,31S	1.5
1893	Pit-N	124	529	129	179	14	11	3	79	75	25	.338	.422	.423	127	24	37			.869	-6	*O-111,S-12/2	1.0
1894	*NY-N	137	519	109	172	22	4	7	104	55	22	.331	.400	.430	101	2	43			.914	-2	*O-137	-0.7
1895	NY-N	131	521	113	177	23	19	8	103	57	29	.340	.408	.503	137	29	32			.914	-3	*O-131/P-1	1.3
1896	NY-N	133	562	136	197	18	**21**	5	74	55	36	.351	.410	.484	139	32	39			.952	4	*O-133/P-2	2.1
1897	NY-N	129	564	117	186	22	9	3	64	40		.330	.375	.417	112	10	50			.937	9	*O-129	0.8
1898	NY-N	156	654	129	204	28	16	2	68	59		.312	.372	.413	129	24	36			.917	-2	*O-156	1.0
1899	NY-N	151	604	117	182	21	3	2	58	74		.301	.378	.356	106	8	31			.932	3	*O-151	-0.1
1900	NY-N	141	571	114	180	30	7	1	51	50		.315	.371	.398	118	14	**45**			.939	10	*O-141/P-1	1.2
1901	NY-N	135	543	82	182	23	6	1	47	51		.335	.396	.405	138	28	24			.941	4	*O-135/P-1	2.1
1902	NY-N	24	88	14	23	1	2	0	7	17		.261	.381	.318	117	3	6			.925	2	O-24	-0.4
1903	NY-N	84	280	42	72	6	1	0	28	28		.257	.327	.286	72	-9	14			.959	-6	O-75	-1.9
Total	17	1984	8021	1639	2532	285	161	69	1014	868	305	.316	.385	.417	121	245	583			.915	-6	*O-1827/P-93,S231	11.1

■ JOHN VANN
Vann, John Silas b: 6/7/1893, Fairland, Okla. d: 6/10/58, Shreveport, La.   BR/TR,   Deb: 6/11/13

YEAR	TM/L	G	AB	R	H	2B	3B	HR	RBI	BB	SO	AVG	OBP	SLG	PRO+	BR/A	SB	CS	SBR	FA	FR	G/POS	TPR
1913	StL-N	1	1	0	0	0	0	0	0	0	1	.000	.000	.000	-99	-0	0			.000	0	H	0.0

■ JAY Van NOY
Van Noy, Jay Lowell b: 11/4/28, Garland, Utah   BL/TR, 6'1", 200 lbs.   Deb: 6/18/51

YEAR	TM/L	G	AB	R	H	2B	3B	HR	RBI	BB	SO	AVG	OBP	SLG	PRO+	BR/A	SB	CS	SBR	FA	FR	G/POS	TPR
1951	StL-N	6	7	1	0	0	0	0	0	1	6	.000	.125	.000	-63	-2	0	0	0	1.000	-0	/O-1	-0.2

■ MAURICE Van ROBAYS
Van Robays, Maurice Rene "Bomber" b: 11/15/14, Detroit, Mich. d: 3/1/65, Detroit, Mich.   BR/TR, 6'0.5", 190 lbs.   Deb: 9/7/39

YEAR	TM/L	G	AB	R	H	2B	3B	HR	RBI	BB	SO	AVG	OBP	SLG	PRO+	BR/A	SB	CS	SBR	FA	FR	G/POS	TPR
1939	Pit-N	27	105	13	33	9	0	2	16	6	10	.314	.351	.457	118	2	0			.919	-4	O-25/3-1	-0.2
1940	Pit-N	145	572	82	156	27	7	11	116	33	58	.273	.316	.402	98	-3	2			.963	-4	*O-143/1-1	-1.5
1941	Pit-N	129	457	62	129	23	5	4	78	41	29	.282	.343	.381	104	2	0			.974	7	*O-121	0.2
1942	Pit-N	100	328	29	76	13	5	1	46	30	24	.232	.298	.311	76	-10	0			.986	5	O-84	-1.0
1943	Pit-N	69	236	32	68	17	7	1	35	18	19	.288	.344	.432	119	5	0			.940	-3	O-60	-0.1
1946	Pit-N	59	146	14	31	5	3	1	12	11	15	.212	.272	.308	63	-7	0			.955	-5	O-37/1-2	-1.5
Total	6	529	1844	232	493	94	27	20	303	139	155	.267	.321	.380	97	-11	2			.966	-3	O-470/1-3,3	-4.1

■ ANDY Van SLYKE
Van Slyke, Andrew James b: 12/21/60, Utica, N.Y.   BL/TR, 6'2", 192 lbs.   Deb: 6/17/83

YEAR	TM/L	G	AB	R	H	2B	3B	HR	RBI	BB	SO	AVG	OBP	SLG	PRO+	BR/A	SB	CS	SBR	FA	FR	G/POS	TPR
1983	StL-N	101	309	51	81	15	5	8	38	46	64	.262	.360	.421	115	7	21	7	2	.974	-10	O-69,3-30/1	-0.3
1984	StL-N	137	361	45	88	16	4	7	50	63	71	.244	.356	.368	107	5	28	5	5	1.000	-12	O-81,3-32,1	-0.5
1985	*StL-N	146	424	61	110	25	6	13	55	47	54	.259	.336	.439	116	9	34	6	7	.996	-2	*O-142/1-2	1.0
1986	StL-N	137	418	48	113	23	7	13	61	47	85	.270	.345	.452	119	10	21	8	2	.969	3	*O-110,1-38	1.1
1987	Pit-N	157	564	93	165	36	11	21	82	56	122	.293	.361	.507	126	20	34	8	5	.988	10	*O-150/1-1	3.0
1988	Pit-N★	154	587	101	169	23	**15**	25	100	57	126	.288	.352	.506	146	33	30	9	4	.991	17	*O-152	5.1
1989	Pit-N	130	476	64	113	18	9	9	53	47	100	.237	.310	.370	97	-2	16	4	2	.989	14	*O-123/1-2	1.1
1990	*Pit-N	136	493	67	140	26	6	17	77	66	89	.284	.370	.465	133	23	14	4	2	.976	3	*O-133	2.5
1991	*Pit-N	138	491	87	130	24	7	17	83	71	85	.265	.362	.446	128	19	10	3	1	.996	1	*O-135	1.9
1992	*Pit-N★	154	614	103	**199**	45	12	14	89	58	99	.324	.386	.505	152	41	12	3	2	.989	11	*O-154	5.4
1993	Pit-N†	83	323	42	100	13	4	8	50	24	40	.310	.361	.449	116	7	11	2	2	.995	3	O-78	1.0
1994	Pit-N	105	374	41	92	18	3	6	30	52	72	.246	.341	.358	83	-8	7	0	2	.992	6	O-99	-0.3
Total	12	1578	5434	803	1500	282	89	158	768	634	1007	.276	.354	.440	122	163	238	59	36	.988	44	*O-1426/1-82,3	21.0

■ IKE Van ZANDT
Van Zandt, Charles Isaac b: 1877, Brooklyn, N.Y. d: 9/14/08, Nashua, N.H.   BL,   Deb: 8/5/01

YEAR	TM/L	G	AB	R	H	2B	3B	HR	RBI	BB	SO	AVG	OBP	SLG	PRO+	BR/A	SB	CS	SBR	FA	FR	G/POS	TPR
1901	NY-N	3	6	1	1	0	0	0	0	0	0	.167	.167	.167	-3	-1	0			.333	-2	/P-2,O-1	-0.1
1904	Chi-N	3	11	0	0	0	0	0	0	0	0	.000	.000	.000	-99	-0	0			1.000	0	/O-3	0.0

YEAR	TM/L	G	AB	R	H	2B	3B	HR	RBI	BB	SO	AVG	OBP	SLG	PRO+	BR/A	SB	CS	SBR	FA	FR	G/POS	TPR
1905	StL-A	94	322	31	75	15	1	1	20		7	.233	.252	.295	77	-10	7			.878	-11	O-75/P-1,1	-2.7
Total	3	100	339	32	76	15	1	1	20		7	.224	.242	.283	69	-13	7			.872	-13	/O-79,P-3,1	-3.1

■ DICK Van ZANT
Van Zant, Richard "Foghorn Dick" b: 11/1864, Indiana d: 8/6/12, Wayne Co., Ind. Deb: 10/4/1888

YEAR	TM/L	G	AB	R	H	2B	3B	HR	RBI	BB	SO	AVG	OBP	SLG	PRO+	BR/A	SB	CS	SBR	FA	FR	G/POS	TPR
1888	Cle-a	10	31	1	8	1	0	0	1		1	.258	.303	.290	93	-0	1			.784	0	3-10	0.0

■ EDDIE VARGAS
Vargas, Hediberto (Rodriguez) b: 2/23/59, Guanica, P.R. BR/TR, 6'4", 205 lbs. Deb: 9/8/82

YEAR	TM/L	G	AB	R	H	2B	3B	HR	RBI	BB	SO	AVG	OBP	SLG	PRO+	BR/A	SB	CS	SBR	FA	FR	G/POS	TPR
1982	Pit-N	8	8	1	3	1	0	0	3	0	2	.375	.375	.500	139	0	0	0	0	1.000	0	/1-5	0.0
1984	Pit-N	18	31	3	7	2	0	0	2	3	5	.226	.294	.290	65	-1	0	0	0	.982	-0	1-13	-0.2
Total	2	26	39	4	10	3	0	0	5	3	7	.256	.310	.333	80	-1	0	0	0	.986	-0	/1-18	-0.2

■ BUCK VARNER
Varner, Glen Gann b: 8/17/30, Hixson, Tenn. BL/TR, 5'10", 170 lbs. Deb: 9/19/52

YEAR	TM/L	G	AB	R	H	2B	3B	HR	RBI	BB	SO	AVG	OBP	SLG	PRO+	BR/A	SB	CS	SBR	FA	FR	G/POS	TPR
1952	Was-A	2	4	0	0	0	0	0	0	1	1	.000	.200	.000	-43	-1	0	0	0	1.000	-0	/O-1	-0.1

■ PETE VARNEY
Varney, Richard Fred b: 4/10/49, Roxbury, Mass. BR/TR, 6'3", 235 lbs. Deb: 8/26/73

YEAR	TM/L	G	AB	R	H	2B	3B	HR	RBI	BB	SO	AVG	OBP	SLG	PRO+	BR/A	SB	CS	SBR	FA	FR	G/POS	TPR
1973	Chi-A	5	4	0	0	0	0	0	0	1	0	.000	.200	.000	-38	-1	0	0	0	1.000	0	/C-5	0.0
1974	Chi-A	9	28	1	7	0	0	0	2	1	8	.250	.276	.250	51	-2	0	0	0	.981	1	/C-9	0.0
1975	Chi-A	36	107	12	29	5	1	2	8	6	28	.271	.316	.393	98	-1	2	0	1	.988	-1	C-34/D-2	0.0
1976	Chi-A	14	41	5	10	2	0	3	5	2	9	.244	.279	.512	128	1	0	0	0	.988	1	C-14	0.3
	Atl-N	5	10	0	1	0	0	0	0	0	2	.100	.100	.100	-41	-2	0	0	0	1.000	-1	/C-5	-0.2
Total	4	69	190	18	47	7	1	5	15	10	47	.247	.289	.374	86	-4	2	0	1	.988	-1	/C-67,D-2	0.1

■ GARY VARSHO
Varsho, Gary Andrew b: 6/20/61, Marshfield, Wis. BL/TR, 5'11", 190 lbs. Deb: 7/6/88

YEAR	TM/L	G	AB	R	H	2B	3B	HR	RBI	BB	SO	AVG	OBP	SLG	PRO+	BR/A	SB	CS	SBR	FA	FR	G/POS	TPR
1988	Chi-N	46	73	6	20	3	0	0	5	1	6	.274	.284	.315	69	-3	5	0	2	.906	-2	O-18	-0.4
1989	Chi-N	61	87	10	16	4	2	0	6	4	13	.184	.220	.276	38	-7	3	0	1	.929	-3	O-21	-1.0
1990	Chi-N	46	48	10	12	0	1	1	6	1	6	.250	.265	.333	59	-3	2	0	1	1.000	-1	/O-3	-0.3
1991	*Pit-N	99	187	23	51	11	2	4	23	19	34	.273	.346	.417	115	4	9	2	2	.989	-4	O-54/1-3	0.0
1992	*Pit-N	103	162	22	36	6	3	4	22	10	32	.222	.267	.370	80	-5	5	4	5	.984	-5	O-44	-1.1
1993	Cin-N	77	95	8	22	6	0	2	11	9	19	.232	.305	.358	77	-3	1	0	0	1.000	-2	O-22	-0.5
1994	Pit-N	67	82	15	21	8	2	0	5	4	19	.256	.307	.402	83	-2	0	1	-1	.926	-10	O-36/1-1	-1.3
Total	7	499	734	94	178	40	10	10	73	48	129	.243	.294	.365	81	-19	25	5	5	.966	-26	O-198/1-4	-4.6

■ JIM VATCHER
Vatcher, James Ernest b: 5/27/66, Santa Monica, Cal. BR/TR, 5'9", 165 lbs. Deb: 5/30/90

YEAR	TM/L	G	AB	R	H	2B	3B	HR	RBI	BB	SO	AVG	OBP	SLG	PRO+	BR/A	SB	CS	SBR	FA	FR	G/POS	TPR
1990	Phi-N	36	46	5	12	1	0	1	4	4	6	.261	.320	.348	84	-1	0	0	0	1.000	-6	O-24	-0.8
	Atl-N	21	27	2	7	1	1	0	3	1	9	.259	.286	.370	75	-1	0	0	0	1.000	-1	/O-6	-0.2
	Yr	57	73	7	19	2	1	1	7	5	15	.260	.308	.356	80	-2	0	0	0	1.000	-7	O-30	-1.0
1991	SD-N	17	20	3	4	0	0	0	2	4	6	.200	.333	.200	52	-1	1	0	0	.900	-2	O-11	-0.3
1992	SD-N	13	16	1	4	1	0	0	2	3	6	.250	.368	.313	93	-0	0	0	0	1.000	-2	O-13	-0.2
Total	3	87	109	11	27	3	1	1	11	12	27	.248	.322	.321	77	-3	1	0	0	.980	-11	/O-54	-1.5

■ GLENN VAUGHAN
Vaughan, Glenn Edward "Sparky" b: 2/15/44, Compton, Cal. BB/TR, 5'11", 170 lbs. Deb: 9/20/63

YEAR	TM/L	G	AB	R	H	2B	3B	HR	RBI	BB	SO	AVG	OBP	SLG	PRO+	BR/A	SB	CS	SBR	FA	FR	G/POS	TPR
1963	Hou-N	9	30	1	5	0	0	0	0	2	5	.167	.219	.167	14	-3	1	0	0	.914	-3	/S-9,3-1	-0.7

■ ARKY VAUGHAN
Vaughan, Joseph Floyd b: 3/9/12, Clifty, Ark. d: 8/30/52, Eagleville, Cal. BL/TR, 5'10.5", 175 lbs. Deb: 4/17/32 H

YEAR	TM/L	G	AB	R	H	2B	3B	HR	RBI	BB	SO	AVG	OBP	SLG	PRO+	BR/A	SB	CS	SBR	FA	FR	G/POS	TPR
1932	Pit-N	129	497	71	158	15	10	4	61	39	26	.318	.375	.412	113	11	10			.934	-20	*S-128	0.1
1933	Pit-N	152	573	85	180	29	**19**	9	97	64	23	.314	.388	.478	146	35	3			.945	-9	*S-152	3.8
1934	Pit-N★	149	558	115	186	41	11	12	94	**94**	38	.333	**.431**	.511	148	41	10			.952	3	*S-149	**5.1**
1935	Pit-N★	137	499	108	192	34	10	19	99	**97**	18	**.385**	**.491**	**.607**	187	67	4			.950	-11	*S-137	**6.1**
1936	Pit-N☆	156	568	**122**	190	30	11	9	78	**118**	21	.335	**.453**	.474	146	44	6			.945	-11	*S-156	4.1
1937	Pit-N★	126	469	71	151	17	**17**	5	72	54	22	.322	.394	.463	132	22	7			.956	0	*S-108,O-12	2.8
1938	Pit-N☆	148	541	88	174	35	5	7	68	104	21	.322	.433	.444	140	36	14			.961	18	*S-147	**6.4**
1939	Pit-N★	152	595	94	182	30	11	6	62	70	20	.306	.385	.424	119	18	12			.962	9	*S-152	3.9
1940	Pit-N★	156	594	**113**	178	40	**15**	7	95	88	25	.300	.393	.453	134	30	12			.942	8	*S-155/3-2	**5.1**
1941	Pit-N★	106	374	69	118	20	7	6	38	50	13	.316	.399	.455	141	21	8			.958	-12	S-97/3-3	1.7
1942	Bro-N★	128	495	82	137	18	4	2	49	51	17	.277	.348	.341	100	1	8			.959	-10	*3-119/S-5,2	-0.8
1943	Bro-N	149	610	**112**	186	39	6	5	66	60	13	.305	.370	.413	126	20	**20**			.965	-24	S-99,3-55	0.4
1947	*Bro-N	64	126	24	41	5	2	2	25	27	11	.325	.444	.444	132	7	4			1.000	1	O-22,3-10	0.7
1948	Bro-N	65	123	19	30	3	0	3	22	21	8	.244	.354	.341	86	-2	0			1.000	1	O-26/3-8	-0.2
Total	14	1817	6622	1173	2103	356	128	96	926	937	276	.318	.406	.453	136	352	118			.951	-59	*S-1485,3-197/O2	39.2

■ FRED VAUGHN
Vaughn, Frederick Thomas "Muscles" b: 10/18/18, Coalinga, Cal. d: 3/2/64, Near Lake Wales, Fla. BR/TR, 5'10", 185 lbs. Deb: 8/20/44

YEAR	TM/L	G	AB	R	H	2B	3B	HR	RBI	BB	SO	AVG	OBP	SLG	PRO+	BR/A	SB	CS	SBR	FA	FR	G/POS	TPR
1944	Was-A	30	109	10	28	2	1	1	21	9	24	.257	.319	.321	87	-2	2	2	-1	.942	-2	2-26/3-3	-0.3
1945	Was-A	80	268	28	63	7	4	1	25	23	48	.235	.298	.302	81	-7	0	3	-2	.946	-5	2-76/S-1	-1.0
Total	2	110	377	38	91	9	5	2	46	32	72	.241	.304	.308	83	-9	2	5	-2	.945	-6	2-102/3-3,S	-1.3

■ GREG VAUGHN
Vaughn, Gregory Lamont b: 7/3/65, Sacramento, Cal. BR/TR, 6', 195 lbs. Deb: 8/10/89

YEAR	TM/L	G	AB	R	H	2B	3B	HR	RBI	BB	SO	AVG	OBP	SLG	PRO+	BR/A	SB	CS	SBR	FA	FR	G/POS	TPR
1989	Mil-A	38	113	18	30	3	0	5	23	13	23	.265	.341	.425	116	2	4	1	1	.943	-3	O-24,D-13	-0.1
1990	Mil-A	120	382	51	84	26	2	17	61	33	91	.220	.284	.432	98	-3	7	4	-0	.967	-1	*O-106/D-8	-0.6
1991	Mil-A	145	542	81	132	24	5	27	98	62	125	.244	.322	.456	116	10	2	2	-1	.994	13	*O-135/D-10	1.8
1992	Mil-A	141	501	77	114	18	2	23	78	60	123	.228	.316	.409	104	2	15	15	-5	.990	3	*O-131/D-7	-0.2
1993	Mil-A★	154	569	97	152	28	2	30	97	89	118	.267	.371	.482	129	24	10	7	-1	.986	4	O-94,D-58	2.1
1994	Mil-A	95	370	59	94	24	1	19	55	51	93	.254	.346	.478	107	4	9	5	-0	.982	0	O-81,D-14	0.1
Total	6	693	2477	383	606	123	12	121	412	308	573	.245	.331	.451	113	39	47	34	6	.984	16	*O-571,D-110	3.1

■ FARMER VAUGHN
Vaughn, Harry Francis b: 3/1/1864, Ruraldale, Ohio d: 2/21/14, Cincinnati, Ohio BR/TR, 6'3", 177 lbs. Deb: 10/7/1886

YEAR	TM/L	G	AB	R	H	2B	3B	HR	RBI	BB	SO	AVG	OBP	SLG	PRO+	BR/A	SB	CS	SBR	FA	FR	G/POS	TPR
1886	Cin-a	1	3	0	0	0	0	0	0			.000	.250	.000	-19	-0				.917	1	/C-1	0.0
1888	Lou-a	51	189	15	37	4	2	1	21	4		.196	.216	.254	52	-10	4			.863	-2	O-28,C-25	-1.0
1889	Lou-a	90	360	39	86	11	5	3	45	7	41	.239	.253	.322	65	-18	13			.900	3	C-54,O-20,1/3	-1.0
1890	NY-P	44	166	27	44	7	0	1	22	10	9	.265	.307	.325	63	-10	6			.877	-12	C-30,O-12/32	-1.6
1891	Cin-a	51	175	21	45	7	1	1	14	14	15	.257	.316	.326	71	-6	7			.923	7	C-44/O-6,13P	0.3
	Mil-a	25	99	13	33	7	0	0	9	4	5	.333	.359	.404	98	-2	1			.924	2	C-20/1-4,O	0.2
	Yr	76	274	34	78	14	1	1	23	18	20	.285	.331	.354	85	-8	8			.923	9	C-64/O-7,13P	0.5
1892	Cin-N	91	346	45	88	10	5	2	50	16	13	.254	.295	.329	90	-5	10			.929	-13	C-67,1-14,O/3	-1.3
1893	Cin-N	121	483	68	135	17	12	1	108	35	17	.280	.332	.371	85	-12	16			**.969**	1	C-80,O-23,1	-0.5
1894	Cin-N	72	284	50	88	15	5	8	64	12	11	.310	.338	.482	92	-6	5			.918	-1	C-43,1-27/OS	-0.2
1895	Cin-N	92	334	60	102	23	5	1	47	17	10	.305	.339	.413	90	-7	15			.934	11	C-77,1-15/32	0.9
1896	Cin-N	114	433	71	127	20	9	2	66	16	7	.293	.320	.395	82	-14	7			.984	5	1-57,C-57	-0.3
1897	Cin-N	54	199	21	58	13	5	0	30	2		.291	.299	.407	80	-7	2			.986	-0	1-35,C-15	-0.5
1898	Cin-N	78	275	35	84	8	5	1	46	11		.305	.339	.389	101	-3	4			.979	-3	1-39/C-33	-0.9
1899	Cin-N	31	108	9	19	1	0	0	2	3		.176	.198	.185	5	-14	4			.982	3	1-21/C-7,O	-0.9
Total	13	915	3454	474	946	147	53	21	525	151	128	.274	.307	.365	80	-112	92			.926	-0	C-553,1-253,O/3S2P	-5.9

■ MO VAUGHN
Vaughn, Maurice Samuel b: 12/15/67, Norwalk, Conn. BL/TR, 6'1", 225 lbs. Deb: 6/27/91

YEAR	TM/L	G	AB	R	H	2B	3B	HR	RBI	BB	SO	AVG	OBP	SLG	PRO+	BR/A	SB	CS	SBR	FA	FR	G/POS	TPR
1991	Bos-A	74	219	21	57	12	0	4	32	26	43	.260	.344	.370	93	-2	2	1	0	.985	-2	1-49,D-16	-0.7
1992	Bos-A	113	355	42	83	16	2	13	57	47	67	.234	.328	.400	97	-2	3	3	-1	.982	-2	1-85,D-20	-1.1
1993	Bos-A	152	539	86	160	34	1	29	101	79	130	.297	.395	.525	136	28	4	3	-1	.987	-9	*1-131,D-19	0.7

YEAR	TM/L	G	AB	R	H	2B	3B	HR	RBI	BB	SO	AVG	OBP	SLG	PRO+	BR/A	SB	CS	SBR	FA	FR	G/POS	TPR
1994	Bos-A	111	394	65	122	25	1	26	82	57	112	.310	.410	.576	141	25	4	4	-1	.989	-5	*1-106/D-1	0.9
Total	4	450	1507	214	422	87	4	72	272	209	352	.280	.376	.486	123	50	13	11	-3	.986	-17	1-371/D-56	-0.2

■ BOBBY VAUGHN
Vaughn, Robert   b: 6/4/1885, Stamford, N.Y.   d: 4/11/65, Seattle, Wash.   BR/TR, 5'9", 150 lbs.   Deb: 6/12/09

YEAR	TM/L	G	AB	R	H	2B	3B	HR	RBI	BB	SO	AVG	OBP	SLG	PRO+	BR/A	SB	CS	SBR	FA	FR	G/POS	TPR
1909	NY-A	5	14	1	2	0	0	0	0	1		.143	.200	.143	8	-1	1			.882	-3	/2-4,S-1	-0.5
1915	StL-F	144	521	69	146	19	9	0	32	58	38	.280	.356	.351	85	-10	24			.953	-8	*2-127,S-12/3	-1.7
Total	2	149	535	70	148	19	9	0	32	59	38	.277	.352	.346	83	-11	25			.951	-11	2-131/S-13,3	-2.2

■ BOBBY VEACH
Veach, Robert Hayes   b: 6/29/1888, Island, Ky.   d: 8/7/45, Detroit, Mich.   BL/TR, 5'11", 160 lbs.   Deb: 8/6/12

YEAR	TM/L	G	AB	R	H	2B	3B	HR	RBI	BB	SO	AVG	OBP	SLG	PRO+	BR/A	SB	CS	SBR	FA	FR	G/POS	TPR
1912	Det-A	23	79	8	27	5	1	0	15	5		.342	.388	.430	138	4	2			.927	2	O-22	0.5
1913	Det-A	137	491	54	132	22	10	0	64	53	19	.269	.346	.354	107	4	22			.917	-5	*O-135	-0.7
1914	Det-A	149	531	56	146	19	14	1	72	50	29	.275	.341	.369	110	6	20	20	-6	.965	3	*O-145	-0.4
1915	Det-A	152	569	81	178	**40**	10	3	**112**	68	43	.313	.390	.434	140	27	16	19	-7	.975	2	*O-152	1.6
1916	Det-A	150	566	92	173	33	15	3	91	52	41	.306	.367	.433	135	23	24	15	-2	.967	4	*O-150	1.9
1917	Det-A	154	571	79	182	31	12	8	**103**	61	44	.319	.393	.457	160	40	21			.956	5	*O-154	4.0
1918	Det-A	127	499	59	139	21	13	3	**78**	35	23	.279	.331	.391	123	11	21			.977	3	*O-127/P-1	0.8
1919	Det-A	139	538	87	**191**	45	17	3	101	33	33	.355	.398	.519	160	40	19			.967	11	*O-138	4.3
1920	Det-A	154	612	92	188	39	15	11	113	36	22	.307	.353	.474	121	15	11	7	-1	.967	15	*O-154	1.6
1921	Det-A	150	612	110	207	43	13	16	128	48	31	.338	.387	.529	133	28	14	10	-2	.974	15	*O-149	2.8
1922	Det-A	155	618	96	202	34	13	9	126	42	27	.327	.377	.468	123	20	9	1	2	.982	8	*O-154	1.8
1923	Det-A	114	293	45	94	13	3	2	39	29	21	.321	.388	.406	111	5	10	3	1	.943	-14	O-85	-1.1
1924	Bos-A	142	519	77	153	35	9	5	99	47	18	.295	.359	.426	102	0	5	5	-2	.956	-1	*O-130	-1.1
1925	Bos-A	1	5	0	1	0	0	0	2	1		.200	.333	.200	38	-0	0	0	0	1.000	0	/O-1	0.0
	NY-A	56	116	13	41	10	2	0	15	8	0	.353	.400	.474	123	4	1	4	-2	.957	-7	O-33	-0.6
	*Was-A	18	37	4	9	3	0	0	8	3		.243	.300	.324	60	-2	0	0	0	.923	-3	O-11	-0.5
	Yr	75	158	17	51	13	2	0	25	12	4	.323	.374	.430	106	1	1	4	-2	.952	-10	O-45	-1.1
Total	14	1821	6656	953	2063	393	147	64	1166	571	367	.310	.370	.442	127	225	195	84		.964	39	*O-1740/P-1	14.9

■ PEEK-A-BOO VEACH
Veach, William Walter   b: 6/15/1862, Indianapolis, Ind   d: 11/12/37, Indianapolis, Ind.   Deb: 8/24/1884

YEAR	TM/L	G	AB	R	H	2B	3B	HR	RBI	BB	SO	AVG	OBP	SLG	PRO+	BR/A	SB	CS	SBR	FA	FR	G/POS	TPR
1884	KC-U	27	82	9	11	1	0	1		9		.134	.220	.183	12	-10				.833	-1	O-14,P-12/21	-0.6
1887	Lou-a	1	3	0	0	0	0	0		1		.000	.250	.000	-26	-0	0			.750	-0	/P-1	0.0
1890	Cle-N	64	238	24	56	10	5	0	32	33	28	.235	.336	.319	93	-1	9			.971	6	1-64	0.1
	Pit-N	8	30	6	9	1	1	2	5	8	3	.300	.447	.600	231	5	0			.968	1	/1-8	0.5
	Yr	72	268	30	65	11	6	2	37	41	31	.243	.349	.351	107	4	9			.971	7	1-72	0.6
Total	3	100	353	39	76	12	6	3	37	51	31	.215	.319	.309	85	-6	9			.971	6	/1-73,O-14,P2	0.0

■ COOT VEAL
Veal, Orville Inman   b: 7/9/32, Sandersville, Ga.   BR/TR, 6'1", 165 lbs.   Deb: 7/30/58

YEAR	TM/L	G	AB	R	H	2B	3B	HR	RBI	BB	SO	AVG	OBP	SLG	PRO+	BR/A	SB	CS	SBR	FA	FR	G/POS	TPR
1958	Det-A	58	207	29	53	10	2	0	16	14	21	.256	.306	.324	69	-9	1	1	-0	.981	-8	S-58	-1.3
1959	Det-A	77	89	12	18	1	0	1	15	8	7	.202	.276	.247	42	-7	0	1	0	.962	10	S-72	0.5
1960	Det-A	27	64	8	19	5	1	0	8	11	7	.297	.400	.406	115	2	0	0	0	.988	-2	S-22/3-3,2	0.1
1961	Was-A	69	218	21	44	10	0	0	8	19	29	.202	.275	.248	41	-18	1	8	-5	.974	0	S-63	-1.7
1962	Pit-N	1	1	0	0	0	0	0	0	0	1	.000	.000	.000	-99	-0	0	0	0	.000	0	H	0.0
1963	Det-A	15	32	5	7	0	0	0	4	4	4	.219	.306	.219	48	-2	0	0	0	.980	4	S-12	0.2
Total	6	247	611	75	141	26	3	1	51	56	69	.231	.301	.288	59	-34	2	9	-5	.976	4	S-227/3-3,2	-2.2

■ JESUS VEGA
Vega, Jesus Anthony (Morales)   b: 10/14/55, Bayamon, P.R.   BR/TR, 6'1", 176 lbs.   Deb: 9/5/79

YEAR	TM/L	G	AB	R	H	2B	3B	HR	RBI	BB	SO	AVG	OBP	SLG	PRO+	BR/A	SB	CS	SBR	FA	FR	G/POS	TPR
1979	Min-A	4	7	0	0	0	0	0	0	0	2	.000	.000	.000	-96	-2	0	0	0	.000	0	/H	-0.2
1980	Min-A	12	30	3	5	0	0	0	4	3	7	.167	.242	.167	13	-4	1	0	0	1.000	0	/1-2,D-9	-0.3
1982	Min-A	71	199	23	53	6	0	5	29	8	19	.266	.295	.372	80	-6	6	1	1	.974	-1	D-39,1-18/O	-0.8
Total	3	87	236	26	58	6	0	5	33	11	28	.246	.279	.335	65	-11	7	1	2	.975	-1	/D-48,1-20,O	-1.3

■ RANDY VELARDE
Velarde, Randy Lee   b: 11/24/62, Midland, Tex.   BR/TR, 6' ", 185 lbs.   Deb: 8/20/87

YEAR	TM/L	G	AB	R	H	2B	3B	HR	RBI	BB	SO	AVG	OBP	SLG	PRO+	BR/A	SB	CS	SBR	FA	FR	G/POS	TPR
1987	NY-A	8	22	1	4	0	0	0	0	0	6	.182	.182	.182	-3	-3	0	0	0	.933	0	/S-8	-0.3
1988	NY-A	48	115	18	20	6	0	5	12	8	24	.174	.240	.357	65	-6	1	1	-0	.967	8	2-24,S-14,3	0.4
1989	NY-A	33	100	12	34	4	2	2	11	7	14	.340	.389	.480	145	6	3	0	-2	.954	2	3-27/S-9	0.6
1990	NY-A	95	229	21	48	6	2	5	19	20	53	.210	.276	.319	66	-11	0	3	-2	.945	9	3-74,S-15/02D	-0.2
1991	NY-A	80	184	19	45	11	1	1	15	18	43	.245	.322	.332	81	-4	3	1	0	.935	-4	3-50,S-31/O	0.4
1992	NY-A	121	412	57	112	24	1	7	46	38	78	.272	.336	.386	103	5	7	2	1	.974	-8	S-75,3-26,O/2	-0.1
1993	NY-A	85	226	28	68	13	2	7	24	18	39	.301	.363	.469	126	8	2	2	-1	.932	-1	O-50,S-26,3/D	0.7
1994	NY-A	77	280	47	78	16	1	9	34	22	61	.279	.340	.439	106	2	4	2	0	.944	1	S-49,3-27/O2	0.6
Total	8	547	1568	203	409	80	9	36	162	131	318	.261	.325	.392	97	-7	17	14	-3	.932	19	3-231,S-227/O2D	2.1

■ GUILLERMO VELASQUEZ
Velasquez, Guillermo (Burgara)   b: 4/23/68, Mexicali, Mexico   BL/TR, 6'3", 220 lbs.   Deb: 9/14/92

YEAR	TM/L	G	AB	R	H	2B	3B	HR	RBI	BB	SO	AVG	OBP	SLG	PRO+	BR/A	SB	CS	SBR	FA	FR	G/POS	TPR
1992	SD-N	15	23	1	7	0	0	1	5	1	7	.304	.333	.435	114	0	0	0	0	.933	-1	/1-3,O-2	-0.1
1993	SD-N	79	143	7	30	2	0	3	20	13	35	.210	.276	.287	50	-10	0	0	0	.984	-1	1-38/O-6	-1.4
Total	2	94	166	8	37	2	0	4	25	14	42	.223	.283	.307	58	-10	0	0	0	.981	-2	/1-41,O-8	-1.5

■ FREDDIE VELAZQUEZ
Velazquez, Federico Antonio (Velasquez)   b: 12/6/37, Santo Domingo, D.R.   BR/TR, 6'1", 185 lbs.   Deb: 4/20/69

YEAR	TM/L	G	AB	R	H	2B	3B	HR	RBI	BB	SO	AVG	OBP	SLG	PRO+	BR/A	SB	CS	SBR	FA	FR	G/POS	TPR
1969	Sea-A	6	16	1	2	2	0	0	2	1	3	.125	.176	.250	18	-2	0	0	0	1.000	-1	/C-5	-0.2
1973	Atl-N	15	23	2	8	1	0	1	3	1	3	.348	.375	.391	105	0	0	0	0	.975	2	C-11	0.2
Total	2	21	39	3	10	3	0	1	5	2	6	.256	.293	.333	71	-2	0	0	0	.985	1	/C-16	0.0

■ OTTO VELEZ
Velez, Otoniel (Franceschi)   b: 11/29/50, Ponce, P.R.   BR/TR, 6', 195 lbs.   Deb: 9/4/73

YEAR	TM/L	G	AB	R	H	2B	3B	HR	RBI	BB	SO	AVG	OBP	SLG	PRO+	BR/A	SB	CS	SBR	FA	FR	G/POS	TPR
1973	NY-A	23	77	9	15	4	0	2	7	15	24	.195	.326	.325	87	-1	0	1	-1	.959	1	O-23	-0.2
1974	NY-A	27	67	9	14	1	1	2	10	15	24	.209	.354	.343	104	1	0	0	0	.986	-4	1-21/O-3,3	-0.4
1975	NY-A	6	8	0	2	0	0	0	1	2	0	.250	.400	.250	90	0	0	0	0	1.000	-0	/1-1,D-1	0.0
1976	*NY-A	49	94	11	25	6	0	2	10	23	26	.266	.410	.394	137	6	0	0	0	.979	-3	O-24/1-8,3D	0.2
1977	Tor-A	120	360	50	92	19	3	16	62	65	87	.256	.371	.458	123	13	4	2	0	.973	0	O-79,D-28	0.9
1978	Tor-A	91	248	29	66	14	2	9	38	45	41	.266	.383	.448	130	11	1	3	-2	.982	7	O-74/1-1,D	1.4
1979	Tor-A	99	274	45	79	21	0	15	48	46	45	.288	.396	.529	145	18	0	1	-1	.971	-5	O-73/1-6,D	0.9
1980	Tor-A	104	357	54	96	12	3	20	62	54	86	.269	.368	.487	126	13	0	0	0	.975	0	D-97/1-3	1.0
1981	Tor-A	80	240	32	51	9	2	11	28	55	60	.213	.366	.404	114	6	3	3	-2	1.000	-0	D-74/1-1	0.1
1982	Tor-A	28	52	4	10	1	0	1	5	13	15	.192	.354	.269	68	-2	1	0	0	.000	0	D-24	-0.3
1983	Cle-A	10	25	1	2	0	0	0	1	3	6	.080	.179	.080	-25	-4	0	0	0	.000	0	/D-8	-0.5
Total	11	637	1802	244	452	87	11	78	272	336	414	.251	.372	.441	122	61	6	10	-4	.973	-4	O-276,D-255/13	3.1

■ PAT VELTMAN
Veltman, Arthur Patrick   b: 3/24/06, Mobile, Ala.   d: 10/1/80, San Antonio, Tex.   BR/TR, 6', 175 lbs.   Deb: 4/17/26

YEAR	TM/L	G	AB	R	H	2B	3B	HR	RBI	BB	SO	AVG	OBP	SLG	PRO+	BR/A	SB	CS	SBR	FA	FR	G/POS	TPR
1926	Chi-A	5	4	1	1	0	0	0		1	0	.250	.400	.250	75	-0	0	0	0	1.000	0	/S-1	0.0
1928	NY-N	1	3	1	1	0	1	0		1	0	.333	.500	1.000	282	1	0			1.000	0	/O-1	0.1
1929	NY-N	2	1	1	0	0	0	0	2	0		.000	.667	.000	81	0	0			1.000	0	/C-1	0.0
1931	Bos-N	1	1	0	0	0	0	0		0		.000	.000	.000	-99	-0	0			.000	0	H	0.0
1932	NY-N	2	1	0	0	0	0	0		0		.000	.000	.000	-99	-0	0			.000	0	H	0.0
1934	Pit-N	12	28	1	3	0	0	0	2	0	1	.107	.107	.107	-41	-6	0			1.000	-2	C-11	-0.7
Total	6	23	38	4	5	0	1	0	4	2	1	.132	.214	.184	-7	-5	0	<u>0</u>		1.000	-2	/C-12,O-1,S	-0.6

YEAR	TM/L	G	AB	R	H	2B	3B	HR	RBI	BB	SO	AVG	OBP	SLG	PRO+	BR/A	SB	CS	SBR	FA	FR	G/POS	TPR

■ MAX VENABLE
Venable, William McKinley b: 6/6/57, Phoenix, Ariz. BL/TR, 5'10", 185 lbs. Deb: 4/8/79

1979	SF-N	55	85	12	14	1	1	0	3	10	18	.165	.260	.200	29	-8	3	3	-1	.914	-5	O-25	-1.5
1980	SF-N	64	138	13	37	5	0	0	10	15	22	.268	.340	.304	83	-3	8	2	1	1.000	-5	O-40	-0.9
1981	SF-N	18	32	2	6	0	2	0	1	4	3	.188	.278	.313	68	-1	3	1	0	1.000	0	/O-5	-0.1
1982	SF-N	71	125	17	28	2	1	1	7	7	16	.224	.265	.280	53	-8	9	3	1	.986	-4	O-53	-1.2
1983	SF-N	94	228	28	50	7	4	6	27	22	34	.219	.296	.364	85	-5	15	2	3	.993	3	O-66	-0.1
1984	Mon-N	38	71	7	17	2	0	2	7	3	7	.239	.280	.352	80	-2	1	0	0	1.000	-4	O-27	-0.7
1985	Cin-N	77	135	21	39	12	3	0	10	6	17	.289	.319	.422	101	-0	11	3	2	1.000	-1	O-39	-0.1
1986	Cin-N	108	147	17	31	7	1	2	15	17	24	.211	.293	.313	64	-7	7	2	1	.969	-10	O-57	-1.8
1987	Cin-N	7	7	2	1	0	0	0	2	0	0	.143	.143	.143	-23	-1	0	0	0	1.000	-1	/O-4	-0.2
1989	Cal-A	20	53	7	19	4	0	0	4	1	16	.358	.370	.434	128	1	0	0	0	1.000	-1	O-13	-0.1
1990	Cal-A	93	189	26	49	9	3	4	21	24	31	.259	.343	.402	110	3	5	1	1	.975	-12	O-77/D-1	-1.0
1991	Cal-A	82	187	24	46	8	2	3	21	11	30	.246	.295	.358	80	-5	2	1	0	.967	-11	O-65/D-3	-1.8
Total	12	727	1397	176	337	57	17	18	128	120	218	.241	.304	.345	81	-37	64	18	8	.982	-54	O-471/D-4	-9.5

■ ROBIN VENTURA
Ventura, Robin Mark b: 7/14/67, Santa Maria, Cal. BL/TR, 6'1", 185 lbs. Deb: 9/12/89

1989	Chi-A	16	45	5	8	3	0	0	7	8	6	.178	.315	.244	61	-2	0	0	0	.962	2	3-16	0.0
1990	Chi-A	150	493	48	123	17	1	5	54	55	53	.249	.326	.318	83	-10	1	4	-2	.939	-0	*3-147/1-1	-1.2
1991	Chi-A	157	606	92	172	25	1	23	100	80	67	.284	.371	.442	127	24	2	4	-2	.959	1	*3-151,1-31	2.3
1992	Chi-A★	157	592	85	167	38	1	16	93	93	71	.282	.380	.431	128	25	2	4	-2	.957	24	*3-157/1-2	4.6
1993	*Chi-A	157	554	85	145	27	1	22	94	105	82	.262	.382	.433	121	20	1	6	-3	.965	-5	*3-155/1-4	1.2
1994	Chi-A	109	401	57	113	15	1	18	78	61	69	.282	.379	.459	116	11	3	1	0	.935	-4	*3-108/1-3,S	0.7
Total	6	746	2691	372	728	125	5	84	426	402	348	.271	.368	.414	115	66	9	19	-9	.953	17	3-734/1-41,S	7.6

▶ VINCE VENTURA
Ventura, Vincent b: 4/18/17, New York, N.Y. BR/TR, 6'1.5", 190 lbs. Deb: 5/8/45

1945	Was-A	18	58	4	12	0	0	0	2	4	4	.207	.258	.207	39	-5	0	0	0	.886	-1	O-15	-0.7

■ EMIL VERBAN
Verban, Emil Matthew "Dutch" or "Antelope" b: 8/27/15, Lincoln, Ill. d: 6/8/89, Quincy, Ill. BR/TR, 5'11", 165 lbs. Deb: 4/18/44

1944	*StL-N	146	498	51	128	14	2	0	43	19	14	.257	.287	.293	62	-25	0			.968	-6	*2-146	-2.4
1945	StL-N†	155	597	59	166	22	8	0	72	19	15	.278	.304	.342	77	-19	4			.978	-19	*2-155	-2.9
1946	StL-N	1	1	0	0	0	0	0	0	0	0	.000	.000	.000	-96	-0	0			.000	0	H	
	Phi-N★	138	473	44	130	17	5	0	34	21	18	.275	.306	.332	83	-12	5			.963	-3	*2-138	-0.6
	Yr	139	474	44	130	17	5	0	34	21	18	.274	.305	.331	83	-12	5			.963	-3	*2-138	-0.6
1947	Phi-N★	155	540	50	154	14	8	0	42	23	8	.285	.316	.341	77	-18	5			.982	17	*2-155	0.9
1948	Phi-N	55	169	14	39	5	1	0	11	11	5	.231	.282	.272	51	-11	4			.975	-4	2-54	-1.3
	Chi-N	56	248	37	73	15	1	1	16	4	7	.294	.308	.375	88	-5	4			.964	6	2-56	0.4
	Yr	111	417	51	112	20	2	1	27	15	12	.269	.297	.333	72	-17	4			.969	2	2-110	-0.9
1949	Chi-N	98	343	38	99	11	1	0	22	8	2	.289	.309	.327	72	-14	3			.965	3	2-88	-0.7
1950	Chi-N	45	37	7	4	1	0	0	3	3	5	.108	.175	.135	-17	-6	0			.966	6	/2-8,S-3,3O	-0.1
	Bos-N	4	5	1	0	0	0	0	0	0	0	.000	.000	.000	-99	-1	0			.833	1	/2-2	0.0
	Yr	49	42	8	4	1	0	0	3	3	5	.095	.156	.119	-27	-8	0			.927	7	2-10/S-3,3O	-0.1
Total	7	853	2911	301	793	99	26	1	241	108	74	.272	.301	.325	73	-113	21			.971	1	2-802/S-3,O3	-6.7

■ GENE VERBLE
Verble, Gene Kermit "Satchel" b: 6/29/28, Concord, N.C. BR/TR, 5'10", 163 lbs. Deb: 4/17/51

1951	Was-A	68	177	16	36	3	2	0	15	18	10	.203	.277	.243	42	-14	1	1	-0	.978	-2	S-28,2-19/3	-1.3
1953	Was-A	13	21	4	4	0	0	0	2	2	1	.190	.261	.190	24	-2	0	0	0	1.000	2	/S-8	0.0
Total	2	81	198	20	40	3	2	0	17	20	11	.202	.275	.237	40	-16	1	1	-0	.981	1	/S-36,2-19,3	-1.3

■ FRANK VERDI
Verdi, Frank Michael b: 6/2/26, Brooklyn, N.Y. BR/TR, 5'10.5", 170 lbs. Deb: 5/10/53

1953	NY-A	1	0	0	0	0	0	0	0	0	0	—	—	—	—	0	0	0	0	.000	0	/S-1	0.0

■ JOHNNY VERGEZ
Vergez, John Louis b: 7/9/06, Oakland, Cal. d: 7/15/91, Davis, Cal. BR/TR, 5'8", 165 lbs. Deb: 4/14/31

1931	NY-N	152	565	67	157	24	2	13	81	29	65	.278	.320	.396	94	-6	11			.932	-3	*3-152	0.0
1932	NY-N	118	376	42	98	21	3	6	43	25	36	.261	.310	.380	86	-8	1			.935	5	*3-111/S-1	0.5
1933	NY-N	123	458	57	124	21	6	16	72	39	66	.271	.332	.448	123	13	1			.928	-14	*3-123	0.7
1934	NY-N	108	320	31	64	18	1	7	27	28	55	.200	.269	.328	60	-19	1			.943	10	*3-104	-0.6
1935	Phi-N	148	546	56	136	27	4	9	63	46	67	.249	.312	.363	73	-21	8			.953	-7	*3-148/S-2	-2.2
1936	Phi-N	15	40	4	11	2	0	1	5	3	11	.275	.326	.400	86	-1	0			.964	0	3-12	0.0
	StL-N	8	18	1	3	1	0	0	1	1	3	.167	.211	.222	17	-2	0			.929	0	/3-8	-0.2
	Yr	23	58	5	14	3	0	1	6	4	14	.241	.290	.345	66	-3	0			.952	0	3-20	-0.2
Total	6	672	2323	258	593	114	16	52	292	171	303	.255	.311	.385	87	-44	22			.939	-8	3-658/S-3	-1.7

■ MICKEY VERNON
Vernon, James Barton b: 4/22/18, Marcus Hook, Pa. BL/TL, 6'2", 180 lbs. Deb: 7/8/39 MC

1939	Was-A	76	276	23	71	15	4	1	30	24	28	.257	.317	.351	76	-10	1	1	-0	.985	-3	1-75	-2.0
1940	Was-A	5	19	0	3	0	0	0	0	0	3	.158	.158	.158	-19	-3	0	0	0	1.000	0	/1-4	-0.4
1941	Was-A	138	531	73	159	27	11	9	93	43	51	.299	.352	.443	114	9	9	3	1	.992	-6	*1-132	-0.6
1942	Was-A	151	621	76	168	34	6	9	86	59	63	.271	.337	.388	104	3	25	6	4	.982	-8	*1-151	-1.1
1943	Was-A	145	553	89	148	29	8	7	70	67	55	.268	.357	.387	122	16	24	8	2	.990	-11	*1-143	0.0
1946	Was-A★	148	587	88	207	51	8	8	85	49	64	.353	.403	.508	163	47	14	10	-2	.990	-1	*1-147	3.6
1947	Was-A	154	600	77	159	29	12	7	85	49	42	.265	.320	.388	99	-3	12	12	-4	.987	-4	*1-154	-1.7
1948	Was-A★	150	558	78	135	27	7	3	48	54	43	.242	.310	.332	73	-23	15	11	-2	.989	5	*1-150	-2.1
1949	Cle-A	153	584	72	170	27	4	18	83	58	51	.291	.357	.443	113	9	9	7	-2	.991	19	*1-153	2.4
1950	Cle-A	28	90	8	17	0	0	0	10	12	10	.189	.284	.189	24	-10	2	0	1	.996	1	1-25	-0.8
	Was-A	90	327	47	100	17	3	9	65	50	29	.306	.404	.459	127	14	6	1	1	.990	1	1-85	1.3
	Yr	118	417	55	117	17	3	9	75	62	39	.281	.379	.400	104	4	8	1	2	.991	3	*1-110	0.5
1951	Was-A	141	546	69	160	30	7	9	87	53	45	.293	.358	.423	112	9	7	6	-2	.994	-4	*1-137	-0.3
1952	Was-A	154	569	71	143	33	9	10	80	89	66	.251	.353	.394	111	9	7	7	-2	.993	1	*1-153	0.2
1953	Was-A★	152	608	101	205	43	11	15	115	63	57	.337	.403	.518	151	43	4	6	-2	.992	-3	*1-152	3.1
1954	Was-A★	151	597	90	173	33	14	20	97	61	61	.290	.360	.492	140	29	1	4	-2	.992	-9	*1-148	1.1
1955	Was-A★	150	538	74	162	23	8	14	85	74	50	.301	.389	.452	133	25	4	4	-2	.994	-6	*1-144	0.6
1956	Bos-A★	119	403	67	125	28	4	15	84	57	40	.310	.405	.511	125	15	1	0	0	.989	-3	*1-108	0.5
1957	Bos-A	102	270	36	65	18	1	7	38	41	35	.241	.351	.393	97	-0	0	0	0	.992	4	1-70	-0.1
1958	Cle-A★	119	355	49	104	22	3	8	55	44	56	.293	.374	.439	126	13	0	4	-2	.987	-2	1-96	0.4
1959	Mil-N	74	91	8	20	4	0	3	14	7	20	.220	.283	.363	77	-3	0	0	0	.983	1	1-10/O-4	-0.3
1960	Pit-N	9	8	0	1	0	0	0	1	0	1	.125	.222	.125	-2	-1	0	0	0	.000	0	H	-0.1
Total	20	2409	8731	1196	2495	490	120	172	1311	955	869	.286	.359	.428	116	186	137	90	-13	.990	-32	*1-2237/O-4	3.7

■ ZOILO VERSALLES
Versalles, Zoilo Casanova (Rodriguez) "Zorro" b: 12/18/39, Veldado, Cuba BR/TR, 5'10", 150 lbs. Deb: 8/1/59

1959	Was-A	29	59	4	9	0	0	1	4	5	15	.153	.219	.203	17	-7	1	0	0	.943	3	S-29	-0.2
1960	Was-A	15	45	2	6	2	2	0	4	2	5	.133	.170	.267	16	-5	0	0	0	.935	-2	S-15	-0.6
1961	Min-A	129	510	65	143	25	5	7	53	25	61	.280	.315	.390	83	-13	16	9	-1	.952	-2	*S-129	-0.5
1962	Min-A	160	568	69	137	18	9	17	67	37	71	.241	.290	.373	74	-22	5	5	-2	.970	32	*S-160	2.3
1963	Min-A★	159	621	74	162	31	13	10	54	33	66	.261	.303	.401	94	-6	7	4	-0	.961	-2	*S-159	0.3
1964	Min-A	160	659	94	171	33	10	20	64	42	88	.259	.312	.431	103	2	14	4	2	.957	-17	*S-160	-0.2

YEAR	TM/L	G	AB	R	H	2B	3B	HR	RBI	BB	SO	AVG	OBP	SLG	PRO+	BR/A	SB	CS	SBR	FA	FR	G/POS	TPR
1965	*Min-A★	160	666	**126**	182	**45**	**12**	19	77	41	122	.273	.322	.462	115	11	27	5	**5**	.950	2	*S-160	3.1
1966	Min-A	137	543	73	135	20	6	7	36	40	85	.249	.288	.346	82	-12	10	12	-4	.942	-17	*S-135	-2.2
1967	Min-A	160	581	63	116	16	7	6	50	33	113	.200	.250	.282	53	-34	5	3	-0	.958	2	*S-159	-1.9
1968	LA-N	122	403	29	79	16	3	2	24	26	84	.196	.245	.266	57	-22	6	4	-1	.954	8	*S-119	-0.3
1969	Cle-A	72	217	21	49	11	1	1	13	21	47	.226	.300	.300	66	-10	3	1	-0	.975	-11	2-46,3-30/S	-1.8
	Was-A	31	75	9	20	2	1	0	6	3	13	.267	.304	.320	79	-2	1	0	0	.935	-1	S-13/2-6,3	-0.2
	Yr	103	292	30	69	13	2	1	19	24	60	.236	.301	.305	69	-12	4	1	1	.978	-12	2-52,3-35,S	-2.0
1971	Atl-N	66	194	21	37	11	0	5	22	11	40	.191	.234	.325	53	-12	2	1	0	.902	-14	3-30,S-24/2	-2.6
Total	12	1400	5141	650	1246	230	63	95	471	318	810	.242	.292	.367	82	-133	97	48		.956	-20	*S-1265/3-65,2	-4.8

■ TOM VERYZER
Veryzer, Thomas Martin b: 2/11/53, Port Jefferson, N.Y. BR/TR, 6'1", 185 lbs. Deb: 8/14/73

YEAR	TM/L	G	AB	R	H	2B	3B	HR	RBI	BB	SO	AVG	OBP	SLG	PRO+	BR/A	SB	CS	SBR	FA	FR	G/POS	TPR
1973	Det-A	18	20	1	6	0	1	0	2	2	4	.300	.364	.400	108	0	0	0	0	.857	-5	S-18	-0.4
1974	Det-A	22	55	4	13	2	0	2	9	5	8	.236	.300	.382	92	-1	0	0	0	.927	-10	S-20	-0.9
1975	Det-A	128	404	37	102	13	1	5	48	23	76	.252	.301	.327	74	-14	2	6	-3	.960	-4	*S-128	-0.8
1976	Det-A	97	354	31	83	8	2	1	25	21	44	.234	.289	.277	64	-16	1	4	-2	.966	-1	S-97	-0.8
1977	Det-A	125	350	31	69	12	1	2	28	16	44	.197	.232	.254	31	-33	0	1	-1	.969	10	*S-124	-1.1
1978	Cle-A	130	421	48	114	18	4	1	32	13	36	.271	.301	.340	81	-11	1	2	-1	.963	-4	*S-129	-0.1
1979	Cle-A	149	449	41	99	9	3	0	34	34	54	.220	.281	.254	45	-34	2	5	-2	.974	4	*S-148	-1.6
1980	Cle-A	109	358	28	97	12	0	2	28	10	25	.271	.306	.321	72	-14	0	5	-3	.971	-1	*S-108	-0.5
1981	Cle-A	75	221	13	54	4	0	0	14	10	10	.244	.280	.262	58	-12	1	1	0	.970	-7	S-75	-1.1
1982	NY-N	40	54	6	18	2	0	0	4	3	4	.333	.368	.370	108	1	1	0	0	.962	-1	2-26,S-16	0.1
1983	Chi-N	59	88	5	18	3	0	1	3	3	13	.205	.237	.273	37	-8	0	0	0	.978	7	S-28,3-17	0.1
1984	*Chi-N	44	74	5	14	1	0	0	4	3	11	.189	.259	.203	29	-7	0	0	0	.966	-2	S-36/3-5,2	-0.7
Total	12	996	2848	250	687	84	12	14	231	143	329	.241	.285	.294	61	-148	9	23	-11	.966	-14	S-927/2-30,3	-7.8

■ ERNIE VICK
Vick, Henry Arthur b: 7/2/1900, Toledo, Ohio d: 7/16/80, Ann Arbor, Mich. BR/TR, 5'9.5", 185 lbs. Deb: 6/29/22

YEAR	TM/L	G	AB	R	H	2B	3B	HR	RBI	BB	SO	AVG	OBP	SLG	PRO+	BR/A	SB	CS	SBR	FA	FR	G/POS	TPR
1922	StL-N	3	6	1	2	2	0	0	0	0	0	.333	.333	.667	159	0	0	0	0	.875	-0	/C-3	0.0
1924	StL-N	16	23	2	8	1	0	0	0	3	3	.348	.423	.391	122	1	0	0	0	.974	3	C-16	0.4
1925	StL-N	14	32	3	6	2	1	0	3	3	1	.188	.257	.313	44	-3	0	0	0	.929	0	/C-9	-0.2
1926	StL-N	24	51	6	10	2	0	0	4	3	4	.196	.241	.235	27	-5	0	0	0	.944	-1	C-23	-0.5
Total	4	57	112	12	26	7	1	0	7	9	8	.232	.289	.313	58	-7	0	0	0	.944	2	/C-51	-0.3

■ SAMMY VICK
Vick, Samuel Bruce b: 4/12/1895, Batesville, Miss. d: 8/17/86, Memphis, Tenn. BR/TR, 5'10.5", 163 lbs. Deb: 9/20/17

YEAR	TM/L	G	AB	R	H	2B	3B	HR	RBI	BB	SO	AVG	OBP	SLG	PRO+	BR/A	SB	CS	SBR	FA	FR	G/POS	TPR
1917	NY-A	10	36	4	10	3	0	0	2	1	0	.278	.297	.361	100	-0	2			.882	-1	O-10	-0.2
1918	NY-A	2	3	1	2	0	0	0	1	0	0	.667	.667	.667	296	0	0			.000	-1	/O-1	0.0
1919	NY-A	106	407	59	101	15	9	2	27	35	55	.248	.308	.344	82	-10	9			.952	-4	*O-100	-2.3
1920	NY-A	51	118	21	26	7	1	0	11	14	20	.220	.313	.297	60	-7	1	1	-0	.949	-4	O-33	-1.3
1921	Bos-A	44	77	5	20	3	1	0	9	1	10	.260	.269	.325	52	-6	0	1	-1	1.000	-1	O-14	-0.8
Total	5	213	641	90	159	28	11	2	50	51	91	.248	.305	.335	76	-22	12	2		.951	-11	O-158	-4.6

■ GEORGE VICO
Vico, George Steve "Sam" b: 8/9/23, San Fernando, Cal. d: 1/13/94, Redondo Beach, Cal. BL/TR, 6'4", 200 lbs. Deb: 4/20/48

YEAR	TM/L	G	AB	R	H	2B	3B	HR	RBI	BB	SO	AVG	OBP	SLG	PRO+	BR/A	SB	CS	SBR	FA	FR	G/POS	TPR
1948	Det-A	144	521	50	139	23	9	8	58	39	39	.267	.326	.392	88	-11	2	2	-1	.988	-3	*1-142	-1.5
1949	Det-A	67	142	15	27	5	2	4	18	21	17	.190	.311	.338	72	-6	0	0	0	.985	2	1-53	-0.4
Total	2	211	663	65	166	28	11	12	76	60	56	.250	.323	.380	85	-17	2	2	-1	.987	-1	1-195	-1.9

■ JOSE VIDAL
Vidal, Jose (Nicolas) "Papito" b: 4/3/40, Batey Lechugas, D.R. BR/TR, 6', 190 lbs. Deb: 9/5/66

YEAR	TM/L	G	AB	R	H	2B	3B	HR	RBI	BB	SO	AVG	OBP	SLG	PRO+	BR/A	SB	CS	SBR	FA	FR	G/POS	TPR
1966	Cle-A	17	32	4	6	1	1	0	3	5	11	.188	.297	.281	67	-1	0	1	-1	1.000	-1	O-11	-0.3
1967	Cle-A	16	34	4	4	0	0	0	0	7	12	.118	.268	.118	17	-3	0	1	-1	1.000	-0	O-10	-0.6
1968	Cle-A	37	54	5	9	0	0	2	5	2	15	.167	.196	.278	43	-4	3	0	1	1.000	-5	O-26/1-1	-1.0
1969	Sea-A	18	26	7	5	0	1	1	2	4	8		.323	.385	99	-0	1	1	-0	.917	-0	/O-6	-0.1
Total	4	88	146	20	24	1	2	3	10	18				.260	53	-8	4	3	-1	.985	-7	/O-53,1-1	-2.0

■ HECTOR VILLANUEVA
Villanueva, Hector (Balasquide) b: 10/...s, P.R. BR/TR, 6'1", 220 lbs. Deb: 6/1/90

YEAR	TM/L	G	AB	R	H	2B	3B	HR	RBI	BB	SO	AVG	OBP	SLG	PRO+	BR/A	SB	CS	SBR	FA	FR	G/POS	TPR
1990	Chi-N	52	114	14	31	4	1	7	18	4	2			.509	112	1	1	0	0	.991	-4	C-23,1-14	-0.2
1991	Chi-N	71	192	23	53	10	1	13	32	21				.542	140	9	0	0	0	.979	-9	C-55/1-6	0.4
1992	Chi-N	51	112	9	17	6	0	2	13	1...				.259	37	-9	0	0	0	.978	6	C-28/1-6	-0.2
1993	StL-N	17	55	7	8	1	0	3	9					.327	40	-5	0	0	0	1.000	-1	C-17	-0.5
Total	4	191	473	53	109	21	2	25	72					.442	98	-4	1	0	0	.984	-8	C-123/1-26	-0.5

■ FERNANDO VINA
Vina, Fernando b: 4/16/69, Sacramen... ...70 lbs. Deb: 4/10/93

YEAR	TM/L	G	AB	R	H	2B	3B	HR	RBI	BB	SO	AVG	OBP	SLG	PRO+	BR/A	SB	CS	SBR	FA	FR	G/POS	TPR
1993	Sea-A	24	45	5	10	2	0	0	2			...7		.267	61	-2	6	0	2	1.000	6	2-16/S-4,D	0.6
1994	NY-N	79	124	20	31	6	0	0	6	12			.372	.298	77	-3	3	1	0	.979	2	2-13,3-12/SO	0.0
Total	2	103	169	25	41	8	0	0	8	16			.360	.290	73	-5	9	1	2	.991	8	/2-29,S-13,30D	0.6

■ CHARLIE VINSON
Vinson, Charles Anthony "Chuck" b: 1/5/44, Washington, D.C. BL/TL, 6'3", 207 lbs. Deb: 9/19/66

YEAR	TM/L	G	AB	R	H	2B	3B	HR	RBI	BB	SO	AVG	OBP	SLG	PRO+	BR/A	SB	CS	SBR	FA	FR	G/POS	TPR
1966	Cal-A	13	22	3	4	2	0	1	6	5	9	.182	.357	.409	123	1	0	0	0	1.000	-1	1-11	0.0

■ RUBE VINSON
Vinson, Ernest Augustus b: 3/20/1879, Dover, Del. d: 10/12/51, Chester, Pa. 5'9", 168 lbs. Deb: 9/27/04

YEAR	TM/L	G	AB	R	H	2B	3B	HR	RBI	BB	SO	AVG	OBP	SLG	PRO+	BR/A	SB	CS	SBR	FA	FR	G/POS	TPR
1904	Cle-A	15	49	12	15	1	0	0	2		10	.306	.433	.327	143	3	2			1.000	3	O-15	0.6
1905	Cle-A	39	134	12	26	3	1	0	9		7	.194	.245	.231	51	-7	4			.930	-3	O-36	-1.4
1906	Chi-A	10	24	2	6	0	0	0	3		2	.250	.308	.250	77	-1	1			.600	-3	/O-7	-0.4
Total	3	64	207	26	47	4	1	0	14		19	.227	.301	.256	77	-5	7			.919	-3	/O-58	-1.2

■ JIM VIOX
Viox, James Harry b: 12/30/1890, Lockland, Ohio d: 1/6/69, Erlanger, Ky. BR/TR, 5'7", 150 lbs. Deb: 5/9/12

YEAR	TM/L	G	AB	R	H	2B	3B	HR	RBI	BB	SO	AVG	OBP	SLG	PRO+	BR/A	SB	CS	SBR	FA	FR	G/POS	TPR
1912	Pit-N	33	70	8	13	2	3	1	7	3	9	.186	.219	.343	53	-5	2			.957	-4	3-10/S-8,O2	-0.9
1913	Pit-N	137	492	86	156	32	8	2	65	64	28	.317	.399	.427	142	29	14			.959	-43	*2-124,S-10	-1.6
1914	Pit-N	143	506	52	134	18	5	1	57	63	33	.265	.351	.326	106	6	9			.939	-25	*2-138/S-2,O	-2.2
1915	Pit-N	150	503	56	129	17	8	2	45	75	31	.256	.357	.334	111	10	12	8	-1	.954	-23	*2-134,3-13/O	-1.3
1916	Pit-N	43	132	12	33	7	2	1	17	11	17	.250	.340	.326	104	1	2			.937	-16	2-25,3-11	-1.6
Total	5	506	1703	214	465	76	24	7	191	222	112	.273	.361	.358	116	41	39	8		.949	-111	2-422/3-34,SO	-7.6

■ BILL VIRDON
Virdon, William Charles b: 6/9/31, Hazel Park, Mich. BL/TR, 6', 175 lbs. Deb: 4/12/55 MC

YEAR	TM/L	G	AB	R	H	2B	3B	HR	RBI	BB	SO	AVG	OBP	SLG	PRO+	BR/A	SB	CS	SBR	FA	FR	G/POS	TPR
1955	StL-N	144	534	58	150	18	6	17	68	36	64	.281	.327	.433	100	-1	2	4	-2	.966	-0	*O-142	-1.0
1956	StL-N	24	71	10	15	2	0	2	9	5	8	.211	.273	.324	60	-4	0	1	-1	.982	-1	O-24	-0.7
	Pit-N	133	509	67	170	21	10	8	37	33	63	.334	.376	.462	126	19	6	6	-2	.989	4	*O-130	1.4
	Yr	157	580	77	185	23	10	10	46	38	71	.319	.363	.445	118	14	6	7	-2	.988	3	*O-154	0.7
1957	Pit-N	144	561	59	141	28	11	8	50	33	69	.251	.293	.383	82	-15	3	3	-1	.986	12	*O-141	-1.3
1958	Pit-N	144	604	75	161	24	11	9	46	52	70	.267	.326	.387	90	-9	5	3	-0	.993	11	*O-143	-0.6
1959	Pit-N	144	519	67	132	24	2	8	41	55	65	.254	.328	.355	83	-12	7	4	-0	.979	**24**	*O-144	0.4
1960	*Pit-N	120	409	60	108	16	9	8	40	40	44	.264	.330	.406	99	-0	8	2	1	.983	7	*O-109	0.3
1961	Pit-N	146	599	81	156	22	8	9	58	49	45	.260	.316	.369	81	-16	5	8	-3	.985	11	*O-145	-1.7
1962	Pit-N	156	663	82	164	27	**10**	6	47	36	65	.247	.287	.345	69	-30	5	13	-6	.976	6	*O-156	-4.0
1963	Pit-N	142	554	58	149	22	6	8	43	33	55	.269	.322	.372	99	-1	1		1	.988	6	*O-142	0.1
1964	Pit-N	145	473	59	115	11	3	3	27	30	48	.243	.288	.298	66	-21	1	5	-3	.976	-7	*O-134	-3.9
1965	Pit-N	135	481	58	134	22	5	4	24	30	49	.279	.322	.370	94	-4	4	3	-1	.970	-2	*O-128	-1.3

YEAR	TM/L	G	AB	R	H	2B	3B	HR	RBI	BB	SO	AVG	OBP	SLG	PRO+	BR/A	SB	CS	SBR	FA	FR	G/POS	TPR
1968	Pit-N	6	3	1	1	0	0	1	2	0	2	.333	.333	1.333	388	1	0	0	0	1.000	-1	/O-4	-0.1
Total	12	1583	5980	735	1596	237	81	91	502	442	647	.267	.318	.379	89	-95	47	54	-18	.982	69	*O-1542	-12.9

■ OZZIE VIRGIL
Virgil, Osvaldo Jose Jr. b: 12/7/56, Mayaguez, P.R. BR/TR, 6'1", 205 lbs. Deb: 10/5/80 F

YEAR	TM/L	G	AB	R	H	2B	3B	HR	RBI	BB	SO	AVG	OBP	SLG	PRO+	BR/A	SB	CS	SBR	FA	FR	G/POS	TPR
1980	Phi-N	1	5	1	1	1	0	0	0	0	1	.200	.200	.400	60	-0	0	0	0	1.000	-1	/C-1	-0.1
1981	Phi-N	6	6	0	0	0	0	0	0	0	2	.000	.000	.000	-96	-2	0	0	0	1.000	0	/C-1	-0.2
1982	Phi-N	49	101	11	24	6	0	3	8	10	26	.238	.306	.386	91	-1	0	1	-1	.964	4	C-35	0.3
1983	*Phi-N	55	140	11	30	7	0	6	23	8	34	.214	.272	.393	83	-4	0	2	-1	.966	-5	C-51	-0.8
1984	Phi-N	141	456	61	119	21	2	18	68	45	91	.261	.334	.434	113	7	1	1	-0	.992	-3	*C-137	1.0
1985	Phi-N★	131	426	47	105	16	5	19	55	49	85	.246	.331	.432	109	5	0	0	0	.994	-4	*C-120	0.7
1986	Atl-N	114	359	45	80	9	0	15	48	63	73	.223	.345	.373	93	-2	1	0	0	.984	14	*C-111	2.0
1987	Atl-N★	123	429	57	106	13	1	27	72	47	81	.247	.331	.471	104	2	0	1	-1	.989	-2	*C-122	0.8
1988	Atl-N	107	320	23	82	10	0	9	31	22	54	.256	.314	.372	92	-3	2	0	1	.990	-11	C-96	-0.8
1989	Tor-A	9	11	2	2	1	0	1	2	4	3	.182	.400	.545	167	1	0	0	0	1.000	-0	/C-1,D-6	0.1
1990	Tor-A	3	5	0	0	0	0	0	0	0	0	.000	.000	.000	-98	-1	0	0	0	1.000	-0	/C-2,D-1	-0.1
Total	11	739	2258	258	549	84	6	98	307	248	453	.243	.326	.416	101	1	4	5	-2	.987	-8	C-677/D-7	2.9

■ OZZIE VIRGIL
Virgil, Osvaldo Jose Sr. (Pichardo) b: 5/17/33, Montecristi, D.R. BR/TR, 6', 175 lbs. Deb: 9/23/56 FC

YEAR	TM/L	G	AB	R	H	2B	3B	HR	RBI	BB	SO	AVG	OBP	SLG	PRO+	BR/A	SB	CS	SBR	FA	FR	G/POS	TPR
1956	NY-N	3	12	2	5	1	1	0	2	0	0	.417	.417	.667	186	1	0	0	0	.800	-2	/3-3	0.0
1957	NY-N	96	226	26	53	9	2	4	24	14	27	.235	.279	.305	57	-14	2	3	-1	.926	9	3-62,O-24/S	-0.6
1958	Det-A	49	193	19	47	10	2	3	19	8	20	.244	.274	.363	69	-9	1	0	0	.981	3	3-49	-0.5
1960	Det-A	62	132	16	30	4	2	3	13	4	14	.227	.250	.356	60	-8	1	1	-0	.974	8	3-42/2-8,SC	0.1
1961	Det-A	20	30	1	4	0	0	1	1	1	5	.133	.161	.233	4	-4	0	0	0	.938	-1	/3-9,C-3,2S	-0.5
	KC-A	11	21	1	3	0	0	0	0	0	3	.143	.143	.143	-23	-4	0	0	0	.818	0	/3-4,C-3	-0.3
	Yr	31	51	2	7	0	0	1	1	1	8	.137	.154	.196	-7	-8	0	0	0	.889	-1	3-13/C-6,2S	-0.8
1962	Bal-A	1	0	0	0	0	0	0	0	1	0	—	1.000	—	209	0	0	0	0	.000	0	H	0.0
1965	Pit-N	39	49	3	13	2	0	1	5	2	10	.265	.294	.367	85	-1	0	0	0	1.000	2	C-15/3-7,2	0.1
1966	SF-N	42	89	7	19	2	0	2	9	4	12	.213	.247	.303	51	-6	1	1	-0	.984	0	C-13,3-13/12O	-0.6
1969	SF-N	1	0	0	0	0	0	0	0	0	0	.000	.000	.000	-99	-0	0	0	0	.000	0	H	0.0
Total	9	324	753	75	174	19	7	14	73	34	91	.231	.264	.331	59	-43	6	5	-1	.951	19	3-189/C-35,O2S1	-2.3

■ JAKE VIRTUE
Virtue, Jacob Kitchline "Guesses" b: 3/2/1865, Philadelphia, Pa. d: 2/3/43, Camden, N.J. BB/TL, 5'9.5", 165 lbs. Deb: 7/21/1890

YEAR	TM/L	G	AB	R	H	2B	3B	HR	RBI	BB	SO	AVG	OBP	SLG	PRO+	BR/A	SB	CS	SBR	FA	FR	G/POS	TPR
1890	Cle-N	62	223	39	68	6	5	2	25	49	15	.305	.432	.404	147	16	9			.982	0	1-62	1.2
1891	Cle-N	139	517	82	135	19	14	2	72	75	40	.261	.363	.364	107	6	15			.972	-10	*1-139	-1.0
1892	*Cle-N	147	557	98	157	15	20	2	89	84	68	.282	.380	.391	128	20	14			.984	-1	*1-147	0.8
1893	Cle-N	97	378	87	100	16	10	1	60	54	14	.265	.358	.368	88	-7	11			.975	1	1-73,O-13/S3P	-0.7
1894	Cle-N	29	89	15	23	4	1	0	10	13	3	.258	.359	.326	64	-5	1			.885	-2	O-21/2-3,1P	-0.6
Total	5	474	1764	321	483	60	50	7	256	275	140	.274	.376	.376	111	30	50			.978	-15	1-423/O-34,3S2P	-0.3

◪ JOE VISNER
Visner, Joseph Paul (b: Joseph Paul Vezina) b: 9/27/1859, Minneapolis, Minn. d: 6/17/45, Fosston, Minn. BL/TR, 5'11", 180 lbs. Deb: 7/4/1885

YEAR	TM/L	G	AB	R	H	2B	3B	HR	RBI	BB	SO	AVG	OBP	SLG	PRO+	BR/A	SB	CS	SBR	FA	FR	G/POS	TPR
1885	Bal-a	4	13	2	3	0	0	0		0	2	.231	.333	.231	82	-0				.750	-1	/O-4	-0.1
1889	*Bro-a	80	295	56	76	12	10	8	68	36	36	.258	.346	.447	125	9	13			.871	-16	C-53,O-29	-0.2
1890	Pit-P	127	521	110	138	15	**22**	3	71	76	44	.265	.367	.395	113	12	18			.893	-6	*O-127	0.2
1891	Was-a	18	68	13	19	2	3	1	7	8	7	.279	.355	.441	134	3	2			.806	-2	O-17/C-1,3	0.0
	StL-a	6	27	2	4	0	1	0	1	0	3	.148	.148	.222	5	-4	0			1.000	0	/O-6	-0.3
	Yr	24	95	15	23	2	4	1	8	8	10	.242	.301	.379	94	-1	2			.846	-2	O-23/C-1,3	-0.3
Total	4	235	924	183	240	29	36	12	147	122	90	.260	.353	.408	114	20	33			.892	-25	O-183/C-54,3	-0.4

■ JOE VITELLI
Vitelli, Antonio Joseph b: 4/12/08, McKees Rocks, Pa. d: 2/7/67, Pittsburgh, Pa. BR/TR, 6'1", 195 lbs. Deb: 5/30/44

YEAR	TM/L	G	AB	R	H	2B	3B	HR	RBI	BB	SO	AVG	OBP	SLG	PRO+	BR/A	SB	CS	SBR	FA	FR	G/POS	TPR
1944	Pit-N	4	3	0	0	0	0	0	0	0	0	.000	.000	.000	-96	-1	0			.750	0	/P-4	0.0
1945	Pit-N	1	0	1	0	0	0	0	0	0	0	—	—	—	—	0	0			.000	0	R	0.0
Total	2	5	3	1	0	0	0	0	0	0	0	.000	.000	.000	-96	-1	0			.750	0	/P-4	0.0

■ OSSIE VITT
Vitt, Oscar Joseph b: 1/4/1890, San Francisco, Cal. d: 1/31/63, Oakland, Cal. BR/TR, 5'10", 150 lbs. Deb: 4/11/12 M

YEAR	TM/L	G	AB	R	H	2B	3B	HR	RBI	BB	SO	AVG	OBP	SLG	PRO+	BR/A	SB	CS	SBR	FA	FR	G/POS	TPR
1912	Det-A	76	273	39	67	4	4	0	19	18		.245	.297	.289	70	-11	17			.929	0	O-28,3-24,2	-1.2
1913	Det-A	99	359	45	86	11	3	2	33	31	18	.240	.304	.304	79	-10	5			.960	5	2-78,3-17/O	-0.6
1914	Det-A	66	195	35	49	7	0	0	8	31	8	.251	.354	.287	90	-1	10	8	-2	.964	14	2-36,3-16/OS	-0.1
1915	Det-A	152	560	116	140	18	13	1	48	80	22	.250	.348	.334	99	-0	26	18	-3	**.964**	14	*3-151/2-2	1.9
1916	Det-A	153	597	88	135	17	12	0	42	75	28	.226	.314	.295	80	-14	18			**.964**	28	*3-151/S-2	2.1
1917	Det-A	140	512	65	130	13	6	0	47	56	15	.254	.329	.303	93	-3	18			.940	-17	*3-140	-2.0
1918	Det-A	81	267	29	64	5	2	0	17	32	6	.240	.321	.273	83	-5	5			.953	4	3-66/2-9,O	0.1
1919	Bos-A	133	469	64	114	10	3	0	40	44	11	.243	.309	.277	69	-18	9			**.970**	14	*3-133	0.1
1920	Bos-A	87	296	50	65	10	4	1	28	43	10	.220	.321	.291	66	-14	5	4	-1	.986	-6	3-64,2-21	-1.7
1921	Bos-A	78	232	29	44	11	1	0	13	45	13	.190	.321	.246	48	-17	1	2	-1	.962	-4	3-71/O-3,1	-1.6
Total	10	1065	3760	560	894	106	48	4	295	455	131	.238	.322	.295	80	-93	114	32		.960	40	3-833,2-161/OS1	-3.0

■ JOSE VIZCAINO
Vizcaino, Jose Luis (Pimental) b: 3/26/68, San Cristobal, D.R. BB/TR, 6'1", 150 lbs. Deb: 9/10/89

YEAR	TM/L	G	AB	R	H	2B	3B	HR	RBI	BB	SO	AVG	OBP	SLG	PRO+	BR/A	SB	CS	SBR	FA	FR	G/POS	TPR
1989	LA-N	7	10	2	2	0	0	0	0	0	1	.200	.200	.200	15	-1	0	0	0	.882	2	/S-5	0.1
1990	LA-N	37	51	3	14	1	1	0	2	4	8	.275	.327	.333	85	-1	1	1	-0	.956	3	S-11/2-6	0.2
1991	Chi-N	93	145	7	38	5	0	0	10	5	18	.262	.287	.297	61	-7	2	1	0	.947	5	3-57,S-33/2	0.1
1992	Chi-N	86	285	25	64	10	4	1	17	14	35	.225	.261	.298	57	-16	3	0	1	.969	2	S-50,3-29/2	-1.1
1993	Chi-N	151	551	74	158	19	4	4	54	46	71	.287	.345	.358	90	-7	12	9	-2	.968	4	S-81,3-44,2	0.6
1994	NY-N	103	410	47	105	13	3	3	33	33	62	.256	.315	.324	67	-20	1	11	-6	.970	-12	*S-102	-3.0
Total	6	477	1452	158	381	48	12	8	116	102	195	.262	.313	.329	73	-52	19	22	-8	.968	9	S-282,3-130/2	-3.1

■ OMAR VIZQUEL
Vizquel, Omar Enrique (Gonzalez) b: 4/24/67, Caracas, Venez. BB/TR, 5'9", 155 lbs. Deb: 4/3/89

YEAR	TM/L	G	AB	R	H	2B	3B	HR	RBI	BB	SO	AVG	OBP	SLG	PRO+	BR/A	SB	CS	SBR	FA	FR	G/POS	TPR
1989	Sea-A	143	387	45	85	7	3	1	20	28	40	.220	.273	.261	50	-25	1	4	-2	.971	11	*S-143	-0.7
1990	Sea-A	81	255	19	63	3	2	2	18	18	22	.247	.297	.298	66	-11	4	1	1	.980	-3	S-81	-0.7
1991	Sea-A	142	426	42	98	16	4	1	41	45	37	.230	.304	.293	66	-19	7	2	1	.980	24	*S-138/2-1	1.5
1992	Sea-A	136	483	49	142	20	4	0	21	32	38	.294	.340	.352	94	-4	15	13	-3	**.989**	0	*S-136	0.3
1993	Sea-A	158	560	68	143	14	2	2	31	50	71	.255	.321	.298	67	-25	12	14	-5	.980	23	*S-155/D-2	0.5
1994	Cle-A	69	286	39	78	10	1	1	33	23	23	.273	.327	.325	66	-14	13	4	2	.981	-1	S-69	-0.7
Total	6	729	2397	262	609	70	16	7	164	196	231	.254	.312	.305	69	-99	52	38	-7	.980	54	S-722/D-2,2	0.2

■ OTTO VOGEL
Vogel, Otto Henry b: 10/26/1899, Mendota, Ill. d: 7/19/69, Iowa City, Iowa BR/TR, 6', 195 lbs. Deb: 6/5/23

YEAR	TM/L	G	AB	R	H	2B	3B	HR	RBI	BB	SO	AVG	OBP	SLG	PRO+	BR/A	SB	CS	SBR	FA	FR	G/POS	TPR
1923	Chi-N	41	81	10	17	0	1	6	7	11	.210	.297	.272	51	-6	2	3	-1	.929	-2	O-24/3-1	-1.0
1924	Chi-N	70	172	28	46	11	2	1	24	10	26	.267	.319	.372	84	-4	4	4	-1	.956	0	O-53/3-2	-0.7
Total	2	111	253	38	63	11	3	2	30	17	37	.249	.312	.340	73	-10	6	7	-2	.948	-2	/O-77,3-3	-1.7

■ JACK VOIGT
Voigt, John David b: 5/17/66, Sarasota, Fla. BR/TR, 6'1", 175 lbs. Deb: 8/3/92

YEAR	TM/L	G	AB	R	H	2B	3B	HR	RBI	BB	SO	AVG	OBP	SLG	PRO+	BR/A	SB	CS	SBR	FA	FR	G/POS	TPR
1992	Bal-A	1	0	0	0	0	0	0	0	0	0					0	0	0	0	.000	0	/R	0.0
1993	Bal-A	64	152	32	45	11	1	6	23	25	33	.296	.395	.500	133	8	1	0	0	.987	-1	O-43/1-5,3D	0.5
1994	Bal-A	59	141	15	34	5	0	3	20	18	25	.241	.331	.340	69	-6	0	0	0	.989	-4	O-54/1-6,D	-1.0
Total	3	124	293	47	79	16	1	9	43	43	58	.270	.365	.423	102	2	1	0	0	.988	-5	/O-97,D-11,13	-0.5

YEAR	TM/L	G	AB	R	H	2B	3B	HR	RBI	BB	SO	AVG	OBP	SLG	PRO+	BR/A	SB	CS	SBR	FA	FR	G/POS	TPR

■ CLYDE VOLLMER   Vollmer, Clyde Frederick   b: 9/24/21, Cincinnati, Ohio   BR/TR, 6'1", 190 lbs.   Deb: 5/31/42

YEAR	TM/L	G	AB	R	H	2B	3B	HR	RBI	BB	SO	AVG	OBP	SLG	PRO+	BR/A	SB	CS	SBR	FA	FR	G/POS	TPR
1942	Cin-N	12	43	2	4	0	0	1	4	1	5	.093	.114	.163	-20	-7	0			1.000	1	O-11	-0.6
1946	Cin-N	9	22	1	4	0	0	1	1	1	3	.182	.217	.182	14	-2	2			1.000	-3	/O-7	-0.6
1947	Cin-N	78	155	19	34	10	0	1	13	9	18	.219	.267	.303	51	-11	0			.984	-7	O-66	-2.0
1948	Cin-N	7	9	0	1	0	0	0	0	1	1	.111	.200	.111	-14	-1	0			.000	-1	/O-2	-0.2
	Was-A	1	5	1	2	0	0	0	0	0	1	.400	.400	.400	116	0	0	0	0	1.000	0	/O-1	0.0
1949	Was-A	129	443	58	112	17	1	14	59	53	62	.253	.335	.391	94	-6	1	2	-1	.982	4	*O-114	-0.7
1950	Was-A	6	14	4	4	0	0	0	1	2	3	.286	.375	.286	75	-0	1	0	0	1.000	0	/O-3	0.0
	Bos-A	57	169	35	48	10	0	7	37	21	35	.284	.363	.467	102	-0	1	0	0	.954	-2	O-39	-0.3
	Yr	63	183	39	52	10	0	7	38	23	38	.284	.364	.454	100	-0	2	0	1	.957	-1	O-42	-0.3
1951	Bos-A	115	386	66	97	9	2	22	85	55	66	.251	.346	.456	105	2	0	0	0	.986	-1	*O-106	-0.2
1952	Bos-A	90	250	35	66	12	4	11	50	39	47	.264	.370	.476	124	8	2	2	-1	1.000	-1	O-70	0.4
1953	Bos-A	1	0	0	0	0	0	0	0	1	0	—	1.000	—	180	0	0	0	0	.000	0	H	0.0
	Was-A	118	408	54	106	15	3	11	74	48	59	.260	.342	.392	100	0	0	2	-1	.979	7	*O-106	0.2
	Yr	119	408	54	106	15	3	11	74	49	59	.260	.343	.392	101	0	0	2	-1	.979	7	*O-106	0.2
1954	Was-A	62	117	8	30	4	0	2	15	12	28	.256	.331	.342	89	-2	0	0	0	1.000	-3	O-26	-0.6
Total	10	685	2021	283	508	77	10	69	339	243	328	.251	.335	.402	95	-19	7	6		.984	-3	O-551	-4.6

■ FRITZ Von KOLNITZ   Von Kolnitz, Alfred Holmes   b: 5/20/1893, Charleston, S.C.   d: 3/18/48, Mount Pleasant, S.C.   BR/TR, 5'10.5", 175 lbs.   Deb: 4/18/14

YEAR	TM/L	G	AB	R	H	2B	3B	HR	RBI	BB	SO	AVG	OBP	SLG	PRO+	BR/A	SB	CS	SBR	FA	FR	G/POS	TPR
1914	Cin-N	41	104	8	23	2	0	0	6	6	16	.221	.270	.240	51	-6	4			.914	-4	3-20,O-11/C1	-1.1
1915	Cin-N	50	78	6	15	4	1	0	6	7	11	.192	.259	.269	59	-4	1	3	-2	.933	-6	3-18/S-6,1CO	-1.2
1916	Chi-A	24	44	1	10	3	0	0	7	2	6	.227	.261	.295	66	-2	0			.909	-5	3-13	-0.7
Total	3	115	226	15	48	9	1	0	19	15	33	.212	.264	.261	56	-12	5	3		.918	-15	/3-51,O-12,S1C	-3.0

■ JOE VOSMIK   Vosmik, Joseph Franklin   b: 4/4/10, Cleveland, Ohio   d: 1/27/62, Cleveland, Ohio   BR/TR, 6', 185 lbs.   Deb: 9/13/30

YEAR	TM/L	G	AB	R	H	2B	3B	HR	RBI	BB	SO	AVG	OBP	SLG	PRO+	BR/A	SB	CS	SBR	FA	FR	G/POS	TPR
1930	Cle-A	9	26	1	6	2	0	0	4	1	1	.231	.259	.308	42	-2	0	0	0	.933	1	/O-5	-0.2
1931	Cle-A	149	591	80	189	36	14	7	117	38	30	.320	.363	.464	110	7	7	7	-2	.970	6	*O-147	0.1
1932	Cle-A	153	621	106	194	39	12	10	97	58	42	.312	.376	.462	109	8	2	3	-1	.989	24	*O-153	1.9
1933	Cle-A	119	438	53	115	20	10	4	56	42	13	.263	.331	.381	84	-10	0	2	-1	.985	6	*O-113	-1.1
1934	Cle-A	104	405	71	138	33	2	6	78	35	10	.341	.393	.477	122	13	1	1	-0	.976	-2	*O-104	0.6
1935	Cle-A★	152	620	93	**216**	**47**	**20**	10	110	59	30	.348	.408	.537	140	36	2	1	0	.986	1	*O-150	2.9
1936	Cle-A	138	506	76	145	29	7	7	94	79	21	.287	.383	.413	96	-2	5	1	1	.978	-1	*O-136	-0.6
1937	StL-A	144	594	81	193	47	9	4	93	49	38	.325	.377	.455	108	7	2	3	-1	.972	8	*O-143	0.8
1938	Bos-A	146	621	121	**201**	37	6	9	86	59	26	.324	.384	.446	103	3	0	3	-2	.978	3	*O-146	-0.1
1939	Bos-A	145	554	89	153	29	6	7	84	66	33	.276	.356	.388	87	-10	3	4	-1	.974	-4	*O-144	-1.9
1940	Bro-N	116	404	45	114	14	6	1	42	22	21	.282	.321	.354	81	-10	0			.976	0	O-99	-1.5
1941	Bro-N	25	56	0	11	0	0	0	4	4	4	.196	.250	.196	26	-5	0			1.000	-5	O-18	-1.2
1944	Was-A	14	36	2	7	2	0	0	9	2	3	.194	.237	.250	41	-3	0	0	0	1.000	-2	O-12	-0.6
Total	13	1414	5472	818	1682	335	92	65	874	514	272	.307	.369	.438	104	29	23	24		.979	34	*O-1370	-0.9

■ ALEX VOSS   Voss, Alexander   b: 5/16/1858, Roswell, Ga.   d: 8/31/06, Cincinnati, Ohio   BR/TR, 6'1", 180 lbs.   Deb: 4/17/1884

YEAR	TM/L	G	AB	R	H	2B	3B	HR	RBI	BB	SO	AVG	OBP	SLG	PRO+	BR/A	SB	CS	SBR	FA	FR	G/POS	TPR
1884	Was-U	63	245	33	47	9	0	0			5	.192	.208	.229	19	-27				.848	4	P-27,3-16,10/S	-1.6
	KC-U	14	45	1	4	0	0	0				.089	.089	.089	-59	-10				.867	1	/O-8,P-7	-0.4
	Yr	77	290	34	51	9	0	0			5	.176	.190	.207	8	-36				.859	5	P-34,O-21,31/S	-2.0

■ BILL VOSS   Voss, William Edward   b: 10/31/43, Glendale, Cal.   BL/TL, 6'2", 160 lbs.   Deb: 9/14/65

YEAR	TM/L	G	AB	R	H	2B	3B	HR	RBI	BB	SO	AVG	OBP	SLG	PRO+	BR/A	SB	CS	SBR	FA	FR	G/POS	TPR
1965	Chi-A	11	33	4	6	1	0	0	3	3	5	.182	.250	.333	68	-1	0	0	0	1.000	-1	O-10	-0.4
1966	Chi-A	2	2	0	0	0	0	0	0	0	2	.000	.000	.000	-99	-1	0	0	0	1.000	-0	/O-1	-0.1
1967	Chi-A	13	22	4	2	0	0	0	0	1	1	.091	.091	.091	-48	-4	1	1	-0	1.000	-2	O-11	-0.7
1968	Chi-A	61	167	14	26	2	1	2	15	16	34	.156	.238	.216	38	-12	5	3	-0	.963	-4	O-55	-2.2
1969	Cal-A	133	349	33	91	11	4	2	40	35	40	.261	.328	.332	90	-5	5	3	-0	.995	1	*O-111/1-2	-0.9
1970	Cal-A	80	181	21	44	4	3	3	30	23	18	.243	.335	.348	92	-2	2	1	0	.979	2	O-55	-0.2
1971	Mil-A	97	275	31	69	4	0	10	30	24	45	.251	.313	.375	95	-2	2	2	-1	.987	-4	O-79	-1.1
1972	Mil-A	27	36	1	3	1	0	0	1	5	4	.083	.195	.111	-7	-5	0	1	-1	.929	-3	O-11	-0.9
	Oak-A	40	97	10	22	5	1	1	5	9	16	.227	.299	.330	92	-2	0	0	0	1.000	-1	O-34	-0.4
	Yr	67	133	11	25	6	1	1	6	14	20	.188	.270	.271	64	-8	0	1	-1	.987	-4	O-45	-1.3
	StL-N	11	15	1	4	2	0	0	3	2	2	.267	.353	.400	115	0	0	0	0	1.000	-0	/O-2	0.0
Total	8	475	1177	119	267	29	10	19	127	117	167	.227	.300	.317	78	-33	15	11	-2	.986	-11	O-369/1-2	-6.9

■ PHIL VOYLES   Voyles, Philip Vance   b: 5/12/1900, Murphy, N.C.   d: 11/3/72, Marlborough, Mass.   BL/TR, 5'11.5", 175 lbs.   Deb: 9/4/29

YEAR	TM/L	G	AB	R	H	2B	3B	HR	RBI	BB	SO	AVG	OBP	SLG	PRO+	BR/A	SB	CS	SBR	FA	FR	G/POS	TPR
1929	Bos-N	20	68	9	16	0	2	0	14	6	8	.235	.297	.294	49	-5	0			.922	-2	O-20	-0.8

■ GEORGE VUKOVICH   Vukovich, George Stephen   b: 6/24/56, Chicago, Ill.   BL/TR, 6', 198 lbs.   Deb: 4/13/80

YEAR	TM/L	G	AB	R	H	2B	3B	HR	RBI	BB	SO	AVG	OBP	SLG	PRO+	BR/A	SB	CS	SBR	FA	FR	G/POS	TPR
1980	*Phi-N	78	58	6	13	1	1	0	8	6	9	.224	.297	.276	58	-3	0	0	0	.933	-9	O-28	-1.3
1981	*Phi-N	20	26	5	10	0	0	1	4	1	0	.385	.407	.500	150	2	1	0	0	1.000	-2	/O-9	0.0
1982	Phi-N	123	335	41	91	18	2	6	42	32	47	.272	.335	.391	100	0	2	9	-5	.977	-6	*O-102	-1.3
1983	Cle-A	124	312	31	77	13	2	3	44	24	37	.247	.305	.330	72	-12	3	4	-2	.986	-13	*O-122	-2.9
1984	Cle-A	134	437	38	133	22	5	9	60	34	61	.304	.356	.439	117	10	1	4	-2	.994	14	*O-130	1.8
1985	Cle-A	149	434	43	106	22	0	6	45	30	75	.244	.295	.350	76	-14	2	2	-1	.988	-7	*O-137	-2.6
Total	6	628	1602	164	430	76	10	27	203	127	229	.268	.324	.379	92	-18	9	19	-9	.987	-22	O-528	-6.3

■ JOHN VUKOVICH   Vukovich, John Christopher   b: 7/31/47, Sacramento, Cal.   BR/TR, 6'1", 190 lbs.   Deb: 9/11/70   MC

YEAR	TM/L	G	AB	R	H	2B	3B	HR	RBI	BB	SO	AVG	OBP	SLG	PRO+	BR/A	SB	CS	SBR	FA	FR	G/POS	TPR
1970	Phi-N	3	8	1	1	0	0	0	0	1	2	.125	.222	.125	-5	-1	0	0	0	.778	1	/S-2,3-1	0.0
1971	Phi-N	74	217	11	36	5	0	6	14	12	34	.166	.213	.189	15	-24	2	1	0	.956	10	3-74	-1.6
1973	Mil-A	55	128	10	16	3	0	2	9	9	40	.125	.182	.195	7	-16	0	2	-1	.948	-4	3-40,1-13/S	-2.2
1974	Mil-A	38	80	5	15	1	0	3	11	1	16	.188	.198	.313	45	-6	2	1	0	.945	-2	S-12,3-12,2/1	-0.2
1975	Cin-N	31	38	4	8	3	0	0	2	4	5	.211	.286	.289	59	-2	0	0	0	.925	7	3-31	0.5
1976	Phi-N	4	8	2	1	0	0	1	2	0	2	.125	.125	.500	69	-0	0	0	0	1.000	-0	/3-4,1-1	-0.1
1977	Phi-N	2	2	0	0	0	0	0	0	0	0	.000	.000	.000	-96	-1	0	0	0	.000	0	H	-0.1
1979	Phi-N	10	15	0	3	1	0	0	1	0	3	.200	.200	.267	25	-2	0	0	0	1.000	0	/3-7,2-3	0.0
1980	Phi-N	49	62	4	10	1	1	0	5	2	9	.161	.200	.210	14	-7	0	1	-1	.958	7	3-34/2-9,S1	-0.8
1981	Phi-N	11	1	0	0	0	0	0	0	0	0	.000	.000	.000	-96	-0	0	0	0	.800	1	/3-9,1-1,2	0.0
Total	10	277	559	37	90	14	1	6	44	29	109	.161	.205	.222	20	-59	4	5	-2	.951	18	3-212/2-24,1S	-4.5

■ FRANK WADDEY   Waddey, Frank Orum   b: 8/21/05, Memphis, Tenn.   d: 10/21/90, Knoxville, Tenn.   BL/TL, 5'10.5", 185 lbs.   Deb: 4/16/31

YEAR	TM/L	G	AB	R	H	2B	3B	HR	RBI	BB	SO	AVG	OBP	SLG	PRO+	BR/A	SB	CS	SBR	FA	FR	G/POS	TPR
1931	StL-A	14	22	3	6	1	0	0	2	2	3	.273	.333	.318	70	-1	0	0	0	1.000	-3	/O-7	-0.4

■ HAM WADE   Wade, Abraham Lincoln   b: 12/20/1880, Spring City, Pa.   d: 7/21/68, Riverside, N.J.   BR/TR, 5'8", 155 lbs.   Deb: 9/9/07

YEAR	TM/L	G	AB	R	H	2B	3B	HR	RBI	BB	SO	AVG	OBP	SLG	PRO+	BR/A	SB	CS	SBR	FA	FR	G/POS	TPR
1907	NY-N	1	0	0	0	0	0	0	0	0	0	—	1.000	—	208	0	0	0		1.000	0	/O-1	0.0

■ GALE WADE   Wade, Galeard Lee   b: 1/20/29, Hollister, Mo.   BL/TR, 6'1.5", 185 lbs.   Deb: 4/11/55

YEAR	TM/L	G	AB	R	H	2B	3B	HR	RBI	BB	SO	AVG	OBP	SLG	PRO+	BR/A	SB	CS	SBR	FA	FR	G/POS	TPR
1955	Chi-N	9	33	5	6	1	0	1	4	1	3	.182	.270	.303	52	-2	0	0	0	.867	-2	/O-9	-0.5
1956	Chi-N	10	12	0	0	0	0	0	1	0	0	.000	.077	.000	-78	-3	0	0	0	.875	-0	/O-3	-0.4
Total	2	19	45	5	6	1	0	1	5	1	3	.133	.220	.222	18	-5	0	0	0	.870	-2	/O-12	-0.9

YEAR	TM/L	G	AB	R	H	2B	3B	HR	RBI	BB	SO	AVG	OBP	SLG	PRO+	BR/A	SB	CS	SBR	FA	FR	G/POS	TPR

■ RIP WADE
Wade, Richard Frank   b: 1/12/1898, Duluth, Minn.   d: 6/16/57, Sandstone, Minn.   BL/TR, 5'11", 174 lbs.   Deb: 4/19/23

1923	Was-A	33	69	8	16	2	2	2	14	5	10	.232	.284	.406	84	-2	0	0	0	.967	-2	O-19	-0.5

■ WOODY WAGENHORST
Wagenhorst, Ellwood Otto   b: 6/3/1863, Kutztown, Pa.   d: 2/12/46, Washington, D.C.   Deb: 6/25/1888

1888	Phi-N	2	8	2	1	0	0	0	0	0	1	.125	.125	.125	-19	-1	0			.800	-1	/3-2	-0.2

■ BUTTS WAGNER
Wagner, Albert   b: 9/17/1869, Mansfield, Pa.   d: 11/26/28, Pittsburgh, Pa.   BR/TR, 5'10", 170 lbs.   Deb: 4/27/1898   F

1898	Was-N	63	223	20	50	11	2	1	31	14		.224	.279	.305	67	-10	4			.833	-11	3-39,O-10/S2	-1.9
	Bro-N	11	38	2	9	1	1	0	3	2		.237	.275	.316	69	-2	0			.813	-3	3-11	-0.4
	Yr	74	261	22	59	12	3	1	34	16		.226	.279	.307	68	-12	4			.828	-14	3-50,O-10/S2	-2.3

■ HEINIE WAGNER
Wagner, Charles F.   b: 9/23/1880, New York, N.Y.   d: 3/20/43, New Rochelle, N.Y.   BR/TR, 5'9", 183 lbs.   Deb: 7/1/02   MC

1902	NY-N	17	56	4	12	1	0	0	2	0		.214	.214	.232	38	-4	3			.862	-3	S-17	-0.6
1906	Bos-A	9	32	1	9	0	0	0	4	1		.281	.303	.281	83	-1	2			.943	1	/2-9	0.1
1907	Bos-A	111	385	29	82	10	4	2	21	31		.213	.275	.275	76	-10	20			.931	5	*S-109/2-1,3	-0.2
1908	Bos-A	153	526	62	130	11	5	1	46	27		.247	.288	.293	86	-8	20			.939	32	*S-153	3.0
1909	Bos-A	124	430	53	110	16	7	1	49	35		.256	.316	.333	103	1	18			.933	14	*S-123/2-1	2.0
1910	Bos-A	142	491	61	134	26	7	1	52	44		.273	.335	.360	115	8	26			.927	-12	*S-140	0.2
1911	Bos-A	80	261	34	67	13	8	1	38	29		.257	.340	.379	101	0	15			.946	-4	2-40,S-32	-0.2
1912	*Bos-A	144	504	75	138	25	6	2	68	62		.274	.358	.359	100	1	21			.922	-13	*S-144	0.0
1913	Bos-A	110	365	43	83	14	8	2	34	40	29	.227	.316	.326	86	-7	9			.938	4	*S-105/2-4	0.7
1915	Bos-A	84	267	38	64	11	2	0	29	37	34	.240	.330	.296	93	-1	8	4	0	.927	-16	2-79/3-1,O	-1.7
1916	Bos-A	6	8	2	4	1	0	0	0	3	0	.500	.636	.625	278	2	2			1.000	2	/3-4,2-1,S	0.5
1918	Bos-A	3	8	0	1	0	0	0	0	1	0	.125	.222	.125	5	-1	0			.900	-0	/2-2,3-1	-0.1
Total	12	983	3333	402	834	128	47	10	343	310	63	.250	.319	.326	95	-19	144	4		.928	11	S-824,2-137/3O	3.7

■ HAL WAGNER
Wagner, Harold Edward   b: 7/2/15, E.Riverton, N.J.   d: 8/7/79, Riverside, N.J.   BL/TR, 6', 165 lbs.   Deb: 10/3/37

1937	Phi-A	1	0	0	0	0	0	0	0	0	0	—	—	—	—	0	0	0	0	1.000	0	/C-1	0.0
1938	Phi-A	33	88	10	20	2	1	0	8	8	9	.227	.299	.273	45	-7	0	0	0	.972	-1	/C-30	-0.7
1939	Phi-A	5	8	0	1	0	0	0	0	0	3	.125	.125	.125	-37	-2	0	0	0	1.000	2	/C-5	0.0
1940	Phi-A	34	75	9	19	5	1	0	10	11	6	.253	.356	.347	85	-1	0	0	0	.964	3	C-28	0.3
1941	Phi-A	46	131	18	29	8	2	1	15	19	9	.221	.320	.336	75	-5	1	0	0	.976	2	C-42	0.1
1942	Phi-A☆	104	288	26	68	17	1	1	30	24	29	.236	.304	.313	74	-10	1	0	0	.986	-2	C-94	-0.6
1943	Phi-A	111	289	22	69	17	1	1	26	36	17	.239	.327	.315	89	-4	3	3	-1	.980	-8	C-99	-0.7
1944	Phi-A	5	4	0	1	0	0	0	0	0	0	.250	.250	.250	44	-0	0	0	0	1.000	0	/C-1	0.0
	Bos-A	66	223	21	74	13	4	1	38	29	14	.332	.418	.439	147	15	1	1	-0	.970	0	C-64	1.9
	Yr	71	227	21	75	13	4	1	38	29	14	.330	.415	.436	145	15	1	1	-0	.971	0	C-65	1.9
1946	*Bos-A★	117	370	39	85	12	2	6	52	69	32	.230	.354	.322	85	-5	3	1	-0	.983	-7	*C-116	-0.6
1947	Bos-A	21	65	5	15	3	0	0	6	9	5	.231	.324	.277	63	-3	0	0	-0	.978	-1	C-21	-0.3
	Det-A	71	191	19	55	10	0	5	33	28	16	.288	.382	.419	119	5	0	1	-1	.990	-4	C-71	0.5
	Yr	92	256	24	70	13	0	5	39	37	21	.273	.367	.383	105	2	0	1	-1	.987	-5	C-92	0.2
1948	Det-A	54	109	10	22	3	0	0	10	20	11	.202	.326	.229	48	-8	1	0	0	.989	-4	C-52	-0.8
	Phi-N	3	4	0	0	0	0	0	0	0	0	.000	.000	.000	-99	-1	0			1.000	1	/C-1	0.0
1949	Phi-N	1	4	0	0	0	0	0	0	0	1	.000	.000	.000	-99	-1	0			.750	-1	/C-1	-0.2
Total	12	672	1849	179	458	90	12	15	228	253	152	.248	.343	.334	87	-27	10	6		.981	-21	C-626	-1.1

■ HONUS WAGNER
Wagner, John Peter "The Flying Dutchman"   b: 2/24/1874, Mansfield, Pa.   d: 12/6/55, Carnegie, Pa.   BR/TR, 5'11", 200 lbs.   Deb: 7/19/1897   FMCH

1897	Lou-N	61	237	37	80	17	4	2	39	15		.338	.379	.468	127	9	19			.908	3	O-52/2-9	0.7
1898	Lou-N	151	588	80	176	29	3	10	105	31		.299	.341	.410	117	10	27			.972	-4	1-75,3-65,2	0.7
1899	Lou-N	147	571	98	192	43	13	7	113	40		.336	.391	.494	142	31	37			.928	1	3-75,O-61/21	2.6
1900	*Pit-N	135	527	107	201	**45**	**22**	4	100	41		**.381**	**.434**	**.573**	**175**	52	38			.965	-8	*O-118/3-9,21P	3.3
1901	Pit-N	140	549	101	194	37	11	6	**126**	53		.353	.417	.494	159	41	**49**			.918	10	S-61,O-54,3/2	5.1
1902	Pit-N	136	534	**105**	176	**30**	16	3	**91**	43		.330	.394	**.463**	**159**	**36**	**42**			1.000	8	O-61,S-44,1/P2	4.4
1903	*Pit-N	129	512	97	182	30	**19**	5	101	44		**.355**	.414	.518	160	39	46			.933	25	*S-111,O-12/1	**6.3**
1904	Pit-N	132	490	97	171	**44**	14	4	75	59		**.349**	**.423**	**.520**	**186**	50	**53**			.929	-6	*S-121/O-8,12	4.8
1905	Pit-N	147	548	114	199	32	14	6	101	54		**.363**	.427	.505	173	49	57			.935	20	*S-145/O-2	7.3
1906	Pit-N	142	516	**103**	175	**38**	9	2	71	58		**.339**	.416	.459	166	40	53			.941	24	*S-137/O-2,3	7.3
1907	Pit-N	142	515	98	180	**38**	14	6	82	46		**.350**	**.408**	**.513**	**186**	49	**61**			.938	4	*S-138/1-4	**6.3**
1908	Pit-N	151	568	100	**201**	**39**	**19**	10	**109**	54		**.354**	**.415**	**.542**	**205**	**65**	**53**			.943	-7	*S-151	**7.0**
1909	*Pit-N	137	495	92	168	**39**	10	5	**100**	66		**.339**	**.420**	.489	**168**	**39**	35			.940	6	*S-136/O-1	5.2
1910	Pit-N	150	556	90	**178**	34	4	4	81	59	47	.320	.390	.432	132	22	24			.935	3	*S-138,1-11/2	3.2
1911	Pit-N	130	473	87	158	23	16	9	89	67	34	**.334**	.423	.507	154	35	20			.932	4	*S-101,1-28/O	**4.5**
1912	Pit-N	145	558	91	181	35	20	7	**102**	59	38	.324	.395	.496	145	34	26			**.962**	23	*S-143	**6.6**
1913	Pit-N	114	413	51	124	18	4	3	56	26	40	.300	.349	.385	114	7	21			**.962**	13	*S-105	3.1
1914	Pit-N	150	552	60	139	15	9	1	50	51	51	.252	.317	.317	93	-5	23			**.950**	7	*S-132,3-17/1	1.4
1915	Pit-N	156	566	68	155	32	17	6	78	39	64	.274	.325	.422	127	16	22	15	-2	.948	-5	*S-131,2-12,1	2.1
1916	Pit-N	123	432	45	124	15	9	1	39	34	36	.287	.350	.370	120	11	11			.942	-15	S-92,1-24/2	0.1
1917	Pit-N	74	230	15	61	7	1	0	24	24	17	.265	.337	.304	94	-1	5			.985	-4	1-47,3-18/2SM	-0.7
Total	21	2792	10430	1736	3415	640	252	101	1732	963	327	.327	.391	.466	150	631	722	15		.940	101	*S-1887,O-372,13/2P	81.3

■ JOE WAGNER
Wagner, Joseph Bernard   b: 4/24/1889, New York, N.Y.   d: 11/15/48, Bronx, N.Y.   BR/TR, 5'11", 165 lbs.   Deb: 4/25/15

1915	Cin-N	75	197	17	35	5	2	0	13	8	35	.178	.210	.223	31	-17	4	6	-2	.961	6	2-46,S-12/3	-1.4

■ LEON WAGNER
Wagner, Leon Lamar   b: 5/13/34, Chattanooga, Tenn.   BL/TR, 6'1", 195 lbs.   Deb: 6/22/58

1958	SF-N	74	221	31	70	9	0	13	35	18	34	.317	.371	.534	139	12	1	0	0	.949	-0	O-57	0.9
1959	SF-N	87	129	20	29	4	3	5	22	25	24	.225	.363	.419	110	2	0	0	0	.941	-2	O-28	0.0
1960	StL-N	39	98	12	21	2	0	4	11	17	17	.214	.336	.357	83	-2	0	1	0	.963	1	O-32	-0.4
1961	LA-A	133	453	74	127	19	2	28	79	48	65	.280	.353	.517	116	9	5	1	1	.971	-0	*O-116	0.5
1962	LA-A★	160	612	96	164	21	5	37	107	50	87	.268	.326	.500	123	17	7	5	-1	.972	-7	*O-156	0.0
1963	LA-A★	149	550	73	160	11	1	26	90	49	73	.291	.356	.456	134	24	5	7	-3	.960	-2	*O-141	1.3
1964	Cle-A	163	641	94	162	19	2	31	100	56	121	.253	.319	.434	108	6	14	2	3	.959	-1	*O-163	0.0
1965	Cle-A	144	517	91	152	18	1	28	79	60	52	.294	.371	.495	143	29	12	2	2	.957	-9	*O-134	1.7
1966	Cle-A	150	549	70	153	20	0	23	66	46	69	.279	.336	.441	121	14	5	2	1	.990	-8	*O-139	0.0
1967	Cle-A	135	433	56	105	15	1	15	54	37	76	.242	.320	.386	107	4	3	3	-1	.980	-7	*O-117	-1.1
1968	Cle-A	38	49	5	9	4	0	0	6	6	6	.184	.273	.265	65	-2	0	0	0	.500	-3	O-10	-0.7
	Chi-A	69	162	14	46	8	0	1	18	21	31	.284	.366	.352	117	4	2	1	0	.941	-8	O-46	-0.7
	Yr	107	211	19	55	12	0	1	24	27	37	.261	.345	.332	106	2	2	1	0	.895	-11	O-56	-1.4
1969	SF-N	11	12	0	4	0	0	0	2	2	1	.333	.467	.333	130	1	0	0	0	1.000	0	/O-1	0.1
Total	12	1352	4426	636	1202	150	15	211	669	435	656	.272	.343	.455	121	117	54	24	2	.964	-44	*O-1140	1.6

■ MARK WAGNER
Wagner, Mark Duane   b: 3/4/54, Conneaut, Ohio   BR/TR, 6'1", 175 lbs.   Deb: 8/20/76

1976	Det-A	39	115	9	30	2	3	0	12	6	18	.261	.298	.330	81	-3	0	2	-1	.947	10	S-39	1.0
1977	Det-A	22	48	4	7	0	1	3	8	3	12	.146	.226	.250	28	-5	0	1	-1	.923	-1	S-21/2-1	-0.5
1978	Det-A	39	109	10	26	1	2	0	6	3	11	.239	.272	.284	55	-6	1	0	0	.964	-6	S-35/2-4	-0.9

YEAR	TM/L	G	AB	R	H	2B	3B	HR	RBI	BB	SO	AVG	OBP	SLG	PRO+	BR/A	SB	CS	SBR	FA	FR	G/POS	TPR
1979	Det-A	75	146	16	40	3	0	1	13	16	25	.274	.346	.315	77	-4	3	2	-0	.974	7	S-41,2-29/3	0.6
1980	Det-A	45	72	5	17	1	0	0	3	7	11	.236	.304	.250	52	-4	0	1	-1	.935	2	S-28/3-9,2	-0.1
1981	Tex-A	50	85	15	22	4	1	1	14	8	13	.259	.323	.365	103	0	1	1	-0	.964	2	S-43/2-4,3	0.5
1982	Tex-A	60	179	14	43	4	1	0	8	10	28	.240	.280	.274	56	-11	1	0	0	.955	-0	S-60	-0.5
1983	Tex-A	2	2	0	0	0	0	0	0	0	1	.000	.000	.000	-99	-1	0	0	0	1.000	1	/S-2	0.1
1984	Oak-A	82	87	8	20	5	1	0	12	7	11	.230	.287	.310	70	-4	2	0	1	.951	12	S-57,3-15/2PD	1.0
Total	9	414	843	81	205	20	9	3	71	61	130	.243	.297	.299	66	-38	8	7	-2	.953	25	S-326/2-52,3DP	1.2

■ BILL WAGNER
Wagner, William Joseph   b: 1/2/1894, Jesup, Iowa   d: 1/11/51, Waterloo, Iowa   BR/TR, 6', 187 lbs.   Deb: 7/16/14

YEAR	TM/L	G	AB	R	H	2B	3B	HR	RBI	BB	SO	AVG	OBP	SLG	PRO+	BR/A	SB	CS	SBR	FA	FR	G/POS	TPR
1914	Pit-N	3	1	0	0	0	0	0	0	0	0	.000	.000	.000	-99	-0	0			1.000	0	/C-3	0.0
1915	Pit-N	5	5	0	0	0	0	0	0	1	2	.000	.167	.000	-48	-1	0			1.000	2	/C-3	0.1
1916	Pit-N	19	38	2	9	0	2	0	2	5	8	.237	.326	.342	104	0	0			.936	2	C-15	0.3
1917	Pit-N	53	151	15	31	7	2	0	9	11	22	.205	.264	.278	64	-6	1			.958	-4	C-37,1-12	-0.9
1918	Bos-N	13	47	2	10	0	0	1	7	4	5	.213	.275	.277	71	-2	0			.917	-5	C-13	-0.6
Total	5	93	242	19	50	7	4	1	18	21	37	.207	.273	.281	69	-9	1			.947	-5	/C-71,1-12	-1.1

■ KERMIT WAHL
Wahl, Kermit Emerson   b: 11/18/22, Columbia, S.Dak.   d: 9/16/87, Tucson, Ariz.   BR/TR, 5'11", 170 lbs.   Deb: 6/23/44

YEAR	TM/L	G	AB	R	H	2B	3B	HR	RBI	BB	SO	AVG	OBP	SLG	PRO+	BR/A	SB	CS	SBR	FA	FR	G/POS	TPR
1944	Cin-N	4	1	0	0	0	0	0	0	0	0	.000	.000	.000	-99	-0	0			.000	0	/3-1	0.0
1945	Cin-N	71	194	18	39	8	2	0	10	23	22	.201	.284	.263	54	-12	2			.948	5	2-32,S-31/3	-0.3
1947	Cin-N	39	81	8	14	0	0	1	4	6	12	.173	.239	.210	20	-9	0			.964	0	3-20/S-9,2	-0.3
1950	Phi-A	89	280	26	72	12	3	2	27	30	30	.257	.331	.343	74	-11	1	1	-0	.946	11	3-61,S-18/2	0.0
1951	Phi-A	20	59	4	11	2	0	0	6	9	5	.186	.294	.220	40	-5	0	0	0	.967	2	3-18	-0.3
	StL-A	8	27	2	9	1	1	0	3	0	3	.333	.333	.444	106	0	0	0	0	.950	1	/3-6	0.0
	Yr	28	86	6	20	3	1	0	9	9	8	.233	.305	.291	60	-5	0	0	0	.962	3	3-24	-0.3
Total	5	231	642	58	145	23	6	3	50	68	72	.226	.302	.294	60	-37	3	1		.949	25	3-113/S-58,2	-0.9

■ EDDIE WAITKUS
Waitkus, Edward Stephen   b: 9/4/19, Cambridge, Mass.   d: 9/15/72, Jamaica Plain, Mass.   BL/TL, 6'1", 175 lbs.   Deb: 4/15/41

YEAR	TM/L	G	AB	R	H	2B	3B	HR	RBI	BB	SO	AVG	OBP	SLG	PRO+	BR/A	SB	CS	SBR	FA	FR	G/POS	TPR
1941	Chi-N	12	28	1	5	0	0	0	0	0	3	.179	.207	.179	10	-3	0			.949	-1	/1-9	-0.5
1946	Chi-N	113	441	50	134	24	5	4	55	23	14	.304	.340	.408	114	6	3			.996	4	*1-106	0.4
1947	Chi-N	130	514	60	150	28	6	2	35	32	17	.292	.336	.381	94	-5	3			.994	8	*1-126	-0.2
1948	Chi-N★	139	562	87	166	27	10	7	44	43	19	.295	.348	.416	110	7	11			.992	7	*1-116,O-20	1.1
1949	Phi-N†	54	209	41	64	16	3	1	28	33	12	.306	.403	.426	126	9	3			.994	1	1-54	0.9
1950	*Phi-N	154	641	102	182	32	5	2	44	55	29	.284	.341	.359	86	-12	3			.993	-2	*1-154	-1.8
1951	Phi-N	145	610	65	157	27	4	1	46	53	22	.257	.317	.320	73	-23	0	3	-2	.992	-2	*1-144	-3.4
1952	Phi-N	146	499	51	144	29	4	2	49	64	23	.289	.371	.375	108	7	2	2	-1	.991	-2	*1-146	0.0
1953	Phi-N	81	247	24	72	9	2	1	16	13	23	.291	.330	.356	79	-7	1	1	-0	.989	-1	1-59	-1.1
1954	Bal-A	95	311	35	88	17	4	2	33	28	25	.283	.344	.383	107	2	0	1	-1	1.000	6	1-78	-0.2
1955	Bal-A	38	85	2	22	1	0	0	9	11	10	.259	.344	.294	78	-2	2	0	1	.974	-2	1-26	-0.5
	Phi-N	33	107	10	30	5	0	2	14	17	7	.280	.379	.383	105	1	0	1	-1	.996	0	1-31	-0.1
Total	11	1140	4254	528	1214	215	44	24	373	372	204	.285	.344	.374	96	-21	28	8		.993	10	*1-1049/O-20	-5.4

■ CHARLIE WAITT
Waitt, Charles C.   b: 10/14/1853, Hallowell, Me.   d: 10/21/12, San Francisco, Cal.   5'11", 165 lbs.   Deb: 5/25/1875

YEAR	TM/L	G	AB	R	H	2B	3B	HR	RBI	BB	SO	AVG	OBP	SLG	PRO+	BR/A	SB	CS	SBR	FA	FR	G/POS	TPR
1875	StL-n	31	118	14	25	9	0	0				.212	.225	.288	84	-1						O-29/1-2	-0.1
1877	Chi-N	10	41	2	4	0	0	0	2	0	3	.098	.098	.098	-34	-6				.793	2	O-10	-0.4
1882	Bal-a	72	250	19	39	4	0	0		13		.156	.198	.172	28	-17				.874	0	*O-72	-1.6
1883	Phi-N	1	3	0	1	0	0	0		0	1	.333	.333	.333	114	0				.333	-1	/O-1	-0.1
Total	3	83	294	21	44	4	0	0	2	13	4	.150	.186	.163	18	-24				.855	1	/O-83	-2.1

■ DON WAKAMATSU
Wakamatsu, Wilbur Donald   b: 2/22/63, Hood River, Ore.   BR/TR, 6'2", 200 lbs.   Deb: 5/22/91

YEAR	TM/L	G	AB	R	H	2B	3B	HR	RBI	BB	SO	AVG	OBP	SLG	PRO+	BR/A	SB	CS	SBR	FA	FR	G/POS	TPR
1991	Chi-A	18	31	2	7	0	0	0	1	6	.226	.250	.226	33	-3	0	0	0	1.000	-0	C-18	-0.3

■ HOWARD WAKEFIELD
Wakefield, Howard John   b: 4/2/1884, Bucyrus, Ohio   d: 4/16/41, Chicago, Ill.   BR/TR, 6'1", 205 lbs.   Deb: 9/18/05   F

YEAR	TM/L	G	AB	R	H	2B	3B	HR	RBI	BB	SO	AVG	OBP	SLG	PRO+	BR/A	SB	CS	SBR	FA	FR	G/POS	TPR
1905	Cle-A	10	26	3	4	0	0	0	1	0		.154	.185	.154	8	-3	0			.926	-3	/C-8	-0.5
1906	Was-A	77	211	17	59	9	2	1	21	7		.280	.303	.355	111	2	6			.946	-15	C-60	-0.8
1907	Cle-A	26	37	4	5	2	0	0	3	3		.135	.200	.189	24	-3	0			.930	-0	C-11	-0.3
Total	3	113	274	24	68	11	2	1	25	10		.248	.277	.314	89	-4	6			.943	-18	/C-79	-1.6

■ DICK WAKEFIELD
Wakefield, Richard Cummings   b: 5/6/21, Chicago, Ill.   d: 8/26/85, Redford, Mich.   BL/TR, 6'4", 210 lbs.   Deb: 6/26/41   F

YEAR	TM/L	G	AB	R	H	2B	3B	HR	RBI	BB	SO	AVG	OBP	SLG	PRO+	BR/A	SB	CS	SBR	FA	FR	G/POS	TPR
1941	Det-A	7	7	0	1	0	0	0	0	0	1	.143	.143	.143	-22	-1	0	0	0	1.000	-0	/O-1	-0.1
1943	Det-A★	155	633	91	200	38	8	7	79	62	60	.316	.377	.434	127	21	4	5	-2	.959	-6	*O-155	0.6
1944	Det-A	78	276	53	98	15	5	12	53	55	29	.355	.464	.576	186	33	2	2	-1	.963	-4	O-78	2.5
1946	Det-A	111	396	64	106	11	5	12	59	59	55	.268	.364	.412	110	6	3	5	-2	.964	0	*O-104	-0.1
1947	Det-A	112	368	59	104	15	5	8	51	80	44	.283	.412	.416	127	17	4	4	-2	.950	-2	*O-101	0.7
1948	Det-A	110	322	50	89	20	5	11	53	70	55	.276	.406	.472	129	15	0	1	-1	.948	0	O-86	1.0
1949	Det-A	59	126	17	26	3	1	6	19	32	24	.206	.367	.389	100	4	0	0	0	1.000	0	O-32	0.0
1950	NY-A	3	2	0	1	0	0	0	1	1	0	.500	.667	.500	208	1	0	0	0	.000	0	H	0.0
1952	NY-N	3	2	0	0	0	0	0	0	1	1	.000	.333	.000	-0	-0	0	0	0	.000	0	H	0.0
Total	9	638	2132	334	625	102	29	56	315	360	270	.293	.396	.447	130	92	10	17	-7	.959	-11	O-557	4.6

■ MATT WALBECK
Walbeck, Matthew Lovick   b: 10/2/69, Sacramento, Cal.   BB/TR, 5'11", 195 lbs.   Deb: 4/7/93

YEAR	TM/L	G	AB	R	H	2B	3B	HR	RBI	BB	SO	AVG	OBP	SLG	PRO+	BR/A	SB	CS	SBR	FA	FR	G/POS	TPR
1993	Chi-N	11	30	2	6	2	0	1	6	1	6	.200	.226	.367	56	-2	0	0	0	1.000	-0	C-11	-0.2
1994	Min-A	97	338	31	69	12	0	5	35	17	37	.204	.246	.284	36	-32	1	1	-0	.993	-7	C-95/D-1	-3.2
Total	2	108	368	33	75	14	0	6	41	18	43	.204	.245	.291	38	-34	1	1	-0	.993	-7	C-106/D-1	-3.4

■ ED WALCZAK
Walczak, Edwin Joseph "Husky"   b: 9/21/18, Artic, R.I.   BR/TR, 5'11", 180 lbs.   Deb: 9/3/45

YEAR	TM/L	G	AB	R	H	2B	3B	HR	RBI	BB	SO	AVG	OBP	SLG	PRO+	BR/A	SB	CS	SBR	FA	FR	G/POS	TPR
1945	Phi-N	20	57	6	12	3	0	0	2	6	9	.211	.286	.263	55	-3	0			.966	1	2-17/S-2	-0.2

■ FRED WALDEN
Walden, Thomas Fred   b: 6/25/1890, Fayette, Mo.   d: 9/27/55, Jefferson Barracks, Mo.   BR/TR,   Deb: 6/3/12

YEAR	TM/L	G	AB	R	H	2B	3B	HR	RBI	BB	SO	AVG	OBP	SLG	PRO+	BR/A	SB	CS	SBR	FA	FR	G/POS	TPR
1912	StL-A	1	0	0	0	0	0	0	0	0	0	—	—	—	—	0	0			.000	-1	/C-1	-0.1

■ IRV WALDRON
Waldron, Irving J.   b: 1/21/1876, Hillside, N.Y.   d: 7/22/44, Worcester, Mass.   BR/TR,   Deb: 4/25/01

YEAR	TM/L	G	AB	R	H	2B	3B	HR	RBI	BB	SO	AVG	OBP	SLG	PRO+	BR/A	SB	CS	SBR	FA	FR	G/POS	TPR
1901	Mil-A	62	266	48	79	8	6	0	29	16		.297	.342	.372	103	1	12			.883	-2	O-62	-0.5
	Was-A	79	332	54	107	14	3	0	23	22		.322	.368	.383	110	5	8			.955	-5	O-78	-0.5
	Yr	141	598	102	186	22	9	0	52	38		.311	.356	.378	107	6	20			.923	-7	*O-140	-1.0

■ JIM WALEWANDER
Walewander, James   b: 5/2/62, Chicago, Ill.   BB/TR, 5'10", 160 lbs.   Deb: 5/31/87

YEAR	TM/L	G	AB	R	H	2B	3B	HR	RBI	BB	SO	AVG	OBP	SLG	PRO+	BR/A	SB	CS	SBR	FA	FR	G/POS	TPR
1987	Det-A	53	54	24	13	3	1	1	4	7	6	.241	.328	.389	93	-0	2	1	0	1.000	15	2-24,3-17/SD	1.4
1988	Det-A	88	175	23	37	5	0	0	6	12	26	.211	.262	.240	43	-13	11	4	1	.977	14	2-61/S-8,3D	0.4
1990	NY-A	9	5	1	1	1	0	0	0	0		.200	.200	.400	64	-0	1	1	-0	1.000	1	/2-2,3-2,SD	0.1
1993	Cal-A	12	8	2	1	0	0	0	0	5	1	.125	.462	.125	64	0	1	1	-0	1.000	5	/S-6,2-2,D	0.1
Total	4	162	242	50	52	9	1	1	14	24	33	.215	.286	.273	57	-14	15	7	0	.982	37	/2-89,D-22,3S	2.4

■ RUBE WALKER
Walker, Albert Bluford   b: 5/16/26, Lenoir, N.C.   d: 12/12/92, Morganton, N.C.   BL/TR, 6'1", 185 lbs.   Deb: 4/20/48   C

YEAR	TM/L	G	AB	R	H	2B	3B	HR	RBI	BB	SO	AVG	OBP	SLG	PRO+	BR/A	SB	CS	SBR	FA	FR	G/POS	TPR
1948	Chi-N	79	171	17	47	8	0	5	26	24	17	.275	.371	.409	115	4	0			.980	-3	C-44	0.4
1949	Chi-N	56	172	11	42	4	1	3	22	9	18	.244	.282	.331	66	-9	0			.964	-5	C-43	-1.1
1950	Chi-N	74	213	19	49	7	1	6	16	18	34	.230	.290	.357	70	-10	0			.975	1	C-62	-0.6

YEAR	TM/L	G	AB	R	H	2B	3B	HR	RBI	BB	SO	AVG	OBP	SLG	PRO+	BR/A	SB	CS	SBR	FA	FR	G/POS	TPR
1951	Chi-N	37	107	9	25	4	0	2	5	12	13	.234	.311	.327	71	-4	0	0	0	.969	-4	C-31	-0.7
	Bro-N	36	74	6	18	4	0	2	9	6	14	.243	.300	.378	80	-2	0	0	0	.972	-5	C-23	-0.6
	Yr	73	181	15	43	8	0	4	14	18	27	.238	.307	.348	74	-7	0	0	0	.970	-9	C-54	-1.3
1952	Bro-N	46	139	9	36	8	0	1	19	8	17	.259	.304	.338	77	-4	0	0	0	.987	5	C-40	0.3
1953	Bro-N	43	95	5	23	6	0	3	9	7	11	.242	.301	.400	79	-3	0	0	0	.978	1	C-28	-0.1
1954	Bro-N	50	155	12	28	7	0	5	23	24	17	.181	.294	.323	59	-10	0	0	0	.996	1	C-47	-0.6
1955	Bro-N	48	103	6	26	5	0	2	13	15	11	.252	.347	.359	86	-2	1	0	0	.987	2	C-35	0.1
1956	*Bro-N	54	146	5	31	6	1	3	20	7	18	.212	.248	.329	50	-10	0	1	-1	.986	-1	C-43	-1.1
1957	Bro-N	60	166	12	30	8	0	2	23	15	33	.181	.249	.265	35	-15	2	0	1	.992	-6	C-50	-1.9
1958	LA-N	25	44	3	5	2	0	1	5	7	10	.114	.204	.227	14	-6	0	0	0	.985	-2	C-20	-0.7
Total	11	608	1585	114	360	69	3	35	192	150	213	.227	.296	.341	68	-71	3	1		.982	-15	C-466	-6.6

■ TONY WALKER
Walker, Anthony Bruce b: 7/1/59, San Diego, Cal.   BR/TR, 6'2", 205 lbs.   Deb: 4/8/86

YEAR	TM/L	G	AB	R	H	2B	3B	HR	RBI	BB	SO	AVG	OBP	SLG	PRO+	BR/A	SB	CS	SBR	FA	FR	G/POS	TPR
1986	Hou-N	84	90	19	20	7	0	2	10	11	15	.222	.307	.367	87	-2	11	3	2	.986	-14	O-68	-1.5

■ FRANK WALKER
Walker, Charles Franklin b: 9/22/1894, Enoree, S.C.   d: 9/16/74, Bristol, Tenn.   BR/TR, 5'11", 165 lbs.   Deb: 9/6/17

YEAR	TM/L	G	AB	R	H	2B	3B	HR	RBI	BB	SO	AVG	OBP	SLG	PRO+	BR/A	SB	CS	SBR	FA	FR	G/POS	TPR
1917	Det-A	2	2	0	0	0	0	0	0	0	1	.000	.000	.000	-99	-0	0			.000	0	H	-0.1
1918	Det-A	55	167	10	33	10	3	1	20	7	29	.198	.234	.311	67	-8	3			.922	-2	O-45	-1.4
1920	Phi-A	24	91	10	21	2	2	0	10	5	14	.231	.286	.297	54	-6	0	2	-1	.983	-1	O-24	-1.0
1921	Phi-A	19	66	6	15	3	0	1	6	8	11	.227	.311	.318	60	-4	1	0	0	.961	1	O-19	-0.4
1925	NY-N	39	81	12	18	1	0	1	5	9	11	.222	.308	.272	51	-6	1	1	-0	.960	-1	O-21	-0.8
Total	5	139	407	38	87	16	5	3	41	29	66	.214	.273	.300	58	-24	5	3		.949	-4	O-109	-3.7

■ TILLY WALKER
Walker, Clarence William b: 9/4/1887, Telford, Tenn.   d: 9/20/59, Chattanooga, Tenn   BR/TR, 5'11", 165 lbs.   Deb: 4/12/11

YEAR	TM/L	G	AB	R	H	2B	3B	HR	RBI	BB	SO	AVG	OBP	SLG	PRO+	BR/A	SB	CS	SBR	FA	FR	G/POS	TPR
1911	Was-A	95	356	44	99	6	4	2	39	15		.278	.311	.334	82	-10	12			.917	-3	O-94	-1.6
1912	Was-A	39	110	22	30	2	1	0	9	8		.273	.333	.309	83	-2	11			.837	-3	O-34/2-1	-0.6
1913	StL-A	23	85	7	25	4	1	0	11	2	9	.294	.310	.365	100	-0	5			.911	-0	O-23	-0.2
1914	StL-A	151	517	67	154	24	16	6	78	51	72	.298	.365	.441	148	28	29	17	-2	.972	16	*O-145	3.9
1915	StL-A	144	510	53	137	20	7	5	49	36	77	.269	.323	.365	110	4	20	17	-4	.940	15	*O-139	0.8
1916	*Bos-A	128	467	68	124	29	11	3	46	23	45	.266	.303	.394	109	-2	14			.959	-4	*O-128	-0.9
1917	Bos-A	106	337	41	83	18	7	2	37	25	38	.246	.300	.359	102	-1	6			.972	6	O-96	0.0
1918	Phi-A	114	414	56	122	20	0	**11**	48	41	44	.295	.360	.423	135	16	8			.953	5	*O-109	1.6
1919	Phi-A	125	456	47	133	30	6	10	64	26	41	.292	.330	.450	116	7	8			.933	-4	*O-115	-0.4
1920	Phi-A	149	585	79	157	23	7	17	82	41	59	.268	.321	.419	94	-8	8	3	1	.940	6	*O-149	-1.2
1921	Phi-A	142	556	89	169	32	5	23	101	73	41	.304	.389	.522	125	21	3	5	-2	.955	9	*O-142	1.6
1922	Phi-A	153	565	111	160	31	4	37	99	61	67	.283	.357	.549	130	21	4	3	-1	.956	-2	*O-148	0.8
1923	Phi-A	52	109	12	30	5	2	2	16	14	11	.275	.368	.413	104	1	1	2	-1	1.000	-2	O-26	-0.3
Total	13	1421	5067	696	1423	244	71	118	679	416	504	.281	.339	.427	115	80	129	47		.949	41	*O-1348/2-1	3.5

■ CHICO WALKER
Walker, Cleotha b: 11/25/57, Jackson, Miss.   BB/TR, 5'9", 179 lbs.   Deb: 9/2/80

YEAR	TM/L	G	AB	R	H	2B	3B	HR	RBI	BB	SO	AVG	OBP	SLG	PRO+	BR/A	SB	CS	SBR	FA	FR	G/POS	TPR
1980	Bos-A	19	57	3	12	0	0	1	5	6	10	.211	.297	.263	52	-4	3	2	-0	.958	1	2-11/D-7	-0.3
1981	Bos-A	6	17	3	6	0	0	0	2	1	2	.353	.389	.353	108	0	0	2	-1	1.000	-2	/2-5	0.1
1983	Bos-A	4	5	2	2	0	2	0	1	0	0	.400	.400	1.200	299	1	0	0	0	1.000	0	/O-3	0.1
1984	Bos-A	3	2	0	0	0	0	0	1	0	1	.000	.000	.000	-96	-1	0	0	0	1.000	0	/2-1	-0.1
1985	Chi-N	21	12	3	1	0	0	0	0	0	5	.083	.083	.083	-48	-2	1	0	0	1.000	-2	/O-6,2-2	-0.4
1986	Chi-N	28	101	21	28	3	2	1	7	10	20	.277	.342	.376	91	-1	15	4	2	.956	-5	O-26	-0.5
1987	Chi-N	47	105	15	21	4	0	0	7	12	23	.200	.282	.238	38	-9	11	4	1	.974	-5	O-33/3-2	-1.4
1988	Cal-A	33	78	8	12	1	0	0	2	6	15	.154	.214	.167	8	-9	2	1	0	.933	-2	O-17/2-7,3	-1.2
1991	Chi-N	124	374	51	96	10	1	6	34	33	57	.257	.317	.337	80	-9	13	5	1	.929	-23	3-57,O-53/2	-3.4
1992	Chi-N	19	26	2	3	0	0	0	2	3	4	.115	.207	.115	-6	-4	1	0	0	1.000	0	/O-6,2-2,3	-0.4
	NY-N	107	227	24	70	12	1	4	36	24	46	.308	.375	.423	127	8	14	1	4	.971	-7	3-36,2-16,O	0.5
	Yr	126	253	26	73	12	1	4	38	27	50	.289	.357	.391	113	5	15	1	4	.960	-7	3-38,O-21,2	0.1
1993	NY-N	115	213	18	48	7	1	9	14	29	212	.225	.308	.338	63	-11	7	0	2	.976	-4	2-24,3-23,O	-1.3
Total	11	526	1217	150	299	37	7	17	116	109	212	.246	.308	.329	75	-41	67	19	9	.968	-49	O-174,3-122/2D	-8.7

■ DUANE WALKER
Walker, Duane Allen b: 3/13/57, Pasadena, Tex.   BL/TL, 6', 185 lbs.   Deb: 5/25/82

YEAR	TM/L	G	AB	R	H	2B	3B	HR	RBI	BB	SO	AVG	OBP	SLG	PRO+	BR/A	SB	CS	SBR	FA	FR	G/POS	TPR
1982	Cin-N	86	239	26	52	10	0	5	22	27	58	.218	.302	.322	73	-8	9	3	1	.992	0	O-69	-0.9
1983	Cin-N	109	225	14	53	12	1	2	29	20	43	.236	.298	.324	70	-9	6	3	0	.956	0	O-60	-1.1
1984	Cin-N	83	195	35	57	10	3	10	28	33	35	.292	.395	.528	150	14	7	3	0	.950	-5	O-68	0.8
1985	Cin-N	37	48	5	8	2	1	2	6	6	18	.167	.259	.375	72	-2	1	0	0	.882	-1	O-10	-0.3
	Tex-A	53	132	14	23	2	0	5	11	15	29	.174	.264	.303	54	-8	2	1	0	1.000	1	O-32,D-10	-0.8
1988	StL-N	24	22	1	4	1	0	0	3	2	7	.182	.250	.227	38	-2	0	0	0	.000	-2	/O-4,1-1	-0.4
Total	5	392	861	95	197	37	5	24	99	103	190	.229	.313	.367	86	-16	25	10	2	.967	-6	O-243/D-10,1	-2.7

■ ERNIE WALKER
Walker, Ernest Robert b: 9/17/1890, Blossburg, Ala.   d: 4/1/65, Pell City, Ala.   BL/TR, 6', 165 lbs.   Deb: 4/13/13   F

YEAR	TM/L	G	AB	R	H	2B	3B	HR	RBI	BB	SO	AVG	OBP	SLG	PRO+	BR/A	SB	CS	SBR	FA	FR	G/POS	TPR
1913	StL-A	7	14	0	3	0	0	0	2	0	5	.214	.214	.214	26	-1	0			1.000	-0	/O-2	-0.2
1914	StL-A	74	131	19	39	5	3	1	14	13	26	.298	.366	.405	137	6	6	4	-1	.960	-6	O-38	-0.3
1915	StL-A	50	109	15	23	4	2	0	9	23	32	.211	.348	.284	93	0	5	8	-3	.881	-6	O-33	-1.1
Total	3	131	254	34	65	9	5	1	25	36	63	.256	.351	.343	112	4	11	12		.928	-12	/O-73	-1.6

■ DIXIE WALKER
Walker, Fred "The People's Cherce" b: 9/24/10, Villa Rica, Ga.   d: 5/17/82, Birmingham, Ala.   BL/TR, 6'1", 175 lbs.   Deb: 4/28/31   FC

YEAR	TM/L	G	AB	R	H	2B	3B	HR	RBI	BB	SO	AVG	OBP	SLG	PRO+	BR/A	SB	CS	SBR	FA	FR	G/POS	TPR
1931	NY-A	2	10	1	3	2	0	1	0	0	4	.300	.300	.500	113	0	0	0	0	1.000	-0	/O-2	0.0
1933	NY-A	98	328	68	90	15	7	15	51	26	28	.274	.330	.500	125	9	2	2	-1	.962	5	O-77	0.9
1934	NY-A	17	17	2	2	0	0	0	0	1	3	.118	.167	.118	-27	-3	0	0	0	1.000	-0	/O-1	-0.3
1935	NY-A	8	13	1	2	1	0	0	1	0	1	.154	.154	.231	-2	-2	0	0	0	.750	-1	/O-2	-0.2
1936	NY-A	6	20	3	7	0	2	1	5	1	3	.350	.381	.700	167	2	1	1	-0	1.000	-0	/O-5	0.0
	Chi-A	26	70	12	19	2	0	0	11	14	6	.271	.400	.300	73	-2	1	0	0	1.000	0	O-17	-0.2
	Yr	32	90	15	26	2	2	1	16	15	9	.289	.396	.389	92	-1	2	1	-0	1.000	-0	O-22	-0.2
1937	Chi-A	154	593	105	179	28	**16**	9	95	78	26	.302	.384	.449	109	9	1	2	-1	.952	-10	*O-154	-0.6
1938	Det-A	127	454	84	140	27	6	6	43	65	32	.308	.396	.434	120	3	5	4	-1	.979	-9	*O-114	-1.0
1939	Det-A	43	154	30	47	4	5	6	19	15	8	.305	.367	.474	106	4	4	1	1	.970	4	O-37	0.4
	Bro-N	61	225	27	63	6	4	2	38	20	10	.280	.339	.369	87	-4	3			.968	2	O-59	-0.4
1940	Bro-N	143	556	75	171	37	6	6	66	42	21	.308	.357	.435	111	8	3			.973	2	*O-136	0.3
1941	*Bro-N	148	531	88	165	32	9	9	71	70	25	.311	.391	.452	131	23	4			.976	11	*O-146	2.7
1942	Bro-N	118	393	57	114	28	1	6	54	47	15	.290	.367	.412	126	13	1			.986	-1	*O-110	0.7
1943	Bro-N★	138	540	83	163	32	6	9	71	49	24	.302	.363	.411	123	16	3			.969	3	*O-136	1.2
1944	Bro-N★	147	535	77	191	37	8	13	91	72	27	**.357**	.434	.529	173	53	6			.962	-3	*O-140	4.4
1945	Bro-N†	154	607	102	182	42	9	8	**124**	75	16	.300	.381	.438	128	24	6			.992	12	*O-153	2.8
1946	Bro-N★	150	576	80	184	29	9	9	116	67	28	.319	.391	.448	136	28	14			.969	-8	*O-149	1.4
1947	*Bro-N★	148	529	77	162	31	3	9	94	97	26	.306	.415	.427	119	19	6			.964	-8	*O-147	0.3
1948	Pit-N	129	408	39	129	19	3	6	54	52	18	.316	.393	.392	111	8	1			.977	-12	*O-112	-1.0
1949	Pit-N	88	181	26	51	4	1	1	18	26	11	.282	.372	.331	88	-2	0			.984	-4	O-39/1-3	-0.8
Total	18	1905	6740	1037	2064	376	96	105	1023	817	325	.306	.383	.437	121	202	59	10		.972	-16	*O-1736/1-3	10.6

YEAR	TM/L	G	AB	R	H	2B	3B	HR	RBI	BB	SO	AVG	OBP	SLG	PRO+	BR/A	SB	CS	SBR	FA	FR	G/POS	TPR

■ GEE WALKER
Walker, Gerald Holmes b: 3/19/08, Gulfport, Miss. d: 3/20/81, Whitfield, Miss. BR/TR, 5'11", 188 lbs. Deb: 4/14/31 FC

YEAR	TM/L	G	AB	R	H	2B	3B	HR	RBI	BB	SO	AVG	OBP	SLG	PRO+	BR/A	SB	CS	SBR	FA	FR	G/POS	TPR
1931	Det-A	59	189	20	56	17	2	1	28	14	21	.296	.345	.423	98	-1	10	7	-1	.953	-3	O-44	-0.8
1932	Det-A	127	480	71	155	32	6	8	78	13	38	.323	.345	.465	104	1	30	6	5	.949	4	*O-116	0.3
1933	Det-A	127	483	68	135	29	7	9	64	15	49	.280	.304	.424	89	-10	26	9	2	.942	-1	*O-113	-1.3
1934	*Det-A	98	347	54	104	19	2	6	39	19	20	.300	.340	.418	94	-4	20	9	1	.947	2	O-80	-0.4
1935	*Det-A	98	362	52	109	22	6	7	53	15	21	.301	.329	.453	104	0	6	4	-1	.954	-3	O-85	-0.6
1936	Det-A	134	550	105	194	55	5	12	93	23	30	.353	.387	.536	125	19	17	8	0	.948	5	*O-125	1.7
1937	Det-A†	151	635	105	213	42	4	18	113	41	74	.335	.380	.499	117	15	23	7	3	.956	-6	*O-151	0.6
1938	Chi-A	120	442	69	135	23	6	16	87	38	32	.305	.360	.493	109	5	9	4	0	.958	-5	*O-107	-0.4
1939	Chi-A	149	598	95	174	30	11	13	111	28	43	.291	.330	.443	94	-8	17	6	2	.967	9	*O-147	-0.2
1940	Was-A	140	595	87	175	29	7	13	96	24	58	.294	.325	.432	101	-2	21	4	4	.967	-2	*O-140	-0.7
1941	Cle-A	121	445	56	126	26	11	6	48	18	46	.283	.313	.431	100	-3	12	6	0	.982	8	*O-105	-0.2
1942	Cin-N	119	422	40	97	20	2	5	50	31	44	.230	.290	.322	79	-12	11			.973	4	*O-110	-1.4
1943	Cin-N	114	429	48	105	23	2	2	54	12	38	.245	.270	.329	74	-16	6			.980	-6	*O-106	-2.9
1944	Cin-N	121	478	56	133	21	3	5	62	23	48	.278	.318	.366	96	-4	7			.967	-7	*O-117	-1.8
1945	Cin-N	106	316	28	80	11	2	2	21	16	38	.253	.289	.320	71	-13	8			.962	-7	O-67/3-3	-2.4
Total	15	1784	6771	954	1991	399	76	124	997	330	600	.294	.331	.430	99	-32	223	70		.961	-7	*O-1613/3-3	-10.5

■ GREG WALKER
Walker, Gregory Lee b: 10/6/59, Douglas, Ga. BL/TR, 6'3", 210 lbs. Deb: 9/18/82

YEAR	TM/L	G	AB	R	H	2B	3B	HR	RBI	BB	SO	AVG	OBP	SLG	PRO+	BR/A	SB	CS	SBR	FA	FR	G/POS	TPR
1982	Chi-A	11	17	3	7	2	1	2	7	2	3	.412	.474	1.000	292	4	0	0	0	.000	0	/D-4	0.4
1983	*Chi-A	118	307	32	83	16	3	10	55	28	57	.270	.335	.440	107	3	2	1	0	.985	-7	1-59,D-21	-0.8
1984	Chi-A	136	442	62	130	29	2	24	75	35	66	.294	.349	.532	134	19	8	5	-1	.995	-5	*1-101,D-21	0.7
1985	Chi-A	163	601	77	155	38	4	24	92	44	100	.258	.311	.454	102	0	5	2	0	.994	-3	*1-151/D-7	-1.1
1986	Chi-A	78	282	37	78	10	6	13	51	29	44	.277	.348	.493	122	9	8	1	2	.993	-1	1-77/D-1	0.1
1987	Chi-A	157	566	85	145	33	2	27	94	75	112	.256	.348	.465	110	9	2	1	0	.994	-14	*1-154/D-3	-1.6
1988	Chi-A	99	377	45	93	22	1	8	42	29	77	.247	.306	.374	90	-6	0	1	-1	.993	-14	1-98	-2.9
1989	Chi-A	77	233	25	49	14	0	5	26	23	50	.210	.290	.335	77	-7	0	0	0	.987	-6	1-48,D-23	-1.7
1990	Chi-A	2	5	0	1	0	0	0	0	0	2	.200	.200	.200	12	-1	0	0	0	1.000	0	/1-1,D-1	0.0
	Bal-A	14	34	2	5	0	0	0	2	3	9	.147	.237	.147	10	-4	1	0	0	.000	0	D-11	-0.4
	Yr	16	39	2	6	0	0	0	2	3	11	.154	.233	.154	10	-5	1	0	0	1.000	0	D-12/1-1	-0.4
Total	9	855	2864	368	746	164	19	113	444	268	520	.260	.328	.449	108	26	19	12	-2	.993	-49	1-689/D-92	-7.3

■ HARRY WALKER
Walker, Harry William "Harry The Hat" b: 10/22/16, Pascagoula, Miss. BL/TR, 6'2", 190 lbs. Deb: 9/25/40 FMC

YEAR	TM/L	G	AB	R	H	2B	3B	HR	RBI	BB	SO	AVG	OBP	SLG	PRO+	BR/A	SB	CS	SBR	FA	FR	G/POS	TPR
1940	StL-N	7	27	2	5	2	0	0	6	0	2	.185	.185	.259	20	-3	0			1.000	2	/O-7	-0.1
1941	StL-N	7	15	3	4	1	0	0	1	2	1	.267	.353	.333	88	-0	0			.875	-1	/O-5	-0.2
1942	*StL-N	74	191	38	60	12	2	0	16	11	14	.314	.355	.398	112	2	2			.968	-1	O-56/2-2	-0.1
1943	*StL-N★	148	564	76	166	28	6	2	53	40	24	.294	.341	.376	102	1	5			.965	-6	*O-144/2-1	-1.3
1946	*StL-N	112	346	53	82	14	6	3	27	30	29	.237	.300	.338	77	-11	12			.974	-7	O-92/1-8	-1.1
1947	StL-N	10	25	2	5	1	0	0	0	4	2	.200	.310	.240	46	-2	0			.938	-2	O-10	-0.4
	Phi-N★	130	488	79	181	28	16	1	41	59	37	.371	.443	.500	156	41	13			.966	14	*O-127/1-4	4.6
	Yr	140	513	81	186	29	**16**	1	41	63	39	**.363**	.436	.487	150	39	13			.964	12	*O-137/1-4	4.2
1948	Phi-N	112	332	34	97	11	2	2	23	33	30	.292	.358	.355	95	-1	4			.981	2	O-81/1-4,3	-0.4
1949	Chi-N	42	159	20	42	6	3	1	14	11	6	.264	.312	.358	81	-4	2			.947	-3	O-39	-1.0
	Cin-N	86	314	53	100	15	2	1	23	34	17	.318	.385	.389	107	4	4			.963	2	O-77/1-1	0.2
	Yr	128	473	73	142	21	5	2	37	45	23	.300	.361	.378	99	-0	6			.959	-2	*O-116/1-1	-0.8
1950	StL-N	60	150	17	31	5	0	0	7	18	12	.207	.292	.240	40	-13	0			.969	-1	O-46/1-2	-1.5
1951	StL-N	8	26	2	8	1	0	0	2	2	1	.308	.357	.346	90	-0	0	0	0	1.000	-1	/O-6,1-1	-0.2
1955	StL-N	11	14	2	5	2	0	0	1	1	0	.357	.400	.500	137	1	0	0	0	1.000	-1	/O-1,M	0.2
Total	11	807	2651	385	786	126	37	10	214	245	175	.296	.358	.383	103	15	42	0		.968	10	O-691/1-20,23	-1.3

■ HUB WALKER
Walker, Harvey Willos b: 8/17/06, Gulfport, Miss. d: 11/26/82, San Jose, Cal. BL/TR, 5'10.5", 175 lbs. Deb: 4/15/31 F

YEAR	TM/L	G	AB	R	H	2B	3B	HR	RBI	BB	SO	AVG	OBP	SLG	PRO+	BR/A	SB	CS	SBR	FA	FR	G/POS	TPR
1931	Det-A	90	252	27	72	13	1	0	16	23	25	.286	.355	.345	82	-6	10	1	2	.961	-0	O-66	-0.7
1935	Det-A	9	25	4	4	3	0	0	1	3	4	.160	.250	.280	38	-2	0			1.000	-0	/O-7	-0.3
1936	Cin-N	92	258	49	71	18	1	4	23	35	32	.275	.366	.399	113	5	8			.970	4	O-73/C-1,1	-0.1
1937	Cin-N	78	221	33	55	9	4	1	19	34	24	.249	.349	.339	92	-1	7			.993	4	O-58/2-3	0.0
1945	*Det-A	28	23	4	3	0	0	0	1	9	4	.130	.375	.130	46	-1	1	0	0	1.000	-2	/O-7	-0.3
Total	5	297	779	117	205	43	6	5	60	104	89	.263	.354	.353	92	-5	26	1		.975	-4	O-211/2-3,1C	-1.4

■ JOHNNY WALKER
Walker, John Miles b: 12/11/1896, Toulon, Ill. d: 8/19/76, Hollywood, Fla. BR/TR, 6', 175 lbs. Deb: 9/19/19

YEAR	TM/L	G	AB	R	H	2B	3B	HR	RBI	BB	SO	AVG	OBP	SLG	PRO+	BR/A	SB	CS	SBR	FA	FR	G/POS	TPR
1919	Phi-A	3	9	0	0	0	0	0	0	0	0	.000	.000	.000	-99	-2	0			.941	-0	/C-3	-0.2
1920	Phi-A	9	22	0	5	1	0	0	5	0	1	.227	.227	.273	32	-2	0	0	0	.960	-1	/C-6	-0.2
1921	Phi-A	113	423	41	109	14	5	2	46	9	29	.258	.278	.329	54	-30	5	0	2	.989	-6	1-99/C-7	-3.5
Total	3	125	454	41	114	15	5	2	51	9	32	.251	.270	.319	50	-35	5	0	2	.968	-7	/1-99,C-16	-3.9

■ SPEED WALKER
Walker, Joseph Richard b: 1/23/1898, Munhall, Pa. d: 6/20/59, W.Mifflin, Pa. BR/TR, 6', 170 lbs. Deb: 9/15/23

YEAR	TM/L	G	AB	R	H	2B	3B	HR	RBI	BB	SO	AVG	OBP	SLG	PRO+	BR/A	SB	CS	SBR	FA	FR	G/POS	TPR
1923	StL-N	2	7	1	2	0	0	0	0	0	1	.286	.286	.286	52	-0	0	0	0	1.000	-0	/1-2	-0.1

■ LARRY WALKER
Walker, Larry Kenneth Robert b: 12/1/66, Maple Ridge, B.C., Canada BL/TR, 6'2", 185 lbs. Deb: 8/16/89

YEAR	TM/L	G	AB	R	H	2B	3B	HR	RBI	BB	SO	AVG	OBP	SLG	PRO+	BR/A	SB	CS	SBR	FA	FR	G/POS	TPR
1989	Mon-N	20	47	4	8	0	0	0	4	5	13	.170	.264	.170	26	-4	1	1	-0	1.000	0	O-15	-0.5
1990	Mon-N	133	419	59	101	18	3	19	51	49	112	.241	.328	.434	112	6	21	7	2	.985	9	*O-124	1.5
1991	Mon-N	137	487	59	141	30	2	16	64	42	102	.290	.352	.458	128	17	14	9	-1	.991	9	*O-102,1-39	2.1
1992	Mon-N★	143	528	85	159	31	4	23	93	41	97	.301	.358	.506	143	28	18	6	2	.993	14	*O-139	4.4
1993	Mon-N	138	490	85	130	24	5	22	86	80	76	.265	.375	.469	119	15	29	7	5	.979	4	*O-132/1-4	2.6
1994	Mon-N	103	395	76	127	**44**	2	19	86	47	74	.322	.399	.587	150	29	15	5	2	.973	4	O-68,1-35	2.9
Total	6	674	2366	368	666	147	16	99	384	264	474	.281	.360	.483	129	91	98	35	8	.986	45	O-580/1-78	13.0

■ FLEET WALKER
Walker, Moses Fleetwood b: 10/7/1856, Mt.Pleasant, Ohio d: 5/11/24, Cleveland, Ohio BR/TR, 159 lbs. Deb: 5/1/1884 F

YEAR	TM/L	G	AB	R	H	2B	3B	HR	RBI	BB	SO	AVG	OBP	SLG	PRO+	BR/A	SB	CS	SBR	FA	FR	G/POS	TPR
1884	Tol-a	42	152	23	40	2	3	0	8			.263	.325	.316	106	1				.887	-6	C-41/O-1	-0.1

■ OSCAR WALKER
Walker, Oscar b: 3/18/1854, Brooklyn, N.Y. d: 5/20/1889, Brooklyn, N.Y. BL/TL, 5'10", 166 lbs. Deb: 9/17/1875

YEAR	TM/L	G	AB	R	H	2B	3B	HR	RBI	BB	SO	AVG	OBP	SLG	PRO+	BR/A	SB	CS	SBR	FA	FR	G/POS	TPR
1875	Atl-n	1	2	0	0	0	0	0			1	.000	.333	.000	30	-0						/O-1	0.0
1879	Buf-N	72	287	35	79	15	6	1	35	8	38	.275	.295	.380	118	5				.946	3	*1-72	0.5
1880	Buf-N	34	126	12	29	4	2	1	15	6	18	.230	.265	.317	95	-1				.917	-2	1-24,O-11	-0.4
1882	StL-a	76	318	48	76	15	7	**7**			10	.239	.262	.396	115	4				.846	8	*O-75/2-1,1	1.0
1884	Bro-a	95	382	59	103	12	8	2			9	.270	.292	.359	110	4				.868	0	O-59,1-36	-0.1
1885	Bal-a	4	13	1	0	0	0	0			0	.000	.000	.000	-99	-3				.667	0	/O-4	-0.4
Total	5	281	1126	155	287	46	23	11	50	33	56	.255	.278	.366	109	9				.850	8	O-149,1-133/2	0.6

■ WALT WALKER
Walker, Walter S. b: 3/12/1860, Berlin, Mich. d: 2/28/22, Pontiac, Mich. TR, 5'10.5", 162 lbs. Deb: 5/8/1884

YEAR	TM/L	G	AB	R	H	2B	3B	HR	RBI	BB	SO	AVG	OBP	SLG	PRO+	BR/A	SB	CS	SBR	FA	FR	G/POS	TPR
1884	Det-N	1	4	1	1	0	0	0	0	0	0	.250	.250	.250	61	-0				.750	-1	C-1	-0.1

■ WELDAY WALKER
Walker, Welday Wilberforce b: 6/1859, Steubenville, Ohio d: 11/23/37, Steubenville, Ohio Deb: 7/15/1884 F

YEAR	TM/L	G	AB	R	H	2B	3B	HR	RBI	BB	SO	AVG	OBP	SLG	PRO+	BR/A	SB	CS	SBR	FA	FR	G/POS	TPR
1884	Tol-a	5	18	1	4	1	0	0			0	.222	.222	.278	60	-1				.667	-1	/O-5	-0.2

YEAR	TM/L	G	AB	R	H	2B	3B	HR	RBI	BB	SO	AVG	OBP	SLG	PRO+	BR/A	SB	CS	SBR	FA	FR	G/POS	TPR

■ CURT WALKER
Walker, William Curtis b: 7/3/1896, Beeville, Tex. d: 12/9/55, Beeville, Tex. BL/TR, 5'9.5", 170 lbs. Deb: 9/17/19

YEAR	TM/L	G	AB	R	H	2B	3B	HR	RBI	BB	SO	AVG	OBP	SLG	PRO+	BR/A	SB	CS	SBR	FA	FR	G/POS	TPR
1919	NY-A	1	1	0	0	0	0	0	0	0	0	.000	.000	.000	-99	-0	0			.000	0	H	0.0
1920	NY-N	8	14	0	1	0	0	0	0	1	3	.071	.133	.071	-41	-3	0	0	0	1.000	-1	/O-4	-0.4
1921	NY-N	64	192	30	55	13	5	3	35	15	8	.286	.338	.453	107	2	4	3	-1	.978	1	O-58	-0.2
	Phi-N	21	77	11	26	2	1	0	8	5	5	.338	.378	.390	96	-0	0	2	-1	.970	-5	O-21	-0.8
	Yr	85	269	41	81	15	6	3	43	20	13	.301	.349	.435	104	1	4	5	-2	.976	-4	O-79	-1.0
1922	Phi-N	148	581	102	196	36	11	12	89	56	46	.337	.399	.499	119	16	11	4	1	.955	5	*O-147	1.1
1923	Phi-N	140	527	66	148	26	5	5	66	45	31	.281	.337	.378	79	-16	12	12	-4	.947	5	*O-137/1-1	-2.3
1924	Phi-N	24	71	11	21	6	1	1	8	7	4	.296	.359	.451	103	0	0	1	-1	.900	-4	O-20	-0.5
	Cin-N	109	397	55	119	21	10	4	46	44	15	.300	.371	.433	117	10	7	5	-1	.978	0	*O-109	0.2
	Yr	133	468	66	140	27	11	5	54	51	19	.299	.369	.436	114	10	7	6	-2	.969	-4	*O-129	-0.3
1925	Cin-N	145	509	86	162	22	16	6	71	57	31	.318	.387	.460	118	15	14	11	-2	.983	4	*O-141	0.5
1926	Cin-N	155	571	83	175	24	20	6	78	60	31	.306	.372	.450	124	19	3			.961	4	*O-152	1.2
1927	Cin-N	146	527	60	154	16	10	6	80	47	19	.292	.350	.395	102	2	5			.957	3	*O-141	-0.5
1928	Cin-N	123	427	64	119	15	12	6	73	49	14	.279	.354	.412	101	1	19			.955	4	*O-122	-0.3
1929	Cin-N	141	492	76	154	28	15	7	83	85	17	.313	.416	.474	126	23	17			.969	-6	*O-138	0.7
1930	Cin-N	134	472	74	145	26	11	8	51	64	30	.307	.391	.460	110	9	4			.965	-6	*O-120	-0.5
Total	12	1359	4858	718	1475	235	117	64	688	535	254	.304	.374	.440	110	77	96	38		.963	2	*O-1310/1-1	-1.8

■ HOWARD WALL
Wall, Howard Deb: 9/13/1873

YEAR	TM/L	G	AB	R	H	2B	3B	HR	RBI	BB	SO	AVG	OBP	SLG	PRO+	BR/A	SB	CS	SBR	FA	FR	G/POS	TPR
1873	Was-n	1	4	1	1	0	0	0	0	0	0	.250	.250	.250	49	-0						/S-1	0.0

■ JOE WALL
Wall, Joseph Francis "Gummy" b: 7/24/1873, Brooklyn, N.Y. d: 7/17/36, Brooklyn, N.Y. BL/TL, Deb: 9/22/01

YEAR	TM/L	G	AB	R	H	2B	3B	HR	RBI	BB	SO	AVG	OBP	SLG	PRO+	BR/A	SB	CS	SBR	FA	FR	G/POS	TPR
1901	NY-N	4	8	0	4	0	0	0	1	0		.500	.500	.500	198	2	1	0		1.000	-3	/C-2,O-1	-0.1
1902	NY-N	6	14	2	5	2	0	0	0	2		.357	.438	.500	191	2	0			1.000	-0	/O-3	0.1
	Bro-N	5	18	0	3	0	0	0	0	3		.167	.318	.167	50	-1	0			.893	-3	/C-5	-0.4
	Yr	11	32	2	8	2	0	0	0	5		.250	.368	.313	110	1	0			.893	-3	/C-5,O-3	-0.3
Total	2	15	40	2	12	2	0	0	1	5		.300	.391	.350	127	2	0			.903	-6	/C-7,O-4	-0.4

■ JACK WALLACE
Wallace, Clarence Eugene b: 8/6/1890, Winnfield, La. d: 10/15/60, Winnfield, La. BR/TR, 5'10.5", 175 lbs. Deb: 9/27/15

YEAR	TM/L	G	AB	R	H	2B	3B	HR	RBI	BB	SO	AVG	OBP	SLG	PRO+	BR/A	SB	CS	SBR	FA	FR	G/POS	TPR
1915	Chi-N	2	7	1	2	0	0	0	1	0	2	.286	.375	.286	101	0	0			1.000	2	/C-2	0.2

■ DON WALLACE
Wallace, Donald Allen b: 8/25/40, Sapulpa, Okla. BL/TR, 5'8", 165 lbs. Deb: 4/12/67

YEAR	TM/L	G	AB	R	H	2B	3B	HR	RBI	BB	SO	AVG	OBP	SLG	PRO+	BR/A	SB	CS	SBR	FA	FR	G/POS	TPR
1967	Cal-A	23	6	2	0	0	0	0	0	3	2	.000	.333	.000	6	-1	0	1	-1	1.000	2	/2-4,1-1,3	0.1

■ DOC WALLACE
Wallace, Frederick Renshaw "Jesse" b: 9/30/1893, Church Hill, Md. d: 12/31/64, Haverford, Pa. BR/TR, 5'6.5", 135 lbs. Deb: 5/2/19

YEAR	TM/L	G	AB	R	H	2B	3B	HR	RBI	BB	SO	AVG	OBP	SLG	PRO+	BR/A	SB	CS	SBR	FA	FR	G/POS	TPR
1919	Phi-N	2	4	0	1	0	0	0	0	0	0	.250	.250	.250	47	-0	0			.875	0	/S-2	0.0

■ JIM WALLACE
Wallace, James L. b: 11/14/1881, Boston, Mass. d: 5/16/53, Revere, Mass. BL/TL, 5'9", 150 lbs. Deb: 8/24/05

YEAR	TM/L	G	AB	R	H	2B	3B	HR	RBI	BB	SO	AVG	OBP	SLG	PRO+	BR/A	SB	CS	SBR	FA	FR	G/POS	TPR
1905	Pit-N	7	29	3	6	1	0	0	3	3		.207	.281	.241	55	-2	2			.929	1	/O-7	-0.1

■ BOBBY WALLACE
Wallace, Rhoderick John b: 11/4/1873, Pittsburgh, Pa. d: 11/3/60, Torrance, Cal. BR/TR, 5'8", 170 lbs. Deb: 9/15/1894 MUCH

YEAR	TM/L	G	AB	R	H	2B	3B	HR	RBI	BB	SO	AVG	OBP	SLG	PRO+	BR/A	SB	CS	SBR	FA	FR	G/POS	TPR
1894	Cle-N	4	13	0	2	1	0	0	1	0	1	.154	.154	.231	-8	-2	0			1.000	1	/P-4	0.0
1895	Cle-N	30	98	16	21	2	3	0	10	6	17	.214	.274	.296	44	-9	0			.910	3	P-30	0.0
1896	*Cle-N	45	149	19	35	6	3	1	17	11	21	.235	.287	.336	60	-9	2			.950	-2	O-23,P-22/1	-0.8
1897	Cle-N	130	516	99	173	33	21	4	112	48		.335	.394	.504	129	19	14			.928	4	*3-130/O-1	2.2
1898	Cle-N	154	593	81	160	25	13	3	99	63		.270	.344	.371	106	5	7			.936	17	*3-141,2-13	2.3
1899	StL-N	151	577	91	170	28	14	12	108	54		.295	.357	.454	119	13	17			.919	39	*S-100,3-52	5.3
1900	StL-N	126	485	70	130	25	9	4	70	40		.268	.328	.381	96	-4	7			.934	3	*S-126/3-1	0.8
1901	StL-N	134	550	69	178	34	15	2	91	20		.324	.351	.451	138	24	15			.929	30	*S-134	6.2
1902	StL-A	133	494	71	141	32	9	1	63	45		.285	.350	.393	107	5	18			.948	11	*S-131/P-1,O	2.2
1903	StL-A	135	511	63	136	21	7	1	54	28		.266	.309	.341	97	-2	10			.924	18	*S-135	2.3
1904	StL-A	139	541	57	149	29	4	2	69	42		.275	.330	.355	124	15	20			.947	8	*S-139	3.0
1905	StL-A	156	587	67	159	25	9	1	59	45		.271	.324	.349	120	12	13			.935	19	*S-156	3.8
1906	StL-A	139	476	64	123	21	7	2	67	58		.258	.344	.345	121	13	24			.949	3	*S-138	2.2
1907	StL-A	147	538	56	138	20	7	0	70	54		.257	.327	.320	107	5	16			.941	5	*S-147	1.9
1908	StL-A	137	487	59	123	24	4	1	60	52		.253	.327	.324	111	7	5			.951	18	*S-137	3.1
1909	StL-A	116	403	36	96	12	6	0	35	38		.238	.310	.278	92	-3	7			.946	11	S-87,3-29	1.2
1910	StL-A	138	508	47	131	19	7	0	37	49		.258	.324	.323	110	6	12			.948	22	S-99,3-39	3.6
1911	StL-A	125	410	35	95	12	2	0	31	46		.232	.312	.271	66	-18	8			.943	2	*S-124/2-1M	-0.8
1912	StL-A	100	323	39	78	14	5	0	31	43		.241	.332	.316	89	-4	3			.942	8	S-87,3-10/2M	1.2
1913	StL-A	55	147	11	31	5	0	0	21	14	16	.211	.293	.245	59	-7	1			.931	-5	S-39/3-7	-1.0
1914	StL-A	26	73	3	16	2	1	0	5	5	13	.219	.269	.274	66	-3	1	1	-0	.889	-11	S-19/3-2	-1.5
1915	StL-A	9	13	1	3	2	0	0	4	5	0	.231	.444	.385	154	1	0	1	-1	.848	1	/S-9	0.2
1916	StL-A	14	18	0	5	0	0	0	1	2	1	.278	.350	.278	93	-0				.958	5	/3-9,S-5	0.6
1917	StL-N	8	10	0	1	0	0	0	2	0	1	.100	.100	.100	-40	-2	0			1.000	-1	/3-5,S-2	-0.3
1918	StL-N	32	98	3	15	1	0	0	4	6	9	.153	.202	.163	12	-10	1			.959	2	2-17,S-12/3	-0.8
Total	25	2383	8618	1057	2309	391	143	34	1121	774	79	.268	.332	.358	106	53	201	2		.938	212	*S-1826,3-426/P201	36.9

■ TIM WALLACH
Wallach, Timothy Charles b: 9/14/57, Huntington Park, Cal. BR/TR, 6'3", 200 lbs. Deb: 9/6/80

YEAR	TM/L	G	AB	R	H	2B	3B	HR	RBI	BB	SO	AVG	OBP	SLG	PRO+	BR/A	SB	CS	SBR	FA	FR	G/POS	TPR
1980	Mon-N	5	11	1	2	0	0	1	2	1	5	.182	.250	.455	93	-0	0	0	0	1.000	-1	/O-3,1-1	-0.2
1981	*Mon-N	71	212	19	50	9	1	4	13	15	37	.236	.299	.344	81	-5	0	1	-1	1.000	-4	O-35,1-16,3	-1.3
1982	Mon-N	158	596	89	160	31	3	28	97	36	81	.268	.314	.471	115	9	6	4	-1	.948	-6	*3-156/O-2,1	-0.1
1983	Mon-N	156	581	54	156	33	3	19	70	55	97	.269	.338	.434	113	9	0	3	-2	.956	-7	*3-156	-0.2
1984	Mon-N★	160	582	55	143	25	4	18	72	50	101	.246	.313	.395	102	0	3	7	-3	.959	16	*3-160/S-1	1.1
1985	Mon-N★	155	569	70	148	36	3	22	81	38	79	.260	.312	.450	117	10	9	9	-3	.967	37	*3-154	4.3
1986	Mon-N	134	480	50	112	22	1	18	71	44	72	.233	.311	.396	94	-5	8	4	0	.958	15	*3-132	0.8
1987	Mon-N★	153	593	89	177	**42**	4	26	123	37	98	.298	.347	.514	121	16	9	5	-0	.952	-0	*3-150/P-1	1.3
1988	Mon-N	159	592	52	152	**32**	5	12	69	38	88	.257	.305	.389	93	-6	2	6	-3	.962	12	*3-153/2-1	0.2
1989	Mon-N★	154	573	76	159	**42**	0	13	77	58	81	.277	.345	.419	116	12	3	7	-3	.958	6	*3-153/P-1	1.7
1990	Mon-N★	161	626	69	185	37	5	21	98	42	80	.296	.343	.471	126	20	6	9	-4	.954	4	*3-161	2.2
1991	Mon-N	151	577	60	130	22	1	13	73	50	100	.225	.294	.334	77	-18	2	4	-2	**.968**	6	*3-149	-1.3
1992	Mon-N	150	537	53	120	29	1	9	59	50	90	.223	.299	.331	79	-15	2	2	-1	.964	18	3-85,1-71	-0.2
1993	LA-N	133	477	42	106	19	1	12	62	32	70	.222	.275	.342	68	-23	0	3	-1	.958	0	*3-130/1-1	-2.4
1994	LA-N	113	414	68	116	21	1	23	78	46	80	.280	.358	.502	129	16	0	2	-1	.959	-10	*3-113	0.6
Total	15	2013	7420	847	1916	400	33	239	1045	592	1159	.258	.319	.418	104	22	50	65	-24	.959	87	*3-1867/1-90,OP2S	6.5

■ JACK WALLAESA
Wallaesa, John b: 8/31/19, Easton, Pa. d: 12/27/86, Easton, Pa. BB/TR, 6'3", 191 lbs. Deb: 9/22/40

YEAR	TM/L	G	AB	R	H	2B	3B	HR	RBI	BB	SO	AVG	OBP	SLG	PRO+	BR/A	SB	CS	SBR	FA	FR	G/POS	TPR
1940	Phi-A	6	20	0	3	0	0	0	2	0	2	.150	.150	.150	-22	-4	0	0	0	.903	1	/S-6	-0.2
1942	Phi-A	36	117	13	30	4	1	2	13	8	26	.256	.315	.359	90	-2	0	1	-1	.920	-7	S-36	-0.8
1946	Phi-A	63	194	16	38	4	2	5	11	14	47	.196	.250	.314	57	-12	1	0	0	.916	-16	S-59	-2.6
1947	Chi-A	81	205	25	40	9	1	7	32	23	51	.195	.279	.351	78	-7	2	4	-1	.968	13	S-27,O-22/3	0.6
1948	Chi-A	33	48	2	9	0	0	1	3	1	12	.188	.204	.250	21	-6	0	0	0	1.000	-0	/S-5,O-1	-0.5
Total	5	219	584	56	120	17	4	15	61	46	138	.205	.267	.325	65	-30	3	3	-1	.933	-10	S-133/O-23,3	-3.5

YEAR	TM/L	G	AB	R	H	2B	3B	HR	RBI	BB	SO	AVG	OBP	SLG	PRO+	BR/A	SB	CS	SBR	FA	FR	G/POS	TPR

■ **NORM WALLEN**   Wallen, Norman Edward (b: Norman Edward Walentoski)   b: 2/13/17, Milwaukee, Wis.   BR/TR, 5'11.5", 175 lbs.   Deb: 4/20/45

| 1945 | Bos-N | 4 | 15 | 1 | 2 | 0 | 1 | 0 | 1 | 1 | 1 | .133 | .188 | .267 | 25 | -2 | 0 | | | .800 | -2 | /3-4 | -0.3 |

■ **TY WALLER**   Waller, Elliott Tyrone   b: 3/14/57, Fresno, Cal.   BR/TR, 6', 180 lbs.   Deb: 9/6/80

1980	StL-N	5	12	3	1	0	0	0	1	5	1	.083	.154	.083	-31	-2	0	0	0	1.000	-2	/3-5	-0.5
1981	Chi-N	30	71	10	19	2	1	3	13	4	18	.268	.307	.451	108	0	2	0	1	.978	-2	3-22/2-3,O	-0.2
1982	Chi-N	17	21	4	5	0	0	0	1	2	5	.238	.304	.238	52	-1	0	0	0	1.000	-2	/O-7,3-1	-0.3
1987	Hou-N	11	6	1	1	1	0	0	0	0	3	.167	.167	.333	30	-1	0	0	0	1.000	-1	/O-3	-0.1
Total	4	63	110	18	26	3	1	3	14	7	31	.236	.282	.364	78	-4	2	0	1	.961	-7	/3-28,O-13,2	-1.1

■ **DENNY WALLING**   Walling, Dennis Martin   b: 4/17/54, Neptune, N.J.   BL/TR, 6'1", 185 lbs.   Deb: 9/7/75

1975	Oak-A	6	8	0	1	1	0	0	0	0	4	.125	.125	.250	4	-1	0	0	0	1.000	-1	/O-3	-0.2
1976	Oak-A	3	11	1	3	0	0	0	0	0	3	.273	.273	.273	63	-1	0	0	0	.889	-1	/O-3	-0.1
1977	Hou-N	6	21	1	6	0	1	0	6	2	4	.286	.348	.381	105	0	0	1	-1	1.000	-1	/O-5	0.0
1978	Hou-N	120	247	30	62	11	3	3	36	30	24	.251	.335	.356	101	0	9	2	1	.980	2	O-78	0.1
1979	Hou-N	82	147	21	48	8	4	3	31	17	21	.327	.396	.497	151	10	3	2	-0	.985	-3	O-42	0.6
1980	*Hou-N	100	284	30	85	6	5	3	29	35	26	.299	.376	.380	123	9	4	3	-1	.989	-7	1-63,O-19	-0.2
1981	*Hou-N	65	158	23	37	8	0	5	23	28	17	.234	.349	.367	109	2	2	1	0	.990	-1	1-27,O-27	-0.4
1982	Hou-N	85	146	22	30	4	1	1	14	23	19	.205	.314	.267	69	-6	4	2	0	1.000	-4	O-32,1-20	-1.1
1983	Hou-N	100	135	24	40	5	3	3	19	15	16	.296	.367	.444	132	6	2	2	-1	.992	-4	1-42,3-13,O	0.0
1984	Hou-N	87	249	37	70	11	5	3	31	16	28	.281	.327	.402	112	3	7	1	2	.956	-1	3-52,1-16/O	0.2
1985	Hou-N	119	345	44	93	20	1	7	45	25	26	.270	.319	.394	101	-0	5	2	0	.938	-2	3-51,1-46,O	-0.5
1986	*Hou-N	130	382	54	119	23	1	13	58	36	31	.312	.371	.479	136	18	1	1	-0	.960	2	*3-102,O-11/1	1.8
1987	Hou-N	110	325	45	92	21	4	5	33	39	37	.283	.360	.418	110	5	5	1	1	.948	-3	3-79,1-16/O	-0.1
1988	Hou-N	65	176	19	43	10	2	1	20	15	18	.244	.304	.341	88	-3	1	0	0	.950	9	3-51/1-3,O	0.6
	StL-N	19	58	3	13	3	0	0	1	2	7	.224	.250	.276	50	-4	1	0	0	1.000	-2	O-11/3-5,1	-0.7
	Yr	84	234	22	56	13	2	1	21	17	25	.239	.291	.325	79	-7	2	0	0	.941	6	3-56,O-12/1	-0.1
1989	StL-N	69	79	9	24	7	0	1	11	14	12	.304	.409	.430	136	4	0	0	0	.969	-2	1-20/3-9,O	0.2
1990	StL-N	78	127	7	28	5	0	1	19	8	15	.220	.267	.283	51	-8	0	0	0	1.000	1	1-15,3-11/O	-0.9
1991	Tex-A	24	44	1	4	1	0	0	2	3	8	.091	.184	.114	-16	-7	0	0	0	.950	-3	3-14/O-5	-1.0
1992	Hou-N	3	3	1	1	0	0	0	0	0	0	.333	.333	.333	94	-0	0	0	0	.000	0	/H	0.0
Total	18	1271	2945	372	799	142	30	49	380	308	316	.271	.341	.390	107	29	44	18	2	.947	-25	3-387,O-290,1	-1.7

■ **JOE WALLIS**   Wallis, Harold Joseph   b: 1/9/52, E.St.Louis, Ill.   BB/TR, 5'10", 195 lbs.   Deb: 9/2/75

1975	Chi-N	16	56	9	16	2	1	4	5	4	14	.286	.344	.446	113	1	2	0	1	1.000	-0	O-15	0.1
1976	Chi-N	121	338	51	86	11	5	5	21	33	62	.254	.323	.361	86	-6	3	9	-5	.976	2	O-90	-1.3
1977	Chi-N	56	80	14	20	3	0	2	8	16	25	.250	.375	.363	89	-1	0	1	-1	.974	-8	O-35	-1.0
1978	Chi-N	28	55	7	17	2	1	1	6	5	13	.309	.367	.436	110	1	0	2	-1	1.000	-4	O-25	-0.5
	Oak-A	85	279	28	66	16	1	6	26	26	42	.237	.302	.366	91	-4	1	4	-2	.980	3	O-80/D-1	-0.7
1979	Oak-A	23	78	6	11	2	0	1	3	10	18	.141	.247	.205	25	-8	1	0	0	1.000	-1	O-23	-1.0
Total	5	329	886	115	216	36	9	16	68	95	174	.244	.318	.359	86	-17	7	16	-8	.982	-9	O-268/D-1	-4.4

■ **LEE WALLS**   Walls, Ray Lee   b: 1/6/33, San Diego, Cal.   d: 10/11/93, Los Angeles, Cal.   BR/TR, 6'3", 205 lbs.   Deb: 4/21/52   C

1952	Pit-N	32	80	6	15	0	1	2	5	8	22	.188	.261	.287	51	-5	0	0	0	1.000	0	O-19	-0.6
1956	Pit-N	143	474	72	130	20	11	11	54	50	83	.274	.346	.432	110	7	3	5	-2	.967	6	*O-133/3-1	0.4
1957	Pit-N	8	22	3	4	1	0	0	0	2	5	.182	.250	.227	30	-2	1	0	0	1.000	1	/O-7	-0.2
	Chi-N	117	366	42	88	10	5	6	33	27	67	.240	.294	.344	72	-15	5	3	-0	.984	-5	O-94/3-1	-2.6
	Yr	125	388	45	92	11	5	6	33	29	72	.237	.292	.338	70	-17	6	3	-0	.985	-4	*O-101/3-1	-2.8
1958	Chi-N★	136	513	80	156	19	3	24	72	47	62	.304	.371	.493	128	21	4	4	-1	.992	5	*O-132	1.8
1959	Chi-N	120	354	43	91	18	3	8	33	42	73	.257	.344	.393	97	-1	0	2	-1	.967	-8	*O-119	-1.5
1960	Cin-N	29	84	12	23	3	2	1	7	17	20	.274	.396	.393	115	2	2	0	1	.960	1	O-24/1-2	0.2
	Phi-N	65	181	19	36	6	1	3	19	14	32	.199	.256	.293	50	-13	3	2	-1	.947	-9	3-34,O-13/1	-2.4
	Yr	94	265	31	59	3	3	4	26	31	52	.223	.304	.325	72	-10	5	2	0	.958	-8	O-37,3-34/1	-2.2
1961	Phi-N	91	261	32	73	6	4	8	30	19	48	.280	.329	.425	99	-1	2	2	-1	.987	-6	1-28,3-26,O	-1.0
1962	LA-N	60	109	9	29	3	1	7	17	10	21	.266	.328	.312	77	-3	1	0	0	.929	-4	O-17,1-11/3	-0.8
1963	LA-N	64	86	12	20	1	0	3	11	7	25	.233	.290	.349	89	-1	0	0	0	1.000	-2	O-18/1-5,3	-0.4
1964	LA-N	37	28	1	5	1	0	0	3	2	12	.179	.233	.214	29	-3	0	0	0	1.000	-2	/O-6,C-1	-0.5
Total	10	902	2558	331	670	88	31	66	284	245	470	.262	.330	.394	96	-14	21	18	-5	.977	-23	O-599/3-68,1C	-7.6

■ **AUSTIN WALSH**   Walsh, Austin Edward   b: 9/1/1891, Cambridge, Mass.   d: 1/26/55, Glendale, Cal.   BL/TL, 5'11", 175 lbs.   Deb: 4/19/14

| 1914 | Chi-F | 57 | 121 | 14 | 29 | 6 | 1 | 1 | 10 | 4 | 25 | .240 | .264 | .331 | 57 | -9 | 0 | | | 1.000 | -3 | O-30 | -1.3 |

■ **JIMMY WALSH**   Walsh, James Charles   b: 9/22/1885, Kallila, Ireland   d: 7/3/62, Syracuse, N.Y.   BL/TR, 5'10.5", 170 lbs.   Deb: 8/26/12

1912	Phi-A	31	107	11	27	8	2	0	15	12		.252	.328	.364	101	0	7			.947	-2	O-30	-0.1
1913	Phi-A	97	303	56	77	16	5	0	27	38	40	.254	.341	.340	102	1	15			.961	1	O-90	-0.2
1914	NY-A	43	136	13	26	1	3	1	11	29	21	.191	.333	.265	80	-2	6	9	-4	.977	-1	O-41	-0.9
	*Phi-A	68	216	35	51	11	6	3	36	30	27	.236	.340	.384	123	6	6	12	-5	.966	-0	O-56/1-3,3S	-0.2
	Yr	111	352	48	77	12	9	4	47	59	48	.219	.337	.338	106	4	12	21	-9	.971	-1	O-97/1-3,3S	-1.1
1915	Phi-A	117	417	48	86	15	5	1	20	57	64	.206	.306	.278	78	-11	22	12	-1	.976	7	*O-109/3-2,1	-1.0
1916	Phi-A	114	390	42	91	13	6	1	27	54	36	.233	.330	.305	95	-1	27	14	-0	.939	-0	*O-113/1-1	-0.9
	*Bos-A	14	17	5	3	1	0	0	2	4	2	.176	.333	.235	71	-0	3	2	-0	1.000	-3	/O-6,3-2	-0.4
	Yr	128	407	47	94	14	6	1	29	58	38	.231	.330	.302	94	-2	30	16	-1	.940	-3	*O-119/3-2,1	-1.3
1917	Bos-A	57	185	25	49	6	3	0	12	25	14	.265	.352	.330	109	3	6			.982	-0	O-47	0.0
Total	6	541	1771	235	410	71	31	6	150	249	204	.232	.330	.317	96	-4	92	49		.964	5	O-492/3-7,1S	-3.7

■ **JOHN WALSH**   Walsh, John Gabriel   b: 3/25/1879, Wilkes-Barre, Pa.   d: 4/25/47, Jamaica, N.Y.   BR/TR, 5'8.5", 162 lbs.   Deb: 6/22/03

| 1903 | Phi-N | 1 | 3 | 0 | 0 | 0 | 0 | 0 | 0 | 0 | 0 | .000 | .000 | .000 | -99 | -1 | 0 | | | 1.000 | -0 | /3-1 | -0.1 |

■ **JOE WALSH**   Walsh, Joseph Francis   b: 10/14/1886, Minersville, Pa.   d: 1/6/67, Buffalo, N.Y.   BR/TR, 6'2", 170 lbs.   Deb: 10/8/10

1910	NY-A	1	4	0	2	1	0	0	2	0	0	.500	.500	.750	275	1	0			1.000	-1	/C-1	-0.3
1911	NY-A	4	9	2	2	1	0	0	0	0	0	.222	.222	.333	51	-1	0			1.000	-3	/C-4	-0.3
Total	2	5	13	2	4	2	0	0	2	0	0	.308	.308	.462	114	0	0			1.000	-4	/C-5	-0.3

■ **JOE WALSH**   Walsh, Joseph Patrick "Tweet"   b: 3/13/17, Roxbury, Mass.   BR/TR, 5'10", 155 lbs.   Deb: 7/1/38

| 1938 | Bos-N | 4 | 8 | 0 | 0 | 0 | 0 | 0 | 0 | 0 | 2 | .000 | .000 | .000 | -99 | -2 | 0 | | | .900 | -2 | /S-4 | -0.4 |

■ **JOE WALSH**   Walsh, Joseph R. "Reddy"   b: 11/5/1864, Chicago, Ill.   d: 8/8/11, Omaha, Neb.   BL/TR,   Deb: 9/3/1891

| 1891 | Bal-a | 26 | 100 | 14 | 21 | 0 | 1 | 1 | 10 | 6 | 18 | .210 | .255 | .260 | 47 | -7 | 4 | | | .865 | 6 | S-13,2-13 | 0.0 |

■ **DEE WALSH**   Walsh, Leo Thomas   b: 3/28/1890, St.Louis, Mo.   d: 7/14/71, St.Louis, Mo.   BB/TR, 5'9.5", 165 lbs.   Deb: 4/10/13

1913	StL-A	23	53	9	9	0	1	0	5	6	11	.170	.302	.208	51	-3	3			.933	2	S-22/3-1	0.1
1914	StL-A	7	23	1	2	0	0	0	1	2	4	.087	.160	.087	-27	-4	1	1	-0	.919	-0	/S-7	-0.4
1915	StL-A	59	150	13	33	5	0	0	6	14	25	.220	.308	.253	71	-5	6	6	-2	.951	1	O-45/3-2,P2S	-0.8
Total	3	89	226	22	44	5	1	0	12	22	40	.195	.292	.226	56	-11	10	7		.924	3	/O-45,S-30,32P	-1.1

YEAR	TM/L	G	AB	R	H	2B	3B	HR	RBI	BB	SO	AVG	OBP	SLG	PRO+	BR/A	SB	CS	SBR	FA	FR	G/POS	TPR

■ JIMMY WALSH
Walsh, Michael Timothy "Runt" b: 3/25/1886, Lima, Ohio d: 1/21/47, Baltimore, Md. BR/TR, 5'9", 174 lbs. Deb: 4/25/10

YEAR	TM/L	G	AB	R	H	2B	3B	HR	RBI	BB	SO	AVG	OBP	SLG	PRO+	BR/A	SB	CS	SBR	FA	FR	G/POS	TPR
1910	Phi-N	88	242	28	60	8	3	3	31	25	38	.248	.323	.343	91	-3	5			.947	-2	2-26,O-26/S3	-0.6
1911	Phi-N	94	289	29	78	20	3	1	31	21	30	.270	.324	.370	93	-4	5			.962	-6	O-48,2-14/S3CP1	-1.1
1912	Phi-N	51	150	16	40	6	3	2	19	8	20	.267	.304	.387	83	-4	3			.944	0	2-31,3-12/C	-0.4
1913	Phi-N	26	30	3	10	4	0	0	5	1	5	.333	.355	.467	128	1	1			1.000	-1	/2-6,S-3,3O	0.0
1914	Bal-F	120	428	54	132	25	4	10	65	22	56	.308	.345	.456	103	0	18			.932	3	*3-113/2-1,SO	0.7
1915	Bal-F	106	401	43	121	20	1	9	60	21	44	.302	.340	.424	100	-1	12			.936	-9	*3-106	-0.6
	StL-F	17	31	5	6	1	0	0	1	3	4	.194	.306	.226	41	-2	1			.913	-1	/3-9	-0.3
	Yr	123	432	48	127	21	1	9	61	24	48	.294	.337	.410	96	-4	13			.934	-10	*3-115	-0.9
Total	6	502	1571	178	447	84	14	25	212	101	197	.285	.332	.404	96	-13	45			.925	-14	3-253/2-78,OSC1P	-2.3

■ TOM WALSH
Walsh, Thomas Joseph b: 2/28/1885, Davenport, Iowa d: 3/16/63, Naples, Fla. BR/TR, 5'11", 170 lbs. Deb: 8/15/06

YEAR	TM/L	G	AB	R	H	2B	3B	HR	RBI	BB	SO	AVG	OBP	SLG	PRO+	BR/A	SB	CS	SBR	FA	FR	G/POS	TPR
1906	Chi-N	2	1	0	0	0	0	0	0	0	0	.000	.000	.000	-95	-0	0			1.000	0	/C-2	0.0

■ WALT WALSH
Walsh, Walter William b: 4/30/1897, Newark, N.J. d: 1/15/66, Avon By The Sea, N.J. BR/TR, 5'11", 170 lbs. Deb: 5/4/20

YEAR	TM/L	G	AB	R	H	2B	3B	HR	RBI	BB	SO	AVG	OBP	SLG	PRO+	BR/A	SB	CS	SBR	FA	FR	G/POS	TPR
1920	Phi-N	2	0	0	0	0	0	0	0	0	0	—	—	—	—	0	0	0	0	.000	0	R	0.0

■ ROXY WALTERS
Walters, Alfred John b: 11/5/1892, San Francisco, Cal. d: 6/3/56, Alameda, Cal. BR/TR, 5'8.5", 160 lbs. Deb: 9/16/15

YEAR	TM/L	G	AB	R	H	2B	3B	HR	RBI	BB	SO	AVG	OBP	SLG	PRO+	BR/A	SB	CS	SBR	FA	FR	G/POS	TPR
1915	NY-A	2	3	0	1	0	0	0	0	0	0	.333	.333	.333	100	-0				1.000	2	/C-2	0.2
1916	NY-A	66	203	13	54	9	3	0	23	14	42	.266	.320	.340	96	-1	2			.974	17	C-65	2.2
1917	NY-A	61	171	16	45	2	0	0	14	9	22	.263	.304	.275	76	-5	2			.968	11	C-57	1.1
1918	NY-A	64	191	18	38	5	1	0	12	9	18	.199	.239	.236	42	-14	3			.953	-5	C-50/O-9	-1.8
1919	Bos-A	48	135	7	26	2	0	0	9	7	15	.193	.259	.207	33	-12	1			.982	5	C-47	-0.4
1920	Bos-A	88	258	25	51	11	1	0	28	30	21	.198	.303	.248	49	-18	2	2	-1	.980	8	C-85/1-2	-0.5
1921	Bos-A	54	169	17	34	4	1	0	14	10	11	.201	.254	.237	27	-19	3	0	1	.990	15	C-54	-0.4
1922	Bos-A	38	98	4	19	2	0	0	6	6	8	.194	.240	.214	19	-12	0	0	0	.967	6	C-36	-0.4
1923	Bos-A	40	104	9	26	4	0	0	5	2	6	.250	.264	.288	45	-8	0	2	-1	.974	7	C-36/2-1	-0.2
1924	Cle-A	32	74	10	19	2	0	0	5	10	6	.257	.345	.284	63	-4	0	1	-1	.979	6	C-25/2-7	0.2
1925	Cle-A	5	20	0	4	0	0	0	0	0	2	.200	.200	.200	2	-3	0	0	0	1.000	-0	/C-5	-0.3
Total	11	498	1426	119	317	41	6	0	116	97	151	.222	.281	.259	51	-96	13	5		.975	70	C-462/O-9,21	0.1

■ DAN WALTERS
Walters, Daniel Gene b: 8/15/66, Brunswick, Maine BR/TR, 6'4", 225 lbs. Deb: 6/1/92

YEAR	TM/L	G	AB	R	H	2B	3B	HR	RBI	BB	SO	AVG	OBP	SLG	PRO+	BR/A	SB	CS	SBR	FA	FR	G/POS	TPR
1992	SD-N	57	179	14	45	11	1	4	22	10	28	.251	.298	.391	92	-2	1	0	0	.992	7	C-55	0.8
1993	SD-N	27	94	6	19	3	0	1	10	7	13	.202	.257	.266	40	-8	0	0	0	.970	-3	C-26	-0.9
Total	2	84	273	20	64	14	1	5	32	17	41	.234	.284	.348	73	-10	1	0	0	.985	4	/C-81	-0.1

■ FRED WALTERS
Walters, Fred James "Whale" b: 9/4/12, Laurel, Miss. d: 2/1/80, Laurel, Miss. BR/TR, 6'1", 210 lbs. Deb: 4/17/45

YEAR	TM/L	G	AB	R	H	2B	3B	HR	RBI	BB	SO	AVG	OBP	SLG	PRO+	BR/A	SB	CS	SBR	FA	FR	G/POS	TPR
1945	Bos-A	40	93	2	16	2	0	0	5	10	9	.172	.252	.194	29	-8	1	1	-0	.993	6	C-38	-0.1

■ KEN WALTERS
Walters, Kenneth Rogers b: 11/11/33, Fresno, Cal. BR/TR, 6'1", 180 lbs. Deb: 4/12/60

YEAR	TM/L	G	AB	R	H	2B	3B	HR	RBI	BB	SO	AVG	OBP	SLG	PRO+	BR/A	SB	CS	SBR	FA	FR	G/POS	TPR
1960	Phi-N	124	426	42	102	10	0	8	37	16	50	.239	.269	.319	60	-24	4	3	-1	.988	6	*O-119	-2.5
1961	Phi-N	86	180	23	41	8	2	2	14	5	25	.228	.253	.328	53	-12	2	2	-1	.975	-6	O-56/1-5,3	-2.1
1963	Cin-N	49	75	6	14	2	0	1	7	4	14	.187	.237	.253	40	-6	0	2	-1	.889	-5	O-21/1-1	-1.3
Total	3	259	681	71	157	20	2	11	58	25	89	.231	.261	.314	56	-42	6	7	-2	.979	-5	O-196/1-6,3	-5.9

■ BUCKY WALTERS
Walters, William Henry b: 4/19/09, Philadelphia, Pa. d: 4/20/91, Abington, Pa. BR/TR, 6'1", 180 lbs. Deb: 9/18/31 MC

YEAR	TM/L	G	AB	R	H	2B	3B	HR	RBI	BB	SO	AVG	OBP	SLG	PRO+	BR/A	SB	CS	SBR	FA	FR	G/POS	TPR
1931	Bos-N	9	38	2	8	2	0	0	4	0	3	.211	.211	.263	28	-4	0			.947	0	/3-6,2-3	-0.3
1932	Bos-N	22	75	8	14	3	1	0	4	2	18	.187	.208	.253	24	-8	0			.910	2	3-22	-0.5
1933	Bos-A	52	195	27	50	8	3	4	28	19	24	.256	.326	.390	90	-3	1	1	-0	.940	1	3-43/2-7	0.1
1934	Bos-A	23	88	10	19	4	4	4	18	3	12	.216	.242	.489	79	-4	0	0	0	.906	3	3-23	0.3
	Phi-N	83	300	36	78	20	3	4	38	19	54	.260	.308	.387	75	-11	1			.950	-7	3-80/2-3,P	-1.4
1935	Phi-N	49	96	14	24	2	1	0	6	9	12	.250	.314	.292	58	-6	0			1.000	1	P-24/O-5,23	-0.2
1936	Phi-N	64	121	12	29	10	1	1	16	7	15	.240	.281	.364	66	-6	0			.974	9	P-40/2-1,3	0.0
1937	Phi-N★	56	137	15	38	6	0	1	16	5	16	.277	.303	.343	69	-6	1			.988	5	P-37/3-8	-0.1
1938	Phi-N	15	35	6	10	2	0	1	3	1	5	.286	.306	.429	103	-0	1			.955	0	P-12	0.0
	Cin-N	36	64	10	9	1	0	0	5	7	18	.141	.236	.156	10	-8	0			.981	2	P-27	0.0
	Yr	51	99	16	19	3	0	1	8	8	23	.192	.259	.253	42	-8	1			.973	3	P-39	0.0
1939	*Cin-N☆	40	120	16	39	8	1	1	16	5	12	.325	.357	.433	111	2	1			.979	4	P-39	0.0
1940	*Cin-N★	37	117	11	24	3	0	1	18	4	14	.205	.231	.256	34	-11	2			.945	-1	P-36	0.0
1941	Cin-N★	39	106	6	20	6	0	0	9	7	13	.189	.239	.245	36	-9	0			.977	2	P-37	0.0
1942	Cin-N★	40	99	13	24	6	1	2	13	3	13	.242	.265	.384	89	-2	0			.961	1	P-34/O-1	-0.1
1943	Cin-N	37	90	11	24	7	1	1	12	6	15	.267	.313	.400	107	0	1			.971	1	P-34	0.0
1944	*Cin-N★	37	107	9	30	4	0	2	13	8	18	.280	.330	.318	86	-2	2			1.000	1	P-34	0.0
1945	Cin-N	24	61	11	14	3	0	2	8	3	14	.230	.266	.426	93	-1	2			.975	-0	P-22	0.0
1946	Cin-N	24	55	6	7	2	0	0	5	4	12	.127	.186	.164	-0	-7	2			.940	2	P-20	0.0
1947	Cin-N	20	45	3	12	2	0	0	4	2	13	.267	.298	.311	62	-2	0			.962	-1	P-20	0.0
1948	Cin-N	7	15	1	4	0	0	0	2	0	2	.267	.267	.267	46	-1	0			1.000	1	/P-7,M	0.0
1950	Bos-N	1	2	0	0	0	0	0	0	0	0	.000	.000	.000	-99	-1	0			1.000	-0	/P-1	0.0
Total	19	715	1966	227	477	99	16	23	234	114	303	.243	.286	.344	69	-90	12	1		.974	28	P-428,3-184/2O	-2.2

■ DANNY WALTON
Walton, Daniel James "Mickey" b: 7/14/47, Los Angeles, Cal. BR/TR, 6', 200 lbs. Deb: 4/20/68

YEAR	TM/L	G	AB	R	H	2B	3B	HR	RBI	BB	SO	AVG	OBP	SLG	PRO+	BR/A	SB	CS	SBR	FA	FR	G/POS	TPR
1968	Hou-N	2	2	0	0	0	0	0	0	0	1	.000	.000	.000	-99	-0	0	0	1	.000	0	H	-0.1
1969	Sea-A	23	92	12	20	1	2	3	10	5	26	.217	.280	.370	82	-3	2	0	1	.976	-1	O-23	-0.4
1970	Mil-A	117	397	32	102	20	1	17	66	51	126	.257	.350	.441	116	9	2	3	-1	.965	-6	*O-114	-0.4
1971	Mil-A	30	69	5	14	3	0	2	9	7	22	.203	.286	.333	76	-2	0	0	0	.923	-4	O-19/3-1	-0.7
	NY-A	5	14	1	2	0	0	1	2	0	7	.143	.143	.357	40	-1	0	0	0	1.000	-1	/O-4	-0.2
	Yr	35	83	6	16	3	0	3	11	7	29	.193	.264	.337	71	-3	0	0	0	.933	-5	O-23/3-1	-0.9
1973	Min-A	37	96	13	17	1	1	4	8	17	28	.177	.301	.333	75	-3	0	0	0	1.000	-3	O-18,D-11/3	-0.7
1975	Min-A	42	63	4	11	2	0	1	8	4	18	.175	.224	.254	34	-6	0	0	0	.962	-1	/1-7,C-2,D	-0.7
1976	LA-N	18	15	0	2	0	0	0	2	0	5	.133	.188	.133	-8	-2	0	0	0	.000	0	H	-0.3
1977	Hou-N	13	21	0	4	0	0	0	1	0	5	.190	.190	.190	3	-3	0	0	0	.956	-0	/1-5	-0.3
1980	Tex-A	10	10	2	2	0	0	0	3	3	5	.200	.385	.200	67	-0	0	0	0	.000	0	/D-1	0.0
Total	9	297	779	69	174	27	4	28	107	88	240	.223	.310	.376	90	-12	4	3	-1	.966	-15	O-178/D-18,1C3	-3.8

■ JEROME WALTON
Walton, Jerome O'Terrell b: 7/8/65, Newnan, Ga. BR/TR, 6'1", 175 lbs. Deb: 4/4/89

YEAR	TM/L	G	AB	R	H	2B	3B	HR	RBI	BB	SO	AVG	OBP	SLG	PRO+	BR/A	SB	CS	SBR	FA	FR	G/POS	TPR
1989	*Chi-N	116	475	64	139	23	3	5	46	27	77	.293	.339	.385	99	-1	24	7	3	.990	4	*O-115	0.3
1990	Chi-N	101	392	63	103	16	2	2	21	50	70	.263	.352	.329	82	-8	14	7	0	.977	3	O-98	-0.8
1991	Chi-N	123	270	42	59	13	1	5	17	19	55	.219	.277	.330	67	-12	7	3	0	.983	-10	*O-101	-2.5
1992	Chi-N	30	55	7	7	1	0	0	1	9	13	.127	.273	.164	26	-5	1	2	-1	.944	-3	O-24	-1.0
1993	Cal-N	5	2	0	0	0	0	0	0	0	1	.000	.333	.000	-2	-0	0	0	0	1.000	0	H	0.0
1994	Cin-N	46	68	10	21	4	1	1	9	4	12	.309	.347	.412	98	-0	1	3	-2	1.000	-6	O-26/1-7	-0.8
Total	6	421	1262	188	329	56	7	13	94	110	229	.261	.327	.347	84	-26	48	22	1	.982	-13	O-365/1-7,D	-4.8

■ REGGIE WALTON
Walton, Reginald Sherard b: 10/24/52, Kansas City, Mo. BR/TR, 6'3", 205 lbs. Deb: 6/13/80

YEAR	TM/L	G	AB	R	H	2B	3B	HR	RBI	BB	SO	AVG	OBP	SLG	PRO+	BR/A	SB	CS	SBR	FA	FR	G/POS	TPR
1980	Sea-A	31	83	8	23	6	0	2	9	3	10	.277	.310	.422	98	-1	2	2	-1	.929	-2	O-17,D-11	-0.4

YEAR	TM/L	G	AB	R	H	2B	3B	HR	RBI	BB	SO	AVG	OBP	SLG	PRO+	BR/A	SB	CS	SBR	FA	FR	G/POS	TPR
1981	Sea-A	12	6	1	0	0	0	0	0	1	2	.000	.143	.000	-54	-1	0	0	0	.000	-2	/O-4,D-1	-0.3
1982	Pit-N	13	15	1	3	1	0	0	0	1	1	.200	.294	.267	56	-1	0	0	0	.000	-1	/O-2	-0.2
Total 3		56	104	10	26	7	0	2	9	5	13	.250	.297	.375	83	-3	2	2	-1	.929	-5	/O-23,D-12	-0.9

■ BILL WAMBSGANSS
Wambsganss, William Adolph b: 3/19/1894, Cleveland, Ohio d: 12/8/85, Lakewood, Ohio BR/TR, 5'11", 175 lbs. Deb: 8/4/14

YEAR	TM/L	G	AB	R	H	2B	3B	HR	RBI	BB	SO	AVG	OBP	SLG	PRO+	BR/A	SB	CS	SBR	FA	FR	G/POS	TPR
1914	Cle-A	43	143	12	31	6	2	0	12	8	24	.217	.277	.287	67	-6	2	7	-4	.921	-1	S-36/2-4	-0.8
1915	Cle-A	121	375	30	73	4	4	0	21	36	50	.195	.272	.227	48	-23	8	9	-3	.938	7	2-78,3-35	-1.9
1916	Cle-A	136	475	57	117	14	4	0	45	41	40	.246	.313	.293	77	-13	13			.925	-8	*S-106,2-24/3	-1.6
1917	Cle-A	141	499	52	127	17	6	0	43	37	42	.255	.315	.313	85	-9	16			.951	15	*2-137/1-3	1.4
1918	Cle-A	87	315	34	93	15	2	0	40	21	21	.295	.345	.356	102	0	16			.952	-2	2-87	0.4
1919	Cle-A	139	526	60	146	17	6	2	60	32	24	.278	.323	.344	82	-13	18			.963	11	2-139	0.5
1920	*Cle-A	153	560	83	138	16	11	1	55	54	26	.244	.316	.317	66	-28	9	18	-8	.960	8	2-153	-2.1
1921	Cle-A	107	410	80	117	28	5	2	47	44	27	.285	.359	.393	90	-6	13	7	-0	.963	-18	*2-103/3-2	-2.0
1922	Cle-A	142	538	89	141	22	6	0	47	60	26	.262	.341	.325	74	-19	17	10	-1	.961	-9	*2-125,S-16	-2.4
1923	Cle-A	101	345	59	100	20	4	1	59	43	15	.290	.373	.380	99	0	10	9	-2	.963	5	2-86/3-4,S	0.4
1924	Bos-A	156	632	93	174	41	5	0	49	54	33	.275	.336	.356	79	-21	14	8	-1	.963	14	*2-156	-0.5
1925	Bos-A	111	360	50	83	12	4	1	41	52	21	.231	.329	.294	59	-22	3	5	-2	.957	4	*2-103/1-6	-1.7
1926	Phi-A	54	54	11	19	3	0	0	1	8	8	.352	.444	.407	116	2	1	1	-0	.923	0	S-17/2-8	0.2
Total 13		1491	5237	710	1359	215	59	7	520	490	357	.259	.328	.327	78	-157	140	74		.958	26	*2-1203,S-177/31	-10.1

■ LLOYD WANER
Waner, Lloyd James "Little Poison" b: 3/16/06, Harrah, Okla. d: 7/22/82, Oklahoma City, Okla. BL/TR, 5'9", 150 lbs. Deb: 4/12/27 FH

YEAR	TM/L	G	AB	R	H	2B	3B	HR	RBI	BB	SO	AVG	OBP	SLG	PRO+	BR/A	SB	CS	SBR	FA	FR	G/POS	TPR
1927	*Pit-N	150	629	133	223	17	6	2	27	37	23	.355	.396	.410	108	9	14			.976	-1	*O-150/2-1	-0.2
1928	Pit-N	152	659	121	221	22	14	5	61	40	13	.335	.377	.434	107	7	8			.980	7	*O-152	0.3
1929	Pit-N	151	662	134	234	28	20	5	74	37	20	.353	.395	.479	113	13	6			.987	16	*O-151	1.7
1930	Pit-N	68	260	32	94	8	3	1	36	5	5	.362	.376	.427	93	-2	3			.983	2	O-65	-0.5
1931	Pit-N	154	681	90	214	25	13	4	57	39	16	.314	.352	.407	104	4	7			.979	18	*O-153/2-1	1.2
1932	Pit-N	134	565	90	188	27	11	2	38	31	11	.333	.367	.430	116	12	6			.986	12	*O-131	1.6
1933	Pit-N	121	500	59	138	14	5	0	26	22	8	.276	.307	.324	80	-13	3			.982	1	*O-114	-1.9
1934	Pit-N	140	611	95	173	27	6	1	48	38	12	.283	.326	.352	80	-17	6			.979	12	*O-139	-1.1
1935	Pit-N	122	537	83	166	22	14	0	46	22	10	.309	.336	.402	95	-5	1			.989	6	*O-121	-0.3
1936	Pit-N	106	414	67	133	13	8	1	31	31	5	.321	.369	.399	104	3	1			.984	1	O-92	0.0
1937	Pit-N	129	537	80	177	23	4	1	45	34	12	.330	.370	.393	107	6	3			.988	6	*O-123	0.8
1938	Pit-N☆	147	619	79	194	25	7	5	57	28	11	.313	.343	.401	103	2	5			.986	2	*O-144	-0.1
1939	Pit-N	112	379	49	108	15	3	0	24	17	13	.285	.321	.340	79	-11	0			.992	6	O-92/3-1	-0.8
1940	Pit-N	72	166	30	43	3	0	0	3	5	5	.259	.285	.277	56	-10	2			.989	-1	O-42	-1.3
1941	Pit-N	3	4	2	1	0	0	0	1	2	0	.250	.500	.250	116	0	0			1.000	0	/O-1	0.1
	Bos-N	19	51	7	21	1	0	0	4	2	0	.412	.434	.431	151	3	1			.969	-1	/O-15	0.2
	Cin-N	55	164	17	42	4	1	0	6	8	0	.256	.291	.293	64	-8	0			.986	-3	O-44	-1.4
	Yr	77	219	26	64	5	1	0	11	12	0	.292	.329	.324	85	-4	1			.981	-4	O-60	-1.1
1942	Phi-N	101	287	23	75	7	3	0	10	16	6	.261	.300	.307	82	-7	0			.967	-1	O-75	-1.2
1944	Bro-N	15	14	3	4	1	0	0	1	3	0	.286	.412	.286	101	0	0			1.000	-2	/O-4	-0.2
	Pit-N	19	14	2	5	0	0	0	2	0	0	.357	.438	.357	120	1	0			1.000	-2	/O-7	-0.2
	Yr	34	28	5	9	0	0	0	3	5	0	.321	.424	.321	110	1	0			1.000	-4	O-11	-0.4
1945	Pit-N	23	19	5	5	0	0	0	1	1	3	.263	.300	.263	55	-1	0			1.000	-0	/O-3	-0.1
Total 18		1993	7772	1201	2459	281	118	27	598	420	173	.316	.353	.393	99	-13	67			.983	76	*O-1818/2-2,3	-3.4

■ PAUL WANER
Waner, Paul Glee "Big Poison" b: 4/16/03, Harrah, Okla. d: 8/29/65, Sarasota, Fla. BL/TL, 5'8.5", 153 lbs. Deb: 4/13/26 FCH

YEAR	TM/L	G	AB	R	H	2B	3B	HR	RBI	BB	SO	AVG	OBP	SLG	PRO+	BR/A	SB	CS	SBR	FA	FR	G/POS	TPR
1926	Pit-N	144	536	101	180	35	22	8	79	66	19	.336	.413	.528	144	34	11			.976	8	*O-139	3.1
1927	*Pit-N	155	623	114	237	42	18	9	131	60	14	.380	.437	.549	152	46	5			.980	8	*O-143,1-14	4.2
1928	Pit-N	152	602	142	223	50	19	6	86	77	16	.370	.446	.547	152	48	6			.975	5	*O-131,1-24	4.0
1929	Pit-N	151	596	131	200	43	15	15	100	89	24	.336	.424	.534	133	32	15			.986	2	*O-143/1-7	2.1
1930	Pit-N	145	589	117	217	32	18	8	77	57	18	.368	.428	.525	128	29	18			.959	-3	*O-143	1.4
1931	Pit-N	150	559	88	180	35	10	6	70	73	21	.322	.404	.453	131	27	6			.976	15	*O-138,1-10	3.1
1932	Pit-N	154	630	107	215	62	10	8	82	56	24	.341	.397	.510	144	39	13			.974	3	*O-154	3.2
1933	Pit-N★	154	618	101	191	38	16	7	70	60	20	.309	.372	.456	136	29	5			.981	5	*O-154	2.7
1934	Pit-N★	146	599	122	217	32	16	14	90	68	24	.362	.429	.539	154	47	8			.985	7	*O-145	4.6
1935	Pit-N★	139	549	98	176	29	12	11	78	61	22	.321	.392	.477	128	23	2			.983	3	*O-136	2.0
1936	Pit-N	148	585	107	218	53	9	5	94	74	29	.373	.446	.520	156	48	7			.960	9	*O-145	4.9
1937	Pit-N★	154	619	94	219	30	9	5	74	63	34	.354	.413	.441	132	30	4			.970	1	*O-150/1-3	2.5
1938	Pit-N	148	625	77	175	31	6	6	69	47	28	.280	.331	.378	94	-5	3			.977	-3	*O-147	-1.3
1939	Pit-N	125	461	62	151	30	6	3	45	35	18	.328	.375	.438	120	13	0			.978	2	*O-106	1.1
1940	Pit-N	89	238	52	69	16	1	1	32	23	14	.290	.352	.378	102	1	0			.985	-5	O-45/1-8	-0.7
1941	Bro-N	11	35	5	6	0	0	0	4	8	0	.171	.326	.171	41	-2	0			.923	-2	/O-9	-0.5
	Bos-N	95	294	40	82	10	2	2	46	47	14	.279	.384	.347	110	6	1			.965	-4	O-77/1-7	-0.3
	Yr	106	329	45	88	10	2	2	50	55	14	.267	.372	.328	102	3	1			.961	-6	O-86/1-7	-0.8
1942	Bos-N	114	333	43	86	17	1	1	39	62	20	.258	.376	.324	108	1	2			.969	-8	O-94	-0.7
1943	Bro-N	82	225	29	70	6	1	0	26	35	9	.311	.400	.396	132	5	0			.960	-1	O-57	0.7
1944	Bro-N	83	136	16	39	4	1	0	16	27	7	.287	.405	.331	111	4	0			.983	-2	O-32	0.0
	NY-A	9	7	1	1	0	0	0	1	2	1	.143	.333	.143	37	-0	1	0	0	.000	0	H	0.0
1945	NY-A	1	1	0	0	0	0	0	0	1	0	—	1.000	—	191	0	0			.000	0	H	0.0
Total 20		2549	9459	1627	3152	605	191	113	1309	1091	376	.333	.404	.473	133	464	104	0		.975	40	*O-2288/1-73	36.1

■ JACK WANNER
Wanner, Clarence Curtis "Johnny" b: 11/29/1885, Geneseo, Ill. d: 5/28/19, Geneseo, Ill. BR/TR, 5'11.5", 190 lbs. Deb: 9/28/09

YEAR	TM/L	G	AB	R	H	2B	3B	HR	RBI	BB	SO	AVG	OBP	SLG	PRO+	BR/A	SB	CS	SBR	FA	FR	G/POS	TPR
1909	NY-A	3	8	0	1	0	0	0	0	2		.125	.300	.125	35	-0	1			.600	-2	/S-2	-0.3

■ PEE-WEE WANNINGER
Wanninger, Paul Louis b: 12/12/02, Birmingham, Ala. d: 3/7/81, N.Augusta, S.C. BL/TR, 5'7", 150 lbs. Deb: 4/22/25

YEAR	TM/L	G	AB	R	H	2B	3B	HR	RBI	BB	SO	AVG	OBP	SLG	PRO+	BR/A	SB	CS	SBR	FA	FR	G/POS	TPR
1925	NY-A	117	403	35	95	13	6	1	22	11	34	.236	.256	.305	43	-36	3	5	-2	.944	-6	*S-111/3-3,2	-3.1
1927	Bos-A	18	60	4	12	0	0	0	3	5	6	.200	.284	.200	28	-6	2	4	-2	.890	-4	S-15	-0.8
	Cin-N	28	93	14	23	2	2	0	8	6	7	.247	.293	.312	64	-5	0			.953	6	S-28	0.4
Total 2		163	556	53	130	15	8	1	31	23	43	.234	.266	.295	45	-47	5	9		.941	-1	S-154/3-3,2	-3.5

■ AARON WARD
Ward, Aaron Lee b: 8/28/1896, Booneville, Ark. d: 1/30/61, New Orleans, La. BR/TR, 5'10.5", 160 lbs. Deb: 8/14/17

YEAR	TM/L	G	AB	R	H	2B	3B	HR	RBI	BB	SO	AVG	OBP	SLG	PRO+	BR/A	SB	CS	SBR	FA	FR	G/POS	TPR
1917	NY-A	8	26	0	3	0	0	0	1	1	5	.115	.148	.115	-19	-4	0			.926	-2	/S-7	-0.7
1918	NY-A	20	32	2	4	1	0	0	1	2	7	.125	.176	.156	0	-4	0			.941	4	S-12/O-4,2	0.0
1919	NY-A	27	34	5	7	2	0	0	2	5	6	.206	.308	.265	61	-2	0			1.000	2	/1-5,3-3,S2	0.0
1920	NY-A	127	496	62	127	18	7	11	54	33	84	.256	.304	.387	79	-17	7	5	-1	.965	22	*3-114,S-12	1.1
1921	*NY-A	153	556	77	170	30	10	5	75	42	68	.306	.363	.423	98	-2	6	4	-3	.961	19	*2-124,3-33	1.8
1922	*NY-A	154	558	69	149	19	5	7	68	45	64	.267	.328	.357	77	-19	6	4	-2	.974	3	*2-152/3-2	-1.3
1923	*NY-A	152	567	79	161	26	11	10	82	50	65	.284	.351	.422	101	-0	8	8	-2	.980	14	*2-152	1.2
1924	NY-A	120	400	42	101	13	10	8	66	40	45	.253	.326	.387	85	-11	4	4	-2	.973	8	*2-120/S-1	-0.4
1925	NY-A	125	439	41	108	22	3	4	38	49	49	.246	.326	.337	70	-20	1	4	-2	.966	-11	*2-113,3-3,2	-0.4
1926	NY-A	22	31	5	10	2	0	0	5	5	8	.323	.364	.387	97	-0	0			1.000	-4	/2-4,3-1	-0.4
1927	Chi-A	145	463	75	125	25	8	5	56	63	56	.270	.360	.391	97	-1	6	5	-1	.963	-19	*2-139/3-6	-1.6

YEAR	TM/L	G	AB	R	H	2B	3B	HR	RBI	BB	SO	AVG	OBP	SLG	PRO+	BR/A	SB	CS	SBR	FA	FR	G/POS	TPR
1928	Cle-A	6	9	0	1	0	0	0	0	1	2	.111	.200	.111	-16	-2	0	0	0	.818	2	/3-3,S-2,2	0.1
Total	12	1059	3611	457	966	158	54	50	446	339	457	.268	.335	.383	85	-81	36	38		.970	36	2-809,3-172/S10	-3.1

■ CHUCK WARD
Ward, Charles William b: 7/30/1894, St.Louis, Mo. d: 4/4/69, Indian Rocks, Fla. BR/TR, 5'11.5", 170 lbs. Deb: 4/11/17

YEAR	TM/L	G	AB	R	H	2B	3B	HR	RBI	BB	SO	AVG	OBP	SLG	PRO+	BR/A	SB	CS	SBR	FA	FR	G/POS	TPR
1917	Pit-N	125	423	25	100	12	3	0	43	32	43	.236	.302	.279	76	-11	5			.912	-27	*S-112/2-8,3	-3.7
1918	Bro-N	2	6	0	2	0	0	0	3	0	0	.333	.333	.333	104	-0	0			1.000	-1	/3-2	-0.1
1919	Bro-N	45	150	7	35	1	2	0	8	7	11	.233	.277	.267	62	-7	0			.920	-6	3-45	-1.2
1920	Bro-N	19	71	7	11	1	0	0	4	3	3	.155	.200	.169	6	-8	1	0	0	.928	-9	S-19	-1.7
1921	Bro-N	12	28	1	2	1	0	0	0	4	2	.071	.188	.107	-19	-5	0	0	0	.937	4	S-12	0.0
1922	Bro-N	33	91	12	25	5	1	0	14	5	8	.275	.320	.352	74	-4	1	1	-0	.934	-3	S-31/3-2	-0.4
Total	6	236	769	52	175	20	6	0	72	51	67	.228	.286	.269	63	-35	7	1		.919	-41	S-174/3-54,2	-7.1

■ CHRIS WARD
Ward, Chris Gilbert b: 5/18/49, Oakland, Cal. BL/TL, 6', 180 lbs. Deb: 9/10/72

YEAR	TM/L	G	AB	R	H	2B	3B	HR	RBI	BB	SO	AVG	OBP	SLG	PRO+	BR/A	SB	CS	SBR	FA	FR	G/POS	TPR
1972	Chi-N	1	1	0	0	0	0	0	0	0	0	.000	.000	.000	-90	-0	0	0	0	.000	0	H	0.0
1974	Chi-N	92	137	8	28	4	0	1	15	18	13	.204	.297	.255	53	-8	0	2	-1	.977	1	O-22/1-6	-0.9
Total	2	93	138	8	28	4	0	1	15	18	13	.203	.295	.254	52	-8	0	2	-1	.977	1	/O-22,1-6	-0.9

■ PIGGY WARD
Ward, Frank Gray b: 4/16/1867, Chambersburg, Pa. d: 10/24/12, Altoona, Pa. TR, 5'9.5", 196 lbs. Deb: 6/12/1883

YEAR	TM/L	G	AB	R	H	2B	3B	HR	RBI	BB	SO	AVG	OBP	SLG	PRO+	BR/A	SB	CS	SBR	FA	FR	G/POS	TPR
1883	Phi-N	1	5	0	0	0	0	0	0	0	2	.000	.000	.000	-99	-1				1.000	-1	/3-1	-0.2
1889	Phi-N	7	25	0	4	1	0	0	4	0	7	.160	.160	.200	0	-3	1			.848	-2	/2-6,O-1	-0.5
1891	Pit-N	6	18	3	6	0	0	0	2	3	3	.333	.455	.333	134	1	3			.833	-1	/O-5	0.0
1892	Bal-N	56	186	28	54	6	5	1	33	31	18	.290	.403	.392	137	10	10			.892	1	O-43/2-7,SC	0.9
1893	Bal-N	11	49	11	12	1	3	0	5	5	2	.245	.327	.388	88	-1	4			.846	-1	/O-9,1-2	-0.2
	Cin-N	42	150	44	42	4	1	0	10	37	10	.280	.440	.320	101	3	27			.827	-2	O-40/1-1	-0.1
	Yr	53	199	55	54	5	4	0	15	42	12	.271	.415	.337	99	2	31			.832	-3	O-49/1-3	-0.3
1894	Was-N	98	347	86	105	11	7	0	36	80	31	.303	.419	.375	103	9	41			.900	-23	2-79,O-12/S3	-0.9
Total	6	221	780	172	223	23	16	1	90	156	73	.286	.419	.360	106	17	86			.852	-29	O-110/2-92,S13C	-1.0

■ GARY WARD
Ward, Gary Lamell b: 12/6/53, Los Angeles, Cal. BR/TR, 6'2", 202 lbs. Deb: 9/3/79

YEAR	TM/L	G	AB	R	H	2B	3B	HR	RBI	BB	SO	AVG	OBP	SLG	PRO+	BR/A	SB	CS	SBR	FA	FR	G/POS	TPR
1979	Min-A	10	14	2	4	0	0	0	1	3	3	.286	.412	.286	89	-0	0	1	-1	1.000	-1	/O-5	-0.1
1980	Min-A	13	41	11	19	6	2	1	10	3	6	.463	.500	.780	228	7	0	0	0	1.000	-2	O-12	0.4
1981	Min-A	85	295	42	78	7	6	3	29	28	48	.264	.328	.359	92	-3	5	2	0	.975	6	O-80/D-2	0.0
1982	Min-A	152	570	85	165	33	7	28	91	37	105	.289	.334	.519	127	19	13	1	3	.989	13	*O-150/D-2	3.0
1983	Min-A★	157	623	76	173	34	5	19	88	44	98	.278	.328	.440	105	4	8	1	2	.978	**26**	*O-152/D-2	2.6
1984	Tex-A	155	602	97	171	21	7	21	79	55	95	.284	.344	.447	113	10	7	5	-1	.987	12	*O-148/D-5	1.7
1985	Tex-A★	154	593	77	170	28	7	15	70	39	97	.287	.332	.433	106	4	26	7	4	.969	2	*O-153/D-1	0.5
1986	Tex-A	105	380	54	120	15	2	5	51	31	72	.316	.373	.405	109	6	12	8	-1	.996	13	*O-104/D-1	1.4
1987	NY-A	146	529	65	131	22	1	16	78	33	101	.248	.293	.384	78	-17	9	1	2	.985	-4	O-94,D-36,1	-2.3
1988	NY-A	91	231	26	52	8	0	4	24	24	41	.225	.304	.312	73	-8	0	1	-1	.992	-4	O-54,1-11/3D	-1.5
1989	NY-A	8	17	3	5	1	0	0	1	3	5	.294	.400	.353	115	1	0	0	0	1.000	-1	/O-6,D-1	-0.1
	Det-A	105	275	24	69	10	2	9	29	21	54	.251	.304	.400	99	-1	1	3	-2	.990	0	O-51,1-26,D	-0.6
	Yr	113	292	27	74	11	2	9	30	24	59	.253	.310	.397	100	-1	1	3	-2	.991	-1	O-57,D-27,1	-0.7
1990	Det-A	106	309	32	79	11	2	9	46	30	55	.256	.324	.392	98	-1	2	0	1	.988	-4	O-85,D-13/1	-0.7
Total	12	1287	4479	594	1236	196	41	130	597	351	775	.276	.330	.425	104	20	83	30	7	.984	55	*O-1094/D-98,13	4.3

■ JIM WARD
Ward, James H. H. b: 3/2/1855, Boston, Mass. d: 6/4/1886, Boston, Mass. Deb: 8/3/1876

YEAR	TM/L	G	AB	R	H	2B	3B	HR	RBI	BB	SO	AVG	OBP	SLG	PRO+	BR/A	SB	CS	SBR	FA	FR	G/POS	TPR
1876	Phi-N	1	4	1	2	0	0	0	1	0	1	.500	.500	.500	236	1				.750	-0	/C-1	0.0

■ RUBE WARD
Ward, John Andrew b: 2/6/1879, New Lexington, Ohio d: 1/17/45, Akron, Ohio Deb: 4/28/02

YEAR	TM/L	G	AB	R	H	2B	3B	HR	RBI	BB	SO	AVG	OBP	SLG	PRO+	BR/A	SB	CS	SBR	FA	FR	G/POS	TPR
1902	Bro-N	13	31	4	9	1	0	0	2	2		.290	.333	.323	102	-0	0			.850	-1	O-11	-0.2

■ JOHN WARD
Ward, John E. b: Washington, D.C. Deb: 5/23/1884

YEAR	TM/L	G	AB	R	H	2B	3B	HR	RBI	BB	SO	AVG	OBP	SLG	PRO+	BR/A	SB	CS	SBR	FA	FR	G/POS	TPR
1884	Was-U	1	4	0	1	0	0	0		0	0	.250	.250	.250	38	-0				.000	-1	/O-1	-0.1

■ JAY WARD
Ward, John Francis b: 9/9/38, Brookfield, Mo. BR/TR, 6'1", 185 lbs. Deb: 5/6/63   C

YEAR	TM/L	G	AB	R	H	2B	3B	HR	RBI	BB	SO	AVG	OBP	SLG	PRO+	BR/A	SB	CS	SBR	FA	FR	G/POS	TPR
1963	Min-A	9	15	0	1	0	0	0	2	1	5	.067	.125	.133	-27	-3	0	0	0	1.000	-1	/3-4,O-1	-0.3
1964	Min-A	12	31	4	7	2	0	0	2	6	13	.226	.351	.290	80	-1	0	0	0	.977	0	/2-9,O-3	0.0
1970	Cin-N	6	3	0	0	0	0	0	0	2	1	.000	.400	.000	17	-0	0	0	0	1.000	-0	/3-2,1-1,2	0.0
Total	3	27	49	4	8	3	0	0	4	9	19	.163	.293	.224	46	-3	0	0	0	.977	-1	/2-10,3-6,O1	-0.3

■ JOHN WARD
Ward, John Montgomery b: 3/3/1860, Bellefonte, Pa. d: 3/4/25, Augusta, Ga. BL/TR, 5'9", 165 lbs. Deb: 7/15/1878   MH

YEAR	TM/L	G	AB	R	H	2B	3B	HR	RBI	BB	SO	AVG	OBP	SLG	PRO+	BR/A	SB	CS	SBR	FA	FR	G/POS	TPR
1878	Pro-N	37	138	14	27	5	4	1	15	2	13	.196	.207	.312	69	-5				.866	2	P-37	0.0
1879	Pro-N	83	364	71	104	9	4	2	41	7	14	.286	.299	.349	115	6				.938	3	*P-70,3-16/O	0.1
1880	Pro-N	86	356	53	81	12	2	0	27	6	16	.228	.240	.272	76	-9				.983	14	*P-70,3-25/OM	0.7
1881	Pro-N	85	357	56	87	18	6	0	53	5	10	.244	.254	.328	83	-7				.887	6	O-40,P-39,S	-0.3
1882	Pro-N	83	355	58	87	10	3	1	39	13	22	.245	.272	.299	83	-7				.824	10	O-50,P-33/S	0.1
1883	NY-N	88	380	76	97	18	7	7	54	8	25	.255	.271	.395	100	-0				.859	19	O-56,P-34/3S2	1.3
1884	NY-N	113	482	98	122	8	2	6	51	28	47	.253	.294	.322	91	-5				.847	8	O-59,2-47/PM	0.2
1885	NY-N	111	446	72	101	8	9	0	37	17	39	.226	.255	.285	75	-12				.904	6	*S-111	-0.4
1886	NY-N	122	491	82	134	17	5	2	81	19	25	.273	.300	.340	93	-5	36			.870	-3	*S-122	-0.6
1887	NY-N	129	545	114	184	16	5	1	53	29	12	.338	.375	.391	119	15	**111**			**.919**	30	*S-129	3.9
1888	*NY-N	122	510	70	128	14	5	4	49	9	13	.251	.265	.310	84	-10	38			.857	-3	*S-122	-1.0
1889	*NY-N	114	479	87	143	13	4	1	67	27	7	.299	.339	.349	92	-5	62			.890	6	*S-108/2-7	0.6
1890	Bro-P	128	561	134	189	15	12	4	60	51	22	.337	.394	.428	113	8	63			.878	21	*S-128,M	2.9
1891	Bro-N	105	441	85	122	13	5	0	39	36	10	.277	.335	.329	94	-3	57			.878	-0	*S-87,2-18M	0.3
1892	Bro-N	148	614	109	163	13	3	1	47	39	19	.265	.355	.301	103	6	**88**			.920	3	*2-148,M	1.1
1893	NY-N	135	588	129	193	27	9	2	77	47	5	.328	.379	.415	111	8	46			.918	7	*2-134,M	1.5
1894	*NY-N	136	540	100	143	13	6	0	77	34	6	.265	.310	.306	49	-45	39			.924	5	*2-136,M	-2.6
Total	17	1825	7647	1408	2105	231	96	26	867	420	326	.275	.314	.341	93	-68	540			.885	133	S-826,2-491,PO/3	7.8

■ JOE WARD
Ward, Joseph A. b: 9/2/1884, Philadelphia, Pa. d: 8/11/34, Philadelphia, Pa. TR, Deb: 4/24/06

YEAR	TM/L	G	AB	R	H	2B	3B	HR	RBI	BB	SO	AVG	OBP	SLG	PRO+	BR/A	SB	CS	SBR	FA	FR	G/POS	TPR
1906	Phi-N	35	129	12	38	8	6	0	11	5		.295	.321	.450	140	5	2			.929	-6	3-27/2-3,S	0.0
1909	NY-A	9	28	3	5	0	0	0	0	1		.179	.233	.179	30	-2	2			.846	-5	/2-7,1-1	-0.9
	Phi-N	74	184	21	49	8	2	0	23	9		.266	.304	.332	96	-1	7			.944	-10	2-48/S-8,1O	-1.3
1910	Phi-N	48	124	11	18	2	1	0	13	3	11	.145	.178	.177	4	-15	1			.975	2	1-32/S-1,3	-1.5
Total	3	166	465	47	110	18	9	0	47	18	11	.237	.271	.314	78	-14	12			.929	-20	/2-58,1-38,3SO	-3.7

■ HAP WARD
Ward, Joseph Nichols b: 11/15/1885, Leesburg, N.J. d: 9/13/79, Elmer, N.J. Deb: 5/18/12

YEAR	TM/L	G	AB	R	H	2B	3B	HR	RBI	BB	SO	AVG	OBP	SLG	PRO+	BR/A	SB	CS	SBR	FA	FR	G/POS	TPR
1912	Det-A	1	2	0	0	0	0	0	0	0	0	.000	.000	.000	-99	-1	0			1.000	0	/O-1	0.0

■ KEVIN WARD
Ward, Kevin Michael b: 9/28/61, Lansdale, Pa. BR/TR, 6'1", 195 lbs. Deb: 5/10/91

YEAR	TM/L	G	AB	R	H	2B	3B	HR	RBI	BB	SO	AVG	OBP	SLG	PRO+	BR/A	SB	CS	SBR	FA	FR	G/POS	TPR
1991	SD-N	44	107	13	26	7	2	2	8	9	27	.243	.308	.402	95	-1	1	4	-2	.982	-2	O-33	-0.6
1992	SD-N	81	147	12	29	5	0	3	12	14	38	.197	.276	.293	60	-8	2	3	-1	.946	-6	O-51	-1.7
Total	2	125	254	25	55	12	2	5	20	23	65	.217	.289	.339	75	-9	3	7	-3	.961	-9	/O-84	-2.3

YEAR	TM/L	G	AB	R	H	2B	3B	HR	RBI	BB	SO	AVG	OBP	SLG	PRO+	BR/A	SB	CS	SBR	FA	FR	G/POS	TPR

■ PETE WARD
Ward, Peter Thomas b: 7/26/39, Montreal, Que., Can BL/TR, 6'1", 200 lbs. Deb: 9/21/62 C

1962	Bal-A	8	21	1	3	2	0	0	2	4	5	.143	.280	.238	44	-2	0	0	0	1.000	-0	/O-6	-0.2
1963	Chi-A	157	600	80	177	34	6	22	84	52	77	.295	.356	.482	135	27	7	6	-2	.923	-5	*3-154/2-1,S	2.1
1964	Chi-A	144	539	61	152	28	3	23	94	56	76	.282	.352	.473	131	22	1	1	-0	.958	13	*3-138	3.4
1965	Chi-A	138	507	62	125	25	3	10	57	56	83	.247	.329	.367	104	2	4	2	-2	.952	9	*3-134/2-1	0.7
1966	Chi-A	84	251	22	55	7	1	3	28	24	49	.219	.295	.291	74	-8	3	1	0	.989	-2	O-59,3-16/1	-1.4
1967	Chi-A	146	467	49	109	16	2	18	62	61	109	.233	.336	.392	119	12	3	2	-0	.991	-17	O-89,1-39,3	-1.3
1968	Chi-A	125	399	43	86	15	0	15	50	76	85	.216	.335	.366	117	11	4	3	-1	.946	-9	3-77,1-31,O	-0.1
1969	Chi-A	105	199	22	49	7	0	6	32	33	38	.246	.362	.372	101	1	0	0	0	.994	-2	1-25,3-21/O	-0.3
1970	NY-A	66	77	5	20	2	2	1	18	9	17	.260	.337	.377	102	0	0	0	0	1.000	-1	1-13	-0.1
Total	9	973	3060	345	776	136	17	98	427	371	539	.254	.342	.405	116	65	20	17	-4	.945	-14	3-562,O-185,1/2S	2.8

■ PRESTON WARD
Ward, Preston Meyer b: 7/24/27, Columbia, Mo. BL/TR, 6'3", 198 lbs. Deb: 4/20/48

1948	Bro-N	42	146	9	38	9	2	1	21	15	23	.260	.329	.370	86	-3	0			.990	-2	1-38	-0.5
1950	Chi-N	80	285	31	72	11	2	6	33	27	42	.253	.317	.368	81	-8	3			.995	10	1-76	0.0
1953	Chi-N	33	100	10	23	5	0	4	12	18	21	.230	.347	.400	92	-1	3	1	0	.961	-7	O-27/1-7	-0.8
	Pit-N	88	281	35	59	7	1	8	27	44	39	.210	.319	.327	69	-12	1	3	-2	.991	4	1-78	-1.2
	Yr	121	381	45	82	12	1	12	39	62	60	.215	.327	.346	76	-13	4	4	-1	.991	-2	1-85,O-27	-2.0
1954	Pit-N	117	360	37	97	16	2	7	48	39	61	.269	.341	.383	90	-5	0	0	0	.984	5	1-48,O-42,3	-0.4
1955	Pit-N	84	179	16	38	7	4	5	25	22	22	.212	.299	.380	80	-6	0	0	0	.998	2	1-48/O-1	-0.6
1956	Pit-N	16	30	3	10	0	1	1	11	6	4	.333	.444	.500	157	3	0	0	0	1.000	-5	/3-5,O-5	-0.2
	Cle-A	87	150	18	38	10	0	6	21	16	20	.253	.325	.440	98	-1	0	0	0	.988	2	1-60,O-17	-0.1
1957	Cle-A	10	11	2	2	1	0	0	0	0	2	.182	.182	.273	23	-1	0	0	0	1.000	-1	/1-1	-0.1
1958	Cle-A	48	148	22	50	3	1	4	21	10	27	.338	.384	.453	133	6	0	1	-1	.957	-3	3-24,1-21	0.2
	KC-A	81	268	28	68	10	1	6	24	27	36	.254	.322	.366	87	-5	0	1	-1	.989	-7	1-39,3-34/O	-1.5
	Yr	129	416	50	118	13	2	10	45	37	63	.284	.344	.397	103	2	0	2	-1	.992	-10	1-60,3-58/O	-1.3
1959	KC-A	58	109	8	27	4	1	2	19	7	12	.248	.293	.358	76	-4	0	0	0	.982	-3	1-22/O-1	-0.8
Total	9	744	2067	219	522	83	15	50	262	231	315	.253	.328	.380	88	-36	7	6		.992	-3	1-438/O-95,3	-6.0

■ TURNER WARD
Ward, Turner Max b: 4/11/65, Orlando, Fla. BB/TR, 6'2", 200 lbs. Deb: 9/10/90

1990	Cle-A	14	46	10	16	2	1	1	10	3	8	.348	.388	.500	147	3	3	0	1	.957	0	O-13/D-1	0.4
1991	Cle-A	40	100	11	23	7	0	0	5	10	16	.230	.300	.300	66	-4	0	0	0	1.000	-2	O-38	-0.7
	Tor-A	8	13	1	4	0	0	0	2	1	2	.308	.357	.308	83	-0	0	0	0	1.000	-1	/O-6	-0.2
	Yr	48	113	12	27	7	0	0	7	11	18	.239	.306	.301	68	-5	0	0	0	1.000	0	O-44	-0.9
1992	Tor-A	18	29	7	10	3	0	1	3	4	4	.345	.424	.552	164	3	0	1	-1	1.000	-1	O-12	0.1
1993	Tor-A	72	167	20	32	4	2	4	28	23	26	.192	.293	.311	62	-9	3	3	-1	.990	-7	O-65/1-1	-1.7
1994	Mil-A	102	367	55	85	15	2	9	45	52	68	.232	.332	.357	76	-13	6	2	1	.985	3	O-99/3-1	-1.0
Total	5	254	722	104	170	31	5	15	93	93	124	.235	.326	.355	79	-21	12	6	0	.988	-8	O-233/3-1,1D	-3.1

■ BUZZY WARES
Wares, Clyde Ellsworth b: 3/23/1886, Vandalia, Mich. d: 5/26/64, South Bend, Ind. BR/TR, 5'10", 150 lbs. Deb: 9/15/13 C

1913	StL-A	11	35	5	10	2	0	0	1	1	3	.286	.306	.343	92	-1	2			.973	-4	/2-9	-0.5
1914	StL-A	81	215	20	45	10	1	0	23	28	35	.209	.300	.265	73	-7	10	10	-3	.903	-2	S-68/2-8	-0.7
Total	2	92	250	25	55	12	1	0	24	29	38	.220	.301	.276	76	-7	12	10		.973	-6	/S-68,2-17	-1.2

■ FRED WARNER
Warner, Frederick John Rodney b: 1855, Philadelphia, Pa. d: 2/13/1886, Philadelphia, Pa. 5'7", 155 lbs. Deb: 4/30/1875

1875	Cen-n	14	57	11	14	1	0	0		1		.246	.259	.263	88	-0						O-14	0.0
1876	Phi-N	1	3	0	0	0	0	0	0	0	0	.000	.000	.000	-99	-1				.600	-0	/O-1	-0.1
1878	Ind-N	43	165	19	41	4	0	0	10	2	15	.248	.257	.273	86	-2				.907	-3	*S-41/O-2	-0.3
1879	Cle-N	76	316	32	77	11	4	0	22	2	20	.244	.248	.304	82	-6				.827	3	O-54,O-21/1	-0.5
1883	Phi-N	39	141	13	32	6	1	0	13	5	21	.227	.253	.284	69	-5				.775	-9	3-38/O-1	-1.2
1884	Bro-a	84	352	40	78	4	0	1		17		.222	.259	.241	64	-13				.824	-6	*3-84	-1.7
Total	5	243	977	104	228	25	5	1	45	26	56	.233	.254	.272	73	-27				.815	-18	3-176/S-41,O1	-3.8

■ HOOKS WARNER
Warner, Hoke Hayden b: 5/22/1894, Del Rio, Tex. d: 2/19/47, San Francisco, Cal BL/TR, 5'10.5", 170 lbs. Deb: 8/21/16

1916	Pit-N	44	168	12	40	1	1	2	14	6	19	.238	.264	.292	70	-6	6			.899	-11	3-42/2-1	-1.9
1917	Pit-N	3	5	0	1	0	0	0	0	0	1	.200	.200	.200	22	-0	0			1.000	1	/3-1	0.1
1919	Pit-N	6	8	0	1	0	0	0	2	3	1	.125	.364	.125	48	-0	0			.818	1	/3-3	0.0
1921	Chi-A	14	38	4	8	1	0	0	3	2	1	.211	.268	.237	35	-3	1	1	-0	.957	-1	3-10	-0.4
Total	4	67	219	16	50	2	1	2	19	11	22	.228	.268	.274	61	-10	7	1		.906	-10	/3-56,2-1	-2.2

■ JOHN WARNER
Warner, John Joseph b: 8/15/1872, New York, N.Y. d: 12/21/43, Far Rockaway, N.Y. BL/TR, 5'11", 165 lbs. Deb: 4/23/1895

1895	Bos-N	3	7	2	1	0	0	0	1	1	0	.143	.333	.143	24	-1	0			.917	1	/C-3	0.0
	Lou-N	67	232	20	62	4	2	1	20	11	16	.267	.320	.315	68	-11	10			.931	-10	C-64/1-3,2	-1.2
	Yr	70	239	22	63	4	2	1	21	12	16	.264	.320	.310	67	-11	10			.930	-10	C-67/1-3,2	-1.2
1896	Lou-N	33	110	9	25	1	1	0	10	10	10	.227	.303	.255	50	-8	3			.939	9	C-32/1-1	0.4
	NY-N	19	54	9	14	1	0	0	3	3	7	.259	.310	.278	57	-3	1			.922	-1	C-19	-0.2
	Yr	52	164	18	39	2	1	0	13	13	17	.238	.306	.262	52	-11	4			.934	9	C-51/1-1	0.2
1897	NY-N	110	397	50	109	6	3	2	51	26		.275	.344	.320	78	-11	8			.952	16	*C-110	1.4
1898	NY-N	110	373	40	96	14	5	0	42	22		.257	.316	.322	86	-7	9			.968	15	*C-109/O-1	1.7
1899	NY-N	88	293	38	78	8	1	0	19	15		.266	.315	.300	72	-11	15			.952	12	C-82/1-3	0.7
1900	NY-N	34	108	15	27	4	0	0	13	8		.250	.319	.287	71	-4	1			.948	3	C-31	0.1
1901	NY-N	87	291	19	70	6	1	0	20	3		.241	.268	.268	58	-16	3			.967	-3	C-84	-1.1
1902	Bos-A	65	222	19	52	5	7	0	12	13		.234	.286	.320	66	-11	0			.979	4	C-64	0.0
1903	NY-N	89	285	38	81	8	5	0	34	7		.284	.322	.347	87	-5	5			**.986**	12	C-85	1.4
1904	NY-N	86	287	29	57	5	1	1	15	14		.199	.253	.233	48	-17	7			**.982**	2	C-86	-0.7
1905	StL-N	41	137	9	35	2	2	1	12	6		.255	.301	.321	88	-2	2			.958	3	C-41	0.5
	Det-A	36	119	12	24	3	2	0	7	8		.202	.252	.269	65	-5	2			.974	6	C-36	0.0
1906	Det-A	50	153	15	37	4	2	0	10	12		.242	.326	.294	92	-1	4			.978	9	C-49	1.3
	Was-A	32	103	5	21	4	1	1	9	2		.204	.226	.291	65	-5	3			.968	9	C-32	0.8
	Yr	82	256	20	58	8	3	1	19	14		.227	.288	.293	82	-5	7			.974	18	C-81	2.1
1907	Was-A	72	207	11	53	5	0	0	17	12		.256	.306	.280	95	-1	3			.971	-8	C-64	-0.4
1908	Was-A	51	116	8	28	2	1	0	8	8		.241	.313	.276	100	0	7			.982	1	C-41/1-1	0.5
Total	14	1073	3494	348	870	81	35	6	303	181	33	.249	.303	.297	74	-118	83			.966	74	*C-1032/1-8,O2	5.2

■ JACKIE WARNER
Warner, John Joseph b: 8/1/43, Monrovia, Cal. BR/TR, 6', 180 lbs. Deb: 4/12/66

1966	Cal-A	45	123	22	26	4	1	7	16	9	55	.211	.265	.431	99	-1	0	0	0	.984	-2	O-37	-0.4

■ JACK WARNER
Warner, John Ralph b: 8/29/03, Evansville, Ind. d: 3/13/86, Mt.Vernon, Ill. BR/TR, 5'9.5", 165 lbs. Deb: 9/24/25

1925	Det-A	10	39	7	13	0	0	0	2	3	6	.333	.381	.333	84	-1	0	0	0	1.000	-2	3-10	-0.2
1926	Det-A	100	311	41	78	8	6	0	34	38	24	.251	.342	.315	71	-12	8	4	0	.956	-4	3-95/S-3	-1.0
1927	Det-A	139	559	78	149	22	9	1	45	47	45	.267	.330	.343	74	-21	14	4	0	.947	-5	*3-138	-1.7
1928	Det-A	75	206	33	44	4	4	0	13	16	15	.214	.274	.272	43	-17	4	4	-1	.944	6	3-52/S-7	-0.9
1929	Bro-N	17	62	3	17	2	0	0	4	7	6	.274	.348	.306	65	-2	3			.945	-2	S-17	-0.3
1930	Bro-N	21	25	4	8	1	0	0	0	2	7	.320	.370	.360	79	-1	1			1.000	2	/3-8	0.1

YEAR	TM/L	G	AB	R	H	2B	3B	HR	RBI	BB	SO	AVG	OBP	SLG	PRO+	BR/A	SB	CS	SBR	FA	FR	G/POS	TPR
1931	Bro-N	9	4	2	2	0	0	0	0	1	1	.500	.600	.500	200	1	0			1.000	2	/S-2,3-1	0.3
1933	Phi-N	107	340	31	76	15	1	0	22	28	33	.224	.285	.274	53	-20	1			.973	3	2-71,3-30/S	-1.2
Total	8	478	1546	199	387	52	20	1	120	142	137	.250	.319	.312	65	-75	31	12		.950	0	3-334/2-71,S	-4.9

■ HAL WARNOCK
Warnock, Harold Charles b: 1/6/12, New York, N.Y. BL/TR, 6'2", 180 lbs. Deb: 9/2/35

YEAR	TM/L	G	AB	R	H	2B	3B	HR	RBI	BB	SO	AVG	OBP	SLG	PRO+	BR/A	SB	CS	SBR	FA	FR	G/POS	TPR
1935	StL-A	6	7	1	2	2	0	0	0	0	3	.286	.286	.571	112	0	0	0	0	1.000	-1	/O-2	-0.1

■ BENNIE WARREN
Warren, Bennie Louis b: 3/2/12, Elk City, Okla. d: 5/11/94, Oklahoma City, Okla. BR/TR, 6'1", 184 lbs. Deb: 9/13/39

YEAR	TM/L	G	AB	R	H	2B	3B	HR	RBI	BB	SO	AVG	OBP	SLG	PRO+	BR/A	SB	CS	SBR	FA	FR	G/POS	TPR
1939	Phi-N	18	56	4	13	0	0	1	7	7	7	.232	.317	.286	65	-3	0			.958	-4	C-17	-0.5
1940	Phi-N	106	289	33	71	6	1	12	34	40	46	.246	.339	.398	107	3	1			.975	-4	C-97/1-1	0.6
1941	Phi-N	121	345	34	74	13	2	9	35	44	66	.214	.309	.342	86	-6	0			.973	-4	*C-110	-0.2
1942	Phi-N	90	225	19	47	6	3	7	20	24	36	.209	.288	.356	92	-3	0			.972	-2	C-78/1-1	0.1
1946	NY-N	39	69	7	11	1	1	4	8	14	21	.159	.301	.377	91	-1	0			.965	1	C-30	0.2
1947	NY-N	3	5	0	1	0	0	0	1	0	0	.200	.200	.200	6	-1	0			1.000	-1	/C-3	-0.1
Total	6	377	989	97	217	26	7	33	104	129	177	.219	.313	.360	92	-11	1			.972	-13	C-335/1-2	0.1

■ BILL WARREN
Warren, William Hackney "Hack" b: 2/11/1883, Missouri d: 1/28/60, Whiteville, Tenn. BR/TR, 5'8", 165 lbs. Deb: 4/30/14

YEAR	TM/L	G	AB	R	H	2B	3B	HR	RBI	BB	SO	AVG	OBP	SLG	PRO+	BR/A	SB	CS	SBR	FA	FR	G/POS	TPR
1914	Ind-F	26	50	5	12	2	0	0	5	5	7	.240	.309	.280	48	-4	2			.931	-5	C-23	-0.8
1915	New-F	5	3	0	1	0	0	0	1	0	0	.333	.333	.333	83	-0	0			1.000	-1	/C-1,1-1	0.0
Total	2	31	53	5	13	2	0	0	6	5	7	.245	.310	.283	50	-4	2			.932	-5	/C-24,1-1	-0.8

■ RABBIT WARSTLER
Warstler, Harold Burton b: 9/13/03, N.Canton, Ohio d: 5/31/64, N.Canton, Ohio BR/TR, 5'7.5", 150 lbs. Deb: 7/24/30

YEAR	TM/L	G	AB	R	H	2B	3B	HR	RBI	BB	SO	AVG	OBP	SLG	PRO+	BR/A	SB	CS	SBR	FA	FR	G/POS	TPR
1930	Bos-A	54	162	16	30	2	3	1	13	20	21	.185	.275	.253	36	-16	2		-1	.947	-3	S-54	-1.3
1931	Bos-A	66	181	20	44	5	3	0	10	15	27	.243	.308	.304	65	-9	2	3	-1	.933	1	2-42,S-19/3	-0.5
1932	Bos-A	115	388	26	82	15	5	0	34	22	43	.211	.259	.276	40	-35	9	6	-1	.939	**28**	*S-107	0.1
1933	Bos-A	92	322	44	70	13	1	1	17	42	36	.217	.308	.273	55	-20	2	4	-2	.951	1	S-87	-1.4
1934	Phi-A	117	419	56	99	19	3	1	36	51	30	.236	.321	.303	64	-22	9	3	1	.969	16	*2-107/S-2	0.1
1935	Phi-A	138	496	62	124	20	7	3	59	56	53	.250	.326	.337	72	-20	8	4	0	.959	2	*2-136/3-2	-0.7
1936	Phi-A	66	236	27	59	8	6	1	24	36	16	.250	.354	.347	75	-9	0	0	0	.973	11	2-66	0.6
	Bos-N	74	304	27	64	6	0	0	17	22	33	.211	.266	.230	37	-27	2			.948	13	S-74	-0.9
1937	Bos-N	149	555	57	124	20	3	0	36	51	62	.223	.291	.276	60	-31	4			.942	-11	*S-149	-3.1
1938	Bos-N	142	467	37	108	10	4	0	40	48	38	.231	.303	.270	65	-22	3			.937	-7	S-135/2-7	-1.9
1939	Bos-N	114	342	34	83	11	3	0	24	24	31	.243	.292	.292	62	-19	2			.953	5	S-49,2-43,3	-1.1
1940	Bos-N	33	57	6	12	0	0	0	4	10	5	.211	.328	.211	54	-3	0			.974	-1	2-24/3-2,S	-0.3
	Chi-N	45	159	19	36	4	1	1	18	18	10	.226	.263	.283	52	-11	1			.939	-1	S-28,2-17	-0.9
	Yr	78	216	25	48	4	1	1	22	18	24	.222	.282	.264	53	-14	1			.960	-2	2-41,S-29/3	-1.2
Total	11	1205	4088	431	935	133	36	11	332	405	414	.229	.300	.287	59	-243	42	22		.942	49	S-705,2-442/3	-11.3

■ CARL WARWICK
Warwick, Carl Wayne b: 2/27/37, Dallas, Tex. BR/TL, 5'10", 170 lbs. Deb: 4/11/61

YEAR	TM/L	G	AB	R	H	2B	3B	HR	RBI	BB	SO	AVG	OBP	SLG	PRO+	BR/A	SB	CS	SBR	FA	FR	G/POS	TPR
1961	LA-N	19	11	2	1	0	0	0	1	2	3	.091	.231	.091	-9	-2	0	0	0	1.000	-4	O-12	-0.6
	StL-N	55	152	27	38	6	2	4	16	24	33	.250	.329	.395	83	-4	3	0	1	.970	-5	O-48	-1.1
	Yr	74	163	29	39	6	2	4	17	20	36	.239	.322	.374	77	-5	3	0	1	.970	-10	O-60	-1.7
1962	StL-N	13	23	4	8	0	0	1	4	2	2	.348	.400	.478	123	1	2	0	1	1.000	-1	O-10	0.0
	Hou-N	130	477	63	124	17	1	16	60	38	77	.260	.315	.400	98	-3	2	3	-1	.986	1	*O-128	-1.1
	Yr	143	500	67	132	17	1	17	64	40	79	.264	.319	.404	98	-3	4	3	-1	.986	-0	*O-138	-1.1
1963	Hou-N	150	528	49	134	19	5	7	47	49	70	.254	.320	.348	98	-1	3	3	-1	.988	-2	*O-141/1-2	-1.3
1964	*StL-N	88	158	14	41	7	1	3	15	11	30	.259	.308	.373	83	-3	2	0	1	.933	-6	O-49	-1.1
1965	StL-N	50	77	3	12	2	1	0	6	4	18	.156	.198	.208	13	-9	1	0	0	.960	-3	O-21/1-4	-1.3
	Bal-A	9	14	3	0	0	0	0	0	3	2	.000	.176	.000	-44	-3	0	0	0	1.000	-1	/O-3	-0.4
1966	Chi-N	16	22	3	5	0	0	0	0	0	6	.227	.227	.227	27	-2	0	0	0	1.000	-2	O-10	-0.4
Total	6	530	1462	168	363	51	10	31	149	127	241	.248	.309	.360	87	-26	13	6	0	.980	-24	O-422/1-6	-7.3

■ BILL WARWICK
Warwick, Firmin Newton b: 11/26/1897, Philadelphia, Pa. d: 12/19/84, San Antonio, Tex. BR/TR, 6'0.5", 180 lbs. Deb: 7/18/21

YEAR	TM/L	G	AB	R	H	2B	3B	HR	RBI	BB	SO	AVG	OBP	SLG	PRO+	BR/A	SB	CS	SBR	FA	FR	G/POS	TPR
1921	Pit-N	1	1	0	0	0	0	0	0	0	0	.000	.000	.000	-97	-0	0	0		.500	-1	/C-1	0.0
1925	StL-N	13	41	8	12	1	2	1	6	5	5	.293	.370	.488	114	1	0	1	-1	1.000	-4	C-13	-0.3
1926	StL-N	9	14	0	5	0	0	0	2	0	2	.357	.357	.357	89	-0	0	0		.923	2	/C-9	0.2
Total	3	23	56	8	17	1	2	1	8	5	7	.304	.361	.446	105	0	0	1		.954	-2	/C-23	-0.1

■ JIMMY WASDELL
Wasdell, James Charles b: 5/15/14, Cleveland, Ohio d: 8/6/83, New Port Richey, Fla. BL/TL, 5'11", 185 lbs. Deb: 9/3/37

YEAR	TM/L	G	AB	R	H	2B	3B	HR	RBI	BB	SO	AVG	OBP	SLG	PRO+	BR/A	SB	CS	SBR	FA	FR	G/POS	TPR
1937	Was-A	32	110	13	28	4	4	2	12	7	13	.255	.299	.418	82	-4	1		-1	.995	-0	1-21/O-7	-0.7
1938	Was-A	53	140	19	33	2	1	2	16	12	12	.236	.296	.307	55	-10	5	2	0	.996	-1	1-26/O-6	-1.3
1939	Was-A	29	109	12	33	5	1	0	13	9	16	.303	.361	.367	94	-1	3	1	0	.964	-2	1-28	-0.6
1940	Was-A	10	35	3	3	1	0	0	0	2	7	.086	.135	.114	-37	-7	0	0	0	1.000	-1	/1-8	-0.9
	Bro-N	77	230	35	64	14	4	3	37	18	24	.278	.333	.413	99	-1	4			.947	-7	O-42,1-17	-1.1
1941	*Bro-N	94	265	39	79	14	3	4	48	16	15	.298	.345	.419	110	3	2			.956	-6	O-54,1-15	-0.8
1942	Pit-N	122	409	44	106	11	2	3	38	47	22	.259	.337	.318	90	-4	1			.957	-3	O-97/1-7	-1.4
1943	Pit-N	4	2	0	1	0	0	0	1	2	0	.500	.750	.500	256	1	0			.000	0	H	0.1
	Phi-N	141	522	54	136	19	6	4	67	46	22	.261	.323	.343	96	-3	6			.988	-8	1-82,O-56	-2.0
	Yr	145	524	54	137	19	6	4	68	46	22	.261	.326	.344	97	-2	6			.988	-8	1-82,O-56	-1.9
1944	Phi-N	133	451	47	125	23	3	3	40	45	17	.277	.344	.355	100	1	0			.980	-9	*O-121/1-4	-1.5
1945	Phi-N	134	500	65	150	19	8	7	60	32	11	.300	.346	.412	113	7	7			.967	-2	O-65,1-63	-0.2
1946	Phi-N	26	51	7	13	0	0	0	5	2	2	.255	.309	.392	101	-0	2			.923	-2	O-11/1-2	-0.3
	Cle-A	32	41	1	11	0	0	0	4	4	4	.268	.333	.268	74	-1	1	0	0	.939	-2	1-4,O-3	0.0
1947	Cle-A	1	1	0	0	0	0	0	0	0	0	.000	.000	.000	-99	-0	0	0	0	.000	0	H	0.0
Total	11	888	2866	339	782	109	34	29	341	243	165	.273	.332	.365	96	-20	29	4		.966	-45	O-462,1-277	-11.0

■ LINK WASEM
Wasem, Lincoln William b: 1/30/11, Birmingham, Ohio d: 3/6/79, S.Laguna, Cal. BR/TR, 5'9.5", 180 lbs. Deb: 5/5/37

YEAR	TM/L	G	AB	R	H	2B	3B	HR	RBI	BB	SO	AVG	OBP	SLG	PRO+	BR/A	SB	CS	SBR	FA	FR	G/POS	TPR
1937	Bos-N	2	1	0	0	0	0	0	0	0	0	.000	.000	.000	-99	-0				1.000	0	/C-2	0.0

■ LIBE WASHBURN
Washburn, Libeus b: 6/16/1874, Lyme, N.H. d: 3/22/40, Malone, N.Y. BB/TL, 5'10", 180 lbs. Deb: 5/30/02

YEAR	TM/L	G	AB	R	H	2B	3B	HR	RBI	BB	SO	AVG	OBP	SLG	PRO+	BR/A	SB	CS	SBR	FA	FR	G/POS	TPR
1902	NY-N	6	9	1	4	0	0	0	0	0	0	.444	.615	.444	229	2	1			1.000	-1	/O-3	0.1
1903	Phi-N	8	18	1	3	0	0	0	1	1		.167	.167	.167	8	-2	0			1.000	-1	/P-4,O-2	-0.1
Total	2	14	27	2	7	0	0	0	1	3		.259	.375	.259	89	-0	1			1.000	-1	/O-5,P-4	0.0

■ CLAUDELL WASHINGTON
Washington, Claudell b: 8/31/54, Los Angeles, Cal. BL/TL, 6', 190 lbs. Deb: 7/5/74

YEAR	TM/L	G	AB	R	H	2B	3B	HR	RBI	BB	SO	AVG	OBP	SLG	PRO+	BR/A	SB	CS	SBR	FA	FR	G/POS	TPR
1974	*Oak-A	73	221	16	63	10	5	0	19	13	44	.285	.328	.376	109	2	6	8	-3	.985	-1	D-38,O-32	-0.5
1975	*Oak-A★	148	590	86	182	24	7	10	77	32	80	.308	.349	.424	120	14	40	15	3	.978	-3	*O-148	0.8
1976	Oak-A	134	490	65	126	20	6	5	53	30	90	.257	.304	.353	96	-4	37	20	-1	.963	-2	*O-126/D-4	-1.3
1977	Tex-A	129	521	63	148	31	2	12	68	25	112	.284	.321	.420	99	-2	21	8	2	.978	-1	*O-127/D-1	-0.7
1978	Tex-A	12	42	1	7	0	0	0	2	1	12	.167	.186	.167	-0	-6	0	1	-1	.917	-1	/O-7,D-4	-0.8
	Chi-A	86	314	33	83	16	5	6	31	12	57	.264	.294	.404	94	-4	5	5	-2	.959	-2	O-82/D-1	-1.1
	Yr	98	356	34	90	16	5	6	33	13	69	.253	.281	.376	83	-9	5	6	-2	.957	-3	O-89/D-5	-1.9
1979	Chi-A	131	471	79	132	33	5	13	66	29	63	.280	.325	.454	108	4	19	11	-1	.974	4	*O-122	0.1
1980	Chi-A	32	90	15	26	4	2	1	12	5	19	.289	.333	.411	103	-0	8	5	0	.933	-2	O-23/D-2	-0.2
	NY-N	79	284	38	78	16	4	10	42	20	63	.275	.325	.465	121	7	17	5	2	.978	2	O-70	0.8

YEAR	TM/L	G	AB	R	H	2B	3B	HR	RBI	BB	SO	AVG	OBP	SLG	PRO+	BR/A	SB	CS	SBR	FA	FR	G/POS	TPR
1981	Atl-N	85	320	37	93	22	3	5	37	15	47	.291	.330	.425	110	3	12	6	0	.993	2	O-79	0.2
1982	*Atl-N	150	563	94	150	24	6	16	80	50	107	.266	.333	.416	104	3	33	10	4	.950	-4	*O-139	-0.2
1983	Atl-N	134	496	75	138	24	8	9	44	35	103	.278	.326	.413	96	-3	31	9	4	.974	2	*O-128	-0.1
1984	Atl-N★	120	416	62	119	21	2	17	61	59	77	.286	.376	.469	127	16	21	9	1	.967	-5	*O-107	0.8
1985	Atl-N	122	398	62	110	14	6	15	43	40	66	.276	.344	.455	115	7	14	4	2	.962	-14	O-99	-0.8
1986	Atl-N	40	137	17	37	11	0	5	14	14	26	.270	.338	.460	112	2	4	7	-3	.957	-5	O-38	-0.8
	NY-A	54	135	19	32	5	0	6	16	7	33	.237	.285	.407	87	-3	6	1	1	.985	-6	O-39	-0.8
1987	NY-A	102	312	42	87	17	0	9	44	27	54	.279	.336	.420	100	-0	10	1	2	.988	5	O-72,D-13	0.0
1988	NY-A	126	455	62	140	22	3	11	64	24	74	.308	.345	.442	120	11	15	6	1	.984	2	*O-117	1.0
1989	Cal-A	110	418	53	114	18	4	13	42	27	84	.273	.315	.428	111	5	13	5	1	.975	-3	*O-100/D-7	0.1
1990	Cal-A	12	34	3	6	1	0	1	3	2	8	.176	.222	.294	44	-3	1	0	0	1.000	1	/O-9	-0.2
	NY-A	33	80	4	13	1	1	0	6	2	17	.162	.183	.200	7	-10	3	1	0	1.000	1	O-21/D-2	-1.0
	Yr	45	114	7	19	2	1	1	9	4	25	.167	.195	.228	18	-13	4	1	1	1.000	2	O-30/D-2	-1.2
Total	17	1912	6787	926	1884	334	69	164	824	468	1266	.278	.328	.420	106	40	312	134	13	.973	-37	*O-1685/D-72	-4.7

■ HERB WASHINGTON
Washington, Herbert Lee   b: 11/16/51, Belzoni, Miss.   BR/TR, 6', 170 lbs.   Deb: 4/4/74

YEAR	TM/L	G	AB	R	H	2B	3B	HR	RBI	BB	SO	AVG	OBP	SLG	PRO+	BR/A	SB	CS	SBR	FA	FR	G/POS	TPR
1974	*Oak-A	92	0	29	0	0	0	0	0	0	0	—	—	—		0	29	16	-1	.000	0	R	-0.3
1975	Oak-A	13	0	4	0	0	0	0	0	0	0	—	—	—		0	2	1	0	.000	0	R	0.0
Total	2	105	0	33	0	0	0	0	0	0	0	—	—	—		0	31	17	-1		0	-0,-0	-0.3

■ LA RUE WASHINGTON
Washington, La Rue   b: 9/7/53, Long Beach, Cal.   BR/TR, 6', 170 lbs.   Deb: 9/7/78

YEAR	TM/L	G	AB	R	H	2B	3B	HR	RBI	BB	SO	AVG	OBP	SLG	PRO+	BR/A	SB	CS	SBR	FA	FR	G/POS	TPR
1978	Tex-A	3	3	0	0	0	0	0	0	0	1	.000	.000	.000	-99	-1	0	0	0	1.000	2	/2-2,D-1	0.1
1979	Tex-A	25	18	5	5	0	0	0	2	4	0	.278	.409	.278	90	0	2	1	0	1.000	-3	O-13/3-1	-0.3
Total	2	28	21	5	5	0	0	0	2	4	1	.238	.360	.238	67	-1	2	1	0	1.000	-1	/O-13,2-2,3D	-0.2

■ RON WASHINGTON
Washington, Ronald   b: 4/29/52, New Orleans, La.   BR/TR, 5'11", 163 lbs.   Deb: 9/10/77

YEAR	TM/L	G	AB	R	H	2B	3B	HR	RBI	BB	SO	AVG	OBP	SLG	PRO+	BR/A	SB	CS	SBR	FA	FR	G/POS	TPR
1977	LA-N	10	19	4	7	0	0	0	1	0	2	.368	.400	.368	108	0	1	1	-0	.857	-2	S-10	-0.1
1981	Min-A	28	84	8	19	3	1	0	5	4	14	.226	.270	.286	56	-5	4	1	1	.951	6	S-26/O-2	0.4
1982	Min-A	119	451	48	122	17	6	5	39	14	29	.271	.292	.368	78	-14	3	3	-1	.972	-44	S-91,2-37/3	-5.1
1983	Min-A	99	317	28	78	7	3	4	26	22	50	.246	.297	.325	69	-13	10	5	0	.962	-17	S-81,2-14/3D	-2.2
1984	Min-A	88	197	25	58	11	5	3	23	4	31	.294	.312	.447	102	0	1	1	1	.978	-16	S-71/2-9,3D	-1.2
1985	Min-A	70	135	24	37	6	4	1	14	8	15	.274	.315	.400	89	-2	5	1	1	.951	-4	S-31,2-24/31D	-0.3
1986	Min-A	48	74	15	19	3	0	4	11	3	21	.257	.286	.459	96	-1	1	2	-1	.917	0	2-16,D-15/S3	-0.2
1987	Bal-A	26	79	7	16	3	1	1	6	1	15	.203	.213	.304	36	-7	0	1	-1	1.000	0	3-20/2-3,OSD	-0.6
1988	Cle-A	69	223	30	57	14	2	2	21	9	35	.256	.300	.363	82	-5	3	5	-1	.933	-14	S-54/3-8,2D	-1.6
1989	Hou-N	7	7	1	1	1	0	0	0	0	4	.143	.143	.286	20	-1	0	0	0	.000	-0	/2-1,3-1	-0.1
Total	10	564	1586	190	414	65	22	20	146	65	266	.261	.294	.368	79	-49	28	18	-2	.958	-88	S-372,2-111/3DO1	-11.0

■ GEORGE WASHINGTON
Washington, Sloan Vernon "Vern"   b: 6/4/07, Linden, Tex.   d: 2/17/85, Linden, Tex.   BL/TR, 5'11.5", 190 lbs.   Deb: 4/17/35

YEAR	TM/L	G	AB	R	H	2B	3B	HR	RBI	BB	SO	AVG	OBP	SLG	PRO+	BR/A	SB	CS	SBR	FA	FR	G/POS	TPR
1935	Chi-A	108	339	40	96	22	3	8	47	10	18	.283	.310	.437	89	-7	1	0	0	.974	0	O-79	-0.9
1936	Chi-A	20	49	6	8	2	0	1	5	1	4	.163	.180	.265	8	-7	0	0	0	.938	-2	O-12	-0.8
Total	2	128	388	46	104	24	3	9	52	11	22	.268	.294	.415	78	-15	1	0	0	.970	-2	/O-91	-1.7

■ U L WASHINGTON
Washington, U L   b: 10/27/53, Stringtown, Okla.   BB/TR, 5'11", 175 lbs.   Deb: 9/6/77

YEAR	TM/L	G	AB	R	H	2B	3B	HR	RBI	BB	SO	AVG	OBP	SLG	PRO+	BR/A	SB	CS	SBR	FA	FR	G/POS	TPR
1977	KC-A	10	20	0	4	1	1	0	1	5	4	.200	.360	.350	94	-0	1	0	0	.872	0	/S-9	0.1
1978	KC-A	69	129	10	34	2	1	0	9	10	20	.264	.317	.295	71	-5	12	6	0	.927	-11	S-49,2-19/D	-1.2
1979	KC-A	101	268	32	68	12	5	2	25	20	44	.254	.306	.358	77	-9	10	7	-1	.970	1	S-50,2-46/3	-0.2
1980	*KC-A	153	549	79	150	16	11	6	53	53	78	.273	.337	.375	94	-4	20	7	2	.957	-26	*S-152	-1.1
1981	KC-A	98	339	40	77	19	1	2	29	41	43	.227	.311	.307	79	-8	10	10	-3	.973	-21	S-98	-2.4
1982	KC-A	119	437	64	125	19	3	10	60	38	48	.286	.343	.412	106	2	23	7	3	.961	-11	*S-117/D-1	0.7
1983	KC-A	144	547	76	129	19	6	5	41	48	78	.236	.299	.320	70	-22	40	7	8	.947	-10	*S-140/D-1	-1.0
1984	*KC-A	63	170	18	38	6	0	1	10	14	31	.224	.283	.276	55	-10	4	6	-2	.961	0	S-61	-0.7
1985	Mon-N	68	193	24	48	9	4	1	17	15	33	.249	.303	.352	88	-4	6	3	0	.978	-14	2-43/S-9,3	-1.2
1986	Pit-N	72	135	14	27	0	4	0	10	15	27	.200	.280	.259	49	-9	6	0	2	.947	-8	S-51/2-3	-1.2
1987	Pit-N	10	10	1	3	0	0	0	0	2	3	.300	.417	.300	93	0	0	0	0	.833	-0	/S-1,3-1	0.0
Total	11	907	2797	358	703	103	36	27	255	261	409	.251	.315	.343	82	-67	132	53	8	.956	-95	S-737,2-111/3D	-8.2

■ MARK WASINGER
Wasinger, Mark Thomas   b: 8/4/61, Monterey, Cal.   BR/TR, 6', 165 lbs.   Deb: 5/27/86

YEAR	TM/L	G	AB	R	H	2B	3B	HR	RBI	BB	SO	AVG	OBP	SLG	PRO+	BR/A	SB	CS	SBR	FA	FR	G/POS	TPR
1986	SD-N	3	8	0	0	0	0	0	1	0	2	.000	.000	.000	-99	-2	0	0	0	.500	-1	/3-3,2-1	-0.4
1987	SF-N	44	80	16	22	3	0	1	3	8	14	.275	.341	.350	88	-1	2	0	1	.973	3	3-21,2-10/S	0.2
1988	SF-N	3	2	1	0	0	0	0	0	0	0	.000	.000	.000	-99	-1	0	0	0	.000	0	/3-1	-0.1
Total	3	50	90	17	22	3	0	1	4	8	16	.244	.306	.311	68	-4	2	0	1	.907	2	/3-25,2-11,S	-0.3

■ FRED WATERMAN
Waterman, Frederick A.   b: 12/1845, New York, N.Y.   d: 12/16/1899, Cincinnati, Ohio   5'7.5", 148 lbs.   Deb: 5/5/1871

YEAR	TM/L	G	AB	R	H	2B	3B	HR	RBI	BB	SO	AVG	OBP	SLG	PRO+	BR/A	SB	CS	SBR	FA	FR	G/POS	TPR
1871	Oly-n	32	158	46	50	7	4	0	17	10	0	.316	.357	.411	127	7	11					*3-27/C-6	0.3
1872	Oly-n	9	44	13	18	1	1	0	6	0	0	.409	.409	.477	181	4						/3-7,C-2	0.2
1873	Was-n	15	80	20	28	3	3	0	10	1	1	.350	.358	.463	144	4						/S-9,O-4,3	0.3
1875	Chi-n	5	20	2	6	0	0	0	0	0	0	.300	.300	.300	107	0						/3-4,2-1	0.0
Total	4 n	61	302	81	102	11	8	0	11			.338	.361	.427	137	15						/3-40,S-9,CO2	0.8

■ JOHN WATHAN
Wathan, John David   b: 10/4/49, Cedar Rapids, Iowa   BR/TR, 6'2", 205 lbs.   Deb: 5/26/76   MC

YEAR	TM/L	G	AB	R	H	2B	3B	HR	RBI	BB	SO	AVG	OBP	SLG	PRO+	BR/A	SB	CS	SBR	FA	FR	G/POS	TPR
1976	*KC-A	27	42	5	12	1	0	0	5	2	5	.286	.333	.310	88	-1	2	-1		.984	-1	C-23/1-3	-0.2
1977	*KC-A	55	119	18	39	5	3	2	21	5	8	.328	.355	.471	122	3	2	0	1	.993	-2	C-35/1-5,D	0.2
1978	*KC-A	67	190	19	57	10	1	2	28	3	12	.300	.325	.395	99	-1	2	1	0	1.000	1	1-47,C-21	-0.2
1979	KC-A	90	199	26	41	7	3	2	28	7	24	.206	.233	.302	42	-16	2	1	0	.993	-2	1-49,C-23,D/O	-2.0
1980	*KC-A	126	453	57	138	14	7	6	58	50	42	.305	.377	.406	114	10	17	3	3	.982	-11	C-77,O-35,1	0.4
1981	KC-A	89	301	24	76	9	3	1	19	19	23	.252	.301	.312	78	-9	11	6	-0	.979	-11	C-73,O-16/1	-1.8
1982	KC-A	121	448	79	121	11	3	5	51	48	46	.270	.343	.328	85	-7	36	9	5	.980	-17	*C-120/1-3	-1.5
1983	KC-A	128	437	49	107	18	3	2	32	27	56	.245	.290	.314	66	-20	28	7	4	.985	-4	C-92,1-37/O	-1.8
1984	*KC-A	97	171	17	31	7	1	2	10	21	34	.181	.271	.269	50	-12	6	6	2	.975	5	C-59,1-33/OD	-0.7
1985	*KC-A	60	145	11	34	8	1	1	9	17	15	.234	.319	.324	76	-4	1	1	0	.986	12	C-49/1-6,D	0.9
Total	10	860	2505	305	656	90	25	21	261	199	265	.262	.320	.343	83	-56	105	36	10	.982	-31	C-572,1-196/OD	-6.7

■ DAVE WATKINS
Watkins, David Roger   b: 3/15/44, Owensboro, Ky.   BR/TR, 5'10", 185 lbs.   Deb: 4/9/69

YEAR	TM/L	G	AB	R	H	2B	3B	HR	RBI	BB	SO	AVG	OBP	SLG	PRO+	BR/A	SB	CS	SBR	FA	FR	G/POS	TPR
1969	Phi-N	69	148	17	26	2	1	4	12	22	53	.176	.291	.284	63	-7	2	3	-1	.981	-5	C-54/O-5,3	-1.2

■ GEORGE WATKINS
Watkins, George Archibald   b: 6/4/1900, Freestone Co., Tex   d: 6/1/70, Houston, Tex.   BL/TR, 6', 175 lbs.   Deb: 4/15/30

YEAR	TM/L	G	AB	R	H	2B	3B	HR	RBI	BB	SO	AVG	OBP	SLG	PRO+	BR/A	SB	CS	SBR	FA	FR	G/POS	TPR
1930	*StL-N	119	391	85	146	32	7	17	87	24	49	.373	.415	.621	141	25	5			.956	-6	O-89,1-13/2	1.1
1931	*StL-N	131	503	93	145	30	13	13	51	31	66	.288	.336	.477	112	7	15			.958	-6	*O-129	-0.7
1932	StL-N	127	458	67	143	35	3	9	63	45	46	.312	.384	.461	122	15	18			.949	3	*O-120	1.0
1933	StL-N	138	525	66	146	24	5	5	62	39	62	.278	.342	.371	98	-0	11			.953	1	*O-135	-0.7
1934	NY-N	105	296	38	73	18	3	6	33	24	34	.247	.316	.389	90	-5	2			.944	-10	O-81	-1.2
1935	Phi-N	150	600	80	162	25	5	17	76	40	78	.270	.320	.413	87	-12	3			.958	5	*O-148	-1.2
1936	Phi-N	19	70	7	17	4	0	2	5	5	13	.243	.293	.386	74	-3	2			.889	-3	O-17	-0.6
	Bro-N	105	364	54	93	24	6	4	43	38	34	.255	.334	.387	93	-4	5			.969	-4	O-98	-1.1

YEAR	TM/L	G	AB	R	H	2B	3B	HR	RBI	BB	SO	AVG	OBP	SLG	PRO+	BR/A	SB	CS	SBR	FA	FR	G/POS	TPR
	Yr	124	434	61	110	28	6	6	48	43	47	.253	.328	.387	90	-6		7		.959	-7	*O-115	-1.7
Total	7	894	3207	490	925	192	42	73	420	246	382	.288	.347	.443	105	24		61		.954	-20	O-817/1-13,2	-3.9

■ **ED WATKINS**   Watkins, James Edward b: 6/21/1877, Philadelphia, Pa. d: 3/29/33, Kelvin, Ariz. Deb: 9/6/02

YEAR	TM/L	G	AB	R	H	2B	3B	HR	RBI	BB	SO	AVG	OBP	SLG	PRO+	BR/A	SB	CS	SBR	FA	FR	G/POS	TPR
1902	Phi-N	1	3	0	0	0	0	0	0	0	1	.000	.250	.000	-22	-0	0			1.000	-0	/O-1	-0.1

■ **BILL WATKINS**   Watkins, William Henry b: 5/5/1858, Brantford, Ont., Can d: 6/9/37, Port Huron, Mich. 5'10", 156 lbs. Deb: 8/1/1884 M

| 1884 | Ind-a | 34 | 127 | 16 | 26 | 4 | 0 | 0 | | 5 | | .205 | .241 | .236 | 58 | -6 | | | | .845 | -6 | 3-23/2-9,SM | -1.0 |

■ **NEAL WATLINGTON**   Watlington, Julius Neal b: 12/25/22, Yanceyville, N.C. BL/TR, 6', 195 lbs. Deb: 7/10/53

| 1953 | Phi-A | 21 | 44 | 4 | 7 | 1 | 0 | 0 | 3 | 3 | 8 | .159 | .213 | .182 | 7 | -6 | 0 | 1 | -1 | .978 | 0 | /C-9 | -0.6 |

■ **ART WATSON**   Watson, Arthur Stanhope "Watty" b: 1/11/1884, Jeffersonville, Ind. d: 5/9/50, Buffalo, N.Y. BL/TR, 5'10", 175 lbs. Deb: 5/19/14

1914	Bro-F	22	46	7	13	4	1	1	3	1	6	.283	.298	.478	100	-0				.977	2	C-18	0.3
1915	Bro-F	9	19	4	5	0	3	0	1	3	4	.263	.364	.579	151	1	0			.957	-3	/C-7	-0.1
	Buf-F	22	30	6	14	1	0	1	13	0	4	.467	.467	.600	180	3	0			.778	-4	/C-6,O-1	-0.1
	Yr	31	49	10	19	1	3	1	14	3	8	.388	.423	.592	168	4	0			.878	-7	C-13/O-1	-0.2
Total	2	53	95	17	32	5	4	2	17	4	14	.337	.364	.537	135	4	0			.946	-5	/C-31,O-1	0.1

■ **JOHNNY WATSON**   Watson, John Thomas b: 1/16/08, Tazewell, Va. d: 4/29/65, Huntington, W.Va. BL/TR, 6', 175 lbs. Deb: 9/26/30

| 1930 | Det-A | 4 | 12 | 1 | 3 | 2 | 0 | 0 | 3 | 1 | 2 | .250 | .308 | .417 | 80 | -0 | 0 | | | .933 | -1 | /S-4 | -0.1 |

■ **BOB WATSON**   Watson, Robert Jose "Bull" b: 4/10/46, Los Angeles, Cal. BR/TR, 6'2", 205 lbs. Deb: 9/9/66 C

1966	Hou-N	1	1	0	0	0	0	0	0	0	0	.000	.000	.000	-99	-0	0	0	0	.000	0	H	0.0
1967	Hou-N	6	14	1	3	0	0	1	2	0	3	.214	.214	.429	82	-0	0	0	0	.958	0	/1-3	-0.1
1968	Hou-N	45	140	13	32	7	0	2	8	13	32	.229	.299	.321	88	-2	1	0	0	.885	-5	O-40	-1.0
1969	Hou-N	20	40	3	11	3	0	0	3	6	5	.275	.396	.350	113	1	0	0	0	1.000	-1	/O-6,1-5,C	0.0
1970	Hou-N	97	327	48	89	19	2	11	61	24	59	.272	.330	.443	110	3	1	1	-0	.992	-8	1-83/C-6,O	-1.2
1971	Hou-N	129	468	49	135	17	3	9	67	41	56	.288	.348	.395	113	8	0	3	-2	.985	-10	O-87,1-45	-1.3
1972	Hou-N	147	548	74	171	27	4	16	86	53	83	.312	.381	.464	142	30	1	1	-2	.978	-6	*O-143/1-2	1.8
1973	Hou-N★	158	573	97	179	24	3	16	94	85	73	.312	.405	.449	137	31	1	4	-2	.969	-1	*O-142,1-26/C	2.2
1974	Hou-N	150	524	69	156	19	4	11	67	60	61	.298	.373	.412	125	18	3	4	-2	.981	-10	*O-140,1-35	0.1
1975	Hou-N★	132	485	67	157	27	1	18	85	40	50	.324	.379	.495	152	32	3	5	-2	.993	-2	*1-118/O-9	2.1
1976	Hou-N	157	585	76	183	31	3	16	102	62	64	.313	.382	.458	151	38	3	3	-1	.990	-2	*1-155	2.6
1977	Hou-N	151	554	77	160	38	6	22	110	57	69	.289	.362	.498	141	30	5	0	2	.994	12	*1-146	3.5
1978	Hou-N	139	461	51	133	25	4	14	79	51	57	.289	.364	.451	137	22	3	1	0	.992	10	*1-128	2.6
1979	Hou-N	49	163	15	39	4	0	3	18	16	23	.239	.307	.319	75	-6	0	0	0	.993	3	1-44	-0.6
	Bos-A	84	312	48	105	19	4	13	53	29	33	.337	.402	.548	145	20	3	2	-0	.988	2	1-58,D-26	1.7
1980	*NY-A	130	469	62	144	25	3	13	68	48	56	.307	.373	.456	128	18	2	1	0	.990	-2	*1-104,D-21	1.0
1981	*NY-A	59	156	15	33	3	3	6	12	24	17	.212	.317	.385	103	1	0	0	0	.997	-1	1-50/D-6	-0.3
1982	NY-A	7	17	3	4	3	0	0	3	3	0	.235	.350	.412	110	0	0	0	0	1.000	-1	/1-6,D-1	-0.1
	Atl-N	57	114	16	28	3	1	5	22	14	20	.246	.328	.421	104	1	1	1	-0	1.000	-4	1-27/O-2	-0.5
1983	Atl-N	65	149	14	46	9	0	6	37	18	23	.309	.383	.490	131	6	0	2	-1	.984	-3	1-34	0.0
1984	Atl-N	49	85	4	18	4	0	2	12	9	12	.212	.287	.329	68	-4	0	0	0	.983	1	1-19	-0.4
Total	19	1832	6185	802	1826	307	41	184	989	653	796	.295	.367	.447	130	247	27	28	-9	.991	-26	*1-1088,O-570/DC	12.1

■ **ALLIE WATT**   Watt, Albert Bailey b: 12/12/1899, Philadelphia, Pa. d: 3/15/68, Norfolk, Va. BR/TR, 5'8", 154 lbs. Deb: 10/3/20 F

| 1920 | Was-A | 1 | 1 | 0 | 1 | 1 | 0 | 0 | 1 | 0 | 0 | 1.000 | 1.000 | 2.000 | 700 | 1 | 0 | 0 | 0 | 1.000 | 0 | /2-1 | 0.1 |

■ **JOHNNY WATWOOD**   Watwood, John Clifford "Lefty" b: 8/17/05, Alexander City, Ala. d: 3/1/80, Goodwater, Ala. BL/TL, 6'1", 186 lbs. Deb: 4/16/29

1929	Chi-A	85	278	33	84	12	6	2	28	22	21	.302	.355	.410	98	-1	6	3	0	.942	-2	O-77	-0.7
1930	Chi-A	133	427	75	129	25	4	2	51	52	35	.302	.382	.393	100	2	5	7	-3	.989	3	1-62,O-52	-0.7
1931	Chi-A	128	367	51	104	16	6	1	47	56	30	.283	.380	.368	103	4	9	3	1	.944	3	*O-102/1-4	0.2
1932	Chi-A	13	49	5	15	2	0	0	0	1	3	.306	.333	.347	82	-1	0	0	0	.960	-2	O-13	-0.4
	Bos-A	95	266	26	66	11	0	0	30	20	11	.248	.301	.289	55	-17	7	4	-0	.945	-1	O-46,1-18	-2.2
	Yr	108	315	31	81	13	0	0	30	21	14	.257	.306	.298	59	-19	7	4	-0	.948	-4	O-59,1-18	-2.6
1933	Bos-A	13	30	2	4	0	0	0	2	3	3	.133	.212	.133	-7	-5	0	0	0	.950	-1	/O-9	-0.5
1939	Phi-N	2	6	0	1	0	0	0	0	0	0	.167	.167	.167	-11	-1	0			.933	-1	/1-2	-0.2
Total	6	469	1423	192	403	66	16	5	158	154	103	.283	.356	.363	89	-19	27	17		.948	-0	O-299/1-86	-4.5

■ **BOB WAY**   Way, Robert Clinton b: 4/2/06, Emlenton, Pa. d: 6/20/74, Pittsburgh, Pa. BR/TR, 5'10.5", 168 lbs. Deb: 4/12/27

| 1927 | Chi-A | 5 | 3 | 1 | 1 | 0 | 0 | 0 | 1 | 0 | 0 | .333 | .333 | .333 | 75 | -0 | 0 | 0 | 0 | 1.000 | 0 | /2-1 | 0.0 |

■ **ROY WEATHERLY**   Weatherly, Cyril Roy "Stormy" b: 2/25/15, Warren, Tex. d: 1/19/91, Woodville, Tex. BL/TR, 5'6.5", 170 lbs. Deb: 6/27/36

1936	Cle-A	84	349	64	117	28	6	8	53	16	29	.335	.364	.519	115	6	3	8	-4	.973	4	O-84	0.3
1937	Cle-A	53	134	19	27	4	0	5	13	6	14	.201	.246	.343	47	-12	1	1	-0	.964	-3	O-38/3-1	-1.5
1938	Cle-A	83	210	32	55	14	3	2	18	14	14	.262	.308	.386	74	-9	8	5	-1	.975	-1	O-55	-1.1
1939	Cle-A	95	323	43	100	16	6	1	32	19	23	.310	.348	.406	95	-3	7	2	1	.961	-8	O-76	-1.1
1940	Cle-A	135	578	90	175	35	11	12	59	27	26	.303	.335	.464	108	4	9	8	-2	.969	6	*O-135	0.1
1941	Cle-A	102	363	59	105	21	5	3	37	32	20	.289	.350	.399	103	1	2	5	-2	.968	-8	O-88	-1.4
1942	Cle-A	128	473	61	122	23	7	5	39	35	25	.258	.310	.368	96	-5	8	13	-5	.991	2	*O-117	-1.4
1943	*NY-A	77	280	37	74	8	3	7	28	18	9	.264	.311	.389	104	0	4	7	-3	.983	-2	O-68	-0.9
1946	NY-A	2	2	0	1	0	0	0	0	0	0	.500	.500	.500	178	0	0	0	0	.000	0	H	0.0
1950	NY-N	52	69	10	18	3	0	0	11	13	10	.261	.378	.391	102	1	0			1.000	-1	O-15	-0.1
Total	10	811	2781	415	794	152	44	43	290	180	170	.286	.331	.418	99	-16	42	49		.975	-10	O-676/3-1	-7.1

■ **ART WEAVER**   Weaver, Arthur Coggshall "Six O'Clock" b: 4/7/1879, Wichita, Kan. d: 3/23/17, Denver, Colo. TR, 6'1", 160 lbs. Deb: 9/14/02

1902	StL-N	11	33	2	6	2	0	0	3	1		.182	.206	.242	40	-2	0			.983	2	C-11	0.0
1903	StL-N	16	49	4	12	0	0	0	5	4		.245	.302	.245	58	-3	1			.969	-3	C-16	0.2
	Pit-N	16	48	8	11	0	1	0	3	2		.229	.260	.271	50	-3	0			.978	-1	C-11/1-5	-0.3
	Yr	32	97	12	23	0	1	0	8	6		.237	.282	.258	54	-6	1			.972	-2	C-27/1-5	-0.1
1905	StL-A	28	92	5	11	2	1	0	3	1		.120	.129	.163	-8	-11	0			.962	5	C-28	-0.4
1908	Chi-A	15	35	1	7	1	0	0	1	1		.200	.222	.229	47	-2	0			.953	-5	C-15	-0.7
Total	4	86	257	20	47	5	2	0	15	9		.183	.211	.218	31	-22	1			.967	4	/C-81,1-5	-1.2

■ **BUCK WEAVER**   Weaver, George Daniel b: 8/18/1890, Pottstown, Pa. d: 1/31/56, Chicago, Ill. BR/TR, 5'11", 170 lbs. Deb: 4/11/12

1912	Chi-A	147	523	55	117	21	8	1	43	9		.224	.245	.300	58	-31	12			.915	-6	*S-147	-2.5
1913	Chi-A	151	533	51	145	17	8	4	52	15	60	.272	.302	.356	94	-7	20			.929	34	*S-151	4.2
1914	Chi-A	136	541	64	133	20	9	2	28	20	40	.246	.279	.327	83	-14	14	20	-8	.928	5	*S-134	-0.6
1915	Chi-A	148	563	83	151	18	11	3	49	32	58	.268	.316	.355	98	-4	24	20	-5	.939	1	*S-148	0.4
1916	Chi-A	151	582	78	132	27	8	3	38	30	48	.227	.280	.309	76	-19	22	13	-11	.941	7	3-85,S-66	-0.7
1917	*Chi-A	118	447	64	127	16	5	3	32	27	29	.284	.332	.362	110	4	19			.949	9	*3-107,S-10	1.7
1918	Chi-A	112	420	37	126	12	5	0	29	11	24	.300	.323	.352	103	-1	20			.941	-0	S-98,3-11/2	0.4
1919	*Chi-A	140	571	89	169	33	9	3	75	11	21	.296	.315	.401	100	-0	22			.963	3	3-97,S-43	0.4
1920	Chi-A	151	629	102	208	34	8	2	74	28	23	.331	.365	.420	107	6	19	17	-5	.933	-10	*3-127,S-25	-0.1
Total	9	1254	4809	623	1308	198	69	21	420	183	303	.272	.307	.355	92	-68	172	70		.935	39	S-822,3-427/2	3.2

YEAR	TM/L	G	AB	R	H	2B	3B	HR	RBI	BB	SO	AVG	OBP	SLG	PRO+	BR/A	SB	CS	SBR	FA	FR	G/POS	TPR

■ JIM WEAVER
Weaver, James Francis b: 10/10/59, Kingston, N.Y. BL/TL, 6'3", 190 lbs. Deb: 4/10/85

YEAR	TM/L	G	AB	R	H	2B	3B	HR	RBI	BB	SO	AVG	OBP	SLG	PRO+	BR/A	SB	CS	SBR	FA	FR	G/POS	TPR
1985	Det-A	12	7	2	1	1	0	0	0	1	4	.143	.250	.286	47	-1	0	1	-1	1.000	-2	/O-4,D-4	-0.3
1987	Sea-A	7	4	2	0	0	0	0	0	2	3	.000	.333	.000	-1	-1	1	1	-0	1.000	-1	/O-4	-0.1
1989	SF-N	12	20	2	4	3	0	0	2	0	7	.200	.200	.350	56	-1	1	0	0	1.000	-1	/O-8	-0.3
Total	3	31	31	6	5	4	0	0	2	3	14	.161	.235	.290	47	-1	2	2	-1	1.000	-4	/O-16,D-4	-0.7

■ FARMER WEAVER
Weaver, William B. b: 3/23/1865, Parkersburg, W.Va. d: 1/23/43, Akron, Ohio BL, Deb: 9/16/1888

YEAR	TM/L	G	AB	R	H	2B	3B	HR	RBI	BB	SO	AVG	OBP	SLG	PRO+	BR/A	SB	CS	SBR	FA	FR	G/POS	TPR
1888	Lou-a	26	112	12	28	1	1	0	8	3		.250	.276	.277	79	-3	12			.878	-2	O-26	-0.5
1889	Lou-a	124	499	62	145	17	6	0	60	40	22	.291	.352	.349	102	2	21			.918	-1	*O-123/C-2,32	-0.1
1890	*Lou-a	130	557	101	161	27	9	3		29		.289	.333	.386	115	8	45			.933	-1	*O-127/S-2,3	0.2
1891	Lou-a	135	565	76	160	25	7	1	55	33	23	.283	.335	.358	99	-2	30			.956	17	*O-132/C-4	0.9
1892	Lou-N	138	551	58	140	15	4	0	57	40	17	.254	.315	.296	92	-4	30			.902	-11	*O-122,C-15/1	-1.8
1893	Lou-N	106	439	79	128	17	7	2	49	27	12	.292	.348	.376	100	-0	17			.913	-1	O-85,C-21	-0.3
1894	Lou-N	64	244	19	54	5	2	3	24	7	11	.221	.249	.295	33	-27	3			.958	-0	O-35,C-17,1/2	-2.2
	Pit-N	30	115	16	40	7	2	0	24	6	1	.348	.405	.443	105	1	4			.943	-10	C-14,S-12/3O	-0.5
	Yr	94	359	35	94	12	4	3	48	13	12	.262	.301	.343	58	-25	7			.947	-10	O-36,C-31,S1/32	-2.7
Total	7	753	3082	423	856	114	38	9	277	185	86	.278	.330	.348	95	-25	162			.927	-9	O-651/C-73,S132	-4.3

■ SKEETER WEBB
Webb, James Laverne b: 11/4/09, Meridian, Miss. d: 7/8/86, Meridian, Miss. BR/TR, 5'9.5", 150 lbs. Deb: 7/20/32

YEAR	TM/L	G	AB	R	H	2B	3B	HR	RBI	BB	SO	AVG	OBP	SLG	PRO+	BR/A	SB	CS	SBR	FA	FR	G/POS	TPR
1932	StL-N	1	0	0	0	0	0	0	0	0	0	—	—	—	—	0	0			.000	0	/S-1	0.0
1938	Cle-A	20	58	11	16	2	0	0	2	8	7	.276	.364	.310	72	-7	1	0	0	.964	5	S-13/3-3,2	-0.3
1939	Cle-A	81	269	28	71	14	1	2	26	15	24	.264	.305	.346	68	-13	1	1	-0	.932	-9	S-81	-1.4
1940	Chi-A	84	334	33	79	11	2	1	29	30	33	.237	.299	.290	53	-23	3	6	-3	.969	-10	2-74/S-7,3	-2.8
1941	Chi-A	29	84	7	16	2	0	0	6	3	9	.190	.227	.214	18	-10	1	0	0	.940	6	2-18/S-5,3	-0.3
1942	Chi-A	32	94	5	16	2	1	0	4	4	13	.170	.204	.213	18	-10	1	2	-1	.961	2	2-29	-0.9
1943	Chi-A	58	213	15	50	5	2	0	22	6	19	.235	.256	.277	56	-12	5	4	-1	.953	-3	2-54	-1.4
1944	Chi-A	139	513	44	108	19	6	0	30	20	39	.211	.242	.271	47	-37	7	3	0	.944	-5	*S-135/2-5	-3.2
1945	*Det-A	118	407	43	81	12	6	0	21	30	35	.199	.254	.238	41	-31	8	7	-2	.957	23	*S-104,2-11	-0.2
1946	Det-A	64	169	12	37	1	1	0	17	9	18	.219	.258	.237	37	-14	3	3	-1	.972	15	2-50/S-8	0.3
1947	Det-A	50	79	13	16	3	0	0	6	7	9	.203	.267	.241	41	-6	3	0	1	.992	12	2-30/S-6	0.8
1948	Phi-A	23	54	5	8	2	0	0	3	0	9	.148	.148	.185	-12	-9	0	0	0	1.000	3	/2-9,S-8	-0.5
Total	12	699	2274	216	498	73	15	3	166	132	215	.219	.263	.268	46	-168	33	26		.946	32	S-368,2-282/3	-9.9

■ EARL WEBB
Webb, William Earl b: 9/17/1897, Bon Air, Tenn. d: 5/23/65, Jamestown, Tenn. BL/TR, 6'1", 185 lbs. Deb: 8/13/25

YEAR	TM/L	G	AB	R	H	2B	3B	HR	RBI	BB	SO	AVG	OBP	SLG	PRO+	BR/A	SB	CS	SBR	FA	FR	G/POS	TPR
1925	NY-N	4	3	0	0	0	0	0	0	1	1	.000	.250	.000	-31	-1	0	0	0	.000	0	H	-0.1
1927	Chi-N	102	332	58	100	18	4	14	52	48	31	.301	.391	.506	138	18	3			.959	2	O-86	1.4
1928	Chi-N	62	140	22	35	7	3	3	23	14	17	.250	.318	.407	90	-3	0			.986	2	O-31	-0.3
1930	Bos-A	127	449	61	145	30	6	16	66	44	56	.323	.385	.523	133	22	2	1	0	.959	-5	*O-116	0.7
1931	Bos-A	151	589	96	196	67	3	14	103	70	51	.333	.404	.528	151	43	2	2	-1	.948	-2	*O-151	2.8
1932	Bos-A	52	192	23	54	9	1	5	27	25	15	.281	.364	.417	105	2	0	0	0	.964	-3	O-50/1-2	-0.4
	Det-A	88	338	49	97	19	8	3	51	39	18	.287	.361	.417	97	-1	1	1	-0	.955	0	O-85	-0.6
	Yr	140	530	72	151	28	9	8	78	64	33	.285	.362	.417	100	0	1	1	-0	.958	-2	*O-135/1-2	-1.0
1933	Det-A	6	11	1	3	0	0	0	3	3	0	.273	.429	.273	87	0	0	0	0	1.000	-1	/O-2	-0.1
	Chi-A	58	107	16	31	5	0	1	8	16	13	.290	.382	.364	103	1	0	0	0	1.000	-4	O-16,1-10	-0.4
	Yr	64	118	17	34	5	0	1	11	19	13	.288	.387	.356	101	1	0	0	0	1.000	-5	O-18,1-10	-0.4
Total	7	650	2161	326	661	155	25	56	333	260	202	.306	.381	.478	125	82	8	4		.958	-11	O-537/1-12	3.0

■ BILL WEBB
Webb, William Joseph b: 6/25/1895, Chicago, Ill. d: 1/12/43, Chicago, Ill. BR/TR, 5'10", 161 lbs. Deb: 9/17/17 C

YEAR	TM/L	G	AB	R	H	2B	3B	HR	RBI	BB	SO	AVG	OBP	SLG	PRO+	BR/A	SB	CS	SBR	FA	FR	G/POS	TPR
1917	Pit-N	5	15	1	3	0	0	0	0	2	3	.200	.294	.200	51	-1	0			1.000	1	/2-4,S-1	0.0

■ HARRY WEBER
Weber, Harry b: Indianapolis, Ind. Deb: 7/22/1884

YEAR	TM/L	G	AB	R	H	2B	3B	HR	RBI	BB	SO	AVG	OBP	SLG	PRO+	BR/A	SB	CS	SBR	FA	FR	G/POS	TPR
1884	Ind-a	3	8	0	0	0	0	0		0		.000	.111	.000	-62	-1				.794	1	/C-3	0.0

■ JOE WEBER
Weber, Joseph Edward b: 2/15/1862, Hamilton, Ont., Canada d: 12/15/21, Hamilton, Ont., Canada Deb: 5/30/1884

YEAR	TM/L	G	AB	R	H	2B	3B	HR	RBI	BB	SO	AVG	OBP	SLG	PRO+	BR/A	SB	CS	SBR	FA	FR	G/POS	TPR
1884	Det-N	2	8	0	0	0	0	0	0	0	2	.000	.000	.000	-99	-2				.750	0	/O-2	-0.2

■ LENNY WEBSTER
Webster, Leonard Irell b: 2/10/65, New Orleans, La. BR/TR, 5'9", 185 lbs. Deb: 9/1/89

YEAR	TM/L	G	AB	R	H	2B	3B	HR	RBI	BB	SO	AVG	OBP	SLG	PRO+	BR/A	SB	CS	SBR	FA	FR	G/POS	TPR
1989	Min-A	14	20	3	6	2	0	0	1	3	2	.300	.391	.400	116	1	0	0	0	1.000	-2	C-14	-0.1
1990	Min-A	2	6	1	2	1	0	0	0	1	1	.333	.429	.500	149	0	0	0	0	1.000	-1	/C-2	0.0
1991	Min-A	18	34	7	10	1	0	3	8	6	10	.294	.400	.588	162	3	0	0	0	.986	4	C-17	0.7
1992	Min-A	53	118	10	33	10	1	1	13	9	11	.280	.331	.407	102	0	0	2	-1	.995	1	C-49/D-1	0.2
1993	Min-A	49	106	14	21	2	0	1	8	11	8	.198	.274	.245	40	-9	1	0	0	1.000	3	C-45/D-1	-0.3
1994	Mon-N	57	143	13	39	10	0	5	23	16	24	.273	.370	.448	110	2	0	0	0	.996	-1	C-46	0.3
Total	6	193	427	48	111	26	1	10	53	46	56	.260	.340	.396	96	-2	1	2	-1	.996	5	C-173/D-2	0.8

■ MITCH WEBSTER
Webster, Mitchell Dean b: 5/16/59, Larned, Kan. BB/TL, 6', 185 lbs. Deb: 9/2/83

YEAR	TM/L	G	AB	R	H	2B	3B	HR	RBI	BB	SO	AVG	OBP	SLG	PRO+	BR/A	SB	CS	SBR	FA	FR	G/POS	TPR
1983	Tor-A	11	11	2	2	0	0	0	0	1	1	.182	.250	.182	20	-1	0	0	0	1.000	-3	/O-7,D-2	-0.4
1984	Tor-A	26	22	9	5	2	1	0	4	1	7	.227	.261	.409	79	-1	0	0	0	.875	-3	O-10/1-1,D	-0.3
1985	Tor-A	4	1	0	0	0	0	0	0	0	0	.000	.000	.000	-98	-0	0	1	-1	.000	-1	/O-2,D-2	-0.2
	Mon-N	74	212	32	58	8	2	11	30	20	33	.274	.336	.486	135	9	15	9	-1	.993	-5	O-64	0.1
1986	Mon-N	151	576	89	167	31	13	8	49	57	78	.290	.358	.431	117	14	36	15	2	.977	4	*O-146	1.5
1987	Mon-N	156	588	101	165	30	8	15	63	70	95	.281	.363	.435	107	7	33	10	4	.982	1	*O-153	0.6
1988	Mon-N	81	259	33	66	5	2	6	13	36	37	.255	.357	.313	90	-2	12	10	-2	.994	-3	O-71	-1.0
	Chi-N	70	264	36	70	11	6	4	26	19	50	.265	.322	.398	101	0	10	4	1	.971	2	O-65	0.1
	Yr	151	523	69	136	16	8	6	39	55	87	.260	.340	.356	95	-2	22	14	-2	.982	-1	*O-136	-0.9
1989	*Chi-N	98	272	40	70	12	4	3	19	30	55	.257	.333	.364	92	-2	14	2	4	.965	-1	O-74	-0.3
1990	Cle-A	128	437	58	110	20	6	12	55	20	61	.252	.289	.407	93	-6	22	6	3	.991	9	*O-118/1-3,D	0.4
1991	Cle-A	13	32	2	4	0	0	0	0	5	8	.125	.200	.125	-8	-5	2	2	-1	1.000	-1	O-10	-0.6
	Pit-N	36	97	9	17	3	4	1	9	9	21	.175	.245	.320	59	-0	6	0	0	.963	2	O-29	-0.8
	LA-N	58	74	12	21	5	1	1	10	9	21	.284	.361	.419	122	2	0	1	-0	1.000	-8	O-36/1-1	-0.8
	Yr	94	171	21	38	8	5	2	19	18	52	.222	.296	.363	86	-3	6	1	-0	.978	-10	O-65/1-1	-1.6
1992	LA-N	135	262	33	70	12	5	6	35	27	49	.267	.340	.420	116	2	11	5	0	.977	-12	O-90	-0.9
1993	LA-N	88	172	26	42	6	2	2	14	11	24	.244	.297	.337	74	-7	4	6	-2	.950	-9	O-56	-1.9
1994	LA-N	82	84	12	23	4	0	4	12	8	13	.274	.344	.464	115	2	1	2	-1	1.000	-12	O-48	-1.1
Total	12	1211	3363	498	890	149	54	69	339	321	564	.265	.334	.403	102	10	160	73	4	.980	-43	O-979/D-16,1	-5.6

■ RAY WEBSTER
Webster, Ramon Alberto b: 8/31/42, Colon, Panama BL/TL, 6', 185 lbs. Deb: 4/11/67

YEAR	TM/L	G	AB	R	H	2B	3B	HR	RBI	BB	SO	AVG	OBP	SLG	PRO+	BR/A	SB	CS	SBR	FA	FR	G/POS	TPR
1967	KC-A	122	360	41	92	15	4	11	51	32	44	.256	.320	.411	118	7	5	3	-0	.989	-3	1-83,O-15	-0.1
1968	Oak-A	66	196	17	42	11	1	3	23	12	24	.214	.260	.327	81	-5	3	0	-0	.988	-1	1-55	-1.1
1969	Oak-A	64	77	5	20	0	1	1	13	12	8	.260	.367	.325	99	-0	3	0	0	.981	1	1-13	0.1
1970	SD-N	95	116	12	30	3	0	2	11	11	12	.259	.323	.336	80	-3	1	0	-0	.981	-1	1-15/O-1	-0.6
1971	SD-N	10	8	0	1	0	0	0	1	0	3	.125	.125	.125	26	-1	0	0	0	.000	0	H	-0.1
	Oak-A	7	5	0	0	0	0	0	0	0	0	.000	.000	.000	-99	-1	0	0	0	.000	0	H	-0.1
	Chi-N	16	16	1	5	2	0	0	0	1	3	.313	.353	.438	107	0	0	0	0	1.000	0	/1-1	-0.1
Total	5	380	778	76	190	31	6	17	98	70	94	.244	.309	.365	99	-3	9	4	0	.989	-4	1-168/O-16	-1.9

YEAR	TM/L	G	AB	R	H	2B	3B	HR	RBI	BB	SO	AVG	OBP	SLG	PRO+	BR/A	SB	CS	SBR	FA	FR	G/POS	TPR

■ RAY WEBSTER Webster, Raymond George b: 11/15/37, Grass Valley, Cal. BR/TR, 6', 175 lbs. Deb: 4/17/59

1959	Cle-A	40	74	10	15	2	1	2	10	5	7	.203	.253	.338	63	-4	1	0	0	.929	0	2-24/3-4	-0.3
1960	Bos-A	7	3	1	0	0	0	0	1	1	0	.000	.250	.000	-25	-1	0	0	0	1.000	1	/2-1	0.0
Total	2	47	77	11	15	2	1	2	11	6	7	.195	.253	.325	59	-5	1	0	0	.931	1	/2-25,3-4	-0.3

■ PETE WECKBECKER Weckbecker, Peter b: 8/30/1864, Butler, Pa. d: 5/16/35, Hampton, Va. 5'7", 150 lbs. Deb: 10/5/1889

1889	Ind-N	1	1	0	0	0	0	0	2	0	0	.000	.000	.000	-98	-0				1.000	0	/C-1	0.0
1890	*Lou-a	32	101	17	24	1	0	0		8	0	.238	.300	.248	63	-4	7			.941	1	C-32	-0.1
Total	2	33	102	17	24	1	0	0	2	8	0	.235	.297	.245	61	-5	7			.941	1	/C-33	-0.1

■ ERIC WEDGE Wedge, Eric Michael b: 1/27/68, Fort Wayne, Ind. BR/TR, 6'3", 215 lbs. Deb: 10/5/91

1991	Bos-A	1	1	0	1	0	0	0	0	0	0	1.000	1.000	1.000	434	0	0	0	0	.000	0	/D-1	0.0
1992	Bos-A	27	68	11	17	2	0	5	11	13	18	.250	.370	.500	133	3	0	0	0	1.000	-0	D-20/C-5	0.2
1993	Col-N	9	11	2	2	0	0	0	1	0	4	.182	.182	.182	-2	-2	0	0	0	1.000	1	/C-1	-0.1
1994	Bos-A	2	6	0	0	0	0	0	0	1	3	.000	.143	.000	-55	-1	0	0	0	.000	0	/D-2	-0.1
Total	4	39	86	13	20	2	0	5	12	14	25	.233	.340	.430	104	1	0	0	0	1.000	0	/D-23,C-6	0.0

■ BERT WEEDEN Weeden, Charles Albert b: 12/21/1882, Northwood, N.H. d: 1/7/39, Northwood, N.H. BL/TL, 6', 200 lbs. Deb: 6/4/11

| 1911 | Bos-N | 1 | 1 | 0 | 0 | 0 | 0 | 0 | 0 | 0 | 0 | .000 | .000 | .000 | -93 | -0 | 0 | | | .000 | 0 | H | 0.0 |

■ JOHNNY WEEKLY Weekly, Johnny b: 6/14/37, Waterproof, La. d: 11/24/74, Walnut Creek, Cal. BR/TR, 6' ", 200 lbs. Deb: 4/13/62

1962	Hou-N	13	26	3	5	1	0	2	2	7	4	.192	.364	.462	129	1	0	0	0	1.000	-1	/O-7	0.0
1963	Hou-N	34	80	4	18	3	0	3	14	7	14	.225	.295	.375	98	-0	0	0	0	1.000	1	O-23	-0.1
1964	Hou-N	6	15	0	2	0	0	0	3	1	3	.133	.188	.133	-8	-2	0	0	0	1.000	1	/O-5	-0.2
Total	3	53	121	7	25	4	0	5	19	15	21	.207	.299	.364	92	-1	0	0	0	1.000	1	/O-35	-0.3

■ JOHN WEHNER Wehner, John Paul b: 6/29/67, Pittsburgh, Pa. BR/TR, 6'3", 204 lbs. Deb: 7/17/91

1991	Pit-N	37	106	15	36	7	0	0	7	7	17	.340	.381	.406	123	3	3	0	1	.936	7	3-36	1.2
1992	*Pit-N	55	123	11	22	6	0	0	4	12	22	.179	.252	.228	37	-10	3	0	1	.961	5	3-34,1-13/2	-0.6
1993	Pit-N	29	35	3	5	0	0	0	6	10	10	.143	.268	.143	14	-4	0	0	0	1.000	-1	O-13/2-3,3	-0.5
1994	Pit-N	2	4	1	1	1	0	0	3	0	1	.250	.250	.500	90	-0	0	0	0	1.000	0	/3-1	0.0
Total	4	123	268	30	64	14	0	0	14	25	50	.239	.304	.291	68	-11	6	0	2	.949	11	/3-74,O-13,12	0.1

■ STUMP WEIDMAN Weidman, George E. b: 2/17/1861, Rochester, N.Y. d: 3/2/05, New York, N.Y. BR/TR, 5'7.5", 165 lbs. Deb: 8/26/1880 U

1880	Buf-N	23	78	8	8	1	0	0	3	2	11	.103	.125	.115	-18	-9				.893	-3	P-17,O-13	-0.5
1881	Det-N	13	47	8	12	1	0	0	5	2	2	.255	.286	.277	75	-1				1.000	-2	P-13	0.0
1882	Det-N	50	193	20	42	7	1	0	20	2	19	.218	.226	.264	57	-9				.906	0	P-46/O-6,S	0.0
1883	Det-N	79	313	34	58	6	1	1	24	4	38	.185	.196	.220	27	-26				.909	-2	P-52,O-35/2	-1.2
1884	Det-N	81	300	24	49	6	0	0	26	13	41	.163	.198	.183	22	-26				.846	-3	O-53,P-26/S2	-1.9
1885	Det-N	44	153	7	24	2	1	1	14	8	32	.157	.199	.203	30	-12				.869	-5	P-38/O-7,2	-0.3
1886	KC-N	51	179	13	30	2	0	0	7	5	46	.168	.190	.179	12	-19	3			.936	3	P-51/O-3	-0.1
1887	Det-N	21	82	12	17	2	0	0	11	3	3	.207	.235	.232	29	-8	6			.837	-1	P-21/O-2	-0.1
	NY-a	14	46	5	7	1	1	0		4		.152	.220	.217	23	-5	2			.882	2	P-12/O-3	0.0
	NY-N	1	3	0	1	0	0	0	0	0		.333	.333	.333	90	-0				.500	-0	/P-1	0.0
1888	NY-N	2	7	1	0	0	0	0	1	2	1	.000	.222	.000	-24	-1	0			.714	-0	/P-2	0.0
Total	9	379	1401	132	248	28	4	2	111	45	193	.177	.203	.207	28	-115	11			.885	-10	P-279,O-122/2S	-4.1

■ RALPH WEIGEL Weigel, Ralph Richard "Wig" b: 10/2/21, Coldwater, Ohio d: 4/15/92, Memphis, Tenn. BR/TR, 6'1", 180 lbs. Deb: 9/18/46

1946	Cle-A	6	12	0	2	0	0	0	0	2	.167	.167	.167	-7	-2	1	0	0	1.000	-1	/C-6	-0.3
1948	Chi-A	66	163	8	38	7	3	0	26	13	18	.233	.294	.313	64	-9	1	2	-1	.969	-7	C-39/O-2	-1.4
1949	Was-A	34	60	4	14	2	0	0	4	8	6	.233	.324	.267	58	-3	0	1	-1	.985	1	C-21	-0.3
Total	3	106	235	12	54	9	3	0	30	21	26	.230	.296	.294	59	-14	2	3	-1	.976	-8	/C-66,O-2	-2.0

■ PODGE WEIHE Weihe, John Garibaldi b: 11/13/1862, Cincinnati, Ohio d: 4/15/14, Cincinnati, Ohio BR/TR, 5'11", 175 lbs. Deb: 8/6/1883

1883	Cin-a	1	4	1	1	0	0	0		0		.250	.250	.250	58	-0				1.000	0	/O-1	0.0
1884	Ind-a	63	256	29	65	13	2	4		9		.254	.279	.367	112	3				.860	-0	O-58/2-4,1	0.2
Total	2	64	260	30	66	13	2	4		9		.254	.279	.365	111	3				.864	0	/O-59,2-4,1	0.2

■ DICK WEIK Weik, Richard Henry "Legs" b: 11/17/27, Waterloo, Iowa d: 4/21/91, Harvey, Ill. BR/TR, 6'3.5", 184 lbs. Deb: 9/8/48

1948	Was-A	3	4	1	3	0	1	0	0	0	0	.750	.750	1.250	439	1	0	0	0	1.000	-0	/P-3	0.0
1949	Was-A	28	28	3	5	0	0	0	2	1	8	.179	.207	.179	2	-4	0	0	0	.964	1	P-27	0.0
1950	Was-A	14	13	0	2	0	0	0	0	0	3	.154	.154	.154	-22	-2	0	0	0	1.000	-1	P-14	0.0
	Cle-A	11	5	0	1	1	0	0	0	0	4	.200	.200	.400	52	-0	0	0	0	1.000	1	P-11	0.0
	Yr	25	18	0	3	1	0	0	0	0	7	.167	.167	.222	-1	-3	0	0	0	1.000	-1	P-25	0.0
1953	Cle-A	1	0	1	0	0	0	0	0	0	0	—	—	—		0	0	0	0	.000	0	R	0.0
	Det-A	12	2	1	1	1	0	0	1	0	1	.500	.500	1.000	300	1	0	0	0	1.000	0	P-12	0.0
	Yr	13	2	2	1	1	0	0	1	0	1	.500	.500	1.000	301	1	0	0	0	1.000	0	P-12	0.0
1954	Det-A	9	1	0	0	0	0	0	0	0	0	.000	.000	.000	-99	-0	0	0	0	.500	-1	/P-9	0.0
Total	5	78	53	6	12	2	1	0	3	1	16	.226	.241	.302	43	-5	0	0	0	.958	-2	/P-76	0.0

■ ELMER WEINGARTNER Weingartner, Elmer William "Dutch" b: 8/13/18, Cleveland, Ohio BR/TR, 5'11", 178 lbs. Deb: 4/19/45

| 1945 | Cle-A | 20 | 39 | 5 | 9 | 1 | 0 | 0 | 1 | 1 | 3 | .231 | .302 | .256 | 66 | -2 | 0 | 0 | 0 | .871 | -3 | S-20 | -0.4 |

■ PHIL WEINTRAUB Weintraub, Philip "Mickey" b: 10/12/07, Chicago, Ill. d: 6/21/87, Palm Springs, Cal BL/TL, 6'1", 195 lbs. Deb: 9/5/33

1933	NY-N	8	15	3	3	0	0	1	1	3	2	.200	.333	.400	110	0	0			.667	-3	/O-6	-0.3
1934	NY-N	31	74	13	26	2	0	0	15	15	10	.351	.461	.378	130	4	0			.944	-4	O-20	0.0
1935	NY-N	64	112	18	27	3	3	1	6	17	13	.241	.341	.348	87	-2	0			.975	-3	1-19/O-7	-0.6
1937	Cin-N	49	177	27	48	10	4	3	20	19	25	.271	.345	.424	113	3	1			.976	-3	O-47	-0.1
	NY-N	6	9	3	3	2	0	0	1	1	1	.333	.400	.556	155	-0	0			1.000	-0	/O-1	0.0
	Yr	55	186	30	51	12	4	3	21	20	26	.274	.348	.430	115	4	1			.976	-3	O-48	-0.1
1938	Phi-N	100	351	51	109	23	2	4	45	64	43	.311	.422	.422	137	21	1			.988	2	1-98	1.2
1944	NY-N	104	361	55	114	18	9	13	77	59	59	.316	.412	.524	162	31	0			.992	3	1-99	2.9
1945	NY-N	82	283	45	77	9	1	10	42	54	29	.272	.389	.417	122	10	2			.993	3	1-77	0.8
Total	7	444	1382	215	407	67	19	32	207	232	182	.295	.398	.440	133	69	4			.990	-4	1-293/O-81	3.9

■ AL WEIS Weis, Albert John b: 4/2/38, Franklin Square, N.Y BB/TR, 6', 170 lbs. Deb: 9/15/62

1962	Chi-A	7	12	2	1	0	0	0	0	2	3	.083	.267	.083	-1	-2	1	0	0	.882	-1	/S-4,2-1,3	-0.2
1963	Chi-A	99	210	41	57	9	0	0	18	18	37	.271	.335	.314	85	-4	15	1	4	.990	14	2-48,S-27/3	1.9
1964	Chi-A	133	328	36	81	4	4	2	23	22	41	.247	.300	.302	70	-13	22	7	2	.966	12	*2-116/S-9,O	0.9
1965	Chi-A	103	135	29	40	4	3	1	12	12	22	.296	.362	.393	122	4	4	1	1	.975	25	2-74/S-7,3O	3.4
1966	Chi-A	129	187	20	29	4	0	0	9	17	50	.155	.233	.187	24	-18	3	4	-2	.987	37	2-96,S-18	2.2
1967	Chi-A	50	53	9	13	2	0	0	4	1	7	.245	.273	.283	67	-2	3	3	-1	.986	11	2-32,S-13	1.0
1968	NY-N	90	274	20	47	6	0	1	14	21	63	.172	.236	.204	33	-22	3	3	-1	.958	7	S-59,2-29/3	-1.0
1969	*NY-N	103	247	20	53	3	2	2	23	15	51	.215	.260	.291	49	-16	3	1	-1	.960	13	S-52,2-43/3	0.3
1970	NY-N	75	121	20	25	7	1	1	11	7	21	.207	.256	.306	50	-9	1	1	-0	.952	2	2-44,S-15	-0.4

YEAR	TM/L	G	AB	R	H	2B	3B	HR	RBI	BB	SO	AVG	OBP	SLG	PRO+	BR/A	SB	CS	SBR	FA	FR	G/POS	TPR
1971	NY-N	11	11	3	0	0	0	0	1	2	4	.000	.154	.000	-54	-2	0	0	0	1.000	1	/2-5,3-2	-0.2
Total	10	800	1578	195	346	45	11	7	115	117	299	.219	.279	.275	59	-84	55	22	3	.975	121	2-488,S-204/3O	7.9

■ **BUTCH WEIS**   Weis, Arthur John   b: 3/2/01, St.Louis, Mo.   BL/TL, 5'11", 180 lbs.   Deb: 4/15/22

YEAR	TM/L	G	AB	R	H	2B	3B	HR	RBI	BB	SO	AVG	OBP	SLG	PRO+	BR/A	SB	CS	SBR	FA	FR	G/POS	TPR
1922	Chi-N	2	2	2	1	0	0	0	0	0	0	.500	.500	.500	156	0	0	0	0	.000	0	H	0.0
1923	Chi-N	22	26	2	6	1	0	0	2	5	8	.231	.355	.269	67	-1	0	1	-1	1.000	-1	/O-6	-0.3
1924	Chi-N	37	133	19	37	8	1	0	23	15	14	.278	.356	.353	90	-1	4	5	-2	.978	6	O-36	0.0
1925	Chi-N	67	180	16	48	5	3	0	25	23	22	.267	.350	.361	81	-5	2	4	-2	.964	-5	O-47	-1.3
Total	4	128	341	39	92	14	4	0	50	43	44	.270	.353	.352	84	-7	6	10	-4	.973	0	/O-89	-1.6

■ **BUD WEISER**   Weiser, Harry Budson   b: 1/8/1891, Shamokin, Pa.   d: 7/31/61, Shamokin, Pa.   BR/TR, 5'11", 165 lbs.   Deb: 4/29/15

YEAR	TM/L	G	AB	R	H	2B	3B	HR	RBI	BB	SO	AVG	OBP	SLG	PRO+	BR/A	SB	CS	SBR	FA	FR	G/POS	TPR
1915	Phi-N	37	64	6	9	2	0	0	8	7	12	.141	.236	.172	24	-6	2	2	-1	.897	-5	O-20	-1.4
1916	Phi-N	4	10	1	3	1	0	0	1	0	3	.300	.300	.400	110	0	0			1.000	-1	/O-4	-0.1
Total	2	41	74	7	12	3	0	0	9	7	15	.162	.244	.203	36	-6	2	2		.912	-6	/O-24	-1.5

■ **GARY WEISS**   Weiss, Gary Lee   b: 12/27/55, Brenham, Tex.   BB/TR, 5'10", 170 lbs.   Deb: 9/13/80

YEAR	TM/L	G	AB	R	H	2B	3B	HR	RBI	BB	SO	AVG	OBP	SLG	PRO+	BR/A	SB	CS	SBR	FA	FR	G/POS	TPR
1980	LA-N	8	0	2	0	0	0	0	0	0	0	—	—	—		0	0	0	0	.000	0	/R	0.0
1981	LA-N	14	19	2	2	0	0	0	1	1	4	.105	.150	.105	-28	-3	0	0	0	.920	-1	S-13	-0.4
Total	2	22	19	4	2	0	0	0	1	1	4	.105	.150	.105	-28	-3	0	0	0	.920	-1	/S-13	-0.4

■ **JOE WEISS**   Weiss, Joseph Harold   b: 1/27/1894, Chicago, Ill.   d: 7/7/67, Cedar Rapids, Iowa   BR/TR, 6', 165 lbs.   Deb: 8/29/15

YEAR	TM/L	G	AB	R	H	2B	3B	HR	RBI	BB	SO	AVG	OBP	SLG	PRO+	BR/A	SB	CS	SBR	FA	FR	G/POS	TPR
1915	Chi-F	29	85	6	19	1	2	0	11	3	24	.224	.250	.282	45	-7	0			.992	-1	1-29	-1.0

■ **WALT WEISS**   Weiss, Walter William   b: 11/28/63, Tuxedo, N.Y.   BB/TR, 6', 175 lbs.   Deb: 7/12/87

YEAR	TM/L	G	AB	R	H	2B	3B	HR	RBI	BB	SO	AVG	OBP	SLG	PRO+	BR/A	SB	CS	SBR	FA	FR	G/POS	TPR
1987	Oak-A	16	26	3	12	4	0	0	1	2	2	.462	.500	.615	208	4	1	2	-1	.974	5	S-11/D-2	0.8
1988	*Oak-A	147	452	44	113	17	3	3	39	35	56	.250	.317	.321	82	-10	4	4	-1	.979	10	*S-147	1.0
1989	*Oak-A	84	236	30	55	11	0	3	21	21	39	.233	.298	.318	76	-7	6	1	1	.953	-14	S-84	-1.5
1990	Oak-A	138	445	50	118	17	1	2	35	46	53	.265	.339	.321	89	-5	9	3	1	.979	-26	S-137	-2.0
1991	Oak-A	40	133	15	30	6	1	0	13	12	14	.226	.290	.286	63	-7	6	0	2	.970	-10	S-40	-1.2
1992	*Oak-A	103	316	36	67	5	2	0	21	43	39	.212	.308	.241	59	-16	6	3	0	.956	-14	*S-103	-2.4
1993	Fla-N	158	500	50	133	14	2	1	39	79	73	.266	.369	.308	79	-11	7	3	0	.977	-18	*S-153	-1.7
1994	Col-N	110	423	58	106	11	4	1	32	56	58	.251	.338	.303	59	-25	12	7	-1	.973	3	*S-110	-1.3
Total	8	796	2531	286	634	85	13	10	201	294	334	.250	.333	.306	75	-78	51	23	2	.972	-64	S-785/D-2	-8.3

■ **JOHNNY WELAJ**   Welaj, John Ludwig   b: 5/27/14, Moss Creek, Pa.   BR/TR, 6', 164 lbs.   Deb: 5/2/39

YEAR	TM/L	G	AB	R	H	2B	3B	HR	RBI	BB	SO	AVG	OBP	SLG	PRO+	BR/A	SB	CS	SBR	FA	FR	G/POS	TPR
1939	Was-A	63	201	23	55	11	2	1	33	13	20	.274	.318	.363	80	-7	13	2	3	.975	-4	O-55	-0.9
1940	Was-A	88	215	31	55	9	0	3	21	19	20	.256	.322	.340	77	-7	8	7	-2	.978	-1	O-53	-1.2
1941	Was-A	49	96	16	20	4	0	0	5	6	16	.208	.255	.250	36	-9	3	1	0	.979	-0	O-19	-1.0
1943	Phi-A	93	281	45	68	16	1	0	15	15	17	.242	.280	.306	72	-11	12	5	1	.960	-3	O-72	-1.5
Total	4	293	793	115	198	40	3	4	74	53	73	.250	.298	.323	71	-34	36	15	2	.970	-5	O-199	-4.6

■ **CURT WELCH**   Welch, Curtis Benton   b: 2/11/1862, E.Liverpool, Ohio   d: 8/29/1896, E.Liverpool, Ohio   BR/TR, 5'10", 175 lbs.   Deb: 5/1/1884

YEAR	TM/L	G	AB	R	H	2B	3B	HR	RBI	BB	SO	AVG	OBP	SLG	PRO+	BR/A	SB	CS	SBR	FA	FR	G/POS	TPR
1884	Tol-a	109	425	61	95	24	5	0		10		.224	.248	.304	76	-12				.888	16	*O-107/2-2,C1	0.2
1885	*StL-a	112	432	84	117	18	8	3		23		.271	.355	.370	112	5				.946	14	*O-112	1.4
1886	*StL-a	138	563	114	158	31	13	2		29		.281	.332	.393	121	11	59			.952	14	*O-138/2-2	1.9
1887	*StL-a	131	544	98	151	32	7	3		25		.278	.322	.379	86	-15	89			.941	19	*O-123/2-8,1	0.2
1888	Phi-a	136	549	125	155	22	8	1	61	33		.282	.355	.357	129	20	95			.952	4	*O-135/2-3	1.9
1889	Phi-a	125	516	134	140	39	6	0	39	67	30	.271	.355	.370	114	13	66			.923	8	*O-125	1.5
1890	Phi-a	103	396	100	106	21	4	2		49		.268	.392	.356	123	16	64			.919	14	*O-103/P-1	2.2
	Bal-a	19	68	16	9	4	0	0		9		.132	.253	.191	30	-6	8			.974	2	O-17/1-2	-0.4
	Yr	122	464	116	115	25	4	2		58		.248	.372	.332	109	9	72			.926	16	*O-120/1-2,P	1.8
1891	Bal-a	132	514	122	138	22	10	3	55	77	42	.268	.400	.368	119	17	50			.946	19	*O-113,2-21/S	2.8
1892	Bal-N	63	237	42	56	1	3	1	22	36	9	.236	.363	.278	92	-0	14			.905	-4	O-63	-0.6
	Cin-N	25	94	14	19	0	2	1	7	7	8	.202	.299	.277	75	-3	7			.925	-0	O-25	-0.4
	Yr	88	331	56	75	1	5	2	29	43	17	.227	.345	.278	88	-3	21			.911	-4	O-88	-1.0
1893	Lou-N	14	47	5	8	1	0	0	2	16	1	.170	.400	.191	64	-1	1			.912	-0	O-14	-0.1
Total	10	1107	4385	915	1152	215	66	16	186	381	93	.263	.345	.353	107	45	453			.933	107	*O-1075/2-36,1SCP	10.6

■ **FRANK WELCH**   Welch, Frank Tiguer "Bugger"   b: 8/10/1897, Birmingham, Ala.   d: 7/25/57, Birmingham, Ala.   BR/TR, 5'9", 175 lbs.   Deb: 9/9/19

YEAR	TM/L	G	AB	R	H	2B	3B	HR	RBI	BB	SO	AVG	OBP	SLG	PRO+	BR/A	SB	CS	SBR	FA	FR	G/POS	TPR
1919	Phi-A	15	54	5	9	1	1	2	7	7	10	.167	.262	.333	66	-3	0			.909	4	O-15	-0.4
1920	Phi-A	100	360	43	93	17	5	4	40	26	41	.258	.312	.367	78	-12	2	9	-5	.937	-6	O-97	-2.9
1921	Phi-A	115	403	48	115	18	6	7	45	34	43	.285	.347	.412	92	-5	6	0	2	.943	3	*O-104	-0.8
1922	Phi-A	114	375	43	97	17	3	11	49	40	40	.259	.335	.408	90	-6	3	4	-2	.949	-0	*O-104	-1.5
1923	Phi-A	125	421	56	125	19	9	4	55	48	40	.297	.344	.413	106	4	1	4	-2	.967	3	*O-117	-0.2
1924	Phi-A	94	293	47	85	13	2	5	31	35	27	.290	.372	.399	98	-1	2	3	-1	.985	1	O-74	-0.5
1925	Phi-A	85	202	40	56	5	4	4	41	29	14	.277	.373	.401	90	-3	2	1	0	.968	-3	O-57	-0.8
1926	Phi-A	75	174	26	49	8	1	4	23	26	9	.282	.381	.408	100	0	2	5	-2	.975	-5	O-49	-1.0
1927	Bos-A	15	28	2	5	2	0	0	4	5	1	.179	.303	.250	46	-2	0	2	-1	1.000	2	/O-6	-0.2
Total	9	738	2310	310	634	100	31	41	295	250	225	.274	.350	.398	92	-27	18	28		.955	-5	O-623	-8.3

■ **HERB WELCH**   Welch, Herbert M. "Dutch"   b: 10/19/1898, Roellen, Tenn.   d: 4/13/67, Memphis, Tenn.   BL/TR, 5'6", 154 lbs.   Deb: 9/15/25

YEAR	TM/L	G	AB	R	H	2B	3B	HR	RBI	BB	SO	AVG	OBP	SLG	PRO+	BR/A	SB	CS	SBR	FA	FR	G/POS	TPR
1925	Bos-A	13	38	2	11	0	1	0	2	0	6	.289	.289	.342	60	-1	0			.893	5	S-13	0.4

■ **TUB WELCH**   Welch, James T.   b: 7/3/1866, St.Louis, Mo.   TR, 5'11", 230 lbs.   Deb: 6/12/1890

YEAR	TM/L	G	AB	R	H	2B	3B	HR	RBI	BB	SO	AVG	OBP	SLG	PRO+	BR/A	SB	CS	SBR	FA	FR	G/POS	TPR
1890	Tol-a	35	108	15	31	3	1	1		8		.287	.358	.361	109	1	7			.930	0	C-25,1-10	0.2
1895	Lou-N	47	153	18	37	4	1	1	8	13	7	.242	.310	.301	62	-8	2			.888	-1	C-28,1-20	-0.5
Total	2	82	261	33	68	7	2	2	8	21	7	.261	.330	.326	80	-7	9			.911	-1	/C-53,1-30	-0.3

■ **MILT WELCH**   Welch, Milton Edward   b: 7/26/24, Farmersville, Ill   BR/TR, 5'10", 175 lbs.   Deb: 6/5/45

YEAR	TM/L	G	AB	R	H	2B	3B	HR	RBI	BB	SO	AVG	OBP	SLG	PRO+	BR/A	SB	CS	SBR	FA	FR	G/POS	TPR
1945	Det-A	2	0	0	0	0	0	0	0	0	1	.000	.000	.000	-94	-0	0	0	0	1.000	0	/C-1	0.0

■ **HARRY WELCHONCE**   Welchonce, Harry Monroe "Welch"   b: 11/20/1883, North Point, Pa.   d: 2/26/77, Arcadia, Cal.   BL/TR, 6', 170 lbs.   Deb: 4/17/11

YEAR	TM/L	G	AB	R	H	2B	3B	HR	RBI	BB	SO	AVG	OBP	SLG	PRO+	BR/A	SB	CS	SBR	FA	FR	G/POS	TPR
1911	Phi-N	26	66	9	14	4	0	0	6	7	8	.212	.288	.273	56	-4	0			.929	-3	O-17	-0.8

■ **MIKE WELDAY**   Welday, Lyndon Earl   b: 12/19/1879, Conway, Iowa   d: 5/28/42, Leavenworth, Kan.   BL/TL,   Deb: 4/21/07

YEAR	TM/L	G	AB	R	H	2B	3B	HR	RBI	BB	SO	AVG	OBP	SLG	PRO+	BR/A	SB	CS	SBR	FA	FR	G/POS	TPR
1907	Chi-A	24	35	2	8	1	1	0	0	6		.229	.341	.314	113	1	0			.938	-3	O-15	-0.2
1909	Chi-A	29	74	3	14	0	0	0	5	4		.189	.231	.189	34	-5	2			.886	1	O-20	-0.6
Total	2	53	109	5	22	1	1	0	5	10		.202	.269	.229	60	-5	2			.900	-2	/O-35	-0.8

■ **OLLIE WELF**   Welf, Oliver Henry   b: 1/17/1889, Cleveland, Ohio   d: 6/15/67, Cleveland, Ohio   BR/TL, 5'9", 160 lbs.   Deb: 8/30/16

YEAR	TM/L	G	AB	R	H	2B	3B	HR	RBI	BB	SO	AVG	OBP	SLG	PRO+	BR/A	SB	CS	SBR	FA	FR	G/POS	TPR
1916	Cle-A	1	0	0	0	0	0	0	0	0	0	—	—	—		0	0			.000	0	R	0.0

■ **BRAD WELLMAN**   Wellman, Brad Eugene   b: 8/17/59, Lodi, Cal.   BR/TR, 6', 170 lbs.   Deb: 9/4/82

YEAR	TM/L	G	AB	R	H	2B	3B	HR	RBI	BB	SO	AVG	OBP	SLG	PRO+	BR/A	SB	CS	SBR	FA	FR	G/POS	TPR
1982	SF-N	6	4	1	1	0	0	0	0	0	0	.250	.250	.250	40	-0	0	0	0	1.000	0	/2-2	0.0
1983	SF-N	82	182	15	39	3	0	1	16	22	39	.214	.299	.247	55	-11	5	3	-0	.965	2	2-74/S-2	-0.7
1984	SF-N	93	265	23	60	9	1	2	25	19	41	.226	.278	.291	62	-14	10	5	0	.977	16	2-54,S-34/3	0.7

YEAR	TM/L	G	AB	R	H	2B	3B	HR	RBI	BB	SO	AVG	OBP	SLG	PRO+	BR/A	SB	CS	SBR	FA	FR	G/POS	TPR
1985	SF-N	71	174	16	41	11	1	0	16	4	33	.236	.269	.310	65	-9	5	2	0	.983	-2	2-36,3-25/S	-1.1
1986	SF-N	12	13	0	2	0	0	0	1	1	2	.154	.214	.154	3	-2	0	0	0	1.000	-0	/S-8,2-1,3	-0.2
1987	LA-N	3	4	1	1	0	0	0	1	0	1	.250	.250	.250	34	-0	0	0	0	1.000	-0	/2-1,S-1,3	0.0
1988	KC-A	71	107	11	29	3	0	1	6	6	23	.271	.322	.327	81	-3	1	2	-1	.972	15	2-46,S-15/3D	1.3
1989	KC-A	103	178	30	41	4	0	2	12	7	36	.230	.263	.287	55	-11	5	3	-0	.995	19	2-64,S-34/3D	1.1
Total	8	441	927	97	214	30	2	6	77	59	176	.231	.282	.287	61	-48	26	15	-1	.978	50	2-278/S-97,3D	1.1

◼ BOB WELLMAN
Wellman, Robert Joseph b: 7/15/25, Norwood, Ohio BR/TR, 6'4", 210 lbs. Deb: 9/23/48

YEAR	TM/L	G	AB	R	H	2B	3B	HR	RBI	BB	SO	AVG	OBP	SLG	PRO+	BR/A	SB	CS	SBR	FA	FR	G/POS	TPR
1948	Phi-A	4	10	1	2	0	1	0	0	3	2	.200	.385	.400	109	0	0	0	0	1.000	0	/1-2,O-1	0.0
1950	Phi-A	11	15	1	5	0	0	1	1	0	3	.333	.333	.533	121	0	0	0	0	1.000	-0	/O-2	0.0
Total	2	15	25	2	7	0	1	1	1	3	5	.280	.357	.480	117	1	0	0	0	.889	0	/O-3,1-2	0.0

◼ GREG WELLS
Wells, Gregory De Wayne b: 4/25/54, McIntosh, Ala. BR/TR, 6'5", 218 lbs. Deb: 8/10/81

YEAR	TM/L	G	AB	R	H	2B	3B	HR	RBI	BB	SO	AVG	OBP	SLG	PRO+	BR/A	SB	CS	SBR	FA	FR	G/POS	TPR
1981	Tor-A	32	73	7	18	5	0	0	5	5	12	.247	.295	.315	71	-3	0	2	-1	.994	-0	1-22/D-3	-0.5
1982	Min-A	15	54	5	11	1	2	0	3	1	8	.204	.218	.296	39	-5	0	0	0	.962	-2	1-10/D-5	-0.7
Total	2	47	127	12	29	6	2	0	8	6	20	.228	.263	.307	58	-7	0	2	-1	.983	-2	/1-32,D-8	-1.2

◼ JAKE WELLS
Wells, Jacob b: 8/9/1863, Memphis, Tenn. d: 3/16/27, Hendersonville, N.C. BR/TR, 5'11", 167 lbs. Deb: 8/10/1888

YEAR	TM/L	G	AB	R	H	2B	3B	HR	RBI	BB	SO	AVG	OBP	SLG	PRO+	BR/A	SB	CS	SBR	FA	FR	G/POS	TPR
1888	Det-N	16	57	5	9	1	0	0	2	0	5	.158	.158	.175	6	-6	0			.917	5	C-16	0.0
1890	StL-a	30	105	17	25	3	0	0		10		.238	.333	.267	67	-5	1			.941	2	C-28/O-3	-0.1
Total	2	46	162	22	34	4	0	0	2	10	5	.210	.277	.235	50	-11	1			.932	6	/C-44,O-3	-0.1

◼ LEO WELLS
Wells, Leo Donald b: 7/18/17, Kansas City, Kan. BR/TR, 5'9", 170 lbs. Deb: 4/16/42

YEAR	TM/L	G	AB	R	H	2B	3B	HR	RBI	BB	SO	AVG	OBP	SLG	PRO+	BR/A	SB	CS	SBR	FA	FR	G/POS	TPR
1942	Chi-A	35	62	8	12	2	0	1	4	4	5	.194	.242	.274	46	-5	1	0	0	1.000	11	S-12/3-6	0.7
1946	Chi-A	45	127	11	24	4	1	1	11	12	34	.189	.259	.260	47	-9	3	4	-2	.942	8	3-38/S-2	-0.3
Total	2	80	189	19	36	6	1	2	15	16	39	.190	.254	.265	47	-14	4	4	-1	.938	19	/3-44,S-14	0.4

◼ JIMMY WELSH
Welsh, James Daniel b: 10/9/02, Denver, Colo. d: 10/30/70, Oakland, Cal. BL/TR, 6'1", 174 lbs. Deb: 4/14/25

YEAR	TM/L	G	AB	R	H	2B	3B	HR	RBI	BB	SO	AVG	OBP	SLG	PRO+	BR/A	SB	CS	SBR	FA	FR	G/POS	TPR
1925	Bos-N	122	484	69	151	25	8	7	63	20	24	.312	.350	.440	110	5	7	4	-0	.960	6	*O-116/2-3	0.4
1926	Bos-N	134	490	69	136	18	11	3	57	33	28	.278	.333	.378	100	-1	6			.965	10	*O-129	0.0
1927	Bos-N	131	497	72	143	26	7	9	54	23	27	.288	.332	.423	109	4	11			.969	13	*O-129/1-1	0.9
1928	NY-N	124	476	77	146	22	5	9	54	29	30	.307	.357	.431	104	3	4			.981	-0	*O-117	-0.5
1929	NY-N	38	129	25	32	7	0	2	8	9	3	.248	.331	.349	69	-6	3			.940	-6	O-35	-1.4
	Bos-N	53	186	24	54	8	7	2	16	13	9	.290	.350	.441	98	-1	1			.979	9	O-51	0.4
	Yr	91	315	49	86	15	7	4	24	22	12	.273	.342	.403	86	-7	4			.970	2	O-86	-1.0
1930	Bos-N	113	422	51	116	21	9	3	36	29	23	.275	.327	.389	75	-18	5			.980	11	*O-110	-1.3
Total	6	715	2684	387	778	127	47	35	288	156	144	.290	.340	.411	98	-14	37	4		.971	42	O-687/2-3,1	-1.5

◼ LEW WENDELL
Wendell, Lewis Charles b: 3/22/1892, New York, N.Y. d: 7/11/53, Brooklyn, N.Y. BR/TR, 5'11", 178 lbs. Deb: 6/10/15

YEAR	TM/L	G	AB	R	H	2B	3B	HR	RBI	BB	SO	AVG	OBP	SLG	PRO+	BR/A	SB	CS	SBR	FA	FR	G/POS	TPR
1915	NY-N	20	36	0	8	1	1	0	5	2	7	.222	.263	.306	76	-1	0			.920	-5	C-18	-0.6
1916	NY-N	2	2	0	0	0	0	0	0	0	2	.000	.000	.000	-99	-0	0			.000	0	H	-0.1
1924	Phi-N	21	32	3	8	1	0	0	2	3	5	.250	.314	.281	54	-2	0	0	0	1.000	-1	C-17	-0.3
1925	Phi-N	18	26	0	2	0	0	0	3	1	3	.077	.111	.077	-47	-6	0			.909	-1	/C-9	-0.6
1926	Phi-N	1	4	0	0	0	0	0	0	0	0	.000	.000	.000	-95	-1	0			.333	-1	/C-1	-0.2
Total	5	62	100	3	18	2	1	0	10	6	17	.180	.226	.220	23	-10	0		0	.925	-8	/C-45	-1.8

◼ JACK WENTZ
Wentz, John George (b: John George Wernz) b: 3/4/1863, Louisville, Ky. d: 9/14/07, Louisville, Ky. BR/TR, 5'10.5", 175 lbs. Deb: 4/15/1891

YEAR	TM/L	G	AB	R	H	2B	3B	HR	RBI	BB	SO	AVG	OBP	SLG	PRO+	BR/A	SB	CS	SBR	FA	FR	G/POS	TPR
1891	Lou-a	1	4	0	1	0	0	0	0	0	0	.250	.250	.250	44	-0	0			.667	-1	/2-1	-0.1

◼ STAN WENTZEL
Wentzel, Stanley Aaron b: 1/13/17, Lorane, Pa. d: 11/28/91, St.Lawrence, Pa. BR/TR, 6'1", 200 lbs. Deb: 9/23/45

YEAR	TM/L	G	AB	R	H	2B	3B	HR	RBI	BB	SO	AVG	OBP	SLG	PRO+	BR/A	SB	CS	SBR	FA	FR	G/POS	TPR
1945	Bos-N	4	19	3	4	0	1	0	6	0	3	.211	.211	.316	45	-1	1			1.000	-1	/O-4	-0.3

◼ JULIE WERA
Wera, Julian Valentine b: 2/9/02, Winona, Minn. d: 12/12/75, Rochester, Minn. BR/TR, 5'8", 164 lbs. Deb: 4/14/27

YEAR	TM/L	G	AB	R	H	2B	3B	HR	RBI	BB	SO	AVG	OBP	SLG	PRO+	BR/A	SB	CS	SBR	FA	FR	G/POS	TPR
1927	NY-A	38	42	7	10	3	0	1	8	1	5	.238	.273	.381	70	-2	0	0	0	1.000	3	3-19	0.1
1929	NY-A	5	12	1	5	0	0	0	2	1	1	.417	.462	.417	137	1	0	0	0	1.000	-1	/3-4	0.0
Total	2	43	54	8	15	3	0	1	10	2	6	.278	.316	.389	85	-1	0	0	0	1.000	2	/3-23	0.1

◼ BILLY WERBER
Werber, William Murray b: 6/20/08, Berwyn, Md. BR/TR, 5'10", 170 lbs. Deb: 6/25/30

YEAR	TM/L	G	AB	R	H	2B	3B	HR	RBI	BB	SO	AVG	OBP	SLG	PRO+	BR/A	SB	CS	SBR	FA	FR	G/POS	TPR
1930	NY-A	4	14	5	4	0	0	0	2	3	1	.286	.412	.286	84	-0	0	0		.955	1	/S-3,3-1	0.1
1933	NY-A	3	2	0	0	0	0	0	0	0	0	.000	.000	.000	-99	-0	0	0	0	.000	0	/3-1	0.0
	Bos-A	108	425	64	110	30	6	3	39	33	39	.259	.312	.379	83	-11	15	5		.910	-17	S-71,3-38/2	-1.8
	Yr	111	427	64	110	30	6	3	39	33	39	.258	.311	.377	82	-12	15	5	3	.910	-17	S-71,3-39/2	-1.9
1934	Bos-A	152	623	129	200	41	10	11	67	77	37	.321	.397	.472	115	14	40	15	3	.941	20	*3-130,S-22	4.0
1935	Bos-A	124	462	84	118	30	3	14	61	69	41	.255	.357	.424	95	-4	29	7	5	.942	17	*3-123	2.1
1936	Bos-A	145	535	89	147	29	6	10	67	89	37	.275	.382	.407	90	-8	23	13	-1	.935	-12	*3-101,O-45/2	-1.7
1937	Phi-A	128	493	85	144	31	4	7	70	74	39	.292	.386	.414	103	3	35	13	3	.958	0	*3-125/O-3	1.0
1938	Phi-A	134	499	92	129	22	7	11	69	93	37	.259	.371	.397	96	-1	19	15	-3	.935	0	*3-134	-0.2
1939	*Cin-N	147	599	115	173	35	5	5	57	91	46	.289	.388	.389	109	11	15			.933	13	*3-147	2.5
1940	*Cin-N	143	584	105	162	35	5	12	48	68	40	.277	.361	.416	113	11	16			.962	3	*3-143	1.7
1941	Cin-N	109	418	59	100	9	2	4	46	53	24	.205	.308	.299	77	-11	14			.959	13	*3-107	0.4
1942	NY-N	98	370	51	76	9	2	1	13	51	22	.205	.308	.249	64	-15	9			.927	10	3-93	-0.4
Total	11	1295	5024	875	1363	271	50	78	539	701	363	.271	.364	.392	97	-10	215	68		.944	49	*3-1143/S-96,O2	7.6

◼ PERRY WERDEN
Werden, Percival Wheritt b: 7/21/1865, St.Louis, Mo. d: 1/9/34, Minneapolis, Minn. BR/TR, 6'2", 220 lbs. Deb: 4/24/1884

YEAR	TM/L	G	AB	R	H	2B	3B	HR	RBI	BB	SO	AVG	OBP	SLG	PRO+	BR/A	SB	CS	SBR	FA	FR	G/POS	TPR
1884	StL-U	18	76	7	18	2	0	0		2		.237	.256	.263	40	-6				.893	-1	P-16/O-6	-0.2
1888	Was-N	3	10	0	3	0	0	0	2	1	4	.300	.364	.300	120	0	0			.857	-0	/O-3	0.0
1890	Tol-a	128	498	113	147	22	20	6		78		.295	.404	.456	149	32	59			.972	5	*1-124/O-5	2.7
1891	Bal-a	139	552	102	160	20	18	6	104	52	59	.290	.363	.424	124	15	46			.980	1	*1-139	0.7
1892	StL-N	149	598	73	154	22	6	8	84	59	52	.258	.328	.355	112	9	20			.982	12	*1-149	1.2
1893	StL-N	125	500	73	138	22	29	1	94	49	25	.276	.349	.442	109	4	11			.968	3	*1-124/O-1	0.3
1897	Lou-N	131	506	76	153	21	14	5	83	40		.302	.366	.429	113	9	14			.984	18	*1-131	2.4
Total	7	693	2740	444	773	109	87	26	367	281	140	.282	.359	.414	119	63	150			.978	38	1-667/P-16,O	7.1

◼ JOHNNY WERHAS
Werhas, John Charles "Peaches" b: 2/7/38, Highland Park, Mich. BR/TR, 6'2", 200 lbs. Deb: 4/14/64

YEAR	TM/L	G	AB	R	H	2B	3B	HR	RBI	BB	SO	AVG	OBP	SLG	PRO+	BR/A	SB	CS	SBR	FA	FR	G/POS	TPR
1964	LA-N	29	83	6	16	2	1	0	8	13	12	.193	.302	.241	59	-4	0	0	0	.952	4	3-28	-0.1
1965	LA-N	4	3	1	0	0	0	0	0	1	2	.000	.250	.000	-24	-0	0	0	0	1.000	-0	/1-1	-0.1
1967	LA-N	7	7	0	1	0	0	0	0	0	3	.143	.143	.143	-20	-1	0	0	0	.000	0	H	-0.1
	Cal-A	49	75	8	12	1	1	2	6	10	22	.160	.267	.280	64	-3	0	0	0	.963	1	3-30/1-4,O	-0.3
Total	3	89	168	15	29	3	2	2	14	24	39	.173	.280	.250	57	-9	0	0	0	.956	4	/3-58,1-5,O	-0.6

◼ DON WERNER
Werner, Donald Paul b: 3/8/53, Appleton, Wis. BR/TR, 6'1", 185 lbs. Deb: 9/2/75

YEAR	TM/L	G	AB	R	H	2B	3B	HR	RBI	BB	SO	AVG	OBP	SLG	PRO+	BR/A	SB	CS	SBR	FA	FR	G/POS	TPR
1975	Cin-N	7	8	0	1	0	0	0	0	0	0	.125	.222	.125	-2	-1	0	0	0	.923	0	/C-7	-0.1
1976	Cin-N	3	4	0	2	1	0	0	1	1	1	.500	.600	.750	275	1	0	0	0	1.000	1	/C-3	0.2
1977	Cin-N	10	23	3	4	0	0	1	3	1	3	.174	.240	.435	75	-1	0	1	-1	1.000	1	C-10	0.0
1978	Cin-N	50	113	7	17	2	1	0	8	14	30	.150	.250	.186	23	-11	0	0	0	.987	5	C-49	-0.6
1980	Cin-N	24	64	2	11	2	0	0	5	7	10	.172	.264	.203	32	-6	1	0	0	.962	1	C-24	-0.4

YEAR	TM/L	G	AB	R	H	2B	3B	HR	RBI	BB	SO	AVG	OBP	SLG	PRO+	BR/A	SB	CS	SBR	FA	FR	G/POS	TPR
1981	Tex-A	2	8	1	2	0	0	0	0	0	2	.250	.250	.250	47	-1	0	1	-1	.000	0	/D-2	-0.1
1982	Tex-A	22	59	4	12	2	0	0	3	3	7	.203	.242	.237	34	-5	0	0	0	.980	1	C-22	-0.4
Total	7	118	279	17	49	7	1	2	24	24	53	.176	.256	.229		-24	2	2	-1	.979	9	C-115/D-2	-1.4

■ JOE WERRICK
Werrick, Joseph Abraham b: 10/25/1861, St.Paul, Minn. d: 5/10/43, St.Peter, Minn. BR/TR, 5'9", 151 lbs. Deb: 9/27/1884

YEAR	TM/L	G	AB	R	H	2B	3B	HR	RBI	BB	SO	AVG	OBP	SLG	PRO+	BR/A	SB	CS	SBR	FA	FR	G/POS	TPR
1884	StP-U	9	27	3	2	0	0	0		1		.074	.107	.074	-92	-8				.756	-0	/S-9	-0.8
1886	Lou-a	136	561	75	140	20	14	3		33		.250	.294	.351	96	-6	19			.853	-1	*3-136	-0.3
1887	Lou-a	136	533	90	152	21	13	7		38		.285	.336	.413	106	2	49			.831	-0	*3-136	0.4
1888	Lou-a	111	413	49	89	12	7	0	51	30		.215	.274	.278	79	-9	15			.811	-13	3-89,S-11/2O	-1.8
Total	4	392	1534	217	383	53	34	10	51	102		.250	.300	.348	94	-21	83			.834	-14	3-361/S-20,2O	-2.5

■ DON WERT
Wert, Donald Ralph b: 7/29/38, Strasburg, Pa. BR/TR, 5'9", 165 lbs. Deb: 5/11/63

YEAR	TM/L	G	AB	R	H	2B	3B	HR	RBI	BB	SO	AVG	OBP	SLG	PRO+	BR/A	SB	CS	SBR	FA	FR	G/POS	TPR
1963	Det-A	78	251	31	65	6	2	7	25	24	51	.259	.329	.382	95	-1	3	3	-1	.957	3	3-47,2-21/S	0.4
1964	Det-A	148	525	63	135	18	5	9	55	50	74	.257	.329	.362	91	-6	3	4	-2	.965	0	*3-142/S-4	-0.9
1965	Det-A	162	609	81	159	22	2	12	54	73	71	.261	.343	.363	100	1	5	6	-2	**.976**	5	*3-161/S-3,2	0.0
1966	Det-A	150	559	56	150	20	2	11	70	64	69	.268	.346	.370	103	4	6	3	0	.972	-18	*3-150	-1.9
1967	Det-A	142	534	60	137	23	2	6	40	44	59	.257	.321	.341	93	-4	1	1	0	.978	-5	*3-140/S-1	-1.1
1968	*Det-A★	150	536	44	107	15	1	12	37	37	79	.200	.258	.299	66	-22	0	3	-2	.966	-6	*3-150/S-2	-3.5
1969	Det-A	132	423	46	95	11	1	14	50	49	60	.225	.307	.355	81	-11	3	1	0	.966	-0	*3-129	-1.1
1970	Det-A	128	363	34	79	13	0	6	33	44	56	.218	.309	.303	69	-15	1	3	-2	.953	-2	*3-117/2-2	-2.0
1971	Was-A	20	40	2	2	1	0	0	2	4	10	.050	.156	.075	-35	-7	0	0	0	1.000	-4	/S-7,3-7,2	-1.1
Total	9	1110	3840	417	929	129	15	77	366	389	529	.242	.317	.343	87	-61	22	24	-8	.968	-27	*3-1043/S-25,2	-11.2

■ DENNIS WERTH
Werth, Dennis Dean b: 12/29/52, Lincoln, Ill. BR/TR, 6'1", 200 lbs. Deb: 9/17/79

YEAR	TM/L	G	AB	R	H	2B	3B	HR	RBI	BB	SO	AVG	OBP	SLG	PRO+	BR/A	SB	CS	SBR	FA	FR	G/POS	TPR
1979	NY-A	3	4	1	1	0	0	0	0	0	0	.250	.250	.250	36	-0	0	0	0	1.000	0	/1-1	0.0
1980	NY-A	39	65	15	20	3	0	3	12	12	19	.308	.416	.492	150	5	0	1	0	1.000	-2	1-12/O-8,C3D	0.2
1981	NY-A	34	55	7	6	1	0	0	1	12	12	.109	.269	.127	18	-5	1	0	-1	1.000	4	1-19/O-8,CD	-0.6
1982	KC-A	41	15	5	2	0	0	0	2	4	2	.133	.316	.133	29	-1	0	0	0	.990	2	1-35/C-2	0.1
Total	4	117	139	28	29	4	0	3	15	28	33	.209	.341	.302	82	-1	1	1	-0	.996	1	/1-67,O-16,DC3	-0.3

■ DEL WERTZ
Wertz, Dwight Lyman Moody b: 10/11/1888, Canton, Ohio d: 5/26/58, Sarasota, Fla. BR/TR, 5'10", 160 lbs. Deb: 5/23/14

YEAR	TM/L	G	AB	R	H	2B	3B	HR	RBI	BB	SO	AVG	OBP	SLG	PRO+	BR/A	SB	CS	SBR	FA	FR	G/POS	TPR
1914	Buf-F	3	0	1	0	0	0	0	0	0	0					0	0	0	0	1.000	0	/S-1	0.0

■ VIC WERTZ
Wertz, Victor Woodrow b: 2/9/25, York, Pa. d: 7/7/83, Detroit, Mich. BL/TR, 6', 186 lbs. Deb: 4/15/47

YEAR	TM/L	G	AB	R	H	2B	3B	HR	RBI	BB	SO	AVG	OBP	SLG	PRO+	BR/A	SB	CS	SBR	FA	FR	G/POS	TPR
1947	Det-A	102	333	60	96	22	4	6	44	47	66	.288	.376	.432	121	10	2	0	1	.965	-2	O-83	0.4
1948	Det-A	119	391	49	97	19	9	7	67	48	70	.248	.335	.396	92	-6	2	0	0	.954	1	O-98	-1.0
1949	Det-A★	155	608	96	185	26	6	20	133	80	61	.304	.385	.465	124	20	2	3	-1	.981	2	*O-155	1.3
1950	Det-A	149	559	99	172	37	4	27	123	91	55	.308	.408	.533	135	29	0	1	-1	.967	-8	*O-145	1.3
1951	Det-A★	138	501	86	143	24	4	27	94	78	61	.285	.383	.511	139	27	0	3	-2	.989	5	*O-131	2.3
1952	Det-A☆	85	285	46	70	15	3	17	51	46	44	.246	.352	.498	134	12	1	0	0	.986	3	O-79	1.2
	StL-A	37	130	22	45	5	0	6	19	23	20	.346	.444	.523	164	12	0	0	0	.955	-3	O-36	0.8
	Yr	122	415	68	115	20	3	23	70	69	64	.277	.381	.506	143	24	1	0	0	.976	0	*O-115	2.0
1953	StL-A	128	440	61	118	18	6	19	70	72	44	.268	.376	.466	124	15	1	4	-2	.974	7	*O-121	1.6
1954	Bal-A	29	94	5	19	1	0	1	13	11	17	.202	.286	.245	50	-6	0	0	0	.963	2	O-27	-0.6
	*Cle-A	94	295	33	81	14	2	14	48	34	40	.275	.350	.478	123	8	0	2	-1	.989	2	1-83/O-5	0.5
	Yr	123	389	38	100	15	2	15	61	45	57	.257	.334	.422	106	2	0	2	-1	.989	4	1-83,O-32	-0.1
1955	Cle-A	74	257	30	65	11	2	14	55	32	33	.253	.338	.475	112	3	1	1	-0	.984	-3	1-63/O-9	-0.4
1956	Cle-A	136	481	65	127	22	0	32	106	75	87	.264	.369	.509	127	18	0	0	0	.991	1	*1-133	1.0
1957	Cle-A★	144	515	84	145	21	0	28	105	78	88	.282	.378	.485	136	26	2	3	-1	.988	-2	*1-139	1.5
1958	Cle-A	25	43	5	12	1	0	3	12	5	7	.279	.354	.512	139	2	0	0	0	.980	4	/1-8	0.2
1959	Bos-A	94	247	38	68	13	0	7	49	22	32	.275	.339	.413	101	0	0	0	0	.992	2	1-64	-0.2
1960	Bos-A	131	443	45	125	22	0	19	103	37	54	.282	.339	.460	110	5	0	2	-1	.987	3	*1-117	-0.1
1961	Bos-A	99	317	33	83	16	2	11	60	38	43	.262	.345	.429	103	1	0	0	0	.991	3	1-86	-0.2
	Det-A	8	6	1	1	0	0	0	1	0	1	.167	.167	.167	-10	-1	0	0	0	.000	0	H	-0.2
	Yr	107	323	34	84	16	2	11	61	38	44	.260	.342	.424	101	0	0	0	0	.991	3	1-86	-0.3
1962	Det-A	74	105	7	34	2	0	5	18	5	13	.324	.360	.486	121	3	0	0	0	.988	0	1-16	0.2
1963	Det-A	6	5	0	0	0	0	0	0	0	1	.000	.000	.000	-97	-1	0	0	0	.000	0	H	-0.1
	Min-A	35	44	3	6	0	0	3	7	6	5	.136	.240	.341	59	-3	0	0	0	1.000	0	/1-6	-0.2
	Yr	41	49	3	6	0	0	3	7	6	6	.122	.218	.306	44	-4	0	0	0	1.000	0	/1-6	-0.3
Total	17	1862	6099	867	1692	289	42	266	1178	828	842	.277	.366	.469	121	177	9	19	-9	.973	12	O-889,1-715	9.4

■ JIM WESSINGER
Wessinger, James Michael b: 9/25/55, Utica, N.Y. BR/TR, 5'10", 165 lbs. Deb: 8/4/79

YEAR	TM/L	G	AB	R	H	2B	3B	HR	RBI	BB	SO	AVG	OBP	SLG	PRO+	BR/A	SB	CS	SBR	FA	FR	G/POS	TPR
1979	Atl-N	10	7	2	0	0	0	0	0	1	4	.000	.125	.000	-59	-2	0	0	0	.833	1	/2-2	-0.1

■ MAX WEST
West, Max Edward b: 11/28/16, Dexter, Mo. BL/TR, 6'1.5", 182 lbs. Deb: 4/19/38

YEAR	TM/L	G	AB	R	H	2B	3B	HR	RBI	BB	SO	AVG	OBP	SLG	PRO+	BR/A	SB	CS	SBR	FA	FR	G/POS	TPR
1938	Bos-N	123	418	47	98	16	5	10	63	38	38	.234	.300	.368	92	-6	5			.986	-9	*O-109/1-7	-1.9
1939	Bos-N	130	449	67	128	26	6	19	82	51	55	.285	.364	.497	139	23	1			.974	-7	*O-124	1.2
1940	Bos-N★	139	524	72	137	27	5	7	72	65	54	.261	.344	.372	103	3	2			.975	1	*O-102,1-36	-0.5
1941	Bos-N	138	484	63	134	28	4	12	68	72	68	.277	.373	.426	130	20	5			.981	6	*O-132	1.9
1942	Bos-N	134	452	54	115	22	0	16	56	68	59	.254	.354	.409	126	15	4			.991	-1	1-85,O-50	0.7
1946	Bos-N	1	1	0	0	0	0	0	0	1	0	.000	.000	.000	-99	-0	0			1.000	-0	/1-1	0.0
	Cin-N	72	202	16	43	13	0	5	18	32	36	.213	.323	.351	95	-1	1			.952	1	O-58	-0.5
	Yr	73	203	16	43	13	0	5	18	32	37	.212	.322	.350	94	-2	1			.952	1	O-58/1-1	-0.5
1948	Pit-N	87	146	19	26	4	0	8	21	27	29	.178	.310	.370	82	-4	1			.991	-1	1-32,O-16	-0.8
Total	7	824	2676	338	681	136	20	77	380	353	340	.254	.344	.407	114	50	19			.975	-15	O-591,1-161	0.1

■ BUCK WEST
West, Milton Douglas b: 8/29/1860, Spring Mill, Ohio d: 1/13/29, Mansfield, Ohio BL/TR, 5'10", 200 lbs. Deb: 8/24/1884

YEAR	TM/L	G	AB	R	H	2B	3B	HR	RBI	BB	SO	AVG	OBP	SLG	PRO+	BR/A	SB	CS	SBR	FA	FR	G/POS	TPR
1884	Cin-a	33	131	20	32	2	8	1		2		.244	.256	.405	107	0				.825	-6	O-33	-0.5
1890	Cle-N	37	151	20	37	6	1	2	29	7	11	.245	.283	.338	82	-4	4			.831	-1	O-37	-0.6
Total	2	70	282	40	69	8	9	3	29	9	11	.245	.271	.369	94	-4	4			.828	-7	/O-70	-1.1

■ DICK WEST
West, Richard Thomas b: 11/24/15, Louisville, Ky. BR/TR, 6'2", 180 lbs. Deb: 9/28/38

YEAR	TM/L	G	AB	R	H	2B	3B	HR	RBI	BB	SO	AVG	OBP	SLG	PRO+	BR/A	SB	CS	SBR	FA	FR	G/POS	TPR
1938	Cin-N	1	1	0	0	0	0	0	0	0	0	.000	.000	.000	-99	-0	0			.000	0	H	0.0
1939	Cin-N	8	19	1	4	0	0	0	4	1	4	.211	.250	.211	25	-2	0			1.000	-1	/O-5,C-1	-0.3
1940	Cin-N	7	28	4	11	2	0	1	6	0	2	.393	.393	.571	161	3	1			1.000	-1	/C-7	0.0
1941	Cin-N	67	172	15	37	5	1	1	17	6	23	.215	.246	.285	49	-12	4			.970	-3	C-64	-1.2
1942	Cin-N	33	79	9	14	3	0	1	8	5	13	.177	.226	.253	40	-6	0			.989	3	C-17/O-6	-0.3
1943	Cin-N	3	0	1	0	0	0	0				—	—	—			0			.000	0	R	0.0
Total	6	119	299	30	66	10	2	4	35	12	42	.221	.253	.298	55	-18	6			.977	-4	/C-89,O-11	-1.8

■ SAM WEST
West, Samuel Filmore b: 10/5/04, Longview, Tex. d: 11/23/85, Lubbock, Tex. BL/TL, 5'11", 165 lbs. Deb: 4/17/27 C

YEAR	TM/L	G	AB	R	H	2B	3B	HR	RBI	BB	SO	AVG	OBP	SLG	PRO+	BR/A	SB	CS	SBR	FA	FR	G/POS	TPR
1927	Was-A	38	67	9	16	4	1	0	6	8	8	.239	.320	.328	69	-3	1	0	0	.939	-1	O-18	-0.5
1928	Was-A	125	378	59	114	30	7	3	40	20	23	.302	.338	.442	104	1	5	6	-2	**.996**	-10	*O-116	-1.7
1929	Was-A	142	510	60	136	16	8	3	75	45	41	.267	.326	.347	73	-20	9	8	-2	.978	15	*O-139	-1.6
1930	Was-A	120	411	75	135	22	10	6	67	37	34	.328	.385	.474	116	10	5	5	-2	.972	3	*O-118	0.4

YEAR	TM/L	G	AB	R	H	2B	3B	HR	RBI	BB	SO	AVG	OBP	SLG	PRO+	BR/A	SB	CS	SBR	FA	FR	G/POS	TPR
1931	Was-A	132	526	77	175	43	13	3	91	30	37	.333	.369	.481	121	14	6	8	-3	.990	21	*O-127	2.2
1932	Was-A	146	554	88	159	27	12	6	83	48	57	.287	.345	.412	96	-4	4	5	-2	.979	19	*O-143	0.5
1933	StL-A★	133	517	93	155	25	12	11	48	59	49	.300	.373	.458	112	8	10	8	-2	.988	8	*O-127	0.8
1934	StL-A★	122	482	90	157	22	10	9	55	62	55	.326	.403	.469	115	11	3	5	-2	.972	7	*O-120	1.0
1935	StL-A☆	138	527	93	158	37	4	10	70	75	46	.300	.388	.442	109	8	1	6	-3	**.989**	17	*O-135	1.5
1936	StL-A	152	533	78	148	26	4	7	70	94	70	.278	.386	.381	87	-8	2	0	1	.983	9	*O-148	-0.4
1937	StL-A★	122	457	68	150	37	4	7	58	46	28	.328	.390	.473	115	11	1	1	-0	.987	12	*O-105	1.7
1938	StL-A	44	165	17	51	8	2	1	27	14	9	.309	.363	.400	91	-2	1	0	0	.971	-3	O-41	-0.6
	Was-A	92	344	51	104	19	5	5	47	33	21	.302	.363	.430	105	2	1	1	-0	.983	-3	O-85	-0.3
	Yr	136	509	68	155	27	7	6	74	47	30	.305	.363	.420	100	-0	2	1	-0	.979	-6	*O-126	-0.9
1939	Was-A	115	390	52	110	20	8	3	52	67	29	.282	.387	.397	109	7	1	1	-0	.992	3	O-89,1-17	0.5
1940	Was-A	57	99	7	25	6	1	1	18	16	13	.253	.357	.364	93	-1	0	2	-1	.990	-1	1-12/O-9	-0.4
1941	Was-A	26	37	3	10	0	0	0	6	11	2	.270	.438	.270	95	1	1	0	0	1.000	-0	/O-8	0.0
1942	Chi-A	49	151	14	35	5	0	0	25	31	18	.232	.363	.265	80	-2	2	0	1	.983	-3	O-45	-0.7
Total	16	1753	6148	934	1838	347	101	75	838	696	540	.299	.371	.425	103	34	53	56	-18	.983	93	*O-1573/1-29	2.4

■ MAX WEST
West, Walter Maxwell b: 7/14/04, Sunset, Tex. d: 4/25/71, Houston, Tex. BR/TR, 5'11", 165 lbs. Deb: 9/18/28

YEAR	TM/L	G	AB	R	H	2B	3B	HR	RBI	BB	SO	AVG	OBP	SLG	PRO+	BR/A	SB	CS	SBR	FA	FR	G/POS	TPR
1928	Bro-N	7	21	4	6	1	1	0	1	4	1	.286	.400	.429	118	1	0			.882	1	/O-6	0.2
1929	Bro-N	5	8	1	2	1	0	0	1	1	0	.250	.333	.375	77	-0	0			1.000	-1	/O-2	-0.1
Total	2	12	29	5	8	2	1	0	2	5	1	.276	.382	.414	107	0	0			.895	1	/O-8	0.1

■ BILLY WEST
West, William Nelson b: 8/21/1840, Philadelphia, Pa. Deb: 5/22/1874

YEAR	TM/L	G	AB	R	H	2B	3B	HR	RBI	BB	SO	AVG	OBP	SLG	PRO+	BR/A	SB	CS	SBR	FA	FR	G/POS	TPR
1874	Atl-n	9	35	4	7	1	0	0			1	.200	.222	.229	50	-2						2-10	-0.2
1876	NY-N	1	4	0	0	0	0	0	0	0	0	.000	.000	.000	-99	-1				1.000	-0	/2-1	-0.1

■ OSCAR WESTERBERG
Westerberg, Oscar William b: 7/8/1882, Alameda, Cal. d: 4/17/09, Alameda, Cal. BB/TR Deb: 9/5/07

YEAR	TM/L	G	AB	R	H	2B	3B	HR	RBI	BB	SO	AVG	OBP	SLG	PRO+	BR/A	SB	CS	SBR	FA	FR	G/POS	TPR
1907	Bos-N	2	6	0	2	0	0	0	1	1		.333	.429	.333	139	0	0			1.000	-1	/S-2	0.0

■ JIM WESTLAKE
Westlake, James Patrick b: 7/3/30, Sacramento, Cal. BL/TL, 6'1", 190 lbs. Deb: 4/16/55 F

YEAR	TM/L	G	AB	R	H	2B	3B	HR	RBI	BB	SO	AVG	OBP	SLG	PRO+	BR/A	SB	CS	SBR	FA	FR	G/POS	TPR
1955	Phi-N	1	1	0	0	0	0	0	0	0	1	.000	.000	.000	-99	-0	0	0	0	.000	0	H	0.0

■ WALLY WESTLAKE
Westlake, Waldon Thomas b: 11/8/20, Gridley, Cal. BR/TR, 6', 186 lbs. Deb: 4/15/47 F

YEAR	TM/L	G	AB	R	H	2B	3B	HR	RBI	BB	SO	AVG	OBP	SLG	PRO+	BR/A	SB	CS	SBR	FA	FR	G/POS	TPR
1947	Pit-N	112	407	59	111	17	4	17	69	27	63	.273	.324	.459	103	-0	5			.988	4	*O-109	-0.2
1948	Pit-N	132	428	78	122	10	6	17	65	46	40	.285	.360	.456	117	10	2			.976	-0	*O-125	0.3
1949	Pit-N	147	525	77	148	24	8	23	104	45	69	.282	.345	.490	118	12	6			.982	5	*O-143	1.0
1950	Pit-N	139	477	69	136	15	6	24	95	48	78	.285	.359	.493	118	11	1			**.991**	4	*O-123	1.0
1951	Pit-N	50	181	28	51	4	0	16	45	9	26	.282	.323	.569	131	7	0	1	-1	.908	5	3-34,O-11	1.0
	StL-N★	73	267	36	68	8	5	6	39	24	42	.255	.325	.390	91	-4	1	2	-1	.982	2	O-68	-0.5
	Yr	123	448	64	119	12	5	22	84	33	68	.266	.324	.462	107	3	1	3	-2	.984	7	O-79,3-34	0.5
1952	StL-N	21	74	7	16	3	0	0	10	8	11	.216	.293	.257	53	-5	1	1	-0	1.000	6	O-15	0.1
	Cin-N	59	183	29	37	4	0	3	14	31	29	.202	.324	.273	67	-7	0	2	-1	.992	-2	O-56	-1.2
	Yr	80	257	36	53	7	0	3	24	39	40	.206	.315	.268	63	-12	1	3	-2	.995	5	O-71	-1.1
	Cle-A	29	69	11	16	4	1	1	9	8	16	.232	.312	.362	93	-1	1	0	0	1.000	-3	O-28	-0.5
1953	Cle-A	82	218	42	72	7	1	9	46	35	29	.330	.427	.495	153	17	2	0	1	.963	-11	O-72	0.5
1954	*Cle-A	85	240	36	63	9	2	11	42	26	37	.262	.340	.454	114	4	0	1	-1	.964	-7	O-70	-0.6
1955	Cle-A	16	20	2	5	1	0	0	1	3	5	.250	.348	.300	73	-1	0	0	0	1.000	-0	/O-7	-0.1
	Bal-A	8	24	0	3	1	0	0	0	6	5	.125	.300	.167	30	-2	0	0	0	1.000	-1	/O-7	-0.4
	Yr	24	44	2	8	2	0	0	1	9	10	.182	.321	.227	49	-3	0	0	0	1.000	-2	O-14	-0.5
1956	Phi-N	4	4	0	0	0	0	0	0	0	3	.000	.200	.000	-41	-1	0	0	0	.000	0	H	-0.1
Total	10	958	3117	474	848	107	33	127	539	317	453	.272	.346	.450	111	41	19	7		.983	1	O-834/3-34	0.3

■ AL WESTON
Weston, Alfred John b: 12/11/05, Lynn, Mass. BR/TR, 6', 195 lbs. Deb: 7/7/29

YEAR	TM/L	G	AB	R	H	2B	3B	HR	RBI	BB	SO	AVG	OBP	SLG	PRO+	BR/A	SB	CS	SBR	FA	FR	G/POS	TPR
1929	Bos-N	3	3	0	0	0	0	0	0	0	2	.000	.000	.000	-99	-1	0			.000	0	H	-0.1

■ WES WESTRUM
Westrum, Wesley Noreen b: 11/28/22, Clearbrook, Minn. BR/TR, 5'11", 185 lbs. Deb: 9/17/47 MC

YEAR	TM/L	G	AB	R	H	2B	3B	HR	RBI	BB	SO	AVG	OBP	SLG	PRO+	BR/A	SB	CS	SBR	FA	FR	G/POS	TPR
1947	NY-N	6	12	1	5	1	0	0	0	0	2	.417	.417	.500	142	1				1.000	0	/C-2	0.1
1948	NY-N	66	125	14	20	3	1	4	16	20	36	.160	.276	.296	54	-8	3			.981	8	C-63	0.3
1949	NY-N	64	169	23	41	4	1	7	28	37	39	.243	.385	.402	111	4	1			.980	-0	C-62	0.7
1950	NY-N	140	437	68	103	13	3	23	71	92	73	.236	.371	.437	111	9	2			**.999**	10	*C-139	2.5
1951	*NY-N	124	361	59	79	12	0	20	70	104	93	.219	.400	.418	119	14	1	0	0	.987	8	*C-122	2.8
1952	NY-N☆	114	322	47	71	11	0	14	43	76	68	.220	.374	.385	110	7	1	2	-1	.978	-4	*C-112	0.8
1953	NY-N☆	107	290	40	65	5	0	12	30	56	73	.224	.352	.366	86	-5	2	0	1	.982	4	*C-106/3-1	0.4
1954	*NY-N	98	246	25	46	3	1	8	27	45	60	.187	.320	.305	63	-13	0	1	-1	.985	12	C-98	0.3
1955	NY-N	69	137	11	29	1	0	4	18	24	18	.212	.333	.307	71	-5	0	1	-1	.987	10	C-68	0.6
1956	NY-N	68	132	10	29	5	2	3	8	25	28	.220	.348	.356	91	-1	0	0	0	.982	13	C-67	1.4
1957	NY-N	63	91	4	15	1	0	1	2	10	24	.165	.255	.209	27	-9	0	1	-1	.966	2	C-63	-0.7
Total	11	919	2322	302	503	59	8	96	315	489	514	.217	.357	.373	95	-6	10	5		.985	64	C-902/3-1	9.2

■ JEFF WETHERBY
Wetherby, Jeffrey Barrett b: 10/18/63, Granada Hills, Cal. BL/TL, 6'2", 195 lbs. Deb: 6/7/89

YEAR	TM/L	G	AB	R	H	2B	3B	HR	RBI	BB	SO	AVG	OBP	SLG	PRO+	BR/A	SB	CS	SBR	FA	FR	G/POS	TPR
1989	Atl-N	52	48	5	10	2	1	1	7	4	6	.208	.269	.354	75	-2	1	0	0	1.000	-2	/O-9	-0.4

■ DUTCH WETZEL
Wetzel, Franklin Burton b: 7/7/1893, Columbus, Ind. d: 3/5/42, Hollywood, Cal. BR/TR, 5'9.5", 177 lbs. Deb: 9/15/20

YEAR	TM/L	G	AB	R	H	2B	3B	HR	RBI	BB	SO	AVG	OBP	SLG	PRO+	BR/A	SB	CS	SBR	FA	FR	G/POS	TPR
1920	StL-A	7	21	5	9	1	1	0	5	4	1	.429	.520	.571	183	3	0	1	-1	.875	-2	/O-6	0.2
1921	StL-A	61	119	16	25	2	0	2	10	9	20	.210	.271	.277	38	-11	0	0	0	.981	-2	/O-27	-1.4
Total	2	68	140	21	34	3	1	2	15	13	21	.243	.312	.321	59	-8	0	1	-1	.957	-2	/O-33	-1.2

■ BILL WHALEY
Whaley, William Carl b: 2/10/1899, Indianapolis, Ind. d: 3/3/43, Indianapolis, Ind. BR/TR, 5'11", 178 lbs. Deb: 4/18/23

YEAR	TM/L	G	AB	R	H	2B	3B	HR	RBI	BB	SO	AVG	OBP	SLG	PRO+	BR/A	SB	CS	SBR	FA	FR	G/POS	TPR
1923	StL-A	23	50	5	12	1	0	0	1	4	2	.240	.309	.320	62	-3	0	0	0	1.000	-0	O-13	-0.4

■ BERT WHALING
Whaling, Albert James b: 6/22/1888, Los Angeles, Cal. d: 1/21/65, Sawtelle, Cal. BR/TR, 6', 185 lbs. Deb: 4/22/13

YEAR	TM/L	G	AB	R	H	2B	3B	HR	RBI	BB	SO	AVG	OBP	SLG	PRO+	BR/A	SB	CS	SBR	FA	FR	G/POS	TPR
1913	Bos-N	79	211	22	51	8	2	0	25	10	32	.242	.283	.299	65	-10	3			**.990**	1	C-77	-0.3
1914	Bos-N	60	172	18	36	7	0	0	12	21	28	.209	.303	.250	65	-7	2			.981	12	C-59	1.0
1915	Bos-N	72	190	10	42	6	2	0	13	8	38	.221	.264	.274	66	-8	0	1	-1	.986	1	C-69	-0.3
Total	3	211	573	50	129	21	4	0	50	39	98	.225	.283	.276	65	-25	5	1		.986	14	C-205	0.4

■ MACK WHEAT
Wheat, McKinley Davis b: 6/9/1893, Polo, Mo. d: 8/14/79, Los Banos, Cal. BR/TR, 5'11.5", 167 lbs. Deb: 4/14/15 F

YEAR	TM/L	G	AB	R	H	2B	3B	HR	RBI	BB	SO	AVG	OBP	SLG	PRO+	BR/A	SB	CS	SBR	FA	FR	G/POS	TPR
1915	Bro-N	8	14	0	1	0	0	0	0	0	5	.071	.071	.071	-56	-3	0			.957	-0	/C-8	-0.3
1916	Bro-N	2	2	0	0	0	0	0	0	0	1	.000	.000	.000	-97	-0	0			1.000	0	/C-2	-0.3
1917	Bro-N	29	60	2	8	1	0	0	0	1	12	.133	.161	.150	-4	-7	1			.968	1	C-18/O-9	-0.7
1918	Bro-N	57	157	11	34	7	1	3		8	24	.217	.255	.293	67	-6	2			.966	-1	C-38/O-7	-0.6
1919	Bro-N	41	112	5	23	3	0	0	8	2	22	.205	.246	.232	43	-8	1			.944	-4	C-38	-0.9
1920	Phi-N	78	230	15	52	10	3	3	20	9	35	.226	.261	.335	67	-10	3	1	0	.961	9	C-74	0.4
1921	Phi-N	10	27	1	5	2	1	0	3	1		.185	.241	.333	47	-2	0			.980	5	/C-9	0.3
Total	7	225	602	34	123	21	4	6	35	19	102	.204	.241	.279	47	-37	7	1		.961	9	C-187/O-16	-1.8

YEAR	TM/L	G	AB	R	H	2B	3B	HR	RBI	BB	SO	AVG	OBP	SLG	PRO+	BR/A	SB	CS	SBR	FA	FR	G/POS	TPR

■ ZACK WHEAT   Wheat, Zachary Davis "Buck"   b: 5/23/1888, Hamilton, Mo.   d: 3/11/72, Sedalia, Mo.   BL/TR, 5'10", 170 lbs.   Deb: 9/11/09   FH

YEAR	TM/L	G	AB	R	H	2B	3B	HR	RBI	BB	SO	AVG	OBP	SLG	PRO+	BR/A	SB	CS	SBR	FA	FR	G/POS	TPR
1909	Bro-N	26	102	15	31	7	3	0	4	6		.304	.343	.431	145	5	1			.952	2	O-26	0.6
1910	Bro-N	156	606	78	172	36	15	2	55	47	80	.284	.341	.403	120	13	16			.962	6	*O-156	1.2
1911	Bro-N	140	534	55	153	26	13	5	76	29	58	.287	.332	.412	112	6	21			.955	-3	*O-136	-0.4
1912	Bro-N	123	453	70	138	28	7	8	65	39	40	.305	.367	.450	128	16	16			.968	3	*O-120	1.2
1913	Bro-N	138	535	64	161	28	10	7	58	25	45	.301	.335	.430	114	8	19			.978	9	*O-135	1.1
1914	Bro-N	145	533	66	170	26	9	9	89	47	50	.319	.377	.452	143	27	20			.962	18	*O-144	4.2
1915	Bro-N	146	528	64	136	15	12	5	66	52	42	.258	.330	.360	107	5	21	14	-2	.953	10	*O-144	0.7
1916	*Bro-N	149	568	76	177	32	13	9	73	43	49	.312	.366	**.461**	149	32	19			.975	9	*O-149	3.8
1917	Bro-N	109	362	38	113	15	11	1	41	20	18	.312	.352	.423	133	13	5			.979	6	O-98	1.7
1918	Bro-N	105	409	39	137	15	3	0	51	16	17	**.335**	.369	.386	131	14	9			.979	4	*O-105	1.4
1919	Bro-N	137	536	70	159	23	11	5	62	33	27	.297	.344	.409	123	14	15			.971	-1	*O-137	0.4
1920	*Bro-N	148	583	89	191	26	13	9	73	48	21	.328	.385	.463	138	29	8	10	-4	.971	-4	*O-148	1.1
1921	Bro-N	148	568	91	182	31	10	14	85	44	22	.320	.372	.484	121	16	11	8	-2	.965	-4	*O-148	-0.1
1922	Bro-N	152	600	92	201	29	12	16	112	45	22	.335	.388	.503	129	25	9	6	-1	**.991**	2	*O-152	1.4
1923	Bro-N	98	349	63	131	13	5	6	65	23	12	.375	.417	.510	148	24	3	3	-1	.908	-11	O-87	0.6
1924	Bro-N	141	566	92	212	41	8	14	97	49	18	.375	.428	.549	165	52	3	4	-2	.965	5	*O-139	4.5
1925	Bro-N	150	616	125	221	42	14	14	103	45	22	.359	.403	.541	143	38	3	1	0	.962	0	*O-149	2.7
1926	Bro-N	111	411	68	119	31	2	5	35	21	14	.290	.326	.411	99	-2	4			.955	2	*O-102	-0.8
1927	Phi-A	88	247	34	80	12	1	1	38	18	5	.324	.379	.393	95	-1	2	3	-1	.983	-3	O-62	-0.8
Total	19	2410	9106	1289	2884	476	172	132	1248	650	559̲	.317	.367	.450	129	335	205	49		.966	50	*O-2337	24.5

■ WOODY WHEATON   Wheaton, Elwood Pierce   b: 10/3/14, Philadelphia, Pa.   BL/TL, 5'8.5", 160 lbs.   Deb: 9/28/43

YEAR	TM/L	G	AB	R	H	2B	3B	HR	RBI	BB	SO	AVG	OBP	SLG	PRO+	BR/A	SB	CS	SBR	FA	FR	G/POS	TPR
1943	Phi-A	7	30	2	6	2	0	0	2	3	2	.200	.294	.267	65	-1	0	0	0	1.000	1	/O-7	-0.1
1944	Phi-A	30	59	1	11	2	0	0	5	5	3	.186	.250	.220	35	-5	1	2	-1	1.000	2	P-11/O-8	-0.2
Total	2	37	89	3	17	4	0	0	7	8	5	.191	.265	.236	45	-6	1	2	-1	.981	3	/O-15,P-11	-0.3

■ DON WHEELER   Wheeler, Donald Wesley "Scott"   b: 9/29/22, Minneapolis, Minn   BR/TR, 5'10", 175 lbs.   Deb: 4/23/49

YEAR	TM/L	G	AB	R	H	2B	3B	HR	RBI	BB	SO	AVG	OBP	SLG	PRO+	BR/A	SB	CS	SBR	FA	FR	G/POS	TPR
1949	Chi-A	67	192	17	46	9	2	1	22	27	19	.240	.333	.323	76	-6	2	0	1	.976	3	C-58	0.0

■ ED WHEELER   Wheeler, Edward   b: 6/15/1878, Sherman, Mich.   d: 8/15/60, Ft.Worth, Tex.   BB/TR, 5'10", 160 lbs.   Deb: 5/10/02

YEAR	TM/L	G	AB	R	H	2B	3B	HR	RBI	BB	SO	AVG	OBP	SLG	PRO+	BR/A	SB	CS	SBR	FA	FR	G/POS	TPR
1902	Bro-N	30	96	4	12	0	0	0	5	3		.125	.152	.125	-14	-13	1			.863	-3	3-11,2-10/S	-1.6

■ ED WHEELER   Wheeler, Edward Raymond   b: 5/24/15, Los Angeles, Cal.   d: 8/4/83, Centralia, Wash.   BR/TR, 5'9", 160 lbs.   Deb: 4/19/45

YEAR	TM/L	G	AB	R	H	2B	3B	HR	RBI	BB	SO	AVG	OBP	SLG	PRO+	BR/A	SB	CS	SBR	FA	FR	G/POS	TPR
1945	Cle-A	46	72	12	14	2	0	0	1	8	13	.194	.275	.222	47	-5	1	1	-0	.912	-6	3-14,S-11/2	-1.1

■ GEORGE WHEELER   Wheeler, George Harrison "Heavy"   b: 11/10/1881, Shelburn, Ind.   d: 6/14/18, Clinton, Ind.   BL/TR, 5'9.5", 180 lbs.   Deb: 7/27/10

YEAR	TM/L	G	AB	R	H	2B	3B	HR	RBI	BB	SO	AVG	OBP	SLG	PRO+	BR/A	SB	CS	SBR	FA	FR	G/POS	TPR
1910	Cin-N	3	3	0	0	0	0	0	0	0	2	.000	.000	.000	-99	-1	0			.000	0	H	-0.1

■ HARRY WHEELER   Wheeler, Harry Eugene   b: 3/3/1858, Versailles, Ind.   d: 10/9/1900, Cincinnati, Ohio   BR/TR, 5'11", 165 lbs.   Deb: 6/19/1878   M

YEAR	TM/L	G	AB	R	H	2B	3B	HR	RBI	BB	SO	AVG	OBP	SLG	PRO+	BR/A	SB	CS	SBR	FA	FR	G/POS	TPR
1878	Pro-N	7	27	7	4	0	0	0	1	2	15	.148	.207	.148	18	-2				.975	-2	/P-7	0.0
1879	Cin-N	1	3	0	0	0	0	0	0	0	2	.000	.000	.000	-99	-1				1.000	0	/O-1,P-1	-0.1
1880	Cle-N	1	4	0	1	0	0	0	0	0		.250	.250	.250	72	-0				1.000	0	/O-1	0.0
	Cin-N	17	65	1	6	2	0	0	2	0	15	.092	.092	.123	-28	-8				.750	1	O-17	-0.8
	Yr	18	69	1	7	2	0	0	2	0	15	.101	.101	.130	-22	-8				.759	1	O-18	-0.8
1882	Cin-a	76	344	59	86	11	11	1		7		.250	.265	.355	102	-1				.808	-5	*O-64,1-12/P	-0.7
1883	Col-a	82	371	42	84	6	7	0		6		.226	.239	.280	72	-10				.803	-2	*O-82/2-1,P	-1.2
1884	StL-a	5	19	0	5	2	0	0		1		.263	.300	.368	113	0				.600	-1	/O-5	-0.1
	KC-U	14	62	11	16	1	0	0		3		.258	.292	.274	63	-3				.769	0	O-13/P-1M	-0.3
	CP-U	37	158	29	36	5	3	1		4		.228	.247	.316	52	-11				.774	-5	O-37	-1.4
	Bal-U	17	69	3	18	2	0	0		0		.261	.261	.290	45	-5				.815	-1	O-17	-0.6
	Yr	68	289	43	70	8	3	1		7		.242	.260	.301	52	-19				.781	-5	O-67/P-1	-2.3
Total	6	257	1122	152	256	29	21	2	3	23	32̲	.228	.244	.297	69	-41				.791	-14	O-237/P-14,12	-5.2

■ DICK WHEELER   Wheeler, Richard (b: Richard Wheeler Maynard)   b: 1/14/1898, Keene, N.H.   d: 2/12/62, Lexington, Mass.   BR/TR, 5'11", 185 lbs.   Deb: 6/17/18

YEAR	TM/L	G	AB	R	H	2B	3B	HR	RBI	BB	SO	AVG	OBP	SLG	PRO+	BR/A	SB	CS	SBR	FA	FR	G/POS	TPR
1918	StL-N	3	6	0	0	0	0	0	0	0	3	.000	.000	.000	-99	-1	0			.000	-1	/O-2	-0.3

■ BOBBY WHEELOCK   Wheelock, Warren H.   b: 8/6/1864, Charlestown, Mass.   d: 3/13/28, Boston, Mass.   BR/TR, 5'8", 160 lbs.   Deb: 5/19/1887

YEAR	TM/L	G	AB	R	H	2B	3B	HR	RBI	BB	SO	AVG	OBP	SLG	PRO+	BR/A	SB	CS	SBR	FA	FR	G/POS	TPR
1887	Bos-N	48	166	32	42	4	2	1	15	15	15	.253	.315	.337	81	-4	20			.878	-7	O-28,S-20/2	-0.9
1890	Col-a	52	190	24	45	6	1	1		25		.237	.326	.295	89	-2	34			.885	-1	S-52	0.0
1891	Col-a	136	498	82	114	15	1	0	39	78	55	.229	.336	.263	76	-12	52			.899	19	*S-136	1.3
Total	3	236	854	138	201	25	4	3	54̲	118	70̲	.235	.330	.285	80	-18	106			.894	11	S-208/O-28,2	0.4

■ JIMMY WHELAN   Whelan, James Francis   b: 5/11/1890, Kansas City, Mo.   d: 11/29/29, Dayton, Ohio   BR/TR, 5'8.5", 165 lbs.   Deb: 4/24/13

YEAR	TM/L	G	AB	R	H	2B	3B	HR	RBI	BB	SO	AVG	OBP	SLG	PRO+	BR/A	SB	CS	SBR	FA	FR	G/POS	TPR
1913	StL-N	1	1	0	0	0	0	0	0	0	0	.000	.000	.000	-99	-0	0			.000	0	H	0.0

■ TOM WHELAN   Whelan, Thomas Joseph   b: 1/3/1894, Lynn, Mass.   d: 6/26/57, Boston, Mass.   BR/TR, 5'11", 175 lbs.   Deb: 8/13/20

YEAR	TM/L	G	AB	R	H	2B	3B	HR	RBI	BB	SO	AVG	OBP	SLG	PRO+	BR/A	SB	CS	SBR	FA	FR	G/POS	TPR
1920	Bos-N	1	0	0	0	0	0	0	0	0	1	.000	.500	.000	54	0	0	0	0	1.000	0	/1-1	0.0

■ PETE WHISENANT   Whisenant, Thomas Peter   b: 12/14/29, Asheville, N.C.   BR/TR, 6'2", 200 lbs.   Deb: 4/16/52   C

YEAR	TM/L	G	AB	R	H	2B	3B	HR	RBI	BB	SO	AVG	OBP	SLG	PRO+	BR/A	SB	CS	SBR	FA	FR	G/POS	TPR
1952	Bos-N	24	52	3	10	2	0	0	7	4	13	.192	.250	.231	35	-5	1	1	-0	.973	2	O-14	-0.3
1955	StL-N	58	115	10	22	5	1	2	9	5	29	.191	.225	.304	39	-10	2	0	1	.964	-1	O-40	-1.2
1956	Chi-N	103	314	37	75	16	3	11	46	24	53	.239	.295	.414	89	-5	8	2	1	.992	6	O-93	-0.3
1957	Cin-N	67	90	18	19	3	2	5	11	5	24	.211	.253	.456	80	-3	0	1	-1	.982	-9	O-43	-1.4
1958	Cin-N	85	203	33	48	9	2	11	40	18	37	.236	.299	.463	93	-3	3	0	1	1.000	-1	O-66/2-1	-0.6
1959	Cin-N	36	71	13	17	2	0	5	11	8	18	.239	.316	.479	105	0	0	0	0	.966	-2	O-21	-0.3
1960	Cin-N	1	1	0	0	0	0	0	0	0	0	.000	.000	.000	-98	-0	0	0	0	.000	0	H	0.0
	Cle-A	7	6	0	1	0	0	0	0	1	2	.167	.167	.167	-10	-1	0	0	0	1.000	-1	/O-2	-0.2
	Was-A	58	115	19	26	9	0	9	19	19	14	.226	.336	.383	95	-1	2	1	0	1.000	-9	O-47	-1.2
	Yr	65	121	19	27	9	0	9	19	19	16	.223	.329	.372	90	-2	2	1	0	1.000	-10	O-49	-1.4
1961	Min-A	10	6	1	0	0	0	0	1	0	2	.000	.143	.000	-55	-1	0	0	0	1.000	-2	/O-5	-0.3
	Cin-N	26	15	6	3	0	0	1	1	2	4	.200	.294	.200	34	-1	1	0	0	1.000	-4	O-12/C-1,3	-0.5
Total	8	475	988	140	221	46	8	37	134	86	196	.224	.287	.399	80	-30	17	5	2	.988	-20	O-343/3-1,C2	-6.3

■ LARRY WHISENTON   Whisenton, Larry   b: 7/3/56, St.Louis, Mo.   BL/TL, 6'1", 190 lbs.   Deb: 9/17/77

YEAR	TM/L	G	AB	R	H	2B	3B	HR	RBI	BB	SO	AVG	OBP	SLG	PRO+	BR/A	SB	CS	SBR	FA	FR	G/POS	TPR
1977	Atl-N	4	4	1	1	0	0	0	1	0	3	.250	.250	.250	31	-0	0	0	0	.000	0	H	-0.1
1978	Atl-N	6	16	1	3	1	0	0	2	1	2	.188	.235	.250	32	-1	0	0	0	1.000	0	/O-4	-0.2
1979	Atl-N	13	37	3	9	2	1	0	4	4	8	.243	.300	.351	72	-1	1	0	0	1.000	3	O-13	0.1
1981	Atl-N	9	5	1	1	0	0	0	0	2	1	.200	.429	.200	81	-1	0	0	0	.000	-1	/O-2	-0.1
1982	*Atl-N	84	143	21	34	7	2	4	17	23	33	.238	.343	.399	103	1	2	2	-1	.964	-2	O-34	-0.3
Total	5	116	205	27	48	10	3	4	24	29	42	.234	.329	.371	80	-1	3	2	-0	.968	-1	/O-53	-0.6

■ LEW WHISTLER   Whistler, Lewis W. (b: Lewis Wissler)   b: 3/10/1868, St.Louis, Mo.   d: 12/30/59, St.Louis, Mo.   TR, 5'10.5", 178 lbs.   Deb: 8/7/1890

YEAR	TM/L	G	AB	R	H	2B	3B	HR	RBI	BB	SO	AVG	OBP	SLG	PRO+	BR/A	SB	CS	SBR	FA	FR	G/POS	TPR
1890	NY-N	45	170	27	49	9	7	2	29	20	37	.288	.366	.459	140	8	8			.982	-2	1-45	0.4
1891	NY-N	72	265	39	65	8	7	3	38	24	45	.245	.315	.362	101	0	4			.852	-16	S-33,O-22/123	-1.3

YEAR	TM/L	G	AB	R	H	2B	3B	HR	RBI	BB	SO	AVG	OBP	SLG	PRO+	BR/A	SB	CS	SBR	FA	FR	G/POS	TPR
1892	Bal-N	52	209	32	47	6	6	2	21	18	22	.225	.296	.340	90	-3	12			.973	-1	1-51/O-1	-0.7
	Lou-N	80	285	42	67	4	7	5	34	30	45	.235	.312	.351	109	3	14			.978	-2	1-72,2-10	-0.2
	Yr	132	494	74	114	10	13	7	55	48	67	.231	.305	.346	101	-0	26			.976	-3	*1-123,2-10/O	-0.9
1893	Lou-N	13	47	5	10	1	1	0	9	5	5	.213	.302	.277	59	-3	1			.946	-0	1-13	-0.3
	StL-N	10	38	5	9	1	0	0	2	3	2	.237	.293	.263	48	-3	0			.923	-1	/O-9,1-1	-0.4
	Yr	23	85	10	19	2	1	0	11	8	7	.224	.298	.271	54	-6	1			.949	-2	1-14/O-9	-0.7
Total	4	272	1014	150	247	29	28	12	133	100	156	.244	.318	.363	103	3	39			.976	-22	1-189/S-33,023	-2.5

■ LOU WHITAKER
Whitaker, Louis Rodman   b: 5/12/57, Brooklyn, N.Y.   BL/TR, 5'11", 160 lbs.   Deb: 9/9/77

YEAR	TM/L	G	AB	R	H	2B	3B	HR	RBI	BB	SO	AVG	OBP	SLG	PRO+	BR/A	SB	CS	SBR	FA	FR	G/POS	TPR
1977	Det-A	11	32	5	8	1	0	0	2	4	6	.250	.333	.281	66	-1	2	2	-1	1.000	-3	/2-9	-0.5
1978	Det-A	139	484	71	138	12	7	3	58	61	65	.285	.366	.357	101	3	7	7	-2	.978	12	*2-136/D-2	2.3
1979	Det-A	127	423	75	121	14	8	3	42	78	66	.286	.398	.378	107	8	20	10	0	.986	2	*2-126	1.8
1980	Det-A	145	477	68	111	19	1	1	45	73	79	.233	.335	.283	69	-18	8	4	0	.985	-3	*2-143	-1.2
1981	Det-A	109	335	48	88	14	4	5	36	40	42	.263	.343	.373	103	2	5	3	-0	.985	6	*2-108	1.4
1982	Det-A	152	560	76	160	22	8	15	65	48	58	.286	.343	.434	111	8	11	3	2	**.988**	12	*2-149/D-1	3.0
1983	Det-A★	161	643	94	206	40	6	12	72	67	70	.320	.385	.457	134	31	17	10	-1	.983	-13	*2-160	2.4
1984	*Det-A★	143	558	90	161	25	1	13	56	62	63	.289	.360	.407	112	10	6	5	-1	.979	-11	*2-142	0.3
1985	Det-A★	152	609	102	170	29	8	21	73	80	56	.279	.365	.456	124	21	6	4	-1	.984	-16	*2-150	1.0
1986	Det-A★	144	584	95	157	26	6	20	73	63	70	.269	.340	.437	110	8	13	8	-1	.984	-1	*2-141	1.1
1987	*Det-A†	149	604	110	160	38	6	16	59	71	108	.265	.343	.427	107	7	13	5	1	.976	-14	*2-148	0.0
1988	Det-A	115	403	54	111	18	2	12	55	66	61	.275	.377	.419	128	17	2	0	1	.984	-23	*2-110	-0.1
1989	Det-A	148	509	77	128	21	1	28	85	89	59	.251	.366	.462	135	25	6	3	0	.985	-1	*2-146/D-2	2.9
1990	Det-A	132	472	75	112	22	2	18	60	74	71	.237	.341	.407	107	5	8	2	1	.991	12	*2-130/D-1	2.1
1991	Det-A	138	470	94	131	26	2	23	78	90	45	.279	.397	.489	142	29	4	2	0	**.994**	-11	*2-135/D-3	2.1
1992	Det-A	130	453	77	126	26	0	19	71	81	46	.278	.389	.461	137	24	6	4	-1	.984	-15	*2-119,D-10	1.2
1993	Det-A	119	383	72	111	32	1	9	67	78	46	.290	.415	.449	133	22	3	3	-1	.981	14	*2-110	3.6
1994	Det-A	92	322	67	97	21	2	12	43	41	47	.301	.382	.491	124	12	2	0	1	.970	-3	2-83/D-5	1.1
Total	18	2306	8321	1350	2296	406	65	230	1040	1166	1058	.276	.366	.423	116	213	139	75	-3	.984	-58	*2-2245/D-24	24.5

■ STEVE WHITAKER
Whitaker, Stephen Edward   b: 5/7/43, Tacoma, Wash.   BL/TR, 6'1", 187 lbs.   Deb: 8/23/66

YEAR	TM/L	G	AB	R	H	2B	3B	HR	RBI	BB	SO	AVG	OBP	SLG	PRO+	BR/A	SB	CS	SBR	FA	FR	G/POS	TPR
1966	NY-A	31	114	15	28	3	2	7	15	9	24	.246	.306	.491	130	4	0	0	0	.955	-0	O-31	0.3
1967	NY-A	122	441	37	107	12	3	11	50	23	89	.243	.285	.358	92	-6	2	5	-2	.982	6	*O-114	-0.9
1968	NY-A	28	60	3	7	2	0	0	3	8	18	.117	.221	.150	14	-6	0	1	-1	.917	-1	O-14	-1.0
1969	Sea-A	69	116	15	29	2	1	6	13	12	29	.250	.346	.440	114	2	2	0	1	.962	-2	O-39	-0.1
1970	SF-N	16	27	3	3	1	0	0	4	2	14	.111	.172	.148	-13	-4	0	0	0	.857	-2	/O-9	-0.7
Total	5	266	758	73	174	20	6	24	85	54	174	.230	.285	.367	92	-10	4	6	-2	.967	0	O-207	-2.4

■ FUZZ WHITE
White, Albert Eugene   b: 6/27/18, Springfield, Mo.   BL/TR, 6', 175 lbs.   Deb: 9/17/40

YEAR	TM/L	G	AB	R	H	2B	3B	HR	RBI	BB	SO	AVG	OBP	SLG	PRO+	BR/A	SB	CS	SBR	FA	FR	G/POS	TPR
1940	StL-A	2	2	0	0	0	0	0	0	0	0	.000	.000	.000	-98	-1	0	0	0	.000	0	H	-0.1
1947	NY-N	7	13	3	3	0	0	0	0	0	0	.231	.231	.231	23	-1	0			1.000	0	/O-5	-0.2
Total	2	9	15	3	3	0	0	0	0	0	0	.200	.200	.200	6	-2	0	0		1.000	0	/O-5	-0.3

■ C. B. WHITE
White, C. B.   b: Wakeman, Ohio   Deb: 6/1/1883

YEAR	TM/L	G	AB	R	H	2B	3B	HR	RBI	BB	SO	AVG	OBP	SLG	PRO+	BR/A	SB	CS	SBR	FA	FR	G/POS	TPR
1883	Phi-N	1	1	0	0	0	0	0	0	0	0	.000	.000	.000	-99	-0				.667	0	/S-1,3-1	0.0

■ CHARLIE WHITE
White, Charles   b: 8/12/28, Kinston, N.C.   BL/TR, 5'11", 192 lbs.   Deb: 4/18/54

YEAR	TM/L	G	AB	R	H	2B	3B	HR	RBI	BB	SO	AVG	OBP	SLG	PRO+	BR/A	SB	CS	SBR	FA	FR	G/POS	TPR
1954	Mil-N	50	93	14	22	4	0	1	8	9	8	.237	.304	.312	65	-5	0	0	0	.981	-2	C-28	-0.6
1955	Mil-N	12	30	3	7	1	0	0	4	5	7	.233	.361	.267	74	-1	0	0	0	1.000	-2	C-10	-0.2
Total	2	62	123	17	29	5	0	1	12	14	15	.236	.319	.301	67	-6	0	0	0	.986	-4	/C-38	-0.8

■ DERRICK WHITE
White, Derrick Ramon   b: 10/12/69, San Rafael, Cal.   BR/TR, 6'1", 220 lbs.   Deb: 7/22/93

YEAR	TM/L	G	AB	R	H	2B	3B	HR	RBI	BB	SO	AVG	OBP	SLG	PRO+	BR/A	SB	CS	SBR	FA	FR	G/POS	TPR
1993	Mon-N	17	49	6	11	3	0	2	4	2	12	.224	.269	.408	75	-2	2	0	1	.993	-0	1-17	-0.3

■ DEVON WHITE
White, Devon Markes   b: 12/29/62, Kingston, Jamaica   BB/TR, 6'2", 180 lbs.   Deb: 9/2/85

YEAR	TM/L	G	AB	R	H	2B	3B	HR	RBI	BB	SO	AVG	OBP	SLG	PRO+	BR/A	SB	CS	SBR	FA	FR	G/POS	TPR
1985	Cal-A	21	7	7	1	0	0	0	0	1	3	.143	.333	.143	37	-1	3	1	0	1.000	-5	O-16	-0.5
1986	*Cal-A	29	51	8	12	1	1	1	3	6	8	.235	.316	.353	83	-1	6	0	2	.961	-3	O-28	-0.3
1987	Cal-A	159	639	103	168	33	5	24	87	39	135	.263	.307	.443	99	-3	32	11	3	.980	14	*O-159	0.8
1988	Cal-A	122	455	76	118	22	2	11	51	23	84	.259	.298	.389	89	-5	17	8	0	.976	15	*O-116	0.7
1989	Cal-A★	156	636	86	156	18	13	12	56	31	129	.245	.283	.371	84	-15	44	16	4	.989	15	*O-154/D-1	-0.1
1990	Cal-A	125	443	57	96	17	3	11	44	44	116	.217	.292	.343	79	-13	21	6	3	.972	8	*O-122	-0.5
1991	*Tor-A	156	642	110	181	40	10	17	60	55	135	.282	.345	.455	115	12	33	10	3	**.998**	17	*O-156	2.9
1992	*Tor-A	153	641	98	159	26	7	17	60	47	133	.248	.303	.390	89	-10	37	4	9	.985	15	*O-152/D-1	1.0
1993	*Tor-A★	146	598	116	163	42	6	15	52	57	127	.273	.343	.438	108	6	34	4	8	.993	13	*O-145	2.3
1994	Tor-A	100	403	67	109	24	6	13	49	21	80	.270	.315	.457	95	-4	11	3	2	.978	8	O-98	0.3
Total	10	1167	4515	728	1163	223	53	121	462	324	950	.258	.312	.411	96	-35	238	63	34	.984	98	*O-1146/D-2	6.6

■ DON WHITE
White, Donald William   b: 1/8/19, Everett, Wash.   d: 6/15/87, Carlsbad, Cal.   BR/TR, 6'1", 195 lbs.   Deb: 4/19/48

YEAR	TM/L	G	AB	R	H	2B	3B	HR	RBI	BB	SO	AVG	OBP	SLG	PRO+	BR/A	SB	CS	SBR	FA	FR	G/POS	TPR
1948	Phi-A	86	253	29	62	14	2	1	28	19	16	.245	.303	.328	68	-12	0	1	-1	.957	-4	O-54,3-17	-1.9
1949	Phi-A	57	169	12	36	6	0	0	10	14	12	.213	.273	.249	40	-15	2	0	1	.989	-2	O-48/3-4	-1.8
Total	2	143	422	41	98	20	2	1	38	33	28	.232	.291	.296	57	-27	2	1	0	.971	-6	O-102/3-21	-3.7

■ ED WHITE
White, Edward Perry   b: 4/6/26, Anniston, Ala.   d: 9/28/82, Lakeland, Fla.   BR/TR, 6'2", 200 lbs.   Deb: 9/16/55

YEAR	TM/L	G	AB	R	H	2B	3B	HR	RBI	BB	SO	AVG	OBP	SLG	PRO+	BR/A	SB	CS	SBR	FA	FR	G/POS	TPR
1955	Chi-A	3	4	0	2	0	0	0	0	1	1	.500	.600	.500	193	1	0	0	0	1.000	-0	/O-2	0.0

■ ELDER WHITE
White, Elder Lafayette   b: 12/23/34, Colerain, N.C.   BR/TR, 5'11", 165 lbs.   Deb: 4/10/62

YEAR	TM/L	G	AB	R	H	2B	3B	HR	RBI	BB	SO	AVG	OBP	SLG	PRO+	BR/A	SB	CS	SBR	FA	FR	G/POS	TPR
1962	Chi-N	23	53	4	8	2	0	0		8	11	.151	.274	.189	26	-5	3	0	1	.986	0	S-15/3-1	-0.3

■ ELMER WHITE
White, Elmer   b: 5/23/1850, Caton, N.Y.   d: 3/17/1872, Caton, N.Y.   Deb: 5/4/1871

YEAR	TM/L	G	AB	R	H	2B	3B	HR	RBI	BB	SO	AVG	OBP	SLG	PRO+	BR/A	SB	CS	SBR	FA	FR	G/POS	TPR
1871	Cle-n	15	70	13	18	2	0	0	9	1	6	.257	.268	.286	63	-3	0					O-13/C-2	-0.2

■ FRANK WHITE
White, Frank   b: 9/4/50, Greenville, Miss.   BR/TR, 5'11", 170 lbs.   Deb: 6/12/73   C

YEAR	TM/L	G	AB	R	H	2B	3B	HR	RBI	BB	SO	AVG	OBP	SLG	PRO+	BR/A	SB	CS	SBR	FA	FR	G/POS	TPR
1973	KC-A	51	139	20	31	6	1	0	5	8	23	.223	.265	.281	50	-9	3	1	0	.937	7	S-37,2-11	0.2
1974	KC-A	99	204	19	45	6	3	1	18	5	33	.221	.239	.294	50	-13	3	4	-2	.962	3	2-50,S-29,3/D	1.4
1975	KC-A	111	304	43	76	10	2	7	36	20	39	.250	.286	.365	84	-7	11	3	2	.987	15	2-67,S-42/3CD	1.6
1976	*KC-A	152	446	39	102	17	6	2	46	19	42	.229	.265	.307	67	-19	20	11	-1	.973	**21**	*2-130,S-37	1.2
1977	*KC-A	152	474	59	116	21	5	5	50	25	67	.245	.285	.342	70	-20	23	5	4	**.989**	-3	*2-152/S-4	-0.9
1978	*KC-A	143	461	66	127	24	6	7	50	26	59	.275	.318	.399	98	-2	13	10	-2	.978	-17	*2-140	-1.1
1979	KC-A★	127	467	73	124	26	4	10	48	25	54	.266	.304	.403	87	-9	28	8	4	.982	-22	*2-125	-1.9
1980	*KC-A	154	560	70	148	23	6	7	60	19	69	.264	.291	.357	76	-19	19	6	2	.988	-7	*2-153	-1.5
1981	*KC-A★	94	364	35	91	17	1	9	38	19	50	.250	.287	.376	91	-5	4	2	0	.988	-16	2-93	-1.7
1982	KC-A	145	524	71	156	45	6	11	56	16	65	.298	.326	.469	114	8	10	7	-1	.978	-15	*2-144	0.0
1983	KC-A	146	549	52	143	35	6	11	77	20	51	.260	.286	.406	88	-11	13	5	1	**.990**	9	*2-145	0.6
1984	*KC-A	129	479	58	130	22	5	17	56	27	72	.271	.313	.445	106	3	5	5	-2	.985	13	*2-129	1.9
1985	*KC-A	149	563	62	140	25	1	22	69	28	86	.249	.285	.414	88	-11	10	4	1	.980	14	*2-149	1.0
1986	KC-A★	151	566	76	154	37	6	22	84	43	88	.272	.326	.465	110	6	4	4	-0	.987	-0	*2-151/S-1,3	1.1
1987	KC-A	154	563	67	138	32	2	17	78	51	86	.245	.310	.400	84	-13	1	3	-2	.987	8	*2-152/D-1	0.0

YEAR TM/L	G	AB	R	H	2B	3B	HR	RBI	BB	SO	AVG	OBP	SLG	PRO+	BR/A	SB	CS	SBR	FA	FR	G/POS	TPR
1988 KC-A	150	537	48	126	25	1	8	58	21	67	.235	.269	.330	66	-25	7	3	0	**.994**	7	*2-148/D-3	-1.2
1989 KC-A	135	418	34	107	22	1	2	36	30	52	.256	.309	.328	80	-11	3	2	-0	.985	7	*2-132/O-1	-0.1
1990 KC-A	82	241	20	52	14	1	2	21	10	32	.216	.256	.307	58	-14	1	0	0	.978	1	2-79/O-1	-1.2
Total 18	2324	7859	912	2006	407	58	160	886	412	1035	.255	.295	.383	85	-173	178	83	4	.984	46	*2-2150,S-150/3DOC	-0.6

■ DOC WHITE White, Guy Harris b: 4/9/1879, Washington, D.C. d: 2/19/69, Silver Spring, Md. BL/TL, 6'1", 150 lbs. Deb: 4/22/01

YEAR TM/L	G	AB	R	H	2B	3B	HR	RBI	BB	SO	AVG	OBP	SLG	PRO+	BR/A	SB	CS	SBR	FA	FR	G/POS	TPR
1901 Phi-N	31	98	15	27	3	1	1	10	2		.276	.297	.357	87	-2	1			.951	2	P-31/O-1	0.0
1902 Phi-N	61	179	17	47	3	1	1	15	11		.263	.305	.307	89	-2	5			.931	-2	P-36,O-19	-0.6
1903 Chi-A	38	99	10	20	3	0	0	5	19		.202	.331	.232	74	-2	1			.969	3	P-37/O-1	0.0
1904 Chi-A	33	76	7	12	2	0	0	2	10		.158	.256	.184	42	-5	3			.951	1	P-30/O-2	-0.1
1905 Chi-A	37	90	7	15	4	1	0	7	4		.167	.202	.233	40	-6	3			.960	1	P-36/O-1	0.1
1906 *Chi-A	29	65	11	12	1	1	0	3	13		.185	.321	.231	75	-1	3			.922	2	P-28/O-1	0.0
1907 Chi-A	48	90	12	20	1	0	0	2	12		.222	.314	.233	77	-2	2			**.986**	4	P-46/O-2,2	-0.1
1908 Chi-A	51	109	12	25	1	0	0	10	12		.229	.306	.239	79	-2	4			**.986**	6	P-41/O-3	-0.1
1909 Chi-A	72	192	24	45	1	5	0	7	33		.234	.347	.292	106	3	7			.926	-4	O-40,P-24	-0.3
1910 Chi-A	56	126	14	25	1	2	0	8	14		.198	.279	.238	65	-5	2			.972	1	P-33,O-14	-0.3
1911 Chi-A	39	78	12	20	1	1	0	6	7		.256	.318	.295	74	-3	1			.919	-1	P-34/1-2,O	0.0
1912 Chi-A	32	56	5	7	1	1	0	0	7		.125	.222	.179	15	-6	0			**1.000**	-1	P-32	0.0
1913 Chi-A	20	25	1	3	0	0	0	3	1	1	.120	.214	.120	-2	-3	0			.959	2	P-19/1-1	0.0
Total 13	547	1283	147	278	22	13	2	75	147	1	.217	.298	.259	74	-36	32			.960	14	P-427/O-85,12	-1.4

■ DEACON WHITE White, James Laurie b: 12/7/1847, Caton, N.Y. d: 7/7/39, Aurora, Ill. BL/TR, 5'11", 175 lbs. Deb: 5/4/1871 FM

YEAR TM/L	G	AB	R	H	2B	3B	HR	RBI	BB	SO	AVG	OBP	SLG	PRO+	BR/A	SB	CS	SBR	FA	FR	G/POS	TPR
1871 Cle-n	29	146	40	47	6	5	1	21	4	1	.322	.340	.452	132	7	2					*C-27/2-2	0.4
1872 Cle-n	22	108	21	37	3	2	0	22	4	1	.343	.366	.407	146	6						C-13/2-6,OM	0.4
1873 Bos-n	60	310	79	121	20	8	0	**64**	0	2	.390	.390	.506	149	16						*C-56/O-9	1.2
1874 Bos-n	70	350	75	106	4	7	3		4		.303	.311	.380	112	3						*C-55,O-12/12	0.3
1875 Bos-n	80	372	77	136	20	4	1		2		**.366**	.369	.449	175	26						*C-72/O-7,1	2.4
1876 Chi-N	66	303	66	104	18	1	1	**60**	7	3	.343	.358	.419	141	11				.844	7	*C-63/O-3,13P	1.7
1877 Bos-n	59	266	51	**103**	14	**11**	2	49	8	3	**.387**	**.405**	**.545**	190	26				.963	1	1-35,O-19/C	2.3
1878 Cin-N	61	258	41	81	4	1	0	29	10	5	.314	.340	.337	136	11				.909	-4	*C-48,O-16/3	0.7
1879 Cin-N	78	333	55	110	16	6	1	52	6	9	.330	.342	.423	159	21				.901	2	*C-59,O-21/1M	2.2
1880 Cin-N	35	141	21	42	4	2	0	7	9	7	.298	.340	.355	137	6				.738	-3	O-33/1-3,2	0.1
1881 Buf-N	78	319	58	99	24	4	0	53	9	8	.310	.329	.411	133	12				.943	-9	1-26,2-25,O/3C	0.2
1882 Buf-N	83	337	51	95	17	0	1	33	15	16	.282	.313	.341	108	3				.837	-10	*3-63,C-20	-0.4
1883 Buf-N	94	391	62	114	14	5	0	47	23	18	.292	.331	.353	106	3				.797	-10	*3-77,C-22	-0.6
1884 Buf-N	110	452	82	147	16	11	5	74	32	13	.325	.370	.442	149	25				.825	-7	*3-108/C-3	1.7
1885 Buf-N	98	404	54	118	6	6	0	57	12	11	.292	.313	.337	106	2				.888	1	*3-98	0.4
1886 Det-N	124	491	65	142	19	5	1	76	31	35	.289	.331	.354	106	3	9			.847	-9	*3-124	-0.2
1887 *Det-N	111	449	71	136	20	11	3	75	26	15	.303	.353	.416	109	5	20			.848	-0	*3-106/O-3,1	0.6
1888 Det-N	125	527	75	157	22	5	4	71	21	24	.298	.336	.381	128	16	12			.857	-3	*3-125	1.5
1889 Pit-N	55	225	35	57	10	1	0	26	16	18	.253	.314	.307	82	-5	2			.872	-10	3-52/1-3	-1.2
1890 Buf-P	122	439	62	114	13	4	0	47	67	30	.260	.381	.308	93	2	3			.905	19	3-64,1-57/SP	1.6
Total 5 n	261	1286	292	447	53	26	5	107	14	4	.348	.355	.441	144	58	8					C-223/O-31,21	4.7
Total 15	1299	5335	849	1619	217	73	18	756	292	215	.303	.344	.382	123	138	46			.853	-33	3-826,C-226,1O/2PSD	10.6

■ JERRY WHITE White, Jerome Cardell b: 8/23/52, Shirley, Mass. BB/TR, 5'11", 165 lbs. Deb: 9/16/74

YEAR TM/L	G	AB	R	H	2B	3B	HR	RBI	BB	SO	AVG	OBP	SLG	PRO+	BR/A	SB	CS	SBR	FA	FR	G/POS	TPR
1974 Mon-N	9	10	0	4	1	1	0	2	0	0	.400	.400	.700	193	1	3	0	1	1.000	-2	/O-7	0.0
1975 Mon-N	39	97	14	29	4	1	2	7	10	7	.299	.364	.423	113	2	5	2	0	.976	2	O-30	0.3
1976 Mon-N	114	278	32	68	11	1	2	21	27	31	.245	.316	.313	76	-8	15	7	0	.982	-10	O-92	-2.2
1977 Mon-N	16	21	4	4	0	0	0	1	1	3	.190	.227	.190	14	-3	1	0	0	1.000	-1	/O-8	-0.4
1978 Mon-N	18	10	2	2	0	0	0	0	1	3	.200	.273	.200	34	-1	1	0	0	.000	-1	O-3	-0.2
Chi-N	59	136	22	37	6	0	1	10	23	16	.272	.377	.338	90	-1	4	3	-1	.981	-3	O-54	-0.6
Yr	77	146	24	39	6	0	1	10	24	19	.267	.371	.329	89	-1	5	3	-0	.981	-4	O-57	-0.8
1979 Mon-N	88	138	30	41	7	1	3	18	21	23	.297	.394	.428	125	6	8	4	0	.983	-8	O-43	-0.3
1980 Mon-N	110	214	22	56	9	3	7	23	30	37	.262	.355	.430	118	5	8	7	-2	.946	-12	O-84	-1.0
1981 *Mon-N	59	119	11	26	5	1	3	11	13	17	.218	.295	.353	82	-3	5	2	0	.952	-5	O-39	-0.9
1982 Mon-N	69	115	13	28	6	1	2	13	8	26	.243	.304	.365	85	-1	3	3	-1	1.000	-4	O-37	-0.8
1983 Mon-N	40	34	4	5	1	0	0	0	12	8	.147	.383	.176	60	-1	4	0	1	1.000	-3	O-13	-0.3
1986 StL-N	25	24	1	3	0	0	0	3	2	3	.125	.192	.250	21	-3	0	0	0	1.000	-1	/O-6	-0.4
Total 11	646	1196	155	303	50	9	21	109	148	174	.253	.339	.363	94	-8	57	28	0	.974	-48	O-409	-6.8

■ JACK WHITE White, John Peter b: 8/31/05, New York, N.Y. d: 6/19/71, Flushing, N.Y. BB/TR, 5'7.5", 150 lbs. Deb: 6/22/27

YEAR TM/L	G	AB	R	H	2B	3B	HR	RBI	BB	SO	AVG	OBP	SLG	PRO+	BR/A	SB	CS	SBR	FA	FR	G/POS	TPR
1927 Cin-N	5	4	1	0	0	0	0	0	0	0	.000	.000	.000	-99	-1	0			1.000	0	/2-3,S-2	-0.1
1928 Cin-N	1	3	0	0	0	0	0	0	0	1	.000	.000	.000	-99	-1	0			.833	-1	/2-1	-0.1
Total 2	6	7	1	0	0	0	0	0	0	1	.000	.000	.000	-99	-2	0			.929	-0	/2-4,S-2	-0.2

■ JACK WHITE White, John Wallace b: 1/19/1878, Traders Point, Ind. d: 9/30/63, Indianapolis, Ind BR/TR, 5'6", Deb: 6/26/04

YEAR TM/L	G	AB	R	H	2B	3B	HR	RBI	BB	SO	AVG	OBP	SLG	PRO+	BR/A	SB	CS	SBR	FA	FR	G/POS	TPR
1904 Bos-N	1	5	1	0	0	0	0	0	0		.000	.000	.000	-99	-1	0			1.000	1	/O-1	-0.1

■ JO-JO WHITE White, Joyner Clifford b: 6/1/09, Red Oak, Ga. d: 10/9/86, Tacoma, Wash. BL/TR, 5'11", 165 lbs. Deb: 4/15/32 FMC

YEAR TM/L	G	AB	R	H	2B	3B	HR	RBI	BB	SO	AVG	OBP	SLG	PRO+	BR/A	SB	CS	SBR	FA	FR	G/POS	TPR
1932 Det-A	80	208	25	54	6	3	2	21	22	19	.260	.330	.346	73	-8	6	8	-3	.962	-0	O-48	-1.3
1933 Det-A	91	234	43	59	9	5	2	34	27	26	.252	.337	.359	83	-6	5	5	-2	.977	-0	O-54	-0.9
1934 *Det-A	115	384	97	120	18	5	0	44	69	39	.313	.419	.385	108	9	28	6	**5**	.959	-0	*O-100	0.8
1935 *Det-A	114	412	82	99	13	12	2	32	68	42	.240	.348	.345	83	-10	19	10	-0	.962	-2	O-98	-1.4
1936 Det-A	58	51	11	14	3	0	0	6	9	10	.275	.383	.333	78	-1	2	0	1	.938	-7	O-18	-0.7
1937 Det-A	94	305	50	75	5	7	0	21	50	40	.246	.354	.348	67	-14	12	7	-1	.973	-3	O-82	-1.9
1938 Det-A	78	206	40	54	6	1	0	15	30	15	.262	.359	.301	63	-11	3	4	-2	.967	-0	O-55	-1.2
1943 Phi-A	139	500	69	124	17	7	1	30	61	51	.248	.335	.316	91	-4	12	4	1	.966	-4	*O-133	-1.5
1944 Phi-A	85	267	30	59	4	2	1	21	40	27	.221	.320	.262	71	-8	5	4	-1	.949	-1	O-74/S-1	-1.5
Cin-N	24	85	9	20	2	0	0	5	10	7	.235	.316	.259	65	-4	0			1.000	1	O-23	-0.4
Total 9	878	2652	456	678	83	42	8	229	386	276	.256	.353	.328	82	-57	92	48		.965	-16	O-685/S-1	-10.0

■ MIKE WHITE White, Joyner Michael b: 12/18/38, Detroit, Mich. BR/TR, 5'8", 160 lbs. Deb: 9/21/63 F

YEAR TM/L	G	AB	R	H	2B	3B	HR	RBI	BB	SO	AVG	OBP	SLG	PRO+	BR/A	SB	CS	SBR	FA	FR	G/POS	TPR
1963 Hou-N	3	7	1	2	0	0	0	0	0	0	.286	.286	.286	69	-0	0	0	0	1.000	1	/2-2	0.1
1964 Hou-N	89	280	30	76	11	3	0	27	20	47	.271	.320	.332	89	-4	1	1	0	.978	2	O-72,2-10/3	-0.5
1965 Hou-N	8	9	0	0	0	0	0	1	1	2	.000	.100	.000	-74	-2	0	0	0	1.000	-0	/3-1	-0.3
Total 3	100	296	30	78	11	3	0	27	21	49	.264	.312	.321	84	-7	1	1	0	.985	3	O-72,2-12,3	-0.7

■ MYRON WHITE White, Myron Alan b: 8/1/57, Long Beach, Cal. BL/TL, 5'11", 180 lbs. Deb: 9/4/78

YEAR TM/L	G	AB	R	H	2B	3B	HR	RBI	BB	SO	AVG	OBP	SLG	PRO+	BR/A	SB	CS	SBR	FA	FR	G/POS	TPR
1978 LA-N	7	4	1	2	0	0	0	0	1	1	.500	.500	.500	181	0	0	1	-1	1.000	-1	/O-4	-0.2

■ RONDELL WHITE White, Rondell Bernard b: 2/23/72, Milledgeville, Ga. BR/TR, 6'1", 205 lbs. Deb: 9/1/93

YEAR TM/L	G	AB	R	H	2B	3B	HR	RBI	BB	SO	AVG	OBP	SLG	PRO+	BR/A	SB	CS	SBR	FA	FR	G/POS	TPR
1993 Mon-N	23	73	9	19	3	1	2	15	7	16	.260	.325	.411	91	-1	1	2	-1	1.000	-3	O-21	-0.6
1994 Mon-N	40	97	16	27	10	1	2	13	9	18	.278	.358	.464	110	1	1	1	-0	.946	-3	O-29	-0.2
Total 2	63	170	25	46	13	2	4	28	16	34	.271	.344	.441	102	1	2	3	-1	.971	-6	/O-50	-0.8

YEAR	TM/L	G	AB	R	H	2B	3B	HR	RBI	BB	SO	AVG	OBP	SLG	PRO+	BR/A	SB	CS	SBR	FA	FR	G/POS	TPR

■ ROY WHITE   White, Roy Hilton b: 12/27/43, Los Angeles, Cal.   BB/TR, 5'10", 172 lbs.   Deb: 9/7/65   C

YEAR	TM/L	G	AB	R	H	2B	3B	HR	RBI	BB	SO	AVG	OBP	SLG	PRO+	BR/A	SB	CS	SBR	FA	FR	G/POS	TPR
1965	NY-A	14	42	7	14	2	0	0	3	4	7	.333	.404	.381	125	2	2	1	0	1.000	-1	O-10/2-1	0.1
1966	NY-A	115	316	39	71	13	2	7	20	37	43	.225	.308	.345	91	-4	14	7	0	.957	0	O-82/2-2	-0.7
1967	NY-A	70	214	22	48	8	0	2	18	19	25	.224	.291	.290	75	-7	10	4	1	.968	-6	O-36,3-17	-1.6
1968	NY-A	159	577	89	154	20	7	17	62	73	50	.267	.352	.414	136	25	20	11	-1	.997	10	*O-154	2.9
1969	NY-A★	130	448	55	130	30	5	7	74	81	51	.290	.400	.426	136	25	18	10	-1	.989	11	*O-126	2.9
1970	NY-A☆	162	609	109	180	30	6	22	94	95	66	.296	.391	.473	144	38	24	10	1	.994	7	*O-161	3.9
1971	NY-A	147	524	86	153	22	7	19	84	86	66	.292	.399	.469	154	40	14	7	0	**1.000**	10	*O-145	4.5
1972	NY-A	155	556	76	150	29	0	10	54	**99**	59	.270	.385	.376	131	26	23	7	3	.994	9	*O-162	3.4
1973	NY-A	162	639	88	157	22	3	18	60	78	61	.246	.330	.374	101	1	16	9	-1	.977	4	*O-162	-0.3
1974	NY-A	136	473	68	130	19	8	7	43	67	44	.275	.369	.393	123	16	15	6	1	.993	3	O-67,D-53	1.6
1975	NY-A	148	556	81	161	32	5	12	59	72	50	.290	.373	.430	130	23	16	15	-4	.984	11	*O-135/1-7,D	2.4
1976	*NY-A	156	626	**104**	179	29	3	14	65	83	52	.286	.370	.409	129	24	31	13	2	.987	6	*O-156	2.6
1977	*NY-A	143	519	72	139	25	2	14	52	75	58	.268	.360	.405	109	8	18	11	-1	.981	10	*O-135/D-4	1.1
1978	*NY-A	103	346	44	93	13	3	8	43	42	35	.269	.351	.393	112	6	10	4	1	.992	-4	O-74,D-23	-0.1
1979	NY-A	81	205	24	44	6	0	3	27	23	21	.215	.294	.288	59	-12	2	2	-1	1.000	0	D-29,O-27	-1.4
Total	15	1881	6650	964	1803	300	51	160	758	934	708	.271	.363	.404	122	213	233	117	-0	.988	71	*O-1625,D-111/312	21.3

■ SAMMY WHITE   White, Samuel Charles b: 7/7/28, Wenatchee, Wash.   d: 8/5/91, Princeville, Hawaii   BR/TR, 6'3", 195 lbs.   Deb: 9/26/51

YEAR	TM/L	G	AB	R	H	2B	3B	HR	RBI	BB	SO	AVG	OBP	SLG	PRO+	BR/A	SB	CS	SBR	FA	FR	G/POS	TPR
1951	Bos-A	4	11	0	2	0	0	0	0	0	3	.182	.182	.182	-1	-2	0	0	0	1.000	1	/C-4	-0.1
1952	Bos-A	115	381	35	107	20	2	10	49	16	43	.281	.310	.423	95	-4	2	3	-1	.983	-2	*C-110	-0.2
1953	Bos-A☆	136	476	59	130	34	2	13	64	29	48	.273	.318	.435	96	-4	3	2	-0	.986	9	*C-131	1.0
1954	Bos-A	137	493	46	139	25	2	14	75	21	50	.282	.311	.426	90	-8	1	3	-2	.979	13	*C-133	0.9
1955	Bos-A	143	544	65	142	30	4	11	64	44	58	.261	.324	.392	84	-13	1	2	-1	.984	-0	*C-143	-0.9
1956	Bos-A	114	392	28	96	15	2	5	44	35	40	.245	.307	.332	61	-23	2	1	-0	.984	7	*C-114	-1.0
1957	Bos-A	111	340	24	73	10	1	3	31	25	38	.215	.268	.276	46	-25	0	1	-1	.985	-4	*C-111	-2.7
1958	Bos-A	102	328	25	85	15	3	6	35	21	37	.259	.306	.378	81	-9	1	1	-0	.988	-2	*C-102	-0.6
1959	Bos-A	119	377	34	107	13	4	1	42	23	39	.284	.327	.347	81	-9	4	2	-0	.990	8	*C-119	-0.3
1961	Mil-N	21	63	1	14	1	0	1	5	2	9	.222	.246	.286	43	-5	0	0	-0	.974	4	C-20	0.0
1962	Phi-N	41	97	7	21	4	0	2	12	2	16	.216	.240	.320	50	-7	0	0	-0	.975	5	C-40	-0.1
Total	11	1043	3502	324	916	167	20	66	421	218	381	.262	.307	.377	79	-109	14	15	-5	.984	30	*C-1027	-4.0

■ SAM WHITE   White, Samuel Lambeth b: 8/23/1892, Greater Preston, Yorkshire, England   d: 11/11/29, Philadelphia, Pa.   BL/TR, 6', 185 lbs.   Deb: 9/8/19

YEAR	TM/L	G	AB	R	H	2B	3B	HR	RBI	BB	SO	AVG	OBP	SLG	PRO+	BR/A	SB	CS	SBR	FA	FR	G/POS	TPR
1919	Bos-N	1	1	0	0	0	0	0	0	0	0	.000	.000	.000	-99	-0	0			1.000	2	/C-1	0.1

■ BARNEY WHITE   White, William Barney "Bear" b: 6/25/23, Paris, Tex.   BR/TR, 5'11", 186 lbs.   Deb: 6/5/45

YEAR	TM/L	G	AB	R	H	2B	3B	HR	RBI	BB	SO	AVG	OBP	SLG	PRO+	BR/A	SB	CS	SBR	FA	FR	G/POS	TPR
1945	Bro-N	4	1	2	0	0	0	0	0	1	1	.000	.500	.000	46	0	0			1.000	0	/S-1,3-1	0.0

■ BILL WHITE   White, William De Kova b: 1/28/34, Lakewood, Fla.   BL/TL, 6', 195 lbs.   Deb: 5/7/56

YEAR	TM/L	G	AB	R	H	2B	3B	HR	RBI	BB	SO	AVG	OBP	SLG	PRO+	BR/A	SB	CS	SBR	FA	FR	G/POS	TPR
1956	NY-N	138	508	63	130	23	7	22	59	47	72	.256	.324	.459	108	5	15	8	-0	.989	2	*1-138/O-2	-0.3
1958	SF-N	26	29	5	7	1	0	1	4	7	5	.241	.389	.379	107	1	1	0	0	1.000	-1	/1-3,O-2	0.0
1959	StL-N☆	138	517	77	156	33	9	12	72	34	61	.302	.347	.470	108	5	15	10	-2	.962	-2	O-92,1-71	-0.6
1960	StL-N★	144	554	81	157	27	10	16	79	42	83	.283	.336	.455	105	3	12	6	0	.990	-6	*1-123,O-29	-1.4
1961	StL-N★	153	591	89	169	28	11	20	90	64	84	.286	.357	.472	107	6	8	11	-4	.989	-2	*1-151	-1.4
1962	StL-N	159	614	93	199	31	3	20	102	58	69	.324	.388	.482	120	18	9	7	-2	.993	1	*1-146,O-27	0.8
1963	StL-N★	162	658	106	200	26	8	27	109	59	100	.304	.361	.491	131	25	10	9	-2	.991	-2	*1-162	1.5
1964	*StL-N★	160	631	92	191	37	4	21	102	52	103	.303	.357	.474	121	17	7	6	-2	**.996**	-1	*1-160	0.8
1965	StL-N	148	543	82	157	26	3	24	73	63	86	.289	.367	.481	125	18	3	3	-1	.992	6	*1-144	1.6
1966	Phi-N	159	577	85	159	23	6	22	103	68	109	.276	.355	.451	122	18	16	6	1	**.994**	7	*1-158	1.6
1967	Phi-N	110	308	29	77	6	2	8	33	52	61	.250	.364	.360	107	5	6	1	1	.993	0	1-95	0.1
1968	Phi-N	127	385	34	92	16	2	9	40	39	79	.239	.312	.361	102	1	0	1	-1	.994	4	*1-111	-0.4
1969	StL-N	49	57	7	12	1	0	0	4	11	15	.211	.338	.228	61	-2	1	0	0	1.000	1	1-15	-0.2
Total	13	1673	5972	843	1706	278	65	202	870	596	927	.286	.353	.455	115	120	103	68	-10	.992	8	*1-1477,O-152	2.1

■ BILL WHITE   White, William Dighton b: 5/1/1860, Bridgeport, Ohio   d: 12/29/24, Bellaire, Ohio   TR,   Deb: 5/3/1884

YEAR	TM/L	G	AB	R	H	2B	3B	HR	RBI	BB	SO	AVG	OBP	SLG	PRO+	BR/A	SB	CS	SBR	FA	FR	G/POS	TPR
1884	Pit-a	74	291	25	66	7	10	0			13	.227	.262	.320	87	-4				.807	-11	S-60,3-10/O	-1.4
1886	Lou-a	135	557	96	143	17	10	1			37	.257	.304	.329	93	-7	14			.871	17	*S-135/P-1	1.0
1887	Lou-a	132	512	85	129	7	9	2			47	.252	.315	.313	74	-18	41			.869	22	*S-132	0.4
1888	Lou-a	49	198	35	55	6	5	1	30		7	.278	.313	.374	122	4	15			.816	-3	S-38,3-11	0.3
	*StL-a	76	275	31	48	2	3	2	30		21	.175	.238	.225	44	-18	6			.892	-3	S-74/2-2	-1.8
	Yr	125	473	66	103	8	8	3	60		28	.218	.269	.288	74	-15	21			.864	-6	*S-112,3-11/2	-1.5
Total	4	466	1833	272	441	39	37	6	60		125	.241	.292	.312	82	-43	76			.860	22	S-439/3-21,O2P	-1.5

■ BILL WHITE   White, William Edward b: Milner, Ga.   Deb: 6/21/1879

YEAR	TM/L	G	AB	R	H	2B	3B	HR	RBI	BB	SO	AVG	OBP	SLG	PRO+	BR/A	SB	CS	SBR	FA	FR	G/POS	TPR
1879	Pro-N	1	4	1	1	0	0	0	0	0	1	.250	.250	.250	67	-0				1.000	0	/1-1	0.0

■ WARREN WHITE   White, William Warren (a.k.a. William Warren)   d: 3/3/1898,   5'10.5", 170 lbs.   Deb: 6/17/1871   M

YEAR	TM/L	G	AB	R	H	2B	3B	HR	RBI	BB	SO	AVG	OBP	SLG	PRO+	BR/A	SB	CS	SBR	FA	FR	G/POS	TPR
1871	Oly-n	1	4	0	0	0	0	0	0	0	0	.000	.000	.000	-99	-1	0					/2-1	-0.1
1872	Nat-n	10	45	7	12	0	0	0	3	0		.267	.267	.267	55	-3						3-9,S-1	-0.3
1873	Was-n	39	160	29	43	3	5	0	18	0	1	.269	.269	.350	83	-3						*3-37/S-3	-0.3
1874	Bal-n	45	212	20	56	1	0	0			1	.264	.268	.269	72	-6						*3-45,M	-0.5
1875	Chi-n	69	285	37	71	9	0	0				.249	.249	.281	82	-5						*3-61/S-4,O2	-0.5
1884	Was-U	4	18	2	1	0	0	0				.056	.056	.056	-72	-4				.692	-1	/3-2,S-1,2	-0.5
Total	5 n	164	706	93	182	13	5	0	21	1	1	.258	.259	.290	76	-19						3-152/S-8,O2	-1.7

■ ED WHITED   Whited, Edward Morris b: 2/9/64, Bristol, Pa.   BR/TR, 6'3", 195 lbs.   Deb: 7/5/89

YEAR	TM/L	G	AB	R	H	2B	3B	HR	RBI	BB	SO	AVG	OBP	SLG	PRO+	BR/A	SB	CS	SBR	FA	FR	G/POS	TPR
1989	Atl-N	36	74	5	12	3	0	1	4	6	15	.162	.225	.243	33	-6	1	0	0	.914	-0	3-29/1-3	-0.7

■ BURGESS WHITEHEAD   Whitehead, Burgess Urquhart "Whitey" b: 6/29/10, Tarboro, N.C.   d: 11/25/93, Windsor, N.C.   BR/TR, 5'10.5", 160 lbs.   Deb: 4/30/33

YEAR	TM/L	G	AB	R	H	2B	3B	HR	RBI	BB	SO	AVG	OBP	SLG	PRO+	BR/A	SB	CS	SBR	FA	FR	G/POS	TPR
1933	StL-N	12	7	2	2	0	0	0	0	0	1	.286	.286	.286	60	-0				1.000	0	/S-9,2-3	0.0
1934	*StL-N	100	332	55	92	13	5	1	24	12	19	.277	.310	.355	73	-13	5			.962	-1	2-48,S-29,3	-0.9
1935	StL-N★	107	338	45	89	10	2	0	33	11	14	.263	.289	.305	57	-20	5			.980	5	2-80/3-8,S	-1.0
1936	*NY-N	154	632	99	176	31	3	4	47	29	32	.278	.317	.356	82	-16	14			.969	29	*2-153	2.3
1937	*NY-N★	152	574	64	164	15	6	5	52	28	32	.286	.323	.359	84	-13	7			**.974**	26	*2-152	2.3
1939	NY-N	95	335	31	80	6	3	2	24	24	19	.239	.290	.293	59	-19	1			.970	21	2-91/S-4,3	0.7
1940	NY-N	133	568	68	160	16	4	4	36	26	17	.282	.319	.340	81	-15	9			.947	13	3-74,2-57/S	0.3
1941	NY-N	116	403	41	92	15	4	1	23	14	10	.228	.258	.293	54	-25	7			.970	-0	*2-104/3-1	-1.9
1946	Pit-N	55	127	10	28	1	2	0	5	6	6	.220	.261	.260	47	-9	3			.963	-6	2-30/3-4,S	-1.4
Total	9	924	3316	415	883	100	31	17	245	150	138	.266	.304	.331	72	-130	51			.972	86	2-718,3-116/S	0.4

■ MILT WHITEHEAD   Whitehead, Milton P. b: 1862, Canada   d: 8/15/01, Highland, Cal.   BB,   Deb: 4/20/1884

YEAR	TM/L	G	AB	R	H	2B	3B	HR	RBI	BB	SO	AVG	OBP	SLG	PRO+	BR/A	SB	CS	SBR	FA	FR	G/POS	TPR
1884	StL-U	99	393	61	83	15	1	1			8	.211	.227	.262	31	-37				.803	-11	*S-94/O-2,P23	-4.2
	KC-U	5	22	2	3	0	0	0				.136	.136	.136	-30	-4				.857	-1	/2-3,C-1,S3	-0.4
	Yr	104	415	63	86	15	1	1			8	.207	.222	.255	29	-41				.804	-12	S-95/2-4,O3,PC	-4.6

YEAR	TM/L	G	AB	R	H	2B	3B	HR	RBI	BB	SO	AVG	OBP	SLG	PRO+	BR/A	SB	CS	SBR	FA	FR	G/POS	TPR

■ GIL WHITEHOUSE
Whitehouse, Gilbert Arthur b: 10/15/1893, Somerville, Mass. d: 2/14/26, Brewer, Me. BB/TR, 5'10", 170 lbs. Deb: 6/20/12

1912	Bos-N	2	3	0	0	0	0	0	0	0	3	.000	.000	.000	-98	-1	0			.667	-1	/C-2	-0.2
1915	New-F	35	120	16	27	6	2	0	9	6	16	.225	.268	.308	57	-8	3			.949	-1	O-28/P-1,C	-1.1
Total	2	37	123	16	27	6	2	0	9	6	19	.220	.262	.301	53	-9	3			.846	-2	/O-28,C-3,P	-1.3

■ GURDON WHITELEY
Whiteley, Gurdon W. b: 10/5/1859, Ashaway, R.I. d: 11/24/24, Cranston, R.I. 5'11", 190 lbs. Deb: 8/7/1884

1884	Cle-N	8	34	4	5	0	0	0	0	1	8	.147	.171	.147	1	-4				.800	1	/O-8	-0.3
1885	Bos-N	33	135	14	25	2	2	1	7	1	25	.185	.191	.252	44	-9				.781	-2	O-32/C-1	-1.0
Total	2	41	169	18	30	2	2	1	7	2	33	.178	.187	.231	34	-12				.785	-1	/O-40,C-1	-1.3

■ GEORGE WHITEMAN
Whiteman, George "Lucky" b: 12/23/1882, Peoria, Ill. d: 2/10/47, Houston, Tex. BR/TR, 5'7", 160 lbs. Deb: 9/13/07

1907	Bos-A	4	12	0	2	0	0	0	1	0	1	.167	.167	.167	6	-1	0			1.000	-1	/O-2	-0.2
1913	NY-A	11	32	8	11	3	1	0	2	7	2	.344	.462	.500	181	4	2			.938	1	O-11	0.5
1918	*Bos-A	71	214	24	57	14	0	1	28	20	9	.266	.335	.346	107	2	9			.935	-11	O-69	-1.5
Total	3	86	258	32	70	17	1	1	31	27	11	.271	.345	.357	113	4	11			.936	-11	/O-82	-1.2

■ MARK WHITEN
Whiten, Mark Anthony b: 11/25/66, Pensacola, Fla. BB/TR, 6'3", 210 lbs. Deb: 7/12/90

1990	Tor-A	33	88	12	24	1	1	2	7	7	14	.273	.326	.375	94	-1	2	0	1	1.000	2	O-30/D-2	0.1
1991	Tor-A	46	149	12	33	4	3	2	19	11	35	.221	.280	.329	65	-7	0	1	-1	1.000	3	O-42	-0.6
	Cle-A	70	258	34	66	14	4	7	26	19	50	.256	.312	.422	100	-0	4	2	0	.962	11	O-67/D-3	0.9
	Yr	116	407	46	99	18	7	9	45	30	85	.243	.300	.388	87	-8	4	3	-1	.975	14	*O-109/D-3	0.3
1992	Cle-A	148	508	73	129	19	4	9	43	72	102	.254	.349	.360	101	2	16	12	-2	.980	13	*O-144/D-2	1.0
1993	StL-N	152	562	81	142	13	4	25	99	58	110	.253	.325	.423	100	-0	15	8	-0	.971	1	*O-148	-0.3
1994	StL-N	92	334	57	98	18	2	14	53	37	75	.293	.366	.485	124	12	10	5	0	.964	15	O-90	2.4
Total	5	541	1899	269	492	69	18	59	247	204	386	.259	.333	.408	102	5	47	28	-3	.974	44	O-521/D-7	3.5

■ FRED WHITFIELD
Whitfield, Fred Dwight b: 1/7/38, Vandiver, Ala. BL/TL, 6'1", 190 lbs. Deb: 5/27/62

1962	StL-N	73	158	20	42	7	1	8	34	7	30	.266	.301	.475	95	-2	1	0	0	.987	1	1-38	-0.2
1963	Cle-A	109	346	44	87	17	3	21	54	24	61	.251	.307	.500	123	9	0	1	-1	.987	-3	1-92	0.1
1964	Cle-A	101	293	29	79	13	1	10	29	12	58	.270	.303	.423	100	-1	0	5	-3	.992	-2	1-79	-0.9
1965	Cle-A	132	468	49	137	23	1	26	90	16	42	.293	.319	.513	131	16	2	2	-1	.993	4	*1-122	1.4
1966	Cle-A	137	502	59	121	15	2	27	78	27	76	.241	.285	.440	105	1	1	2	-1	.991	-4	*1-132	-1.3
1967	Cle-A	100	257	24	56	10	0	9	31	25	45	.218	.290	.362	91	-1	0	3	-2	.993	4	1-66	-0.5
1968	Cin-N	87	171	15	44	8	0	6	32	9	29	.257	.302	.409	105	1	0	3	-2	.981	-1	1-41	-0.5
1969	Cin-N	74	74	2	11	0	0	1	8	18	27	.149	.315	.189	42	-5	0	0	0	.985	1	1-14	-0.5
1970	Mon-N	4	15	0	1	0	0	0	0	1	3	.067	.125	.067	-47	-3	0	0	0	.976	2	/1-4	-0.2
Total	9	817	2284	242	578	93	8	108	356	139	371	.253	.301	.443	107	14	7	16	-8	.990	3	1-588	-2.6

■ TERRY WHITFIELD
Whitfield, Terry Bertland b: 1/12/53, Blythe, Cal. BL/TR, 6'1", 197 lbs. Deb: 9/29/74

1974	NY-A	2	5	0	1	0	0	0	0	0	0	.200	.200	.200	16	-1	0	0	0	.000	-1	/O-1	-0.1
1975	NY-A	28	81	9	22	1	1	0	7	1	17	.272	.280	.309	68	-4	1	0	0	.978	0	O-25/D-1	-0.4
1976	NY-A	1	0	0	0	0	0	0	0	0	0	—	—	—	—	0	0	0	0	.000	-1	/O-1	-0.1
1977	SF-N	114	326	41	93	21	3	7	36	20	46	.285	.330	.433	103	2	1	2	-1	.972	-3	O-84	-0.6
1978	SF-N	149	488	70	141	20	2	10	32	33	69	.289	.337	.400	109	5	5	11	-5	.988	0	*O-140	-0.6
1979	SF-N	133	394	52	113	20	4	5	44	36	47	.287	.353	.396	111	6	5	4	-1	.957	2	*O-106	0.3
1980	SF-N	118	321	38	95	16	2	4	26	20	44	.296	.339	.396	107	3	4	2	0	.987	-0	O-95	-0.1
1984	LA-N	87	180	15	44	8	0	4	18	17	35	.244	.313	.356	88	-3	1	4	-2	.988	-5	O-58	-1.1
1985	*LA-N	79	104	8	27	7	0	3	16	6	27	.260	.300	.413	101	-0	1	1	0	.926	-5	O-28	-0.6
1986	LA-N	19	14	0	1	0	0	0	0	5	3	.071	.316	.071	14	-1	0	0	0	1.000	-0	/O-1	-0.2
Total	10	730	1913	233	537	93	12	33	179	138	288	.281	.332	.394	103	6	18	24	-9	.976	-12	O-539/D-1	-3.5

■ ED WHITING
Whiting, Edward C. (a.k.a. Harry Zieber) b: 1860, Philadelphia, Pa. BL/TR, 188 lbs. Deb: 5/2/1882

1882	Bal-a	74	308	43	80	14	5	0		7		.260	.276	.338	115	5				.834	-7	*C-72/1-3,O	0.0
1883	Lou-a	58	240	35	70	16	4	2		9		.292	.317	.417	145	12				.884	-8	C-50/O-6,231	0.6
1884	Lou-a	42	157	16	35	7	3	0		9		.223	.274	.306	93	-1				.891	-2	C-40/O-2,1	0.1
1886	Was-N	6	21	0	0	0	0	0	0	1	12	.000	.045	.000	-90	-2	0			.919	-3	/C-6	-0.6
Total	4	180	726	94	185	37	12	2	0	26	12	.255	.282	.347	114	12	0			.866	-20	C-168/O-10,123	0.1

■ DICK WHITMAN
Whitman, Dick Corwin b: 11/9/20, Woodburn, Ore. BL/TR, 5'11", 170 lbs. Deb: 4/16/46

1946	Bro-N	104	265	39	69	15	3	2	31	22	19	.260	.317	.362	92	-3	5			1.000	-2	O-85	-0.9
1947	Bro-N	4	10	1	4	0	0	0	2	1	0	.400	.455	.400	124	0	0			1.000	0	/O-3	0.0
1948	Bro-N	60	165	24	48	13	0	0	20	14	12	.291	.346	.370	91	-2	4			.990	-1	O-48	-0.5
1949	*Bro-N	23	49	8	9	2	0	0	2	4	4	.184	.245	.224	26	-5	0			.952	-1	O-11	-0.7
1950	*Phi-N	75	132	21	33	7	0	0	12	10	10	.250	.317	.303	65	-6	1			.983	-4	O-32	-1.1
1951	Phi-N	19	17	0	2	0	0	0	0	0	1	.118	.118	.118	-37	-3	0			.000	-3	/O-6	-0.6
Total	6	285	638	93	165	37	3	2	67	51	46	.259	.316	.335	78	-20	10	0		.992	-11	O-185	-3.8

■ FRANK WHITMAN
Whitman, Walter Franklin "Hooker" b: 8/15/24, Marengo, Ind. BR/TR, 6'2", 175 lbs. Deb: 6/30/46

1946	Chi-A	17	16	7	1	0	0	0	1	2	6	.063	.211	.063	-22	-3	0	1	-1	1.000	4	/S-6,1-1,2	0.1
1948	Chi-A	3	6	0	0	0	0	0	0	0	3	.000	.000	.000	-99	-2	0	0	0	.500	-1	/S-1	-0.3
Total	2	20	22	7	1	0	0	0	1	2	9	.045	.160	.045	-43	-4	0	1	-1	.885	3	/S-7,2-1,1	-0.2

■ DAN WHITMER
Whitmer, Daniel Charles b: 11/23/55, Redlands, Cal. BR/TR, 6'3", 195 lbs. Deb: 7/20/80 C

1980	Cal-A	48	87	8	21	3	0	0	7	4	21	.241	.275	.276	53	-6	1	0	0	1.000	4	C-48	0.0
1981	Tor-A	7	9	0	1	1	0	0	0	1	2	.111	.200	.222	20	-1	0	0	0	1.000	1	/C-7	0.0
Total	2	55	96	8	22	4	0	0	7	5	23	.229	.267	.271	49	-7	1	0	0	1.000	5	/C-55	0.0

■ DARRELL WHITMORE
Whitmore, Darrell Lamont b: 11/18/68, Front Royal, Va. BL/TR, 6'1", 210 lbs. Deb: 6/25/93

1993	Fla-N	76	250	24	51	8	2	4	19	10	72	.204	.249	.300	44	-20	4	2	0	.979	2	O-69	-2.0
1994	Fla-N	9	22	1	5	1	0	0	3	5	.227	.320	.273	54	-1	0	1	-1	1.000	1	/O-6	-0.1
Total	2	85	272	25	56	9	2	4	19	13	77	.206	.255	.298	45	-22	4	3	-1	.981	2	/O-75	-2.1

■ PINKY WHITNEY
Whitney, Arthur Carter b: 1/2/05, San Antonio, Tex. d: 9/1/87, Center, Tex. BR/TR, 5'10", 165 lbs. Deb: 4/11/28

1928	Phi-N	151	585	73	176	35	4	10	103	36	30	.301	.342	.426	96	-4	3			.955	3	*3-149	0.7
1929	Phi-N	154	612	89	200	43	14	8	115	61	35	.327	.390	.482	108	7	7			.967	21	*3-154	3.1
1930	Phi-N	149	606	87	207	41	5	8	117	40	41	.342	.383	.465	97	-3	3			.965	20	*3-148	2.3
1931	Phi-N	130	501	64	144	36	5	9	74	30	38	.287	.331	.433	96	-4	6			.948	-6	*3-128	-0.2
1932	Phi-N	154	624	93	186	33	11	13	124	35	66	.298	.335	.449	97	-4	4			.960	5	*3-151/2-5	1.2
1933	Phi-N	31	121	12	32	4	0	3	19	8	8	.264	.310	.372	83	-3	1			.963	-4	3-30	-0.6
	Bos-N	100	382	42	94	17	2	8	49	25	23	.246	.296	.364	95	-4	2			.971	1	3-85,2-18	0.4
	Yr	131	503	54	126	21	2	11	68	33	31	.250	.299	.366	92	-6	3			.969	-4	3-115,2-18	-0.2
1934	Bos-N	146	563	58	146	26	2	12	79	25	54	.259	.294	.377	85	-14	3			.968	3	*3-111,2-36/S	-0.5
1935	Bos-N	126	458	41	125	23	4	4	60	24	36	.273	.312	.367	89	-8	5			.958	6	3-74,2-49	0.4
1936	Bos-N	10	40	1	7	0	0	0	5	2	4	.175	.233	.175	12	-5				.971	1	3-10	-0.3
	Phi-N★	114	411	44	121	17	3	6	59	37	33	.294	.354	.394	92	-5	2			.955	10	*3-111/2-1	0.9

YEAR	TM/L	G	AB	R	H	2B	3B	HR	RBI	BB	SO	AVG	OBP	SLG	PRO+	BR/A	SB	CS	SBR	FA	FR	G/POS	TPR
	Yr	124	451	45	128	17	3	6	64	39	37	.284	.343	.375	86	-9	2			.956	11	*3-121/2-1	0.6
1937	Phi-N	138	487	56	166	19	4	8	79	43	44	.341	.395	.446	118	13	6			.982	4	*3-130	2.0
1938	Phi-N	102	300	27	83	9	1	3	38	27	22	.277	.336	.343	90	-4	0			.934	-2	3-75/1-4,2	-0.5
1939	Phi-N	34	75	9	14	0	1	1	6	7	4	.187	.256	.253	38	-7	0			.991	1	1-12/2-8,3	-0.7
Total	12	1539	5765	696	1701	303	56	93	927	400	438	.295	.343	.415	96	-43	45			.961	63	*3-1358,2-119/1S	8.2

■ ART WHITNEY
Whitney, Arthur Wilson b: 1/16/1858, Brockton, Mass. d: 8/15/43, Lowell, Mass. BR/TR, 5'8", 155 lbs. Deb: 5/1/1880 F

YEAR	TM/L	G	AB	R	H	2B	3B	HR	RBI	BB	SO	AVG	OBP	SLG	PRO+	BR/A	SB	CS	SBR	FA	FR	G/POS	TPR
1880	Wor-N	76	302	38	67	13	5	1	36	9	15	.222	.244	.308	79	-7				.860	-1	*3-76	-0.6
1881	Det-N	58	214	23	39	7	5	0	9	7	15	.182	.208	.262	45	-13				.849	7	*3-58	-0.5
1882	Pro-N	11	40	2	3	0	0	0	1	2	11	.075	.119	.075	-36	-6				.784	-2	S-11	-0.7
	Det-N	31	115	10	21	0	0	0	4	1	12	.183	.190	.183	20	-10				.854	1	3-22/S-8,P	-0.6
	Yr	42	155	12	24	0	0	0	5	3	23	.155	.171	.155	5	-16				.854	-1	3-22,S-19/P	-1.3
1884	Pit-a	23	94	10	28	4	0	0		1		.298	.305	.340	109	1				.916	4	3-21/O-1,S	0.4
1885	Pit-a	90	373	53	87	10	4	0		16		.233	.267	.282	74	-11				.918	-14	*S-75/3-8,2O	-2.1
1886	Pit-a	136	511	70	122	13	4	0		51		.239	.315	.280	87	-6	15			.906	11	*3-95,S-42/P	0.7
1887	Pit-N	119	431	57	112	11	4	1	51	55	18	.260	.346	.304	87	-4	10			.924	-4	*3-119	-0.5
1888	*NY-N	90	328	28	72	1	4	1	28	8	22	.220	.240	.256	59	-15	7			.887	7	3-90	-0.7
1889	*NY-N	129	473	71	103	12	2	1	59	56	39	.218	.303	.258	57	-26	19			.882	-5	*3-129/P-1	-1.8
1890	NY-P	119	442	71	97	12	3	0	45	64	19	.219	.322	.260	52	-31	8			.865	-12	3-88,S-31	-3.1
1891	Cin-a	93	347	42	69	6	1	3	33	31	20	.199	.270	.248	44	-27	8			.903	-5	3-93	-2.4
	StL-a	3	11	0	0	0	0	0	0	1	2	.000	.083	.000	-66	-2	0			.867	2	/3-3	-0.1
	Yr	96	358	42	69	6	1	3	33	32	22	.193	.265	.240	41	-29	8			.902	-3	3-96	-2.5
Total	11	978	3681	475	820	89	32	6	266	302	173	.223	.285	.269	64	-158	67			.888	-6	3-802,S-168/P2O	-12.0

■ FRANK WHITNEY
Whitney, Frank Thomas "Jumbo" b: 2/18/1856, Brockton, Mass. d: 10/30/43, Baltimore, Md. BR/TR, 5'7.5", 152 lbs. Deb: 5/17/1876 F

YEAR	TM/L	G	AB	R	H	2B	3B	HR	RBI	BB	SO	AVG	OBP	SLG	PRO+	BR/A	SB	CS	SBR	FA	FR	G/POS	TPR
1876	Bos-N	34	139	27	33	7	1	0	15	1	3	.237	.243	.302	79	-3				.818	3	O-34/2-1	-0.1

■ JIM WHITNEY
Whitney, James Evans "Grasshopper Jim" b: 11/10/1857, Conklin, N.Y. d: 5/21/1891, Binghamton, N.Y. BL/TR, 6'2", 172 lbs. Deb: 5/2/1881

YEAR	TM/L	G	AB	R	H	2B	3B	HR	RBI	BB	SO	AVG	OBP	SLG	PRO+	BR/A	SB	CS	SBR	FA	FR	G/POS	TPR
1881	Bos-N	75	282	37	72	17	3	0	32	19	18	.255	.302	.337	106	3				.808	-9	*P-66,O-15/1	-0.5
1882	Bos-N	61	251	49	81	18	7	5	48	24	13	.323	.382	.510	183	24				.886	-3	P-49/O-9,1	-0.1
1883	Bos-N	96	409	78	115	27	10	3	57	25	29	.281	.323	.433	124	11				.921	-4	P-62,O-40/1	0.0
1884	Bos-N	66	270	41	70	17	5	3	40	16	38	.259	.301	.393	117	5				1.000	-1	P-38,O-15,1/3	-0.4
1885	Bos-N	72	290	35	68	8	4	0	36	17	24	.234	.277	.290	86	-4				.901	5	P-51,O-17/1	-0.3
1886	KC-N	67	247	26	59	13	3	2	23	29	39	.239	.319	.340	94	-2	5			.927	6	P-46,O-22/3	-0.1
1887	Was-N	54	201	29	53	9	6	2	22	18	24	.264	.324	.398	105	2	10			.905	2	P-47/O-7	-0.2
1888	Was-N	42	141	13	24	0	0	1	17	7	20	.170	.209	.191	30	-11	3			.882	-2	P-39/O-3,1	-0.2
1889	Ind-N	10	32	6	12	4	1	0	4	5	6	.375	.474	.563	185	4	2			1.000	-1	/P-9,O-1	0.0
1890	Phi-a	7	21	3	5	0	0	0		1		.238	.273	.238	52	-1				.900	-1	/P-6,O-1	0.0
Total	10	550	2144	316	559	113	39	18	279	161	211	.261	.313	.375	112	30	20			.900	-9	P-413,O-130/13	-1.8

■ ERNIE WHITT
Whitt, Leo Ernest b: 6/13/52, Detroit, Mich. BL/TR, 6'2", 200 lbs. Deb: 9/12/76

YEAR	TM/L	G	AB	R	H	2B	3B	HR	RBI	BB	SO	AVG	OBP	SLG	PRO+	BR/A	SB	CS	SBR	FA	FR	G/POS	TPR
1976	Bos-A	8	18	4	4	2	0	1	3	2	2	.222	.300	.500	117	0	0	0	0	1.000	-1	/C-8	0.0
1977	Tor-A	23	41	4	7	3	0	0	6	2	12	.171	.209	.244	23	-4	0	0	0	1.000	1	C-14	-0.3
1978	Tor-A	2	4	0	0	0	0	0	0	1	1	.000	.200	.000	-38	-1	0	0	0	1.000	0	/C-1	0.0
1980	Tor-A	106	295	23	70	12	2	6	34	22	30	.237	.290	.353	72	-12	1	3	-2	.986	6	*C-105	-0.4
1981	Tor-A	74	195	16	46	9	0	1	16	20	30	.236	.307	.297	70	-7	5	2	0	.991	9	C-72	0.5
1982	Tor-A	105	284	28	74	14	2	11	42	26	34	.261	.323	.440	98	-1	3	1	0	.982	1	C-98/D-1	0.3
1983	Tor-A	123	344	53	88	15	2	17	56	50	55	.256	.350	.459	114	7	1	1	-0	.992	6	*C-119	1.7
1984	Tor-A	124	315	35	75	12	1	15	46	43	49	.238	.331	.425	104	2	0	3	-2	.994	12	*C-118	1.7
1985	*Tor-A★	139	412	55	101	21	2	19	64	47	59	.245	.324	.444	105	2	3	6	-3	.988	6	*C-134	1.1
1986	Tor-A	131	395	48	106	19	2	16	56	35	39	.268	.328	.448	106	3	0	1	-1	.991	-4	*C-129	0.6
1987	Tor-A	135	446	57	120	24	1	19	75	44	50	.269	.336	.455	105	3	0	1	-1	.994	6	*C-131	1.6
1988	Tor-A	127	398	63	100	11	2	16	70	61	38	.251	.352	.410	112	8	4	2	0	.994	-6	*C-123	1.1
1989	*Tor-A	129	385	42	101	24	1	11	53	52	53	.262	.350	.416	117	9	5	4	-1	.992	-2	*C-115/D-8	1.3
1990	Atl-N	67	180	14	31	8	0	2	10	23	27	.172	.266	.250	40	-14	0	2	-1	.991	2	C-59	-1.1
1991	Bal-A	35	62	5	15	2	0	0	3	8	12	.242	.329	.274	71	-2	0	0	0	1.000	-1	C-20/D-2	-0.2
Total	15	1328	3774	447	938	176	15	134	534	436	491	.249	.327	.410	98	-9	22	26	-9	.991	36	*C-1246/D-11	7.9

■ POSSUM WHITTED
Whitted, George Bostic b: 2/4/1890, Durham, N.C. d: 10/16/62, Wilmington, N.C. BR/TR, 5'8.5", 168 lbs. Deb: 9/16/12

YEAR	TM/L	G	AB	R	H	2B	3B	HR	RBI	BB	SO	AVG	OBP	SLG	PRO+	BR/A	SB	CS	SBR	FA	FR	G/POS	TPR
1912	StL-N	12	46	7	12	3	0	0	7	3	5	.261	.306	.326	75	-2	1			.857	-3	3-12	-0.5
1913	StL-N	123	404	44	89	10	5	0	38	31	44	.220	.282	.270	59	-21	9			.989	5	0-41,S-38,3/21	-1.5
1914	StL-N	20	31	3	4	1	0	0	1	0	3	.129	.129	.161	-14	-4	1			.889	-3	/3-5,O-3,2	-0.8
	*Bos-N	66	218	36	57	11	4	2	31	18	18	.261	.326	.376	109	2	10			.967	4	0-38,2-15/13S	0.5
	Yr	86	249	39	61	12	4	2	32	18	21	.245	.304	.349	95	-2	11			.957	1	0-41,2-16/31S	-0.3
1915	*Phi-N	128	448	46	126	17	3	1	43	29	47	.281	.328	.339	101	0	24	15	-2	.978	4	*O-119/1-7	-0.4
1916	Phi-N	147	526	68	148	20	12	6	68	19	46	.281	.309	.399	113	6	29	17	-2	.964	5	*O-136,1-16	0.2
1917	Phi-N	149	553	69	155	24	9	3	70	30	56	.280	.317	.373	107	3	10			.977	4	*O-141,1-10/32	0.2
1918	Phi-N	24	86	7	21	4	0	0	3	4	10	.244	.278	.291	69	-3	4			.982	0	0-22/1-1	-0.2
1919	Phi-N	78	289	32	72	14	1	3	32	14	20	.249	.284	.336	80	-7	5			.955	0	0-47,2-26/1	-1.0
	Pit-N	35	131	15	51	7	7	0	21	6	4	.389	.420	.550	183	13	7			.988	3	1-33/3-2,O	1.5
	Yr	113	420	47	123	21	8	3	53	20	24	.293	.327	.402	112	5	12			.955	3	0-48,1-35,2/3	0.5
1920	Pit-N	134	494	53	129	11	12	1	74	35	36	.261	.314	.338	85	-10	11	11	-3	.961	-3	*3-125,1-10/O	-1.1
1921	Pit-N	108	403	60	114	23	7	7	63	26	21	.283	.328	.427	96	-3	5	10	-5	.988	9	*O-102/1-7	-0.6
1922	Bro-N	1	0	0	0	0	0	0	0	0	0	.000	.000	.000	-99	-0	0	0	0	.000	0	H	0.0
Total	11	1025	3630	440	978	145	60	23	451	215	310	.269	.313	.361	95	-27	116	53		.975	27	0-651,3-177/12S	-3.9

■ FLOYD WICKER
Wicker, Floyd Euliss b: 9/12/43, Burlington, N.C. BL/TR, 6'2", 175 lbs. Deb: 6/23/68

YEAR	TM/L	G	AB	R	H	2B	3B	HR	RBI	BB	SO	AVG	OBP	SLG	PRO+	BR/A	SB	CS	SBR	FA	FR	G/POS	TPR
1968	StL-N	5	4	2	2	0	0	0	0	0	0	.500	.500	.500	204	0	0	0	0	.000	0	H	0.1
1969	Mon-N	41	39	2	4	0	0	0	2	2	20	.103	.146	.103	-29	-7	0	0	0	1.000	-2	O-11	-1.0
1970	Mil-A	15	41	3	8	1	0	1	3	1	8	.195	.214	.293	38	-4	0	0	0	1.000	-1	O-12	-0.5
1971	Mil-A	11	8	0	1	0	0	0	0	2	0	.125	.300	.125	24	-1	0	0	0	.000	0	H	-0.1
	SF-N	9	21	3	3	0	0	0	1	2	5	.143	.250	.143	14	-2	0	0	0	1.000	1	/O-7	-0.2
Total	4	81	113	10	18	1	0	1	6	7	33	.159	.215	.195	15	-13	0	0	0	1.000	-3	/O-30	-1.7

■ AL WICKLAND
Wickland, Albert b: 1/27/1888, Chicago, Ill. d: 3/14/80, Port Washington, Wis. BL/TL, 5'7", 155 lbs. Deb: 8/21/13

YEAR	TM/L	G	AB	R	H	2B	3B	HR	RBI	BB	SO	AVG	OBP	SLG	PRO+	BR/A	SB	CS	SBR	FA	FR	G/POS	TPR
1913	Cin-N	26	79	7	17	5	5	0	8	6	19	.215	.279	.405	94	-1	3			.983	1	O-24	-0.1
1914	Chi-F	157	536	74	148	31	10	6	68	81	58	.276	.375	.405	108	-1	17			.962	-1	*O-157	-0.1
1915	Chi-F	30	86	11	21	2	2	1	5	13	11	.244	.343	.349	91	-1	3			.946	-2	O-24	-0.4
	Pit-F	110	389	63	117	12	8	1	30	52	47	.301	.386	.380	106	5	23			.968	4	*O-109	0.4
	Yr	140	475	74	138	14	10	2	35	65	58	.291	.378	.375	104	4	26			.966	2	*O-133	0.0
1918	Bos-N	95	332	55	87	7	13	4	32	53	39	.262	.367	.398	139	17	12			.975	3	O-95	1.6
1919	NY-A	26	46	9	7	1	0	0	5	2	10	.152	.188	.174	2	-6	0			1.000	-4	O-15	-1.1
Total	5	444	1468	212	397	58	38	12	144	207	184	.270	.364	.386	109	22	58			.968	-1	O-424	0.3

YEAR	TM/L	G	AB	R	H	2B	3B	HR	RBI	BB	SO	AVG	OBP	SLG	PRO+	BR/A	SB	CS	SBR	FA	FR	G/POS	TPR

■ TOM WIEDENBAUER Wiedenbauer, Thomas John b: 11/5/58, Menomonie, Wis. BR/TR, 6'1", 180 lbs. Deb: 9/14/79

| 1979 | Hou-N | 4 | 6 | 0 | 4 | 1 | 0 | 0 | 2 | 0 | 2 | .667 | .667 | .833 | 326 | 2 | 0 | 0 | 0 | 1.000 | -1 | /O-3 | 0.1 |

■ TOM WIEGHAUS Wieghaus, Thomas Robert b: 2/1/57, Chicago Heights, Ill BR/TR, 6', 195 lbs. Deb: 10/4/81

1981	Mon-N	1	1	0	0	0	0	0	0	0	0	.000	.000	.000	-99	-0	0	0	0	1.000	1	/C-1	0.1
1983	Mon-N	1	0	0	0	0	0	0	0	0	0	—	—	—	—	0	0	0	0	1.000	-0	/C-1	0.0
1984	Hou-N	6	10	0	0	0	0	0	1	1	3	.000	.091	.000	-78	-2	0	0	0	1.000	2	/C-6	0.0
Total	3	8	11	0	0	0	0	0	1	1	3	.000	.083	.000	-80	-3	0	0	0	1.000	3	/C-8	0.1

■ WHITEY WIETELMANN Wietelmann, William Frederick b: 3/15/19, Zanesville, Ohio BB/TR, 6', 170 lbs. Deb: 9/6/39 C

1939	Bos-N	23	69	2	14	1	0	0	5	2	9	.203	.225	.217	21	-8	1			.953	2	S-22/2-1	-0.5
1940	Bos-N	35	41	3	8	1	0	0	1	5	5	.195	.283	.220	43	-3	0			.962	3	2-15/3-9,S	0.0
1941	Bos-N	16	33	1	3	0	0	0	0	1	5	.091	.118	.091	-43	-6	0			1.000	3	2-10/S-5,3	-0.3
1942	Bos-N	13	34	4	7	2	0	0	0	4	5	.206	.289	.265	64	-1	0			.941	-1	S-11/2-1	-0.1
1943	Bos-N	153	534	33	115	14	1	0	39	46	40	.215	.281	.245	53	-31	9			.957	20	*S-153	0.0
1944	Bos-N	125	417	46	100	18	1	2	32	33	25	.240	.300	.302	67	-18	0			.954	-6	*S-103,2-23/3	-1.6
1945	Bos-N	123	428	53	116	15	3	4	33	39	27	.271	.335	.348	89	-6	4			.972	3	2-87,S-39/3P	0.4
1946	Bos-N	44	78	7	16	0	0	0	5	14	8	.205	.326	.205	52	-4	0			.915	-6	S-16/3-8,2P	-0.9
1947	Pit-N	48	128	21	30	4	1	1	7	12	10	.234	.305	.305	59	-7	0			.885	-13	S-22,2-14/31	-1.9
Total	9	580	1762	170	409	55	6	7	122	156	131	.232	.298	.282	63	-85	14			.952	4	S-374,2-155/3P1	-4.9

■ ALAN WIGGINS Wiggins, Alan Anthony b: 2/17/58, Los Angeles, Cal. d: 1/6/91, Los Angeles, Cal. BB/TR, 6'2", 160 lbs. Deb: 9/4/81

1981	SD-N	15	14	4	5	0	0	0	1	0	1	.357	.400	.357	125	0	2	0	1	.750	-1	/O-4	0.0
1982	SD-N	72	254	40	65	3	3	1	15	13	19	.256	.295	.303	71	-10	33	6	6	.967	1	O-68/2-1	-0.5
1983	SD-N	144	503	83	139	20	2	0	22	65	43	.276	.360	.324	94	-2	66	13	12	.992	-1	*O-105,1-45	0.4
1984	*SD-N	158	596	106	154	19	7	3	34	75	57	.258	.344	.329	90	-6	70	21	8	.962	-29	*2-157	-2.2
1985	SD-N	10	37	3	2	1	0	0	0	2	4	.054	.103	.081	-49	-7	0	1	-1	1.000	-3	/2-9	-1.2
	Bal-A	76	298	43	85	11	4	0	21	29	16	.285	.353	.349	96	-1	30	13	1	.960	-24	2-76	-2.1
1986	Bal-A	71	239	30	60	3	1	0	11	22	20	.251	.314	.272	62	-12	21	7	2	.978	-19	2-66/D-1	-2.6
1987	Bal-A	85	306	37	71	4	2	1	15	28	34	.232	.299	.268	53	-20	20	7	2	.983	-0	D-44,2-33/O	-1.7
Total	7	631	2247	346	581	61	19	5	118	235	193	.259	.331	.309	80	-57	242	68	32	.967	-76	2-342,O-182/D1	-9.9

■ DEL WILBER Wilber, Delbert Quentin "Babe" b: 2/24/19, Lincoln Park, Mich. BR/TR, 6'3", 200 lbs. Deb: 4/21/46 MC

1946	StL-N	4	4	0	0	0	0	0	1	0	1	.000	.200	.000	-39	-1	0			1.000	1	/C-4	0.0
1947	StL-N	51	99	7	23	8	1	0	12	5	13	.232	.269	.333	57	-6	0			.983	1	C-34	-0.4
1948	StL-N	27	58	5	11	0	0	0	10	4	9	.190	.242	.224	25	-6	0			.949	-3	C-26	-0.8
1949	StL-N	2	4	0	1	0	0	0	0	0	1	.250	.250	.250	33	-0	0			1.000	0	/C-2	0.0
1951	Phi-N	84	245	30	68	7	3	8	34	17	26	.278	.324	.429	102	0	0	1	-1	.978	4	C-73	0.6
1952	Phi-N	2	2	0	0	0	0	0	0	0	1	.000	.000	.000	-99	-1	0	0	0	.000	0	H	-0.1
	Bos-A	47	135	7	36	10	1	3	23	7	20	.267	.308	.422	94	-2	1	0	0	.995	1	C-39	0.1
1953	Bos-A	58	112	16	27	6	1	7	29	6	21	.241	.286	.500	103	-0	0	0	0	.980	-3	C-28/1-2	-0.2
1954	Bos-A	24	61	2	8	2	1	1	7	4	6	.131	.185	.246	15	-7	0	0	0	.950	-5	C-18	-1.3
Total	8	299	720	67	174	35	7	19	115	44	96	.242	.287	.389	79	-23	1	1		.978	-4	C-224/1-2	-2.1

■ CLAUDE WILBORN Wilborn, Claude Edward b: 9/1/12, Woodsdale, N.C. d: 11/13/92, Roxboro, N.C. BL/TR, 6'1", 180 lbs. Deb: 9/8/40

| 1940 | Bos-N | 5 | 7 | 0 | 0 | 0 | 0 | 0 | 0 | 0 | 1 | .000 | .000 | .000 | -99 | -2 | 0 | | | .500 | -1 | /O-3 | -0.4 |

■ TED WILBORN Wilborn, Thaddeus Iglehart b: 12/16/58, Waco, Tex. BB/TR, 6', 165 lbs. Deb: 4/5/79

1979	Tor-A	22	12	3	0	0	0	0	0	1	7	.000	.077	.000	-76	-3	0	1	-1	.875	-2	/O-7	-0.5
1980	NY-A	8	8	2	2	0	0	0	1	0	1	.250	.250	.250	38	-1	0	0	0	1.000	1	/O-3	0.0
Total	2	30	20	5	2	0	0	0	1	1	8	.100	.143	.100	-33	-4	0	1	-1	.933	-1	/O-10	-0.5

■ WILEY Wiley Deb: 6/23/1884

| 1884 | Was-U | 1 | 4 | 0 | 0 | 0 | 0 | 0 | | 0 | | .000 | .000 | .000 | -99 | -1 | | | | .333 | -1 | /3-1 | -0.2 |

■ ROB WILFONG Wilfong, Robert Donald b: 9/1/53, Pasadena, Cal. BL/TR, 6'1", 185 lbs. Deb: 4/10/77

1977	Min-A	73	171	22	42	1	1	1	13	17	26	.246	.321	.281	67	-7	10	4	1	.959	4	2-66/D-1	0.0
1978	Min-A	92	199	23	53	8	0	1	11	19	27	.266	.336	.322	84	-4	8	4	0	.986	6	2-80/D-5	0.7
1979	Min-A	140	419	71	131	22	6	9	59	29	54	.313	.360	.458	115	8	11	4	1	.979	21	*2-133/O-3	3.6
1980	Min-A	131	416	55	103	16	5	8	45	34	61	.248	.309	.368	79	-12	10	6	-1	.995	-4	*2-120/O-6	-1.1
1981	Min-A	93	305	32	75	11	3	3	19	29	43	.246	.311	.331	80	-8	2	4	-2	.980	4	2-93	-0.1
1982	Min-A	25	81	7	13	1	0	0	5	7	13	.160	.236	.173	14	-9	0	2	-1	.980	-0	2-22	-1.0
	*Cal-A	55	102	17	25	4	2	1	11	7	17	.245	.294	.353	77	-3	4	0	1	.982	9	2-28/3-5,OSD	0.7
	Yr	80	183	24	38	5	2	1	16	14	30	.208	.268	.273	49	-13	4	2	0	.981	9	2-50/3-5,OSD	-0.3
1983	Cal-A	65	177	17	45	7	1	2	17	10	25	.254	.294	.339	74	-6	2	0	-1	.995	12	2-39,3-13/SD	0.6
1984	Cal-A	108	307	31	76	13	2	6	33	20	53	.248	.298	.362	82	-8	3	2	0	.975	3	2-97/S-4,D	-0.2
1985	Cal-A	83	217	16	41	3	0	4	13	16	32	.189	.245	.258	38	-19	4	1	1	.986	21	2-69/D-2	0.5
1986	*Cal-A	92	288	25	63	11	3	3	33	16	34	.219	.265	.309	56	-18	4	4	-2	.982	9	2-90	-0.8
1987	SF-N	2	8	2	1	0	0	1	2	1	2	.125	.222	.500	89	-0	1	0	0	.833	-2	/2-2	-0.2
Total	11	959	2690	318	668	97	23	39	261	205	387	.248	.305	.345	77	-86	54	33	-4	.982	80	2-839/3-18,SOD	2.7

■ SPIDER WILHELM Wilhelm, Charles Ernest b: 5/23/29, Baltimore, Md. d: 10/20/92, Venice, Fla. BR/TR, 5'9", 170 lbs. Deb: 9/6/53

| 1953 | Phi-A | 7 | 7 | 1 | 2 | 1 | 0 | 0 | 0 | 0 | 3 | .286 | .286 | .429 | 87 | -0 | 0 | 0 | 0 | .875 | -0 | /S-6 | 0.0 |

■ JIM WILHELM Wilhelm, James Webster b: 9/20/52, San Rafael, Cal. BR/TR, 6'3", 190 lbs. Deb: 9/4/78

1978	SD-N	10	19	2	7	2	0	0	4	0	2	.368	.400	.474	155	1	1	0	0	1.000	-3	O-10	-0.1
1979	SD-N	39	103	8	25	4	3	0	8	12	12	.243	.257	.340	65	-5	1	1	-0	.985	0	O-30	-0.6
Total	2	49	122	10	32	6	3	0	12	12	14	.262	.280	.361	79	-4	2	1	-0	.987	-2	/O-40	-0.7

■ JOE WILHOIT Wilhoit, Joseph William b: 12/20/1885, Hiawatha, Kan. d: 9/25/30, Santa Barbara, Cal. BL/TR, 6'2", 175 lbs. Deb: 4/12/16

1916	Bos-N	116	383	44	88	13	4	2	38	27	45	.230	.282	.300	82	-8	18			.979	2	*O-108	-1.4
1917	Bos-N	54	186	20	51	5	0	1	10	17	15	.274	.335	.317	107	2	5			.928	3	O-52	-0.4
	Pit-N	9	10	0	2	0	0	0	0	1	1	.200	.273	.200	44	-1	0			1.000	-0	/O-3,1-1	-0.1
	*NY-N	34	50	9	17	2	2	0	8	8	5	.340	.431	.460	179	5	0			1.000	-2	O-11	0.3
	Yr	97	246	29	70	7	2	1	18	26	21	.285	.353	.341	118	6	5			.941	3	O-66/1-1	-0.2
1918	NY-N	64	135	13	37	3	3	0	15	17	14	.274	.355	.341	115	3	4			.975	-8	O-55	-0.7
1919	Bos-A	6	18	7	6	0	0	0	2	5	2	.333	.478	.333	138	1	1			1.000	-1	/O-5	0.0
Total	4	283	782	93	201	23	9	3	73	75	82	.257	.323	.321	101	2	28			.969	-11	O-234/1-1	-2.3

■ DENNEY WILIE Wilie, Dennis Ernest b: 9/22/1890, Mt.Calm, Tex. d: 6/20/66, Hayward, Cal. BL/TL, 5'8", 155 lbs. Deb: 7/27/11

1911	StL-N	28	51	10	12	3	1	0	3	8	11	.235	.361	.333	97	0	3			1.000	-3	O-15	-0.3
1912	StL-N	30	48	2	11	0	1	0	6	7	9	.229	.351	.271	73	-1	0			.917	-3	O-16	-0.5
1915	Cle-A	45	131	14	33	4	1	2	10	26	18	.252	.384	.344	115	4	2	6	-3	.910	-2	O-35	-0.4
Total	3	103	230	26	56	7	3	2	19	41	38	.243	.372	.326	102	2	5	6		.925	-8	/O-66	-1.2

YEAR	TM/L	G	AB	R	H	2B	3B	HR	RBI	BB	SO	AVG	OBP	SLG	PRO+	BR/A	SB	CS	SBR	FA	FR	G/POS	TPR

■ HARRY WILKE　　Wilke, Henry Joseph　b: 12/14/1900, Cincinnati, Ohio　d: 6/21/91, Hamilton, Ohio　BR/TR, 5'10.5", 171 lbs.　Deb: 5/12/27

1927	Chi-N	3	9	0	0	0	0	0	0	0	1	.000	.000	.000	-99	-3	0			1.000	0	/3-3	-0.2

■ CURTIS WILKERSON　　Wilkerson, Curtis Vernon　b: 4/26/61, Petersburg, Va.　BB/TR, 5'9", 158 lbs.　Deb: 9/10/83

1983	Tex-A	16	35	7	6	0	1	0	1	2	5	.171	.216	.229	23	-4	3	0	1	1.000	2	/S-9,2-2,3	0.0
1984	Tex-A	153	484	47	120	12	0	1	26	22	72	.248	.283	.279	55	-29	12	10	-2	.944	-28	*S-116,2-47	-4.9
1985	Tex-A	129	360	35	88	11	6	0	22	22	63	.244	.295	.308	65	-17	14	7	0	.957	3	*S-110,2-19/D	-0.4
1986	Tex-A	110	236	27	56	10	3	0	15	11	42	.237	.274	.305	56	-14	9	7	-2	.968	15	2-60,S-56/D	0.3
1987	Tex-A	85	138	28	37	5	3	2	14	6	16	.268	.308	.391	84	-3	6	3	0	.946	11	S-33,2-28,3/D	0.9
1988	Tex-A	117	338	41	99	12	5	0	28	26	43	.293	.347	.358	95	-2	9	4	0	.970	10	2-87,S-24,3/D	1.3
1989	*Chi-N	77	160	18	39	4	2	1	10	8	33	.244	.280	.313	64	-7	4	2	0	.881	4	3-26,2-15/SO	-0.3
1990	Chi-N	77	186	21	41	5	1	0	16	7	36	.220	.249	.258	37	-16	2	2	-1	.888	-4	3-52,2-14/SO	-2.1
1991	*Pit-N	85	191	20	36	9	1	2	18	15	40	.188	.248	.277	48	-13	2	1	0	.992	3	2-30,S-15,3	-0.9
1992	KC-A	111	296	27	74	10	1	2	29	18	47	.250	.295	.311	68	-13	18	7	1	.968	-4	S-69,2-39/3D	-1.1
1993	KC-A	12	28	1	4	0	0	0	0	1	6	.143	.172	.143	-13	-4	2	0	1	1.000	-1	2-10/S-4	-0.4
Total	11	972	2452	272	600	78	23	8	179	138	403	.245	.288	.305	63	-123	81	43	-2	.957	11	S-444,2-351,3/DO	-7.6

■ RICK WILKINS　　Wilkins, Richard David　b: 6/4/67, Jacksonville, Fla.　BL/TR, 6'2", 210 lbs.　Deb: 6/6/91

1991	Chi-N	86	203	21	45	9	0	6	22	19	56	.222	.307	.355	82	-5	3	3	-1	.993	9	C-82	0.7
1992	Chi-N	83	244	20	66	9	1	8	22	28	53	.270	.346	.414	111	9	0	2	-1	.993	10	C-73	1.8
1993	Chi-N	136	446	78	135	23	1	30	73	50	99	.303	.377	.561	149	30	2	1	0	.996	7	*C-133	4.3
1994	Chi-N	100	313	44	71	25	2	7	39	40	86	.227	.318	.387	85	-7	4	3	-1	.993	-5	C-95/1-2	-0.7
Total	4	405	1206	163	317	66	4	51	156	137	294	.263	.343	.451	113	22	9	9	-3	.994	21	C-383/1-2	6.1

■ BOBBY WILKINS　　Wilkins, Robert Linwood　b: 8/11/22, Denton, N.C.　BR/TR, 5'9", 165 lbs.　Deb: 4/18/44

1944	Phi-A	24	25	7	6	0	0	0	3	1	4	.240	.296	.240	55	-1	0	0		.943	5	/S-9	0.4
1945	Phi-A	62	154	22	40	6	0	0	4	10	17	.260	.305	.299	76	-5	2	4	-2	.923	0	S-40/O-4	-0.4
Total	2	86	179	29	46	6	0	0	7	11	21	.257	.304	.291	73	-6	2	4	-2	.926	5	/S-49,O-4	0.0

■ ED WILKINSON　　Wilkinson, Edward Henry　b: 6/20/1890, Jacksonville, Ore　d: 4/9/18, Tucson, Ariz.　BR/TR, 6', 170 lbs.　Deb: 7/4/11

1911	NY-A	10	13	2	3	0	0	0	1	0		.231	.231	.231	27	-1	0			.800	-1	/O-3,2-1	-0.2

■ BOB WILL　　Will, Robert Lee "Butch"　b: 7/15/31, Berwyn, Ill.　BL/TL, 5'10.5", 175 lbs.　Deb: 4/16/57

1957	Chi-N	70	112	13	25	3	0	1	10	5	21	.223	.256	.277	44	-9	1	0	0	.963	-5	O-30	-1.5
1958	Chi-N	6	4	1	1	0	0	0	0	2	0	.250	.500	.250	108	0	0	0	0	.000	0	/O-1	0.0
1960	Chi-N	138	475	58	121	20	9	6	53	47	54	.255	.323	.373	91	-6	1	5	-3	.992	2	*O-121	-1.3
1961	Chi-N	86	113	9	29	9	0	0	8	15	19	.257	.344	.336	80	-3	0	1	-1	1.000	-6	O-30/1-1	-1.0
1962	Chi-N	87	92	6	22	3	0	2	15	13	22	.239	.333	.337	78	-3	0	0	0	1.000	-1	/O-9	-0.4
1963	Chi-N	23	23	0	4	0	0	0	1	3	1	.174	.208	.174	11	-3	0	0	0	1.000	0	/1-1	-0.3
Total	6	410	819	87	202	35	9	9	87	83	119	.247	.317	.344	80	-22	2	6	-3	.988	-10	O-191/1-2	-4.5

■ JERRY WILLARD　　Willard, Gerald Duane　b: 3/14/60, Oxnard, Cal.　BL/TR, 6'2", 195 lbs.　Deb: 4/11/84

1984	Cle-A	87	246	21	55	8	1	10	37	26	55	.224	.298	.386	86	-5	1	0	0	.981	-1	C-76/D-1	-0.2
1985	Cle-A	104	300	39	81	13	0	7	36	28	59	.270	.334	.383	97	-1	0	0	0	.990	0	C-96/D-1	0.4
1986	Oak-A	75	161	17	43	7	0	4	26	22	28	.267	.362	.385	112	3	0	1	-1	.994	-11	C-71/D-1	-0.5
1987	Oak-A	7	6	1	1	0	0	0	0	2	1	.167	.375	.167	55	-0	0	0	0	1.000	-0	/1-1,3-1,D	-0.1
1990	Chi-A	3	3	0	0	0	0	0	0	0	2	.000	.000	.000	-99	-1	0	0	0	.000	0	/C-1	-0.1
1991	*Atl-N	17	14	1	3	0	0	1	4	2	5	.214	.313	.429	100	-0	0	0	0	1.000	1	/C-1	0.0
1992	Atl-N	26	23	2	8	1	0	2	7	1	3	.348	.375	.652	175	2	0	0	0	1.000	0	/C-1	0.3
	Mon-N	21	25	0	3	0	0	0	1	1	7	.120	.154	.120	-22	-4	0	0	0	.952	0	/1-5	-0.4
	Yr	47	48	2	11	1	0	2	8	2	10	.229	.260	.375	76	-2	0	0	0	.952	1	/1-5,C-1	-0.1
1994	Sea-A	6	5	1	1	0	0	1	3	1	1	.200	.333	.800	177	1	0	0	0	.000	-0	/C-1,D-1	0.0
Total	8	346	783	82	195	29	1	25	114	83	161	.249	.323	.384	95	-5	1	1	-0	.988	-11	C-247/D-7,13	-0.6

■ RIP WILLIAMS　　Williams, Alva Mitchel "Buff"　b: 1/31/1882, Carthage, Ill.　d: 7/23/33, Keokuk, Iowa　BR/TR, 5'11.5", 187 lbs.　Deb: 4/12/11

1911	Bos-A	95	284	36	68	8	5	0	31	24		.239	.314	.303	73	-10	9			.975	1	1-57,C-38	-0.6
1912	Was-A	61	157	14	50	11	4	0	22	7		.318	.352	.439	125	4	2			.978	4	C-48	1.2
1913	Was-A	66	106	9	30	6	2	1	12	9	16	.283	.339	.406	115	2	3			.985	-4	C-18/1-9,O	-0.1
1914	Was-A	81	169	17	47	6	4	1	22	13	19	.278	.341	.379	112	2	2	2	-1	.975	-5	C-44/1-8,O	0.0
1915	Was-A	91	197	14	48	8	4	0	31	18	20	.244	.320	.325	91	-2	4	3	-1	.967	8	C-40,1-15/3	0.8
1916	Was-A	76	202	16	54	10	2	0	20	15	19	.267	.324	.337	100	-0	5			.982	-9	1-34,C-23/3	-0.9
1918	Cle-A	28	71	5	17	2	2	0	7	9	6	.239	.325	.324	87	-1	2			.980	-2	1-21/C-1	-0.4
Total	7	498	1186	111	314	51	23	2	145	95	80	.265	.328	.352	97	-6	27	5		.977	-6	C-212,1-144/O3	-0.0

■ ART WILLIAMS　　Williams, Arthur Franklin　b: 8/26/1877, Somerville, Mass.　d: 5/16/41, Arlington, Va.　TR ,　Deb: 5/7/02

1902	Chi-N	47	160	17	37	3	0	0	14	15		.231	.309	.250	75	-4	9			.917	-3	O-24,1-19	-0.9

■ GUS WILLIAMS　　Williams, August Joseph "Gloomy Gus"　b: 5/7/1888, Omaha, Neb.　d: 4/16/64, Sterling, Ill.　BL/TL, 6', 185 lbs.　Deb: 4/12/11　F

1911	StL-A	9	26	1	7	3	0	0	4	0		.269	.296	.385	93	-0	0			.867	-1	/O-7	-0.2
1912	StL-A	64	216	32	63	13	7	2	32	27		.292	.370	.444	138	10	18			.930	2	O-62	0.9
1913	StL-A	148	538	72	147	21	16	5	53	57	87	.273	.346	.400	121	13	31			.951	4	*O-143	1.1
1914	StL-A	144	499	51	126	19	6	4	47	36	120	.253	.308	.339	98	-3	35	20	-2	.933	-2	*O-142	-0.9
1915	StL-A	45	119	15	24	2	2	1	11	6	16	.202	.246	.277	59	-7	11	1	3	.949	-5	O-35	-1.1
Total	5	410	1398	171	367	58	31	12	147	126	223	.263	.327	.374	110	14	95	21		.939	2	O-389	-0.2

■ BERNIE WILLIAMS　　Williams, Bernabe (Figueroa)　b: 9/13/68, San Juan, P.R.　BB/TR, 6'2", 180 lbs.　Deb: 7/7/91

1991	NY-A	85	320	43	76	19	4	3	34	48	57	.238	.339	.350	91	-3	10	5	0	.979	6	O-85	0.0
1992	NY-A	62	261	39	73	14	2	5	26	29	36	.280	.354	.406	113	5	7	6	-2	.995	6	O-62	1.1
1993	NY-A	139	567	67	152	31	4	12	68	53	106	.268	.335	.400	100	-0	9	9	-3	.989	6	*O-139	-0.1
1994	NY-A	108	408	80	118	29	1	12	57	61	54	.289	.386	.453	124	16	16	9	-1	.990	5	*O-107	1.6
Total	4	394	1556	229	419	93	11	32	185	191	253	.269	.353	.405	106	17	42	29	-5	.988	24	O-393	2.6

■ BERNIE WILLIAMS　　Williams, Bernard　b: 10/8/48, Alameda, Cal.　BR/TR, 6'1", 175 lbs.　Deb: 9/7/70

1970	SF-N	7	16	2	5	2	0	0	1	2	1	.313	.389	.438	122	1	1	1	-0	1.000	1	/O-6	0.1
1971	SF-N	35	73	8	13	1	0	1	5	12	24	.178	.294	.233	52	-4	1	1	-0	.933	-5	O-27	-1.1
1972	SF-N	46	68	12	13	3	1	3	9	7	22	.191	.267	.397	85	-2	0	0	0	1.000	2	O-15	-0.1
1974	SD-N	14	15	1	2	0	0	0	0	0	6	.133	.133	.133	-26	-2	0	0	0	1.000	-1	/O-3	-0.4
Total	4	102	172	23	33	6	1	4	15	21	53	.192	.280	.308	66	-8	2	2	-1	.974	-3	/O-51	-1.5

■ BILLY WILLIAMS　　Williams, Billy Leo　b: 6/15/38, Whistler, Ala.　BL/TR, 6'1", 175 lbs.　Deb: 8/6/59　CH

1959	Chi-N	18	33	0	5	0	1	0	2	1	7	.152	.176	.212	3	-5	0	0	0	1.000	-0	O-10	-0.5
1960	Chi-N	12	47	4	13	0	2	2	7	5	12	.277	.346	.489	127	2	0	0	0	.962	0	O-12	0.1
1961	Chi-N	146	529	75	147	20	7	25	86	45	70	.278	.340	.484	114	10	6	0	0	.954	2	*O-135	0.2
1962	Chi-N★	159	618	94	184	22	8	22	91	70	72	.298	.373	.466	119	17	9	9	-3	.967	16	*O-159	2.0
1963	Chi-N	161	612	87	175	36	9	25	95	68	78	.286	.359	.497	136	29	7	6	-2	.987	16	*O-160	3.7

YEAR	TM/L	G	AB	R	H	2B	3B	HR	RBI	BB	SO	AVG	OBP	SLG	PRO+	BR/A	SB	CS	SBR	FA	FR	G/POS	TPR
1964	Chi-N★	162	645	100	201	39	2	33	98	59	84	.312	.371	.532	145	38	10	7	-1	.950	1	*O-162	3.0
1965	Chi-N★	164	645	115	203	39	6	34	108	65	76	.315	.380	.552	155	46	10	1	2	.968	0	*O-164	4.3
1966	Chi-N	162	648	100	179	23	5	29	91	69	61	.276	.350	.461	122	19	6	3	0	.976	8	*O-162	2.0
1967	Chi-N	162	634	92	176	21	12	28	84	68	67	.278	.349	.481	129	24	6	3	0	.989	-3	*O-162	1.3
1968	Chi-N★	163	642	91	185	30	8	30	98	48	53	.288	.340	.500	140	29	4	1	1	.967	-11	*O-163	1.1
1969	Chi-N	163	642	103	188	33	10	21	95	59	70	.293	.356	.474	116	12	3	2	-0	.957	2	*O-159	0.5
1970	Chi-N	161	636	137	205	34	4	42	129	72	65	.322	.393	.586	142	35	7	1	2	.989	8	*O-160	3.6
1971	Chi-N	157	594	86	179	27	5	28	93	77	44	.301	.384	.505	131	24	7	5	-1	.977	7	*O-154	2.4
1972	Chi-N★	150	574	95	191	34	6	37	122	62	59	.333	.403	.606	166	48	3	1	0	.984	-3	*O-144/1-5	4.1
1973	Chi-N★	156	576	72	166	22	2	20	86	76	72	.288	.372	.438	115	13	4	3	1	.985	12	*O-138,1-19	1.7
1974	Chi-N	117	404	55	113	22	0	16	68	67	44	.280	.383	.453	128	16	4	5	-2	.986	2	1-65,O-43	1.1
1975	*Oak-A	155	520	68	127	20	1	23	81	76	68	.244	.343	.419	117	12	0	0	0	.971	-0	*D-145/1-7	0.8
1976	Oak-A	120	351	36	74	12	0	11	41	58	44	.211	.323	.339	98	0	4	2	0	.000	-0	*D-106/O-1	-0.0
Total	18	2488	9350	1410	2711	434	88	426	1475	1045	1046	.290	.364	.492	131	371	90	49	-2	.973	52	*O-2088,D-251/1	31.1

■ DALLAS WILLIAMS
Williams, Dallas McKinley b: 2/28/58, Brooklyn, N.Y.   BL/TL, 5'11", 165 lbs.   Deb: 9/19/81

YEAR	TM/L	G	AB	R	H	2B	3B	HR	RBI	BB	SO	AVG	OBP	SLG	PRO+	BR/A	SB	CS	SBR	FA	FR	G/POS	TPR
1981	Bal-A	2	2	0	1	0	0	0	0	0	0	.500	.500	.500	189	0	0	0	0	1.000	-0	/O-1	0.0
1983	Cin-N	18	36	2	2	0	0	0	1	3	6	.056	.128	.056	-46	-7	0	0	0	1.000	-1	O-12	-0.9
Total	2	20	38	2	3	0	0	0	1	3	6	.079	.146	.079	-35	-7	0	0	0	1.000	-2	/O-13	-0.9

■ DANA WILLIAMS
Williams, Dana Lamont b: 3/20/63, Weirton, W.Va.   BR/TR, 5'10", 170 lbs.   Deb: 6/21/89

YEAR	TM/L	G	AB	R	H	2B	3B	HR	RBI	BB	SO	AVG	OBP	SLG	PRO+	BR/A	SB	CS	SBR	FA	FR	G/POS	TPR
1989	Bos-A	8	5	1	1	1	0	0	0	0	1	.200	.333	.400	100	0	0	0	0	1.000	-0	/O-1,D-2	0.0

■ DAVEY WILLIAMS
Williams, David Carlous b: 11/2/27, Dallas, Tex.   BR/TR, 5'10", 160 lbs.   Deb: 9/16/49   C

YEAR	TM/L	G	AB	R	H	2B	3B	HR	RBI	BB	SO	AVG	OBP	SLG	PRO+	BR/A	SB	CS	SBR	FA	FR	G/POS	TPR
1949	NY-N	13	50	7	12	1	1	1	5	7	4	.240	.333	.360	86	-1	0			.953	-10	2-13	-1.1
1951	*NY-N	30	64	17	17	1	0	2	8	5	8	.266	.319	.375	85	-1	1	1	-0	1.000	2	2-22	0.1
1952	NY-N	138	540	70	137	26	3	13	55	48	63	.254	.324	.385	95	-4	2	3	-1	.973	-15	*2-138	-1.4
1953	NY-N★	112	340	51	101	11	2	3	34	44	19	.297	.382	.368	95	-1	2	5	-2	.982	0	2-95	0.2
1954	*NY-N	142	544	65	121	18	3	9	46	43	33	.222	.285	.316	56	-35	1	1	-0	.982	-7	*2-142	-3.3
1955	NY-N	82	247	25	62	4	1	4	15	17	17	.251	.305	.324	67	-12	0	2	-1	.968	-8	2-71	-1.6
Total	6	517	1785	235	450	61	10	32	163	164	144	.252	.321	.351	79	-54	6	12		.978	-38	2-481	-7.1

■ DEWEY WILLIAMS
Williams, Dewey Edgar "Dee" b: 2/5/16, Durham, N.C.   BR/TR, 6', 160 lbs.   Deb: 6/28/44

YEAR	TM/L	G	AB	R	H	2B	3B	HR	RBI	BB	SO	AVG	OBP	SLG	PRO+	BR/A	SB	CS	SBR	FA	FR	G/POS	TPR
1944	Chi-N	79	262	23	63	7	2	0	27	23	18	.240	.302	.282	65	-12	2			.981	4	C-77	-0.3
1945	*Chi-N	59	100	16	28	2	2	2	5	13	13	.280	.363	.400	114	2	0			.978	2	C-54	0.6
1946	Chi-N	4	5	0	1	0	0	0	0	0	2	.200	.200	.200	14	-1	0			1.000	0	/C-2	-0.1
1947	Chi-N	3	2	0	0	0	0	0	0	0	1	.000	.000	.000	-99	-1	0			.000	0	/C-1	-0.1
1948	Cin-N	48	95	9	16	2	0	1	5	10	18	.168	.248	.221	29	-10	0			.961	-3	C-47	-1.1
Total	5	193	464	48	108	11	4	3	37	46	52	.233	.302	.293	67	-20	2			.976	3	C-181	-0.9

■ EARL WILLIAMS
Williams, Earl Baxter b: 1/27/03, Cumberland Gap, Tenn.   d: 3/10/58, Knoxville, Tenn.   BR/TR, 6'0.5", 185 lbs.   Deb: 5/27/28

YEAR	TM/L	G	AB	R	H	2B	3B	HR	RBI	BB	SO	AVG	OBP	SLG	PRO+	BR/A	SB	CS	SBR	FA	FR	G/POS	TPR
1928	Bos-N	3	2	0	0	0	0	0	0	0	1	.000	.000	.000	-99	-1	0			1.000	0	/C-1	-0.1

■ EARL WILLIAMS
Williams, Earl Craig b: 7/14/48, Newark, N.J.   BR/TR, 6'3", 220 lbs.   Deb: 9/13/70

YEAR	TM/L	G	AB	R	H	2B	3B	HR	RBI	BB	SO	AVG	OBP	SLG	PRO+	BR/A	SB	CS	SBR	FA	FR	G/POS	TPR
1970	Atl-N	10	19	4	7	4	0	1	6	3	4	.368	.455	.579	165	2	0	0	0	1.000	1	/1-4,3-3	0.3
1971	Atl-N	145	497	64	129	14	1	33	87	42	80	.260	.326	.491	121	12	0	1	-1	.981	-8	C-72,3-42,1	0.4
1972	Atl-N	151	565	72	146	24	2	28	87	62	118	.258	.338	.457	113	9	0	0	0	.980	-19	*C-116,3-21,1	-0.7
1973	*Bal-A	132	459	58	109	18	1	22	83	66	107	.237	.337	.425	114	9	0	2	-1	.987	-9	C-95,1-42/D	0.0
1974	*Bal-A	118	413	47	105	16	0	14	52	40	79	.254	.330	.395	111	6	0	2	-1	.983	-14	C-75,1-47/D	-0.9
1975	Atl-N	111	383	42	92	13	0	11	50	34	63	.240	.307	.360	82	-10	0	0	0	.989	-5	1-90,C-11	-2.1
1976	Atl-N	61	184	18	39	3	0	9	26	19	33	.212	.289	.375	82	-5	0	0	0	.995	-9	C-38,1-17	-1.4
	Mon-N	61	190	17	45	10	2	8	29	14	32	.237	.289	.437	100	-1	0	0	0	.981	6	1-47,C-13	0.3
	Yr	122	374	35	84	13	2	17	55	33	65	.225	.289	.406	91	-6	0	0	0	.986	-2	1-64,C-51	-1.1
1977	Oak-A	100	348	39	84	13	0	13	38	18	58	.241	.288	.391	84	-8	2	0	1	.989	-4	D-45,C-36,1	-1.3
Total	8	889	3058	361	756	115	6	138	457	298	574	.247	.321	.424	105	14	2	5	-2	.984	-60	C-456,1-327/3D	-5.4

■ EDDIE WILLIAMS
Williams, Edward Laquan b: 11/1/64, Shreveport, La.   BR/TR, 6', 175 lbs.   Deb: 4/18/86

YEAR	TM/L	G	AB	R	H	2B	3B	HR	RBI	BB	SO	AVG	OBP	SLG	PRO+	BR/A	SB	CS	SBR	FA	FR	G/POS	TPR
1986	Cle-A	5	7	2	1	0	0	0	0	0	3	.143	.143	.143	-22	-1	0	0	0	.000	-2	/O-4	-0.3
1987	Cle-A	22	64	9	11	4	0	1	4	9	19	.172	.284	.281	50	-5	0	0	0	.982	2	3-22	-0.3
1988	Cle-A	10	21	3	4	0	0	0	1	0	3	.190	.227	.190	18	-2	0	0	0	1.000	3	3-10	0.0
1989	Chi-A	66	201	25	55	8	0	3	10	18	31	.274	.345	.358	101	1	1	2	-1	.909	1	3-65	0.1
1990	SD-N	14	42	5	12	3	0	3	4	5	6	.286	.362	.571	151	3	0	1	-1	.897	-1	3-13	0.1
1994	SD-N	49	175	32	58	11	1	11	42	15	26	.331	.394	.594	154	14	0	1	-1	.988	-2	1-46/3-1	0.7
Total	6	166	510	76	141	26	1	18	62	47	88	.276	.348	.437	113	9	1	4	-2	.929	1	3-111/1-46,O	0.3

■ DIB WILLIAMS
Williams, Edwin Dibrell b: 1/19/10, Greenbrier, Ark.   d: 4/2/92, Searcy, Ark.   BR/TR, 5'11.5", 175 lbs.   Deb: 4/27/30

YEAR	TM/L	G	AB	R	H	2B	3B	HR	RBI	BB	SO	AVG	OBP	SLG	PRO+	BR/A	SB	CS	SBR	FA	FR	G/POS	TPR
1930	Phi-A	67	191	24	50	10	3	3	22	15	19	.262	.322	.393	77	-7	2	1	0	.951	4	2-39,S-19/3	0.0
1931	*Phi-A	86	294	41	79	12	2	6	40	19	21	.269	.313	.384	78	-10	2	0	1	.931	7	S-72,2-10/O	0.5
1932	Phi-A	62	215	30	54	10	1	4	24	22	23	.251	.329	.363	76	-8	0	1	-1	.952	7	2-53/S-3	0.1
1933	Phi-A	115	408	52	118	20	5	11	73	32	35	.289	.342	.444	106	3	0	0	0	.921	-9	S-84,2-29/1	0.0
1934	Phi-A	66	205	25	56	10	1	2	17	21	18	.273	.341	.361	84	-5	1	0	0	.956	-0	2-53/S-2	-0.2
1935	Phi-A	4	10	0	1	0	0	0	0	0	1	.100	.100	.100	-49	-2	0	0	0	1.000	-2	/2-2	-0.4
	Bos-A	75	251	26	63	12	4	0	25	24	23	.251	.319	.335	65	-13	2	0	1	.952	-5	3-30,2-29,S/1	-1.4
	Yr	79	261	26	64	12	4	0	25	24	24	.245	.311	.326	61	-15	2	0	1	.973	-7	2-31,3-30,S/1	-1.8
Total	6	475	1574	198	421	74	12	29	201	133	140	.267	.327	.385	82	-43	7	3	0	.955	1	2-215,S-195/310	-1.4

■ DENNY WILLIAMS
Williams, Evon Daniel b: 12/13/1899, Portland, Ore.   d: 3/23/29, San Clemente, Cal.   BL/TR, 5'8.5", 150 lbs.   Deb: 4/15/21

YEAR	TM/L	G	AB	R	H	2B	3B	HR	RBI	BB	SO	AVG	OBP	SLG	PRO+	BR/A	SB	CS	SBR	FA	FR	G/POS	TPR
1921	Cin-N	10	7	0	0	0	0	0	0	0	0	.000	.000	.000	-99	-2	0			1.000	-0	/O-1	-0.3
1924	Bos-A	25	85	17	31	3	0	0	4	10	5	.365	.438	.400	117	3	3	3	-1	.972	-2	O-19	-0.1
1925	Bos-A	69	218	28	50	1	3	0	13	17	11	.229	.285	.261	39	-20	5	6	-3	.953	-2	O-52	-2.7
1928	Bos-A	16	18	1	4	0	0	0	1	1	3	.222	.263	.222	29	-2	0	0	0	1.000	-2	/O-6	-0.4
Total	4	120	328	46	85	4	3	0	18	28	19	.259	.319	.290	56	-21	5	10	-5	.959	-7	/O-78	-3.5

■ CY WILLIAMS
Williams, Fred b: 12/21/1887, Wadena, Ind.   d: 4/23/74, Eagle River, Wis.   BL/TL, 6'2", 180 lbs.   Deb: 7/18/12

YEAR	TM/L	G	AB	R	H	2B	3B	HR	RBI	BB	SO	AVG	OBP	SLG	PRO+	BR/A	SB	CS	SBR	FA	FR	G/POS	TPR
1912	Chi-N	28	62	3	15	0	1	0	6	6	14	.242	.309	.290	65	-3	2			1.000	-2	O-22	-0.6
1913	Chi-N	49	156	17	35	3	3	4	32	5	26	.224	.262	.359	76	-6	5			.976	-5	O-44	-1.2
1914	Chi-N	55	94	12	19	2	2	0	5	13	13	.202	.312	.266	73	-3	2			.941	3	O-27	-0.7
1915	Chi-N	151	518	59	133	22	6	13	64	26	49	.257	.305	.398	112	5	15	10	-2	.968	4	*O-149	0.2
1916	Chi-N	118	405	55	113	19	9	12	66	51	64	.279	.372	.459	140	19	6			.989	-4	*O-116	1.1
1917	Chi-N	138	468	53	113	22	4	5	42	38	78	.241	.308	.338	91	-5	8			.960	12	*O-136	0.0
1918	Phi-N	94	351	49	97	14	1	6	39	27	30	.276	.337	.373	109	4	10			.968	-0	O-91	-0.1
1919	Phi-N	109	435	54	121	21	1	9	39	30	43	.278	.335	.393	111	5	9			.970	-4	*O-108	0.2
1920	Phi-N	148	590	88	192	36	10	15	72	32	45	.325	.360	.497	139	28	18	12	-2	.972	10	*O-147	2.6
1921	Phi-N	146	562	67	180	28	6	18	75	30	32	.320	.357	.488	112	9	5	15	-8	.979	16	*O-146	0.6
1922	Phi-N	151	584	98	180	30	6	26	92	74	49	.308	.392	.514	120	17	11	14	-5	.973	2	*O-150	0.3

YEAR	TM/L	G	AB	R	H	2B	3B	HR	RBI	BB	SO	AVG	OBP	SLG	PRO+	BR/A	SB	CS	SBR	FA	FR	G/POS	TPR
1923	Phi-N	136	535	98	157	22	3	**41**	114	59	57	.293	.371	.576	131	21	11	10	-3	.981	-3	*O-135	0.6
1924	Phi-N	148	558	101	183	31	11	24	93	67	49	.328	.403	.552	137	28	7	12	-5	.962	-3	*O-145	1.1
1925	Phi-N	107	314	78	104	11	5	13	60	53	34	.331	.435	.522	132	17	4	9	-4	.989	-5	O-96	0.2
1926	Phi-N	107	336	63	116	13	4	18	53	38	35	.345	.418	**.568**	155	26	2			.963	-8	O-93	1.2
1927	Phi-N	131	492	86	135	18	2	**30**	98	61	57	.274	.365	.502	128	19	0			.970	1	*O-130	1.2
1928	Phi-N	99	238	31	61	9	0	12	37	54	34	.256	.400	.445	117	8	0			1.000	-2	O-69	0.1
1929	Phi-N	66	65	11	19	2	0	5	21	22	9	.292	.471	.554	144	5	0			.966	-0	O-11	0.4
1930	Phi-N	21	17	1	8	2	0	0	2	4	3	.471	.571	.588	169	2	0			1.000	-1	/O-3	0.1
Total	19	2002	6780	1024	1981	306	74	251	1005	690	721	.292	.365	.470	123	197	115	82		.973	15	*O-1818	7.3

■ PAPA WILLIAMS
Williams, Fred b: 7/17/13, Meridian, Miss. d: 11/2/93, Meridian, Miss. BR/TR, 6'1", 200 lbs. Deb: 4/19/45

YEAR	TM/L	G	AB	R	H	2B	3B	HR	RBI	BB	SO	AVG	OBP	SLG	PRO+	BR/A	SB	CS	SBR	FA	FR	G/POS	TPR
1945	Cle-A	16	19	0	4	0	0	0	0	1	2	.211	.250	.211	36	-2	0	0	0	1.000	0	/1-3	-0.1

■ GEORGE WILLIAMS
Williams, George b: 10/23/39, Detroit, Mich. BR/TR, 5'11", 165 lbs. Deb: 7/16/61

YEAR	TM/L	G	AB	R	H	2B	3B	HR	RBI	BB	SO	AVG	OBP	SLG	PRO+	BR/A	SB	CS	SBR	FA	FR	G/POS	TPR
1961	Phi-N	17	36	4	9	0	0	0	1	4	4	.250	.325	.250	56	-2	0	0	0	.967	2	2-15	0.1
1962	Hou-N	5	8	1	3	1	0	0	2	0	1	.375	.375	.500	143	0	0	0	0	1.000	0	/2-3	0.1
1964	KC-A	37	91	10	19	6	0	0	2	6	12	.209	.265	.275	49	-6	0	0	0	.970	-3	2-20/S-2,3O	-0.8
Total	3	59	135	15	31	7	0	0	5	10	17	.230	.288	.281	56	-8	0	0	0	.970	-1	/2-38,O-2,3S	-0.6

■ GERALD WILLIAMS
Williams, Gerald Floyd b: 8/10/66, New Orleans, La. BR/TR, 6'2", 190 lbs. Deb: 9/15/92

YEAR	TM/L	G	AB	R	H	2B	3B	HR	RBI	BB	SO	AVG	OBP	SLG	PRO+	BR/A	SB	CS	SBR	FA	FR	G/POS	TPR
1992	NY-A	15	27	7	8	2	0	3	6	0	3	.296	.296	.704	174	2	2	0	1	.913	-1	O-12	0.2
1993	NY-A	42	67	11	10	2	3	0	6	1	14	.149	.186	.269	21	-8	2	0	1	.956	-8	O-37/D-1	-1.6
1994	NY-A	57	86	19	25	8	0	4	13	4	17	.291	.322	.523	121	2	1	3	-2	.957	-11	O-43/D-2	-1.0
Total	3	114	180	37	43	12	3	7	25	5	34	.239	.267	.456	92	-3	5	3	-0	.948	-20	/O-92,D-3	-2.4

■ HARRY WILLIAMS
Williams, Harry Peter b: 6/23/1890, Omaha, Neb. d: 12/21/63, Huntington Park, Cal. BR/TR, 6'1.5", 200 lbs. Deb: 8/7/13 F

YEAR	TM/L	G	AB	R	H	2B	3B	HR	RBI	BB	SO	AVG	OBP	SLG	PRO+	BR/A	SB	CS	SBR	FA	FR	G/POS	TPR
1913	NY-A	27	82	18	21	3	1	1	12	15	10	.256	.378	.354	114	2	6			.981	-2	1-27	0.0
1914	NY-A	59	178	9	29	5	2	1	17	26	26	.163	.287	.230	56	-9	3	6	-3	.976	-5	1-58	-2.1
Total	2	86	260	27	50	8	3	2	29	41	36	.192	.316	.269	75	-7	9	6		.977	-7	/1-85	-2.1

■ JIM WILLIAMS
Williams, James Alfred b: 4/29/47, Zachary, La. BR/TR, 6'2", 190 lbs. Deb: 9/8/69

YEAR	TM/L	G	AB	R	H	2B	3B	HR	RBI	BB	SO	AVG	OBP	SLG	PRO+	BR/A	SB	CS	SBR	FA	FR	G/POS	TPR
1969	SD-N	13	25	4	7	1	0	0	2	3	11	.280	.357	.320	95	-0	0	0	0	.900	-0	/O-6	-0.1
1970	SD-N	11	14	4	4	0	0	0	0	1	3	.286	.333	.286	70	-1	1	0	0	1.000	-1	/O-6	-0.1
Total	2	24	39	8	11	1	0	0	2	4	14	.282	.349	.308	86	-1	1	0	0	.938	-2	/O-12	-0.2

■ JIMY WILLIAMS
Williams, James Francis b: 10/4/43, Santa Maria, Cal. BR/TR, 5'10", 170 lbs. Deb: 4/26/66 MC

YEAR	TM/L	G	AB	R	H	2B	3B	HR	RBI	BB	SO	AVG	OBP	SLG	PRO+	BR/A	SB	CS	SBR	FA	FR	G/POS	TPR
1966	StL-N	13	11	1	3	0	0	0	1	1	5	.273	.333	.273	71	-0	0	0	0	1.000	-2	/S-7,2-3	-0.2
1967	StL-N	1	2	0	0	0	0	0	0	0	1	.000	.000	.000	-99	-1	0	0	0	1.000	1	/S-1	0.0
Total	2	14	13	1	3	0	0	0	1	1	6	.231	.286	.231	46	-1	0	0	0	1.000	-1	/S-8,2-3	-0.2

■ JIMMY WILLIAMS
Williams, James Thomas b: 12/20/1876, St.Louis, Mo. d: 1/16/65, St.Petersburg, Fla BR/TR, 5'9", 175 lbs. Deb: 4/15/1899

YEAR	TM/L	G	AB	R	H	2B	3B	HR	RBI	BB	SO	AVG	OBP	SLG	PRO+	BR/A	SB	CS	SBR	FA	FR	G/POS	TPR
1899	Pit-N	152	617	126	219	28	**27**	9	116	60		.355	.417	.532	160	50	26			.902	7	*3-152	5.2
1900	*Pit-N	106	416	73	110	15	11	5	68	32		.264	.323	.389	95	-4	18			.889	6	*3-103/S-4	0.3
1901	Bal-A	130	501	113	159	26	**21**	7	96	56		.317	.388	.495	138	25	21			.935	-2	*3-130	2.5
1902	Bal-A	125	498	83	156	27	**21**	8	83	36		.313	.361	.500	131	19	14			.945	4	*2-104,3-19/1	2.5
1903	NY-A	132	502	60	134	30	12	3	82	39		.267	.326	.392	108	5	9			**.957**	16	*2-132	2.6
1904	NY-A	146	559	62	147	31	7	2	74	38		.263	.314	.354	106	4	14			.951	17	*2-146	2.7
1905	NY-A	129	470	54	107	20	8	6	62	50		.228	.306	.343	95	-3	14			**.964**	5	*2-129	0.3
1906	NY-A	139	501	62	139	25	7	3	77	44		.277	.342	.373	112	7	8			.958	11	*2-139	2.0
1907	NY-A	139	504	53	136	17	11	2	63	35		.270	.319	.359	107	3	14			.966	-1	*2-139	0.1
1908	StL-A	148	539	63	127	20	7	4	53	55		.236	.310	.321	104	3	7			.963	5	*2-148	0.8
1909	StL-A	110	374	32	73	3	6	0	22	29		.195	.257	.235	60	-17	6			.962	-6	*2-109	-2.9
Total	11	1456	5481	781	1507	242	138	49	796	474		.275	.337	.396	114	90	151			.955	62	*2-1176,3-274/S1	16.1

■ KEN WILLIAMS
Williams, Kenneth Roy b: 6/28/1890, Grants Pass, Ore. d: 1/22/59, Grants Pass, Ore. BL/TR, 6', 170 lbs. Deb: 7/14/15

YEAR	TM/L	G	AB	R	H	2B	3B	HR	RBI	BB	SO	AVG	OBP	SLG	PRO+	BR/A	SB	CS	SBR	FA	FR	G/POS	TPR
1915	Cin-N	71	219	22	53	10	4	0	16	15	20	.242	.297	.324	86	-4	4	3	-1	.948	2	O-62	-0.6
1916	Cin-N	10	27	1	3	0	0	0	1	2	5	.111	.172	.111	-12	-4	1			.955	1	O-10	-0.3
1918	StL-A	2	1	0	0	0	0	0	1	1	0	.000	.500	.000	53	0	0			.000	0	H	0.0
1919	StL-A	65	227	32	68	10	5	6	35	26	25	.300	.376	.467	133	10	7			.937	4	O-63	1.0
1920	StL-A	141	521	90	160	34	13	10	72	41	26	.307	.362	.480	118	12	18	8	1	.961	8	*O-138	1.0
1921	StL-A	146	547	115	190	31	7	24	117	74	42	.347	.429	.561	142	35	20	17	-4	.932	7	*O-145	2.5
1922	StL-A	153	585	128	194	34	11	**39**	**155**	74	31	.332	.413	.627	162	51	37	20	-1	.970	20	*O-153	4.4
1923	StL-A	147	555	106	198	37	12	29	91	79	32	.357	.439	.623	168	54	18	17	-5	.967	11	*O-145	4.7
1924	StL-A	114	398	78	129	21	4	18	84	69	17	.324	.425	.533	137	23	20	11	-1	.968	6	*O-109	1.9
1925	StL-A	102	411	83	136	31	5	25	105	37	14	.331	.390	**.613**	144	24	10	5	0	.955	5	*O-102	2.0
1926	StL-A	108	347	55	97	15	7	17	74	39	23	.280	.354	.510	118	7	5	4	-1	.948	1	O-92/2-1	0.1
1927	StL-A	131	423	70	136	23	6	17	74	57	30	.322	.403	.525	135	21	9	7	-2	.965	6	*O-113	1.8
1928	Bos-A	133	462	59	140	25	1	8	67	37	15	.303	.356	.413	104	2	4	9	-4	.971	-3	*O-127	-1.3
1929	Bos-A	74	139	21	48	14	2	3	21	15	7	.345	.409	.540	146	9	1	5	-3	.963	-5	O-39/1-2	0.0
Total	14	1397	4862	860	1552	285	77	196	913	566	287	.319	.393	.530	136	241	154	106		.958	48	*O-1298/1-2,2	17.2

■ KENNY WILLIAMS
Williams, Kenneth Royal b: 4/6/64, Berkeley, Cal. BR/TR, 6'2", 187 lbs. Deb: 9/2/86

YEAR	TM/L	G	AB	R	H	2B	3B	HR	RBI	BB	SO	AVG	OBP	SLG	PRO+	BR/A	SB	CS	SBR	FA	FR	G/POS	TPR
1986	Chi-A	15	31	2	4	0	0	1	1	1	11	.129	.182	.226	10	-4	1	1	-0	1.000	0	O-10/D-1	-0.4
1987	Chi-A	116	391	48	110	18	2	11	50	10	83	.281	.315	.422	91	-6	21	10	-0	.981	6	*O-115	-0.3
1988	Chi-A	73	220	18	35	4	2	8	28	10	64	.159	.223	.305	46	-16	6	5	-1	.959	-4	O-38,3-32/D	-2.3
1989	Det-A	94	258	29	53	5	1	6	23	18	63	.205	.270	.302	63	-13	9	4	0	.979	-4	O-87/1-1,D	-1.1
1990	Det-A	57	83	10	11	2	0	0	5	3	24	.133	.172	.157	-7	-12	2	2	-1	1.000	-3	O-47/D-6	-1.7
	Tor-A	49	72	13	14	6	1	0	8	7	18	.194	.275	.306	61	-4	7	2	1	1.000	-7	O-30/D-9	-1.0
	Yr	106	155	23	25	8	1	0	13	10	42	.161	.222	.226	25	-16	9	4	0	1.000	-10	O-77,D-15	-2.7
1991	Tor-A	13	29	5	6	2	0	1	3	4	5	.207	.324	.379	90	-0	1	0	0	1.000	-0	/O-9,D-2	0.0
	Mon-N	34	70	11	19	5	2	1	9	1	18	.271	.311	.400	100	-0	2	1	0	.957	1	O-24	0.0
Total	6	451	1154	136	252	42	8	27	119	56	290	.218	.271	.339	66	-55	49	25	-0	.981	-3	O-360/3-32,D1	-6.8

■ MARK WILLIAMS
Williams, Mark Westley b: 7/28/53, Elmira, N.Y. BL/TL, 6', 180 lbs. Deb: 5/20/77

YEAR	TM/L	G	AB	R	H	2B	3B	HR	RBI	BB	SO	AVG	OBP	SLG	PRO+	BR/A	SB	CS	SBR	FA	FR	G/POS	TPR
1977	Oak-A	3	2	0	0	0	0	0	1	1	1	.000	.333	.000	0	-0	0	0	0	1.000	-0	/O-1	0.0

■ MATT WILLIAMS
Williams, Matthew Derrick b: 11/28/65, Bishop, Cal. BR/TR, 6'2", 205 lbs. Deb: 4/11/87

YEAR	TM/L	G	AB	R	H	2B	3B	HR	RBI	BB	SO	AVG	OBP	SLG	PRO+	BR/A	SB	CS	SBR	FA	FR	G/POS	TPR
1987	SF-N	84	245	28	46	9	2	8	21	16	68	.188	.240	.339	54	-17	4	3	-1	.975	20	S-70,3-17	0.7
1988	SF-N	52	156	17	32	6	1	8	19	8	41	.205	.253	.410	91	-3	0	1	-1	.967	10	3-43,S-14	0.7
1989	*SF-N	84	292	31	59	18	1	18	50	14	72	.202	.244	.455	98	-3	1	2	-1	.961	6	3-73,S-30	0.4
1990	SF-N	159	617	87	171	27	2	33	**122**	33	138	.277	.321	.488	124	17	7	4	-0	.959	4	*3-159	2.2
1991	SF-N	157	589	72	158	24	5	34	98	33	128	.268	.314	.499	129	19	5	5	-2	.964	9	*3-155/S-4	2.8
1992	SF-N	146	529	58	120	13	5	20	66	39	109	.227	.287	.384	94	-7	7	7	-2	.945	7	*3-144	-0.2
1993	SF-N	145	579	105	170	33	4	38	110	27	80	.294	.330	.561	137	27	1	3	-2	.970	3	*3-144	2.8

YEAR	TM/L	G	AB	R	H	2B	3B	HR	RBI	BB	SO	AVG	OBP	SLG	PRO+	BR/A	SB	CS	SBR	FA	FR	G/POS	TPR
1994	SF-N★	112	445	74	119	16	3	**43**	96	33	87	.267	.321	.607	140	22	1	0	0	.963	9	*3-110	3.1
Total	8	939	3452	472	875	146	23	202	582	203	723	.253	.301	.485	116	55	26	25	-7	.960	69	3-845,S-118	12.5

■ OTTO WILLIAMS
Williams, Otto George b: 11/2/1877, Newark, N.J. d: 3/19/37, Omaha, Neb. BR/TR, 5'8", 165 lbs. Deb: 10/5/02 C

YEAR	TM/L	G	AB	R	H	2B	3B	HR	RBI	BB	SO	AVG	OBP	SLG	PRO+	BR/A	SB	CS	SBR	FA	FR	G/POS	TPR
1902	StL-N	2	5	0	2	0	0	0	2	1		.400	.500	.400	185	1	1			.813	1	/S-2	0.2
1903	StL-N	53	187	10	38	4	2	0	9	9		.203	.240	.246	40	-15	6			.885	-5	S-52/2-1	-1.7
	Chi-N	38	130	14	29	5	0	0	13	4		.223	.246	.262	46	-9	8			.937	5	S-26/2-7,13	-0.3
	Yr	91	317	24	67	9	2	0	22	13		.211	.242	.252	42	-24	14			.904	0	S-78/2-8,13	-2.0
1904	Chi-N	57	185	21	37	4	1	0	8	13		.200	.256	.232	51	-10	9			.973	-0	0-21,1-11,S/23	-1.2
1906	Was-N	20	51	3	7	0	0	0	2	2		.137	.185	.137	1	-6	0			.897	0	/S-8,2-6,13	-0.6
Total	4	170	558	48	113	13	3	0	34	29		.203	.244	.237	43	-40	24			.905	1	/S-98,0-21,213	-3.6

■ REGGIE WILLIAMS
Williams, Reginald Bernard b: 5/5/66, Laurens, S.C. BB/TR, 6'1", 180 lbs. Deb: 9/8/92

YEAR	TM/L	G	AB	R	H	2B	3B	HR	RBI	BB	SO	AVG	OBP	SLG	PRO+	BR/A	SB	CS	SBR	FA	FR	G/POS	TPR
1992	Cal-A	14	26	5	6	1	1	0	2	1	10	.231	.259	.346	68	-1	0	2	-1	1.000	-1	O-12/D-2	-0.4

■ REGGIE WILLIAMS
Williams, Reginald Dewayne b: 8/29/60, Memphis, Tenn. BR/TR, 5'11", 185 lbs. Deb: 9/2/85

YEAR	TM/L	G	AB	R	H	2B	3B	HR	RBI	BB	SO	AVG	OBP	SLG	PRO+	BR/A	SB	CS	SBR	FA	FR	G/POS	TPR
1985	LA-N	22	9	4	3	0	0	0	0	0	4	.333	.333	.333	90	-0	1	0	0	.900	-3	O-15	-0.3
1986	LA-N	128	303	35	84	14	2	4	32	23	57	.277	.332	.376	102	0	9	3	1	.984	-16	*O-124	-1.8
1987	LA-N	39	36	6	4	0	0	0	4	5	9	.111	.220	.111	-9	-6	1	1	-0	.913	-8	O-30	-1.4
1988	Cle-A	11	31	7	7	2	0	1	3	0	6	.226	.226	.387	66	-1	0	0	0	1.000	-2	O-11	-0.4
Total	4	200	379	52	98	16	2	5	39	28	76	.259	.313	.351	87	-7	11	4	1	.974	-29	O-180	-3.9

■ DICK WILLIAMS
Williams, Richard Hirschfeld b: 5/7/29, St.Louis, Mo. BR/TR, 6', 190 lbs. Deb: 6/10/51 MC

YEAR	TM/L	G	AB	R	H	2B	3B	HR	RBI	BB	SO	AVG	OBP	SLG	PRO+	BR/A	SB	CS	SBR	FA	FR	G/POS	TPR
1951	Bro-N	23	60	5	12	3	1	1	5	4	10	.200	.250	.333	54	-4	0	0	0	1.000	-2	O-15	-0.6
1952	Bro-N	36	68	13	21	4	1	0	11	2	10	.309	.329	.397	99	-0	0	0	0	1.000	-4	O-25/1-1,3	-0.2
1953	*Bro-N	30	55	4	12	2	0	2	5	3	10	.218	.271	.364	62	-3	0	0	0	.923	-7	O-24	-1.1
1954	Bro-N	16	34	5	5	0	0	1	2	2	7	.147	.194	.235	11	-5	0	0	0	1.000	-4	O-14	-0.9
1956	Bro-N	7	7	0	2	0	0	0	0	0	1	.286	.286	.286	50	-0	0	0	0	.000	0	H	0.0
	Bal-A	87	353	45	101	18	4	11	37	30	40	.286	.342	.453	117	7	5	5	-2	.990	-3	O-81,1-10,2/3	-0.2
1957	Bal-A	47	167	16	39	10	2	1	17	14	21	.234	.293	.335	76	-6	0	1	-1	1.000	4	O-26,3-15,1	-0.8
	Cle-A	67	205	33	58	7	0	6	17	12	19	.283	.326	.405	99	-1	3	4	-2	.973	-3	O-37,3-19	-0.7
	Yr	114	372	49	97	17	2	7	34	26	40	.261	.311	.374	89	-7	3	5	-2	.984	-2	O-63,3-34,1	-1.5
1958	Bal-A	128	409	36	113	17	0	4	32	37	47	.276	.339	.347	94	-3	0	6	-4	1.000	-9	O-70,3-45,1/2	-2.0
1959	KC-A	130	488	72	130	33	1	16	75	28	60	.266	.313	.436	102	-0	4	1	1	.957	-8	3-80,1-32,O/2	-1.1
1960	KC-A	127	420	47	121	31	0	12	65	39	68	.288	.350	.448	113	7	0	0	0	.951	5	3-57,1-34,O	0.9
1961	Bal-A	103	310	37	64	15	2	8	24	20	38	.206	.255	.345	61	-19	0	0	0	.968	-10	O-75,1-20/3	-3.6
1962	Bal-A	82	178	20	44	7	1	1	18	14	26	.247	.306	.315	72	-7	0	0	0	1.000	-2	O-29,1-21/3	-1.2
1963	Bos-A	79	136	15	35	8	0	2	12	15	25	.257	.331	.360	91	-1	0	0	0	.976	-6	3-17,1-11/O	-0.9
1964	Bos-A	61	69	10	11	2	0	5	11	7	10	.159	.247	.406	74	-3	0	0	0	1.000	5	1-21,3-13/O	0.2
Total	13	1023	2959	358	768	157	12	70	331	227	392	.260	.315	.392	92	-38	12	21	-9	.989	-46	0-456,3-257,1/2	-12.2

■ RINALDO WILLIAMS
Williams, Rinaldo Lewis b: 12/18/1893, Santa Cruz, Cal. d: 4/24/66, Cottonwood, Ariz. BL/TR, Deb: 10/8/14

YEAR	TM/L	G	AB	R	H	2B	3B	HR	RBI	BB	SO	AVG	OBP	SLG	PRO+	BR/A	SB	CS	SBR	FA	FR	G/POS	TPR
1914	Bro-F	4	15	1	4	2	0	0	0	0		.267	.267	.400	72	-1	0			.923	-0	/3-4	-0.1

■ BOB WILLIAMS
Williams, Robert Elias b: 4/27/1884, Monday, Ohio d: 8/6/62, Nelsonville, Ohio BR/TR, 6', 190 lbs. Deb: 7/3/11

YEAR	TM/L	G	AB	R	H	2B	3B	HR	RBI	BB	SO	AVG	OBP	SLG	PRO+	BR/A	SB	CS	SBR	FA	FR	G/POS	TPR
1911	NY-A	20	47	3	9	2	0	0	8	5		.191	.269	.234	38	-4	1			.942	-1	C-20	-0.3
1912	NY-A	20	44	7	6	1	0	0	3	9		.136	.283	.159	26	-4	0			.930	-2	C-20	-0.5
1913	NY-A	6	19	0	3	0	0	0	0	1	3	.158	.200	.158	5	-2	0			.971	0	/C-6	-0.2
Total	3	46	110	10	18	3	0	0	11	15	3	.164	.264	.191	28	-10	1			.941	-2	/C-46	-1.0

■ TED WILLIAMS
Williams, Theodore Samuel "The Kid', "The Thumper" or "The Splendid Splinter"
b: 8/30/18, San Diego, Cal. BL/TR, 6'3", 205 lbs. Deb: 4/20/39 MH

YEAR	TM/L	G	AB	R	H	2B	3B	HR	RBI	BB	SO	AVG	OBP	SLG	PRO+	BR/A	SB	CS	SBR	FA	FR	G/POS	TPR
1939	Bos-A	149	565	131	185	44	11	31	**145**	107	64	.327	.436	.609	158	51	2	1	0	.945	2	*O-149	4.3
1940	Bos-A★	144	561	**134**	193	43	14	23	113	96	54	.344	**.442**	.594	159	52	4	4	-1	.960	1	*O-143/P-1	4.0
1941	Bos-A★	143	456	**135**	185	33	3	**37**	120	**145**	27	**.406**	**.551**	**.735**	**232**	**98**	2	4	-2	.961	-5	*O-133	**7.9**
1942	Bos-A★	150	522	**141**	186	34	5	**36**	137	**145**	51	**.356**	**.499**	**.648**	**214**	**87**	3	2	-0	.988	3	*O-150	**8.1**
1946	*Bos-A★	150	514	**142**	176	37	8	38	123	**156**	44	.342	**.497**	**.667**	**211**	**85**	0	0	0	.971	-0	*O-150	**7.9**
1947	Bos-A★	156	528	**125**	181	40	9	**32**	114	**162**	47	**.343**	**.499**	**.634**	**199**	**79**	0	1	-0	.975	1	*O-156	**7.2**
1948	Bos-A★	137	509	124	188	**44**	3	25	127	**126**	41	**.369**	**.497**	**.615**	**185**	**68**	4	0	1	.983	0	*O-134	5.8
1949	Bos-A★	155	566	**150**	194	**39**	3	**43**	**159**	**162**	48	.343	**.490**	**.650**	**187**	**77**	1	1	-0	.983	3	*O-155	**6.7**
1950	Bos-A★	89	334	82	106	24	1	28	97	82	21	.317	.452	.647	163	32	3	0	1	.956	-4	O-86	2.4
1951	Bos-A★	148	531	109	169	28	4	30	126	**144**	45	.318	**.464**	.556	159	**49**	-1	1	-1	.988	1	*O-147	**4.5**
1952	Bos-A	6	10	2	4	0	1	1	3	2	2	.400	.500	.900	264	2	0	0	0	1.000	-0	/O-2	0.2
1953	Bos-A†	37	91	17	37	6	0	13	34	19	10	.407	.509	.901	261	20	0	1	-1	.970	-4	O-26	1.5
1954	Bos-A★	117	386	93	133	23	1	29	89	**136**	32	.345	**.516**	.635	193	**58**	0	0	0	.982	-3	*O-115	**5.0**
1955	Bos-A★	98	320	77	114	21	3	28	83	91	24	.356	.501	.703	203	50	2	0	1	.989	-1	O-93	4.4
1956	Bos-A★	136	400	71	138	28	2	24	82	102	39	.345	**.479**	.605	164	41	0	0	0	.973	-2	*O-110	3.0
1957	Bos-A★	132	420	96	163	28	1	38	87	119	43	**.388**	**.528**	**.731**	**227**	82	0	1	-1	.995	-3	*O-125	7.1
1958	Bos-A★	129	411	81	135	23	2	26	85	98	49	**.328**	**.462**	.584	174	46	1	0	0	.957	-12	*O-114	2.9
1959	Bos-A★	103	272	32	69	15	0	10	43	52	27	.254	.377	.419	113	6	0	0	0	.970	-8	O-76	-0.5
1960	Bos-A★	113	310	56	98	15	0	29	72	75	41	.316	.454	.645	187	40	1	1	0	.993	-2	O-87	3.3
Total	19	2292	7706	1798	2654	525	71	521	1839	2019	709	.344	.483	.634	186	1024	24	17	-3	.974	-34	*O-2151/P-1	85.7

■ WALT WILLIAMS
Williams, Walter Allen "No-Neck" b: 12/19/43, Brownwood, Tex. BR/TR, 5'6", 185 lbs. Deb: 4/21/64 C

YEAR	TM/L	G	AB	R	H	2B	3B	HR	RBI	BB	SO	AVG	OBP	SLG	PRO+	BR/A	SB	CS	SBR	FA	FR	G/POS	TPR
1964	Hou-N	10	9	1	0	0	0	0	0	0	2	.000	.000	.000	-99	-2	1	0	0	1.000	-1	/O-5	-0.3
1967	Chi-A	104	275	35	66	16	3	3	15	17	20	.240	.289	.353	92	-3	3	2	-0	.983	-2	O-73	-1.0
1968	Chi-A	63	133	6	32	6	0	1	8	4	17	.241	.273	.308	75	-4	0	1	-1	1.000	-2	O-34	-1.0
1969	Chi-A	135	471	59	143	22	1	3	32	26	33	.304	.344	.374	96	-3	6	2	1	.985	2	*O-111	-0.6
1970	Chi-A	110	315	43	79	18	1	9	15	19	30	.251	.298	.343	73	-12	3	3	-1	.949	-5	O-79	-1.5
1971	Chi-A	114	361	43	106	17	3	8	35	24	27	.294	.346	.424	114	6	5	5	-2	1.000	2	O-90/3-1	-0.2
1972	Chi-A	77	221	22	55	7	1	2	11	13	20	.249	.291	.317	79	-6	6	1	1	.990	1	O-57/3-1	-0.7
1973	Cle-A	104	350	43	101	15	1	8	38	14	29	.289	.318	.406	101	-1	9	4	0	.970	5	O-61,D-26	0.1
1974	NY-A	43	53	5	6	0	0	0	3	1	10	.113	.130	.113	-31	-9	1	0	0	.955	-6	O-24/D-3	-1.6
1975	NY-A	82	185	27	52	5	1	5	16	8	23	.281	.321	.400	106	1	0	1	-1	.982	-3	O-31,D-17/2	-0.4
Total	10	842	2373	284	640	106	11	33	173	126	211	.270	.311	.365	91	-33	34	19	-5	.981	-6	O-565/D-46,23	-7.2

■ WASH WILLIAMS
Williams, Washington J. b: Philadelphia, Pa. d: 1/1890, Philadelphia, Pa. 5'11", 180 lbs. Deb: 8/5/1884

YEAR	TM/L	G	AB	R	H	2B	3B	HR	RBI	BB	SO	AVG	OBP	SLG	PRO+	BR/A	SB	CS	SBR	FA	FR	G/POS	TPR
1884	Ric-a	2	8	0	2	0	0	0		0	0	.250	.250	.250	64	-0				.500	-1	/O-2	-0.1
1885	Chi-N	1	4	0	1	0	0	0		0	0	.250	.250	.250	54	-0				.500	-0	/O-1,P-1	-0.1
Total	2	3	12	0	3	0	0	0		0	0	.250	.250	.250	61	-1				.500	-1	/O-3,P-1	-0.2

■ BILLY WILLIAMS
Williams, William b: 6/13/33, Newberry, S.C. BL/TR, 6'3", 195 lbs. Deb: 8/15/69

YEAR	TM/L	G	AB	R	H	2B	3B	HR	RBI	BB	SO	AVG	OBP	SLG	PRO+	BR/A	SB	CS	SBR	FA	FR	G/POS	TPR
1969	Sea-A	4	10	1	0	0	0	0	0	1	3	.000	.167	.000	-51	-2	0	0	0	1.000	1	/O-3	-0.2

YEAR	TM/L	G	AB	R	H	2B	3B	HR	RBI	BB	SO	AVG	OBP	SLG	PRO+	BR/A	SB	CS	SBR	FA	FR	G/POS	TPR

■ WOODY WILLIAMS
Williams, Woodrow Wilson b: 8/22/12, Pamplin, Va. BR/TR, 5'11", 175 lbs. Deb: 9/5/38

YEAR	TM/L	G	AB	R	H	2B	3B	HR	RBI	BB	SO	AVG	OBP	SLG	PRO+	BR/A	SB	CS	SBR	FA	FR	G/POS	TPR
1938	Bro-N	20	51	6	17	1	1	0	6	4	1	.333	.382	.392	111	1	1			.931	-7	S-18/3-1	-0.5
1943	Cin-N	30	69	8	26	2	1	0	11	1	3	.377	.386	.435	139	3	0			.986	1	2-12/3-7,S	0.5
1944	Cin-N	155	653	73	157	23	3	1	35	44	24	.240	.290	.289	66	-30	7			.971	15	*2-155	-0.6
1945	Cin-N	133	482	46	114	14	0	0	27	39	24	.237	.296	.266	58	-27	6			.969	-10	*2-133	-2.9
Total	4	338	1255	133	314	40	5	1	79	88	52	.250	.301	.292	69	-52	14			.971	-1	2-300/S-23,3	-3.5

■ NED WILLIAMSON
Williamson, Edward Nagle b: 10/24/1857, Philadelphia, Pa. d: 3/3/1894, Willow Springs, Ark BR/TR, 5'11", 210 lbs. Deb: 5/1/1878

YEAR	TM/L	G	AB	R	H	2B	3B	HR	RBI	BB	SO	AVG	OBP	SLG	PRO+	BR/A	SB	CS	SBR	FA	FR	G/POS	TPR
1878	Ind-N	63	250	31	58	10	2	1	19	5	15	.232	.247	.300	91	-2				.867	-4	*3-63	-0.3
1879	Chi-N	80	320	66	94	20	13	1	36	24	31	.294	.343	.447	149	16				.871	17	*3-70/1-6,C	3.2
1880	Chi-N	75	311	65	78	20	2	0	31	15	26	.251	.285	.328	101	-0				.893	12	*3-63,C-11/2	1.4
1881	Chi-N	82	343	56	92	12	6	1	48	19	19	.268	.307	.347	100	-0				.909	22	*3-76/2-4,PSC	2.2
1882	Chi-N	83	348	66	98	27	4	3	60	27	21	.282	.333	.408	130	11				.881	16	*3-83/P-1	2.6
1883	Chi-N	98	402	83	111	49	5	2	59	22	48	.276	.314	.438	118	8				.807	18	*3-97/C-3,P	2.1
1884	Chi-N	107	417	84	116	18	8	27	84	42	56	.278	.344	.554	164	28				.861	24	*3-99,C-10/P	4.7
1885	*Chi-N	113	407	87	97	16	5	3	65	75	60	.238	.357	.324	106	2				.892	12	*3-113/P-2,C	1.5
1886	*Chi-N	121	430	69	93	17	8	6	58	80	71	.216	.339	.335	92	-6	13			.869	-2	*S-121/C-4,P	-0.6
1887	Chi-N	127	439	77	117	20	14	9	78	73	57	.267	.377	.437	111	5	45			.890	-31	*S-127/P-1	-2.1
1888	Chi-N	132	452	75	113	9	14	8	73	65	71	.250	.352	.385	126	14	25			.884	-12	*S-132	0.5
1889	Chi-N	47	173	16	41	3	1	1	30	23	22	.237	.340	.283	71	-6	2			.844	-24	S-47	-2.4
1890	Chi-P	73	261	34	51	7	3	2	26	36	35	.195	.311	.268	53	-17	3			.809	-20	3-52,S-21	-2.8
Total	13	1201	4553	809	1159	228	85	64	667	506	532	.255	.332	.384	112	54	88			.866	28	3-716,S-450/CP21	10.0

■ HOWIE WILLIAMSON
Williamson, Nathaniel Howard b: 12/23/04, Little Rock, Ark. d: 8/15/69, Texarkana, Ark. BL/TL, 6', 170 lbs. Deb: 7/7/28

YEAR	TM/L	G	AB	R	H	2B	3B	HR	RBI	BB	SO	AVG	OBP	SLG	PRO+	BR/A	SB	CS	SBR	FA	FR	G/POS	TPR
1928	StL-N	10	9	0	2	0	0	0	0	1	4	.222	.300	.222	38	-1	0			.000	0	H	-0.1

■ JULIUS WILLIGROD
Willigrod, Julius b: Iowa d: 11/27/06, San Francisco, Cal BL , Deb: 7/15/1882

YEAR	TM/L	G	AB	R	H	2B	3B	HR	RBI	BB	SO	AVG	OBP	SLG	PRO+	BR/A	SB	CS	SBR	FA	FR	G/POS	TPR
1882	Det-N	1	3	0	1	0	0	0	1	0	1	.333	.333	.333	115	0				1.000	-1	/S-1	0.0
	Cle-N	9	36	5	5	1	1	0	2	3	7	.139	.205	.222	38	-2				.813	-3	/O-9	-0.5
	Yr	10	39	5	6	1	1	0	3	3	8	.154	.214	.231	44	-2				.813	-3	/O-9,S-1	-0.5

■ HUGH WILLINGHAM
Willingham, Thomas Hugh b: 5/30/06, Dalhart, Tex. d: 6/15/88, ElReno, Okla. BR/TR, 6', 180 lbs. Deb: 9/13/30

YEAR	TM/L	G	AB	R	H	2B	3B	HR	RBI	BB	SO	AVG	OBP	SLG	PRO+	BR/A	SB	CS	SBR	FA	FR	G/POS	TPR
1930	Chi-A	3	4	2	1	0	0	0	2	1		.250	.500	.250	100	1	0			1.000	-0	/2-1	0.0
1931	Phi-N	23	35	5	9	2	1	1	3	2	9	.257	.297	.457	93	-1	0			.875	0	/S-8,3-2,O	0.0
1932	Phi-N	4	2	0	0	0	0	0	0	0	0	.000	.000	.000	-89	-0	0			.000	0	H	-0.1
1933	Phi-N	1	1	0	0	0	0	0	0	0	1	.000	.000	.000	-89	-0	0			.000	0	H	0.0
Total	4	31	42	7	10	2	1	1	3	4	10	.238	.304	.405	82	-1	0	0		.875	-0	/S-8,3-2,O2	-0.1

■ WILLS
Wills Deb: 5/14/1884

YEAR	TM/L	G	AB	R	H	2B	3B	HR	RBI	BB	SO	AVG	OBP	SLG	PRO+	BR/A	SB	CS	SBR	FA	FR	G/POS	TPR
1884	Was-a	4	15	1	2	2	0	0		0		.133	.133	.267	31	-1				.889	2	/O-4	0.1
	KC-U	5	21	2	3	1	0	0		0		.143	.143	.190	-12	-3				1.000	1	/O-5	-0.3
Total	1	9	36	3	5	3	0	0		0		.139	.139	.222	4	-4				.938	2	/O-9	-0.2

■ DAVE WILLS
Wills, Davis Bowles b: 1/26/1877, Charlottesville, Va. d: 10/12/59, Washington, D.C. BL/TL, Deb: 6/8/1899

YEAR	TM/L	G	AB	R	H	2B	3B	HR	RBI	BB	SO	AVG	OBP	SLG	PRO+	BR/A	SB	CS	SBR	FA	FR	G/POS	TPR
1899	Lou-N	24	94	15	21	3	1	0	12	2		.223	.240	.277	41	-8	1			.957	-3	1-24	-1.0

■ BUMP WILLS
Wills, Elliott Taylor b: 7/27/52, Washington, D.C. BB/TR, 5'9", 177 lbs. Deb: 4/7/77 F

YEAR	TM/L	G	AB	R	H	2B	3B	HR	RBI	BB	SO	AVG	OBP	SLG	PRO+	BR/A	SB	CS	SBR	FA	FR	G/POS	TPR
1977	Tex-A	152	541	87	155	28	6	9	62	65	96	.287	.363	.410	109	8	28	12	1	.982	3	*2-150/S-2,1D	2.3
1978	Tex-A	157	539	78	135	17	4	9	57	63	91	.250	.333	.347	91	-5	52	14	7	.981	21	*2-156	3.5
1979	Tex-A	146	543	90	148	21	3	5	46	53	58	.273	.342	.350	88	-8	35	11	4	.976	7	*2-146	1.3
1980	Tex-A	146	578	102	152	31	5	5	58	51	71	.263	.326	.360	90	-7	34	9	5	.984	19	*2-144	2.5
1981	Tex-A	102	410	51	103	13	2	4	41	32	49	.251	.307	.307	82	-10	12	9	4	.983	9	*2-101/D-1	0.4
1982	Chi-N	128	419	64	114	18	4	6	38	46	76	.272	.351	.377	101	2	35	10	5	.963	-18	*2-103	-0.7
Total	6	831	3030	472	807	128	24	36	302	310	441	.266	.338	.360	94	-20	196	65	20	.979	40	2-800/D-2,S1	9.3

■ MAURY WILLS
Wills, Maurice Morning b: 10/2/32, Washington, D.C. BB/TR, 5'11", 170 lbs. Deb: 6/6/59 FM

YEAR	TM/L	G	AB	R	H	2B	3B	HR	RBI	BB	SO	AVG	OBP	SLG	PRO+	BR/A	SB	CS	SBR	FA	FR	G/POS	TPR
1959	*LA-N	83	242	27	63	5	2	0	7	13	27	.260	.298	.298	55	-15	7	3	0	.966	2	S-82	-0.7
1960	LA-N	148	516	75	152	15	2	0	27	35	47	.295	.343	.331	80	-13	50	12	8	.945	21	*S-145	2.7
1961	LA-N★	148	613	105	173	12	10	1	31	59	50	.282	.346	.339	76	-19	35	15	2	.959	12	*S-148	0.6
1962	LA-N★	165	695	130	208	13	10	6	48	51	57	.299	.349	.373	100	-0	104	13	23	.956	-5	*S-165	3.3
1963	*LA-N☆	134	527	83	159	19	3	0	34	44	48	.302	.357	.349	112	8	40	19	1	.959	-5	*S-109,3-33	1.3
1964	LA-N	158	630	81	173	15	5	2	34	41	73	.275	.319	.324	88	-11	53	17	6	.963	-8	*S-149/3-6	-0.2
1965	*LA-N★	158	650	92	186	14	7	0	33	40	64	.286	.331	.329	93	-6	94	31	10	.970	21	*S-155	3.7
1966	*LA-N★	143	594	60	162	14	2	1	39	34	60	.273	.314	.308	80	-16	38	24	-3	.967	9	*S-139/3-4	0.3
1967	Pit-N	149	616	92	186	12	9	3	45	31	44	.302	.336	.365	100	0	29	10	3	.948	9	*3-144/S-2	1.2
1968	Pit-N	153	627	76	174	12	6	0	31	45	57	.278	.327	.316	95	-3	52	21	3	.957	-9	*3-141,S-10	-0.9
1969	Mon-N	47	189	23	42	3	0	0	8	20	21	.222	.297	.238	51	-12	15	6	1	.950	-3	S-46/2-1	-0.9
	LA-N	104	434	57	129	7	8	4	39	39	40	.297	.357	.378	114	8	25	15	-1	.969	7	*S-104	2.6
	Yr	151	623	80	171	10	8	4	47	59	61	.274	.338	.335	94	-5	40	21	-1	.963	4	*S-150/2-1	1.7
1970	LA-N	132	522	77	141	19	3	0	34	50	34	.270	.334	.318	79	-15	28	13	1	.959	-19	*S-126/3-4	-1.9
1971	LA-N	149	601	73	169	14	3	3	44	40	44	.281	.326	.329	92	-7	15	8	-0	.978	1	*S-144/3-4	1.3
1972	LA-N	71	132	16	17	3	1	0	4	10	18	.129	.190	.167	2	-17	1	1	-0	.984	-4	S-31,3-26	-1.9
Total	14	1942	7588	1067	2134	177	71	20	458	552	684	.281	.331	.331	88	-118	586	208	51	.963	30	*S-1555,3-362/2	10.5

■ KID WILLSON
Willson, Frank Hoxie b: 11/3/1895, Bloomington, Neb. d: 4/17/64, Union Gap, Wash. BL/TL, 6'1", 190 lbs. Deb: 7/2/18

YEAR	TM/L	G	AB	R	H	2B	3B	HR	RBI	BB	SO	AVG	OBP	SLG	PRO+	BR/A	SB	CS	SBR	FA	FR	G/POS	TPR
1918	Chi-A	4	1	2	0	0	0	0	0	1	1	.000	.500	.000	50	0	0			.000	0	H	0.0
1927	Chi-A	7	10	1	1	0	0	0	1	0	2	.100	.100	.100	-49	-2	0	0	0	1.000	0	/O-2	-0.2
Total	2	11	11	3	1	0	0	0	1	1	3	.091	.167	.091	-31	-2	0	0	0	1.000	0	/O-2	-0.2

■ WALT WILMOT
Wilmot, Walter Robert b: 10/18/1863, Plover, Wis. d: 2/1/29, Chicago, Ill. BB/TR, Deb: 4/20/1888

YEAR	TM/L	G	AB	R	H	2B	3B	HR	RBI	BB	SO	AVG	OBP	SLG	PRO+	BR/A	SB	CS	SBR	FA	FR	G/POS	TPR
1888	Was-N	119	473	61	106	16	9	4	43	23	55	.224	.263	.321	91	-5	46			.872	11	*O-119	0.3
1889	Was-N	108	432	88	125	19	19	9	57	51	32	.289	.367	.484	146	26	40			.927	15	*O-108	3.2
1890	Chi-N	139	571	114	159	15	13	13	99	64	44	.278	.353	.419	120	12	76			.938	13	*O-139	1.8
1891	StL-N	121	498	102	139	14	10	11	71	55	21	.279	.357	.414	124	15	42			.922	-5	*O-121	0.5
1892	Chi-N	92	380	47	82	7	7	2	35	40	20	.216	.297	.287	76	-11	31			.903	-2	O-92	-1.2
1893	Chi-N	94	392	69	118	14	14	3	61	40	8	.301	.367	.431	113	7	39			.873	-0	*O-93	0.1
1894	Chi-N	133	597	134	197	45	12	5	130	35	23	.330	.368	.471	96	-7	74			.872	-7	*O-133	-1.8
1895	Chi-N	108	466	86	132	16	6	8	72	30	19	.283	.327	.395	80	-16	28			.914	4	*O-108	-1.7
1897	NY-N	11	34	8	9	2	0	1	4	2		.265	.306	.412	91	-1	1			.938	0	/O-9	-0.1
1898	NY-N	35	138	16	33	4	2	2	22	9		.239	.286	.341	82	-4	4			.886	-5	O-34	-1.1
Total	10	960	3981	725	1100	152	92	58	594	349	222	.276	.337	.404	105	16	381			.903	28	O-956	0.0

■ ARCHIE WILSON
Wilson, Archie Clifton b: 11/25/23, Los Angeles, Cal. BR/TR, 5'11", 175 lbs. Deb: 9/18/51

YEAR	TM/L	G	AB	R	H	2B	3B	HR	RBI	BB	SO	AVG	OBP	SLG	PRO+	BR/A	SB	CS	SBR	FA	FR	G/POS	TPR
1951	NY-A	4	4	0	0	0	0	0	0	0	0	.000	.200	.000	-44	-1	0	0	0	1.000	-0	/O-2	-0.1
1952	NY-A	3	2	0	1	0	0	0	0	0	0	.500	.500	.500	190	0	0	0	0	.000	0	H	0.0

YEAR	TM/L	G	AB	R	H	2B	3B	HR	RBI	BB	SO	AVG	OBP	SLG	PRO+	BR/A	SB	CS	SBR	FA	FR	G/POS	TPR
	Was-A	26	96	8	20	2	3	0	14	5	11	.208	.255	.292	54	-6	0	0	0	.971	1	O-24	-0.7
	Bos-A	18	38	1	10	3	0	0	2	2	3	.263	.300	.342	73	-1	0	0	0	.944	-2	O-13	-0.4
	Yr	47	136	9	31	5	3	0	17	7	14	.228	.271	.309	61	-8	0	0	0	.966	-1	O-37	-1.1
Total	2	51	140	9	31	5	3	0	17	7	14	.221	.268	.300	58	-8	0	0	0	.967	-1	/O-39	-1.2

■ ART WILSON
Wilson, Arthur Earl "Dutch" b: 12/11/1885, Macon, Ill. d: 6/12/60, Chicago, Ill. BR/TR, 5'8", 170 lbs. Deb: 9/29/08

YEAR	TM/L	G	AB	R	H	2B	3B	HR	RBI	BB	SO	AVG	OBP	SLG	PRO+	BR/A	SB	CS	SBR	FA	FR	G/POS	TPR
1908	NY-N	1	0	0	0	0	0	0	0	0		—	—	—		0	0			.000	0	R	0.0
1909	NY-N	19	42	4	10	2	1	0	5	4		.238	.304	.333	96	-0	0			.985	-4	C-19	-0.4
1910	NY-N	26	52	10	14	4	1	0	5	9	6	.269	.387	.385	125	2	2			.975	-1	C-25/1-1	0.3
1911	*NY-N	66	109	17	33	9	1	1	17	19	12	.303	.411	.431	132	5	6			.963	-6	C-64	0.3
1912	*NY-N	65	121	17	35	6	0	3	19	13	14	.289	.358	.413	107	1	2			.960	1	C-61	0.5
1913	*NY-N	54	79	5	15	0	1	0	8	11	11	.190	.289	.215	45	-5	1			.965	6	C-49	0.3
1914	Chi-F	137	440	78	128	31	8	10	64	70	80	.291	.394	.466	130	20	13			.974	14	*C-132	4.6
1915	Chi-F	96	269	44	82	11	2	7	31	65	38	.305	.442	.439	144	21	8			.980	6	C-87	2.1
1916	Pit-N	53	128	11	33	5	2	1	12	13	27	.258	.331	.352	109	2	4			.981	-9	C-39	-0.5
	Chi-N	36	114	5	22	3	1	0	5	6	14	.193	.233	.237	40	-8	1			.953	-4	C-34	-1.1
	Yr	89	242	16	55	8	3	1	17	19	41	.227	.286	.298	76	-7	5			.967	-13	C-73	-1.6
1917	Chi-N	81	211	17	45	9	2	2	25	32	36	.213	.322	.303	86	-3	6			.968	7	C-75	1.2
1918	Bos-N	89	280	15	69	8	4	2	19	24	31	.246	.310	.289	87	-4	5			.977	-10	C-85	-0.8
1919	Bos-N	71	191	14	49	7	1	0	16	25	19	.257	.346	.309	102	1	2			.977	-2	C-64/1-1	0.5
1920	Bos-N	16	19	0	1	0	0	0	0	1	1	.053	.143	.053	-44	-4	0	0	0	1.000	-2	/3-6,C-2	-0.5
1921	Cle-A	2	1	0	0	0	0	0	0	0	0	.000	.000	.000	-99	-0	0	0	0	1.000	0	/C-2	0.0
Total	14	812	2056	237	536	96	22	24	226	292	289	.261	.357	.364	106	28	50	0		.972	-18	C-738/3-6,1	6.5

■ ARTIE WILSON
Wilson, Arthur Lee b: 10/28/20, Springfield, Ala. BL/TR, 5'10", 162 lbs. Deb: 4/18/51

YEAR	TM/L	G	AB	R	H	2B	3B	HR	RBI	BB	SO	AVG	OBP	SLG	PRO+	BR/A	SB	CS	SBR	FA	FR	G/POS	TPR
1951	NY-N	19	22	2	4	0	0	0	1	2	1	.182	.250	.182	18	-2	2	0	1	1.000	3	/2-3,S-3,1	0.1

■ CHARLIE WILSON
Wilson, Charles Woodrow "Swamp Baby" b: 1/13/05, Clinton, S.C. d: 12/19/70, Rochester, N.Y. BB/TR, 5'10.5", 178 lbs. Deb: 4/14/31

YEAR	TM/L	G	AB	R	H	2B	3B	HR	RBI	BB	SO	AVG	OBP	SLG	PRO+	BR/A	SB	CS	SBR	FA	FR	G/POS	TPR
1931	Bos-N	16	58	7	11	4	0	1	11	3	5	.190	.230	.310	45	-5	0			.917	-2	3-14	-0.6
1932	StL-N	24	96	7	19	3	3	1	2	3	8	.198	.222	.323	43	-8	0			.935	-7	S-24	-1.2
1933	StL-N	1	1	0	0	0	0	0	0	0	1	.000	.000	.000	-95	-0	0			.000	0	/S-1	0.0
1935	StL-N	16	31	1	10	0	0	0	1	2	2	.323	.364	.323	83	-1	0			.933	-1	/3-8	-0.1
Total	4	57	186	15	40	7	3	2	14	8	16	.215	.247	.317	50	-13	0			.935	-10	/S-25,3-22	-1.9

■ CRAIG WILSON
Wilson, Craig b: 11/28/64, Annapolis, Md. BR/TR, 5'11", 175 lbs. Deb: 9/6/89

YEAR	TM/L	G	AB	R	H	2B	3B	HR	RBI	BB	SO	AVG	OBP	SLG	PRO+	BR/A	SB	CS	SBR	FA	FR	G/POS	TPR
1989	StL-N	6	4	1	1	0	0	0	1	1	2	.250	.400	.250	87	-0	0	0	0	.500	-0	/3-2	0.0
1990	StL-N	55	121	13	30	2	0	0	7	8	14	.248	.295	.264	55	-7	0	2	-1	.971	-0	3-13,O-13/21	-0.9
1991	StL-N	60	82	5	14	2	0	0	13	6	10	.171	.227	.195	20	-9	0	0	-0	.905	-1	3-12/O-5,12	-1.1
1992	StL-N	61	106	6	33	6	0	0	13	10	18	.311	.371	.368	113	2	1	2	-1	.970	-3	3-18,2-11/O	-0.2
1993	KC-A	21	49	6	13	1	0	1	3	7	6	.265	.357	.347	85	-1	1	1	-0	1.000	-1	3-15/2-1,O	-0.4
Total	5	203	362	31	91	11	0	1	37	32	50	.251	.312	.290	68	-15	2	5	-2	.957	-8	/3-60,2-24,O1	-2.6

■ DAN WILSON
Wilson, Daniel Allen b: 3/25/69, Arlington Heights, Ill. BR/TR, 6'3", 190 lbs. Deb: 9/7/92

YEAR	TM/L	G	AB	R	H	2B	3B	HR	RBI	BB	SO	AVG	OBP	SLG	PRO+	BR/A	SB	CS	SBR	FA	FR	G/POS	TPR
1992	Cin-N	12	25	2	9	1	0	0	3	3	8	.360	.429	.400	132	1	0	0	0	1.000	0	/C-9	0.2
1993	Cin-N	36	76	6	17	3	0	0	8	9	16	.224	.306	.263	54	-5	0	0	0	.994	-0	C-35	-0.4
1994	Sea-A	91	282	24	61	14	2	3	27	10	57	.216	.246	.312	42	-25	1	2	-1	.986	6	C-91	-1.4
Total	3	139	383	32	87	18	2	3	38	22	81	.227	.271	.308	50	-28	1	2	-1	.988	6	C-135	-1.6

■ EDDIE WILSON
Wilson, Edward Francis b: 9/7/09, Hamden, Conn. d: 4/11/79, Hamden, Conn. BL/TL, 5'11", 165 lbs. Deb: 6/21/36

YEAR	TM/L	G	AB	R	H	2B	3B	HR	RBI	BB	SO	AVG	OBP	SLG	PRO+	BR/A	SB	CS	SBR	FA	FR	G/POS	TPR
1936	Bro-N	52	173	28	60	8	1	3	25	14	25	.347	.402	.457	129	7	3			.926	-5	O-47	0.0
1937	Bro-N	36	54	11	12	4	1	1	8	17	14	.222	.408	.389	116	2	1			.966	-3	O-21	-0.2
Total	2	88	227	39	72	12	2	4	33	31	39	.317	.404	.441	126	10	4			.936	-9	/O-68	-0.2

■ FRANK WILSON
Wilson, Francis Edward "Squash" b: 4/20/01, Malden, Mass. d: 11/25/74, Leicester, Mass. BL/TR, 6', 185 lbs. Deb: 6/20/24

YEAR	TM/L	G	AB	R	H	2B	3B	HR	RBI	BB	SO	AVG	OBP	SLG	PRO+	BR/A	SB	CS	SBR	FA	FR	G/POS	TPR
1924	Bos-N	61	215	20	51	7	0	1	15	23	22	.237	.311	.284	63	-11	3	4	-2	.973	3	O-55	-1.3
1925	Bos-N	12	31	3	13	1	1	0	0	4	1	.419	.486	.516	171	4	2	1	0	1.000	1	O-10	0.3
1926	Bos-N	87	236	22	56	11	3	0	23	20	21	.237	.300	.309	70	-10	3			.934	-2	O-56	-1.3
1928	Cle-A	2	1	0	0	0	0	0	0	1	0	.000	.500	.000	41	0	0	0	0	.000	0	H	-0.2
	StL-A	6	5	1	0	0	0	0	0	0	0	.000	.000	.000	-97	-1	0	0	0	.000	-0	/O-1	-0.2
	Yr	8	6	1	0	0	0	0	0	1	0	.000	.143	.000	-58	-1	0	0	0	.000	-0	/O-1	-0.2
Total	4	168	488	46	120	19	4	1	38	48	44	.246	.315	.307	72	-19	8	5		.958	4	O-122	-2.5

■ TUG WILSON
Wilson, George Archer b: 1860, Brooklyn, N.Y. d: 11/28/14, New York, N.Y. Deb: 5/9/1884

YEAR	TM/L	G	AB	R	H	2B	3B	HR	RBI	BB	SO	AVG	OBP	SLG	PRO+	BR/A	SB	CS	SBR	FA	FR	G/POS	TPR
1884	Bro-a	24	82	13	19	4	0	0	5			.232	.276	.280	81	-2				.826	-3	O-12,C-10/12	-0.4

■ SQUANTO WILSON
Wilson, George Francis b: 3/29/1889, Old Town, Me. d: 3/26/67, Winthrop, Maine BB/TR, 5'9.5", 170 lbs. Deb: 10/2/11

YEAR	TM/L	G	AB	R	H	2B	3B	HR	RBI	BB	SO	AVG	OBP	SLG	PRO+	BR/A	SB	CS	SBR	FA	FR	G/POS	TPR
1911	Det-A	5	16	2	3	0	0	0	0	2		.188	.278	.188	29	-1	0			.900	-1	/C-5	-0.2
1914	Bos-A	1	0	0	0	0	0	0	0	0	0	—	—	—		0	0			.000	0	/1-1	0.0
Total	2	6	16	2	3	0	0	0	0	2	0	.188	.278	.188	29	-1	0			.900	-1	/C-5,1-1	-0.2

■ ICEHOUSE WILSON
Wilson, George Peacock b: 9/14/12, Maricopa, Cal. d: 10/13/73, Moraga, Cal. BR/TR, 6', 186 lbs. Deb: 5/31/34

YEAR	TM/L	G	AB	R	H	2B	3B	HR	RBI	BB	SO	AVG	OBP	SLG	PRO+	BR/A	SB	CS	SBR	FA	FR	G/POS	TPR
1934	Det-A	1	1	0	0	0	0	0	0	0	0	.000	.000	.000	-99	-0	0	0	0	.000	0	H	0.0

■ GEORGE WILSON
Wilson, George Washington "Teddy" b: 8/30/25, Cherryville, N.C. d: 10/29/74, Gastonia, N.C. BL/TR, 6'1.5", 185 lbs. Deb: 4/15/52

YEAR	TM/L	G	AB	R	H	2B	3B	HR	RBI	BB	SO	AVG	OBP	SLG	PRO+	BR/A	SB	CS	SBR	FA	FR	G/POS	TPR
1952	Chi-A	8	9	0	1	0	0	0	0	1	2	.111	.200	.111	-12	-1	0	0	0	1.000	0	/O-1	-0.1
	NY-N	62	112	9	27	7	0	2	16	3	14	.241	.261	.357	69	-5	0	0	0	.923	-3	O-21/1-2	-0.9
1953	NY-N	11	8	0	1	0	0	0	0	3	0	.125	.364	.125	34	-1	0	0	0	.000	0	H	-0.1
1956	NY-N	53	68	5	9	1	0	1	2	5	14	.132	.192	.191	3	-9	0	0	0	1.000	0	/O-8	-1.0
	*NY-A	11	12	1	2	0	0	0	1	2	2	.167	.333	.167	37	-1	0	0	0	.750	-2	/O-6	-0.3
Total	3	145	209	15	40	8	0	3	19	14	32	.191	.246	.273	41	-17	0	0	0	.932	-5	/O-36,1-2	-2.4

■ GLENN WILSON
Wilson, Glenn Dwight b: 12/22/58, Baytown, Tex. BR/TR, 6'1", 190 lbs. Deb: 4/15/82

YEAR	TM/L	G	AB	R	H	2B	3B	HR	RBI	BB	SO	AVG	OBP	SLG	PRO+	BR/A	SB	CS	SBR	FA	FR	G/POS	TPR
1982	Det-A	84	322	39	94	15	1	12	34	15	51	.292	.323	.457	111	4	2	3	-1	.987	7	O-80/D-4	0.8
1983	Det-A	144	503	55	135	25	6	11	65	25	79	.268	.307	.408	97	-3	1	1	-0	.988	-7	*O-143	-1.5
1984	Phi-N	132	341	28	82	21	3	6	31	17	56	.240	.279	.372	80	-10	7	1	2	.968	-12	*O-109/3-4	-2.4
1985	Phi-N★	161	608	73	167	39	5	14	102	35	117	.275	.314	.424	102	-0	7	4	-0	.968	20	*O-158	1.6
1986	Phi-N	155	584	70	158	30	4	15	84	42	91	.271	.324	.413	98	-2	5	1	1	.989	21	*O-154	1.5
1987	Phi-N	154	569	55	150	21	2	14	54	38	82	.264	.311	.381	80	-17	3	6	-3	.968	15	*O-154/P-1	-0.9
1988	Sea-A	78	284	28	71	10	1	3	17	15	52	.250	.288	.324	68	-12	1	1	-0	.980	1	O-75/D-2	-1.5
	Pit-N	37	126	11	34	5	0	3	18	9	18	.270	.292	.381	93	-2	0			.985	-1	O-35	-0.1
1989	Pit-N	100	330	42	93	20	4	9	49	32	39	.282	.347	.448	130	12	1	4	-2	.977	1	O-85,1-10	0.9
	Hou-N	28	102	8	22	6	2	0	15	9	19	.216	.252	.333	68	-5	0	1	-0	.966	5	O-25	-0.1
	Yr	128	432	50	115	26	6	9	64	41	58	.266	.326	.421	116	8	1	5	-2	.974	6	*O-110,1-10	0.8
1990	Hou-N	118	368	42	90	14	0	10	55	26	64	.245	.296	.364	83	-9	0	3	-2	.975	7	*O-108/1-1	-0.6
1993	Pit-N	10	14	0	2	0	0	0	0	0	9	.143	.143	.143	-23	-2	0			.875	0	/O-5	-0.2
Total	10	1201	4151	451	1098	209	26	98	521	253	672	.265	.309	.398	93	-46	27	25	-7	.977	57	*O-1131/1-11,D3P	-2.8

YEAR	TM/L	G	AB	R	H	2B	3B	HR	RBI	BB	SO	AVG	OBP	SLG	PRO+	BR/A	SB	CS	SBR	FA	FR	G/POS	TPR

■ GRADY WILSON
Wilson, Grady Herbert b: 11/23/22, Columbus, Ga. BR/TR, 6'0.5", 170 lbs. Deb: 5/15/48

| 1948 | Pit-N | 12 | 10 | 1 | 1 | 1 | 0 | 0 | 1 | 0 | 3 | .100 | .100 | .200 | -20 | -2 | 0 | | | .846 | 1 | /S-7 | -0.1 |

■ HENRY WILSON
Wilson, Henry C. b: 4/8/1877, Baltimore, Md. Deb: 10/12/1898

| 1898 | Bal-N | 1 | 2 | 0 | 0 | 0 | 0 | 0 | 0 | 0 | 1 | .000 | .333 | .000 | -2 | -0 | 0 | | | 1.000 | 0 | /C-1 | 0.0 |

■ JIMMIE WILSON
Wilson, James "Ace" b: 7/23/1900, Philadelphia, Pa. d: 5/31/47, Bradenton, Fla. BR/TR, 6'1.5", 200 lbs. Deb: 4/17/23 MC

1923	Phi-N	85	252	27	66	9	0	1	25	4	17	.262	.276	.310	49	-19	4	2	0	.960	-3	C-69/O-2	-1.9
1924	Phi-N	95	280	32	78	16	3	6	39	17	12	.279	.322	.421	87	-6	5	4	-1	.968	5	C-82/1-2,O	0.3
1925	Phi-N	108	335	42	110	19	3	3	54	32	25	.328	.390	.430	100	1	5	3	-0	.982	-9	C-89/O-1	-0.3
1926	Phi-N	90	279	40	85	10	2	4	32	25	20	.305	.362	.398	99	-0	3			.950	2	C-79	0.5
1927	Phi-N	128	443	50	122	15	2	2	45	34	15	.275	.330	.332	77	-14	13			.975	-19	*C-124	-2.4
1928	Phi-N	21	70	11	21	4	1	0	13	9	8	.300	.380	.386	97	-0	3			.990	2	C-20	0.3
	*StL-N	120	411	45	106	26	2	2	50	45	24	.258	.333	.345	76	-14	9			.983	1	*C-120	-0.3
	Yr	141	481	56	127	30	3	2	63	54	32	.264	.340	.351	79	-14	12			.985	2	*C-140	0.0
1929	StL-N	120	394	59	128	27	8	4	71	43	19	.325	.394	.464	111	7	4			.972	5	*C-119	2.0
1930	*StL-N	107	362	54	115	25	7	1	58	28	17	.318	.368	.434	90	-6	8			.987	10	C-99	1.2
1931	*StL-N	115	383	45	105	20	2	0	51	28	15	.274	.332	.337	77	-12	5			.985	11	*C-110	0.6
1932	StL-N	92	274	36	68	16	2	2	28	15	18	.248	.290	.343	67	-13	9			.982	2	C-75/1-3,2	-0.7
1933	StL-N★	113	369	34	94	17	0	1	45	23	33	.255	.300	.309	71	-14	6			.982	2	*C-107	-0.6
1934	Phi-N	91	277	25	81	11	0	3	35	14	10	.292	.326	.365	75	-10	1			.987	-0	C-77/1-1,2M	-0.4
1935	Phi-N★	93	290	38	81	20	0	1	37	19	19	.279	.326	.359	76	-10	4			.982	8	C-78/2-1M	0.2
1936	Phi-N	85	230	25	64	12	0	1	27	12	21	.278	.314	.343	70	-10	5			.960	-6	C-63/1-1M	-1.3
1937	Phi-N	39	87	15	24	3	0	1	8	6	4	.276	.323	.345	75	-3	1			.978	-1	C-22/1-2M	-0.3
1938	Phi-N	3	2	0	0	0	0	0	0	0	0	.000	.000	.000	-99	-1	0			1.000	0	/C-1,M	0.0
1939	Cin-N	4	3	0	1	0	0	0	0	0	1	.333	.333	.333	79	-0	0			.000	-0	/C-1	0.0
1940	*Cin-N	16	37	2	9	2	0	0	6	3	3	.243	.282	.297	59	-2	1			.982	3	C-16	-0.0
Total	18	1525	4778	580	1358	252	32	32	621	356	280	.284	.336	.370	82	-123	86	9		.977	11	*C-1351/1-9,O2	-2.9

■ GARY WILSON
Wilson, James Garrett b: 1/12/1877, Baltimore, Md. d: 5/1/69, Randallstown, Md. BR/TR, 5'7", 168 lbs. Deb: 9/27/02

| 1902 | Bos-A | 2 | 8 | 0 | 1 | 0 | 0 | 0 | 1 | 0 | | .125 | .125 | .125 | -30 | -1 | 0 | | | .800 | 0 | /2-2 | -0.1 |

■ JIM WILSON
Wilson, James George b: 12/29/60, Corvallis, Ore. BR/TR, 6'3", 230 lbs. Deb: 9/13/85

1985	Cle-A	4	14	2	5	0	0	0	4	1	3	.357	.400	.357	110	0	0	0	0	1.000	-1	/1-2,D-2	-0.1
1989	Sea-A	5	8	0	0	0	0	0	0	0	3	.000	.000	.000	-97	-2	0	0	0	.000	0	/D-5	-0.2
Total	2	9	22	2	5	0	0	0	4	1	6	.227	.261	.227	36	-2	0	0	0	1.000	-1	/D-7,1-2	-0.3

■ CHIEF WILSON
Wilson, John Owen b: 8/21/1883, Austin, Tex. d: 2/22/54, Bertram, Tex. BL/TR, 6'2", 185 lbs. Deb: 4/15/08

1908	Pit-N	144	529	47	120	8	7	3	42	22		.227	.260	.285	74	-16	12			.955	1	*O-144	-2.5
1909	*Pit-N	154	569	64	155	22	12	4	59	19		.272	.303	.374	102	-2	17			.957	6	*O-154	-0.2
1910	Pit-N	146	536	59	148	14	13	4	50	21	68	.276	.312	.373	94	-6	8			.972	3	*O-146	-1.1
1911	Pit-N	148	544	72	163	34	12	12	107	41	55	.300	.353	.472	125	15	10			.977	7	*O-146	1.5
1912	Pit-N	152	583	80	175	19	36	11	95	35	67	.300	.342	.513	134	22	16			.961	1	*O-152	1.6
1913	Pit-N	155	580	71	154	12	14	10	73	32	62	.266	.307	.386	102	-1	9			.969	6	*O-155	-0.2
1914	StL-N	154	580	64	150	27	12	9	73	32	66	.259	.302	.393	107	2	14			.983	17	*O-154	1.4
1915	StL-N	107	348	33	96	13	6	3	39	19	43	.276	.321	.374	110	3	8	15	-7	.984	12	*O-105	0.5
1916	StL-N	120	355	30	85	8	2	3	32	20	46	.239	.289	.299	81	-8	4			.955	-11	*O-113	-2.7
Total	9	1280	4624	520	1246	157	114	59	571	241	407	.269	.311	.391	105	9	98	15		.968	42	*O-1269	-1.7

■ LES WILSON
Wilson, Lester Wilbur "Tug" b: 7/15/1885, Gratiot County, Mich. d: 4/4/69, Edmonds, Wash. BL/TR, 5'11", 170 lbs. Deb: 7/15/11

| 1911 | Bos-A | 5 | 7 | 0 | 0 | 0 | 0 | 0 | 0 | 0 | 2 | .000 | .222 | .000 | -36 | -1 | 0 | | | 1.000 | -1 | /O-3 | -0.2 |

■ HACK WILSON
Wilson, Lewis Robert b: 4/26/1900, Ellwood City, Pa. d: 11/23/48, Baltimore, Md. BR/TR, 5'6", 190 lbs. Deb: 9/29/23 H

1923	NY-N	3	10	0	2	0	0	0	0	0	1	.200	.200	.200	6	-1	0	0	0	.857	-1	/O-3	-0.2
1924	*NY-N	107	383	62	113	19	12	10	57	44	46	.295	.369	.486	131	16	4	3	-1	.967	-7	*O-103	0.2
1925	NY-N	62	180	28	43	7	4	6	30	21	33	.239	.322	.422	92	-3	5	2	0	.975	-11	O-50	-1.5
1926	Chi-N	142	529	97	170	36	8	21	109	69	61	.321	.406	.539	150	38	10			.973	2	*O-140	3.0
1927	Chi-N	146	551	119	175	30	12	30	129	71	70	.318	.401	.579	160	45	13			.967	-1	*O-146	3.5
1928	Chi-N	145	520	89	163	32	9	31	120	77	94	.313	.404	.588	159	44	4			.960	-10	*O-143	2.3
1929	*Chi-N	150	574	135	198	30	5	39	159	78	83	.345	.425	.618	155	49	3			.970	-3	*O-150	3.2
1930	Chi-N	155	585	146	208	35	6	56	190	105	84	.356	.454	.723	177	74	3			.951	-7	*O-155	4.8
1931	Chi-N	112	395	66	103	22	4	13	61	63	69	.261	.362	.435	112	7	1			.978	-5	*O-103	-0.5
1932	Bro-N	135	481	77	143	37	5	23	123	51	85	.297	.366	.538	142	28	2			.955	-9	*O-125	1.1
1933	Bro-N	117	360	41	96	13	2	9	54	52	50	.267	.359	.389	119	10	7			.963	-7	O-90/2-5	-0.1
1934	Bro-N	67	172	24	45	5	0	6	27	40	33	.262	.401	.395	120	7	0			.974	-3	O-43	0.2
	Phi-N	7	20	0	2	0	0	0	3	3	4	.100	.217	.100	-11	-3	0			1.000	-1	/O-6	-0.4
	Yr	74	192	24	47	5	0	6	30	43	37	.245	.383	.365	105	3	0			.977	-4	O-49	-0.2
Total	12	1348	4760	884	1461	266	67	244	1062	674	713	.307	.395	.545	145	311	52	5		.965	-62	*O-1257/2-5	15.6

■ TACK WILSON
Wilson, Michael b: 5/16/55, Shreveport, La. BR/TR, 5'10", 185 lbs. Deb: 4/9/83

1983	Min-A	5	4	4	1	1	0	0	1	0	0	.250	.250	.500	97	-0	0	0	0	1.000	-0	/O-1,D-2	0.0
1987	Cal-A	7	2	5	1	0	0	0	0	1	0	.500	.667	.500	224	1	0	0	0	1.000	-1	/O-4,D-2	-0.1
Total	2	12	6	9	2	1	0	0	1	1	0	.333	.429	.500	150	1	0	0	0	1.000	-2	/O-5,D-4	-0.1

■ NIGEL WILSON
Wilson, Nigel Edward b: 1/12/70, Oshawa, Ont., Can. BL/TL, 6'1", 185 lbs. Deb: 9/8/93

| 1993 | Fla-N | 7 | 16 | 0 | 0 | 0 | 0 | 0 | 0 | 0 | 11 | .000 | .000 | .000 | -95 | -4 | 0 | 0 | 0 | 1.000 | -0 | /O-3 | -0.5 |

■ PARKE WILSON
Wilson, Parke Asel b: 10/26/1867, Keithsburg, Ill. d: 12/20/34, Hermosa Beach, Cal BR/TR, 5'11", 166 lbs. Deb: 7/19/1893

1893	NY-N	31	114	16	28	4	1	2	21	7	9	.246	.289	.351	70	-6	5			.969	-7	C-31	-0.8
1894	NY-N	49	175	35	58	5	5	1	32	14	5	.331	.387	.434	99	-0	8			.841	-9	C-34,1-15	-0.5
1895	NY-N	67	238	32	56	9	0	0	30	14	16	.235	.281	.273	44	-20	11			.938	3	C-53,1-11/3	-1.0
1896	NY-N	75	253	33	60	2	0	0	23	13	14	.237	.277	.245	39	-22	9			.936	-4	C-71/1-2	-1.5
1897	NY-N	46	154	29	46	9	3	0	22	15		.299	.365	.396	104	1	5			.929	-2	C-30,1-10/O2	0.2
1898	NY-N	1	4	0	0	0	0	0	0	0	0	.000	.000	.000	-99	-1	0			1.000	0	/O-1	-0.1
1899	NY-N	97	328	49	88	8	6	0	42	43		.268	.360	.329	93	-1	16			.925	-8	C-31,1-29,S3/0	-0.5
Total	7	366	1266	194	336	37	15	3	170	106	44	.265	.327	.325	73	-49	54			.926	-27	C-250/1-67,S3O2	-4.2

■ BOB WILSON
Wilson, Robert b: 2/22/25, Dallas, Tex. d: 4/23/85, Dallas, Tex. BR/TR, 5'11", 197 lbs. Deb: 5/17/58

| 1958 | LA-N | 3 | 5 | 0 | 1 | 0 | 0 | 0 | 0 | 0 | 0 | .200 | .200 | .200 | 6 | -1 | 0 | 0 | 0 | 1.000 | -0 | /O-1 | -0.1 |

■ RED WILSON
Wilson, Robert James b: 3/7/29, Milwaukee, Wis. BR/TR, 6', 200 lbs. Deb: 9/22/51

1951	Chi-A	4	11	1	3	1	0	0	0	1	2	.273	.333	.364	90	-0	0	0	0	1.000	-1	/C-4	-0.1
1952	Chi-A	2	3	0	0	0	0	0	0	0	1	.000	.000	.000	-99	-1	0	0	0	1.000	1	/C-2	0.0
1953	Chi-A	71	164	21	41	6	1	0	16	26	12	.250	.353	.299	75	-5	2	3	-1	.981	10	C-63	0.6
1954	Chi-A	8	20	2	4	0	1	0	1	1	2	.200	.238	.350	58	-1	0	0	0	1.000	4	/C-8	0.3

YEAR	TM/L	G	AB	R	H	2B	3B	HR	RBI	BB	SO	AVG	OBP	SLG	PRO+	BR/A	SB	CS	SBR	FA	FR	G/POS	TPR
	Det-A	54	170	22	48	11	1	2	22	27	12	.282	.381	.394	115	4	3	1	0	.996	2	C-53	0.9
	Yr	62	190	24	52	11	1	3	23	28	14	.274	.367	.389	108	3	3	1	0	.997	6	C-61	1.2
1955	Det-A	78	241	26	53	9	0	2	17	26	23	.220	.296	.282	57	-14	1	2	-1	.984	-6	C-72	-1.9
1956	Det-A	78	228	32	66	12	2	7	38	42	18	.289	.400	.452	124	9	2	1	0	.991	3	C-78	1.5
1957	Det-A	60	180	21	43	8	1	3	13	25	19	.239	.341	.344	86	-3	2	3	-1	1.000	1	C-60	-0.1
1958	Det-A	103	298	31	89	13	1	3	29	35	30	.299	.376	.379	101	2	10	0	3	.992	7	*C-101	1.8
1959	Det-A	67	228	28	60	17	2	4	35	10	23	.263	.300	.408	88	-4	2	2	-1	.988	2	C-64	0.0
1960	Det-A	45	134	17	29	4	0	1	14	16	14	.216	.300	.269	54	-8	3	0	1	.980	-0	C-45	-0.5
	Cle-A	32	88	5	19	3	0	1	10	6	7	.216	.274	.284	53	-6	0	0	0	.989	7	C-30	0.3
	Yr	77	222	22	48	7	0	2	24	22	21	.216	.290	.275	53	-14	3	0	1	.984	7	C-75	-0.2
Total	10	602	1765	206	455	84	8	24	189	215	163	.258	.341	.355	87	-28	25	12	0	.990	31	C-580	2.8

■ MIKE WILSON
Wilson, Samuel Marshall   b: 12/2/1896, Edge Hill, Pa.   d: 5/16/78, Boynton Beach, Fla   BR/TR, 5'10.5", 160 lbs.   Deb: 6/4/21

YEAR	TM/L	G	AB	R	H	2B	3B	HR	RBI	BB	SO	AVG	OBP	SLG	PRO+	BR/A	SB	CS	SBR	FA	FR	G/POS	TPR
1921	Pit-N	5	4	0	0	0	0	0	0	0	0	.000	.000	.000	-97	-1	0	0	0	.833	0	/C-5	-0.1

■ NEIL WILSON
Wilson, Samuel O'Neil   b: 6/14/35, Lexington, Tenn.   BL/TR, 6'1", 175 lbs.   Deb: 4/17/60

YEAR	TM/L	G	AB	R	H	2B	3B	HR	RBI	BB	SO	AVG	OBP	SLG	PRO+	BR/A	SB	CS	SBR	FA	FR	G/POS	TPR
1960	SF-N	6	10	0	0	0	0	0	0	0	1	.000	.091	.000	-77	-2	0	0	0	.958	0	/C-6	-0.2

■ TOM WILSON
Wilson, Thomas G. "Slats"   b: 6/3/1890, Fleming, Kan.   d: 3/7/53, San Pedro, Cal.   BB/TR, 6'1.5", 160 lbs.   Deb: 9/8/14

YEAR	TM/L	G	AB	R	H	2B	3B	HR	RBI	BB	SO	AVG	OBP	SLG	PRO+	BR/A	SB	CS	SBR	FA	FR	G/POS	TPR
1914	Was-A	1	1	0	0	0	0	0	0	0	0	.000	.000	.000	-96	-0	0	0	0	.000	0	/C-1	0.0

■ BILL WILSON
Wilson, William Donald   b: 11/6/28, Central City, Neb.   BR/TR, 6'2", 200 lbs.   Deb: 9/24/50

YEAR	TM/L	G	AB	R	H	2B	3B	HR	RBI	BB	SO	AVG	OBP	SLG	PRO+	BR/A	SB	CS	SBR	FA	FR	G/POS	TPR
1950	Chi-A	3	6	0	0	0	0	0	0	0	2	.000	.250	.000	-33	-1	0	0	0	1.000	-1	/O-2	-0.2
1953	Chi-A	9	17	1	1	0	0	0	1	0	7	.059	.111	.059	-51	-4	0	0	0	1.000	0	/O-3	-0.4
1954	Chi-A	20	35	4	6	1	0	2	5	7	5	.171	.310	.371	83	-1	0	1	-1	.943	-2	O-19	-0.4
	Phi-A	94	323	43	77	10	1	15	33	39	59	.238	.335	.415	104	-1	1	2	-1	.989	8	O-91	0.5
	Yr	114	358	47	83	11	1	17	38	46	64	.232	.333	.411	102	0	1	3	-2	.984	6	*O-110	0.1
1955	KC-A	98	273	39	61	12	0	15	38	24	63	.223	.289	.432	91	-5	1	1	-0	.969	-3	O-82/P-1	-1.2
Total	4	224	654	87	145	23	1	32	77	72	136	.222	.308	.407	92	-10	2	4	-2	.979	3	O-197/P-1	-1.7

■ BILL WILSON
Wilson, William G.   b: 10/28/1867, Hannibal, Mo.   d: 5/9/24, St.Paul, Minn.   TR ,   Deb: 4/30/1890

YEAR	TM/L	G	AB	R	H	2B	3B	HR	RBI	BB	SO	AVG	OBP	SLG	PRO+	BR/A	SB	CS	SBR	FA	FR	G/POS	TPR
1890	Pit-N	83	304	30	65	11	3	0	21	22	50	.214	.271	.270	65	-13	5			.874	2	C-38,O-25,1/S	-0.8
1897	Lou-N	105	381	43	81	12	4	1	41	18		.213	.257	.273	41	-33	9			.940	-1	*C-103/3-1	-1.9
1898	Lou-N	29	102	5	17	1	2	1	13	5		.167	.213	.245	32	-9	3			.895	-4	C-28/1-1	-1.0
Total	3	217	787	78	163	24	9	2	75	45	50	.207	.257	.268	49	-56	17			.912	-3	C-169/O-25,13S	-3.7

■ MOOKIE WILSON
Wilson, William Hayward   b: 2/9/56, Bamberg, S.C.   BB/TR, 5'10", 170 lbs.   Deb: 9/2/80

YEAR	TM/L	G	AB	R	H	2B	3B	HR	RBI	BB	SO	AVG	OBP	SLG	PRO+	BR/A	SB	CS	SBR	FA	FR	G/POS	TPR
1980	NY-N	27	105	16	26	5	3	0	4	12	19	.248	.325	.352	91	-1	7	7	-2	.973	2	O-26	-0.3
1981	NY-N	92	328	49	89	8	8	3	14	20	59	.271	.317	.372	96	-2	24	12	0	.983	6	O-80	0.1
1982	NY-N	159	639	90	178	25	9	5	55	32	102	.279	.315	.369	91	-8	58	16	8	.988	17	*O-156	1.3
1983	NY-N	152	638	91	176	25	6	7	51	18	103	.276	.300	.367	85	-15	54	16	7	.984	13	*O-148	0.0
1984	NY-N	154	587	88	162	28	10	10	54	26	90	.276	.309	.409	102	-1	46	9	8	.990	17	*O-146	2.1
1985	NY-N	93	337	56	93	16	8	6	26	28	48	.276	.332	.424	113	5	24	9	2	.964	2	O-83	0.7
1986	*NY-N	123	381	61	110	17	5	9	45	32	72	.289	.345	.430	116	8	25	7	3	.979	-6	*O-114	0.2
1987	*NY-N	124	385	58	115	19	7	9	34	35	85	.299	.360	.455	120	11	21	6	3	.963	-8	*O-109	0.3
1988	*NY-N	112	378	61	112	17	5	8	41	27	63	.296	.346	.431	128	13	15	4	2	.976	-7	*O-104	0.6
1989	NY-N	80	249	22	51	10	1	3	18	10	47	.205	.238	.289	53	-16	7	4	-0	.975	-3	O-71	-2.2
	*Tor-A	54	238	32	71	9	1	2	17	3	37	.298	.314	.370	93	-3	12	1	3	.991	-3	O-54	-0.5
1990	*Tor-A	147	588	81	156	36	4	3	51	31	102	.265	.302	.355	82	-15	23	4	5	.992	8	*O-141/D-6	-0.6
1991	*Tor-A	86	241	26	58	12	4	2	28	8	35	.241	.280	.349	70	-10	11	3	2	.973	-1	O-41,D-34	-1.2
Total	12	1403	5094	731	1397	227	71	67	438	282	866	.274	.315	.386	96	-35	327	98	39	.982	38	*O-1273/D-40	0.5

■ WILLIE WILSON
Wilson, Willie James   b: 7/9/55, Montgomery, Ala.   BB/TR, 6'3", 195 lbs.   Deb: 9/4/76

YEAR	TM/L	G	AB	R	H	2B	3B	HR	RBI	BB	SO	AVG	OBP	SLG	PRO+	BR/A	SB	CS	SBR	FA	FR	G/POS	TPR
1976	KC-A	12	6	0	1	0	0	0	0	0	2	.167	.167	.167	-2	-1	2	1	0	.875	-2	/O-6	-0.2
1977	KC-A	13	34	10	11	2	0	0	1	1	8	.324	.343	.382	97	-0	6	3	0	.960	-9	/O-9,D-2	0.0
1978	*KC-A	127	198	43	43	8	2	0	16	16	33	.217	.282	.278	57	-11	46	12	7	.978	-14	*O-112/D-6	-2.1
1979	KC-A	154	588	113	185	18	13	6	49	28	92	.315	.353	.420	106	4	83	12	18	.985	15	*O-152	2.9
1980	*KC-A	161	705	133	230	28	15	3	49	28	81	.326	.357	.421	112	11	79	10	18	.988	22	*O-159	4.3
1981	*KC-A	102	439	54	133	10	7	1	32	18	42	.303	.336	.364	103	1	34	8	5	.987	22	*O-101	2.6
1982	KC-A★	136	585	87	194	19	15	3	46	26	81	.332	.366	.431	118	14	37	11	5	.987	15	*O-135	2.9
1983	KC-A★	137	576	90	159	22	8	2	33	33	75	.276	.316	.352	84	-13	59	8	13	.975	1	*O-136	-0.3
1984	*KC-A	128	541	81	163	24	9	2	44	39	56	.301	.352	.390	104	3	47	5	11	.990	10	*O-128	2.1
1985	*KC-A	141	605	87	168	25	21	4	43	29	94	.278	.316	.408	96	-4	43	11	6	.995	3	*O-140	0.0
1986	KC-A	156	631	77	170	20	7	9	44	31	97	.269	.313	.366	82	-16	34	8	5	.993	5	*O-155	-1.0
1987	KC-A	146	610	97	170	18	15	4	30	32	88	.279	.321	.377	82	-16	59	11	11	.997	3	*O-143/D-2	-0.6
1988	KC-A	147	591	81	155	17	11	1	37	22	106	.262	.291	.333	74	-21	35	7	6	.989	-0	*O-142	-2.0
1989	KC-A	112	383	58	97	17	7	3	43	27	78	.253	.304	.358	86	-7	24	6	4	.977	-3	*O-108/D-1	-1.0
1990	KC-A	115	307	49	89	13	3	2	42	30	57	.290	.357	.371	106	3	24	6	4	1.000	-6	*O-106/D-1	-0.1
1991	Oak-A	113	294	38	70	14	4	0	28	18	43	.238	.291	.313	71	-12	20	5	3	.983	-4	O-87/D-9	-1.4
1992	*Oak-A	132	396	38	107	15	5	0	37	35	65	.270	.331	.333	91	-4	28	8	4	.981	7	*O-120/D-5	0.4
1993	Chi-N	105	221	29	57	11	3	1	11	11	40	.258	.302	.348	75	-8	7	2	1	.991	-18	O-82	-2.7
1994	Chi-N	17	21	4	5	0	0	0	0	6	6	.238	.273	.429	81	-1	0	0	0	1.000	-3	O-10	-0.4
Total	19	2154	7731	1169	2207	281	147	41	585	425	1144	.285	.328	.376	93	-77	668	134	120	.987	53	*O-2031/D-26	3.4

■ ED WINCENIAK
Winceniak, Edward Joseph   b: 4/16/29, Chicago, Ill.   BR/TR, 5'9", 165 lbs.   Deb: 4/25/56

YEAR	TM/L	G	AB	R	H	2B	3B	HR	RBI	BB	SO	AVG	OBP	SLG	PRO+	BR/A	SB	CS	SBR	FA	FR	G/POS	TPR
1956	Chi-N	15	17	1	2	1	0	0	0	1	3	.118	.167	.118	-22	-3	0	0	0	.889	-0	/3-4,2-1	-0.3
1957	Chi-N	17	50	5	12	3	0	1	8	2	9	.240	.269	.360	68	-2	0	0	0	1.000	-3	/S-5,3-4,2	-0.5
Total	2	32	67	6	14	3	0	1	8	3	12	.209	.243	.299	45	-5	0	0	0	.955	-3	/3-8,S-5,2	-0.8

■ GORDIE WINDHORN
Windhorn, Gordon Ray   b: 12/19/33, Watseka, Ill.   BR/TR, 6'1", 185 lbs.   Deb: 9/10/59

YEAR	TM/L	G	AB	R	H	2B	3B	HR	RBI	BB	SO	AVG	OBP	SLG	PRO+	BR/A	SB	CS	SBR	FA	FR	G/POS	TPR
1959	NY-A	7	11	0	0	0	0	0	0	0	3	.000	.000	.000	-99	-3	0	0	0	1.000	-1	/O-4	-0.4
1961	LA-N	34	33	10	8	2	1	2	6	4	3	.242	.324	.545	115	1	0	1	-1	.944	-2	O-17	-0.3
1962	KC-A	14	19	1	3	1	0	0	1	0	3	.158	.158	.211	-2	-3	0	0	0	1.000	-2	/O-7	-0.4
	LA-A	40	45	9	8	6	0	0	1	7	10	.178	.288	.311	63	-2	1	1	-0	1.000	-7	O-27	-1.0
	Yr	54	64	10	11	7	0	0	2	7	13	.172	.254	.281	44	-5	1	1	-0	1.000	-9	O-34	-1.4
Total	3	95	108	20	19	9	1	2	8	11	19	.176	.252	.333	55	-7	1	2	-1	.981	-12	/O-55	-2.1

■ BILL WINDLE
Windle, Willis Brewer   b: 12/13/04, Galena, Kan.   d: 12/8/81, Corpus Christi, Tex   BL/TL, 5'11.5", 170 lbs.   Deb: 9/27/28

YEAR	TM/L	G	AB	R	H	2B	3B	HR	RBI	BB	SO	AVG	OBP	SLG	PRO+	BR/A	SB	CS	SBR	FA	FR	G/POS	TPR
1928	Pit-N	1	1	1	1	1	0	0	0	0	0	1.000	1.000	2.000	641	1	0			1.000	0	/1-1	0.1
1929	Pit-N	2	2	1	0	0	0	0	0	0	1	.000	.000	.000	-98	-0	0			1.000	-0	/1-2	0.0
Total	2	3	2	1	1	1	0	0	0	0	1	.500	.500	1.000	264	0	0			1.000	-0	/1-3	0.1

■ ROBBIE WINE
Wine, Robert Paul Jr.   b: 7/13/62, Norristown, Pa.   BR/TR, 6'2", 190 lbs.   Deb: 9/2/86   F

YEAR	TM/L	G	AB	R	H	2B	3B	HR	RBI	BB	SO	AVG	OBP	SLG	PRO+	BR/A	SB	CS	SBR	FA	FR	G/POS	TPR
1986	Hou-N	9	12	2	3	1	0	0	0	1	4	.250	.308	.333	79	-0	0	0	0	1.000	3	/C-8	0.3

YEAR	TM/L	G	AB	R	H	2B	3B	HR	RBI	BB	SO	AVG	OBP	SLG	PRO+	BR/A	SB	CS	SBR	FA	FR	G/POS	TPR
1987	Hou-N	14	29	1	3	1	0	0	0	1	10	.103	.133	.138	-29	-5	0	0	0	.979	-1	C-12	-0.6
Total	2	23	41	3	6	2	0	0	0	2	14	.146	.186	.195	2	-6	0	0	0	.988	2	/C-20	-0.3

■ BOBBY WINE   Wine, Robert Paul Sr. b: 9/17/38, New York, N.Y. BR/TR, 6'1", 187 lbs. Deb: 9/20/60 FMC

YEAR	TM/L	G	AB	R	H	2B	3B	HR	RBI	BB	SO	AVG	OBP	SLG	PRO+	BR/A	SB	CS	SBR	FA	FR	G/POS	TPR
1960	Phi-N	4	14	1	2	0	0	0	0	0	2	.143	.143	.143	-22	-2	0	0	0	1.000	0	/S-4	-0.2
1962	Phi-N	112	311	30	76	15	0	4	25	11	49	.244	.270	.331	62	-17	2	0	1	.979	7	S-89,3-20	-0.3
1963	Phi-N	142	418	29	90	14	3	6	44	14	83	.215	.242	.306	58	-23	1	3	-2	.971	15	*S-132/3-8	-0.2
1964	Phi-N	126	283	28	60	8	3	4	34	25	37	.212	.276	.304	64	-13	1	0	0	.965	7	*S-108,3-16	0.0
1965	Phi-N	139	394	31	90	8	1	5	33	31	69	.228	.285	.292	64	-19	0	0	0	.967	22	*S-135/1-4	1.2
1966	Phi-N	46	89	8	21	5	0	0	5	6	13	.236	.292	.292	63	-4	0	1	-1	.974	12	S-40/O-2	0.9
1967	Phi-N	135	363	27	69	12	5	2	28	29	77	.190	.250	.267	48	-25	3	2	-0	.980	29	*S-134/1-2	1.6
1968	Phi-N	27	71	5	12	3	0	2	7	6	17	.169	.234	.296	58	-4	0	0	0	.972	3	S-25/3-1	0.2
1969	Mon-N	121	370	23	74	8	1	3	25	28	49	.200	.256	.251	43	-28	0	0	0	.949	17	*S-118/1-1,3	0.1
1970	Mon-N	159	501	40	116	21	3	3	51	39	94	.232	.288	.303	59	-29	0	1	-1	.976	20	*S-159	0.7
1971	Mon-N	119	340	25	68	9	0	1	16	25	46	.200	.255	.235	39	-27	0	0	0	.982	2	*S-119	-1.2
1972	Mon-N	34	18	2	4	1	0	0	0	0	2	.222	.222	.278	41	-1	0	0	0	1.000	5	3-21/S-4,2	0.4
Total	12	1164	3172	249	682	104	16	30	268	214	538	.215	.265	.286	54	-194	7	7	-2	.971	137	*S-1067/3-67,102	3.2

■ RALPH WINEGARNER   Winegarner, Ralph Lee b: 10/29/09, Benton, Kan. d: 4/14/88, Wichita, Kan. BR/TR, 6', 182 lbs. Deb: 9/20/30 C

YEAR	TM/L	G	AB	R	H	2B	3B	HR	RBI	BB	SO	AVG	OBP	SLG	PRO+	BR/A	SB	CS	SBR	FA	FR	G/POS	TPR
1930	Cle-A	5	22	5	10	1	0	0	2	1	7	.455	.478	.500	143	2	0	0	0	.857	1	/3-5	0.2
1932	Cle-A	7	7	1	1	0	0	0	0	0	5	.143	.143	.143	-24	-1	0	0	0	.750	-0	/P-5	0.0
1934	Cle-A	32	51	9	10	2	0	1	5	3	11	.196	.241	.294	37	-5	0	0	0	1.000	1	P-22/O-1	0.0
1935	Cle-A	65	84	11	26	4	1	3	17	9	12	.310	.376	.488	120	2	1	1	-0	.944	2	P-25/O-4,31	0.2
1936	Cle-A	18	16	0	2	0	0	0	2	1	6	.125	.176	.125	-24	-3	0	0	0	1.000	-0	/P-9	0.0
1949	StL-A	9	5	2	2	0	0	1	2	1	2	.400	.500	1.000	280	1	0	0	0	1.000	-0	/P-9	0.0
Total	6	136	185	28	51	7	1	5	28	15	43	.276	.330	.405	86	-4	1	1	-0	.952	2	/P-70,3-8,O1	0.4

■ DAVE WINFIELD   Winfield, David Mark b: 10/3/51, St.Paul, Minn. BR/TR, 6'6", 220 lbs. Deb: 6/19/73

YEAR	TM/L	G	AB	R	H	2B	3B	HR	RBI	BB	SO	AVG	OBP	SLG	PRO+	BR/A	SB	CS	SBR	FA	FR	G/POS	TPR
1973	SD-N	56	141	9	39	4	1	3	12	12	19	.277	.333	.383	107	1	0	0	0	.956	-1	O-36/1-1	-0.2
1974	SD-N	145	498	57	132	18	4	20	75	40	96	.265	.321	.438	116	8	9	7	-2	.960	7	*O-131	0.8
1975	SD-N	143	509	74	136	20	2	15	76	69	82	.267	.358	.403	118	13	23	4	5	.972	10	*O-138	2.2
1976	SD-N	137	492	81	139	26	4	13	69	65	78	.283	.370	.431	138	24	26	7	4	.982	12	*O-134	3.6
1977	SD-N★	157	615	104	169	29	7	25	92	58	75	.275	.337	.467	126	19	16	7	1	.972	20	*O-156	3.4
1978	SD-N★	158	587	88	181	30	5	24	97	55	81	.308	.370	.499	153	39	21	9	1	.979	-19	*O-154/1-2	1.5
1979	SD-N★	159	597	97	184	27	10	34	**118**	85	71	.308	.396	.558	**167**	55	15	9	-1	.986	11	*O-157	**5.9**
1980	SD-N★	162	558	89	154	25	6	20	87	79	83	.276	.368	.450	135	27	23	7	3	.987	-4	*O-159	2.0
1981	*NY-A★	105	388	52	114	25	1	13	68	43	41	.294	.366	.464	140	20	11	1	3	.985	-6	*O-102/D-1	1.4
1982	NY-A★	140	539	84	151	24	8	37	106	45	64	.280	.336	.560	143	29	5	3	-0	.974	12	*O-135/D-4	3.7
1983	NY-A★	152	598	99	169	26	8	32	116	58	77	.283	.348	.513	139	30	15	6	1	.978	-11	*O-151	1.5
1984	NY-A★	141	567	106	193	34	4	19	100	53	71	.340	.397	.515	156	43	6	4	-1	.994	2	*O-140	4.0
1985	NY-A★	155	633	105	174	34	6	26	114	52	96	.275	.330	.471	119	15	19	7	2	.991	12	*O-152/D-2	2.2
1986	NY-A★	154	565	90	148	31	5	24	104	77	106	.262	.352	.462	121	17	6	5	-1	.984	5	*O-145/3-2,D	1.5
1987	NY-A★	156	575	83	158	22	1	27	97	76	96	.275	.359	.457	116	14	5	6	-2	.989	-4	*O-145/D-8	0.2
1988	NY-A★	149	559	96	180	37	2	25	107	69	88	.322	.398	.530	159	44	9	4	0	.989	-3	*O-141/D-4	3.7
1990	NY-A	20	61	7	13	3	0	2	6	4	13	.213	.273	.361	75	-2	0	0	0	1.000	-3	O-12/D-7	-0.5
	Cal-A	112	414	63	114	18	2	19	72	48	68	.275	.352	.466	130	16	0	1	-1	.989	-5	*O-108/D-3	0.7
	Yr	132	475	70	127	21	2	21	78	52	81	.267	.342	.453	122	14	0	1	-1	.989	-8	*O-120,D-10	0.2
1991	Cal-A	150	568	75	149	27	4	28	86	56	109	.262	.330	.472	119	13	7	2	1	.990	-1	*O-115/D-34	0.9
1992	*Tor-A	156	583	92	169	33	3	26	108	82	89	.290	.378	.491	136	28	2	3	-1	1.000	1	*D-130,O-26	2.3
1993	Min-A	143	547	72	148	27	2	21	76	45	106	.271	.325	.442	104	2	2	3	-1	1.000	0	*D-105,O-31/1	-0.4
1994	Min-A	77	294	35	74	15	3	10	43	31	51	.252	.323	.425	91	-5	2	1	0	1.000	0	D-76/O-1	-0.7
Total	21	2927	10888	1658	3088	535	88	463	1829	1202	1660	.284	.356	.476	131	448	222	96	9	.982	34	*O-2469,D-380/13	39.7

■ AL WINGO   Wingo, Absalom Holbrook "Red" b: 5/6/1898, Norcross, Ga. d: 10/9/64, Detroit, Mich. BL/TR, 5'11", 180 lbs. Deb: 9/9/19 F

YEAR	TM/L	G	AB	R	H	2B	3B	HR	RBI	BB	SO	AVG	OBP	SLG	PRO+	BR/A	SB	CS	SBR	FA	FR	G/POS	TPR
1919	Phi-A	15	59	9	18	1	3	0	2	4	12	.305	.349	.424	115	1	0			.815	-3	O-15	-0.3
1924	Det-A	78	150	21	43	12	2	1	26	21	13	.287	.374	.413	105	1	2	5	-2	.925	-8	O-43	-1.1
1925	Det-A	130	440	104	163	34	10	5	68	69	31	.370	.456	.527	151	37	14	13	-4	.971	-3	*O-122	3.1
1926	Det-A	108	298	45	84	19	0	1	45	52	32	.282	.389	.356	94	-1	4	2	0	.923	4	O-74/3-2	-0.2
1927	Det-A	75	137	15	32	8	2	0	20	25	14	.234	.352	.321	74	-5	1	0	0	.891	-3	O-34	-0.9
1928	Det-A	87	242	30	69	13	2	2	30	40	17	.285	.389	.380	101	2	2	2	-1	.968	-3	O-71	-0.6
Total	6	493	1326	224	409	87	19	9	191	211	119	.308	.404	.423	114	36	23	22		.944	-6	O-359/3-2	-0.0

■ ED WINGO   Wingo, Edmond Armand (b: Edmond Armand La Riviere)
b: 10/8/1895, St.Anne De Bellevue, Que., Canada d: 12/5/64, Lachine, Que., Can. BR/TR, 5'6", 145 lbs. Deb: 10/2/20

YEAR	TM/L	G	AB	R	H	2B	3B	HR	RBI	BB	SO	AVG	OBP	SLG	PRO+	BR/A	SB	CS	SBR	FA	FR	G/POS	TPR
1920	Phi-A	1	4	0	1	0	0	0	1	0	0	.250	.250	.250	32	-0	0	0	0	1.000	1	/C-1	0.0

■ IVEY WINGO   Wingo, Ivey Brown b: 7/8/1890, Gainesville, Ga. d: 3/1/41, Waycross, Ga.. BL/TR, 5'10", 160 lbs. Deb: 4/20/11 FMC

YEAR	TM/L	G	AB	R	H	2B	3B	HR	RBI	BB	SO	AVG	OBP	SLG	PRO+	BR/A	SB	CS	SBR	FA	FR	G/POS	TPR
1911	StL-N	25	57	4	12	2	0	0	3	3	7	.211	.250	.246	40	-5	0			.916	-3	C-18	-0.3
1912	StL-N	100	310	38	82	18	8	2	44	23	45	.265	.317	.394	96	-3	8			.957	4	C-92	0.9
1913	StL-N	112	307	25	78	5	5	2	35	17	41	.254	.295	.342	83	-8	18			.945	-4	C-98/1-5,O	-0.4
1914	StL-N	80	237	24	71	8	5	4	26	18	17	.300	.352	.426	132	9	15			.958	-3	C-70/O-4	1.2
1915	Cin-N	119	339	26	75	11	6	3	29	13	33	.221	.250	.316	69	-14	10	11	-4	.966	3	C-98/O-1	-0.8
1916	Cin-N	119	347	30	85	8	11	2	40	25	27	.245	.298	.349	100	-0	4			.958	7	*C-107,M	1.6
1917	Cin-N	121	399	37	106	16	11	2	39	25	13	.266	.311	.376	115	6	9			.967	-5	*C-120	1.2
1918	Cin-N	100	323	35	82	15	6	0	31	19	18	.254	.297	.337	95	-3	6			.973	-6	C-93/O-5	-0.1
1919	*Cin-N	76	245	30	67	12	0	0	27	23	19	.273	.336	.371	115	5	4			.969	3	C-75	1.6
1920	Cin-N	108	364	32	96	11	5	2	38	19	13	.264	.300	.338	84	-8	6	4	-1	.958	-10	*C-107/2-2	-1.2
1921	Cin-N	97	295	20	79	7	6	3	38	21	14	.268	.319	.363	84	-7	3	2	-0	.959	5	C-92/O-1	0.3
1922	Cin-N	80	260	24	74	13	3	3	45	23	11	.285	.343	.392	91	-4	1	4	-2	.964	4	C-78	-0.3
1923	Cin-N	61	171	10	45	9	2	1	24	9	11	.263	.304	.357	75	-6	1	1	0	.969	3	C-57	-0.1
1924	Cin-N	66	192	21	55	5	4	1	23	14	8	.286	.338	.370	91	-2	1	1	-1	.989	5	C-65/1-1	0.5
1925	Cin-N	55	146	6	30	7	0	0	12	11	8	.205	.261	.253	33	-15	1	2	-1	.965	3	C-55	-0.9
1926	Cin-N	7	10	0	2	0	0	0	1	1	0	.200	.333	.200	48	-1	0			1.000	-0	/C-7	-0.0
1929	Cin-N	1	1	0	0	0	0	0	0	0	0	.000	.000	.000	-99	-0	0			.000	0	/C-1	0.0
Total	17	1327	4003	362	1039	147	81	25	455	264	285	.260	.307	.355	91	-56	87	25		.962	11	*C-1233/O-12,12	3.6

■ GEORGE WINKELMAN   Winkelman, George Edward b: 2/18/1865, Washington, D.C. d: 5/19/60, Washington, D.C. BL/TL, Deb: 8/4/1883

YEAR	TM/L	G	AB	R	H	2B	3B	HR	RBI	BB	SO	AVG	OBP	SLG	PRO+	BR/A	SB	CS	SBR	FA	FR	G/POS	TPR
1883	Lou-a	4	13	2	0	0	0	0		0	1	.000	.071	.000	-81	-3				.625	0	/O-4	-0.2
1886	Was-N	1	5	0	1	0	0	0	0	0	0	.200	.200	.200	23	-0	0			.000	-1	/O-1,P-1	0.0
Total	2	5	18	2	1	0	0	0	0	1	1	.056	.105	.056	-51	-3	0			.625	-1	/O-5,P-1	-0.2

■ HERM WINNINGHAM   Winningham, Herman Son b: 12/1/61, Orangeburg, S.C. BL/TR, 5'11", 185 lbs. Deb: 9/1/84

YEAR	TM/L	G	AB	R	H	2B	3B	HR	RBI	BB	SO	AVG	OBP	SLG	PRO+	BR/A	SB	CS	SBR	FA	FR	G/POS	TPR
1984	NY-N	14	27	5	11	1	1	0	5	1	7	.407	.429	.519	167	2	2	1	0	1.000	-4	O-10	-0.2
1985	Mon-N	125	312	30	74	6	5	3	21	28	72	.237	.300	.317	77	-10	20	9	1	.983	-4	*O-116	-1.7
1986	Mon-N	90	185	23	40	6	3	4	11	18	51	.216	.286	.346	74	-7	12	7	-1	.980	-7	O-66/S-1	-1.7

YEAR	TM/L	G	AB	R	H	2B	3B	HR	RBI	BB	SO	AVG	OBP	SLG	PRO+	BR/A	SB	CS	SBR	FA	FR	G/POS	TPR
1987	Mon-N	137	347	34	83	20	3	4	41	34	68	.239	.307	.349	71	-14	29	10	3	.975	-8	*O-131	-2.2
1988	Mon-N	47	90	10	21	2	1	0	6	12	18	.233	.324	.278	71	-3	4	5	-2	.982	-3	O-30	-0.9
	Cin-N	53	113	6	26	1	3	0	15	5	27	.230	.263	.292	57	-6	8	3	1	1.000	-3	O-42	-1.1
	Yr	100	203	16	47	3	4	0	21	17	45	.232	.291	.286	63	-9	12	8	-1	.992	-7	O-72	-2.0
1989	Cin-N	115	251	40	63	11	3	3	13	24	50	.251	.316	.355	88	-4	14	5	1	.980	-7	O-85	-1.1
1990	*Cin-N	84	160	20	41	8	5	3	17	14	31	.256	.316	.425	98	-1	6	4	-1	1.000	-9	O-64	-1.2
1991	Cin-N	98	169	17	38	6	1	1	4	11	40	.225	.272	.290	56	-10	4	4	-1	.953	-8	O-66	-2.1
1992	Bos-A	105	234	27	55	8	1	1	14	10	53	.235	.266	.291	52	-15	6	5	-1	.975	-4	O-67/D-6	-2.2
Total	9	868	1888	212	452	69	26	19	147	157	417	.239	.298	.334	74	-67	105	53	-0	.980	-58	O-677/D-6,S	-14.4

■ TOM WINSETT
Winsett, John Thomas "Long Tom" b: 11/24/09, McKenzie, Tenn. d: 7/87, Memphis, Tenn. BL/TR, 6'2", 190 lbs. Deb: 4/20/30

YEAR	TM/L	G	AB	R	H	2B	3B	HR	RBI	BB	SO	AVG	OBP	SLG	PRO+	BR/A	SB	CS	SBR	FA	FR	G/POS	TPR
1930	Bos-A	1	1	0	0	0	0	0	0	0	1	.000	.000	.000	-99	-0	0	0	0	.000	0	H	0.0
1931	Bos-A	64	76	6	15	1	0	1	7	4	21	.197	.247	.250	33	-8	0	0	0	1.000	0	/O-8	-0.8
1933	Bos-A	6	12	1	1	0	0	0	0	1	6	.083	.154	.083	-36	-2	0	0	0	1.000	-2	/O-4	-0.4
1935	StL-N	7	12	2	6	1	0	0	2	2	3	.500	.571	.583	203	2	0			.000	-1	/O-2	0.1
1936	Bro-N	22	85	13	20	7	0	1	18	11	14	.235	.330	.353	83	-2	0			1.000	1	O-21	-0.1
1937	Bro-N	118	350	32	83	15	5	5	42	45	64	.237	.329	.351	84	-7	3			.960	1	*O-101/P-1	-0.9
1938	Bro-N	12	30	6	9	1	0	1	7	6	4	.300	.417	.433	131	2	0			.882	-2	/O-9	0.0
Total	7	230	566	60	134	25	5	8	76	69	113	.237	.325	.341	79	-16	3	0		.963	-2	O-145/P-1	-2.1

■ MATT WINTERS
Winters, Matthew Littleton b: 3/18/60, Buffalo, N.Y. BL/TR, 6'3", 215 lbs. Deb: 5/30/89

YEAR	TM/L	G	AB	R	H	2B	3B	HR	RBI	BB	SO	AVG	OBP	SLG	PRO+	BR/A	SB	CS	SBR	FA	FR	G/POS	TPR
1989	KC-A	42	107	14	25	6	0	2	9	14	23	.234	.322	.346	89	-1				.939	-4	O-31/D-3	-0.6

■ KETTLE WIRTS
Wirts, Elwood Vernon b: 10/31/1897, Consumne, Cal. d: 7/12/68, Sacramento, Cal. BR/TR, 5'11", 170 lbs. Deb: 7/20/21

YEAR	TM/L	G	AB	R	H	2B	3B	HR	RBI	BB	SO	AVG	OBP	SLG	PRO+	BR/A	SB	CS	SBR	FA	FR	G/POS	TPR
1921	Chi-N	7	11	0	2	0	0	0	1	0	3	.182	.182	.182	-3	-2	0	0	0	1.000	1	/C-5	-0.1
1922	Chi-N	31	58	7	10	2	0	1	6	12	15	.172	.314	.259	48	-4	0	0	0	.968	-5	C-27	-0.8
1923	Chi-N	5	5	2	1	0	0	0	1	2	0	.200	.429	.200	71	-0	0	0	0	1.000	1	/C-3	0.1
1924	Chi-A	6	12	0	1	0	0	0	0	2	2	.083	.214	.083	-22	-2	1	0	0	1.000	1	/C-5	-0.1
Total	4	49	86	9	14	2	0	1	8	16	20	.163	.294	.221	35	-8	1	0	0	.981	-3	/C-40	-0.9

■ HUGHIE WISE
Wise, Hugh Edward b: 3/9/06, Campbellsville, Ky. d: 7/21/87, Plantation, Fla. BB/TR, 6', 178 lbs. Deb: 9/26/30

YEAR	TM/L	G	AB	R	H	2B	3B	HR	RBI	BB	SO	AVG	OBP	SLG	PRO+	BR/A	SB	CS	SBR	FA	FR	G/POS	TPR
1930	Det-A	2	6	0	2	0	0	0	0	0	0	.333	.333	.333	68	-0	0	0	0	1.000	1	/C-2	0.1

■ CASEY WISE
Wise, Kendall Cole b: 9/8/32, Lafayette, Ind. BB/TR, 6', 170 lbs. Deb: 4/16/57

YEAR	TM/L	G	AB	R	H	2B	3B	HR	RBI	BB	SO	AVG	OBP	SLG	PRO+	BR/A	SB	CS	SBR	FA	FR	G/POS	TPR
1957	Chi-N	43	106	12	19	3	1	0	7	11	14	.179	.256	.226	32	-10	0	0	0	.940	3	2-31/S-5	-0.5
1958	*Mil-N	31	71	8	14	1	0	0	4	8	9	.197	.240	.211	23	-8	1	1	-0	1.000	0	2-10/S-7,3	-0.7
1959	Mil-N	22	76	11	13	2	0	1	5	5	5	.171	.267	.237	39	-7	0	0	0	.989	-7	2-20/S-5	-1.3
1960	Det-A	30	68	6	10	0	2	2	5	4	9	.147	.194	.294	29	-7	1	0	0	.983	3	2-17,S-10/3	-0.3
Total	4	126	321	37	56	6	3	3	17	29	36	.174	.243	.240	31	-32	2	1	0	.968	-2	/2-78,S-27,3	-2.8

■ NICK WISE
Wise, Nicholas Joseph b: 6/15/1866, Boston, Mass. d: 1/15/23, Boston, Mass. BR/TR, 5'11", 194 lbs. Deb: 6/20/1888

YEAR	TM/L	G	AB	R	H	2B	3B	HR	RBI	BB	SO	AVG	OBP	SLG	PRO+	BR/A	SB	CS	SBR	FA	FR	G/POS	TPR
1888	Bos-N	1	3	0	0	0	0	0	0	0	0	.000	.000	.000	-98	-0				.000	-0	/O-1,C-1	-0.1

■ SAM WISE
Wise, Samuel Washington "Modoc" b: 8/18/1857, Akron, Ohio d: 1/22/10, Akron, Ohio BL/TR, 5'10.5", 170 lbs. Deb: 7/30/1881

YEAR	TM/L	G	AB	R	H	2B	3B	HR	RBI	BB	SO	AVG	OBP	SLG	PRO+	BR/A	SB	CS	SBR	FA	FR	G/POS	TPR
1881	Det-N	1	4	0	2	0	0	0	0	0	2	.500	.500	.500	207	0				.571	-0	/3-1	0.0
1882	Bos-N	78	298	44	66	11	4	4	34	5	45	.221	.234	.326	77	-8				.852	-13	*S-72/3-6	-1.5
1883	Bos-N	96	406	73	110	25	7	4	58	13	74	.271	.294	.397	105	2				.823	-2	*S-96	0.1
1884	Bos-N	114	426	60	91	15	9	4	41	25	104	.214	.257	.319	81	-9				.884	6	*S-107/2-7	-0.2
1885	Bos-N	107	424	71	120	20	10	4	46	25	61	.283	.323	.406	139	18				.858	13	*S-79,2-22/O	3.1
1886	Bos-N	96	387	71	112	19	12	6	72	33	61	.289	.345	.432	140	19	31			.956	-24	1-57,2-20,S/O	-1.0
1887	Bos-N	113	467	103	156	27	17	9	92	36	44	.334	.390	.522	151	32	43			.869	-6	S-72,O-27,2	2.2
1888	Bos-N	105	417	66	100	19	12	4	40	34	66	.240	.306	.372	113	6	33			.888	10	S-89/3-6,102	1.7
1889	Was-N	121	472	79	118	15	8	4	62	61	62	.250	.341	.341	97	-0	24			.916	-23	2-72,S-26,3O	-1.6
1890	Buf-P	119	505	95	148	29	11	6	102	46	45	.293	.359	.430	120	14	19			.906	5	*2-119	2.1
1891	Bal-a	103	388	70	96	14	5	1	48	62	52	.247	.364	.317	94	-1	33			.888	-13	*2-99/S-4	-0.8
1893	Was-N	122	521	102	162	27	17	5	77	49	27	.311	.375	.457	124	16	20			.924	14	*2-91,3-31	2.7
Total	12	1175	4715	834	1281	221	112	49	672	389	643	.272	.332	.397	115	90	203			.859	-33	S-563,2-448/130	6.8

■ PHIL WISNER
Wisner, Philip N. b: 7/1869, Washington, D.C. d: 7/5/36, Washington, D.C. TR, Deb: 8/30/1895

YEAR	TM/L	G	AB	R	H	2B	3B	HR	RBI	BB	SO	AVG	OBP	SLG	PRO+	BR/A	SB	CS	SBR	FA	FR	G/POS	TPR
1895	Was-N	1	0	0	0	0	0	0	0	0	0	—	—	—	—	0	0			.250	-1	/S-1	0.0

■ DAVE WISSMAN
Wissman, David Alvin b: 2/17/41, Greenfield, Mass. BL/TR, 6'2", 178 lbs. Deb: 9/15/64

YEAR	TM/L	G	AB	R	H	2B	3B	HR	RBI	BB	SO	AVG	OBP	SLG	PRO+	BR/A	SB	CS	SBR	FA	FR	G/POS	TPR
1964	Pit-N	16	27	2	4	0	0	0	0	1	9	.148	.179	.148	-7	-4	0	0	0	1.000	-1	O-10	-0.6

■ TEX WISTERZIL
Wisterzil, George John b: 3/7/1891, Detroit, Mich. d: 6/27/64, San Antonio, Tex. BR/TR, 5'9.5", 150 lbs. Deb: 4/14/14

YEAR	TM/L	G	AB	R	H	2B	3B	HR	RBI	BB	SO	AVG	OBP	SLG	PRO+	BR/A	SB	CS	SBR	FA	FR	G/POS	TPR
1914	Bro-F	149	534	54	137	18	10	0	66	34	47	.257	.314	.328	67	-27	17			**.956**	16	*3-149	-0.6
1915	Bro-F	36	106	13	33	3	3	0	21	21	7	.311	.438	.396	125	5	8			.949	3	3-31	1.0
	Chi-F	7	20	3	4	1	0	0	2	0	3	.200	.304	.250	52	-1	0			.955	0	/3-6	-0.1
	StL-F	8	24	1	5	1	0	0	4	2	2	.208	.296	.250	45	-2	2			.939	2	/3-8	0.1
	Chi-F	42	144	12	36	3	1	0	14	5	10	.250	.280	.285	54	-10	2			.968	8	3-42	0.1
	Yr	93	294	29	78	8	4	0	39	31	21	.265	.345	.320	81	-7	12			.958	14	3-87	1.0
Total	2	242	828	83	215	26	14	0	105	65	68	.260	.326	.325	72	-34	29			.957	29	3-236	0.4

■ MICKEY WITEK
Witek, Nicholas Joseph b: 12/19/15, Luzerne, Pa. d: 8/24/90, Kingston, Pa. BR/TR, 5'10", 170 lbs. Deb: 4/16/40

YEAR	TM/L	G	AB	R	H	2B	3B	HR	RBI	BB	SO	AVG	OBP	SLG	PRO+	BR/A	SB	CS	SBR	FA	FR	G/POS	TPR
1940	NY-N	119	433	34	111	7	0	3	31	24	17	.256	.295	.293	62	-22	2			.958	**19**	S-89,2-32	0.7
1941	NY-N	26	94	11	34	5	0	1	16	4	2	.362	.388	.447	132	4	0			.933	2	2-23	0.7
1942	NY-N	148	553	72	144	19	6	5	48	36	20	.260	.306	.344	89	-9	2			**.978**	-1	*2-147	0.0
1943	NY-N	153	622	68	195	17	6	6	55	41	23	.314	.356	.370	109	7	1			.967	16	*2-153	3.3
1946	NY-N	82	284	32	75	13	2	4	29	28	11	.264	.330	.366	97	-1	1			.962	-12	2-42,3-35	-1.1
1947	NY-N	51	160	22	35	4	1	3	17	15	12	.219	.286	.313	58	-10	1			.983	11	2-40/3-3	0.4
1949	NY-A	1	1	0	1	0	0	0	0	0	0	1.000	1.000	1.000	430	0	0	0	0	.000	0	H	0.0
Total	7	580	2147	239	595	65	9	22	196	148	84	.277	.324	.347	90	-30	7	0		.969	34	2-437/S-89,3	4.0

■ FRANK WITHROW
Withrow, Frank Blaine "Kid" b: 6/14/1891, Greenwood, Mo. d: 9/5/66, Omaha, Neb. BR/TR, 5'11.5", 187 lbs. Deb: 4/15/20

YEAR	TM/L	G	AB	R	H	2B	3B	HR	RBI	BB	SO	AVG	OBP	SLG	PRO+	BR/A	SB	CS	SBR	FA	FR	G/POS	TPR
1920	Phi-N	48	132	8	24	4	1	0	12	6	26	.182	.239	.227	33	-11	0			.973	3	C-48	-0.5
1922	Phi-N	10	21	3	7	2	0	0	3	5	5	.333	.417	.429	108	-0	0			.909	1	/C-8	0.2
Total	2	58	153	11	31	6	1	0	15	11	31	.203	.265	.255	45	-11	0	0	0	.965	4	/C-56	-0.3

■ CORKY WITHROW
Withrow, Raymond Wallace b: 11/28/37, High Coal, W.Va. BR/TR, 6'3.5", 197 lbs. Deb: 9/6/63

YEAR	TM/L	G	AB	R	H	2B	3B	HR	RBI	BB	SO	AVG	OBP	SLG	PRO+	BR/A	SB	CS	SBR	FA	FR	G/POS	TPR
1963	StL-N	6	9	0	0	0	0	0	0	1	2	.000	.000	.000	-91	-2	0	0	0	1.000	-0	/O-2	-0.3

■ RON WITMEYER
Witmeyer, Ronald Herman b: 6/28/67, West Islip, N.Y. BL/TL, 6'3", 215 lbs. Deb: 8/25/91

YEAR	TM/L	G	AB	R	H	2B	3B	HR	RBI	BB	SO	AVG	OBP	SLG	PRO+	BR/A	SB	CS	SBR	FA	FR	G/POS	TPR
1991	Oak-A	11	19	0	1	0	0	0	0	0	5	.053	.053	.053	-75	-4	0	0	0	1.000	0	/1-8	-0.5

YEAR	TM/L	G	AB	R	H	2B	3B	HR	RBI	BB	SO	AVG	OBP	SLG	PRO+	BR/A	SB	CS	SBR	FA	FR	G/POS	TPR

■ WHITEY WITT Witt, Lawton Walter (b: Ladislaw Waldemar Wittkowski)
b: 9/28/1895, Orange, Mass. d: 7/14/88, Salem Co., N.J. BL/TR, 5'7", 150 lbs. Deb: 4/12/16

YEAR	TM/L	G	AB	R	H	2B	3B	HR	RBI	BB	SO	AVG	OBP	SLG	PRO+	BR/A	SB	CS	SBR	FA	FR	G/POS	TPR
1916	Phi-A	143	563	64	138	16	15	2	36	55	71	.245	.315	.337	101	-1	19			.902	-1	*S-142	0.7
1917	Phi-A	128	452	62	114	13	4	0	28	65	45	.252	.346	.299	98	1	12			.935	5	*S-111/O-7,3	1.2
1919	Phi-A	122	460	56	123	15	6	0	33	46	26	.267	.334	.326	85	-9	11			.972	-3	O-59,2-56/3	-1.3
1920	Phi-A	65	218	29	70	11	3	1	25	27	16	.321	.396	.413	113	5	2	3	-1	.960	-8	O-50,2-10/S	-0.8
1921	Phi-A	154	629	100	198	31	11	4	45	77	52	.315	.390	.418	106	7	16	15	-4	.959	-2	*O-154	-1.5
1922	*NY-A	140	528	98	157	11	6	4	40	**89**	29	.297	.400	.364	98	3	5	8	-3	.976	-5	*O-139	-1.5
1923	*NY-A	146	596	113	187	18	10	6	56	67	42	.314	.386	.408	107	8	2	7	-4	**.979**	2	*O-144	-0.3
1924	NY-A	147	600	88	178	26	5	1	36	45	20	.297	.346	.362	83	-15	9	7	-2	.976	-1	*O-144	-2.6
1925	NY-A	31	40	9	8	2	1	0	0	6	2	.200	.304	.300	55	-3	1	1	-0	1.000	4	O-10	-0.4
1926	Bro-N	63	85	13	22	1	1	0	3	12	6	.259	.351	.294	76	-2	1			.920	-2	O-22	-0.5
Total	10	1139	4171	632	1195	144	62	18	302	489	309	.287	.362	.364	97	-6	78	41		.971	-15	O-729,S-255/23	-6.5

■ JERRY WITTE Witte, Jerome Charles b: 7/30/15, St.Louis, Mo. BR/TR, 6'1", 190 lbs. Deb: 9/10/46

YEAR	TM/L	G	AB	R	H	2B	3B	HR	RBI	BB	SO	AVG	OBP	SLG	PRO+	BR/A	SB	CS	SBR	FA	FR	G/POS	TPR
1946	StL-A	18	73	7	14	2	0	2	4	0	18	.192	.192	.301	35	-7	0	0	0	.967	-2	1-18	-1.1
1947	StL-A	34	99	4	14	2	1	2	12	11	22	.141	.227	.242	30	-10	0	0	0	.983	-1	1-27	-1.3
Total	2	52	172	11	28	4	1	4	16	11	40	.163	.213	.267	32	-16	0	0	0	.977	-4	/1-45	-2.4

■ JOHN WOCKENFUSS Wockenfuss, Johnny Bilton b: 2/27/49, Welch, W.Va. BR/TR, 6', 190 lbs. Deb: 8/11/74

YEAR	TM/L	G	AB	R	H	2B	3B	HR	RBI	BB	SO	AVG	OBP	SLG	PRO+	BR/A	SB	CS	SBR	FA	FR	G/POS	TPR
1974	Det-A	13	29	1	4	1	0	0	2	3	2	.138	.219	.172	13	-3	0	0	0	.932	-1	C-13	-0.4
1975	Det-A	35	118	15	27	6	3	4	13	10	15	.229	.289	.432	97	-1	0	0	0	.982	4	C-34	0.4
1976	Det-A	60	144	18	32	7	2	3	10	17	14	.222	.309	.361	92	-1	0	3	-2	.941	-7	C-59	-1.0
1977	Det-A	53	164	26	45	8	1	9	25	14	18	.274	.331	.500	117	3	0	0	0	.985	-7	C-37/O-9,D	-0.2
1978	Det-A	71	187	23	53	5	0	7	22	21	14	.283	.359	.422	116	4	0	1	-1	.978	-8	O-60/D-2	-0.7
1979	Det-A	87	231	27	61	9	1	15	46	18	40	.264	.323	.506	116	4	2	2	-1	.996	1	1-31,C-20,D/O	0.3
1980	Det-A	126	372	56	102	13	2	16	65	68	64	.274	.391	.449	126	16	1	4	-2	.983	-5	1-52,D-28,CO	1.1
1981	Det-A	70	172	20	37	4	0	9	25	28	22	.215	.325	.395	103	1	0	0	0	.984	-3	D-39,1-25/CO	-0.5
1982	Det-A	70	193	28	58	9	0	8	32	29	21	.301	.392	.472	135	10	0	0	0	.981	-3	C-24,1-17,DO/3	0.6
1983	Det-A	92	245	32	66	8	1	9	44	31	37	.269	.351	.420	114	5	1	1	-0	1.000	4	D-39,C-29,1/3O	0.8
1984	Phi-N	86	180	20	52	3	1	6	24	30	24	.289	.390	.417	125	7	1	0	0	.996	1	1-39,C-21/3	-0.4
1985	Phi-N	32	37	1	6	0	0	0	2	8	7	.162	.311	.162	35	-3	0	0	0	1.000	-1	/1-7,C-2	-0.4
Total	12	795	2072	267	543	73	11	86	310	277	278	.262	.351	.432	114	42	5	11	-5	.972	-27	C-269,1-184,DO/3	1.2

■ ANDY WOEHR Woehr, Andrew Emil b: 2/4/1896, Fort Wayne, Ind. d: 7/24/90, Fort Wayne, Ind. BR/TR, 5'11", 165 lbs. Deb: 9/15/23

YEAR	TM/L	G	AB	R	H	2B	3B	HR	RBI	BB	SO	AVG	OBP	SLG	PRO+	BR/A	SB	CS	SBR	FA	FR	G/POS	TPR
1923	Phi-N	13	41	3	14	2	0	0	3	1	1	.341	.357	.390	87	-1	0	0	0	.975	3	3-13	0.3
1924	Phi-N	50	152	11	33	4	5	0	17	5	8	.217	.252	.309	44	-12	2	2	-1	.920	-5	3-44/2-1	-1.5
Total	2	63	193	14	47	6	5	0	20	6	9	.244	.274	.326	53	-13	2	2	-1	.935	-2	/3-57,2-1	-1.2

■ JOE WOERLIN Woerlin, Joseph b: 10/9/1864, France d: 6/22/19, St.Louis, Mo. Deb: 7/21/1895

YEAR	TM/L	G	AB	R	H	2B	3B	HR	RBI	BB	SO	AVG	OBP	SLG	PRO+	BR/A	SB	CS	SBR	FA	FR	G/POS	TPR
1895	Was-N	1	3	1	1	0	0	0	0	0	0	.333	.333	.333	73	-0	0			1.000	-1	/S-1	0.0

■ JIM WOHLFORD Wohlford, James Eugene b: 2/28/51, Visalia, Cal. BR/TR, 5'11", 175 lbs. Deb: 9/1/72

YEAR	TM/L	G	AB	R	H	2B	3B	HR	RBI	BB	SO	AVG	OBP	SLG	PRO+	BR/A	SB	CS	SBR	FA	FR	G/POS	TPR
1972	KC-A	15	25	3	6	1	0	0	0	2	6	.240	.321	.280	80	-1	0	0	0	.950	-2	/2-8	-0.3
1973	KC-A	45	109	21	29	1	3	2	10	11	12	.266	.333	.385	95	-1	1	1	-0	1.000	3	D-19,O-13	0.1
1974	KC-A	143	501	55	136	16	7	2	44	39	74	.271	.328	.343	88	-7	16	13	-3	.982	1	*O-138/D-1	-1.6
1975	KC-A	116	353	45	90	10	5	0	30	34	37	.255	.322	.312	78	-10	12	7	-1	.953	-6	*O-102/D-4	-2.0
1976	*KC-A	107	293	47	73	10	2	1	24	29	24	.249	.319	.307	83	-6	22	16	-3	.975	-1	O-93/2-1,D	-1.3
1977	Mil-A	129	391	41	97	16	3	2	36	21	49	.248	.288	.320	66	-19	17	16	-5	.981	-2	*O-125/2-1,D	-2.9
1978	Mil-A	46	118	16	35	7	2	1	19	6	16	.297	.331	.415	108	1	3	2	-0	.982	-5	O-35/D-4	-0.5
1979	Mil-A	63	175	19	46	13	1	1	17	8	28	.263	.295	.366	77	-6	6	2	1	.969	-2	O-55/D-5	-0.9
1980	SF-N	91	193	17	54	6	4	1	24	13	23	.280	.329	.368	96	-1	1	4	-2	.989	-2	O-49/3-1	-0.7
1981	SF-N	50	68	4	11	3	0	1	7	4	9	.162	.208	.250	30	-6	0	0	0	1.000	-3	O-10	-1.0
1982	SF-N	97	250	37	64	12	1	2	25	30	36	.256	.336	.336	89	-3	8	3	1	.992	-2	O-72	-0.6
1983	Mon-N	83	141	7	39	8	0	1	14	5	14	.277	.301	.355	82	-4	0	1	-0	.988	-11	O-61	-1.6
1984	Mon-N	95	213	20	64	13	2	5	29	14	19	.300	.344	.451	127	7	3	0	1	.989	-2	O-59/3-2	0.4
1985	Mon-N	70	125	9	24	5	1	1	15	16	18	.192	.284	.272	60	-7	0	2	-1	1.000	-5	O-43	-1.4
1986	Mon-N	70	94	10	25	4	2	1	9	9	17	.266	.330	.383	97	-0	0	2	-1	1.000	-5	G-22/3-6	-0.5
Total	15	1220	3049	349	793	125	33	21	305	241	376	.260	.316	.343	85	-62	89	68	-14	.980	-41	O-877/D-37,23	-14.8

■ JOHN WOJCIK Wojcik, John Joseph b: 4/6/42, Olean, N.Y. BL/TR, 6', 175 lbs. Deb: 9/9/62

YEAR	TM/L	G	AB	R	H	2B	3B	HR	RBI	BB	SO	AVG	OBP	SLG	PRO+	BR/A	SB	CS	SBR	FA	FR	G/POS	TPR
1962	KC-A	16	43	8	13	4	0	0	9	13	4	.302	.474	.395	131	3	3	0	1	1.000	-1	O-12	0.2
1963	KC-A	19	59	7	11	0	0	0	2	8	8	.186	.284	.186	33	-5	2	0	1	1.000	0	O-17	-0.5
1964	KC-A	6	22	1	3	0	0	0	0	2	8	.136	.208	.136	-2	-3	0	0	0	1.000	0	/O-6	-0.4
Total	3	41	124	16	27	4	0	0	11	23	20	.218	.345	.250	64	-5	5	0	2	1.000	-1	/O-35	-0.7

■ RAY WOLF Wolf, Raymond Bernard "Grandpa" b: 7/15/04, Chicago, Ill. d: 10/6/79, Fort Worth, Tex. BR/TR, 5'11", 175 lbs. Deb: 7/27/27

YEAR	TM/L	G	AB	R	H	2B	3B	HR	RBI	BB	SO	AVG	OBP	SLG	PRO+	BR/A	SB	CS	SBR	FA	FR	G/POS	TPR
1927	Cin-N	1	1	0	0	0	0	0	0	0	0	.000	.000	.000	-99	-0	0			1.000	-0	/1-1	0.0

■ JIMMY WOLF Wolf, William Van Winkle "Chicken" b: 5/12/1862, Louisville, Ky. d: 5/16/03, Louisville, Ky. BR/TR, 5'9", 190 lbs. Deb: 5/2/1882 M

YEAR	TM/L	G	AB	R	H	2B	3B	HR	RBI	BB	SO	AVG	OBP	SLG	PRO+	BR/A	SB	CS	SBR	FA	FR	G/POS	TPR
1882	Lou-a	78	318	46	95	11	8	0		9		.299	.318	.384	144	14				.902	-2	*O-70/S-9,1P	1.1
1883	Lou-a	98	389	59	102	17	9	1		5		.262	.272	.360	110	4				.890	17	*O-78,C-20/S2	1.9
1884	Lou-a	110	486	79	146	24	11	3		4		.300	.310	.414	140	20				.884	0	*O-101,C-11/S31	1.7
1885	Lou-a	112	483	79	141	23	17	1		11		.292	.309	.416	128	13				.917	-0	*O-111/C-2,3P	0.9
1886	Lou-a	130	545	93	148	17	12	3		27		.272	.310	.363	105	-0	23			.934	9	*O-122/1-8,C2P	0.5
1887	Lou-a	137	569	103	160	27	13	2		34		.281	.331	.385	97	-4	45			.940	8	*O-128,1-11	0.1
1888	Lou-a	128	538	80	154	28	11	0	67	25		.286	.320	.379	126	15	41			.886	7	O-85,S-39/3C1	1.8
1889	Lou-a	130	546	72	159	20	9	3	57	29	34	.291	.333	.377	104	2	18			.946	-1	O-88,1-16,2S/3M	-0.1
1890	*Lou-a	134	543	100	**197**	29	11	4		43		**.363**	.421	.479	169	46	46			.939	-2	*O-123,3-12	3.6
1891	Lou-a	138	537	67	136	17	8	1	82	42	36	.253	.317	.320	83	-12	13			.918	5	*O-133/1-5,3	-1.0
1892	StL-N	3	14	1	2	0	0	0	1	0	1	.143	.143	.143	-14	-2	0			1.000	-1	/O-3	-0.3
Total	11	1198	4968	779	1440	213	109	18	207	229	71	.290	.327	.387	118	97	186			.918	41	*O-1042/S-64,1C32P	10.2

■ HARRY WOLFE Wolfe, Harold "Whitey" b: 11/24/1890, Massachusetts d: 7/28/71, Fort Wayne, Ind. BR/TR, 5'8", 160 lbs. Deb: 4/15/17

YEAR	TM/L	G	AB	R	H	2B	3B	HR	RBI	BB	SO	AVG	OBP	SLG	PRO+	BR/A	SB	CS	SBR	FA	FR	G/POS	TPR
1917	Chi-N	9	5	1	2	0	0	0	1	1	1	.400	.500	.400	164	1	0			1.000	0	/O-2,S-1	0.1
	Pit-N	3	5	0	0	0	0	0	1	1	4	.000	.167	.000	-45	-1	0			.875	1	/2-1,S-1	0.0
	Yr	12	10	1	2	0	0	0	1	2	5	.200	.333	.200	61	-0	0			1.000	1	/O-2,S-2,2	0.1

■ LARRY WOLFE Wolfe, Laurence Marcy b: 3/2/53, Melbourne, Fla. BR/TR, 5'11", 170 lbs. Deb: 9/16/77

YEAR	TM/L	G	AB	R	H	2B	3B	HR	RBI	BB	SO	AVG	OBP	SLG	PRO+	BR/A	SB	CS	SBR	FA	FR	G/POS	TPR
1977	Min-A	8	25	3	6	1	0	0	6	1	2	.240	.269	.280	51	-2	0	0	0	1.000	0	/3-8	-0.2
1978	Min-A	88	235	25	55	10	1	3	25	36	27	.234	.336	.323	85	-4	0	1	-1	.953	6	3-81/S-7	0.1
1979	Bos-A	47	78	12	19	4	0	3	15	17	21	.244	.385	.410	109	1	0	0	0	.963	6	2-27/3-9,SC1	0.8
1980	Bos-A	18	23	3	3	1	0	1	4	0	3	.130	.130	.304	15	-3	0	0	0	1.000	1	3-14/D-4	-0.2
Total	4	161	361	43	83	16	1	7	50	54	53	.230	.332	.338	84	-7	0	1	-1	.957	13	3-112/2-27,SD1C	0.5

YEAR	TM/L	G	AB	R	H	2B	3B	HR	RBI	BB	SO	AVG	OBP	SLG	PRO+	BR/A	SB	CS	SBR	FA	FR	G/POS	TPR

■ POLLY WOLFE Wolfe, Roy Chamberlain b: 9/1/1888, Knoxville, Ill. d: 11/21/38, Morris, Ill. BL/TR, 5'10", 170 lbs. Deb: 9/22/12

1912	Chi-A	1	1	0	0	0	0	0	0	0		.000	.000	.000	-99	-0	0			.000	0	H	0.0
1914	Chi-A	8	28	0	6	0	0	0	0	3	6	.214	.290	.214	53	-2	1	1	-0	.875	-1	/O-7	-0.4
Total	2	9	29	0	6	0	0	0	0	3	6	.207	.281	.207	47	-2	1	1		.875	-1	/O-7	-0.4

■ ABE WOLSTENHOLME Wolstenholme, Abraham Lincoln b: 3/4/1861, Philadelphia, Pa. d: 3/4/16, Philadelphia, Pa. Deb: 6/4/1883

| 1883 | Phi-N | 3 | 11 | 0 | 1 | 1 | 0 | 0 | 0 | 0 | | .091 | .091 | .182 | -22 | -2 | | | | .727 | -3 | /C-2,O-1 | -0.4 |

■ HARRY WOLTER Wolter, Harry Meigs b: 7/11/1884, Monterey, Cal. d: 7/7/70, Palo Alto, Cal. BL/TL, 5'10", 175 lbs. Deb: 5/14/07

1907	Cin-N	4	15	1	2	0	0	0	1	0		.133	.133	.133	-16	-2	0			1.000	-0	/O-4	-0.3
	Pit-N	1	1	0	0	0	0	0	0	0		.000	.000	.000	-99	-0	0			.000	-0	/P-1	0.0
	StL-N	16	47	4	16	0	0	0	6	3		.340	.380	.340	130	2	1			.962	3	O-12/P-3	0.5
	Yr	21	63	5	18	0	0	0	7	3		.286	.318	.286	91	-1	1			.969	3	O-16/P-4	0.2
1909	Bos-A	54	122	14	30	2	4	2	10	9		.246	.298	.377	110	1	2			.978	-1	1-17,P-11/O	0.1
1910	NY-A	135	479	84	128	15	9	4	42	66		.267	.364	.361	120	13	39			.940	-3	*O-129/1-2	0.4
1911	NY-A	122	434	78	132	17	15	4	36	62		.304	.396	.440	125	15	28			.951	4	*O-113/1-2	1.3
1912	NY-A	12	32	8	11	2	1	0	1	10		.344	.512	.469	171	2	4			.923	-1	/O-9	0.2
1913	NY-A	127	425	53	108	18	6	2	43	80	50	.254	.377	.339	109	9	13			.946	-7	*O-121	-0.4
1917	Chi-N	117	353	44	88	15	7	0	28	38	40	.249	.324	.331	94	-2	7			.942	-4	O-97/1-1	-1.2
Total	7	588	1908	286	515	69	42	12	167	268	90	.270	.365	.369	114	39	95			.941	-10	O-494/1-22,P	0.6

■ HARRY WOLVERTON Wolverton, Harry Sterling "Fighting Harry" b: 12/6/1873, Mt. Vernon, Ohio d: 2/4/37, Oakland, Cal. BL/TR, 5'11", 205 lbs. Deb: 9/25/1898 M

1898	Chi-N	13	49	4	16	1	0	0	7	3		.327	.353	.347	101	0	1			.848	3	3-13	0.3
1899	Chi-N	99	389	50	111	14	11	1	49	30		.285	.350	.386	105	2	14			.860	-6	3-98/S-1	-0.2
1900	Chi-N	3	11	2	2	0	0	0	0	2		.182	.308	.182	38	-1	1			.875	-2	/3-3	-0.2
	Phi-N	101	383	42	108	10	8	3	58	20		.282	.323	.373	92	-5	4			.881	-9	*3-101	-1.3
	Yr	104	394	44	110	10	8	3	58	22		.279	.322	.368	91	-6	5			.881	-11	3-104	-1.5
1901	Phi-N	93	379	42	117	15	4	0	43	22		.309	.356	.369	108	4	13			.921	3	3-93	0.8
1902	Was-A	59	249	35	62	8	3	1	23	13		.249	.292	.317	68	-11	8			.904	3	3-59	-0.7
	Phi-N	34	136	12	40	3	2	0	16	9		.294	.347	.346	114	2	3			.931	9	3-34	1.2
1903	Phi-N	123	494	72	152	13	12	0	53	18		.308	.342	.383	110	5	10			.941	1	*3-123	0.7
1904	Phi-N	102	398	43	106	15	5	0	49	26		.266	.321	.329	105	-2	18			.925	1	*3-102	0.7
1905	Bos-N	122	463	38	104	15	7	2	55	23		.225	.276	.300	73	-16	10			.934	4	*3-122	0.4
1912	NY-A	34	50	6	15	1	1	0	4	2		.300	.340	.360	94	-0	1			.821	-1	/3-8,M	-0.1
Total	9	783	3001	346	833	95	53	7	352	166		.278	.326	.352	96	-17	83			.909	6	3-756/S-1	0.4

■ TONY WOMACK Womack, Anthony Darrell b: 9/25/69, Chatham, Va. BL/TR, 5'9", 160 lbs. Deb: 9/10/93

1993	Pit-N	15	24	5	2	0	0	0	0	3	3	.083	.185	.083	-25	-4	2	0	1	.971	5	/S-6	0.2
1994	Pit-N	5	12	4	4	0	0	0	1	2	3	.333	.429	.333	103	0	0	0	0	.750	-3	/2-3,S-2	-0.3
Total	2	20	36	9	6	0	0	0	1	5	6	.167	.268	.167	19	-4	2	0	1	.973	2	/S-8,2-3	-0.1

■ SID WOMACK Womack, Sidney Kirk "Tex" b: 10/2/1896, Greensburg, La. d: 8/28/58, Jackson, Miss. BR/TR, 5'10.5", 185 lbs. Deb: 8/15/26

| 1926 | Bos-N | 1 | 3 | 0 | 0 | 0 | 0 | 0 | 1 | 0 | | .000 | .000 | .000 | -99 | -1 | 0 | | | 1.000 | 0 | /C-1 | -0.1 |

■ WOOD Wood Deb: 9/30/1874

| 1874 | Bal-n | 1 | 6 | 0 | 0 | 0 | 0 | 0 | 0 | 0 | | .000 | .000 | .000 | -99 | -1 | | | | | | /2-1 | -0.1 |

■ DOC WOOD Wood, Charles Spencer b: 2/28/1900, Batesville, Miss. d: 11/3/74, New Orleans, La. BR/TR, 5'10", 150 lbs. Deb: 7/21/23

| 1923 | Phi-A | 3 | 3 | 0 | 1 | 0 | 0 | 0 | 0 | 0 | | .333 | .333 | .333 | 75 | -0 | 0 | 0 | 0 | .833 | 1 | /S-3 | 0.1 |

■ TED WOOD Wood, Edward Robert b: 1/4/67, Mansfield, Ohio BL/TL, 6'2", 178 lbs. Deb: 9/4/91

1991	SF-N	10	25	0	3	0	0	0	1	2	11	.120	.185	.120	-13	-4	0	0	0	.909	-1	/O-8	-0.6
1992	SF-N	24	58	5	12	2	0	1	3	6	15	.207	.292	.293	70	-2	0	0	0	.972	1	O-16	-0.2
1993	Mon-N	13	26	4	5	1	0	0	3	3	3	.192	.276	.231	36	-2	0	0	0	1.000	-1	/O-8	-0.3
Total	3	47	109	9	20	3	0	1	7	11	29	.183	.264	.239	42	-8	0	0	0	.968	-1	/O-32	-1.1

■ FRED WOOD Wood, Fred S. b: 1863, Hamilton, Ont., Canada d: 8/23/33, New York, N.Y. 5'5", 150 lbs. Deb: 5/14/1884 F

1884	Det-N	12	42	4	2	0	0	0	1	3	18	.048	.111	.048	-51	-7				.889	-1	/C-7,O-6,S	-0.7
1885	Buf-N	1	4	0	1	0	0	0	0	0		.250	.250	.250	60	-0				.833	-0	/C-1	0.0
Total	2	13	46	4	3	0	0	0	1	3	18	.065	.122	.065	-41	-7				.883	-1	/C-8,O-6,S	-0.7

■ GEORGE WOOD Wood, George A. "Dandy" b: 11/9/1858, Boston, Mass. d: 4/4/24, Harrisburg, Pa. BL/TR, 5'10.5", 175 lbs. Deb: 5/1/1880 MU

1880	Wor-N	81	327	37	80	16	5	2	28	10	37	.245	.267	.324	91	-4				.887	-7	*O-80/3-2,1	-1.3
1881	Det-N	80	337	54	100	18	9	2	32	19	32	.297	.334	.421	131	11				.862	-2	*O-80	0.7
1882	Det-N	84	375	69	101	12	12	7	29	14	30	.269	.296	.421	127	11				.884	2	*O-84	1.2
1883	Det-N	99	441	81	133	26	11	5	47	25	37	.302	.339	.444	142	23				.876	9	*O-99/P-1	2.6
1884	Det-N	114	473	79	119	16	10	8	29	39	75	.252	.309	.378	122	13				.896	3	*O-114/3-1	1.3
1885	Det-N	82	362	62	105	19	8	5	28	13	19	.290	.315	.428	138	14				.885	0	O-70,3-12/SP	1.2
1886	Phi-N	106	450	81	123	18	15	4	50	23	75	.273	.309	.407	115	7	9			.904	-5	*O-97/S-6,3	0.0
1887	Phi-N	113	491	118	142	22	19	14	66	40	51	.289	.350	.497	125	14	19			.873	-10	*O-104/S-3,32	0.3
1888	Phi-N	106	433	67	99	19	6	5	51	39	44	.229	.303	.342	100	0	20			.905	0	*O-104/3-2,P	-0.3
1889	Phi-N	97	422	77	106	21	4	5	53	53	33	.251	.336	.355	86	-9	17			.915	-4	O-92/S-6,P	-1.3
	Bal-a	3	10	1	2	0	0	0	1	0	2	.200	.200	.200	14	-1	1			1.000	0	/O-3	-0.1
1890	Phi-P	132	539	115	156	20	14	9	102	51	35	.289	.360	.429	108	4	20			.895	14	*O-132/3-1	1.1
1891	Phi-a	132	528	105	163	18	14	3	61	72	52	.309	.399	.413	128	20	22			.939	7	*O-122/3-6,SM	2.1
1892	Bal-N	21	76	9	17	1	1	0	10	10	8	.224	.330	.263	78	-2	1			.911	2	O-21	0.0
	Cin-N	30	107	10	21	2	4	0	14	10	17	.196	.271	.290	71	-4	4			.863	-2	O-30	-0.6
	Yr	51	183	19	38	3	5	0	24	20	25	.208	.296	.279	74	-6	5			.885	1	O-51	-0.6
Total	13	1280	5371	965	1467	228	132	68	601	418	547	.273	.329	.403	116	98	113			.895	10	*O-1232/3-30,SP21	6.9

■ HARRY WOOD Wood, Harold Austin b: 2/10/1881, Waterville, Maine d: 5/18/55, Bethesda, Md. BL/TR, 5'10", 155 lbs. Deb: 4/19/03

| 1903 | Cin-N | 2 | 3 | 0 | 0 | 0 | 0 | 0 | 0 | 1 | | .000 | .250 | .000 | -24 | -0 | 0 | | | .000 | -1 | /O-2 | -0.1 |

■ JAKE WOOD Wood, Jacob b: 6/22/37, Elizabeth, N.J. BR/TR, 6'1", 170 lbs. Deb: 4/11/61

1961	Det-A	162	663	96	171	17	14	11	69	58	141	.258	.321	.376	83	-16	30	9	4	.969	-27	*2-162	-2.1
1962	Det-A	111	367	68	83	10	5	8	30	33	59	.226	.292	.346	68	-17	24	3	5	.950	-31	2-90	-3.3
1963	Det-A	85	351	50	95	11	2	11	27	24	61	.271	.330	.407	102	1	18	5	3	.958	-11	2-81/3-1	-1.0
1964	Det-A	64	125	11	29	2	1	1	7	4	24	.232	.256	.304	54	-8	9	1	2	.989	-1	1-11,2-10/3O	-1.0
1965	Det-A	58	104	12	30	3	0	2	7	10	19	.288	.357	.375	107	1	3	3	-1	.977	-2	2-20/1-1,S3	0.0
1966	Det-A	98	230	39	58	9	3	2	27	28	48	.252	.336	.343	94	-1	9	4	-1	.968	-13	2-52/3-4,1	-1.2
1967	Det-A	14	20	2	1	1	0	0	0	0	7	.050	.095	.100	-41	-3	1	0	0	1.000	-0	/1-2,2-2	-0.4
	Cin-N	16	17	1	2	1	0	0	1	2	3	.118	.167	.118	-15	-3	1	1	0	1.000	0	/O-2	-0.3
Total	7	608	1877	279	469	53	26	35	168	159	362	.250	.313	.362	82	-46	79	23	10	.963	-85	2-417/1-16,3OS	-8.3

YEAR	TM/L	G	AB	R	H	2B	3B	HR	RBI	BB	SO	AVG	OBP	SLG	PRO+	BR/A	SB	CS	SBR	FA	FR	G/POS	TPR

■ JIMMY WOOD   Wood, James Leon b: 12/1/1844, Brooklyn, N.Y. d: 11/30/1886, TR, 5'8.5", 150 lbs. Deb: 5/8/1871 M

1871	Chi-n	28	135	45	51	10	6	1	29	11	3	.378	.425	.563	163	9	18					*2-28,M	0.4
1872	Tro-n	25	116	40	38	9	3	2	27	2	1	.328	.339	.509	155	7						2-25,M	0.4
	Eck-n	7	30	10	6	1	1	0	0	4	1	.200	.294	.300	98	1						2-7,M	0.0
	Yr	32	146	50	44	10	4	2	27	6	2	.301	.329	.466	145	8						2-32	0.4
1873	Phi-n	42	209	67	67	11	1	0	27	8	1	.321	.346	.383	110	2						*2-42,M	-0.1
Total	3 n	102	490	162	162	31	11	3	83	25	6	.331	.363	.457	136	19						2-102	0.7

■ JOE WOOD   Wood, Joe "Smokey Joe" (b: Howard Ellsworth Wood) b: 10/25/1889, Kansas City, Mo. d: 7/27/85, West Haven, Conn BR/TR, 5'11", 180 lbs. Deb: 8/24/08 F

1908	Bos-A	6	7	1	0	0	0	0				.000	.000	.000	-97	-1	0			.889	-0	/P-6	0.0
1909	Bos-A	24	55	4	9	0	1	0	3	2		.164	.207	.200	28	-5	0			.971	-4	P-24	0.0
1910	Bos-A	35	69	9	18	2	1	1	5	5		.261	.311	.362	108	0	0			.975	2	P-35	0.0
1911	Bos-A	44	88	15	23	4	2	2	11	10		.261	.343	.420	114	1	1			.947	2	P-44	0.0
1912	*Bos-A	43	124	16	36	13	1	1	13	11		.290	.348	.435	118	2	0			.974	8	P-43	0.0
1913	Bos-A	24	56	10	15	5	0	0	10	4	7	.268	.317	.357	95	-1	1			.955	4	P-23	0.0
1914	Bos-A	21	43	2	6	1	0	0	1	3	14	.140	.213	.163	13	-5	0			1.000	1	P-18	0.0
1915	Bos-A	29	54	6	14	1	1	1	7	5	10	.259	.322	.370	111	0	1	1	-0	.982	1	P-25	0.0
1917	Cle-A	10	6	1	0	0	0	0	0	0		.000	.000	.000	-93	-1	0			1.000	0	/P-5	0.0
1918	Cle-A	119	422	41	125	22	4	5	66	36	38	.296	.356	.403	118	8	8			.962	0	O-95,2-19/1	0.5
1919	Cle-A	72	192	30	49	10	6	0	27	32	21	.255	.367	.370	101	1	3			.932	-8	O-64/P-1	-1.1
1920	*Cle-A	61	137	25	37	11	2	1	30	25	16	.270	.390	.401	107	2	1	1	-0	.987	-6	O-55/P-1	-0.7
1921	Cle-A	66	194	32	71	16	5	4	60	25	17	.366	.438	.562	151	15	2	0	1	.973	-13	O-64	-0.1
1922	Cle-A	142	505	74	150	33	8	8	92	50	63	.297	.367	.442	109	7	5	1	1	.960	2	*O-141	0.0
Total	14	696	1952	266	553	118	31	23	325	208	189	.283	.357	.411	110	25	23	3		.962	-11	O-419,P-225/21	-1.4

■ JOE WOOD   Wood, Joseph Perry "J.P." or "Little Joe" b: 10/3/19, Houston, Tex. d: 3/25/85, Houston, Tex. BR/TR, 5'9.5", 160 lbs. Deb: 5/2/43

1943	Det-A	60	164	22	53	4	4	1	17	6	13	.323	.347	.415	114	2	2	2	-1	.896	-16	2-22,3-18	-1.4

■ KEN WOOD   Wood, Kenneth Lanier b: 7/1/24, Lincolnton, N.C. BR/TR, 6', 200 lbs. Deb: 4/28/48

1948	StL-A	10	24	2	2	0	1	0	2	1	4	.083	.120	.167	-24	-4	0	0	0	1.000	1	/O-5	-0.4
1949	StL-A	7	6	0	0	0	0	0	0	1	2	.000	.143	.000	-58	-1	0	0	0	.000	-1	/O-3	-0.3
1950	StL-A	128	369	42	83	24	0	13	62	38	58	.225	.299	.396	74	-17	0	4	-2	.952	-2	O-94	-2.3
1951	StL-A	109	333	40	79	19	0	15	44	27	49	.237	.296	.429	92	-6	1	2	-1	.959	-4	*O-100	-1.4
1952	Bos-A	15	20	0	2	0	0	0	0	3	4	.100	.217	.100	-9	-3	0	0	0	.889	-4	O-13	-0.7
	Was-A	61	210	26	50	8	6	6	32	30	21	.238	.333	.419	112	-1	0	1	-1	.954	9	O-56	0.9
	Yr	76	230	26	52	8	6	6	32	33	25	.226	.323	.391	99	-1	0	1	-1	.951	5	O-69	0.2
1953	Was-A	12	33	0	7	1	0	0	3	2	3	.212	.257	.242	36	-3	0	0	0	1.000	1	/O-7	-0.3
Total	6	342	995	110	223	52	7	34	143	102	141	.224	.298	.393	81	-31	1	7	-4	.956	-1	O-278	-4.5

■ BOB WOOD   Wood, Robert Lynn b: 7/28/1865, Thorn Hill, Ohio d: 5/22/43, Churchill, Ohio BR/TR, 5'8.5", 153 lbs. Deb: 5/2/1898

1898	Cin-N	39	109	14	30	6	0	0	16	9		.275	.331	.330	84	-2	1			.943	1	C-29/O-1,1	0.1
1899	Cin-N	62	194	34	61	11	7	0	24	25		.314	.406	.443	131	9	3			.937	-10	C-53/O-2,31	0.3
1900	Cin-N	45	139	17	37	8	1	0	22	10		.266	.320	.338	84	-3	3			.967	-6	C-18,3-15/O	-0.7
1901	Cle-A	98	346	45	101	23	3	1	49	12		.292	.327	.384	101	-0	6			.952	-1	C-84/3-4,012S	0.7
1902	Cle-A	81	258	23	76	18	2	0	40	27		.295	.375	.380	114	6	1			.940	-8	C-52,1-16/O23	0.4
1904	Det-A	49	175	15	43	6	2	1	17	5		.246	.271	.320	89	-3	1			.974	10	C-47	1.3
1905	Det-A	8	24	1	2	1	0	0	0	1		.083	.120	.125	-22	-3	0			.886	-0	/C-7	-0.3
Total	7	382	1245	149	350	73	15	2	168	89		.281	.339	.369	102	3	15			.951	-14	C-290/3-22,102S	1.8

■ ROY WOOD   Wood, Roy Winton "Woody" b: 8/29/1892, Monticello, Ark. d: 4/6/74, Fayetteville, Ark. BR/TR, 6', 175 lbs. Deb: 6/16/13

1913	Pit-N	14	35	4	10	4	0	0	2	1	8	.286	.306	.400	105	0	0			.895	-1	/O-8,1-1	0.1
1914	Cle-A	72	220	24	52	6	3	1	15	13	26	.236	.300	.305	79	-6	6	9	-4	.946	-1	O-40,1-20	-1.3
1915	Cle-A	33	78	5	15	2	1	0	3	2	13	.192	.232	.244	41	-6	1	2	-1	.990	-2	1-21/O-2	-0.9
Total	3	119	333	33	77	12	4	1	20	16	47	.231	.285	.300	73	-12	7	11		.936	-4	/O-50,1-42	-2.1

■ LARRY WOODALL   Woodall, Charles Lawrence b: 7/26/1894, Staunton, Va. d: 5/16/63, Cambridge, Mass. BR/TR, 5'9", 165 lbs. Deb: 5/20/20 C

1920	Det-A	18	49	4	12	1	0	0	5	2	6	.245	.275	.265	45	-4	1	0	0	.988	2	C-15	-0.1
1921	Det-A	46	80	10	29	4	1	0	14	6	7	.363	.407	.438	117	2	1	0	0	.966	-7	C-25	-0.4
1922	Det-A	50	125	19	43	2	2	0	18	8	11	.344	.388	.392	107	2	0	1	-1	.977	-10	C-40	-0.7
1923	Det-A	71	148	20	41	12	2	1	19	22	9	.277	.371	.405	106	2	2	1	0	.983	-5	C-60	-0.1
1924	Det-A	67	165	23	51	9	2	0	25	21	5	.309	.387	.388	102	1	0	0	0	.986	0	C-62	0.4
1925	Det-A	75	171	20	35	4	1	0	13	24	8	.205	.303	.240	39	-15	0	0	0	.967	-7	C-75	-1.8
1926	Det-A	67	146	18	34	5	0	0	15	15	2	.233	.304	.267	49	-11	0	0	0	.979	-4	C-59	-1.1
1927	Det-A	88	246	28	69	8	6	0	39	37	9	.280	.375	.362	90	-2	9	1	2	**.997**	4	C-86	0.8
1928	Det-A	65	186	19	39	7	1	0	13	24	10	.210	.300	.258	47	-14	3	1	0	.992	4	C-62	-0.4
1929	Det-A	1	1	0	0	0	0	0	0	0	0	.000	.000	.000	-99	-0	0	0	0	.000	0	H	0.0
Total	10	548	1317	161	353	52	15	1	161	159	67	.268	.347	.333	77	-40	16	4	2	.984	-22	C-484	-3.4

■ DARRELL WOODARD   Woodard, Darrell Lee b: 12/10/56, Wilmar, Ark. BR/TR, 5'11", 160 lbs. Deb: 8/6/78

1978	Oak-A	33	9	10	0	0	0	0	0	1	1	.000	.100	.000	-73	-2	3	4	-2	.964	9	2-14/3-1,D	0.5

■ MIKE WOODARD   Woodard, Michael Cary b: 3/2/60, Melrose Park, Ill. BL/TR, 5'9", 155 lbs. Deb: 9/11/85

1985	SF-N	24	82	12	20	1	0	0	9	5	3	.244	.287	.256	56	-5	6	1	1	.990	-5	2-23	-0.9
1986	SF-N	48	79	14	20	2	1	1	5	10	9	.253	.337	.342	92	-1	7	2	1	.986	-2	2-23/S-2,3	-0.1
1987	SF-N	10	19	0	4	1	0	0	1	0	1	.211	.211	.263	26	-2	0	0	0	1.000	2	/2-8	0.0
1988	Chi-A	18	45	3	6	0	1	0	4	1	5	.133	.170	.178	-2	-6	1	1	-0	.975	4	2-14/D-2	-0.2
Total	4	100	225	29	50	4	2	1	19	16	18	.222	.277	.271	55	-14	14	4	1	.985	-1	/2-68,D-2,3S	-1.2

■ RED WOODHEAD   Woodhead, James b: 7/9/1851, Chelsea, Mass. d: 9/7/1881, Boston, Mass. 5'6", 160 lbs. Deb: 4/15/1873

1873	Mar-n	1	5	1	0	0	0	0	0	0	0	.000	.000	.000	-99	-1						/S-1	-0.1
1879	Syr-N	34	131	4	21	1	0	0	2	0	23	.160	.160	.168	9	-12				.792	-7	3-34	-1.7

■ GENE WOODLING   Woodling, Eugene Richard b: 8/16/22, Akron, Ohio BL/TR, 5'9.5", 195 lbs. Deb: 9/23/43 C

1943	Cle-A	8	25	5	8	2	1	0	6	2	1	.320	.346	.600	186	2	0	0	0	1.000	-1	/O-6	0.2
1946	Cle-A	61	133	8	25	1	4	0	9	16	13	.188	.280	.256	54	-8	1	2	-1	1.000	-3	O-37	-1.4
1947	Pit-N	22	79	7	21	2	0	0	10	7	5	.266	.326	.342	75	-3	0			.968	3	O-21	-0.2
1949	*NY-A	112	296	60	80	13	7	5	44	52	21	.270	.381	.412	110	5	2	2	-1	.982	-10	O-98	-1.0
1950	*NY-A	122	449	81	127	20	10	6	60	70	31	.283	.381	.412	106	5	5	3	-0	.993	10	*O-116	1.0
1951	*NY-A	120	420	65	118	15	8	15	71	62	37	.281	.373	.462	130	17	0	4	-3	.993	1	*O-116	1.1
1952	*NY-A	122	408	58	116	12	12	6	63	59	31	.309	.397	.473	151	28	1	4	-3	**.996**	6	*O-118	2.8
1953	*NY-A	125	395	64	121	26	4	10	58	82	29	.306	**.429**	.468	147	30	2	7	-4	**.996**	4	*O-119	2.6
1954	NY-A	97	304	40	76	12	5	3	40	53	24	.250	.361	.352	99	3	3	4	-2	.983	-1	O-89	-0.5
1955	Bal-A	47	145	22	32	6	3	2	18	24	18	.221	.335	.352	91	-2	1	1	-0	1.000	-8	O-44	-1.2
	Cle-A	79	259	33	72	15	5	6	35	36	15	.278	.372	.402	104	3	2	4	-2	.993	-3	O-70	-0.5
	Yr	126	404	55	104	21	3	8	53	60	33	.257	.359	.384	100	1	3	5	-2	.995	-11	*O-114	-1.7

YEAR	TM/L	G	AB	R	H	2B	3B	HR	RBI	BB	SO	AVG	OBP	SLG	PRO+	BR/A	SB	CS	SBR	FA	FR	G/POS	TPR
1956	Cle-A	100	317	56	83	17	0	8	38	69	29	.262	.398	.391	107	6	2	6	-3	.981	-0	O-85	-0.2
1957	Cle-A	133	430	74	138	25	2	19	78	64	35	.321	.412	.521	155	34	0	5	-3	.992	11	*O-113	3.5
1958	Bal-A	133	413	57	114	16	1	15	65	66	49	.276	.378	.429	128	18	4	2	0	.974	-10	*O-116	0.1
1959	Bal-A★	140	440	63	132	22	2	14	77	78	35	.300	.405	.455	139	26	1	1	-0	.981	-13	*O-124	0.8
1960	Bal-A	140	435	68	123	18	3	11	62	84	40	.283	.403	.414	123	18	3	0	1	.995	-3	*O-124	1.0
1961	Was-A	110	342	39	107	16	4	10	57	50	24	.313	.404	.471	135	18	1	0	0	.988	-3	O-90	1.1
1962	Was-A	44	107	19	30	4	0	5	16	24	5	.280	.421	.458	138	7	1	0	0	.953	-4	O-30	0.1
	NY-N	81	190	18	52	8	1	5	24	24	22	.274	.358	.405	103	1	0	0	0	.986	-4	O-48	-0.5
Total	17	1796	5587	830	1585	257	63	147	830	921	479	.284	.388	.431	123	206	29	45		.989	-29	*O-1566	8.8

■ SAM WOODRUFF
Woodruff, Orville Francis   b: 12/27/1876, Chilo, Ohio   d: 7/22/37, Cincinnati, Ohio   BR/TR, 5'9", 160 lbs.   Deb: 4/14/04

YEAR	TM/L	G	AB	R	H	2B	3B	HR	RBI	BB	SO	AVG	OBP	SLG	PRO+	BR/A	SB	CS	SBR	FA	FR	G/POS	TPR
1904	Cin-N	87	306	20	58	14	3	0	20	19		.190	.244	.255	50	-19	9			.932	-4	3-61,2-17/SO	-2.1
1910	Cin-N	21	61	6	9	1	0	0	2	7	8	.148	.235	.164	18	-6	2			.933	-1	3-17/2-4	-0.7
Total	2	108	367	26	67	15	3	0	22	26	8	.183	.242	.240	45	-25	11			.932	-5	/3-78,2-21,SO	-2.8

■ PETE WOODRUFF
Woodruff, Peter Frank   b: 6/1873, New York   BR/TR,   Deb: 9/19/1899

YEAR	TM/L	G	AB	R	H	2B	3B	HR	RBI	BB	SO	AVG	OBP	SLG	PRO+	BR/A	SB	CS	SBR	FA	FR	G/POS	TPR
1899	NY-N	20	61	11	15	1	1	2	7	9		.246	.343	.393	105	0	3			1.000	-1	O-19/1-1	-0.2

■ AL WOODS
Woods, Alvis   b: 8/8/53, Oakland, Cal.   BL/TL, 6'3", 195 lbs.   Deb: 4/7/77

YEAR	TM/L	G	AB	R	H	2B	3B	HR	RBI	BB	SO	AVG	OBP	SLG	PRO+	BR/A	SB	CS	SBR	FA	FR	G/POS	TPR
1977	Tor-A	122	440	58	125	17	4	6	35	36	38	.284	.338	.382	94	-3	8	7	-2	.969	-2	*O-115/D-4	-1.2
1978	Tor-A	62	220	19	53	12	3	3	25	11	23	.241	.280	.364	78	-7	1	2	-1	.978	3	O-60	-0.7
1979	Tor-A	132	436	57	121	24	4	5	36	40	28	.278	.340	.385	94	-3	6	4	-1	.967	3	*O-127	-0.5
1980	Tor-A	109	373	54	112	18	2	15	47	37	35	.300	.365	.480	124	12	4	4	-1	.991	6	O-88,D-13	1.3
1981	Tor-A	85	288	20	71	15	0	1	21	19	31	.247	.293	.309	69	-11	3	4	-2	.973	-7	O-77/D-2	-1.4
1982	Tor-A	85	201	20	47	11	1	3	24	21	20	.234	.306	.343	71	-8	1	3	-2	.970	-7	O-64,D-10	-1.8
1986	Min-A	23	28	5	9	1	0	2	8	3	5	.321	.387	.571	153	2	0	0	0	.000	0	/D-7	0.2
Total	7	618	1986	233	538	98	14	35	196	167	180	.271	.328	.387	93	-19	23	24	-8	.974	6	O-531/D-36	-4.1

■ GARY WOODS
Woods, Gary Lee   b: 7/20/54, Santa Barbara, Cal   BR/TR, 6'2", 190 lbs.   Deb: 9/14/76

YEAR	TM/L	G	AB	R	H	2B	3B	HR	RBI	BB	SO	AVG	OBP	SLG	PRO+	BR/A	SB	CS	SBR	FA	FR	G/POS	TPR
1976	Oak-A	6	8	0	1	0	0	0	0	0	3	.125	.125	.125	-28	-1	0	0	0	1.000	-1	/O-4,D-1	-0.2
1977	Tor-A	60	227	21	49	9	1	0	17	7	38	.216	.246	.264	38	-19	5	4	-1	.994	3	O-60	-2.0
1978	Tor-A	8	19	1	3	1	0	0	0	1	1	.158	.200	.211	15	-2	1	0	0	1.000	-0	/O-6	-0.2
1980	*Hou-N	19	53	8	20	5	0	2	15	2	9	.377	.400	.585	186	6	1	0	0	1.000	2	O-14	0.4
1981	*Hou-N	54	110	10	23	4	1	0	12	11	22	.209	.281	.264	58	-6	2	1	0	.984	-3	O-40	-1.0
1982	Chi-N	117	245	28	66	15	1	4	30	21	48	.269	.327	.388	97	-1	3	3	-1	1.000	-14	*O-103	-1.9
1983	Chi-N	93	190	25	46	9	0	4	22	15	27	.242	.298	.353	76	-6	5	3	-0	.971	-11	O-73/2-1	-2.0
1984	*Chi-N	87	98	13	23	4	1	3	10	15	21	.235	.336	.388	94	-1	2	1	0	1.000	-13	O-62/2-3	-1.5
1985	Chi-N	81	82	11	20	3	0	0	4	14	18	.244	.354	.280	72	-3	0	1	-1	1.000	-13	O-56	-1.8
Total	9	525	1032	117	251	50	4	13	110	86	187	.243	.303	.337	76	-34	19	13	-2	.992	-54	O-418/2-4,D	-10.2

■ JIM WOODS
Woods, James Jerome "Woody"   b: 9/17/39, Chicago, Ill.   BR/TR, 6', 175 lbs.   Deb: 9/27/57

YEAR	TM/L	G	AB	R	H	2B	3B	HR	RBI	BB	SO	AVG	OBP	SLG	PRO+	BR/A	SB	CS	SBR	FA	FR	G/POS	TPR
1957	Chi-N	2	0	1	0	0	0	0	0	0	0	—	—	—		0	0	0	0	.000	0	R	0.0
1960	Phi-N	11	34	4	6	0	0	1	3	3	13	.176	.243	.265	39	-3	0	0	0	.939	2	3-11	-0.1
1961	Phi-N	23	48	6	11	3	0	2	9	4	15	.229	.302	.417	89	-1	0	0	0	.968	-1	3-15	-0.1
Total	3	36	82	11	17	3	0	3	12	7	28	.207	.278	.354	69	-4	0	0	0	.953	1	/3-26	-0.2

■ RON WOODS
Woods, Ronald Lawrence   b: 2/1/43, Hamilton, Ohio   BR/TR, 5'10", 173 lbs.   Deb: 4/22/69

YEAR	TM/L	G	AB	R	H	2B	3B	HR	RBI	BB	SO	AVG	OBP	SLG	PRO+	BR/A	SB	CS	SBR	FA	FR	G/POS	TPR
1969	Det-A	17	15	3	4	0	0	1	3	2	3	.267	.353	.467	122	0	0	0	0	1.000	-2	/O-7	-0.2
	NY-A	72	171	18	30	5	2	1	7	22	29	.175	.273	.246	48	-12	2	0	1	1.000	-3	O-67	-1.8
	Yr	89	186	21	34	5	2	2	10	24	32	.183	.280	.263	54	-11	2	0	1	1.000	-5	O-74	-2.0
1970	NY-A	95	225	30	51	5	3	8	27	33	35	.227	.326	.382	100	-0	4	2	0	.974	-6	O-78	-1.0
1971	NY-A	25	32	4	8	1	0	1	2	4	2	.250	.333	.375	107	0	0	0	0	.929	-1	/O-9	-0.1
	Mon-N	51	138	26	41	7	3	1	17	19	18	.297	.382	.413	125	5	0	2	-1	.989	-1	O-45	0.1
1972	Mon-N	97	221	21	57	5	1	10	31	22	33	.258	.325	.425	110	2	3	3	-1	.991	-11	O-73	-1.3
1973	Mon-N	135	318	45	73	11	3	3	31	56	44	.230	.345	.311	80	-7	12	6	0	.977	-9	*O-114	-2.0
1974	Mon-N	90	127	15	26	0	0	1	12	17	17	.205	.303	.228	48	-8	6	5	-1	.987	-12	O-61	-2.4
Total	6	582	1247	162	290	34	12	26	130	175	171	.233	.328	.342	87	-19	27	18	-3	.984	-45	O-454	-8.7

■ TRACY WOODSON
Woodson, Tracy Michael   b: 10/5/62, Richmond, Va.   BR/TR, 6'3", 215 lbs.   Deb: 4/7/87

YEAR	TM/L	G	AB	R	H	2B	3B	HR	RBI	BB	SO	AVG	OBP	SLG	PRO+	BR/A	SB	CS	SBR	FA	FR	G/POS	TPR
1987	LA-N	53	136	14	31	8	1	1	11	9	21	.228	.286	.324	63	-7	1	1	-0	.958	-1	3-45/1-7	-1.0
1988	*LA-N	65	173	15	43	4	1	3	15	7	32	.249	.282	.335	79	-5	1	2	-1	.938	-5	3-41,1-25	-1.3
1989	LA-N	4	6	0	0	0	0	0	0	0	1	.000	.000	.000	-99	-2	0	0	0	1.000	0	/3-1	-0.2
1992	StL-N	31	114	9	35	8	0	1	22	3	10	.307	.331	.404	110	1	0	0	0	.945	-6	3-26/1-3	-0.6
1993	StL-N	62	77	4	16	2	0	0	2	1	14	.208	.218	.234	21	-9	1	0	0	.909	2	3-28,1-11	-0.7
Total	5	215	506	42	125	22	2	5	50	20	78	.247	.281	.328	70	-22	2	3	-1	.943	-10	3-141/1-46	-3.8

■ WOODY WOODWARD
Woodward, William Frederick   b: 9/23/42, Miami, Fla.   BR/TR, 6'2", 185 lbs.   Deb: 9/9/63

YEAR	TM/L	G	AB	R	H	2B	3B	HR	RBI	BB	SO	AVG	OBP	SLG	PRO+	BR/A	SB	CS	SBR	FA	FR	G/POS	TPR
1963	Mil-N	10	2	1	0	0	0	0	0	0	0	.000	.000	.000	-99	-1	0	0	0	1.000	3	/S-5	0.2
1964	Mil-N	77	115	18	24	2	1	0	11	6	28	.209	.260	.243	43	-9	0	1	-1	.958	13	2-40,S-18/31	0.6
1965	Mil-N	112	265	17	55	7	4	0	11	10	50	.208	.236	.264	41	-21	2	2	-1	.977	11	*S-107/2-8	-0.6
1966	Atl-N	144	455	46	120	23	3	0	43	37	54	.264	.325	.327	81	-11	2	4	-1	.973	-6	2-79,S-73	-0.7
1967	Atl-N	136	429	30	97	15	2	0	25	37	51	.226	.289	.270	62	-21	0	6	-4	.982	9	*2-120,S-16	-0.7
1968	Atl-N	12	24	2	4	1	0	0	3	1	6	.167	.200	.208	23	-2	0	0	0	.973	3	/S-6,3-2,2	0.2
	Cin-N	56	119	13	29	2	0	0	10	7	23	.244	.297	.261	64	-5	2	0	0	.968	-3	S-41/2-9,1	-0.5
	Yr	68	143	15	33	3	0	0	11	8	29	.231	.281	.252	58	-7	2	0	1	.969	-1	S-47,2-10/31	-0.3
1969	Cin-N	97	241	36	63	12	0	0	15	24	40	.261	.333	.311	77	-7	3	2	-0	.966	-2	S-93/2-2	0.0
1970	*Cin-N	100	264	23	59	8	3	1	14	20	21	.223	.283	.288	53	-17	2	1	-1	.973	2	S-77,3-20,2/1	-0.8
1971	Cin-N	136	273	22	66	9	1	0	18	27	28	.242	.310	.282	70	-10	2	2	0	.987	-5	S-85,3-63/2	-0.6
Total	9	880	2187	208	517	79	14	1	148	169	301	.236	.295	.287	64	-103	14	15	-5	.974	23	S-521,2-278/31	-2.9

■ JUNIOR WOOTEN
Wooten, Earl Hazwell   b: 1/16/24, Pelzer, S.C.   BR/TL, 5'11", 160 lbs.   Deb: 9/16/47

YEAR	TM/L	G	AB	R	H	2B	3B	HR	RBI	BB	SO	AVG	OBP	SLG	PRO+	BR/A	SB	CS	SBR	FA	FR	G/POS	TPR
1947	Was-A	6	24	0	2	0	0	0	1	0	4	.083	.083	.083	-55	-5	1	0	0	.905	-1	/O-6	-0.6
1948	Was-A	88	258	34	66	8	3	1	23	24	21	.256	.324	.322	74	-10	2	1	0	.979	1	O-73/1-6,P	-1.2
Total	2	94	282	34	68	8	3	1	24	24	25	.241	.305	.301	64	-15	3	1	0	.972	1	/O-79,1-6,P	-1.8

■ FAVEL WORDSWORTH
Wordsworth, Favel Perry   b: 12/22/1850, New York, N.Y.   d: 8/12/1888, New York, N.Y.   Deb: 4/28/1873

YEAR	TM/L	G	AB	R	H	2B	3B	HR	RBI	BB	SO	AVG	OBP	SLG	PRO+	BR/A	SB	CS	SBR	FA	FR	G/POS	TPR
1873	Res-n	12	42	5	10	1	0	0	3	2	1	.238	.273	.262	63	-2						S-11/O-1	-0.1

■ CHUCK WORKMAN
Workman, Charles Thomas   b: 1/6/15, Leeton, Mo.   d: 1/3/53, Kansas City, Mo.   BL/TR, 6', 175 lbs.   Deb: 9/18/38

YEAR	TM/L	G	AB	R	H	2B	3B	HR	RBI	BB	SO	AVG	OBP	SLG	PRO+	BR/A	SB	CS	SBR	FA	FR	G/POS	TPR
1938	Cle-A	2	5	1	2	0	0	0	0	0	0	.400	.400	.400	103	0	0	0	0	.500	-0	/O-1	0.0
1941	Cle-A	9	4	2	0	0	0	0	0	0	0	.000	.000	.000	-45	-1	0	0	0	.000	0	H	-0.1
1943	Bos-N	153	615	71	153	17	1	10	67	53	72	.249	.311	.328	86	-11	12			.988	6	*O-149/1-3,3	-1.5
1944	Bos-N	140	418	46	87	18	3	11	53	42	41	.208	.287	.344	74	-15	4			.983	-3	*O-103,3-19	-2.3
1945	Bos-N	139	514	77	141	16	2	25	87	51	58	.274	.347	.459	122	14	9			.910	-17	*3-107,O-24	-0.1
1946	Bos-N	25	48	5	8	2	0	2	7	3	11	.167	.231	.333	58	-3	0			.920	-1	O-12	-0.5

YEAR	TM/L	G	AB	R	H	2B	3B	HR	RBI	BB	SO	AVG	OBP	SLG	PRO+	BR/A	SB	CS	SBR	FA	FR	G/POS	TPR
	Pit-N	58	145	11	32	4	1	4	16	11	19	.221	.280	.303	64	-7	2			1.000	6	O-40/3-1	-0.3
	Yr	83	193	16	40	6	1	4	23	14	30	.207	.268	.311	63	-10	2			.986	5	O-52/3-1	-0.8
Total	6	526	1749	213	423	57	7	50	230	161	202	.242	.311	.368	91	-24	24	0		.985	-8	O-329,3-128/1	-4.8

■ HANK WORKMAN
Workman, Henry Kilgariff b: 2/5/26, Los Angeles, Cal. BL/TR, 6'1", 185 lbs. Deb: 9/4/50

YEAR	TM/L	G	AB	R	H	2B	3B	HR	RBI	BB	SO	AVG	OBP	SLG	PRO+	BR/A	SB	CS	SBR	FA	FR	G/POS	TPR
1950	NY-A	2	5	1	1	0	0	0	0	0	1	.200	.200	.200	3	-1	0	0	0	1.000	-0	/1-1	-0.1

■ HERB WORTH
Worth, Herbert b: 5/2/1847, Brooklyn, N.Y. d: 4/27/14, Brooklyn, N.Y. Deb: 7/29/1872

YEAR	TM/L	G	AB	R	H	2B	3B	HR	RBI	BB	SO	AVG	OBP	SLG	PRO+	BR/A	SB	CS	SBR	FA	FR	G/POS	TPR
1872	Atl-n	1	6	1	1	1	0	0	1	0	0	.167	.167	.333	43	-1						/O-1	0.0

■ CRAIG WORTHINGTON
Worthington, Craig Richard b: 4/17/65, Los Angeles, Cal. BR/TR, 6', 200 lbs. Deb: 4/26/88

YEAR	TM/L	G	AB	R	H	2B	3B	HR	RBI	BB	SO	AVG	OBP	SLG	PRO+	BR/A	SB	CS	SBR	FA	FR	G/POS	TPR
1988	Bal-A	26	81	5	15	2	0	2	4	9	24	.185	.267	.284	56	-5	1	0	0	.961	1	3-26	-0.4
1989	Bal-A	145	497	57	123	23	0	15	70	61	114	.247	.335	.384	105	4	1	2	-1	.951	-10	*3-145	-0.6
1990	Bal-A	133	425	46	96	17	0	8	44	63	96	.226	.330	.322	86	-7	1	2	-1	.945	-12	*3-131/D-2	-1.9
1991	Bal-A	31	102	11	23	3	0	4	12	12	14	.225	.313	.373	93	-1	0	1	-1	.975	-3	3-30	-0.4
1992	Cle-A	9	24	0	4	0	0	0	2	2	4	.167	.231	.167	13	-3	0	1	-1	.857	2	/3-9	-0.2
Total	5	344	1129	119	261	45	0	29	132	147	252	.231	.324	.348	91	-11	3	6	-3	.949	-22	3-341/D-2	-3.5

■ RED WORTHINGTON
Worthington, Robert Lee b: 4/24/06, Alhambra, Cal. d: 12/8/63, Sepulveda, Cal. BR/TR, 5'11", 170 lbs. Deb: 4/14/31

YEAR	TM/L	G	AB	R	H	2B	3B	HR	RBI	BB	SO	AVG	OBP	SLG	PRO+	BR/A	SB	CS	SBR	FA	FR	G/POS	TPR
1931	Bos-N	128	491	47	143	25	10	4	44	26	38	.291	.328	.407	100	-1	1			**.988**	-3	*O-124	-1.3
1932	Bos-N	105	435	62	132	35	8	8	61	15	24	.303	.330	.476	118	9	1			.987	-1	*O-104	0.1
1933	Bos-N	17	45	3	7	4	0	0	1	3	3	.156	.174	.244	20	-5	0			.900	-1	O-10	-0.7
1934	Bos-N	41	65	6	16	5	0	0	6	6	5	.246	.319	.323	78	-2	0			.920	-1	O-11	-0.3
	StL-N	1	1	0	0	0	0	0	0	0	1	.000	.000	.000	-94	-0	0			.000	0	H	0.0
	Yr	42	66	6	16	5	0	0	6	6	6	.242	.315	.318	75	-2	0			.920	-1	O-11	-0.3
Total	4	292	1037	118	298	69	18	12	111	48	71	.287	.321	.423	103	1	2			.981	-7	O-249	-2.2

■ CHUCK WORTMAN
Wortman, William Lewis b: 1/5/1892, Baltimore, Md. d: 8/19/77, Las Vegas, Nev. BR/TR, 5'7", 150 lbs. Deb: 7/20/16

YEAR	TM/L	G	AB	R	H	2B	3B	HR	RBI	BB	SO	AVG	OBP	SLG	PRO+	BR/A	SB	CS	SBR	FA	FR	G/POS	TPR
1916	Chi-N	69	234	17	47	4	2	2	16	18	22	.201	.258	.261	54	-13	4			.908	-21	S-69	-3.5
1917	Chi-N	75	190	24	33	4	1	0	9	18	23	.174	.245	.205	36	-14	6			.918	-8	S-65/2-1,3	-2.2
1918	*Chi-N	17	17	4	2	0	0	1	3	1	2	.118	.167	.294	39	-1	3			.864	2	/2-8,S-4	0.1
Total	3	161	441	45	82	8	3	3	28	37	47	.186	.249	.238	46	-28	13			.913	-27	S-138/2-9,3	-5.6

■ RON WOTUS
Wotus, Ronald Allan b: 3/3/61, Colchester, Conn. BR/TR, 6'1", 164 lbs. Deb: 9/3/83

YEAR	TM/L	G	AB	R	H	2B	3B	HR	RBI	BB	SO	AVG	OBP	SLG	PRO+	BR/A	SB	CS	SBR	FA	FR	G/POS	TPR
1983	Pit-N	5	3	0	0	0	0	0	0	0	1	.000	.000	.000	-98	-1	0	0	0	1.000	1	/S-2,2-1	0.0
1984	Pit-N	27	55	4	12	6	0	0	2	6	8	.218	.295	.327	75	-2	0	0	0	.976	9	S-17/2-7	0.9
Total	2	32	58	4	12	6	0	0	2	6	9	.207	.281	.310	66	-3	0	0	0	.976	10	/S-19,2-8	0.9

■ JIMMY WOULFE
Woulfe, James Joseph b: 11/25/1859, New Orleans, La. d: 12/20/24, New Orleans, La. TR, 5'11", Deb: 5/16/1884

YEAR	TM/L	G	AB	R	H	2B	3B	HR	RBI	BB	SO	AVG	OBP	SLG	PRO+	BR/A	SB	CS	SBR	FA	FR	G/POS	TPR
1884	Cin-a	8	34	3	5	0	1	0		1		.147	.171	.206	22	-3				.625	-3	/O-7,3-1	-0.6
	Pit-a	15	53	7	6	1	0	0		0		.113	.113	.132	-20	-7				.893	1	O-15	-0.6
	Yr	23	87	10	11	1	1	0		1		.126	.136	.161	-3	-10				.795	-2	O-22/3-1	-1.2

■ AL WRIGHT
Wright, Albert Edgar "A-1" b: 11/11/12, San Francisco, Cal BR/TR, 6'1.5", 170 lbs. Deb: 4/25/33

YEAR	TM/L	G	AB	R	H	2B	3B	HR	RBI	BB	SO	AVG	OBP	SLG	PRO+	BR/A	SB	CS	SBR	FA	FR	G/POS	TPR
1933	Bos-N	4	1	0	1	0	0	0	0	0	0	1.000	1.000	1.000	515	1	0			.500	-0	/2-3	0.0

■ AB WRIGHT
Wright, Albert Owen b: 11/16/05, Terlton, Okla. BR/TR, 6'1.5", 190 lbs. Deb: 4/20/35

YEAR	TM/L	G	AB	R	H	2B	3B	HR	RBI	BB	SO	AVG	OBP	SLG	PRO+	BR/A	SB	CS	SBR	FA	FR	G/POS	TPR
1935	Cle-A	67	160	17	38	11	1	2	18	10	17	.237	.291	.356	65	-9	2	1	0	.984	-8	O-47	-1.7
1944	Bos-N	71	195	20	50	9	0	7	35	18	31	.256	.326	.410	102	0	0			.968	-4	O-47	-0.6
Total	2	138	355	37	88	20	1	9	53	28	48	.248	.310	.386	85	-9	2	1		.974	-11	/O-94	-2.3

■ CY WRIGHT
Wright, Ceylon b: 8/16/1893, Minneapolis, Minn. d: 11/7/47, Hines, Ill. BL/TR, 5'9", 150 lbs. Deb: 6/30/16

YEAR	TM/L	G	AB	R	H	2B	3B	HR	RBI	BB	SO	AVG	OBP	SLG	PRO+	BR/A	SB	CS	SBR	FA	FR	G/POS	TPR
1916	Chi-A	8	18	0	0	0	0	0	0	1	7	.000	.053	.000	-83	-4	0			.844	-1	/S-8	-0.5

■ GLENN WRIGHT
Wright, Forest Glenn "Buckshot" b: 2/6/01, Archie, Mo. d: 4/6/84, Olathe, Kan. BR/TR, 5'11", 170 lbs. Deb: 4/15/24

YEAR	TM/L	G	AB	R	H	2B	3B	HR	RBI	BB	SO	AVG	OBP	SLG	PRO+	BR/A	SB	CS	SBR	FA	FR	G/POS	TPR
1924	Pit-N	153	616	80	177	28	18	7	111	27	52	.287	.318	.425	96	-5	14	6	1	.946	11	*S-153	2.3
1925	*Pit-N	153	614	97	189	32	10	18	121	31	32	.308	.341	.480	100	-2	7	-3		.939	0	*S-153/3-1	1.1
1926	Pit-N	119	458	73	141	15	15	8	77	19	26	.308	.335	.459	106	2	6			.927	-13	*S-116	0.2
1927	*Pit-N	143	570	78	160	26	4	9	105	39	46	.281	.328	.358	85	-13	4			.942	-17	*S-143	-1.5
1928	Pit-N	108	407	63	126	20	8	8	66	21	53	.310	.343	.457	103	1	3			.927	-24	*S-101/1-1,O	-1.1
1929	Bro-N	24	25	4	5	0	0	1	6	3	6	.200	.286	.320	51	-2	0			.667	-3	/S-3	-0.4
1930	Bro-N	135	532	83	171	28	12	22	126	32	70	.321	.360	.543	116	11	2			.964	-2	*S-134	2.2
1931	Bro-N	77	268	36	76	9	4	9	32	14	35	.284	.324	.448	106	1	1			.942	6	S-75	1.4
1932	Bro-N	127	446	50	122	31	5	11	60	12	57	.274	.293	.439	96	-4	1			.939	8	*S-122/1-2	1.3
1933	Bro-N	71	192	19	49	13	0	1	18	11	24	.255	.299	.339	85	-4	1			.936	-4	S-51/1-9,3	-0.6
1935	Chi-A	9	25	1	3	1	0	0	1	0	6	.120	.120	.160	-27	-5	0			.943	0	/2-7	-0.4
Total	11	1119	4153	584	1219	203	76	94	723	209	407	.294	.328	.447	99	-19	38	13		.941	-37	*S-1051/1-12,230	4.5

■ GEORGE WRIGHT
Wright, George b: 1/28/1847, Yonkers, N.Y. d: 8/21/37, Boston, Mass. BR/TR, 5'9.5", 150 lbs. Deb: 5/5/1871 FMH

YEAR	TM/L	G	AB	R	H	2B	3B	HR	RBI	BB	SO	AVG	OBP	SLG	PRO+	BR/A	SB	CS	SBR	FA	FR	G/POS	TPR
1871	Bos-n	16	80	33	33	7	5	0	11	6	1	.412	.453	.625	200	10	9					S-15/1-1	0.6
1872	Bos-n	48	255	87	87	16	5	2	33	3	1	.341	.349	.467	141	10						*S-48	0.9
1873	Bos-n	59	325	99	126	13	7	3	48	2	8	.388	.402	.498	151	17						*S-59	1.0
1874	Bos-n	60	313	76	106	11	15	2		7		.339	.353	.489	156	18						*S-60	1.2
1875	Bos-n	79	406	105	135	18	7	1		2		.333	.336	.419	154	20						*S-79/P-2	1.4
1876	Bos-N	70	335	72	100	18	6	1	34	8	9	.299	.315	.397	134	11				.888	13	*S-68/2-2,P	2.1
1877	Bos-N	61	290	58	80	15	1	0	35	9	15	.276	.298	.334	95	-2				.878	9	*2-58/S-3	0.8
1878	Bos-N	59	267	35	60	5	1	0	12	6	22	.225	.242	.251	58	-13				**.947**	11	*S-59	0.1
1879	Pro-N	85	388	79	107	15	10	1	42	13	20	.276	.299	.374	122	9				.924	21	*S-85,M	3.2
1880	Bos-N	1	4	2	1	0	0	0	0	0	0	.250	.250	.250	72	-0				1.000	-0	/S-1	0.0
1881	Bos-N	7	25	4	5	0	0	0	3	1		.200	.286	.200	58	-1				.963	-3	/S-7	-0.3
1882	Pro-N	46	185	14	30	1	2	0	9	4	36	.162	.180	.189	19	-16				.873	-7	S-46	-2.0
Total	5 n	262	1379	400	487	65	39	8	92	26	4	.353	.365	.474	154	75						S-261/P-2,1	5.1
Total	7	329	1494	264	383	54	20	2	132	43	103	.256	.277	.323	93	-11				.911	42	S-269/2-60,P	3.9

■ GEORGE WRIGHT
Wright, George De Witt b: 12/22/58, Oklahoma City, Okla BB/TR, 5'11", 180 lbs. Deb: 4/10/82

YEAR	TM/L	G	AB	R	H	2B	3B	HR	RBI	BB	SO	AVG	OBP	SLG	PRO+	BR/A	SB	CS	SBR	FA	FR	G/POS	TPR
1982	Tex-A	150	557	69	147	20	5	11	50	30	77	.264	.305	.377	91	-8	3	7	-3	.981	11	*O-149	-0.5
1983	Tex-A	162	634	79	175	28	6	18	80	41	82	.276	.322	.424	106	3	8	7	-2	.985	10	*O-161	0.7
1984	Tex-A	101	383	40	93	19	4	9	48	15	54	.243	.275	.384	78	-13	0	2	-1	.983	-3	O-80,D-18	-2.0
1985	Tex-A	109	363	21	69	13	0	2	18	25	49	.190	.242	.242	33	-33	4	7	-3	.991	-1	*O-102/D-4	-4.1
1986	Tex-A	49	106	9	23	3	1	2	7	4	23	.217	.252	.311	53	-7	3	5	-2	.969	-5	O-42	-1.5
	Mon-N	56	117	12	22	5	0	0	5	11	28	.188	.264	.265	47	-9	1	1	-0	1.000	-2	O-32	-1.3
Total	5	627	2160	231	529	88	18	42	208	126	314	.245	.289	.361	78	-66	19	29	-12	.984	10	O-566/D-22	-8.7

■ JOE WRIGHT
Wright, Joseph S. b: 1873, Pittsburgh, Pa. BL/TL, 5'8", 175 lbs. Deb: 7/14/1895

YEAR	TM/L	G	AB	R	H	2B	3B	HR	RBI	BB	SO	AVG	OBP	SLG	PRO+	BR/A	SB	CS	SBR	FA	FR	G/POS	TPR
1895	Lou-N	60	228	30	63	10	4	1	30	12	28	.276	.315	.368	81	-7	7			.963	-2	O-60	-1.1
1896	Lou-N	2	7	0	2	0	0	0	0	0	1	.286	.286	.286	53	-0	0			1.000	-0	/O-2	-0.1

YEAR	TM/L	G	AB	R	H	2B	3B	HR	RBI	BB	SO	AVG	OBP	SLG	PRO+	BR/A	SB	CS	SBR	FA	FR	G/POS	TPR
	Pit-N	15	52	5	16	2	1	0	6	1	2	.308	.321	.385	89	-1	1			.958	-2	O-12/3-1	-0.3
	Yr	17	59	5	18	2	1	0	6	1	3	.305	.317	.373	85	-1	1			.962	-2	O-14/3-1	-0.4
Total	2	77	287	35	81	12	5	1	36	13	31	.282	.316	.369	82	-8	8			.963	-5	/O-74,3-1	-1.5

■ PAT WRIGHT   Wright, Patrick Francis   b: 7/5/1865, Pottsville, Pa.   d: 5/29/43, Springfield, Ill.   BB/TR, 6'2", 190 lbs.   Deb: 7/11/1890

YEAR	TM/L	G	AB	R	H	2B	3B	HR	RBI	BB	SO	AVG	OBP	SLG	PRO+	BR/A	SB	CS	SBR	FA	FR	G/POS	TPR
1890	Chi-N	1	2	0	0	0	0	0	0	0	1	.000	.333	.000	-1	-0	0			1.000	0	/2-1	0.0

■ SAM WRIGHT   Wright, Samuel   b: 11/25/1848, New York, N.Y.   d: 5/6/28, Boston, Mass.   BR/TR, 5'7.5", 146 lbs.   Deb: 4/21/1875   F

YEAR	TM/L	G	AB	R	H	2B	3B	HR	RBI	BB	SO	AVG	OBP	SLG	PRO+	BR/A	SB	CS	SBR	FA	FR	G/POS	TPR
1875	NH-n	33	128	10	24	4	0	0			1	.188	.194	.219	49	-6						S-33	-0.6
1876	Bos-N	2	8	0	1	0	0	0	0	0	0	.125	.125	.125	-16	-1				.778	-0	/S-2	-0.1
1880	Cin-N	9	34	0	3	0	0	0	0	0	0	.088	.088	.088	-40	-5				.889	-2	/S-9	-0.6
1881	Bos-N	1	4	0	1	0	0	0	0	0	0	.250	.250	.250	60	-0				.667	-1	/S-1	-0.1
Total	3	12	46	0	5	0	0	0	0	0	5	.109	.109	.109	-27	-6				.843	-3	/S-12	-0.8

■ TAFFY WRIGHT   Wright, Taft Shedron   b: 8/10/11, Tabor City, N.C.   d: 10/22/81, Orlando, Fla.   BL/TR, 5'10", 180 lbs.   Deb: 4/18/38

YEAR	TM/L	G	AB	R	H	2B	3B	HR	RBI	BB	SO	AVG	OBP	SLG	PRO+	BR/A	SB	CS	SBR	FA	FR	G/POS	TPR
1938	Was-A	100	263	37	92	18	10	2	36	13	17	.350	.389	.517	134	13	1	2	-1	.982	-4	O-60	0.5
1939	Was-A	129	499	77	154	29	11	4	93	38	19	.309	.359	.435	110	6	1	2	-1	.950	-3	*O-123	-0.2
1940	Chi-A	147	581	79	196	31	9	5	88	43	25	.337	.385	.448	114	12	4	7	-3	.963	-4	*O-144	-0.2
1941	Chi-A	136	513	71	165	35	5	10	97	60	27	.322	.399	.468	130	23	5	4	-1	.973	-2	*O-134	-0.2
1942	Chi-A	85	300	43	100	13	5	0	47	48	9	.333	.432	.410	141	19	1	8	-5	.968	-1	O-81	1.1
1946	Chi-A	115	422	46	116	19	4	7	52	42	17	.275	.342	.389	108	4	10	3	1	.991	-3	*O-107	-0.3
1947	Chi-A	124	401	48	130	13	4	4	54	48	17	.324	.398	.387	123	14	8	6	-1	.971	-4	*O-100	0.4
1948	Chi-A	134	455	50	127	15	6	4	61	38	18	.279	.341	.365	91	-7	2	1	0	.987	1	O-114	-1.2
1949	Phi-A	59	149	14	35	2	5	2	25	16	6	.235	.321	.356	82	-4	0	0	0	.970	-0	O-35	-0.6
Total	9	1029	3583	465	1115	175	55	38	553	346	155	.311	.376	.423	116	80	32	33	-10	.972	-21	O-898	0.5

■ TOM WRIGHT   Wright, Thomas Everette   b: 9/22/23, Shelby, N.C.   BL/TR, 5'11.5", 180 lbs.   Deb: 9/15/48

YEAR	TM/L	G	AB	R	H	2B	3B	HR	RBI	BB	SO	AVG	OBP	SLG	PRO+	BR/A	SB	CS	SBR	FA	FR	G/POS	TPR
1948	Bos-A	3	2	1	1	0	0	0	0	0	0	.500	.500	1.500	400	1	0	0	0	.000	0	H	0.1
1949	Bos-A	5	4	1	1	1	0	0	1	1	1	.250	.400	.500	128	0	0	0	0	.000	0	H	0.0
1950	Bos-A	54	107	17	34	7	0	0	20	6	18	.318	.360	.383	82	-3	0	0	0	.953	-2	O-24	-0.6
1951	Bos-A	28	63	8	14	1	1	1	9	11	8	.222	.347	.317	73	-2	0	0	0	.950	-4	O-18	-0.6
1952	StL-A	29	66	6	16	0	0	1	6	12	20	.242	.359	.288	79	-1	1	1	-0	.976	1	O-18	-0.2
	Chi-A	60	132	15	34	10	2	1	21	16	16	.258	.342	.386	102	0	1	0	0	.969	-2	O-34	-0.2
	Yr	89	198	21	50	10	2	2	27	28	36	.253	.348	.354	94	-1	2	1	-0	.971	-1	O-52	-0.4
1953	Chi-A	77	132	14	33	5	3	2	25	12	21	.250	.322	.379	86	-3	0	0	0	.978	-5	O-33	-0.9
1954	Was-A	76	171	13	42	4	4	1	17	18	38	.246	.325	.333	85	-4	0	0	0	1.000	-2	O-43	-0.7
1955	Was-A	7	7	0	0	0	0	0	0	0	1	.000	.000	.000	-99	-2	0	0	0	.000	0	H	-0.2
1956	Was-A	2	1	0	0	0	0	0	0	0	0	.000	.000	.000	-99	-0	0	0	0	.000	0	H	0.0
Total	9	341	685	75	175	28	11	6	99	76	123	.255	.336	.355	85	-14	2	1	0	.977	-13	O-170	-3.3

■ DICK WRIGHT   Wright, Willard James   b: 5/5/1890, Worcester, N.Y.   d: 1/24/52, Bethlehem, Pa.   BR/TR, 5'10", 170 lbs.   Deb: 6/30/15

YEAR	TM/L	G	AB	R	H	2B	3B	HR	RBI	BB	SO	AVG	OBP	SLG	PRO+	BR/A	SB	CS	SBR	FA	FR	G/POS	TPR
1915	Bro-F	4	5	0	0	0	0	0	0	0	0	.000	.000	.000	-99	-1	0			.833	-1	/C-3	-0.2

■ BILL WRIGHT   Wright, William Hiram   Deb: 9/16/1887

YEAR	TM/L	G	AB	R	H	2B	3B	HR	RBI	BB	SO	AVG	OBP	SLG	PRO+	BR/A	SB	CS	SBR	FA	FR	G/POS	TPR
1887	Was-N	1	3	0	2	0	0	0	0	0	0	.667	.667	.667	286	1	0			.778	-0	/C-1	0.0

■ HARRY WRIGHT   Wright, William Henry   b: 1/10/1835, Sheffield, England   d: 10/3/1895, Atlantic City, N.J.   BR/TR, 5'9.5", 157 lbs.   Deb: 5/5/1871   FMH

YEAR	TM/L	G	AB	R	H	2B	3B	HR	RBI	BB	SO	AVG	OBP	SLG	PRO+	BR/A	SB	CS	SBR	FA	FR	G/POS	TPR
1871	Bos-n	31	147	42	44	5	2	0	26	13	2	.299	.356	.361	103	1	7					*O-30/P-9,SM	0.2
1872	Bos-n	48	208	39	54	6	0	0	22	9	2	.260	.290	.288	75	-7						*O-48/P-7M	-0.2
1873	Bos-n	58	266	57	67	8	3	2	33	10	3	.252	.290	.327	72	-11						*O-58/P-12M	-0.5
1874	Bos-n	40	184	44	56	9	2	2		4		.304	.319	.408	123	4						*O-40/P-6,CM	0.4
1875	Bos-n	1	4	1	1	0	0	0		0		.250	.250	.250	71	-0						/O-1,M	0.0
1876	Bos-N	1	3	0	0	0	0	0	0	0	0	.000	.000	.000	-98	-1				.000	-0	/O-1,M	-0.1
1877	Bos-N	1	4	0	0	0	0	0	0	0	1	.000	.000	.000	-97	-1				.667	1	/O-1,M	-0.1
Total	5 n	178	809	183	222	28	7	4	81	36	7	.274	.305	.341	89	-14						O-177/P-34,CS	0.0
Total	2	2	7	0	0	0	0	0	0	0	2	.000	.000	.000	-97	-1				.667	1	/O-2	-0.1

■ RASTY WRIGHT   Wright, William Smith   b: 1/31/1863, Birmingham, Mich.   d: 10/14/22, Duluth, Minn.   BL, 6'1", 185 lbs.   Deb: 4/17/1890

YEAR	TM/L	G	AB	R	H	2B	3B	HR	RBI	BB	SO	AVG	OBP	SLG	PRO+	BR/A	SB	CS	SBR	FA	FR	G/POS	TPR
1890	Syr-a	88	348	82	106	10	6	0	69			.305	.428	.368	150	29	30			.907	4	O-88	2.5
	Cle-N	13	45	7	5	1	0	0	2	12	4	.111	.298	.133	27	-4	3			.917	-1	O-13	-0.4
Total	1	101	393	89	111	11	6	0	2	81	4	.282	.412	.341	135	25	33			.908	3	O-101	2.1

■ RUSS WRIGHTSTONE   Wrightstone, Russell Guy   b: 3/18/1893, Bowmansdale, Pa.   d: 2/25/69, Harrisburg, Pa.   BL/TR, 5'10.5", 176 lbs.   Deb: 4/19/20

YEAR	TM/L	G	AB	R	H	2B	3B	HR	RBI	BB	SO	AVG	OBP	SLG	PRO+	BR/A	SB	CS	SBR	FA	FR	G/POS	TPR
1920	Phi-N	76	206	23	54	6	1	3	17	10	25	.262	.303	.345	82	-5	3	2	-0	.934	6	3-56/S-2,2	0.3
1921	Phi-N	109	372	59	110	13	4	9	51	18	20	.296	.332	.425	92	-5	4	4	-1	.922	4	3-54,O-37/2	-0.1
1922	Phi-N	99	331	56	101	18	6	5	33	28	17	.305	.365	.441	98	-2	4	5	-2	.973	13	3-40,S-35/1	1.4
1923	Phi-N	119	392	59	107	21	7	5	57	21	19	.273	.315	.416	82	-12	5	2	0	.942	-4	3-72,S-21/2	-0.7
1924	Phi-N	118	388	55	119	24	4	7	58	27	15	.307	.363	.443	102	1	5	4	-1	.944	-8	3-97/2-9,SO	-0.7
1925	Phi-N	92	286	48	99	18	5	14	61	19	18	.346	.389	.591	135	14	0	3	-2	.937	-19	0-45,S-12,32/1	-0.8
1926	Phi-N	112	368	55	113	23	1	7	57	27	11	.307	.356	.432	106	3	0			.977	-0	1-53,3-37,2/O	0.2
1927	Phi-N	141	533	62	163	24	5	6	75	48	20	.306	.365	.403	104	4	0			.989	-1	*1-136/2-1,3	-0.4
1928	Phi-N	33	91	7	19	5	1	1	11	14	5	.209	.321	.319	65	-4	0			.936	-4	O-26/1-4	-1.0
	NY-N	30	25	3	4	0	1	1	5	3	2	.160	.250	.280	38	-2	0			1.000	0	/1-2	-0.2
	Yr	63	116	10	23	5	1	2	16	17	7	.198	.306	.310	60	-7	0			.936	-4	O-26/1-6	-1.2
Total	9	929	2992	427	889	152	34	60	425	215	152	.297	.349	.431	99	-9	35	20		.942	-12	3-368,1-203,O/S2	-1.4

■ ZEKE WRIGLEY   Wrigley, George Watson   b: 1/18/1874, Philadelphia, Pa.   d: 9/28/52, Philadelphia, Pa.   5'8.5", 150 lbs.   Deb: 8/31/1896

YEAR	TM/L	G	AB	R	H	2B	3B	HR	RBI	BB	SO	AVG	OBP	SLG	PRO+	BR/A	SB	CS	SBR	FA	FR	G/POS	TPR
1896	Was-N	5	9	1	1	0	0	0	0	1	1	.111	.200	.111	-17	-2	0			.909	3	/2-3,S-1	0.1
1897	Was-N	104	388	65	110	14	8	3	64	21		.284	.320	.384	86	-9	5			.885	-2	O-36,S-33,3/2	-1.0
1898	Was-N	111	400	50	98	9	10	2	39	20		.245	.283	.333	76	-14	10			.895	11	S-97,2-11/O3	0.2
1899	NY-N	4	15	1	3	0	0	0	1	1		.200	.250	.200	25	-2	1			.818	-1	/3-5	-0.3
	Bro-N	15	49	4	10	2	2	0	11	3		.204	.250	.327	56	-3	2			.870	-4	S-14/3-1	-0.5
	Yr	19	64	5	13	2	2	0	12	4		.203	.250	.297	49	-5	3			.870	-4	S-14/3-6	-0.8
Total	4	239	861	121	222	25	20	5	117	46	1	.258	.296	.351	78	-29	18			.892	7	S-145/O-39,32	-1.5

■ RICK WRONA   Wrona, Richard James   b: 12/10/63, Tulsa, Okla.   BR/TR, 6'1", 185 lbs.   Deb: 9/3/88

YEAR	TM/L	G	AB	R	H	2B	3B	HR	RBI	BB	SO	AVG	OBP	SLG	PRO+	BR/A	SB	CS	SBR	FA	FR	G/POS	TPR
1988	Chi-N	4	6	0	0	0	0	0	0	0	0	.000	.000	.000	-96	-1	0	0	0	1.000	1	/C-2	0.0
1989	*Chi-N	38	92	11	26	2	1	2	14	2	21	.283	.305	.391	91	-1	0	0	0	.983	2	C-37	0.2
1990	Chi-N	16	29	3	5	0	0	0	2	1	11	.172	.226	.172	10	-3	1	0	0	.970	3	C-16	0.0
1992	Cin-N	11	23	0	4	1	0	0	3	1	6	.174	.174	.174	-1	-3	0	0	0	.965	3	C-10/1-1	0.0
1993	Chi-A	4	8	1	1	0	0	0	0	0	1	.125	.125	.125	-33	-1	0	0	0	1.000	1	/C-4	-0.2
1994	Mil-A	6	10	2	5	4	0	0	3	1	0	.500	.545	1.200	326	3	0	0	0	.923	-1	/C-5,1-1	0.2
Total	6	79	168	16	41	7	1	4	22	5	40	.244	.270	.345	68	-6	1	0	0	.976	7	/C-74,1-2	0.2

■ YATS WUESTLING   Wuestling, George   b: 10/18/03, St.Louis, Mo.   d: 4/26/70, St.Louis, Mo.   BR/TR, 5'11", 167 lbs.   Deb: 6/15/29

YEAR	TM/L	G	AB	R	H	2B	3B	HR	RBI	BB	SO	AVG	OBP	SLG	PRO+	BR/A	SB	CS	SBR	FA	FR	G/POS	TPR
1929	Det-A	54	150	13	30	4	1	0	16	9	24	.200	.250	.240	27	-16	1	3	-2	.943	-2	S-52/2-1,3	-1.4

YEAR	TM/L	G	AB	R	H	2B	3B	HR	RBI	BB	SO	AVG	OBP	SLG	PRO+	BR/A	SB	CS	SBR	FA	FR	G/POS	TPR
1930	Det-A	4	9	0	0	0	0	0	0	2	3	.000	.182	.000	-48	-2	0	0	0	.842	1	/S-4	-0.1
	NY-A	25	58	5	11	0	1	0	3	4	14	.190	.242	.224	20	-7	0	1	-1	.918	4	S-21/3-3	-0.2
	Yr	29	67	5	11	0	1	0	3	6	17	.164	.233	.194	10	-9	0	1	-1	.904	5	S-25/3-3	-0.3
Total	2	83	217	18	41	4	2	0	19	15	41	.189	.245	.226	21	-26	1	4	-2	.931	2	/S-77,3-4,2	-1.7

■ JOE WYATT
Wyatt, Loral John b: 4/6/1900, Petersburg, Ind. d: 12/5/70, Oblong, Ill. BR/TR, 6'1", 175 lbs. Deb: 9/11/24

YEAR	TM/L	G	AB	R	H	2B	3B	HR	RBI	BB	SO	AVG	OBP	SLG	PRO+	BR/A	SB	CS	SBR	FA	FR	G/POS	TPR
1924	Cle-A	4	12	1	2	0	0	0	1	2	1	.167	.286	.167	18	-1	0	0	0	.833	-1	/O-4	-0.3

■ REN WYLIE
Wylie, James Renwick b: 12/14/1861, Elizabeth, Pa. d: 8/17/51, Wilkinsburg, Pa. BR/TR, 5'11", 155 lbs. Deb: 8/11/1882

YEAR	TM/L	G	AB	R	H	2B	3B	HR	RBI	BB	SO	AVG	OBP	SLG	PRO+	BR/A	SB	CS	SBR	FA	FR	G/POS	TPR
1882	Pit-a	1	3	0	0	0	0	0		0		.000	.000	.000	-99	-1				1.000	0	/O-1	0.0

■ FRANK WYMAN
Wyman, Frank H. b: 5/10/1862, Haverhill, Mass. d: 2/4/16, Everett, Mass. Deb: 6/10/1884

YEAR	TM/L	G	AB	R	H	2B	3B	HR	RBI	BB	SO	AVG	OBP	SLG	PRO+	BR/A	SB	CS	SBR	FA	FR	G/POS	TPR
1884	KC-U	30	124	16	27	4	0	0		3		.218	.236	.250	37	-11				.743	5	O-25/P-3,13	-0.5
	CP-U	2	8	1	3	0	0	0		0		.375	.375	.375	105	0				.846	-0	/1-2	-0.1
	Yr	32	132	17	30	4	0	0		3		.227	.244	.258	42	-10				.743	4	O-25/1-5,P3	-0.6

■ BUTCH WYNEGAR
Wynegar, Harold Delano b: 3/14/56, York, Pa. BB/TR, 6', 194 lbs. Deb: 4/9/76

YEAR	TM/L	G	AB	R	H	2B	3B	HR	RBI	BB	SO	AVG	OBP	SLG	PRO+	BR/A	SB	CS	SBR	FA	FR	G/POS	TPR
1976	Min-A★	149	534	58	139	21	2	10	69	79	63	.260	.358	.363	108	8	0	0	0	.978	-10	*C-137,D-15	0.2
1977	Min-A★	144	532	76	139	22	3	10	79	68	61	.261	.347	.370	97	-1	2	3	-1	.993	-11	*C-142/3-1	-0.9
1978	Min-A	135	454	36	104	22	1	4	45	47	42	.229	.310	.308	73	-15	1	0	0	.988	-3	*C-131/3-1	-1.5
1979	Min-A	149	504	74	136	20	0	7	57	74	36	.270	.366	.351	91	-4	2	2	-1	.992	-4	*C-146	-0.4
1980	Min-A	146	486	61	124	18	3	5	57	63	36	.255	.343	.335	81	-11	3	1	0	.988	4	*C-142/D-1	-0.2
1981	Min-A	47	150	11	37	5	0	1	10	17	9	.247	.327	.280	72	-5	0	1	-1	.995	-1	C-37/D-9	-0.5
1982	Min-A	24	86	9	18	4	0	1	8	10	12	.209	.292	.291	59	-5	0	0	0	.986	-2	C-24	-0.5
	NY-A	63	191	27	56	8	1	3	20	40	21	.293	.418	.393	126	9	0	1	-1	.993	-1	C-62	1.1
	Yr	87	277	36	74	12	1	4	28	50	33	.267	.381	.361	106	4	0	1	-1	.991	-2	C-86	0.6
1983	NY-A	94	301	40	89	18	0	6	42	52	29	.296	.401	.429	133	16	1	1	-0	.985	-13	*C-93	0.7
1984	NY-A	129	442	48	118	13	1	6	45	65	35	.267	.361	.342	99	2	1	4	-2	.993	-4	*C-126	0.3
1985	NY-A	102	309	27	69	15	0	5	32	64	43	.223	.357	.320	89	-2	0	0	0	.990	2	C-96	0.4
1986	NY-A	61	194	19	40	4	1	7	29	30	21	.206	.313	.345	80	-5	0	0	0	.994	-2	C-57	-0.3
1987	Cal-A	31	92	4	19	2	0	0	5	9	13	.207	.277	.228	37	-8	0	0	0	.994	3	C-28/D-1	-0.4
1988	Cal-A	27	55	8	14	4	1	0	6	5	8	.255	.349	.418	117	1	0	0	0	.981	-0	C-26	0.2
Total	13	1301	4330	498	1102	176	15	65	506	626	428	.255	.351	.347	93	-20	10	13	-5	.989	-43	*C-1247/D-26,3	-1.8

■ EARLY WYNN
Wynn, Early "Gus" b: 1/6/20, Hartford, Ala. BB/TR, 6', 200 lbs. Deb: 9/13/39 CH

YEAR	TM/L	G	AB	R	H	2B	3B	HR	RBI	BB	SO	AVG	OBP	SLG	PRO+	BR/A	SB	CS	SBR	FA	FR	G/POS	TPR
1939	Was-A	3	6	0	1	0	0	0	1	1	1	.167	.286	.167	20	-1	0	0	0	1.000	-1	/P-3	0.0
1941	Was-A	5	15	1	2	1	0	0	0	0	5	.133	.133	.200	-14	-2	0	0	0	.917	0	/P-5	0.0
1942	Was-A	30	69	4	15	2	0	0	7	3	13	.217	.250	.246	40	-6	0	0	0	.953	-1	P-30	0.0
1943	Was-A	38	98	6	29	3	1	1	11	1	11	.296	.303	.378	102	-0	0	0	0	.947	-2	P-37	0.0
1944	Was-A	43	92	4	19	2	0	1	9	3	21	.207	.232	.261	42	-7	0	0	0	.972	-2	P-33	0.0
1946	Was-A	25	47	4	15	2	0	1	9	5	7	.319	.385	.426	134	2	0	0	0	.962	-0	P-17	0.0
1947	Was-A	54	120	6	33	6	0	2	13	1	19	.275	.281	.375	84	-3	0	0	0	.980	-1	P-33	0.0
1948	Was-A	73	106	9	23	3	1	0	16	14	22	.217	.308	.264	55	-7	0	0	0	.950	-1	P-33	0.0
1949	Cle-A	35	70	3	10	1	0	1	7	4	10	.143	.189	.200	3	-10	0	0	0	1.000	1	P-26	0.0
1950	Cle-A	39	77	12	18	5	1	2	10	10	12	.234	.322	.403	87	-2	0	0	0	.932	0	P-32	0.0
1951	Cle-A	41	108	8	20	8	1	1	13	7	9	.185	.235	.306	48	-9	0	0	0	.982	-1	P-37	0.0
1952	Cle-A	44	99	5	22	2	0	0	10	9	15	.222	.287	.242	52	-6	0	0	0	.943	-1	P-42	0.0
1953	Cle-A	37	91	11	25	2	0	3	10	7	17	.275	.327	.396	97	-1	0	0	0	1.000	-1	P-36	0.0
1954	*Cle-A	40	93	10	17	3	0	0	4	7	13	.183	.240	.215	25	-10	0	0	0	.957	-3	P-40	0.0
1955	Cle-A★	34	84	8	15	3	0	1	7	6	17	.179	.233	.250	29	-9	0	0	0	.944	-3	P-32	0.0
1956	Cle-A★	38	101	5	23	5	0	1	15	7	22	.228	.278	.307	53	-7	1	0	0	.955	1	P-38	0.0
1957	Cle-A★	40	86	4	10	0	0	0	4	11	23	.116	.216	.116	-7	-13	0	0	0	1.000	-1	P-40	0.0
1958	Chi-A★	40	75	7	15	1	0	0	11	10	25	.200	.294	.213	43	-6	0	0	0	1.000	-2	P-40	0.0
1959	*Chi-A★	37	90	11	22	7	0	2	8	9	18	.244	.320	.389	95	-1	0	0	0	.957	-1	P-37	0.0
1960	Chi-A★	36	75	8	15	2	1	1	7	14	17	.200	.333	.293	72	-3	0	0	0	.972	-2	P-36	0.0
1961	Chi-A	17	37	4	6	0	0	0	2	3	11	.162	.225	.162	5	-5	0	0	0	1.000	-2	P-17	0.0
1962	Chi-A	27	54	5	7	1	0	0	2	7	17	.130	.230	.148	4	-7	0	0	0	1.000	-2	P-27	0.0
1963	Cle-A	20	11	1	3	0	0	0	0	2	5	.273	.385	.273	89	-0	0	0	0	1.000	-0	P-20	0.0
Total	23	796	1704	136	365	59	5	17	173	141	330	.214	.275	.285	54	-111	1	0	0	.967	-25	P-691	0.0

■ JIM WYNN
Wynn, James Sherman b: 3/12/42, Hamilton, Ohio BR/TR, 5'9", 170 lbs. Deb: 7/10/63

YEAR	TM/L	G	AB	R	H	2B	3B	HR	RBI	BB	SO	AVG	OBP	SLG	PRO+	BR/A	SB	CS	SBR	FA	FR	G/POS	TPR
1963	Hou-N	70	250	31	61	10	5	4	27	30	53	.244	.325	.372	107	2	4	2	0	.963	-2	O-53,S-21/3	-0.2
1964	Hou-N	67	219	19	49	7	0	5	18	24	58	.224	.303	.324	81	-5	5	5	-2	.958	5	O-64	-0.5
1965	Hou-N	157	564	90	155	30	7	22	73	84	126	.275	.374	.470	146	36	43	4	11	.978	20	*O-155	6.1
1966	Hou-N	105	418	62	107	21	1	18	62	41	81	.256	.324	.440	118	9	13	10	-2	.978	11	*O-104	1.3
1967	Hou-N★	158	594	102	148	29	3	37	107	74	137	.249	.334	.495	139	29	16	4	2	.968	9	*O-157	3.4
1968	Hou-N	156	542	85	146	23	5	26	67	90	131	.269	.378	.474	158	40	11	17	-7	.988	15	*O-153	4.5
1969	Hou-N	149	495	113	133	17	1	33	87	148	142	.269	.440	.507	168	53	23	7	3	.985	11	*O-149	6.0
1970	Hou-N	157	554	82	156	32	2	27	88	106	96	.282	.398	.493	143	36	24	5	4	.987	10	*O-151	4.2
1971	Hou-N	123	404	38	82	16	0	7	45	56	63	.203	.303	.295	72	-14	10	5	0	.988	2	*O-116	-2.0
1972	Hou-N	145	542	117	148	29	3	24	90	103	99	.273	.391	.470	147	36	17	7	1	.983	6	*O-144	3.9
1973	Hou-N	139	481	90	106	14	5	20	55	91	102	.220	.349	.395	106	6	14	11	-2	.986	3	*O-133	0.4
1974	*LA-N★	150	535	104	145	17	4	32	108	108	104	.271	.393	.497	154	41	18	15	-4	.992	11	*O-148	4.3
1975	LA-N★	130	412	80	102	16	0	18	58	110	77	.248	.407	.417	135	25	7	3	0	.983	-1	*O-120	2.0
1976	Atl-N	148	449	75	93	19	1	17	66	127	111	.207	.382	.367	107	9	16	6	1	.971	11	*O-138	1.6
1977	NY-A	30	77	7	11	2	1	1	3	15	16	.143	.283	.234	43	-6	1	0	0	1.000	2	D-15/O-8	-0.5
	Mil-A	36	117	10	23	3	1	0	10	17	31	.197	.299	.239	49	-8	3	0	1	.967	-1	O-17,D-15	-0.9
	Yr	66	194	17	34	5	2	1	13	32	47	.175	.292	.237	46	-14	4	0	1	.981	1	D-30,O-25	-1.4
Total	15	1920	6653	1105	1665	285	39	291	964	1224	1427	.250	.369	.436	129	289	225	101	7	.981	110	*O-1810/D-30,S3	33.2

■ MARVELL WYNNE
Wynne, Marvell b: 12/17/59, Chicago, Ill. BL/TL, 5'11", 185 lbs. Deb: 6/15/83

YEAR	TM/L	G	AB	R	H	2B	3B	HR	RBI	BB	SO	AVG	OBP	SLG	PRO+	BR/A	SB	CS	SBR	FA	FR	G/POS	TPR
1983	Pit-N	103	366	66	89	16	2	7	26	38	52	.243	.319	.355	85	-7	12	10	-2	.983	-0	*O-102	-1.4
1984	Pit-N	154	653	77	174	24	11	0	39	42	81	.266	.311	.337	82	-16	24	19	-4	.990	5	*O-154	-2.1
1985	Pit-N	103	337	21	69	18	2	1	18	18	48	.205	.247	.258	42	-26	10	5	0	.987	6	*O-99	-2.5
1986	SD-N	137	288	34	76	19	2	7	37	15	45	.264	.303	.417	98	-2	11	11	-3	.986	-11	*O-125	-1.9
1987	SD-N	98	188	17	47	8	2	2	24	20	37	.250	.322	.346	80	-5	11	6	-0	.981	-11	O-71	-1.7
1988	SD-N	128	333	37	88	13	4	11	42	31	62	.264	.327	.426	117	7	3	4	-2	.987	-11	*O-113	-1.0
1989	SD-N	105	294	19	74	11	1	6	35	12	41	.252	.283	.357	82	-8	4	1	1	.971	-7	O-96	-1.7
	*Chi-N	20	48	8	9	2	1	1	4	1	7	.188	.220	.333	52	-3	2	0	1	.944	-2	O-13	-0.6
	Yr	125	342	27	83	13	2	7	39	13	48	.243	.275	.354	77	-11	6	1	1	.968	-10	*O-109	-2.3
1990	Chi-N	92	186	21	38	8	2	4	19	14	25	.204	.264	.333	59	-11	3	2	-0	.991	-9	O-66	-2.2
Total	8	940	2693	300	664	107	28	40	244	191	398	.247	.298	.352	81	-72	80	58	-11	.985	-41	O-839	-15.1

■ JOHNNY WYROSTEK
Wyrostek, John Barney b: 7/12/19, Fairmont City, Ill. d: 12/12/86, St. Louis, Mo. BL/TR, 6'2", 180 lbs. Deb: 9/10/42

YEAR	TM/L	G	AB	R	H	2B	3B	HR	RBI	BB	SO	AVG	OBP	SLG	PRO+	BR/A	SB	CS	SBR	FA	FR	G/POS	TPR
1942	Pit-N	9	35	0	4	0	1	0	3	2	1	.114	.184	.171	4	-4	0			1.000	1	/O-8	-0.4

YEAR	TM/L	G	AB	R	H	2B	3B	HR	RBI	BB	SO	AVG	OBP	SLG	PRO+	BR/A	SB	CS	SBR	FA	FR	G/POS	TPR
1943	Pit-N	51	79	7	12	3	0	0	1	3	15	.152	.183	.190	7	-9	0			.919	-5	O-20/3-2,12	-1.6
1946	Phi-N	145	545	73	153	30	4	6	45	70	42	.281	.366	.383	116	12	7			.981	17	*O-142	2.4
1947	Phi-N	128	454	68	124	24	7	5	51	61	45	.273	.364	.390	104	4	7			.971	1	*O-126	-0.2
1948	Cin-N	136	512	74	140	24	9	17	76	52	63	.273	.344	.455	119	12	7			.977	4	*O-130	0.8
1949	Cin-N	134	474	54	118	20	4	9	46	58	63	.249	.333	.365	86	-9	7			.971	1	*O-129	-1.4
1950	Cin-N★	131	509	70	145	34	5	8	76	52	38	.285	.357	.418	103	2	1			.980	-2	*O-129/1-4	-0.5
1951	Cin-N★	142	537	52	167	31	3	2	61	54	54	.311	.376	.391	105	5	2	1	0	.970	-7	*O-139	-0.7
1952	Cin-N	30	106	12	25	1	3	1	10	18	7	.236	.347	.330	89	-1	1	2	-1	1.000	2	O-29/1-1	-0.1
	Phi-N	98	321	45	88	16	3	1	37	44	26	.274	.363	.352	100	2	1	7	-4	.972	8	O-88	0.2
	Yr	128	427	57	113	17	6	2	47	62	33	.265	.359	.347	97	0	2	9	-5	.980	10	*O-117/1-1	0.1
1953	Phi-N	125	409	42	111	14	2	6	47	38	43	.271	.339	.359	83	-10	0	3	-2	.962	2	*O-110	-1.3
1954	Phi-N	92	259	28	62	12	4	3	28	29	39	.239	.318	.351	74	-10	0	0	0	.990	-5	O-55,1-22	-1.7
Total	11	1221	4240	525	1149	209	45	58	481	482	437	.271	.349	.383	98	-5	33	13		.975	16	*O-1105/1-28,32	-4.5

■ HENRY YAIK

Yaik, Henry b: 3/1/1864, Detroit, Mich. d: 9/21/35, Detroit, Mich. 5'11", 185 lbs. Deb: 10/3/1888

YEAR	TM/L	G	AB	R	H	2B	3B	HR	RBI	BB	SO	AVG	OBP	SLG	PRO+	BR/A	SB	CS	SBR	FA	FR	G/POS	TPR
1888	Pit-N	2	6	0	2	0	0	0	1	1	0	.333	.429	.333	158	0	0			.625	2	/O-1,C-1	0.2

■ AD YALE

Yale, William M. b: 4/17/1870, Bristol, Conn. d: 4/27/48, Bridgeport, Conn. Deb: 9/18/05

YEAR	TM/L	G	AB	R	H	2B	3B	HR	RBI	BB	SO	AVG	OBP	SLG	PRO+	BR/A	SB	CS	SBR	FA	FR	G/POS	TPR
1905	Bro-N	4	13	1	1	0	0	0	1	1		.077	.143	.077	-37	-2	0			1.000	-0	/1-4	-0.3

■ HUGH YANCY

Yancy, Hugh b: 10/16/49, Sarasota, Fla. BR/TR, 5'11", 170 lbs. Deb: 7/5/72

YEAR	TM/L	G	AB	R	H	2B	3B	HR	RBI	BB	SO	AVG	OBP	SLG	PRO+	BR/A	SB	CS	SBR	FA	FR	G/POS	TPR
1972	Chi-A	3	9	0	1	0	0	0	0	0	0	.111	.111	.111	-33	-1	0	1	-1	1.000	0	/3-3	-0.2
1974	Chi-A	1	0	0	0	0	0	0	0	0	0	—	—	—	—	-0	0	0	0	.000	0	/D-1	0.0
1976	Chi-A	3	10	0	1	1	0	0	0	0	3	.100	.100	.200	-14	-1	0	0	0	1.000	-1	/2-3	-0.2
Total	3	7	19	0	2	1	0	0	0	0	3	.105	.105	.158	-23	-3	0	1	-1	1.000	-1	/2-3,3-3,D	-0.4

■ GEORGE YANKOWSKI

Yankowski, George Edward b: 11/19/22, Cambridge, Mass. BR/TR, 6', 180 lbs. Deb: 8/17/42

YEAR	TM/L	G	AB	R	H	2B	3B	HR	RBI	BB	SO	AVG	OBP	SLG	PRO+	BR/A	SB	CS	SBR	FA	FR	G/POS	TPR
1942	Phi-A	6	13	0	2	1	0	0	2	0	2	.154	.154	.231	7	-2	0	0		1.000	0	/C-6	-0.1
1949	Chi-A	12	18	0	3	1	0	0	2	0	2	.167	.167	.222	3	-3	0	0		1.000	1	/C-6	-0.1
Total	2	18	31	0	5	2	0	0	4	0	4	.161	.161	.226	5	-4	0	0		1.000	1	/C-12	-0.2

■ GEORGE YANTZ

Yantz, George Webb b: 7/27/1886, Louisville, Ky. d: 2/26/67, Louisville, Ky. BR/TR, 5'6.5", 168 lbs. Deb: 9/30/12

YEAR	TM/L	G	AB	R	H	2B	3B	HR	RBI	BB	SO	AVG	OBP	SLG	PRO+	BR/A	SB	CS	SBR	FA	FR	G/POS	TPR
1912	Chi-N	1	1	0	1	0	0	0	0	0	0	1.000	1.000	1.000	449	0	0			.000	0	/C-1	0.0

■ YAM YARYAN

Yaryan, Clarence Everett b: 11/5/1892, Knowlton, Iowa d: 11/16/64, Birmingham, Ala. BR/TR, 5'10.5", 180 lbs. Deb: 4/23/21

YEAR	TM/L	G	AB	R	H	2B	3B	HR	RBI	BB	SO	AVG	OBP	SLG	PRO+	BR/A	SB	CS	SBR	FA	FR	G/POS	TPR
1921	Chi-A	45	102	11	31	8	2	0	15	9	16	.304	.366	.422	102	0	0	0		.933	-6	C-34	-0.4
1922	Chi-A	36	71	9	14	2	0	2	9	6	10	.197	.269	.310	51	-5	1	0		.966	-1	C-26	-0.5
Total	2	81	173	20	45	10	2	2	24	15	26	.260	.326	.376	81	-5	1	0		.948	-8	/C-60	-0.9

■ CARL YASTRZEMSKI

Yastrzemski, Carl Michael "Yaz" b: 8/22/39, Southampton, N.Y. BL/TR, 5'11", 182 lbs. Deb: 4/11/61 H

YEAR	TM/L	G	AB	R	H	2B	3B	HR	RBI	BB	SO	AVG	OBP	SLG	PRO+	BR/A	SB	CS	SBR	FA	FR	G/POS	TPR
1961	Bos-A	148	583	71	155	31	6	11	80	50	96	.266	.327	.396	90	-9	6	5	-1	.963	1	*O-147	-1.8
1962	Bos-A	160	646	99	191	43	6	19	94	66	82	.296	.364	.469	118	17	7	4	-0	.969	16	*O-160	2.2
1963	Bos-A★	151	570	91	183	40	3	14	68	95	72	.321	.419	.475	145	38	8	5	-1	.980	13	*O-151	4.4
1964	Bos-A	151	567	77	164	29	9	15	67	75	90	.289	.374	.451	122	19	6	5	-1	.973	28	*O-148/3-2	3.9
1965	Bos-A†	133	494	78	154	45	3	20	72	70	58	.312	.398	.536	154	36	7	6	-2	.987	6	*O-130	3.6
1966	Bos-A☆	160	594	81	165	39	2	16	80	84	60	.278	.368	.431	117	14	8	9	-3	.985	17	*O-158	2.2
1967	*Bos-A★	161	579	112	189	31	4	44	121	91	69	.326	.421	.622	189	65	10	8	-2	.978	13	*O-161	7.3
1968	Bos-A★	157	539	90	162	32	2	23	74	119	90	.301	.429	.495	168	50	13	6	-2	.991	17	*O-155/1-3	6.6
1969	Bos-A★	162	603	96	154	28	2	40	111	101	91	.255	.363	.507	134	27	15	7	0	.985	10	*O-143,1-22	2.9
1970	Bos-A★	161	566	125	186	29	0	40	102	128	66	.329	.453	.592	174	62	23	13	-1	.990	1	1-94,O-69	5.2
1971	Bos-A★	148	508	75	129	21	2	15	70	106	60	.254	.384	.392	118	12	8	7	-2	.993	14	*O-146	1.8
1972	Bos-A★	125	455	70	120	18	2	12	68	67	44	.264	.363	.391	118	12	5	4	-1	.974	8	O-83,1-42	1.4
1973	Bos-A†	152	540	82	160	25	4	19	95	105	58	.296	.411	.463	138	30	9	7	-2	.994	-5	*1-107,3-31,O	1.5
1974	Bos-A★	148	515	93	155	25	2	15	79	104	48	.301	.421	.445	139	31	12	7	-1	.997	-7	1-84,O-63/D	1.6
1975	*Bos-A★	149	543	91	146	30	1	14	60	87	67	.269	.372	.405	110	9	8	4	0	.996	-1	*1-140/O-8,D	-0.1
1976	Bos-A	155	546	71	146	23	2	21	102	80	67	.267	.362	.432	118	12	5	6	-1	.998	-8	1-94,O-51,D	-0.7
1977	Bos-A	150	558	99	165	27	3	28	102	73	40	.296	.378	.505	124	18	11	1	3	1.000	14	*O-140/1-7,D	2.8
1978	Bos-A†	144	523	70	145	21	2	17	81	76	44	.277	.367	.423	111	9	4	5	-2	.986	6	O-71,1-50,D	0.6
1979	Bos-A★	147	518	69	140	28	1	21	87	62	46	.270	.351	.450	108	6	3	3	-1	.996	6	D-56,1-51,O	0.4
1980	Bos-A	105	364	49	100	21	1	15	50	44	38	.275	.353	.462	115	8	0	2	-1	1.000	-3	D-49,O-39,1	0.0
1981	Bos-A	91	338	36	83	14	1	7	53	49	28	.246	.341	.355	95	-1	0	1	-1	.992	3	D-48,1-39	-0.3
1982	Bos-A★	131	459	53	126	22	1	16	72	59	50	.275	.360	.431	110	7	0	1	-1	1.000	6	*D-102,1-14/O	0.2
1983	Bos-A★	119	380	38	101	24	0	10	56	54	29	.266	.360	.408	103	3	0	0	0	1.000	-1	*D-107/1-2,O	-0.2
Total	23	3308	11988	1816	3419	646	59	452	1844	1845	1393	.285	.382	.462	128	474	168	116	-19	.981	149	*O-2076,1-765,D/3	45.5

■ AL YATES

Yates, Albert Arthur b: 5/26/45, Jersey City, N.J. BR/TR, 6'2", 210 lbs. Deb: 5/13/71

YEAR	TM/L	G	AB	R	H	2B	3B	HR	RBI	BB	SO	AVG	OBP	SLG	PRO+	BR/A	SB	CS	SBR	FA	FR	G/POS	TPR
1971	Mil-A	24	47	5	13	2	0	1	4	3	7	.277	.320	.383	100	-0	1	0	0	1.000	1	O-12	0.0

■ BERT YEABSLEY

Yeabsley, Robert Watkins b: 12/17/1893, Philadelphia, Pa. d: 2/8/61, Philadelphia, Pa. BR/TR, 5'9.5", 175 lbs. Deb: 5/28/19

YEAR	TM/L	G	AB	R	H	2B	3B	HR	RBI	BB	SO	AVG	OBP	SLG	PRO+	BR/A	SB	CS	SBR	FA	FR	G/POS	TPR
1919	Phi-N	3	0	0	0	0	0	0	0	1	0	—	1.000	—	200	0	0			.000	0	H	0.0

■ GEORGE YEAGER

Yeager, George J. "Doc" b: 6/5/1874, Cincinnati, Ohio d: 7/5/40, Cincinnati, Ohio BR/TR, 5'10", 190 lbs. Deb: 9/25/1896

YEAR	TM/L	G	AB	R	H	2B	3B	HR	RBI	BB	SO	AVG	OBP	SLG	PRO+	BR/A	SB	CS	SBR	FA	FR	G/POS	TPR
1896	Bos-N	2	5	1	1	0	0	0	0	1		.200	.200	.200	5	-1	0			1.000	-0	/1-2	-0.1
1897	*Bos-N	30	95	20	23	2	3	2	15	7		.242	.294	.389	75	-4	2			.970	-4	C-13,O-10/23	-0.2
1898	Bos-N	68	221	37	59	13	1	3	24	16		.267	.328	.376	96	-2	1			.951	-3	C-37,1-17/OS	-0.2
1899	Bos-N	3	8	1	1	0	0	0	0	1		.125	.222	.125	-3	-1	0			1.000	0	/O-2,C-1	-0.1
1901	Cle-A	39	139	13	31	5	0	0	14	4		.223	.250	.259	43	-11	2			.964	3	C-25/1-5,O2	-0.5
	Pit-N	26	91	9	24	7	1	0	10	4		.264	.302	.308	75	-3	1			.971	-2	C-20/3-4,1	-0.5
1902	NY-N	38	108	6	22	2	1	0	9	11		.204	.277	.241	60	-5	1			.946	-1	C-27/1-3,O	-0.3
	Bal-A	11	38	3	7	1	0	0	2	2		.184	.225	.211	20	-4	0			.930	1	C-11	-0.2
Total	6	217	705	90	168	25	6	5	73	45	1	.238	.290	.312	69	-30	7			.953	-4	C-134/1-28,O23S	-1.8

■ JOE YEAGER

Yeager, Joseph F. "Little Joe" b: 8/28/1875, Philadelphia, Pa. d: 7/2/37, Detroit, Mich. BR/TR, 5'10", 160 lbs. Deb: 4/22/1898

YEAR	TM/L	G	AB	R	H	2B	3B	HR	RBI	BB	SO	AVG	OBP	SLG	PRO+	BR/A	SB	CS	SBR	FA	FR	G/POS	TPR
1898	Bro-N	43	134	12	23	5	1	0	15	7		.172	.218	.224	27	-13	1			.908	-8	P-36/O-4,S2	-0.1
1899	Bro-N	23	47	12	9	0	1	0	4	6		.191	.333	.234	55	-3	0			.914	3	S-11,P-10/O3	0.1
1900	Bro-N	3	9	0	3	0	0	0	0	0		.333	.333	.333	79	-0	0			1.000	-1	/P-2,3-1	0.0
1901	Det-A	41	125	18	37	7	1	2	17	4		.296	.343	.416	105	1	3			.919	5	P-26,S-12/2	0.3
1902	Det-A	50	161	17	39	6	5	1	23	5		.242	.282	.360	76	-6	0			.957	-1	P-19,O-13,2/S3	-0.8
1903	Det-A	109	402	36	103	15	6	0	43	18		.256	.303	.323	91	-4	9			.921	-9	*3-107/P-1,S	-1.2
1905	NY-A	115	401	53	107	16	7	0	42	25		.267	.330	.342	102	1	8			.923	-0	3-91,S-21	0.4
1906	NY-A	57	123	20	37	6	1	0	12	13		.301	.407	.366	129	5	3			.905	3	S-22,2-13/3	0.5
1907	StL-A	123	436	32	104	21	7	1	44	31		.239	.294	.326	98	-2	11			.938	7	3-91,2-17,S	0.9
1908	StL-A	10	15	3	5	1	0	0	1	1		.333	.474	.400	183	2	2			1.000	0	/2-4,S-1	0.2
Total	10	574	1853	203	467	77	29	4	201	110		.252	.312	.331	92	-20	37			.927	-4	3-295/P-94,S20	0.3

STEVE YEAGER — Yeager, Stephen Wayne b: 11/24/48, Huntington, W.Va. BR/TR, 6', 190 lbs. Deb: 8/2/72

YEAR	TM/L	G	AB	R	H	2B	3B	HR	RBI	BB	SO	AVG	OBP	SLG	PRO+	BR/A	SB	CS	SBR	FA	FR	G/POS	TPR
1972	LA-N	35	106	18	29	0	1	4	15	16	26	.274	.374	.406	124	4	0	0	0	.984	9	C-35	1.4
1973	LA-N	54	134	18	34	5	0	2	10	15	33	.254	.342	.336	93	-1	1	0	0	.981	5	C-50	0.6
1974	*LA-N	94	316	41	84	16	1	12	41	32	77	.266	.337	.437	120	7	2	2	-1	.992	13	C-93	2.4
1975	LA-N	135	452	34	103	16	1	16	54	40	75	.228	.302	.347	83	-11	2	5	-2	.992	12	*C-135	0.4
1976	LA-N	117	359	42	77	11	3	11	35	30	84	.214	.288	.354	83	-9	3	1	0	.985	9	C-115	0.4
1977	*LA-N	125	387	53	99	21	2	16	55	43	84	.256	.336	.444	108	4	1	3	-2	.977	12	*C-123	1.8
1978	*LA-N	94	228	19	44	7	0	4	23	36	41	.193	.303	.276	63	-11	1	0	0	.988	11	C-91	0.3
1979	LA-N	105	310	33	67	9	2	13	41	29	68	.216	.283	.384	81	-9	1	0	0	.984	11	*C-103	0.6
1980	LA-N	96	227	20	48	8	0	2	20	20	58	.211	.275	.273	55	-14	2	3	-1	.984	4	C-95	-0.9
1981	*LA-N	42	86	5	18	2	0	3	7	6	14	.209	.261	.337	71	-4	0	0	0	.994	1	C-40	-0.2
1982	LA-N	82	196	13	48	5	2	2	18	13	28	.245	.295	.321	74	-7	0	0	0	.990	7	C-76	0.1
1983	*LA-N	113	335	31	68	8	3	15	41	23	57	.203	.256	.379	74	-13	1	1	-0	.985	-6	*C-112	-1.5
1984	LA-N	74	197	16	45	4	0	4	29	20	38	.228	.300	.310	72	-7	1	2	-1	.994	-6	C-65	-1.2
1985	*LA-N	53	121	4	25	4	1	0	9	7	24	.207	.250	.256	43	-9	0	1	-1	.992	-0	C-48	0.0
1986	Sea-A	50	130	10	27	2	0	2	12	12	23	.208	.275	.269	48	-9	0	0	0	1.000	-0	C-49	-0.7
Total	15	1269	3584	357	816	118	16	102	410	342	726	.228	.300	.355	83	-88	14	18	-7	.987	90	*C-1230	3.6

BILL YEATMAN — Yeatman, William Suter b: 3/1839, Alexandria, Va. d: 4/20/01, York, Pa. Deb: 4/20/1872

YEAR	TM/L	G	AB	R	H	2B	3B	HR	RBI	BB	SO	AVG	OBP	SLG	PRO+	BR/A	SB	CS	SBR	FA	FR	G/POS	TPR
1872	Nat-n	1	4	0	0	0	0	0	0	0	0	.000	.000	.000	-86	-1						/O-1	-0.1

ERIC YELDING — Yelding, Eric Girard b: 2/22/65, Montrose, Ala. BR/TR, 5'11", 170 lbs. Deb: 4/9/89

YEAR	TM/L	G	AB	R	H	2B	3B	HR	RBI	BB	SO	AVG	OBP	SLG	PRO+	BR/A	SB	CS	SBR	FA	FR	G/POS	TPR
1989	Hou-N	70	90	19	21	2	0	0	9	7	19	.233	.296	.256	61	-4	11	5	0	1.000	6	S-15,2-13/O	0.3
1990	Hou-N	142	511	69	130	9	5	1	28	39	87	.254	.307	.297	69	-21	64	25	4	.971	-6	O-94,S-40,2/3	-2.2
1991	Hou-N	78	276	19	67	11	1	2	20	13	46	.243	.277	.301	66	-13	11	9	-2	.939	-14	S-72/O-4	-2.5
1992	Hou-N	9	8	1	2	0	0	0	0	0	3	.250	.250	.250	44	-1	0	0	0	.000	-1	/S-2,O-2	-0.2
1993	Chi-N	69	108	14	22	5	1	1	10	11	22	.204	.277	.296	54	-7	3	2	-0	.984	12	2-32/3-7,SO	0.6
Total	5	368	993	122	242	27	7	3	67	70	177	.244	.294	.294	66	-46	89	41	2	.948	-3	S-130,O-109/23	-4.0

ARCHIE YELLE — Yelle, Archie Joseph b: 6/11/1892, Saginaw, Mich. d: 5/2/83, Woodland, Cal. BR/TR, 5'10.5", 170 lbs. Deb: 5/12/17

YEAR	TM/L	G	AB	R	H	2B	3B	HR	RBI	BB	SO	AVG	OBP	SLG	PRO+	BR/A	SB	CS	SBR	FA	FR	G/POS	TPR
1917	Det-A	25	51	4	7	1	0	0	0	5	4	.137	.214	.157	13	-5	0			.975	-1	C-24	-0.6
1918	Det-A	56	144	7	25	3	0	0	7	9	15	.174	.227	.194	28	-13	0			.948	7	C-52	-0.2
1919	Det-A	6	4	1	0	0	0	0	0	1	0	.000	.000	.000	-42	-1	0			.833	-1	/C-6	-0.1
Total	3	87	199	12	32	4	0	0	7	15	19	.161	.223	.181	23	-19	2			.952	5	/C-82	-0.9

STEVE YERKES — Yerkes, Stephen Douglas b: 5/15/1888, Hatboro, Pa. d: 1/31/71, Lansdale, Pa. BR/TR, 5'9", 165 lbs. Deb: 9/29/09

YEAR	TM/L	G	AB	R	H	2B	3B	HR	RBI	BB	SO	AVG	OBP	SLG	PRO+	BR/A	SB	CS	SBR	FA	FR	G/POS	TPR
1909	Bos-A	5	7	0	2	0	0	0	0	0	0	.286	.286	.286	79	-1				1.000	-1	/S-2	-0.1
1911	Bos-A	142	502	70	140	24	3	1	57	52		.279	.354	.345	96	-2	14			.927	-20	*S-116,2-14,3	-1.4
1912	*Bos-A	131	523	73	132	22	6	0	42	41		.252	.312	.317	76	-17	4			.943	-15	*2-131	-3.5
1913	Bos-A	137	483	67	129	29	6	1	48	50	32	.267	.338	.358	101	1	11			.957	-19	*2-129	-2.2
1914	Bos-A	92	293	23	64	17	2	1	23	14	23	.218	.259	.300	68	-13	5	6	-2	.972	4	2-91	-1.3
	Pit-F	39	142	18	48	9	5	1	25	11	13	.338	.386	.493	128	5	2			.974	8	S-39	1.6
1915	Pit-F	121	434	44	125	17	8	1	49	30	27	.288	.337	.371	90	-7	17			.967	-3	*2-114/S-8	-0.8
1916	Chi-N	44	137	12	36	6	2	1	10	9	7	.263	.308	.358	94	-1	1			.919	1	2-41	0.1
Total	7	711	2521	307	676	124	32	6	254	207	102	.268	.328	.350	90	-33	54	6		.956	-45	2-520,S-165/3	-7.6

TOM YEWCIC — Yewcic, Thomas J. "Kibby" b: 5/9/32, Conemaugh, Pa. BR/TR, 5'11", 180 lbs. Deb: 6/27/57

YEAR	TM/L	G	AB	R	H	2B	3B	HR	RBI	BB	SO	AVG	OBP	SLG	PRO+	BR/A	SB	CS	SBR	FA	FR	G/POS	TPR
1957	Det-A	1	1	0	0	0	0	0	0	0	0	.000	.000	.000	-97	-0	0	0	0	.833	1	/C-1	0.0

ED YEWELL — Yewell, Edwin Leonard b: 8/22/1862, Washington, D.C. d: 9/15/40, Washington, D.C. Deb: 5/12/1884

YEAR	TM/L	G	AB	R	H	2B	3B	HR	RBI	BB	SO	AVG	OBP	SLG	PRO+	BR/A	SB	CS	SBR	FA	FR	G/POS	TPR
1884	Was-a	27	93	14	23	3	1	0			1	.247	.263	.301	95	-0				.885	-3	2-11/O-8,3S	-0.2
	Was-U	1	4	0	0	0	0	0				.000	.000	.000	-99	-1				.571	-0	/3-1	-0.1
Total	1	28	97	14	23	3	1	0			1	.237	.253	.289	84	-2				.773	-3	/2-11,3-8,OS	-0.3

JOE YINGLING — Yingling, Joseph Granville b: 7/23/1866, Westminster, Md. d: 10/24/46, Manchester, Md. BR/TL, 5'7.5", 145 lbs. Deb: 5/28/1886

YEAR	TM/L	G	AB	R	H	2B	3B	HR	RBI	BB	SO	AVG	OBP	SLG	PRO+	BR/A	SB	CS	SBR	FA	FR	G/POS	TPR
1886	Was-N	1	2	0	0	0	0	0	0	0	1	.000	.000	.000	-99	-1	0			.500	-0	/P-1	0.0
1894	Phi-N	1	4	0	1	0	0	0	0	0	1	.250	.250	.250	21	-1	0			1.000	-1	/S-1	-0.1
Total	2	2	6	0	1	0	0	0	0	0	2	.167	.167	.167	-14	-1	0			1.000	-1	/S-1,P-1	-0.1

BILL YOHE — Yohe, William Clyde b: 9/2/1878, Mt.Elere, Ill. d: 12/24/38, Bremerton, Wash. TR, 5'8", 180 lbs. Deb: 8/30/09

YEAR	TM/L	G	AB	R	H	2B	3B	HR	RBI	BB	SO	AVG	OBP	SLG	PRO+	BR/A	SB	CS	SBR	FA	FR	G/POS	TPR
1909	Was-A	21	72	6	15	2	0	0	4	3		.208	.240	.236	53	-4	2			.921	3	3-19	0.0

TONY YORK — York, Anthony Batton b: 11/27/12, Irene, Tex. d: 4/18/70, Hillsboro, Tex. BR/TR, 5'10", 165 lbs. Deb: 4/18/44

YEAR	TM/L	G	AB	R	H	2B	3B	HR	RBI	BB	SO	AVG	OBP	SLG	PRO+	BR/A	SB	CS	SBR	FA	FR	G/POS	TPR
1944	Chi-N	28	85	4	20	1	0	0	7	4	11	.235	.270	.247	46	-6	0			.940	10	S-15,3-12	0.5

RUDY YORK — York, Preston Rudolph b: 8/17/13, Ragland, Ala. d: 2/5/70, Rome, Ga. BR/TR, 6'1", 209 lbs. Deb: 8/22/34 MC

YEAR	TM/L	G	AB	R	H	2B	3B	HR	RBI	BB	SO	AVG	OBP	SLG	PRO+	BR/A	SB	CS	SBR	FA	FR	G/POS	TPR
1934	Det-A	3	6	0	1	0	0	0	0	1	3	.167	.286	.167	19	-1	0	0	0	1.000	-0	/C-2	-0.1
1937	Det-A	104	375	72	115	18	3	35	103	41	52	.307	.375	.651	150	25	3	2	-0	.960	-19	C-54,3-41/1	0.9
1938	Det-A★	135	463	85	138	27	2	33	127	92	74	.298	.417	.579	139	28	1	2	-1	.990	-1	*C-116,O-14/1	2.8
1939	Det-A	102	329	66	101	16	1	20	68	42	50	.307	.387	.544	126	12	5	0	-0	.985	-8	C-67,1-19	0.7
1940	*Det-A	155	588	105	186	46	6	33	134	89	88	.316	.410	.583	141	35	3	2	-0	.990	5	*1-155	2.3
1941	Det-A★	155	590	91	153	29	3	27	111	92	88	.259	.360	.456	104	3	3	1	-0	.986	-1	*1-155	-1.0
1942	Det-A★	153	577	81	150	26	4	21	90	73	71	.260	.343	.428	107	5	3	5	-3	.988	15	*1-152	1.0
1943	Det-A★	155	571	90	155	22	11	**34**	**118**	84	88	.271	.366	**.527**	148	33	5	5	-2	.990	18	*1-155	4.3
1944	Det-A☆	151	587	77	161	27	7	18	98	68	73	.276	.353	.439	119	14	5	3	-0	.989	-1	*1-151	1.1
1945	*Det-A	155	595	71	157	25	5	18	87	60	85	.264	.331	.413	109	5	6	6	-2	.988	-2	*1-155	-1.0
1946	*Bos-A★	154	579	78	160	30	6	17	119	86	93	.276	.371	.437	118	15	2	2	-0	.994	6	*1-154	1.2
1947	Bos-A	48	184	16	39	7	0	6	27	22	32	.212	.296	.348	73	-7	0	0	-0	.995	1	1-48	-0.8
	Chi-A☆	102	400	40	97	18	4	15	64	36	55	.243	.305	.420	104	-0	1	0	-0	**.995**	0	*1-150	-0.5
	Yr	150	584	56	136	25	4	21	91	58	87	.233	.302	.397	94	-8	1	0	0	.995	0	*1-150	-1.3
1948	Phi-A	31	51	4	8	0	0	0	6	7	15	.157	.259	.157	12	-6	0	0	0	.988	-1	1-14	-0.7
Total	13	1603	5891	876	1621	291	52	277	1152	792	867	.275	.362	.483	121	160	38	26	-4	.990	16	*1-1263,C-239/30	10.2

TOM YORK — York, Thomas Jefferson b: 7/13/1851, Brooklyn, N.Y. d: 2/17/36, New York, N.Y. BL, 5'9", 165 lbs. Deb: 5/9/1871 MU

YEAR	TM/L	G	AB	R	H	2B	3B	HR	RBI	BB	SO	AVG	OBP	SLG	PRO+	BR/A	SB	CS	SBR	FA	FR	G/POS	TPR
1871	Tro-n	29	145	36	37	5	7	2	23	9	1	.255	.299	.428	104	0	2					*O-29	0.1
1872	Bal-n	51	249	65	64	8	4	1	42	4	1	.257	.269	.333	81	-7						*O-49	-0.3
1873	Bal-n	57	277	70	84	10	5	2	49	3	3	.303	.311	.397	107	2						*O-57	0.3
1874	Phi-n	50	223	36	58	3	8	0			4	.260	.273	.345	92	-2						*O-50	-0.1
1875	Har-n	86	376	68	112	12	7	0			4	.298	.305	.367	125	8						*O-85	0.7
1876	Har-N	67	263	47	68	12	6	1	39	10	4	.259	.286	.369	108	1				.899	2	*O-67	0.2
1877	Har-N	56	237	43	67	16	7	1	37	3	11	.283	.292	.422	137	10				.865	0	*O-56	1.6
1878	Pro-N	62	269	56	83	19	**10**	1	26	8	19	.309	.329	.465	159	16				.873	4	*O-62,M	1.6
1879	Pro-N	81	342	69	106	25	5	1	50	19	28	.310	.346	.421	154	20				.898	-4	*O-81	1.0
1880	Pro-N	53	203	21	43	6	3	0	8	8	29	.212	.242	.276	77	-4				.934	-3	O-53	-0.8
1881	Pro-N	85	316	57	96	23	5	2	47	29	26	.304	.362	.427	150	19				.859	-2	*O-85,M	1.4

YEAR	TM/L	G	AB	R	H	2B	3B	HR	RBI	BB	SO	AVG	OBP	SLG	PRO+	BR/A	SB	CS	SBR	FA	FR	G/POS	TPR
1882	Pro-N	81	321	48	86	23	7	1	40	19	14	.268	.309	.393	123	8				.873	-3	*O-81	0.5
1883	Cle-N	100	381	56	99	29	5	2	46	**37**	55	.260	.325	.378	114	8				.864	0	*O-100	0.6
1884	Bal-a	83	314	64	70	14	7	1	34			.223	.318	.322	105	3				.843	-5	*O-83	-0.4
1885	Bal-a	22	87	6	23	4	2	0	8			.264	.326	.356	117	2				.938	1	O-22	0.2
Total	5 n	273	1270	275	355	38	31	5	114	24	5	.280	.293	.370	104	1						O-270	0.7
Total	10	690	2733	467	741	174	57	10	**303**	175	**186**	.271	.317	.387	126	83				.878	-8	O-690	5.0

■ NED YOST
Yost, Edgar Frederick b: 8/19/55, Eureka, Cal. BR/TR, 6'1", 190 lbs. Deb: 4/12/80

YEAR	TM/L	G	AB	R	H	2B	3B	HR	RBI	BB	SO	AVG	OBP	SLG	PRO+	BR/A	SB	CS	SBR	FA	FR	G/POS	TPR
1980	Mil-A	15	31	0	5	0	0	0	0	0	6	.161	.161	.161	-12	-5	0	0	0	1.000	2	C-15	-0.2
1981	Mil-A	18	27	4	6	0	0	3	3	3	6	.222	.300	.556	150	1	0	0	0	.956	2	C-16	0.4
1982	*Mil-A	40	98	13	27	6	3	1	8	7	20	.276	.324	.429	111	1	3	1	0	.977	-2	C-39/D-1	0.1
1983	Mil-A	61	196	21	44	5	1	6	28	5	36	.224	.244	.352	67	-10	1	0	0	.971	-6	C-61	-1.3
1984	Tex-A	80	242	15	44	4	0	6	25	6	47	.182	.202	.273	29	-23	1	2	-1	.995	-5	C-78	-2.7
1985	Mon-N	5	11	1	2	0	0	0	0	0	0	.182	.182	.182	2	-1	0	0	0	.962	1	/C-5	-0.1
Total	6	219	605	54	128	15	4	16	64	21	117	.212	.238	.329	56	-37	5	3	-0	.982	-8	C-214/D-1	-3.8

■ EDDIE YOST
Yost, Edward Frederick Joseph "The Walking Man" b: 10/13/26, Brooklyn, N.Y. BR/TR, 5'10", 170 lbs. Deb: 8/16/44 MC

YEAR	TM/L	G	AB	R	H	2B	3B	HR	RBI	BB	SO	AVG	OBP	SLG	PRO+	BR/A	SB	CS	SBR	FA	FR	G/POS	TPR
1944	Was-A	7	14	3	2	0	0	0	0	1	2	.143	.200	.143	-1	-2	0	0	0	.917	-1	/3-3,S-2	-0.2
1946	Was-A	8	25	2	2	1	0	0	1	5	5	.080	.233	.120	1	-3	2	1	0	1.000	1	/3-7	-0.3
1947	Was-A	115	428	52	102	17	3	0	14	45	57	.238	.314	.292	71	-16	3	5	-2	.958	-9	*3-114	-2.8
1948	Was-A	145	555	74	138	32	11	2	50	82	51	.249	.349	.357	91	-7	4	3	-1	.966	-13	*3-145	-2.1
1949	Was-A	124	435	57	110	19	2	9	45	91	41	.253	.383	.391	107	7	3	3	-1	.954	-2	*3-122	0.1
1950	Was-A	155	573	114	169	26	2	11	58	**141**	63	.295	.440	.405	123	30	6	6	-2	.954	-2	*3-155	2.2
1951	Was-A☆	154	568	109	161	36	4	12	65	**126**	55	.283	.423	.424	132	32	6	4	-1	.954	-27	*3-152/O-3	0.3
1952	Was-A	157	587	92	137	32	3	12	49	**129**	73	.233	.378	.359	110	13	4	3	-1	.962	-35	*3-157	-2.7
1953	Was-A	152	577	107	157	30	7	9	45	**123**	59	.272	.403	.395	119	21	7	4	-0	.965	-13	*3-152	0.5
1954	Was-A	155	539	101	138	26	4	11	47	**131**	71	.256	.406	.380	123	24	7	3	0	.968	3	*3-155	2.5
1955	Was-A	122	375	64	91	17	5	7	48	95	54	.243	.410	.371	117	15	4	3	-1	.943	-6	*3-107	0.8
1956	Was-A	152	515	94	119	17	2	11	53	**151**	82	.231	.412	.336	100	9	8	5	-1	.963	11	*3-135/O-8	2.0
1957	Was-A	110	414	47	104	13	5	9	37	83	49	.251	.370	.372	104	5	1	11	-6	.952	-11	*3-107	-1.0
1958	Was-A	134	406	55	91	16	0	8	37	81	43	.224	.365	.323	93	-0	3	6	-3	.964	-15	*3-114/O-4,1	-1.8
1959	Det-A	148	521	**115**	145	19	0	21	61	**135**	77	.278	**.437**	.436	133	32	9	2	2	**.962**	-11	*3-146/2-1	2.3
1960	Det-A	143	497	78	129	23	2	14	47	**125**	69	.260	.416	.398	118	19	5	4	-1	.933	-27	*3-142	-1.0
1961	LA-A	76	213	29	43	4	0	3	15	50	48	.202	.358	.263	62	-10	0	1	-1	.964	-10	3-67	-2.0
1962	LA-A	52	104	22	25	9	1	0	10	30	21	.240	.415	.346	111	3	0	2	-1	.950	-3	3-28/1-7	0.0
Total	18	2109	7346	1215	1863	337	56	139	683	1614	920	.254	.395	.371	109	172	72	66	-18	.957	-169	*3-2008/O-15,1S2	-3.2

■ ELMER YOTER
Yoter, Elmer Elsworth b: 6/26/1900, Plainfield, Pa. d: 7/26/66, Camp Hill, Pa. BR/TR, 5'7", 155 lbs. Deb: 9/9/21

YEAR	TM/L	G	AB	R	H	2B	3B	HR	RBI	BB	SO	AVG	OBP	SLG	PRO+	BR/A	SB	CS	SBR	FA	FR	G/POS	TPR
1921	Phi-A	3	3	0	0	0	0	0	0	0	0	.000	.000	.000	-99	-1	0	0	0	.000	0	H	-0.1
1924	Cle-A	19	66	3	18	1	1	0	7	5	8	.273	.324	.318	65	-3	0	0	0	.905	-2	3-19	-0.4
1927	Chi-N	13	27	2	6	1	1	0	5	4	4	.222	.323	.333	76	-1	0	0	0	.947	-1	3-11	-0.1
1928	Chi-N	1	0	0	0	0	0	0	0	0	0	—	—	—	—	0		0		.000	0	/3-1	0.0
Total	4	36	96	5	24	2	2	0	12	9	12	.250	.314	.313	63	-5	0	0	0	.915	-2	/3-31	-0.6

■ DEL YOUNG
Young, Delmer Edward b: 5/11/12, Cleveland, Ohio d: 12/8/79, San Francisco, Cal. BB/TR, 5'11", 168 lbs. Deb: 4/19/37 F

YEAR	TM/L	G	AB	R	H	2B	3B	HR	RBI	BB	SO	AVG	OBP	SLG	PRO+	BR/A	SB	CS	SBR	FA	FR	G/POS	TPR
1937	Phi-N	109	360	36	70	9	2	0	24	18	55	.194	.235	.231	25	-37	6			.950	11	*2-108	-2.0
1938	Phi-N	108	340	27	78	13	2	0	31	20	35	.229	.276	.279	55	-21	0			.933	-2	S-87,2-17	-1.6
1939	Phi-N	77	217	22	57	9	3	2	20	8	24	.263	.289	.364	77	-8	1			.946	-18	S-55,2-17	-2.1
1940	Phi-N	15	33	2	8	0	1	0	1	2	1	.242	.286	.303	65	-2	0			.962	-0	/S-6,2-5	-0.1
Total	4	309	950	87	213	31	7	3	76	48	115	.224	.264	.281	48	-68	7			.938	-9	S-148,2-147	-5.8

■ DEL YOUNG
Young, Delmer John b: 10/24/1885, Macon, Mo. d: 12/17/59, Cleveland, Ohio BL/TR, 5'11", 195 lbs. Deb: 9/24/09 F

YEAR	TM/L	G	AB	R	H	2B	3B	HR	RBI	BB	SO	AVG	OBP	SLG	PRO+	BR/A	SB	CS	SBR	FA	FR	G/POS	TPR
1909	Cin-N	2	7	0	2	0	0	0	1	1		.286	.375	.286	106	0	0			1.000	0	/O-2	0.0
1914	Buf-F	80	174	17	48	5	5	4	22	3	13	.276	.288	.431	83	-6	0			.944	-6	O-41	-1.4
1915	Buf-F	12	15	0	2	0	0	0	1	0		.133	.188	.133	-13	-2	1			.667	-1	/O-3	-0.4
Total	3	94	196	17	52	5	5	4	23	5	13	.265	.284	.403	77	-8	1			.933	-7	/O-46	-1.8

■ DON YOUNG
Young, Donald Wayne b: 10/18/45, Houston, Tex. BR/TR, 6'2", 185 lbs. Deb: 9/9/65

YEAR	TM/L	G	AB	R	H	2B	3B	HR	RBI	BB	SO	AVG	OBP	SLG	PRO+	BR/A	SB	CS	SBR	FA	FR	G/POS	TPR
1965	Chi-N	11	35	1	2	0	0	0	2	0	11	.057	.057	.143	-45	-7	0			.933	-2	O-11	-1.0
1969	Chi-N	101	272	36	65	12	3	6	27	38	74	.239	.343	.371	89	-4	1	5	-3	.975	-4	*O-100	-1.6
Total	2	112	307	37	67	12	3	7	29	38	85	.218	.314	.345	76	-10	1	5	-3	.972	-6	O-111	-2.6

■ ERIC YOUNG
Young, Eric Orlando b: 5/18/67, New Brunswick, N.J. BR/TR, 5'9", 180 lbs. Deb: 7/30/92

YEAR	TM/L	G	AB	R	H	2B	3B	HR	RBI	BB	SO	AVG	OBP	SLG	PRO+	BR/A	SB	CS	SBR	FA	FR	G/POS	TPR
1992	LA-N	49	132	9	34	1	0	1	11	8	9	.258	.300	.288	68	-5	6	1	1	.957	10	2-43	0.7
1993	Col-N	144	490	82	132	16	8	3	42	63	41	.269	.357	.353	78	-15	42	19	1	.962	-11	2-79,O-52	-2.3
1994	Col-N	90	228	37	62	13	1	7	30	38	17	.272	.381	.430	95	-1	18	7	1	.981	5	O-60/2-1	0.0
Total	3	283	850	128	228	30	9	11	83	109	67	.268	.355	.364	82	-21	66	27	4	.960	1	2-123,O-112	-1.6

■ ERNIE YOUNG
Young, Ernest Wesley b: 7/8/69, Chicago, Ill. BR/TR, 6'1", 190 lbs. Deb: 5/17/94

YEAR	TM/L	G	AB	R	H	2B	3B	HR	RBI	BB	SO	AVG	OBP	SLG	PRO+	BR/A	SB	CS	SBR	FA	FR	G/POS	TPR
1994	Oak-A	11	30	2	2	1	0	0	3	1	8	.067	.097	.100	-54	-7	0	0	0	.958	0	O-10/D-1	-0.6

■ GEORGE YOUNG
Young, George Joseph b: 4/1/1890, Brooklyn, N.Y. d: 3/13/50, Brightwaters, N.Y. BL/TR, 6', 185 lbs. Deb: 8/10/13

YEAR	TM/L	G	AB	R	H	2B	3B	HR	RBI	BB	SO	AVG	OBP	SLG	PRO+	BR/A	SB	CS	SBR	FA	FR	G/POS	TPR
1913	Cle-A	2	2	0	0	0	0	0	0	0	0	.000	.000	.000	-97	-0	0			.000	0	H	-0.1

■ GERALD YOUNG
Young, Gerald Anthony b: 10/22/64, Tela, Honduras BB/TR, 6'2", 185 lbs. Deb: 7/8/87

YEAR	TM/L	G	AB	R	H	2B	3B	HR	RBI	BB	SO	AVG	OBP	SLG	PRO+	BR/A	SB	CS	SBR	FA	FR	G/POS	TPR
1987	Hou-N	71	274	44	88	9	2	1	15	26	27	.321	.382	.380	107	4	26	9	2	.980	5	O-67	0.8
1988	Hou-N	149	576	79	148	21	9	0	37	66	66	.257	.336	.325	94	-3	65	27	3	.992	13	*O-145	0.9
1989	Hou-N	146	533	71	124	17	3	0	38	74	60	.233	.328	.276	77	-13	34	25	-5	**.998**	26	*O-143	0.5
1990	Hou-N	57	154	15	27	4	1	1	4	20	34	.175	.270	.234	41	-12	6	3	0	.990	-2	O-50	-1.5
1991	Hou-N	108	142	26	31	3	1	1	11	24	17	.218	.331	.275	77	-4	16	5	2	1.000	-14	O-84	-1.8
1992	Hou-N	74	76	14	14	1	1	0	4	10	11	.184	.279	.224	46	-6	6	2	1	.964	-15	O-57	-2.2
1993	Col-N	19	19	5	1	0	0	0	1	4	1	.053	.217	.053	-20	-3	0	1	-1	.882	-3	O-11	-0.7
1994	StL-N	16	41	5	13	3	2	0	3	9	8	.317	.364	.488	124	1	2	1	0	1.000	-1	O-11	0.0
Total	8	640	1815	259	446	58	19	3	113	227	213	.246	.332	.304	82	-36	155	73	2	.990	9	O-568	-4.0

■ HERMAN YOUNG
Young, Herman John b: 4/14/1886, Boston, Mass. d: 12/13/66, Ipswich, Mass. BR/TR, 5'8", 155 lbs. Deb: 6/11/11

YEAR	TM/L	G	AB	R	H	2B	3B	HR	RBI	BB	SO	AVG	OBP	SLG	PRO+	BR/A	SB	CS	SBR	FA	FR	G/POS	TPR
1911	Bos-N	9	25	2	6	0	0	0	3	4		.240	.269	.240	40	-2	0			.905	4	/3-5,S-3	0.2

■ JOHN YOUNG
Young, John Thomas b: 2/9/49, Los Angeles, Cal. BL/TL, 6'3", 210 lbs. Deb: 9/9/71

YEAR	TM/L	G	AB	R	H	2B	3B	HR	RBI	BB	SO	AVG	OBP	SLG	PRO+	BR/A	SB	CS	SBR	FA	FR	G/POS	TPR
1971	Det-A	2	4	1	2	1	0	0	2	0	0	.500	.500	.750		1	0	0	0	1.000	-0	/1-1	0.0

■ KEVIN YOUNG
Young, Kevin Stacey b: 6/16/69, Alpena, Mich. BR/TR, 6'3", 210 lbs. Deb: 7/12/92

YEAR	TM/L	G	AB	R	H	2B	3B	HR	RBI	BB	SO	AVG	OBP	SLG	PRO+	BR/A	SB	CS	SBR	FA	FR	G/POS	TPR
1992	Pit-N	10	7	2	4	0	0	0	4	2	0	.571	.667	.571	256	2	1	0	0	.750	-1	/3-7,1-1	0.1
1993	Pit-N	141	449	38	106	24	3	6	47	36	82	.236	.306	.343	73	-17	2	2	-1	**.998**	7	*1-135/3-6	-2.1
1994	Pit-N	59	122	15	25	7	2	1	11	8	34	.205	.260	.320	50	-9	0	2	-1	1.000	1	1-37,3-17/O	-1.0
Total	3	210	578	55	135	31	5	7	62	46	116	.234	.301	.341	71	-24	3	4	-2	.998	7	1-173/3-30,O	-3.0

YEAR	TM/L	G	AB	R	H	2B	3B	HR	RBI	BB	SO	AVG	OBP	SLG	PRO+	BR/A	SB	CS	SBR	FA	FR	G/POS	TPR

■ PEP YOUNG　　Young, Lemuel Floyd　b: 8/29/07, Jamestown, N.C.　d: 1/14/62, Jamestown, N.C.　BR/TR, 5'9", 162 lbs.　Deb: 4/25/33

1933	Pit-N	25	20	3	6	1	1	0	0	0	5	.300	.300	.450	112	0	0			1.000	0	/2-1,S-1	0.1
1934	Pit-N	19	17	3	4	0	0	0	2	0	6	.235	.235	.235	26	-2	0			1.000	2	/2-2,S-2	0.1
1935	Pit-N	128	494	60	131	25	10	7	82	21	59	.265	.298	.399	83	-13	2			.952	-12	*2-107/3-6,OS	-1.6
1936	Pit-N	125	475	47	118	23	10	6	77	29	52	.248	.293	.377	77	-16	3			.966	-24	*2-123	-3.1
1937	Pit-N	113	408	43	106	20	3	9	54	26	63	.260	.306	.390	88	-8	4			.942	18	S-45,3-39,2	1.6
1938	Pit-N	149	562	58	156	36	5	4	79	40	64	.278	.329	.381	94	-5	7			.973	**32**	*2-149	3.5
1939	Pit-N	84	293	34	81	14	3	3	29	23	29	.276	.333	.375	92	-4	1			.967	3	2-84	0.4
1940	Pit-N	54	136	19	34	8	2	2	20	12	23	.250	.320	.382	94	-1	1			.909	-5	2-33/S-7,3	-0.4
1941	Cin-N	4	12	2	2	0	0	0	0	0	1	.167	.231	.167	13	-1	0			.923	1	/3-3	-0.1
	StL-N	2	2	0	0	0	0	0	0	0	2	.000	.000	.000	-94	-1	0			.000	0	H	-0.1
	Yr	6	14	2	2	0	0	0	0	0	3	.143	.200	.143	-2	-2	0			.923	1	/3-3	-0.2
1945	StL-N	27	47	5	7	1	0	1	4	1	8	.149	.167	.234	10	-6	0			.978	1	S-11/3-9,2	-0.5
Total	10	730	2466	274	645	128	34	32	347	152	312	.262	.308	.380	85	-56	18			.964	17	2-532/S-70,3O	-0.1

■ MIKE YOUNG　　Young, Michael Darren　b: 3/20/60, Oakland, Cal.　BB/TR, 6'2", 195 lbs.　Deb: 9/14/82

1982	Bal-A	6	2	2	0	0	0	0	0	0	1	.000	.000	.000	-99	-1	0	0	0	1.000	-0	/O-1,D-2	-0.1
1983	Bal-A	25	36	5	6	2	1	0	2	2	8	.167	.237	.278	40	-3	1	0	0	.929	-4	O-22/D-3	-0.7
1984	Bal-A	123	401	59	101	17	2	17	52	58	110	.252	.356	.431	119	12	6	2	1	.982	-9	*O-115/D-1	-0.1
1985	Bal-A	139	450	72	123	22	1	28	81	48	104	.273	.349	.513	136	21	1	5	-3	.975	-0	O-90,D-37	1.5
1986	Bal-A	117	369	43	93	15	1	9	42	49	90	.252	.344	.371	96	-1	3	1	0	.962	2	O-69,D-38	-0.1
1987	Bal-A	110	363	46	87	10	1	16	39	46	91	.240	.328	.405	96	-2	10	7	-1	.975	-3	O-60,D-47	-0.9
1988	Phi-N	75	146	13	33	14	0	1	14	26	43	.226	.347	.342	96	0	0	0	0	.938	-2	O-42	-0.3
	Mil-A	8	14	2	0	0	0	0	0	2	5	.000	.176	.000	-46	-3	0	0	0	.000	-1	/O-2,D-5	-0.4
1989	Cle-A	32	59	2	11	0	0	1	5	6	13	.186	.273	.237	44	-4	1	2	-1	1.000	0	D-15/O-1	-0.6
Total	8	635	1840	244	454	80	6	72	235	237	465	.247	.339	.414	107	20	22	17	-4	.969	-18	O-402,D-148	-1.7

■ BABE YOUNG　　Young, Norman Robert　b: 7/1/15, Astoria, N.Y.　d: 12/25/83, Everett, Mass.　BL/TL, 6'2.5", 185 lbs.　Deb: 9/26/36

1936	NY-N	1	1	0	0	0	0	0	0	0	0	.000	.000	.000	-99	-0	0			.000	0	H	0.0
1939	NY-N	22	75	8	23	4	0	3	14	5	6	.307	.373	.480	127	3	0			.982	-2	1-22	-0.1
1940	NY-N	149	556	75	159	27	4	17	101	69	28	.286	.367	.441	121	16	4			.992	-2	*1-147	0.0
1941	NY-N	152	574	90	152	28	5	25	104	66	39	.265	.346	.462	124	17	1			.986	-4	*1-150	0.2
1942	NY-N	101	287	37	80	17	1	11	59	34	22	.279	.365	.460	140	14	1			.972	-4	O-54,1-18	0.7
1946	NY-N	104	291	30	81	11	0	7	33	30	21	.278	.346	.388	107	3	3			.988	-8	1-49,O-24	-0.9
1947	NY-N	14	14	0	1	0	0	0	0	1	0	.071	.071	.143	-44	-3	0			.000	0	H	-0.3
	Cin-N	95	364	55	103	21	3	14	79	35	26	.283	.349	.473	117	8	0			.990	-2	1-93	0.3
	Yr	109	378	55	104	22	3	14	79	35	27	.275	.340	.460	111	5	0			.990	-2	1-93	0.0
1948	Cin-N	49	130	11	30	7	2	1	12	19	12	.231	.329	.338	84	-3	0			.993	0	1-31/O-1	-0.3
	StL-N	41	111	14	27	5	2	1	13	16	6	.243	.339	.351	82	-3	0			.996	-4	1-35	-0.7
	Yr	90	241	25	57	12	4	2	25	35	18	.237	.333	.344	83	-5	0			.995	-4	1-66/O-1	-1.0
Total	8	728	2403	320	656	121	17	79	415	274	161	.273	.352	.436	117	52	0			.989	-25	1-545/O-79	-1.1

■ RALPH YOUNG　　Young, Ralph Stuart　b: 9/19/1889, Philadelphia, Pa.　d: 1/24/65, Philadelphia, Pa.　BB/TR, 5'5", 165 lbs.　Deb: 4/10/13

1913	NY-A	7	15	2	1	0	0	0	0	3	3	.067	.222	.067	-15	-2	2			.857	1	/S-7	0.0
1915	Det-A	123	378	44	92	6	5	0	31	53	31	.243	.339	.286	83	-7	12	11	-3	.950	8	*2-119	0.0
1916	Det-A	153	528	60	139	16	6	1	45	62	43	.263	.342	.322	96	-2	20	20	-6	.966	-1	*2-146/S-6,3	-0.4
1917	Det-A	141	503	64	116	18	2	1	35	61	35	.231	.317	.280	83	-9	8			.958	8	*2-141	0.7
1918	Det-A	91	298	31	56	7	1	0	21	54	17	.188	.313	.218	63	-11	15			.939	-12	*2-91	-1.9
1919	Det-A	125	456	63	96	13	5	1	25	53	32	.211	.294	.268	60	-24	8			.970	17	*2-120/S-5	-0.1
1920	Det-A	150	594	84	173	21	6	0	33	85	30	.291	.382	.347	96	1	8	13	-5	.969	-11	*2-150	-1.0
1921	Det-A	107	401	70	120	8	3	0	29	69	23	.299	.406	.334	91	-1	11	9	-2	.947	-23	*2-106	-2.2
1922	Phi-A	125	470	62	105	19	2	1	35	55	21	.223	.309	.279	53	-32	8	6	-1	.960	-15	*2-120	-4.4
Total	9	1022	3643	480	898	108	30	4	254	495	235	.247	.339	.296	79	-86	92	<u>59</u>		.959	-28	2-993/S-18,3	-9.3

■ DICK YOUNG　　Young, Richard Ennis　b: 6/3/28, Seattle, Wash.　BL/TR, 5'11", 175 lbs.　Deb: 9/11/51

1951	Phi-N	15	68	7	16	5	0	0	2	3	6	.235	.268	.309	55	-4	0	1	-1	.922	-9	2-15	-1.4
1952	Phi-N	5	9	3	2	1	0	0	0	1	3	.222	.300	.333	76	-0	1	0	0	.900	-0	/2-2	0.0
Total	2	20	77	10	18	6	0	0	2	4	9	.234	.272	.312	58	-5	1	1	-0	.919	-9	/2-17	-1.4

■ BOBBY YOUNG　　Young, Robert George　b: 1/22/25, Granite, Md.　d: 1/28/85, Baltimore, Md.　BL/TR, 6'1", 175 lbs.　Deb: 7/28/48

1948	StL-N	3	1	0	0	0	0	0	0	0	1	.000	.000	.000	-95	-0	0			1.000	0	/3-1	0.0
1951	StL-A	147	611	75	159	13	9	1	31	44	51	.260	.310	.316	67	-28	8	7	-2	.980	1	*2-147	-2.2
1952	StL-A	149	575	59	142	15	9	4	39	56	48	.247	.314	.325	76	-19	3	3	-1	.984	-9	*2-149	-2.2
1953	StL-A	148	537	48	137	22	2	4	25	41	40	.255	.309	.326	70	-22	2	1	0	.977	-17	*2-148	-3.1
1954	Bal-A	130	432	43	106	13	6	4	24	54	42	.245	.331	.331	88	-7	4	4	-1	.976	-14	*2-127	-1.5
1955	Bal-A	59	186	5	37	3	0	1	8	11	23	.199	.244	.231	30	-19	1	4	-2	.985	3	2-58	-1.5
	Cle-A	18	45	7	14	1	1	0	6	1	2	.311	.326	.378	86	-1	0	0	0	.983	7	2-11/3-1	0.6
	Yr	77	231	12	51	4	1	1	14	12	25	.221	.259	.260	42	-19	1	4	-2	.985	9	2-69/3-1	-0.9
1956	Cle-A	1	0	0	0	0	0	0	0	0	0	—	—	—	—	0	0	0	0	.000	0	R	0.0
1958	Phi-N	32	60	7	14	1	1	0	4	1	5	.233	.246	.333	52	-4	0	0	0	.968	-2	2-21	-0.6
Total	8	687	2447	244	609	68	28	15	137	208	212	.249	.308	.318	71	-100	18	<u>19</u>		.980	-32	2-661/3-2	-10.5

■ RUSS YOUNG　　Young, Russell Charles　b: 9/15/02, Bryan, Ohio　d: 5/13/84, Roseville, Cal.　BB/TR, 6', 175 lbs.　Deb: 4/16/31

| 1931 | StL-A | 16 | 34 | 2 | 4 | 0 | 0 | 1 | 2 | 2 | 4 | .118 | .167 | .206 | -3 | -5 | 0 | 0 | 0 | 1.000 | 2 | C-16 | -0.2 |

■ JOEL YOUNGBLOOD　　Youngblood, Joel Randolph　b: 8/28/51, Houston, Tex.　BR/TR, 6', 180 lbs.　Deb: 4/13/76　C

1976	Cin-N	55	57	8	11	1	1	0	1	2	8	.193	.233	.246	35	-5	1	0	0	.938	-1	/O-9,3-6,C2	-0.6
1977	StL-N	25	27	1	5	2	0	0	1	3	5	.185	.267	.259	43	-2	0	2	-1	1.000	-3	O-11/3-6	-0.7
	NY-N	70	182	16	46	11	1	0	11	13	40	.253	.303	.324	72	-7	1	3	-2	.954	2	2-33,O-22,3	-0.6
	Yr	95	209	17	51	13	1	0	12	16	45	.244	.298	.316	67	-10	1	5	-3	1.000	-1	O-33,2-33,3	-1.3
1978	NY-N	113	266	40	67	12	8	7	30	16	39	.252	.297	.436	106	1	4	0	1	.989	2	O-50,2-39/3S	0.4
1979	NY-N	158	590	90	162	37	5	16	60	60	84	.275	.349	.436	117	13	18	13	-2	.985	4	*O-147,2-13,3	1.2
1980	NY-N	146	514	58	142	26	2	8	69	52	69	.276	.345	.381	105	4	14	11	-2	.984	15	*O-121,3-21/2	1.2
1981	NY-N★	43	143	16	50	10	2	4	25	12	19	.350	.408	.531	167	12	2	5	-2	.962	2	O-41	1.1
1982	NY-N	80	202	21	52	12	0	3	21	8	37	.257	.302	.361	85	-4	0	4	-2	.969	-9	O-63/2-8,S3	-1.7
	Mon-N	40	90	16	18	2	0	0	8	9	21	.200	.294	.222	45	-6	2	1	0	1.000	-3	O-35	-1.0
	Yr	120	292	37	70	14	0	3	29	17	58	.240	.300	.318	73	-10	2	5	-2	.979	-12	O-98/2-8,S3	-2.7
1983	SF-N	124	373	59	109	20	3	17	53	33	59	.292	.358	.499	139	19	7	4	-0	.948	-30	2-64,3-28,O	-1.1
1984	SF-N	134	469	50	119	17	1	10	51	48	86	.254	.328	.358	96	-2	5	6	-2	.887	-26	*3-117,O-11/2	-3.4
1985	SF-N	95	230	24	62	6	0	4	24	30	37	.270	.356	.348	103	2	3	2	-0	.955	-0	O-56/3-1	-0.1
1986	SF-N	97	184	20	47	12	0	5	24	15	38	.255	.310	.402	105	1	1	1	-0	1.000	-3	O-45/1-7,32S	-0.2
1987	SF-N	69	91	9	23	3	0	3	11	5	13	.253	.299	.385	83	-2	1	1	-0	1.000	-3	O-22/3-2	-0.6
1988	SF-N	83	123	12	31	4	0	0	16	10	17	.252	.313	.285	76	-4	1	1	-0	.980	-11	O-45	-1.7

YEAR	TM/L	G	AB	R	H	2B	3B	HR	RBI	BB	SO	AVG	OBP	SLG	PRO+	BR/A	SB	CS	SBR	FA	FR	G/POS	TPR
1989	Cin-N	76	118	13	25	5	0	3	13	13	21	.212	.301	.331	78	-3	0	1	-1	.970	-10	O-45	-1.6
Total	14	1408	3659	453	969	180	23	80	422	332	589	.265	.332	.392	103	15	60	55	-15	.981	-78	O-745,3-218,2/1SC	-10.1

■ HENRY YOUNGMAN
Youngman, Henry b: 1865, Indiana, Pa. d: 1/24/36, Pittsburgh, Pa. TR, Deb: 4/19/1890

YEAR	TM/L	G	AB	R	H	2B	3B	HR	RBI	BB	SO	AVG	OBP	SLG	PRO+	BR/A	SB	CS	SBR	FA	FR	G/POS	TPR
1890	Pit-N	13	47	6	6	1	1	0	4	6	9	.128	.226	.191	25	-4	1			.750	-2	/3-7,2-6	-0.5

■ ROSS YOUNGS
Youngs, Ross Middlebrook "Pep" (b: Royce Middlebrook Youngs)
b: 4/10/1897, Shiner, Tex. d: 10/22/27, San Antonio, Tex. BL/TR, 5'8", 162 lbs. Deb: 9/25/17 H

YEAR	TM/L	G	AB	R	H	2B	3B	HR	RBI	BB	SO	AVG	OBP	SLG	PRO+	BR/A	SB	CS	SBR	FA	FR	G/POS	TPR
1917	NY-N	7	26	5	9	2	3	0	1	1	5	.346	.370	.654	218	3	1			1.000	1	/O-7	0.4
1918	NY-N	121	474	70	143	16	8	1	25	44	49	.302	.368	.376	129	18	10			.950	-6	*O-120/2-7	0.5
1919	NY-N	130	489	73	152	31	7	2	43	51	47	.311	.384	.415	142	26	24			.942	2	*O-130	2.1
1920	NY-N	153	581	92	204	27	14	6	78	75	55	.351	.427	.477	161	48	18	18	-5	.935	3	*O-153	3.6
1921	*NY-N	141	504	90	165	24	16	3	102	71	47	.327	.411	.456	129	24	21	17	-4	.978	-4	*O-137	0.6
1922	*NY-N	149	559	105	185	34	10	7	86	55	50	.331	.398	.465	121	18	17	9	-0	.942	-4	*O-147	1.1
1923	*NY-N	152	596	121	200	33	12	3	87	73	36	.336	.412	.446	128	27	13	19	-8	.959	1	*O-152	1.0
1924	*NY-N	133	526	112	187	33	12	10	74	77	31	.356	.441	.521	161	49	11	9	-2	.955	-1	*O-132/2-3	3.6
1925	NY-N	130	500	82	132	24	6	6	53	66	51	.264	.354	.372	89	-7	17	11	-2	.952	-6	*O-127/2-3	-2.1
1926	NY-N	95	372	62	114	12	5	4	43	37	19	.306	.372	.398	109	5	21			.974	2	O-94	0.0
Total	10	1211	4627	812	1491	236	93	42	592	550	390	.322	.399	.441	131	212	153	83		.953	-4	*O-1199/2-12	10.8

■ EDDIE YOUNT
Yount, Floyd Edwin b: 12/19/16, Newton, N.C. d: 10/26/73, Newton, N.C. BR/TR, 6'1", 185 lbs. Deb: 9/9/37

YEAR	TM/L	G	AB	R	H	2B	3B	HR	RBI	BB	SO	AVG	OBP	SLG	PRO+	BR/A	SB	CS	SBR	FA	FR	G/POS	TPR
1937	Phi-A	4	7	1	2	0	0	0	1	0	1	.286	.286	.286	45	-1	0	0	0	1.000	-0	/O-2	-0.1
1939	Pit-N	2	2	0	0	0	0	0	0	1	0	.000	.000	.000	-99	-1	0			.000	0	H	-0.1
Total	2	6	9	1	2	0	0	0	1	0	3	.222	.222	.222	14	-1	0	0		1.000	-0	/O-2	-0.2

■ ROBIN YOUNT
Yount, Robin R b: 9/16/55, Danville, Ill. BR/TR, 6', 170 lbs. Deb: 4/5/74 F

YEAR	TM/L	G	AB	R	H	2B	3B	HR	RBI	BB	SO	AVG	OBP	SLG	PRO+	BR/A	SB	CS	SBR	FA	FR	G/POS	TPR
1974	Mil-A	107	344	48	86	14	5	3	26	12	46	.250	.277	.346	79	-10	7	7	-2	.962	-11	*S-107	-1.1
1975	Mil-A	147	558	67	149	28	2	8	52	33	69	.267	.309	.367	90	-8	12	4	1	.939	-23	*S-145	-1.5
1976	Mil-A	161	638	59	161	19	3	2	54	38	69	.252	.294	.301	76	-20	16	11	-2	.963	-5	*S-161/O-1	-0.7
1977	Mil-A	154	605	66	174	34	4	4	49	41	80	.288	.335	.377	94	-5	16	7	1	.964	-9	*S-153	0.4
1978	Mil-A	127	502	66	147	23	9	9	71	24	43	.293	.326	.428	110	5	16	5	2	.959	22	*S-125	4.5
1979	Mil-A	149	577	72	154	26	5	8	51	35	52	.267	.310	.371	83	-15	11	8	-2	.969	5	*S-149	0.6
1980	Mil-A★	143	611	121	179	49	10	23	87	26	67	.293	.323	.519	131	22	20	5	3	.961	0	*S-133/D-9	4.0
1981	*Mil-A	96	377	50	103	15	5	10	49	22	37	.273	.317	.419	116	6	4	1	1	.985	28	S-93/D-3	4.5
1982	*Mil-A★	156	635	129	210	46	12	29	114	54	63	.331	.384	.578	171	59	14	3		.969	-4	*S-154/D-1	7.0
1983	Mil-A★	149	578	102	178	42	10	17	80	72	58	.308	.387	.503	155	44	12	5	1	.973	-5	*S-139/D-8	5.2
1984	Mil-A	160	624	105	186	27	7	16	80	67	67	.298	.367	.441	127	24	14	4	2	.971	15	*S-120,D-39	5.0
1985	Mil-A	122	466	76	129	26	3	15	68	49	56	.277	.348	.442	115	10	10	4	1	.970	4	*O-108,D-12/1	1.0
1986	Mil-A	140	522	82	163	31	7	9	46	62	73	.312	.389	.450	124	19	14	5	1	.997	12	*O-131/1-3,D	2.6
1987	Mil-A	158	635	99	198	25	9	21	103	76	94	.312	.386	.479	124	23	19	9	0	.987	8	*O-150/D-8	2.5
1988	Mil-A	162	621	92	190	38	11	13	91	63	63	.306	.373	.465	132	27	22	6	4	.996	15	*O-158/D-4	4.1
1989	Mil-A	160	614	101	195	38	9	21	103	63	71	.318	.387	.511	153	42	19	3	4	.981	4	*O-157/D-1	4.6
1990	Mil-A	158	587	98	145	17	5	17	77	78	89	.247	.341	.380	102	3	15	8	-0	.991	6	*O-157/D-1	0.5
1991	Mil-A	130	503	66	131	20	4	10	77	54	79	.260	.337	.376	99	0	6	4	-1	.994	6	*O-117,D-13	0.0
1992	Mil-A	150	557	71	147	40	3	8	77	53	81	.264	.331	.390	103	2	15	6	1	.995	2	*O-139,D-11	0.2
1993	Mil-A	127	454	62	117	25	3	8	51	44	93	.258	.330	.379	91	-5	9	2	2	.997	4	*O-114/1-7,D	-0.3
Total	20	2856	11008	1632	3142	583	126	251	1406	966	1350	.285	.346	.430	115	223	271	105	18	.964	71	*S-1479,O-1218,D/1	43.1

■ JEFF YURAK
Yurak, Jeffrey Lynn b: 2/26/54, Pasadena, Cal. BB/TR, 6'3", 195 lbs. Deb: 9/15/78

YEAR	TM/L	G	AB	R	H	2B	3B	HR	RBI	BB	SO	AVG	OBP	SLG	PRO+	BR/A	SB	CS	SBR	FA	FR	G/POS	TPR
1978	Mil-A	5	5	0	0	0	0	0	1	0	0	.000	.167	.000	-49	-1	0	0	0	1.000	0	/O-1	-0.1

■ SAL YVARS
Yvars, Salvador Anthony b: 2/20/24, New York, N.Y. BR/TR, 5'10", 187 lbs. Deb: 9/27/47

YEAR	TM/L	G	AB	R	H	2B	3B	HR	RBI	BB	SO	AVG	OBP	SLG	PRO+	BR/A	SB	CS	SBR	FA	FR	G/POS	TPR
1947	NY-N	1	5	1	1	0	0	0	0	0	2	.200	.200	.200	6	-1	0			1.000	-0	/C-1	-0.1
1948	NY-N	15	38	4	8	1	0	1	6	3	1	.211	.286	.316	62	-2	0			1.000	3	C-15	0.1
1949	NY-N	3	8	0	0	0	0	0	0	1	1	.000	.111	.000	-68	-2	0			1.000	1	/C-2	-0.1
1950	NY-N	9	14	0	2	0	0	0	1	1	2	.143	.200	.143	-8	-2	0			.963	2	/C-9	0.0
1951	*NY-N	25	41	9	13	2	0	2	3	5	7	.317	.417	.512	147	3	0			.942	-3	/C-23	0.0
1952	NY-N	66	151	15	37	3	0	4	18	10	16	.245	.296	.344	77	-5	0			.988	7	C-59	0.4
1953	NY-N	23	47	1	13	0	0	1	7	1	7	.277	.370	.277	71	-2	0			1.000	1	C-20	-0.1
	StL-N	30	57	4	14	2	0	1	6	4	6	.246	.306	.333	67	-3	0	1	-1	.989	2	C-26	-0.0
	Yr	53	104	5	27	2	0	1	7	11	7	.260	.336	.308	69	-4	0	1	-1	.994	3	C-46	-0.1
1954	StL-N	38	57	8	14	2	0	1	8	6	5	.246	.328	.421	93	-1	1	0		1.000	-2	C-21	-0.2
Total	8	210	418	41	102	12	0	10	42	37	41	.244	.315	.344	76	-14	1	1		.987	10	C-176	0.0

■ ELMER ZACHER
Zacher, Elmer Henry "Silver" b: 9/17/1883, Buffalo, N.Y. d: 12/20/44, Buffalo, N.Y. BR/TR, 5'9", 190 lbs. Deb: 4/30/10

YEAR	TM/L	G	AB	R	H	2B	3B	HR	RBI	BB	SO	AVG	OBP	SLG	PRO+	BR/A	SB	CS	SBR	FA	FR	G/POS	TPR
1910	NY-N	1	0	0	0	0	0	0	0	0		—	—	—	—		0	0		1.000	-0	/O-1	0.0
	StL-N	47	132	7	28	5	1	0	10	10	19	.212	.278	.265	61	-7	3			.966	3	O-36/2-1	-0.6
	Yr	48	132	7	28	5	1	0	10	10	19	.212	.278	.265	61	-7	3			.966	2	O-37/2-1	-0.6

■ FRED ZAHNER
Zahner, Frederick Joseph b: 6/5/1870, Louisville, Ky. d: 7/24/1900, Louisville, Ky. Deb: 7/23/1894

YEAR	TM/L	G	AB	R	H	2B	3B	HR	RBI	BB	SO	AVG	OBP	SLG	PRO+	BR/A	SB	CS	SBR	FA	FR	G/POS	TPR
1894	Lou-N	13	45	7	9	0	1	0	3	3	5	.200	.250	.244	21	-6	2			.778	-5	C-10/O-2,1	-0.8
1895	Lou-N	21	49	7	11	1	1	0	6	6	4	.224	.321	.286	61	-3	0			.824	-6	C-21	-0.6
Total	2	34	94	14	20	1	2	0	9	9	9	.213	.288	.266	42	-8	2			.805	-11	/C-31,O-2,1	-1.4

■ FRANKIE ZAK
Zak, Frank Thomas b: 2/22/22, Passaic, N.J. d: 2/6/72, Passaic, N.J. BR/TR, 5'10", 150 lbs. Deb: 4/21/44

YEAR	TM/L	G	AB	R	H	2B	3B	HR	RBI	BB	SO	AVG	OBP	SLG	PRO+	BR/A	SB	CS	SBR	FA	FR	G/POS	TPR
1944	Pit-N☆	87	160	33	48	3	1	0	11	22	18	.300	.385	.331	99	1	6			.948	6	S-67	1.0
1945	Pit-N	15	28	2	4	2	0	0	3	3	5	.143	.226	.214	22	-3	0			.971	1	S-10/2-1	-0.2
1946	Pit-N	21	20	8	4	0	0	0	1	0	0	.200	.238	.200	24	-2	0			.929	9	S-10	0.7
Total	3	123	208	43	56	5	1	0	14	26	23	.269	.350	.303	82	-4	6			.948	15	/S-87,2-1	1.5

■ JACK ZALUSKY
Zalusky, John Francis b: 6/22/1879, Minneapolis, Minn d: 8/11/35, Minneapolis, Minn. BR/TR, 5'11.5", 172 lbs. Deb: 9/4/03

YEAR	TM/L	G	AB	R	H	2B	3B	HR	RBI	BB	SO	AVG	OBP	SLG	PRO+	BR/A	SB	CS	SBR	FA	FR	G/POS	TPR
1903	NY-A	7	16	2	5	0	0	0		1	1	.313	.353	.313	95	-0	0			1.000	-0	/C-6,1-1	-0.1

■ EDUARDO ZAMBRANO
Zambrano, Eduardo Jose (Guerra) b: 2/1/66, Maracaibo, Venez. BR/TR, 6'2", 175 lbs. Deb: 9/19/93

YEAR	TM/L	G	AB	R	H	2B	3B	HR	RBI	BB	SO	AVG	OBP	SLG	PRO+	BR/A	SB	CS	SBR	FA	FR	G/POS	TPR
1993	Chi-N	8	17	1	5	0	0	0	2	1	3	.294	.333	.294	71	-1	0	0		1.000	-2	/O-4,1-2	-0.3
1994	Chi-N	67	116	17	30	7	0	6	18	16	29	.259	.353	.474	116	3	2	1	0	.944	-4	O-27/1-9,3	-0.2
Total	2	75	133	18	35	7	0	6	20	17	32	.263	.351	.451	111	2	2	1	0	.946	-6	/O-31,1-11,3	-0.5

■ JOE ZAPUSTAS
Zapustas, Joseph John b: 7/25/07, Boston, Mass. BR/TR, 6'1", 185 lbs. Deb: 9/28/33

YEAR	TM/L	G	AB	R	H	2B	3B	HR	RBI	BB	SO	AVG	OBP	SLG	PRO+	BR/A	SB	CS	SBR	FA	FR	G/POS	TPR
1933	Phi-A	2	5	0	1	0	0	0	0	0	0	.200	.200	.200	4	-0	0			1.000	-1	/O-2	-0.1

■ JOSE ZARDON
Zardon, Jose Antonio (Sanchez) "Guineo" b: 5/20/23, Havana, Cuba BR/TR, 6', 150 lbs. Deb: 4/18/45

YEAR	TM/L	G	AB	R	H	2B	3B	HR	RBI	BB	SO	AVG	OBP	SLG	PRO+	BR/A	SB	CS	SBR	FA	FR	G/POS	TPR
1945	Was-A	54	131	13	38	5	3	0	17	7	9	.290	.326	.374	112	3	1			.972	-1	O-43	-0.1

■ AL ZARILLA
Zarilla, Allen Lee "Zeke" b: 5/1/19, Los Angeles, Cal. BL/TR, 5'11", 180 lbs. Deb: 6/30/43 C

YEAR	TM/L	G	AB	R	H	2B	3B	HR	RBI	BB	SO	AVG	OBP	SLG	PRO+	BR/A	SB	CS	SBR	FA	FR	G/POS	TPR
1943	StL-A	70	228	27	58	7	1	2	17	17	20	.254	.309	.320	82	-5	1	1	-0	.962	-2	O-60	-1.1

YEAR	TM/L	G	AB	R	H	2B	3B	HR	RBI	BB	SO	AVG	OBP	SLG	PRO+	BR/A	SB	CS	SBR	FA	FR	G/POS	TPR
1944	*StL-A	100	288	43	86	13	6	6	45	29	33	.299	.375	.448	127	10	1	1	-0	.977	-2	O-79	0.4
1946	StL-A	125	371	46	96	14	9	4	43	27	37	.259	.311	.377	87	-7	3	5	-2	.973	3	*O-107	-1.1
1947	StL-A	127	380	34	85	15	6	3	38	40	45	.224	.303	.318	71	-15	3	6	-3	.986	-10	*O-110	-3.5
1948	StL-A★	144	529	78	174	39	3	12	74	48	48	.329	.389	.482	128	19	11	6	-0	.962	-9	*O-136	0.3
1949	StL-A	15	56	10	14	1	0	1	6	8	2	.250	.354	.321	76	-2	1	1	-0	1.000	-5	O-15	-0.8
	Bos-A	124	474	68	133	32	4	9	71	48	51	.281	.352	.422	97	-3	4	4	-1	.984	-2	*O-122	-1.2
	Yr	139	530	78	147	33	4	10	77	56	53	.277	.352	.411	95	-5	5	5	-2	.985	-7	*O-137	-2.0
1950	Bos-A	130	471	92	153	32	10	9	74	76	47	.325	.423	.493	122	17	2	3	-1	.976	-4	*O-128	0.6
1951	Chi-A	120	382	56	98	21	2	10	60	60	57	.257	.363	.401	109	5	2	4	-2	.983	-12	*O-117	-1.2
1952	Chi-A	39	99	14	23	4	1	2	7	14	6	.232	.333	.354	90	-1	1	0	0	.974	-6	O-32	-0.8
	StL-A	48	130	20	31	6	0	1	9	27	15	.238	.373	.308	88	-1	2	1	0	.976	0	O-35	-0.2
	Bos-A	21	60	9	11	0	1	2	8	7	8	.183	.269	.317	58	-4	2	0	1	.941	-1	O-19	-0.5
	Yr	108	289	43	65	10	2	5	24	48	29	.225	.339	.325	83	-6	5	1	1	.968	-7	O-86	-1.5
1953	Bos-A	57	67	11	13	2	0	0	4	14	13	.194	.333	.224	50	-4	0	1	-1	.947	-5	O-18	-1.0
Total	10	1120	3535	507	975	186	43	61	456	415	382	.276	.357	.405	102	10	33	33	-10	.974	-53	O-978	-10.1

■ NORM ZAUCHIN
Zauchin, Norbert Henry b: 11/17/29, Royal Oak, Mich. BR/TR, 6'4.5", 220 lbs. Deb: 9/23/51

YEAR	TM/L	G	AB	R	H	2B	3B	HR	RBI	BB	SO	AVG	OBP	SLG	PRO+	BR/A	SB	CS	SBR	FA	FR	G/POS	TPR
1951	Bos-A	5	12	0	2	1	0	0	0	0	4	.167	.167	.250	11	-2	0	1	-1	.957	-0	/1-4	-0.2
1955	Bos-A	130	477	65	114	10	0	27	93	69	105	.239	.339	.430	97	-3	3	0	1	**.995**	1	*1-126	-0.8
1956	Bos-A	44	84	12	18	2	0	2	11	14	22	.214	.333	.310	63	-4	0	0	0	.990	-1	1-31	-0.6
1957	Bos-A	52	91	11	24	3	0	3	14	9	13	.264	.343	.396	96	0	0	0	0	.972	0	1-36	-0.2
1958	Was-A	96	303	35	69	8	2	15	37	38	68	.228	.316	.416	101	0	2	0	1	.995	2	1-91	-0.4
1959	Was-A	19	71	11	15	4	0	3	4	7	14	.211	.291	.394	87	-1	0	0	1	.995	-2	1-19	-0.5
Total	6	346	1038	134	242	28	2	50	159	137	226	.233	.327	.408	93	-11	5	1	1	.993	0	1-307	-2.7

■ ZAY
Zay Deb: 10/7/1886

YEAR	TM/L	G	AB	R	H	2B	3B	HR	RBI	BB	SO	AVG	OBP	SLG	PRO+	BR/A	SB	CS	SBR	FA	FR	G/POS	TPR
1886	Bal-a	1	1	0	0	0	0	0		0	0	.000	.000	.000	-99	-0	0			.000	-0	/O-1,P-1	0.0

■ JOE ZDEB
Zdeb, Joseph Edmund b: 6/27/53, Compton, Ill. BR/TR, 5'11", 185 lbs. Deb: 4/7/77

YEAR	TM/L	G	AB	R	H	2B	3B	HR	RBI	BB	SO	AVG	OBP	SLG	PRO+	BR/A	SB	CS	SBR	FA	FR	G/POS	TPR
1977	*KC-A	105	195	26	58	5	2	2	23	16	23	.297	.351	.374	97	-1	6	5	-1	.970	-18	O-93/3-1,D	-2.2
1978	KC-A	60	127	18	32	2	3	0	11	7	18	.252	.291	.315	69	-5	3	0	1	.957	-9	O-52/2-1,3D	-1.6
1979	KC-A	15	23	3	4	1	1	0	0	2	4	.174	.240	.304	45	-2	1	0	0	1.000	-1	/O-9	-0.3
Total	3	180	345	47	94	8	6	2	34	25	45	.272	.322	.348	83	-8	10	5	0	.967	-29	O-154/D-5,32	-4.1

■ DAVE ZEARFOSS
Zearfoss, David William Tilden b: 1/1/1868, Schenectady, N.Y. d: 9/12/45, Wilmington, Del. TR, 5'9". Deb: 4/17/1896

YEAR	TM/L	G	AB	R	H	2B	3B	HR	RBI	BB	SO	AVG	OBP	SLG	PRO+	BR/A	SB	CS	SBR	FA	FR	G/POS	TPR
1896	NY-N	19	60	5	13	1	1	0	6	5	5	.217	.288	.267	48	-4	2			.893	-4	C-19	-0.5
1897	NY-N	5	10	1	3	0	1	0	0	0	0	.300	.300	.500	112	0	0			.880	2	/C-5	0.2
1898	NY-N	1	1	0	1	0	0	0	0	0	0	1.000	1.000	1.000	489	0	0			1.000	1	/C-1	0.1
1904	StL-N	27	80	7	17	2	0	0	9		10	.213	.300	.237	70	-2	0			.966	-2	C-25	-0.2
1905	StL-N	20	51	2	8	0	1	0	2		4	.157	.218	.196	24	-5	0			.966	-0	C-19	-0.4
Total	5	72	202	15	42	3	3	0	17	19	5	.208	.279	.252	56	-11	2			.943	-3	/C-69	-0.8

■ GEORGE ZEBER
Zeber, George William b: 8/29/50, Ellwood City, Pa. BB/TR, 5'11", 170 lbs. Deb: 5/7/77

YEAR	TM/L	G	AB	R	H	2B	3B	HR	RBI	BB	SO	AVG	OBP	SLG	PRO+	BR/A	SB	CS	SBR	FA	FR	G/POS	TPR
1977	*NY-A	25	65	8	21	3	0	3	10	9	11	.323	.405	.508	149	5	0	0	0	.961	1	2-21/S-2,3D	0.7
1978	NY-A	3	6	0	0	0	0	0	0	0	0	.000	.000	.000	-99	-2	0	0	0	.750	-1	/2-1	-0.3
Total	2	28	71	8	21	3	0	3	10	9	11	.296	.375	.465	129	3	0	0	0	.953	-0	/2-22,3-2,SD	0.4

■ ROLLIE ZEIDER
Zeider, Rollie Hubert "Bunions" b: 11/16/1883, Auburn, Ind. d: 9/12/67, Garrett, Ind. BR/TR, 5'10", 162 lbs. Deb: 4/14/10

YEAR	TM/L	G	AB	R	H	2B	3B	HR	RBI	BB	SO	AVG	OBP	SLG	PRO+	BR/A	SB	CS	SBR	FA	FR	G/POS	TPR
1910	Chi-A	136	498	57	108	9	2	0	31	62		.217	.305	.243	75	-12	49			.931	-2	2-87,S-45/3	-1.6
1911	Chi-A	73	217	39	55	3	0	2	21	29		.253	.347	.295	82	-4	28			.997	-5	1-29,S-17,3/2	-0.8
1912	Chi-A	130	420	57	103	12	10	1	42	50		.245	.330	.329	91	-4	47			.979	6	1-66,3-56/S	0.1
1913	Chi-A	16	20	4	7	0	0	0	2	4	1	.350	.458	.350	139	1	3			1.000	2	/3-6,1-3,2	0.4
	NY-N	50	159	15	37	2	0	0	12	25	9	.233	.341	.245	72	-4	3			.901	-14	S-24,2-19/13	-1.8
	Yr	66	179	19	44	2	0	0	14	29	10	.246	.354	.257	79	-3	6			.901	-11	S-24,2-20/31	-1.4
1914	Chi-F	119	452	60	124	13	2	1	36	44	28	.274	.344	.319	77	-15	35			.936	-0	*3-117/S-1	-1.1
1915	Chi-F	129	494	65	112	22	2	0	34	43	24	.227	.297	.279	58	-30	16			.941	-4	2-83,3-30,S	-2.8
1916	Chi-N	98	345	29	81	11	2	1	22	26	26	.235	.294	.287	71	-11	9			.928	-8	3-55,2-33/OS1	-1.9
1917	Chi-N	108	354	36	86	14	2	0	27	28	30	.243	.302	.294	77	-9	17			.901	-21	S-48,3-26,2/10	-3.0
1918	*Chi-N	82	251	31	56	3	2	0	26	23	20	.223	.288	.251	63	-10	16			.956	-11	2-79/1-1,3	-1.9
Total	9	941	3210	393	769	89	22	5	253	334	138	.240	.315	.286	74	-99	223			.945	-52	2-335,3-307,S1/O	-14.4

■ TODD ZEILE
Zeile, Todd Edward b: 9/9/65, Van Nuys, Cal. BR/TR, 6'1", 190 lbs. Deb: 8/18/89

YEAR	TM/L	G	AB	R	H	2B	3B	HR	RBI	BB	SO	AVG	OBP	SLG	PRO+	BR/A	SB	CS	SBR	FA	FR	G/POS	TPR
1989	StL-N	28	82	7	21	3	1	1	8	9	14	.256	.330	.354	92	-1	0	0	0	.971	-2	C-23	-0.1
1990	StL-N	144	495	62	121	25	3	15	57	67	77	.244	.337	.398	101	1	2	4	-2	.988	-11	*C-105,3-24,1/O	-0.6
1991	StL-N	155	565	76	158	36	3	11	81	62	94	.280	.356	.412	115	12	17	11	-2	.943	-7	*3-154	0.4
1992	StL-N	126	439	51	113	18	4	7	48	68	70	.257	.357	.364	108	6	7	10	-4	.960	-7	*3-124	-0.5
1993	StL-N	157	571	82	158	36	1	17	103	70	76	.277	.356	.433	112	10	5	4	-1	.923	-5	*3-153	0.5
1994	StL-N	113	415	62	111	25	1	19	75	52	56	.267	.353	.470	117	10	1	3	-2	.960	3	*3-112	1.1
Total	6	723	2567	340	682	143	13	70	372	328	387	.266	.351	.413	110	39	32	32	-10	.942	-28	3-567,C-128/1O	0.8

■ BART ZELLER
Zeller, Barton Wallace b: 7/22/41, Chicago Heights, Ill. BR/TR, 6'1", 185 lbs. Deb: 5/21/70 C

YEAR	TM/L	G	AB	R	H	2B	3B	HR	RBI	BB	SO	AVG	OBP	SLG	PRO+	BR/A	SB	CS	SBR	FA	FR	G/POS	TPR
1970	StL-N	1	0	0	0	0	0	0	0	0	0	—	—	—	—	0	0	0	0	1.000	-0	/C-1	0.0

■ GUS ZERNIAL
Zernial, Gus Edward "Ozark Ike" b: 6/27/23, Beaumont, Tex. BR/TR, 6'2.5", 210 lbs. Deb: 4/19/49

YEAR	TM/L	G	AB	R	H	2B	3B	HR	RBI	BB	SO	AVG	OBP	SLG	PRO+	BR/A	SB	CS	SBR	FA	FR	G/POS	TPR
1949	Chi-A	73	198	29	63	17	2	5	38	15	26	.318	.366	.500	132	8	0	1	-1	1.000	-5	O-46	0.0
1950	Chi-A	143	543	75	152	16	4	29	93	38	110	.280	.330	.484	110	3	0	2	-1	.969	2	*O-137	-0.2
1951	Chi-A	4	19	2	2	0	0	0	4	2	2	.105	.190	.105	-19	-3	0	0	0	.933	1	/O-4	-0.2
	Phi-A	139	552	90	151	30	5	33	129	61	99	.274	.350	.525	132	21	2	2	-1	.974	10	*O-138	2.4
	Yr	143	571	92	153	30	5	**33**	129	63	101	.268	.345	.511	127	18	2	2	-1	.972	11	*O-142	2.2
1952	Phi-A	145	549	76	144	15	1	29	100	70	87	.262	.347	.452	114	9	5	1	0	.972	-1	*O-141	0.4
1953	Phi-A★	147	556	85	158	21	3	42	108	57	79	.284	.355	.559	138	27	4	0	1	.972	13	*O-141	3.5
1954	Phi-A	97	336	42	84	8	2	14	62	30	60	.250	.319	.411	98	-2	0	0	0	.953	-1	O-90/1-2	-0.7
1955	KC-A	120	413	62	105	9	3	30	84	30	90	.254	.309	.508	116	6	1	0	0	.964	8	*O-103	0.9
1956	KC-A	109	272	36	61	12	0	16	44	33	66	.224	.317	.445	99	-2	2	0	1	.984	-1	O-69	-0.3
1957	KC-A	131	437	56	103	20	1	27	69	34	84	.236	.292	.471	104	-5	0	1	1	.952	-0	*O-113/1-1	-0.8
1958	Det-A	66	124	8	40	7	1	5	23	6	25	.323	.354	.516	127	4	0	0	0	.939	-2	O-24	0.1
1959	Det-A	60	132	11	30	4	0	7	26	7	27	.227	.266	.417	80	-3	0	0	0	.972	-3	1-32/O-1	-0.9
Total	11	1234	4131	572	1093	159	22	237	776	383	755	.265	.331	.486	115	66	15	7	0	.968	24	*O-1007/1-35	4.2

■ CHARLIE ZIEGLER
Ziegler, Charles W. b: 1/13/1875, Canton, Ohio d: 4/18/04, Canton, Ohio Deb: 9/23/1899

YEAR	TM/L	G	AB	R	H	2B	3B	HR	RBI	BB	SO	AVG	OBP	SLG	PRO+	BR/A	SB	CS	SBR	FA	FR	G/POS	TPR
1899	Cle-N	2	8	2	2	0	0	0	0	0	0	.250	.250	.250	40	-1	0			.750	-1	/S-1,2-1	-0.2
1900	Phi-N	3	11	0	3	0	0	0	0	0	1	.273	.273	.273	51	-1	0			.889	-1	/3-3	-0.2
Total	2	5	19	2	5	0	0	0	0	0	1	.263	.263	.263	47	-1	0			.889	-2	/3-3,2-1,S	-0.4

YEAR	TM/L	G	AB	R	H	2B	3B	HR	RBI	BB	SO	AVG	OBP	SLG	PRO+	BR/A	SB	CS	SBR	FA	FR	G/POS	TPR

■ BENNY ZIENTARA　Zientara, Benedict Joseph　b: 2/14/20, Chicago, Ill.　d: 4/16/85, Lake Elsinore, Cal.　BR/TR, 5'9", 165 lbs.　Deb: 9/11/41

1941	Cin-N	9	21	3	6	0	0	0	2	1	3	.286	.318	.286	71	-1	0			.914	1	/2-6	0.1
1946	Cin-N	78	280	26	81	10	2	0	16	14	11	.289	.323	.339	91	-4	3			.970	24	2-39,3-36	2.4
1947	Cin-N	117	418	60	108	18	1	2	24	23	23	.258	.297	.321	64	-22	2			.976	-17	*2-100,3-13	-3.2
1948	Cin-N	74	187	17	35	1	2	0	7	12	11	.187	.236	.214	23	-20	0			.990	12	2-60/3-3,S	-0.5
Total	4	278	906	106	230	29	5	2	49	50	48	.254	.293	.304	64	-46	5			.976	20	2-205/3-52,S	-1.2

■ BILL ZIES　Zies, William　BL　Deb: 8/9/1891

| 1891 | StL-a | 2 | 3 | 0 | 1 | 0 | 0 | 0 | 0 | 0 | 0 | .333 | .333 | .333 | 79 | -0 | 0 | | | 1.000 | 0 | /C-2 | 0.0 |

■ CHIEF ZIMMER　Zimmer, Charles Louis　b: 11/23/1860, Marietta, Ohio　d: 8/22/49, Cleveland, Ohio　BR/TR, 6', 190 lbs.　Deb: 7/18/1884　MU

1884	Det-N	8	29	0	2	1	0	0	0	1	14	.069	.100	.103	-38	-4				.830	-1	/C-6,O-2	-0.5
1886	NY-a	6	19	1	3	0	0	0		1		.158	.238	.158	26	-2	0			.893	3	/C-6	0.2
1887	Cle-a	14	52	9	12	5	0	0		4		.231	.298	.327	76	-2	1			.923	-4	C-12/1-2	-0.4
1888	Cle-a	65	212	27	51	11	4	0	22	18		.241	.312	.330	109	3	15			.917	7	C-59/O-3,1S	1.3
1889	Cle-N	84	259	47	67	9	9	1	21	44	35	.259	.368	.375	110	5	14			.931	7	C-81/1-3	1.6
1890	Cle-N	125	444	54	95	16	6	2	57	46	54	.214	.303	.291	75	-14	15			.937	12	*C-125	0.9
1891	Cle-N	116	440	55	112	21	4	3	69	33	49	.255	.312	.341	87	-9	15			.936	18	*C-116/3-1	1.8
1892	*Cle-N	111	413	63	108	29	13	1	64	32	47	.262	.325	.402	115	6	18			.938	11	*C-111	2.3
1893	Cle-N	57	227	27	70	13	7	2	41	16	15	.308	.357	.454	108	1	4			.968	8	C-56/3-1	1.1
1894	Cle-N	90	341	55	97	20	5	4	65	17	31	.284	.328	.408	74	-16	14			.963	10	C-89	0.2
1895	*Cle-N	88	315	60	107	21	2	5	56	33	30	.340	.417	.467	121	10	14			.975	9	C-84/1-3	2.1
1896	*Cle-N	91	336	46	93	18	3	3	46	31	48	.277	.354	.375	87	-7	4			.972	9	*C-91/3-1	1.0
1897	Cle-N	80	294	50	93	22	3	0	40	25		.316	.378	.412	103	1	8			.976	7	C-80	1.4
1898	Cle-N	20	63	5	15	2	0	0	4	5		.238	.304	.270	66	-3	2			.970	4	C-19	0.3
1899	Cle-N	20	73	9	25	1	2	1	14	5		.342	.407	.479	154	5	1			.957	-1	C-20	0.5
	Lou-N	75	262	43	78	11	3	2	29	22		.298	.370	.385	107	3	9			.985	1	C-62,1-11	0.9
	Yr	95	335	52	103	13	4	4	43	27		.307	.378	.406	117	8	10			.978	0	C-82,1-11	1.4
1900	*Pit-N	82	271	27	80	7	10	0	35	17		.295	.361	.395	108	3	4			.961	5	C-78/1-2	1.4
1901	Pit-N	69	236	17	52	7	3	0	21	20		.220	.292	.275	63	-11	6			.975	-7	C-68	-1.0
1902	Pit-N	42	142	13	38	4	2	0	17	11		.268	.338	.324	101	0	4			.969	-1	C-41/1-1	0.4
1903	Phi-N	37	118	9	26	3	1	1	19	9		.220	.292	.288	68	-5	3			.968	4	C-35,M	0.3
Total	19	1280	4546	617	1224	222	76	26	620	390	323	.269	.339	.369	95	-35	151			.952	102	*C-1239/1-25,O3S	15.8

■ DON ZIMMER　Zimmer, Donald William　b: 1/17/31, Cincinnati, Ohio　BR/TR, 5'9", 177 lbs.　Deb: 7/2/54　MC

1954	Bro-N	24	33	3	6	0	1	0	0	3	8	.182	.270	.242	34	-3	2	0	1	.939	3	S-13	0.1
1955	*Bro-N	88	280	38	67	10	1	15	50	19	66	.239	.292	.443	89	-5	5	3	-0	.976	9	2-62,S-21/3	0.9
1956	Bro-N	17	20	4	6	1	0	0	2	0	7	.300	.333	.350	78	-1	0	1	-1	.944	3	/S-8,3-2	0.1
1957	Bro-N	84	269	23	59	9	1	6	19	16	63	.219	.263	.327	52	-18	1	3	-2	.957	9	3-39,S-37/2	-0.6
1958	LA-N	127	455	52	119	15	2	17	60	28	92	.262	.306	.415	86	-10	14	2	3	.965	33	*S-114,3-12/2O	3.5
1959	*LA-N	97	249	21	41	7	1	4	28	37	56	.165	.275	.249	38	-22	3	1	0	.972	2	S-88/3-5,2	-1.3
1960	Chi-N	132	368	37	95	16	7	6	35	27	56	.258	.309	.389	90	-5	8	6	-1	.980	6	2-75,3-45/SO	0.6
1961	Chi-N★	128	477	57	120	25	4	13	40	25	70	.252	.292	.403	81	-14	5	1	1	.973	0	*2-116/3-5,O	-0.1
1962	NY-N	14	52	3	4	1	0	0	1	3	10	.077	.127	.096	-38	-10	0	1	-1	.961	5	3-14	-0.6
	Cin-N	63	192	16	48	11	2	2	16	14	30	.250	.304	.359	75	-7	1	2	-1	.949	-1	3-43,2-17/S	-0.7
	Yr	77	244	19	52	12	2	2	17	17	40	.213	.267	.303	51	-17	1	3	-2	.952	4	3-57,2-17/S	-1.3
1963	LA-N	22	23	4	5	1	0	1	2	3	10	.217	.308	.391	107	0	0	0	0	.933	2	3-10/2-1,S	0.2
	Was-A	83	298	37	74	12	1	13	44	18	57	.248	.296	.426	100	-1	3	2	-0	.935	3	3-78/2-2	0.2
1964	Was-A	121	341	38	84	16	2	12	38	27	94	.246	.302	.411	96	-2	1	3	-2	.955	-13	3-87/O-4,C2	-1.9
1965	Was-A	95	226	20	45	6	1	5	17	26	59	.199	.287	.252	56	-13	2	0	1	.966	-7	C-33,3-26,2	-1.9
Total	12	1095	3283	353	773	130	22	91	352	246	678	.235	.291	.372	76	-112	45	25	-2	.941	53	3-375,2-294,S/CO	-1.5

■ EDDIE ZIMMERMAN　Zimmerman, Edward Desmond　b: 1/4/1883, Oceanic, N.J.　d: 5/6/45, Emmaus, Pa.　BR/TR, 5'9", 160 lbs.　Deb: 9/29/06

1906	StL-N	5	14	0	3	0	0	0	0	0	0	.214	.214	.214	35	-1	0			.929	-0	/3-5	-0.1
1911	Bro-N	122	417	31	77	10	7	3	36	34	37	.185	.249	.264	46	-32	9			.961	3	*3-122	-2.7
Total	2	127	431	31	80	10	7	3	37	34	37	.186	.248	.262	45	-33	9			.960	3	3-127	-2.8

■ JERRY ZIMMERMAN　Zimmerman, Gerald Robert　b: 9/21/34, Omaha, Neb.　BR/TR, 6'2", 185 lbs.　Deb: 4/14/61　C

1961	*Cin-N	76	204	8	42	5	0	0	10	11	21	.206	.253	.230	29	-20	1	1	-0	.975	3	C-76	-1.5
1962	Min-A	34	62	8	17	4	0	0	7	3	5	.274	.318	.339	74	-2	0	0	0	.992	2	C-34	0.1
1963	Min-A	39	56	3	13	1	0	0	3	2	8	.232	.259	.250	43	-4	0	0	0	1.000	4	C-39	0.2
1964	Min-A	63	120	6	24	4	0	0	12	10	15	.200	.278	.225	42	-9	0	0	0	.993	6	C-63	-0.2
1965	*Min-A	83	154	8	33	1	1	1	11	12	23	.214	.275	.253	49	-10	0	0	0	.997	12	C-82	0.5
1966	Min-A	60	119	11	30	4	1	1	15	15	23	.252	.341	.328	88	-1	0	0	0	.996	9	C-59	1.0
1967	Min-A	104	234	13	39	3	0	1	12	22	49	.167	.244	.192	28	-20	0	1	-1	.992	15	*C-104	-0.2
1968	Min-A	24	45	3	5	1	0	0	2	3	10	.111	.184	.133	-3	-5	0	0	0	.991	5	C-24	0.1
Total	8	483	994	60	203	22	2	3	72	78	154	.204	.270	.239	43	-73	1	2	-1	.991	58	C-481	0.0

■ HEINIE ZIMMERMAN　Zimmerman, Henry　b: 2/9/1887, New York, N.Y.　d: 3/14/69, New York, N.Y.　BR/TR, 5'11.5", 176 lbs.　Deb: 9/8/07

1907	*Chi-N	5	9	0	2	1	0	0	0	1	0	.222	.222	.333	70	-0	0			.789	1	/2-4,S-1,O	0.1
1908	Chi-N	46	113	17	33	4	1	0	9	1		.292	.298	.345	101	-0	2			.923	-10	2-20/O-8,S3	-1.2
1909	Chi-N	65	183	23	50	9	0	2	21	3		.273	.285	.344	93	-3	7			.945	-8	2-31,S-12/3	-1.1
1910	*Chi-N	99	335	35	95	16	6	3	38	20	36	.284	.326	.394	111	3	7			.948	-10	2-32,S-26,3/01	-0.7
1911	Chi-N	143	535	80	164	22	17	9	85	25	50	.307	.343	.462	124	14	23			.946	-1	*2-108,3-20,1	1.1
1912	Chi-N	145	557	95	207	41	14	14	99	38	60	.372	.418	.571	169	50	23			.916	2	3-121,1-22	5.1
1913	Chi-N	127	447	69	140	28	12	9	95	41	40	.313	.379	.490	147	26	18			.912	5	*3-125	3.4
1914	Chi-N	146	564	75	167	36	4	4	87	20	46	.296	.326	.424	123	12	17			.897	-21	*3-118,S-15,2	-0.3
1915	Chi-N	139	520	65	138	28	11	3	62	21	33	.265	.300	.379	105	1	19	13	-2	.943	-9	*2-100,3-36/S	-0.8
1916	Chi-N	107	398	54	116	25	5	6	64	16	31	.291	.324	.425	116	6	15	12	-3	.932	7	3-85,2-14/S	1.9
	NY-N	40	151	22	41	4	0	0	19	7	10	.272	.304	.298	90	-2	9	8	-2	.943	-3	3-40/2-1	-0.4
	Yr	147	549	76	157	29	5	6	83	23	43	.286	.318	.390	110	5	24	20	-5	.935	4	*3-125,2-15/S	1.5
1917	*NY-N	150	585	61	174	22	9	7	102	16	43	.297	.317	.391	121	11	13			.947	13	*3-149/2-5	3.0
1918	NY-N	121	463	43	126	19	10	1	56	13	23	.272	.294	.363	102	-1	14			.955	-4	*3-100,1-19	-0.5
1919	NY-N	123	444	56	113	20	6	4	58	21	30	.255	.296	.354	96	-3	8			.940	-1	*3-123	0.1
Total	13	1456	5304	695	1566	275	105	58	796	242	404	.295	.331	.419	121	114	175	33		.928	-38	3-945,2-327/S10	9.7

■ ROY ZIMMERMAN　Zimmerman, Roy Franklin　b: 9/13/16, Pine Grove, Pa.　BL/TL, 6'2", 187 lbs.　Deb: 9/2/45

| 1945 | NY-N | 27 | 98 | 14 | 27 | 1 | 0 | 5 | 15 | 5 | 16 | .276 | .330 | .439 | 111 | 1 | 1 | | | .988 | -2 | 1-25/O-1 | -0.3 |

■ BILL ZIMMERMAN　Zimmerman, William H.　b: 1/20/1889, Kengen, Germany　d: 10/4/52, Newark, N.J.　BR/TR, 5'8.5", 172 lbs.　Deb: 4/14/15

| 1915 | Bro-N | 22 | 57 | 3 | 16 | 2 | 0 | 0 | 7 | 4 | 8 | .281 | .328 | .316 | 93 | -0 | 1 | | | .864 | -4 | O-18 | -0.6 |

■ FRANK ZINN　Zinn, Frank　b: 12/21/1865, Phoenixville, Pa.　d: 5/12/36, Manayunk, Pa.　5'8", 150 lbs.　Deb: 4/18/1888

| 1888 | Phi-a | 2 | 7 | 0 | 0 | 0 | 0 | 0 | 0 | 0 | 1 | .000 | .125 | .000 | -59 | -1 | 0 | | | .938 | -1 | /C-2 | -0.1 |

YEAR	TM/L	G	AB	R	H	2B	3B	HR	RBI	BB	SO	AVG	OBP	SLG	PRO+	BR/A	SB	CS	SBR	FA	FR	G/POS	TPR

■ GUY ZINN Zinn, Guy b: 2/13/1887, Hallbrook, W.Va. d: 10/6/49, Clarksburg, W.Va. BL/TR, 5'10.5", 170 lbs. Deb: 9/11/11

1911	NY-A	9	27	5	4	0	2	0	1	4		.148	.281	.296	57	-2	0			.923	-0	/O-8	-0.2
1912	NY-A	106	401	56	105	15	10	6	55	50		.262	.345	.394	105	2	17			.893	-12	*O-106	-1.5
1913	Bos-N	36	138	15	41	8	2	1	15	4	23	.297	.322	.406	105	0	3			.948	4	O-35	0.3
1914	Bal-F	61	225	30	63	10	6	3	25	16	26	.280	.336	.418	92	-3	6			.935	-5	O-57	-1.1
1915	Bal-F	102	312	30	84	18	3	5	43	35	28	.269	.343	.394	94	-3	2			.949	-5	O-88	-1.2
Total	5	314	1103	136	297	51	23	15	139	109	77	.269	.338	.398	98	-6	28			.927	-17	O-294	-3.7

■ BUD ZIPFEL Zipfel, Marion Sylvester b: 11/18/38, Belleville, Ill. BL/TR, 6'3", 200 lbs. Deb: 7/26/61

1961	Was-A	50	170	17	34	7	5	4	18	15	49	.200	.265	.371	69	-8	1	1	-0	.983	-4	1-44	-1.7
1962	Was-A	68	184	21	44	4	1	6	21	17	43	.239	.307	.370	82	-5	1	2	-1	.976	-2	1-26,O-23	-1.1
Total	2	118	354	38	78	11	6	10	39	32	92	.220	.287	.370	76	-13	2	3	-1	.981	-7	/1-70,O-23	-2.8

■ RICHIE ZISK Zisk, Richard Walter b: 2/6/49, Brooklyn, N.Y. BR/TR, 6'1", 208 lbs. Deb: 9/8/71

1971	Pit-N	7	15	2	3	1	0	1	2	4	7	.200	.368	.467	136	1	0	0	0	1.000	-1	/O-6	0.0
1972	Pit-N	17	37	4	7	3	0	0	4	7	10	.189	.318	.270	70	-1	0	0	0	.938	-2	O-12	-0.4
1973	Pit-N	103	333	44	108	23	7	10	54	21	63	.324	.364	.526	148	20	0	0	0	.987	2	O-84	1.9
1974	*Pit-N	149	536	75	168	30	3	17	100	65	91	.313	.388	.476	146	33	1	1	-0	.985	9	*O-141	3.6
1975	*Pit-N	147	504	69	146	27	3	20	75	68	109	.290	.376	.474	136	25	0	1	-1	.975	1	*O-140	2.0
1976	Pit-N	155	581	91	168	35	2	21	89	52	96	.289	.348	.465	128	20	1	0	0	.987	9	*O-152	2.4
1977	Chi-A★	141	531	78	154	17	6	30	101	55	98	.290	.360	.514	135	25	0	4	-2	.982	6	*O-109,D-28	2.3
1978	Tex-A★	140	511	68	134	19	1	22	85	58	76	.262	.341	.432	116	11	3	3	-1	.988	-2	O-90,D-49	0.2
1979	Tex-A	144	503	69	132	21	1	18	64	57	75	.262	.338	.416	103	2	1	1	-0	.972	-4	*O-134	-0.8
1980	Tex-A	135	448	48	130	17	1	19	77	39	72	.290	.347	.460	123	13	0	2	-1	.980	-3	D-86,O-37	0.5
1981	Sea-A	94	357	42	111	12	1	16	43	28	63	.311	.366	.485	138	17	0	2	-1	.000	0	D-93	1.3
1982	Sea-A	131	503	61	147	28	1	21	62	49	89	.292	.356	.477	123	15	2	1	0	.000	0	*D-130	1.1
1983	Sea-A	90	285	30	69	12	0	12	36	30	61	.242	.314	.411	94	-3	0	0	0	.000	0	D-84	-0.6
Total	13	1453	5144	681	1477	245	26	207	792	533	910	.287	.355	.466	126	176	8	15	-7	.981	14	O-905,D-470	13.5

■ BILLY ZITZMANN Zitzmann, William Arthur b: 11/19/1895, Long Island City, N.Y. d: 5/29/85, Passaic, N.J. BR/TR, 5'10.5", 175 lbs. Deb: 4/17/19

1919	Pit-N	11	26	5	5	1	0	0	2	0	6	.192	.192	.231	26	-2	2			.917	-2	/O-8	-0.5
	Cin-N	2	1	0	0	0	0	0	0	0	0	.000	.000	.000	-99	-0	0			.000	-1	/O-1	-0.1
	Yr	13	27	5	5	1	0	0	2	0	6	.185	.185	.222	22	-3	2			.917	-2	/O-9	-0.6
1925	Cin-N	104	301	53	76	13	3	0	21	35	22	.252	.342	.316	71	-12	11	11	-3	.959	-14	O-89/S-1	-3.3
1926	Cin-N	53	94	21	23	2	1	0	3	6	7	.245	.304	.287	61	-5	3			.965	-3	O-31	-1.0
1927	Cin-N	88	232	47	66	10	4	0	24	20	18	.284	.352	.362	94	-1	9			.958	-9	O-60/S-8,3	-1.3
1928	Cin-N	101	266	53	79	9	3	3	33	13	22	.297	.337	.387	90	-4	13			.958	-6	O-78/3-1	-1.5
1929	Cin-N	47	84	18	19	3	0	0	6	9	10	.226	.309	.262	45	-7	4			.940	-3	O-22/1-5	-1.0
Total	6	406	1004	197	268	38	11	3	89	83	85	.267	.333	.336	77	-32	42	11		.956	-37	O-289/S-9,13	-8.7

■ EDDIE ZOSKY Zosky, Edward James b: 2/10/68, Whittier, Cal. BR/TR, 6', 175 lbs. Deb: 9/2/91

1991	Tor-A	18	27	2	4	1	1	0	2	0	8	.148	.148	.259	10	-3	0	0	0	1.000	1	S-18	-0.1
1992	Tor-A	8	7	1	2	0	1	0	1	0	2	.286	.286	.571	129	0	0	0	0	.923	1	/S-8	0.1
Total	2	26	34	3	6	1	2	0	3	0	10	.176	.176	.324	34	-3	0	0	0	.980	2	/S-26	0.0

■ BOB ZUPCIC Zupcic, Robert b: 8/18/66, Pittsburgh, Pa. BR/TR, 6'4", 220 lbs. Deb: 9/7/91

1991	Bos-A	18	25	3	4	0	0	1	3	1	6	.160	.192	.280	28	-3	0	0	0	.875	-5	O-16	-0.7
1992	Bos-A	124	392	46	108	19	1	3	43	25	60	.276	.325	.352	84	-8	2	2	-1	.977	-2	*O-114/D-5	-1.3
1993	Bos-A	141	286	40	69	24	2	2	26	27	54	.241	.311	.360	75	-10	5	2	0	.979	-19	*O-122/D-5	-3.0
1994	Bos-A	4	4	0	0	0	0	0	0	0	1	.000	.000	.000	-94	-1	0	1	-1	1.000	-0	/O-2,D-1	-0.2
	Chi-A	32	88	10	18	4	1	1	8	4	16	.205	.239	.307	40	-8	0	0	0	1.000	-1	O-28/3-2,1	-0.9
	Yr	36	92	10	18	4	1	1	8	4	17	.196	.229	.293	34	-9	0	1	-1	1.000	-1	O-30/3-2,D1	-1.1
Total	4	319	795	99	199	47	4	7	80	57	137	.250	.305	.346	73	-30	7	5	-1	.977	-27	O-282/D-11,31	-6.1

■ FRANK ZUPO Zupo, Frank Joseph "Noodles" b: 8/29/39, San Francisco, Cal. BL/TR, 5'11", 182 lbs. Deb: 7/1/57

1957	Bal-A	10	12	2	1	0	0	0	0	1	4	.083	.154	.083	-36	-2	0	0	0	.913	0	/C-8	-0.2
1958	Bal-A	1	2	0	0	0	0	0	0	0	0	.000	.000	.000	-99	-1	0	0	0	1.000	0	/C-1	0.0
1961	Bal-A	5	4	1	2	1	0	0	0	1	1	.500	.600	.750	268	1	0	0	0	1.000	0	/C-4	0.1
Total	3	16	18	3	3	1	0	0	0	2	6	.167	.250	.222	31	-2	0	0	0	.941	1	/C-13	-0.1

■ PAUL ZUVELLA Zuvella, Paul b: 10/31/58, San Mateo, Cal. BR/TR, 6', 178 lbs. Deb: 9/4/82

1982	Atl-N	2	1	0	0	0	0	0	0	0	0	.000	.000	.000	-96	-0	0	0	0	.800	1	/S-1	0.1
1983	Atl-N	3	5	0	0	0	0	0	0	2	1	.000	.375	.000	11	-0	0	0	0	.750	-2	/S-2	-0.2
1984	Atl-N	11	25	2	5	1	0	0	1	3	3	.200	.259	.240	38	-2	0	0	0	1.000	1	/2-6,S-6	-0.1
1985	Atl-N	81	190	16	48	8	1	0	4	16	14	.253	.311	.305	69	-8	2	0	1	.986	9	2-42,S-33/3	0.5
1986	NY-A	21	48	2	4	1	0	0	2	5	4	.083	.170	.104	-24	-8	0	0	0	.966	4	S-21	-0.3
1987	NY-A	14	34	2	6	0	0	0	0	0	4	.176	.176	.176	-6	-5	0	0	0	1.000	-1	/2-7,S-6,3	-0.6
1988	Cle-A	51	130	9	30	5	1	0	7	8	13	.231	.275	.285	56	-8	0	0	0	.959	-3	S-49	-0.8
1989	Cle-A	24	58	10	16	2	0	2	6	1	11	.276	.300	.414	98	-0	0	0	0	.963	-3	S-15/3-5,D	-0.3
1991	KC-A	2	0	0	0	0	0	0	0	0	0	—	—	—	—		0	0	0	.000	0	/3-2	0.0
Total	9	209	491	41	109	17	2	2	20	34	50	.222	.275	.277	52	-32	2	0	1	.959	5	S-133/2-55,3D	-1.7

■ DUTCH ZWILLING Zwilling, Edward Harrison b: 11/2/1888, St.Louis, Mo. d: 3/27/78, LaCrescenta, Cal. BL/TL, 5'6.5", 160 lbs. Deb: 8/14/10 C

1910	Chi-A	27	87	7	16	5	0	0	5	11		.184	.283	.241	67	-3	1			.940	-2	O-27	-0.7
1914	Chi-F	154	592	91	185	38	8	**16**	95	46	68	.313	.363	.485	126	18	21			.962	2	*O-154	1.4
1915	Chi-F	150	548	65	157	32	7	13	**94**	67	65	.286	.366	.442	123	16	24			.979	8	*O-148/1-3	1.8
1916	Chi-N	35	53	4	6	1	0	1	8	4	6	.113	.175	.189	11	-6	0			1.000	0	O-10	-0.9
Total	4	366	1280	167	364	76	15	30	202	128	139	.284	.351	.438	116	26	46			.969	6	O-339/1-3	1.6

The Pitcher Register

The Pitcher Register consists of the central pitching statistics of every man who has pitched in major league play since 1871, *without exception*. Pitcher batting is expressed in Batting Runs in the Pitcher Batting column, and in the newly added columns for base hits and batting average. Pitcher defense is expressed in Fielding Runs in the Pitcher Defense column.

The pitchers are listed alphabetically by surname and, when more than one pitcher bears the name, alphabetically by *given* name—not by "use name," by which we mean the name he may have had applied to him during his playing career. This is the standard method of alphabetizing used in other biographical reference works, and in the case of baseball it makes it easier to find a lesser-known player with a common surname like Smith or Johnson. This method also jibes with that employed in the Team Roster and Annual Record where, for example, Charles "Old Hoss" Radbourn is shown not as the puzzling O. Radbourn or H. Radbourn, as some reference books have it, but as C. Radbourn. On the whole, we have been conservative in ascribing nicknames, doing so only when the player was in fact known by that name during his playing days.

Each person in the Pitcher Register can be found by finding the Pitcher Register list in the Contents and selecting the title whose names alphabetically surround the surname of pitcher you desire. Pitcher batting and pitcher defense, because the win-denominated numbers they produce are so small, are not sorted for single-season leaders (although the all-time leaders in these categories, single season and lifetime, will be found in the separate section called "All-Time Leaders"). Symbols denoting All Star Game selection and/or play appear to the right of the team/league column. An additional finding aid is an asterisk alongside the team for which a player appeared in postseason competition, thus making for easy cross-reference to the earlier sections on postseason play.

The record of a man who pitched in more than one season is given in one line for each season, plus a career total line. If he pitched for more than one team in a given year, his totals for each team are given on separate lines; and if the teams for which he pitched in his "traded year" are in the same league, then his full record is stated in both separate and combined fashion. (In the odd case of a man playing for three or more clubs in one year, with some of these clubs being in the same league, the combined total line will reflect only his play in that one league.) A man who pitched in only one year has no additional career total line since it would be identical to his seasonal listing.

In *Total Baseball 1*, fractional innings were calculated for teams in the Annual Record but were rounded off to the nearest whole inning for individuals, in accordance with baseball scoring practice. In 1981, this rounding-off procedure cost Sammy Stewart of Baltimore an ERA title, as Oakland's Steve McCatty won the crown despite having a higher ERA when fractional innings were counted; this singular occurrence led to a change in baseball scoring practice. In the first edition our data base conformed to the 1976-1982 practice for all of pitching history, excepting those men who pitched only one-third of an inning in an entire season. In the second edition of Total Baseball we recalculated all fractional innings pitched: look for a superscript figure, either a one or a two, in the IP column to indicate thirds of innings.

Pitching records for the National Association are included in the Pitcher Register because the editors, like most baseball historians, regard it as a major league, inasmuch as it was the only professional league of its day and supplied the National League of 1876 with most of its personnel. In this edition of *Total Baseball*, we benefit from the SABR research project referred to in the Introduction to the Annual Record—which to date has produced games started, complete games, shutouts, saves, innings pitched, hits, bases on balls and, for 1871-1873, strikeouts, earned runs, and ERA. For the years 1874-1875 we have estimated ERA based on the teams' average of 40 percent of runs allowed being earned. In future editions of *Total Baseball* we may have actual earned-run data, but for now this estimation produces reasonable results. Unless Major League Baseball reverses the position it adopted in 1969 and restores the NA to official major league status, we will continue the practice of carrying separate totals for the National Association rather than integrating them into the career marks of those pitchers whose major league tenures began before 1876 and concluded in that year or after it.

Gaps remain elsewhere in the official record of baseball and in the ongoing process of sabermetric reconstruction. The reader will note occasional blank elements in biographical lines; these are not typographical lapses but signs that the information does not exist or has not yet been found. However, unlike the case of batting records, there are no incomplete statistical columns for pitchers except in the National Association years of 1874-1875 and Pitcher Defense 1871-1875. Where official statistics did not exist or the raw data have not survived, as with batters facing pitchers before 1908 in the American League and before 1903 in the National, we have constructed figures from the available raw data. For example, to obtain a pitcher's BFP—Batters Facing Pitchers—for calculating Opponents' On Base Percentage or Batting Average, we have subtracted league base hits from league at-bats, divided by league innings pitched, multiplied by the pitcher's innings and added his hits and walks allowed and hit-by-pitch, if available. Research in this area continues, and we hope one day to eliminate the need for inferential data all the way back to 1871.

For a key to the team and league abbreviations used in the Pitcher Register go to the last entry of the Contents. For a guide to the other procedures and abbreviations employed in the Pitcher Register, review the comments on the prodigiously extended pitching record below.

YEAR TM/L	W	L	PCT	G	GS	CG	SH	SV	IP	H	HR	BB	SO	RAT	ERA	ERA+	OAV	OOB	BH	AVG	PB	PR	/A	PD	TPI
● **RIP VAN WINKLE**									Van Winkle, Rip "Half Moon" (Also Played in 1874 as Geoffrey Crayon)																
									b: 4/30/1820, Plattekill, N.Y. d: 12/12/80, Hudson, N.Y. BL/TL, 5'5", 145 lbs. Deb: 5/7/1874 MUCHF ♦																
1874 Bos-n	27	30	.474	57	57	56	1	0	498	502	5	18		9.4	*3.90*	104	.258	.270	40	.167	-3	5	3		-0.1
1875 Wes-n	29	22	.569	52	51	50	2	1	450	491	4	25		10.3	4.02	106	.260	.272	50	.200	1	7	7		0.5
1883 Bal-a	5	18	.217	27	23	19	0	1	196	207	7	76	77	13.0	3.44	101	.274	.340	18	.180	-0	-3	1	0	-0.1
1884 Was-U	0	1	.000	1	1	1	0	0	8	10	0	2	3	13.5	4.50	110	.309	.349	0	.000	1	-0	-0	0	0.0
KC-U	5	2	.714	8	6	5	0	0	52	66	0	9	14	13.0	4.33	104	.312	.340	9	.250	2	3	1	0	0.1
Yr	5	3	.625	7	7	6	0	0	60	76	0	11	17	13.0	4.35	104	.311	.341	9	.225	2	3	1	0	0.1
1890 Cin-P	0	0	—	1	1	1	0	0	0	5	2	2	0	∞	∞	-97	1.000	1.000	1	.250	0	-2	-2	0	-0.2
1907 NY-N	16	13	.552	35	34	18	0	2	251	224	19	78	170	10.8	2.76	126	.236	.293	30	.250	1	17	20	2	2.2
1908 NY-N	16	12	.571	36	35	14	1	5	278	224	15	48	205	8.8	2.20	130	.215	.250	25	.200	1	24	20	-3	2.2
1909 NY-N	25	7	.781	36	35	18	0	5	273	202	24	82	208		2.21	164	.201	.261	20	.147	-1	42	43	1	4.2
1910 NY-N	18	12	.600	37	36	19	0	2	291	230	21	83	283	9.4	2.81	135	.211	.267	38	.277	4	40	32	1	3.6
1911 NY-N	20	10	.667	36	35	21	0	4	286	210	18	61	289	8.6	1.76	188	.202	.246	40	.296	4	54	49	-1	5.5
1912 NY-N	21	12	.636	35	35	13	0	3	262	215	23	77	249	10.0	2.92	116	.219	.275	34	.281	3	18	14	1	1.7
1913 NY-N	19	10	.655	36	36	18	0	3	290	219	23	64	251	8.8	2.08	184	.202	.247	31	.263	2	51	56	2	5.9
1914 Ind-F	11	11	.500	32	32	12	0	5	236	199	19	75	201	10.4	3.20	126	.226	.287	22	.227	-1	11	22	1	2.2
1915 NY-N	22	9	.710	36	36	15	0	5	280	217	11	88	243	9.8	2.38	155	.211	.274	33	.311	3	39	41	1	4.2
1936 NY-N☆	7	3	.700	13	13	5	0	3	96	79	7	28	72	10.0	3.00	140	.218	.274	11	.196	1	10	13	3	1.5
Bos-A	5	7	.417	16	16	1	0	0	104	114	8	29	72	12.4	3.81	112	.271	.318	20	.189	0	4	5	-2	0.7
1967 *Bos-A★	0	1	.000	1	1	0	0	0	⅓	5	2	1	1	180.0	108.00	1200	.833	.857	0	.000	0	-2	-2	0	-0.2
Total 2 n	56	52	.519	109	108	106	3	1	948	993	9	43		9.8	3.96	105	.259	.271	90	.184	-2	12	7		0.4
Total 14	190	128	.597	384	375	180	1	38	2903	2486	199	803	2338	10.2	2.76	134	.224	.285	294	.224	23	304	313	6	33.6

Looking at the biographical line for any pitcher, we see first his use name in full capitals, then his given name and nickname (and any other name he may have used or been born with, such as the matronymic of a Latin American player). His date and place of birth follow "b" and his date and place of death follow "d"; years through 1900 are expressed fully, in four digits, and years after 1900 are expressed in only their last two digits. Then come his manner of batting and throwing, abbreviated for a left-handed batter who throws right as BL/TR (a switch-hitter would be shown as BB for "bats both" and a switch thrower as TB for "throws both"). Next, and for most pitchers last, is the pitcher's debut date in the major leagues.

Some pitchers continue in major league baseball after their pitching days are through, as managers, coaches, or even umpires. A pitcher whose biographical line concludes with an M can also be located in the Manager Roster; one whose line bears a C will be listed in the Coach Roster; and one with a U occupies a place in the Umpire Roster. (In the last case we have placed a U on the biographical line only for those pitchers who umpired in at least six games in a year, for in the nineteenth century—and especially in the years of the National Association—there were literally hundreds of players who were pressed into service as umpires for a game or two; it would be misleading to accord such pitchers the same code we give to Bob Emslie or Bill Dinneen.) The select few who have been enshrined in the Baseball Hall of Fame are noted with an H. They are also listed in the Hall of Fame Roster found toward the end of Bill Deane's "Awards and Honors" essay. An F in this line denotes family connection—father-son-grandfather-grandson or brother.

A black diamond appears at the end of the biographical line for pitchers who also appear in the Player Register by virtue of their having played in 100 or more games at another position, including pinch hitter, or having played more than half of their total major league games at another position, or having played more games at a position other than pitcher in at least one year.

The explanations for the statistical column heads follow; for more technical information about formulas and calculations, see the Glossary. The vertical rules in the column-header line separate the stats into six logical groupings: year, team, league; wins and losses; game-related counting stats; inning-related counting stats; basic calculated averages; pitcher batting; sabermetric figures of more complex calculation; and run-denominated Linear Weights stats for pitching, fielding, and Total Pitcher Index.

Note that the TPI (Total Pitcher Index) in this edition differs from those in earlier volumes, because for players who were both batters and pitchers, the method of allocating Wins between TPI and TPR (Total Player Rating) was improved. Previously, if a pitcher pitched in over half his games, all his batting was included with his pitcher rating (TPI); if he pitched in less than half his games, his Batting Wins were thrown over to his batter rating (TPR), with his TPI including only his Pitching Wins and Pitcher Defense. The new method prorates batting proportionally with the number of games pitched. In addition, fielding ratings at nonpitching positions for players who pitched in over half their games, previously omitted, are now part of the Total Baseball Ranking. In any case, the TPR values of batter-pitchers should remain about the same. Thus in 1918, Babe Ruth now has a batter rating of 2.6 Wins and a pitcher rating of 2.9 (total 5.5). In previous editions his marks used to be 4.1 and 1.0, respectively, or 5.1 overall, with none of his batting counted in with his pitching record even though he pitched 20 of 95 games. The large jump in his pitcher rating is because now his pitcher batting is compared against average batting for pitchers.

Also—and this is a key difference—the formula for Total Pitcher Index has been revised to employ the Relief Ranking formula (see Glossary) for all pitchers, not just relievers. The principal effect will be to calculate Pitcher Wins for relievers instead of Adjusted Pitcher Runs, as was formerly the case. The TPI will still be the sum of pitching, batting, fielding, and baserunning runs, but the

Pitcher Runs will be expressed as Ranking Runs rather than Adjusted Pitching Runs. Check the Glossary for the specifics, but the net effect will be to raise the TPIs of relief closers and, to a lesser extent, starters who average a high number of innings per start, and to lower somewhat the TPIs of mopup relievers (few saves, few decisions) and starters with many no-decision games.

Taken out from the Pitcher Register of earlier editions are the following statistics: Hits Per Game and Bases on Balls Per Game (still available in the Annual Record and Leaders sections, and now stated in combined fashion as Ratio); Strikeouts Per Game (still available in the Annual Record and Leaders sections and, in any event, fairly evident from a glance at the SO and IP columns); Park Factor for pitchers (still available from the Annual Record); Clutch Pitching Index, newly developed for Total Baseball but which we have judged to be of lesser interest and value than the more established sabermetric measures (still, it is present in the Annual Record and Leaders sections); and Wins Above Team, a stat that has so many cautions associated with it that we judged it to be of little value when applied to all the pitchers shown in the Register.

Finally, we have made an upward adjustment to overall league performance in the Federal League of 1914-15 and the Union Association of 1884 (thus lowering individual ratings), because while both leagues are regarded as major leagues, there can be no doubt that their caliber of play was not equivalent to that in the rival leagues of those years. Suffice it to say here that league earned run averages were reduced by 20 percent for the UA and 10 percent for the FL. A full explanantion of the adjustment procedure may be found in the Glossary, under "League Performance."

YEAR	Year in which a man pitched (When a space in the column is blank, this indicates that the man pitched for two or more clubs in the last year stated in the column; if those clubs were in the same league, then the man will also have a combined total line, beginning with the abbreviation "Yr" placed in the TM/L column.)
*	Denotes postseason play, World Series or League Championship Series.
Yr	Year's totals for pitching with two or more clubs in same league (see comments for YEAR)
★	Named to All Star Game, played
☆	Named to All Star Game, did not play
†	Named to All Star Game, replaced because of injury
TM/L	Team and League (see comments for YEAR)
W	Wins
L	Losses
PCT	Win Percentage (Wins divided by decisions)
G	Games pitched
GS	Games Started
CG	Complete Games
SH	Shutouts (Complete-game shutouts only)

SV	Saves (Employing definition in force at the time, and 1969 definition for years prior to 1969)
IP	Innings Pitched (Fractional innings included, as discussed above)
H	Hits allowed
HR	Home Runs allowed
BB	Bases on Balls allowed
SO	Strikeouts
RAT	Ratio (Hits allowed plus walks allowed per nine innings)
ERA	Earned Run Average (In a handful of cases, a pitcher will have faced one or more batters for his full season's work yet failed to retire any of them [thus having an innings-pitched figure of zero]; if any of the men he put on base came around to score earned runs, these runs produced an infinite ERA, expressed in the pitcher's record as ∞. (see Van Winkle's 1890 season)
ERA$^+$	Adjusted Earned Run Average normalized to league average and adjusted for home-park factor. (See comments for /A.)
OAV	Opponents' Batting Average
OOB	Opponents' On Base Percentage
BH	Base Hits (as a batter)
AVG	Batting Average
PB	Pitcher Batting (Expressed in Batting Runs. Pitcher Batting is park-adjusted and weighted, for those who played primarily at other positions, by the ratio of games pitched to games played. For more technical data about Runs Per Win and Batting Run formulas, see Glossary.)
PR	Pitching Runs (Linear Weights measure of runs saved *beyond* what a league-average pitcher might have saved, defined as zero. New to this edition, the formula used to calculate Relief Ranking is now employed for all pitchers; this creates small differences for starters but large differences for relievers, especially closers [see Glossary for further detail]. Occasionally the curious figure of – 0 will appear in this column, or in the columns of other Linear Weights measures of batting, fielding, and the TPI. This "negative zero" figure signifies a run contribution that falls below the league average, but to so small a degree that it cannot be said to have cost the team a run.
/A	Adjusted (This signifies that the stat to the immediate left, in this instance Pitching Runs, is here normalized to league average and adjusted for home-park factor. A mark of 100 is a league-average performance, and superior marks exceed 100. An innovation for this edition is to use three-year averages for pitching park factors. If a team moved, or the park changed dramatically, then two-year averages are employed; if the park was used for only one year, then of course only that run-scoring data is used.)
PD	Pitcher Defense (Expressed in Fielding Runs. See comment above on PB and see Glossary.)

TPI   Total Pitcher Index (The sum, expressed in wins beyond league average, of a pitcher's Pitching Runs, [now expressed as Ranking Runs—see Glossary] Batting Runs—in the AL since 1973—and Fielding Runs, all divided by the Runs Per Win factor for that year—which is generally around 10, historically in the 9–11 range; see Glossary.)

Total   For players whose careers include play in the National Association as well as other major leagues, two totals are given, as described above and as illustrated in Rip Van Winkle's record, where the record of his years in the National Association is shown alongside the notation "Total 2 n," where *2* stands for the number of years totaled and *n* stands for National Association. For players whose careers began in 1876 or later, the lifetime record is shown alongside the notation "Total x," where *x* stands for the number of post-1875 years totaled.

YEAR	TM/L	W	L	PCT	G	GS	CG	SH	SV	IP	H	HR	BB	SO	RAT	ERA	ERA+	OAV	OOB	BH	AVG	PB	PR	/A	PD	TPI

● DON AASE   Aase, Donald William b: 9/8/54, Orange, Cal. BR/TR, 6'3", 210 lbs. Deb: 7/26/77

1977	Bos-A	6	2	.750	13	13	4	2	0	92¹	85	6	19	49	10.2	3.12	144	.244	.285	0	—	0	10	14	-0	1.0
1978	Cal-A	11	8	.579	29	29	6	1	0	178²	185	14	80	93	13.4	4.03	90	.270	.348	0	—	0	-5	-8	-0	-0.7
1979	*Cal-A	9	10	.474	37	28	7	1	2	185¹	200	19	77	96	13.5	4.81	85	.277	.347	0	—	0	-12	-15	-2	-1.4
1980	Cal-A	8	13	.381	40	21	5	1	2	175	193	13	66	74	13.4	4.06	97	.287	.351	0	—	0	-1	-3	-1	-0.3
1981	Cal-A	4	4	.500	39	0	0	0	11	65¹	56	4	24	38	11.0	2.34	156	.234	.304	0	—	0	10	9	-0	1.5
1982	Cal-A	3	3	.500	24	0	0	0	4	52	45	5	23	40	11.8	3.46	117	.243	.327	0	—	0	4	3	-0	0.4
1984	Cal-A	4	1	.800	23	0	0	0	8	39	30	1	19	28	11.3	1.62	246	.221	.316	0	—	0	10	10	-0	1.8
1985	Bal-A	10	6	.625	54	0	0	0	14	88	83	6	35	67	12.2	3.78	106	.258	.332	0	—	0	4	2	-0	0.5
1986	Bal-A★	6	7	.462	66	0	0	0	34	81²	71	6	28	67	11.0	2.98	139	.234	.298	0	—	0	11	11	-0	2.6
1987	Bal-A	1	0	1.000	7	0	0	0	2	8	8	1	4	3	13.5	2.25	195	.276	.364	0	—	0	2	2	-0	0.5
1988	Bal-A	0	0	—	35	0	0	0	2	46²	40	4	37	28	14.9	4.05	96	.240	.377	0	—	0	-0	-1	-1	0.5
1989	NY-N	1	5	.167	49	0	0	0	2	59¹	56	5	26	34	12.6	3.94	83	.245	.324	0	.000	-1	-3	-4	-0	-0.5
1990	LA-N	3	1	.750	32	0	0	0	3	38	33	5	19	24	12.3	4.97	74	.232	.323	0	—	0	-5	-6	-1	-0.7
Total	13	66	60	.524	448	91	22	5	82	1109¹	1085	89	457	641	12.6	3.80	103	.259	.333	0	.000	-1	23	15	-5	4.7

● BERT ABBEY   Abbey, Bert Wood b: 11/29/1869, Essex, Vt. d: 6/11/62, Essex Junction, Vt. BR/TR, 5'11", 175 lbs. Deb: 6/14/1892

1892	Was-N	5	18	.217	27	23	19	0	1	195²	207	7	76	77	13.3	3.45	94	.261	.330	9	.120	-3	-4	-4	2	-0.5
1893	Chi-N	2	4	.333	7	7	5	0	0	56	74	1	20	6	15.8	5.46	85	.309	.372	6	.231	-0	-5	-5	0	-0.4
1894	Chi-N	2	7	.222	11	11	10	0	0	92	119	3	37	24	15.6	5.18	108	.310	.375	5	.128	-5	1	4	-1	-0.2
1895	Chi-N	0	1	.000	1	1	1	0	0	8	10	0	2	3	14.6	4.50	113	.301	.359	1	.333	-0	1	1	0	0.1
	Bro-N	5	2	.714	8	6	5	0	0	52	66	0	9	14	13.5	4.33	102	.304	.341	5	.263	1	3	1	1	0.2
	Yr	5	3	.625	9	7	6	0	0	60	76	0	11	17	13.5	4.35	103	.303	.340	6	.273	1	3	1	1	0.3
1896	Bro-N	8	8	.500	25	18	12	0	0	164¹	210	7	48	37	14.6	5.15	80	.308	.361	12	.190	-0	-14	-19	-2	-1.5
Total	5	22	40	.355	79	66	52	0	1	568	686	18	192	161	14.3	4.52	92	.292	.352	38	.169	-8	-19	-23	0	-2.3

● CHARLIE ABBEY   Abbey, Charles S. b: 10/14/1866, Falls City, Neb. d: 4/27/26, San Francisco, Cal. BL, 5'8.5", 169 lbs. Deb: 8/16/1893 ◆

| 1896 | Was-N | 0 | 0 | — | 1 | 0 | 0 | 0 | 0 | 2 | 6 | 0 | 0 | 0 | 27.0 | 4.50 | 98 | .511 | .511 | 79 | .262 | 0 | -0 | -0 | -0 | 0.0 |

● JIM ABBOTT   Abbott, James Anthony b: 9/19/67, Flint, Mich. BL/TL, 6'3", 200 lbs. Deb: 4/8/89

1989	Cal-A	12	12	.500	29	29	4	2	0	181¹	190	13	74	115	13.3	3.92	97	.274	.347	0	—	0	-1	-2	-1	-0.2
1990	Cal-A	10	14	.417	33	33	4	1	0	211²	246	16	72	105	13.7	4.51	85	.295	.355	0	—	0	-14	-16	1	-1.5
1991	Cal-A	18	11	.621	34	34	5	1	0	243	222	14	73	158	11.1	2.89	142	.244	.304	0	—	0	33	33	3	4.1
1992	Cal-A	7	15	.318	29	29	7	0	0	211	208	12	68	130	11.9	2.77	144	.263	.325	0	—	0	27	28	2	3.0
1993	NY-A	11	14	.440	32	32	4	1	0	214	221	14	73	95	12.5	4.37	95	.271	.334	0	—	0	-1	-5	1	-0.1
1994	NY-A	9	8	.529	24	24	2	0	0	160¹	167	9	64	90	13.1	4.55	97	.273	.344	0	—	0	5	-2	0	0.2
Total	6	67	74	.475	181	181	26	5	0	1221¹	1254	101	424	693	12.5	3.78	107	.270	.334	0	—	0	48	36	7	5.5

● KYLE ABBOTT   Abbott, Lawrence Kyle b: 2/18/68, Newburyport, Mass. BL/TL, 6'4", 200 lbs. Deb: 9/10/91

1991	Cal-A	1	2	.333	5	3	0	0	0	19²	22	2	13	12	16.5	4.58	91	.301	.414	0	—	0	-1	-1	0	-0.1
1992	Phi-N	1	14	.067	31	19	0	0	0	133¹	147	20	45	88	13.0	5.13	68	.283	.341	2	.069	-1	-24	-24	-1	-2.8
Total	2	2	16	.111	36	22	0	0	0	153	169	22	58	100	13.5	5.06	71	.285	.351	2	.069	-1	-25	-25	-1	-2.9

● DAN ABBOTT   Abbott, Leander Franklin "Big Dan" b: 3/16/1862, Portage, Ohio d: 2/13/30, Ottawa Lake, Mich. BR/TR, 5'11", 190 lbs. Deb: 4/19/1890

| 1890 | Tol-a | 0 | 2 | .000 | 3 | 1 | 1 | 0 | 1 | 13 | 19 | 0 | 8 | 1 | 19.4 | 6.23 | 63 | .330 | .421 | 1 | .143 | 0 | -3 | -3 | 1 | -0.4 |

● PAUL ABBOTT   Abbott, Paul David b: 9/15/67, Van Nuys, Cal. BR/TR, 6'3", 185 lbs. Deb: 8/21/90

1990	Min-A	0	5	.000	7	7	0	0	0	34²	37	0	28	25	17.1	5.97	70	.282	.412	0	—	0	-8	-7	-1	-1.1
1991	Min-A	3	1	.750	15	3	0	0	0	47¹	38	5	36	43	14.1	4.75	90	.232	.370	0	—	0	-3	-3	-0	-0.5
1992	Min-A	0	0	—	6	0	0	0	0	11	12	1	5	13	14.7	3.27	124	.279	.367	0	—	0	1	1	1	-0.1
1993	Cle-A	0	1	.000	5	5	0	0	0	18¹	19	5	11	7	14.7	6.38	68	.260	.357	0	—	0	-4	-4	0	-0.2
Total	4	3	7	.300	33	15	0	0	0	111¹	106	11	80	88	15.2	5.25	80	.258	.381	0	—	0	-15	-13	-0	-1.9

● GLENN ABBOTT   Abbott, William Glenn b: 2/16/51, Little Rock, Ark. BR/TR, 6'6", 200 lbs. Deb: 7/29/73

1973	Oak-A	1	0	1.000	5	3	1	0	0	18²	16	3	7	6	11.1	3.86	92	.225	.295	0	—	0	-0	-1	-0	0.0
1974	Oak-A	5	7	.417	19	17	3	0	0	96	89	4	34	38	11.8	3.00	111	.247	.317	0	—	0	7	3	-0	0.4
1975	*Oak-A	5	5	.500	30	15	3	1	0	114¹	109	16	50	51	12.7	4.25	85	.253	.333	0	—	0	-6	-8	-1	-0.5
1976	Oak-A	2	4	.333	19	10	0	0	0	62¹	87	6	16	27	15.0	5.49	61	.333	.374	0	—	0	-14	-15	-0	-1.1
1977	Sea-A	12	13	.480	36	34	7	0	0	204¹	212	32	56	100	12.3	4.45	92	.270	.328	0	—	0	-9	-8	-0	-0.9
1978	Sea-A	7	15	.318	29	28	8	1	0	155¹	191	22	44	67	13.7	5.27	72	.303	.350	0	—	0	-26	-25	-0	-3.1
1979	Sea-A	4	10	.286	23	19	3	0	0	116²	138	18	30	25	13.8	5.17	84	.301	.358	0	—	0	-12	-11	-0	-1.2
1980	Sea-A	12	12	.500	31	31	9	2	0	215	228	27	49	78	11.7	4.10	101	.272	.315	0	—	0	-2	1	2	0.3
1981	Sea-A	4	9	.308	22	20	1	0	0	130¹	127	14	28	35	10.7	3.94	98	.258	.298	0	—	0	-4	-1	-0	-0.4
1983	Sea-A	5	3	.625	14	14	2	0	0	82¹	103	9	15	38	13.3	4.59	93	.311	.349	0	—	0	-5	-3	-1	-0.5
	Det-A	2	1	.667	7	7	1	1	0	46²	43	5	7	11	9.6	1.93	203	.244	.273	0	—	0	11	10	-1	0.7
	Yr	7	4	.636	21	21	3	1	0	129	146	14	22	49	11.7	3.63	114	.285	.314	0	—	0	6	7	-1	0.2
1984	Det-A	3	4	.429	13	8	1	0	0	44	62	9	8	8	14.7	5.93	66	.326	.360	0	—	0	-9	-10	0	-1.3
Total	11	62	83	.428	248	206	37	5	0	1286	1405	162	352	484	12.5	4.39	89	.280	.331	0	—	0	-69	-67	-0	-7.6

● AL ABER   Aber, Albert Julius "Lefty" b: 7/31/27, Cleveland, Ohio d: 5/20/93, Garfield Heights, Ohio BL/TL, 6'2", 195 lbs. Deb: 9/15/50

1950	Cle-A	1	0	1.000	1	1	1	0	0	9	5	0	4	4	9.0	2.00	217	.167	.265	0	.000	0	3	2	-0	0.2
1953	Cle-A	1	1	.500	6	0	0	0	0	6	6	0	9	4	22.5	7.50	50	.240	.441	0	—	1	-2	-2	-0	-0.6
	Det-A	4	3	.571	17	10	2	0	0	66²	63	6	41	34	14.0	4.45	91	.260	.367	3	.130	-1	-3	-3	1	-0.3
	Yr	5	4	.556	23	10	2	0	0	72²	69	3	50	38	14.7	4.71	86	.258	.375	3	.130	-1	-6	-5	1	-0.9
1954	Det-A	5	11	.313	32	18	4	0	3	124²	121	8	40	54	11.8	3.97	93	.257	.320	5	.128	-1	-3	-4	1	-0.6
1955	Det-A	6	3	.667	39	1	0	0	3	80	86	9	28	37	12.8	3.37	114	.275	.334	1	.059	-2	5	4	1	0.3
1956	Det-A	4	4	.500	42	0	0	0	7	63	65	7	25	21	13.1	3.43	120	.270	.343	3	.300	1	5	5	0	0.7
1957	Det-A	3	3	.500	28	0	0	0	1	37	46	6	11	11	13.9	6.81	57	.315	.367	1	.125	-0	-12	-12	1	-1.8
	KC-A	0	0	—	3	0	0	0	0	3	6	0	2	2	24.0	12.00	33	.400	.471	1	1.000	0	-3	-3	0	0.1
	Yr	3	3	.500	31	0	0	0	1	40	52	6	13	13	14.6	7.20	54	.317	.367	2	.222	0	-15	-15	1	-1.7
Total	6	24	25	.490	168	30	7	0	14	389¹	398	29	160	169	13.0	4.18	93	.269	.342	14	.140	-3	-11	-13	3	-2.0

● BILL ABERNATHIE   Abernathie, William Edward b: 1/30/29, Torrance, Cal. BR/TR, 5'10", 190 lbs. Deb: 9/27/52

| 1952 | Cle-A | 0 | 0 | — | 1 | 0 | 0 | 0 | 1 | 2 | 4 | 1 | 1 | 0 | 22.5 | 13.50 | 25 | .444 | .500 | 0 | .000 | -0 | -2 | -2 | -0 | -0.2 |

● TED ABERNATHY   Abernathy, Talmadge Lafayette b: 10/30/21, Bynum, N.C. BR/TR, 6'2", 210 lbs. Deb: 9/19/42

1942	Phi-A	0	0	—	1	0	0	0	0	2²	2	0	3	1	16.9	10.13	37	.222	.417	0	—	0	-2	-2	0	0.0
1943	Phi-A	0	3	.000	5	2	1	0	0	14²	24	0	13	10	22.7	12.89	26	.353	.457	1	.250	0	-16	-15	0	-2.3
1944	Phi-A	0	0	—	1	0	0	0	0	3	5	0	1	2	18.0	3.00	116	.417	.462	0	.000	-0	0	0	0	0.0
Total	3	0	3	.000	7	2	1	0	0	20¹	31	0	17	13	21.2	11.07	31	.348	.453	1	.200	0	-17	-17	0	-2.3

● TED ABERNATHY   Abernathy, Theodore Wade b: 3/6/33, Stanley, N.C. BR/TR, 6'4", 215 lbs. Deb: 4/13/55

1955	Was-A	5	9	.357	40	14	3	2	0	119¹	136	6	67	79	15.8	5.96	64	.294	.392	4	.154	-1	-26	-28	1	-2.9
1956	Was-A	1	3	.250	5	4	2	0	0	30¹	35	2	10	18	13.6	4.15	104	.292	.351	2	.182	-0	0	1	2	0.2
1957	Was-A	2	10	.167	26	16	2	0	0	85	100	9	65	50	17.9	6.78	57	.314	.437	4	.167	-1	-28	-27	1	-3.2

YEAR	TM/L	W	L	PCT	G	GS	CG	SH	SV	IP	H	HR	BB	SO	RAT	ERA	ERA+	OAV	OOB	BH	AVG	PB	PR	/A	PD	TPI
1960	Was-A	0	0	—	2	0	0	0	0	3	4	0	4	1	24.0	12.00	32	.308	.471	1	1.000	0	-3	-3	-0	0.1
1963	Cle-A	7	2	.778	43	0	0	0	12	59¹	54	4	29	47	12.6	2.88	126	.251	.340	2	.400	1	5	5	2	1.3
1964	Cle-A	2	6	.250	53	0	0	0	11	72²	66	5	46	57	14.1	4.33	83	.247	.362	0	.000	-1	-6	-6	3	-0.6
1965	Chi-N	4	6	.400	84	0	0	0	31	136¹	113	7	56	104	11.5	2.57	143	.227	.311	3	.167	0	15	17	4	2.6
1966	Chi-N	1	3	.250	20	0	0	0	4	27²	26	4	17	18	14.6	6.18	60	.255	.372	0	.000	-0	-8	-8	2	-1.2
	Atl-N	4	4	.500	38	0	0	0	4	65¹	58	5	36	42	12.9	3.86	94	.247	.347	2	.250	1	-2	-2	1	-0.1
	Yr	5	7	.417	58	0	0	0	8	93	84	9	53	60	13.3	4.55	80	.248	.349	2	.167	0	-10	-9	2	-1.3
1967	Cin-N	6	3	.667	70	0	0	0	28	106¹	63	3	41	88	9.2	1.27	295	.170	.261	1	.059	-1	25	29	2	4.5
1968	Cin-N	10	7	.588	78	0	0	0	13	134²	111	9	55	64	11.4	2.47	128	.228	.312	0	.000	-0	8	10	3	1.9
1969	Chi-N	4	3	.571	56	0	0	0	3	85¹	75	8	42	55	12.4	3.16	127	.234	.325	2	.250	0	4	8	2	1.0
1970	Chi-N	0	0	—	11	0	0	0	1	9	9	0	5	2	15.0	2.00	225	.281	.395	0	—	0	2	3	0	0.1
	StL-N	1	0	1.000	11	0	0	0	1	18¹	15	0	12	8	14.7	2.95	140	.246	.395	0	.000	-0	2	2	1	0.2
	Yr	1	0	1.000	22	0	0	0	2	27¹	24	0	17	10	14.5	2.63	161	.255	.386	0	.000	-0	4	5	1	0.3
	KC-A	9	3	.750	36	0	0	0	12	55²	41	3	38	49	12.9	2.59	144	.209	.340	3	.214	0	7	7	0	1.9
1971	KC-A	4	6	.400	63	0	0	0	23	81	60	3	50	55	12.9	2.56	134	.210	.339	1	.077	-1	8	8	2	1.6
1972	KC-A	3	4	.429	45	0	0	0	5	58¹	44	2	19	28	10.2	1.70	179	.210	.284	0	.000	-1	9	9	1	1.3
Total	14	63	69	.477	681	34	7	2	148	1147²	1010	70	592	765	12.9	3.46	106	.241	.341	25	.138	-4	12	26	27	8.7

● WOODY ABERNATHY
Abernathy, Virgil Woodrow b: 2/1/15, Forest City, N.C. BL/TL, 6′, 170 lbs. Deb: 7/28/46

YEAR	TM/L	W	L	PCT	G	GS	CG	SH	SV	IP	H	HR	BB	SO	RAT	ERA	ERA+	OAV	OOB	BH	AVG	PB	PR	/A	PD	TPI
1946	NY-N	1	1	.500	15	1	0	0	1	40	32	5	10	6	9.4	3.37	102	.232	.284	0	.000	-1	0	0	-1	-0.2
1947	NY-N	0	0	—	1	0	0	0	0	2	4	0	1	0	22.5	9.00	40	.400	.455	0	—	0	-1	-1	-0	0.0
Total	2	1	1	.500	16	1	0	0	1	42	36	5	11	6	10.1	3.64	95	.243	.296	0	.000	-1	-1	-1	-1	-0.2

● HARRY ABLES
Ables, Harry Terrell "Hans" b: 10/4/1884, Terrell, Tex. d: 2/8/51, San Antonio, Tex. BR/TL, 6′2.5″, 200 lbs. Deb: 9/4/05

YEAR	TM/L	W	L	PCT	G	GS	CG	SH	SV	IP	H	HR	BB	SO	RAT	ERA	ERA+	OAV	OOB	BH	AVG	PB	PR	/A	PD	TPI
1905	StL-A	0	3	.000	6	3	1	0	0	30²	37	0	13	11	14.7	3.82	67	.299	.366	0	.000	-1	-4	-4	-1	-0.6
1909	Cle-A	1	1	.500	5	3	3	0	0	29²	26	1	10	24	11.2	2.12	120	.226	.294	0	.000	-1	1	1	-1	-0.2
1911	NY-A	0	1	.000	3	2	0	0	0	11	16	0	7	6	18.8	9.82	37	.333	.418	0	.000	-1	-8	-8	-0	-0.6
Total	3	1	5	.167	14	8	4	0	0	71¹	79	1	30	41	13.9	4.04	67	.276	.346	0	.000	-4	-11	-11	-2	-1.4

● GEORGE ABRAMS
Abrams, George Allen b: 11/9/1899, Seattle, Wash. d: 12/5/86, Clearwater, Fla. BR/TR, 5′9″, 170 lbs. Deb: 4/19/23

YEAR	TM/L	W	L	PCT	G	GS	CG	SH	SV	IP	H	HR	BB	SO	RAT	ERA	ERA+	OAV	OOB	BH	AVG	PB	PR	/A	PD	TPI
1923	Cin-N	0	0	—	3	0	0	0	0	4²	10	0	3	1	27.0	9.64	40	.500	.583	1	1.000	0	-3	-3	-0	0.0

● JOHNNY ABREGO
Abrego, Johnny Ray b: 7/4/62, Corpus Christi, Tex BR/TR, 6′, 185 lbs. Deb: 9/4/85

YEAR	TM/L	W	L	PCT	G	GS	CG	SH	SV	IP	H	HR	BB	SO	RAT	ERA	ERA+	OAV	OOB	BH	AVG	PB	PR	/A	PD	TPI
1985	Chi-N	1	1	.500	6	5	0	0	0	24	32	3	12	13	16.5	6.38	63	.352	.427	0	.000	-1	-7	-6	0	-0.5

● JIM ACKER
Acker, James Justin b: 9/24/58, Freer, Tex. BR/TR, 6′2″, 212 lbs. Deb: 4/7/83

YEAR	TM/L	W	L	PCT	G	GS	CG	SH	SV	IP	H	HR	BB	SO	RAT	ERA	ERA+	OAV	OOB	BH	AVG	PB	PR	/A	PD	TPI
1983	Tor-A	5	1	.833	38	5	0	0	1	97²	103	7	38	44	13.7	4.33	99	.273	.352	0	—	0	-3	-0	1	-0.1
1984	Tor-A	3	5	.375	32	3	0	0	1	72	79	3	25	33	13.8	4.38	94	.286	.358	0	—	0	-3	-2	-0	-0.5
1985	*Tor-A	7	2	.778	61	0	0	0	10	86¹	86	7	43	42	13.8	3.23	130	.268	.360	0	—	0	9	9	1	1.2
1986	Tor-A	2	4	.333	23	5	0	0	0	60	63	6	22	32	13.1	4.35	97	.281	.351	0	—	0	-1	-1	0	0.0
	Atl-N	3	8	.273	21	14	0	0	0	95	100	7	26	37	12.0	3.79	105	.274	.324	3	.107	-1	-1	2	1	0.2
1987	Atl-N	4	9	.308	68	0	0	0	14	114²	109	11	51	68	12.9	4.16	104	.253	.338	3	.214	-1	-1	2	1	0.5
1988	Atl-N	0	4	.000	21	1	0	0	0	42	45	6	14	25	12.9	4.71	78	.280	.341	2	.400	1	-6	-5	0	-0.3
1989	Atl-N	0	6	.000	59	0	0	0	2	97²	84	5	20	68	9.7	2.67	137	.237	.280	1	.143	-0	9	11	1	0.7
	*Tor-A	2	1	.667	14	0	0	0	1	28¹	24	1	12	24	11.8	1.59	237	.235	.322	0	—	0	7	7	1	0.9
1990	Tor-A	4	4	.500	59	0	0	0	1	91²	91	9	30	54	13.4	3.83	103	.281	.341	0	—	0	1	1	1	0.2
1991	*Tor-A	3	5	.375	54	4	0	0	1	88¹	77	16	36	44	11.7	5.20	81	.238	.318	0	—	0	-11	-10	-0	-0.8
1992	Sea-A	0	0	—	17	0	0	0	0	30²	45	4	11	11	16.7	5.28	75	.338	.393	0	—	0	-5	-4	-0	0.0
Total	10	33	49	.402	467	32	0	0	30	904¹	918	82	329	482	12.7	3.97	102	.267	.337	9	.167	-0	-5	10	8	2.0

● TOM ACKER
Acker, Thomas James b: 3/7/30, Paterson, N.J. BR/TR, 6′4″, 215 lbs. Deb: 4/20/56

YEAR	TM/L	W	L	PCT	G	GS	CG	SH	SV	IP	H	HR	BB	SO	RAT	ERA	ERA+	OAV	OOB	BH	AVG	PB	PR	/A	PD	TPI
1956	Cin-N	4	3	.571	29	1	1	1	1	83²	97	7	29	54	9.8	2.37	168	.201	.277	1	.053	-1	13	15	1	1.2
1957	Cin-N	10	5	.667	49	6	1	0	4	108²	122	16	41	67	14.2	4.97	83	.293	.368	1	.053	-1	-13	-10	-0	-1.5
1958	Cin-N	4	3	.571	38	10	3	0	1	124²	126	10	43	90	12.4	4.55	91	.266	.331	2	.067	-1	-8	-6	-2	-0.6
1959	Cin-N	1	2	.333	37	6	0	0	2	63¹	57	10	37	45	13.9	4.12	98	.246	.359	1	.111	-0	-1	-0	-1	-0.2
Total	4	19	13	.594	153	23	5	1	8	380¹	365	43	150	256	12.6	4.12	99	.257	.335	5	.065	-3	-10	-1	-2	-1.1

● FRITZ ACKLEY
Ackley, Florian Frederick b: 4/10/37, Hayward, Wis. BL/TR, 6′1.5″, 202 lbs. Deb: 9/21/63

YEAR	TM/L	W	L	PCT	G	GS	CG	SH	SV	IP	H	HR	BB	SO	RAT	ERA	ERA+	OAV	OOB	BH	AVG	PB	PR	/A	PD	TPI
1963	Chi-A	1	0	1.000	2	2	0	0	0	13	7	2	7	11	9.7	2.08	169	.167	.286	1	.200	0	2	2	0	0.1
1964	Chi-A	0	0	—	3	2	0	0	0	6¹	10	2	4	6	19.9	8.53	41	.345	.424	1	1.000	1	-3	-4	0	0.1
Total	2	1	0	1.000	5	4	0	0	0	19¹	17	4	11	17	13.0	4.19	83	.239	.341	2	.333	1	-1	-2	1	0.3

● CY ACOSTA
Acosta, Cecilio (Miranda) b: 11/22/46, Sabino, Mexico BR/TR, 5′10″, 165 lbs. Deb: 6/4/72

YEAR	TM/L	W	L	PCT	G	GS	CG	SH	SV	IP	H	HR	BB	SO	RAT	ERA	ERA+	OAV	OOB	BH	AVG	PB	PR	/A	PD	TPI
1972	Chi-A	3	0	1.000	26	0	0	0	5	34²	25	2	17	28	10.9	1.56	201	.210	.309	0	.000	-0	6	6	-1	0.7
1973	Chi-A	10	6	.625	48	0	0	0	18	97	66	8	39	60	10.4	2.23	178	.193	.289	0	.000	-0	17	19	-1	3.7
1974	Chi-A	0	3	.000	27	0	0	0	3	45²	43	3	18	19	13.0	3.74	100	.256	.346	0	.000	-0	-1	-0	0	-0.1
1975	Phi-N	0	0	—	6	0	0	0	1	8²	9	2	3	2	12.5	6.23	60	.273	.333	0	—	0	-3	-2	-0	-0.1
Total	4	13	9	.591	107	0	0	0	27	186	143	15	77	109	11.2	2.66	140	.216	.309	0	.000	-0	20	22	-2	4.3

● ED ACOSTA
Acosta, Eduardo Elixbet b: 3/9/44, Boquete, Panama BB/TR, 6′5″, 215 lbs. Deb: 9/7/70

YEAR	TM/L	W	L	PCT	G	GS	CG	SH	SV	IP	H	HR	BB	SO	RAT	ERA	ERA+	OAV	OOB	BH	AVG	PB	PR	/A	PD	TPI
1970	Pit-N	0	0	—	3	0	0	0	1	2²	5	1	2	1	27.0	13.50	29	.417	.533	0	—	0	-3	-3	-0	-0.2
1971	SD-N	3	3	.500	8	6	3	1	0	46	43	4	7	16	9.8	2.74	120	.246	.275	0	.000	-2	4	3	-1	0.1
1972	SD-N	3	6	.333	46	2	0	0	0	89	105	7	30	53	14.0	4.45	74	.302	.362	1	.083	-0	-10	-11	-1	-1.2
Total	3	6	9	.400	57	8	3	1	1	137²	153	12	39	70	12.8	4.05	81	.286	.339	1	.034	-2	-9	-11	-1	-1.3

● JOSE ACOSTA
Acosta, Jose "Acostica" b: 3/4/1891, Havana, Cuba d: 11/16/77, Havana, Cuba BR/TR, 5′6″, 134 lbs. Deb: 7/28/20 F

YEAR	TM/L	W	L	PCT	G	GS	CG	SH	SV	IP	H	HR	BB	SO	RAT	ERA	ERA+	OAV	OOB	BH	AVG	PB	PR	/A	PD	TPI
1920	Was-A	5	4	.556	17	5	4	1	1	82²	92	1	26	9	12.8	4.03	93	.290	.344	6	.240	1	-2	-3	-3	-0.4
1921	Was-A	5	4	.556	33	7	2	0	3	115²	148	4	36	30	14.3	4.36	94	.317	.366	2	.067	-2	-1	-3	-1	-0.5
1922	Chi-A	0	2	.000	5	1	0	0	0	15	25	4	6	6	18.6	8.40	48	.417	.470	1	.200	-0	-7	-7	-0	-0.8
Total	3	10	10	.500	55	13	6	1	4	213¹	265	9	68	45	14.0	4.51	88	.314	.365	9	.150	-1	-10	-13	-4	-1.7

● MARK ACRE
Acre, Mark Robert b: 9/16/68, Concord, Cal. BR/TR, 6′8″, 235 lbs. Deb: 5/13/94

YEAR	TM/L	W	L	PCT	G	GS	CG	SH	SV	IP	H	HR	BB	SO	RAT	ERA	ERA+	OAV	OOB	BH	AVG	PB	PR	/A	PD	TPI
1994	Oak-A	5	1	.833	34	0	0	0	0	34¹	24	4	23	21	12.6	3.41	130	.202	.336	0	—	0	5	4	0	1.1

● ACE ADAMS
Adams, Ace Townsend b: 3/2/12, Willows, Cal. BR/TR, 5′10.5″, 182 lbs. Deb: 4/15/41

YEAR	TM/L	W	L	PCT	G	GS	CG	SH	SV	IP	H	HR	BB	SO	RAT	ERA	ERA+	OAV	OOB	BH	AVG	PB	PR	/A	PD	TPI
1941	NY-N	4	1	.800	38	0	0	0	1	71	84	3	35	18	15.2	4.82	77	.304	.385	1	.083	-1	-9	-9	-1	-0.8
1942	NY-N	7	4	.636	61	0	0	0	11	88	69	1	31	33	10.2	1.84	183	.223	.293	4	.100	-1	14	15	0	2.3
1943	NY-N☆	11	7	.611	70	3	1	0	9	140¹	121	5	55	46	11.4	2.82	122	.236	.311	4	.125	9	10	-1	1.1
1944	NY-N	8	11	.421	65	4	1	0	13	137²	149	8	58	32	13.8	4.25	86	.279	.354	3	.103	-2	-10	-9	-2	-1.6
1945	NY-N	11	9	.550	65	0	0	0	15	113	109	7	44	39	12.3	3.42	114	.252	.324	3	.188	0	5	6	1	1.3
1946	NY-N	0	1	.000	3	0	0	0	0	2²	9	2	1	2	33.8	16.88	20	.500	.526	0	—	0	-4	-4	0	-1.1
Total	6	41	33	.554	302	7	2	0	49	552²	541	26	224	171	12.6	3.47	104	.260	.334	12	.121	-4	5	9	-2	1.2

● BABE ADAMS
Adams, Charles Benjamin b: 5/18/1882, Tipton, Ind. d: 7/27/68, Silver Spring, Md BL/TR, 5′11.5″, 185 lbs. Deb: 4/18/06

YEAR	TM/L	W	L	PCT	G	GS	CG	SH	SV	IP	H	HR	BB	SO	RAT	ERA	ERA+	OAV	OOB	BH	AVG	PB	PR	/A	PD	TPI
1906	StL-N	0	1	.000	1	1	0	0	0	4	9	0	2	0	24.8	13.50	19	.474	.524	0	.000	-0	-5	-5	0	-0.8
1907	Pit-N	0	2	.000	4	3	1	0	0	22	40	1	3	11	18.8	6.95	35	.408	.442	2	.286	0	-11	-11	0	-0.8

YEAR TM/L	W	L	PCT	G	GS	CG	SH	SV	IP	H	HR	BB	SO	RAT	ERA	ERA+	OAV	OOB	BH	AVG	PB	PR	/A	PD	TPI
1909 *Pit-N	12	3	.800	25	12	7	3	2	130	88	0	23	65	7.9	1.11	246	.196	.240	2	.051	-3	22	23	-1	2.5
1910 Pit-N	18	9	.667	34	30	16	3	0	245	217	4	60	101	10.4	2.24	138	.240	.291	16	.193	1	22	23	-5	2.0
1911 Pit-N	22	12	.647	40	37	24	6	0	293¹	253	5	42	133	9.3	2.33	147	.237	.271	26	.252	4	35	36	-8	3.5
1912 Pit-N	11	8	.579	28	21	11	2	0	170¹	169	4	35	63	10.9	2.91	112	.262	.303	12	.226	4	10	7	-2	0.8
1913 Pit-N	21	10	.677	43	37	24	4	0	313²	271	8	49	144	9.2	2.15	140	.235	.267	33	.289	9	37	30	-1	3.7
1914 Pit-N	13	16	.448	40	35	19	3	1	283	253	5	39	91	9.5	2.51	105	.244	.276	11	.165	1	9	4	-2	0.3
1915 Pit-N	14	14	.500	40	30	17	2	2	245	229	6	34	62	9.7	2.87	95	.252	.280	12	.141	-2	-3	-4	-0	-0.7
1916 Pit-N	2	9	.182	16	10	4	1	0	72¹	91	2	12	22	13.2	5.72	47	.320	.355	6	.273	2	-25	-24	0	-3.2
1918 Pit-N	1	1	.500	3	3	2	0	0	22²	15	0	4	6	7.5	1.19	241	.197	.237	3	.333	1	4	4	-1	0.5
1919 Pit-N	17	10	.630	34	29	23	6	1	263¹	213	1	23	92	8.2	1.98	152	.220	.241	17	.185	-0	27	30	-4	2.7
1920 Pit-N	17	13	.567	35	33	19	8	2	263	240	6	18	84	8.9	2.16	149	.244	.259	13	.146	-5	29	31	-2	2.8
1921 Pit-N	14	5	.737	25	20	11	2	0	160	155	4	18	55	9.7	2.64	145	.251	.272	16	.254	3	20	21	-2	2.5
1922 Pit-N	8	11	.421	27	19	12	4	0	171¹	191	1	15	39	11.0	3.57	114	.287	.307	16	.286	4	10	10	1	1.4
1923 Pit-N	13	7	.650	26	22	11	0	1	158²	196	8	25	38	12.6	4.42	91	.309	.336	15	.273	5	-7	-7	-0	-0.7
1924 Pit-N	3	1	.750	9	3	2	0	0	39²	31	1	3	5	7.7	1.13	338	.209	.225	2	.182	-0	12	12	-1	1.0
1925 *Pit-N	6	5	.545	33	10	3	0	3	101¹	129	7	17	18	13.2	5.42	82	.306	.338	7	.226	0	-13	-11	-2	-1.2
1926 Pit-N	2	3	.400	19	0	0	0	3	36²	51	5	8	7	14.5	6.14	64	.347	.381	2	.222	-0	-9	-9	-1	-1.3
Total 19	194	140	.581	482	355	206	44	15	2995¹	2841	68	430	1036	10.0	2.76	118	.253	.284	216	.212	24	161	161	-32	15.0

● **RED ADAMS**   Adams, Charles Dwight   b: 10/7/21, Parlier, Cal.   BR/TR, 6', 185 lbs.   Deb: 5/5/46   C

1946 Chi-N	0	1	.000	8	0	0	0	0	12	18	1	7	8	18.8	8.25	40	.353	.431	0	.000	-0	-6	-7	1	-0.5

● **DAN ADAMS**   Adams, Daniel Leslie "Rube"   b: 6/19/1887, St.Louis, Mo.   d: 10/6/64, St.Louis, Mo.   BR/TR, 5'11.5", 165 lbs.   Deb: 5/22/14

1914 KC-F	4	9	.308	36	14	6	0	3	136	141	3	52	38	13.2	3.51	79	.273	.347	7	.152	-2	-9	-11	-1	-1.3
1915 KC-F	0	2	.000	11	2	0	0	0	35	41	3	13	16	14.1	4.63	57	.301	.367	1	.111	-1	-7	-8	0	-0.5
Total 2	4	11	.267	47	16	6	0	3	171	182	5	65	54	13.4	3.74	74	.279	.351	8	.145	-2	-17	-19	-1	-1.8

● **JOE ADAMS**   Adams, Joseph Edward   b: 10/28/1877, Cowden, Ill.   d: 10/8/52, Montgomery City, Mo   BR/TL, 6', 190 lbs.   Deb: 4/26/02

1902 StL-N	0	0	—	1	0	0	0	0	4	9	0	2	0	27.0	9.00	30	.442	.513	0	—	-0	-3	-3	1	0.0

● **KARL ADAMS**   Adams, Karl Tutwiler "Rebel"   b: 8/11/1891, Columbus, Ga.   d: 9/17/67, Everett, Wash.   BR/TR, 6'2", 170 lbs.   Deb: 4/19/14

1914 Cin-N	0	0	—	4	0	0	0	0	8	14	0	5	5	21.4	9.00	33	.424	.500	1	.500	-0	-6	-5	0	0.1
1915 Chi-N	1	9	.100	26	12	3	0	0	107	105	5	43	57	12.6	4.71	59	.267	.342	0	.000	-4	-23	-23	0	-2.4
Total 2	1	9	.100	30	12	3	0	0	115	119	5	48	62	13.2	5.01	56	.279	.355	1	.031	-4	-29	-28	0	-2.3

● **RICK ADAMS**   Adams, Reuben Alexander   b: 12/23/1878, Paris, Tex.   d: 3/10/55, Paris, Tex.   BL/TL, 6', 165 lbs.   Deb: 7/13/05

1905 Was-A	2	5	.286	11	6	3	1	0	62²	63	1	24	25	13.6	3.59	74	.263	.349	4	.174	0	-6	-7	0	-0.6

● **BOB ADAMS**   Adams, Robert Andrew   b: 1/20/07, Birmingham, Ala.   d: 3/6/70, Jacksonville, Fla.   BR/TR, 6'0.5", 165 lbs.   Deb: 9/27/31

1931 Phi-N	0	1	.000	1	1	0	0	0	6	14	0	1	3	22.5	9.00	47	.424	.441	0	.000	-0	-3	-3	-0	-0.4
1932 Phi-N	0	0	—	4	0	0	0	0	6	7	0	2	2	13.5	1.50	294	.318	.375	0	—	-0	2	2	0	0.0
Total 2	0	1	.000	5	1	0	0	0	12	21	0	3	5	18.0	5.25	82	.382	.414	0	.000	-0	-2	-1	0	-0.4

● **BOB ADAMS**   Adams, Robert Burdette   b: 7/24/01, Holyoke, Mass.   BR/TR, 5'11", 168 lbs.   Deb: 9/22/25

1925 Bos-A	0	0	—	2	0	0	0	0	5²	10	1	3	1	20.6	7.94	57	.417	.481	1	.333	0	-2	-2	1	0.1

● **WILLIE ADAMS**   Adams, William John Irvin   b: 9/27/1890, Clearfield, Pa.   d: 6/18/37, Albany, N.Y.   BR/TR, 6'4", 180 lbs.   Deb: 6/30/12

1912 StL-A	2	3	.400	13	5	0	0	0	46¹	50	0	19	16	13.8	3.88	85	.284	.360	0	.000	-2	-3	-3	-1	-0.6
1913 StL-A	0	0	—	4	0	0	0	0	9	12	1	4	5	19.0	10.00	29	.286	.388	0	.000	-0	-7	-7	-0	0.0
1914 Pit-F	1	1	.500	15	2	1	0	2	55¹	70	4	22	14	15.1	3.74	77	.326	.391	1	.067	-1	-5	-5	-1	-0.5
1918 Phi-A	5	12	.294	32	14	7	2	0	169	164	2	97	39	14.5	4.42	66	.272	.383	8	.140	-3	-31	-28	1	-2.9
1919 Phi-A	0	0	—	1	0	0	0	0	4²	7	1	2	0	19.3	3.86	89	.389	.476	0	.000	-0	-0	-0	-0	0.0
Total 5	8	16	.333	65	21	8	0	2	284¹	303	8	144	74	14.8	4.37	69	.287	.383	9	.102	-6	-46	-43	-2	-4.0

● **MIKE ADAMSON**   Adamson, John Michael   b: 9/13/47, San Diego, Cal.   BR/TR, 6'2", 185 lbs.   Deb: 7/1/67

1967 Bal-A	0	1	.000	3	2	0	0	0	9²	9	1	12	8	19.6	8.38	38	.257	.447	1	.500	1	-6	-6	-0	-0.5
1968 Bal-A	0	2	.000	2	2	0	0	0	7²	9	2	4	4	15.3	9.39	31	.281	.361	1	.333	1	-5	-6	-0	-1.1
1969 Bal-A	0	1	.000	6	0	0	0	0	8	10	0	6	2	18.0	4.50	79	.357	.471	0	.000	-0	-1	-1	1	-0.1
Total 3	0	4	.000	11	4	0	0	0	25¹	28	3	22	14	17.8	7.46	43	.295	.427	2	.333	1	-12	-12	-0	-1.7

● **GRADY ADKINS**   Adkins, Grady Emmett "Butcher Boy"   b: 6/29/1897, Jacksonville, Ark.   d: 3/31/66, Little Rock, Ark.   BR/TR, 5'11", 175 lbs.   Deb: 4/13/28

1928 Chi-A	10	16	.385	36	27	14	0	1	224²	235	12	89	54	13.2	3.73	109	.278	.351	10	.143	-3	8	8	-1	0.4
1929 Chi-A	2	11	.154	31	15	5	0	0	138¹	168	12	67	24	15.4	5.33	80	.303	.379	11	.239	-5	-17	-16	2	-0.8
Total 2	12	27	.308	67	42	19	0	1	363	403	24	156	78	14.0	4.34	95	.288	.363	21	.181	-1	-9	-8	1	-0.4

● **DEWEY ADKINS**   Adkins, John Dewey   b: 5/11/18, Norcatur, Kan.   BR/TR, 6'2", 195 lbs.   Deb: 9/19/42

1942 Was-A	0	0	—	1	1	0	0	0	6¹	7	0	6	3	18.5	9.95	37	.259	.394	1	.500	0	-4	-4	-0	0.0
1943 Was-A	0	0	—	7	0	0	0	0	10¹	9	0	5	1	12.2	2.61	123	.250	.341	0	—	0	1	1	-1	-0.1
1949 Chi-N	2	4	.333	30	5	1	0	0	82¹	98	10	39	43	15.0	5.68	71	.298	.372	4	.200	1	-15	-15	1	-0.7
Total 3	2	4	.333	38	6	1	0	0	99	114	10	50	47	14.9	5.64	70	.291	.371	5	.227	1	-19	-19	0	-0.8

● **DOC ADKINS**   Adkins, Merle Theron   b: 8/5/1872, Troy, Wis.   d: 2/21/34, Durham, N.C.   BR/TR, 5'10.5", 220 lbs.   Deb: 6/24/02

1902 Bos-A	1	1	.500	4	2	1	0	0	20	30	2	3	16.6		4.05	88	.346	.395	2	.222	-0	-1	-1	0	-0.1
1903 NY-A	0	0	—	2	1	0	0	1	7	10	0	5	0	20.6	7.71	40	.334	.445	0	.000	-0	-4	-4	-1	-0.2
Total 2	1	1	.500	6	3	1	0	1	27	40	2	12	3	17.7	5.00	69	.343	.409	2	.167	-1	-5	-5	0	-0.3

● **STEVE ADKINS**   Adkins, Steven Thomas   b: 10/26/64, Chicago, Ill.   BR/TL, 6'6", 210 lbs.   Deb: 9/12/90

1990 NY-A	1	2	.333	5	5	0	0	0	24	19	4	29	14	18.0	6.38	62	.226	.425	0	—	0	-7	-6	-0	-0.7

● **JUAN AGOSTO**   Agosto, Juan Roberto (Gonzalez)   b: 2/23/58, Rio Piedras, P.R.   BL/TL, 6'2", 190 lbs.   Deb: 9/7/81

1981 Chi-A	0	0	—	2	0	0	0	0	5²	5	1	0	3	9.5	4.76	75	.238	.273	0	—	0	-1	-1	0	0.1
1982 Chi-A	0	0	—	1	0	0	0	0	2	7	0	1	0	31.5	18.00	22	.538	.538	0	—	0	-3	-3	0	0.0
1983 *Chi-A	2	2	.500	39	0	0	0	7	41²	41	2	11	29	11.4	4.10	102	.283	.338	0	—	-0	-0	0	0	0.0
1984 Chi-A	2	1	.667	49	0	0	0	1	55¹	54	2	34	26	14.8	3.09	135	.270	.384	0	—	0	6	7	2	0.4
1985 Chi-A	4	3	.571	54	0	0	0	1	60¹	45	3	23	39	10.6	3.58	121	.210	.296	0	—	0	4	5	2	0.7
1986 Chi-A	0	0	.000	9	0	0	0	0	4²	6	0	4	3	19.3	7.71	56	.300	.417	0	—	-0	-2	-2	-0	-0.7
Min-A	1	2	.333	17	1	0	0	1	20¹	43	1	14	9	26.1	8.85	49	.443	.522	0	—	0	-11	-10	1	-1.4
Yr	1	4	.200	26	1	0	0	1	25	49	1	18	12	24.8	8.64	50	.419	.504	0	—	-0	-12	-12	1	-2.1
1987 Hou-N	1	1	.500	27	0	0	0	0	27¹	26	1	10	6	11.9	2.63	149	.248	.313	0	.000	-0	4	4	1	0.4
1988 Hou-N	10	2	.833	75	0	0	0	4	91²	74	6	30	33	10.2	2.26	147	.226	.291	0	.000	-0	12	11	4	1.9
1989 Hou-N	4	5	.444	71	0	0	0	0	83	81	3	32	46	12.5	2.93	116	.256	.329	1	.200	0	5	4	1	0.6
1990 Hou-N	9	8	.529	82	0	0	0	4	92¹	91	4	39	50	13.4	4.29	87	.261	.347	0	.000	-0	-5	-6	2	-0.9
1991 StL-N	5	3	.625	72	0	0	0	2	86	92	4	39	34	14.5	4.81	77	.291	.383	1	.333	1	-11	-10	1	-0.8
1992 StL-N	2	4	.333	22	0	0	0	0	31²	39	2	15	14	14.5	6.25	54	.312	.383	0	—	-0	-10	-10	1	-1.7
Sea-A	0	0	—	17	0	0	0	0	18¹	27	1	4	12	14.7	5.89	67	.346	.370	0	—	0	-4	-4	0	0.0

YEAR	TM/L	W	L	PCT	G	GS	CG	SH	SV	IP	H	HR	BB	SO	RAT	ERA	ERA+	OAV	OOB	BH	AVG	PB	PR	/A	PD	TPI
1993	Hou-N	0	0	—	6	0	0	0	0	6	8	1	0	3	12.0	6.00	65	.308	.308	0	—	0	-1	-1	-0	0.0
Total	13	40	33	.548	543	2	0	0	29	626¹	639	30	248	307	13.2	4.01	94	.272	.349	2	.100	-1	-16	-17	14	-1.4

● RICK AGUILERA　Aguilera, Richard Warren　b: 12/31/61, San Gabriel, Cal.　BR/TR, 6'5", 200 lbs.　Deb: 6/12/85

YEAR	TM/L	W	L	PCT	G	GS	CG	SH	SV	IP	H	HR	BB	SO	RAT	ERA	ERA+	OAV	OOB	BH	AVG	PB	PR	/A	PD	TPI
1985	NY-N	10	7	.588	21	19	2	0	0	122¹	118	8	37	74	11.6	3.24	107	.258	.317	10	.278	3	5	3	-0	0.7
1986	*NY-N	10	7	.588	28	20	2	0	0	141²	145	15	36	104	11.9	3.88	91	.263	.316	8	.157	2	-2	-5	2	-0.2
1987	NY-N	11	3	.786	18	17	1	0	0	115	124	12	33	77	12.5	3.60	105	.276	.330	9	.225	3	6	2	2	0.8
1988	*NY-N	0	4	.000	11	3	0	0	0	24²	29	2	10	16	14.6	6.93	46	.296	.367	1	.250	0	-10	-10	0	-1.4
1989	NY-N	6	6	.500	36	0	0	0	7	69¹	59	3	21	80	10.6	2.34	140	.231	.295	0	.000	-0	9	7	-0	1.3
	Min-A	3	5	.375	11	11	3	0	0	75²	71	5	17	57	10.6	3.21	129	.245	.289	0	—	0	6	8	1	0.8
1990	Min-A	5	3	.625	56	0	0	0	32	65¹	55	5	19	61	10.7	2.76	151	.224	.291	0	—	0	8	10	-1	2.2
1991	*Min-A★	4	5	.444	63	0	0	0	42	69	44	3	30	61	9.8	2.35	182	.183	.277	0	—	0	13	15	-0	3.8
1992	Min-A★	2	6	.250	64	0	0	0	41	66²	60	7	17	52	10.5	2.84	143	.238	.289	0	—	0	8	9	-1	2.1
1993	Min-A★	4	3	.571	65	0	0	0	34	72¹	60	9	14	59	9.3	3.11	140	.223	.264	0	—	0	10	10	1	2.0
1994	Min-A	1	4	.200	44	0	0	0	23	44²	57	7	10	46	13.5	3.63	134	.306	.342	0	—	0	6	6	0	1.2
Total	10	56	53	.514	417	70	8	0	179	866²	822	76	244	687	11.4	3.29	117	.250	.306	28	.203	8	59	54	3	13.3

● HANK AGUIRRE　Aguirre, Henry John　b: 1/31/31, Azusa, Cal.　d: 9/5/94, Bloomfield Hills, Mich.　BR/TL, 6'4", 205 lbs.　Deb: 9/10/55　C

YEAR	TM/L	W	L	PCT	G	GS	CG	SH	SV	IP	H	HR	BB	SO	RAT	ERA	ERA+	OAV	OOB	BH	AVG	PB	PR	/A	PD	TPI
1955	Cle-A	2	0	1.000	4	1	1	1	0	12²	6	0	12	6	12.8	1.42	281	.143	.333	0	.000	-1	4	4	-0	0.4
1956	Cle-A	3	5	.375	16	9	2	1	0	65¹	63	7	27	31	12.5	3.72	113	.253	.329	2	.111	-2	3	4	-1	0.2
1957	Cle-A	1	1	.500	10	1	0	0	0	20¹	26	0	13	9	17.3	5.75	65	.317	.411	0	.000	-1	-4	-5	-0	-0.5
1958	Det-A	3	4	.429	44	3	0	0	5	69²	67	5	27	38	12.3	3.75	108	.255	.326	3	.214	0	0	2	1	0.3
1959	Det-A	0	0	—	3	0	0	0	0	2²	4	0	3	3	23.6	3.38	120	.364	.500	0	0	0	0	0	0	0.0
1960	Det-A	5	3	.625	37	6	1	0	10	94²	75	7	30	80	10.3	2.85	139	.217	.286	1	.036	-3	11	12	-2	0.7
1961	Det-A	4	4	.500	45	0	0	0	8	55¹	44	5	38	32	13.7	3.25	126	.224	.356	0	.000	-1	5	5	-1	0.7
1962	Det-A★	16	8	.667	42	22	11	2	3	216	162	14	65	156	9.7	2.21	184	.205	.269	2	.027	-8	42	45	-3	3.7
1963	Det-A	14	15	.483	38	33	14	3	0	225²	222	25	68	134	11.9	3.67	102	.256	.316	10	.132	-1	-2	-3	-3	-0.3
1964	Det-A	5	10	.333	32	27	8	0	1	161²	134	15	59	88	11.2	3.79	97	.223	.301	3	.057	-4	-3	-2	-3	-0.9
1965	Det-A	14	10	.583	32	32	10	2	0	208¹	185	24	60	141	11.0	3.59	97	.236	.298	6	.086	-2	-3	-3	-1	-0.7
1966	Det-A	3	9	.250	30	14	2	0	0	103²	104	14	26	50	11.5	3.82	91	.260	.310	3	.120	0	-4	-4	-2	-0.6
1967	Det-A	0	1	.000	31	1	0	0	0	41¹	34	2	17	33	11.1	2.40	136	.219	.297	1	.500	1	4	4	0	0.2
1968	LA-N	1	2	.333	25	0	0	0	3	39¹	32	0	13	25	11.0	0.69	403	.227	.306	0	.000	-0	10	9	-1	0.8
1969	Chi-N	1	0	1.000	41	0	0	0	1	45	45	2	12	19	11.8	2.60	155	.269	.326	2	.400	1	5	5	1	0.3
1970	Chi-N	3	0	1.000	17	0	0	0	1	14	13	3	9	11	14.8	4.50	100	.250	.371	0	.000	-0	-1	-0	-0	-0.1
Total	16	75	72	.510	447	149	44	9	33	1375²	1216	123	479	856	11.4	3.24	116	.236	.307	33	.085	-21	67	79	-16	4.2

● EDDIE AINSMITH　Ainsmith, Edward Wilbur "Dorf"　b: 2/4/1892, Cambridge, Mass.　d: 9/6/81, Ft.Lauderdale, Fla　BR/TR, 5'11", 180 lbs.　Deb: 8/9/10　♦

YEAR	TM/L	W	L	PCT	G	GS	CG	SH	SV	IP	H	HR	BB	SO	RAT	ERA	ERA+	OAV	OOB	BH	AVG	PB	PR	/A	PD	TPI
1913	Was-A	0	0	—	1	0	0	0	0	0¹	2	0	0	0	54.0	54.00	5	.667	.667	49	.214	0	-2	-2	0	0.0

● RALEIGH AITCHISON　Aitchison, Raleigh Leonidas　b: 12/5/1887, Tyndall, S.D.　d: 9/26/58, Columbus, Kan.　BR/TL, 5'11.5", 175 lbs.　Deb: 4/19/11

YEAR	TM/L	W	L	PCT	G	GS	CG	SH	SV	IP	H	HR	BB	SO	RAT	ERA	ERA+	OAV	OOB	BH	AVG	PB	PR	/A	PD	TPI
1911	Bro-N	0	1	.000	1	0	0	0	0	1¹	1	0	1	0	13.5	0.00	—	.200	.333	0	—	0	1	0	-0	0.4
1914	Bro-N	12	7	.632	26	17	8	3	0	172¹	156	4	60	87	11.4	2.66	107	.244	.312	10	.196	1	2	4	-3	0.2
1915	Bro-N	0	4	.000	7	5	2	0	0	32²	36	3	6	14	12.1	4.96	56	.267	.308	0	.000	-0	-8	-8	0	-0.9
Total	3	12	12	.500	34	22	10	3	0	206¹	193	7	67	101	11.6	3.01	95	.247	.311	10	.169	1	-5	-4	-3	-0.3

● JACK AKER　Aker, Jackie Delane　b: 7/13/40, Tulare, Cal.　BR/TR, 6'2", 190 lbs.　Deb: 5/3/64　C

YEAR	TM/L	W	L	PCT	G	GS	CG	SH	SV	IP	H	HR	BB	SO	RAT	ERA	ERA+	OAV	OOB	BH	AVG	PB	PR	/A	PD	TPI
1964	KC-A	0	1	.000	9	0	0	0	0	16¹	17	6	10	7	18.2	8.82	43	.266	.412	0	.000	-0	-9	-9	1	-0.5
1965	KC-A	4	3	.571	34	0	0	0	3	51¹	45	3	18	26	11.6	3.16	111	.242	.319	0	.000	-1	2	2	1	0.3
1966	KC-A	8	4	.667	66	0	0	0	32	113	81	7	28	68	8.9	1.99	171	.201	.258	2	.095	-1	18	18	3	3.4
1967	KC-A	3	8	.273	57	0	0	0	12	88	87	9	32	65	12.5	4.30	74	.264	.334	1	.125	-0	-10	-11	2	-1.5
1968	Oak-A	4	4	.500	54	0	0	0	11	74²	72	6	33	44	13.4	4.10	69	.258	.349	1	.143	-0	-9	-11	-0	-1.5
1969	Sea-A	0	2	.000	15	0	0	0	3	16²	25	4	13	9	21.1	7.56	48	.357	.464	0	.000	0	-7	-7	1	-1.0
	NY-A	8	4	.667	38	0	0	0	11	65²	51	4	22	40	10.6	2.06	169	.217	.295	1	.111	-0	11	10	2	2.4
	Yr	8	6	.571	53	0	0	0	14	82¹	76	8	35	47	12.6	3.17	111	.248	.333	1	.100	-0	4	3	2	1.4
1970	NY-A	4	2	.667	41	0	0	0	16	70	57	3	20	36	10.4	2.06	171	.226	.293	1	.063	-1	13	11	-0	1.4
1971	NY-A	4	4	.500	41	0	0	0	4	55²	48	3	26	24	12.0	2.59	125	.238	.325	0	.000	-0	5	4	1	0.7
1972	NY-A	0	0	—	4	0	0	0	0	6	5	0	3	1	13.5	3.00	98	.238	.360	0	—	-0	-0	1	1	0.1
	Chi-N	6	6	.500	48	0	0	0	17	67	65	4	23	36	12.5	2.96	129	.259	.333	0	.000	-0	4	6	2	1.7
1973	Chi-N	4	5	.444	47	0	0	0	12	63²	76	8	23	25	14.3	4.10	96	.308	.371	0	.000	-0	-3	-1	2	-0.1
1974	Atl-N	0	1	.000	17	0	0	0	0	16²	17	3	9	7	14.0	3.78	100	.298	.394	0	.000	-0	-0	-0	0	0.0
	NY-N	2	1	.667	24	0	0	0	2	41¹	33	4	14	18	10.7	3.48	102	.213	.287	1	.500	1	1	0	-1	0.0
	Yr	2	2	.500	41	0	0	0	2	58	50	7	23	25	11.6	3.57	102	.234	.314	1	.333	1	0	-0	-0	0.0
Total	11	47	45	.511	495	0	0	0	123	746	679	64	274	404	12.0	3.28	105	.247	.324	7	.076	-5	14	13	13	5.4

● DARREL AKERFELDS　Akerfelds, Darrel Wayne　b: 6/12/62, Denver, Colo.　BR/TR, 6'2", 210 lbs.　Deb: 8/1/86

YEAR	TM/L	W	L	PCT	G	GS	CG	SH	SV	IP	H	HR	BB	SO	RAT	ERA	ERA+	OAV	OOB	BH	AVG	PB	PR	/A	PD	TPI
1986	Oak-A	0	0	—	2	0	0	0	0	5¹	7	2	3	5	16.9	6.75	57	.304	.385	0	—	0	-2	-2	0	0.0
1987	Cle-A	2	6	.250	16	13	1	0	0	74²	84	18	38	42	15.5	6.75	67	.284	.378	0	—	0	-19	-18	-0	-1.7
1989	Tex-A	0	1	.000	6	0	0	0	0	11	11	1	5	9	13.1	3.27	121	.250	.327	0	—	0	1	1	0	0.1
1990	Phi-N	5	2	.714	71	0	0	0	3	93	65	10	54	42	11.8	3.77	101	.201	.320	1	.167	-0	0	0	-1	0.0
1991	Phi-N	2	1	.667	30	0	0	0	0	49²	49	5	27	31	14.3	5.26	70	.257	.357	0	.000	-0	-9	-9	1	-0.5
Total	5	9	10	.474	125	13	1	0	3	233²	216	36	127	129	13.7	5.08	79	.246	.350	1	.111	-0	-28	-28	0	-2.1

● JERRY AKERS　Akers, Albert Earl　b: 11/1/1887, Shelbyville, Ind.　d: 5/15/79, Bay Pines, Fla.　BR/TR, 5'11", 175 lbs.　Deb: 5/4/12

YEAR	TM/L	W	L	PCT	G	GS	CG	SH	SV	IP	H	HR	BB	SO	RAT	ERA	ERA+	OAV	OOB	BH	AVG	PB	PR	/A	PD	TPI
1912	Was-A	1	1	.500	5	1	0	0	0	20¹	24	1	15	11	18.1	4.87	68	.300	.423	2	.333	0	-4	-3	-1	-0.4

● GIBSON ALBA　Alba, Gibson Alberto (Rosado)　b: 1/18/60, Santiago, D.R.　BL/TL, 6'2", 160 lbs.　Deb: 5/3/88

YEAR	TM/L	W	L	PCT	G	GS	CG	SH	SV	IP	H	HR	BB	SO	RAT	ERA	ERA+	OAV	OOB	BH	AVG	PB	PR	/A	PD	TPI
1988	StL-N	0	0	—	3	0	0	0	0	3¹	1	0	2	3	8.1	2.70	129	.091	.231	0	—	0	0	0	-0	0.0

● JOE ALBANESE　Albanese, Joseph Peter　b: 6/26/33, New York, N.Y.　BR/TR, 6'3", 215 lbs.　Deb: 7/18/58

YEAR	TM/L	W	L	PCT	G	GS	CG	SH	SV	IP	H	HR	BB	SO	RAT	ERA	ERA+	OAV	OOB	BH	AVG	PB	PR	/A	PD	TPI
1958	Was-A	0	0	—	6	0	0	0	0	6	8	1	2	3	15.0	4.50	85	.348	.400	1	—	-0	-0	-0	-1	0.0

● CY ALBERTS　Alberts, Frederick Joseph　b: 1/14/1882, Grand Rapids, Mich　d: 8/27/17, Fort Wayne, Ind.　BR/TR, 6', 230 lbs.　Deb: 9/17/10

YEAR	TM/L	W	L	PCT	G	GS	CG	SH	SV	IP	H	HR	BB	SO	RAT	ERA	ERA+	OAV	OOB	BH	AVG	PB	PR	/A	PD	TPI
1910	StL-N	1	2	.333	4	3	2	0	0	27²	35	1	20	10	17.9	6.18	48	.330	.437	0	.000	-0	-10	-10	-1	-1.0

● ED ALBOSTA　Albosta, Edward John "Rube"　b: 10/27/18, Saginaw, Mich.　BR/TR, 6'1", 175 lbs.　Deb: 9/3/41

YEAR	TM/L	W	L	PCT	G	GS	CG	SH	SV	IP	H	HR	BB	SO	RAT	ERA	ERA+	OAV	OOB	BH	AVG	PB	PR	/A	PD	TPI
1941	Bro-N	0	2	.000	2	2	0	0	0	13	11	1	8	5	13.2	6.23	59	.239	.352	0	—	-1	-4	-4	0	-0.5
1946	Pit-N	0	6	.000	17	6	0	0	0	39²	41	3	35	19	17.5	6.13	58	.266	.405	1	.125	-0	-12	-11	0	-1.6
Total	2	0	8	.000	19	8	0	0	0	52²	52	4	43	24	16.4	6.15	58	.260	.393	1	.083	-1	-16	-15	0	-2.1

● ED ALBRECHT　Albrecht, Edward Arthur　b: 2/28/29, Affton, Mo.　d: 12/29/79, Cahokia, Ill.　BR/TR, 5'10.5", 165 lbs.　Deb: 10/2/49

YEAR	TM/L	W	L	PCT	G	GS	CG	SH	SV	IP	H	HR	BB	SO	RAT	ERA	ERA+	OAV	OOB	BH	AVG	PB	PR	/A	PD	TPI
1949	StL-A	1	0	1.000	1	1	1	0	0	5	1	0	4	1	9.0	5.40	84	.063	.250	0	.000	-0	-1	-0	0	-0.1
1950	StL-A	0	1	.000	2	1	0	0	0	6²	11	2	7	1	17.6	5.40	92	.250	.419	0	.000	-0	-0	-0	-0	-0.1
Total	2	1	1	.500	3	2	1	0	0	11²	12	2	11	2	13.9	5.40	88	.175	.353	0	—	-0	-1	-0	-0	-0.2

● VIC ALBURY　Albury, Victor　b: 5/12/47, Key West, Fla.　BL/TL, 6', 190 lbs.　Deb: 8/7/73

YEAR	TM/L	W	L	PCT	G	GS	CG	SH	SV	IP	H	HR	BB	SO	RAT	ERA	ERA+	OAV	OOB	BH	AVG	PB	PR	/A	PD	TPI
1973	Min-A	1	0	1.000	14	0	0	0	0	23¹	13	1	19	13	12.3	2.70	147	.169	.333	0	—	0	3	3	-1	0.0

YEAR	TM/L	W	L	PCT	G	GS	CG	SH	SV	IP	H	HR	BB	SO	RAT	ERA	ERA+	OAV	OOB	BH	AVG	PB	PR	/A	PD	TPI
1974	Min-A	8	9	.471	32	22	4	1	0	164	159	19	80	85	13.4	4.12	91	.259	.350	0	—	0	-9	-7	-1	-0.7
1975	Min-A	6	7	.462	32	15	2	0	1	135	115	16	97	72	14.4	4.53	85	.237	.368	0	.000	0	-11	-10	1	-0.9
1976	Min-A	3	1	.750	23	0	0	0	0	50¹	51	0	24	23	13.8	3.58	101	.271	.360	0	—	0	-0	-0	-0	-0.1
Total	4	18	17	.514	101	37	6	1	1	372²	338	36	220	193	13.8	4.11	92	.247	.357	0	.000	0	-18	-13	-1	-1.7

● SANTO ALCALA
Alcala, Santo (b: Santo Anibal (Alcala))   b: 12/23/52, San Pedro De Macoris, D.R.   BR/TR, 6'5", 195 lbs.   Deb: 4/10/76

YEAR	TM/L	W	L	PCT	G	GS	CG	SH	SV	IP	H	HR	BB	SO	RAT	ERA	ERA+	OAV	OOB	BH	AVG	PB	PR	/A	PD	TPI
1976	Cin-N	11	4	.733	30	21	3	1	0	132	131	12	67	67	13.7	4.70	74	.261	.352	6	.140	-0	-18	-18	-1	-2.0
1977	Cin-N	1	1	.500	7	2	0	0	0	15²	22	1	7	9	17.2	5.74	68	.349	.423	0	.000	-0	-3	-3	0	-0.4
	Mon-N	2	6	.250	31	10	0	0	2	101²	104	12	47	64	13.5	4.69	81	.263	.344	2	.080	-1	-9	-10	-1	-1.0
	Yr	3	7	.300	38	12	0	0	2	117¹	126	13	54	73	14.0	4.83	79	.273	.352	2	.071	-1	-12	-13	-1	-1.4
Total	2	14	11	.560	68	33	3	1	2	249¹	257	25	121	140	13.9	4.76	77	.268	.353	8	.113	-2	-30	-31	-2	-3.4

● DALE ALDERSON
Alderson, Dale Leonard   b: 3/9/18, Belden, Neb.   d: 2/12/82, Garden Grove, Cal.   BR/TR, 5'10", 190 lbs.   Deb: 9/18/43

YEAR	TM/L	W	L	PCT	G	GS	CG	SH	SV	IP	H	HR	BB	SO	RAT	ERA	ERA+	OAV	OOB	BH	AVG	PB	PR	/A	PD	TPI
1943	Chi-N	0	1	.000	4	2	0	0	0	14	21	2	3	4	15.4	6.43	52	.356	.387	0	.000	-0	-5	-5	0	-0.3
1944	Chi-N	0	0	—	12	1	0	0	0	21²	31	2	9	7	16.6	6.65	53	.344	.404	0	.000	-1	-7	-7	1	0.0
Total	2	0	1	.000	16	3	0	0	0	35²	52	4	12	11	16.5	6.56	53	.349	.398	0	.000	-1	-12	-12	0	-0.3

● SCOTT ALDRED
Aldred, Scott Phillip   b: 6/12/68, Flint, Mich.   BL/TL, 6'4", 195 lbs.   Deb: 9/9/90

YEAR	TM/L	W	L	PCT	G	GS	CG	SH	SV	IP	H	HR	BB	SO	RAT	ERA	ERA+	OAV	OOB	BH	AVG	PB	PR	/A	PD	TPI
1990	Det-A	1	2	.333	4	3	0	0	0	14¹	13	0	10	7	15.1	3.77	105	.265	.400	0	—	0	0	0	-0	0.0
1991	Det-A	2	4	.333	11	11	1	0	0	57¹	58	9	30	35	13.8	5.18	80	.266	.355	0	—	0	-7	-7	0	-0.6
1992	Det-A	3	8	.273	16	13	0	0	0	65	80	12	33	34	16.1	6.78	58	.307	.391	0	—	0	-21	-20	1	-2.8
1993	Col-N	0	0	—	5	0	0	0	0	6²	10	1	9	5	27.0	10.80	44	.357	.526	0	—	0	-5	-4	0	0.0
	Mon-N	1	0	1.000	3	0	0	0	0	5¹	9	1	1	4	16.9	6.75	62	.375	.400	0	—	0	-2	-2	0	-0.2
	Yr	1	0	1.000	8	0	0	0	0	12	19	2	10	9	21.8	9.00	50	.358	.460	0	—	0	-7	-6	0	-0.2
Total	4	7	14	.333	39	27	1	0	0	148²	170	23	83	85	15.6	6.05	67	.293	.386	0	—	0	-34	-33	0	-3.6

● JAY ALDRICH
Aldrich, Jay Robert   b: 4/14/61, Alexandria, La.   BR/TR, 6'3", 210 lbs.   Deb: 6/5/87

YEAR	TM/L	W	L	PCT	G	GS	CG	SH	SV	IP	H	HR	BB	SO	RAT	ERA	ERA+	OAV	OOB	BH	AVG	PB	PR	/A	PD	TPI
1987	Mil-A	3	1	.750	31	0	0	0	0	58¹	71	8	13	22	13.3	4.94	93	.306	.348	0	—	0	-3	-2	-1	-0.4
1989	Mil-A	1	0	1.000	16	0	0	0	0	26	24	3	13	12	13.2	3.81	101	.253	.349	0	—	0	0	0	0	0.1
	Atl-N	1	2	.333	8	0	0	0	0	12¹	7	0	6	7	9.5	2.19	167	.167	.271	0	.000	-0	2	2	-0	0.4
1990	Bal-A	1	2	.333	7	0	0	0	0	12	17	1	7	5	18.0	8.25	46	.327	.407	0	—	0	-6	-6	0	-1.3
Total	3	6	5	.545	62	0	0	0	0	108²	119	12	39	46	13.3	4.72	89	.283	.348	0	.000	-0	-7	-6	-1	-1.2

● VIC ALDRIDGE
Aldridge, Victor Eddington   b: 10/25/1893, Indian Springs, Ind.   d: 4/17/73, Terre Haute, Ind.   BR/TR, 5'9.5", 175 lbs.   Deb: 4/15/17

YEAR	TM/L	W	L	PCT	G	GS	CG	SH	SV	IP	H	HR	BB	SO	RAT	ERA	ERA+	OAV	OOB	BH	AVG	PB	PR	/A	PD	TPI
1917	Chi-N	6	6	.500	30	6	1	1	2	106²	100	1	37	44	11.7	3.12	93	.252	.319	4	.138	-2	-5	-3	3	-0.2
1918	Chi-N	0	1	.000	3	0	0	0	0	12¹	11	0	6	10	12.4	1.46	191	.275	.370	1	.333	0	2	2	-0	0.2
1922	Chi-N	16	15	.516	36	34	20	2	0	258¹	287	14	56	66	12.4	3.52	119	.286	.332	26	.260	3	17	20	1	2.5
1923	Chi-N	16	9	.640	30	30	15	2	0	217	209	17	67	64	11.5	3.48	115	.251	.307	19	.268	3	12	12	-1	1.5
1924	Chi-N	15	12	.556	32	32	20	1	0	244¹	261	10	80	74	12.8	3.50	112	.279	.341	15	.176	-3	10	11	-0	0.7
1925	*Pit-N	15	7	.682	30	26	14	1	0	213¹	218	15	74	88	12.5	3.63	123	.269	.334	20	.233	-1	15	20	-3	1.3
1926	Pit-N	10	13	.435	30	26	12	1	1	190	204	7	73	61	13.3	4.07	97	.279	.348	16	.225	-1	-5	-3	-2	-0.6
1927	*Pit-N	15	10	.600	35	34	17	1	1	239¹	248	16	74	86	12.3	4.25	97	.270	.328	21	.219	-0	-9	-4	-3	-0.7
1928	NY-N	4	7	.364	22	17	3	0	2	119¹	133	7	45	33	13.7	4.83	81	.285	.352	11	.275	2	-11	-12	-1	-0.9
Total	9	97	80	.548	248	205	102	8	6	1600²	1671	87	512	526	12.5	3.76	107	.273	.333	133	.229	2	26	44	-7	3.8

● DOYLE ALEXANDER
Alexander, Doyle Lafayette   b: 9/4/50, Cordova, Ala.   BR/TR, 6'3", 205 lbs.   Deb: 6/26/71

YEAR	TM/L	W	L	PCT	G	GS	CG	SH	SV	IP	H	HR	BB	SO	RAT	ERA	ERA+	OAV	OOB	BH	AVG	PB	PR	/A	PD	TPI
1971	LA-N	6	6	.500	17	12	4	0	0	92¹	105	6	18	30	12.1	3.80	85	.282	.317	9	.273	3	-3	-6	-1	-0.5
1972	Bal-A	6	8	.429	35	9	2	2	2	106¹	78	5	30	49	9.2	2.45	125	.203	.262	2	.080	-1	7	7	2	1.1
1973	*Bal-A	12	8	.600	29	26	10	0	0	174²	169	19	52	63	11.7	3.86	97	.258	.319	0	—	0	-1	-3	1	-0.1
1974	Bal-A	6	9	.400	30	12	2	0	0	114¹	127	7	43	40	13.7	4.01	86	.290	.359	0	—	0	-5	-7	3	-0.5
1975	Bal-A	8	8	.500	32	11	3	1	1	133¹	127	7	47	46	11.8	3.04	116	.251	.316	0	—	0	11	7	2	1.0
1976	Bal-A	3	4	.429	11	6	2	1	0	64¹	58	3	24	17	11.5	3.50	94	.247	.317	0	—	0	0	-2	1	0.2
	*NY-A	10	5	.667	19	19	5	2	0	136²	114	9	39	41	10.3	3.29	104	.229	.289	0	—	0	3	2	-2	0.0
	Yr	13	9	.591	30	25	7	3	0	201	172	12	63	58	10.7	3.36	100	.234	.297	0	—	0	4	-0	-1	0.2
1977	Tex-A	17	11	.607	34	34	12	1	0	237	221	24	82	82	11.6	3.65	112	.246	.311	0	—	0	11	11	1	1.4
1978	Tex-A	9	10	.474	31	28	7	1	0	191	198	6	71	81	12.7	3.86	97	.270	.336	0	—	0	-2	-3	2	-0.1
1979	Tex-A	5	7	.417	23	18	0	0	0	113¹	114	9	69	50	14.6	4.45	93	.268	.371	0	—	0	-3	-4	2	-0.1
1980	Atl-N	14	11	.560	35	35	7	1	0	231²	227	20	74	114	11.8	4.20	89	.256	.316	15	.181	-15	-12	3	-0.8
1981	SF-N	11	7	.611	24	24	1	1	0	152¹	156	11	44	77	11.9	2.89	118	.263	.316	9	.176	1	10	9	-2	1.0
1982	NY-A	1	7	.125	16	11	0	0	0	66²	81	14	14	26	12.8	6.08	66	.298	.332	0	—	0	-15	-15	-0	-1.5
1983	NY-A	0	2	.000	8	5	0	0	0	28¹	31	6	7	14	12.1	6.35	61	.277	.319	0	—	0	-7	-8	-0	-0.3
	Tor-A	7	6	.538	17	15	5	0	0	116²	126	14	26	46	11.8	3.93	109	.279	.319	0	—	0	2	5	0	0.2
	Yr	7	8	.467	25	20	5	0	0	145	157	20	33	63	11.9	4.41	96	.278	.319	0	—	0	-6	-3	0	-0.1
1984	Tor-A	17	6	**.739**	36	35	11	2	0	261²	238	21	59	139	10.3	3.13	131	.242	.287	0	—	0	25	28	-0	2.2
1985	*Tor-A	17	10	.630	36	36	6	1	0	260²	268	28	67	142	11.8	3.45	122	.266	.315	0	—	0	20	22	0	2.1
1986	Tor-A	5	4	.556	17	17	3	0	0	111	120	18	20	65	11.7	4.46	95	.273	.310	0	—	0	-3	-3	-1	-0.3
	Atl-N	6	6	.500	17	17	2	0	0	117¹	135	9	17	74	11.7	3.84	104	.287	.312	8	.211	1	-2	2	-1	0.2
1987	Atl-N	5	10	.333	16	16	3	0	0	117²	115	21	27	64	11.0	4.13	105	.257	.302	1	.029	-3	-1	3	-2	-0.1
	*Det-A	9	0	1.000	11	11	3	3	0	88¹	63	3	26	44	9.1	1.53	276	.201	.263	0	—	0	29	26	0	3.0
1988	Det-A☆	14	11	.560	34	34	5	1	0	229	260	30	46	126	12.2	4.32	88	.282	.320	0	—	0	-9	-13	-3	-1.5
1989	Det-A	6	18	.250	33	33	5	1	0	223	245	28	76	95	13.2	4.44	86	.280	.341	0	—	0	-14	-15	0	-1.4
Total	19	194	174	.527	561	464	98	18	3	3367²	3376	324	978	1528	11.8	3.76	102	.261	.316	44	.166	1	38	32	7	5.2

● GERALD ALEXANDER
Alexander, Gerald Paul   b: 3/26/68, Baton Rouge, La.   BR/TR, 5'11", 190 lbs.   Deb: 9/9/90

YEAR	TM/L	W	L	PCT	G	GS	CG	SH	SV	IP	H	HR	BB	SO	RAT	ERA	ERA+	OAV	OOB	BH	AVG	PB	PR	/A	PD	TPI
1990	Tex-A	0	0	—	3	2	0	0	0	7	14	0	5	8	25.7	7.71	77	.438	.526	0	—	0	-3	-3	0	0.0
1991	Tex-A	5	3	.625	30	9	0	0	0	89¹	93	11	48	50	14.5	5.24	77	.272	.366	0	—	0	-11	-12	0	-0.9
1992	Tex-A	1	0	1.000	3	0	0	0	0	1²	5	1	1	1	32.4	27.00	14	.500	.545	0	—	0	-4	-4	0	-1.7
Total	3	6	3	.667	36	11	0	0	0	98	112	12	54	59	15.6	5.79	69	.292	.385	0	—	0	-19	-19	0	-2.6

● PETE ALEXANDER
Alexander, Grover Cleveland   b: 2/26/1887, Elba, Neb.   d: 11/4/50, St.Paul, Neb.   BR/TR, 6'1", 185 lbs.   Deb: 4/15/11   H

YEAR	TM/L	W	L	PCT	G	GS	CG	SH	SV	IP	H	HR	BB	SO	RAT	ERA	ERA+	OAV	OOB	BH	AVG	PB	PR	/A	PD	TPI
1911	Phi-N	**28**	13	.683	48	37	**31**	**7**	3	367	285	5	129	227	10.3	2.57	134	**.219**	.293	24	.174	-2	34	35	1	3.6
1912	Phi-N	19	17	.528	46	34	25	3	3	310¹	289	11	105	**195**	11.6	2.81	129	.251	.317	19	.186	0	21	28	1	3.1
1913	Phi-N	22	8	.733	47	36	23	**9**	2	306¹	288	9	75	159	10.8	2.79	120	.254	.302	13	.126	-4	14	19	2	1.4
1914	Phi-N	**27**	15	.643	46	39	**32**	6	1	355	327	6	76	**214**	10.5	2.38	123	.244	.290	32	.234	2	16	22	4	3.3
1915	*Phi-N	**31**	10	**.756**	49	42	**36**	**12**	3	376¹	253	3	64	241	7.8	**1.22**	**225**	**.191**	**.234**	22	.169	0	**64**	**64**	7	**8.6**
1916	Phi-N	**33**	12	.733	48	45	**38**	**16**	3	389	323	6	50	167	8.9	**1.55**	**171**	.230	.262	33	.239	8	**46**	48	1	**7.3**
1917	Phi-N	**30**	13	.698	45	44	**34**	**8**	0	388	336	4	56	**200**	9.2	1.83	153	.234	.266	30	.216	4	**38**	42	2	**5.9**
1918	Chi-N	2	1	.667	3	3	3	1	0	26	19	1	3	15	8.3	1.73	161	.207	.240	1	.100	-1	4	3	0	0.3
1919	Chi-N	16	11	.593	30	27	20	**9**	1	235	180	3	38	121	8.3	**1.72**	**167**	**.211**	.245	12	.171	1	31	30	5	4.4
1920	Chi-N	**27**	14	.659	46	40	**33**	7	5	363¹	335	8	69	**173**	10.0	**1.91**	**168**	.248	.285	27	.229	4	**50**	52	2	**7.1**
1921	Chi-N	15	13	.536	31	29	21	**3**	1	252	286	10	33	77	11.4	3.39	113	.296	.320	29	.305	6	11	12	-1	1.8
1922	Chi-N	16	13	.552	33	31	20	1	1	245²	283	14	34	48	11.7	3.63	113	.286	.311	16	.176	-2	13	14	3	1.7
1923	Chi-N	22	12	.647	39	36	26	3	2	305	308	11	30	72	**10.0**	3.19	126	.259	**.277**	24	.216	0	28	28	4	3.2
1924	Chi-N	12	5	.706	21	20	12	0	0	169¹	183	9	25	33	11.1	3.03	129	.272	.299	15	.231	4	16	16	2	1.7
1925	Chi-N	15	11	.577	32	30	20	1	0	236	270	14	29	63	11.5	3.39	127	.288	.312	19	.241	3	23	24	-2	2.3

YEAR	TM/L	W	L	PCT	G	GS	CG	SH	SV	IP	H	HR	BB	SO	RAT	ERA	ERA+	OAV	OOB	BH	AVG	PB	PR	/A	PD	TPI
1926	Chi-N	3	3	.500	7	7	4	0	0	52	55	0	7	12	10.7	3.46	111	.270	.294	7	.467	3	2	2	1	0.6
	*StL-N	9	7	.563	23	16	11	2	2	148¹	136	8	24	35	9.8	2.91	134	.242	.276	6	.120	-4	15	16	-0	1.3
	Yr	12	10	.545	30	23	15	2	2	200¹	191	8	31	47	10.1	3.05	127	.250	.281	13	.200	-1	17	19	1	1.9
1927	StL-N	21	10	.677	37	30	22	2	3	268	261	11	38	48	10.1	2.52	157	.258	.286	23	.245	3	42	43	1	5.2
1928	*StL-N	16	9	.640	34	31	18	1	2	243²	262	15	37	59	11.1	3.36	119	.277	.306	25	.291	4	17	17	-1	2.1
1929	StL-N	9	8	.529	22	19	8	0	0	132	149	10	23	33	11.8	3.89	120	.285	.317	2	.049	-4	12	11	2	1.0
1930	Phi-N	0	3	.000	9	3	0	0	0	21²	40	5	6	6	19.1	9.14	60	.396	.430	0	.000	-0	-10	-9	-1	-1.0
Total	20	373	208	.642	696	599	437	90	32	5190	4868	164	951	2198	10.2	2.56	135	.250	.288	378	.209	24	484	522	31	64.9

● BOB ALEXANDER
Alexander, Robert Somerville b: 8/7/22, Vancouver, B.C., Can d: 4/7/93, Oceanside, Cal. BR/TR, 6'2.5", 205 lbs. Deb: 4/11/55

YEAR	TM/L	W	L	PCT	G	GS	CG	SH	SV	IP	H	HR	BB	SO	RAT	ERA	ERA+	OAV	OOB	BH	AVG	PB	PR	/A	PD	TPI
1955	Bal-A	1	0	1.000	4	0	0	0	0	4	8	0	2	0	24.8	13.50	28	.444	.524	0	—	-0	-4	-4	-0	-0.9
1957	Cle-A	0	1	.000	5	0	0	0	0	7	10	0	5	1	20.6	9.00	41	.357	.471	0	.000	-0	-4	-4	-0	-0.6
Total	2	1	1	.500	9	0	0	0	0	11	18	0	7	1	22.1	10.64	35	.391	.491	0	.000	-0	-8	-8	-1	-1.5

● BRIAN ALLARD
Allard, Brian Marshall b: 1/3/58, Spring Valley, Ill. BR/TR, 6'1", 175 lbs. Deb: 8/8/79

YEAR	TM/L	W	L	PCT	G	GS	CG	SH	SV	IP	H	HR	BB	SO	RAT	ERA	ERA+	OAV	OOB	BH	AVG	PB	PR	/A	PD	TPI
1979	Tex-A	1	3	.250	7	4	2	0	0	33¹	36	4	13	14	13.2	4.32	96	.283	.350	0	—	0	-0	-1	-0	0.0
1980	Tex-A	0	1	.000	5	2	0	0	0	14¹	13	0	10	10	15.1	5.65	69	.236	.364	0	—	0	-3	-3	-0	-0.1
1981	Sea-A	3	2	.600	7	7	1	0	0	48	48	5	8	20	10.5	3.75	103	.265	.296	0	—	0	-0	1	-0	-0.1
Total	3	4	6	.400	19	13	3	0	0	95²	97	9	31	44	12.1	4.23	94	.267	.327	0	—	0	-3	-3	-1	-0.2

● FRANK ALLEN
Allen, Frank Leon b: 8/26/1889, Newbern, Ala. d: 7/30/33, Gainesville, Ala. BR/TL, 5'9", 175 lbs. Deb: 4/24/12

YEAR	TM/L	W	L	PCT	G	GS	CG	SH	SV	IP	H	HR	BB	SO	RAT	ERA	ERA+	OAV	OOB	BH	AVG	PB	PR	/A	PD	TPI
1912	Bro-N	3	9	.250	20	15	5	1	0	109	119	1	57	58	14.6	3.63	92	.285	.373	6	.167	2	-3	-3	-0	-0.1
1913	Bro-N	4	18	.182	34	25	11	0	2	174²	144	6	81	82	12.1	2.83	116	.231	.329	7	.137	-1	7	9	-3	0.7
1914	Bro-N	8	14	.364	36	21	10	1	0	171¹	165	6	57	68	11.8	3.10	92	.265	.330	6	.128	0	-6	-5	-1	-0.7
	Pit-F	1	0	1.000	1	1	0	0	0	7	9	0	3	0	11.6	5.14	56	.321	.321	1	.500	1	-2	-2	-0	-0.1
1915	Pit-F	23	13	.639	41	37	24	6	0	283¹	230	9	100	127	10.8	2.51	108	.227	.304	7	.079	-6	7	6	-1	0.1
1916	Bos-N	8	2	.800	19	14	7	2	1	113	102	1	31	63	10.9	2.07	120	.244	.302	7	.206	3	7	5	-1	0.7
1917	Bos-N	3	11	.214	29	14	2	0	0	112	124	3	47	56	14.2	3.94	65	.297	.376	5	.172	2	-15	-17	-2	-2.1
Total	6	50	67	.427	180	127	60	10	3	970¹	893	26	373	457	12.1	2.93	98	.252	.330	39	.135	1	-5	-7	-8	-1.5

● JOHN ALLEN
Allen, John Marshall b: 10/27/1890, Berkeley Springs, W.Va. d: 9/24/67, Hagerstown, Md. BR/TR, 6'1", 170 lbs. Deb: 6/2/14

YEAR	TM/L	W	L	PCT	G	GS	CG	SH	SV	IP	H	HR	BB	SO	RAT	ERA	ERA+	OAV	OOB	BH	AVG	PB	PR	/A	PD	TPI
1914	Bal-F	0	1	—	1	0	0	0	0	2	2	0	2	2	22.5	18.00	17	.286	.500	0	—	0	-3	-3	0	0.0

● JOHNNY ALLEN
Allen, John Thomas b: 9/30/05, Lenoir, N.C. d: 3/29/59, St.Petersburg, Fla BR/TR, 6', 180 lbs. Deb: 4/19/32

YEAR	TM/L	W	L	PCT	G	GS	CG	SH	SV	IP	H	HR	BB	SO	RAT	ERA	ERA+	OAV	OOB	BH	AVG	PB	PR	/A	PD	TPI
1932	*NY-A	17	4	.810	33	21	13	3	4	192	162	10	76	109	11.4	3.70	110	.228	.306	9	.123	-2	17	8	-1	0.5
1933	NY-A	15	7	.682	35	24	10	1	1	184²	171	9	87	119	12.8	4.39	89	.242	.328	13	.181	0	-2	-10	-1	-1.1
1934	NY-A	5	2	.714	13	10	4	0	0	71²	62	3	32	54	12.1	2.89	141	.227	.313	5	.192	1	13	9	0	0.9
1935	NY-A	13	6	.684	23	23	12	2	0	167	149	11	58	113	11.4	3.61	112	.238	.307	15	.224	1	16	8	1	1.0
1936	Cle-A	20	10	.667	36	31	19	4	1	243	234	6	97	165	12.3	3.44	146	.256	.328	14	.161	-3	43	43	2	4.5
1937	Cle-A	15	1	.938	24	20	14	0	0	173	157	4	60	87	11.5	2.55	181	.244	.313	6	.090	-7	40	40	1	2.7
1938	Cle-A★	14	8	.636	30	27	13	0	0	200	189	15	81	112	12.3	4.18	111	.246	.321	20	.253	4	13	10	2	1.5
1939	Cle-A	9	7	.563	28	26	9	2	0	175	199	9	56	79	13.3	4.58	96	.291	.347	16	.225	1	-3	-3	0	0.1
1940	Cle-A	9	8	.529	32	17	5	3	5	138²	126	3	48	62	11.5	3.44	123	.243	.311	10	.208	0	15	12	-0	1.4
1941	StL-A	2	5	.286	20	9	2	0	1	67	89	4	29	27	16.1	6.58	65	.319	.387	3	.136	0	-18	-17	-0	-1.6
	*Bro-N	3	0	1.000	11	4	1	0	0	57¹	46	6	12	21	7.8	2.51	146	.188	.234	1	.050	-2	7	7	0	0.1
1942	Bro-N	10	6	.625	27	15	5	1	3	118	106	11	39	50	11.2	3.20	102	.238	.302	7	.179	-0	1	0	0	0.1
1943	Bro-N	5	1	.833	17	1	0	0	1	38	42	3	25	15	16.3	4.26	79	.280	.390	3	.429	2	-4	-4	-0	-0.4
	NY-N	1	3	.250	15	0	0	0	2	41	37	4	14	24	11.2	3.07	112	.245	.309	0	.000	-2	1	2	1	0.1
	Yr	6	4	.600	32	1	0	0	3	79	79	7	39	39	13.4	3.65	93	.260	.345	3	.143	-0	-2	-1	-0	-0.3
1944	NY-N	4	7	.364	18	13	2	1	0	84	88	7	24	33	12.2	4.07	90	.260	.313	2	.083	-2	-4	-4	-1	-0.8
Total	13	142	75	.654	352	241	109	17	18	1950¹	1849	104	738	1070	12.1	3.75	113	.249	.321	124	.173	-8	138	102	6	8.9

● LLOYD ALLEN
Allen, Lloyd Cecil b: 5/8/50, Merced, Cal. BR/TR, 6'1", 185 lbs. Deb: 9/1/69

YEAR	TM/L	W	L	PCT	G	GS	CG	SH	SV	IP	H	HR	BB	SO	RAT	ERA	ERA+	OAV	OOB	BH	AVG	PB	PR	/A	PD	TPI
1969	Cal-A	0	1	.000	4	1	0	0	0	10	5	1	10	5	13.5	5.40	65	.147	.341	1	.500	1	-2	-2	1	-0.1
1970	Cal-A	1	1	.500	8	2	0	0	0	24	23	0	11	12	13.1	2.63	138	.261	.350	0	—	-0	3	3	-0	0.1
1971	Cal-A	4	6	.400	54	1	0	0	15	94	75	4	40	72	11.0	2.49	130	.221	.303	5	.294	2	10	8	0	1.4
1972	Cal-A	3	7	.300	42	6	0	0	5	85¹	76	7	55	53	14.1	3.48	84	.240	.357	2	.118	-1	-4	-5	-1	-0.9
1973	Cal-A	0	0	—	5	0	0	0	1	8²	15	0	5	4	20.8	10.38	34	.417	.488	0	—	0	-6	-7	-0	-0.2
	Tex-A	0	6	.000	23	5	0	0	1	41	58	3	39	25	22.2	9.22	40	.326	.459	0	—	0	-25	-25	-1	-3.2
	Yr	0	6	.000	28	5	0	0	2	49²	73	3	44	29	22.1	9.42	39	.338	.460	0	—	0	-31	-32	-1	-3.4
1974	Tex-A	0	1	.000	14	0	0	0	0	22	24	2	18	18	17.6	6.55	54	.276	.406	0	—	0	-7	-7	-1	-0.4
	Chi-A	0	1	.000	6	2	0	0	0	7	7	0	12	3	25.7	10.29	36	.259	.500	0	—	0	-5	-5	-0	-0.7
	Yr	0	2	.000	20	2	0	0	0	29	31	2	30	21	19.2	7.45	48	.265	.419	0	—	0	-12	-12	-1	-1.1
1975	Chi-A	0	2	.000	3	0	0	0	0	5¹	8	2	6	2	23.6	11.81	33	.348	.483	0	—	0	-5	-5	0	-1.3
Total	7	8	25	.242	159	19	0	0	22	297¹	291	19	196	194	15.1	4.69	70	.258	.373	8	.200	2	-41	-46	-0	-5.3

● MYRON ALLEN
Allen, Myron Smith "Zeke" b: 3/22/1854, Kingston, N.Y. d: 3/8/24, Kingston, N.Y. BR/TR, 5'8", 150 lbs. Deb: 7/19/1883 ◆

YEAR	TM/L	W	L	PCT	G	GS	CG	SH	SV	IP	H	HR	BB	SO	RAT	ERA	ERA+	OAV	OOB	BH	AVG	PB	PR	/A	PD	TPI
1883	NY-N	0	1	.000	1	1	1	0	0	8	8	0	3	0	12.4	1.13	275	.276	.344	0	.000	-1	2	2	-0	0.1
1887	Cle-a	1	0	1.000	2	0	0	0	0	9²	9	0	3	1	12.1	0.93	466	.243	.317	128	.276	0	4	4	-0	0.3
1888	KC-a	0	2	.000	2	2	2	0	0	18	17	0	1	2	10.0	2.50	137	.240	.271	29	.213	0	1	1	0	0.3
Total	3	1	3	.250	5	3	3	0	0	35²	34	0	7	3	11.1	1.77	205	.249	.300	157	.259	-0	7	7	0	0.7

● NEIL ALLEN
Allen, Neil Patrick b: 1/24/58, Kansas City, Kan. BR/TR, 6'2", 190 lbs. Deb: 4/15/79

YEAR	TM/L	W	L	PCT	G	GS	CG	SH	SV	IP	H	HR	BB	SO	RAT	ERA	ERA+	OAV	OOB	BH	AVG	PB	PR	/A	PD	TPI
1979	NY-N	6	10	.375	50	5	0	0	8	99	100	4	47	65	13.4	3.55	103	.268	.350	0	.000	-2	2	1	0	0.0
1980	NY-N	7	10	.412	59	0	0	0	22	97¹	87	7	40	79	11.7	3.70	96	.244	.320	2	.143	-0	-1	-2	-1	-0.5
1981	NY-N	7	6	.538	43	0	0	0	18	66²	64	4	26	50	12.2	2.97	117	.259	.330	1	.200	1	4	4	1	1.1
1982	NY-N	3	7	.300	50	0	0	0	19	64²	65	5	30	59	13.4	3.06	119	.266	.349	1	.167	1	4	4	-0	0.9
1983	NY-N	2	7	.222	21	4	1	1	2	54	57	6	36	32	15.5	4.50	81	.278	.386	0	.000	-1	-5	-5	-0	-1.0
	StL-N	10	6	.625	25	18	4	2	0	121²	122	6	48	74	12.6	3.70	98	.265	.335	5	.128	-1	-1	-1	-0	-0.2
	Yr	12	13	.480	46	22	5	3	2	175²	179	12	84	106	13.5	3.94	90	.268	.351	5	.102	-2	-6	-6	-1	-1.2
1984	StL-N	9	6	.600	57	0	0	0	3	119	105	6	49	66	11.6	3.55	98	.239	.315	6	.240	0	0	-1	1	0.1
1985	StL-N	1	4	.200	17	1	0	0	1	29	32	3	17	16	15.5	5.59	63	.283	.382	0	.000	-0	-7	-7	-0	-1.2
	NY-A	1	0	1.000	17	0	0	0	1	29¹	26	1	13	16	12.0	2.76	145	.234	.315	0	—	0	5	4	0	0.3
1986	Chi-A	7	2	.778	22	7	2	2	0	113	101	8	38	57	11.2	3.82	113	.244	.311	0	—	0	4	5	0	0.3
1987	Chi-A	0	7	.000	15	10	0	0	0	49²	74	6	26	28	18.5	7.07	65	.365	.442	0	—	0	-14	-14	-0	-1.6
	NY-A	0	1	.000	8	1	0	0	0	24²	23	2	10	16	12.0	3.65	120	.242	.314	0	—	0	2	2	-0	0.1
	Yr	0	8	.000	23	11	0	0	0	74¹	97	8	36	42	16.1	5.93	76	.321	.393	0	—	0	-12	-12	-1	-1.5
1988	NY-A	5	3	.625	41	2	0	0	1	117¹	121	14	37	61	12.3	3.84	103	.268	.326	0	—	0	2	2	-0	-0.1
1989	Cle-A	0	1	.000	3	0	0	0	0	3	8	1	0	3	24.0	15.00	26	.500	.500	0	—	0	-4	-4	0	-0.4
Total	11	58	70	.453	434	59	7	6	75	988¹	985	73	417	611	12.8	3.88	97	.264	.339	15	.130	-1	-9	-11	-3	-2.9

● BOB ALLEN
Allen, Robert Earl "Thin Man" b: 7/2/14, Smithville, Tenn. BR/TR, 6'1", 165 lbs. Deb: 9/19/37

YEAR	TM/L	W	L	PCT	G	GS	CG	SH	SV	IP	H	HR	BB	SO	RAT	ERA	ERA+	OAV	OOB	BH	AVG	PB	PR	/A	PD	TPI
1937	Phi-N	0	1	.000	3	1	0	0	0	12	18	2	8	8	19.5	6.75	64	.321	.406	1	.333	0	-4	-3	-1	-0.3

YEAR TM/L	W	L	PCT	G	GS	CG	SH	SV	IP	H	HR	BB	SO	RAT	ERA	ERA+	OAV	OOB	BH	AVG	PB	PR	/A	PD	TPI

● **BOB ALLEN**   Allen, Robert Gray b: 10/23/37, Tatum, Tex.   BL/TL, 6'2", 185 lbs.   Deb: 4/14/61

1961 Cle-A	3	2	.600	48	0	0	0	3	81²	96	7	40	42	15.1	3.75	105	.294	.373	2	.167	0	3	2	-0	0.1
1962 Cle-A	1	1	.500	30	0	0	0	4	30²	29	5	25	23	15.8	5.87	66	.250	.383	0	.000	-1	-6	-7	0	-0.6
1963 Cle-A	1	2	.333	43	0	0	0	5	56	58	5	29	51	14.1	4.66	78	.266	.355	1	.200	-0	-6	-6	0	-0.4
1966 Cle-A	2	2	.500	36	0	0	0	5	51¹	56	2	13	33	12.4	4.21	82	.273	.323	1	.111	-0	-4	-4	1	-0.4
1967 Cle-A	0	5	.000	47	0	0	0	5	54¹	49	4	25	50	12.4	2.98	110	.243	.329	0	—	-0	2	2	0	0.3
Total 5	7	12	.368	204	0	0	0	19	274	288	23	132	199	14.0	4.11	89	.270	.353	4	.129	-1	-13	-14	2	-1.0

● **DANA ALLISON**   Allison, Dana Eric b: 8/14/66, Front Royal, Va.   BR/TL, 6'3", 215 lbs.   Deb: 4/9/91

| 1991 Oak-A | 1 | 1 | .500 | 11 | 0 | 0 | 0 | 0 | 11 | 16 | 1 | 0 | 5 | 17.2 | 7.36 | 52 | .381 | .447 | 0 | — | 0 | -4 | -4 | -0 | -0.6 |

● **DOUG ALLISON**   Allison, Douglas L. b: 7/1845, Philadelphia, Pa.   d: 12/19/16, Washington, D.C.   BR/TR, 5'10.5", 160 lbs.   Deb: 5/5/1871   F♦

| 1878 Pro-N | 0 | 0 | — | 1 | 0 | 0 | 0 | 0 | 5 | 11 | 0 | 1 | 0 | 21.6 | 1.80 | 123 | .440 | .462 | 22 | .289 | 0 | 0 | 0 | -0 | 0.0 |

● **MACK ALLISON**   Allison, Mack Pendleton b: 1/23/1887, Owensboro, Ky.   d: 3/13/64, Mount Vernon, Mo.   BR/TR, 6'1", 185 lbs.   Deb: 9/13/11

1911 StL-A	2	1	.667	3	3	3	0	0	26¹	24	0	5	2	10.6	2.05	165	.253	.304	2	.200	-0	4	4	-1	0.3
1912 StL-A	6	17	.261	31	20	11	1	1	169	171	4	49	43	12.0	3.62	92	.269	.327	7	.135	-3	-6	-6	-1	-1.1
1913 StL-A	1	3	.250	11	4	3	0	0	51¹	52	0	13	12	11.9	2.28	129	.287	.345	0	.000	-2	4	4	-2	-0.1
Total 3	9	21	.300	45	27	17	1	1	246²	247	4	67	57	11.9	3.17	102	.271	.328	9	.118	-6	2	2	-4	-0.9

● **LUIS ALOMA**   Aloma, Luis (Barba) "Witto" b: 7/23/23, Havana, Cuba   BR/TR, 6'2", 195 lbs.   Deb: 4/19/50

1950 Chi-A	7	2	.778	42	0	0	0	4	87²	77	6	53	49	13.4	3.80	118	.234	.342	1	.067	-2	8	7	-0	0.4
1951 Chi-A	6	0	1.000	25	1	1	1	3	69¹	52	3	24	25	10.1	1.82	222	.215	.291	7	.350	2	18	17	-2	1.5
1952 Chi-A	3	1	.750	25	0	0	0	6	40	42	5	11	18	12.1	4.27	85	.278	.331	0	.000	-1	-3	-3	-0	-0.5
1953 Chi-A	2	0	1.000	24	0	0	0	2	38¹	41	7	23	23	15.0	4.70	86	.283	.381	0	.000	-1	-3	-3	-0	-0.2
Total 4	18	3	.857	116	1	1	1	15	235¹	212	21	111	115	12.5	3.44	120	.245	.333	8	.167	-2	20	18	-2	1.2

● **MATTY ALOU**   Alou, Mateo Rojas (b: Mateo Rojas (Alou)) b: 12/22/38, Haina, D.R.   BL/TL, 5'9", 160 lbs.   Deb: 9/26/60   F♦

| 1965 SF-N | 0 | 0 | — | 1 | 0 | 0 | 0 | 0 | 3 | 3 | 0 | 3 | 0 | 18.0 | 0.00 | — | .333 | .400 | 75 | .231 | 0 | 1 | 1 | -0 | 0.1 |

● **PORFI ALTAMIRANO**   Altamirano, Porfirio (Ramirez) b: 5/17/52, Darillo, Nic.   BR/TR, 6', 175 lbs.   Deb: 5/9/82

1982 Phi-N	5	1	.833	29	0	0	0	2	39	41	2	14	26	12.9	4.15	88	.281	.348	1	.250	0	-2	-2	0	-0.3
1983 Phi-N	2	3	.400	31	0	0	0	2	41¹	38	9	15	24	12.0	3.70	96	.255	.331	0	.000	-0	-0	-1	0	-0.1
1984 Chi-N	0	0	—	5	0	0	0	0	11¹	8	2	1	7	7.1	4.76	82	.195	.214	0	.000	-0	-1	-1	0	0.0
Total 3	7	4	.636	65	0	0	0	4	91²	87	13	30	57	11.8	4.03	91	.259	.325	1	.125	-0	-4	-4	0	-0.4

● **ERNIE ALTEN**   Alten, Ernest Matthias "Lefty" b: 12/1/1894, Avon, Ohio   d: 9/9/81, Napa, Cal.   BR/TL, 6', 175 lbs.   Deb: 4/17/20

| 1920 Det-A | 0 | 1 | .000 | 14 | 1 | 0 | 0 | 0 | 23 | 40 | 2 | 9 | 4 | 19.6 | 9.00 | 41 | .392 | .446 | 0 | .000 | -1 | -13 | -13 | 0 | -0.5 |

● **NICK ALTROCK**   Altrock, Nicholas b: 9/15/1876, Cincinnati, Ohio   d: 1/20/65, Washington, D.C.   BB/TL, 5'10", 197 lbs.   Deb: 7/14/1898   C♦

1898 Lou-N	3	3	.500	11	7	6	0	0	70	89	2	21	13	14.5	4.50	79	.307	.360	7	.241	-0	-7	-7	2	-0.3
1902 Bos-A	0	2	.000	3	2	1	0	0	18	19	0	7	5	13.5	2.00	179	.271	.346	0	.000	-1	3	3	1	0.3
1903 Bos-A	0	1	.000	1	1	1	0	0	8	13	0	4	3	19.1	9.00	34	.363	.427	2	.667	1	-5	-5	1	-0.3
Chi-A	4	3	.571	12	8	6	1	0	71	59	4	19	19	10.3	2.15	130	.226	.286	9	.300	2	6	5	3	1.1
Yr	4	4	.500	13	9	7	1	0	79	72	4	23	22	11.2	2.85	99	.242	.303	11	.333	4	1	-0	4	0.8
1904 Chi-A	19	14	.576	38	36	31	6	1	307	274	2	48	87	9.5	2.96	83	.240	.272	22	.198	1	-12	-17	4	-1.3
1905 Chi-A	23	12	.657	38	34	31	3	0	315²	274	3	63	97	9.7	1.88	131	.235	.275	14	.125	-3	27	21	8	2.9
1906 *Chi-A	20	13	.606	38	30	25	4	0	287²	269	0	42	99	9.8	2.06	123	.251	.281	16	.160	-1	20	15	4	2.1
1907 Chi-A	7	13	.350	30	21	15	1	2	213²	210	3	31	61	10.2	2.57	93	.259	.288	13	.181	1	-0	-4	5	0.2
1908 Chi-A	5	7	.417	23	13	8	1	2	136	127	2	18	21	9.7	2.71	85	.248	.276	10	.204	1	-5	-6	5	0.1
1909 Chi-A	0	1	.000	1	1	1	0	0	9	16	0	1	2	17.0	5.00	47	.485	.500	0	.000	-0	-3	-3	0	-0.3
Was-A	1	3	.250	9	5	2	0	0	38	55	0	5	9	14.4	5.45	45	.333	.357	1	.053	-1	-13	-13	0	-1.3
Yr	1	4	.200	10	6	3	0	0	47	71	0	6	11	14.9	5.36	45	.359	.380	1	.045	-1	-15	-15	1	-1.6
1912 Was-A	0	1	.000	1	0	0	0	0	1	2	0	2	0	27.0	18.00	19	.400	.429	0	.000	-0	-2	-2	-0	-0.9
1913 Was-A	0	0	—	4	0	0	0	0	9	7	0	4	2	12.0	5.00	59	.184	.279	0	.000	-0	-2	-2	0	-0.3
1914 Was-A	0	0	—	1	0	0	0	0	1	3	0	0	0	27.0	0.00	—	.750	.750	0	—	0	-0	-0	-0	0.0
1915 Was-A	0	0	—	3	0	0	0	0	3	7	0	1	2	24.0	9.00	33	.438	.471	0	.000	-0	-2	-2	-0	-0.3
1918 Was-A	1	2	.333	5	3	1	0	0	24	24	1	6	5	11.6	3.00	91	.279	.333	1	.125	0	-1	-1	0	0.0
1919 Was-A	0	0	—	1	0	0	0	0	0	4	0	0	0	—	∞	—	1.000	1.000	0	—	0	-4	-4	0	-0.3
1924 Was-A	0	0	—	1	0	0	0	0	2	4	0	0	0	18.0	0.00	—	.500	.500	1	1.000	1	1	1	0	0.1
Total 16	83	75	.525	218	161	128	16	6	1514	1455	17	272	425	10.4	2.67	95	.254	.291	97	.176	1	3	-20	34	1.9

● **JOSE ALVAREZ**   Alvarez, Jose Lino b: 4/12/56, Tampa, Fla.   BR/TR, 5'10", 170 lbs.   Deb: 10/1/81

1981 Atl-N	0	0	—	1	0	0	0	0	2	0	0	2	0	9.0	0.00	—	.000	.000	0	—	0	1	1	-0	0.0
1982 Atl-N	0	0	—	7	0	0	0	0	7²	7	1	2	6	11.7	4.70	79	.308	.357	0	—	0	-1	-1	-0	0.0
1988 Atl-N	5	6	.455	60	0	0	0	3	102¹	88	7	53	81	12.9	2.99	123	.240	.346	3	.375	1	5	8	1	1.1
1989 Atl-N	3	3	.500	30	0	0	0	2	50¹	44	4	24	45	12.3	2.86	128	.237	.327	0	.000	-0	4	4	1	0.6
Total 4	8	9	.471	98	0	0	0	5	162¹	140	12	79	134	12.5	2.99	123	.240	.337	3	.273	1	9	12	2	1.7

● **WILSON ALVAREZ**   Alvarez, Wilson Eduardo (Fuenmayor) b: 3/24/70, Maracaibo, Venez.   BL/TL, 6'1", 175 lbs.   Deb: 7/24/89

1989 Tex-A	0	1	.000	1	1	0	0	0	0	3	2	2	0	—	∞	—	1.000	1.000	0	—	0	-3	-3	0	-0.3
1991 Chi-A	3	2	.600	10	9	2	1	0	56¹	47	9	29	32	12.1	3.51	113	.230	.326	0	—	0	4	3	-0	0.3
1992 Chi-A	5	3	.625	34	9	0	0	1	100¹	103	12	65	66	15.4	5.20	74	.272	.384	0	—	0	-14	-15	-0	-1.1
1993 *Chi-A	15	8	.652	31	31	1	1	0	207²	168	14	122	155	12.9	2.95	142	.230	.346	0	—	0	32	28	-0	2.9
1994 Chi-A★	12	8	.600	24	24	1	0	0	161²	147	16	62	108	11.6	3.45	136	.241	.311	0	—	0	24	22	0	2.5
Total 5	35	22	.614	100	74	5	3	1	526	468	53	280	361	13.0	3.64	117	.243	.342	0	—	0	42	36	-1	4.3

● **RED AMES**   Ames, Leon Kessling b: 8/2/1882, Warren, Ohio   d: 10/8/36, Warren, Ohio   BB/TR, 5'10.5", 185 lbs.   Deb: 9/14/03

1903 NY-N	2	0	1.000	2	2	2	1	0	14	5	0	8	14	8.4	1.29	260	.114	.250	0	.000	-1	3	3	-1	0.3
1904 NY-N	4	6	.400	16	13	11	1	3	115	94	2	38	93	10.6	2.27	120	.222	.291	5	.125	-1	6	6	0	0.3
1905 *NY-N	22	8	.733	34	31	21	2	0	262²	220	8	105	198	11.2	2.74	107	.230	.308	14	.144	-1	8	6	1	0.5
1906 NY-N	12	10	.545	31	25	15	1	1	203¹	166	1	93	156	11.6	2.66	98	.223	.312	4	.066	-3	-0	-1	3	-0.1
1907 NY-N	10	12	.455	39	26	17	2	1	233¹	184	4	108	146	11.6	2.16	115	.219	.315	12	.174	2	8	8	3	1.3
1908 NY-N	7	4	.636	18	15	5	0	1	114¹	96	0	27	81	9.8	1.81	133	.232	.281	7	.194	-0	7	7	1	0.9
1909 NY-N	15	10	.600	34	26	20	2	1	244	217	6	81	156	11.1	2.69	95	.241	.306	6	.074	-5	-2	-4	7	-0.2
1910 NY-N	12	11	.522	33	23	13	3	0	190¹	161	6	63	94	10.9	2.22	133	.237	.308	11	.177	-1	17	16	4	2.1
1911 *NY-N	11	10	.524	34	23	13	1	2	205	170	6	54	118	10.0	2.68	126	.223	.277	6	.094	-3	16	16	3	1.4
1912 *NY-N	11	5	.688	33	22	9	2	2	179	194	3	35	83	11.7	2.46	137	.281	.320	13	.224	1	19	18	2	1.8
1913 NY-N	2	1	.667	8	5	2	0	1	41²	35	3	8	30	9.5	2.16	144	.241	.286	2	.154	-1	5	4	2	0.5
Cin-N	11	13	.458	31	24	12	1	2	187¹	185	7	70	80	12.5	2.88	113	.265	.336	6	.102	-4	7	8	0	0.5
Yr	13	14	.481	39	29	14	1	3	229	220	10	78	110	11.9	2.75	117	.261	.327	8	.111	-5	12	12	2	1.0
1914 Cin-N	15	23	.395	47	36	18	3	6	297	274	6	94	126	11.3	2.64	111	.248	.311	12	.108	-4	5	10	4	1.3
1915 Cin-N	2	4	.333	17	7	4	1	0	68	82	3	24	26	14.0	4.50	64	.311	.368	1	.050	-1	-13	-12	1	-1.1
StL-N	9	3	.750	15	14	8	2	1	113¹	93	1	32	48	9.9	2.46	113	.226	.282	4	.114	-2	4	4	2	0.4
Yr	11	7	.611	32	21	12	3	1	181¹	175	3	56	74	11.5	3.23	87	.259	.316	5	.091	-3	-10	-8	2	-0.7

YEAR TM/L	W	L	PCT	G	GS	CG	SH	SV	IP	H	HR	BB	SO	RAT	ERA	ERA+	OAV	OOB	BH	AVG	PB	PR	/A	PD	TPI
1916 StL-N	11	16	.407	45	25	10	2	8	228	225	3	57	98	11.3	2.64	100	.263	.313	12	.176	-0	-1	0	-2	-0.2
1917 StL-N	15	10	.600	43	19	10	2	3	209	189	2	57	62	10.7	2.71	99	.249	.304	12	.188	2	-0	-0	4	0.7
1918 StL-N	9	14	.391	27	25	17	0	1	206²	192	1	52	68	10.8	2.31	117	.252	.304	10	.156	-1	10	9	-1	0.9
1919 StL-N	3	5	.375	23	6	1	0	1	70	88	1	25	19	14.7	4.89	57	.314	.373	4	.222	-0	-15	-16	-2	-2.0
Phi-N	0	2	.000	3	2	1	0	1	16	26	0	3	4	16.3	6.19	52	.400	.426	2	.400	1	-6	-5	0	-0.6
Yr	3	7	.300	26	8	2	0	2	86	114	1	28	23	14.9	5.13	56	.329	.380	6	.261	1	-21	-22	-2	-2.6
Total 17	183	167	.523	533	369	209	26	36	3198	2896	42	1034	1702	11.2	2.63	108	.245	.310	143	.141	-21	77	77	32	8.7

● DOC AMOLE   Amole, Morris George b: 7/5/1878, Coatesville, Pa. d: 3/7/12, Wilmington, Del. BR/TL, 5'9", 165 lbs. Deb: 8/19/1897

YEAR TM/L	W	L	PCT	G	GS	CG	SH	SV	IP	H	HR	BB	SO	RAT	ERA	ERA+	OAV	OOB	BH	AVG	PB	PR	/A	PD	TPI
1897 Bal-N	4	4	.500	11	7	6	0	0	70	67	0	17	19	11.6	2.57	162	.250	.309	3	.107	-3	14	12	0	0.9
1898 Was-N	0	6	.000	7	5	4	0	0	49¹	83	0	22	11	20.3	7.84	47	.370	.440	2	.100	-2	-23	-23	1	-2.1
Total 2	4	10	.286	18	12	10	0	0	119¹	150	0	39	30	15.2	4.75	84	.305	.370	5	.104	-4	-10	-10	1	-1.2

● VICENTE AMOR   Amor, Vicente (Alvarez) b: 8/8/32, Havana, Cuba BR/TR, 6'3", 182 lbs. Deb: 4/16/55

YEAR TM/L	W	L	PCT	G	GS	CG	SH	SV	IP	H	HR	BB	SO	RAT	ERA	ERA+	OAV	OOB	BH	AVG	PB	PR	/A	PD	TPI
1955 Chi-N	0	1	.000	4	0	0	0	0	6	11	0	3	3	21.0	4.50	91	.407	.467	0	—	0	-0	-0	1	0.0
1957 Cin-N	1	2	.333	9	4	1	0	0	27¹	39	2	10	9	16.8	5.93	69	.345	.408	1	.167	-0	-6	-6	-0	-0.6
Total 2	1	3	.250	13	4	1	0	0	33¹	50	2	13	12	17.6	5.67	72	.357	.419	1	.167	-0	-7	-6	1	-0.6

● WALTER ANCKER   Ancker, Walter b: 4/10/1894, New York, N.Y. d: 2/13/54, Englewood, N.J. BR/TR, 6'1", 190 lbs. Deb: 9/3/15

YEAR TM/L	W	L	PCT	G	GS	CG	SH	SV	IP	H	HR	BB	SO	RAT	ERA	ERA+	OAV	OOB	BH	AVG	PB	PR	/A	PD	TPI
1915 Phi-A	0	0		4	1	0	0	0	17²	19	1	17	4	19.9	3.57	82	.279	.443	0	.000	-1	-1	-1	0	-0.1

● LARRY ANDERSEN   Andersen, Larry Eugene b: 5/6/53, Portland, Ore. BR/TR, 6'3", 205 lbs. Deb: 9/5/75

YEAR TM/L	W	L	PCT	G	GS	CG	SH	SV	IP	H	HR	BB	SO	RAT	ERA	ERA+	OAV	OOB	BH	AVG	PB	PR	/A	PD	TPI
1975 Cle-A	0	0		3	0	0	0	0	5²	4	0	2	4	9.5	4.76	79	.200	.273	0	—	0	-1	-1	0	0.0
1977 Cle-A	0	1	.000	11	0	0	0	0	14¹	10	1	9	8	11.9	3.14	126	.200	.322	0	—	0	1	1	1	0.2
1979 Cle-A	0	0		8	0	0	0	0	16²	25	3	4	7	15.7	7.56	56	.357	.392	0	—	0	-6	-6	0	0.0
1981 Sea-A	3	3	.500	41	0	0	0	5	67²	57	4	18	40	10.2	2.66	145	.228	.285	0	—	0	7	9	-0	0.7
1982 Sea-A	0	0	—	40	1	0	0	1	79²	100	16	23	32	14.3	5.99	71	.311	.364	0	—	0	-17	-15	1	-0.1
1983 *Phi-N	1	0	1.000	17	0	0	0	0	26¹	19	0	9	14	9.6	2.39	149	.200	.269	0	.000	-0	4	3	0	0.1
1984 Phi-N	3	7	.300	64	0	0	0	4	90²	85	5	25	54	10.9	2.38	152	.248	.299	0	.000	-0	12	13	0	1.4
1985 Phi-N	3	3	.500	57	0	0	0	3	73	78	5	26	50	13.2	4.32	85	.274	.341	0	.000	-0	-6	-5	2	-0.3
1986 Phi-N	0	0	—	10	0	0	0	0	12²	19	1	0	9	15.6	4.26	90	.388	.423	0	—	-0	-1	-1	0	0.0
*Hou-N	2	1	.667	38	0	0	0	1	64²	64	2	23	33	12.2	2.78	129	.266	.344	0	.000	-1	7	6	0	0.2
Yr	2	1	.667	48	0	0	0	1	77¹	83	2	26	42	12.8	3.03	120	.294	.356	0	.000	-1	6	5	0	0.2
1987 Hou-N	9	5	.643	67	0	0	0	5	101²	95	7	41	94	12.2	3.45	113	.246	.322	1	.167	0	7	5	-0	0.7
1988 Hou-N	2	4	.333	53	0	0	0	5	82²	82	3	20	66	11.2	2.94	113	.254	.299	2	.333	1	5	3	0	0.3
1989 Hou-N	4	4	.500	60	0	0	0	3	87²	63	2	24	85	8.9	1.54	220	.198	.254	1	.333	0	19	18	1	1.8
1990 Hou-N	5	2	.714	50	0	0	0	6	73²	61	2	24	68	10.5	1.95	190	.229	.296	0	.000	-0	15	14	1	1.7
*Bos-A	0	0	—	15	0	0	0	1	22	18	0	2	25	9.0	1.23	332	.220	.256	0	—	-0	7	7	-1	-0.2
1991 SD-N	3	4	.429	38	0	0	0	13	47	39	0	13	40	10.0	2.30	165	.231	.286	0	.000	-0	7	8	0	1.7
1992 SD-N	1	1	.500	34	0	0	0	2	35	26	2	8	35	9.0	3.34	107	.202	.254	0	.000	0	1	1	0	0.1
1993 *Phi-N	3	2	.600	64	0	0	0	1	61²	54	4	21	67	11.1	2.92	136	.233	.299	1	1.000	0	8	7	-1	0.5
1994 Phi-N	1	2	.333	29	0	0	0	0	32²	33	2	15	27	13.2	4.41	94	.256	.333	0	—	0	-1	-1	-0	-0.1
Total 17	40	39	.506	699	1	0	0	49	995¹	932	58	311	758	11.4	3.15	119	.249	.309	5	.132	-0	68	67	5	8.7

● ALLAN ANDERSON   Anderson, Allan Lee b: 1/7/64, Lancaster, Ohio BL/TL, 6', 186 lbs. Deb: 6/11/86

YEAR TM/L	W	L	PCT	G	GS	CG	SH	SV	IP	H	HR	BB	SO	RAT	ERA	ERA+	OAV	OOB	BH	AVG	PB	PR	/A	PD	TPI
1986 Min-A	3	6	.333	21	10	1	0	0	84¹	106	11	30	51	14.6	5.55	78	.316	.374	0	—	0	-13	-12	0	-1.0
1987 Min-A	1	0	1.000	4	2	0	0	0	12¹	20	3	10	3	21.9	10.95	42	.392	.492	0	—	0	-9	-9	-0	-0.7
1988 Min-A	16	9	.640	30	30	3	1	0	202¹	199	14	37	83	10.8	2.45	166	.261	.301	0	—	0	34	36	1	4.5
1989 Min-A	17	10	.630	33	33	4	1	0	196²	214	15	53	69	12.5	3.80	109	.275	.327	0	.000	-0	2	7	-1	0.9
1990 Min-A	7	18	.280	31	31	5	1	0	188²	214	20	39	82	12.3	4.53	92	.289	.329	0	—	0	-13	-8	2	-1.1
1991 Min-A	5	11	.313	29	22	2	0	0	134¹	148	24	42	51	13.1	4.96	86	.281	.340	0	.000	-0	-13	-10	-0	-1.1
Total 6	49	54	.476	148	128	15	3	0	818²	901	87	211	339	12.5	4.11	101	.282	.331	0	.000	-0	-12	5	2	1.5

● RED ANDERSON   Anderson, Arnold Revola b: 6/19/12, Lawton, Iowa d: 8/7/72, Sioux City, Iowa BR/TR, 6'3", 210 lbs. Deb: 9/19/37

YEAR TM/L	W	L	PCT	G	GS	CG	SH	SV	IP	H	HR	BB	SO	RAT	ERA	ERA+	OAV	OOB	BH	AVG	PB	PR	/A	PD	TPI
1937 Was-A	0	1	.000	2	1	0	0	0	10²	11	0	11	3	19.4	6.75	66	.282	.451	0	—	-0	-3	-3	0	-0.2
1940 Was-A	1	1	.500	2	2	0	0	0	14	12	0	5	3	10.9	3.86	108	.245	.315	3	.600	1	1	0	0	0.2
1941 Was-A	4	6	.400	32	6	1	0	0	112	127	7	53	34	14.7	4.18	97	.296	.377	8	.258	2	-0	-2	-1	0.0
Total 3	5	8	.385	36	9	3	0	0	136²	150	7	69	40	14.7	4.35	94	.290	.378	11	.282	3	-2	-4	-1	0.0

● BRIAN ANDERSON   Anderson, Brian James b: 4/16/72, Portsmouth, Va. BL/TL, 6'1", 190 lbs. Deb: 9/10/93

YEAR TM/L	W	L	PCT	G	GS	CG	SH	SV	IP	H	HR	BB	SO	RAT	ERA	ERA+	OAV	OOB	BH	AVG	PB	PR	/A	PD	TPI
1993 Cal-A	0	0	—	4	1	0	0	0	11¹	11	1	2	4	10.3	3.97	113	.256	.289	0	—	0	0	1	-0	-0.3
1994 Cal-A	7	5	.583	18	18	0	0	0	101²	120	13	27	47	13.5	5.22	95	.300	.352	0	—	0	-5	-3	-0	-0.4
Total 2	7	5	.583	22	19	0	0	0	113	131	14	29	51	13.1	5.10	97	.296	.346	0	—	0	-4	-2	-0	-0.7

● DAVE ANDERSON   Anderson, David S. b: 10/10/1868, Chester, Pa. d: 3/22/1897, Chester, Pa. TL , Deb: 8/24/1889

YEAR TM/L	W	L	PCT	G	GS	CG	SH	SV	IP	H	HR	BB	SO	RAT	ERA	ERA+	OAV	OOB	BH	AVG	PB	PR	/A	PD	TPI
1889 Phi-N	0	1	.000	5	2	1	0	0	23	30	2	14	8	17.2	7.43	59	.306	.392	2	.182	-0	-9	-8	0	-0.3
1890 Phi-N	1	1	.500	3	2	1	0	0	19¹	31	0	11	7	20.0	7.45	49	.351	.429	1	.111	-1	-8	-8	0	-0.7
Pit-N	2	11	.154	13	13	13	0	0	108	116	2	49	41	14.3	4.67	71	.246	.350	3	.071	-5	-13	-16	4	-1.6
Yr	3	12	.200	16	15	14	0	0	127¹	147	2	60	48	15.1	5.09	66	.280	.361	4	.078	-6	-21	-25	4	-2.3
Total 2	3	13	.188	21	17	15	0	0	150¹	177	4	74	56	15.5	5.45	64	.284	.368	6	.097	-6	-30	-33	4	-2.6

● JOHN ANDERSON   Anderson, John Charles b: 11/23/32, St.Paul, Minn. BR/TR, 6'1", 190 lbs. Deb: 8/17/58

YEAR TM/L	W	L	PCT	G	GS	CG	SH	SV	IP	H	HR	BB	SO	RAT	ERA	ERA+	OAV	OOB	BH	AVG	PB	PR	/A	PD	TPI
1958 Phi-N	0	0	—	5	1	0	0	0	16	26	5	4	9	17.4	7.88	50	.361	.403	0	.000	-0	-7	-7	-0	0.0
1960 Bal-A	0	0	—	4	0	0	0	0	4²	8	0	4	1	23.1	13.50	28	.444	.545	0	—	0	-5	-5	0	0.0
1962 StL-N	0	0	—	5	0	0	0	1	6¹	4	0	3	9	9.9	1.42	300	.182	.280	0	—	0	1	1	0	0.0
Hou-N	0	0	—	10	0	0	0	0	17²	26	1	3	6	14.8	5.09	73	.338	.363	0	.000	-0	-2	-3	1	0.0
Yr	0	0	—	15	0	0	0	1	24	30	1	6	9	13.5	4.13	94	.300	.340	0	.000	-0	-0	-1	0	0.0
Total 3	0	0	—	24	1	0	0	1	44²	64	6	14	19	15.9	6.45	60	.339	.387	0	.000	-0	-12	-13	-0	0.0

● FRED ANDERSON   Anderson, John Frederick b: 12/11/1885, Calahaln, N.C. d: 11/8/57, Winston-Salem, N.C. BR/TR, 6'2", 180 lbs. Deb: 9/25/09

YEAR TM/L	W	L	PCT	G	GS	CG	SH	SV	IP	H	HR	BB	SO	RAT	ERA	ERA+	OAV	OOB	BH	AVG	PB	PR	/A	PD	TPI
1909 Bos-A	0	0	—	1	1	0	0	0	8	3	0	1	5	4.5	1.13	222	.115	.148	0	.000	-0	1	1	0	0.0
1913 Bos-A	0	6	.000	10	8	4	0	0	57¹	84	0	21	32	16.6	5.97	49	.350	.405	1	.050	-2	-19	-19	-0	-2.0
1914 Buf-F	13	15	.464	37	28	21	2	0	260¹	243	8	64	144	10.7	3.08	96	.249	.297	17	.189	-3	-6	-3	-1	-0.7
1915 Buf-F	19	13	.594	36	28	14	5	0	240	192	5	72	142	10.0	2.51	111	.222	.285	12	.150	-5	6	8	-1	0.4
1916 NY-N	9	13	.409	38	27	13	2	2	188	206	7	38	98	11.9	3.40	72	.277	.316	8	.138	-0	-16	-20	-2	-2.7
1917 *NY-N	8	8	.500	38	18	8	1	3	162	122	1	34	69	8.8	1.44	177	.209	.255	3	.071	-3	23	20	-1	1.7
1918 NY-N	4	2	.667	18	4	2	1	3	70²	62	1	17	24	10.3	2.67	98	.246	.299	0	.000	-3	1	-0	3	0.0
Total 7	53	57	.482	178	114	62	11	8	986¹	912	22	247	514	10.7	2.75	96	.248	.298	41	.131	-16	-11	-15	-2	-3.3

● BUD ANDERSON   Anderson, Karl Adam b: 5/27/56, Westbury, N.Y. BR/TR, 6'3", 210 lbs. Deb: 6/11/82

YEAR TM/L	W	L	PCT	G	GS	CG	SH	SV	IP	H	HR	BB	SO	RAT	ERA	ERA+	OAV	OOB	BH	AVG	PB	PR	/A	PD	TPI
1982 Cle-A	3	4	.429	25	5	1	0	0	80²	84	4	30	44	12.8	3.35	122	.268	.334	0	—	0	7	7	-0	0.5
1983 Cle-A	1	6	.143	39	1	0	0	7	68¹	64	8	32	32	12.6	4.08	104	.255	.339	0	—	0	-0	1	-1	0.0
Total 2	4	10	.286	64	6	1	0	7	149	148	12	62	76	12.7	3.68	113	.262	.337	0	—	0	6	8	-1	0.5

● LARRY ANDERSON   Anderson, Lawrence Dennis b: 12/3/52, Maywood, Cal. BR/TR, 6'3", 190 lbs. Deb: 9/25/74

YEAR TM/L	W	L	PCT	G	GS	CG	SH	SV	IP	H	HR	BB	SO	RAT	ERA	ERA+	OAV	OOB	BH	AVG	PB	PR	/A	PD	TPI
1974 Mil-A	0	0	—	2	0	0	0	0	2¹	2	0	1	3	11.6	0.00	—	.250	.333	0	—	0	1	1	0	0.0

YEAR	TM/L	W	L	PCT	G	GS	CG	SH	SV	IP	H	HR	BB	SO	RAT	ERA	ERA+	OAV	OOB	BH	AVG	PB	PR	/A	PD	TPI
1975	Mil-A	1	0	1.000	8	1	1	1	0	30¹	36	3	6	13	12.5	5.04	76	.298	.331	0	—	0	-4	-4	0	-0.1
1977	Chi-A	1	3	.250	6	0	0	0	0	8²	10	1	15	7	26.0	9.35	44	.286	.500	0	—	0	-5	-5	-0	-1.8
Total	3	2	3	.400	16	1	1	1	0	41¹	48	4	22	23	15.2	5.66	68	.293	.376	0	—	0	-8	-8	0	-1.9

● MIKE ANDERSON
Anderson, Michael Allen b: 6/22/51, Florence, S.C. BR/TR, 6'2", 200 lbs. Deb: 9/2/71 F♦

YEAR	TM/L	W	L	PCT	G	GS	CG	SH	SV	IP	H	HR	BB	SO	RAT	ERA	ERA+	OAV	OOB	BH	AVG	PB	PR	/A	PD	TPI
1979	Phi-N	0	0	—	1	0	0	0	0	1	2	0	0	2	18.0	0.00	—	.400	.400	18	.231	0	0	0	0	0.0

● MIKE ANDERSON
Anderson, Michael James b: 7/30/66, Austin, Tex. BR/TR, 6'3", 200 lbs. Deb: 9/7/93

YEAR	TM/L	W	L	PCT	G	GS	CG	SH	SV	IP	H	HR	BB	SO	RAT	ERA	ERA+	OAV	OOB	BH	AVG	PB	PR	/A	PD	TPI
1993	Cin-N	0	0	—	3	0	0	0	0	5¹	12	3	3	4	25.3	18.56	22	.444	.500	0	.000	-0	-9	-9	0	0.0

● CRAIG ANDERSON
Anderson, Norman Craig b: 7/1/38, Washington, D.C. BR/TR, 6'2", 205 lbs. Deb: 6/23/61

YEAR	TM/L	W	L	PCT	G	GS	CG	SH	SV	IP	H	HR	BB	SO	RAT	ERA	ERA+	OAV	OOB	BH	AVG	PB	PR	/A	PD	TPI
1961	StL-N	4	3	.571	25	0	0	0	1	38²	38	3	12	21	11.9	3.26	135	.255	.315	3	.333	1	3	5	0	0.9
1962	NY-N	3	17	.150	50	14	2	0	4	131¹	150	18	63	62	14.9	5.35	78	.278	.359	3	.094	-2	-20	-17	3	-2.3
1963	NY-N	0	2	.000	3	2	0	0	0	9¹	17	0	3	6	19.3	8.68	40	.362	.400	1	.333	0	-6	-5	0	-0.9
1964	NY-N	0	1	.000	4	1	0	0	0	13	21	0	3	5	16.6	5.54	65	.382	.414	0	.000	0	-3	-3	0	-0.2
Total	4	7	23	.233	82	17	2	0	5	192¹	226	21	81	94	14.6	5.10	81	.286	.357	7	.149	-1	-26	-20	3	-2.5

● RICK ANDERSON
Anderson, Richard Arlen b: 11/29/56, Everett, Wash. BR/TR, 6', 175 lbs. Deb: 6/9/86

YEAR	TM/L	W	L	PCT	G	GS	CG	SH	SV	IP	H	HR	BB	SO	RAT	ERA	ERA+	OAV	OOB	BH	AVG	PB	PR	/A	PD	TPI
1986	NY-N	2	1	.667	15	5	0	0	1	49²	45	3	11	21	10.1	2.72	130	.245	.287	1	.091	-1	6	5	-1	0.2
1987	KC-A	0	2	.000	6	2	0	0	0	13	26	6	9	12	25.6	13.85	33	.394	.481	0	—	0	-14	-13	0	-1.6
1988	KC-A	2	1	.667	7	3	0	0	0	34	41	3	9	9	13.5	4.24	94	.308	.357	0	—	0	-1	-1	-1	-0.2
Total	3	4	4	.500	28	10	0	0	1	96²	112	6	29	42	13.4	4.75	81	.292	.347	1	.091	-1	-9	-10	-1	-1.6

● RICK ANDERSON
Anderson, Richard Lee b: 12/25/53, Inglewood, Cal. d: 6/23/89, Wilmington, Cal. BR/TR, 6'2", 210 lbs. Deb: 9/18/79

YEAR	TM/L	W	L	PCT	G	GS	CG	SH	SV	IP	H	HR	BB	SO	RAT	ERA	ERA+	OAV	OOB	BH	AVG	PB	PR	/A	PD	TPI
1979	NY-A	0	0	—	1	0	0	0	0	2¹	1	0	4	0	19.3	3.86	106	.167	.500	0	—	0	0	0	1	0.1
1980	Sea-A	0	0	—	5	2	0	0	0	9²	8	1	10	7	16.8	3.72	111	.229	.400	0	—	0	0	0	-0	-0.1
Total	2	0	0	—	6	2	0	0	0	12	9	1	14	7	17.3	3.75	110	.220	.418	0	—	0	0	0	0	0.0

● BOB ANDERSON
Anderson, Robert Carl b: 9/29/35, E.Chicago, Ind. BR/TR, 6'4.5", 210 lbs. Deb: 7/31/57

YEAR	TM/L	W	L	PCT	G	GS	CG	SH	SV	IP	H	HR	BB	SO	RAT	ERA	ERA+	OAV	OOB	BH	AVG	PB	PR	/A	PD	TPI
1957	Chi-N	0	1	.000	8	0	0	0	0	16¹	20	2	8	7	16.0	7.71	50	.317	.403	0	.000	-1	-7	-7	0	-0.4
1958	Chi-N	3	3	.500	17	8	2	0	0	65²	61	3	29	51	12.5	3.97	99	.255	.338	2	.118	-1	-0	-0	0	-0.1
1959	Chi-N	12	13	.480	37	36	7	1	0	235¹	245	21	77	113	12.5	4.13	96	.272	.333	6	.075	-4	-5	-5	1	-0.8
1960	Chi-N	9	11	.450	38	30	5	0	1	203²	201	26	68	115	12.2	4.11	92	.255	.320	12	.169	0	-8	-8	1	-0.6
1961	Chi-N	7	10	.412	57	12	1	0	8	152	162	14	56	96	13.0	4.26	98	.275	.340	6	.143	0	-4	-1	4	0.2
1962	Chi-N	2	7	.222	57	4	0	0	0	107²	111	9	60	82	14.7	5.02	83	.266	.364	3	.130	-1	-13	-10	0	-0.9
1963	Det-A	3	1	.750	32	3	0	0	0	60	58	5	21	38	12.8	3.30	113	.258	.337	4	.444	2	2	3	-0	0.3
Total	7	36	46	.439	246	93	15	1	13	840²	858	80	319	502	12.9	4.26	93	.266	.337	33	.134	-4	-34	-29	5	-2.3

● SCOTT ANDERSON
Anderson, Scott Richard b: 8/1/62, Corvallis, Ore. BR/TR, 6'6", 190 lbs. Deb: 4/8/87

YEAR	TM/L	W	L	PCT	G	GS	CG	SH	SV	IP	H	HR	BB	SO	RAT	ERA	ERA+	OAV	OOB	BH	AVG	PB	PR	/A	PD	TPI
1987	Tex-A	0	1	.000	8	0	0	0	0	11¹	17	0	8	6	20.6	9.53	47	.347	.448	0	—	0	-6	-6	1	-0.4
1990	Mon-N	0	1	.000	4	3	0	0	0	18	12	1	5	16	8.5	3.00	122	.188	.246	0	.000	-0	2	1	-0	0.0
Total	2	0	2	.000	12	3	0	0	0	29¹	29	1	13	22	13.2	5.52	72	.257	.339	0	.000	-0	-5	-5	0	-0.4

● VARNEY ANDERSON
Anderson, Varney Samuel "Varn" b: 6/18/1866, Geneva, Ill. d: 11/5/41, Rockford, Ill. BR/TR, 5'10", 165 lbs. Deb: 8/1/1889

YEAR	TM/L	W	L	PCT	G	GS	CG	SH	SV	IP	H	HR	BB	SO	RAT	ERA	ERA+	OAV	OOB	BH	AVG	PB	PR	/A	PD	TPI
1889	Ind-N	0	1	.000	2	1	1	0	0	12	13	0	9	3	18.8	4.50	93	.268	.413	0	.000	-1	-1	-0	0	-0.1
1894	Was-N	0	2	.000	2	2	2	0	0	14	15	0	6	3	14.1	7.07	74	.271	.353	3	.429	1	-3	-3	-0	-0.2
1895	Was-N	9	16	.360	29	25	18	0	0	204²	288	13	97	35	17.4	5.89	81	.327	.400	28	.289	3	-25	-25	1	-1.8
1896	Was-N	0	1	.000	2	2	1	0	0	9	23	0	3	0	26.0	13.00	34	.471	.502	1	.600	1	-9	-9	-1	-0.6
Total	4	9	20	.310	35	30	22	0	0	239²	339	13	115	41	17.6	6.16	78	.328	.402	34	.298	4	-37	-37	0	-2.7

● WALTER ANDERSON
Anderson, Walter Carl "Lefty" b: 9/25/1897, Grand Rapids, Mich. d: 1/6/90, Battle Creek, Mich. BL/TL, 6'2", 160 lbs. Deb: 5/14/17

YEAR	TM/L	W	L	PCT	G	GS	CG	SH	SV	IP	H	HR	BB	SO	RAT	ERA	ERA+	OAV	OOB	BH	AVG	PB	PR	/A	PD	TPI
1917	Phi-A	0	0	—	14	2	0	0	0	38²	32	0	21	10	12.6	3.03	91	.246	.355	3	.429	1	-2	-1	-0	0.1
1919	Phi-A	1	0	1.000	3	0	0	0	0	14	13	0	8	10	14.1	3.86	89	.245	.355	0	.000	-1	-1	-1	0	-0.1
Total	2	1	0	1.000	17	2	0	0	0	52²	45	0	29	20	13.0	3.25	90	.246	.355	3	.273	0	-3	-2	0	0.1

● BILL ANDERSON
Anderson, William Edward "Lefty" b: 11/28/1895, Boston, Mass. d: 3/13/83, Medford, Mass. BR/TL, 6'1", 165 lbs. Deb: 9/10/25

YEAR	TM/L	W	L	PCT	G	GS	CG	SH	SV	IP	H	HR	BB	SO	RAT	ERA	ERA+	OAV	OOB	BH	AVG	PB	PR	/A	PD	TPI
1925	Bos-N	0	0	—	2	0	0	0	0	2²	5	0	2	1	23.6	10.13	40	.500	.583	0	.000	-0	-2	-2	-0	0.0

● WINGO ANDERSON
Anderson, Wingo Charlie b: 8/13/1886, Alvarado, Tex. d: 12/19/50, Fort Worth, Tex. BL/TL, 5'10.5", 150 lbs. Deb: 4/16/10

YEAR	TM/L	W	L	PCT	G	GS	CG	SH	SV	IP	H	HR	BB	SO	RAT	ERA	ERA+	OAV	OOB	BH	AVG	PB	PR	/A	PD	TPI
1910	Cin-N	0	0	—	7	2	0	0	0	17¹	16	0	17	11	17.7	4.67	62	.258	.425	1	.200	-0	-3	-3	-1	-0.1

● JOHN ANDRE
Andre, John Edward b: 1/3/23, Brockton, Mass. d: 11/25/76, Centerville, Mass. BL/TR, 6'4", 200 lbs. Deb: 4/16/55

YEAR	TM/L	W	L	PCT	G	GS	CG	SH	SV	IP	H	HR	BB	SO	RAT	ERA	ERA+	OAV	OOB	BH	AVG	PB	PR	/A	PD	TPI
1955	Chi-N	0	1	.000	22	3	0	0	0	45	45	7	28	19	14.8	5.80	70	.259	.365	1	.111	-1	-9	-9	-0	-0.3

● ELBERT ANDREWS
Andrews, Elbert De Vore b: 12/11/01, Greenwood, S.C. d: 11/25/79, Greenwood, S.C. BL/TR, 6', 175 lbs. Deb: 5/1/25

YEAR	TM/L	W	L	PCT	G	GS	CG	SH	SV	IP	H	HR	BB	SO	RAT	ERA	ERA+	OAV	OOB	BH	AVG	PB	PR	/A	PD	TPI
1925	Phi-A	0	0	—	6	0	0	0	0	8	12	0	11	0	25.9	10.13	46	.375	.535	0	—	0	-5	-5	-0	0.0

● HUB ANDREWS
Andrews, Herbert Carl b: 8/31/22, Burbank, Okla. BR/TR, 6', 170 lbs. Deb: 4/20/47

YEAR	TM/L	W	L	PCT	G	GS	CG	SH	SV	IP	H	HR	BB	SO	RAT	ERA	ERA+	OAV	OOB	BH	AVG	PB	PR	/A	PD	TPI
1947	NY-N	0	0	—	7	0	0	0	0	8²	14	1	4	2	18.7	6.23	65	.368	.429	0	—	0	-2	-2	0	0.0
1948	NY-N	0	0	—	1	0	0	0	0	3	3	0	0	0	9.0	0.00	—	.300	.300	0	—	0	1	1	0	0.0
Total	2	0	0	—	8	0	0	0	0	11²	17	1	4	2	16.2	4.63	87	.354	.404	0	—	0	-1	-1	0	0.0

● IVY ANDREWS
Andrews, Ivy Paul "Poison" b: 5/6/07, Dora, Ala. d: 11/24/70, Birmingham, Ala. BR/TR, 6'1", 200 lbs. Deb: 8/15/31

YEAR	TM/L	W	L	PCT	G	GS	CG	SH	SV	IP	H	HR	BB	SO	RAT	ERA	ERA+	OAV	OOB	BH	AVG	PB	PR	/A	PD	TPI
1931	NY-A	2	0	1.000	7	3	1	0	0	34¹	39	3	8	10	11.5	4.19	95	.273	.314	2	.182	0	1	-1	-0	0.0
1932	NY-A	2	1	.667	4	1	1	0	0	24²	20	0	9	7	10.6	1.82	223	.215	.284	2	.222	1	7	6	0	0.8
	Bos-A	8	6	.571	25	19	8	0	0	141²	144	4	53	30	12.6	3.81	118	.262	.329	7	.137	-3	11	11	-1	0.5
	Yr	10	7	.588	29	20	9	0	0	166¹	164	4	62	37	12.3	3.52	126	.255	.322	9	.150	-2	18	17	-0	1.3
1933	Bos-A	7	13	.350	34	17	5	0	1	140	157	8	61	37	14.1	4.95	88	.279	.350	9	.214	-0	-10	-9	-1	-1.2
1934	StL-A	4	11	.267	43	13	2	0	3	139	166	4	65	51	15.0	4.66	107	.301	.375	14	.350	3	-3	5	-2	0.6
1935	StL-A	13	7	.650	50	20	10	0	1	213¹	231	6	53	43	12.0	3.54	135	.273	.317	9	.132	-5	22	30	-2	1.7
1936	StL-A	7	12	.368	36	25	11	0	1	191¹	221	19	50	33	12.7	4.84	111	.286	.330	10	.169	-1	4	11	-2	0.7
1937	Cle-A	3	4	.429	20	4	1	1	0	59²	76	3	9	16	12.8	4.37	105	.311	.336	3	.250	-1	2	2	-1	0.0
	*NY-A	3	2	.600	11	5	3	1	1	49	49	2	17	17	12.1	3.12	142	.259	.320	1	.067	-1	8	7	0	0.6
	Yr	6	6	.500	31	9	4	2	1	108²	125	5	26	33	12.5	3.81	119	.289	.329	4	.148	-1	10	9	-0	0.7
1938	NY-A	1	3	.250	19	1	1	0	0	48	51	3	17	13	12.8	3.00	151	.268	.329	2	.167	-0	10	8	0	0.7
Total	8	50	59	.459	249	108	43	2	8	1041	1151	59	342	257	12.9	4.14	115	.279	.335	59	.185	-6	51	70	-9	4.4

● JOHN ANDREWS
Andrews, John Richard b: 2/9/49, Monterey Park, Cal. BL/TL, 5'10", 175 lbs. Deb: 4/8/73

YEAR	TM/L	W	L	PCT	G	GS	CG	SH	SV	IP	H	HR	BB	SO	RAT	ERA	ERA+	OAV	OOB	BH	AVG	PB	PR	/A	PD	TPI
1973	StL-N	1	1	.500	16	0	0	0	0	18¹	16	3	11	5	13.3	4.42	82	.235	.342	1	.500	0	-2	-2	-0	-0.2

● NATE ANDREWS
Andrews, Nathan Hardy b: 9/30/13, Pembroke, N.C. d: 4/26/91, Winston-Salem, N.C. BR/TR, 6', 195 lbs. Deb: 5/1/37

YEAR	TM/L	W	L	PCT	G	GS	CG	SH	SV	IP	H	HR	BB	SO	RAT	ERA	ERA+	OAV	OOB	BH	AVG	PB	PR	/A	PD	TPI
1937	StL-N	0	0	—	4	0	0	0	0	9	12	1	3	6	15.0	4.00	100	.324	.375	0	—	0	-0	-0	0	0.1
1939	StL-N	1	2	.333	11	1	0	0	0	16	24	0	12	6	20.3	6.75	61	.343	.439	0	.000	-0	-5	-5	-0	-0.8
1940	Cle-A	0	1	1.000	6	0	0	0	0	12	16	1	6	3	16.5	6.00	70	.327	.400	0	—	0	-2	-2	-0	-0.1
1941	Cle-A	0	0	—	2	0	0	0	0	2¹	3	0	2	1	19.3	11.57	34	.300	.417	0	—	0	-2	-2	-0	0.0
1943	Bos-N	14	20	.412	36	34	23	3	0	283²	253	11	75	80	10.6	2.57	133	.238	.291	14	.156	-0	26	27	2	3.4
1944	Bos-N☆	16	15	.516	37	34	16	2	2	257¹	263	14	74	76	11.9	3.22	119	.261	.312	10	.114	-4	11	17	1	1.8

YEAR	TM/L	W	L	PCT	G	GS	CG	SH	SV	IP	H	HR	BB	SO	RAT	ERA	ERA+	OAV	OOB	BH	AVG	PB	PR	/A	PD	TPI
1945	Bos-N	7	12	.368	21	19	8	0	0	137^2	160	9	52	26	13.9	4.58	84	.295	.356	9	.209	0	-12	-11	-0	-1.4
1946	Cin-N	2	4	.333	7	7	3	0	0	43^1	50	2	8	13	12.3	3.95	85	.281	.316	1	.071	-1	-3	-3	-0	-0.5
	NY-N	1	0	1.000	3	2	0	0	0	12	17	2	4	5	15.8	6.00	57	.362	.412	1	.500	-1	-3	-3	-0	-0.2
	Yr	3	4	.429	10	9	3	0	0	55^1	67	4	12	18	12.8	4.39	77	.296	.332	2	.125	-0	-6	-6	-0	-0.7
Total 8		41	54	.432	127	97	50	5	2	773^1	798	40	236	216	12.1	3.46	106	.265	.321	35	.146	-4	10	17	4	2.3

● **FRED ANDRUS** Andrus, Frederick Hotham b: 8/23/1850, Washington, Mich. d: 11/10/37, Detroit, Mich. BR/TR, 6'2", 185 lbs. Deb: 7/25/1876 ♦

YEAR	TM/L	W	L	PCT	G	GS	CG	SH	SV	IP	H	HR	BB	SO	RAT	ERA	ERA+	OAV	OOB	BH	AVG	PB	PR	/A	PD	TPI
1884	Chi-N	1	0	1.000	1	1	1	0	0	9	11	1	2	2	13.0	2.00	157	.297	.333	1	.200	0	1	1	0	0.1

● **JOAQUIN ANDUJAR** Andujar, Joaquin b: 12/21/52, San Pedro De Macoris, D.R. BB/TR, 6', 180 lbs. Deb: 4/8/76

YEAR	TM/L	W	L	PCT	G	GS	CG	SH	SV	IP	H	HR	BB	SO	RAT	ERA	ERA+	OAV	OOB	BH	AVG	PB	PR	/A	PD	TPI
1976	Hou-N	9	10	.474	28	25	9	4	0	172^1	163	8	75	59	12.5	3.60	89	.255	.334	8	.140	-0	-2	-8	-1	-0.9
1977	Hou-N☆	11	8	.579	26	25	4	1	0	158^2	149	11	64	69	12.3	3.69	97	.251	.328	10	.189	2	4	-2	2	0.2
1978	Hou-N	5	7	.417	35	13	2	0	1	110^2	88	3	58	55	12.2	3.42	97	.224	.330	3	.130	-0	2	-1	2	0.1
1979	Hou-N★	12	12	.500	46	23	8	0	4	194	168	7	88	77	12.0	3.43	102	.233	.319	5	.088	-0	6	2	4	0.6
1980	*Hou-N	3	8	.273	35	14	0	0	2	122	132	8	43	75	12.9	3.91	84	.277	.337	5	.172	2	-4	-8	1	-0.3
1981	Hou-N	2	3	.400	9	3	0	0	0	23^2	29	2	12	18	15.6	4.94	67	.296	.373	0	.000	-0	-4	-4	-1	-0.9
	StL-N	6	1	.857	11	8	1	0	0	55^1	56	4	11	19	10.9	3.74	95	.265	.302	0	.000	-2	-2	-1	-0	-0.3
	Yr	8	4	.667	20	11	1	0	0	79	85	6	23	37	12.3	4.10	85	.273	.323	0	.000	-2	-5	-5	-0	-1.2
1982	*StL-N	15	10	.600	38	37	9	5	0	265^2	237	11	50	137	10.0	2.47	146	.240	.282	15	.158	-1	33	34	2	3.2
1983	StL-N	6	16	.273	39	34	5	2	1	225	215	23	75	125	11.7	4.16	87	.253	.316	6	.082	-3	-13	-14	5	-1.0
1984	StL-N†	20	14	.588	36	36	12	4	0	261^1	218	20	70	147	10.2	3.34	104	.229	.286	11	.131	3	7	4	3	1.0
1985	*StL-N†	21	12	.636	38	38	10	2	0	269^2	265	15	82	112	11.9	3.40	104	.260	.322	10	.106	-2	6	-4	1	0.2
1986	Oak-A	12	7	.632	28	26	7	1	1	155^1	139	23	56	72	11.5	3.82	101	.239	.310	0	—	0	6	1	0	0.1
1987	Oak-A	3	5	.375	13	13	1	0	0	60^2	63	11	26	32	13.6	6.08	68	.269	.350	0	—	0	-11	-13	0	-1.3
1988	Hou-N	2	5	.286	23	10	0	0	0	78^2	94	9	21	35	13.7	4.00	83	.297	.350	4	.211	2	-5	-6	0	-0.3
Total 13		127	118	.518	405	305	68	19	9	2153	2016	155	731	1032	11.7	3.58	98	.250	.316	77	.127	-1	24	-13	18	0.4

● **NORM ANGELINI** Angelini, Norman Stanley b: 9/24/47, San Francisco, Cal. BL/TL, 5'11", 175 lbs. Deb: 7/22/72

YEAR	TM/L	W	L	PCT	G	GS	CG	SH	SV	IP	H	HR	BB	SO	RAT	ERA	ERA+	OAV	OOB	BH	AVG	PB	PR	/A	PD	TPI
1972	KC-A	2	1	.667	21	0	0	0	2	16	13	1	12	16	14.6	2.25	135	.228	.371	0	.000	-0	1	1	-0	0.3
1973	KC-A	0	0	—	7	0	0	0	1	3^2	2	0	7	3	22.1	4.91	84	.200	.529	0	—	0	-0	-0	-0	-0.1
Total 2		2	1	.667	28	0	0	0	3	19^2	15	1	19	19	16.0	2.75	117	.224	.402	0	.000	-0	1	1	-0	0.2

● **CAP ANSON** Anson, Adrian Constantine b: 4/11/1852, Marshalltown, Iowa d: 4/14/22, Chicago, Ill. BR/TR, 6', 227 lbs. Deb: 5/6/1871 MH♦

YEAR	TM/L	W	L	PCT	G	GS	CG	SH	SV	IP	H	HR	BB	SO	RAT	ERA	ERA+	OAV	OOB	BH	AVG	PB	PR	/A	PD	TPI
1883	Chi-N	0	0	—	2	0	0	0	1	3	1	0	1	0	6.0	0.00	—	.091	.167	127	.308	1	1	1	0	0.1
1884	Chi-N	0	1	.000	1	0	0	0	0	1	3	2	1	0	36.0	18.00	17	.375	.444	159	.335	0	-2	-2	0	-0.9
Total 2		0	1	.000	3	0	0	0	1	4	4	2	1	0	13.5	4.50	71	.211	.286	2995	.329	1	-1	-1	0	-0.8

● **JOHNNY ANTONELLI** Antonelli, John August b: 4/12/30, Rochester, N.Y. BL/TL, 6', 190 lbs. Deb: 7/4/48

YEAR	TM/L	W	L	PCT	G	GS	CG	SH	SV	IP	H	HR	BB	SO	RAT	ERA	ERA+	OAV	OOB	BH	AVG	PB	PR	/A	PD	TPI
1948	Bos-N	0	0	—	4	0	0	0	1	4	2	0	3	0	11.3	2.25	170	.143	.294	0	—	0	1	1	0	0.1
1949	Bos-N	3	7	.300	22	10	3	1	0	96	99	6	42	48	13.4	3.56	106	.273	.351	3	.120	-1	5	2	-1	0.0
1950	Bos-N	2	3	.400	20	6	2	1	0	57^2	81	9	22	33	16.7	5.93	65	.335	.399	2	.125	-1	-11	-13	0	-1.0
1953	Mil-N	12	12	.500	31	26	11	2	1	175^1	167	15	71	131	12.3	3.18	123	.242	.314	11	.177	0	22	14	1	1.9
1954	*NY-N★	21	7	**.750**	39	37	18	**6**	2	258^2	209	22	94	152	10.7	**2.30**	**176**	**.219**	.293	16	.163	0	**51**	**50**	2	**5.5**
1955	NY-N	14	16	.467	38	34	14	2	1	235^1	206	24	82	143	11.4	3.33	121	.234	.307	17	.207	0	19	18	1	2.6
1956	NY-N★	20	13	.606	41	36	15	5	1	258^1	225	20	75	145	10.6	2.86	132	.234	.292	14	.157	1	26	27	1	3.6
1957	NY-N☆	12	18	.400	40	38	8	3	0	212^1	228	19	67	114	12.6	3.77	104	.276	.333	11	.153	3	-3	4	-2	0.6
1958	SF-N☆	16	13	.552	41	34	13	0	3	241^2	216	31	87	143	11.4	3.28	116	.239	.308	19	.226	4	18	14	-3	1.7
1959	SF-N★	19	10	.655	40	38	17	**4**	1	282	247	29	76	165	10.4	3.10	123	.233	.286	16	.158	1	27	22	-1	2.2
1960	SF-N	6	7	.462	41	10	1	1	11	112^1	106	7	47	57	12.4	3.77	92	.253	.331	4	.235	2	-0	-4	-1	-0.3
1961	Cle-A	0	4	.000	11	7	0	0	0	48	68	8	18	23	16.3	6.56	60	.338	.395	4	.267	1	-14	-14	1	-0.8
	Mil-N	1	0	1.000	9	0	0	0	0	10^2	16	2	3	8	16.0	7.59	49	.340	.380	0	.000	-0	-4	-5	-0	-0.4
Total 12		126	110	.534	377	268	102	25	21	1992^1	1870	185	687	1162	11.7	3.34	116	.247	.313	121	.178	15	141	118	-1	15.7

● **BOB APODACA** Apodaca, Robert John b: 1/31/50, Los Angeles, Cal. BR/TR, 5'11", 170 lbs. Deb: 9/18/73

YEAR	TM/L	W	L	PCT	G	GS	CG	SH	SV	IP	H	HR	BB	SO	RAT	ERA	ERA+	OAV	OOB	BH	AVG	PB	PR	/A	PD	TPI
1973	NY-N	0	0	—	1	0	0	0	0	2	0	0	2	0	—	∞	—	—	1.000	0	—	0	-1	-1	0	-0.1
1974	NY-N	6	6	.500	35	8	1	0	3	103	92	7	42	54	11.9	3.50	102	.241	.319	3	.120	0	1	1	-1	0.1
1975	NY-N	3	4	.429	46	0	0	0	13	84^2	66	4	28	45	10.0	1.49	232	.222	.289	4	.364	2	20	18	2	2.6
1976	NY-N	3	7	.300	43	3	0	0	5	89^2	71	4	29	45	10.3	2.81	117	.223	.293	0	.125	0	7	5	1	0.7
1977	NY-N	4	8	.333	59	0	0	0	5	84	83	7	30	53	12.2	3.43	109	.255	.319	1	.167	-0	4	3	1	0.5
Total 5		16	25	.390	184	11	1	0	26	361^1	312	22	131	197	11.2	2.86	123	.236	.307	10	.172	2	32	26	4	3.8

● **LUIS APONTE** Aponte, Luis Eduardo (Yuripe) b: 6/14/53, ElTigre, Venez. BR/TR, 6', 185 lbs. Deb: 9/4/80

YEAR	TM/L	W	L	PCT	G	GS	CG	SH	SV	IP	H	HR	BB	SO	RAT	ERA	ERA+	OAV	OOB	BH	AVG	PB	PR	/A	PD	TPI
1980	Bos-A	0	0	—	4	0	0	0	0	7	6	0	2	1	10.3	1.29	328	.250	.308	0	—	0	2	2	0	-0.2
1981	Bos-A	1	0	1.000	7	0	0	0	1	15^2	11	0	3	11	8.0	0.57	674	.208	.250	0	—	0	5	6	1	0.4
1982	Bos-A	2	2	.500	40	0	0	0	3	85	78	5	25	44	10.9	3.18	136	.246	.301	0	—	0	8	11	2	0.5
1983	Bos-A	5	4	.556	34	0	0	0	3	62	74	7	23	32	14.4	3.63	120	.301	.365	0	—	0	3	5	1	0.7
1984	Cle-A	1	0	1.000	25	0	0	0	3	50^1	53	5	15	25	12.3	4.11	99	.269	.324	0	—	0	-1	-0	-1	-0.1
Total 5		9	6	.600	110	0	0	0	7	220	222	17	68	113	12.0	3.27	129	.265	.323	0	—	0	18	23	3	1.3

● **KEVIN APPIER** Appier, Robert Kevin b: 12/6/67, Lancaster, Cal. BR/TR, 6'2", 180 lbs. Deb: 6/14/89

YEAR	TM/L	W	L	PCT	G	GS	CG	SH	SV	IP	H	HR	BB	SO	RAT	ERA	ERA+	OAV	OOB	BH	AVG	PB	PR	/A	PD	TPI
1989	KC-A	1	4	.200	6	5	0	0	0	21^2	24	3	12	10	19.1	9.14	47	.374	.447	0	—	0	-13	-13	-1	-2.2
1990	KC-A	12	8	.600	32	24	3	0	0	185^2	179	13	54	127	11.6	2.76	139	.252	.310	0	—	0	24	22	-0	2.3
1991	KC-A	13	10	.565	34	31	6	3	0	207^2	205	13	61	158	11.6	3.42	120	.255	.309	0	—	0	15	16	0	1.7
1992	KC-A	15	8	.652	30	30	3	0	0	208^1	167	10	68	150	10.2	2.46	165	.217	.282	0	—	0	34	37	0	3.8
1993	KC-A	18	8	.692	34	34	5	1	0	238^2	183	8	81	186	10.0	**2.56**	**179**	.212	.280	0	—	0	**47**	**53**	-2	4.8
1994	KC-A	7	6	.538	23	23	0	0	0	155	137	11	63	145	11.8	3.83	135	.240	.320	0	—	0	17	23	0	1.4
Total 6		66	44	.600	159	147	18	7	0	1017	905	58	339	776	11.1	3.09	139	.238	.302	0	—	0	124	138	-2	11.8

● **FRED APPLEGATE** Applegate, Frederick Romaine b: 5/9/1879, Williamsport, Pa. d: 4/21/68, Williamsport, Pa. BR/TR, 6'2", 180 lbs. Deb: 9/30/04

YEAR	TM/L	W	L	PCT	G	GS	CG	SH	SV	IP	H	HR	BB	SO	RAT	ERA	ERA+	OAV	OOB	BH	AVG	PB	PR	/A	PD	TPI
1904	Phi-A	1	2	.333	3	3	3	0	0	21	29	0	8	12	16.3	6.43	42	.328	.390	2	.286	0	-9	-9	0	-1.0

● **ED APPLETON** Appleton, Edward Samuel "Whitey" b: 2/29/1892, Arlington, Tex. d: 1/27/32, Arlington, Tex. BR/TR, 6'0.5", 173 lbs. Deb: 4/16/15

YEAR	TM/L	W	L	PCT	G	GS	CG	SH	SV	IP	H	HR	BB	SO	RAT	ERA	ERA+	OAV	OOB	BH	AVG	PB	PR	/A	PD	TPI
1915	Bro-N	4	10	.286	34	10	5	0	0	138^1	133	3	66	50	13.5	3.32	84	.263	.357	7	.159	-0	-9	-8	-1	-0.9
1916	Bro-N	1	2	.333	14	3	1	0	1	47	49	1	18	14	13.0	3.06	88	.278	.349	2	.167	-0	-2	-2	-1	-0.3
Total 2		5	12	.294	48	13	6	0	1	185^1	182	4	84	64	13.4	3.25	85	.267	.355	9	.161	-0	-11	-10	-2	-1.2

● **PETE APPLETON** Appleton, Peter William "Jake" (a.k.a. Jablonowski In 1927-33) b: 5/20/04, Terryville, Conn. d: 1/18/74, Trenton, N.J. BR/TR, 5'11", 180 lbs. Deb: 9/14/27

YEAR	TM/L	W	L	PCT	G	GS	CG	SH	SV	IP	H	HR	BB	SO	RAT	ERA	ERA+	OAV	OOB	BH	AVG	PB	PR	/A	PD	TPI
1927	Cin-N	2	1	.667	6	2	1	0	0	29^2	29	0	17	3	14.0	1.82	208	.261	.359	6	.545	2	7	6	1	0.9
1928	Cin-N	3	4	.429	31	1	0	0	0	82^2	101	7	22	20	13.6	4.68	84	.311	.358	10	.323	3	-6	-7	2	0.0
1930	Cle-A	8	7	.533	39	7	2	0	1	118^2	122	8	53	45	13.7	4.02	120	.274	.357	8	.200	-1	8	11	2	1.2
1931	Cle-A	4	4	.500	29	3	0	0	0	79^2	100	2	29	25	14.7	4.63	100	.293	.350	5	.208	0	-2	-0	0	0.0
1932	Cle-A	0	0	—	4	0	0	0	0	5	11	1	4	1	25.2	16.20	29	.407	.467	0	—	0	-7	-6	0	0.0
	Bos-A	0	3	.000	11	3	0	0	0	46	49	2	26	15	15.1	4.11	109	.265	.362	3	.176	-0	-5	-4	2	0.3
	Yr	0	3	.000	15	3	0	0	0	51	60	3	29	16	16.1	5.29	85	.283	.374	3	.176	-0	-5	-4	2	0.3

YEAR TM/L	W	L	PCT	G	GS	CG	SH	SV	IP	H	HR	BB	SO	RAT	ERA	ERA+	OAV	OOB	BH	AVG	PB	PR	/A	PD	TPI
1933 NY-A	0	0	—	1	0	0	0	0	2	3	0	1	0	18.0	0.00	—	.375	.444	0	—	0	1	1	0	0.0
1936 Was-A	14	9	.609	38	20	12	1	3	201²	199	7	77	77	12.5	3.53	135	.254	.324	19	.250	2	34	28	1	3.0
1937 Was-A	8	15	.348	35	18	7	4	2	168	167	16	72	62	13.1	4.39	101	.260	.339	11	.186	-2	4	1	3	0.2
1938 Was-A	7	9	.438	43	10	5	0	5	164¹	175	12	61	62	13.0	4.60	98	.270	.333	15	.254	3	3	-2	-0	0.1
1939 Was-A	5	10	.333	40	4	2	0	6	102²	104	7	48	50	13.7	4.56	95	.265	.351	4	.160	-1	1	-2	-0	-0.4
1940 Chi-A	4	0	1.000	25	0	0	0	5	57²	54	8	28	21	13.0	5.62	78	.248	.336	3	.176	-0	-8	-8	-0	-0.7
1941 Chi-A	0	3	.000	13	0	0	0	1	27¹	27	4	17	12	15.1	5.27	78	.257	.371	1	.250	0	-3	-4	-0	-0.3
1942 Chi-A	0	0	—	4	0	0	0	0	4²	2	0	3	2	9.6	3.86	93	.133	.278	0	—	0	-0	-0	-0	0.0
StL-A	1	1	.500	14	0	0	0	2	27¹	25	1	11	12	11.9	2.96	125	.243	.316	1	.167	1	2	2	1	0.4
Yr	1	1	.500	18	0	0	0	2	32	27	1	14	14	11.5	3.09	119	.229	.311	1	.167	1	2	2	1	0.4
1945 StL-A	0	0	—	2	0	0	0	0	2¹	3	0	7	1	38.6	15.43	23	.273	.556	0	—	0	-3	-3	0	-0.1
Was-A	1	0	1.000	6	2	1	0	1	21¹	16	1	11	12	11.4	3.38	92	.211	.310	1	.200	-0	-0	-1	-0	-0.1
Yr	1	0	1.000	8	2	1	0	1	23²	19	1	18	13	14.1	4.56	69	.218	.352	1	.200	-0	-3	-4	0	-0.1
Total 14	57	66	.463	341	71	34	6	26	1141	1187	76	486	420	13.4	4.30	104	.264	.343	87	.233	7	33	19	12	4.6

● **LUIS AQUINO** Aquino, Luis Antonio (Colon) b: 5/19/64, Santurce, P.R. BR/TR, 6′, 195 lbs. Deb: 8/8/86

YEAR TM/L	W	L	PCT	G	GS	CG	SH	SV	IP	H	HR	BB	SO	RAT	ERA	ERA+	OAV	OOB	BH	AVG	PB	PR	/A	PD	TPI
1986 Tor-A	1	1	.500	7	0	0	0	0	11¹	14	2	3	5	13.5	6.35	66	.304	.347	0	—	0	-3	-3	-0	-0.4
1988 KC-A	1	0	1.000	7	5	1	1	0	29	33	1	17	11	15.8	2.79	143	.282	.378	0	—	0	4	4	-0	0.1
1989 KC-A	6	8	.429	34	16	2	1	0	141¹	148	6	35	68	11.9	3.50	110	.271	.320	0	—	0	6	5	1	0.6
1990 KC-A	4	1	.800	20	3	1	0	0	68¹	59	6	27	28	11.9	3.16	121	.237	.321	0	—	0	6	5	0	0.4
1991 KC-A	8	4	.667	38	18	1	0	3	157	152	10	47	80	11.6	3.44	120	.253	.311	0	—	0	11	12	0	0.9
1992 KC-A	3	6	.333	15	13	0	0	0	67²	81	5	20	11	13.6	4.52	90	.303	.354	0	—	0	-4	-4	1	-0.5
1993 Fla-N	6	8	.429	38	13	0	0	0	110²	115	6	40	67	13.0	3.42	126	.276	.346	2	.080	-2	8	11	4	1.5
1994 Fla-N	2	1	.667	29	1	0	0	0	50²	39	3	22	22	11.4	3.73	121	.210	.303	1	.167	-0	3	4	1	0.3
Total 8	31	29	.517	188	69	5	3	3	636	641	39	211	292	12.4	3.58	114	.264	.328	3	.097	-2	30	35	6	2.9

● **FRED ARCHER** Archer, Frederick Marvin "Lefty" b: 3/7/10, Johnson City, Tenn. d: 10/31/81, Charlotte, N.C. BL/TL, 6′, 193 lbs. Deb: 9/5/36

YEAR TM/L	W	L	PCT	G	GS	CG	SH	SV	IP	H	HR	BB	SO	RAT	ERA	ERA+	OAV	OOB	BH	AVG	PB	PR	/A	PD	TPI
1936 Phi-A	2	3	.400	6	5	2	0	0	36²	41	3	15	14	14.5	6.38	80	.289	.369	4	.267	0	-5	-5	-0	-0.5
1937 Phi-A	0	0	—	1	0	0	0	0	3	4	0	0	2	12.0	6.00	79	.333	.333	0	—	0	-0	-0	0	0.0
Total 2	2	3	.400	7	5	2	0	0	39²	45	3	15	11	14.3	6.35	80	.292	.366	4	.267	0	-6	-6	0	-0.5

● **JIM ARCHER** Archer, James William b: 5/25/32, Max Meadows, Va. BR/TL, 6′, 190 lbs. Deb: 4/30/61

YEAR TM/L	W	L	PCT	G	GS	CG	SH	SV	IP	H	HR	BB	SO	RAT	ERA	ERA+	OAV	OOB	BH	AVG	PB	PR	/A	PD	TPI
1961 KC-A	9	15	.375	39	27	9	2	5	205¹	204	11	60	110	11.8	3.20	131	.257	.313	4	.063	-5	19	22	-0	2.0
1962 KC-A	0	1	.000	18	1	0	0	0	27²	40	8	10	12	16.3	9.43	45	.342	.394	1	1.000	0	-17	-16	-0	-0.5
Total 2	9	16	.360	57	28	9	2	5	233	244	19	70	122	12.3	3.94	106	.268	.323	5	.078	-4	2	6	-1	1.5

● **RUGGER ARDIZOIA** Ardizoia, Rinaldo Joseph b: 11/20/19, Oleggio, Italy BR/TR, 5′11″, 180 lbs. Deb: 4/30/47

YEAR TM/L	W	L	PCT	G	GS	CG	SH	SV	IP	H	HR	BB	SO	RAT	ERA	ERA+	OAV	OOB	BH	AVG	PB	PR	/A	PD	TPI
1947 NY-A	0	0	—	1	0	0	0	0	2	4	1	1	0	22.5	9.00	39	.500	.556	0	—	0	-1	-1	0	0.0

● **FRANK ARELLANES** Arellanes, Frank Julian b: 1/28/1882, Santa Cruz, Cal. d: 12/13/18, San Jose, Cal. BR/TR, 6′, 180 lbs. Deb: 7/28/08

YEAR TM/L	W	L	PCT	G	GS	CG	SH	SV	IP	H	HR	BB	SO	RAT	ERA	ERA+	OAV	OOB	BH	AVG	PB	PR	/A	PD	TPI
1908 Bos-A	4	3	.571	11	8	6	1	0	79	60	1	18	33	9.2	1.82	135	.213	.267	5	.167	0	5	6	-1	0.4
1909 Bos-A	16	12	.571	45	28	17	1	8	230²	192	3	43	82	9.4	2.18	114	.229	.270	13	.167	-1	8	8	0	0.9
1910 Bos-A	4	7	.364	18	13	2	0	0	100	106	1	24	33	12.0	2.88	89	.283	.332	6	.176	0	-4	-4	-0	-0.4
Total 3	24	22	.522	74	49	25	2	8	409²	358	5	85	148	10.0	2.28	110	.239	.285	24	.169	-1	9	10	-1	0.9

● **RUDY ARIAS** Arias, Rodolfo (Martinez) b: 6/6/31, Las Villas, Cuba BL/TL, 5′10″, 165 lbs. Deb: 4/10/59

YEAR TM/L	W	L	PCT	G	GS	CG	SH	SV	IP	H	HR	BB	SO	RAT	ERA	ERA+	OAV	OOB	BH	AVG	PB	PR	/A	PD	TPI
1959 Chi-A	2	0	1.000	34	0	0	0	2	44	49	7	20	28	14.3	4.09	92	.277	.354	0	.000	-1	-1	-2	1	-0.1

● **DON ARLICH** Arlich, Donald Louis b: 2/15/43, Wayne, Mich. BL/TL, 6′2″, 185 lbs. Deb: 10/2/65

YEAR TM/L	W	L	PCT	G	GS	CG	SH	SV	IP	H	HR	BB	SO	RAT	ERA	ERA+	OAV	OOB	BH	AVG	PB	PR	/A	PD	TPI
1965 Hou-N	0	0	—	1	1	0	0	0	6	5	0	1	0	9.0	3.00	112	.227	.261	0	.000	-0	0	0	-0	0.0
1966 Hou-N	0	1	.000	7	0	0	0	0	4	11	0	4	1	36.0	15.75	22	.478	.571	0	.000	-0	-5	-5	-0	-1.2
Total 2	0	1	.000	8	1	0	0	0	10	16	0	5	1	19.8	8.10	42	.356	.431	0	.000	-0	-5	-5	-0	-1.2

● **STEVE ARLIN** Arlin, Stephen Ralph b: 9/25/45, Seattle, Wash. BR/TR, 6′3.5″, 195 lbs. Deb: 6/17/69

YEAR TM/L	W	L	PCT	G	GS	CG	SH	SV	IP	H	HR	BB	SO	RAT	ERA	ERA+	OAV	OOB	BH	AVG	PB	PR	/A	PD	TPI
1969 SD-N	0	1	.000	4	1	0	0	0	10²	13	2	9	9	18.6	9.28	38	.289	.407	0	.000	-0	-7	-7	-0	-0.6
1970 SD-N	1	0	1.000	2	2	1	0	0	12²	11	0	8	13	13.5	2.84	140	.244	.358	0	.000	-1	2	2	0	0.1
1971 SD-N	9	19	.321	36	34	10	4	0	227²	211	8	103	156	12.7	3.48	95	.244	.329	9	.123	-0	-5	-5	-1	-0.8
1972 SD-N	10	21	.323	38	37	12	3	0	250	217	19	122	159	12.5	3.60	91	.237	.332	11	.153	3	-4	-9	-0	-0.8
1973 SD-N	11	14	.440	34	27	7	3	0	180	196	26	72	98	13.4	5.10	68	.278	.346	10	.167	1	-29	-33	-1	-3.9
1974 SD-N	1	7	.125	16	12	1	0	1	64	85	5	37	18	17.4	5.91	60	.326	.413	2	.111	-1	-16	-17	-0	-2.0
Cle-A	2	5	.286	11	10	1	0	0	43²	59	1	22	20	16.7	6.60	55	.333	.407	0	—	0	-14	-14	-1	-2.0
Total 6	34	67	.337	141	123	32	11	1	788²	792	61	373	463	13.5	4.33	78	.263	.348	32	.139	1	-69	-82	-3	-10.0

● **ORVILLE ARMBRUST** Armbrust, Orville Martin b: 3/2/10, Beirne, Ark. d: 10/2/67, Mobile, Ala. BR/TR, 5′10″, 195 lbs. Deb: 9/18/34

YEAR TM/L	W	L	PCT	G	GS	CG	SH	SV	IP	H	HR	BB	SO	RAT	ERA	ERA+	OAV	OOB	BH	AVG	PB	PR	/A	PD	TPI
1934 Was-A	1	0	1.000	3	2	0	0	0	12²	10	1	3	3	9.2	2.13	203	.208	.255	0	.000	-1	3	3	1	0.2

● **HOWARD ARMSTRONG** Armstrong, Howard Elmer b: 12/2/1889, E.Claridon, Ohio d: 3/8/26, Canisteo, N.Y. BR/TR, 5′9″, 165 lbs. Deb: 9/30/11

YEAR TM/L	W	L	PCT	G	GS	CG	SH	SV	IP	H	HR	BB	SO	RAT	ERA	ERA+	OAV	OOB	BH	AVG	PB	PR	/A	PD	TPI
1911 Phi-A	0	1	.000	1	0	0	0	0	3	3	0	1	0	12.0	—	—	.273	.333	0	.000	-0	1	1	0	0.4

● **JACK ARMSTRONG** Armstrong, Jack William b: 3/7/65, Englewood, N.J. BR/TR, 6′5″, 220 lbs. Deb: 6/21/88

YEAR TM/L	W	L	PCT	G	GS	CG	SH	SV	IP	H	HR	BB	SO	RAT	ERA	ERA+	OAV	OOB	BH	AVG	PB	PR	/A	PD	TPI
1988 Cin-N	4	7	.364	14	13	0	0	0	65¹	63	8	38	45	13.9	5.79	62	.256	.356	2	.095	-1	-17	-16	1	-2.4
1989 Cin-N	2	3	.400	9	8	0	0	0	42²	40	5	21	23	12.9	4.64	78	.245	.332	0	.000	-1	-5	-5	0	-0.6
1990 *Cin-N★	12	9	.571	29	27	2	1	0	166	151	9	59	110	11.7	3.42	115	.241	.313	5	.106	-2	7	10	0	1.0
1991 Cin-N	7	13	.350	27	24	1	0	0	139²	158	25	54	93	13.8	5.48	69	.293	.359	4	.093	-2	-28	-26	-0	-3.4
1992 Cle-A	6	15	.286	35	23	1	0	0	166²	176	23	67	114	13.3	4.64	84	.269	.340	0	—	0	-13	-14	1	-1.3
1993 Fla-N	9	17	.346	36	33	0	0	0	196¹	210	29	78	118	13.5	4.49	96	.271	.343	10	.152	-2	-10	-4	-0	-0.6
1994 Tex-A	0	1	.000	2	2	0	0	0	10	9	3	2	7	9.9	3.60	126	.231	.268	0	—	0	1	1	0	0.4
Total 7	40	65	.381	152	130	4	1	0	786²	807	102	319	510	13.1	4.58	87	.265	.338	21	.114	-6	-65	-54	2	-6.9

● **MIKE ARMSTRONG** Armstrong, Michael Dennis b: 3/7/54, Glen Cove, N.Y. BR/TR, 6′3″, 206 lbs. Deb: 8/12/80

YEAR TM/L	W	L	PCT	G	GS	CG	SH	SV	IP	H	HR	BB	SO	RAT	ERA	ERA+	OAV	OOB	BH	AVG	PB	PR	/A	PD	TPI
1980 SD-N	0	0	—	11	0	0	0	0	14¹	16	3	13	14	18.2	5.65	61	.296	.433	0	.000	-0	-3	-4	-0	-0.1
1981 SD-N	0	2	.000	10	0	0	0	0	12	14	1	11	9	18.8	6.00	54	.311	.446	0	.000	-0	-3	-4	-0	-0.6
1982 KC-A	5	5	.500	52	0	0	0	6	112²	88	9	43	75	10.7	3.20	128	.215	.295	0	—	0	11	11	-1	0.9
1983 KC-A	10	7	.588	58	0	0	0	0	102²	86	11	45	52	11.7	3.86	106	.228	.315	0	—	0	3	3	0	0.4
1984 NY-A	3	2	.600	36	0	0	0	1	54¹	47	6	26	43	12.1	3.48	109	.239	.327	0	—	0	3	2	0	0.5
1985 NY-A	0	0	—	9	0	0	0	0	14²	9	4	2	11	6.8	3.07	130	.173	.204	0	—	0	2	2	0	0.1
1986 NY-A	0	1	.000	7	1	0	0	0	8²	13	4	5	8	18.7	9.35	44	.351	.429	0	—	0	-5	-5	-0	-0.4
1987 Cle-A	1	0	1.000	14	0	0	0	0	18²	27	4	10	9	17.8	8.68	52	.333	.407	0	—	0	-9	-9	-0	-0.5
Total 8	19	17	.528	197	1	0	0	11	338	300	42	155	221	12.3	4.10	97	.240	.326	0	.000	-0	-2	-4	-3	0.3

● **SCOTT ARNOLD** Arnold, Scott Gentry b: 8/18/62, Lexington, Ky. BR/TR, 6′2″, 210 lbs. Deb: 4/7/88

YEAR TM/L	W	L	PCT	G	GS	CG	SH	SV	IP	H	HR	BB	SO	RAT	ERA	ERA+	OAV	OOB	BH	AVG	PB	PR	/A	PD	TPI
1988 StL-N	0	0	—	6	0	0	0	0	6²	9	0	4	8	17.6	5.40	64	.321	.406	0	—	0	-1	-1	0	0.0

● **TONY ARNOLD** Arnold, Tony Dale b: 5/3/59, ElPaso, Tex. BR/TR, 5′11″, 170 lbs. Deb: 8/9/86

YEAR TM/L	W	L	PCT	G	GS	CG	SH	SV	IP	H	HR	BB	SO	RAT	ERA	ERA+	OAV	OOB	BH	AVG	PB	PR	/A	PD	TPI
1986 Bal-A	0	2	.000	11	0	0	0	0	25¹	25	0	11	7	12.8	3.55	116	.278	.356	0	—	0	2	2	1	0.3

YEAR	TM/L	W	L	PCT	G	GS	CG	SH	SV	IP	H	HR	BB	SO	RAT	ERA	ERA+	OAV	OOB	BH	AVG	PB	PR	/A	PD	TPI
1987	Bal-A	0	0	—	27	0	0	0	0	53	71	8	17	18	15.3	5.77	76	.330	.385	0	—	0	-8	-8	2	0.2
Total	2	0	2	.000	38	0	0	0	0	78¹	96	8	28	25	14.5	5.06	85	.315	.376	0	—	0	-6	-6	3	0.5

● BRAD ARNSBERG
Arnsberg, Bradley James b: 8/20/63, Seattle, Wash. BR/TR, 6'4", 205 lbs. Deb: 9/6/86

YEAR	TM/L	W	L	PCT	G	GS	CG	SH	SV	IP	H	HR	BB	SO	RAT	ERA	ERA+	OAV	OOB	BH	AVG	PB	PR	/A	PD	TPI
1986	NY-A	0	0	—	2	1	0	0	0	8	13	1	1	3	15.8	3.38	121	.342	.359	0	—	0	1	1	-0	0.0
1987	NY-A	1	3	.250	6	2	0	0	0	19¹	22	5	13	14	16.3	5.59	77	.289	.393	0	—	0	-2	-3	1	-0.4
1989	Tex-A	2	1	.667	16	1	0	0	1	48	45	6	22	26	13.1	4.13	96	.247	.338	0	—	0	-1	-1	1	0.0
1990	Tex-A	6	1	.857	53	0	0	0	5	62²	56	4	33	44	13.1	2.15	182	.235	.333	0	—	0	12	12	1	1.6
1991	Tex-A	0	1	.000	9	0	0	0	0	9²	10	5	5	8	14.0	8.38	48	.256	.341	0	—	0	-5	-5	-0	-0.4
1992	Cle-A	0	0	—	8	0	0	0	0	10²	13	6	11	5	21.9	11.81	33	.317	.481	0	—	0	-9	-9	-0	0.1
Total	6	9	6	.600	94	4	0	0	6	158¹	159	27	85	100	14.3	4.26	94	.259	.356	0	—	0	-5	-5	2	0.9

● ORIE ARNTZEN
Arntzen, Orie Edgar "Old Folks" b: 10/18/09, Beverly, Ill. d: 1/28/70, Cedar Rapids, Iowa BR/TR, 6'1", 200 lbs. Deb: 4/20/43

YEAR	TM/L	W	L	PCT	G	GS	CG	SH	SV	IP	H	HR	BB	SO	RAT	ERA	ERA+	OAV	OOB	BH	AVG	PB	PR	/A	PD	TPI
1943	Phi-A	4	13	.235	32	20	9	0	0	164¹	172	5	69	66	13.5	4.22	81	.277	.354	8	.160	-1	-17	-15	-3	-1.9

● RENE AROCHA
Arocha, Rene (Magaly) b: 2/24/66, Havana, Cuba BR/TR, 6', 180 lbs. Deb: 4/9/93

YEAR	TM/L	W	L	PCT	G	GS	CG	SH	SV	IP	H	HR	BB	SO	RAT	ERA	ERA+	OAV	OOB	BH	AVG	PB	PR	/A	PD	TPI
1993	StL-N	11	8	.579	32	29	1	0	0	188	197	20	31	96	11.1	3.78	105	.271	.304	6	.103	-2	5	4	-1	0.1
1994	StL-N	4	4	.500	45	7	1	1	11	83	94	9	21	62	12.9	4.01	101	.286	.336	1	.111	0	2	1	-0	0.1
Total	2	15	12	.556	77	36	2	1	11	271	291	29	52	158	11.6	3.85	104	.276	.314	7	.104	-2	7	4	-1	0.2

● GERRY ARRIGO
Arrigo, Gerald William b: 6/12/41, Chicago, Ill. BL/TL, 6'1", 195 lbs. Deb: 6/12/61

YEAR	TM/L	W	L	PCT	G	GS	CG	SH	SV	IP	H	HR	BB	SO	RAT	ERA	ERA+	OAV	OOB	BH	AVG	PB	PR	/A	PD	TPI
1961	Min-A	0	1	.000	7	2	0	0	0	9²	9	0	10	6	19.6	10.24	41	.265	.457	1	.500	0	-7	-6	0	-0.5
1962	Min-A	0	0	—	1	0	0	0	0	1	3	0	1	1	36.0	18.00	23	.600	.667	0	—	0	-2	-2	0	0.0
1963	Min-A	1	2	.333	5	1	0	0	0	15²	12	2	4	13	9.2	2.87	127	.211	.262	0	.000	-0	1	1	0	0.2
1964	Min-A	7	4	.636	41	12	2	1	1	105¹	97	11	45	96	12.3	3.84	93	.244	.324	5	.172	1	-3	-3	0	-0.2
1965	Cin-N	2	4	.333	27	5	0	0	2	54	75	4	30	43	17.8	6.17	61	.342	.426	2	.167	1	-16	-15	-1	-1.7
1966	Cin-N	0	0	—	3	0	0	0	0	7¹	7	2	3	3	12.3	4.91	79	.250	.323	0	.000	-0	-1	-1	-0	0.0
	NY-N	3	3	.500	17	5	0	0	0	43¹	47	5	16	28	13.1	3.74	97	.276	.339	5	.500	3	-1	-0	1	0.3
	Yr	3	3	.500	20	5	0	0	0	50²	54	7	19	31	13.0	3.91	94	.273	.336	5	.455	3	-2	-1	0	0.3
1967	Cin-N	6	6	.500	32	5	1	1	1	74	61	6	35	56	12.2	3.16	119	.232	.331	4	.211	1	2	5	-2	0.7
1968	Cin-N	12	10	.545	36	31	5	1	0	205¹	181	13	77	140	11.5	3.33	95	.237	.310	5	.075	-2	-8	-4	1	-0.5
1969	Cin-N	4	7	.364	20	16	1	0	0	91	89	9	61	35	15.6	4.15	91	.256	.379	5	.161	0	-6	-4	-2	-0.7
1970	Chi-A	0	3	.000	5	3	0	0	0	13¹	24	4	9	12	22.3	12.83	30	.393	.471	0	.000	-0	-13	-13	-0	-2.2
Total	10	35	40	.467	194	80	9	3	4	620	605	56	291	433	13.3	4.14	85	.258	.345	27	.151	2	-52	-42	-3	-4.6

● FERNANDO ARROYO
Arroyo, Fernando b: 3/21/52, Sacramento, Cal. BR/TR, 6'3", 195 lbs. Deb: 6/28/75

YEAR	TM/L	W	L	PCT	G	GS	CG	SH	SV	IP	H	HR	BB	SO	RAT	ERA	ERA+	OAV	OOB	BH	AVG	PB	PR	/A	PD	TPI
1975	Det-A	2	1	.667	14	2	1	0	0	53¹	56	5	22	25	13.3	4.56	88	.272	.345	0	—	0	-5	-3	1	-0.1
1977	Det-A	8	18	.308	38	28	8	1	0	209¹	227	23	52	60	12.0	4.17	103	.278	.321	0	—	0	-3	3	6	0.6
1978	Det-A	0	0	—	2	0	0	0	0	4¹	8	1	0	1	18.7	8.31	47	.400	.429	0	—	0	-2	-2	-0	-0.1
1979	Det-A	1	1	.500	6	0	0	0	0	12	17	3	4	7	15.8	8.25	52	.340	.389	0	—	0	-5	-5	0	-0.8
1980	Min-A	6	6	.500	21	11	1	1	0	92¹	97	7	32	27	12.8	4.68	93	.273	.337	0	—	0	-7	-3	-1	-1.0
1981	Min-A	7	10	.412	23	19	2	0	0	128¹	144	11	34	39	12.8	3.93	100	.290	.342	0	—	0	-4	0	0	-0.3
1982	Min-A	0	1	.000	6	0	0	0	0	13²	17	2	6	4	15.1	5.27	81	.321	.390	0	—	0	-2	-2	1	-0.2
	Oak-A	0	0	—	10	0	0	0	0	22¹	23	4	7	9	12.5	5.24	75	.271	.333	0	—	0	-3	-3	0	0.3
	Yr	0	1	.000	16	0	0	0	0	36	40	6	13	13	13.5	5.25	77	.288	.353	0	—	0	-5	-5	1	0.1
1986	Oak-A	0	0	—	1	0	0	0	0	1	0	0	3	0	—	—	—	—	1.000	0	—	0	0	0	0	0.5
Total	8	24	37	.393	121	60	12	2	0	535²	589	56	160	172	12.8	4.44	94	.283	.337	0	—	0	-30	-16	7	-1.1

● LUIS ARROYO
Arroyo, Luis Enrique b: 2/18/27, Penuelas, P.R. BL/TL, 5'8", 190 lbs. Deb: 4/20/55

YEAR	TM/L	W	L	PCT	G	GS	CG	SH	SV	IP	H	HR	BB	SO	RAT	ERA	ERA+	OAV	OOB	BH	AVG	PB	PR	/A	PD	TPI
1955	StL-N☆	11	8	.579	35	24	9	1	0	159	162	22	63	68	12.8	4.19	97	.261	.331	13	.232	1	-3	-2	-2	-0.4
1956	Pit-N	3	3	.500	18	2	1	0	0	28²	36	5	12	17	15.1	4.71	80	.298	.361	2	.500	1	-3	-3	0	-0.5
1957	Pit-N	3	11	.214	54	10	0	0	1	130²	151	19	31	101	13.0	4.68	81	.282	.329	5	.156	-1	-12	-13	-2	-1.5
:959	Cin-N	1	0	1.000	10	0	0	0	0	13²	17	0	11	8	18.4	3.95	103	.321	.438	0	.000	-0	-0	0	0	0.0
1960	*NY-A	5	1	.833	29	0	0	0	7	40²	30	2	22	29	11.5	2.88	125	.207	.311	0	.000	-0	5	3	0	0.0
1961	*NY-A☆	15	5	.750	65	0	0	0	29	119	83	5	49	87	10.2	2.19	169	.199	.288	7	.280	2	24	20	-1	4.3
1962	NY-A	1	3	.250	27	0	0	0	7	33²	33	5	17	21	13.6	4.81	78	.262	.354	2	.500	1	-3	-4	-1	-0.6
1963	NY-A	1	1	.500	6	0	0	0	0	6	12	0	3	5	22.5	13.50	26	.444	.500	0	—	0	-7	-7	-0	-1.8
Total	8	40	32	.556	244	36	10	1	44	531¹	524	58	208	336	12.6	3.93	98	.256	.329	29	.227	2	2	-5	-5	0.0

● RUDY ARROYO
Arroyo, Rudolph b: 6/19/50, New York, N.Y. BL/TL, 6'2", 195 lbs. Deb: 6/1/71

YEAR	TM/L	W	L	PCT	G	GS	CG	SH	SV	IP	H	HR	BB	SO	RAT	ERA	ERA+	OAV	OOB	BH	AVG	PB	PR	/A	PD	TPI
1971	StL-N	0	1	.000	9	0	0	0	0	11²	18	2	5	5	17.7	5.40	67	.375	.434	0	.000	-0	-3	-2	-0	-0.2

● HARRY ARUNDEL
Arundel, Harry b: 2/1855, Philadelphia, Pa. d: 3/25/04, Cleveland, Ohio TR, 5'6", 145 lbs. Deb: 7/19/1875

YEAR	TM/L	W	L	PCT	G	GS	CG	SH	SV	IP	H	HR	BB	SO	RAT	ERA	ERA+	OAV	OOB	BH	AVG	PB	PR	/A	PD	TPI
1875	Atl-n	0	1	.000	1	1	0	0	0	1¹	6	0	1	0	47.3	13.50	17	.429	.467	0	.000	-1	-2	-2		-0.7
1882	Pit-a	4	10	.286	14	14	13	0	0	120	155	3	23	47	13.4	4.65	56	.293	.323	10	.189	0	-26	-27	5	-2.0
1884	Pro-N	1	0	1.000	1	1	1	0	0	9	8	0	4	4	12.0	1.00	282	.250	.333	1	.333	0	2	2	-0	0.2
Total	2	5	10	.333	15	15	14	0	0	129	163	3	27	51	13.3	4.40	60	.291	.324	11	.196	0	-24	-25	5	-1.8

● KEN ASH
Ash, Kenneth Lowther b: 9/16/01, Anmoore, W.Va. d: 11/15/79, Clarksburg, W.Va. BR/TR, 5'11", 165 lbs. Deb: 4/17/25

YEAR	TM/L	W	L	PCT	G	GS	CG	SH	SV	IP	H	HR	BB	SO	RAT	ERA	ERA+	OAV	OOB	BH	AVG	PB	PR	/A	PD	TPI
1925	Chi-A	0	0	—	2	0	0	0	0	4	7	2	0	0	15.8	9.00	46	.389	.389	0	—	0	-2	-2	-0	0.0
1928	Cin-N	3	3	.500	8	5	2	0	0	36	43	1	13	6	14.3	6.50	61	.314	.377	1	.071	-1	-10	-10	0	-1.4
1929	Cin-N	1	5	.167	29	7	2	0	2	82	91	2	30	26	13.8	4.83	95	.292	.363	3	.143	-1	-1	-2	-0	-0.3
1930	Cin-N	2	0	1.000	16	1	1	0	0	39¹	37	1	16	15	12.1	3.43	141	.268	.344	2	.182	-1	7	6	1	0.3
Total	4	6	8	.429	55	13	5	0	2	161¹	178	6	59	47	13.6	4.96	90	.294	.363	6	.130	-3	-6	-9	1	-1.4

● ANDY ASHBY
Ashby, Andrew Jason b: 7/11/67, Kansas City, Mo. BR/TR, 6'5", 180 lbs. Deb: 6/10/91

YEAR	TM/L	W	L	PCT	G	GS	CG	SH	SV	IP	H	HR	BB	SO	RAT	ERA	ERA+	OAV	OOB	BH	AVG	PB	PR	/A	PD	TPI
1991	Phi-N	1	5	.167	8	8	0	0	0	42	41	5	19	26	13.5	6.00	61	.256	.346	1	.083	-1	-11	-11	0	-1.4
1992	Phi-N	1	3	.250	10	8	0	0	0	37	42	6	21	24	15.6	7.54	46	.290	.383	1	.091	-0	-17	-17	0	-1.6
1993	Col-N	0	4	.000	20	9	0	0	1	54	89	6	32	33	20.7	8.50	56	.377	.458	4	.267	-1	-27	-22	1	-1.4
	SD-N	3	6	.333	12	12	0	0	0	69	79	14	24	44	13.6	5.48	75	.295	.355	1	.048	-1	-11	-10	-1	-1.2
	Yr	3	10	.231	32	21	0	0	1	123	168	19	56	77	16.5	6.80	65	.329	.397	5	.139	-1	-38	-33	1	-2.6
1994	SD-N	6	11	.353	24	24	4	0	1	164¹	145	16	43	121	10.5	3.40	124	.233	.286	8	.163	-1	15	15	0	1.4
Total	4	11	29	.275	74	61	4	0	1	366¹	396	46	139	248	13.4	5.26	79	.277	.345	15	.139	-2	-50	-46	1	-4.2

● PAUL ASSENMACHER
Assenmacher, Paul Andre b: 12/10/60, Detroit, Mich. BL/TL, 6'3", 195 lbs. Deb: 4/12/86

YEAR	TM/L	W	L	PCT	G	GS	CG	SH	SV	IP	H	HR	BB	SO	RAT	ERA	ERA+	OAV	OOB	BH	AVG	PB	PR	/A	PD	TPI
1986	Atl-N	7	3	.700	61	0	0	0	7	68¹	61	5	26	56	11.5	2.50	159	.241	.312	0	.000	-0	9	11	1	2.0
1987	Atl-N	1	1	.500	52	0	0	0	2	54²	58	8	24	39	13.7	5.10	85	.260	.335	0	.000	-0	-6	-5	-1	-0.3
1988	Atl-N	8	7	.533	64	0	0	0	5	79¹	72	4	32	71	11.9	3.06	120	.251	.328	1	.333	1	3	5	0	1.2
1989	Atl-N	1	3	.250	49	0	0	0	0	57²	55	7	16	64	11.2	3.59	102	.249	.303	0	.000	-0	-1	0	0	0.0
	*Chi-N	2	1	.667	14	0	0	0	0	19	19	1	12	15	14.7	5.21	72	.275	.383	0	.000	-0	-4	-3	0	-0.5
	Yr	3	4	.429	63	0	0	0	0	76²	74	3	28	79	12.0	3.99	92	.253	.318	0	.000	-0	-4	-3	0	-0.5
1990	Chi-N	7	2	.778	74	1	0	0	10	103	90	6	36	95	11.1	2.80	146	.239	.308	0	.000	-1	11	15	1	1.5
1991	Chi-N	7	8	.467	75	0	0	0	15	102²	85	9	31	117	10.4	3.24	120	.223	.287	1	.250	1	5	7	-1	1.2
1992	Chi-N	4	4	.500	70	0	0	0	8	68	72	6	26	67	13.4	4.10	88	.271	.342	0	.000	-0	-5	-4	-0	-0.6
1993	Chi-N	2	1	.667	46	0	0	0	0	38²	44	5	13	34	13.3	3.49	114	.288	.343	1	.500	2	2	-0	1	0.1

YEAR	TM/L	W	L	PCT	G	GS	CG	SH	SV	IP	H	HR	BB	SO	RAT	ERA	ERA+	OAV	OOB	BH	AVG	PB	PR	/A	PD	TPI
	NY-A	2	2	.500	26	0	0	0	0	17¹	10	0	9	11	10.4	3.12	133	.175	.299	0	—	0	2	2	-0	0.4
1994	Chi-A	1	2	.333	44	0	0	0	1	33	26	2	13	29	10.9	3.55	132	.224	.308	0	—	0	5	4	0	0.4
Total	9	42	34	.553	575	1	0	0	48	641²	592	53	238	598	11.8	3.44	115	.246	.317	3	.083	-0	23	36	0	5.4

● PEDRO ASTACIO
Astacio, Pedro Julio (Pura) b: 11/28/69, Hato Mayor, D.R.   BR/TR, 6'2", 174 lbs.   Deb: 7/3/92

YEAR	TM/L	W	L	PCT	G	GS	CG	SH	SV	IP	H	HR	BB	SO	RAT	ERA	ERA+	OAV	OOB	BH	AVG	PB	PR	/A	PD	TPI
1992	LA-N	5	5	.500	11	11	4	4	0	82	80	1	20	43	11.2	1.98	174	.255	.304	3	.125	-1	14	13	-0	1.6
1993	LA-N	14	9	.609	31	31	3	2	0	186¹	165	14	68	122	11.5	3.57	107	.239	.312	10	.161	-1	10	5	-1	0.3
1994	LA-N	6	8	.429	23	23	3	1	0	149	142	18	47	108	11.7	4.29	92	.252	.314	3	.064	-3	-1	-6	-1	-0.8
Total	3	25	22	.532	65	65	10	7	0	417¹	387	33	135	273	11.5	3.52	108	.247	.311	16	.120	-5	22	13	-2	1.1

● KEITH ATHERTON
Atherton, Keith Rowe b: 2/19/59, Mathews, Va.   BR/TR, 6'4", 200 lbs.   Deb: 7/14/83

YEAR	TM/L	W	L	PCT	G	GS	CG	SH	SV	IP	H	HR	BB	SO	RAT	ERA	ERA+	OAV	OOB	BH	AVG	PB	PR	/A	PD	TPI
1983	Oak-A	2	5	.286	29	0	0	0	4	68¹	53	7	23	40	10.1	2.77	139	.215	.285	0	.000	0	10	8	-1	0.8
1984	Oak-A	7	6	.538	57	0	0	0	2	104	110	13	39	58	13.1	4.33	86	.274	.341	0	—	0	-4	-7	-2	-1.0
1985	Oak-A	4	7	.364	56	0	0	0	3	104²	89	17	42	77	11.3	4.30	90	.231	.306	0	—	0	-2	-5	-2	-0.2
1986	Oak-A	1	2	.333	13	0	0	0	0	15¹	18	2	11	8	17.0	5.87	66	.295	.403	0	—	0	-3	-3	-0	-0.2
	Min-A	5	8	.385	47	0	0	0	10	81²	82	9	35	59	13.0	3.75	115	.264	.340	0	—	0	4	5	-0	0.7
	Yr	6	10	.375	60	0	0	0	10	97	100	11	46	67	13.6	4.08	104	.267	.349	0	—	0	1	2	-0	0.5
1987	*Min-A	7	5	.583	59	0	0	0	2	79¹	81	10	30	51	13.0	4.54	102	.262	.335	0	—	0	-1	-1	-0	0.1
1988	Min-A	7	5	.583	49	0	0	0	3	74	65	10	22	43	10.8	3.41	119	.235	.296	0	—	0	5	5	-0	0.7
1989	Cle-A	0	3	.000	32	0	0	0	0	39	48	7	13	14	14.1	4.15	95	.293	.345	0	—	0	-1	-1	-1	-0.2
Total	7	33	41	.446	342	0	0	0	26	566¹	546	75	215	349	12.3	3.99	101	.253	.324	0	.000	0	8	3	-6	0.6

● TOMMY ATKINS
Atkins, Francis Montgomery b: 12/9/1887, Ponca, Neb.   d: 5/7/56, Cleveland, Ohio   BL/TL, 5'10.5", 165 lbs.   Deb: 10/2/09

YEAR	TM/L	W	L	PCT	G	GS	CG	SH	SV	IP	H	HR	BB	SO	RAT	ERA	ERA+	OAV	OOB	BH	AVG	PB	PR	/A	PD	TPI
1909	Phi-A	0	0	—	1	1	0	0	0	6	6	0	5	4	16.5	4.50	53	.261	.393	0	.000	0	-1	-1	0	-0.1
1910	Phi-A	3	2	.600	15	3	2	0	2	57	53	0	23	29	12.2	2.68	88	.254	.330	2	.118	-1	-1	-2	0	-0.3
Total	2	3	2	.600	16	4	2	0	2	63	59	0	28	33	12.6	2.86	83	.254	.337	2	.105	-1	-2	-3	0	-0.3

● JAMES ATKINS
Atkins, James Curtis b: 3/10/21, Birmingham, Ala.   BL/TR, 6'3", 205 lbs.   Deb: 9/29/50

YEAR	TM/L	W	L	PCT	G	GS	CG	SH	SV	IP	H	HR	BB	SO	RAT	ERA	ERA+	OAV	OOB	BH	AVG	PB	PR	/A	PD	TPI
1950	Bos-A	0	0	—	1	0	0	0	0	4²	4	1	4	0	17.4	3.86	127	.235	.409	0	.000	-0	0	1	-0	0.0
1952	Bos-A	0	1	.000	3	1	0	0	0	10¹	11	0	7	2	15.7	3.48	113	.275	.383	2	.667	1	0	1	0	0.1
Total	2	0	1	.000	4	1	0	0	0	15	15	1	11	2	16.2	3.60	118	.263	.391	2	.400	0	1	1	0	0.1

● AL ATKINSON
Atkinson, Albert Wright b: 3/9/1861, Clinton, Ill.   d: 6/17/52, Elkhorn Township, Mo.   BR/TR, 5'11.5", 165 lbs.   Deb: 5/1/1884

YEAR	TM/L	W	L	PCT	G	GS	CG	SH	SV	IP	H	HR	BB	SO	RAT	ERA	ERA+	OAV	OOB	BH	AVG	PB	PR	/A	PD	TPI
1884	Phi-a	11	11	.500	22	22	20	1	0	184	180	3	41	93	10.6	4.21	80	.244	.274	16	.193	-1	-20	-17	0	-1.7
	CP-U	6	10	.375	16	16	16	1	0	140	127	1	21	104	9.5	2.76	88	.226	.254	14	.206	-5	-5	-5	1	-0.9
	Bal-U	3	5	.375	8	8	8	1	0	69²	60	4	12	50	9.3	2.33	115	.217	.249	4	.138	-4	1	3	0	-0.1
	Yr	9	15	.375	24	24	24	1	0	209²	187	5	33	154	9.4	2.62	96	.223	.252	18	.186	-9	-4	-2	1	-1.0
1886	Phi-a	25	17	.595	45	45	44	1	0	396²	414	11	101	154	12.2	3.95	89	.256	.308	18	.122	-6	-22	-20	-2	-2.4
1887	Phi-a	6	8	.429	15	15	11	0	0	124²	156	2	54	34	15.6	5.92	72	.292	.364	12	.203	-1	-22	-23	1	-1.8
Total	3	51	51	.500	106	106	99	3	0	915	943	21	209	435	11.7	3.96	85	.251	.297	64	.165	-16	-68	-61	-1	-6.9

● BILL ATKINSON
Atkinson, William Cecil Glenn b: 10/4/54, Chatham, Ont., Can.   BL/TR, 5'7", 165 lbs.   Deb: 9/18/76

YEAR	TM/L	W	L	PCT	G	GS	CG	SH	SV	IP	H	HR	BB	SO	RAT	ERA	ERA+	OAV	OOB	BH	AVG	PB	PR	/A	PD	TPI
1976	Mon-N	0	0	—	4	0	0	0	0	5	3	0	1	4	7.2	0.00	—	.176	.222	0	—	0	2	2	0	0.0
1977	Mon-N	7	2	.778	55	0	0	0	7	83¹	72	12	29	56	10.9	3.35	114	.234	.300	1	.200	-0	5	4	1	0.6
1978	Mon-N	2	2	.500	29	0	0	0	3	45¹	45	5	28	32	14.7	4.37	81	.268	.376	2	.500	1	-4	-4	0	-0.3
1979	Mon-N	2	0	1.000	10	0	0	0	1	13²	9	0	4	7	8.6	1.98	186	.170	.228	0	.000	-0	3	3	-0	0.3
Total	4	11	4	.733	98	0	0	0	11	147¹	129	17	62	99	11.7	3.42	108	.236	.315	3	.300	1	6	5	1	0.6

● DON AUGUST
August, Donald Glenn b: 7/3/63, Inglewood, Cal.   BR/TR, 6'3", 190 lbs.   Deb: 6/2/88

YEAR	TM/L	W	L	PCT	G	GS	CG	SH	SV	IP	H	HR	BB	SO	RAT	ERA	ERA+	OAV	OOB	BH	AVG	PB	PR	/A	PD	TPI
1988	Mil-A	13	7	.650	24	22	6	1	0	148¹	137	12	48	66	11.2	3.09	129	.245	.305	0	—	0	14	15	2	2.1
1989	Mil-A	12	12	.500	31	25	2	1	0	142¹	175	17	58	51	14.9	5.31	72	.302	.368	0	—	0	-23	-23	-1	-3.3
1990	Mil-A	0	3	.000	5	0	0	0	0	11	13	0	4	3	14.7	6.55	59	.295	.367	0	—	0	-3	-3	-0	-0.7
1991	Mil-A	9	8	.529	28	23	1	1	0	138¹	166	18	47	62	14.1	5.47	73	.301	.359	0	—	0	-21	-23	-0	-2.3
Total	4	34	30	.531	88	70	9	3	0	440	491	47	158	181	13.4	4.64	85	.283	.345	0	—	0	-33	-35	4	-4.2

● JERRY AUGUSTINE
Augustine, Gerald Lee b: 7/24/52, Kewaunee, Wis.   BL/TL, 6', 185 lbs.   Deb: 9/9/75

YEAR	TM/L	W	L	PCT	G	GS	CG	SH	SV	IP	H	HR	BB	SO	RAT	ERA	ERA+	OAV	OOB	BH	AVG	PB	PR	/A	PD	TPI
1975	Mil-A	2	0	1.000	5	3	1	0	0	26²	24	2	12	8	13.2	3.04	126	.274	.361	0	—	0	2	2	-0	0.1
1976	Mil-A	9	12	.429	39	24	5	3	0	171²	167	9	56	59	11.9	3.30	106	.261	.324	0	—	0	4	4	-2	0.3
1977	Mil-A	12	18	.400	33	33	10	1	0	209	222	23	72	68	12.8	4.48	91	.277	.339	0	—	0	-10	-10	-1	-1.2
1978	Mil-A	13	12	.520	35	30	9	2	0	188¹	204	14	61	59	12.9	4.54	83	.280	.339	0	—	0	-16	-16	2	-1.7
1979	Mil-A	9	6	.600	43	2	0	0	5	85²	95	6	30	41	13.2	3.47	120	.284	.344	0	—	0	7	7	-2	1.0
1980	Mil-A	4	3	.571	39	1	0	0	2	69²	83	5	36	22	15.6	4.52	86	.301	.385	0	—	0	-4	-5	-0	-0.4
1981	Mil-A	2	2	.500	27	2	0	0	2	61¹	75	4	18	26	13.8	4.26	80	.300	.349	0	—	0	-4	-6	-1	-0.3
1982	Mil-A	1	3	.250	20	2	1	0	0	62	63	13	26	22	13.2	5.08	74	.267	.345	0	—	0	-7	-9	-1	-0.2
1983	Mil-A	3	3	.500	34	7	1	0	2	64¹	89	11	25	40	16.1	5.74	65	.328	.387	0	—	0	-12	-14	-0	-1.3
1984	Mil-A	0	0	—	4	0	0	0	0	5¹	4	0	4	3	15.2	0.00	—	.211	.375	0	—	0	2	2	0	0.2
Total	10	55	59	.482	279	104	27	6	11	944	1028	87	340	348	13.2	4.23	90	.281	.346	0	—	0	-37	-45	-3	-3.7

● ELDON AUKER
Auker, Eldon Le Roy "Submarine" b: 9/21/10, Norcatur, Kan.   BR/TR, 6'2", 194 lbs.   Deb: 8/10/33

YEAR	TM/L	W	L	PCT	G	GS	CG	SH	SV	IP	H	HR	BB	SO	RAT	ERA	ERA+	OAV	OOB	BH	AVG	PB	PR	/A	PD	TPI
1933	Det-A	3	3	.500	15	6	2	1	0	55	55	3	25	17	14.7	5.24	82	.285	.363	2	.118	-1	-6	-6	-1	-0.7
1934	*Det-A	15	7	.682	43	18	10	2	1	205	234	3	56	86	12.9	3.42	128	.288	.336	11	.149	-2	24	22	3	2.1
1935	*Det-A	18	7	**.720**	36	25	13	2	0	195	213	13	61	63	13.1	3.83	109	.279	.340	16	.216	1	14	7	1	1.0
1936	Det-A	13	16	.448	35	31	14	2	0	215¹	263	11	83	66	14.6	4.89	101	.302	.365	24	.308	7	4	1	5	1.2
1937	Det-A	17	9	.654	39	32	19	1	1	252²	250	13	97	73	12.6	3.88	120	.260	.351	18	.198	4	21	22	5	2.9
1938	Det-A	11	10	.524	27	24	12	1	0	160²	184	14	56	46	13.7	5.27	95	.284	.346	5	.088	-4	-9	-5	3	-0.8
1939	Bos-A	9	10	.474	31	25	6	1	0	151	183	13	61	43	14.6	5.36	88	.294	.358	12	.226	2	-12	-11	2	-0.8
1940	StL-A	16	11	.593	38	35	20	2	0	263²	299	17	96	78	13.6	3.96	116	.281	.342	19	.213	3	12	18	2	2.1
1941	StL-A	14	15	.483	34	33	15	2	0	216	268	20	85	60	14.6	5.50	78	.303	.365	10	.125	-3	-32	-29	1	-3.3
1942	StL-A	14	13	.519	35	34	17	2	0	249	273	16	86	62	13.1	4.08	91	.277	.337	14	.161	-1	-12	-11	-1	-1.1
Total	10	130	101	.563	333	261	126	14	2	1963²	2230	129	706	594	13.6	4.42	101	.285	.347	131	.187	6	3	11	21	2.8

● JOE AUSANIO
Ausanio, Joseph John b: 12/9/65, Kingston, N.Y.   BR/TR, 6'1", 205 lbs.   Deb: 7/14/94

YEAR	TM/L	W	L	PCT	G	GS	CG	SH	SV	IP	H	HR	BB	SO	RAT	ERA	ERA+	OAV	OOB	BH	AVG	PB	PR	/A	PD	TPI
1994	NY-A	2	1	.667	13	0	0	0	0	15²	16	3	6	15	12.6	5.17	86	.254	.319	0	—	0	-1	-1	0	0.0

● DENNIS AUST
Aust, Dennis Kay b: 11/25/40, Tecumseh, Neb.   BR/TR, 5'11", 180 lbs.   Deb: 9/6/65

YEAR	TM/L	W	L	PCT	G	GS	CG	SH	SV	IP	H	HR	BB	SO	RAT	ERA	ERA+	OAV	OOB	BH	AVG	PB	PR	/A	PD	TPI
1965	StL-N	0	0	—	6	0	0	0	1	7¹	6	0	2	7	9.8	4.91	78	.214	.267	0	.000	-0	-1	-1	0	0.0
1966	StL-N	0	1	.000	9	0	0	0	1	9²	12	1	6	7	16.8	6.52	55	.308	.400	0	.000	-0	-3	-3	-0	-0.4
Total	2	0	1	.000	15	0	0	0	2	17	18	1	8	14	13.8	5.82	64	.269	.347	0	.000	-0	-4	-4	0	-0.4

● JIM AUSTIN
Austin, James Parker b: 12/7/63, Farmville, Va.   BR/TR, 6'2", 200 lbs.   Deb: 7/4/91

YEAR	TM/L	W	L	PCT	G	GS	CG	SH	SV	IP	H	HR	BB	SO	RAT	ERA	ERA+	OAV	OOB	BH	AVG	PB	PR	/A	PD	TPI
1991	Mil-A	0	0	—	5	0	0	0	0	8²	8	1	11	3	22.8	8.31	48	.276	.512	0	—	0	-4	-4	0	0.1
1992	Mil-A	5	2	.714	47	0	0	0	0	58¹	38	2	32	30	11.1	1.85	207	.191	.309	0	—	0	14	13	-1	1.5
1993	Mil-A	1	2	.333	31	0	0	0	0	33	28	3	13	15	11.5	3.82	111	.230	.309	0	—	0	2	2	0	0.1
Total	3	6	4	.600	83	0	0	0	0	100	74	6	56	48	12.2	3.06	130	.211	.330	0	—	0	11	10	-1	1.7

YEAR	TM/L	W	L	PCT	G	GS	CG	SH	SV	IP	H	HR	BB	SO	RAT	ERA	ERA+	OAV	OOB	BH	AVG	PB	PR	/A	PD	TPI

● **RICK AUSTIN**　　Austin, Rick Gerald　b: 10/27/46, Seattle, Was.　BR/TL, 6'4", 190 lbs.　Deb: 6/21/70

1970	Cle-A	2	5	.286	31	8	1	1	3	67²	74	10	26	53	13.7	4.79	83	.281	.353	2	.111	0	-8	-6	1	-0.5
1971	Cle-A	0	0	—	23	0	0	0	1	23	25	3	20	20	18.8	5.09	75	.291	.440	0	.000	-0	-4	-3	0	0.0
1975	Mil-A	2	3	.400	32	0	0	0	2	40	32	3	32	30	14.6	4.05	95	.222	.367	0	—	0	-1	-1	-1	-0.2
1976	Mil-A	0	0	—	3	0	0	0	0	5¹	10	1	0	3	18.6	5.06	69	.435	.458	0	—	0	-1	-1	0	0.0
Total	4	4	8	.333	89	8	1	1	6	136	141	17	78	106	15.0	4.63	84	.273	.377	2	.105	0	-14	-11	1	-0.7

● **AL AUTRY**　　Autry, Albert　b: 2/29/52, Modesto, Cal.　BR/TR, 6'5", 225 lbs.　Deb: 9/14/76

| 1976 | Atl-N | 1 | 0 | 1.000 | 1 | 1 | 0 | 0 | 0 | 5 | 4 | 2 | 3 | 3 | 12.6 | 5.40 | 70 | .222 | .333 | 0 | .000 | -0 | -1 | -1 | -0 | -0.2 |

● **STEVE AVERY**　　Avery, Steven Thomas　b: 4/14/70, Trenton, Mich.　BL/TL, 6'4", 180 lbs.　Deb: 6/13/90

1990	Atl-N	3	11	.214	21	20	1	1	0	99	121	7	45	75	15.3	5.64	72	.302	.375	4	.133	-1	-20	-18	2	-2.1
1991	*Atl-N	18	8	.692	35	35	3	1	0	210¹	189	21	65	137	11.0	3.38	115	.240	.300	17	.215	3	7	12	-0	1.8
1992	*Atl-N	11	11	.500	35	35	2	2	0	233²	216	14	71	129	11.1	3.20	114	.246	.302	13	.171	2	8	12	-0	1.2
1993	*Atl-N★	18	6	.750	35	35	3	1	0	223¹	216	14	43	125	10.4	2.94	136	.261	.297	12	.160	1	27	27	2	2.9
1994	Atl-N	8	3	.727	24	24	1	0	0	151²	127	15	55	122	11.0	4.04	103	.227	.301	5	.102	-2	3	2	0	0.0
Total	5	58	39	.598	150	149	10	5	0	918	869	71	279	588	11.3	3.58	110	.252	.309	51	.165	3	25	35	4	3.8

● **JAY AVREA**　　Avrea, James Epherium　b: 7/6/20, Cleburne, Tex.　d: 6/26/87, Dallas, Tex.　BR/TR, 6'1.5", 175 lbs.　Deb: 4/22/50

| 1950 | Cin-N | 0 | 0 | — | 2 | 0 | 0 | 0 | 0 | 5¹ | 6 | 0 | 3 | 2 | 15.2 | 3.38 | 125 | .273 | .360 | 0 | .000 | -0 | 1 | 1 | -0 | 0.0 |

● **BOBBY AYALA**　　Ayala, Robert Joseph　b: 7/8/69, Ventura, Cal.　BR/TR, 6'2", 190 lbs.　Deb: 9/5/92

1992	Cin-N	2	1	.667	5	5	0	0	0	29	33	1	13	23	14.6	4.34	83	.297	.376	0	—	-1	-3	-2	1	-0.2
1993	Cin-N	7	10	.412	43	9	0	0	3	98	106	16	45	65	14.5	5.60	72	.274	.360	2	.095	-1	-17	-17	-1	-2.9
1994	Sea-A	4	3	.571	46	0	0	0	18	56²	42	2	26	76	10.8	2.86	172	.203	.292	0	—	0	12	13	0	2.2
Total	3	13	14	.481	94	14	0	0	21	183²	181	19	84	164	13.4	4.56	93	.257	.343	2	.067	-2	-7	-7	-0	-0.9

● **JAKE AYDELOTT**　　Aydelott, Jacob Stuart　b: 7/6/1861, N.Manchester, Ind.　d: 10/22/26, Detroit, Mich.　6', 180 lbs.　Deb: 5/15/1884

1884	Ind-a	5	7	.417	12	12	11	0	0	106	129	6	29	30	13.4	4.92	67	.282	.324	5	.114	-3	-20	-19	-2	-2.0
1886	Phi-a	0	2	.000	2	2	2	0	0	18	21	0	12	5	16.5	4.00	88	.304	.407	0	.000	-1	-1	-1	-0	-0.2
Total	2	5	9	.357	14	14	13	0	0	124	150	0	41	35	13.9	4.79	69	.285	.336	5	.100	-4	-21	-20	-2	-2.2

● **BILL AYERS**　　Ayers, William Oscar　b: 9/27/19, Newnan, Ga.　d: 9/24/80, Newnan, Ga.　BR/TR, 6'3", 185 lbs.　Deb: 4/17/47

| 1947 | NY-N | 0 | 3 | .000 | 13 | 4 | 0 | 0 | 1 | 35¹ | 46 | 7 | 14 | 22 | 15.5 | 8.15 | 50 | .322 | .386 | 2 | .250 | 0 | -16 | -16 | 1 | -1.2 |

● **DOC AYERS**　　Ayers, Yancy Wyatt　b: 5/20/1890, Fancy Gap, Va.　d: 5/26/68, Pulaski, Va.　BR/TR, 6'1", 185 lbs.　Deb: 9/9/13

1913	Was-A	1	1	.500	4	2	1	1	1	17²	12	0	4	17	8.7	1.53	193	.182	.239	0	.000	-1	3	3	1	0.3
1914	Was-A	12	15	.444	49	32	8	3	3	265¹	221	5	54	148	9.6	2.54	111	.238	.286	14	.169	-0	6	8	-2	0.6
1915	Was-A	14	9	.609	40	16	8	2	3	211¹	178	1	38	96	9.5	2.21	134	.234	.276	12	.190	-1	17	18	-4	1.2
1916	Was-A	5	9	.357	43	17	7	0	2	157	173	4	52	69	13.1	3.78	74	.285	.346	6	.140	-2	-17	-17	-4	-2.2
1917	Was-A	11	10	.524	40	15	12	3	1	207²	192	3	59	78	11.2	2.17	121	.256	.317	13	.206	-0	11	11	-1	1.0
1918	Was-A	10	12	.455	40	24	11	4	3	219²	215	2	63	67	11.7	2.83	96	.261	.319	10	.152	-2	-1	-2	-0	-0.5
1919	Was-A	0	6	.000	11	5	0	0	1	43²	52	0	17	12	15.0	2.89	111	.317	.395	5	.417	2	2	2	1	0.4
	Det-A	5	3	.625	24	5	3	1	0	93²	88	2	31	32	11.7	2.69	119	.254	.320	3	.125	-1	6	5	-0	0.3
	Yr	5	9	.357	35	10	3	1	1	137¹	140	2	48	44	12.5	2.75	116	.272	.337	8	.222	0	7	7	0	0.7
1920	Det-A	7	14	.333	46	23	8	3	1	208²	217	6	62	103	12.4	3.88	96	.280	.340	9	.153	-2	-2	-4	-0	-0.6
1921	Det-A	0	0	—	2	1	0	0	0	4	9	0	2	0	24.8	9.00	47	.450	.500	0	—	0	-2	-2	-0	0.0
Total	9	65	79	.451	299	140	58	17	15	1428²	1357	23	382	622	11.3	2.84	105	.259	.315	72	.171	-8	22	21	-10	0.5

● **BOB AYRAULT**　　Ayrault, Robert Cunningham　b: 4/27/66, South Lake Tahoe, Cal.　BR/TR, 6'4", 230 lbs.　Deb: 6/7/92

1992	Phi-N	2	2	.500	30	0	0	0	0	43¹	32	0	17	27	10.4	3.12	112	.209	.292	0	—	0	2	2	0	0.2
1993	Phi-N	2	0	1.000	10	0	0	0	0	10¹	18	1	10	8	25.3	9.58	41	.375	.492	0	.000	-0	-6	-6	-0	-1.1
	Sea-A	1	1	.500	14	0	0	0	0	19²	18	1	6	7	11.0	3.20	137	.254	.312	0	—	0	2	3	0	0.2
Total	2	5	3	.625	54	0	0	0	0	73¹	68	2	33	42	12.6	4.05	94	.250	.336	0	.000	-0	-2	-2	-0	-0.7

● **BOB BABCOCK**　　Babcock, Robert Ernest　b: 8/25/49, New Castle, Pa.　BR/TR, 6'5", 210 lbs.　Deb: 7/22/79

1979	Tex-A	0	0	—	4	0	0	0	0	5¹	7	1	7	6	23.6	10.13	41	.318	.483	0	—	0	-4	-4	0	0.0
1980	Tex-A	1	2	.333	19	0	0	0	0	23¹	20	3	8	15	11.6	4.63	84	.238	.319	0	—	0	-2	-2	-0	-0.2
1981	Tex-A	1	1	.500	16	0	0	0	0	28²	21	2	16	18	11.9	2.20	158	.219	.336	0	—	0	5	4	-0	0.3
Total	3	2	3	.400	39	0	0	0	0	57¹	48	6	31	39	12.9	3.92	94	.238	.347	0	—	0	-0	-1	-0	0.1

● **JOHNNY BABICH**　　Babich, John Charles　b: 5/14/13, Albion, Cal.　BR/TR, 6'1.5", 185 lbs.　Deb: 6/19/34

1934	Bro-N	7	11	.389	25	19	7	0	1	135	148	5	51	62	13.4	4.20	93	.281	.347	7	.140	-3	-2	-4	2	-0.6
1935	Bro-N	7	14	.333	37	24	7	2	0	143¹	191	7	52	55	15.4	6.66	60	.317	.373	9	.184	-0	-42	-43	0	-5.1
1936	Bos-N	0	0	—	3	0	0	0	0	6	11	1	6	1	27.0	10.50	37	.440	.563	0	.000	-0	-4	-4	0	0.0
1940	Phi-A	14	13	.519	31	30	16	1	0	229¹	222	16	80	94	11.9	3.73	119	.248	.310	10	.116	-6	17	18	0	1.4
1941	Phi-A	2	7	.222	16	14	4	0	0	78¹	85	9	31	19	13.7	6.09	69	.281	.353	10	.400	4	-17	-17	1	-1.1
Total	5	30	45	.400	112	87	34	3	1	592	657	38	220	231	13.5	4.93	85	.279	.343	36	.171	-5	-49	-50	3	-5.4

● **LES BACKMAN**　　Backman, Lester John　b: 3/20/1888, Cleves, Ohio　d: 11/8/75, Cincinnati, Ohio　BR/TR, 6'0.5", 195 lbs.　Deb: 7/3/09

1909	StL-N	3	11	.214	21	14	8	0	0	128¹	146	1	39	35	13.2	4.14	61	.302	.357	4	.103	-1	-22	-23	-0	-2.5
1910	StL-N	6	7	.462	26	11	4	0	2	116	117	4	53	41	13.3	3.03	98	.265	.346	4	.114	0	0	-1	-0	-0.1
Total	2	9	18	.333	47	25	12	0	2	244¹	263	5	92	76	13.3	3.61	76	.284	.352	8	.108	-1	-22	-24	-1	-2.6

● **EDDIE BACON**　　Bacon, Edgar Suter　b: 4/8/1895, Franklin Co., Ky.　d: 10/2/63, Louisville, Ky.　Deb: 8/13/17　◆

| 1917 | Phi-A | 0 | 0 | — | 1 | 0 | 0 | 0 | 0 | 6 | 5 | 0 | 7 | 0 | 18.0 | 6.00 | 46 | .238 | .429 | 3 | .500 | 1 | -2 | -2 | 1 | 0.3 |

● **MIKE BACSIK**　　Bacsik, Michael James　b: 4/1/52, Dallas, Tex.　BR/TR, 6'1", 185 lbs.　Deb: 6/15/75

1975	Tex-A	1	2	.333	7	3	0	0	0	26²	28	3	6	13	12.8	3.71	101	.275	.339	0	—	0	0	0	-0	0.0
1976	Tex-A	3	2	.600	23	0	0	0	0	55	66	3	26	21	15.4	4.25	84	.308	.388	0	—	0	-4	-4	-1	-0.4
1977	Tex-A	0	0	—	2	0	0	0	0	2¹	9	1	0	1	34.7	19.29	21	.563	.563	0	—	0	-4	-4	0	0.0
1979	Min-A	4	2	.667	31	0	0	0	0	65²	61	6	29	33	12.3	4.39	100	.249	.328	0	—	0	-1	-0	-0	-0.1
1980	Min-A	0	0	—	10	0	0	0	0	23	26	1	11	9	14.5	4.30	101	.286	.363	0	—	0	-1	0	-0	-0.1
Total	5	8	6	.571	73	3	0	0	0	172²	190	12	75	77	14.0	4.43	91	.284	.359	0	—	0	-10	-8	-1	-0.6

● **FRED BACZEWSKI**　　Baczewski, Frederic John "Lefty"　b: 5/15/26, St.Paul, Minn.　d: 11/14/76, Culver City, Cal.　BL/TL, 6'2.5", 185 lbs.　Deb: 4/26/53

1953	Chi-N	0	0	—	9	0	0	0	0	10	20	1	6	3	24.3	6.30	71	.435	.509	1	.500	-2	-2	-0	0.0
	Cin-N	11	4	.733	24	18	10	1	1	138¹	125	13	52	58	11.6	3.45	126	.244	.315	8	.178	-0	13	14	-3	1.1
	Yr	11	4	.733	33	18	10	1	1	148¹	145	14	58	61	12.4	3.64	120	.259	.330	9	.191	0	11	12	-3	1.1
1954	Cin-N	6	6	.500	29	22	4	1	0	130	159	22	53	43	14.7	5.26	80	.305	.370	3	.071	-3	-17	-15	-1	-1.7
1955	Cin-N	0	0	—	1	0	0	0	0	1	2	2	0	0	18.0	18.00	24	.400	.400	0	—	-2	-2	-0	0.0
Total	3	17	10	.630	63	40	14	2	1	279¹	306	38	111	104	13.5	4.45	96	.282	.351	12	.135	-3	-8	-5	-4	-0.6

● **LORE BADER**　　Bader, Lore Verne "King"　b: 4/27/1888, Bader, Ill.　d: 6/2/73, LeRoy, Kan.　BL/TR, 6', 175 lbs.　Deb: 9/30/12　C

| 1912 | NY-N | 2 | 0 | 1.000 | 2 | 1 | 1 | 0 | 0 | 10 | 9 | 0 | 6 | 3 | 14.4 | 0.90 | 376 | .250 | .372 | 0 | .000 | -0 | 3 | 3 | 0 | 0.5 |
| 1917 | Bos-A | 2 | 0 | 1.000 | 15 | 1 | 0 | 0 | 1 | 38¹ | 48 | 1 | 18 | 14 | 15.7 | 2.35 | 110 | .306 | .381 | 3 | .300 | 1 | 1 | 1 | 1 | 0.2 |

YEAR TM/L	W	L	PCT	G	GS	CG	SH	SV	IP	H	HR	BB	SO	RAT	ERA	ERA+	OAV	OOB	BH	AVG	PB	PR	/A	PD	TPI
1918 Bos-A	1	3	.250	5	4	2	1	0	27	26	1	12	10	13.7	3.33	81	.271	.369	1	.111	-1	-2	-2	-1	-0.5
Total 3	5	3	.625	22	6	3	1	1	75¹	83	2	36	27	14.8	2.51	109	.287	.376	4	.182	-0	2	2	-0	0.2

● **ED BAECHT**   Baecht, Edward Joseph b: 5/15/07, Paden, Okla. d: 8/15/57, Grafton, Ill.   BR/TR, 6'3", 195 lbs. Deb: 4/24/26

YEAR TM/L	W	L	PCT	G	GS	CG	SH	SV	IP	H	HR	BB	SO	RAT	ERA	ERA+	OAV	OOB	BH	AVG	PB	PR	/A	PD	TPI
1926 Phi-N	2	0	1.000	28	1	1	0	0	56	73	4	28	14	16.4	6.11	68	.324	.402	2	.143	-1	-14	-12	2	-0.3
1927 Phi-N	0	1	.000	1	1	0	0	0	6	12	0	2	0	21.0	12.00	34	.429	.467	0	.000	-0	-5	-5	0	-0.6
1928 Phi-N	1	1	.500	9	1	0	0	0	24	37	1	9	10	17.3	6.00	71	.385	.438	1	.143	-0	-5	-5	0	-0.3
1931 Chi-N	2	4	.333	22	6	2	0	0	67	64	1	32	34	14.0	3.76	103	.250	.351	5	.278	1	1	1	1	0.2
1932 Chi-N	0	0	—	1	0	0	0	0	1	1	0	1	0	18.0	0.00	—	.333	.500	0	—	0	0	-0	0	0.0
1937 StL-A	0	0	—	3	0	0	0	0	6¹	13	3	6	3	29.8	12.79	38	.419	.538	0	.000	-0	-6	-6	0	0.0
Total 6	5	6	.455	64	9	3	0	0	160¹	200	9	78	61	16.2	5.56	73	.313	.397	8	.190	-1	-29	-27	3	-1.0

● **JIM BAGBY**   Bagby, James Charles Jacob Jr. b: 9/8/16, Cleveland, Ohio d: 9/2/88, Marietta, Ga.   BR/TR, 6'2", 170 lbs. Deb: 4/18/38 F

YEAR TM/L	W	L	PCT	G	GS	CG	SH	SV	IP	H	HR	BB	SO	RAT	ERA	ERA+	OAV	OOB	BH	AVG	PB	PR	/A	PD	TPI
1938 Bos-A	15	11	.577	43	25	10	1	2	198²	218	9	90	73	14.1	4.21	117	.283	.360	13	.191	-1	13	16	2	1.9
1939 Bos-A	5	5	.500	21	11	3	0	0	80	119	7	36	35	17.7	7.09	67	.347	.412	10	.294	3	-22	-21	-0	-1.9
1940 Bos-A	10	16	.385	36	21	6	1	2	182²	217	15	83	57	14.8	4.73	95	.296	.368	15	.203	-0	-7	-5	0	-0.6
1941 Cle-A	9	15	.375	33	27	12	0	2	200²	214	10	76	53	13.3	4.04	98	.273	.341	18	.243	2	-2	-2	2	0.1
1942 Cle-A☆	17	9	.654	38	35	16	4	1	270²	267	19	64	54	11.0	2.96	117	.258	.302	18	.189	1	21	15	0	1.5
1943 Cle-A☆	17	14	.548	36	33	16	3	1	273	248	15	70	70	10.9	3.10	100	.240	.296	30	.268	4	6	0	2	0.9
1944 Cle-A	4	5	.444	13	10	2	0	0	79	101	2	34	12	15.8	4.33	76	.312	.384	7	.226	1	-8	-9	-0	-0.8
1945 Cle-A	8	11	.421	25	19	11	3	1	159¹	171	3	59	38	13.1	3.73	87	.279	.344	17	.293	3	-6	-8	-3	-0.3
1946 *Bos-A	7	6	.538	21	11	6	1	0	106²	117	4	49	16	14.1	3.71	99	.279	.356	5	.119	-2	-2	-1	-0	-0.3
1947 Pit-N	5	4	.556	37	6	2	0	0	115²	143	14	37	23	14.4	4.67	90	.304	.361	7	.219	1	-8	-6	1	-0.2
Total 10	97	96	.503	303	198	84	13	9	1666¹	1815	98	608	431	13.2	3.96	97	.278	.342	140	.226	12	-11	-23	10	0.3

● **JIM BAGBY**   Bagby, James Charles Jacob Sr. "Sarge" b: 10/5/1889, Barnett, Ga. d: 7/28/54, Marietta, Ga.   BB/TR, 6', 170 lbs. Deb: 4/22/12 F

YEAR TM/L	W	L	PCT	G	GS	CG	SH	SV	IP	H	HR	BB	SO	RAT	ERA	ERA+	OAV	OOB	BH	AVG	PB	PR	/A	PD	TPI
1912 Cin-N	2	1	.667	5	1	0	0	0	17¹	17	2	9	10	13.5	3.12	108	.270	.361	0	.000	-1	2	3	-0	0.2
1916 Cle-A	16	16	.500	48	27	14	3	5	272²	253	2	67	88	10.8	2.61	115	.251	.303	15	.167	-1	7	12	-3	1.1
1917 Cle-A	23	13	.639	49	37	26	8	7	320²	277	6	83	83	10.0	1.96	144	.235	.283	25	.231	2	25	31	-3	3.8
1918 Cle-A	17	16	.515	45	31	23	2	6	271¹	274	0	78	57	11.7	2.69	112	.276	.330	21	.212	-0	3	10	-2	1.0
1919 Cle-A	17	11	.607	35	32	21	0	3	241¹	258	6	44	61	11.4	2.80	120	.275	.310	23	.258	5	12	15	-0	2.1
1920 *Cle-A	31	12	.721	48	38	30	3	0	339²	338	9	79	73	11.2	2.89	132	.266	.311	33	.252	6	34	34	-7	3.8
1921 Cle-A	14	12	.538	40	26	13	0	4	191²	238	14	49	37	13.4	4.70	91	.308	.348	15	.197	-1	-9	-9	-2	-1.4
1922 Cle-A	4	5	.444	25	10	4	0	1	98¹	134	5	39	25	16.1	6.32	63	.340	.404	11	.262	3	-25	-25	-1	-0.9
1923 Pit-N	3	2	.600	21	6	2	0	3	68²	95	6	25	16	15.9	5.24	76	.336	.392	1	.050	-2	-9	-9	-1	-0.9
Total 9	127	88	.591	316	208	133	16	29	1821²	1884	47	458	450	11.7	3.11	110	.273	.321	144	.218	11	38	62	-15	7.8

● **STAN BAHNSEN**   Bahnsen, Stanley Raymond b: 12/15/44, Council Bluffs, Ia.   BR/TR, 6'2", 203 lbs. Deb: 9/9/66

YEAR TM/L	W	L	PCT	G	GS	CG	SH	SV	IP	H	HR	BB	SO	RAT	ERA	ERA+	OAV	OOB	BH	AVG	PB	PR	/A	PD	TPI
1966 NY-A	1	1	.500	4	3	1	0	1	23	15	3	7	16	8.6	3.52	94	.181	.244	1	.143	-0	-0	-1	-0	-0.1
1968 NY-A	17	12	.586	37	34	10	1	0	267¹	216	14	68	162	9.6	2.05	141	.221	.273	4	.049	-4	27	25	-2	2.2
1969 NY-A	9	16	.360	40	33	5	2	1	220²	222	28	90	130	12.7	3.83	91	.260	.331	5	.083	-3	-5	-9	-1	-1.2
1970 NY-A	14	11	.560	36	35	6	2	0	232²	227	23	75	116	11.8	3.33	106	.256	.316	11	.149	-0	10	5	1	0.5
1971 NY-A	14	12	.538	36	34	14	3	0	242	221	20	72	110	11.1	3.35	97	.248	.308	12	.152	-1	3	-3	3	0.0
1972 Chi-A	21	16	.568	43	41	5	1	0	252¹	263	22	73	157	12.2	3.60	87	.268	.323	14	.152	-1	-15	-13	2	-1.8
1973 Chi-A	18	21	.462	42	42	14	4	0	282¹	290	20	117	120	13.1	3.57	111	.269	.343	0	—	0	8	12	2	1.8
1974 Chi-A	12	15	.444	38	35	10	1	0	216¹	230	17	110	102	14.3	4.70	79	.277	.364	0	—	0	-26	-23	1	-2.6
1975 Chi-A	4	6	.400	12	12	2	0	0	67¹	78	9	40	31	16.2	6.01	64	.291	.389	0	—	0	-17	-16	-0	-2.0
Oak-A	6	7	.462	21	16	2	0	0	100	88	2	37	49	11.5	3.24	112	.238	.313	0	.000	0	6	4	0	0.5
Yr	10	13	.435	33	28	4	0	0	167¹	166	11	77	80	13.2	4.36	85	.259	.342	0	.000	0	-11	-12	-0	-1.5
1976 Oak-A	8	7	.533	35	14	1	1	0	143	124	13	43	82	10.6	3.34	101	.232	.292	0	—	0	3	0	1	0.1
1977 Oak-A	1	2	.333	11	2	0	0	1	22	24	5	13	21	15.5	6.14	66	.286	.388	0	—	0	-5	-5	-0	-0.7
Mon-N	8	9	.471	23	22	3	1	0	127¹	142	14	38	58	12.7	4.81	79	.283	.333	5	.119	-1	-13	-14	-0	-1.7
1978 Mon-N	1	5	.167	44	1	0	0	7	75	74	9	31	44	12.6	3.84	92	.261	.334	1	.091	-1	-2	-3	-0	-0.4
1979 Mon-N	3	1	.750	55	0	0	0	5	94¹	80	10	42	71	11.6	3.15	116	.236	.320	1	.071	-0	6	5	-0	0.3
1980 Mon-N	7	6	.538	57	0	0	0	4	91¹	80	7	33	48	11.1	3.05	117	.235	.302	1	.111	1	6	5	-0	0.3
1981 *Mon-N	2	1	.667	25	3	0	0	1	49	45	7	24	28	12.9	4.96	70	.247	.338	1	.111	-0	-8	-7	-0	-0.7
1982 Cal-A	0	1	.000	7	0	0	0	0	9²	13	0	8	5	19.6	4.66	87	.310	.420	0	—	0	-1	-1	-0	-0.1
Phi-N	0	0	—	8	0	0	0	0	13¹	8	0	3	9	7.4	1.35	271	.182	.234	0	—	0	3	3	-0	0.0
Total 16	146	149	.495	574	327	73	16	20	2529	2440	223	924	1359	12.1	3.60	97	.255	.323	56	.117	-9	-20	-35	4	-5.1

● **ED BAHR**   Bahr, Edson Garfield b: 10/16/19, Rouleau, Sask., Canada   BR/TR, 6'1.5", 172 lbs. Deb: 5/1/46

YEAR TM/L	W	L	PCT	G	GS	CG	SH	SV	IP	H	HR	BB	SO	RAT	ERA	ERA+	OAV	OOB	BH	AVG	PB	PR	/A	PD	TPI
1946 Pit-N	8	6	.571	27	14	7	2	0	136²	128	8	52	44	12.2	2.63	134	.254	.330	8	.178	-1	12	14	-0	1.3
1947 Pit-N	3	5	.375	19	11	1	0	0	82¹	82	5	43	25	14.0	4.59	92	.263	.358	2	.087	-2	-5	-3	-1	-0.6
Total 2	11	11	.500	46	25	8	2	0	219	210	13	95	69	12.9	3.37	112	.257	.341	10	.147	-3	7	10	-1	0.7

● **GROVER BAICHLEY**   Baichley, Grover Cleveland b: 1/7/1890, Toledo, Ill. d: 6/30/56, San Jose, Cal.   BR/TR, 5'9.5", 165 lbs. Deb: 8/24/14

YEAR TM/L	W	L	PCT	G	GS	CG	SH	SV	IP	H	HR	BB	SO	RAT	ERA	ERA+	OAV	OOB	BH	AVG	PB	PR	/A	PD	TPI
1914 StL-A	0	0	—	4	0	0	0	0	7	9	0	3	3	15.4	5.14	53	.346	.414	0	.000	-0	-2	-2	0	0.0

● **SCOTT BAILES**   Bailes, Scott Alan b: 12/18/61, Chillicothe, Ohio   BL/TL, 6'2", 175 lbs. Deb: 4/9/86

YEAR TM/L	W	L	PCT	G	GS	CG	SH	SV	IP	H	HR	BB	SO	RAT	ERA	ERA+	OAV	OOB	BH	AVG	PB	PR	/A	PD	TPI
1986 Cle-A	10	10	.500	62	10	0	0	7	112²	123	12	43	60	13.3	4.95	84	.276	.342	0	—	0	-10	-10	-1	-1.7
1987 Cle-A	7	8	.467	39	17	0	0	6	120¹	145	21	47	65	14.7	4.64	98	.296	.362	0	—	0	-2	-2	-0	-0.2
1988 Cle-A	9	14	.391	37	21	5	2	0	145	149	22	46	53	12.2	4.90	84	.266	.324	0	—	0	-15	-13	-0	-1.9
1989 Cle-A	5	9	.357	34	11	0	0	0	113²	116	7	29	47	11.7	4.28	93	.269	.320	0	—	0	-5	-4	-0	-0.5
1990 Cal-A	2	0	1.000	27	0	0	0	0	35¹	46	8	20	16	17.1	6.37	60	.315	.401	0	—	0	-10	-10	-1	-0.3
1991 Cal-A	1	2	.333	42	0	0	0	0	51²	41	5	22	41	11.7	4.18	98	.218	.313	0	—	0	-0	-0	-0	-0.0
1992 Cal-A	3	1	.750	32	0	0	0	0	38²	59	7	28	25	20.5	7.45	53	.351	.447	0	—	0	-15	-15	-0	-1.4
Total 7	37	44	.457	273	59	5	2	13	617¹	679	82	235	307	13.6	4.93	84	.280	.347	0	—	0	-57	-54	-0	-6.0

● **SWEETBREADS BAILEY**   Bailey, Abraham Lincoln b: 2/12/1895, Joliet, Ill. d: 9/27/39, Joliet, Ill.   BR/TR, 6', 184 lbs. Deb: 5/23/19

YEAR TM/L	W	L	PCT	G	GS	CG	SH	SV	IP	H	HR	BB	SO	RAT	ERA	ERA+	OAV	OOB	BH	AVG	PB	PR	/A	PD	TPI
1919 Chi-N	3	5	.375	21	5	0	0	0	71¹	75	2	20	19	12.4	3.15	91	.288	.346	7	.389	3	-2	-2	2	0.3
1920 Chi-N	1	2	.333	21	1	0	0	0	36²	55	1	11	8	16.7	7.12	45	.359	.410	1	.143	-0	-16	-16	1	-1.2
1921 Chi-N	0	0	—	3	0	0	0	0	5	6	0	2	2	16.2	3.60	106	.300	.391	0	—	0	0	0	0	0.0
Bro-N	0	0	—	7	0	0	0	0	24¹	35	1	9	6	15.9	5.18	75	.368	.417	0	—	0	-4	-3	-0	-0.1
Yr	0	0	—	10	0	0	0	0	29¹	41	1	9	8	15.6	4.91	79	.353	.405	0	.000	-0	-4	-3	-0	-0.1
Total 3	4	7	.364	52	6	0	0	0	137¹	171	4	40	35	14.3	4.59	69	.324	.379	8	.267	2	-22	-22	2	-1.0

● **HARVEY BAILEY**   Bailey, Harvey Francis b: 11/24/1876, Adrian, Mich. d: 7/10/22, Toledo, Ohio   TL, 6', Deb: 6/30/1899

YEAR TM/L	W	L	PCT	G	GS	CG	SH	SV	IP	H	HR	BB	SO	RAT	ERA	ERA+	OAV	OOB	BH	AVG	PB	PR	/A	PD	TPI
1899 Bos-N	6	4	.600	12	11	8	0	0	86²	83	7	35	26	12.9	3.95	105	.252	.335	8	.235	0	-1	2	-1	0.1
1900 Bos-N	0	0	—	4	1	0	0	0	20	24	0	11	9	16.6	4.95	83	.296	.394	2	.222	0	-3	-2	1	0.1
Total 2	6	4	.600	16	12	8	0	0	106²	107	7	46	35	13.6	4.13	100	.261	.347	10	.233	0	-4	-0	-0	0.2

● **HOWARD BAILEY**   Bailey, Howard L b: 7/31/57, Grand Haven, Mich.   BR/TL, 6', 195 lbs. Deb: 4/12/81

YEAR TM/L	W	L	PCT	G	GS	CG	SH	SV	IP	H	HR	BB	SO	RAT	ERA	ERA+	OAV	OOB	BH	AVG	PB	PR	/A	PD	TPI
1981 Det-A	1	4	.200	9	5	0	0	0	36²	45	4	13	17	15.0	7.36	51	.308	.377	0	—	0	-15	-15	1	-1.7
1982 Det-A	0	0	—	8	0	0	0	1	10	6	0	2	3	7.2	0.00	—	.182	.229	0	—	0	5	5	0	0.1

YEAR TM/L	W	L	PCT	G	GS	CG	SH	SV	IP	H	HR	BB	SO	RAT	ERA	ERA+	OAV	OOB	BH	AVG	PB	PR	/A	PD	TPI
1983 Det-A	5	5	.500	33	3	0	0	0	72	69	11	25	21	12.0	4.88	80	.255	.322	0	—	0	-7	-8	0	-0.9
Total 3	6	9	.400	50	8	0	0	1	118²	120	15	40	41	12.5	5.23	74	.267	.333	0	—	0	-17	-18	1	-2.5

● **JIM BAILEY**   Bailey, James Hopkins b: 12/16/34, Strawberry Plains, Tenn. BB/TL, 6'2.5", 210 lbs. Deb: 9/10/59 F

YEAR TM/L	W	L	PCT	G	GS	CG	SH	SV	IP	H	HR	BB	SO	RAT	ERA	ERA+	OAV	OOB	BH	AVG	PB	PR	/A	PD	TPI
1959 Cin-N	0	1	.000	3	1	0	0	0	11²	17	1	6	7	18.5	6.17	66	.333	.414	0	.000	-0	-3	-3	-0	-0.3

● **KING BAILEY**   Bailey, Leonard C. b: 11/1870, Virginia BL/TL, 6' ", 185 lbs. Deb: 9/21/1895

YEAR TM/L	W	L	PCT	G	GS	CG	SH	SV	IP	H	HR	BB	SO	RAT	ERA	ERA+	OAV	OOB	BH	AVG	PB	PR	/A	PD	TPI
1895 Cin-N	1	0	1.000	1	1	1	0	0	8	13	0	0	0	15.8	5.63	88	.359	.376	2	.500	1	-1	-1	0	0.0

● **CORY BAILEY**   Bailey, Phillip Cory b: 1/24/71, Marion, Ill. BR/TR, 6'1", 210 lbs. Deb: 9/1/93

YEAR TM/L	W	L	PCT	G	GS	CG	SH	SV	IP	H	HR	BB	SO	RAT	ERA	ERA+	OAV	OOB	BH	AVG	PB	PR	/A	PD	TPI
1993 Bos-A	0	1	.000	11	0	0	0	0	15²	12	0	12	11	13.8	3.45	134	.231	.375	0	—	0	2	2	1	-0.3
1994 Bos-A	0	1	.000	5	0	0	0	0	4¹	10	2	3	4	27.0	12.46	41	.476	.542	0	—	0	-4	-4	0	-1.0
Total 2	0	2	.000	16	0	0	0	0	20	22	2	15	15	16.6	5.40	88	.301	.420	0	—	0	-2	-1	1	-1.3

● **STEVE BAILEY**   Bailey, Steven John b: 2/12/42, Bronx, N.Y. BR/TR, 6'1", 194 lbs. Deb: 4/14/67

YEAR TM/L	W	L	PCT	G	GS	CG	SH	SV	IP	H	HR	BB	SO	RAT	ERA	ERA+	OAV	OOB	BH	AVG	PB	PR	/A	PD	TPI
1967 Cle-A	2	5	.286	32	1	0	0	2	64²	62	5	42	46	14.9	3.90	84	.259	.377	0	.000	-1	-5	-5	0	-0.6
1968 Cle-A	0	1	.000	2	1	0	0	0	5	4	1	2	1	10.8	3.60	82	.235	.316	0	—	0	-0	-0	-0	-0.1
Total 2	2	6	.250	34	2	0	0	2	69²	66	6	44	47	14.6	3.88	84	.258	.373	0	.000	-1	-5	-5	-0	-0.7

● **BILL BAILEY**   Bailey, William F. b: 4/12/1889, Ft.Smith, Ark. d: 11/2/26, Houston, Tex. BL/TL, 5'11", 165 lbs. Deb: 9/17/07

YEAR TM/L	W	L	PCT	G	GS	CG	SH	SV	IP	H	HR	BB	SO	RAT	ERA	ERA+	OAV	OOB	BH	AVG	PB	PR	/A	PD	TPI
1907 StL-A	4	1	.800	6	5	3	0	0	48¹	39	0	15	17	10.8	2.42	104	.223	.299	3	.150	-1	1	1	-1	-0.2
1908 StL-A	3	5	.375	22	12	7	0	0	106²	85	2	50	42	11.6	3.04	79	.220	.314	3	.088	-1	-8	-8	-2	-1.1
1909 StL-A	9	10	.474	32	20	17	1	0	199	174	2	75	114	11.5	2.44	99	.248	.325	22	.286	5	1	-1	-1	0.5
1910 StL-A	3	18	.143	34	20	13	0	0	192¹	186	2	97	90	13.7	3.32	74	.262	.359	13	.206	0	-17	-18	-1	-2.0
1911 StL-A	0	3	.000	7	2	2	0	0	31²	42	1	16	8	17.1	4.55	74	.339	.423	0	.000	-2	-4	-4	0	-0.5
1912 StL-A	0	1	.000	3	2	0	0	0	10²	15	0	10	2	21.1	9.28	36	.341	.463	1	.500	-1	-7	-7	-1	-0.5
1914 Bal-F	7	9	.438	19	18	10	1	0	128²	106	2	68	131	12.7	3.08	99	.230	.338	7	.163	-1	-3	-1	3	0.1
1915 Bal-F	6	19	.240	36	23	11	2	0	190¹	179	8	115	98	14.3	4.63	62	.255	.366	15	.231	-0	-40	-37	-1	-4.6
Chi-F	3	1	.750	5	5	3	3	0	33¹	23	1	10	24	8.9	2.16	116	.202	.266	2	.222	1	2	1	1	0.2
Yr	9	20	.310	41	28	14	5	0	223²	202	9	125	122	13.2	4.27	66	.245	.344	17	.230	-0	-38	-36	-1	-4.4
1918 Det-A	1	2	.333	8	4	1	0	0	37²	53	0	26	13	19.1	5.97	45	.368	.468	1	.077	-1	-13	-14	1	-1.1
1921 StL-N	2	5	.286	19	6	3	1	0	74	95	1	22	20	14.5	4.26	86	.330	.381	2	.091	-2	-4	-5	1	-0.5
1922 StL-N	0	2	.000	12	0	0	0	0	31²	38	1	23	11	17.3	5.40	72	.325	.436	2	.286	-0	-5	-5	1	-0.2
Total 11	38	76	.333	203	117	70	8	0	1084¹	1035	20	527	570	13.3	3.57	77	.261	.354	71	.194	-3	-97	-98	-1	-9.9

● **BOB BAILOR**   Bailor, Robert Michael b: 7/10/51, Connellsville, Pa. BR/TR, 5'11", 170 lbs. Deb: 9/6/75 C♦

YEAR TM/L	W	L	PCT	G	GS	CG	SH	SV	IP	H	HR	BB	SO	RAT	ERA	ERA+	OAV	OOB	BH	AVG	PB	PR	/A	PD	TPI
1980 Tor-A	0	0	—	3	0	0	0	0	2¹	4	0	1	0	19.3	7.71	56	.364	.417	82	.236	2	-1	-1	-0	0.0

● **LOREN BAIN**   Bain, Herbert Loren b: 7/4/22, Staples, Minn. BR/TR, 6', 190 lbs. Deb: 6/23/45

YEAR TM/L	W	L	PCT	G	GS	CG	SH	SV	IP	H	HR	BB	SO	RAT	ERA	ERA+	OAV	OOB	BH	AVG	PB	PR	/A	PD	TPI
1945 NY-N	0	0	—	3	0	0	0	0	8	10	1	4	1	16.9	7.88	50	.323	.417	1	.333	0	-4	-4	-0	0.0

● **DOUG BAIR**   Bair, Charles Douglas b: 8/22/49, Defiance, Ohio BR/TR, 6', 180 lbs. Deb: 9/13/76

YEAR TM/L	W	L	PCT	G	GS	CG	SH	SV	IP	H	HR	BB	SO	RAT	ERA	ERA+	OAV	OOB	BH	AVG	PB	PR	/A	PD	TPI
1976 Pit-N	0	0	—	4	0	0	0	0	6¹	4	0	5	4	12.8	5.68	61	.174	.321	0	—	0	-2	-2	-0	0.0
1977 Oak-A	4	6	.400	45	0	0	0	8	83¹	78	11	57	68	14.6	3.46	116	.253	.370	0	—	0	6	5	1	0.9
1978 Cin-N	7	6	.538	70	0	0	0	28	100¹	87	6	38	91	11.2	1.97	196	.236	.307	2	.143	-0	18	18	1	3.3
1979 *Cin-N	11	7	.611	65	0	0	0	16	94¹	93	7	51	86	14.0	4.29	87	.256	.353	0	.000	-1	-6	-6	-1	-1.4
1980 Cin-N	3	6	.333	61	0	0	0	6	85	91	7	39	62	13.9	4.24	84	.277	.355	0	.000	-0	-6	-6	2	-0.6
1981 StL-N	2	2	.500	24	0	0	0	0	39	42	5	17	16	13.6	5.77	62	.271	.343	1	.333	1	-10	-10	-1	-0.9
StL-N	2	0	1.000	11	0	0	0	1	15²	13	0	2	14	8.6	3.45	103	.224	.250	0	.000	-0	0	0	-0	0.0
Yr	4	2	.667	35	0	0	0	1	54²	55	5	19	30	12.2	5.10	70	.258	.319	1	.167	1	-10	-9	-1	-0.9
1982 *StL-N	5	3	.625	63	0	0	0	8	91²	69	7	36	68	10.4	2.55	142	.211	.291	1	.077	-1	11	11	0	1.1
1983 StL-N	1	1	.500	26	0	0	0	4	29²	24	4	13	21	11.2	3.03	119	.224	.308	0	.000	-0	2	2	-0	0.1
Det-A	7	3	.700	27	1	0	0	4	55²	51	8	19	39	11.5	3.88	101	.242	.307	0	—	0	1	0	-0	0.2
1984 *Det-A	5	3	.625	47	1	0	0	4	93²	82	10	36	57	11.3	3.75	105	.238	.310	0	—	0	3	2	1	0.3
1985 Det-A	2	0	1.000	21	3	0	0	0	49	54	3	25	30	14.7	6.24	65	.281	.367	0	—	0	-11	-12	1	-0.3
StL-N	—	—	—	2	0	0	0	0	2	1	0	2	0	13.5	0.00	—	.167	.375	0	—	0	1	1	-0	0.0
1986 Oak-A	2	3	.400	31	0	0	0	0	45	37	5	18	40	11.0	3.00	129	.224	.301	0	—	0	6	4	0	1.1
1987 Phi-N	2	0	1.000	11	0	0	0	0	13²	17	4	5	10	14.5	5.93	72	.309	.367	0	.000	-0	-3	-3	-0	-0.1
1988 Tor-A	0	0	—	10	0	0	0	0	13¹	14	2	3	8	11.5	4.05	97	.280	.321	0	—	0	-0	-0	-0	0.0
1989 Pit-N	2	3	.400	44	0	0	0	1	67¹	52	9	28	56	10.7	2.27	148	.211	.292	1	.200	0	9	8	1	0.7
1990 Pit-N	0	0	—	22	0	0	0	0	24¹	30	3	11	19	15.2	4.81	75	.306	.376	0	.000	-0	-3	-3	0	0.0
Total 15	55	43	.561	584	5	0	0	81	909¹	839	86	405	689	12.4	3.63	103	.246	.328	5	.096	-2	15	10	2	4.1

● **BOB BAIRD**   Baird, Robert Allen b: 1/16/40, Knoxville, Tenn. d: 4/11/74, Chattanooga, Tenn. BL/TL, 6'4", 195 lbs. Deb: 9/3/62

YEAR TM/L	W	L	PCT	G	GS	CG	SH	SV	IP	H	HR	BB	SO	RAT	ERA	ERA+	OAV	OOB	BH	AVG	PB	PR	/A	PD	TPI
1962 Was-A	0	1	.000	3	3	0	0	0	10²	13	0	8	3	17.7	6.75	60	.310	.420	0	.000	-0	-3	-3	-0	-0.3
1963 Was-A	0	3	.000	5	3	0	0	0	11²	12	1	7	7	15.4	7.71	48	.261	.370	1	.333	0	-5	-5	-0	-1.1
Total 2	0	4	.000	8	6	0	0	0	22¹	25	1	15	10	16.5	7.25	53	.284	.394	1	.167	-0	-9	-8	-1	-1.4

● **JERSEY BAKELY**   Bakely, Edward Enoch (b: Edward Enoch Bakley) b: 4/17/1864, Blackwood, N.J. d: 2/17/15, Philadelphia, Pa. BR/TR, Deb: 5/11/1883

YEAR TM/L	W	L	PCT	G	GS	CG	SH	SV	IP	H	HR	BB	SO	RAT	ERA	ERA+	OAV	OOB	BH	AVG	PB	PR	/A	PD	TPI
1883 Phi-a	5	3	.625	8	8	7	0	0	61¹	65	0	12	14	11.3	3.23	108	.255	.288	5	.192	1	1	2	-0	0.2
1884 Phi-U	14	25	.359	39	38	38	1	0	344²	390	0	76	204	12.2	4.47	52	.267	.303	22	.132	-16	-77	-82	-3	-8.2
Wil-U	0	2	.000	2	2	2	0	0	17	24	0	1	9	13.2	4.24	63	.312	.321	0	—	0	-3	-3	-0	-0.3
KC-U	2	3	.400	5	5	3	0	0	33	29	0	4	13	9.0	2.45	91	.220	.243	3	.150	-2	-0	-1	-1	-0.3
Yr	16	30	.348	46	45	43	1	0	394²	443	0	81	226	11.9	4.29	54	.265	.299	25	.130	-18	-81	-86	-4	-8.8
1888 Cle-a	25	33	.431	61	61	60	4	0	532²	518	14	128	212	11.2	2.97	104	.246	.294	26	.134	-6	5	7	-1	0.1
1889 Cle-N	12	22	.353	36	34	33	2	0	304¹	296	9	106	105	12.1	2.96	136	.247	.313	15	.135	-1	36	36	2	3.4
1890 Cle-P	12	25	.324	43	38	32	0	0	326¹	412	13	147	67	15.6	4.47	89	.295	.365	28	.203	-2	-9	-18	-3	-1.8
1891 Was-a	2	10	.167	13	12	11	0	0	104¹	127	6	60	32	16.6	6.35	70	.290	.383	10	.222	-0	-19	-19	-2	-1.7
Bal-a	4	2	.667	8	6	5	0	0	59	48	1	30	13	12.1	2.29	163	.215	.310	2	.095	-0	9	10	-1	0.8
Yr	6	12	.333	21	18	16	0	0	163¹	175	7	90	45	14.7	4.24	88	.262	.351	12	.182	-0	-9	-9	-3	-0.9
Total 6	76	125	.378	215	204	191	7	0	1782²	1909	43	564	669	12.7	3.66	91	.262	.318	111	.153	-26	-57	-68	-9	-7.8

● **DAVE BAKENHASTER**   Bakenhaster, David Lee b: 3/5/45, Columbus, O. BR/TR, 5'10", 168 lbs. Deb: 6/20/64

YEAR TM/L	W	L	PCT	G	GS	CG	SH	SV	IP	H	HR	BB	SO	RAT	ERA	ERA+	OAV	OOB	BH	AVG	PB	PR	/A	PD	TPI
1964 StL-N	0	0	—	2	0	0	0	0	3	9	1	1	0	30.0	6.00	63	.474	.500	0	—	0	-1	-1	0	0.0

● **AL BAKER**   Baker, Albert Jones b: 2/28/06, Batesville, Miss. d: 11/6/82, Kenedy, Tex. BR/TR, 5'11", 170 lbs. Deb: 8/20/38

YEAR TM/L	W	L	PCT	G	GS	CG	SH	SV	IP	H	HR	BB	SO	RAT	ERA	ERA+	OAV	OOB	BH	AVG	PB	PR	/A	PD	TPI
1938 Bos-A	0	0	—	3	0	0	0	0	7²	13	2	2	2	18.8	9.39	53	.371	.421	0	.000	-1	-4	-4	-0	-0.1

● **BOCK BAKER**   Baker, Charles "Smiling Bock" b: 7/17/1878, Troy, N.Y. d: 8/17/40, New York, N.Y. TL, 5'9", 181 lbs. Deb: 4/28/01

YEAR TM/L	W	L	PCT	G	GS	CG	SH	SV	IP	H	HR	BB	SO	RAT	ERA	ERA+	OAV	OOB	BH	AVG	PB	PR	/A	PD	TPI
1901 Cle-A	0	1	.000	1	1	1	0	0	8	23	0	6	0	33.8	5.63	68	.499	.565	0	.000	-0	-2	-2	-0	-0.2
Phi-A	0	1	.000	1	1	0	0	0	6	6	0	6	0	18.0	10.50	36	.257	.409	1	.333	-0	-5	-4	-0	-0.5
Yr	0	2	.000	2	2	1	0	0	14	29	0	12	0	26.4	7.71	47	.412	.498	1	.143	-1	-6	-6	-0	-0.7

● **ERNIE BAKER**   Baker, Earnest Gould b: 8/8/1875, Concord, Mich. d: 10/25/45, Homer, Mich. BR/TR, 5'10", 160 lbs. Deb: 8/18/05

YEAR TM/L	W	L	PCT	G	GS	CG	SH	SV	IP	H	HR	BB	SO	RAT	ERA	ERA+	OAV	OOB	BH	AVG	PB	PR	/A	PD	TPI
1905 Cin-N	0	0	—	1	0	0	0	0	4	7	1	0	1	18.0	4.50	73	.412	.444	0	.000	-0	-1	-1	-0	-0.1

YEAR TM/L	W	L	PCT	G	GS	CG	SH	SV	IP	H	HR	BB	SO	RAT	ERA	ERA+	OAV	OOB	BH	AVG	PB	PR	/A	PD	TPI
● **JESSE BAKER** Baker, Jesse Ormond b: 6/3/1888, Anderson Island, Wash. d: 9/26/72, Tacoma, Wash. BL/TL, 5'11", 188 lbs. Deb: 4/23/11																									
1911 Chi-A	2	7	.222	22	8	3	0	1	94	101	3	30	51	12.9	3.93	82	.288	.351	3	.103	-2	-6	-7	1	-0.7
● **KIRTLEY BAKER** Baker, Kirtley "Whitey" b: 6/24/1869, Aurora, Ind. d: 4/15/27, Covington, Ky. BR/TR, 5'9", 160 lbs. Deb: 5/7/1890 ◆																									
1890 Pit-N	3	19	.136	25	21	19	2	0	178¹	209	11	86	76	15.9	5.60	59	.283	.374	10	.147	-1	-40	-46	-0	-4.3
1893 Bal-N	3	8	.273	15	12	8	0	0	91²	138	5	58	26	19.7	8.44	56	.337	.426	17	.298	2	-38	-38	3	-2.7
1894 Bal-N	0	1	.000	1	0	0	0	0	0	1	0	2	0	—	∞	—	1.000	1.000	0	.000	-0	-5	-5	-0	-0.3
1898 Was-N	2	3	.400	6	5	4	0	0	47	56	1	18	7	14.2	3.06	120	.293	.354	5	.278	2	3	3	-1	0.4
1899 Was-N	1	7	.125	11	6	3	0	0	54	79	3	22	6	17.8	6.83	57	.340	.411	3	.158	-1	-18	-18	2	-1.9
Total 5	9	38	.191	58	44	34	2	0	371	483	20	186	115	17.0	6.28	60	.307	.392	35	.211	1	-99	-103	4	-8.8
● **NEAL BAKER** Baker, Neal Vernon b: 4/30/04, LaPorte, Tex. d: 1/5/82, Houston, Tex. BR/TR, 6'1", 175 lbs. Deb: 6/26/27																									
1927 Phi-A	0	0	—	5	2	0	0	0	17¹	27	2	7	3	17.7	5.71	75	.365	.420	1	.167	-0	-3	-3	0	0.0
● **NORM BAKER** Baker, Norman Leslie b: 10/14/1863, Philadelphia, Pa. d: 2/20/49, Hurffville, N.J. Deb: 5/21/1883																									
1883 Pit-a	0	2	.000	3	3	2	0	0	19	24	0	11	5	16.6	3.32	97	.289	.373	0	.000	-2	-0	-0	-1	-0.2
1885 Lou-a	13	12	.520	25	24	24	1	0	217	210	3	69	79	12.0	3.40	95	.241	.304	18	.207	-1	-4	-4	-2	-0.6
1890 Bal-a	1	1	.500	2	2	2	0	0	17	16	0	6	10	11.6	3.71	109	.241	.304	0	.000	-1	1	0	0	0.0
Total 3	14	15	.483	30	29	28	1	0	253	250	3	86	94	12.3	3.42	96	.245	.309	18	.170	-3	-3	-4	-2	-0.8
● **STEVE BAKER** Baker, Steven Byrne b: 8/30/56, Eugene, Ore. BR/TR, 6', 185 lbs. Deb: 5/25/78																									
1978 Det-A	2	4	.333	15	10	0	0	0	63¹	66	6	42	39	15.3	4.55	85	.276	.384	0	—	0	-6	-5	-1	-0.7
1979 Det-A	1	7	.125	21	12	0	0	1	84	97	13	51	54	16.5	6.64	65	.296	.400	0	—	0	-23	-22	-1	-2.0
1982 Oak-A	1	1	.500	5	3	0	0	0	25²	30	3	4	14	11.9	4.56	86	.288	.315	0	—	0	-1	-2	-0	-0.2
1983 Oak-A	3	3	.500	35	1	0	0	5	54	59	4	26	23	14.5	4.33	89	.282	.367	0	—	0	-2	-3	-1	-0.2
StL-N	0	1	.000	8	0	0	0	0	10	10	0	4	1	13.5	1.80	201	.286	.375	0	—	0	2	2	0	0.2
Total 4	7	16	.304	84	26	0	0	6	237	262	26	127	131	15.1	5.13	78	.286	.379	0	—	0	-29	-29	-3	-2.7
● **TOM BAKER** Baker, Thomas Calvin "Rattlesnake" b: 6/11/13, Nursery, Tex. d: 1/3/91, Fort Worth, Tex. BR/TR, 6'1.5", 180 lbs. Deb: 8/15/35																									
1935 Bro-N	1	0	1.000	11	1	1	0	0	42	48	2	20	10	14.6	4.29	93	.277	.352	9	.474	4	-1	-1	-1	0.2
1936 Bro-N	1	8	.111	35	8	2	0	2	87²	98	3	48	35	15.2	4.72	88	.288	.379	7	.233	1	-7	-6	0	-0.4
1937 Bro-N	0	1	.000	7	0	0	0	0	8¹	14	1	5	2	21.6	8.64	47	.378	.465	0	—	0	-4	-4	0	-0.4
NY-N	1	0	1.000	13	0	0	0	0	31	30	0	16	11	13.4	4.06	96	.262	.359	2	.222	-1	-1	-0	-1	-0.1
Yr	1	1	.500	20	0	0	0	0	39¹	44	1	21	13	14.9	5.03	78	.293	.380	2	.222	-1	-5	-5	-0	-0.5
1938 NY-N	0	0	—	2	0	0	0	0	4	5	0	3	0	18.0	6.75	56	.313	.421	0	—	0	-1	-1	0	0.0
Total 4	3	9	.250	68	9	3	0	2	173	195	6	92	58	15.1	4.73	85	.288	.375	18	.310	5	-14	-13	-1	-0.7
● **TOM BAKER** Baker, Thomas Henry b: 5/6/34, Port Townsend, Wash. d: 3/9/80, Port Townsend, Wash BL/TL, 6', 195 lbs. Deb: 8/2/63																									
1963 Chi-N	0	1	.000	10	1	0	0	0	18	20	2	7	14	14.0	3.00	117	.282	.354	0	.000	-0	1	1	0	0.0
● **MIKE BALAS** Balas, Mitchell Francis (b: Mitchell Francis Balaski) b: 5/17/10, Lowell, Mass. BR/TR, 6', 195 lbs. Deb: 4/27/38																									
1938 Bos-N	0	0	—	1	0	0	0	0	1¹	3	0	0	0	20.3	6.75	51	.375	.375	0	—	0	-0	-0	-0	0.0
● **JACK BALDSCHUN** Baldschun, Jack Edward b: 10/16/36, Greenville, O. BR/TR, 6', 190 lbs. Deb: 4/28/61																									
1961 Phi-N	5	3	.625	65	0	0	0	3	99²	90	7	49	59	13.0	3.88	105	.243	.339	0	.000	-1	2	2	0	0.1
1962 Phi-N	12	7	.632	67	0	0	0	13	112²	95	6	58	95	12.4	2.96	131	.231	.328	1	.063	-1	12	11	1	2.1
1963 Phi-N	11	7	.611	65	0	0	0	16	113²	99	7	42	89	11.4	2.30	141	.232	.306	0	.000	-2	13	12	1	2.2
1964 Phi-N	6	9	.400	71	0	0	0	21	118¹	111	8	40	96	11.7	3.12	111	.246	.312	4	.250	1	6	5	1	1.1
1965 Phi-N	5	8	.385	65	0	0	0	6	99	102	4	42	67	13.5	3.82	91	.273	.352	0	.000	-1	-3	-4	1	-0.6
1966 Cin-N	1	5	.167	42	0	0	0	0	57¹	71	4	25	44	15.7	5.49	71	.318	.397	1	.333	-0	-12	-10	0	-0.9
1967 Cin-N	0	0	—	9	0	0	0	0	13	15	0	9	12	16.6	4.15	90	.283	.387	0	.000	-0	-1	-1	-0	0.0
1969 SD-N	7	2	.778	61	0	0	0	1	77	80	7	29	67	13.0	4.79	74	.264	.332	1	.250	1	-10	-11	-0	-1.2
1970 SD-N	1	0	1.000	12	0	0	0	0	13¹	24	2	4	12	18.9	10.13	39	.375	.412	0	—	0	-9	-9	-0	-0.6
Total 9	48	41	.539	457	0	0	0	60	704	687	45	298	555	12.9	3.69	98	.257	.336	7	.090	-3	-3	-5	4	2.2
● **LADY BALDWIN** Baldwin, Charles Busted b: 4/8/1859, Oramel, N.Y. d: 3/7/37, Hastings, Mich. BL/TL, 5'11", 160 lbs. Deb: 9/30/1884 ◆																									
1884 Mil-U	1	1	.500	2	2	2	0	0	17	7	0	1	21	4.2	2.65	50	.117	.131	6	.222	-0	-0	-2	-0	-0.2
1885 Det-N	11	9	.550	21	20	19	1	1	179¹	137	2	28	135	**8.3**	1.86	153	**.197**	**.228**	30	.242	3	19	20	2	2.4
1886 Det-N	**42**	13	.764	56	56	55	**7**	0	487	371	11	100	**323**	**8.7**	2.24	148	**.202**	**.243**	41	.201	3	58	58	4	6.1
1887 *Det-N	13	10	.565	24	24	24	1	0	211	225	8	61	60	12.4	3.84	105	.269	.323	23	.271	3	6	5	1	0.6
1888 Det-N	3	3	.500	6	6	5	0	0	53	76	5	16	26	15.6	5.43	51	.322	.365	6	.261	2	-15	-16	-1	-1.3
1890 Bro-N	1	0	1.000	2	1	0	0	0	7²	15	0	4	4	22.3	7.04	49	.398	.456	0	.000	-0	-3	-3	-0	-0.3
Buf-P	2	5	.286	7	7	7	0	0	62	90	5	24	13	17.0	4.50	91	.325	.385	8	.286	1	-2	-3	-0	-0.1
Total 6	73	41	.640	118	116	112	9	1	1017	921	31	233	582	10.3	2.85	118	.232	.276	114	.231	12	63	58	5	7.2
● **KID BALDWIN** Baldwin, Clarence Geoghan b: 11/1/1864, Newport, Ky. d: 7/10/1897, Cincinnati, Ohio BR/TR, 5'6", 147 lbs. Deb: 7/27/1884 ◆																									
1885 Cin-a	0	0	—	2	1	0	0	0	4	5	0	6	1	24.8	9.00	36	.294	.478	17	.135	-4	-3	-3	0	0.0
● **DAVE BALDWIN** Baldwin, David George b: 3/30/38, Tucson, Ariz. BR/TR, 6'2", 200 lbs. Deb: 9/6/66																									
1966 Was-A	0	0	—	4	0	0	0	0	7	8	0	4	4	11.6	3.86	90	.267	.290	0	—	0	-0	-0	-0	0.0
1967 Was-A	2	4	.333	58	0	0	0	12	68²	53	2	20	52	10.1	1.70	186	.215	.285	0	.000	-0	12	11	1	1.6
1968 Was-A	0	2	.000	40	0	0	0	5	42	40	7	12	30	11.1	4.07	72	.260	.313	0	.000	-1	-5	-5	1	-0.4
1969 Was-A	2	4	.333	43	0	0	0	4	66²	57	4	34	51	13.0	4.05	86	.236	.342	0	.000	-1	-3	-4	-0	-0.6
1970 Mil-A	2	1	.667	28	0	0	0	1	35¹	25	4	18	26	11.0	2.55	149	.205	.307	1	.500	0	5	5	2	0.7
1973 Chi-A	0	0	—	3	0	0	0	0	4	7	0	1	1	19.8	3.60	110	.368	.478	0	—	0	0	0	0	0.0
Total 6	6	11	.353	176	0	0	0	22	224²	190	17	89	164	11.5	3.08	108	.234	.316	1	.067	-1	8	6	4	1.3
● **HARRY BALDWIN** Baldwin, Howard Edward b: 6/3/1900, Baltimore, Md. d: 1/23/58, Baltimore, Md. BR/TR, 5'11", 160 lbs. Deb: 5/4/24																									
1924 *NY-N	3	1	.750	10	2	1	0	0	33²	42	5	11	14	14.2	4.28	86	.309	.361	4	.364	1	-2	-2	-0	-0.2
1925 NY-N	0	0	—	1	0	0	0	0	1	3	0	1	0	36.0	9.00	45	.500	.571	0	—	0	-1	-1	0	0.0
Total 2	3	1	.750	11	2	1	0	0	34²	45	5	12	14	14.8	4.41	83	.317	.370	4	.364	1	-2	-3	-0	-0.2
● **MARK BALDWIN** Baldwin, Marcus Elmore "Fido" b: 10/29/1863, Pittsburgh, Pa. d: 11/10/29, Pittsburgh, Pa. BR/TR, 6', 190 lbs. Deb: 5/2/1887																									
1887 Chi-N	18	17	.514	40	39	35	1	**1**	334	329	23	122	164	12.6	3.40	132	.248	.319	26	.187	-4	25	41	-3	2.6
1888 Chi-N	13	15	.464	30	30	27	2	0	251	241	13	99	157	12.7	2.76	110	.249	.327	16	.151	-1	7	7	2	0.8
1889 Col-a	27	34	.443	**63**	59	54	6	1	**513²**	458	9	274	**368**	13.2	3.61	100	.231	.331	39	.188	-1	14	1	1	0.2
1890 Chi-P	**34**	24	.586	**59**	57	**54**	1	0	**501**	498	10	249	**211**	13.7	3.31	131	.248	.336	45	.209	-1	52	58	4	5.2
1891 Pit-N	22	28	.440	53	50	48	2	0	437²	385	10	227	197	13.1	2.76	119	.227	.327	27	.153	-3	29	26	1	2.1
1892 Pit-N	26	27	.491	56	53	45	2	0	440¹	447	11	194	157	13.6	3.47	95	.253	.334	18	.101	-12	-9	-9	-2	-2.1
1893 Pit-N	0	0	—	1	1	0	0	0	2¹	6	0	1	0	27.0	11.57	39	.465	.503	0	.000	-0	-2	-2	0	0.0
NY-N	16	20	.444	45	39	33	2	2	331¹	335	6	141	100	13.3	4.10	114	.255	.332	17	.127	-11	21	20	-3	0.5
Yr	16	20	.444	46	40	33	2	**2**	333²	341	6	142	100	13.4	4.15	112	.257	.334	17	.126	-11	19	19	-3	0.5
Total 7	156	165	.486	347	328	296	14	4	2811¹	2699	82	1307	1354	13.2	3.36	114	.244	.330	188	.162	-32	132	142	0	9.3
● **O. F. BALDWIN** Baldwin, Orson F. b: 11/3/1881, Carson City, Mich. d: 2/16/42, Los Angeles, Cal. TR, 185 lbs. Deb: 9/6/08																									
1908 StL-N	1	3	.250	4	4	0	0	0	14²	16	0	11	5	18.4	6.14	38	.302	.448	0	.000	-1	-6	-6	-0	-1.5

YEAR	TM/L	W	L	PCT	G	GS	CG	SH	SV	IP	H	HR	BB	SO	RAT	ERA	ERA+	OAV	OOB	BH	AVG	PB	PR	/A	PD	TPI
● RICK BALDWIN	Baldwin, Rickey Alan b: 6/1/53, Fresno, Cal. BL/TR, 6'3", 180 lbs. Deb: 4/10/75																								
1975	NY-N	3	5	.375	54	0	0	0	6	97¹	97	4	34	54	12.5	3.33	104	.263	.332	3	.200	0	3	1	1	0.2
1976	NY-N	0	0	—	11	0	0	0	0	22²	14	0	10	9	10.3	2.38	138	.189	.302	1	.333	0	3	2	0	0.0
1977	NY-N	1	2	.333	40	0	0	0	1	62²	62	6	31	23	14.1	4.45	84	.265	.363	2	.500	1	-4	-5	1	-0.1
Total	3	4	7	.364	105	0	0	0	7	182²	173	10	75	86	12.8	3.60	98	.256	.339	6	.273	1	2	-1	1	0.1
● JEFF BALLARD	Ballard, Jeffrey Scott b: 8/13/63, Billings, Mont. BL/TL, 6'2", 198 lbs. Deb: 5/9/87																								
1987	Bal-A	2	8	.200	14	14	0	0	0	69²	100	15	35	27	17.4	6.59	67	.344	.414	0	—	0	-17	-17	0	-1.8
1988	Bal-A	8	12	.400	25	25	6	1	0	153¹	167	15	42	41	12.6	4.40	89	.278	.332	0	—	0	-7	-9	-2	-1.0
1989	Bal-A	18	8	.692	35	35	4	1	0	215¹	240	16	57	62	12.6	3.43	111	.287	.336	0	—	0	11	9	4	1.6
1990	Bal-A	2	11	.154	44	17	0	0	0	133¹	152	22	42	50	13.3	4.93	77	.289	.345	0	—	0	-15	-17	0	-1.3
1991	Bal-A	6	12	.333	26	22	0	0	0	123²	153	16	28	37	13.3	5.60	71	.302	.341	0	—	0	-21	-23	-1	-2.7
1993	Pit-N	4	1	.800	25	5	0	0	0	53²	70	3	15	16	14.6	4.86	83	.332	.382	4	.364	1	-5	-5	1	-0.2
1994	Pit-N	1	1	.500	28	0	0	0	2	24¹	32	5	10	11	15.9	6.66	64	.323	.391	1	.500	0	-7	-7	-0	-0.6
Total	7	41	53	.436	197	118	10	2	2	773¹	914	92	229	244	13.5	4.71	83	.298	.350	5	.385	2	-60	-68	2	-6.0
● JAY BALLER	Baller, Jay Scot b: 10/6/60, Stayton, Ore. BR/TR, 6'7", 225 lbs. Deb: 9/19/82																								
1982	Phi-N	0	0	—	4	1	0	0	0	8	7	1	2	7	11.3	3.38	109	.226	.294	0	—	0	0	-0	-0	0.0
1985	Chi-N	2	3	.400	20	4	0	0	1	52	52	8	17	31	12.1	3.46	115	.260	.321	0	.000	-1	1	3	-0	0.2
1986	Chi-N	2	4	.333	36	0	0	0	5	53²	58	7	28	42	14.8	5.37	75	.275	.365	0	.000	-1	-10	-8	-1	-1.1
1987	Chi-N	0	1	.000	23	0	0	0	0	29¹	38	4	20	27	17.8	6.75	63	.325	.423	1	1.000	0	-9	-8	-0	-0.2
1990	KC-A	0	1	.000	3	0	0	0	0	2¹	4	1	2	1	27.0	15.43	25	.364	.500	0	—	0	-3	-3	-0	-0.9
1992	Phi-N	0	0	—	8	0	0	0	0	11	10	5	10	9	16.4	8.18	43	.250	.400	0	—	0	-6	-6	-0	0.0
Total	6	4	9	.308	94	5	0	0	6	156¹	169	26	79	117	14.6	5.24	77	.277	.365	1	.071	-1	-26	-21	-2	-2.0
● MARK BALLINGER	Ballinger, Mark Alan b: 1/31/49, Glendale, Cal. BR/TR, 6'6", 205 lbs. Deb: 8/6/71																								
1971	Cle-A	1	2	.333	18	0	0	0	0	34²	30	3	13	25	11.4	4.67	82	.233	.308	1	.200	-0	-5	-3	-0	-0.3
● WIN BALLOU	Ballou, Noble Winfield b: 11/30/1897, Mount Morgan, Ky. d: 1/30/63, San Francisco, Cal BR/TL, 5'10.5", 170 lbs. Deb: 8/24/25																								
1925	*Was-A	1	1	.500	10	1	1	0	0	27²	38	1	13	13	16.6	4.55	93	.342	.411	1	.143	-0	-1	-0	-1	-0.1
1926	StL-A	11	10	.524	43	14	5	0	2	154	186	12	71	59	15.3	4.79	90	.311	.387	2	.048	-3	-13	-9	3	-1.0
1927	StL-A	5	6	.455	21	11	4	0	0	90¹	105	4	46	17	15.1	4.78	91	.309	.393	1	.036	-4	-6	-4	-0	-0.8
1929	Bro-N	2	3	.400	25	1	0	0	0	57²	69	5	38	20	16.7	6.71	69	.304	.404	1	.063	-2	-13	-13	2	-0.9
Total	4	19	20	.487	99	27	10	0	2	329²	398	22	168	109	15.6	5.11	86	.312	.394	5	.054	-9	-33	-27	5	-2.8
● TONY BALSAMO	Balsamo, Anthony Fred b: 11/21/37, Brooklyn, N.Y. BR/TR, 6'2", 185 lbs. Deb: 4/14/62																								
1962	Chi-N	0	1	.000	18	0	0	0	0	29¹	34	1	20	27	16.9	6.44	64	.293	.401	1	.200	-0	-8	-7	1	-0.1
● GEORGE BAMBERGER	Bamberger, George Irvin b: 8/1/25, Staten Island, N.Y. BR/TR, 6', 175 lbs. Deb: 4/19/51 MC																								
1951	NY-N	0	0	—	2	0	0	0	0	2	4	2	2	1	27.0	18.00	22	.444	.545	0	—	0	-3	-3	-0	0.0
1952	NY-N	0	0	—	5	0	0	0	0	4	6	1	6	0	27.0	9.00	41	.353	.522	0	—	0	-2	-2	-0	0.0
1959	Bal-A	0	0	—	3	1	0	0	1	8¹	15	1	2	2	18.4	7.56	50	.405	.436	0	.000	-0	-3	-3	0	-0.1
Total	3	0	0	—	10	1	0	0	1	14¹	25	4	10	3	22.0	9.42	40	.397	.479	0	.000	-0	-9	-9	-0	-0.1
● SAL BANDO	Bando, Salvatore Leonard b: 2/13/44, Cleveland, O. BR/TR, 6', 205 lbs. Deb: 9/3/66 FC♦																								
1979	Mil-A	0	0	—	1	0	0	0	0	3	3	0	0	0	9.0	6.00	69	.231	.231	117	.246	1	-1	-1	-0	0.0
● EDDIE BANE	Bane, Edward Norman b: 3/22/52, Chicago, Ill. BR/TL, 5'9", 160 lbs. Deb: 7/4/73																								
1973	Min-A	0	5	.000	23	6	0	0	2	60¹	64	5	30	42	14.0	4.92	80	.270	.359	0	—	0	-7	-6	1	-0.7
1975	Min-A	3	1	.750	4	4	0	0	0	28¹	28	2	15	14	14.0	2.86	135	.262	.358	0	—	0	3	3	-1	0.2
1976	Min-A	4	7	.364	17	15	1	0	0	79¹	92	6	39	24	14.9	5.11	71	.290	.368	0	—	0	-14	-13	-2	-2.0
Total	3	7	13	.350	44	25	1	0	2	168	182	13	84	80	14.4	4.66	81	.278	.363	0	—	0	-19	-17	-1	-2.5
● DICK BANEY	Baney, Richard Lee b: 11/1/46, Fullerton, Cal. BR/TR, 6', 185 lbs. Deb: 7/11/69																								
1969	Sea-A	1	0	1.000	9	1	0	0	0	18²	18	2	9	13	13.5	3.86	94	.292	.354	0	.000	-0	-0	-0	-0	-0.1
1973	Cin-N	2	1	.667	11	1	0	0	2	30²	26	1	6	17	10.6	2.93	116	.234	.298	2	.222	1	2	2	-1	0.1
1974	Cin-N	1	0	1.000	22	1	0	0	1	41	51	4	17	12	14.9	5.49	64	.305	.370	0	.000	-1	-9	-9	-1	-0.4
Total	3	4	1	.800	42	3	0	0	3	90¹	98	7	30	38	13.2	4.28	81	.280	.344	2	.125	-0	-7	-8	-3	-0.4
● DAN BANKHEAD	Bankhead, Daniel Robert b: 5/3/20, Empire, Ala. d: 5/2/76, Houston, Tex. BR/TR, 6'1", 184 lbs. Deb: 8/26/47																								
1947	*Bro-N	0	0	—	4	0	0	0	1	10	15	1	8	6	21.6	7.20	57	.341	.453	1	.250	1	-3	-3	-0	0.0
1950	Bro-N	9	4	.692	41	12	2	1	3	129¹	119	16	88	96	14.5	5.50	75	.252	.371	9	.231	1	-19	-20	-1	-1.8
1951	Bro-N	0	1	.000	7	1	0	0	0	14	27	5	14	9	26.4	15.43	25	.422	.526	0	.000	-0	-18	-18	-1	-1.1
Total	3	9	5	.643	52	13	2	1	4	153¹	161	22	110	111	16.1	6.52	63	.277	.395	10	.222	2	-41	-41	-1	-2.9
● SCOTT BANKHEAD	Bankhead, Michael Scott b: 7/31/63, Raleigh, N.C. BR/TR, 5'10", 175 lbs. Deb: 5/25/86																								
1986	KC-A	8	9	.471	24	17	0	0	0	121	121	14	37	94	12.0	4.61	92	.259	.318	0	—	0	-6	-5	-0	-0.7
1987	Sea-A	9	8	.529	27	25	2	0	0	149¹	168	35	37	95	12.5	5.42	87	.283	.329	0	—	0	-16	-12	-2	-1.5
1988	Sea-A	7	9	.438	21	21	2	1	0	135	115	8	38	102	10.4	3.07	136	.224	.278	0	—	0	13	16	-1	1.7
1989	Sea-A	14	6	.700	33	33	3	2	0	210¹	187	19	63	140	10.8	3.34	121	.239	.298	0	—	0	13	16	-2	1.3
1990	Sea-A	0	2	.000	4	4	0	0	0	13	18	2	7	10	11.08	36	.333	.410	0	—	0	-10	-10	-0	-1.3
1991	Sea-A	3	6	.333	17	9	0	0	0	60²	73	8	21	28	14.2	4.90	84	.297	.357	0	—	0	-5	-5	-0	-0.7
1992	Cin-N	10	4	.714	54	0	0	0	1	70²	57	4	29	53	11.3	2.93	123	.218	.304	2	.222	0	5	5	-2	0.9
1993	Bos-A	2	1	.667	40	0	0	0	0	64¹	59	7	29	47	12.3	3.50	132	.250	.332	0	—	0	6	8	-1	0.2
1994	Bos-A	3	2	.600	27	0	0	0	0	37²	34	5	12	25	11.0	4.54	113	.239	.299	0	—	0	0	0	0	0.0
Total	9	56	47	.544	247	109	7	3	1	862	832	102	273	594	11.7	4.09	104	.252	.312	2	.222	0	0	16	-9	-0.1
● BILL BANKS	Banks, William John (b: William John Yerrick) b: 2/26/1874, Danville, Pa. d: 9/8/36, Danville, Pa. BR/TR, 5'11", 150 lbs. Deb: 9/27/1895																								
1895	Bos-N	1	0	1.000	1	1	0	0	0	7	7	0	4	4	14.1	0.00	—	.256	.352	0	.000	-1	4	4	0	0.5
1896	Bos-N	0	3	.000	4	3	2	0	0	23	42	2	13	6	22.3	10.57	43	.389	.463	3	.273	0	-16	-15	-1	-1.4
Total	2	1	3	.250	5	4	2	0	0	30	49	2	17	10	20.4	8.10	58	.362	.441	3	.214	-1	-12	-11	-1	-0.9
● WILLIE BANKS	Banks, Willie Anthony b: 2/27/69, Jersey City, N.J. BR/TR, 6'1", 190 lbs. Deb: 7/31/91																								
1991	Min-A	1	1	.500	5	3	0	0	0	17¹	12	1	12	16	17.1	5.71	75	.288	.388	0	—	0	-3	-3	-1	-0.6
1992	Min-A	4	4	.500	16	12	0	0	0	71	80	6	37	37	15.1	5.70	71	.288	.375	0	—	0	-14	-13	-0	-1.5
1993	Min-A	11	12	.478	31	30	0	0	0	171¹	186	17	78	138	14.0	4.04	108	.280	.358	0	—	0	5	6	-1	0.6
1994	Chi-N	8	12	.400	23	23	1	1	0	138¹	139	16	56	91	12.8	5.40	76	.261	.333	5	.122	-1	-18	-20	-2	-2.6
Total	4	24	29	.453	75	68	1	1	0	398	426	40	183	282	13.9	4.88	86	.275	.354	5	.122	-1	-30	-30	-4	-4.1
● FLOYD BANNISTER	Bannister, Floyd Franklin b: 6/10/55, Pierre, S.D. BL/TL, 6'1", 195 lbs. Deb: 4/19/77																								
1977	Hou-N	8	9	.471	24	23	4	1	0	142²	138	11	68	112	13.2	4.04	88	.254	.341	9	.188	0	-2	-7	-1	-0.9
1978	Hou-N	3	9	.250	28	16	2	2	0	110¹	120	13	63	94	15.0	4.81	69	.280	.374	5	.161	0	-15	-18	-2	-2.0
1979	Sea-A	10	15	.400	30	30	2	1	0	182¹	185	20	68	115	12.7	4.05	108	.260	.328	0	—	0	3	6	-2	0.4
1980	Sea-A	9	13	.409	32	32	8	0	0	217²	200	24	66	155	11.1	3.47	119	.239	.296	0	—	0	14	16	-1	1.4
1981	Sea-A	9	9	.500	21	20	5	1	0	121¹	128	14	39	85	12.6	4.45	87	.268	.327	0	—	PB	-11	-8	-1	-1.3
1982	Sea-A★	12	13	.480	35	35	5	3	0	247	225	32	77	**209**	11.1	3.43	124	.243	.303	0	—	0	18	22	-1	1.9

YEAR TM/L	W	L	PCT	G	GS	CG	SH	SV	IP	H	HR	BB	SO	RAT	ERA	ERA+	OAV	OOB	BH	AVG	PB	PR	/A	PD	TPI
1983 *Chi-A	16	10	.615	34	34	5	2	0	217¹	191	19	71	193	10.9	3.35	125	.233	.295	0	—	0	17	20	-1	1.9
1984 Chi-A	14	11	.560	34	33	4	0	0	218	211	30	80	152	12.3	4.83	86	.252	.322	0	.000	0	-20	-16	-2	-1.8
1985 Chi-A	10	14	.417	34	34	4	1	0	210²	211	30	100	198	13.5	4.87	89	.261	.346	0	—	0	-17	-13	-1	-1.5
1986 Chi-A	10	14	.417	28	27	6	1	0	165¹	162	17	48	92	11.5	3.54	122	.259	.314	0	—	0	12	14	-1	1.7
1987 Chi-A	16	11	.593	34	34	11	2	0	228²	216	38	49	124	10.4	3.58	128	.246	.286	0	—	0	22	25	-3	2.3
1988 KC-A	12	13	.480	31	31	2	0	0	189¹	182	22	68	113	12.1	4.33	92	.248	.316	0	—	0	-8	-7	-0	-0.9
1989 KC-A	4	1	.800	14	14	0	0	0	75¹	87	8	18	35	12.7	4.66	83	.290	.332	0	—	0	-7	-7	1	-0.3
1991 Cal-A	0	0	—	16	0	0	0	0	25	25	5	10	16	12.6	3.96	104	.266	.337	0	—	0	0	0	-1	0.0
1992 Tex-A	1	1	.500	36	0	0	0	0	37	39	3	21	30	15.3	6.32	60	.281	.387	0	—	0	-10	-10	-0	-0.3
Total 15	134	143	.484	431	363	62	16	0	2388	2320	291	846	1723	12.1	4.06	101	.253	.319	14	.175	1	-3	16	-15	0.6

● JIMMY BANNON
Bannon, James Henry "Foxy Grandpa"   b: 5/5/1871, Amesbury, Mass.   d: 3/24/48, Glen Rock, N.J.   BR/TR, 5'5", 160 lbs.   Deb: 6/15/1893   F♦

YEAR TM/L	W	L	PCT	G	GS	CG	SH	SV	IP	H	HR	BB	SO	RAT	ERA	ERA+	OAV	OOB	BH	AVG	PB	PR	/A	PD	TPI
1893 StL-N	0	1	.000	1	1	0	0	0	4	10	1	5	1	38.3	22.50	21	.458	.590	36	.336	0	-8	-8	-0	-1.0
1894 Bos-N	0	0	—	1	0	0	0	0	2	4	1	1	0	22.5	0.00	—	.410	.465	166	.336	0	1	1	0	0.0
1895 Bos-N	0	0	—	1	0	0	0	0	3	4	0	2	1	18.0	6.00	85	.315	.408	171	.350	0	-0	-0	0	0.0
Total 3	0	1	.000	3	1	0	0	0	9	18	2	8	2	28.0	12.00	42	.406	.516	459	.320	1	-7	-7	-0	-1.0

● JACK BANTA
Banta, John Kay   b: 6/24/25, Hutchinson, Kan.   BL/TR, 6'2.5", 175 lbs.   Deb: 9/18/47

YEAR TM/L	W	L	PCT	G	GS	CG	SH	SV	IP	H	HR	BB	SO	RAT	ERA	ERA+	OAV	OOB	BH	AVG	PB	PR	/A	PD	TPI
1947 Bro-N	0	1	.000	3	1	0	0	0	7²	7	1	4	3	14.1	7.04	59	.226	.333	0	.000	-0	-3	-2	1	-0.2
1948 Bro-N	0	1	.000	2	1	0	0	0	3¹	5	1	2	1	27.0	8.10	49	.385	.556	0	.000	-0	-2	-2	-0	-0.4
1949 *Bro-N	10	6	.625	48	12	2	1	3	152¹	125	12	68	97	11.8	3.37	122	.223	.314	5	.109	-2	11	12	1	1.1
1950 Bro-N	4	4	.500	16	5	1	0	2	41¹	39	2	36	15	17.0	4.35	94	.252	.402	2	.167	-0	-1	-1	-1	-0.3
Total 4	14	12	.538	69	19	3	1	5	204²	176	15	113	116	13.1	3.78	108	.232	.339	7	.115	-2	6	7	0	0.2

● STEVE BARBER
Barber, Stephen David   b: 2/22/39, Takoma Park, Md.   BL/TL, 6', 200 lbs.   Deb: 4/21/60

YEAR TM/L	W	L	PCT	G	GS	CG	SH	SV	IP	H	HR	BB	SO	RAT	ERA	ERA+	OAV	OOB	BH	AVG	PB	PR	/A	PD	TPI
1960 Bal-A	10	7	.588	36	27	6	1	2	181²	148	10	113	112	13.1	3.22	118	.226	.343	3	.056	-4	13	12	0	0.7
1961 Bal-A	18	12	.600	37	34	14	8	1	248¹	194	13	130	150	11.8	3.33	115	.218	.319	13	.162	2	19	14	4	2.2
1962 Bal-A	9	6	.600	28	19	5	2	0	140¹	145	9	61	89	13.3	3.46	107	.262	.337	3	.071	-2	8	4	1	0.3
1963 Bal-A†	20	13	.606	39	36	11	2	0	258²	253	12	92	180	12.1	2.75	126	.258	.324	12	.138	-0	25	21	2	2.8
1964 Bal-A	9	13	.409	36	26	4	0	1	157	144	15	81	118	13.3	3.84	93	.248	.347	7	.149	1	-4	-5	3	-0.3
1965 Bal-A	15	10	.600	37	32	7	2	0	220²	177	16	81	130	10.6	2.69	129	.224	.297	5	.077	-2	19	19	1	2.1
1966 Bal-A☆	10	5	.667	25	22	5	3	0	133¹	104	6	49	91	10.5	2.30	145	.218	.294	3	.068	-3	17	15	1	1.5
1967 Bal-A	4	9	.308	15	15	1	1	0	74²	47	5	61	48	13.6	4.10	77	.185	.353	2	.091	-1	-7	-8	0	-1.3
NY-A	6	9	.400	17	17	3	1	0	97²	103	4	54	70	14.7	4.05	77	.278	.375	5	.172	1	-9	-10	-1	-1.4
Yr	10	18	.357	32	32	4	2	0	172¹	150	9	115	118	14.0	4.07	77	.238	.358	7	.137	0	-16	-18	-0	-2.7
1968 NY-A	6	5	.545	20	19	3	1	0	128¹	127	7	64	87	13.6	3.23	90	.256	.345	2	.051	-1	-4	-5	0	-0.5
1969 Sea-A	4	7	.364	25	16	0	0	0	86¹	99	9	48	69	15.4	4.80	76	.292	.381	5	.200	1	-11	-11	0	-1.2
1970 Chi-N	0	1	.000	5	0	0	0	0	5²	10	0	6	3	25.4	9.53	47	.417	.533	0	—	0	-3	-3	-0	-0.5
Atl-N	0	1	.000	5	2	0	0	0	14²	17	3	5	11	14.1	4.91	87	.288	.354	1	.250	0	-1	-1	-0	-0.1
Yr	0	2	.000	10	2	0	0	0	20¹	27	3	11	14	17.3	6.20	70	.325	.411	1	.250	0	-5	-4	-0	-0.6
1971 Atl-N	3	1	.750	39	3	0	0	2	75	92	6	25	40	14.3	4.80	77	.301	.357	2	.154	-1	-9	-9	0	-0.5
1972 Atl-N	0	0	—	5	0	0	0	0	15²	18	1	6	11	14.4	5.74	66	.290	.362	1	.200	1	-4	-3	1	0.1
Cal-A	4	4	.500	34	3	0	0	2	58	37	4	30	34	10.6	2.02	144	.188	.298	1	.143	1	7	6	-1	0.9
1973 Cal-A	3	2	.600	50	1	0	0	4	89¹	90	5	32	58	12.6	3.53	101	.265	.333	0	—	0	3	0	-1	0.5
1974 SF-N	0	1	.000	13	0	0	0	1	13²	13	0	12	13	16.5	5.27	72	.255	.397	0	—	0	-3	-2	-1	-0.2
Total 15	121	106	.533	466	272	59	21	13	1999	1818	125	950	1309	12.7	3.36	105	.245	.334	65	.115	-6	54	34	10	5.1

● STEVE BARBER
Barber, Steven Lee   b: 3/13/48, Grand Rapids, Mich.   BR/TR, 6'1", 190 lbs.   Deb: 4/9/70

YEAR TM/L	W	L	PCT	G	GS	CG	SH	SV	IP	H	HR	BB	SO	RAT	ERA	ERA+	OAV	OOB	BH	AVG	PB	PR	/A	PD	TPI
1970 Min-A	0	0	—	18	0	0	0	2	27¹	26	1	18	14	15.1	4.61	81	.263	.387	0	.000	-0	-3	-3	-0	-0.1
1971 Min-A	1	0	1.000	4	2	0	0	0	11²	8	2	13	4	16.2	6.17	58	.190	.382	0	.000	-1	-4	-3	-0	-0.3
Total 2	1	0	1.000	22	2	0	0	2	39	34	3	31	18	15.5	5.08	72	.241	.385	0	.000	-1	-6	-6	-1	-0.4

● FRANK BARBERICH
Barberich, Frank Frederick   b: 2/3/1882, Newtown, N.Y.   d: 5/1/65, Ocala, Fla.   BB/TR, 5'10.5", 175 lbs.   Deb: 9/17/07

YEAR TM/L	W	L	PCT	G	GS	CG	SH	SV	IP	H	HR	BB	SO	RAT	ERA	ERA+	OAV	OOB	BH	AVG	PB	PR	/A	PD	TPI
1907 Bos-N	1	1	.500	2	2	1	0	0	12¹	19	0	5	1	17.5	5.84	44	.358	.414	0	.000	-0	-5	-5	-0	-0.7
1910 Bos-A	0	0	—	2	0	0	0	0	5	7	0	2	0	16.2	7.20	35	.350	.409	0	.000	-0	-3	-3	0	0.0
Total 2	1	1	.500	4	2	1	0	0	17¹	26	0	7	1	17.1	6.23	41	.356	.412	0	.000	-0	-7	-7	-0	-0.7

● CURT BARCLAY
Barclay, Curtis Cordell   b: 8/22/31, Chicago, Ill.   d: 3/25/85, Missoula, Montana   BR/TR, 6'3", 210 lbs.   Deb: 4/21/57

YEAR TM/L	W	L	PCT	G	GS	CG	SH	SV	IP	H	HR	BB	SO	RAT	ERA	ERA+	OAV	OOB	BH	AVG	PB	PR	/A	PD	TPI
1957 NY-N	9	9	.500	37	28	5	2	0	183	196	21	48	67	12.1	3.44	114	.274	.321	11	.190	0	9	10	3	1.2
1958 SF-N	1	0	1.000	6	1	0	0	0	16	16	3	5	6	13.5	2.81	136	.258	.343	4	.667	2	2	2	0	0.3
1959 SF-N	0	0	—	1	0	0	0	0	0¹	2	0	2	0	108.0	54.00	7	.500	.667	0	—	0	-2	-2	-0	0.0
Total 3	10	9	.526	44	29	5	2	0	199¹	214	24	55	73	12.4	3.48	113	.274	.325	15	.234	2	9	10	3	1.5

● RAY BARE
Bare, Raymond Douglas   b: 4/15/49, Miami, Fla.   d: 3/29/94, Miami, Fla.   BR/TR, 6'2", 195 lbs.   Deb: 7/30/72

YEAR TM/L	W	L	PCT	G	GS	CG	SH	SV	IP	H	HR	BB	SO	RAT	ERA	ERA+	OAV	OOB	BH	AVG	PB	PR	/A	PD	TPI
1972 StL-N	0	1	.000	14	0	0	0	0	16²	18	0	6	5	13.0	0.54	630	.281	.343	0	—	0	5	5	-0	0.4
1974 StL-N	1	2	.333	10	3	0	0	0	24¹	22	2	9	6	12.6	5.92	60	.281	.347	1	.200	-0	-6	-6	1	-0.6
1975 Det-A	8	13	.381	29	21	6	1	0	150²	174	10	47	71	13.3	4.48	90	.293	.346	0	—	0	-12	-8	2	-1.1
1976 Det-A	7	8	.467	30	21	3	2	0	134	157	13	51	59	14.0	4.63	80	.293	.354	0	—	0	-17	-14	1	-1.4
1977 Det-A	0	2	.000	5	4	0	0	0	14¹	24	3	7	4	19.5	12.56	34	.381	.443	0	—	0	-14	-13	1	-1.6
Total 5	16	26	.381	88	49	9	3	1	340	398	28	120	145	13.7	4.79	84	.290	.354	1	.200	-0	-43	-36	4	-4.3

● JOHN BARFIELD
Barfield, John David   b: 10/15/64, Pine Bluff, Ark.   BL/TL, 6'1", 185 lbs.   Deb: 9/7/89

YEAR TM/L	W	L	PCT	G	GS	CG	SH	SV	IP	H	HR	BB	SO	RAT	ERA	ERA+	OAV	OOB	BH	AVG	PB	PR	/A	PD	TPI
1989 Tex-A	0	1	.000	4	2	0	0	0	11²	15	0	4	9	14.7	6.17	64	.319	.373	0	—	0	-3	-3	-0	-0.3
1990 Tex-A	4	3	.571	33	0	0	0	1	44¹	42	2	13	17	11.4	4.67	84	.268	.327	0	—	0	-4	-4	0	-0.5
1991 Tex-A	4	4	.500	28	9	0	0	1	83¹	96	11	22	27	12.7	4.54	89	.289	.333	0	—	0	-4	-5	-0	-0.4
Total 3	8	8	.500	65	11	0	0	2	139¹	153	13	39	53	12.5	4.72	85	.285	.335	0	—	0	-11	-11	-0	-1.2

● CLYDE BARFOOT
Barfoot, Clyde Raymond "Foots"   b: 7/8/1891, Richmond, Va.   d: 3/11/71, Highland Park, Cal   BR/TR, 6', 170 lbs.   Deb: 4/13/22

YEAR TM/L	W	L	PCT	G	GS	CG	SH	SV	IP	H	HR	BB	SO	RAT	ERA	ERA+	OAV	OOB	BH	AVG	PB	PR	/A	PD	TPI
1922 StL-N	4	5	.444	42	2	1	0	2	117²	139	2	30	19	13.7	4.21	92	.307	.363	12	.353	5	-1	-4	1	0.2
1923 StL-N	3	3	.500	33	2	1	1	1	101¹	112	7	27	23	12.4	3.73	105	.289	.337	7	.189	-1	3	2	0	0.0
1926 Det-A	1	2	.333	11	1	0	0	2	31¹	42	4	9	7	14.6	4.88	83	.318	.362	1	.200	-0	-3	-3	1	-0.2
Total 3	8	10	.444	86	5	2	1	5	250¹	293	13	66	49	13.3	4.10	95	.301	.353	20	.263	4	-1	-5	1	0.0

● GREG BARGAR
Bargar, Greg Robert   b: 1/27/59, Inglewood, Cal.   BR/TR, 6'2", 185 lbs.   Deb: 7/17/83

YEAR TM/L	W	L	PCT	G	GS	CG	SH	SV	IP	H	HR	BB	SO	RAT	ERA	ERA+	OAV	OOB	BH	AVG	PB	PR	/A	PD	TPI
1983 Mon-N	2	0	1.000	8	3	0	0	0	20	23	6	8	9	14.4	6.75	53	.271	.340	1	.167	-0	-7	-7	-1	-0.7
1984 Mon-N	0	1	.000	3	1	0	0	0	8	8	1	7	2	16.9	7.88	43	.286	.429	0	.000	-0	-4	-4	-0	-0.4
1986 StL-N	0	2	.000	22	0	0	0	0	27¹	36	3	10	12	16.1	5.60	65	.330	.402	0	.000	-0	-6	-6	1	-0.4
Total 3	2	3	.400	33	4	0	0	0	55¹	67	10	25	23	15.6	6.34	57	.302	.382	1	.111	-0	-16	-17	0	-1.5

● CY BARGER
Barger, Eros Bolivar   b: 5/18/1885, Jamestown, Ky.   d: 9/23/64, Columbia, Ky.   BL/TR, 6', 160 lbs.   Deb: 8/30/06

YEAR TM/L	W	L	PCT	G	GS	CG	SH	SV	IP	H	HR	BB	SO	RAT	ERA	ERA+	OAV	OOB	BH	AVG	PB	PR	/A	PD	TPI
1906 NY-A	0	0	—	2	1	0	0	1	5¹	7	0	3	3	16.9	10.13	29	.319	.401	1	.333	0	-4	-4	-0	-0.2
1907 NY-A	0	0	—	1	0	0	0	0	6	4	0	5	1	18.0	3.00	93	.372	.372	0	.0	0	-0	-0	-1	-0.1
1910 Bro-N	15	15	.500	35	30	25	2	1	271²	267	2	107	87	12.6	2.88	105	.275	.351	24	.231	-8	5	5	2	1.0
1911 Bro-N	11	15	.423	30	30	21	1	0	217¹	224	4	71	60	12.5	3.52	95	.279	.342	33	.228	1	-3	-4	1	-0.2
1912 Bro-N	1	9	.100	16	11	6	0	0	94	120	4	42	30	15.9	5.46	61	.326	.401	7	.189	-0	-21	-22	1	-1.9

YEAR TM/L	W	L	PCT	G	GS	CG	SH	SV	IP	H	HR	BB	SO	RAT	ERA	ERA+	OAV	OOB	BH	AVG	PB	PR	/A	PD	TPI
1914 Pit-F	10	16	.385	33	26	18	1	1	228¹	252	7	63	70	12.7	4.34	66	.290	.342	17	.205	-1	-37	-37	-2	-4.0
1915 Pit-F	9	8	.529	34	13	8	1	6	153	130	1	47	47	10.6	2.29	118	.238	.303	15	.278	2	7	7	-1	0.9
Total 7	46	63	.422	151	111	78	5	9	975²	1010	18	334	297	12.7	3.56	85	.280	.346	97	.227	5	-54	-56	-0	-4.5

● **LEN BARKER**   Barker, Leonard Harold b: 7/7/55, Fort Knox, Ky.   BR/TR, 6'5", 225 lbs.   Deb: 9/14/76

YEAR TM/L	W	L	PCT	G	GS	CG	SH	SV	IP	H	HR	BB	SO	RAT	ERA	ERA+	OAV	OOB	BH	AVG	PB	PR	/A	PD	TPI
1976 Tex-A	1	0	1.000	2	2	1	0	0	15	7	0	6	7	9.0	2.40	149	.149	.273	0	—	0	2	2	-0	0.1
1977 Tex-A	4	1	.800	15	3	0	0	1	47¹	36	1	24	51	11.6	2.66	153	.217	.319	0	—	0	7	7	1	0.8
1978 Tex-A	1	5	.167	29	0	0	0	4	52¹	63	6	29	33	16.2	4.82	78	.304	.395	0	—	0	-6	-6	-0	-0.7
1979 Cle-A	6	6	.500	29	19	2	0	0	137¹	146	6	70	93	14.3	4.92	87	.277	.364	0	—	0	-11	-10	-1	-0.9
1980 Cle-A	19	12	.613	36	36	8	1	0	246¹	237	17	92	**187**	12.1	4.17	98	.252	.320	0	—	0	-4	-3	-2	-0.5
1981 Cle-A★	8	7	.533	22	22	9	3	0	154¹	150	7	46	**127**	11.5	3.91	93	.249	.303	0	—	0	-4	-5	-0	-0.4
1982 Cle-A	15	11	.577	33	33	10	1	0	244²	211	18	88	187	11.1	3.90	105	.232	.301	0	—	0	5	5	-0	0.5
1983 Cle-A	8	13	.381	24	24	4	1	0	149²	150	16	52	105	12.3	5.11	83	.266	.330	0	—	0	-17	-15	-1	-2.0
Atl-N	1	3	.250	6	6	0	0	0	33	31	0	14	21	12.3	3.82	102	.248	.324	1	.125	-0	-1	0	1	0.1
1984 Atl-N	7	8	.467	21	20	1	0	0	126¹	120	10	38	95	11.4	3.85	100	.254	.312	2	.053	-1	-4	0	3	0.2
1985 Atl-N	2	9	.182	20	18	0	0	0	73²	84	10	37	47	14.9	6.35	61	.288	.370	-2	.000	-2	-23	-21	-1	-3.0
1987 Mil-A	2	1	.667	11	11	0	0	0	43²	54	6	17	22	15.0	5.36	85	.303	.371	0	—	0	-4	-4	-0	-0.4
Total 11	74	76	.493	248	194	35	7	5	1323²	1289	96	513	975	12.4	4.34	93	.256	.327	3	.048	-3	-59	-48	-1	-6.2

● **JEFF BARKLEY**   Barkley, Jeffrey Carver b: 11/21/59, Hickory, N.C.   BB/TR, 6'3", 185 lbs.   Deb: 9/16/84

YEAR TM/L	W	L	PCT	G	GS	CG	SH	SV	IP	H	HR	BB	SO	RAT	ERA	ERA+	OAV	OOB	BH	AVG	PB	PR	/A	PD	TPI
1984 Cle-A	0	0	—	3	0	0	0	0	4	6	0	1	4	15.8	6.75	67	.353	.389	0	—	0	-1	-1	0	-0.1
1985 Cle-A	0	3	.000	21	0	0	0	1	41	37	5	15	30	11.4	5.27	78	.243	.311	0	—	0	-5	-5	0	-0.3
Total 2	0	3	.000	24	0	0	0	1	45	43	5	16	34	11.8	5.40	76	.254	.319	0	—	0	-6	-6	0	-0.4

● **MIKE BARLOW**   Barlow, Michael Roswell b: 4/30/48, Stamford, N.Y.   BL/TR, 6'6", 215 lbs.   Deb: 6/18/75

YEAR TM/L	W	L	PCT	G	GS	CG	SH	SV	IP	H	HR	BB	SO	RAT	ERA	ERA+	OAV	OOB	BH	AVG	PB	PR	/A	PD	TPI
1975 StL-N	0	0	—	9	0	0	0	0	7²	11	0	3	2	17.6	4.70	80	.355	.429	0	—	0	-1	-1	-0	0.0
1976 Hou-N	2	2	.500	16	0	0	0	0	22	27	0	17	11	18.0	4.50	71	.318	.431	0	.000	-0	-2	-3	1	-0.5
1977 Cal-A	4	2	.667	20	1	0	0	1	59	53	5	27	25	12.8	4.58	86	.249	.344	0	—	0	-3	-4	0	-0.1
1978 Cal-A	0	0	—	1	0	0	0	0	2	3	0	0	1	13.5	4.50	80	.375	.375	0	—	0	-0	-0	-0	0.0
1979 *Cal-A	1	1	.500	35	0	0	0	0	86	106	8	30	33	14.7	5.13	79	.314	.376	0	—	0	-9	-10	0	0.0
1980 Tor-A	3	1	.750	40	1	0	0	5	55	57	4	21	19	13.1	4.09	105	.273	.345	0	—	0	-0	-1	-0	-0.1
1981 Tor-A	0	0	—	12	0	0	0	0	15	22	1	6	5	19.2	4.20	94	.338	.427	0	—	0	-1	-0	0	-0.1
Total 7	10	6	.625	133	2	0	0	6	246²	279	16	104	96	14.5	4.63	86	.294	.373	0	.000	-0	-17	-18	0	-0.7

● **CHARLIE BARNABE**   Barnabe, Charles Edward b: 6/12/1900, Russell Gulch, Colo.   d: 8/16/77, Waco, Tex.   BL/TL, 5'11.5", 164 lbs.   Deb: 4/14/27

YEAR TM/L	W	L	PCT	G	GS	CG	SH	SV	IP	H	HR	BB	SO	RAT	ERA	ERA+	OAV	OOB	BH	AVG	PB	PR	/A	PD	TPI
1927 Chi-A	0	5	.000	17	4	1	0	0	61	86	2	20	5	16.4	5.31	76	.351	.411	3	.158	1	-8	-9	1	-0.4
1928 Chi-A	0	2	.000	7	2	0	0	0	9²	17	0	0	3	16.8	6.52	62	.395	.409	4	.500	2	-3	-3	1	-0.2
Total 2	0	7	.000	24	6	1	0	0	70²	103	2	20	8	16.4	5.48	74	.358	.411	7	.259	3	-11	-11	1	-0.6

● **BRIAN BARNES**   Barnes, Brian Keith b: 3/25/67, Roanoke Rapids, N.C.   BL/TL, 5'9", 170 lbs.   Deb: 9/14/90

YEAR TM/L	W	L	PCT	G	GS	CG	SH	SV	IP	H	HR	BB	SO	RAT	ERA	ERA+	OAV	OOB	BH	AVG	PB	PR	/A	PD	TPI
1990 Mon-N	1	1	.500	4	4	1	0	0	28	25	2	7	23	10.3	2.89	126	.236	.283	0	.000	-1	3	2	0	0.1
1991 Mon-N	5	8	.385	28	27	1	0	0	160	135	16	84	117	12.7	4.22	86	.233	.336	4	.082	-1	-10	-11	1	-0.7
1992 Mon-N	6	6	.500	21	17	0	0	0	100	77	9	46	65	11.3	2.97	117	.213	.307	8	.276	2	6	6	0	0.9
1993 Mon-N	2	6	.250	52	8	0	0	3	100	105	9	48	60	13.8	4.41	95	.274	.355	3	.150	-0	-4	-3	-0	-0.2
1994 Cle-A	0	1	.000	6	0	0	0	0	13¹	12	2	15	5	18.2	5.40	91	.235	.409	0	—	0	-1	-1	0	-0.2
LA-N	0	0	—	5	0	0	0	0	5	10	1	4	5	25.2	7.20	55	.400	.483	0	—	0	-2	-2	-0	0.0
Total 5	14	22	.389	116	56	2	0	3	406¹	364	39	204	275	12.8	3.94	95	.242	.335	15	.140	1	-7	-8	1	-0.1

● **FRANK BARNES**   Barnes, Frank b: 8/26/26, Longwood, Miss.   BR/TR, 6', 170 lbs.   Deb: 9/22/57

YEAR TM/L	W	L	PCT	G	GS	CG	SH	SV	IP	H	HR	BB	SO	RAT	ERA	ERA+	OAV	OOB	BH	AVG	PB	PR	/A	PD	TPI
1957 StL-N	0	1	.000	3	1	0	0	0	10	13	0	9	5	19.8	4.50	88	.317	.440	0	.000	-0	-1	-1	-0	-0.1
1958 StL-N	1	1	.500	8	1	0	0	0	19	19	3	16	17	17.5	7.58	54	.260	.407	1	.167	-0	-8	-7	-0	-0.7
1960 StL-N	0	1	.000	4	1	0	0	1	7²	8	1	9	8	21.1	3.52	116	.267	.450	0	.000	-0	0	0	-0	0.0
Total 3	1	3	.250	15	3	0	0	1	36²	40	4	34	30	18.9	5.89	69	.278	.425	1	.100	-1	-8	-7	-1	-0.8

● **FRANK BARNES**   Barnes, Frank Samuel "Lefty" b: 1/9/1900, Dallas, Tex.   d: 9/27/67, Houston, Tex.   BL/TL, 6'2.5", 195 lbs.   Deb: 4/18/29

YEAR TM/L	W	L	PCT	G	GS	CG	SH	SV	IP	H	HR	BB	SO	RAT	ERA	ERA+	OAV	OOB	BH	AVG	PB	PR	/A	PD	TPI
1929 Det-A	0	1	.000	4	1	0	0	0	5	10	3	3	0	25.2	7.20	60	.400	.483	0	.000	-0	-2	-2	-0	-0.3
1930 NY-A	0	1	.000	2	2	0	0	0	12¹	13	0	13	2	19.7	8.03	54	.283	.450	2	.333	1	-5	-5	1	-0.1
Total 2	0	2	.000	6	3	0	0	0	17¹	23	3	16	2	21.3	7.79	55	.324	.461	2	.286	1	-6	-7	2	-0.4

● **JESSE BARNES**   Barnes, Jesse Lawrence "Nubby"   b: 8/26/1892, Perkins, Okla.   d: 9/9/61, Santa Rosa, N.Mex.   BL/TR, 6', 170 lbs.   Deb: 7/30/15   F

YEAR TM/L	W	L	PCT	G	GS	CG	SH	SV	IP	H	HR	BB	SO	RAT	ERA	ERA+	OAV	OOB	BH	AVG	PB	PR	/A	PD	TPI
1915 Bos-N	3	0	1.000	9	3	2	0	0	45¹	41	1	10	16	10.9	1.39	186	.244	.302	3	.176	-1	7	6	-1	0.3
1916 Bos-N	6	15	.286	33	18	9	3	1	163	154	3	37	55	10.8	2.37	105	.254	.302	9	.188	0	4	2	4	0.7
1917 Bos-N	13	21	.382	50	33	27	2	1	295	261	3	50	107	9.6	2.68	95	.241	.277	24	.238	1	-4	-3	3	0.3
1918 NY-N	6	1	.857	9	9	4	2	0	54²	53	0	13	12	10.9	1.81	145	.255	.299	4	.222	-0	6	5	2	0.9
1919 NY-N	**25**	9	.735	38	34	23	4	1	295²	263	8	35	92	9.1	2.40	117	.236	.260	32	.267	5	17	13	3	2.4
1920 NY-N	20	15	.571	43	34	23	2	0	292²	271	9	56	63	10.1	2.64	113	.250	.288	22	.204	-2	16	11	3	1.3
1921 *NY-N	15	9	.625	42	31	15	1	6	258²	298	13	44	56	12.0	3.10	118	.299	.331	19	.207	-1	20	16	1	1.4
1922 *NY-N	13	8	.619	37	30	14	2	0	212²	236	10	38	52	11.7	3.51	114	.278	.311	14	.182	-1	14	12	3	1.2
1923 NY-N	3	1	.750	12	4	1	0	1	36	48	1	13	12	15.3	6.25	61	.329	.384	3	.273	-0	-9	-10	1	-0.8
Bos-N	10	14	.417	31	23	12	5	2	195¹	204	8	43	41	11.4	2.76	144	.270	.310	10	.147	-4	27	27	3	2.9
Yr	13	15	.464	43	27	13	5	3	231¹	252	9	56	53	12.0	3.31	120	.280	.322	13	.165	-4	18	17	4	2.1
1924 Bos-N	15	20	.429	37	32	21	**4**	0	267²	292	7	53	49	11.6	3.23	118	.284	.319	20	.222	-1	19	18	1	2.1
1925 Bos-N	11	16	.407	32	28	17	0	0	216¹	255	14	63	55	13.3	4.53	88	.297	.346	16	.198	-1	-6	-13	-2	-1.5
1926 Bro-N	10	11	.476	31	24	10	1	1	158	204	6	35	29	13.7	5.24	73	.321	.358	14	.237	-0	-25	-25	-0	-2.9
1927 Bro-N	2	10	.167	18	10	2	0	0	78²	106	5	25	14	15.0	5.72	69	.331	.380	5	.217	-0	-16	-15	-0	-2.0
Total 13	152	150	.503	422	313	180	26	13	2569²	2686	88	515	653	11.3	3.22	104	.273	.310	195	.214	1	74	41	20	6.3

● **JUNIE BARNES**   Barnes, Junie Shoaf "Lefty" b: 12/1/11, Linwood, N.C.   d: 12/31/63, Jacksonville, N.C.   BL/TL, 5'11.5", 170 lbs.   Deb: 9/12/34

YEAR TM/L	W	L	PCT	G	GS	CG	SH	SV	IP	H	HR	BB	SO	RAT	ERA	ERA+	OAV	OOB	BH	AVG	PB	PR	/A	PD	TPI
1934 Cin-N	0	0	—	2	0	0	0	0	0¹	0	0	1	0	27.0	0.00	—	.000	.500	0	—	0	0	0	0	0.0

● **RICH BARNES**   Barnes, Richard Monroe b: 7/21/59, Palm Beach, Fla.   BR/TL, 6'4", 186 lbs.   Deb: 7/18/82

YEAR TM/L	W	L	PCT	G	GS	CG	SH	SV	IP	H	HR	BB	SO	RAT	ERA	ERA+	OAV	OOB	BH	AVG	PB	PR	/A	PD	TPI
1982 Chi-A	0	2	.000	6	2	0	0	1	17	21	1	4	6	14.3	4.76	85	.292	.346	0	—	0	-1	-1	-0	-0.1
1983 Cle-A	1	1	.500	4	2	0	0	0	11²	18	0	10	2	21.6	6.94	61	.375	.483	0	—	0	-4	-4	-0	-0.7
Total 2	1	3	.250	10	4	0	0	1	28²	39	1	14	8	17.3	5.65	73	.325	.404	0	—	0	-5	-5	-0	-0.8

● **BOB BARNES**   Barnes, Robert Avery "Lefty" b: 1/6/02, Washburn, Ill.   BL/TL, 5'11.5", 150 lbs.   Deb: 7/8/24

YEAR TM/L	W	L	PCT	G	GS	CG	SH	SV	IP	H	HR	BB	SO	RAT	ERA	ERA+	OAV	OOB	BH	AVG	PB	PR	/A	PD	TPI
1924 Chi-A	0	0	—	2	0	0	0	0	4²	14	1	0	1	27.0	19.29	21	.519	.519	0	.000	-0	-8	-8	-0	0.0

● **ROSS BARNES**   Barnes, Roscoe Charles b: 5/8/1850, Mount Morris, Ill.   d: 2/5/15, Chicago, Ill.   BR/TR, 5'8.5", 145 lbs.   Deb: 5/5/1871   U◆

YEAR TM/L	W	L	PCT	G	GS	CG	SH	SV	IP	H	HR	BB	SO	RAT	ERA	ERA+	OAV	OOB	BH	AVG	PB	PR	/A	PD	TPI
1876 Chi-N	0	0	—	1	0	0	0	0	1¹	7	0	0	0	47.3	20.25	12	.538	.538	138	.429	1	-3	-3	0	0.0

● **VIRGIL BARNES**   Barnes, Virgil Jennings "Zeke" b: 3/5/1897, Ontario, Kan.   d: 7/24/58, Wichita, Kan.   BR/TR, 6', 165 lbs.   Deb: 9/25/19   F

YEAR TM/L	W	L	PCT	G	GS	CG	SH	SV	IP	H	HR	BB	SO	RAT	ERA	ERA+	OAV	OOB	BH	AVG	PB	PR	/A	PD	TPI
1919 NY-N	0	0	—	1	0	0	0	0	2	6	0	1	1	31.5	18.00	16	.545	.583	0	—	0	-3	-3	0	0.0
1920 NY-N	0	0	—	1	1	0	0	0	7	9	1	2	2	12.9	3.86	78	.310	.333	0	.000	-0	-1	-1	0	-0.1
1922 NY-N	1	0	1.000	22	3	1	0	2	51²	46	1	11	16	9.9	3.48	115	.243	.285	2	.167	-1	4	3	0	0.1
1923 *NY-N	2	3	.400	22	6	2	0	1	53	59	2	19	16	13.2	3.91	98	.285	.345	0	.000	-2	1	0	-0	-0.2

YEAR TM/L	W	L	PCT	G	GS	CG	SH	SV	IP	H	HR	BB	SO	RAT	ERA	ERA+	OAV	OOB	BH	AVG	PB	PR	/A	PD	TPI
1924 *NY-N	16	10	.615	35	29	15	1	3	229¹	239	10	57	59	11.6	3.06	120	.270	.314	14	.182	-2	21	15	2	1.6
1925 NY-N	15	11	.577	32	27	17	1	2	221²	242	9	53	53	12.0	3.53	114	.281	.323	9	.101	-9	18	12	0	0.4
1926 NY-N	8	13	.381	31	25	9	2	1	185	183	4	56	54	11.8	2.87	131	.261	.318	3	.054	-7	20	18	-1	1.1
1927 NY-N	14	11	.560	35	29	12	2	2	228²	251	14	51	66	12.0	3.98	97	.283	.325	9	.108	-7	-1	-3	-1	-1.1
1928 NY-N	3	3	.500	10	9	3	1	0	55¹	71	3	18	11	14.5	5.04	78	.330	.382	2	.091	-2	-6	-7	-1	-0.9
Bos-N	2	7	.222	16	10	1	0	0	60¹	86	3	26	7	16.7	5.82	67	.344	.406	1	.059	-2	-12	-13	-1	-1.8
Yr	5	10	.333	26	19	4	1	0	115²	157	6	44	18	15.6	5.45	72	.338	.395	3	.077	-3	-19	-20	-1	-2.7
Total 9	61	59	.508	205	135	58	7	11	1094	1192	46	293	275	12.3	3.66	105	.282	.329	40	.108	-31	38	22	1	-0.9

● REX BARNEY
Barney, Rex Edward b: 12/19/24, Omaha, Neb. BR/TR, 6'3", 185 lbs. Deb: 8/18/43

YEAR TM/L	W	L	PCT	G	GS	CG	SH	SV	IP	H	HR	BB	SO	RAT	ERA	ERA+	OAV	OOB	BH	AVG	PB	PR	/A	PD	TPI
1943 Bro-N	2	2	.500	9	8	1	0	0	45¹	36	4	41	23	15.7	6.35	53	.217	.378	1	.056	-2	-15	-15	-0	-1.4
1946 Bro-N	2	5	.286	16	9	1	0	0	53²	46	2	51	36	16.3	5.87	58	.240	.399	4	.235	1	-15	-15	-0	-1.7
1947 *Bro-N	5	2	.714	28	9	0	0	0	77²	66	4	59	36	14.7	4.75	87	.240	.378	3	.111	-1	-6	-5	-1	-0.6
1948 Bro-N	15	13	.536	44	34	12	4	0	246²	193	17	122	138	11.7	3.10	129	.217	.315	14	.167	-2	23	25	-4	1.9
1949 *Bro-N	9	8	.529	38	20	6	2	1	140²	108	15	89	80	12.8	4.41	93	.216	.338	10	.213	-0	-6	-5	-3	-0.8
1950 Bro-N	2	1	.667	20	1	0	0	0	33²	25	6	48	23	20.0	6.42	64	.214	.449	1	.125	0	-9	-9	-1	-0.7
Total 6	35	31	.530	155	81	20	6	1	597²	474	48	410	336	13.5	4.31	91	.221	.350	33	.164	-4	-26	-24	-9	-3.3

● EDGAR BARNHART
Barnhart, Edgar Vernon b: 9/16/04, Providence, Mo. d: 9/14/84, Columbia, Mo. BL/TR, 5'10", 160 lbs. Deb: 9/23/24

YEAR TM/L	W	L	PCT	G	GS	CG	SH	SV	IP	H	HR	BB	SO	RAT	ERA	ERA+	OAV	OOB	BH	AVG	PB	PR	/A	PD	TPI
1924 StL-A	0	0	—	1	0	0	0	0	1	0	0	2	0	18.0	0.00	—	.000	.400	0	—	0	1	0	0.0

● LES BARNHART
Barnhart, Leslie Earl "Barney" b: 2/23/05, Hoxie, Kan. d: 10/7/71, Scottsdale, Ariz. BR/TR, 6', 180 lbs. Deb: 9/22/28

YEAR TM/L	W	L	PCT	G	GS	CG	SH	SV	IP	H	HR	BB	SO	RAT	ERA	ERA+	OAV	OOB	BH	AVG	PB	PR	/A	PD	TPI
1928 Cle-A	0	1	.000	2	1	0	0	0	9	13	1	4	1	17.0	7.00	59	.325	.386	1	.500	-1	-3	-3	-1	-0.3
1930 Cle-A	1	0	1.000	1	1	0	0	0	8¹	12	0	4	1	17.3	6.48	74	.364	.432	0	.000	-1	-2	-2	-0	-0.2
Total 2	1	1	.500	3	2	0	0	0	17¹	25	1	8	2	17.1	6.75	66	.342	.407	1	.200	-0	-5	-4	-0	-0.5

● GEORGE BARNICLE
Barnicle, George Bernard "Barney" b: 8/26/17, Fitchburg, Mass. d: 10/10/90, Largo, Fla. BR/TR, 6'2", 175 lbs. Deb: 9/6/39

YEAR TM/L	W	L	PCT	G	GS	CG	SH	SV	IP	H	HR	BB	SO	RAT	ERA	ERA+	OAV	OOB	BH	AVG	PB	PR	/A	PD	TPI
1939 Bos-N	2	2	.500	6	1	0	0	0	18¹	16	1	8	15	11.8	4.91	75	.235	.316	0	.000	-1	-2	-2	0	-0.5
1940 Bos-N	1	0	1.000	13	2	1	0	0	32²	28	1	31	11	17.9	7.44	50	.233	.414	0	.000	-1	-13	-14	1	-0.5
1941 Bos-N	0	1	.000	1	1	0	0	0	6²	5	0	4	2	13.5	6.75	53	.238	.385	0	.000	-0	-2	-2	0	-0.3
Total 3	3	3	.500	20	4	1	0	0	57²	49	2	43	28	15.5	6.55	56	.234	.382	0	.000	-2	-17	-18	1	-1.3

● ED BARNOWSKI
Barnowski, Edward Anthony b: 8/23/43, Scranton, Pa. BR/TR, 6'2", 195 lbs. Deb: 9/8/65

YEAR TM/L	W	L	PCT	G	GS	CG	SH	SV	IP	H	HR	BB	SO	RAT	ERA	ERA+	OAV	OOB	BH	AVG	PB	PR	/A	PD	TPI
1965 Bal-A	0	0	—	4	0	0	0	0	4¹	3	0	7	6	20.8	2.08	167	.200	.455	0	—	0	1	1	-0	0.0
1966 Bal-A	0	0	—	2	0	0	0	0	3	4	0	1	2	15.0	3.00	111	.364	.417	0	—	0	0	0	0	0.0
Total 2	0	0	—	6	0	0	0	0	7¹	7	0	8	8	18.4	2.45	139	.269	.441	0	—	0	1	1	-0	0.0

● SALOME BAROJAS
Barojas, Salome (Romero) b: 6/16/57, Cordoba, Mex. BR/TR, 5'9", 188 lbs. Deb: 4/11/82

YEAR TM/L	W	L	PCT	G	GS	CG	SH	SV	IP	H	HR	BB	SO	RAT	ERA	ERA+	OAV	OOB	BH	AVG	PB	PR	/A	PD	TPI
1982 Chi-A	6	6	.500	61	0	0	0	21	106²	96	9	46	56	12.1	3.54	114	.244	.324	0	—	0	6	6	3	1.2
1983 *Chi-A	3	3	.500	52	0	0	0	12	87¹	70	2	32	38	11.0	2.47	169	.224	.306	0	—	0	15	17	0	1.4
1984 Chi-A	3	2	.600	24	0	0	0	1	39¹	48	3	19	18	15.3	4.58	91	.310	.385	0	—	0	-3	-2	1	-0.3
Sea-A	6	5	.545	19	14	0	0	1	95¹	88	12	41	37	12.5	3.97	101	.249	.332	0	—	0	1	0	1	0.1
Yr	9	7	.563	43	14	0	0	2	134²	136	15	60	55	13.3	4.14	97	.268	.349	0	—	0	-2	-2	2	-0.2
1985 Sea-A	0	5	.000	17	4	0	0	0	52²	65	6	33	27	16.7	5.98	70	.305	.398	0	—	0	-11	-10	0	-0.9
1988 Phi-N	0	0	—	6	0	0	0	0	8²	7	1	8	1	15.6	8.31	43	.250	.417	0	—	0	-5	-5	-0	0.0
Total 5	18	21	.462	179	18	0	0	35	390	374	33	179	177	13.0	3.95	103	.257	.342	0	—	0	4	6	5	1.5

● JIM BARR
Barr, James Leland b: 2/10/48, Lynwood, Cal. BR/TR, 6'3", 205 lbs. Deb: 7/31/71

YEAR TM/L	W	L	PCT	G	GS	CG	SH	SV	IP	H	HR	BB	SO	RAT	ERA	ERA+	OAV	OOB	BH	AVG	PB	PR	/A	PD	TPI
1971 *SF-N	1	1	.500	17	0	0	0	0	35¹	33	3	5	16	9.9	3.57	95	.254	.287	0	.000	-0	-0	-1	1	0.0
1972 SF-N	8	10	.444	44	18	8	2	2	179	166	16	41	86	10.6	2.87	122	.246	.292	9	.184	1	12	12	1	1.4
1973 SF-N	11	17	.393	41	33	8	3	2	231¹	240	24	49	88	11.4	3.81	100	.268	.310	10	.152	-1	-4	0	-1	-0.1
1974 SF-N	13	9	.591	44	27	11	5	2	239²	223	17	47	84	10.2	2.74	139	.251	.293	18	.254	4	23	28	1	3.1
1975 SF-N	13	14	.481	35	33	12	2	0	244	244	17	58	77	11.3	3.06	124	.265	.310	9	.118	-3	15	20	3	2.2
1976 SF-N	15	12	.556	37	37	8	3	0	252¹	260	9	60	75	11.5	2.89	126	.266	.310	12	.162	2	17	21	3	2.8
1977 SF-N	12	16	.429	38	38	6	2	0	234¹	286	18	56	97	13.3	4.76	82	.306	.347	10	.132	-2	-22	-27	-3	-2.3
1978 SF-N	8	11	.421	32	25	5	2	1	163	180	7	35	44	11.9	3.53	98	.281	.319	5	.100	-3	1	-2	0	-0.4
1979 Cal-A	10	12	.455	36	25	5	0	0	197	217	22	55	69	12.6	4.20	97	.287	.338	0	—	0	-0	-3	2	-0.4
1980 Cal-A	1	4	.200	24	7	0	0	0	68	90	12	23	22	15.4	5.56	71	.323	.380	0	—	0	-12	-12	-0	-0.8
1982 SF-N	4	3	.571	53	9	1	1	2	128²	125	9	20	36	10.4	3.29	109	.262	.297	8	.250	1	4	4	0	0.4
1983 SF-N	5	3	.625	53	0	0	0	2	92²	106	7	20	47	12.3	3.98	89	.294	.332	2	.133	-0	-4	-5	0	-0.4
Total 12	101	112	.474	454	252	64	20	12	2065¹	2170	161	469	741	11.6	3.56	105	.273	.316	83	.162	-0	31	42	12	6.0

● BOB BARR
Barr, Robert Alexander b: 3/12/08, Newton, Mass. BR/TR, 6', 175 lbs. Deb: 9/11/35

YEAR TM/L	W	L	PCT	G	GS	CG	SH	SV	IP	H	HR	BB	SO	RAT	ERA	ERA+	OAV	OOB	BH	AVG	PB	PR	/A	PD	TPI
1935 Bro-N	0	0	—	2	0	0	0	0	2¹	5	0	2	0	27.0	3.86	103	.385	.467	0	—	0	0	0	-0	0.0

● BOB BARR
Barr, Robert McClelland b: 12/1856, Washington, D.C. d: 3/11/30, Washington, D.C. BR/TR, 6'1", 192 lbs. Deb: 6/23/1883

YEAR TM/L	W	L	PCT	G	GS	CG	SH	SV	IP	H	HR	BB	SO	RAT	ERA	ERA+	OAV	OOB	BH	AVG	PB	PR	/A	PD	TPI
1883 Pit-a	6	18	.250	26	23	19	0	1	203¹	263	5	28	81	12.9	4.38	73	.294	.316	35	.246	3	-24	-26	1	-2.1
1884 Was-a	9	23	.281	32	32	32	2	0	281	311	9	31	138	11.4	3.46	88	.258	.284	20	.148	-2	-7	-13	-1	-1.4
Ind-a	3	11	.214	16	16	15	0	0	132	160	2	19	69	12.5	4.98	66	.275	.304	12	.185	0	-25	-25	-1	-2.1
Yr	12	34	.261	48	48	47	2	0	413	471	11	50	207	11.5	3.94	79	.262	.284	32	.160	-2	-32	-38	-2	-3.5
1886 Was-N	3	18	.143	22	22	21	1	0	190²	216	7	54	80	12.7	4.30	76	.273	.320	13	.165	-2	-21	-21	-1	-2.1
1890 Roc-a	28	24	.538	57	54	52	3	0	493¹	458	7	219	209	12.6	3.25	110	.239	.321	36	.179	-1	34	17	3	1.6
1891 NY-N	0	4	.000	5	4	2	0	0	27	47	1	12	11	20.7	5.33	60	.368	.434	1	.091	-0	-6	-6	0	-0.7
Total 5	49	98	.333	158	151	141	6	1	1327¹	1455	31	363	588	12.6	3.83	87	.264	.313	117	.185	-3	-49	-74	1	-6.8

● STEVE BARR
Barr, Steven Charles b: 9/8/51, St.Louis, Mo. BL/TL, 6'4", 200 lbs. Deb: 10/1/74

YEAR TM/L	W	L	PCT	G	GS	CG	SH	SV	IP	H	HR	BB	SO	RAT	ERA	ERA+	OAV	OOB	BH	AVG	PB	PR	/A	PD	TPI
1974 Bos-A	1	0	1.000	1	1	1	0	0	9	7	0	6	3	13.0	4.00	96	.212	.333	0	—	0	-0	-0	0	-0.4
1975 Bos-A	0	1	.000	3	2	0	0	0	7	11	1	7	2	23.1	2.57	158	.367	.486	0	—	0	1	1	-0	-0.5
1976 Tex-A	2	6	.250	20	10	3	0	0	67²	70	10	44	27	15.2	5.59	64	.269	.375	0	—	0	-16	-15	0	-1.6
Total 3	3	7	.300	24	13	4	0	0	83²	88	11	57	32	15.6	5.16	71	.272	.382	0	—	0	-15	-14	0	-2.5

● RED BARRETT
Barrett, Charles Henry b: 2/14/15, Santa Barbara, Cal d: 7/28/90, Wilson, N.C. BR/TR, 5'11", 183 lbs. Deb: 9/15/37

YEAR TM/L	W	L	PCT	G	GS	CG	SH	SV	IP	H	HR	BB	SO	RAT	ERA	ERA+	OAV	OOB	BH	AVG	PB	PR	/A	PD	TPI
1937 Cin-N	0	0	—	1	0	0	0	0	6¹	5	0	2	1	9.9	1.42	263	.227	.292	0	.000	-0	2	2	-0	-0.1
1938 Cin-N	2	0	1.000	6	2	0	0	0	28²	28	2	5	3	13.5	3.14	116	.257	.347	1	.143	-0	2	2	-0	0.0
1939 Cin-N	0	0	—	2	0	0	0	0	5¹	5	0	1	1	10.1	1.69	227	.263	.300	0	.000	-0	2	2	-0	0.0
1940 Cin-N	1	0	1.000	3	0	0	0	0	2²	5	0	1	1	20.3	6.75	56	.455	.500	0	—	0	-1	-1	0	-0.3
1943 Bos-N	12	18	.400	38	31	14	3	0	255	240	11	63	64	10.8	3.18	107	.250	.298	11	.136	-4	6	7	1	0.4
1944 Bos-N	9	16	.360	42	30	11	1	2	230¹	257	13	63	54	12.6	4.06	94	.285	.329	13	.173	-1	-12	-6	2	-0.6
1945 Bos-N	2	3	.400	9	5	2	0	2	38	43	6	16	13	14.2	4.74	81	.281	.353	2	.222	-4	-4	-4	1	-0.4
StL-N†	21	9	.700	36	29	22	3	0	246²	244	12	38	63	10.3	2.74	137	.256	.285	10	.112	-5	29	28	-1	2.5
Yr	23	12	.657	45	34	24	3	2	284²	287	18	54	76	10.8	3.00	125	.259	.302	12	.122	-5	25	24	0	2.1
1946 StL-N	3	2	.600	28	7	1	0	1	67	75	5	24	22	13.6	4.03	86	.282	.346	1	.059	-1	-5	-4	1	-0.4
1947 Bos-N	11	12	.478	36	30	12	3	1	210²	200	16	52	53	10.9	3.55	110	.244	.292	8	.111	4	12	8	0	0.5
1948 *Bos-N	7	8	.467	34	13	3	0	0	128¹	132	9	26	40	11.1	3.65	105	.268	.305	7	.179	-1	4	3	1	0.3

YEAR	TM/L	W	L	PCT	G	GS	CG	SH	SV	IP	H	HR	BB	SO	RAT	ERA	ERA+	OAV	OOB	BH	AVG	PB	PR	/A	PD	TPI
1949	Bos-N	1	1	.500	23	0	0	0	0	44¹	58	4	10	17	14.2	5.68	66	.326	.368	1	.200	-0	-8	-9	1	-0.3
Total	11	69	69	.500	253	149	67	11	7	1263¹	1292	78	312	333	11.5	3.53	105	.264	.309	54	.136	-16	28	26	5	1.6

● FRANK BARRETT
Barrett, Francis Joseph "Red" b: 7/1/13, Ft.Lauderdale, Fla BR/TR, 6'2", 173 lbs. Deb: 10/1/39

YEAR	TM/L	W	L	PCT	G	GS	CG	SH	SV	IP	H	HR	BB	SO	RAT	ERA	ERA+	OAV	OOB	BH	AVG	PB	PR	/A	PD	TPI
1939	StL-N	0	1	.000	1	0	0	0	0	1²	1	0	1	3	10.8	5.40	76	.167	.286	0	—	0	-0	-0	0	-0.1
1944	Bos-A	8	7	.533	38	2	0	0	8	90¹	93	5	42	40	13.5	3.69	92	.271	.352	4	.143	-1	-3	-3	-0	-0.6
1945	Bos-A	4	3	.571	37	0	0	0	3	86	77	0	29	35	11.1	2.62	130	.249	.314	5	.250	-1	7	8	-1	0.7
1946	Bos-A	2	4	.333	23	0	0	0	0	35¹	35	2	17	12	13.5	5.09	67	.252	.338	0	.000	-1	-7	-7	1	-1.0
1950	Pit-N	1	2	.333	5	0	0	0	0	4¹	5	1	1	0	12.5	4.15	106	.357	.400	0	—	0	-0	0	0	0.1
Total	5	15	17	.469	104	2	0	0	12	217²	211	8	90	90	12.5	3.51	98	.260	.336	9	.167	-1	-2	-2	1	-0.9

● TIM BARRETT
Barrett, Timothy Wayne b: 1/24/61, Huntingburg, Ind. BL/TR, 6'1", 185 lbs. Deb: 7/18/88

YEAR	TM/L	W	L	PCT	G	GS	CG	SH	SV	IP	H	HR	BB	SO	RAT	ERA	ERA+	OAV	OOB	BH	AVG	PB	PR	/A	PD	TPI
1988	Mon-N	0	0	—	4	0	0	0	1	9¹	10	2	2	5	11.6	5.79	62	.270	.308	0	.000	-0	-2	-2	0	-0.1

● DICK BARRETT
Barrett, Tracy Souter "Kewpie Dick" (a.k.a. Richard Oliver 1933 And Richard Oliver Barrett 1934-43)
b: 9/28/06, Montoursville, Pa d: 10/30/66, Seattle, Wash. BR/TR, 5'9", 175 lbs. Deb: 6/27/33

YEAR	TM/L	W	L	PCT	G	GS	CG	SH	SV	IP	H	HR	BB	SO	RAT	ERA	ERA+	OAV	OOB	BH	AVG	PB	PR	/A	PD	TPI
1933	Phi-A	4	4	.500	15	7	3	0	0	70¹	74	2	49	26	15.9	5.76	74	.272	.385	6	.286	2	-12	-12	0	-0.9
1934	Bos-N	1	3	.250	15	3	0	0	0	32¹	50	2	12	14	17.3	6.68	57	.365	.416	1	.143	-0	-9	-10	1	-1.0
1943	Chi-N	0	4	.000	15	4	0	0	0	45	52	2	28	20	16.2	4.80	70	.291	.389	1	.111	-1	-7	-7	-0	-0.7
	Phi-N	10	9	.526	23	20	10	2	1	169¹	137	5	51	65	10.1	2.39	141	.221	.282	7	.143	-1	19	18	0	2.2
	Yr	10	13	.435	38	24	10	2	1	214¹	189	7	79	85	11.3	2.90	116	.236	.306	8	.138	-1	12	11	0	1.5
1944	Phi-N	12	18	.400	37	27	11	1	0	221¹	223	7	88	74	12.8	3.86	94	.262	.333	16	.216	2	-6	-6	2	-0.3
1945	Phi-N	8	20	.286	36	30	8	0	1	190²	217	11	92	72	14.9	5.38	71	.281	.363	9	.145	-1	-33	-33	1	-4.2
Total	5	35	58	.376	141	91	32	3	2	729	753	29	320	271	13.4	4.28	86	.266	.343	40	.180	1	-49	-50	4	-4.9

● BILL BARRETT
Barrett, William Joseph "Whispering Bill" b: 5/28/1900, Cambridge, Mass. d: 1/26/51, Cambridge, Mass. BR/TR, 6', 175 lbs. Deb: 5/13/21 ◆

YEAR	TM/L	W	L	PCT	G	GS	CG	SH	SV	IP	H	HR	BB	SO	RAT	ERA	ERA+	OAV	OOB	BH	AVG	PB	PR	/A	PD	TPI
1921	Phi-A	1	0	1.000	4	0	0	0	0	5	2	0	9	2	19.8	7.20	62	.133	.458	7	.233	0	-2	-2	0	-0.2

● FRANCISCO BARRIOS
Barrios, Francisco Javier (Jimenez)
b: 6/10/53, Hermosillo, Mex. d: 4/9/82, Hermosillo, Mexico BR/TR, 6'3", 195 lbs. Deb: 8/18/74

YEAR	TM/L	W	L	PCT	G	GS	CG	SH	SV	IP	H	HR	BB	SO	RAT	ERA	ERA+	OAV	OOB	BH	AVG	PB	PR	/A	PD	TPI
1974	Chi-A	0	0	—	2	0	0	0	0	2	7	0	2	2	40.5	27.00	14	.538	.600	0	—	0	-5	-5	-0	-0.2
1976	Chi-A	5	9	.357	35	14	6	0	3	141²	136	13	46	81	11.8	4.32	83	.255	.318	0	—	0	-13	-12	-1	-1.3
1977	Chi-A	14	7	.667	33	31	9	0	0	231¹	241	22	58	119	11.8	4.12	99	.267	.315	0	—	0	-2	-1	-1	-0.1
1978	Chi-A	9	15	.375	33	32	9	2	0	195²	180	13	85	79	12.5	4.05	94	.246	.330	0	—	0	-6	-5	2	-0.4
1979	Chi-A	8	3	.727	15	15	2	0	0	94²	98	9	33	28	12.0	3.61	118	.242	.314	0	—	0	6	7	-0	0.6
1980	Chi-A	1	1	.500	3	3	0	0	0	16¹	21	4	8	2	16.5	4.96	81	.323	.405	0	—	0	-2	-2	-0	-0.2
1981	Chi-A	1	3	.250	8	7	1	0	0	36¹	45	3	14	12	14.9	3.96	90	.292	.355	0	—	0	-1	-2	-0	-0.2
Total	7	38	38	.500	129	102	27	2	3	718	718	64	246	323	12.4	4.15	94	.260	.326	0	—	0	-22	-20	-1	-1.8

● FRANK BARRON
Barron, Frank John b: 8/6/1890, St.Marys, W.Va. d: 9/18/64, St.Marys, W.Va. BL/TL, 6'1", 175 lbs. Deb: 8/19/14

YEAR	TM/L	W	L	PCT	G	GS	CG	SH	SV	IP	H	HR	BB	SO	RAT	ERA	ERA+	OAV	OOB	BH	AVG	PB	PR	/A	PD	TPI
1914	Was-A	0	0	—	1	0	0	0	0	1	1	0	0	1	9.0	0.00	—	.333	.333	0	—	0	0	0	0	0.0

● ED BARRY
Barry, Edward "Jumbo" b: 10/2/1882, Madison, Wis. d: 6/19/20, Montague, Mass. TL, 6'3", 185 lbs. Deb: 8/21/05

YEAR	TM/L	W	L	PCT	G	GS	CG	SH	SV	IP	H	HR	BB	SO	RAT	ERA	ERA+	OAV	OOB	BH	AVG	PB	PR	/A	PD	TPI
1905	Bos-A	1	2	.333	7	5	2	0	0	40²	38	2	15	18	12.6	2.88	94	.249	.332	1	.091	-0	-1	-1	-2	-0.3
1906	Bos-A	3	3	.000	3	3	3	0	0	21	23	2	5	10	13.3	6.00	46	.281	.345	1	.111	-0	-8	-8	0	-0.9
1907	Bos-A	0	1	.000	2	2	1	0	0	17¹	13	1	5	6	9.9	2.08	124	.210	.280	0	.000	-0	1	1	-0	0.0
Total	3	1	6	.143	12	10	6	0	0	79	74	5	25	34	12.2	3.53	76	.250	.325	2	.087	-1	-8	-7	-2	-1.2

● HARDIN BARRY
Barry, Hardin "Finn" b: 3/26/1891, Susanville, Cal. d: 11/5/69, Carson City, Nev. BR/TR, 6', 185 lbs. Deb: 6/21/12

YEAR	TM/L	W	L	PCT	G	GS	CG	SH	SV	IP	H	HR	BB	SO	RAT	ERA	ERA+	OAV	OOB	BH	AVG	PB	PR	/A	PD	TPI
1912	Phi-A	0	0	—	3	0	0	0	0	13	18	0	4	3	15.9	7.62	40	.360	.418	0	.000	-0	-6	-7	-0	-0.1

● TOM BARRY
Barry, Thomas Arthur b: 4/10/1879, St.Louis, Mo. d: 6/4/46, St.Louis, Mo. TR, 5'9", 155 lbs. Deb: 4/15/04

YEAR	TM/L	W	L	PCT	G	GS	CG	SH	SV	IP	H	HR	BB	SO	RAT	ERA	ERA+	OAV	OOB	BH	AVG	PB	PR	/A	PD	TPI
1904	Phi-N	0	1	.000	1	1	0	0	0	0²	6	0	1	1	94.5	40.50	7	.667	.700	0	—	0	-3	-3	0	-1.7

● BOB BARTHELSON
Barthelson, Robert Edward b: 7/15/24, New Haven, Conn. BR/TR, 6', 185 lbs. Deb: 7/4/44

YEAR	TM/L	W	L	PCT	G	GS	CG	SH	SV	IP	H	HR	BB	SO	RAT	ERA	ERA+	OAV	OOB	BH	AVG	PB	PR	/A	PD	TPI
1944	NY-N	1	1	.500	7	1	0	0	0	9²	13	2	5	4	16.8	4.66	79	.310	.383	0	—	0	-1	-1	-0	-0.2

● JOHN BARTHOLD
Barthold, John Francis "Hans" b: 4/14/1882, Philadelphia, Pa. d: 11/4/46, Fairview Village, Pa. BB/TR, 5'11", 180 lbs. Deb: 5/17/04

YEAR	TM/L	W	L	PCT	G	GS	CG	SH	SV	IP	H	HR	BB	SO	RAT	ERA	ERA+	OAV	OOB	BH	AVG	PB	PR	/A	PD	TPI
1904	Phi-A	0	0	—	4	0	0	0	0	10²	12	0	8	5	17.7	5.06	53	.284	.410	1	.333	1	-3	-A	-0	0.1

● LES BARTHOLOMEW
Bartholomew, Lester Justin b: 4/4/03, Madison, Wis. d: 9/19/72, Barrington, Ill. BR/TL, 5'11.5", 195 lbs. Deb: 4/11/28

YEAR	TM/L	W	L	PCT	G	GS	CG	SH	SV	IP	H	HR	BB	SO	RAT	ERA	ERA+	OAV	OOB	BH	AVG	PB	PR	/A	PD	TPI
1928	Pit-N	0	0	—	6	0	0	0	0	22²	31	2	9	6	15.9	7.15	57	.356	.417	1	.143	-0	-8	-8	-0	0.0
1932	Chi-A	0	0	—	3	0	0	0	0	5¹	5	0	6	1	18.6	5.06	85	.250	.423	0	.000	-0	-0	-0	0	0.0
Total	2	0	0	—	9	0	0	0	0	28	36	2	15	7	16.4	6.75	61	.336	.418	1	.125	-0	-8	-8	-0	0.0

● BILL BARTLEY
Bartley, William Jackson b: 1/8/1885, Cincinnati, Ohio d: 5/17/65, Cincinnati, Ohio BR/TR, 5'11.5", 190 lbs. Deb: 9/15/03

YEAR	TM/L	W	L	PCT	G	GS	CG	SH	SV	IP	H	HR	BB	SO	RAT	ERA	ERA+	OAV	OOB	BH	AVG	PB	PR	/A	PD	TPI
1903	NY-N	0	0	—	1	0	0	0	0	3	3	0	4	2	21.0	0.00	—	.273	.467	0	.000	-0	1	1	0	0.0
1906	Phi-A	0	0	—	3	0	0	0	1	8²	10	0	6	6	16.6	9.35	29	.292	.398	1	.333	1	-6	-6	1	-0.4
1907	Phi-A	0	1	.000	15	3	2	0	0	56¹	44	0	19	16	10.1	2.24	117	.217	.284	2	.095	-2	2	2	-0	-0.2
Total	3	0	1	.000	19	3	2	0	1	68	57	0	29	24	11.4	3.04	87	.230	.311	3	.120	-1	-3	-3	0	0.0

● SHAWN BARTON
Barton, Shawn Edward b: 5/14/63, Los Angeles, Cal. BR/TL, 6'3", 195 lbs. Deb: 8/6/92

YEAR	TM/L	W	L	PCT	G	GS	CG	SH	SV	IP	H	HR	BB	SO	RAT	ERA	ERA+	OAV	OOB	BH	AVG	PB	PR	/A	PD	TPI
1992	Sea-A	0	1	.000	14	0	0	0	0	12¹	10	1	7	4	12.4	2.92	136	.238	.347	0	—	0	1	1	0	0.1

● CHARLIE BARTSON
Bartson, Charles Franklin b: 3/13/1865, Peoria, Ill. d: 6/9/36, Peoria, Ill. 6', 170 lbs. Deb: 5/14/1890

YEAR	TM/L	W	L	PCT	G	GS	CG	SH	SV	IP	H	HR	BB	SO	RAT	ERA	ERA+	OAV	OOB	BH	AVG	PB	PR	/A	PD	TPI
1890	Chi-P	8	10	.444	25	19	16	0	1	188	222	8	66	47	14.4	4.26	102	.281	.347	13	.173	-2	-1	2	4	0.3

● JIM BASKETTE
Baskette, James Blaine "Big Jim" b: 12/10/1887, Athens, Tenn. d: 7/30/42, Athens, Tenn. BR/TR, 6'2", 185 lbs. Deb: 9/22/11

YEAR	TM/L	W	L	PCT	G	GS	CG	SH	SV	IP	H	HR	BB	SO	RAT	ERA	ERA+	OAV	OOB	BH	AVG	PB	PR	/A	PD	TPI
1911	Cle-A	1	2	.333	4	2	2	0	0	21¹	21	0	9	8	13.1	3.38	101	.273	.356	2	.333	1	-0	0	-0	0.0
1912	Cle-A	8	4	.667	29	11	7	1	1	116	109	2	46	51	12.6	3.18	107	.252	.334	5	.125	-1	2	3	-3	-0.1
1913	Cle-A	0	0	—	2	1	0	0	0	4²	8	0	2	0	19.3	5.79	52	.400	.455	1	1.000	1	-1	-1	0	0.1
Total	3	9	6	.600	35	14	9	1	1	142	138	2	57	59	12.9	3.30	103	.261	.342	8	.170	1	2	2	-3	0.0

● NORM BASS
Bass, Norman Delaney b: 1/21/39, Laurel, Miss. BR/TR, 6'3", 205 lbs. Deb: 4/23/61

YEAR	TM/L	W	L	PCT	G	GS	CG	SH	SV	IP	H	HR	BB	SO	RAT	ERA	ERA+	OAV	OOB	BH	AVG	PB	PR	/A	PD	TPI
1961	KC-A	11	11	.500	40	23	6	2	0	170²	164	17	82	74	13.2	4.69	89	.255	.343	7	.119	-2	-13	-10	-3	-1.6
1962	KC-A	2	6	.250	22	10	0	0	0	75¹	96	7	46	33	17.0	6.09	69	.317	.407	1	.045	-2	-18	-16	1	-1.5
1963	KC-A	0	0	—	3	1	0	0	0	7²	11	2	9	4	23.5	11.74	38	.333	.476	0	.000	-0	-7	-7	0	0.0
Total	3	13	17	.433	65	34	6	2	0	253²	271	26	137	111	14.6	5.32	79	.277	.368	8	.098	-4	-37	-32	-2	-3.1

● DICK BASS
Bass, Richard William b: 7/7/06, Rogersville, Tenn. d: 2/3/89, Graceville, Fla. BR/TR, 6'2", 175 lbs. Deb: 9/21/39

YEAR	TM/L	W	L	PCT	G	GS	CG	SH	SV	IP	H	HR	BB	SO	RAT	ERA	ERA+	OAV	OOB	BH	AVG	PB	PR	/A	PD	TPI
1939	Was-A	0	1	.000	1	1	0	0	0	8	7	0	6	1	15.8	6.75	64	.241	.389	0	.000	-0	-2	-2	-0	-0.2

● CHARLIE BASTIAN
Bastian, Charles J. b: 7/4/1860, Philadelphia, Pa. d: 1/18/32, Pennsauken, N.J. BR/TR, 5'6.5", 145 lbs. Deb: 8/18/1884 ◆

YEAR	TM/L	W	L	PCT	G	GS	CG	SH	SV	IP	H	HR	BB	SO	RAT	ERA	ERA+	OAV	OOB	BH	AVG	PB	PR	/A	PD	TPI
1884	Wil-U	0	0	—	1	0	0	0	0	6	6	0	2	0	12.0	3.00	89	.243	.243	12	.200	-0	-0	-0	-0	0.0

● JOE BATCHELDER
Batchelder, Joseph Edmund "Win" b: 7/11/1898, Wenham, Mass. d: 5/5/89, Beverly, Mass. BR/TL, 5'7", 165 lbs. Deb: 9/29/23

YEAR	TM/L	W	L	PCT	G	GS	CG	SH	SV	IP	H	HR	BB	SO	RAT	ERA	ERA+	OAV	OOB	BH	AVG	PB	PR	/A	PD	TPI
1923	Bos-N	1	0	1.000	4	1	0	0	0	9	12	1	2	2	14.0	7.00	57	.353	.389	0	.000	0	-3	-3	-0	-0.3
1924	Bos-N	0	0	—	3	0	0	0	0	4²	4	0	2	2	11.6	3.86	99	.235	.316	0	.000	-0	-0	0	0	0.0

YEAR TM/L	W	L	PCT	G	GS	CG	SH	SV	IP	H	HR	BB	SO	RAT	ERA	ERA+	OAV	OOB	BH	AVG	PB	PR	/A	PD	TPI
1925 Bos-N	0	0	—	4	0	0	0	0	7	10	0	1	2	14.1	5.14	78	.357	.379	0	.000	-0	-1	-1	0	0.0
Total 3	1	0	1.000	11	1	1	0	0	20²	26	2	4	6	13.5	5.66	70	.329	.369	0	.000	-0	-4	-4	0	-0.3

● **RICH BATCHELOR**   Batchelor, Richard Anthony b: 4/8/67, Florence, S.C. BR/TR, 6'1", 195 lbs. Deb: 9/3/93

YEAR TM/L	W	L	PCT	G	GS	CG	SH	SV	IP	H	HR	BB	SO	RAT	ERA	ERA+	OAV	OOB	BH	AVG	PB	PR	/A	PD	TPI
1993 StL-N	0	0	—	9	0	0	0	0	10	14	1	3	4	15.3	8.10	49	.359	.405	0	.000	-0	-5	-5	-0	0.0

● **DICK BATES**   Bates, Charles Richard b: 10/7/45, McArthur, Ohio BL/TR, 6', 190 lbs. Deb: 4/27/69

YEAR TM/L	W	L	PCT	G	GS	CG	SH	SV	IP	H	HR	BB	SO	RAT	ERA	ERA+	OAV	OOB	BH	AVG	PB	PR	/A	PD	TPI
1969 Sea-A	0	0	—	1	0	0	0	0	1²	3	1	3	3	32.4	27.00	13	.375	.545	0	—	0	-4	-4	0	0.0

● **FRANK BATES**   Bates, Creed Frank b: Chattanooga, Tenn. Deb: 10/7/1898

YEAR TM/L	W	L	PCT	G	GS	CG	SH	SV	IP	H	HR	BB	SO	RAT	ERA	ERA+	OAV	OOB	BH	AVG	PB	PR	/A	PD	TPI
1898 Cle-N	2	1	.667	4	4	4	0	0	29	30	0	11	5	13.0	3.10	117	.265	.335	1	.111	0	2	2	-0	0.1
1899 StL-N	0	0	—	2	0	0	0	0	8²	7	0	5	0	12.5	1.04	383	.221	.327	1	.333	1	3	3	-0	0.0
Cle-N	1	18	.053	20	19	17	0	0	153	239	6	105	13	21.6	7.24	51	.355	.458	14	.215	1	-57	-60	-0	-5.3
Yr	1	18	.053	22	19	17	0	0	161²	246	6	110	13	21.1	6.90	54	.349	.452	15	.221	2	-55	-58	-0	-5.3
Total 2	3	19	.136	26	23	21	0	0	190²	276	6	121	18	19.9	6.33	58	.337	.437	16	.208	2	-53	-56	-0	-5.2

● **JOHN BATES**   Bates, John William b: 5/28/1868, Ohio d: 3/24/19, Oakland, Cal. Deb: 8/25/1889

YEAR TM/L	W	L	PCT	G	GS	CG	SH	SV	IP	H	HR	BB	SO	RAT	ERA	ERA+	OAV	OOB	BH	AVG	PB	PR	/A	PD	TPI
1889 KC-a	0	1	.000	1	1	1	0	0	8	15	0	5	3	22.5	13.50	31	.387	.458	0	.000	-1	-9	-8	-0	-0.7

● **MIGUEL BATISTA**   Batista, Miguel Jerez (Decartes) b: 2/19/71, Santo Domingo, D.R. BR/TR, 6', 160 lbs. Deb: 4/11/92

YEAR TM/L	W	L	PCT	G	GS	CG	SH	SV	IP	H	HR	BB	SO	RAT	ERA	ERA+	OAV	OOB	BH	AVG	PB	PR	/A	PD	TPI
1992 Pit-N	0	0	—	1	0	0	0	0	2	4	1	3	1	31.5	9.00	38	.400	.538	0	—	0	-1	-1	-0	0.0

● **JOE BATTIN**   Battin, Joseph V. b: 11/11/1851, Philadelphia, Pa. d: 12/10/37, Akron, Ohio BR/TR, Deb: 8/11/1871 MU♦

YEAR TM/L	W	L	PCT	G	GS	CG	SH	SV	IP	H	HR	BB	SO	RAT	ERA	ERA+	OAV	OOB	BH	AVG	PB	PR	/A	PD	TPI
1877 StL-N	0	0	—	1	0	0	0	0	3²	3	0	1	1	9.8	4.91	53	.200	.250	45	.199	0	-1	-1	-0	0.0
1883 Pit-a	0	0	—	2	0	0	0	0	4	9	0	1	0	22.5	2.25	143	.420	.446	83	.214	0	0	0	-0	0.0
Total 2	0	0	—	3	0	0	0	0	7²	12	0	2	1	16.4	3.52	83	.330	.364	313	.218	0	-0	-1	-0	0.0

● **CHRIS BATTON**   Batton, Christopher Sean b: 8/24/54, Los Angeles, Cal. BR/TR, 6'4", 195 lbs. Deb: 9/19/76

YEAR TM/L	W	L	PCT	G	GS	CG	SH	SV	IP	H	HR	BB	SO	RAT	ERA	ERA+	OAV	OOB	BH	AVG	PB	PR	/A	PD	TPI
1976 Oak-A	0	0	—	2	1	0	0	0	4	5	1	3	4	18.0	9.00	44	.313	.421	0	—	0	-2	-3	-0	0.1

● **LOU BAUER**   Bauer, Louis Walter b: 11/30/1898, Egg Harbor City, N.J. d: 2/4/79, Pomona, N.J. BR/TR, 6', 175 lbs. Deb: 8/13/18

YEAR TM/L	W	L	PCT	G	GS	CG	SH	SV	IP	H	HR	BB	SO	RAT	ERA	ERA+	OAV	OOB	BH	AVG	PB	PR	/A	PD	TPI
1918 Phi-A	0	0	—	1	0	0	0	0	0	0	0	2	0	—	∞	—	—	1.000	0	—	0	-1	-1	0	-0.1

● **AL BAUERS**   Bauers, Albert J. b: 1850, Columbus, Ohio d: 9/6/13, Wilkes-Barre, Pa. TL, Deb: 9/22/1884 U

YEAR TM/L	W	L	PCT	G	GS	CG	SH	SV	IP	H	HR	BB	SO	RAT	ERA	ERA+	OAV	OOB	BH	AVG	PB	PR	/A	PD	TPI
1884 Col-a	1	2	.333	3	3	3	0	0	25	22	1	14	13	13.0	4.68	65	.224	.321	3	.273	0	-4	-5	0	-0.4
1886 StL-N	0	4	.000	4	4	3	0	0	28²	31	1	27	13	18.2	5.97	54	.267	.406	2	.167	-1	-8	-9	-1	-1.0
Total 2	1	6	.143	7	7	6	0	0	53²	53	2	41	26	15.8	5.37	58	.248	.369	5	.217	-0	-12	-13	-1	-1.4

● **RUSS BAUERS**   Bauers, Russell Lee b: 5/10/14, Townsend, Wis. BL/TR, 6'3", 195 lbs. Deb: 8/20/36

YEAR TM/L	W	L	PCT	G	GS	CG	SH	SV	IP	H	HR	BB	SO	RAT	ERA	ERA+	OAV	OOB	BH	AVG	PB	PR	/A	PD	TPI
1936 Pit-N	0	0	—	1	1	0	0	0	1¹	2	0	4	0	47.3	33.75	12	.500	.778	0	—	0	-4	-4	-0	0.0
1937 Pit-N	13	6	.684	34	19	11	2	1	187²	174	2	80	118	12.4	2.88	134	.245	.325	15	.217	1	22	21	3	2.3
1938 Pit-N	13	14	.481	40	34	12	2	3	243	207	7	99	117	11.6	3.07	124	.233	.314	21	.239	4	19	20	-3	2.1
1939 Pit-N	2	4	.333	15	8	1	0	1	53²	46	4	25	12	12.1	3.35	114	.240	.330	4	.211	-0	3	3	-1	0.2
1940 Pit-N	0	2	.000	15	2	0	0	0	30²	42	4	18	11	18.2	7.63	50	.323	.413	2	.286	-0	-13	-13	-0	-0.7
1941 Pit-N	1	3	.250	8	5	1	0	0	37¹	40	1	25	20	15.7	5.54	65	.267	.371	5	.357	1	-8	-8	-1	-0.8
1946 Chi-N	2	1	.667	15	2	2	0	1	43¹	45	1	19	22	13.5	3.53	94	.273	.351	3	.300	1	-1	-1	-0	0.1
1950 StL-A	0	0	—	1	0	0	0	0	2	6	0	1	0	31.5	4.50	110	.600	.636	0	—	0	0	0	0	0.0
Total 8	31	30	.508	129	71	27	4	6	599	562	17	271	300	12.7	3.53	107	.250	.334	50	.242	7	19	17	-2	3.2

● **FRANK BAUMANN**   Baumann, Frank Matt "The Beau" b: 7/1/33, St.Louis, Mo. BL/TL, 6'1", 210 lbs. Deb: 7/31/55

YEAR TM/L	W	L	PCT	G	GS	CG	SH	SV	IP	H	HR	BB	SO	RAT	ERA	ERA+	OAV	OOB	BH	AVG	PB	PR	/A	PD	TPI
1955 Bos-A	2	1	.667	7	5	0	0	0	34	38	3	17	27	14.8	5.82	74	.281	.366	3	.231	-0	-7	-6	0	-0.4
1956 Bos-A	2	1	.667	7	1	0	0	0	24²	22	3	14	18	13.1	3.28	141	.234	.333	3	.333	1	2	4	-1	0.4
1957 Bos-A	1	0	1.000	4	1	0	0	0	12	13	1	3	7	12.8	3.75	106	.277	.333	1	.500	0	0	0	-0	0.0
1958 Bos-A	2	2	.500	10	7	2	0	0	52¹	56	4	27	31	15.0	4.47	90	.276	.372	3	.214	1	-4	-3	-1	-0.2
1959 Bos-A	6	4	.600	26	10	2	0	1	95²	96	11	55	48	14.3	4.05	100	.259	.357	6	.207	1	-2	0	1	0.1
1960 Chi-A	13	6	.684	47	20	7	2	3	185¹	169	11	53	71	10.8	**2.67**	142	.247	.302	8	.154	1	25	23	-2	2.1
1961 Chi-A	10	13	.435	53	23	5	1	3	187²	249	22	59	75	14.9	5.61	70	.318	.368	16	.262	6	-33	-35	-3	-3.1
1962 Chi-A	7	6	.538	40	10	3	1	4	119²	117	10	36	55	11.7	3.38	115	.258	.316	8	.267	4	8	7	0	1.2
1963 Chi-A	2	1	.667	24	1	0	0	1	50¹	52	2	17	31	12.3	3.04	125	.265	.324	1	.091	-0	3	3	0	0.1
1964 Chi-A	0	3	.000	22	0	0	0	0	32	40	4	16	19	15.8	6.19	56	.320	.397	0	.000	-0	-9	-10	-0	-1.0
1965 Chi-N	0	1	.000	4	0	0	0	0	3²	4	0	3	2	17.2	7.36	50	.286	.412	0	—	0	-2	-1	0	-0.4
Total 11	45	38	.542	244	78	19	4	13	797¹	856	70	300	384	13.2	4.11	95	.276	.342	49	.218	14	-19	-19	-2	-1.2

● **GEORGE BAUMGARDNER**   Baumgardner, George Washington b: 7/22/1891, Barboursville, W.Va. d: 12/13/70, Barboursville, W.Va. BL/TR, 5'11", 178 lbs. Deb: 4/14/12

YEAR TM/L	W	L	PCT	G	GS	CG	SH	SV	IP	H	HR	BB	SO	RAT	ERA	ERA+	OAV	OOB	BH	AVG	PB	PR	/A	PD	TPI
1912 StL-A	11	13	.458	30	27	18	2	0	218¹	222	1	79	102	12.9	3.38	98	.274	.346	11	.145	-0	-2	-2	-0	-0.1
1913 StL-A	10	19	.345	38	31	23	2	1	253¹	267	6	84	78	12.8	3.13	94	.283	.348	13	.167	2	-5	-5	-2	-0.5
1914 StL-A	14	13	.519	45	18	9	3	3	183²	152	3	84	93	12.0	2.79	97	.229	.323	7	.132	-1	-1	-2	-1	-0.5
1915 StL-A	0	2	.000	7	1	1	0	0	22¹	29	0	11	6	16.1	4.43	65	.358	.435	0	.000	-1	-4	-4	-1	-0.4
1916 StL-A	1	0	1.000	4	2	0	0	0	8	12	0	5	4	19.1	7.88	35	.364	.447	0	.000	-0	-4	-5	-1	-0.6
Total 5	36	47	.434	124	79	51	7	4	685²	682	10	263	283	12.8	3.22	93	.269	.345	31	.144	-0	-16	-17	-2	-2.1

● **ROSS BAUMGARTEN**   Baumgarten, Ross b: 5/27/55, Highland Park, Ill. BL/TL, 6'1", 180 lbs. Deb: 8/16/78

YEAR TM/L	W	L	PCT	G	GS	CG	SH	SV	IP	H	HR	BB	SO	RAT	ERA	ERA+	OAV	OOB	BH	AVG	PB	PR	/A	PD	TPI
1978 Chi-A	2	2	.500	7	4	1	1	0	23	29	3	9	15	15.3	5.87	65	.315	.382	0	—	0	-5	-5	-0	-0.8
1979 Chi-A	13	8	.619	28	28	4	3	0	190²	175	18	83	72	12.2	3.54	120	.243	.322	0	—	0	14	15	-0	1.5
1980 Chi-A	2	12	.143	24	23	3	1	0	136	127	10	52	66	11.9	3.44	117	.256	.327	0	—	0	9	9	2	1.1
1981 Chi-A	5	9	.357	19	19	2	1	0	101²	101	9	40	52	12.6	4.07	88	.260	.331	0	—	0	-5	-6	-0	-0.7
1982 Pit-N	0	5	.000	12	10	0	0	0	44	60	3	27	17	17.8	6.55	57	.347	.435	1	.083	-1	-14	-14	0	-1.5
Total 5	22	36	.379	90	84	10	6	0	495¹	492	43	211	222	12.8	4.00	100	.263	.339	1	.083	-1	-1	-1	2	-0.4

● **HARRY BAUMGARTNER**   Baumgartner, Harry E. b: 10/8/1892, S.Pittsburg, Tenn. d: 12/3/30, Augusta, Ga. BR/TR, 5'11", 175 lbs. Deb: 9/6/20

YEAR TM/L	W	L	PCT	G	GS	CG	SH	SV	IP	H	HR	BB	SO	RAT	ERA	ERA+	OAV	OOB	BH	AVG	PB	PR	/A	PD	TPI
1920 Det-A	0	1	.000	9	0	0	0	0	18	18	1	6	7	12.0	4.00	93	.273	.333	1	.250	0	-0	-1	0	0.0

● **STAN BAUMGARTNER**   Baumgartner, Stanwood Fulton b: 12/14/1894, Houston, Tex. d: 10/4/55, Philadelphia, Pa. BL/TL, 6', 175 lbs. Deb: 6/26/14

YEAR TM/L	W	L	PCT	G	GS	CG	SH	SV	IP	H	HR	BB	SO	RAT	ERA	ERA+	OAV	OOB	BH	AVG	PB	PR	/A	PD	TPI
1914 Phi-N	2	2	.500	15	3	2	1	0	60¹	60	0	16	24	11.6	3.28	90	.270	.325	1	.053	-1	-3	-2	-1	-0.4
1915 Phi-N	0	0	.000	16	1	0	0	0	48¹	38	2	23	27	11.5	2.42	113	.226	.323	1	.083	-0	2	2	1	0.1
1916 Phi-N	0	0	—	1	0	0	0	0	4	5	0	1	0	13.5	2.25	118	.333	.375	0	.000	-0	0	-0	0	0.0
1921 Phi-N	3	6	.333	22	7	2	0	0	66²	80	6	30	13	17.1	7.02	60	.355	.404	6	.200	-0	-24	-21	-1	-2.4
1922 Phi-N	1	1	.500	6	1	0	0	0	9²	18	1	5	2	21.4	6.52	72	.409	.469	1	.333	-0	-3	-3	-0	-0.3
1924 Phi-A	13	6	.684	36	16	12	1	4	181	181	6	73	45	12.8	2.88	**149**	.271	.347	13	.217	-0	27	28	-2	2.5
1925 Phi-A	6	3	.667	37	11	2	1	3	113¹	120	2	35	18	12.9	3.57	130	.275	.338	7	.233	-0	10	14	-1	0.9
1926 Phi-A	1	1	.500	10	1	0	0	0	22¹	28	2	10	6	15.3	4.03	103	.326	.396	1	.333	-0	0	0	-0	0.0
Total 8	26	21	.553	143	40	18	3	7	505²	553	19	185	129	13.4	3.70	109	.287	.354	30	.190	-2	9	19	-3	0.5

● **GEORGE BAUSEWINE**   Bausewine, George W. b: 3/22/1869, Philadelphia, Pa. d: 7/29/47, Norristown, Pa. 6'2", 207 lbs. Deb: 9/14/1889 U

YEAR TM/L	W	L	PCT	G	GS	CG	SH	SV	IP	H	HR	BB	SO	RAT	ERA	ERA+	OAV	OOB	BH	AVG	PB	PR	/A	PD	TPI
1889 Phi-a	1	4	.200	7	6	6	0	0	55¹	64	1	33	18	17.2	3.90	97	.281	.393	1	.048	-2	-0	-1	0	-0.2

YEAR	TM/L	W	L	PCT	G	GS	CG	SH	SV	IP	H	HR	BB	SO	RAT	ERA	ERA+	OAV	OOB	BH	AVG	PB	PR	/A	PD	TPI
● ED BAUTA				Bauta, Eduardo (Galvez) b: 1/6/35, Florida, Cuba BR/TR, 6'3", 200 lbs. Deb: 7/6/60																					
1960	StL-N	0	0		9	0	0	0	1	15²	14	4	11	6	14.9	6.32	65	.237	.366	0	.000	-0	-4	-4	-0	-0.1
1961	StL-N	2	0	1.000	13	0	0	0	5	19¹	12	2	5	12	7.9	1.40	315	.171	.227	2	.500	1	6	6	-0	1.1
1962	StL-N	1	0	1.000	20	0	0	0	1	32¹	28	5	21	25	13.9	5.01	85	.239	.360	1	.250	-0	-4	-3	-0	-0.1
1963	StL-N	3	4	.429	38	0	0	0	3	52²	55	2	21	30	13.3	3.93	90	.279	.355	0	.000	-1	-4	-2	-1	-0.5
	NY-N	0	0		9	0	0	0	0	19	22	0	9	13	14.7	5.21	67	.289	.365	0	.000	-0	-4	-4	-0	0.0
	Yr	3	4	.429	47	0	0	0	3	71²	77	2	30	43	13.4	4.27	83	.278	.358	0	.000	-1	-8	-6	-1	-0.5
1964	NY-N	0	2	.000	8	0	0	0	1	10	17	1	3	3	18.0	5.40	66	.395	.435	0	—	-0	-2	-2	-0	-0.4
Total	5	6	6	.500	97	0	0	0	11	149	148	14	70	89	13.4	4.35	89	.263	.349	3	.176	-0	-13	-8	-1	-0.0
● JOSE BAUTISTA				Bautista, Jose Joaquin (Arias) b: 7/25/64, Bani, D.R. BR/TR, 6'1", 205 lbs. Deb: 4/9/88																					
1988	Bal-A	6	15	.286	33	25	3	0	0	171²	171	21	45	76	11.7	4.30	91	.258	.311	0	—	0	-6	-8	-1	-0.7
1989	Bal-A	3	4	.429	15	10	0	0	0	78	84	17	15	30	11.5	5.31	71	.274	.310	0	—	0	-12	-13	-1	-1.1
1990	Bal-A	1	0	1.000	22	0	0	0	0	26²	28	4	7	15	11.8	4.05	94	.272	.318	0	—	-0	-0	-1	-0	-0.1
1991	Bal-A	0	1	.000	5	0	0	0	0	5¹	13	1	5	3	32.1	16.88	23	.464	.559	0	—	0	-8	-8	-0	-1.1
1993	Chi-N	10	3	.769	58	7	1	0	2	111²	105	11	27	63	11.0	2.82	141	.250	.303	4	.190	0	15	14	1	1.7
1994	Chi-N	4	5	.444	58	0	0	0	1	69¹	75	10	17	45	12.3	3.89	106	.284	.335	0	.000	-0	2	2	-0	0.2
Total	6	24	28	.462	191	42	4	0	3	462²	476	64	116	232	11.8	4.18	94	.267	.317	4	.174	-0	-9	-13	-1	-1.1
● BILL BAYNE				Bayne, William Lear "Beverly" b: 4/18/1899, Pittsburgh, Pa. d: 5/22/81, St.Louis, Mo. BL/TL, 5'9", 160 lbs. Deb: 9/20/19																					
1919	StL-A	1	1	.500	2	1	0	0	0	12	16	0	6	6	16.5	5.25	63	.320	.393	2	.400	0	-3	-3	0	-0.3
1920	StL-A	5	6	.455	18	13	6	1	0	99²	102	3	41	38	13.5	3.70	106	.279	.363	6	.171	-2	1	-2	-2	-0.2
1921	StL-A	11	5	.688	47	14	6	1	3	164	167	8	80	82	13.8	4.72	95	.270	.358	18	.300	5	-8	-4	-1	0.0
1922	StL-A	4	5	.444	26	9	3	0	2	92²	86	5	37	38	12.8	4.56	91	.249	.338	7	.233	-1	-5	-4	-2	-0.6
1923	StL-A	2	2	.500	19	2	0	0	0	46	49	4	31	15	16.2	4.50	93	.287	.405	3	.231	0	-3	-2	-1	0.2
1924	StL-A	1	3	.250	22	3	0	0	0	50²	47	4	29	20	14.9	4.44	102	.250	.373	6	.429	2	-1	0	-1	0.2
1928	Cle-A	2	5	.286	37	6	3	0	3	108²	128	3	43	39	15.0	5.13	81	.309	.388	11	.367	3	-13	-12	2	-0.4
1929	Bos-A	5	5	.500	27	6	3	0	0	84¹	111	9	29	26	15.8	6.72	64	.326	.392	8	.320	2	-23	-23	1	-1.9
1930	Bos-A	0	0	—	1	0	0	0	0	4	5	1	1	1	13.5	4.50	102	.294	.333	1	.500	0	0	0	0	0.0
Total	9	31	32	.492	199	55	21	2	8	662	711	37	297	259	14.4	4.84	87	.283	.370	62	.290	10	-55	-45	-3	-3.4
● WALTER BEALL				Beall, Walter Esau b: 7/29/1899, Washington, D.C. d: 1/28/59, Suitland, Md. BR/TR, 5'10", 178 lbs. Deb: 9/3/24																					
1924	NY-A	2	0	1.000	4	2	0	0	0	23	19	2	17	18	14.1	3.52	118	.237	.371	1	.143	-1	2	2	-1	0.0
1925	NY-A	0	1	.000	8	1	0	0	0	11¹	11	0	19	8	26.2	12.71	34	.282	.541	0	.000	-1	-10	-11	0	-0.8
1926	NY-A	2	4	.333	20	9	1	0	1	81²	71	2	68	56	16.0	3.53	109	.240	.392	3	.136	0	4	3	1	0.3
1927	NY-A	0	0	—	1	0	0	0	0	1	1	0	0	0	9.0	9.00	43	.333	.333	0	—	0	-1	-1	-0	0.0
1929	Was-A	1	0	1.000	7	0	0	0	0	7	8	0	7	3	19.3	3.86	110	.348	.500	0	—	-1	0	0	0	0.0
Total	5	5	5	.500	36	12	1	0	1	124	110	4	111	85	16.7	4.43	90	.249	.410	4	.114	-1	-4	-6	0	-0.5
● ALEX BEAM				Beam, Alexander Rodger b: 11/21/1870, Johnstown, Pa. d: 4/17/38, Nogales, Ariz. Deb: 5/25/1889																					
1889	Pit-N	1	1	.500	2	2	2	0	0	18	11	0	15	1	13.0	6.50	58	.171	.328	1	.167	0	-5	-6	-0	-0.4
● ERNIE BEAM				Beam, Ernest Joseph b: 3/17/1867, Mansfield, Ohio d: 9/12/18, Mansfield, Ohio TR , 6'0.5", 185 lbs. Deb: 5/2/1895																					
1895	Phi-N	0	2	.000	9	1	1	0	**3**	24²	33	1	25	3	21.5	11.31	42	.316	.452	2	.182	-1	-18	-18	-0	-1.4
● CHARLIE BEAMON				Beamon, Charles Alfonso Sr. b: 12/25/34, Oakland, Cal. BR/TR, 5'11", 195 lbs. Deb: 9/26/56 F																					
1956	Bal-A	2	0	1.000	2	1	1	1	0	13	9	0	8	14	11.8	1.38	283	.191	.309	0	.000	-1	4	4	0	0.5
1957	Bal-A	0	0	—	4	1	0	0	0	8²	8	1	7	5	16.6	5.19	69	.229	.372	0	.000	-0	-1	-2	-0	0.0
1958	Bal-A	1	3	.250	21	3	0	0	0	49²	47	3	21	26	13.4	4.35	83	.266	.363	0	.000	-1	-3	-4	2	-0.2
Total	3	3	3	.500	27	5	1	1	0	71¹	64	4	36	45	13.5	3.91	93	.247	.354	0	.000	-2	-1	-2	2	0.3
● BELVE BEAN				Bean, Beveric Benton "Bill" b: 4/23/05, Mullin, Tex. d: 6/1/88, Comanche, Tex. BR/TR, 6'1.5", 197 lbs. Deb: 5/30/30																					
1930	Cle-A	3	3	.500	23	3	1	0	2	74¹	99	7	32	19	15.9	5.45	89	.331	.396	9	.346	2	-7	-5	0	-0.2
1931	Cle-A	0	1	.000	4	0	0	0	0	7	11	0	4	3	20.6	6.43	72	.379	.471	0	.000	-0	-2	-1	0	-0.2
1933	Cle-A	1	2	.333	27	2	0	0	0	70¹	80	6	20	41	12.9	5.25	85	.300	.351	4	.182	-1	-8	-6	1	-0.2
1934	Cle-A	5	1	.833	21	1	0	0	0	51¹	53	2	21	20	13.5	3.86	118	.265	.344	3	.200	0	4	4	1	0.5
1935	Cle-A	0	0	—	1	0	0	0	0	1	2	1	0	0	18.0	9.00	50	.400	.400	0	—	0	-1	-0	-0	-0.0
	Was-A	2	0	1.000	10	2	0	0	0	31	43	5	19	6	18.0	7.26	60	.339	.425	3	.375	2	-10	-10	-0	-0.4
	Yr	2	0	1.000	11	2	0	0	0	32	45	6	19	6	18.0	7.31	59	.341	.424	3	.375	2	-10	-11	-1	-0.4
Total	5	11	7	.611	86	8	1	0	2	235	288	21	96	89	14.9	5.32	86	.311	.378	19	.264	4	-22	-19	1	-0.5
● DAVE BEARD				Beard, Charles David b: 10/2/59, Atlanta, Ga. BL/TR, 6'5", 215 lbs. Deb: 7/16/80																					
1980	Oak-A	0	1	.000	13	0	0	0	0	16	12	0	7	12	11.3	3.38	112	.218	.317	0	—	0	1	1	-0	0.4
1981	*Oak-A	1	1	.500	8	0	0	0	3	13	9	1	4	15	9.7	2.77	126	.191	.269	0	—	0	1	1	0	0.2
1982	Oak-A	10	9	.526	54	2	0	0	11	91²	85	9	35	73	11.9	3.44	114	.244	.315	0	—	0	6	5	-0	1.3
1983	Oak-A	5	5	.500	43	0	0	0	10	61	55	8	36	40	13.7	5.61	69	.246	.355	0	—	0	-10	-12	-1	-1.9
1984	Sea-A	3	2	.600	43	0	0	0	5	76	88	15	33	40	14.8	5.80	69	.291	.369	0	—	0	-15	-15	-1	-1.0
1985	Chi-N	0	0	—	9	0	0	0	0	12²	16	2	7	4	16.3	6.39	62	.314	.397	0	—	0	-4	-3	0	0.0
1989	Det-A	0	2	.000	2	1	0	0	0	5¹	7	2	2	1	20.3	5.06	75	.375	.444	0	—	0	-1	-1	-0	-0.2
Total	7	19	20	.487	172	3	0	0	30	275²	274	37	124	185	13.3	4.70	83	.261	.344	0	—	0	-21	-25	-2	-1.2
● MIKE BEARD				Beard, Michael Richard b: 6/21/50, Little Rock, Ark. BL/TL, 6'1", 185 lbs. Deb: 9/7/74																					
1974	Atl-N	0	0	—	6	0	0	0	0	9¹	5	1	7	7	6.8	2.89	131	.156	.206	0	—	0	1	1	0	0.0
1975	Atl-N	4	0	1.000	34	2	0	0	0	70¹	71	4	28	27	12.9	3.20	118	.265	.339	1	.111	-0	3	4	0	0.2
1976	Atl-N	0	2	.000	30	0	0	0	1	33²	38	1	14	8	13.9	4.28	89	.299	.369	0	.000	-0	-3	-2	1	0.0
1977	Atl-N	0	0	—	4	0	0	0	0	4²	14	3	2	1	30.9	9.64	46	.452	.485	0	—	0	-3	-3	-0	-0.2
Total	4	4	2	.667	74	2	0	0	1	118	128	9	45	43	13.4	3.74	102	.279	.348	1	.100	-0	-2	1	1	0.2
● RALPH BEARD				Beard, Ralph William b: 2/11/29, Cincinnati, Ohio BR/TR, 6'5", 200 lbs. Deb: 6/29/54																					
1954	StL-N	0	4	.000	13	10	0	0	0	58	62	7	28	17	14.3	3.72	110	.278	.364	1	.059	-1	2	2	-1	-0.1
● GENE BEARDEN				Bearden, Henry Eugene b: 9/5/20, Lexa, Ark. BL/TL, 6'3", 204 lbs. Deb: 5/10/47																					
1947	Cle-A	0	0	—	1	0	0	0	0	0¹	2	0	1	0	81.0	81.00	4	.667	.750	0	—	0	-3	-3	0	0.0
1948	*Cle-A	20	7	.741	37	29	15	6	1	229²	187	9	106	80	11.6	**2.43**	**167**	.229	.320	23	.256	5	47	**42**	3	5.5
1949	Cle-A	8	8	.500	32	19	5	0	0	127	140	6	92	41	16.6	5.10	78	.286	.401	5	.111	-3	-13	-16	4	-1.6
1950	Cle-A	1	3	.250	14	3	0	0	0	45¹	57	5	32	10	17.7	6.15	70	.328	.432	2	.154	-1	-8	-9	-1	-0.7
	Was-A	3	5	.375	12	6	4	0	0	68¹	81	1	33	20	15.3	4.21	107	.297	.377	5	.227	1	3	2	1	0.3
	Yr	4	8	.333	26	12	4	0	0	113²	138	6	65	30	16.2	4.99	89	.309	.399	7	.200	2	-5	-7	-0	-0.4
1951	Was-A	0	0	—	1	1	0	0	0	2²	6	0	2	1	27.0	16.88	24	.429	.500	0	—	-0	-4	-4	-0	0.0
	Det-A	3	4	.429	37	4	2	1	0	106	112	6	58	38	14.5	4.33	96	.275	.366	6	.188	1	-2	-2	0	0.0
	Yr	3	4	.429	38	5	2	1	0	108²	118	6	60	39	14.8	4.64	90	.280	.371	6	.188	1	-6	-6	-0	0.0
1952	StL-A	7	8	.467	34	16	3	0	0	150²	158	10	73	45	14.2	4.30	91	.270	.357	23	.354	6	-10	-6	1	0.1
1953	Chi-A	3	3	.500	25	3	0	0	0	58¹	48	5	30	24	12.5	2.93	137	.223	.327	4	.190	-1	7	7	-0	0.6
Total	7	45	38	.542	193	84	29	7	1	788¹	791	48	435	259	14.1	3.96	103	.266	.361	68	.236	10	17	12	7	4.2

● GARY BEARE
Beare, Gary Ray b: 8/22/52, San Diego, Cal. BR/TR, 6'4", 205 lbs. Deb: 9/7/76

YEAR TM/L	W	L	PCT	G	GS	CG	SH	SV	IP	H	HR	BB	SO	RAT	ERA	ERA+	OAV	OOB	BH	AVG	PB	PR	/A	PD	TPI
1976 Mil-A	2	3	.400	6	5	2	0	0	41	43	4	15	32	12.7	3.29	106	.274	.337	0	—	0	1	1	-0	0.2
1977 Mil-A	3	3	.500	17	6	0	0	0	58^{2}	63	6	38	32	15.6	6.44	63	.276	.382	0	—	0	-16	-15	2	-1.2
Total 2	5	6	.455	23	11	2	0	0	99^{2}	106	10	53	64	14.4	5.15	74	.275	.364	0	—	0	-15	-15	1	-1.0

● LARRY BEARNARTH
Bearnarth, Lawrence Donald b: 9/11/41, New York, N.Y. BR/TR, 6'2", 203 lbs. Deb: 4/16/63 C

YEAR TM/L	W	L	PCT	G	GS	CG	SH	SV	IP	H	HR	BB	SO	RAT	ERA	ERA+	OAV	OOB	BH	AVG	PB	PR	/A	PD	TPI
1963 NY-N	3	8	.273	58	2	0	0	4	126^{1}	127	7	47	48	12.8	3.42	102	.268	.340	6	.200	1	-2	1	2	0.5
1964 NY-N	5	5	.500	44	1	0	0	3	78	79	6	38	31	13.7	4.15	86	.271	.360	2	.143	-0	-5	-5	3	-0.4
1965 NY-N	3	5	.375	40	3	0	0	0	60^{2}	75	6	28	16	15.9	4.60	77	.304	.384	1	.111	-0	-7	-7	0	-0.8
1966 NY-N	2	3	.400	29	1	0	0	0	54^{2}	59	11	20	27	13.2	4.45	82	.281	.346	1	.111	-0	-5	-5	1	-0.3
1971 Mil-A	0	0	—	2	0	0	0	0	3	10	1	2	2	36.0	18.00	18	.556	.600	0	—	0	-5	-5	0	0.0
Total 5	13	21	.382	173	7	0	0	8	322^{2}	350	31	135	124	13.9	4.13	86	.282	.358	10	.161	1	-24	-21	7	-1.0

● KEVIN BEARSE
Bearse, Kevin Gerard b: 11/7/65, Jersey City, N.J. BL/TL, 6'2", 195 lbs. Deb: 4/15/90

YEAR TM/L	W	L	PCT	G	GS	CG	SH	SV	IP	H	HR	BB	SO	RAT	ERA	ERA+	OAV	OOB	BH	AVG	PB	PR	/A	PD	TPI
1990 Cle-A	0	2	.000	3	3	0	0	0	7^{2}	16	2	5	2	27.0	12.91	30	.421	.511	0	—	0	-8	-8	-0	-1.4

● CHRIS BEASLEY
Beasley, Christopher Charles b: 6/23/62, Jackson, Tenn. BR/TR, 6'2", 190 lbs. Deb: 7/20/91

YEAR TM/L	W	L	PCT	G	GS	CG	SH	SV	IP	H	HR	BB	SO	RAT	ERA	ERA+	OAV	OOB	BH	AVG	PB	PR	/A	PD	TPI
1991 Cal-A	0	1	.000	22	0	0	0	0	26^{2}	26	2	10	14	12.5	3.38	122	.257	.330	0	—	0	2	2	0	0.1

● ED BEATIN
Beatin, Ebenezer Ambrose b: 8/10/1866, Baltimore, Md. d: 5/9/25, Baltimore, Md. BR/TL, 5'9", 162 lbs. Deb: 8/2/1887

YEAR TM/L	W	L	PCT	G	GS	CG	SH	SV	IP	H	HR	BB	SO	RAT	ERA	ERA+	OAV	OOB	BH	AVG	PB	PR	/A	PD	TPI
1887 Det-N	1	1	.500	2	2	2	0	0	18	13	2	6		11.0	4.00	101	.203	.301	1	.000	-1	0	0	-0	-0.1
1888 Det-N	5	7	.417	12	12	12	1	0	107	111	6	16	44	10.9	2.86	97	.251	.280	14	.250	5	-0	-1	0	0.4
1889 Cle-N	20	15	.571	36	36	35	3	0	317^{2}	316	12	141	126	13.1	3.57	113	.251	.330	14	.116	-5	16	16	-1	0.9
1890 Cle-N	22	30	.423	54	54	53	1	0	474^{1}	518	11	186	155	13.6	3.83	93	.269	.339	27	.141	-9	-14	-13	3	-1.7
1891 Cle-N	0	3	.000	5	4	2	0	0	29	39	1	21	4	20.5	5.28	66	.310	.432	1	.077	-1	-6	-6	-0	-0.6
Total 5	48	56	.462	109	108	104	5	0	946	997	32	372	335	13.3	3.68	99	.262	.332	56	.144	-12	-4	-4	1	-1.1

● JIM BEATTIE
Beattie, James Louis b: 7/4/54, Hampton, Va. BR/TR, 6'6", 220 lbs. Deb: 4/25/78

YEAR TM/L	W	L	PCT	G	GS	CG	SH	SV	IP	H	HR	BB	SO	RAT	ERA	ERA+	OAV	OOB	BH	AVG	PB	PR	/A	PD	TPI
1978 *NY-A	6	9	.400	25	22	0	0	0	128	123	8	51	65	12.8	3.73	97	.255	.336	0	—	0	1	-2	1	-0.1
1979 NY-A	3	6	.333	15	13	1	1	0	76	85	5	41	32	14.9	5.21	78	.294	.382	0	—	0	-8	-10	1	-0.8
1980 Sea-A	5	15	.250	33	29	3	0	0	187^{1}	205	19	98	67	14.7	4.85	85	.286	.375	0	—	0	-17	-15	0	-1.4
1981 Sea-A	3	2	.600	13	9	0	0	1	66^{2}	59	2	18	36	10.7	2.97	130	.232	.288	0	—	0	5	7	0	0.5
1982 Sea-A	8	12	.400	28	26	6	1	0	172^{1}	149	13	65	140	11.2	3.34	127	.233	.305	0	—	0	14	17	1	1.7
1983 Sea-A	10	15	.400	30	29	8	2	0	196^{2}	197	12	66	132	12.2	3.84	111	.259	.321	0	—	0	5	9	3	1.1
1984 Sea-A	12	16	.429	32	32	12	2	0	211	206	13	75	119	12.2	3.41	117	.260	.328	0	—	0	14	13	1	1.9
1985 Sea-A	5	6	.455	18	15	1	1	0	70^{1}	93	9	33	45	16.5	7.29	58	.316	.391	0	—	0	-25	-24	-1	-3.2
1986 Sea-A	0	6	.000	9	7	0	0	0	40^{1}	57	7	14	24	16.5	6.02	70	.341	.402	0	—	0	-8	-8	1	-1.0
Total 9	52	87	.374	203	182	31	7	1	1148^{2}	1174	88	461	660	13.0	4.17	98	.267	.341	0	—	0	-20	-12	7	-1.3

● BLAINE BEATTY
Beatty, Gordon Blaine b: 4/25/64, Victoria, Tex. BL/TL, 6'2", 185 lbs. Deb: 9/16/89

YEAR TM/L	W	L	PCT	G	GS	CG	SH	SV	IP	H	HR	BB	SO	RAT	ERA	ERA+	OAV	OOB	BH	AVG	PB	PR	/A	PD	TPI
1989 NY-N	0	0	—	2	1	0	0	0	6	5	1	2	3	10.5	1.50	218	.217	.280	1	.500	0	1	1	0	0.0
1991 NY-N	0	0	—	5	0	0	0	0	9^{2}	9	0	4	7	12.1	2.79	130	.250	.325	0	—	0	1	1	0	0.0
Total 2	0	0	—	7	1	0	0	0	15^{2}	14	1	6	10	11.5	2.30	152	.237	.308	1	.500	0	2	2	0	0.0

● JOHNNY BEAZLEY
Beazley, John Andrew "Nig" b: 5/25/18, Nashville, Tenn. d: 4/21/90, Nashville, Tenn. BR/TR, 6'1.5", 190 lbs. Deb: 9/28/41

YEAR TM/L	W	L	PCT	G	GS	CG	SH	SV	IP	H	HR	BB	SO	RAT	ERA	ERA+	OAV	OOB	BH	AVG	PB	PR	/A	PD	TPI
1941 StL-N	1	0	1.000	1	1	0	0	0	9	10	0	3	4	13.0	1.00	376	.294	.351	0	—	-0	3	3	-0	0.3
1942 *StL-N	21	6	.778	43	23	13	3	3	215^{1}	181	4	73	91	10.7	2.13	161	.226	.293	10	.137	-1	28	31	0	4.0
1946 *StL-N	7	5	.583	19	18	5	0	0	103	109	6	55	36	14.7	4.46	77	.275	.368	8	.242	1	-12	-11	-1	-1.2
1947 Bos-N	2	0	1.000	9	2	2	0	0	28^{2}	30	1	19	12	15.4	4.40	89	.273	.380	0	.000	-1	-1	-2	0	-0.2
1948 Bos-N	0	1	.000	3	2	0	0	0	16	19	2	7	4	14.6	4.50	85	.284	.351	0	.000	-1	-1	-1	0	-0.1
1949 Bos-N	0	0	—	1	0	0	0	0	2	0	0	0	0	0.00	0.00	—	.000	.000	0	—	0	1	1	0	0.0
Total 6	31	12	.721	76	46	21	3	3	374	349	13	157	147	12.3	3.01	116	.247	.325	18	.150	-1	18	20	-1	2.8

● BUCK BECANNON
Becannon, James Melvin b: 8/22/1859, New York, N.Y. d: 11/5/23, New York, N.Y. 5'10", 165 lbs. Deb: 10/15/1884 ◆

YEAR TM/L	W	L	PCT	G	GS	CG	SH	SV	IP	H	HR	BB	SO	RAT	ERA	ERA+	OAV	OOB	BH	AVG	PB	PR	/A	PD	TPI
1884 *NY-a	1	0	1.000	1	1	1	0	0	6	2	0	2	6	6.0	1.50	208	.091	.167	0	.000	-0	1	1	0	0.1
1885 NY-a	2	8	.200	10	10	10	0	0	85	108	5	24	15	14.5	6.25	47	.296	.348	10	.303	2	-28	-31	0	-2.4
Total 2	3	8	.273	11	11	11	0	0	91	110	5	26	15	13.9	5.93	50	.284	.337	10	.244	2	-27	-30	0	-2.3

● GEORGE BECHTEL
Bechtel, George A. b: 1848, Philadelphia, Pa. 5'11", 165 lbs. Deb: 5/20/1871 ◆

YEAR TM/L	W	L	PCT	G	GS	CG	SH	SV	IP	H	HR	BB	SO	RAT	ERA	ERA+	OAV	OOB	BH	AVG	PB	PR	/A	PD	TPI
1871 Ath-n	1	2	.333	3	3	2	0	0	26	43	0	11	1	18.7	7.96	51	.319	.370	33	.351	1	-11	-11		-0.7
1873 Phi-n	0	2	.000	3	2	1	0	0	16	27	0	2	0	16.3	4.50	73	.318	.333	63	.244	0	-2	-2		-0.2
1874 Phi-n	1	3	.250	6	4	4	0	0	42	64	0	0	0	13.7	3.86	79	.320	.320	44	.291	-4	-4	-4		-0.2
1875 Cen-n	2	12	.143	14	14	14	0	0	126	170	0	3	0	12.4	3.93	61	.277	.281	17	.274	3	-21	-21		-1.5
Ath-n	3	1	.750	4	4	4	0	0	36	45	0	3	0	12.0	2.25	117	.298	.312	46	.280	1	1	2		0.2
Yr	5	13	.278	18	18	18	0	0	162	215	0	6	0	12.3	3.56	69	.281	.287	63	.279	3	-20	-20		-1.3
Total 4 n	7	20	.259	30	27	25	0	0	246	349	0	19	1	13.5	4.13	59	.295	.306	277	.284	6	-46	-46		-2.4

● GEORGE BECK
Beck, Ernest George B. b: 2/21/1890, South Bend, Ind. d: 10/29/73, South Bend, Ind. BR/TR, 5'11", 165 lbs. Deb: 5/15/14

YEAR TM/L	W	L	PCT	G	GS	CG	SH	SV	IP	H	HR	BB	SO	RAT	ERA	ERA+	OAV	OOB	BH	AVG	PB	PR	/A	PD	TPI
1914 Cle-A	0	0	—	1	0	0	0	0	1	1	0	1	0	18.0	0.00	—	.250	.400	0	—	0	0	0	-0	0.0

● FRANK BECK
Beck, Frank J. (b: Frank J. Hengstebeck) b: 4/29/1860, Poughkeepsie, N.Y. d: 2/8/41, Detroit, Mich. TR, 5'9", 141 lbs. Deb: 5/2/1884 ◆

YEAR TM/L	W	L	PCT	G	GS	CG	SH	SV	IP	H	HR	BB	SO	RAT	ERA	ERA+	OAV	OOB	BH	AVG	PB	PR	/A	PD	TPI
1884 Pit-a	0	3	.000	3	3	3	0	0	25	33	0	6	11	15.8	6.12	55	.306	.370	4	.333	1	-8	-8	0	-0.6
Bal-U	0	2	.000	2	2	1	0	0	9	17	0	4	7	21.0	8.00	34	.378	.429	2	.100	-1	-6	-5	0	-0.8
Total 1	0	5	.000	5	5	4	0	0	34	50	0	10	18	17.2	6.62	48	.327	.387	6	.188	-0	-14	-13	0	-1.4

● RICH BECK
Beck, Richard Henry b: 1/21/41, Pasco, Wash. BB/TR, 6'3", 190 lbs. Deb: 9/14/65

YEAR TM/L	W	L	PCT	G	GS	CG	SH	SV	IP	H	HR	BB	SO	RAT	ERA	ERA+	OAV	OOB	BH	AVG	PB	PR	/A	PD	TPI
1965 NY-A	2	1	.667	3	3	1	1	0	21	22	1	7	10	12.4	2.14	159	.275	.333	0	.000	-0	3	3	0	0.4

● ROD BECK
Beck, Rodney Roy b: 8/3/68, Burbank, Cal. BR/TR, 6'1", 215 lbs. Deb: 5/6/91

YEAR TM/L	W	L	PCT	G	GS	CG	SH	SV	IP	H	HR	BB	SO	RAT	ERA	ERA+	OAV	OOB	BH	AVG	PB	PR	/A	PD	TPI
1991 SF-N	1	1	.500	31	0	0	0	1	52^{1}	53	4	13	38	11.5	3.78	95	.273	.322	1	.500	0	-1	-1	0	0.0
1992 SF-N	3	3	.500	65	0	0	0	17	92	62	4	15	87	7.7	1.76	188	.190	.230	0	.500	1	18	16	-0	1.7
1993 SF-N★	3	1	.750	76	0	0	0	48	79^{1}	57	11	13	86	8.3	2.16	181	.201	.243	0	.000	0	17	15	-1	2.7
1994 SF-N★	2	4	.333	48	0	0	0	28	48^{2}	49	10	13	39	11.5	2.77	145	.261	.308	0	.000	-0	8	7	-0	1.5
Total 4	9	9	.500	220	0	0	0	94	272^{1}	221	29	54	250	9.3	2.45	150	.223	.267	2	.182	1	42	37	-1	5.9

● BOOM-BOOM BECK
Beck, Walter William b: 10/16/04, Decatur, Ill. d: 5/7/87, Champaign, Ill. BR/TR, 6'2", 200 lbs. Deb: 9/22/24 C

YEAR TM/L	W	L	PCT	G	GS	CG	SH	SV	IP	H	HR	BB	SO	RAT	ERA	ERA+	OAV	OOB	BH	AVG	PB	PR	/A	PD	TPI
1924 StL-A	0	0	—	1	0	0	0	0	1	2	0	1	0	27.0	0.00	—	.667	.750	0	—	0	0	0	-0	0.0
1927 StL-A	1	0	1.000	3	1	1	0	0	11^{1}	15	0	5	6	16.7	5.56	78	.333	.412	1	.250	-0	-2	-2	0	-0.1
1928 StL-A	2	3	.400	16	4	2	0	0	49	52	4	20	17	14.0	4.41	95	.289	.373	6	.429	1	-2	-2	-0	0.0
1933 Bro-N	12	20	.375	43	35	15	3	1	257	270	9	69	89	12.3	3.54	91	.267	.321	18	.189	-0	-6	-9	-0	-1.1
1934 Bro-N	2	6	.250	22	9	2	0	0	57	72	6	32	24	17.2	7.42	53	.301	.395	4	.235	1	-21	-22	1	-2.4
1939 Phi-N	7	14	.333	34	16	12	0	3	182^{2}	203	11	64	77	13.3	4.73	85	.284	.345	9	.132	-3	-16	-15	-1	-1.8
1940 Phi-N	4	9	.308	29	15	4	0	0	129^{1}	147	6	49	44	13.7	4.31	90	.286	.349	2	.056	-3	-7	-6	1	-0.7
1941 Phi-N	1	9	.100	19	11	1	0	0	95^{1}	104	8	35	34	13.3	4.63	80	.283	.341	3	.120	-1	-5	-5	0	0.0
1942 Phi-N	0	0	—	26	0	0	0	0	53	69	4	20	10	14.8	4.75	70	.324	.378	4	.333	1	-8	-9	-0	-0.1
1943 Phi-N	0	0	—	4	0	0	0	0	13^{2}	24	1	5	3	20.4	9.88	34	.393	.456	2	.500	1	-10	-10	-0	0.0

YEAR TM/L	W	L	PCT	G	GS	CG	SH	SV	IP	H	HR	BB	SO	RAT	ERA	ERA+	OAV	OOB	BH	AVG	PB	PR	/A	PD	TPI
1944 Det-A	1	2	.333	28	0	0	0	1	74	67	5	27	25	11.8	3.89	92	.243	.317	7	.318	2	-4	-3	-2	-0.1
1945 Cin-N	2	4	.333	11	5	2	0	1	47²	42	0	12	9	10.4	3.40	111	.236	.288	3	.214	-0	2	2	0	0.2
Pit-N	6	1	.857	14	5	4	0	0	63	54	2	14	20	9.7	2.14	184	.234	.278	2	.125	-1	12	13	-0	1.2
Yr	8	5	.615	25	10	6	0	1	110²	96	2	26	29	9.9	2.68	144	.234	.280	5	.167	-1	14	15	-0	1.4
Total 12	38	69	.355	265	100	44	3	6	1034	1121	63	342	352	13.1	4.30	86	.277	.340	61	.187	-2	-72	-71	-5	-6.3

● **CHARLIE BECKER**   Becker, Charles S. "Buck" b: 10/14/1888, Washington, D.C.   d: 7/30/28, Washington, D.C.   BL/TL, 6'2", 180 lbs.   Deb: 8/2/11

YEAR TM/L	W	L	PCT	G	GS	CG	SH	SV	IP	H	HR	BB	SO	RAT	ERA	ERA+	OAV	OOB	BH	AVG	PB	PR	/A	PD	TPI
1911 Was-A	3	5	.375	11	5	5	1	0	71¹	80	2	23	31	13.9	4.04	81	.268	.335	5	.227	-0	-5	-6	-0	-0.6
1912 Was-A	0	0	—	4	0	0	0	0	9	8	0	6	5	14.0	3.00	111	.258	.378	1	.500	0	0	0	-0	0.0
Total 2	3	5	.375	15	5	5	1	0	80¹	88	2	29	36	13.9	3.92	84	.267	.340	6	.250	-0	-5	-6	-1	-0.6

● **BOB BECKER**   Becker, Robert Charles b: 8/15/1875, Syracuse, N.Y.   d: 10/11/51, Syracuse, N.Y.   TL ,   Deb: 9/6/1897

YEAR TM/L	W	L	PCT	G	GS	CG	SH	SV	IP	H	HR	BB	SO	RAT	ERA	ERA+	OAV	OOB	BH	AVG	PB	PR	/A	PD	TPI
1897 Phi-N	0	2	.000	5	2	2	0	0	24	32	0	7	10	15.0	5.63	75	.317	.367	1	.111	-0	-3	-4	-0	-0.3
1898 Phi-N	0	0	—	1	0	0	0	0	5	6	0	5	0	19.8	10.80	32	.295	.434	0	.000	-0	-4	-4	-0	0.0
Total 2	0	2	.000	6	2	2	0	0	29	38	0	12	10	15.8	6.52	62	.313	.380	1	.100	-0	-7	-8	-0	-0.3

● **JAKE BECKLEY**   Beckley, Jacob Peter "Eagle Eye" b: 8/4/1867, Hannibal, Mo.   d: 6/25/18, Kansas City, Mo.   BL/TL, 5'10", 200 lbs.   Deb: 6/20/1888   H◆

YEAR TM/L	W	L	PCT	G	GS	CG	SH	SV	IP	H	HR	BB	SO	RAT	ERA	ERA+	OAV	OOB	BH	AVG	PB	PR	/A	PD	TPI
1902 Cin-N	0	1	.000	1	1	0	0	0	4	9	0	1	2	22.5	6.75	44	.442	.468	175	.330	0	-2	-2	1	-0.2

● **JIM BECKMAN**   Beckman, James Joseph (b: Reinhardt Boeckman) b: 3/1/05, Cincinnati, Ohio   d: 12/5/74, Montgomery, Ohio   BR/TR, 5'10", 172 lbs.   Deb: 7/27/27

YEAR TM/L	W	L	PCT	G	GS	CG	SH	SV	IP	H	HR	BB	SO	RAT	ERA	ERA+	OAV	OOB	BH	AVG	PB	PR	/A	PD	TPI
1927 Cin-N	0	1	.000	4	1	0	0	0	12¹	18	2	6	0	18.2	5.84	65	.340	.417	0	.000	-0	-3	-3	-1	-0.3
1928 Cin-N	0	1	.000	6	0	0	0	0	15¹	19	1	9	4	16.4	5.87	67	.306	.394	0	.000	-0	-3	-3	-0	-0.3
Total 2	0	2	.000	10	1	0	0	0	27²	37	3	15	4	17.2	5.86	66	.322	.405	0	.000	-0	-6	-6	-1	-0.6

● **BILL BECKMANN**   Beckmann, William Aloysius b: 12/8/07, Clayton, Mo.   d: 1/2/90, Florissant, Mo.   BR/TR, 6', 175 lbs.   Deb: 5/2/39

YEAR TM/L	W	L	PCT	G	GS	CG	SH	SV	IP	H	HR	BB	SO	RAT	ERA	ERA+	OAV	OOB	BH	AVG	PB	PR	/A	PD	TPI
1939 Phi-A	7	11	.389	27	19	7	2	0	155¹	198	15	41	20	13.9	5.39	87	.312	.355	13	.250	0	-13	-12	-2	-1.2
1940 Phi-A	8	4	.667	34	9	6	2	1	127¹	132	11	35	47	11.9	4.17	107	.265	.314	8	.205	-1	3	4	-2	0.1
1941 Phi-A	5	9	.357	22	15	4	0	1	130	141	11	33	28	12.2	4.57	92	.270	.315	9	.191	0	-6	-6	-3	-0.8
1942 Phi-A	0	1	.000	5	1	0	0	0	20¹	24	1	9	10	14.6	7.08	53	.289	.359	2	.500	-1	-8	-7	-1	-0.2
StL-N	1	0	1.000	2	0	0	0	0	7	4	0	1	3	6.4	0.00	—	.200	.238	0	.000	-0	3	3	0	0.4
Total 4	21	25	.457	90	44	17	4	2	440	499	38	119	108	12.7	4.79	92	.284	.330	32	.224	1	-22	-18	-7	-1.7

● **JOE BECKWITH**   Beckwith, Thomas Joseph b: 1/28/55, Opelika, Ala.   BL/TR, 6'3", 200 lbs.   Deb: 7/21/79

YEAR TM/L	W	L	PCT	G	GS	CG	SH	SV	IP	H	HR	BB	SO	RAT	ERA	ERA+	OAV	OOB	BH	AVG	PB	PR	/A	PD	TPI
1979 LA-N	1	2	.333	17	0	0	0	2	37¹	42	4	15	28	13.7	4.34	84	.284	.350	0	.000	-1	-3	-3	-0	-0.3
1980 LA-N	3	3	.500	38	0	0	0	0	59²	60	1	23	40	12.7	1.96	178	.263	.333	0	.000	0	11	10	-1	0.9
1982 LA-N	2	1	.667	19	1	0	0	1	40	38	2	14	33	11.7	2.70	128	.252	.315	0	.000	-1	4	3	-1	0.1
1983 *LA-N	3	4	.429	42	3	0	0	1	71	73	5	35	50	13.8	3.55	101	.264	.348	1	.200	-1	1	0	1	0.1
1984 KC-A	8	4	.667	49	1	0	0	1	100²	92	13	25	75	10.6	3.40	119	.247	.298	0	—	0	7	7	-0	0.8
1985 *KC-A	1	5	.167	49	0	0	0	0	95	99	9	32	80	12.7	4.07	102	.269	.333	0	—	0	1	1	0	0.1
1986 LA-N	0	0	—	15	0	0	0	2	18¹	28	5	6	13	16.7	6.87	50	.350	.395	0	—	0	-6	-7	-1	-0.1
Total 7	18	19	.486	229	5	0	0	7	422	432	39	150	319	12.6	3.54	107	.266	.331	1	.053	-1	14	12	-0	1.5

● **JULIO BECQUER**   Becquer, Julio (Villegas) b: 12/20/31, Havana, Cuba   BL/TL, 5'11.5", 178 lbs.   Deb: 9/13/55   ◆

YEAR TM/L	W	L	PCT	G	GS	CG	SH	SV	IP	H	HR	BB	SO	RAT	ERA	ERA+	OAV	OOB	BH	AVG	PB	PR	/A	PD	TPI
1960 Was-A	0	0	—	1	0	0	0	0	1	1	1	0	0	9.0	9.00	43	.250	.250	75	.252	0	-1	-1	-0	0.0
1961 Min-A	0	0	—	1	0	0	0	0	1¹	4	0	1	0	33.8	20.25	21	.500	.556	20	.238	0	-2	-2	-0	0.0
Total 2	0	0	—	2	0	0	0	0	2¹	5	1	1	0	23.1	15.43	26	.417	.462	238	.244	0	-3	-3	-0	0.0

● **PHIL BEDGOOD**   Bedgood, Phillip Burlette b: 3/8/1898, Harrison, Ga.   d: 11/8/27, Fort Pierce, Fla.   BB/TR, 6'3", 218 lbs.   Deb: 9/20/22

YEAR TM/L	W	L	PCT	G	GS	CG	SH	SV	IP	H	HR	BB	SO	RAT	ERA	ERA+	OAV	OOB	BH	AVG	PB	PR	/A	PD	TPI
1922 Cle-A	1	0	1.000	1	1	0	0	0	9	7	0	4	5	14.0	4.00	100	.233	.378	0	.000	-0	0	0	-0	0.0
1923 Cle-A	0	2	.000	9	2	0	0	0	18²	16	0	14	7	15.4	5.30	75	.246	.395	1	.250	-0	-3	-3	-0	-0.2
Total 2	1	2	.333	10	3	1	0	0	27²	23	0	18	12	15.0	4.88	82	.242	.390	1	.167	-0	-3	-3	-0	-0.2

● **HUGH BEDIENT**   Bedient, Hugh Carpenter b: 10/23/1889, Gerry, N.Y.   d: 7/21/65, Jamestown, N.Y.   BR/TR, 6', 185 lbs.   Deb: 4/26/12

YEAR TM/L	W	L	PCT	G	GS	CG	SH	SV	IP	H	HR	BB	SO	RAT	ERA	ERA+	OAV	OOB	BH	AVG	PB	PR	/A	PD	TPI
1912 *Bos-A	20	9	.690	41	28	19	0	2	231	206	6	55	122	10.3	2.92	116	.240	.288	14	.192	1	10	12	1	1.6
1913 Bos-A	15	14	.517	43	28	15	1	5	259	255	0	67	122	11.4	2.78	106	.261	.312	10	.125	-3	4	5	-4	-0.3
1914 Bos-A	8	12	.400	42	16	7	1	2	177¹	187	4	45	70	12.0	3.60	75	.281	.331	5	.100	-2	-17	-18	-1	-2.3
1915 Buf-F	16	18	.471	53	30	16	2	10	269¹	284	5	69	106	11.9	3.17	88	.274	.321	9	.108	-5	-13	-11	-2	-2.2
Total 4	59	53	.527	179	102	57	4	19	936²	932	15	236	420	11.4	3.08	96	.263	.312	38	.133	-9	-16	-12	-5	-3.2

● **ANDY BEDNAR**   Bednar, Andrew Jackson b: 8/16/08, Streator, Ill.   d: 11/26/37, Graham, Tex.   BR/TR, 5'10.5", 180 lbs.   Deb: 9/6/30

YEAR TM/L	W	L	PCT	G	GS	CG	SH	SV	IP	H	HR	BB	SO	RAT	ERA	ERA+	OAV	OOB	BH	AVG	PB	PR	/A	PD	TPI
1930 Pit-N	0	0	—	2	0	0	0	0	1¹	4	0	1	1	33.8	27.00	18	.500	.556	—	0	-3	-3	0	0.0	
1931 Pit-N	0	0	—	3	0	0	0	0	4	10	1	0	2	22.5	11.25	34	.476	.476	0	—	0	-3	-3	0	0.0
Total 2	0	0	—	5	0	0	0	0	5¹	14	1	1	3	25.3	15.19	27	.483	.500	0	—	0	-7	-7	0	0.0

● **STEVE BEDROSIAN**   Bedrosian, Stephen Wayne b: 12/6/57, Methuen, Mass.   BR/TR, 6'3", 200 lbs.   Deb: 8/14/81

YEAR TM/L	W	L	PCT	G	GS	CG	SH	SV	IP	H	HR	BB	SO	RAT	ERA	ERA+	OAV	OOB	BH	AVG	PB	PR	/A	PD	TPI
1981 Atl-N	1	2	.333	15	1	0	0	0	24¹	15	2	15	9	11.5	4.44	81	.169	.295	0	.000	-0	-3	-2	-0	-0.3
1982 *Atl-N	8	6	.571	64	3	0	0	11	137²	102	7	57	123	10.7	2.42	154	.206	.293	1	.038	-2	18	20	-0	2.1
1983 Atl-N	9	10	.474	70	1	0	0	19	120	100	11	51	114	11.6	3.60	108	.229	.315	2	.105	-1	0	4	0	0.6
1984 Atl-N	9	6	.600	40	4	0	0	11	83²	65	5	33	81	10.6	2.37	163	.210	.289	2	.118	-1	11	14	-1	2.7
1985 Atl-N	7	15	.318	37	37	0	0	0	206²	198	17	111	134	13.7	3.83	100	.254	.351	5	.078	-4	-6	0	-2	-0.5
1986 Phi-N	8	6	.571	68	0	0	0	29	90¹	79	12	34	82	11.3	3.39	114	.232	.301	1	.200	-0	3	5	-1	1.0
1987 Phi-N★	5	3	.625	65	0	0	0	40	89	79	11	28	74	10.9	2.83	150	.237	.298	0	.000	-0	12	14	0	2.4
1988 Phi-N	6	6	.500	57	0	0	0	28	74¹	75	6	27	61	12.3	3.75	95	.257	.320	0	.000	-0	-3	-2	-0	-0.4
1989 Phi-N	2	3	.400	28	0	0	0	6	33²	21	7	17	24	10.4	3.21	110	.183	.293	0	—	0	1	1	-0	0.4
*SF-N	1	4	.200	40	0	0	0	17	51	35	5	22	34	10.1	2.65	127	.192	.279	1	.167	-0	5	4	-1	0.6
Yr	3	7	.300	68	0	0	0	23	84²	56	12	39	58	10.1	2.87	120	.187	.280	1	.167	-0	6	5	-1	0.8
1990 SF-N	9	9	.500	68	0	0	0	17	79¹	72	6	44	43	13.4	4.20	87	.241	.342	2	.500	1	-4	-5	-1	-1.1
1991 *Min-A	5	3	.625	56	0	0	0	6	77¹	70	11	35	44	12.6	4.42	96	.243	.331	0	—	0	-3	-1	-1	-0.3
1993 Atl-N	5	2	.714	49	0	0	0	0	49²	34	4	14	33	9.1	1.63	246	.194	.262	0	.000	0	13	13	0	1.6
1994 Atl-N	0	2	.000	46	0	0	0	0	46	41	4	18	43	11.9	3.33	125	.243	.323	1	.500	0	5	4	-0	0.2
Total 13	75	77	.493	703	46	0	0	184	1163	986	108	506	899	11.7	3.31	116	.229	.314	15	.098	-7	52	69	-8	8.8

● **FRED BEEBE**   Beebe, Frederick Leonard b: 12/31/1880, Lincoln, Neb.   d: 10/30/57, Elgin, Ill.   BR/TR, 6'1", 190 lbs.   Deb: 4/17/06

YEAR TM/L	W	L	PCT	G	GS	CG	SH	SV	IP	H	HR	BB	SO	RAT	ERA	ERA+	OAV	OOB	BH	AVG	PB	PR	/A	PD	TPI
1906 Chi-N	6	1	.857	14	6	4	0	1	70	56	1	32	55	12.0	2.70	98	.210	.306	3	.103	-1	-1	-0	-1	-0.3
StL-N	9	9	.500	20	19	16	4	0	160²	115	0	68	116	10.8	3.02	87	.208	.305	10	.172	0	-7	-7	-0	-0.8
Yr	15	10	.600	34	25	20	4	1	230²	171	2	100	**171**	10.9	2.93	90	.207	.300	13	.149	-1	-7	-6	-1	-1.1
1907 StL-N	7	19	.269	31	29	24	4	0	238¹	192	1	109	141	11.7	2.72	92	.230	.326	11	.128	-3	-7	-6	-1	-0.8
1908 StL-N	5	13	.278	29	19	12	0	0	174¹	134	0	66	72	10.5	2.63	90	**.193**	.267	7	.125	-2	-5	-5	2	-0.6
1909 StL-N	15	21	.417	44	34	18	6	0	287²	256	5	104	105	11.5	2.82	90	.229	.299	18	.167	-4	-7	-9	-3	-1.3
1910 Cin-N	12	14	.462	35	26	13	1	0	214¹	193	3	94	93	12.3	3.07	95	.246	.333	12	.164	-2	-6	-6	1	-0.3
1911 Phi-N	3	3	.500	9	8	2	0	0	48¹	52	2	24	20	14.7	4.47	77	.297	.391	1	.263	-2	-6	-6	1	-0.3
1916 Cle-A	5	3	.625	20	12	5	0	2	100²	92	1	37	32	11.6	2.41	125	.251	.321	6	.214	1	5	7	-0	0.6
Total 7	62	83	.428	202	153	93	9	4	1294¹	1090	17	534	634	11.6	2.86	93	.227	.311	72	.158	-8	-28	-30	6	-3.8

● **ED BEECHER**   Beecher, Edward H. b: 7/2/1860, Guilford, Conn.   d: 9/12/35, Hartford, Conn.   BL/TL, 5'10", 185 lbs.   Deb: 6/28/1887   ◆

YEAR TM/L	W	L	PCT	G	GS	CG	SH	SV	IP	H	HR	BB	SO	RAT	ERA	ERA+	OAV	OOB	BH	AVG	PB	PR	/A	PD	TPI
1890 Buf-P	0	0	—	1	0	0	0	0	6	10	0	3	0	19.5	12.00	34	.356	.418	159	.297	0	-5	-5	-0	0.0

YEAR TM/L	W	L	PCT	G	GS	CG	SH	SV	IP	H	HR	BB	SO	RAT	ERA	ERA+	OAV	OOB	BH	AVG	PB	PR	/A	PD	TPI
● **ROY BEECHER** Beecher, Leroy "Colonel" b: 5/10/1884, Swanton, Ohio d: 10/11/52, Toledo, Ohio BL/TR, 6'2", 180 lbs. Deb: 9/29/07																								
1907 NY-N	0	2	.000	2	2	2	0	0	14	17	0	6	5	14.8	2.57	96	.293	.359	0	.000	-1	-0	-0	-0	-0.1
1908 NY-N	0	0	—	2	0	0	0	1	5²	11	0	3	0	22.2	7.94	30	.440	.500	1	.333	1	-4	-3	0	-0.1
Total 2	0	2	.000	4	2	2	0	1	19²	28	0	9	5	16.9	4.12	60	.337	.402	1	.125	-0	-4	-4	0	-0.2
● **FRED BEENE** Beene, Freddy Ray b: 11/24/42, Angleton, Tex. BB/TR, 5'9", 160 lbs. Deb: 9/18/68																								
1968 Bal-A	0	0	—	1	0	0	0	0	1	2	0	1	1	27.0	9.00	33	.500	.600	0	—	0	-1	-1	0	0.0
1969 Bal-A	0	0	—	2	0	0	0	0	2²	2	0	1	0	10.1	0.00	—	.200	.273	0	—	0	1	1	0	0.0
1970 Bal-A	0	0	—	4	0	0	0	0	6	8	1	5	4	19.5	6.00	61	.320	.433	0	—	0	-2	-2	0	0.0
1972 NY-A	1	3	.250	29	1	0	0	3	57²	55	3	24	37	12.5	2.34	126	.256	.333	0	.000	-1	5	4	0	0.2
1973 NY-A	6	0	1.000	19	4	0	0	1	91	67	5	27	49	9.4	1.68	218	.209	.273	0	—	0	22	20	1	1.6
1974 NY-A	0	0	—	6	0	0	0	1	10	9	1	2	10	10.8	2.70	129	.231	.286	0	—	0	1	1	0	0.2
Cle-A	4	4	.500	32	0	0	0	2	73	68	7	26	35	11.7	4.93	73	.246	.314	0	—	0	-11	-11	1	-1.0
Yr	4	4	.500	38	0	0	0	3	83	77	8	28	45	11.5	4.66	77	.244	.307	0	—	0	-10	-10	1	-0.8
1975 Cle-A	1	0	1.000	19	1	0	0	1	46²	63	4	25	20	17.6	6.94	54	.323	.408	0	—	0	-16	-16	0	-0.4
Total 7	12	7	.632	112	6	0	0	8	288	274	21	111	156	12.3	3.63	97	.253	.326	0	.000	-1	-1	-4	2	0.6
● **ANDY BEENE** Beene, Ramon Andrew b: 10/13/56, Freeport, Tex. BR/TR, 6'3", 205 lbs. Deb: 9/22/83																								
1983 Mil-A	0	0	—	1	0	0	0	0	2	3	0	1	0	18.0	4.50	83	.333	.400	0	—	0	-0	-0	-0	0.8
1984 Mil-A	0	2	.000	5	3	0	0	0	18²	28	1	9	11	18.8	11.09	35	.350	.429	0	—	0	-15	-15	0	-1.0
Total 2	0	2	.000	6	3	0	0	0	20²	31	1	10	11	18.7	10.45	37	.348	.426	0	—	0	-15	-15	0	-0.2
● **CLARENCE BEERS** Beers, Clarence Scott b: 12/9/18, ElDorado, Kan. BR/TR, 6', 175 lbs. Deb: 5/2/48																								
1948 StL-N	0	0	—	1	0	0	0	0	0²	3	0	1	0	54.0	13.50	30	.500	.571	0	—	0	-1	-1	-0	-0.1
● **JOE BEGGS** Beggs, Joseph Stanley "Fireman" b: 11/4/10, Rankin, Pa. d: 7/19/83, Indianapolis, Ind BR/TR, 6'1", 182 lbs. Deb: 4/19/38																								
1938 NY-A	3	2	.600	14	9	4	0	0	58¹	69	7	20	8	13.7	5.40	84	.299	.355	5	.250	1	-4	-6	2	-0.2
1940 *Cin-N	12	3	.800	37	1	0	0	7	76²	68	1	21	25	10.6	2.00	190	.243	.298	4	.190	-0	16	15	1	3.3
1941 Cin-N	4	3	.571	37	0	0	0	5	57	57	2	27	19	13.3	3.79	95	.313	.402	3	.300	1	-1	-1	0	-0.1
1942 Cin-N	6	5	.545	38	0	0	0	8	88²	65	4	33	24	10.0	2.13	154	.206	.283	0	.000	-3	12	11	3	1.6
1943 Cin-N	7	6	.538	39	4	0	2	6	115¹	121	6	25	28	11.4	2.34	142	.276	.315	5	.143	-1	13	12	1	1.5
1944 Cin-N	1	0	1.000	1	1	1	0	0	9	8	0	0	2	8.0	2.00	174	.222	.222	0	.000	-0	2	1	0	0.1
1946 Cin-N	12	10	.545	28	22	14	2	1	190	175	15	39	38	10.2	2.32	144	.247	.287	14	.222	2	23	22	1	2.9
1947 Cin-N	0	3	.000	11	4	0	0	0	32¹	42	4	6	11	13.4	5.29	78	.316	.345	1	.091	-1	-4	-4	1	-0.4
NY-N	3	3	.500	32	0	0	0	2	66	81	6	18	23	13.6	4.23	96	.300	.346	1	.077	-1	-1	-1	-0	-0.2
Yr	3	6	.333	43	4	0	0	2	98¹	123	10	24	34	13.5	4.58	89	.305	.346	2	.083	-2	-6	-5	0	-0.6
1948 NY-N	0	0	—	1	0	0	0	0	0¹	1	0	1	0	54.0	0.00	—	.667	.667	0	—	0	0	0	0	0.0
Total 9	48	35	.578	238	41	23	4	29	693²	688	39	189	178	11.4	2.96	122	.265	.316	33	.167	-3	55	50	8	8.5
● **ED BEGLEY** Begley, Edward N. (b: Edward N. Bagley) b: 1863, New York, N.Y. d: 7/24/19, Waterbury, Conn. Deb: 5/3/1884																								
1884 NY-N	12	18	.400	31	30	30	0	0	266	296	9	99	104	13.4	4.16	72	.263	.323	22	.182	-3	-35	-35	-2	-3.4
1885 NY-a	4	9	.308	15	14	10	0	0	115	131	5	48	44	14.6	4.93	60	.278	.355	9	.173	-0	-21	-25	1	-2.1
Total 2	16	27	.372	46	44	40	0	0	381	427	14	147	148	13.7	4.39	68	.268	.333	31	.179	-3	-56	-60	-1	-5.5
● **PETIE BEHAN** Behan, Charles Frederick b: 12/11/1887, Dallas City, Pa. d: 1/22/57, Bradford, Pa. BR/TR, 5'10", 160 lbs. Deb: 9/16/21																								
1921 Phi-N	0	1	.000	2	2	1	0	0	10²	17	0	1	3	15.2	5.91	72	.354	.367	0	.000	-1	-3	-2	0	-0.2
1922 Phi-N	4	2	.667	7	5	3	1	0	47¹	49	3	14	13	12.2	2.47	189	.259	.314	5	.250	-0	9	12	-1	1.3
1923 Phi-N	3	12	.200	31	17	5	0	2	131	182	11	57	27	16.5	5.50	84	.336	.401	8	.186	-2	-22	-13	-1	-1.5
Total 3	7	15	.318	40	24	9	1	2	189	248	14	72	43	15.3	4.76	97	.319	.378	13	.194	-3	-16	-3	-2	-0.4
● **RICK BEHENNA** Behenna, Richard Kipp b: 3/6/60, Miami, Fla. BR/TR, 6'2", 170 lbs. Deb: 4/12/83																								
1983 Atl-N	3	3	.500	14	6	0	0	0	37¹	37	7	12	17	12.1	4.58	85	.255	.316	4	.333	2	-4	-3	-0	-0.3
Cle-A	0	2	.000	5	4	0	0	0	26	22	0	14	9	12.8	4.15	102	.232	.336	0	—	0	-0	0	0	-0.2
1984 Cle-A	0	3	.000	3	3	0	0	0	9²	17	5	8	6	24.2	13.97	29	.386	.491	0	—	0	-11	-11	0	-2.1
1985 Cle-A	0	2	.000	4	4	0	0	0	19²	29	3	8	4	16.9	7.78	53	.354	.411	0	—	0	-8	-8	-1	-0.7
Total 3	3	10	.231	26	17	0	0	0	92²	105	15	42	36	14.6	6.12	66	.287	.365	4	.333	2	-23	-21	-1	-3.3
● **MEL BEHNEY** Behney, Melvin Brian b: 9/2/47, Newark, N.J. BL/TL, 6'2", 180 lbs. Deb: 8/14/70																								
1970 Cin-N	0	2	.000	5	1	0	0	0	10	15	1	8	2	20.7	4.50	90	.341	.442	0	.000	-0	-1	-1	-0	-0.1
● **HANK BEHRMAN** Behrman, Henry Bernard b: 6/27/21, Brooklyn, N.Y. d: 1/20/87, New York, N.Y. BR/TR, 5'11", 174 lbs. Deb: 4/17/46																								
1946 Bro-N	11	5	.688	47	11	2	0	4	150²	138	3	69	78	12.5	2.93	115	.241	.325	4	.095	-3	8	8	-2	0.3
1947 *Bro-N	0	0	—	2	0	0	0	0	3²	3	1	4	2	17.2	9.82	42	.231	.412	0	—	0	-2	-2	-0	-0.1
Pit-N	0	2	.000	10	2	0	0	0	24²	33	6	17	11	19.0	9.12	46	.347	.456	0	.000	-1	-14	-13	-1	-1.1
*Bro-N	5	3	.625	38	6	0	0	8	88¹	94	9	44	31	14.1	5.30	78	.274	.357	6	.231	1	-12	-11	-1	-1.2
Yr	5	5	.500	50	8	0	0	8	116²	130	16	65	44	15.0	6.25	66	.287	.376	6	.188	-0	-28	-27	-2	-2.3
1948 Bro-N	5	4	.556	34	4	2	1	7	91	95	7	42	42	13.8	4.05	99	.268	.350	3	.107	-2	-1	-1	-0	-0.3
1949 NY-N	3	3	.500	43	4	1	1	0	71¹	64	5	52	25	14.6	4.92	81	.239	.363	1	.077	-1	-7	-7	-0	-0.6
Total 4	24	17	.585	174	27	5	2	19	429²	427	31	228	189	13.9	4.40	87	.259	.352	14	.122	-5	-28	-28	-5	-2.9
● **TIM BELCHER** Belcher, Timothy Wayne b: 10/19/61, Mount Gilead, Ohio BR/TR, 6'3", 210 lbs. Deb: 9/6/87																								
1987 LA-N	4	2	.667	6	5	0	0	0	34	30	2	7	23	9.8	2.38	166	.240	.280	2	.200	0	6	6	-0	1.0
1988 *LA-N	12	6	.667	36	27	4	1	4	179²	143	8	51	152	9.8	2.91	115	.217	.275	4	.071	-2	11	8	-1	0.6
1989 LA-N	15	12	.556	39	30	**10**	**8**	1	230	182	20	80	200	10.5	2.82	121	.217	.291	7	.100	-2	17	15	-2	1.4
1990 LA-N	9	9	.500	24	24	5	2	0	153	136	17	48	102	10.9	4.00	91	.240	.302	7	.163	-4	-6	-2	-2	-0.7
1991 LA-N	10	9	.526	33	33	2	1	0	209¹	189	17	75	156	11.4	2.62	137	.240	.307	8	.119	-3	25	23	-2	1.6
1992 Cin-N	15	14	.517	35	34	2	1	0	227²	201	17	80	149	11.2	3.91	92	.238	.307	8	.105	-2	-10	-8	-0	-1.2
1993 Cin-N	9	6	.600	22	22	4	2	0	137	134	11	47	101	12.4	4.47	90	.254	.324	10	.200	1	-6	-7	-1	-0.7
*Chi-A	3	5	.375	12	11	1	0	0	71²	64	8	27	34	11.6	4.40	95	.242	.314	0	—	0	-1	-2	-1	-0.2
1994 Det-A	7	15	.318	25	25	3	0	0	162	192	21	78	76	15.2	5.89	81	.290	.368	0	—	0	-20	-20	0	-2.2
Total 8	84	78	.519	232	211	31	16	5	1404¹	1271	114	493	993	11.5	3.69	102	.241	.309	46	.124	-5	19	10	-8	-0.4
● **STAN BELINDA** Belinda, Stanley Peter b: 8/6/66, Huntingdon, Pa. BR/TR, 6'3", 185 lbs. Deb: 9/8/89																								
1989 Pit-N	0	1	.000	8	0	0	0	0	10¹	13	0	2	10	13.1	6.10	55	.295	.326	0	—	0	-3	-3	-0	-0.3
1990 *Pit-N	3	4	.429	55	0	0	0	8	58¹	48	4	29	55	12.0	3.55	102	.227	.324	0	.000	-1	2	0	-1	-0.1
1991 *Pit-N	7	5	.583	60	0	0	0	16	78¹	50	10	35	71	10.2	3.45	104	.184	.286	0	.000	-0	2	1	-1	0.1
1992 *Pit-N	6	4	.600	59	0	0	0	18	71¹	58	8	29	57	11.0	3.15	109	.223	.301	2	.667	0	1	3	-2	0.4
1993 Pit-N	3	1	.750	40	0	0	0	19	42¹	35	4	11	30	10.0	3.61	112	.224	.280	0	.000	0	2	2	-0	0.3
KC-A	1	1	.500	23	0	0	0	0	27¹	30	2	6	25	12.2	4.28	107	.280	.325	0	—	0	0	1	-0	0.0
1994 KC-A	2	2	.500	37	0	0	0	1	49	47	6	24	37	14.0	5.14	101	.250	.350	0	—	0	-2	0	-0	-0.1
Total 6	22	18	.550	282	0	0	0	62	337	281	34	136	285	11.5	3.82	102	.227	.310	2	.125	-0	4	3	-4	0.3
● **BO BELINSKY** Belinsky, Robert b: 12/7/36, New York, N.Y. BL/TL, 6'2", 191 lbs. Deb: 4/18/62																								
1962 LA-A	10	11	.476	33	31	5	3	1	187¹	149	12	122	145	13.6	3.56	109	.216	.344	10	.167	1	9	6	-0	0.7
1963 LA-A	2	9	.182	13	13	2	0	0	76²	78	12	35	60	13.7	5.75	60	.262	.347	2	.074	-2	-18	-20	1	-2.5

YEAR	TM/L	W	L	PCT	G	GS	CG	SH	SV	IP	H	HR	BB	SO	RAT	ERA	ERA+	OAV	OOB	BH	AVG	PB	PR	/A	PD	TPI
1964	LA-A	9	8	.529	23	22	4	1	0	135¹	120	8	49	91	11.6	2.86	115	.240	.315	4	.095	-1	11	6	-1	0.5
1965	Phi-N	4	9	.308	30	14	3	0	1	109²	103	13	48	71	12.9	4.84	71	.248	.334	6	.188	1	-16	-17	-1	-2.0
1966	Phi-N	0	2	.000	9	1	0	0	0	15¹	14	3	5	8	12.9	2.93	123	.250	.344	1	.333	0	1	1	0	0.2
1967	Hou-N	3	9	.250	27	18	0	0	0	115¹	112	12	54	80	13.6	4.68	71	.255	.347	3	.077	-1	-17	-18	-2	-2.1
1969	Pit-N	0	3	.000	8	3	0	0	0	17²	17	1	14	15	16.8	4.58	76	.266	.412	0	.000	-0	-2	-2	-0	-0.4
1970	Cin-N	0	0	—	3	0	0	0	0	8	10	0	6	6	18.0	4.50	90	.294	.400	1	1.000	1	-0	-0	-0	0.1
Total	8	28	51	.354	146	102	14	4	2	665¹	603	61	333	476	13.2	4.10	86	.241	.340	27	.131	-2	-32	-43	-4	-5.5

● CHARLIE BELL
Bell, Charles C. b: 8/12/1868, Cincinnati, Ohio d: 2/7/37, Cincinnati, Ohio TR , Deb: 10/13/1889 F♦

YEAR	TM/L	W	L	PCT	G	GS	CG	SH	SV	IP	H	HR	BB	SO	RAT	ERA	ERA+	OAV	OOB	BH	AVG	PB	PR	/A	PD	TPI
1889	KC-a	1	0	1.000	1	1	1	0	0	9	4	0	3	3	8.0	1.00	418	.130	.231	1	.167	0	3	3	1	0.4
1891	Lou-a	2	6	.250	10	9	8	0	0	77	93	4	20	16	14.1	4.68	78	.289	.346	1	.036	-2	-8	-9	-2	-1.0
	Cin-a	1	0	1.000	1	1	1	0	0	9	2	0	3	1	6.0	0.00	—	.070	.183	2	.500	0	4	4	0	0.5
	Yr	3	6	.333	11	10	9	0	0	86	95	4	23	17	12.5	4.19	88	.265	.311	3	.094	-2	-4	-5	-1	-0.5
Total	2	4	6	.400	12	11	10	0	0	95	99	4	26	20	12.8	3.88	97	.259	.323	4	.105	-2	-2	-1	-1	-0.1

● ERIC BELL
Bell, Eric Alvin b: 10/27/63, Modesto, Cal. BL/TL, 6'3", 195 lbs. Deb: 9/24/85

YEAR	TM/L	W	L	PCT	G	GS	CG	SH	SV	IP	H	HR	BB	SO	RAT	ERA	ERA+	OAV	OOB	BH	AVG	PB	PR	/A	PD	TPI
1985	Bal-A	0	0	—	4	0	0	0	0	5²	4	1	4	4	12.7	4.76	85	.200	.333	0	—	0	-0	-0	0	0.1
1986	Bal-A	1	2	.333	4	4	0	0	0	23¹	23	4	14	18	14.3	5.01	82	.258	.359	0	—	0	-2	-2	-1	-0.3
1987	Bal-A	10	13	.435	33	29	2	0	0	165	174	32	78	111	13.9	5.45	81	.271	.351	0	—	0	-18	-19	-1	-2.3
1991	Cle-A	4	0	1.000	10	0	0	0	0	18	5	0	5	7	5.5	0.50	830	.091	.180	0	—	0	7	7	-0	1.6
1992	Cle-A	0	2	.000	7	1	0	0	0	15¹	22	1	9	10	18.8	7.63	51	.349	.438	0	—	0	-6	-6	1	-0.6
1993	Hou-N	0	1	.000	10	0	0	0	0	7¹	10	0	2	2	14.7	6.14	63	.313	.353	0	—	0	-2	-2	-0	-0.3
Total	6	15	18	.455	68	34	2	0	0	234²	238	38	112	152	13.6	5.18	83	.264	.348	0	—	0	-22	-23	-2	-1.8

● GARY BELL
Bell, Gary b: 11/17/36, San Antonio, Tex. BR/TR, 6'1", 198 lbs. Deb: 6/1/58

YEAR	TM/L	W	L	PCT	G	GS	CG	SH	SV	IP	H	HR	BB	SO	RAT	ERA	ERA+	OAV	OOB	BH	AVG	PB	PR	/A	PD	TPI
1958	Cle-A	12	10	.545	33	23	10	0	1	182	141	17	73	110	10.8	3.31	110	.213	.296	11	.196	2	9	7	-2	0.7
1959	Cle-A	16	11	.593	44	28	12	1	5	234	208	28	105	136	12.2	4.04	91	.238	.323	18	.240	3	-5	-9	-2	-0.9
1960	Cle-A★	9	10	.474	28	23	6	2	1	154²	139	15	82	109	13.3	4.13	90	.242	.344	7	.149	-0	-4	-7	1	-0.7
1961	Cle-A	12	16	.429	34	34	11	2	0	228¹	214	32	100	163	12.6	4.10	96	.245	.326	16	.198	1	-2	-4	1	-0.4
1962	Cle-A	10	9	.526	57	6	1	0	12	107²	104	14	52	80	13.3	4.26	91	.264	.354	5	.208	1	-4	-5	-1	-0.8
1963	Cle-A	8	5	.615	58	7	0	0	5	119	91	13	52	91	11.1	2.95	123	.208	.298	3	.115	-1	9	9	1	1.0
1964	Cle-A	8	6	.571	56	2	0	0	5	106	106	15	53	89	13.8	4.33	83	.260	.351	6	.375	2	-8	-9	-1	-1.0
1965	Cle-A	6	5	.545	60	0	0	0	17	103²	86	7	52	90	12.2	3.04	115	.226	.319	1	.063	-0	5	5	-1	0.6
1966	Cle-A☆	14	15	.483	40	37	12	0	0	254	211	19	79	194	10.4	3.22	107	.228	.291	10	.132	-1	6	6	2	0.8
1967	Cle-A	1	5	.167	9	9	1	0	0	60²	50	7	24	39	11.1	3.71	88	.234	.314	0	.000	-2	-3	-3	1	-0.4
	*Bos-A	12	8	.600	29	24	8	0	3	165¹	143	16	47	115	10.6	3.16	110	.231	.290	12	.203	1	1	6	-1	0.8
	Yr	13	13	.500	38	33	9	0	3	226	193	23	71	154	10.7	3.31	104	.231	.295	12	.162	-1	-2	3	0	0.4
1968	Bos-A☆	11	11	.500	35	27	9	3	1	191²	177	7	68	103	11.3	3.12	101	.239	.308	13	.220	2	-3	1	0	0.3
1969	Sea-A	2	6	.250	13	11	1	1	2	61¹	76	8	34	30	16.4	4.70	77	.305	.393	3	.214	1	-7	-7	0	-0.7
	Chi-A	0	0	—	23	2	0	0	0	38²	48	8	23	26	17.0	6.28	61	.308	.403	0	.000	-0	-11	-10	0	0.0
	Yr	2	6	.250	36	13	1	1	2	100	124	16	57	56	16.5	5.31	70	.302	.390	3	.158	1	-19	-18	0	-0.7
Total	12	121	117	.508	519	233	71	9	51	2015	1794	206	842	1378	12.0	3.68	98	.239	.320	105	.185	9	-17	-18	-3	-0.7

● GEORGE BELL
Bell, George Glenn "Farmer" b: 11/2/1874, Greenwood, N.Y. d: 12/25/41, New York, N.Y. BR/TR, 6', 195 lbs. Deb: 4/17/07

YEAR	TM/L	W	L	PCT	G	GS	CG	SH	SV	IP	H	HR	BB	SO	RAT	ERA	ERA+	OAV	OOB	BH	AVG	PB	PR	/A	PD	TPI
1907	Bro-N	8	16	.333	35	27	20	3	1	263²	222	1	77	88	10.4	2.25	104	.238	.300	8	.095	-2	6	3	2	0.3
1908	Bro-N	4	15	.211	29	21	12	2	1	155¹	162	3	45	63	12.1	3.59	65	.270	.324	8	.170	1	-21	-22	1	-2.4
1909	Bro-N	16	15	.516	33	30	29	6	1	256	236	6	73	95	11.0	2.71	96	.251	.307	15	.167	1	-3	-3	2	-0.1
1910	Bro-N	10	27	.270	44	36	25	6	1	310	267	6	82	102	10.2	2.64	115	.241	.296	13	.134	-4	13	13	-3	0.7
1911	Bro-N	5	6	.455	19	12	6	2	0	101	123	2	28	28	13.6	4.28	78	.315	.364	4	.121	-1	-10	-11	2	-1.0
Total	5	43	79	.352	160	126	92	17	4	1086	1010	16	305	376	11.0	2.85	94	.254	.310	48	.137	-6	-14	-20	4	-2.5

● HI BELL
Bell, Herman S b: 7/16/1897, Mt.Sherman, Ky. d: 6/7/49, Glendale, Cal. BR/TR, 6', 185 lbs. Deb: 4/16/24

YEAR	TM/L	W	L	PCT	G	GS	CG	SH	SV	IP	H	HR	BB	SO	RAT	ERA	ERA+	OAV	OOB	BH	AVG	PB	PR	/A	PD	TPI
1924	StL-N	3	8	.273	28	11	5	0	1	113¹	124	5	29	29	12.5	4.92	77	.292	.344	2	.065	-1	-13	-14	0	-1.5
1926	*StL-N	6	6	.500	27	7	3	0	2	85	82	1	17	27	11.0	3.18	123	.255	.296	3	.120	-1	6	7	-1	0.6
1927	StL-N	1	3	.250	25	1	0	0	0	57¹	71	5	22	31	14.8	3.92	101	.317	.381	1	.091	-1	-0	0	-0	-0.1
1929	StL-N	0	2	.000	7	0	0	0	0	13	19	1	4	4	15.9	6.92	67	.339	.383	0	.000	-0	-3	-3	-0	-0.5
1930	*StL-N	3	4	.571	39	9	2	0	8	115¹	143	4	23	42	13.1	3.90	129	.299	.334	2	.077	-3	14	14	1	0.7
1932	NY-N	8	4	.667	35	10	3	0	2	120	132	12	16	25	11.3	3.68	101	.280	.307	3	.088	-2	3	0	-1	-0.3
1933	*NY-N	6	5	.545	38	7	1	1	5	105¹	100	4	20	24	10.4	2.05	157	.246	.285	4	.138	-1	15	14	-1	1.3
1934	NY-N	4	3	.571	22	2	0	0	6	54	72	2	12	9	14.3	3.67	105	.319	.358	2	.105	-1	2	1	-1	0.0
Total	8	32	34	.485	221	47	14	1	24	663¹	743	34	143	191	12.2	3.69	107	.285	.326	17	.096	-12	23	19	-4	0.2

● JERRY BELL
Bell, Jerry Houston b: 10/6/47, Madison, Tenn. BB/TR, 6'4", 190 lbs. Deb: 9/6/71

YEAR	TM/L	W	L	PCT	G	GS	CG	SH	SV	IP	H	HR	BB	SO	RAT	ERA	ERA+	OAV	OOB	BH	AVG	PB	PR	/A	PD	TPI
1971	Mil-A	2	1	.667	8	0	0	0	0	14²	10	0	6	8	9.8	3.07	113	.200	.286	—	—	0	1	1	-0	0.1
1972	Mil-A	5	1	.833	25	3	0	0	0	70²	50	1	33	20	11.0	1.66	183	.209	.313	1	.071	-1	11	11	1	0.9
1973	Mil-A	9	9	.500	31	25	8	0	1	183²	185	14	70	57	12.7	3.97	95	.263	.334	0	—	0	-3	-4	1	-0.1
1974	Mil-A	1	0	1.000	5	0	0	0	0	14	17	2	5	4	14.1	2.57	141	.315	.373	0	—	0	2	2	-0	0.1
Total	4	17	11	.607	69	28	8	0	1	283	262	17	114	89	12.2	3.28	109	.250	.329	1	.071	-1	10	9	1	1.0

● RALPH BELL
Bell, Ralph Albert "Lefty" b: 11/6/1890, Kohoka, Mo. d: 10/18/59, Burlington, Iowa BL/TL, 5'11.5", 170 lbs. Deb: 7/16/12

YEAR	TM/L	W	L	PCT	G	GS	CG	SH	SV	IP	H	HR	BB	SO	RAT	ERA	ERA+	OAV	OOB	BH	AVG	PB	PR	/A	PD	TPI
1912	Chi-A	0	0	—	3	0	0	0	0	6	8	1	8	5	24.0	9.00	36	.333	.500	0	.000	-0	-4	-4	0	0.0

● BILL BELL
Bell, William Samuel "Ding Dong" b: 10/24/33, Goldsboro, N.C. d: 10/11/62, Durham, N.C. BR/TR, 6'3", 200 lbs. Deb: 9/5/52

YEAR	TM/L	W	L	PCT	G	GS	CG	SH	SV	IP	H	HR	BB	SO	RAT	ERA	ERA+	OAV	OOB	BH	AVG	PB	PR	/A	PD	TPI
1952	Pit-N	0	1	.000	4	1	0	0	0	15²	16	3	13	4	16.7	4.60	87	.254	.382	0	—	-0	-2	-1	0	-0.1
1955	Pit-N	0	0	—	1	0	0	0	0	1	0	0	1	0	9.0	0.00	—	.000	.250	0	—	0	0	-0	0	0.0
Total	2	0	1	.000	5	1	0	0	0	16²	16	3	14	4	16.2	4.32	93	.242	.375	0	.000	-0	-1	-1	0	-0.1

● CHIEF BENDER
Bender, Charles Albert b: 5/5/1884, Crow Wing Co., Minn d: 5/22/54, Philadelphia, Pa. BR/TR, 6'2", 185 lbs. Deb: 4/20/03 CH

YEAR	TM/L	W	L	PCT	G	GS	CG	SH	SV	IP	H	HR	BB	SO	RAT	ERA	ERA+	OAV	OOB	BH	AVG	PB	PR	/A	PD	TPI
1903	Phi-A	17	14	.548	36	33	29	2	0	270	239	6	65	127	11.0	3.07	100	.237	.299	22	.183	-1	-3	-0	-3	-0.2
1904	Phi-A	10	11	.476	29	20	18	4	0	203²	167	1	59	149	10.2	2.87	93	.225	.285	18	.228	3	-6	-4	-2	-0.4
1905	*Phi-A	18	11	.621	35	23	18	4	0	229	193	5	90	142	11.6	2.83	94	.230	.313	20	.217	2	-4	-4	3	-0.1
1906	Phi-A	15	10	.600	36	27	24	0	3	238¹	208	5	48	159	10.0	2.53	108	.238	.284	25	.253	7	4	5	-1	1.3
1907	Phi-A	16	8	.667	33	24	20	4	0	219¹	185	1	34	112	9.1	2.05	127	.231	.265	23	.230	3	12	14	-2	1.7
1908	Phi-A	8	9	.471	18	17	14	2	1	138²	121	1	21	85	9.4	1.75	146	.236	.270	11	.220	2	10	13	-2	1.8
1909	Phi-A	18	8	.692	34	29	24	5	1	250	196	1	45	161	8.9	1.66	145	.214	.254	20	.215	4	23	21	2	2.9
1910	*Phi-A	23	5	.821	30	28	25	3	0	250	182	1	47	155	8.6	1.58	150	.207	.255	25	.269	8	26	22	2	3.8
1911	*Phi-A	17	5	.773	31	24	16	2	3	216¹	198	2	58	114	10.8	2.16	146	.252	.307	13	.165	-3	28	24	1	2.0
1912	Phi-A	13	8	.619	27	19	12	1	2	171	169	1	33	90	10.7	2.74	113	.277	.315	9	.150	-1	11	7	-2	0.4
1913	*Phi-A	21	10	.677	48	21	14	2	13	236²	208	2	59	135	10.3	2.21	125	.228	.277	12	.154	0	19	15	-2	1.9
1914	*Phi-A	17	3	.850	28	23	14	7	2	179	159	4	55	107	10.6	2.26	115	.240	.299	9	.145	-1	10	7	-0	0.8
1915	Bal-F	4	16	.200	26	23	15	0	1	178¹	198	5	37	89	12.2	3.99	72	.298	.342	16	.267	3	-25	-22	-1	-2.1
1916	Phi-N	7	7	.500	27	13	4	0	3	122²	137	3	34	43	13.3	3.74	71	.287	.347	12	.279	4	-15	-15	2	-1.3
1917	Phi-N	8	2	.800	20	10	8	4	2	113	84	1	26	43	9.3	1.67	168	.205	.277	8	.205	1	13	14	2	1.3
1925	Chi-A	0	0	—	1	0	0	0	0	1	1	1	1	0	18.0	18.00	23	.333	.500	0	—	0	-2	-2	-0	0.0
Total	16	212	127	.625	459	334	255	40	34	3017	2645	40	712	1711	10.3	2.46	111	.239	.291	243	.212	33	101	95	-5	13.8

YEAR	TM/L	W	L	PCT	G	GS	CG	SH	SV	IP	H	HR	BB	SO	RAT	ERA	ERA+	OAV	OOB	BH	AVG	PB	PR	/A	PD	TPI

● **ANDY BENES**   Benes, Andrew Charles   b: 8/20/67, Evansville, Ind.   BR/TR, 6'6", 235 lbs.   Deb: 8/11/89

1989	SD-N	6	3	.667	10	10	0	0	0	66²	51	7	31	66	11.2	3.51	100	.213	.305	6	.250	2	-0	-0	0	0.2
1990	SD-N	10	11	.476	32	31	2	0	0	192¹	177	18	69	140	11.6	3.60	106	.242	.309	6	.100	-2	4	5	-3	0.0
1991	SD-N	15	11	.577	33	33	4	1	0	223	194	23	59	167	10.4	3.03	125	.232	.286	2	.032	-2	16	19	-1	1.9
1992	SD-N	13	14	.481	34	34	2	2	0	231¹	230	14	61	169	11.5	3.35	107	.264	.316	10	.149	2	4	6	0	0.9
1993	SD-N★	15	15	.500	34	34	4	2	0	230²	200	23	86	179	11.3	3.78	109	.232	.305	9	.125	-0	7	9	-3	0.7
1994	SD-N	6	14	.300	25	25	2	2	0	172¹	155	20	51	**189**	10.8	3.86	109	.237	.294	8	.163	-0	7	6	1	0.8
Total	6	65	68	.489	168	167	14	7	0	1116¹	1007	105	357	910	11.1	3.51	110	.240	.302	41	.123	-1	37	45	-5	4.5

● **RAY BENGE**   Benge, Raymond Adelphia   b: 4/22/02, Jacksonville, Tex.   BR/TR, 5'9.5", 160 lbs.   Deb: 9/26/25

1925	Cle-A	1	0	1.000	2	2	1	1	0	11²	9	0	3	3	9.3	1.54	286	.205	.255	2	.400	0	4	4	-1	0.3
1926	Cle-A	1	0	1.000	8	0	0	0	0	11²	15	0	4	3	14.7	3.86	105	.313	.365	1	.333	0	0	0	0	0.1
1928	Phi-N	8	18	.308	40	28	12	1	1	201²	219	15	88	68	13.9	4.55	94	.286	.363	12	.207	-0	-13	-6	-2	-0.9
1929	Phi-N	11	15	.423	38	27	9	2	4	199	255	24	77	78	15.2	6.29	83	.323	.385	15	.203	-3	-35	-24	-3	-3.0
1930	Phi-N	11	15	.423	38	29	14	0	1	225²	305	22	81	70	15.4	5.70	96	.328	.382	18	.205	-3	-18	-6	-1	-0.9
1931	Phi-N	14	18	.438	38	31	16	2	2	247	251	12	61	117	11.6	3.17	134	.262	.310	18	.205	-2	19	30	-2	3.3
1932	Phi-N	13	12	.520	41	28	13	2	6	222¹	247	15	58	89	12.5	4.05	109	.281	.329	13	.173	-3	-4	9	-1	0.6
1933	Bro-N	10	17	.370	37	30	16	2	1	228²	238	11	55	74	11.8	3.42	94	.268	.315	14	.184	-0	-2	-5	-3	-0.9
1934	Bro-N	14	12	.538	36	32	14	1	0	227	252	11	61	64	12.5	4.32	90	.272	.319	15	.169	-2	-7	-11	-1	-1.3
1935	Bro-N	9	9	.500	23	17	5	1	1	124²	142	12	47	39	13.7	4.48	89	.289	.353	9	.191	-1	-6	-7	-2	-1.1
1936	Bos-N	7	9	.438	21	19	2	0	0	115	161	6	38	32	15.7	5.79	66	.333	.382	6	.140	-3	-23	-25	-2	-3.2
	Phi-N	1	4	.200	15	6	0	0	1	45²	70	3	19	13	17.5	4.73	96	.350	.406	0	.000	-1	-4	-1	-2	-0.4
	Yr	8	13	.381	36	25	2	0	1	160²	231	9	57	45	16.1	5.49	73	.337	.388	6	.113	-4	-26	-26	-4	-3.6
1938	Cin-N	1	1	.500	9	0	0	0	2	15¹	13	1	6	5	11.2	4.11	89	.228	.302	1	.333	0	-1	-1	-0	-0.1
Total	12	101	130	.437	346	249	102	12	19	1875¹	2177	132	598	655	13.5	4.52	95	.292	.347	124	.188	-17	-89	-46	-18	-7.5

● **ARMANDO BENITEZ**   Benitez, Armando German   b: 11/3/72, Ramon Santana, D.R.   BR/TR, 6'4", 180 lbs.   Deb: 7/28/94

| 1994 | Bal-A | 0 | 0 | — | 3 | 0 | 0 | 0 | 0 | 10 | 8 | 0 | 4 | 14 | 11.7 | 0.90 | 564 | .216 | .310 | 0 | | | 0 | 4 | 5 | 0 | -0.1 |

● **HENRY BENN**   Benn, Henry Omer   b: 1/25/1890, Viola, Wis.   d: 6/4/67, Madison, Wis.   BR/TR, 6', 190 lbs.   Deb: 9/24/14

| 1914 | Cle-A | 0 | 0 | — | 1 | 0 | 0 | 0 | 0 | 1 | 0 | 0 | 1 | 0 | — | — | — | .000 | .000 | 0 | | | 0 | 0 | -0 | 0.0 |

● **DAVE BENNETT**   Bennett, David Hans   b: 11/7/45, Berkeley, Cal.   BR/TR, 6'5", 195 lbs.   Deb: 6/12/64   F

| 1964 | Phi-N | 0 | 0 | — | 1 | 0 | 0 | 0 | 0 | 1 | 2 | 0 | 1 | 0 | 18.0 | 9.00 | 39 | .400 | .400 | 0 | | | 0 | -1 | -1 | 0 | 0.0 |

● **DENNIS BENNETT**   Bennett, Dennis John   b: 10/5/39, Oakland, Cal.   BL/TL, 6'5", 205 lbs.   Deb: 5/12/62   F

1962	Phi-N	9	9	.500	31	24	7	2	3	174²	144	17	68	149	11.2	3.81	102	.224	.304	8	.127	-1	3	1	-1	0.0
1963	Phi-N	9	5	.643	23	16	6	1	1	119¹	102	12	33	82	10.5	2.64	122	.231	.290	9	.225	3	9	8	0	1.3
1964	Phi-N	12	14	.462	41	32	7	2	1	208	222	23	58	125	12.3	3.68	94	.280	.333	13	.197	3	-3	-5	-1	-0.3
1965	Bos-A	5	7	.417	34	18	3	0	0	141²	152	15	53	85	13.4	4.38	85	.279	.350	7	.179	2	-15	-10	-1	-0.7
1966	Bos-A	3	3	.500	16	13	0	0	0	75	75	9	23	47	11.9	3.24	117	.261	.318	3	.130	1	2	5	-1	0.4
1967	Bos-A	4	3	.571	13	11	4	1	0	69²	72	12	22	34	12.4	3.88	90	.268	.328	3	.120	-0	-5	-3	-0	-0.4
	NY-N	1	1	.500	8	6	0	0	0	26¹	37	4	7	14	15.4	5.13	66	.336	.381	2	.250	-0	-5	-5	-0	-0.3
1968	Cal-A	0	5	.000	16	7	1	0	1	48¹	46	6	17	36	12.5	3.54	82	.250	.327	1	.077	-1	-3	-3	1	-0.4
Total	7	43	47	.478	182	127	28	6	6	863	850	98	281	572	12.1	3.69	96	.260	.324	46	.166	7	-18	-13	-2	-0.5

● **FRANK BENNETT**   Bennett, Francis Allen "Chip"   b: 10/27/04, Mardela Springs, Md.   d: 3/18/66, New Castle, Del.   BR/TR, 5'10.5", 163 lbs.   Deb: 9/17/27

1927	Bos-A	0	1	.000	4	1	0	0	0	12¹	15	0	6	1	15.3	2.92	145	.333	.412	0	.000	-1	2	2	0	0.1
1928	Bos-A	0	0	—	1	0	0	0	0	1	1	0	0	0	9.0	0.00	—	.250	.250	0	—	0	0	0	0	0.0
Total	2	0	1	.000	5	1	0	0	0	13¹	16	0	6	1	14.9	2.70	156	.327	.400	0	.000	-1	2	2	0	0.1

● **ALLEN BENSON**   Benson, Allen Wilbert "Bullet Ben"   b: 7/12/08, Hurley, S.Dak.   BR/TR, 6'1", 185 lbs.   Deb: 8/19/34

| 1934 | Was-A | 0 | 1 | .000 | 2 | 2 | 0 | 0 | 0 | 9² | 19 | 0 | 5 | 4 | 24.2 | 12.10 | 36 | .413 | .491 | 0 | .000 | -0 | -8 | -8 | -0 | -0.7 |

● **CY BENTLEY**   Bentley, Clytus G.   b: 11/23/1850, East Haven, Conn.   d: 2/26/1873, Middletown, Conn.   Deb: 4/26/1872

| 1872 | Man-n | 2 | 15 | .118 | 18 | 17 | 16 | 0 | 0 | 154 | 273 | 4 | 12 | 5 | 16.7 | 6.14 | 60 | .319 | .329 | 27 | .235 | -0 | -41 | -42 | | -2.8 |

● **JACK BENTLEY**   Bentley, John Needles   b: 3/8/1895, Sandy Spring, Md.   d: 10/24/69, Olney, Md.   BL/TL, 5'11.5", 200 lbs.   Deb: 9/6/13   ♦

1913	Was-A	1	0	1.000	3	1	0	0	1	11	5	0	2	5	5.7	0.00	—	.147	.194	0	.000	-0	4	4	0	0.4
1914	Was-A	5	7	.417	30	11	3	2	**4**	125¹	110	3	53	55	11.9	2.37	119	.249	.334	11	.275	2	5	6	-1	0.8
1915	Was-A	0	2	.000	4	2	0	0	0	11¹	8	0	3	4	8.7	0.79	374	.200	.256	0	.000	-0	3	3	-0	0.4
1916	Was-A	0	0	—	2	0	0	0	0	1¹	0	0	1	1	6.8	0.00	—	.000	.250	0	—	0	0	0	0	0.0
1923	*NY-N	13	8	.619	31	26	12	1	3	183	198	10	67	80	13.3	4.48	85	.277	.343	38	.427	16	-10	-13	-1	0.0
1924	*NY-N	16	5	.762	28	24	13	1	1	188	196	11	56	60	12.3	3.78	97	.273	.329	26	.265	4	2	-2	-1	0.0
1925	NY-N	11	9	.550	28	22	11	0	0	157	200	10	59	47	14.9	5.04	80	.323	.383	30	.303	6	-14	-18	-1	-0.9
1926	Phi-N	0	2	.000	7	3	0	0	0	25¹	37	2	10	7	16.7	8.17	51	.327	.382	62	.258	1	-12	-11	-0	-0.7
	NY-N	0	0	—	1	0	0	0	0	2	0	0	2	1	9.0	0.00	—	.000	.250	1	.250	-0	1	1	0	0.0
	Yr	0	2	.000	8	3	0	0	0	27¹	37	2	12	8	16.1	7.57	54	.311	.374	63	.258	1	-11	-11	-0	-0.7
1927	NY-N	0	0	—	4	0	0	0	0	9²	7	1	10	3	16.8	2.79	138	.206	.400	2	.222	1	1	1	0	0.1
Total	9	46	33	.582	138	89	39	4	9	714	761	37	263	259	13.1	4.01	91	.280	.346	170	.291	28	-20	-28	-3	0.1

● **AL BENTON**   Benton, John Alton   b: 3/18/11, Noble, Okla.   d: 4/14/68, Lynwood, Cal.   BR/TR, 6'4", 215 lbs.   Deb: 4/18/34

1934	Phi-A	7	9	.438	32	21	7	0	1	155	145	7	88	58	13.6	4.88	90	.249	.349	6	.109	-4	-7	-9	0	-1.1
1935	Phi-A	3	4	.429	27	9	0	0	0	78¹	110	7	47	42	18.2	7.70	59	.328	.413	1	.040	-3	-28	-27	-1	-2.3
1938	Det-A	5	3	.625	29	19	6	0	0	95¹	93	10	39	33	12.6	3.30	151	.259	.333	4	.121	-3	16	18	1	1.1
1939	Det-A	6	8	.429	37	16	3	0	5	150	182	11	58	67	14.5	4.56	107	.294	.355	4	.091	-4	1	5	0	0.4
1940	Det-A	6	10	.375	42	0	0	0	17	79¹	93	5	36	50	14.6	4.42	107	.294	.366	0	.000	-3	-0	3	-0	0.4
1941	Det-A☆	15	6	.714	38	14	7	1	7	157²	130	11	65	63	11.3	2.97	153	**.221**	.302	3	.060	-5	21	28	0	3.1
1942	Det-A★	7	13	.350	35	30	9	1	2	226²	210	9	84	110	11.7	2.90	136	.246	.314	5	.075	-5	19	26	-1	1.6
1945	*Det-A	13	8	.619	31	27	12	5	3	191²	175	7	63	76	11.3	2.02	174	.241	.303	4	.063	-6	29	32	2	3.2
1946	Det-A	11	7	.611	28	15	6	1	1	140²	132	9	58	60	12.2	3.65	100	.245	.319	9	.184	-1	-2	0	1	0.0
1947	Det-A	6	7	.462	36	14	4	0	3	133	147	11	61	33	14.1	4.40	86	.288	.365	6	.154	-2	-10	-9	-0	-1.1
1948	Det-A	2	2	.500	30	0	0	0	3	44¹	45	4	36	18	16.6	5.68	77	.273	.406	2	.182	-0	-7	-6	0	-0.6
1949	Cle-A	9	6	.600	40	11	4	2	10	135²	116	7	51	41	11.1	2.12	188	.238	.312	5	.132	-2	31	28	-2	2.9
1950	Cle-A	4	2	.667	36	0	0	0	6	63	57	7	30	26	12.6	3.57	121	.243	.331	1	.083	-1	7	5	-1	0.4
1952	Bos-A	4	3	.571	24	0	0	0	6	37²	37	1	17	22	12.9	2.39	165	.268	.348	0	.000	-1	9	7	-0	1.0
Total	14	98	88	.527	455	167	58	10	66	1688¹	1672	106	733	697	12.9	3.66	115	.259	.336	50	.098	-39	74	102	-1	8.9

● **RUBE BENTON**   Benton, John Clebon   b: 6/27/1887, Clinton, N.C.   d: 12/12/37, Dothan, Ala.   BL/TL, 6'1", 190 lbs.   Deb: 6/28/10

1910	Cin-N	0	1	.000	12	2	0	0	0	38	44	1	23	15	16.1	4.74	62	.282	.378	1	.091	-1	-7	-8	1	-0.2
1911	Cin-N	3	3	.500	11	6	5	0	0	44²	44	0	23	28	14.1	2.01	164	.270	.370	2	.143	-0	7	6	-1	0.7
1912	Cin-N	18	20	.474	**50**	39	22	2	2	302	304	9	118	162	13.5	3.10	108	.278	.356	14	.135	-6	10	9	2	0.5
1913	Cin-N	11	7	.611	23	22	9	1	0	144¹	140	4	60	68	13.0	3.49	93	.265	.350	10	.208	1	-5	-4	-1	-0.4
1914	Cin-N	16	18	.471	41	31	16	3	2	271	223	3	95	121	10.9	2.96	99	.228	.303	13	.143	-3	-5	-1	0	-0.4
1915	Cin-N	6	13	.316	35	21	6	2	4	176¹	165	2	67	83	12.6	3.32	86	.257	.340	11	.208	-0	-11	-9	2	-0.8

YEAR TM/L	W	L	PCT	G	GS	CG	SH	SV	IP	H	HR	BB	SO	RAT	ERA	ERA+	OAV	OOB	BH	AVG	PB	PR	/A	PD	TPI
NY-N	3	5	.375	10	7	3	0	0	60²	57	0	9	26	10.5	2.82	91	.253	.297	5	.217	1	-0	-2	-0	-0.1
Yr	9	18	.333	45	28	9	2	5	237	222	2	76	109	11.5	3.19	87	.252	.315	16	.211	1	-12	-11	2	-0.9
1916 NY-N	16	8	.667	38	29	15	3	2	238²	210	5	58	115	10.5	2.87	85	.241	.296	7	.090	-4	-7	-11	-1	-1.8
1917 *NY-N	15	9	.625	35	25	14	3	3	215	190	5	41	70	10.0	2.72	94	.238	.281	12	.167	-1	-0	-4	-2	-0.8
1918 NY-N	1	2	.333	3	3	2	0	0	24	17	0	3	9	7.5	1.88	140	.202	.230	1	.143	1	2	2	0	0.4
1919 NY-N	17	11	.607	35	28	11	1	2	209	181	5	52	53	10.2	2.63	107	.237	.289	13	.194	-1	7	4	-1	0.4
1920 NY-N	9	16	.360	33	25	12	4	2	193¹	222	8	31	52	11.9	3.03	99	.291	.321	6	.092	-7	2	-1	4	-0.3
1921 NY-N	5	2	.714	18	9	3	1	0	72	72	2	17	11	11.1	2.88	128	.266	.309	3	.143	-1	7	6	-1	0.4
1923 Cin-N	14	10	.583	33	26	15	0	1	219	243	10	57	59	12.5	3.66	106	.284	.333	23	.287	4	8	5	1	0.9
1924 Cin-N	7	9	.438	32	15	6	1	1	162²	166	2	46	42	10.7	2.77	136	.266	.297	12	.261	2	20	18	1	2.0
1925 Cin-N	9	10	.474	33	16	6	1	1	164²	182	3	34	36	13.3	4.05	102	.301	.340	9	.200	1	4	1	-1	0.1
Total 15	150	144	.510	437	304	145	24	21	2517¹	2472	52	712	950	11.7	3.09	102	.261	.319	142	.172	-14	33	13	4	0.6

● LARRY BENTON
Benton, Lawrence James   b: 11/20/1897, St.Louis, Mo.   d: 4/3/53, Amberley, Ohio   BR/TR, 5'11", 165 lbs.   Deb: 4/25/23

YEAR TM/L	W	L	PCT	G	GS	CG	SH	SV	IP	H	HR	BB	SO	RAT	ERA	ERA+	OAV	OOB	BH	AVG	PB	PR	/A	PD	TPI
1923 Bos-N	5	9	.357	35	9	1	0	0	128	141	4	57	42	14.2	4.99	80	.293	.373	5	.161	-1	-14	-14	1	-1.3
1924 Bos-N	5	7	.417	30	13	4	0	1	128	129	4	64	41	13.8	4.15	92	.274	.365	3	.091	-3	-4	-5	-0	-0.7
1925 Bos-N	14	7	.667	31	21	16	2	1	183¹	170	6	70	49	11.9	3.09	130	.249	.320	14	.241	2	24	19	-1	2.0
1926 Bos-N	14	14	.500	43	27	12	1	1	231²	244	10	81	103	12.9	3.85	92	.280	.346	12	.154	-4	-1	-8	-3	-1.4
1927 Bos-N	4	2	.667	11	10	3	0	0	60¹	72	3	27	25	15.1	4.48	83	.310	.387	4	.222	1	-4	-5	-1	-0.4
NY-N	13	5	.722	29	23	8	1	2	173	183	9	54	65	12.4	3.95	98	.275	.331	8	.160	-2	-1	-4	-0	-0.4
Yr	17	7	.708	40	33	11	1	2	233¹	255	12	81	90	13.0	4.09	93	.284	.344	12	.176	-1	-4	-7	-1	-0.8
1928 NY-N	25	9	.735	42	35	28	2	4	310¹	299	14	71	90	10.7	2.73	143	.258	.300	16	.143	-3	44	41	-0	3.9
1929 NY-N	11	17	.393	39	30	14	3	3	237	276	16	61	63	12.8	4.14	111	.297	.340	9	.105	-6	15	12	1	0.7
1930 NY-N	1	3	.250	8	4	1	0	1	30	42	8	14	16	16.8	7.80	61	.323	.389	3	.300	-1	-9	-10	-0	-1.0
Cin-N	7	12	.368	35	22	9	0	1	177²	246	7	45	47	14.7	5.12	94	.337	.375	11	.177	-2	-3	-6	-3	-0.9
Yr	8	15	.348	43	26	10	0	2	207²	288	15	59	63	15.0	5.50	87	.334	.377	14	.194	-0	-12	-16	-3	-1.9
1931 Cin-N	10	15	.400	38	23	12	2	0	204¹	246	6	53	35	12.9	3.35	112	.299	.343	11	.167	-1	12	9	1	1.0
1932 Cin-N	6	13	.316	35	21	7	0	2	179²	201	10	27	35	11.4	4.31	90	.285	.311	11	.204	0	-9	-9	-1	-0.9
1933 Cin-N	10	11	.476	34	19	7	2	2	152²	160	5	36	33	11.7	3.71	91	.271	.316	9	.170	-1	-6	-5	-2	-1.0
1934 Cin-N	0	1	.000	16	1	0	0	2	29	53	1	7	5	18.6	6.52	63	.393	.423	2	.286	0	-8	-8	-0	-0.3
1935 Bos-N	2	3	.400	29	0	0	0	0	72	103	6	24	21	16.0	6.88	53	.338	.388	4	.200	-1	-23	-25	-1	-1.5
Total 13	127	128	.498	455	258	122	13	22	2297	2559	109	691	670	12.8	4.03	98	.288	.341	122	.165	-17	14	-16	-8	-2.2

● SID BENTON
Benton, Sidney Wright   b: 8/4/1895, Buckner, Ark.   d: 3/8/77, Fayetteville, Ark.   BR/TR, 6'1", 170 lbs.   Deb: 4/18/22

YEAR TM/L	W	L	PCT	G	GS	CG	SH	SV	IP	H	HR	BB	SO	RAT	ERA	ERA+	OAV	OOB	BH	AVG	PB	PR	/A	PD	TPI
1922 StL-N	0	0	—	1	0	0	0	0	0	0	0	0	2	0	—	—	—	1.000	0	—	0	0	0	0	0.0

● JOE BENZ
Benz, Joseph Louis "Blitzen" or "Butcher Boy"   b: 1/21/1886, New Alsace, Ind.   d: 4/22/57, Chicago, Ill.   BR/TR, 6'1.5", 196 lbs.   Deb: 8/16/11

YEAR TM/L	W	L	PCT	G	GS	CG	SH	SV	IP	H	HR	BB	SO	RAT	ERA	ERA+	OAV	OOB	BH	AVG	PB	PR	/A	PD	TPI
1911 Chi-A	3	2	.600	12	6	1	0	0	55²	52	0	13	28	10.8	2.26	142	.251	.302	1	.059	-2	7	6	1	0.4
1912 Chi-A	13	17	.433	42	31	12	3	0	238²	231	5	70	97	11.7	2.90	110	.259	.319	10	.132	-5	11	8	1	0.5
1913 Chi-A	7	10	.412	33	17	6	1	1	151	146	1	59	79	12.3	2.74	107	.254	.325	1	.180	-1	3	3	4	0.7
1914 Chi-A	14	19	.424	48	35	16	4	2	283¹	245	4	66	142	9.9	2.26	119	.236	.282	12	.130	-3	15	14	6	2.0
1915 Chi-A	15	11	.577	39	28	17	2	0	238¹	209	4	43	81	9.6	2.11	141	.238	.276	10	.127	-5	22	23	3	2.2
1916 Chi-A	9	5	.643	28	9	6	4	0	142	108	0	32	57	9.1	2.03	136	.214	.265	3	.065	-4	13	12	1	0.8
1917 Chi-A	7	3	.700	19	13	7	2	0	94²	76	1	23	25	9.6	2.47	108	.220	.272	5	.167	-1	2	2	0	0.1
1918 Chi-A	8	8	.500	29	17	10	1	0	154	156	1	28	30	10.9	2.63	104	.269	.304	11	.216	-1	3	2	3	0.5
1919 Chi-A	0	0	—	1	0	0	0	0	2	2	0	0	0	9.0	0.00	—	.250	.250	0	—	0	1	1	0	0.0
Total 9	76	75	.503	251	163	75	17	3	1359²	1225	16	334	539	10.5	2.43	119	.243	.294	61	.138	-21	76	70	19	7.2

● JASON BERE
Bere, Jason Phillip   b: 5/26/71, Cambridge, Mass.   BR/TR, 6'3", 185 lbs.   Deb: 5/27/93

YEAR TM/L	W	L	PCT	G	GS	CG	SH	SV	IP	H	HR	BB	SO	RAT	ERA	ERA+	OAV	OOB	BH	AVG	PB	PR	/A	PD	TPI
1993 *Chi-A	12	5	.706	24	24	1	0	0	142²	109	12	81	129	12.3	3.47	120	.210	.323	0	—	0	13	11	-0	1.4
1994 Chi-A★	12	2	.857	24	24	1	0	0	141²	119	17	80	127	12.7	3.81	123	.229	.333	0	—	0	16	14	0	1.2
Total 2	24	7	.774	48	48	1	0	0	284¹	228	29	161	256	12.5	3.64	122	.220	.328	0	—	0	29	25	-0	2.6

● JUAN BERENGUER
Berenguer, Juan Bautista   b: 11/30/54, Aguadulce, Pan.   BR/TR, 5'11", 215 lbs.   Deb: 8/17/78

YEAR TM/L	W	L	PCT	G	GS	CG	SH	SV	IP	H	HR	BB	SO	RAT	ERA	ERA+	OAV	OOB	BH	AVG	PB	PR	/A	PD	TPI
1978 NY-N	0	2	.000	5	3	0	0	0	13	17	1	11	8	20.1	8.31	42	.327	.453	0	.000	-0	-7	-7	-0	-1.0
1979 NY-N	1	1	.500	5	5	0	0	0	30²	28	2	12	25	12.0	2.93	124	.252	.331	1	.143	0	3	2	-1	0.1
1980 NY-N	0	1	.000	6	0	0	0	0	9¹	9	1	10	7	18.3	5.79	61	.250	.413	0	—	0	-2	-2	-0	-0.2
1981 KC-A	0	4	.000	8	3	0	0	0	19²	22	4	16	20	18.3	8.69	41	.289	.426	0	—	0	-11	-11	-1	-1.9
Tor-A	2	9	.182	12	11	1	0	0	71	62	7	35	29	12.7	4.31	91	.235	.331	0	—	0	-5	-3	-1	-0.6
Yr	2	13	.133	20	14	1	0	0	90²	84	11	51	49	13.7	5.26	73	.243	.346	0	—	0	-16	-14	-2	-2.5
1982 Det-A	0	0	—	2	1	0	0	0	6²	5	0	9	8	18.9	6.75	60	.200	.412	0	—	0	-2	-2	-0	-0.4
1983 Det-A	9	5	.643	37	19	2	1	1	157²	110	19	71	129	10.7	3.14	124	.193	.289	0	—	0	16	13	-2	1.0
1984 Det-A	11	10	.524	31	27	2	1	0	168¹	146	14	79	118	12.3	3.48	113	.232	.323	0	—	0	10	8	-1	0.8
1985 Det-A	5	6	.455	31	13	0	0	0	95	96	12	48	82	13.7	5.59	73	.259	.346	0	—	0	-15	-16	1	-1.6
1986 SF-N	2	3	.400	46	4	0	0	4	73¹	64	4	44	72	13.5	2.70	130	.242	.354	1	.143	-0	8	7	-1	0.4
1987 *Min-A	8	1	.889	47	5	0	0	4	112	100	10	47	110	11.8	3.94	117	.238	.315	0	—	0	6	8	-1	0.4
1988 Min-A	8	4	.667	57	1	0	0	2	100	74	7	61	99	12.2	3.96	103	.207	.325	0	—	0	1	1	0	0.0
1989 Min-A	9	3	.750	56	0	0	0	3	106	96	11	47	93	12.3	3.48	119	.246	.330	0	—	0	5	8	-1	0.4
1990 Min-A	8	5	.615	51	0	0	0	0	100¹	85	9	58	77	13.0	3.41	122	.232	.340	0	—	0	6	8	-2	0.4
1991 Atl-N	0	3	.000	49	0	0	0	17	64¹	43	6	20	53	9.2	2.24	174	.189	.263	0	.000	-1	10	12	-0	1.2
1992 Atl-N	3	1	.750	28	0	0	0	0	33¹	35	7	16	19	14.0	5.13	71	.269	.354	0	.000	-0	-6	-5	-0	-0.7
KC-A	1	4	.200	19	2	0	0	0	44²	42	5	20	26	12.7	5.64	72	.247	.330	0	—	0	-8	-8	-0	-0.8
Total 15	67	62	.519	490	95	5	2	32	1205¹	1034	116	604	975	12.5	3.90	103	.232	.328	2	.083	-1	7	14	-11	-1.5

● BRUCE BERENYI
Berenyi, Bruce Michael   b: 8/21/54, Bryan, Ohio   BR/TR, 6'3", 215 lbs.   Deb: 7/5/80

YEAR TM/L	W	L	PCT	G	GS	CG	SH	SV	IP	H	HR	BB	SO	RAT	ERA	ERA+	OAV	OOB	BH	AVG	PB	PR	/A	PD	TPI
1980 Cin-N	2	2	.500	6	6	0	0	0	27²	34	1	23	19	18.5	7.81	46	.318	.438	0	.000	-1	-13	-13	-0	-1.6
1981 Cin-N	9	6	.600	21	20	5	3	0	126	97	3	77	106	12.4	3.50	101	.211	.324	8	.190	1	-0	-1	-1	0.1
1982 Cin-N	9	18	.333	34	34	4	1	0	222¹	208	8	96	157	12.4	3.36	110	.255	.335	15	.242	3	6	8	2	1.5
1983 Cin-N	9	14	.391	32	31	4	1	0	186¹	173	9	102	151	13.4	3.86	98	.247	.345	12	.218	2	-5	-1	3	0.3
1984 Cin-N	3	7	.300	13	11	0	0	0	51	63	4	42	53	18.5	6.00	63	.306	.423	1	.063	-1	-14	-13	0	-2.2
NY-N	9	6	.600	19	19	0	0	0	115	100	6	53	81	12.1	3.76	94	.238	.325	9	.243	2	-2	-3	-1	-0.3
Yr	12	13	.480	32	30	0	0	0	166	163	10	95	134	14.0	4.45	81	.260	.358	10	.189	1	-16	-15	-1	-2.5
1985 NY-N	1	0	1.000	3	3	0	0	0	13²	8	0	4	8	12.5	2.63	131	.170	.328	1	.250	0	1	1	1	0.2
1986 NY-N	2	2	.500	4	4	0	0	0	39²	47	5	22	30	15.9	6.35	56	.299	.389	0	.000	-1	-12	-12	-0	-1.2
Total 7	44	55	.444	142	131	13	5	0	781²	730	32	425	607	13.4	4.03	91	.251	.347	46	.197	4	-38	-32	3	-3.2

● HEINIE BERGER
Berger, Charles   b: 1/7/1882, LaSalle, Ill.   d: 2/10/54, Lakewood, Ohio   TR, 5'9",   Deb: 5/6/07

YEAR TM/L	W	L	PCT	G	GS	CG	SH	SV	IP	H	HR	BB	SO	RAT	ERA	ERA+	OAV	OOB	BH	AVG	PB	PR	/A	PD	TPI
1907 Cle-A	3	3	.500	14	7	5	1	0	87¹	74	0	20	50	9.8	2.99	84	.231	.279	5	.179	0	-4	-5	-1	-0.5
1908 Cle-A	13	8	.619	29	24	16	0	0	199¹	152	1	66	101	10.0	2.12	113	.219	.290	8	.108	-4	6	6	-0	0.1
1909 Cle-A	13	14	.481	34	29	19	4	1	247	221	2	58	162	10.6	2.73	94	.256	.312	11	.133	-1	-7	-5	-0	-0.7
1910 Cle-A	3	4	.429	13	8	2	0	0	65¹	57	0	32	24	12.7	3.03	85	.243	.341	3	.143	-1	-4	-3	-1	-0.5
Total 4	32	29	.525	90	68	42	5	1	599	504	3	176	337	10.5	2.60	96	.238	.303	27	.131	-6	-9	-7	-2	-1.6

● SEAN BERGMAN
Bergman, Sean Frederick   b: 4/11/70, Joliet, Ill.   BR/TR, 6'4", 205 lbs.   Deb: 7/7/93

YEAR TM/L	W	L	PCT	G	GS	CG	SH	SV	IP	H	HR	BB	SO	RAT	ERA	ERA+	OAV	OOB	BH	AVG	PB	PR	/A	PD	TPI
1993 Det-A	1	4	.200	9	6	1	0	0	39²	47	6	23	19	16.1	5.67	76	.294	.386	0	—	0	-6	-6	0	-0.6

YEAR	TM/L	W	L	PCT	G	GS	CG	SH	SV	IP	H	HR	BB	SO	RAT	ERA	ERA+	OAV	OOB	BH	AVG	PB	PR	/A	PD	TPI
1994	Det-A	2	1	.667	3	3	0	0	0	17²	22	2	7	12	15.3	5.60	85	.301	.370	0	—	0	-2	-2	0	-0.2
Total	2	3	5	.375	12	9	1	0	0	57¹	69	8	30	31	15.9	5.65	78	.296	.381	0	—	0	-8	-8	0	-0.8

● **JACK BERLY**   Berly, John Chambers b: 5/24/03, Natchitoches, La.   d: 6/26/77, Houston, Tex.   BR/TR, 5'11.5", 190 lbs.   Deb: 4/22/24

YEAR	TM/L	W	L	PCT	G	GS	CG	SH	SV	IP	H	HR	BB	SO	RAT	ERA	ERA+	OAV	OOB	BH	AVG	PB	PR	/A	PD	TPI
1924	StL-N	0	0	—	4	0	0	0	0	8	8	2	4	2	13.5	5.63	67	.267	.353	0	.000	-0	-2	-2	0	0.0
1931	NY-N	7	8	.467	27	11	4	1	0	111¹	114	6	51	45	13.7	3.88	95	.270	.354	6	.171	-1	-0	2	1	-0.2
1932	Phi-N	1	2	.333	21	1	1	0	2	46	61	4	21	15	16.2	7.63	58	.333	.405	0	—	-1	-19	-16	1	-1.1
1933	Phi-N	2	3	.400	13	6	1	1	0	50	62	5	22	4	15.5	5.04	76	.307	.381	4	.308	0	-9	-7	1	-0.5
Total	4	10	13	.435	65	18	6	2	2	215¹	245	17	98	66	14.6	5.02	78	.292	.371	10	.167	-2	-30	-27	3	-1.8

● **VICTOR BERNAL**   Bernal, Victor Hugo b: 10/6/53, Los Angeles, Cal.   BR/TR, 6'1", 175 lbs.   Deb: 4/6/77

YEAR	TM/L	W	L	PCT	G	GS	CG	SH	SV	IP	H	HR	BB	SO	RAT	ERA	ERA+	OAV	OOB	BH	AVG	PB	PR	/A	PD	TPI
1977	SD-N	1	1	.500	15	0	0	0	0	20¹	23	4	9	6	14.2	5.31	67	.287	.360	0	.000	-0	-3	-4	-0	-0.4

● **DWIGHT BERNARD**   Bernard, Dwight Vern b: 5/31/52, Mt.Vernon, Ill.   BR/TR, 6'2", 170 lbs.   Deb: 6/29/78

YEAR	TM/L	W	L	PCT	G	GS	CG	SH	SV	IP	H	HR	BB	SO	RAT	ERA	ERA+	OAV	OOB	BH	AVG	PB	PR	/A	PD	TPI
1978	NY-N	1	4	.200	30	1	0	0	0	48	54	4	27	26	15.2	4.31	81	.297	.388	1	.200	0	-4	-4	0	-0.4
1979	NY-N	0	3	.000	32	1	0	0	0	44	59	2	26	20	17.4	4.70	77	.331	.417	0	—	0	-5	-5	0	-0.3
1981	*Mil-A	0	0	—	6	0	0	0	0	5	5	0	6	1	19.8	3.60	95	.263	.440	0	—	0	0	-0	-0	0.1
1982	*Mil-A	3	1	.750	47	0	0	0	6	79	78	4	27	45	12.1	3.76	101	.263	.326	0	—	0	3	0	-1	0.1
Total	4	4	8	.333	115	2	0	0	6	176	196	10	86	92	14.5	4.14	88	.290	.371	1	.200	0	-6	-9	-1	-0.5

● **JOE BERNARD**   Bernard, Joseph Carl "J.C." b: 3/24/1882, Brighton, Ill.   d: 9/22/60, Springfield, Ill   BR/TR, 6'1", 175 lbs.   Deb: 9/23/09

YEAR	TM/L	W	L	PCT	G	GS	CG	SH	SV	IP	H	HR	BB	SO	RAT	ERA	ERA+	OAV	OOB	BH	AVG	PB	PR	/A	PD	TPI
1909	StL-N	0	0	—	1	0	0	0	0	1	1	0	2	2	27.0	0.00	—	.250	.500	0	—	0	1	1	-0	0.1

● **BILL BERNHARD**   Bernhard, William Henry "Strawberry Bill" b: 3/16/1871, Clarence, N.Y.   d: 3/30/49, San Diego, Cal.   BB/TR, 6'1", 205 lbs.   Deb: 4/24/1899

YEAR	TM/L	W	L	PCT	G	GS	CG	SH	SV	IP	H	HR	BB	SO	RAT	ERA	ERA+	OAV	OOB	BH	AVG	PB	PR	/A	PD	TPI
1899	Phi-N	6	6	.500	21	12	10	1	0	132¹	120	3	36	23	11.0	2.65	139	.242	.301	13	.241	0	18	15	-0	1.2
1900	Phi-N	15	10	.600	32	27	20	0	1	218²	284	3	74	49	14.9	4.77	76	.313	.368	14	.154	-5	-26	-28	1	-2.9
1901	Phi-A	17	10	.630	31	27	26	1	0	257	328	6	50	58	13.3	4.52	84	.307	.339	20	.187	-1	-24	-21	4	-1.6
1902	Phi-A	1	0	1.000	1	1	1	0	0	9	7	0	3	1	10.0	1.00	367	.215	.282	0	.000	-1	3	3	-1	0.1
	Cle-A	17	5	.773	27	24	22	3	1	217	169	4	34	57	8.6	2.20	157	.216	.253	18	.200	-1	33	30	1	2.8
	Yr	18	5	**.783**	28	25	23	3	1	226	176	4	37	58	**8.7**	2.15	161	**.216**	**.254**	18	.191	-2	36	33	1	2.9
1903	Cle-A	14	6	.700	20	19	18	3	0	165²	151	1	21	60	9.3	2.12	135	.242	.267	12	.185	-1	16	14	1	1.6
1904	Cle-A	23	13	.639	38	37	35	4	0	320²	323	3	55	137	10.7	2.13	119	.263	.296	22	.177	-1	17	14	1	1.4
1905	Cle-A	7	13	.350	22	19	17	0	0	174¹	185	5	34	66	11.4	3.36	79	.273	.309	6	.087	-6	-13	-14	0	-2.1
1906	Cle-A	16	15	.516	31	30	23	2	0	255¹	235	4	47	85	10.1	2.54	103	.248	.287	21	.212	0	4	2	2	0.7
1907	Cle-A	0	4	.000	8	4	3	0	0	42	58	0	11	19	14.8	3.21	78	.329	.369	3	.200	0	-3	-3	-0	-0.3
Total	9	116	82	.586	231	200	175	14	3	1792	1860	26	365	545	11.3	3.04	102	.268	.307	129	.180	-13	23	11	7	0.9

● **WALTER BERNHARDT**   Bernhardt, Walter Jacob b: 5/20/1893, Pleasant Village, Pa.   d: 7/26/58, Watertown, N.Y.   BR/TR, 6'2", 175 lbs.   Deb: 7/16/18

YEAR	TM/L	W	L	PCT	G	GS	CG	SH	SV	IP	H	HR	BB	SO	RAT	ERA	ERA+	OAV	OOB	BH	AVG	PB	PR	/A	PD	TPI
1918	NY-A	0	0	—	1	0	0	0	0	0²	0	0	0	0	0.0	—	—	.000	.000	0	—	0	0	0	0	0.0

● **JOE BERRY**   Berry, Jonas Arthur "Jittery Joe" b: 12/16/04, Huntsville, Ark.   d: 9/27/58, Anaheim, Cal.   BL/TR, 5'10.5", 145 lbs.   Deb: 9/6/42

YEAR	TM/L	W	L	PCT	G	GS	CG	SH	SV	IP	H	HR	BB	SO	RAT	ERA	ERA+	OAV	OOB	BH	AVG	PB	PR	/A	PD	TPI
1942	Chi-N	0	0	—	2	0	0	0	0	2	7	0	2	1	40.5	18.00	18	.538	.600	0	—	0	-3	-3	0	0.0
1944	Phi-A	10	8	.556	53	0	0	0	**12**	111¹	78	4	23	44	8.3	1.94	179	.192	.238	3	.120	-1	18	**19**	2	3.6
1945	Phi-A	8	7	.533	**52**	0	0	0	5	130¹	114	6	38	51	10.5	2.35	146	.232	.287	5	.143	-1	**15**	16	1	2.0
1946	Phi-A	0	1	.000	5	0	0	0	0	13	15	1	3	5	13.2	2.77	128	.288	.339	1	.333	0	1	1	0	0.1
	Cle-A	3	6	.333	21	0	0	0	1	37¹	32	4	21	16	12.8	3.38	98	.235	.338	2	.286	0	1	-0	-1	-0.1
	Yr	3	7	.300	26	0	0	0	1	50¹	47	5	24	21	12.7	3.22	105	.249	.333	3	.300	1	2	1	-0	0.0
Total	4	21	22	.488	133	0	0	0	18	294	246	14	87	117	10.3	2.45	140	.224	.282	11	.157	-2	31	32	3	5.6

● **FRANK BERTAINA**   Bertaina, Frank Louis b: 4/14/44, San Francisco, Cal.   BL/TL, 5'11", 180 lbs.   Deb: 8/1/64

YEAR	TM/L	W	L	PCT	G	GS	CG	SH	SV	IP	H	HR	BB	SO	RAT	ERA	ERA+	OAV	OOB	BH	AVG	PB	PR	/A	PD	TPI
1964	Bal-A	1	0	1.000	6	4	1	1	0	26	18	3	13	18	10.7	2.77	129	.198	.298	0	.000	-1	2	2	0	0.1
1965	Bal-A	0	0	—	2	1	0	0	0	6	9	0	4	5	19.5	6.00	58	.360	.448	0	.000	-0	-2	-2	0	-0.1
1966	Bal-A	2	5	.286	16	9	0	0	0	63¹	52	3	36	46	13.1	3.13	107	.226	.341	2	.105	-1	2	1	-2	-0.1
1967	Bal-A	1	1	.500	5	2	0	0	0	21²	17	4	14	19	12.9	3.32	95	.224	.344	1	.111	-0	-0	-0	-1	-0.1
	Was-A	6	5	.545	18	17	4	4	0	95²	90	8	37	67	11.9	2.92	108	.251	.322	2	.057	-3	3	3	-1	0.0
	Yr	7	6	.538	23	19	4	4	0	117¹	107	12	51	86	12.1	2.99	106	.246	.325	3	.068	-3	3	2	-1	-0.1
1968	Was-A	7	13	.350	27	23	1	0	0	127¹	133	8	52	80	14.7	4.66	63	.273	.369	5	.132	-0	-24	-25	-1	-3.7
1969	Was-A	1	3	.250	14	5	0	0	0	35²	43	8	23	25	16.7	6.56	53	.291	.386	4	.364	2	-12	-12	-0	-1.0
	Bal-A	0	0	—	3	0	0	0	0	6	1	0	3	5	6.0	0.00	—	.063	.211	1	1.000	1	2	2	-0	0.0
	Yr	1	3	.250	17	5	0	0	0	41²	44	8	26	30	15.1	5.62	62	.267	.366	5	.417	3	-9	-10	-0	-0.9
1970	StL-N	1	2	.333	8	5	0	0	0	31¹	36	1	15	14	14.6	3.16	130	.293	.370	1	.143	-0	3	3	-0	0.3
Total	7	19	29	.396	99	66	6	5	0	413	399	42	214	280	13.6	3.84	85	.257	.350	16	.127	-1	-24	-27	-2	-4.4

● **LEFTY BERTRAND**   Bertrand, Roman Mathias b: 2/28/09, Cobden, Minn.   BR/TL, 6', 180 lbs.   Deb: 4/15/36

YEAR	TM/L	W	L	PCT	G	GS	CG	SH	SV	IP	H	HR	BB	SO	RAT	ERA	ERA+	OAV	OOB	BH	AVG	PB	PR	/A	PD	TPI
1936	Phi-N	0	0	—	2	0	0	0	0	3	3	1	2	1	22.5	9.00	50	.333	.455	0	—	0	-1	-1	-0	-0.1

● **FRED BESANA**   Besana, Frederick Cyril b: 4/5/31, Lincoln, Cal.   BR/TL, 6'3.5", 200 lbs.   Deb: 4/18/56

YEAR	TM/L	W	L	PCT	G	GS	CG	SH	SV	IP	H	HR	BB	SO	RAT	ERA	ERA+	OAV	OOB	BH	AVG	PB	PR	/A	PD	TPI
1956	Bal-A	1	0	1.000	7	2	0	0	0	17²	22	6	14	7	19.4	5.60	70	.310	.437	0	.000	-0	-3	-3	1	-0.1

● **HERMAN BESSE**   Besse, Herman A. b: 8/16/11, St.Louis, Mo.   d: 8/13/72, Los Angeles, Cal.   BL/TL, 6'2", 190 lbs.   Deb: 4/19/40

YEAR	TM/L	W	L	PCT	G	GS	CG	SH	SV	IP	H	HR	BB	SO	RAT	ERA	ERA+	OAV	OOB	BH	AVG	PB	PR	/A	PD	TPI
1940	Phi-A	0	3	.000	17	5	0	0	0	53	70	10	34	19	18.2	8.83	50	.315	.413	5	.263	2	-26	-26	-1	-1.1
1941	Phi-A	2	0	1.000	6	2	1	0	0	19²	28	4	12	8	18.3	10.07	42	.329	.412	1	.200	-0	-13	-13	0	-1.0
1942	Phi-A	2	9	.182	30	14	4	0	1	133	163	7	69	78	16.0	6.16	61	.300	.383	12	.226	-2	-37	-35	-2	-2.6
1943	Phi-A	1	1	.500	5	1	0	0	0	16¹	14	2	4	3	12.7	3.31	103	.295	.348	0	.000	-1	-0	-0	-0	-0.1
1946	Phi-A	0	2	.000	7	3	0	0	1	20²	19	1	9	10	12.2	5.23	68	.247	.326	0	.000	-0	-4	-4	-0	-0.4
Total	5	5	15	.250	65	25	5	0	2	242²	298	24	128	118	16.1	6.79	58	.302	.386	18	.200	2	-80	-77	-3	-5.2

● **DON BESSENT**   Bessent, Fred Donald b: 3/13/31, Jacksonville, Fla.   d: 7/7/90, Jacksonville, Fla.   BR/TR, 6', 175 lbs.   Deb: 7/17/55

YEAR	TM/L	W	L	PCT	G	GS	CG	SH	SV	IP	H	HR	BB	SO	RAT	ERA	ERA+	OAV	OOB	BH	AVG	PB	PR	/A	PD	TPI
1955	*Bro-N	8	1	.889	24	2	1	0	3	63¹	51	7	21	29	10.2	2.70	150	.220	.285	2	.100	-2	9	10	-0	1.2
1956	*Bro-N	4	3	.571	38	0	0	0	9	79¹	63	5	31	52	10.7	2.50	159	.221	.297	2	.111	-1	11	13	-1	1.2
1957	Bro-N	1	3	.250	27	0	0	0	0	44	58	5	19	24	15.8	5.73	73	.328	.393	1	.250	0	-9	-8	-0	-0.7
1958	LA-N	1	0	1.000	19	0	0	0	0	24¹	24	3	17	13	15.5	3.33	123	.270	.393	0	.000	-0	2	2	1	0.1
Total	4	14	7	.667	108	2	1	0	12	211	196	20	88	118	12.2	3.33	122	.250	.327	5	.114	-3	13	17	-1	1.8

● **KARL BEST**   Best, Karl Jon b: 3/6/59, Aberdeen, Was.   BR/TR, 6'4", 210 lbs.   Deb: 8/19/83

YEAR	TM/L	W	L	PCT	G	GS	CG	SH	SV	IP	H	HR	BB	SO	RAT	ERA	ERA+	OAV	OOB	BH	AVG	PB	PR	/A	PD	TPI
1983	Sea-A	0	1	.000	4	0	0	0	0	5¹	14	2	5	3	35.4	13.50	32	.483	.583	0	—	0	-6	-5	-0	-1.0
1984	Sea-A	1	1	.500	7	0	0	0	0	6	7	0	0	6	10.5	3.00	133	.292	.292	0	—	0	1	1	-0	0.3
1985	Sea-A	2	1	.667	15	0	0	0	4	32¹	25	1	6	32	8.9	1.95	216	.207	.250	0	—	0	8	8	-0	0.9
1986	Sea-A	2	3	.400	26	0	0	0	1	35²	35	3	21	23	14.4	4.04	105	.255	.358	0	—	0	1	1	-1	0.0
1988	Min-A	0	0	—	11	0	0	0	0	12	15	1	7	9	16.5	4.50	—	.306	.393	0	—	0	-3	-3	-0	-0.1
Total	5	5	6	.455	61	0	0	0	5	91¹	96	7	39	73	13.7	4.04	104	.267	.345	0	—	0	1	2	-2	0.1

● **JIM BETHKE**   Bethke, James Charles b: 11/5/46, Falls City, Neb.   BR/TR, 6'3", 185 lbs.   Deb: 4/12/65

YEAR	TM/L	W	L	PCT	G	GS	CG	SH	SV	IP	H	HR	BB	SO	RAT	ERA	ERA+	OAV	OOB	BH	AVG	PB	PR	/A	PD	TPI
1965	NY-N	2	0	1.000	25	0	0	0	0	40	41	3	22	19	15.5	4.27	83	.266	.379	0	.000	-0	-3	-3	1	-0.1

YEAR TM/L	W	L	PCT	G	GS	CG	SH	SV	IP	H	HR	BB	SO	RAT	ERA	ERA+	OAV	OOB	BH	AVG	PB	PR	/A	PD	TPI
● **JEFF BETTENDORF**				Bettendorf, Jeffrey Allen b: 12/10/60, Lompoc, Cal. BR/TR, 6'3", 180 lbs. Deb: 4/8/84																					
1984 Oak-A	0	0	—	3	0	0	0	1	9²	9	3	5	5	13.0	4.66	80	.243	.333	0	—	0	-1	-1	-0	0.4
● **HARRY BETTS**				Betts, Harold Matthew "Chubby" or "Ginger" b: 6/19/1881, Alliance, Ohio d: 5/22/46, San Antonio, Tex. BR/TR, 5'10", 200 lbs. Deb: 9/22/03																					
1903 StL-N	0	1	.000	1	1	1	0	0	9	11	0	5	2	18.0	10.00	33	.297	.409	0	.000	-0	-7	-7	-0	-0.5
1913 Cin-N	0	0	—	1	0	0	0	0	3¹	1	0	3	0	13.5	2.70	120	.143	.455	0	.000	-0	0	0	-0	0.0
Total 2	0	1	.000	2	1	1	0	0	12¹	12	0	8	2	16.8	8.03	41	.273	.418	0	.000	-1	-7	-7	-0	-0.5
● **HUCK BETTS**				Betts, Walter Martin b: 2/18/1897, Millsboro, Del. d: 6/13/87, Millsboro, Del. BR/TR, 5'11", 170 lbs. Deb: 4/26/20																					
1920 Phi-N	1	1	.500	27	4	1	0	0	88¹	86	3	33	18	12.3	3.57	96	.261	.332	2	.080	-2	-4	-1	-1	-0.3
1921 Phi-N	3	7	.300	32	2	1	0	4	100²	141	8	14	28	14.2	4.47	95	.337	.365	8	.267	0	-8	-3	-0	-0.2
1922 Phi-N	1	0	1.000	7	0	0	0	0	15	23	3	8	4	18.6	9.60	49	.348	.419	0	.000	-0	-9	-8	-0	-0.5
1923 Phi-N	2	4	.333	19	4	3	0	1	84¹	100	7	14	18	12.6	3.09	149	.314	.351	3	.097	-3	9	14	0	0.6
1924 Phi-N	7	10	.412	37	9	2	0	2	144¹	160	8	42	46	12.9	4.30	104	.286	.341	7	.156	-2	-7	3	-2	-0.1
1925 Phi-N	4	5	.444	35	7	1	0	1	97¹	146	10	38	28	17.3	5.55	86	.342	.400	10	.294	2	-14	-8	1	-0.4
1932 Bos-N	13	11	.542	31	27	16	3	1	221²	229	9	35	32	10.7	2.80	134	.267	.295	19	.241	2	27	24	-2	2.4
1933 Bos-N	11	11	.500	35	26	17	2	4	242	225	9	55	40	10.4	2.79	110	.248	.290	17	.224	1	15	7	4	1.4
1934 Bos-N	17	10	.630	40	27	10	2	3	213	258	17	42	69	12.8	4.06	94	.296	.330	13	.188	1	-0	-6	-2	-0.7
1935 Bos-N	2	9	.182	44	19	2	1	0	159²	213	9	40	40	14.4	5.47	69	.321	.362	7	.159	-0	-26	-30	1	-1.7
Total 10	61	68	.473	307	125	53	8	16	1366¹	1581	83	321	323	12.7	3.93	98	.292	.334	86	.197	-2	-18	-9	-0	0.5
● **BILL BEVENS**				Bevens, Floyd Clifford b: 10/21/16, Hubbard, Ore. d: 10/26/91, Salem, Ore. BR/TR, 6'3.5", 210 lbs. Deb: 5/12/44																					
1944 NY-A	4	1	.800	8	5	3	0	0	43²	44	4	16	12	12.0	2.68	130	.273	.331	1	.063	-2	4	4	-0	0.2
1945 NY-A	13	9	.591	29	25	14	2	0	184	174	12	68	76	11.9	3.67	94	.254	.322	7	.111	-4	-6	-4	1	-0.9
1946 NY-A	16	13	.552	31	31	18	3	0	249²	213	11	78	120	10.5	2.23	154	.232	.293	7	.083	-4	35	34	-4	3.0
1947 *NY-A	7	13	.350	28	23	11	1	0	165	167	13	77	77	13.4	3.82	93	.264	.345	7	.121	-3	-2	-5	-0	-0.9
Total 4	40	36	.526	96	84	46	6	0	642¹	598	40	236	289	11.7	3.08	113	.250	.318	22	.100	-13	31	29	-4	1.4
● **LOU BEVIL**				Bevil, Louis Eugene (b: Louis Eugene Bevilacqua) b: 11/27/22, Nelson, Ill. d: 2/1/73, Dixon, Ill. BB/TR, 5'11.5", 190 lbs. Deb: 9/2/42																					
1942 Was-A	0	1	.000	4	1	0	0	0	9²	9	0	11	2	19.6	6.52	56	.265	.457	0	.000	-0	-3	-3	-0	-0.3
● **BEN BEVILLE**				Beville, Clarence Benjamin b: 8/28/1877, Colusa, Cal. d: 1/5/37, Yountville, Cal. BR/TR, 5'9", 190 lbs. Deb: 5/24/01																					
1901 Bos-A	0	2	.000	2	2	1	0	0	9	8	0	9	1	18.0	4.00	96	.235	.409	2	.286	0	-0	-0	-0	-0.1
● **JIM BIBBY**				Bibby, James Blair b: 10/29/44, Franklinton, N.C. BR/TR, 6'5", 235 lbs. Deb: 9/4/72																					
1972 StL-N	1	3	.250	6	6	0	0	0	40¹	29	4	19	28	10.9	3.35	102	.206	.304	1	.125	0	0	0	-0	0.1
1973 StL-N	0	2	.000	6	3	0	0	0	16	19	2	17	12	21.4	9.56	38	.306	.469	0	.000	0	-10	-11	0	-1.1
Tex-A	9	10	.474	26	23	11	2	1	180¹	121	14	106	155	11.6	3.24	115	**.192**	.314	0	—	0	11	10	-2	0.8
1974 Tex-A	19	19	.500	41	41	11	5	0	264	255	25	113	149	12.9	4.74	75	.255	.336	0	—	0	-33	-34	1	-4.3
1975 Tex-A	2	6	.250	12	12	4	1	0	68¹	73	2	28	31	13.6	5.00	75	.274	.348	0	—	0	-9	-9	-1	-1.0
Cle-A	5	9	.357	24	12	2	0	1	112²	99	7	50	62	11.9	3.20	118	.235	.316	0	—	0	7	7	1	0.9
Yr	7	15	.318	36	24	6	1	1	181	172	9	78	93	12.4	3.88	97	.248	.324	0	—	0	-2	-2	-0	-0.1
1976 Cle-A	13	7	.650	34	21	4	3	1	163¹	162	6	56	84	12.1	3.20	109	.266	.329	0	—	0	6	5	-1	0.5
1977 Cle-A	12	13	.480	37	30	9	2	2	206²	197	17	73	141	11.9	3.57	110	.250	.317	0	—	0	11	9	-2	0.8
1978 Pit-N	8	7	.533	34	14	3	2	1	107	100	10	39	72	11.9	3.53	105	.246	.315	4	.129	1	1	2	0	0.4
1979 *Pit-N	12	4	.750	34	17	4	1	0	137²	110	9	47	103	10.5	2.81	138	.218	.290	8	.178	2	14	16	-2	1.8
1980 Pit-N★	19	6	**.760**	35	34	6	1	0	238¹	210	20	88	144	11.5	3.32	110	.238	.312	12	.156	2	7	8	-2	0.8
1981 Pit-N	6	3	.667	14	14	2	2	0	93²	79	4	26	48	10.3	2.50	144	.225	.282	4	.143	1	10	11	-1	1.1
1983 Pit-N	5	12	.294	29	12	0	0	2	78	92	10	51	44	16.6	6.69	55	.297	.398	2	.111	-1	-27	-26	-0	-5.1
1984 Tex-A	0	0	—	8	0	0	0	0	16¹	19	1	10	6	16.0	4.41	94	.297	.392	0	—	0	-1	-0	-0	-0.1
Total 12	111	101	.524	340	239	56	19	8	1722²	1565	131	723	1079	12.2	3.76	98	.243	.323	31	.148	5	-11	-11	-8	-4.4
● **VERN BICKFORD**				Bickford, Vernon Edgell b: 8/17/20, Hellier, Ky. d: 5/6/60, Concord, Va. BR/TR, 6', 185 lbs. Deb: 4/24/48																					
1948 *Bos-N	11	5	.688	33	22	10	1	1	146	125	9	63	60	11.8	3.27	117	.226	.309	10	.204	1	11	9	-1	0.9
1949 Bos-N★	16	11	.593	37	36	15	2	0	230²	246	20	106	101	14.0	4.25	89	.273	.354	15	.185	-1	-5	-12	2	-1.1
1950 Bos-N	19	14	.576	40	39	**27**	2	0	311²	293	25	122	126	12.2	3.47	111	.248	.321	16	.138	-4	23	13	1	0.7
1951 Bos-N	11	9	.550	25	20	12	3	0	164²	146	7	76	76	12.5	3.12	118	.240	.330	6	.115	-2	15	10	3	1.2
1952 Bos-N	7	12	.368	26	22	7	1	0	161¹	165	7	64	62	12.9	3.74	97	.269	.340	9	.176	-0	-0	-2	1	-0.2
1953 Mil-N	2	5	.286	20	9	2	0	1	58	60	8	35	25	15.1	5.28	74	.279	.385	1	.067	-1	-6	-9	1	-0.4
1954 Bal-A	0	1	.000	1	1	0	0	0	4	5	0	1	0	13.5	9.00	40	.333	.375	0	—	0	-2	-2	-0	-0.4
Total 7	66	57	.537	182	149	73	9	2	1076¹	1040	76	467	450	12.8	3.71	102	.254	.335	57	.156	-7	36	7	3	0.2
● **DAN BICKHAM**				Bickham, Daniel Denison b: 10/31/1864, Dayton, Ohio d: 3/3/51, Dayton, Ohio BR/TR, 5'10", 160 lbs. Deb: 8/13/1886																					
1886 Cin-a	1	0	1.000	1	1	1	0	0	9	13	0	3	6	16.0	3.00	117	.351	.400	1	.333	0	0	1	-0	0.1
● **CHARLIE BICKNELL**				Bicknell, Charles Stephen "Bud" b: 7/27/28, Plainfield, N.J. BR/TR, 5'11", 170 lbs. Deb: 4/22/48																					
1948 Phi-N	0	1	.000	17	1	0	0	0	25²	29	5	17	5	16.1	5.96	66	.287	.390	0	.000	-1	-6	-6	-1	-0.3
1949 Phi-N	0	0	—	13	0	0	0	0	28¹	32	3	17	4	16.2	7.62	52	.291	.395	0	.000	1	-11	-12	-0	0.0
Total 2	0	1	.000	30	1	0	0	0	54	61	8	34	9	16.2	6.83	58	.289	.393	0	.000	-0	-17	-17	-1	-0.3
● **MIKE BIELECKI**				Bielecki, Michael Joseph b: 7/31/59, Baltimore, Md. BR/TR, 6'3", 200 lbs. Deb: 9/14/84																					
1984 Pit-N	0	0	—	4	0	0	0	0	4¹	4	0	1	0	8.3	0.00	—	.250	.250	0	—	0	2	2	0	0.0
1985 Pit-N	2	3	.400	12	7	0	0	0	45²	45	5	31	22	15.2	4.53	79	.257	.372	0	.000	-1	-5	-5	1	-0.5
1986 Pit-N	6	11	.353	31	27	0	0	0	148²	149	10	83	83	14.2	4.66	82	.262	.358	3	.063	-3	-16	-14	-1	-1.8
1987 Pit-N	2	3	.400	8	8	2	0	0	45²	43	6	12	25	11.0	4.73	87	.250	.303	1	.063	-0	-3	-3	-0	-0.4
1988 Chi-N	2	2	.500	19	5	0	0	0	48¹	55	4	16	33	13.2	3.35	108	.284	.338	1	.100	-0	1	1	-0	0.0
1989 *Chi-N	18	7	**.720**	33	33	4	3	0	212¹	187	16	81	147	11.4	3.14	120	.237	.308	3	.043	-5	8	15	-1	1.0
1990 Chi-N	8	11	.421	36	29	0	0	0	168	188	13	70	103	14.1	4.93	83	.286	.361	7	.163	-0	-21	-16	3	-1.4
1991 Chi-N	13	11	.542	39	25	0	0	0	172	169	18	54	72	11.8	4.50	86	.262	.321	3	.065	-2	-16	-12	-1	-1.7
Atl-N	0	0	—	2	0	0	0	0	1²	2	0	2	2	21.6	0.00	—	.286	.444	0	—	0	1	1	0	0.0
Yr	13	11	.542	41	25	0	0	0	173²	171	18	56	74	11.8	4.46	87	.259	.317	3	.065	-2	-15	-11	-1	-1.7
1992 Atl-N	2	4	.333	19	14	1	1	0	80²	77	2	27	62	11.7	2.57	143	.254	.317	1	.125	-1	8	10	1	0.7
1993 Cle-A	4	5	.444	13	13	0	0	0	68²	90	8	23	38	15.1	5.90	73	.310	.365	0	—	0	-12	-12	-0	-1.2
1994 Atl-N	2	0	1.000	19	0	0	0	0	27	26	2	12	18	13.7	4.00	104	.277	.360	0	.000	-0	1	0	0	0.0
Total 11	59	57	.509	235	162	7	4	1	1023	1037	84	411	607	12.9	4.17	93	.265	.337	21	.078	-14	-52	-32	3	-5.3
● **HARRY BIEMILLER**				Biemiller, Harry Lee b: 10/9/1897, Baltimore, Md. d: 5/25/65, Orlando, Fla. BR/TR, 6'1", 171 lbs. Deb: 8/26/20																					
1920 Was-A	1	0	1.000	5	2	1	0	0	17	21	1	13	10	18.0	4.76	78	.318	.430	0	.000	-1	-2	-1	1	-0.1
1925 Cin-N	0	1	.000	23	1	0	0	2	47	45	2	21	9	14.0	4.02	102	.280	.386	0	.000	-0	1	0	2	0.1
Total 2	1	1	.500	28	3	1	0	2	64	66	3	34	19	15.0	4.22	95	.291	.399	0	.000	-1	-1	-1	2	0.0
● **LOU BIERBAUER**				Bierbauer, Louis W. b: 9/28/1865, Erie, Pa. d: 1/31/26, Erie, Pa. BL/TR, 5'8", 140 lbs. Deb: 4/17/1886 ♦																					
1886 Phi-a	0	0	—	2	0	0	0	0	10²	9	0	5	5	11.0	4.22	83	.178	.260	118	.226	-0	-1	-1	-1	0.0
1887 Phi-a	0	0	—	1	0	0	0	0	1	0	0	0	0	0.00	—	.000	.000	144	.272	0	0	0	0	0.1

YEAR	TM/L	W	L	PCT	G	GS	CG	SH	SV	IP	H	HR	BB	SO	RAT	ERA	ERA+	OAV	OOB	BH	AVG	PB	PR	/A	PD	TPI
1888	Phi-a	0	0	—	1	0	0	0	0	3	5	0	0	3	15.0	0.00	—	.358	.358	143	.267	0	1	1	-0	0.0
Total	3	0	0	—	4	0	0	0	1	14²	13	0	5	5	11.0	3.07	112	.210	.269	1521	.267	0	1	1	-1	0.1

● **LYLE BIGBEE**   Bigbee, Lyle Randolph "Al"   b: 8/22/1893, Sweet Home, Ore.   d: 8/5/42, Portland, Ore.   BL/TR, 6', 180 lbs.   Deb: 4/15/20   F♦

YEAR	TM/L	W	L	PCT	G	GS	CG	SH	SV	IP	H	HR	BB	SO	RAT	ERA	ERA+	OAV	OOB	BH	AVG	PB	PR	/A	PD	TPI
1920	Phi-A	0	3	.000	12	2	0	0	0	45	66	5	25	12	18.2	8.00	50	.369	.446	14	.187	0	-21	-20	0	-1.1
1921	Pit-N	0	0	—	5	0	0	0	0	8	4	0	4	1	9.0	1.13	341	.154	.267	0	.000	-0	2	2	-0	0.0
Total	2	0	3	.000	17	2	0	0	0	53	70	5	29	13	16.8	6.96	57	.341	.423	14	.182	-0	-19	-17	0	-1.1

● **CHARLIE BIGGS**   Biggs, Charles Orval   b: 9/15/06, French Lick, Ind.   d: 5/24/54, French Lick, Ind.   BR/TR, 6'1", 185 lbs.   Deb: 9/3/32

YEAR	TM/L	W	L	PCT	G	GS	CG	SH	SV	IP	H	HR	BB	SO	RAT	ERA	ERA+	OAV	OOB	BH	AVG	PB	PR	/A	PD	TPI
1932	Chi-A	1	1	.500	6	4	0	0	0	24²	32	2	12	1	17.1	6.93	62	.314	.402	1	.111	-0	-7	-7	-0	-0.5

● **LARRY BIITTNER**   Biittner, Lawrence David   b: 7/27/45, Pocahontas, Ia.   BL/TL, 6'2", 205 lbs.   Deb: 7/17/70   ♦

YEAR	TM/L	W	L	PCT	G	GS	CG	SH	SV	IP	H	HR	BB	SO	RAT	ERA	ERA+	OAV	OOB	BH	AVG	PB	PR	/A	PD	TPI
1977	Chi-N	0	0	—	1	0	0	0	0	1¹	5	3	1	3	40.5	40.50	11	.556	.600	147	.298	-0	-5	-5	0	0.0

● **JIM BILBREY**   Bilbrey, James Melvin   b: 4/20/24, Rickman, Tenn.   d: 12/26/85, Toledo, Ohio   BR/TR, 6'2.5", 205 lbs.   Deb: 5/17/49

YEAR	TM/L	W	L	PCT	G	GS	CG	SH	SV	IP	H	HR	BB	SO	RAT	ERA	ERA+	OAV	OOB	BH	AVG	PB	PR	/A	PD	TPI
1949	StL-A	0	0	—	1	0	0	0	0	1	1	0	3	0	36.0	18.00	25	.250	.571			0	-2	-1	0	0.0

● **EMIL BILDILLI**   Bildilli, Emil "Hill Billy"   b: 9/16/12, Diamond, Ind.   d: 9/16/46, Hartford City, Ind.   BR/TL, 5'10", 170 lbs.   Deb: 8/24/37

YEAR	TM/L	W	L	PCT	G	GS	CG	SH	SV	IP	H	HR	BB	SO	RAT	ERA	ERA+	OAV	OOB	BH	AVG	PB	PR	/A	PD	TPI
1937	StL-A	0	1	.000	4	1	0	0	0	8	12	1	3	2	16.9	10.13	48	.353	.405	0	.000	-0	-5	-5	1	-0.4
1938	StL-A	1	2	.333	5	3	2	0	0	21²	33	3	11	11	18.3	7.06	70	.359	.427	2	.250	-0	-5	-5	-0	-0.5
1939	StL-A	1	1	.500	2	2	2	0	0	19	21	0	6	8	12.8	3.32	147	.266	.318	0	.000	-0	3	3	0	0.3
1940	StL-A	2	4	.333	28	11	3	0	1	97	113	12	52	32	15.5	5.57	82	.298	.386	6	.200	-1	-13	-11	3	-0.4
1941	StL-A	0	0	—	2	0	0	0	0	2¹	5	0	3	2	30.9	11.57	37	.417	.533	0		0	-2	-2	0	0.0
Total	5	4	8	.333	41	17	7	0	1	148	184	16	75	55	15.9	5.84	80	.309	.388	8	.178	-2	-22	-19	4	-1.0

● **HARRY BILLIARD**   Billiard, Harry Pree "Pree"   b: 11/11/1883, Monroe, Ind.   d: 6/3/23, Wooster, Ohio   BR/TR, 6', 190 lbs.   Deb: 7/31/08

YEAR	TM/L	W	L	PCT	G	GS	CG	SH	SV	IP	H	HR	BB	SO	RAT	ERA	ERA+	OAV	OOB	BH	AVG	PB	PR	/A	PD	TPI
1908	NY-A	0	0	—	6	0	0	0	0	17	15	1	14	10	18.0	2.65	94	.234	.410	1	.200	-0	-0	-0	-1	-0.1
1914	Ind-F	8	7	.533	32	16	5	0	2	125²	117	4	63	45	13.4	3.72	84	.257	.356	7	.184	-1	-12	-8	-2	-1.3
1915	New-F	0	1	.000	14	2	0	0	1	28¹	32	0	28	7	20.0	5.72	45	.291	.447	2	.333	-1	-9	-10	1	-0.3
Total	3	8	8	.500	52	18	5	0	3	171	164	5	105	62	14.9	3.95	75	.260	.379	10	.204	-2	-22	-19	-2	-1.7

● **JACK BILLINGHAM**   Billingham, John Eugene   b: 2/21/43, Orlando, Fla.   BR/TR, 6'4", 215 lbs.   Deb: 4/11/68

YEAR	TM/L	W	L	PCT	G	GS	CG	SH	SV	IP	H	HR	BB	SO	RAT	ERA	ERA+	OAV	OOB	BH	AVG	PB	PR	/A	PD	TPI
1968	LA-N	3	0	1.000	50	1	0	0	8	70²	54	0	30	46	11.0	2.17	128	.215	.304	0	.000	0	6	5	1	0.4
1969	Hou-N	6	7	.462	52	4	1	0	2	82²	92	12	29	71	13.7	4.25	83	.290	.359	1	.071	-0	-6	-6	-0	-1.0
1970	Hou-N	13	9	.591	46	24	8	1	0	187²	190	10	63	134	12.6	3.98	97	.259	.326	6	.103	-2	1	-2	1	-0.3
1971	Hou-N	10	16	.385	33	33	8	3	0	228¹	205	9	68	139	11.4	3.39	99	.243	.311	9	.123	-3	2	-1	0	-0.4
1972	*Cin-N	12	12	.500	36	31	8	4	1	217²	197	18	64	137	11.1	3.18	101	.241	.301	5	.070	-4	7	1	-1	-0.4
1973	*Cin-N☆	19	10	.655	40	40	16	7	0	293¹	257	20	95	155	11.1	3.04	112	.236	.303	6	.065	-5	20	12	2	0.8
1974	Cin-N	19	11	.633	36	35	8	1	0	212¹	233	16	64	103	12.8	3.94	88	.288	.345	5	.075	-5	-8	-11	1	-1.9
1975	*Cin-N	15	10	.600	33	32	5	0	0	208	222	22	76	79	13.3	4.11	87	.279	.348	7	.108	-1	-11	-12	-2	-1.6
1976	*Cin-N	12	10	.545	34	29	5	2	1	177	190	17	62	76	13.0	4.32	81	.279	.343	14	.237	-1	-16	-16	-1	-1.6
1977	Cin-N	10	10	.500	36	23	3	2	0	161²	195	16	56	76	14.5	5.23	75	.306	.371	9	.161	-1	-24	-23	2	-2.4
1978	Det-A	15	8	.652	30	30	10	4	0	201²	218	16	65	59	13.0	3.88	100	.284	.346	0	—	0	-3	-0	-1	-0.2
1979	Det-A	10	7	.588	35	19	2	0	3	158	163	13	60	59	13.1	3.30	111	.275	.348	0		0	16	18	-1	1.7
1980	Det-A	0	0	—	8	0	0	0	0	7¹	11	1	6	3	20.9	7.36	56	.355	.459	0		0	-3	-3	-0	-0.1
	Bos-A	1	3	.250	7	4	0	0	0	24¹	45	6	12	4	22.6	11.10	38	.413	.488	0		0	-19	-19	-0	-2.4
	Yr	1	3	.250	15	4	0	0	0	31²	56	7	18	7	22.2	10.23	41	.397	.479	0		0	-22	-21	-0	-2.5
Total	13	145	113	.562	476	305	74	27	15	2230²	2272	176	750	1141	12.6	3.83	94	.268	.335	62	.111	-17	-37	-59	-0	-9.4

● **JOSH BILLINGS**   Billings, Haskell Clark   b: 9/27/07, New York, N.Y.   d: 12/26/83, Greenbrae, Cal.   BR/TR, 5'11", 180 lbs.   Deb: 8/17/27

YEAR	TM/L	W	L	PCT	G	GS	CG	SH	SV	IP	H	HR	BB	SO	RAT	ERA	ERA+	OAV	OOB	BH	AVG	PB	PR	/A	PD	TPI
1927	Det-A	5	4	.556	10	9	5	0	0	67	64	3	39	18	14.6	4.84	87	.259	.373	7	.259	-0	-5	-5	-1	-0.5
1928	Det-A	5	10	.333	21	16	4	0	0	110²	118	4	59	48	14.8	5.12	80	.276	.371	10	.286	3	-13	-12	-0	-1.2
1929	Det-A	0	1	.000	8	0	0	0	0	19¹	27	0	9	1	17.2	5.12	84	.365	.440	0	.000	-1	-2	-2	1	-0.1
Total	3	10	15	.400	39	25	8	1	0	197	209	7	107	67	15.0	5.03	83	.279	.378	17	.250	2	-20	-19	0	-1.8

● **DOUG BIRD**   Bird, James Douglas   b: 3/5/50, Corona, Cal.   BR/TR, 6'4", 180 lbs.   Deb: 4/29/73

YEAR	TM/L	W	L	PCT	G	GS	CG	SH	SV	IP	H	HR	BB	SO	RAT	ERA	ERA+	OAV	OOB	BH	AVG	PB	PR	/A	PD	TPI
1973	KC-A	4	4	.500	54	0	0	0	20	102¹	81	10	30	83	9.9	2.99	137	.217	.279	0		0	9	13	-2	1.0
1974	KC-A	7	6	.538	55	1	1	0	10	92¹	100	6	27	62	12.5	2.73	140	.286	.339	0		0	9	11	1	1.8
1975	KC-A	9	6	.600	51	4	0	0	11	105¹	100	7	40	81	12.1	3.25	119	.258	.331	0		0	6	7	-1	1.0
1976	*KC-A	12	10	.545	39	27	2	1	2	197²	191	17	31	107	10.2	3.37	104	.251	.283	0		0	3	3	-2	0.1
1977	*KC-A	11	4	.733	53	5	0	0	14	118¹	110	14	29	83	11.6	3.88	104	.270	.319	0		0	2	2	-1	0.2
1978	*KC-A	6	6	.500	40	6	0	0	1	98²	110	8	31	48	13.0	5.29	72	.284	.340	0		0	-17	-16	-0	-1.9
1979	Phi-N	2	0	1.000	32	1	0	0	0	61	73	7	16	33	13.4	5.16	74	.305	.354	1	.167	-0	-10	-9	-1	-0.4
1980	NY-A	3	0	1.000	22	1	0	0	1	50²	47	3	14	17	11.0	2.66	147	.257	.313	0		0	8	7	1	0.5
1981	NY-A	5	1	.833	17	4	0	0	0	53¹	58	5	16	28	12.5	2.70	132	.280	.332	0		0	6	5	0	0.6
	Chi-N	4	5	.444	12	12	2	1	0	75¹	72	5	16	34	10.6	3.58	103	.254	.297	2	.100	-1	-1	1	-1	-0.1
1982	Chi-N	9	14	.391	35	33	2	1	0	191	230	26	30	71	12.4	5.14	73	.297	.325	8	.143	-2	-33	-30	-2	-3.5
1983	Bos-A	4	4	.200	22	6	0	0	1	67²	91	14	16	33	14.5	6.65	65	.324	.365	0		0	-19	-17	-0	-1.3
Total	11	73	60	.549	432	100	8	3	60	1213²	1273	122	296	680	11.8	3.99	96	.272	.319	11	.134	-2	-36	-23	-8	-2.0

● **RED BIRD**   Bird, James Edward   b: 4/25/1890, Stephenville, Tex.   d: 3/23/72, Murfreesboro, Ark.   BL/TL, 5'11", 170 lbs.   Deb: 9/17/21

YEAR	TM/L	W	L	PCT	G	GS	CG	SH	SV	IP	H	HR	BB	SO	RAT	ERA	ERA+	OAV	OOB	BH	AVG	PB	PR	/A	PD	TPI
1921	Was-A	0	0	—	1	0	0	0	0	5	5	0	1	2	12.6	5.40	76	.294	.368	0	.000	-0	-1	-1	0	0.0

● **MIKE BIRKBECK**   Birkbeck, Michael Lawrence   b: 3/10/61, Orrville, Ohio   BR/TR, 6'1", 190 lbs.   Deb: 8/17/86

YEAR	TM/L	W	L	PCT	G	GS	CG	SH	SV	IP	H	HR	BB	SO	RAT	ERA	ERA+	OAV	OOB	BH	AVG	PB	PR	/A	PD	TPI
1986	Mil-A	1	1	.500	7	4	0	0	0	22	24	6	12	13	14.7	4.50	96	.282	.371	0		0	-1	-0	-0	-0.1
1987	Mil-A	1	4	.200	10	10	1	0	0	45	63	8	19	25	16.4	6.20	74	.335	.396	0		0	-9	-8	1	-0.7
1988	Mil-A	10	8	.556	23	23	0	0	0	124	141	10	37	64	13.0	4.72	84	.285	.336	0		0	-10	-10	2	-1.1
1989	Mil-A	0	4	.000	9	9	1	0	0	44²	57	4	22	31	16.5	5.44	71	.310	.392	0		0	-8	-8	-0	-0.7
1992	NY-N	0	1	.000	1	1	0	0	0	7	12	3	1	2	16.7	9.00	39	.387	.406	0	.000	-0	-4	-4	0	-0.5
Total	5	12	18	.400	50	47	2	0	0	242²	297	25	91	135	14.5	5.23	78	.302	.364	0	.000	-0	-32	-31	2	-3.1

● **RALPH BIRKOFER**   Birkofer, Ralph Joseph "Lefty"   b: 11/5/08, Cincinnati, Ohio   d: 3/16/71, Cincinnati, Ohio   BL/TL, 5'11", 213 lbs.   Deb: 4/25/33

YEAR	TM/L	W	L	PCT	G	GS	CG	SH	SV	IP	H	HR	BB	SO	RAT	ERA	ERA+	OAV	OOB	BH	AVG	PB	PR	/A	PD	TPI
1933	Pit-N	4	2	.667	9	8	3	1	0	50²	43	1	17	20	10.8	2.31	144	.229	.296	7	.318	1	6	6	-0	0.8
1934	Pit-N	11	12	.478	41	24	11	0	1	204	227	11	66	71	13.1	4.10	100	.277	.335	17	.227	1	-1	-0	-2	-0.4
1935	Pit-N	9	7	.563	37	18	8	1	1	150¹	173	5	42	80	13.2	4.07	101	.283	.335	14	.241	2	-1	1	-3	0.0
1936	Pit-N	7	5	.583	34	13	2	0	0	109¹	130	4	41	44	14.5	4.69	86	.295	.362	9	.220	0	-8	-8	-3	-1.0
1937	Bro-N	0	2	.000	11	1	0	0	0	29²	45	3	9	9	16.4	6.67	60	.341	.383	2	.273	1	-9	-9	-1	-0.5
Total	5	31	28	.525	132	64	24	2	2	544	618	24	175	224	13.4	4.19	96	.282	.340	50	.242	5	-13	-10	-8	-0.8

● **BABE BIRRER**   Birrer, Werner Joseph   b: 7/4/28, Buffalo, N.Y.   BR/TR, 6', 195 lbs.   Deb: 6/5/55

YEAR	TM/L	W	L	PCT	G	GS	CG	SH	SV	IP	H	HR	BB	SO	RAT	ERA	ERA+	OAV	OOB	BH	AVG	PB	PR	/A	PD	TPI
1955	Det-A	4	3	.571	36	3	1	0	3	80¹	77	9	29	28	11.9	4.15	93	.248	.313	3	.158	2	-2	-3	-1	-0.1
1956	Bal-A	0	0	—	4	0	0	0	0	5¹	9	0	1	1	16.9	6.75	58	.360	.385	0	.000	-0	-2	-2	-0	0.0
1958	LA-N	0	0	—	16	0	0	0	1	34	43	4	7	16	13.5	4.50	91	.309	.347	4	.571	-2	-2	-1	0	0.1
Total	3	4	3	.571	56	3	1	0	4	119²	129	13	37	45	12.6	4.36	90	.272	.326	7	.259	4	-5	-6	-1	-0.1

YEAR	TM/L	W	L	PCT	G	GS	CG	SH	SV	IP	H	HR	BB	SO	RAT	ERA	ERA+	OAV	OOB	BH	AVG	PB	PR	/A	PD	TPI
● TIM BIRTSAS	Birtsas, Timothy Dean b: 9/5/60, Pontiac, Mich. BL/TL, 6'7", 240 lbs. Deb: 5/3/85																									
1985	Oak-A	10	6	.625	29	25	2	0	0	141¹	124	18	91	94	13.9	4.01	96	.238	.354	0	—	0	2	-2	-3	-0.3
1986	Oak-A	0	0	—	2	0	0	0	0	2	2	1	4	1	27.0	22.50	17	.286	.545	0	—	0	-4	-4	-0	0.2
1988	Cin-N	1	3	.250	36	4	0	0	0	64¹	61	6	24	38	12.3	4.20	85	.250	.325	0	.000	-1	-5	-4	-1	-0.5
1989	Cin-N	2	2	.500	42	1	0	0	1	69²	68	5	27	57	12.7	3.75	96	.261	.337	1	.250	-1	-2	-1	1	0.0
1990	Cin-N	1	3	.250	29	0	0	0	0	51¹	69	7	24	41	16.5	3.86	102	.325	.397	0	.000	-0	0	0	0	0.0
Total 5		14	14	.500	138	30	2	0	1	328²	324	37	170	231	13.8	4.08	93	.260	.354	1	.056	-0	-10	-11	-4	-0.6
● FRANK BISCAN	Biscan, Frank Stephen "Porky" b: 3/13/20, Mt.Olive, Ill. d: 5/22/59, St.Louis, Mo. BL/TL, 5'11", 190 lbs. Deb: 5/3/42																									
1942	StL-A	0	1	.000	11	0	0	0	1	27	13	1	11	10	8.0	2.33	159	.143	.235	0	.000	-0	4	4	0	0.1
1946	StL-A	1	1	.500	16	0	0	0	1	22²	28	3	22	9	19.9	5.16	72	.318	.455	0	.000	-0	-4	-4	-0	-0.4
1948	StL-A	6	7	.462	47	4	1	0	2	98²	129	3	71	45	19.1	6.11	75	.322	.435	5	.192	1	-20	-17	0	-1.9
Total 3		7	9	.438	74	4	1	0	4	148¹	170	4	104	64	17.2	5.28	81	.294	.409	5	.143	-0	-20	-17	0	-2.2
● CHARLIE BISHOP	Bishop, Charles Tuller b: 1/1/24, Atlanta, Ga. d: 7/5/93, Lawrenceville, Ga. BR/TR, 6'2", 195 lbs. Deb: 8/22/52																									
1952	Phi-A	2	2	.500	6	5	1	0	0	30²	29	2	24	17	15.6	6.46	61	.238	.363	1	.111	-0	-9	-9	0	-0.9
1953	Phi-A	3	14	.176	39	20	1	1	2	160²	174	15	86	66	14.8	5.66	76	.282	.375	5	.089	-4	-30	-24	2	-2.5
1954	Phi-A	4	6	.400	20	12	4	0	1	96	98	10	50	34	14.3	4.41	89	.275	.372	4	.121	-2	-7	-5	-2	-0.8
1955	KC-A	1	0	1.000	4	0	0	0	0	6²	6	1	8	4	23.0	5.40	77	.261	.500	1	.500	0	-1	-1	-0	-0.1
Total 4		10	22	.313	69	37	6	1	3	294	307	28	168	121	14.9	5.33	77	.275	.376	11	.110	-6	-47	-39	1	-4.3
● JIM BISHOP	Bishop, James Morton b: 1/28/1898, Montgomery City, Mo. d: 9/20/73, Montgomery City, Mo. BR/TR, 6', 195 lbs. Deb: 4/26/23																									
1923	Phi-N	0	3	.000	15	0	0	0	1	32²	48	2	11	5	17.1	6.34	73	.353	.413	0	.000	-2	-8	-6	1	-0.6
1924	Phi-N	0	1	.000	7	1	0	0	0	16²	24	3	7	3	16.7	6.48	69	.348	.408	1	.200	-0	-5	-4	0	-0.2
Total 2		0	4	.000	22	1	0	0	1	49¹	72	5	18	8	17.0	6.39	71	.351	.412	1	.067	-2	-13	-10	1	-0.8
● LLOYD BISHOP	Bishop, Lloyd Clifton b: 4/25/1890, Conway Springs, Kan. d: 6/18/68, Wichita, Kan. BR/TR, 6', 180 lbs. Deb: 9/5/14																									
1914	Cle-A	0	1	.000	3	1	0	0	0	8	14	0	3	1	19.1	5.63	51	.389	.436	0	—	-0	-3	-2	-0	-0.3
● BILL BISHOP	Bishop, William Henry "Lefty" b: 10/22/1900, Houtzdale, Pa. d: 2/14/56, St.Joseph, Mo. BL/TL, 5'8", 170 lbs. Deb: 9/15/21																									
1921	Phi-A	0	0	—	2	0	0	0	0	7	8	0	10	4	23.1	9.00	50	.267	.450	0	.000	-1	-4	-4	0	0.0
● BILL BISHOP	Bishop, William Robinson b: 12/27/1869, Adamsburg, Pa. d: 12/15/32, Pittsburgh, Pa. Deb: 9/13/1886																									
1886	Pit-a	0	1	.000	2	2	2	0	0	17	17	0	11	4	15.4	3.18	107	.221	.326	1	.143	-1	1	0	-1	-0.1
1887	Pit-N	0	3	.000	3	3	3	0	0	27	45	2	22	4	23.0	13.33	29	.354	.457	0	.000	-1	-28	-28	-0	-1.9
1889	Chi-N	0	0	—	2	0	0	0	2	3	6	0	6	1	36.0	18.00	23	.403	.575	0	—	0	-5	-5	-0	-0.5
Total 3		0	4	.000	7	5	5	0	2	47	68	2	39	9	21.1	9.96	37	.311	.422	1	.059	-2	-32	-33	-1	-2.5
● HI BITHORN	Bithorn, Hiram Gabriel (Sosa) b: 3/18/16, Santurce, P.R. d: 1/1/52, ElMante, Mex. BR/TR, 6'1", 200 lbs. Deb: 4/15/42																									
1942	Chi-N	9	14	.391	38	16	9	0	2	171¹	191	8	81	65	14.3	3.68	87	.296	.374	7	.123	-1	-7	-9	-1	-1.4
1943	Chi-N	18	12	.600	39	30	19	7	2	249²	227	8	65	86	10.6	2.60	129	.244	.294	16	.174	-0	22	21	1	2.6
1946	Chi-N	6	5	.545	26	7	2	1	1	86²	97	5	25	34	12.7	3.84	86	.283	.332	5	.179	-0	-4	-5	-0	-0.7
1947	Chi-A	1	0	1.000	2	0	0	0	0	2	2	0	0	0	9.0	0.00	—	.286	.286	0	—	1	1	0	0	0.4
Total 4		34	31	.523	105	53	30	8	5	509²	517	21	171	185	12.2	3.16	104	.268	.328	28	.158	-2	12	7	-0	0.9
● JOE BITKER	Bitker, Joseph Anthony b: 2/12/64, Glendale, Cal. BR/TR, 6'1", 175 lbs. Deb: 7/31/90																									
1990	Oak-A	0	0	—	1	0	0	0	0	3	1	0	1	2	6.0	0.00	—	.111	.200	0	—	0	1	1	0	0.2
	Tex-A	0	0	—	5	0	0	0	0	9	7	0	3	6	11.0	3.00	131	.212	.297	0	—	0	1	1	0	0.0
	Yr	0	0	—	6	0	0	0	0	12	8	0	4	8	9.8	2.25	172	.190	.277	0	—	0	2	2	0	0.2
1991	Tex-A	1	0	1.000	9	0	0	0	0	14²	17	4	8	16	15.3	6.75	60	.274	.357	0	—	0	-4	-4	-0	-0.2
Total 2		1	0	1.000	15	0	0	0	0	26²	25	4	12	24	12.8	4.73	84	.240	.325	0	—	0	-2	-2	0	0.0
● JEFF BITTIGER	Bittiger, Jeffrey Scott b: 4/13/62, Jersey City, N.J. BR/TR, 5'10", 175 lbs. Deb: 9/2/86																									
1986	Phi-N	1	1	.500	3	3	0	0	0	14²	16	2	7	8	14.7	5.52	70	.271	.358	1	.333	1	-3	-3	0	-0.2
1987	Min-A	1	0	1.000	3	1	0	0	0	8¹	11	2	0	5	13.0	5.40	85	.314	.333	0	—	0	-1	-1	-0	-0.1
1988	Chi-A	2	4	.333	25	7	0	0	0	61²	59	11	29	33	12.8	4.23	94	.255	.338	0	—	0	-2	-2	-1	-0.2
1989	Chi-A	0	1	.000	2	1	0	0	0	9²	9	2	6	1	14.0	6.52	58	.257	.366	0	—	0	-3	-3	-0	-0.3
Total 4		4	6	.400	33	12	0	0	0	94¹	95	17	42	53	13.3	4.77	84	.264	.344	1	.333	1	-8	-8	-1	-0.7
● JIM BIVIN	Bivin, James Nathaniel b: 12/11/09, Jackson, Miss. d: 11/7/82, Pueblo, Colo. BR/TR, 6', 155 lbs. Deb: 4/16/35																									
1935	Phi-N	2	9	.182	47	14	0	0	1	161²	220	20	65	54	16.0	5.79	78	.316	.377	7	.146	-1	-32	-23	-1	-1.5
● DAVE BLACK	Black, David b: 4/19/1892, Chicago, Ill. d: 10/27/36, Pittsburgh, Pa. BL/TR, 6'2", 175 lbs. Deb: 5/2/14																									
1914	Chi-F	1	0	1.000	8	1	0	0	0	21	28	1	4	19	11.5	6.12	43	.311	.340	2	.286	1	-9	-10	0	-0.3
1915	Chi-F	6	7	.462	25	10	2	0	0	121¹	104	3	33	43	10.6	2.45	103	.241	.304	4	.108	-3	4	1	2	-0.1
	Bal-F	1	3	.250	8	4	1	0	0	34	32	2	15	10	13.0	3.71	77	.260	.350	3	.250	0	-4	-3	1	-0.3
	Yr	7	10	.412	33	14	3	0	0	155¹	136	5	48	53	10.8	2.72	95	.243	.305	7	.143	-3	0	-2	2	-0.4
1923	Bos-A	0	0	—	2	0	0	0	0	1	2	0	0	0	18.0	0.00	—	.500	.500	0	—	0	0	-0	0	0.0
Total 3		8	10	.444	43	15	4	0	0	181¹	166	6	52	72	11.2	3.18	82	.256	.319	9	.161	-2	-8	-11	2	-0.7
● DON BLACK	Black, Donald Paul b: 7/20/16, Salix, Iowa d: 4/21/59, Cuyahoga Falls, O. BR/TR, 6', 185 lbs. Deb: 4/24/43																									
1943	Phi-A	6	16	.273	33	26	12	1	1	208	193	8	110	65	13.4	4.20	81	.247	.344	13	.188	-1	-21	-19	0	-1.9
1944	Phi-A	10	12	.455	29	27	8	0	0	177¹	177	6	75	78	13.0	4.06	86	.259	.336	11	.186	-1	-12	-11	-0	-1.4
1945	Phi-A	5	11	.313	26	18	0	0	0	125¹	154	5	69	47	16.0	5.17	66	.307	.391	6	.162	-2	-25	-24	-1	-3.1
1946	Cle-A	1	2	.333	18	4	0	0	0	43²	45	5	21	15	13.8	4.53	73	.273	.358	2	.200	0	-5	-6	1	-0.3
1947	Cle-A	10	12	.455	30	28	8	3	0	190²	177	17	85	72	12.4	3.92	89	.249	.330	12	.182	-1	-5	-9	1	-1.0
1948	Cle-A	2	2	.500	18	10	1	0	0	52	57	5	40	16	17.0	5.37	76	.282	.403	3	.200	-0	-6	-8	0	-0.5
Total 6		34	55	.382	154	113	37	4	1	797	803	46	400	293	13.7	4.35	80	.264	.352	47	.184	-4	-74	-76	0	-8.2
● BUD BLACK	Black, Harry Ralston b: 6/30/57, San Mateo, Cal. BL/TL, 6'2", 180 lbs. Deb: 9/5/81																									
1981	Sea-A	0	0	—	2	0	0	0	0	1	2	0	3	0	45.0	0.00	—	.500	.714	0	—	0	0	0	0	-0.2
1982	KC-A	4	6	.400	22	14	0	0	0	88¹	92	10	34	40	13.1	4.58	89	.269	.340	0	—	0	-5	-5	-0	-0.5
1983	KC-A	10	7	.588	24	24	3	0	0	161¹	159	19	43	58	11.4	3.79	107	.257	.308	0	—	0	5	5	2	0.7
1984	*KC-A	17	12	.586	35	35	8	1	0	257	226	22	64	140	10.3	3.12	129	.233	**.283**	0	—	0	25	26	3	3.1
1985	*KC-A	10	15	.400	33	33	5	2	0	205²	216	11	59	122	12.4	4.33	96	.268	.324	0	—	0	-4	-4	-1	-0.5
1986	KC-A	5	10	.333	56	4	0	0	9	121	100	14	43	68	11.2	3.20	133	.225	.303	0	—	0	13	14	1	1.8
1987	KC-A	8	6	.571	29	18	0	0	1	122¹	126	16	35	61	12.2	3.60	126	.265	.322	0	—	0	12	13	-0	1.3
1988	KC-A	2	1	.667	17	0	0	0	0	22	23	2	11	19	13.9	4.91	81	.267	.351	0	—	0	-2	-2	-0	-0.3
	Cle-A	2	3	.400	16	7	0	0	1	59	59	6	23	44	13.1	5.03	82	.262	.341	0	—	0	-7	-6	1	-0.4
	Yr	4	4	.500	33	7	0	0	1	81	82	8	34	63	13.3	5.00	82	.264	.344	0	—	0	-9	-8	0	-0.7
1989	Cle-A	12	11	.522	33	32	6	3	0	222¹	213	14	52	88	10.8	3.36	118	.252	.296	0	—	0	13	15	-1	1.4
1990	Cle-A	11	10	.524	29	29	5	2	0	191	171	17	58	103	11.0	3.53	111	.236	.296	0	—	0	8	8	-0	0.8
	Tor-A	2	1	.667	3	3	0	0	0	15²	12	0	3	3	8.0	4.02	98	.189	.246	0	—	0	-0	-1	-0	0.0
	Yr	13	11	.542	32	32	5	2	0	206²	183	17	61	106	10.6	3.57	110	.230	.286	0	—	0	8	8	0	0.8
1991	SF-N	12	16	.429	34	34	3	3	0	214¹	201	25	71	104	11.6	3.99	90	.251	.315	13	.183	1	-7	-10	2	-0.9

YEAR TM/L	W	L	PCT	G	GS	CG	SH	SV	IP	H	HR	BB	SO	RAT	ERA	ERA+	OAV	OOB	BH	AVG	PB	PR	/A	PD	TPI
1992 SF-N	10	12	.455	28	28	2	1	0	177	178	23	59	82	12.1	3.97	83	.263	.323	3	.056	-3	-9	-13	1	-1.6
1993 SF-N	8	2	.800	16	16	0	0	0	93²	89	13	33	45	11.9	3.56	110	.256	.325	9	.243	2	5	4	1	0.7
1994 SF-N	4	2	.667	10	10	0	0	0	54¹	50	9	16	28	11.4	4.47	90	.245	.309	1	.059	-0	-3	-3	-0	-0.4
Total 14	117	114	.506	387	286	32	12	11	2006	1915	209	607	1005	11.5	3.77	105	.251	.311	26	.145	-1	44	42	9	5.0

● JOE BLACK
Black, Joseph b: 2/8/24, Plainfield, N.J. BR/TR, 6'2", 220 lbs. Deb: 5/1/52

YEAR TM/L	W	L	PCT	G	GS	CG	SH	SV	IP	H	HR	BB	SO	RAT	ERA	ERA+	OAV	OOB	BH	AVG	PB	PR	/A	PD	TPI
1952 *Bro-N	15	4	.789	56	2	1	0	15	142¹	102	9	41	85	9.1	2.15	169	.201	.262	5	.139	-1	**25**	**24**	-2	3.3
1953 *Bro-N	6	3	.667	34	3	0	0	5	72²	74	12	27	42	12.6	5.33	80	.259	.325	4	.235	0	-8	-9	-0	-1.1
1954 Bro-N	0	0	—	5	0	0	0	0	7	11	3	5	3	20.6	11.57	35	.355	.444	0	—	0	-6	-6	-0	0.0
1955 Bro-N	1	0	1.000	6	0	0	0	0	15¹	15	1	5	9	11.7	2.93	138	.273	.333	1	.333	0	2	2	-0	0.1
Cin-N	5	2	.714	32	11	1	0	3	102¹	106	13	25	54	11.5	4.22	100	.263	.306	3	.100	-2	-2	0	-0	-0.3
Yr	6	2	.750	38	11	1	0	3	117²	121	14	30	63	11.5	4.05	104	.264	.309	4	.121	-2	-0	2	-1	-0.2
1956 Cin-N	3	2	.600	32	0	0	0	2	61²	61	11	25	27	12.6	4.52	88	.256	.327	0	.000	-1	-5	-4	-1	-0.5
1957 Was-A	0	1	.000	7	0	0	0	0	12²	22	4	1	2	16.3	7.11	55	.393	.404	0	—	0	-5	-5	-0	-0.3
Total 6	30	12	.714	172	16	2	0	25	414	391	53	129	222	11.3	3.91	102	.248	.306	13	.135	-5	1	3	-3	1.2

● BOB BLACK
Black, Robert Benjamin b: 12/10/1862, Cincinnati, Ohio d: 3/21/33, Sioux City, Iowa Deb: 8/19/1884 ♦

YEAR TM/L	W	L	PCT	G	GS	CG	SH	SV	IP	H	HR	BB	SO	RAT	ERA	ERA+	OAV	OOB	BH	AVG	PB	PR	/A	PD	TPI
1884 KC-U	4	9	.308	16	15	13	0	0	123	127	1	17	93	10.5	3.22	69	.249	.273	36	.247	1	-11	-13	2	-0.8

● BUD BLACK
Black, William Carroll b: 7/9/32, St.Louis, Mo. BR/TR, 6'3", 197 lbs. Deb: 9/13/52

YEAR TM/L	W	L	PCT	G	GS	CG	SH	SV	IP	H	HR	BB	SO	RAT	ERA	ERA+	OAV	OOB	BH	AVG	PB	PR	/A	PD	TPI
1952 Det-A	0	1	.000	2	0	0	0	0	8	14	0	5	0	21.4	10.13	38	.389	.463	0	.000	-0	-6	-6	-0	-0.6
1955 Det-A	1	1	.500	3	2	1	1	0	14	12	0	8	7	14.1	1.29	299	.231	.355	1	.250	0	4	4	0	0.6
1956 Det-A	1	1	.500	5	1	0	0	0	10	10	2	5	7	13.5	3.60	114	.256	.341	0	.000	-0	1	1	0	0.1
Total 3	2	3	.400	10	5	1	1	0	32	36	2	18	14	15.8	4.22	93	.283	.381	1	.111	-1	-1	-1	0	0.1

● CHARLIE BLACKBURN
Blackburn, Foster Edwin b: 1/6/1895, Chicago, Ill. d: 3/9/84, New Port Richey, Fla. BR/TR, 6'1", 165 lbs. Deb: 4/17/15

YEAR TM/L	W	L	PCT	G	GS	CG	SH	SV	IP	H	HR	BB	SO	RAT	ERA	ERA+	OAV	OOB	BH	AVG	PB	PR	/A	PD	TPI
1915 KC-F	0	1	.000	7	2	0	0	0	15²	19	2	13	7	18.4	8.62	31	.306	.427	0	.000	-1	-10	-10	0	-0.6
1921 Chi-A	0	0	—	1	0	0	0	0	1	0	0	1	0	9.0	0.00	—	.000	.333	0	—	0	0	0	-0	0.0
Total 2	0	1	.000	8	2	0	0	0	16²	19	2	14	7	17.8	8.10	34	.297	.423	0	.000	-1	-10	-10	0	-0.6

● GEORGE BLACKBURN
Blackburn, George W. "Smiling George" b: 9/21/1871, Ozark, Mo. TR, 5'11", 184 lbs. Deb: 7/6/1897

YEAR TM/L	W	L	PCT	G	GS	CG	SH	SV	IP	H	HR	BB	SO	RAT	ERA	ERA+	OAV	OOB	BH	AVG	PB	PR	/A	PD	TPI
1897 Bal-N	2	2	.500	5	4	3	0	0	33	34	2	11	12	12.8	6.82	61	.264	.332	1	.077	-2	-9	-10	-0	-1.0

● JIM BLACKBURN
Blackburn, James Ray "Bones" b: 6/19/24, Warsaw, Ky. d: 10/26/69, Cincinnati, Ohio BR/TR, 6'4", 175 lbs. Deb: 7/24/48

YEAR TM/L	W	L	PCT	G	GS	CG	SH	SV	IP	H	HR	BB	SO	RAT	ERA	ERA+	OAV	OOB	BH	AVG	PB	PR	/A	PD	TPI
1948 Cin-N	0	2	.000	16	0	0	0	0	32¹	38	1	14	10	14.5	4.18	94	.302	.371	0	.000	-0	-1	-1	0	-0.1
1951 Cin-N	0	0	—	2	0	0	0	0	3²	8	3	2	1	29.5	17.18	24	.444	.545	0	—	0	-5	-5	0	0.0
Total 2	0	2	.000	18	0	0	0	0	36	46	4	16	11	16.0	5.50	71	.319	.395	0	.000	-0	-6	-6	-0	-0.1

● RON BLACKBURN
Blackburn, Ronald Hamilton b: 4/23/35, Mt.Airy, N.C. BR/TR, 6'0.5", 160 lbs. Deb: 4/15/58

YEAR TM/L	W	L	PCT	G	GS	CG	SH	SV	IP	H	HR	BB	SO	RAT	ERA	ERA+	OAV	OOB	BH	AVG	PB	PR	/A	PD	TPI
1958 Pit-N	2	1	.667	38	2	0	0	3	63²	61	7	27	31	12.9	3.39	114	.261	.345	2	.286	1	4	3	1	0.4
1959 Pit-N	1	1	.500	26	0	0	0	1	44¹	50	5	15	19	13.6	3.65	106	.286	.349	1	.200	1	1	1	-1	0.1
Total 2	3	2	.600	64	2	0	0	4	108	111	12	42	50	13.2	3.50	110	.271	.346	2	.250	2	5	4	0	0.5

● LENA BLACKBURNE
Blackburne, Russell Aubrey "Slats"
b: 10/23/1886, Clifton Heights, Pa. d: 2/29/68, Riverside, N.J. BR/TR, 5'11", 160 lbs. Deb: 4/14/10 MC♦

YEAR TM/L	W	L	PCT	G	GS	CG	SH	SV	IP	H	HR	BB	SO	RAT	ERA	ERA+	OAV	OOB	BH	AVG	PB	PR	/A	PD	TPI
1929 Chi-A	0	0	—	1	0	0	0	0	0¹	1	0	0	0	27.0	0.00	—	1.000	1.000	0	—	0	0	0	0	0.0

● EWELL BLACKWELL
Blackwell, Ewell "The Whip" b: 10/23/22, Fresno, Cal. BR/TR, 6'6", 195 lbs. Deb: 4/21/42

YEAR TM/L	W	L	PCT	G	GS	CG	SH	SV	IP	H	HR	BB	SO	RAT	ERA	ERA+	OAV	OOB	BH	AVG	PB	PR	/A	PD	TPI
1942 Cin-N	0	0	—	2	0	0	0	0	3	3	0	3	1	18.0	6.00	55	.231	.375	0	.000	-0	-1	-1	0	0.0
1946 Cin-N★	9	13	.409	33	25	10	5	0	194¹	160	1	79	100	11.3	2.45	136	.226	.307	6	.107	-3	21	19	4	2.3
1947 Cin-N★	**22**	8	.733	33	33	**23**	6	0	273	227	10	95	**193**	10.7	2.47	166	.234	.304	13	.123	-5	48	49	5	**5.2**
1948 Cin-N★	7	9	.438	22	20	4	1	1	138²	134	12	52	114	12.3	4.54	86	.251	.323	11	.229	1	-9	-10	4	-0.5
1949 Cin-N	5	5	.500	30	4	0	0	1	76²	80	7	34	55	13.7	4.23	99	.271	.352	4	.211	-0	-2	-0	1	0.1
1950 Cin-N★	17	15	.531	40	32	18	0	1	261	203	12	112	188	11.3	2.97	143	**.210**	.301	13	.146	-2	34	37	2	**4.3**
1951 Cin-N★	16	15	.516	38	32	11	2	2	232²	204	16	97	120	12.0	3.44	118	.233	.315	24	.293	7	13	16	0	2.9
1952 Cin-N	3	12	.200	23	17	3	0	0	102	107	6	60	48	15.2	5.38	70	.275	.379	5	.156	-0	-19	-18	-0	-2.4
*NY-A	1	0	1.000	5	2	0	0	1	16	12	0	12	7	13.5	0.56	591	.203	.338	1	.200	-0	6	5	-0	0.4
1953 NY-A	2	0	1.000	8	4	0	0	1	19²	17	2	13	11	14.2	3.66	101	.233	.356	0	—	-1	1	1	-0	-0.1
1955 KC-A	0	1	.000	2	0	0	0	0	4	3	1	5	2	20.3	6.75	62	.250	.500	0	—	0	-1	-1	-0	-0.3
Total 10	82	78	.512	236	169	69	15	10	1321	1150	67	562	839	12.0	3.30	120	.235	.319	77	.174	-3	91	96	16	11.9

● GEORGE BLAEHOLDER
Blaeholder, George Franklin b: 1/26/04, Orange, Cal. d: 12/29/47, Garden Grove, Cal. BR/TR, 5'11", 175 lbs. Deb: 4/20/25

YEAR TM/L	W	L	PCT	G	GS	CG	SH	SV	IP	H	HR	BB	SO	RAT	ERA	ERA+	OAV	OOB	BH	AVG	PB	PR	/A	PD	TPI
1925 StL-A	0	0	—	2	0	0	0	0	2	6	3	1	1	36.0	31.50	18	.600	.667	0	—	0	-6	-6	-0	0.0
1927 StL-A	0	1	.000	1	1	1	0	0	9	8	1	4	2	13.0	5.00	87	.258	.361	1	.333	0	-1	-1	0	0.0
1928 StL-A	10	15	.400	38	26	9	1	3	214¹	235	23	52	87	12.1	4.37	96	.280	.324	15	.211	2	-8	-4	5	0.2
1929 StL-A	14	15	.483	42	24	13	4	2	222	237	18	61	72	12.1	4.18	106	.275	.323	9	.122	-1	2	6	6	0.9
1930 StL-A	11	13	.458	37	23	10	1	4	191¹	235	20	46	70	13.3	4.61	106	.303	.343	12	.185	-1	6	6	-1	0.4
1931 StL-A	11	15	.423	35	32	13	1	0	226¹	280	15	56	79	13.4	4.53	102	.295	.335	11	.143	-3	-4	3	3	0.3
1932 StL-A	14	14	.500	42	36	16	1	0	258¹	304	19	76	80	13.3	4.70	103	.290	.340	12	.136	-4	-6	4	0	0.1
1933 StL-A	15	19	.441	38	36	14	2	0	255²	283	24	69	63	12.4	4.72	99	.280	.326	14	.182	-1	-12	-2	3	0.0
1934 StL-A	14	18	.438	39	33	14	1	3	234¹	276	16	68	66	13.2	4.22	118	.296	.343	7	.093	-5	7	20	0	1.9
1935 StL-A	1	1	.500	6	2	0	0	0	17²	25	3	6	10	15.8	7.13	67	.342	.392	0	.000	-1	-5	-5	1	-0.4
Phi-A	6	10	.375	23	22	10	1	0	149	173	10	49	22	13.4	3.99	114	.289	.343	2	.043	-6	8	9	2	0.4
Yr	7	11	.389	29	24	10	1	0	166²	198	13	55	22	13.7	4.32	106	.295	.348	2	.040	-7	3	5	2	0.0
1936 Cle-A	8	4	.667	35	16	6	1	0	134¹	158	21	47	30	13.9	5.09	99	.295	.356	6	.130	-3	-1	-2	2	-0.2
Total 11	104	125	.454	338	251	106	14	12	1914¹	2220	173	535	572	13.0	4.54	103	.290	.337	89	.142	-25	-26	30	20	3.6

● DENNIS BLAIR
Blair, Dennis Herman b: 6/5/54, Middletown, Ohio BR/TR, 6'5", 182 lbs. Deb: 5/26/74

YEAR TM/L	W	L	PCT	G	GS	CG	SH	SV	IP	H	HR	BB	SO	RAT	ERA	ERA+	OAV	OOB	BH	AVG	PB	PR	/A	PD	TPI
1974 Mon-N	11	7	.611	22	22	4	1	0	146	113	7	72	76	11.7	3.27	117	.210	.308	6	.118	-2	6	9	3	1.2
1975 Mon-N	8	15	.348	30	27	1	0	0	163¹	150	14	106	82	14.3	3.80	101	.251	.366	7	.143	-1	-3	-0	-1	-0.2
1976 Mon-N	0	2	.000	5	4	1	0	0	15²	21	1	11	9	19.5	4.02	92	.300	.410	0	—	0	-1	-1	-0	-0.1
1980 SD-N	0	1	.000	5	1	0	0	0	14	18	3	3	11	13.5	6.43	53	.310	.344	1	.200	0	-4	-5	-1	-0.3
Total 4	19	25	.432	62	54	6	1	0	339	302	25	192	178	13.4	3.69	103	.239	.344	14	.128	-4	3	4	1	0.6

● WILLIE BLAIR
Blair, William Allen b: 12/18/65, Paintsville, Ky. BR/TR, 6'1", 185 lbs. Deb: 4/11/90

YEAR TM/L	W	L	PCT	G	GS	CG	SH	SV	IP	H	HR	BB	SO	RAT	ERA	ERA+	OAV	OOB	BH	AVG	PB	PR	/A	PD	TPI
1990 Tor-A	3	5	.375	27	6	0	0	0	68²	66	4	28	43	12.5	4.06	97	.250	.324	0	—	0	-1	-1	-0	-0.3
1991 Cle-A	2	3	.400	11	5	0	0	0	36	58	7	10	13	17.3	6.75	62	.377	.418	0	—	0	-11	-10	0	-1.3
1992 Hou-N	5	7	.417	29	8	0	0	0	78²	74	9	25	48	11.6	4.00	84	.249	.312	1	.059	-1	-4	-6	-1	-1.0
1993 Col-N	6	10	.375	46	18	0	0	0	146	184	20	42	84	14.1	4.75	100	.306	.354	4	.111	-2	-11	0	-0	-0.2
1994 Col-N	0	5	.000	47	1	0	0	3	77²	91	9	39	68	16.3	5.79	86	.308	.391	0	.000	-0	-14	-7	-1	-0.6
Total 5	16	30	.348	160	38	0	0	3	407	480	45	144	256	14.0	4.86	89	.294	.355	5	.085	-3	-41	-25	-4	-3.4

● BILL BLAIR
Blair, William Ellsworth b: 9/17/1863, Pittsburgh, Pa. d: 2/22/1890, Pittsburgh, Pa. BL/TL, 5'8.5", 172 lbs. Deb: 7/19/1888

YEAR TM/L	W	L	PCT	G	GS	CG	SH	SV	IP	H	HR	BB	SO	RAT	ERA	ERA+	OAV	OOB	BH	AVG	PB	PR	/A	PD	TPI
1888 Phi-a	1	3	.250	4	4	3	0	0	31	29	0	8	16	11.0	2.61	114	.239	.291	4	.308	1	2	1	1	0.3

YEAR	TM/L	W	L	PCT	G	GS	CG	SH	SV	IP	H	HR	BB	SO	RAT	ERA	ERA+	OAV	OOB	BH	AVG	PB	PR	/A	PD	TPI

● DICK BLAISDELL   Blaisdell, Howard Carleton b: 6/18/1862, Bradford, Mass.   d: 8/20/1886, Malden, Mass.   Deb: 7/9/1884

| 1884 | KC-U | 0 | 3 | .000 | 3 | 3 | 3 | 0 | 0 | 26 | 49 | 0 | 4 | 8 | 18.3 | 8.65 | 26 | .377 | .396 | 5 | .313 | 0 | -18 | -19 | -1 | -1.4 |

● ED BLAKE   Blake, Edward James b: 12/23/25, E.St.Louis, Ill.   BR/TR, 5'11", 175 lbs.   Deb: 5/1/51

1951	Cin-N	0	0	—	3	0	0	0	0	4	10	3	1	1	24.8	11.25	36	.476	.500	0	—	0	-3	-3	0	0.0
1952	Cin-N	0	0	—	2	0	0	0	0	3	3	0	0	0	9.0	0.00	—	.250	.250	0	—	0	1	1	0	0.0
1953	Cin-N	0	0	—	1	0	0	0	0	0	1	0	1	0	—	∞	—	1.000	1.000	0	—	0	-2	-2	0	-0.2
1957	KC-A	0	0	—	2	0	0	0	0	1²	1	1	2	0	16.2	5.40	73	.167	.375	0	—	0	-0	-0	-0	0.0
Total	4	0	0	—	8	0	0	0	0	8²	15	4	4	1	19.7	8.31	48	.375	.432	0	—	0	-4	-4	1	-0.2

● SHERIFF BLAKE   Blake, John Frederick b: 9/17/1899, Ansted, W.Va.   d: 10/31/82, Beckley, W.Va.   BB/TR, 6', 180 lbs.   Deb: 6/29/20

1920	Pit-N	0	0	—	6	0	0	0	0	13¹	21	3	6	7	18.9	8.10	40	.368	.438	1	.250	-0	-7	-7	0	0.0
1924	Chi-N	6	6	.500	29	11	4	0	1	106¹	123	3	44	42	14.3	4.57	85	.299	.370	9	.290	1	-8	-8	1	-0.6
1925	Chi-N	10	18	.357	36	31	14	0	2	231¹	260	17	114	93	14.7	4.86	89	.287	.370	12	.152	-4	-15	-14	0	-1.8
1926	Chi-N	11	12	.478	39	27	11	4	1	197²	204	7	92	95	13.8	3.60	107	.280	.366	14	.215	-1	5	5	2	0.7
1927	Chi-N	13	14	.481	32	27	13	2	0	224¹	238	3	82	64	13.0	3.29	117	.282	.348	16	.193	-2	16	14	3	1.6
1928	Chi-N	17	11	.607	34	29	16	4	1	240²	209	4	101	78	11.7	2.47	156	.240	.321	19	.216	0	41	37	-2	3.8
1929	*Chi-N	14	13	.519	35	30	13	1	1	218¹	244	8	103	70	14.4	4.29	108	.291	.370	14	.173	-2	10	8	-2	0.5
1930	Chi-N	10	14	.417	34	24	7	0	0	186²	213	14	99	80	15.2	4.82	101	.291	.378	15	.227	-1	3	1	3	0.3
1931	Chi-N	0	4	.000	16	5	0	0	0	50	64	4	26	29	16.4	5.22	74	.312	.392	8	.500	3	-8	-8	1	-0.2
	Phi-N	4	5	.444	14	9	1	0	1	71	90	2	35	31	16.2	5.58	76	.305	.384	6	.240	0	-13	-11	2	-0.9
	Yr	4	9	.308	30	14	1	0	1	121	154	6	61	60	16.2	5.43	75	.307	.386	14	.341	3	-21	-18	3	-1.1
1937	StL-A	2	2	.500	15	1	0	0	1	36²	55	5	20	12	18.4	7.61	63	.350	.424	1	.100	-1	-12	-11	0	-1.1
	StL-N	0	3	.000	14	2	2	0	0	43²	45	1	18	20	13.0	3.71	107	.271	.342	3	.300	1	1	1	0	0.2
Total	10	87	102	.460	304	196	81	11	8	1620	1766	68	740	621	14.1	4.13	101	.284	.363	118	.211	-6	12	9	9	2.5

● AL BLANCHE   Blanche, Prosby Albert (b: Prosper Belangio) b: 9/21/09, Somerville, Mass.   BR/TR, 6', 178 lbs.   Deb: 8/23/35

1935	Bos-N	0	0	—	6	0	0	0	0	17¹	14	0	4	9	9.9	1.56	243	.230	.288	1	.167	-0	5	4	0	0.0
1936	Bos-N	0	1	.000	11	0	0	0	1	16	20	1	8	4	16.3	6.19	62	.303	.387	1	.250	0	-4	-4	1	-0.2
Total	2	0	1	.000	17	0	0	0	1	33¹	34	1	13	8	13.0	3.78	101	.268	.340	2	.200	0	1	0	1	-0.2

● GIL BLANCO   Blanco, Gilbert Henry b: 12/15/45, Phoenix, Ariz.   BL/TL, 6'5", 205 lbs.   Deb: 4/24/65

1965	NY-A	1	1	.500	17	1	0	0	0	20¹	16	1	12	14	12.8	3.98	85	.232	.354	0	—	0	-1	-1	-1	-0.2
1966	KC-A	2	4	.333	11	6	0	0	0	38¹	31	3	36	21	16.7	4.70	72	.237	.415	2	.167	-0	-5	-6	0	-0.8
Total	2	3	5	.375	28	6	0	0	0	58²	47	4	48	35	15.3	4.45	76	.235	.395	2	.167	-0	-7	-7	-0	-1.0

● FRED BLANDING   Blanding, Frederick James "Fritz" b: 2/8/1888, Redlands, Cal.   d: 7/16/50, Salem, Va.   BR/TR, 6', 185 lbs.   Deb: 9/15/10

1910	Cle-A	2	2	.500	6	5	4	1	0	45¹	43	0	12	25	11.7	2.78	93	.254	.319	2	.111	-1	-1	-1	-1	-0.3
1911	Cle-A	7	11	.389	29	16	11	0	2	176	190	5	60	80	13.1	3.68	93	.283	.347	17	.262	2	-7	-5	-0	-0.3
1912	Cle-A	18	14	.563	39	31	23	1	1	262	259	4	79	75	11.7	2.92	117	.267	.324	21	.226	1	12	14	0	1.8
1913	Cle-A	15	10	.600	41	22	14	3	0	215	234	6	72	63	12.9	2.55	119	.282	.341	21	.244	4	9	12	-2	1.5
1914	Cle-A	3	9	.250	29	12	5	0	1	116	133	0	54	35	14.6	3.96	73	.301	.378	4	.103	-2	-16	-14	-1	-1.5
Total	5	45	46	.495	144	86	57	5	4	814¹	859	15	277	278	12.7	3.13	102	.279	.341	65	.216	4	-3	6	-2	1.2

● FRED BLANK   Blank, Frederick August b: 6/18/1874, DeSoto, Mo.   d: 2/5/36, St.Louis, Mo.   BL/TL, 6'0.5", 175 lbs.   Deb: 6/20/1894

| 1894 | Cin-N | 0 | 1 | .000 | 1 | 1 | 1 | 0 | 0 | 8 | 5 | 0 | 9 | 1 | 15.8 | 4.50 | 124 | .178 | .378 | 0 | .000 | -1 | 1 | 1 | 1 | 0.1 |

● HOMER BLANKENSHIP   Blankenship, Homer "Si" b: 8/4/02, Bonham, Tex.   d: 6/22/74, Longview, Tex.   BR/TR, 6', 185 lbs.   Deb: 9/6/22   F

1922	Chi-A	0	0	—	4	0	0	0	0	13	21	1	5	3	18.0	4.85	84	.389	.441	0	.000	-1	-1	-0	-0.1
1923	Chi-A	1	1	.500	4	0	0	0	1	5	9	0	1	1	18.0	3.60	110	.429	.455	0	—	0	0	0	0	0.1
1928	Pit-N	0	2	.000	5	2	1	0	0	21²	27	1	9	6	15.0	5.82	70	.321	.387	3	.375	1	-4	-4	1	-0.2
Total	3	1	3	.250	13	2	1	0	1	39²	57	2	15	10	16.3	5.22	78	.358	.414	3	.250	0	-5	-5	1	-0.2

● KEVIN BLANKENSHIP   Blankenship, Kevin De Wayne b: 1/26/63, Anaheim, Cal.   BR/TR, 6', 180 lbs.   Deb: 9/20/88

1988	Atl-N	0	1	.000	2	2	0	0	0	10²	7	0	7	5	12.7	3.38	109	.194	.341	0	.000	0	0	0	-0	0.0
	Chi-N	1	0	1.000	1	1	0	0	0	5	7	2	1	4	14.4	7.20	50	.318	.348	0	.000	0	-2	-2	-0	-0.4
	Yr	1	1	.500	3	3	0	0	0	15²	14	2	8	9	12.6	4.60	79	.237	.328	0	.000	-1	-2	-2	-1	-0.4
1989	Chi-N	0	0	—	2	0	0	0	0	5¹	4	0	2	2	10.1	1.69	223	.200	.273	0	.000	0	1	1	-0	0.0
1990	Chi-N	0	2	.000	3	2	0	0	0	12¹	13	1	6	5	13.9	5.84	70	.265	.345	0	.000	0	-3	-2	0	-0.4
Total	3	1	3	.250	8	5	0	0	0	33¹	31	3	16	16	13.0	4.59	83	.244	.333	0	.000	0	-4	-3	-1	-0.8

● TED BLANKENSHIP   Blankenship, Theodore b: 5/10/01, Bonham, Tex.   d: 1/14/45, Atoka, Okla.   BR/TR, 6'1", 170 lbs.   Deb: 7/2/22   F

1922	Chi-A	8	10	.444	24	15	7	0	1	127²	124	4	47	42	12.2	3.81	107	.266	.335	7	.171	-1	3	4	0	0.4
1923	Chi-A	9	14	.391	44	23	9	1	0	204²	219	8	100	57	14.2	4.35	91	.287	.372	16	.211	2	-8	-9	-1	-0.8
1924	Chi-A	7	6	.538	25	11	7	0	1	129¹	167	3	38	36	14.3	5.01	82	.317	.364	15	.326	6	-11	-13	-2	-0.8
1925	Chi-A	17	8	.680	40	23	16	3	1	232	218	11	69	81	11.1	3.03	137	.253	.308	18	.205	2	35	29	-4	2.5
1926	Chi-A	13	10	.565	29	26	15	1	1	209¹	217	13	65	66	12.2	3.61	107	.273	.328	10	.132	-2	10	6	-2	0.1
1927	Chi-A	12	17	.414	37	34	11	3	0	236²	280	14	74	51	13.5	5.06	80	.299	.352	15	.188	3	-24	-27	-3	-2.6
1928	Chi-A	9	11	.450	27	22	8	0	0	158	186	9	80	36	15.3	4.61	88	.306	.388	10	.169	-0	-10	-10	-2	-1.4
1929	Chi-A	0	2	.000	8	3	0	0	0	18¹	28	3	9	7	18.2	8.84	48	.359	.425	1	.250	-0	-9	-9	-1	-0.9
1930	Chi-A	2	1	.667	7	1	0	0	0	15²	23	0	7	2	19.0	9.20	50	.311	.443	1	.200	-0	-7	-7	-1	-1.2
Total	9	77	79	.494	241	156	73	8	4	1330²	1462	63	489	378	13.3	4.29	94	.287	.351	93	.196	7	-22	-36	-15	-4.7

● CY BLANTON   Blanton, Darrell Elijah b: 7/6/08, Waurika, Okla.   d: 9/13/45, Norman, Okla.   BL/TR, 5'11.5", 180 lbs.   Deb: 9/23/34

1934	Pit-N	0	1	.000	1	1	0	0	0	8	5	1	4	5	11.3	3.38	122	.161	.278	0	.000	0	1	1	0	0.1
1935	Pit-N	18	13	.581	35	31	23	4	1	254¹	220	3	55	142	9.8	2.58	159	.229	.272	13	.134	-4	41	43	2	4.7
1936	Pit-N	13	15	.464	44	32	15	4	3	235²	235	9	55	127	11.2	3.51	115	.257	.301	13	.155	-3	13	14	1	1.3
1937	Pit-N★	14	12	.538	36	34	14	4	0	242²	250	13	76	143	12.3	3.30	117	.266	.324	14	.165	-0	17	15	-0	1.4
1938	Pit-N	11	7	.611	29	25	10	1	0	172²	190	13	46	80	12.4	3.70	103	.281	.329	13	.203	-1	2	2	0	0.2
1939	Pit-N	2	3	.400	10	6	2	0	0	42	45	4	10	11	11.8	4.29	90	.266	.307	4	.286	1	-2	-2	-0	-0.2
1940	Phi-N	3	4	.571	13	10	5	0	0	77	82	7	21	24	12.2	4.32	90	.272	.322	2	.083	-1	-4	-4	0	-0.2
1941	Phi-N☆	6	13	.316	28	25	7	1	0	163²	186	11	57	64	13.5	4.51	82	.284	.344	6	.118	-2	-16	-15	-3	-2.0
1942	Phi-N	0	4	.000	6	3	0	0	0	22¹	30	3	13	15	17.7	5.64	59	.345	.436	1	.125	-0	-6	-6	0	-1.0
Total	9	68	71	.489	202	167	75	14	4	1218¹	1243	64	337	611	11.8	3.55	110	.262	.314	66	.154	-11	45	49	2	4.2

● WADE BLASINGAME   Blasingame, Wade Allen b: 11/22/43, Deming, N.Mex.   BL/TL, 6'1", 185 lbs.   Deb: 9/17/63

1963	Mil-N	0	0	—	2	0	0	0	0	2	9	0	2	6	27.0	12.00	27	.467	.529	0	—	0	-3	-3	0	0.0
1964	Mil-N	9	5	.643	28	13	3	1	2	116²	113	15	51	70	12.9	4.24	83	.257	.334	7	.175	3	-9	-9	0	-0.7
1965	Mil-N	16	10	.615	38	36	10	1	1	224²	200	17	116	117	12.9	3.77	94	.244	.341	15	.185	1	-6	-6	1	-0.4
1966	Atl-N	3	7	.300	16	12	0	0	0	67²	71	5	25	34	13.0	5.32	68	.272	.340	6	.217	1	-13	-13	-0	-1.6
1967	Atl-N	0	1	.000	10	0	0	0	0	25¹	27	1	21	20	17.4	4.62	72	.287	.422	1	.200	-0	-4	-4	0	-0.0
	Hou-N	4	7	.364	15	14	0	0	0	77	91	9	27	46	14.0	5.96	56	.298	.359	4	.182	2	-22	-23	-0	-2.7
	Yr	5	7	.417	25	14	0	0	0	102¹	118	10	48	66	14.8	5.63	59	.295	.373	5	.172	2	-26	-26	0	-2.7
1968	Hou-N	1	2	.333	22	2	0	0	1	36	45	3	10	22	13.8	4.75	62	.308	.353	0	.000	0	-7	-7	1	-0.5
1969	Hou-N	5	5	.000	26	5	0	0	0	52	66	4	33	33	17.5	5.37	66	.306	.402	0	.000	-1	-10	-11	0	-1.1

YEAR TM/L	W	L	PCT	G	GS	CG	SH	SV	IP	H	HR	BB	SO	RAT	ERA	ERA+	OAV	OOB	BH	AVG	PB	PR	/A	PD	TPI
1970 Hou-N	3	3	.500	13	13	1	0	0	77²	76	4	23	55	11.7	3.48	112	.261	.320	2	.083	-0	5	3	0	0.3
1971 Hou-N	9	11	.450	30	28	2	0	0	158¹	177	11	45	93	13.4	4.60	73	.285	.346	10	.204	4	-20	-22	1	-2.0
1972 Hou-N	0	0	—	10	0	0	0	0	8¹	4	1	8	9	15.1	8.64	39	.148	.378	0	—	0	-5	-5	0	0.0
NY-A	0	1	.000	12	1	0	0	0	17	14	5	11	7	13.8	4.24	70	.250	.382	0	.000	0	-2	-2	1	0.0
Total 10	46	51	.474	222	128	16	2	5	863²	891	75	372	512	13.5	4.52	77	.271	.350	44	.166	14	-96	-101	4	-8.5

● STEVE BLASS
Blass, Stephen Robert   b: 4/18/42, Canaan, Conn.   BR/TR, 6′, 165 lbs.   Deb: 5/10/64

YEAR TM/L	W	L	PCT	G	GS	CG	SH	SV	IP	H	HR	BB	SO	RAT	ERA	ERA+	OAV	OOB	BH	AVG	PB	PR	/A	PD	TPI
1964 Pit-N	5	8	.385	24	13	3	1	0	104²	107	9	45	67	13.2	4.04	87	.266	.341	2	.067	-1	-6	-6	0	-0.8
1966 Pit-N	11	7	.611	34	25	1	0	0	155²	173	12	46	76	12.8	3.87	92	.284	.336	12	.231	-1	-5	-5	-3	-0.7
1967 Pit-N	6	8	.429	32	16	2	0	0	126²	126	12	47	72	12.4	3.55	95	.261	.329	5	.128	-1	-3	-3	0	-0.3
1968 Pit-N	18	6	**.750**	33	31	12	7	0	220¹	191	13	57	132	10.3	2.12	138	.234	.288	11	.138	-1	21	20	-1	2.1
1969 Pit-N	16	10	.615	38	32	9	0	2	210	207	21	86	147	12.8	4.46	78	.258	.335	21	.250	6	-20	-23	3	-1.8
1970 Pit-N	10	12	.455	31	31	6	1	0	196²	187	14	73	120	12.1	3.52	111	.254	.326	8	.114	-2	11	8	0	0.6
1971 *Pit-N	15	8	.652	33	33	12	**5**	0	240	226	16	68	136	11.1	2.85	119	.249	.303	10	.120	-3	16	14	1	1.1
1972 *Pit-N★	19	8	.704	33	32	11	2	0	249²	227	18	84	117	11.4	2.49	134	.246	.311	15	.183	1	27	23	2	2.9
1973 Pit-N	3	9	.250	23	18	1	0	0	88²	109	11	84	27	20.8	9.85	36	.313	.462	10	.417	4	-61	-62	1	-6.3
1974 Pit-N	0	0	—	1	0	0	0	0	5	7	2	7	2	21.6	9.00	38	.238	.429	0	.000	0	-3	-3	0	0.0
Total 10	103	76	.575	282	231	57	16	2	1597¹	1558	128	597	896	12.4	3.63	94	.258	.328	94	.172	4	-21	-37	3	-3.2

● STEVE BLATERIC
Blateric, Stephen Lawrence   b: 3/20/44, Denver, Colo.   BR/TR, 6′3″, 200 lbs.   Deb: 9/17/71

YEAR TM/L	W	L	PCT	G	GS	CG	SH	SV	IP	H	HR	BB	SO	RAT	ERA	ERA+	OAV	OOB	BH	AVG	PB	PR	/A	PD	TPI
1971 Cin-N	0	0	—	2	0	0	0	0	2²	5	2	0	4	20.3	13.50	25	.385	.429	0	—	0	-3	-3	0	0.0
1972 NY-A	0	0	—	1	0	0	0	0	4	2	0	0	4	4.5	0.00	—	.143	.143	0	.000	-0	1	1	0	0.0
1975 Cal-A	0	0	—	2	0	0	0	0	4¹	9	0	1	5	20.8	6.23	57	.429	.455	0	—	0	-1	-1	-0	0.4
Total 3	0	0	—	5	0	0	0	0	11	16	2	1	13	14.7	5.73	57	.333	.360	0	.000	-0	-3	-3	0	0.4

● HENRY BLAUVELT
Blauvelt, Henry Russell   b: 4/8/1873, Nyack, N.Y.   d: 12/28/26, Portland, Ore.   Deb: 6/22/1890

YEAR TM/L	W	L	PCT	G	GS	CG	SH	SV	IP	H	HR	BB	SO	RAT	ERA	ERA+	OAV	OOB	BH	AVG	PB	PR	/A	PD	TPI
1890 Roc-a	0	0	—	2	0	0	0	0	12¹	19	0	8	5	19.7	10.22	35	.342	.425	3	.500	1	-9	-9	0	0.1

● GARY BLAYLOCK
Blaylock, Gary Nelson   b: 10/11/31, Clarkton, Mo.   BR/TR, 6′, 196 lbs.   Deb: 4/10/59   C

YEAR TM/L	W	L	PCT	G	GS	CG	SH	SV	IP	H	HR	BB	SO	RAT	ERA	ERA+	OAV	OOB	BH	AVG	PB	PR	/A	PD	TPI
1959 StL-N	4	5	.444	26	12	3	0	0	100	117	14	43	61	14.6	5.13	83	.298	.371	4	.118	0	-13	-10	1	-0.7
NY-A	0	1	.000	15	1	0	0	0	25²	30	0	15	20	16.1	3.51	104	.306	.404	1	.500	1	1	0	-0	0.0
Total 1	4	6	.400	41	13	3	0	0	125²	147	14	58	81	14.9	4.80	86	.300	.377	5	.139	1	-12	-10	1	-0.7

● BOB BLAYLOCK
Blaylock, Robert Edward   b: 6/28/35, Chattanooga, Okla   BR/TR, 6′1″, 185 lbs.   Deb: 7/22/56

YEAR TM/L	W	L	PCT	G	GS	CG	SH	SV	IP	H	HR	BB	SO	RAT	ERA	ERA+	OAV	OOB	BH	AVG	PB	PR	/A	PD	TPI
1956 StL-N	1	6	.143	14	6	0	0	0	41	45	7	24	39	15.1	6.37	59	.276	.369	1	.091	-1	-12	-12	0	-1.8
1959 StL-N	0	1	.000	3	1	0	0	0	9	8	1	3	3	11.0	4.00	106	.229	.289	-0	.000	-0	-0	0	0	0.0
Total 2	1	7	.125	17	7	0	0	0	50	53	8	27	42	14.4	5.94	65	.268	.356	1	.083	-1	-12	-12	0	-1.8

● RAY BLEMKER
Blemker, Raymond   b: 8/9/37, Huntingburg, Ind.   d: 2/15/94, Evansville, Ind   BR/TL, 5′11″, 190 lbs.   Deb: 7/3/60

YEAR TM/L	W	L	PCT	G	GS	CG	SH	SV	IP	H	HR	BB	SO	RAT	ERA	ERA+	OAV	OOB	BH	AVG	PB	PR	/A	PD	TPI
1960 KC-A	0	0	—	1	0	0	0	0	1²	3	1	2	0	32.4	27.00	15	.375	.545	0	—	0	-4	-4	-0	0.0

● CLARENCE BLETHEN
Blethen, Clarence Waldo "Climax"   b: 7/11/1893, Dover-Foxcroft, Maine   d: 4/11/73, Frederick, Md.   BL/TR, 5′11″, 165 lbs.   Deb: 9/17/23

YEAR TM/L	W	L	PCT	G	GS	CG	SH	SV	IP	H	HR	BB	SO	RAT	ERA	ERA+	OAV	OOB	BH	AVG	PB	PR	/A	PD	TPI
1923 Bos-A	0	0	—	5	0	0	0	0	17²	29	4	9	7	18.3	7.13	58	.382	.434	0	.000	-1	-6	-6	-1	-0.2
1929 Bro-N	0	0	—	2	0	0	0	0	2	4	0	3	0	31.5	9.00	51	.444	.583	0	—	-0	-1	-1	0	0.0
Total 2	0	0	—	7	0	0	0	0	19²	33	4	10	2	19.7	7.32	57	.388	.453	0	.000	-1	-7	-7	-1	-0.2

● BOB BLEWETT
Blewett, Robert Lawrence   b: 6/28/1877, Fond Du Lac, Wis.   d: 3/17/58, Sedro Woolley, Wash.   BL/TL, 5′11″, 170 lbs.   Deb: 6/17/02

YEAR TM/L	W	L	PCT	G	GS	CG	SH	SV	IP	H	HR	BB	SO	RAT	ERA	ERA+	OAV	OOB	BH	AVG	PB	PR	/A	PD	TPI
1902 NY-N	0	2	.000	5	3	2	0	0	28	39	0	7	8	15.1	4.82	58	.329	.371	0	.000	-1	-6	-6	-1	-0.6

● ELMER BLISS
Bliss, Elmer Ward   b: 3/9/1875, Penfield, Pa.   d: 3/18/62, Bradford, Pa.   BL/TR, 6′, 180 lbs.   Deb: 9/28/03   ♦

YEAR TM/L	W	L	PCT	G	GS	CG	SH	SV	IP	H	HR	BB	SO	RAT	ERA	ERA+	OAV	OOB	BH	AVG	PB	PR	/A	PD	TPI
1903 NY-A	1	0	1.000	1	0	0	0	0	7	4	0	3	5.1		0.00	—	.167	.167	0	.000	-0	2	2	-0	0.3

● TERRY BLOCKER
Blocker, Terry Fennell   b: 8/18/59, Columbia, S.C.   BL/TL, 6′2″, 195 lbs.   Deb: 4/11/85   ♦

YEAR TM/L	W	L	PCT	G	GS	CG	SH	SV	IP	H	HR	BB	SO	RAT	ERA	ERA+	OAV	OOB	BH	AVG	PB	PR	/A	PD	TPI
1989 Atl-N	0	0	—	1	0	0	0	0	1	0	0	2	18.0		0.00	—	.000	.500	7	.226	0	0	0	0	0.0

● JOE BLONG
Blong, Joseph Myles   b: 9/17/1853, St.Louis, Mo.   d: 9/16/1892, St.Louis, Mo.   BR/TR,   Deb: 5/4/1875   ♦

YEAR TM/L	W	L	PCT	G	GS	CG	SH	SV	IP	H	HR	BB	SO	RAT	ERA	ERA+	OAV	OOB	BH	AVG	PB	PR	/A	PD	TPI
1875 RS-n	3	12	.200	15	15	12	1	0	129	169	0	2		11.9	3.35	72	.285	.287	10	.147	-4	-13	-13		-1.4
1876 StL-N	0	0	—	1	0	0	0	0	4	2	0	1	0	6.8	0.00	—	.154	.214	62	.235	-0	1	1	0	0.0
1877 StL-N	10	9	.526	25	21	17	0	0	187¹	203	0	38	51	11.6	2.74	95	.262	.296	47	.216	1	-3	-2	-2	-0.4
Total 2	10	9	.526	26	21	17	0	0	191¹	205	0	39	51	11.5	2.68	97	.260	.295	109	.226	1	-2	-1	-1	-0.4

● VIDA BLUE
Blue, Vida Rochelle   b: 7/28/49, Mansfield, La.   BB/TL, 6′, 189 lbs.   Deb: 7/20/69

YEAR TM/L	W	L	PCT	G	GS	CG	SH	SV	IP	H	HR	BB	SO	RAT	ERA	ERA+	OAV	OOB	BH	AVG	PB	PR	/A	PD	TPI
1969 Oak-A	1	1	.500	12		0	0	1	42	49	13	18	24	14.4	6.64	52	.290	.358	0	.000	-0	-14	-15	-1	-0.8
1970 Oak-A	2	0	1.000	6	6	2	2	0	38²	20	0	12	35	7.7	2.09	169	.152	.228	3	.200	2	7	6	0	0.5
1971 *Oak-A★	24	8	.750	39	39	24	**8**	0	312	209	19	88	301	**8.7**	**1.82**	183	**.189**	**.252**	12	.118	-2	57	53	-4	4.9
1972 Oak-A	6	10	.375	25	23	5	4	0	151	117	11	48	111	9.9	2.80	101	.215	.280	2	.044	-2	4	1	-2	-0.4
1973 *Oak-A	20	9	.690	37	37	13	4	0	263²	214	26	105	158	11.0	3.28	108	.224	.303	0	.000	0	16	8	-2	0.5
1974 *Oak-A	17	15	.531	40	40	12	1	0	282¹	246	17	98	174	11.0	3.25	102	.236	.303	0	—	0	11	2	-5	-0.1
1975 *Oak-A★	22	11	.667	39	38	13	2	1	278	243	21	99	189	11.2	3.01	120	.236	.307	0	—	0	24	19	-2	2.0
1976 Oak-A	18	13	.581	37	37	20	6	0	298¹	268	9	63	166	10.0	2.35	143	.239	.280	0	—	0	**39**	33	-3	3.1
1977 Oak-A†	14	19	.424	38	38	16	1	0	279²	284	25	86	157	11.9	3.83	105	.264	.319	0	.000	-1	7	6	-1	0.5
1978 SF-N★	18	10	.643	35	35	9	4	0	258	233	12	70	171	10.6	2.79	124	.246	.298	6	.076	-2	23	19	-2	2.0
1979 SF-N	14	14	.500	34	34	10	0	0	237	246	23	111	138	13.6	5.01	70	.272	.352	10	.120	-1	-34	-40	2	-3.9
1980 SF-N†	14	10	.583	31	31	10	3	0	224	202	14	61	129	10.6	2.97	119	.242	.294	5	.074	-4	16	14	2	1.3
1981 SF-N★	8	6	.571	18	18	1	0	0	124²	97	7	54	63	11.0	2.45	140	.217	.303	7	.200	2	14	14	2	2.0
1982 KC-A	13	12	.520	31	31	6	2	0	181	163	20	80	103	12.1	3.78	108	.238	.318	0	—	0	6	6	-0	0.7
1983 KC-A	0	5	.000	19	14	1	0	0	85¹	96	12	35	53	14.0	6.01	68	.286	.357	0	—	0	-18	-18	-1	-1.0
1985 SF-N	8	8	.500	33	20	1	0	0	131	115	17	80	103	13.5	4.47	77	.240	.350	4	.133	1	-13	-15	0	-1.6
1986 SF-N	10	10	.500	28	28	0	0	0	156²	137	19	77	100	12.3	3.27	107	.239	.329	4	.093	1	8	4	-1	0.5
Total 17	209	161	.565	502	473	143	37	2	3343¹	2939	263	1185	2175	11.2	3.27	108	.237	.305	53	.104	-1	152	95	-17	10.2

● JIM BLUEJACKET
Bluejacket, James (b: James Smith)   b: 7/8/1887, Adair, Okla.   d: 3/26/47, Pekin, Ill.   BR/TR, 6′2.5″, 200 lbs.   Deb: 8/6/14   F

YEAR TM/L	W	L	PCT	G	GS	CG	SH	SV	IP	H	HR	BB	SO	RAT	ERA	ERA+	OAV	OOB	BH	AVG	PB	PR	/A	PD	TPI
1914 Bro-F	4	5	.444	17	3	1	1	1	67	77	2	19	29	12.9	3.76	76	.302	.350	3	.136	-5	-7	-7	1	-0.8
1915 Bro-F	10	11	.476	24	21	10	2	1	162²	155	7	75	48	12.7	3.15	86	.258	.340	8	.131	-5	-8	-8	-4	-1.8
1916 Cin-N	0	1	.000	3	2	0	0	0	7	12	0	3	1	19.3	7.71	34	.400	.455	0	.000	-0	-4	-4	-0	-0.6
Total 3	14	17	.452	44	30	13	3	1	236²	244	4	97	78	13.0	3.46	80	.275	.347	11	.129	-6	-18	-18	-3	-3.2

● CLINT BLUME
Blume, Clinton Willis   b: 10/17/1898, Brooklyn, N.Y.   d: 6/12/73, Islip, N.Y.   BR/TR, 5′11″, 175 lbs.   Deb: 9/30/22

YEAR TM/L	W	L	PCT	G	GS	CG	SH	SV	IP	H	HR	BB	SO	RAT	ERA	ERA+	OAV	OOB	BH	AVG	PB	PR	/A	PD	TPI
1922 NY-N	1	0	1.000	1	1	1	0	0	9	7	0	1	2	8.0	1.00	400	.212	.235	1	1.000	1	3	3	-1	0.4
1923 NY-N	2	0	1.000	12	1	0	0	0	24	22	0	20	2	16.5	3.75	102	.265	.419	0	.000	-0	1	1	-0	-0.1
Total 2	3	0	1.000	13	2	1	0	0	33	29	0	21	4	14.2	3.00	129	.250	.374	1	.167	1	4	3	-1	0.3

● BERT BLYLEVEN
Blyleven, Rik Aalbert   b: 4/6/51, Zeist, Holland   BR/TR, 6′3″, 207 lbs.   Deb: 6/5/70

YEAR TM/L	W	L	PCT	G	GS	CG	SH	SV	IP	H	HR	BB	SO	RAT	ERA	ERA+	OAV	OOB	BH	AVG	PB	PR	/A	PD	TPI
1970 *Min-A	10	9	.526	27	25	5	1	0	164	143	17	47	135	10.5	3.18	117	.232	.289	7	.140	-1	10	10	-2	0.8
1971 Min-A	16	15	.516	38	38	17	5	0	278¹	267	21	59	224	10.7	2.81	126	.255	.298	12	.132	-3	20	23	-0	2.2
1972 Min-A	17	17	.500	39	38	11	3	0	287¹	247	22	69	228	10.2	2.73	118	.233	.286	15	.160	-1	11	15	1	2.0

YEAR	TM/L	W	L	PCT	G	GS	CG	SH	SV	IP	H	HR	BB	SO	RAT	ERA	ERA+	OAV	OOB	BH	AVG	PB	PR	/A	PD	TPI
1973	Min-A★	20	17	.541	40	40	25	**9**	0	325	296	16	67	258	10.3	2.52	**157**	.242	.287	0	—	0	**47**	**52**	-2	5.7
1974	Min-A	17	17	.500	37	37	19	3	0	281	244	14	77	249	10.6	2.66	141	.233	.292	0	—	0	30	34	0	4.0
1975	Min-A	15	10	.600	35	35	20	3	0	275²	219	24	84	233	10.0	3.00	128	.219	.283	0	—	0	24	26	3	2.5
1976	Min-A	4	5	.444	12	12	4	0	0	95¹	101	3	35	75	13.2	3.12	116	.283	.354	0	—	0	4	5	0	0.5
	Tex-A	9	11	.450	24	24	14	6	0	202¹	182	11	46	144	10.5	2.76	130	.242	.293	0	—	0	17	19	2	2.0
	Yr	13	16	.448	36	36	18	6	0	297²	283	14	81	219	11.2	2.87	125	.254	.309	0	—	0	21	24	2	2.5
1977	Tex-A	14	12	.538	30	30	15	5	0	234²	181	20	69	182	**9.9**	2.72	150	.214	.279	0	—	0	35	35	0	3.8
1978	Pit-N	14	10	.583	34	34	11	4	0	243²	217	17	66	182	10.7	3.03	122	.235	.290	11	.129	-2	15	18	1	1.6
1979	*Pit-N	12	5	.706	37	37	4	0	0	237¹	238	21	92	172	12.7	3.60	108	.265	.338	9	.129	-3	3	7	-2	0.0
1980	Pit-N	8	13	.381	34	32	5	2	0	216²	219	20	59	168	11.5	3.82	95	.262	.311	5	.082	-4	-5	-4	-0	-0.8
1981	Cle-A	11	7	.611	20	20	9	1	0	159¹	145	9	40	107	10.7	2.88	126	.245	.298	0	—	0	14	13	-2	1.4
1982	Cle-A	2	2	.500	4	4	0	0	0	20¹	16	2	11	19	12.0	4.87	84	.211	.310	0	—	0	-2	-2	0	-0.3
1983	Cle-A	7	10	.412	24	24	5	0	0	156¹	160	8	44	123	12.3	3.91	108	.267	.328	0	—	0	3	6	1	0.6
1984	Cle-A	19	7	.731	33	32	12	4	0	245	204	19	74	170	10.4	2.87	143	.224	.287	0	—	0	31	33	0	3.4
1985	Cle-A★	9	11	.450	23	23	15	4	0	179²	163	14	49	129	11.0	3.26	127	.240	.298	0	—	0	18	18	-1	1.7
	Min-A	8	5	.615	14	14	9	1	0	114	101	9	26	77	10.2	3.00	147	.237	.284	0	—	0	15	18	-0	1.8
	Yr	17	16	.515	37	37	**24**	**5**	0	293²	264	23	75	**206**	10.5	3.16	134	.236	.286	0	—	0	32	35	-1	3.5
1986	Min-A	17	14	.548	36	36	16	3	0	**271²**	262	50	58	215	10.9	4.01	107	.250	.295	0	—	0	5	9	-1	0.8
1987	*Min-A	15	12	.556	37	37	8	1	0	267	249	46	101	196	12.1	4.01	115	.249	.323	0	—	0	13	18	2	1.7
1988	Min-A	10	17	.370	33	33	7	0	0	207¹	240	21	51	145	13.3	5.43	75	.294	.348	0	—	0	-34	-31	-1	-3.6
1989	Cal-A	17	5	.773	33	33	8	**5**	0	241	225	14	44	131	10.3	2.73	140	.248	.289	0	—	0	31	29	1	2.7
1990	Cal-A	8	7	.533	23	23	2	0	0	134	163	15	25	69	13.1	5.24	73	.303	.342	0	—	0	-20	-21	0	-2.0
1992	Cal-A	8	12	.400	25	24	1	0	0	133	150	17	29	70	12.5	4.74	84	.285	.329	0	—	0	-12	-11	-1	-1.6
Total	22	287	250	.534	692	685	242	60	0	4970	4632	430	1322	3701	11.1	3.31	117	.247	.303	59	.131	-13	271	319	1	30.9

● MIKE BLYZKA
Blyzka, Michael John b: 12/25/28, Hamtramck, Mich. BR/TR, 5'11.5", 190 lbs. Deb: 4/21/53

YEAR	TM/L	W	L	PCT	G	GS	CG	SH	SV	IP	H	HR	BB	SO	RAT	ERA	ERA+	OAV	OOB	BH	AVG	PB	PR	/A	PD	TPI
1953	StL-A	2	6	.250	33	9	2	0	0	94¹	110	6	56	23	15.8	6.39	66	.292	.383	0	.000	-3	-25	-23	-1	-2.0
1954	Bal-A	1	5	.167	37	0	0	0	1	86¹	83	2	51	35	14.0	4.69	76	.254	.354	2	.133	-1	-9	-11	0	-0.8
Total	2	3	11	.214	70	9	2	0	1	180²	193	8	107	58	14.9	5.58	70	.274	.370	2	.053	-4	-34	-34	-0	-2.8

● CHARLIE BOARDMAN
Boardman, Charles Louis b: 4/27/1893, Seneca Falls, N.Y. d: 8/10/68, Sacramento, Cal. BL/TL, 6'2.5", 194 lbs. Deb: 9/26/13

YEAR	TM/L	W	L	PCT	G	GS	CG	SH	SV	IP	H	HR	BB	SO	RAT	ERA	ERA+	OAV	OOB	BH	AVG	PB	PR	/A	PD	TPI
1913	Phi-A	0	2	.000	2	2	1	0	0	9	10	0	6	4	16.0	2.00	138	.294	.400	0	.000	-0	1	-0	0.1
1914	Phi-A	0	0	—	2	0	0	0	0	7¹	10	0	4	2	17.2	4.91	53	.357	.438	0	.000	-0	-2	-2	-0	0.0
1915	StL-N	1	0	1.000	3	1	1	0	0	19	12	0	15	7	12.8	2.84	98	.188	.342	2	.286	-0	-0	-0	-0	0.0
Total	3	1	2	.333	7	3	2	0	0	35¹	32	0	25	13	14.5	3.06	90	.254	.377	2	.167	-1	-1	-1	0.1

● RANDY BOCKUS
Bockus, Randy Walter b: 10/5/60, Canton, Ohio BL/TR, 6'2", 190 lbs. Deb: 9/10/86

YEAR	TM/L	W	L	PCT	G	GS	CG	SH	SV	IP	H	HR	BB	SO	RAT	ERA	ERA+	OAV	OOB	BH	AVG	PB	PR	/A	PD	TPI
1986	SF-N	0	0	—	5	0	0	0	0	7	6	1	6	4	16.7	2.57	137	.241	.371	0	.000	-0	1	1	1	0.0
1987	SF-N	1	0	1.000	12	0	0	0	0	17¹	17	2	4	9	10.9	3.63	106	.266	.309	0	.000	-0	1	0	-0	0.0
1988	SF-N	1	1	.500	20	0	0	0	0	32	35	2	13	18	13.8	4.78	68	.297	.371	1	.167	-0	-5	-5	-0	-0.3
1989	Det-A	0	0	—	2	0	0	0	0	5¹	7	0	2	2	15.2	5.06	75	.333	.391	0	.000	-0	-1	-1	-0	0.0
Total	4	2	1	.667	39	0	0	0	0	61²	66	5	25	33	13.4	4.23	83	.284	.357	1	.125	-0	-4	-5	1	-0.3

● MIKE BODDICKER
Boddicker, Michael James b: 8/23/57, Cedar Rapids, Iowa BR/TR, 5'11", 172 lbs. Deb: 10/4/80

YEAR	TM/L	W	L	PCT	G	GS	CG	SH	SV	IP	H	HR	BB	SO	RAT	ERA	ERA+	OAV	OOB	BH	AVG	PB	PR	/A	PD	TPI
1980	Bal-A	0	1	.000	1	1	0	0	0	7¹	6	1	5	4	13.5	6.14	64	.207	.324	0	—	0	-2	-2	-0	-0.2
1981	Bal-A	0	0	—	2	0	0	0	0	5²	6	1	2	2	12.7	4.76	76	.261	.320	0	—	0	-1	-1	-0	0.0
1982	Bal-A	1	0	1.000	7	0	0	0	0	25²	25	2	12	20	13.0	3.51	115	.258	.339	0	—	0	2	2	0	0.1
1983	*Bal-A	16	8	.667	27	26	10	**5**	0	179	141	13	52	120	9.7	2.77	143	**.216**	.274	0	—	0	26	24	3	3.4
1984	Bal-A☆	**20**	11	.645	34	34	16	4	0	261¹	218	23	81	128	10.5	**2.79**	139	.228	.292	0	—	0	**35**	31	6	**4.2**
1985	Bal-A	12	17	.414	32	32	9	2	0	203¹	227	16	89	135	14.2	4.07	99	.286	.361	0	—	0	2	-1	6	0.4
1986	Bal-A	14	12	.538	33	33	7	0	0	218¹	214	30	74	175	12.3	4.70	88	.255	.323	0	—	0	-13	-14	3	-1.0
1987	Bal-A	10	12	.455	33	33	7	2	0	226	212	29	78	152	11.8	4.18	105	.248	.316	0	—	0	7	5	4	0.8
1988	Bal-A	6	12	.333	21	21	4	0	0	147	149	14	51	100	12.9	3.86	101	.265	.338	0	—	0	2	1	-1	0.0
	*Bos-A	7	3	.700	15	14	1	1	0	89	85	3	26	56	11.5	2.63	156	.257	.317	0	—	0	13	15	2	1.8
	Yr	13	15	.464	36	35	5	1	0	236	234	17	77	156	12.0	3.39	117	.256	.316	0	—	0	15	15	1	1.8
1989	Bos-A	15	11	.577	34	34	3	2	0	211²	217	19	71	145	12.7	4.00	103	.267	.333	0	—	0	-3	2	1	0.4
1990	*Bos-A	17	8	.680	34	34	4	0	0	228	225	16	69	143	12.0	3.36	121	.258	.319	0	—	0	14	18	1	1.0
1991	KC-A	12	12	.500	30	29	1	0	0	180²	188	13	59	79	13.0	4.08	101	.272	.340	0	—	0	0	1	2	0.3
1992	KC-A	1	4	.200	29	8	0	0	3	86²	92	5	37	47	14.2	4.98	81	.269	.354	0	—	0	-10	-9	1	-0.5
1993	Mil-A	3	5	.375	10	10	1	0	0	54	77	6	15	24	16.0	5.67	75	.338	.389	0	—	0	-8	-9	-0	-1.0
Total	14	134	116	.536	342	309	63	16	3	2123²	2082	188	721	1330	12.2	3.80	107	.257	.325	0	—	0	64	65	28	10.6

● GEORGE BOEHLER
Boehler, George Henry b: 1/2/1892, Lawrenceburg, Ind. d: 6/23/58, Lawrenceburg, Ind BR/TR, 6'2", 180 lbs. Deb: 9/13/12

YEAR	TM/L	W	L	PCT	G	GS	CG	SH	SV	IP	H	HR	BB	SO	RAT	ERA	ERA+	OAV	OOB	BH	AVG	PB	PR	/A	PD	TPI
1912	Det-A	0	2	.000	5	4	2	0	0	32	50	0	14	15	18.6	6.47	50	.365	.431	1	.100	-1	-11	-11	1	-0.6
1913	Det-A	0	1	.000	1	1	1	0	0	8	11	0	6	2	21.4	6.75	43	.355	.487	1	.333	1	-3	-3	1	-0.3
1914	Det-A	2	3	.400	18	6	2	0	0	63	54	1	48	37	15.7	3.57	79	.242	.394	3	.176	1	-6	-5	-0	-0.4
1915	Det-A	1	1	.500	8	0	0	0	0	15	19	0	4	7	14.4	1.80	168	.328	.381	3	.750	2	2	2	-0	-0.3
1916	Det-A	1	1	.500	5	2	1	0	0	13¹	12	0	9	8	15.5	4.73	61	.261	.404	0	.000	-0	-3	-3	1	-0.3
1920	StL-A	1	0	1.000	7	1	0	0	0	7	10	1	4	2	18.0	7.71	51	.303	.378	0	.000	-0	-3	-3	-0	-0.3
1921	StL-A	0	0	—	2	0	0	0	0	1	1	0	0	0	9.0	0.00	—	.500	.500	0	—	0	0	0	-0	0.0
1923	Pit-N	1	3	.250	10	3	1	0	0	28¹	33	1	26	12	19.1	6.04	66	.314	.455	3	.300	1	-6	-6	-0	-0.7
1926	Bro-N	1	0	1.000	10	1	0	0	0	34²	42	1	23	10	17.7	4.41	87	.302	.412	3	.250	0	-2	-2	-1	-0.1
Total	9	6	12	.333	61	18	7	0	0	202¹	232	4	134	93	17.1	4.71	70	.300	.415	14	.233	3	-33	-32	1	-2.3

● JOE BOEHLING
Boehling, John Joseph b: 3/20/1891, Richmond, Va. d: 9/8/41, Richmond, Va. BL/TL, 5'11", 168 lbs. Deb: 6/20/12

YEAR	TM/L	W	L	PCT	G	GS	CG	SH	SV	IP	H	HR	BB	SO	RAT	ERA	ERA+	OAV	OOB	BH	AVG	PB	PR	/A	PD	TPI
1912	Was-A	0	0	—	3	0	0	0	0	5	4	0	2	2	21.6	7.20	46	.235	.480	0	—	0	-2	-2	0	0.0
1913	Was-A	17	7	.708	38	25	18	3	4	235¹	197	3	82	110	11.0	2.14	138	.229	.303	19	.221	1	21	21	2	2.6
1914	Was-A	12	8	.600	27	24	14	2	1	196	180	4	76	91	12.2	3.03	93	.258	.339	17	.239	4	-6	-5	2	0.1
1915	Was-A	14	13	.519	40	32	14	2	0	229¹	217	5	119	108	13.5	3.22	92	.255	.352	13	.173	0	-7	-6	2	-0.4
1916	Was-A	9	11	.450	27	19	7	2	0	139²	134	1	54	52	12.3	3.09	90	.260	.333	7	.171	1	-4	-5	4	-0.2
	Cle-A	2	4	.333	12	9	3	0	0	60²	63	0	23	18	13.1	2.67	113	.281	.353	5	.263	1	1	1	1	0.4
	Yr	11	15	.423	39	28	10	2	0	200¹	197	1	77	70	12.4	2.97	96	.265	.336	12	.200	1	-3	-2	4	0.2
1917	Cle-A	1	6	.143	12	7	1	0	0	46¹	50	1	16	11	13.4	4.66	61	.291	.361	3	.188	-0	-10	-9	-0	-1.4
1920	Cle-A	0	1	.000	3	2	0	0	0	13	16	0	10	4	18.0	4.85	78	.333	.448	2	.500	1	-2	-2	-0	0.0
Total	7	55	50	.524	162	118	57	9	5	925¹	861	13	386	396	12.5	2.97	98	.254	.337	66	.212	7	-10	-5	11	1.1

● LARRY BOERNER
Boerner, Lawrence Hyer b: 1/21/05, Staunton, Va. d: 10/16/69, Staunton, Va. BR/TR, 6'4.5", 175 lbs. Deb: 6/30/32

YEAR	TM/L	W	L	PCT	G	GS	CG	SH	SV	IP	H	HR	BB	SO	RAT	ERA	ERA+	OAV	OOB	BH	AVG	PB	PR	/A	PD	TPI
1932	Bos-A	0	4	.000	21	5	0	0	0	61	71	2	37	19	16.4	5.02	90	.302	.404	0	.000	-3	-4	-4	0	-0.4

● JOE BOEVER
Boever, Joseph Martin b: 10/4/60, Kirkwood, Mo. BR/TR, 6'1", 200 lbs. Deb: 7/19/85

YEAR	TM/L	W	L	PCT	G	GS	CG	SH	SV	IP	H	HR	BB	SO	RAT	ERA	ERA+	OAV	OOB	BH	AVG	PB	PR	/A	PD	TPI
1985	StL-N	0	0	—	13	0	0	0	0	16¹	17	3	4	20	11.6	4.41	80	.270	.313	0	—	0	-1	-2	-0	0.0
1986	StL-N	0	1	.000	11	0	0	0	0	21²	19	2	11	8	13.3	1.66	219	.232	.323	1	.500	0	5	5	-0	0.2
1987	Atl-N	1	0	1.000	14	0	0	0	0	18¹	29	4	12	18	20.1	7.36	59	.367	.451	0	—	0	-7	-6	-0	-0.3
1988	Atl-N	0	2	.000	16	0	0	0	1	20¹	12	1	7	6	6.2	1.77	208	.182	.206	0	—	0	4	4	0	0.5
1989	Atl-N	4	11	.267	66	0	0	0	21	82¹	78	6	34	68	12.4	3.94	93	.252	.328	0	.000	-0	-4	-3	1	-0.5

YEAR TM/L	W	L	PCT	G	GS	CG	SH	SV	IP	H	HR	BB	SO	RAT	ERA	ERA+	OAV	OOB	BH	AVG	PB	PR	/A	PD	TPI
1990 Atl-N	1	3	.250	33	0	0	0	8	42¹	40	6	35	35	15.9	4.68	86	.252	.387	0	.000	-0	-4	-3	-1	-0.5
Phi-N	2	3	.400	34	0	0	0	6	46	37	0	16	40	10.4	2.15	178	.215	.282	0	.000	-0	8	9	0	1.1
Yr	3	6	.333	67	0	0	0	14	88¹	77	6	51	75	13.0	3.36	117	.231	.333	0	—	0	4	6	-1	0.6
1991 Phi-N	3	5	.375	68	0	0	0	0	98¹	90	10	54	89	13.2	3.84	95	.245	.341	1	.333	0	-2	-2	-1	-0.2
1992 Hou-N	3	6	.333	**81**	0	0	0	2	111¹	103	3	45	67	12.3	2.51	134	.248	.327	0	.000	-1	12	11	0	0.8
1993 Oak-A	4	2	.667	42	0	0	0	0	79¹	87	8	33	49	14.1	3.86	86	.280	.356	0	—	0	4	2	0	0.5
Det-A	2	1	.667	19	0	0	0	3	23	14	1	11	14	9.8	2.74	156	.179	.281	0	—	0	4	4	-0	0.6
Yr	6	3	.667	61	0	0	0	3	102¹	101	9	44	63	12.8	3.61	114	.255	.330	0	—	0	8	6	-0	1.1
1994 Det-A	9	2	.818	46	0	0	0	3	81¹	80	12	37	49	13.2	3.98	120	.263	.347	0	—	0	7	7	0	0.9
Total 10	29	36	.446	443	0	0	0	44	640²	606	56	293	464	12.8	3.51	110	.252	.336	2	.125	-1	27	26	-1	3.1

● **JOHN BOGART**   Bogart, John Renzie "Big John"   b: 9/21/1900, Bloomsburg, Pa.   d: 12/7/86, Clarence, N.Y.   BR/TR, 6'2", 195 lbs.   Deb: 9/17/20

YEAR TM/L	W	L	PCT	G	GS	CG	SH	SV	IP	H	HR	BB	SO	RAT	ERA	ERA+	OAV	OOB	BH	AVG	PB	PR	/A	PD	TPI
1920 Det-A	2	1	.667	4	2	0	0	0	23²	16	0	18	5	12.9	3.04	122	.195	.340	2	.250	-0	2	2	-1	0.1

● **RAY BOGGS**   Boggs, Raymond Joseph "Lefty"   b: 12/12/04, Reamsville, Kan.   d: 11/27/89, Grand Junction, Colo.   BL/TL, 6'0.5", 170 lbs.   Deb: 9/1/28

YEAR TM/L	W	L	PCT	G	GS	CG	SH	SV	IP	H	HR	BB	SO	RAT	ERA	ERA+	OAV	OOB	BH	AVG	PB	PR	/A	PD	TPI
1928 Bos-N	0	0	—	4	0	0	0	0	5	2	0	7	2	21.6	5.40	72	.167	.545	0	—	0	-1	-1	-0	0.0

● **TOMMY BOGGS**   Boggs, Thomas Winton   b: 10/25/55, Poughkeepsie, N.Y.   BR/TR, 6'2", 200 lbs.   Deb: 7/19/76

YEAR TM/L	W	L	PCT	G	GS	CG	SH	SV	IP	H	HR	BB	SO	RAT	ERA	ERA+	OAV	OOB	BH	AVG	PB	PR	/A	PD	TPI
1976 Tex-A	1	7	.125	13	13	3	0	0	90¹	87	7	34	36	12.2	3.49	103	.257	.326	0	—	0	0	1	-1	-0.1
1977 Tex-A	0	3	.000	6	6	0	0	0	27¹	40	1	12	15	17.5	5.93	69	.351	.417	0	—	0	-6	-6	-0	-0.6
1978 Atl-N	2	8	.200	16	12	1	1	0	59	80	8	26	21	16.3	6.71	60	.323	.389	3	.167	0	-21	-17	-2	-2.7
1979 Atl-N	0	2	.000	3	3	0	0	0	12²	21	0	4	1	18.5	6.39	63	.362	.413	1	.250	0	-4	-3	-0	-0.4
1980 Atl-N	12	9	.571	32	26	4	3	0	192¹	180	14	46	84	10.8	3.42	109	.249	.298	10	.159	-2	4	7	-2	0.3
1981 Atl-N	3	13	.188	25	24	2	0	0	142²	140	11	54	81	12.4	4.10	87	.265	.336	7	.152	-1	-10	-8	-1	-1.0
1982 Atl-N	2	2	.500	10	10	0	0	0	46¹	43	2	22	29	13.0	3.30	113	.253	.336	4	.235	-1	2	2	-0	0.2
1983 Atl-N	0	0	—	5	0	0	0	0	6¹	11	1	5	5	12.8	5.68	68	.320	.346	0	—	0	-1	-1	-0	0.0
1985 Tex-A	0	0	—	4	0	0	0	0	7	13	3	2	6	19.3	11.57	37	.382	.417	0	—	0	-6	-6	-0	0.0
Total 9	20	44	.313	114	94	10	4	0	584	612	47	201	278	12.7	4.22	89	.273	.337	25	.169	-2	-41	-31	-5	-4.3

● **WARREN BOGLE**   Bogle, Warren Frederick   b: 10/19/46, Passaic, N.J.   BL/TL, 6'4", 220 lbs.   Deb: 7/31/68

YEAR TM/L	W	L	PCT	G	GS	CG	SH	SV	IP	H	HR	BB	SO	RAT	ERA	ERA+	OAV	OOB	BH	AVG	PB	PR	/A	PD	TPI
1968 Oak-A	0	0	—	16	1	0	0	0	23	26	3	8	26	13.3	4.30	65	.283	.340	0	.000	-1	-3	-4	1	0.0

● **BRIAN BOHANON**   Bohanon, Brian Edward   b: 8/1/68, Denton, Tex.   BL/TL, 6'2", 210 lbs.   Deb: 4/10/90

YEAR TM/L	W	L	PCT	G	GS	CG	SH	SV	IP	H	HR	BB	SO	RAT	ERA	ERA+	OAV	OOB	BH	AVG	PB	PR	/A	PD	TPI
1990 Tex-A	0	3	.000	11	6	0	0	0	34	40	6	18	15	15.9	6.62	59	.296	.387	0	—	0	-10	-10	1	-0.7
1991 Tex-A	4	3	.571	11	11	1	0	0	61¹	66	4	23	34	13.4	4.84	83	.274	.342	0	—	0	-5	-6	-1	-0.5
1992 Tex-A	1	1	.500	18	7	0	0	0	45²	57	7	25	29	16.4	6.31	60	.297	.381	0	—	0	-12	-13	-0	-0.3
1993 Tex-A	4	4	.500	36	8	0	0	0	92²	107	8	46	45	15.2	4.76	87	.296	.382	0	—	0	-5	-6	-1	-0.1
1994 Tex-A	2	2	.500	11	5	0	0	0	37¹	51	7	8	26	14.5	7.23	63	.321	.357	0	—	0	-10	-11	-0	-0.6
Total 5	11	13	.458	87	37	1	0	0	271	321	32	120	149	15.0	5.61	73	.295	.370	0	—	0	-42	-46	1	-2.2

● **PAT BOHEN**   Bohen, Leo Ignatius   b: 9/30/1891, Oakland, Iowa   d: 4/8/42, Napa, Cal.   BR/TR, 5'10.5", 155 lbs.   Deb: 10/1/13

YEAR TM/L	W	L	PCT	G	GS	CG	SH	SV	IP	H	HR	BB	SO	RAT	ERA	ERA+	OAV	OOB	BH	AVG	PB	PR	/A	PD	TPI
1913 Phi-A	0	1	.000	1	1	1	0	0	8	3	0	2	5	5.6	1.13	246	.115	.179	0	.000	-0	2	1	-0	0.1
1914 Pit-N	0	0	—	1	0	0	0	0	1	2	0	2	0	45.0	18.00	15	.500	.714	0	.000	-0	-2	-2	-0	0.0
Total 2	0	1	.000	2	1	1	0	0	9	5	0	4	5	10.0	3.00	92	.167	.286	0	.000	-1	-0	-0	-0	0.1

● **CHARLIE BOHN**   Bohn, Charles   b: 1857, Cleveland, Ohio   d: 8/1/03, Cleveland, Ohio   BR/TR, 5'9", 165 lbs.   Deb: 6/20/1882   ♦

YEAR TM/L	W	L	PCT	G	GS	CG	SH	SV	IP	H	HR	BB	SO	RAT	ERA	ERA+	OAV	OOB	BH	AVG	PB	PR	/A	PD	TPI
1882 Lou-a	1	1	.500	2	2	2	0	0	18	21	0	3	1	12.0	3.00	83	.273	.300	2	.154	-0	-1	-1	0	-0.1

● **JOHN BOHNET**   Bohnet, John Kelly   b: 1/18/61, Pasadena, Cal.   BB/TL, 6', 175 lbs.   Deb: 5/10/82

YEAR TM/L	W	L	PCT	G	GS	CG	SH	SV	IP	H	HR	BB	SO	RAT	ERA	ERA+	OAV	OOB	BH	AVG	PB	PR	/A	PD	TPI
1982 Cle-A	0	0	—	3	3	0	0	0	11²	11	4	7	4	14.7	6.94	59	.250	.365	0	—	0	-4	-4	0	0.0

● **DAN BOITANO**   Boitano, Danny Jon   b: 3/22/53, Sacramento, Cal.   BR/TR, 6', 185 lbs.   Deb: 10/1/78

YEAR TM/L	W	L	PCT	G	GS	CG	SH	SV	IP	H	HR	BB	SO	RAT	ERA	ERA+	OAV	OOB	BH	AVG	PB	PR	/A	PD	TPI
1978 Phi-N	0	0	—	1	0	0	0	0	1	0	0	1	0	9.0	.000	—	.000	.250	0	—	0	0	0	0	0.0
1979 Mil-A	0	0	—	5	0	0	0	0	6	6	1	3	5	13.5	1.50	278	.273	.360	0	—	0	2	2	0	0.1
1980 Mil-A	0	1	.000	11	0	0	0	0	17²	26	7	6	11	16.8	8.15	47	.342	.398	0	—	0	-8	-8	0	-0.2
1981 NY-N	2	1	.667	15	0	0	0	0	16¹	21	5	7	8	15.4	5.51	63	.309	.373	0	—	0	-4	-4	0	-0.6
1982 Tex-A	0	0	—	19	0	0	0	0	30¹	33	5	13	28	14.2	5.34	72	.280	.361	0	—	0	-4	-5	-0	0.2
Total 5	2	2	.500	51	0	0	0	0	71¹	86	18	28	52	15.0	5.68	67	.300	.372	0	—	0	-14	-15	0	-0.6

● **DICK BOKELMANN**   Bokelmann, Richard Werner   b: 10/26/26, Arlington Heights, Ill.   BR/TR, 6'0.5", 180 lbs.   Deb: 8/3/51

YEAR TM/L	W	L	PCT	G	GS	CG	SH	SV	IP	H	HR	BB	SO	RAT	ERA	ERA+	OAV	OOB	BH	AVG	PB	PR	/A	PD	TPI
1951 StL-N	3	3	.500	20	1	0	0	3	52¹	49	2	31	22	13.9	3.78	105	.245	.349	0	.000	-2	1	1	-1	-0.1
1952 StL-N	0	1	.000	11	0	0	0	0	12²	20	0	7	5	19.2	9.24	40	.357	.429	0	—	0	-8	-8	1	-0.5
1953 StL-N	0	0	—	3	0	0	0	0	3	4	0	0	0	12.0	6.00	71	.308	.308	0	—	0	-1	-1	0	0.0
Total 3	3	4	.429	34	1	0	0	3	68	73	2	38	27	14.8	4.90	80	.271	.364	0	.000	-2	-7	-7	0	-0.6

● **JOE BOKINA**   Bokina, Joseph   b: 4/4/10, Northampton, Mass.   d: 10/25/91, Chattanooga, Tenn.   BR/TR, 6', 184 lbs.   Deb: 4/16/36

YEAR TM/L	W	L	PCT	G	GS	CG	SH	SV	IP	H	HR	BB	SO	RAT	ERA	ERA+	OAV	OOB	BH	AVG	PB	PR	/A	PD	TPI
1936 Was-A	0	2	.000	5	1	0	0	0	8¹	15	0	6	5	22.7	8.64	55	.395	.477	0	.000	-0	-3	-4	-0	-0.7

● **BERNIE BOLAND**   Boland, Bernard Anthony   b: 1/21/1892, Rochester, N.Y.   d: 9/12/73, Detroit, Mich.   BR/TR, 5'8.5", 168 lbs.   Deb: 4/14/15

YEAR TM/L	W	L	PCT	G	GS	CG	SH	SV	IP	H	HR	BB	SO	RAT	ERA	ERA+	OAV	OOB	BH	AVG	PB	PR	/A	PD	TPI
1915 Det-A	13	7	.650	45	18	8	1	2	202²	167	2	75	72	11.0	3.11	98	.230	.307	11	.175	-1	-4	-2	0	-0.2
1916 Det-A	10	3	.769	46	9	5	1	3	130¹	111	1	73	59	13.0	3.94	73	.240	.349	8	.250	2	-16	-15	-3	-1.7
1917 Det-A	16	11	.593	43	28	13	3	6	238	192	0	95	89	11.1	2.68	99	.226	.308	4	.056	-5	-1	-1	-0	-0.7
1918 Det-A	14	10	.583	29	25	14	4	0	204	176	1	67	63	11.0	2.65	101	.236	.304	12	.174	0	3	0	-1	-0.1
1919 Det-A	14	16	.467	35	30	18	1	1	242²	222	7	80	71	11.3	3.04	105	.253	.318	8	.108	-3	5	4	-2	0.0
1920 Det-A	0	2	.000	4	3	1	0	0	17¹	23	0	14	4	20.3	7.79	48	.348	.476	1	.143	-0	-8	-8	0	-0.7
1921 StL-A	1	4	.200	7	1	0	0	0	27	34	2	28	6	21.0	9.33	48	.309	.453	1	.100	-1	-15	-15	0	-2.0
Total 7	68	53	.562	209	119	59	10	12	1062	925	13	432	364	11.7	3.25	91	.241	.322	45	.138	-8	-35	-36	-5	-5.4

● **BILL BOLDEN**   Bolden, William Horace "Big Bill"   b: 5/9/1893, Dandridge, Tenn.   d: 12/8/66, Jefferson City, Tenn.   BR/TR, 6'4", 200 lbs.   Deb: 6/27/19

YEAR TM/L	W	L	PCT	G	GS	CG	SH	SV	IP	H	HR	BB	SO	RAT	ERA	ERA+	OAV	OOB	BH	AVG	PB	PR	/A	PD	TPI
1919 StL-N	0	1	.000	3	1	0	0	0	12	17	0	4	4	16.5	5.25	53	.340	.400	1	.333	-0	-3	-3	0	-0.2

● **STEW BOLEN**   Bolen, Stewart O'Neal   b: 10/12/02, Jackson, Ala.   d: 8/30/69, Mobile, Ala.   BL/TL, 5'11", 180 lbs.   Deb: 4/15/26

YEAR TM/L	W	L	PCT	G	GS	CG	SH	SV	IP	H	HR	BB	SO	RAT	ERA	ERA+	OAV	OOB	BH	AVG	PB	PR	/A	PD	TPI
1926 StL-A	0	0	—	5	0	0	0	0	14²	21	2	6	7	16.6	6.14	70	.356	.415	2	.500	1	-3	-3	-0	0.0
1927 StL-A	0	1	.000	3	1	1	0	0	9²	14	0	5	7	17.7	8.38	52	.368	.442	1	.333	0	-5	-4	0	-0.3
1931 Phi-N	3	12	.200	28	16	3	0	0	98²	125	9	63	55	16.8	6.39	66	.297	.399	5	.156	-1	-28	-23	-3	-3.1
1932 Phi-N	0	0	—	5	0	0	0	0	16	18	0	10	3	16.9	2.81	157	.281	.395	1	.143	-0	2	3	-0	-0.1
Total 4	3	13	.188	41	17	3	0	0	139	170	7	84	72	16.8	6.09	70	.306	.403	9	.196	-0	-34	-28	-0	-3.5

● **BOBBY BOLIN**   Bolin, Bobby Donald   b: 1/29/39, Hickory Grove, S.C.   BR/TR, 6'4", 200 lbs.   Deb: 4/18/61

YEAR TM/L	W	L	PCT	G	GS	CG	SH	SV	IP	H	HR	BB	SO	RAT	ERA	ERA+	OAV	OOB	BH	AVG	PB	PR	/A	PD	TPI
1961 SF-N	2	2	.500	37	1	0	0	5	48	37	6	37	48	14.4	3.19	120	.210	.356	2	.286	0	5	3	-1	0.3
1962 *SF-N	7	3	.700	41	5	2	0	5	92	84	10	35	74	12.1	3.62	105	.243	.321	6	.261	2	3	2	-1	0.3
1963 SF-N	10	6	.625	47	12	6	2	0	137¹	128	13	57	134	12.6	3.28	98	.242	.324	5	.143	2	0	-1	-2	-0.2
1964 SF-N	6	9	.400	38	23	5	3	1	174²	143	16	77	146	11.9	3.25	110	.220	.313	6	.100	1	6	6	-1	0.5
1965 SF-N	14	6	.700	45	13	2	0	4	163	125	17	56	135	10.2	2.76	130	.214	.288	5	.167	1	14	15	-2	1.8
1966 SF-N	11	10	.524	36	34	10	4	1	224¹	174	25	70	143	10.2	2.89	127	.211	.281	13	.171	3	18	19	-2	1.9
1967 SF-N	6	8	.429	37	15	0	0	0	120	120	16	50	69	13.0	4.88	67	.258	.333	8	.242	2	-20	-21	-1	-2.2

YEAR	TM/L	W	L	PCT	G	GS	CG	SH	SV	IP	H	HR	BB	SO	RAT	ERA	ERA+	OAV	OOB	BH	AVG	PB	PR	/A	PD	TPI
1968	SF-N	10	5	.667	34	19	6	3	0	176²	128	9	46	126	9.1	1.99	148	.200	.258	5	.091	-1	20	19	-1	1.5
1969	SF-N	7	7	.500	30	22	2	0	0	146¹	149	17	49	102	12.6	4.43	79	.260	.326	6	.154	3	-14	-15	-1	-1.1
1970	Mil-A	5	11	.313	32	20	3	0	1	132	131	20	67	81	13.8	4.91	77	.256	.346	7	.194	-1	-18	-16	-1	-1.7
	Bos-A	2	0	1.000	6	0	0	0	2	8	2	0	5	8	9.0	0.00	—	.080	.258	0	.000	-0	3	4	0	1.1
	Yr	7	11	.389	38	20	3	0	3	140	133	20	72	89	13.2	4.63	82	.243	.332	7	.189	2	-14	-13	-1	-0.6
1971	Bos-A	5	3	.625	52	0	0	0	6	69²	74	7	24	51	12.7	4.26	87	.273	.332	3	.250	-0	-6	-4	-1	-0.6
1972	Bos-A	0	1	.000	21	0	0	0	5	30²	24	3	11	27	10.6	2.93	109	.209	.283	0	.000	0	1	0	-0	0.1
1973	Bos-A	3	4	.429	39	0	0	0	15	53¹	45	5	13	31	10.5	2.70	149	.232	.284	0		0	7	8	1	1.6
Total	13	88	75	.540	495	164	32	10	50	1576	1364	164	597	1175	11.5	3.40	103	.231	.308	69	.163	15	18	19	-13	3.2

● **GREG BOLLO** Bollo, Gregory Gene b: 11/16/43, Detroit, Mich. BR/TR, 6'4", 183 lbs. Deb: 5/9/65

YEAR	TM/L	W	L	PCT	G	GS	CG	SH	SV	IP	H	HR	BB	SO	RAT	ERA	ERA+	OAV	OOB	BH	AVG	PB	PR	/A	PD	TPI
1965	Chi-A	0	0	—	15	0	0	0	0	22²	12	5	9	16	9.1	3.57	89	.152	.256	0	—	0	-0	-1	0	0.0
1966	Chi-A	0	1	.000	3	1	0	0	0	7	7	0	3	4	14.1	2.57	123	.269	.367	0	.000	-0	1	0	-0	0.0
Total	2	0	1	.000	18	1	0	0	0	29²	19	5	12	20	10.3	3.34	96	.181	.283	0	.000	0	-0	-0	0	0.0

● **RODNEY BOLTON** Bolton, Rodney Earl b: 9/23/68, Chattanooga, Tenn. BR/TR, 6'2", 190 lbs. Deb: 4/10/93

YEAR	TM/L	W	L	PCT	G	GS	CG	SH	SV	IP	H	HR	BB	SO	RAT	ERA	ERA+	OAV	OOB	BH	AVG	PB	PR	/A	PD	TPI
1993	Chi-A	2	6	.250	9	8	0	0	0	42¹	55	4	16	17	15.3	7.44	56	.314	.375	0	—	0	-15	-15	1	-2.0

● **TOM BOLTON** Bolton, Thomas Edward b: 5/6/62, Nashville, Tenn. BL/TL, 6'3", 175 lbs. Deb: 5/17/87

YEAR	TM/L	W	L	PCT	G	GS	CG	SH	SV	IP	H	HR	BB	SO	RAT	ERA	ERA+	OAV	OOB	BH	AVG	PB	PR	/A	PD	TPI
1987	Bos-A	1	0	1.000	29	0	0	0	0	61²	83	5	27	49	16.3	4.38	104	.329	.399	0	—	0	1	1	0	-0.2
1988	Bos-A	1	3	.250	28	0	0	0	1	30¹	35	1	14	21	14.5	4.75	87	.285	.358	0	—	0	-3	-2	1	-0.5
1989	Bos-A	0	4	.000	4	4	0	0	0	17¹	21	1	10	9	16.1	8.31	49	.292	.378	0	—	0	-9	-8	-0	-1.8
1990	*Bos-A	10	5	.667	21	16	3	0	0	119²	111	6	47	65	12.1	3.38	120	.251	.327	0	—	0	7	9	1	0.7
1991	Bos-A	8	9	.471	25	19	0	0	0	110	136	16	51	64	15.4	5.24	82	.308	.381	0	—	0	-14	-11	-1	-1.9
1992	Bos-A	1	2	.333	21	1	0	0	0	29	34	0	14	23	15.5	3.41	123	.286	.370	0	—	0	2	3	0	-0.2
	Cin-N	3	3	.500	16	8	0	0	0	46¹	52	9	23	27	15.0	5.24	69	.284	.370	0	.000	-1	-9	-8	0	-1.1
1993	Det-A	6	6	.500	43	8	0	0	0	102²	113	5	45	66	14.5	4.47	96	.282	.364	0	—	0	-2	-2	0	-0.1
1994	Bal-A	1	2	.333	22	0	0	0	0	23¹	29	3	13	12	16.2	5.40	94	.309	.393	0	—	0	-2	-1	0	-0.4
Total	8	31	34	.477	209	56	3	0	1	540¹	614	46	244	336	14.6	4.56	93	.289	.366	0	.000	-1	-28	-20	2	-5.5

● **MARK BOMBACK** Bomback, Mark Vincent b: 4/14/53, Portsmouth, Va. BR/TR, 5'11", 170 lbs. Deb: 9/12/78

YEAR	TM/L	W	L	PCT	G	GS	CG	SH	SV	IP	H	HR	BB	SO	RAT	ERA	ERA+	OAV	OOB	BH	AVG	PB	PR	/A	PD	TPI
1978	Mil-A	0	0	—	2	0	0	0	0	1²	5	1	1	1	32.4	16.20	23	.500	.545	0	—	0	-2	-2	-0	-0.4
1980	NY-N	10	8	.556	36	25	2	1	0	162²	191	17	49	68	13.5	4.09	87	.297	.350	10	.233	3	-9	-10	2	-0.4
1981	Tor-A	5	5	.500	20	11	0	0	0	90¹	84	6	35	33	12.0	3.89	101	.251	.323	0	—	0	-2	1	0	0.1
1982	Tor-A	1	5	.167	16	8	0	0	0	59²	87	10	25	22	17.3	6.03	74	.343	.408	0	—	0	-13	-10	0	-1.3
Total	4	16	18	.471	74	45	2	1	0	314¹	367	34	110	124	13.9	4.47	86	.295	.356	10	.233	3	-27	-22	3	-1.6

● **TOMMY BOND** Bond, Thomas Henry b: 4/2/1856, Granard, Ireland d: 1/24/41, Boston, Mass. BR/TR, 5'7.5", 160 lbs. Deb: 5/5/1874 MU♦

YEAR	TM/L	W	L	PCT	G	GS	CG	SH	SV	IP	H	HR	BB	SO	RAT	ERA	ERA+	OAV	OOB	BH	AVG	PB	PR	/A	PD	TPI
1874	Atl-n	22	32	.407	55	55	55	1	0	497	609	16	10		11.2	*3.19*	88	.268	.271	54	.219	-2	-10	-21		-1.5
1875	Har-n	19	16	.543	40	39	37	6	0	352	301	3	10		8.0	*1.56*	**166**	.215	.220	78	.270	3	35	40		3.5
1876	Har-N	31	13	.705	45	45	45	6	0	408	355	2	13	88	8.1	1.68	141	.220	.227	50	.275	1	29	32	5	3.2
1877	Bos-N	**40**	17	**.702**	58	58	58	**6**	0	521	530	5	36	170	9.8	2.11	133	**.261**	.249	59	.228	-4	**41**	41	3	3.5
1878	Bos-N	**40**	19	**.678**	**59**	59	**57**	**9**	0	532²	571	5	33	**182**	10.2	2.06	115	.269	.280	50	.212	-4	15	18	2	1.3
1879	Bos-N	43	19	.694	64	64	59	**11**	0	555¹	543	8	24	155	**9.2**	**1.96**	**126**	.251	.259	62	.241	2	33	**32**	7	**3.8**
1880	Bos-N	26	29	.473	63	57	49	3	0	493	559	1	45	118	11.0	2.67	85	.274	.290	62	.220	-2	-16	-22	10	-1.4
1881	Bos-N	0	3	.000	3	3	3	0	0	25¹	40	3	2	2	14.9	4.26	62	.360	.372	4	.200	-0	-4	-5	1	-0.4
1882	Wor-N	0	1	.000	2	2	0	0	0	12¹	12	0	7	2	13.9	4.38	71	.218	.306	4	.133	-1	-2	-2	-0	-0.2
1884	Bos-U	13	9	.591	23	21	19	0	0	189	185	4	11	128	9.5	3.00	79	.239	.253	48	.296	-0	-12	-13	3	-1.0
	Ind-a	0	5	.000	5	5	5	0	0	43	62	5	4	15	14.2	5.65	58	.310	.310	3	.130	-1	-11	-11	-1	-1.1
Total	2 n	41	48	.461	95	94	92	7	0	849	910	19	20		9.9	*2.51*	109	.248	.252	132	.246	2	25	21		2.0
Total	8	193	115	.627	322	314	294	35	0	2779²	2857	32	178	860	9.8	2.25	110	.255	.267	340	.236	2	71	70	30	7.7

● **RICKY BONES** Bones, Ricardo Ricky b: 4/7/69, Salinas, P.R. BR/TR, 5'10", 175 lbs. Deb: 8/11/91

YEAR	TM/L	W	L	PCT	G	GS	CG	SH	SV	IP	H	HR	BB	SO	RAT	ERA	ERA+	OAV	OOB	BH	AVG	PB	PR	/A	PD	TPI
1991	SD-N	4	6	.400	11	11	0	0	0	54	57	3	18	31	12.5	4.83	79	.269	.326	1	.077	-0	-7	-6	-1	-1.2
1992	Mil-A	9	10	.474	31	28	0	0	0	163¹	169	27	48	65	12.5	4.57	84	.264	.324	0	—	0	-12	-13	-1	-1.4
1993	Mil-A	11	11	.500	32	31	3	0	0	203²	222	28	63	63	12.9	4.86	87	.278	.336	0	—	0	-12	-14	-1	-1.2
1994	Mil-A☆	10	9	.526	24	24	4	1	0	170²	166	17	45	57	11.3	3.43	144	.255	.306	0	—	0	26	28	0	2.7
Total	4	34	36	.486	98	94	7	1	0	591²	614	75	174	216	12.3	4.37	98	.266	.323	1	.077	-0	-5	-5	-3	-1.1

● **JULIO BONETTI** Bonetti, Julio Giacomo b: 7/14/11, Genoa, Italy d: 6/17/52, Belmont, Cal. BR/TR, 6', 180 lbs. Deb: 4/22/37

YEAR	TM/L	W	L	PCT	G	GS	CG	SH	SV	IP	H	HR	BB	SO	RAT	ERA	ERA+	OAV	OOB	BH	AVG	PB	PR	/A	PD	TPI
1937	StL-A	4	11	.267	28	16	7	0	1	143¹	190	13	60	43	15.8	5.84	83	.321	.385	7	.149	-2	-19	-16	2	-1.3
1938	StL-A	2	3	.400	17	0	0	0	0	28¹	41	1	13	7	17.2	6.35	78	.350	.415	0	.000	-1	-5	-4	-0	-0.7
1940	Chi-N	0	0	—	1	0	0	0	0	1¹	3	0	4	0	47.3	20.25	19	.429	.636	0	—	0	-2	-2	-0	0.0
Total	3	6	14	.300	46	16	7	0	1	173	234	14	77	50	16.3	6.03	80	.327	.394	7	.127	-3	-27	-23	2	-2.0

● **HANK BONEY** Boney, Henry Tate "Haney" b: 10/28/03, Wallace, N.C. BR/TR, 5'11", 176 lbs. Deb: 6/28/27

YEAR	TM/L	W	L	PCT	G	GS	CG	SH	SV	IP	H	HR	BB	SO	RAT	ERA	ERA+	OAV	OOB	BH	AVG	PB	PR	/A	PD	TPI
1927	NY-N	0	0	—	3	0	0	0	0	4	4	0	2	0	13.5	2.25	171	.267	.353	0	—	0	1	1	-0	0.0

● **TINY BONHAM** Bonham, Ernest Edward b: 8/16/13, Ione, Cal. d: 9/15/49, Pittsburgh, Pa. BR/TR, 6'2", 215 lbs. Deb: 8/8/40

YEAR	TM/L	W	L	PCT	G	GS	CG	SH	SV	IP	H	HR	BB	SO	RAT	ERA	ERA+	OAV	OOB	BH	AVG	PB	PR	/A	PD	TPI
1940	NY-A	9	3	.750	12	12	10	3	0	99¹	83	4	13	37	8.7	1.90	212	.224	.250	7	.189	0	27	24	-2	2.5
1941	*NY-A	9	6	.600	23	14	7	1	2	126²	118	12	31	43	10.7	2.98	132	.246	.294	8	.160	-1	16	13	-3	1.1
1942	*NY-A☆	21	5	**.808**	28	27	**22**	**6**	0	226	199	11	24	71	**8.9**	2.27	152	.237	**.259**	9	.122	-2	**35**	29	-4	2.6
1943	*NY-A☆	15	8	.652	28	26	17	4	1	225²	197	13	52	71	10.0	2.27	142	.236	.282	15	.197	0	26	24	-5	2.0
1944	NY-A	12	9	.571	26	25	17	1	0	213²	228	14	41	54	11.3	2.99	116	.273	.307	10	.133	-3	10	12	-3	0.5
1945	NY-A	8	11	.421	23	23	12	0	0	180²	186	11	22	42	10.4	3.29	105	.265	.288	15	.238	3	2	4	-3	0.3
1946	NY-A	5	8	.385	18	14	6	2	3	104²	97	6	23	30	10.3	3.70	93	.243	.284	4	.129	-0	-2	-3	-2	-0.6
1947	Pit-N	11	8	.579	33	18	7	3	3	149²	167	17	35	63	12.3	3.85	110	.277	.319	7	.156	-0	3	6	-3	0.4
1948	Pit-N	6	10	.375	22	20	7	0	2	135²	145	18	42	44	11.3	4.31	94	.276	.310	8	.163	-2	-5	-4	-4	-0.9
1949	Pit-N	7	4	.636	18	14	5	1	0	89	81	11	23	25	10.5	4.25	99	.246	.295	1	.045	-1	-0	-2	-3	-0.3
Total	10	103	72	.589	231	193	110	21	9	1551	1501	117	287	478	10.4	3.06	120	.254	.289	84	.161	-7	110	105	-29	7.6

● **BILL BONHAM** Bonham, William Gordon b: 10/1/48, Glendale, Cal. BR/TR, 6'3", 195 lbs. Deb: 4/7/71

YEAR	TM/L	W	L	PCT	G	GS	CG	SH	SV	IP	H	HR	BB	SO	RAT	ERA	ERA+	OAV	OOB	BH	AVG	PB	PR	/A	PD	TPI
1971	Chi-N	2	1	.667	33	2	0	0	0	60	63	6	36	41	15.6	4.65	85	.281	.392	2	.167	-0	-8	-5	1	-0.1
1972	Chi-N	1	1	.500	19	4	0	0	4	57²	54	6	25	49	12.8	3.12	122	.260	.340	4	.286	1	2	4	0	0.4
1973	Chi-N	7	5	.583	44	15	3	0	6	152	126	10	64	121	11.5	3.02	131	.230	.315	4	.093	-3	11	16	4	1.4
1974	Chi-N	11	22	.333	44	36	10	2	1	242²	246	13	109	191	13.4	3.86	99	.263	.343	12	.143	-3	-6	-1	5	0.1
1975	Chi-N	13	15	.464	38	36	7	2	0	229¹	254	15	109	165	14.4	4.71	81	.281	.361	15	.183	-0	-28	-22	1	-2.3
1976	Chi-N	9	13	.409	32	31	3	0	0	196	215	11	96	110	14.4	4.27	90	.283	.365	13	.200	1	-17	-9	0	-0.8
1977	Chi-N	10	13	.435	34	34	1	0	0	214²	207	15	82	134	12.2	4.36	101	.254	.324	15	.231	1	-11	3	3	0.5
1978	Cin-N	11	5	.688	23	23	0	0	0	140¹	151	9	50	83	13.0	3.53	101	.276	.337	8	.186	2	1	0	3	0.6
1979	Cin-N	9	7	.563	29	29	2	0	0	175²	173	14	60	72	12.3	3.79	98	.261	.330	8	.140	-1	-1	-2	0	-0.2
1980	Cin-N	2	1	.667	4	4	0	0	0	19	21	1	5	23	12.3	4.74	75	.276	.321	0	—	0	-2	-2	-0	-0.2
Total	10	75	83	.475	300	214	27	4	11	1487¹	1512	98	636	985	13.2	4.01	97	.266	.343	81	.172	-2	-59	-20	18	-0.8

YEAR TM/L	W	L	PCT	G	GS	CG	SH	SV	IP	H	HR	BB	SO	RAT	ERA	ERA+	OAV	OOB	BH	AVG	PB	PR	/A	PD	TPI
● **JOE BONIKOWSKI** Bonikowski, Joseph Peter b: 1/16/41, Philadelphia, Pa. BR/TR, 6', 175 lbs. Deb: 4/12/62																									
1962 Min-A	5	7	.417	30	13	3	0	2	99²	95	6	38	45	12.1	3.88	105	.255	.325	4	.148	-1	1	2	1	0.3
● **BILL BONNESS** Bonness, William John "Lefty" b: 12/15/23, Cleveland, Ohio d: 12/3/77, Detroit, Mich. BR/TL, 6'4", 200 lbs. Deb: 9/26/44																									
1944 Cle-A	0	1	.000	2	1	0	0	0	7	11	0	5	1	23.1	7.71	43	.367	.486	0	.000	-0	-3	-3	0	-0.4
● **GUS BONO** Bono, Adlai Wendell b: 8/29/1894, Doe Run, Mo. d: 12/3/48, Dearborn, Mich. BR/TR, 5'11", 175 lbs. Deb: 9/13/20																									
1920 Was-A	0	2	.000	4	1	0	0	0	12¹	17	0	6	4	16.8	8.76	43	.315	.383	0	.000	-0	-7	-7	0	-0.9
● **GREG BOOKER** Booker, Gregory Scott b: 6/22/60, Lynchburg, Va. BR/TR, 6'6", 233 lbs. Deb: 9/11/83																									
1983 SD-N	0	1	.000	6	1	0	0	0	11²	18	2	9	5	20.8	7.71	45	.375	.474	0	.000	-0	-5	-5	-0	-0.4
1984 *SD-N	1	1	.500	32	1	0	0	0	57¹	67	4	27	28	14.8	3.30	108	.295	.370	2	.286	1	2	2	0	0.1
1985 SD-N	0	1	.000	17	0	0	0	0	22¹	20	3	17	7	15.3	6.85	52	.247	.384	0	.000	-0	-8	-8	-0	-0.4
1986 SD-N	1	0	1.000	9	0	0	0	0	11	10	0	4	7	11.5	1.64	223	.233	.298	0	—	0	3	2	-0	0.2
1987 SD-N	1	1	.500	44	0	0	0	1	68¹	62	5	30	17	12.5	3.16	125	.246	.333	0	.000	-1	7	6	-0	0.1
1988 SD-N	2	2	.500	34	2	0	0	0	63²	68	5	19	43	12.4	3.39	100	.278	.332	2	.250	1	0	0	1	0.1
1989 SD-N	0	1	.000	11	0	0	0	0	19	15	2	10	8	11.8	4.26	82	.224	.325	0	—	0	-2	-2	-0	-0.1
Min-A	0	0	—	6	0	0	0	0	8²	11	1	2	3	13.5	4.15	100	.306	.342	0	—	0	-0	-0	1	-0.5
1990 SF-N	0	0	—	2	0	0	0	0	2	7	0	1	1	31.5	13.50	27	.538	.538	0	—	0	-2	-2	-0	0.0
Total 8	5	7	.417	161	4	0	0	1	264	278	22	118	119	13.7	3.89	94	.275	.353	4	.174	1	-6	-7	1	-0.9
● **RED BOOLES** Booles, Seabron Jesse b: 7/14/1880, Bernice, La. d: 3/16/55, Monroe, La. BL/TL, 5'10", 150 lbs. Deb: 7/30/09																									
1909 Cle-A	0	1	.000	3	2	2	0	0	22²	20	0	8	6	11.5	1.99	129	.235	.309	1	.167	0	1	1	-0	0.1
● **DANNY BOONE** Boone, Daniel Hugh b: 1/14/54, Long Beach, Cal. BL/TL, 5'8", 150 lbs. Deb: 4/11/81 F																									
1981 SD-N	1	0	1.000	37	0	0	0	2	63¹	63	2	21	43	12.1	2.84	115	.267	.329	2	.500	1	5	3	1	0.3
1982 SD-N	1	0	1.000	10	0	0	0	1	16	21	2	3	8	13.5	5.63	61	.323	.353	1	.200	0	-4	-4	-0	-0.2
Hou-N	0	1	.000	10	0	0	0	1	12²	7	1	4	4	7.8	3.55	93	.171	.244	0	.000	-0	0	-0	0	0.0
Yr	1	1	.500	20	0	0	0	2	28²	28	3	7	12	11.0	4.71	72	.264	.310	1	.167	0	-4	-4	0	-0.2
1990 Bal-A	0	0	—	4	1	0	0	0	9²	12	1	3	2	14.9	2.79	136	.308	.372	0	—	0	1	1	0	0.3
Total 3	2	1	.667	61	1	0	0	4	101²	103	6	31	57	12.0	3.36	99	.270	.329	3	.300	1	2	-0	1	0.4
● **GEORGE BOONE** Boone, George Morris b: 3/1/1871, Louisville, Ky. d: 9/24/10, Louisville, Ky. Deb: 4/23/1891																									
1891 Lou-a	0	0	—	4	1	0	0	1	15	15	0	9	4	14.4	7.80	47	.252	.350	2	.333	0	-7	-7	-0	-0.1
● **DAN BOONE** Boone, James Albert b: 1/19/1895, Samantha, Ala. d: 5/11/68, Tuscaloosa, Ala. BR/TR, 6'2", 190 lbs. Deb: 9/10/19																									
1919 Phi-A	0	1	.000	3	2	0	0	0	14²	24	0	10	1	20.9	6.75	51	.375	.459	0	.000	-1	-6	-5	1	-0.3
1921 Det-A	0	0	—	1	0	0	0	0	2	1	0	2	0	13.5	0.00	—	.200	.429	1	1.000	0	1	1	0	0.0
1922 Cle-A	4	6	.400	11	10	4	2	0	75¹	87	3	19	9	12.8	4.06	99	.298	.343	5	.192	-1	-0	-0	1	-0.1
1923 Cle-A	4	6	.400	27	4	2	0	0	70¹	93	3	31	15	16.3	6.01	66	.322	.393	4	.211	0	-16	-16	3	-1.6
Total 4	8	13	.381	42	16	6	2	0	162¹	205	6	62	25	15.0	5.10	77	.315	.378	9	.180	-1	-21	-21	4	-2.0
● **AMOS BOOTH** Booth, Amos Smith "Darling" b: 9/14/1853, Cincinnati, O. d: 7/1/21, Miamisburg, Ohio BR/TR, 5'9", 159 lbs. Deb: 4/25/1876 ♦																									
1876 Cin-N	0	1	.000	3	1	0	0	0	9²	22	0	0	0	20.5	9.31	44	.431	.431	71	.261	-0	-8	-8	-0	-0.6
1877 Cin-N	1	7	.125	12	8	6	0	0	86	114	1	13	18	13.3	3.56	74	.296	.319	27	.172	-1	-7	-9	-1	-0.8
Total 2	1	8	.111	15	9	6	0	0	95²	136	1	13	18	14.0	4.14	63	.312	.332	98	.224	-1	-15	-16	-1	-1.4
● **EDDIE BOOTH** Booth, Edward H. b: Brooklyn, N.Y. Deb: 4/26/1872 ♦																									
1876 NY-N	0	0	—	1	0	0	0	0	5	16	0	0	0	28.8	10.80	20	.471	.471	49	.215	-0	-5	-5	-0	0.0
● **JOHN BOOZER** Boozer, John Morgan b: 7/6/38, Columbia, S.C. d: 1/24/86, Lexington, S.C. BR/TR, 6'3", 205 lbs. Deb: 7/22/62																									
1962 Phi-N	0	0	—	9	0	0	0	0	20¹	22	3	10	13	14.2	5.75	67	.282	.364	0	.000	-0	-4	-4	-0	0.0
1963 Phi-N	3	4	.429	26	8	2	0	1	83	67	11	33	69	11.0	2.93	110	.227	.307	3	.143	-0	3	3	-2	0.0
1964 Phi-N	3	4	.429	22	3	0	0	2	60¹	64	6	18	51	12.5	5.07	68	.271	.328	1	.077	-1	-10	-11	1	-1.2
1966 Phi-N	0	0	—	2	2	0	0	0	5¹	8	1	3	5	18.6	6.75	53	.348	.423	0	—	0	-2	-2	0	0.0
1967 Phi-N	5	4	.556	28	7	1	0	1	74²	86	6	24	48	13.4	4.10	83	.292	.347	4	.211	1	-6	-6	-0	-0.6
1968 Phi-N	2	2	.500	38	0	0	0	5	68²	76	3	15	49	12.2	3.67	82	.279	.322	1	.111	-0	-5	-5	-0	-0.4
1969 Phi-N	1	2	.333	46	2	0	0	6	82	91	12	36	47	13.9	4.28	83	.283	.356	3	.333	1	-6	-7	-1	-0.3
Total 7	14	16	.467	171	22	3	0	15	394¹	414	42	139	282	12.8	4.09	82	.272	.336	12	.162	-0	-30	-31	-2	-2.5
● **PEDRO BORBON** Borbon, Pedro (Rodriguez) b: 12/2/46, Valverde, Mao, D.R. BR/TR, 6'2", 185 lbs. Deb: 4/9/69 F																									
1969 Cal-A	2	3	.400	22	6	1	0	0	41	55	5	11	20	15.4	6.15	57	.324	.378	0	.000	-0	-12	-12	-0	-1.4
1970 Cin-N	0	2	.000	12	1	0	0	0	17¹	21	2	6	6	15.6	6.75	60	.309	.390	0	.000	-0	-5	-5	2	-0.4
1971 Cin-N	0	0	—	3	0	0	0	0	4¹	3	1	1	4	8.3	4.15	81	.200	.250	0	—	0	-0	-0	-0	0.0
1972 *Cin-N	8	3	.727	62	2	0	0	11	122	115	3	32	48	11.1	3.17	101	.254	.307	1	.048	-1	4	1	-1	-0.1
1973 *Cin-N	11	4	.733	80	0	0	0	14	121	137	4	35	60	12.9	2.16	158	.298	.349	5	.333	1	**20**	17	-0	2.6
1974 Cin-N	10	7	.588	73	0	0	0	14	139	133	11	32	53	10.9	3.24	108	.255	.303	6	.192	-0	6	4	-0	0.4
1975 *Cin-N	9	5	.643	67	0	0	0	5	125	145	6	21	29	12.2	2.95	122	.301	.334	7	.292	2	9	9	-1	1.1
1976 *Cin-N	4	3	.571	69	1	0	0	8	121	135	4	31	53	12.6	3.35	105	.292	.342	4	.222	0	2	2	-0	0.1
1977 Cin-N	10	5	.667	73	0	0	0	18	127	131	6	24	60	11.2	3.19	123	.268	.307	4	.182	0	10	10	-2	1.3
1978 Cin-N	8	2	.800	62	0	0	0	4	99¹	102	6	27	35	12.0	4.98	71	.274	.328	2	.182	0	-16	-16	-0	-1.7
1979 Cin-N	2	2	.500	30	0	0	0	2	44²	48	5	8	23	11.3	3.43	109	.277	.309	2	.333	0	2	2	0	0.2
SF-N	4	3	.571	30	0	0	0	3	46	56	7	13	26	13.5	4.89	71	.303	.348	1	.333	0	-6	-7	-1	-1.1
Yr	6	5	.545	60	0	0	0	5	90²	104	9	21	49	12.4	4.17	87	.287	.326	3	.333	1	-4	-6	-1	-0.9
1980 StL-N	1	0	1.000	10	0	0	0	0	19	17	3	10	4	12.8	3.79	97	.250	.346	1	.250	0	-0	-0	-0	0.0
Total 12	69	39	.639	593	4	0	0	80	1026²	1098	63	251	409	12.1	3.52	101	.280	.328	32	.205	2	14	3	-4	1.0
● **PEDRO BORBON** Borbon, Pedro Felix (Marte) b: 11/15/67, Mao, D.R. BR/TL, 6'1", 205 lbs. Deb: 10/2/92 F																									
1992 Atl-N	0	1	.000	2	0	0	0	0	1¹	2	0	1	1	20.3	6.75	54	.333	.429	0	—	0	-0	-0	0	-0.3
1993 Atl-N	0	0	—	3	0	0	0	0	1²	3	0	3	2	32.4	21.60	19	.429	.600	0	—	0	-3	-3	-0	0.0
Total 2	0	1	.000	5	0	0	0	0	3	5	0	4	3	27.0	15.00	26	.385	.529	0	—	0	-4	-4	-0	-0.3
● **GEORGE BORCHERS** Borchers, George Benard "Chief" b: 4/18/1869, Sacramento, Cal. d: 10/24/38, Sacramento, Cal. BB/TR, 5'10", 180 lbs. Deb: 5/18/1888																									
1888 Chi-N	4	4	.500	10	10	7	1	0	67	67	2	29	26	13.7	3.49	87	.251	.338	2	.061	-2	-5	-5	-0	-0.5
1895 Lou-N	0	1	.000	1	1	0	0	0	0²	1	0	3	0	54.0	27.00	17	.341	.674	0	—	0	-2	-2	-0	-1.1
Total 2	4	5	.444	11	11	7	1	0	67²	68	2	32	26	14.1	3.72	82	.252	.344	2	.061	-2	-6	-5	-0	-1.6
● **JOE BORDEN** Borden, Joseph Emley (a.k.a. Joseph Emley Josephs In 1875) b: 5/9/1854, Jacobstown, N.J. d: 10/14/29, Yeadon, Pa. BR/TR, 5'9", 140 lbs. Deb: 7/24/1875																									
1875 Phi-n	2	4	.333	7	7	7	2	0	66	47	0	7		**7.4**	1.64	154	**.181**	**.203**	3	.107	-3	6	6		0.2
1876 Bos-N	11	12	.478	29	24	16	2	1	218¹	257	4	51	34	12.7	2.89	78	.276	.313	25	.207	-3	-14	-15	-2	-1.7
● **RICH BORDI** Bordi, Richard Albert b: 4/18/59, San Francisco, Cal. BR/TR, 6'7", 220 lbs. Deb: 7/16/80																									
1980 Oak-A	0	0	—	1	0	0	0	0	2	4	0	0	0	18.0	4.50	84	.400	.400	0	—	0	-0	-0	-0	0.0
1981 Oak-A	0	0	—	2	0	0	0	0	2	1	0	1	0	9.0	0.00	—	.143	.250	0	—	0	1	1	-0	0.0
1982 Sea-A	0	2	.000	7	2	0	0	0	13	18	4	1	10	13.8	8.31	51	.310	.333	0	—	0	-6	-6	-0	-0.9

YEAR	TM/L	W	L	PCT	G	GS	CG	SH	SV	IP	H	HR	BB	SO	RAT	ERA	ERA+	OAV	OOB	BH	AVG	PB	PR	/A	PD	TPI
1983	Chi-N	0	2	.000	11	1	0	0	1	25¹	34	4	12	20	16.3	4.97	76	.321	.390	0	.000	-0	-4	-3	0	-0.3
1984	Chi-N	5	2	.714	31	7	0	0	4	83¹	78	11	20	41	10.6	3.46	113	.242	.287	1	.053	-1	1	4	-1	0.2
1985	NY-A	6	8	.429	51	3	0	0	2	98	95	5	29	64	11.5	3.21	124	.253	.308	0	—	0	10	9	-1	1.2
1986	Bal-A	6	4	.600	52	1	0	0	3	107	105	13	41	83	12.6	4.46	93	.254	.327	0	—	0	-3	-4	1	-0.2
1987	NY-A	3	1	.750	16	1	0	0	0	33	42	7	12	23	14.7	7.64	57	.309	.365	0	—	0	-12	-12	-1	-1.2
1988	Oak-A	0	1	.000	2	2	0	0	0	7²	6	0	5	6	12.9	4.70	80	.214	.333	0	—	0	-1	-1	-0	-0.1
Total 9		20	20	.500	173	17	0	0	10	371¹	383	42	121	247	12.4	4.34	93	.263	.322	1	.043	-2	-13	-12	-2	-1.3

● BILL BORDLEY
Bordley, William Clarke b: 1/9/58, Los Angeles, Cal. BR/TL, 6'3", 185 lbs. Deb: 6/30/80

YEAR	TM/L	W	L	PCT	G	GS	CG	SH	SV	IP	H	HR	BB	SO	RAT	ERA	ERA+	OAV	OOB	BH	AVG	PB	PR	/A	PD	TPI
1980	SF-N	2	3	.400	8	6	0	0	0	30²	34	3	21	11	16.1	4.70	75	.288	.396	1	.167	0	-4	-4	1	-0.5

● PAUL BORIS
Boris, Paul Stanley b: 12/13/55, Irvington, N.J. BR/TR, 6'2", 200 lbs. Deb: 5/21/82

YEAR	TM/L	W	L	PCT	G	GS	CG	SH	SV	IP	H	HR	BB	SO	RAT	ERA	ERA+	OAV	OOB	BH	AVG	PB	PR	/A	PD	TPI
1982	Min-A	1	2	.333	23	0	0	0	0	49²	46	8	19	30	12.1	3.99	106	.246	.322	0	—	0	1	1	-0	-0.2

● FRANK BORK
Bork, Frank Bernard b: 7/13/40, Buffalo, N.Y. BR/TL, 6'2", 175 lbs. Deb: 4/15/64

YEAR	TM/L	W	L	PCT	G	GS	CG	SH	SV	IP	H	HR	BB	SO	RAT	ERA	ERA+	OAV	OOB	BH	AVG	PB	PR	/A	PD	TPI
1964	Pit-N	2	2	.500	33	2	0	0	2	42	51	6	11	31	13.5	4.07	86	.295	.341	1	.200	0	-2	-3	0	-0.2

● TOM BORLAND
Borland, Thomas Bruce "Spike" b: 2/14/33, ElDorado, Kan. BL/TL, 6'3", 172 lbs. Deb: 5/15/60

YEAR	TM/L	W	L	PCT	G	GS	CG	SH	SV	IP	H	HR	BB	SO	RAT	ERA	ERA+	OAV	OOB	BH	AVG	PB	PR	/A	PD	TPI
1960	Bos-A	0	4	.000	26	4	0	0	3	51	67	4	23	32	15.9	6.53	62	.322	.390	0	.000	-2	-15	-14	0	-1.3
1961	Bos-A	0	0	—	1	0	0	0	0	1	3	0	0	0	27.0	18.00	23	.500	.500	0	—	0	-2	-2	-0	0.0
Total 2		0	4	.000	27	4	0	0	3	52	70	4	23	32	16.1	6.75	60	.327	.392	0	.000	-2	-17	-16	0	-1.3

● TOBY BORLAND
Borland, Toby Shawn b: 5/29/69, Quitman, La. BR/TR, 6'6", 186 lbs. Deb: 5/27/94

YEAR	TM/L	W	L	PCT	G	GS	CG	SH	SV	IP	H	HR	BB	SO	RAT	ERA	ERA+	OAV	OOB	BH	AVG	PB	PR	/A	PD	TPI
1994	Phi-N	1	0	1.000	24	0	0	0	1	34¹	31	1	14	26	12.8	2.36	175	.248	.343	0	.000	-0	7	7	-0	0.1

● HANK BOROWY
Borowy, Henry Ludwig b: 5/12/16, Bloomfield, N.J. BR/TR, 6', 175 lbs. Deb: 4/18/42

YEAR	TM/L	W	L	PCT	G	GS	CG	SH	SV	IP	H	HR	BB	SO	RAT	ERA	ERA+	OAV	OOB	BH	AVG	PB	PR	/A	PD	TPI
1942	*NY-A	15	4	.789	25	21	13	4	1	178¹	157	6	66	85	11.3	2.52	136	.233	.301	11	.157	-1	22	18	1	1.9
1943	*NY-A	14	9	.609	29	27	14	3	0	217¹	195	11	72	113	11.1	2.82	114	.241	.305	15	.203	3	12	10	1	1.4
1944	NY-A★	17	12	.586	35	30	19	3	2	252²	224	15	88	107	11.1	2.64	132	.236	.301	12	.133	-3	22	24	2	2.5
1945	NY-A†	10	5	.667	18	18	7	1	0	132¹	107	6	58	35	11.3	3.13	111	.221	.305	11	.220	1	3	5	1	0.8
	*Chi-N	11	2	.846	15	14	11	1	1	122¹	105	2	47	47	11.2	2.13	171	.231	.303	7	.171	0	23	21	-1	2.1
1946	Chi-N	12	10	.545	32	28	8	1	0	201	220	9	61	95	12.6	3.76	88	.274	.326	13	.181	1	-8	-10	0	-0.9
1947	Chi-N	8	12	.400	40	25	7	1	2	183	190	19	63	75	12.5	4.38	90	.267	.328	7	.125	-1	-6	-9	0	-0.9
1948	Chi-N	5	10	.333	39	17	2	1	1	127	156	9	49	50	14.5	4.89	80	.308	.369	8	.222	2	-13	-14	2	-1.1
1949	Phi-N	12	12	.500	28	28	12	1	0	193¹	188	19	63	43	11.7	4.19	94	.259	.319	13	.213	3	-3	-5	-2	-0.4
1950	Phi-N	0	0	—	3	0	0	0	0	6¹	5	0	4	3	12.8	5.68	71	.250	.375	0	—	0	-1	-1	0	0.0
	Pit-N	1	3	.250	11	3	0	0	0	25¹	32	6	9	9	14.9	6.39	69	.311	.372	1	.167	-0	-6	-6	0	-0.8
	Yr	1	3	.250	14	3	0	0	0	31²	37	6	13	12	14.5	6.25	69	.301	.372	1	.167	-0	-7	-7	0	-0.8
	Det-A	1	1	.500	13	2	1	0	0	32²	23	6	16	12	10.7	3.31	142	.205	.305	1	.143	-0	5	5	-0	0.2
1951	Det-A	2	2	.500	26	1	0	0	0	45¹	58	3	27	16	17.1	6.95	60	.314	.404	0	.000	-1	-14	-14	1	-1.1
Total 10		108	82	.568	314	214	94	16	7	1717	1660	108	623	690	12.0	3.50	104	.254	.320	99	.173	3	35	24	5	3.7

● CHRIS BOSIO
Bosio, Christopher Louis b: 4/3/63, Carmichael, Cal. BR/TR, 6'3", 235 lbs. Deb: 8/3/86

YEAR	TM/L	W	L	PCT	G	GS	CG	SH	SV	IP	H	HR	BB	SO	RAT	ERA	ERA+	OAV	OOB	BH	AVG	PB	PR	/A	PD	TPI
1986	Mil-A	0	4	.000	10	4	0	0	0	34²	41	9	13	29	14.0	7.01	62	.293	.353	0	—	0	-11	-10	0	-1.1
1987	Mil-A	11	8	.579	46	19	2	1	2	170	187	18	50	150	12.6	5.24	87	.276	.327	0	—	0	-15	-13	1	-1.3
1988	Mil-A	7	15	.318	38	22	9	1	6	182	190	13	38	84	11.4	3.36	118	.268	.307	0	—	0	12	13	3	1.8
1989	Mil-A	15	10	.600	33	33	8	2	0	234²	225	16	48	173	10.7	2.95	130	.249	.291	0	—	0	24	23	1	2.5
1990	Mil-A	4	9	.308	20	20	4	1	0	132²	131	15	38	76	11.7	4.00	97	.258	.313	0	—	0	-1	-2	2	0.0
1991	Mil-A	14	10	.583	32	32	5	1	0	204²	187	15	58	117	11.1	3.25	122	.244	.304	0	—	0	19	16	-1	1.8
1992	Mil-A	16	6	.727	33	33	4	2	0	231¹	223	21	44	120	10.5	3.62	106	.254	.293	0	—	0	8	6	0	0.7
1993	Sea-A	9	9	.500	29	24	3	1	1	164¹	138	14	59	119	11.1	3.45	128	.229	.304	0	—	0	16	17	0	1.7
1994	Sea-A	4	10	.286	19	19	4	0	0	125	137	15	40	67	12.9	4.32	114	.277	.333	0	—	0	7	8	0	0.7
Total 9		80	81	.497	260	206	39	9	9	1479¹	1459	136	388	935	11.4	3.77	109	.257	.308	0	—	0	59	57	7	6.8

● SHAWN BOSKIE
Boskie, Shawn Kealoha b: 3/28/67, Hawthorne, Nev. BR/TR, 6'3", 205 lbs. Deb: 5/20/90

YEAR	TM/L	W	L	PCT	G	GS	CG	SH	SV	IP	H	HR	BB	SO	RAT	ERA	ERA+	OAV	OOB	BH	AVG	PB	PR	/A	PD	TPI
1990	Chi-N	5	6	.455	15	15	1	0	0	97²	99	8	31	49	12.1	3.69	111	.265	.323	8	.222	1	1	4	0	0.6
1991	Chi-N	4	9	.308	28	20	0	0	0	129	150	14	52	62	14.4	5.23	74	.294	.364	7	.171	2	-22	-19	1	-1.5
1992	Chi-N	5	11	.313	23	18	0	0	0	91²	96	14	36	39	13.4	5.01	72	.284	.360	5	.185	1	-15	-14	1	-2.1
1993	Chi-N	5	3	.625	39	2	0	0	0	65²	63	7	21	39	12.5	3.43	116	.258	.335	2	.273	1	4	4	-1	0.4
1994	Chi-N	0	0	—	2	0	0	0	0	3²	3	0	0	2	7.4	0.00	—	.214	.214	0	—	0	2	2	0	0.1
	Phi-N	4	6	.400	18	14	1	0	0	84¹	85	14	29	59	12.5	5.23	79	.258	.323	3	.115	1	-10	-10	0	-0.9
	Yr	4	6	.400	20	14	1	0	0	88	88	14	29	61	12.3	5.01	82	.256	.319	3	.115	1	-8	-9	1	-0.9
	Sea-A	0	1	.000	2	1	0	0	0	2²	4	1	1	0	16.9	6.75	73	.333	.385	0	—	0	-1	-1	0	-0.3
Total 5		23	36	.390	127	70	2	0	0	474²	500	58	170	250	13.1	4.59	86	.274	.343	26	.184	6	-40	-34	2	-3.8

● DICK BOSMAN
Bosman, Richard Allen b: 2/17/44, Kenosha, Wis. BR/TR, 6'3", 208 lbs. Deb: 6/1/66 C

YEAR	TM/L	W	L	PCT	G	GS	CG	SH	SV	IP	H	HR	BB	SO	RAT	ERA	ERA+	OAV	OOB	BH	AVG	PB	PR	/A	PD	TPI
1966	Was-A	2	6	.250	13	7	0	0	0	39	60	4	12	20	16.6	7.62	45	.361	.404	3	.250	0	-18	-18	-1	-3.1
1967	Was-A	3	1	.750	7	7	2	1	0	51¹	38	3	10	25	8.4	1.75	180	.204	.245	3	.200	0	8	8	-1	0.7
1968	Was-A	2	9	.182	46	10	0	0	1	139	139	9	35	63	11.5	3.69	79	.262	.312	6	.200	1	-11	-12	-0	-0.9
1969	Was-A	14	5	.737	31	26	5	2	1	193	156	11	39	99	9.2	**2.19**	**158**	.220	.262	6	.094	-1	31	27	1	2.7
1970	Was-A	16	12	.571	36	34	7	3	0	230²	212	16	71	134	11.1	3.00	118	.245	.304	11	.138	-2	18	14	0	1.4
1971	Was-A	12	16	.429	35	35	7	1	0	236²	245	29	71	113	12.2	3.73	89	.272	.329	7	.093	-2	-7	-11	-2	-1.6
1972	Tex-A	8	10	.444	29	29	1	1	0	173¹	183	11	48	105	12.3	3.63	83	.273	.327	5	.094	-2	-11	-12	1	-1.3
1973	Tex-A	2	5	.286	7	7	1	1	0	40¹	42	6	17	14	13.4	4.24	88	.268	.343	0	—	0	-2	-2	-0	-0.4
	Cle-A	1	8	.111	22	17	2	0	0	97	130	19	29	41	15.3	6.22	63	.320	.374	0	—	0	-26	-25	-1	-2.1
	Yr	3	13	.188	29	24	3	1	0	137¹	172	25	46	55	14.7	5.64	69	.304	.363	0	—	0	-28	-27	-1	-2.5
1974	Cle-A	7	5	.583	25	18	2	1	0	127¹	126	13	29	56	11.0	4.10	88	.255	.298	0	—	0	-7	-7	-2	-0.8
1975	Cle-A	2	0	.000	6	3	0	0	0	28²	33	3	8	11	13.8	4.08	93	.292	.355	0	—	0	-1	-1	-0	-0.1
	*Oak-A	11	4	.733	22	21	2	0	0	122²	112	12	24	67	10.2	3.52	103	.240	.281	0	—	0	3	1	1	0.2
	Yr	11	6	.647	28	24	2	0	0	151¹	145	15	32	53	10.7	3.63	101	.248	.290	0	—	0	1	1	1	0.1
1976	Oak-A	4	2	.667	27	15	0	0	0	112	118	13	19	34	11.1	4.10	82	.274	.306	0	—	0	-7	-9	0	-0.4
Total 11		82	85	.491	306	229	29	10	2	1591	1594	149	412	757	11.5	3.67	93	.261	.312	41	.125	-5	-29	-46	-5	-5.7

● MEL BOSSER
Bosser, Melvin Edward b: 2/8/20, Johnstown, Pa. BR/TR, 6', 173 lbs. Deb: 4/29/45

YEAR	TM/L	W	L	PCT	G	GS	CG	SH	SV	IP	H	HR	BB	SO	RAT	ERA	ERA+	OAV	OOB	BH	AVG	PB	PR	/A	PD	TPI
1945	Cin-N	2	0	1.000	7	2	0	0	0	16	9	0	17	3	14.6	3.38	111	.158	.351	0	.000	-1	1	1	-0	0.0

● ANDY BOSWELL
Boswell, Andrew Cottrell b: 9/5/1874, New Gretna, N.J. d: 2/3/36, Ocean City, N.J. 6'1", 165 lbs. Deb: 5/10/1895

YEAR	TM/L	W	L	PCT	G	GS	CG	SH	SV	IP	H	HR	BB	SO	RAT	ERA	ERA+	OAV	OOB	BH	AVG	PB	PR	/A	PD	TPI
1895	NY-N	2	2	.500	5	4	3	0	0	34	41	1	22	18	17.5	5.82	80	.294	.401	2	.188	-1	-4	-4	-1	-0.5
	Was-N	1	2	.333	6	3	3	0	0	30	44	1	19	12	19.5	6.00	80	.336	.428	4	.286	0	-4	-4	-0	-0.3
	Yr	3	4	.429	11	7	6	0	0	64	85	2	41	30	18.0	5.91	80	.311	.404	7	.233	-1	-8	-8	-1	-0.8

● DAVE BOSWELL
Boswell, David Wilson b: 1/20/45, Baltimore, Md. BR/TR, 6'3", 185 lbs. Deb: 9/18/64

YEAR	TM/L	W	L	PCT	G	GS	CG	SH	SV	IP	H	HR	BB	SO	RAT	ERA	ERA+	OAV	OOB	BH	AVG	PB	PR	/A	PD	TPI
1964	Min-A	2	0	1.000	4	4	0	0	0	23¹	21	4	12	25	12.7	4.24	84	.236	.327	2	.222	0	-2	-1	1	-0.1
1965	*Min-A	6	5	.545	27	12	1	0	0	106	77	20	46	85	10.9	3.40	105	.204	.298	12	.316	4	1	2	-1	0.5
1966	Min-A	12	5	.706	28	21	8	1	0	169¹	120	19	65	173	10.1	3.14	115	.197	.280	9	.143	-1	6	9	1	0.8
1967	Min-A	14	12	.538	37	32	11	3	0	222²	162	14	107	204	11.2	3.27	106	.202	.302	16	.219	4	-1	5	-1	0.8

YEAR	TM/L	W	L	PCT	G	GS	CG	SH	SV	IP	H	HR	BB	SO	RAT	ERA	ERA+	OAV	OOB	BH	AVG	PB	PR	/A	PD	TPI
1968	Min-A	10	13	.435	34	28	7	2	0	190	148	19	87	143	11.5	3.32	93	.213	.307	14	.233	5	-7	-5	-2	-0.3
1969	*Min-A	20	12	.625	39	38	10	0	0	256¹	215	18	99	190	11.3	3.23	113	.226	.304	16	.170	3	11	12	-2	1.5
1970	Min-A	3	7	.300	18	15	0	0	0	68²	80	12	44	45	16.5	6.42	58	.292	.394	4	.160	-0	-21	-21	-1	-2.7
1971	Det-A	0	0	—	3	0	0	0	0	4¹	3	0	6	3	18.7	6.23	58	.200	.429	0	—	-0	-1	-1	0	0.0
	Bal-A	1	2	.333	15	1	0	0	0	24²	32	4	15	14	17.1	4.38	77	.305	.392	1	.200	0	-3	-3	0	-0.3
	Yr	1	2	.333	18	1	0	0	0	29	35	4	21	17	17.4	4.66	73	.289	.394	1	.200	0	-4	-4	0	-0.3
Total 8		68	56	.548	205	151	37	6	0	1065¹	858	110	481	882	11.6	3.52	99	.219	.310	74	.202	13	-17	-4	-4	0.2

● DEREK BOTELHO
Botelho, Derek Wayne   b:8/2/56, Long Beach, Cal.   BR/TR, 6'2", 180 lbs.   Deb:7/18/82

YEAR	TM/L	W	L	PCT	G	GS	CG	SH	SV	IP	H	HR	BB	SO	RAT	ERA	ERA+	OAV	OOB	BH	AVG	PB	PR	/A	PD	TPI
1982	KC-A	2	1	.667	8	4	0	0	0	24	25	4	8	12	12.4	4.13	99	.275	.333	0	—	0	-0	-0	-0	0.0
1985	Chi-N	1	3	.250	11	7	1	0	0	44	52	8	23	23	15.8	5.32	75	.299	.387	2	.143	-0	-8	-6	-0	-0.6
Total 2		3	4	.429	19	11	1	0	0	68	77	12	31	35	14.6	4.90	82	.291	.369	2	.143	-0	-9	-7	-1	-0.6

● RICKY BOTTALICO
Bottalico, Richard Paul   b:8/26/69, New Britain, Conn.   BL/TR, 6'1", 200 lbs.   Deb:7/29/94

YEAR	TM/L	W	L	PCT	G	GS	CG	SH	SV	IP	H	HR	BB	SO	RAT	ERA	ERA+	OAV	OOB	BH	AVG	PB	PR	/A	PD	TPI
1994	Phi-N	0	0	—	3	0	0	0	0	3	3	0	1	3	12.0	0.00	—	.250	.308	0	—	0	1	1	-0	0.0

● KENT BOTTENFIELD
Bottenfield, Kent Dennis   b:11/14/68, Portland, Ore.   BB/TR, 6'3", 225 lbs.   Deb:7/6/92

YEAR	TM/L	W	L	PCT	G	GS	CG	SH	SV	IP	H	HR	BB	SO	RAT	ERA	ERA+	OAV	OOB	BH	AVG	PB	PR	/A	PD	TPI
1992	Mon-N	1	2	.333	10	4	0	0	0	32¹	26	1	11	14	10.6	2.23	156	.217	.288	3	.375	1	5	4	-1	0.5
1993	Mon-N	2	5	.286	23	11	0	0	0	83	93	11	33	33	14.2	4.12	101	.288	.363	4	.167	-0	-1	-0	-0	-0.0
	Col-N	3	5	.375	14	14	1	0	0	76²	86	13	38	30	14.7	6.10	78	.302	.386	7	.269	1	-18	-11	2	-0.8
	Yr	5	10	.333	37	25	1	0	0	159²	179	24	71	63	14.1	5.07	88	.292	.366	11	.220	1	-18	-11	2	-0.8
1994	Col-N	3	1	.750	15	1	0	0	1	24²	28	1	10	15	14.6	5.84	85	.283	.360	0	.000	-0	-4	-2	-1	-0.4
	SF-N	0	0	—	1	0	0	0	0	1²	5	1	0	0	27.0	10.80	37	.556	.556	0	—	-0	-1	-1	-0	0.0
	Yr	3	1	.750	16	1	0	0	1	26¹	33	2	10	15	14.7	6.15	80	.300	.358	0	.000	-0	-6	-4	-1	-0.4
Total 3		9	13	.409	63	30	1	0	2	218¹	238	27	92	92	14.0	4.78	91	.285	.362	14	.237	1	-19	-10	0	-0.7

● RALPH BOTTING
Botting, Ralph Wayne   b:5/12/55, Houlton, Maine   BL/TL, 6', 195 lbs.   Deb:6/28/79

YEAR	TM/L	W	L	PCT	G	GS	CG	SH	SV	IP	H	HR	BB	SO	RAT	ERA	ERA+	OAV	OOB	BH	AVG	PB	PR	/A	PD	TPI
1979	Cal-A	2	0	1.000	12	1	0	0	0	29²	46	6	15	22	18.8	8.80	46	.362	.434	0	—	0	-15	-16	-0	-0.9
1980	Cal-A	0	3	.000	6	6	0	0	0	26¹	40	1	13	12	18.1	5.81	68	.348	.414	0	—	0	-5	-6	-0	-0.5
Total 2		2	3	.400	18	7	0	0	0	56	86	7	28	34	18.5	7.39	54	.355	.424	0	—	0	-20	-21	-0	-1.4

● BOB BOTZ
Botz, Robert Allen   b:4/28/35, Milwaukee, Wis.   BR/TR, 5'11", 170 lbs.   Deb:5/8/62

YEAR	TM/L	W	L	PCT	G	GS	CG	SH	SV	IP	H	HR	BB	SO	RAT	ERA	ERA+	OAV	OOB	BH	AVG	PB	PR	/A	PD	TPI
1962	LA-A	2	1	.667	35	0	0	0	2	63	71	7	11	24	12.0	3.43	113	.285	.321	0	.000	-1	4	3	-1	-0.1

● DENIS BOUCHER
Boucher, Denis   b:3/7/68, Montreal, Que., Can.   BR/TL, 6'1", 195 lbs.   Deb:4/12/91

YEAR	TM/L	W	L	PCT	G	GS	CG	SH	SV	IP	H	HR	BB	SO	RAT	ERA	ERA+	OAV	OOB	BH	AVG	PB	PR	/A	PD	TPI
1991	Tor-A	0	3	.000	7	7	0	0	0	35¹	39	6	16	16	14.5	4.58	92	.279	.361	0	—	0	-2	-1	1	-0.2
	Cle-A	1	4	.200	5	5	0	0	0	22²	35	6	8	13	17.1	8.34	50	.350	.398	0	—	0	-11	-11	0	-1.7
	Yr	1	7	.125	12	12	0	0	0	58	74	12	24	29	15.2	6.05	69	.305	.367	0	—	0	-13	-12	1	-1.9
1992	Cle-A	2	2	.500	8	7	0	0	0	41	48	9	20	17	15.1	6.37	61	.302	.383	0	—	0	-11	-11	-1	-0.9
1993	Mon-N	3	1	.750	5	5	0	0	0	28¹	24	1	3	14	8.6	1.91	219	.229	.250	1	.167	0	7	7	-0	1.0
1994	Mon-N	0	1	.000	10	2	0	0	0	18²	24	6	7	17	14.9	6.75	63	.324	.383	1	.333	1	-5	-5	0	-0.2
Total 4		6	11	.353	35	26	0	0	0	146	170	28	54	77	14.0	5.42	76	.294	.357	2	.222	1	-22	-21	0	-2.0

● CARL BOULDIN
Bouldin, Carl Edward   b:9/17/39, Germantown, Ky.   BB/TR, 6'2", 180 lbs.   Deb:9/2/61

YEAR	TM/L	W	L	PCT	G	GS	CG	SH	SV	IP	H	HR	BB	SO	RAT	ERA	ERA+	OAV	OOB	BH	AVG	PB	PR	/A	PD	TPI
1961	Was-A	0	1	.000	2	1	0	0	0	3¹	9	0	2	2	29.7	16.20	25	.500	.550	0	.000	-0	-5	-5	-0	-0.9
1962	Was-A	1	2	.333	6	3	0	0	0	20	26	0	9	12	16.2	5.85	69	.321	.396	0	.000	-1	-4	-4	-0	-0.6
1963	Was-A	2	2	.500	10	3	0	0	0	23¹	31	3	8	10	15.0	5.79	64	.307	.358	0	.000	-1	-6	-6	-0	-0.9
1964	Was-A	0	3	.000	9	3	0	0	0	25	30	2	11	12	15.5	5.40	69	.294	.374	0	.000	-0	-5	-5	-0	-0.6
Total 4		3	8	.273	27	10	1	0	0	71²	96	5	30	36	16.2	6.15	62	.318	.385	0	.000	-2	-19	-19	0	-3.0

● JAKE BOULTES
Boultes, Jacob John   b:8/6/1884, St.Louis, Mo.   d:12/24/55, St.Louis, Mo.   TR, 6'3",   Deb:4/18/07

YEAR	TM/L	W	L	PCT	G	GS	CG	SH	SV	IP	H	HR	BB	SO	RAT	ERA	ERA+	OAV	OOB	BH	AVG	PB	PR	/A	PD	TPI
1907	Bos-N	5	9	.357	24	12	11	0	0	139²	140	4	50	49	12.8	2.71	94	.266	.338	9	.132	-2	-4	-2	4	0.0
1908	Bos-N	3	5	.375	17	5	1	0	0	74²	80	7	8	28	10.7	3.01	80	.274	.296	3	.143	-0	-5	-5	-0	-0.7
1909	Bos-N	0	0	—	1	0	0	0	0	8	9	2	0	1	11.3	6.75	42	.290	.313	1	.333	0	-4	-3	-0	0.0
Total 3		8	14	.364	42	17	12	0	0	222¹	229	10	58	78	12.0	2.96	85	.269	.324	13	.141	-2	-13	-11	4	-0.7

● JIM BOUTON
Bouton, James Alan   b:3/8/39, Newark, N.J.   BR/TR, 6', 185 lbs.   Deb:4/22/62

YEAR	TM/L	W	L	PCT	G	GS	CG	SH	SV	IP	H	HR	BB	SO	RAT	ERA	ERA+	OAV	OOB	BH	AVG	PB	PR	/A	PD	TPI
1962	NY-A	7	7	.500	36	16	3	1	2	133	124	9	59	71	12.4	3.99	94	.254	.334	2	.063	-2	-0	-4	0	-0.5
1963	*NY-A★	21	7	.750	40	30	12	6	1	249¹	191	18	87	148	10.1	2.53	139	.212	.284	6	.072	-6	31	27	-1	2.3
1964	*NY-A	18	13	.581	38	37	11	4	0	271¹	227	32	60	125	9.7	3.02	120	.225	.273	13	.130	-3	18	18	-3	1.3
1965	NY-A	4	15	.211	30	25	2	0	0	151¹	158	23	60	97	13.3	4.82	71	.269	.342	4	.093	-0	-23	-24	-0	-2.8
1966	NY-A	3	8	.273	24	19	3	0	0	120¹	117	13	38	65	11.7	2.69	123	.257	.315	4	.105	-2	10	8	1	0.7
1967	NY-A	1	0	1.000	17	1	0	0	0	44¹	47	5	18	31	13.4	4.67	67	.275	.347	0	.000	-0	-7	-8	-0	-0.2
1968	NY-A	1	1	.500	12	3	1	0	0	44	49	5	9	24	12.3	3.68	79	.287	.330	0	.000	-0	-3	-4	1	-0.1
1969	Sea-A	2	1	.667	57	1	0	0	1	92	77	9	38	68	11.4	3.91	93	.219	.299	0	.000	-1	-3	-3	1	-0.1
	Hou-N	0	2	.000	16	1	0	0	0	30²	32	1	12	33	13.5	4.11	86	.267	.330	0	.000	-0	-2	-2	0	-0.2
1970	Hou-N	4	6	.400	29	6	1	0	0	73¹	84	5	33	49	14.5	5.40	72	.285	.359	6	.353	-2	-11	-12	-0	-1.3
1978	Atl-N	1	3	.250	5	5	0	0	0	29	25	4	21	10	14.3	4.97	82	.234	.359	0	.000	-1	-4	-3	-0	-0.5
Total 10		62	63	.496	304	144	34	11	6	1238²	1131	127	435	720	11.5	3.57	99	.243	.311	35	.101	-13	5	-5	-1	-1.4

● RYAN BOWEN
Bowen, Ryan Eugene   b:2/10/68, Hanford, Cal.   BR/TR, 6', 185 lbs.   Deb:7/22/91

YEAR	TM/L	W	L	PCT	G	GS	CG	SH	SV	IP	H	HR	BB	SO	RAT	ERA	ERA+	OAV	OOB	BH	AVG	PB	PR	/A	PD	TPI
1991	Hou-N	6	4	.600	14	13	0	0	0	71²	73	4	36	49	14.1	5.15	68	.268	.360	4	.182	1	-12	-13	-2	-1.6
1992	Hou-N	0	7	.000	11	9	0	0	0	33²	48	8	30	22	21.4	10.96	31	.333	.455	1	.111	-0	-28	-28	-1	-4.6
1993	Fla-N	8	12	.400	27	27	1	0	0	156¹	156	11	87	98	14.1	4.42	90	.263	.360	6	.118	-1	-7	-0	-0	-0.3
1994	Fla-N	1	5	.167	8	8	1	0	0	47¹	50	9	19	32	13.5	4.94	91	.273	.348	5	.357	2	-4	-2	-1	-0.2
Total 4		15	28	.349	60	57	3	1	0	309¹	327	32	172	201	14.8	5.38	75	.274	.370	16	.167	2	-50	-46	-4	-6.7

● CY BOWEN
Bowen, Sutherland McCoy   b:2/17/1871, Kingston, Ind.   d:1/25/25, Greensburg, Ind.   BR/TR, 6', 175 lbs.   Deb:4/28/1896

YEAR	TM/L	W	L	PCT	G	GS	CG	SH	SV	IP	H	HR	BB	SO	RAT	ERA	ERA+	OAV	OOB	BH	AVG	PB	PR	/A	PD	TPI
1896	NY-N	0	1	.000	2	1	1	0	0	12	12	0	9	3	18.0	6.00	70	.258	.411	1	.333	0	-2	-2	0	-0.1

● FRANK BOWERMAN
Bowerman, Frank Eugene "Mike"   b:12/5/1868, Romeo, Mich.   d:11/30/48, Romeo, Mich.   BR/TR, 6'2", 190 lbs.   Deb:8/24/1895   M♦

YEAR	TM/L	W	L	PCT	G	GS	CG	SH	SV	IP	H	HR	BB	SO	RAT	ERA	ERA+	OAV	OOB	BH	AVG	PB	PR	/A	PD	TPI
1904	NY-N	0	0	—	1	0	0	0	0	1	3	0	1	0	36.0	9.00	30	.429	.500	67	.232	0	-1	-1	-0	0.0

● STEW BOWERS
Bowers, Stewart Cole "Doc"   b:2/26/15, New Freedom, Pa.   BB/TR, 6', 170 lbs.   Deb:8/5/35   ♦

YEAR	TM/L	W	L	PCT	G	GS	CG	SH	SV	IP	H	HR	BB	SO	RAT	ERA	ERA+	OAV	OOB	BH	AVG	PB	PR	/A	PD	TPI
1935	Bos-A	2	1	.667	10	2	1	0	0	23²	26	1	17	16	16.4	3.42	139	.283	.394	1	.200	0	3	3	0	0.4
1936	Bos-A	0	0	—	5	0	0	0	0	5²	10	1	2	0	19.1	9.53	56	.370	.414	0	—	0	-3	-3	0	0.0
Total 2		2	1	.667	15	2	1	0	0	29¹	36	2	19	16	16.9	4.60	106	.303	.399	1	.200	0	-0	-1	-0	0.4

● GRANT BOWLER
Bowler, Grant Tierney "Moose"   b:10/24/07, Denver, Col.   d:6/25/68, Denver, Colo.   BR/TR, 6', 190 lbs.   Deb:8/21/31

YEAR	TM/L	W	L	PCT	G	GS	CG	SH	SV	IP	H	HR	BB	SO	RAT	ERA	ERA+	OAV	OOB	BH	AVG	PB	PR	/A	PD	TPI
1931	Chi-A	0	1	.000	13	3	1	0	0	35¹	40	1	24	15	16.3	5.35	80	.288	.393	1	.100	-0	-4	-4	-1	-0.2
1932	Chi-A	0	0	—	4	0	0	0	0	6¹	15	1	3	2	25.6	15.63	28	.484	.529	0	.000	-0	-8	-8	-0	-0.2
Total 2		0	1	.000	17	3	1	0	0	41²	55	2	27	17	17.7	6.91	62	.324	.416	1	.083	-1	-12	-12	-1	-0.2

● CHARLIE BOWLES
Bowles, Charles James   b:3/15/17, Norwood, Mass.   BR/TR, 6'3", 180 lbs.   Deb:9/25/43

YEAR	TM/L	W	L	PCT	G	GS	CG	SH	SV	IP	H	HR	BB	SO	RAT	ERA	ERA+	OAV	OOB	BH	AVG	PB	PR	/A	PD	TPI
1943	Phi-A	1	1	.500	2	2	2	0	0	18	17	0	4	6	10.5	3.00	113	.258	.300	-1	.125	-1	1	1	0	0.0

YEAR TM/L	W	L	PCT	G	GS	CG	SH	SV	IP	H	HR	BB	SO	RAT	ERA	ERA+	OAV	OOB	BH	AVG	PB	PR	/A	PD	TPI
1945 Phi-A	0	3	.000	8	4	1	0	0	33¹	35	3	23	11	15.7	5.13	67	.273	.384	5	.238	0	-7	-6	0	-0.5
Total 2	1	4	.200	10	6	3	0	0	51¹	52	3	27	17	13.9	4.38	78	.268	.357	6	.207	-0	-6	-5	0	-0.5

● EMMETT BOWLES   Bowles, Emmett Jerome "Chief" b: 8/2/1898, Wanette, Okla. d: 9/3/59, Flagstaff, Ariz. BR/TR, 6', 180 lbs. Deb: 9/12/22

| 1922 Chi-A | 0 | 0 | — | 1 | 0 | 0 | 0 | 0 | 1 | 2 | 0 | 1 | 0 | 27.0 | 27.00 | 15 | .500 | .600 | 0 | — | 0 | -3 | -3 | -0 | 0.0 |

● ABE BOWMAN   Bowman, Alvah Edson b: 1/25/1893, Greenup, Ill. d: 10/11/79, Longview, Tex. BR/TR, 6'1", 190 lbs. Deb: 5/19/14

1914 Cle-A	2	7	.222	22	10	2	1	0	72²	74	0	45	27	15.2	4.46	65	.277	.389	1	.048	-2	-14	-13	-0	-1.7
1915 Cle-A	0	1	.000	2	1	0	0	0	1¹	1	0	3	0	27.0	20.25	15	.250	.571	0	—	0	-3	-3	1	-1.2
Total 2	2	8	.200	24	11	2	1	0	74	75	0	48	27	15.4	4.74	61	.277	.393	1	.048	-2	-16	-15	-0	-2.9

● JOE BOWMAN   Bowman, Joseph Emil b: 6/17/10, Kansas City, Kan. d: 11/22/90, Kansas City, Mo. BL/TR, 6'2", 190 lbs. Deb: 4/18/32 ♦

1932 Phi-A	0	1	.000	7	0	0	0	0	11	14	2	6	4	18.8	8.18	55	.318	.434	1	1.000	0	-5	-4	1	-0.2
1934 NY-N	5	4	.556	30	10	3	0	3	107¹	119	9	36	36	13.2	3.61	107	.279	.338	5	.172	0	5	3	-0	0.2
1935 Phi-N	7	10	.412	33	17	6	1	1	148¹	157	13	56	58	13.2	4.25	107	.269	.337	13	.194	0	-4	5	-0	0.5
1936 Phi-N	9	20	.310	40	28	12	0	1	203²	243	14	53	80	13.4	5.04	90	.289	.336	15	.195	-1	-23	-17	-2	-1.7
1937 Pit-N	8	8	.500	30	19	7	0	1	128	161	11	35	38	13.9	4.57	85	.306	.351	10	.213	2	-9	-10	-0	-1.0
1938 Pit-N	3	4	.429	17	1	0	0	1	60	68	2	20	25	13.2	4.65	82	.285	.340	7	.333	2	-6	-6	-1	-0.5
1939 Pit-N	10	14	.417	37	27	10	1	1	184²	217	15	43	58	13.0	4.48	86	.292	.336	33	.344	12	-12	-13	-0	-0.3
1940 Pit-N	9	10	.474	32	24	10	0	2	187²	209	10	66	57	13.5	4.46	85	.274	.337	22	.244	9	-13	-14	-0	-0.3
1941 Pit-N	3	2	.600	18	7	1	1	1	69¹	77	3	28	22	13.8	2.99	121	.278	.346	8	.258	1	5	5	-0	0.5
1944 Bos-A	12	8	.600	26	24	10	1	0	168¹	175	14	64	53	12.9	4.81	71	.269	.336	20	.200	3	-26	-26	-2	-2.7
1945 Bos-A	0	2	.000	3	3	0	0	0	11²	18	1	9	6	20.8	9.26	37	.360	.458	2	.222	0	-8	-8	-0	-1.0
Cin-N	11	13	.458	25	24	15	1	0	185²	198	8	68	71	13.2	3.59	105	.270	.338	5	.070	-5	4	4	-2	-0.2
Total 11	77	96	.445	298	184	74	5	11	1465²	1656	102	484	502	13.4	4.40	89	.282	.341	141	.221	24	-89	-77	-7	-6.7

● BOB BOWMAN   Bowman, Robert James b: 10/3/10, Keystone, W.Va. d: 9/4/72, Bluefield, W.Va. BR/TR, 5'10.5", 160 lbs. Deb: 4/21/39

1939 StL-N	13	5	.722	51	15	4	2	9	169¹	141	8	60	78	10.7	2.60	158	.232	.302	4	.085	-3	25	28	-1	2.7
1940 StL-N	7	5	.583	28	17	7	0	0	114¹	118	9	43	43	13.0	4.33	92	.267	.337	2	.061	-2	-6	-4	-0	-0.7
1941 NY-N	6	7	.462	29	6	2	0	1	80¹	100	10	36	25	15.3	5.71	65	.302	.372	1	.048	-1	-19	-18	1	-2.6
1942 Chi-N	0	0	—	1	0	0	0	0	1	1	0	0	0	9.0	0.00	—	.250	.250	0	—	0	0	-0	-0	0.0
Total 4	26	17	.605	109	38	13	2	10	365	360	27	139	146	12.5	3.82	104	.260	.330	7	.069	-5	0	6	-1	-0.6

● BOB BOWMAN   Bowman, Robert Leroy b: 5/10/31, Laytonville, Cal. BR/TR, 6'1", 195 lbs. Deb: 4/16/55 ♦

| 1959 Phi-N | 0 | 1 | .000 | 5 | 0 | 0 | 0 | 0 | 6 | 5 | 1 | 5 | 0 | 15.0 | 6.00 | 68 | .227 | .370 | 10 | .127 | -0 | -1 | -1 | 0 | -0.2 |

● ROGER BOWMAN   Bowman, Roger Clinton b: 8/18/27, Amsterdam, N.Y. BR/TL, 6', 175 lbs. Deb: 9/22/49

1949 NY-N	0	0	—	2	2	0	0	0	6¹	6	1	7	4	18.5	4.26	93	.261	.433	0	.000	-0	-0	-1	1	0.0
1951 NY-N	2	4	.333	9	5	0	0	0	26¹	35	2	22	24	19.8	6.15	64	.297	.411	0	.000	-0	-6	-7	-1	-1.3
1952 NY-N	0	0	—	2	1	0	0	0	3	6	0	3	3	30.0	12.00	31	.429	.556	0	.000	-0	-3	-3	-0	-0.7
1953 Pit-N	0	4	.000	30	2	0	0	0	65¹	65	9	29	36	13.1	4.82	93	.261	.341	2	.286	-4	-4	-3	0	-0.1
1955 Pit-N	0	3	.000	7	2	0	0	0	16²	25	2	10	8	19.4	8.64	48	.347	.434	1	.500	-0	-9	-8	0	-1.2
Total 5	2	11	.154	50	12	0	0	0	117²	137	14	71	75	16.2	5.81	73	.288	.385	3	.167	-0	-22	-20	1	-2.6

● SUMNER BOWMAN   Bowman, Sumner Sallade b: 2/9/1867, Millersburg, Pa. d: 1/11/54, Millersburg, Pa. BL/TL, 6', 160 lbs. Deb: 6/11/1890

1890 Phi-N	0	0	—	1	1	0	0	0	8	11	0	2	0	15.8	7.88	46	.317	.371	2	.500	1	-4	-4	-0	0.0
Pit-N	2	5	.286	9	7	6	0	0	70²	100	1	50	22	20.5	6.62	50	.323	.435	10	.278	2	-24	-26	-0	-1.7
Yr	2	5	.286	10	8	6	0	0	78²	111	1	52	22	19.9	6.75	49	.322	.426	12	.308	3	-28	-30	-0	-1.7
1891 Phi-a	2	5	.286	8	8	8	0	0	68	73	0	37	22	15.2	3.44	111	.265	.362	13	.241	0	2	3	-1	0.2
Total 2	4	10	.286	18	16	14	0	0	146²	184	1	89	46	17.8	5.22	68	.297	.400	25	.266	3	-26	-27	-1	-1.5

● TED BOWSFIELD   Bowsfield, Edward Oliver b: 1/10/35, Vernon, B.C., Canada BR/TL, 6'1", 190 lbs. Deb: 7/20/58

1958 Bos-A	4	2	.667	16	10	2	0	0	65²	58	3	36	38	13.0	3.84	104	.233	.332	4	.154	-1	-1	1	1	0.1
1959 Bos-A	0	1	.000	5	2	0	0	0	9	16	2	9	4	25.0	15.00	27	.390	.500	0	.000	-0	-11	-11	-0	-1.0
1960 Bos-A	1	2	.333	17	2	0	0	2	21	20	1	13	18	14.6	5.14	79	.260	.374	1	.250	-0	-3	-3	1	-0.3
Cle-A	3	4	.429	11	6	1	1	0	40²	47	1	20	14	14.8	5.09	73	.296	.374	1	.100	-0	-5	-6	1	-0.9
Yr	4	6	.400	28	8	1	1	2	61²	67	2	33	32	14.6	5.11	75	.280	.368	2	.143	-0	-8	-9	1	-1.2
1961 LA-A	11	8	.579	41	21	4	1	0	157	154	18	63	88	12.5	3.73	121	.255	.327	7	.137	-1	5	14	-1	1.3
1962 LA-A	9	8	.529	34	25	1	0	1	139	154	12	40	52	12.7	4.40	88	.277	.328	6	.162	-1	-7	-8	-3	-0.6
1963 KC-A	5	7	.417	41	11	2	1	3	111¹	115	14	47	67	13.3	4.45	88	.269	.345	1	.043	-1	-10	-7	2	-0.6
1964 KC-A	4	7	.364	50	9	2	1	0	118²	135	12	31	46	12.9	4.10	90	.285	.334	2	.095	-1	-6	-4	-0	-0.4
Total 7	37	39	.487	215	86	12	4	6	662¹	699	63	259	326	13.2	4.35	93	.270	.339	22	.127	-3	-38	-24	-1	-2.9

● OIL CAN BOYD   Boyd, Dennis Ray b: 10/6/59, Meridian, Miss. BR/TR, 6'1", 155 lbs. Deb: 9/13/82

1982 Bos-A	0	1	.000	3	1	0	0	0	8¹	11	2	2	2	14.0	5.40	80	.314	.351	0	—	0	-1	-1	-0	-0.1
1983 Bos-A	4	8	.333	15	13	5	0	0	98²	103	9	23	43	11.6	3.28	132	.269	.312	0	—	0	9	12	-1	0.8
1984 Bos-A	12	12	.500	29	26	10	3	0	197²	207	18	53	134	11.9	4.37	95	.269	.317	0	—	0	-8	-5	2	-0.3
1985 Bos-A	15	13	.536	35	35	13	3	0	272¹	273	26	67	154	11.4	3.70	116	.265	.308	0	—	0	13	18	3	1.9
1986 *Bos-A	16	10	.615	30	30	10	0	0	214¹	222	32	45	129	11.3	3.78	110	.265	.304	0	—	0	9	9	1	1.1
1987 Bos-A	1	3	.250	7	7	2	0	0	36²	47	6	9	12	14.2	5.89	77	.315	.363	0	—	0	-6	-6	1	-0.5
1988 Bos-A	9	7	.563	23	23	1	0	0	129²	147	25	41	71	13.2	5.34	77	.289	.344	0	—	0	-20	-18	-1	-2.1
1989 Bos-A	3	2	.600	10	10	0	0	0	59	57	8	19	26	11.6	4.42	93	.253	.311	0	—	0	-4	-2	1	-0.3
1990 Mon-N	10	6	.625	31	31	3	3	0	190²	164	19	52	113	10.3	2.93	125	.233	.289	3	.051	-4	18	15	-1	0.6
1991 Mon-N	6	8	.429	19	19	1	1	0	120¹	115	9	40	82	11.6	3.52	103	.256	.316	3	.083	-1	2	1	-1	-0.1
Tex-A	2	7	.222	12	12	0	0	0	62	81	12	17	33	14.2	6.68	60	.311	.356	0	—	0	-18	-18	-2	-2.2
Total 10	78	77	.503	214	207	43	10	0	1389²	1427	166	368	799	11.7	4.04	101	.266	.315	6	.063	-5	-5	5	3	-1.2

● JAKE BOYD   Boyd, Jacob Henry b: 1/19/1874, Martinsburg, W.Va. d: 8/12/32, Gettysburg, Pa. TL, 160 lbs. Deb: 9/20/1894 ♦

1894 Was-N	0	3	.000	3	3	3	0	0	19	37	1	14	3	24.6	8.53	62	.403	.487	3	.143	-1	-7	-7	0	-0.7
1895 Was-N	2	11	.154	14	12	10	0	0	85¹	126	1	35	16	18.0	7.07	68	.337	.409	42	.268	2	-22	-21	1	-2.1
1896 Was-N	1	2	.333	4	2	0	0	0	32	45	0	15	6	16.9	6.75	65	.329	.418	1	.077	-1	-8	-8	0	-0.6
Total 3	3	16	.158	21	17	13	0	0	136²	208	2	64	25	19.1	7.20	66	.346	.423	46	.241	0	-37	-37	2	-3.4

● GARY BOYD   Boyd, Gary Lee b: 8/22/46, Pasadena, Cal. BR/TR, 6'4", 200 lbs. Deb: 8/1/69

| 1969 Cle-A | 0 | 2 | .000 | 8 | 3 | 0 | 0 | 0 | 11 | 8 | 1 | 14 | 9 | 18.0 | 9.00 | 42 | .205 | .415 | 0 | .000 | 0 | -7 | -6 | -0 | -1.0 |

● RAY BOYD   Boyd, Raymond C. b: 2/11/1887, Hortonville, Ind. d: 2/11/20, Hortonville, Ind. BR/TR, 5'10", 160 lbs. Deb: 9/24/10

1910 StL-A	0	2	.000	3	2	1	0	0	14¹	16	0	5	6	13.8	4.40	56	.286	.355	1	.200	-0	-3	-3	-1	-0.5
1911 Cin-N	2	2	.500	7	4	3	0	1	44	34	0	19	20	11.3	2.66	124	.206	.296	1	.083	-0	4	3	-0	0.2
Total 2	2	4	.333	10	6	4	0	1	58¹	50	0	24	26	11.9	3.09	101	.226	.310	2	.118	-0	1	0	-1	-0.3

● BILL BOYD   Boyd, William J. b: 12/22/1852, New York, N.Y. d: 9/30/12, Jamaica, N.Y. Deb: 4/22/1872 MU♦

| 1875 Atl-n | 0 | 0 | — | 1 | 1 | 0 | 0 | 0 | 1² | 4 | 0 | 0 | 0 | 21.6 | 5.40 | 43 | .444 | .444 | 44 | .297 | 0 | -1 | -1 | | 0.0 |

● CLOYD BOYER   Boyer, Cloyd Victor "Junior" b: 9/1/27, Alba, Mo. BR/TR, 6'1", 188 lbs. Deb: 4/23/49 FC

| 1949 StL-N | 0 | 0 | — | 4 | 1 | 0 | 0 | 0 | 3¹ | 5 | 0 | 7 | 0 | 32.4 | 10.80 | 39 | .357 | .571 | 0 | — | 0 | -3 | -2 | 0 | 0.0 |

YEAR TM/L	W	L	PCT	G	GS	CG	SH	SV	IP	H	HR	BB	SO	RAT	ERA	ERA+	OAV	OOB	BH	AVG	PB	PR	/A	PD	TPI
1950 StL-N	7	7	.500	36	14	6	1	1	120¹	105	15	49	82	11.7	3.52	122	.233	.312	6	.182	0	8	10	0	1.1
1951 StL-N	2	5	.286	19	8	1	0	1	63¹	68	9	46	40	16.6	5.26	75	.286	.408	4	.200	0	-9	-9	-2	-1.1
1952 StL-N	6	6	.500	23	14	4	2	0	110¹	108	11	47	44	13.0	4.24	88	.258	.338	8	.211	-2	-6	-6	-2	-0.6
1955 KC-A	5	5	.500	30	11	2	0	0	98¹	107	21	69	32	16.7	6.22	67	.282	.402	2	.069	-2	-25	-22	-1	-2.2
Total 5	20	23	.465	112	48	13	3	2	395²	393	56	218	198	14.3	4.73	86	.262	.362	20	.167	1	-34	-30	-4	-2.8

● HENRY BOYLE
Boyle, Henry J. "Handsome Henry"   b: 9/20/1860, Philadelphia, Pa.   d: 5/25/32, Philadelphia, Pa.   TR , Deb: 7/9/1884 ♦

YEAR TM/L	W	L	PCT	G	GS	CG	SH	SV	IP	H	HR	BB	SO	RAT	ERA	ERA+	OAV	OOB	BH	AVG	PB	PR	/A	PD	TPI
1884 StL-U	15	3	.833	19	16	16	1	0	150	118	3	10	88	7.7	1.74	138	.202	.215	68	.260	-1	12	11	-1	0.8
1885 StL-N	16	24	.400	42	39	39	1	0	366²	346	2	100	133	10.9	2.75	100	.239	.288	52	.202	1	3	-0	-1	0.0
1886 StL-N	9	15	.375	25	24	23	2	0	210	183	5	46	101	9.8	1.76	184	.220	.261	27	.250	4	36	34	1	3.9
1887 Ind-N	13	24	.351	38	38	37	0	0	328	356	11	69	85	12.0	3.65	114	.265	.307	27	.191	-1	15	18	-4	1.2
1888 Ind-N	15	22	.405	37	37	36	3	0	323	315	11	58	98	10.7	3.26	91	.245	.283	18	.144	-3	-15	-11	3	-1.1
1889 Ind-N	21	23	.477	46	45	38	2	0	378²	422	14	95	97	12.6	3.92	106	.273	.321	38	.245	5	4	11	-5	1.1
Total 6	89	111	.445	207	199	189	10	0	1756¹	1740	46	378	602	11.0	3.06	110	.247	.289	230	.219	5	56	61	-7	5.9

● HARRY BOYLES
Boyles, Harry "Stretch"   b: 11/29/11, Granite City, Ill.   BR/TR, 6'5", 185 lbs.   Deb: 8/3/38

YEAR TM/L	W	L	PCT	G	GS	CG	SH	SV	IP	H	HR	BB	SO	RAT	ERA	ERA+	OAV	OOB	BH	AVG	PB	PR	/A	PD	TPI
1938 Chi-A	0	4	.000	9	2	1	0	0	29¹	31	2	25	18	17.8	5.22	94	.263	.400	1	.125	-1	-1	-1	1	-0.1
1939 Chi-A	0	0	—	2	0	0	0	0	3¹	4	0	6	1	27.0	10.80	44	.308	.526	0	.000	-0	-2	-2	-0	0.0
Total 2	0	4	.000	11	2	1	0	0	32²	35	2	31	19	18.7	5.79	84	.267	.415	1	.111	-1	-4	-3	1	-0.1

● GENE BRABENDER
Brabender, Eugene Mathew   b: 8/16/41, Madison, Wis.   BR/TR, 6'5.5", 225 lbs.   Deb: 5/11/66

YEAR TM/L	W	L	PCT	G	GS	CG	SH	SV	IP	H	HR	BB	SO	RAT	ERA	ERA+	OAV	OOB	BH	AVG	PB	PR	/A	PD	TPI
1966 Bal-A	4	3	.571	31	1	0	0	2	71	57	4	29	62	11.0	3.55	94	.229	.312	1	.077	-1	-1	-2	0	-0.2
1967 Bal-A	6	4	.600	14	14	3	1	0	94	77	6	23	71	9.7	3.35	94	.220	.270	2	.071	-1	-1	-2	-0	-0.3
1968 Bal-A	6	7	.462	37	15	3	2	3	125	116	9	48	92	12.0	3.31	88	.248	.322	3	.086	-0	-5	-5	-1	-0.7
1969 Sea-A	13	14	.481	40	29	7	1	0	202¹	193	26	103	139	13.7	4.36	83	.254	.353	9	.129	-1	-17	-16	-3	-2.4
1970 Mil-A	6	15	.286	29	21	2	0	1	128²	127	8	79	76	14.5	6.02	63	.255	.359	4	.098	-2	-33	-32	-0	-4.7
Total 5	35	43	.449	151	80	15	4	6	621	570	53	282	440	12.6	4.25	80	.245	.332	19	.102	-5	-56	-58	-3	-8.3

● JACK BRACKEN
Bracken, John James   b: 4/14/1881, Cleveland, Ohio   d: 7/16/54, Highland Park, Mich.   BR/TR, 5'11", 175 lbs.   Deb: 8/7/01

YEAR TM/L	W	L	PCT	G	GS	CG	SH	SV	IP	H	HR	BB	SO	RAT	ERA	ERA+	OAV	OOB	BH	AVG	PB	PR	/A	PD	TPI
1901 Cle-A	4	8	.333	12	12	12	0	0	100	137	4	31	18	16.0	6.21	57	.322	.381	10	.227		-28	-30	-1	-2.6

● JOHN BRACKENRIDGE
Brackenridge, John Givler   b: 12/24/1880, Harrisburg, Pa.   d: 3/20/53, Harrisburg, Pa.   BR/TR, 6',   Deb: 4/15/04

YEAR TM/L	W	L	PCT	G	GS	CG	SH	SV	IP	H	HR	BB	SO	RAT	ERA	ERA+	OAV	OOB	BH	AVG	PB	PR	/A	PD	TPI
1904 Phi-N	0	1	.000	7	1	0	0	0	34	37	4	16	11	15.1	5.56	48	.298	.396	2	.154	-0	-11	-11	2	-0.1

● DON BRADEY
Bradey, Donald Eugene   b: 10/4/34, Charlotte, N.C.   BR/TR, 5'9", 180 lbs.   Deb: 9/25/64

YEAR TM/L	W	L	PCT	G	GS	CG	SH	SV	IP	H	HR	BB	SO	RAT	ERA	ERA+	OAV	OOB	BH	AVG	PB	PR	/A	PD	TPI
1964 Hou-N	0	2	.000	3	1	0	0	0	2¹	6	0	3	2	34.7	19.29	18	.429	.529	0		0	-4	-4	-0	-2.2

● LARRY BRADFORD
Bradford, Larry   b: 12/21/49, Chicago, Ill.   BR/TL, 6'1", 200 lbs.   Deb: 9/24/77

YEAR TM/L	W	L	PCT	G	GS	CG	SH	SV	IP	H	HR	BB	SO	RAT	ERA	ERA+	OAV	OOB	BH	AVG	PB	PR	/A	PD	TPI
1977 Atl-N	0	0	—	2	0	0	0	0	2²	3	1	0	1	10.1	3.38	132	.273	.273	0	—	0	0	0	0	0.0
1979 Atl-N	1	0	1.000	21	0	0	0	2	19	11	0	10	11	10.4	0.95	427	.172	.293	0	.000	-0	6	7	0	0.5
1980 Atl-N	3	4	.429	56	0	0	0	4	55¹	49	3	22	32	11.7	2.44	153	.243	.320	0	.000	-0	7	8	-0	1.1
1981 Atl-N	2	0	1.000	25	0	0	0	1	26²	26	1	12	14	12.8	3.71	96	.268	.349	1	1.000	0	-1	-0	0	0.0
Total 4	6	4	.600	104	0	0	0	7	103²	89	5	44	58	11.7	2.52	150	.238	.321	1	.200	-0	13	14	1	1.6

● BILL BRADFORD
Bradford, William D   b: 8/28/21, Choctaw, Ark.   BR/TR, 6'2", 180 lbs.   Deb: 4/24/56

YEAR TM/L	W	L	PCT	G	GS	CG	SH	SV	IP	H	HR	BB	SO	RAT	ERA	ERA+	OAV	OOB	BH	AVG	PB	PR	/A	PD	TPI
1956 KC-A	0	0	—	1	0	0	0	0	2	2	2	1	0	13.5	9.00	48	.250	.333	0		0	-1	-1	0	0.0

● FRED BRADLEY
Bradley, Fred Langdon   b: 7/31/20, Parsons, Kan.   BR/TR, 6'1", 180 lbs.   Deb: 5/1/48

YEAR TM/L	W	L	PCT	G	GS	CG	SH	SV	IP	H	HR	BB	SO	RAT	ERA	ERA+	OAV	OOB	BH	AVG	PB	PR	/A	PD	TPI
1948 Chi-A	0	0	—	8	0	0	0	0	15²	11	2	4	2	9.2	4.60	93	.190	.254	0	.000	-0	-1	-1	0	0.0
1949 Chi-A	0	0	—	1	1	0	0	0	2	4	0	3	0	31.5	13.50	31	.444	.583	0	.000	-0	-2	-2	0	0.0
Total 2	0	0	—	9	1	0	0	0	17²	15	2	7	2	11.7	5.60	76	.224	.307	0	.000	-0	-3	-3	0	0.0

● FOGHORN BRADLEY
Bradley, George H.   b: 7/1/1855, Milford, Mass.   d: 4/3/1900, Philadelphia, Pa.   BR/TR,   Deb: 8/23/1876   U

YEAR TM/L	W	L	PCT	G	GS	CG	SH	SV	IP	H	HR	BB	SO	RAT	ERA	ERA+	OAV	OOB	BH	AVG	PB	PR	/A	PD	TPI
1876 Bos-N	9	10	.474	22	21	16	1	1	173¹	201	1	16	16	11.3	2.49	91	.263	.279	19	.232	-1	-4	-5	-1	-0.5

● GEORGE BRADLEY
Bradley, George Washington "Grin"   b: 7/13/1852, Reading, Pa.   d: 10/2/31, Philadelphia, Pa.   BR/TR, 5'10.5", 175 lbs.   Deb: 5/4/1875 ♦

YEAR TM/L	W	L	PCT	G	GS	CG	SH	SV	IP	H	HR	BB	SO	RAT	ERA	ERA+	OAV	OOB	BH	AVG	PB	PR	/A	PD	TPI
1875 StL-n	33	26	.559	60	60	57	4	0	535²	538	3	16		9.3	2.05	108	.240	.245	62	.244	7	24	10		1.5
1876 StL-N	45	19	.703	64	64	63	16	0	573	470	3	38	103	8.0	1.23	174	.211	.224	66	.249	4	69	58	1	5.8
1877 Chi-N	18	23	.439	50	44	35	2	0	394	452	4	39	59	11.2	3.31	90	.269	.286	52	.243	-0	-22	-15	1	-1.3
1879 Tro-N	13	40	.245	54	54	53	3	0	487	590	12	26	133	11.4	2.85	88	.275	.284	62	.247	4	-19	-19	4	-0.7
1880 Pro-N	13	8	.619	28	20	16	4	1	196	158	0	6	54	7.5	1.38	160	.210	.217	70	.227	1	22	18	1	1.9
1881 Cle-N	2	4	.333	6	6	5	0	0	51	70	2	3	6	12.9	3.88	67	.320	.329	60	.249	0	-6	-7	-1	-0.7
1882 Cle-N	9	9	.400	18	16	15	0	0	147	164	5	22	32	11.4	3.73	75	.264	.289	21	.183	-3	-14	-15	3	-1.2
1883 Phi-a	16	7	.696	26	23	22	0	0	214¹	215	7	22	56	10.0	3.15	110	.244	.263	73	.234	0	4	8	-1	0.5
1884 Cin-U	25	15	.625	41	38	36	3	0	342	350	7	23	168	9.8	2.71	95	.248	.260	43	.190	-12	-10	-6	2	-1.4
Total 8	138	125	.525	287	265	245	28	1	2404¹	2469	42	179	611	9.9	2.50	103	.248	.262	456	.228	-5	23	19	11	2.9

● HERB BRADLEY
Bradley, Herbert Theodore   b: 1/3/03, Agenda, Kan.   d: 10/16/59, Clay Center, Kan.   BR/TR, 6', 170 lbs.   Deb: 5/9/27

YEAR TM/L	W	L	PCT	G	GS	CG	SH	SV	IP	H	HR	BB	SO	RAT	ERA	ERA+	OAV	OOB	BH	AVG	PB	PR	/A	PD	TPI
1927 Bos-A	1	1	.500	6	2	2	0	0	23	16	0	7	6	9.8	3.13	135	.198	.278	3	.429	1	3	3	-0	0.3
1928 Bos-A	0	3	.000	15	5	1	0	0	47¹	64	2	16	14	15.6	7.23	57	.339	.396	2	.154	-1	-17	-16	1	-0.8
1929 Bos-A	0	0	—	3	0	0	0	0	4	7	1	2	0	20.3	6.75	63	.438	.500	0	.000	-0	-1	-1	0	0.0
Total 3	1	4	.200	24	7	3	1	0	74¹	87	3	25	20	14.0	5.93	70	.304	.368	5	.238	-0	-15	-15	1	-0.5

● BERT BRADLEY
Bradley, Steven Bert   b: 12/23/56, Athens, Ga.   BB/TR, 6'1", 190 lbs.   Deb: 9/3/83

YEAR TM/L	W	L	PCT	G	GS	CG	SH	SV	IP	H	HR	BB	SO	RAT	ERA	ERA+	OAV	OOB	BH	AVG	PB	PR	/A	PD	TPI
1983 Oak-A	0	0	—	6	0	0	0	0	8¹	14	1	4	3	19.4	6.48	59	.400	.462	0	—	0	-2	-2	1	0.1

● TOM BRADLEY
Bradley, Thomas William   b: 3/16/47, Asheville, N.C.   BR/TR, 6'3", 185 lbs.   Deb: 9/9/69

YEAR TM/L	W	L	PCT	G	GS	CG	SH	SV	IP	H	HR	BB	SO	RAT	ERA	ERA+	OAV	OOB	BH	AVG	PB	PR	/A	PD	TPI
1969 Cal-A	1	0	1.000	3	0	0	0	0	2	9	1	0	2	40.5	27.00	13	.600	.600	0	—	0	-5	-5	0	-1.8
1970 Cal-A	2	5	.286	17	11	1	1	0	69²	71	3	33	53	13.6	4.13	87	.270	.354	3	.167	0	-3	-4	-0	-0.3
1971 Chi-A	15	15	.500	45	39	7	6	2	285²	273	16	74	206	11.0	2.96	121	.248	.297	15	.156	-1	16	20	-2	1.8
1972 Chi-A	15	14	.517	40	40	11	2	0	260	225	19	65	209	10.1	2.98	116	.231	.280	12	.132	-2	2	4	-0	0.2
1973 SF-N	13	12	.520	35	34	6	1	0	224	212	26	69	136	11.4	3.90	98	.246	.304	15	.195	-1	-6	-2	-2	-0.3
1974 SF-N	8	11	.421	30	21	2	0	0	134¹	152	16	52	72	13.7	5.16	74	.282	.346	2	.075	-2	-23	-20	-1	-2.9
1975 SF-N	2	3	.400	13	6	0	0	0	42	57	6	18	13	16.3	6.21	61	.326	.392	0	.000	-1	-12	-11	0	-1.2
Total 7	55	61	.474	183	151	27	10	2	1017²	999	86	311	691	11.7	3.72	96	.254	.311	48	.145	-5	-31	-19	-5	-4.5

● BILL BRADLEY
Bradley, William Joseph   b: 2/13/1878, Cleveland, Ohio   d: 3/11/54, Cleveland, Ohio   BR/TR, 6', 185 lbs.   Deb: 8/26/1899   M♦

YEAR TM/L	W	L	PCT	G	GS	CG	SH	SV	IP	H	HR	BB	SO	RAT	ERA	ERA+	OAV	OOB	BH	AVG	PB	PR	/A	PD	TPI
1901 Cle-A	0	0	—	1	0	0	0	0	1	4	0	0	0	36.0	0.00	—	.581	.581	151	.293	0	0	-0	0	0.0

● JOE BRADSHAW
Bradshaw, Joe Siah   b: 8/17/1897, Roellen, Tenn.   d: 1/30/85, Tavares, Fla.   BR/TR, 6'2.5", 200 lbs.   Deb: 5/9/29

YEAR TM/L	W	L	PCT	G	GS	CG	SH	SV	IP	H	HR	BB	SO	RAT	ERA	ERA+	OAV	OOB	BH	AVG	PB	PR	/A	PD	TPI
1929 Bro-N	0	0	—	2	0	0	0	0	4	3	0	4	1	20.3	4.50	103	.231	.474	0		0	0	0	0	0.0

● NEAL BRADY
Brady, Cornelius Joseph   b: 3/4/1897, Covington, Ky.   d: 6/19/47, Fort Mitchell, Ky   BR/TR, 6'0.5", 197 lbs.   Deb: 9/25/15

YEAR TM/L	W	L	PCT	G	GS	CG	SH	SV	IP	H	HR	BB	SO	RAT	ERA	ERA+	OAV	OOB	BH	AVG	PB	PR	/A	PD	TPI
1915 NY-A	0	0	—	2	1	0	0	0	8²	9	0	7	6	16.6	3.12	94	.281	.410	-1		-0	-0	-0	-1	-0.1
1917 NY-A	1	0	1.000	2	1	0	0	0	9	6	0	5	4	11.0	2.00	134	.188	.242	1	.500	1	1	1	0	0.2
1925 Cin-N	1	3	.250	20	3	2	0	1	63²	73	4	20	12	13.7	4.66	88	.289	.350	6	.240	1	-3	-4	2	-0.1
Total 3	2	3	.400	24	5	2	0	1	81¹	88	4	32	22	13.7	4.20	91	.278	.351	7	.226	1	-2	-3	1	0.0

YEAR	TM/L	W	L	PCT	G	GS	CG	SH	SV	IP	H	HR	BB	SO	RAT	ERA	ERA+	OAV	OOB	BH	AVG	PB	PR	/A	PD	TPI

● **JIM BRADY**   Brady, James Joseph "Diamond Jim" b: 3/2/36, Jersey City, N.J.   BL/TL, 6'2", 185 lbs. Deb: 5/12/56

| 1956 | Det-A | 0 | 0 | — | 6 | 0 | 0 | 0 | 0 | 6¹ | 15 | 3 | 11 | 3 | 36.9 | 28.42 | 14 | .484 | .619 | 0 | — | 0 | -17 | -17 | 0 | 0.0 |

● **KING BRADY**   Brady, James Ward b: 5/28/1881, Elmer, N.J. d: 8/21/47, Albany, N.Y.   BR/TR, 6', 190 lbs. Deb: 9/21/05

1905	Phi-N	1	1	.500	2	2	2	0	0	13	19	0	3	3	14.5	3.46	84	.333	.356	1	.200	-0	-1	-1	-0	-0.1
1906	Pit-N	1	1	.500	3	2	1	0	0	23	30	0	4	14	13.3	2.35	114	.313	.340	1	.100	-1	1	1	-1	-0.1
1907	Pit-N	0	0	—	1	0	0	0	0	2	2	0	1	0	13.5	0.00	—	.286	.375	0	—	0	1	1	-0	0.0
1908	Bos-A	1	0	1.000	1	1	1	1	0	9	8	0	0	3	8.0	0.00	—	.242	.242	0	.000	-0	2	2	-0	0.2
1912	Bos-N	0	0	—	1	0	0	0	0	2²	5	0	3	0	27.0	20.25	18	.313	.421	0	.000	-0	-5	-5	0	0.0
Total	5	3	2	.600	8	5	4	1	0	49²	64	0	10	20	13.4	3.08	89	.306	.338	2	.111	-1	-2	-2	-1	0.0

● **BILL BRADY**   Brady, William Aloysius "King" b: 8/18/1889, New York, N.Y.   TR, 6'2", Deb: 7/9/12

| 1912 | Bos-N | 0 | 0 | — | 1 | 0 | 0 | 0 | 0 | 1 | 2 | 0 | 0 | 0 | 18.0 | 0.00 | — | .500 | .500 | 0 | — | 0 | 0 | 0 | 0 | 0.0 |

● **DICK BRAGGINS**   Braggins, Richard Realf b: 12/25/1879, Mercer, Pa. d: 8/16/63, Lake Wales, Fla.   BR/TR, 5'11", 170 lbs. Deb: 5/16/01

| 1901 | Cle-A | 1 | 2 | .333 | 4 | 3 | 2 | 0 | 0 | 32 | 44 | 1 | 15 | 1 | 16.9 | 4.78 | 74 | .323 | .394 | 2 | .154 | -1 | -4 | -4 | 0 | -0.4 |

● **ASA BRAINARD**   Brainard, Asa "Count" b: 1841, Albany, N.Y. d: 12/29/1888, Denver, Colo.   TR, 5'8.5", 150 lbs. Deb: 5/5/1871 ♦

1871	Oly-n	12	15	.444	30	30	30	0	0	264	361	4	37	13	13.6	4.50	93	.288	.308	30	.224	-6	-8	-10		-0.9
1872	Oly-n	2	7	.222	9	9	9	0	0	79	147	0	5	11	17.3	6.38	56	.332	.339	16	.390	4	-23	-24		-1.3
	Man-n	0	2	.000	2	2	1	0	0	8	14	1	0	0	15.8	7.88	47	.286	.286	5	.200	-0	-4	-4		-0.5
	Yr	2	9	.182	11	11	10	0	0	87	161	1	5	11	17.2	6.52	56	.327	.334	21	.318	4	-27	-28		-1.8
1873	Bal-n	5	7	.417	14	14	12	0	0	108²	182	0	9	3	15.8	4.14	79	.323	.334	18	.261	1	-11	-11		-0.7
1874	Bal-n	5	22	.185	29	27	25	0	0	239	403	1	27		16.2	4.93	62	.326	.341	50	.253	-0	-51	-50		-3.7
Total	4 n	24	53	.312	84	82	77	0	0	698²	1107	6	78	17	15.3	4.84	63	.312	.327	119	.255	-2	-143	-140		-7.1

● **AL BRAITHWOOD**   Braithwood, Alfred b: 2/15/1892, Braceville, Ill. d: 11/24/60, Rowlesburg, W.Va.   BR/TL, 6'1.5", 145 lbs. Deb: 9/1/15

| 1915 | Pit-F | 0 | 0 | — | 2 | 0 | 0 | 0 | 0 | 3 | 0 | 0 | 0 | 2 | 0.0 | 0.00 | — | .000 | .000 | 0 | — | 0 | 1 | 1 | -0 | 0.0 |

● **ERV BRAME**   Brame, Ervin Beckham b: 10/12/01, Big Rock, Tenn. d: 11/22/49, Hopkinsville, Ky.   BL/TR, 6'2", 190 lbs. Deb: 4/14/28

1928	Pit-N	7	4	.636	24	11	6	0	0	95²	110	5	44	22	14.6	5.08	80	.291	.366	13	.265	4	-12	-11	-1	-0.8
1929	Pit-N	16	11	.593	37	28	19	1	0	229²	250	17	71	68	12.6	4.55	105	.278	.331	36	.310	12	4	6	-4	1.2
1930	Pit-N	17	8	.680	32	29	**22**	0	1	235²	291	21	56	55	13.4	4.70	106	.305	.346	41	.353	11	7	7	-3	1.3
1931	Pit-N	9	13	.409	26	21	15	0	1	179²	211	14	45	33	12.8	4.21	91	.295	.336	26	.274	6	-7	-7	-2	-0.4
1932	Pit-N	3	1	.750	23	3	0	0	0	51	84	6	16	10	17.6	7.41	51	.305	.407	5	.250	1	-20	-20	-1	-1.4
Total	5	52	37	.584	142	92	62	3	1	791²	946	63	232	188	13.5	4.76	94	.298	.347	121	.306	33	-27	-25	-11	-0.1

● **RALPH BRANCA**   Branca, Ralph Theodore Joseph "Hawk" b: 1/6/26, Mt.Vernon, N.Y.   BR/TR, 6'3", 220 lbs. Deb: 6/12/44

1944	Bro-N	0	2	.000	21	1	0	0	1	44²	46	2	32	16	16.7	7.05	50	.274	.405	0	.000	-1	-17	-17	-0	-0.9
1945	Bro-N	5	6	.455	16	15	7	0	1	109²	73	4	79	69	12.5	3.04	124	.189	.327	4	.100	-3	9	9	0	0.6
1946	Bro-N	3	1	.750	24	10	2	2	3	67¹	62	4	41	42	13.8	3.88	87	.246	.352	2	.111	-0	-3	-4	-1	-0.3
1947	*Bro-N☆	21	12	.636	43	36	15	4	1	280	251	22	98	148	11.4	2.67	155	.240	.309	12	.124	-3	43	46	-4	4.4
1948	Bro-N★	14	9	.609	36	28	11	1	1	215²	189	24	80	122	11.4	3.51	114	.232	.304	15	.203	1	11	12	-4	0.8
1949	*Bro-N☆	13	5	.722	34	27	9	2	1	186²	181	21	91	109	13.2	4.39	93	.253	.339	5	.081	-2	-7	-6	-4	-1.1
1950	Bro-N	7	9	.438	43	15	5	0	7	142	152	24	55	100	13.1	4.69	93	.271	.336	4	.118	1	-9	-9	-1	-1.0
1951	Bro-N	13	12	.520	42	27	13	3	3	204	180	19	85	118	11.8	3.26	120	.237	.316	11	.175	-1	16	15	-3	1.4
1952	Bro-N	4	2	.667	16	7	2	0	0	61	52	8	21	26	11.4	3.84	95	.232	.309	3	.158	-0	-1	-1	-1	-0.2
1953	Bro-N	0	0	—	7	0	0	0	0	11	15	4	5	9	18.0	9.82	43	.341	.431	0	—	0	-7	-7	0	0.0
	Det-A	4	7	.364	17	14	7	0	1	102	98	7	31	50	11.6	4.15	98	.253	.311	4	.118	-1	-2	-1	-1	-0.3
1954	Det-A	3	3	.500	17	5	0	0	0	45¹	63	10	30	15	18.9	5.76	64	.330	.426	4	.308	2	-10	-10	-1	-1.1
	NY-A	1	0	1.000	5	3	0	0	0	12²	9	0	13	7	16.3	2.84	121	.209	.404	2	.500	1	1	1	0	0.1
	Yr	4	3	.571	22	8	0	0	0	58	72	10	43	22	15.2	5.12	71	.304	.413	6	.353	2	-9	-10	-1	-1.0
1956	Bro-N	0	0	—	1	0	0	0	0	2	1	0	2	2	13.5	0.00	—	.143	.333	0	—	1	1	1	0	0.0
Total	12	88	68	.564	322	188	71	12	19	1484	1372	149	663	829	12.5	3.79	104	.245	.328	66	.142	-6	25	27	-18	2.4

● **HARVEY BRANCH**   Branch, Harvey Alfred b: 2/8/39, Memphis, Tenn.   BR/TL, 6', 175 lbs. Deb: 9/18/62

| 1962 | StL-N | 0 | 1 | .000 | 1 | 1 | 0 | 0 | 0 | 5 | 5 | 1 | 5 | 2 | 18.0 | 5.40 | 79 | .263 | .417 | 0 | .000 | -0 | -1 | -1 | -0 | -0.1 |

● **NORM BRANCH**   Branch, Norman Downs "Red" b: 3/22/15, Spokane, Wash. d: 11/21/71, Navasota, Tex.   BR/TR, 6'3", 200 lbs. Deb: 5/5/41

1941	NY-A	5	1	.833	27	0	0	0	2	47	37	2	26	28	12.1	2.87	137	.224	.330	0	.000	-1	7	6	1	0.6
1942	NY-A	0	1	.000	10	0	0	0	2	15²	18	3	16	13	19.5	6.32	54	.290	.436	1	.333	0	-5	-5	0	-0.4
Total	2	5	2	.714	37	0	0	0	4	62²	55	5	42	41	13.3	3.73	102	.242	.361	1	.077	-1	2	1	1	0.2

● **ROY BRANCH**   Branch, Roy b: 7/12/53, St.Louis, Mo.   BR/TR, 6', 175 lbs. Deb: 9/11/79

| 1979 | Sea-A | 0 | 1 | .000 | 2 | 2 | 0 | 0 | 0 | 11¹ | 12 | 2 | 7 | 6 | 15.1 | 7.94 | 55 | .273 | .373 | 0 | — | 0 | -5 | -5 | -0 | -0.4 |

● **CHICK BRANDOM**   Brandom, Chester Milton b: 3/31/1887, Coldwater, Kan. d: 10/7/58, Santa Ana, Cal.   BR/TR, 5'8", 161 lbs. Deb: 9/3/08

1908	Pit-N	1	0	1.000	3	1	1	0	1	17	13	0	4	8	9.5	0.53	435	.228	.290	1	.143	-0	3	3	0	0.3
1909	Pit-N	1	0	1.000	13	2	0	0	2	40²	33	0	10	21	9.7	1.11	246	.239	.295	1	.100	-1	7	7	1	0.3
1915	New-F	1	1	.500	16	1	1	0	0	50¹	55	0	15	15	12.7	3.40	75	.293	.348	2	.200	-1	-4	-5	-1	-0.1
Total	3	3	1	.750	32	4	2	0	3	108	101	0	29	44	11.1	2.08	124	.264	.320	4	.148	-2	6	6	2	0.5

● **BUCKY BRANDON**   Brandon, Darrell G b: 7/8/40, Nacogdoches, Tex.   BR/TR, 6'2", 200 lbs. Deb: 4/19/66

1966	Bos-A	8	8	.500	40	17	5	2	2	157²	129	13	70	101	11.6	3.31	115	.222	.310	8	.182	1	2	9	0	1.1
1967	Bos-A	5	11	.313	39	19	2	0	3	157²	147	21	59	96	12.2	4.17	84	.245	.320	8	.186	1	-16	-12	-0	-1.2
1968	Bos-A	0	0	—	8	0	0	0	0	12²	19	1	9	10	20.6	6.39	49	.333	.433	0	.000	-0	-5	-5	0	0.0
1969	Sea-A	0	1	.000	8	1	0	0	0	15	15	4	16	10	19.8	8.40	43	.302	.423	0	—	0	-8	-8	-0	-0.5
	Min-A	0	0	—	3	0	0	0	0	3¹	5	1	3	1	21.6	2.70	135	.357	.471	0	—	0	0	0	-0	0.0
	Yr	0	1	.000	11	1	0	0	0	18¹	20	5	19	11	19.1	7.36	49	.263	.411	0	.000	-0	-8	-8	-0	-0.5
1971	Phi-N	6	6	.500	52	0	0	0	4	83	81	5	47	44	13.9	3.90	90	.266	.362	2	.154	-0	-4	-4	-1	-0.6
1972	Phi-N	7	7	.500	42	6	0	0	2	104¹	106	9	46	67	13.3	3.45	104	.268	.353	1	.067	-1	0	2	-2	-0.3
1973	Phi-N	2	4	.333	36	0	0	0	2	56¹	54	5	25	25	13.1	5.43	70	.261	.349	1	.200	-1	-11	-10	-1	-1.1
Total	7	28	37	.431	228	43	7	2	13	590	556	59	275	354	13.0	4.04	90	.250	.339	20	.164	-1	-42	-27	-2	-2.4

● **ED BRANDT**   Brandt, Edward Arthur "Big Ed" b: 2/17/05, Spokane, Wash. d: 11/1/44, Spokane, Wash.   BL/TL, 6'1", 190 lbs. Deb: 4/26/28

1928	Bos-N	9	21	.300	38	31	12	1	0	225¹	234	22	109	84	14.0	5.07	77	.273	.359	17	.243	5	-27	-29	2	-2.6
1929	Bos-N	8	13	.381	38	26	11	0	0	167²	196	12	83	50	15.2	5.53	85	.302	.385	15	.234	2	-15	-16	2	-1.2
1930	Bos-N	4	11	.267	41	13	4	1	1	147¹	168	15	59	65	13.9	5.01	99	.291	.356	12	.240	1	-1	-1	2	0.1
1931	Bos-N	18	11	.621	33	29	23	3	2	250	228	11	77	112	11.1	2.92	130	.244	.304	21	.256	5	26	24	3	3.6
1932	Bos-N	16	16	.500	35	31	19	2	1	254	271	11	57	79	11.8	3.97	95	.275	.318	19	.207	-0	-3	-6	1	-0.8
1933	Bos-N	18	14	.563	41	32	23	4	4	287²	256	10	77	104	10.5	2.60	118	.245	.298	30	.309	9	24	15	-0	2.7
1934	Bos-N	16	14	.533	40	28	20	3	5	255	249	13	83	106	11.9	3.53	108	.254	.315	23	.240	4	15	8	-3	1.1
1935	Bos-N	5	19	.208	29	25	12	0	0	174²	224	12	66	61	15.0	5.00	76	.319	.378	13	.210	-0	-19	-24	1	-2.6
1936	Bro-N	11	13	.458	38	29	12	1	2	234	246	14	65	76	12.1	3.50	118	.268	.319	16	.190	1	14	16	-2	1.3
1937	Pit-N	11	10	.524	35	25	7	2	2	176¹	177	11	67	74	13.2	3.11	124	.263	.332	10	.169	1	16	15	1	1.8

YEAR TM/L	W	L	PCT	G	GS	CG	SH	SV	IP	H	HR	BB	SO	RAT	ERA	ERA+	OAV	OOB	BH	AVG	PB	PR	/A	PD	TPI
1938 Pit-N	5	4	.556	24	14	5	0	0	96¹	93	3	35	38	12.0	3.46	110	.250	.314	11	.297	2	4	4	-1	0.5
Total 11	121	146	.453	378	278	150	18	17	2268¹	2342	134	778	877	12.5	3.86	101	.269	.332	187	.236	30	34	5	6	4.2

● **BILL BRANDT**   Brandt, William George b: 3/21/15, Aurora, Ind. d: 5/16/68, Fort Wayne, Ind.   BR/TR, 5'8.5", 170 lbs. Deb: 9/20/41

YEAR TM/L	W	L	PCT	G	GS	CG	SH	SV	IP	H	HR	BB	SO	RAT	ERA	ERA+	OAV	OOB	BH	AVG	PB	PR	/A	PD	TPI
1941 Pit-N	0	1	.000	2	1	0	0	0	7	5	0	3	0	10.3	3.86	94	.200	.286	0	.000	-0	-0	-0	-0	-0.1
1942 Pit-N	1	1	.500	3	3	1	0	0	16¹	23	1	5	4	15.4	4.96	68	.343	.389	1	.143	-0	-3	-3	-0	-0.4
1943 Pit-N	4	1	.800	29	3	0	0	0	57¹	57	3	19	17	12.1	3.14	111	.248	.308	1	.143	-0	2	2	-0	0.1
Total 3	5	3	.625	34	7	1	0	0	80²	85	4	27	21	12.6	3.57	97	.264	.323	2	.133	-1	-2	-1	-1	-0.4

● **CLIFF BRANTLEY**   Brantley, Clifford b: 4/12/68, Staten Island, N.Y.   BR/TR, 6'1", 190 lbs. Deb: 9/3/91

YEAR TM/L	W	L	PCT	G	GS	CG	SH	SV	IP	H	HR	BB	SO	RAT	ERA	ERA+	OAV	OOB	BH	AVG	PB	PR	/A	PD	TPI
1991 Phi-N	2	2	.500	6	5	0	0	0	31²	26	0	19	25	13.4	3.41	107	.228	.348	0	.000	-1	1	1	0	0.0
1992 Phi-N	2	6	.250	28	9	0	0	0	76¹	71	6	58	32	15.7	4.60	76	.251	.386	3	.214	1	-9	-9	0	-0.8
Total 2	4	8	.333	34	14	0	0	0	108	97	6	77	57	15.0	4.25	83	.244	.375	3	.136	0	-8	-9	0	-0.8

● **JEFF BRANTLEY**   Brantley, Jeffrey Hoke b: 9/5/63, Florence, Ala.   BR/TR, 5'11", 180 lbs. Deb: 8/5/88

YEAR TM/L	W	L	PCT	G	GS	CG	SH	SV	IP	H	HR	BB	SO	RAT	ERA	ERA+	OAV	OOB	BH	AVG	PB	PR	/A	PD	TPI
1988 SF-N	0	1	.000	9	1	0	0	1	20²	22	2	6	11	12.6	5.66	65	.275	.333	1	.500	-0	-5	-6	1	-0.2
1989 *SF-N	7	1	.875	59	1	0	0	0	97¹	101	10	37	69	12.9	4.07	83	.271	.340	1	.083	-1	-6	-8	0	-0.6
1990 SF-N★	5	3	.625	55	0	0	0	19	86²	77	3	33	61	11.7	1.56	234	.240	.317	2	.286	1	22	20	0	2.9
1991 SF-N	5	2	.714	67	0	0	0	15	95¹	78	8	52	81	12.7	2.45	146	.225	.335	0	.000	-0	13	12	-1	1.2
1992 SF-N	7	7	.500	56	4	0	0	7	91²	67	8	45	86	11.3	2.95	112	.207	.310	1	.111	0	6	4	-1	0.5
1993 SF-N	5	6	.455	53	12	0	0	0	113²	112	19	46	76	13.1	4.28	91	.259	.340	3	.107	-1	-3	-5	-2	-0.7
1994 Cin-N	6	6	.500	50	0	0	0	15	65¹	46	6	28	63	10.2	2.48	168	.200	.289	0	.000	-0	13	12	0	2.7
Total 7	35	26	.574	349	18	0	0	57	570²	503	56	247	447	12.2	3.15	115	.239	.325	8	.125	-1	39	30	-2	5.8

● **KITTY BRASHEAR**   Brashear, Norman C. b: 8/27/1877, Mansfield, Ohio d: 12/22/34, Los Angeles, Cal. BR/TR,   Deb: 6/25/1899 F

YEAR TM/L	W	L	PCT	G	GS	CG	SH	SV	IP	H	HR	BB	SO	RAT	ERA	ERA+	OAV	OOB	BH	AVG	PB	PR	/A	PD	TPI
1899 Lou-N	1	0	1.000	3	0	0	0	0	8	8	0	2	5	12.4	4.50	86	.260	.326	1	.500	-1	-1	-1	0	0.0

● **JOHN BRAUN**   Braun, John Paul b: 12/26/39, Madison, Wis.   BR/TR, 6'5", 218 lbs. Deb: 10/2/64

YEAR TM/L	W	L	PCT	G	GS	CG	SH	SV	IP	H	HR	BB	SO	RAT	ERA	ERA+	OAV	OOB	BH	AVG	PB	PR	/A	PD	TPI
1964 Mil-N	0	0	—	1	0	0	0	0	2	2	0	1	1	13.5	5.00		.286	.375	-0		1	1	-0	0.0

● **GARLAND BRAXTON**   Braxton, Edgar Garland b: 6/10/1900, Snow Camp, N.C. d: 2/25/66, Norfolk, Va.   BB/TL, 5'11", 152 lbs. Deb: 5/27/21

YEAR TM/L	W	L	PCT	G	GS	CG	SH	SV	IP	H	HR	BB	SO	RAT	ERA	ERA+	OAV	OOB	BH	AVG	PB	PR	/A	PD	TPI
1921 Bos-N	1	3	.250	17	2	0	0	0	37¹	44	0	17	16	15.2	4.82	76	.310	.391	0	.000	-1	-4	-5	1	-0.5
1922 Bos-N	1	2	.333	25	4	2	0	0	66²	75	3	24	15	13.9	3.38	118	.286	.355	-2	.063	-2	5	5	-1	0.0
1925 NY-A	1	1	.500	3	2	0	0	0	19¹	26	1	5	11	14.9	6.52	65	.338	.386	2	.333	0	-5	-5	0	-0.4
1926 NY-A	5	1	.833	37	1	0	0	2	67¹	71	1	19	30	12.0	2.67	144	.275	.325	6	.300	1	10	9	0	0.9
1927 Was-A	10	9	.526	58	2	0	0	13	155¹	144	5	33	96	10.4	2.95	138	.246	.289	9	.231	0	20	19	-2	2.2
1928 Was-A	13	11	.542	38	24	15	2	6	218¹	177	7	44	94	9.3	2.51	160	.222	.267	9	.125	-4	37	36	0	3.5
1929 Was-A	12	10	.545	37	20	9	0	4	182	219	6	51	59	13.5	4.85	88	.299	.346	8	.148	-1	-12	-12	-1	-1.5
1930 Was-A	3	2	.600	15	0	0	0	5	27¹	22	3	9	7	10.2	3.29	140	.222	.287	-0	.000	-1	4	4	-1	0.6
Chi-A	4	10	.286	19	10	2	0	1	90²	127	9	33	44	16.0	6.45	72	.333	.388	2	.087	-2	-18	-18	-1	-2.5
Yr	7	12	.368	34	10	2	0	6	118	149	12	42	51	14.6	5.72	81	.310	.367	2	.071	-2	-14	-14	-2	-1.9
1931 Chi-A	0	3	.000	17	3	0	0	1	47¹	71	1	23	28	18.3	6.85	62	.338	.409	1	.091	-1	-13	-13	-1	-0.8
StL-A	0	0	—	11	1	0	0	0	18	27	2	10	7	19.0	10.50	44	.370	.452	2	.667	1	-12	-12	-0	0.1
Yr	0	3	.000	28	4	0	0	1	65¹	98	3	33	35	18.2	7.85	56	.344	.414	3	.214	0	-25	-25	-0	-0.7
1933 StL-A	1	0	1.000	5	1	0	0	0	8¹	11	0	8	5	21.6	9.72	48	.289	.426	0	.000	-0	-5	-5	-0	-0.5
Total 10	50	53	.485	282	70	28	2	32	938	1014	38	276	412	12.6	4.13	101	.278	.332	40	.156	-8	8	2	-5	1.1

● **AL BRAZLE**   Brazle, Alpha Eugene "Cotton" b: 10/19/13, Loyal, Okla. d: 10/24/73, Grand Junction, Colo.   BL/TL, 6'2", 185 lbs. Deb: 7/25/43

YEAR TM/L	W	L	PCT	G	GS	CG	SH	SV	IP	H	HR	BB	SO	RAT	ERA	ERA+	OAV	OOB	BH	AVG	PB	PR	/A	PD	TPI
1943 *StL-N	8	2	.800	13	9	4	1	0	88	74	0	29	26	10.5	1.53	219	.231	.295	9	.281	2	18	18	0	2.4
1946 *StL-N	11	10	.524	37	15	6	2	0	153¹	152	1	55	58	12.3	3.29	105	.261	.327	11	.212	-0	2	3	0	0.3
1947 StL-N	14	8	.636	44	19	7	0	4	168	186	7	48	85	12.6	2.84	146	.284	.335	14	.219	1	23	24	3	3.4
1948 StL-N	10	6	.625	42	23	6	2	1	156¹	171	8	50	55	12.7	3.80	108	.281	.335	8	.145	-2	3	5	3	0.6
1949 StL-N	14	8	.636	39	25	9	1	0	206¹	208	18	61	75	12.0	3.18	131	.263	.321	11	.134	-4	20	22	-0	1.7
1950 StL-N	11	9	.550	46	12	3	0	6	164²	188	12	80	47	14.9	4.10	105	.296	.378	13	.213	-1	1	4	-1	0.3
1951 StL-N	5	5	.545	56	8	5	0	7	154¹	139	13	60	66	11.9	3.09	128	.245	.322	5	.109	-3	15	15	-2	0.6
1952 StL-N	12	5	.706	46	6	3	1	16	109¹	75	7	42	55	9.7	2.72	137	.198	.280	4	.125	-1	12	12	-2	1.9
1953 StL-N	6	7	.462	60	0	0	0	18	92	101	8	43	57	14.3	4.21	101	.281	.360	5	.333	1	1	1	2	0.1
1954 StL-N	5	4	.556	58	0	0	0	8	84¹	93	10	24	30	12.8	4.16	99	.288	.343	0	.000	-1	-1	-0	-1	-0.3
Total 10	97	64	.602	441	117	47	7	60	1376²	1387	84	492	554	12.4	3.31	120	.266	.332	80	.177	-9	93	103	3	11.3

● **HARRY BRECHEEN**   Brecheen, Harry David "Harry The Cat" b: 10/14/14, Broken Bow, Okla.   BL/TL, 5'10", 160 lbs. Deb: 4/22/40 C

YEAR TM/L	W	L	PCT	G	GS	CG	SH	SV	IP	H	HR	BB	SO	RAT	ERA	ERA+	OAV	OOB	BH	AVG	PB	PR	/A	PD	TPI
1940 StL-N	0	0	—	3	0	0	0	0	3¹	2	0	2	4	10.8	0.00	—	.167	.286	-0		1	1	0	0.0
1943 *StL-N	9	6	.600	29	13	8	1	4	135¹	98	4	39	68	9.3	2.26	149	.206	.270	8	.190	1	17	17	1	2.1
1944 *StL-N	16	5	.762	30	22	13	3	0	189¹	174	8	46	88	10.6	2.85	124	.242	.290	11	.162	1	16	14	-0	1.5
1945 StL-N	15	4	.789	24	18	13	2	3	157¹	136	5	44	63	10.6	2.52	149	.238	.298	7	.123	-1	22	21	-1	2.3
1946 *StL-N	15	15	.500	36	30	14	5	3	231¹	212	8	67	117	11.0	2.49	139	.244	.301	11	.133	-3	24	25	2	3.1
1947 StL-N★	16	11	.593	29	28	18	1	1	223¹	220	20	66	89	11.6	3.30	125	.260	.316	20	.241	5	19	21	1	2.9
1948 StL-N☆	20	7	.741	33	30	21	7	1	233¹	193	6	49	149	9.4	2.24	183	.222	.265	12	.146	-1	45	48	1	5.5
1949 StL-N	14	11	.560	32	31	14	2	1	214²	207	18	65	88	11.7	3.35	124	.252	.312	21	.273	5	16	19	-1	2.5
1950 StL-N	8	11	.421	27	23	12	2	1	163¹	151	18	45	69	11.0	3.80	113	.244	.298	14	.241	3	6	9	-0	1.2
1951 StL-N	8	4	.667	24	16	5	0	2	138²	134	11	54	57	12.3	3.25	122	.256	.327	12	.218	2	11	11	-0	1.1
1952 StL-N	7	5	.583	25	13	4	1	2	100¹	82	12	28	54	10.1	3.32	112	.223	.283	6	.207	1	5	4	2	0.9
1953 StL-A	5	13	.278	26	16	3	0	1	117¹	122	7	31	44	12.0	3.07	137	.269	.320	7	.179	-1	12	15	2	2.3
Total 12	133	92	.591	318	240	125	25	18	1907²	1731	117	536	901	10.9	2.92	133	.242	.298	129	.192	11	194	205	6	25.4

● **BILL BRECKINRIDGE**   Breckinridge, William Robertson b: 10/16/07, Tulsa, Okla. d: 8/23/58, Tulsa, Okla. BR/TR, 5'11", 175 lbs. Deb: 6/30/29

YEAR TM/L	W	L	PCT	G	GS	CG	SH	SV	IP	H	HR	BB	SO	RAT	ERA	ERA+	OAV	OOB	BH	AVG	PB	PR	/A	PD	TPI
1929 Phi-A	0	0	—	3	1	0	0	0	10	10	0	16	2	23.4	8.10	52	.270	.491	0	.000	-1	-4	-4	-1	-0.1

● **FRED BREINING**   Breining, Fred Lawrence b: 11/15/55, San Francisco, Cal.   BR/TR, 6'4", 185 lbs. Deb: 9/4/80

YEAR TM/L	W	L	PCT	G	GS	CG	SH	SV	IP	H	HR	BB	SO	RAT	ERA	ERA+	OAV	OOB	BH	AVG	PB	PR	/A	PD	TPI
1980 SF-N	0	0	—	5	0	0	0	0	6²	8	0	4	3	17.6	5.40	65	.333	.448	0	—	0	-1	-1	-0	0.0
1981 SF-N	5	2	.714	45	1	0	0	0	77²	66	4	38	37	12.3	2.55	135	.243	.340	1	.000	-1	8	8	0	0.6
1982 SF-N	11	6	.647	54	9	2	0	0	143¹	146	6	52	98	12.5	3.08	117	.269	.334	6	.207	-1	8	8	1	1.2
1983 SF-N	11	12	.478	32	32	6	0	0	202²	202	15	60	117	11.9	3.82	93	.259	.316	10	.149	1	-4	-6	-1	-0.6
1984 Mon-N	0	0	—	4	0	0	0	0	6²	4	0	5	5	12.2	1.35	254	.190	.346	0	.000	-0	2	2	-0	0.0
Total 5	27	20	.574	140	42	8	0	0	437	426	25	159	260	12.2	3.34	106	.260	.329	16	.148	-1	12	10	-0	1.2

● **ALONZO BREITENSTEIN**   Breitenstein, Alonzo b: 11/9/1857, Utica, N.Y. d: 6/19/32, Utica, N.Y. Deb: 7/7/1883

YEAR TM/L	W	L	PCT	G	GS	CG	SH	SV	IP	H	HR	BB	SO	RAT	ERA	ERA+	OAV	OOB	BH	AVG	PB	PR	/A	PD	TPI
1883 Phi-N	0	1	.000	1	1	0	0	0	8	8	0	2	0	18.0	9.00	34	.320	.370	0	.000	-0	-3	-3	-0	-0.5

● **TED BREITENSTEIN**   Breitenstein, Theodore P. "Theo" b: 6/1/1869, St.Louis, Mo. d: 5/3/35, St.Louis, Mo.   BL/TL, 5'9", 167 lbs. Deb: 4/28/1891

YEAR TM/L	W	L	PCT	G	GS	CG	SH	SV	IP	H	HR	BB	SO	RAT	ERA	ERA+	OAV	OOB	BH	AVG	PB	PR	/A	PD	TPI
1891 StL-a	2	0	1.000	6	1	1	1	1	28²	15	2	14	13	9.1	2.20	191	.150	.254	1	.000	-3	5	6	-1	0.2
1892 StL-N	9	19	.321	39	32	28	1	1	282¹	280	8	148	126	13.8	4.69	68	.248	.339	16	.122	-3	-44	-47	3	-3.7
1893 StL-N	19	24	.442	48	42	38	1	1	382²	359	16	152	102	12.3	3.18	149	.241	.316	29	.181	-5	63	66	2	5.5
1894 StL-N	27	23	.540	56	56	46	1	0	447¹	497	21	191	140	14.1	4.79	113	.284	.352	40	.220	-1	27	31	3	2.6
1895 StL-N	19	30	.388	54	50	46	1	0	429²	458	16	178	127	13.6	4.44	109	.267	.343	42	.193	-7	16	19	3	1.3
1896 StL-N	18	26	.409	44	43	37	1	0	339²	376	12	138	114	13.8	4.48	97	.278	.347	42	.259	3	-4	-5	4	0.1

YEAR	TM/L	W	L	PCT	G	GS	CG	SH	SV	IP	H	HR	BB	SO	RAT	ERA	ERA+	OAV	OOB	BH	AVG	PB	PR	/A	PD	TPI
1897	Cin-N	23	12	.657	40	39	32	2	0	320¹	345	3	91	98	12.5	3.62	126	.273	.326	33	.266	3	25	33	-0	3.1
1898	Cin-N	20	14	.588	39	37	32	3	0	315²	313	2	123	68	12.7	3.42	112	.257	.330	26	.215	1	7	15	3	1.7
1899	Cin-N	13	9	.591	26	24	21	0	0	210²	219	2	71	59	12.8	3.59	109	.268	.333	37	.352	9	6	8	-0	1.5
1900	Cin-N	10	10	.500	24	20	18	1	0	192¹	205	4	79	39	13.9	3.65	101	.272	.352	24	.190	-0	1	0	2	0.2
1901	StL-N	0	3	.000	3	3	1	0	0	15	24	1	14	3	22.8	6.60	48	.358	.469	2	.333	0	-5	-6	1	-0.8
Total	11	160	170	.485	379	341	300	12	3	2964¹	3091	79	1203	889	13.3	4.04	109	.265	.338	291	.216	-3	96	121	20	11.7

● AD BRENNAN
Brennan, Addison Foster   b: 7/18/1881, LaHarpe, Kan.   d: 1/7/62, Kansas City, Mo.   BL/TL, 5'11", 170 lbs.   Deb: 5/19/10

YEAR	TM/L	W	L	PCT	G	GS	CG	SH	SV	IP	H	HR	BB	SO	RAT	ERA	ERA+	OAV	OOB	BH	AVG	PB	PR	/A	PD	TPI
1910	Phi-N	2	0	1.000	19	5	2	0	0	73¹	72	2	28	28	12.6	2.33	134	.264	.339	7	.280	1	6	6	-2	0.1
1911	Phi-N	2	1	.667	5	3	1	0	0	22²	22	0	12	12	13.9	3.57	96	.259	.357	2	.222	-0	-0	-0	0	0.0
1912	Phi-N	11	9	.550	27	19	13	1	2	174	185	4	49	78	12.3	3.57	102	.274	.326	15	.254	-4	-3	1	2	0.7
1913	Phi-N	14	12	.538	40	25	12	1	1	207	204	5	46	94	11.1	2.39	139	.268	.314	11	.164	-2	19	22	0	2.5
1914	Chi-F	5	5	.500	16	11	5	1	0	85²	84	6	21	31	11.2	3.57	74	.256	.305	8	.250	1	-7	-9	-1	-0.9
1915	Chi-F	3	9	.250	19	13	7	2	0	106	117	4	30	40	13.1	3.74	67	.287	.346	5	.185	0	-12	-14	-2	-1.7
1918	Was-A	0	0	—	2	1	0	0	0	5¹	7	0	5	0	21.9	5.06	54	.241	.371	0	.000	-0	-1	-1	0	0.0
	Cle-A	0	0	—	1	0	0	0	0	3	3	0	3	0	18.0	3.00	100	.333	.500	0	—	-0	-0	-0	-0	0.0
	Yr	0	0	—	3	1	0	0	0	8¹	10	0	8	0	19.4	4.32	65	.256	.383	0	.000	-0	-1	-1	0	0.0
Total	7	37	36	.507	129	77	40	5	3	677	694	21	194	283	12.1	3.11	102	.270	.327	48	.218	4	1	4	-2	0.7

● DON BRENNAN
Brennan, James Donald   b: 12/2/03, Augusta, Maine   d: 4/26/53, Boston, Mass.   BR/TR, 6', 210 lbs.   Deb: 4/16/33

YEAR	TM/L	W	L	PCT	G	GS	CG	SH	SV	IP	H	HR	BB	SO	RAT	ERA	ERA+	OAV	OOB	BH	AVG	PB	PR	/A	PD	TPI
1933	NY-A	5	1	.833	18	10	3	0	3	85	92	4	47	46	14.7	4.98	78	.275	.365	7	.259	2	-7	-10	1	-0.4
1934	Cin-N	4	3	.571	28	7	2	0	0	78	89	3	35	31	14.4	3.81	107	.290	.364	5	.227	0	2	2	-1	0.2
1935	Cin-N	5	5	.500	38	5	2	1	5	114¹	101	4	44	48	11.7	3.15	126	.242	.320	3	.100	-1	11	11	-2	0.6
1936	Cin-N	5	2	.714	41	4	0	0	9	94¹	117	2	35	40	14.6	4.39	87	.305	.364	2	.080	-3	-4	-6	-0	-0.8
1937	Cin-N	1	1	.500	10	0	0	0	0	16	25	1	10	1	19.7	6.75	55	.347	.427	0	.000	-1	-5	-5	0	-0.6
	*NY-N	1	0	1.000	6	0	0	0	0	9¹	12	0	9	1	21.2	6.75	58	.316	.458	0	.000	-0	-3	-3	0	-0.3
	Yr	2	1	.667	16	0	0	0	0	25¹	37	1	19	7	20.3	6.75	56	.336	.438	0	.000	-1	-8	-8	0	-0.9
Total	5	21	12	.636	141	26	7	1	19	397	436	14	180	172	14.1	4.19	94	.281	.358	17	.155	-2	-5	-12	-2	-1.3

● TOM BRENNAN
Brennan, Thomas Martin   b: 10/30/52, Chicago, Ill.   BR/TR, 6'1", 180 lbs.   Deb: 9/5/81

YEAR	TM/L	W	L	PCT	G	GS	CG	SH	SV	IP	H	HR	BB	SO	RAT	ERA	ERA+	OAV	OOB	BH	AVG	PB	PR	/A	PD	TPI
1981	Cle-A	2	2	.500	7	6	1	0	0	48¹	49	5	14	15	11.7	3.17	114	.259	.310	0	—	0	3	2	1	0.3
1982	Cle-A	4	2	.667	30	4	0	0	2	92²	112	9	10	46	12.0	4.27	95	.300	.322	0	—	0	-2	-2	0	-0.1
1983	Cle-A	2	2	.500	11	5	1	1	0	39²	45	5	8	21	12.3	3.86	110	.288	.327	0	—	0	1	2	0	0.1
1984	Chi-A	0	1	.000	4	1	0	0	0	6²	8	1	3	3	14.9	4.05	103	.308	.379	0	—	-0	0	0	0	0.0
1985	LA-N	1	3	.250	12	4	0	0	0	31²	41	0	11	17	14.8	7.39	47	.333	.388	1	.125	-0	-13	-14	1	-1.4
Total	5	9	10	.474	64	20	2	1	2	219	255	20	46	102	12.5	4.40	89	.294	.332	1	.125	-0	-12	-12	3	-1.1

● WILLIAM BRENNAN
Brennan, William Raymond   b: 1/15/63, Tampa, Fla.   BR/TR, 6'3", 200 lbs.   Deb: 7/19/88

YEAR	TM/L	W	L	PCT	G	GS	CG	SH	SV	IP	H	HR	BB	SO	RAT	ERA	ERA+	OAV	OOB	BH	AVG	PB	PR	/A	PD	TPI
1988	LA-N	0	1	.000	4	2	0	0	0	9¹	13	0	6	7	18.3	6.75	49	.342	.432	0	.000	-0	-3	-4	0	-0.3
1993	Chi-N	2	1	.667	8	1	0	0	0	15	16	2	8	11	15.0	4.20	95	.291	.391	0	.000	-0	-0	-0	0	0.0
Total	2	2	2	.500	12	3	0	0	0	24¹	29	2	14	18	16.3	5.18	72	.312	.407	0	.000	-0	-4	-4	0	-0.3

● JIM BRENNEMAN
Brenneman, James Leroy   b: 2/13/41, San Diego, Cal.   BR/TR, 6'2", 180 lbs.   Deb: 7/9/65

YEAR	TM/L	W	L	PCT	G	GS	CG	SH	SV	IP	H	HR	BB	SO	RAT	ERA	ERA+	OAV	OOB	BH	AVG	PB	PR	/A	PD	TPI
1965	NY-A	0	0	—	3	0	0	0	0	2	5	1	3	2	36.0	18.00	—	.455	.571	0	—	0	-3	-3	-0	0.0

● BERT BRENNER
Brenner, Delbert Henry "Dutch"   b: 7/18/1887, Minneapolis, Minn   d: 4/11/71, St.Louis Park, Minn.   BR/TR, 6', 175 lbs.   Deb: 9/21/12

YEAR	TM/L	W	L	PCT	G	GS	CG	SH	SV	IP	H	HR	BB	SO	RAT	ERA	ERA+	OAV	OOB	BH	AVG	PB	PR	/A	PD	TPI
1912	Cle-A	1	0	1.000	2	1	0	0	0	13	14	0	4	3	12.5	2.77	123	.286	.340	0	.000	-1	1	1	0	0.0

● LYNN BRENTON
Brenton, Lynn Davis "Buck" or "Herb"   b: 10/7/1890, Peoria, Ill.   d: 10/14/68, Los Angeles, Cal.   BR/TR, 5'10", 165 lbs.   Deb: 8/10/13

YEAR	TM/L	W	L	PCT	G	GS	CG	SH	SV	IP	H	HR	BB	SO	RAT	ERA	ERA+	OAV	OOB	BH	AVG	PB	PR	/A	PD	TPI
1913	Cle-A	0	0	—	1	0	0	0	0	2	4	0	2	1	18.0	9.00	34	.400	.400	0	—	-1	-1	-1	-0	0.0
1915	Cle-A	2	3	.400	11	5	1	1	0	51	60	1	20	18	14.5	3.35	91	.308	.378	2	.118	-1	-2	-2	-1	-0.4
1920	Cin-N	2	1	.667	5	1	0	1	1	18¹	17	0	4	14	10.3	4.91	62	.236	.276	2	.250	-0	-4	-4	2	-0.5
1921	Cin-N	1	8	.111	17	9	2	0	1	60	80	0	17	19	14.7	4.05	88	.342	.389	2	.133	-0	-2	-3	2	-0.2
Total	4	5	12	.294	34	15	4	1	2	131¹	161	1	41	52	14.0	3.97	83	.315	.369	6	.150	-1	-9	-10	3	-1.1

● ROGER BRESNAHAN
Bresnahan, Roger Philip "The Duke Of Tralee"   b: 6/11/1879, Toledo, Ohio   d: 12/4/44, Toledo, Ohio   BR/TR, 5'9", 200 lbs.   Deb: 8/27/1897   MCH ◆

YEAR	TM/L	W	L	PCT	G	GS	CG	SH	SV	IP	H	HR	BB	SO	RAT	ERA	ERA+	OAV	OOB	BH	AVG	PB	PR	/A	PD	TPI
1897	Was-N	4	0	1.000	6	5	3	1	0	41	52	1	10	12	14.3	3.95	110	.306	.356	6	.375	1	2	2	0	0.2
1901	Bal-N	0	1	.000	2	1	0	0	0	6	10	0	4	3	21.0	6.00	64	.366	.447	79	.268	0	-2	-1	0	-0.2
1910	StL-N	0	0	—	1	0	0	0	0	3¹	6	0	1	0	18.9	0.00	—	.400	.438	65	.278	0	1	1	1	0.1
Total	3	4	1	.800	9	6	3	1	0	50¹	68	1	15	15	15.4	3.93	107	.321	.374	1252	.279	2	1	1	0	0.1

● RUBE BRESSLER
Bressler, Raymond Bloom   b: 10/23/1894, Coder, Pa.   d: 11/7/66, Cincinnati, Ohio   BR/TL, 6', 187 lbs.   Deb: 4/24/14   ◆

YEAR	TM/L	W	L	PCT	G	GS	CG	SH	SV	IP	H	HR	BB	SO	RAT	ERA	ERA+	OAV	OOB	BH	AVG	PB	PR	/A	PD	TPI
1914	Phi-A	10	4	.714	29	10	8	1	2	147²	112	1	56	96	10.5	1.77	148	.220	.302	11	.216	4	16	14	-2	1.5
1915	Phi-A	4	17	.190	32	20	7	1	0	178¹	183	3	118	69	15.5	5.20	56	.283	.399	8	.145	1	-45	-45	0	-4.5
1916	Phi-A	0	2	.000	4	2	0	0	0	15	16	0	14	8	19.2	6.60	43	.296	.457	1	.200	1	-6	-6	-0	-0.7
1917	Cin-N	0	0	—	2	1	0	0	0	9	15	0	5	2	20.0	6.00	44	.429	.500	1	.200	-0	-3	-3	-0	-0.3
1918	Cin-N	8	5	.615	17	13	10	0	0	128	124	3	39	37	11.5	2.46	108	.261	.318	17	.274	4	4	3	3	1.1
1919	Cin-N	2	4	.333	13	4	1	0	0	41²	37	1	8	13	9.7	3.46	80	.248	.287	34	.206	2	-3	-1	0	-0.3
1920	Cin-N	2	0	1.000	10	2	1	1	0	20¹	24	0	2	4	11.5	1.77	172	.300	.317	8	.267	0	3	3	0	0.3
Total	7	26	32	.448	107	52	27	3	2	540	511	8	242	229	12.8	3.40	81	.262	.348	1170	.301	12	-34	-38	1	-2.6

● HERB BRETT
Brett, Herbert James "Duke"   b: 5/23/1900, Lawrenceville, Va.   d: 11/25/74, St.Petersburg, Fla   BR/TR, 6', 175 lbs.   Deb: 8/8/24

YEAR	TM/L	W	L	PCT	G	GS	CG	SH	SV	IP	H	HR	BB	SO	RAT	ERA	ERA+	OAV	OOB	BH	AVG	PB	PR	/A	PD	TPI
1924	Chi-N	0	0	—	1	1	0	0	0	5¹	6	0	7	1	21.9	5.06	77	.300	.481	0	.000	-0	-1	-1	-0	-0.1
1925	Chi-N	1	1	.500	10	1	0	0	0	17¹	12	0	3	6	8.3	3.63	119	.194	.242	0	.000	-0	1	1	1	0.2
Total	2	1	1	.500	11	2	0	0	0	22²	18	0	10	7	11.5	3.97	106	.220	.312	0	.000	-0	1	1	1	0.2

● KEN BRETT
Brett, Kenneth Alven   b: 9/18/48, Brooklyn, N.Y.   BL/TL, 5'11", 195 lbs.   Deb: 9/27/67   F

YEAR	TM/L	W	L	PCT	G	GS	CG	SH	SV	IP	H	HR	BB	SO	RAT	ERA	ERA+	OAV	OOB	BH	AVG	PB	PR	/A	PD	TPI
1967	*Bos-A	0	0	—	1	0	0	0	0	2	3	0	0	2	13.5	4.50	77	.375	.375	0	—	0	-0	-0	-0	0.0
1969	Bos-A	2	3	.400	8	8	0	0	0	39¹	41	6	22	23	15.1	5.26	72	.275	.379	3	.300	2	-7	-6	0	-0.5
1970	Bos-A	8	9	.471	41	14	1	0	2	139¹	118	17	79	155	12.9	4.07	97	.223	.327	13	.317	6	-6	-2	1	0.5
1971	Bos-A	0	3	.000	29	2	0	0	0	59	57	7	35	57	14.2	5.34	69	.253	.356	2	.200	-0	-12	-11	0	-0.6
1972	Mil-A	7	12	.368	26	22	2	1	0	133	121	13	49	74	11.6	4.53	67	.242	.311	10	.227	4	-22	-22	-2	-3.0
1973	Phi-N	13	9	.591	31	25	10	3	0	211²	206	19	74	111	11.9	3.44	110	.259	.322	20	.250	8	5	8	2	1.9
1974	*Pit-N★	13	9	.591	27	27	10	3	0	191	192	9	51	96	11.8	3.30	104	.257	.308	27	.310	11	7	3	0	1.5
1975	*Pit-N	9	5	.643	23	16	4	1	0	118	110	10	43	47	11.8	3.36	106	.250	.320	12	.231	4	3	2	0	0.7
1976	NY-A	0	0	—	2	0	0	0	1	2¹	2	0	0	1	7.7	0.00	—	.222	.222	0	—	0	1	1	0	0.1
	Chi-A	10	12	.455	27	26	16	1	2	200²	171	5	76	91	11.2	3.32	107	.234	.308	1	.083	2	4	4	2	0.6
	Yr	10	12	.455	29	26	16	1	2	203	173	5	76	92	11.2	3.28	109	.233	.307	1	.083	2	5	6	2	0.7
1977	Chi-A	6	4	.600	13	13	2	0	0	82²	101	10	15	39	12.7	5.01	82	.305	.337	0	—	-0	-9	-8	-0	-0.9
	Cal-A	7	10	.412	21	21	5	0	0	142	157	15	38	41	12.6	4.25	92	.287	.337	0	—	-0	-3	-5	2	-0.0
	Yr	13	14	.481	34	34	7	0	0	224²	258	25	53	80	12.6	4.53	88	.293	.335	0	—	-0	-12	-14	2	-0.9
1978	Cal-A	3	5	.375	31	10	1	1	1	100	100	7	42	43	12.9	4.95	73	.262	.336	0	—	-0	-13	-15	2	-0.7
1979	Min-A	0	0	—	9	0	0	0	0	12²	16	1	6	3	15.6	4.97	88	.320	.393	0	—	0	-1	-1	0	-0.3
	LA-N	4	3	.571	30	0	0	0	2	47	52	1	12	13	12.4	3.45	105	.277	.323	3	.273	0	1	1	2	0.4

YEAR TM/L	W	L	PCT	G	GS	CG	SH	SV	IP	H	HR	BB	SO	RAT	ERA	ERA+	OAV	OOB	BH	AVG	PB	PR	/A	PD	TPI
1980 KC-A	0	0	—	8	0	0	0	1	13¹	8	0	5	4	9.5	0.00	—	.174	.269	0	—	0	6	6	0	0.1
1981 KC-A	1	1	.500	22	0	0	0	2	32¹	35	2	14	7	13.9	4.18	86	.282	.360	0	—	0	-2	-2	0	-0.1
Total 14	83	85	.494	349	184	51	8	11	1526¹	1490	127	562	807	12.2	3.93	93	.257	.325	91	.262	35	-47	-46	8	-0.3

● **MARV BREUER** Breuer, Marvin Howard "Baby Face" b: 4/29/14, Rolla, Mo. d: 1/17/91, Rolla, Mo. BR/TR, 6'2", 185 lbs. Deb: 5/4/39

YEAR TM/L	W	L	PCT	G	GS	CG	SH	SV	IP	H	HR	BB	SO	RAT	ERA	ERA+	OAV	OOB	BH	AVG	PB	PR	/A	PD	TPI
1939 NY-A	0	0	—	1	0	0	0	0	1	2	0	1	0	27.0	9.00	48	.667	.750	0	—	0	-0	-1	0	0.0
1940 NY-A	8	9	.471	27	22	10	0	0	164	175	20	61	71	13.0	4.55	89	.267	.329	2	.037	-5	-3	-10	-1	-1.3
1941 *NY-A	9	7	.563	26	18	7	1	2	141	131	10	49	77	11.6	4.09	96	.243	.308	4	.087	-3	1	-2	-1	-0.6
1942 *NY-A	8	9	.471	27	19	6	0	1	164¹	157	11	37	72	10.7	3.07	112	.252	.295	3	.056	-3	11	7	-2	0.1
1943 NY-A	0	1	.000	5	1	0	0	0	14	22	0	6	6	18.0	8.36	39	.349	.406	1	.333	-0	-8	-8	0	-0.5
Total 5	25	26	.490	86	60	23	1	3	484¹	487	41	154	226	12.0	4.03	94	.258	.315	10	.064	-11	0	-13	-3	-2.3

● **JIM BREWER** Brewer, James Thomas b: 11/17/37, Merced, Cal. d: 11/16/87, Tyler, Tex. BL/TL, 6'2", 195 lbs. Deb: 7/17/60 C

YEAR TM/L	W	L	PCT	G	GS	CG	SH	SV	IP	H	HR	BB	SO	RAT	ERA	ERA+	OAV	OOB	BH	AVG	PB	PR	/A	PD	TPI
1960 Chi-N	0	3	.000	5	4	0	0	0	21²	25	2	6	7	13.3	5.82	65	.272	.323	1	.167	0	-5	-5	0	-0.6
1961 Chi-N	1	7	.125	36	11	0	0	0	86²	116	17	21	57	14.3	5.82	72	.321	.360	4	.182	0	-17	-16	-2	-1.4
1962 Chi-N	0	1	.000	6	1	0	0	0	5²	10	2	3	1	20.6	9.53	44	.435	.500	0	—	0	-4	-3	0	-0.5
1963 Chi-N	3	2	.600	29	1	0	0	0	49²	59	10	15	35	13.4	4.89	72	.294	.343	0	.000	0	-9	-8	-1	-0.8
1964 LA-N	4	3	.571	34	5	1	1	1	93	79	5	25	63	10.1	3.00	108	.232	.284	6	.273	2	6	2	-1	0.2
1965 *LA-N	3	2	.600	19	2	0	0	0	49¹	33	1	28	31	11.1	1.82	179	.196	.311	0	.000	-1	9	8	0	0.8
1966 *LA-N	0	2	.000	13	0	0	0	2	22	17	0	11	8	11.5	3.68	90	.221	.318	0	—	0	-0	-1	0	-0.1
1967 LA-N	5	4	.556	30	11	0	0	1	100²	78	9	31	74	9.8	2.68	116	.218	.283	1	.045	-1	8	5	-1	0.2
1968 LA-N	8	3	.727	54	0	0	0	14	76¹	59	5	33	75	10.8	2.48	112	.219	.304	2	.222	0	4	2	0	0.5
1969 LA-N	7	6	.538	59	0	0	0	20	88¹	71	5	41	92	11.8	2.55	131	.221	.317	1	.091	0	10	8	0	1.5
1970 LA-N	7	6	.538	58	0	0	0	24	89	66	10	33	91	10.0	3.13	122	.207	.281	1	.083	-0	9	7	0	1.3
1971 LA-N	6	5	.545	55	0	0	0	22	81¹	55	4	24	66	8.7	1.88	172	.194	.257	3	.333	1	14	12	1	2.6
1972 LA-N	8	7	.533	51	0	0	0	17	78¹	41	6	25	69	7.8	1.26	264	.157	.236	0	.000	0	19	18	-0	4.5
1973 LA-N★	4	8	.429	56	0	0	0	20	71²	58	8	25	56	10.4	3.01	114	.229	.299	2	.400	1	5	3	0	0.9
1974 *LA-N	4	4	.500	24	0	0	0	0	39¹	29	5	10	26	8.9	2.52	135	.207	.260	0	.000	-1	5	4	-1	0.7
1975 LA-N	3	1	.750	21	0	0	0	2	33	44	2	13	21	15.5	5.18	66	.333	.393	0	.000	0	-6	-7	0	-0.8
Cal-A	1	0	1.000	21	0	0	0	5	34²	27	3	11	22	12.7	1.82	195	.279	.333	0	—	0	8	7	-1	0.9
1976 Cal-A	3	1	.750	13	0	0	0	0	20	20	0	6	16	11.7	2.70	123	.256	.310	0	—	0	2	1	0	0.3
Total 17	69	65	.515	584	35	1	1	132	1040²	898	92	360	810	11.0	3.07	111	.236	.303	21	.150	1	59	38	-4	10.2

● **JACK BREWER** Brewer, John Herndon "Buddy" b: 7/21/19, Los Angeles, Cal. BR/TR, 6'2", 170 lbs. Deb: 7/15/44

YEAR TM/L	W	L	PCT	G	GS	CG	SH	SV	IP	H	HR	BB	SO	RAT	ERA	ERA+	OAV	OOB	BH	AVG	PB	PR	/A	PD	TPI
1944 NY-N	1	4	.200	14	7	2	0	0	55	66	8	16	21	13.9	5.56	66	.288	.343	4	.211	0	-12	-12	-1	-1.0
1945 NY-N	8	6	.571	28	21	8	0	0	159²	162	14	58	49	12.6	3.83	102	.260	.326	10	.179	-1	-1	1	-3	-0.3
1946 NY-N	0	0	—	1	0	0	0	0	2	3	0	2	3	22.5	13.50	25	.333	.455	0	—	0	-2	-2	-0	0.0
Total 3	9	10	.474	43	28	10	0	0	216²	231	22	76	73	13.0	4.36	88	.268	.332	14	.187	-1	-15	-12	-3	-1.3

● **ROD BREWER** Brewer, Rodney Lee b: 2/24/66, Eustis, Fla. BL/TL, 6'3", 210 lbs. Deb: 9/5/90 ♦

YEAR TM/L	W	L	PCT	G	GS	CG	SH	SV	IP	H	HR	BB	SO	RAT	ERA	ERA+	OAV	OOB	BH	AVG	PB	PR	/A	PD	TPI
1993 StL-N	0	0	—	1	0	0	0	0	1	3	1	2	1	45.0	45.00	9	.500	.625	42	.286	0	-5	-5	0	0.0

● **TOM BREWER** Brewer, Thomas Austin b: 9/3/31, Wadesboro, N.C. BR/TR, 6'1", 175 lbs. Deb: 4/18/54

YEAR TM/L	W	L	PCT	G	GS	CG	SH	SV	IP	H	HR	BB	SO	RAT	ERA	ERA+	OAV	OOB	BH	AVG	PB	PR	/A	PD	TPI
1954 Bos-A	10	9	.526	33	23	7	0	0	162²	152	15	95	69	14.1	4.65	88	.249	.356	16	.267	3	-17	-10	-2	-1.0
1955 Bos-A	11	10	.524	31	28	9	2	0	192²	198	21	87	91	13.7	4.20	102	.263	.346	11	.151	-2	-5	2	3	0.3
1956 Bos-A★	19	9	.679	32	32	15	4	0	244¹	200	14	112	127	11.7	3.50	132	.220	.325	28	.298	4	18	30	4	4.1
1957 Bos-A	16	13	.552	32	32	15	2	0	238¹	225	24	93	128	12.3	3.85	103	.250	.325	19	.202	-1	-2	4	6	0.9
1958 Bos-A	12	12	.500	33	32	10	1	0	227¹	227	21	93	124	13.0	3.72	108	.259	.335	16	.195	-0	1	7	4	1.1
1959 Bos-A	10	12	.455	36	32	11	3	2	215¹	219	14	88	121	12.9	3.76	108	.265	.338	8	.111	-4	2	7	4	0.7
1960 Bos-A	10	15	.400	34	29	8	1	1	186²	220	13	72	60	14.4	4.82	84	.301	.338	12	.194	-0	-20	-16	3	-1.7
1961 Bos-A	3	2	.600	10	9	0	0	0	42	37	4	29	13	14.1	3.43	122	.242	.363	4	.286	1	3	3	1	0.6
Total 8	91	82	.526	241	217	75	13	3	1509¹	1478	126	669	733	13.1	4.00	104	.257	.338	114	.207	1	-19	27	22	5.0

● **BILLY BREWER** Brewer, William Robert b: 4/15/68, Fort Worth, Tex. BL/TL, 6'1", 175 lbs. Deb: 4/8/93

YEAR TM/L	W	L	PCT	G	GS	CG	SH	SV	IP	H	HR	BB	SO	RAT	ERA	ERA+	OAV	OOB	BH	AVG	PB	PR	/A	PD	TPI
1993 KC-A	2	2	.500	46	0	0	0	0	39	31	6	20	28	11.8	3.46	132	.230	.329	0	—	0	4	5	-1	0.0
1994 KC-A	4	1	.800	50	0	0	0	3	38²	28	4	16	25	10.7	2.56	202	.207	.301	0	—	0	10	11	0	1.4
Total 2	6	3	.667	96	0	0	0	3	77²	59	10	36	53	11.2	3.01	162	.219	.315	0	—	0	13	16	-1	1.4

● **ALAN BRICE** Brice, Alan Healey b: 10/1/37, New York, N.Y. BR/TR, 6'5", 215 lbs. Deb: 9/22/61

YEAR TM/L	W	L	PCT	G	GS	CG	SH	SV	IP	H	HR	BB	SO	RAT	ERA	ERA+	OAV	OOB	BH	AVG	PB	PR	/A	PD	TPI
1961 Chi-A	0	1	.000	3	0	0	0	0	3¹	4	0	3	3	18.9	0.00	—	.308	.438	0	—	0	1	1	-0	0.4

● **RALPH BRICKNER** Brickner, Ralph Harold "Brick" b: 5/2/25, Cincinnati, Ohio d: 5/9/94, Port Jefferson, N.Y. BR/TR, 6'3.5", 215 lbs. Deb: 5/4/52

YEAR TM/L	W	L	PCT	G	GS	CG	SH	SV	IP	H	HR	BB	SO	RAT	ERA	ERA+	OAV	OOB	BH	AVG	PB	PR	/A	PD	TPI
1952 Bos-A	3	1	.750	14	1	0	0	1	33	32	1	11	9	11.7	2.18	181	.264	.326	2	.250	1	5	6	-1	0.8

● **MARSHALL BRIDGES** Bridges, Marshall "Sheriff" b: 6/2/31, Jackson, Miss. d: 9/3/90, Jackson, Miss. BB/TL, 6'1", 180 lbs. Deb: 6/17/59

YEAR TM/L	W	L	PCT	G	GS	CG	SH	SV	IP	H	HR	BB	SO	RAT	ERA	ERA+	OAV	OOB	BH	AVG	PB	PR	/A	PD	TPI
1959 StL-N	6	3	.667	27	4	1	0	1	76	67	10	37	76	12.3	4.26	99	.240	.329	5	.217	2	-3	-0	-2	0.0
1960 StL-N	2	2	.500	20	1	0	0	1	31¹	33	2	16	27	14.4	3.45	119	.266	.355	0	.000	-0	1	2	-0	0.2
Cin-N	4	0	1.000	14	0	0	0	2	25¹	14	1	7	26	7.5	1.07	359	.161	.223	1	.250	0	8	8	-0	1.4
Yr	6	2	.750	34	1	0	0	3	56²	47	3	23	53	11.1	2.38	167	.220	.295	1	.100	-0	9	10	-1	1.6
1961 Cin-N	0	1	.000	13	0	0	0	0	20²	26	4	11	17	16.5	7.84	52	.317	.404	0	.000	-0	-9	-9	-0	-0.4
1962 *NY-A	8	4	.667	52	0	0	0	18	71²	49	4	48	66	12.2	3.14	119	.194	.323	0	.000	-0	7	5	2	1.0
1963 NY-A	2	1	.667	23	0	0	0	1	33	27	2	30	35	15.8	3.82	92	.237	.400	0	—	0	-1	-1	-2	0.1
1964 Was-A	0	3	.000	17	0	0	0	2	30	37	3	17	16	16.2	5.70	65	.303	.388	0	.000	-0	-7	-7	-0	-0.7
1965 Was-A	1	2	.333	40	0	0	0	0	57¹	62	3	25	39	13.7	2.67	130	.268	.340	1	.143	0	5	5	0	0.3
Total 7	23	15	.605	206	5	1	0	25	345¹	315	29	191	302	13.3	3.75	102	.244	.343	7	.119	-0	1	3	1	1.9

● **TOMMY BRIDGES** Bridges, Thomas Jefferson Davis b: 12/28/06, Gordonsville, Tenn. d: 4/19/68, Nashville, Tenn. BR/TR, 5'10.5", 155 lbs. Deb: 8/13/30 C

YEAR TM/L	W	L	PCT	G	GS	CG	SH	SV	IP	H	HR	BB	SO	RAT	ERA	ERA+	OAV	OOB	BH	AVG	PB	PR	/A	PD	TPI
1930 Det-A	3	2	.600	8	5	2	0	0	37²	28	4	23	17	12.2	4.06	118	.215	.333	3	.300	1	2	3	-0	0.4
1931 Det-A	8	16	.333	35	23	8	2	0	173	182	13	108	105	15.1	4.99	92	.263	.363	8	.148	-2	-12	-8	-1	-1.2
1932 Det-A	14	12	.538	34	26	10	**4**	1	201	174	14	119	108	13.2	3.36	140	.233	.339	11	.164	-1	25	30	1	3.2
1933 Det-A	14	12	.538	33	28	17	2	2	233	192	8	110	120	11.9	3.09	140	**.226**	.319	16	.205	2	31	32	1	3.5
1934 *Det-A☆	22	11	.667	36	35	23	3	1	275	249	16	104	151	11.7	3.67	120	.241	.312	12	.122	-4	25	22	-2	1.7
1935 *Det-A☆	21	10	.677	36	34	23	4	1	274¹	277	22	113	**163**	12.9	3.51	119	.259	.332	26	.239	3	29	20	-1	2.1
1936 Det-A†	**23**	11	.676	39	38	26	5	0	294²	289	21	115	**175**	12.5	3.60	137	.255	.326	25	.212	0	47	44	2	4.4
1937 Det-A★	15	12	.556	34	31	18	3	0	245¹	267	15	91	138	13.2	4.07	115	.274	.338	23	.240	2	15	16	1	1.3
1938 Det-A	13	9	.591	25	20	13	0	1	151	171	14	58	101	13.8	4.59	109	.287	.353	7	.130	-1	3	7	-1	0.6
1939 Det-A★	17	7	.708	29	26	14	2	2	198	186	11	61	129	11.5	3.50	140	.243	.304	14	.197	-0	25	31	-0	3.3
1940 *Det-A☆	12	9	.571	29	28	12	2	0	197²	171	11	88	133	11.8	3.37	141	.229	.311	12	.176	-2	22	30	-1	2.6
1941 Det-A	9	12	.429	25	22	10	1	0	147²	128	10	70	90	12.1	3.41	133	.233	.320	4	.085	-3	12	9	2	1.8
1942 Det-A	9	7	.563	23	22	11	2	1	174	164	6	61	97	11.8	2.74	144	.246	.313	6	.095	-2	18	23	1	1.9
1943 Det-A	12	7	.632	25	22	11	2	2	191²	159	9	61	124	10.3	2.39	147	.226	.287	14	.219	2	19	24	-1	2.6
1945 Det-A	1	0	1.000	9	1	0	0	0	11	14	2	2	6	13.1	3.27	107	.311	.340	0	.000	0	-0	0	0	0.0
1946 Det-A	1	1	.500	9	1	0	0	1	21¹	24	5	8	17	13.9	5.91	62	.279	.347	0	.000	0	-6	-5	0	-0.5
Total 16	194	138	.584	424	362	200	33	10	2826¹	2675	181	1192	1674	12.4	3.57	126	.248	.325	181	.180	-5	256	291	-3	28.7

YEAR TM/L	W	L	PCT	G	GS	CG	SH	SV	IP	H	HR	BB	SO	RAT	ERA	ERA+	OAV	OOB	BH	AVG	PB	PR	/A	PD	TPI

● BUTTONS BRIGGS
Briggs, Herbert Theodore b: 7/8/1875, Poughkeepsie, N.Y. d: 2/18/11, Cleveland, Ohio BR/TR, 6'1", 180 lbs. Deb: 4/23/1896

YEAR TM/L	W	L	PCT	G	GS	CG	SH	SV	IP	H	HR	BB	SO	RAT	ERA	ERA+	OAV	OOB	BH	AVG	PB	PR	/A	PD	TPI
1896 Chi-N	12	8	.600	26	21	19	0	1	194	202	6	108	84	15.1	4.31	105	.266	.369	10	.128	-6	1	5	-3	-0.4
1897 Chi-N	4	17	.190	22	22	21	0	0	186²	246	6	85	60	16.4	5.26	85	.315	.388	13	.160	-6	-20	-16	-1	-2.0
1898 Chi-N	1	3	.250	4	4	3	0	0	30	38	0	10	14	14.7	5.70	63	.306	.363	6	.429	2	-7	-7	-0	-0.6
1904 Chi-N	19	11	.633	34	30	28	3	3	277	252	3	77	112	10.9	2.05	139	.240	.304	16	.170	-0	21	19	-4	1.6
1905 Chi-N	8	8	.500	20	20	13	5	0	168	141	1	52	68	10.7	2.14	139	.237	.304	3	.053	-4	16	16	-2	0.7
Total 5	44	47	.484	106	97	84	8	4	855²	879	16	332	338	13.1	3.41	104	.268	.342	48	.148	-15	12	14	-10	-0.7

● JOHN BRIGGS
Briggs, Jonathan Tift b: 1/24/34, Natoma, Cal. BR/TR, 5'10", 175 lbs. Deb: 4/17/56

YEAR TM/L	W	L	PCT	G	GS	CG	SH	SV	IP	H	HR	BB	SO	RAT	ERA	ERA+	OAV	OOB	BH	AVG	PB	PR	/A	PD	TPI
1956 Chi-N	0	0	—	3	0	0	0	0	5¹	5	1	4	1	20.3	1.69	223	.238	.429	0	—	0	1	1	0	0.0
1957 Chi-N	0	1	.000	3	0	0	0	0	4¹	7	2	3	1	20.8	12.46	31	.368	.455	0	—	0	-4	-4	-0	-0.8
1958 Chi-N	5	5	.500	20	17	3	1	0	95²	99	12	45	46	13.6	4.52	87	.270	.352	9	.257	2	-6	-6	-1	-0.5
1959 Cle-A	0	1	.000	4	1	0	0	0	12²	12	1	3	5	10.7	2.13	173	.245	.288	0	.000	-0	2	2	-0	0.1
1960 Cle-A	4	2	.667	21	2	0	0	1	36¹	32	4	15	19	11.9	4.46	84	.250	.333	1	.125	-0	-2	-3	-1	-0.6
KC-A	0	2	.000	8	1	0	0	0	11¹	19	3	12	8	24.6	12.71	31	.380	.500	0	.000	-0	-11	-11	-0	-1.6
Yr	4	4	.500	29	3	0	0	1	47²	51	7	27	27	14.7	6.42	59	.282	.375	1	.091	-1	-13	-14	-1	-2.2
Total 5	9	11	.450	59	21	3	1	1	165²	174	23	82	80	14.2	5.00	77	.275	.363	10	.208	1	-20	-21	-2	-3.4

● NELSON BRILES
Briles, Nelson Kelley b: 8/5/43, Dorris, Cal. BR/TR, 5'11", 200 lbs. Deb: 4/19/65

YEAR TM/L	W	L	PCT	G	GS	CG	SH	SV	IP	H	HR	BB	SO	RAT	ERA	ERA+	OAV	OOB	BH	AVG	PB	PR	/A	PD	TPI
1965 StL-N	3	3	.500	37	2	0	0	4	82¹	79	4	26	52	12.1	3.50	110	.258	.328	2	.133	-0	0	3	-1	0.1
1966 StL-N	4	15	.211	49	17	0	0	6	154	162	14	54	100	13.0	3.21	112	.279	.348	3	.079	-2	7	6	1	0.7
1967 *StL-N	14	5	.737	49	14	4	2	6	155¹	139	8	40	94	10.7	2.43	135	.236	.290	6	.150	-0	16	15	-2	1.8
1968 *StL-N	19	11	.633	33	33	13	4	0	243²	251	18	55	141	11.6	2.81	103	.266	.311	11	.138	1	5	2	-2	0.1
1969 StL-N	15	13	.536	36	33	10	3	0	227²	218	17	63	126	11.2	3.52	102	.251	.303	8	.105	-1	2	1	-1	-0.1
1970 StL-N	6	7	.462	30	19	1	1	0	106²	129	14	36	59	14.1	6.24	66	.297	.353	7	.179	1	-26	-25	-2	-2.7
1971 *Pit-N	8	4	.667	37	14	4	2	1	136	131	12	35	76	11.2	3.04	109	.250	.301	10	.256	4	6	5	-1	0.7
1972 *Pit-N	14	11	.560	28	27	9	2	0	195²	185	14	43	120	10.5	3.08	108	.249	.291	11	.157	-0	8	5	-1	0.6
1973 Pit-N	14	13	.519	33	33	7	1	0	218²	201	19	51	94	10.4	2.84	124	.244	.288	14	.194	3	20	16	0	2.3
1974 KC-A	5	7	.417	18	17	3	0	0	103	118	9	21	41	12.3	4.02	95	.293	.331	0	—	0	-5	-2	-1	-0.7
1975 KC-A	6	6	.500	24	16	3	0	2	112	127	19	25	73	12.6	4.26	90	.285	.330	0	—	0	-6	-5	-0	-0.6
1976 Tex-A	11	9	.550	32	31	7	1	1	210	224	17	47	98	11.7	3.26	110	.273	.314	0	—	0	6	8	-3	0.3
1977 Tex-A	6	4	.600	28	15	2	1	1	108¹	114	13	30	57	12.5	4.24	96	.275	.333	0	—	0	-2	-2	-1	-0.3
Bal-A	0	0	—	2	0	0	0	1	8	5	2	0	2	11.3	6.75	56	.294	.294	0	—	0	-1	-1	-0	-0.1
Yr	6	4	.600	30	15	2	1	1	112¹	119	15	30	59	11.9	4.33	94	.271	.318	0	—	0	-3	-3	-1	-0.3
1978 Bal-A	4	4	.500	16	8	1	0	0	68	61	6	21	30	13.4	4.64	75	.279	.351	0	—	0	-1	-1	-0	-1.0
Total 14	129	112	.535	452	279	64	17	22	2111²	2141	186	547	1163	11.7	3.44	102	.264	.314	72	.154	5	25	19	-14	1.2

● FRANK BRILL
Brill, Francis Hasbrouck (b: Francis Hasbrouck Briell) b: 3/30/1864, Astoria, N.Y. d: 11/19/44, Flushing, N.Y. BR/TR, 5'8", 155 lbs. Deb: 6/23/1884

YEAR TM/L	W	L	PCT	G	GS	CG	SH	SV	IP	H	HR	BB	SO	RAT	ERA	ERA+	OAV	OOB	BH	AVG	PB	PR	/A	PD	TPI
1884 Det-N	2	10	.167	12	12	12	1	0	103	148	7	26	18	15.2	5.50	53	.312	.348	6	.136	-3	-29	-30	-2	-2.9

● JIM BRILLHEART
Brillheart, James Benson b: 9/28/03, Dublin, Va. d: 9/2/72, Radford, Va. BR/TL, 5'11", 170 lbs. Deb: 4/17/22

YEAR TM/L	W	L	PCT	G	GS	CG	SH	SV	IP	H	HR	BB	SO	RAT	ERA	ERA+	OAV	OOB	BH	AVG	PB	PR	/A	PD	TPI
1922 Was-A	4	6	.400	31	10	3	0	1	119²	120	3	72	47	15.0	3.61	107	.275	.388	3	.083	-4	6	3	-2	-0.3
1923 Was-A	0	1	.000	12	0	0	0	0	18	27	1	12	8	20.0	7.00	54	.360	.455	0	—	-0	-6	-6	-0	-0.3
1927 Chi-N	4	2	.667	32	12	4	0	0	128²	140	4	38	36	12.7	4.13	94	.286	.343	1	.023	-5	-3	-4	-1	-0.8
1931 Bos-A	0	0	—	11	1	0	0	0	19²	27	2	15	7	19.2	5.49	78	.325	.429	2	.500	2	-2	-3	1	0.2
Total 4	8	9	.471	86	23	7	0	1	286	314	10	137	98	14.6	4.19	93	.290	.376	6	.070	-8	-6	-9	-2	-1.2

● BRAD BRINK
Brink, Bradford Albert b: 1/20/65, Roseville, Cal. BR/TR, 6'2", 195 lbs. Deb: 5/17/92

YEAR TM/L	W	L	PCT	G	GS	CG	SH	SV	IP	H	HR	BB	SO	RAT	ERA	ERA+	OAV	OOB	BH	AVG	PB	PR	/A	PD	TPI
1992 Phi-N	0	4	.000	8	7	0	0	0	41¹	53	2	13	16	14.6	4.14	84	.308	.360	1	.083	-0	-3	-3	-0	-0.3
1993 Phi-N	0	0	—	2	0	0	0	0	6	3	1	3	6	9.0	3.00	132	.143	.250	0	.000	-0	1	1	0	0.1
1994 SF-N	0	0	—	4	0	0	0	0	8¹	4	1	4	3	8.6	1.08	372	.143	.250	0	.000	-0	3	3	0	0.0
Total 3	0	4	.000	14	7	0	0	0	55²	60	4	20	27	13.1	3.56	102	.271	.335	1	.071	-1	1	0	-0	-0.3

● JOHN BRISCOE
Briscoe, John Eric b: 9/22/67, LaGrange, Ill. BR/TR, 6'3", 185 lbs. Deb: 4/18/91

YEAR TM/L	W	L	PCT	G	GS	CG	SH	SV	IP	H	HR	BB	SO	RAT	ERA	ERA+	OAV	OOB	BH	AVG	PB	PR	/A	PD	TPI
1991 Oak-A	0	0	—	11	0	0	0	0	14	12	3	10	9	14.1	7.07	54	.235	.361	0	—	0	-5	-5	-0	0.3
1992 Oak-A	0	1	.000	2	0	0	0	0	7	12	0	4	9	27.0	6.43	58	.400	.538	0	—	0	-2	-2	-0	-0.2
1993 Oak-A	1	0	1.000	17	0	0	0	0	24²	26	2	26	24	19.0	8.03	51	.277	.433	0	—	0	-10	-11	-0	0.1
1994 Oak-A	4	2	.667	37	0	0	0	0	49¹	31	7	39	45	13.0	4.01	111	.185	.341	0	—	0	4	2	0	0.3
Total 4	5	3	.625	67	0	0	0	0	95	81	12	84	82	15.7	5.68	74	.236	.388	0	—	0	-12	-16	-0	0.5

● LOU BRISSIE
Brissie, Leland Victor b: 6/5/24, Anderson, S.C. BL/TL, 6'4", 215 lbs. Deb: 9/28/47

YEAR TM/L	W	L	PCT	G	GS	CG	SH	SV	IP	H	HR	BB	SO	RAT	ERA	ERA+	OAV	OOB	BH	AVG	PB	PR	/A	PD	TPI
1947 Phi-A	0	1	.000	1	1	0	0	0	7	9	1	5	4	18.0	6.43	59	.310	.412	0	.000	-0	-2	-2	0	-0.3
1948 Phi-A	14	10	.583	39	25	11	0	5	194	202	6	95	127	13.9	4.13	104	.269	.352	18	.237	0	3	3	-2	0.2
1949 Phi-A★	16	11	.593	34	29	18	0	3	229¹	220	20	118	118	13.5	4.28	96	.251	.344	24	.267	3	-2	-4	-4	-0.5
1950 Phi-A	7	19	.269	46	31	15	2	8	246	237	22	117	101	13.1	4.02	113	.253	.338	15	.172	-3	15	14	-0	1.1
1951 Phi-A	0	2	.000	2	2	0	0	0	13¹	20	0	8	3	18.9	6.75	63	.357	.438	1	.200	-0	-4	-4	-0	-0.5
Cle-A	4	3	.571	54	4	1	0	9	112¹	90	5	61	50	12.3	3.20	118	.223	.329	6	.261	0	11	7	-2	0.4
Yr	4	5	.444	56	6	1	0	9	125²	110	5	69	53	13.0	3.58	107	.239	.342	7	.250	0	8	4	-2	-0.1
1952 Cle-A	3	2	.600	42	1	0	0	2	82²	76	5	34	28	11.1	3.48	96	.221	.299	3	.250	1	-2	-1	-1	-0.1
1953 Cle-A	0	0	—	16	0	0	0	2	13	21	2	13	5	23.5	7.62	49	.389	.507	0	—	0	-5	-6	-0	-0.2
Total 7	44	48	.478	234	93	45	2	29	897²	867	61	451	436	13.4	4.07	102	.254	.343	67	.227	1	19	18	-7	0.3

● JIM BRITT
Britt, James Edward b: 2/25/1856, Brooklyn, N.Y. d: 2/28/23, San Francisco, Cal Deb: 5/2/1872

YEAR TM/L	W	L	PCT	G	GS	CG	SH	SV	IP	H	HR	BB	SO	RAT	ERA	ERA+	OAV	OOB	BH	AVG	PB	PR	/A	PD	TPI
1872 Atl-n	9	28	.243	37	37	37	0	0	336	561	6	19	13	15.5	5.06	91	.323	.331	39	.248	-8	-50	-17		-1.6
1873 Atl-n	17	36	.321	54	54	51	1	0	480²	696	6	40	15	13.8	3.89	78	.300	.320	47	.196	-3	-34	-46		-3.2
Total 2 n	26	64	.289	91	91	88	1	0	816²	1257	12	59	28	14.5	4.38	69	.310	.320	86	.217	-11	-102	-122		-4.8

● JACK BRITTIN
Brittin, John Albert b: 3/4/24, Athens, Ill. d: 1/5/94, Springfield, Ill. BR/TR, 5'11", 175 lbs. Deb: 9/15/50

YEAR TM/L	W	L	PCT	G	GS	CG	SH	SV	IP	H	HR	BB	SO	RAT	ERA	ERA+	OAV	OOB	BH	AVG	PB	PR	/A	PD	TPI
1950 Phi-N	0	0	—	3	0	0	0	0	4	3	0	3	3	11.3	4.50	90	.143	.294	0	—	0	-0	-0	0	0.0
1951 Phi-N	0	0	—	3	0	0	0	0	4	5	0	6	3	24.8	9.00	43	.294	.478	0	—	0	-2	-2	-0	0.0
Total 2	0	0	—	6	0	0	0	0	8	7	0	9	6	18.0	6.75	58	.226	.400	0	—	0	-2	-2	-0	0.0

● JIM BRITTON
Britton, James Allan b: 3/25/44, N.Tonawanda, N.Y. BR/TR, 6'5", 225 lbs. Deb: 9/20/67

YEAR TM/L	W	L	PCT	G	GS	CG	SH	SV	IP	H	HR	BB	SO	RAT	ERA	ERA+	OAV	OOB	BH	AVG	PB	PR	/A	PD	TPI
1967 Atl-N	0	2	.000	2	2	0	0	0	13¹	15	2	2	4	11.5	6.08	55	.278	.304	0	.000	-0	-4	-4	-0	-0.6
1968 Atl-N	4	6	.400	34	9	2	2	0	90	81	1	34	61	11.7	3.10	97	.245	.320	3	.143	-0	-1	-1	-0	-0.3
1969 *Atl-N	7	5	.583	24	13	2	1	1	88	69	10	49	60	12.1	3.78	95	.218	.323	4	.190	-2	-2	-1	-2	-0.3
1971 Mon-N	2	3	.400	16	6	0	0	0	45²	49	10	27	23	15.4	5.72	62	.274	.375	0	.000	-1	-11	-11	-1	-1.3
Total 4	13	16	.448	76	30	4	3	1	237	214	23	112	148	12.5	4.03	83	.243	.332	7	.127	-2	-18	-18	-2	-2.4

● TONY BRIZZOLARA
Brizzolara, Anthony John b: 1/14/57, Santa Monica, Cal. BR/TR, 6'5", 215 lbs. Deb: 5/19/79

YEAR TM/L	W	L	PCT	G	GS	CG	SH	SV	IP	H	HR	BB	SO	RAT	ERA	ERA+	OAV	OOB	BH	AVG	PB	PR	/A	PD	TPI
1979 Atl-N	6	9	.400	20	19	2	0	0	107¹	131	6	33	64	14.2	5.28	77	.303	.356	1	.029	-3	-18	-15	0	-2.1
1983 Atl-N	1	0	1.000	14	0	0	0	0	20¹	22	2	6	17	12.4	3.54	109	.278	.329	0	—	0	0	1	-0	0.0
1984 Atl-N	1	2	.333	10	4	0	0	0	29	33	4	13	17	14.3	5.28	73	.284	.357	0	.000	-1	-5	-5	0	-0.5
Total 3	8	11	.421	44	23	2	0	1	156²	188	12	52	98	14.0	5.06	79	.297	.353	1	.024	-4	-24	-19	-0	-2.6

● JOHNNY BROACA
Broaca, John Joseph b: 10/3/09, Lawrence, Mass. d: 5/16/85, Lawrence, Mass. BR/TR, 5'11", 190 lbs. Deb: 6/2/34

YEAR TM/L	W	L	PCT	G	GS	CG	SH	SV	IP	H	HR	BB	SO	RAT	ERA	ERA+	OAV	OOB	BH	AVG	PB	PR	/A	PD	TPI
1934 NY-A	12	9	.571	26	24	13	1	0	177¹	203	9	65	74	13.7	4.16	98	.284	.344	2	.030	-7	7	-2	-2	-1.0
1935 NY-A	15	7	.682	29	27	14	2	0	201	199	16	79	78	12.4	3.58	113	.254	.323	12	.150	-4	19	10	-3	0.3
1936 NY-A	12	7	.632	37	27	12	1	3	206	235	16	90	84	13.2	4.24	110	.284	.337	9	.110	-6	18	10	-2	-0.1
1937 NY-A	1	4	.200	7	6	3	0	0	44	58	5	17	9	15.3	4.70	94	.324	.383	0	.000	-2	-0	-1	-1	-0.4
1939 Cle-A	4	2	.667	22	2	0	0	0	46	53	5	28	13	15.8	4.70	94	.288	.382	0	.000	-2	-0	-1	-0	-0.3
Total 5	44	29	.603	121	86	42	4	3	674¹	748	51	255	258	13.4	4.08	105	.278	.341	23	.091	-21	44	15	-8	-1.5

● PETE BROBERG
Broberg, Peter Sven b: 3/2/50, W.Palm Beach, Fla. BR/TR, 6'3", 205 lbs. Deb: 6/20/71

YEAR TM/L	W	L	PCT	G	GS	CG	SH	SV	IP	H	HR	BB	SO	RAT	ERA	ERA+	OAV	OOB	BH	AVG	PB	PR	/A	PD	TPI
1971 Was-A	5	9	.357	18	18	7	1	0	124²	104	10	53	89	12.1	3.47	95	.228	.322	5	.114	0	-0	-2	-1	-0.3
1972 Tex-A	5	12	.294	39	25	3	2	1	176¹	153	14	85	133	12.8	4.29	70	.237	.338	4	.078	-2	-24	-25	1	-2.5
1973 Tex-A	5	9	.357	22	20	6	1	0	118²	130	8	66	57	15.2	5.61	66	.283	.379	0	—	0	-24	-25	-0	-2.6
1974 Tex-A	0	4	.000	12	2	0	0	0	29	29	7	13	15	13.3	8.07	44	.264	.347	0	—	0	-14	-15	-1	-1.6
1975 Mil-A	14	16	.467	38	32	7	2	0	220¹	219	17	106	100	13.9	4.13	93	.263	.357	0	—	0	-9	-7	-0	-0.9
1976 Mil-A	1	7	.125	20	11	1	0	0	92¹	99	5	72	28	17.1	4.97	70	.281	.409	0	—	0	-15	-15	-1	-1.3
1977 Chi-N	1	2	.333	22	0	0	0	0	36	34	8	18	20	13.0	4.75	92	.256	.344	0	.000	-1	-3	-1	-0	-0.2
1978 Oak-A	10	12	.455	35	26	2	0	0	165²	174	16	65	94	13.1	4.62	79	.269	.338	0	—	0	-16	-18	1	-2.0
Total 8	41	71	.366	206	134	26	6	1	963	942	85	478	536	13.8	4.56	78	.259	.353	9	.089	-3	-105	-109	-0	-11.4

● DOUG BROCAIL
Brocail, Douglas Keith b: 5/16/67, Clearfield, Pa. BL/TR, 6'5", 220 lbs. Deb: 9/8/92

YEAR TM/L	W	L	PCT	G	GS	CG	SH	SV	IP	H	HR	BB	SO	RAT	ERA	ERA+	OAV	OOB	BH	AVG	PB	PR	/A	PD	TPI
1992 SD-N	0	0	—	3	3	0	0	0	14	17	2	5	15	14.1	6.43	56	.298	.355	1	.200	-0	-5	-4	-0	0.0
1993 SD-N	4	13	.235	24	24	0	0	0	128¹	143	16	42	70	13.3	4.56	91	.282	.342	6	.182	-0	-7	-6	-0	-0.7
1994 SD-N	0	0	—	12	0	0	0	0	17	21	1	5	11	14.8	5.82	72	.304	.368	0	.000	-0	-3	-3	-0	0.0
Total 3	4	13	.235	39	27	0	0	0	159¹	181	19	52	96	13.5	4.86	84	.286	.346	7	.175	-0	-15	-14	-0	-0.7

● LEW BROCKETT
Brockett, Lewis Albert "King" b: 7/23/1880, Brownsville, Ill. d: 9/19/60, Norris City, Ill. BR/TR, 5'10.5", 168 lbs. Deb: 4/25/07

YEAR TM/L	W	L	PCT	G	GS	CG	SH	SV	IP	H	HR	BB	SO	RAT	ERA	ERA+	OAV	OOB	BH	AVG	PB	PR	/A	PD	TPI
1907 NY-A	1	2	.333	8	4	1	0	0	46¹	41	1	26	13	16.7	6.22	45	.308	.397	4	.182	-0	-19	-18	-1	-1.2
1909 NY-A	10	8	.556	26	18	10	3	1	170	148	3	59	70	11.3	2.12	119	.245	.318	17	.283	3	7	8	4	1.7
1911 NY-A	2	4	.333	16	8	2	0	0	75¹	73	3	39	25	14.0	4.66	77	.256	.356	12	.308	2	-11	-9	1	-0.4
Total 3	13	14	.481	50	30	13	3	1	291²	279	7	124	108	12.8	3.43	83	.259	.343	33	.273	5	-23	-19	3	0.1

● DICK BRODOWSKI
Brodowski, Richard Stanley b: 7/26/32, Bayonne, N.J. BR/TR, 6'2", 190 lbs. Deb: 6/15/52

YEAR TM/L	W	L	PCT	G	GS	CG	SH	SV	IP	H	HR	BB	SO	RAT	ERA	ERA+	OAV	OOB	BH	AVG	PB	PR	/A	PD	TPI
1952 Bos-A	5	5	.500	20	12	4	0	0	114²	111	12	50	42	12.9	4.40	90	.252	.333	8	.205	1	-9	-6	-0	-0.4
1955 Bos-A	1	0	1.000	16	0	0	0	0	32	36	5	25	10	17.4	5.63	76	.295	.419	5	.500	3	-6	-5	1	0.2
1956 Was-A	0	3	.000	7	3	1	0	0	17²	31	5	12	8	21.9	9.17	47	.397	.478	0	.000	-1	-10	-10	-0	-1.3
1957 Was-A	0	1	.000	6	0	0	0	0	11¹	12	2	10	4	18.3	11.12	35	.261	.404	0	.000	-0	-9	-9	0	-0.7
1958 Cle-A	1	0	1.000	5	0	0	0	0	10	3	0	6	12	8.1	0.00	—	.100	.250	0	—	-0	4	4	-0	0.4
1959 Cle-A	2	2	.500	18	0	0	0	5	30	19	3	21	9	12.9	1.80	205	.181	.333	2	.333	1	7	6	-1	1.0
Total 6	9	11	.450	72	15	5	0	5	215²	212	27	124	85	14.4	4.76	84	.258	.361	15	.242	3	-23	-19	0	-0.8

● ERNIE BROGLIO
Broglio, Ernest Gilbert b: 8/27/35, Berkeley, Cal. BR/TR, 6'2", 200 lbs. Deb: 4/11/59

YEAR TM/L	W	L	PCT	G	GS	CG	SH	SV	IP	H	HR	BB	SO	RAT	ERA	ERA+	OAV	OOB	BH	AVG	PB	PR	/A	PD	TPI
1959 StL-N	7	12	.368	35	25	6	3	0	181¹	174	20	89	133	13.1	4.72	90	.250	.335	6	.098	-3	-15	-10	1	-1.1
1960 StL-N	21	9	.700	52	24	9	3	0	226¹	172	18	100	188	10.9	2.74	149	.213	.301	14	.206	2	26	34	1	4.8
1961 StL-N	9	12	.429	29	26	7	2	0	174²	166	19	75	113	12.5	4.12	107	.248	.325	9	.145	-2	-5	-1	0	0.3
1962 StL-N	12	9	.571	34	30	11	4	0	222¹	193	22	93	132	11.7	3.00	143	.237	.316	10	.139	-2	23	31	1	2.6
1963 StL-N	18	8	.692	39	35	11	5	0	250	202	24	90	145	10.7	2.99	119	.216	.287	10	.112	-3	8	16	0	1.3
1964 StL-N	3	5	.375	11	11	3	1	0	69¹	61	7	36	36	11.9	3.50	109	.247	.317	2	.095	-0	0	2	-0	0.2
Chi-N	4	7	.364	18	16	3	0	1	100¹	111	12	30	46	12.6	4.04	92	.281	.332	10	.286	-1	-6	-4	-1	-0.2
Yr	7	12	.368	29	27	6	1	1	169²	176	19	56	82	12.3	3.82	98	.267	.324	12	.214	2	-5	-1	-2	0.0
1965 Chi-N	1	6	.143	26	6	0	0	0	50²	63	7	46	22	19.4	6.93	53	.313	.441	0	.000	-0	-19	-18	-1	-2.4
1966 Chi-N	2	6	.250	15	11	2	0	1	62¹	70	14	38	34	15.6	6.35	58	.290	.387	7	.368	3	-19	-19	2	-1.7
Total 8	77	74	.510	259	184	52	18	2	1337¹	1216	143	587	849	12.2	3.74	107	.242	.322	68	.158	-2	-3	39	1	3.8

● KEN BRONDELL
Brondell, Kenneth Leroy b: 10/17/21, Bradshaw, Neb. BR/TR, 6'1", 195 lbs. Deb: 5/3/44

YEAR TM/L	W	L	PCT	G	GS	CG	SH	SV	IP	H	HR	BB	SO	RAT	ERA	ERA+	OAV	OOB	BH	AVG	PB	PR	/A	PD	TPI
1944 NY-N	0	1	.000	7	2	1	0	0	19¹	27	3	8	1	16.3	8.38	44	.329	.389	0	.000	-1	-10	-10	-1	-0.6

● JEFF BRONKEY
Bronkey, Jacob Jeffrey b: 9/18/65, Kabul, Afghanistan BR/TR, 6'3", 215 lbs. Deb: 5/2/93

YEAR TM/L	W	L	PCT	G	GS	CG	SH	SV	IP	H	HR	BB	SO	RAT	ERA	ERA+	OAV	OOB	BH	AVG	PB	PR	/A	PD	TPI
1993 Tex-A	1	1	.500	21	0	0	0	0	36	39	4	11	18	12.8	4.00	104	.285	.342	0	.000	0	1	1	1	0.1
1994 Mil-A	1	1	.500	16	0	0	0	0	20²	29	3	12	13	13.9	4.35	113	.247	.344	0	—	0	1	1	0	0.1
Total 2	2	2	.500	37	0	0	0	0	56²	59	7	23	31	13.2	4.13	107	.271	.343	0	.000	0	2	2	1	0.2

● JIM BRONSTAD
Bronstad, James Warren b: 6/22/36, Ft.Worth, Tex. BR/TR, 6'3", 196 lbs. Deb: 6/7/59

YEAR TM/L	W	L	PCT	G	GS	CG	SH	SV	IP	H	HR	BB	SO	RAT	ERA	ERA+	OAV	OOB	BH	AVG	PB	PR	/A	PD	TPI
1959 NY-A	0	3	.000	16	3	0	0	2	29¹	34	2	13	14	14.7	5.22	70	.288	.364	0	.000	-0	-4	-5	0	-0.6
1963 Was-A	1	3	.250	25	0	0	0	0	57¹	66	9	22	22	14.0	5.65	66	.297	.363	0	.000	-1	-13	-12	1	-0.9
1964 Was-A	0	1	.000	4	0	0	0	0	7	10	0	2	9	15.4	5.14	72	.345	.387	0	—	0	-1	-1	-0	-0.2
Total 3	1	7	.125	45	3	0	0	2	93²	110	11	37	45	14.3	5.48	67	.298	.365	0	.000	-2	-18	-19	2	-1.7

● IKE BROOKENS
Brookens, Edward Dwain b: 1/3/49, Chambersburg, Pa. BR/TR, 6'5", 170 lbs. Deb: 6/17/75

YEAR TM/L	W	L	PCT	G	GS	CG	SH	SV	IP	H	HR	BB	SO	RAT	ERA	ERA+	OAV	OOB	BH	AVG	PB	PR	/A	PD	TPI
1975 Det-A	0	0	—	3	0	0	0	0	10¹	11	3	5	8	14.8	5.23	77	.282	.378	0	—	0	-2	-1	-0	-0.1

● HARRY BROOKS
Brooks, Harry Frank b: 11/30/1865, Philadelphia, Pa. d: 12/5/45, Philadelphia, Pa. Deb: 7/24/1886 ◆

YEAR TM/L	W	L	PCT	G	GS	CG	SH	SV	IP	H	HR	BB	SO	RAT	ERA	ERA+	OAV	OOB	BH	AVG	PB	PR	/A	PD	TPI
1886 NY-a	0	1	.000	1	1	0	0	0	2	5	0	2	0	49.5	36.00	9	.429	.478	0	—	-0	-7	-7	-0	-1.5

● JIM BROSNAN
Brosnan, James Patrick b: 10/24/29, Cincinnati, O. BR/TR, 6'4", 210 lbs. Deb: 4/15/54

YEAR TM/L	W	L	PCT	G	GS	CG	SH	SV	IP	H	HR	BB	SO	RAT	ERA	ERA+	OAV	OOB	BH	AVG	PB	PR	/A	PD	TPI
1954 Chi-N	1	0	1.000	18	0	0	0	0	33¹	44	9	18	17	17.0	9.45	44	.331	.414	1	.125	-0	-20	-19	1	-0.4
1956 Chi-N	5	9	.357	30	10	1	1	1	95	95	9	45	51	13.3	3.79	100	.270	.353	4	.182	-0	-0	-0	-1	-0.1
1957 Chi-N	5	5	.500	41	5	1	0	0	98²	79	11	46	73	11.5	3.38	115	.219	.310	5	.250	2	6	5	1	0.8
1958 Chi-N	3	4	.429	8	8	2	0	0	51²	41	3	29	24	12.2	3.14	125	.225	.332	2	.105	-1	5	4	1	0.6
StL-N	8	4	.667	33	12	2	0	7	115	107	10	50	65	12.4	3.44	120	.248	.330	3	.097	-1	6	9	0	0.9
Yr	11	8	.579	41	20	4	0	7	166²	148	13	79	89	12.3	3.35	121	.241	.329	5	.100	-2	11	13	1	1.5
1959 StL-N	1	3	.250	20	1	0	0	2	33	34	5	15	18	13.6	4.91	86	.276	.360	2	.286	1	-4	-2	1	-0.1
Cin-N	8	3	.727	26	9	1	1	2	83¹	79	7	26	56	11.9	3.35	121	.248	.314	1	.043	-2	6	7	1	0.7
Yr	9	6	.600	46	10	1	1	4	116¹	113	12	41	74	12.3	3.79	108	.255	.324	3	.100	-1	2	4	1	0.6
1960 Cin-N	7	2	.778	57	2	0	0	12	99	79	4	22	62	9.2	2.36	162	.225	.271	3	.200	2	15	16	2	2.0
1961 *Cin-N	10	4	.714	53	0	0	0	16	80	77	7	18	40	10.7	3.04	134	.249	.291	2	.154	-0	9	9	1	1.9
1962 Cin-N	4	4	.500	48	0	0	0	13	64²	76	8	18	51	13.1	3.34	120	.292	.338	0	.000	-1	4	5	0	0.7
1963 Cin-N	0	1	.000	6	0	0	0	0	4²	8	1	3	4	21.2	7.71	43	.421	.500	0	—	0	-2	-2	0	-0.4
Chi-A	3	8	.273	45	0	0	0	14	73	71	7	22	46	11.5	2.84	124	.263	.318	4	.308	1	6	5	-0	1.1
Total 9	55	47	.539	385	47	7	2	67	831¹	790	80	312	507	12.4	3.54	111	.254	.324	27	.153	-1	31	36	3	7.7

● TERRY BROSS
Bross, Terrence Paul b: 3/30/66, ElPaso, Tex. BR/TR, 6'9", 234 lbs. Deb: 9/4/91

YEAR TM/L	W	L	PCT	G	GS	CG	SH	SV	IP	H	HR	BB	SO	RAT	ERA	ERA+	OAV	OOB	BH	AVG	PB	PR	/A	PD	TPI
1991 NY-N	0	0	—	8	0	0	0	0	10	7	1	3	5	9.0	1.80	202	.200	.263	0	—	0	2	2	-0	0.0
1993 SF-N	0	0	—	2	0	0	0	0	2	3	1	1	1	18.0	9.00	43	.333	.400	0	—	0	-1	-1	-0	0.0
Total 2	0	0	—	10	0	0	0	0	12	10	2	4	6	10.5	3.00	123	.227	.292	0	.000	0	1	1	-1	0.0

YEAR TM/L	W	L	PCT	G	GS	CG	SH	SV	IP	H	HR	BB	SO	RAT	ERA	ERA+	OAV	OOB	BH	AVG	PB	PR	/A	PD	TPI

● FRANK BROSSEAU   Brosseau, Franklin Lee b: 7/31/44, Drayton, N.D.   BR/TR, 6'1", 180 lbs.   Deb: 9/10/69

1969 Pit-N	0	0	—	2	0	0	0	0	1²	2	0	2	2	21.6	10.80	32	.286	.444	0	—	0	-1	-1	0	0.0
1971 Pit-N	0	0	—	1	0	0	0	0	2	1	0	0	0	4.5	0.00	—	.200	.200	0	—	0	1	1	0	0.0
Total 2	0	0	—	3	0	0	0	0	3²	3	0	2	2	12.3	4.91	70	.250	.357	0	—	0	-1	-1	0	0.0

● DAN BROUTHERS   Brouthers, Dennis Joseph "Big Dan" b: 5/8/1858, Sylvan Lake, N.Y.   d: 8/2/32, E.Orange, N.J.   BL/TL, 6'2", 207 lbs.   Deb: 6/23/1879 H♦

1879 Tro-N	0	2	.000	3	2	2	0	0	21	35	0	8	6	18.4	5.57	45	.343	.391	46	.274	1	-7	-7	-1	-0.5
1883 Buf-N	0	0	—	1	0	0	0	0	2	9	0	3	2	54.0	31.50	10	.643	.706	159	.374	1	-6	-6	-0	0.0
Total 2	0	2	.000	4	2	2	0	0	23	44	0	11	8	21.5	7.83	33	.379	.433	2296	.342	1	-13	-13	-1	-0.5

● SCOTT BROW   Brow, Scott John b: 3/17/69, Butte, Mont.   BR/TR, 6'3", 200 lbs.   Deb: 4/28/93

1993 Tor-A	1	1	.500	6	3	0	0	0	18	19	2	10	7	15.0	6.00	72	.275	.375	0	—	0	-3	-3	1	-0.2
1994 Tor-A	0	3	.000	18	0	0	0	2	29	34	4	19	15	16.8	5.90	82	.288	.391	0	—	0	-4	-3	0	-0.4
Total 2	1	4	.200	24	3	0	0	2	47	53	6	29	22	16.1	5.94	78	.283	.385	0	—	0	-7	-7	1	-0.6

● FRANK BROWER   Brower, Frank Willard "Turkeyfoot" b: 3/26/1893, Gainesville, Va.   d: 11/20/60, Baltimore, Md.   BL/TR, 6'2", 180 lbs.   Deb: 8/14/20 ♦

| 1924 Cle-A | 0 | 0 | — | 4 | 0 | 0 | 0 | 0 | 9² | 7 | 0 | 4 | 0 | 11.2 | 0.93 | 459 | .212 | .316 | 30 | .280 | 1 | 4 | 4 | -0 | 0.0 |

● ALTON BROWN   Brown, Alton Leo "Deacon" b: 4/16/25, Norfolk, Va.   BR/TR, 6'2", 195 lbs.   Deb: 4/21/51

| 1951 Was-A | 0 | 0 | — | 7 | 0 | 0 | 0 | 0 | 11² | 14 | 1 | 12 | 2 | 20.8 | 9.26 | 46 | .298 | .450 | 0 | .000 | -0 | -7 | -7 | -0 | 0.0 |

● BOARDWALK BROWN   Brown, Carroll William b: 2/20/1887, Woodbury, N.J.   d: 2/8/77, Burlington, N.J.   BR/TR, 6'1.5", 178 lbs.   Deb: 9/27/11

1911 Phi-A	0	1	.000	2	1	1	0	0	12	12	0	2	6	10.5	4.50	70	.267	.298	0	.000	-1	-2	-2	0	-0.2
1912 Phi-A	13	11	.542	34	24	15	3	0	199	204	2	87	64	13.6	3.66	84	.283	.367	11	.145	-3	-8	-13	3	-1.4
1913 Phi-A	17	11	.607	43	35	11	3	1	235¹	200	6	87	70	11.4	2.94	94	.219	.294	13	.159	-1	-0	-5	-2	-0.9
1914 Phi-A	1	6	.143	15	8	2	0	0	66	64	1	26	20	12.3	4.09	64	.268	.340	0	.000	-2	-10	-11	0	-1.3
NY-A	5	5	.500	20	14	8	0	1	122¹	123	2	42	57	12.2	3.24	85	.271	.334	8	.182	1	-7	-6	3	-0.1
Yr	6	11	.353	35	22	10	0	1	188¹	187	3	68	77	12.2	3.54	77	.270	.336	8	.125	-0	-17	-17	3	-1.4
1915 NY-A	2	6	.250	19	11	5	0	1	96²	95	4	47	34	13.7	4.10	72	.275	.370	6	.188	-1	-12	-12	-0	-1.1
Total 5	38	40	.487	133	93	42	6	3	731¹	698	15	291	251	12.5	3.47	83	.257	.334	38	.147	-6	-39	-49	4	-5.0

● CHARLIE BROWN   Brown, Charles E. b: 1878, Baltimore, Md.   TL , 6', 180 lbs.   Deb: 8/4/1897

| 1897 Cle-N | 1 | 2 | .333 | 4 | 4 | 2 | 0 | 0 | 24¹ | 30 | 2 | 17 | 8 | 19.2 | 7.77 | 58 | .300 | .427 | 3 | .273 | 0 | -9 | -9 | -0 | -0.8 |

● BUSTER BROWN   Brown, Charles Edward "Yank" b: 8/31/1881, Boone, Iowa   d: 2/9/14, Sioux City, Iowa   BR/TR, 6', 180 lbs.   Deb: 6/22/05

1905 StL-N	8	11	.421	23	21	17	3	0	178²	172	6	62	57	12.3	2.97	100	.260	.332	6	.092	-3	1	0	3	0.0
1906 StL-N	8	16	.333	32	27	21	0	0	238¹	208	2	112	109	12.5	2.64	99	.234	.327	14	.165	0	-0	-0	2	0.2
1907 StL-N	1	6	.143	9	8	6	0	0	63²	57	2	45	17	15.1	3.39	74	.263	.401	7	.269	2	-7	-6	2	-0.3
Phi-N	9	6	.600	21	16	13	4	0	130	118	3	56	38	12.5	2.42	100	.246	.333	10	.189	2	1	-0	-1	0.1
Yr	10	12	.455	30	24	19	4	0	193²	175	5	101	55	13.1	2.74	89	.250	.349	17	.215	3	-6	-6	1	-0.2
1908 Phi-N	0	0	—	3	0	0	0	0	7	9	0	5	3	19.3	2.57	94	.346	.469	1	.200	-0	-0	-0	1	0.1
1909 Phi-N	0	0	—	7	1	0	0	0	25	22	1	16	10	14.0	3.24	80	.259	.382	0	.000	-1	-2	-2	0	-0.1
Bos-N	4	8	.333	18	17	8	2	0	123¹	108	1	56	32	12.5	3.14	90	.244	.339	7	.146	-2	-7	-4	1	-0.5
Yr	4	8	.333	25	18	8	2	0	148¹	130	2	72	42	12.7	3.16	88	.246	.344	7	.123	-3	-9	-6	1	-0.6
1910 Bos-N	9	23	.281	46	29	16	1	2	263	251	4	94	88	11.9	2.67	125	.268	.337	16	.198	0	11	19	1	2.5
1911 Bos-N	8	18	.308	42	25	13	0	2	241	258	11	116	76	14.3	4.29	89	.284	.371	21	.250	3	-24	-13	0	-0.9
1912 Bos-N	4	15	.211	31	21	12	0	0	168¹	146	7	66	68	11.4	4.01	89	.239	.315	13	.213	1	-11	-8	0	-0.7
1913 Bos-N	0	0	—	2	0	0	0	0	13¹	19	0	3	3	16.2	4.73	70	.396	.453	0	.000	-0	-2	-2	-0	0.0
Total 9	51	103	.331	234	165	106	10	4	1451²	1368	36	631	501	12.8	3.21	96	.258	.343	95	.182	3	-41	-18	8	0.4

● CURLY BROWN   Brown, Charles Roy "Lefty" b: 12/9/1888, Spring Hill, Kan.   d: 6/10/68, Spring Hill, Kan.   BL/TL, 5'10.5", 165 lbs.   Deb: 9/8/11

1911 StL-A	1	2	.333	3	2	2	0	0	23	22	0	5	8	11.0	2.74	123	.247	.295	0	.000	-1	2	2	0	0.0
1912 StL-A	1	3	.250	16	4	2	1	0	64²	69	0	35	28	14.9	4.87	68	.277	.373	5	.208	-0	-11	-11	-3	-0.9
1913 StL-A	1	1	.500	2	2	2	0	0	14	12	0	4	3	10.3	2.57	114	.245	.302	2	.400	1	1	1	-0	0.1
1915 Cin-N	0	2	.000	7	3	0	0	0	27	26	6	13	11	11.3	4.67	61	.245	.298	4	.364	1	-6	-5	-1	-0.4
Total 4	3	8	.273	28	11	6	1	0	128²	129	2	50	52	12.9	4.20	76	.262	.337	11	.224	0	-15	-14	-4	-1.2

● CLINT BROWN   Brown, Clinton Harold b: 7/8/03, Blackash, Pa.   d: 12/31/55, Rocky River, Ohio   BL/TR, 6'1", 190 lbs.   Deb: 9/27/28

1928 Cle-A	0	1	.000	2	1	1	0	0	11	14	0	2	3	13.1	4.91	84	.304	.333	1	.200	-0	-1	-1	0	-0.1
1929 Cle-A	0	2	.000	3	1	1	0	0	16¹	18	0	6	1	13.2	3.31	134	.286	.348	0	.000	-1	2	2	1	0.2
1930 Cle-A	11	13	.458	35	31	16	3	1	213²	271	14	51	54	13.7	4.97	97	.314	.356	18	.247	2	-8	-3	2	0.0
1931 Cle-A	11	15	.423	39	33	12	2	0	233¹	284	10	55	50	13.1	4.71	98	.295	.333	15	.172	-2	-8	-2	4	0.0
1932 Cle-A	15	12	.556	37	32	21	1	1	262²	298	14	50	59	12.1	4.08	116	.279	.314	25	.250	6	12	19	2	2.4
1933 Cle-A	11	12	.478	33	23	10	2	1	185	202	10	34	47	11.6	3.41	130	.276	.310	9	.145	-3	18	21	3	2.4
1934 Cle-A	4	3	.571	17	2	0	0	1	50¹	83	3	14	15	17.3	5.90	77	.359	.396	5	.294	1	-8	-8	-0	-0.8
1935 Cle-A	4	3	.571	23	5	1	0	2	49	61	3	14	20	14.0	5.14	88	.300	.349	2	.200	-0	-4	-3	1	-0.4
1936 Chi-A	6	2	.750	38	5	0	0	5	83	106	5	24	19	14.4	4.99	104	.315	.366	4	.160	-0	0	2	0	0.2
1937 Chi-A	7	7	.500	**53**	0	0	0	**18**	100	92	7	36	51	11.6	3.42	135	.242	.309	4	.222	1	**13**	**13**	1	2.3
1938 Chi-A	1	3	.250	9	0	0	0	2	13²	16	2	7	2	16.5	4.61	106	.333	.439	1	.500	1	0	1	0	0.3
1939 Chi-A	11	10	.524	**61**	0	0	0	18	118¹	127	8	27	41	11.7	3.88	122	.281	.322	4	.211	1	10	11	2	2.3
1940 Chi-A	4	6	.400	37	0	0	0	10	66	75	5	16	22	12.7	3.68	120	.284	.330	1	.071	-1	5	5	0	0.8
1941 Cle-A	3	3	.500	41	0	0	0	5	74¹	73	3	28	22	12.8	3.27	120	.279	.348	2	.118	0	7	6	3	0.8
1942 Cle-A	1	1	.500	7	0	0	0	0	9	16	2	2	4	19.0	6.00	57	.356	.396	0	.000	-0	-2	-3	-0	-0.6
Total 15	89	93	.489	434	130	62	8	64	1485²	1740	84	368	410	12.9	4.26	109	.291	.335	91	.199	5	37	60	19	9.8

● CURT BROWN   Brown, Curtis Steven b: 1/15/60, Ft.Lauderdale, Fla.   BR/TR, 6'5", 200 lbs.   Deb: 6/10/83

1983 Cal-A	1	1	.500	10	0	0	0	0	16	25	1	4	7	16.3	7.31	55	.368	.403	0	—	0	-6	-6	-0	-0.6
1984 NY-A	1	1	.500	13	0	0	0	0	16²	18	1	4	10	11.9	2.70	140	.281	.324	0	—	0	2	2	0	0.3
1986 Mon-N	0	1	.000	6	0	0	0	0	12	15	0	2	4	12.8	3.00	123	.319	.347	0	.000	-0	1	1	0	0.1
1987 Mon-N	0	1	.000	5	0	0	0	0	7	10	2	4	6	18.0	7.71	54	.333	.412	0	—	0	-3	-3	0	-0.3
Total 4	2	4	.333	34	0	0	0	0	51²	68	4	14	27	14.3	4.88	80	.325	.368	0	.000	-0	-5	-6	-0	-0.5

● ED BROWN   Brown, Edward P. b: Chicago, Ill.   TR , 178 lbs.   Deb: 8/19/1882 ♦

1882 StL-a	0	0	—	1	0	0	0	0	2	2	0	1	0	9.0	0.00	—	.243	.243	11	.183	-0	1	1	-0	0.0
1884 Tol-a	0	1	.000	1	1	1	0	0	9	19	0	4	2	24.0	9.00	38	.396	.453	27	.176	-0	-6	-6	-0	-0.4
Total 2	0	1	.000	2	1	1	0	0	11	21	0	4	2	21.3	7.36	45	.374	.425	38	.178	-0	-5	-5	-0	-0.4

● ELMER BROWN   Brown, Elmer Young "Shook" b: 3/25/1883, Southport, Ind.   d: 1/23/55, Indianapolis, Ind.   BL/TR, 5'11.5", 172 lbs.   Deb: 9/16/11

1911 StL-A	1	1	.500	5	3	1	1	0	16²	16	0	14	5	16.2	6.48	52	.242	.375	1	.125	-1	-6	-6	1	-0.6
1912 StL-A	5	8	.385	23	13	2	1	0	120¹	122	2	42	45	13.2	2.99	111	.280	.359	6	.167	-1	4	4	-1	0.3
1913 Bro-N	0	0	—	3	1	0	0	0	13	6	0	10	6	11.8	2.08	159	.158	.347	0	.000	-1	2	2	-0	-0.1
1914 Bro-N	1	2	.333	11	4	1	0	0	36²	33	2	23	22	15.5	3.93	73	.402	.563	1	.083	-1	-5	-4	1	-0.4
1915 Bro-N	0	0	—	1	0	0	0	0	2	4	0	3	1	31.5	9.00	31	.500	.636	0	—	0	-1	-1	0	0.0
Total 5	7	11	.389	43	21	4	2	0	188²	181	4	92	79	14.0	3.48	93	.287	.395	8	.133	-3	-6	-5	0	-0.8

YEAR TM/L	W	L	PCT	G	GS	CG	SH	SV	IP	H	HR	BB	SO	RAT	ERA	ERA+	OAV	OOB	BH	AVG	PB	PR	/A	PD	TPI
● **HAL BROWN**			Brown, Hector Harold "Skinny"			b: 12/11/24, Greensboro, N.C.				BR/TR, 6'2", 182 lbs.		Deb: 4/19/51		C										
1951 Chi-A	0	0	—	3	0	0	0	1	8²	15	3	4	4	19.7	9.35	43	.385	.442	2	1.000	1	-5	-5	0	0.0
1952 Chi-A	2	3	.400	24	8	1	0	0	72¹	82	8	21	31	12.8	4.23	86	.284	.332	3	.158	1	-4	-5	-0	-0.2
1953 Bos-A	11	6	.647	30	25	6	1	0	166¹	177	16	57	62	12.7	4.65	90	.269	.327	5	.293	5	-12	-8	-0	-0.4
1954 Bos-A	1	8	.111	40	5	1	0	0	118	126	6	41	66	13.0	4.12	100	.269	.331	3	.125	-0	-5	-0	1	0.0
1955 Bos-A	1	0	1.000	2	0	0	0	0	4	2	0	2	2	9.0	2.25	191	.143	.250	1	1.000	0	1	1	-0	0.2
Bal-A	0	4	.000	15	5	1	0	0	57	51	5	26	26	12.2	4.11	93	.241	.324	0	.000	-1	-1	-2	-1	-0.3
Yr	1	4	.200	17	5	1	0	0	61	53	5	28	28	12.0	3.98	97	.235	.319	1	.059	-1	-0	-1	-1	-0.1
1956 Bal-A	9	7	.563	35	14	4	1	2	151²	142	18	37	57	10.7	4.04	97	.247	.294	8	.190	1	2	-2	0	0.0
1957 Bal-A	7	8	.467	25	20	7	2	1	150	132	17	37	62	10.3	3.90	92	.236	.285	10	.208	2	-2	-5	-1	-0.4
1958 Bal-A	7	5	.583	19	17	4	2	1	96²	96	9	20	44	10.8	3.07	117	.259	.297	4	.148	-0	7	6	-0	0.6
1959 Bal-A	11	9	.550	31	21	2	0	3	164	158	16	32	81	10.5	3.79	100	.252	.290	2	.048	-3	1	-0	-1	-0.3
1960 Bal-A	12	5	.706	30	20	6	1	0	159	155	14	22	66	**10.1**	3.06	125	.258	**.286**	8	.182	3	14	13	-1	1.5
1961 Bal-A	10	6	.625	27	23	6	3	1	166²	153	14	33	61	10.1	3.19	121	.247	.286	7	.140	-0	16	12	-0	1.0
1962 Bal-A	6	4	.600	22	11	0	0	1	85²	88	12	21	25	11.8	4.10	90	.268	.318	8	.286	2	-1	-4	-1	-0.4
NY-A	0	1	.000	2	1	0	0	0	6²	9	3	2	2	14.9	6.75	56	.333	.379	0	.000	-0	-2	-2	-0	-0.3
Yr	6	5	.545	24	12	0	0	1	92¹	97	15	23	27	11.7	4.29	86	.270	.314	8	.276	1	-3	-6	-1	-0.7
1963 Hou-N	5	11	.313	26	20	6	3	0	141¹	137	14	8	68	9.2	3.31	95	.255	.266	4	.093	-2	-0	-2	-3	-0.7
1964 Hou-N	3	15	.167	27	21	3	0	1	132	154	18	26	53	12.4	3.95	86	.292	.327	5	.128	-1	-6	-8	-2	-1.2
Total 14	85	92	.480	358	211	47	13	11	1680	1677	173	389	710	11.1	3.81	98	.260	.303	82	.169	8	2	-11	-10	-0.9
● **JACKIE BROWN**			Brown, Jackie Gene		b: 5/31/43, Holdenville, Okla.				BR/TR, 6'1", 195 lbs.		Deb: 7/2/70		FC											
1970 Was-A	2	2	.500	24	5	1	0	0	57	49	8	37	47	13.6	3.95	90	.231	.345	2	.154	-0	-1	-2	-1	-0.3
1971 Was-A	3	4	.429	14	9	0	0	0	47	60	9	27	21	16.9	5.94	56	.316	.404	2	.133	-0	-13	-14	1	-1.8
1973 Tex-A	5	5	.500	25	3	2	1	2	66²	82	7	25	45	14.7	3.92	95	.309	.373	0	—	0	-1	-1	-1	-0.3
1974 Tex-A	13	12	.520	35	26	9	2	0	216²	219	13	74	134	12.3	3.57	100	.265	.329	0	—	0	1	-0	-1	-0.1
1975 Tex-A	5	5	.500	17	7	2	1	0	70¹	70	7	35	35	13.7	4.22	89	.266	.357	0	—	0	-3	-4	-2	-0.6
Cle-A	1	2	.333	25	3	1	0	1	69¹	72	9	29	41	13.1	4.28	88	.276	.348	0	—	0	-4	-4	-0	-0.2
Yr	6	7	.462	42	10	3	1	1	139²	142	16	64	76	13.3	4.25	89	.269	.349	0	—	0	-7	-8	-2	-0.8
1976 Cle-A	9	11	.450	32	27	5	2	0	180	193	14	55	104	12.8	4.25	82	.276	.335	0	—	0	-15	-15	-1	-1.6
1977 Mon-N	9	12	.429	42	25	6	2	0	185²	189	15	71	89	12.8	4.51	84	.264	.334	7	.125	-2	-12	-14	-2	-1.9
Total 7	47	53	.470	214	105	26	8	3	892²	934	82	353	516	13.2	4.18	87	.272	.343	11	.131	-3	-48	-55	-7	-6.8
● **KEVIN BROWN**			Brown, James Kevin		b: 3/14/65, Milledgeville, Ga.				BR/TR, 6'4", 195 lbs.		Deb: 9/30/86													
1986 Tex-A	1	0	1.000	1	1	0	0	0	5	6	0	0	4	10.8	3.60	119	.316	.316	0	—	0	0	0	0	0.1
1988 Tex-A	1	1	.500	4	4	1	0	0	23¹	33	3	8	12	16.2	4.24	96	.330	.385	0	—	0	-1	-0	-0	-0.1
1989 Tex-A	12	9	.571	28	28	7	0	0	191	167	10	70	104	11.4	3.35	118	.234	.305	0	—	0	11	13	3	1.7
1990 Tex-A	12	10	.545	26	26	6	2	0	180	175	13	60	88	11.9	3.60	109	.255	.318	0	.000	0	6	6	-0	0.7
1991 Tex-A	9	12	.429	33	33	0	0	0	210²	233	17	90	96	14.4	4.40	92	.284	.364	0	—	0	-7	-9	1	-0.7
1992 Tex-A★	21	11	.656	35	35	11	1	0	**265²**	262	11	76	173	11.8	3.32	114	.260	.318	0	—	0	18	14	2	1.9
1993 Tex-A	15	12	.556	34	34	12	3	0	233	228	14	74	142	12.2	3.59	115	.252	.319	0	—	0	19	14	4	2.0
1994 Tex-A	7	9	.438	26	25	3	0	0	170	218	18	50	123	14.5	4.82	94	.314	.365	0	—	0	-0	-5	-0	-0.1
Total 8	78	64	.549	187	186	40	6	0	1278²	1322	85	428	742	12.7	3.81	106	.267	.332	0	.000	0	47	34	9	5.5
● **JIM BROWN**			Brown, James W. H.		b: 12/12/1860, Clinton Co., Pa.		d: 4/6/08, Williamsport, Pa.				Deb: 4/17/1884	♦												
1884 Alt-U	1	9	.100	11	11	7	0	0	74	99	0	36	39	16.4	5.35	50	.301	.370	22	.250	-2	-24	-22	0	-2.2
NY-N	0	1	.000	1	1	1	0	0	9	10	0	8	2	18.0	5.00	60	.263	.391	0	.000	-1	-2	-2	-0	-0.2
StP-U	1	4	.200	6	6	4	1	0	36	43	1	14	20	14.3	3.75	35	.277	.337	5	.313	4	-5	-10	-0	-0.8
1886 Phi-a	0	1	.000	1	1	1	0	0	8¹	9	0	3	4	13.0	3.24	108	.265	.324	0	.000	-1	0	0	-0	0.0
Total 2	2	15	.118	19	19	13	1	0	127¹	161	1	61	65	15.7	4.74	50	.289	.360	27	.245	1	-31	-34	0	-3.2
● **JOHN BROWN**			Brown, John J. "Ad"		b: Trenton, N.J.		Deb: 8/11/1897																	
1897 Bro-N	0	1	.000	1	1	0	0	0	5	7	0	4	0	25.2	7.20	57	.328	.494	1	.500	0	-2	-2	0	-0.2
● **JOPHERY BROWN**			Brown, Jophery Clifford		b: 1/22/45, Grambling, La.		Deb: 9/21/68																	
1968 Chi-N	0	0	—	1	0	0	0	0	2	2	0	1	0	13.5	4.50	70	.286	.375	0	—	0	-0	-0	0	0.03
● **JOE BROWN**			Brown, Joseph E.		b: 4/4/1859, Warren, Pa.		d: 6/28/1888, Warren, Pa.		5'10", 162 lbs.		Deb: 8/16/1884	♦												
1884 Chi-N	4	2	.667	7	6	5	0	0	50	56	4	27	11	11.3	4.68	67	.258	.281	13	.213	-1	-9	-9	-0	-0.9
1885 Bal-a	0	4	.000	4	4	4	0	0	38	52	0	9	13	13.3	5.68	57	.306	.322	3	.158	-1	-10	-10	-0	-0.9
Total 2	4	6	.400	11	10	9	0	0	88	108	4	11	36	12.2	5.11	62	.279	.299	16	.200	-2	-20	-19	-1	-1.8
● **JOE BROWN**			Brown, Joseph Henry		b: 7/3/1900, Little Rock, Ark.		d: 3/7/50, Los Angeles, Cal.		BR/TR, 6', 176 lbs.		Deb: 5/17/27													
1927 Chi-A	0	0	—	1	1	0	0	0	0	2	0	1	0	∞	—	1.000	1.000	0	—	0	-3	-3	0	-0.2
● **KEITH BROWN**			Brown, Keith Edward		b: 2/14/64, Flagstaff, Ariz.		BB/TR, 6'4", 215 lbs.		Deb: 8/25/88															
1988 Cin-N	2	1	.667	4	3	0	0	0	16¹	14	1	4	6	9.9	2.76	130	.237	.286	0	.000	-0	1	1	0	0.2
1990 Cin-N	0	0	—	8	0	0	0	0	11¹	12	2	3	8	11.9	4.76	83	.286	.333	0	—	0	-1	-1	0	0.0
1991 Cin-N	0	0	—	11	0	0	0	0	12	15	0	6	4	15.8	2.25	169	.306	.382	0	—	0	2	2	0	0.0
1992 Cin-N	0	1	.000	2	2	0	0	0	8	10	2	5	5	16.9	4.50	80	.313	.405	0	.000	-0	-1	-1	-0	-0.1
Total 4	2	2	.500	25	5	0	0	0	47²	51	5	18	23	13.0	3.40	110	.280	.345	0	.000	-1	1	2	-0	0.1
● **KEVIN BROWN**			Brown, Kevin Dewayne		b: 3/5/66, Oroville, Cal.		BL/TL, 6'1", 185 lbs.		Deb: 7/27/90															
1990 NY-N	0	0	—	2	0	0	0	0	2	1	0	2	1	13.5	0.00	—	.250	.333	0	—	0	1	1	0	0.0
Mil-A	1	1	.500	5	3	0	0	0	21	14	1	7	12	9.4	2.57	151	.182	.259	0	—	0	3	3	1	0.3
1991 Mil-A	2	4	.333	15	10	0	0	0	63²	66	6	34	30	14.3	5.51	72	.270	.362	0	—	0	-10	-11	-0	-0.8
1992 Sea-A	0	0	—	2	0	0	0	0	3	4	1	2	1	21.0	9.00	44	.333	.467	0	—	0	-2	-2	0	-0.1
Total 3	3	5	.375	24	13	0	0	0	89²	86	8	45	44	13.3	4.82	82	.252	.343	0	—	0	-8	-9	1	-0.5
● **LEW BROWN**			Brown, Lewis J. "Blower"		b: 2/1/1858, Leominster, Mass.		d: 1/16/1889, Boston, Mass.		BR/TR, 5'10.5", 185 lbs.		Deb: 6/17/1876	♦												
1878 Pro-N	0	0	—	1	0	0	0	0	1	0	0	4	0	36.0	18.00	12	.000	.500	74	.305	-2	-2	-2	-0	0.0
1884 Bos-U	0	0	—	1	0	0	0	1	1	6	0	1	0	63.0	36.00	7	.659	.692	75	.231	-0	-4	-4	-0	-0.6
Total 2	0	0	—	2	0	0	0	1	2	6	0	5	0	49.5	27.00	8	.458	.607	379	.248	0	-5	-5	0	-0.6
● **LLOYD BROWN**			Brown, Lloyd Andrew "Gimpy"		b: 12/25/04, Beeville, Tex.		d: 1/14/74, Opa-Locka, Fla.		BL/TL, 5'9", 170 lbs.		Deb: 7/17/25													
1925 Bro-N	0	3	.000	17	5	1	0	0	63¹	79	1	25	23	15.1	4.12	101	.319	.385	2	.087	-2	1	0	0	-0.2
1928 Was-A	4	4	.500	27	10	2	0	1	107	112	7	40	38	13.0	4.04	99	.273	.341	5	.161	0	0	-0	3	0.3
1929 Was-A	8	7	.533	40	15	7	1	0	168	186	7	69	48	13.7	4.18	101	.297	.368	11	.220	3	1	1	2	0.5
1930 Was-A	16	12	.571	38	22	10	1	0	197	220	6	59	59	13.2	4.25	108	.293	.354	14	.215	2	9	8	3	1.4
1931 Was-A	15	14	.517	42	32	15	1	0	258²	256	13	79	79	11.7	3.20	134	.257	.311	22	.229	3	34	31	1	3.4
1932 Was-A	15	12	.556	46	24	10	2	5	202²	239	11	55	63	13.4	4.44	97	.296	.342	7	-10	-5	1	-3	1	-0.7
1933 StL-A	1	6	.143	8	6	2	0	0	39	57	1	17	7	17.1	7.15	65	.350	.411	3	.273	-1	-12	-11	1	-1.4
Bos-A	8	11	.421	33	21	9	2	1	163¹	180	4	64	37	13.4	4.02	109	.281	.347	16	.281	6	5	6	4	1.7
Yr	9	17	.346	41	27	15	2	1	202¹	237	5	81	44	14.1	4.63	96	.295	.360	19	.279	-8	-4	5	0.3	
1934 Cle-A	5	10	.333	38	15	5	0	2	117	116	7	51	30	13.0	3.85	118	.263	.342	7	.233	1	8	9	0	1.2

YEAR TM/L	W	L	PCT	G	GS	CG	SH	SV	IP	H	HR	BB	SO	RAT	ERA	ERA+	OAV	OOB	BH	AVG	PB	PR	/A	PD	TPI
1935 Cle-A	8	7	.533	42	8	4	2	4	122	123	6	37	45	12.0	3.61	125	.265	.323	4	.108	-2	**11**	**12**	1	1.2
1936 Cle-A	8	10	.444	24	16	12	1	1	140¹	166	13	45	34	13.7	4.17	121	.294	.349	10	.222	2	14	14	1	1.7
1937 Cle-A	3	6	.250	31	5	2	0	0	77	107	4	27	32	16.0	6.55	70	.329	.386	4	.167	-1	-16	-17	1	-1.4
1940 Phi-N	1	3	.250	18	2	0	0	3	37²	58	3	16	16	17.7	6.21	63	.354	.411	1	.077	-1	-10	-10	0	-1.2
Total 12	91	105	.464	404	181	77	10	21	1693	1899	83	590	510	13.3	4.20	105	.288	.348	106	.192	6	45	42	19	6.5

● **MACE BROWN**   Brown, Mace Stanley b: 5/21/09, North English, Ia.   BR/TR, 6'1", 190 lbs.   Deb: 5/21/35 C

YEAR TM/L	W	L	PCT	G	GS	CG	SH	SV	IP	H	HR	BB	SO	RAT	ERA	ERA+	OAV	OOB	BH	AVG	PB	PR	/A	PD	TPI
1935 Pit-N	4	1	.800	18	5	2	0	0	72²	84	5	22	28	13.1	3.59	114	.287	.337	4	.167	-0	3	4	2	0.4
1936 Pit-N	10	11	.476	47	10	3	0	3	165	178	8	55	56	12.8	3.87	105	.275	.332	10	.167	-2	3	3	1	0.3
1937 Pit-N	7	2	.778	50	2	0	0	7	107²	109	2	45	60	13.0	4.18	92	.261	.334	9	.300	-2	-3	-4	-1	-0.2
1938 Pit-N★	15	9	.625	**51**	2	0	0	5	132²	155	5	44	55	13.5	3.80	100	.294	.349	5	.132	-2	-0	-0	-0	-0.2
1939 Pit-N	9	13	.409	47	19	8	1	7	200¹	232	8	52	71	12.8	3.37	114	.293	.338	7	.109	-4	12	10	1	0.8
1940 Pit-N	10	9	.526	48	17	5	1	**7**	173	181	5	49	73	12.1	3.49	109	.267	.318	6	.115	-1	7	6	1	0.7
1941 Pit-N	0	0	—	1	0	0	0	0	1¹	2	0	0	0	13.5	0.00	—	.333	.333	0	—	0	1	1	0	0.0
Bro-N	3	2	.600	24	0	0	0	3	42²	31	3	26	22	12.2	3.16	116	.208	.330	0	.000	-1	2	2	1	0.3
Yr	3	2	.600	25	0	0	0	3	44	33	3	26	22	12.3	3.07	119	.213	.330	0	.000	-1	3	3	1	0.3
1942 Bos-A	9	3	.750	34	0	0	0	6	60¹	56	4	28	20	12.5	3.43	109	.255	.339	1	.067	-1	2	1	0	0.4
1943 Bos-A	6	6	.500	**49**	0	0	0	9	93¹	71	2	51	40	11.8	2.12	156	.222	.329	1	.059	-1	**12**	**12**	0	1.7
1946 *Bos-A	3	1	.750	18	0	0	0	1	26¹	26	2	16	10	14.4	2.05	179	.268	.372	0	.000	-1	4	5	1	0.7
Total 10	76	57	.571	387	55	18	2	48	1075¹	1125	44	388	435	12.7	3.46	110	.271	.335	43	.137	-11	43	43	6	4.9

● **MARK BROWN**   Brown, Mark Anthony b: 7/13/59, Bellows Falls, Vt.   BB/TR, 6'2", 190 lbs.   Deb: 8/9/84

YEAR TM/L	W	L	PCT	G	GS	CG	SH	SV	IP	H	HR	BB	SO	RAT	ERA	ERA+	OAV	OOB	BH	AVG	PB	PR	/A	PD	TPI
1984 Bal-A	1	2	.333	9	0	0	0	0	23	22	2	7	10	11.7	3.91	99	.256	.319	0	—	0	-0	-0	-0	0.0
1985 Min-A	0	0	—	6	0	0	0	0	15²	21	1	7	5	16.1	6.89	64	.333	.400	0	—	0	-5	-4	-0	-0.1
Total 2	1	2	.333	15	0	0	0	0	38²	43	3	14	15	13.5	5.12	80	.289	.354	0	—	0	-5	-4	-1	-0.1

● **MIKE BROWN**   Brown, Michael Gary b: 3/4/59, Camden County, N.J.   BR/TR, 6'2", 195 lbs.   Deb: 9/16/82

YEAR TM/L	W	L	PCT	G	GS	CG	SH	SV	IP	H	HR	BB	SO	RAT	ERA	ERA+	OAV	OOB	BH	AVG	PB	PR	/A	PD	TPI
1982 Bos-A	1	0	1.000	3	0	0	0	0	6	7	0	1	4	12.0	0.00	—	.304	.333	0	—	0	3	3	-0	0.4
1983 Bos-A	6	6	.500	19	18	3	1	0	104	110	12	43	35	13.4	4.67	93	.276	.350	0	—	0	-7	-4	-1	-0.5
1984 Bos-A	1	8	.111	15	11	0	0	0	67	104	9	19	32	16.9	6.85	61	.347	.391	0	—	0	-21	-20	-0	-2.3
1985 Bos-A	0	0	—	2	1	0	0	0	3¹	9	0	3	3	32.4	21.60	20	.500	.571	0	—	0	-6	-6	-0	-0.1
1986 Bos-A	4	4	.500	15	10	0	0	0	57¹	72	10	25	32	15.4	5.34	78	.316	.386	0	—	0	-7	-7	0	-0.9
Sea-A	0	2	.000	6	2	0	0	0	15²	19	4	11	9	17.2	7.47	57	.302	.405	0	—	0	-6	-6	-0	-0.6
Yr	4	6	.400	21	12	0	0	0	73	91	14	36	41	15.7	5.79	72	.308	.384	0	—	0	-13	-13	1	-1.5
1987 Sea-A	0	0	—	1	0	0	0	0	0¹	3	0	0	0	81.0	54.00	9	.750	.750	0	—	0	-2	-2	-0	-0.2
Total 6	12	20	.375	61	42	3	1	0	253²	324	35	102	115	15.3	5.75	74	.313	.378	0	—	0	-47	-42	0	-4.2

● **MORDECAI BROWN**   Brown, Mordecai Peter Centennial "Three Finger" or "Miner"
b: 10/19/1876, Nyesville, Ind.   d: 2/14/48, Terre Haute, Ind.   BB/TR, 5'10", 175 lbs.   Deb: 4/19/03 MH

YEAR TM/L	W	L	PCT	G	GS	CG	SH	SV	IP	H	HR	BB	SO	RAT	ERA	ERA+	OAV	OOB	BH	AVG	PB	PR	/A	PD	TPI
1903 StL-N	9	13	.409	26	24	19	1	0	201	231	7	59	83	13.3	2.60	126	.293	.347	15	.195	-0	15	15	2	1.6
1904 Chi-N	15	10	.600	26	23	21	4	1	212¹	155	1	50	81	**8.9**	1.86	143	**.199**	**.253**	19	.213	1	21	19	-1	2.3
1905 Chi-N	18	12	.600	30	24	24	4	0	249	219	3	44	89	9.5	2.17	138	.235	.271	13	.140	-1	23	23	-0	2.4
1906 *Chi-N	26	6	.813	36	32	27	**9**	3	277¹	198	1	61	144	**8.5**	**1.04**	254	.202	**.252**	20	.204	1	**49**	**49**	2	**6.8**
1907 *Chi-N	20	6	.769	34	27	20	6	1	233	180	2	40	107	8.7	1.39	179	.221	.262	13	.153	-0	28	29	4	**4.0**
1908 *Chi-N	29	9	.763	44	31	27	9	**5**	312¹	214	1	49	123	7.7	1.47	160	.195	.232	25	.207	1	31	31	-1	4.1
1909 *Chi-N	27	9	.750	**50**	34	**32**	8	7	**342²**	246	1	53	172	8.0	1.31	194	.202	.239	22	.176	1	**49**	**47**	-1	5.4
1910 *Chi-N	25	14	.641	46	31	**27**	6	7	295¹	256	3	64	143	**9.9**	1.86	155	.232	**.277**	18	.175	-0	39	34	3	4.9
1911 Chi-N	21	11	.656	**53**	27	21	0	**13**	270	267	5	55	129	10.9	2.80	118	.262	.303	23	.253	5	18	15	-4	1.9
1912 Chi-N	5	6	.455	15	8	5	2	0	88²	92	2	20	34	11.5	2.64	126	.274	.317	9	.290	2	8	7	-2	0.8
1913 Cin-N	11	12	.478	39	16	11	1	6	173¹	174	7	44	41	11.4	2.91	112	.277	.325	11	.204	-0	6	7	-1	0.7
1914 StL-F	12	6	.667	26	18	13	2	0	175	172	7	43	81	11.2	3.29	92	.254	.302	15	.254	-2	-8	-5	-2	-0.6
Bro-F	2	5	.286	9	8	5	0	0	57²	63	1	18	32	12.6	4.21	68	.276	.329	4	.211	-1	-9	-9	-0	-1.0
Yr	14	11	.560	35	26	18	2	0	232²	235	8	61	113	11.4	3.52	85	.259	.306	19	.244	-3	-16	-13	-3	-1.6
1915 Chi-F	17	8	.680	35	25	17	3	4	236¹	189	6	64	95	9.9	2.09	120	.220	.279	24	.293	5	17	11	3	2.0
1916 Chi-N	2	3	.400	12	4	2	0	0	48¹	52	1	9	21	12.1	3.91	74	.289	.337	4	.250	0	-7	-5	-0	-0.5
Total 14	239	130	.648	481	332	271	55	49	3172¹	2708	43	673	1375	9.8	2.06	137	.233	.278	235	.206	15	279	267	1	34.8

● **MYRL BROWN**   Brown, Myrl Lincoln b: 10/10/1894, Waynesboro, Pa.   d: 2/23/81, Harrisburg, Pa.   BR/TR, 5'11", 172 lbs.   Deb: 8/19/22

YEAR TM/L	W	L	PCT	G	GS	CG	SH	SV	IP	H	HR	BB	SO	RAT	ERA	ERA+	OAV	OOB	BH	AVG	PB	PR	/A	PD	TPI
1922 Pit-N	3	1	.750	7	5	2	0	0	34²	42	2	13	9	14.3	5.97	68	.296	.355	3	.273	1	-7	-7	1	-0.6

● **NORM BROWN**   Brown, Norman b: 2/1/19, Evergreen, N.C.   BB/TR, 6'3", 180 lbs.   Deb: 10/3/43

YEAR TM/L	W	L	PCT	G	GS	CG	SH	SV	IP	H	HR	BB	SO	RAT	ERA	ERA+	OAV	OOB	BH	AVG	PB	PR	/A	PD	TPI
1943 Phi-A	0	0	—	1	1	0	0	0	7	5	0	0	1	6.4	0.00	—	.185	.185	0	.000	-0	3	3	0	0.0
1946 Phi-A	0	1	.000	4	0	0	0	0	7¹	8	2	6	3	17.2	6.14	58	.267	.389	0	—	-0	-2	-2	-0	-0.3
Total 2	0	1	.000	5	1	0	0	0	14¹	13	2	6	4	11.9	3.14	111	.228	.302	0	.000	-0	0	1	0	-0.3

● **PAUL BROWN**   Brown, Paul Dwayne b: 6/18/41, Ft.Smith, Ark.   BR/TR, 6'1", 190 lbs.   Deb: 7/23/61 F

YEAR TM/L	W	L	PCT	G	GS	CG	SH	SV	IP	H	HR	BB	SO	RAT	ERA	ERA+	OAV	OOB	BH	AVG	PB	PR	/A	PD	TPI
1961 Phi-N	0	1	.000	5	1	0	0	0	10	13	3	8	1	19.8	8.10	50	.325	.449	1	.500	0	-5	-4	-0	-0.4
1962 Phi-N	0	6	.000	23	9	0	0	1	63²	74	9	33	29	15.5	5.94	65	.298	.387	2	.154	0	-14	-15	-1	-1.3
1963 Phi-N	0	1	.000	6	2	0	0	0	15¹	16	1	5	10	12.9	4.11	79	.238	.314	1	.500	0	-1	-1	0	0.0
1968 Phi-N	0	0	—	2	0	0	0	0	4	6	1	1	4	15.8	9.00	33	.353	.389	0	—	0	-3	-3	-0	-0.0
Total 4	0	8	.000	36	12	0	0	1	93	108	14	47	45	15.6	6.00	63	.293	.382	4	.235	1	-23	-23	-0	-1.7

● **RAY BROWN**   Brown, Paul Percival b: 1/31/1889, Chicago, Ill.   d: 5/29/55, Los Angeles, Cal.   BR/TR, 6'1", 172 lbs.   Deb: 9/29/09

YEAR TM/L	W	L	PCT	G	GS	CG	SH	SV	IP	H	HR	BB	SO	RAT	ERA	ERA+	OAV	OOB	BH	AVG	PB	PR	/A	PD	TPI
1909 Chi-N	1	0	1.000	1	1	1	0	0	9	5	0	4	2	9.0	2.00	127	.172	.273	0	.000	-0	1	1	-0	0.0

● **STUB BROWN**   Brown, Richard P. b: 8/3/1870, Baltimore, Md.   d: 3/11/48, Baltimore, Md.   TL, 6'2", 220 lbs.   Deb: 8/15/1893

YEAR TM/L	W	L	PCT	G	GS	CG	SH	SV	IP	H	HR	BB	SO	RAT	ERA	ERA+	OAV	OOB	BH	AVG	PB	PR	/A	PD	TPI
1893 Bal-N	0	0	—	2	0	0	0	0	9	13	0	5	0	19.0	6.00	79	.328	.416	1	.200	-0	-1	-1	-0	-0.1
1894 Bal-N	4	0	1.000	9	6	3	0	0	49²	59	4	24	8	15.2	4.89	112	.292	.370	2	.087	-4	2	3	-1	-0.2
1897 Cin-N	0	1	.000	2	1	1	0	0	13	17	1	8	2	17.3	4.15	110	.313	.401	0	.000	-1	0	1	-0	-0.1
Total 3	4	1	.800	13	7	4	0	0	71²	89	4	37	10	16.1	4.90	106	.301	.382	3	.091	-5	1	2	-1	-0.4

● **BOB BROWN**   Brown, Robert Murray b: 4/1/11, Dorchester, Mass.   d: 8/3/90, Pembroke, Mass.   BR/TR, 6'0.5", 190 lbs.   Deb: 4/21/30

YEAR TM/L	W	L	PCT	G	GS	CG	SH	SV	IP	H	HR	BB	SO	RAT	ERA	ERA+	OAV	OOB	BH	AVG	PB	PR	/A	PD	TPI
1930 Bos-N	0	0	—	3	0	0	0	0	6	10	4	8	1	27.0	10.50	47	.417	.563	0	.000	-0	-4	-4	0	0.0
1931 Bos-N	0	1	.000	6¹	6¹	1	0	0	6¹	9	1	8	3	17.1	8.53	44	.375	.444	1	.500	-0	-3	-3	-0	-0.4
1932 Bos-N	14	7	.667	35	28	9	0	1	213	187	6	104	110	12.4	3.30	114	.238	.329	13	.194	-0	14	11	-1	0.9
1933 Bos-N	0	0	—	5	0	0	0	0	6²	6	0	3	3	12.2	2.70	114	.250	.333	0	.000	-0	0	0	-0	0.0
1934 Bos-N	1	3	.250	16	8	2	1	0	58¹	59	4	36	21	15.1	5.71	67	.262	.371	5	.238	-0	-11	-12	-1	-0.8
1935 Bos-N	1	8	.111	15	10	2	1	0	65	79	2	36	19	15.7	6.37	59	.302	.386	2	.105	-1	-17	-19	-1	-2.3
1936 Bos-N	0	2	.000	2	2	0	0	0	8¹	10	1	3	5	14.0	5.40	71	.278	.333	0	.000	-0	-1	-1	-0	-0.3
Total 7	16	21	.432	79	49	13	2	1	363²	360	11	193	159	13.8	4.48	84	.261	.354	21	.183	-2	-22	-28	-3	-2.9

● **SCOTT BROWN**   Brown, Scott Edward b: 8/30/56, DeQuincy, La.   BR/TR, 6'2", 220 lbs.   Deb: 8/11/81

YEAR TM/L	W	L	PCT	G	GS	CG	SH	SV	IP	H	HR	BB	SO	RAT	ERA	ERA+	OAV	OOB	BH	AVG	PB	PR	/A	PD	TPI
1981 Cin-N	1	0	1.000	10	0	0	0	0	13	16	1	7	7	11.8	2.77	128	.314	.327	0	.000	-0	1	1	-0	0.1

● **STEVE BROWN**   Brown, Steven Elbert b: 2/12/57, San Francisco, Cal.   BR/TR, 6'5", 200 lbs.   Deb: 8/1/83

YEAR TM/L	W	L	PCT	G	GS	CG	SH	SV	IP	H	HR	BB	SO	RAT	ERA	ERA+	OAV	OOB	BH	AVG	PB	PR	/A	PD	TPI
1983 Cal-A	2	3	.400	12	4	2	1	0	46	45	4	16	23	11.9	3.52	114	.256	.318	0	—	0	3	3	-0	0.2

YEAR	TM/L	W	L	PCT	G	GS	CG	SH	SV	IP	H	HR	BB	SO	RAT	ERA	ERA+	OAV	OOB	BH	AVG	PB	PR	/A	PD	TPI
1984	Cal-A	0	1	.000	3	3	0	0	0	11	16	0	9	5	20.5	9.00	44	.340	.446	0	—	0	-6	-6	-0	-0.5
Total	2	2	4	.333	15	7	2	1	0	57	61	4	25	28	13.6	4.58	87	.274	.347	0	—	0	-3	-4	-0	-0.3

● **TOM BROWN**   Brown, Thomas Dale   b: 8/10/49, Lafayette, La.   BR/TR, 6'1", 170 lbs.   Deb: 9/14/78

YEAR	TM/L	W	L	PCT	G	GS	CG	SH	SV	IP	H	HR	BB	SO	RAT	ERA	ERA+	OAV	OOB	BH	AVG	PB	PR	/A	PD	TPI
1978	Sea-A	0	0	—	6	0	0	0	0	13	14	2	4	8	12.5	4.15	92	.286	.340	0	—	0	-1	-1	0	0.0

● **TOM BROWN**   Brown, Thomas Tarlton   b: 9/21/1860, Liverpool, England   d: 10/25/27, Washington, D.C.   BL/TR, 5'10", 168 lbs.   Deb: 7/6/1882   MU♦

YEAR	TM/L	W	L	PCT	G	GS	CG	SH	SV	IP	H	HR	BB	SO	RAT	ERA	ERA+	OAV	OOB	BH	AVG	PB	PR	/A	PD	TPI
1882	Bal-a	0	0	—	2	0	0	0	0	8¹	13	0	6	2	20.5	1.08	255	.334	.423	55	.304	1	1	2	-1	0.0
1883	Col-a	0	1	.000	3	1	1	0	0	14	14	0	10	6	15.4	5.79	53	.244	.356	115	.274	1	-4	-4	-1	-0.3
1884	Col-a	2	1	.667	4	0	0	0	0	19	27	0	7	5	16.1	7.11	43	.281	.330	123	.273	1	-8	-9	-1	-1.0
1885	Pit-a	0	0	—	2	0	0	0	0	6	0	0	3	2	9.0	3.00	107	.000	.207	134	.307	1	0	0	-0	0.0
1886	Pit-a	0	0	—	1	0	0	0	0	2	2	0	5	1	31.5	9.00	38	.125	.333	131	.285	1	-1	-1	-0	-0.0
Total	5	2	2	.500	12	1	1	0	0	49¹	56	0	31	16	16.4	5.29	57	.242	.339	1952	.265	4	-12	-12	-2	-1.3

● **JUMBO BROWN**   Brown, Walter George   b: 4/30/07, Greene, R.I.   d: 10/2/66, Freeport, N.Y.   BR/TR, 6'4", 295 lbs.   Deb: 8/26/25

YEAR	TM/L	W	L	PCT	G	GS	CG	SH	SV	IP	H	HR	BB	SO	RAT	ERA	ERA+	OAV	OOB	BH	AVG	PB	PR	/A	PD	TPI
1925	Chi-N	0	0	—	2	0	0	0	0	6	5	0	4	0	13.5	3.00	144	.217	.333	0	.000	-0	1	1	0	0.0
1927	Cle-A	0	2	.000	8	0	0	0	0	18²	19	3	26	8	22.2	6.27	67	.284	.489	2	.667	1	-4	-4	0	-0.2
1928	Cle-A	0	1	.000	5	0	0	0	0	14²	19	0	15	12	20.9	6.75	61	.365	.507	2	.667	1	-4	-4	-0	-0.1
1932	NY-A	5	2	.714	19	3	3	1	1	55²	58	1	30	31	14.6	4.53	90	.270	.364	4	.174	-1	-0	-3	1	-0.2
1933	NY-A	7	5	.583	21	8	1	0	0	74	78	3	52	55	15.8	5.23	74	.269	.380	5	.179	-1	-8	-11	-0	-1.5
1935	NY-A	6	5	.545	20	8	3	1	0	87¹	94	2	37	41	13.5	3.61	112	.279	.350	10	.313	3	8	4	-0	0.8
1936	NY-A	1	4	.200	20	3	0	0	0	64	93	4	29	19	17.2	5.91	79	.352	.416	0	.000	-3	-6	-9	1	-0.8
1937	Cin-N	1	0	1.000	4	1	0	0	0	9²	16	0	3	4	17.7	8.38	45	.390	.432	0	.000		-5	-5	-0	-0.5
	NY-N	1	0	1.000	4	0	0	0	0	8²	5	0	5	4	10.4	1.04	374	.172	.294	0	—	0	3	3	1	0.4
	Yr	2	0	1.000	8	1	0	0	0	18¹	21	0	8	8	14.2	4.91	78	.300	.372	0	.000	-0	-2	-2	0	-0.1
1938	NY-N	5	3	.625	43	0	0	0	5	90	65	5	28	42	9.4	1.80	209	.204	.271	3	.188	1	**20**	**20**	-1	1.8
1939	NY-N	4	0	1.000	31	0	0	0	7	56¹	69	1	25	24	15.2	4.15	95	.304	.375	4	.364	1	-1	-1	0	0.0
1940	NY-N	2	4	.333	41	0	0	0	**7**	55¹	49	5	25	31	12.0	3.42	114	.232	.314	1	.100	-1	3	3	-1	0.2
1941	NY-N	1	5	.167	31	0	0	0	**8**	57	49	2	21	30	11.1	3.32	111	.238	.308	1	.111	-1	2	2	-1	0.2
Total	12	33	31	.516	249	23	7	2	29	597¹	619	26	300	301	13.9	4.07	99	.271	.357	32	.204	2	7	-4	-0	0.1

● **WALTER BROWN**   Brown, Walter Irving   b: 4/23/15, Jamestown, N.Y.   d: 2/3/91, Westfield, N.Y.   BR/TR, 5'11", 175 lbs.   Deb: 5/16/47

YEAR	TM/L	W	L	PCT	G	GS	CG	SH	SV	IP	H	HR	BB	SO	RAT	ERA	ERA+	OAV	OOB	BH	AVG	PB	PR	/A	PD	TPI
1947	StL-A	1	0	1.000	19	0	0	0	0	46	54	3	33	13	16.8	4.89	79	.294	.394	0	.000	1	-6	-5	-0	-0.2

● **CAL BROWNING**   Browning, Calvin Duane   b: 3/16/38, Burns Flat, Okla.   BL/TL, 5'11", 190 lbs.   Deb: 6/12/60

YEAR	TM/L	W	L	PCT	G	GS	CG	SH	SV	IP	H	HR	BB	SO	RAT	ERA	ERA+	OAV	OOB	BH	AVG	PB	PR	/A	PD	TPI
1960	StL-N	0	0	—	1	0	0	0	0	0²	5	1	0	0	81.0	40.50	10	.714	.750	0	—	0	-3	-3	-0	-0.3

● **FRANK BROWNING**   Browning, Frank "Dutch"   b: 10/29/1882, Falmouth, Ky.   d: 5/19/48, San Antonio, Tex.   BR/TR, 5'5", 145 lbs.   Deb: 4/16/10

YEAR	TM/L	W	L	PCT	G	GS	CG	SH	SV	IP	H	HR	BB	SO	RAT	ERA	ERA+	OAV	OOB	BH	AVG	PB	PR	/A	PD	TPI
1910	Det-A	2	2	.500	11	6	2	0	3	49	51	0	16	16	11.2	2.57	102	.262	.298	0	.000	-2	0	0	1	0.0

● **PETE BROWNING**   Browning, Louis Rogers "The Gladiator"   b: 6/17/1861, Louisville, Ky.   d: 9/10/05, Louisville, Ky.   BR/TR, 6', 180 lbs.   Deb: 5/2/1882   ♦

YEAR	TM/L	W	L	PCT	G	GS	CG	SH	SV	IP	H	HR	BB	SO	RAT	ERA	ERA+	OAV	OOB	BH	AVG	PB	PR	/A	PD	TPI
1884	Lou-a	0	1	.000	1	1	0	0	0	0¹	2	0	2	0	135.0	54.00	6	1.000	1.000	150	.336	1	-2	-2	0	-1.9

● **TOM BROWNING**   Browning, Thomas Leo   b: 4/28/60, Casper, Wyoming   BL/TL, 6'1", 190 lbs.   Deb: 9/9/84

YEAR	TM/L	W	L	PCT	G	GS	CG	SH	SV	IP	H	HR	BB	SO	RAT	ERA	ERA+	OAV	OOB	BH	AVG	PB	PR	/A	PD	TPI
1984	Cin-N	1	0	1.000	3	3	0	0	0	23¹	27	0	5	14	12.3	1.54	245	.303	.340	1	.143	-0	5	6	0	0.2
1985	Cin-N	20	9	.690	38	38	6	4	0	261¹	242	29	73	155	11.0	3.55	107	.245	.299	17	.193	2	1	7	-2	0.8
1986	Cin-N	14	13	.519	39	39	4	2	0	243¹	225	26	70	147	10.9	3.81	102	.245	.299	14	.163	-1	-3	2	-3	-0.2
1987	Cin-N	10	13	.435	32	31	2	0	0	183	201	41	61	117	13.1	5.02	85	.284	.345	8	.154	0	-19	-16	-2	-1.8
1988	Cin-N	18	5	.783	36	36	5	2	0	250²	205	36	64	124	9.9	3.41	105	.224	.280	12	.145	0	1	5	-3	0.2
1989	Cin-N	15	12	.556	37	37	9	2	0	249²	241	31	64	118	11.1	3.39	106	.255	.304	7	.090	-3	3	6	-1	0.1
1990	*Cin-N	15	9	.625	35	35	2	1	0	227²	235	24	52	99	11.5	3.80	104	.266	.311	7	.093	-3	-0	4	-2	-0.2
1991	Cin-N☆	14	14	.500	36	36	1	0	0	230¹	241	32	56	115	11.8	4.18	91	.266	.312	12	.171	-1	-13	-10	-3	-1.3
1992	Cin-N	6	5	.545	16	16	0	0	0	87	108	6	28	33	14.3	5.07	71	.311	.366	7	.226	1	-15	-14	0	-1.5
1993	Cin-N	7	7	.500	21	20	0	0	0	114	159	15	20	53	14.2	4.74	85	.333	.361	8	.216	2	-9	-9	1	-0.6
1994	Cin-N	3	1	.750	7	7	2	1	0	40²	34	8	13	22	10.6	4.20	99	.222	.287	2	.143	-0	0	-0	-0	-0.1
Total	11	123	88	.583	300	298	31	12	0	1911	1918	234	506	997	11.6	3.92	98	.262	.312	95	.153	2	-48	-20	-15	-4.4

● **BRUCE BRUBAKER**   Brubaker, Bruce Ellsworth   b: 12/29/41, Harrisburg, Pa.   BR/TR, 6'1", 198 lbs.   Deb: 4/15/67

YEAR	TM/L	W	L	PCT	G	GS	CG	SH	SV	IP	H	HR	BB	SO	RAT	ERA	ERA+	OAV	OOB	BH	AVG	PB	PR	/A	PD	TPI
1967	LA-N	0	0	—	1	0	0	0	0	1¹	3	1	0	2	20.3	20.25	15	.429	.429	0	—	0	-3	-3	0	0.0
1970	Mil-A	0	0	—	1	0	0	0	0	2	2	1	1	0	13.5	9.00	42	.250	.333	0	—	0	-1	-1	-0	0.0
Total	2	0	0	—	2	0	0	0	0	3¹	5	2	1	2	16.2	13.50	26	.333	.375	0	—	0	-4	-4	0	0.0

● **LOU BRUCE**   Bruce, Louis R.   b: 1/16/1877, St.Regis, N.Y.   d: 2/9/68, Ilion, N.Y.   BL/TR, 5'5", 145 lbs.   Deb: 6/22/04   ♦

YEAR	TM/L	W	L	PCT	G	GS	CG	SH	SV	IP	H	HR	BB	SO	RAT	ERA	ERA+	OAV	OOB	BH	AVG	PB	PR	/A	PD	TPI
1904	Phi-A	0	0	—	2	0	0	0	0	11	11	1	2	2	10.6	4.91	55	.261	.295	27	.267	0	-3	-3	0	0.1

● **BOB BRUCE**   Bruce, Robert James   b: 5/16/33, Detroit, Mich.   BR/TR, 6'3", 210 lbs.   Deb: 9/14/59

YEAR	TM/L	W	L	PCT	G	GS	CG	SH	SV	IP	H	HR	BB	SO	RAT	ERA	ERA+	OAV	OOB	BH	AVG	PB	PR	/A	PD	TPI
1959	Det-A	0	1	.000	2	1	0	0	0	2	2	1	3	1	22.5	9.00	45	.250	.455	0	—	0	-1	-1	-0	-0.4
1960	Det-A	4	7	.364	34	15	1	0	0	130	127	16	56	76	13.0	3.74	106	.250	.331	7	.179	0	2	3	1	0.3
1961	Det-A	1	2	.333	14	6	0	0	0	44²	57	6	24	25	16.7	4.43	92	.320	.407	1	.111	0	-2	-2	-1	-0.2
1962	Hou-N	10	9	.526	32	27	6	4	0	175	164	16	82	135	13.3	4.06	92	.248	.342	11	.200	5	-2	-6	-0	-0.1
1963	Hou-N	5	9	.357	30	25	1	1	0	170¹	162	7	60	123	12.2	3.59	88	.250	.321	7	.127	-2	-6	-8	-1	-0.6
1964	Hou-N	15	9	.625	35	29	9	4	0	202¹	191	14	33	135	10.1	2.76	124	.246	.279	12	.190	2	18	15	-0	2.0
1965	Hou-N	9	18	.333	35	34	7	1	0	229²	241	22	38	145	11.3	3.72	90	.270	.307	9	.122	-1	-5	-9	0	-1.1
1966	Hou-N	3	13	.188	25	23	1	0	0	129²	160	16	29	71	13.7	5.34	64	.301	.346	3	.077	-2	-25	-28	0	-3.2
1967	Atl-N	2	3	.400	12	7	1	0	1	38²	42	3	15	22	13.5	4.89	68	.269	.337	2	.167	0	-7	-7	-1	-0.9
Total	9	49	71	.408	219	167	26	6	1	1122¹	1146	95	340	733	12.3	3.85	91	.263	.323	52	.150	6	-28	-43	-2	-4.2

● **FRED BRUCKBAUER**   Bruckbauer, Frederick John   b: 5/27/38, New Ulm, Minn.   BR/TR, 6'1", 185 lbs.   Deb: 4/25/61

YEAR	TM/L	W	L	PCT	G	GS	CG	SH	SV	IP	H	HR	BB	SO	RAT	ERA	ERA+	OAV	OOB	BH	AVG	PB	PR	/A	PD	TPI
1961	Min-A	0	0	—	1	0	0	0	0	0	3	0	1	0	—	∞	—	1.000	1.000	0	—	0	-3	-3	-0	-0.3

● **ANDY BRUCKMILLER**   Bruckmiller, Andrew   b: 1/1/1882, McKeesport, Pa.   d: 1/12/70, McKeesport, Pa.   BR/TR, 5'11", 175 lbs.   Deb: 6/26/05

YEAR	TM/L	W	L	PCT	G	GS	CG	SH	SV	IP	H	HR	BB	SO	RAT	ERA	ERA+	OAV	OOB	BH	AVG	PB	PR	/A	PD	TPI
1905	Det-A	0	0	—	1	0	0	0	0	1	4	0	1	1	45.0	27.00	10	.586	.639	0	.000	-0	-3	-3	-0	0.0

● **MIKE BRUHERT**   Bruhert, Michael Edwin   b: 6/24/51, Jamaica, N.Y.   BR/TR, 6'6", 220 lbs.   Deb: 4/9/78

YEAR	TM/L	W	L	PCT	G	GS	CG	SH	SV	IP	H	HR	BB	SO	RAT	ERA	ERA+	OAV	OOB	BH	AVG	PB	PR	/A	PD	TPI
1978	NY-N	4	11	.267	27	22	1	1	0	133²	171	6	34	56	13.9	4.78	73	.317	.359	3	.075	-3	-18	-19	-0	-2.2

● **DUFF BRUMLEY**   Brumley, Duff Lechaun   b: 8/25/70, Cleveland, Tenn.   BR/TR, 6'4", 195 lbs.   Deb: 6/1/94

YEAR	TM/L	W	L	PCT	G	GS	CG	SH	SV	IP	H	HR	BB	SO	RAT	ERA	ERA+	OAV	OOB	BH	AVG	PB	PR	/A	PD	TPI
1994	Tex-A	0	0	—	2	0	0	0	0	3¹	6	1	5	4	29.7	16.20	28	.400	.550	0	—	0	-4	-4	0	0.0

● **GREG BRUMMETT**   Brummett, Gregory Scott   b: 4/20/67, Wichita, Kan.   BR/TR, 6', 180 lbs.   Deb: 5/29/93

YEAR	TM/L	W	L	PCT	G	GS	CG	SH	SV	IP	H	HR	BB	SO	RAT	ERA	ERA+	OAV	OOB	BH	AVG	PB	PR	/A	PD	TPI
1993	SF-N	2	3	.400	8	8	0	0	0	46	53	9	13	20	12.9	4.70	83	.294	.342	0	.000	-1	-3	-4	-0	-0.5
	Min-A	2	1	.667	5	5	0	0	0	26²	29	3	15	10	14.9	5.74	76	.299	.393	0	—	-0	-4	-4	-1	-0.4
Total	1	4	4	.500	13	13	0	0	0	72²	82	12	28	30	13.6	5.08	80	.296	.361	0	.000	-1	-8	-8	-1	-0.9

● **JACK BRUNER**   Bruner, Jack Raymond   b: 7/1/24, Waterloo, Iowa   BL/TL, 6'1", 185 lbs.   Deb: 9/16/49

YEAR	TM/L	W	L	PCT	G	GS	CG	SH	SV	IP	H	HR	BB	SO	RAT	ERA	ERA+	OAV	OOB	BH	AVG	PB	PR	/A	PD	TPI
1949	Chi-A	1	2	.333	4	2	0	0	0	7²	10	0	8	4	21.1	8.22	51	.357	.500	0	.000	-0	-3	-3	-0	-1.1
1950	Chi-A	0	0	—	9	0	0	0	0	12¹	7	0	14	8	16.1	3.65	123	.184	.415	0	—	0	1	1	-0	0.0

YEAR	TM/L	W	L	PCT	G	GS	CG	SH	SV	IP	H	HR	BB	SO	RAT	ERA	ERA+	OAV	OOB	BH	AVG	PB	PR	/A	PD	TPI
	StL-A	1	2	.333	13	1	0	0	1	35	36	4	23	16	15.7	4.63	107	.267	.381	0	.000	-1	-0	1	-1	-0.1
	Yr	1	2	.333	22	1	0	0	1	47¹	43	4	37	24	15.6	4.37	110	.247	.385	0	.000	-1	1	2	-1	-0.1
Total	2	2	4	.333	26	3	0	0	1	55	53	4	45	28	16.5	4.91	96	.264	.406	0	.000	-1	-2	-1	-1	-1.2

● **ROY BRUNER**   Bruner, Walter Roy   b: 2/10/17, Cecilia, Ky.   d: 11/30/86, St.Matthews, Ky.   BR/TR, 6', 165 lbs.   Deb: 9/14/39

YEAR	TM/L	W	L	PCT	G	GS	CG	SH	SV	IP	H	HR	BB	SO	RAT	ERA	ERA+	OAV	OOB	BH	AVG	PB	PR	/A	PD	TPI
1939	Phi-N	0	4	.000	4	4	2	0	0	27	38	3	11	17	17.0	6.67	60	.339	.408	1	.111	-1	-8	-8	-1	-1.0
1940	Phi-N	0	0	—	2	0	0	0	0	6¹	5	2	6	4	15.6	5.68	69	.227	.393	0	.500	-0	-1	-1	0	0.1
1941	Phi-N	0	3	.000	13	1	0	0	0	29¹	37	1	25	13	19.0	4.91	75	.336	.459	0	.000	-0	-4	-4	-1	-0.5
Total	3	0	7	.000	19	5	2	0	0	62²	80	6	44	28	17.8	5.74	67	.328	.431	2	.118	-1	-14	-13	-1	-1.4

● **GEORGE BRUNET**   Brunet, George Stuart "Lefty"   b: 6/8/35, Houghton, Mich.   d: 10/25/91, Poza Rica, Mex.   BR/TL, 6'1", 210 lbs.   Deb: 9/14/56

YEAR	TM/L	W	L	PCT	G	GS	CG	SH	SV	IP	H	HR	BB	SO	RAT	ERA	ERA+	OAV	OOB	BH	AVG	PB	PR	/A	PD	TPI
1956	KC-A	0	0	—	6	1	0	0	0	9	10	1	11	5	21.0	7.00	62	.286	.457	0	.000	-0	-3	-3	0	0.0
1957	KC-A	0	1	.000	4	2	0	0	0	11¹	13	2	4	3	13.5	5.56	71	.277	.333	0	.000	-0	-2	-2	-0	-0.2
1959	KC-A	0	0	—	2	0	0	0	0	4²	10	2	7	7	34.7	11.57	35	.435	.581	0	—	0	-4	-4	1	0.1
1960	KC-A	0	2	.000	3	2	0	0	0	10¹	12	0	10	4	20.0	4.35	91	.308	.460	0	.000	-0	-1	-0	1	0.0
	Mil-N	2	0	1.000	17	6	0	0	0	49²	53	6	22	39	13.8	5.07	68	.275	.352	1	.091	-1	-7	-9	0	-0.4
1961	Mil-N	0	0	—	5	0	0	0	0	5	7	1	2	0	16.2	5.40	69	.412	.474	0	—	-1	-1	-1	0	0.0
1962	Hou-N	2	4	.333	17	11	0	0	0	54	62	2	21	36	13.8	4.50	83	.291	.355	1	.059	-1	-3	-5	1	-0.5
1963	Hou-N	0	3	.000	5	2	0	0	0	12²	24	2	6	11	21.3	7.11	44	.393	.448	0	.000	-0	-5	-6	0	-1.1
	Bal-A	0	1	.000	16	0	0	0	1	20	25	3	9	13	15.7	5.40	64	.301	.376	0	.000	-0	-4	-4	0	-0.2
1964	LA-A	2	2	.500	10	7	0	0	0	42¹	38	2	25	36	13.4	3.61	91	.237	.341	2	.182	0	-2	-2	0	-0.1
1965	Cal-A	9	11	.450	41	26	8	3	2	197	149	9	69	141	10.1	2.56	133	.209	.282	3	.054	-2	20	18	-1	1.4
1966	Cal-A	13	13	.500	41	32	8	2	0	212	183	21	106	148	12.5	3.31	101	.234	.329	7	.103	-3	3	1	-0	0.0
1967	Cal-A	11	19	.367	40	37	7	2	1	250	203	19	90	165	10.7	3.31	95	.223	.295	6	.077	-4	-2	-5	-2	-1.2
1968	Cal-A	13	17	.433	39	36	8	5	0	245¹	191	23	68	132	9.6	2.86	102	.215	.273	6	.081	-3	3	1	-2	-0.5
1969	Cal-A	6	7	.462	23	19	2	2	0	100²	98	15	39	56	12.3	3.84	91	.255	.325	1	.037	-1	-2	-4	-1	-0.7
	Sea-A	2	5	.286	12	11	2	0	0	63²	70	11	28	37	13.9	5.37	68	.280	.353	3	.150	1	-12	-12	1	-1.1
	Yr	8	12	.400	35	30	4	2	0	164¹	168	26	67	93	12.9	4.44	80	.264	.334	4	.085	-0	-15	-16	-0	-1.8
1970	Was-A	8	6	.571	24	20	2	1	0	118	124	10	48	67	13.2	4.42	80	.275	.346	6	.158	1	-9	-11	-1	-1.2
	Pit-N	1	1	.500	12	1	0	0	0	16²	19	1	9	17	15.7	2.70	144	.311	.408	0	.000	-0	2	2	0	0.2
1971	StL-N	0	1	.000	7	0	0	0	0	9¹	12	3	7	4	18.3	5.79	62	.316	.422	1	.333	0	-2	-2	-0	-0.2
Total	15	69	93	.426	324	213	39	15	4	1431²	1303	133	581	921	12.0	3.62	92	.244	.320	37	.089	-14	-31	-46	-4	-5.7

● **TOM BRUNO**   Bruno, Thomas Michael   b: 1/26/53, Chicago, Ill.   BR/TR, 6'5", 210 lbs.   Deb: 8/1/76

YEAR	TM/L	W	L	PCT	G	GS	CG	SH	SV	IP	H	HR	BB	SO	RAT	ERA	ERA+	OAV	OOB	BH	AVG	PB	PR	/A	PD	TPI
1976	KC-A	1	0	1.000	12	0	0	0	0	17¹	20	3	9	11	15.1	6.75	52	.290	.372	0	—	0	-6	-6	-0	-0.4
1977	Tor-A	0	1	.000	12	0	0	0	0	18¹	30	4	13	9	21.6	7.85	53	.366	.458	0	—	0	-8	-7	-0	-0.4
1978	StL-N	4	3	.571	18	3	0	0	1	49²	38	3	17	33	10.0	1.99	176	.209	.276	1	.083	-1	9	8	-1	1.1
1979	StL-N	2	3	.400	27	1	0	0	0	38¹	37	1	22	27	14.3	4.23	89	.253	.359	1	.200	0	-2	-2	-0	-0.2
Total	4	7	7	.500	69	4	0	0	1	123²	125	11	61	80	13.8	4.22	87	.261	.348	2	.118	-1	-7	-7	-1	0.1

● **WARREN BRUSSTAR**   Brusstar, Warren Scott   b: 2/2/52, Oakland, Cal.   BR/TR, 6'3", 200 lbs.   Deb: 5/6/77

YEAR	TM/L	W	L	PCT	G	GS	CG	SH	SV	IP	H	HR	BB	SO	RAT	ERA	ERA+	OAV	OOB	BH	AVG	PB	PR	/A	PD	TPI
1977	*Phi-N	7	2	.778	46	0	0	0	3	71¹	64	7	24	46	11.2	2.65	151	.250	.317	0	.000	-1	10	11	1	1.4
1978	*Phi-N	6	3	.667	58	0	0	0	0	88²	74	0	30	60	10.9	2.33	153	.239	.312	1	.143	0	12	12	2	1.4
1979	Phi-N	1	0	1.000	13	0	0	0	1	14¹	23	1	4	3	17.0	6.91	55	.383	.422	0	—	0	-5	-5	0	-0.4
1980	*Phi-N	2	2	.500	26	0	0	0	0	38²	42	3	13	21	12.8	3.72	102	.286	.344	0	.000	-0	-1	0	0	0.0
1981	*Phi-N	0	1	.000	14	0	0	0	0	12¹	12	0	10	8	16.8	4.38	83	.250	.390	0	—	0	-1	-1	0	-0.1
1982	Phi-N	2	3	.400	22	0	0	0	2	22²	31	2	5	11	14.7	4.76	77	.348	.389	0	.000	-0	-3	-3	0	-0.6
	Chi-A	2	0	1.000	10	0	0	0	0	18¹	19	2	3	8	11.3	3.44	117	.257	.295	0	—	0	1	1	0	0.2
1983	Chi-N	3	1	.750	50	0	0	0	1	80¹	67	1	37	46	11.9	2.35	161	.234	.326	0	.000	0	11	13	0	0.6
1984	*Chi-N	1	1	.500	41	0	0	0	3	63²	57	4	21	36	11.2	3.11	126	.247	.312	1	.200	1	3	6	-0	0.3
1985	Chi-N	4	3	.571	51	0	0	0	4	74¹	87	8	36	34	15.3	6.05	66	.292	.374	1	.143	0	-20	-17	-2	-1.9
Total	9	28	16	.636	340	0	0	0	14	484²	476	28	183	273	12.5	3.51	109	.265	.337	3	.094	-1	8	17	2	0.9

● **CLAY BRYANT**   Bryant, Claiborne Henry   b: 11/16/11, Madison Heights, Va.   BR/TR, 6'2.5", 195 lbs.   Deb: 4/19/35   C

YEAR	TM/L	W	L	PCT	G	GS	CG	SH	SV	IP	H	HR	BB	SO	RAT	ERA	ERA+	OAV	OOB	BH	AVG	PB	PR	/A	PD	TPI
1935	Chi-N	1	2	.333	9	1	0	0	2	22²	34	1	7	13	16.3	5.16	76	.358	.402	2	.333	2	-3	-3	-0	-0.2
1936	Chi-N	1	2	.333	26	0	0	0	0	57¹	57	0	24	35	13.0	3.30	121	.259	.337	5	.417	1	**5**	**4**	1	0.4
1937	Chi-N	9	3	.750	38	10	4	1	3	135¹	117	1	78	75	13.0	4.26	94	.232	.336	14	.311	-5	-5	-4	-3	-0.2
1938	*Chi-N	19	11	.633	44	30	17	3	2	270¹	235	6	125	**135**	12.0	3.10	124	.235	.321	24	.226	4	21	22	-3	2.4
1939	Chi-N	2	1	.667	4	4	2	0	0	31¹	42	3	14	9	16.4	5.74	69	.307	.375	3	.214	0	-6	-6	-1	-0.5
1940	Chi-N	0	1	.000	8	0	0	0	0	26¹	26	2	14	5	13.7	4.78	78	.265	.357	3	.333	1	-3	-3	0	0.0
Total	6	32	20	.615	129	45	23	4	7	543¹	511	13	262	272	12.9	3.73	104	.249	.335	51	.266	13	8	10	-6	1.9

● **RON BRYANT**   Bryant, Ronald Raymond   b: 11/12/47, Redlands, Cal.   BB/TL, 6', 190 lbs.   Deb: 9/29/67

YEAR	TM/L	W	L	PCT	G	GS	CG	SH	SV	IP	H	HR	BB	SO	RAT	ERA	ERA+	OAV	OOB	BH	AVG	PB	PR	/A	PD	TPI
1967	SF-N	0	0	—	1	0	0	0	0	4	3	0	0	9	9.0	4.50	73	.200	.250	0	.000	-0	-1	-1	-0	0.0
1969	SF-N	4	3	.571	16	8	0	0	1	57²	60	8	25	30	13.6	4.37	80	.271	.351	3	.188	1	-5	-6	-0	-0.6
1970	SF-N	5	8	.385	34	11	1	0	0	96	103	7	38	66	13.4	4.78	83	.274	.344	3	.111	-0	-8	-9	1	-1.0
1971	*SF-N	7	10	.412	27	22	3	2	0	140	146	9	49	79	12.7	3.79	90	.272	.336	10	.200	1	-5	-6	0	-0.6
1972	SF-N	14	7	.667	35	28	11	4	0	214	176	20	77	107	10.7	2.90	120	.224	.295	12	.171	1	13	14	-4	0.9
1973	SF-N	**24**	12	.667	41	39	8	0	0	270	240	23	115	143	12.1	3.53	108	.234	.316	16	.168	1	4	9	0	1.2
1974	SF-N	3	15	.167	41	23	0	0	0	126²	142	11	68	75	15.2	5.61	68	.286	.376	4	.129	-1	-28	-26	0	-3.4
1975	StL-N	0	1	.000	10	0	0	0	0	8²	20	2	7	7	28.0	16.62	23	.444	.519	0	.000	0	-13	-12	0	-1.2
Total	8	57	56	.504	205	132	23	6	1	917	890	80	379	509	12.7	4.02	91	.254	.331	48	.165	0	-42	-36	-4	-4.7

● **T.R. BRYDEN**   Bryden, Thomas Ray   b: 1/17/59, Moses Lake, Wash.   BR/TR, 6'4", 190 lbs.   Deb: 4/10/86

YEAR	TM/L	W	L	PCT	G	GS	CG	SH	SV	IP	H	HR	BB	SO	RAT	ERA	ERA+	OAV	OOB	BH	AVG	PB	PR	/A	PD	TPI
1986	Cal-A	2	1	.667	16	0	0	0	0	34¹	38	4	21	25	16.0	6.55	63	.290	.396	0	—	0	-9	-9	0	-0.6

● **TOD BRYNAN**   Brynan, Charles Ruley   b: 7/1863, Philadelphia, Pa.   d: 5/10/25, Philadelphia, Pa.   BR/TR,   Deb: 6/22/1888

YEAR	TM/L	W	L	PCT	G	GS	CG	SH	SV	IP	H	HR	BB	SO	RAT	ERA	ERA+	OAV	OOB	BH	AVG	PB	PR	/A	PD	TPI
1888	Chi-N	2	1	.667	3	3	3	0	0	25	29	2	7	11	13.7	6.48	47	.271	.328	2	.182	0	-10	-9	-0	-0.9
1891	Bos-N	0	1	.000	1	1	0	0	0	1	4	0	3	0	63.0	54.00	7	.572	.701	0	—	0	-6	-6	-0	-1.9
Total	2	2	2	.500	4	4	3	0	0	26	33	2	10	11	15.6	8.31	37	.289	.357	2	.182	0	-16	-15	-1	-2.8

● **JIM BUCHANAN**   Buchanan, James Forrest   b: 7/1/1876, Chatham Hill, Va.   d: 6/15/49, Norfolk, Neb.   BL/TR, 5'10", 165 lbs.   Deb: 4/16/05

YEAR	TM/L	W	L	PCT	G	GS	CG	SH	SV	IP	H	HR	BB	SO	RAT	ERA	ERA+	OAV	OOB	BH	AVG	PB	PR	/A	PD	TPI
1905	StL-A	5	9	.357	22	15	12	1	**2**	141¹	149	2	27	54	11.6	3.50	73	.272	.308	7	.152	-0	-13	-15	0	-1.5

● **BOB BUCHANAN**   Buchanan, Robert Gordon   b: 5/3/61, Ridley Park, Pa.   BL/TL, 6'1", 185 lbs.   Deb: 7/13/85

YEAR	TM/L	W	L	PCT	G	GS	CG	SH	SV	IP	H	HR	BB	SO	RAT	ERA	ERA+	OAV	OOB	BH	AVG	PB	PR	/A	PD	TPI
1985	Cin-N	1	0	1.000	14	0	0	0	0	16	25	4	9	3	19.1	8.44	45	.368	.442	0	.000	-0	-9	-8	0	-0.5
1989	KC-A	0	0	—	2	0	0	0	0	3¹	5	1	3	3	21.6	16.20	24	.333	.444	0	—	0	-5	-5	0	0.0
Total	2	1	0	1.000	16	0	0	0	0	19¹	30	5	12	6	19.6	9.78	39	.361	.442	0	.000	-0	-13	-13	0	-0.5

● **GARY BUCKELS**   Buckels, Gary Scott   b: 7/22/65, LaMirada, Cal.   BR/TR, 6', 185 lbs.   Deb: 7/23/94

YEAR	TM/L	W	L	PCT	G	GS	CG	SH	SV	IP	H	HR	BB	SO	RAT	ERA	ERA+	OAV	OOB	BH	AVG	PB	PR	/A	PD	TPI
1994	StL-N	0	1	.000	10	0	0	0	0	12	8	2	7	9	11.3	2.25	181	.186	.300	0	.000	-0	3	2	0	0.2

● **GARLAND BUCKEYE**   Buckeye, Garland Maiers "Gob"   b: 10/16/1897, Heron Lake, Minn.   d: 11/14/75, Stone Lake, Wis.   BB/TL, 6', 260 lbs.   Deb: 6/19/18

YEAR	TM/L	W	L	PCT	G	GS	CG	SH	SV	IP	H	HR	BB	SO	RAT	ERA	ERA+	OAV	OOB	BH	AVG	PB	PR	/A	PD	TPI
1918	Was-A	0	0	—	3	0	0	0	0	6	6	0	6	2	40.5	18.00	15	.333	.600	0	—	0	-3	-3	0	0.0
1925	Cle-A	13	8	.619	30	18	11	1	0	153	161	3	58	49	13.2	3.65	121	.267	.338	14	.226	2	13	13	-1	1.7
1926	Cle-A	6	9	.400	32	18	5	1	0	165²	160	3	69	36	12.8	3.10	131	.264	.345	12	.200	2	17	18	-2	1.4

YEAR	TM/L	W	L	PCT	G	GS	CG	SH	SV	IP	H	HR	BB	SO	RAT	ERA	ERA+	OAV	OOB	BH	AVG	PB	PR	/A	PD	TPI
1927	Cle-A	10	17	.370	35	25	13	2	1	204²	231	6	74	38	13.6	3.96	106	.296	.360	19	.268	3	4	6	-1	0.8
1928	Cle-A	1	5	.167	9	6	0	0	0	35	58	2	5	6	16.7	6.69	62	.389	.417	1	.111	-1	-10	-10	-0	-1.4
	NY-N	0	0	—	1	0	0	0	0	3²	9	1	2	3	27.0	14.73	27	.409	.458	1	.500	1	-4	-4	0	0.1
Total	5	30	39	.435	108	67	29	4	1	564	622	15	214	134	13.6	3.91	108	.287	.356	47	.230	7	16	19	-3	2.6

● ED BUCKINGHAM
Buckingham, Edward Taylor b: 5/12/1874, Metuchen, N.J. d: 7/30/42, Bridgeport, Conn. Deb: 8/30/1895

YEAR	TM/L	W	L	PCT	G	GS	CG	SH	SV	IP	H	HR	BB	SO	RAT	ERA	ERA+	OAV	OOB	BH	AVG	PB	PR	/A	PD	TPI
1895	Was-N	0	0	—	1	1	0	0	0	3	6	0	2	1	24.0	6.00	80	.408	.479	0	.000	-0	-0	-0	-0	0.0

● JESS BUCKLES
Buckles, Jesse Robert "Jim" b: 5/20/1890, LaVerne, Cal. d: 8/2/75, Westminster, Cal. BL/TL, 6'2.5", 205 lbs. Deb: 9/17/16

YEAR	TM/L	W	L	PCT	G	GS	CG	SH	SV	IP	H	HR	BB	SO	RAT	ERA	ERA+	OAV	OOB	BH	AVG	PB	PR	/A	PD	TPI
1916	NY-A	0	0	—	2	0	0	0	0	4	3	0	1	0	9.0	2.25	128	.188	.235	0	.000	-0	0	0	-0	0.0

● JOHN BUCKLEY
Buckley, John Edward b: 3/20/1869, Marlborough, Mass. d: 5/3/42, Westborough, Mass. BL/TR, 6'1", 200 lbs. Deb: 7/15/1890

YEAR	TM/L	W	L	PCT	G	GS	CG	SH	SV	IP	H	HR	BB	SO	RAT	ERA	ERA+	OAV	OOB	BH	AVG	PB	PR	/A	PD	TPI
1890	Buf-P	1	3	.250	4	4	4	0	0	34	49	5	16	4	17.2	7.68	53	.323	.388	0	.000	-2	-13	-14	0	-1.1

● MIKE BUDNICK
Budnick, Michael Joe b: 9/15/19, Astoria, Ore. BR/TR, 6'1", 200 lbs. Deb: 4/18/46

YEAR	TM/L	W	L	PCT	G	GS	CG	SH	SV	IP	H	HR	BB	SO	RAT	ERA	ERA+	OAV	OOB	BH	AVG	PB	PR	/A	PD	TPI
1946	NY-N	2	3	.400	35	7	1	1	3	88¹	75	13	48	36	12.5	3.16	109	.231	.330	6	.300	3	2	3	1	0.5
1947	NY-N	0	0	—	7	1	0	0	0	12	16	0	10	6	19.5	10.50	39	.314	.426	1	.250	0	-9	-9	0	0.0
Total	2	2	3	.400	42	8	1	1	3	100¹	91	13	58	42	13.4	4.04	87	.242	.343	7	.292	3	-6	-6	1	0.5

● CHARLIE BUFFINTON
Buffinton, Charles G. b: 6/14/1861, Fall River, Mass. d: 9/23/07, Fall River, Mass. BR/TR, 6'1", 180 lbs. Deb: 5/17/1882   M◆

YEAR	TM/L	W	L	PCT	G	GS	CG	SH	SV	IP	H	HR	BB	SO	RAT	ERA	ERA+	OAV	OOB	BH	AVG	PB	PR	/A	PD	TPI
1882	Bos-N	2	3	.400	5	5	4	1	0	42	53	2	14	17	14.4	4.07	70	.296	.347	13	.260	0	-5	-6	1	-0.5
1883	Bos-N	25	14	.641	43	41	34	4	1	333	346	4	51	188	10.7	3.03	102	.254	.281	81	.238	0	4	3	-1	0.1
1884	Bos-N	48	16	.750	67	67	63	8	0	587	506	15	76	417	8.9	2.15	135	.219	.244	94	.267	12	54	48	3	5.7
1885	Bos-N	22	27	.449	51	50	49	6	0	434¹	425	10	112	242	11.1	2.88	93	.246	.292	81	.240	5	-3	-9	6	0.0
1886	Bos-N	7	10	.412	18	17	16	0	0	151	203	4	39	47	14.4	4.59	70	.308	.346	51	.290	4	-21	-23	-1	-1.8
1887	Phi-N	21	17	.553	40	38	35	1	0	332¹	352	16	92	160	12.1	3.66	116	.264	.313	72	.268	2	15	21	7	2.6
1888	Phi-N	28	17	.622	46	46	43	6	0	400¹	324	6	59	199	8.7	1.91	155	.213	.244	29	.181	-1	42	47	10	**5.8**
1889	Phi-N	28	16	.636	47	43	37	2	0	380	390	10	121	153	12.2	3.24	130	.257	.315	32	.208	-3	33	47	2	4.3
1890	Phi-P	19	15	.559	36	33	28	0	1	283¹	312	8	126	89	14.1	3.81	112	.268	.343	41	.273	4	13	15	1	1.6
1891	Bos-a	29	9	**.763**	48	43	33	2	0	363²	303	8	120	158	**10.6**	2.55	137	.219	**.284**	34	.188	-0	47	38	6	3.6
1892	Bal-N	4	8	.333	13	13	9	0	0	97	130	4	36	30	16.6	4.92	70	.309	.381	15	.349	4	-18	-16	2	-1.1
Total	11	233	152	.605	414	396	351	30	3	3404	3344	87	856	1700	11.2	2.96	114	.246	.292	543	.245	27	162	161	35	20.3

● BOB BUHL
Buhl, Robert Ray b: 8/12/28, Saginaw, Mich. BR/TR, 6'2", 190 lbs. Deb: 4/17/53

YEAR	TM/L	W	L	PCT	G	GS	CG	SH	SV	IP	H	HR	BB	SO	RAT	ERA	ERA+	OAV	OOB	BH	AVG	PB	PR	/A	PD	TPI
1953	Mil-N	13	8	.619	30	18	8	3	0	154¹	133	9	73	83	12.2	2.97	132	.235	.326	6	.113	-3	23	16	1	1.8
1954	Mil-N	2	7	.222	31	14	2	1	3	110¹	117	5	65	57	15.0	4.00	93	.277	.376	1	.032	-3	1	-3	-0	-0.6
1955	Mil-N	13	11	.542	38	27	11	1	1	201²	168	13	109	117	12.4	3.21	117	.227	.327	6	.105	-4	18	12	-1	0.9
1956	Mil-N	18	8	.692	38	33	13	2	0	216²	190	18	105	86	12.3	3.32	104	.236	.326	7	.096	-4	11	3	0	0.0
1957	*Mil-N	18	7	**.720**	34	31	14	2	0	216²	191	15	121	117	13.0	2.74	128	.241	.341	6	.082	-3	27	18	-2	1.4
1958	Mil-N	5	2	.714	11	10	3	0	1	73	74	5	30	27	12.9	3.45	102	.260	.332	5	.200	0	4	1	1	0.2
1959	Mil-N	15	9	.625	31	25	12	**4**	0	198	181	19	74	105	11.7	2.86	124	.243	.313	4	.057	-5	24	15	3	1.5
1960	Mil-N★	16	9	.640	36	33	11	2	0	238²	202	23	103	121	11.6	3.09	111	.229	.312	14	.157	-4	18	9	3	1.0
1961	Mil-N	9	10	.474	32	28	9	1	0	188¹	180	23	98	77	13.5	4.11	91	.256	.351	4	.067	-4	-2	-8	1	-1.0
1962	Mil-N	0	1	.000	1	1	0	0	0	2	6	0	4	1	45.0	22.50	17	.545	.667	0	.000	-0	-4	-4	-0	-1.1
	Chi-N	12	13	.480	34	30	8	1	0	212	204	23	94	109	12.9	3.69	112	.255	.338	0	.000	-6	6	11	-2	0.4
	Yr	12	14	.462	35	31	8	1	0	214	210	23	98	110	13.2	3.87	107	.259	.343	0	.000	-6	2	7	-2	-0.7
1963	Chi-N	11	14	.440	37	34	9	0	0	226	219	24	62	108	11.3	3.38	104	.259	.312	8	.108	-3	-2	3	1	0.1
1964	Chi-N	15	14	.517	36	35	11	3	0	227²	208	22	68	107	11.1	3.83	94	.244	.303	7	.096	-2	-8	-3	2	-0.3
1965	Chi-N	13	11	.542	32	31	2	0	0	184¹	207	26	57	92	12.9	4.39	84	.284	.335	4	.060	-6	-17	-15	0	-2.2
1966	Chi-N	0	0	—	1	1	0	0	0	2¹	4	1	1	1	19.3	15.43	24	.400	.455	0	.000	-0	-3	-3	0	0.0
	Phi-N	6	8	.429	32	18	1	0	1	132	156	10	39	59	13.6	4.77	75	.298	.351	4	.098	-2	-17	-17	1	-1.8
	Yr	6	8	.429	33	19	1	0	1	134¹	160	11	40	60	13.7	4.96	73	.299	.352	4	.095	-2	-20	-20	1	-1.8
1967	Phi-N	0	0	—	3	0	0	0	0	3	6	2	2	1	24.0	12.00	28	.462	.533	0	—	-2	-3	-3	0	-0.2
Total	15	166	132	.557	457	369	111	20	6	2587	2446	238	1105	1268	12.5	3.55	103	.251	.330	76	.089	-43	75	36	8	0.3

● DE WAYNE BUICE
Buice, De Wayne Allison b: 8/20/57, Lynwood, Cal. BR/TR, 6', 170 lbs. Deb: 4/25/87

YEAR	TM/L	W	L	PCT	G	GS	CG	SH	SV	IP	H	HR	BB	SO	RAT	ERA	ERA+	OAV	OOB	BH	AVG	PB	PR	/A	PD	TPI
1987	Cal-A	6	7	.462	57	0	0	0	17	114	87	6	40	109	10.2	3.39	127	.213	.287	0	—	0	13	11	0	1.5
1988	Cal-A	2	4	.333	32	0	0	0	3	41¹	45	5	19	38	13.9	5.88	66	.287	.364	0	—	0	-9	-9	0	-1.2
1989	Tor-A	1	0	1.000	7	0	0	0	0	17	13	2	13	10	13.8	5.82	65	.220	.361	0	—	0	-4	-4	0	-0.2
Total	3	9	11	.450	96	0	0	0	20	172¹	145	19	72	157	11.4	4.23	98	.232	.314	0	—	0	1	-2	0	0.1

● CY BUKER
Buker, Cyril Owen b: 2/5/19, Greenwood, Wis. BL/TR, 5'11", 190 lbs. Deb: 5/17/45

YEAR	TM/L	W	L	PCT	G	GS	CG	SH	SV	IP	H	HR	BB	SO	RAT	ERA	ERA+	OAV	OOB	BH	AVG	PB	PR	/A	PD	TPI
1945	Bro-N	7	2	.778	42	4	0	0	5	87¹	90	2	45	48	14.0	3.30	114	.268	.356	3	.188	-0	5	4	-1	0.4

● JIM BULLINGER
Bullinger, James Eric b: 8/21/65, New Orleans, La. BR/TR, 6'2", 185 lbs. Deb: 5/27/92

YEAR	TM/L	W	L	PCT	G	GS	CG	SH	SV	IP	H	HR	BB	SO	RAT	ERA	ERA+	OAV	OOB	BH	AVG	PB	PR	/A	PD	TPI
1992	Chi-N	2	8	.200	39	9	1	0	7	85	72	9	54	36	13.8	4.66	77	.233	.354	5	.250	2	-11	-10	2	-0.9
1993	Chi-N	1	0	1.000	15	0	0	0	1	16²	18	1	9	10	14.6	4.32	92	.277	.365	0	.000	-1	-1	-1	-0	-0.1
1994	Chi-N	6	2	.750	33	10	1	0	2	100	87	6	34	72	11.0	3.60	114	.235	.300	3	.136	1	7	6	-1	0.4
Total	3	9	10	.474	87	19	2	0	10	201²	177	16	97	118	12.5	4.11	95	.238	.329	8	.186	2	-5	-5	1	-0.6

● RED BULLOCK
Bullock, Malton Joseph b: 10/12/11, Biloxi, Miss. d: 6/27/88, Pascagoula, Miss. BL/TL, 6'1", 192 lbs. Deb: 5/19/36

YEAR	TM/L	W	L	PCT	G	GS	CG	SH	SV	IP	H	HR	BB	SO	RAT	ERA	ERA+	OAV	OOB	BH	AVG	PB	PR	/A	PD	TPI
1936	Phi-A	0	2	.000	12	2	0	0	0	16²	19	0	37	7	30.2	14.04	36	.271	.523	0	.000	-1	-17	-17	0	-1.5

● WALLY BUNKER
Bunker, Wallace Edward b: 1/25/45, Seattle, Wash. BR/TR, 6'2", 197 lbs. Deb: 9/29/63

YEAR	TM/L	W	L	PCT	G	GS	CG	SH	SV	IP	H	HR	BB	SO	RAT	ERA	ERA+	OAV	OOB	BH	AVG	PB	PR	/A	PD	TPI
1963	Bal-A	0	1	.000	1	1	0	0	0	4	10	1	3	1	29.3	13.50	26	.476	.542	1	.500	0	-4	-4	-0	-0.7
1964	Bal-A	19	5	**.792**	29	29	12	1	0	214	161	17	62	96	9.5	2.69	133	.207	.269	5	.069	-2	22	21	1	2.2
1965	Bal-A	10	8	.556	34	27	4	1	2	189	170	16	58	84	11.0	3.38	103	.242	.303	4	.073	-1	2	2	-1	-0.1
1966	*Bal-A	10	6	.625	29	24	4	0	0	142²	151	16	48	89	12.7	4.29	78	.269	.329	5	.104	-0	-14	-15	-1	-1.7
1967	Bal-A	3	7	.300	29	9	1	0	1	88	83	7	31	51	11.9	4.09	77	.254	.322	2	.077	-2	-8	-9	1	-1.1
1968	Bal-A	0	1	.000	18	10	2	1	0	71	59	4	14	44	9.4	2.41	121	.225	.267	2	.111	-0	5	4	-0	0.1
1969	KC-A	12	11	.522	35	31	10	1	2	222²	198	29	62	130	10.7	3.23	114	.238	.294	10	.143	0	10	11	3	1.5
1970	KC-A	2	11	.154	24	15	2	1	0	121²	109	16	50	59	11.8	4.22	89	.238	.313	2	.065	-0	-7	-6	-1	-0.8
1971	KC-A	2	3	.400	7	6	1	0	0	32¹	35	7	6	15	11.4	5.01	68	.271	.304	0	.000	-1	-6	-6	-0	-0.8
Total	9	60	52	.536	206	152	34	5	5	1085¹	976	113	334	569	11.0	3.51	99	.240	.300	31	.094	-5	-3	-3	1	-1.5

● JIM BUNNING
Bunning, James Paul David b: 10/23/31, Southgate, Ky. BR/TR, 6'3", 195 lbs. Deb: 7/20/55

YEAR	TM/L	W	L	PCT	G	GS	CG	SH	SV	IP	H	HR	BB	SO	RAT	ERA	ERA+	OAV	OOB	BH	AVG	PB	PR	/A	PD	TPI
1955	Det-A	3	5	.375	15	8	0	0	1	51	59	8	32	37	16.6	6.35	60	.291	.395	3	.200	-0	-14	-14	0	-1.9
1956	Det-A	5	1	.833	15	3	0	0	1	53¹	55	8	28	34	14.0	3.71	111	.257	.343	6	.333	2	3	2	-1	0.4
1957	Det-A★	**20**	8	.714	45	30	14	1	1	**267¹**	214	33	72	182	10.0	2.69	143	.218	.279	20	.213	3	**33**	**35**	-5	3.3
1958	Det-A	14	12	.538	35	34	10	3	0	219²	188	28	79	177	11.3	3.52	115	.228	.304	14	.187	-1	6	12	-3	1.0
1959	Det-A★	17	13	.567	40	35	14	1	1	249²	220	37	75	**201**	11.0	3.89	104	.234	.298	17	.191	1	-1	-5	-5	0.1
1960	Det-A	11	14	.440	36	34	10	3	0	252	217	20	64	**201**	10.4	2.79	**142**	.236	.293	13	.160	-2	**30**	**33**	-1	2.6
1961	Det-A★	17	11	.607	38	37	12	4	1	268	232	25	71	194	10.5	3.19	128	.229	.285	13	.130	-4	25	27	-2	2.0
1962	Det-A★	19	10	.655	41	35	12	2	6	258	262	28	74	184	12.2	3.59	113	.261	.320	23	.242	4	11	14	-5	1.3
1963	Det-A★	12	13	.480	39	35	6	1	1	248¹	245	38	69	196	11.6	3.88	97	.254	.307	13	.155	-1	-7	-4	-2	-0.6
1964	Phi-N★	19	8	.704	41	39	13	5	2	284¹	248	23	46	219	9.7	2.63	132	.233	.274	12	.121	-2	29	27	-4	1.8

YEAR	TM/L	W	L	PCT	G	GS	CG	SH	SV	IP	H	HR	BB	SO	RAT	ERA	ERA+	OAV	OOB	BH	AVG	PB	PR	/A	PD	TPI
1965	Phi-N	19	9	.679	39	39	15	7	0	291	253	23	62	268	10.1	2.60	133	.232	.281	22	.214	4	30	28	0	3.1
1966	Phi-N★	19	14	.576	43	41	16	5	1	314	260	26	55	252	9.6	2.41	149	.223	.270	19	.179	1	42	41	-3	4.1
1967	Phi-N	17	15	.531	40	40	16	6	0	302¹	241	18	73	253	9.7	2.29	149	.217	.273	17	.163	2	36	38	-3	4.1
1968	Pit-N	4	14	.222	27	26	3	1	0	160	168	14	48	95	12.6	3.88	75	.272	.333	5	.098	-2	-16	-17	-3	-2.2
1969	Pit-N	10	9	.526	25	25	4	0	0	156	147	10	49	124	11.7	3.81	92	.249	.313	2	.043	-3	-4	-6	-3	-1.3
	LA-N	3	1	.750	9	9	1	0	0	56¹	65	5	10	33	12.1	3.36	98	.288	.321	2	.111	-1	-0	-1	-0.2	
	Yr	13	10	.565	34	34	5	0	0	212¹	212	15	59	157	11.5	3.69	93	.257	.307	4	.062	-4	-2	-6	-4	-1.5
1970	Phi-N	10	15	.400	34	33	4	0	0	219	233	19	56	147	12.2	4.11	97	.274	.325	9	.127	-2	-2	-3	-1	-0.6
1971	Phi-N	5	12	.294	29	16	1	0	1	110	126	11	37	58	13.8	5.48	64	.297	.362	3	.120	0	-25	-24	-0	-3.4
Total	17	224	184	.549	591	519	151	40	16	3760¹	3433	372	1000	2855	11.0	3.27	114	.242	.299	213	.167	-1	179	192	-41	13.6

● **DAVE BURBA**   Burba, David Allen   b: 7/7/66, Dayton, Ohio   BR/TR, 6'4", 220 lbs.   Deb: 9/8/90

YEAR	TM/L	W	L	PCT	G	GS	CG	SH	SV	IP	H	HR	BB	SO	RAT	ERA	ERA+	OAV	OOB	BH	AVG	PB	PR	/A	PD	TPI
1990	Sea-A	0	0	—	6	0	0	0	0	8	8	0	2	4	12.4	4.50	88	.267	.333	0	—	0	-1	-0	0	0.0
1991	Sea-A	2	2	.500	22	2	0	0	0	36²	34	6	14	16	11.8	3.68	112	.245	.314	0	—	0	2	2	-0	0.1
1992	SF-N	2	7	.222	23	11	0	0	0	70²	80	4	31	47	14.4	4.97	67	.287	.362	1	.067	-1	-11	-13	-1	-1.7
1993	SF-N	10	3	.769	54	5	0	0	0	95¹	95	14	37	88	12.7	4.25	92	.265	.338	5	.294	2	-2	-4	0	-0.3
1994	SF-N	3	6	.333	57	0	0	0	0	74	59	5	45	84	13.4	4.38	92	.221	.346	0	.000	-0	-1	-3	-1	-0.4
Total	5	17	18	.486	162	18	0	0	1	284²	276	29	129	239	13.2	4.39	87	.257	.343	6	.171	1	-14	-18	-2	-2.3

● **BILL BURBACH**   Burbach, William David   b: 8/22/47, Dickeyville, Wis.   BR/TR, 6'4", 215 lbs.   Deb: 4/11/69

YEAR	TM/L	W	L	PCT	G	GS	CG	SH	SV	IP	H	HR	BB	SO	RAT	ERA	ERA+	OAV	OOB	BH	AVG	PB	PR	/A	PD	TPI
1969	NY-A	6	8	.429	31	24	2	1	0	140²	112	15	102	82	13.8	3.65	95	.219	.351	4	.100	-1	-0	-3	-1	-0.4
1970	NY-A	0	2	.000	4	4	0	0	0	16²	23	2	9	10	17.8	10.26	34	.324	.407	0	.000	-1	-12	-12	-0	-1.2
1971	NY-A	0	1	.000	2	0	0	0	0	3¹	6	0	5	3	29.7	10.80	30	.400	.550	0	.000	-0	-3	-3	-0	-0.7
Total	3	6	11	.353	37	28	2	1	0	160²	141	17	116	95	14.6	4.48	78	.236	.363	4	.085	-2	-15	-18	-1	-2.3

● **LARRY BURCHART**   Burchart, Larry Wayne   b: 2/8/46, Tulsa, Okla.   BR/TR, 6'3", 205 lbs.   Deb: 4/10/69

YEAR	TM/L	W	L	PCT	G	GS	CG	SH	SV	IP	H	HR	BB	SO	RAT	ERA	ERA+	OAV	OOB	BH	AVG	PB	PR	/A	PD	TPI
1969	Cle-A	0	2	.000	29	0	0	0	0	42¹	42	2	24	26	14.2	4.25	89	.266	.366	0	—	0	-3	-2	-1	-0.2

● **FRED BURCHELL**   Burchell, Frederick Duff   b: 7/14/1879, Perth Amboy, N.J.   d: 11/20/51, Jordan, N.Y.   BR/TL, 5'11", 190 lbs.   Deb: 4/17/03

YEAR	TM/L	W	L	PCT	G	GS	CG	SH	SV	IP	H	HR	BB	SO	RAT	ERA	ERA+	OAV	OOB	BH	AVG	PB	PR	/A	PD	TPI
1903	Phi-N	0	3	.000	6	3	2	0	0	44	48	0	14	12	13.1	2.86	114	.293	.356	3	.188	-1	2	2	-0	0.0
1907	Bos-A	0	1	.000	2	1	0	0	0	10	8	0	2	6	9.9	2.70	96	.221	.281	1	.200	-0	-0	-0	-0	0.0
1908	Bos-A	10	8	.556	31	19	9	0	0	179²	161	2	65	94	11.9	2.96	83	.247	.326	17	.246	1	-11	-10	-2	-1.1
1909	Bos-A	3	3	.500	10	5	1	0	0	52	51	1	11	12	11.1	2.94	85	.271	.318	3	.158	-0	-3	-3	1	-0.3
Total	4	13	15	.464	49	28	12	0	0	285²	268	3	92	124	11.8	2.93	89	.258	.328	24	.220	-0	-12	-10	-2	-1.4

● **FREDDIE BURDETTE**   Burdette, Freddie Thomason   b: 9/15/36, Moultrie, Ga.   BR/TR, 6'1", 170 lbs.   Deb: 9/5/62

YEAR	TM/L	W	L	PCT	G	GS	CG	SH	SV	IP	H	HR	BB	SO	RAT	ERA	ERA+	OAV	OOB	BH	AVG	PB	PR	/A	PD	TPI
1962	Chi-N	0	0	—	8	0	0	0	1	9²	5	2	8	5	12.1	3.72	111	.161	.333	0	.000	-0	0	0	-0	0.0
1963	Chi-N	0	0	—	4	0	0	0	0	4²	5	1	2	1	13.5	3.86	91	.313	.389	0	—	0	-0	0	-0	0.0
1964	Chi-N	1	0	1.000	18	0	0	0	0	20	17	2	10	4	12.6	3.15	118	.243	.346	1	1.000	-0	1	1	-0	0.1
Total	3	1	0	1.000	30	0	0	0	1	34¹	27	5	20	10	12.6	3.41	112	.231	.348	1	.500	0	1	2	-0	0.1

● **LEW BURDETTE**   Burdette, Selva Lewis   b: 11/22/26, Nitro, W.Va.   BR/TR, 6'2", 190 lbs.   Deb: 9/26/50   C

YEAR	TM/L	W	L	PCT	G	GS	CG	SH	SV	IP	H	HR	BB	SO	RAT	ERA	ERA+	OAV	OOB	BH	AVG	PB	PR	/A	PD	TPI
1950	NY-A	0	0	—	2	0	0	0	0	1¹	3	0	4	0	20.3	6.75	64	.500	.500	0	—	0	-0	-0	0	0.0
1951	Bos-N	0	0	—	3	0	0	0	0	4¹	6	0	5	1	24.9	6.23	59	.375	.545	0	.000	-0	-1	-1	0	0.0
1952	Bos-N	6	11	.353	45	9	5	0	7	137	138	8	47	47	12.3	3.61	100	.265	.328	4	.114	-0	2	-0	1	0.0
1953	Mil-N	15	5	.750	46	13	6	1	8	175	177	7	56	58	12.2	3.24	121	.264	.326	9	.170	-1	20	13	2	1.5
1954	Mil-N	15	14	.517	38	32	13	4	0	238	224	17	62	79	11.0	2.76	135	.251	.302	7	.089	-5	35	26	1	2.5
1955	Mil-N	13	8	.619	42	33	11	2	0	230	253	25	73	70	13.0	4.03	93	.280	.337	20	.233	3	0	-7	2	-0.1
1956	Mil-N	19	10	.655	39	35	16	6	1	256¹	234	22	52	110	10.1	**2.70**	128	.241	.282	16	.186	1	30	22	1	2.6
1957	*Mil-N★	17	9	.654	37	33	14	1	0	256²	260	25	59	78	11.3	3.72	94	.264	.307	13	.148	1	5	-6	2	-0.3
1958	*Mil-N	20	10	**.667**	40	36	19	0	0	275¹	279	18	50	113	10.9	2.91	121	.264	.301	24	.242	9	**32**	19	3	3.1
1959	Mil-N★	**21**	15	.583	41	39	20	4	1	289²	312	38	38	105	10.9	4.07	87	.273	.297	21	.202	6	-4	-17	0	-1.3
1960	Mil-N	19	13	.594	45	32	**18**	4	4	275²	277	19	35	83	10.3	3.36	102	.260	.287	16	.176	5	12	2	5	1.2
1961	Mil-N	18	11	.621	40	36	14	3	0	272¹	295	31	33	92	10.9	4.00	94	.273	.296	21	.204	5	1	-8	2	0.0
1962	Mil-N	10	9	.526	37	19	6	1	2	143²	172	26	23	59	12.3	4.89	78	.294	.327	9	.176	-0	-15	-17	1	-1.9
1963	Mil-N	6	5	.545	15	13	4	1	0	84	71	15	24	28	10.3	3.64	88	.228	.285	1	.038	-0	-3	-4	-0	-0.6
	StL-N	3	8	.273	21	14	3	0	2	98	106	6	16	45	11.8	3.77	94	.278	.319	3	.097	-1	-5	-2	-2	-0.5
	Yr	9	13	.409	36	27	7	1	2	182	177	21	40	73	11.1	3.71	92	.255	.302	4	.070	-2	-9	-6	-2	-1.1
1964	StL-N	1	0	1.000	8	0	0	0	0	10	10	1	3	3	11.7	1.80	211	.256	.310	0	.000	-0	2	2	-0	0.2
	Chi-N	9	9	.500	28	17	8	2	0	131	152	15	19	40	11.8	4.88	76	.292	.319	12	.279	6	-20	-17	2	-1.4
	Yr	10	9	.526	36	17	8	2	0	141	162	16	22	43	11.8	4.66	80	.289	.317	12	.273	6	-18	-15	2	-1.2
1965	Chi-N	0	2	.000	7	3	0	0	0	20¹	26	3	4	5	13.7	5.31	69	.299	.337	2	.333	1	-4	-4	-0	-0.2
	Phi-N	3	3	.500	19	9	1	1	0	70²	95	5	17	23	14.9	5.48	63	.329	.376	6	.300	1	-15	-16	0	-1.1
	Yr	3	5	.375	26	12	1	1	0	91	121	8	21	28	14.5	5.44	65	.321	.365	8	.308	2	-19	-20	0	-1.3
1966	Cal-A	7	2	.778	54	0	0	0	5	79²	80	4	12	27	10.5	3.39	99	.268	.298	1	.125	-0	-0	-0	-1	-0.1
1967	Cal-A	1	0	1.000	19	0	0	0	0	18²	16	4	0	8	8.3	4.91	64	.232	.243	-0	—	0	-3	-4	-0	-0.2
Total	18	203	144	.585	626	373	158	33	31	3067¹	3186	289	628	1074	11.4	3.66	99	.268	.308	185	.183	30	68	-18	19	3.4

● **BILL BURDICK**   Burdick, William Byron   b: 10/11/1859, Austin, Minn.   d: 10/23/49, Spokane, Wash.   BR/TR,   Deb: 7/23/1888

YEAR	TM/L	W	L	PCT	G	GS	CG	SH	SV	IP	H	HR	BB	SO	RAT	ERA	ERA+	OAV	OOB	BH	AVG	PB	PR	/A	PD	TPI
1888	Ind-N	10	10	.500	20	20	20	0	0	176	168	12	43	55	11.1	2.81	105	.242	.292	10	.147	-2	1	3	-0	0.0
1889	Ind-N	2	4	.333	10	4	2	0	1	45²	58	7	13	16	14.0	4.53	92	.300	.344	2	.118	-0	-3	-2	-0	-0.2
Total	2	12	14	.462	30	24	22	0	1	221²	226	19	56	71	11.7	3.17	101	.255	.304	12	.141	-2	-2	1	-0	-0.2

● **TOM BURGMEIER**   Burgmeier, Thomas Henry   b: 8/2/43, St.Paul, Minn.   BL/TL, 5'11", 185 lbs.   Deb: 4/10/68   C

YEAR	TM/L	W	L	PCT	G	GS	CG	SH	SV	IP	H	HR	BB	SO	RAT	ERA	ERA+	OAV	OOB	BH	AVG	PB	PR	/A	PD	TPI
1968	Cal-A	1	4	.200	56	2	0	0	5	72²	65	5	24	33	11.0	4.33	67	.250	.313	0	.000	0	-11	-12	4	-0.6
1969	KC-A	3	1	.750	31	0	0	0	0	54	67	5	21	23	14.8	4.17	88	.316	.380	3	.167	-0	-3	-3	2	0.0
1970	KC-A	6	6	.500	41	0	0	0	1	68¹	59	6	23	43	10.8	3.16	118	.236	.300	2	.143	-0	4	4	2	0.9
1971	KC-A	9	7	.563	67	0	0	0	17	88¹	71	3	30	44	11.0	1.73	198	.223	.303	5	.250	2	17	17	3	4.4
1972	KC-A	6	2	.750	51	0	0	0	9	55¹	67	0	33	18	16.4	4.23	72	.313	.407	4	.333	1	-7	-7	1	-1.2
1973	KC-A	0	0	—	6	0	0	0	1	10	13	2	4	4	16.2	5.40	76	.310	.383	0	—	0	-2	-1	-0	-0.4
1974	Min-A	5	3	.625	50	0	0	0	4	91²	92	7	26	34	11.8	4.52	83	.270	.325	0	—	0	-9	-8	3	-0.6
1975	Min-A	5	8	.385	46	0	0	0	11	75²	76	7	23	41	11.9	3.09	125	.264	.321	0	—	0	6	6	0	1.2
1976	Min-A	8	1	.889	57	0	0	0	1	115¹	95	11	29	45	9.8	2.50	144	.226	.279	0	—	0	13	14	2	1.1
1977	Min-A	6	4	.600	61	0	0	0	7	97¹	113	15	33	35	13.7	5.09	78	.299	.358	0	—	0	-11	-12	1	-1.1
1978	Bos-A	2	1	.667	35	1	0	0	4	61¹	74	7	23	24	14.7	4.40	93	.302	.369	0	—	0	-4	-2	1	-0.2
1979	Bos-A	3	2	.600	44	0	0	0	9	88²	89	8	16	60	11.1	2.74	161	.263	.304	0	—	0	15	16	1	0.6
1980	Bos-A☆	5	4	.556	62	0	0	0	24	99	87	3	20	54	9.9	2.00	211	.241	.285	0	—	0	22	24	3	3.8
1981	Bos-A	4	5	.444	32	0	0	0	6	59²	61	5	17	35	12.4	2.87	135	.268	.329	0	—	0	5	7	1	1.0
1982	Bos-A	7	0	1.000	40	0	0	0	2	102¹	98	6	21	40	10.7	2.29	188	.259	.303	0	—	0	20	21	1	1.4
1983	Oak-A	6	7	.462	49	0	0	0	6	96	89	2	32	39	11.3	2.81	137	.244	.305	0	—	0	13	11	2	1.7
1984	Oak-A	3	0	1.000	17	0	0	0	2	23	15	2	8	8	9.0	2.35	159	.190	.264	0	—	0	4	4	0	0.8
Total	17	79	55	.590	745	3	0	0	102	1258²	1231	94	384	584	11.8	3.23	118	.261	.321	14	.212	2	72	81	27	12.8

● **ENRIQUE BURGOS**   Burgos, Enrique (Calles)   b: 10/7/65, Chorrera, Panama   BL/TL, 6'4", 195 lbs.   Deb: 7/15/93

YEAR	TM/L	W	L	PCT	G	GS	CG	SH	SV	IP	H	HR	BB	SO	RAT	ERA	ERA+	OAV	OOB	BH	AVG	PB	PR	/A	PD	TPI
1993	KC-A	0	1	.000	5	0	0	0	0	5	5	0	6	6	21.6	9.00	51	.238	.429	0	—	0	-3	-2	0	-0.8

YEAR TM/L	W	L	PCT	G	GS	CG	SH	SV	IP	H	HR	BB	SO	RAT	ERA	ERA+	OAV	OOB	BH	AVG	PB	PR	/A	PD	TPI

● **SANDY BURK** Burk, Charles Sanford b: 4/22/1887, Columbus, Ohio d: 10/11/34, Brooklyn, N.Y. BR/TR, 5'8", 155 lbs. Deb: 9/12/10

YEAR TM/L	W	L	PCT	G	GS	CG	SH	SV	IP	H	HR	BB	SO	RAT	ERA	ERA+	OAV	OOB	BH	AVG	PB	PR	/A	PD	TPI
1910 Bro-N	0	3	.000	4	3	1	0	0	19¹	17	0	27	14	21.4	6.05	50	.258	.484	0	.000	-1	-6	-6	0	-0.9
1911 Bro-N	1	3	.250	13	7	1	0	0	58	54	1	47	15	16.1	5.12	65	.261	.405	2	.105	-1	-11	-12	0	-0.8
1912 Bro-N	0	0	—	2	0	0	0	0	8¹	9	0	3	2	13.0	3.24	103	.273	.333	1	.250	0	0	0	0	0.0
StL-N	1	3	.250	12	4	2	0	1	44²	37	0	12	17	10.1	2.42	142	.236	.294	0	.000	-2	5	5	-1	0.2
Yr	1	3	.250	14	4	2	0	1	53	46	0	15	19	10.5	2.55	134	.242	.301	1	.067	-1	5	5	-1	0.2
1913 StL-N	0	2	.000	19	5	0	0	1	70	81	1	33	29	15.4	5.14	63	.290	.377	2	.091	-2	-15	-15	-0	-0.6
1915 Pit-F	2	0	1.000	2	2	1	0	0	18	8	0	11	9	9.5	1.00	271	.140	.279	1	.167	-0	3	3	-1	0.2
Total 5	4	11	.267	52	21	5	0	2	218¹	206	2	133	86	14.5	4.25	76	.258	.372	6	.090	-6	-24	-24	-2	-1.8

● **ELMER BURKART** Burkart, Elmer Robert "Swede" b: 2/1/17, Torresdale, Pa. BR/TR, 6'2", 190 lbs. Deb: 9/14/36

YEAR TM/L	W	L	PCT	G	GS	CG	SH	SV	IP	H	HR	BB	SO	RAT	ERA	ERA+	OAV	OOB	BH	AVG	PB	PR	/A	PD	TPI
1936 Phi-N	0	0	—	2	0	0	0	0	7²	4	0	12	2	18.8	3.52	129	.160	.432	0	.000	-0	0	1	0	0.0
1937 Phi-N	0	0	—	7	0	0	0	0	16	20	0	9	4	16.3	6.19	70	.323	.408	0	.000	-1	-4	-3	0	-0.1
1938 Phi-N	0	1	.000	2	1	1	0	0	10	12	0	3	1	14.4	4.50	86	.286	.348	0	.000	-0	-1	-1	-0	-0.1
1939 Phi-N	1	0	1.000	5	0	0	0	0	8¹	11	0	2	2	14.0	4.32	93	.344	.382	1	1.000	1	-0	-0	-0	-0.1
Total 4	1	1	.500	16	3	1	0	0	42	47	0	26	9	15.9	4.93	85	.292	.394	1	.083	-1	-5	-3	-0	-0.2

● **JAMES BURKE** Burke, James b: Attleboro, Mass. Deb: 6/10/1882

YEAR TM/L	W	L	PCT	G	GS	CG	SH	SV	IP	H	HR	BB	SO	RAT	ERA	ERA+	OAV	OOB	BH	AVG	PB	PR	/A	PD	TPI
1882 Buf-N	0	1	.000	1	1	0	0	0	4	10	0	0	0	22.5	11.25	26	.435	.435	0	.000	-1	-4	-4	1	-0.6
1883 Buf-N	0	0	—	1	1	0	0	0	8	9	0	3	1	13.5	5.63	56	.243	.300	1	.200	-0	-2	-2	-0	-0.0
1884 Bos-U	19	15	.559	38	36	34	0	0	322	326	10	31	255	10.0	2.85	84	.246	.263	41	.223	-7	-15	-17	-4	-2.3
Total 3	19	16	.543	40	38	34	0	0	334	345	10	34	256	10.2	3.02	80	.249	.267	42	.218	-8	-21	-23	-4	-2.9

● **JOHN BURKE** Burke, John Patrick b: 1/27/1877, Hazleton, Pa. d: 8/4/50, Jersey City, N.J. BR/TR, Deb: 6/27/02 ♦

YEAR TM/L	W	L	PCT	G	GS	CG	SH	SV	IP	H	HR	BB	SO	RAT	ERA	ERA+	OAV	OOB	BH	AVG	PB	PR	/A	PD	TPI
1902 NY-N	0	1	.000	2	1	1	0	0	14	21	0	3	3	15.4	5.79	48	.345	.376	2	.154	-0	-5	-5	0	-0.3

● **BOBBY BURKE** Burke, Robert James "Lefty" b: 1/23/07, Joliet, Ill. d: 2/8/71, Joliet, Ill. BL/TL, 6'0.5", 150 lbs. Deb: 4/16/27

YEAR TM/L	W	L	PCT	G	GS	CG	SH	SV	IP	H	HR	BB	SO	RAT	ERA	ERA+	OAV	OOB	BH	AVG	PB	PR	/A	PD	TPI
1927 Was-A	3	2	.600	36	6	1	0	0	100	91	6	32	20	11.7	3.96	103	.245	.316	3	.125	-2	2	1	0	-0.2
1928 Was-A	2	4	.333	26	7	2	1	0	85¹	87	1	18	27	11.3	3.90	103	.277	.320	5	.250	1	1	1	0	0.2
1929 Was-A	6	8	.429	37	17	4	0	0	141	154	6	55	51	13.6	4.79	89	.279	.349	6	.140	-3	-8	-9	-2	-1.2
1930 Was-A	3	4	.429	24	4	2	0	3	74¹	62	2	29	35	11.4	3.63	127	.229	.310	4	.174	-1	8	8	-1	0.5
1931 Was-A	8	3	.727	30	13	3	1	2	128²	124	6	50	38	12.3	4.27	101	.255	.327	10	.213	-0	2	0	0	0.0
1932 Was-A	3	6	.333	22	10	2	0	0	91	98	4	44	32	14.1	5.14	84	.272	.353	5	.200	-0	-7	-8	-1	-0.8
1933 Was-A	4	3	.571	25	6	4	1	0	64	64	1	31	28	13.6	3.23	129	.256	.343	4	.235	0	7	7	0	0.7
1934 Was-A	8	8	.500	37	15	7	1	0	168	155	2	72	52	12.2	3.21	134	.245	.323	13	.228	2	24	21	0	1.9
1935 Was-A	1	8	.111	15	10	2	0	0	66¹	90	7	27	16	16.1	7.46	58	.327	.391	4	.182	-0	-22	-23	1	-2.4
1937 Phi-N	0	0	—	2	0	0	0	0	0	1	0	2	0	∞	∞	—	.500	.750	0	—	0	-1	-1	0	-0.1
Total 10	38	46	.452	254	88	27	4	5	918²	926	35	360	299	12.8	4.29	99	.263	.336	54	.194	-3	6	3	-3	-1.4

● **STEVE BURKE** Burke, Steven Michael b: 3/5/55, Stockton, Cal. BB/TR, 6'2", 200 lbs. Deb: 9/10/77

YEAR TM/L	W	L	PCT	G	GS	CG	SH	SV	IP	H	HR	BB	SO	RAT	ERA	ERA+	OAV	OOB	BH	AVG	PB	PR	/A	PD	TPI
1977 Sea-A	0	1	.000	6	0	0	0	0	15²	12	0	7	6	10.9	2.87	143	.226	.317	0	—	0	2	2	0	0.2
1978 Sea-A	0	1	.000	18	0	0	0	0	49	46	2	24	16	13.0	3.49	109	.258	.350	0	—	0	1	2	0	0.1
Total 2	0	2	.000	24	0	0	0	0	64²	58	2	31	22	12.5	3.34	116	.251	.342	0	—	0	4	4	0	0.3

● **TIM BURKE** Burke, Timothy Philip b: 2/19/59, Omaha, Neb. BR/TR, 6'3", 205 lbs. Deb: 4/8/85

YEAR TM/L	W	L	PCT	G	GS	CG	SH	SV	IP	H	HR	BB	SO	RAT	ERA	ERA+	OAV	OOB	BH	AVG	PB	PR	/A	PD	TPI
1985 Mon-N	9	4	.692	**78**	0	0	0	8	120¹	86	9	44	87	10.2	2.39	142	.204	.290	1	.100	-0	**16**	13	1	1.6
1986 Mon-N	9	7	.563	68	2	0	0	4	101¹	103	7	46	82	13.6	2.93	126	.262	.345	0	.000	-0	9	9	1	1.4
1987 Mon-N	7	0	1.000	55	0	0	0	18	91	64	3	17	58	8.0	1.19	354	.196	.235	0	.000	-0	**29**	**30**	1	3.5
1988 Mon-N	3	5	.375	61	0	0	0	18	82	84	7	25	42	12.3	3.40	106	.272	.332	0	.000	-0	0	2	0	0.3
1989 Mon-N★	9	3	.750	68	0	0	0	28	84²	68	6	22	54	9.6	2.55	138	.225	.278	0	.000	-0	9	9	1	2.1
1990 Mon-N	3	3	.500	58	0	0	0	20	75	71	6	21	47	11.3	2.52	145	.247	.303	1	.167	0	11	9	2	1.5
1991 Mon-N	3	4	.429	37	0	0	0	5	46	41	3	14	25	11.5	4.11	88	.243	.316	0	.000	-0	-2	-3	0	-0.4
NY-N	3	3	.500	35	0	0	0	1	55²	55	5	12	34	10.8	2.75	132	.255	.294	0	.000	-1	6	6	1	0.6
Yr	6	7	.462	72	0	0	0	6	101²	96	8	26	59	10.8	3.36	108	.246	.293	0	.000	-1	4	3	1	0.2
1992 NY-N	1	2	.333	15	0	0	0	0	15²	26	1	3	7	16.7	5.74	60	.366	.392	0	—	0	-4	-4	0	-0.7
NY-A	2	2	.500	23	0	0	0	0	27²	26	2	15	8	13.7	3.25	120	.250	.350	0	—	0	2	2	1	0.4
Total 8	49	33	.598	498	2	0	0	102	699¹	624	49	219	444	11.1	2.72	135	.240	.294	2	.045	-2	76	74	7	10.3

● **BILL BURKE** Burke, William R. b: 11/1865, Cincinnati, Ohio d: 3/17/39, Atchison, Kan. 6', 200 lbs. Deb: 7/20/1887

YEAR TM/L	W	L	PCT	G	GS	CG	SH	SV	IP	H	HR	BB	SO	RAT	ERA	ERA+	OAV	OOB	BH	AVG	PB	PR	/A	PD	TPI
1887 Det-N	0	1	.000	2	2	1	0	0	15	21	0	5	3	16.8	6.00	67	.318	.384	2	.250	-0	-3	-3	-0	-0.2

● **BILLY BURKE** Burke, William Ignatius b: 7/11/1889, Clinton, Mass. d: 2/9/67, Worcester, Mass. BL/TL, 5'10", 165 lbs. Deb: 4/30/10

YEAR TM/L	W	L	PCT	G	GS	CG	SH	SV	IP	H	HR	BB	SO	RAT	ERA	ERA+	OAV	OOB	BH	AVG	PB	PR	/A	PD	TPI
1910 Bos-N	1	0	1.000	19	1	0	0	0	64	68	1	29	22	13.9	4.08	82	.302	.387	4	.190	-1	-7	-5	-1	-0.2
1911 Bos-N	0	1	.000	2	1	0	0	0	3¹	6	0	5	1	29.7	18.90	20	.429	.579	1	1.000	0	-6	-6	-0	-1.1
Total 2	1	1	.500	21	2	0	0	0	67¹	74	1	34	23	14.7	4.81	70	.310	.400	5	.227	-0	-13	-11	-2	-1.3

● **JESSE BURKETT** Burkett, Jesse Cail "Crab" b: 12/4/1868, Wheeling, W.Va. d: 5/27/53, Worcester, Mass. BL/TL, 5'8", 155 lbs. Deb: 4/22/1890 CH♦

YEAR TM/L	W	L	PCT	G	GS	CG	SH	SV	IP	H	HR	BB	SO	RAT	ERA	ERA+	OAV	OOB	BH	AVG	PB	PR	/A	PD	TPI
1890 NY-N	3	10	.231	21	12	6	0	0	118	134	3	92	82	18.3	5.57	63	.277	.407	124	.309	8	-26	-27	2	-1.7
1894 Cle-N	0	0	—	1	0	0	0	0	4	6	0	1	0	15.8	4.50	121	.342	.378	187	.358	0	0	0	0	-0.0
1902 StL-A	0	1	.000	1	0	0	0	0	1	4	0	1	2	45.0	9.00	39	.585	.638	169	.306	0	-1	-1	0	-0.4
Total 3	3	11	.214	23	12	6	0	0	123	144	3	94	84	18.4	5.56	64	.284	.409	2850	.338	9	-26	-27	2	-2.1

● **JOHN BURKETT** Burkett, John David b: 11/28/64, New Brighton, Pa. BR/TR, 6'2", 205 lbs. Deb: 9/15/87

YEAR TM/L	W	L	PCT	G	GS	CG	SH	SV	IP	H	HR	BB	SO	RAT	ERA	ERA+	OAV	OOB	BH	AVG	PB	PR	/A	PD	TPI
1987 SF-N	0	0	—	3	0	0	0	0	6	7	2	3	5	16.5	4.50	85	.304	.407	0	.000	-0	-0	-0	0	0.0
1990 SF-N	14	7	.667	33	32	2	0	1	204	201	18	61	118	11.7	3.79	96	.257	.314	3	.048	-3	-0	-3	-1	-0.7
1991 SF-N	12	11	.522	36	34	3	1	0	206²	223	19	60	131	12.8	4.18	86	.277	.335	5	.091	-1	-11	-14	-1	-1.6
1992 SF-N	13	9	.591	32	32	3	0	0	189²	194	13	45	107	11.5	3.84	86	.264	.310	1	.018	-3	-7	-11	-3	-1.8
1993 SF-N★	**22**	7	.759	34	34	2	1	0	231²	224	18	40	145	10.7	3.65	107	.255	.296	9	.118	-1	10	7	1	0.8
1994 SF-N	6	8	.429	25	25	0	0	0	159¹	176	14	36	85	12.4	3.62	111	.286	.332	3	.059	-4	11	7	0	0.2
Total 6	67	42	.615	163	157	10	3	1	997¹	1025	84	245	591	11.8	3.83	99	.267	.317	21	.070	-13	2	-15	-2	-3.1

● **KEN BURKHART** Burkhart, Kenneth William (b: Kenneth William Burkhardt) b: 11/18/16, Knoxville, Tenn. BR/TR, 6'1", 190 lbs. Deb: 4/21/45 U

YEAR TM/L	W	L	PCT	G	GS	CG	SH	SV	IP	H	HR	BB	SO	RAT	ERA	ERA+	OAV	OOB	BH	AVG	PB	PR	/A	PD	TPI
1945 StL-N	18	8	.692	42	22	12	4	2	217¹	206	9	66	67	11.4	2.90	129	.251	.309	13	.181	1	22	20	-1	2.2
1946 StL-N	6	3	.667	25	13	5	2	2	100	111	4	36	32	13.4	2.88	120	.282	.348	5	.147	-0	6	6	-2	0.4
1947 StL-N	3	6	.333	34	6	1	0	1	95	108	13	23	44	12.8	5.21	79	.292	.340	3	.125	-1	-12	-11	1	-1.0
1948 StL-N	0	0	—	20	0	0	0	1	37¹	50	4	14	16	15.9	5.54	74	.331	.395	1	.250	0	-7	-6	1	-0.7
Cin-N	0	3	.000	16	0	0	0	0	41²	42	3	16	14	12.7	6.91	57	.255	.324	3	.333	2	-14	-14	-0	-0.7
Yr	0	3	.000	36	0	0	0	1	79	92	7	30	30	14.0	6.27	64	.289	.352	4	.308	2	-20	-20	0	-0.7
1949 Cin-N	0	0	—	11	0	0	0	1	28¹	29	2	10	8	12.4	3.18	132	.282	.345	2	.286	0	3	3	0	0.1
Total 5	27	20	.574	148	41	18	6	7	519²	546	35	165	181	12.5	3.84	99	.273	.332	27	.180	2	-2	-1	-2	1.0

● **WALLY BURNETTE** Burnette, Wallace Harper b: 6/20/29, Blairs, Va. BR/TR, 6'0.5", 178 lbs. Deb: 7/15/56

YEAR TM/L	W	L	PCT	G	GS	CG	SH	SV	IP	H	HR	BB	SO	RAT	ERA	ERA+	OAV	OOB	BH	AVG	PB	PR	/A	PD	TPI
1956 KC-A	6	8	.429	18	14	4	1	0	121¹	115	13	39	54	11.6	2.89	150	.252	.314	2	.051	-4	17	19	-1	1.5
1957 KC-A	7	12	.368	38	9	1	0	1	113	115	8	44	57	12.7	4.30	92	.268	.338	8	.250	1	-6	-4	2	-0.4

YEAR	TM/L	W	L	PCT	G	GS	CG	SH	SV	IP	H	HR	BB	SO	RAT	ERA	ERA+	OAV	OOB	BH	AVG	PB	PR	/A	PD	TPI
1958	KC-A	1	1	.500	12	4	0	0	0	28¹	29	2	14	11	13.7	3.49	112	.264	.347	1	.167	0	1	1	-1	0.0
Total	3	14	21	.400	68	27	5	1	1	262²	259	23	97	122	12.3	3.56	116	.260	.328	11	.143	-4	11	16	1	1.1

● DENNIS BURNS
Burns, Dennis b: 5/24/1898, Tiff City, Mo. d: 5/21/69, Tulsa, Okla. BR/TR, 5'10", 180 lbs. Deb: 9/22/23

YEAR	TM/L	W	L	PCT	G	GS	CG	SH	SV	IP	H	HR	BB	SO	RAT	ERA	ERA+	OAV	OOB	BH	AVG	PB	PR	/A	PD	TPI
1923	Phi-A	2	1	.667	4	3	2	0	0	27	21	1	7	8	9.3	2.00	205	.210	.262	1	.111	-1	6	6	-0	0.6
1924	Phi-A	6	8	.429	37	17	7	0	1	154	191	3	68	26	15.2	5.08	84	.314	.384	6	.143	-2	-15	-14	-0	-1.3
Total	2	8	9	.471	41	20	9	0	1	181	212	4	75	34	14.3	4.62	92	.299	.367	7	.137	-3	-9	-7	-0	-0.7

● FARMER BURNS
Burns, James "Slab" b: Ashtabula, Ohio TR , 5'7", 168 lbs. Deb: 7/6/01

YEAR	TM/L	W	L	PCT	G	GS	CG	SH	SV	IP	H	HR	BB	SO	RAT	ERA	ERA+	OAV	OOB	BH	AVG	PB	PR	/A	PD	TPI
1901	StL-N	0	0	—	1	0	0	0	0	1	2	0	1	0	36.0	9.00	35	.411	.583	0	—	0	-1	-1	-0	0.0

● DICK BURNS
Burns, Richard Simon b: 12/26/1863, Holyoke, Mass. d: 11/16/37, Holyoke, Mass. BL/TL, 5'7", 140 lbs. Deb: 5/3/1883 ◆

YEAR	TM/L	W	L	PCT	G	GS	CG	SH	SV	IP	H	HR	BB	SO	RAT	ERA	ERA+	OAV	OOB	BH	AVG	PB	PR	/A	PD	TPI
1883	Det-N	2	12	.143	17	13	13	0	0	127²	172	8	33	30	14.5	4.51	69	.301	.339	26	.186	-2	-19	-20	-0	-1.8
1884	Cin-U	23	15	.605	40	40	34	1	0	329²	298	7	47	167	9.4	2.46	104	.225	.252	107	.306	3	-1	4	0	0.6
1885	StL-N	0	0	—	1	0	0	0	0	3	3	0	0	2	9.0	9.00	31	.250	.250	12	.222	0	-2	-2	1	0.1
Total	3	25	27	.481	58	53	47	1	0	460¹	473	15	80	199	10.2	3.07	89	.248	.278	145	.267	2	-22	-18	1	-1.1

● BRITT BURNS
Burns, Robert Britt b: 6/8/59, Houston, Tex. BL/TL, 6'5", 218 lbs. Deb: 8/5/78

YEAR	TM/L	W	L	PCT	G	GS	CG	SH	SV	IP	H	HR	BB	SO	RAT	ERA	ERA+	OAV	OOB	BH	AVG	PB	PR	/A	PD	TPI
1978	Chi-A	0	2	.000	2	2	0	0	0	7²	14	2	3	3	20.0	12.91	29	.378	.425	0	—	0	-8	-8	0	-1.3
1979	Chi-A	0	0	—	6	0	0	0	0	5	10	1	1	2	19.8	5.40	79	.435	.458	0	—	0	-1	-1	-0	-0.2
1980	Chi-A	15	13	.536	34	32	11	1	0	238	213	17	63	133	10.6	2.84	142	.241	.295	0	—	0	32	31	-1	3.5
1981	Chi-A☆	10	6	.625	24	23	5	1	0	156²	139	14	49	108	11.1	2.64	135	.238	.303	0	—	0	18	16	-4	1.3
1982	Chi-A	13	5	.722	28	28	5	1	0	169¹	168	12	67	116	12.6	4.04	100	.257	.329	0	—	0	1	-0	-3	-0.3
1983	*Chi-A	10	11	.476	29	26	8	4	0	173²	165	14	55	115	11.7	3.58	117	.249	.311	0	—	0	9	12	-2	1.0
1984	Chi-A	4	12	.250	34	16	2	0	3	117	130	7	45	85	13.8	5.00	83	.280	.349	0	—	0	-13	-11	-0	-1.4
1985	Chi-A	18	11	.621	36	34	8	1	0	227	206	26	79	172	11.4	3.96	109	.242	.308	0	—	0	5	9	-1	0.8
Total	8	70	60	.538	193	161	39	11	3	1094¹	1045	93	362	734	11.8	3.66	111	.251	.315	0	—	0	42	49	-11	3.6

● TOM BURNS
Burns, Thomas Everett b: 3/30/1857, Honesdale, Pa. d: 3/19/02, Jersey City, N.J. BR/TR, 5'7", 152 lbs. Deb: 5/1/1880 MU◆

YEAR	TM/L	W	L	PCT	G	GS	CG	SH	SV	IP	H	HR	BB	SO	RAT	ERA	ERA+	OAV	OOB	BH	AVG	PB	PR	/A	PD	TPI
1880	Chi-N	0	0	—	1	0	0	0	0	1¹	2	0	2	1	27.0	0.00	—	.250	.400	103	.309	0	0	0	0	0.0

● OYSTER BURNS
Burns, Thomas P. b: 9/6/1864, Philadelphia, Pa. d: 11/11/28, Brooklyn, N.Y. BR/TR, 5'8", 183 lbs. Deb: 8/18/1884 ◆

YEAR	TM/L	W	L	PCT	G	GS	CG	SH	SV	IP	H	HR	BB	SO	RAT	ERA	ERA+	OAV	OOB	BH	AVG	PB	PR	/A	PD	TPI
1884	Bal-a	0	0	—	2	0	0	0	1	9	12	0	6	6	14.0	3.00	116	.343	.378	39	.298	1	0	0	-0	0.0
1885	Bal-a	7	4	.636	15	11	10	1	3	105²	112	4	21	30	12.4	3.58	91	.266	.321	74	.231	3	-4	-4	-1	-0.2
1887	Bal-a	1	0	1.000	3	0	0	0	0	11¹	16	0	4	2	18.3	9.53	43	.291	.371	188	.341	2	-7	-7	-1	-0.4
1888	Bal-a	0	1	.000	5	0	0	0	0	12²	12	0	3	2	10.7	4.26	70	.241	.284	97	.298	2	-2	-2	-0	-0.1
Total	4	8	5	.615	25	11	10	1	4	138²	152	2	30	40	12.9	4.09	81	.271	.326	1389	.300	7	-12	-12	-2	-0.7

● TODD BURNS
Burns, Todd Edward b: 7/6/63, Maywood, Cal. BR/TR, 6'2", 186 lbs. Deb: 5/31/88

YEAR	TM/L	W	L	PCT	G	GS	CG	SH	SV	IP	H	HR	BB	SO	RAT	ERA	ERA+	OAV	OOB	BH	AVG	PB	PR	/A	PD	TPI
1988	*Oak-A	8	2	.800	17	14	2	0	1	102²	93	8	34	57	11.2	3.16	120	.241	.304	0	—	0	9	7	-1	0.8
1989	*Oak-A	6	5	.545	50	2	0	0	8	96¹	66	3	28	49	8.9	2.24	164	.196	.260	0	—	0	18	15	-1	2.0
1990	*Oak-A	3	3	.500	43	2	0	0	0	78²	78	8	32	43	12.6	2.97	125	.263	.334	0	—	0	8	6	-1	0.7
1991	Oak-A	1	0	1.000	9	0	0	0	0	13¹	10	2	8	3	12.2	3.38	114	.217	.333	0	—	0	1	1	0	0.4
1992	Tex-A	3	5	.375	35	10	0	0	1	103	97	8	32	55	11.6	3.84	99	.248	.311	0	—	0	1	-1	-1	-0.1
1993	Tex-A	0	4	.000	25	5	0	0	0	65	63	6	32	31	13.4	4.57	91	.253	.343	0	—	0	-2	-3	-1	-1.0
	StL-N	0	4	.000	24	0	0	0	0	30²	32	3	9	10	12.0	6.16	64	.274	.325	0	.000	-0	-7	-7	-1	-1.0
Total	6	21	23	.477	203	33	2	0	13	489²	439	43	175	252	11.4	3.47	110	.241	.310	0	.000	-0	28	19	-6	2.8

● BILL BURNS
Burns, William Thomas "Sleepy Bill" b: 1/29/1880, San Saba, Tex. d: 6/6/53, Ramona, Cal. BB/TL, 6'2", 195 lbs. Deb: 4/18/08

YEAR	TM/L	W	L	PCT	G	GS	CG	SH	SV	IP	H	HR	BB	SO	RAT	ERA	ERA+	OAV	OOB	BH	AVG	PB	PR	/A	PD	TPI
1908	Was-A	6	11	.353	23	19	11	2	0	165	135	3	18	55	8.6	1.69	135	.229	.257	8	.148	-1	13	11	3	1.4
1909	Was-A	1	1	.500	6	4	1	0	0	29¹	25	0	7	13	10.7	1.23	198	.229	.294	2	.182	-0	4	4	0	0.3
	Chi-A	7	13	.350	23	19	10	3	0	168	161	2	34	50	10.9	2.04	115	.264	.312	10	.172	2	8	6	1	1.0
	Yr	8	14	.364	29	23	11	3	0	197¹	186	2	41	63	10.7	1.92	123	.258	.305	12	.174	1	12	10	1	1.3
1910	Chi-A	0	0	—	1	0	0	0	0	0¹	0	0	1	0	27.0	0.00	—	.000	.500	0	—	0	0	0	0	0.0
	Cin-N	8	13	.381	31	21	13	2	0	178²	183	3	49	57	12.3	3.48	84	.273	.333	16	.262	2	-9	-11	-0	-0.9
1911	Cin-N	1	0	1.000	6	3	0	0	0	17²	17	1	3	5	11.7	3.06	108	.254	.315	3	.429	2	1	0	1	0.3
	Phi-N	6	10	.375	21	14	8	3	1	121	132	5	26	47	12.2	3.42	101	.287	.333	6	.150	-1	-0	0	2	0.0
	Yr	7	10	.412	27	17	8	3	2	138²	149	6	29	52	11.9	3.38	102	.281	.326	9	.191	0	1	0	3	0.3
1912	Det-A	1	4	.200	6	5	2	0	0	38²	52	0	9	6	14.7	5.35	61	.338	.382	3	.231	1	-9	-9	-0	-0.8
Total	5	30	52	.366	117	85	45	10	2	718²	705	14	147	233	11.1	2.72	100	.265	.313	48	.197	5	8	1	7	1.3

● PETE BURNSIDE
Burnside, Peter Willits b: 7/2/30, Evanston, Ill. BR/TL, 6'2", 190 lbs. Deb: 9/20/55

YEAR	TM/L	W	L	PCT	G	GS	CG	SH	SV	IP	H	HR	BB	SO	RAT	ERA	ERA+	OAV	OOB	BH	AVG	PB	PR	/A	PD	TPI
1955	NY-N	1	0	1.000	2	2	1	0	0	12²	10	1	9	2	13.5	2.84	142	.204	.328	1	.200	0	2	2	-0	0.1
1957	NY-N	1	4	.200	10	9	1	1	0	30²	47	5	13	18	17.9	8.80	45	.356	.418	0	.000	-1	-17	-17	-0	-2.3
1958	SF-N	0	0	—	6	1	0	0	0	10²	20	3	5	4	21.1	6.75	56	.400	.455	0	—	0	-3	-3	-0	0.0
1959	Det-A	1	3	.250	30	0	0	0	1	62	55	7	25	49	11.9	3.77	108	.237	.317	0	.000	-1	1	2	0	0.1
1960	Det-A	7	7	.500	31	15	2	0	2	113²	122	14	50	71	13.9	4.28	93	.277	.356	4	.148	-1	-5	-4	-1	-0.6
1961	Was-A	4	9	.308	33	16	4	2	2	113¹	106	11	51	56	12.7	4.53	89	.251	.335	2	.059	-3	-6	-6	-1	-1.0
1962	Was-A	5	11	.313	40	20	6	0	2	149²	152	20	51	74	12.3	4.45	91	.263	.325	2	.057	-3	-8	-7	-2	-1.1
1963	Bal-A	0	1	.000	6	1	0	0	0	7¹	11	0	2	6	17.2	4.91	71	.344	.400	0	.000	-0	-1	-1	-0	-0.2
	Was-A	0	1	.000	38	1	0	0	0	67¹	84	12	24	23	14.4	6.15	60	.308	.364	1	.091	-0	-19	-18	-1	-0.4
	Yr	0	2	.000	44	1	0	0	0	74²	95	12	26	29	14.6	6.03	61	.310	.364	1	.083	-1	-20	-19	-2	-0.6
Total	8	19	36	.345	196	64	14	3	7	567¹	607	73	230	303	13.5	4.81	82	.275	.347	10	.076	-8	-57	-53	-6	-5.4

● SHELDON BURNSIDE
Burnside, Sheldon John b: 12/22/54, South Bend, Ind. BR/TL, 6'5", 200 lbs. Deb: 9/4/78

YEAR	TM/L	W	L	PCT	G	GS	CG	SH	SV	IP	H	HR	BB	SO	RAT	ERA	ERA+	OAV	OOB	BH	AVG	PB	PR	/A	PD	TPI
1978	Det-A	0	0	—	2	0	0	0	0	4	4	0	2	3	13.5	9.00	43	.250	.333	0	—	0	-2	-2	-0	-0.2
1979	Det-A	1	1	.500	10	0	0	0	0	21¹	28	4	8	13	15.6	6.33	68	.333	.398	0	—	0	-5	-5	0	-0.6
1980	Cin-N	1	0	1.000	7	0	0	0	0	4²	6	1	1	2	13.5	1.93	185	.333	.368	0	.000	-0	1	1	1	0.2
Total	3	2	1	.667	19	0	0	0	0	30	38	5	11	18	15.0	6.00	69	.322	.385	0	—	0	-6	-6	1	-0.6

● GEORGE BURPO
Burpo, George Harvie b: 6/19/22, Jenkins, Ky. BR/TL, 6', 195 lbs. Deb: 6/9/46

YEAR	TM/L	W	L	PCT	G	GS	CG	SH	SV	IP	H	HR	BB	SO	RAT	ERA	ERA+	OAV	OOB	BH	AVG	PB	PR	/A	PD	TPI
1946	Cin-N	0	0	—	2	0	0	0	0	2¹	4	0	5	1	34.7	15.43	22	.400	.600	0	—	0	-3	-3	-0	0.0

● HARRY BURRELL
Burrell, Harry J. b: 5/26/1869, Bethel, Vt. d: 12/11/14, Omaha, Neb. BR/TR, Deb: 9/13/1891

YEAR	TM/L	W	L	PCT	G	GS	CG	SH	SV	IP	H	HR	BB	SO	RAT	ERA	ERA+	OAV	OOB	BH	AVG	PB	PR	/A	PD	TPI
1891	StL-a	4	2	.667	7	4	3	0	0	43	51	4	21	19	15.5	4.81	87	.285	.366	5	.227	-0	-5	-3	-0	-0.4

● AL BURRIS
Burris, Alva Burton b: 1/28/1874, Warwick, Md. d: 3/24/38, Salisbury, Md. BR/TR, Deb: 6/22/1894

YEAR	TM/L	W	L	PCT	G	GS	CG	SH	SV	IP	H	HR	BB	SO	RAT	ERA	ERA+	OAV	OOB	BH	AVG	PB	PR	/A	PD	TPI
1894	Phi-N	0	0	—	1	0	0	0	0	5	14	0	2	0	28.8	18.00	28	.493	.526	2	.500	1	-7	-7	0	0.0

● RAY BURRIS
Burris, Bertram Ray b: 8/22/50, Idabel, Okla. BR/TR, 6'5", 200 lbs. Deb: 4/8/73 C

YEAR	TM/L	W	L	PCT	G	GS	CG	SH	SV	IP	H	HR	BB	SO	RAT	ERA	ERA+	OAV	OOB	BH	AVG	PB	PR	/A	PD	TPI
1973	Chi-N	1	1	.500	31	1	0	0	2	64²	65	6	27	57	12.8	2.92	135	.261	.333	1	.143	0	5	7	1	0.3
1974	Chi-N	3	5	.375	40	4	0	0	1	75	91	8	26	40	14.5	6.60	58	.300	.363	1	.077	-1	-25	-23	-1	-2.5
1975	Chi-N	15	10	.600	36	35	8	2	0	238¹	259	26	73	108	12.7	4.12	93	.281	.339	5	.081	-1	-13	-7	-4	-1.0
1976	Chi-N	15	13	.536	37	36	10	4	0	249	251	22	70	112	11.8	3.11	124	.263	.317	9	.111	-4	11	21	0	1.9
1977	Chi-N	14	16	.467	39	39	5	1	0	221	270	29	67	105	13.8	4.72	85	.305	.356	12	.174	1	-20	-/8	3	-0.7
1978	Chi-N	7	13	.350	40	32	4	1	1	198²	210	15	79	94	13.5	4.76	85	.274	.349	7	.115	-1	-26	-16	2	-1.5

YEAR	TM/L	W	L	PCT	G	GS	CG	SH	SV	IP	H	HR	BB	SO	RAT	ERA	ERA+	OAV	OOB	BH	AVG	PB	PR	/A	PD	TPI
1979	Chi-N	0	0	—	14	0	0	0	0	21²	23	0	15	14	16.2	6.23	66	.284	.402	0	.000	0	-6	-5	0	0.1
	NY-A	1	3	.250	15	0	0	0	0	27²	40	5	10	19	16.3	6.18	66	.342	.394	0	—	0	-6	-6	-0	-0.6
	NY-N	0	2	.000	4	4	0	0	0	21²	21	2	6	10	11.6	3.32	109	.247	.304	1	.167	-0	1	1	0	0.1
1980	NY-N	7	13	.350	29	29	1	0	0	170¹	181	20	54	83	12.6	4.02	88	.277	.336	5	.098	-2	-8	-9	-1	-1.3
1981	*Mon-N	9	7	.563	22	21	4	0	0	135²	117	9	41	52	10.7	3.05	114	.235	.297	7	.189	1	7	7	1	0.7
1982	Mon-N	4	14	.222	37	15	2	0	2	123²	143	14	53	55	14.4	4.73	77	.297	.369	5	.179	1	-16	-15	-1	-2.0
1983	Mon-N	4	7	.364	40	17	2	1	0	154	139	13	56	100	11.5	3.68	97	.244	.314	9	.231	3	-1	-2	0	0.2
1984	Oak-A	13	10	.565	34	28	5	1	0	211²	193	15	90	93	12.4	3.15	119	.244	.327	0	—	0	20	14	-3	1.1
1985	Mil-A	9	13	.409	29	28	6	0	0	170¹	182	25	53	81	12.6	4.81	87	.272	.328	0	—	0	-13	-12	-1	-1.4
1986	StL-N	4	5	.444	23	10	0	0	0	82	92	13	32	34	14.0	5.60	65	.287	.359	4	.148	0	-17	-18	-1	-1.8
1987	Mil-A	2	2	.500	10	2	0	0	0	23	33	4	12	8	17.6	5.87	78	.351	.425	0	—	0	-4	-3	0	-0.6
Total	15	108	134	.446	480	302	47	10	4	2188¹	2310	221	764	1065	12.9	4.17	93	.274	.338	76	.151	-1	-110	-75	-6	-9.0

● JOHN BURROWS
Burrows, John   b: 10/30/13, Winnfield, La.   d: 4/27/87, Coal Run, Ohio   BR/TL, 5'10", 200 lbs.   Deb: 4/25/43

YEAR	TM/L	W	L	PCT	G	GS	CG	SH	SV	IP	H	HR	BB	SO	RAT	ERA	ERA+	OAV	OOB	BH	AVG	PB	PR	/A	PD	TPI
1943	Phi-A	0	1	.000	4	1	0	0	0	7²	8	0	9	3	21.1	8.22	41	.276	.462	0	.000	-0	-4	-4	-0	-0.5
	Chi-N	0	2	.000	23	1	0	0	2	32²	25	0	16	18	11.8	3.86	87	.205	.307	2	.667	1	-2	-2	0	0.0
1944	Chi-N	0	0	—	3	0	0	0	0	3	7	0	3	1	30.0	18.00	20	.467	.556	0	—	0	-5	-5	0	0.0
Total	2	0	3	.000	30	2	0	0	2	43¹	40	0	28	22	14.7	5.61	60	.241	.360	2	.500	1	-11	-11	0	-0.5

● TERRY BURROWS
Burrows, Terry Dale   b: 11/28/68, Lake Charles, La.   BL/TL, 6'1", 185 lbs.   Deb: 6/12/94

YEAR	TM/L	W	L	PCT	G	GS	CG	SH	SV	IP	H	HR	BB	SO	RAT	ERA	ERA+	OAV	OOB	BH	AVG	PB	PR	/A	PD	TPI
1994	Tex-A	0	0	—	1	0	0	0	0	1	1	1	1	1	18.0	9.00	50	.250	.400	0	—	0	-0	-0	0	0.5

● JIM BURTON
Burton, Jim Scott   b: 10/27/49, Royal Oak, Mich.   BR/TL, 6'3", 195 lbs.   Deb: 6/10/75

YEAR	TM/L	W	L	PCT	G	GS	CG	SH	SV	IP	H	HR	BB	SO	RAT	ERA	ERA+	OAV	OOB	BH	AVG	PB	PR	/A	PD	TPI
1975	*Bos-A	1	2	.333	29	4	0	0	1	53	58	6	19	39	13.1	2.89	141	.276	.336	0	—	0	5	7	0	-0.3
1977	Bos-A	0	0	—	1	0	0	0	0	2²	2	0	1	3	10.1	0.00	—	.200	.273	0	—	0	1	1	-0	-0.7
Total	2	1	2	.333	30	4	0	0	1	55²	60	6	20	42	12.9	2.75	149	.273	.333	0	—	0	6	8	-0	-1.0

● MOE BURTSCHY
Burtschy, Edward Frank   b: 4/18/22, Cincinnati, Ohio   BR/TR, 6'3", 208 lbs.   Deb: 6/17/50

YEAR	TM/L	W	L	PCT	G	GS	CG	SH	SV	IP	H	HR	BB	SO	RAT	ERA	ERA+	OAV	OOB	BH	AVG	PB	PR	/A	PD	TPI
1950	Phi-A	0	1	.000	9	1	0	0	0	19	22	2	21	12	20.8	7.11	64	.289	.449	0	.000	-0	-5	-5	-0	-0.2
1951	Phi-A	0	0	—	7	0	0	0	0	17	18	0	12	4	16.4	5.29	81	.277	.397	1	.333	0	-2	-2	0	0.0
1954	Phi-A	5	4	.556	46	0	0	0	4	94²	80	7	53	54	13.4	3.80	103	.234	.350	2	.118	-1	-1	1	0	0.0
1955	KC-A	2	0	1.000	7	0	0	0	0	11¹	17	0	10	9	22.2	10.32	40	.354	.475	1	.333	0	-8	-8	-0	-1.1
1956	KC-A	3	1	.750	21	0	0	0	0	43¹	41	6	30	18	15.4	3.95	110	.263	.392	1	.125	-1	1	2	2	0.3
Total	5	10	6	.625	90	1	0	0	4	185¹	178	15	126	97	15.4	4.71	88	.259	.385	5	.139	-1	-15	-12	1	-1.0

● DENNIS BURTT
Burtt, Dennis Allen   b: 11/29/57, San Diego, Cal.   BB/TR, 6', 180 lbs.   Deb: 9/4/85

YEAR	TM/L	W	L	PCT	G	GS	CG	SH	SV	IP	H	HR	BB	SO	RAT	ERA	ERA+	OAV	OOB	BH	AVG	PB	PR	/A	PD	TPI
1985	Min-A	2	2	.500	5	2	0	0	0	28¹	20	2	7	9	8.6	3.81	116	.200	.252	0	—	0	1	2	0	0.1
1986	Min-A	0	0	—	3	0	0	0	0	2	7	1	3	1	45.0	31.50	14	.538	.625	0	—	0	-6	-6	-0	-0.1
Total	2	2	2	.500	8	2	0	0	0	30¹	27	3	10	10	11.0	5.64	78	.239	.301	0	—	0	-5	-4	0	0.0

● DICK BURWELL
Burwell, Richard Matthew   b: 1/23/40, Alton, Ill.   BR/TR, 6'1", 190 lbs.   Deb: 9/13/60

YEAR	TM/L	W	L	PCT	G	GS	CG	SH	SV	IP	H	HR	BB	SO	RAT	ERA	ERA+	OAV	OOB	BH	AVG	PB	PR	/A	PD	TPI
1960	Chi-N	0	0	—	3	1	0	0	0	9²	11	2	7	1	17.7	5.59	68	.306	.432	1	.333	0	-2	-2	-0	0.0
1961	Chi-N	0	0	—	2	0	0	0	0	4	6	0	4	0	22.5	9.00	46	.375	.500	0	.000	-0	-2	-2	0	0.0
Total	2	0	0	—	5	1	0	0	0	13²	17	2	11	1	19.1	6.59	59	.327	.453	1	.250	0	-4	-4	0	0.0

● BILL BURWELL
Burwell, William Edwin   b: 3/27/1895, Jarbalo, Kan.   d: 6/11/73, Ormond Beach, Fla   BL/TR, 5'11", 175 lbs.   Deb: 5/1/20   MC

YEAR	TM/L	W	L	PCT	G	GS	CG	SH	SV	IP	H	HR	BB	SO	RAT	ERA	ERA+	OAV	OOB	BH	AVG	PB	PR	/A	PD	TPI
1920	StL-A	6	4	.600	33	2	0	0	4	113¹	133	5	42	30	14.2	3.65	107	.303	.369	7	.167	-2	2	3	-0	0.1
1921	StL-A	2	4	.333	33	3	1	0	2	84¹	102	2	29	17	14.2	5.12	87	.309	.368	6	.240	-0	-8	-6	-1	-0.1
1928	Pit-N	1	0	1.000	4	1	0	0	0	20²	18	2	8	2	11.3	5.23	78	.234	.306	2	.222	-0	-3	-3	0	-0.1
Total	3	9	8	.529	70	6	1	0	6	218¹	253	9	79	49	13.9	4.37	95	.299	.363	15	.197	-2	-9	-5	-1	-0.5

● STEVE BUSBY
Busby, Steven Lee   b: 9/29/49, Burbank, Cal.   BR/TR, 6'2", 205 lbs.   Deb: 9/8/72

YEAR	TM/L	W	L	PCT	G	GS	CG	SH	SV	IP	H	HR	BB	SO	RAT	ERA	ERA+	OAV	OOB	BH	AVG	PB	PR	/A	PD	TPI
1972	KC-A	3	1	.750	5	5	3	0	0	40	28	1	8	31	8.1	1.57	192	.200	.243	3	.200	0	7	6	-1	0.7
1973	KC-A	16	15	.516	37	37	7	1	0	238¹	246	18	105	174	13.5	4.23	97	.271	.350	0	—	0	-11	-3	2	-0.7
1974	KC-A☆	22	14	.611	38	38	20	3	0	292¹	284	14	92	198	11.9	3.39	113	.258	.320	0	—	0	8	14	3	1.5
1975	KC-A★	18	12	.600	34	34	18	3	0	260¹	233	18	81	160	11.0	3.08	125	.242	.303	0	—	0	20	22	4	2.6
1976	KC-A	3	3	.500	13	13	1	0	0	71²	58	7	49	29	13.8	4.40	80	.218	.346	0	—	0	-7	-7	-0	-0.6
1978	KC-A	1	0	1.000	7	5	0	0	0	21¹	24	2	15	10	17.3	7.59	50	.282	.402	0	—	0	-9	-9	-0	-0.6
1979	KC-A	6	6	.500	22	12	4	0	0	94¹	71	10	64	45	12.9	3.63	118	.220	.349	0	—	0	6	7	2	0.8
1980	KC-A	1	3	.250	11	6	0	0	0	42¹	59	3	19	12	17.0	6.17	66	.335	.406	0	—	0	-10	-10	-0	-0.9
Total	8	70	54	.565	167	150	53	7	0	1060²	1003	73	433	659	12.4	3.72	105	.253	.330	3	.200	0	4	20	10	2.8

● DON BUSCHHORN
Buschhorn, Donald Lee   b: 4/29/46, Independence, Mo.   BR/TR, 6', 170 lbs.   Deb: 5/15/65

YEAR	TM/L	W	L	PCT	G	GS	CG	SH	SV	IP	H	HR	BB	SO	RAT	ERA	ERA+	OAV	OOB	BH	AVG	PB	PR	/A	PD	TPI
1965	KC-A	0	1	.000	12	3	0	0	0	31	36	7	8	9	13.1	4.35	80	.295	.344	2	.500	1	-3	-3	-0	0.0

● GUY BUSH
Bush, Guy Terrell "The Mississippi Mudcat"   b: 8/23/01, Aberdeen, Miss.   d: 7/2/85, Shannon, Miss.   BR/TR, 6', 175 lbs.   Deb: 9/17/23

YEAR	TM/L	W	L	PCT	G	GS	CG	SH	SV	IP	H	HR	BB	SO	RAT	ERA	ERA+	OAV	OOB	BH	AVG	PB	PR	/A	PD	TPI
1923	Chi-N	0	0	—	1	0	0	0	0	1	1	0	2	0	9.0	0.00	—	.250	.250	0	—	0	0	0	0	0.0
1924	Chi-N	2	5	.286	16	8	4	0	0	80²	91	7	24	36	13.1	4.02	97	.285	.339	4	.154	-1	-1	-1	-2	-0.4
1925	Chi-N	6	13	.316	42	15	5	0	4	182	213	15	52	76	13.3	4.30	101	.300	.350	11	.193	-2	-1	0	4	0.2
1926	Chi-N	13	9	.591	35	16	7	2	2	157¹	149	3	42	32	11.1	2.86	134	.258	.311	8	.167	-2	17	17	-1	1.9
1927	Chi-N	10	10	.500	36	22	9	1	2	193¹	177	3	79	62	12.2	3.03	128	.250	.330	8	.123	-4	19	18	0	1.3
1928	Chi-N	15	6	.714	42	24	9	2	2	204¹	229	10	86	61	14.1	3.83	100	.293	.367	6	.082	-6	4	0	-1	-0.6
1929	*Chi-N	18	7	.720	**50**	29	18	2	**8**	270²	277	16	107	82	12.9	3.66	126	.265	.335	15	.165	-4	32	29	0	2.0
1930	Chi-N	15	10	.600	46	25	11	0	3	225	291	22	86	75	15.2	6.20	79	.316	.376	22	.282	3	-31	-33	1	-2.5
1931	Chi-N	16	8	.667	39	24	14	1	2	180¹	190	9	66	54	12.9	4.49	86	.268	.332	7	.123	-3	-13	-13	4	-1.3
1932	*Chi-N	19	11	.633	40	30	15	1	0	238²	262	13	70	73	12.8	3.21	118	.278	.332	15	.179	0	18	15	1	1.8
1933	Chi-N	20	12	.625	41	32	20	4	2	259	261	9	68	84	11.5	2.75	119	.257	.306	11	.125	-1	17	14	4	2.1
1934	Chi-N	18	10	.643	40	27	15	1	2	209¹	213	15	54	75	11.5	3.83	101	.262	.309	16	.229	1	5	1	1	0.3
1935	Pit-N	11	11	.500	41	25	8	1	2	204¹	237	16	40	42	12.4	4.32	95	.285	.321	8	.127	-1	-7	-5	-1	-0.6
1936	Pit-N	1	3	.250	16	0	0	0	2	34²	49	3	11	10	15.6	5.97	68	.336	.382	3	.333	-1	-8	-7	1	-0.7
	Bos-N	4	5	.444	15	11	5	0	0	90¹	98	2	20	28	11.8	3.39	113	.281	.320	3	.120	-1	6	4	1	0.4
	Yr	5	8	.385	31	11	5	0	2	125	147	5	31	38	12.8	4.10	95	.297	.338	6	.176	-0	-1	-3	1	-0.3
1937	Bos-N	8	15	.348	32	20	11	1	1	180²	201	8	48	56	12.4	3.54	101	.282	.328	6	.111	-2	8	1	1	0.0
1938	StL-N	0	1	.000	6	0	0	0	0	6	6	1	2	1	13.5	4.50	88	.286	.286	0	—	0	-0	-0	-0	-0.1
1945	Cin-N	0	0	—	4	0	0	0	0	4¹	5	0	3	1	16.6	8.31	45	.278	.381	0	—	0	-2	-2	0	-0.1
Total	17	176	136	.564	542	308	151	16	34	2722	2950	152	859	850	12.7	3.86	103	.277	.334	143	.161	-22	64	40	12	3.7

● JOE BUSH
Bush, Leslie Ambrose "Bullet Joe"   b: 11/27/1892, Brainerd, Minn.   d: 11/1/74, Ft.Lauderdale, Fla.   BR/TR, 5'9", 173 lbs.   Deb: 9/30/12

YEAR	TM/L	W	L	PCT	G	GS	CG	SH	SV	IP	H	HR	BB	SO	RAT	ERA	ERA+	OAV	OOB	BH	AVG	PB	PR	/A	PD	TPI
1912	Phi-A	0	0	—	1	1	0	0	0	8	14	0	4	3	20.3	7.88	39	.368	.429	2	.500	1	-4	-4	-0	0.1
1913	*Phi-A	15	6	.714	39	16	6	1	3	200¹	199	3	66	81	12.1	3.82	72	.248	.310	11	.157	-0	-20	-23	4	-2.0
1914	*Phi-A	16	12	.571	38	22	14	2	3	206	196	3	81	109	11.9	3.06	85	.242	.322	14	.189	2	-7	-10	-0	-1.2
1915	Phi-A	5	15	.250	25	18	8	0	0	145²	137	3	89	89	14.2	4.14	71	.263	.375	7	.143	-3	-19	-20	0	-2.7
1916	Phi-A	15	24	.385	40	33	25	8	0	286²	222	8	130	157	11.1	2.57	111	.219	.310	14	.140	-4	8	9	5	1.4
1917	Phi-A	11	17	.393	37	31	17	4	2	233¹	207	3	111	121	12.3	2.47	111	.241	.328	16	.200	1	5	7	0	1.1
1918	*Bos-A	15	15	.500	36	31	26	7	2	272²	241	3	91	125	11.1	2.11	127	.242	.307	27	.276	6	20	17	3	3.1

YEAR TM/L	W	L	PCT	G	GS	CG	SH	SV	IP	H	HR	BB	SO	RAT	ERA	ERA+	OAV	OOB	BH	AVG	PB	PR	/A	PD	TPI
1919 Bos-A	0	0	—	3	2	0	0	0	9	11	0	4	3	15.0	5.00	60	.324	.395	2	.400	1	-2	-2	0	0.1
1920 Bos-A	15	15	.500	35	32	18	0	1	243^2	287	3	94	88	14.4	4.25	86	.300	.369	25	.245	2	-12	-16	3	-1.4
1921 Bos-A	16	9	.640	37	32	21	3	1	254^1	244	10	93	96	12.1	3.50	121	.260	.330	39	.325	6	22	20	1	2.7
1922 *NY-A	26	7	**.788**	39	30	20	0	3	255^5	240	16	85	92	11.5	3.31	121	.252	.314	31	.326	8	21	20	1	3.1
1923 *NY-A	19	15	.559	37	30	22	3	0	275^2	263	7	117	125	12.6	3.43	115	.260	.340	31	.274	1	17	16	1	2.6
1924 NY-A	17	16	.515	39	31	19	3	1	252	262	9	109	80	13.5	3.57	116	.273	.352	42	.339	14	18	16	2	3.4
1925 StL-A	14	14	.500	33	28	15	2	0	208^2	230	18	91	63	13.9	5.09	92	.284	.357	26	.255	3	-16	-10	2	-0.4
1926 Was-A	1	8	.111	12	11	3	0	0	71^1	83	6	35	27	15.5	6.69	58	.292	.380	7	.233	1	-21	-22	0	-2.2
Pit-N	6	6	.500	19	11	9	2	3	110^2	97	7	35	38	10.9	3.01	131	.236	.299	13	.265	2	10	11	-1	1.3
1927 Pit-N	1	2	.333	5	3	0	0	0	6^2	14	1	5	1	25.7	13.50	30	.412	.487	3	.600	1	-7	-7	0	-2.1
NY-N	1	1	.500	3	2	1	0	0	12	18	1	5	6	17.3	7.50	51	.340	.397	2	.500	1	-5	-5	-0	-0.6
Yr	2	3	.400	8	5	1	0	0	18^2	32	2	10	7	20.3	9.64	41	.368	.433	5	.556	2	-12	-12	0	-2.7
1928 Phi-A	2	1	.667	11	2	1	0	1	35^1	39	1	18	15	14.8	5.09	79	.300	.389	1	.067	-1	-4	-4	1	-0.4
Total 17	195	183	.516	489	366	225	35	20	3087^1	2992	96	1263	1319	12.6	3.51	99	.259	.335	313	.253	49	4	-8	21	5.9

● JACK BUSHELMAN
Bushelman, John Francis b: 8/29/1885, Cincinnati, Ohio d: 10/26/55, Roanoke, Va. BR/TR, 6'2", 175 lbs. Deb: 10/5/09

YEAR TM/L	W	L	PCT	G	GS	CG	SH	SV	IP	H	HR	BB	SO	RAT	ERA	ERA+	OAV	OOB	BH	AVG	PB	PR	/A	PD	TPI
1909 Cin-N	0	1	.000	1	1	1	0	0	7	7	1	4	3	14.1	2.57	101	.241	.333	0	.000	-0	0	0	-0	-0.1
1911 Bos-A	0	1	.000	3	1	1	0	0	12	8	0	10	5	14.3	3.00	109	.186	.352	0	.000	-0	0	0	-0	-0.1
1912 Bos-A	1	0	1.000	3	0	0	0	0	7^2	9	0	5	5	16.4	4.70	72	.310	.412	0	.000	-0	-1	-1	0	-0.1
Total 3	1	2	.333	7	2	2	0	0	26^2	24	1	19	13	14.9	3.38	93	.238	.364	0	.000	-1	-1	-1	-0	-0.2

● FRANK BUSHEY
Bushey, Francis Clyde b: 8/1/06, Wheaton, Kan. d: 3/18/72, Topeka, Kan. BR/TR, 6', 180 lbs. Deb: 9/17/27

YEAR TM/L	W	L	PCT	G	GS	CG	SH	SV	IP	H	HR	BB	SO	RAT	ERA	ERA+	OAV	OOB	BH	AVG	PB	PR	/A	PD	TPI
1927 Bos-A	0	0	—	1	0	0	0	0	1^1	2	0	2	0	27.0	6.75	63	.500	.667	0	—	-0	-0	-0	0	0.0
1930 Bos-A	0	1	.000	11	0	0	0	0	30	34	1	15	4	15.3	6.30	73	.306	.398	1	.111	-1	-6	-6	0	-0.2
Total 2	0	1	.000	12	0	0	0	0	31^1	36	1	17	4	15.8	6.32	73	.313	.410	1	.111	-1	-6	-6	0	-0.2

● CHRIS BUSHING
Bushing, Christopher Shaun b: 11/4/67, Rockville Centre, N.Y. BR/TR, 6', 190 lbs. Deb: 9/3/93

YEAR TM/L	W	L	PCT	G	GS	CG	SH	SV	IP	H	HR	BB	SO	RAT	ERA	ERA+	OAV	OOB	BH	AVG	PB	PR	/A	PD	TPI
1993 Cin-N	0	0	—	6	0	0	0	0	4^1	9	1	4	3	27.0	12.46	32	.450	.542	0	—	0	-4	-4	-0	0.0

● TOM BUSKEY
Buskey, Thomas William b: 2/20/47, Harrisburg, Pa. BR/TR, 6'3", 220 lbs. Deb: 8/5/73

YEAR TM/L	W	L	PCT	G	GS	CG	SH	SV	IP	H	HR	BB	SO	RAT	ERA	ERA+	OAV	OOB	BH	AVG	PB	PR	/A	PD	TPI
1973 NY-A	0	1	.000	8	0	0	0	1	16^2	18	2	4	4	12.4	5.40	68	.286	.338	0	—	0	-3	-3	-0	0.0
1974 NY-A	0	1	.000	4	0	0	0	1	5^2	10	1	3	3	22.2	6.35	59	.400	.483	0	—	0	-2	-2	-0	-0.2
Cle-A	2	6	.250	51	0	0	0	17	93	93	10	33	40	12.3	3.19	113	.263	.327	0	—	0	4	4	1	0.7
Yr	2	7	.222	55	0	0	0	18	98^2	103	11	36	43	12.8	3.38	107	.271	.336	0	—	0	3	3	1	0.5
1975 Cle-A	5	3	.625	50	0	0	0	7	77	69	4	29	29	11.6	2.57	147	.252	.326	0	—	0	10	10	2	1.4
1976 Cle-A	5	4	.556	39	0	0	0	7	94^1	88	9	34	32	11.9	3.63	96	.256	.328	0	—	0	-1	-1	1	0.0
1977 Cle-A	0	0	—	21	0	0	0	0	34	45	6	8	15	14.3	5.29	74	.313	.353	0	—	0	-5	-5	-0	0.2
1978 Tor-A	0	1	.000	8	0	0	0	0	13^1	14	1	5	7	12.8	3.38	116	.275	.339	0	—	0	1	1	1	0.0
1979 Tor-A	6	10	.375	44	0	0	0	7	78^2	74	10	25	44	11.4	3.43	126	.249	.310	0	—	0	7	8	2	1.7
1980 Tor-A	3	1	.750	33	0	0	0	0	66^2	68	11	26	34	12.7	4.45	97	.278	.347	0	—	0	-3	-1	-0	-0.4
Total 8	21	27	.438	258	0	0	0	34	479^1	479	57	167	212	12.3	3.66	105	.267	.332	0	—	0	9	11	5	3.4

● MAX BUTCHER
Butcher, Albert Maxwell b: 9/21/10, Holden, W.Va. d: 9/15/57, Man, W.Va. BR/TR, 6'2", 220 lbs. Deb: 4/20/36

YEAR TM/L	W	L	PCT	G	GS	CG	SH	SV	IP	H	HR	BB	SO	RAT	ERA	ERA+	OAV	OOB	BH	AVG	PB	PR	/A	PD	TPI
1936 Bro-N	6	6	.500	38	15	5	0	2	147^2	154	11	59	55	13.0	3.96	104	.268	.337	6	.125	-3	1	3	-2	-0.2
1937 Bro-N	11	15	.423	39	24	8	1	0	191^2	203	12	75	57	13.4	4.27	94	.280	.354	10	.161	-1	-8	-5	3	-0.4
1938 Bro-N	5	4	.556	24	8	3	0	2	72^2	104	9	39	21	17.8	6.56	59	.334	.410	4	.160	0	-22	-21	1	-2.3
Phi-N	4	8	.333	12	12	11	0	0	98^1	94	6	31	29	11.6	2.93	133	.253	.314	9	.257	1	9	10	0	1.3
Yr	9	12	.429	36	20	14	0	2	171	198	15	70	50	14.2	4.47	87	.290	.358	13	.217	1	-13	-11	2	-1.0
1939 Phi-N	2	13	.133	19	16	3	0	0	104^1	131	10	51	27	15.8	5.61	71	.308	.383	7	.184	-1	-20	-19	-2	-2.5
Pit-N	4	4	.500	14	12	5	2	0	86^2	104	2	23	21	13.2	3.43	112	.297	.340	3	.097	-2	5	4	2	0.3
Yr	6	17	.261	33	28	8	2	0	191	235	12	74	48	14.6	4.62	85	.302	.363	10	.145	-3	-15	-15	-0	-2.2
1940 Pit-N	8	9	.471	35	24	6	2	2	136^1	161	13	46	40	13.7	6.01	63	.290	.346	15	.300	4	-33	-33	1	-3.2
1941 Pit-N	17	12	.586	33	32	19	0	0	236	249	11	66	61	12.1	3.05	118	.265	.314	15	.183	-1	15	15	0	1.7
1942 Pit-N	5	8	.385	24	18	9	0	1	150^2	144	7	44	49	11.3	2.93	116	.247	.303	7	.143	-2	6	8	0	0.5
1943 Pit-N	10	8	.556	33	21	10	2	1	193^2	191	6	57	45	11.6	2.60	134	.262	.317	10	.164	-1	17	19	0	1.6
1944 Pit-N	13	11	.542	35	27	13	5	1	199	216	8	46	43	11.9	3.12	119	.273	.314	12	.190	-1	11	13	3	1.7
1945 Pit-N	10	8	.556	28	20	12	2	0	169^1	184	5	46	37	12.4	3.03	130	.277	.328	12	.222	-1	15	17	1	1.8
Total 10	95	106	.473	334	229	104	14	9	1786^1	1935	100	583	485	12.8	3.73	101	.276	.333	110	.184	-6	-3	11	8	0.3

● JOHN BUTCHER
Butcher, John Daniel b: 3/8/57, Glendale, Cal. BR/TR, 6'4", 190 lbs. Deb: 9/8/80

YEAR TM/L	W	L	PCT	G	GS	CG	SH	SV	IP	H	HR	BB	SO	RAT	ERA	ERA+	OAV	OOB	BH	AVG	PB	PR	/A	PD	TPI
1980 Tex-A	3	3	.500	6	6	1	0	0	35^1	34	2	13	27	12.0	4.08	96	.248	.313	0	—	0	-0	-1	0	0.2
1981 Tex-A	1	2	.333	5	3	1	1	0	27^2	18	0	8	19	8.5	1.63	213	.186	.248	0	—	0	6	6	0	0.9
1982 Tex-A	1	5	.167	18	13	2	0	1	94^1	102	10	34	39	13.2	4.87	80	.280	.345	0	—	0	-8	-10	2	-0.4
1983 Tex-A	6	6	.500	38	6	1	1	5	123	128	8	41	58	12.4	3.51	114	.270	.329	0	—	0	8	7	0	0.8
1984 Min-A	13	11	.542	34	34	8	1	0	225	242	18	53	83	12.0	3.44	122	.276	.320	0	—	0	14	19	-1	1.6
1985 Min-A	11	14	.440	34	33	8	2	0	207^2	239	24	43	92	12.5	4.98	88	.289	.328	0	—	0	-19	-13	0	-1.5
1986 Min-A	0	3	.000	16	10	1	0	0	70	82	11	24	29	13.8	6.30	68	.294	.352	0	—	0	-17	-16	0	-0.7
Cle-A	1	5	.167	13	8	1	1	0	50^2	86	6	13	16	18.1	6.93	60	.381	.421	0	—	0	-15	-16	-1	-1.5
Yr	1	8	.111	29	18	2	1	0	120^2	168	17	37	45	15.5	6.56	65	.330	.379	0	—	0	-32	-31	-1	-2.2
Total 7	36	49	.424	164	113	23	6	6	833^2	931	79	229	363	12.7	4.42	94	.284	.334	0	—	0	-32	-24	1	-0.6

● MIKE BUTCHER
Butcher, Michael Dana b: 5/10/65, Davenport, Iowa BR/TR, 6'1", 200 lbs. Deb: 7/6/92

YEAR TM/L	W	L	PCT	G	GS	CG	SH	SV	IP	H	HR	BB	SO	RAT	ERA	ERA+	OAV	OOB	BH	AVG	PB	PR	/A	PD	TPI
1992 Cal-A	2	2	.500	19	0	0	0	0	27^2	29	3	13	24	14.3	3.25	122	.264	.352	0	—	0	2	2	-0	0.3
1993 Cal-A	1	0	1.000	23	0	0	0	8	28^1	21	2	15	24	12.1	2.86	158	.204	.317	0	—	0	5	5	-1	0.4
1994 Cal-A	2	1	.667	33	0	0	0	1	29^2	31	2	23	19	17.0	6.67	75	.274	.406	0	—	0	-6	-6	0	-0.7
Total 3	5	3	.625	75	0	0	0	9	85^2	81	7	51	67	14.5	4.31	104	.248	.360	0	—	0	1	2	-1	0.0

● SAL BUTERA
Butera, Salvatore Philip b: 9/25/52, Richmond Hill, N.Y BR/TR, 6', 190 lbs. Deb: 4/10/80 ◆

YEAR TM/L	W	L	PCT	G	GS	CG	SH	SV	IP	H	HR	BB	SO	RAT	ERA	ERA+	OAV	OOB	BH	AVG	PB	PR	/A	PD	TPI
1985 Mon-N	0	0	—	1	0	0	0	0	1	0	0	0	0	0.0	0.00	—	.000	.000	24	.200	0	0	0	-0	0.3
1986 Cin-N	0	0	—	1	0	0	0	0	1	0	0	1	1	9.0	0.00	—	.000	.250	27	.239	0	0	0	-0	0.0
Total 2	0	0	—	2	0	0	0	0	2	0	0	1	1	4.5	0.00	—	.000	.143	182	.227	0	1	1	-0	0.0

● BILL BUTLAND
Butland, Wilburn Rue b: 3/22/18, Terre Haute, Ind. BR/TL, 6'5", 185 lbs. Deb: 5/29/40

YEAR TM/L	W	L	PCT	G	GS	CG	SH	SV	IP	H	HR	BB	SO	RAT	ERA	ERA+	OAV	OOB	BH	AVG	PB	PR	/A	PD	TPI
1940 Bos-A	1	2	.333	3	3	1	0	0	21	27	0	10	5	15.9	5.57	81	.307	.378	0	.000	-1	-3	-3	1	-0.3
1942 Bos-A	7	1	.875	23	10	6	2	1	111^1	85	8	33	46	9.8	2.51	149	.206	.270	1	.036	-1	14	15	0	1.0
1946 Bos-A	1	0	1.000	5	2	0	0	0	16^1	23	3	13	10	19.8	11.02	33	.343	.450	1	.250	0	-14	-13	0	-0.7
1947 Bos-A	0	0	—	1	0	0	0	0	2	3	0	0	1	13.5	4.50	86	.333	.333	0	—	0	-0	-0	-0	0.0
Total 4	9	3	.750	32	15	7	2	1	150^2	138	11	56	62	11.8	3.88	99	.240	.310	2	.051	-2	-2	-1	1	0.0

● CECIL BUTLER
Butler, Cecil Dean "Slewfoot" b: 10/23/37, Dallas, Ga. BR/TR, 6'4", 195 lbs. Deb: 4/23/62

YEAR TM/L	W	L	PCT	G	GS	CG	SH	SV	IP	H	HR	BB	SO	RAT	ERA	ERA+	OAV	OOB	BH	AVG	PB	PR	/A	PD	TPI
1962 Mil-N	2	0	1.000	9	2	1	0	0	31	26	4	9	22	10.2	2.61	145	.217	.271	0	.000	-1	5	4	0	0.2
1964 Mil-N	0	0	—	2	0	0	0	0	4^1	7	2	0	2	14.5	8.31	94	.368	.368	0	—	0	-2	-2	0	0.0
Total 2	2	0	1.000	11	2	1	0	0	35^1	33	6	9	24	10.7	3.31	114	.237	.284	0	.000	-1	2	2	0	0.2

YEAR	TM/L	W	L	PCT	G	GS	CG	SH	SV	IP	H	HR	BB	SO	RAT	ERA	ERA+	OAV	OOB	BH	AVG	PB	PR	/A	PD	TPI

● CHARLIE BUTLER   Butler, Charles Thomas   b: 5/12/06, Green Cove Springs, Fla.   d: 5/10/64, Brunswick, Ga.   BR/TL, 6'1.5", 210 lbs.   Deb: 5/1/33

| 1933 | Phi-N | 0 | 0 | — | 1 | 0 | 0 | 0 | 0 | 1 | 1 | 0 | 2 | 0 | 27.0 | 9.00 | 42 | .250 | .500 | 0 | — | 0 | -1 | -1 | -0 | 0.0 |

● IKE BUTLER   Butler, Isaac Burr   b: 8/22/1873, Langston, Mich.   d: 3/17/48, Oakland, Cal.   TR, 6', 175 lbs.   Deb: 8/5/02

| 1902 | Bal-A | 1 | 10 | .091 | 16 | 14 | 12 | 0 | 0 | 116¹ | 168 | 1 | 45 | 13 | 16.6 | 5.34 | 71 | .338 | .395 | 6 | .113 | -3 | -23 | -20 | -1 | -1.9 |

● BILL BUTLER   Butler, William Franklin   b: 3/12/47, Hyattsville, Md.   BL/TL, 6'2", 210 lbs.   Deb: 4/9/69

1969	KC-A	9	10	.474	34	29	5	4	0	193²	174	15	91	156	12.5	3.90	94	.240	.328	3	.050	-4	-6	-5	-3	-1.1
1970	KC-A	4	12	.250	25	25	2	1	0	140²	117	17	87	75	13.1	3.77	99	.229	.342	2	.045	-3	-1	-1	-2	-0.6
1971	KC-A	1	2	.333	14	6	0	0	0	44¹	45	6	18	32	12.8	3.45	99	.268	.339	1	.083	-1	0	-0	-0	-0.1
1972	Cle-A	0	0	—	6	2	0	0	0	11²	9	1	10	6	14.7	1.54	208	.220	.373	0	.000	-0	2	2	-0	0.0
1974	Min-A	4	6	.400	26	12	2	0	1	98²	91	9	56	79	13.5	4.10	91	.251	.353	0	—	0	-5	-4	-2	-0.8
1975	Min-A	5	4	.556	23	8	1	0	0	81²	100	12	35	55	14.9	5.95	65	.301	.368	0	—	0	-20	-19	-0	-2.0
1977	Min-A	0	1	.000	6	4	0	0	0	21	19	5	15	5	15.0	6.86	58	.244	.372	0	—	0	-7	-7	-1	-0.2
Total	7	23	35	.397	134	86	10	5	1	591²	555	65	312	408	13.3	4.21	88	.250	.345	6	.051	-7	-37	-33	-9	-4.8

● TOM BUTTERS   Butters, Thomas Arden   b: 4/8/38, Delaware, O.   BR/TR, 6'2", 195 lbs.   Deb: 9/8/62

1962	Pit-N	0	0	—	4	0	0	0	0	6	5	0	6	10	18.0	1.50	262	.238	.429	0	—	0	2	2	-0	0.0
1963	Pit-N	0	0	—	6	1	0	0	0	16¹	15	1	8	11	13.8	4.41	75	.259	.368	1	.333	0	-2	-2	-0	0.0
1964	Pit-N	2	2	.500	28	4	0	0	0	64¹	52	5	37	58	12.5	2.38	148	.221	.327	2	.182	0	8	8	-1	0.4
1965	Pit-N	0	1	.000	5	0	0	0	0	9	9	2	5	6	14.0	7.00	50	.250	.341	0	—	0	-3	-3	-0	-0.4
Total	4	2	3	.400	43	5	0	0	0	95²	81	6	56	85	13.2	3.10	113	.231	.342	3	.200	0	4	4	-1	0.0

● FRANK BUTTERY   Buttery, Frank   b: 5/13/1851, Silvermine, Conn.   d: 12/16/02, Silvermine, Conn.   Deb: 4/26/1872 ♦

| 1872 | Man-n | 3 | 2 | .600 | 6 | 5 | 5 | 0 | 0 | 49 | 81 | 0 | 1 | 6 | 15.1 | 5.14 | 71 | .331 | .333 | 25′ | .269 | -0 | -8 | -8 | | -0.5 |

● RALPH BUXTON   Buxton, Ralph Stanley "Buck"   b: 6/7/11, Weyburn, Sask., Canada   d: 1/6/88, San Leandro, Cal.   BR/TR, 5'11.5", 163 lbs.   Deb: 9/11/38

1938	Phi-A	0	1	.000	5	0	0	0	0	9¹	12	1	5	9	16.4	4.82	100	.324	.405	0	.000	-0	-0	-0	-0	0.0
1949	NY-A	0	1	.000	14	0	0	0	2	26²	22	3	16	14	12.8	4.05	100	.229	.339	0	.000	-0	-0	-0	-1	-0.1
Total	2	0	2	.000	19	0	0	0	2	36	34	4	21	23	13.8	4.25	100	.256	.357	0	.000	-1	0	-0	-0	-0.1

● JOHN BUZHARDT   Buzhardt, John William   b: 8/17/36, Prosperity, S.C.   BR/TR, 6'2", 198 lbs.   Deb: 9/10/58

1958	Chi-N	3	0	1.000	6	2	1	0	0	24¹	16	2	7	9	8.5	1.85	212	.184	.245	1	.125	-0	6	6	1	0.7
1959	Chi-N	4	5	.444	31	10	1	1	0	101¹	107	12	29	33	12.2	4.97	79	.271	.322	2	.069	-1	-12	-12	1	-1.0
1960	Phi-N	5	16	.238	30	29	5	0	0	200¹	198	14	73	92	12.0	3.86	100	.259	.321	10	.161	-1	-2	0	-1	-0.1
1961	Phi-N	6	18	.250	41	27	6	1	0	202¹	200	28	65	92	12.1	4.49	91	.263	.326	6	.105	-2	-10	-9	0	-1.2
1962	Chi-A	8	12	.400	28	25	8	2	0	152¹	156	16	59	64	12.9	4.19	93	.264	.335	6	.118	-2	-4	-5	2	-0.6
1963	Chi-A	9	4	.692	19	18	6	3	0	126¹	100	8	31	59	9.7	2.42	145	.216	.273	4	.083	-3	17	15	1	1.4
1964	Chi-A	10	8	.556	31	25	8	3	0	160	150	13	35	97	10.6	2.98	116	.250	.295	11	.204	2	11	8	0	1.2
1965	Chi-A	13	8	.619	32	30	4	1	1	188²	167	12	56	108	11.0	3.01	106	.242	.305	7	.125	0	10	4	-1	0.3
1966	Chi-A	6	11	.353	33	22	5	4	1	150¹	144	13	30	66	10.7	3.83	83	.248	.289	5	.116	-1	-7	-11	3	-1.0
1967	Chi-A	3	9	.250	28	7	0	0	0	88²	100	11	37	33	14.5	3.96	78	.294	.373	4	.200	0	-7	-8	0	-1.1
	Bal-A	0	1	.000	7	1	0	0	0	11²	14	1	5	7	14.7	4.63	68	.298	.365	0	.000	-0	-2	-2	0	-0.1
	Yr	3	10	.231	35	8	0	0	0	100¹	114	12	42	40	14.0	4.04	77	.288	.356	4	.190	-0	-9	-10	1	-1.2
	Hou-N	0	0	—	1	0	0	0	0	0²	0	0	0	0	0.0	0.00	—	.000	.000	0	—	0	0	0	0	0.0
1968	Hou-N	4	4	.500	39	4	0	0	5	83²	73	0	35	37	12.0	3.12	95	.239	.325	4	.250	1	-1	-2	1	0.0
Total	11	71	96	.425	326	200	44	15	7	1490²	1425	130	457	678	11.6	3.66	97	.253	.314	60	.135	-7	-1	-16	7	-1.5

● BUD BYERLY   Byerly, Eldred William   b: 10/26/20, Webster Groves, Mo   BR/TR, 6'2.5", 185 lbs.   Deb: 9/26/43

1943	StL-N	1	0	1.000	2	2	0	0	0	13	14	0	5	6	13.2	3.46	97	.280	.345	0	.000	-0	-0	-0	-0	-0.1
1944	*StL-N	2	2	.500	9	4	2	0	0	42¹	37	2	20	13	12.1	3.40	104	.228	.313	2	.167	-0	1	1	1	0.1
1945	StL-N	4	5	.444	33	8	2	0	0	95	111	3	41	39	14.5	4.74	79	.288	.358	5	.217	1	-10	-10	2	-0.6
1950	Cin-N	0	1	.000	4	1	0	0	0	14²	12	1	4	5	9.8	2.45	173	.218	.271	0	.000	-0	3	3	-0	0.3
1951	Cin-N	2	1	.667	40	0	0	0	0	66	69	6	25	28	13.1	3.27	125	.267	.337	0	.000	-0	5	6	1	0.3
1952	Cin-N	0	1	.000	12	2	0	0	0	24²	29	1	9	14	13.1	5.11	74	.309	.356	1	.200	-0	-4	-4	0	-0.2
1956	Was-A	2	4	.333	25	0	0	0	4	51²	45	4	14	19	10.6	2.96	146	.243	.303	1	.091	-1	7	7	1	0.9
1957	Was-A	6	6	.500	47	0	0	0	6	95	94	6	22	39	11.1	3.13	125	.264	.309	1	.067	-1	7	8	1	1.1
1958	Was-A	2	0	1.000	17	0	0	0	1	24	34	4	11	13	17.3	6.75	56	.347	.418	0	.000	-0	-8	-8	-0	-0.7
	Bos-A	1	2	.333	18	0	0	0	0	30¹	31	1	7	16	11.6	1.78	225	.272	.320	0	.000	-1	7	7	0	0.6
	Yr	3	2	.600	35	0	0	0	1	54¹	65	5	18	29	13.9	3.98	99	.302	.359	0	—	-1	-0	-0	-0	-0.1
1959	SF-N	1	0	1.000	11	0	0	0	0	13	11	2	5	4	11.1	1.38	275	.234	.308	0	—	0	4	4	1	0.3
1960	SF-N	1	0	1.000	19	0	0	0	2	22	32	3	6	13	16.0	5.32	65	.340	.386	0	.000	-0	-4	-4	-0	-0.3
Total	11	22	22	.500	237	17	4	0	14	491²	519	34	167	209	12.7	3.70	105	.273	.335	10	.118	-4	8	10	4	1.5

● HARRY BYRD   Byrd, Harry Gladwin   b: 2/3/25, Darlington, S.C.   d: 5/14/85, Darlington, S.C.   BR/TR, 6'1", 188 lbs.   Deb: 4/21/50

1950	Phi-A	0	0	—	6	0	0	0	0	10²	25	3	9	2	30.4	16.88	27	.481	.571	0	.000	-0	-15	-15	-0	0.0
1952	Phi-A	15	15	.500	37	28	15	3	2	228¹	244	12	98	116	13.4	3.31	120	.274	.351	10	.133	-3	9	16	0	1.8
1953	Phi-A	11	20	.355	40	37	11	2	0	236²	279	23	115	122	15.5	5.51	78	.294	.379	18	.222	-1	-40	-32	-1	-3.8
1954	NY-A	9	7	.563	25	21	5	1	0	132¹	131	10	43	52	12.3	2.99	115	.258	.324	9	.196	1	11	7	-0	0.7
1955	Bal-A	3	2	.600	14	8	1	1	1	65¹	64	7	28	25	13.6	4.55	84	.261	.354	3	.158	-0	-4	-5	-1	-0.4
	Chi-A	4	6	.400	25	12	1	1	1	91	85	10	30	44	11.6	4.65	85	.251	.315	2	.067	-3	-7	-7	-0	-1.0
	Yr	7	8	.467	39	20	2	2	2	156¹	149	17	58	69	12.0	4.61	85	.251	.320	5	.102	-3	-11	-12	-1	-1.4
1956	Chi-A	0	1	.000	3	1	0	0	0	4¹	6	1	2	0	17.0	10.38	39	.474	.565	0	.000	-0	-3	-3	-0	-0.6
1957	Det-A	4	3	.571	37	1	0	0	5	59	53	6	28	20	12.7	3.36	115	.249	.342	0	.000	-1	3	3	-0	0.3
Total	7	46	54	.460	187	108	33	8	9	827²	890	71	355	381	14.0	4.35	91	.277	.356	42	.160	-8	-46	-36	-3	-3.0

● JEFF BYRD   Byrd, Jeffrey Alan   b: 11/11/56, LaMesa, Cal.   BR/TR, 6'3", 195 lbs.   Deb: 6/20/77

| 1977 | Tor-A | 2 | 13 | .133 | 17 | 17 | 1 | 0 | 0 | 87¹ | 98 | 5 | 68 | 40 | 17.1 | 6.18 | 68 | .286 | .404 | 0 | — | 0 | -21 | -19 | 1 | -2.8 |

● JERRY BYRNE   Byrne, Gerald Wilford   b: 2/2/07, Parnell, Mich.   d: 8/11/55, Lansing, Mich.   BR/TR, 6', 170 lbs.   Deb: 8/31/29

| 1929 | Chi-A | 0 | 1 | .000 | 3 | 1 | 0 | 0 | 0 | 7¹ | 11 | 0 | 6 | 1 | 20.9 | 7.36 | 58 | .379 | .486 | 0 | .000 | -0 | -3 | -3 | -0 | -0.3 |

● TOMMY BYRNE   Byrne, Thomas Joseph   b: 12/31/19, Baltimore, Md.   BL/TL, 6'1", 182 lbs.   Deb: 4/27/43

1943	NY-A	2	1	.667	11	2	0	0	0	31²	28	1	35	22	18.8	6.54	49	.248	.437	1	.091	-0	-11	-12	0	-1.0
1946	NY-A	0	1	.000	4	1	0	0	0	9¹	7	1	8	5	15.4	5.79	60	.194	.356	2	.222	-0	-2	-2	-0	-0.2
1947	NY-A	0	0	—	4	1	0	0	0	4¹	2	0	4	2	22.8	4.15	85	.294	.478	0	—	0	-0	-0	-0	0.0
1948	NY-A	8	5	.615	31	11	5	1	2	133²	79	8	101	93	12.7	3.30	124	.172	.332	15	.326	6	15	12	-1	1.5
1949	*NY-A	15	7	.682	32	30	12	3	0	196	125	11	179	129	14.6	3.72	109	**.183**	.362	16	.193	1	10	7	-3	0.5
1950	NY-A☆	15	9	.625	31	31	10	0	0	203¹	188	23	160	118	16.2	4.74	91	.245	.387	22	.272	7	-4	-10	-2	-0.5
1951	NY-A	2	1	.667	9	3	0	0	0	21	16	0	36	14	23.6	6.86	56	.213	.482	2	.222	1	-6	-7	-0	-0.8
	StL-A	4	10	.286	19	17	7	2	0	122²	104	5	114	57	16.9	3.82	115	.235	.404	16	.281	3	4	8	-1	1.1
	Yr	6	11	.353	28	20	7	2	0	143²	120	5	150	71	17.7	4.26	101	.230	.413	18	.273	4	-2	1	-1	0.3
1952	StL-A	7	14	.333	29	24	14	0	0	196	182	16	160	122	14.0	4.68	84	.247	.388	21	.250	3	-22	-17	-4	-1.5
1953	Chi-A	2	0	1.000	6	5	2	0	0	16	18	0	26	4	24.8	10.13	40	.295	.506	3	.167	1	-11	-11	-0	-1.0
	Was-A	0	5	.000	6	5	2	0	0	33²	35	3	22	22	15.5	4.28	91	.276	.387	1	.059	-1	-1	-1	-0	-0.2

YEAR	TM/L	W	L	PCT	G	GS	CG	SH	SV	IP	H	HR	BB	SO	RAT	ERA	ERA+	OAV	OOB	BH	AVG	PB	PR	/A	PD	TPI
	Yr	2	5	.286	12	11	2	0	0	49²	53	3	48	26	18.5	6.16	64	.282	.430	4	.114	-0	-12	-12	1	-1.2
1954	NY-A	3	2	.600	5	5	4	1	0	40	36	1	19	24	12.4	2.70	127	.240	.325	7	.368	4	5	3	0	0.9
1955	*NY-A	16	5	.762	27	22	9	3	2	160	137	12	87	76	13.0	3.15	119	.237	.344	16	.205	4	14	11	-1	1.6
1956	*NY-A	7	3	.700	37	8	1	0	6	109²	108	9	72	52	14.9	3.36	115	.262	.374	14	.269	6	10	6	1	1.2
1957	*NY-A	4	6	.400	30	4	1	0	2	84²	70	8	60	57	14.6	4.36	82	.227	.364	7	.189	-0	-5	-7	-1	-0.5
Total	13	85	69	.552	281	170	65	12	12	1362	1138	98	1037	766	14.9	4.11	97	.229	.371	143	.238	41	-5	-20	-11	1.1

● MARTY BYSTROM
Bystrom, Martin Eugene b: 7/26/58, Coral Gables, Fla.   BR/TR, 6'5", 200 lbs.   Deb: 9/7/80

YEAR	TM/L	W	L	PCT	G	GS	CG	SH	SV	IP	H	HR	BB	SO	RAT	ERA	ERA+	OAV	OOB	BH	AVG	PB	PR	/A	PD	TPI
1980	*Phi-N	5	0	1.000	6	5	1	0	0	36	26	1	9	21	8.8	1.50	252	.195	.246	1	.071	-1	8	9	1	1.4
1981	Phi-N	4	3	.571	9	9	1	0	0	53²	55	3	16	24	12.1	3.35	108	.264	.320	2	.118	-1	1	2	1	0.1
1982	Phi-N	5	6	.455	19	16	1	0	0	89	93	2	35	50	13.4	4.85	76	.277	.354	3	.125	-0	-12	-12	-1	-1.5
1983	*Phi-N	6	9	.400	24	23	1	1	0	119¹	136	6	44	87	14.1	4.60	77	.285	.353	9	.237	2	-13	-14	-1	-1.5
1984	Phi-N	4	4	.500	11	11	0	0	0	56²	66	5	22	36	14.0	5.08	71	.283	.345	3	.158	-0	-9	-9	-0	-1.2
	NY-A	2	2	.500	7	7	0	0	0	39¹	34	3	13	24	11.0	2.97	127	.230	.296	0	—	0	4	4	1	0.6
1985	NY-A	3	2	.600	8	8	0	0	0	41	44	8	19	16	14.0	5.71	70	.280	.362	0	—	0	-7	-8	-0	-0.6
Total	6	29	26	.527	84	79	4	2	0	435	454	28	158	258	13.0	4.26	86	.268	.336	18	.161	0	-28	-28	-1	-2.7

● GREG CADARET
Cadaret, Gregory James b: 2/27/62, Detroit, Mich.   BL/TL, 6'3", 205 lbs.   Deb: 7/5/87

YEAR	TM/L	W	L	PCT	G	GS	CG	SH	SV	IP	H	HR	BB	SO	RAT	ERA	ERA+	OAV	OOB	BH	AVG	PB	PR	/A	PD	TPI
1987	Oak-A	6	2	.750	29	0	0	0	0	39²	37	6	24	30	14.1	4.54	91	.252	.360	0	—	0	-0	-2	1	0.3
1988	*Oak-A	5	2	.714	58	0	0	0	3	71²	60	2	36	64	12.2	2.89	131	.226	.320	0	—	0	9	7	0	0.7
1989	Oak-A	0	0	—	26	0	0	0	0	27²	21	0	19	14	13.0	2.28	162	.214	.342	0	—	0	5	4	1	0.1
	NY-A	5	5	.500	20	13	3	1	0	92¹	109	7	38	66	14.5	4.58	84	.298	.367	0	—	0	-7	-7	0	-0.7
	Yr	5	5	.500	46	13	3	1	0	120	130	7	57	80	14.2	4.05	94	.279	.360	0	—	0	-2	-3	1	-0.6
1990	NY-A	5	4	.556	54	6	0	0	3	121¹	120	8	64	80	13.7	4.15	96	.268	.361	0	—	0	-3	-2	2	0.0
1991	NY-A	8	6	.571	68	5	0	0	3	121²	110	8	59	105	12.6	3.62	114	.246	.337	0	—	0	6	7	1	0.8
1992	NY-A	4	8	.333	46	11	1	1	1	103²	104	12	74	73	15.6	4.25	92	.267	.387	0	—	0	-4	-4	1	-0.3
1993	Cin-N	2	1	.667	34	0	0	0	1	32²	40	3	23	23	17.6	4.96	81	.305	.413	0	.000	-0	-3	-3	-0	-0.3
	KC-A	1	1	.500	13	0	0	0	0	15¹	14	0	7	2	12.9	2.93	156	.264	.361	0	—	0	2	3	0	0.3
1994	Tor-A	0	1	.000	21	0	0	0	0	20	24	4	17	15	18.4	5.85	82	.289	.410	0	—	0	-2	-2	0	-0.1
	Det-A	1	0	1.000	17	0	0	0	0	20	17	0	16	14	14.8	3.60	132	.227	.363	0	—	0	3	3	0	0.2
	Yr	1	1	.500	38	0	0	0	2	40	41	4	33	29	16.6	4.72	101	.259	.387	0	—	0	0	0	0	0.1
Total	8	37	30	.552	386	35	4	2	13	666	656	50	377	486	14.1	3.99	101	.262	.361	0	.000	-0	5	3	6	1.0

● LEON CADORE
Cadore, Leon Joseph "Caddy" b: 11/20/1890, Chicago, Ill.   d: 3/16/58, Spokane, Wash.   BR/TR, 6'1", 190 lbs.   Deb: 4/28/15

YEAR	TM/L	W	L	PCT	G	GS	CG	SH	SV	IP	H	HR	BB	SO	RAT	ERA	ERA+	OAV	OOB	BH	AVG	PB	PR	/A	PD	TPI
1915	Bro-N	0	2	.000	7	2	1	0	0	21	28	0	8	12	16.3	5.57	50	.337	.409	0	.000	-1	-7	-7	0	-0.7
1916	Bro-N	0	0	—	1	0	0	0	0	6	10	0	0	2	15.0	4.50	60	.370	.370	0	.000	-0	-1	-1	0	0.0
1917	Bro-N	13	13	.500	37	30	21	1	3	264	231	3	63	115	10.3	2.45	114	.241	.292	24	.261	5	8	10	-2	1.4
1918	Bro-N	1	0	1.000	2	1	1	0	0	17	10	0	2	5	4.8	0.53	526	.115	.164	0	.000	-0	4	4	0	0.2
1919	Bro-N	14	12	.538	35	27	16	3	0	250²	228	5	39	94	9.8	2.37	125	.245	.280	14	.161	-3	15	17	-3	1.0
1920	*Bro-N	15	14	.517	35	30	16	4	0	254¹	256	4	56	79	11.1	2.62	122	.270	.313	20	.220	2	15	17	1	2.3
1921	Bro-N	13	14	.481	35	30	12	1	0	211²	243	17	46	79	12.5	4.17	93	.292	.334	14	.187	-1	-9	-7	-1	-1.0
1922	Bro-N	8	15	.348	29	21	13	0	0	190¹	224	13	57	49	13.3	4.35	94	.299	.349	19	.268	4	-5	-6	-3	-0.5
1923	Bro-N	4	1	.800	8	4	3	0	0	36	39	2	13	5	13.0	3.25	119	.291	.354	1	.077	-1	3	3	-1	0.1
	Chi-A	0	1	1.000	1	1	0	0	0	2¹	6	0	2	3	30.9	23.14	17	.500	.571	0	—	0	-5	-5	-0	-1.1
1924	NY-N	0	0	—	2	0	0	0	0	4	2	0	3	2	11.3			.154	.313	0	—	0	2	2	0	0.0
Total	10	68	72	.486	192	147	83	10	3	1257¹	1273	44	289	445	11.4	3.14	106	.269	.314	92	.208	5	19	27	-8	1.7

● CHARLIE CADY
Cady, Charles B. b: 12/1865, Chicago, Ill.   d: 6/7/09, Kankakee, Ill.   5'11", 180 lbs.   Deb: 9/5/1883   ◆

YEAR	TM/L	W	L	PCT	G	GS	CG	SH	SV	IP	H	HR	BB	SO	RAT	ERA	ERA+	OAV	OOB	BH	AVG	PB	PR	/A	PD	TPI
1883	Cle-N	0	1	.000	1	1	1	0	0	8	13	0	4	6	19.1	7.88	40	.361	.425	0	.000	-1	-4	-4	-0	-0.4
1884	CP-U	3	1	.750	4	4	4	0	0	35	37	0	13	15	12.9	2.83	86	.254	.315	2	.100	-1	-2	-2	-0	-0.3
Total	2	3	2	.600	5	5	5	0	0	43	50	0	17	20	14.0	3.77	68	.275	.337	2	.059	-2	-6	-6	-0	-0.7

● JOHN CAHILL
Cahill, John Patrick Francis "Patsy" b: 4/30/1865, San Francisco, Cal.   d: 10/31/01, Pleasanton, Cal.   BR/TR, 5'7.5", 168 lbs.   Deb: 5/31/1884   ◆

YEAR	TM/L	W	L	PCT	G	GS	CG	SH	SV	IP	H	HR	BB	SO	RAT	ERA	ERA+	OAV	OOB	BH	AVG	PB	PR	/A	PD	TPI
1884	Col-a	1	0	1.000	2	1	1	0	0	16	15	0	4	1	12.4	5.06	60	.211	.282	46	.219	0	-3	-4	-0	-0.2
1886	StL-N	1	0	1.000	2	0	0	0	0	12	11	0	3	2	10.5	3.00	108	.268	.318	92	.199	0	0	0	0	0.0
1887	Ind-N	0	2	.000	6	1	1	0	0	22	40	2	19	5	25.0	14.32	29	.430	.535	54	.205	-1	-25	-25	-1	-1.6
Total	3	2	2	.500	10	2	2	0	0	50	66	2	26	8	17.5	8.64	41	.322	.411	192	.205	-1	-28	-28	-1	-1.8

● LES CAIN
Cain, Leslie b: 1/13/48, San Luis Obispo, Cal.   BL/TL, 6'1", 200 lbs.   Deb: 4/28/68

YEAR	TM/L	W	L	PCT	G	GS	CG	SH	SV	IP	H	HR	BB	SO	RAT	ERA	ERA+	OAV	OOB	BH	AVG	PB	PR	/A	PD	TPI
1968	Det-A	1	0	1.000	8	4	0	0	0	24	25	1	20	13	16.9	3.00	100	.269	.398	1	.143	-0	-0	0	0	0.1
1970	Det-A	12	7	.632	29	29	6	0	0	180²	167	16	98	156	13.5	3.84	97	.247	.349	11	.162	0	-2	-2	-0	-0.2
1971	Det-A	10	9	.526	26	26	3	1	0	144²	121	14	91	118	13.6	4.35	82	.228	.348	8	.145	-0	-14	-12	-1	-1.6
1972	Det-A	0	3	.000	5	5	0	0	0	23²	18	2	16	16	12.9	3.80	83	.209	.333	1	.143	-0	-2	-2	-0	-0.3
Total	4	23	19	.548	68	64	8	1	0	373	331	32	225	303	13.7	3.98	90	.233	.351	21	.153	-0	-19	-16	-1	-2.0

● SUGAR CAIN
Cain, Merritt Patrick b: 4/5/07, Macon, Ga.   d: 4/3/75, Atlanta, Ga.   BL/TR, 5'11", 190 lbs.   Deb: 4/15/32

YEAR	TM/L	W	L	PCT	G	GS	CG	SH	SV	IP	H	HR	BB	SO	RAT	ERA	ERA+	OAV	OOB	BH	AVG	PB	PR	/A	PD	TPI
1932	Phi-A	3	4	.429	10	6	3	0	0	45	42	1	28	24	14.0	5.00	90	.256	.365	3	.250	1	-3	-2	-0	-0.3
1933	Phi-A	13	12	.520	38	32	16	1	1	218	244	18	137	43	15.9	4.25	101	.280	.379	16	.200	-1	1	1	-1	-0.1
1934	Phi-A	9	17	.346	36	32	15	0	0	230²	235	15	128	66	14.3	4.41	99	.266	.360	13	.159	-3	2	-1	-1	-0.4
1935	Phi-A	0	5	.000	6	5	0	0	0	26	39	1	19	5	20.1	6.58	69	.382	.479	0	.000	-1	-6	-6	0	-1.0
	StL-A	9	8	.529	31	24	8	0	0	167²	197	7	104	68	16.4	5.26	91	.290	.388	11	.193	-2	-15	-9	-3	-1.2
	Yr	9	13	.409	37	29	8	0	0	193²	236	8	123	73	16.9	5.44	88	.302	.400	11	.169	-4	-21	-15	-3	-2.2
1936	StL-A	1	1	.500	4	3	1	0	0	16¹	20	0	9	8	16.0	6.61	81	.286	.367	2	.286	-0	-3	-2	-0	-0.2
	Chi-A	14	10	.583	30	26	14	1	0	195¹	228	18	75	42	14.2	4.75	110	.293	.359	7	.103	-4	6	10	-3	0.4
	Yr	15	11	.577	34	29	15	1	0	211²	248	18	84	50	14.3	4.89	107	.292	.360	9	.120	-4	3	8	-3	0.2
1937	Chi-A	4	2	.667	18	6	1	0	0	68²	88	7	51	17	18.2	6.16	75	.325	.432	4	.182	-1	-12	-12	-0	-0.9
1938	Chi-A	0	1	.000	5	0	0	0	0	19²	26	0	18	6	20.1	4.58	107	.321	.444	0	.000	-1	0	1	-1	-0.2
Total	7	53	60	.469	178	137	58	2	1	987¹	1119	67	569	279	15.5	4.83	96	.287	.380	56	.163	-13	-29	-21	-9	-3.9

● BOB CAIN
Cain, Robert Max "Sugar" b: 10/16/24, Longford, Kan.   BL/TL, 6', 165 lbs.   Deb: 9/18/49   ◆

YEAR	TM/L	W	L	PCT	G	GS	CG	SH	SV	IP	H	HR	BB	SO	RAT	ERA	ERA+	OAV	OOB	BH	AVG	PB	PR	/A	PD	TPI
1949	Chi-A	0	0	—	6	0	0	0	0	11	7	0	5	5	9.8	2.45	170	.179	.273	0	.000	0	2	2	-0	0.0
1950	Chi-A	9	12	.429	34	23	11	1	2	171²	153	12	109	77	14.0	3.93	114	.244	.361	12	.197	-0	12	11	0	1.1
1951	Chi-A	1	2	.333	4	4	1	0	0	26¹	25	2	13	14	13.4	3.76	107	.248	.350	3	.333	1	1	1	-0	0.1
	Det-A	11	10	.524	35	22	6	1	2	149¹	135	14	82	58	13.7	4.70	89	.239	.347	13	.245	2	-10	-9	-0	-0.9
	Yr	12	12	.500	39	26	7	1	2	175²	160	15	95	61	13.6	4.56	91	.240	.344	16	.258	3	-9	-8	-0	-0.8
1952	StL-A	12	10	.545	29	27	8	1	2	170	169	15	62	70	12.3	4.13	95	.264	.331	8	.138	-1	-9	-4	-2	-0.8
1953	StL-A	4	10	.286	32	13	1	0	1	99²	129	8	45	36	15.8	6.23	67	.310	.379	6	.200	-1	-25	-22	-2	-2.9
Total	5	37	44	.457	140	89	27	3	8	628	618	50	316	249	13.7	4.50	93	.259	.351	42	.196	0	-27	-21	-4	-3.4

● CHARLIE CALDWELL
Caldwell, Charles William "Chuck" b: 8/2/01, Bristol, Va.   d: 11/1/57, Princeton, N.J.   BR/TR, 5'10", 180 lbs.   Deb: 7/7/25

YEAR	TM/L	W	L	PCT	G	GS	CG	SH	SV	IP	H	HR	BB	SO	RAT	ERA	ERA+	OAV	OOB	BH	AVG	PB	PR	/A	PD	TPI
1925	NY-A	0	0	—	3	0	0	0	0	2²	7	0	3	1	33.8	16.88	25	.467	.556	0	.000	-0	-4	-4	-0	0.0

● EARL CALDWELL
Caldwell, Earl Welton "Teach" b: 4/9/05, Sparks, Tex.   d: 9/15/81, Mission, Tex.   BR/TR, 6'1", 178 lbs.   Deb: 9/8/28

YEAR	TM/L	W	L	PCT	G	GS	CG	SH	SV	IP	H	HR	BB	SO	RAT	ERA	ERA+	OAV	OOB	BH	AVG	PB	PR	/A	PD	TPI
1928	Phi-N	1	4	.200	5	5	1	0	0	34²	46	5	17	6	16.4	5.71	75	.348	.423	1	.111	-0	-7	-6	0	-0.7
1935	StL-A	3	2	.600	6	5	2	1	0	36²	34	2	17	5	12.5	3.68	130	.245	.327	2	.182	-0	3	5	1	0.6

YEAR TM/L	W	L	PCT	G	GS	CG	SH	SV	IP	H	HR	BB	SO	RAT	ERA	ERA+	OAV	OOB	BH	AVG	PB	PR	/A	PD	TPI
1936 StL-A	7	16	.304	41	25	10	2	2	189	252	15	83	59	16.7	6.00	90	.319	.394	11	.190	-1	-20	-13	-1	-1.4
1937 StL-A	0	0	—	9	2	0	0	0	29	39	3	13	8	16.8	6.83	71	.317	.391	2	.222	0	-7	-6	0	0.0
1945 Chi-A	6	7	.462	27	11	5	1	4	105¹	108	8	37	45	12.6	3.59	92	.265	.331	8	.216	-0	-3	-3	3	-0.1
1946 Chi-A	13	4	.765	39	0	0	0	8	90²	60	2	29	42	8.9	2.08	164	.186	.255	3	.167	1	**14**	**13**	1	3.0
1947 Chi-A	1	4	.200	40	0	0	0	8	54¹	53	4	30	22	13.9	3.64	100	.261	.359	0	.000	-0	-4	-5	-0	-0.2
1948 Chi-A	1	5	.167	25	1	0	0	3	39	53	3	22	10	17.8	5.31	80	.335	.423	0	.000	-0	-4	-5	-0	-0.7
Bos-A	1	1	.500	8	0	0	0	0	9	11	2	11	5	23.0	13.00	34	.333	.511	1	.333	0	-9	-9	-0	-1.5
Yr	2	6	.250	33	1	0	0	3	48	64	5	33	15	18.4	6.75	63	.332	.432	1	.125	-0	-13	-13	-1	-2.2
Total 8	33	43	.434	200	49	18	5	25	587²	656	44	259	202	14.4	4.69	92	.284	.363	28	.178	-2	-32	-25	3	-1.0

● RALPH CALDWELL
Caldwell, Ralph Grant "Lefty" b: 1/18/1884, Philadelphia, Pa. d: 8/5/69, W.Trenton, N.J. BL/TL, 5'9", 155 lbs. Deb: 9/10/04

YEAR TM/L	W	L	PCT	G	GS	CG	SH	SV	IP	H	HR	BB	SO	RAT	ERA	ERA+	OAV	OOB	BH	AVG	PB	PR	/A	PD	TPI
1904 Phi-N	2	2	.500	6	5	5	0	0	41	40	1	15	30	12.5	4.17	64	.242	.313	8	.444	3	-7	-7	0	-0.3
1905 Phi-N	1	3	.250	7	2	1	0	1	34	44	1	7	29	14.3	4.24	69	.321	.367	0	.000	-2	-5	-5	-1	-0.8
Total 2	3	5	.375	13	7	6	0	1	75	84	2	22	59	13.3	4.20	66	.278	.337	8	.242	1	-11	-12	-1	-1.1

● MIKE CALDWELL
Caldwell, Ralph Michael b: 1/22/49, Tarboro, N.C. BR/TL, 6', 185 lbs. Deb: 9/4/71

YEAR TM/L	W	L	PCT	G	GS	CG	SH	SV	IP	H	HR	BB	SO	RAT	ERA	ERA+	OAV	OOB	BH	AVG	PB	PR	/A	PD	TPI
1971 SD-N	1	0	1.000	6	0	0	0	0	6²	4	0	3	5	9.5	0.00	—	.174	.269	1	1.000	1	3	2	0	0.5
1972 SD-N	7	11	.389	42	20	4	2	2	163²	183	10	49	102	13.0	4.01	82	.282	.337	7	.140	-1	-10	-13	5	-1.1
1973 SD-N	5	14	.263	55	13	3	1	10	149	146	6	53	86	12.1	3.74	93	.260	.326	5	.143	-1	-1	-5	2	-0.5
1974 SF-N	14	5	.737	31	27	6	2	0	189¹	176	17	63	83	11.6	2.95	129	.249	.314	9	.143	-2	14	18	4	2.0
1975 SF-N	7	13	.350	38	21	4	0	1	163¹	194	16	48	53	13.6	4.79	79	.296	.348	7	.159	-0	-21	-18	2	-1.9
1976 SF-N	1	7	.125	50	9	0	0	2	107¹	145	5	20	55	14.0	4.86	75	.324	.356	3	.158	-0	-16	-15	1	-1.0
1977 Cin-N	0	0	—	14	0	0	0	1	24²	25	1	8	11	12.0	4.01	98	.260	.317	2	.500	2	-0	-0	-0	0.1
Mil-A	5	8	.385	24	12	2	0	0	94¹	101	6	36	38	13.3	4.58	89	.271	.338	0	—	0	-5	-5	3	-0.4
1978 Mil-A	22	9	.710	37	34	**23**	6	1	293¹	258	14	54	131	9.8	2.36	159	.234	.274	0	—	0	46	45	1	5.0
1979 Mil-A	16	6	**.727**	30	30	16	4	0	235	252	18	39	89	11.3	3.29	126	.278	.311	0	—	0	24	23	5	2.4
1980 Mil-A	13	11	.542	34	33	11	2	1	225¹	248	29	56	74	12.2	4.03	96	.285	.330	0	—	0	-0	-4	0	-0.4
1981 *Mil-A	11	9	.550	24	23	3	0	0	144¹	151	16	38	41	11.8	3.93	87	.272	.319	0	—	0	-4	-8	-0	-1.0
1982 *Mil-A	17	13	.567	35	34	12	3	0	258	269	30	58	75	11.4	3.91	97	.271	.311	0	—	0	5	-4	2	0.1
1983 Mil-A	12	11	.522	32	32	10	2	0	228¹	269	35	51	58	12.7	4.53	82	.296	.334	0	—	0	-12	-20	-0	-1.5
1984 Mil-A	6	13	.316	26	19	4	1	0	126	160	11	21	34	13.0	4.64	83	.314	.343	0	—	0	-9	-11	1	-1.4
Total 14	137	130	.513	475	307	98	23	18	2408²	2581	218	597	939	12.0	3.81	99	.276	.322	34	.157	-2	11	-14	24	0.9

● RAY CALDWELL
Caldwell, Raymond Benjamin "Rube" or "Slim" b: 4/26/1888, Corydon, Pa. d: 8/17/67, Salamanca, N.Y. BL/TR, 6'2", 190 lbs. Deb: 9/9/10 ♦

YEAR TM/L	W	L	PCT	G	GS	CG	SH	SV	IP	H	HR	BB	SO	RAT	ERA	ERA+	OAV	OOB	BH	AVG	PB	PR	/A	PD	TPI
1910 NY-A	1	0	1.000	6	2	1	0	1	19¹	19	1	9	17	13.0	3.72	71	.260	.341	0	.000	-1	-3	-2	0	-0.3
1911 NY-A	14	14	.500	41	26	19	1	1	255	240	7	79	145	11.7	3.35	107	.260	.327	40	.272	3	-0	7	-3	0.8
1912 NY-A	8	16	.333	30	26	13	3	0	183¹	196	1	67	95	13.2	4.47	80	.277	.344	18	.237	1	-23	-18	1	-1.7
1913 NY-A	9	8	.529	27	16	15	2	1	164¹	131	5	60	87	11.0	2.41	124	.219	.299	28	.289	3	10	11	-1	1.7
1914 NY-A	17	9	.654	31	23	22	5	1	213	153	4	51	92	8.8	1.94	142	.205	.260	22	.195	1	19	19	-2	2.5
1915 NY-A	19	16	.543	36	35	31	3	0	305	266	6	107	130	11.2	2.89	101	.244	.315	35	.243	8	2	1	-3	0.6
1916 NY-A	5	12	.294	21	18	14	1	0	165²	142	6	65	76	11.7	2.99	97	.243	.327	19	.204	-0	-3	-2	-1	-0.3
1917 NY-A	13	16	.448	32	29	21	1	0	236	199	8	76	102	10.7	2.86	94	.234	.302	32	.258	6	-5	-5	-1	0.3
1918 NY-A	9	8	.529	24	21	14	1	1	176²	173	6	59	120	12.0	3.06	93	.261	.325	44	.291	-4	-5	-4	-3	-0.1
1919 Bos-A	7	4	.636	18	12	6	1	0	86¹	92	1	31	23	13.1	3.96	76	.279	.346	13	.271	1	-7	-9	-2	-1.0
Cle-A	5	1	.833	6	6	4	1	0	52²	33	1	19	24	9.2	1.71	196	.181	.266	8	.348	2	9	10	-1	1.3
Yr	12	5	.706	24	18	10	2	0	139	125	2	50	47	11.5	3.11	101	.243	.312	21	.296	4	2	1	-3	0.3
1920 *Cle-A	20	10	.667	34	33	20	1	0	237²	286	9	63	80	13.4	3.86	98	.303	.350	19	.213	-2	-3	-3	-0	-0.5
1921 Cle-A	6	6	.500	32	12	4	1	0	147	159	7	49	76	12.9	4.90	87	.275	.333	11	.208	0	-10	-10	-0	-0.8
Total 12	133	120	.526	343	259	184	21	9	2242	2089	59	738	1006	11.6	3.22	99	.253	.319	289	.248	31	-20	-4	-19	2.5

● JEFF CALHOUN
Calhoun, Jeffrey Wilton b: 4/11/58, LaGrange, Ga. BL/TL, 6'2", 190 lbs. Deb: 9/2/84

YEAR TM/L	W	L	PCT	G	GS	CG	SH	SV	IP	H	HR	BB	SO	RAT	ERA	ERA+	OAV	OOB	BH	AVG	PB	PR	/A	PD	TPI
1984 Hou-N	0	1	.000	9	0	0	0	0	15¹	5	0	2	11	4.1	1.17	283	.100	.135	0	—	0	4	4	-0	0.2
1985 Hou-N	2	5	.286	44	0	0	0	4	63²	56	2	24	47	11.3	2.54	136	.243	.315	0	.000	-0	7	6	0	0.8
1986 *Hou-N	1	0	1.000	20	0	0	0	0	26²	28	3	12	14	13.5	3.71	97	.264	.339	0	—	0	-0	-1	-1	-0.1
1987 Phi-N	3	1	.750	42	0	0	0	1	42²	25	1	26	31	11.0	1.48	287	.168	.295	0	.000	-0	12	13	1	1.2
1988 Phi-N	0	0	—	3	0	0	0	0	2¹	6	2	1	1	27.0	15.43	23	.462	.500	0	—	0	-3	-3	-0	0.0
Total 5	6	7	.462	118	0	0	0	5	150²	120	8	65	104	11.1	2.51	147	.219	.303	0	.000	-0	21	20	-0	2.1

● FRED CALIGIURI
Caligiuri, Frederick John b: 10/22/18, W.Hickory, Pa. BR/TR, 6', 190 lbs. Deb: 9/3/41

YEAR TM/L	W	L	PCT	G	GS	CG	SH	SV	IP	H	HR	BB	SO	RAT	ERA	ERA+	OAV	OOB	BH	AVG	PB	PR	/A	PD	TPI
1941 Phi-A	2	2	.500	5	5	4	0	0	43	43	2	14	7	12.3	2.93	143	.257	.312	4	.200	1	6	6	-1	0.5
1942 Phi-A	0	3	.000	13	2	0	0	1	36²	45	2	18	20	16.0	6.38	59	.300	.382	1	.083	-0	-11	-11	-0	-0.9
Total 2	2	5	.286	18	7	4	0	1	79²	90	4	32	27	14.0	4.52	89	.277	.345	5	.156	1	-5	-5	-1	-0.4

● WILL CALIHAN
Calihan, William T. b: 1867, Oswego, N.Y. d: 12/20/17, Rochester, N.Y. 5'8", 150 lbs. Deb: 4/17/1890

YEAR TM/L	W	L	PCT	G	GS	CG	SH	SV	IP	H	HR	BB	SO	RAT	ERA	ERA+	OAV	OOB	BH	AVG	PB	PR	/A	PD	TPI
1890 Roc-a	18	15	.545	37	36	31	0	0	296¹	276	4	125	127	12.7	3.28	109	.239	.322	23	.145	-3	19	9	3	0.8
1891 Phi-a	6	6	.500	13	11	11	0	0	112	151	7	47	28	16.9	6.43	59	.312	.387	11	.196	-1	-34	-32	2	-2.4
Total 2	24	21	.533	50	47	42	0	0	408¹	427	11	172	155	13.8	4.14	88	.261	.341	34	.158	-5	-14	-23	4	-1.6

● BEN CALLAHAN
Callahan, Benjamin Franklin b: 5/19/57, Mt.Airy, N.C. BR/TR, 6'7", 230 lbs. Deb: 6/22/83

YEAR TM/L	W	L	PCT	G	GS	CG	SH	SV	IP	H	HR	BB	SO	RAT	ERA	ERA+	OAV	OOB	BH	AVG	PB	PR	/A	PD	TPI
1983 Oak-A	1	2	.333	4	2	0	0	0	9¹	18	0	5	2	22.2	12.54	37	.400	.460	0	—	0	-9	-9	0	-1.8

● NIXEY CALLAHAN
Callahan, James Joseph b: 3/18/1874, Fitchburg, Mass. d: 10/4/34, Boston, Mass. BR/TR, 5'10.5", 180 lbs. Deb: 5/12/1894 M♦

YEAR TM/L	W	L	PCT	G	GS	CG	SH	SV	IP	H	HR	BB	SO	RAT	ERA	ERA+	OAV	OOB	BH	AVG	PB	PR	/A	PD	TPI
1894 Phi-N	1	2	.333	9	2	1	0	2	33²	64	3	17	9	23.0	9.89	52	.398	.470	5	.238	-1	-19	-18	1	-1.3
1897 Chi-N	12	9	.571	23	22	21	1	0	189²	221	6	55	52	13.5	4.03	111	.289	.343	105	.292	3	6	9	1	1.2
1898 Chi-N	20	10	.667	31	31	30	2	0	274¹	267	6	71	73	11.4	2.46	146	.253	.307	43	.262	4	35	34	1	3.9
1899 Chi-N	21	12	.636	35	34	33	3	0	294¹	327	5	76	77	13.1	3.06	123	.281	.338	39	.260	4	26	23	5	3.0
1900 Chi-N	13	16	.448	32	32	32	2	0	285¹	347	5	74	77	14.0	3.82	94	.299	.353	27	.235	2	-4	-7	6	0.2
1901 Chi-A	15	8	.652	27	22	20	1	0	215¹	195	4	50	72	10.6	2.42	144	.239	.290	39	.331	8	30	25	3	3.9
1902 Chi-A	16	14	.533	35	31	29	2	0	282¹	287	8	89	75	12.3	3.60	94	.264	.326	51	.234	3	-1	-7	6	0.2
1903 Chi-A	1	2	.333	3	3	3	0	0	28	40	0	5	12	14.8	4.50	62	.334	.366	128	.292	1	-5	-5	1	-0.1
Total 8	99	73	.576	195	177	169	11	2	1603	1748	33	437	445	12.8	3.39	109	.276	.332	901	.273	25	70	54	26	10.8

● JIM CALLAHAN
Callahan, James W. b: Moberly, Mo. Deb: 9/3/1898

YEAR TM/L	W	L	PCT	G	GS	CG	SH	SV	IP	H	HR	BB	SO	RAT	ERA	ERA+	OAV	OOB	BH	AVG	PB	PR	/A	PD	TPI
1898 StL-N	0	2	.000	2	2	1	0	0	8¹	18	2	7	2	29.2	16.20	23	.430	.530	0	.000	-1	-12	-11	0	-1.6

● JOE CALLAHAN
Callahan, Joseph Thomas b: 10/8/16, E.Boston, Mass. d: 5/24/49, S.Boston, Mass. BR/TR, 6'2", 170 lbs. Deb: 9/13/39

YEAR TM/L	W	L	PCT	G	GS	CG	SH	SV	IP	H	HR	BB	SO	RAT	ERA	ERA+	OAV	OOB	BH	AVG	PB	PR	/A	PD	TPI
1939 Bos-N	1	0	1.000	4	1	1	0	0	17¹	17	0	3	6	10.9	3.12	119	.250	.292	0	.000	-0	2	1	0	0.1
1940 Bos-N	0	2	.000	6	2	0	0	0	15	20	1	13	3	19.8	10.20	36	.351	.471	0	.000	-1	-11	-11	1	-1.2
Total 2	1	2	.333	10	3	1	0	0	32¹	37	1	16	11	15.0	6.40	58	.296	.380	0	.000	-1	-9	-10	1	-1.1

● RAY CALLAHAN
Callahan, Raymond James "Pat" b: 8/29/1891, Ashland, Wis. d: 1/23/73, Olympia, Wash. BL/TL, 5'10.5", 170 lbs. Deb: 9/12/15

YEAR TM/L	W	L	PCT	G	GS	CG	SH	SV	IP	H	HR	BB	SO	RAT	ERA	ERA+	OAV	OOB	BH	AVG	PB	PR	/A	PD	TPI
1915 Cin-N	0	0	—	3	0	0	0	0	7	12	1	4	2	18.5	8.53	34	.364	.382	1	.333	-0	-4	-4	-0	0.0

● DICK CALMUS
Calmus, Richard Lee b: 1/7/44, Los Angeles, Cal. BR/TR, 6'4", 187 lbs. Deb: 4/22/63

YEAR TM/L	W	L	PCT	G	GS	CG	SH	SV	IP	H	HR	BB	SO	RAT	ERA	ERA+	OAV	OOB	BH	AVG	PB	PR	/A	PD	TPI
1963 LA-N	3	1	.750	21	1	0	0	0	44	32	3	16	25	9.8	2.66	114	.204	.277	0	.000	-1	3	2	-1	0.0

YEAR TM/L	W	L	PCT	G	GS	CG	SH	SV	IP	H	HR	BB	SO	RAT	ERA	ERA+	OAV	OOB	BH	AVG	PB	PR	/A	PD	TPI
1967 Chi-N	0	0	—	1	1	0	0	0	4¹	5	2	0	1	10.4	8.31	43	.278	.278	1	.500	0	-2	-2	0	0.0
Total 2	3	1	.750	22	2	0	0	0	48¹	37	5	16	26	9.9	3.17	97	.211	.277	1	.125	-0	1	-1	-1	0.0

● **MARK CALVERT**   Calvert, Mark b: 9/29/56, Tulsa, Okla. BR/TR, 6'1", 195 lbs. Deb: 4/17/83

YEAR TM/L	W	L	PCT	G	GS	CG	SH	SV	IP	H	HR	BB	SO	RAT	ERA	ERA+	OAV	OOB	BH	AVG	PB	PR	/A	PD	TPI
1983 SF-N	1	4	.200	18	4	0	0	0	37¹	46	2	34	14	20.0	6.27	56	.307	.444	0	.000	-1	-11	-11	1	-1.4
1984 SF-N	2	4	.333	10	5	1	0	0	32	40	4	9	14	14.1	5.06	69	.303	.352	0	.000	-1	-5	-6	0	-1.0
Total 2	3	8	.273	28	9	1	0	0	69¹	86	6	43	19	17.3	5.71	62	.305	.404	0	.000	-1	-16	-17	1	-2.4

● **PAUL CALVERT**   Calvert, Paul Leo Emile b: 10/6/17, Montreal, Que., Can. BR/TR, 6', 185 lbs. Deb: 9/24/42

YEAR TM/L	W	L	PCT	G	GS	CG	SH	SV	IP	H	HR	BB	SO	RAT	ERA	ERA+	OAV	OOB	BH	AVG	PB	PR	/A	PD	TPI
1942 Cle-A	0	0	—	1	0	0	0	0	2	0	0	2	2	9.0	0.00	—	.000	.286	0	—	0	1	1	-0	0.0
1943 Cle-A	0	0	—	5	0	0	0	0	8¹	6	0	6	2	14.0	4.32	72	.200	.351	0	.000	-0	-1	-1	0	0.0
1944 Cle-A	1	3	.250	35	4	0	0	0	77	89	4	38	31	14.8	4.56	72	.289	.367	4	.267	1	-10	-11	2	-0.2
1945 Cle-A	0	0	—	1	0	0	0	0	1¹	4	0	2	1	27.0	13.50	24	.429	.500	0	—	-0	-2	-2	0	0.0
1949 Was-A	6	17	.261	34	23	5	0	1	160²	175	11	86	52	14.7	5.43	78	.279	.368	7	.137	-2	-22	-21	3	-2.5
1950 Det-A	2	2	.500	32	0	0	0	4	51¹	71	7	25	14	17.2	6.31	74	.324	.398	0	.000	-1	-10	-9	1	-0.7
1951 Det-A	0	0	—	1	0	0	0	0	1	0	0	1	0	9.0	0.00	—	.250	.250	0	—	0	0	0	0	0.0
Total 7	9	22	.290	109	27	5	0	5	301²	345	22	158	102	15.2	5.31	76	.287	.373	11	.149	-2	-43	-43	5	-3.4

● **ERNIE CAMACHO**   Camacho, Ernest Carlos b: 2/1/55, Salinas, Cal. BR/TR, 6'1", 180 lbs. Deb: 5/22/80

YEAR TM/L	W	L	PCT	G	GS	CG	SH	SV	IP	H	HR	BB	SO	RAT	ERA	ERA+	OAV	OOB	BH	AVG	PB	PR	/A	PD	TPI
1980 Oak-A	0	0	—	5	0	0	0	0	11²	20	2	5	9	20.1	6.94	54	.364	.426	0	—	0	-4	-4	-0	0.0
1981 Pit-N	0	1	.000	7	3	0	0	0	21²	23	0	15	11	15.8	4.98	72	.295	.409	0	.000	-0	-4	-3	-0	-0.2
1983 Cle-A	0	1	.000	4	0	0	0	0	5¹	5	1	2	2	13.5	5.06	84	.250	.348	0	—	0	-1	-0	-0	-0.3
1984 Cle-A	5	9	.357	69	0	0	0	23	100	83	6	37	48	10.9	2.43	168	.229	.303	0	—	0	17	18	-0	3.3
1985 Cle-A	0	1	.000	2	0	0	0	0	3¹	4	0	1	2	13.5	8.10	51	.333	.385	0	—	0	-1	-1	0	-0.3
1986 Cle-A	2	4	.333	51	0	0	0	20	57¹	60	1	31	36	14.6	4.08	101	.269	.363	0	—	0	1	0	1	0.1
1987 Cle-A	0	1	.000	15	0	0	0	1	13²	21	1	5	9	19.1	9.22	49	.350	.426	0	—	0	-7	-7	1	-0.5
1988 Hou-N	0	3	.000	13	0	0	0	1	17²	25	1	12	13	18.8	7.64	43	.352	.446	0	.000	-0	-8	-8	0	-1.4
1989 SF-N	3	0	1.000	13	0	0	0	0	16¹	10	1	11	14	11.6	2.76	122	.175	.309	0	.000	-0	1	1	0	0.3
1990 SF-N	0	0	—	8	0	0	0	0	10	10	1	3	8	11.7	3.60	101	.256	.310	0	—	0	0	-0	0	0.0
StL-N	0	0	—	6	0	0	0	0	5²	7	2	6	7	20.6	7.94	48	.318	.464	0	—	0	-3	-3	0	0.0
Yr	0	0	—	14	0	0	0	0	15²	17	3	9	15	14.9	5.17	72	.279	.371	0	—	0	-2	-3	-0	0.0
Total 10	10	20	.333	193	3	0	0	45	262²	268	16	128	159	13.8	4.21	94	.268	.356	0	.000	-1	-8	-8	1	1.0

● **FRED CAMBRIA**   Cambria, Frederick Dennis b: 1/22/48, Cambria Heights, N.Y. BR/TR, 6'2", 195 lbs. Deb: 8/26/70

YEAR TM/L	W	L	PCT	G	GS	CG	SH	SV	IP	H	HR	BB	SO	RAT	ERA	ERA+	OAV	OOB	BH	AVG	PB	PR	/A	PD	TPI
1970 Pit-N	1	2	.333	6	5	0	0	0	33¹	37	2	12	14	13.5	3.51	111	.272	.336	2	.200	1	2	1	0	0.2

● **JACK CAMERON**   Cameron, John William "Happy Jack" b: 9/1884, Nova Scotia, Can. d: 8/17/51, Boston, Mass. Deb: 9/13/06 ♦

YEAR TM/L	W	L	PCT	G	GS	CG	SH	SV	IP	H	HR	BB	SO	RAT	ERA	ERA+	OAV	OOB	BH	AVG	PB	PR	/A	PD	TPI
1906 Bos-N	0	0	—	2	1	0	0	0	6	4	0	6	2	15.0	0.00	—	.211	.400	11	.180	-0	2	2	0	0.0

● **HARRY CAMNITZ**   Carnnitz, Henry Richardson b: 10/26/1884, McKinney, Ky. d: 1/6/51, Louisville, Ky. BR/TR, 6'1", 168 lbs. Deb: 4/14/09 F

YEAR TM/L	W	L	PCT	G	GS	CG	SH	SV	IP	H	HR	BB	SO	RAT	ERA	ERA+	OAV	OOB	BH	AVG	PB	PR	/A	PD	TPI
1909 Pit-N	0	0	—	1	0	0	0	0	4	6	0	1	1	15.8	4.50	61	.353	.389	0	.000	-1	-1	-1	0	0.0
1911 StL-N	1	0	1.000	2	0	0	0	0	2	0	1	2	0	4.5	0.00	—	.000	.143	0	—	0	1	1	-0	0.4
Total 2	1	0	1.000	3	0	0	0	0	6	6	0	2	3	12.0	3.00	98	.261	.320	0	.000	-0	-0	-0	-0	0.4

● **HOWIE CAMNITZ**   Camnitz, Samuel Howard "Red" b: 8/22/1881, Covington, Ky. d: 3/2/60, Louisville, Ky. BR/TR, 5'9", 169 lbs. Deb: 4/22/04 F

YEAR TM/L	W	L	PCT	G	GS	CG	SH	SV	IP	H	HR	BB	SO	RAT	ERA	ERA+	OAV	OOB	BH	AVG	PB	PR	/A	PD	TPI
1904 Pit-N	1	4	.200	10	2	2	0	0	49	48	0	20	21	13.0	4.22	65	.259	.341	1	.063	-1	-8	-8	-1	-1.0
1906 Pit-N	1	0	1.000	2	1	1	1	0	9	6	0	5	5	11.0	2.00	134	.188	.297	0	.000	-0	1	1	-0	0.0
1907 Pit-N	13	8	.619	31	19	15	4	1	180	135	0	59	85	9.9	2.15	113	.211	.281	3	.050	-5	6	6	-0	0.0
1908 Pit-N	16	9	.640	38	26	17	3	2	236²	182	6	69	118	9.7	1.56	148	.210	.272	6	.083	-3	21	20	-1	1.7
1909 *Pit-N	25	6	**.806**	41	30	20	6	3	283	207	1	68	133	9.0	1.62	168	.211	.267	12	.138	-3	31	35	-3	3.7
1910 Pit-N	12	13	.480	38	31	16	1	2	260	246	6	61	120	11.0	3.22	96	.256	.308	11	.125	-3	-5	-3	-2	-0.9
1911 Pit-N	20	15	.571	40	33	18	1	1	267²	245	8	84	139	11.2	3.13	110	.248	.309	12	.143	-3	8	9	-3	0.4
1912 Pit-N	22	12	.647	41	32	22	2	2	276²	256	8	82	121	11.4	2.83	115	.251	.315	23	.235	1	18	13	-3	1.2
1913 Pit-N	6	17	.261	36	21	5	1	2	192¹	203	7	84	64	13.8	3.74	81	.282	.363	9	.153	-1	-12	-16	1	-1.8
Phi-N	3	3	.500	9	5	1	0	1	49	49	2	23	21	13.6	3.67	91	.268	.356	1	.063	-1	-3	-2	-1	-0.5
Yr	9	20	.310	45	26	6	1	3	241¹	252	9	107	85	13.5	3.73	83	.277	.354	10	.133	-3	-14	-17	-0	-2.3
1914 Pit-F	14	19	.424	36	34	20	1	1	262	256	14	90	82	12.2	3.23	89	.258	.324	14	.161	-5	-10	-11	-5	-2.1
1915 Pit-F	0	0	—	4	2	0	0	0	20	19	1	6	6	13.5	4.50	64	.257	.353	0	.000	-1	-4	-4	-1	-0.2
Total 11	133	106	.556	326	236	137	20	15	2085¹	1852	41	656	915	11.1	2.75	106	.242	.307	92	.136	-24	44	40	-18	0.5

● **RICK CAMP**   Camp, Rick Lamar b: 6/10/53, Trion, Ga. BR/TR, 6', 198 lbs. Deb: 9/15/76

YEAR TM/L	W	L	PCT	G	GS	CG	SH	SV	IP	H	HR	BB	SO	RAT	ERA	ERA+	OAV	OOB	BH	AVG	PB	PR	/A	PD	TPI
1976 Atl-N	0	1	.000	5	1	0	0	0	11¹	13	0	2	6	11.9	6.35	60	.302	.333	0	.000	-0	-4	-3	1	-0.2
1977 Atl-N	6	3	.667	54	0	0	0	10	78²	89	6	47	51	15.7	4.00	111	.283	.377	0	.000	-1	-1	4	-0	0.4
1978 Atl-N	2	4	.333	42	4	0	0	6	74¹	99	5	32	23	16.2	3.75	108	.329	.399	0	.000	-1	-1	2	-0	0.1
1980 Atl-N	6	4	.600	77	0	0	0	22	108¹	92	3	29	33	10.4	1.91	196	.235	.294	1	.111	-0	20	22	4	3.4
1981 Atl-N	9	3	.750	48	0	0	0	17	76	68	5	12	47	9.6	1.78	202	.239	.272	0	.000	-1	14	**15**	1	3.1
1982 *Atl-N	11	13	.458	51	21	3	0	5	177¹	199	18	52	68	12.8	3.65	102	.291	.342	1	.024	-3	-1	0	1	-0.1
1983 Atl-N	10	9	.526	40	16	1	0	0	140	146	16	38	61	12.1	3.79	102	.270	.323	3	.077	-2	-3	1	0	0.0
1984 Atl-N	8	6	.571	31	21	1	0	0	148²	134	11	63	89	12.1	3.27	118	.245	.325	5	.111	-2	5	10	0	0.7
1985 Atl-N	4	6	.400	66	2	0	0	3	127²	130	8	61	49	13.8	3.95	97	.263	.349	3	.231	1	-5	-1	-2	-0.2
Total 9	56	49	.533	414	65	5	0	57	942¹	970	72	336	407	12.7	3.37	114	.269	.335	13	.074	-8	25	51	3	7.2

● **KID CAMP**   Camp, Winfield Scott b: 1870, Columbus, Ohio d: 3/2/1895, Omaha, Neb. TR, 6', 160 lbs. Deb: 5/3/1892 F

YEAR TM/L	W	L	PCT	G	GS	CG	SH	SV	IP	H	HR	BB	SO	RAT	ERA	ERA+	OAV	OOB	BH	AVG	PB	PR	/A	PD	TPI
1892 Pit-N	0	1	.000	4	1	1	0	0	23	31	4	9	6	16.0	6.26	53	.310	.373	1	.091	-1	-8	-8	-1	-0.5
1894 Chi-N	0	1	.000	3	2	2	0	0	22	34	0	12	6	19.2	6.55	86	.349	.426	0	.000	-3	-3	-2	0	-0.2
Total 2	0	2	.000	7	3	3	0	0	45	65	4	21	12	17.6	6.40	69	.329	.399	1	.045	-4	-11	-10	-1	-0.7

● **BERT CAMPANERIS**   Campaneris, Dagoberto (Blanco) "Campy" (b: Dagoberto Campania (Blanco)) b: 3/9/42, Pueblo Nuevo, Cuba BR/TR, 5'10", 160 lbs. Deb: 7/23/64 ♦

YEAR TM/L	W	L	PCT	G	GS	CG	SH	SV	IP	H	HR	BB	SO	RAT	ERA	ERA+	OAV	OOB	BH	AVG	PB	PR	/A	PD	TPI
1965 KC-A	0	0	—	1	0	0	0	0	1	1	0	2	1	27.0	9.00	39	.333	.600	156	.270	0	-1	-1	0	0.0

● **ARCHIE CAMPBELL**   Campbell, Archibald Stewart "Iron Man" b: 10/20/03, Maplewood, N.J. d: 12/22/89, Sparks, Nevada BR/TR, 6', 180 lbs. Deb: 4/21/28

YEAR TM/L	W	L	PCT	G	GS	CG	SH	SV	IP	H	HR	BB	SO	RAT	ERA	ERA+	OAV	OOB	BH	AVG	PB	PR	/A	PD	TPI
1928 NY-A	0	1	.000	13	1	0	0	2	24	30	0	11	9	15.4	5.25	72	.288	.357	1	.250	-1	-3	-4	-1	-0.3
1929 Was-A	0	0	—	4	0	0	0	0	4	10	1	5	1	33.8	15.75	27	.500	.600	0	—	0	-5	-5	-0	-0.9
1930 Cin-N	2	4	.333	23	3	1	0	4	58	71	2	31	19	16.0	5.43	89	.311	.396	4	.267	-3	-4	-2	2	-0.2
Total 3	2	6	.250	40	4	1	0	6	86	111	3	47	29	16.6	5.86	77	.315	.398	5	.263	0	-11	-13	2	-1.4

● **DAVE CAMPBELL**   Campbell, David Alan b: 9/3/51, Princeton, Ind. BR/TR, 6'3", 210 lbs. Deb: 5/6/77

YEAR TM/L	W	L	PCT	G	GS	CG	SH	SV	IP	H	HR	BB	SO	RAT	ERA	ERA+	OAV	OOB	BH	AVG	PB	PR	/A	PD	TPI
1977 Atl-N	0	6	.000	65	0	0	0	13	88²	78	7	33	42	11.6	3.05	146	.239	.315	1	.083	-1	9	14	-2	1.1
1978 Atl-N	4	4	.500	53	0	0	0	1	69¹	67	10	49	45	15.7	4.80	84	.258	.385	0	—	0	-9	-6	0	-0.7
Total 2	4	10	.286	118	0	0	0	14	158	145	17	82	87	13.4	3.82	112	.247	.348	1	.083	-1	-1	8	-2	0.4

● **HUGH CAMPBELL**   Campbell, Hugh F. b: 1846, Scotland d: 3/1/1881, Elizabeth, N.J. Deb: 4/28/1873 F

YEAR TM/L	W	L	PCT	G	GS	CG	SH	SV	IP	H	HR	BB	SO	RAT	ERA	ERA+	OAV	OOB	BH	AVG	PB	PR	/A	PD	TPI
1873 Res-n	2	16	.111	19	18	18	0	0	165	250	7	7	5	14.0	2.84	118	.296	.302	13	.151	-5	8	9		0.4

YEAR TM/L	W	L	PCT	G	GS	CG	SH	SV	IP	H	HR	BB	SO	RAT	ERA	ERA+	OAV	OOB	BH	AVG	PB	PR	/A	PD	TPI

● JIM CAMPBELL   Campbell, James Marcus b: 5/19/66, Santa Maria, Cal. BL/TL, 5'11", 175 lbs. Deb: 8/21/90

| 1990 KC-A | 1 | 0 | 1.000 | 2 | 2 | 0 | 0 | 0 | 9² | 15 | 1 | 1 | 2 | 14.9 | 8.38 | 46 | .349 | .364 | 0 | — | 0 | -5 | -5 | -0 | -0.3 |

● JOHN CAMPBELL   Campbell, John Millard b: 9/13/07, Washington, D.C. BR/TR, 6'1.5", 184 lbs. Deb: 7/23/33

| 1933 Was-A | 0 | 0 | — | 1 | 0 | 0 | 0 | 0 | 1 | 1 | 0 | 1 | 0 | 18.0 | 0.00 | — | .200 | .333 | 0 | — | 0 | 0 | 0 | -0 | 0.0 |

● KEVIN CAMPBELL   Campbell, Kevin Wade b: 12/6/64, Marianna, Ark. BR/TR, 6'2", 255 lbs. Deb: 7/19/91

1991 Oak-A	1	0	1.000	14	0	0	0	0	23	13	4	14	16	11.0	2.74	140	.167	.301	0	—	0	3	3	0	0.2
1992 Oak-A	2	3	.400	32	5	0	0	1	65	66	4	45	38	15.4	5.12	73	.267	.380	0	—	0	-9	-10	-1	-0.7
1993 Oak-A	0	0	—	11	0	0	0	0	16	20	1	11	9	18.0	7.31	56	.313	.421	0	—	0	-5	-6	-0	0.0
1994 Min-A	1	0	1.000	14	0	0	0	0	24²	20	2	5	15	9.5	2.92	166	.233	.283	0	—	0	5	5	0	0.2
Total 4	4	3	.571	71	5	0	0	1	128²	119	11	75	78	13.8	4.55	88	.251	.356	0	—	0	-5	-8	-1	-0.3

● MIKE CAMPBELL   Campbell, Michael Thomas b: 2/17/64, Seattle, Wash. BR/TR, 6'3", 210 lbs. Deb: 7/4/87

1987 Sea-A	1	4	.200	9	9	1	0	0	49¹	41	9	25	35	12.4	4.74	99	.224	.324	0	—	0	-2	-0	0	-0.4
1988 Sea-A	6	10	.375	20	20	2	0	0	114²	128	18	43	63	13.4	5.89	71	.280	.342	0	—	0	-24	-22	-1	-2.8
1989 Sea-A	1	2	.333	5	5	0	0	0	21	28	4	10	6	16.3	7.29	55	.301	.369	0	—	0	-8	-8	-0	-1.1
1992 Tex-A	1	1	.000	1	0	0	0	0	3²	3	1	2	2	13.2	9.82	39	.231	.333	0	—	0	-2	-2	-0	-0.4
1994 SD-N	1	1	.500	3	2	0	0	0	8¹	13	5	5	10	19.4	12.96	32	.351	.429	1	.333	0	-8	-8	-0	-1.3
Total 5	9	18	.333	38	36	3	0	0	197	213	37	85	116	13.7	6.12	70	.272	.345	1	.333	0	-44	-40	-1	-6.0

● BILLY CAMPBELL   Campbell, William James b: 11/5/1873, Pittsburgh, Pa. d: 10/6/57, Cincinnati, Ohio BL/TL, 5'10", 165 lbs. Deb: 4/17/05

1905 StL-N	1	1	.500	2	2	0	0	2	17	27	0	7	2	18.0	7.41	40	.365	.420	1	.143	-0	-8	-8	1	-0.7
1907 Cin-N	3	0	1.000	3	3	3	0	0	21	19	0	3	4	9.4	2.14	121	.244	.272	1	.250	1	1	1	1	0.2
1908 Cin-N	12	13	.480	35	24	19	2	2	221¹	203	3	44	73	10.5	2.60	89	.252	.299	6	.083	-3	-6	-7	4	-0.8
1909 Cin-N	7	11	.389	30	15	7	0	2	148¹	162	0	39	37	12.7	2.67	97	.288	.344	6	.140	-1	-1	-1	2	0.0
Total 4	23	25	.479	70	44	31	2	4	407²	411	3	93	116	11.5	2.80	88	.270	.320	15	.115	-4	-15	-16	8	-1.3

● BILL CAMPBELL   Campbell, William Richard b: 8/9/48, Highland Park, Mich. BR/TR, 6'3", 190 lbs. Deb: 7/14/73

1973 Min-A	3	3	.500	28	2	0	0	7	51²	44	5	20	42	11.3	3.14	126	.226	.301	0	—	0	4	5	0	0.4
1974 Min-A	8	7	.533	63	0	0	0	19	120¹	109	4	55	89	12.4	2.62	143	.242	.327	0	—	0	13	15	1	2.2
1975 Min-A	4	6	.400	47	7	2	1	5	121	119	13	46	76	12.4	3.79	102	.262	.333	0	.000	0	-0	1	1	0.1
1976 Min-A	17	5	**.773**	78	0	0	0	20	167²	145	9	62	115	11.4	3.01	120	.234	.309	0	—	0	10	11	-0	1.5
1977 Bos-A★	13	9	.591	69	0	0	0	31	140	112	13	60	114	11.4	2.96	152	.224	.313	0	—	0	17	24	2	3.9
1978 Bos-A	7	5	.583	29	0	0	0	4	50²	62	3	17	47	14.0	3.91	105	.308	.362	0	—	0	-1	1	1	-0.1
1979 Bos-A	3	4	.429	41	0	0	0	9	54²	55	5	23	25	13.0	4.28	103	.262	.338	0	—	0	-0	1	1	0.1
1980 Bos-A	4	0	1.000	23	0	0	0	0	41¹	44	1	22	17	14.4	4.79	88	.284	.373	0	—	0	-3	-3	-1	-0.4
1981 Bos-A	1	1	.500	30	0	0	0	7	48¹	45	5	20	37	12.1	3.17	122	.245	.319	0	—	0	3	4	0	0.2
1982 Chi-N	3	6	.333	62	0	0	0	8	100	89	6	40	71	11.6	3.69	101	.245	.319	1	.143	-0	-1	0	2	0.3
1983 Chi-N	6	8	.429	82	0	0	0	8	122¹	128	9	49	97	13.1	4.49	84	.275	.346	1	.100	-1	-12	-9	-2	-1.0
1984 Phi-N	6	5	.545	57	0	0	0	1	81¹	68	2	35	52	11.4	3.43	106	.222	.302	0	.000	0	1	2	-1	0.1
1985 *StL-N	5	3	.625	50	0	0	0	4	64¹	55	5	21	41	10.9	3.50	101	.230	.298	2	.333	1	1	0	-1	0.0
1986 Det-A	3	6	.333	34	0	0	0	3	55²	46	5	21	37	11.0	3.88	106	.230	.306	0	—	0	2	1	-1	0.2
1987 Mon-N	0	0	—	7	0	0	0	0	10	18	2	4	4	19.8	8.10	52	.360	.407	0	.000	0	-4	-4	0	0.0
Total 15	83	68	.550	700	9	2	1	126	1229¹	1139	82	495	864	12.1	3.54	110	.248	.324	4	.154	1	28	49	5	7.5

● CARDELL CAMPER   Camper, Cardell b: 7/6/52, Boley, Okla. BR/TR, 6'3", 208 lbs. Deb: 9/11/77

| 1977 Cle-A | 1 | 0 | 1.000 | 3 | 1 | 0 | 0 | 0 | 9¹ | 7 | 0 | 4 | 9 | 10.6 | 3.86 | 102 | .200 | .282 | 0 | — | 0 | 0 | 0 | -0 | 0.2 |

● SAL CAMPFIELD   Campfield, William Holton b: 2/19/1868, Meadville, Pa. d: 5/16/52, Meadville, Pa. BR/TR, 6'0.5", Deb: 5/15/1896

| 1896 NY-N | 1 | 1 | .500 | 6 | 2 | 2 | 0 | 0 | 27 | 31 | 1 | 6 | 6 | 13.0 | 4.00 | 105 | .286 | .335 | 2 | .167 | -0 | 1 | 1 | -1 | 0.0 |

● SAL CAMPISI   Campisi, Salvatore John b: 8/11/42, Brooklyn, N.Y. BR/TR, 6'2", 210 lbs. Deb: 8/15/69

1969 StL-N	1	0	1.000	7	0	0	0	0	9²	4	0	6	7	9.3	0.93	384	.121	.256	0	—	0	3	3	0	0.3
1970 StL-N	2	2	.500	37	0	0	0	4	49¹	53	2	37	26	17.0	2.92	141	.282	.408	0	.000	-0	6	7	-0	0.6
1971 Min-A	0	0	—	6	0	0	0	0	4¹	5	1	4	2	18.7	4.15	86	.294	.429	0	—	0	-0	0	0	0.0
Total 3	3	2	.600	50	0	0	0	4	63¹	62	3	47	35	15.9	2.70	148	.261	.389	0	.000	-0	9	9	0	0.9

● HUGH CANAVAN   Canavan, Hugh Edward "Hugo" b: 5/13/1897, Worcester, Mass. d: 9/4/67, Boston, Mass. BL/TL, 5'8", 160 lbs. Deb: 4/23/18

| 1918 Bos-N | 0 | 4 | .000 | 11 | 3 | 3 | 0 | 0 | 46² | 70 | 0 | 15 | 18 | 17.4 | 6.36 | 42 | .366 | .427 | 2 | .095 | -0 | -19 | -19 | 1 | -1.4 |

● JOHN CANDELARIA   Candelaria, John Robert "Candy Man" b: 11/6/53, New York, N.Y. BL/TL, 6'7", 232 lbs. Deb: 6/8/75

1975 *Pit-N	8	6	.571	18	18	4	1	0	120²	95	8	36	95	9.9	2.76	128	.212	.273	6	.140	-0	12	10	-1	1.0
1976 Pit-N	16	7	.696	32	31	11	4	1	220	173	22	60	138	9.6	3.15	111	.216	.273	14	.184	3	9	8	-1	1.1
1977 Pit-N☆	20	5	**.800**	33	33	6	1	0	230²	197	29	50	133	9.7	**2.34**	**170**	.232	.276	18	.225	4	**40**	42	-2	4.7
1978 Pit-N	12	11	.522	30	29	3	1	1	189	191	15	49	94	11.7	3.24	114	.261	.312	9	.173	1	7	10	-2	1.3
1979 *Pit-N	14	9	.609	33	30	8	0	0	207	201	25	41	101	10.7	3.22	121	.253	.292	9	.132	-1	12	15	0	1.5
1980 Pit-N	11	14	.440	35	34	7	0	1	233¹	246	14	50	97	11.5	4.01	90	.276	.317	15	.195	2	-11	-10	-1	-0.8
1981 Pit-N	2	2	.500	6	6	0	0	0	40²	42	3	11	14	11.7	3.54	101	.271	.319	3	.231	-0	-0	-0	-0	0.0
1982 Pit-N	12	7	.632	31	30	1	1	1	174²	166	13	37	133	10.7	2.94	126	.255	.299	12	.222	3	13	15	-1	1.8
1983 Pit-N	15	8	.652	33	32	3	1	1	197²	191	15	45	157	10.8	3.23	115	.257	.302	9	.138	0	9	10	-2	0.9
1984 Pit-N	12	11	.522	33	28	3	1	2	185¹	179	19	34	133	10.4	2.72	132	.256	.291	8	.129	1	18	18	-2	2.1
1985 Pit-N	2	4	.333	37	0	0	0	9	54¹	57	7	14	47	11.9	3.64	98	.275	.324	0	.000	0	-0	-0	-0	-0.1
Cal-A	7	3	.700	13	13	1	1	0	71	70	7	24	53	12.3	3.80	108	.262	.330	0	—	0	3	2	-1	0.3
1986 *Cal-A	10	2	.833	16	16	1	1	0	91²	68	4	26	81	9.5	2.55	161	.206	.270	0	—	0	17	16	-1	1.9
1987 Cal-A	8	6	.571	20	20	0	0	0	116²	127	17	20	74	11.4	4.71	91	.279	.311	0	—	0	-3	-5	-2	-0.2
NY-N	2	0	1.000	3	3	0	0	0	12¹	17	1	3	10	14.6	5.84	65	.333	.370	1	.200	-0	-2	-3	0	-0.4
1988 NY-A	13	7	.650	25	24	6	2	1	157	150	24	23	121	10.0	3.38	116	.248	.302	0	—	0	10	10	0	1.2
1989 NY-A	3	3	.500	10	6	1	0	0	49	49	8	12	37	11.2	5.14	76	.258	.302	0	—	0	-7	-7	-0	-0.8
Mon-N	0	2	.000	12	0	0	0	0	16¹	17	3	4	14	11.6	3.31	107	.283	.328	0	—	0	0	0	-0	0.0
1990 Min-A	7	3	.700	34	1	0	0	4	58¹	55	9	9	44	9.9	3.39	122	.244	.274	0	—	0	3	5	-1	0.8
Tor-A	0	3	.000	13	2	0	0	1	21¹	32	2	11	19	19.0	5.48	72	.356	.437	0	—	0	-4	-4	1	-0.4
Yr	7	6	.538	47	3	0	0	5	79²	87	11	20	63	12.3	3.95	104	.274	.321	0	—	0	-0	1	-0	0.4
1991 LA-N	1	1	.500	59	0	0	0	2	33²	31	3	11	38	11.2	3.74	96	.252	.313	0	—	0	-0	-1	-1	-0.1
1992 LA-N	2	5	.286	50	0	0	0	5	25¹	20	1	13	23	11.7	2.84	121	.220	.317	0	—	0	2	2	0	0.6
1993 Pit-N	0	3	.000	24	0	0	0	1	19²	29	3	9	17	16.0	8.24	48	.313	.389	0	—	0	-9	-9	-1	-1.4
Total 19	177	122	.592	600	356	54	13	29	2525²	2399	245	592	1673	10.8	3.33	114	.251	.298	104	.174	15	117	126	-13	15.0

● MILO CANDINI   Candini, Mario Cain b: 8/3/17, Manteca, Cal. BR/TR, 6', 187 lbs. Deb: 5/1/43

1943 Was-A	11	7	.611	28	21	8	3	1	166	144	3	65	67	11.4	2.49	128	.238	.313	9	.161	-1	15	13	1	1.4
1944 Was-A	6	7	.462	28	10	4	2	1	103	110	3	49	31	14.0	4.11	79	.276	.357	10	.313	3	-8	-10	-0	-0.9
1946 Was-A	2	0	1.000	9	0	0	0	0	21²	15	1	4	6	7.9	2.08	161	.192	.232	2	.333	1	4	4	-0	0.4
1947 Was-A	3	4	.429	38	2	0	0	1	87	96	6	35	31	13.6	5.17	70	.273	.339	3	.167	-0	-14	-14	0	-1.0
1948 Was-A	2	3	.400	35	4	1	0	3	94¹	96	1	63	23	15.3	5.15	84	.267	.378	8	.364	3	-9	-8	-0	-0.2
1949 Was-A	0	0	—	3	0	0	0	1	5²	4	0	1	1	7.9	4.76	89	.200	.238	1	1.000	0	-0	-0	-0	0.0

YEAR TM/L	W	L	PCT	G	GS	CG	SH	SV	IP	H	HR	BB	SO	RAT	ERA	ERA+	OAV	OOB	BH	AVG	PB	PR	/A	PD	TPI
1950 Phi-N	1	0	1.000	18	0	0	0	0	30	32	2	15	10	14.1	2.70	150	.281	.364	1	.167	-0	5	4	1	0.2
1951 Phi-N	1	0	1.000	15	0	0	0	0	30	33	3	18	14	15.3	6.00	64	.275	.370	1	.333	1	-7	-7	0	-0.1
Total 8	26	21	.553	174	37	13	5	8	537²	530	18	250	183	13.1	3.92	92	.259	.341	35	.243	7	-15	-19	1	-0.2

● TOM CANDIOTTI
Candiotti, Thomas Caesar b: 8/31/57, Walnut Creek, Cal. BR/TR, 6'3", 205 lbs. Deb: 8/8/83

YEAR TM/L	W	L	PCT	G	GS	CG	SH	SV	IP	H	HR	BB	SO	RAT	ERA	ERA+	OAV	OOB	BH	AVG	PB	PR	/A	PD	TPI
1983 Mil-A	4	4	.500	10	8	2	1	0	55²	62	4	16	21	12.9	3.23	116	.291	.346	0	—	0	5	3	-1	0.5
1984 Mil-A	2	2	.500	8	6	0	0	0	32¹	38	5	10	23	13.4	5.29	73	.277	.327	0	—	0	-5	-5	-1	-0.6
1986 Cle-A	16	12	.571	36	34	17	3	0	252¹	234	18	106	167	12.4	3.57	116	.246	.326	0	—	0	17	16	3	1.9
1987 Cle-A	7	18	.280	32	32	7	2	0	201²	193	28	93	111	12.9	4.78	95	.250	.333	0	—	0	-7	-6	0	-0.6
1988 Cle-A	14	8	.636	31	31	11	1	0	216²	225	15	53	137	11.8	3.28	125	.272	.321	0	—	0	16	20	2	2.1
1989 Cle-A	13	10	.565	31	31	4	0	0	206	188	10	55	124	10.8	3.10	128	.242	.295	0	—	0	18	20	4	2.5
1990 Cle-A	15	11	.577	31	29	3	1	0	202	207	23	55	128	11.9	3.65	107	.263	.316	0	—	0	6	6	3	1.0
1991 Cle-A	7	6	.538	15	15	3	0	0	108¹	88	6	28	86	9.8	2.24	185	.218	.272	0	—	0	22	23	-0	2.7
*Tor-A	6	7	.462	19	19	3	0	0	129²	114	6	45	81	11.3	2.98	141	.236	.306	0	—	0	16	18	0	1.7
Yr	13	13	.500	34	34	6	0	0	238	202	12	73	167	10.6	2.65	158	.225	.287	0	—	0	38	41	-0	4.4
1992 LA-N	11	15	.423	32	30	6	2	0	203²	177	13	63	152	10.7	3.00	115	.237	.299	6	.107	-1	11	10	1	1.2
1993 LA-N	8	10	.444	33	32	2	0	0	213²	192	12	71	155	11.3	3.12	122	.241	.308	8	.133	-1	22	17	-0	1.2
1994 LA-N	7	7	.500	23	22	5	0	0	153	149	9	54	102	12.2	4.12	96	.259	.328	7	.140	-1	2	-3	1	-0.2
Total 11	110	110	.500	301	289	63	10	0	1975	1867	149	649	1287	11.7	3.46	116	.250	.314	21	.127	-3	123	118	13	13.4

● JOHN CANEIRA
Caneira, John Cascaes b: 10/7/52, Waterbury, Conn. BR/TR, 6'3", 180 lbs. Deb: 9/10/77

YEAR TM/L	W	L	PCT	G	GS	CG	SH	SV	IP	H	HR	BB	SO	RAT	ERA	ERA+	OAV	OOB	BH	AVG	PB	PR	/A	PD	TPI
1977 Cal-A	2	2	.500	6	4	0	0	0	28²	27	5	16	17	13.5	4.08	96	.252	.350	0	—	0	-0	-1	-1	0.2
1978 Cal-A	0	0	—	2	0	0	0	0	7²	8	2	3	0	12.9	7.04	51	.286	.355	0	—	0	-3	-3	-0	0.1
Total 2	2	2	.500	8	6	0	0	0	36¹	35	7	19	17	13.4	4.71	82	.259	.351	0	—	0	-3	-3	-1	0.3

● JOHN CANGELOSI
Cangelosi, John Anthony b: 3/10/63, Brooklyn, N.Y. BB/TL, 5'8", 150 lbs. Deb: 6/3/85 ◆

YEAR TM/L	W	L	PCT	G	GS	CG	SH	SV	IP	H	HR	BB	SO	RAT	ERA	ERA+	OAV	OOB	BH	AVG	PB	PR	/A	PD	TPI
1988 Pit-N	0	0	—	1	0	0	0	0	2	1	0	0	0	4.5	0.00	—	.143	.143	30	.254	0	1	1	-0	0.0

● JOSE CANO
Cano, Joselito (Soriano) b: 3/7/62, Boca De Soco, D.R. BR/TR, 6'3", 175 lbs. Deb: 8/28/89

YEAR TM/L	W	L	PCT	G	GS	CG	SH	SV	IP	H	HR	BB	SO	RAT	ERA	ERA+	OAV	OOB	BH	AVG	PB	PR	/A	PD	TPI
1989 Hou-N	1	1	.500	6	3	0	0	0	23	24	2	7	8	12.1	5.09	67	.267	.320	0	.000	-1	-4	-4	-0	-0.4

● JOSE CANSECO
Canseco, Jose (Capas) b: 7/2/64, Havana, Cuba BR/TR, 6'3", 240 lbs. Deb: 9/2/85 F◆

YEAR TM/L	W	L	PCT	G	GS	CG	SH	SV	IP	H	HR	BB	SO	RAT	ERA	ERA+	OAV	OOB	BH	AVG	PB	PR	/A	PD	TPI
1993 Tex-A	0	0	—	1	0	0	0	0	1	2	0	3	0	45.0	27.00	15	.500	.714	59	.255	1	-3	-3	0	0.0

● GUY CANTRELL
Cantrell, Guy Dewey "Gunner" b: 4/9/04, Clarita, Okla. d: 1/31/61, McAlester, Okla. BR/TR, 6', 190 lbs. Deb: 8/18/25

YEAR TM/L	W	L	PCT	G	GS	CG	SH	SV	IP	H	HR	BB	SO	RAT	ERA	ERA+	OAV	OOB	BH	AVG	PB	PR	/A	PD	TPI
1925 Bro-N	1	0	1.000	14	3	1	0	0	36	42	0	14	13	14.3	3.00	139	.294	.361	0	—	-1	5	5	1	0.1
1927 Bro-N	0	0	—	6	0	0	0	0	10	10	0	6	5	14.4	2.70	147	.250	.348	1	.333	0	1	1	0	0.0
Phi-A	0	2	.000	2	2	2	0	0	18	25	0	7	7	16.0	5.00	85	.338	.395	1	.167	-0	-2	-1	0	-0.2
1930 Det-A	1	5	.167	16	2	1	0	0	35	38	5	20	20	15.2	5.66	85	.271	.366	0	.000	-2	-4	-3	1	-0.5
Total 3	2	7	.222	38	7	4	0	0	99	115	5	47	45	14.9	4.27	103	.290	.368	2	.074	-3	1	1	2	-0.6

● BEN CANTWELL
Cantwell, Benjamin Caldwell b: 4/13/02, Milan, Tenn. d: 12/4/62, Salem, Mo. BR/TR, 6'1", 168 lbs. Deb: 8/19/27

YEAR TM/L	W	L	PCT	G	GS	CG	SH	SV	IP	H	HR	BB	SO	RAT	ERA	ERA+	OAV	OOB	BH	AVG	PB	PR	/A	PD	TPI
1927 NY-N	1	1	.500	5	2	1	0	0	19²	26	1	2	6	13.3	4.12	94	.313	.337	2	.250	0	-0	-1	-0	-0.1
1928 NY-N	1	0	1.000	7	1	0	0	1	18¹	20	1	4	0	12.3	4.42	89	.282	.329	2	.500	1	-1	-1	1	0.1
Bos-N	3	3	.500	22	9	3	0	0	90	112	7	36	18	15.0	5.10	77	.304	.369	5	.172	-1	-11	-12	1	-0.7
Yr	4	3	.571	29	10	3	0	1	108¹	132	8	40	18	14.5	4.98	78	.300	.361	7	.212	-0	-12	-13	2	-0.6
1929 Bos-N	4	13	.235	27	20	8	0	2	157	171	11	52	25	12.9	4.47	105	.280	.338	9	.180	0	4	4	0	0.7
1930 Bos-N	9	15	.375	31	21	10	0	2	173¹	213	15	45	43	13.4	4.88	101	.312	.355	19	.302	2	2	1	4	0.7
1931 Bos-N	7	9	.438	33	16	9	2	2	156¹	160	4	34	32	11.2	3.63	104	.262	.301	13	.228	0	4	3	3	0.6
1932 Bos-N	13	11	.542	37	9	3	1	5	146	133	6	33	33	10.5	2.96	127	.247	.296	14	.280	2	15	13	3	2.6
1933 Bos-N	20	10	.667	40	29	18	2	2	254²	242	12	54	57	10.6	2.62	117	.249	.291	12	.141	-1	20	13	4	1.8
1934 Bos-N	5	11	.313	27	19	6	1	5	143¹	163	8	34	45	12.5	4.33	88	.285	.327	12	.279	1	-4	-8	2	-0.5
1935 Bos-N	4	25	.138	39	24	13	0	0	210²	235	15	44	34	12.0	4.61	82	.282	.320	19	.284	4	-14	-19	2	-1.7
1936 Bos-N	9	9	.500	34	12	4	0	2	133¹	127	8	35	42	11.2	3.04	126	.252	.306	8	.195	-1	15	12	3	1.7
1937 NY-N	0	1	1.000	1	1	0	0	0	4	6	1	1	1	15.8	9.00	43	.375	.412	0	—	0	-2	-2	0	-0.4
Bro-N	0	0	—	13	0	0	0	0	27¹	32	1	8	12	13.2	4.61	88	.288	.336	1	.167	-2	-2	-2	2	-0.2
Yr	0	1	.000	14	1	0	0	0	31¹	38	2	9	13	13.5	5.17	78	.299	.346	1	.167	-2	-4	-4	2	-0.2
Total 11	76	108	.413	316	163	75	6	21	1534	1640	90	382	348	12.0	3.91	100	.275	.321	116	.231	8	25	-2	28	5.0

● MIKE CANTWELL
Cantwell, Michael Joseph b: 1/15/1896, Washington, D.C. d: 1/5/53, Oteen, N.C. BL/TL, 5'10", 155 lbs. Deb: 8/17/16 F

YEAR TM/L	W	L	PCT	G	GS	CG	SH	SV	IP	H	HR	BB	SO	RAT	ERA	ERA+	OAV	OOB	BH	AVG	PB	PR	/A	PD	TPI
1916 NY-A	0	0	—	1	0	0	0	0	2	0	0	2	0	9.0	0.00	—	.000	.333	0	—	0	1	1	-0	0.0
1919 Phi-N	1	3	.250	5	3	2	0	0	27¹	36	1	9	6	15.5	5.60	58	.343	.405	2	.222	-0	-8	-7	-1	-1.0
1920 Phi-N	0	3	.000	5	1	0	0	0	23¹	25	1	15	8	16.6	3.86	89	.284	.406	1	.143	-1	-2	-1	0	-0.2
Total 3	1	6	.143	11	4	2	0	0	52²	61	2	26	14	15.7	4.61	71	.310	.404	3	.188	-1	-9	-8	-1	-1.2

● TOM CANTWELL
Cantwell, Thomas Aloysius b: 12/23/1888, Washington, D.C. d: 4/1/68, Washington, D.C. BL/TR, 6', 170 lbs. Deb: 5/19/09 F

YEAR TM/L	W	L	PCT	G	GS	CG	SH	SV	IP	H	HR	BB	SO	RAT	ERA	ERA+	OAV	OOB	BH	AVG	PB	PR	/A	PD	TPI
1909 Cin-N	1	0	1.000	6	1	1	0	0	21²	16	0	7	7	10.0	1.66	157	.205	.279	3	.600	1	2	2	-0	0.3
1910 Cin-N	0	0	—	2	0	0	0	0	1¹	2	0	3	0	33.8	13.50	22	.400	.625	0	—	0	-2	-2	-0	0.0
Total 2	1	0	1.000	8	1	1	0	0	23	18	0	10	7	11.3	2.35	112	.217	.309	3	.600	1	1	1	-0	0.3

● MIKE CAPEL
Capel, Michael Lee b: 10/13/61, Marshall, Tex. BR/TR, 6'1", 175 lbs. Deb: 5/7/88

YEAR TM/L	W	L	PCT	G	GS	CG	SH	SV	IP	H	HR	BB	SO	RAT	ERA	ERA+	OAV	OOB	BH	AVG	PB	PR	/A	PD	TPI
1988 Chi-N	2	1	.667	22	0	0	0	0	29¹	34	5	13	19	15.3	4.91	73	.293	.379	0	.000	-0	-5	-4	-0	-0.5
1990 Mil-A	0	0	—	2	0	0	0	0	0¹	6	0	1	1	216.0	135.00	3	.857	.889	0	—	0	-5	-5	-0	-0.5
1991 Hou-N	1	3	.250	25	0	0	0	3	32²	33	3	15	23	13.2	3.03	116	.266	.345	0	—	0	2	2	0	0.2
Total 3	3	4	.429	49	0	0	0	3	62¹	73	8	29	43	15.3	4.62	77	.296	.379	0	.000	-0	-7	-7	-0	-0.3

● DOUG CAPILLA
Capilla, Douglas Edmund b: 1/7/52, Honolulu, Hawaii BL/TL, 5'8", 175 lbs. Deb: 9/12/76

YEAR TM/L	W	L	PCT	G	GS	CG	SH	SV	IP	H	HR	BB	SO	RAT	ERA	ERA+	OAV	OOB	BH	AVG	PB	PR	/A	PD	TPI
1976 StL-N	1	0	1.000	7	0	0	0	0	8¹	8	0	4	5	13.0	5.40	65	.242	.324	0	—	0	-2	-2	0	-0.2
1977 StL-N	0	0	—	2	0	0	0	0	2¹	2	0	2	1	15.4	15.43	25	.222	.364	0	—	0	-3	-3	0	-0.2
Cin-N	7	8	.467	22	16	1	0	0	106¹	94	10	59	74	13.1	4.23	93	.237	.338	2	.059	-3	-4	-4	-1	-0.8
Yr	7	8	.467	24	16	1	0	0	108²	96	10	61	75	13.2	4.47	88	.236	.339	2	.059	-3	-7	-7	-1	-0.8
1978 Cin-N	0	1	.000	6	3	0	0	0	11	14	1	11	9	20.5	9.82	36	.318	.455	0	—	0	-8	-8	-0	-0.7
1979 Cin-N	1	0	1.000	5	0	0	0	0	6¹	7	1	5	0	18.5	8.53	44	.269	.406	1	1.000	0	-3	-3	0	-0.2
Chi-N	0	1	.000	13	0	0	0	0	17¹	14	1	16	12	10.9	2.60	159	.206	.280	0	—	0	2	3	0	0.2
Yr	1	1	.500	18	0	0	0	0	23²	21	2	12	12	12.5	4.18	98	.221	.308	1	1.000	0	-1	-0	1	-0.2
1980 Chi-N	2	8	.200	39	11	0	0	0	89²	82	7	51	51	13.7	4.12	95	.253	.360	4	.190	-0	-5	-2	1	-0.1
1981 Chi-N	1	0	1.000	42	0	0	0	0	51	52	1	34	28	15.5	3.18	116	.284	.402	0	.000	0	2	3	0	0.0
Total 6	12	18	.400	136	31	1	0	0	292¹	273	21	173	178	14.0	4.34	89	.252	.359	7	.115	-3	-21	-15	0	-2.0

● GEORGE CAPPUZZELLO
Cappuzzello, George Angelo b: 1/15/54, Youngstown, Ohio BR/TL, 6', 175 lbs. Deb: 5/31/81

YEAR TM/L	W	L	PCT	G	GS	CG	SH	SV	IP	H	HR	BB	SO	RAT	ERA	ERA+	OAV	OOB	BH	AVG	PB	PR	/A	PD	TPI
1981 Det-A	1	1	.500	18	3	0	1	1	33²	28	2	18	19	12.8	3.48	108	.222	.329	0	—	0	1	1	-0	0.0
1982 Hou-N	0	1	.000	17	0	0	0	0	19¹	16	2	7	13	12.1	2.79	119	.232	.329	0	.000	-0	2	1	0	0.1
Total 2	1	2	.333	35	3	0	1	1	53	44	4	25	32	12.6	3.23	112	.226	.329	0	.000	-0	2	2	0	0.1

● BUZZ CAPRA
Capra, Lee William b: 10/1/47, Chicago, Ill. BR/TR, 5'10", 168 lbs. Deb: 9/15/71

YEAR TM/L	W	L	PCT	G	GS	CG	SH	SV	IP	H	HR	BB	SO	RAT	ERA	ERA+	OAV	OOB	BH	AVG	PB	PR	/A	PD	TPI
1971 NY-N	0	1	.000	3	0	0	0	0	5¹	3	0	5	6	13.5	8.44	40	.167	.348	0	.000	-0	-3	-3	0	-0.5

YEAR	TM/L	W	L	PCT	G	GS	CG	SH	SV	IP	H	HR	BB	SO	RAT	ERA	ERA+	OAV	OOB	BH	AVG	PB	PR	/A	PD	TPI
1972	NY-N	3	2	.600	14	6	0	0	0	53	50	7	27	45	13.1	4.58	73	.253	.342	3	.250	1	-7	-7	1	-0.4
1973	NY-N	2	7	.222	24	0	0	0	4	42	35	4	28	35	13.9	3.86	94	.233	.361	0	.000	0	-1	-1	0	-0.2
1974	Atl-N☆	16	8	.667	39	27	11	5	1	217	163	13	84	137	10.4	**2.28**	**166**	**.208**	.287	11	.164	0	32	36	-3	3.7
1975	Atl-N	4	7	.364	12	12	5	0	0	78¹	77	8	28	35	12.2	4.25	89	.257	.322	1	.043	-2	-5	-4	1	-0.7
1976	Atl-N	0	1	.000	5	0	0	0	0	9¹	9	0	6	4	14.5	8.68	44	.265	.375	0	—	0	-5	-5	0	-0.5
1977	Atl-N	6	11	.353	45	16	0	0	0	139¹	142	28	80	100	14.6	5.36	83	.263	.362	4	.111	-2	-22	-14	-1	-1.7
Total	7	31	37	.456	142	61	16	5	5	544¹	479	60	258	362	12.4	3.87	100	.237	.326	19	.135	-2	-12	1	-1	-0.3

● PAT CARAWAY   Caraway, Cecil Bradford Patrick b: 9/26/05, Erath Co., Tex. d: 6/9/74, ElPaso, Tex. BL/TL, 6'4", 175 lbs. Deb: 4/19/30

YEAR	TM/L	W	L	PCT	G	GS	CG	SH	SV	IP	H	HR	BB	SO	RAT	ERA	ERA+	OAV	OOB	BH	AVG	PB	PR	/A	PD	TPI
1930	Chi-A	10	10	.500	38	21	9	1	1	193¹	194	11	57	83	11.8	3.86	120	.267	.323	11	.172	-1	17	16	3	1.6
1931	Chi-A	10	24	.294	51	32	11	1	2	220	268	17	101	55	15.4	6.22	68	.295	.370	14	.194	-1	-45	-48	-1	-6.1
1932	Chi-A	2	6	.250	19	9	1	0	0	64²	80	6	37	13	16.7	6.82	63	.304	.396	3	.143	-1	-17	-18	0	-1.8
Total	3	22	40	.355	108	62	21	2	3	478	542	34	195	151	14.1	5.35	83	.286	.356	28	.178	-3	-45	-50	2	-6.3

● JOHN CARDEN   Carden, John Bruton b: 5/19/21, Killeen, Tex. d: 2/8/49, Mexia, Tex. BR/TR, 6'5", 210 lbs. Deb: 5/18/46

YEAR	TM/L	W	L	PCT	G	GS	CG	SH	SV	IP	H	HR	BB	SO	RAT	ERA	ERA+	OAV	OOB	BH	AVG	PB	PR	/A	PD	TPI
1946	NY-N	0	0	—	1	0	0	0	0	2	4	0	4	1	40.5	22.50	15	.400	.600	0	—	0	-4	-4	-0	0.0

● CONRAD CARDINAL   Cardinal, Conrad Seth b: 3/30/42, Brooklyn, N.Y. BR/TR, 6'1", 190 lbs. Deb: 4/11/63

YEAR	TM/L	W	L	PCT	G	GS	CG	SH	SV	IP	H	HR	BB	SO	RAT	ERA	ERA+	OAV	OOB	BH	AVG	PB	PR	/A	PD	TPI
1963	Hou-N	0	1	.000	6	1	0	0	0	13¹	15	0	7	7	14.9	6.08	52	.283	.367	0	.000	-0	-4	-4	0	-0.3

● BEN CARDONI   Cardoni, Armand Joseph "Big Ben" b: 8/21/20, Jessup, Pa. d: 4/2/69, Jessup, Pa. BR/TR, 6'3", 195 lbs. Deb: 8/22/43

YEAR	TM/L	W	L	PCT	G	GS	CG	SH	SV	IP	H	HR	BB	SO	RAT	ERA	ERA+	OAV	OOB	BH	AVG	PB	PR	/A	PD	TPI
1943	Bos-N	0	0	—	11	0	0	0	1	28	38	1	14	5	17.0	6.43	53	.336	.414	0	.000	-1	-9	-9	-0	-0.2
1944	Bos-N	0	6	.000	22	5	1	0	0	75²	83	5	37	24	14.4	3.93	97	.284	.367	4	.235	-0	-3	-1	-1	-0.1
1945	Bos-N	0	0	—	3	0	0	0	0	4	6	0	3	5	22.5	9.00	43	.300	.417	0	—	0	-2	-2	-0	0.0
Total	3	0	6	.000	36	5	1	0	1	107²	127	6	54	34	15.4	4.76	78	.299	.382	4	.167	-1	-14	-13	-1	-0.3

● DON CARDWELL   Cardwell, Donald Eugene b: 12/7/35, Winston-Salem, N.C. BR/TR, 6'4", 210 lbs. Deb: 4/21/57

YEAR	TM/L	W	L	PCT	G	GS	CG	SH	SV	IP	H	HR	BB	SO	RAT	ERA	ERA+	OAV	OOB	BH	AVG	PB	PR	/A	PD	TPI
1957	Phi-N	4	8	.333	30	19	5	1	1	128¹	122	17	42	92	11.8	4.91	78	.251	.316	7	.200	1	-15	-16	-1	-1.2
1958	Phi-N	3	6	.333	16	14	3	0	0	107²	99	16	37	77	11.5	4.51	88	.241	.307	8	.211	1	-7	-7	0	-0.4
1959	Phi-N	9	10	.474	25	22	5	1	0	153	135	22	65	106	12.0	4.06	101	.238	.320	3	.055	-3	-2	1	-3	-0.5
1960	Phi-N	1	2	.333	5	4	0	0	0	28¹	28	4	11	21	12.7	4.45	87	.262	.336	2	.250	-2	-2	-0	0	0.0
	Chi-N	8	14	.364	31	26	6	1	0	177	166	19	68	129	12.2	4.37	86	.249	.323	14	.203	3	-12	-12	-2	-1.1
	Yr	9	16	.360	36	30	6	1	0	205¹	194	23	79	150	12.2	4.38	87	.250	.324	16	.208	5	-14	-13	-2	-1.1
1961	Chi-N	15	14	.517	39	38	13	3	0	259¹	243	22	88	156	11.8	3.82	110	.246	.314	10	.105	-1	6	10	2	1.2
1962	Chi-N	7	16	.304	41	29	6	1	4	195²	205	27	60	104	12.6	4.92	84	.267	.327	9	.148	-0	-21	-17	1	-1.7
1963	Pit-N	13	15	.464	33	32	7	2	0	213²	195	21	52	112	11.1	3.07	107	.245	.305	6	.085	-2	5	5	-1	0.4
1964	Pit-N	1	2	.333	4	4	1	1	0	19¹	15	1	7	10	11.6	2.79	126	.217	.316	1	.143	-0	2	2	0	0.3
1965	Pit-N	13	10	.565	37	34	12	2	0	240¹	214	21	59	107	10.7	3.18	110	.239	.295	12	.162	3	10	9	2	1.3
1966	Pit-N	6	6	.500	32	14	1	0	1	101²	112	15	27	60	12.8	4.60	78	.282	.337	3	.103	-1	-11	-12	2	-1.1
1967	NY-N	5	9	.357	26	16	3	3	0	118¹	112	8	39	71	12.0	3.57	95	.249	.319	6	.158	2	-3	-2	2	0.2
1968	NY-N	7	13	.350	29	25	5	1	0	179²	156	9	50	82	10.8	2.96	102	.233	.296	3	.049	-3	1	2	0	0.2
1969	*NY-N	8	10	.444	30	21	4	0	0	152¹	145	15	47	60	11.6	3.01	121	.252	.314	8	.170	1	10	11	2	1.6
1970	NY-N	0	2	.000	16	1	0	0	0	25	31	3	6	8	14.4	6.48	62	.316	.374	0	.000	-1	-7	-7	0	-0.5
	Atl-N	2	1	.667	16	1	0	0	0	23	31	5	13	16	17.6	9.00	48	.326	.413	2	.400	1	-13	-12	1	-1.2
	Yr	2	3	.400	32	2	1	0	0	48	62	8	19	24	15.4	7.69	54	.312	.374	2	.200	-0	-19	-19	1	-1.7
Total	14	102	138	.425	410	301	72	17	7	2122²	2009	225	671	1211	11.8	3.92	95	.250	.315	94	.135	2	-59	-47	10	-2.7

● TEX CARLETON   Carleton, James Otto b: 8/19/06, Comanche, Tex. d: 1/11/77, Fort Worth, Tex. BB/TR, 6'1.5", 180 lbs. Deb: 4/17/32

YEAR	TM/L	W	L	PCT	G	GS	CG	SH	SV	IP	H	HR	BB	SO	RAT	ERA	ERA+	OAV	OOB	BH	AVG	PB	PR	/A	PD	TPI
1932	StL-N	10	13	.435	44	22	9	3	0	196¹	198	12	70	113	12.4	4.08	96	.261	.326	9	.150	-2	-4	-3	2	-0.3
1933	StL-N	17	11	.607	44	33	15	4	3	277	263	15	97	147	11.8	3.38	103	.249	.315	17	.187	1	-1	3	-1	0.3
1934	*StL-N	16	11	.593	40	31	16	0	2	240²	260	14	52	103	11.9	4.26	99	.271	.314	17	.193	1	-5	-1	0	-0.1
1935	*Chi-N	11	8	.579	31	22	8	0	1	171	169	17	60	84	12.2	3.89	101	.257	.322	8	.129	-3	2	1	2	0.0
1936	Chi-N	14	10	.583	35	26	12	**4**	1	197¹	204	14	67	88	12.6	3.65	109	.268	.332	14	.233	6	8	7	2	1.6
1937	Chi-N	16	8	.667	32	27	18	4	0	208¹	183	10	94	105	12.1	3.15	126	.236	.321	12	.169	1	18	19	1	2.2
1938	*Chi-N	10	9	.526	33	24	9	0	0	167²	213	11	74	80	15.8	5.42	71	.307	.381	15	.231	3	-30	-30	-0	-2.7
1940	Bro-N	6	6	.500	34	17	4	1	2	149	140	12	47	88	11.5	3.81	105	.245	.305	8	.186	-0	1	3	1	0.1
Total	8	100	76	.568	293	202	91	16	9	1607¹	1630	105	561	808	12.5	3.91	100	.261	.326	100	.185	6	-13	-0	6	1.1

● CISCO CARLOS   Carlos, Francisco Manuel b: 9/17/40, Monrovia, Cal. BR/TR, 6'3", 205 lbs. Deb: 8/25/67

YEAR	TM/L	W	L	PCT	G	GS	CG	SH	SV	IP	H	HR	BB	SO	RAT	ERA	ERA+	OAV	OOB	BH	AVG	PB	PR	/A	PD	TPI
1967	Chi-A	2	0	1.000	8	7	1	1	0	41²	23	0	9	27	7.1	0.86	359	.161	.216	1	.063	-1	11	10	0	0.4
1968	Chi-A	4	14	.222	29	21	6	2	0	122¹	121	13	37	57	12.4	3.90	78	.258	.326	2	.065	-1	-13	-12	2	-1.7
1969	Chi-A	4	3	.571	25	0	0	0	0	49¹	52	4	23	28	14.6	5.66	68	.274	.367	0	.000	-1	-11	-10	1	-1.3
	Was-A	1	1	.500	6	4	0	0	0	17²	23	2	6	5	14.8	4.58	76	.348	.403	1	.200	1	-2	-2	0	-0.1
	Yr	5	4	.556	31	8	0	0	0	67	75	6	29	33	14.0	5.37	70	.287	.359	1	.067	-0	-13	-12	1	-1.4
1970	Was-A	0	0	—	5	0	0	0	0	6	3	0	4	2	10.5	1.50	237	.150	.292	0	—	0	1	1	0	0.2
Total	4	11	18	.379	73	36	1	1	0	237	222	19	79	119	12.0	3.72	88	.250	.322	4	.065	-3	-13	-12	3	-2.7

● DON CARLSEN   Carlsen, Donald Herbert b: 10/15/26, Chicago, Ill. BR/TR, 6'1", 175 lbs. Deb: 4/28/48

YEAR	TM/L	W	L	PCT	G	GS	CG	SH	SV	IP	H	HR	BB	SO	RAT	ERA	ERA+	OAV	OOB	BH	AVG	PB	PR	/A	PD	TPI
1948	Chi-N	0	0	—	1	0	0	0	0	1	5	0	1	1	63.0	36.00	11	.625	.700	0	—	0	-4	-4	0	0.0
1951	Pit-N	2	3	.400	7	6	2	0	0	43	50	4	14	20	13.6	4.19	101	.292	.349	4	.250	-1	-1	0	-1	0.0
1952	Pit-N	0	1	.000	5	1	0	0	0	10	20	1	5	2	22.5	10.80	37	.417	.472	1	.333	1	-8	-8	1	-0.6
Total	3	2	4	.333	13	7	2	0	0	54	75	5	21	23	16.2	6.00	70	.330	.390	5	.263	-0	-12	-11	0	-0.6

● HAL CARLSON   Carlson, Harold Gust b: 5/17/1892, Rockford, Ill. d: 5/28/30, Chicago, Ill. BR/TR, 6', 180 lbs. Deb: 4/13/17

YEAR	TM/L	W	L	PCT	G	GS	CG	SH	SV	IP	H	HR	BB	SO	RAT	ERA	ERA+	OAV	OOB	BH	AVG	PB	PR	/A	PD	TPI
1917	Pit-N	7	11	.389	34	17	9	1	1	161¹	140	0	49	68	10.8	2.90	98	.241	.304	6	.122	-2	-3	-1	2	-0.2
1918	Pit-N	0	1	.000	3	2	0	0	0	12	12	1	5	5	12.8	3.75	77	.286	.362	1	.200	-0	-1	-1	-0	-0.1
1919	Pit-N	8	10	.444	22	14	7	1	0	141	114	0	39	49	9.9	2.23	135	.243	.303	7	.163	-1	11	12	1	1.7
1920	Pit-N	14	13	.519	39	31	16	3	3	246²	262	4	63	62	12.1	3.36	96	.281	.331	23	.271	3	-6	-4	-5	-0.6
1921	Pit-N	4	8	.333	31	10	6	0	4	109²	121	6	37	20	12.0	4.27	90	.290	.330	10	.294	1	-6	-5	1	-0.4
1922	Pit-N	9	12	.429	39	18	6	0	2	145¹	193	10	58	64	15.8	5.70	72	.323	.386	15	.268	3	-26	-26	3	-2.7
1923	Pit-N	0	0	—	4	0	0	0	0	13¹	19	2	2	4	14.9	4.73	85	.358	.393	0	.000	-0	-1	-1	0	0.0
1924	Phi-N	8	17	.320	38	24	12	1	2	203²	267	9	55	66	14.4	4.86	92	.329	.374	21	.276	2	-22	-9	1	-0.8
1925	Phi-N	13	14	.481	35	32	18	**4**	0	234	281	19	80	80	13.0	4.23	113	.298	.338	17	.183	-2	1	14	-1	1.1
1926	Phi-N	17	12	.586	35	34	20	3	0	267¹	293	6	47	55	11.5	3.23	128	.283	.313	23	.240	2	18	27	-4	2.6
1927	Phi-N	4	5	.444	11	9	4	0	1	63²	80	7	18	13	13.9	5.23	79	.316	.362	6	.240	0	-9	-8	-1	-1.0
	Chi-N	12	8	.600	27	22	15	2	0	184²	201	9	27	27	11.2	3.17	122	.280	.307	11	.164	-3	15	14	-0	1.0
	Yr	16	13	.552	38	31	19	2	1	248	281	16	45	40	11.9	3.70	106	.289	.322	17	.185	-3	6	6	-1	0.0
1928	Chi-N	3	2	.600	20	5	2	0	4	56¹	74	4	15	11	14.2	5.91	65	.329	.371	5	.263	0	-12	-13	0	-1.1
1929	*Chi-N	11	5	.688	31	14	6	2	2	111²	131	8	31	35	13.1	5.16	90	.292	.340	9	.231	-0	-5	-7	-2	-0.6
1930	Chi-N	4	2	.667	8	6	2	1	0	51²	68	5	14	14	14.5	5.05	97	.313	.358	5	.250	0	-0	-1	1	0.0
Total	14	114	120	.487	377	238	121	17	19	2002	2256	93	498	590	12.5	3.97	99	.291	.337	159	.223	4	-49	-8	-0	-1.1

● LEON CARLSON   Carlson, Leon Alton "Swede" b: 2/17/1895, Jamestown, N.Y. d: 9/15/61, Jamestown, N.Y. BR/TR, 6'3", 195 lbs. Deb: 5/31/20

YEAR	TM/L	W	L	PCT	G	GS	CG	SH	SV	IP	H	HR	BB	SO	RAT	ERA	ERA+	OAV	OOB	BH	AVG	PB	PR	/A	PD	TPI
1920	Was-A	0	0	—	3	0	0	0	0	12¹	14	1	2	3	11.7	3.65	102	.292	.320	1	.167	-0	0	0	-0	-0.1

YEAR	TM/L	W	L	PCT	G	GS	CG	SH	SV	IP	H	HR	BB	SO	RAT	ERA	ERA+	OAV	OOB	BH	AVG	PB	PR	/A	PD	TPI

● STEVE CARLTON   Carlton, Steven Norman "Lefty" b: 12/22/44, Miami, Fla.   BL/TL, 6'4", 210 lbs. Deb: 4/12/65 H

YEAR	TM/L	W	L	PCT	G	GS	CG	SH	SV	IP	H	HR	BB	SO	RAT	ERA	ERA+	OAV	OOB	BH	AVG	PB	PR	/A	PD	TPI
1965	StL-N	0	0	—	15	2	0	0	0	25	27	3	8	21	13.0	2.52	153	.287	.350	0	.000	-0	3	4	1	0.0
1966	StL-N	3	3	.500	9	9	2	1	0	52	56	2	18	25	12.8	3.12	115	.280	.339	4	.267	1	3	3	0	0.4
1967	*StL-N	14	9	.609	30	28	11	2	1	193	173	10	62	168	11.1	2.98	110	.238	.300	11	.153	1	8	6	0	0.8
1968	*StL-N★	13	11	.542	34	33	10	5	0	231²	214	11	61	162	10.8	2.99	97	.246	.298	12	.164	2	-0	-2	-1	-0.1
1969	StL-N★	17	11	.607	31	31	12	2	0	236¹	185	15	93	210	10.7	2.17	165	.216	.295	17	.213	5	37	37	-1	4.9
1970	StL-N	10	19	.345	34	33	13	2	0	253²	239	25	109	193	12.4	3.73	110	.251	.329	16	.200	2	9	11	-1	1.2
1971	StL-N☆	20	9	.690	37	36	18	4	0	273¹	275	23	98	172	12.4	3.56	101	.262	.328	17	.177	1	-3	1	-0	0.2
1972	Phi-N★	**27**	10	.730	41	41	**30**	8	0	**346**	257	17	87	**310**	9.0	**1.97**	**182**	.206	.259	23	.197	4	**57**	**62**	-2	**7.4**
1973	Phi-N	13	20	.394	40	40	**18**	3	0	293¹	293	29	113	223	12.5	3.90	97	.260	.329	16	.160	1	-8	-3	-1	-0.4
1974	Phi-N☆	16	13	.552	39	39	17	1	0	291	249	21	136	**240**	12.1	3.22	117	.234	.323	25	.245	2	13	18	-1	1.9
1975	Phi-N	15	14	.517	37	37	14	3	0	255¹	217	24	104	192	11.4	3.56	105	.233	.312	14	.156	-0	2	5	-1	0.4
1976	*Phi-N	20	7	**.741**	35	35	13	2	0	252²	224	19	72	195	10.6	3.13	113	.237	.291	20	.217	2	10	12	-4	0.4
1977	*Phi-N☆	**23**	10	.697	36	36	17	2	0	283	229	25	89	198	10.2	2.64	151	.223	.288	26	.268	8	40	43	1	6.0
1978	*Phi-N	16	13	.552	34	34	12	3	0	247¹	228	30	63	161	10.7	2.84	126	.246	.297	25	.291	7	20	20	1	3.3
1979	Phi-N★	18	11	.621	35	35	13	4	0	251	202	25	89	213	10.6	3.62	106	.219	.292	21	.223	3	3	6	-1	0.9
1980	*Phi-N☆	**24**	9	.727	38	38	13	3	0	**304**	243	15	90	**286**	9.9	2.34	**162**	.218	.278	19	.188	-1	**43**	**49**	-1	**5.3**
1981	*Phi-N☆	13	4	.765	24	24	10	1	0	190	152	9	62	179	10.2	2.42	150	.222	.288	9	.134	-0	23	26	-1	2.2
1982	Phi-N★	**23**	11	.676	38	38	**19**	6	0	295²	253	17	86	**286**	10.3	3.10	118	.232	.289	22	.218	4	16	18	-1	2.4
1983	*Phi-N	15	16	.484	37	37	8	3	0	283²	277	20	84	275	11.5	3.11	115	.258	.314	19	.196	3	16	14	-1	1.7
1984	Phi-N	13	7	.650	33	33	1	0	0	229	214	14	79	163	11.5	3.58	102	.246	.309	16	.190	2	0	1	-3	0.0
1985	Phi-N	1	8	.111	16	16	0	0	0	92	84	6	53	48	13.4	3.33	111	.249	.350	5	.179	0	3	4	1	0.4
1986	Phi-N	4	8	.333	16	16	0	0	0	83	102	15	45	62	15.9	6.18	62	.297	.379	7	.206	1	-23	-21	-1	-2.7
	SF-N	1	3	.250	6	6	0	0	0	30	36	4	16	18	15.9	5.10	69	.303	.390	2	.182	1	-5	-5	1	-0.5
	Yr	5	11	.313	22	22	0	0	0	113	138	19	61	80	15.9	5.89	64	.297	.380	9	.200	2	-27	-27	-0	-3.2
	Chi-A	4	3	.571	10	10	0	0	0	63¹	58	6	25	40	11.8	3.69	117	.252	.325	0	—	0	3	4	-1	0.1
1987	Cle-A	5	9	.357	23	14	3	0	1	109	111	17	63	71	14.5	5.37	84	.266	.364	0	—	0	-11	-10	-0	-1.2
	Min-A	1	5	.167	9	7	0	0	0	43	54	7	23	20	16.5	6.70	69	.310	.397	0	—	0	-11	-10	-0	-1.3
	Yr	6	14	.300	32	21	3	0	1	152	165	24	86	91	15.0	5.74	79	.276	.369	0	—	0	-22	-20	-0	-2.5
1988	Min-A	0	1	.000	4	1	0	0	0	9²	20	5	5	5	23.3	16.76	24	.408	.463	0	—	0	-14	-14	-0	-1.1
Total	24	329	244	.574	741	709	254	55	2	5217¹	4672	414	1833	4136	11.3	3.22	115	.240	.308	346	.201	49	236	277	-18	33.2

● DON CARMAN   Carman, Donald Wayne b: 8/14/59, Oklahoma City, Okla BL/TL, 6'3", 195 lbs. Deb: 10/1/83

YEAR	TM/L	W	L	PCT	G	GS	CG	SH	SV	IP	H	HR	BB	SO	RAT	ERA	ERA+	OAV	OOB	BH	AVG	PB	PR	/A	PD	TPI
1983	Phi-N	0	0	—	1	0	0	0	1	1	0	0	1	0	0.0	0.00	—	.000	.000	0	—	0	0	0	0	0.1
1984	Phi-N	0	1	.000	11	0	0	0	0	13¹	14	2	6	16	13.5	5.40	67	.255	.328	0	.000	-0	-3	-3	-0	-0.2
1985	Phi-N	9	4	.692	71	0	0	0	7	86¹	52	6	38	87	9.6	2.08	177	.178	.277	0	.000	-0	14	15	0	2.5
1986	Phi-N	10	5	.667	50	14	2	1	1	134¹	113	11	52	98	11.3	3.22	120	.234	.313	0	.000	-3	7	9	2	0.9
1987	Phi-N	13	11	.542	35	35	3	2	0	211	194	34	69	125	11.4	4.22	100	.244	.308	5	.082	-3	-3	-0	-4	-0.6
1988	Phi-N	10	14	.417	36	32	2	0	0	201¹	211	20	70	116	12.7	4.29	83	.270	.333	3	.048	-5	-19	-16	-3	-2.6
1989	Phi-N	5	15	.250	49	20	0	0	0	149¹	152	21	86	81	14.5	5.24	68	.260	.358	1	.029	-3	-29	-28	-1	-3.9
1990	Phi-N	6	2	.750	59	1	0	0	0	86²	69	13	38	58	11.5	4.15	92	.218	.310	3	.273	1	-3	-3	0	-0.2
1991	Cin-N	0	2	.000	28	0	0	0	0	36	42	8	19	15	15.0	5.25	72	.284	.375	0	.000	-1	-6	-6	0	-0.3
1992	Tex-A	0	0	—	2	0	0	0	0	2¹	4	0	2	2	15.4	7.71	49	.364	.364	0	—	0	-1	-1	-0	0.0
Total	10	53	54	.495	342	102	7	3	11	921²	849	115	378	598	12.2	4.11	92	.245	.323	12	.057	-14	-42	-32	-5	-4.3

● CHET CARMICHAEL   Carmichael, Chester Keller b: 1/9/1888, Muncie, Ind. d: 8/22/60, Rochester, N.Y. BR/TR, 5'11.5", 200 lbs. Deb: 9/5/09

YEAR	TM/L	W	L	PCT	G	GS	CG	SH	SV	IP	H	HR	BB	SO	RAT	ERA	ERA+	OAV	OOB	BH	AVG	PB	PR	/A	PD	TPI
1909	Cin-N	0	0	—	2	0	0	0	0	7	9	0	3	2	18.0	0.00	—	.321	.424	0	.000	-0	2	2	-0	-0.1

● EDDIE CARNETT   Carnett, Edwin Elliott "Lefty" b: 10/21/16, Springfield, Mo. BL/TL, 6', 185 lbs. Deb: 4/19/41 ♦

YEAR	TM/L	W	L	PCT	G	GS	CG	SH	SV	IP	H	HR	BB	SO	RAT	ERA	ERA+	OAV	OOB	BH	AVG	PB	PR	/A	PD	TPI
1941	Bos-N	0	0	—	2	0	0	0	0	1¹	4	0	3	2	47.3	20.25	18	.500	.636	0	—	0	-2	-2	0	0.0
1944	Chi-A	0	0	—	2	0	0	0	0	2	3	1	0	1	13.5	9.00	38	.333	.333	126	.276	1	-1	-1	0	0.0
1945	Cle-A	0	0	—	2	0	0	0	0	2	0	0	0	1	0.0	0.00	—	.000	.000	16	.219	0	1	1	-0	0.0
Total	3	0	0	—	6	0	0	0	0	5¹	7	1	3	4	16.9	8.44	40	.304	.385	142	.268	1	-3	-3	0	0.0

● PAT CARNEY   Carney, Patrick Joseph "Doc" b: 8/7/1876, Holyoke, Mass. d: 1/9/53, Worcester, Mass. BL/TL, 6', 200 lbs. Deb: 9/20/01 ♦

YEAR	TM/L	W	L	PCT	G	GS	CG	SH	SV	IP	H	HR	BB	SO	RAT	ERA	ERA+	OAV	OOB	BH	AVG	PB	PR	/A	PD	TPI
1902	Bos-N	0	1	.000	2	1	0	0	0	5	6	1	3	3	18.0	9.00	31	.297	.413	141	.270	0	-3	-3	-0	-0.6
1903	Bos-N	4	5	.444	10	9	9	0	0	78	93	2	31	29	14.5	4.04	79	.284	.349	94	.240	2	-7	-7	-0	-0.6
1904	Bos-N	0	4	.000	4	2	1	0	0	26¹	40	1	12	5	18.1	5.81	47	.364	.431	57	.204	0	-9	-9	-0	-1.1
Total	3	4	10	.286	16	12	10	0	0	109¹	139	4	46	37	15.6	4.69	66	.303	.372	308	.247	2	-19	-20	-1	-2.3

● CRIS CARPENTER   Carpenter, Cris Howell b: 4/5/65, St.Augustine, Fla. BR/TR, 6'1", 195 lbs. Deb: 5/14/88

YEAR	TM/L	W	L	PCT	G	GS	CG	SH	SV	IP	H	HR	BB	SO	RAT	ERA	ERA+	OAV	OOB	BH	AVG	PB	PR	/A	PD	TPI
1988	StL-N	2	3	.400	8	8	1	0	0	47²	56	3	9	24	12.5	4.72	74	.298	.333	2	.143	-0	-7	-7	-0	-0.7
1989	StL-N	4	4	.500	36	5	0	0	0	68	70	4	26	35	13.0	3.18	114	.262	.332	4	.444	1	2	3	-0	0.5
1990	StL-N	0	0	—	4	0	0	0	0	8	5	2	2	6	7.9	4.50	85	.167	.219	0	.000	-0	-1	-1	-0	0.0
1991	StL-N	10	4	.714	59	0	0	0	0	66	53	6	20	47	10.0	4.23	88	.220	.280	1	.333	1	-4	-4	-0	-0.7
1992	StL-N	5	4	.556	73	0	0	0	1	88	69	10	27	46	10.2	2.97	114	.220	.291	1	.333	-0	5	4	-1	0.4
1993	Fla-N	0	1	.000	29	0	0	0	0	37¹	29	1	13	26	10.6	2.89	149	.212	.289	0	—	0	5	6	1	0.2
	Tex-A	4	1	.800	27	0	0	0	1	32	35	4	12	27	13.8	4.22	98	.289	.363	0	—	0	0	-0	-0	0.0
1994	Tex-A	2	5	.286	47	0	0	0	5	59	69	6	20	27	13.6	5.03	90	.291	.346	0	—	0	-2	-3	0	0.0
Total	7	27	22	.551	283	13	1	0	7	406	386	37	129	250	11.7	3.83	100	.252	.314	8	.267	1	-0	-1	-1	-0.3

● LEW CARPENTER   Carpenter, Lewis Emmett b: 8/16/13, Woodstock, Ga. d: 4/25/79, Marietta, Ga. BR/TR, 6'2", 195 lbs. Deb: 5/1/43

YEAR	TM/L	W	L	PCT	G	GS	CG	SH	SV	IP	H	HR	BB	SO	RAT	ERA	ERA+	OAV	OOB	BH	AVG	PB	PR	/A	PD	TPI
1943	Was-A	0	0	—	4	0	0	0	0	3¹	1	0	4	1	16.2	0.00	—	.125	.462	0	—	0	1	1	-0	0.0

● PAUL CARPENTER   Carpenter, Paul Calvin b: 8/12/1894, Granville, Ohio d: 3/14/68, Newark, Ohio BR/TR, 5'11", 165 lbs. Deb: 7/26/16

YEAR	TM/L	W	L	PCT	G	GS	CG	SH	SV	IP	H	HR	BB	SO	RAT	ERA	ERA+	OAV	OOB	BH	AVG	PB	PR	/A	PD	TPI
1916	Pit-N	0	0	—	5	0	0	0	0	7²	8	0	4	5	14.1	1.17	229	.258	.343	0	.000	-0	1	1	0	0.0

● BOB CARPENTER   Carpenter, Robert Louis b: 12/12/17, Chicago, Ill. BR/TR, 6'3", 195 lbs. Deb: 9/12/40

YEAR	TM/L	W	L	PCT	G	GS	CG	SH	SV	IP	H	HR	BB	SO	RAT	ERA	ERA+	OAV	OOB	BH	AVG	PB	PR	/A	PD	TPI
1940	NY-N	2	0	1.000	5	3	2	0	0	33	29	2	14	25	11.7	2.73	142	.238	.316	1	.100	-0	4	4	-0	0.2
1941	NY-N	11	6	.647	29	19	8	1	2	131²	138	15	42	42	12.4	3.83	97	.265	.323	7	.156	-0	-3	-2	-3	-0.5
1942	NY-N	11	10	.524	28	25	12	2	0	185²	192	13	51	53	11.8	3.15	107	.263	.312	12	.185	-1	3	4	-3	0.1
1946	NY-N	1	3	.250	12	6	1	0	0	39	37	7	18	13	12.7	4.85	71	.245	.325	1	.100	-0	-6	-6	-1	-0.7
1947	NY-N	0	0	—	2	0	0	0	0	3	5	0	3	0	24.0	12.00	34	.385	.500	0	—	0	-3	-3	0	0.0
	Chi-N	0	1	.000	4	1	0	0	0	7¹	10	1	4	1	17.2	4.91	80	.323	.400	1	1.000	-0	-1	-1	0	0.0
	Yr	0	1	.000	6	1	0	0	0	10¹	15	1	7	1	19.2	6.97	57	.341	.431	1	1.000	-0	-3	-3	0	0.0
Total	5	25	20	.556	80	54	23	4	2	399²	411	38	132	134	12.3	3.60	98	.262	.321	22	.168	-1	-5	-3	-6	-0.9

● FRANK CARPIN   Carpin, Frank Dominic b: 9/14/38, Brooklyn, N.Y. BL/TL, 5'10", 172 lbs. Deb: 5/25/65

YEAR	TM/L	W	L	PCT	G	GS	CG	SH	SV	IP	H	HR	BB	SO	RAT	ERA	ERA+	OAV	OOB	BH	AVG	PB	PR	/A	PD	TPI
1965	Pit-N	3	1	.750	39	0	0	0	4	39²	35	6	24	27	14.1	3.18	111	.243	.363	0	—	0	2	1	0	0.3
1966	Hou-N	1	0	1.000	10	0	0	0	0	6	9	0	6	2	22.5	7.50	46	.346	.469	0	—	0	-3	-3	-0	-0.5
Total	2	4	1	.800	49	0	0	0	4	45²	44	6	30	29	15.2	3.74	93	.259	.379	0	.000	-0	-1	-1	1	-0.2

● HECTOR CARRASCO   Carrasco, Hector (Pacheco) b: 10/22/69, San Pedro De Macoris, D.R. BR/TR, 6'2", 175 lbs. Deb: 4/4/94

YEAR	TM/L	W	L	PCT	G	GS	CG	SH	SV	IP	H	HR	BB	SO	RAT	ERA	ERA+	OAV	OOB	BH	AVG	PB	PR	/A	PD	TPI
1994	Cin-N	5	6	.455	45	0	0	0	6	56¹	42	3	30	41	11.8	2.24	186	.210	.319	0	.000	-1	12	12	-0	2.3

YEAR TM/L	W	L	PCT	G	GS	CG	SH	SV	IP	H	HR	BB	SO	RAT	ERA	ERA+	OAV	OOB	BH	AVG	PB	PR	/A	PD	TPI
● **ALEX CARRASQUEL**				Carrasquel, Alejandro Eloy (Aparicio) b: 7/24/12, Caracas, Venez. d: 8/19/69, Caracas, Venez. BR/TR, 6'1", 182 lbs. Deb: 4/23/39																				
1939 Was-A	5	9	.357	40	17	7	0	2	159¹	165	7	68	41	13.2	4.69	93	.266	.340	7	.167	1	-1	-6	0	-0.3
1940 Was-A	6	2	.750	28	0	0	0	0	48	42	4	29	19	13.3	4.88	86	.240	.348	0	.000	-1	-3	-4	0	-0.6
1941 Was-A	6	2	.750	35	5	4	0	2	96²	103	7	49	30	14.2	3.44	117	.095	.364	2	.095	0	8	6	4	0.9
1942 Was-A	7	7	.500	35	15	7	1	4	152¹	161	7	53	40	12.7	3.43	107	.267	.327	6	.136	-0	4	4	1	0.5
1943 Was-A	11	7	.611	39	13	4	1	5	144¹	160	3	54	48	13.4	3.68	87	.279	.342	8	.186	1	-6	-8	1	-0.8
1944 Was-A	8	7	.533	43	7	3	0	2	134	143	8	50	35	13.1	3.43	95	.273	.342	7	.194	1	0	-3	1	0.0
1945 Was-A	7	5	.583	35	7	5	2	1	122²	105	5	40	38	10.6	2.71	114	.228	.289	3	.083	-2	9	5	-0	0.3
1949 Chi-A	0	0	—	3	0	0	0	0	3²	8	1	4	1	29.5	14.73	28	.421	.522	0	—	0	-4	-4	0	-0.0
Total 8	50	39	.562	258	64	30	4	16	861	887	42	347	252	13.0	3.73	98	.265	.335	33	.144	0	6	-9	8	-0.0
● **AMALIO CARRENO**				Carreno, Amalio Rafael (Adrian) b: 4/11/64, Chacachacare, Ven. BR/TR, 6', 170 lbs. Deb: 7/7/91																				
1991 Phi-N	0	0	—	3	0	0	0	0	3¹	5	1	3	2	27.0	16.20	23	.333	.500	0	.000	-0	-5	-5	-0	0.0
● **BILL CARRICK**				Carrick, William Martin "Doughnut Bill" b: 9/5/1873, Erie, Pa. d: 3/7/32, Philadelphia, Pa. TR , Deb: 7/30/1898																				
1898 NY-N	3	1	.750	5	4	4	0	0	39²	39	0	21	10	14.7	3.40	102	.255	.364	3	.167	-1	1	0	1	0.0
1899 NY-N	16	27	.372	44	43	**40**	3	0	361²	485	4	122	60	15.6	4.65	81	.320	.378	18	.138	-6	-32	-36	2	-3.7
1900 NY-N	19	22	.463	**45**	41	32	1	0	341²	415	7	92	63	13.7	3.53	102	.299	.348	20	.174	-3	6	3	-0	0.0
1901 Was-A	14	22	.389	42	37	34	0	0	324	367	12	93	70	13.3	3.75	98	.282	.339	20	.159	-5	-3	-3	0	-0.7
1902 Was-A	11	17	.393	31	30	28	0	0	257²	344	10	72	36	14.8	4.86	76	.320	.368	20	.185	-2	-37	-33	-3	-3.3
Total 5	63	89	.414	167	155	138	4	0	1324²	1650	33	400	239	14.4	4.14	89	.304	.359	81	.163	-16	-64	-68	-0	-7.7
● **DON CARRITHERS**				Carrithers, Donald George b: 9/15/49, Lynwood, Cal. BR/TR, 6'2", 180 lbs. Deb: 8/1/70																				
1970 SF-N	2	1	.667	11	2	0	0	0	22	31	5	14	14	18.4	7.36	54	.333	.421	0	.000	-0	-8	-8	-0	-1.0
1971 *SF-N	5	3	.625	22	12	2	1	1	80¹	77	6	37	41	13.0	4.03	84	.254	.339	3	.176	0	-5	-6	-1	-0.5
1972 SF-N	4	8	.333	25	14	2	0	1	90	108	10	42	42	15.5	5.80	60	.296	.376	6	.207	1	-23	-23	0	-2.8
1973 SF-N	1	2	.333	25	3	0	0	0	58	64	2	35	36	16.0	4.81	79	.278	.383	4	.250	0	-7	-6	1	-0.1
1974 Mon-N	5	2	.714	22	3	0	0	0	60	56	6	17	31	11.4	3.00	128	.249	.310	4	.286	0	4	3	-0	0.8
1975 Mon-N	5	3	.625	19	14	5	2	0	101	90	7	38	37	11.8	3.30	116	.240	.317	6	.176	0	4	6	2	0.7
1976 Mon-N	6	12	.333	34	19	2	0	0	140¹	153	9	78	71	15.3	4.43	84	.286	.384	4	.108	-1	-14	-11	1	-1.3
1977 Min-A	0	1	.000	7	0	0	0	0	14¹	16	2	6	3	14.4	6.91	58	.271	.348	0	—	0	-5	-5	-0	-0.2
Total 8	28	32	.467	165	67	11	3	3	566	595	47	267	275	14.1	4.45	83	.272	.358	27	.176	0	-55	-48	5	-4.4
● **CLAY CARROLL**				Carroll, Clay Palmer "Hawk" b: 5/2/41, Clanton, Ala. BR/TR, 6'1", 200 lbs. Deb: 9/2/64																				
1964 Mil-N	2	0	1.000	11	0	0	0	1	20¹	15	1	3	17	8.0	1.77	199	.200	.231	0	.000	-0	4	4	1	0.5
1965 Mil-N	0	1	.000	19	1	0	0	1	34²	35	3	13	16	12.7	4.41	80	.269	.340	0	.000	-1	-3	-3	-0	-0.2
1966 Atl-N	8	7	.533	**73**	3	0	0	11	144¹	127	8	29	67	10.0	2.37	154	.236	.280	3	.100	-2	20	20	1	2.3
1967 Atl-N	6	12	.333	42	7	1	0	0	93	111	6	29	35	13.8	5.52	60	.304	.360	1	.063	-1	-22	-23	1	-4.0
1968 Atl-N	0	1	.000	10	0	0	0	0	22¹	26	1	6	10	12.9	4.84	62	.310	.356	0	.000	-0	-5	-5	0	-0.2
Cin-N	7	7	.500	58	1	0	0	17	121²	102	3	32	61	10.4	2.29	138	.230	.290	6	.250	1	9	12	1	2.2
Yr	7	8	.467	68	1	0	0	17	144	128	4	38	71	10.8	2.69	117	.242	.300	6	.207	1	5	7	2	2.0
1969 Cin-N	12	6	.667	71	4	0	0	7	150²	149	9	78	90	14.0	3.52	107	.262	.358	6	.207	-0	1	4	3	1.0
1970 *Cin-N	9	4	.692	65	0	0	0	16	104¹	104	4	27	63	11.5	2.59	156	.259	.309	1	.071	-1	17	17	1	2.6
1971 Cin-N☆	10	4	.714	61	0	0	0	15	93²	78	5	42	64	11.7	2.50	134	.234	.324	1	.100	-1	10	9	4	2.0
1972 *Cin-N☆	6	4	.600	**65**	0	0	0	**37**	96	89	5	32	51	11.4	2.25	143	.256	.321	2	.182	0	13	10	1	2.2
1973 *Cin-N	8	8	.500	53	0	0	0	14	92²	111	5	34	41	14.6	3.69	92	.307	.374	3	.214	-0	-0	-3	1	-0.5
1974 Cin-N	12	5	.706	57	3	0	0	6	100²	96	3	30	46	11.3	2.15	163	.256	.311	3	.167	-1	16	15	2	2.8
1975 *Cin-N	7	5	.583	56	2	0	0	7	96¹	93	7	32	44	12.0	2.62	137	.255	.320	0	.000	-2	11	10	-1	1.1
1976 Chi-A	4	4	.500	29	0	0	0	6	77¹	67	1	24	38	10.8	2.56	139	.242	.307	0	—	0	8	9	0	1.0
1977 StL-N	4	2	.667	51	0	0	0	4	90	77	8	24	34	10.2	2.50	154	.238	.293	1	.091	-1	14	13	1	1.0
Chi-A	1	3	.250	8	0	0	0	1	11¹	14	3	4	4	14.3	4.76	86	.311	.367	0	—	-0	-1	-0	-0	-0.3
1978 Pit-N	0	0	—	2	0	0	0	0	4	2	0	3	0	11.3	2.25	164	.143	.294	0	—	0	1	1	0	0.0
Total 15	96	73	.568	731	28	1	0	143	1353¹	1296	67	442	681	11.8	2.94	120	.257	.321	27	.130	-5	93	90	17	13.5
● **ED CARROLL**				Carroll, Edgar Fleischer b: 7/27/07, Baltimore, Md. d: 10/13/84, Rossville, Md. BR/TR, 6'3", 185 lbs. Deb: 5/1/29																				
1929 Bos-A	1	0	1.000	24	3	0	0	0	67¹	77	6	20	13	13.5	5.61	76	.291	.349	1	.063	-2	-10	-10	0	-0.3
● **OWNIE CARROLL**				Carroll, Owen Thomas b: 11/11/02, Kearny, N.J. d: 6/8/75, Orange, N.J. BR/TR, 5'10.5", 165 lbs. Deb: 6/20/25																				
1925 Det-A	2	2	.500	10	4	1	0	0	40²	46	1	28	12	16.8	3.76	114	.293	.406	6	.375	1	3	2	-2	0.2
1927 Det-A	10	6	.625	31	15	8	0	0	172	186	5	73	41	13.9	3.98	106	.281	.358	12	.174	-2	3	4	2	0.3
1928 Det-A	16	12	.571	34	28	19	2	2	231	219	6	87	51	12.2	3.27	126	.262	.337	19	.194	-0	20	21	1	2.4
1929 Det-A	9	17	.346	34	26	12	0	1	202	249	10	86	54	15.3	4.63	93	.310	.383	17	.230	2	-9	-8	2	-0.5
1930 Det-A	0	5	.000	6	3	0	0	0	20¹	30	3	9	4	17.3	10.62	45	.333	.394	1	.143	-1	-13	-13	0	-2.2
NY-A	0	1	.000	10	1	0	0	0	32²	49	2	18	8	19.6	6.61	65	.374	.464	2	.200	-0	-7	-8	1	-0.1
Yr	0	6	.000	16	4	0	0	0	53	79	5	27	12	18.7	8.15	55	.357	.437	3	.176	-0	-21	-22	1	-2.3
Cin-N	0	1	.000	3	2	1	0	0	14	17	3	9	0	12.9	4.50	107	.309	.345	1	.200	-0	1	1	0	0.0
1931 Cin-N	3	9	.250	29	12	4	0	0	107¹	135	6	51	24	15.9	5.53	67	.314	.392	7	.206	-0	-20	-21	1	-1.9
1932 Cin-N	10	19	.345	32	26	15	0	1	210	245	7	44	55	12.8	4.50	86	.286	.328	16	.208	2	-14	-15	-1	-1.7
1933 Bro-N	13	15	.464	33	31	11	0	0	226¹	248	6	45	42	12.3	3.78	85	.281	.327	11	.149	-1	-11	-14	3	-1.4
1934 Bro-N	1	3	.250	26	5	1	0	1	74¹	100	9	33	17	17.2	6.42	61	.342	.406	6	.240	1	-19	-21	3	-0.6
Total 9	64	90	.416	248	153	71	2	5	1330²	1532	61	486	311	14.0	4.43	89	.294	.359	98	.200	-4	-68	-72	11	-5.5
● **DICK CARROLL**				Carroll, Richard Thomas "Shadow" b: 7/21/1884, Cleveland, Ohio d: 11/22/45, Cleveland, Ohio BR/TR, 6'2" Deb: 9/25/09																				
1909 NY-A	0	0	—	2	1	0	0	0	5	7	1	1	1	14.4	3.60	70	.292	.320	1	.500	0	-1	-1	-0	0.0
● **TOM CARROLL**				Carroll, Thomas Michael b: 11/5/52, Utica, N.Y. BL/TR, 6'3", 190 lbs. Deb: 7/7/74																				
1974 Cin-N	4	3	.571	16	13	0	0	0	78¹	68	11	44	37	12.9	3.68	95	.231	.331	4	.154	-1	-1	-2	-1	-0.3
1975 Cin-N	4	1	.800	12	7	0	0	0	47	52	1	26	14	15.3	4.98	72	.284	.379	0	.000	-1	-7	-7	-1	-0.9
Total 2	8	4	.667	28	20	0	0	0	125¹	120	12	70	51	13.8	4.16	85	.252	.350	4	.100	-2	-8	-9	-2	-1.2
● **KID CARSEY**				Carsey, Wilfred b: 10/22/1870, New York, N.Y. d: 3/29/60, Miami, Fla. BL/TR, 5'7", 168 lbs. Deb: 4/8/1891 ♦																				
1891 Was-a	14	37	.275	54	53	46	1	0	415	513	17	161	174	15.2	4.99	75	.294	.362	28	.150	-5	-58	-57	6	-5.1
1892 Phi-N	19	16	.543	43	36	30	1	0	317²	320	6	104	76	12.4	3.12	104	.251	.314	20	.153	-3	6	5	2	0.3
1893 Phi-N	20	15	.571	39	35	30	1	1	318¹	375	7	124	50	14.6	4.81	95	.285	.355	27	.186	-7	-5	-8	2	-1.2
1894 Phi-N	18	12	.600	35	31	26	0	0	277	349	22	102	41	15.2	5.56	92	.304	.370	34	.272	4	-7	-14	2	-0.7
1895 Phi-N	24	16	.600	44	40	35	0	1	342¹	460	14	118	64	15.7	4.92	97	.317	.376	41	.291	5	-5	-1	-3	-0.3
1896 Phi-N	11	11	.500	27	21	18	1	1	187¹	273	4	72	36	17.0	5.62	77	.337	.397	18	.222	1	-26	-27	1	-2.2
1897 Phi-N	2	1	.667	4	4	2	0	0	28	35	0	16	1	16.7	5.14	82	.303	.393	3	.231	-0	-3	-3	-0	-0.3
StL-N	3	8	.273	12	11	11	0	0	99	133	5	31	14	15.3	6.00	73	.319	.372	13	.302	2	-19	-18	1	-1.2
Yr	5	9	.357	16	15	13	0	0	127	168	5	47	15	15.5	5.81	75	.315	.376	16	.286	2	-21	-20	1	-1.5
1898 StL-N	2	12	.143	20	13	10	0	0	123²	177	2	37	10	16.3	6.33	60	.333	.387	21	.200	-0	-37	-35	2	-3.0
1899 Cle-N	1	8	.111	10	9	8	0	0	77²	109	2	21	11	15.6	5.68	65	.330	.379	10	.278	-1	-16	-17	1	-1.3
Was-N	1	2	.333	4	3	2	0	0	29	27	0	7	3	9.9	3.72	105	.247	.280	0	.000	-2	0	1	1	-0.1
Yr	2	10	.167	14	12	10	0	0	106²	136	2	28	14	13.9	5.15	73	.308	.351	10	.213	-1	-15	-17	2	-1.4

YEAR	TM/L	W	L	PCT	G	GS	CG	SH	SV	IP	H	HR	BB	SO	RAT	ERA	ERA+	OAV	OOB	BH	AVG	PB	PR	/A	PD	TPI
1901	Bro-N	1	0	1.000	2	0	0	0	0	7	9	1	3	4	16.7	10.29	33	.310	.393	0	.000	-0	-5	-5	-0	-0.6
Total	10	116	138	.457	294	256	218	4	3	2222	2780	80	796	484	15.0	4.95	85	.300	.363	221	.213	-8	-175	-183	14	-15.7

● **AL CARSON**   Carson, Albert James "Soldier" b: 8/22/1882, Chicago, Ill. d: 11/26/62, San Diego, Cal. TR , Deb: 5/6/10

YEAR	TM/L	W	L	PCT	G	GS	CG	SH	SV	IP	H	HR	BB	SO	RAT	ERA	ERA+	OAV	OOB	BH	AVG	PB	PR	/A	PD	TPI
1910	Chi-N	0	0	—	2	0	0	0	0	6²	6	0	1	2	9.5	4.05	71	.240	.269	0	.000	0	-1	-1	0	0.0

● **ANDY CARTER**   Carter, Andrew Godfrey b: 11/9/68, Philadelphia, Pa. BL/TL, 6'5", 200 lbs. Deb: 5/3/94

YEAR	TM/L	W	L	PCT	G	GS	CG	SH	SV	IP	H	HR	BB	SO	RAT	ERA	ERA+	OAV	OOB	BH	AVG	PB	PR	/A	PD	TPI
1994	Phi-N	0	2	.000	20	0	0	0	0	34¹	34	5	12	18	13.6	4.46	93	.268	.359	0	.000	-1	-1	-1	-1	-0.2

● **ARNOLD CARTER**   Carter, Arnold Lee "Hook" or "Lefty" b: 3/14/18, Rainelle, W.Va. d: 4/12/89, Louisville, Ky. BL/TL, 5'10", 170 lbs. Deb: 4/29/44

YEAR	TM/L	W	L	PCT	G	GS	CG	SH	SV	IP	H	HR	BB	SO	RAT	ERA	ERA+	OAV	OOB	BH	AVG	PB	PR	/A	PD	TPI
1944	Cin-N	11	7	.611	33	18	9	3	3	148²	143	1	40	33	11.3	2.60	134	.256	.309	12	.250	5	17	15	1	2.4
1945	Cin-N	2	4	.333	13	6	2	1	0	46²	54	2	13	4	13.3	3.09	122	.286	.338	3	.176	0	4	3	0	0.5
Total	2	13	11	.542	46	24	11	4	3	195¹	197	3	53	37	11.7	2.72	131	.264	.317	15	.231	5	20	18	1	2.9

● **NICK CARTER**   Carter, Conrad Powell b: 5/19/1879, Oatlands, Va. d: 11/23/61, Grasonville, Md. BL/TR, 5'8", 126 lbs. Deb: 4/14/08

YEAR	TM/L	W	L	PCT	G	GS	CG	SH	SV	IP	H	HR	BB	SO	RAT	ERA	ERA+	OAV	OOB	BH	AVG	PB	PR	/A	PD	TPI
1908	Phi-A	2	5	.286	14	4	2	0	0	60²	58	1	17	17	11.4	2.97	86	.270	.329	2	.100	-2	-4	-3	1	-0.4

● **JEFF CARTER**   Carter, Jeffrey Allen b: 12/3/64, Tampa, Fla. BR/TR, 6'3", 195 lbs. Deb: 7/31/91

YEAR	TM/L	W	L	PCT	G	GS	CG	SH	SV	IP	H	HR	BB	SO	RAT	ERA	ERA+	OAV	OOB	BH	AVG	PB	PR	/A	PD	TPI
1991	Chi-A	0	1	.000	5	2	0	0	0	12	8	1	5	2	9.8	5.25	76	.182	.265	0		0	-2	-2	-0	-0.2

● **LARRY CARTER**   Carter, Larry Gene b: 5/22/65, Charleston, W.Va. BR/TR, 6'5", 195 lbs. Deb: 9/6/92

YEAR	TM/L	W	L	PCT	G	GS	CG	SH	SV	IP	H	HR	BB	SO	RAT	ERA	ERA+	OAV	OOB	BH	AVG	PB	PR	/A	PD	TPI
1992	SF-N	1	5	.167	6	6	0	0	0	33	34	6	18	21	14.2	4.64	71	.270	.361	2	.200	1	-4	-5	-1	-0.8

● **PAUL CARTER**   Carter, Paul Warren "Nick" b: 5/1/1894, Lake Park, Ga. d: 9/11/84, Lake Park, Ga. BL/TR, 6'3", 175 lbs. Deb: 9/15/14

YEAR	TM/L	W	L	PCT	G	GS	CG	SH	SV	IP	H	HR	BB	SO	RAT	ERA	ERA+	OAV	OOB	BH	AVG	PB	PR	/A	PD	TPI
1914	Cle-A	1	3	.250	5	4	1	0	0	24²	35	0	5	9	14.6	2.92	99	.340	.370	0	.000	-1	-0	-0	-0	-0.1
1915	Cle-A	1	1	.500	11	2	2	0	0	42	44	1	18	14	13.3	3.21	95	.272	.344	3	.214	1	-1	-1	1	0.1
1916	Chi-N	2	2	.500	8	5	2	0	0	36	26	1	17	14	10.8	2.75	106	.203	.297	2	.167	-0	-1	1	1	0.2
1917	Chi-N	5	8	.385	23	13	6	2	0	113¹	115	2	19	34	10.9	3.26	89	.276	.313	6	.171	-0	-7	-5	-1	-0.7
1918	Chi-N	3	2	.600	21	4	1	0	2	73	78	2	19	13	12.1	2.71	103	.290	.339	6	.240	0	0	1	2	0.2
1919	Chi-N	5	4	.556	28	7	2	0	1	85	81	1	28	17	11.8	2.65	109	.252	.316	7	.269	1	3	2	-0	0.3
1920	Chi-N	3	6	.333	31	8	2	0	2	106	131	3	36	14	14.6	4.67	69	.324	.387	6	.171	-1	-18	-17	-2	-1.7
Total	7	20	26	.435	127	43	16	2	7	480	510	10	142	115	12.4	3.32	89	.283	.339	30	.195	-1	-24	-19	1	-1.7

● **SOL CARTER**   Carter, Solomon Mobley "Buck" b: 12/23/08, Picayune, Miss. BR/TR, 6', 178 lbs. Deb: 4/15/31

YEAR	TM/L	W	L	PCT	G	GS	CG	SH	SV	IP	H	HR	BB	SO	RAT	ERA	ERA+	OAV	OOB	BH	AVG	PB	PR	/A	PD	TPI
1931	Phi-A	0	0	—	2	0	0	0	0	2¹	1	0	4	1	19.3	19.29	23	.143	.455	0		0	-4	-4	1	0.0

● **BOB CARUTHERS**   Caruthers, Robert Lee "Parisian Bob" b: 1/5/1864, Memphis, Tenn. d: 8/5/11, Peoria, Ill. BL/TR, 5'7", 138 lbs. Deb: 9/7/1884 MU♦

YEAR	TM/L	W	L	PCT	G	GS	CG	SH	SV	IP	H	HR	BB	SO	RAT	ERA	ERA+	OAV	OOB	BH	AVG	PB	PR	/A	PD	TPI
1884	StL-a	7	2	.778	13	7	7	0	0	82²	61	1	15	58	8.6	2.61	125	.189	.232	21	.256	2	6	6	-1	0.6
1885	*StL-a	**40**	13	**.755**	53	53	53	6	0	482¹	430	3	57	190	9.4	**2.07**	**158**	.230	.260	50	.225	6	**63**	**64**	0	6.6
1886	*StL-a	30	14	.682	44	43	42	2	0	387¹	323	3	86	166	9.7	2.32	148	.217	.263	106	.334	26	48	48	-2	6.8
1887	*StL-a	29	9	**.763**	39	39	39	2	0	341	337	6	61	74	10.9	3.30	138	.247	.287	130	.357	20	38	47	7	6.2
1888	Bro-a	29	15	.659	44	43	42	4	0	391²	337	4	53	140	9.2	2.39	125	.224	.255	77	.230	10	29	26	1	3.5
1889	*Bro-a	**40**	11	**.784**	56	50	46	**7**	1	445	444	16	104	118	11.3	3.13	119	.252	.298	43	.250	17	35	29	2	4.2
1890	*Bro-N	23	11	.676	37	33	30	1	0	300	292	9	87	64	11.7	3.09	111	.247	.306	63	.265	11	16	12	3	2.2
1891	Bro-N	18	14	.563	38	32	29	2	1	297	323	7	107	69	13.4	3.12	106	.267	.333	48	.281	11	7	6	1	1.7
1892	StL-N	2	10	.167	16	10	10	0	1	101¹	131	10	27	21	14.5	5.84	55	.301	.350	142	.277	6	-29	-30	0	-2.4
Total	9	218	99	.688	340	310	298	24	3	2828²	2678	59	597	900	10.7	2.83	123	.240	.285	694	.282	111	214	206	11	29.4

● **CHUCK CARY**   Cary, Charles Douglas b: 3/3/60, Whittier, Cal. BL/TL, 6'4", 210 lbs. Deb: 8/22/85

YEAR	TM/L	W	L	PCT	G	GS	CG	SH	SV	IP	H	HR	BB	SO	RAT	ERA	ERA+	OAV	OOB	BH	AVG	PB	PR	/A	PD	TPI
1985	Det-A	0	1	.000	16	0	0	0	2	23²	16	2	8	22	9.9	3.42	119	.190	.277	0	—	0	2	2	-0	0.1
1986	Det-A	1	1	.333	22	0	0	0	0	31²	33	3	15	21	13.6	3.41	121	.273	.353	0	—	0	3	3	-0	0.2
1987	Atl-N	1	1	.500	13	0	0	0	1	16²	17	3	4	15	11.9	3.78	115	.266	.319	0	.000	-0	1	1	-0	0.1
1988	Atl-N	0	0	—	7	0	0	0	0	8¹	8	1	4	7	14.0	6.48	57	.250	.351	0	—	0	-3	-3	-0	-0.1
1989	NY-A	4	4	.500	22	11	2	0	0	99¹	78	13	29	79	9.7	3.26	119	.209	.266	0	—	0	7	7	-2	0.4
1990	NY-A	6	12	.333	28	27	2	0	0	156²	155	21	55	134	12.1	4.19	95	.260	.323	0	—	0	-5	-4	-1	-0.5
1991	NY-A	1	6	.143	10	9	0	0	0	53¹	61	6	32	34	15.7	5.91	70	.285	.378	0	—	0	-11	-10	-0	-1.2
1993	Chi-A	1	0	1.000	16	0	0	0	0	20²	12	1	11	10	15.7	5.23	80	.286	.396	0	—	0	-2	-2	0	0.1
Total	8	14	26	.350	134	47	4	0	3	410¹	390	50	158	322	12.2	4.17	96	.250	.322	0	.000	-0	-9	-7	-4	-0.8

● **SCOTT CARY**   Cary, Scott Russell "Red" b: 4/11/23, Kendallville, Ind. BL/TL, 5'11.5", 168 lbs. Deb: 5/1/47

YEAR	TM/L	W	L	PCT	G	GS	CG	SH	SV	IP	H	HR	BB	SO	RAT	ERA	ERA+	OAV	OOB	BH	AVG	PB	PR	/A	PD	TPI
1947	Was-A	3	1	.750	23	3	1	0	0	54²	73	5	20	25	15.5	5.93	63	.312	.369	1	.077	-1	-13	-13	-1	-1.0

● **JERRY CASALE**   Casale, Jerry Joseph b: 9/27/33, Brooklyn, N.Y. BR/TR, 6'2", 200 lbs. Deb: 9/14/58

YEAR	TM/L	W	L	PCT	G	GS	CG	SH	SV	IP	H	HR	BB	SO	RAT	ERA	ERA+	OAV	OOB	BH	AVG	PB	PR	/A	PD	TPI
1958	Bos-A	0	0	—	2	0	0	0	0	3	1	0	2	3	9.0	0.00	—	.111	.273	0	—	0	1	1	0	0.0
1959	Bos-A	13	8	.619	31	26	9	3	0	179²	162	20	89	93	12.8	4.31	94	.238	.331	10	.169	3	-9	-5	-4	-0.7
1960	Bos-A	2	9	.182	29	14	1	0	0	96¹	113	14	67	54	16.9	6.17	66	.294	.400	9	.273	3	-25	-23	-0	-2.0
1961	LA-A	1	5	.167	13	7	0	0	0	42²	52	9	25	35	16.5	6.54	69	.297	.388	6	.462	3	-12	-10	-0	-0.9
	Det-A	0	0	—	3	1	0	0	0	12	15	3	3	6	13.5	5.25	78	.313	.353	0	.000	-0	-2	-2	0	-0.1
	Yr	1	5	.167	16	8	0	0	0	54²	67	12	28	41	15.6	6.26	71	.298	.375	6	.375	3	-14	-11	-0	-0.9
1962	Det-A	1	2	.333	18	1	0	0	0	36²	33	5	18	16	12.5	4.66	87	.236	.323	0	.000	-1	-3	-2	0	-0.2
Total	5	17	24	.415	96	49	10	3	1	370¹	376	51	204	207	14.3	5.08	81	.262	.356	25	.216	7	-49	-40	-5	-3.8

● **JOE CASCARELLA**   Cascarella, Joseph Thomas "Crooning Joe" b: 6/28/07, Philadelphia, Pa. BR/TR, 5'10.5", 175 lbs. Deb: 4/17/34

YEAR	TM/L	W	L	PCT	G	GS	CG	SH	SV	IP	H	HR	BB	SO	RAT	ERA	ERA+	OAV	OOB	BH	AVG	PB	PR	/A	PD	TPI
1934	Phi-A	12	15	.444	42	22	9	2	1	194¹	214	8	104	71	14.9	4.68	94	.288	.377	6	.094	-4	-4	-6	2	-0.9
1935	Phi-A	1	6	.143	9	3	1	0	0	32¹	29	1	22	15	14.2	5.29	86	.252	.372	1	.125	-1	-3	-3	2	-0.4
	Bos-A	0	3	.000	6	4	0	0	0	17	25	3	11	9	19.1	6.88	69	.329	.414	0	.000	-0	-5	-4	0	-0.6
	Yr	1	9	.100	15	7	1	0	0	49¹	54	4	33	24	15.9	5.84	79	.283	.388	1	.100	-1	-8	-7	2	-1.0
1936	Bos-A	0	2	.000	10	1	0	0	0	20²	27	0	9	7	15.7	6.97	76	.329	.396	0	.000	-1	-4	-4	0	-0.3
	Was-A	9	8	.529	22	16	7	1	1	139¹	147	7	54	34	13.4	4.07	117	.276	.349	7	.143	-2	15	11	-2	0.7
	Yr	9	10	.474	32	17	7	1	1	160	174	7	63	41	13.7	4.44	109	.283	.355	7	.132	-3	11	7	-2	0.4
1937	Was-A	0	5	.000	10	4	1	0	0	32¹	50	3	23	10	20.6	8.07	55	.347	.440	2	.222	-0	-12	-13	0	-1.6
	Cin-N	1	2	.333	11	3	2	0	1	43²	44	1	20	16	13.6	3.92	95	.263	.349	1	.091	-1	-0	-1	-0	-0.1
1938	Cin-N	4	7	.364	33	1	0	0	0	61	56	2	22	30	13.0	4.57	80	.275	.336	1	.167	-0	-5	-6	0	-1.2
Total	5	27	48	.360	143	54	20	3	8	540²	602	25	267	192	14.6	4.84	91	.287	.370	20	.121	-9	-19	-26	1	-4.4

● **CHARLIE CASE**   Case, Charles Emmett b: 9/7/1879, Smith Landing, O. d: 4/16/64, Clermont, Ohio BR/TR, 6', 170 lbs. Deb: 7/5/01

YEAR	TM/L	W	L	PCT	G	GS	CG	SH	SV	IP	H	HR	BB	SO	RAT	ERA	ERA+	OAV	OOB	BH	AVG	PB	PR	/A	PD	TPI
1901	Cin-N	1	2	.333	3	3	3	0	0	27	34	0	6	13	13.3	4.67	69	.305	.341	1	.100	-1	-4	-4	-0	-0.5
1904	Pit-N	10	5	.667	18	17	14	3	0	141	129	0	31	49	10.5	2.94	93	.243	.290	9	.170	1	-3	-3	1	-0.2
1905	Pit-N	11	11	.500	31	24	18	3	1	217	202	2	66	57	11.7	2.57	117	.251	.319	7	.103	-2	10	10	-3	0.5
1906	Pit-N	1	1	.500	2	2	1	0	0	11	8	0	3	5	11.5	5.73	47	.190	.292	1	.500	1	-4	-4	0	-0.5
Total	4	23	19	.548	54	46	36	6	1	396	373	2	108	114	11.4	2.93	99	.250	.310	18	.135	-1	-0	-1	-3	-0.7

● **DAN CASEY**   Casey, Daniel Maurice b: 11/20/1862, Binghamton, N.Y. d: 2/8/43, Washington, D.C. BR/TL, 6', 180 lbs. Deb: 8/18/1884 F

YEAR	TM/L	W	L	PCT	G	GS	CG	SH	SV	IP	H	HR	BB	SO	RAT	ERA	ERA+	OAV	OOB	BH	AVG	PB	PR	/A	PD	TPI
1884	Wil-U	1	1	.500	2	2	2	0	0	18	23	0	4	10	13.5	1.00	266	.291	.325	1	.167	-1	3	3	-0	0.2
1885	Det-N	4	8	.333	12	12	12	1	0	104	105	4	31	79	12.1	3.29	86	.256	.315	5	.116	-3	-5	-5	1	-0.7
1886	Phi-N	24	18	.571	44	44	39	1	0	369	326	8	104	193	10.5	2.41	137	.223	.275	23	.152	-5	37	36	-1	2.9

YEAR TM/L	W	L	PCT	G	GS	CG	SH	SV	IP	H	HR	BB	SO	RAT	ERA	ERA+	OAV	OOB	BH	AVG	PB	PR	/A	PD	TPI
1887 Phi-N	28	13	.683	45	45	43	4	0	390¹	377	15	115	119	11.7	**2.86**	**148**	.246	.305	27	.165	-11	53	60	-2	3.7
1888 Phi-N	14	18	.438	33	33	31	2	0	285²	298	6	48	108	11.1	3.15	94	.259	.291	18	.153	-4	-10	-6	1	-0.9
1889 Phi-N	6	10	.375	20	20	15	1	0	152²	170	4	72	65	14.7	3.77	115	.273	.356	15	.221	-2	4	10	0	0.7
1890 Syr-a	19	22	.463	45	42	40	2	0	360²	365	8	165	169	13.6	4.14	88	.255	.337	26	.162	-4	-11	-24	2	-2.3
Total 7	96	90	.516	201	198	182	14	0	1680¹	1664	42	543	743	12.0	3.18	113	.249	.309	115	.162	-27	71	75	1	3.6

● HUGH CASEY
Casey, Hugh Thomas b: 10/14/13, Atlanta, Ga. d: 7/3/51, Atlanta, Ga. BR/TR, 6'1", 207 lbs. Deb: 4/29/35

YEAR TM/L	W	L	PCT	G	GS	CG	SH	SV	IP	H	HR	BB	SO	RAT	ERA	ERA+	OAV	OOB	BH	AVG	PB	PR	/A	PD	TPI
1935 Chi-N	0	0	—	13	0	0	0	0	25²	29	2	14	10	15.1	3.86	102	.279	.364	1	.167	-0	0	0	0	0.0
1939 Bro-N	15	10	.600	40	25	15	0	1	227¹	228	13	54	79	11.6	2.93	137	.260	.311	15	.203	0	25	28	2	3.1
1940 Bro-N	11	8	.579	44	10	5	2	2	154	136	13	51	53	11.3	3.62	110	.237	.306	9	.250	2	4	6	1	1.0
1941 *Bro-N	14	11	.560	45	18	4	1	7	162	155	8	57	61	11.8	3.89	94	.251	.316	6	.120	-1	-5	-4	2	-0.6
1942 Bro-N	6	3	.667	50	2	0	0	13	112	91	3	44	54	11.0	2.25	145	.221	.300	4	.148	-0	13	13	-1	1.2
1946 Bro-N	11	5	.688	46	1	0	0	5	99²	101	2	33	31	12.3	1.99	170	.267	.329	3	.136	-1	**16**	**15**	3	2.9
1947 *Bro-N	10	4	.714	46	0	0	0	18	76²	75	7	29	40	12.4	3.99	104	.260	.331	1	.056	-1	1	1	0	0.1
1948 Bro-N	3	0	1.000	22	0	0	0	0	36	59	6	17	7	19.5	8.00	50	.391	.459	0	—	-1	-16	-16	-0	-1.6
1949 Pit-N	4	1	.800	33	0	0	0	5	38²	50	4	14	9	15.1	4.66	90	.314	.374	1	.333	0	-3	-2	-2	-0.4
NY-A	1	0	1.000	4	0	0	0	0	7²	11	0	5	8	22.3	8.22	49	.324	.452	0	.000	-0	-3	-4	-0	-0.4
Total 9	75	42	.641	343	56	24	3	55	939²	935	58	321	349	12.3	3.45	110	.260	.325	40	.164	-2	32	38	6	5.3

● BILL CASEY
Casey, William B. b: St.Louis, Mo. Deb: 8/17/1887

YEAR TM/L	W	L	PCT	G	GS	CG	SH	SV	IP	H	HR	BB	SO	RAT	ERA	ERA+	OAV	OOB	BH	AVG	PB	PR	/A	PD	TPI
1887 Phi-a	0	0	—	1	0	0	0	0	1	4	0	1	0	45.0	18.00	24	.667	.714	0	—	0	-2	-2	-0	0.0

● CARL CASHION
Cashion, Jay Carl b: 6/6/1891, Mecklenburg Co, N.C. d: 11/17/35, Lake Millicent, Wis. BL/TR, 6'2", 200 lbs. Deb: 8/4/11

YEAR TM/L	W	L	PCT	G	GS	CG	SH	SV	IP	H	HR	BB	SO	RAT	ERA	ERA+	OAV	OOB	BH	AVG	PB	PR	/A	PD	TPI
1911 Was-A	1	5	.167	11	9	5	0	0	71¹	67	4	47	26	15.3	4.16	79	.220	.338	12	.324	2	-6	-7	1	-0.2
1912 Was-A	10	6	.625	26	17	13	1	1	170¹	150	4	103	84	13.6	3.17	105	.250	.365	22	.214	2	3	3	-1	0.5
1913 Was-A	1	1	.500	4	3	0	0	0	9	7	0	14	3	24.0	6.00	49	.269	.558	3	.250	0	-3	-3	0	-0.5
1914 Was-A	0	1	.000	2	1	0	0	0	5	4	0	6	1	19.8	10.80	26	.250	.478	0	.000	-0	-4	-4	0	-0.7
Total 4	12	13	.480	43	30	18	1	1	255²	228	8	170	114	14.6	3.70	89	.241	.366	37	.242	5	-11	-11	1	-0.9

● LARRY CASIAN
Casian, Lawrence Paul b: 10/28/65, Lynwood, Cal. BR/TL, 6', 170 lbs. Deb: 9/9/90

YEAR TM/L	W	L	PCT	G	GS	CG	SH	SV	IP	H	HR	BB	SO	RAT	ERA	ERA+	OAV	OOB	BH	AVG	PB	PR	/A	PD	TPI
1990 Min-A	2	1	.667	5	3	0	0	0	22¹	26	2	4	11	12.1	3.22	129	.306	.337	0	—	0	2	2	-0	0.3
1991 Min-A	0	0	—	15	0	0	0	0	18¹	28	4	7	6	17.7	7.36	58	.354	.414	0	—	0	-7	-6	0	-0.3
1992 Min-A	1	0	1.000	6	0	0	0	0	6²	7	1	2	2	10.8	2.70	150	.259	.286	0	—	0	1	1	0	-0.1
1993 Min-A	5	3	.625	54	0	0	0	1	56²	59	1	14	31	11.8	3.02	144	.268	.315	0	—	0	8	8	-1	1.0
1994 Min-A	1	3	.250	33	0	0	0	0	40²	57	11	12	18	15.7	7.08	69	.343	.394	0	—	0	-10	-10	-0	-0.9
Cle-A	2	2	.000	7	0	0	0	0	8¹	16	1	4	2	21.6	8.64	57	.421	.476	0	—	0	-4	-3	-0	-0.9
Yr	1	5	.167	40	0	0	0	0	49	73	12	16	20	16.3	7.35	66	.351	.397	0	—	0	-14	-13	0	-1.8
Total 5	9	9	.500	120	3	0	0	2	153	193	19	42	70	14.1	4.94	90	.314	.362	0	—	0	-10	-8	-0	-0.9

● CRAIG CASKEY
Caskey, Craig Douglas b: 12/11/49, Visalia, Cal. BB/TL, 5'11", 185 lbs. Deb: 7/19/73

YEAR TM/L	W	L	PCT	G	GS	CG	SH	SV	IP	H	HR	BB	SO	RAT	ERA	ERA+	OAV	OOB	BH	AVG	PB	PR	/A	PD	TPI
1973 Mon-N	0	0	—	9	1	0	0	0	14¹	15	3	4	6	12.6	5.65	67	.278	.339	0	.000	-0	-3	-3	0	0.0

● ED CASSIAN
Cassian, Edwin b: Connecticut 5'8", 160 lbs. Deb: 6/26/1891

YEAR TM/L	W	L	PCT	G	GS	CG	SH	SV	IP	H	HR	BB	SO	RAT	ERA	ERA+	OAV	OOB	BH	AVG	PB	PR	/A	PD	TPI
1891 Phi-N	1	3	.250	6	4	3	0	0	38	40	0	16	10	14.0	2.84	120	.260	.342	2	.118	-1	2	2	1	0.1
Was-a	2	4	.333	7	5	5	0	0	53	73	4	35	14	19.2	5.60	67	.316	.417	9	.346	2	-11	-11	0	-0.7
Total 1	3	7	.300	13	9	8	0	0	91	113	4	51	24	17.0	4.45	81	.294	.388	11	.256	1	-9	-9	1	-0.6

● JOHN CASSIDY
Cassidy, John P. b: 1857, Brooklyn, N.Y. d: 7/2/1891, Brooklyn, N.Y. BR/TL, 5'8", 168 lbs. Deb: 4/24/1875 ◆

YEAR TM/L	W	L	PCT	G	GS	CG	SH	SV	IP	H	HR	BB	SO	RAT	ERA	ERA+	OAV	OOB	BH	AVG	PB	PR	/A	PD	TPI
1875 Atl-n	1	20	.048	30	22	18	0	0	214²	278	6	12	12	12.2	3.98	58	.276	.284	29	.176	-2	-36	-40	—	-3.0
1877 Har-N	1	1	.500	2	2	2	0	0	18	24	0	1	2	12.5	5.00	49	.320	.329	95	.378	1	-4	-5	-0	-0.4

● GEORGE CASTER
Caster, George Jasper "Ug" b: 8/4/07, Colton, Cal. d: 12/18/55, Lakewood, Cal. BR/TR, 6'1.5", 180 lbs. Deb: 9/10/34

YEAR TM/L	W	L	PCT	G	GS	CG	SH	SV	IP	H	HR	BB	SO	RAT	ERA	ERA+	OAV	OOB	BH	AVG	PB	PR	/A	PD	TPI
1934 Phi-A	3	2	.600	5	3	2	0	0	37	32	3	14	15	11.9	3.41	129	.235	.320	4	.267	0	4	4	1	0.6
1935 Phi-A	1	4	.200	25	1	0	0	1	63¹	86	8	37	24	17.8	6.25	73	.322	.408	5	.227	0	-13	-12	2	-0.7
1937 Phi-A	12	19	.387	34	33	19	3	0	231²	227	23	107	100	13.1	4.43	106	.258	.339	19	.211	-1	5	7	0	0.8
1938 Phi-A	16	20	.444	42	40	20	2	1	281¹	310	25	117	112	13.8	4.35	111	.277	.347	20	.198	-1	14	15	-2	1.6
1939 Phi-A	9	9	.500	28	17	7	1	0	136	144	16	45	59	12.7	4.90	96	.276	.337	9	.209	-1	-4	-3	0	-0.4
1940 Phi-A	4	19	.174	36	24	11	0	2	178¹	234	16	69	75	15.4	6.56	68	.312	.372	8	.129	-3	-43	-42	-1	-4.7
1941 StL-A	3	7	.300	32	9	3	0	0	104¹	105	12	37	36	12.4	5.00	86	.259	.324	3	.103	-0	-10	-8	1	-0.8
1942 StL-A	8	2	.800	39	0	0	0	5	80	62	3	39	34	11.7	2.81	132	.217	.317	1	.067	-1	8	8	1	1.0
1943 StL-A	6	8	.429	35	0	0	0	8	76¹	69	4	41	43	13.1	2.12	157	.246	.345	3	.136	-1	10	10	0	2.1
1944 StL-A	6	6	.500	42	0	0	0	12	81	91	5	33	46	13.8	2.44	147	.284	.351	5	.250	0	9	10	-0	1.9
1945 StL-A	1	2	.333	10	0	0	0	0	15²	20	0	7	9	15.5	6.89	51	.308	.375	1	.333	0	-6	-6	-0	-1.1
*Det-A	5	1	.833	22	0	0	0	2	51¹	47	3	27	23	13.3	3.86	91	.250	.350	2	.182	-0	-3	-2	-0	-0.2
Yr	6	3	.667	32	0	0	0	3	67	67	3	34	32	13.8	4.57	77	.265	.356	3	.214	-0	-9	-8	-1	-1.3
1946 Det-A	2	1	.667	26	0	0	0	4	41¹	42	1	24	19	14.6	5.66	65	.264	.364	1	.143	-0	-10	-9	1	-0.8
Total 12	76	100	.432	376	127	62	6	39	1377²	1469	121	597	595	13.7	4.54	96	.273	.349	81	.184	-7	-39	-27	2	-0.7

● TONY CASTILLO
Castillo, Antonio Jose (Jimenez) b: 3/1/63, Quibor, Venez. BL/TL, 5'10", 177 lbs. Deb: 8/14/88

YEAR TM/L	W	L	PCT	G	GS	CG	SH	SV	IP	H	HR	BB	SO	RAT	ERA	ERA+	OAV	OOB	BH	AVG	PB	PR	/A	PD	TPI
1988 Tor-A	1	0	1.000	14	0	0	0	0	15	10	2	2	14	7.2	3.00	131	.200	.231	0	—	0	2	2	0	0.1
1989 Tor-A	1	1	.500	17	0	0	0	0	17²	23	0	10	10	17.3	6.11	62	.333	.425	0	—	0	-4	-5	-0	-0.4
Atl-N	0	1	.000	12	0	0	0	0	9¹	7	0	4	5	11.6	4.82	76	.222	.300	0	.000	-0	-1	-1	0	-0.1
1990 Atl-N	5	1	.833	52	3	0	0	1	76²	93	5	20	64	13.4	4.23	95	.302	.347	1	.143	0	-4	-2	1	0.0
1991 Atl-N	1	1	.500	7	0	0	0	0	8²	13	3	5	8	18.7	7.27	53	.342	.419	0	—	0	-3	-3	-0	-0.7
NY-N	1	0	1.000	10	3	0	0	0	23²	27	1	6	10	12.5	1.90	191	.281	.324	0	.000	-0	5	5	1	0.2
Yr	2	1	.667	17	3	0	0	0	32¹	40	4	11	18	14.2	3.34	111	.299	.352	0	.000	-0	1	1	0	-0.5
1993 *Tor-A	3	2	.600	51	0	0	0	0	50²	44	4	22	28	11.7	3.38	128	.242	.324	0	—	0	5	5	0	0.5
1994 Tor-A	5	2	.714	41	0	0	0	0	68	66	7	28	43	12.8	2.51	192	.260	.340	0	—	0	17	17	0	1.5
Total 6	17	8	.680	204	6	0	0	3	269²	284	22	97	182	12.9	3.60	117	.275	.340	1	.083	-0	16	18	2	1.1

● MANNY CASTILLO
Castillo, Esteban Manuel Antonio (Cabrera) b: 4/1/57, Santo Domingo, D.R. BB/TR, 5'9", 160 lbs. Deb: 9/1/80 ◆

YEAR TM/L	W	L	PCT	G	GS	CG	SH	SV	IP	H	HR	BB	SO	RAT	ERA	ERA+	OAV	OOB	BH	AVG	PB	PR	/A	PD	TPI
1983 Sea-A	0	0	—	1	0	0	0	0	2²	8	3	2	0	40.5	23.63	18	.533	.632	42	.207	1	-6	-6	-0	0.0

● FRANK CASTILLO
Castillo, Frank Anthony b: 4/1/69, ElPaso, Tex. BR/TR, 6'1", 180 lbs. Deb: 6/27/91

YEAR TM/L	W	L	PCT	G	GS	CG	SH	SV	IP	H	HR	BB	SO	RAT	ERA	ERA+	OAV	OOB	BH	AVG	PB	PR	/A	PD	TPI
1991 Chi-N	6	7	.462	18	18	4	0	0	111²	107	5	33	73	11.3	4.35	89	.252	.306	5	.143	-0	-8	-6	0	-0.7
1992 Chi-N	10	11	.476	33	33	0	0	0	205¹	179	19	63	135	10.9	3.46	104	.232	.295	6	.092	-2	1	3	-1	0.0
1993 Chi-N	5	8	.385	29	25	2	0	0	141¹	162	20	39	84	13.4	4.84	82	.293	.349	7	.163	-0	-13	-13	3	-0.9
1994 Chi-N	2	1	.667	4	4	1	0	0	23	25	3	5	19	11.7	4.30	96	.278	.316	0	.000	-1	-0	-0	-0	-0.1
Total 4	23	27	.460	84	80	7	0	0	481¹	473	47	140	311	11.7	4.11	93	.257	.315	18	.118	-4	-20	-16	1	-1.7

● JUAN CASTILLO
Castillo, Juan Francisco (Azdura) b: 6/23/70, Caracas, Venez. BR/TR, 6'5", 205 lbs. Deb: 7/26/94

YEAR TM/L	W	L	PCT	G	GS	CG	SH	SV	IP	H	HR	BB	SO	RAT	ERA	ERA+	OAV	OOB	BH	AVG	PB	PR	/A	PD	TPI
1994 NY-N	0	0	—	2	2	0	0	0	11²	17	2	5	12	17.0	6.94	61	.362	.423	1	.200	0	-4	-3	1	0.1

● BOBBY CASTILLO
Castillo, Robert Ernie b: 4/18/55, Los Angeles, Cal. BR/TR, 5'10", 170 lbs. Deb: 9/10/77

YEAR TM/L	W	L	PCT	G	GS	CG	SH	SV	IP	H	HR	BB	SO	RAT	ERA	ERA+	OAV	OOB	BH	AVG	PB	PR	/A	PD	TPI
1977 LA-N	1	0	1.000	6	1	0	0	0	11¹	12	2	2	7	11.1	3.97	96	.279	.311	BH	.000	-0	-0	-0	0	0.0
1978 LA-N	0	4	.000	18	0	0	0	1	34	28	2	33	30	16.1	3.97	88	.239	.407	0	.000	-1	-1	-2	0	-0.3

YEAR	TM/L	W	L	PCT	G	GS	CG	SH	SV	IP	H	HR	BB	SO	RAT	ERA	ERA+	OAV	OOB	BH	AVG	PB	PR	/A	PD	TPI
1979	LA-N	2	0	1.000	19	0	0	0	7	24¹	26	0	13	25	14.8	1.11	328	.277	.370	1	.000	-0	7	7	0	1.0
1980	LA-N	8	6	.571	61	0	0	0	5	98¹	70	4	45	60	10.6	2.75	127	.206	.301	1	.111	-0	9	8	1	1.3
1981	*LA-N	2	4	.333	34	1	0	0	5	50²	50	5	24	35	13.1	5.33	62	.262	.344	4	.444	2	-10	-11	-1	-1.4
1982	Min-A	13	11	.542	40	25	6	1	0	218¹	194	26	85	123	11.5	3.66	116	.241	.313	0	—	0	10	14	-2	1.2
1983	Min-A	8	12	.400	27	25	3	0	0	158¹	170	17	65	90	13.4	4.77	89	.278	.348	0	—	0	-13	-9	1	-1.0
1984	Min-A	2	1	.667	10	2	0	0	0	25¹	14	2	19	7	11.7	1.78	237	.177	.337	0	—	0	6	7	-0	0.6
1985	*LA-N	2	2	.500	35	5	0	0	0	68	59	9	41	57	13.4	5.43	64	.230	.339	1	.100	-0	-14	-15	0	-0.8
Total	9	38	40	.487	250	59	9	1	18	689	623	67	327	434	12.5	3.94	99	.246	.333	6	.154	0	-6	-2	-1	0.6

● **SLICK CASTLEMAN**   Castleman, Clydell   b: 9/8/13, Donelson, Tenn.   BR/TR, 6′, 185 lbs.   Deb: 5/9/34

YEAR	TM/L	W	L	PCT	G	GS	CG	SH	SV	IP	H	HR	BB	SO	RAT	ERA	ERA+	OAV	OOB	BH	AVG	PB	PR	/A	PD	TPI
1934	NY-N	1	0	1.000	7	1	0	0	0	16²	18	1	10	5	15.1	5.40	72	.277	.373	1	.250	1	-2	-3	1	0.0
1935	NY-N	15	6	.714	29	25	9	1	0	173²	186	14	64	64	13.0	4.09	94	.268	.330	12	.179	-0	-1	-5	1	-0.4
1936	*NY-N	4	7	.364	29	12	2	1	1	111²	148	6	56	54	16.8	5.64	69	.323	.403	5	.128	-1	-20	-22	1	-1.9
1937	NY-N	11	6	.647	23	23	10	2	0	160¹	148	19	33	78	10.2	3.31	117	.247	.287	4	.070	-5	11	10	-3	0.3
1938	NY-N	4	5	.444	21	14	4	0	0	90²	108	4	37	18	14.7	4.17	90	.296	.365	3	.097	-1	-4	-4	-1	-0.6
1939	NY-N	1	2	.333	12	4	0	0	0	33²	36	1	23	6	15.8	4.54	86	.286	.396	3	.333	1	-2	-2	-1	-0.2
Total	6	36	26	.581	121	79	25	4	1	586²	644	45	223	225	13.4	4.25	91	.279	.345	28	.135	-6	-19	-25	-2	-2.8

● **ROY CASTLETON**   Castleton, Royal Eugene   b: 7/26/1885, Salt Lake City, Utah   d: 6/24/67, Los Angeles, Cal.   BR/TL, 5′11″, 167 lbs.   Deb: 4/16/07

YEAR	TM/L	W	L	PCT	G	GS	CG	SH	SV	IP	H	HR	BB	SO	RAT	ERA	ERA+	OAV	OOB	BH	AVG	PB	PR	/A	PD	TPI
1907	NY-A	1	1	.500	3	2	1	0	0	16	11	1	3	7	7.9	2.81	100	.196	.237	0	.000	-1	-0	-0	-0	-0.1
1909	Cin-N	1	1	.500	4	1	1	0	0	14	14	0	6	5	14.1	1.93	135	.275	.373	2	.667	1	1	1	0	0.3
1910	Cin-N	1	2	.333	4	2	1	0	0	13²	15	0	6	1	14.5	3.29	89	.288	.373	0	.000	-1	-0	-1	0	-0.2
Total	3	3	4	.429	11	5	3	0	0	43²	40	1	15	13	12.0	2.68	104	.252	.328	2	.154	-0	0	0	0	0.0

● **PAUL CASTNER**   Castner, Paul Henry "Lefty"   b: 2/16/1897, St.Paul, Minn.   d: 3/3/86, St.Paul, Minn.   BL/TL, 5′11″, 187 lbs.   Deb: 8/6/23

YEAR	TM/L	W	L	PCT	G	GS	CG	SH	SV	IP	H	HR	BB	SO	RAT	ERA	ERA+	OAV	OOB	BH	AVG	PB	PR	/A	PD	TPI
1923	Chi-A	0	0	—	6	0	0	0	0	10	14	0	5	0	17.1	6.30	63	.326	.396	0	.000	-0	-3	-3	0	0.0

● **BILL CASTRO**   Castro, William Radhames (Checo)   b: 12/13/53, Santiago, D.R.   BR/TR, 5′11″, 170 lbs.   Deb: 8/20/74   C

YEAR	TM/L	W	L	PCT	G	GS	CG	SH	SV	IP	H	HR	BB	SO	RAT	ERA	ERA+	OAV	OOB	BH	AVG	PB	PR	/A	PD	TPI
1974	Mil-A	0	0	—	8	0	0	0	0	18	19	2	5	10	12.0	4.50	80	.264	.312	0	—	0	-2	-2	0	0.0
1975	Mil-A	3	2	.600	18	5	0	0	1	75	78	3	17	25	11.6	2.52	152	.271	.316	0	—	0	10	11	0	0.7
1976	Mil-A	4	6	.400	39	0	0	0	8	70¹	70	4	19	23	11.8	3.45	101	.265	.322	0	—	0	1	-0	-0	0.2
1977	Mil-A	8	6	.571	51	0	0	0	13	69¹	76	7	23	28	13.1	4.15	98	.293	.356	0	—	0	-1	-1	1	0.0
1978	Mil-A	5	4	.556	42	0	0	0	8	49²	43	2	14	17	11.4	1.81	207	.234	.309	0	—	0	11	11	0	2.3
1979	Mil-A	3	1	.750	39	0	0	0	6	44¹	40	2	13	10	10.8	2.03	205	.244	.299	0	—	0	11	11	-0	1.1
1980	Mil-A	2	4	.333	56	0	0	0	8	84¹	89	4	17	32	11.5	2.77	139	.274	.314	0	—	0	12	10	1	1.2
1981	NY-A	1	1	.500	11	0	0	0	0	19	26	2	5	4	14.7	3.79	94	.329	.369	0	—	0	-0	-0	0	-0.0
1982	KC-A	3	2	.600	21	4	0	0	1	75²	72	8	20	37	11.2	3.45	118	.243	.296	0	—	0	5	5	-1	0.2
1983	KC-A	2	0	1.000	18	0	0	0	0	40²	51	4	12	17	15.0	6.64	61	.300	.364	0	—	0	-12	-12	0	-0.5
Total	10	31	26	.544	303	9	0	0	45	546¹	564	36	145	203	12.0	3.33	117	.268	.322	0	—	0	35	34	0	5.2

● **ELI CATES**   Cates, Eli Eldo   b: 1/26/1877, Greensfork, Ind.   d: 5/29/64, Anderson, Ind.   BR/TR, 5′9.5″, 175 lbs.   Deb: 4/20/08   ♦

YEAR	TM/L	W	L	PCT	G	GS	CG	SH	SV	IP	H	HR	BB	SO	RAT	ERA	ERA+	OAV	OOB	BH	AVG	PB	PR	/A	PD	TPI
1908	Was-A	4	8	.333	19	10	7	0	0	114²	112	3	32	33	11.4	2.51	91	.261	.314	11	.186	1	-1	-3	1	0.0

● **TED CATHER**   Cather, Theodore Physick   b: 5/20/1889, Chester, Pa.   d: 4/9/45, Elkton, Md.   BR/TR, 5′10.5″, 178 lbs.   Deb: 9/23/12   ♦

YEAR	TM/L	W	L	PCT	G	GS	CG	SH	SV	IP	H	HR	BB	SO	RAT	ERA	ERA+	OAV	OOB	BH	AVG	PB	PR	/A	PD	TPI
1913	StL-N	0	0	—	1	0	0	0	0	0¹	1	0	2	0	108.0	54.00	6	.500	.800	39	.213	0	-2	-2	0	0.0

● **HARDIN CATHEY**   Cathey, Hardin "Lil Abner"   b: 7/6/19, Burns, Tenn.   BR/TR, 6′4″, 190 lbs.   Deb: 4/16/42

YEAR	TM/L	W	L	PCT	G	GS	CG	SH	SV	IP	H	HR	BB	SO	RAT	ERA	ERA+	OAV	OOB	BH	AVG	PB	PR	/A	PD	TPI
1942	Was-A	1	1	.500	12	2	0	0	0	30¹	44	1	16	8	17.8	7.42	49	.341	.414	3	.375	1	-13	-13	-0	-0.7

● **KEEFE CATO**   Cato, John Keefe   b: 5/6/58, Yonkers, N.Y.   BR/TR, 6′1″, 185 lbs.   Deb: 6/13/83

YEAR	TM/L	W	L	PCT	G	GS	CG	SH	SV	IP	H	HR	BB	SO	RAT	ERA	ERA+	OAV	OOB	BH	AVG	PB	PR	/A	PD	TPI
1983	Cin-N	1	0	1.000	4	0	0	0	0	3²	2	0	1	3	7.4	2.45	155	.154	.214	0	—	0	0	1	-0	0.1
1984	Cin-N	0	1	.000	8	0	0	0	1	15²	22	5	4	12	14.9	8.04	47	.344	.382	2	.500	1	-8	-7	0	-0.4
Total	2	1	1	.500	12	0	0	0	1	19¹	24	5	5	15	13.5	6.98	54	.312	.354	2	.500	1	-7	-7	0	-0.3

● **JOHN CATTANACH**   Cattanach, John Leckie   b: 5/10/1863, Providence, R.I.   d: 11/10/26, Providence, R.I.   5′10″, 190 lbs.   Deb: 6/5/1884

YEAR	TM/L	W	L	PCT	G	GS	CG	SH	SV	IP	H	HR	BB	SO	RAT	ERA	ERA+	OAV	OOB	BH	AVG	PB	PR	/A	PD	TPI
1884	Pro-N	0	0	—	1	1	0	0	0	5	2	0	4	2	10.8	9.00	31	.100	.250	0	.000	-1	-3	-3	-0	-0.1
	StL-U	1	1	.500	2	2	2	0	0	17	12	0	4	13	8.5	2.12	113	.185	.232	0	.000	-2	1	1	0	-0.1
Total	1	1	1	.500	3	3	2	0	0	22	14	0	8	15	9.0	3.68	68	.165	.237	0	.000	-2	-3	-3	-0	-0.2

● **BILL CAUDILL**   Caudill, William Holland   b: 7/13/56, Santa Monica, Cal.   BR/TR, 6′1″, 210 lbs.   Deb: 5/12/79

YEAR	TM/L	W	L	PCT	G	GS	CG	SH	SV	IP	H	HR	BB	SO	RAT	ERA	ERA+	OAV	OOB	BH	AVG	PB	PR	/A	PD	TPI
1979	Chi-N	1	7	.125	29	12	0	0	0	90	89	16	41	104	13.4	4.80	86	.255	.340	1	.059	-1	-11	-7	1	-0.7
1980	Chi-N	4	6	.400	72	0	0	0	1	127²	100	10	59	112	11.3	2.19	179	.223	.314	2	.222	0	20	**25**	-1	1.8
1981	Chi-N	1	5	.167	30	10	0	0	0	71	87	4	31	45	15.2	5.83	63	.301	.373	2	.143	0	-18	-17	-1	-1.4
1982	Sea-A	12	9	.571	70	0	0	0	26	95²	65	9	35	111	9.5	2.35	180	.192	.270	0	—	0	18	20	-1	**5.1**
1983	Sea-A	2	8	.200	63	0	0	0	26	72²	70	10	38	73	13.6	4.71	90	.257	.353	0	—	0	-5	-4	-1	-1.1
1984	Oak-A★	9	7	.563	68	0	0	0	36	96¹	77	4	31	89	10.1	2.71	138	.218	.281	0	.000	0	14	11	-2	2.5
1985	Tor-A	4	6	.400	67	0	0	0	14	69¹	53	9	35	46	11.7	2.99	141	.209	.310	0	—	0	9	9	-1	1.5
1986	Tor-A	2	4	.333	40	0	0	0	2	36¹	36	6	17	32	13.6	6.19	68	.254	.342	0	—	0	-8	-8	-1	-1.4
1987	Oak-A	0	0	—	6	0	0	0	1	8	10	3	1	8	12.4	9.00	46	.294	.314	0	—	0	-4	-4	-0	0.1
Total	9	35	52	.402	445	24	0	0	106	667	587	81	288	620	12.0	3.68	110	.237	.320	5	.122	-1	14	26	-7	6.4

● **RED CAUSEY**   Causey, Cecil Algernon   b: 8/11/1893, Georgetown, Fla.   d: 11/11/60, Avon Park, Fla.   BR/TR, 6′1″, 160 lbs.   Deb: 4/26/18

YEAR	TM/L	W	L	PCT	G	GS	CG	SH	SV	IP	H	HR	BB	SO	RAT	ERA	ERA+	OAV	OOB	BH	AVG	PB	PR	/A	PD	TPI
1918	NY-N	11	6	.647	29	18	10	2	2	158¹	143	2	42	48	10.9	2.79	94	.245	.304	6	.125	-3	-0	-3	-1	-0.7
1919	NY-N	9	3	.750	19	16	6	0	0	105	99	5	38	25	11.9	3.69	76	.251	.320	5	.132	-1	-9	-10	-1	-1.3
	Bos-N	4	5	.444	10	10	3	0	0	69	81	1	20	14	13.3	4.57	63	.308	.359	2	.095	-2	-13	-13	0	-1.7
	Yr	13	8	.619	29	26	9	0	0	174	180	6	58	39	12.4	4.03	70	.273	.333	7	.119	-3	-22	-23	-1	-3.0
1920	Phi-N	7	14	.333	35	26	11	1	3	181¹	203	4	79	30	14.2	4.32	79	.299	.376	11	.186	-2	-24	-18	-2	-2.4
1921	Phi-N	3	3	.500	7	7	4	0	0	50²	54	8	11	8	12.4	2.84	149	.294	.335	3	.150	-1	5	8	-0	0.8
	NY-N	1	1	.500	7	1	0	0	0	14²	13	0	6	1	11.7	2.45	149	.228	.302	1	.333	0	2	2	-0	0.2
	Yr	4	4	.500	14	8	4	0	0	65¹	71	4	17	9	12.1	2.76	149	.278	.324	4	.174	-1	7	10	-0	1.0
1922	NY-N	4	3	.571	24	2	1	0	0	70²	69	2	34	13	13.1	3.18	126	.262	.347	5	.238	-0	7	6	1	0.6
Total	5	39	35	.527	131	80	35	3	6	649²	666	18	230	139	12.6	3.59	89	.273	.340	33	.157	-9	-31	-29	-3	-4.5

● **PUG CAVET**   Cavet, Tiller H.   b: 12/26/1889, McGregor, Tex.   d: 8/4/66, San Luis Obispo, Cal.   BL/TL, 6′3″, 176 lbs.   Deb: 4/25/11

YEAR	TM/L	W	L	PCT	G	GS	CG	SH	SV	IP	H	HR	BB	SO	RAT	ERA	ERA+	OAV	OOB	BH	AVG	PB	PR	/A	PD	TPI
1911	Det-A	0	0	—	1	0	0	0	0	4	6	0	1	1	15.8	4.50	77	.316	.360	0	.000	-0	-1	-0	0	0.0
1914	Det-A	7	7	.500	31	14	6	1	2	151¹	129	2	44	51	10.8	2.44	115	.238	.306	5	.106	-2	5	6	1	0.5
1915	Det-A	4	2	.667	17	7	2	0	1	71	83	1	22	26	13.6	4.06	75	.300	.355	6	.250	1	-9	-8	-0	-0.5
Total	3	11	9	.550	49	22	8	1	3	226¹	218	3	67	78	11.8	2.98	97	.260	.323	11	.153	-0	-4	-2	1	0.0

● **JOSE CECENA**   Cecena, Jose Isabel (Lugo)   b: 8/20/63, Ciudad Obregon, Mexico   BR/TR, 5′11″, 180 lbs.   Deb: 4/6/88

YEAR	TM/L	W	L	PCT	G	GS	CG	SH	SV	IP	H	HR	BB	SO	RAT	ERA	ERA+	OAV	OOB	BH	AVG	PB	PR	/A	PD	TPI
1988	Tex-A	0	0	—	22	0	0	0	0	26¹	20	2	23	27	15.4	4.78	85	.213	.378	0	—	0	-2	-2	-0	-0.1

● **ART CECCARELLI**   Ceccarelli, Arthur Edward "Chic"   b: 4/2/30, New Haven, Conn.   BR/TL, 6′, 190 lbs.   Deb: 5/3/55

YEAR	TM/L	W	L	PCT	G	GS	CG	SH	SV	IP	H	HR	BB	SO	RAT	ERA	ERA+	OAV	OOB	BH	AVG	PB	PR	/A	PD	TPI
1955	KC-A	4	7	.364	31	16	3	1	0	123²	123	20	71	68	14.1	5.31	79	.258	.354	3	.079	-3	-19	-16	-2	-1.7
1956	KC-A	0	1	.000	3	2	0	0	0	10	13	3	4	2	16.2	7.20	60	.317	.391	0	.000	-0	-3	-3	1	-0.2
1957	Bal-A	0	5	.000	20	8	1	0	0	58	62	3	31	30	14.7	4.50	80	.278	.371	0	.000	-2	-5	-6	-1	-0.7

YEAR	TM/L	W	L	PCT	G	GS	CG	SH	SV	IP	H	HR	BB	SO	RAT	ERA	ERA+	OAV	OOB	BH	AVG	PB	PR	/A	PD	TPI
1959	Chi-N	5	5	.500	18	15	4	2	0	102	95	19	37	56	11.7	4.76	83	.245	.312	3	.091	-1	-9	-9	-1	-1.0
1960	Chi-N	0	0	—	7	1	0	0	0	13	16	1	4	10	13.8	5.54	68	.296	.345	0	—	0	-3	-3	-0	0.0
Total	5	9	18	.333	79	42	8	3	0	306²	309	46	147	166	13.5	5.05	79	.261	.345	6	.068	-6	-38	-37	-3	-3.6

● REX CECIL
Cecil, Rex Rolston b: 10/8/16, Lindsay, Okla. d: 10/30/66, Long Beach, Cal. BL/TR, 6'3", 195 lbs. Deb: 8/13/44

YEAR	TM/L	W	L	PCT	G	GS	CG	SH	SV	IP	H	HR	BB	SO	RAT	ERA	ERA+	OAV	OOB	BH	AVG	PB	PR	/A	PD	TPI
1944	Bos-A	4	5	.444	11	9	4	0	0	61	72	5	33	33	15.6	5.16	66	.286	.371	5	.278	2	-12	-12	-0	-1.4
1945	Bos-A	2	5	.286	7	7	1	0	0	45	46	4	27	30	14.6	5.20	66	.261	.360	6	.300	1	-9	-9	1	-1.1
Total	2	6	10	.375	18	16	5	0	0	106	118	9	60	63	15.2	5.18	66	.276	.366	11	.289	1	-21	-21	-0	-2.5

● PETE CENTER
Center, Marvin Earl b: 4/22/12, Hazel Green, Ky. BR/TR, 6'4", 190 lbs. Deb: 9/11/42

YEAR	TM/L	W	L	PCT	G	GS	CG	SH	SV	IP	H	HR	BB	SO	RAT	ERA	ERA+	OAV	OOB	BH	AVG	PB	PR	/A	PD	TPI
1942	Cle-A	0	0	—	1	0	0	0	0	3¹	7	0	4	0	32.4	16.20	21	.438	.571	0	.000	-0	-5	-5	-0	0.0
1943	Cle-A	1	2	.333	24	1	0	0	1	42¹	29	3	18	10	10.0	2.76	112	.201	.290	0	.000	-1	3	2	-1	0.0
1945	Cle-A	6	3	.667	31	8	2	0	1	85²	89	2	28	34	12.4	3.99	81	.270	.329	2	.091	-2	-6	-7	-2	-1.1
1946	Cle-A	0	2	.000	21	0	0	0	1	29	29	2	20	6	15.5	4.97	67	.269	.388	0	.000	-0	-5	-5	-0	-0.4
Total	4	7	7	.500	77	9	2	0	3	160¹	154	7	70	50	12.7	4.10	79	.258	.338	2	.065	-3	-13	-16	-3	-1.5

● RICK CERONE
Cerone, Richard Aldo b: 5/19/54, Newark, N.J. BR/TR, 5'11", 192 lbs. Deb: 8/17/75 ♦

YEAR	TM/L	W	L	PCT	G	GS	CG	SH	SV	IP	H	HR	BB	SO	RAT	ERA	ERA+	OAV	OOB	BH	AVG	PB	PR	/A	PD	TPI
1987	NY-A	0	0	—	2	0	0	0	0	2	0	0	1	1	4.5			.000	.143	69	.243	2	1	1	-0	0.0

● JOHN CERUTTI
Cerutti, John Joseph b: 4/28/60, Albany, N.Y. BL/TL, 6'2", 200 lbs. Deb: 9/1/85

YEAR	TM/L	W	L	PCT	G	GS	CG	SH	SV	IP	H	HR	BB	SO	RAT	ERA	ERA+	OAV	OOB	BH	AVG	PB	PR	/A	PD	TPI
1985	Tor-A	0	2	.000	4	1	0	0	0	6²	10	1	4	5	20.3	5.40	78	.323	.417	0		0	-1	-1	0	-0.3
1986	Tor-A	9	4	.692	34	20	2	1	1	145¹	150	25	47	89	12.3	4.15	102	.268	.326	0		0	0	0	0	0.0
1987	Tor-A	11	4	.733	44	21	2	0	0	151¹	144	30	59	92	12.1	4.40	102	.251	.322	0		0	1	2	-2	-0.1
1988	Tor-A	6	7	.462	46	12	0	0	1	123²	120	12	42	65	12.0	3.13	126	.256	.322	0		0	11	11	3	1.4
1989	*Tor-A	11	11	.500	33	31	3	1	0	205¹	214	19	53	69	12.0	3.07	123	.273	.323	0		0	19	16	3	2.0
1990	Tor-A	9	9	.500	30	23	0	0	0	140	162	23	49	49	13.8	4.76	83	.297	.359	0		0	-13	-13	-0	-1.5
1991	Det-A	3	6	.333	38	8	1	0	2	88²	94	9	37	29	13.5	4.57	91	.276	.351	0		0	-5	-4	1	-0.3
Total	7	49	43	.533	229	116	8	2	4	861	894	119	291	398	12.6	3.94	103	.271	.333	0		0	13	12	4	1.2

● RAY CHADWICK
Chadwick, Ray Charles b: 11/17/62, Durham, N.C. BB/TR, 6'2", 180 lbs. Deb: 7/29/86

YEAR	TM/L	W	L	PCT	G	GS	CG	SH	SV	IP	H	HR	BB	SO	RAT	ERA	ERA+	OAV	OOB	BH	AVG	PB	PR	/A	PD	TPI
1986	Cal-A	0	5	.000	7	7	0	0	0	27¹	39	5	15	9	18.1	7.24	57	.336	.417		—	0	-9	-10	0	-1.3

● LEON CHAGNON
Chagnon, Leon Wilbur "Shag" b: 9/28/02, Pittsfield, N.H. d: 7/30/53, Amesbury, Mass. BR/TR, 6', 182 lbs. Deb: 10/5/29

YEAR	TM/L	W	L	PCT	G	GS	CG	SH	SV	IP	H	HR	BB	SO	RAT	ERA	ERA+	OAV	OOB	BH	AVG	PB	PR	/A	PD	TPI
1929	Pit-N	0	0	—	1	1	0	0	0	7	11	1	1	4	15.4	9.00	53	.333	.353	0	.000	-0	-3	-3	0	0.0
1930	Pit-N	3	0	1.000	18	4	3	0	0	62	92	9	23	27	17.4	6.82	73	.355	.418	4	.200	-1	-13	-13	0	-0.5
1932	Pit-N	9	6	.600	30	10	4	1	0	128	140	10	34	52	12.4	3.94	97	.276	.324	9	.225	-2	-1	-2	-2	-0.2
1933	Pit-N	6	4	.600	39	5	1	0	1	100	100	2	17	35	10.8	3.69	90	.259	.296	1	.048	-2	-4	-4	-1	-0.7
1934	Pit-N	4	1	.800	33	1	0	0	1	58	68	5	24	19	14.4	4.81	86	.288	.356	3	.231	0	-5	-4	1	-0.2
1935	NY-N	2	0	1.000	14	1	0	0	1	38¹	32	7	5	16	8.7	3.52	109	.232	.259	0	.000	-0	2	1	0	0.0
Total	6	19	16	.543	135	22	8	1	3	393¹	443	34	104	153	12.8	4.51	87	.284	.333	17	.162	-2	-24	-25	-1	-1.6

● BOB CHAKALES
Chakales, Robert Edward "Chick" b: 8/10/27, Asheville, N.C. BR/TR, 6'1", 185 lbs. Deb: 4/21/51

YEAR	TM/L	W	L	PCT	G	GS	CG	SH	SV	IP	H	HR	BB	SO	RAT	ERA	ERA+	OAV	OOB	BH	AVG	PB	PR	/A	PD	TPI
1951	Cle-A	3	4	.429	17	10	2	1	0	68¹	80	3	43	32	16.2	4.74	80	.292	.388	7	.350	2	-5	-7	-0	-0.5
1952	Cle-A	1	2	.333	5	1	0	0	0	12	19	2	8	7	20.3	9.75	34	.388	.474	2	.500	1	-8	-9	-1	-1.6
1953	Cle-A	0	2	.000	7	3	1	0	0	27	28	2	10	6	13.0	2.67	141	.283	.355	2	.286	1	4	3	0	0.3
1954	Cle-A	2	0	1.000	3	0	0	0	0	10¹	4	0	12	3	13.9	0.87	422	.114	.340	1	.333	1	3	3	-0	0.7
	Bal-A	3	7	.300	38	6	0	0	0	89¹	81	8	43	44	12.6	3.73	96	.245	.333	8	.364	2	-0	-1	0	0.1
	Yr	5	7	.417	41	6	0	0	0	99²	85	8	55	47	12.7	3.43	105	.232	.334	9	.360	3	3	2	-0	0.8
1955	Chi-A	0	0	—	7	0	0	0	0	12¹	11	2	6	6	12.4	1.46	271	.256	.347	0	.000	-1	3	3	0	0.0
	Was-A	2	3	.400	29	0	0	0	0	54²	55	4	25	28	13.3	5.27	73	.263	.345	0	.000	-1	-8	-9	1	-0.8
	Yr	2	3	.400	36	0	0	0	0	67	66	6	31	34	13.2	4.57	84	.262	.345	0	.000	-1	-5	-5	1	-0.8
1956	Was-A	4	4	.500	43	1	0	0	4	96	94	8	57	33	14.4	4.03	107	.268	.375	3	.150	-1	1	3	1	0.3
1957	Was-A	0	1	.000	4	2	0	0	0	18¹	20	2	10	12	14.7	5.40	72	.274	.361	1	.143	0	-3	-3	0	-0.1
	Bos-A	0	2	.000	18	0	0	0	0	32	53	5	11	16	18.3	8.16	49	.379	.428	2	.667	1	-16	-15	-1	-1.1
	Yr	0	3	.000	22	2	0	0	0	50¹	73	7	21	28	17.0	7.15	55	.341	.403	3	.300	1	-19	-18	-0	-1.2
Total	7	15	25	.375	171	23	3	1	10	420¹	445	31	225	187	14.5	4.54	85	.277	.369	26	.271	5	-28	-31	1	-2.7

● GEORGE CHALMERS
Chalmers, George W. "Dut" b: 6/7/1888, Edinburgh, Scot. d: 8/5/60, Bronx, N.Y. BR/TR, 6'1", 189 lbs. Deb: 9/21/10

YEAR	TM/L	W	L	PCT	G	GS	CG	SH	SV	IP	H	HR	BB	SO	RAT	ERA	ERA+	OAV	OOB	BH	AVG	PB	PR	/A	PD	TPI
1910	Phi-N	1	1	.500	4	3	2	0	0	22	21	0	11	12	13.5	5.32	59	.280	.379	1	.143	-0	-6	-5	1	-0.3
1911	Phi-N	13	10	.565	38	22	11	3	4	208²	196	5	101	101	13.0	3.11	111	.256	.346	13	.178	-1	7	8	-1	0.6
1912	Phi-N	3	4	.429	12	8	3	0	0	57²	64	4	37	22	16.1	3.28	111	.296	.404	3	.188	-0	1	-2	-0	0.0
1913	Phi-N	3	10	.231	26	14	4	0	1	116	133	3	51	46	14.7	4.81	69	.296	.374	7	.212	-1	-21	-19	1	-1.9
1914	Phi-N	0	3	.000	3	2	1	0	0	18	23	0	15	6	19.5	5.50	53	.324	.448	0	.000	-1	-5	-5	0	-0.8
1915	*Phi-N	8	9	.471	26	20	13	1	1	170¹	159	3	45	82	10.8	2.48	110	.255	.305	10	.169	-0	5	5	1	0.4
1916	Phi-N	1	4	.200	12	8	2	0	0	53²	49	2	19	21	11.7	3.19	88	.243	.315	0	.000	-2	-3	-3	0	-0.5
Total	7	29	41	.414	121	77	36	4	6	646¹	645	17	279	290	13.1	3.41	93	.269	.348	34	.163	-5	-22	-18	1	-2.5

● CRAIG CHAMBERLAIN
Chamberlain, Craig Philip b: 2/2/57, Hollywood, Cal. BR/TR, 6'1", 190 lbs. Deb: 8/12/79

YEAR	TM/L	W	L	PCT	G	GS	CG	SH	SV	IP	H	HR	BB	SO	RAT	ERA	ERA+	OAV	OOB	BH	AVG	PB	PR	/A	PD	TPI
1979	KC-A	4	4	.500	10	10	4	0	0	69²	68	7	18	30	11.2	3.75	114	.261	.311	0	—	0	4	4	-2	0.2
1980	KC-A	0	1	.000	5	0	0	0	0	9¹	10	3	5	3	14.5	6.75	60	.270	.357	0	—	0	-3	-3	0	-0.3
Total	2	4	5	.444	15	10	4	0	0	79	78	10	23	33	11.6	4.10	103	.262	.317	0	—	0	1	1	-2	-0.1

● ELTON CHAMBERLAIN
Chamberlain, Elton P. "Icebox" b: 11/5/1867, Buffalo, N.Y. d: 9/22/29, Baltimore, Md. BR/TB, 5'9", 168 lbs. Deb: 9/13/1886

YEAR	TM/L	W	L	PCT	G	GS	CG	SH	SV	IP	H	HR	BB	SO	RAT	ERA	ERA+	OAV	OOB	BH	AVG	PB	PR	/A	PD	TPI
1886	Lou-a	0	3	.000	4	4	4	0	0	31¹	39	0	17	18	16.1	6.61	55	.287	.366	3	.158	-0	-11	-10	-0	-0.7
1887	Lou-a	18	16	.529	36	36	35	1	0	309	340	8	117	118	13.7	3.79	116	.274	.343	26	.198	-3	17	21	1	1.5
1888	Lou-a	14	9	.609	24	24	21	1	0	196	177	2	59	119	11.3	2.53	122	.232	.297	18	.191	-0	12	12	1	1.4
	*StL-a	11	2	.846	14	14	13	1	0	112	61	1	27	57	7.6	1.61	203	.154	.220	5	.100	-3	18	21	-1	1.7
	Yr	25	11	.694	38	38	34	2	0	308	238	3	86	176	9.6	2.19	143	.204	.262	23	.160	-3	30	33	0	3.1
1889	StL-a	32	15	.681	53	51	44	3	1	421²	376	8	165	202	11.9	2.97	142	.231	.309	34	.199	-2	41	59	-3	4.7
1890	StL-a	3	1	.750	5	5	3	0	0	35	47	3	11	26	14	18.8	5.91	73	.312	.413	2	.133	-1	-8	-6	0	-0.6
	Col-a	12	6	.667	25	21	19	6	0	175	128	2	70	114	10.6	2.21	162	.198	.284	15	.231	3	32	27	-2	2.4
	Yr	15	7	.682	30	26	22	**6**	0	210	175	5	81	140	11.9	2.83	131	.220	.310	17	.213	2	24	21	-2	1.8
1891	Phi-a	22	23	.489	49	46	44	0	0	405²	397	10	206	204	13.6	4.22	91	.248	.338	33	.188	2	-22	-18	0	-1.4
1892	Cin-N	19	23	.452	52	49	43	2	0	406¹	391	8	170	169	12.8	3.39	96	.251	.322	36	.225	3	-5	-4		-0.6
1893	Cin-N	16	12	.571	34	27	19	1	0	241	288	3	112	59	14.0	3.73	128	.258	.345	19	.196	-3	25	28	-2	2.0
1894	Cin-N	10	9	.526	23	22	18	1	0	177²	220	10	91	57	16.4	5.77	96	.301	.387	22	.314	4	-9	-4	-1	-0.1
1896	Cle-N	0	1	.000	2	2	1	0	0	11	21	1	6	5	22.1	7.36	62	.399	.461	0	.000	-0	-4	-3	-0	-0.3
Total	10	157	120	.567	321	301	264	16	1	2521²	2445	63	1065	1133	12.9	3.57	112	.247	.327	213	.203	-2	88	119	-11	10.0

● BILL CHAMBERLAIN
Chamberlain, William Vincent b: 4/21/09, Stoughton, Mass. d: 2/6/94, Brockton, Mass. BR/TL, 5'10.5", 173 lbs. Deb: 8/2/32

YEAR	TM/L	W	L	PCT	G	GS	CG	SH	SV	IP	H	HR	BB	SO	RAT	ERA	ERA+	OAV	OOB	BH	AVG	PB	PR	/A	PD	TPI
1932	Chi-A	0	5	.000	12	5	0	0	0	41¹	39	3	25	11	13.9	4.57	95	.250	.354	1	.100	-1	-0	-1	-1	-0.2

● CLIFF CHAMBERS
Chambers, Clifford Day "Lefty" b: 1/10/22, Portland, Ore. BL/TL, 6'3", 208 lbs. Deb: 4/24/48

YEAR	TM/L	W	L	PCT	G	GS	CG	SH	SV	IP	H	HR	BB	SO	RAT	ERA	ERA+	OAV	OOB	BH	AVG	PB	PR	/A	PD	TPI
1948	Chi-N	2	9	.182	29	12	3	1	0	103²	100	4	48	51	13.1	4.43	88	.254	.339	4	.133	-1	-5	-6	0	-0.6
1949	Pit-N	13	7	.650	34	21	10	1	0	177¹	186	16	58	93	12.6	3.96	106	.268	.329	13	.236	3	2	5	1	0.9
1950	Pit-N	12	15	.444	37	33	11	2	0	249¹	262	18	92	93	13.0	4.30	102	.265	.332	26	.289	7	-4	2	-2	0.7

YEAR	TM/L	W	L	PCT	G	GS	CG	SH	SV	IP	H	HR	BB	SO	RAT	ERA	ERA+	OAV	OOB	BH	AVG	PB	PR	/A	PD	TPI
1951	Pit-N	3	6	.333	10	10	2	1	0	59²	64	5	31	19	14.9	5.58	76	.276	.371	7	.333	2	-11	-9	-2	-1.1
	StL-N	11	6	.647	21	16	9	1	0	129¹	120	13	56	45	12.2	3.83	104	.251	.329	8	.163	0	2	2	-2	0.1
	Yr	14	12	.538	31	26	11	2	0	189	184	18	87	64	12.9	4.38	92	.257	.338	15	.214	2	-9	-7	-3	-1.0
1952	StL-N	4	4	.500	26	13	2	1	1	98¹	110	8	33	47	13.3	4.12	90	.285	.344	9	.281	3	-4	-4	0	-0.6
1953	StL-N	3	6	.333	32	8	0	0	0	79²	82	7	43	26	14.2	4.86	88	.266	.358	2	.118	-1	-5	-5	0	-0.6
Total	6	48	53	.475	189	113	37	7	1	897¹	924	70	361	374	13.1	4.29	96	.266	.338	69	.235	13	-26	-16	-4	-0.6

● JOHNNIE CHAMBERS
Chambers, Johnnie Monroe b: 9/10/11, Copperhill, Tenn d: 5/11/77, Palatka, Fla. BL/TR, 6', 185 lbs. Deb: 5/4/37

YEAR	TM/L	W	L	PCT	G	GS	CG	SH	SV	IP	H	HR	BB	SO	RAT	ERA	ERA+	OAV	OOB	BH	AVG	PB	PR	/A	PD	TPI
1937	StL-N	0	0	—	2	0	0	0	0	2	5	0	2	1	31.5	18.00	22	.455	.538	0	—	0	-3	-3	-0	0.0

● ROME CHAMBERS
Chambers, Richard Jerome b: 8/31/1875, Weaverville, N.C. d: 8/30/02, Weaverville, N.C. BL/TL, 6'2", 173 lbs. Deb: 5/7/00

| 1900 | Bos-N | 0 | 0 | — | 1 | 0 | 0 | 0 | 1 | 4 | 5 | 0 | 5 | 2 | 22.5 | 11.25 | 37 | .305 | .467 | 0 | .000 | -0 | -3 | -3 | -0 | -0.2 |

● BILL CHAMBERS
Chambers, William Christopher b: 9/13/1889, Cameron, W.Va. d: 3/27/62, Fort Wayne, Ind. BR/TR, 5'9", 185 lbs. Deb: 7/11/10

| 1910 | StL-N | 0 | 0 | — | 1 | 0 | 0 | 0 | 0 | 1 | 1 | 0 | 0 | 0 | 9.0 | 0.00 | — | .250 | .250 | 0 | — | 0 | 0 | 0 | -0 | 0.0 |

● BILL CHAMPION
Champion, Buford Billy b: 9/18/47, Shelby, N.C. BR/TR, 6'4", 188 lbs. Deb: 6/4/69

YEAR	TM/L	W	L	PCT	G	GS	CG	SH	SV	IP	H	HR	BB	SO	RAT	ERA	ERA+	OAV	OOB	BH	AVG	PB	PR	/A	PD	TPI
1969	Phi-N	5	10	.333	23	20	4	2	1	116²	130	7	63	70	15.1	5.01	71	.286	.376	6	.171	0	-18	-19	1	-2.1
1970	Phi-N	0	2	.000	7	1	0	0	0	14	21	3	10	12	20.6	9.00	44	.375	.478	0	.000	-0	-8	-8	0	-0.9
1971	Phi-N	3	5	.375	37	9	0	0	0	108²	100	5	48	49	12.5	4.39	80	.249	.334	3	.111	-1	-11	-10	1	-0.8
1972	Phi-N	4	14	.222	30	22	4	0	0	132²	155	11	54	54	14.2	5.09	71	.301	.368	5	.147	0	-24	-22	1	-2.7
1973	Mil-A	5	8	.385	37	11	2	0	1	136¹	139	10	62	67	13.5	3.70	104	.267	.350	0	—	0	2	1	2	0.5
1974	Mil-A	11	4	.733	31	23	2	0	0	161²	168	12	49	60	12.1	3.62	100	.270	.323	0	—	-0	-0	-0	-1	-0.1
1975	Mil-A	6	6	.500	27	13	3	1	0	110	125	11	55	40	14.7	5.89	65	.290	.370	0	—	0	-26	-25	1	-2.4
1976	Mil-A	0	1	.000	10	3	0	0	0	24¹	35	0	13	8	18.1	7.03	50	.361	.441	0	—	0	-9	-10	1	-0.2
Total	8	34	50	.405	202	102	13	3	2	804¹	873	64	354	360	13.9	4.69	78	.282	.358	14	.141	-1	-95	-93	4	-8.7

● DEAN CHANCE
Chance, Wilmer Dean b: 6/1/41, Wayne, O. BR/TR, 6'3", 200 lbs. Deb: 9/11/61

YEAR	TM/L	W	L	PCT	G	GS	CG	SH	SV	IP	H	HR	BB	SO	RAT	ERA	ERA+	OAV	OOB	BH	AVG	PB	PR	/A	PD	TPI
1961	LA-A	0	2	.000	5	4	0	0	0	18¹	33	0	5	11	19.1	6.87	66	.412	.453	0	.000	-1	-6	-5	1	-0.4
1962	LA-A	14	10	.583	50	24	6	2	8	206²	195	14	66	127	11.6	2.96	130	.250	.313	4	.062	-5	23	21	1	2.0
1963	LA-A	13	18	.419	45	35	6	2	3	248	229	10	90	168	11.9	3.19	107	.243	.316	12	.150	-1	12	6	1	0.8
1964	LA-A★	20	9	.690	46	35	15	11	4	278¹	194	7	86	207	9.1	1.65	199	.195	.261	7	.079	-5	61	51	-2	4.7
1965	Cal-A	15	10	.600	36	33	10	4	0	258²	197	12	101	164	12.2	3.15	108	.208	.328	7	.093	-4	8	6	3	0.8
1966	Cal-A	12	17	.414	41	37	11	2	1	259²	206	18	114	180	11.3	3.08	109	.222	.312	2	.026	-6	10	8	2	0.4
1967	Min-A★	20	14	.588	41	39	18	5	1	283²	244	17	68	220	10.1	2.73	127	.229	.279	3	.033	-6	16	23	2	2.4
1968	Min-A	16	16	.500	43	39	15	6	1	292	224	15	63	234	9.2	2.53	122	.211	.261	5	.054	-6	15	18	3	1.8
1969	*Min-A	5	4	.556	20	15	1	0	0	88¹	76	6	35	50	11.7	2.95	124	.233	.315	1	.042	-1	7	7	-1	0.4
1970	Cle-A	9	8	.529	45	19	1	1	4	155	172	18	59	109	13.8	4.24	93	.287	.357	3	.071	-3	-9	-5	-1	-0.9
	NY-N	0	1	.000	3	0	0	0	1	2	3	0	2	0	22.5	13.50	30	.500	.625	0	—	0	-2	-2	0	-0.1
1971	Det-A	4	6	.400	31	14	0	0	0	89²	91	5	50	64	14.6	3.51	102	.265	.364	0	.000	-2	-1	1	-0	-0.2
Total	11	128	115	.527	406	294	83	33	23	2147¹	1864	122	739	1534	11.2	2.92	119	.234	.305	44	.066	-37	134	131	8	10.8

● ED CHANDLER
Chandler, Edward Oliver b: 2/17/22, Pinson, Ala. BR/TR, 6'2", 190 lbs. Deb: 4/18/47

| 1947 | Bro-N | 0 | 1 | .000 | 15 | 1 | 0 | 0 | 1 | 29² | 31 | 7 | 12 | 8 | 13.0 | 6.37 | 65 | .263 | .331 | 0 | .000 | -0 | -8 | -7 | 0 | -0.3 |

● SPUD CHANDLER
Chandler, Spurgeon Ferdinand b: 9/12/07, Commerce, Ga. d: 1/9/90, S.Pasadena, Fla. BR/TR, 6', 181 lbs. Deb: 5/6/37 C

YEAR	TM/L	W	L	PCT	G	GS	CG	SH	SV	IP	H	HR	BB	SO	RAT	ERA	ERA+	OAV	OOB	BH	AVG	PB	PR	/A	PD	TPI
1937	NY-A	7	4	.636	12	10	6	2	0	82¹	79	8	20	31	10.9	2.84	156	.253	.300	4	.133	-2	16	15	2	1.7
1938	NY-A	14	5	.737	23	23	14	2	0	172	183	7	47	36	12.1	4.03	103	.271	.320	14	.203	2	15	10	4	1.5
1939	NY-A	3	0	1.000	11	0	0	0	0	19	26	0	9	4	16.6	2.84	153	.329	.398	2	.400	1	4	3	1	0.6
1940	NY-A	8	7	.533	27	24	6	1	0	172	184	12	60	56	13.1	4.60	88	.275	.341	9	.150	1	-4	-11	3	-0.4
1941	*NY-A	10	4	.714	28	20	11	4	4	163²	146	5	60	60	11.3	3.19	123	.239	.307	11	.183	-1	17	13	3	1.3
1942	*NY-A★	16	5	.762	24	24	17	3	0	200²	176	13	74	74	11.4	2.38	145	.237	.309	15	.211	4	29	24	3	3.2
1943	*NY-A☆	20	4	.833	30	30	20	5	0	253	197	5	54	134	9.1	1.64	197	.215	.261	25	.258	7	47	44	3	5.7
1944	NY-A	0	0	—	1	1	0	0	0	6	6	1	1	1	12.0	4.50	77	.300	.364	0	.000	-0	-1	-1	0	0.0
1945	NY-A	2	1	.667	4	4	2	1	0	31	30	2	7	12	10.7	4.65	75	.250	.291	4	.333	1	-4	-4	-0	-0.3
1946	NY-A☆	20	8	.714	34	32	20	6	2	257¹	200	7	90	138	10.2	2.10	164	.218	.288	14	.149	4	40	39	4	4.8
1947	*NY-A☆	9	5	.643	17	16	13	2	0	128	100	4	41	68	9.9	2.46	144	.214	.277	12	.245	4	18	15	3	2.5
Total	11	109	43	.717	211	184	109	26	6	1485	1327	64	463	614	11.0	2.84	132	.240	.301	110	.201	17	176	149	27	20.6

● ESTY CHANEY
Chaney, Esty Clyon b: 1/29/1891, Hadley, Pa. d: 2/5/52, Cleveland, Ohio BR/TR, 5'11", 170 lbs. Deb: 8/2/13

YEAR	TM/L	W	L	PCT	G	GS	CG	SH	SV	IP	H	HR	BB	SO	RAT	ERA	ERA+	OAV	OOB	BH	AVG	PB	PR	/A	PD	TPI
1913	Bos-A	0	0	—	1	0	0	0	0	1	1	0	2	0	27.0	9.00	33	.200	.429	0	—	0	-1	-1	-0	0.0
1914	Bro-F	0	0	—	1	0	0	0	0	4	7	0	2	1	20.3	6.75	43	.389	.450	0	.000	-0	-2	-2	-0	0.0
Total	2	0	0	—	2	0	0	0	0	5	8	0	4	1	21.6	7.20	40	.348	.444	0	.000	-0	-2	-2	-0	0.0

● DARRIN CHAPIN
Chapin, Darrin John b: 2/1/66, Warren, Ohio BR/TR, 6', 170 lbs. Deb: 9/21/91

1991	NY-A	0	1	.000	3	0	0	0	0	5¹	3	0	6	5	15.2	5.06	82	.158	.360	0	—	0	-1	-1	0	-0.1
1992	Phi-N	0	0	—	1	0	0	0	0	2	2	1	0	1	9.0	9.00	39	.250	.250	0	—	0	-1	-1	0	0.0
Total	2	0	1	.000	4	0	0	0	0	7¹	5	1	6	6	13.5	6.14	65	.185	.333	0	—	0	-2	-2	0	-0.1

● TINY CHAPLIN
Chaplin, James Bailey b: 7/13/05, Los Angeles, Cal. d: 3/25/39, National City, Cal BR/TR, 6'1", 195 lbs. Deb: 4/13/28

1928	NY-N	0	2	.000	12	1	0	0	0	24	27	0	8	13	13.1	4.50	87	.284	.340	0	.000	-1	-1	-2	-1	-0.2
1930	NY-N	2	6	.250	19	8	3	0	1	73	89	8	16	20	13.4	5.18	91	.305	.349	2	.105	-0	-2	-4	0	-0.3
1931	NY-N	3	0	1.000	16	3	1	0	1	42¹	39	2	16	7	12.1	3.19	116	.242	.318	2	.182	0	3	2	-1	0.1
1936	Bos-N	10	15	.400	40	31	14	0	2	231²	273	21	62	86	13.1	4.12	93	.294	.340	17	.202	-0	-3	-7	2	-0.6
Total	4	15	23	.395	87	43	18	0	4	371	428	31	102	118	13.1	4.25	94	.290	.340	21	.176	-2	-2	-10	1	-1.0

● ED CHAPMAN
Chapman, Edwin Volney b: 11/28/05, Courtland, Miss. BB/TR, 6'1", 185 lbs. Deb: 8/6/33

| 1933 | Was-A | 0 | 0 | — | 6 | 1 | 0 | 0 | 0 | 9 | 10 | 2 | 4 | 2 | 12.0 | 8.00 | 52 | .270 | .308 | 0 | .000 | -0 | -4 | -4 | -0 | -0.1 |

● FRED CHAPMAN
Chapman, Frederick Joseph b: 11/24/1872, Little Cooley, Pa. d: 12/14/57, Union City, Pa. BR/TR, 5'8", 165 lbs. Deb: 7/22/1887

| 1887 | Phi-a | 0 | 0 | — | 1 | 1 | 1 | 0 | 0 | 5 | 8 | 0 | 2 | 4 | 18.0 | 7.20 | 60 | .364 | .417 | 0 | .000 | -0 | -2 | -2 | -0 | 0.0 |

● BEN CHAPMAN
Chapman, William Benjamin b: 12/25/08, Nashville, Tenn. d: 7/7/93, Hoover, Ala. BR/TR, 6', 190 lbs. Deb: 4/15/30 MC♦

1944	Bro-N	5	3	.625	11	9	6	0	0	79¹	75	4	33	37	12.6	3.40	104	.242	.321	14	.368	1	2	1	-2	0.6
1945	Bro-N	3	3	.500	10	7	2	0	0	53²	64	3	32	23	16.6	5.53	68	.296	.394	3	.136	-1	-10	-11	1	-1.0
	Phi-N	0	0	—	3	0	0	0	0	7	7	0	6	4	16.7	7.71	50	.259	.394	16	.314	0	-3	-3	-0	-0.1
	Yr	3	3	.500	13	7	2	0	0	60²	71	3	38	27	16.2	5.79	65	.289	.384	19	.260	-0	-13	-14	1	-1.0
1946	Phi-N	0	0	—	1	0	0	0	0	1	1	0	0	1	9.0	0.00	—	.200	.200	0	.000	0	0	0	0	0.0
Total	3	8	6	.571	25	16	8	0	0	141	147	7	71	65	14.3	4.40	83	.263	.353	1958	.302	6	-11	-12	-1	-0.4

● BILL CHAPPELLE
Chappelle, William Hogan "Big Bill" b: 3/22/1884, Waterloo, N.Y. d: 12/31/44, Mineola, N.Y. BR/TR, 6'2", 206 lbs. Deb: 8/20/08

1908	Bos-N	2	4	.333	13	7	3	1	0	70¹	60	0	17	23	10.4	1.79	135	.233	.290	1	.048	-1	4	5	1	0.4
1909	Bos-N	1	1	.500	5	3	2	0	0	29	31	0	11	8	13.0	1.86	152	.279	.350	4	.364	2	2	3	1	0.6
	Cin-N	0	0	—	1	0	0	0	1	4	5	0	2	0	18.0	2.25	116	.278	.381	0	.000	-0	0	-0	-0	-0
	Yr	1	1	.500	6	3	2	0	1	33	36	0	13	8	13.6	1.91	146	.277	.347	4	.333	2	3	3	1	0.6

YEAR	TM/L	W	L	PCT	G	GS	CG	SH	SV	IP	H	HR	BB	SO	RAT	ERA	ERA+	OAV	OOB	BH	AVG	PB	PR	/A	PD	TPI
1914	Bro-F	4	2	.667	16	6	4	0	0	74¹	71	1	29	31	12.5	3.15	91	.255	.332	0	.000	-4	-2	-2	-1	-0.7
Total 3		7	7	.500	35	16	9	1	1	177²	167	1	59	62	11.9	2.38	113	.251	.321	5	.089	-3	5	6	1	0.3

● NORM CHARLTON
Charlton, Norman Wood b: 1/6/63, Fort Polk, La.   BB/TL, 6'3", 195 lbs.   Deb: 8/19/88

YEAR	TM/L	W	L	PCT	G	GS	CG	SH	SV	IP	H	HR	BB	SO	RAT	ERA	ERA+	OAV	OOB	BH	AVG	PB	PR	/A	PD	TPI
1988	Cin-N	4	5	.444	10	10	0	0	0	61¹	60	6	20	39	12.0	3.96	90	.256	.320	0	.000	-1	-4	-3	-0	-0.5
1989	Cin-N	8	3	.727	69	0	0	0	0	95¹	67	5	40	98	10.3	2.93	123	.197	.285	0	.000	-1	6	7	-0	0.7
1990	*Cin-N	12	9	.571	56	16	1	1	2	154¹	131	10	70	117	12.0	2.74	144	.231	.320	5	.135	0	18	21	1	2.8
1991	Cin-N	3	5	.375	39	11	0	0	1	108¹	92	6	34	77	11.0	2.91	131	.236	.307	1	.043	-2	9	11	1	0.7
1992	Cin-N★	4	2	.667	64	0	0	0	26	81¹	79	7	26	90	12.0	2.99	120	.262	.326	1	.200	0	5	6	-1	0.8
1993	Sea-A	1	3	.250	34	0	0	0	18	34²	22	4	17	48	10.1	2.34	188	.179	.279	0	—	0	8	8	-0	1.7
Total 6		32	27	.542	272	37	1	1	47	535¹	451	38	207	469	11.3	2.96	128	.231	.310	7	.082	-0	42	49	-0	6.2

● PETE CHARTON
Charton, Frank Lane b: 12/21/42, Jackson, Tenn.   BL/TR, 6'2", 190 lbs.   Deb: 4/19/64

YEAR	TM/L	W	L	PCT	G	GS	CG	SH	SV	IP	H	HR	BB	SO	RAT	ERA	ERA+	OAV	OOB	BH	AVG	PB	PR	/A	PD	TPI
1964	Bos-A	0	2	.000	25	5	0	0	0	65	67	12	24	37	12.7	5.26	63	.275	.342	1	.100	-0	-12	-10	2	-0.2

● HAL CHASE
Chase, Harold Homer "Prince Hal" b: 2/13/1883, Los Gatos, Cal.   d: 5/18/47, Colusa, Cal.   BR/TL, 6', 175 lbs.   Deb: 4/14/05 M♦

YEAR	TM/L	W	L	PCT	G	GS	CG	SH	SV	IP	H	HR	BB	SO	RAT	ERA	ERA+	OAV	OOB	BH	AVG	PB	PR	/A	PD	TPI
1908	NY-A	0	0	—	1	0	0	0	0	1	1	0	0	0	—	.000	—	.000	.000	104	.257	0	0	0	0	0.0

● KEN CHASE
Chase, Kendall Fay "Lefty" b: 10/6/13, Oneonta, N.Y.   d: 1/16/85, Oneonta, N.Y.   BL/TL, 6'2", 210 lbs.   Deb: 4/23/36

YEAR	TM/L	W	L	PCT	G	GS	CG	SH	SV	IP	H	HR	BB	SO	RAT	ERA	ERA+	OAV	OOB	BH	AVG	PB	PR	/A	PD	TPI
1936	Was-A	0	0	—	1	1	0	0	0	2¹	2	0	4	1	23.1	11.57	41	.250	.500	1	1.000	1	-2	-2	-0	0.0
1937	Was-A	4	3	.571	14	9	8	0	0	76¹	74	4	60	43	15.8	4.13	107	.257	.385	1	.034	-4	4	3	-0	-0.2
1938	Was-A	9	10	.474	32	21	7	0	1	150	151	4	113	64	16.1	5.58	81	.268	.394	10	.208	1	-13	-18	1	-1.7
1939	Was-A	10	19	.345	32	31	15	1	0	232	215	10	114	118	12.8	3.80	114	.243	.330	15	.169	-3	21	14	0	1.3
1940	Was-A	15	17	.469	35	34	20	1	0	261²	260	14	143	129	14.0	3.23	129	.261	.357	15	.163	-1	33	27	-1	2.8
1941	Was-A	6	18	.250	33	30	8	1	0	205²	228	11	115	98	15.1	5.08	80	.280	.371	11	.149	-2	-21	-24	1	-2.4
1942	Bos-A	5	1	.833	13	10	4	0	0	80¹	82	5	41	34	13.8	3.81	98	.263	.348	6	.182	1	-1	-1	-1	-0.1
1943	Bos-A	4	4	.000	7	5	0	0	0	27¹	36	0	30	9	21.7	6.91	48	.316	.458	1	.091	-4	-11	-11	0	-1.4
	NY-N	4	12	.250	21	20	4	1	0	129¹	140	7	74	86	15.0	4.11	84	.275	.369	9	.214	0	-10	-9	-1	-1.2
Total 8		53	84	.387	188	160	62	4	1	1165	1188	55	694	582	14.7	4.27	97	.265	.365	69	.165	-8	-0	-19	-0	-2.9

● JIM CHATTERTON
Chatterton, James M. b: 10/14/1864, Brooklyn, N.Y.   d: 12/15/44, Tewksbury, Mass.   Deb: 6/7/1884 ♦

YEAR	TM/L	W	L	PCT	G	GS	CG	SH	SV	IP	H	HR	BB	SO	RAT	ERA	ERA+	OAV	OOB	BH	AVG	PB	PR	/A	PD	TPI
1884	KC-U	0	1	.000	1	1	0	0	0	5	11	0	2	1	23.4	3.60	62	.414	.455	2	.133	-0	-1	-1	0	-0.1

● NESTOR CHAVEZ
Chavez, Nestor Isais (Silva) b: 7/6/47, Chacao, Venez.   d: 3/16/69, Maracaibo, Venez.   BR/TR, 6', 170 lbs.   Deb: 9/9/67

YEAR	TM/L	W	L	PCT	G	GS	CG	SH	SV	IP	H	HR	BB	SO	RAT	ERA	ERA+	OAV	OOB	BH	AVG	PB	PR	/A	PD	TPI
1967	SF-N	1	0	1.000	2	0	0	0	0	5	4	0	3	4	12.6	0.00	—	.211	.318	0	.000	-0	2	2	0	0.4

● DAVE CHEADLE
Cheadle, David Baird b: 2/19/52, Greensboro, N.C.   BL/TL, 6'2", 203 lbs.   Deb: 9/16/73

YEAR	TM/L	W	L	PCT	G	GS	CG	SH	SV	IP	H	HR	BB	SO	RAT	ERA	ERA+	OAV	OOB	BH	AVG	PB	PR	/A	PD	TPI
1973	Atl-N	0	1	.000	2	0	0	0	0	2	2	1	3	2	22.5	18.00	22	.250	.455	0	—	0	-3	-3	-0	-1.1

● CHARLIE CHECH
Chech, Charles William b: 4/27/1878, Madison, Wis.   d: 1/31/38, Los Angeles, Cal.   BR/TR, 5'11.5", 190 lbs.   Deb: 4/14/05

YEAR	TM/L	W	L	PCT	G	GS	CG	SH	SV	IP	H	HR	BB	SO	RAT	ERA	ERA+	OAV	OOB	BH	AVG	PB	PR	/A	PD	TPI
1905	Cin-N	14	14	.500	39	25	20	1	0	267²	300	4	77	79	13.0	2.89	114	.288	.344	17	.191	1	3	12	-0	1.2
1906	Cin-N	1	4	.200	11	5	5	0	3	66	59	1	24	17	12.1	2.32	119	.243	.326	5	.200	1	2	3	0	0.4
1908	Cle-A	11	7	.611	27	20	14	4	0	165²	136	3	34	51	9.6	1.74	138	.229	.279	5	.104	-1	12	12	1	1.4
1909	Bos-A	7	5	.583	17	13	6	1	0	106²	107	2	27	40	11.7	2.95	85	.260	.314	3	.083	-2	-6	-5	-0	-0.9
Total 4		33	30	.524	94	63	45	6	3	606	602	10	162	187	11.8	2.52	113	.263	.320	30	.152	-1	12	21	1	2.1

● VIRGIL CHEEVES
Cheeves, Virgil Earl "Chief" b: 2/12/01, Oklahoma City, Okla.   d: 5/5/79, Dallas, Tex.   BR/TR, 6', 195 lbs.   Deb: 9/7/20

YEAR	TM/L	W	L	PCT	G	GS	CG	SH	SV	IP	H	HR	BB	SO	RAT	ERA	ERA+	OAV	OOB	BH	AVG	PB	PR	/A	PD	TPI
1920	Chi-N	0	0	—	5	2	0	0	0	18	16	0	7	3	11.5	3.50	92	.250	.324	0	.000	-0	-1	-1	-1	-0.1
1921	Chi-N	11	12	.478	37	22	9	1	0	163	192	8	47	39	13.7	4.64	82	.309	.366	8	.167	-2	-15	-15	-3	-2.2
1922	Chi-N	12	11	.522	39	23	9	1	2	182²	195	9	76	40	13.8	4.09	103	.281	.360	13	.210	1	0	2	-1	0.2
1923	Chi-N	3	4	.429	19	8	0	0	0	71¹	89	8	37	13	16.3	6.18	65	.314	.399	4	.174	-1	-17	-17	-1	-1.6
1924	Cle-A	0	0	—	8	1	0	0	0	17¹	26	2	17	2	22.8	7.79	55	.388	.518	1	.250	-1	-7	-7	0	0.0
1927	NY-N	0	0	—	3	0	0	0	0	6¹	8	1	4	1	17.1	4.26	90	.333	.429	0	—	0	-0	-0	0	0.0
Total 6		26	27	.491	111	56	18	2	2	458²	526	28	188	98	14.5	4.73	84	.300	.375	26	.184	-1	-40	-38	-5	-3.7

● ITALO CHELINI
Chelini, Italo Vincent "Chilly" or "Lefty"
b: 10/10/14, San Francisco, Cal   d: 8/25/72, San Francisco, Cal   BL/TL, 5'10.5", 175 lbs.   Deb: 9/12/35

YEAR	TM/L	W	L	PCT	G	GS	CG	SH	SV	IP	H	HR	BB	SO	RAT	ERA	ERA+	OAV	OOB	BH	AVG	PB	PR	/A	PD	TPI
1935	Chi-A	0	0	—	2	0	0	0	0	5	7	1	4	1	21.6	12.60	37	.350	.480	1	.500	0	-5	-4	0	0.0
1936	Chi-A	4	3	.571	18	6	5	0	0	83²	100	8	30	16	14.0	4.95	105	.291	.348	5	.156	-1	1	2	-1	-0.1
1937	Chi-A	0	1	.000	4	0	0	0	0	8²	15	2	0	3	16.6	10.38	44	.405	.421	0	.000	0	-6	-6	-0	-0.5
Total 3		4	4	.500	24	6	5	0	0	97¹	122	11	34	20	14.6	5.83	88	.304	.362	6	.171	-1	-9	-8	-1	-0.6

● LARRY CHENEY
Cheney, Laurance Russell b: 5/2/1886, Belleville, Kan.   d: 1/6/69, Daytona Beach, Fla.   BR/TR, 6'1.5", 185 lbs.   Deb: 9/9/11

YEAR	TM/L	W	L	PCT	G	GS	CG	SH	SV	IP	H	HR	BB	SO	RAT	ERA	ERA+	OAV	OOB	BH	AVG	PB	PR	/A	PD	TPI
1911	Chi-N	1	0	1.000	3	1	0	0	0	10	8	0	3	11	9.9	0.00	—	.229	.289	1	.250	0	4	4	1	0.5
1912	Chi-N	26	10	.722	42	37	28	4	0	303¹	262	5	111	140	11.3	2.85	117	.234	.307	24	.226	5	19	16	-2	2.0
1913	Chi-N	21	14	.600	54	36	25	2	11	305	271	7	98	136	11.1	2.57	124	.241	.306	20	.192	2	22	21	-0	2.6
1914	Chi-N	20	18	.526	50	40	21	6	5	311¹	239	9	140	157	11.2	2.54	109	.215	.308	18	.180	3	9	8	1	1.4
1915	Chi-N	8	9	.471	25	18	6	1	0	131¹	120	1	55	68	12.3	3.56	78	.246	.327	6	.150	-1	-12	-11	2	-1.4
	Bro-N	0	2	.000	5	4	1	0	0	27	16	0	17	11	11.7	1.67	167	.174	.315	1	.143	0	3	3	0	0.3
	Yr	8	11	.421	30	22	7	1	0	158¹	136	1	72	79	11.9	3.24	86	.233	.319	7	.149	-1	-9	-8	2	-1.1
1916	*Bro-N	18	12	.600	41	32	15	5	0	253	178	5	105	166	10.4	1.92	140	.198	.289	9	.114	-3	20	21	-1	2.3
1917	Bro-N	8	12	.400	35	24	14	1	2	210¹	185	4	73	102	11.3	2.35	119	.239	.309	14	.206	2	8	10	-1	1.2
1918	Bro-N	11	13	.458	32	21	15	0	1	200²	177	2	74	83	11.7	3.00	93	.241	.319	16	.242	2	-5	-5	1	-0.2
1919	Bro-N	1	3	.250	9	4	2	0	0	39	45	1	14	14	14.1	4.15	72	.300	.367	2	.182	0	-5	-5	-0	-0.6
	Bos-N	2	2	.000	8	2	0	0	0	33	35	0	15	13	13.6	3.55	81	.294	.373	2	.182	0	-2	-3	0	-0.1
	Phi-N	2	5	.286	9	6	1	0	0	57¹	69	2	28	25	15.4	4.55	71	.315	.395	2	.095	-2	-10	-8	-1	-1.2
	Yr	3	10	.231	26	12	7	0	0	129¹	149	3	57	52	14.4	4.18	73	.304	.378	6	.140	-2	-18	-16	-1	-1.9
Total 9		116	100	.537	313	225	132	20	19	1881¹	1605	36	733	926	11.5	2.70	109	.234	.313	115	.186	4	49	52	0	6.8

● TOM CHENEY
Cheney, Thomas Edgar b: 10/14/34, Morgan, Ga.   BR/TR, 6', 180 lbs.   Deb: 4/21/57

YEAR	TM/L	W	L	PCT	G	GS	CG	SH	SV	IP	H	HR	BB	SO	RAT	ERA	ERA+	OAV	OOB	BH	AVG	PB	PR	/A	PD	TPI
1957	StL-N	0	1	.000	4	3	0	0	0	9	6	0	15	10	21.0	5.00	79	.207	.477	0	.000	-1	-1	-1	0	-0.1
1959	StL-N	0	1	.000	11	2	0	0	0	11²	17	2	11	8	23.1	6.94	61	.354	.492	0	—	0	-4	-4	0	-0.3
1960	*Pit-N	2	2	.500	11	8	1	0	0	52	44	5	33	35	13.3	3.98	94	.238	.353	3	.176	0	-1	-1	-2	-0.2
1961	Pit-N	0	0	—	1	0	0	0	0	1	4	0	1	0	—	∞	—	.500	.833	0	—	0	-4	-4	-0	-0.3
	Was-A	1	3	.250	10	7	0	0	0	29²	32	8	26	20	17.6	8.80	46	.283	.417	4	.500	-1	-16	-16	-1	-1.6
1962	Was-A	7	9	.438	37	23	8	3	1	173¹	134	12	97	147	12.1	3.17	127	.213	.320	3	.063	-3	15	17	0	1.1
1963	Was-A	8	9	.471	23	21	7	4	0	136¹	99	14	40	97	9.2	2.71	127	.202	.264	5	.109	-3	14	15	-2	1.3
1964	Was-A	1	3	.250	8	7	0	0	0	48²	45	10	13	25	10.7	3.70	100	.245	.294	3	.250	-2	-1	-1	0	-0.1
1966	Was-A	0	1	.000	3	1	0	0	0	5¹	1	0	9	3	18.6	5.06	68	.222	.440	0	—	0	-1	-1	0	-0.1
Total 8		19	29	.396	115	71	13	8	2	466	382	53	245	345	12.2	3.77	103	.225	.325	18	.135	-3	2	5	-4	-0.2

● JACK CHESBRO
Chesbro, John Dwight "Happy Jack" b: 6/5/1874, N.Adams, Mass.   d: 11/6/31, Conway, Mass.   BR/TR, 5'9", 180 lbs.   Deb: 7/12/1899 CH

YEAR	TM/L	W	L	PCT	G	GS	CG	SH	SV	IP	H	HR	BB	SO	RAT	ERA	ERA+	OAV	OOB	BH	AVG	PB	PR	/A	PD	TPI
1899	Pit-N	6	9	.400	19	17	15	0	0	149	165	3	59	28	14.2	4.11	93	.280	.357	9	.155	-3	-4	-5	-3	-0.9
1900	Pit-N	15	13	.536	32	26	20	0	1	215²	220	4	79	56	13.0	3.67	99	.264	.336	15	.216	-1	-1	-1	-2	-0.4
1901	Pit-N	21	10	.677	36	28	26	6	1	287²	261	4	52	129	10.2	2.38	137	.240	.284	25	.216	3	30	28	-3	2.7
1902	Pit-N	28	6	.824	35	33	31	8	1	286¹	242	1	62	136	10.2	2.17	126	.229	.285	20	.179	-2	19	18	-2	1.6

YEAR	TM/L	W	L	PCT	G	GS	CG	SH	SV	IP	H	HR	BB	SO	RAT	ERA	ERA+	OAV	OOB	BH	AVG	PB	PR	/A	PD	TPI
1903	NY-A	21	15	.583	40	36	33	1	0	324²	300	7	74	147	10.6	2.77	113	.245	.293	23	.185	-1	7	13	2	1.4
1904	NY-A	**41**	12	**.774**	55	51	**48**	6	0	**454²**	338	4	88	239	8.6	1.82	149	**.208**	.252	41	.236	6	39	**45**	5	**6.9**
1905	NY-A	19	15	.559	41	38	24	3	0	303¹	262	5	71	156	10.1	2.20	134	.234	.284	21	.188	0	16	25	1	3.0
1906	NY-A	23	17	.575	49	42	24	4	1	325	314	2	75	152	11.0	2.96	100	.257	.305	26	.208	-1	-10	0	-0	-0.1
1907	NY-A	10	10	.500	30	25	17	1	0	206	192	0	46	78	10.7	2.53	110	.249	.296	15	.197	-1	0	6	-0	0.3
1908	NY-A	14	20	.412	45	31	20	3	1	288²	271	6	67	124	11.0	2.93	85	.251	.303	18	.176	-2	-17	-14	1	-1.9
1909	NY-A	0	4	.000	9	4	2	0	0	49²	70	2	13	17	15.6	6.34	40	.347	.394	3	.176	-0	-21	-21	1	-1.5
	Bos-A	0	1	.000	1	1	0	0	0	6	7	1	4	3	16.5	4.50	56	.318	.423	1	.500	0	-1	-1	-0	-0.2
	Yr	0	5	.000	10	5	2	0	0	55²	77	3	17	20	15.2	6.14	41	.339	.385	4	.211	-0	-23	-22	1	-1.7
Total	11	198	132	.600	392	332	260	35	5	2896²	2642	39	690	1265	10.7	2.68	111	.244	.296	217	.197	-2	59	97	-2	11.1

● **BOB CHESNES**   Chesnes, Robert Vincent b: 5/6/21, Oakland, Cal. d: 5/23/79, Everett, Wash. BB/TR, 6', 180 lbs. Deb: 5/6/48

YEAR	TM/L	W	L	PCT	G	GS	CG	SH	SV	IP	H	HR	BB	SO	RAT	ERA	ERA+	OAV	OOB	BH	AVG	PB	PR	/A	PD	TPI
1948	Pit-N	14	6	.700	25	23	15	0	0	194¹	180	13	90	69	12.7	3.57	114	.247	.333	25	.275	7	8	11	3	2.1
1949	Pit-N	7	13	.350	27	25	8	1	1	145¹	153	15	82	49	14.9	5.88	71	.276	.374	17	.250	6	-30	-27	3	-2.4
1950	Pit-N	3	3	.500	9	7	2	0	0	39	44	7	17	12	14.8	5.54	79	.293	.376	2	.154	-0	-6	-5	2	-0.5
Total	3	24	22	.522	61	55	25	1	1	378²	377	35	189	130	13.7	4.66	89	.263	.354	44	.256	12	-27	-21	8	-0.8

● **MITCH CHETKOVICH**   Chetkovich, Mitchell b: 7/21/17, Fairpoint, Ohio d: 8/24/71, Grass Valley, Cal. BR/TR, 6'3.5", 208 lbs. Deb: 4/19/45

YEAR	TM/L	W	L	PCT	G	GS	CG	SH	SV	IP	H	HR	BB	SO	RAT	ERA	ERA+	OAV	OOB	BH	AVG	PB	PR	/A	PD	TPI
1945	Phi-N	0	0	—	4	0	0	0	0	3	2	0	3	0	15.0	0.00	—	.182	.357	0	—	0	1	1	-0	0.0

● **TONY CHEVEZ**   Chevez, Silvio Antonio (b: Silvio Antonio Aguilera (Chevez)) b: 6/20/54, Telica, Nicaragua BR/TR, 5'11", 177 lbs. Deb: 5/31/77

YEAR	TM/L	W	L	PCT	G	GS	CG	SH	SV	IP	H	HR	BB	SO	RAT	ERA	ERA+	OAV	OOB	BH	AVG	PB	PR	/A	PD	TPI
1977	Bal-A	0	0	—	4	0	0	0	0	8	10	3	8	7	22.5	12.38	31	.294	.455	0	—	0	-7	-8	-0	0.5

● **SCOTT CHIAMPARINO**   Chiamparino, Scott Michael b: 8/22/66, San Mateo, Cal. BR/TR, 6'2", 190 lbs. Deb: 9/5/90

YEAR	TM/L	W	L	PCT	G	GS	CG	SH	SV	IP	H	HR	BB	SO	RAT	ERA	ERA+	OAV	OOB	BH	AVG	PB	PR	/A	PD	TPI
1990	Tex-A	1	2	.333	6	6	0	0	0	37²	36	1	12	19	11.9	2.63	149	.250	.316	0	—	0	5	5	-1	0.3
1991	Tex-A	1	0	1.000	5	5	0	0	0	22¹	26	1	12	8	15.3	4.03	100	.295	.380	0	—	0	-0	-1	-1	-0.1
1992	Tex-A	0	4	.000	4	4	0	0	0	25¹	25	2	5	13	10.7	3.55	107	.260	.297	0	—	0	1	1	-1	0.3
Total	3	2	6	.250	15	15	0	0	0	85¹	87	4	29	40	12.4	3.27	120	.265	.329	0	—	0	7	6	-2	0.5

● **FLOYD CHIFFER**   Chiffer, Floyd John b: 4/20/56, Glen Cove, N.Y. BR/TR, 6'2", 185 lbs. Deb: 4/7/82

YEAR	TM/L	W	L	PCT	G	GS	CG	SH	SV	IP	H	HR	BB	SO	RAT	ERA	ERA+	OAV	OOB	BH	AVG	PB	PR	/A	PD	TPI
1982	SD-N	4	3	.571	51	0	0	0	4	79¹	73	9	34	48	12.6	2.95	116	.247	.333	0	.000	-1	6	4	-0	0.3
1983	SD-N	0	2	.000	15	0	0	0	1	22²	17	0	10	15	10.7	3.18	110	.210	.297	0	.000	-0	1	1	-0	0.1
1984	SD-N	1	0	1.000	15	1	0	0	0	28	42	1	16	20	18.6	7.71	46	.347	.423	0	.000	-0	-13	-13	-1	-0.5
Total	3	5	5	.500	81	1	0	0	5	130	132	10	60	83	13.6	4.02	86	.266	.349	0	.000	-1	-6	-8	-1	-0.1

● **HARRY CHILD**   Child, Harry Stephen Patrick (b: Harry Stephen Patrick Chesley)
b: 5/23/05, Baltimore, Md. d: 11/8/72, Alexandria, Va. BB/TR, 5'11", 187 lbs. Deb: 7/16/30

YEAR	TM/L	W	L	PCT	G	GS	CG	SH	SV	IP	H	HR	BB	SO	RAT	ERA	ERA+	OAV	OOB	BH	AVG	PB	PR	/A	PD	TPI
1930	Was-A	0	0	—	5	0	0	0	0	10	10	1	5	5	13.5	6.30	73	.263	.349	1	.250	-0	-2	-2	0	0.0

● **BILL CHILDERS**   Childers, William b: St.Louis, Mo. Deb: 7/27/1895

YEAR	TM/L	W	L	PCT	G	GS	CG	SH	SV	IP	H	HR	BB	SO	RAT	ERA	ERA+	OAV	OOB	BH	AVG	PB	PR	/A	PD	TPI
1895	Lou-N	0	0	—	1	0	0	0	0	0	2	0	6	0	—	∞	—	1.000	1.000	0	—	0	-6	-6	0	-0.4

● **ROCKY CHILDRESS**   Childress, Rodney Osborne b: 2/18/62, Santa Rosa, Cal. BR/TR, 6'2", 195 lbs. Deb: 5/17/85

YEAR	TM/L	W	L	PCT	G	GS	CG	SH	SV	IP	H	HR	BB	SO	RAT	ERA	ERA+	OAV	OOB	BH	AVG	PB	PR	/A	PD	TPI
1985	Phi-N	0	1	.000	16	1	0	0	0	33¹	45	3	9	14	14.6	6.21	59	.326	.367	1	.167	-0	-10	-9	-0	-0.3
1986	Phi-N	0	0	—	2	0	0	0	0	2²	4	0	1	1	16.9	6.75	57	.364	.417	0	—	0	-1	-1	-0	0.0
1987	Hou-N	1	2	.333	32	0	0	0	0	48¹	46	4	18	26	11.9	2.98	131	.260	.328	0	.000	-0	6	5	-0	0.2
1988	Hou-N	1	0	1.000	11	0	0	0	0	23¹	26	3	9	24	13.9	6.17	54	.280	.350	1	.250	-0	-7	-7	-1	-0.3
Total	4	2	3	.400	61	1	0	0	0	107²	121	10	37	65	13.3	4.76	78	.289	.348	2	.167	-0	-12	-13	-1	-0.4

● **BOB CHIPMAN**   Chipman, Robert Howard "Mr. Chips" b: 10/11/18, Brooklyn, N.Y. d: 11/8/73, Huntington, N.Y. BL/TL, 6'2", 190 lbs. Deb: 9/28/41

YEAR	TM/L	W	L	PCT	G	GS	CG	SH	SV	IP	H	HR	BB	SO	RAT	ERA	ERA+	OAV	OOB	BH	AVG	PB	PR	/A	PD	TPI
1941	Bro-N	1	0	1.000	1	0	0	0	0	5	3	0	1	3	7.2	0.00	—	.150	.190	0	.000	-0	2	2	-0	0.4
1942	Bro-N	0	0	—	2	0	0	0	0	1¹	1	0	2	1	20.3	0.00	—	.250	.500	0	—	0	0	0	-0	0.0
1943	Bro-N	0	0	—	1	0	0	0	0	1²	2	0	2	0	21.6	0.00	—	.400	.571	0	—	0	1	1	-0	0.0
1944	Bro-N	3	1	.750	11	3	1	0	0	36¹	38	1	24	20	15.4	4.21	84	.270	.376	2	.182	-0	-2	-3	-0	-0.3
	Chi-N	9	9	.500	26	21	8	1	2	129	147	9	40	41	13.0	3.49	101	.288	.340	5	.104	-3	2	1	-0	-0.2
	Yr	12	10	.545	37	24	9	1	2	165¹	185	10	64	61	13.6	3.65	97	.284	.348	7	.119	-3	-1	-2	-0	-0.5
1945	*Chi-N	4	5	.444	25	10	3	1	0	72	63	4	34	29	12.3	3.50	104	.230	.317	3	.176	1	2	1	1	0.2
1946	Chi-N	6	5	.545	34	10	5	3	2	109¹	103	8	54	40	13.0	3.13	106	.251	.344	2	.061	-3	3	2	-2	-0.2
1947	Chi-N	7	6	.538	32	17	5	1	0	134²	135	6	66	51	13.4	3.68	107	.264	.348	4	.091	-3	6	4	1	0.2
1948	Chi-N	2	1	.667	34	3	0	0	4	60¹	73	5	24	16	14.5	3.58	109	.293	.355	4	.250	1	3	2	1	0.4
1949	Chi-N	7	8	.467	38	11	3	1	1	113¹	110	7	63	46	13.9	3.97	102	.248	.343	3	.125	-1	1	1	-1	-0.1
1950	Bos-N	7	7	.500	27	12	4	0	1	124	127	10	37	40	12.2	4.43	87	.262	.319	6	.154	-1	-4	-8	-3	-1.1
1951	Bos-N	4	3	.571	33	0	0	0	0	52	59	5	19	17	13.8	4.85	76	.284	.349	1	.100	-1	-5	-7	-0	-1.0
1952	Bos-N	1	1	.500	29	0	0	0	0	41²	28	6	20	16	10.4	2.81	129	.188	.284	2	.400	0	4	4	0	0.3
Total	12	51	46	.526	293	87	29	7	14	880²	889	60	386	322	13.1	3.72	100	.261	.338	32	.128	-8	13	1	-2	-1.4

● **STEVE CHITREN**   Chitren, Stephen Vincent b: 6/8/67, Tokyo, Japan BR/TR, 6', 180 lbs. Deb: 9/15/90

YEAR	TM/L	W	L	PCT	G	GS	CG	SH	SV	IP	H	HR	BB	SO	RAT	ERA	ERA+	OAV	OOB	BH	AVG	PB	PR	/A	PD	TPI
1990	Oak-A	1	0	1.000	8	0	0	0	0	17²	7	0	4	19	5.6	1.02	365	.117	.172	0	—	0	6	5	-0	0.4
1991	Oak-A	1	4	.200	56	0	0	0	4	60¹	59	8	32	47	14.2	4.33	89	.258	.358	0	—	0	-2	-3	-0	-0.3
Total	2	2	4	.333	64	0	0	0	4	78	66	8	36	66	12.2	3.58	106	.228	.322	0	—	0	4	2	-0	0.1

● **NELSON CHITTUM**   Chittum, Nelson Boyd b: 3/25/33, Harrisonburg, Va. BR/TR, 6'1", 180 lbs. Deb: 8/17/58

YEAR	TM/L	W	L	PCT	G	GS	CG	SH	SV	IP	H	HR	BB	SO	RAT	ERA	ERA+	OAV	OOB	BH	AVG	PB	PR	/A	PD	TPI
1958	StL-N	0	1	.000	13	2	0	0	0	29¹	31	5	7	13	12.0	6.44	64	.265	.312	1	.250	0	-8	-8	0	-0.2
1959	Bos-A	3	0	1.000	21	0	0	0	0	30¹	29	0	11	12	11.9	1.19	342	.266	.333	1	.200	0	9	10	1	1.0
1960	Bos-A	0	0	—	6	0	0	0	0	8¹	8	0	6	5	15.1	4.32	94	.242	.359	0	.000	-0	-0	-0	0	-0.0
Total	3	3	1	.750	40	2	0	0	0	68	68	5	24	30	12.3	3.84	106	.263	.327	2	.200	0	0	2	1	0.8

● **BOB CHLUPSA**   Chlupsa, Robert Joseph b: 9/16/45, New York, N.Y. BR/TR, 6'7", 215 lbs. Deb: 7/16/70

YEAR	TM/L	W	L	PCT	G	GS	CG	SH	SV	IP	H	HR	BB	SO	RAT	ERA	ERA+	OAV	OOB	BH	AVG	PB	PR	/A	PD	TPI
1970	StL-N	0	2	.000	14	0	0	0	0	16¹	26	2	9	10	19.3	8.82	47	.366	.438	0	—	0	-9	-9	1	-0.8
1971	StL-N	0	0	—	4	0	0	0	0	2	3	0	1	1	13.5	9.00	40	.333	.333	0	—	0	-1	-1	0	-0.0
Total	2	0	2	.000	18	0	0	0	0	18¹	29	2	9	11	18.7	8.84	46	.363	.427	0	—	0	-10	-10	1	-0.8

● **DON CHOATE**   Choate, Donald Leon b: 7/2/38, Potosi, Mo. BR/TR, 6', 185 lbs. Deb: 9/12/60

YEAR	TM/L	W	L	PCT	G	GS	CG	SH	SV	IP	H	HR	BB	SO	RAT	ERA	ERA+	OAV	OOB	BH	AVG	PB	PR	/A	PD	TPI
1960	SF-N	0	0	—	4	0	0	0	0	8	7	0	4	7	12.4	2.25	155	.233	.324	0	—	0	1	1	0	0.0

● **CHIEF CHOUNEAU**   Chouneau, William (b: William Cadreau) b: 9/2/1889, Cloquet, Minn. d: 9/17/48, Cloquet, Minn. BR/TR, 5'9", 150 lbs. Deb: 10/9/10

YEAR	TM/L	W	L	PCT	G	GS	CG	SH	SV	IP	H	HR	BB	SO	RAT	ERA	ERA+	OAV	OOB	BH	AVG	PB	PR	/A	PD	TPI
1910	Chi-A	0	1	.000	1	1	0	0	0	5¹	7	0	1	1	11.8	3.38	71	.292	.292	0	.000	1	-1	-1	-0	-0.1

● **MIKE CHRIS**   Chris, Michael b: 10/8/57, Santa Monica, Cal. BL/TL, 6'3", 180 lbs. Deb: 7/31/79

YEAR	TM/L	W	L	PCT	G	GS	CG	SH	SV	IP	H	HR	BB	SO	RAT	ERA	ERA+	OAV	OOB	BH	AVG	PB	PR	/A	PD	TPI
1979	Det-A	3	3	.500	13	8	0	0	0	39	46	3	21	31	15.5	6.92	62	.297	.381	0	—	0	-12	-11	1	-1.4
1982	SF-N	0	2	.000	9	6	0	0	0	26	23	2	26	10	17.3	4.85	74	.245	.413	1	.143	-0	-4	-4	1	-0.2
1983	SF-N	0	0	—	7	0	0	0	0	13¹	16	1	16	15	23.0	8.10	44	.308	.486	0	.000	-0	-7	-7	-0	-0.1
Total	3	3	5	.375	29	14	0	0	0	78¹	85	6	63	56	17.2	6.43	61	.282	.411	1	.111	-0	-22	-22	1	-1.7

● **GARY CHRISTENSON**   Christenson, Gary Richard b: 5/5/53, Mineola, N.Y. BL/TL, 6'5", 200 lbs. Deb: 9/1/79

YEAR	TM/L	W	L	PCT	G	GS	CG	SH	SV	IP	H	HR	BB	SO	RAT	ERA	ERA+	OAV	OOB	BH	AVG	PB	PR	/A	PD	TPI
1979	KC-A	0	0	—	6	0	0	0	0	10²	10	1	2	4	10.1	3.38	126	.250	.286	0	—	0	1	1	0	0.0

YEAR TM/L	W	L	PCT	G	GS	CG	SH	SV	IP	H	HR	BB	SO	RAT	ERA	ERA+	OAV	OOB	BH	AVG	PB	PR	/A	PD	TPI
1980 KC-A	3	0	1.000	24	0	0	0	1	31¹	35	4	18	16	15.8	5.17	78	.278	.377	0	—	0	-4	-4	1	-0.4
Total 2	3	0	1.000	30	0	0	0	1	42	45	5	20	20	14.4	4.71	87	.271	.356	0	—	0	-3	-3	1	-0.4

● LARRY CHRISTENSON
Christenson, Larry Richard b: 11/10/53, Everett, Wash. BR/TR, 6'4", 215 lbs. Deb: 4/13/73

YEAR TM/L	W	L	PCT	G	GS	CG	SH	SV	IP	H	HR	BB	SO	RAT	ERA	ERA+	OAV	OOB	BH	AVG	PB	PR	/A	PD	TPI
1973 Phi-N	1	4	.200	10	9	1	0	0	34¹	53	3	20	11	19.4	6.55	58	.366	.446	0	.000	-1	-11	-11	-0	-1.4
1974 Phi-N	1	1	.500	10	1	0	0	2	23	20	2	15	18	13.7	4.30	88	.241	.357	0	.000	-1	-2	-1	-0	-0.2
1975 Phi-N	11	6	.647	29	26	5	2	1	171²	149	12	45	88	10.2	3.67	102	.236	.288	14	.246	5	-1	1	-3	0.4
1976 Phi-N	13	8	.619	32	29	2	0	0	168²	199	8	42	54	12.9	3.68	96	.297	.339	10	.196	4	-3	-3	-3	-0.2
1977 *Phi-N	19	6	.760	34	34	5	1	0	219¹	229	21	69	118	12.5	4.06	98	.268	.327	10	.135	1	-4	-2	-2	-0.3
1978 *Phi-N	13	14	.481	33	33	9	3	0	228	209	16	47	131	10.1	3.24	110	.244	.284	5	.075	-2	9	8	-0	0.7
1979 Phi-N	5	10	.333	19	17	2	0	0	106	118	9	30	53	12.7	4.50	85	.291	.342	5	.290	5	-9	-8	-0	-0.6
1980 *Phi-N	5	1	.833	14	14	0	0	0	73²	62	4	27	49	11.2	4.03	94	.227	.304	7	.368	3	-4	-2	1	0.3
1981 *Phi-N	4	7	.364	20	15	0	0	1	106²	108	8	30	70	11.7	3.54	102	.267	.319	3	.100	-1	-1	-1	-1	-0.1
1982 Phi-N	9	10	.474	33	33	3	0	0	223	212	15	53	145	10.8	3.47	106	.253	.300	5	.075	-3	3	5	-1	0.0
1983 Phi-N	2	4	.333	9	9	0	0	0	48¹	42	2	17	44	11.2	3.91	91	.233	.303	1	.059	-1	-2	-2	1	-0.2
Total 11	83	71	.539	243	220	27	6	4	1402²	1401	100	395	781	11.7	3.79	98	.262	.315	64	.150	10	-24	-12	-8	-1.6

● CLAY CHRISTIANSEN
Christiansen, Clay C. b: 6/28/58, Wichita, Kan. BR/TR, 6'5", 205 lbs. Deb: 5/10/84

YEAR TM/L	W	L	PCT	G	GS	CG	SH	SV	IP	H	HR	BB	SO	RAT	ERA	ERA+	OAV	OOB	BH	AVG	PB	PR	/A	PD	TPI
1984 NY-A	2	4	.333	24	1	0	0	2	38²	50	4	12	27	14.7	6.05	63	.309	.360	0	—	0	-9	-10	-0	-1.4

● MIKE CHRISTOPHER
Christopher, Michael Wayne b: 11/3/63, Petersburg, Va. BR/TR, 6'5", 205 lbs. Deb: 9/10/91

YEAR TM/L	W	L	PCT	G	GS	CG	SH	SV	IP	H	HR	BB	SO	RAT	ERA	ERA+	OAV	OOB	BH	AVG	PB	PR	/A	PD	TPI
1991 LA-N	0	0	—	3	0	0	0	0	4	2	0	3	2	11.3	0.00	—	.167	.333	0	—	0	2	2	0	0.0
1992 Cle-A	0	0	—	10	0	0	0	0	18	17	2	10	13	13.5	3.00	130	.254	.351	0	—	0	2	2	-0	0.1
1993 Cle-A	0	0	—	9	0	0	0	0	11²	14	3	2	8	12.3	3.86	112	.286	.314	0	—	0	1	1	-0	0.0
Total 3	0	0	—	22	0	0	0	0	33²	33	5	15	23	12.8	2.94	136	.258	.336	0	—	0	4	4	-0	0.1

● RUSS CHRISTOPHER
Christopher, Russell Ormand b: 9/12/17, Richmond, Cal. d: 12/5/54, Richmond, Cal. BR/TR, 6'3", 180 lbs. Deb: 4/14/42 F

YEAR TM/L	W	L	PCT	G	GS	CG	SH	SV	IP	H	HR	BB	SO	RAT	ERA	ERA+	OAV	OOB	BH	AVG	PB	PR	/A	PD	TPI
1942 Phi-A	4	13	.235	30	18	10	0	1	165	154	8	99	58	14.0	3.82	99	.254	.362	5	.089	-3	-3	-1	6	0.2
1943 Phi-A	5	8	.385	24	15	5	0	2	133	120	3	58	56	12.2	3.45	98	.242	.325	7	.156	-1	-2	-1	8	0.6
1944 Phi-A	14	14	.500	35	24	13	1	1	215¹	200	6	63	84	11.4	2.97	117	.245	.306	18	.222	3	11	12	5	2.6
1945 Phi-A†	13	13	.500	33	27	17	2	2	227¹	213	9	75	100	11.8	3.17	108	.251	.319	13	.171	-1	5	7	7	1.5
1946 Phi-A	5	7	.417	30	13	1	0	0	119¹	119	5	44	79	12.5	4.30	82	.254	.322	5	.139	-0	-11	-10	4	-0.5
1947 Phi-A	10	7	.588	44	0	0	0	12	80²	70	4	33	33	11.5	2.90	131	.236	.313	2	.125	-0	7	8	1	2.0
1948 *Cle-A	3	2	.600	45	0	0	0	**17**	59	55	3	27	14	12.5	2.90	140	.247	.328	0	.000	-0	9	8	0	1.0
Total 7	54	64	.458	241	97	46	3	35	999²	931	38	399	424	12.2	3.37	106	.248	.325	50	.158	-3	17	24	31	7.4

● BUBBA CHURCH
Church, Emory Nicholas b: 9/12/24, Birmingham, Ala. BR/TR, 6', 180 lbs. Deb: 4/30/50

YEAR TM/L	W	L	PCT	G	GS	CG	SH	SV	IP	H	HR	BB	SO	RAT	ERA	ERA+	OAV	OOB	BH	AVG	PB	PR	/A	PD	TPI
1950 Phi-N	8	6	.571	31	18	8	2	1	142	113	12	56	50	10.7	2.73	149	.225	.303	8	.182	0	22	21	-0	1.9
1951 Phi-N	15	11	.577	38	33	15	4	1	247	246	17	90	104	12.3	3.53	109	.261	.326	22	.256	5	12	9	-2	1.1
1952 Phi-N	0	0	—	2	1	0	0	0	5	11	0	1	3	23.4	10.80	34	.440	.481	0	.000	-0	-4	-4	0	0.0
Cin-N	5	9	.357	29	22	5	1	0	153¹	173	21	48	47	13.1	4.34	87	.301	.358	12	.240	3	-10	-10	-1	-0.6
Yr	5	9	.357	31	23	5	1	0	158¹	184	21	49	50	13.4	4.55	83	.306	.361	12	.235	3	-14	-14	-1	-0.6
1953 Cin-N	3	3	.500	11	7	2	0	0	43²	55	9	19	12	15.7	5.98	73	.318	.392	4	.267	1	-8	-8	-0	-0.8
Chi-N	4	5	.444	27	11	1	0	1	104¹	115	16	49	47	14.3	5.00	89	.276	.355	7	.212	1	-8	-6	-1	-0.5
Yr	7	8	.467	38	18	3	0	1	148	170	25	68	59	14.6	5.29	84	.288	.363	11	.229	2	-17	-14	-1	-1.3
1954 Chi-N	1	3	.250	7	3	1	0	0	14²	21	8	13	8	20.9	9.82	43	.350	.466	0	.000	-1	-9	-9	0	-2.0
1955 Chi-N	0	0	—	2	0	0	0	1	3¹	4	1	1	3	13.5	5.40	76	.286	.333	0	.000	-0	-1	-0	0	-0.1
Total 6	36	37	.493	147	95	32	7	4	713¹	738	84	277	274	12.9	4.10	97	.272	.342	53	.226	9	-7	-8	-4	-1.0

● LEN CHURCH
Church, Leonard b: 3/21/42, Chicago, Ill. d: 4/22/88, Richardson, Tex. BB/TR, 6', 190 lbs. Deb: 8/27/66

YEAR TM/L	W	L	PCT	G	GS	CG	SH	SV	IP	H	HR	BB	SO	RAT	ERA	ERA+	OAV	OOB	BH	AVG	PB	PR	/A	PD	TPI
1966 Chi-N	0	1	.000	4	0	0	0	0	6	10	1	7	3	25.5	7.50	49	.400	.531	0	.000	-0	-3	-3	0	-0.4

● CHUCK CHURN
Churn, Clarence Nottingham b: 2/1/30, Bridgetown, Va. BR/TR, 6'3", 205 lbs. Deb: 4/18/57

YEAR TM/L	W	L	PCT	G	GS	CG	SH	SV	IP	H	HR	BB	SO	RAT	ERA	ERA+	OAV	OOB	BH	AVG	PB	PR	/A	PD	TPI
1957 Pit-N	0	0	—	5	0	0	0	0	8¹	9	1	4	4	14.0	4.32	88	.333	.419	0	.000	-0	-0	-0	1	0.1
1958 Cle-A	0	0	—	6	0	0	0	0	8²	12	1	5	4	17.7	6.23	59	.343	.425	0	—	0	-2	-2	-0	0.0
1959 *LA-N	3	2	.600	14	0	0	0	1	30²	28	2	10	24	11.4	4.99	85	.255	.322	1	.167	-0	-4	-3	0	-0.3
Total 3	3	2	.600	25	0	0	0	1	47²	49	4	19	32	13.0	5.10	79	.285	.359	1	.143	-0	-6	-6	1	-0.2

● MARK CIARDI
Ciardi, Mark Thomas b: 8/19/61, New Brunswick, N.J. BR/TR, 6' ", 180 lbs. Deb: 4/9/87

YEAR TM/L	W	L	PCT	G	GS	CG	SH	SV	IP	H	HR	BB	SO	RAT	ERA	ERA+	OAV	OOB	BH	AVG	PB	PR	/A	PD	TPI
1987 Mil-A	1	1	.500	4	3	0	0	0	16¹	26	6	9	8	19.3	9.37	49	.361	.432	0	—	0	-9	-9	0	-0.9

● AL CICOTTE
Cicotte, Alva Warren "Bozo" b: 12/23/29, Melvindale, Mich. d: 11/29/82, Westland, Mich. BR/TR, 6'3", 185 lbs. Deb: 4/22/57

YEAR TM/L	W	L	PCT	G	GS	CG	SH	SV	IP	H	HR	BB	SO	RAT	ERA	ERA+	OAV	OOB	BH	AVG	PB	PR	/A	PD	TPI
1957 NY-A	2	2	.500	20	2	0	0	2	65¹	57	5	30	36	12.1	3.03	118	.237	.325	3	.150	-0	6	4	0	0.2
1958 Was-A	0	3	.000	8	4	0	0	0	28	36	3	14	14	16.1	4.82	79	.316	.391	2	.200	-0	-3	-3	-1	-0.4
Det-A	3	1	.750	14	2	0	0	0	43	50	1	15	21	13.6	3.56	113	.307	.365	3	.176	-1	1	2	1	0.3
Yr	3	4	.429	22	6	0	0	0	71	86	4	29	35	14.6	4.06	97	.309	.375	5	.185	-1	-2	-1	1	-0.1
1959 Cle-A	3	1	.750	26	1	0	0	1	44	46	4	25	23	14.9	5.32	69	.299	.403	1	.333	1	-7	-8	0	-0.6
1961 StL-N	2	6	.250	29	7	0	0	1	75	83	16	34	51	14.3	5.28	83	.283	.362	6	.286	1	-10	-7	0	-0.6
1962 Hou-N	0	0	—	5	0	0	0	0	4²	8	1	1	4	17.4	3.86	97	.381	.409	0	—	0	0	-0	-0	0.0
Total 5	10	13	.435	102	16	0	0	4	260	280	30	119	149	14.0	4.36	90	.284	.364	15	.211	0	-14	-12	1	-1.1

● EDDIE CICOTTE
Cicotte, Edward Victor "Knuckles" b: 6/19/1884, Springwells, Mich. d: 5/5/69, Detroit, Mich. BB/TR, 5'9", 175 lbs. Deb: 9/3/05

YEAR TM/L	W	L	PCT	G	GS	CG	SH	SV	IP	H	HR	BB	SO	RAT	ERA	ERA+	OAV	OOB	BH	AVG	PB	PR	/A	PD	TPI
1905 Det-A	1	1	.500	3	1	1	0	0	18	25	0	5	6	15.0	3.50	78	.330	.371	3	.429	-1	-2	-2	-1	-0.2
1908 Bos-A	11	12	.478	39	24	17	2	2	207¹	198	0	59	95	11.6	2.43	101	.261	.323	17	.236	-2	-1	1	0	0.4
1909 Bos-A	13	5	.722	27	17	10	1	2	159²	117	3	56	82	9.8	1.97	127	.210	.283	11	.224	3	9	9	-0	1.4
1910 Bos-A	15	11	.577	36	30	20	3	0	250	213	4	86	104	11.2	2.74	93	.233	.308	12	.141	-1	-6	-5	3	-0.4
1911 Bos-A	11	15	.423	35	25	16	1	0	220	236	6	73	106	12.8	2.82	116	.282	.342	10	.141	-2	13	11	1	1.0
1912 Bos-A	1	3	.250	9	6	2	0	0	46	58	0	15	20	14.5	5.67	60	.319	.374	2	.154	0	-12	-12	-1	-0.8
Chi-A	9	7	.563	20	18	13	1	0	152	159	3	37	70	11.6	2.84	113	.277	.320	13	.245	1	8	6	2	1.0
Yr	10	10	.500	29	24	15	1	0	198	217	3	52	90	12.2	3.50	93	.286	.332	15	.227	1	-4	-6	3	0.2
1913 Chi-A	18	12	.600	41	30	18	4	1	268	224	2	73	121	10.1	1.58	185	.226	.281	13	.143	-3	40	40	7	5.2
1914 Chi-A	11	16	.407	45	30	15	4	3	269¹	220	0	72	122	9.9	2.04	132	.232	.288	14	.163	-1	21	19	7	2.7
1915 Chi-A	13	12	.520	39	26	15	1	3	223¹	216	2	48	106	10.9	3.02	99	.261	.306	14	.209	1	-2	-1	0	0.0
1916 Chi-A	15	7	**.682**	44	19	11	2	5	187	138	1	70	91	10.1	1.78	155	.218	.296	12	.211	2	22	20	1	2.9
1917 *Chi-A	**28**	12	.700	49	35	29	7	4	346²	246	2	70	150	8.3	**1.53**	174	.203	**.248**	20	.179	1	**44**	**43**	-1	**5.4**
1918 Chi-A	12	19	.387	38	30	24	1	2	266	275	2	40	104	10.7	2.77	99	.271	.300	14	.163	2	0	-1	-0	0.0
1919 *Chi-A	**29**	7	**.806**	40	35	30	5	1	306²	256	5	49	110	9.0	1.82	175	.228	.261	20	.202	-1	48	46	-4	5.2
1920 Chi-A	21	10	.677	37	35	28	4	2	303¹	316	6	74	87	11.6	3.26	115	.275	.320	22	.196	-3	18	17	0	1.4
Total 14	208	149	.583	502	361	249	35	25	3223¹	2897	32	827	1374	10.5	2.38	123	.245	.298	197	.186	4	200	195	15	25.2

● PETE CIMINO
Cimino, Peter William b: 10/17/42, Philadelphia, Pa. BR/TR, 6'2", 195 lbs. Deb: 9/22/65

YEAR TM/L	W	L	PCT	G	GS	CG	SH	SV	IP	H	HR	BB	SO	RAT	ERA	ERA+	OAV	OOB	BH	AVG	PB	PR	/A	PD	TPI
1965 Min-A	0	0	—	1	0	0	0	0	1	0	0	0	0	0.0	0.00	—	.000	.000	—	—	0	0	0	-0	0.0
1966 Min-A	2	5	.286	35	0	0	0	4	64²	53	4	30	57	11.7	2.92	123	.222	.311	0	.000	-0	4	5	-1	0.5
1967 Cal-A	3	3	.500	46	1	0	0	1	88¹	73	12	31	80	10.8	3.26	96	.229	.301	5	.417	2	-0	-1	-1	-0.1

YEAR	TM/L	W	L	PCT	G	GS	CG	SH	SV	IP	H	HR	BB	SO	RAT	ERA	ERA+	OAV	OOB	BH	AVG	PB	PR	/A	PD	TPI
1968	Cal-A	0	0	—	4	0	0	0	0	7	7	0	4	2	14.1	2.57	113	.259	.355	0	—	0	0	-0	-0	0.0
Total	4	5	8	.385	86	1	0	0	5	161	133	16	65	139	11.2	3.07	108	.226	.306	5	.278	1	4	4	-2	0.4

● **FRANK CIMORELLI**   Cimorelli, Frank Thomas   b: 8/2/68, Poughkeepsie, N.Y.   BR/TR, 6′, 175 lbs.   Deb: 4/30/94

YEAR	TM/L	W	L	PCT	G	GS	CG	SH	SV	IP	H	HR	BB	SO	RAT	ERA	ERA+	OAV	OOB	BH	AVG	PB	PR	/A	PD	TPI
1994	StL-N	0	0	—	11	0	0	0	1	13¹	20	0	10	1	21.6	8.78	46	.345	.457	0	.000	-0	-7	-7	-1	-0.2

● **LOU CIOLA**   Ciola, Louis Alexander   b: 9/6/22, Norfolk, Va.   d: 10/18/81, Austin, Minn.   BR/TR, 5′9″, 165 lbs.   Deb: 7/25/43

YEAR	TM/L	W	L	PCT	G	GS	CG	SH	SV	IP	H	HR	BB	SO	RAT	ERA	ERA+	OAV	OOB	BH	AVG	PB	PR	/A	PD	TPI
1943	Phi-A	1	3	.250	12	3	2	0	0	43²	48	2	22	7	14.6	5.56	61	.273	.357	3	.167	-1	-11	-11	-0	-1.0

● **GALEN CISCO**   Cisco, Galen Bernard   b: 3/7/36, St.Marys, Ohio   BR/TR, 5′11″, 215 lbs.   Deb: 6/11/61   C

YEAR	TM/L	W	L	PCT	G	GS	CG	SH	SV	IP	H	HR	BB	SO	RAT	ERA	ERA+	OAV	OOB	BH	AVG	PB	PR	/A	PD	TPI
1961	Bos-A	2	4	.333	17	8	0	0	0	52¹	67	5	28	26	16.3	6.71	62	.325	.406	1	.100	-0	-16	-15	-0	-1.5
1962	Bos-A	4	7	.364	48	9	1	0	0	83	95	11	50	43	16.0	6.72	61	.292	.392	2	.080	-1	-25	-24	1	-2.6
	NY-N	1	1	.500	4	2	1	0	0	19¹	15	0	11	13	13.5	3.26	128	.208	.337	0	.000	-1	2	2	-0	0.1
1963	NY-N	7	15	.318	51	17	1	0	0	155²	165	15	64	81	13.6	4.34	80	.273	.349	5	.132	-0	-18	-15	-2	-2.0
1964	NY-N	6	19	.240	36	25	5	2	0	191²	182	17	54	78	11.4	3.62	99	.256	.313	6	.111	-0	-2	-1	2	0.1
1965	NY-N	4	8	.333	35	17	1	1	0	112¹	119	12	51	58	13.7	4.49	79	.272	.349	7	.259	2	-12	-12	-2	-1.1
1967	Bos-A	0	1	.000	11	0	0	0	1	22¹	21	4	8	8	11.7	3.63	96	.266	.333	0	.000	-0	-1	-0	0	-0.1
1969	KC-A	1	1	.500	15	0	0	0	1	22¹	17	4	15	18	12.9	3.63	102	.215	.340	0	—	-0	-0	0	0	0.1
Total	7	25	56	.309	192	78	9	3	2	659	681	68	281	325	13.4	4.56	81	.271	.349	21	.128	-0	-72	-64	1	-7.0

● **RALPH CITARELLA**   Citarella, Ralph Alexander   b: 2/7/58, East Orange, N.J.   BR/TR, 6′, 180 lbs.   Deb: 9/13/83

YEAR	TM/L	W	L	PCT	G	GS	CG	SH	SV	IP	H	HR	BB	SO	RAT	ERA	ERA+	OAV	OOB	BH	AVG	PB	PR	/A	PD	TPI
1983	StL-N	0	0	—	6	0	0	0	0	11	9	0	3	4	9.0	1.64	221	.205	.262	0	.000	-0	2	2	-0	0.0
1984	StL-N	0	1	.000	10	2	0	0	0	22¹	20	0	7	15	12.1	3.63	96	.238	.319	1	.250	-0	-0	-0	0	0.0
1987	Chi-A	0	0	—	5	0	0	0	0	11	13	4	4	9	15.5	7.36	62	.302	.388	0	—	0	-4	-3	-0	-0.1
Total	3	0	1	.000	21	2	0	0	0	44¹	41	4	14	28	12.2	4.06	93	.247	.324	1	.200	-0	-1	-1	0	-0.1

● **BOBBY CLACK**   Clack, Robert S. "Gentlemanly Bob" (b: Robert S. Clark)   b: 6/1850, England   d: 10/22/33, Danvers, Mass.   BR/TR, 5′9″, 153 lbs.   Deb: 5/13/1874 ◆

YEAR	TM/L	W	L	PCT	G	GS	CG	SH	SV	IP	H	HR	BB	SO	RAT	ERA	ERA+	OAV	OOB	BH	AVG	PB	PR	/A	PD	TPI
1876	Cin-N	0	0	—	1	0	0	0	0	2	2	0	0	0	9.0	4.50	49	.250	.250	19	.161	-0	-0	-1	0	0.0

● **JIM CLANCY**   Clancy, James   b: 12/18/55, Chicago, Ill.   BR/TR, 6′4″, 220 lbs.   Deb: 7/26/77

YEAR	TM/L	W	L	PCT	G	GS	CG	SH	SV	IP	H	HR	BB	SO	RAT	ERA	ERA+	OAV	OOB	BH	AVG	PB	PR	/A	PD	TPI
1977	Tor-A	4	9	.308	13	13	4	1	0	76²	80	7	47	44	14.9	5.05	83	.280	.381	0	—	0	-8	-7	1	-1.0
1978	Tor-A	10	12	.455	31	30	7	0	0	193²	199	10	91	106	13.5	4.09	96	.270	.351	0	—	0	-7	-4	1	-0.4
1979	Tor-A	2	7	.222	12	11	2	0	0	63²	65	8	31	33	13.6	5.51	79	.272	.356	0	—	0	-9	-8	0	-1.0
1980	Tor-A	13	16	.448	34	34	15	2	0	250²	217	19	128	152	12.5	3.30	130	.233	.327	0	—	0	20	28	-0	2.7
1981	Tor-A	6	12	.333	22	22	2	0	0	125	126	12	64	56	14.0	4.90	80	.262	.355	0	—	0	-17	-13	-3	-2.1
1982	Tor-A★	16	14	.533	40	40	11	3	0	266²	251	26	77	139	11.1	3.71	121	.248	.302	0	—	0	11	23	-2	0.8
1983	Tor-A	15	11	.577	34	34	11	1	0	223	238	23	61	99	12.1	3.91	110	.271	.319	0	—	0	4	10	-2	0.8
1984	Tor-A	13	15	.464	36	36	5	0	0	219²	249	25	88	118	13.9	5.12	80	.287	.355	0	—	0	-28	-25	0	-2.7
1985	*Tor-A	9	6	.600	23	23	1	0	0	128²	117	15	37	66	10.8	3.78	111	.241	.295	0	—	0	5	6	-1	0.6
1986	Tor-A	14	14	.500	34	34	6	3	0	219¹	202	24	63	126	11.0	3.94	107	.243	.299	0	—	0	6	7	1	0.8
1987	Tor-A	15	11	.577	37	37	5	1	0	241¹	234	24	80	180	11.7	3.54	127	.255	.315	0	—	0	24	25	2	2.6
1988	Tor-A	11	13	.458	36	31	4	0	1	196¹	207	26	47	118	12.1	4.49	87	.272	.322	0	—	0	-11	-12	-1	-1.4
1989	Hou-N	7	14	.333	33	26	1	0	0	147	155	13	66	91	13.5	5.08	67	.269	.344	6	.146	-0	-26	-28	-3	-3.8
1990	Hou-N	2	8	.200	33	10	0	0	1	76	100	4	33	44	16.1	6.51	57	.322	.392	3	.214	-0	-23	-24	1	-2.7
1991	Hou-N	0	3	.000	30	0	0	0	5	55	37	5	20	33	9.3	2.78	126	.193	.269	0	.000	-0	6	4	-1	0.2
	*Atl-N	3	2	.600	24	0	0	0	3	34²	36	3	14	17	13.2	5.71	68	.267	.340	0	.000	-0	-8	-7	0	-1.1
	Yr	3	5	.375	54	0	0	0	8	89²	73	8	34	50	10.8	3.91	93	.222	.297	0	.000	-1	-2	-3	-1	-0.9
Total	15	140	167	.456	472	381	74	11	10	2517¹	2513	244	947	1422	12.5	4.23	98	.261	.329	9	.148	-0	-62	-26	-8	-6.4

● **BRYAN CLARK**   Clark, Bryan Donald   b: 7/12/56, Madera, Cal.   BL/TL, 6′2″, 185 lbs.   Deb: 4/11/81

YEAR	TM/L	W	L	PCT	G	GS	CG	SH	SV	IP	H	HR	BB	SO	RAT	ERA	ERA+	OAV	OOB	BH	AVG	PB	PR	/A	PD	TPI
1981	Sea-A	2	5	.286	29	9	1	0	2	93¹	92	3	55	52	14.3	4.34	89	.261	.363	0	—	0	-7	-5	1	-0.3
1982	Sea-A	5	2	.714	37	5	1	1	0	114²	104	6	58	70	12.7	2.75	154	.241	.331	0	—	0	17	19	1	1.2
1983	Sea-A	7	10	.412	41	17	2	0	0	162¹	160	14	72	76	13.0	3.94	108	.261	.342	0	—	0	2	6	3	0.8
1984	Tor-A	1	2	.333	20	3	0	0	0	45²	66	6	22	21	17.5	5.91	69	.342	.412	0	—	0	-10	-9	1	-0.4
1985	Cle-A	3	4	.429	31	3	0	0	2	62²	78	8	34	44	16.1	6.32	65	.311	.393	0	—	0	-15	-15	1	-1.5
1986	Chi-A	0	0	—	5	0	0	0	0	8	8	0	2	5	11.3	4.50	96	.276	.323	0	—	0	-0	-0	-0	-0.1
1987	Chi-A	0	0	—	11	0	0	0	0	18²	17	1	8	8	13.0	2.41	190	.297	.375	0	—	0	4	4	-1	-0.1
1990	Sea-A	2	0	1.000	12	0	0	0	0	11	9	0	10	3	15.5	3.27	121	.237	.396	0	—	0	1	1	0	0.2
Total	8	20	23	.465	186	37	4	1	4	516¹	536	38	261	259	14.0	4.15	100	.272	.359	0	—	0	-8	1	7	-0.2

● **ED CLARK**   Clark, Edward C.   b: Cincinnati, Ohio   Deb: 7/4/1886

YEAR	TM/L	W	L	PCT	G	GS	CG	SH	SV	IP	H	HR	BB	SO	RAT	ERA	ERA+	OAV	OOB	BH	AVG	PB	PR	/A	PD	TPI
1886	Phi-a	0	1	.000	1	1	1	0	0	8	10	2	2	2	15.8	6.75	52	.294	.368	0	.000	-0	-3	-3	-0	-0.3
1891	Col-a	0	0	—	1	0	0	0	0	2	2	0	0	1	9.0	0.00	—	.252	.252	0	.000	-0	1	1	0	0.1
Total	2	0	1	.000	2	1	1	0	0	10	12	2	2	3	14.4	5.40	65	.286	.348	0	.000	-0	-2	-2	-0	-0.3

● **GEORGE CLARK**   Clark, George Myron   b: 5/19/1891, Smithland, Iowa   d: 11/14/40, Sioux City, Iowa   BR/TL, 6′, 190 lbs.   Deb: 5/16/13

YEAR	TM/L	W	L	PCT	G	GS	CG	SH	SV	IP	H	HR	BB	SO	RAT	ERA	ERA+	OAV	OOB	BH	AVG	PB	PR	/A	PD	TPI
1913	NY-A	0	1	.000	11	1	0	0	0	19	22	1	19	5	20.8	9.00	33	.272	.427	2	.500	1	-13	-13	-0	-0.5

● **GINGER CLARK**   Clark, Harvey Daniel   b: 3/7/1879, Wooster, Ohio   d: 5/10/43, Lake Charles, La.   BR/TR, 5′11″, 165 lbs.   Deb: 8/11/02

YEAR	TM/L	W	L	PCT	G	GS	CG	SH	SV	IP	H	HR	BB	SO	RAT	ERA	ERA+	OAV	OOB	BH	AVG	PB	PR	/A	PD	TPI
1902	Cle-A	1	0	1.000	1	0	0	0	0	6	10	0	3	1	21.0	6.00	57	.370	.451	2	.500	1	-2	-2	-0	-0.1

● **MARK CLARK**   Clark, Mark Willard   b: 5/12/68, Bath, Ill.   BR/TR, 6′5″, 225 lbs.   Deb: 9/6/91

YEAR	TM/L	W	L	PCT	G	GS	CG	SH	SV	IP	H	HR	BB	SO	RAT	ERA	ERA+	OAV	OOB	BH	AVG	PB	PR	/A	PD	TPI
1991	StL-N	1	1	.500	7	2	0	0	0	22¹	17	3	11	13	11.3	4.03	92	.215	.311	0	.000	-1	-1	-1	-0	-0.2
1992	StL-N	3	10	.231	20	20	1	1	0	113¹	117	12	36	44	12.2	4.45	76	.265	.321	5	.139	-1	-12	-13	-2	-1.7
1993	Cle-A	7	5	.583	26	15	1	0	0	109¹	119	18	25	57	11.9	4.28	101	.279	.321	0	—	0	0	1	-2	-0.1
1994	Cle-A	11	3	.786	20	20	4	1	0	127¹	133	14	40	60	12.5	3.82	129	.273	.333	0	—	0	14	16	0	1.4
Total	4	22	19	.537	73	57	6	2	0	372¹	386	47	112	174	12.2	4.16	101	.269	.325	5	.116	-1	2	2	-4	-0.6

● **MIKE CLARK**   Clark, Michael John   b: 2/12/22, Camden, N.J.   BR/TR, 6′4″, 190 lbs.   Deb: 7/27/52

YEAR	TM/L	W	L	PCT	G	GS	CG	SH	SV	IP	H	HR	BB	SO	RAT	ERA	ERA+	OAV	OOB	BH	AVG	PB	PR	/A	PD	TPI
1952	StL-N	2	0	1.000	12	4	0	0	0	25¹	32	2	14	10	16.3	6.04	61	.311	.393	0	.000	-1	-6	-7	-0	-0.5
1953	StL-N	1	0	1.000	23	2	0	0	1	35²	46	2	21	17	17.4	4.79	89	.315	.408	0	.000	-1	-2	-2	1	-0.1
Total	2	3	0	1.000	35	6	0	0	1	61	78	4	35	27	17.0	5.31	76	.313	.402	0	.000	-1	-9	-9	1	-0.6

● **SPIDER CLARK**   Clark, Owen F.   b: 9/16/1867, Brooklyn, N.Y.   d: 2/8/1892, Brooklyn, N.Y.   TR, 5′10″, 150 lbs.   Deb: 5/2/1889 ◆

YEAR	TM/L	W	L	PCT	G	GS	CG	SH	SV	IP	H	HR	BB	SO	RAT	ERA	ERA+	OAV	OOB	BH	AVG	PB	PR	/A	PD	TPI
1890	Buf-P	0	0	—	1	0	0	0	0	4	8	0	2	2	22.5	6.75	61	.399	.453	69	.265	0	-1	-1	-0	0.0

● **PHIL CLARK**   Clark, Philip James   b: 10/3/32, Albany, Ga.   BR/TR, 6′3″, 210 lbs.   Deb: 4/15/58

YEAR	TM/L	W	L	PCT	G	GS	CG	SH	SV	IP	H	HR	BB	SO	RAT	ERA	ERA+	OAV	OOB	BH	AVG	PB	PR	/A	PD	TPI
1958	StL-N	0	1	.000	7	0	0	0	1	7²	11	2	3	1	16.4	3.52	117	.355	.412	0	.000	-0	0	1	-0	0.0
1959	StL-N	0	1	.000	7	0	0	0	0	7	8	0	8	5	20.6	12.86	33	.286	.444	0	—	0	-7	-7	-0	-0.8
Total	2	0	2	.000	14	0	0	0	1	14²	19	2	11	6	18.4	7.98	52	.322	.429	0	.000	-0	-7	-6	-0	-0.8

● **RICKEY CLARK**   Clark, Rickey Charles   b: 3/21/46, Mt.Clemens, Mich.   BR/TR, 6′2″, 170 lbs.   Deb: 4/22/67

YEAR	TM/L	W	L	PCT	G	GS	CG	SH	SV	IP	H	HR	BB	SO	RAT	ERA	ERA+	OAV	OOB	BH	AVG	PB	PR	/A	PD	TPI
1967	Cal-A	12	11	.522	32	30	11	1	0	174	144	15	69	81	11.3	2.59	121	.224	.305	2	.040	-4	12	11	1	1.1
1968	Cal-A	1	11	.083	21	17	0	0	0	94¹	74	4	54	60	12.3	3.53	82	.217	.326	3	.107	-1	-6	-6	1	-0.9
1969	Cal-A	0	0	—	6	1	0	0	0	9²	12	2	7	6	17.7	5.59	62	.300	.404	1	.500	1	-2	-2	-1	0.0
1971	Cal-A	2	1	.667	11	7	1	1	1	44	36	6	28	28	13.5	2.86	113	.220	.340	4	.267	1	3	2	-1	0.2

YEAR	TM/L	W	L	PCT	G	GS	CG	SH	SV	IP	H	HR	BB	SO	RAT	ERA	ERA+	OAV	OOB	BH	AVG	PB	PR	/A	PD	TPI
1972	Cal-A	4	9	.308	26	15	2	0	1	109²	105	10	55	61	13.3	4.51	64	.261	.352	3	.097	-1	-18	-20	1	-2.3
Total	5	19	32	.373	96	70	4	2	2	431²	371	37	213	236	12.4	3.38	90	.233	.328	13	.103	-5	-10	-16	1	-1.9

● **BOB CLARK**   Clark, Robert William   b: 8/22/1897, Newport, Pa.   d: 5/18/44, Carlsbad, N.Mex.   BR/TR, 6'3", 188 lbs.   Deb: 5/26/20

1920	Cle-A	1	2	.333	11	2	2	1	0	42	59	0	13	8	15.6	3.43	111	.383	.435	2	.200	-0	2	2	-0	0.0
1921	Cle-A	0	0	—	5	0	0	0	0	9¹	23	2	6	2	28.9	14.46	29	.511	.577	0	.000	-1	-11	-11	-0	-0.1
Total	2	1	2	.333	16	2	2	1	0	51¹	82	2	19	10	18.1	5.44	71	.412	.468	2	.154	-1	-9	-9	-1	-0.1

● **TERRY CLARK**   Clark, Terry Lee   b: 10/18/60, Los Angeles, Cal.   BR/TR, 6'2", 190 lbs.   Deb: 7/7/88

1988	Cal-A	6	6	.500	15	15	2	1	0	94	120	8	31	39	14.5	5.07	76	.323	.375		0		-12	-13	0	-1.2
1989	Cal-A	0	2	.000	4	2	0	0	0	11	13	0	3	7	13.1	4.91	78	.310	.356		0		-1	-1	0	-0.2
1990	Hou-N	0	0	—	1	1	0	0	0	4	9	0	3	2	27.0	13.50	27	.429	.500	1	.500	0	-4	-4	-0	-0.1
Total	3	6	8	.429	20	18	2	1	0	109	142	8	37	48	14.8	5.37	72	.326	.379	1	.500	0	-17	-18	-0	-1.4

● **OTIE CLARK**   Clark, William Otis   b: 5/22/18, Boscobel, Wis.   BR/TR, 6'1.5", 190 lbs.   Deb: 4/17/45

1945	Bos-A	4	4	.500	12	9	4	1	0	82	86	6	19	20	11.6	3.07	111	.268	.311	5	.208	0	3	3	-2	0.1

● **WATTY CLARK**   Clark, William Watson "Lefty"   b: 5/16/02, St.Joseph, La.   d: 3/4/72, Clearwater, Fla.   BL/TL, 6'0.5", 175 lbs.   Deb: 5/28/24

1924	Cle-A	1	3	.250	12	1	0	0	0	25²	38	0	14	6	18.9	7.01	61	.345	.429	2	.222		-8	-8	-0	-1.0
1927	Bro-N	7	2	.778	27	3	1	0	2	73²	74	2	19	32	11.4	2.32	171	.265	.312	3	.143	-1	13	13	0	1.5
1928	Bro-N	12	9	.571	40	19	10	0	3	194²	193	4	50	85	11.3	2.68	148	.259	.306	10	.152	-2	28	28	1	2.7
1929	Bro-N	16	19	.457	41	36	19	3	1	279	295	14	71	140	11.9	3.74	123	.270	.316	16	.165	-3	30	27	-0	2.5
1930	Bro-N	13	13	.500	44	24	9	1	6	200	209	20	38	81	11.1	4.18	117	.271	.306	14	.206	-0	17	16	0	1.9
1931	Bro-N	14	10	.583	34	28	16	3	1	233¹	243	4	52	96	11.4	3.20	119	.267	.308	21	.250	4	17	16	-3	1.6
1932	Bro-N	20	12	.625	40	36	19	2	0	273	282	10	49	99	11.0	3.49	109	.264	.299	21	.216	1	12	10	1	1.3
1933	Bro-N	2	4	.333	11	8	4	1	1	50²	61	6	14	12	12.4	4.80	67	.303	.333	2	.154	-0	-8	-9	-1	-1.0
	NY-N	3	4	.429	16	5	0	0	0	44	58	3	11	11	14.3	4.70	68	.317	.359	3	.273	1	-7	-7	1	-0.9
	Yr	5	8	.385	27	13	4	1	1	94²	119	5	17	25	13.0	4.75	68	.307	.338	5	.208	1	-15	-16	0	-1.9
1934	NY-N	1	2	.333	5	4	1	0	0	18²	23	5	6	6	13.5	6.75	57	.295	.337	1	.167	-0	-6	-6	-0	-0.7
	Bro-N	2	0	1.000	17	1	0	0	0	25¹	40	0	9	10	17.8	5.33	73	.345	.397	1	.125	-1	-4	-4	-0	-0.4
	Yr	3	2	.600	22	5	1	0	0	44	63	5	14	16	16.0	5.93	66	.325	.373	2	.143	-0	-9	-10	-0	-1.1
1935	Bro-N	13	8	.619	33	25	11	1	0	207	215	11	28	35	10.6	3.30	120	.264	.289	14	.177	-0	16	15	2	1.6
1936	Bro-N	7	11	.389	33	16	1	1	0	120	162	11	28	28	14.3	4.43	93	.316	.351	9	.231	-0	-5	-4	-0	-0.5
1937	Bro-N	0	0	—	2	0	0	0	0	2¹	4	0	3	0	27.0	7.71	52	.308	.438		0		-1	-1	0	0.0
Total	12	111	97	.534	355	206	91	14	16	1747¹	1897	86	383	643	11.8	3.66	112	.275	.315	117	.196	1	96	87	1	8.6

● **LEFTY CLARKE**   Clarke, Alan Thomas   b: 3/8/1896, Clarksville, Md.   d: 3/11/75, Cheverly, Md.   BB/TL, 5'11", 180 lbs.   Deb: 10/2/21

1921	Cin-N	0	1	.000	1	1	1	0	0	5	7	0	2	1	16.2	5.40	66	.304	.360	0	.000	-0	-1	-1	-0	-0.2

● **HENRY CLARKE**   Clarke, Henry Tefft   b: 8/28/1875, Bellevue, Neb.   d: 3/28/50, Colorado Springs, Colo.   BR/TR,   Deb: 6/26/1897 ◆

1897	Cle-N	0	4	.000	5	4	3	0	0	30²	32	4	12	3	13.8	6.16	73	.267	.348	7	.280	0	-6	-6	-1	-0.6
1898	Chi-N	1	0	1.000	1	1	1	0	0	9	8	0	5	1	14.0	2.00	179	.237	.352	1	.250	0	2	2	-0	0.2
Total	2	1	4	.200	6	5	4	0	0	39²	40	4	17	4	13.8	5.22	82	.260	.349	8	.276	0	-5	-4	-1	-0.4

● **RUFE CLARKE**   Clarke, Rufus Rivers   b: 4/13/1900, Estill, S.C.   d: 2/8/83, Columbia, S.C.   BR/TR, 6'1", 203 lbs.   Deb: 9/3/23   F

1923	Det-A	1	1	.500	5	0	0	0	0	6	6	0	6	2	19.5	4.50	86	.300	.481	0	—	0	-0	-0	0	-0.1
1924	Det-A	0	0	—	2	0	0	0	0	5¹	3	0	5	1	15.2	3.38	122	.158	.360	0	.000	-0	1	0	-0	0.0
Total	2	1	1	.500	7	0	0	0	0	11	9	0	11	3	17.5	3.97	100	.231	.423	0	.000	-0	0	0	0	-0.1

● **STAN CLARKE**   Clarke, Stanley Martin   b: 8/9/60, Toledo, Ohio   BL/TL, 6'1", 180 lbs.   Deb: 6/7/83

1983	Tor-A	1	1	.500	10	0	0	0	0	11	10	2	5	7	12.3	3.27	131	.256	.341	0		0	1	1	0	0.0
1985	Tor-A	0	0	—	4	0	0	0	0	4	3	1	2	2	11.3	4.50	94	.214	.313	0		0	-0	-0	0	-0.0
1986	Tor-A	0	1	.000	10	0	0	0	0	12²	18	4	10	9	19.9	9.24	46	.375	.483	0		0	-7	-7	0	-0.5
1987	Sea-A	2	2	.500	22	0	0	0	0	23	31	7	10	13	16.0	5.48	86	.333	.398	0		0	-3	-2	-0	-0.4
1989	KC-A	0	2	.000	2	2	0	0	0	7	14	2	4	2	23.1	15.43	25	.438	.500	0		0	-9	-9	-0	-1.5
1990	StL-N	0	0	—	2	0	0	0	0	3¹	2	0	0	3	5.4	2.70	141	.167	.167	0		0	0	0	-0	0.0
Total	6	3	6	.333	50	2	0	0	0	61	78	16	31	36	16.1	6.79	64	.328	.405	0		0	-18	-17	-0	-2.4

● **WEBBO CLARKE**   Clarke, Vibert Ernesto   b: 6/8/28, Colon, Panama   d: 6/14/70, Cristobal, C.Z.   BL/TL, 6', 165 lbs.   Deb: 9/4/55

1955	Was-A	0	0	—	7	2	0	0	0	21¹	17	2	14	9	13.1	4.64	83	.221	.341	1	.167	-0	-2	-2	0	0.0

● **DAD CLARKE**   Clarke, William H.   b: 1/7/1865, Oswego, N.Y.   d: 6/3/11, Lorain, Ohio   BB/TR,   Deb: 4/23/1888

1888	Chi-N	1	0	1.000	2	1	1	0	0	16	23	2	6	6	17.4	5.06	60	.315	.383	2	.286	2	-4	-4	0	0.0
1891	Col-a	1	2	.333	4	3	2	0	0	21	30	4	16	2	20.1	6.86	50	.324	.429	1	.111	-0	-7	-8	-0	-0.8
1894	NY-N	3	4	.429	15	6	5	0	1	84	114	3	26	15	15.3	4.93	106	.320	.372	8	.216	-0	4	3	-0	0.1
1895	NY-N	18	15	.545	37	30	27	1	1	281²	336	5	60	67	13.0	3.39	137	.292	.333	29	.240	-2	44	39	-3	3.1
1896	NY-N	17	24	.415	48	40	33	1	1	351	431	9	60	66	12.9	4.26	99	.300	.333	30	.204	-4	4	-2	-3	-0.8
1897	NY-N	2	1	.667	6	4	2	0	0	31	43	1	11	10	16.3	6.10	68	.326	.386	1	.167	-1	-6	-7	-0	-0.6
	Lou-N	2	4	.333	7	6	6	0	0	54²	74	3	10	7	14.2	3.95	108	.320	.354	5	.227	-1	2	2	-0	0.1
	Yr	4	5	.444	13	10	8	0	0	85²	117	4	21	17	14.7	4.73	89	.321	.361	8	.200	-8	-4	-5	-0	-0.5
1898	Lou-N	0	1	.000	1	1	1	0	0	9	10	1	2	1	14.0	5.00	72	.279	.322	0		0	-1	-1	-0	-0.2
Total	7	44	51	.463	120	92	77	2	3	848¹	1061	24	191	174	13.6	4.17	106	.302	.344	78	.214	-6	35	23	-6	0.9

● **DAD CLARKSON**   Clarkson, Arthur Hamilton   b: 8/31/1866, Cambridge, Mass.   d: 2/5/11, Somerville, Mass.   BR/TR, 5'10", 165 lbs.   Deb: 8/20/1891   F

1891	NY-N	1	2	.333	5	2	1	0	0	28	24	0	18	11	14.5	2.89	111	.223	.350	4	.444	1	1	1	0	0.3
1892	Bos-N	1	0	1.000	1	1	0	0	0	7	5	3	0	1	10.3	1.29	273	.192	.276	0	.000	-0	2	2	0	0.2
1893	StL-N	12	9	.571	24	21	17	1	0	186¹	194	4	79	37	13.9	3.48	136	.260	.342	10	.133	-5	25	26	1	1.8
1894	StL-N	8	17	.320	32	32	24	1	0	233¹	318	9	117	46	17.2	6.36	85	.321	.399	16	.182	-4	-27	-25	1	-2.0
1895	StL-N	1	6	.143	7	7	7	0	0	61	91	4	26	9	17.6	7.38	66	.340	.402	1	.043	-3	-18	-17	-1	-1.6
	Bal-N	12	3	.800	20	14	10	0	0	142	169	5	64	23	15.0	3.87	123	.291	.365	8	.140	-4	14	14	2	0.9
	Yr	13	9	.591	27	21	17	0	0	203	260	12	90	32	15.7	4.92	97	.306	.375	9	.112	-7	-3	-3	1	-0.7
1896	Bal-N	4	2	.667	7	4	3	0	0	47	72	1	18	7	17.6	4.98	86	.348	.405	2	.278	-0	-3	-4	-0	-0.4
Total	6	39	39	.500	96	81	63	2	0	704²	873	26	325	133	15.8	4.90	99	.299	.376	44	.161	-14	-6	-3	2	-0.8

● **JOHN CLARKSON**   Clarkson, John Gibson   b: 7/1/1861, Cambridge, Mass.   d: 2/4/09, Belmont, Mass.   BR/TR, 5'10", 155 lbs.   Deb: 5/2/1882   FH

1882	Wor-N	1	2	.333	3	3	2	0	0	24	49	0	4	9	19.1	4.50	69	.392	.402	4	.364	1	-4	-4	0	-0.3
1884	Chi-N	10	3	.769	14	13	12	0	0	118	94	10	25	102	9.1	2.14	147	.208	.262	22	.262	4	11	11	-3	1.0
1885	*Chi-N	**53**	16	.768	**70**	70	**68**	**10**	0	**623**	497	21	97	**308**	8.6	1.85	164	.208	.239	61	.216	2	**67**	**82**	8	**8.9**
1886	*Chi-N	36	17	.679	55	55	50	3	0	466²	419	20	86	313	9.7	2.41	151	.229	.264	49	.233	4	47	**64**	6	6.5
1887	Chi-N	**38**	21	.644	60	**59**	56	2	0	**523**	513	20	92	237	10.5	3.08	146	.246	.281	52	.242	3	58	82	9	**8.3**
1888	Bos-N	33	20	.623	54	54	53	3	0	**483¹**	448	17	119	223	10.7	2.76	103	.236	.284	40	.195	3	5	5	3	0.9
1889	Bos-N	**49**	19	**.721**	**73**	72	**68**	8	1	**620**	589	16	203	**284**	**11.7**	**2.73**	153	.243	**.306**	54	.206	0	**89**	**99**	11	**10.1**
1890	Bos-N	26	18	.591	44	44	43	2	0	383	370	14	140	138	12.4	3.27	115	.246	.317	13	.249	13	13	21	-3	2.0
1891	Bos-N	33	19	.635	55	51	47	3	**3**	460²	435	18	154	141	11.8	2.79	131	.240	.305	42	.225	3	28	44	4	4.8
1892	Bos-N	8	6	.571	16	16	15	4	0	145²	115	4	60	48	11.1	2.35	150	.208	.292	13	.228	7	15	19	0	1.7
	*Cle-N	17	10	.630	29	28	27	1	1	243¹	235	4	72	91	11.5	2.55	133	.244	.299	14	.139	-5	20	23	-1	1.5

YEAR	TM/L	W	L	PCT	G	GS	CG	SH	SV	IP	H	HR	BB	SO	RAT	ERA	ERA+	OAV	OOB	BH	AVG	PB	PR	/A	PD	TPI
	Yr	25	16	.610	45	44	42	5	1	389	350	8	132	139	11.2	2.48	139	.230	.293	27	.171	-4	35	41	-1	3.2
1893	Cle-N	16	17	.485	36	35	31	0	0	295	358	11	95	62	14.0	4.45	110	.291	.344	27	.206	-4	7	14	3	1.1
1894	Cle-N	8	10	.444	22	18	13	1	0	150²	173	6	46	28	13.1	4.42	124	.285	.335	11	.200	-3	15	17	2	1.4
Total	12	328	178	.648	531	518	485	37	5	4536¹	4295	161	1191	1978	11.0	2.81	134	.240	.291	432	.219	9	371	480	46	48.7

● WALTER CLARKSON
Clarkson, Walter Hamilton b: 11/3/1878, Cambridge, Mass. d: 10/10/46, Cambridge, Mass. BR/TR, 5'10", 150 lbs. Deb: 7/2/04 F

YEAR	TM/L	W	L	PCT	G	GS	CG	SH	SV	IP	H	HR	BB	SO	RAT	ERA	ERA+	OAV	OOB	BH	AVG	PB	PR	/A	PD	TPI
1904	NY-A	1	2	.333	13	4	2	0	1	66¹	63	3	25	43	13.3	5.02	54	.251	.343	7	.269	2	-18	-17	-1	-0.8
1905	NY-A	3	3	.500	9	4	3	0	0	46	40	1	13	35	10.8	3.91	75	.235	.297	1	.053	-2	-6	-5	-1	-0.9
1906	NY-A	9	4	.692	32	16	9	3	0	151	135	6	55	64	11.6	2.32	128	.242	.316	8	.157	-1	6	11	-1	0.7
1907	NY-A	1	1	.500	5	2	0	0	0	17¹	19	1	8	3	15.1	6.23	45	.280	.373	2	.286	0	-7	-7	0	-0.7
	Cle-A	4	6	.400	17	10	9	1	0	90²	77	1	29	32	10.8	1.99	127	.232	.299	1	.036	-3	6	5	-0	0.1
	Yr	5	7	.417	22	12	9	1	0	108	96	2	37	35	11.3	2.67	96	.239	.308	3	.086	-3	-1	-1	-0	-0.6
1908	Cle-A	0	0	—	2	1	0	0	0	3¹	6	0	2	1	27.0	10.80	22	.400	.526	1	1.000	0	-3	-3	-0	0.0
Total	5	18	16	.529	78	37	23	4	1	374²	340	12	132	178	11.9	3.17	88	.244	.320	20	.152	-4	-23	-16	-4	-1.6

● BILL CLARKSON
Clarkson, William Henry "Blackie" b: 9/27/1898, Portsmouth, Va. d: 8/27/71, Raleigh, N.C. BR/TR, 5'11", 160 lbs. Deb: 5/2/27

YEAR	TM/L	W	L	PCT	G	GS	CG	SH	SV	IP	H	HR	BB	SO	RAT	ERA	ERA+	OAV	OOB	BH	AVG	PB	PR	/A	PD	TPI
1927	NY-N	3	9	.250	26	7	2	0	2	86²	92	3	52	28	15.1	4.36	88	.280	.380	1	.050	-1	-4	-5	0	-0.7
1928	NY-N	0	0	—	4	0	0	0	0	5²	10	0	1	3	17.5	7.94	49	.455	.478	0	—	0	-2	-3	-0	-0.5
	Bos-N	0	2	.000	19	1	0	0	0	34²	53	2	22	8	19.7	6.75	58	.349	.434	0	.000	-0	-11	-11	1	-0.5
	Yr	0	2	.000	23	1	0	0	0	40¹	63	2	23	11	19.4	6.92	57	.362	.439	0	.000	-0	-13	-13	1	-0.5
1929	Bos-N	0	1	.000	2	1	0	0	0	7	16	0	4	0	25.7	10.29	45	.485	.541	1	.500	0	-4	-4	0	-0.4
Total	3	3	12	.200	51	9	2	0	2	134	171	5	79	39	16.9	5.44	72	.319	.408	2	.080	-1	-22	-23	1	-1.6

● MARTY CLARY
Clary, Martin Keith b: 4/3/62, Detroit, Mich. BR/TR, 6'4", 190 lbs. Deb: 9/5/87

YEAR	TM/L	W	L	PCT	G	GS	CG	SH	SV	IP	H	HR	BB	SO	RAT	ERA	ERA+	OAV	OOB	BH	AVG	PB	PR	/A	PD	TPI
1987	Atl-N	0	1	.000	7	1	0	0	0	14²	20	2	4	7	15.3	6.14	71	.328	.379	0	.000	-0	-3	-3	-0	-0.2
1989	Atl-N	4	3	.571	18	17	2	1	0	108²	103	6	31	30	11.2	3.15	116	.249	.303	5	.161	0	4	6	0	0.5
1990	Atl-N	1	10	.091	33	14	0	0	0	101²	128	9	39	44	14.9	5.67	71	.308	.368	0	.000	-3	-21	-18	1	-2.0
Total	3	5	14	.263	58	32	2	1	0	225	251	17	74	81	13.1	4.48	86	.282	.339	5	.083	-2	-20	-15	1	-1.7

● GOWELL CLASET
Claset, Gowell Sylvester "Lefty" b: 11/26/07, Battle Creek, Mich d: 3/8/81, St.Petersburg, Fla. BB/TL, 6'3.5", 210 lbs. Deb: 4/12/33

YEAR	TM/L	W	L	PCT	G	GS	CG	SH	SV	IP	H	HR	BB	SO	RAT	ERA	ERA+	OAV	OOB	BH	AVG	PB	PR	/A	PD	TPI
1933	Phi-A	2	0	1.000	8	1	0	0	0	11¹	23	1	11	1	27.0	9.53	45	.426	.523	1	.500	1	-7	-7	0	-0.8

● FRITZ CLAUSEN
Clausen, Frederick William b: 4/26/1869, New York, N.Y. d: 2/11/60, Memphis, Tenn. BR/TL, 5'11", 190 lbs. Deb: 7/23/1892

YEAR	TM/L	W	L	PCT	G	GS	CG	SH	SV	IP	H	HR	BB	SO	RAT	ERA	ERA+	OAV	OOB	BH	AVG	PB	PR	/A	PD	TPI
1892	Lou-N	9	13	.409	24	24	24	2	0	200	181	3	87	94	12.2	3.06	100	.232	.311	13	.155	-3	5	0	-1	-0.3
1893	Lou-N	1	4	.200	5	5	3	0	0	33	41	2	22	4	17.5	6.00	73	.296	.396	3	.214	-1	-5	-6	0	-0.7
	Chi-N	6	2	.750	10	9	8	0	1	76	71	1	39	31	13.6	3.08	150	.240	.338	4	.121	-3	13	13	0	0.8
	Yr	7	6	.538	15	14	11	0	1	109	112	3	61	35	14.7	3.96	115	.257	.355	7	.149	-4	8	7	0	0.1
1894	Chi-N	0	1	.000	1	1	0	0	0	4¹	5	0	3	1	16.6	10.38	54	.286	.391	0	.000	-0	-2	-2	0	-0.3
1896	Lou-N	0	2	.000	2	2	1	0	0	11	17	1	6	4	21.3	6.55	66	.350	.452	0	.000	-0	-3	-3	-0	-0.4
Total	4	16	22	.421	42	41	36	2	1	324¹	315	7	157	134	13.4	3.58	101	.246	.334	20	.147	-8	8	2	-0	-0.9

● AL CLAUSS
Clauss, Albert Stanley "Lefty" b: 6/24/1891, New Haven, Conn. d: 9/13/52, New Haven, Conn. BR/TL, 5'10.5", 178 lbs. Deb: 4/22/13

YEAR	TM/L	W	L	PCT	G	GS	CG	SH	SV	IP	H	HR	BB	SO	RAT	ERA	ERA+	OAV	OOB	BH	AVG	PB	PR	/A	PD	TPI
1913	Det-A	0	1	.000	5	1	0	0	0	13¹	11	0	12	1	16.9	4.73	62	.220	.391	0	.000	-1	-3	-3	-0	-0.3

● DANNY CLAY
Clay, Danny Bruce b: 10/24/61, Sun Valley, Cal. BR/TR, 6'1", 190 lbs. Deb: 5/1/88

YEAR	TM/L	W	L	PCT	G	GS	CG	SH	SV	IP	H	HR	BB	SO	RAT	ERA	ERA+	OAV	OOB	BH	AVG	PB	PR	/A	PD	TPI
1988	Phi-N	0	1	.000	17	0	0	0	0	24	27	5	21	12	18.0	6.00	59	.303	.436	0	.000	-0	-7	-7	-1	-0.3

● KEN CLAY
Clay, Kenneth Earl b: 4/6/54, Lynchburg, Va. BR/TR, 6'3", 195 lbs. Deb: 6/7/77

YEAR	TM/L	W	L	PCT	G	GS	CG	SH	SV	IP	H	HR	BB	SO	RAT	ERA	ERA+	OAV	OOB	BH	AVG	PB	PR	/A	PD	TPI
1977	*NY-A	2	3	.400	21	3	0	0	1	55²	53	6	24	20	12.6	4.37	90	.251	.331	0	—	0	-2	-3	0	-0.2
1978	*NY-A	3	4	.429	28	6	0	0	0	75²	89	3	21	32	13.3	4.28	85	.291	.340	0	—	0	-4	-6	-1	-0.5
1979	NY-A	1	7	.125	32	5	0	0	2	78¹	88	12	25	28	13.2	5.40	75	.291	.350	0	—	0	-10	-12	0	-1.1
1980	Tex-A	3	2	.400	8	8	0	0	0	43	43	4	29	17	15.7	4.60	85	.256	.375	0	—	0	-3	-3	-1	-0.3
1981	Sea-A	2	7	.222	22	14	0	0	0	101	116	10	42	32	14.3	4.63	83	.294	.366	0	—	0	-11	-9	-2	-0.9
Total	5	10	24	.294	111	36	0	0	3	353²	389	35	141	129	13.8	4.68	83	.281	.353	0	—	0	-30	-32	-3	-3.0

● MARK CLEAR
Clear, Mark Alan b: 5/27/56, Los Angeles, Cal. BR/TR, 6'4", 215 lbs. Deb: 4/4/79

YEAR	TM/L	W	L	PCT	G	GS	CG	SH	SV	IP	H	HR	BB	SO	RAT	ERA	ERA+	OAV	OOB	BH	AVG	PB	PR	/A	PD	TPI
1979	*Cal-A★	11	5	.688	52	0	0	0	14	109	87	4	68	98	13.0	3.63	112	.219	.337	0	—	0	7	5	-1	0.8
1980	Cal-A	11	11	.500	58	0	0	0	9	106¹	82	2	65	105	12.9	3.30	119	.216	.338	0	—	0	9	7	-1	1.6
1981	Bos-A	8	3	.727	34	0	0	0	9	76²	69	11	51	82	14.3	4.11	94	.239	.357	0	—	0	-4	-2	-1	-0.5
1982	Bos-A☆	14	9	.609	55	0	0	0	14	105	92	11	61	109	13.7	3.00	144	.238	.352	0	—	0	13	15	-0	3.5
1983	Bos-A	4	5	.444	48	0	0	0	4	96	101	10	68	81	16.1	6.28	69	.273	.390	0	—	0	-24	-21	-1	-2.2
1984	Bos-A	8	3	.727	47	0	0	0	8	67	47	2	70	76	16.0	4.03	103	.198	.385	0	—	0	-0	1	0	0.1
1985	Bos-A	1	3	.250	41	0	0	0	3	55²	45	1	50	55	16.2	3.72	115	.225	.392	0	—	0	3	3	1	0.3
1986	Mil-A	5	5	.500	59	0	0	0	16	73²	53	4	36	85	11.0	2.20	197	.201	.299	0	—	0	16	17	-0	2.9
1987	Mil-A	8	5	.615	58	1	0	0	6	78¹	70	9	55	81	14.9	4.48	102	.239	.368	0	—	0	-0	1	1	0.2
1988	Mil-A	1	0	1.000	25	0	0	0	0	29	23	4	21	26	13.7	2.79	142	.215	.344	0	—	0	4	4	-0	0.4
1990	Cal-A	0	0	—	4	0	0	0	0	7²	5	0	9	6	18.8	5.87	65	.200	.444	0	—	0	-2	-2	-0	-0.3
Total	11	71	49	.592	481	1	0	0	83	804¹	674	60	554	804	14.1	3.85	109	.228	.357	0	—	0	21	30	-3	6.7

● JOE CLEARY
Cleary, Joseph Christopher "Fire" b: 12/3/18, Cork, Ireland BR/TR, 5'9", 150 lbs. Deb: 8/4/45

YEAR	TM/L	W	L	PCT	G	GS	CG	SH	SV	IP	H	HR	BB	SO	RAT	ERA	ERA+	OAV	OOB	BH	AVG	PB	PR	/A	PD	TPI
1945	Was-A	0	0	—	1	0	0	0	0	0¹	5	0	3	1	216.0	189.00	2	.833	.889	0	—	0	-7	-7	0	0.0

● ROGER CLEMENS
Clemens, William Roger b: 8/4/62, Dayton, Ohio BR/TR, 6'4", 215 lbs. Deb: 5/15/84

YEAR	TM/L	W	L	PCT	G	GS	CG	SH	SV	IP	H	HR	BB	SO	RAT	ERA	ERA+	OAV	OOB	BH	AVG	PB	PR	/A	PD	TPI
1984	Bos-A	9	4	.692	21	20	5	1	0	133¹	146	13	29	126	11.9	4.32	94	.271	.311	0	—	0	-5	-2	0	-0.3
1985	Bos-A	7	5	.583	15	15	3	1	0	98¹	83	5	37	74	11.3	3.29	130	.228	.304	0	—	0	9	11	0	1.2
1986	*Bos-A★	24	4	.857	33	33	10	1	0	254	179	21	67	238	8.9	2.48	168	.195	.253	0	—	0	48	48	-1	4.9
1987	Bos-A	20	9	.690	36	36	18	7	0	281²	248	19	83	256	10.9	2.97	153	.235	.296	0	—	0	46	49	-2	4.4
1988	*Bos-A★	18	12	.600	35	35	14	8	0	264	217	17	62	291	9.7	2.93	140	.220	.270	0	—	0	30	35	-2	3.3
1989	Bos-A	17	11	.607	35	35	8	3	0	253¹	215	20	93	230	11.2	3.13	131	.231	.307	0	—	0	21	27	-1	2.6
1990	*Bos-A☆	21	6	.778	31	31	7	4	0	228¹	193	7	54	209	10.0	1.93	211	.228	.280	0	—	0	50	54	1	6.7
1991	Bos-A★	18	10	.643	35	35	13	4	0	271¹	219	15	65	241	9.6	2.62	164	.221	.272	0	—	0	44	51	1	4.8
1992	Bos-A★	18	11	.621	32	32	11	5	0	246²	203	11	62	208	10.0	2.41	175	.224	.280	0	—	0	42	49	-0	5.8
1993	Bos-A	11	14	.440	29	29	2	1	0	191²	175	17	67	160	11.9	4.46	103	.244	.318	0	—	0	-3	3	-1	0.3
1994	Bos-A	9	7	.563	24	24	3	1	0	170²	124	15	71	168	10.5	2.85	181	.203	.291	0	—	0	37	43	0	3.2
Total	11	172	93	.649	326	325	94	36	0	2393¹	2002	160	690	2201	10.4	2.93	147	.226	.287	0	—	0	321	368	-4	36.9

● BILL CLEMENSEN
Clemensen, William Melville b: 6/20/19, New Brunswick, N.J. d: 2/18/94, Alta, Cal. BR/TR, 6'1", 193 lbs. Deb: 5/22/39

YEAR	TM/L	W	L	PCT	G	GS	CG	SH	SV	IP	H	HR	BB	SO	RAT	ERA	ERA+	OAV	OOB	BH	AVG	PB	PR	/A	PD	TPI
1939	Pit-N	1	0	1.000	12	1	0	0	0	27	32	0	20	13	18.3	7.33	52	.311	.437	2	.333	1	-10	-10	1	-0.1
1941	Pit-N	1	0	1.000	2	1	1	0	0	13	7	0	7	4	9.7	2.77	130	.159	.275	0	.000	-1	1	1	-0	0.0
1946	Pit-N	0	0	—	1	0	0	0	0	2	0	0	0	2	0.0	0.00	—	.000	.000	0	—	-0	1	1	-0	0.0
Total	3	1	0	1.000	15	2	1	0	0	42	39	0	27	19	14.8	5.57	67	.255	.377	2	.200	0	-8	-8	1	-0.1

● PAT CLEMENTS
Clements, Patrick Brian b: 2/2/62, McCloud, Cal. BR/TL, 6', 180 lbs. Deb: 4/9/85

YEAR	TM/L	W	L	PCT	G	GS	CG	SH	SV	IP	H	HR	BB	SO	RAT	ERA	ERA+	OAV	OOB	BH	AVG	PB	PR	/A	PD	TPI
1985	Cal-A	5	0	1.000	41	0	0	0	0	62	47	4	25	19	10.7	3.34	123	.218	.305	0	—	0	6	5	1	0.5
	Pit-N	0	2	.000	27	0	0	0	2	34¹	39	2	15	17	14.2	3.67	97	.289	.360	B	.333	0	-0	-0	-1	-0.1
1986	Pit-N	0	4	.000	65	0	0	0	2	61	53	1	32	31	12.8	2.80	137	.251	.355	0	.000	-1	6	7	1	0.5

YEAR	TM/L	W	L	PCT	G	GS	CG	SH	SV	IP	H	HR	BB	SO	RAT	ERA	ERA+	OAV	OOB	BH	AVG	PB	PR	/A	PD	TPI
1987	NY-A	3	3	.500	55	0	0	0	7	80	91	4	30	36	13.9	4.95	89	.299	.368	0	—	0	-4	-5	1	-0.3
1988	NY-A	0	0	—	6	1	0	0	0	8¹	12	1	4	3	17.3	6.48	61	.343	.410	0	—	0	-2	-2	0	0.1
1989	SD-N	4	1	.800	23	1	0	0	0	39	39	4	15	18	12.5	3.92	89	.267	.335	0	.000	-1	-2	-2	0	-0.3
1990	SD-N	0	0	—	9	0	0	0	0	13	20	1	7	6	18.7	4.15	92	.357	.429	0	—	0	-1	-0	0	0.0
1991	SD-N	1	0	1.000	12	0	0	0	0	14¹	13	0	9	8	13.8	3.77	101	.255	.367	0	.000	-0	-0	0	0	0.0
1992	SD-N	2	1	.667	27	0	0	0	0	23²	25	0	12	11	14.8	2.66	134	.281	.379	0	.000	0	2	2	1	0.3
	Bal-A	2	0	1.000	23	0	0	0	0	24²	23	0	11	9	13.1	3.28	122	.258	.353	0	—	0	2	2	1	0.2
Total	8	17	11	.607	288	2	0	0	12	360¹	362	17	160	158	13.3	3.77	105	.272	.355	1	.059	-1	6	7	4	0.9

● LANCE CLEMONS
Clemons, Lance Levis   b: 7/6/47, Philadelphia, Pa.   BL/TL, 6'2", 205 lbs.   Deb: 8/12/71

YEAR	TM/L	W	L	PCT	G	GS	CG	SH	SV	IP	H	HR	BB	SO	RAT	ERA	ERA+	OAV	OOB	BH	AVG	PB	PR	/A	PD	TPI
1971	KC-A	1	0	1.000	10	3	0	0	0	24	26	2	12	20	14.6	4.13	83	.263	.348	2	.286	2	-2	-2	0	0.2
1972	StL-N	0	1	.000	3	1	0	0	0	5¹	8	1	5	2	23.6	10.13	34	.364	.500	0	.000	-0	-4	-4	0	-0.6
1974	Bos-A	1	0	1.000	6	0	0	0	0	6¹	8	1	4	1	18.5	9.95	39	.296	.406	0	—	0	-4	-4	0	-0.6
Total	3	2	1	.667	19	4	0	0	0	35²	42	4	21	23	16.7	6.06	58	.284	.384	2	.250	2	-10	-10	0	-1.0

● REGGIE CLEVELAND
Cleveland, Reginald Leslie   b: 5/23/48, Swift Current, Sask., Canada   BR/TR, 6'1", 195 lbs.   Deb: 10/1/69

YEAR	TM/L	W	L	PCT	G	GS	CG	SH	SV	IP	H	HR	BB	SO	RAT	ERA	ERA+	OAV	OOB	BH	AVG	PB	PR	/A	PD	TPI
1969	StL-N	0	0	—	1	1	0	0	0	4	7	0	1	3	18.0	9.00	40	.368	.400	0	.000	-0	-2	-2	-0	0.0
1970	StL-N	0	4	.000	16	1	0	0	0	26	31	3	18	22	17.0	7.62	54	.298	.402	1	.250	0	-10	-10	-1	-1.4
1971	StL-N	12	12	.500	34	34	10	2	0	222	238	20	53	148	12.0	4.01	90	.271	.317	14	.171	-1	-14	-10	-0	-1.1
1972	StL-N	14	15	.483	33	33	11	3	0	230²	229	21	60	153	11.5	3.94	86	.258	.308	17	.239	3	-13	-14	-1	-1.5
1973	StL-N	14	10	.583	32	32	6	3	0	224	211	13	61	122	11.1	3.01	121	.246	.300	17	.230	4	16	16	-2	1.8
1974	Bos-A	12	14	.462	41	27	0	0	0	221¹	234	25	69	103	12.7	4.31	89	.271	.332	0	—	0	-17	-12	1	-1.2
1975	*Bos-A	13	9	.591	31	20	3	1	0	170²	173	19	52	78	12.0	4.43	92	.263	.320	0	—	0	-12	-7	-0	-0.8
1976	Bos-A	10	9	.526	41	14	3	0	2	170	159	6	61	76	11.9	3.07	127	.246	.315	0	—	0	8	16	-0	0.8
1977	Bos-A	11	8	.579	36	27	9	1	2	190¹	211	20	43	85	12.2	4.26	105	.281	.323	0	—	0	-4	5	-1	-0.1
1978	Bos-A	0	1	.000	1	0	0	0	0	0¹	1	0	0	0	27.0	0.00	—	.333	.333	0	—	0	0	0	0	0.2
	Tex-A	5	7	.417	53	0	0	0	12	75²	65	5	23	46	10.8	3.09	121	.236	.301	0	—	0	6	5	0	1.0
	Yr	5	8	.385	54	0	0	0	12	76	66	5	23	46	10.9	3.08	122	.237	.302	0	—	0	6	6	0	1.2
1979	Mil-A	1	5	.167	29	1	0	0	4	55	77	6	23	22	16.4	6.71	62	.344	.405	0	—	0	-15	-16	-1	-1.8
1980	Mil-A	11	9	.550	45	13	5	2	4	154¹	150	9	46	54	11.9	3.73	104	.254	.317	0	—	0	5	2	-1	0.3
1981	Mil-A	2	3	.400	35	0	0	0	1	64²	57	5	30	18	12.2	5.15	66	.239	.327	0	—	0	-11	-12	-1	-1.0
Total	13	105	106	.498	428	203	57	12	25	1809	1843	152	543	930	12.1	4.01	95	.264	.321	49	.211	6	-63	-38	-9	-4.8

● TEX CLEVENGER
Clevenger, Truman Eugene   b: 7/9/32, Visalia, Cal.   BR/TR, 6'1", 180 lbs.   Deb: 4/18/54

YEAR	TM/L	W	L	PCT	G	GS	CG	SH	SV	IP	H	HR	BB	SO	RAT	ERA	ERA+	OAV	OOB	BH	AVG	PB	PR	/A	PD	TPI
1954	Bos-A	2	4	.333	23	8	1	0	0	67²	67	9	29	43	13.0	4.79	86	.262	.341	3	.214	0	-8	-5	0	-0.4
1956	Was-A	0	0	—	20	1	0	0	0	31²	33	4	21	17	15.3	5.40	80	.264	.370	0	.000	-0	-4	-4	-0	-0.3
1957	Was-A	7	6	.538	52	9	2	0	8	139²	139	11	47	75	12.2	4.19	93	.261	.326	7	.212	1	-6	-5	1	-0.2
1958	Was-A	9	9	.500	**55**	4	0	0	6	124	119	12	50	70	12.3	4.35	88	.251	.324	3	.136	0	-8	-7	3	-0.8
1959	Was-A	8	5	.615	50	7	2	0	8	117¹	114	9	51	71	12.8	3.91	100	.256	.335	4	.174	1	-1	0	4	0.5
1960	Was-A	5	11	.313	53	11	1	0	7	128²	150	10	49	49	14.1	4.20	93	.280	.363	2	.091	-1	-5	-4	-1	-0.7
1961	LA-A	2	1	.667	12	0	0	0	1	16	13	1	13	11	14.6	1.69	267	.220	.361	0	.000	-0	4	5	1	1.0
	NY-A	1	1	.500	21	0	0	0	0	31²	35	3	21	14	16.2	4.83	77	.287	.396	1	.250	1	-3	-4	1	-0.1
	Yr	3	2	.600	33	0	0	0	1	47²	48	4	34	25	15.7	3.78	105	.265	.384	1	.143	0	1	1	1	0.9
1962	NY-A	2	0	1.000	21	0	0	0	0	38	36	3	17	11	12.8	2.84	132	.248	.331	0	.000	-0	5	4	0	0.1
Total	8	36	37	.493	307	40	6	2	30	694²	706	62	298	361	13.2	4.18	94	.265	.342	20	.157	1	-26	-20	8	-0.6

● STEW CLIBURN
Cliburn, Stewart Walker   b: 12/19/56, Jackson, Miss.   BR/TR, 6', 195 lbs.   Deb: 9/17/84   F

YEAR	TM/L	W	L	PCT	G	GS	CG	SH	SV	IP	H	HR	BB	SO	RAT	ERA	ERA+	OAV	OOB	BH	AVG	PB	PR	/A	PD	TPI
1984	Cal-A	0	0	—	1	0	0	0	0	2	3	0	1	1	18.0	13.50	29	.333	.400	0	—	0	-2	-2	0	0.0
1985	Cal-A	9	3	.750	44	0	0	0	6	99	87	5	26	48	10.4	2.09	197	.241	.294	0	—	0	23	22	1	2.9
1988	Cal-A	4	2	.667	40	1	0	0	0	84	83	11	32	42	13.0	4.07	95	.266	.346	0	—	0	-1	-2	0	-0.1
Total	3	13	5	.722	85	1	0	0	6	185	173	16	59	91	11.6	3.11	128	.254	.320	0	—	0	20	18	2	3.0

● JIM CLINTON
Clinton, James Lawrence "Big Jim"   b: 8/10/1850, New York, N.Y.   d: 9/3/21, Brooklyn, N.Y.   BR/TR, 5'8.5", 174 lbs.   Deb: 5/18/1872   MU♦

YEAR	TM/L	W	L	PCT	G	GS	CG	SH	SV	IP	H	HR	BB	SO	RAT	ERA	ERA+	OAV	OOB	BH	AVG	PB	PR	/A	PD	TPI
1875	Atl-n	1	14	.067	17	14	9	0	0	123	146	0	8		11.3	3.22	71	.268	.279	10	.123	-5	-10	-13		-1.4
1876	Lou-N	0	1	.000	1	1	1	0	0	9	12	0	1	1	12.0	6.00	45	.279	.279	22	.338	0	-4	-3	0	-0.2

● TONY CLONINGER
Cloninger, Tony Lee   b: 8/13/40, Lincoln Co., N.C.   BR/TR, 6', 210 lbs.   Deb: 6/15/61   C

YEAR	TM/L	W	L	PCT	G	GS	CG	SH	SV	IP	H	HR	BB	SO	RAT	ERA	ERA+	OAV	OOB	BH	AVG	PB	PR	/A	PD	TPI
1961	Mil-N	7	2	.778	19	10	3	0	0	84	84	16	33	51	12.6	5.25	71	.258	.328	5	.167	-0	-11	-14	1	-1.3
1962	Mil-N	8	3	.727	24	15	4	1	0	111	113	10	46	69	13.0	4.30	88	.264	.337	4	.103	-2	-4	-6	0	-0.7
1963	Mil-N	9	11	.450	41	18	4	2	1	145¹	131	17	63	100	12.1	3.78	85	.239	.320	5	.135	-0	-8	-9	-2	-1.4
1964	Mil-N	19	14	.576	38	34	15	3	2	242²	206	20	82	163	10.8	3.56	99	.231	.298	21	.241	3	-1	-1	-0	0.2
1965	Mil-N	24	11	.686	40	38	16	1	1	279	247	20	119	211	11.9	3.29	107	.236	.316	17	.162	2	8	7	-1	0.9
1966	Atl-N	14	11	.560	39	38	11	1	1	257²	253	29	116	178	13.1	4.12	88	.258	.340	26	.234	10	-15	-14	-0	-0.3
1967	Atl-N	4	7	.364	16	16	1	0	0	76²	85	13	31	55	13.6	5.17	64	.285	.353	5	.200	1	-15	-16	-1	-2.0
1968	Atl-N	1	3	.250	8	8	0	0	0	19	15	0	11	7	12.3	4.26	70	.227	.338	0	.000	-0	-3	-3	0	-0.6
	Cin-N	4	3	.571	17	17	2	2	0	91¹	81	7	48	65	13.0	4.04	78	.233	.331	7	.206	3	-11	-9	-0	-0.4
	Yr	5	6	.455	25	18	2	2	0	110¹	96	7	59	72	12.9	4.08	77	.231	.331	7	.184	3	-13	-12	-1	-1.0
1969	Cin-N	11	17	.393	35	34	6	2	0	189²	184	24	103	103	13.9	5.03	75	.250	.346	12	.167	1	-30	-27	-2	-3.6
1970	*Cin-N	9	7	.563	30	18	0	1	0	148	136	10	76	58	13.3	3.83	105	.249	.347	10	.213	4	3	2	-0	0.3
1971	Cin-N	3	6	.333	28	8	1	0	0	97¹	79	12	49	51	12.2	3.88	86	.230	.332	7	.259	1	-5	-6	-0	-0.3
1972	StL-N	0	2	.000	17	0	0	0	0	26	29	2	19	11	17.0	5.19	66	.293	.412	0	.000	-0	-5	-5	1	-0.3
Total	12	113	97	.538	352	247	63	13	6	1767²	1643	180	798	1120	12.6	4.07	88	.247	.330	119	.192	21	-96	-98	-2	-9.0

● AL CLOSTER
Closter, Alan Edward   b: 6/15/43, Creighton, Neb.   BL/TL, 6'2", 190 lbs.   Deb: 4/19/66

YEAR	TM/L	W	L	PCT	G	GS	CG	SH	SV	IP	H	HR	BB	SO	RAT	ERA	ERA+	OAV	OOB	BH	AVG	PB	PR	/A	PD	TPI
1966	Was-A	0	0	—	1	0	0	0	0	0¹	1	0	2	0	81.0	0.00	—	.500	.750	0	—	0	0	0	0	0.0
1971	NY-A	2	2	.500	14	1	0	0	0	28¹	33	4	13	22	15.2	5.08	64	.289	.372	0	.000	-1	-5	-6	1	-0.8
1972	NY-A	0	0	—	2	0	0	0	0	2¹	2	1	4	2	23.1	11.57	25	.250	.500	0	.000	-0	-2	-2	0	-0.2
1973	Atl-N	0	0	—	4	0	0	0	0	4¹	7	1	4	2	22.8	14.54	27	.389	.500	0	—	0	-5	-5	0	-0.5
Total	4	2	2	.500	21	1	0	0	0	35¹	43	6	23	26	17.3	6.62	50	.303	.407	0	.000	-1	-12	-13	1	-0.8

● ED CLOUGH
Clough, Edgar George "Big Ed" or "Spec"   b: 10/28/06, Wiconisco, Pa.   d: 1/30/44, Harrisburg, Pa.   BL/TL, 6', 188 lbs.   Deb: 8/28/24   ♦

YEAR	TM/L	W	L	PCT	G	GS	CG	SH	SV	IP	H	HR	BB	SO	RAT	ERA	ERA+	OAV	OOB	BH	AVG	PB	PR	/A	PD	TPI
1925	StL-N	0	1	.000	3	1	0	0	0	10	11	1	5	3	15.3	8.10	53	.289	.386	1	.250	-0	-4	-4	-0	-0.4
1926	StL-N	0	0	—	1	0	0	0	0	2	5	0	3	0	40.5	22.50	17	.556	.692	0	—	0	-4	-4	-0	0.0
Total	2	0	1	.000	4	1	0	0	0	12	16	1	8	3	19.5	10.50	40	.340	.456	1	.105	-0	-8	-8	-0	-0.4

● BILL CLOWERS
Clowers, William Perry   b: 8/14/1898, San Marcos, Tex.   d: 1/13/78, Sweeny, Tex.   BL/TL, 5'11", 175 lbs.   Deb: 7/20/26

YEAR	TM/L	W	L	PCT	G	GS	CG	SH	SV	IP	H	HR	BB	SO	RAT	ERA	ERA+	OAV	OOB	BH	AVG	PB	PR	/A	PD	TPI
1926	Bos-A	0	0	—	2	0	0	0	0	1²	2	0	0	0	10.8	—	—	.333	.333	0	—	0	1	1	0	0.0

● BRYAN CLUTTERBUCK
Clutterbuck, Bryan Richard   b: 12/17/59, Detroit, Mich.   BR/TR, 6'4", 223 lbs.   Deb: 7/18/86

YEAR	TM/L	W	L	PCT	G	GS	CG	SH	SV	IP	H	HR	BB	SO	RAT	ERA	ERA+	OAV	OOB	BH	AVG	PB	PR	/A	PD	TPI
1986	Mil-A	0	1	.000	20	0	0	0	0	56²	68	8	16	38	13.7	4.29	101	.296	.347	0	—	0	-1	0	-0	0.0
1989	Mil-A	2	5	.286	14	11	1	0	0	67¹	73	11	16	29	11.9	4.14	93	.269	.310	0	—	0	-2	-2	-2	-0.4
Total	2	2	6	.250	34	11	1	0	0	124	141	19	32	67	12.7	4.21	96	.281	.327	0	—	0	-3	-2	-2	-0.4

● DAVID CLYDE
Clyde, David Eugene   b: 4/22/55, Kansas City, Kan.   BL/TL, 6'1", 185 lbs.   Deb: 6/27/73

YEAR	TM/L	W	L	PCT	G	GS	CG	SH	SV	IP	H	HR	BB	SO	RAT	ERA	ERA+	OAV	OOB	BH	AVG	PB	PR	/A	PD	TPI
1973	Tex-A	4	8	.333	18	18	0	0	0	93¹	106	8	54	74	15.8	5.01	74	.293	.390	0	—	0	-12	-13	-0	-1.3

YEAR TM/L	W	L	PCT	G	GS	CG	SH	SV	IP	H	HR	BB	SO	RAT	ERA	ERA+	OAV	OOB	BH	AVG	PB	PR	/A	PD	TPI
1974 Tex-A	3	9	.250	28	21	4	0	0	117	129	14	47	52	13.8	4.38	81	.286	.359	0	—	0	-10	-11	-2	-1.2
1975 Tex-A	0	1	.000	1	1	0	0	0	7	6	0	6	2	15.4	2.57	146	.273	.429	0	—	0	1	1	-0	0.1
1978 Cle-A	8	11	.421	28	25	5	0	0	153¹	166	4	60	83	13.4	4.28	87	.280	.350	0	—	0	-9	-9	-1	-1.1
1979 Cle-A	3	4	.429	9	8	1	0	0	45²	50	7	13	17	12.6	5.91	72	.279	.332	0	—	0	-9	-8	-0	-1.1
Total 5	18	33	.353	84	73	10	0	0	416¹	457	33	180	228	14.0	4.63	81	.285	.361	0	—	0	-39	-41	-4	-4.6

● **TOM CLYDE** Clyde, Thomas Knox b: 8/17/23, Wachapreague, Va. BR/TR, 6'3", 195 lbs. Deb: 5/31/43

YEAR TM/L	W	L	PCT	G	GS	CG	SH	SV	IP	H	HR	BB	SO	RAT	ERA	ERA+	OAV	OOB	BH	AVG	PB	PR	/A	PD	TPI
1943 Phi-A	0	0	—	4	0	0	0	0	6	7	1	4	0	18.0	9.00	38	.304	.429	0	.000	-0	-4	-4	-0	-0.1

● **ANDY COAKLEY** Coakley, Andrew James (a.k.a. Jack McAllister In 1902)
b: 11/20/1882, Providence, R.I. d: 9/27/63, New York, N.Y. BL/TR, 6', 165 lbs. Deb: 9/17/02

YEAR TM/L	W	L	PCT	G	GS	CG	SH	SV	IP	H	HR	BB	SO	RAT	ERA	ERA+	OAV	OOB	BH	AVG	PB	PR	/A	PD	TPI
1902 Phi-A	2	1	.667	3	3	3	0	0	27	25	0	9	9	12.0	2.67	138	.246	.320	3	.375	1	3	3	0	0.5
1903 Phi-A	0	3	.000	6	3	2	0	0	37²	48	2	11	20	14.6	5.50	56	.309	.362	3	.200	-0	-11	-10	-0	-0.8
1904 Phi-A	4	3	.571	8	8	7	2	0	62	48	1	23	33	10.6	1.89	142	.215	.294	2	.087	-2	5	5	-0	0.3
1905 *Phi-A	18	8	.692	35	31	21	3	0	255	227	2	73	145	10.8	1.84	145	.240	.298	13	.138	-3	23	23	-1	1.9
1906 Phi-A	7	8	.467	22	16	10	0	0	149	144	0	44	59	11.5	3.14	87	.257	.314	7	.143	-2	-7	-7	-3	-1.1
1907 Cin-N	17	16	.515	37	30	21	1	1	265¹	269	1	79	89	12.0	2.34	111	.274	.332	6	.071	-6	4	8	-3	0.0
1908 Cin-N	8	18	.308	32	28	20	4	2	242²	219	3	64	61	10.7	1.86	124	.249	.303	7	.092	-4	14	12	-4	0.4
Chi-N	2	0	1.000	4	3	2	1	0	20¹	14	0	6	7	8.9	0.89	266	.192	.253	0	.000	-1	3	3	-0	0.2
Yr	10	18	.357	36	31	22	5	2	262²	233	3	70	68	10.4	1.78	130	.244	.295	7	.085	-5	17	15	-5	0.6
1909 Chi-N	0	1	.000	1	1	0	0	0	2	7	0	3	1	45.0	18.00	14	.583	.667	0	—	0	-3	-3	0	-1.0
1911 NY-A	0	1	.000	2	1	1	0	0	11²	20	0	2	4	17.0	5.40	67	.377	.400	1	.250	0	-3	-2	0	-0.2
Total 5	58	59	.496	150	124	87	11	3	1072¹	1021	9	314	428	11.4	2.35	111	.256	.314	42	.117	-16	28	32	-12	0.2

● **JIM COATES** Coates, James Alton b: 8/4/32, Farnham, Va. BR/TR, 6'4", 192 lbs. Deb: 9/21/56

YEAR TM/L	W	L	PCT	G	GS	CG	SH	SV	IP	H	HR	BB	SO	RAT	ERA	ERA+	OAV	OOB	BH	AVG	PB	PR	/A	PD	TPI
1956 NY-A	0	0	—	2	0	0	0	0	2	1	0	4	0	27.0	13.50	29	.167	.545	0	—	0	-2	-2	0	-0.1
1959 NY-A	6	1	.857	37	4	2	0	0	100¹	89	10	36	64	11.5	2.87	127	.234	.305	2	.095	-1	11	9	0	0.4
1960 *NY-A★	13	3	.813	35	18	6	2	1	149¹	139	16	66	73	12.5	4.28	84	.248	.330	12	.250	4	-7	-12	-2	-1.0
1961 *NY-A	11	5	.688	43	11	4	1	5	141¹	128	15	53	80	12.0	3.44	108	.243	.321	1	.029	-3	9	4	-0	0.1
1962 *NY-A	7	6	.538	50	6	0	0	6	117²	119	9	50	67	13.3	4.44	84	.263	.343	4	.125	-1	-6	-9	-2	-1.3
1963 Was-A	2	4	.333	20	2	0	0	0	44¹	51	4	21	31	15.2	5.28	70	.297	.383	0	.000	-1	-8	-8	-0	-1.0
Cin-N	0	0	—	9	0	0	0	0	16¹	21	3	6	11	15.4	5.51	61	.313	.378	0	.000	-0	-4	-4	0	-0.1
1965 Cal-A	2	0	1.000	17	0	0	0	3	28	23	1	16	15	12.5	3.54	96	.228	.333	0	.000	-0	-0	-0	-0	-0.1
1966 Cal-A	1	1	.500	9	4	1	1	0	31²	32	3	10	16	11.9	3.98	84	.258	.313	1	.091	-1	-2	-2	-0	-0.2
1967 Cal-A	1	2	.333	25	1	0	0	0	52¹	47	5	23	39	12.7	4.30	73	.244	.336	1	.333	1	-6	-7	0	-0.3
Total 9	43	22	.662	247	46	13	4	15	683¹	650	65	286	396	12.7	4.00	90	.252	.332	21	.131	-3	-15	-30	-4	-3.4

● **GEORGE COBB** Cobb, George Woodworth b: 9/25/1865, Independence, Ia. d: 8/19/26, Pomona, Cal. 6', 168 lbs. Deb: 4/15/1892

YEAR TM/L	W	L	PCT	G	GS	CG	SH	SV	IP	H	HR	BB	SO	RAT	ERA	ERA+	OAV	OOB	BH	AVG	PB	PR	/A	PD	TPI
1892 Bal-N	10	37	.213	53	47	42	0	0	394¹	495	21	140	159	14.9	4.86	71	.295	.356	36	.209	5	-69	-63	2	-5.3

● **HERB COBB** Cobb, Herbert Edward b: 8/6/04, Pinetops, N.C. d: 1/8/80, Tarboro, N.C. BR/TR, 5'11", 150 lbs. Deb: 4/21/29

YEAR TM/L	W	L	PCT	G	GS	CG	SH	SV	IP	H	HR	BB	SO	RAT	ERA	ERA+	OAV	OOB	BH	AVG	PB	PR	/A	PD	TPI
1929 StL-A	0	0	—	1	0	0	0	0	1	3	1	0	0	36.0	36.00	12	.600	.667	—		0	-4	-4	-0	-0.1

● **TY COBB** Cobb, Tyrus Raymond "The Georgia Peach" b: 12/18/1886, Narrows, Ga. d: 7/17/61, Atlanta, Ga. BL/TR, 6'1", 175 lbs. Deb: 8/30/05 MH♦

YEAR TM/L	W	L	PCT	G	GS	CG	SH	SV	IP	H	HR	BB	SO	RAT	ERA	ERA+	OAV	OOB	BH	AVG	PB	PR	/A	PD	TPI
1918 Det-A	0	0	—	2	0	0	0	0	4	6	0	2	0	18.0	4.50	59	.400	.471	161	.382	-1	-1	-0	0.0
1925 Det-A	0	0	—	1	0	0	0	1	1	0	0	0	0	0.00	—	.000	.000	157	.378	1	0	0	0	0.1
Total 2	0	0	—	3	0	0	0	1	5	6	0	2	0	14.4	3.60	83	.333	.400	4189	.366	2	-0	-0	0	0.1

● **JAIME COCANOWER** Cocanower, James Stanley b: 2/14/57, San Juan, P.R. BR/TR, 6'4", 200 lbs. Deb: 9/7/83

YEAR TM/L	W	L	PCT	G	GS	CG	SH	SV	IP	H	HR	BB	SO	RAT	ERA	ERA+	OAV	OOB	BH	AVG	PB	PR	/A	PD	TPI
1983 Mil-A	2	0	1.000	5	3	1	0	0	30	21	1	12	8	10.2	1.80	208	.200	.288	0	—	0	8	6	0	0.7
1984 Mil-A	8	16	.333	33	27	1	0	0	174²	188	13	78	65	14.2	4.02	96	.279	.362	0	—	0	-1	-3	1	-0.2
1985 Mil-A	6	8	.429	24	15	3	1	0	116¹	122	6	73	44	15.7	4.33	96	.274	.386	0	—	0	-2	-2	0	-0.2
1986 Mil-A	0	1	.000	17	2	0	0	0	44²	40	1	38	22	16.1	4.43	98	.248	.398	0	—	0	-1	-1	1	0.1
Total 4	16	25	.390	79	47	5	1	0	365²	371	21	201	139	14.6	3.99	100	.268	.369	0	—	0	3	0	3	0.4

● **GOAT COCHRAN** Cochran, Alvah Jackson "Al" or "Goat" b: 1/31/1891, Concord, Ga. d: 5/23/47, Atlanta, Ga. BR/TR, 5'10", 175 lbs. Deb: 8/25/15

YEAR TM/L	W	L	PCT	G	GS	CG	SH	SV	IP	H	HR	BB	SO	RAT	ERA	ERA+	OAV	OOB	BH	AVG	PB	PR	/A	PD	TPI
1915 Cin-N	0	0	—	1	0	0	0	0	2	5	0	1	22.5	9.00	32	.455	.455	0	—	0	-1	-1	-0	0.0

● **GENE COCREHAM** Cocreham, Eugene b: 11/14/1884, Luling, Tex. d: 12/27/45, Luling, Tex. BR/TR, 6'3.5", 192 lbs. Deb: 9/25/13

YEAR TM/L	W	L	PCT	G	GS	CG	SH	SV	IP	H	HR	BB	SO	RAT	ERA	ERA+	OAV	OOB	BH	AVG	PB	PR	/A	PD	TPI
1913 Bos-N	0	1	.000	1	1	0	0	0	8¹	13	0	4	3	19.4	7.56	43	.371	.450	0	.000	-1	-4	-4	-0	-0.4
1914 Bos-N	3	4	.429	15	3	1	0	0	44²	48	2	27	15	15.1	4.84	57	.296	.397	1	.100	-0	-10	-10	-1	-1.7
1915 Bos-N	0	0	—	1	0	0	0	0	1²	3	0	0	0	16.2	5.40	48	.429	.429	0	—	0	-0	-1	-0	0.0
Total 3	3	5	.375	17	4	1	0	0	54²	64	2	31	18	15.8	5.27	54	.314	.407	1	.071	-1	-15	-15	-2	-2.1

● **CHRIS CODIROLI** Codiroli, Christopher Allen b: 3/26/58, Oxnard, Cal. BR/TR, 6'1", 160 lbs. Deb: 9/11/82

YEAR TM/L	W	L	PCT	G	GS	CG	SH	SV	IP	H	HR	BB	SO	RAT	ERA	ERA+	OAV	OOB	BH	AVG	PB	PR	/A	PD	TPI
1982 Oak-A	1	2	.333	3	3	0	0	0	16²	16	1	4	5	10.8	4.32	90	.246	.290	0	—	0	-0	-1	0	-0.0
1983 Oak-A	12	12	.500	37	31	7	2	1	205²	208	17	72	85	12.6	4.46	86	.264	.331	0	—	0	-9	-14	-2	-1.5
1984 Oak-A	6	4	.600	28	14	1	0	1	89¹	111	16	34	44	14.9	5.84	64	.304	.368	0	—	0	-18	-21	-0	-2.0
1985 Oak-A	14	14	.500	37	37	4	0	0	226	228	23	78	111	12.3	4.46	86	.259	.321	0	—	0	-8	-15	-1	-1.7
1986 Oak-A	5	8	.385	16	16	1	0	0	91²	91	15	38	46	13.4	4.03	96	.250	.324	0	—	0	2	-2	1	-0.1
1987 Oak-A	0	0	—	3	3	0	0	0	11¹	12	1	8	4	16.7	8.74	47	.273	.396	0	—	0	-5	-6	-0	-0.7
1988 Cle-A	0	4	.000	14	2	0	0	0	19¹	32	2	10	12	20.9	9.31	44	.372	.455	0	—	0	-11	-11	-0	-2.2
1990 KC-A	0	1	.000	6	2	0	0	0	10¹	13	1	17	8	29.6	9.58	40	.325	.557	0	—	0	-7	-7	-0	-0.6
Total 8	38	47	.447	144	108	13	2	3	670¹	711	76	261	312	13.4	4.87	79	.270	.341	0	—	0	-58	-76	-2	-8.8

● **SLICK COFFMAN** Coffman, George David b: 12/11/10, Veto, Ala. BR/TR, 6', 155 lbs. Deb: 5/21/37 F

YEAR TM/L	W	L	PCT	G	GS	CG	SH	SV	IP	H	HR	BB	SO	RAT	ERA	ERA+	OAV	OOB	BH	AVG	PB	PR	/A	PD	TPI
1937 Det-A	7	5	.583	28	5	1	0	0	101	121	8	39	22	14.5	4.37	107	.295	.361	5	.172	0	3	3	-1	0.3
1938 Det-A	4	4	.500	39	6	1	0	2	95²	120	6	48	31	15.8	6.02	83	.310	.386	4	.167	-0	-13	-11	-1	-0.9
1939 Det-A	2	1	.667	23	1	0	0	0	42¹	51	4	22	10	15.7	6.38	77	.295	.378	0	.000	-0	-8	-7	0	-0.5
1940 StL-A	2	2	.500	31	4	1	0	1	74²	108	5	23	26	15.8	6.27	73	.334	.379	3	.200	-1	-16	-14	-1	-0.6
Total 4	15	12	.556	121	16	3	0	3	313²	400	23	132	89	15.4	5.60	85	.309	.375	12	.164	-0	-34	-28	-1	-1.7

● **KEVIN COFFMAN** Coffman, Kevin Reese b: 1/19/65, Austin, Tex. BR/TR, 6'2", 175 lbs. Deb: 9/5/87

YEAR TM/L	W	L	PCT	G	GS	CG	SH	SV	IP	H	HR	BB	SO	RAT	ERA	ERA+	OAV	OOB	BH	AVG	PB	PR	/A	PD	TPI
1987 Atl-N	2	3	.400	5	5	0	0	0	25¹	31	2	22	14	19.9	4.62	94	.313	.452	1	.100	-0	-2	-1	1	-0.1
1988 Atl-N	2	6	.250	18	11	0	0	0	67	62	3	54	31	16.1	5.78	64	.251	.393	5	.227	2	-17	-16	0	-1.5
1990 Chi-N	0	2	.000	8	2	0	0	0	18¹	26	0	19	9	22.1	11.29	36	.333	.464	1	.200	0	-15	-15	1	-1.3
Total 3	4	11	.267	31	18	0	0	0	110²	119	5	95	47	18.6	6.42	61	.281	.420	7	.189	1	-34	-31	2	-2.9

● **DICK COFFMAN** Coffman, Samuel Richard b: 12/18/06, Veto, Ala. d: 3/24/72, Athens, Ala. BR/TR, 6'2", 195 lbs. Deb: 4/28/27 F

YEAR TM/L	W	L	PCT	G	GS	CG	SH	SV	IP	H	HR	BB	SO	RAT	ERA	ERA+	OAV	OOB	BH	AVG	PB	PR	/A	PD	TPI
1927 Was-A	0	1	.000	5	2	0	0	0	16	20	2	4	5	13.5	3.38	120	.313	.353	1	.333	0	1	1	0	0.1
1928 StL-A	4	5	.444	29	7	3	0	1	85²	122	7	37	25	16.8	6.09	69	.359	.423	1	.043	-3	-20	-18	-1	-1.9
1929 StL-A	1	1	.500	27	3	1	1	0	52²	61	3	14	11	13.3	5.98	74	.295	.348	0	.000	-1	-10	-9	0	-0.4
1930 StL-A	8	13	.308	38	30	12	1	1	196	250	16	69	54	14.9	5.14	95	.311	.369	9	.136	-1	-11	-6	0	-1.1
1931 StL-A	9	13	.409	32	17	11	2	1	169¹	159	10	51	39	11.3	3.88	119	.241	.298	4	.078	-5	9	14	-2	1.0
1932 StL-A	5	3	.625	9	6	3	0	0	61	66	4	21	14	13.1	3.10	157	.277	.341	1	.045	-2	9	12	-1	1.1
Was-A	1	6	.143	22	9	2	1	0	76¹	92	2	31	17	14.6	4.83	89	.307	.373	2	.091	-1	-3	-4	-1	-0.5

YEAR TM/L	W	L	PCT	G	GS	CG	SH	SV	IP	H	HR	BB	SO	RAT	ERA	ERA+	OAV	OOB	BH	AVG	PB	PR	/A	PD	TPI
Yr	6	9	.400	31	15	5	1	0	137¹	158	5	52	31	13.8	4.06	112	.293	.356	3	.068	-3	6	7	-2	0.6
1933 StL-A	3	7	.300	21	13	3	1	1	81	114	9	39	19	17.2	5.89	79	.329	.399	1	.037	-3	-14	-11	0	-1.4
1934 StL-A	9	10	.474	40	21	6	1	3	173	212	11	59	55	14.2	4.53	110	.303	.358	11	.216	-1	-1	9	0	0.8
1935 StL-A	5	11	.313	41	18	5	0	2	143²	206	14	46	34	15.9	6.14	78	.335	.383	6	.146	-1	-27	-21	-1	-2.2
1936 *NY-N	7	5	.583	42	2	0	0	7	101²	119	7	23	26	12.7	3.90	100	.296	.337	4	.200	-0	1	0	1	0.1
1937 *NY-N	8	3	.727	42	1	0	0	3	80	93	4	31	30	14.4	3.04	128	.289	.359	7	.368	2	**8**	**8**	0	1.3
1938 NY-N	8	4	.667	**51**	3	1	1	**12**	111¹	116	3	21	21	11.3	3.48	108	.268	.306	2	.071	-3	4	4	-2	0.0
1939 NY-N	1	2	.333	28	0	0	0	3	38	50	1	6	9	14.0	3.08	128	.316	.353	0	.000	-1	4	4	-0	0.2
1940 Bos-N	1	5	.167	31	0	0	0	3	48¹	63	4	11	11	14.2	5.40	69	.323	.365	1	.083	-1	-8	-9	-1	-1.2
1945 Phi-N	2	1	.667	14	0	0	0	0	26¹	39	0	2	2	14.0	5.13	75	.351	.363	1	.250	-0	-4	-4	-1	-0.2
Total 15	72	95	.431	472	132	47	8	38	1460¹	1782	92	463	372	14.1	4.65	96	.302	.357	51	.127	-22	-61	-33	-2	-4.3

● DICK COGAN
Cogan, Richard Henry   b: 12/5/1871, Paterson, N.J.   d: 5/2/48, Paterson, N.J.   BR/TR, 5'7", 150 lbs.   Deb: 5/10/1897

YEAR TM/L	W	L	PCT	G	GS	CG	SH	SV	IP	H	HR	BB	SO	RAT	ERA	ERA+	OAV	OOB	BH	AVG	PB	PR	/A	PD	TPI
1897 Bal-N	0	0	—	1	0	0	0	0	2	4	0	2	0	31.5	13.50	31	.411	.549	0	.000	-0	-2	-2	-0	0.0
1899 Chi-N	2	3	.400	5	5	5	0	0	44	54	1	24	9	16.8	4.30	87	.301	.396	5	.200	1	-2	-3	-1	-0.2
1900 NY-N	0	0	—	2	0	0	0	0	8	10	0	6	1	18.0	6.75	54	.305	.413	1	.125	-0	-3	-3	-0	0.0
Total 3	2	3	.400	8	5	5	0	0	54	68	1	32	10	17.5	5.00	75	.307	.406	6	.176	0	-7	-8	-1	-0.2

● HY COHEN
Cohen, Hyman   b: 1/29/31, Brooklyn, N.Y.   BR/TR, 6'5", 220 lbs.   Deb: 4/17/55

YEAR TM/L	W	L	PCT	G	GS	CG	SH	SV	IP	H	HR	BB	SO	RAT	ERA	ERA+	OAV	OOB	BH	AVG	PB	PR	/A	PD	TPI
1955 Chi-N	0	0	—	7	1	0	0	0	17	28	2	10	4	20.6	7.94	51	.378	.459	0	.000	-0	-7	-7	-0	-0.6

● SYD COHEN
Cohen, Sydney Harry   b: 5/7/08, Baltimore, Md.   d: 4/9/88, El Paso, Tex.   BB/TL, 5'11", 180 lbs.   Deb: 9/18/34   F

YEAR TM/L	W	L	PCT	G	GS	CG	SH	SV	IP	H	HR	BB	SO	RAT	ERA	ERA+	OAV	OOB	BH	AVG	PB	PR	/A	PD	TPI
1934 Was-A	1	1	.500	3	2	2	0	0	18	25	2	6	6	15.5	7.50	58	.333	.383	3	.273	0	-6	-6	1	-0.4
1936 Was-A	0	2	.000	19	1	0	0	1	36	44	4	14	21	15.3	5.25	91	.303	.377	0	.000	-1	-1	-2	2	0.0
1937 Was-A	2	4	.333	33	0	0	0	4	55	64	1	17	22	13.3	3.11	142	.299	.351	2	.143	-1	9	8	2	0.9
Total 3	3	7	.300	55	3	2	0	5	109	133	7	37	49	14.3	4.54	100	.306	.365	5	.152	-2	2	-0	5	0.5

● ROCKY COLAVITO
Colavito, Rocco Domenico   b: 8/10/33, New York, N.Y.   BR/TR, 6'3", 190 lbs.   Deb: 9/10/55   C◆

YEAR TM/L	W	L	PCT	G	GS	CG	SH	SV	IP	H	HR	BB	SO	RAT	ERA	ERA+	OAV	OOB	BH	AVG	PB	PR	/A	PD	TPI
1958 Cle-A	0	0	—	1	0	0	0	0	3	0	0	3	1	9.0	0.00	—	.000	.273	148	.303	1	1	1	0	0.0
1968 NY-A	1	0	1.000	1	0	0	0	0	2²	1	0	2	1	10.1	0.00	—	.111	.273	20	.220	0	1	1	-0	0.4
Total 2	1	0	1.000	2	0	0	0	0	5²	1	0	5	2	9.5	0.00	—	.059	.273	1730	.266	1	2	2	0	0.4

● VINCE COLBERT
Colbert, Vincent Norman   b: 12/20/45, Washington, D.C.   BR/TR, 6'4", 200 lbs.   Deb: 5/19/70

YEAR TM/L	W	L	PCT	G	GS	CG	SH	SV	IP	H	HR	BB	SO	RAT	ERA	ERA+	OAV	OOB	BH	AVG	PB	PR	/A	PD	TPI
1970 Cle-A	1	1	.500	23	0	0	0	2	31	37	4	16	17	15.7	7.26	55	.298	.383	0	.000	-0	-12	-11	0	-0.8
1971 Cle-A	7	6	.538	50	10	2	0	2	142²	140	11	71	74	13.7	3.97	96	.265	.356	4	.138	-0	-8	-2	-0	-0.2
1972 Cle-A	1	7	.125	22	11	1	1	0	74²	74	8	38	36	14.3	4.58	70	.267	.370	4	.200	-1	-13	-11	0	-1.1
Total 3	9	14	.391	95	21	3	1	4	248¹	251	23	125	127	14.1	4.57	80	.270	.365	8	.157	0	-33	-25	1	-2.1

● JIM COLBORN
Colborn, James William   b: 5/22/46, Santa Paula, Cal.   BR/TR, 6', 191 lbs.   Deb: 7/13/69

YEAR TM/L	W	L	PCT	G	GS	CG	SH	SV	IP	H	HR	BB	SO	RAT	ERA	ERA+	OAV	OOB	BH	AVG	PB	PR	/A	PD	TPI
1969 Chi-N	1	0	1.000	6	2	0	0	0	14²	15	2	9	4	15.3	3.07	131	.283	.397	0	.000	-0	1	2	0	0.1
1970 Chi-N	3	1	.750	34	6	0	0	4	72²	88	3	23	50	13.9	3.59	125	.298	.351	1	.067	-1	4	7	1	0.4
1971 Chi-N	0	1	.000	14	0	0	0	0	10¹	18	1	3	2	18.3	6.97	56	.383	.420	0	—	0	-4	-3	0	-0.3
1972 Mil-A	7	7	.500	39	12	4	1	0	147²	135	14	43	97	11.0	3.11	97	.245	.302	3	.081	-1	-1	-1	-1	-0.4
1973 Mil-A☆	20	12	.625	43	36	22	4	1	314¹	297	21	87	135	11.1	3.18	118	.251	.304	—	—	0	22	20	2	2.2
1974 Mil-A	10	13	.435	33	31	10	1	0	224	230	27	60	83	11.9	4.06	89	.268	.320	—	—	0	-11	-11	0	-1.0
1975 Mil-A	11	13	.458	36	29	8	1	2	206³	215	18	65	79	12.4	4.27	90	.270	.329	—	—	0	-11	-10	-1	-1.0
1976 Mil-A	9	15	.375	32	32	7	0	0	225²	232	20	54	101	11.5	3.71	94	.268	.312	—	—	0	-5	-5	-0	-0.6
1977 KC-A	18	14	.563	36	35	6	1	0	239	233	22	81	103	12.3	3.62	112	.255	.324	—	—	0	12	11	1	1.4
1978 KC-A	1	2	.333	8	3	0	0	0	28¹	31	4	12	8	14.3	4.76	80	.282	.363	—	—	0	-3	-3	-1	-0.3
Sea-A	3	10	.231	20	19	3	0	0	114¹	125	21	38	26	13.3	5.35	71	.279	.343	—	—	0	-20	-20	3	-1.7
Yr	4	12	.250	28	22	3	0	0	142²	156	25	50	34	13.4	5.24	73	.279	.344	—	—	0	-23	-23	3	-2.0
Total 10	83	88	.485	301	204	60	8	7	1597¹	1619	153	475	688	12.0	3.80	98	.265	.322	4	.073	-3	-17	-14	7	-1.2

● TOM COLCOLOUGH
Colcolough, Thomas Bernard   b: 10/8/1870, Charleston, S.C.   d: 12/10/19, Charleston, S.C.   BR/TR, 5'10.5", 180 lbs.   Deb: 8/1/1893

YEAR TM/L	W	L	PCT	G	GS	CG	SH	SV	IP	H	HR	BB	SO	RAT	ERA	ERA+	OAV	OOB	BH	AVG	PB	PR	/A	PD	TPI
1893 Pit-N	1	0	1.000	8	3	1	0	**2**	43²	45	1	32	7	15.9	4.12	110	.258	.373	2	.143	-0	3	2	-1	0.0
1894 Pit-N	8	5	.615	22	14	11	0	0	148²	207	5	70	29	17.1	7.08	74	.326	.397	14	.200	-3	-29	-30	0	-1.9
1895 Pit-N	1	1	.500	6	5	2	0	0	35¹	38	1	21	15	16.3	5.60	81	.271	.385	5	.333	3	-3	-4	0	0.0
1899 NY-N	4	5	.444	11	8	7	0	0	81²	85	1	41	14	14.2	3.97	95	.268	.357	10	.270	1	-1	-2	1	0.0
Total 4	14	11	.560	47	30	21	0	2	309¹	375	8	164	65	16.1	5.67	82	.296	.382	31	.228	1	-31	-35	0	-1.9

● BERT COLE
Cole, Albert George   b: 7/1/1896, San Francisco, Cal.   d: 5/30/75, San Mateo, Cal.   BL/TL, 6'1", 180 lbs.   Deb: 4/19/21

YEAR TM/L	W	L	PCT	G	GS	CG	SH	SV	IP	H	HR	BB	SO	RAT	ERA	ERA+	OAV	OOB	BH	AVG	PB	PR	/A	PD	TPI
1921 Det-A	7	4	.636	20	11	7	1	1	109²	134	3	36	22	14.3	4.27	100	.305	.363	13	.283	3	0	0	-1	0.2
1922 Det-A	1	6	.143	23	5	2	1	0	79¹	105	4	39	21	16.4	4.88	80	.313	.387	4	.160	-1	-7	-9	0	-0.7
1923 Det-A	13	5	.722	52	13	6	1	5	163	183	9	61	32	13.7	4.14	93	.284	.351	14	.255	2	-3	-5	-1	-0.4
1924 Det-A	3	9	.250	28	11	2	1	2	109¹	135	4	35	16	14.3	4.69	88	.314	.371	10	.270	1	-6	-7	1	-0.5
1925 Det-A	2	3	.400	14	2	1	0	1	33²	44	2	15	7	16.0	5.88	73	.336	.408	3	.273	-0	-6	-6	1	-0.7
Cle-A	1	1	.500	13	2	0	0	1	44	55	1	25	9	16.6	6.14	72	.322	.411	2	.154	-0	-9	-8	-0	-0.4
Yr	3	4	.429	27	4	1	0	2	77²	99	3	40	16	16.2	6.03	73	.327	.407	5	.208	-0	-14	-14	0	-1.1
1927 Chi-A	1	4	.200	27	2	0	0	0	66²	79	3	19	12	13.6	4.72	86	.309	.363	3	.167	-0	-4	-5	2	-0.3
Total 6	28	32	.467	177	46	18	4	10	605²	735	26	230	119	14.6	4.67	87	.305	.370	49	.239	5	-34	-40	2	-2.8

● DAVE COLE
Cole, David Bruce   b: 8/29/30, Williamsport, Md.   BR/TR, 6'2", 175 lbs.   Deb: 9/9/50

YEAR TM/L	W	L	PCT	G	GS	CG	SH	SV	IP	H	HR	BB	SO	RAT	ERA	ERA+	OAV	OOB	BH	AVG	PB	PR	/A	PD	TPI
1950 Bos-N	0	1	.000	4	0	0	0	0	8	7	0	8	3	12.4	1.13	342	.259	.355	0	.000	-0	3	2	-0	0.2
1951 Bos-N	2	4	.333	23	7	1	0	0	67²	64	3	64	33	17.3	4.26	86	.254	.409	6	.353	4	-2	-4	0	0.0
1952 Bos-N	1	1	.500	22	3	0	0	0	44²	38	2	42	22	16.7	4.03	90	.241	.409	0	.000	-1	-1	-2	0	-0.2
1953 Mil-N	0	1	.000	10	0	0	0	0	14²	17	1	14	13	19.0	8.59	46	.279	.413	1	.500	1	-7	-8	-0	-0.3
1954 Chi-N	3	8	.273	18	14	3	0	0	84	74	7	62	37	14.7	5.36	78	.241	.370	6	.214	1	-12	-11	-0	-1.1
1955 Phi-N	0	3	.000	7	3	0	0	0	18¹	21	3	14	6	17.2	6.38	62	.304	.422	1	.200	-0	-5	-5	0	-0.7
Total 6	6	18	.250	84	27	4	0	0	237¹	221	16	199	119	16.2	4.93	79	.253	.395	14	.230	5	-25	-27	1	-2.1

● ED COLE
Cole, Edward William (b: Edward William Kisleauskas)   b: 3/22/09, Wilkes-Barre, Pa.   BR/TR, 5'11", 170 lbs.   Deb: 4/22/38

YEAR TM/L	W	L	PCT	G	GS	CG	SH	SV	IP	H	HR	BB	SO	RAT	ERA	ERA+	OAV	OOB	BH	AVG	PB	PR	/A	PD	TPI
1938 StL-A	1	5	.167	36	6	1	0	3	88²	116	8	48	26	17.2	5.18	96	.313	.399	3	.143	-1	-4	-2	-1	-0.3
1939 StL-A	0	2	.000	6	0	0	0	0	6¹	8	1	6	5	19.9	7.11	68	.308	.438	0	.000	-0	-2	-2	0	-0.4
Total 2	1	7	.125	42	6	1	0	3	95	124	9	54	31	17.3	5.31	94	.312	.401	3	.136	-2	-6	-4	-1	-0.7

● KING COLE
Cole, Leonard Leslie   b: 4/15/1886, Toledo, Iowa   d: 1/6/16, Bay City, Mich.   BR/TR, 6'1", 170 lbs.   Deb: 10/6/09

YEAR TM/L	W	L	PCT	G	GS	CG	SH	SV	IP	H	HR	BB	SO	RAT	ERA	ERA+	OAV	OOB	BH	AVG	PB	PR	/A	PD	TPI
1909 Chi-N	1	1	.500	1	1	1	1	0	9	6	0	3	4	9.0	0.00	—	.194	.265	3	.750	2	3	3	-0	0.7
1910 *Chi-N	20	4	**.833**	33	29	21	4	1	239²	174	2	130	114	11.8	**1.80**	**160**	**.211**	.325	21	.231	2	33	29	-1	3.0
1911 Chi-N	18	7	.720	32	27	13	2	0	221¹	188	3	99	101	12.0	3.13	106	.236	.328	12	.152	-2	7	4	-2	0.0
1912 Chi-N	1	2	.333	8	3	0	0	0	19	36	2	8	9	21.8	10.89	31	.409	.469	2	.400	1	-16	-16	0	-1.9
Pit-N	2	2	.500	12	4	2	0	0	49	61	1	18	11	14.9	6.43	51	.330	.395	2	.133	-1	-16	-17	-0	-1.3
Yr	3	4	.429	20	7	2	0	0	68	97	3	26	20	16.5	7.68	43	.353	.413	4	.200	0	-32	-33	-0	-3.2
1914 NY-A	11	9	.550	33	15	8	2	0	141²	151	6	51	43	12.9	3.30	84	.288	.352	3	.048	-3	-9	-3	-1	-1.9
1915 NY-A	3	3	.500	10	6	2	0	0	51	41	2	22	19	11.6	3.18	92	.224	.317	1	.077	-1	-1	-1	0	-0.3
Total 6	56	27	.675	129	85	47	9	2	730²	657	13	331	298	12.5	3.12	97	.250	.340	43	.173	-2	-0	-7	-6	-1.7

YEAR	TM/L	W	L	PCT	G	GS	CG	SH	SV	IP	H	HR	BB	SO	RAT	ERA	ERA+	OAV	OOB	BH	AVG	PB	PR	/A	PD	TPI

● VICTOR COLE   Cole, Victor Alexander b: 1/23/68, Leningrad, Russia BB/TR, 5'10", 160 lbs. Deb: 6/6/92

| 1992 | Pit-N | 0 | 2 | .000 | 8 | 4 | 0 | 0 | 0 | 23 | 23 | 1 | 14 | 12 | 14.5 | 5.48 | 63 | .261 | .363 | 0 | .000 | -0 | -5 | -5 | 0 | -0.5 |

● JOHN COLEMAN   Coleman, John b: Bristol, Pa. TR, Deb: 6/23/1890

| 1890 | Phi-N | 0 | 1 | .000 | 1 | 1 | 0 | 0 | 0 | 1² | 4 | 0 | 3 | 2 | 37.8 | 21.60 | 17 | .448 | .586 | 0 | — | 0 | -3 | -3 | -0 | -1.0 |

● JOHN COLEMAN   Coleman, John b: 1874, Lees Summit, Mo. TL , 5'10", 174 lbs. Deb: 9/25/1895

| 1895 | StL-N | 0 | 1 | .000 | 1 | 1 | 1 | 0 | 0 | 8 | 12 | 1 | 8 | 5 | 23.6 | 13.50 | 36 | .341 | .475 | 1 | .200 | -0 | -8 | -8 | 0 | -0.6 |

● JOHN COLEMAN   Coleman, John Francis b: 3/6/1863, Saratoga Springs, N.Y. d: 5/31/22, Detroit, Mich. BL/TR, 5'9.5", 170 lbs. Deb: 5/1/1883 ◆

1883	Phi-N	12	48	.200	65	61	59	3	0	538¹	772	17	48	159	13.7	4.87	63	.309	.322	83	.234	4	-103	-106	1	-8.1
1884	Phi-N	5	15	.250	21	19	14	1	0	154¹	216	9	22	37	13.9	4.90	61	.308	.329	42	.246	2	-33	-33	1	-2.9
	Phi-a	0	2	.000	3	2	2	0	0	21	28	0	2	5	14.6	3.43	99	.304	.347	22	.206	-0	-0	-0	-0	0.0
1885	Phi-a	2	2	.500	8	3	3	0	0	60¹	82	0	5	12	13.0	3.43	100	.366	.380	119	.299	2	-1	-0	-0	0.2
1886	Phi-a	1	1	.500	3	1	1	0	0	20²	18	1	5	2	10.5	2.61	134	.225	.279	121	.246	0	2	2	-0	0.2
1889	Phi-a	3	2	.600	5	5	4	0	0	34	38	2	14	6	14.0	2.91	130	.274	.345	1	.053	-2	4	3	1	0.2
1890	Pit-N	0	2	.000	2	1	1	0	0	14	28	1	6	3	21.9	9.64	34	.403	.451	2	.182	-0	-9	-10	-0	-0.9
Total	6	23	72	.242	107	93	84	4	0	842²	1182	30	102	224	13.8	4.68	67	.311	.330	645	.257	7	-142	-144	3	-11.3

● JOE COLEMAN   Coleman, Joseph Howard b: 2/3/47, Boston, Mass. BR/TR, 6'3", 195 lbs. Deb: 9/28/65 FC

1965	Was-A	2	0	1.000	2	2	2	0	0	18	9	0	8	7	8.5	1.50	232	.153	.254	0	.000	-1	4	4	1	0.5
1966	Was-A	1	0	1.000	1	1	1	0	0	9	6	0	2	4	8.0	2.00	173	.188	.235	0	.000	-0	1	1	0	0.2
1967	Was-A	8	9	.471	28	22	3	0	0	134	154	6	47	77	14.1	4.63	68	.291	.359	2	.056	-1	-21	-22	-2	-2.9
1968	Was-A	12	16	.429	33	33	12	2	0	223	212	19	51	139	11.1	3.27	89	.250	.302	9	.129	-1	-7	-9	-1	-1.3
1969	Was-A	12	13	.480	40	36	12	4	1	247²	222	26	100	182	11.9	3.27	106	.243	.322	9	.107	-2	10	5	1	0.3
1970	Was-A	8	12	.400	39	29	6	1	0	218²	199	25	89	152	11.6	3.58	99	.233	.311	8	.119	2	3	-1	0	0.2
1971	Det-A	20	9	.690	39	38	16	3	0	286	241	17	96	236	10.8	3.15	114	.229	.298	9	.094	-3	10	14	-2	0.8
1972	*Det-A†	19	14	.576	40	39	9	3	0	280	216	23	110	222	10.8	2.80	112	.214	.297	2	.110	-2	8	11	-1	0.9
1973	Det-A	23	15	.605	40	40	13	2	0	288¹	283	32	93	202	12.0	3.53	116	.258	.322	0	—	0	9	18	-0	1.9
1974	Det-A	14	12	.538	41	41	11	2	0	285²	272	30	158	177	13.9	4.32	88	.254	.356	0	—	0	-22	-16	-2	-1.3
1975	Det-A	10	18	.357	31	31	6	1	0	201	234	27	85	125	14.7	5.55	72	.291	.366	0	—	0	-40	-34	0	-4.1
1976	Det-A	2	5	.286	12	12	1	0	0	66²	80	1	34	38	16.1	4.86	76	.308	.398	0	—	0	-10	-9	2	-0.7
	Chi-N	2	8	.200	39	4	0	0	2	79	72	9	35	42	12.4	4.10	94	.246	.330	2	.154	-0	-5	-2	-0	-0.3
1977	Oak-A	4	4	.500	43	12	2	0	0	127²	114	11	49	55	11.6	2.96	136	.241	.314	0	—	0	16	15	-0	0.8
1978	Oak-A	3	0	1.000	10	0	0	0	0	19²	12	1	5	4	7.8	1.37	265	.185	.243	0	—	0	5	5	0	0.8
	Tor-A	2	0	1.000	31	0	0	0	0	60²	67	6	30	28	14.5	4.60	85	.286	.370	0	—	0	-6	-5	-1	-0.3
	Yr	5	0	1.000	41	0	0	0	0	80¹	79	7	35	32	12.9	3.81	101	.263	.342	0	—	0	-0	-0	-1	0.5
1979	SF-N	0	0	—	5	0	0	0	0	3²	3	0	2	0	14.7	0.00	—	.231	.375	0	—	0	2	1	0	0.0
	Pit-N	0	0	—	10	0	0	0	0	20²	29	1	9	14	17.0	6.10	64	.326	.394	1	.200	0	-5	-5	-1	0.0
	Yr	0	0	—	15	0	0	0	0	24¹	32	1	11	14	16.3	5.18	74	.308	.379	1	.200	0	-4	-4	-1	0.0
Total	15	142	135	.513	484	340	94	18	7	2569¹	2416	234	1003	1728	12.3	3.70	97	.250	.327	49	.106	-10	-48	-28	-2	-4.4

● JOE COLEMAN   Coleman, Joseph Patrick b: 7/30/22, Medford, Mass. BR/TR, 6'2.5", 200 lbs. Deb: 9/19/42 F

1942	Phi-A	0	1	.000	1	0	0	0	0	6	8	0	1	0	13.5	3.00	126	.308	.333	0	.000	-1	0	1	-0	0.0
1946	Phi-A	0	2	.000	4	2	0	0	0	13	19	1	8	8	18.7	5.54	64	.345	.429	2	.400	1	-3	-3	-0	-0.4
1947	Phi-A	6	12	.333	32	21	9	2	1	160¹	171	17	62	65	13.1	4.32	88	.275	.341	7	.146	-1	-11	-9	-2	-1.3
1948	Phi-A★	14	13	.519	33	29	13	3	0	215²	224	11	90	86	13.1	4.09	105	.269	.341	9	.122	-4	5	5	-1	0.0
1949	Phi-A	13	14	.481	33	30	18	1	1	240	249	12	127	109	14.2	3.86	107	.271	.361	14	.177	0	9	7	-5	0.3
1950	Phi-A	0	5	.000	15	6	2	0	0	54	74	9	50	12	20.7	8.50	54	.332	.454	1	.059	-1	-24	-24	-2	-1.9
1951	Phi-A	1	6	.143	28	9	1	0	1	96¹	117	12	59	34	16.7	5.98	72	.305	.402	7	.259	1	-20	-18	-1	-1.2
1953	Phi-A	3	4	.429	21	9	2	1	0	90	85	8	49	18	13.5	4.00	107	.254	.352	8	.286	1	-0	3	-2	0.2
1954	Bal-A	13	17	.433	33	32	15	4	0	221¹	184	16	96	103	11.5	3.50	102	.232	.317	13	.176	2	6	6	1	0.7
1955	Bal-A	0	1	.000	6	2	0	0	0	11²	19	5	10	4	23.1	10.80	35	.373	.484	2	.667	1	-9	-9	-0	-0.6
	Det-A	2	1	.667	17	0	0	0	3	25¹	22	1	14	7	13.5	3.20	120	.239	.346	3	.750	1	2	2	0	0.4
	Yr	2	2	.500	23	2	0	0	3	37	41	6	24	11	16.1	5.59	69	.281	.386	5	.714	3	-7	-7	-0	-0.2
Total	10	52	76	.406	223	140	60	11	6	1134	1172	92	566	444	13.9	4.38	92	.271	.357	66	.182	2	-44	-44	-12	-3.8

● PERCY COLEMAN   Coleman, Pierce D. b: 10/15/1876, Mason, Ohio d: 2/16/48, Van Nuys, Cal. Deb: 7/2/1897

1897	StL-N	1	2	.333	12	4	2	0	0	57¹	99	0	32	10	21.7	8.16	54	.376	.456	6	.214	-1	-25	-24	1	-0.9
1898	Cin-N	0	1	.000	1	1	1	0	0	9	13	0	3	2	17.0	3.00	128	.335	.397	0	.000	-1	1	1	-0	0.0
Total	2	1	3	.250	13	5	3	0	0	66¹	112	0	35	12	21.0	7.46	58	.370	.449	6	.194	-1	-24	-23	0	-0.9

● RIP COLEMAN   Coleman, Walter Gary b: 7/31/31, Troy, N.Y. BL/TL, 6'2", 185 lbs. Deb: 8/15/55

1955	*NY-A	2	1	.667	10	6	0	0	0	29	40	1	16	15	17.7	5.28	71	.331	.413	2	.200	1	-4	-5	0	-0.4
1956	NY-A	3	5	.375	29	9	0	0	2	88¹	97	6	42	42	14.3	3.67	105	.285	.366	1	.042	-3	5	2	0	-0.1
1957	KC-A	0	7	.000	19	6	1	1	0	41	53	5	25	15	17.1	5.93	67	.325	.415	0	.000	-1	-10	-9	0	-1.4
1959	KC-A	2	10	.167	29	11	2	0	2	81	85	8	34	54	13.3	4.56	88	.273	.347	2	.080	-2	-6	-5	-0	-0.9
	Bal-A	0	0	—	3	0	0	0	0	4	4	0	2	4	13.5	0.00	—	.267	.353	0	—	0	2	2	1	0.1
	Yr	2	10	.167	32	11	2	0	2	85	89	8	36	58	13.2	4.34	92	.271	.342	2	.080	-2	-5	-3	1	-0.8
1960	Bal-A	0	2	.000	5	1	0	0	0	4	4	1	5	0	31.5	11.25	30	.444	.583	0	.000	-0	-3	-3	0	-1.3
Total	5	7	25	.219	95	33	3	1	5	247¹	287	21	124	130	15.1	4.58	85	.296	.379	5	.072	-5	-17	-18	2	-4.0

● ALLAN COLLAMORE   Collamore, Allan Edward b: 6/5/1887, Worcester, Mass. d: 8/8/80, Battle Creek, Mich. BR/TR, 6', 170 lbs. Deb: 4/15/11

1911	Phi-A	0	1	.000	2	0	0	0	0	2	6	0	3	1	49.5	36.00	9	.600	.733	0	—	0	-7	-7	-0	-1.9
1914	Cle-A	3	7	.300	27	8	3	0	0	105¹	100	3	49	32	13.2	3.25	89	.264	.357	3	.094	-2	-6	-4	-1	-0.7
1915	Cle-A	2	5	.286	11	6	5	2	0	64¹	52	1	22	15	10.4	2.38	128	.235	.305	4	.174	0	4	5	1	0.6
Total	3	5	13	.278	40	14	8	2	0	171²	158	4	74	48	12.6	3.30	89	.259	.347	7	.127	-1	-9	-7	-0	-2.0

● HAP COLLARD   Collard, Earl Clinton b: 8/29/1898, Williams, Ariz. d: 7/9/68, Jamestown, Cal. BR/TR, 6', 170 lbs. Deb: 4/23/27

1927	Cle-A	0	0	—	4	0	0	0	0	5¹	8	0	3	2	18.6	5.06	83	.333	.407	0	—	0	-1	-1	0	0.0
1928	Cle-A	0	0	—	1	0	0	0	0	4	4	0	4	1	18.0	2.25	184	.250	.400	1	1.000	0	1	1	-0	0.0
1930	Phi-N	6	12	.333	30	15	4	0	0	127	188	15	39	25	16.3	6.80	80	.350	.397	9	.205	-2	-26	-19	1	-2.1
Total	3	6	12	.333	35	15	4	0	0	136¹	200	15	46	28	16.4	6.60	81	.347	.398	10	.222	-1	-26	-19	1	-2.1

● ORLIN COLLIER   Collier, Orlin Edward b: 2/17/07, E.Prairie, Mo. d: 9/9/44, Memphis, Tenn. BR/TR, 5'11.5", 180 lbs. Deb: 9/11/31

| 1931 | Det-A | 0 | 1 | .000 | 2 | 2 | 0 | 0 | 0 | 11 | 17 | 0 | 7 | 3 | 20.9 | 7.84 | 59 | .362 | .444 | 0 | .000 | -0 | -4 | -4 | -0 | -0.3 |

● HARRY COLLIFLOWER   Colliflower, James Harry "Collie" b: 3/11/1869, Petersville, Md. d: 8/12/61, Washington, D.C. BL/TL, 5'11.5", 175 lbs. Deb: 7/21/1899 U

| 1899 | Cle-N | 1 | 11 | .083 | 14 | 12 | 11 | 0 | 0 | 98 | 152 | 6 | 41 | 8 | 18.7 | 8.17 | 45 | .353 | .423 | 23 | .303 | 2 | -47 | -49 | 0 | -4.0 |

● DAN COLLINS   Collins, Daniel Thomas b: 7/12/1854, St.Louis, Mo. d: 9/21/1883, New Orleans, La. Deb: 6/8/1874 ◆

| 1874 | Chi-n | 1 | 1 | .500 | 2 | 2 | 1 | 0 | 0 | 11 | 21 | 0 | 2 | | 18.8 | 5.73 | 53 | .368 | .390 | 1 | .083 | -1 | -3 | -3 | | -0.4 |

● DON COLLINS   Collins, Donald Edward b: 9/15/52, Lyons, Ga. BR/TL, 6'2", 195 lbs. Deb: 5/4/77

| 1977 | Atl-N | 3 | 9 | .250 | 40 | 6 | 0 | 0 | 2 | 70² | 82 | 8 | 41 | 27 | 15.8 | 5.09 | 87 | .299 | .392 | 0 | .000 | -1 | -9 | -5 | -1 | -1.1 |

YEAR TM/L	W	L	PCT	G	GS	CG	SH	SV	IP	H	HR	BB	SO	RAT	ERA	ERA+	OAV	OOB	BH	AVG	PB	PR	/A	PD	TPI
1980 Cle-A	0	0	—	4	0	0	0	0	6	9	0	7	0	24.0	7.50	54	.346	.485	0	—	0	-2	-2	-0	0.0
Total 2	3	9	.250	44	6	0	0	2	76²	91	8	48	27	16.4	5.28	84	.303	.401	0	.000	-1	-12	-7	-1	-1.1

● **RIP COLLINS**   Collins, Harry Warren b: 2/26/1896, Weatherford, Tex. d: 5/27/68, Bryan, Tex.   BR/TR, 6'1", 205 lbs. Deb: 4/19/20

YEAR TM/L	W	L	PCT	G	GS	CG	SH	SV	IP	H	HR	BB	SO	RAT	ERA	ERA+	OAV	OOB	BH	AVG	PB	PR	/A	PD	TPI
1920 NY-A	14	8	.636	36	18	10	2	1	187¹	171	6	79	66	12.7	3.22	119	.247	.337	8	.129	-4	12	13	-1	0.8
1921 *NY-A	11	5	.688	28	16	7	2	0	137¹	158	6	78	64	16.1	5.44	78	.293	.392	1	.196	-1	-18	-18	-1	-2.0
1922 Bos-A	14	11	.560	32	29	15	3	0	210²	219	4	103	69	14.2	3.76	109	.274	.364	12	.158	-3	7	8	-1	0.5
1923 Det-A	3	7	.300	17	14	3	1	0	92¹	104	3	22	25	13.3	4.87	79	.284	.342	3	.111	-2	-9	-10	0	-1.1
1924 Det-A	14	7	.667	34	30	11	1	0	216	199	6	63	75	11.1	3.21	128	.249	.307	11	.145	-5	25	22	0	1.4
1925 Det-A	6	11	.353	26	20	5	0	0	140	149	7	52	33	13.3	4.56	94	.281	.352	5	.119	-4	-3	-4	4	-0.4
1926 Det-A	8	8	.500	30	13	5	3	1	122	128	4	44	44	13.2	2.73	149	.278	.350	6	.154	-1	17	18	1	2.2
1927 Det-A	13	7	.650	30	25	10	1	0	172²	207	5	59	37	14.3	4.69	90	.312	.375	11	.204	0	-11	-9	5	-0.5
1929 StL-A	11	6	.647	26	20	10	1	1	155¹	162	16	73	47	14.0	4.00	111	.270	.355	17	.274	1	4	7	0	1.1
1930 StL-A	9	7	.563	35	20	6	1	2	171²	168	11	63	75	12.4	4.35	112	.259	.330	7	.130	-2	6	10	-0	0.6
1931 StL-A	5	5	.500	17	14	2	0	0	107	130	5	38	34	14.2	3.79	122	.307	.366	5	.147	-1	7	10	1	0.9
Total 11	108	82	.568	311	219	84	15	5	1712¹	1795	73	674	569	13.4	3.99	106	.275	.351	96	.165	-18	38	45	9	3.5

● **ORTH COLLINS**   Collins, Orth Stein "Buck" b: 4/27/1880, Lafayette, Ind. d: 12/13/49, Ft.Lauderdale, Fla BL/TR, 6', 150 lbs. Deb: 6/1/04 ♦

YEAR TM/L	W	L	PCT	G	GS	CG	SH	SV	IP	H	HR	BB	SO	RAT	ERA	ERA+	OAV	OOB	BH	AVG	PB	PR	/A	PD	TPI
1909 Was-A	0	0	—	1	0	0	0	0	1	0	0	0	1	0.0	0.00	—	.000	.000	0	.000	-0	0	0	-0	0.0

● **PHIL COLLINS**   Collins, Philip Eugene "Fidgety Phil" b: 8/27/01, Chicago, Ill. d: 8/14/48, Chicago, Ill. BR/TR, 5'11", 175 lbs. Deb: 10/7/23

YEAR TM/L	W	L	PCT	G	GS	CG	SH	SV	IP	H	HR	BB	SO	RAT	ERA	ERA+	OAV	OOB	BH	AVG	PB	PR	/A	PD	TPI
1923 Chi-N	1	0	1.000	1	1	0	0	0	5	8	0	1	2	16.2	3.60	111	.400	.429	0	.000	-0	0	0	1	0.1
1929 Phi-N	9	7	.563	43	11	3	0	5	153¹	172	18	83	61	15.2	5.75	90	.284	.374	11	.190	-0	-18	-10	-1	-1.0
1930 Phi-N	16	11	.593	47	25	17	1	3	239	287	22	86	87	14.4	4.78	114	.299	.363	22	.253	3	5	18	-2	1.8
1931 Phi-N	12	16	.429	42	27	16	2	4	240¹	268	14	83	73	13.3	3.86	110	.283	.344	16	.168	-4	0	10	1	0.8
1932 Phi-N	14	12	.538	43	21	6	0	3	184¹	231	14	65	66	14.7	5.27	84	.314	.375	18	.265	2	-29	-18	-0	-2.0
1933 Phi-N	8	13	.381	42	13	5	1	**6**	151	178	9	57	40	14.4	4.11	93	.293	.360	7	.132	-2	-13	-5	-1	-1.1
1934 Phi-N	13	18	.419	45	32	15	0	1	254	277	30	87	72	13.0	4.18	113	.273	.333	15	.170	-5	-3	15	-3	0.9
1935 Phi-N	0	2	.000	3	3	0	0	0	14²	24	5	9	4	20.3	11.66	39	.348	.423	0	.000	-1	-12	-12	0	-1.2
StL-N	7	6	.538	26	8	2	0	2	82²	96	6	26	18	13.6	4.57	90	.290	.347	4	.160	-1	-5	-4	-1	-0.8
Yr	7	8	.467	29	11	2	0	2	97¹	120	11	35	22	14.6	5.64	74	.300	.361	4	.129	-2	-18	-16	-1	-2.0
Total 8	80	85	.485	292	141	64	4	24	1324¹	1541	125	497	423	14.1	4.66	100	.291	.356	93	.193	-8	-75	-3	-7	-2.5

● **RAY COLLINS**   Collins, Raymond Williston b: 2/11/1887, Colchester, Vt. d: 1/9/70, Burlington, Vt. BL/TL, 6'1", 185 lbs. Deb: 7/19/09

YEAR TM/L	W	L	PCT	G	GS	CG	SH	SV	IP	H	HR	BB	SO	RAT	ERA	ERA+	OAV	OOB	BH	AVG	PB	PR	/A	PD	TPI
1909 Bos-A	4	3	.571	12	8	4	2	0	73²	70	2	18	31	10.8	2.81	89	.269	.317	3	.130	-0	-3	-3	1	-0.2
1910 Bos-A	13	11	.542	35	26	18	4	1	244²	205	4	41	109	9.4	1.62	158	.229	.264	15	.179	-1	25	25	-4	2.1
1911 Bos-A	11	12	.478	31	24	14	0	1	194²	184	1	44	86	10.7	2.40	136	.256	.302	9	.150	-0	20	19	-3	1.7
1912 *Bos-A	13	8	.619	27	24	17	4	0	199¹	192	4	42	82	10.7	2.53	135	.256	.297	11	.169	-0	17	19	-3	1.6
1913 Bos-A	19	8	.704	30	30	19	3	0	246²	242	3	37	88	10.3	2.63	112	.263	.293	12	.150	-2	8	9	-4	0.7
1914 Bos-A	20	13	.606	39	30	16	6	0	272¹	252	3	56	72	10.2	2.51	107	.258	.298	11	.139	-0	7	5	-6	0.0
1915 Bos-A	4	7	.364	25	9	2	0	2	104²	101	1	31	43	11.4	4.30	65	.261	.317	8	.286	5	-16	-18	-3	-1.7
Total 7	84	62	.575	199	151	90	19	4	1336	1246	15	269	511	10.3	2.51	115	.254	.294	69	.165	6	59	58	-22	4.2

● **JACKIE COLLUM**   Collum, Jack Dean b: 6/21/27, Victor, Ia. BL/TL, 5'7", 163 lbs. Deb: 9/21/51

YEAR TM/L	W	L	PCT	G	GS	CG	SH	SV	IP	H	HR	BB	SO	RAT	ERA	ERA+	OAV	OOB	BH	AVG	PB	PR	/A	PD	TPI
1951 StL-N	2	1	.667	3	2	1	1	0	17	11	0	10	5	11.1	1.59	250	.204	.328	3	.429	1	4	4	0	1.0
1952 StL-N	0	0	—	2	0	0	0	0	3	2	0	1	0	9.0	0.00	—	.200	.273	0	—	1	1	1	0	0.0
1953 StL-N	0	0	—	7	0	0	0	0	11¹	15	1	4	5	15.1	6.35	67	.326	.380	0	.000	-0	-3	-3	1	0.1
Cin-N	7	11	.389	30	12	4	1	3	124²	123	8	39	51	12.1	3.75	116	.263	.328	10	.278	3	7	8	1	1.4
Yr	7	11	.389	37	12	4	1	3	136	138	9	43	56	12.4	3.97	109	.269	.333	10	.256	2	5	6	2	1.5
1954 Cin-N	7	3	.700	36	2	1	0	0	79	86	8	32	28	14.0	3.76	112	.283	.361	3	.231	2	3	4	3	0.9
1955 Cin-N	9	8	.529	32	17	5	0	1	134	128	17	37	49	11.2	3.63	117	.254	.308	10	.250	2	6	9	-0	1.3
1956 StL-N	6	2	.750	38	1	0	0	7	60	63	6	27	17	13.8	4.20	90	.281	.364	3	.214	1	-3	-3	1	-0.3
1957 Chi-N	1	1	.500	9	0	0	0	1	10²	9	0	9	7	15.2	6.75	57	.211	.375	0	—	0	-3	-3	-0	-0.6
Bro-N	0	0	—	3	0	0	0	0	4¹	7	1	1	3	16.6	8.31	50	.368	.400	0	—	0	-2	-2	-0	-0.1
Yr	1	1	.500	12	0	0	0	1	15	15	1	10	10	15.0	7.20	55	.254	.362	0	—	0	-6	-5	-0	-0.6
1958 LA-N	0	0	—	2	0	0	0	0	3¹	4	0	2	1	16.2	8.10	51	.308	.400	0	—	0	-2	-2	-0	-0.3
1962 Min-A	0	2	.000	8	3	0	0	0	15¹	29	1	11	5	23.5	11.15	37	.414	.494	0	.000	-0	-12	-12	0	-1.3
Cle-A	0	0	—	1	0	0	0	0	1¹	4	0	0	1	27.0	13.50	29	.571	.571	0	—	0	-1	-1	0	-0.0
Yr	0	2	.000	9	3	0	0	0	16²	33	1	11	6	23.8	11.34	36	.418	.489	0	.000	-0	-14	-13	0	-1.3
Total 9	32	28	.533	171	37	11	2	12	464	480	44	173	171	13.0	4.15	101	.273	.344	29	.246	8	-4	1	6	2.5

● **DICK COLPAERT**   Colpaert, Richard Charles b: 1/3/44, Fraser, Mich. BR/TR, 5'10", 182 lbs. Deb: 7/21/70

YEAR TM/L	W	L	PCT	G	GS	CG	SH	SV	IP	H	HR	BB	SO	RAT	ERA	ERA+	OAV	OOB	BH	AVG	PB	PR	/A	PD	TPI
1970 Pit-N	1	0	1.000	8	0	0	0	0	10²	9	3	8	6	14.3	5.91	66	.237	.370	0	—	0	-2	-2	-0	-0.2

● **LOYD COLSON**   Colson, Loyd Albert b: 11/4/47, Wellington, Tex. BR/TR, 6'1", 190 lbs. Deb: 9/25/70

YEAR TM/L	W	L	PCT	G	GS	CG	SH	SV	IP	H	HR	BB	SO	RAT	ERA	ERA+	OAV	OOB	BH	AVG	PB	PR	/A	PD	TPI
1970 NY-A	0	0	—	1	0	0	0	0	2	3	0	3	2	13.5	4.50	78	.333	.333	0	—	-0	-0	-0	-0	0.0

● **LARRY COLTON**   Colton, Lawrence Robert b: 6/8/42, Los Angeles, Cal. BL/TR, 6'3", 200 lbs. Deb: 5/6/68

YEAR TM/L	W	L	PCT	G	GS	CG	SH	SV	IP	H	HR	BB	SO	RAT	ERA	ERA+	OAV	OOB	BH	AVG	PB	PR	/A	PD	TPI
1968 Phi-N	0	0	—	1	0	0	0	0	2	3	0	0	4	13.5	4.50	67	.333	.333	0	—	-0	-0	-0	-0	0.0

● **GEOFF COMBE**   Combe, Geoffrey Wade b: 2/1/56, Melrose, Mass. BR/TR, 6'2", 185 lbs. Deb: 9/2/80

YEAR TM/L	W	L	PCT	G	GS	CG	SH	SV	IP	H	HR	BB	SO	RAT	ERA	ERA+	OAV	OOB	BH	AVG	PB	PR	/A	PD	TPI
1980 Cin-N	0	0	—	4	0	0	0	0	6²	9	0	4	10	17.6	10.80	33	.346	.433	0	—	0	-5	-5	-0	0.0
1981 Cin-N	1	0	1.000	14	0	0	0	0	17²	27	3	10	9	18.8	7.64	46	.370	.446	0	—	0	-8	-8	-0	-0.5
Total 2	1	0	1.000	18	0	0	0	0	24¹	36	3	14	19	18.5	8.51	42	.364	.442	0	—	0	-13	-13	-0	-0.5

● **PAT COMBS**   Combs, Patrick Dennis b: 10/29/66, Newport, R.I. BL/TL, 6'3", 200 lbs. Deb: 9/5/89

YEAR TM/L	W	L	PCT	G	GS	CG	SH	SV	IP	H	HR	BB	SO	RAT	ERA	ERA+	OAV	OOB	BH	AVG	PB	PR	/A	PD	TPI
1989 Phi-N	4	0	1.000	6	6	1	1	0	38²	36	2	6	30	9.8	2.09	169	.248	.278	2	.167	0	6	6	-1	0.7
1990 Phi-N	10	10	.500	32	31	3	2	0	183¹	179	12	86	108	13.2	4.07	94	.257	.342	9	.150	0	-6	-5	-0	-0.5
1991 Phi-N	2	6	.250	14	13	1	0	0	64¹	64	7	43	41	15.2	4.90	75	.254	.367	2	.133	1	-9	-9	-0	-1.0
1992 Phi-N	1	1	.500	4	4	0	0	0	18²	20	0	12	11	15.4	7.71	44	.278	.381	1	.125	1	-9	-9	1	-0.7
Total 4	17	17	.500	56	54	5	3	0	305	299	21	147	190	13.3	4.22	88	.257	.343	14	.147	2	-17	-16	-1	-1.5

● **JORGE COMELLAS**   Comellas, Jorge (Pous) "Pancho" b: 12/7/16, Havana, Cuba BR/TR, 6', 190 lbs. Deb: 4/19/45

YEAR TM/L	W	L	PCT	G	GS	CG	SH	SV	IP	H	HR	BB	SO	RAT	ERA	ERA+	OAV	OOB	BH	AVG	PB	PR	/A	PD	TPI
1945 Chi-N	0	2	.000	7	1	0	0	0	16	12	1	6	6	12.8	4.50	81	.244	.333	0	.000	-0	-1	-1	1	-0.1

● **STEVE COMER**   Comer, Steven Michael b: 1/13/54, Minneapolis, Minn. BB/TR, 6'3", 205 lbs. Deb: 4/15/78 C

YEAR TM/L	W	L	PCT	G	GS	CG	SH	SV	IP	H	HR	BB	SO	RAT	ERA	ERA+	OAV	OOB	BH	AVG	PB	PR	/A	PD	TPI
1978 Tex-A	11	5	.688	30	11	3	2	1	117¹	107	5	37	65	11.1	2.30	163	.249	.310	0	—	0	19	19	1	2.6
1979 Tex-A	17	12	.586	36	36	6	1	0	242¹	230	24	84	86	12.0	3.68	113	.252	.320	0	—	0	14	13	-0	1.4
1980 Tex-A	2	4	.333	12	11	0	0	0	41²	65	5	22	9	19.2	7.99	49	.367	.443	0	—	0	-18	-19	-0	-2.2
1981 Tex-A	8	2	.800	36	1	0	0	6	77¹	70	1	31	22	11.9	2.56	135	.241	.317	0	—	0	9	8	1	1.3
1982 Tex-A	1	6	.143	37	3	1	0	6	97	133	11	36	23	15.9	5.10	76	.342	.400	0	—	0	-11	-13	-0	-0.8
1983 Phi-N	1	0	1.000	3	1	0	0	0	8²	11	0	3	1	14.5	5.19	69	.314	.368	0	.000	-0	-2	-2	-0	-0.2
1984 Cle-A	4	8	.333	22	20	1	0	0	117¹	146	11	39	39	14.5	5.68	72	.309	.366	0	—	0	-22	-21	-0	-1.99
Total 7	44	37	.543	176	83	11	3	13	701²	762	57	252	245	13.2	4.13	95	.281	.347	0	.000	-0	-10	-15	1	0.2

YEAR	TM/L	W	L	PCT	G	GS	CG	SH	SV	IP	H	HR	BB	SO	RAT	ERA	ERA+	OAV	OOB	BH	AVG	PB	PR	/A	PD	TPI

● CHARLIE COMISKEY Comiskey, Charles Albert "Commy" or "The Old Roman" b: 8/15/1859, Chicago, Ill. d: 10/26/31, Eagle River, Wis. BR/TR, 6', 180 lbs. Deb: 5/2/1882 MH♦

1882	StL-a	0	1	.000	2	1	1	0	0	8	12	0	3	2	16.9	0.00	—	.325	.376	80	.243	0	2	2	0	0.3
1884	StL-a	0	0	—	1	0	0	0	0	4	1	0	0	4	2.3	2.25	145	.059	.059	110	.239	0	0	0	-0	0.0
1889	StL-a	0	0	—	1	0	0	0	0	0¹	0	0	0	0	0.0	0.00	—	.000	.000	168	.286	0	0	0	-0	0.0
Total	3	0	1	.000	4	1	1	0	0	12¹	13	0	3	6	11.7	0.73	410	.237	.277	1531	.264	0	3	3	-0	0.3

● JACK COMPTON Compton, Harry Leroy b: 3/9/1882, Lancaster, Ohio d: 7/4/74, Lancaster, Ohio BR/TR, 5'9", 157 lbs. Deb: 9/7/11

| 1911 | Cin-N | 0 | 1 | .000 | 8 | 3 | 0 | 0 | 1 | 25¹ | 19 | 0 | 15 | 6 | 12.4 | 3.91 | 85 | .204 | .321 | 2 | .333 | 0 | -1 | -2 | -0 | -0.1 |

● CLINT COMPTON Compton, Robert Clinton b: 11/1/50, Montgomery, Ala. BL/TL, 5'11", 185 lbs. Deb: 10/3/72

| 1972 | Chi-N | 0 | 0 | — | 1 | 0 | 0 | 0 | 0 | 2 | 2 | 0 | 2 | 0 | 18.0 | 9.00 | 42 | .286 | .444 | 0 | — | 0 | -1 | -1 | -0 | 0.0 |

● KEITH COMSTOCK Comstock, Keith Martin b: 12/23/55, San Francisco, Cal. BL/TL, 6', 175 lbs. Deb: 4/3/84

1984	Min-A	0	0	—	4	0	0	0	0	6¹	6	2	4	2	14.2	8.53	49	.261	.370	0	—	-0	-3	-3	0	-0.2
1987	SF-N	2	0	1.000	15	0	0	0	1	20²	19	1	10	21	12.6	3.05	126	.253	.341	0	.000	-0	2	2	0	0.2
	SD-N	0	1	.000	26	0	0	0	0	36	33	4	21	38	13.5	5.50	72	.252	.355	0	.000	-0	-6	-6	-1	-0.2
	Yr	2	1	.667	41	0	0	0	1	56²	52	5	31	59	13.2	4.61	85	.251	.349	0	.000	-0	-3	-4	-1	0.0
1988	SD-N	0	0	—	7	0	0	0	0	8	8	1	7	4	14.2	6.75	50	.250	.314	0	—	0	-3	-3	0	0.0
1989	Sea-A	1	2	.333	31	0	0	0	0	25²	26	2	10	22	12.6	2.81	144	.268	.336	0	—	0	3	3	-0	0.2
1990	Sea-A	7	4	.636	60	0	0	0	2	56	40	4	26	50	10.6	2.89	137	.206	.300	0	—	0	6	7	1	1.3
1991	Sea-A	0	0	—	1	0	0	0	0	0¹	2	0	1	0	81.0	54.00	8	.667	.750	0	—	0	-2	-2	0	0.0
Total	6	10	7	.588	144	0	0	0	3	153	134	14	75	142	12.3	4.06	97	.231	.332	0	.000	-0	-2	-2	-0	1.3

● RALPH COMSTOCK Comstock, Ralph Remick "Commy" b: 11/24/1890, Sylvania, Ohio d: 9/13/66, Toledo, Ohio BR/TR, 5'10", 168 lbs. Deb: 8/26/13

1913	Det-A	2	5	.286	10	7	1	0	1	60¹	70	0	16	37	16.0	5.37	54	.344	.384	5	.227	1	-16	-16	0	-1.6
1915	Bos-A	1	0	1.000	3	0	0	0	0	9	10	2	2	1	12.0	2.00	139	.294	.333	0	.000	0	1	1	0	0.1
	Pit-F	3	3	.500	12	7	3	0	2	52²	44	3	7	18	8.9	3.25	83	.237	.268	0	.000	-2	-3	-3	-0	-0.6
1918	Pit-N	5	6	.455	15	8	6	0	1	81	78	0	14	44	10.4	3.67	96	.259	.297	5	.192	-0	-2	-1	-0	-0.2
Total	3	11	14	.440	40	22	10	0	4	203	222	5	39	100	11.7	3.72	76	.284	.321	10	.152	-2	-21	-20	-0	-2.3

● DAVE CONCEPCION Concepcion, David Ismael (Benitez) b: 6/17/48, Aragua, Venez. BR/TR, 6'1", 180 lbs. Deb: 4/6/70 ♦

| 1988 | Cin-N | 0 | 0 | — | 1 | 0 | 0 | 0 | 0 | 1¹ | 2 | 0 | 1 | 0 | 13.5 | 0.00 | — | .333 | .333 | 39 | .198 | 0 | 1 | 1 | 0 | 0.0 |

● DAVID CONE Cone, David Brian b: 1/2/63, Kansas City, Mo. BL/TR, 6'1", 185 lbs. Deb: 6/8/86

1986	KC-A	0	0	—	11	0	0	0	0	22²	29	4	13	21	17.1	5.56	76	.309	.398	0	—	0	-3	-3	-0	-0.1
1987	NY-N	5	6	.455	21	13	1	0	1	99¹	87	11	44	68	12.3	3.71	102	.239	.329	2	.065	-1	4	1	-0	-0.1
1988	*NY-N★	20	3	.870	35	28	8	4	0	231¹	178	10	80	213	10.2	2.22	145	.213	.285	12	.150	-1	32	26	-1	2.5
1989	NY-N	14	8	.636	34	33	7	2	0	219²	183	20	74	190	10.7	3.52	93	.223	.290	18	.234	4	-1	-6	-2	-0.4
1990	NY-N	14	10	.583	31	30	6	2	0	211²	177	21	65	**233**	10.3	3.23	116	.226	.286	14	.200	3	13	12	0	1.6
1991	NY-N	14	14	.500	34	34	5	2	0	232²	204	13	73	**241**	10.9	3.29	111	.235	.298	9	.125	-1	10	9	0	1.0
1992	NY-N★	13	7	.650	27	27	7	5	0	196²	162	12	82	214	11.6	2.88	120	.223	.309	6	.092	-2	14	13	0	1.1
	*Tor-A	4	3	.571	8	7	0	0	0	53	39	3	29	47	12.1	2.55	160	.206	.321	0	—	0	8	9	-1	1.1
1993	KC-A	11	14	.440	34	34	6	1	0	254	205	20	114	191	11.7	3.33	137	.223	.315	0	—	0	28	35	-1	3.0
1994	KC-A★	16	5	.762	23	23	4	3	0	171²	130	15	54	132	10.0	2.94	176	.209	.279	0	—	0	36	43	0	**4.6**
Total	9	111	70	.613	258	229	44	19	1	1692²	1394	127	628	1550	11.0	3.12	123	.224	.300	61	.154	5	140	134	-6	14.3

● BOB CONE Cone, Robert Earl b: 2/27/1894, Galveston, Tex. d: 5/24/55, Galveston, Tex. BR/TR, 6'2", 172 lbs. Deb: 7/25/15

| 1915 | Phi-A | 0 | 0 | — | 1 | 1 | 0 | 0 | 0 | 0² | 5 | 0 | 0 | 0 | 67.5 | 40.50 | 7 | .714 | .714 | 0 | — | 0 | -3 | -3 | -0 | 0.0 |

● DICK CONGER Conger, Richard b: 4/3/21, Los Angeles, Cal. d: 2/16/70, Los Angeles, Cal. BR/TR, 6', 185 lbs. Deb: 4/22/40

1940	Det-A	1	0	1.000	2	0	0	0	0	3	2	0	3	1	15.0	3.00	159	.200	.385	0	—	0	0	1	-0	0.2
1941	Pit-N	0	0	—	2	1	0	0	0	4	3	0	3	2	13.5	0.00	—	.214	.353	0	—	0	2	2	-0	0.2
1942	Pit-N	0	0	—	2	1	0	0	0	8¹	9	0	5	3	15.1	2.16	157	.290	.389	0	.000	-0	1	1	1	0.0
1943	Phi-N	2	7	.222	13	10	2	0	0	54²	72	3	24	18	16.6	6.09	55	.327	.406	1	.063	-1	-16	-17	-0	-2.4
Total	4	3	7	.300	19	12	2	0	0	70	86	3	35	24	16.2	5.14	67	.313	.400	1	.053	-1	-13	-13	-0	-2.2

● ALLEN CONKWRIGHT Conkwright, Allen Howard "Red" b: 12/4/1896, Sedalia, Mo. d: 7/30/91, LaMesa, Cal. BR/TR, 5'10", 170 lbs. Deb: 9/16/20

| 1920 | Det-A | 2 | 1 | .667 | 5 | 3 | 0 | 0 | 0 | 19¹ | 29 | 0 | 16 | 4 | 20.9 | 6.98 | 53 | .397 | .506 | 1 | .200 | 1 | -7 | -7 | 0 | -0.9 |

● GENE CONLEY Conley, Donald Eugene b: 11/10/30, Muskogee, Okla. BR/TR, 6'8", 225 lbs. Deb: 4/17/52

1952	Bos-N	0	3	.000	4	3	0	0	0	12²	23	4	9	6	24.2	7.82	46	.397	.493	2	.400	1	-6	-6	-0	-1.1
1954	Mil-N★	14	9	.609	28	27	12	2	0	194¹	171	17	79	113	11.9	2.96	126	.240	.322	12	.156	-2	24	16	-1	1.5
1955	Mil-N★	11	7	.611	22	21	10	0	0	158	152	23	52	107	11.7	4.16	90	.254	.315	11	.204	-1	-2	-7	-0	-0.8
1956	Mil-N	8	9	.471	31	19	5	1	3	158²	169	16	52	68	12.7	3.13	111	.276	.335	7	.156	-1	11	6	-1	0.5
1957	*Mil-N	9	9	.500	35	18	6	1	1	148	133	9	64	61	12.1	3.16	111	.244	.325	9	.196	1	12	6	-0	0.7
1958	Mil-N	0	6	.000	26	7	0	0	2	72	89	8	17	53	13.8	4.88	72	.309	.356	3	.188	1	-7	-11	-0	-0.8
1959	Phi-N★	12	7	.632	25	22	12	3	1	180	159	13	42	102	10.1	3.00	**137**	.235	.281	16	.239	2	19	22	-0	2.5
1960	Phi-N	8	14	.364	29	25	9	2	0	183²	192	10	42	117	11.6	3.68	105	.272	.314	8	.127	-1	2	4	-2	0.2
1961	Bos-A	11	14	.440	33	30	9	2	0	199²	229	23	65	113	13.4	4.91	85	.287	.343	16	.219	4	-20	-17	-1	-1.5
1962	Bos-A	15	14	.517	34	33	9	2	1	241²	238	28	68	134	11.6	3.95	105	.256	.310	18	.207	3	1	5	-1	0.8
1963	Bos-A	3	4	.429	9	9	0	0	0	40²	51	4	21	14	16.2	6.64	57	.305	.386	3	.200	-1	-14	-13	-1	-1.9
Total	11	91	96	.487	276	214	69	13	9	1588²	1606	162	511	888	12.2	3.82	101	.264	.324	105	.192	8	20	6	-6	0.1

● ED CONLEY Conley, Edward J. b: 7/10/1864, Sandwich, Mass. d: 10/16/1894, Cumberland, R.I. 5'11.5", Deb: 7/20/1884

| 1884 | Pro-N | 4 | 4 | .500 | 8 | 8 | 8 | 1 | 0 | 71 | 63 | 4 | 22 | 33 | 10.8 | 2.15 | 131 | .223 | .280 | 4 | .143 | -2 | 7 | 5 | -1 | 0.2 |

● SNIPE CONLEY Conley, James Patrick b: 4/25/1894, Cressona, Pa. d: 1/7/78, DeSoto, Tex. BR/TR, 5'11.5", 179 lbs. Deb: 5/20/14

1914	Bal-F	4	6	.400	35	11	4	2	1	125	112	4	47	86	11.9	2.52	120	.259	.340	4	.114	-3	5	7	-1	0.1
1915	Bal-F	1	4	.200	25	6	4	0	0	86	97	5	32	40	13.9	4.29	67	.314	.386	6	.250	1	-15	-14	-1	-0.7
1918	Cin-N	2	0	1.000	5	0	0	0	1	13²	17	2	5	2	14.5	5.27	51	.321	.379	1	.250	0	-4	-4	0	-0.6
Total	3	7	10	.412	65	17	8	2	2	224²	226	9	84	128	12.8	3.36	88	.284	.360	11	.175	-1	-14	-10	-1	-1.2

● BOB CONLEY Conley, Robert Burns b: 2/1/34, Mousie, Ky. BR/TR, 6'1", 188 lbs. Deb: 9/11/58

| 1958 | Phi-N | 0 | 0 | — | 2 | 2 | 0 | 0 | 0 | 8¹ | 9 | 0 | 4 | 0 | 10.8 | 7.56 | 52 | .273 | .294 | 0 | .000 | -0 | -3 | -3 | -0 | 0.0 |

● BERT CONN Conn, Albert Thomas b: 9/22/1879, Philadelphia, Pa. d: 11/2/44, Philadelphia, Pa. TR , Deb: 9/16/1898 ♦

1898	Phi-N	0	1	.000	1	1	0	0	0	7	13	1	2	3	19.3	6.43	53	.393	.428	1	.333	1	-2	-2	-0	-0.2
1900	Phi-N	0	2	.000	4	1	0	0	0	17¹	29	0	16	2	26.5	8.31	44	.370	.508	3	.333	1	-9	-9	-1	-0.8
Total	2	0	3	.000	5	2	1	0	0	24¹	42	1	18	5	24.4	7.77	46	.377	.487	4	.267	1	-11	-11	-1	-1.0

● SARGE CONNALLY Connally, George Walter b: 8/31/1898, McGregor, Tex. d: 1/27/78, Temple, Tex. BR/TR, 5'11", 170 lbs. Deb: 9/10/21

1921	Chi-A	0	1	.000	2	2	2	0	0	22¹	29	0	10	6	16.1	6.45	66	.330	.404	4	.500	2	-5	-5	-0	-0.5
1923	Chi-A	0	0	—	3	0	0	0	0	8²	7	0	12	3	20.8	6.23	64	.241	.476	1	.333	0	-2	-2	-0	-0.3
1924	Chi-A	7	13	.350	44	13	6	0	6	160	177	4	68	55	14.3	4.05	102	.290	.369	11	.220	-1	3	1	-2	0.3
1925	Chi-A	6	7	.462	40	2	0	0	2	104²	122	2	58	45	15.6	4.64	89	.310	.402	7	.250	1	-3	-6	3	-0.3

YEAR TM/L	W	L	PCT	G	GS	CG	SH	SV	IP	H	HR	BB	SO	RAT	ERA	ERA+	OAV	OOB	BH	AVG	PB	PR	/A	PD	TPI
1926 Chi-A	6	5	.545	31	8	5	0	3	108¹	128	0	35	47	13.7	3.16	122	.300	.356	5	.156	-1	10	9	2	0.9
1927 Chi-A	10	15	.400	43	18	11	1	5	198¹	217	8	83	58	14.0	4.08	99	.292	.370	22	.328	4	1	-1	1	0.4
1928 Chi-A	2	5	.286	28	5	1	0	2	74¹	89	1	29	28	14.8	4.84	84	.313	.385	2	.105	-1	-7	-7	-0	-0.7
1929 Chi-A	0	0	—	11	0	0	0	0	11¹	13	0	8	3	16.7	4.76	90	.317	.429	0	—	0	-1	-1	-0	0.0
1931 Cle-A	5	5	.500	17	9	5	0	1	85²	87	7	50	37	15.0	4.20	110	.256	.361	5	.185	-0	2	4	-0	0.4
1932 Cle-A	8	6	.571	35	7	4	-1	3	112¹	119	6	42	32	13.1	4.33	110	.266	.333	7	.175	-0	2	5	0	0.6
1933 Cle-A	5	3	.625	41	3	1	0	1	103	112	4	49	30	14.3	4.89	91	.271	.353	6	.231	1	-7	-5	-2	-0.5
1934 Cle-A	0	0	—	5	0	0	0	0	5¹	4	0	5	1	15.2	5.06	90	.222	.391	0	.000	-0	-0	-0	0	0.0
Total 12	49	60	.450	303	67	33	2	31	994¹	1104	32	449	345	14.4	4.30	98	.288	.368	70	.233	5	-7	-8	5	1.1

● **BILL CONNELLY**   Connelly, William Wirt "Wild Bill" b: 6/29/25, Alberta, Va. d: 11/27/80, Richmond, Va.   BL/TR, 6', 175 lbs.   Deb: 8/22/45

YEAR TM/L	W	L	PCT	G	GS	CG	SH	SV	IP	H	HR	BB	SO	RAT	ERA	ERA+	OAV	OOB	BH	AVG	PB	PR	/A	PD	TPI
1945 Phi-A	1	1	.500	2	1	0	0	0	8	7	0	8	0	16.9	4.50	76	.259	.429	0	.000	0	-1	-1	-0	-0.2
1950 Chi-A	0	0	—	2	0	0	0	0	2¹	5	1	1	0	23.1	11.57	39	.455	.500	0	—	0	-2	-2	-0	0.0
Det-A	0	0	—	2	0	0	0	0	4	4	1	2	1	13.5	6.75	69	.250	.333	0	.000	0	-1	-1	0	0.0
Yr	0	0	—	4	0	0	0	0	6¹	9	2	3	1	17.1	8.53	54	.333	.400	0	.000	0	-3	-3	0	0.0
1952 NY-N	5	0	1.000	11	4	0	0	0	31²	22	4	25	22	13.4	4.55	81	.208	.359	4	.364	3	-3	-3	1	-0.1
1953 NY-N	0	1	.000	8	2	0	0	0	20¹	33	4	17	11	22.1	11.07	39	.371	.472	0	.000	-1	-15	-15	-0	-0.7
Total 4	6	2	.750	25	7	0	0	0	66¹	71	10	53	34	16.8	6.92	57	.285	.411	4	.211	3	-22	-22	-0	-1.0

● **ED CONNOLLY**   Connolly, Edward Joseph Jr. b: 12/3/39, Brooklyn, N.Y.   BL/TL, 6'1", 190 lbs.   Deb: 4/19/64 F

YEAR TM/L	W	L	PCT	G	GS	CG	SH	SV	IP	H	HR	BB	SO	RAT	ERA	ERA+	OAV	OOB	BH	AVG	PB	PR	/A	PD	TPI
1964 Bos-A	4	11	.267	27	15	1	1	0	80²	80	3	64	73	16.7	4.91	79	.261	.398	3	.167	0	-12	-9	-1	-1.7
1967 Cle-A	2	1	.667	15	4	0	0	0	49¹	63	6	34	45	17.9	7.48	44	.315	.417	2	.182	0	-23	-23	-0	-1.3
Total 2	6	12	.333	42	19	1	1	0	130	143	9	98	118	17.2	5.88	62	.282	.405	5	.172	0	-35	-33	-2	-3.0

● **JOHN CONNOR**   Connor, John b: 8/1854, Scotland d: 10/13/32, Boston, Mass.   Deb: 7/26/1884

YEAR TM/L	W	L	PCT	G	GS	CG	SH	SV	IP	H	HR	BB	SO	RAT	ERA	ERA+	OAV	OOB	BH	AVG	PB	PR	/A	PD	TPI
1884 Bos-N	1	4	.200	7	7	7	0	0	60	70	1	18	29	13.2	3.15	92	.275	.322	2	.080	-3	-1	-2	0	-0.3
1885 Buf-N	0	1	.000	1	1	1	0	0	9	14	0	2	0	16.0	4.00	75	.378	.410	0	.000	-0	-1	-1	-1	-0.2
Lou-a	1	3	.250	4	4	4	0	0	35	43	0	12	19	14.7	4.89	66	.295	.356	2	.143	-1	-6	-6	-1	-0.7
Total 2	2	8	.200	12	12	12	0	0	104	127	1	32	48	13.9	3.81	79	.290	.341	4	.095	-4	-9	-9	-1	-1.2

● **JOE CONNORS**   Connors, Joseph P. b: Paterson, N.J.   Deb: 5/3/1884 ◆

YEAR TM/L	W	L	PCT	G	GS	CG	SH	SV	IP	H	HR	BB	SO	RAT	ERA	ERA+	OAV	OOB	BH	AVG	PB	PR	/A	PD	TPI
1884 Alt-U	0	1	.000	1	1	1	0	0	9	18	0	5	0	23.0	7.00	38	.391	.451	1	.091	-1	-5	-4	0	-0.4
KC-U	0	1	.000	2	1	1	0	0	12	24	1	0	1	18.0	4.50	50	.391	.391	1	.091	-1	-3	-3	-1	-0.3
Yr	0	2	.000	3	2	2	0	0	21	42	1	5	1	20.1	5.57	43	.391	.418	2	.091	-2	-7	-7	-0	-0.7

● **BILL CONNORS**   Connors, William Joseph b: 11/2/41, Schenectady, N.Y.   BR/TR, 6'1", 180 lbs.   Deb: 5/3/66 C

YEAR TM/L	W	L	PCT	G	GS	CG	SH	SV	IP	H	HR	BB	SO	RAT	ERA	ERA+	OAV	OOB	BH	AVG	PB	PR	/A	PD	TPI
1966 Chi-N	0	1	.000	11	0	0	0	0	16	20	4	7	3	15.2	7.31	54	.308	.375	0	—	0	-7	-6	-0	-0.4
1967 NY-N	0	0	—	6	1	0	0	0	13	8	3	5	13	9.7	6.23	54	.170	.264	0	.000	-0	-4	-4	-0	-0.1
1968 NY-N	0	1	.000	9	0	0	0	0	14	21	0	7	8	18.6	9.00	34	.339	.414	1	1.000	1	-9	-9	0	-0.6
Total 3	0	2	.000	26	1	0	0	0	43	49	7	19	24	14.7	7.53	45	.282	.359	1	.500	1	-20	-20	-0	-1.1

● **TED CONOVAR**   Conovar, Theodore "Huck" b: 3/10/1868, Lexington, Ky. d: 7/27/10, Paris, Ky.   BR/TR, 5'10.5", 165 lbs.   Deb: 5/26/1889

YEAR TM/L	W	L	PCT	G	GS	CG	SH	SV	IP	H	HR	BB	SO	RAT	ERA	ERA+	OAV	OOB	BH	AVG	PB	PR	/A	PD	TPI
1889 Cin-a	0	0	—	1	0	0	0	1	2	4	0	2	1	27.0	13.50	29	.403	.503	0	—	0	-2	-2	-0	-0.2

● **TIM CONROY**   Conroy, Timothy James b: 4/3/60, McKeesport, Pa.   BL/TL, 5'11", 185 lbs.   Deb: 6/23/78

YEAR TM/L	W	L	PCT	G	GS	CG	SH	SV	IP	H	HR	BB	SO	RAT	ERA	ERA+	OAV	OOB	BH	AVG	PB	PR	/A	PD	TPI
1978 Oak-A	0	0	—	2	2	0	0	0	4²	3	0	9	0	25.1	7.71	47	.188	.500	0	—	0	-2	-2	-0	0.1
1982 Oak-A	2	2	.500	5	5	1	0	0	25¹	20	1	18	17	13.5	3.55	110	.222	.352	0	—	0	1	1	-0	0.2
1983 Oak-A	7	10	.412	39	18	3	1	0	162¹	141	17	98	112	13.4	3.94	98	.232	.340	0	—	0	2	-1	-2	-0.2
1984 Oak-A	1	6	.143	38	14	0	0	0	93	82	11	63	69	14.2	5.23	72	.236	.356	0	—	0	-13	-15	-1	-0.9
1985 Oak-A	0	1	.000	16	2	0	0	0	25¹	22	3	15	8	13.5	4.26	90	.237	.349	0	—	0	-0	-1	-0	0.0
1986 StL-N	5	11	.313	25	21	1	0	0	115¹	122	15	56	79	14.1	5.23	70	.275	.360	4	.138	1	-19	-20	-1	-2.5
1987 StL-N	3	2	.600	10	9	0	0	0	40²	48	0	25	22	16.4	5.53	75	.306	.404	0	—	-2	-7	-6	-1	-0.8
Total 7	18	32	.360	135	71	5	1	0	466²	438	47	284	307	14.1	4.69	81	.249	.357	4	.091	-1	-37	-46	-6	-4.1

● **JIM CONSTABLE**   Constable, Jimmy Lee "Sheriff" b: 6/14/33, Jonesborough, Tenn.   BB/TL, 6'1", 185 lbs.   Deb: 6/24/56

YEAR TM/L	W	L	PCT	G	GS	CG	SH	SV	IP	H	HR	BB	SO	RAT	ERA	ERA+	OAV	OOB	BH	AVG	PB	PR	/A	PD	TPI
1956 NY-N	0	0	—	3	0	0	0	0	4¹	9	0	7	1	35.3	14.54	26	.429	.586	0	—	0	-5	-5	-0	0.0
1957 NY-N	1	1	.500	16	0	0	0	0	28¹	27	2	7	13	12.1	2.86	138	.262	.333	0	.000	-0	3	3	-0	0.1
1958 SF-N	1	0	1.000	9	0	0	0	1	8	10	1	3	4	14.6	5.63	68	.323	.382	1	1.000	1	-1	-2	1	-0.1
Cle-A	0	1	.000	6	2	0	0	0	9¹	17	1	4	3	21.2	11.57	32	.415	.478	2	1.000	1	-8	-8	-0	-0.2
Was-A	0	1	.000	15	2	0	0	0	27²	29	3	15	25	14.6	4.88	78	.271	.366	1	.250	0	-3	-3	-1	-0.1
Yr	0	2	.000	21	4	0	0	1	37	46	4	19	28	16.1	6.57	57	.309	.391	3	.500	1	-12	-11	-1	-0.8
1962 Mil-N	1	1	.500	3	2	1	1	0	18	14	1	4	12	9.0	2.00	190	.222	.269	0	.000	-0	4	4	-0	0.4
1963 SF-N	0	0	—	4	0	0	0	0	2¹	3	0	1	1	15.4	3.86	83	.333	.400	0	—	0	-0	-0	-0	0.0
Total 5	3	4	.429	56	6	1	1	2	98	109	8	41	59	14.4	4.87	78	.291	.371	4	.235	2	-11	-11	-1	-0.4

● **SANDY CONSUEGRA**   Consuegra, Sandalio Simeon (Castello) b: 9/3/20, Potrerillos, Cuba   BR/TR, 5'10", 165 lbs.   Deb: 6/10/50

YEAR TM/L	W	L	PCT	G	GS	CG	SH	SV	IP	H	HR	BB	SO	RAT	ERA	ERA+	OAV	OOB	BH	AVG	PB	PR	/A	PD	TPI
1950 Was-A	7	8	.467	21	18	8	2	2	124²	132	6	57	38	13.7	4.40	102	.270	.347	7	.175	-1	2	1	0	0.1
1951 Was-A	7	8	.467	40	12	5	0	3	146	140	10	63	31	12.5	4.01	102	.251	.338	10	.233	-0	2	1	1	0.2
1952 Was-A	6	0	1.000	30	2	0	0	5	73²	80	2	27	19	13.1	3.05	116	.276	.338	3	.176	0	5	4	-1	0.3
1953 Was-A	0	0	—	4	0	0	0	0	5	9	0	4	0	23.4	10.80	36	.391	.481	0	—	0	-4	-4	0	0.0
Chi-A	7	5	.583	29	13	5	1	3	124	122	9	28	30	11.0	2.54	158	.258	.302	2	.057	-4	20	20	3	1.9
Yr	7	5	.583	33	13	5	1	3	129	131	9	32	30	11.5	2.86	141	.264	.311	2	.057	-4	16	17	3	1.9
1954 Chi-A★	16	3	**.842**	39	17	3	2	3	154	142	9	35	31	10.3	2.69	139	.248	.292	11	.229	1	18	18	1	2.4
1955 Chi-A	6	5	.545	44	7	3	0	7	126¹	120	4	18	35	10.0	2.64	150	.256	.286	3	.103	-2	19	18	-0	1.5
1956 Chi-A	1	2	.333	28	1	0	0	0	38¹	45	0	11	7	13.4	5.17	79	.296	.348	0	.000	-1	-4	-5	-0	-0.5
Bal-A	1	1	.500	4	1	0	0	0	8²	10	2	2	1	12.5	4.15	94	.294	.333	1	.500	0	-0	-0	0	0.0
Yr	2	3	.400	32	2	0	0	0	47	55	2	13	8	13.0	4.98	82	.293	.338	1	.167	-0	-4	-5	-0	-0.5
1957 Bal-A	0	0	—	5	0	0	0	0	5	4	0	2	0	7.2	1.80	200	.211	.211	0	—	0	1	1	0	0.0
NY-N	0	0	—	4	0	0	0	0	3²	7	1	1	1	19.6	2.45	160	.389	.421	0	—	0	1	1	0	0.0
Total 8	51	32	.614	248	71	24	5	26	809¹	811	43	246	193	11.8	3.37	119	.262	.318	37	.170	-5	59	57	4	5.9

● **NARDI CONTRERAS**   Contreras, Arnaldo Juan b: 9/19/51, Tampa, Fla.   BB/TR, 6'2", 193 lbs.   Deb: 5/23/80

YEAR TM/L	W	L	PCT	G	GS	CG	SH	SV	IP	H	HR	BB	SO	RAT	ERA	ERA+	OAV	OOB	BH	AVG	PB	PR	/A	PD	TPI
1980 Chi-A	0	0	—	8	0	0	0	0	13²	18	1	7	8	17.8	5.93	68	.333	.429	0	—	0	-3	-3	0	0.0

● **JIM CONVERSE**   Converse, James Daniel b: 8/17/71, San Francisco, Cal.   BL/TR, 5'9", 180 lbs.   Deb: 5/22/93

YEAR TM/L	W	L	PCT	G	GS	CG	SH	SV	IP	H	HR	BB	SO	RAT	ERA	ERA+	OAV	OOB	BH	AVG	PB	PR	/A	PD	TPI
1993 Sea-A	1	3	.250	4	4	0	0	0	20¹	23	0	14	10	16.4	5.31	83	.295	.402	0	—	0	-2	-2	1	-0.3
1994 Sea-A	0	5	.000	13	8	0	0	0	48²	73	5	40	39	21.1	8.69	56	.353	.460	0	—	0	-21	-20	0	-1.7
Total 2	1	8	.111	17	12	0	0	0	69	96	5	54	49	19.7	7.70	57	.337	.444	0	—	0	-23	-23	1	-2.0

● **JIM CONWAY**   Conway, James P. b: Clifton, Pa.   TR,   Deb: 5/5/1884 F

YEAR TM/L	W	L	PCT	G	GS	CG	SH	SV	IP	H	HR	BB	SO	RAT	ERA	ERA+	OAV	OOB	BH	AVG	PB	PR	/A	PD	TPI
1884 Bro-a	3	9	.250	13	13	10	0	0	105¹	132	4	15	25	12.8	4.44	75	.289	.316	6	.128	-4	-14	-13	-2	-1.6
1885 Phi-a	0	1	.000	2	1	1	0	0	12¹	19	0	2	0	15.3	7.30	47	.358	.382	0	.000	-0	-6	-5	-0	-0.4
1889 KC-a	19	19	.500	41	37	33	0	0	335	334	12	90	115	11.8	3.25	129	.252	.306	31	.208	-6	22	35	1	2.7
Total 3	22	29	.431	56	52	44	0	0	452²	485	16	107	140	12.1	3.64	109	.264	.311	37	.183	-10	3	16	-1	0.7

YEAR	TM/L	W	L	PCT	G	GS	CG	SH	SV	IP	H	HR	BB	SO	RAT	ERA	ERA+	OAV	OOB	BH	AVG	PB	PR	/A	PD	TPI

● **JERRY CONWAY**   Conway, Jerome Patrick   b: 6/7/01, Holyoke, Mass.   d: 4/16/80, Holyoke, Mass.   BL/TL, 6'2", 190 lbs.   Deb: 8/31/20

| 1920 | Was-A | 0 | 0 | — | 1 | 0 | 0 | 0 | 0 | 2 | 1 | 0 | 1 | 0 | 9.0 | 0.00 | — | .167 | .286 | 0 | — | 0 | 1 | 1 | -0 | 0.0 |

● **PETE CONWAY**   Conway, Peter J.   b: 10/30/1866, Burmont, Pa.   d: 1/13/03, Clifton Heights, Pa.   BR/TR, 5'10.5", 162 lbs.   Deb: 8/10/1885   F♦

1885	Buf-N	10	17	.370	27	27	26	1	0	210	256	10	44	94	12.9	4.67	64	.287	.320	10	.111	-4	-43	-39	1	-4.2
1886	KC-N	5	15	.250	23	20	19	0	0	180	236	6	61	81	14.9	5.75	66	.294	.343	47	.242	0	-49	-39	-2	-3.4
	Det-N	6	5	.545	11	11	11	0	0	91	93	1	25	35	11.7	3.36	99	.255	.303	8	.186	1	-1	-0	-0	-0.1
	Yr	11	20	.355	34	31	30	0	0	271	329	7	86	116	13.8	4.95	73	.282	.331	55	.232	1	-49	-40	-2	-3.5
1887	*Det-N	8	9	.471	17	17	16	0	0	146	132	3	47	40	11.3	2.90	140	.235	.300	22	.232	0	19	19	3	1.9
1888	Det-N	30	14	.682	45	45	43	4	0	391	315	11	57	176	8.9	2.26	123	.208	**.243**	46	.275	15	26	22	3	3.9
1889	Pit-N	2	1	.667	3	3	2	0	0	22	26	1	16	2	17.2	4.91	76	.285	.392	1	.100	0	-2	-3	0	-0.2
Total	5	61	61	.500	126	123	117	5	0	1040	1058	32	250	428	11.5	3.59	90	.250	.295	134	.224	12	-50	-42	4	-2.1

● **DICK CONWAY**   Conway, Richard Butler   b: 4/25/1865, Lowell, Mass.   d: 9/9/26, Lowell, Mass.   BL/TR, 5'7.5", 140 lbs.   Deb: 7/22/1886   F

1886	Bal-a	2	7	.222	9	9	8	0	0	76²	106	6	43	64	17.8	6.81	50	.312	.394	7	.206	0	-29	-29	2	-2.2
1887	Bos-N	9	15	.375	26	26	25	0	0	222¹	249	10	86	45	13.8	4.66	87	.276	.343	36	.248	2	-14	-15	1	-1.0
1888	Bos-N	4	2	.667	6	6	6	0	0	53	49	2	8	12	10.4	2.38	120	.240	.282	4	.160	1	3	3	0	0.2
Total	3	15	24	.385	41	41	39	0	0	352	404	18	137	121	14.2	4.78	78	.279	.347	47	.230	1	-40	-41	2	-3.0

● **JOE CONZELMAN**   Conzelman, Joseph Harrison   b: 7/14/1885, Bristol, Conn.   d: 4/17/79, Mountain Brook, Ala.   BR/TR, 6', 170 lbs.   Deb: 5/1/13

1913	Pit-N	0	1	.000	3	2	1	0	0	15	13	0	5	9	11.4	1.20	251	.245	.322	0	.000	-1	3	3	0	0.1
1914	Pit-N	5	6	.455	33	9	4	1	2	101	88	2	40	39	11.7	2.94	90	.254	.337	3	.111	-2	-2	-3	2	-0.4
1915	Pit-N	1	1	.500	18	1	0	0	0	47¹	41	0	20	22	12.2	3.42	80	.248	.340	1	.091	-1	-4	-4	1	-0.2
Total	3	6	8	.429	54	12	5	1	2	163¹	142	2	65	70	11.8	2.92	93	.252	.336	4	.095	-3	-2	-4	2	-0.5

● **ANDY COOK**   Cook, Andrew Bernard   b: 8/30/67, Memphis, Tenn.   BR/TR, 6'5", 215 lbs.   Deb: 5/9/93

| 1993 | NY-A | 0 | 1 | .000 | 4 | 0 | 0 | 0 | 0 | 5¹ | 4 | 1 | 7 | 4 | 18.6 | 5.06 | 82 | .200 | .407 | 0 | — | 0 | -0 | -1 | 0 | 0.0 |

● **DENNIS COOK**   Cook, Dennis Bryan   b: 10/4/62, LaMarque, Tex.   BL/TL, 6'3", 185 lbs.   Deb: 9/12/88

1988	SF-N	2	1	.667	4	4	1	1	0	22	9	1	11	13	8.2	2.86	114	.125	.241	0	.000	1	1	1	-1	0.1
1989	SF-N	1	0	1.000	2	2	1	0	0	15	13	1	5	9	10.8	1.80	187	.245	.310	1	.167	1	3	3	0	0.3
	Phi-N	6	8	.429	21	16	1	1	0	106	97	17	33	58	11.2	3.99	89	.243	.304	8	.222	1	-6	-5	-1	-0.7
	Yr	7	8	.467	23	18	2	1	0	121	110	18	38	67	11.2	3.72	95	.243	.305	9	.214	2	-3	-3	-1	-0.4
1990	Phi-N	8	3	.727	42	13	2	1	1	141²	132	13	54	58	11.9	3.56	107	.250	.322	13	.310	4	4	4	-0	0.7
	LA-N	1	1	.500	5	3	0	0	0	14¹	23	7	2	6	15.7	7.53	49	.365	.385	2	.286	1	-6	-6	0	-0.6
	Yr	9	4	.692	47	16	2	1	1	156	155	20	56	64	12.2	3.92	97	.259	.323	15	.306	5	-2	-2	-0	0.1
1991	LA-N	1	0	1.000	20	1	0	0	0	17²	12	0	7	8	9.7	0.51	705	.203	.288	0	.000	-0	6	6	0	0.3
1992	Cle-A	5	7	.417	32	25	1	0	0	158	156	29	50	96	11.8	3.82	102	.255	.314	0	—	0	2	2	-2	-0.1
1993	Cle-A	5	5	.500	25	6	0	0	0	54	62	9	16	34	13.3	5.67	76	.295	.351	0	—	0	-8	-8	-1	-1.3
1994	Chi-A	3	1	.750	38	0	0	0	0	33	29	4	14	26	11.7	3.55	132	.230	.307	0	—	0	5	4	0	0.4
Total	7	32	26	.552	189	70	6	3	1	561²	533	81	192	308	11.7	3.85	100	.251	.316	24	.250	7	1	0	-4	-0.9

● **EARL COOK**   Cook, Earl Davis   b: 12/10/08, Stouffville, Ont., Canada   BR/TR, 6', 195 lbs.   Deb: 9/12/41

| 1941 | Det-A | 0 | 0 | — | 1 | 0 | 0 | 0 | 0 | 2 | 4 | 0 | 1 | 0 | 18.0 | 4.50 | 101 | .400 | .400 | 0 | — | 0 | -0 | 0 | -0 | 0.0 |

● **GLEN COOK**   Cook, Glen Patrick   b: 9/8/59, Buffalo, N.Y.   BR/TR, 5'11", 180 lbs.   Deb: 6/23/85

| 1985 | Tex-A | 2 | 3 | .400 | 9 | 7 | 0 | 0 | 0 | 40 | 53 | 12 | 18 | 19 | 16.6 | 9.45 | 45 | .327 | .404 | 0 | — | 0 | -24 | -23 | -1 | -2.3 |

● **MIKE COOK**   Cook, Michael Horace   b: 8/14/63, Charleston, S.C.   BR/TR, 6'3", 200 lbs.   Deb: 7/1/86

1986	Cal-A	0	2	.000	5	1	0	0	0	9	13	3	7	6	20.0	9.00	46	.333	.435	0	—	0	-5	-5	0	-0.8
1987	Cal-A	1	2	.333	16	1	0	0	0	34¹	34	7	18	27	13.6	5.50	78	.264	.354	0	—	0	-4	-5	1	-0.2
1988	Cal-A	0	1	.000	3	0	0	0	0	3²	4	0	1	2	14.7	4.91	79	.308	.400	0	—	0	-0	-0	-0	-0.1
1989	Min-A	0	1	.000	15	0	0	0	0	21¹	22	1	17	15	16.9	5.06	82	.268	.400	0	—	0	-3	-2	-1	-0.6
1993	Bal-A	0	0	—	2	0	0	0	0	3	1	0	2	3	9.0	0.00	—	.091	.231	0	—	0	1	1	-0	-0.1
Total	5	1	6	.143	41	2	0	0	0	71¹	74	11	45	53	15.3	5.55	76	.270	.377	0	—	0	-11	-11	0	-1.8

● **ROLLIN COOK**   Cook, Rollin Edward   b: 10/5/1890, Toledo, Ohio   d: 8/11/75, Toledo, Ohio   BR/TR, 5'9", 152 lbs.   Deb: 7/6/15

| 1915 | StL-A | 0 | 0 | — | 5 | 0 | 0 | 0 | 0 | 13² | 16 | 0 | 9 | 7 | 17.1 | 7.24 | 40 | .276 | .382 | 1 | .250 | 0 | -7 | -7 | 0 | -0.7 |

● **RON COOK**   Cook, Ronald Wayne   b: 7/11/47, Jefferson, Tex.   BL/TL, 6'1", 175 lbs.   Deb: 4/10/70

1970	Hou-N	4	4	.500	41	7	0	0	2	82¹	80	4	42	50	13.7	3.72	104	.274	.371	4	.235	2	3	1	-0	0.3
1971	Hou-N	0	4	.000	5	4	0	0	0	25²	23	2	8	10	11.2	4.91	69	.237	.302	2	.250	0	-4	-4	0	-0.6
Total	2	4	8	.333	46	11	0	0	2	108	103	6	50	60	13.1	4.00	94	.265	.354	6	.240	2	-1	-3	-0	-0.3

● **STEVE COOKE**   Cooke, Steven Montague   b: 1/14/70, Lihue, Hawaii   BR/TL, 6'6", 220 lbs.   Deb: 7/28/92

1992	Pit-N	2	0	1.000	11	0	0	0	0	23	22	2	4	10	10.2	3.52	98	.253	.286	1	.333	0	-0	-0	-0	0.0
1993	Pit-N	10	10	.500	32	32	3	1	0	210²	207	22	59	132	11.5	3.89	104	.258	.312	11	.155	-1	4	4	-2	0.0
1994	Pit-N	4	11	.267	25	23	2	0	0	134¹	157	21	46	74	13.9	5.02	84	.298	.360	8	.190	-0	-12	-12	-1	-1.2
Total	3	16	21	.432	68	55	5	1	1	368	386	45	109	216	12.3	4.28	95	.273	.328	20	.172	-0	-9	-8	-4	-1.2

● **DANNY COOMBS**   Coombs, Daniel Bernard   b: 3/23/42, Lincoln, Me.   BR/TL, 6'5", 210 lbs.   Deb: 9/27/63

1963	Hou-N	0	0	—	1	0	0	0	0	0¹	3	0	0	0	81.0	27.00	12	.750	.750	0	—	0	-1	-1	0	0.0
1964	Hou-N	1	1	.500	7	1	0	0	0	18	21	1	10	14	16.0	5.00	68	.300	.395	0	.000	-0	-3	-3	-0	-0.4
1965	Hou-N	0	2	.000	26	3	0	0	0	47	54	3	23	35	15.3	4.79	70	.292	.379	1	.111	-0	-7	-7	1	-0.2
1966	Hou-N	0	0	—	2	0	0	0	0	2²	4	0	2	3	13.5	3.38	101	.333	.333	0	.000	-0	0	-0	0	0.0
1967	Hou-N	3	0	1.000	6	2	0	0	0	24¹	21	0	9	23	11.1	3.33	99	.233	.303	1	.125	0	0	0	0	0.0
1968	Hou-N	4	3	.571	40	2	0	0	2	46²	50	0	17	29	13.5	3.28	90	.286	.350	4	.400	1	-2	-2	1	-0.1
1969	Hou-N	0	1	.000	8	0	0	0	0	8	12	0	2	3	16.9	6.75	52	.364	.417	0	.000	-0	-3	-3	0	-0.4
1970	SD-N	10	14	.417	35	27	5	2	0	188¹	185	12	76	105	12.6	3.30	121	.256	.329	5	.096	-2	16	14	-2	1.3
1971	SD-N	1	6	.143	19	7	0	0	0	57²	81	10	25	37	16.5	6.24	53	.327	.388	3	.214	1	-18	-19	1	-1.9
Total	9	19	27	.413	144	42	10	2	2	393	433	26	162	249	13.8	4.08	88	.280	.351	14	.140	-0	-17	-21	0	-1.7

● **JACK COOMBS**   Coombs, John Wesley "Colby Jack"   b: 11/18/1882, LeGrand, Iowa   d: 4/15/57, Palestine, Tex.   BB/TR, 6', 185 lbs.   Deb: 7/5/06   MC♦

1906	Phi-A	10	10	.500	23	18	13	1	0	173	149	0	68	90	11.4	2.50	109	.229	.312	16	.239	1	4	4	0	0.7
1907	Phi-A	6	9	.400	23	17	10	2	2	132²	109	2	64	73	12.3	3.12	84	.226	.328	8	.167	-1	-8	-8	0	-1.0
1908	Phi-A	7	5	.583	26	18	10	0	0	153	130	6	64	80	11.6	2.00	128	.233	.316	56	.255	4	7	10	0	1.1
1909	Phi-A	12	11	.522	30	24	18	6	1	205²	156	1	73	97	10.3	2.32	104	.213	.289	14	.169	1	4	0	0	0.3
1910	*Phi-A	**31**	9	.775	**45**	38	35	**13**	1	353	248	0	115	224	9.4	1.30	183	.201	.273	29	.220	4	48	42	-5	4.8
1911	*Phi-A	**28**	12	.700	47	40	26	1	2	336²	360	8	119	185	13.2	3.53	89	.280	.348	45	.319	14	-7	-14	-3	-0.5
1912	Phi-A	21	10	.677	40	32	23	1	2	262¹	227	5	94	120	11.4	3.29	93	.241	.316	28	.255	6	-1	-6	-1	-0.1
1913	Phi-A	0	0	—	2	1	0	0	0	5¹	11	0	2	1	20.3	10.13	27	.440	.444	1	.333	1	-2	-2	-0	-0.2
1914	Phi-A	0	1	.000	2	2	0	0	0	8	8	0	3	1	13.5	4.50	58	.267	.353	3	.273	0	-2	-2	-0	-0.2
1915	Bro-N	15	10	.600	29	24	17	2	0	195²	166	1	91	66	12.6	2.58	108	.236	.337	21	.280	4	4	4	-4	0.5
1916	*Bro-N	13	8	.619	27	20	10	3	0	159	136	3	44	47	10.3	2.66	101	.239	.296	11	.180	-0	6	6	-6	-0.6
1917	Bro-N	7	11	.389	31	14	9	0	0	141	147	4	40	34	13.0	3.96	71	.284	.355	10	.227	2	-20	-18	-3	-2.4

YEAR	TM/L	W	L	PCT	G	GS	CG	SH	SV	IP	H	HR	BB	SO	RAT	ERA	ERA+	OAV	OOB	BH	AVG	PB	PR	/A	PD	TPI
1918	Bro-N	8	14	.364	27	20	16	2	0	189	191	10	49	44	11.5	3.81	73	.266	.315	19	.168	-0	-22	-22	-3	-2.7
1920	Det-A	0	0	—	2	0	0	0	0	5²	7	0	2	1	14.3	3.18	117	.318	.375	0	.000	-0	0	0	-0	0.0
Total	14	158	110	.590	354	269	187	35	8	2320	2034	38	841	1052	11.5	2.78	99	.241	.316	261	.235	36	4	-8	-25	-0.1

● BOBBY COOMBS
Coombs, Raymond Franklin   b: 2/2/08, Goodwins Mills, Me.   d: 10/21/91, Ogunquit, Me.   BR/TR, 5'9.5", 160 lbs.   Deb: 6/8/33

YEAR	TM/L	W	L	PCT	G	GS	CG	SH	SV	IP	H	HR	BB	SO	RAT	ERA	ERA+	OAV	OOB	BH	AVG	PB	PR	/A	PD	TPI
1933	Phi-A	0	1	.000	21	0	0	0	2	31¹	47	4	20	8	19.2	7.47	57	.348	.432	2	.400	1	-11	-11	-0	-0.4
1943	NY-N	0	1	.000	9	0	0	0	0	16	33	1	8	5	23.1	12.94	27	.423	.477	0	.000	0	-17	-17	-0	-0.9
Total	2	0	2	.000	30	0	0	0	2	47¹	80	5	28	13	20.5	9.32	43	.376	.448	2	.286	1	-28	-28	-0	-1.3

● WILLIAM COON
Coon, William K.   b: 3/21/1855, Pennsylvania   d: 8/30/15, Burlington, N.J.   Deb: 9/4/1875 ♦

YEAR	TM/L	W	L	PCT	G	GS	CG	SH	SV	IP	H	HR	BB	SO	RAT	ERA	ERA+	OAV	OOB	BH	AVG	PB	PR	/A	PD	TPI
1876	Phi-N	0	0	—	2	0	0	0	0	7	9	0	0	0	11.6	5.14	47	.257	.257	50	.227	-0	-2	-2	-0	0.0

● JOHNNY COONEY
Cooney, John Walter   b: 3/18/01, Cranston, R.I.   d: 7/8/86, Sarasota, Fla.   BR/TL, 5'10", 165 lbs.   Deb: 4/19/21   FMC♦

YEAR	TM/L	W	L	PCT	G	GS	CG	SH	SV	IP	H	HR	BB	SO	RAT	ERA	ERA+	OAV	OOB	BH	AVG	PB	PR	/A	PD	TPI
1921	Bos-N	0	1	.000	8	1	0	0	0	20²	19	3	10	9	12.6	3.92	93	.241	.326	1	.200	-0	-0	-1	0	0.0
1922	Bos-N	1	2	.333	4	3	1	0	0	25	19	0	6	7	9.4	2.16	185	.224	.283	0	.000	-1	5	5	0	0.4
1923	Bos-N	3	5	.375	23	8	5	2	0	98	92	3	22	23	10.7	3.31	121	.246	.293	25	.379	4	8	7	-2	0.7
1924	Bos-N	8	9	.471	34	19	12	2	2	181	176	4	50	67	11.4	3.18	120	.260	.314	33	.254	2	14	13	-1	1.1
1925	Bos-N	14	14	.500	31	29	20	2	0	245²	267	18	50	65	11.7	3.48	115	.274	.312	33	.320	5	22	14	1	2.4
1926	Bos-N	3	3	.500	19	8	3	1	0	83¹	99	8	20	15	15.3	4.00	89	.320	.387	38	.302	3	-2	-4	0	0.1
1928	Bos-N	3	7	.300	24	6	2	0	1	89²	106	7	31	18	13.8	4.32	91	.303	.360	7	.171	-0	-3	-4	3	-0.1
1929	Bos-N	2	3	.400	14	2	1	0	3	45	57	0	22	11	15.8	5.00	94	.315	.389	23	.319	2	-1	-2	1	0.1
1930	Bos-N	0	0	—	7	0	0	0	0	7	16	1	2	1	25.7	18.00	27	.471	.526	0	.000	-1	-10	-10	-0	0.0
Total	9	34	44	.436	159	76	44	7	6	795¹	858	41	223	224	12.4	3.72	106	.278	.331	965	.286	15	32	19	4	4.7

● BOB COONEY
Cooney, Robert Daniel   b: 7/12/07, Glens Falls, N.Y.   d: 5/4/76, Glens Falls, N.Y.   BR/TR, 5'11", 160 lbs.   Deb: 9/6/31

YEAR	TM/L	W	L	PCT	G	GS	CG	SH	SV	IP	H	HR	BB	SO	RAT	ERA	ERA+	OAV	OOB	BH	AVG	PB	PR	/A	PD	TPI
1931	StL-A	0	3	.000	5	4	1	0	0	39¹	46	1	20	13	15.3	4.12	113	.291	.374	5	.385	1	1	2	-0	0.2
1932	StL-A	1	2	.333	23	3	1	0	1	71	94	8	36	23	16.7	6.97	70	.324	.402	0	.000	-3	-20	-17	-2	-1.0
Total	2	1	5	.167	28	7	2	0	1	110¹	140	9	56	36	16.2	5.95	80	.313	.393	5	.143	-2	-19	-14	-2	-0.8

● BILL COONEY
Cooney, William A. "Cush"   b: 4/7/1883, Boston, Mass.   d: 11/6/28, Roxbury, Mass.   TR ,   Deb: 9/22/09 ♦

YEAR	TM/L	W	L	PCT	G	GS	CG	SH	SV	IP	H	HR	BB	SO	RAT	ERA	ERA+	OAV	OOB	BH	AVG	PB	PR	/A	PD	TPI
1909	Bos-N	0	0	—	3	0	0	0	0	6¹	4	0	2	3	8.5	1.42	199	.182	.250	3	.300	0	1	1	-0	0.0

● WILBUR COOPER
Cooper, Arley Wilbur   b: 2/24/1892, Bearsville, W.Va.   d: 8/7/73, Encino, Cal.   BR/TL, 5'11", 175 lbs.   Deb: 8/29/12

YEAR	TM/L	W	L	PCT	G	GS	CG	SH	SV	IP	H	HR	BB	SO	RAT	ERA	ERA+	OAV	OOB	BH	AVG	PB	PR	/A	PD	TPI
1912	Pit-N	3	0	1.000	6	4	3	2	0	38	32	1	15	30	11.1	1.66	197	.227	.301	2	.154	-0	7	7	-0	0.4
1913	Pit-N	5	3	.625	30	9	3	1	0	93	98	0	45	39	14.0	3.29	92	.276	.361	2	.077	-1	-1	-3	-2	-0.5
1914	Pit-N	16	15	.516	40	34	19	0	1	266²	246	6	79	102	11.1	2.13	125	.254	.313	19	.207	-1	20	16	0	2.0
1915	Pit-N	5	16	.238	38	21	11	1	4	185²	180	4	52	71	11.7	3.30	83	.262	.323	7	.117	-3	-11	-12	1	-1.5
1916	Pit-N	12	11	.522	42	23	16	2	2	246	189	4	74	111	9.8	1.87	144	.215	.279	17	.215	2	21	22	-1	2.2
1917	Pit-N	17	11	.607	40	34	23	7	1	297²	276	4	54	99	10.1	2.36	120	.258	.297	21	.204	2	12	16	-3	1.5
1918	Pit-N	19	14	.576	38	29	26	2	3	273¹	219	2	65	117	9.7	2.11	136	.223	.279	23	.242	3	20	23	-2	3.1
1919	Pit-N	19	13	.594	35	32	27	4	1	286²	229	10	74	106	10.0	2.67	113	.225	.287	29	.287	6	8	11	-5	1.4
1920	Pit-N	24	15	.615	44	37	28	3	2	327	307	4	52	114	10.2	2.39	134	.253	.290	25	.221	1	27	30	-3	3.2
1921	Pit-N	22	14	.611	38	38	29	2	0	327	341	9	80	134	11.9	3.25	118	.272	.320	31	.254	4	19	21	-3	2.2
1922	Pit-N	23	14	.622	41	37	27	4	0	294²	330	13	61	129	12.2	3.18	128	.286	.326	29	.269	9	30	29	-2	4.0
1923	Pit-N	17	19	.472	39	38	26	1	0	294²	331	11	71	77	12.6	3.57	112	.288	.335	28	.262	4	14	14	-1	1.7
1924	Pit-N	20	14	.588	38	35	25	4	1	268²	296	13	40	62	11.4	3.28	117	.283	.313	36	.346	10	17	17	-4	2.5
1925	Chi-N	12	14	.462	32	26	13	0	0	212¹	249	18	61	41	13.3	4.28	101	.291	.341	17	.207	1	-0	1	-2	-0.1
1926	Chi-N	2	1	.667	8	8	3	2	0	55	65	6	21	18	14.1	4.42	87	.311	.374	7	.389	3	-4	-4	-1	-0.2
	Det-A	0	4	.000	8	3	0	0	0	13²	27	0	9	2	25.7	11.20	36	.443	.534	0	.000	-1	-11	-11	0	-2.4
Total	15	216	178	.548	517	408	279	35	14	3480	3415	103	853	1252	11.3	2.89	116	.262	.312	293	.239	39	168	180	-26	19.7

● CAL COOPER
Cooper, Calvin Asa   b: 8/11/22, Great Falls, S.C.   BR/TR, 6'2.5", 180 lbs.   Deb: 9/14/48

YEAR	TM/L	W	L	PCT	G	GS	CG	SH	SV	IP	H	HR	BB	SO	RAT	ERA	ERA+	OAV	OOB	BH	AVG	PB	PR	/A	PD	TPI
1948	Was-A	0	0	—	1	0	0	0	0	1	5	1	0	0	54.0	45.00	10	.625	.667	0	—	0	-5	-5	-0	0.0

● DON COOPER
Cooper, Donald James   b: 1/15/57, New York, N.Y.   BR/TR, 6'1", 185 lbs.   Deb: 4/9/81

YEAR	TM/L	W	L	PCT	G	GS	CG	SH	SV	IP	H	HR	BB	SO	RAT	ERA	ERA+	OAV	OOB	BH	AVG	PB	PR	/A	PD	TPI
1981	Min-A	1	5	.167	27	2	0	0	0	58²	61	9	32	33	14.4	4.30	92	.274	.367	0	—	0	-4	-2	-1	-0.6
1982	Min-A	0	1	.000	6	1	0	0	0	11¹	14	0	11	5	19.9	9.53	45	.311	.446	0	—	0	-7	-7	-0	-0.7
1983	Tor-A	0	0	—	4	0	0	0	0	5¹	8	3	0	5	13.5	6.75	64	.348	.348	0	—	0	-2	-1	-0	-0.5
1985	NY-A	0	0	—	7	0	0	0	0	10	12	2	3	4	13.5	5.40	74	.300	.349	0	—	0	-1	-2	-0	-0.3
Total	4	1	6	.143	44	3	0	0	0	85¹	95	14	46	47	15.0	5.27	76	.287	.376	0	—	0	-14	-12	-2	-1.6

● GUY COOPER
Cooper, Guy Evans "Rebel"   b: 1/28/1893, Rome, Ga.   d: 8/2/51, Santa Monica, Cal.   BB/TR, 6'1", 185 lbs.   Deb: 5/2/14

YEAR	TM/L	W	L	PCT	G	GS	CG	SH	SV	IP	H	HR	BB	SO	RAT	ERA	ERA+	OAV	OOB	BH	AVG	PB	PR	/A	PD	TPI
1914	NY-A	0	0	—	1	0	0	0	0	3	3	0	2	3	15.0	9.00	31	.273	.385	-0		-2	-2	0		0.0
	Bos-A	1	0	1.000	9	1	0	0	0	22	23	1	9	5	14.3	5.32	51	.299	.393	0	.000	-1	-6	-6	-1	-0.5
	Yr	1	0	1.000	10	1	0	0	0	25	26	1	11	8	14.4	5.76	47	.295	.392	0	.000	-1	-8	-8	-1	-0.5
1915	Bos-A	0	0	—	1	0	0	0	0	2	0	0	2	0	9.0	0.00	—	.000	.286	0	—	0	1	1	-0	0.0
Total	2	1	0	1.000	11	1	0	0	0	27	26	1	13	8	14.0	5.33	51	.280	.385	0	.000	-1	-8	-8	-1	-0.5

● MORT COOPER
Cooper, Morton Cecil   b: 3/2/13, Atherton, Mo.   d: 11/17/58, Little Rock, Ark.   BR/TR, 6'2", 210 lbs.   Deb: 9/14/38   F

YEAR	TM/L	W	L	PCT	G	GS	CG	SH	SV	IP	H	HR	BB	SO	RAT	ERA	ERA+	OAV	OOB	BH	AVG	PB	PR	/A	PD	TPI
1938	StL-N	2	1	.667	4	3	1	0	1	23²	17	1	12	11	11.4	3.04	130	.195	.300	2	.222	0	2	2	1	0.4
1939	StL-N	12	6	.667	45	26	7	2	4	210²	208	6	97	130	13.1	3.25	127	.260	.342	16	.232	3	16	20	-3	1.6
1940	StL-N	11	12	.478	38	29	16	3	0	230²	225	12	86	95	12.3	3.63	110	.253	.321	13	.157	-2	6	9	-2	0.4
1941	StL-N	13	9	.591	29	25	12	0	0	186²	175	6	69	118	11.9	3.91	96	.244	.313	13	.186	-0	-6	-3	-1	-0.5
1942	*StL-N★	22	7	.759	37	35	22	10	0	278²	207	9	68	152	9.0	1.78	193	.204	.258	19	.184	-0	48	51	-3	5.0
1943	*StL-N★	21	8	.724	37	32	24	6	3	274	228	5	79	141	10.2	2.30	148	.226	.286	17	.170	-1	33	32	-2	3.2
1944	*StL-N★	22	7	.759	34	33	22	7	1	252¹	227	6	60	97	10.4	2.46	143	.239	.288	19	.202	2	32	30	-5	3.0
1945	StL-N	2	0	1.000	4	3	1	0	0	23²	20	1	7	14	10.6	1.52	246	.227	.292	2	.333	1	6	6	-1	0.5
	Bos-N†	7	4	.636	20	11	4	1	1	78	77	4	27	45	12.1	3.35	115	.257	.320	6	.231	1	4	4	0	0.7
	Yr	9	4	.692	24	14	5	1	1	101²	97	5	34	59	11.7	2.92	130	.249	.311	8	.250	2	10	10	-0	1.2
1946	Bos-N☆	13	11	.542	28	27	15	4	0	199	181	16	39	83	9.9	3.12	110	.239	.276	14	.209	1	6	7	-3	0.6
1947	Bos-N	2	5	.286	10	7	2	0	0	46²	48	2	13	15	12.2	4.05	96	.271	.328	0	.000	-1	-0	-1	-0	-0.3
	NY-N	1	5	.167	8	8	2	0	0	36²	51	7	13	12	15.1	7.12	57	.323	.374	6	.429	4	-12	-12	-1	-1.4
	Yr	3	10	.231	18	15	4	0	0	83¹	99	9	26	27	13.5	5.40	74	.294	.344	6	.222	2	-12	-13	-2	-1.7
1949	Chi-N	0	0	—	1	0	0	0	0	0	2	1	1	0	—	∞	—	1.000	1.000	0	—	0	-3	-3	-0	-0.3
Total	11	128	75	.631	295	239	128	33	14	1840²	1666	85	571	913	11.1	2.97	123	.240	.300	127	.194	6	132	143	-20	12.9

● PAT COOPER
Cooper, Orge Patterson   b: 11/26/17, Albemarle, N.C.   d: 3/15/93, Charlotte, N.C.   BR/TR, 6'3", 180 lbs.   Deb: 5/11/46 ♦

YEAR	TM/L	W	L	PCT	G	GS	CG	SH	SV	IP	H	HR	BB	SO	RAT	ERA	ERA+	OAV	OOB	BH	AVG	PB	PR	/A	PD	TPI
1946	Phi-A	0	0	—	1	0	0	0	0	1	1	0	1	0	18.0	0.00	—	.250	.400							

● MAYS COPELAND
Copeland, Mays   b: 8/31/13, Mountain View, Ark.   d: 11/29/82, Indio, Cal.   BR/TR, 6', 180 lbs.   Deb: 4/27/35

YEAR	TM/L	W	L	PCT	G	GS	CG	SH	SV	IP	H	HR	BB	SO	RAT	ERA	ERA+	OAV	OOB	BH	AVG	PB	PR	/A	PD	TPI
1935	StL-N	0	0	—	1	0	0	0	0	0²	2	0	0	1	27.0	13.50	30	.667	.667	0	—	0	-1	-1	-0	0.0

● HENRY COPPOLA
Coppola, Henry Peter   b: 8/6/12, E.Douglas, Mass.   d: 7/10/90, Norfolk, Mass.   BR/TR, 5'11", 175 lbs.   Deb: 4/19/35

YEAR	TM/L	W	L	PCT	G	GS	CG	SH	SV	IP	H	HR	BB	SO	RAT	ERA	ERA+	OAV	OOB	BH	AVG	PB	PR	/A	PD	TPI
1935	Was-A	3	4	.429	19	5	2	1	0	59¹	72	6	29	19	15.5	5.92	73	.300	.378	1	.071	-0	-10	-11	-0	-1.1
1936	Was-A	0	0	—	6	0	0	0	0	14	17	1	12	2	18.6	4.50	106	.315	.439	1	.333	1	1	0	-0	0.1
Total	2	3	4	.429	25	5	2	1	1	73¹	89	7	41	21	16.1	5.65	78	.303	.390	2	.118	0	-9	-10	-0	-1.0

YEAR	TM/L	W	L	PCT	G	GS	CG	SH	SV	IP	H	HR	BB	SO	RAT	ERA	ERA+	OAV	OOB	BH	AVG	PB	PR	/A	PD	TPI

● DOUG CORBETT Corbett, Douglas Mitchell b: 11/4/52, Sarasota, Fla. BR/TR, 6'1", 185 lbs. Deb: 4/10/80

1980	Min-A	8	6	.571	73	0	0	0	23	136¹	102	7	42	89	9.6	1.98	220	.213	.278	0	—	0	**31**	**36**	3	4.6
1981	Min-A☆	2	6	.250	**54**	0	0	0	17	87²	80	5	34	60	11.7	2.57	154	.239	.309	0	—	0	11	13	2	1.7
1982	Min-A	0	2	.000	10	0	0	0	3	22	27	3	10	15	15.1	5.32	80	.300	.370	0	—	0	-3	-3	1	-0.4
	Cal-A	1	7	.125	33	0	0	0	8	57	46	8	25	37	11.2	5.05	80	.223	.307	0	—	0	-6	-6	0	-0.9
	Yr	1	9	.100	43	0	0	0	11	79	73	11	35	52	12.3	5.13	80	.247	.326	0	—	0	-9	-9	1	-1.3
1983	Cal-A	1	1	.500	11	0	0	0	0	17¹	26	1	4	18	16.1	3.63	110	.351	.392	0	—	0	1	1	-0	0.1
1984	Cal-A	5	1	.833	45	1	0	0	4	85	76	2	30	48	11.4	2.12	187	.244	.314	0	—	0	18	17	0	1.4
1985	Cal-A	3	3	.500	30	0	0	0	0	46	49	7	20	24	13.7	4.89	84	.274	.350	0	—	0	-4	-4	0	-0.4
1986	*Cal-A	4	2	.667	46	0	0	0	10	78²	66	11	22	36	10.2	3.66	112	.231	.288	0	—	0	5	4	1	0.6
1987	Bal-A	0	2	.000	11	0	0	0	1	23	25	5	13	16	14.9	7.83	56	.281	.373	0	—	0	-9	-9	1	-0.6
Total	8	24	30	.444	313	1	0	0	66	553	497	49	200	343	11.4	3.32	125	.242	.312	0	—	0	43	50	8	6.1

● JOE CORBETT Corbett, Joseph A. b: 12/4/1875, San Francisco, Cal. d: 5/2/45, San Francisco, Cal. BR/TR, 5'10", Deb: 8/23/1895

1895	Was-N	0	2	.000	3	3	3	0	0	19	26	3	9	3	17.5	5.68	84	.321	.402	2	.133	-1	-2	-2	0	-0.2
1896	*Bal-N	3	0	1.000	8	3	3	0	0	41	31	0	17	28	11.6	2.20	195	.208	.311	6	.273	1	10	9	-1	0.6
1897	*Bal-N	24	8	.750	37	37	34	1	0	313	330	2	115	149	13.4	3.11	134	.269	.342	37	.247	-0	42	37	2	3.1
1904	StL-N	5	8	.385	14	14	12	0	0	108²	110	2	51	68	14.0	4.39	61	.240	.327	9	.209	1	-20	-20	0	-2.0
Total	4	32	18	.640	62	57	52	1	1	481²	497	7	192	248	13.5	3.42	113	.259	.338	54	.235	1	30	24	2	1.5

● SHERMAN CORBETT Corbett, Sherman Stanley b: 11/3/62, New Braunfels, Tex. BL/TL, 6'4", 205 lbs. Deb: 5/29/88

1988	Cal-A	2	1	.667	34	0	0	0	1	45²	47	2	23	28	13.8	4.14	93	.273	.359	0	—	0	-1	-1	-0	0.0
1989	Cal-A	0	0	—	4	0	0	0	0	5¹	3	1	1	3	6.8	3.38	113	.158	.200	0	—	0	0	0	-0	0.0
1990	Cal-A	0	0	—	4	0	0	0	0	5	8	0	3	2	19.8	9.00	42	.364	.440	0	—	0	-3	-3	-0	0.0
Total	3	2	1	.667	42	0	0	0	1	56	58	3	27	33	13.2	4.50	86	.272	.354	0	—	0	-3	-4	-1	0.0

● RAY CORBIN Corbin, Alton Ray b: 2/12/49, Live Oak, Fla. BR/TR, 6'2", 200 lbs. Deb: 4/6/71

1971	Min-A	8	11	.421	52	11	2	0	3	140¹	141	19	70	83	13.7	4.10	87	.265	.353	7	.206	1	-10	-9	1	-1.0
1972	Min-A	8	9	.471	31	19	5	3	0	161²	135	12	53	150	10.8	2.62	123	.230	.300	4	.082	-2	8	11	-2	0.7
1973	Min-A	8	5	.615	51	7	1	0	14	148¹	124	7	60	83	11.5	3.03	130	.229	.311	0	—	0	13	15	-1	1.4
1974	Min-A	7	6	.538	29	15	1	0	0	112¹	133	8	40	50	14.1	5.29	71	.294	.356	0	—	0	-21	-19	1	-2.1
1975	Min-A	5	7	.417	18	11	3	0	0	89²	105	13	38	49	14.6	5.12	75	.295	.366	0	—	0	-13	-13	1	-1.5
Total	5	36	38	.486	181	63	12	3	17	652¹	638	59	261	348	12.7	3.84	95	.258	.334	11	.133	-2	-23	-14	-0	-2.5

● ARCHIE CORBIN Corbin, Archie Ray b: 12/30/67, Beaumont, Tex. BR/TR, 6'4", 190 lbs. Deb: 9/10/91

| 1991 | KC-A | 0 | 0 | — | 2 | 0 | 0 | 0 | 0 | 2¹ | 3 | 0 | 2 | 1 | 19.3 | 3.86 | 107 | .300 | .417 | 0 | — | 0 | 0 | 0 | -0 | 0.0 |

● JACK CORCORAN Corcoran, John H. b: 1860, Lowell, Mass. Deb: 5/1/1884 ◆

| 1884 | Bro-a | 0 | 0 | — | 1 | 0 | 0 | 0 | 0 | 1 | 0 | 0 | 1 | 0 | 9.0 | 0.00 | — | .000 | .091 | 39 | .211 | 0 | 0 | 0 | -0 | 0.0 |

● LARRY CORCORAN Corcoran, Lawrence J. b: 8/10/1859, Brooklyn, N.Y. d: 10/14/1891, Newark, N.J. BL/TB, 120 lbs. Deb: 5/1/1880 F◆

1880	Chi-N	43	14	.754	63	60	57	4	2	536¹	404	6	99	**268**	8.4	1.95	124	.199	.236	66	.231	-0	25	28	6	3.1
1881	Chi-N	**31**	14	.689	45	44	43	4	0	396²	380	10	78	150	10.4	2.31	118	.242	.278	42	.222	-1	20	19	-2	1.4
1882	Chi-N	27	12	**.692**	39	39	38	5	0	355²	281	5	63	170	**8.7**	**1.95**	**147**	**.200**	**.234**	35	.207	-2	38	36	1	3.1
1883	Chi-N	34	20	.630	56	53	51	3	0	473²	483	7	82	216	10.3	2.49	128	.247	.277	55	.209	-1	34	37	1	3.3
1884	Chi-N	35	23	.603	60	59	57	7	0	516²	473	35	116	272	10.3	2.40	130	.229	.270	61	.243	2	33	42	7	4.6
1885	Chi-N	5	2	.714	7	7	6	1	0	59¹	63	2	24	10	13.2	3.64	83	.259	.326	6	.273	2	-5	-4	0	-0.3
	NY-N	2	1	.667	3	3	2	0	0	25	24	1	11	10	12.6	2.88	93	.245	.321	5	.357	1	-0	-1	1	0.1
	Yr	7	3	.700	10	10	8	1	0	84¹	87	3	35	20	13.0	3.42	86	.255	.324	11	.306	3	-6	-5	1	-0.2
1886	Was-N	0	1	.000	2	1	1	0	0	14	16	0	4	3	12.9	5.79	57	.271	.317	15	.185	0	-4	-4	-0	-0.2
1887	Ind-N	0	2	.000	2	2	1	0	0	15	23	3	19	4	26.4	12.60	33	.338	.494	2	.200	-0	-14	-14	0	-1.1
Total	8	177	89	.665	277	268	256	22	2	2392¹	2147	69	496	1103	10.0	2.36	122	.226	.264	287	.223	1	127	139	14	14.0

● MIKE CORCORAN Corcoran, Michael b: Brooklyn, N.Y. Deb: 7/15/1884 F

| 1884 | Chi-N | 0 | 1 | .000 | 1 | 1 | 1 | 0 | 0 | 9 | 16 | 1 | 7 | 2 | 23.0 | 4.00 | 78 | .372 | .460 | 0 | .000 | -0 | -1 | -1 | -0 | -0.1 |

● ED COREY Corey, Edward Norman "Ike" (b: Abraham Simon Cohen) b: 7/13/1899, Chicago, Ill. d: 9/17/70, Kenosha, Wis. BR/TR, 6', 170 lbs. Deb: 7/2/18

| 1918 | Chi-A | 0 | 0 | — | 1 | 0 | 0 | 0 | 0 | 2 | 2 | 0 | 1 | 0 | 13.5 | 4.50 | 61 | .333 | .429 | 0 | .000 | -0 | -0 | -0 | 0 | 0.0 |

● FRED COREY Corey, Frederick Harrison b: 1857, S.Kingston, R.I. d: 11/27/12, Providence, R.I. BR/TR, Deb: 5/1/1878 ◆

1878	Pro-N	1	2	.333	5	5	2	0	0	23	22	0	7	7	11.3	2.35	94	.250	.305	3	.143	-1	-0	-0	-1	-0.1
1880	Wor-N	8	9	.471	25	17	9	2	2	148¹	131	6	16	47	8.9	2.43	107	.219	.239	24	.174	-3	-1	-3	-3	-0.2
1881	Wor-N	6	15	.286	23	21	20	1	0	188²	231	3	31	33	12.5	3.72	81	.299	.326	45	.222	-1	-20	-15	-1	-1.5
1882	Wor-N	1	13	.071	21	14	12	0	0	139	180	5	19	36	12.9	3.56	87	.286	.307	63	.247	0	-10	-7	1	-0.4
1883	Phi-a	10	7	.588	18	16	15	0	0	148¹	182	3	24	42	12.5	3.40	102	.283	.309	77	.258	2	-2	1	1	0.3
1885	Phi-a	1	0	1.000	1	1	1	0	0	9	18	2	1	3	19.0	7.00	49	.419	.432	94	.245	0	-4	-4	0	-0.3
Total	6	27	46	.370	93	74	59	3	2	656¹	764	19	98	168	11.8	3.32	91	.276	.300	427	.246	-3	-36	-21	-2	-2.2

● POP CORKHILL Corkhill, John Stewart b: 4/11/1858, Parkesburg, Pa. d: 4/4/21, Pennsauken, N.J. BL/TR, 5'10", 180 lbs. Deb: 5/1/1883 ◆

1884	Cin-a	1	0	1.000	1	0	0	0	0	5	1	0	2	4	5.4	1.80	185	.063	.167	124	.274	0	1	1	-0	0.1
1885	Cin-a	1	4	.200	8	1	0	0	1	37	36	1	12	10	11.4	3.65	89	.243	.296	111	.252	1	-2	-2	0	-0.1
1886	Cin-a	0	0	—	1	0	0	0	0	0²	1	0	0	1	13.5	13.50	26	.125	.125	143	.265	0	-1	-1	0	0.0
1887	Cin-a	1	0	1.000	5	0	0	0	0	14²	22	0	5	3	16.6	5.52	79	.324	.370	168	.311	1	-2	-2	-0	-0.1
1888	Cin-a	0	0	—	2	0	0	0	1	5	8	1	0	1	14.4	10.80	29	.349	.349	133	.271	0	-4	-4	-0	-0.2
Total	5	3	4	.429	17	1	0	0	2	62¹	68	3	17	21	12.4	4.62	76	.259	.306	1120	.254	3	-8	-8	-1	-0.3

● MIKE CORKINS Corkins, Michael Patrick b: 5/25/46, Riverside, Cal. BR/TR, 6'1", 200 lbs. Deb: 9/8/69

1969	SD-N	1	3	.250	6	4	0	0	0	17	27	3	8	13	18.5	8.47	42	.370	.432	0	.000	0	-9	-9	0	-1.7
1970	SD-N	5	6	.455	24	18	1	0	0	111	109	11	79	75	15.6	4.62	86	.258	.379	8	.216	2	-7	-8	-1	-0.6
1971	SD-N	0	0	—	8	0	0	0	0	13	14	1	6	16	13.8	3.46	95	.280	.357	0	.000	0	0	-0	-0	0.0
1972	SD-N	6	9	.400	47	9	2	1	6	140	125	14	62	108	12.3	3.54	93	.240	.325	9	.237	3	-1	-4	-0	-0.1
1973	SD-N	5	8	.385	47	11	2	0	3	122	130	12	61	82	14.9	4.50	77	.274	.370	7	.212	4	-11	-14	-2	-1.2
1974	SD-N	2	2	.500	25	2	0	0	0	56¹	53	5	32	41	13.7	4.79	74	.255	.357	0	.000	-0	-7	-8	-1	-0.6
Total	6	19	28	.404	157	44	5	1	9	459¹	458	46	248	335	14.2	4.39	81	.262	.360	24	.202	10	-36	-43	-4	-4.2

● RHEAL CORMIER Cormier, Rheal Paul b: 4/23/67, Moncton, N.B., Can. BL/TL, 5'10", 185 lbs. Deb: 8/15/91

1991	StL-N	4	5	.444	11	10	2	0	0	67²	74	5	8	38	11.2	4.12	90	.277	.303	5	.238	1	-3	-3	-1	-0.4
1992	StL-N	10	10	.500	31	30	3	0	0	186	194	15	33	117	11.2	3.68	92	.269	.306	6	.102	-2	-4	-6	1	-0.7
1993	StL-N	7	6	.538	38	21	1	0	0	145¹	163	18	27	75	12.0	4.33	91	.284	.321	11	.234	2	-5	-6	0	-0.2
1994	StL-N	3	2	.600	7	7	0	0	0	39²	40	6	7	26	11.3	5.45	75	.256	.301	4	.286	1	-5	-6	-1	-0.6
Total	4	24	23	.511	87	68	6	0	0	438²	471	44	75	256	11.5	4.12	89	.274	.310	26	.184	2	-17	-21	0	-1.9

● MARDIE CORNEJO Cornejo, Nieves Mardie b: 8/5/51, Wellington, Kan. BR/TR, 6'3", 200 lbs. Deb: 4/8/78

| 1978 | NY-N | 4 | 2 | .667 | 25 | 0 | 0 | 0 | 3 | 36² | 37 | 1 | 14 | 17 | 13.3 | 2.45 | 142 | .285 | .367 | 0 | — | 0 | 5 | 4 | -0 | 0.7 |

YEAR TM/L	W	L	PCT	G	GS	CG	SH	SV	IP	H	HR	BB	SO	RAT	ERA	ERA+	OAV	OOB	BH	AVG	PB	PR	/A	PD	TPI
● **JEFF CORNELL** Cornell, Jeffery Ray b: 2/10/57, Kansas City, Mo. BB/TR, 5'11", 170 lbs. Deb: 6/2/84																								
1984 SF-N	1	3	.250	23	0	0	0	0	38¹	51	4	22	19	17.4	6.10	57	.340	.428	0	.000	-0	-11	-11	-1	-1.2
● **BRAD CORNETT** Cornett, Brad Byron b: 2/4/69, Lamesa, Tex. BR/TR, 6'3", 190 lbs. Deb: 6/8/94																								
1994 Tor-A	1	3	.250	9	4	0	0	0	31	40	1	11	22	15.7	6.68	72	.331	.400	0	—	0	-6	-6	0	-0.7
● **TERRY CORNUTT** Cornutt, Terry Stanton b: 10/2/52, Roseburg, Ore. BR/TR, 6'2", 195 lbs. Deb: 4/9/77																								
1977 SF-N	1	2	.333	28	1	0	0	0	44¹	38	4	22	23	12.2	3.86	101	.229	.319	0	.000	-0	0	0	-1	-0.1
1978 SF-N	0	0	—	1	0	0	0	0	3	1	0	0	0	3.0	0.00	—	.100	.100	0	—	0	1	1	-0	0.0
Total 2	1	2	.333	29	1	0	0	0	47¹	39	4	22	23	11.6	3.61	107	.222	.308	0	.000	-0	1	1	-1	-0.1
● **ED CORREA** Correa, Edwin Josue (Andino) b: 4/29/66, Hato Rey, P.R. BR/TR, 6'2", 192 lbs. Deb: 9/18/85																								
1985 Chi-A	1	0	1.000	5	1	0	0	0	10¹	11	2	11	10	19.2	6.97	62	.275	.431	0	—	-0	-3	-3	-0	-0.6
1986 Tex-A	12	14	.462	32	32	4	2	0	202¹	167	15	126	189	13.2	4.23	102	.223	.337	0	—	0	-1	2	3	0.3
1987 Tex-A	3	5	.375	15	15	0	0	0	70	83	17	52	61	17.9	7.59	59	.296	.414	0	—	0	-24	-24	-0	-2.2
Total 3	16	19	.457	52	48	4	2	0	282²	261	34	189	260	14.6	5.16	84	.244	.361	0	—	0	-29	-26	2	-2.5
● **FRANK CORRIDON** Corridon, Frank J. "Fiddler" b: 11/25/1880, Newport, R.I. d: 2/21/41, Syracuse, N.Y. BR/TR, 6', 170 lbs. Deb: 4/15/04																								
1904 Chi-N	5	5	.500	12	10	9	0	0	100¹	88	2	37	34	11.8	3.05	87	.240	.321	13	.224	-0	-3	-4	3	-0.1
Phi-N	6	5	.545	12	11	11	1	0	94¹	88	2	28	44	11.8	2.19	122	.250	.320	6	.171	-0	6	5	3	0.8
Yr	11	10	.524	24	21	20	1	0	194²	176	4	65	78	11.5	2.64	101	.242	.312	19	.204	0	2	1	6	0.7
1905 Phi-N	10	12	.455	35	26	18	1	1	212	203	2	57	79	11.7	3.48	84	.257	.319	15	.208	4	-11	-13	2	-0.6
1907 Phi-N	18	14	.563	37	32	23	3	2	274	228	0	89	131	10.7	2.46	98	.230	.299	16	.165	0	-1	5	0	0.4
1908 Phi-N	14	10	.583	27	24	18	1	0	208¹	178	0	48	50	10.0	2.51	97	.239	.290	9	.123	-2	-3	-2	3	-0.1
1909 Phi-N	11	7	.611	27	19	11	3	0	171	147	0	61	69	11.3	2.11	124	.242	.318	11	.186	0	9	9	5	1.6
1910 StL-N	6	14	.300	30	18	9	0	3	156	168	1	55	51	13.4	3.81	78	.283	.353	10	.196	-0	-13	-14	3	-1.5
Total 6	70	67	.511	180	140	99	10	7	1216	1100	7	375	458	11.4	2.80	95	.247	.315	80	.180	3	-16	-20	24	0.5
● **JIM CORSI** Corsi, James Bernard b: 9/9/61, Newton, Mass. BR/TR, 6'1", 210 lbs. Deb: 6/28/88																								
1988 Oak-A	0	1	.000	11	0	0	0	0	21¹	20	1	6	10	11.0	3.80	100	.260	.313	0	—	0	-0	-0	-0	0.1
1989 Oak-A	1	2	.333	22	0	0	0	0	38¹	26	2	10	21	8.7	1.88	196	.194	.255	0	—	0	9	8	-0	0.6
1991 Hou-N	0	5	.000	47	0	0	0	0	77²	76	6	23	53	11.5	3.71	95	.259	.312	0	.000	-0	-2	-2	1	0.0
1992 *Oak-A	4	2	.667	32	0	0	0	0	44	44	2	18	19	12.7	1.43	261	.273	.346	0	—	0	12	11	1	1.7
1993 Fla-N	0	2	.000	15	0	0	0	0	20¹	28	1	10	7	16.8	6.64	65	.337	.409	0	—	0	-6	-5	0	-0.4
Total 5	5	12	.294	127	0	0	0	0	201²	194	12	67	110	11.7	3.17	117	.259	.321	0	.000	-0	15	12	2	2.0
● **BARRY CORT** Cort, Barry Lee b: 4/15/56, Toronto, Ont., Can. BR/TR, 6'5", 210 lbs. Deb: 4/22/77																								
1977 Mil-A	1	1	.500	7	3	1	0	0	24¹	25	1	9	17	12.9	3.33	122	.281	.354	0	—	0	2	2	0	0.2
● **AL CORWIN** Corwin, Elmer Nathan b: 12/3/26, Newburgh, N.Y. BR/TR, 6'1", 170 lbs. Deb: 7/25/51																								
1951 *NY-N	5	1	.833	15	8	3	1	1	59	49	7	21	30	10.7	3.66	107	.222	.289	1	.050	-2	2	2	-2	-0.2
1952 NY-N	6	1	.857	21	7	1	0	2	67²	59	5	36	36	12.5	2.66	139	.237	.335	2	.095	-1	8	8	-1	0.6
1953 NY-N	6	4	.600	48	7	2	1	0	106²	122	17	68	49	16.3	4.98	86	.290	.393	9	.281	4	-8	-8	-1	-0.4
1954 NY-N	1	3	.250	20	0	0	0	0	31¹	35	4	14	14	14.1	4.02	100	.297	.371	0	.000	-0	0	0	-1	-0.1
1955 NY-N	0	1	.000	13	0	0	0	0	24²	24	3	17	13	15.3	4.01	100	.263	.375	0	.000	-0	0	0	-0	-0.1
Total 5	18	10	.643	117	22	6	2	5	289¹	289	36	156	142	13.9	3.98	101	.263	.356	12	.152	0	2	1	-6	-0.2
● **MIKE COSGROVE** Cosgrove, Michael John b: 2/17/51, Phoenix, Ariz. BL/TL, 6'1", 180 lbs. Deb: 9/10/72																								
1972 Hou-N	0	1	.000	7	1	0	0	1	13²	16	2	3	7	12.5	4.61	73	.286	.322	0	—	-0	-2	-2	-1	-0.2
1973 Hou-N	1	1	.500	13	0	0	0	0	10	11	1	8	2	17.1	1.80	202	.282	.404	0	—	0	2	2	-0	0.3
1974 Hou-N	7	3	.700	45	0	0	0	2	90	76	2	39	47	11.6	3.50	99	.232	.316	1	.056	-1	1	-0	-1	-0.2
1975 Hou-N	1	2	.333	32	3	1	0	5	71¹	62	2	37	32	12.5	3.03	111	.245	.341	2	.154	0	5	3	0	0.2
1976 Hou-N	3	4	.429	22	16	1	1	0	89²	106	6	58	34	16.7	5.52	58	.303	.405	2	.087	-1	-20	-23	-0	-1.7
Total 5	12	11	.522	119	20	2	1	8	274²	271	13	145	122	13.7	4.03	83	.264	.357	5	.089	-2	-14	-21	-2	-1.6
● **JIM COSMAN** Cosman, James Henry b: 2/19/43, Brockport, N.Y. BR/TR, 6'4.5", 211 lbs. Deb: 10/2/66																								
1966 StL-N	1	0	1.000	1	1	1	1	0	9	2	0	2	6	5.0	0.00	—	.074	.167	0	.000	-0	4	4	-0	0.4
1967 StL-N	1	0	1.000	10	5	0	0	0	31¹	21	2	24	11	14.4	3.16	104	.198	.370	1	.125	-0	1	0	-1	-0.1
1970 Chi-N	0	0	—	1	0	0	0	0	1	3	1	1	0	36.0	27.00	17	.600	.667	0	—	0	-3	-2	-0	-0.2
Total 3	2	0	1.000	12	6	1	1	0	41¹	26	3	27	16	12.8	3.05	111	.188	.345	1	.091	-1	2	2	-1	0.3
● **JOHN COSTELLO** Costello, John Reilly b: 12/24/60, Bronx, N.Y. BR/TR, 6'1", 190 lbs. Deb: 6/2/88																								
1988 StL-N	5	2	.714	36	0	0	0	1	49²	44	3	25	38	12.5	1.81	192	.235	.325	0	.000	-0	9	9	-1	1.2
1989 StL-N	5	4	.556	48	0	0	0	3	62¹	48	5	20	40	10.1	3.32	109	.213	.283	0	.000	-1	1	2	-1	0.1
1990 StL-N	0	0	—	4	0	0	0	0	4¹	7	1	1	1	18.7	6.23	61	.368	.429	0	—	0	-1	-1	-0	0.0
Mon-N	0	0	—	4	0	0	0	0	6¹	5	2	1	1	8.5	5.68	64	.208	.240	0	—	0	-1	-1	-0	0.0
Yr	0	0	—	8	0	0	0	0	10²	12	3	2	2	11.8	5.91	63	.273	.304	0	—	0	-3	-3	-0	0.0
1991 SD-N	1	0	1.000	27	0	0	0	0	35	37	2	17	24	13.9	3.09	123	.276	.358	0	.000	-0	3	3	-0	0.0
Total 4	11	6	.647	119	0	0	0	4	157²	141	13	64	104	11.9	2.97	122	.239	.317	0	.000	-1	10	11	-3	1.3
● **DAN COTTER** Cotter, Daniel Joseph b: 4/14/1867, Boston, Mass. d: 9/4/35, Boston, Mass. BR/TR, Deb: 7/16/1890																								
1890 Buf-P	0	1	.000	1	1	1	0	0	9	18	1	7	0	25.0	14.00	29	.399	.480	0	.000	-1	-10	-10	-0	-0.7
● **ENSIGN COTTRELL** Cottrell, Ensign Stover b: 8/29/1888, Hoosick Falls, N.Y d: 2/27/47, Syracuse, N.Y. BL/TL, 5'9.5", 173 lbs. Deb: 6/21/11																								
1911 Pit-N	0	0	—	1	0	0	0	0	1	4	0	1	0	45.0	9.00	38	.667	.714	0	—	0	-1	-1	-0	0.0
1912 Chi-N	0	0	—	1	0	0	0	0	4	8	0	1	1	20.3	9.00	37	.444	.474	0	.000	-0	-2	-3	-0	0.0
1913 Phi-A	1	0	1.000	2	1	1	0	0	10	15	0	2	6	15.3	5.40	51	.326	.354	1	.250	1	-3	-3	-0	-0.2
1914 Bos-N	0	1	.000	1	0	0	0	0	1	2	0	3	1	45.0	9.00	31	.333	.556	0	—	0	-1	-1	-0	-0.5
1915 NY-A	0	1	.000	7	0	0	0	0	21¹	29	2	7	7	15.6	3.38	87	.330	.385	0	.000	-1	-1	-1	-0	-0.1
Total 5	1	2	.333	12	2	2	0	0	37¹	58	2	14	12	17.6	4.82	61	.354	.408	1	.083	-1	-8	-8	-0	-0.8
● **JOHNNY COUCH** Couch, John Daniel b: 3/31/1891, Vaughn, Mont. d: 12/8/75, San Mateo, Cal. BL/TR, 6', 180 lbs. Deb: 4/11/17																								
1917 Det-A	0	0	—	3	0	0	0	0	13¹	14	0	3	4	9.5	2.70	98	.255	.269	0	.000	-0	-0	0	0	0.0
1922 Cin-N	16	9	.640	43	34	18	2	1	264	301	13	56	45	12.3	3.89	103	.289	.328	12	.132	-3	6	3	1	0.0
1923 Cin-N	2	7	.222	19	8	1	0	0	69¹	98	2	15	14	14.7	5.97	65	.344	.377	4	.174	-1	-15	-16	-1	-1.9
Phi-N	2	4	.333	11	7	2	0	0	65	91	4	21	18	15.9	5.26	87	.335	.389	6	.250	-1	-9	-5	-0	-0.5
Yr	4	11	.267	30	15	3	0	0	134¹	189	6	36	32	15.3	5.63	75	.339	.383	10	.213	-1	-24	-21	-1	-2.4
1924 Phi-N	4	8	.333	37	6	3	0	0	137	170	13	39	23	13.8	4.73	94	.306	.352	10	.204	-1	-13	-4	-1	-0.3
1925 Phi-N	5	6	.455	34	7	2	1	0	94¹	112	9	39	11	14.5	5.44	88	.298	.365	5	.161	-2	-12	-7	1	-0.7
Total 5	29	34	.460	147	62	26	3	6	643	785	41	171	112	13.5	4.63	91	.304	.350	37	.167	-6	-43	-29	2	-3.4
● **MIKE COUCHEE** Couchee, Michael Eugene b: 12/4/57, San Jose, Cal. BR/TR, 6', 190 lbs. Deb: 4/5/83																								
1983 SD-N	0	1	.000	8	0	0	0	0	14	12	1	6	5	11.6	5.14	68	.214	.290	1	.500	0	-2	-3	-0	-0.2
● **ED COUGHLIN** Coughlin, Edward E. b: 8/5/1861, Hartford, Conn. d: 12/25/52, Hartford, Conn. Deb: 5/15/1884 ♦																								
1884 Buf-N	0	0	—	1	1	0	0	0	0	3	0	0	0	—	∞	—	.600	.600	1	.250	-0	-3	-3	0	-0.2

YEAR TM/L	W	L	PCT	G	GS	CG	SH	SV	IP	H	HR	BB	SO	RAT	ERA	ERA+	OAV	OOB	BH	AVG	PB	PR	/A	PD	TPI
● ROSCOE COUGHLIN							Coughlin, William Edward b: 3/15/1868, Walpole, Mass. d: 3/20/51, Chelsea, Mass. TR, 5′10″, 160 lbs. Deb: 4/22/1890																	
1890 Chi-N	4	6	.400	11	10	10	0	0	95	102	3	40	29	13.8	4.26	86	.266	.342	10	.256	1	-7	-6	1	-0.4
1891 NY-N	3	4	.429	8	7	6	0	0	61	74	5	23	22	14.8	3.84	83	.289	.354	3	.130	1	-3	-4	1	-0.2
Total 2	7	10	.412	19	17	16	0	0	156	176	8	63	51	14.2	4.10	85	.275	.347	13	.210	2	-11	-11	2	-0.6
● FRITZ COUMBE							Coumbe, Frederick Nicholas b: 12/13/1889, Antrim, Pa. d: 3/21/78, Paradise, Cal. BL/TL, 6′, 152 lbs. Deb: 4/22/14																	
1914 Bos-A	1	2	.333	17	5	1	0	1	62¹	49	0	16	17	9.4	1.44	186	.222	.274	2	.111	-1	9	9	0	0.4
Cle-A	1	5	.167	14	5	2	0	0	55¹	59	0	16	22	12.8	3.25	89	.288	.351	6	.261	1	-3	-2	1	-0.1
Yr	2	7	.222	31	10	3	0	1	117²	108	0	32	39	11.0	2.29	121	.254	.312	8	.195	0	6	6	1	0.3
1915 Cle-A	4	7	.364	30	12	4	1	2	114	123	1	37	37	12.6	3.47	88	.294	.355	10	.270	1	-7	-5	3	-0.2
1916 Cle-A	7	5	.583	29	13	7	2	0	120¹	121	1	27	39	11.1	2.02	149	.279	.323	1	.057	-3	11	13	5	1.5
1917 Cle-A	8	6	.571	34	10	4	1	5	134¹	119	0	35	30	10.5	2.14	132	.251	.307	6	.154	-1	8	10	3	1.3
1918 Cle-A	13	7	.650	30	17	9	0	3	150	164	4	52	41	13.0	3.06	98	.286	.347	12	.214	-1	-5	-1	5	0.3
1919 Cle-A	1	1	.500	8	2	0	0	1	23²	32	2	9	7	15.6	5.32	63	.348	.406	3	.500	1	-6	-5	0	-0.3
1920 Cin-N	0	1	.000	3	0	0	0	0	14²	17	0	4	7	12.9	4.91	62	.304	.350	3	.231	1	-3	-3	0	-0.1
1921 Cin-N	3	4	.429	28	6	3	0	1	86²	89	2	21	12	11.5	3.22	111	.280	.326	8	.320	1	5	3	2	0.7
Total 8	38	38	.500	193	70	30	4	13	761¹	773	10	217	212	11.9	2.80	108	.277	.332	52	.206	-1	10	20	20	3.5
● HARRY COURTNEY							Courtney, Henry Seymour b: 11/19/1898, Asheville, N.C. d: 12/11/54, Lyme, Conn. BL/TL, 6′4″, 185 lbs. Deb: 9/13/19																	
1919 Was-A	3	0	1.000	4	3	2	1	0	26¹	25	0	19	6	15.0	2.73	117	.269	.393	2	.200	-1	1	1	-1	0.0
1920 Was-A	8	11	.421	37	24	10	1	0	188	223	6	77	48	14.8	4.74	79	.298	.371	16	.232	4	-20	-21	-3	-1.8
1921 Was-A	6	9	.400	30	15	3	0	1	132²	159	7	71	26	16.1	5.63	73	.305	.397	14	.298	2	-20	-22	-0	-1.9
1922 Was-A	0	1	.000	5	0	0	0	0	10	11	0	9	4	18.0	3.60	107	.306	.444	0	.000	-1	0	0	-0	0.0
Chi-A	5	6	.455	18	11	5	0	0	86²	100	5	37	28	14.3	4.98	82	.299	.371	9	.273	3	-9	-9	-1	-0.7
Yr	5	7	.417	23	11	5	0	0	96²	111	5	46	32	14.7	4.84	84	.300	.379	9	.243	2	-9	-8	-1	-0.7
Total 4	22	27	.449	94	53	20	2	1	443²	518	18	213	112	15.2	4.91	79	.299	.382	41	.252	7	-47	-50	-5	-4.4
● HARRY COVELESKI							Coveleski, Harry Frank "The Giant Killer" (b: Harry Frank Kowalewski)																	
							b: 4/23/1886, Shamokin, Pa. d: 8/4/50, Shamokin, Pa. BB/TL, 6′, 180 lbs. Deb: 9/10/07 F																	
1907 Phi-N	1	0	1.000	4	0	0	0	0	20	10	0	3	6	6.3	0.00	—	.147	.194	0	.000	-0	5	5	0	0.2
1908 Phi-N	4	1	.800	6	5	5	2	0	43²	29	0	12	22	8.9	1.24	196	.196	.265	2	.133	-0	5	6	1	0.8
1909 Phi-N	6	10	.375	24	17	8	2	1	121²	109	0	49	56	12.1	2.74	95	.247	.329	4	.108	-2	-2	-2	1	-0.4
1910 Cin-N	1	1	.500	7	4	2	0	0	39¹	35	1	42	27	18.5	5.26	55	.246	.431	1	.063	-1	-10	-10	1	-0.5
1914 Det-A	22	12	.647	44	36	23	5	2	303²	251	4	100	124	10.8	2.49	113	.227	.298	23	.242	5	8	11	7	2.3
1915 Det-A	22	13	.629	50	38	20	1	4	312²	271	2	87	150	10.9	2.45	124	.233	.298	18	.175	-2	17	20	4	2.4
1916 Det-A	21	11	.656	44	39	22	3	2	324¹	278	6	63	108	9.8	1.97	145	.237	.282	25	.212	1	31	32	4	3.9
1917 Det-A	4	6	.400	16	11	0	0	0	69	70	0	14	15	11.2	2.61	101	.265	.307	5	.227	-0	0	0	2	0.1
1918 Det-A	0	1	.000	3	1	1	0	0	14	17	0	6	3	14.8	3.86	69	.315	.383	1	.250	1	-2	-2	1	-0.1
Total 9	81	55	.596	198	151	83	13	9	1248	1070	13	376	511	10.8	2.39	118	.235	.301	79	.189	-0	55	61	20	8.8
● STAN COVELESKI							Coveleski, Stanley Anthony (b: Stanislaus Kowalewski)																	
							b: 7/13/1889, Shamokin, Pa. d: 3/20/84, South Bend, Ind. BR/TR, 5′11″, 166 lbs. Deb: 9/10/12 FH																	
1912 Phi-A	2	1	.667	5	2	2	1	0	21	18	0	4	9	9.9	3.43	90	.231	.277	1	.143	-0	-0	-1	-1	-0.2
1916 Cle-A	15	13	.536	45	27	11	1	3	232	247	6	58	76	11.9	3.41	88	.278	.323	13	.173	-0	-15	-10	2	-1.1
1917 Cle-A	19	14	.576	45	36	24	9	4	298¹	202	3	94	133	9.0	1.81	157	.194	.261	13	.134	-4	28	34	-4	3.1
1918 Cle-A	22	13	.629	38	33	25	2	1	311	261	2	76	87	9.9	1.82	165	.229	.279	21	.191	-3	33	41	-0	4.6
1919 Cle-A	24	12	.667	43	34	24	4	4	286	286	2	60	118	11.0	2.61	128	.267	.308	20	.213	4	20	23	3	3.6
1920 *Cle-A	24	14	.632	41	38	26	3	2	315	284	6	65	133	10.1	2.49	153	.243	.285	25	.225	3	46	46	3	5.9
1921 Cle-A	23	13	.639	43	40	28	2	2	315	341	6	84	99	12.3	3.37	126	.280	.329	18	.155	-8	32	31	7	3.2
1922 Cle-A	17	14	.548	35	33	21	3	2	276²	292	14	64	98	11.6	3.32	121	.274	.316	10	.101	-7	22	21	1	1.5
1923 Cle-A	13	14	.481	33	31	17	5	2	228	251	8	42	54	11.6	2.76	143	.282	.316	7	.089	-8	31	30	3	2.9
1924 Cle-A	15	16	.484	37	33	18	2	0	240¹	286	6	73	58	13.6	4.04	106	.294	.346	11	.134	-5	5	6	-0	0.2
1925 *Was-A	20	5	.800	32	32	15	3	0	241	230	7	73	58	11.4	2.84	149	.255	.312	9	.111	-8	42	37	0	2.6
1926 Was-A	14	11	.560	36	34	11	3	1	245¹	272	6	81	50	12.9	3.12	124	.286	.342	17	.207	1	25	20	1	2.1
1927 Was-A	2	1	.667	5	4	0	0	0	14¹	13	0	6	3	13.2	3.14	129	.250	.350	2	.333	0	2	1	-0	0.3
1928 NY-A	5	1	.833	12	8	2	0	0	58	72	5	20	5	14.3	5.74	66	.323	.379	1	.053	-1	-11	-13	1	-1.2
Total 14	215	142	.602	450	385	224	38	21	3082	3055	66	802	981	11.4	2.89	128	.262	.311	168	.159	-34	259	276	16	27.5
● CHET COVINGTON							Covington, Chester Rogers "Chesty" b: 11/6/10, Cairo, Ill. d: 6/11/76, Pembroke Park, Fla. BB/TL, 6′2″, 195 lbs. Deb: 4/23/44																	
1944 Phi-N	1	1	.500	19	0	0	0	0	38²	46	2	8	13	12.6	4.66	78	.297	.331	0	.000	-1	-4	-4	-0	-0.3
● TEX COVINGTON							Covington, William Wilkes b: 3/19/1887, Henryville, Tenn. d: 12/10/31, Denison, Tex. BL/TR, 6′1″, 175 lbs. Deb: 4/25/11 F																	
1911 Det-A	7	1	.875	17	6	5	0	0	83²	94	2	33	29	14.7	4.09	86	.297	.381	6	.188	-1	-7	-6	-1	-0.7
1912 Det-A	3	4	.429	14	9	2	1	0	63¹	58	0	30	19	12.9	4.12	79	.253	.347	2	.133	0	-6	-6	-1	-0.6
Total 2	10	5	.667	31	15	7	1	0	147	152	2	63	48	14.0	4.10	82	.278	.367	8	.170	-1	-13	-12	-2	-1.3
● JOE COWLEY							Cowley, Joseph Alan b: 8/15/58, Lexington, Ky. BR/TR, 6′5″, 210 lbs. Deb: 4/13/82																	
1982 Atl-N	1	2	.333	17	8	0	0	0	52¹	53	6	16	27	12.0	4.47	83	.265	.323	3	.200	-0	-5	-4	-0	-0.2
1984 NY-A	9	2	.818	16	11	3	1	0	83¹	75	12	31	71	11.7	3.56	106	.234	.305	0	—	0	4	2	0	0.6
1985 NY-A	12	6	.667	30	26	1	0	0	159²	132	29	85	97	12.6	3.95	101	.224	.328	0	—	0	4	1	-1	0.2
1986 Chi-A	11	11	.500	27	27	4	0	0	162¹	133	20	83	132	12.1	3.88	111	.223	.321	0	—	0	5	8	-1	0.9
1987 Phi-N	0	4	.000	5	4	0	0	0	11²	14	2	17	5	30.9	15.43	27	.389	.548	1	.333	-1	-15	-15	-1	-3.2
Total 5	33	25	.569	95	76	8	1	0	469¹	414	69	232	332	12.7	4.20	96	.235	.329	4	.222	1	-7	-6	-1	-1.7
● DANNY COX							Cox, Danny Bradford b: 9/21/59, Northampton, England BR/TR, 6′4″, 235 lbs. Deb: 8/6/83																	
1983 StL-N	3	6	.333	12	12	0	0	0	83	92	6	23	36	12.5	3.25	111	.286	.333	2	.074	-2	3	3	1	0.2
1984 StL-N	9	11	.450	29	27	1	1	0	156¹	171	9	54	70	13.4	4.03	86	.289	.355	7	.132	0	-8	-10	1	-1.1
1985 *StL-N	18	9	.667	35	35	10	4	0	241	226	19	64	131	10.9	2.88	123	.251	.303	12	.152	1	19	18	-1	1.9
1986 StL-N	12	13	.480	32	32	8	0	0	220	189	14	60	108	10.3	2.90	125	.234	.289	5	.077	-3	20	18	-5	1.1
1987 *StL-N	11	9	.550	31	31	2	0	0	199²	224	17	71	101	13.5	3.88	107	.290	.352	8	.116	-2	4	6	-1	0.3
1988 StL-N	3	8	.273	13	13	0	0	0	86	89	6	25	47	12.0	3.98	98	.272	.326	1	.043	-2	-5	-5	0	-0.7
1991 Phi-N	4	6	.400	23	17	0	0	0	102¹	98	14	39	46	12.1	4.57	80	.258	.329	3	.103	-1	-10	-10	-1	-1.0
1992 Phi-N	2	2	.500	9	7	0	0	0	38¹	46	3	19	30	15.3	5.40	65	.296	.376	1	.091	0	-8	-8	1	-0.8
*Pit-N	3	1	.750	16	0	0	0	3	24¹	20	2	8	18	10.4	3.33	103	.225	.289	0	.000	-0	0	0	-0	-0.0
Yr	5	3	.625	25	7	0	0	3	62²	66	5	27	48	13.4	4.60	76	.269	.342	1	.071	0	-8	-8	0	-0.8
1993 *Tor-A	7	6	.538	44	0	0	0	2	83²	73	8	29	84	11.0	3.12	138	.230	.294	0	—	0	11	11	-1	1.5
1994 Tor-A	1	1	.500	10	0	0	0	0	18²	7	0	7	14	7.2	1.45	334	.113	.214	0	—	0	7	7	0	0.9
Total 10	73	72	.503	254	174	21	5	8	1253	1235	98	399	685	11.9	3.51	106	.261	.321	39	.109	-9	34	30	-6	2.3
● ERNIE COX							Cox, Ernest Thompson b: 2/19/1894, Birmingham, Ala. d: 4/29/74, Birmingham, Ala. BL/TR, 6′1″, 180 lbs. Deb: 5/5/22																	
1922 Chi-A	0	0	—	1	0	0	0	0	1	1	0	2	0	27.0	18.00	23	.250	.500	0	—	0	-2	-2	-0	0.0
● GEORGE COX							Cox, George Melvin b: 11/15/04, Sherman, Tex. BR/TR, 6′1″, 170 lbs. Deb: 4/12/28																	
1928 Chi-A	1	2	.333	26	2	0	0	0	89	110	6	39	22	15.3	5.26	77	.313	.385	2	.077	-2	-12	-12	2	-0.4

YEAR TM/L	W	L	PCT	G	GS	CG	SH	SV	IP	H	HR	BB	SO	RAT	ERA	ERA+	OAV	OOB	BH	AVG	PB	PR	/A	PD	TPI
● **GLENN COX**					Cox, Glenn Melvin			b: 2/3/31, Montebello, Cal.			BR/TR, 6'2", 210 lbs.			Deb: 9/20/55											
1955 KC-A	0	2	.000	2	2	0	0	0	2¹	11	0	1	2	46.3	30.86	14	.611	.632	0	.000	-0	-7	-7	-0	-2.7
1956 KC-A	0	2	.000	3	3	1	0	0	23¹	15	2	22	6	14.3	4.24	102	.203	.385	0	.000	-1	-0	0	-1	-0.2
1957 KC-A	1	0	1.000	10	0	0	0	0	14¹	18	1	9	8	17.0	5.02	79	.321	.415	0	.000	0	-2	-2	0	-0.1
1958 KC-A	0	0	—	2	0	0	0	0	3²	6	1	3	1	22.1	9.82	40	.400	.500	0	—	0	-2	-2	-0	0.0
Total 4	1	4	.200	17	5	1	0	0	43²	50	4	35	17	17.5	6.39	65	.307	.429	0	.000	-1	-12	-11	-1	-3.0
● **CASEY COX**					Cox, Joseph Casey			b: 7/3/41, Long Beach, Cal.			BR/TR, 6'5", 200 lbs.			Deb: 4/15/66											
1966 Was-A	4	5	.444	66	0	0	0	7	113	104	6	35	46	11.4	3.50	99	.250	.314	0	.000	-1	-1	-1	-0	-0.1
1967 Was-A	7	4	.636	54	0	0	0	1	73	67	2	21	32	11.3	2.96	107	.250	.314	0	.000	-0	2	2	0	0.2
1968 Was-A	0	1	.000	4	0	0	0	0	7²	7	0	0	4	8.2	2.35	124	.250	.250	0	—	0	1	0	-0	0.0
1969 Was-A	12	7	.632	52	13	4	0	0	171²	161	15	64	73	11.8	2.78	125	.251	.320	5	.106	-2	16	13	-1	1.1
1970 Was-A	8	12	.400	37	30	1	0	1	192¹	211	27	44	68	12.1	4.45	80	.285	.329	7	.121	-2	-16	-19	-2	-2.2
1971 Was-A	5	7	.417	54	11	0	0	7	124¹	131	9	40	43	12.9	3.98	83	.273	.338	2	.077	-1	-7	-9	-1	-1.2
1972 Tex-A	3	5	.375	35	4	0	0	4	65¹	73	7	26	27	13.8	4.41	68	.277	.344	1	.111	1	-10	-10	-0	-1.3
NY-A	0	1	.000	5	1	0	0	0	11²	13	0	3	4	13.9	4.63	64	.289	.360	0	—	-0	-2	-2	-0	-0.2
Yr	3	6	.333	40	5	0	0	4	77	86	7	29	31	13.7	4.44	68	.276	.341	1	.111	1	-12	-12	-0	-1.5
1973 NY-A	0	0	—	1	0	0	0	0	3	5	0	1	0	24.0	6.00	61	.357	.471	0	—	0	-1	-1	0	0.1
Total 8	39	42	.481	308	59	5	0	20	762	772	66	234	297	12.2	3.70	91	.266	.327	15	.099	-6	-17	-27	-3	-3.6
● **LES COX**					Cox, Leslie Warren			b: 8/14/05, Junction, Tex.			d: 10/14/34, San Angelo, Tex.			BR/TR, 6', 164 lbs.			Deb: 9/11/26							
1926 Chi-A	0	1	.000	2	0	0	0	0	5	6	2	5	3	19.8	5.40	72	.261	.393	1	.500	0	-1	-1	-0	-0.2
● **RED COX**					Cox, Plateau Rex			b: 2/16/1895, Laurel Springs, N.C.			d: 10/15/84, Roanoke, Va.			BL/TR, 6'2", 190 lbs.			Deb: 4/17/20							
1920 Det-A	0	0	—	3	0	0	0	0	5	9	0	3	1	21.6	5.40	69	.375	.444	0	.000	-0	-1	-1	-0	0.0
● **TERRY COX**					Cox, Terry Lee			b: 3/30/49, Odessa, Tex.			BR/TR, 6'5", 215 lbs.			Deb: 9/7/70									
1970 Cal-A	0	0	—	3	0	0	0	0	2¹	4	0	3	1	15.4	3.86	94	.400	.400	—	0	—	0	-0	-0	0.0
● **BILL COX**					Cox, William Donald			b: 6/23/13, Ashmore, Ill.			d: 2/16/88, Charleston, Ill.			BR/TR, 6'1", 185 lbs.			Deb: 6/6/36						
1936 StL-N	0	0	—	2	0	0	0	0	2²	4	0	1	1	16.9	6.75	58	.333	.385	0	—	0	-1	-1	-0	0.0
1937 Chi-A	1	0	1.000	3	2	1	1	0	12²	9	0	5	8	9.9	0.71	648	.200	.280	1	.250	0	6	5	-0	0.4
1938 Chi-A	0	2	.000	7	1	0	0	0	11²	11	0	13	5	18.5	6.94	70	.244	.414	0	.000	-0	-3	-3	-0	-0.4
StL-A	1	4	.200	22	7	1	0	0	63	81	8	35	16	16.6	7.00	71	.315	.397	1	.059	-1	-15	-14	0	-1.0
Yr	1	6	.143	29	8	1	0	0	74²	92	8	48	21	16.9	6.99	71	.305	.400	1	.053	-2	-18	-17	0	-1.4
1939 StL-A	0	2	.000	4	2	1	0	0	9¹	10	0	8	8	17.4	9.64	50	.256	.383	0	.000	-0	-5	-5	1	-0.8
1940 StL-A	0	1	.000	12	0	0	0	0	17¹	23	3	12	7	18.2	7.27	63	.333	.432	0	.000	-0	-6	-5	-0	-0.2
Total 5	2	9	.182	50	12	3	1	0	116²	138	11	74	45	16.4	6.56	74	.296	.392	2	.080	-2	-24	-22	1	-2.0
● **BILL COYLE**					Coyle, William Claude			b: Pittsburgh, Pa.	TR ,		Deb: 7/7/1893														
1893 Bos-N	0	1	.000	2	1	0	0	0	8	14	1	3	2	19.1	9.00	55	.372	.418	0	.000	-0	-4	-4	-0	-0.4
● **CHARLIE COZART**					Cozart, Charles Rhubin			b: 10/17/19, Lenoir, N.C.			BR/TL, 6', 190 lbs.			Deb: 4/17/45									
1945 Bos-N	1	0	1.000	5	0	0	0	0	8	10	2	15	4	28.1	10.13	38	.303	.521	0	.000	-0	-6	-6	1	-0.5
● **ROY CRABB**					Crabb, James Roy			b: 8/23/1890, Monticello, Iowa			d: 3/30/40, Lewistown, Mont.			BR/TR, 5'11", 160 lbs.			Deb: 8/10/12						
1912 Chi-A	0	1	.000	2	1	0	0	0	8²	6	0	4	3	10.4	1.04	308	.214	.313	0	.000	-0	2	2	0	0.2
Phi-A	2	4	.333	7	7	3	0	0	43¹	48	0	17	12	14.3	3.74	82	.287	.367	0	.000	-3	-2	-3	0	-0.6
Yr	2	5	.286	9	8	3	0	0	52	54	0	21	15	13.7	3.29	94	.277	.359	0	.000	-3	0	-1	0	-0.4
● **GEORGE CRABLE**					Crable, George E.			b: 12/1885, Nebraska			BL/TL, 6'1", 190 lbs.			Deb: 8/3/10									
1910 Bro-N	0	0	—	2	1	1	0	0	7¹	5	0	5	3	14.7	4.91	62	.217	.400	0	.000	-0	-2	-2	0	0.0
● **WALT CRADDOCK**					Craddock, Walter Anderson			b: 3/25/32, Pax, W.Va.			d: 7/6/80, Parma Heights, O.			BR/TL, 5'11.5", 176 lbs.			Deb: 9/3/55						
1955 KC-A	0	2	.000	4	2	0	0	0	15	14	3	10	9	16.8	7.80	54	.300	.400	0	.000	-1	-6	-6	-0	-0.7
1956 KC-A	0	2	.000	2	1	0	0	0	9¹	9	1	10	8	18.3	6.75	64	.265	.432	0	.000	-0	-3	-3	-0	-0.5
1958 KC-A	0	3	.000	23	1	0	0	0	36²	41	4	20	22	15.2	5.89	66	.289	.380	0	.000	-0	-9	-8	0	-0.6
Total 3	0	7	.000	29	4	0	0	0	61	68	8	40	39	16.1	6.49	62	.288	.394	0	.000	-1	-18	-17	0	-1.8
● **MOLLY CRAFT**					Craft, Maurice Montague			b: 11/28/1895, Portsmouth, Va.			d: 10/25/78, Los Angeles, Cal.			BR/TR, 6'2", 165 lbs.			Deb: 8/8/16					
1916 Was-A	0	1	.000	2	1	1	0	0	11	12	0	6	9	14.7	3.27	85	.316	.409	0	.000	-0	-1	-1	0	0.0
1917 Was-A	0	0	—	8	0	0	0	1	14	17	0	8	6	16.1	3.86	88	.315	.403	1	.500	-0	-2	-2	0	0.0
1918 Was-A	0	0	—	3	0	0	0	0	7	5	0	1	5	7.7	1.29	212	.208	.240	0	.000	-0	1	1	0	0.0
1919 Was-A	0	3	.000	16	2	0	0	1	48²	59	2	18	17	14.6	3.88	83	.309	.374	2	.111	-2	-4	-4	-0	-0.4
Total 4	0	4	.000	29	3	1	0	2	80²	93	2	33	33	14.3	3.57	84	.303	.374	3	.115	-2	-5	-5	1	-0.4
● **HOWARD CRAGHEAD**					Craghead, Howard Oliver "Judge"			b: 5/25/08, Selma, Cal.			d: 7/15/62, San Diego, Cal.			BR/TR, 6'2", 200 lbs.			Deb: 4/30/31				
1931 Cle-A	0	0	—	4	0	0	0	0	5²	8	0	2	2	15.9	6.35	73	.320	.370	0	—	0	-1	-1	0	0.0
1933 Cle-A	0	0	—	11	0	0	0	0	17¹	19	1	10	9	15.6	6.23	71	.292	.395	0	.000	-0	-4	-3	0	0.0
Total 2	0	0	—	15	0	0	0	0	23	27	1	12	11	15.7	6.26	72	.300	.388	0	.000	-0	-5	-5	0	0.0
● **GEORGE CRAIG**					Craig, George McCarthy "Lefty"			b: 11/15/1887, Philadelphia, Pa.			d: 4/23/11, Indianapolis, Ind.	TL,		Deb: 7/19/07							
1907 Phi-A	0	0	—	2	0	0	0	0	1²	2	0	3	0	37.8	10.80	24	.299	.599	—	0	—	-0	-2	-2	-0	0.0
● **PETE CRAIG**					Craig, Peter Joel			b: 7/10/40, LaSalle, Ontario, Canada			BL/TR, 6'5", 220 lbs.			Deb: 9/6/64									
1964 Was-A	0	0	—	2	1	0	0	0	1²	8	1	4	0	64.8	48.60	8	.667	.750	0	—	0	-8	-8	-0	0.0
1965 Was-A	0	3	.000	3	3	0	0	0	14¹	18	1	8	2	16.3	8.16	43	.321	.406	2	.667	1	-7	-7	1	-1.1
1966 Was-A	0	0	—	1	0	0	0	0	2	2	0	1	1	13.5	4.50	77	.250	.333	0	—	0	-1	-1	-0	0.0
Total 3	0	3	.000	6	4	0	0	0	18	28	2	13	3	20.5	11.50	30	.368	.461	2	.667	1	-16	-16	0	-1.1
● **ROGER CRAIG**					Craig, Roger Lee			b: 2/17/30, Durham, N.C.			BR/TR, 6'4", 191 lbs.			Deb: 7/17/55	MC						
1955 *Bro-N	5	3	.625	21	10	3	0	2	90²	81	8	43	48	12.4	2.78	146	.238	.325	2	.077	-2	13	13	-1	0.8
1956 *Bro-N	12	11	.522	35	32	8	2	1	199	169	25	87	109	11.8	3.71	107	.231	.316	1	.016	-5	1	6	-2	-0.2
1957 Bro-N	6	9	.400	32	13	1	0	0	111²	102	18	47	69	12.2	4.61	90	.249	.329	4	.138	-1	-9	-5	-1	-0.7
1958 LA-N	2	1	.667	9	2	1	0	0	32	30	3	12	16	11.8	4.50	91	.242	.309	0	.000	-1	-2	-1	-1	-0.3
1959 *LA-N	11	5	.688	29	17	7	4	0	152²	122	13	45	76	9.9	2.06	205	.217	.276	3	.058	-4	32	**37**	-1	3.2
1960 LA-N	8	3	.727	21	15	6	1	0	115²	99	8	43	69	11.3	3.27	121	.230	.305	2	.056	-2	4	6	0	0.5
1961 LA-N	5	6	.455	40	14	2	0	2	112²	130	22	52	63	14.9	6.15	71	.288	.367	4	.148	-0	-27	-23	-1	-2.2
1962 NY-N	10	24	.294	42	33	13	0	3	233¹	261	35	70	118	13.0	4.51	93	.288	.343	4	.053	-5	-15	-9	4	-1.3
1963 NY-N	5	22	.185	46	31	14	0	2	236	249	28	58	108	11.9	3.78	92	.267	.314	6	.087	-3	-13	8	3	-0.8
1964 *StL-N	7	9	.438	39	19	3	0	5	166	180	16	35	84	11.9	3.25	117	.279	.317	10	.208	2	5	10	2	1.4
1965 Cin-N	1	4	.200	40	6	0	0	3	64¹	74	6	25	30	14.3	3.64	103	.289	.359	2	.182	-0	-1	-1	-0	0.1
1966 Phi-N	2	1	.667	14	0	0	0	1	22²	31	4	9	15	14.3	5.56	65	.326	.360	4	.235	-1	-5	-5	-1	-0.6
Total 12	74	98	.430	368	186	58	6	19	1536¹	1528	186	522	803	12.2	3.83	104	.259	.323	38	.085	-22	-13	25	4	-0.1

YEAR TM/L	W	L	PCT	G	GS	CG	SH	SV	IP	H	HR	BB	SO	RAT	ERA	ERA+	OAV	OOB	BH	AVG	PB	PR	/A	PD	TPI

● JERRY CRAM   Cram, Gerald Allen b: 12/9/47, Los Angeles, Cal.   BR/TR, 6′, 180 lbs.   Deb: 9/3/69

1969 KC-A	0	1	.000	5	2	0	0	0	16²	15	0	6	10	11.3	3.24	114	.231	.296	0	.000	-0	1	1	-0	0.0
1974 NY-N	0	1	.000	10	0	0	0	0	22¹	22	1	4	8	10.5	1.61	221	.275	.310	1	.333	0	5	5	0	0.2
1975 NY-N	0	1	.000	4	0	0	0	0	5	7	2	2	2	16.2	5.40	64	.333	.391	0	—	0	-1	-1	0	-0.2
1976 KC-A	0	0	—	4	0	0	0	0	4¹	8	0	1	2	18.7	6.23	56	.421	.450	0	—	0	-2	-2	0	0.0
Total 4	0	3	.000	23	2	0	0	0	48¹	52	3	13	22	12.1	2.98	120	.281	.328	1	.167	-0	3	3	0	0.0

● DOC CRAMER   Cramer, Roger Maxwell "Flit" b: 7/22/05, Beach Haven, N.J.   d: 9/9/90, Manahawkin, N.J.   BL/TR, 6′2″, 185 lbs.   Deb: 9/18/29   C◆

| 1938 Bos-A★ | 0 | 0 | — | 1 | 0 | 0 | 0 | 0 | 4 | 3 | 0 | 3 | 1 | 13.5 | 4.50 | 110 | .214 | .353 | 198 | .301 | 0 | 0 | 0 | 0 | 0.0 |

● BILL CRAMER   Cramer, William Wendell b: 5/21/1891, Bedford, Ind.   d: 9/11/66, Fort Wayne, Ind.   BR/TR, 6′, 175 lbs.   Deb: 6/25/12

| 1912 Cin-N | 0 | 0 | — | 1 | 0 | 0 | 0 | 0 | 2¹ | 6 | 0 | 2 | 0 | 23.1 | 0.00 | — | .500 | .500 | 0 | .000 | -0 | 1 | 1 | -0 | 0.0 |

● DOC CRANDALL   Crandall, James Otis b: 10/8/1887, Wadena, Ind.   d: 8/17/51, Bell, Cal.   BR/TR, 5′10.5″, 180 lbs.   Deb: 4/24/08   ◆

1908 NY-N	12	12	.500	32	24	13	0	0	214²	198	3	59	77	11.2	2.93	82	.248	.307	16	.222	5	-14	-12	-1	-1.1
1909 NY-N	6	4	.600	30	7	4	0	6	122	117	5	33	55	11.3	2.88	89	.252	.305	10	.244	3	-4	-4	2	0.1
1910 NY-N	17	4	.810	42	18	13	2	5	207²	194	10	43	73	10.4	2.56	116	.246	.289	25	.342	10	11	9	-1	1.9
1911 *NY-N	15	5	.750	41	15	9	2	5	198²	199	10	51	94	11.6	2.63	128	.256	.307	27	.239	5	17	16	2	2.3
1912 *NY-N	13	7	.650	37	10	7	0	2	162	181	7	35	60	12.1	3.61	94	.286	.326	25	.313	6	-4	-4	-0	0.3
1913 *NY-N	2	4	.333	24	2	1	0	5	55¹	61	2	13	28	12.2	3.09	101	.293	.338	7	.280	2	1	0	1	0.3
*NY-N	2	0	1.000	11	1	1	0	1	42¹	41	1	11	14	11.1	2.55	122	.248	.295	8	.364	3	3	3	1	0.5
Yr	4	4	.500	35	3	2	0	6	97²	102	3	24	42	11.6	2.86	109	.273	.317	15	.319	5	4	3	1	0.8
1914 StL-F	13	9	.591	27	21	18	1	0	196	194	8	52	84	11.4	3.54	86	.256	.305	86	.309	7	-14	-11	-1	-0.4
1915 StL-F	21	15	.583	51	33	22	4	1	312²	307	5	77	117	11.3	2.59	111	.263	.314	40	.284	12	5	10	1	2.6
1916 StL-A	0	0	—	2	0	0	0	0	1¹	7	0	1	0	60.8	27.00	10	.636	.692	1	.083	-0	-4	-4	-0	-0.1
1918 Bos-N	1	2	.333	5	3	3	0	0	34	39	1	4	4	11.6	2.38	113	.307	.333	8	.286	1	1	1	0	0.3
Total 10	102	62	.622	302	134	91	9	25	1546²	1538	52	379	606	11.4	2.92	101	.261	.310	253	.285	54	-1	5	1	6.6

● ED CRANE   Crane, Edward Nicholas "Cannon-Ball" b: 5/27/1862, Boston, Mass.   d: 9/19/1896, Rochester, N.Y.   BR/TR, 5′10.5″, 204 lbs.   Deb: 4/17/1884   ◆

1884 Bos-U	0	2	.000	4	2	1	0	0	18	17	1	6	13	11.5	4.00	60	.233	.291	122	.285	0	-3	-3	1	-0.2
1886 Was-N	1	7	.125	10	8	7	1	0	70	91	5	53	39	18.5	7.20	46	.313	.419	50	.171	-1	-30	-30	0	-2.5
1888 *NY-N	5	6	.455	12	11	11	2	1	92²	70	3	40	58	10.9	2.43	113	.193	.277	6	.162	1	4	3	-1	0.4
1889 *NY-N	14	10	.583	29	25	23	0	0	230	221	10	136	130	14.4	3.68	107	.245	.350	21	.204	3	9	7	-4	0.4
1890 NY-P	16	19	.457	43	35	28	0	0	330¹	323	12	210	117	14.8	4.63	98	.245	.353	46	.315	8	-15	-3	-3	0.0
1891 Cin-a	14	14	.500	32	31	25	1	0	250	216	3	139	122	13.3	**2.45**	**168**	.225	.332	17	.155	-6	35	46	-2	3.5
Cin-N	4	8	.333	15	13	11	1	0	116²	134	3	64	51	15.5	4.09	83	.277	.366	5	.109	-3	-10	-9	0	-1.0
1892 NY-N	16	24	.400	47	43	35	2	1	364¹	350	10	189	174	13.6	3.80	85	.243	.335	40	.245	4	-21	-24	-0	-1.8
1893 NY-N	2	4	.333	10	7	4	0	0	68¹	84	2	41	11	17.3	5.93	79	.293	.393	12	.462	4	-10	-10	-1	-0.3
Bro-N	0	2	.000	2	2	1	0	0	10	19	2	9	5	26.1	13.50	33	.391	.495	2	.400	0	-10	-10	-0	-1.1
Yr	2	6	.250	12	9	5	0	0	78¹	103	4	50	16	17.7	6.89	67	.302	.393	14	.452	5	-19	-20	-1	-1.4
Total 8	72	96	.429	204	177	146	7	2	1550¹	1525	51	887	720	14.3	3.99	95	.247	.347	335	.238	11	-49	-35	-9	-2.5

● LARRY CRAWFORD   Crawford, Charles Lowrie b: 4/27/14, Swissvale, Pa.   BL/TL, 6′1″, 165 lbs.   Deb: 7/21/37

| 1937 Phi-N | 0 | 0 | — | 6 | 0 | 0 | 0 | 0 | 6 | 12 | 2 | 1 | 2 | 19.5 | 15.00 | 29 | .387 | .406 | 0 | — | 0 | -7 | -7 | -0 | 0.0 |

● JIM CRAWFORD   Crawford, James Frederick "Catfish" b: 9/29/50, Chicago, Ill.   BL/TL, 6′3″, 200 lbs.   Deb: 4/6/73

1973 Hou-N	2	4	.333	48	0	0	0	6	70	69	7	33	56	13.4	4.50	81	.256	.341	3	.231	1	-7	-7	-1	-0.5
1975 Hou-N	3	5	.375	44	2	0	0	4	86²	92	6	37	37	13.6	3.63	93	.280	.356	5	.294	2	-0	-3	0	0.0
1976 Det-A	1	8	.111	32	5	1	0	2	109¹	115	4	43	68	13.0	4.53	82	.275	.343	0	—	0	-12	-10	5	-0.6
1977 Det-A	7	8	.467	37	7	0	0	1	126	156	13	50	91	14.8	4.79	90	.300	.373	0	—	0	-10	-7	1	-0.7
1978 Det-A	2	3	.400	39¹	45	3	19	24	39¹	45	3	19	24	15.1	4.35	89	.292	.377	0	—	0	-3	-2	-0	-0.4
Total 5	15	28	.349	181	14	1	0	13	431¹	477	27	182	276	13.9	4.40	86	.285	.357	8	.267	3	-32	-29	6	-2.2

● STEVE CRAWFORD   Crawford, Steven Ray b: 4/29/58, Pryor, Okla.   BR/TR, 6′5″, 225 lbs.   Deb: 9/2/80

1980 Bos-A	2	0	1.000	6	4	0	0	0	32¹	41	3	8	10	13.6	3.62	117	.306	.345	0	—	0	1	2	-0	-0.1
1981 Bos-A	0	5	.000	14	11	0	0	0	57²	69	10	18	29	14.0	4.99	77	.301	.360	0	—	0	-9	-7	-0	-0.6
1982 Bos-A	1	0	1.000	5	0	0	0	0	9	14	0	0	2	14.0	2.00	215	.341	.341	0	—	0	2	2	-0	0.2
1984 Bos-A	5	0	1.000	35	0	0	0	1	62	69	6	21	21	13.2	3.34	125	.286	.346	0	—	0	4	6	-0	0.1
1985 Bos-A	6	5	.545	44	1	0	0	12	91	103	5	28	58	13.0	3.76	114	.289	.340	0	—	0	4	5	1	0.6
1986 *Bos-A	0	2	.000	40	0	0	0	4	57¹	69	5	19	32	13.8	3.92	106	.308	.362	0	—	0	2	2	0	0.1
1987 Bos-A	5	4	.556	29	0	0	0	0	72²	91	13	32	43	15.5	5.33	85	.314	.386	0	—	0	-7	-6	1	-0.7
1989 KC-A	3	1	.750	25	0	0	0	0	54	48	2	19	33	11.7	2.83	136	.242	.318	0	—	0	6	6	2	0.6
1990 KC-A	5	4	.556	46	0	0	0	0	80	79	7	23	54	11.8	4.16	92	.254	.312	0	—	0	-2	-3	1	-0.2
1991 KC-A	3	2	.600	33	0	0	0	1	46²	63	3	18	38	15.2	5.98	69	.311	.373	0	—	0	-10	-10	-0	-1.0
Total 10	30	23	.566	277	16	0	0	19	562²	643	54	186	320	13.5	4.17	99	.290	.348	0	—	0	-8	-3	3	-1.0

● JACK CREEL   Creel, Jack Dalton "Tex" b: 4/23/16, Kyle, Tex.   BR/TR, 6′, 165 lbs.   Deb: 4/22/45

| 1945 StL-N | 5 | 4 | .556 | 26 | 8 | 2 | 0 | 2 | 87 | 78 | 5 | 45 | 34 | 13.3 | 4.14 | 90 | .245 | .349 | 2 | .077 | -2 | -3 | -4 | 0 | -0.5 |

● KEITH CREEL   Creel, Steven Keith b: 2/4/59, Dallas, Tex.   BR/TR, 6′2″, 180 lbs.   Deb: 5/25/82

1982 KC-A	1	4	.200	9	6	0	0	0	41²	43	8	25	13	14.7	5.40	76	.267	.366	0	—	0	-6	-6	0	-0.6
1983 KC-A	2	5	.286	25	10	1	0	0	89¹	116	17	35	31	15.4	6.35	64	.320	.382	0	—	0	-23	-23	-1	-1.6
1985 Cle-A	2	5	.286	15	8	0	0	0	62	73	7	23	31	14.2	4.79	86	.296	.360	0	—	0	-4	-5	-1	-0.5
1987 Tex-A	0	0	—	6	0	0	0	0	9²	12	2	5	5	15.8	4.66	96	.293	.370	0	—	0	-0	-0	0	0.0
Total 4	5	14	.263	55	24	1	0	0	202²	244	34	88	80	14.9	5.60	74	.300	.372	0	—	0	-33	-33	-2	-2.7

● BOB CREMINS   Cremins, Robert Anthony "Lefty" or "Crooked Arm" b: 2/15/06, Pelham Manor, N.Y.   BL/TL, 5′11″, 178 lbs.   Deb: 8/17/27

| 1927 Bos-A | 0 | 0 | — | 4 | 0 | 0 | 0 | 0 | 5¹ | 5 | 0 | 3 | 0 | 13.5 | 5.06 | 83 | .250 | .348 | 0 | — | 0 | -1 | -0 | 0 | 0.0 |

● WALKER CRESS   Cress, Walker James "Foots" b: 3/6/17, Ben Hur, Va.   BR/TR, 6′5″, 205 lbs.   Deb: 4/27/48

1948 Cin-N	0	1	.000	30	2	1	0	0	60	60	2	42	33	15.5	4.50	87	.271	.390	4	.500	2	-4	-4	-1	0.0
1949 Cin-N	0	0	—	3	0	0	0	0	2	2	0	3	0	22.5	0.00	—	.286	.500	0	—	0	1	1	-0	0.0
Total 2	0	1	.000	33	2	1	0	0	62	62	2	45	33	15.7	4.35	90	.272	.394	4	.500	2	-3	-3	-1	0.0

● TIM CREWS   Crews, Stanley Timothy b: 4/3/61, Tampa, Fla.   d: 3/23/93, Orlando, Fla.   BR/TR, 6′, 190 lbs.   Deb: 7/27/87

1987 LA-N	1	1	.500	20	0	0	0	3	29	30	2	8	20	12.4	2.48	160	.268	.328	0	.000	-0	5	5	0	0.4
1988 LA-N	4	0	1.000	42	0	0	0	0	71²	77	3	16	45	11.7	3.14	106	.278	.317	1	.200	0	2	2	-1	0.0
1989 LA-N	0	1	.000	44	0	0	0	0	61²	69	7	23	56	13.7	3.21	106	.284	.351	0	—	0	2	1	-0	0.0
1990 LA-N	4	5	.444	66	2	0	0	5	107¹	98	9	24	76	10.3	2.77	132	.238	.282	0	—	-1	12	11	-1	0.7
1991 LA-N	2	3	.400	60	0	0	0	6	76	75	7	19	53	11.1	3.43	105	.256	.301	0	.000	0	1	0	0	0.1
1992 LA-N	0	3	.000	49	2	0	0	0	78	95	6	20	43	13.5	5.19	66	.310	.357	2	.286	0	-15	-15	-1	-0.6
Total 6	11	13	.458	281	4	0	0	15	423²	444	34	110	293	11.9	3.44	103	.270	.319	3	.136	-0	9	5	-3	0.6

● JERRY CRIDER   Crider, Jerry Stephen b: 9/2/41, Sioux Falls, S.D.   BR/TR, 6′2″, 200 lbs.   Deb: 5/21/69

| 1969 Min-A | 1 | 0 | 1.000 | 21 | 1 | 0 | 0 | 1 | 28² | 31 | 3 | 15 | 16 | 15.1 | 4.71 | 78 | .284 | .381 | 4 | .444 | 2 | -3 | -3 | 0 | 0.1 |

YEAR	TM/L	W	L	PCT	G	GS	CG	SH	SV	IP	H	HR	BB	SO	RAT	ERA	ERA+	OAV	OOB	BH	AVG	PB	PR	/A	PD	TPI
1970	Chi-A	4	7	.364	32	8	0	0	4	91	101	13	34	40	13.5	4.45	88	.288	.354	2	.083	-1	-7	-6	-2	-1.0
Total	2	5	7	.417	53	9	0	0	5	119²	132	16	49	56	13.9	4.51	85	.287	.361	6	.182	1	-11	-9	-2	-0.9

● **CHUCK CRIM**   Crim, Charles Robert b: 7/23/61, Van Nuys, Cal.   BR/TR, 6', 190 lbs.   Deb: 4/8/87

YEAR	TM/L	W	L	PCT	G	GS	CG	SH	SV	IP	H	HR	BB	SO	RAT	ERA	ERA+	OAV	OOB	BH	AVG	PB	PR	/A	PD	TPI
1987	Mil-A	6	8	.429	53	5	0	0	12	130	133	15	39	56	12.1	3.67	125	.266	.323	0	—	0	11	13	-0	1.4
1988	Mil-A	7	6	.538	**70**	0	0	0	9	105	95	11	28	58	10.7	2.91	136	.247	.302	0	—	0	12	12	0	1.6
1989	Mil-A	9	7	.563	**76**	0	0	0	7	117²	114	7	36	59	11.6	2.83	136	.259	.318	0	—	0	14	13	-1	1.7
1990	Mil-A	3	5	.375	67	0	0	0	11	85²	88	7	23	39	11.9	3.47	112	.261	.312	0	—	0	4	4	0	0.5
1991	Mil-A	8	5	.615	66	0	0	0	3	91¹	115	9	25	39	14.0	4.63	86	.305	.351	0	—	0	-5	-7	0	-0.8
1992	Cal-A	7	6	.538	57	0	0	0	1	87	100	11	29	30	14.0	5.17	77	.293	.359	0	—	0	-12	-12	0	-1.6
1993	Cal-A	2	2	.500	11	0	0	0	0	15¹	17	2	5	10	14.1	5.87	77	.298	.375	0	—	0	-3	-2	1	-0.5
1994	Chi-N	5	4	.556	49	1	0	0	2	64¹	69	9	24	43	13.2	4.48	92	.271	.336	0	.000	-0	-2	-3	0	-0.4
Total	8	47	43	.522	449	6	0	0	45	696¹	731	71	209	334	12.4	3.83	106	.272	.329	0	.000	-0	20	19	-0	1.9

● **JACK CRIMIAN**   Crimian, John Melvin b: 2/17/26, Philadelphia, Pa.   BR/TR, 5'10", 180 lbs.   Deb: 7/3/51

YEAR	TM/L	W	L	PCT	G	GS	CG	SH	SV	IP	H	HR	BB	SO	RAT	ERA	ERA+	OAV	OOB	BH	AVG	PB	PR	/A	PD	TPI
1951	StL-N	1	0	1.000	11	0	0	0	1	17	24	3	8	5	16.9	9.00	44	.338	.405	1	.333	0	-10	-10	-0	-0.6
1952	StL-N				5	0	0	0	0	8¹	15	4	4	4	20.5	9.72	38	.417	.475	0	.000	0	-6	-6	-0	0.0
1956	KC-A	4	8	.333	54	7	0	0	3	129	129	19	49	59	12.8	5.51	79	.265	.339	5	.227	1	-19	-17	-0	-1.4
1957	Det-A	0	1	.000	4	0	0	0	0	5²	9	1	4	1	20.6	12.71	30	.375	.464	0	—	0	-6	-6	-0	-0.8
Total	4	5	9	.357	74	7	0	0	4	160	177	27	65	69	13.9	6.36	67	.287	.360	6	.231	1	-40	-38	-1	-2.8

● **DODE CRISS**   Criss, Dode b: 3/12/1885, Sherman, Miss. d: 9/8/55, Sherman, Miss.   BL/TR, 6'2", 200 lbs.   Deb: 4/20/08 ◆

YEAR	TM/L	W	L	PCT	G	GS	CG	SH	SV	IP	H	HR	BB	SO	RAT	ERA	ERA+	OAV	OOB	BH	AVG	PB	PR	/A	PD	TPI
1908	StL-A	0	1	.000	9	1	0	0	0	18	15	1	13	9	15.5	6.50	37	.250	.408	28	.341	1	-8	-8	-1	-0.4
1909	StL-A	1	5	.167	11	6	3	0	0	55¹	53	0	32	43	14.2	3.42	71	.262	.369	14	.292	5	-6	-6	-1	-0.1
1910	StL-A	2	1	.667	6	0	0	0	0	19¹	12	0	9	9	11.6	1.40	177	.176	.309	21	.231	1	2	2	-0	0.5
1911	StL-A	0	2	.000	4	2	0	0	0	18¹	24	0	10	9	17.7	8.35	40	.333	.429	21	.253	1	-10	-10	-0	-0.8
Total	4	3	9	.250	30	9	3	0	0	111	104	1	64	70	14.5	4.38	59	.259	.375	84	.276	8	-22	-22	-1	-0.8

● **BILL CRISTALL**   Cristall, William Arthur "Lefty" b: 9/12/1878, Odessa, Russia d: 1/28/39, Buffalo, N.Y.   BL/TL, 5'7", 145 lbs.   Deb: 9/3/01

YEAR	TM/L	W	L	PCT	G	GS	CG	SH	SV	IP	H	HR	BB	SO	RAT	ERA	ERA+	OAV	OOB	BH	AVG	PB	PR	/A	PD	TPI
1901	Cle-A	1	5	.167	6	6	5	0	0	48¹	54	1	30	12	16.4	4.84	73	.279	.387	7	.350	2	-6	-7	2	-0.3

● **LEO CRISTANTE**   Cristante, Dante Leo b: 12/10/26, Detroit, Mich. d: 8/24/77, Dearborn, Mich.   BR/TR, 6'1", 195 lbs.   Deb: 4/21/51

YEAR	TM/L	W	L	PCT	G	GS	CG	SH	SV	IP	H	HR	BB	SO	RAT	ERA	ERA+	OAV	OOB	BH	AVG	PB	PR	/A	PD	TPI
1951	Phi-N	1	1	.500	10	1	0	0	0	22	28	3	9	6	15.5	4.91	78	.318	.388	1	.167	-0	-2	-3	0	-0.2
1955	Det-A	0	1	.000	20	1	0	0	0	36²	37	1	14	9	12.5	3.19	120	.261	.327	0	.000	-1	3	3	-1	-0.2
Total	2	1	2	.333	30	2	0	0	0	58²	65	4	23	15	13.7	3.84	100	.283	.350	1	.077	-1	1	0	-1	-0.4

● **MORRIE CRITCHLEY**   Critchley, Morris Arthur b: 3/26/1850, New London, Conn. d: 3/6/10, Pittsburgh, Pa.   6'1", 190 lbs.   Deb: 5/8/1882

YEAR	TM/L	W	L	PCT	G	GS	CG	SH	SV	IP	H	HR	BB	SO	RAT	ERA	ERA+	OAV	OOB	BH	AVG	PB	PR	/A	PD	TPI
1882	Pit-a	1	0	1.000	1	1	1	1	0	9	7	0	1	3	8.0	0.00	—	.200	.222	0	.000	-1	3	3	0	0.2
	StL-a	0	4	.000	4	4	4	0	0	34	43	3	7	2	13.2	4.24	66	.289	.321	3	.214	-0	-6	-5	-1	-0.6
	Yr	1	4	.200	5	5	5	1	0	43	50	3	8	5	12.1	3.35	83	.272	.303	3	.158	-1	-3	-3	-1	-0.4

● **CLAUDE CROCKER**   Crocker, Claude Arthur b: 7/20/24, Caroleen, N.C.   BR/TR, 6'2", 185 lbs.   Deb: 8/1/44

YEAR	TM/L	W	L	PCT	G	GS	CG	SH	SV	IP	H	HR	BB	SO	RAT	ERA	ERA+	OAV	OOB	BH	AVG	PB	PR	/A	PD	TPI
1944	Bro-N	0	0	—	2	0	0	0	0	3¹	6	0	5	1	29.7	10.80	33	.400	.550	1	1.000	0	-3	-3	-0	0.1
1945	Bro-N	0	0		1	0	0	0	1	2	2	0	1	1	13.5	0.00	—	.286	.375	0	—	0	1	1	-0	0.1
Total	2	0	0	—	3	0	0	0	1	5¹	8	0	6	2	23.6	6.75	54	.364	.500	1	1.000	0	-2	-2	0	0.2

● **RAY CRONE**   Crone, Raymond Hayes b: 8/7/31, Memphis, Tenn.   BR/TR, 6'2", 185 lbs.   Deb: 4/13/54

YEAR	TM/L	W	L	PCT	G	GS	CG	SH	SV	IP	H	HR	BB	SO	RAT	ERA	ERA+	OAV	OOB	BH	AVG	PB	PR	/A	PD	TPI
1954	Mil-N	1	0	1.000	19	2	1	0	1	49	44	6	19	33	11.8	2.02	184	.247	.323	2	.200	-0	11	9	0	0.2
1955	Mil-N	10	9	.526	33	15	6	1	0	140¹	117	11	42	76	10.2	3.46	108	.227	.285	7	.159	-1	9	5	0	0.4
1956	Mil-N	11	10	.524	35	21	6	0	2	169²	173	19	44	73	11.6	3.87	89	.263	.311	6	.122	1	-2	-8	-1	-0.9
1957	Mil-N	3	1	.750	11	5	2	0	0	42¹	54	8	15	14	14.7	4.46	78	.312	.367	2	.182	1	-3	-5	1	-0.2
	NY-N	4	8	.333	25	17	2	0	1	120²	131	11	40	56	13.0	4.33	91	.272	.331	1	.025	-4	-6	-5	2	-0.6
	Yr	7	9	.438	36	22	4	0	1	163	185	19	55	71	13.4	4.36	88	.282	.340	3	.059	-3	-9	-10	3	-0.8
1958	SF-N	1	2	.333	14	1	0	0	0	24	35	5	13	7	18.0	6.75	56	.354	.429	0	.000	-0	-7	-8	-0	-0.9
Total	5	30	30	.500	137	61	17	1	4	546	554	60	173	260	12.1	3.87	95	.263	.321	18	.115	-2	2	-12	2	-2.0

● **JACK CRONIN**   Cronin, John J. b: 5/26/1874, W.New Brighton, S.I., N.Y. d: 7/12/29, Middletown, N.Y.   BR/TR, 6' ", 200 lbs.   Deb: 8/24/1895

YEAR	TM/L	W	L	PCT	G	GS	CG	SH	SV	IP	H	HR	BB	SO	RAT	ERA	ERA+	OAV	OOB	BH	AVG	PB	PR	/A	PD	TPI
1895	Bro-N				2	0	0	0	2	5	10	0	3	1	23.4	10.80	41	.408	.473	1	.500	1	-3	-4	-0	-0.2
1898	Pit-N	2	2	.500	4	4	2	1	0	28	35	0	8	3	13.8	3.54	101	.304	.349	1	.100	-0	0	0	0	0.0
1899	Cin-N	2	2	.500	5	5	5	0	0	41	56	2	16	9	16.9	5.49	71	.324	.398	2	.118	-1	-7	-7	-1	-0.7
1901	Det-A	13	15	.464	30	28	21	1	0	219²	261	6	42	62	12.9	3.89	99	.292	.331	21	.247	2	-6	-1	-3	-0.2
1902	Det-A	0	0		4	0	0	0	0	17¹	26	1	8	5	19.2	9.35	39	.346	.430	0	.000	-1	-11	-11	-0	-0.1
	Bal-A	3	5	.375	10	8	8	0	0	75²	66	1	24	20	10.7	2.62	144	.235	.296	4	.148	-1	8	10	2	1.1
	Yr	3	5	.375	14	8	8	0	0	93	92	2	32	25	12.0	3.87	97	.257	.317	4	.118	-2	-3	-1	3	1.0
	NY-N	6	4	.455	13	12	11	0	0	114	105	3	18	52	9.7	2.45	115	.245	.275	11	.169	-1	4	5	0	0.3
1903	NY-N	6	4	.600	20	11	8	0	1	115²	130	6	37	50	13.5	3.81	88	.284	.345	9	.196	0	-7	-6	-0	-0.5
1904	Bro-N	12	23	.343	40	34	33	4	0	307	284	10	79	110	11.0	2.70	102	.245	.300	17	.157	-3	1	2	-0	-0.1
Total	7	43	57	.430	128	102	88	6	3	923¹	973	28	235	318	12.1	3.40	96	.270	.321	66	.180	-5	-20	-13	-1	-0.4

● **GEORGE CROSBY**   Crosby, George W. b: 1860, Iowa d: 1/9/13, San Francisco, Cal.   Deb: 5/22/1884

YEAR	TM/L	W	L	PCT	G	GS	CG	SH	SV	IP	H	HR	BB	SO	RAT	ERA	ERA+	OAV	OOB	BH	AVG	PB	PR	/A	PD	TPI
1884	Chi-N	1	2	.333	3	3	3	0	0	28	27	3	12	11	12.5	3.54	89	.227	.298	4	.308	1	-2	-1	1	1

● **KEN CROSBY**   Crosby, Kenneth Stewart b: 12/15/47, New Denver, B.C., Canada   BR/TR, 6'2", 179 lbs.   Deb: 8/5/75

YEAR	TM/L	W	L	PCT	G	GS	CG	SH	SV	IP	H	HR	BB	SO	RAT	ERA	ERA+	OAV	OOB	BH	AVG	PB	PR	/A	PD	TPI
1975	Chi-N	1	0	1.000	9	0	0	0	0	8¹	10	0	7	6	18.4	3.24	119	.294	.415	0	—	0	0	1	0	0.1
1976	Chi-N	0	0	—	7	1	0	0	0	12	20	3	8	5	21.0	12.00	32	.377	.459	1	.500	0	-11	-11	0	0.1
Total	2	1	0	1.000	16	1	0	0	0	20¹	30	3	15	11	19.9	8.41	46	.345	.441	1	.500	1	-11	-10	0	0.1

● **LEM CROSS**   Cross, George Lewis b: 1/9/1872, Sanbornton, N.H. d: 10/9/30, Manchester, N.H.   TR, 5'9", 155 lbs.   Deb: 8/6/1893

YEAR	TM/L	W	L	PCT	G	GS	CG	SH	SV	IP	H	HR	BB	SO	RAT	ERA	ERA+	OAV	OOB	BH	AVG	PB	PR	/A	PD	TPI
1893	Cin-N	0	2	.000	3	3	2	0	0	21	24	3	9	7	14.1	5.57	86	.279	.347	2	.333	1	-2	-2	0	0.0
1894	Cin-N	3	4	.429	8	7	3	0	0	53	94	8	21	11	20.4	8.49	65	.381	.440	6	.231	-1	-19	-17	-1	-1.5
Total	2	3	6	.333	11	10	5	0	0	74	118	11	30	18	18.6	7.66	70	.355	.416	8	.250	-0	-21	-19	-1	-1.5

● **DOUG CROTHERS**   Crothers, Douglas b: 11/16/1859, Natchez, Miss. d: 3/29/07, St.Louis, Mo.   BR/TR,   Deb: 8/3/1884

YEAR	TM/L	W	L	PCT	G	GS	CG	SH	SV	IP	H	HR	BB	SO	RAT	ERA	ERA+	OAV	OOB	BH	AVG	PB	PR	/A	PD	TPI
1884	KC-U	1	2	.333	3	3	3	0	0	25	26	0	6	11	11.5	1.80	124	.251	.291	2	.133	-2	2	1	-1	-0.1
1885	NY-a	7	11	.389	18	18	18	1	0	154	192	4	49	40	14.2	5.08	58	.293	.344	8	.157	0	-31	-36	0	-3.1
Total	2	8	13	.381	21	21	21	1	0	179	218	4	55	51	13.8	4.63	62	.287	.337	10	.152	-2	-30	-35	-0	-3.2

● **BILL CROUCH**   Crouch, Wilmer Elmer b: 8/20/10, Wilmington, Del. d: 12/26/80, Howell, Mich.   BB/TR, 6'1", 180 lbs.   Deb: 5/9/39 F

YEAR	TM/L	W	L	PCT	G	GS	CG	SH	SV	IP	H	HR	BB	SO	RAT	ERA	ERA+	OAV	OOB	BH	AVG	PB	PR	/A	PD	TPI
1939	Bro-N	4	0	1.000	6	3	3	0	0	38¹	37	3	14	10	12.0	2.58	156	.255	.321	2	.133	-1	6	6	-1	0.5
1941	Phi-N	2	3	.400	20	5	1	0	0	59	65	4	17	26	12.5	4.42	84	.286	.336	1	.091	-0	-5	-5	-2	-0.3
	StL-N	1	2	.333	18	4	0	0	6	45	45	2	14	15	11.8	3.00	125	.271	.328	0	.000	-1	3	4	-1	0.1
	Yr	3	5	.375	38	9	1	0	7	104	110	6	31	41	12.2	3.81	98	.280	.333	1	.042	-2	-2	-1	1	-0.2
1945	StL-N	1	0	1.000	6	0	0	0	0	13¹	12	1	7	4	13.5	3.38	111	.255	.360	0	.000	-0	1	1	-0	0.0
Total	3	8	5	.615	50	12	4	0	7	155²	159	10	52	55	12.3	3.47	110	.272	.332	3	.073	-3	4	6	0	0.3

YEAR	TM/L	W	L	PCT	G	GS	CG	SH	SV	IP	H	HR	BB	SO	RAT	ERA	ERA+	OAV	OOB	BH	AVG	PB	PR	/A	PD	TPI

● BILL CROUCH Crouch, William Henry "Skip" b: 12/3/1886, Marshallton, Del. d: 12/22/45, Highland Park, Mich. BL/TL, 6'1", 210 lbs. Deb: 7/12/10 F

| 1910 | StL-A | 0 | 0 | — | 1 | 1 | 1 | 0 | 0 | 8 | 6 | 0 | 7 | 2 | 14.6 | 3.38 | 73 | .231 | .394 | 0 | .000 | -0 | -1 | -1 | -0 | -0.1 |

● ZACH CROUCH Crouch, Zachary Quinn b: 10/26/65, Folsom, Cal. BL/TL, 6'3", 180 lbs. Deb: 6/4/88

| 1988 | Bos-A | 0 | 0 | — | 3 | 0 | 0 | 0 | 0 | 1¹ | 4 | 0 | 2 | 0 | 40.5 | 6.75 | 61 | .571 | .667 | 0 | — | 0 | -0 | -0 | 0 | -0.2 |

● ALVIN CROWDER Crowder, Alvin Floyd "General" b: 1/11/1899, Winston-Salem, N.C d: 4/3/72, Winston-Salem, N.C. BL/TR, 5'10", 170 lbs. Deb: 7/24/26

1926	Was-A	7	4	.636	19	12	6	0	1	100	97	3	60	26	14.3	3.96	98	.261	.367	9	.237	1	1	-1	-1	0.1
1927	Was-A	4	7	.364	15	11	4	2	0	67¹	58	3	42	22	13.6	4.54	89	.232	.347	3	.136	-1	-3	-4	-1	-0.7
	StL-A	3	5	.375	21	8	2	1	3	73²	71	3	42	30	13.9	5.01	87	.260	.361	6	.261	0	-7	-5	-1	-0.6
	Yr	7	12	.368	36	19	6	3	3	141	129	6	84	52	13.7	4.79	88	.246	.351	9	.200	-1	-10	-9	-2	-1.3
1928	StL-A	21	5	**.808**	41	31	19	1	2	244	238	11	91	99	12.2	3.69	114	.258	.325	15	.188	-2	10	14	-5	0.7
1929	StL-A	17	15	.531	40	34	19	4	4	266²	272	22	93	79	12.3	3.92	113	.271	.332	18	.188	-3	10	15	-2	1.1
1930	StL-A	3	7	.300	13	10	5	1	1	77¹	85	11	27	42	13.2	4.66	105	.283	.345	4	.160	-2	0	2	1	0.1
	Was-A	15	9	.625	27	25	20	0	1	202¹	191	6	69	65	11.6	3.60	128	.249	.312	13	.171	-2	24	22	-4	1.7
	Yr	18	16	.529	40	35	25	1	2	279²	276	17	96	107	12.0	3.89	120	.259	.320	17	.168	-4	23	24	-3	1.8
1931	Was-A	18	11	.621	44	26	13	1	2	234¹	255	13	72	85	12.6	3.88	111	.275	.328	19	.216	-1	13	11	-3	0.7
1932	Was-A	**26**	13	.667	50	39	21	3	1	327	319	17	77	103	10.9	3.33	130	.252	.295	27	.221	2	42	36	-2	3.5
1933	*Was-A★	24	15	.615	**52**	35	17	0	4	299¹	311	14	81	110	11.9	3.97	105	.267	.316	19	.186	-1	10	7	-3	0.5
1934	Was-A	4	10	.286	29	13	4	0	3	100²	142	9	38	39	16.1	6.79	64	.326	.380	7	.219	1	-26	-28	-1	-3.2
	*Det-A	5	1	.833	9	9	3	1	0	66²	81	3	20	30	13.6	4.18	105	.295	.342	4	.133	-2	2	2	-1	-0.2
	Yr	9	11	.450	38	22	7	1	3	167¹	223	12	58	69	15.1	5.75	76	.314	.365	11	.177	-1	-23	-26	-2	-3.4
1935	*Det-A	16	10	.615	33	32	16	2	0	241	269	16	67	59	12.7	4.26	98	.285	.335	17	.183	-2	5	-2	-3	-0.7
1936	Det-A	4	3	.571	9	7	1	0	0	44	64	5	21	10	17.4	8.39	59	.342	.409	3	.150	-1	-16	-17	-0	-2.0
Total	11	167	115	.592	402	292	150	16	22	2344¹	2453	136	800	799	12.5	4.12	105	.270	.330	164	.194	-12	64	52	-24	1.0

● CAP CROWELL Crowell, Minot Joy b: 9/5/1892, Roxbury, Mass. d: 9/30/62, Central Falls, R.I. BR/TR, 6'1", 178 lbs. Deb: 6/23/15

1915	Phi-A	2	6	.250	10	8	4	0	0	54¹	56	1	47	15	17.9	5.47	54	.292	.443	5	.227	-0	-15	-15	-0	-2.0
1916	Phi-A	0	5	.000	9	6	1	0	0	39²	43	0	34	15	17.9	4.99	57	.289	.427	-2	.000	-2	-10	-9	-1	-1.3
Total	2	2	11	.154	19	14	5	0	0	94	99	1	81	30	17.9	5.27	55	.290	.436	5	.147	-2	-25	-25	-1	-3.3

● BILLY CROWELL Crowell, William Theodore b: 11/6/1865, Cincinnati, Ohio d: 7/24/35, Ft.Worth, Tex. BR/TR, 5'8.5", 160 lbs. Deb: 4/20/1887

1887	Cle-a	14	31	.311	45	45	45	1	0	389¹	541	9	138	72	16.2	4.88	89	.327	.386	22	.141	-13	-25	-23	-3	-3.1
1888	Cle-a	5	13	.278	18	18	16	0	0	150²	212	8	61	61	16.8	5.79	53	.320	.385	5	.086	-5	-44	-45	-1	-4.4
	Lou-a	0	1	.000	1	1	1	0	0	9	12	1	6	5	19.0	6.00	51	.309	.414	0	.000	-0	-3	-3	-0	-0.2
	Yr	5	14	.263	19	19	17	0	0	159²	224	9	67	66	16.5	5.81	53	.316	.376	5	.082	-5	-49	-48	-0	-4.6
Total	2	19	45	.297	64	64	62	1	0	549	765	18	205	138	16.4	5.15	77	.325	.386	27	.124	-18	-74	-71	-4	-7.7

● WOODY CROWSON Crowson, Thomas Woodrow b: 9/9/18, Fuquay Sprgs., N.C d: 8/14/47, Mayodan, N.C. BR/TR, 6'2", 185 lbs. Deb: 4/17/45

| 1945 | Phi-A | 0 | 0 | — | 1 | 0 | 0 | 0 | 0 | 3 | 2 | 0 | 3 | 2 | 15.0 | 6.00 | 57 | .200 | .385 | 0 | .000 | -0 | -1 | -1 | 0 | 0.0 |

● CAL CRUM Crum, Calvin N. b: 7/27/1890, Cooks Mills, Ill. d: 12/7/45, Tulsa, Okla. BR/TR, 6'1", 175 lbs. Deb: 4/17/17

1917	Bos-N	0	0	—	1	0	0	0	0	1	1	0	1	0	18.0	0.00	—	.250	.400	0	—	0	0	0	0	0.0
1918	Bos-N	0	1	.000	1	1	0	0	0	2¹	6	0	3	0	38.6	15.43	17	.500	.714	0	.000	-0	-3	-3	0	-0.9
Total	2	0	1	.000	2	1	0	0	0	3¹	7	0	4	0	32.4	10.80	24	.500	.632	0	.000	-0	-3	-3	1	-0.9

● ROY CRUMPLER Crumpler, Roy Maxton b: 7/8/1896, Clinton, N.C. d: 10/6/69, Fayetteville, N.C. BL/TL, 6'1", 195 lbs. Deb: 9/16/20

1920	Det-A	1	0	1.000	2	2	1	0	0	13	17	2	11	2	20.1	5.54	67	.315	.439	3	.333	1	-3	-3	-0	-0.1
1925	Phi-N	0	0	—	3	1	0	0	0	4²	8	0	2	1	19.3	7.71	62	.381	.435	0	.000	-0	-2	-2	0	0.0
Total	2	1	0	1.000	5	3	1	0	0	17²	25	2	13	3	19.9	6.11	65	.333	.438	3	.273	1	-4	-4	-0	-0.1

● DICK CRUTCHER Crutcher, Richard Louis b: 11/25/1889, Frankfort, Ky. d: 6/19/52, Frankfort, Ky. BR/TR, 5'9", 148 lbs. Deb: 4/14/14

1914	Bos-N	5	7	.417	33	15	5	1	0	158²	169	4	66	48	13.7	3.46	80	.293	.371	8	.148	-1	-12	-12	1	-0.9
1915	Bos-N	2	2	.500	14	4	1	0	2	43²	50	1	16	17	14.0	4.33	60	.309	.378	3	.231	1	-8	-8	0	-0.7
Total	2	7	9	.438	47	19	6	1	2	202¹	219	5	82	65	13.7	3.65	75	.296	.373	11	.164	-0	-19	-21	1	-1.6

● TODD CRUZ Cruz, Todd Ruben b: 11/23/55, Highland Park, Mich BR/TR, 6', 175 lbs. Deb: 9/4/78 ♦

| 1984 | Bal-A | 0 | 0 | — | 1 | 0 | 0 | 0 | 0 | 1 | 0 | 0 | 0 | 0 | 0.0 | 0.00 | — | .000 | .000 | 31 | .218 | 0 | 0 | 0 | 0 | 0.0 |

● VICTOR CRUZ Cruz, Victor Manuel (b: b: 12/24/57, Rancho Viejo La Vega, D.R. BR/TR, 5'9", 200 lbs. Deb: 6/24/78

1978	Tor-A	7	3	.700	32	0	0	0	9	47¹	28	0	35	51	12.2	1.71	229	.179	.333	0	—	0	11	12	-0	2.8
1979	Cle-A	3	9	.250	61	0	0	0	10	78²	70	10	44	63	13.2	4.23	100	.244	.346	0	—	0	0	0	-2	-0.2
1980	Cle-A	6	7	.462	55	0	0	0	12	86	71	10	27	88	10.6	3.45	118	.229	.297	0	—	0	6	6	-1	0.8
1981	Pit-N	1	1	.500	22	0	0	0	1	34	33	6	15	28	13.0	2.65	136	.264	.348	0	.000	-0	3	4	0	0.2
1983	Tex-A	1	3	.250	17	0	0	0	5	25	16	2	10	18	11.2	1.44	278	.184	.276	0	—	0	7	7	-0	1.4
Total	5	18	23	.439	187	0	0	0	37	271	218	28	131	248	11.8	3.09	131	.226	.323	0	.000	-0	27	28	-4	5.0

● COOKIE CUCCURULLO Cuccurullo, Arthur Joseph b: 2/8/18, Asbury Park, N.J. d: 1/23/83, W.Orange, N.J. BL/TL, 5'10", 168 lbs. Deb: 10/3/43

1943	Pit-N	0	1	.000	1	1	0	0	0	7	10	0	3	3	16.7	6.43	54	.357	.419	0	—	1	-2	-2	0	-0.2
1944	Pit-N	2	1	.667	32	4	0	0	4	106¹	110	5	44	31	13.3	4.06	91	.270	.346	14	.368	5	-5	-4	1	0.4
1945	Pit-N	1	3	.250	29	4	0	0	1	56²	68	2	34	17	16.4	5.24	75	.305	.399	3	.214	-0	-9	-8	0	-0.6
Total	3	3	5	.375	62	9	0	0	5	170	188	7	81	51	14.5	4.55	83	.286	.367	17	.327	5	-17	-15	1	-0.4

● JIM CUDWORTH Cudworth, James Alaric "Cuddy" b: 8/22/1858, Fairhaven, Mass. d: 12/21/43, Middleboro, Mass. BR/TR, 6', 165 lbs. Deb: 7/27/1884 ♦

| 1884 | KC-U | 0 | 0 | — | 2 | 1 | 1 | 0 | 0 | 17 | 19 | 1 | 6 | 3 | 11.6 | 4.24 | 58 | .264 | .294 | 17 | .147 | -1 | -3 | -4 | -1 | -0.1 |

● CHARLIE CUELLAR Cuellar, Jesus Patracis b: 9/24/17, Ybor City, Fla. BR/TR, 5'11", 183 lbs. Deb: 7/2/50

| 1950 | Chi-A | 0 | 0 | — | 2 | 0 | 0 | 0 | 0 | 1¹ | 6 | 0 | 3 | 1 | 60.8 | 33.75 | 13 | .600 | .692 | 0 | — | 0 | -4 | -4 | 0 | -0.4 |

● MIKE CUELLAR Cuellar, Miguel Angel (Santana) b: 5/8/37, Las Villas, Cuba BL/TL, 5'11", 175 lbs. Deb: 4/18/59

1959	Cin-N	0	0	—	2	0	0	0	0	4	7	1	4	0	24.8	15.75	26	.368	.478	0	.000	-0	-5	-5	-0	-0.9
1964	StL-N	5	5	.500	32	7	1	0	4	72	80	8	33	56	14.3	4.50	85	.288	.365	0	.000	-2	-8	-6	1	-0.9
1965	Hou-N	1	4	.200	25	4	0	0	2	56	55	3	21	46	12.4	3.54	95	.262	.332	0	.000	-1	0	-1	0	-0.2
1966	Hou-N	12	10	.545	38	28	11	6	2	227¹	193	10	52	175	9.7	2.22	154	.229	.274	8	.113	-1	35	30	0	2.9
1967	Hou-N★	16	11	.593	36	32	16	3	1	246¹	233	16	63	203	10.9	3.03	109	.248	.296	13	.140	-1	9	8	-0	0.9
1968	Hou-N	8	11	.421	28	24	11	2	1	170²	152	8	45	133	10.4	2.74	108	.237	.289	11	.193	-2	5	4	-0	0.7
1969	Bal-A	23	11	.676	39	39	18	5	0	290²	213	18	79	182	9.1	2.38	149	.204	**.261**	12	.117	-3	**40**	**38**	-6	4.1
1970	*Bal-A☆	24	8	**.750**	40	40	**21**	4	0	297²	273	34	69	190	10.4	3.48	105	.242	.286	10	.089	-4	8	6	-3	-0.2
1971	*Bal-A★	20	9	.690	38	38	21	4	0	292¹	250	30	78	124	10.1	3.08	109	.234	.287	11	.103	-4	12	9	1	0.5
1972	Bal-A	18	12	.600	35	35	17	4	0	248¹	197	21	71	132	9.7	2.57	119	.220	.277	11	.126	-1	13	14	0	1.6
1973	*Bal-A	18	13	.581	38	38	17	4	0	267	265	29	84	140	11.8	3.27	114	.258	.314	0	—	0	16	16	0	1.6
1974	*Bal-A☆	22	10	**.688**	38	38	20	5	0	269¹	253	17	86	106	11.4	3.11	111	.252	.312	0	—	0	15	10	-3	0.9
1975	Bal-A	14	12	.538	36	36	17	5	0	256	229	24	80	106	11.0	3.66	96	.249	.313	0	—	0	3	-4	2	-0.1
1976	Bal-A	4	13	.235	26	19	2	1	0	107	129	8	50	32	15.2	4.96	66	.307	.383	0	—	0	-17	-20	-0	-2.7
1977	Cal-A	0	1	.000	2	1	0	0	0	3¹	9	2	3	3	32.4	18.90	21	.500	.571	0	—	-0	-5	-6	-0	-0.4
Total	15	185	130	.587	453	379	172	36	11	2808	2538	222	822	1632	10.8	3.14	109	.243	.299	76	.115	-13	122	92	-2	8.1

YEAR TM/L	W	L	PCT	G	GS	CG	SH	SV	IP	H	HR	BB	SO	RAT	ERA	ERA+	OAV	OOB	BH	AVG	PB	PR	/A	PD	TPI

● **BOBBY CUELLAR** Cuellar, Robert b: 8/20/52, Alice, Tex. BR/TR, 5'11", 188 lbs. Deb: 9/9/77

| 1977 Tex-A | 0 | 0 | — | 4 | 0 | 0 | 0 | 0 | 6² | 4 | 1 | 2 | 3 | 8.1 | 1.35 | 302 | .182 | .250 | 0 | — | 0 | 2 | 2 | -0 | -0.1 |

● **BERT CUETO** Cueto, Dagoberto (Concepcion) b: 8/14/37, San Luis, Cuba BR/TR, 6'4", 170 lbs. Deb: 6/18/61

| 1961 Min-A | 1 | 3 | .250 | 7 | 5 | 0 | 0 | 0 | 21¹ | 27 | 7 | 10 | 5 | 16.0 | 7.17 | 59 | .300 | .376 | 0 | .000 | -0 | -7 | -7 | 0 | -1.1 |

● **JACK CULLEN** Cullen, John Patrick b: 10/6/39, Newark, N.J. BR/TR, 5'11", 170 lbs. Deb: 9/9/62

1962 NY-A	0	0	—	2	0	0	0	1	3	2	0	2	2	12.0	0.00	—	.182	.308	0	—	0	1	1	-0	0.1
1965 NY-A	3	4	.429	12	9	2	1	0	59	59	2	21	25	12.2	3.05	112	.262	.325	3	.150	-0	3	2	1	0.3
1966 NY-A	1	0	1.000	5	0	0	0	0	11¹	11	0	5	7	12.7	3.97	84	.256	.333	0	.000	-0	-1	-1	-0	-0.1
Total 3	4	4	.500	19	9	2	1	1	73¹	72	2	28	34	12.3	3.07	111	.258	.326	3	.130	-1	3	3	0	0.3

● **NICK CULLOP** Cullop, Henry Nicholas "Tomato Face" b: 10/16/1900, St.Louis, Mo. d: 12/8/78, Westerville, Ohio BR/TR, 6', 200 lbs. Deb: 4/14/26 ♦

| 1927 Cle-A | 0 | 0 | — | 1 | 0 | 0 | 0 | 0 | 1 | 1 | 0 | 3 | 0 | 27.0 | 9.00 | 47 | .600 | .600 | 16 | .235 | 0 | -1 | -1 | -0 | 0.0 |

● **NICK CULLOP** Cullop, Norman Andrew b: 9/17/1887, Chilhowie, Va. d: 4/15/61, Tazewell, Va. BL/TL, 5'11.5", 172 lbs. Deb: 5/20/13

1913 Cle-A	3	7	.300	23	8	4	0	0	97²	105	3	35	30	13.2	4.42	69	.291	.358	4	.129	-1	-16	-15	1	-1.5
1914 Cle-A	0	1	.000	1	0	0	0	0	3¹	4	0	1	3	13.5	2.70	107	.364	.417	0	.000	-0	0	0	-0	0.0
KC-F	14	19	.424	44	36	22	4	1	295²	256	6	87	149	10.8	2.34	119	.235	.299	14	.141	-5	18	14	1	1.1
1915 KC-F	22	11	.667	44	36	22	3	2	302¹	278	8	67	111	10.5	2.44	108	.249	.297	18	.188	-1	10	6	6	1.2
1916 NY-A	13	6	.684	28	22	9	0	1	167	151	4	32	77	10.0	2.05	141	.243	.284	6	.109	-3	14	16	-5	1.0
1917 NY-A	5	9	.357	30	18	5	2	1	146¹	161	2	31	27	11.9	3.32	81	.307	.348	7	.159	-1	-11	-10	-0	-1.1
1921 StL-A	0	2	.000	4	1	0	0	0	11²	18	1	6	3	18.5	8.49	53	.340	.407	0	.000	-0	-5	-5	0	-0.7
Total 6	57	55	.509	174	121	62	9	5	1024	973	24	259	400	11.1	2.73	102	.258	.310	49	.149	-12	10	6	3	0.0

● **BUD CULLOTON** Culloton, Bernard Aloysius b: 5/19/1897, Kingston, N.Y. d: 11/9/76, Kingston, N.Y. BR/TR, 5'11", 180 lbs. Deb: 4/16/25

1925 Pit-N	0	1	.000	9	1	0	0	0	21	19	1	1	3	8.6	2.57	173	.241	.250	0	.000	-0	4	4	-0	0.1
1926 Pit-N	0	0	—	4	0	0	0	0	3²	3	0	6	1	22.1	7.36	53	.214	.450	0	—	-0	-1	-1	0	0.0
Total 2	0	1	.000	13	1	0	0	0	24²	22	1	7	4	10.6	3.28	133	.237	.290	0	.000	-0	3	3	-0	0.1

● **RAY CULP** Culp, Raymond Leonard b: 8/6/41, Elgin, Tex. BR/TR, 6', 200 lbs. Deb: 4/10/63

1963 Phi-N★	14	11	.560	34	30	10	5	0	203¹	148	15	102	176	11.3	2.97	109	.206	.309	9	.136	-0	7	6	-0	0.7
1964 Phi-N	8	7	.533	19	19	3	1	0	135	139	15	56	96	13.3	4.13	84	.263	.340	5	.114	-1	-9	-10	-1	-1.2
1965 Phi-N	14	10	.583	33	30	11	2	0	204¹	188	14	78	134	12.2	3.22	108	.243	.322	6	.088	-2	7	6	-1	0.3
1966 Phi-N	7	4	.636	34	12	1	0	1	110²	106	19	33	100	13.5	5.04	71	.246	.338	2	.077	-2	-18	-18	-1	-1.9
1967 Chi-N	8	11	.421	30	22	4	1	0	152²	138	22	59	111	11.7	3.89	91	.239	.311	5	.098	-1	-9	-6	-1	-0.9
1968 Bos-A	16	6	.727	35	30	11	6	0	216¹	166	18	82	190	10.7	2.91	108	.210	.292	8	.114	-1	2	6	-1	0.4
1969 Bos-A★	17	8	.680	32	32	9	2	0	227	195	25	79	172	11.1	3.81	100	.231	.302	12	.152	1	-5	-0	-0	0.4
1970 Bos-A	17	14	.548	33	33	15	1	0	251¹	211	22	91	197	11.2	3.04	130	.224	.300	12	.124	-3	19	26	-1	2.6
1971 Bos-A	14	16	.467	35	35	12	3	0	242¹	236	21	67	151	11.4	3.60	103	.253	.307	8	.118	-2	-4	2	-2	-0.1
1972 Bos-A	5	8	.385	16	16	4	1	0	105	104	8	53	52	13.7	4.46	72	.260	.351	7	.212	1	-16	-15	0	-1.7
1973 Bos-A	2	6	.250	10	9	0	0	0	50¹	46	9	32	32	14.7	4.47	90	.247	.369	0	—	0	-4	-3	0	-0.4
Total 11	122	101	.547	322	268	80	22	1	1898¹	1677	188	752	1411	11.8	3.58	99	.235	.314	74	.123	-11	-29	-5	-8	-2.2

● **BILL CULP** Culp, William Edward b: 6/11/1887, Bellaire, Ohio d: 9/3/69, Arnold, Pa. BB/TR, 6'1.5", 165 lbs. Deb: 9/8/10

| 1910 Phi-N | 0 | 0 | — | 4 | 0 | 0 | 0 | 1 | 6² | 8 | 0 | 4 | 4 | 16.2 | 8.10 | 39 | .333 | .429 | 0 | .000 | -0 | -4 | -4 | 1 | -0.1 |

● **GEORGE CULVER** Culver, George Raymond b: 7/8/43, Salinas, Cal. BR/TR, 6'2", 185 lbs. Deb: 9/7/66

1966 Cle-A	0	2	.000	5	1	0	0	0	9²	15	1	7	6	21.4	8.38	41	.357	.460	0	.000	-0	-5	-5	-0	-0.9
1967 Cle-A	7	3	.700	53	1	0	0	3	75	71	2	31	41	13.0	3.96	82	.258	.346	1	.250	0	-6	-6	1	-0.7
1968 Cin-N	11	16	.407	42	35	5	2	2	226¹	229	8	84	114	13.0	3.22	98	.264	.339	8	.121	-1	-6	-2	2	-0.1
1969 Cin-N	5	7	.417	32	13	0	0	4	101¹	117	8	52	58	15.8	4.26	88	.291	.384	3	.097	-2	-8	-6	2	-0.7
1970 StL-N	3	3	.500	11	7	2	0	0	56²	64	6	24	23	14.1	4.61	89	.284	.356	3	.176	-0	-4	-3	2	-0.1
Hou-N	3	3	.500	32	0	0	0	3	45	44	1	21	31	13.6	3.20	121	.254	.345	1	.250	-0	4	3	-1	0.4
Yr	6	6	.500	43	7	2	0	3	101²	108	7	45	54	13.8	3.98	101	.270	.348	4	.190	-0	1	0	1	0.3
1971 Hou-N	5	8	.385	59	0	0	0	7	95¹	89	4	38	57	12.2	2.64	127	.257	.334	1	.091	-1	9	8	1	1.2
1972 Hou-N	6	2	.750	45	0	0	0	7	97¹	73	7	43	82	11.2	3.05	110	.212	.309	5	.158	-0	4	3	-0	0.3
1973 LA-N	4	4	.500	28	0	0	0	0	42	45	4	20	23	14.4	3.00	115	.292	.381	0	.000	-0	3	2	1	0.5
Phi-N	3	1	.750	14	0	0	0	0	18²	26	0	15	7	19.8	4.82	79	.342	.451	0	—	0	-2	-2	1	-0.4
Yr	7	5	.583	42	0	0	0	0	60²	71	4	36	30	15.9	3.56	100	.305	.398	0	.000	-0	1	0	1	0.1
1974 Phi-N	1	0	1.000	14	0	0	0	0	21²	20	1	16	9	15.4	6.65	57	.267	.402	0	.000	-0	-7	-7	-0	-0.4
Total 9	48	49	.495	335	57	7	2	23	789	793	42	352	451	13.6	3.62	96	.266	.352	20	.124	-4	-18	-13	8	-0.9

● **JOHN CUMBERLAND** Cumberland, John Sheldon b: 5/10/47, Westbrook, Me. BR/TL, 6', 190 lbs. Deb: 9/27/68

1968 NY-A	0	0	—	1	0	0	0	0	2	3	1	1	1	18.0	9.00	32	.333	.400	0	—	0	-1	-1	0	0.0
1969 NY-A	0	0	—	2	0	0	0	0	4	3	0	4	0	15.8	4.50	77	.231	.412	0	—	-0	-0	-0	0	0.0
1970 NY-A	3	4	.429	15	8	1	0	0	64	62	9	15	38	10.8	3.94	89	.252	.295	1	.059	-1	-2	-3	-1	-0.5
SF-N	2	0	1.000	7	0	0	0	0	11	6	0	4	6	8.2	0.82	486	.158	.238	0	.000	-0	4	4	0	0.6
1971 *SF-N	9	6	.600	45	21	3	2	2	185	153	22	36	65	10.1	2.92	116	.223	.281	7	.119	-2	11	10	-3	0.2
1972 SF-N	4	0	.000	9	6	0	0	0	25	38	6	7	8	16.2	8.64	40	.336	.375	1	.111	-0	-14	-14	-1	-2.1
StL-N	1	1	.500	14	1	0	0	0	21²	23	6	7	7	12.5	6.65	51	.291	.349	0	.000	-1	-8	-8	-1	-0.8
Yr	1	5	.167	23	7	0	0	0	46²	61	12	14	15	14.5	7.71	45	.316	.362	1	.071	-1	-22	-22	-2	-2.9
1974 Cal-A	0	1	.000	17	0	0	0	0	21²	24	2	10	12	14.1	3.74	92	.289	.366	0	—	-0	-1	-0	-0	0.1
Total 6	15	16	.484	110	36	6	2	2	334¹	312	46	103	137	11.2	3.82	90	.246	.303	9	.099	-5	-11	-14	-6	-2.7

● **JOHN CUMMINGS** Cummings, John Russell b: 5/10/69, Torrance, Cal. BL/TL, 6'3", 200 lbs. Deb: 4/10/93

1993 Sea-A	0	6	.000	10	8	1	0	0	46¹	59	6	16	19	15.0	6.02	73	.316	.376	—	—	0	-9	-8	-0	-0.9
1994 Sea-A	2	4	.333	17	8	0	0	0	64	66	7	37	33	14.5	5.63	87	.270	.367	—	—	0	-6	-5	0	-0.4
Total 2	2	10	.167	27	16	1	0	0	110¹	125	13	53	52	14.7	5.79	81	.290	.370	—	—	0	-15	-13	-0	-1.3

● **STEVE CUMMINGS** Cummings, Steven Brent b: 7/15/64, Houston, Tex. BB/TR, 6'2", 200 lbs. Deb: 6/24/89

1989 Tor-A	2	0	1.000	5	2	0	0	0	21	18	1	11	8	12.9	3.00	126	.231	.333	—	—	0	2	2	-0	0.1
1990 Tor-A	0	0	—	6	2	0	0	0	12¹	22	4	5	4	20.4	5.11	77	.431	.491	—	—	0	-2	-2	-0	-0.1
Total 2	2	0	1.000	11	4	0	0	0	33¹	40	5	16	12	15.7	3.78	101	.310	.395	—	—	0	0	0	-0	0.0

● **CANDY CUMMINGS** Cummings, William Arthur b: 10/18/1848, Ware, Mass. d: 5/16/24, Toledo, Ohio BR/TR, 5'9", 120 lbs. Deb: 4/22/1872 H

1872 Mut-n	33	20	.623	55	55	53	3	0	497	600	2	30	43	11.4	2.52	137	.270	.280	52	.206	-4	66	51		3.1
1873 Bal-n	28	14	.667	42	42	42	1	0	382	475	4	33	31	12.0	2.66	122	.274	.287	48	.250	2	25	25		1.9
1874 Phi-n	28	26	.519	54	54	52	1	0	482	602	4	21		11.6	2.88	106	.271	.278	54	.236	-1	7	9		0.5
1875 Har-n	35	12	.745	48	47	46	7	0	417	396	0	6		8.7	1.60	162	.235	.237	44	.199	-5	40	46		3.7
1876 Har-N	16	8	.667	24	24	24	5	0	216	215	0	14	26	9.5	1.67	142	.239	.251	17	.162	-8	15	17	-2	0.6
1877 Cin-N	5	14	.263	19	19	16	0	0	155²	214	2	13	11	13.4	4.34	61	.315	.331	14	.100	-0	-26	-29	0	-2.6
Total 4 n	124	72	.633	199	198	193	14	0	1778	2073	10	90	74	10.9	2.43	128	.264	.272	198	.221	-8	138	135		9.2
Total 2	21	22	.488	43	43	40	5	0	371²	434	2	27	37	11.2	2.78	90	.272	.284	31	.177	-8	-11	-12	-2	-2.0

YEAR TM/L	W	L	PCT	G	GS	CG	SH	SV	IP	H	HR	BB	SO	RAT	ERA	ERA+	OAV	OOB	BH	AVG	PB	PR	/A	PD	TPI

● **BRUCE CUNNINGHAM**   Cunningham, Bruce Lee b: 9/29/05, San Francisco, Cal. d: 3/8/84, Hayward, Cal.   BR/TR, 5'10.5", 165 lbs.   Deb: 5/7/29

YEAR TM/L	W	L	PCT	G	GS	CG	SH	SV	IP	H	HR	BB	SO	RAT	ERA	ERA+	OAV	OOB	BH	AVG	PB	PR	/A	PD	TPI
1929 Bos-N	4	6	.400	17	8	4	0	1	91²	100	7	32	22	13.2	4.52	104	.282	.344	4	.148	-0	2	2	1	0.2
1930 Bos-N	5	6	.455	36	6	2	0	0	106²	121	7	41	28	13.7	5.48	90	.289	.352	6	.194	0	-6	-6	3	-0.2
1931 Bos-N	3	12	.200	33	16	6	1	1	136²	157	7	54	32	14.0	4.48	85	.296	.363	3	.071	-4	-9	-10	4	-1.0
1932 Bos-N	1	0	1.000	18	3	0	0	0	47	50	1	19	21	14.0	3.45	109	.281	.363	2	.222	2	2	2	1	0.3
Total 4	13	24	.351	104	33	12	1	2	382	428	22	146	103	13.7	4.64	93	.289	.356	15	.138	-2	-11	-14	9	-0.7

● **BERT CUNNINGHAM**   Cunningham, Ellsworth Elmer b: 11/25/1865, Wilmington, Del. d: 5/14/52, Cragmere, Del.   BR/TR, 187 lbs.   Deb: 9/15/1887 U

YEAR TM/L	W	L	PCT	G	GS	CG	SH	SV	IP	H	HR	BB	SO	RAT	ERA	ERA+	OAV	OOB	BH	AVG	PB	PR	/A	PD	TPI
1887 Bro-a	0	2	.000	3	3	3	0	0	23	26	0	13	8	16.8	5.09	85	.263	.371	0	.000	-1	-2	-2	-0	-0.2
1888 Bal-a	22	29	.431	51	51	50	0	0	453¹	412	8	157	186	11.9	3.39	88	.233	.307	33	.186	-2	-17	-21	0	-2.1
1889 Bal-a	16	19	.457	39	33	29	0	1	279¹	306	11	141	140	14.9	4.87	81	.270	.358	27	.206	-3	-32	-29	-0	-2.9
1890 Phi-P	3	9	.250	14	11	11	0	0	108²	133	0	67	33	17.1	5.22	82	.289	.387	6	.115	-4	-12	-11	1	-1.1
Buf-P	9	15	.375	25	25	24	2	0	211	251	8	134	78	16.7	5.84	70	.283	.381	23	.228	1	-38	-41	-1	-3.1
Yr	12	24	.333	39	36	35	2	0	319²	384	8	201	111	16.6	5.63	74	.283	.378	29	.190	-4	-50	-52	0	-4.2
1891 Bal-a	11	14	.440	30	25	21	0	0	237²	241	8	138	59	14.8	4.01	93	.254	.355	15	.150	-2	-8	-7	2	-0.6
1895 Lou-N	11	16	.407	31	28	24	1	0	231	299	6	104	49	15.9	4.75	97	.309	.379	30	.300	6	-1	-3	2	0.4
1896 Lou-N	7	14	.333	27	20	17	0	1	189¹	242	6	74	37	15.8	5.09	85	.308	.380	22	.250	3	-15	-16	2	-0.9
1897 Lou-N	14	13	.519	29	27	25	0	0	234²	286	2	72	49	14.2	4.14	103	.298	.355	22	.237	-0	4	3	2	0.5
1898 Lou-N	28	15	.651	44	42	41	0	0	362	387	8	65	34	11.7	3.16	113	.271	.312	32	.229	2	18	17	-1	1.8
1899 Lou-N	17	17	.500	39	37	33	1	0	323²	385	4	75	36	13.2	3.84	101	.295	.340	40	.260	3	1	1	6	0.8
1900 Chi-N	4	3	.571	8	7	7	0	0	64	84	0	21	7	15.3	4.36	92	.315	.374	4	.148	-1	-5	-5	-1	-0.6
1901 Chi-N	0	1	.000	1	1	1	0	0	9	11	0	3	2	14.0	5.00	65	.299	.352	0	.000	-1	-2	-2	-1	-0.2
Total 12	142	167	.460	341	310	286	4	2	2726²	3063	61	1064	718	14.1	4.22	91	.277	.349	254	.217	1	-105	-117	12	-8.1

● **GEORGE CUNNINGHAM**   Cunningham, George Harold b: 7/13/1894, Sturgeon Lake, Minn. d: 3/10/72, Chattanooga, Tenn.   BR/TR, 5'11", 185 lbs.   Deb: 4/14/16 ◆

YEAR TM/L	W	L	PCT	G	GS	CG	SH	SV	IP	H	HR	BB	SO	RAT	ERA	ERA+	OAV	OOB	BH	AVG	PB	PR	/A	PD	TPI
1916 Det-A	7	10	.412	35	14	5	0	2	150¹	146	0	74	68	13.4	2.75	104	.269	.360	11	.268	5	1	2	1	0.9
1917 Det-A	2	7	.222	44	8	4	0	4	139	113	2	51	49	10.9	2.91	91	.227	.304	6	.176	1	-4	-4	0	-0.2
1918 Det-A	6	7	.462	27	14	10	0	1	140	131	0	38	39	11.2	3.15	84	.255	.312	25	.223	3	-6	-8	0	-0.3
1919 Det-A	1	1	.500	17	0	0	0	1	47²	54	0	15	11	14.0	4.91	65	.292	.361	5	.217	2	-9	-9	0	-0.1
Total 4	16	25	.390	123	36	19	0	8	477	444	2	178	167	12.1	3.13	89	.255	.330	47	.224	11	-17	-19	2	0.3

● **MIKE CUNNINGHAM**   Cunningham, Mody b: 6/14/1882, Lancaster, S.C. d: 12/10/69, Lancaster, S.C.   BR/TR, 5'10.5", 175 lbs.   Deb: 8/31/06

YEAR TM/L	W	L	PCT	G	GS	CG	SH	SV	IP	H	HR	BB	SO	RAT	ERA	ERA+	OAV	OOB	BH	AVG	PB	PR	/A	PD	TPI
1906 Phi-A	1	0	1.000	5	1	1	0	0	28	29	1	9	15	12.5	3.21	85	.270	.332	4	.333	1	-2	-2	-0	0.0

● **NIG CUPPY**   Cuppy, George Joseph (b: George Koppe) b: 7/3/1869, Logansport, Ind. d: 7/27/22, Elkhart, Ind.   BR/TR, 5'7", 160 lbs.   Deb: 4/16/1892

YEAR TM/L	W	L	PCT	G	GS	CG	SH	SV	IP	H	HR	BB	SO	RAT	ERA	ERA+	OAV	OOB	BH	AVG	PB	PR	/A	PD	TPI
1892 *Cle-N	28	13	.683	47	42	38	1	1	376	333	9	121	103	11.1	2.51	135	.228	.291	36	.214	0	32	37	3	3.8
1893 Cle-N	17	10	.630	31	30	24	0	0	243²	316	6	75	39	14.8	4.47	109	.305	.357	27	.248	1	5	11	-1	0.9
1894 Cle-N	24	15	.615	43	33	29	3	0	316	381	11	128	65	14.8	4.56	120	.295	.363	35	.259	1	27	32	1	2.9
1895 *Cle-N	26	14	.650	47	40	36	1	2	353	384	9	95	91	12.4	3.54	141	.273	.322	40	.286	7	49	57	4	5.8
1896 *Cle-N	25	14	.641	46	40	35	1	1	358	388	8	75	86	11.8	3.12	146	.274	.314	38	.270	6	50	56	4	5.8
1897 Cle-N	10	6	.625	19	17	13	1	0	138	150	3	26	23	11.8	3.20	141	.275	.314	8	.145	-4	17	20	-1	1.5
1898 Cle-N	9	8	.529	18	15	13	1	0	128	147	4	25	27	12.5	3.30	110	.286	.326	5	.104	-4	4	4	-2	0.0
1899 StL-N	11	8	.579	21	21	18	1	0	171²	203	3	26	25	12.3	3.15	127	.294	.324	13	.186	-3	14	16	0	1.3
1900 Bos-N	8	4	.667	17	13	9	0	1	105¹	107	8	24	23	11.7	3.08	134	.263	.314	11	.262	1	7	12	-1	1.2
1901 Bos-A	4	6	.400	13	11	9	0	0	93¹	111	1	14	22	12.2	4.15	85	.292	.320	10	.204	0	-5	-6	-2	-0.7
Total 10	162	98	.623	302	262	224	9	5	2283	2520	62	609	504	12.6	3.48	127	.275	.325	223	.233	6	200	239	6	22.5

● **SAMMY CURRAN**   Curran, Simon Francis b: 10/30/1874, Dorchester, Mass. d: 5/19/36, Dorchester, Mass.   TL,   Deb: 8/1/02

YEAR TM/L	W	L	PCT	G	GS	CG	SH	SV	IP	H	HR	BB	SO	RAT	ERA	ERA+	OAV	OOB	BH	AVG	PB	PR	/A	PD	TPI
1902 Bos-N	0	0	—	1	0	0	0	0	6²	6	0	0	3	8.1	1.35	209	.240	.240	0	.000	-0	1	1	-0	-0.1

● **LAFAYETTE CURRENCE**   Currence, Delancy Lafayette b: 12/3/51, Rock Hill, S.C.   BB/TL, 5'11", 175 lbs.   Deb: 7/24/75

YEAR TM/L	W	L	PCT	G	GS	CG	SH	SV	IP	H	HR	BB	SO	RAT	ERA	ERA+	OAV	OOB	BH	AVG	PB	PR	/A	PD	TPI
1975 Mil-A	0	2	.000	8	1	0	0	0	18²	25	5	14	7	18.8	7.71	50	.316	.419	0	—	0	-8	-8	-1	-0.8

● **MURPHY CURRIE**   Currie, Archibald Murphy b: 8/31/1893, Fayetteville, N.C. d: 6/22/39, Asheboro, N.C.   BR/TR, 5'11.5", 185 lbs.   Deb: 8/31/16

YEAR TM/L	W	L	PCT	G	GS	CG	SH	SV	IP	H	HR	BB	SO	RAT	ERA	ERA+	OAV	OOB	BH	AVG	PB	PR	/A	PD	TPI
1916 StL-N	0	0	—	6	0	0	0	0	14¹	7	1	9	8	10.0	1.88	140	.149	.286	0	.000	-0	1	1	-1	-0.1

● **CLARENCE CURRIE**   Currie, Clarence Franklin b: 12/30/1878, Glencoe, Ont., Can. d: 7/15/41, Little Chute, Wis   BR/TR,   Deb: 4/25/02

YEAR TM/L	W	L	PCT	G	GS	CG	SH	SV	IP	H	HR	BB	SO	RAT	ERA	ERA+	OAV	OOB	BH	AVG	PB	PR	/A	PD	TPI
1902 Cin-N	3	4	.429	10	7	6	1	0	65¹	70	1	17	20	12.3	3.72	81	.274	.324	2	.083	-2	-7	-5	1	-0.7
StL-N	7	5	.583	15	12	10	2	0	124²	125	0	35	30	12.0	2.60	105	.261	.319	9	.196	-0	3	2	2	0.4
Yr	10	9	.526	25	19	16	3	0	190	195	1	52	50	12.0	2.98	98	.265	.318	11	.157	-2	-4	-3	3	-0.3
1903 StL-N	4	12	.250	22	16	13	1	1	148	155	7	60	52	13.7	4.01	81	.281	.362	4	.085	-3	-12	-12	4	-1.1
Chi-N	1	2	.333	6	3	2	0	1	33¹	35	1	9	9	12.7	2.97	106	.254	.313	5	.417	2	1	1	1	0.3
Yr	5	14	.263	28	19	15	1	2	181¹	190	8	69	61	13.0	3.82	85	.271	.339	9	.153	-1	-11	-12	5	-0.8
Total 2	15	23	.395	53	38	31	4	2	371¹	385	9	121	111	12.8	3.39	89	.270	.336	20	.155	-4	-15	-15	8	-1.1

● **BILL CURRIE**   Currie, William Cleveland b: 11/29/28, Leary, Ga.   BR/TR, 6', 175 lbs.   Deb: 4/13/55

YEAR TM/L	W	L	PCT	G	GS	CG	SH	SV	IP	H	HR	BB	SO	RAT	ERA	ERA+	OAV	OOB	BH	AVG	PB	PR	/A	PD	TPI
1955 Was-A	0	0	—	3	0	0	0	0	4¹	7	3	2	2	20.8	12.46	31	.350	.435	0	—	0	-4	-4	-0	0.0

● **GEORGE CURRY**   Curry, George James "Soldier Boy" b: 12/21/1888, Bridgeport, Conn. d: 10/5/63, Stratford, Conn.   BR/TR, 6', 185 lbs.   Deb: 7/16/11

YEAR TM/L	W	L	PCT	G	GS	CG	SH	SV	IP	H	HR	BB	SO	RAT	ERA	ERA+	OAV	OOB	BH	AVG	PB	PR	/A	PD	TPI
1911 StL-A	0	3	.000	3	3	0	0	0	15²	19	0	24	2	24.7	7.47	45	.339	.538	0	.000	-1	-7	-7	-0	-1.1

● **STEVE CURRY**   Curry, Stephen Thomas b: 9/13/65, Winter Park, Fla.   BR/TR, 6'6", 217 lbs.   Deb: 7/10/88

YEAR TM/L	W	L	PCT	G	GS	CG	SH	SV	IP	H	HR	BB	SO	RAT	ERA	ERA+	OAV	OOB	BH	AVG	PB	PR	/A	PD	TPI
1988 Bos-A	0	1	.000	3	3	0	0	0	11	15	0	14	4	23.7	8.18	50	.357	.518	0	—	0	-5	-5	0	-0.4

● **WES CURRY**   Curry, Wesley b: 4/1/1860, Wilmington, Del. d: 5/19/33, Philadelphia, Pa.   Deb: 8/6/1884 U

YEAR TM/L	W	L	PCT	G	GS	CG	SH	SV	IP	H	HR	BB	SO	RAT	ERA	ERA+	OAV	OOB	BH	AVG	PB	PR	/A	PD	TPI
1884 Ric-a	0	2	.000	2	2	2	0	0	16	15	2	3	1	10.7	5.06	66	.221	.264	2	.250	-0	-3	-3	-0	-0.3

● **CLIFF CURTIS**   Curtis, Clifton Garfield b: 7/3/1883, Delaware, Ohio d: 4/23/43, Utica, Ohio   BR/TR, 6'2", 180 lbs.   Deb: 8/23/09

YEAR TM/L	W	L	PCT	G	GS	CG	SH	SV	IP	H	HR	BB	SO	RAT	ERA	ERA+	OAV	OOB	BH	AVG	PB	PR	/A	PD	TPI
1909 Bos-N	4	5	.444	10	9	8	2	0	83	53	1	30	22	9.2	1.41	200	.191	.275	1	.034	-3	11	13	1	1.3
1910 Bos-N	6	24	.200	43	37	12	2	2	251	251	9	124	75	13.9	3.55	94	.277	.371	12	.146	-4	-14	-6	6	-0.6
1911 Bos-N	1	8	.111	12	9	5	0	1	77	79	4	34	23	13.4	4.44	86	.265	.344	7	.250	-0	-9	-5	1	-0.5
Chi-N	1	2	.333	4	1	0	0	0	7	7	0	5	4	19.3	3.86	86	.241	.405	2	.500	0	-0	-0	-0	-0.1
Phi-N	2	1	.667	8	5	3	1	0	45	45	0	15	13	12.2	2.60	132	.260	.323	4	.267	0	4	4	-0	0.2
Yr	4	11	.267	24	15	8	1	1	129	131	4	54	40	13.0	3.77	97	.259	.332	12	.267	-0	-5	-1	0	-0.4
1912 Phi-N	2	5	.286	10	8	2	0	0	50	55	3	17	20	13.7	3.24	112	.286	.357	0	.000	-2	1	2	1	0.2
Bro-N	4	7	.364	19	9	3	0	0	80	72	4	37	22	12.9	3.94	85	.250	.347	8	.308	1	-5	-5	-0	-0.5
Yr	6	12	.333	29	17	5	0	0	130	127	7	54	42	12.9	3.67	94	.262	.344	8	.195	-1	-4	-3	1	-0.3
1913 Bro-N	8	9	.471	30	16	6	0	2	151²	145	1	55	57	12.3	3.26	101	.255	.328	6	.122	-3	-1	1	2	-0.1
Total 5	28	61	.315	136	94	39	5	6	744²	707	22	317	236	12.8	3.31	101	.259	.344	39	.159	-10	-13	3	9	-0.1

● **JACK CURTIS**   Curtis, Jack Patrick b: 1/11/37, Rhodhiss, N.C.   BL/TL, 5'10", 175 lbs.   Deb: 4/22/61

YEAR TM/L	W	L	PCT	G	GS	CG	SH	SV	IP	H	HR	BB	SO	RAT	ERA	ERA+	OAV	OOB	BH	AVG	PB	PR	/A	PD	TPI
1961 Chi-N	10	13	.435	31	27	6	0	0	180¹	220	23	51	57	13.6	4.89	85	.303	.350	10	.167	3	-17	-14	0	-1.2
1962 Chi-N	0	2	.000	4	4	0	0	0	18	18	2	6	4	12.0	3.50	118	.277	.338	1	.250	-0	1	1	-0	0.1
Mil-N	4	4	.500	30	4	0	0	0	75²	82	8	27	40	13.2	4.16	91	.282	.347	4	.222	2	-2	-3	-1	-0.2
Yr	4	6	.400	34	8	0	0	0	93²	100	10	33	48	13.0	4.04	96	.280	.344	5	.227	2	-1	-2	-1	-0.1

YEAR	TM/L	W	L	PCT	G	GS	CG	SH	SV	IP	H	HR	BB	SO	RAT	ERA	ERA+	OAV	OOB	BH	AVG	PB	PR	/A	PD	TPI
1963	Cle-A	0	0	—	4	0	0	0	0	5	8	0	5	3	25.2	18.00	20	.348	.483	0	—	0	-8	-8	0	-0.3
Total	3	14	19	.424	69	35	6	0	1	279	328	33	89	108	13.6	4.84	84	.297	.352	15	.183	5	-26	-24	-1	-1.3

● JACK CURTIS

Curtis, John Duffield b: 3/9/48, Newton, Mass. BL/TL, 6'2", 185 lbs. Deb: 8/13/70

YEAR	TM/L	W	L	PCT	G	GS	CG	SH	SV	IP	H	HR	BB	SO	RAT	ERA	ERA+	OAV	OOB	BH	AVG	PB	PR	/A	PD	TPI
1970	Bos-A	0	0	—	1	0	0	0	0	2¹	4	1	1	1	19.3	11.57	34	.333	.385	0	—	0	-2	-2	0	0.0
1971	Bos-A	2	2	.500	5	3	1	0	0	26	30	3	6	19	12.5	3.12	119	.291	.330	1	.111	-0	1	2	-1	0.1
1972	Bos-A	11	8	.579	26	21	8	3	0	154¹	161	8	50	106	12.3	3.73	86	.271	.328	5	.094	-2	-12	-9	-0	-1.4
1973	Bos-A	13	13	.500	35	30	10	4	0	221¹	225	24	83	101	12.6	3.58	112	.264	.331	0	6	11	-1	1.0
1974	StL-N	10	14	.417	33	29	5	2	1	195	199	15	83	89	13.1	3.78	94	.267	.342	10	.159	-0	-4	-5	0	-0.6
1975	StL-N	8	9	.471	39	18	4	0	1	146²	151	13	65	67	13.4	3.44	109	.268	.346	8	.211	2	3	5	2	0.9
1976	StL-N	6	11	.353	37	15	3	1	1	134	139	11	65	52	13.7	4.50	79	.276	.359	7	.200	2	-15	-14	0	-1.5
1977	SF-N	3	3	.500	43	9	1	1	1	77	95	5	48	47	16.8	5.49	71	.314	.409	3	.231	1	-14	-14	1	-0.8
1978	SF-N	4	3	.571	46	0	0	0	1	63	60	1	29	38	12.7	3.71	93	.262	.345	0	.000	-0	-1	-2	-0	-0.2
1979	SF-N	10	9	.526	27	18	3	2	0	120²	121	15	42	85	12.2	4.18	84	.257	.318	5	.147	1	-6	-9	-1	-1.3
1980	SD-N	10	8	.556	30	27	6	0	0	187	184	9	67	71	12.2	3.51	98	.262	.329	12	.194	1	2	-2	1	0.0
1981	SD-N	2	6	.250	28	8	0	0	0	66²	70	11	30	31	13.6	5.13	63	.275	.353	1	.077	-1	-12	-14	-0	-1.7
1982	SD-N	8	6	.571	26	18	1	1	0	116¹	121	15	46	54	13.0	4.10	83	.271	.341	11	.297	3	-6	-9	-1	-0.8
	Cal-A	0	1	.000	12	0	0	0	1	12	16	0	3	10	14.3	6.00	68	.320	.358	0	—	-0	-3	-3	-0	-0.3
1983	Cal-A	1	2	.333	37	3	0	0	5	90	89	5	40	36	13.1	3.80	106	.258	.339	0	.000	-0	3	2	-1	0.0
1984	Cal-A	1	2	.333	17	0	0	0	0	28²	30	4	11	18	12.9	4.40	90	.263	.328	0	—	-0	-1	-1	-0	-0.1
Total	15	89	97	.478	438	199	42	14	11	1641	1695	140	669	825	13.0	3.96	91	.270	.341	63	.175	5	-61	-63	-1	-6.7

● VERN CURTIS

Curtis, Vernon Eugene "Turk" b: 5/24/20, Cairo, Ill. d: 6/24/92, Cairo, Ill. BR/TR, 6', 170 lbs. Deb: 9/6/43

YEAR	TM/L	W	L	PCT	G	GS	CG	SH	SV	IP	H	HR	BB	SO	RAT	ERA	ERA+	OAV	OOB	BH	AVG	PB	PR	/A	PD	TPI
1943	Was-A	0	0	—	2	0	0	0	0	4	3	0	6	1	20.3	6.75	47	.200	.429	0	—	0	-2	-2	-0	0.0
1944	Was-A	0	1	.000	3	1	0	0	0	9²	8	0	3	2	10.2	2.79	117	.235	.297	0	.000	-0	1	0	-0	0.0
1946	Was-A	0	0	—	11	0	0	0	0	16¹	19	1	10	7	16.0	7.16	47	.297	.392	0	.000	-0	-7	-7	0	0.0
Total	3	0	1	.000	16	1	0	0	0	30	30	1	19	10	14.7	5.70	58	.265	.371	0	.000	-1	-7	-8	-0	0.0

● ED CUSHMAN

Cushman, Edgar Leander b: 3/27/1852, Eagleville, Ohio d: 9/26/15, Erie, Pa. BR/TL, Deb: 7/6/1883

YEAR	TM/L	W	L	PCT	G	GS	CG	SH	SV	IP	H	HR	BB	SO	RAT	ERA	ERA+	OAV	OOB	BH	AVG	PB	PR	/A	PD	TPI
1883	Buf-N	3	3	.500	7	7	5	0	0	50¹	61	0	17	34	13.9	3.93	81	.285	.338	5	.217	-0	-4	-4	-0	-0.4
1884	Mil-U	4	0	1.000	4	4	4	2	0	36	10	0	3	47	3.3	1.00	132	.082	.104	1	.091	-2	6	1	-1	-0.1
1885	Phi-a	3	7	.300	10	10	10	0	0	87	101	1	17	37	12.5	3.52	98	.269	.306	7	.189	-1	-3	-1	-1	-0.3
	NY-a	8	14	.364	22	22	22	0	0	191	158	2	33	133	9.1	2.78	106	.210	.246	10	.145	-1	10	4	-2	0.1
	Yr	11	21	.344	32	32	32	0	0	278	259	3	50	170	10.1	3.01	103	.229	.263	17	.160	-2	7	3	-3	-0.2
1886	NY-a	17	20	.459	38	37	37	2	0	325²	278	6	99	167	10.4	3.12	109	.220	.277	19	.151	-7	12	10	0	0.3
1887	NY-a	10	15	.400	26	26	25	0	0	220	310	9	83	64	16.4	5.97	71	.325	.384	23	.247	3	-41	-42	-1	-3.1
1890	Tol-a	17	21	.447	40	38	34	0	1	315²	346	5	107	125	13.2	4.19	94	.270	.331	13	.100	-9	-11	-8	-5	-2.0
Total	6	62	80	.437	147	144	137	4	1	1225²	1264	23	359	607	12.1	3.86	92	.254	.308	78	.160	-17	-32	-43	-10	-5.5

● HARVEY CUSHMAN

Cushman, Harvey Barnes b: 7/10/1877, Rockland, Me. d: 12/27/20, Emsworth, Pa. Deb: 8/24/02

YEAR	TM/L	W	L	PCT	G	GS	CG	SH	SV	IP	H	HR	BB	SO	RAT	ERA	ERA+	OAV	OOB	BH	AVG	PB	PR	/A	PD	TPI
1902	Pit-N	0	4	.000	4	4	3	0	0	25²	30	0	31	12	22.1	7.36	37	.291	.463	2	.200	-0	-13	-13	-1	-1.6

● MIKE CVENGROS

Cvengros, Michael John b: 12/1/01, Pana, Ill. d: 8/2/70, Hot Springs, Ark. BL/TL, 5'8", 159 lbs. Deb: 9/30/22

YEAR	TM/L	W	L	PCT	G	GS	CG	SH	SV	IP	H	HR	BB	SO	RAT	ERA	ERA+	OAV	OOB	BH	AVG	PB	PR	/A	PD	TPI
1922	NY-N	0	1	.000	1	1	0	0	0	9	6	1	3	3	10.0	4.00	100	.194	.286	0	.000	-0	0	0	0	0.0
1923	Chi-A	12	13	.480	40	26	14	0	3	214¹	216	6	107	86	14.1	4.41	90	.269	.364	15	.203	-1	-10	-11	0	-1.2
1924	Chi-A	3	12	.200	26	15	2	0	0	105²	119	5	67	36	16.1	5.88	70	.300	.405	6	.200	2	-19	-21	0	-2.2
1925	Chi-A	3	9	.250	22	11	4	0	0	104²	109	7	55	32	14.4	4.30	97	.278	.371	3	.152	-1	1	-2	-0	-0.3
1927	*Pit-N	2	1	.667	23	4	0	0	1	53²	55	3	24	21	13.4	3.35	123	.271	.351	3	.158	-1	3	5	1	0.3
1929	Chi-N	5	4	.556	32	2	0	0	2	64	82	2	29	23	15.8	4.64	99	.319	.390	6	.400	2	1	-0	0	0.2
Total	6	25	40	.385	144	59	21	0	6	551¹	587	24	285	201	14.6	4.59	90	.282	.374	35	.201	1	-24	-28	1	-3.2

● JIM CZAJKOWSKI

Czajkowski, James Mark b: 12/18/63, Parma, Ohio BB/TR, 6'4", 215 lbs. Deb: 7/29/94

YEAR	TM/L	W	L	PCT	G	GS	CG	SH	SV	IP	H	HR	BB	SO	RAT	ERA	ERA+	OAV	OOB	BH	AVG	PB	PR	/A	PD	TPI
1994	Col-N	0	0	—	5	0	0	0	0	8²	9	2	6	2	18.7	4.15	120	.281	.439	0	—	0	1	0	0	0.0

● OMAR DAAL

Daal, Omar Jesus (Cordero) b: 3/1/72, Maracaibo, Venez. BL/TL, 6'3", 160 lbs. Deb: 4/24/93

YEAR	TM/L	W	L	PCT	G	GS	CG	SH	SV	IP	H	HR	BB	SO	RAT	ERA	ERA+	OAV	OOB	BH	AVG	PB	PR	/A	PD	TPI
1993	LA-N	2	3	.400	47	0	0	0	0	35¹	36	5	21	19	14.5	5.09	75	.277	.377	0	—	0	-4	-5	-0	-0.6
1994	LA-N	0	0	—	24	0	0	0	0	13²	12	1	5	9	11.2	3.29	120	.245	.315	0	—	0	1	1	-0	0.0
Total	2	2	3	.400	71	0	0	0	0	49	48	6	26	28	13.6	4.59	84	.268	.361	0	—	0	-3	-4	-0	-0.6

● JOHN D'ACQUISTO

D'Acquisto, John Francis b: 12/24/51, San Diego, Cal. BR/TR, 6'2", 205 lbs. Deb: 9/2/73

YEAR	TM/L	W	L	PCT	G	GS	CG	SH	SV	IP	H	HR	BB	SO	RAT	ERA	ERA+	OAV	OOB	BH	AVG	PB	PR	/A	PD	TPI
1973	SF-N	1	1	.500	7	3	1	0	0	27²	23	4	19	29	13.7	3.58	107	.219	.339	0	.000	-1	0	1	-0	-0.1
1974	SF-N	12	14	.462	38	36	5	1	0	215	182	13	124	167	13.1	3.77	101	.227	.334	8	.113	-1	-4	1	-4	-0.4
1975	SF-N	2	4	.333	10	6	0	0	0	28	29	5	34	22	20.9	10.29	37	.264	.445	0	.000	-0	-21	-20	-1	-3.4
1976	SF-N	3	8	.273	28	19	0	0	0	106	93	5	102	53	16.8	5.35	68	.243	.406	7	.269	2	-22	-20	-1	-1.8
1977	StL-N	0	0	—	3	2	0	0	0	8¹	5	0	7	9	17.3	4.32	89	.185	.421	0	.000	-0	-0	-0	-0	0.0
	SD-N	1	2	.333	17	12	0	0	0	44	49	3	47	45	19.8	6.95	51	.297	.455	0	.000	-0	-15	-17	0	-1.0
	Yr	1	2	.333	20	14	0	0	0	52¹	54	3	57	54	19.3	6.54	55	.278	.444	0	.000	-1	-15	-17	-0	-1.0
1978	SD-N	4	3	.571	45	3	0	0	10	93	60	2	56	104	11.3	2.13	156	.185	.307	4	.190	1	15	12	-1	1.2
1979	SD-N	9	13	.409	51	11	1	1	2	133²	140	15	86	97	15.4	4.92	72	.275	.383	4	.129	1	-18	-21	-2	-3.2
1980	SD-N	2	3	.400	39	0	0	0	0	67	67	2	36	44	14.0	3.76	91	.270	.365	0	.000	-1	0	-0	-0	-0.3
	Mon-N	0	2	.000	11	0	0	0	2	20²	14	0	9	15	10.0	2.18	164	.206	.299	0	—	0	3	3	-0	0.4
	Yr	2	5	.286	50	0	0	0	2	87²	81	2	45	59	12.9	3.39	105	.252	.343	0	.000	-1	2	1	-0	0.1
1981	Cal-A	0	0	—	6	0	0	0	0	19¹	26	2	12	8	18.2	10.71	34	.338	.433	0	—	0	-15	-15	-0	0.0
1982	Oak-A	0	1	.000	11	0	0	0	0	17	20	1	9	7	15.4	5.29	74	.290	.372	0	—	0	-2	-3	-0	0.1
Total	10	34	51	.400	266	92	7	2	15	779²	708	52	544	600	14.7	4.56	79	.245	.368	23	.127	0	-79	-81	-9	-8.5

● JOHN DAGENHARD

Dagenhard, John Douglas b: 4/25/17, Magnolia, Ohio BR/TR, 6'2", 195 lbs. Deb: 9/28/43

YEAR	TM/L	W	L	PCT	G	GS	CG	SH	SV	IP	H	HR	BB	SO	RAT	ERA	ERA+	OAV	OOB	BH	AVG	PB	PR	/A	PD	TPI
1943	Bos-N	1	0	1.000	2	1	1	0	0	11	9	0	4	2	12.3	0.00	—	.225	.326	0	.000	-0	4	4	1	0.5

● PETE DAGLIA

Daglia, Peter George b: 2/28/06, Napa, Cal. d: 3/11/52, Willits, Cal. BR/TR, 6'1", 200 lbs. Deb: 6/8/32

YEAR	TM/L	W	L	PCT	G	GS	CG	SH	SV	IP	H	HR	BB	SO	RAT	ERA	ERA+	OAV	OOB	BH	AVG	PB	PR	/A	PD	TPI
1932	Chi-A	2	4	.333	12	5	2	0	0	50	67	4	20	16	16.4	5.76	75	.324	.394	1	.077	-1	-7	-8	-1	-0.9

● JAY DAHL

Dahl, Jay Steven b: 12/6/45, San Bernardino, Cal. d: 6/20/65, Salisbury, N.C. BB/TL, 5'10", 183 lbs. Deb: 9/27/63

YEAR	TM/L	W	L	PCT	G	GS	CG	SH	SV	IP	H	HR	BB	SO	RAT	ERA	ERA+	OAV	OOB	BH	AVG	PB	PR	/A	PD	TPI
1963	Hou-N	0	1	.000	1	1	0	0	0	2²	7	0	0	0	23.6	16.88	19	.438	.438	0	—	0	-4	-4	-0	-0.9

● JERRY DAHLKE

Dahlke, Jerome Alexander "Joe" b: 6/8/30, Marathon, Wis. BR/TR, 6', 180 lbs. Deb: 5/6/56

YEAR	TM/L	W	L	PCT	G	GS	CG	SH	SV	IP	H	HR	BB	SO	RAT	ERA	ERA+	OAV	OOB	BH	AVG	PB	PR	/A	PD	TPI
1956	Chi-A	0	0	—	5	0	0	0	0	2¹	5	0	6	1	42.4	19.29	21	.455	.647	0	—	0	-4	-4	-0	0.0

● SAM DAILEY

Dailey, Samuel Laurence b: 3/31/04, Oakford, Ill. d: 12/2/79, Columbia, Mo. BL/TR, 5'11", 168 lbs. Deb: 7/4/29

YEAR	TM/L	W	L	PCT	G	GS	CG	SH	SV	IP	H	HR	BB	SO	RAT	ERA	ERA+	OAV	OOB	BH	AVG	PB	PR	/A	PD	TPI
1929	Phi-N	2	2	.500	20	5	0	0	0	51¹	74	5	23	18	17.2	7.54	69	.349	.415	1	.059	-2	-16	-13	-1	-1.1

● VINCE DAILEY

Dailey, Vincent Perry b: 12/25/1864, Osceola, Pa. d: 11/14/19, Hornell, N.Y. 6', 200 lbs. Deb: 4/21/1890 ◆

YEAR	TM/L	W	L	PCT	G	GS	CG	SH	SV	IP	H	HR	BB	SO	RAT	ERA	ERA+	OAV	OOB	BH	AVG	PB	PR	/A	PD	TPI
1890	Cle-N	0	1	.000	2	1	0	0	0	7	12	0	7	0	24.4	7.71	46	.367	.478	71	.289	1	-3	-3	0	-0.3

● BILL DAILEY

Dailey, William Garland b: 5/13/35, Arlington, Va. BR/TR, 6'3", 185 lbs. Deb: 8/17/61

YEAR	TM/L	W	L	PCT	G	GS	CG	SH	SV	IP	H	HR	BB	SO	RAT	ERA	ERA+	OAV	OOB	BH	AVG	PB	PR	/A	PD	TPI
1961	Cle-A	1	0	1.000	12	0	0	0	0	19	16	0	6	7	10.4	0.95	415	.232	.293	0	.000	-0	6	6	0	0.3

YEAR	TM/L	W	L	PCT	G	GS	CG	SH	SV	IP	H	HR	BB	SO	RAT	ERA	ERA+	OAV	OOB	BH	AVG	PB	PR	/A	PD	TPI
1962	Cle-A	2	2	.500	27	0	0	0	1	42²	43	0	17	24	13.1	3.59	108	.270	.348	0	.000	-0	2	1	-0	0.1
1963	Min-A	6	3	.667	66	0	0	0	21	108²	80	9	19	72	8.2	1.99	183	.208	.246	5	.238	-2	20	20	2	3.0
1964	Min-A	1	2	.333	14	0	0	0	0	15¹	23	3	17	6	25.8	8.22	44	.377	.537	0	—	0	-8	-8	0	-1.4
Total	4	10	7	.588	119	0	0	0	22	185²	162	12	59	109	11.0	2.76	135	.241	.308	5	.192	1	20	20	3	2.0

● ED DAILY
Daily, Edward M. b: 9/7/1862, Providence, R.I. d: 10/21/1891, Washington, D.C. BR/TR, 5'10.5", 174 lbs. Deb: 5/4/1885 F♦

YEAR	TM/L	W	L	PCT	G	GS	CG	SH	SV	IP	H	HR	BB	SO	RAT	ERA	ERA+	OAV	OOB	BH	AVG	PB	PR	/A	PD	TPI
1885	Phi-N	26	23	.531	50	50	49	4	0	440	370	12	90	140	9.4	2.21	126	.217	.256	38	.207	-0	30	28	-4	2.4
1886	Phi-N	16	9	.640	27	23	22	1	0	218	211	7	59	95	11.1	3.06	108	.242	.290	70	.227	3	6	6	2	0.8
1887	Phi-N	0	4	.000	6	5	4	0	0	41¹	52	2	25	7	16.8	7.19	59	.289	.376	30	.283	1	-14	-14	1	-0.8
	Was-N	0	1	.000	1	1	1	0	0	7	5	0	6	3	14.1	7.71	53	.208	.367	78	.251	0	-3	-3	0	-0.3
	Yr	0	5	.000	7	6	5	0	0	48¹	57	2	31	10	16.4	7.26	58	.279	.374	108	.259	1	-17	-16	1	-1.1
1888	Was-N	2	7	.222	9	8	8	0	0	73²	88	7	19	20	13.4	4.89	57	.278	.325	102	.225	1	-17	-17	0	-1.5
1889	Col-a	0	0	—	2	0	0	0	1	1²	1	0	4	2	27.0	21.60	17	.168	.503	148	.256	0	-3	-3	-0	-0.4
1890	Bro-a	10	15	.400	27	27	27	0	0	235²	252	3	93	82	13.9	4.05	96	.265	.342	94	.239	3	-5	-4	2	0.1
	NY-N	2	0	1.000	2	1	1	0	0	16	6	0	6	0	9.0	2.25	156	.112	.252	2	.133	-1	2	2	1	0.2
	*Lou-a	6	3	.667	12	10	9	1	0	93	83	2	30	31	11.3	1.94	199	.232	.298	20	.250	2	20	20	2	2.1
1891	Lou-a	4	8	.333	15	14	11	0	0	111¹	149	6	48	27	16.6	5.74	64	.310	.382	16	.250	2	-25	-26	0	-1.9
Total	7	66	70	.485	151	139	132	6	1	1237²	1217	39	380	407	11.9	3.39	98	.246	.305	616	.239	12	-8	-11	5	0.7

● HUGH DAILY
Daily, Hugh Ignatius "One Arm" (b: Harry Criss) b: 1857, Baltimore, Md. BR/TR, 6'2", 180 lbs. Deb: 5/1/1882

YEAR	TM/L	W	L	PCT	G	GS	CG	SH	SV	IP	H	HR	BB	SO	RAT	ERA	ERA+	OAV	OOB	BH	AVG	PB	PR	/A	PD	TPI
1882	Buf-N	15	14	.517	29	29	29	0	0	255²	246	6	70	116	11.1	2.99	98	.234	.282	18	.164	-6	-3	-2	-5	-1.1
1883	Cle-N	23	19	.548	45	43	40	4	0	378²	360	5	99	171	10.9	2.42	130	.243	.291	18	.127	-10	30	31	-1	1.8
1884	CP-U	27	27	.500	56	56	54	5	0	484²	430	11	71	469	9.3	2.43	100	.222	.249	43	.219	-11	1	1	1	-0.8
	Was-U	1	1	.500	2	2	2	0	0	16	16	0	1	14	9.6	2.25	107	.243	.255	0	.000	-1	0	-0	-0	-0.1
	Yr	28	28	.500	58	58	56	5	0	500²	446	11	72	483	9.3	2.43	101	.223	.250	43	.214	-12	1	1	1	-0.9
1885	StL-N	3	8	.273	11	11	10	1	0	91¹	92	5	44	31	13.4	3.94	70	.252	.333	3	.086	-3	-11	-12	-0	-1.4
1886	Was-N	0	6	.000	6	6	6	0	0	49	69	2	40	15	20.0	7.35	45	.332	.440	2	.125	-1	-22	-22	-0	-1.9
1887	Cle-a	4	12	.250	16	16	16	0	0	139²	181	1	44	30	14.7	3.67	118	.311	.362	4	.069	-18	10	10	-1	0.1
Total	6	73	87	.456	165	163	157	10	1	1415	1394	30	369	846	11.2	2.92	101	.245	.291	88	.157	-39	5	6	-6	-3.4

● BRUCE DalCANTON
DalCanton, John Bruce b: 6/15/42, California, Pa. BR/TR, 6'2", 205 lbs. Deb: 9/3/67 C

YEAR	TM/L	W	L	PCT	G	GS	CG	SH	SV	IP	H	HR	BB	SO	RAT	ERA	ERA+	OAV	OOB	BH	AVG	PB	PR	/A	PD	TPI
1967	Pit-N	2	1	.667	8	1	0	0	0	24	19	1	10	13	11.3	1.88	179	.211	.297	2	.333	1	4	4	-1	0.5
1968	Pit-N	1	1	.500	7	0	0	0	2	17	7	0	6	8	7.9	2.12	138	.127	.238	0	.000	-0	2	2	-1	0.1
1969	Pit-N	8	2	.800	57	0	0	0	5	86¹	79	3	49	56	13.3	3.34	105	.252	.353	3	.300	2	2	1	-0	0.4
1970	Pit-N	9	4	.692	41	6	1	0	1	84²	94	7	39	53	14.2	4.57	85	.282	.359	0	.000	-1	-5	-6	-1	-1.0
1971	KC-A	8	6	.571	25	22	2	0	0	141¹	144	8	44	58	12.0	3.44	100	.262	.317	4	.087	-3	-0	-0	-2	-0.4
1972	KC-A	6	6	.500	35	16	1	0	2	132¹	135	7	29	75	11.2	3.40	89	.265	.306	4	.098	-2	-5	-5	-2	-0.9
1973	KC-A	4	3	.571	32	3	1	0	3	97¹	108	8	46	38	14.6	4.81	85	.284	.367	0	—	0	-11	-8	-0	-0.7
1974	KC-A	8	10	.444	31	22	9	2	0	175¹	135	5	82	96	11.4	3.13	122	.211	.306	0	—	0	9	13	-1	1.4
1975	KC-A	0	0	.000	4	2	0	0	0	8²	23	0	7	5	32.2	15.58	25	.479	.554	0	—	0	-11	-11	0	-1.8
	Atl-N	2	7	.222	26	9	0	0	3	67	63	2	24	38	12.5	3.36	112	.248	.327	2	.105	-1	2	3	1	0.4
1976	Atl-N	3	5	.375	42	1	0	0	1	73¹	67	6	42	36	13.6	3.56	106	.244	.348	2	.222	-1	0	2	1	0.3
1977	Chi-A	0	2	.000	8	0	0	0	2	24	20	1	9	9	12.4	3.75	109	.230	.330	0	—	0	1	1	-1	0.0
Total	11	51	49	.510	316	83	15	2	19	931¹	894	48	391	485	12.6	3.67	99	.253	.331	17	.113	-3	-12	-5	-3	-1.7

● GENE DALE
Dale, Emmett Eugene b: 6/16/1889, St.Louis, Mo. d: 3/20/58, St.Louis, Mo. BR/TR, 6'3", 179 lbs. Deb: 9/19/11

YEAR	TM/L	W	L	PCT	G	GS	CG	SH	SV	IP	H	HR	BB	SO	RAT	ERA	ERA+	OAV	OOB	BH	AVG	PB	PR	/A	PD	TPI
1911	StL-N	0	2	.000	5	2	0	0	0	14²	13	0	16	13	19.0	6.75	50	.250	.443	2	.400	1	-5	-5	0	-0.6
1912	StL-N	0	5	.000	19	3	1	0	0	61²	76	4	51	37	19.0	6.57	52	.311	.436	6	.273	1	-22	-22	-1	-1.5
1915	Cin-N	18	17	.514	49	35	20	4	3	296²	256	6	107	104	11.2	2.46	116	.243	.316	20	.220	2	10	13	1	1.7
1916	Cin-N	3	4	.429	17	5	2	0	0	69²	80	3	33	23	14.9	5.17	50	.304	.386	3	.143	-0	-20	-20	1	-1.8
Total	4	21	28	.429	90	45	23	4	3	442²	425	13	207	177	13.1	3.60	81	.263	.352	31	.223	3	-37	-34	-1	-2.2

● BUD DALEY
Daley, Leavitt Leo b: 10/7/32, Orange, Cal. BL/TL, 6'1", 185 lbs. Deb: 9/10/55

YEAR	TM/L	W	L	PCT	G	GS	CG	SH	SV	IP	H	HR	BB	SO	RAT	ERA	ERA+	OAV	OOB	BH	AVG	PB	PR	/A	PD	TPI
1955	Cle-A	0	1	.000	2	1	0	0	0	7	10	1	1	2	14.1	6.43	62	.333	.355	0	.000	-0	-2	-2	0	-0.2
1956	Cle-A	1	0	1.000	14	0	0	0	0	20¹	21	2	14	13	17.7	6.20	68	.273	.417	0	.000	-0	-5	-5	1	-0.1
1957	Cle-A	2	8	.200	34	10	1	0	2	87¹	99	7	40	54	15.4	4.43	84	.279	.368	4	.200	0	-6	-7	1	-0.6
1958	KC-A	2	3	.600	26	5	1	0	0	70²	67	5	19	39	11.7	3.31	118	.249	.313	2	.125	-1	4	5	1	0.3
1959	KC-A★	16	13	.552	39	29	12	2	1	216¹	212	24	62	125	11.9	3.16	127	.257	.317	23	.295	4	17	20	-0	3.1
1960	KC-A★	16	16	.500	37	35	13	1	0	231	234	27	96	126	13.2	4.56	87	.263	.341	12	.160	-1	-18	-15	1	-1.6
1961	KC-A	4	8	.333	16	10	2	0	0	63²	84	6	22	36	15.7	4.95	84	.319	.383	2	.111	-1	-7	-5	1	-0.9
	*NY-A	8	9	.471	23	17	7	0	0	129²	127	17	51	83	12.6	3.96	94	.257	.331	6	.133	-1	-3	-1	-0	-0.6
	Yr	12	17	.414	39	27	9	0	0	193¹	211	23	73	119	13.4	4.28	90	.275	.341	8	.127	-2	-6	-6	-0	-1.5
1962	*NY-A	7	5	.583	43	6	0	0	4	105¹	105	8	21	55	11.2	3.59	104	.258	.303	5	.185	-0	4	2	0	0.2
1963	NY-A	0	0	—	1	0	0	0	1	1	2	0	0	0	18.0	0.00	—	.667	.667	0	—	0	0	0	0	0.1
1964	NY-A	3	2	.600	13	0	0	0	1	35	37	3	25	16	17.0	4.63	78	.274	.402	2	.250	-1	-4	-4	1	-0.4
Total	10	60	64	.484	248	116	36	3	10	967¹	998	100	351	549	13.1	4.03	97	.266	.339	56	.192	3	-15	-14	4	-0.7

● BILL DALEY
Daley, William b: 6/27/1868, Poughkeepsie, N.Y d: 5/4/22, Poughkeepsie, N.Y. TL , Deb: 7/17/1889

YEAR	TM/L	W	L	PCT	G	GS	CG	SH	SV	IP	H	HR	BB	SO	RAT	ERA	ERA+	OAV	OOB	BH	AVG	PB	PR	/A	PD	TPI
1889	Bos-N	3	3	.500	9	7	4	0	0	48	34	1	43	40	14.8	4.31	97	.193	.357	3	.150	-1	-2	-1	3	0.1
1890	Bos-P	18	7	.720	34	25	19	2	2	235	246	8	167	110	16.2	3.60	122	.258	.373	17	.155	-5	17	21	-1	1.1
1891	Bos-a	8	6	.571	19	11	10	0	2	126²	119	6	81	68	14.7	2.98	117	.240	.355	10	.169	-3	10	7	1	0.4
Total	3	29	16	.644	62	43	33	2	4	409²	399	14	291	218	15.6	3.49	117	.245	.366	30	.159	-8	25	27	3	1.6

● MIKE DALTON
Dalton, Michael Edward b: 3/27/63, Palo Alto, Cal. BR/TL, 6', 215 lbs. Deb: 5/31/91

YEAR	TM/L	W	L	PCT	G	GS	CG	SH	SV	IP	H	HR	BB	SO	RAT	ERA	ERA+	OAV	OOB	BH	AVG	PB	PR	/A	PD	TPI
1991	Det-A	0	0	—	4	0	0	0	0	8	12	2	2	4	15.8	3.38	123	.333	.368	0	—	0	1	1	-0	-0.1

● GEORGE DALY
Daly, George Josephs "Pecks" b: 7/28/1887, Buffalo, N.Y. d: 12/12/57, Buffalo, N.Y. BR/TR, 5'10.5", 175 lbs. Deb: 9/26/09

YEAR	TM/L	W	L	PCT	G	GS	CG	SH	SV	IP	H	HR	BB	SO	RAT	ERA	ERA+	OAV	OOB	BH	AVG	PB	PR	/A	PD	TPI
1909	NY-N	0	3	.000	3	3	3	0	0	21	31	0	8	8	17.1	6.00	43	.341	.400	1	.111	-1	-8	-8	-1	-1.1

● BILL DAMMANN
Dammann, William Henry "Wee Willie" b: 8/9/1872, Chicago, Ill. d: 12/6/48, Lynnhaven, Va. BL/TL, 5'7", 155 lbs. Deb: 4/24/1897

YEAR	TM/L	W	L	PCT	G	GS	CG	SH	SV	IP	H	HR	BB	SO	RAT	ERA	ERA+	OAV	OOB	BH	AVG	PB	PR	/A	PD	TPI
1897	Cin-N	6	4	.600	16	11	7	1	0	95	122	1	37	21	15.5	4.74	96	.309	.376	5	.161	-1	-4	-2	1	-0.1
1898	Cin-N	16	10	.615	35	22	16	2	2	224²	277	3	67	51	14.1	3.61	106	.301	.353	16	.195	1	0	6	-3	0.4
1899	Cin-N	2	1	.667	9	5	3	1	1	48	74	0	11	2	16.1	4.88	80	.351	.386	1	.056	-2	-5	-5	0	-0.4
Total	3	24	15	.615	60	38	26	4	3	367²	473	5	115	74	14.7	4.06	99	.310	.363	22	.168	-1	-10	-1	-2	-0.1

● ART DANEY
Daney, Arthur Lee b: 7/9/04, Talihina, Okla. d: 3/11/88, Phoenix, Ariz. BR/TR, 5'11", 165 lbs. Deb: 5/25/28

YEAR	TM/L	W	L	PCT	G	GS	CG	SH	SV	IP	H	HR	BB	SO	RAT	ERA	ERA+	OAV	OOB	BH	AVG	PB	PR	/A	PD	TPI
1928	Phi-A	0	0	—	1	0	0	0	0	1	1	0	0	0	9.0	0.00	—	.250	.250	0	—	0	0	0	0	—

● DAVE DANFORTH
Danforth, David Charles "Dauntless Dave" b: 3/7/1890, Granger, Tex. d: 9/19/70, Baltimore, Md. BL/TL, 6', 167 lbs. Deb: 8/1/11

YEAR	TM/L	W	L	PCT	G	GS	CG	SH	SV	IP	H	HR	BB	SO	RAT	ERA	ERA+	OAV	OOB	BH	AVG	PB	PR	/A	PD	TPI
1911	Phi-A	4	1	.800	14	2	1	0	0	33²	29	1	21	13	13.1	3.74	84	.240	.348	1	.167	-0	-2	-2	-0	-0.3
1912	Phi-A	0	0	—	3	0	0	0	0	20¹	26	0	12	8	16.8	3.98	77	.338	.427	2	.250	-2	-2	-2	0	-0.0
1916	Chi-A	3	3	.545	28	8	1	0	0	93²	87	3	49	62	12.2	3.27	85	.259	.358	2	.087	-1	-5	-5	-1	-0.2
1917	*Chi-A	11	6	.647	50	9	1	1	9	173	155	1	74	79	12.1	2.65	100	.244	.325	6	.130	0	0	0	-3	0.0
1918	Chi-A	6	15	.286	39	11	6	0	2	139	148	1	40	48	12.5	3.43	80	.288	.345	6	.143	-2	-10	-11	0	-1.8
1919	Chi-A	1	2	.333	15	1	0	0	1	41²	58	1	20	17	17.1	7.78	41	.333	.405	1	.111	0	-21	-21	-0	-1.5

YEAR TM/L	W	L	PCT	G	GS	CG	SH	SV	IP	H	HR	BB	SO	RAT	ERA	ERA+	OAV	OOB	BH	AVG	PB	PR	/A	PD	TPI
1922 StL-A	5	2	.714	20	10	3	0	1	79²	93	1	38	48	14.9	3.28	127	.304	.383	2	.087	-2	7	8	-1	0.3
1923 StL-A	16	14	.533	38	26	16	0	1	226¹	221	4	87	96	12.7	3.94	106	.262	.340	15	.211	2	1	6	-1	0.8
1924 StL-A	15	12	.556	41	27	11	1	4	219²	246	16	69	65	13.0	4.51	100	.292	.348	13	.171	-2	-7	0	-3	-0.4
1925 StL-A	7	9	.438	38	15	5	0	2	159	172	19	61	53	13.4	4.36	107	.284	.353	8	.174	-2	1	6	-4	-0.1
Total 10	71	66	.518	286	109	43	2	23	1186	1235	45	455	484	13.1	3.89	95	.277	.349	56	.160	-6	-37	-25	-10	-3.9

● CHUCK DANIEL
Daniel, Charles Edward b: 9/17/33, Bluffton, Ark. BR/TR, 6'2", 195 lbs. Deb: 9/21/57

YEAR TM/L	W	L	PCT	G	GS	CG	SH	SV	IP	H	HR	BB	SO	RAT	ERA	ERA+	OAV	OOB	BH	AVG	PB	PR	/A	PD	TPI
1957 Det-A	0	0	—	1	0	0	0	0	2¹	3	1	0	2	11.6	7.71	50	.333	.333	0	—	0	-1	-1	-0	0.0

● BENNIE DANIELS
Daniels, Bennie b: 6/17/32, Tuscaloosa, Ala. BL/TR, 6'1.5", 193 lbs. Deb: 9/24/57

YEAR TM/L	W	L	PCT	G	GS	CG	SH	SV	IP	H	HR	BB	SO	RAT	ERA	ERA+	OAV	OOB	BH	AVG	PB	PR	/A	PD	TPI
1957 Pit-N	0	1	.000	1	1	0	0	0	7	5	0	3	2	10.3	1.29	295	.208	.296	0	.000	-0	2	2	1	0.3
1958 Pit-N	0	3	.000	8	5	1	0	0	27²	31	3	15	7	15.3	5.53	70	.290	.382	1	.125	-0	-5	-5	1	-0.4
1959 Pit-N	7	9	.438	34	12	0	0	1	100²	115	9	39	67	13.9	5.45	71	.287	.353	9	.310	6	-17	-18	-1	-2.0
1960 Pit-N	1	3	.250	10	6	0	0	0	40¹	52	4	17	16	15.4	7.81	48	.311	.375	3	.188	0	-18	-18	1	-1.5
1961 Was-A	12	11	.522	32	28	12	1	0	212	184	14	80	110	11.3	3.44	117	.237	.311	15	.197	3	14	14	1	1.8
1962 Was-A	7	16	.304	44	21	3	1	2	161¹	172	14	68	66	13.5	4.85	83	.280	.354	6	.130	-1	-16	-15	5	-1.5
1963 Was-A	5	10	.333	35	24	6	1	1	168²	163	19	58	88	11.8	4.38	85	.250	.312	7	.152	1	-14	-12	3	-0.6
1964 Was-A	8	10	.444	33	24	3	2	0	163	147	20	64	73	11.7	3.70	100	.245	.317	6	.128	0	-1	0	3	0.3
1965 Was-A	5	13	.278	33	18	1	0	1	116¹	135	16	39	42	13.5	4.72	74	.290	.345	4	.133	0	-16	-16	-0	-2.3
Total 9	45	76	.372	230	139	26	5	5	997	1004	99	383	471	12.6	4.44	86	.264	.332	51	.170	-6	-72	-69	12	-5.9

● CHARLIE DANIELS
Daniels, Charles L. b: 7/1/1861, Roxbury, Mass. d: 2/9/38, Boston, Mass. Deb: 4/18/1884

YEAR TM/L	W	L	PCT	G	GS	CG	SH	SV	IP	H	HR	BB	SO	RAT	ERA	ERA+	OAV	OOB	BH	AVG	PB	PR	/A	PD	TPI
1884 Bos-U	0	2	.000	2	2	2	0	0	16²	20	0	2	12	11.9	4.32	55	.278	.298	3	.273	0	-3	-4	-0	-0.3

● PETE DANIELS
Daniels, Peter J. "Smiling Pete" b: 4/8/1864, County Cavan, Ireland d: 2/13/28, Indianapolis, Ind. BL/TL, Deb: 4/19/1890

YEAR TM/L	W	L	PCT	G	GS	CG	SH	SV	IP	H	HR	BB	SO	RAT	ERA	ERA+	OAV	OOB	BH	AVG	PB	PR	/A	PD	TPI
1890 Pit-N	1	2	.333	4	4	3	0	0	28	40	1	12	8	17.7	7.07	47	.325	.399	4	.333	1	-11	-12	-0	-0.8
1898 StL-N	1	6	.143	10	6	3	0	0	54²	62	0	14	13	13.0	3.62	105	.283	.335	3	.176	0	-0	1	-0	0.1
Total 2	2	8	.200	14	10	6	0	0	82²	102	1	26	21	14.6	4.79	76	.298	.359	7	.241	1	-11	-11	-0	-0.7

● GEORGE DARBY
Darby, George William "Deacon" b: 2/6/1869, Kansas City, Mo. d: 2/25/37, Sacramento, Cal. BR/TR, 5'10.5", 160 lbs. Deb: 4/28/1893

YEAR TM/L	W	L	PCT	G	GS	CG	SH	SV	IP	H	HR	BB	SO	RAT	ERA	ERA+	OAV	OOB	BH	AVG	PB	PR	/A	PD	TPI
1893 Cin-N	1	1	.500	4	3	2	0	0	29	41	2	18	6	19.2	7.76	62	.323	.419	3	.300	0	-10	-10	1	-0.4

● PAT DARCY
Darcy, Patrick Leonard b: 5/12/50, Troy, Ohio BL/TR, 6'3", 175 lbs. Deb: 9/12/74

YEAR TM/L	W	L	PCT	G	GS	CG	SH	SV	IP	H	HR	BB	SO	RAT	ERA	ERA+	OAV	OOB	BH	AVG	PB	PR	/A	PD	TPI
1974 Cin-N	1	0	1.000	6	2	0	0	0	17	17	2	8	14	13.2	3.71	94	.262	.342	1	.333	0	-0	-0	-0	0.0
1975 *Cin-N	11	5	.688	27	22	1	0	1	130²	134	4	59	46	13.3	3.58	100	.269	.346	4	.085	-3	1	0	-0	-0.3
1976 Cin-N	2	3	.400	11	4	0	0	2	39	41	2	22	15	14.5	6.23	56	.279	.373	2	.182	1	-12	-12	-1	-1.5
Total 3	14	8	.636	44	28	1	0	3	186²	192	8	89	75	13.5	4.15	86	.270	.352	7	.115	-2	-11	-12	-1	-1.8

● ALVIN DARK
Dark, Alvin Ralph "Blackie" b: 1/7/22, Comanche, Okla. BR/TR, 5'11", 185 lbs. Deb: 7/14/46 MC♦

YEAR TM/L	W	L	PCT	G	GS	CG	SH	SV	IP	H	HR	BB	SO	RAT	ERA	ERA+	OAV	OOB	BH	AVG	PB	PR	/A	PD	TPI
1953 NY-N	0	0	—	1	1	0	0	0	1	1	1	0	1	18.0	18.00	24	.250	.400	194	.300	0	-2	-2	-0	0.0

● RON DARLING
Darling, Ronald Maurice b: 8/19/60, Honolulu, Hawaii BR/TR, 6'3", 195 lbs. Deb: 9/6/83

YEAR TM/L	W	L	PCT	G	GS	CG	SH	SV	IP	H	HR	BB	SO	RAT	ERA	ERA+	OAV	OOB	BH	AVG	PB	PR	/A	PD	TPI
1983 NY-N	1	3	.250	5	5	1	0	0	35¹	31	0	17	23	13.0	2.80	129	.248	.352	1	.100	-1	3	3	0	0.3
1984 NY-N	12	9	.571	33	33	2	2	0	205²	179	17	104	136	12.6	3.81	93	.235	.331	10	.149	-1	-5	-6	2	-0.5
1985 NY-N☆	16	6	.727	36	35	4	2	0	248	214	21	114	167	12.0	2.90	119	.235	.323	13	.171	2	19	15	3	1.9
1986 *NY-N	15	6	.714	34	34	4	2	0	237	203	21	81	184	10.9	2.81	126	.234	.302	8	.099	-2	24	19	3	1.8
1987 NY-N	12	8	.600	32	32	2	0	0	207²	183	24	96	167	12.2	4.29	88	.233	.319	8	.123	1	-5	-12	4	-0.6
1988 *NY-N	17	9	.654	34	34	7	4	0	240²	218	24	60	161	10.6	3.25	99	.240	.297	18	.220	6	5	-1	0	0.5
1989 NY-N	14	14	.500	33	33	4	0	0	217¹	214	19	70	153	11.9	3.52	93	.258	.318	9	.123	1	-1	-6	2	-0.5
1990 NY-N	7	9	.438	33	18	1	0	0	126	135	20	44	99	13.1	4.50	83	.273	.338	4	.129	-0	-10	-11	1	-1.1
1991 NY-N	5	6	.455	17	17	0	0	0	102¹	96	9	28	58	11.4	3.87	94	.251	.313	4	.118	-0	-2	-3	-0	-0.3
Mon-N	0	2	.000	3	3	0	0	0	17	25	6	5	11	16.4	7.41	49	.333	.383	1	.167	0	-7	-7	-0	-0.7
Yr	5	8	.385	20	20	0	0	0	119¹	121	15	33	69	11.7	4.37	83	.259	.309	5	.125	-0	-9	-10	-1	-1.0
Oak-A	3	7	.300	12	12	0	0	0	75	64	7	38	60	12.5	4.08	94	.237	.335	0	—	0	0	-2	0	0.2
1992 *Oak-A	15	10	.600	33	33	4	3	0	206¹	198	15	72	99	12.0	3.66	102	.253	.319	0	—	0	6	2	-1	0.3
1993 Oak-A	5	9	.357	31	29	3	0	0	178	198	22	72	95	13.9	5.16	79	.281	.352	0	—	0	-17	-21	-2	-1.4
1994 Oak-A	10	11	.476	25	25	4	0	0	160	162	18	59	108	12.8	4.50	99	.267	.339	0	.000	0	5	-1	0	-0.1
Total 12	132	109	.548	361	343	36	13	0	2256¹	2120	223	860	1521	12.1	3.77	97	.250	.323	76	.144	6	17	-30	13	-0.2

● BOB DARNELL
Darnell, Robert Jack b: 11/6/30, Wewoka, Okla. BR/TR, 5'10", 175 lbs. Deb: 8/10/54

YEAR TM/L	W	L	PCT	G	GS	CG	SH	SV	IP	H	HR	BB	SO	RAT	ERA	ERA+	OAV	OOB	BH	AVG	PB	PR	/A	PD	TPI
1954 Bro-N	0	0	—	6	1	0	0	0	14¹	15	2	7	5	13.8	3.14	130	.278	.361	0	.000	-0	1	2	0	0.0
1956 Bro-N	0	0	—	1	0	0	0	0	1¹	1	0	0	0	6.8	0.00	—	.200	.200	0	—	0	1	1	0	0.0
Total 2	0	0	—	7	1	0	0	0	15²	16	2	7	5	13.2	2.87	142	.271	.348	0	.000	-0	2	2	0	0.0

● MIKE DARR
Darr, Michael Edward b: 3/23/56, Pomona, Cal. BR/TR, 6'4", 190 lbs. Deb: 9/6/77

YEAR TM/L	W	L	PCT	G	GS	CG	SH	SV	IP	H	HR	BB	SO	RAT	ERA	ERA+	OAV	OOB	BH	AVG	PB	PR	/A	PD	TPI
1977 Tor-A	0	1	.000	1	1	0	0	0	1¹	3	1	4	1	54.0	33.75	12	.429	.667	0	—	0	-4	-4	0	-1.5

● GEORGE DARROW
Darrow, George Oliver b: 7/12/03, Beloit, Kan. d: 3/24/83, Sun City, Ariz. BL/TL, 6', 180 lbs. Deb: 4/22/34

YEAR TM/L	W	L	PCT	G	GS	CG	SH	SV	IP	H	HR	BB	SO	RAT	ERA	ERA+	OAV	OOB	BH	AVG	PB	PR	/A	PD	TPI
1934 Phi-N	2	6	.250	17	8	2	0	1	49	57	4	28	14	16.3	5.51	86	.302	.403	2	.133	0	-8	-4	0	-0.6

● BOBBY DARWIN
Darwin, Arthur Bobby Lee b: 2/16/43, Los Angeles, Cal. BR/TR, 6'2", 200 lbs. Deb: 9/30/62 ♦

YEAR TM/L	W	L	PCT	G	GS	CG	SH	SV	IP	H	HR	BB	SO	RAT	ERA	ERA+	OAV	OOB	BH	AVG	PB	PR	/A	PD	TPI
1962 LA-A	0	1	.000	1	1	0	0	0	3¹	8	0	4	6	32.4	10.80	36	.421	.522	0	.000	-0	-3	-3	-0	-0.5
1969 LA-N	0	0	—	3	0	0	0	0	3²	4	0	5	0	27.0	9.82	34	.333	.579	0	—	0	-3	-3	-0	0.0
Total 2	0	1	.000	4	1	0	0	0	7	12	0	9	6	29.6	10.29	35	.387	.548	559	.251	-0	-5	-5	-0	-0.5

● DANNY DARWIN
Darwin, Daniel Wayne b: 10/25/55, Bonham, Tex. BR/TR, 6'3", 190 lbs. Deb: 9/8/78 F

YEAR TM/L	W	L	PCT	G	GS	CG	SH	SV	IP	H	HR	BB	SO	RAT	ERA	ERA+	OAV	OOB	BH	AVG	PB	PR	/A	PD	TPI
1978 Tex-A	1	0	1.000	3	1	0	0	0	8²	11	0	1	8	12.5	4.15	90	.324	.343	0	—	0	-0	-0	-0	-0.1
1979 Tex-A	4	4	.500	20	6	1	0	0	78	50	3	30	58	9.8	4.04	103	.186	.280	0	—	0	2	1	-1	0.0
1980 Tex-A	13	4	.765	53	2	0	0	8	109²	98	4	50	104	12.3	2.63	148	.243	.329	0	—	0	17	15	0	2.6
1981 Tex-A	9	9	.500	22	22	6	2	0	146	115	12	57	98	11.0	3.64	95	.218	.302	0	—	0	-3	-1	-2	-0.2
1982 Tex-A	10	8	.556	56	1	0	0	7	89	95	6	37	61	13.6	3.44	113	.279	.354	0	—	0	6	4	2	1.3
1983 Tex-A	8	13	.381	28	26	9	2	0	183	175	9	62	92	11.8	3.49	115	.250	.313	0	—	0	12	10	-1	1.0
1984 Tex-A	8	12	.400	35	32	5	1	0	223²	249	19	54	123	12.4	3.94	105	.279	.323	0	—	0	1	5	-2	0.1
1985 Mil-A	8	18	.308	39	29	11	1	2	217²	212	34	65	125	11.6	3.80	109	.254	.311	0	—	0	8	9	-3	0.7
1986 Mil-A	6	8	.429	27	14	5	1	0	130¹	120	13	30	80	10.9	3.52	123	.246	.300	0	—	0	9	12	1	1.1
Hou-N	5	2	.714	12	8	1	0	0	54¹	50	9	9	40	9.8	2.32	155	.239	.271	1	.063	-1	8	8	1	0.8
1987 Hou-N	9	10	.474	33	30	3	1	0	195²	184	17	69	134	11.9	3.59	109	.246	.314	12	.182	2	11	7	-2	0.7
1988 Hou-N	8	13	.381	44	20	3	0	3	192	189	20	48	129	11.4	3.84	86	.259	.311	4	.071	-1	-8	-11	2	-1.1
1989 Hou-N	11	4	.733	68	0	0	0	7	122	92	8	33	104	9.4	2.36	143	.212	.271	2	.118	-1	15	14	-1	1.7
1990 Hou-N	11	4	.733	48	17	3	0	2	162³	136	11	31	109	**9.5**	**2.21**	**168**	.225	**.267**	5	.132	1	29	27	-1	2.4
1991 Bos-A	3	6	.333	12	12	0	0	0	68	71	15	15	42	11.9	5.16	83	.263	.311	0	—	0	-8	-7	-0	-0.8
1992 Bos-A	9	9	.500	51	15	2	0	3	161¹	159	11	53	124	12.1	3.96	106	.257	.321	0	—	0	-0	4	-1	0.1
1993 Bos-A	15	11	.577	34	34	2	1	0	229¹	196	31	49	130	**9.7**	3.26	142	.230	**.274**	0	—	0	27	35	-0	3.4
1994 Bos-A	7	5	.583	13	13	0	0	0	75²	101	13	24	54	15.0	6.30	82	.317	.366	0	—	0	-13	-10	0	-1.2
Total 17	145	140	.509	598	282	51	9	32	2447	2303	231	722	1615	11.3	3.56	112	.248	.307	24	.124	-0	116	119	-10	12.3

YEAR	TM/L	W	L	PCT	G	GS	CG	SH	SV	IP	H	HR	BB	SO	RAT	ERA	ERA+	OAV	OOB	BH	AVG	PB	PR	/A	PD	TPI
● JEFF DARWIN					Darwin, Jeffrey Scott b: 7/6/69, Sherman, Tex. BR/TR, 6'3", 180 lbs. Deb: 6/13/94 F																					
1994	Sea-A	0	0	—	2	0	0	0	0	4	7	1	3	1	24.8	13.50	36	.389	.500	0	—	0	-4	-4	0	0.0
● DOUG DASCENZO					Dascenzo, Douglas Craig b: 6/30/64, Cleveland, Ohio BB/TL, 5'7", 150 lbs. Deb: 9/2/88 ◆																					
1990	Chi-N	0	0	—	1	0	0	0	0	1	1	0	0	0	9.0	0.00	—	.333	.333	61	.253	0	0	0	-0	0.0
1991	Chi-N	0	0	—	3	0	0	0	0	4	2	0	2	2	9.0	0.00	—	.154	.267	61	.255	1	2	2	-0	0.0
Total	2	0	0	—	4	0	0	0	0	5	3	0	2	2	9.0	0.00	—	.188	.278	286	.235	1	2	2	-0	0.0
● LEE DASHNER					Dashner, Lee Claire "Lefty" b: 4/25/1887, Renault, Ill. d: 12/16/59, ElDorado, Kan. BB/TL, 5'11.5", 192 lbs. Deb: 8/4/13																					
1913	Cle-A	0	0	—	1	0	0	0	0	1²	0	0	0	2	0.0	5.40	56	.000	.000	0	—	0	-0	-0	-0	0.0
● FRANK DASSO					Dasso, Francis Joseph Nicholas b: 8/31/17, Chicago, Ill. BR/TR, 5'11.5", 185 lbs. Deb: 4/22/45																					
1945	Cin-N	4	5	.444	16	12	6	0	0	95²	89	9	53	39	13.4	3.67	102	.253	.351	5	.161	-1	1	1	0	0.1
1946	Cin-N	0	0	—	2	0	0	0	0	1	2	0	2	1	36.0	27.00	12	.400	.571	0	—	0	-3	-3	0	0.0
Total	2	4	5	.444	18	12	6	0	0	96²	91	9	55	40	13.6	3.91	96	.255	.354	5	.161	-1	-1	-2	0	0.1
● DAN DAUB					Daub, Daniel William "Mickey" b: 1/12/1868, Middletown, Ohio d: 3/25/51, Bradenton, Fla. BR/TR, 5'10", 160 lbs. Deb: 8/31/1892																					
1892	Cin-N	1	2	.333	4	3	2	0	0	25	23	0	13	12	13.7	2.88	113	.235	.336	0	.000	-1	1	1	0	0.0
1893	Bro-N	6	6	.500	12	12	12	0	0	103	104	3	61	25	14.9	3.84	115	.254	.358	8	.190	-2	9	7	3	0.7
1894	Bro-N	10	12	.455	34	27	15	0	0	224	291	7	91	46	16.1	6.11	81	.311	.383	18	.189	-6	-19	-29	-1	-2.4
1895	Bro-N	10	10	.500	25	21	16	0	0	184²	212	4	51	36	13.4	4.29	102	.284	.339	14	.197	-2	12	2	2	0.2
1896	Bro-N	12	11	.522	32	24	18	0	0	225	255	4	63	53	13.6	3.60	115	.283	.335	19	.226	-2	19	13	4	1.5
1897	Bro-N	6	11	.353	19	16	11	0	0	137²	180	8	48	19	15.6	6.08	67	.313	.376	11	.224	2	-27	-30	-0	-2.5
Total	6	45	52	.464	126	103	74	0	0	899¹	1065	26	327	185	14.5	4.75	93	.290	.357	70	.201	-6	-7	-36	8	-2.5
● HOOKS DAUSS					Dauss, George August (b: George August Daus) b: 9/22/1889, Indianapolis, Ind d: 7/27/63, St.Louis, Mo. BR/TR, 5'10.5", 168 lbs. Deb: 9/28/12																					
1912	Det-A	1	1	.500	2	2	2	0	0	17	11	0	9	7	12.2	3.18	103	.186	.324	1	.250	1	0	0	1	0.2
1913	Det-A	13	12	.520	33	29	22	2	1	225	188	4	82	107	11.3	2.48	118	.228	.308	14	.177	3	11	11	-1	1.5
1914	Det-A	18	15	.545	45	35	22	3	4	302	286	3	87	150	11.7	2.86	98	.257	.321	21	.216	6	-4	-2	1	0.4
1915	Det-A	24	13	.649	46	35	27	1	2	309²	261	1	115	132	11.2	2.50	121	.235	.313	15	.146	0	15	18	9	3.2
1916	Det-A	19	12	.613	39	29	18	1	4	238²	220	2	90	95	12.3	3.21	89	.257	.339	16	.222	8	-10	-9	2	-0.1
1917	Det-A	17	14	.548	37	31	22	6	2	270²	243	3	87	102	11.2	2.43	109	.245	.311	11	.126	-1	7	7	4	1.1
1918	Det-A	12	16	.429	33	26	21	1	3	249²	243	4	58	73	11.2	2.99	90	.263	.313	14	.182	3	-6	-9	2	-0.5
1919	Det-A	21	9	.700	34	32	22	2	0	256¹	262	9	63	73	11.6	3.55	90	.267	.315	14	.144	-3	-9	-10	6	-0.8
1920	Det-A	13	21	.382	38	32	18	0	0	270¹	308	11	84	82	13.3	3.56	105	.289	.345	14	.169	1	7	5	8	1.5
1921	Det-A	10	15	.400	32	28	16	0	1	233	275	11	81	68	14.3	4.33	99	.297	.362	23	.261	2	-1	-1	5	0.6
1922	Det-A	13	13	.500	39	25	12	1	4	218²	251	7	59	78	13.0	4.20	92	.289	.339	15	.208	3	-4	-8	1	-0.5
1923	Det-A	21	13	.618	50	39	22	4	3	316	331	10	78	105	11.8	3.62	107	.272	.319	24	.231	5	13	9	2	1.4
1924	Det-A	12	11	.522	40	10	5	0	6	131¹	155	6	40	44	13.4	4.59	90	.302	.354	5	.132	-2	-5	-7	0	-1.2
1925	Det-A	16	11	.593	35	30	16	1	1	228	238	11	85	58	12.9	3.16	136	.272	.339	15	.185	1	31	29	-1	3.0
1926	Det-A	12	6	.667	35	5	0	0	9	124¹	135	6	49	27	13.3	4.20	97	.287	.354	10	.238	4	-2	-0	0	0.1
Total	15	222	182	.550	538	388	245	22	40	3390²	3407	87	1067	1201	12.2	3.30	103	.266	.329	212	.189	32	44	33	38	9.9
● VIC DAVALILLO					Davalillo, Victor Jose (Romero) b: 7/31/36, Cabimas, Venez. BL/TL, 5'7", 155 lbs. Deb: 4/9/63 F◆																					
1969	StL-N	0	0	—	2	0	0	0	0	0	2	0	2	0	∞	—	.1.000	1.000	26	.265	0	-1	-1	0	-0.1
● CLAUDE DAVENPORT					Davenport, Claude Edwin "Big Dave" b: 5/28/1898, Runge, Tex. d: 6/13/76, Corpus Christi, Tex. BR/TR, 6'6", 193 lbs. Deb: 10/2/20 F																					
1920	NY-N	0	0	—	1	0	0	0	0	2	2	1	0	0	13.5	4.50	67	.250	.333	0	.000	-0	-0	-0	-0	0.0
● DAVE DAVENPORT					Davenport, David W. b: 2/20/1890, DeRidder, La. d: 10/16/54, ElDorado, Ark. BR/TR, 6'6", 220 lbs. Deb: 4/17/14 F																					
1914	Cin-N	2	2	.500	10	6	3	1	2	54	38	1	30	22	11.8	2.50	117	.202	.321	2	.111	-1	2	3	-0	0.1
	StL-F	8	13	.381	33	26	13	2	4	215²	204	3	80	142	12.1	3.46	88	.251	.324	6	.088	-6	-14	-10	1	-1.4
1915	StL-F	22	18	.550	55	46	30	10	1	392	300	5	96	229	9.2	2.20	131	.215	.268	12	.092	-11	23	30	-8	0.9
1916	StL-A	12	11	.522	59	31	13	4	2	290²	267	4	100	129	11.6	2.85	96	.256	.326	10	.137	3	-1	-3	-3	-0.3
1917	StL-A	17	17	.500	47	39	20	2	2	280²	273	4	105	100	12.4	3.08	84	.260	.331	9	.098	-6	-13	-15	-1	-2.5
1918	StL-A	10	11	.476	31	22	12	2	1	180	182	0	69	60	12.9	3.25	84	.261	.347	7	.135	1	-9	-10	2	-1.1
1919	StL-A	2	11	.154	24	16	5	0	0	123¹	135	4	41	37	13.0	3.94	84	.280	.339	3	.077	-4	-10	-9	1	-1.1
Total	6	73	83	.468	259	186	96	18	12	1537	1399	22	521	719	11.5	2.93	97	.248	.316	49	.104	-24	-22	-9	-9	-5.2
● LUM DAVENPORT					Davenport, Joubert Lum b: 6/27/1900, Tucson, Ariz. d: 4/21/61, Dallas, Tex. BL/TL, 6'1", 165 lbs. Deb: 5/2/21																					
1921	Chi-A	0	3	.000	13	2	0	0	0	35¹	41	1	32	9	18.8	6.88	62	.318	.457	7	.412	2	-10	-10	-0	-0.6
1922	Chi-A	1	1	.500	9	1	0	0	0	16²	14	2	13	9	14.6	10.80	38	.233	.370	0	.000	-0	-13	-12	-0	-1.2
1923	Chi-A	0	0	—	2	0	0	0	0	4¹	7	0	4	1	22.8	6.23	64	.438	.550	1	1.000	0	-1	-1	0	0.0
1924	Chi-A	0	0	—	1	0	0	0	0	2	1	0	2	1	13.5	0.00	—	.125	.300	0	—	0	1	1	0	0.0
Total	4	1	4	.200	25	3	0	0	0	58¹	63	3	51	20	17.7	7.71	54	.296	.434	8	.381	2	-23	-23	-0	-1.8
● MIKE DAVEY					Davey, Michael Gerard b: 6/2/52, Spokane, Wash. BR/TL, 6'2", 190 lbs. Deb: 8/13/77																					
1977	Atl-N	0	0	—	16	0	0	0	2	16	19	1	9	7	15.8	5.06	88	.302	.389	0	.000	-0	-2	-1	-0	-0.1
1978	Atl-N	0	0	—	3	0	0	0	0	2²	1	0	1	0	6.8	0.00	—	.125	.222	0	—	-0	1	1	-0	0.0
Total	2	0	0	—	19	0	0	0	2	18²	20	1	10	7	14.5	4.34	101	.282	.370	0	.000	-0	-1	-0	-0	-0.1
● RAY DAVIAULT					Daviault, Raymond Joseph Robert b: 5/27/34, Montreal, Que., Can BR/TR, 6'1", 170 lbs. Deb: 4/13/62																					
1962	NY-N	1	5	.167	36	3	0	0	1	81	92	14	48	51	16.0	6.22	67	.288	.388	1	.067	-1	-21	-18	-1	-1.4
● BOB DAVIDSON					Davidson, Robert Banks b: 1/6/63, Bad Kurznach, W.Ger. BR/TR, 6', 185 lbs. Deb: 7/15/89																					
1989	NY-A	0	0	—	1	0	0	0	0	1	1	1	1	0	18.0	18.00	21	.250	.400	0	—	-0	-2	-2	0	0.0
● TED DAVIDSON					Davidson, Thomas Eugene b: 10/4/39, Las Vegas, Nev. BR/TL, 6', 192 lbs. Deb: 7/24/65																					
1965	Cin-N	4	3	.571	24	1	0	0	1	68²	57	5	17	54	10.0	2.23	168	.233	.288	0	.000	-2	10	12	0	1.0
1966	Cin-N	5	4	.556	54	0	0	0	4	85¹	82	11	23	54	11.2	3.90	100	.253	.305	0	.000	-1	-3	-0	-0	-0.2
1967	Cin-N	1	0	1.000	9	0	0	0	0	13	13	0	3	6	11.1	4.15	90	.250	.291	0	—	-0	-1	-1	0	0.0
1968	Cin-N	1	0	1.000	23	0	0	0	0	21²	27	3	7	7	14.1	6.23	51	.307	.358	0	.000	-0	-8	-7	0	-0.4
	Atl-N	0	0	—	4	0	0	0	0	6²	10	2	4	3	18.9	6.75	44	.345	.424	0	—	-0	-3	-3	0	-0.1
	Yr	1	0	1.000	27	0	0	0	0	28¹	37	5	11	10	15.2	6.35	49	.316	.375	0	.000	-0	-11	-10	-0	-0.4
Total	4	11	7	.611	114	1	0	0	5	195¹	189	21	54	124	11.3	3.69	101	.256	.309	0	.000	-3	-5	1	1	0.4
● JERRY DAVIE					Davie, Gerald Lee b: 2/10/33, Detroit, Mich. BR/TR, 6', 180 lbs. Deb: 4/14/59																					
1959	Det-A	2	2	.500	11	5	4	0	0	36²	40	8	17	20	15.0	4.17	97	.265	.355	4	.400	2	-1	-1	0	0.2
● GEORGE DAVIES					Davies, George Washington b: 2/22/1868, Portage, Wis. d: 9/22/06, Waterloo, Wis. 180 lbs. Deb: 8/18/1891																					
1891	Mil-a	7	5	.583	12	12	12	1	0	102	94	2	35	61	11.6	2.65	166	.237	.303	9	.243	1	12	20	-1	1.9
1892	Cle-N	10	16	.385	26	26	23	0	0	215²	201	4	69	95	11.5	2.59	131	.237	.299	12	.138	-5	17	19	3	1.7
1893	Cle-N	0	2	.000	3	3	1	0	0	15	28	1	10	2	22.8	11.40	43	.387	.461	2	.333	-2	-11	-11	-0	-0.9
	NY-N	1	1	.500	5	1	0	0	0	36¹	41	1	13	8	13.4	6.19	75	.276	.334	4	.333	2	-6	-6	0	0.0
	Yr	1	3	.250	8	4	1	0	0	51¹	69	2	23	10	16.1	7.71	61	.312	.377	6	.333	-1	-17	-17	1	-0.9
Total	3	18	24	.429	46	42	37	1	0	369	364	8	127	166	12.2	3.32	116	.248	.312	27	.190	-3	12	22	2	2.7

YEAR TM/L	W	L	PCT	G	GS	CG	SH	SV	IP	H	HR	BB	SO	RAT	ERA	ERA+	OAV	OOB	BH	AVG	PB	PR	/A	PD	TPI
● CHICK DAVIES Davies, Lloyd Garrison b: 3/6/1892, Peabody, Mass. d: 9/5/73, Middletown, Conn. BL/TL, 5'8", 145 lbs. Deb: 7/11/14 ♦
1914 Phi-A	1	0	1.000	1	1	1	0	0	9	8	0	3	4	11.0	1.00	261	.258	.324	11	.239	0	2	2	0	0.3
1915 Phi-A	1	2	.333	4	2	0	0	0	15¹	20	0	12	2	19.4	8.80	33	.339	.458	24	.182	0	-10	-10	1	-1.5
1925 NY-N	0	0	—	2	1	0	0	0	7¹	13	0	4	5	20.9	6.14	66	.361	.425	0	.000	-0	-2	-2	0	0.0
1926 NY-N	2	4	.333	38	1	0	0	6	89	96	3	35	27	13.2	3.94	95	.277	.344	4	.222	1	-1	-2	1	0.0
Total 4	4	6	.400	45	5	1	0	6	120²	137	3	54	38	14.3	4.48	80	.290	.364	39	.193	1	-11	-12	2	-1.2
● CHILI DAVIS Davis, Charles Theodore b: 1/17/60, Kingston, Jamaica BB/TR, 6'3", 195 lbs. Deb: 4/10/81 ♦
1993 Cal-A	0	0	—	1	0	0	0	0	2	0	0	0	0	4.5	0.00	—	.000	.143	139	.243	1	1	1	-0	0.0
● CURT DAVIS Davis, Curtis Benton "Coonskin" b: 9/7/03, Greenfield, Mo. d: 10/13/65, Covina, Cal. BR/TR, 6'2", 185 lbs. Deb: 4/21/34
1934 Phi-N	19	17	.528	**51**	31	18	3	5	274¹	283	14	60	99	11.5	2.95	160	.269	.313	20	.211	-2	34	54	9	**7.8**
1935 Phi-N	16	14	.533	44	27	19	3	2	231	264	14	47	74	12.4	3.66	124	.285	.324	13	.173	-1	9	22	2	2.8
1936 Phi-N	2	4	.333	10	8	3	0	0	60¹	71	6	19	18	13.6	4.62	98	.291	.345	4	.154	-1	-4	-0	0	-0.2
Chi-N★	11	9	.550	24	20	10	0	1	153	146	11	31	52	10.5	3.00	133	.251	.290	8	.151	-2	17	17	3	2.1
Yr	13	13	.500	34	28	13	0	1	213¹	217	17	50	70	11.3	3.46	120	.263	.306	12	.152	-3	13	16	3	1.9
1937 Chi-N	10	5	.667	28	14	8	0	1	123²	138	7	30	32	12.6	4.08	98	.286	.334	12	.300	4	-2	-1	2	0.4
1938 StL-N	12	8	.600	40	21	8	2	3	173¹	187	9	27	36	11.2	3.63	109	.272	.301	13	.228	2	3	6	1	1.0
1939 StL-N☆	22	16	.579	49	31	13	3	7	248	279	13	48	77	12.0	3.63	113	.280	.315	40	.381	12	8	13	1	3.3
1940 StL-N	4	4	.000	14	7	0	0	1	54	73	4	19	12	15.5	5.17	77	.327	.383	0	.000	-0	-8	-7	1	-0.6
Bro-N	8	7	.533	22	18	9	0	2	137	135	13	19	46	10.2	3.81	105	.256	.283	6	.128	-1	1	3	1	0.3
Yr	8	11	.421	36	25	9	0	3	191	208	17	38	58	11.6	4.19	95	.277	.312	6	.091	-3	-7	-4	2	-0.3
1941 *Bro-N	13	7	.650	28	16	10	5	2	154¹	141	6	27	50	9.9	2.97	123	.244	.280	11	.186	2	11	12	4	2.1
1942 Bro-N	15	6	.714	32	26	13	5	2	206	179	10	51	60	10.4	2.36	138	.233	.287	12	.176	-0	22	21	3	2.5
1943 Bro-N	10	13	.435	31	21	8	2	3	164¹	182	8	39	47	12.2	3.78	89	.281	.324	9	.164	-1	-7	-8	2	-0.9
1944 Bro-N	10	11	.476	31	23	12	1	4	194	207	12	39	49	11.6	3.34	106	.270	.310	10	.159	-2	6	5	2	0.5
1945 Bro-N	10	10	.500	24	18	10	0	0	149²	171	9	21	39	11.7	3.25	116	.280	.308	7	.137	-1	9	8	1	1.0
1946 Bro-N	0	0	—	1	0	0	0	0	2	3	1	2	0	27.0	13.50	25	.375	.545	—	0	0	-2	-2	0	0.0
Total 13	158	131	.547	429	281	141	24	33	2325	2459	142	479	684	11.6	3.42	116	.270	.310	165	.203	7	96	139	31	22.1
● DIXIE DAVIS Davis, Frank Talmadge b: 10/12/1890, Wilson Mills, N.C. d: 2/4/44, Raleigh, N.C. BR/TR, 5'11", 155 lbs. Deb: 7/12/12
1912 Cin-N	0	1	.000	7	0	0	0	0	26²	25	0	16	12	14.2	2.70	124	.258	.368	2	.200	-0	2	2	-1	0.0
1915 Chi-A	0	0	—	2	0	0	0	0	3	2	0	2	1	15.0	0.00	—	.250	.455	—	0	1	1	0	0.0
1918 Phi-N	0	2	.000	17	2	1	0	0	47	43	1	30	18	14.0	3.06	98	.247	.358	0	.000	-0	-0	-1	-1	-0.2
1920 StL-L	18	12	.600	38	31	22	0	0	269¹	250	10	149	85	13.6	3.17	123	.256	.359	25	.266	3	19	22	-4	2.0
1921 StL-A	16	16	.500	40	36	20	2	0	265¹	279	12	123	100	14.0	4.44	101	.281	.366	20	.211	-3	-5	1	-1	-0.3
1922 StL-A	11	6	.647	25	25	7	2	0	174¹	162	10	87	65	13.3	4.08	102	.250	.345	8	.136	-3	-1	1	-0	-0.3
1923 StL-A	4	6	.400	19	17	5	1	0	109¹	106	4	63	36	14.3	3.62	115	.259	.365	10	.250	-0	4	7	-2	0.3
1924 StL-A	11	13	.458	29	24	11	5	0	160¹	159	9	72	45	13.3	4.10	110	.263	.347	7	.152	-2	2	7	-1	0.7
1925 StL-A	12	7	.632	35	23	9	0	1	180¹	192	10	106	58	15.2	4.59	102	.279	.380	11	.172	-4	-4	2	1	-0.1
1926 StL-A	3	8	.273	27	7	2	0	1	83	93	7	40	39	14.5	4.66	92	.292	.372	4	.167	-0	-6	-3	-0	-0.5
Total 10	75	71	.514	239	165	77	10	2	1318²	1311	63	688	460	14.0	3.97	107	.267	.362	87	.197	-10	12	39	-10	1.6
● GEORGE DAVIS Davis, George Allen "Iron" b: 3/9/1890, Lancaster, N.Y. d: 6/4/61, Buffalo, N.Y. BB/TR, 5'10.5", 175 lbs. Deb: 7/16/12
1912 NY-A	1	4	.200	10	7	5	0	0	54	61	3	28	22	15.3	6.50	55	.293	.385	2	.111	-1	-19	-17	-2	-1.6
1913 Bos-N	0	0	—	2	0	0	0	0	8	7	1	3	2	13.5	4.50	73	.241	.353	0	.000	-0	-1	-1	-0	-0.1
1914 Bos-N	3	3	.500	9	6	4	1	0	55²	42	1	26	26	11.5	3.40	81	.215	.317	3	.167	-0	-4	-4	-2	-0.6
1915 Bos-N	3	3	.500	15	9	4	0	0	73¹	85	2	19	26	13.3	3.80	68	.304	.356	6	.261	1	-9	-10	0	-0.6
Total 4	7	10	.412	36	22	13	1	0	191	195	7	78	77	13.3	4.48	66	.274	.354	11	.180	-0	-33	-33	-3	-2.9
● STORM DAVIS Davis, George Earl b: 12/26/61, Dallas, Tex. BR/TR, 6'4", 207 lbs. Deb: 4/29/82
1982 Bal-A	8	4	.667	29	8	1	0	0	100²	96	8	28	67	11.1	3.49	116	.257	.308	0	—	0	7	6	-0	0.7
1983 *Bal-A	13	7	.650	34	29	6	1	0	200¹	180	14	64	125	11.1	3.59	110	.238	.299	0	—	0	10	8	-2	0.7
1984 Bal-A	14	9	.609	35	31	10	2	0	225	205	7	71	105	11.2	3.12	124	.247	.310	0	—	0	22	19	-3	1.7
1985 Bal-A	10	8	.556	31	28	8	1	0	175	172	16	70	93	12.5	4.53	89	.256	.327	0	—	0	-7	-10	-1	-0.7
1986 Bal-A	9	12	.429	25	25	2	0	0	154	166	16	49	96	12.6	3.62	114	.275	.330	0	—	0	9	9	-1	1.3
1987 SD-N	2	7	.222	21	10	0	0	0	62²	70	5	36	37	15.5	6.18	64	.280	.375	1	.063	-1	-15	-15	-0	-2.0
Oak-A	1	1	.500	5	5	0	0	0	30¹	28	3	11	28	11.6	3.26	126	.241	.307	0	—	0	4	3	-1	0.0
1988 *Oak-A	16	7	.696	33	33	0	0	0	201²	211	16	91	127	13.5	3.70	102	.274	.352	0	—	0	6	2	-2	0.0
1989 *Oak-A	19	7	.731	31	31	1	0	0	169¹	187	19	68	91	13.7	4.36	84	.288	.358	0	—	0	-9	-13	-2	-1.7
1990 KC-A	7	10	.412	21	20	0	0	0	112	129	9	35	62	13.2	4.74	81	.281	.332	0	—	0	-10	-11	-1	-1.5
1991 KC-A	3	9	.250	51	9	1	1	2	114¹	140	11	46	53	14.7	4.96	83	.306	.370	0	—	0	-11	-11	-1	-1.2
1992 Bal-A	7	3	.700	48	2	0	0	4	89¹	79	5	36	53	11.8	3.43	117	.244	.323	0	—	0	5	6	1	0.7
1993 Oak-A	2	6	.250	19	8	0	0	0	62²	68	5	33	37	14.8	6.18	66	.276	.367	0	—	0	-13	-15	-0	-1.5
Det-A	0	2	.000	24	0	0	0	0	35¹	25	4	15	36	10.4	3.06	140	.198	.289	0	—	0	5	5	0	0.4
Yr	2	8	.200	43	8	0	0	0	98	93	9	48	73	13.0	5.05	82	.247	.334	0	—	0	-8	-10	-0	-1.1
1994 Det-A	2	4	.333	35	0	0	0	0	50	48	3	34	38	13.1	3.56	134	.207	.337	0	—	0	7	6	0	0.7
Total 13	113	96	.541	442	239	30	5	11	1780²	1792	136	687	1048	12.6	4.02	99	.263	.332	1	.063	-1	10	-11	-7	-1.7
● GEORGE DAVIS Davis, George Stacey b: 8/23/1870, Cohoes, N.Y. d: 10/17/40, Philadelphia, Pa. BB/TR, 5'9", 180 lbs. Deb: 4/19/1890 M♦
1891 Cle-N	0	1	.000	3	0	0	0	1	4	8	0	3	4	24.8	15.75	22	.401	.479	165	.289	1	-6	-5	-0	-1.1
● JIM DAVIS Davis, James Bennett b: 9/15/24, Red Bluff, Cal. BB/TL, 6', 180 lbs. Deb: 4/18/54
1954 Chi-N	11	7	.611	46	12	2	0	4	127²	114	12	51	58	11.6	3.52	119	.247	.326	2	.063	-1	8	10	1	1.3
1955 Chi-N	7	11	.389	42	16	0	0	3	133²	122	16	58	62	12.3	4.44	92	.246	.327	1	.027	-4	-6	-5	-1	-1.1
1956 Chi-N	5	7	.417	46	11	2	1	2	120¹	116	11	66	66	13.5	3.66	103	.256	.349	5	.179	-0	1	1	1	0.2
1957 StL-N	0	1	.000	10	0	0	0	1	13²	18	1	6	7	15.8	5.27	75	.340	.407	-0	-2	-2	-0	-0.2	
NY-N	1	0	1.000	10	0	0	0	0	11	13	2	5	6	14.7	6.55	60	.283	.353	1	1.000	-0	-3	-3	-0	-0.2
Yr	1	1	.500	20	0	0	0	1	24²	31	3	11	13	15.3	5.84	68	.310	.378	1	.500	-0	-5	-5	-0	-0.4
Total 4	24	26	.480	154	39	4	1	10	406¹	383	42	179	197	12.7	4.01	100	.253	.337	9	.091	-5	-2	0	1	-0.0
● JOEL DAVIS Davis, Joel Clark b: 1/30/65, Jacksonville, Fla. BL/TR, 6'5", 205 lbs. Deb: 8/11/85
1985 Chi-A	3	3	.500	12	11	1	0	0	71¹	76	6	26	37	12.4	4.16	104	.256	.322	0	—	0	-0	1	-1	-0.4
1986 Chi-A	4	5	.444	19	19	1	0	0	105¹	115	9	51	54	14.3	4.70	92	.280	.361	0	—	0	-6	-5	-1	-0.5
1987 Chi-A	1	5	.167	13	9	1	0	0	55	56	7	29	25	13.9	5.73	80	.264	.353	0	—	0	-8	-7	-1	-0.9
1988 Chi-A	0	1	.000	5	2	0	0	0	16	21	4	5	10	14.6	6.75	58	.328	.377	0	—	0	-5	-5	-0	-0.3
Total 4	8	14	.364	49	41	3	0	0	247²	263	26	111	126	13.7	4.91	89	.273	.349	0	—	0	-19	-15	-3	-2.1
● DAISY DAVIS Davis, John Henry Albert b: 11/28/1858, Boston, Mass. d: 11/5/02, Lynn, Mass. TR, Deb: 5/6/1884
1884 StL-a	10	12	.455	25	24	20	1	0	198¹	196	1	35	143	11.1	2.90	112	.249	.293	15	.172	-2	8	8	-1	0.4
Bos-N	1	3	.250	4	4	3	0	0	31	50	2	8	13	16.8	7.84	37	.355	.389	0	.000	-3	-17	-17	0	-1.6
1885 Bos-N	5	6	.455	11	11	10	1	0	94¹	110	2	28	30	13.2	4.29	63	.280	.328	7	.189	-1	-15	-17	-1	-1.7
Total 2	16	21	.432	40	39	33	2	0	323²	356	5	71	186	12.3	3.78	84	.269	.313	22	.157	-5	-25	-26	-2	-2.9

YEAR	TM/L	W	L	PCT	G	GS	CG	SH	SV	IP	H	HR	BB	SO	RAT	ERA	ERA+	OAV	OOB	BH	AVG	PB	PR	/A	PD	TPI

● **JOHN DAVIS** Davis, John Kirk b: 1/5/63, Chicago, Ill. BR/TR, 6'7", 215 lbs. Deb: 7/24/87

1987	KC-A	5	2	.714	27	0	0	0	2	43²	29	0	26	24	11.7	2.27	201	.195	.322	0	—	0	11	11	0	1.5
1988	Chi-A	2	5	.286	34	1	0	0	1	63²	77	5	50	37	18.5	6.64	60	.297	.419	0	—	0	-19	-19	-0	-1.9
1989	Chi-A	0	1	.000	4	0	0	0	1	6	5	2	2	5	10.5	4.50	85	.217	.280	0	—	0	-0	-0	0	0.1
1990	SD-N	0	1	.000	6	0	0	0	0	9¹	9	1	4	7	12.5	5.79	66	.257	.333	0	.000	-0	-2	-1	-0	-0.2
Total	4	7	9	.438	71	1	0	0	4	122²	120	8	82	73	15.3	4.92	85	.258	.375	0	.000	-0	-11	-10	-0	-0.5

● **BUD DAVIS** Davis, John Wilbur "Country" b: 12/7/1896, Merry Point, Va. d: 5/26/67, Williamsburg, Va. BL/TR, 6', 207 lbs. Deb: 4/19/15

| 1915 | Phi-A | 0 | 2 | .000 | 18 | 2 | 0 | 0 | 0 | 66² | 65 | 1 | 59 | 18 | 17.6 | 4.05 | 72 | .273 | .429 | 8 | .308 | 2 | -8 | -8 | -1 | 0.0 |

● **MARK DAVIS** Davis, Mark William b: 10/19/60, Livermore, Cal. BL/TL, 6'4", 205 lbs. Deb: 9/12/80

1980	Phi-N	0	0	—	2	1	0	0	0	7	4	0	5	5	11.6	2.57	147	.160	.300	1	.500	0	1	1	-0	0.0
1981	Phi-N	1	4	.200	9	9	0	0	0	43	49	7	24	29	15.3	7.74	47	.299	.388	1	.091	-0	-20	-20	-0	-2.0
1983	SF-N	6	4	.600	20	20	2	2	0	111	93	14	50	83	11.8	3.49	101	.227	.315	4	.133	0	2	1	-1	0.0
1984	SF-N	5	17	.227	46	27	1	0	0	174²	201	25	54	124	13.4	5.36	65	.293	.349	6	.130	0	-34	-36	-2	-4.2
1985	SF-N	5	12	.294	77	1	0	0	7	114¹	89	13	41	131	10.5	3.54	97	.219	.295	3	.250	1	1	-1	-1	-0.2
1986	SF-N	5	7	.417	67	2	0	0	4	84¹	63	6	34	90	10.5	2.99	118	.212	.295	1	.125	0	7	5	-0	0.7
1987	SF-N	4	5	.444	20	11	1	0	0	70²	72	9	28	51	13.2	4.71	82	.273	.351	5	.217	2	-5	-7	-1	-0.7
	SD-N	5	3	.625	43	0	0	0	2	62¹	51	5	31	47	12.1	3.18	124	.224	.322	2	.286	0	6	5	0	0.7
	Yr	9	8	.529	63	11	1	0	2	133	123	14	59	98	12.5	3.99	98	.247	.329	7	.233	2	1	-1	-0	0.0
1988	SD-N★	5	10	.333	62	0	0	0	28	98¹	70	2	42	102	10.3	2.01	169	.199	.284	2	.200	1	16	15	2	3.8
1989	SD-N★	4	3	.571	70	0	0	0	44	92²	66	6	31	92	9.6	1.85	189	.200	.273	0	.000	-1	17	17	-1	3.0
1990	KC-A	2	7	.222	53	3	0	0	6	68²	71	9	52	73	16.6	5.11	75	.259	.385	0	—	0	-9	-10	-1	-1.3
1991	KC-A	6	3	.667	29	5	0	0	1	62²	55	6	39	47	13.6	4.45	93	.240	.353	0	—	0	-2	-2	-0	-0.3
1992	KC-A	1	3	.250	13	6	0	0	0	36¹	42	6	28	19	17.3	7.18	56	.294	.409	0	—	0	-13	-13	-0	-1.3
	Atl-N	1	0	1.000	14	0	0	0	0	16²	22	3	13	15	19.4	7.02	52	.314	.429	0	.000	-0	-7	-6	-1	-0.4
1993	Phi-N	1	2	.333	25	0	0	0	0	31¹	35	4	24	28	17.2	5.17	77	.273	.392	1	.333	0	-4	-4	-0	-0.4
	SD-N	0	3	.000	35	0	0	0	4	38¹	44	6	20	42	15.0	3.52	117	.295	.379	0	.000	-0	2	3	0	0.2
	Yr	1	5	.167	60	0	0	0	4	69²	79	10	44	70	15.9	4.26	95	.284	.382	1	.250	0	-2	-2	-0	-0.2
1994	SD-N	0	1	.000	20	0	0	0	0	16¹	24	4	13	15	18.2	8.82	48	.299	.412	0	—	0	-8	-8	-0	-0.4
Total	14	51	84	.378	605	85	4	2	96	1128²	1047	125	529	993	12.8	4.15	88	.248	.335	26	.156	5	-52	-61	-4	-2.8

● **PEACHES DAVIS** Davis, Ray Thomas b: 5/31/05, Glen Rose, Tex. BL/TR, 6'3.5", 190 lbs. Deb: 7/11/36

1936	Cin-N	8	8	.500	26	15	5	0	5	125²	139	7	36	32	12.7	3.58	107	.280	.331	7	.163	-1	6	3	0	0.3
1937	Cin-N	11	13	.458	42	24	11	1	3	218	252	5	51	59	12.6	3.59	104	.295	.337	10	.128	-4	8	3	-3	-0.3
1938	Cin-N	7	12	.368	29	19	11	1	1	167²	193	9	40	28	12.6	3.97	92	.290	.331	15	.246	1	-3	-6	-3	-0.8
1939	Cin-N	1	0	1.000	20	0	0	0	2	30²	43	5	11	4	16.1	6.46	59	.341	.399	1	.333	0	-9	-9	0	-0.3
Total	4	27	33	.450	117	58	27	2	11	542	627	26	138	123	12.8	3.87	96	.293	.337	33	.178	-4	2	-8	-6	-1.1

● **BOB DAVIS** Davis, Robert Edward b: 9/11/33, New York, N.Y. BR/TR, 6', 170 lbs. Deb: 7/26/58

1958	KC-A	0	4	.000	8	4	0	0	0	31	45	5	12	22	17.1	7.84	50	.346	.410	1	.167	-0	-14	-14	0	-1.5
1960	KC-A	0	0	—	21	0	0	0	1	32	31	1	22	28	15.2	3.66	109	.263	.383	1	.250	0	1	1	1	0.1
Total	2	0	4	.000	29	4	0	0	1	63	76	6	34	50	16.1	5.71	69	.306	.396	2	.200	-0	-13	-12	2	-1.4

● **RON DAVIS** Davis, Ronald Gene b: 8/6/55, Houston, Tex. BR/TR, 6'4", 207 lbs. Deb: 7/29/78

1978	NY-A	0	0	—	4	0	0	0	0	2¹	3	0	3	0	23.1	11.57	31	.333	.500	0	—	0	-2	-2	0	0.1
1979	NY-A	14	2	.875	44	0	0	0	9	85¹	84	5	28	43	11.9	2.85	143	.262	.323	0	.000	0	13	12	1	2.3
1980	*NY-A	9	3	.750	53	0	0	0	7	131	121	9	32	65	10.9	2.95	133	.246	.299	0	.000	0	16	14	0	1.4
1981	*NY-A★	4	5	.444	43	0	0	0	6	73	47	6	25	83	8.9	2.71	132	.186	.259	0	—	0	8	7	-1	0.9
1982	Min-A	3	9	.250	63	0	0	0	22	106	106	16	47	89	13.1	4.42	96	.261	.339	0	—	0	-4	-2	-0	-0.4
1983	Min-A	5	8	.385	66	0	0	0	30	89	89	6	33	84	12.6	3.34	127	.266	.338	0	—	0	7	9	-2	1.5
1984	Min-A	7	11	.389	64	0	0	0	29	83	79	11	41	74	13.2	4.55	92	.253	.344	0	—	0	-5	-3	-0	-1.1
1985	Min-A	2	6	.250	57	0	0	0	25	64²	55	7	35	72	13.1	3.48	127	.230	.338	0	—	0	5	7	-0	0.9
1986	Min-A	2	6	.250	36	0	0	0	2	38²	55	7	29	30	20.5	9.08	47	.340	.451	0	—	0	-21	-21	0	-3.9
	Chi-N	0	2	.000	17	0	0	0	0	20	31	3	3	10	15.3	7.65	53	.356	.378	0	.000	-0	-9	-8	-1	-0.8
1987	Chi-N	0	0	—	21	0	0	0	0	32¹	43	5	8	31	15.3	5.85	73	.328	.385	0	—	0	-6	-6	-1	-0.1
	LA-N	0	0	—	4	0	0	0	0	4	7	0	6	1	31.5	6.75	59	.412	.583	0	—	0	-1	-1	0	-0.0
	Yr	0	0	—	25	0	0	0	0	36¹	50	5	18	32	17.1	5.94	71	.336	.411	0	—	0	-8	-7	-0	-0.1
1988	SF-N	1	1	.500	9	0	0	0	0	17¹	15	4	6	15	11.4	4.67	70	.234	.310	0	.000	-0	-2	-3	-0	-0.3
Total	11	47	53	.470	481	0	0	0	130	746²	735	82	300	597	12.7	4.05	101	.260	.336	0	.000	-0	-3	3	-3	0.5

● **STEVE DAVIS** Davis, Steven Kennon b: 8/4/60, San Antonio, Tex. BL/TL, 6'1", 195 lbs. Deb: 8/25/85

1985	Tor-A	2	1	.667	10	5	0	0	0	28	23	5	13	22	11.6	3.54	119	.223	.310	0	—	0	2	2	-0	0.2
1986	Tor-A	0	0	—	3	0	0	0	0	3²	8	2	5	5	31.9	17.18	25	.471	.591	0	—	0	-5	-5	-0	-0.2
1989	Cle-A	1	1	.500	12	0	0	0	0	25²	34	2	14	12	16.8	8.06	49	.318	.397	0	—	0	-12	-12	-0	-0.9
Total	3	3	2	.600	25	5	0	0	0	57¹	65	9	32	39	15.2	6.44	64	.286	.375	0	—	0	-15	-15	-1	-1.1

● **TIM DAVIS** Davis, Timothy Howard b: 7/14/70, Marianna, Fla. BL/TL, 5'11", 165 lbs. Deb: 4/4/94

| 1994 | Sea-A | 2 | 2 | .500 | 42 | 1 | 0 | 0 | 2 | 49¹ | 57 | 4 | 25 | 28 | 15.1 | 4.01 | 122 | .295 | .379 | 0 | — | 0 | 4 | 5 | 0 | 0.4 |

● **WILEY DAVIS** Davis, Wiley Anderson b: 8/1/1875, Seymour, Tenn. d: 9/22/42, Detroit, Mich. BR/TR, 5'10", 165 lbs. Deb: 4/18/1896

| 1896 | Cin-N | 1 | 1 | .500 | 2 | 0 | 0 | 0 | 0 | 4¹ | 8 | 0 | 2 | 1 | 20.8 | 8.31 | 55 | .391 | .446 | 0 | .000 | — | -2 | -2 | 0 | -0.5 |

● **WOODY DAVIS** Davis, Woodrow Wilson "Babe" b: 4/25/13, Nicholls, Ga. BL/TR, 6'1", 200 lbs. Deb: 5/2/38

| 1938 | Det-A | 0 | 0 | — | 2 | 0 | 0 | 0 | 0 | 6 | 3 | 0 | 4 | 1 | 10.5 | 1.50 | 333 | .158 | .304 | 0 | .000 | -0 | 2 | 2 | -0 | 0.0 |

● **MIKE DAVISON** Davison, Michael Lynn b: 8/4/45, Galesburg, Ill. BL/TL, 6'1", 170 lbs. Deb: 10/1/69

1969	SF-N	0	0	—	1	0	0	0	0	2	2	0	0	2	9.0	4.50	78	.250	.250	0	—	-0	-0	-0	-0	0.0
1970	SF-N	3	5	.375	31	0	0	0	1	36	46	4	22	21	17.0	6.50	61	.324	.415	0	.000	0	-10	-10	1	-1.9
Total	2	3	5	.375	32	0	0	0	1	38	48	4	22	23	16.6	6.39	62	.320	.407	0	.000	-0	-10	-10	1	-1.9

● **BILL DAWLEY** Dawley, William Chester b: 2/6/58, Norwich, Conn. BR/TR, 6'4", 240 lbs. Deb: 4/15/83

1983	Hou-N★	6	6	.500	48	0	0	0	14	79²	51	9	22	60	8.4	2.82	120	.185	.247	2	.222	0	7	5	-1	0.8
1984	Hou-N	11	4	.733	60	0	0	0	5	98	82	5	35	47	10.7	1.93	172	.234	.303	3	.333	2	18	15	-1	2.5
1985	Hou-N	5	3	.625	49	0	0	0	2	81	76	7	37	48	12.6	3.56	97	.259	.341	2	.200	0	-1	0	-0	0.0
1986	Chi-A	0	7	.000	46	0	0	0	2	97²	91	10	28	66	11.1	3.32	130	.247	.302	0	.000	0	9	11	-1	0.6
1987	StL-N	5	8	.385	60	0	0	0	2	96²	93	15	38	65	12.3	4.47	93	.259	.332	2	.167	0	-4	-3	-1	-0.3
1988	Phi-N	0	2	.000	8	0	0	0	0	8²	16	3	4	3	20.8	13.50	26	.381	.435	0	—	0	-10	-10	-0	-1.9
1989	Oak-A	0	0	—	4	0	0	0	0	9	11	0	2	3	14.0	4.00	92	.297	.350	0	—	0	-0	-0	-0	0.0
Total	7	27	30	.474	275	0	0	0	25	470²	420	49	166	292	11.3	3.42	109	.243	.311	9	.214	3	21	16	-2	1.7

● **JOE DAWSON** Dawson, Ralph Fenton b: 3/9/1897, Bow, Wash. d: 1/4/78, Longview, Tex. BR/TR, 5'11", 182 lbs. Deb: 7/4/24

1924	Cle-A	1	2	.333	4	4	0	0	0	20¹	24	0	21	7	20.4	6.64	64	.300	.451	2	.286	0	-5	-5	1	-0.6
1927	*Pit-N	3	7	.300	20	7	4	0	0	80²	80	2	32	17	12.5	4.46	92	.268	.338	5	.200	-1	-5	-3	-1	-0.5
1928	Pit-N	7	7	.500	31	7	3	0	0	128²	116	6	56	36	12.1	3.29	123	.242	.322	12	.279	3	10	11	-3	1.2

YEAR TM/L	W	L	PCT	G	GS	CG	SH	SV	IP	H	HR	BB	SO	RAT	ERA	ERA+	OAV	OOB	BH	AVG	PB	PR	/A	PD	TPI
1929 Pit-N	0	1	.000	4	0	0	0	0	8^2	13	2	3	2	16.6	8.31	57	.342	.390	1	.500	1	-3	-3	-0	-0.3
Total 4	11	17	.393	59	18	5	0	3	238^1	233	10	112	62	13.1	4.15	99	.260	.343	20	.260	3	-4	-1	-3	-0.2

● REX DAWSON
Dawson, Rexford Paul b: 2/10/1889, Skagit Co., Wash. d: 10/20/58, Indianapolis, Ind. BL/TR, 6', 185 lbs. Deb: 10/3/13

YEAR TM/L	W	L	PCT	G	GS	CG	SH	SV	IP	H	HR	BB	SO	RAT	ERA	ERA+	OAV	OOB	BH	AVG	PB	PR	/A	PD	TPI
1913 Was-A	0	0	—	1	0	0	0	0	1	1	0	1	0	9.0	0.00	—	.250	.250	0	—	0	0	0	-0	0.0

● PEA RIDGE DAY
Day, Clyde Henry b: 8/26/1899, Pea Ridge, Ark. d: 3/21/34, Kansas City, Mo. BR/TR, 6', 190 lbs. Deb: 9/19/24

YEAR TM/L	W	L	PCT	G	GS	CG	SH	SV	IP	H	HR	BB	SO	RAT	ERA	ERA+	OAV	OOB	BH	AVG	PB	PR	/A	PD	TPI
1924 StL-N	1	1	.500	3	3	1	0	0	17^2	22	0	6	3	14.3	4.58	82	.306	.359	1	.125	-1	-1	-2	-0	-0.3
1925 StL-N	2	4	.333	17	4	1	0	1	40	53	5	7	13	14.2	6.30	69	.325	.364	2	.154	-1	-9	-9	-1	-1.3
1926 Cin-N	0	0	—	4	0	0	0	0	7^1	13	1	2	2	18.4	7.36	50	.406	.441	0	.000	-0	-3	-3	-0	-0.1
1931 Bro-N	2	2	.500	22	2	1	0	1	57^1	75	5	13	30	13.8	4.55	84	.315	.351	4	.222	-0	-4	-5	-1	-0.4
Total 4	5	7	.417	46	9	3	0	2	122^1	163	11	28	48	14.3	5.30	75	.323	.362	7	.171	-2	-18	-18	-2	-2.1

● BILL DAY
Day, William M. b: 7/28/1867, Wilmington, Del. d: 8/16/23, Wilmington, Del. TR, 5'8", 150 lbs. Deb: 8/20/1889

YEAR TM/L	W	L	PCT	G	GS	CG	SH	SV	IP	H	HR	BB	SO	RAT	ERA	ERA+	OAV	OOB	BH	AVG	PB	PR	/A	PD	TPI
1889 Phi-N	0	3	.000	4	3	2	0	0	19	16	0	23	20	18.5	5.21	83	.221	.409	0	.000	-2	-3	-2	-0	-0.4
1890 Phi-N	1	1	.500	4	2	2	0	0	23^2	26	0	12	9	14.5	3.04	120	.271	.352	1	.100	-1	1	2	-1	-0.1
Pit-N	0	6	.000	6	6	6	0	0	50	66	1	24	10	16.4	5.22	63	.308	.381	4	.043	-4	-9	-11	1	-1.1
Yr	1	7	.125	10	8	8	0	0	73^2	92	1	36	19	15.8	4.52	75	.297	.372	2	.061	-5	-8	-9	1	-1.2
Total 2	1	10	.091	14	11	10	0	0	92^2	108	1	59	39	16.3	4.66	77	.282	.380	2	.047	-6	-10	-11	0	-1.6

● KEN DAYLEY
Dayley, Kenneth Grant b: 2/25/59, Jerome, Idaho BL/TL, 6', 175 lbs. Deb: 5/13/82

YEAR TM/L	W	L	PCT	G	GS	CG	SH	SV	IP	H	HR	BB	SO	RAT	ERA	ERA+	OAV	OOB	BH	AVG	PB	PR	/A	PD	TPI
1982 Atl-N	5	6	.455	20	11	0	0	0	71^1	79	9	25	34	13.1	4.54	82	.286	.346	5	.250	1	-7	-6	-2	-1.0
1983 Atl-N	5	8	.385	24	16	0	0	0	104^2	100	12	39	70	12.1	4.30	90	.257	.328	7	.219	1	-8	-5	-2	-0.7
1984 Atl-N	0	3	.000	4	4	0	0	0	18^2	28	1	6	10	16.9	5.30	73	.341	.393	2	.500	1	-4	-3	0	-0.4
StL-N	0	2	.000	3	2	0	0	0	5	16	1	5	0	37.8	18.00	19	.615	.677	0	—	0	-8	-8	-0	-2.1
Yr	0	5	.000	7	6	0	0	0	23^2	44	6	11	10	20.9	7.99	47	.404	.458	2	.500	1	-12	-11	0	-2.5
1985 *StL-N	4	4	.500	57	0	0	0	11	65^1	65	2	18	62	11.4	2.76	128	.263	.313	4	.400	1	6	6	2	1.1
1986 StL-N	0	3	.000	31	0	0	0	5	38^2	42	1	11	33	12.6	3.26	112	.275	.327	1	.200	0	2	2	0	0.2
1987 *StL-N	9	5	.643	53	0	0	0	4	61	52	2	33	63	12.6	2.66	156	.234	.339	0	—	0	10	10	-1	2.2
1988 StL-N	2	7	.222	54	0	0	0	5	55^1	48	2	19	38	11.1	2.77	126	.239	.308	-0	.000	-0	4	4	-0	0.7
1989 StL-N	4	3	.571	71	0	0	0	12	75^1	63	3	30	40	11.1	2.87	127	.228	.304	-1	.000	-1	5	6	-2	0.6
1990 StL-N	4	4	.500	58	0	0	0	2	73^1	63	5	30	51	11.4	3.56	107	.233	.310	0	.000	0	2	2	0	0.1
1991 Tor-A	0	0	—	8	0	0	0	0	4^1	7	0	5	2	27.0	6.23	67	.368	.520		—	0	-1	-1	0	0.0
1993 Tor-A	0	0	—	2	0	0	0	0	0^2	1	0	4	2	67.5	0.00	—	.333	.714	0	—	0	-0	-0	0	0.0
Total 11	33	45	.423	385	33	0	0	39	573^2	564	42	225	406	12.5	3.64	103	.261	.332	17	.210	3	1	7	-5	0.7

● REN DEAGLE
Deagle, Lorenzo Burroughs b: 6/26/1858, New York, N.Y. d: 12/24/36, Kansas City, Mo. BR/TR, 5'9", 190 lbs. Deb: 5/17/1883

YEAR TM/L	W	L	PCT	G	GS	CG	SH	SV	IP	H	HR	BB	SO	RAT	ERA	ERA+	OAV	OOB	BH	AVG	PB	PR	/A	PD	TPI
1883 Cin-a	10	8	.556	18	18	17	1	0	148	136	0	34	48	10.3	2.31	141	.228	.270	9	.129	-5	16	15	-1	0.9
1884 Cin-a	3	1	.750	4	4	4	1	0	34	39	0	9	12	13.0	5.03	66	.322	.374	0	.000	-2	-7	-6	-0	-0.7
Lou-a	4	6	.400	12	12	8	0	0	87^1	80	0	13	23	10.3	2.58	120	.238	.281	6	.133	-3	7	5	1	0.3
Yr	7	7	.500	16	16	12	1	0	121^1	119	0	22	35	11.0	3.26	97	.260	.304	6	.103	-5	-0	-1	1	-0.4
Total 2	17	15	.531	34	34	29	2	0	269^1	255	0	56	83	10.7	2.74	117	.242	.286	15	.117	-9	16	14	-1	0.5

● COT DEAL
Deal, Ellis Fergason b: 1/23/23, Arapaho, Okla. BB/TR, 5'10.5", 185 lbs. Deb: 9/11/47 C

YEAR TM/L	W	L	PCT	G	GS	CG	SH	SV	IP	H	HR	BB	SO	RAT	ERA	ERA+	OAV	OOB	BH	AVG	PB	PR	/A	PD	TPI
1947 Bos-A	0	1	.000	5	2	0	0	0	12^2	20	0	7	6	19.2	9.24	42	.364	.435	2	.500	1	-8	-8	0	-0.5
1948 Bos-A	1	0	1.000	4	0	0	0	0	4	3	0	3	2	13.5			.200	.333	0	—	0	2	2	0	0.5
1950 StL-N	0	0	—	3	0	0	0	0	1	3	0	2	1	45.0	18.00	24	.500	.625	0	—	0	-2	-2	-0	-0.1
1954 StL-N	2	3	.400	33	0	0	0	1	71^2	85	14	36	25	15.7	6.28	65	.297	.383	2	.100	0	-18	-17	-0	-1.1
Total 4	3	4	.429	45	2	0	0	1	89^1	111	14	48	34	16.4	6.55	63	.307	.394	4	.167	1	-25	-24	-0	-1.1

● CHUBBY DEAN
Dean, Alfred Lovill b: 8/24/16, Mt.Airy, N.C. d: 12/21/70, Riverside, Cal. BL/TL, 5'11", 181 lbs. Deb: 4/14/36 ◆

YEAR TM/L	W	L	PCT	G	GS	CG	SH	SV	IP	H	HR	BB	SO	RAT	ERA	ERA+	OAV	OOB	BH	AVG	PB	PR	/A	PD	TPI
1937 Phi-A	1	0	1.000	2	1	0	0	0	9	7	0	6	4	13.0	4.00	118	.219	.342	81	.262	0	1	1	0	0.1
1938 Phi-A	2	1	.667	6	1	0	0	0	23	22	3	15	3	14.5	3.52	137	.250	.359	6	.300	2	3	3	1	0.6
1939 Phi-A	5	8	.385	54	1	0	0	7	116^2	132	8	80	39	16.4	5.25	90	.289	.395	27	.351	8	-8	-7	1	0.2
1940 Phi-A	6	13	.316	30	19	8	1	1	159	220	21	63	38	16.6	6.61	67	.324	.381	26	.289	4	-39	-38	1	-2.9
1941 Phi-A	2	4	.333	18	7	2	0	0	75^2	90	9	35	22	14.9	6.19	68	.294	.367	9	.243	-2	-17	-17	0	-0.9
Cle-A	1	4	.200	8	8	2	0	0	53^1	57	3	24	14	13.7	4.39	90	.282	.358	4	.160	-1	-1	-3	-0	-0.1
Yr	3	8	.273	26	15	4	0	0	129	147	12	59	36	14.4	5.44	79	.289	.363	13	.210	-2	-19	-19	1	-1.0
1942 Cle-A	8	11	.421	27	22	8	0	1	172^2	170	7	66	46	12.3	3.81	91	.261	.329	27	.267	8	-3	-7	-3	-0.2
1943 Cle-A	5	5	.500	17	9	3	0	0	76	83	1	34	29	14.0	4.50	69	.281	.358	9	.196	1	-10	-12	-1	-1.4
Total 7	30	46	.395	162	68	23	1	9	685^2	781	52	323	195	14.5	5.08	79	.288	.364	287	.274	25	-75	-80	-1	-4.6

● DORY DEAN
Dean, Charles Wilson b: 11/6/1852, Cincinnati, Ohio d: 5/4/35, Nashville, Tenn. BR/TR, Deb: 6/22/1876

YEAR TM/L	W	L	PCT	G	GS	CG	SH	SV	IP	H	HR	BB	SO	RAT	ERA	ERA+	OAV	OOB	BH	AVG	PB	PR	/A	PD	TPI
1876 Cin-N	4	26	.133	30	30	26	0	0	262^2	397	1	24	22	14.4	3.73	59	.322	.335	36	.261	1	-42	-45	-1	-3.7

● HARRY DEAN
Dean, James Harry b: 5/12/15, Rockmart, Ga. d: 6/1/60, Rockmart, Ga. BR/TR, 6'4", 185 lbs. Deb: 4/16/41

YEAR TM/L	W	L	PCT	G	GS	CG	SH	SV	IP	H	HR	BB	SO	RAT	ERA	ERA+	OAV	OOB	BH	AVG	PB	PR	/A	PD	TPI
1941 Was-A	0	0	—	2	0	0	0	0	2	2	0	3	0	27.0	4.50	90	.250	.500	0	—	0	-0	-0	-0	0.0

● DIZZY DEAN
Dean, Jay Hanna b: 1/16/10, Lucas, Ark. d: 7/17/74, Reno, Nevada BR/TR, 6'2", 182 lbs. Deb: 9/28/30 FCH

YEAR TM/L	W	L	PCT	G	GS	CG	SH	SV	IP	H	HR	BB	SO	RAT	ERA	ERA+	OAV	OOB	BH	AVG	PB	PR	/A	PD	TPI
1930 StL-N	1	0	1.000	1	1	1	0	0	9	3	0	3	5	6.0	1.00	502	.103	.188	1	.333	0	4	4	1	0.5
1932 StL-N	18	15	.545	46	33	16	4	2	286	280	14	102	191	12.2	3.30	119	.260	.327	25	.258	5	18	20	-1	2.5
1933 StL-N	20	18	.526	**48**	34	**26**	3	4	293	279	11	64	**199**	10.7	3.04	114	.250	.293	19	.181	1	10	14	-5	1.4
1934 *StL-N★	**30**	7	**.811**	50	33	24	**7**	7	311^2	288	14	75	**195**	10.7	2.66	159	.241	.289	29	.246	4	49	54	-2	6.4
1935 StL-N★	28	12	.700	50	36	**29**	3	5	**325^1**	324	16	77	**190**	11.2	3.04	135	.256	.300	30	.234	4	35	38	-5	4.3
1936 StL-N★	24	13	.649	**51**	34	**28**	2	**11**	**315**	310	21	53	**195**	10.5	3.17	124	.253	.285	27	.223	1	30	27	-4	2.8
1937 StL-N★	13	10	.565	27	25	17	4	1	197^1	200	9	33	120	10.7	2.69	148	.259	.291	15	.227	2	27	28	-3	3.0
1938 *Chi-N	7	1	.875	13	10	3	1	0	74^2	63	2	8	22	8.7	1.81	212	.226	.250	5	.192	-0	16	17	-1	1.6
1939 Chi-N	6	4	.600	19	13	7	2	0	96^1	98	4	17	27	10.8	3.36	117	.261	.294	5	.147	-1	6	6	-1	0.4
1940 Chi-N	3	3	.500	10	9	3	0	0	54	68	4	20	18	14.7	5.17	73	.306	.364	4	.222	0	-8	-9	1	-0.7
1941 Chi-N	0	0	—	1	1	0	0	0	1	3	0	1	0	27.0	18.00	19	.429	.429		—	0	-2	-2	0	0.0
1947 StL-A	0	0	—	1	1	0	0	0	4	3	0	1	0	9.0	0.00	—	.231	.286	1	1.000	0	2	2	0	0.0
Total 12	150	83	.644	317	230	154	26	30	1967^1	1919	95	453	1163	11.0	3.02	130	.253	.298	161	.225	15	187	201	-20	22.2

● PAUL DEAN
Dean, Paul Dee "Daffy" b: 8/14/13, Lucas, Ark. d: 3/17/81, Springdale, Ark. BR/TR, 6', 175 lbs. Deb: 4/18/34 F

YEAR TM/L	W	L	PCT	G	GS	CG	SH	SV	IP	H	HR	BB	SO	RAT	ERA	ERA+	OAV	OOB	BH	AVG	PB	PR	/A	PD	TPI
1934 *StL-N	19	11	.633	39	26	16	6	2	233^1	225	19	52	150	10.9	3.43	123	.248	.292	20	.241	1	16	21	-6	1.9
1935 StL-N	19	12	.613	46	33	19	2	5	269^2	261	16	55	143	10.8	3.37	122	.249	.292	12	.133	-5	19	22	-6	1.2
1936 StL-N	5	5	.500	17	14	5	0	1	92	113	3	20	28	13.1	4.60	86	.300	.337	2	.059	-4	-6	-7	-3	-1.3
1937 StL-N	0	0	—	1	1	0	0	0	0	2	0	2	0	—	∞	—	1.000	1.000	0	—		-3	-3	-0	-0.3
1938 StL-N	3	1	.750	5	4	2	1	0	31	37	3	5	14	12.2	2.61	151	.298	.326	2	.182	-0	4	5	-1	0.5
1939 StL-N	0	1	.000	16	2	0	0	0	43	54	4	10	16	13.6	6.07	68	.310	.351	1	.111	-1	-10	-9	-0	-0.3
1940 NY-N	4	4	.500	27	7	2	0	0	99^1	102	8	29	32	12.0	3.90	100	.281	.330	3	.115	-2	-1	-0	-3	-0.2
1941 NY-N	0	0	—	5	0	0	0	0	5^2	8	0	3	4	17.5	3.18	116	.320	.393	0	—	0	0	-0	-0	0.0
1943 StL-A	0	0	—	3	1	0	0	0	13^1	16	0	3	1	13.5	3.38	99	.296	.345	0	.000	-0	-0	-0	-0	-0.1
Total 9	50	34	.595	159	87	44	8	8	787^1	825	53	179	387	11.7	3.75	109	.266	.309	40	.156	-10	20	28	-18	1.3

YEAR	TM/L	W	L	PCT	G	GS	CG	SH	SV	IP	H	HR	BB	SO	RAT	ERA	ERA+	OAV	OOB	BH	AVG	PB	PR	/A	PD	TPI

● WAYLAND DEAN
Dean, Wayland Ogden b: 6/20/02, Richwood, W.Va. d: 4/10/30, Huntington, W.Va. BB/TR, 6'1", 178 lbs. Deb: 4/17/24

YEAR	TM/L	W	L	PCT	G	GS	CG	SH	SV	IP	H	HR	BB	SO	RAT	ERA	ERA+	OAV	OOB	BH	AVG	PB	PR	/A	PD	TPI
1924	*NY-N	6	12	.333	26	20	6	0	0	125²	139	9	45	39	13.5	5.01	73	.280	.346	8	.200	1	-16	-19	3	-2.0
1925	NY-N	10	7	.588	33	14	6	1	1	151¹	169	13	50	53	13.3	4.64	87	.282	.342	12	.235	3	-6	-10	0	-0.7
1926	Phi-N	8	16	.333	33	26	15	1	0	203²	245	9	89	52	14.9	4.91	84	.307	.379	27	.265	5	-24	-17	-1	-1.4
1927	Phi-N	0	1	.000	2	0	0	0	0	3	6	0	2	1	24.0	12.00	34	.500	.571	2	.667	1	-3	-3	0	-0.5
	Chi-N	0	0	—	2	0	0	0	0	2	0	0	2	2	13.5	0.00	—	.000	.429	0	—	0	1	1	0	0.0
	Yr	0	1	.000	4	0	0	0	0	5	6	0	4	3	19.8	7.20	56	.375	.524	2	.667	1	-2	-2	0	-0.5
Total	4	24	36	.400	96	60	27	2	1	485²	559	31	188	147	14.1	4.87	82	.293	.360	49	.250	10	-48	-47	2	-4.6

● DENNIS DeBARR
DeBarr, Dennis Lee b: 1/16/53, Cheyenne, Wyo. BL/TL, 6'2", 190 lbs. Deb: 5/14/77

YEAR	TM/L	W	L	PCT	G	GS	CG	SH	SV	IP	H	HR	BB	SO	RAT	ERA	ERA+	OAV	OOB	BH	AVG	PB	PR	/A	PD	TPI
1977	Tor-A	0	1	.000	14	0	0	0	0	21¹	29	1	8	10	15.6	5.91	71	.337	.394	0	—	0	-4	-4	-0	-0.2

● JOE DeBERRY
DeBerry, Joseph Gaddy b: 11/29/1896, Mt.Gilead, N.C. d: 10/9/44, Southern Pines, N.C BR/TR, 6'1", 175 lbs. Deb: 8/24/20

YEAR	TM/L	W	L	PCT	G	GS	CG	SH	SV	IP	H	HR	BB	SO	RAT	ERA	ERA+	OAV	OOB	BH	AVG	PB	PR	/A	PD	TPI
1920	StL-A	2	4	.333	10	7	3	1	0	54²	65	2	20	12	14.3	4.94	79	.307	.372	3	.167	-1	-7	-6	0	-0.6
1921	StL-A	0	1	.000	10	1	0	0	0	12¹	15	0	10	1	18.2	6.57	68	.300	.417	0	—	-0	-3	-3	0	-0.2
Total	2	2	5	.286	20	8	3	1	0	67	80	2	30	13	15.0	5.24	77	.305	.381	3	.150	-1	-10	-9	0	-0.8

● DAVE DeBUSSCHERE
DeBusschere, David Albert b: 10/16/40, Detroit, Mich. BR/TR, 6'6", 225 lbs. Deb: 4/22/62

YEAR	TM/L	W	L	PCT	G	GS	CG	SH	SV	IP	H	HR	BB	SO	RAT	ERA	ERA+	OAV	OOB	BH	AVG	PB	PR	/A	PD	TPI
1962	Chi-A	0	0	—	12	0	0	0	0	18	5	1	23	8	14.5	2.00	195	.089	.363	0	—	0	4	4	0	0.0
1963	Chi-A	3	4	.429	24	10	1	1	0	84¹	80	9	34	53	12.6	3.09	113	.249	.329	1	.045	-2	5	4	0	0.2
Total	2	3	4	.429	36	10	1	1	0	102¹	85	10	57	61	12.9	2.90	123	.225	.335	1	.045	-2	9	8	0	0.2

● ART DECATUR
Decatur, Arthur Rue b: 1/14/1894, Cleveland, Ohio d: 4/25/66, Talladega, Ala. BR/TR, 6'1", 190 lbs. Deb: 4/15/22

YEAR	TM/L	W	L	PCT	G	GS	CG	SH	SV	IP	H	HR	BB	SO	RAT	ERA	ERA+	OAV	OOB	BH	AVG	PB	PR	/A	PD	TPI
1922	Bro-N	3	4	.429	29	2	1	0	1	87²	87	3	29	31	12.0	2.77	147	.265	.327	2	.080	-2	13	13	-2	0.6
1923	Bro-N	3	3	.500	36	5	2	0	3	97²	101	3	32	25	12.4	2.58	150	.264	.325	0	.000	-3	**15**	14	-2	0.4
1924	Bro-N	10	9	.526	31	10	3	0	1	126¹	156	12	27	38	13.3	4.13	91	.308	.348	5	.114	-4	-4	-5	-2	-1.3
1925	Bro-N	0	0	—	1	0	0	0	0	1	3	0	0	0	27.0	18.00	23	.600	.600	—	0	-2	-2	-0	0.0
	Phi-N	4	13	.235	25	15	4	0	2	128	170	13	35	31	14.6	5.27	91	.316	.360	2	.049	-5	-14	-7	-2	-1.4
	Yr	4	13	.235	26	15	4	0	2	129	173	13	35	31	14.7	5.37	89	.319	.362	2	.049	-5	-16	-9	-2	-1.4
1926	Phi-N	0	0	—	2	1	0	0	0	3	6	0	2	0	24.0	6.00	69	.375	.444	0	.000	-0	-1	-1	-0	0.0
1927	Phi-N	3	5	.375	29	3	0	0	0	94²	130	11	20	27	14.6	7.42	56	.334	.373	6	.222	-8	-37	-35	-2	-2.7
Total	6	23	34	.404	153	36	10	0	7	538¹	653	42	145	152	13.6	4.51	92	.302	.349	15	.094	-14	-29	-23	-10	-4.4

● MARTY DECKER
Decker, Dee Martin b: 6/7/57, Upland, Cal. BR/TR, 5'10", 168 lbs. Deb: 9/20/83

YEAR	TM/L	W	L	PCT	G	GS	CG	SH	SV	IP	H	HR	BB	SO	RAT	ERA	ERA+	OAV	OOB	BH	AVG	PB	PR	/A	PD	TPI
1983	SD-N	0	0	—	4	0	0	0	0	8²	5	1	3	9	9.3	2.08	168	.167	.265	0	—	0	1	1	0	0.0

● JOE DECKER
Decker, George Henry b: 6/16/47, Storm Lake, Ia. BR/TR, 6', 180 lbs. Deb: 9/18/69

YEAR	TM/L	W	L	PCT	G	GS	CG	SH	SV	IP	H	HR	BB	SO	RAT	ERA	ERA+	OAV	OOB	BH	AVG	PB	PR	/A	PD	TPI
1969	Chi-N	1	0	1.000	4	1	0	0	0	12¹	10	0	6	13	11.7	2.92	138	.222	.314	0	.000	-0	1	2	-0	0.1
1970	Chi-N	2	7	.222	24	17	1	0	0	108²	108	12	56	79	13.9	4.64	97	.263	.357	6	.176	1	-7	-2	-1	-0.1
1971	Chi-N	3	2	.600	21	4	0	0	0	45²	62	2	25	37	17.1	4.73	83	.343	.422	2	.250	1	-6	-4	1	-0.3
1972	Chi-N	1	0	1.000	5	1	0	0	0	12²	9	1	4	7	9.2	2.13	179	.188	.250	0	.000	-0	2	2	-0	0.2
1973	Min-A	10	10	.500	29	24	6	3	0	170¹	156	12	88	109	13.7	4.17	95	.260	.352	0	—	0	-7	-4	0	-0.4
1974	Min-A	16	14	.533	37	37	11	1	0	248²	234	24	97	158	12.1	3.29	114	.252	.324	0	—	0	9	13	-2	1.2
1975	Min-A	1	3	.250	10	7	1	0	0	26¹	25	2	36	8	20.8	8.54	45	.260	.462	0	—	0	-14	-14	-0	-1.8
1976	Min-A	2	7	.222	13	12	0	0	0	58	60	3	51	35	17.4	5.28	68	.273	.412	0	—	0	-11	-11	1	-1.5
1979	Sea-A	0	1	.000	9	2	0	0	0	27¹	27	2	14	12	13.5	4.28	102	.255	.342	0	—	0	-0	0	1	0.0
Total	9	36	44	.450	152	105	19	4	0	710	702	58	377	458	13.8	4.17	95	.262	.355	8	.174	-1	-34	-18	-1	-2.7

● JEFF DEDMON
Dedmon, Jeffrey Linden b: 3/4/60, Torrance, Cal. BL/TR, 6'2", 200 lbs. Deb: 9/2/83

YEAR	TM/L	W	L	PCT	G	GS	CG	SH	SV	IP	H	HR	BB	SO	RAT	ERA	ERA+	OAV	OOB	BH	AVG	PB	PR	/A	PD	TPI
1983	Atl-N	0	0	—	5	0	0	0	0	4	10	1	0	3	22.5	13.50	29	.455	.455	0	—	0	-4	-4	0	-0.4
1984	Atl-N	4	3	.571	54	0	0	0	4	81	86	5	35	51	13.7	3.78	102	.277	.354	0	.000	-1	-2	1	2	0.2
1985	Atl-N	6	3	.667	60	0	0	0	0	86	84	5	49	41	14.0	4.08	94	.264	.364	1	.111	-0	-5	-2	3	0.1
1986	Atl-N	6	6	.500	57	0	0	0	3	99²	90	8	39	58	12.0	2.98	133	.242	.320	2	.125	-1	8	11	2	1.4
1987	Atl-N	3	4	.429	53	3	0	0	4	89²	82	8	42	40	12.5	3.91	111	.246	.332	4	.250	1	2	4	1	0.6
1988	Cle-A	1	0	1.000	21	0	0	0	1	33²	35	3	21	17	15.8	4.54	90	.276	.391	0	—	0	-2	-2	1	0.1
Total	6	20	16	.556	250	3	0	0	12	394	387	30	186	210	13.3	3.84	105	.261	.348	7	.149	-0	-3	8	9	2.4

● DUMMY DEEGAN
Deegan, William John b: 11/16/1874, Bronx, N.Y. d: 5/17/57, Bronx, N.Y. Deb: 8/3/01

YEAR	TM/L	W	L	PCT	G	GS	CG	SH	SV	IP	H	HR	BB	SO	RAT	ERA	ERA+	OAV	OOB	BH	AVG	PB	PR	/A	PD	TPI
1901	NY-N	0	1	.000	2	1	1	0	0	17	27	0	6	8	17.5	6.35	52	.357	.404	0	.000	-1	-6	-6	0	-0.3

● JOHN DEERING
Deering, John Thomas b: 6/25/1879, Lynn, Mass. d: 2/15/43, Beverly, Mass. BR/TR, 6', 180 lbs. Deb: 5/12/03

YEAR	TM/L	W	L	PCT	G	GS	CG	SH	SV	IP	H	HR	BB	SO	RAT	ERA	ERA+	OAV	OOB	BH	AVG	PB	PR	/A	PD	TPI
1903	Det-A	3	4	.429	10	8	5	0	0	60²	77	3	24	14	15.1	3.86	75	.308	.371	8	.333	2	-6	-7	-1	-0.5
	NY-A	4	3	.571	9	7	6	1	0	60	59	0	18	14	11.7	3.75	83	.256	.313	1	.043	-3	-5	-4	-1	-0.8
	Yr	7	7	.500	19	15	11	1	0	120²	136	3	42	28	13.4	3.80	79	.283	.342	9	.191	-0	-11	-11	-2	-1.3

● MIKE DEGERICK
Degerick, Michael Arthur b: 4/1/43, New York, N.Y. BR/TR, 6'2", 178 lbs. Deb: 9/4/61

YEAR	TM/L	W	L	PCT	G	GS	CG	SH	SV	IP	H	HR	BB	SO	RAT	ERA	ERA+	OAV	OOB	BH	AVG	PB	PR	/A	PD	TPI
1961	Chi-A	0	0	—	1	0	0	0	0	1²	2	0	1	0	16.2	5.40	72	.400	.500	0	—	0	-0	-0	-0	0.0
1962	Chi-A	0	0	—	1	0	0	0	0	1	1	0	1	0	18.0	0.00	—	.250	.400	0	—	0	0	0	0	0.0
Total	2	0	0	—	2	0	0	0	0	2²	3	0	2	0	16.9	3.38	116	.333	.455	0	—	0	0	0	0	0.0

● PEP DEININGER
Deininger, Otto Charles b: 10/10/1877, Wasseralfingen, Germany d: 9/25/50, Boston, Mass. BL/TL, 5'8.5", 180 lbs. Deb: 4/26/02 ◆

YEAR	TM/L	W	L	PCT	G	GS	CG	SH	SV	IP	H	HR	BB	SO	RAT	ERA	ERA+	OAV	OOB	BH	AVG	PB	PR	/A	PD	TPI
1902	Bos-A	0	0	—	2	1	0	0	0	12	19	3	2	3	22.5	9.75	37	.358	.469	2	.333	1	-8	-8	-1	0.1

● JOSE DeJESUS
DeJesus, Jose Luis b: 1/6/65, Brooklyn, N.Y. BR/TR, 6'5", 175 lbs. Deb: 9/9/88

YEAR	TM/L	W	L	PCT	G	GS	CG	SH	SV	IP	H	HR	BB	SO	RAT	ERA	ERA+	OAV	OOB	BH	AVG	PB	PR	/A	PD	TPI
1988	KC-A	0	1	.000	2	1	0	0	0	2²	6	0	5	2	37.1	27.00	15	.429	.579	0	—	0	-7	-7	-0	-1.5
1989	KC-A	0	0	—	3	1	0	0	0	8	7	1	8	2	16.9	4.50	85	.241	.405	0	—	0	-1	-1	-0	0.0
1990	Phi-N	7	8	.467	22	22	3	1	0	130	97	10	73	87	11.9	3.74	102	.210	.321	3	.079	-1	1	1	-1	0.0
1991	Phi-N	10	9	.526	31	29	3	0	1	181²	147	7	128	118	13.8	3.42	107	.224	.355	8	.129	-1	5	5	-3	0.1
1994	KC-A	3	1	.750	5	4	0	0	0	26²	27	2	13	12	13.5	4.73	110	.276	.360	0	—	0	1	0	0	-0.1
Total	5	20	19	.513	63	57	6	1	1	349	284	20	227	221	13.3	3.84	100	.226	.347	11	.110	-2	-1	-0	-3	-1.5

● TOMMY de la CRUZ
de la Cruz, Tomas (Rivero) b: 9/18/11, Marianao, Cuba d: 9/6/58, Havana, Cuba BR/TR, 6'2", 168 lbs. Deb: 4/20/44

YEAR	TM/L	W	L	PCT	G	GS	CG	SH	SV	IP	H	HR	BB	SO	RAT	ERA	ERA+	OAV	OOB	BH	AVG	PB	PR	/A	PD	TPI
1944	Cin-N	9	9	.500	34	20	9	0	1	191¹	170	9	45	65	10.2	3.25	108	.238	.284	9	.155	-0	8	5	-0	0.4

● JIM DELAHANTY
Delahanty, James Christopher b: 6/20/1879, Cleveland, Ohio d: 10/17/53, Cleveland, Ohio BR/TR, 5'10.5", 170 lbs. Deb: 4/19/01 F◆

YEAR	TM/L	W	L	PCT	G	GS	CG	SH	SV	IP	H	HR	BB	SO	RAT	ERA	ERA+	OAV	OOB	BH	AVG	PB	PR	/A	PD	TPI
1904	Bos-N	0	0	—	1	0	0	0	0	3¹	5	0	1	0	16.2	0.00	—	.357	.400	142	.285	—	1	1	0	0.0
1905	Bos-N	0	0	—	1	1	0	0	0	2	5	1	0	0	22.5	4.50	69	.500	.500	119	.258	—	0	0	0	0.0
Total	2	0	0	—	2	1	0	0	0	5¹	10	1	1	0	18.6	1.69	171	.417	.440	1159	.283	1	1	1	0	0.0

● ART DELANEY
Delaney, Arthur Dewey "Swede" (b: Arthur Dewey Helenius)
b: 1/5/1895, Chicago, Ill. d: 5/2/70, Hayward, Cal. BR/TR, 5'10.5", 178 lbs. Deb: 4/16/24

YEAR	TM/L	W	L	PCT	G	GS	CG	SH	SV	IP	H	HR	BB	SO	RAT	ERA	ERA+	OAV	OOB	BH	AVG	PB	PR	/A	PD	TPI
1924	StL-N	1	0	1.000	8	1	1	0	0	20	19	0	6	2	11.2	1.80	210	.250	.305	2	.286	0	5	4	0	0.3
1928	Bos-N	9	17	.346	39	22	8	0	2	192¹	197	11	56	45	11.9	3.79	103	.267	.319	9	.143	-3	4	3	1	0.3
1929	Bos-N	3	5	.375	20	8	3	1	0	75	103	6	35	17	16.7	6.12	76	.336	.405	3	.143	-1	-12	-12	-1	-1.0
Total	3	13	22	.371	67	31	12	1	2	287¹	319	17	97	64	13.1	4.26	96	.285	.343	14	.154	-2	-3	-5	0	-0.6

YEAR TM/L	W	L	PCT	G	GS	CG	SH	SV	IP	H	HR	BB	SO	RAT	ERA	ERA+	OAV	OOB	BH	AVG	PB	PR	/A	PD	TPI
● **FRANCISCO de la ROSA** de la Rosa, Francisco (Jimenez) b: 3/3/66, LaRomana, D.R. BB/TR, 5'11", 185 lbs. Deb: 9/7/91																								
1991 Bal-A	0	0	—	2	0	0	0	0	4	6	0	2	1	18.0	4.50	88	.353	.421	0	—	-0	-0	-0	-0	0.3
● **JOSE DeLEON** DeLeon, Jose (Chestaro) b: 12/20/60, LaVega, D.R. BR/TR, 6'3", 215 lbs. Deb: 7/23/83																								
1983 Pit-N	7	3	.700	15	15	3	2	0	108	75	5	47	118	10.3	2.83	131	.196	.285	2	.059	-1	10	10	-1	0.8
1984 Pit-N	7	13	.350	30	28	5	1	0	192¹	147	10	92	153	11.3	3.74	96	.214	.310	5	.085	-4	-3	-3	-3	-0.9
1985 Pit-N	2	19	.095	31	25	1	0	3	162²	138	15	89	149	12.7	4.70	76	.231	.334	2	.056	-2	-20	-20	-1	-2.7
1986 Pit-N	1	3	.250	9	1	0	0	1	16¹	17	2	17	11	19.3	8.27	46	.266	.427	0	.000	0	-8	-8	0	-1.7
Chi-A	4	5	.444	13	13	1	0	0	79	49	7	42	68	10.8	2.96	145	.179	.297	0	—	0	11	12	0	1.3
1987 Chi-A	11	12	.478	33	31	2	0	0	206	177	24	97	153	12.4	4.02	114	.230	.324	0	—	0	10	13	-3	0.8
1988 StL-N	13	10	.565	34	34	3	1	0	225¹	198	13	86	208	11.4	3.67	95	.237	.310	10	.139	-0	-6	-5	-2	-0.8
1989 StL-N	16	12	.571	36	36	5	3	0	244²	173	16	80	**201**	9.5	3.05	119	**.197**	.269	8	.096	-4	12	16	-4	0.9
1990 StL-N	7	19	.269	32	32	0	0	0	182²	168	15	86	164	12.8	4.43	86	.246	.335	6	.107	-1	-13	-13	-2	-1.9
1991 StL-N	5	9	.357	28	28	1	0	0	162²	144	15	61	118	11.7	2.71	137	.239	.315	2	.043	-4	18	18	-2	0.9
1992 StL-N	2	7	.222	29	15	0	0	0	102¹	95	7	43	72	12.3	4.57	74	.245	.324	1	.048	-1	-12	-13	-1	-1.3
Phi-N	0	1	.000	3	3	0	0	0	15	16	0	5	7	12.6	3.00	116	.281	.339	2	.400	1	1	1	-0	0.1
Yr	2	8	.200	32	18	0	0	0	117¹	111	7	48	79	12.2	4.37	78	.246	.318	3	.115	-0	-11	-13	-2	-1.2
1993 Phi-N	3	0	1.000	24	0	0	0	0	47	39	5	27	34	13.6	3.26	122	.229	.351	0	.000	-1	4	4	-1	0.1
*Chi-A	0	0	—	11	0	0	0	0	10¹	5	2	3	6	7.8	1.74	240	.152	.243	0	—	0	3	3	-0	0.0
1994 Chi-A	3	2	.600	42	0	0	0	2	67	48	5	31	67	11.4	3.36	140	.200	.307	0	—	0	11	10	-0	0.7
Total 12	81	115	.413	370	264	21	7	6	1821¹	1489	141	806	1529	11.6	3.69	103	.224	.312	38	.091	-16	16	24	-20	-3.7
● **LUIS DeLEON** DeLeon, Luis Antonio (Tricoche) b: 8/19/58, Ponce, P.R. BR/TR, 6'1", 153 lbs. Deb: 9/6/81																								
1981 StL-N	0	1	.000	10	0	0	0	0	15¹	11	1	3	8	8.2	2.35	151	.200	.241	0	.000	-0	2	2	-0	0.1
1982 SD-N	9	5	.643	61	0	0	0	15	102	77	10	16	60	8.3	2.03	169	.212	.247	1	.091	-0	18	16	1	2.8
1983 SD-N	6	6	.500	63	0	0	0	13	111	89	8	27	90	9.5	2.68	130	.224	.275	2	.143	-0	12	10	-2	1.1
1984 SD-N	2	2	.500	32	0	0	0	0	42²	44	12	12	44	12.7	5.48	65	.256	.319	0	.000	-0	-9	-9	-0	-0.8
1985 SD-N	0	3	.000	29	0	0	0	3	38²	39	6	10	31	12.1	4.19	84	.267	.327	1	.200	-0	-3	-3	-0	-0.3
1987 Bal-A	0	2	.000	11	0	0	0	1	20²	19	1	8	13	12.6	4.79	92	.253	.341	0	—	0	-1	-1	-1	0.1
1989 Sea-A	0	0	—	1	1	0	0	0	4	5	1	1	2	15.8	2.25	179	.313	.389	0	—	0	1	1	-0	-0.2
Total 7	17	19	.472	207	1	0	0	32	334¹	284	39	77	248	10.0	3.12	114	.232	.284	4	.114	-0	20	16	-2	2.8
● **FLAME DELHI** Delhi, Lee William b: 11/5/1892, Harqua Hala, Ariz. d: 5/9/66, San Rafael, Cal. BR/TR, 6'2.5", 198 lbs. Deb: 4/16/12																								
1912 Chi-A	0	0	—	1	0	0	0	0	3	7	0	3	2	30.0	9.00	36	.412	.500	0	—	0	-2	-2	0	0.0
● **WHEEZER DELL** Dell, William George b: 6/11/1887, Tuscarora, Nev. d: 8/24/66, Independence, Cal. BR/TR, 6'4", 210 lbs. Deb: 4/22/12																								
1912 StL-N	0	0	—	3	0	0	0	0	2¹	3	0	3	0	23.1	11.57	30	.188	.316	0	—	0	-2	-2	-0	0.0
1915 Bro-N	11	10	.524	40	24	12	4	1	215	166	5	100	94	11.5	2.34	119	.218	.315	10	.152	-1	10	10	0	1.0
1916 *Bro-N	8	9	.471	32	16	9	2	1	155	143	2	43	76	11.0	2.26	118	.256	.314	4	.091	-2	6	7	-1	0.4
1917 Bro-N	0	4	.000	17	4	0	0	1	58	55	3	25	28	12.7	3.72	75	.263	.347	1	.063	-2	-7	-6	-1	-0.7
Total 4	19	23	.452	92	44	21	6	3	430¹	367	10	171	198	11.5	2.55	108	.237	.319	15	.119	-5	7	9	-2	0.7
● **IKE DELOCK** Delock, Ivan Martin b: 11/11/29, Highland Park, Mich BR/TR, 5'11", 175 lbs. Deb: 4/17/52																								
1952 Bos-A	4	9	.308	39	7	1	1	5	95	88	9	50	46	13.3	4.26	92	.245	.341	1	.045	-1	-6	-3	-1	-0.6
1953 Bos-A	3	1	.750	23	1	0	0	1	48²	60	2	20	22	15.2	4.44	95	.308	.378	1	.100	-1	-2	-1	-1	-0.2
1955 Bos-A	9	7	.563	29	18	6	0	3	143²	136	16	61	88	12.6	3.76	114	.247	.326	7	.143	-1	3	8	-1	0.7
1956 Bos-A	13	7	.650	48	8	1	0	9	128¹	122	12	80	105	14.5	4.21	110	.252	.363	3	.103	-2	-1	6	0	0.7
1957 Bos-A	9	8	.529	49	2	0	0	11	94	80	11	45	62	12.3	3.83	104	.232	.323	1	.048	-1	-0	2	-1	0.1
1958 Bos-A	14	8	.636	31	19	9	1	2	160	155	13	56	82	11.9	3.37	119	.252	.315	2	.063	-4	7	11	-1	1.0
1959 Bos-A	11	6	.647	28	17	4	0	0	134¹	120	12	62	55	12.3	2.95	138	.236	.322	3	.064	-3	14	17	-2	1.5
1960 Bos-A	9	10	.474	24	23	3	1	0	129¹	145	21	52	49	14.0	4.73	85	.283	.354	5	.116	-3	-12	-10	-1	-1.6
1961 Bos-A	6	9	.400	28	28	3	1	0	156	185	24	52	80	13.8	4.90	85	.293	.349	5	.104	-2	-15	-13	-2	-1.4
1962 Bos-A	4	5	.444	17	13	4	2	0	86¹	89	10	24	49	11.8	3.75	110	.268	.317	2	.087	-1	2	4	-1	0.1
1963 Bos-A	1	2	.333	6	6	1	0	0	32	31	4	12	23	12.1	4.50	84	.246	.312	0	.000	-1	-3	-3	-0	-0.4
Bal-A	1	3	.250	7	5	0	0	0	30¹	25	7	16	11	12.2	5.04	69	.236	.336	0	—	-0	-5	-5	-0	-0.7
Yr	2	5	.286	13	11	1	0	0	62¹	56	11	28	34	12.1	4.76	76	.240	.322	0	.000	-0	-8	-8	-0	-1.1
Total 11	84	75	.528	329	147	32	6	31	1238	1236	141	530	672	13.0	4.03	102	.259	.336	31	.086	-20	-19	12	-9	-0.8
● **RAMON de los SANTOS** de los Santos, Ramon (Genero) b: 1/19/49, Santo Domingo, D.R. BL/TL, 6'1", 175 lbs. Deb: 8/21/74																								
1974 Hou-N	1	1	.500	12	0	0	0	0	12¹	11	0	9	7	14.6	2.19	158	.234	.357	0	—	0	2	2	0	0.3
● **RICH DeLUCIA** DeLucia, Richard Anthony b: 10/7/64, Reading, Pa. BR/TR, 6', 180 lbs. Deb: 9/8/90																								
1990 Sea-A	1	2	.333	5	5	1	0	0	36	30	2	9	20	9.8	2.00	198	.226	.275	0	—	0	8	8	-1	0.5
1991 Sea-A	12	13	.480	32	31	0	0	0	182	176	31	78	98	12.8	5.09	81	.260	.339	0	—	0	-20	-20	-2	-2.5
1992 Sea-A	3	6	.333	30	11	0	0	1	83²	100	13	35	66	14.7	5.49	72	.293	.362	0	—	0	-14	-14	-1	-1.5
1993 Sea-A	3	6	.333	30	1	0	0	0	42²	46	5	23	48	14.8	4.64	95	.272	.363	0	—	0	-2	-1	1	-0.2
1994 Cin-N	0	0	—	8	0	0	0	0	10²	9	4	5	15	11.8	4.22	99	.214	.298	0	—	0	-0	-0	-0	0.0
Total 5	19	27	.413	105	48	1	0	1	355	361	55	150	247	13.1	4.79	86	.265	.341	0	—	0	-28	-27	-3	-3.7
● **FRED DEMARAIS** Demarais, Frederick b: 11/1/1866, Canada d: 3/6/19, Stamford, Conn. TR, 5'9", 168 lbs. Deb: 7/26/1890																								
1890 Chi-N	0	0	—	1	0	0	0	0	2	1	0	1	1	9.0	0.00	—	.144	.252	0	.000	-0	1	1	0	0.1
● **AL DEMAREE** Demaree, Albert Wentworth b: 9/8/1884, Quincy, Ill. d: 4/30/62, Los Angeles, Cal. BL/TR, 6', 170 lbs. Deb: 9/26/12																								
1912 NY-N	1	0	1.000	2	2	1	1	2	16	17	0	2	11	10.7	1.69	200	.288	.311	0	.000	-1	3	3	0	0.1
1913 *NY-N	13	4	.765	31	24	11	2	2	199²	176	4	38	76	9.9	2.21	141	.243	.286	7	.106	-3	22	20	-3	0.9
1914 NY-N	10	17	.370	38	30	13	2	0	224	219	3	77	89	12.2	3.09	86	.263	.331	9	.132	-2	-8	-11	-1	-1.6
1915 Phi-N	14	11	.560	42	32	26	13	3	209²	201	4	58	92	11.2	3.05	90	.263	.314	12	.176	-0	-7	-5	-3	-1.3
1916 Phi-N	19	14	.576	39	35	25	4	1	285	252	6	48	130	9.7	2.62	101	.242	.281	11	.109	-4	-0	-1	-6	-1.1
1917 Chi-N	5	9	.357	24	18	6	1	1	141¹	125	5	37	43	10.4	2.55	114	.244	.297	5	.122	-1	3	5	1	0.4
NY-N	4	5	.444	15	11	1	0	0	78¹	70	1	17	23	10.1	2.64	97	.239	.283	2	.111	-1	1	-1	0	-0.2
Yr	9	14	.391	39	29	7	1	1	219²	195	6	54	66	10.2	2.58	107	.241	.290	7	.119	-2	3	5	1	0.2
1918 NY-N	8	6	.571	26	14	8	2	1	142	143	5	25	39	10.8	2.47	106	.262	.297	6	.128	-3	5	4	-0	-0.1
1919 Bos-N	6	6	.500	25	13	4	0	3	128	147	3	35	34	12.9	3.80	75	.300	.348	2	.048	-5	-13	-13	-2	-2.0
Total 8	80	72	.526	232	173	84	15	9	1424	1350	34	337	514	10.9	2.77	100	.256	.304	54	.118	-20	6	0	-16	-4.9
● **LARRY DEMERY** Demery, Lawrence Calvin b: 6/4/53, Bakersfield, Cal. BR/TR, 6', 170 lbs. Deb: 6/2/74																								
1974 *Pit-N	6	6	.500	19	15	2	0	0	95¹	95	12	51	51	13.8	4.25	81	.262	.354	5	.152	1	-7	-9	-1	-1.0
1975 *Pit-N	7	5	.583	45	8	1	0	4	114²	95	7	43	59	11.1	2.90	122	.230	.307	3	.125	1	9	8	-1	0.9
1976 Pit-N	10	7	.588	36	15	4	1	0	145	123	8	58	72	11.4	3.17	110	.234	.313	5	.125	-1	5	5	0	0.5
1977 Pit-N	6	5	.545	39	8	0	0	3	90¹	100	13	47	35	14.6	5.08	78	.279	.363	3	.150	0	-12	-11	-0	-1.3
Total 4	29	23	.558	139	46	7	1	7	445¹	413	40	199	217	12.5	3.72	97	.249	.331	16	.137	0	-6	-6	-2	-0.9
● **HARRY DeMILLER** DeMiller, Harry b: 11/12/1867, Wooster, Ohio d: 10/19/28, Santa Ana, Cal. BR/TL, Deb: 8/20/1892																								
1892 Chi-N	1	1	.500	4	2	2	0	0	24	29	1	16	15	17.3	6.38	52	.287	.390	3	.300	1	-8	-8	0	-0.4

YEAR TM/L	W	L	PCT	G	GS	CG	SH	SV	IP	H	HR	BB	SO	RAT	ERA	ERA+	OAV	OOB	BH	AVG	PB	PR	/A	PD	TPI
● **DON DeMOLA** DeMola, Donald John b: 7/5/52, Glen Cove, N.Y. BR/TR, 6'2", 185 lbs. Deb: 4/13/74																									
1974 Mon-N	1	0	1.000	25	1	0	0	0	57²	46	7	21	47	10.5	3.12	123	.223	.295	0	.000	-1	3	5	-1	0.0
1975 Mon-N	4	7	.364	60	0	0	0	1	97²	92	8	42	63	12.7	4.15	92	.251	.335	0	.000	-1	-6	-4	-3	-0.8
Total 2	5	7	.417	85	1	0	0	1	155¹	138	15	63	110	11.9	3.77	102	.241	.321	0	.000	-1	-3	1	-3	-0.8
● **BEN DeMOTT** DeMott, Benyew Harrison b: 4/2/1889, Green Village, N.J. d: 7/5/63, Somerville, N.J. BR/TR, 6', 192 lbs. Deb: 8/12/10																									
1910 Cle-A	0	3	.000	6	4	1	0	0	28¹	45	0	8	13	17.2	5.40	48	.388	.432	3	.167	-0	-9	-9	0	-0.9
1911 Cle-A	0	1	.000	1	1	0	0	0	3²	10	0	2	2	29.5	12.27	28	.588	.632	0	.000	-0	-4	-4	0	-0.6
Total 2	0	4	.000	7	5	1	0	0	32	55	0	10	15	18.6	6.19	43	.414	.458	3	.136	-0	-13	-12	1	-1.5
● **CON DEMPSEY** Dempsey, Cornelius Francis b: 9/16/23, San Francisco, Cal. BR/TR, 6'4", 190 lbs. Deb: 4/28/51																									
1951 Pit-N	0	2	.000	3	2	0	0	0	7	11	2	4	3	19.3	9.00	47	.393	.469	0	.000	-0	-4	-4	0	-0.8
● **RICK DEMPSEY** Dempsey, John Rikard b: 9/13/49, Fayetteville, Tenn. BR/TR, 6', 190 lbs. Deb: 9/23/69 ◆																									
1991 Mil-A	0	0	—	2	0	0	0	0	2	3	0	1	0	18.0	4.50	88	.333	.400	34	.231	2	-0	-0	-0	0.0
◉ **MARK DEMPSEY** Dempsey, Mark Steven b: 12/17/57, Dayton, Ohio BR/TR, 6'6", 220 lbs. Deb: 9/4/82																									
1982 SF-N	0	0	—	3	1	0	0	0	5²	11	1	2	4	20.6	7.94	48	.440	.481	0	.000	-0	-3	-3	0	-0.2
● **BILL DENEHY** Denehy, William Francis b: 3/31/46, Middletown, Conn. BB/TR, 6'3", 200 lbs. Deb: 4/16/67																									
1967 NY-N	1	7	.125	15	8	0	0	0	53²	51	8	29	35	13.4	4.70	72	.248	.340	0	.000	-1	-8	-8	-1	-1.2
1968 Was-A	0	0	—	3	0	0	0	0	2	4	0	4	1	36.0	9.00	32	.444	.615	0	—	0	-1	-1	0	-0.1
1971 Det-A	0	3	.000	31	1	0	0	1	49	47	4	28	27	14.5	4.22	85	.250	.359	0	.000	1	-4	-3	-0	-0.2
Total 3	1	10	.091	49	9	0	0	1	104²	102	12	61	63	14.4	4.56	76	.253	.357	0	.000	-1	-13	-13	-1	-1.4
● **BRIAN DENMAN** Denman, Brian John b: 2/12/56, Minneapolis, Minn. BR/TR, 6'4", 205 lbs. Deb: 8/22/82																									
1982 Bos-A	3	4	.429	9	9	2	1	0	49	55	6	9	9	11.8	4.78	90	.282	.314	0	—	0	-4	-3	0	-0.6
● **DON DENNIS** Dennis, Donald Ray b: 3/3/42, Uniontown, Kan. BR/TR, 6'2", 190 lbs. Deb: 6/18/65																									
1965 StL-N	2	3	.400	41	0	0	0	6	55	47	3	16	29	10.5	2.29	168	.236	.296	2	.400	1	8	9	2	1.3
1966 StL-N	4	2	.667	38	1	0	0	2	59²	73	8	17	25	13.7	4.98	72	.302	.350	1	.083	-1	-9	-9	3	-0.7
Total 2	6	5	.545	79	1	0	0	8	114²	120	11	33	54	12.2	3.69	101	.272	.326	3	.176	-0	-1	0	4	0.6
● **JERRY DENNY** Denny, Jeremiah Dennis (b: Jeremiah Dennis Eldridge) b: 3/16/1859, New York, N.Y. d: 8/16/27, Houston, Tex. BR/TR, 5'11.5", 180 lbs. Deb: 5/2/1881 ◆																									
1888 Ind-N	0	0	—	1	0	0	0	0	4	5	1	4	1	20.3	9.00	33	.278	.409	137	.261	0	-3	-3	-0	0.0
● **JOHN DENNY** Denny, John Allen b: 11/8/52, Prescott, Ariz. BR/TR, 6'3", 190 lbs. Deb: 9/12/74																									
1974 StL-N	0	0	—	2	0	0	0	0	2	3	0	0	1	13.5	0.00	—	.273	.273	0	—	0	1	1	-0	0.0
1975 StL-N	10	7	.588	25	24	3	2	0	136	149	5	51	72	13.4	3.97	95	.280	.346	10	.227	1	-5	-3	2	-0.1
1976 StL-N	11	9	.550	30	30	8	3	0	207	189	11	74	74	11.8	**2.52**	140	.246	.318	15	.224	2	23	**23**	1	2.7
1977 StL-N	8	8	.500	26	26	3	1	0	149²	165	9	62	60	14.0	4.51	85	.281	.355	5	.098	-3	-10	-11	3	-1.0
1978 StL-N	14	11	.560	33	33	11	2	0	234	200	13	74	103	10.8	2.96	119	.238	.304	13	.178	2	16	14	8	2.7
1979 StL-N	8	11	.421	31	31	5	2	0	206	206	24	100	99	13.5	4.85	78	.264	.350	9	.129	-1	-26	-25	2	-2.1
1980 Cle-A	8	6	.571	16	16	4	1	0	108²	116	4	47	59	13.9	4.39	93	.284	.365	0	—	0	-4	-4	1	-0.4
1981 Cle-A	10	6	.625	19	19	6	3	0	145²	139	9	66	94	12.9	3.15	115	.254	.338	0	—	0	8	8	5	1.4
1982 Cle-A	6	11	.353	21	21	5	0	0	138¹	126	11	73	94	13.3	5.01	81	.240	.340	0	—	0	-14	-14	1	-1.4
Phi-N	0	2	.000	4	4	0	0	0	22¹	18	1	10	19	11.3	4.03	91	.217	.301	1	.167	0	-1	-1	1	0.1
1983 *Phi-N	19	6	**.760**	36	36	7	1	0	242²	229	9	53	139	10.6	2.37	150	.250	.294	13	.169	0	**34**	32	1	3.5
1984 Phi-N	7	7	.500	22	22	2	0	0	154²	122	11	29	94	9.0	2.45	148	.214	.257	8	.191	0	20	20	4	2.3
1985 Phi-N	11	14	.440	33	33	6	2	0	230²	252	15	83	123	13.2	3.82	96	.282	.345	10	.123	-2	-6	-4	1	-0.4
1986 Cin-N	11	10	.524	27	27	2	1	0	171¹	179	15	56	115	12.6	4.20	92	.272	.333	12	.222	2	-9	-6	3	-0.3
Total 13	123	108	.532	325	322	62	18	0	2148²	2093	137	778	1146	12.3	3.59	104	.258	.327	97	.170	2	25	30	31	7.0
● **EDDIE DENT** Dent, Elliott Estill b: 12/8/1887, Baltimore, Md. d: 11/25/74, Birmingham, Ala. BR/TR, 6'1", 190 lbs. Deb: 8/31/09																									
1909 Bro-N	2	4	.333	6	5	4	0	0	42	47	2	15	17	13.3	4.29	61	.307	.369	1	.067	-1	-8	-8	-1	-1.2
1911 Bro-N	2	1	.667	5	3	1	0	0	31²	30	0	10	3	11.9	3.69	90	.256	.326	1	.100	-0	-1	-1	0	-0.1
1912 Bro-N	0	0	—	1	0	0	0	0	1	4	0	1	1	45.0	36.00	9	.571	.625	0	.000	-0	-4	-4	0	0.0
Total 3	4	5	.444	12	8	5	0	0	74²	81	2	26	21	13.1	4.46	65	.292	.357	2	.077	-2	-13	-13	-0	-1.3
● **ROGER DENZER** Denzer, Roger "Peaceful Valley" b: 10/5/1871, LeSeur, Minn. d: 9/18/49, LeSeur, Minn. BL/TR, 6', 180 lbs. Deb: 4/24/1897																									
1897 Chi-N	2	8	.200	12	10	8	0	0	94²	125	4	34	17	15.3	5.13	87	.315	.372	6	.154	-3	-9	-7	-1	-0.9
1901 NY-N	2	6	.250	11	9	3	1	0	61²	69	2	5	22	11.1	3.36	99	.281	.301	2	.091	-1	-0	-0	-2	-0.3
Total 2	4	14	.222	23	19	11	1	0	156¹	194	6	39	39	13.6	4.43	90	.302	.346	8	.131	-4	-9	-8	-2	-1.2
● **GEORGE DERBY** Derby, George H. "Jonah" b: 7/6/1857, Webster, Mass. d: 7/4/25, Philadelphia, Pa. BL/TR, 6', 175 lbs. Deb: 5/2/1881																									
1881 Det-N	29	26	.527	56	55	55	**9**	0	494²	505	3	86	**212**	10.8	2.20	132	.251	.281	44	.186	-10	**32**	39	2	**3.0**
1882 Det-N	17	20	.459	40	39	38	3	0	362	386	8	81	182	11.6	3.26	90	.256	.294	29	.195	-6	-14	-13	1	-1.5
1883 Buf-N	2	10	.167	14	13	12	0	1	107²	173	3	15	34	15.7	5.85	54	.334	.353	14	.237	-1	-32	-32	1	-2.6
Total 3	48	56	.462	110	107	105	12	1	964¹	1064	14	182	428	11.6	3.01	98	.263	.295	87	.196	-17	-15	-5	4	-1.1
● **PAUL DERRINGER** Derringer, Samuel Paul "Duke" b: 10/17/06, Springfield, Ky. d: 11/17/87, Sarasota, Fla. BR/TR, 6'3.5", 205 lbs. Deb: 4/16/31																									
1931 *StL-N	18	8	**.692**	35	23	15	4	2	211²	225	9	65	134	12.5	3.36	117	.274	.330	7	.097	-6	12	14	-0	0.9
1932 StL-N	11	14	.440	39	30	14	1	0	233¹	296	6	67	78	14.1	4.05	97	.310	.356	13	.178	-0	-4	-3	-2	-0.5
1933 StL-N	0	2	.000	3	2	1	0	0	17	24	0	9	3	18.0	4.24	82	.353	.436	0	.000	-2	-2	-1	-0	-0.2
Cin-N	7	25	.219	33	31	16	2	1	231	240	4	51	86	11.5	3.23	105	.271	.315	14	.184	-1	3	4	1	0.5
Yr	7	27	.206	36	33	17	2	1	248	264	4	60	89	11.9	3.30	103	.277	.323	14	.173	-2	1	3	1	0.3
1934 Cin-N	15	21	.417	47	31	18	1	4	261	297	6	59	122	12.4	3.59	114	.283	.323	18	.196	0	14	14	-2	1.7
1935 Cin-N★	22	13	.629	45	33	20	2	0	276²	295	13	49	120	11.3	3.51	113	.271	.305	13	.140	-5	16	14	3	1.4
1936 Cin-N	19	19	.500	**51**	37	13	2	5	282¹	331	11	42	121	12.0	4.02	95	.289	.316	18	.200	-1	0	-6	0	-0.8
1937 Cin-N	10	14	.417	43	26	12	1	1	222²	240	7	55	94	11.9	4.04	92	.271	.313	16	.200	1	-3	-8	1	-0.6
1938 Cin-N☆	21	14	.600	41	37	**26**	4	3	**307**	315	20	49	132	10.7	2.93	124	.262	.291	21	.176	-0	29	24	-2	2.4
1939 *Cin-N★	25	7	**.781**	38	35	28	5	0	301	321	15	35	128	10.7	2.93	131	.272	.295	23	.209	0	33	30	-3	2.7
1940 *Cin-N★	20	12	.625	37	37	26	3	0	296²	280	17	48	115	**10.0**	3.06	124	.246	**.276**	18	.167	-2	26	24	-4	1.8
1941 Cin-N★	12	14	.462	29	28	17	2	0	228¹	233	16	54	76	11.3	3.31	109	.266	.309	13	.155	-3	8	7	-1	0.4
1942 Cin-N†	10	11	.476	29	27	13	1	0	208²	203	4	49	68	11.0	3.06	107	.250	.296	9	.132	-2	6	5	-4	-0.1
1943 Chi-N	10	14	.417	32	22	10	2	0	174	184	7	39	75	11.5	3.57	93	.224	.303	13	.224	1	-4	-4	-4	-0.9
1944 Chi-N	7	13	.350	42	16	7	0	3	180	205	13	39	69	12.2	4.15	85	.284	.321	9	.158	-2	-11	-12	-1	-1.5
1945 *Chi-N	16	11	.593	35	30	15	1	0	213²	223	8	51	86	11.6	3.45	106	.265	.308	15	.197	-1	-3	-4	-0	-0.6
Total 15	223	212	.513	579	445	251	32	29	3645	3912	158	761	1507	11.6	3.46	108	.272	.310	220	.175	-20	131	108	-17	7.6
● **JIM DERRINGTON** Derrington, Charles James "Blackie" b: 11/29/39, Compton, Cal. BL/TL, 6'3", 190 lbs. Deb: 9/30/56																									
1956 Chi-A	0	1	.000	1	1	0	0	0	6	9	2	6	3	22.5	7.50	55	.375	.500	1	.500	0	-2	-2	-0	-0.3
1957 Chi-A	0	1	.000	20	5	0	0	0	37	29	5	29	14	14.4	4.86	77	.216	.360	0	.000	-0	-4	-5	-1	-0.3
Total 2	0	2	.000	21	6	0	0	0	43	38	7	35	17	15.5	5.23	72	.241	.381	1	.167	0	-7	-7	-1	-0.6

YEAR	TM/L	W	L	PCT	G	GS	CG	SH	SV	IP	H	HR	BB	SO	RAT	ERA	ERA+	OAV	OOB	BH	AVG	PB	PR	/A	PD	TPI

● JIM DESHAIES Deshaies, James Joseph b: 6/23/60, Massena, N.Y. BL/TL, 6'4", 225 lbs. Deb: 8/7/84

1984	NY-A	0	1	.000	2	2	0	0	0	7	14	1	7	5	27.0	11.57	33	.438	.538	0	—	0	-6	-6	0	-0.7
1985	Hou-N	0	0	—	2	0	0	0	0	3	1	0	0	2	3.0	0.00	—	.100	.100	0	—	0	1	1	-0	0.0
1986	Hou-N	12	5	.706	26	26	1	1	0	144	124	16	59	128	11.6	3.25	111	.234	.313	2	.047	-1	7	6	-2	0.3
1987	Hou-N	11	6	.647	26	25	1	0	0	152	149	22	57	104	12.2	4.62	85	.257	.324	5	.094	-0	-9	-12	-1	-1.2
1988	Hou-N	11	14	.440	31	31	3	2	0	207	164	20	72	127	10.3	3.00	111	.218	.288	3	.048	-4	10	7	-2	0.2
1989	Hou-N	15	10	.600	34	34	6	3	0	225²	180	15	79	153	10.5	2.91	114	.217	.288	9	.120	-2	15	12	-1	0.9
1990	Hou-N	7	12	.368	34	34	2	0	0	209¹	186	21	84	119	12.2	3.78	98	.245	.326	4	.063	-3	0	-2	-1	-0.6
1991	Hou-N	5	12	.294	28	28	1	0	0	161	156	19	72	98	12.8	4.98	70	.259	.339	4	.098	-1	-23	-26	-2	-2.7
1992	SD-N	4	7	.364	15	15	0	0	0	96	92	9	33	46	12.4	3.28	109	.258	.323	6	.207	1	2	3	1	0.5
1993	Min-A	11	13	.458	27	27	1	0	0	167¹	159	24	51	80	11.6	4.41	99	.254	.317	0	—	0	-2	-1	-1	-0.2
	SF-N	2	2	.500	5	4	0	0	0	17	24	2	6	5	16.4	4.24	92	.348	.408	0	.000	-1	-0	-1	-0	-0.2
1994	Min-A	6	12	.333	25	25	0	0	0	130¹	170	30	54	78	15.6	7.39	66	.321	.386	0	—	0	-37	-37	0	-3.9
Total	11	84	94	.472	255	251	15	6	0	1519²	1419	176	574	945	12.0	4.09	92	.250	.322	33	.089	-12	-41	-56	-8	-7.6

● JIMMIE DeSHONG DeShong, James Brooklyn b: 11/30/09, Harrisburg, Pa. d: 10/16/93, Lower Paxton Township, Pa. BR/TR, 5'11", 165 lbs. Deb: 4/12/32

1932	Phi-A	0	0	—	6	0	0	0	0	10	17	3	9	5	24.3	11.70	39	.378	.491	0	.000	-0	-8	-8	0	0.0
1934	NY-A	6	7	.462	31	12	6	0	3	133²	126	6	56	40	12.4	4.11	99	.243	.319	8	.190	2	6	-1	-0	0.1
1935	NY-A	4	1	.800	29	3	0	0	3	69	64	6	33	30	12.9	3.26	124	.242	.331	1	.071	-1	9	6	2	0.5
1936	Was-A	18	10	.643	34	31	16	2	2	223²	255	11	96	59	14.2	4.63	103	.285	.356	15	.190	2	10	4	-2	0.4
1937	Was-A	14	15	.483	37	34	20	0	1	264¹	290	6	124	86	14.2	4.90	90	.280	.359	19	.202	2	-8	-14	-1	-1.0
1938	Was-A	5	8	.385	31	14	1	0	0	131¹	160	11	83	41	16.7	6.58	69	.310	.407	12	.261	3	-26	-30	-2	-2.1
1939	Was-A	0	3	.000	7	6	1	0	0	40²	56	7	31	12	19.3	8.63	50	.337	.442	3	.200	0	-18	-19	1	-1.0
Total	7	47	44	.516	175	100	44	2	9	872²	968	59	432	273	14.6	5.08	87	.281	.363	58	.198	7	-35	-63	3	-3.1

● JOHN DeSILVA DeSilva, John Reed b: 9/30/67, Fort Bragg, Cal. BR/TR, 6', 193 lbs. Deb: 8/15/93

1993	Det-A	0	0	—	1	0	0	0	0	1	2	0	0	0	18.0	9.00	48	.667	.667	0	—	0	-1	-1	-0	0.0
	LA-N	0	0	—	3	0	0	0	0	5¹	6	0	1	6	11.8	6.75	57	.273	.304	0	—	0	-2	-2	-0	0.0
Total	1	0	0	—	4	0	0	0	0	6¹	8	0	1	6	12.8	7.11	55	.320	.346	0	—	0	-2	-2	-0	0.0

● SHORTY DesJARDIEN DesJardien, Paul Raymond b: 8/24/1893, Coffeyville, Kan. d: 3/7/56, Monrovia, Cal. BR/TR, 6'4.5", 205 lbs. Deb: 5/20/16

| 1916 | Cle-A | 0 | 0 | — | 1 | 0 | 0 | 0 | 0 | 1 | 1 | 0 | 1 | 0 | 18.0 | 18.00 | 17 | .200 | .333 | 0 | — | 0 | -2 | -2 | -0 | 0.0 |

● RUBE DESSAU Dessau, Frank Rolland b: 3/29/1883, New Galilee, Pa. d: 5/6/52, York, Pa. BB/TR, 5'11", 175 lbs. Deb: 9/22/07

1907	Bos-N	0	1	.000	2	2	1	0	0	9¹	13	0	10	1	23.1	10.61	24	.394	.545	0	.000	-0	-8	-8	-0	-0.8
1910	Bro-N	2	3	.400	19	0	0	0	1	51¹	67	0	29	24	17.7	5.79	52	.328	.424	1	.067	-1	-16	-16	-1	-1.7
Total	2	2	4	.333	21	2	1	0	1	60²	80	0	39	25	18.5	6.53	45	.338	.443	1	.053	-1	-24	-24	-2	-2.5

● JOHN DETTMER Dettmer, John Franklin b: 3/4/70, Centerville, Ill. BR/TR, 6', 185 lbs. Deb: 6/16/94

| 1994 | Tex-A | 0 | 6 | .000 | 11 | 9 | 0 | 0 | 0 | 54 | 63 | 10 | 20 | 27 | 14.3 | 4.33 | 105 | .286 | .354 | 0 | — | 0 | 3 | 1 | 0 | 0.2 |

● TOM DETTORE Dettore, Thomas Anthony b: 11/17/47, Canonsburg, Pa. BL/TR, 6'4", 200 lbs. Deb: 6/11/73

1973	Pit-N	0	1	.000	12	1	0	0	0	22²	33	1	14	13	19.9	5.96	59	.340	.439	0	.000	-0	-6	-6	-0	-0.3
1974	Chi-N	3	5	.375	16	9	0	0	0	64²	64	4	31	43	14.1	4.18	91	.255	.351	5	.250	1	-4	-3	0	-0.1
1975	Chi-N	5	4	.556	36	5	0	0	0	85¹	88	8	31	46	13.5	5.38	71	.270	.350	6	.250	1	-17	-15	0	-1.3
1976	Chi-N	0	1	.000	4	0	0	0	0	7	11	3	2	4	16.7	10.29	38	.355	.394	0	—	0	-5	-5	-0	-0.6
Total	4	8	11	.421	68	15	0	0	0	179²	196	16	78	106	14.6	5.21	73	.278	.365	11	.229	2	-32	-28	0	-2.3

● MEL DEUTSCH Deutsch, Melvin Elliott b: 7/26/15, Caldwell, Tex. BR/TR, 6'4", 215 lbs. Deb: 4/21/46

| 1946 | Bos-A | 0 | 0 | — | 3 | 0 | 0 | 0 | 0 | 6¹ | 7 | 1 | 3 | 2 | 14.2 | 5.68 | 64 | .280 | .357 | 0 | .000 | -0 | -2 | -1 | -0 | 0.0 |

● CHARLIE DEVENS Devens, Charles b: 1/1/10, Milton, Mass. BR/TR, 6'1", 180 lbs. Deb: 9/24/32

1932	NY-A	1	0	1.000	1	1	1	0	0	9	6	0	4	4	13.0	2.00	204	.200	.351	0	.000	-0	2	2	-0	0.2
1933	NY-A	3	3	.500	14	8	2	0	0	62	59	1	50	23	15.8	4.35	89	.250	.381	2	.095	-1	-1	-3	-1	-0.4
1934	NY-A	1	0	1.000	1	1	1	0	0	11	9	0	5	4	11.5	1.64	248	.225	.311	1	.500	1	3	3	0	0.5
Total	3	5	3	.625	16	10	4	0	0	82	74	1	62	31	14.9	3.73	105	.242	.370	3	.120	0	5	2	-1	0.2

● ADRIAN DEVINE Devine, Paul Adrian b: 12/2/51, Galveston, Tex. BR/TR, 6'4", 205 lbs. Deb: 6/27/73

1973	Atl-N	2	3	.400	24	1	0	0	4	32¹	45	6	12	15	16.4	6.40	61	.338	.401	1	.250	0	-10	-9	-1	-1.5
1975	Atl-N	1	0	1.000	5	2	0	0	0	16¹	19	2	7	8	14.9	4.41	86	.284	.360	0	.000	-1	-1	-1	-0	-0.2
1976	Atl-N	5	6	.455	48	1	0	0	9	73	72	3	26	48	12.2	3.21	118	.255	.320	0	.000	-2	2	5	-1	0.6
1977	Tex-A	11	6	.647	56	2	0	0	15	105²	102	8	31	67	11.7	3.58	114	.259	.319	0	—	0	6	6	2	1.2
1978	Atl-N	5	4	.556	31	6	0	0	0	65¹	84	3	25	26	15.0	5.92	68	.323	.382	1	.091	-1	-17	-14	-1	-1.9
1979	Atl-N	1	2	.333	40	0	0	0	0	66²	84	3	25	26	15.0	3.24	125	.311	.374	0	.000	-1	4	6	-0	0.1
1980	Tex-A	1	1	.500	13	0	0	0	0	28	49	4	9	8	19.0	4.82	81	.377	.421	0	—	0	-2	-3	-0	-0.2
Total	7	26	22	.542	217	12	0	0	31	387¹	455	34	135	194	14.0	4.21	95	.296	.357	2	.049	-3	-19	-9	0	-1.9

● JIM DEVINE Devine, Walter James b: 10/5/1858, Brooklyn, N.Y. d: 1/11/05, Syracuse, N.Y. TL, Deb: 5/9/1883 ◆

| 1883 | Bal-a | 1 | 1 | .500 | 2 | 2 | 1 | 0 | 0 | 11 | 15 | 0 | 1 | 3 | 13.1 | 7.36 | 47 | .305 | .319 | 2 | .222 | -0 | -5 | -5 | -1 | -0.6 |

● HAL DEVINEY Deviney, Harold John b: 4/11/1893, Newton, Mass. d: 1/4/33, Westwood, Mass. BR/TR, Deb: 7/30/20

| 1920 | Bos-A | 0 | 0 | — | 1 | 0 | 0 | 0 | 0 | 3 | 7 | 0 | 2 | 0 | 27.0 | 15.00 | 24 | .500 | .563 | 2 | 1.000 | 2 | -4 | -4 | -0 | 0.2 |

● JIM DEVLIN Devlin, James Alexander b: 1849, Philadelphia, Pa. d: 10/10/1883, Philadelphia, Pa. BR/TR, 5'11", 175 lbs. Deb: 4/21/1873 ◆

1875	Chi-n	7	16	.304	28	24	24	0	0	224	254	0	11		10.6	2.89	87	.255	.263	92	.292	7	-11	-10		-0.2
1876	Lou-N	30	35	.462	**68**	68	**66**	5	0	**622**	566	3	37	**122**	8.7	1.56	174	.224	.235	94	.315	2	51	**80**	1	7.3
1877	Lou-N	35	25	.583	**61**	61	**61**	4	0	**559**	617	4	41	141	10.6	2.25	**147**	.270	.283	72	.269	-2	34	**65**	2	5.9
Total	2	65	60	.520	129	129	127	9	0	1181	1183	7	78	263	9.6	1.89	159	.246	.258	166	.293	1	86	145	3	13.2

● JIM DEVLIN Devlin, James H. b: 4/16/1866, Troy, N.Y. d: 12/14/1900, Troy, N.Y. TL, 5'7", 135 lbs. Deb: 6/28/1886

1886	NY-N	0	0	—	1	0	0	0	0	2	3	0	4	2	31.5	18.00	18	.250	.438	0	.000	-0	-3	-3	0	-0.3
1887	Phi-N	0	2	.000	2	2	2	0	0	18	20	0	10	6	16.5	6.00	71	.267	.375	2	.333	0	-4	-4	0	-0.2
1888	•StL-a	6	5	.545	11	11	10	0	0	90¹	82	3	20	45	11.0	3.19	102	.233	.290	11	.297	2	-1	-1	0	0.2
1889	StL-a	5	3	.625	9	8	5	0	0	60	56	0	24	37	13.1	2.40	176	.239	.329	5	.192	-2	10	12	1	1.3
Total	4	11	10	.524	23	21	17	0	1	170¹	161	3	58	90	12.5	3.38	109	.239	.317	18	.257	1	1	6	2	1.0

● CHARLIE DEWALD Dewald, Charles H. b: 9/1867, Newark, N.J. d: 8/22/04, Cleveland, Ohio TL, Deb: 9/2/1890

| 1890 | Cle-P | 2 | 0 | 1.000 | 2 | 2 | 2 | 0 | 0 | 14 | 13 | 0 | 5 | 6 | 11.6 | 0.64 | 618 | .236 | .299 | 3 | .375 | 1 | 6 | 5 | -0 | 0.6 |

● MARK DEWEY Dewey, Mark Alan b: 1/3/65, Grand Rapids, Mich. BR/TR, 6', 185 lbs. Deb: 8/24/90

1990	SF-N	1	1	.500	14	0	0	0	0	22²	22	1	5	11	10.7	2.78	131	.259	.300	0	.000	0	3	2	0	0.2
1992	NY-N	1	0	1.000	20	0	0	0	0	33¹	37	2	10	24	12.7	4.32	80	.288	.355	0	.000	0	-0	-1	-0	-0.1
1993	Pit-N	1	2	.333	21	0	0	0	7	26²	14	0	10	14	9.1	2.36	171	.157	.265	0	—	0	5	5	0	0.9
1994	Pit-N	2	1	.667	45	0	0	0	0	51¹	61	4	19	30	14.6	3.68	115	.303	.372	1	1.000	0	3	3	-1	0.2
Total	4	5	4	.556	100	0	0	0	8	134	134	7	44	79	12.4	3.43	114	.264	.330	1	.333	1	8	7	-0	1.2

YEAR TM/L	W	L	PCT	G	GS	CG	SH	SV	IP	H	HR	BB	SO	RAT	ERA	ERA+	OAV	OOB	BH	AVG	PB	PR	/A	PD	TPI

● CARLOS DIAZ   Diaz, Carlos Antonio   b: 1/7/58, Kaneohe, Hawaii   BR/TL, 6', 170 lbs.   Deb: 6/30/82

YEAR TM/L	W	L	PCT	G	GS	CG	SH	SV	IP	H	HR	BB	SO	RAT	ERA	ERA+	OAV	OOB	BH	AVG	PB	PR	/A	PD	TPI
1982 Atl-N	3	2	.600	19	0	0	0	1	25¹	31	3	9	16	14.2	4.62	81	.307	.364	0	.000	-0	-3	-3	0	-0.5
NY-N	0	0	—	4	0	0	0	0	3²	6	0	4	0	24.5	0.00	—	.353	.476	0	—	0	1	1	0	0.0
Yr	3	2	.600	23	0	0	0	1	29	37	3	13	16	15.5	4.03	92	.311	.379	0	.000	-0	-1	-1	0	-0.5
1983 NY-N	3	1	.750	54	0	0	0	2	83¹	62	1	35	64	10.6	2.05	177	.211	.297	0	.000	-0	15	15	1	0.8
1984 LA-N	1	0	1.000	37	0	0	0	1	41	47	4	24	36	15.6	5.49	64	.285	.376	0	.000	-0	-9	-9	-1	-0.3
1985 *LA-N	6	3	.667	46	0	0	0	0	79¹	70	7	18	73	10.0	2.61	133	.230	.273	0	.000	-0	9	8	-1	0.7
1986 LA-N	0	0	—	19	0	0	0	0	25¹	33	2	7	18	14.2	4.26	81	.317	.360	0	.000	-0	-2	-2	0	0.0
Total 5	13	6	.684	179	0	0	0	4	258	249	17	97	207	12.1	3.21	111	.253	.320	0	.000	-1	12	10	-0	0.7

● ROB DIBBLE   Dibble, Robert Keith   b: 1/24/64, Bridgeport, Conn.   BL/TR, 6'4", 230 lbs.   Deb: 6/29/88

YEAR TM/L	W	L	PCT	G	GS	CG	SH	SV	IP	H	HR	BB	SO	RAT	ERA	ERA+	OAV	OOB	BH	AVG	PB	PR	/A	PD	TPI
1988 Cin-N	1	1	.500	37	0	0	0	0	59¹	43	2	21	59	9.9	1.82	197	.207	.283	0	.000	-0	11	12	-1	0.2
1989 Cin-N	10	5	.667	74	0	0	0	2	99	62	4	39	141	9.5	2.09	172	.176	.264	0	.000	-1	15	17	-1	2.3
1990 *Cin-N★	8	3	.727	68	0	0	0	11	98	62	3	34	136	8.9	1.74	226	.183	.259	0	.000	-1	**22**	**24**	-0	3.1
1991 Cin-N★	3	5	.375	67	0	0	0	31	82¹	67	5	25	124	10.1	3.17	120	.223	.282	0	.000	-0	5	6	-0	1.0
1992 Cin-N	3	5	.375	63	0	0	0	25	70¹	48	3	31	110	10.4	3.07	117	.193	.287	2	.400	1	3	4	-1	0.8
1993 Cin-N	1	4	.200	45	0	0	0	19	41²	34	8	42	49	16.3	6.48	62	.225	.400	1	1.000	0	-11	-11	0	-2.2
Total 6	26	23	.531	354	0	0	0	88	450²	316	25	192	619	10.3	2.74	137	.198	.287	3	.120	-1	45	51	-3	5.2

● PEDRO DIBUT   Dibut, Pedro (Villafana)   b: 11/18/1892, Cienfuegos, Cuba   d: 12/4/79, Hialeah, Fla.   BR/TR, 5'8", 190 lbs.   Deb: 5/1/24

YEAR TM/L	W	L	PCT	G	GS	CG	SH	SV	IP	H	HR	BB	SO	RAT	ERA	ERA+	OAV	OOB	BH	AVG	PB	PR	/A	PD	TPI
1924 Cin-N	3	0	1.000	7	2	2	0	0	36²	24	1	12	15	8.8	2.21	170	.188	.257	3	.273	1	7	6	1	0.7
1925 Cin-N	0	0	—	1	0	0	0	0	0	3	0	0	0	—	∞	—	1.000	1.000	0	—	0	-2	-2	0	-0.2
Total 2	3	0	1.000	8	2	2	0	0	36²	27	1	12	15	9.6	2.70	139	.206	.273	3	.273	1	5	4	1	0.5

● LEO DICKERMAN   Dickerman, Leo Louis   b: 10/31/1896, DeSoto, Mo.   d: 4/30/82, Atkins, Ark.   BR/TR, 6'4", 192 lbs.   Deb: 4/21/23

YEAR TM/L	W	L	PCT	G	GS	CG	SH	SV	IP	H	HR	BB	SO	RAT	ERA	ERA+	OAV	OOB	BH	AVG	PB	PR	/A	PD	TPI
1923 Bro-N	8	12	.400	35	20	7	1	0	159²	180	4	72	58	14.3	3.72	104	.283	.357	13	.250	3	5	3	2	0.8
1924 Bro-N	0	0	—	7	2	0	0	0	19²	20	0	16	9	17.4	5.49	68	.263	.404	1	.167	-0	-4	-4	0	0.0
StL-N	7	4	.636	18	13	8	1	0	119²	108	6	51	28	12.0	2.41	157	.249	.328	9	.231	1	19	18	0	1.7
Yr	7	4	.636	25	15	8	1	0	139¹	128	6	67	37	12.6	2.84	133	.250	.337	10	.222	1	16	14	1	1.7
1925 StL-N	4	11	.267	29	20	7	2	1	130²	135	10	79	40	14.9	5.58	77	.273	.376	3	.114	-3	-19	-18	4	-1.7
Total 3	19	27	.413	89	55	22	4	1	429²	443	20	218	135	14.0	4.00	99	.270	.358	28	.193	1	2	-1	6	0.8

● GEORGE DICKERSON   Dickerson, George Clark   b: 12/1/1892, Renner, Tex.   d: 7/9/38, Los Angeles, Cal.   BR/TR, 6'1", 170 lbs.   Deb: 8/2/17

YEAR TM/L	W	L	PCT	G	GS	CG	SH	SV	IP	H	HR	BB	SO	RAT	ERA	ERA+	OAV	OOB	BH	AVG	PB	PR	/A	PD	TPI
1917 Cle-A	0	0	—	1	0	0	0	0	1	0	0	0	0	0.00	—	.000	.000	0	—	-0	0	0	-0	0.0

● EMERSON DICKMAN   Dickman, George Emerson   b: 11/12/14, Buffalo, N.Y.   d: 4/27/81, New York, N.Y.   BR/TR, 6'2", 175 lbs.   Deb: 6/27/36

YEAR TM/L	W	L	PCT	G	GS	CG	SH	SV	IP	H	HR	BB	SO	RAT	ERA	ERA+	OAV	OOB	BH	AVG	PB	PR	/A	PD	TPI
1936 Bos-A	0	0	—	1	0	0	0	0	1	2	0	1	2	27.0	9.00	59	.400	.500	0	—	-0	-0	-0	0	0.0
1938 Bos-A	5	5	.500	32	11	3	1	0	104	117	9	54	22	15.1	5.28	93	.288	.377	10	.286	4	-6	-4	-0	-0.6
1939 Bos-A	8	3	.727	48	1	0	0	5	113²	126	10	43	46	13.6	4.43	107	.282	.349	2	.056	-4	2	4	3	0.2
1940 Bos-A	8	6	.571	35	9	2	0	3	100	121	15	38	40	14.7	6.03	75	.291	.356	3	.107	-2	-18	-17	2	-2.1
1941 Bos-A	1	1	.500	9	3	1	0	0	31	37	4	17	16	15.7	6.39	65	.301	.386	1	.091	-1	-8	-8	-1	-0.6
Total 5	22	15	.595	125	24	6	1	8	349²	403	38	153	126	14.6	5.33	88	.288	.363	16	.145	-2	-30	-25	4	-2.5

● JIM DICKSON   Dickson, James Edward   b: 4/20/38, Portland, Ore.   BL/TR, 6'1", 185 lbs.   Deb: 7/2/63

YEAR TM/L	W	L	PCT	G	GS	CG	SH	SV	IP	H	HR	BB	SO	RAT	ERA	ERA+	OAV	OOB	BH	AVG	PB	PR	/A	PD	TPI
1963 Hou-N	0	1	.000	13	0	0	0	2	14²	22	0	2	6	14.7	6.14	51	.344	.364	0	.000	-0	-5	-5	-0	-0.5
1964 Cin-N	1	0	1.000	4	0	0	0	0	5	8	0	5	6	23.4	7.20	50	.444	.565	0	—	0	-2	-2	0	-0.4
1965 KC-A	3	2	.600	68	0	0	0	1	85²	68	6	47	54	12.3	3.47	101	.220	.327	0	.000	-0	-0	-0	-1	-0.1
1966 KC-A	1	0	1.000	24	1	0	0	1	37	37	4	23	20	14.6	5.35	63	.264	.368	1	.250	0	-8	-8	-0	-0.3
Total 4	5	3	.625	109	1	0	0	3	142¹	135	10	77	86	13.5	4.36	79	.254	.351	1	.143	-0	-15	-15	-1	-1.3

● LANCE DICKSON   Dickson, Lance Michael   b: 10/19/69, Fullerton, Cal.   BR/TL, 6', 185 lbs.   Deb: 8/9/90

YEAR TM/L	W	L	PCT	G	GS	CG	SH	SV	IP	H	HR	BB	SO	RAT	ERA	ERA+	OAV	OOB	BH	AVG	PB	PR	/A	PD	TPI
1990 Chi-N	0	3	.000	3	3	0	0	0	13²	20	2	4	4	15.8	7.24	56	.370	.414	0	.000	-0	-5	-5	1	-0.8

● MURRY DICKSON   Dickson, Murry Monroe   b: 8/21/16, Tracy, Mo.   d: 9/21/89, Kansas City, Kan.   BR/TR, 5'10.5", 157 lbs.   Deb: 9/30/39

YEAR TM/L	W	L	PCT	G	GS	CG	SH	SV	IP	H	HR	BB	SO	RAT	ERA	ERA+	OAV	OOB	BH	AVG	PB	PR	/A	PD	TPI
1939 StL-N	0	0	—	1	0	0	0	0	3²	1	0	1	2	4.9	0.00	—	.091	.167	0	.000	-0	2	2	0	0.0
1940 StL-N	0	0	—	1	1	0	0	0	1²	5	0	1	0	32.4	16.20	25	.500	.545	0	—	-0	-2	-2	0	0.0
1942 StL-N	6	3	.667	36	7	2	0	2	120²	91	4	61	66	11.4	2.91	118	.216	.316	8	.190	-0	5	7	1	0.6
1943 *StL-N	8	2	.800	31	7	2	0	0	115²	119	4	49	44	13.1	3.58	94	.269	.343	9	.265	1	-3	-3	-0	-0.2
1946 *StL-N	15	6	.714	47	19	12	2	1	184¹	160	8	56	82	10.7	2.88	120	.234	.295	18	.277	4	11	12	4	2.2
1947 StL-N	13	16	.448	47	25	11	4	3	231²	211	16	88	111	11.7	3.07	135	.243	.315	17	.213	1	25	27	3	3.4
1948 StL-N	12	16	.429	42	29	11	1	1	252¹	257	39	85	113	12.2	4.14	99	.265	.325	27	.281	4	-5	-1	1	0.3
1949 Pit-N	12	14	.462	44	20	11	2	0	224¹	216	17	80	89	12.1	3.29	128	.255	.324	17	.202	0	19	23	5	3.0
1950 Pit-N	10	15	.400	51	22	8	0	3	225	227	26	83	76	12.5	3.80	115	.260	.326	21	.256	3	9	15	2	2.0
1951 Pit-N	20	16	.556	45	35	19	3	2	288²	294	32	101	112	12.5	4.02	105	.262	.327	30	.273	5	-2	7	4	1.7
1952 Pit-N	14	21	.400	43	34	21	2	2	277²	278	26	76	112	11.5	3.57	112	.261	.311	24	.224	2	5	13	4	2.3
1953 Pit-N★	10	19	.345	45	26	10	1	4	200²	240	27	58	88	13.5	4.53	99	.298	.348	7	.115	-4	-5	-1	-0	-0.5
1954 Phi-N	10	20	.333	40	31	12	4	1	226¹	256	31	73	64	13.2	3.78	107	.286	.342	15	.190	-0	7	7	3	1.0
1955 Phi-N	12	11	.522	36	28	12	4	0	216	190	27	82	92	11.5	3.50	113	.238	.312	18	.220	1	13	11	1	1.3
1956 Phi-N	0	3	.000	3	3	0	0	0	23	20	1	2	12	12.5	5.09	76	.241	.337	1	.333	-1	-3	-3	-0	-0.3
StL-N	13	8	.619	28	27	12	3	0	196¹	175	20	57	109	10.7	3.07	123	.240	.296	19	.247	4	15	16	4	2.5
Yr	13	11	.542	31	30	12	3	0	219¹	195	21	69	110	10.9	3.28	115	.240	.301	22	.256	4	12	12	4	2.2
1957 StL-N	5	3	.625	14	13	3	1	0	74	87	8	25	29	13.7	4.14	96	.296	.353	6	.222	1	-2	-1	2	0.1
1958 KC-A	9	5	.643	27	9	3	0	1	99	99	12	31	46	12.0	3.27	119	.258	.317	9	.257	2	5	7	2	1.4
*NY-A	1	2	.333	6	2	0	0	1	20¹	18	4	12	9	13.7	5.75	61	.237	.348	2	.286	0	-4	-5	-0	-0.7
Yr	10	7	.588	33	11	3	0	2	119¹	117	16	43	55	12.1	3.70	104	.253	.318	11	.262	2	1	2	2	0.7
1959 KC-A	2	1	.667	8	0	0	0	1	71	85	9	31	36	14.2	4.94	81	.290	.350	3	.176	-1	-9	-7	-0	-0.4
Total 18	172	181	.487	625	338	149	27	23	3052¹	3029	302	1058	1281	12.2	3.66	110	.260	.323	253	.231	25	81	120	32	19.7

● WALT DICKSON   Dickson, Walter R. "Hickory"   b: 12/3/1878, New Summerfield, Tex.   d: 12/9/18, Ardmore, Okla.   BR/TR, 5'11.5", 175 lbs.   Deb: 4/26/10

YEAR TM/L	W	L	PCT	G	GS	CG	SH	SV	IP	H	HR	BB	SO	RAT	ERA	ERA+	OAV	OOB	BH	AVG	PB	PR	/A	PD	TPI
1910 NY-N	1	0	1.000	12	1	0	0	0	29²	31	1	9	12	12.1	5.46	54	.272	.325	1	.250	0	-8	-8	-1	-0.3
1912 Bos-N	3	19	.136	36	20	9	1	1	189	233	2	61	47	14.1	3.86	93	.320	.375	10	.167	-1	-9	-6	2	-0.6
1913 Bos-N	6	7	.462	19	15	8	0	0	128	118	4	45	47	11.5	3.23	102	.249	.316	8	.178	-1	-0	1	-1	-0.2
1914 Pit-F	9	19	.321	40	32	19	3	1	256²	262	6	74	63	11.9	3.16	91	.273	.327	7	.084	-9	-8	-8	-0	-1.8
1915 Pit-F	7	5	.583	27	11	4	0	1	96²	115	4	33	36	14.0	4.19	65	.316	.376	4	.129	-1	-16	-16	0	-1.9
Total 5	26	50	.342	134	79	40	4	2	700	759	17	222	202	12.7	3.60	86	.288	.345	30	.135	-12	-41	-38	0	-4.8

● GEORGE DIEHL   Diehl, George Krause   b: 2/25/18, Emmaus, Pa.   d: 8/24/86, Kingsport, Tenn.   BR/TR, 6'2", 196 lbs.   Deb: 4/19/42

YEAR TM/L	W	L	PCT	G	GS	CG	SH	SV	IP	H	HR	BB	SO	RAT	ERA	ERA+	OAV	OOB	BH	AVG	PB	PR	/A	PD	TPI
1942 Bos-N	0	0	—	1	0	0	0	0	3²	2	0	2	0	12.3	2.45	136	.167	.333	0	.000	-0	0	0	0	0.0
1943 Bos-N	0	0	—	1	0	0	0	0	4	4	0	3	1	15.8	4.50	76	.267	.389	0	.000	-0	-0	-0	1	0.1
Total 2	0	0	—	2	0	0	0	0	7²	6	0	5	1	14.1	3.52	96	.222	.364	0	.000	-0	0	0	1	0.1

● LARRY DIERKER   Dierker, Lawrence Edward   b: 9/22/46, Hollywood, Cal   BR/TR, 6'4", 215 lbs.   Deb: 9/22/64

YEAR TM/L	W	L	PCT	G	GS	CG	SH	SV	IP	H	HR	BB	SO	RAT	ERA	ERA+	OAV	OOB	BH	AVG	PB	PR	/A	PD	TPI
1964 Hou-N	0	1	.000	3	1	0	0	0	9	7	1	3	5	10.0	2.00	171	.219	.286	0	.000	-0	2	1	-1	0.1
1965 Hou-N	7	8	.467	26	19	3	0	0	146²	135	16	37	109	10.7	3.50	96	.240	.290	5	.100	-1	1	-2	-2	-0.5
1966 Hou-N	10	8	.556	29	28	8	2	0	187	173	17	45	108	10.5	3.18	108	.240	.285	10	.149	1	9	5	-1	0.5

YEAR	TM/L	W	L	PCT	G	GS	CG	SH	SV	IP	H	HR	BB	SO	RAT	ERA	ERA+	OAV	OOB	BH	AVG	PB	PR	/A	PD	TPI
1967	Hou-N	6	5	.545	15	15	4	0	0	99	95	4	25	68	11.0	3.36	98	.252	.300	7	.226	2	0	-1	-1	0.0
1968	Hou-N	12	15	.444	32	32	10	1	0	233^2	206	14	89	161	11.7	3.31	89	.240	.317	5	.068	-3	-9	-9	-2	-1.7
1969	Hou-N★	20	13	.606	39	37	20	4	0	305^1	240	18	72	232	9.2	2.33	152	.214	**.262**	17	.144	-1	43	41	-1	4.3
1970	Hou-N	16	12	.571	37	36	17	2	1	269^2	263	31	82	191	11.7	3.87	100	.254	.313	16	.174	-0	5	0	-1	-0.1
1971	Hou-N†	12	6	.667	24	23	6	2	0	159	150	8	33	91	10.5	2.72	124	.248	.289	4	.074	-3	13	11	0	1.0
1972	Hou-N	15	8	.652	31	31	12	5	0	214^2	209	14	51	115	11.1	3.40	99	.256	.304	13	.167	0	1	-1	-2	-0.3
1973	Hou-N	1	1	.500	14	3	0	0	0	27	27	3	13	18	14.0	4.33	84	.265	.359	0	.000	-0	-2	-2	-0	-0.2
1974	Hou-N	11	10	.524	33	33	7	3	0	223^2	189	18	82	150	11.1	2.90	120	.232	.307	14	.197	1	18	14	0	1.4
1975	Hou-N	14	16	.467	34	34	14	2	0	232	225	24	91	127	12.5	4.00	84	.260	.335	7	.092	-4	-10	-16	-1	-2.4
1976	Hou-N	13	14	.481	28	28	7	4	0	187^2	171	9	72	112	11.9	3.69	86	.243	.319	9	.141	-4	-4	-10	-1	-1.6
1977	StL-N	2	6	.250	11	9	0	0	0	39^1	40	7	16	6	13.3	4.58	84	.267	.345	0	.000	-1	-3	-3	-0	-0.7
Total 14		139	123	.531	356	329	106	25	1	2333^2	2130	184	711	1493	11.1	3.31	103	.243	.303	107	.136	-12	65	29	-12	-0.2

● BILL DIETRICH
Dietrich, William John "Bullfrog" b: 3/29/10, Philadelphia, Pa. d: 6/20/78, Philadelphia, Pa. BR/TR, 6', 185 lbs. Deb: 4/13/33

YEAR	TM/L	W	L	PCT	G	GS	CG	SH	SV	IP	H	HR	BB	SO	RAT	ERA	ERA+	OAV	OOB	BH	AVG	PB	PR	/A	PD	TPI
1933	Phi-A	0	1	.000	8	1	0	0	0	17	13	1	19	4	16.9	5.82	74	.236	.432	1	.333	1	-3	-3	0	0.0
1934	Phi-A	11	12	.478	39	23	14	4	3	207^2	201	12	114	88	13.8	4.68	94	.255	.351	15	.208	3	-4	-7	-2	-0.5
1935	Phi-A	7	13	.350	43	15	8	1	3	185^1	203	7	101	54	14.8	5.39	84	.276	.364	5	.083	-6	-19	-17	-1	-2.2
1936	Phi-A	4	6	.400	21	4	0	0	3	71^2	91	4	40	34	16.5	6.53	78	.305	.388	3	.111	-2	-12	-11	1	-1.3
	Was-A	0	1	.000	5	0	0	0	0	8^1	13	0	6	4	20.5	9.72	49	.351	.442	0	—	0	-4	-5	0	-0.4
	Chi-A	4	4	.500	14	11	6	1	0	82^2	93	8	36	34	14.2	4.68	111	.284	.356	8	.267	1	3	5	-0	0.4
	Yr	8	11	.421	40	15	6	1	3	162^1	197	12	82	77	15.5	5.75	89	.297	.375	11	.193	-1	-13	-11	1	-1.3
1937	Chi-A	8	10	.444	29	20	7	1	1	143^1	162	15	72	62	14.7	4.90	94	.285	.366	8	.182	1	-4	-5	1	-0.3
1938	Chi-A	2	4	.333	8	7	1	0	0	48	49	7	31	11	15.0	5.44	90	.259	.364	1	.063	-1	-3	-3	-0	-0.4
1939	Chi-A	7	8	.467	25	19	2	0	0	127^2	134	14	56	43	13.5	5.22	91	.272	.349	8	.216	2	-8	-7	-1	-0.5
1940	Chi-A	10	6	.625	23	17	6	1	0	149^2	154	10	65	43	13.2	4.03	110	.266	.340	12	.240	3	6	7	-2	0.8
1941	Chi-A	5	8	.385	19	15	4	1	0	109^1	114	7	50	26	13.8	5.35	77	.263	.345	3	.088	0	-15	-15	-2	-1.6
1942	Chi-A	6	11	.353	26	23	6	0	0	160	173	16	70	39	13.9	4.89	74	.277	.355	5	.104	-1	-22	-23	-0	-2.3
1943	Chi-A	12	10	.545	26	26	12	2	0	186^2	180	4	53	52	11.3	2.80	119	.253	.307	8	.143	0	10	11	1	1.5
1944	Chi-A	16	17	.485	36	36	15	2	0	246	269	15	68	70	12.4	3.62	95	.279	.328	9	.117	-3	-5	-5	-1	-1.0
1945	Chi-A	7	10	.412	18	16	6	3	0	122^1	136	4	36	43	12.7	4.19	79	.279	.329	6	.167	0	-11	-12	0	-1.4
1946	Chi-A	3	3	.500	11	9	3	0	1	62	63	4	24	20	12.6	2.61	131	.267	.335	1	.053	-2	6	6	1	0.5
1947	Phi-A	5	2	.714	11	9	2	1	0	60^2	48	0	40	18	13.4	3.12	122	.223	.350	1	.063	-2	4	5	-1	0.3
1948	Phi-A	1	2	.333	4	2	0	0	0	15^1	21	0	9	5	17.6	5.87	73	.356	.441	0	.000	-0	-3	-3	-0	-0.4
Total 16		108	128	.458	366	253	92	17	11	2003^2	2117	128	890	660	13.6	4.48	92	.271	.348	94	.150	-5	-85	-84	-3	-8.8

● DUTCH DIETZ
Dietz, Lloyd Arthur b: 2/9/12, Cincinnati, Ohio d: 10/29/72, Beaumont, Tex. BR/TR, 5'11.5", 180 lbs. Deb: 4/26/40

YEAR	TM/L	W	L	PCT	G	GS	CG	SH	SV	IP	H	HR	BB	SO	RAT	ERA	ERA+	OAV	OOB	BH	AVG	PB	PR	/A	PD	TPI
1940	Pit-N	0	1	.000	4	2	0	0	0	15^1	22	2	4	8	15.3	5.87	65	.355	.394	1	.143	-0	-3	-4	0	-0.3
1941	Pit-N	7	2	.778	33	6	4	1	1	100^1	88	6	33	22	11.0	2.33	155	.233	.298	4	.160	-1	15	14	0	1.2
1942	Pit-N	6	9	.400	40	13	3	0	3	134^1	139	8	57	35	13.2	3.95	86	.268	.342	7	.200	1	-10	-8	-2	-1.1
1943	Pit-N	0	3	.000	8	0	0	0	0	9	12	0	4	4	17.0	6.00	58	.324	.405	0	—	0	-3	-3	1	-0.7
	Phi-N	1	1	.500	21	0	0	0	2	36	42	2	15	10	14.3	6.50	52	.292	.358	1	.167	-0	-12	-13	-0	-0.8
	Yr	1	4	.200	29	0	0	0	2	45	54	2	19	14	14.6	6.40	53	.297	.363	1	.167	-0	-15	-15	-0	-1.5
Total 4		14	16	.467	106	21	7	1	6	295	303	18	113	79	12.8	3.87	90	.266	.334	13	.178	-0	-14	-13	-1	-1.7

● REESE DIGGS
Diggs, Reese Wilson "Diggsy" b: 9/22/15, Mathews, Va. d: 10/30/78, Baltimore, Md. BB/TR, 6'2", 180 lbs. Deb: 9/15/34

YEAR	TM/L	W	L	PCT	G	GS	CG	SH	SV	IP	H	HR	BB	SO	RAT	ERA	ERA+	OAV	OOB	BH	AVG	PB	PR	/A	PD	TPI
1934	Was-A	1	2	.333	4	3	2	0	0	21^1	26	3	15	2	17.3	6.75	64	.313	.418	2	.250	0	-5	-6	-0	-0.6

● JACK DiLAURO
DiLauro, Jack Edward b: 5/3/43, Akron, Ohio BB/TL, 6'2", 185 lbs. Deb: 5/15/69

YEAR	TM/L	W	L	PCT	G	GS	CG	SH	SV	IP	H	HR	BB	SO	RAT	ERA	ERA+	OAV	OOB	BH	AVG	PB	PR	/A	PD	TPI
1969	NY-N	1	4	.200	23	4	0	0	1	63^2	50	4	18	27	9.6	2.40	152	.216	.272	0	.000	-1	8	9	-0	0.5
1970	Hou-N	1	3	.250	42	0	0	0	3	33^2	34	4	17	23	13.6	4.28	91	.262	.347	0	.000	-0	-1	-1	-0	-0.3
Total 2		2	7	.222	65	4	0	0	4	97^1	84	8	35	50	11.0	3.05	122	.232	.300	0	.000	-2	7	7	-1	0.2

● GORDON DILLARD
Dillard, Gordon Lee b: 5/20/64, Salinas, Cal. BL/TL, 6'1", 190 lbs. Deb: 8/12/88

YEAR	TM/L	W	L	PCT	G	GS	CG	SH	SV	IP	H	HR	BB	SO	RAT	ERA	ERA+	OAV	OOB	BH	AVG	PB	PR	/A	PD	TPI
1988	Bal-A	0	0	—	2	1	0	0	0	3	3	1	4	2	21.0	6.00	65	.273	.467	0	—	0	-1	-1	0	0.1
1989	Phi-N	0	0	—	5	0	0	0	0	4	7	0	0	2	15.8	6.75	53	.368	.368	0	—	0	-1	-1	0	0.0
Total 2		0	0	—	7	1	0	0	0	7	10	1	4	4	18.0	6.43	58	.333	.412	0	—	0	-2	-2	0	0.1

● HARLEY DILLINGER
Dillinger, Harley Hugh "Hoke" or "Lefty" b: 10/30/1894, Pomeroy, Ohio d: 1/8/59, Cleveland, Ohio BR/TL, 5'11", 175 lbs. Deb: 8/16/14

YEAR	TM/L	W	L	PCT	G	GS	CG	SH	SV	IP	H	HR	BB	SO	RAT	ERA	ERA+	OAV	OOB	BH	AVG	PB	PR	/A	PD	TPI
1914	Cle-A	0	1	.000	11	2	1	0	0	33^2	41	0	25	11	17.9	4.54	64	.325	.441	0	.000	-1	-7	-6	-1	-0.4

● BILL DILLMAN
Dillman, William Howard b: 5/25/45, Trenton, N.J. BR/TR, 6'2", 180 lbs. Deb: 4/14/67

YEAR	TM/L	W	L	PCT	G	GS	CG	SH	SV	IP	H	HR	BB	SO	RAT	ERA	ERA+	OAV	OOB	BH	AVG	PB	PR	/A	PD	TPI
1967	Bal-A	5	9	.357	32	15	2	1	3	124	115	13	33	69	11.0	4.35	72	.249	.303	5	.161	-0	-15	-17	-1	-2.0
1970	Mon-N	2	3	.400	18	0	0	0	0	30^2	28	4	18	17	13.8	5.28	78	.255	.364	0	.000	-0	-4	-4	0	-0.6
Total 2		7	12	.368	50	15	2	1	3	154^2	143	17	51	86	11.5	4.54	74	.250	.316	5	.152	-1	-20	-21	-1	-2.6

● STEVE DILLON
Dillon, Stephen Edward b: 3/20/43, Yonkers, N.Y. BL/TL, 5'10", 160 lbs. Deb: 9/5/63

YEAR	TM/L	W	L	PCT	G	GS	CG	SH	SV	IP	H	HR	BB	SO	RAT	ERA	ERA+	OAV	OOB	BH	AVG	PB	PR	/A	PD	TPI
1963	NY-N	0	0	—	1	0	0	0	0	1^2	3	0	0	1	16.2	10.80	32	.429	.429	0	—	0	-1	-1	0	0.0
1964	NY-N	0	0	—	2	0	0	0	0	3	4	1	2	2	18.0	9.00	40	.333	.429	0	—	0	-2	-2	0	0.0
Total 2		0	0	—	3	0	0	0	0	4^2	7	1	2	3	17.4	9.64	37	.368	.429	0	—	0	-3	-3	0	0.0

● FRANK DIMICHELE
Dimichele, Frank Lawrence b: 2/16/65, Philadelphia, Pa. BR/TL, 6'3", 205 lbs. Deb: 4/8/88

YEAR	TM/L	W	L	PCT	G	GS	CG	SH	SV	IP	H	HR	BB	SO	RAT	ERA	ERA+	OAV	OOB	BH	AVG	PB	PR	/A	PD	TPI
1988	Cal-A	0	0	—	4	0	0	0	0	8	9	2	7	3	21.2	9.64	40	.265	.333	0	—	0	-3	-3	-0	0.0

● BILL DINNEEN
Dinneen, William Henry "Big Bill" b: 4/5/1876, Syracuse, N.Y. d: 1/13/55, Syracuse, N.Y. BR/TR, 6'1", 190 lbs. Deb: 4/22/1898 U

YEAR	TM/L	W	L	PCT	G	GS	CG	SH	SV	IP	H	HR	BB	SO	RAT	ERA	ERA+	OAV	OOB	BH	AVG	PB	PR	/A	PD	TPI
1898	Was-N	9	16	.360	29	27	22	0	0	218^1	238	6	88	83	14.1	4.00	92	.275	.353	8	.100	-4	-9	-8	0	-1.2
1899	Was-N	14	20	.412	37	35	30	0	0	291	350	6	106	91	14.4	3.93	100	.297	.361	36	.303	5	-2	-0	4	0.8
1900	Bos-N	20	14	.588	40	37	33	1	0	320^2	304	11	105	107	11.7	3.12	133	.250	.314	35	.280	2	21	**36**	2	**3.6**
1901	Bos-N	15	18	.455	37	34	31	0	0	309^1	295	8	77	141	11.0	2.94	123	.250	.299	31	.211	0	13	23	-1	2.1
1902	Bos-A	21	21	.500	42	42	39	2	0	371^1	348	9	99	136	11.0	2.93	122	.248	.302	18	.128	-6	27	27	-6	1.3
1903	*Bos-A	21	13	.618	37	34	32	6	2	299	255	6	66	148	9.8	2.26	134	.230	.276	17	.160	-1	23	26	-1	2.6
1904	Bos-A	23	14	.622	37	37	37	5	0	335^2	283	8	63	153	9.3	2.20	122	.230	.268	25	.208	-0	15	18	-2	1.7
1905	Bos-A	12	14	.462	31	29	23	2	1	243^2	235	7	50	97	10.8	3.73	72	.255	.300	13	.148	-3	-29	-28	0	-3.1
1906	Bos-A	8	19	.296	28	27	22	1	0	218^2	209	4	52	60	10.8	2.92	94	.255	.300	7	.111	-1	-6	-4	-3	-0.9
1907	Bos-A	0	4	.000	5	5	3	0	0	32^2	42	3	8	14	14.3	5.23	49	.314	.361	0	.000	-1	-10	-10	-1	-1.2
	StL-A	7	10	.412	24	16	15	2	4	155^1	153	3	33	38	11.1	2.43	104	.259	.304	10	.204	2	1	3	0	0.0
	Yr	7	14	.333	29	21	18	2	4	188	195	8	41	46	11.5	2.92	87	.269	.312	10	.169	1	-8	-8	-4	-1.2
1908	StL-A	14	7	.667	27	16	11	1	0	167	133	2	39	52	10.2	2.10	114	.231	.300	12	.203	0	5	5	-3	0.4
1909	StL-A	6	7	.462	17	13	8	3	0	112	112	3	29	26	11.4	3.46	70	.267	.316	7	.194	-2	-12	-13	-0	-1.3
Total 12		170	177	.490	391	352	306	23	7	3074^2	2957	78	829	1127	11.3	3.01	107	.254	.308	219	.192	-5	38	71	-15	4.8

● RON DIORIO
Diorio, Ronald Michael b: 7/15/46, Waterbury, Conn. BR/TR, 6'6", 212 lbs. Deb: 8/9/73

YEAR	TM/L	W	L	PCT	G	GS	CG	SH	SV	IP	H	HR	BB	SO	RAT	ERA	ERA+	OAV	OOB	BH	AVG	PB	PR	/A	PD	TPI
1973	Phi-N	0	0	—	23	0	0	0	1	19^1	18	1	6	11	11.2	2.33	163	.257	.316	0	—	0	3	3	-0	0.0
1974	Phi-N	0	0	—	2	0	0	0	0	1	2	1	1	0	27.0	18.00	21	.400	.500	0	—	0	-2	-2	0	0.0
Total 2		0	0	—	25	0	0	0	1	20^1	20	2	7	11	12.0	3.10	122	.267	.329	0	—	0	2	0		0.0

YEAR	TM/L	W	L	PCT	G	GS	CG	SH	SV	IP	H	HR	BB	SO	RAT	ERA	ERA+	OAV	OOB	BH	AVG	PB	PR	/A	PD	TPI

● **FRANK DiPINO**   DiPino, Frank Michael   b: 10/22/56, Syracuse, N.Y.   BL/TL, 6′, 180 lbs.   Deb: 9/14/81

1981	Mil-A	0	0	—	2	0	0	0	0	2¹	0	0	3	3	11.6	0.00	—	.000	.300	0	—	0	1	1	-0	0.2
1982	Hou-N	2	2	.500	6	6	0	0	0	28¹	32	1	11	25	13.7	6.04	55	.302	.368	0	.000	-1	-8	-9	-1	-1.2
1983	Hou-N	3	4	.429	53	0	0	0	20	71¹	52	2	20	67	9.2	2.65	128	.205	.265	1	.167	1	8	6	1	1.1
1984	Hou-N	4	9	.308	57	0	0	0	14	75¹	74	3	36	65	13.3	3.35	99	.260	.345	0	.000	-1	2	-0	0	-0.1
1985	Hou-N	3	7	.300	54	0	0	0	0	76	69	7	43	49	13.5	4.03	86	.248	.353	2	.167	-0	-4	-5	-2	-0.8
1986	Hou-N	1	3	.250	31	0	0	0	3	40¹	27	5	16	27	10.0	3.57	101	.189	.280	1	.200	0	1	0	0	0.1
	Chi-N	2	4	.333	30	0	0	0	0	40	47	6	14	43	13.7	5.17	78	.297	.355	0	.000	-0	-6	-5	1	-0.6
	Yr	3	7	.300	61	0	0	0	3	80¹	74	11	30	70	11.7	4.37	87	.243	.311	1	.167	-0	-6	-5	2	-0.5
1987	Chi-N	3	3	.500	69	0	0	0	4	80	75	7	34	61	12.4	3.15	136	.252	.330	1	.500	-0	8	10	1	0.9
1988	Chi-N	2	3	.400	63	0	0	0	0	90¹	102	6	32	69	13.4	4.98	72	.285	.344	1	.100	-0	-15	-14	-0	-1.0
1989	StL-N	9	0	1.000	67	0	0	0	0	88¹	73	6	20	44	9.5	2.45	148	.227	.273	1	.077	-1	10	12	0	1.1
1990	StL-N	5	2	.714	62	0	0	0	3	81	92	8	31	49	13.8	4.56	84	.294	.359	1	.250	0	-7	-7	1	-0.5
1992	StL-N	0	0	—	9	0	0	0	0	11	9	0	3	8	9.8	1.64	207	.220	.273	1	1.000	0	2	2	0	0.1
1993	KC-A	1	1	.500	11	0	0	0	0	15²	21	2	6	5	16.7	6.89	66	.328	.403	0	—	0	-4	-4	0	-0.6
Total	12	35	38	.479	514	6	0	0	56	700	673	53	269	515	12.2	3.83	96	.256	.328	9	.125	-1	-12	-13	2	-1.3

● **JERRY DiPOTO**   DiPoto, Gerard Peter   b: 5/24/68, Jersey City, N.J.   BR/TR, 6′2″, 200 lbs.   Deb: 5/11/93

1993	Cle-A	4	4	.500	46	0	0	0	11	56¹	57	0	30	41	14.1	2.40	180	.270	.364	0	—	0	12	12	1	2.1
1994	Cle-A	0	0	—	7	0	0	0	0	15²	26	1	10	9	21.3	8.04	61	.406	.493	0	—	0	-6	-5	0	-0.1
Total	2	4	4	.500	53	0	0	0	11	72	83	1	40	50	15.6	3.63	123	.302	.394	0	—	0	6	7	1	2.0

● **GEORGE DISCH**   Disch, George Charles   b: 3/15/1879, Lincoln, Mo.   d: 8/25/50, Rapid City, S.D.   5′11″   Deb: 8/8/05

| 1905 | Det-A | 0 | 2 | .000 | 8 | 3 | 1 | 0 | 0 | 47² | 43 | 1 | 8 | 14 | 10.0 | 2.64 | 104 | .242 | .282 | 2 | .105 | -1 | 0 | 1 | -0 | -0.1 |

● **ALEC DISTASO**   Distaso, Alec John   b: 12/23/48, Los Angeles, Cal.   BR/TR, 6′2″, 200 lbs.   Deb: 4/20/69

| 1969 | Chi-N | 0 | 0 | — | 2 | 0 | 0 | 0 | 0 | 4² | 6 | 0 | 1 | 1 | 13.5 | 3.86 | 104 | .316 | .350 | 0 | — | 0 | -0 | 0 | 0 | 0.0 |

● **ART DITMAR**   Ditmar, Arthur John   b: 4/3/29, Winthrop, Mass.   BR/TR, 6′2″, 196 lbs.   Deb: 4/19/54

1954	Phi-A	1	4	.200	14	5	0	0	0	39¹	50	4	36	14	19.9	6.41	61	.314	.444	1	.125	-0	-12	-11	-0	-1.2
1955	KC-A	12	12	.500	35	22	7	1	1	175¹	180	23	86	79	14.0	5.03	83	.270	.360	13	.210	-0	-21	-17	1	-2.0
1956	KC-A	12	22	.353	44	34	14	2	1	254¹	254	30	108	126	13.1	4.42	98	.262	.340	13	.143	-4	-7	-3	-1	-0.8
1957	*NY-A	8	3	.727	46	11	0	0	6	127¹	128	9	35	64	11.7	3.25	110	.261	.313	7	.200	-0	8	5	-1	0.3
1958	*NY-A	9	8	.529	38	13	4	0	4	139²	124	14	38	52	10.8	3.42	103	.237	.295	11	.250	2	5	2	-2	0.2
1959	*NY-A	13	9	.591	38	25	7	1	1	202	156	17	52	96	9.6	2.90	126	.211	.270	15	.197	2	22	17	-1	1.8
1960	*NY-A	15	9	.625	34	28	8	1	0	200	195	25	56	65	11.3	3.06	117	.256	.308	11	.159	0	18	12	-2	1.1
1961	NY-A	2	3	.400	12	8	1	0	0	54¹	59	9	14	24	12.4	4.64	80	.285	.336	1	.053	-2	-4	-6	-1	-0.6
	KC-A	0	5	.000	20	5	0	0	1	54	60	6	23	19	14.2	5.67	74	.286	.362	2	.167	-0	-10	-9	-0	-0.8
	Yr	2	8	.200	32	13	1	0	1	108¹	119	15	37	43	13.1	5.15	77	.281	.341	3	.097	-2	-14	-14	-1	-1.4
1962	KC-A	2	0	.000	6	5	0	0	0	21²	31	1	13	13	19.1	6.65	64	.323	.414	1	.167	-0	-6	-6	-0	-0.5
Total	9	72	77	.483	287	156	41	5	14	1268	1237	138	461	552	12.3	3.98	97	.256	.326	75	.178	-3	-7	-16	-6	-2.5

● **SONNY DIXON**   Dixon, John Craig   b: 11/5/24, Charlotte, N.C.   BB/TR, 6′2.5″, 205 lbs.   Deb: 4/20/53

1953	Was-A	5	8	.385	43	6	3	0	3	120	123	13	31	40	11.7	3.75	104	.267	.316	4	.154	-0	3	2	1	0.4
1954	Was-A	1	2	.333	16	0	0	0	1	29²	26	3	12	11	11.5	3.03	117	.236	.311	0	.000	-1	2	2	1	0.2
	Phi-A	5	7	.417	38	6	1	0	4	107¹	136	8	27	42	13.9	4.86	80	.308	.352	7	.250	2	-14	-11	3	-0.8
	Yr	6	9	.400	54	6	1	0	5	137	162	11	39	49	13.4	4.47	86	.293	.343	7	.206	1	-11	-10	3	-0.6
1955	KC-A	0	0	—	2	0	0	0	0	1²	3	0	0	0	32.4	16.20	26	.545	.545	0	—	0	-2	-2	0	0.0
1956	NY-A	0	1	.000	3	0	0	0	1	4¹	5	0	5	1	20.8	2.08	186	.294	.455	0	.000	-0	1	1	0	0.2
Total	4	11	18	.379	102	12	4	0	9	263	296	25	75	90	12.9	4.17	93	.284	.335	11	.180	1	-9	-9	6	0.0

● **KEN DIXON**   Dixon, Kenneth John   b: 10/17/60, Monroe, Va.   BB/TR, 5′11″, 166 lbs.   Deb: 9/22/84

1984	Bal-A	0	1	.000	2	2	0	0	0	13	14	1	4	8	12.5	4.15	93	.269	.321	0	—	0	-0	-0	0	0.0
1985	Bal-A	8	4	.667	34	18	3	1	1	162	144	20	64	108	11.7	3.67	110	.237	.312	0	—	0	9	7	-1	0.3
1986	Bal-A	11	13	.458	35	33	2	0	0	202¹	194	33	83	170	12.4	4.58	90	.249	.322	0	—	0	-9	-10	-1	-1.1
1987	Bal-A	7	10	.412	34	15	0	0	5	105	128	31	27	91	13.4	6.43	68	.292	.334	0	—	0	-23	-24	-0	-3.4
Total	4	26	28	.481	105	68	5	1	6	482¹	480	85	178	377	12.4	4.66	89	.256	.322	0	—	0	-24	-28	-2	-4.2

● **STEVE DIXON**   Dixon, Steven Ross   b: 8/3/69, Cincinnati, Ohio   BL/TL, 6′, 190 lbs.   Deb: 9/7/93

1993	StL-N	0	0	—	4	0	0	0	0	2²	7	1	5	2	40.5	33.75	12	.538	.667	0	—	0	-9	-9	0	0.0
1994	StL-N	0	0	—	2	0	0	0	0	2¹	3	0	8	1	42.4	23.14	18	.333	.647	0	—	0	-5	-5	0	0.0
Total	2	0	0	—	6	0	0	0	0	5	10	1	13	3	41.4	28.80	14	.455	.657	0	—	0	-14	-14	0	0.0

● **TOM DIXON**   Dixon, Thomas Earl   b: 4/23/55, Orlando, Fla.   BR/TR, 5′11″, 175 lbs.   Deb: 7/30/77

1977	Hou-N	1	0	1.000	9	4	1	0	0	30¹	40	4	0	15	14.2	3.26	109	.320	.361	0	.000	-1	2	1	0	0.0
1978	Hou-N	7	11	.389	30	19	3	2	1	140	140	8	40	66	11.6	3.99	83	.265	.318	4	.100	-2	-6	-11	-1	-1.5
1979	Hou-N	1	2	.333	19	1	0	0	0	25²	39	2	15	9	18.9	6.66	53	.348	.425	1	1.000	0	-8	-9	1	-0.8
1983	Mon-N	0	1	.000	4	0	0	0	0	3²	6	1	1	4	19.6	9.82	37	.375	.444	0	—	0	-3	-3	-0	-0.6
Total	4	9	14	.391	62	24	4	2	1	199²	225	11	63	94	13.1	4.33	78	.288	.343	5	.104	-2	-15	-21	-0	-2.9

● **BILL DOAK**   Doak, William Leopold "Spittin' Bill"   b: 1/28/1891, Pittsburgh, Pa.   d: 11/26/54, Bradenton, Fla.   BR/TR, 6′0.5″, 165 lbs.   Deb: 9/1/12

1912	Cin-N	0	0	—	1	1	0	0	0	2	4	0	1	0	22.5	4.50	75	.444	.500	0	—	0	-0	-0	-0	0.0
1913	StL-N	2	8	.200	15	12	5	1	0	93	79	4	39	51	11.9	3.10	104	.236	.325	1	.032	-3	1	1	-1	-0.1
1914	StL-N	19	6	.760	36	33	16	7	1	256	193	2	87	118	10.1	**1.72**	**162**	.216	.290	10	.118	-3	30	31	5	3.2
1915	StL-N	16	18	.471	38	36	19	3	1	276	263	4	85	124	11.6	2.64	106	.261	.323	15	.174	1	3	5	7	1.5
1916	StL-N	12	8	.600	29	26	11	2	0	192	177	5	55	82	11.0	2.63	101	.251	.308	8	.129	-2	-0	0	3	0.1
1917	StL-N	16	20	.444	44	37	16	3	2	281²	257	6	85	111	11.2	3.10	87	.250	.312	12	.126	-4	-12	-13	5	-1.6
1918	StL-N	9	15	.375	31	23	16	1	1	211	191	4	60	74	10.9	2.43	111	.249	.306	12	.182	1	8	7	5	1.5
1919	StL-N	13	14	.481	31	29	13	3	0	202²	182	5	55	69	10.6	3.11	90	.246	.299	7	.109	-4	-4	-7	5	-0.9
1920	StL-N	20	12	.625	39	37	20	5	1	270	256	7	80	90	11.4	2.53	118	.253	.312	10	.114	-6	18	14	0	0.9
1921	StL-N	15	6	**.714**	32	28	13	1	1	208²	224	9	37	83	11.4	**2.59**	**142**	.278	.313	10	.143	-3	28	25	2	2.2
1922	StL-N	11	13	.458	37	29	8	2	2	180¹	222	12	69	73	14.7	5.54	70	.311	.374	7	.130	-3	-29	-34	0	-3.9
1923	StL-N	8	13	.381	30	26	7	2	0	185	199	4	69	53	13.2	3.26	120	.279	.346	4	.045	-9	15	13	3	0.8
1924	StL-N	2	1	.667	11	1	0	0	3	22	25	0	14	7	16.0	3.27	116	.313	.415	1	.200	-0	1	1	1	0.2
	Bro-N	11	5	.688	21	16	8	1	0	149¹	130	8	35	32	10.1	3.07	122	.239	.289	10	.179	-0	13	11	3	1.3
	Yr	13	6	.684	32	17	8	1	3	171¹	155	8	49	39	10.9	3.10	121	.249	.307	11	.180	-1	15	12	5	1.5
1927	Bro-N	11	8	.579	27	20	6	1	0	145	153	6	40	32	12.2	3.48	114	.271	.322	6	.128	-3	7	8	1	0.8
1928	Bro-N	3	8	.273	28	12	4	1	3	99¹	104	1	35	12	13.0	3.26	122	.271	.340	4	.111	-2	8	8	3	0.8
1929	StL-N	1	2	.333	3	2	0	0	0	9	17	1	5	3	22.0	12.00	39	.415	.478	0	.000	0	-7	-7	-0	-1.6
Total	16	169	157	.518	453	368	162	34	16	2782²	2676	71	851	1014	11.6	2.98	107	.259	.319	115	.127	-42	80	64	43	5.3

● **WALT DOANE**   Doane, Walter Rudolph   b: 3/12/1887, Bellevue, Idaho   d: 10/19/35, W.Brandywine, Pa.   BL/TR, 6′, 165 lbs.   Deb: 9/20/09   ◆

1909	Cle-A	0	1	.000	1	1	0	0	0	5	10	0	1	2	19.8	5.40	47	.400	.423	1	.111	-0	-2	-2	-0	-0.3
1910	Cle-A	0	0	—	6	0	0	0	0	17²	31	1	8	8	20.4	5.60	46	.413	.476	2	.286	1	-6	-6	-1	0.0
Total	2	0	1	.000	7	1	0	0	0	22²	41	1	9	9	20.3	5.56	46	.410	.464	3	.188	1	-8	-8	-1	-0.3

YEAR	TM/L	W	L	PCT	G	GS	CG	SH	SV	IP	H	HR	BB	SO	RAT	ERA	ERA+	OAV	OOB	BH	AVG	PB	PR	/A	PD	TPI

● JOHN DOBB   Dobb, John Kenneth "Lefty" b: 11/15/01, Muskegon, Mich. d: 7/31/91, Muskegon, Mich. BR/TL, 6'2", 180 lbs. Deb: 8/13/24

| 1924 | Chi-A | 0 | 0 | — | 2 | 0 | 0 | 0 | 0 | 2 | 4 | 0 | 1 | 2 | 22.5 | 9.00 | 46 | .400 | .455 | 0 | — | 0 | -1 | -1 | -0 | 0.0 |

● RAY DOBENS   Dobens, Raymond Joseph "Lefty" b: 7/28/06, Nashua, N.H. d: 4/21/80, Stuart, Fla. BL/TL, 5'8", 175 lbs. Deb: 7/7/29

| 1929 | Bos-A | 0 | 0 | — | 11 | 2 | 0 | 0 | 0 | 28¹ | 32 | 0 | 9 | 4 | 13.3 | 3.81 | 112 | .302 | .362 | 3 | .375 | 1 | 1 | 1 | -1 | 0.0 |

● JESS DOBERNIC   Dobernic, Andrew Joseph b: 11/20/17, Mt.Olive, Ill. BR/TR, 5'10", 170 lbs. Deb: 7/2/39

1939	Chi-A	0	1	.000	4	0	0	0	0	3¹	3	0	6	1	27.0	13.50	35	.231	.500	0	.000	-0	-3	-3	0	-0.7
1948	Chi-N	7	2	.778	54	0	0	0	0	85²	67	8	40	48	11.3	3.15	124	.213	.303	2	.200	-0	8	7	-2	0.5
1949	Chi-N	0	0	—	4	0	0	0	0	4	9	2	4	0	29.3	20.25	20	.450	.542	0	—	0	-7	-7	-0	0.0
	Cin-N	0	0	—	14	0	0	0	0	19¹	28	7	16	6	20.5	9.78	43	.329	.436	0	.000	0	-12	-12	-0	0.0
	Yr	0	0	—	18	0	0	0	0	23¹	37	9	20	6	22.0	11.57	36	.352	.456	0	.000	-0	-20	-19	-0	0.0
Total 3		7	3	.700	76	0	0	0	0	112¹	107	17	66	55	14.0	5.21	76	.247	.349	2	.154	-0	-15	-15	-2	-0.2

● CHUCK DOBSON   Dobson, Charles Thomas b: 1/10/44, Kansas City, Mo. BR/TR, 6'4", 200 lbs. Deb: 4/19/66

1966	KC-A	4	6	.400	14	14	1	0	0	83²	71	7	50	61	13.2	4.09	83	.234	.346	3	.115	-1	-6	-6	-1	-0.7
1967	KC-A	10	10	.500	32	29	4	1	0	197²	172	17	75	110	11.4	3.69	86	.233	.306	13	.181	0	-10	-11	-0	-1.1
1968	Oak-A	12	14	.462	35	34	11	3	0	225¹	197	20	80	168	11.2	3.00	94	.234	.303	15	.200	2	-0	-4	2	-0.2
1969	Oak-A	15	13	.536	35	35	11	1	0	235¹	244	16	80	137	12.4	3.86	89	.270	.330	8	.101	-3	-6	-11	-2	-1.7
1970	Oak-A	16	15	.516	41	40	13	**5**	0	267	230	32	92	149	11.0	3.74	95	.229	.297	11	.118	-3	-1	-6	-2	-1.2
1971	Oak-A	15	5	.750	30	30	7	1	0	189	185	24	71	100	12.2	3.81	88	.259	.327	13	.197	-3	-7	-10	-0	-0.7
1973	Oak-A	0	1	.000	1	1	0	0	0	2¹	6	1	2	3	30.9	7.71	46	.429	.500	0	—	0	-1	-1	-0	-0.3
1974	Cal-A	2	3	.400	5	5	2	0	0	30	39	3	13	16	15.6	5.70	60	.315	.380	0	—	0	-7	-8	-0	-1.0
1975	Cal-A	0	2	.000	9	2	0	0	0	28	30	5	13	14	14.5	6.75	53	.275	.363	0	—	0	-9	-10	-1	-0.7
Total 9		74	69	.517	202	190	49	11	0	1258¹	1174	125	476	758	11.9	3.78	87	.247	.318	63	.153	-2	-48	-68	-1	-7.6

● JOE DOBSON   Dobson, Joseph Gordon "Burrhead" b: 1/20/17, Durant, Okla. d: 6/23/94, Jacksonville, Fla. BR/TR, 6'2", 197 lbs. Deb: 4/26/39

1939	Cle-A	2	3	.400	35	3	0	0	1	78	87	3	51	27	16.0	5.88	75	.290	.395	1	.056	-2	-11	-13	1	-0.8
1940	Cle-A	3	7	.300	40	7	2	1	3	100	101	8	48	57	13.4	4.95	85	.268	.351	3	.125	-1	-6	-8	-0	-0.8
1941	Bos-A	12	5	.706	27	18	7	1	0	134¹	136	8	67	69	13.7	4.49	93	.262	.349	7	.149	0	-5	-5	-2	-0.7
1942	Bos-A	11	9	.550	30	23	10	3	0	182²	155	9	68	72	11.1	3.30	113	.231	.303	10	.145	-1	7	9	2	0.9
1943	Bos-A	7	11	.389	25	20	9	3	0	164¹	144	4	57	72	11.0	3.12	106	.239	.305	5	.096	-3	3	4	-2	-0.2
1946	*Bos-A	13	7	.650	32	24	9	1	0	166²	148	11	68	91	11.7	3.24	113	.234	.309	5	.100	-2	5	8	2	0.9
1947	Bos-A	18	8	.692	33	31	15	1	0	228²	203	16	73	110	10.9	2.95	132	.238	**.299**	16	.208	1	19	24	-2	2.5
1948	Bos-A☆	16	10	.615	38	32	16	5	2	245¹	237	14	92	116	12.1	3.56	123	.253	.320	17	.202	1	20	23	-1	2.2
1949	Bos-A	14	12	.538	33	27	12	2	2	212²	219	12	97	87	13.5	3.85	113	.269	.348	10	.147	-1	8	12	-1	1.1
1950	Bos-A	15	10	.600	39	27	12	1	4	206²	217	15	81	81	13.0	4.18	117	.275	.343	15	.214	1	9	16	1	2.0
1951	Chi-A	7	6	.538	28	21	6	0	3	146²	136	17	51	67	11.5	3.62	111	.248	.312	3	.065	-6	8	7	0	0.0
1952	Chi-A	14	10	.583	29	25	11	3	1	200²	164	11	60	101	10.0	2.51	145	.222	.280	12	.190	1	26	25	-2	2.8
1953	Chi-A	5	5	.500	23	15	3	1	1	100²	96	10	37	50	11.9	3.67	110	.249	.314	2	.069	-2	4	4	-1	0.1
1954	Bos-A	0	0	—	2	0	0	0	0	2²	5	0	1	1	20.3	6.75	61	.385	.429	0	—	0	-1	-1	-0	0.0
Total 14		137	103	.571	414	273	112	22	18	2170	2048	137	851	992	12.1	3.62	112	.250	.322	106	.152	-15	86	105	-5	10.0

● PAT DOBSON   Dobson, Patrick Edward b: 2/12/42, Depew, N.Y. BR/TR, 6'3", 190 lbs. Deb: 5/31/67 C

1967	Det-A	1	2	.333	28	1	0	0	0	49¹	38	6	27	34	12.2	2.92	112	.216	.327	0	.000	-1	2	2	-1	0.0
1968	*Det-A	5	8	.385	47	10	2	1	7	125	89	13	48	93	10.0	2.66	113	.200	.281	4	.143	0	4	5	1	0.7
1969	Det-A	5	10	.333	49	9	1	0	9	105	100	10	39	64	12.0	3.60	104	.253	.322	2	.091	-1	0	0	1	0.1
1970	SD-N	14	15	.483	40	34	8	1	1	251	257	28	78	185	12.2	3.76	106	.265	.322	10	.141	-0	8	6	-0	0.5
1971	*Bal-A	20	8	.714	38	37	18	4	1	282¹	248	24	63	187	10.0	2.90	116	.235	.279	10	.110	-3	18	14	-1	0.9
1972	Bal-A☆	16	18	.471	38	36	13	3	0	268¹	220	13	69	161	9.8	2.65	116	.224	.278	12	.141	-2	12	13	-2	1.3
1973	Atl-N	3	7	.300	12	10	1	1	0	57²	73	1	19	23	14.5	4.99	79	.315	.369	1	.067	-1	-9	-7	-0	-1.2
	NY-A	9	8	.529	22	21	6	1	0	142¹	150	22	34	70	11.8	4.17	88	.266	.311	0	—	0	-6	-8	0	-0.8
1974	NY-A	19	15	.559	39	39	12	2	0	281	282	23	75	157	11.6	3.07	113	.262	.312	0	—	0	17	13	-1	1.4
1975	NY-A	11	14	.440	33	30	7	1	0	207²	205	21	83	129	12.5	4.07	89	.261	.333	0	—	0	-7	-10	-0	-1.1
1976	Cle-A	16	12	.571	35	35	6	0	0	217¹	226	15	65	117	12.1	3.48	100	.272	.327	0	—	0	1	0	-1	0.0
1977	Cle-A	3	12	.200	33	17	0	0	1	131¹	155	23	65	81	14.9	6.14	64	.299	.378	0	—	0	-31	-33	-0	-3.1
Total 11		122	129	.486	414	279	74	14	19	2120¹	2043	197	665	1301	11.5	3.54	100	.263	.314	39	.123	-8	10	-3	-3	-1.3

● GEORGE DOCKINS   Dockins, George Woodrow "Lefty" b: 5/5/17, Clyde, Kan. BL/TL, 6', 175 lbs. Deb: 5/5/45

1945	StL-N	8	6	.571	31	12	5	2	0	126¹	132	4	38	33	12.1	3.21	117	.269	.321	6	.176	1	8	8	1	0.8
1947	Bro-N	0	0	—	4	0	0	0	0	5¹	10	2	2	1	20.3	11.81	35	.400	.444	0	.000	-0	-5	-5	0	0.0
Total 2		8	6	.571	35	12	5	2	0	131²	142	6	40	34	12.4	3.55	106	.275	.327	6	.171	1	4	3	-0	0.8

● SAM DODGE   Dodge, Samuel Edward b: 12/9/1889, Neath, Pa. d: 4/5/66, Utica, N.Y. BR/TR, 6'1", 170 lbs. Deb: 9/24/21

1921	Bos-A	0	0	—	1	0	0	0	0	1	1	0	1	0	18.0	9.00	47	.500	.667	0	—	0	-1	-1	-0	0.0
1922	Bos-A	0	0	—	3	0	0	0	0	6	11	0	3	3	21.0	4.50	91	.379	.438	0	.000	-0	-0	-0	0	0.0
Total 2		0	0	—	4	0	0	0	0	7	12	0	4	3	20.6	5.14	80	.387	.457	0	.000	-0	-1	-1	-0	0.0

● FRED DOE   Doe, Alfred George "Count" b: 4/18/1864, Rockport, Mass. d: 10/4/38, Quincy, Mass. BR/TR, 5'10", 165 lbs. Deb: 8/23/1890

1890	Buf-P	0	1	.000	1	1	1	0	0	6	10	1	0	7	25.5	12.00	34	.356	.485	0	—	-0	-5	-5	0	-0.5
	Pit-P	0	0	—	1	0	0	0	0	4	4	0	2	1	13.5	4.50	87	.249	.332	1	.500	-0	-0	-0	-0	0.0
	Yr	0	1	.000	2	1	1	0	0	10	14	0	9	4	20.7	9.00	45	.317	.433	1	.250	-0	-5	-6	-0	-0.5

● ED DOHENY   Doheny, Edwin Richard b: 11/24/1873, Northfield, Vt. d: 12/29/16, Medfield, Mass. BL/TL, 5'10.5", 165 lbs. Deb: 9/16/1895

1895	NY-N	0	3	.000	3	3	3	0	0	25²	37	2	19	9	20.7	6.66	70	.332	.442	1	.100	-1	-5	-6	-0	-0.5
1896	NY-N	6	7	.462	17	15	9	0	0	108¹	112	3	59	39	14.7	4.49	94	.265	.363	6	.150	-2	-1	-3	-0	-0.5
1897	NY-N	4	4	.500	10	10	10	0	0	85	69	0	45	37	12.9	2.12	196	.220	.333	7	.200	-1	21	19	3	1.6
1898	NY-N	7	19	.269	28	27	23	0	0	213	238	1	101	96	15.2	3.68	95	.280	.370	14	.163	-1	-2	-5	3	-0.3
1899	NY-N	14	17	.452	35	33	30	1	0	265¹	282	2	156	115	16.1	4.51	83	.272	.386	21	.241	-0	-19	-22	5	-1.6
1900	NY-N	4	14	.222	20	18	12	0	0	133²	148	0	96	44	17.9	5.45	66	.280	.411	12	.222	-0	-26	-27	2	-2.7
1901	NY-N	2	5	.286	10	6	6	0	0	74	88	1	17	36	13.5	4.50	73	.293	.344	10	.345	3	-10	-10	-0	-0.5
	Pit-N	6	2	.750	11	10	6	1	0	76²	68	1	22	28	11.2	2.00	164	.236	.302	3	.115	0	11	11	-2	0.9
	Yr	8	7	.533	21	16	12	1	0	150²	156	2	39	64	11.9	3.23	102	.263	.314	13	.236	4	2	1	-1	0.4
1902	Pit-N	16	4	.800	22	21	19	2	0	188¹	161	0	61	75	11.3	2.53	108	.231	.307	12	.156	-2	5	4	-1	0.1
1903	Pit-N	16	8	.667	27	25	22	2	0	222²	209	1	89	75	12.8	3.19	101	.252	.338	19	.209	-1	5	1	5	0.5
Total 9		75	83	.475	183	168	140	6	2	1392²	1412	13	665	567	14.3	3.75	94	.263	.359	111	.198	-3	-24	-37	15	-3.0

● JOHN DOHERTY   Doherty, John Harold b: 6/11/67, New York, N.Y. BR/TR, 6'4", 200 lbs. Deb: 4/8/92

1992	Det-A	7	4	.636	47	11	0	0	3	116	131	4	25	37	12.4	3.88	102	.287	.329	—	0	0	1	1	1	0.2
1993	Det-A	14	11	.560	32	31	3	2	0	184²	205	19	48	63	12.6	4.44	97	.286	.335	—	0	-2	-3	-2	-0.5
1994	Det-A	6	7	.462	18	17	2	0	0	101¹	139	13	26	28	14.9	6.48	73	.337	.380	—	0	-19	-19	0	-1.9
Total 3		27	22	.551	97	59	5	2	3	402	475	36	99	128	13.1	4.79	90	.299	.345	—	0	-21	-21	-0	-2.2

● JOHN DOLAN   Dolan, John b: 9/12/1867, Newport, Ky. d: 5/8/48, Springfield, Ohio TR, 5'10", 170 lbs. Deb: 9/5/1890

| 1890 | Cin-N | 1 | 1 | .500 | 2 | 2 | 2 | 0 | 0 | 18 | 17 | 3 | 10 | 9 | 14.0 | 4.50 | 79 | .242 | .344 | 1 | .125 | -1 | -2 | -2 | -0 | -0.2 |

YEAR	TM/L	W	L	PCT	G	GS	CG	SH	SV	IP	H	HR	BB	SO	RAT	ERA	ERA+	OAV	OOB	BH	AVG	PB	PR	/A	PD	TPI
1891	Col-a	12	11	.522	27	24	19	0	0	203¹	216	8	84	68	13.3	4.16	83	.263	.332	7	.090	-4	-10	-16	-2	-1.9
1892	Was-N	2	2	.500	5	4	3	0	0	37	39	0	15	8	13.4	4.38	74	.260	.331	3	.231	0	-4	-5	-1	-0.4
1893	StL-N	0	1	.000	3	1	1	0	1	17¹	26	1	7	1	17.7	4.15	114	.336	.399	1	.143	0	1	1	-0	0.0
1895	Chi-N	0	1	.000	2	2	1	0	0	11	16	0	6	1	18.8	6.55	78	.334	.419	0	.000	-0	-2	-2	-0	-0.1
Total 5		15	16	.484	39	33	26	0	1	286²	314	12	122	87	13.8	4.30	83	.269	.340	12	.110	-5	-17	-23	-3	-2.6

● COZY DOLAN
Dolan, Patrick Henry b: 12/3/1872, Cambridge, Mass. d: 3/29/07, Louisville, Ky. BL/TL, 5'10", 160 lbs. Deb: 4/26/1895 ♦

YEAR	TM/L	W	L	PCT	G	GS	CG	SH	SV	IP	H	HR	BB	SO	RAT	ERA	ERA+	OAV	OOB	BH	AVG	PB	PR	/A	PD	TPI
1895	Bos-N	11	7	.611	25	21	18	3	1	198¹	215	11	67	47	13.4	4.27	120	.272	.340	20	.241	-1	11	18	4	1.5
1896	Bos-N	1	4	.200	6	5	3	0	0	41	55	1	27	14	18.7	4.83	94	.318	.419	2	.143	-1	-2	-1	-0	-0.3
1905	Bos-N	0	1	.000	2	0	0	0	0	4	7	2	1	1	18.0	9.00	34	.368	.400	119	.275	1	-3	-3	-0	-0.5
1906	Bos-N	0	1	.000	2	0	0	0	0	12	12	1	6	7	13.5	4.50	60	.300	.391	136	.248	-0	-2	-2	-1	-0.2
Total 4		12	13	.480	35	26	21	3	1	255¹	289	15	101	69	14.3	4.44	109	.283	.357	855	.269	-2	4	12	3	0.5

● TOM DOLAN
Dolan, Thomas J. b: 1/10/1859, New York, N.Y. d: 1/16/13, St. Louis, Mo. BR/TR, Deb: 9/30/1879 ♦

YEAR	TM/L	W	L	PCT	G	GS	CG	SH	SV	IP	H	HR	BB	SO	RAT	ERA	ERA+	OAV	OOB	BH	AVG	PB	PR	/A	PD	TPI
1883	StL-a	0	0	—	1	0	0	0	0	4	4	0	0	1	9.0	4.50	90	.244	.244	63	.214	-0	-1	-0	0	0.0

● ART DOLL
Doll, Arthur James "Moose" b: 5/7/13, Chicago, Ill. d: 4/28/78, Calumet City, Ill. BR/TR, 6'1", 190 lbs. Deb: 9/21/35 ♦

YEAR	TM/L	W	L	PCT	G	GS	CG	SH	SV	IP	H	HR	BB	SO	RAT	ERA	ERA+	OAV	OOB	BH	AVG	PB	PR	/A	PD	TPI
1936	Bos-N	0	1	.000	1	1	0	0	0	8	11	1	2	2	15.8	3.38	114	.355	.412	0	.000	-0	1	0	-0	0.0
1938	Bos-N	0	0	—	3	0	0	0	0	4	4	0	3	1	15.8	2.25	153	.286	.412	1	1.000	1	1	1	0	0.1
Total 2		0	1	.000	4	1	0	0	0	12	15	1	5	3	15.8	3.00	123	.333	.412	2	.154	0	1	1	-0	0.1

● RED DONAHUE
Donahue, Francis Rostell b: 1/23/1873, Waterbury, Conn. d: 8/25/13, Philadelphia, Pa. BR/TR, 6', 187 lbs. Deb: 5/6/1893

YEAR	TM/L	W	L	PCT	G	GS	CG	SH	SV	IP	H	HR	BB	SO	RAT	ERA	ERA+	OAV	OOB	BH	AVG	PB	PR	/A	PD	TPI
1893	NY-N	0	0	—	2	0	0	0	1	5	8	1	3	1	23.4	9.00	52	.351	.468	0	.000	-0	-2	-2	-0	-0.1
1895	StL-N	0	1	.000	1	1	1	0	0	8	9	2	3	2	14.6	6.75	72	.280	.359	0	.000	-1	-2	-2	0	-0.2
1896	StL-N	7	24	.226	32	32	28	0	0	267	376	6	98	70	16.4	5.80	75	.329	.389	17	.159	-8	-43	-43	-1	-4.3
1897	StL-N	10	35	.222	**46**	42	**38**	1	1	348	484	16	106	64	15.8	6.13	72	.326	.380	33	.213	-3	-70	-67	5	-6.1
1898	Phi-N	16	17	.485	35	35	33	1	0	284¹	327	7	80	57	13.3	3.55	97	.286	.340	16	.143	-7	2	-3	4	-0.7
1899	Phi-N	21	8	.724	35	31	27	4	0	279	292	6	63	51	11.8	3.39	109	.269	.316	20	.180	-5	15	9	3	0.6
1900	Phi-N	15	10	.600	32	24	21	2	2	240	299	6	50	41	13.4	3.60	100	.304	.344	20	.222	-1	3	0	-1	-0.2
1901	Phi-N	21	13	.618	35	34	34	1	1	304¹	307	2	60	89	11.1	2.60	131	.260	.301	11	.094	-9	24	27	-2	1.6
1902	StL-A	22	11	.667	35	34	33	2	0	316¹	322	7	65	63	11.2	2.76	128	.264	.306	11	.093	-9	29	27	7	2.2
1903	StL-A	8	7	.533	16	15	14	0	0	131	145	0	22	51	11.5	2.75	106	.280	.309	8	.157	-2	3	2	0	0.1
	Cle-A	7	9	.438	16	15	14	4	0	136²	142	3	12	45	10.5	2.44	117	.267	.291	8	.151	-1	8	6	1	0.7
	Yr	15	16	.484	32	30	28	4	0	267²	287	3	34	96	11.0	2.59	111	.273	.300	16	.154	-3	11	9	2	0.8
1904	Cle-A	19	14	.576	35	32	30	6	0	277	281	4	49	127	10.9	2.40	105	.264	.299	17	.168	-1	6	4	2	0.5
1905	Cle-A	6	12	.333	20	18	14	1	0	137²	132	2	25	45	10.6	3.40	77	.253	.294	4	.075	-5	-11	-12	1	-1.8
1906	Det-A	13	14	.481	28	28	26	3	0	241	260	1	54	82	12.0	2.73	101	.278	.323	10	.123	-4	-1	-1	-0	-0.3
Total 13		165	175	.485	368	341	313	25	3	2975¹	3384	61	690	788	12.7	3.61	96	.285	.331	175	.152	-57	-40	-52	19	-8.0

● DEACON DONAHUE
Donahue, John Stephen Michael b: 6/23/20, Chicago, Ill. BR/TR, 6', 180 lbs. Deb: 9/16/43

YEAR	TM/L	W	L	PCT	G	GS	CG	SH	SV	IP	H	HR	BB	SO	RAT	ERA	ERA+	OAV	OOB	BH	AVG	PB	PR	/A	PD	TPI
1943	Phi-N	0	0	—	2	0	0	0	0	4	4	0	1	1	13.5	4.50	75	.235	.316	0	—	0	-0	-1	0	0.0
1944	Phi-N	0	2	.000	6	0	0	0	0	9¹	18	0	2	2	19.3	7.71	47	.429	.455	0	.000	-0	-4	-4	0	-0.8
Total 2		0	2	.000	8	0	0	0	0	13¹	22	0	3	3	17.6	6.75	52	.373	.413	0	.000	-0	-5	-5	0	-0.8

● ATLEY DONALD
Donald, Richard Atley "Swampy" b: 8/19/10, Morton, Miss. d: 10/19/92, West Monroe, La. BL/TR, 6'1", 186 lbs. Deb: 4/21/38

YEAR	TM/L	W	L	PCT	G	GS	CG	SH	SV	IP	H	HR	BB	SO	RAT	ERA	ERA+	OAV	OOB	BH	AVG	PB	PR	/A	PD	TPI
1938	NY-A	0	1	.000	2	2	0	0	0	12	7	0	14	6	16.5	5.25	86	.175	.400	1	.167	-0	1	1	-0	-0.1
1939	NY-A	13	3	.813	24	20	11	2	1	153	144	12	60	55	12.0	3.71	118	.247	.317	15	.250	3	16	11	-1	1.1
1940	NY-A	8	3	.727	24	11	6	1	0	118²	113	11	59	60	13.2	3.03	133	.249	.339	6	.146	-2	18	13	-3	0.6
1941	*NY-A	9	5	.643	22	20	10	0	0	159	141	11	69	71	12.1	3.57	110	.237	.320	5	.081	-4	10	6	-0	0.1
1942	*NY-A	11	3	.786	20	19	10	1	0	147²	133	6	45	53	10.8	3.11	111	.239	.296	9	.148	-1	9	5	-2	0.1
1943	NY-A	6	4	.600	22	15	2	0	0	119¹	134	10	38	57	13.0	4.60	70	.276	.329	6	.128	-2	-17	-18	-2	-1.9
1944	NY-A	13	10	.565	30	19	9	1	0	159	173	13	59	48	13.2	3.34	104	.280	.345	10	.182	-0	2	3	-1	0.2
1945	NY-A	5	4	.556	9	9	6	2	0	63²	62	3	25	19	12.3	2.97	117	.248	.316	5	.208	0	3	4	-2	0.3
Total 8		65	33	.663	153	115	54	6	1	932¹	907	66	369	369	12.4	3.52	107	.253	.325	57	.160	-7	39	24	-11	0.4

● ED DONALDS
Donalds, Edward Alexander "Erston" b: 6/22/1885, Bidwell, Ohio d: 7/3/50, Columbus, Ohio BR/TR, 5'11", 180 lbs. Deb: 9/1/12

YEAR	TM/L	W	L	PCT	G	GS	CG	SH	SV	IP	H	HR	BB	SO	RAT	ERA	ERA+	OAV	OOB	BH	AVG	PB	PR	/A	PD	TPI
1912	Cin-N	1	0	1.000	1	0	0	0	0	4	7	0	0	1	15.8	4.50	75	.438	.438	0	.000	-0	-0	-1	0	-0.1

● MIKE DONLIN
Donlin, Michael Joseph "Turkey Mike" b: 5/30/1878, Peoria, Ill. d: 9/24/33, Hollywood, Cal. BL/TL, 5'9", 170 lbs. Deb: 7/19/1899 ♦

YEAR	TM/L	W	L	PCT	G	GS	CG	SH	SV	IP	H	HR	BB	SO	RAT	ERA	ERA+	OAV	OOB	BH	AVG	PB	PR	/A	PD	TPI
1899	StL-N	0	1	.000	3	1	0	0	0	15¹	15	1	14	6	17.6	7.63	52	.256	.408	86	.323	1	-6	-6	1	-0.2
1902	Cin-N	0	0	—	1	0	0	0	0	1	1	0	0	0	9.0	0.00	—	.260	.260	41	.287	0	0	0	-0	0.0
Total 2		0	1	.000	4	1	0	0	0	16¹	16	1	14	6	17.1	7.16	55	.256	.400	1282	.333	1	-6	-6	1	-0.2

● ED DONNELLY
Donnelly, Edward "Big Ed" or "Ned" (b: Edward O'Donnell)
b: 7/29/1880, Hampton, N.Y. d: 11/28/57, Rutland, Vt. BR/TR, 6'1", 205 lbs. Deb: 9/19/11

YEAR	TM/L	W	L	PCT	G	GS	CG	SH	SV	IP	H	HR	BB	SO	RAT	ERA	ERA+	OAV	OOB	BH	AVG	PB	PR	/A	PD	TPI
1911	Bos-N	3	2	.600	5	4	4	1	0	36²	33	0	9	16	10.8	2.45	156	.236	.291	1	.071	-1	4	6	-0	0.6
1912	Bos-N	5	10	.333	37	18	10	0	0	184¹	225	10	72	67	14.7	4.35	82	.304	.370	19	.275	3	-19	-16	1	-0.8
Total 2		8	12	.400	42	22	14	1	0	221	258	10	81	83	14.1	4.03	90	.293	.357	20	.241	1	-15	-10	1	-0.2

● ED DONNELLY
Donnelly, Edward Vincent b: 12/10/34, Allen, Mich. BR/TR, 6', 175 lbs. Deb: 8/1/59

YEAR	TM/L	W	L	PCT	G	GS	CG	SH	SV	IP	H	HR	BB	SO	RAT	ERA	ERA+	OAV	OOB	BH	AVG	PB	PR	/A	PD	TPI
1959	Chi-N	1	1	.500	9	0	0	0	0	14¹	18	1	9	6	17.0	3.14	126	.305	.397	0	—	0	1	1	0	0.2

● FRANK DONNELLY
Donnelly, Franklin Marion b: 10/7/1869, Tamaroa, Ill. d: 2/3/53, Canton, Ill. 5'6", 180 lbs. Deb: 8/15/1893

YEAR	TM/L	W	L	PCT	G	GS	CG	SH	SV	IP	H	HR	BB	SO	RAT	ERA	ERA+	OAV	OOB	BH	AVG	PB	PR	/A	PD	TPI
1893	Chi-N	3	1	.750	7	5	3	0	**2**	42	51	1	17	6	15.4	5.36	86	.291	.367	8	.444	4	-3	-3	-0	0.1

● BLIX DONNELLY
Donnelly, Sylvester Urban b: 1/21/14, Olivia, Minn. d: 6/20/76, Olivia, Minn. BR/TR, 5'10", 178 lbs. Deb: 5/6/44

YEAR	TM/L	W	L	PCT	G	GS	CG	SH	SV	IP	H	HR	BB	SO	RAT	ERA	ERA+	OAV	OOB	BH	AVG	PB	PR	/A	PD	TPI
1944	*StL-N	2	1	.667	27	4	2	0	2	76¹	64	2	34	45	11.4	2.12	166	.218	.307	1	.063	-1	13	12	1	0.5
1945	StL-N	8	10	.444	31	23	9	4	2	166¹	157	10	87	76	13.5	3.52	106	.250	.346	7	.130	-2	5	4	-4	-0.2
1946	StL-N	1	2	.333	13	0	0	0	0	13²	17	1	10	11	18.4	3.95	87	.347	.467	0	—	0	-1	-1	-0	-0.2
	Phi-N	3	4	.429	12	8	2	1	0	76¹	64	7	24	38	10.6	2.95	116	.220	.284	7	.280	2	4	4	1	0.5
	Yr	4	6	.400	25	8	2	1	0	90	81	8	34	49	11.7	3.10	111	.238	.310	7	.280	2	3	3	1	0.3
1947	Phi-N	4	6	.400	38	10	5	1	5	120²	113	6	46	31	12.1	2.98	134	.265	.340	2	.063	-2	14	14	-0	0.9
1948	Phi-N	5	7	.417	26	19	8	1	2	131²	125	13	49	46	11.9	3.69	107	.261	.330	10	.222	2	4	4	-3	0.3
1949	Phi-N	2	1	.667	23	10	1	0	0	78¹	84	7	40	36	14.4	5.06	78	.284	.382	4	.174	-1	-9	-10	-2	-0.6
1950	Phi-N	2	4	.333	14	1	0	0	0	21	30	5	10	10	17.1	4.29	94	.330	.396	1	.200	-0	-1	-0	0	-0.1
1951	Bos-N	0	1	.000	6	0	0	0	0	7¹	8	1	6	3	18.4	7.36	50	.286	.429	0	.000	-0	-3	-3	0	-0.4
Total 8		27	36	.429	190	75	27	7	12	691²	659	52	306	296	12.8	3.49	109	.257	.340	32	.159	-2	27	24	-8	0.7

● JIM DONOHUE
Donohue, James Thomas b: 10/31/38, St. Louis, Mo. BR/TR, 6'4", 190 lbs. Deb: 4/11/61

YEAR	TM/L	W	L	PCT	G	GS	CG	SH	SV	IP	H	HR	BB	SO	RAT	ERA	ERA+	OAV	OOB	BH	AVG	PB	PR	/A	PD	TPI
1961	Det-A	1	1	.500	14	0	0	0	0	20¹	23	2	15	20	16.8	3.54	116	.287	.400	0	.000	-0	1	-0	0	0.1
	LA-A	4	6	.400	38	7	0	0	5	100¹	93	16	50	79	12.8	4.31	105	.246	.334	4	.148	-1	-3	2	-0	0.1
	Yr	5	7	.417	52	7	0	0	5	120²	116	18	65	99	13.5	4.18	106	.253	.346	4	.143	-1	-2	4	-1	0.2
1562	LA-A	1	0	1.000	12	0	0	0	1	24¹	24	4	11	14	13.7	3.70	104	.258	.349	1	.250	0	1	0	-0	0.1
	Min-A	0	1	.000	6	1	0	0	0	10¹	12	2	6	3	15.7	6.97	59	.324	.419	0	.000	0	-4	-3	0	-0.3
	Yr	1	1	.500	18	1	0	0	1	34²	36	6	17	17	13.8	4.67	84	.273	.356	1	.167	0	-3	-3	-0	-0.1
Total 2		6	8	.429	70	9	0	0	7	155¹	152	24	82	116	13.7	4.29	101	.259	.351	5	.147	-1	-5	1	-1	-0.1

YEAR TM/L	W	L	PCT	G	GS	CG	SH	SV	IP	H	HR	BB	SO	RAT	ERA	ERA+	OAV	OOB	BH	AVG	PB	PR	/A	PD	TPI
● **PETE DONOHUE**				Donohue, Peter Joseph b: 11/5/1900, Athens, Tex. d: 2/23/88, Ft.Worth, Tex. BR/TR, 6'2", 185 lbs. Deb: 7/1/21																				
1921 Cin-N	7	6	.538	21	11	7	0	1	118¹	117	5	26	44	10.9	3.35	107	.263	.304	8	.211	1	6	3	2	0.6
1922 Cin-N	18	9	**.667**	33	30	18	2	1	242	257	7	43	66	11.3	3.12	128	.276	.312	16	.182	-3	26	23	1	2.1
1923 Cin-N	21	15	.583	42	36	19	2	3	274¹	304	3	68	84	12.5	3.38	114	.278	.326	24	.250	3	19	15	1	2.0
1924 Cin-N	16	9	.640	35	32	16	3	0	222¹	248	9	36	72	11.9	3.60	105	.285	.321	14	.192	-0	7	4	-1	0.2
1925 Cin-N	21	14	.600	42	38	**27**	3	2	**301**	310	3	49	78	10.8	3.08	133	.268	.299	32	.294	7	40	34	-3	4.0
1926 Cin-N	**20**	14	.588	47	38	17	**5**	2	285²	298	6	39	73	10.9	3.37	109	.268	.298	33	.311	9	14	10	-3	1.7
1927 Cin-N	6	16	.273	33	24	12	1	1	190²	253	6	32	48	13.5	4.11	92	.328	.356	16	.250	1	-4	-7	0	-0.6
1928 Cin-N	7	11	.389	23	18	8	0	1	150	180	10	32	37	12.9	4.74	83	.309	.348	7	.146	-0	-13	-13	1	-1.3
1929 Cin-N	10	13	.435	32	24	7	0	0	177²	243	12	51	30	15.1	5.42	84	.331	.377	20	.333	4	-14	-17	0	-1.3
1930 Cin-N	1	3	.250	8	5	2	0	1	34¹	53	0	13	4	17.6	6.29	77	.363	.419	1	.100	-1	-5	-6	1	-0.5
NY-N	7	6	.538	18	11	4	0	1	86²	135	6	18	26	16.1	6.13	77	.360	.392	9	.273	1	-11	-13	-2	-1.6
Yr	8	9	.471	26	16	6	0	2	121	188	6	31	30	16.4	6.17	77	.360	.398	10	.233	0	-16	-19	-0	-2.1
1931 NY-N	0	1	.000	4	1	0	0	0	11¹	14	1	4	4	14.3	5.56	66	.311	.367	0	.000	-0	-2	-2	0	-0.2
Cle-A	0	0	—	2	0	0	0	0	5¹	9	1	5	4	23.6	8.44	55	.429	.538	0	.000	-0	-2	-2	-0	0.0
1932 Bos-A	0	1	.000	4	2	0	0	0	12²	18	2	6	1	17.1	7.82	57	.340	.407	0	.000	-0	-5	-5	1	-0.3
Total 12	134	118	.532	344	270	137	16	12	2112¹	2439	68	422	571	12.4	3.87	103	.293	.330	180	.246	21	56	25	-1	4.8
● **LINO DONOSO**				Donoso, Lino (Galeta) b: 9/23/22, Havana, Cuba d: 10/13/90, Veracruz, Mexico BL/TL, 5'11", 160 lbs. Deb: 6/18/55																				
1955 Pit-N	4	6	.400	25	9	3	0	1	95	106	16	35	38	13.5	5.31	78	.287	.351	5	.185	-1	-13	-13	0	-1.2
1956 Pit-N	0	0	—	3	0	0	0	0	1²	2	0	1	1	16.2	0.00	—	.250	.333	0	—	1	1	1	0	0.0
Total 2	4	6	.400	28	9	3	0	1	96²	108	16	36	39	13.5	5.21	79	.286	.350	5	.185	-1	-13	-12	0	-1.2
● **DICK DONOVAN**				Donovan, Richard Edward b: 12/7/27, Boston, Mass. BL/TR, 6'3", 205 lbs. Deb: 4/24/50																				
1950 Bos-N	0	2	.000	10	3	0	0	0	29²	28	4	34	9	19.4	8.19	47	.255	.438	1	.167	1	-13	-14	-0	-0.7
1951 Bos-N	0	0	—	8	2	0	0	0	13²	17	0	11	4	18.4	5.27	70	.298	.412	1	.333	1	-2	-2	0	0.2
1952 Bos-N	0	2	.000	7	2	0	0	1	13	18	1	12	6	22.2	5.54	65	.346	.485	0	.000	-0	-3	-3	1	-0.4
1954 Det-A	0	0	—	2	0	0	0	0	6	9	1	5	2	21.0	10.50	35	.360	.467	0	.000	-0	-5	-5	-0	0.0
1955 Chi-A☆	15	9	.625	29	24	11	5	0	187	186	17	48	88	11.4	3.32	119	.261	.311	17	.224	5	13	13	1	2.1
1956 Chi-A	12	10	.545	34	31	14	3	0	234²	212	22	59	120	10.6	3.64	113	.240	.292	20	.222	18	8	13	12	1.9
1957 Chi-A	16	6	**.727**	28	28	**16**	3	0	220²	203	17	45	88	10.4	2.77	135	.247	.293	12	.145	2	25	24	0	2.5
1958 Chi-A	15	14	.517	34	34	16	4	0	248	240	23	53	127	10.9	3.01	121	.251	.295	9	.112	-1	21	17	-1	1.6
1959 *Chi-A	9	10	.474	31	29	5	1	0	179²	171	15	58	71	11.7	3.66	103	.247	.310	8	.131	1	4	2	-2	0.1
1960 Chi-A	6	1	.857	33	8	0	0	3	78²	87	13	25	30	12.8	5.38	70	.283	.337	3	.130	-0	-13	-14	1	-1.1
1961 Was-A★	10	10	.500	23	22	11	2	0	168²	138	10	35	62	**9.4**	**2.40**	**167**	.224	**.269**	10	.179	2	30	30	-1	3.7
1962 Cle-A★	20	10	.667	34	34	16	**5**	0	250²	255	23	47	94	10.9	3.59	108	.263	.299	16	.180	6	11	8	-1	1.4
1963 Cle-A	11	13	.458	30	30	7	3	0	206	211	27	28	84	10.7	4.24	85	.265	.295	9	.130	-1	-14	-14	-1	-1.7
1964 Cle-A	7	9	.438	30	23	5	0	0	158¹	181	19	29	83	12.1	4.55	79	.290	.324	7	.146	3	-16	-17	1	-1.2
1965 Cle-A	1	3	.250	12	3	0	0	0	22²	32	6	6	12	15.1	5.96	58	.333	.373	0	.000	-1	-6	-6	-0	-1.1
Total 15	122	99	.552	345	273	101	25	5	2017¹	1988	198	495	880	11.3	3.67	104	.258	.306	113	.163	24	45	31	-0	7.3
● **TOM DONOVAN**				Donovan, Thomas Joseph b: 1/1/1873, West Troy, N.Y. d: 3/25/33, Watervliet, N.Y. BR/TR, 6'2", 168 lbs. Deb: 9/10/01 F♦																				
1901 Cle-A	0	0	—	1	0	0	0	0	7	16	0	3	0	27.0	5.14	69	.442	.510	18	.254	0	-1	-1	0	0.0
● **BILL DONOVAN**				Donovan, Willard Earl b: 7/6/16, Maywood, Ill. BB/TL, 6'2", 198 lbs. Deb: 4/19/42																				
1942 Bos-N	3	6	.333	31	10	2	0	0	89¹	97	2	32	23	13.0	3.43	97	.283	.344	6	.240	1	-1	-1	2	0.3
1943 Bos-N	1	0	1.000	7	0	0	0	0	14²	17	0	9	1	16.0	1.84	185	.304	.400	1	.333	0	3	3	1	0.3
Total 2	4	6	.400	38	10	2	0	0	104	114	2	41	24	13.4	3.20	105	.286	.352	7	.250	1	1	2	3	0.6
● **BILL DONOVAN**				Donovan, William Edward "Wild Bill" b: 10/13/1876, Lawrence, Mass. d: 12/9/23, Forsyth, N.Y. BR/TR, 5'11", 190 lbs. Deb: 4/22/1898 M♦																				
1898 Was-N	1	6	.143	17	7	6	0	0	88	88	0	69	36	16.8	3.80	85	.258	.394	17	.165	-1	-7	-7	-0	-0.5
1899 Bro-N	1	2	.333	5	2	2	0	1	25	35	0	13	11	17.3	4.32	91	.330	.403	3	.231	-0	-1	-1	-0	-0.1
1900 Bro-N	1	2	.333	5	4	2	0	0	31	36	0	18	13	16.5	6.68	58	.290	.392	0	.000	-2	-10	-10	1	-0.8
1901 Bro-N	**25**	15	.625	**45**	38	36	2	**3**	351	324	1	152	226	12.4	2.77	121	.244	.325	23	.170	-1	22	23	-1	2.1
1902 Bro-N	17	15	.531	35	33	30	4	1	297²	250	1	111	170	11.1	2.78	99	.228	.303	28	.174	-0	-0	-1	1	0.0
1903 Det-A	17	16	.515	35	34	**34**	4	0	307	247	3	95	187	10.2	2.29	127	.220	.284	30	.242	4	23	21	-3	2.4
1904 Det-A	17	16	.515	34	34	30	3	0	293	251	6	94	137	10.9	2.46	104	.232	.300	38	.271	5	5	3	-0	1.0
1905 Det-A	18	15	.545	34	32	27	5	0	280²	236	2	101	135	11.1	2.60	105	.229	.304	25	.192	1	2	-3	-3	0.4
1906 Det-A	9	15	.375	25	25	22	0	0	211²	221	4	72	85	12.8	3.15	88	.272	.337	11	.121	-11	-9	-7	-0	-1.5
1907 *Det-A	25	4	**.862**	32	28	27	3	1	271	222	3	82	123	10.4	2.19	119	.225	.290	29	.266	7	11	13	-6	1.5
1908 *Det-A	18	7	.720	29	28	25	6	0	242²	210	2	53	141	10.0	2.08	117	.231	.278	13	.159	0	9	9	-6	0.2
1909 *Det-A	8	7	.533	21	17	13	4	2	140¹	121	0	60	76	12.0	2.31	109	.235	.322	9	.200	1	3	3	-2	0.2
1910 Det-A	17	7	.708	26	23	20	0	0	206²	184	4	61	107	11.0	2.44	108	.243	.305	10	.145	-2	2	4	-6	-0.4
1911 Det-A	10	9	.526	20	19	15	1	0	168¹	160	4	64	81	12.1	3.31	104	.250	.321	12	.200	3	3	-5	0.1	
1912 Det-A	1	0	1.000	3	1	0	0	0	10	5	0	2	6	7.2	0.90	362	.147	.216	1	.077	-1	3	3	-0	0.1
1915 NY-A	0	3	.000	9	1	0	0	0	33²	35	1	10	17	12.3	4.81	61	.278	.336	1	.083	-1	-7	-7	-1	-0.7
1916 NY-A	0	0	—	1	0	0	0	0	1	1	0	0	0	18.0	0.00	—	.250	.400	0	—	0	0	0	-0	0.0
1918 Det-A	1	0	1.000	2	1	0	0	0	6	5	0	1	0	9.0	1.50	177	.227	.261	1	.500	-1	1	1	-0	0.2
Total 18	186	139	.572	378	327	289	35	8	2964²	2631	30	1059	1552	11.5	2.69	106	.239	.310	251	.193	9	44	54	-31	4.1
● **JOHN DOPSON**				Dopson, John Robert b: 7/14/63, Baltimore, Md. BL/TR, 6'4", 205 lbs. Deb: 9/4/85																				
1985 Mon-N	0	2	.000	4	3	0	0	0	13	25	4	4	9	20.1	11.08	31	.379	.414	0	.000	0	-11	-11	-0	-1.3
1988 Mon-N	3	11	.214	26	26	1	0	0	168²	150	15	58	101	11.2	3.04	118	.235	.300	3	.059	-3	8	10	-3	0.3
1989 Bos-A	12	8	.600	29	28	2	0	0	169¹	166	14	69	95	12.6	3.99	103	.257	.330	0	—	0	2	3	6	0.5
1990 Bos-A	0	0	—	4	4	0	0	0	17²	13	2	9	9	11.2	2.04	200	.200	.297	0	—	0	4	4	1	0.0
1991 Bos-A	0	0	—	1	0	0	0	0	1	2	0	1	0	27.0	18.00	24	.500	.600	0	—	0	-2	-2	0	0.0
1992 Bos-A	7	11	.389	25	25	0	0	0	141¹	159	17	38	55	12.7	4.08	103	.287	.335	0	—	0	-2	2	1	-0.1
1993 Bos-A	7	11	.389	34	28	1	1	0	155²	170	16	59	89	13.4	4.97	93	.281	.347	0	—	0	-11	-6	1	-0.9
1994 Cal-A	1	4	.200	21	5	0	0	0	58²	67	6	26	33	14.7	6.14	81	.288	.366	0	—	0	-9	-7	0	-0.7
Total 8	30	47	.390	144	119	4	1	1	725¹	752	74	264	386	12.7	4.27	98	.268	.333	3	.055	-3	-25	-8	2	-2.2
● **JOHN DORAN**				Doran, John F. b: 1867, Chicago, Ill. TL, 5'11", 175 lbs. Deb: 4/11/1891																				
1891 Lou-a	5	10	.333	15	14	12	1	0	126	160	3	75	55	17.7	5.43	67	.299	.398	10	.189	-2	-24	-25	-0	-2.3
● **MIKE DORGAN**				Dorgan, Michael Cornelius b: 10/2/1853, Middletown, Conn. d: 4/26/09, Hartford, Conn. BR/TR, 5'9", 180 lbs. Deb: 5/8/1877 FM♦																				
1879 Syr-N	0	0	—	2	0	0	0	0	12	10	0	2	8	11.3	2.25	105	.260	.288	72	.267	0	0	0	0	0.0
1880 Pro-N	0	0	—	1	0	0	0	0	8	4	0	0	4	4.5	1.13	196	.138	.138	79	.246	0	1	1	0	0.0
1883 NY-N	0	1	.000	1	1	1	0	0	7	8	0	6	3	18.0	3.86	80	.286	.412	61	.234	0	-1	-1	-0	-0.1
1884 NY-N	8	6	.571	14	14	12	0	0	113	98	5	51	90	11.9	3.50	85	.215	.294	94	.276	2	-7	-7	1	-0.5
Total 4	8	7	.533	18	15	13	0	0	140	123	5	59	103	11.7	3.28	84	.218	.293	802	.274	3	-6	-6	1	-0.6
● **FRITZ DORISH**				Dorish, Harry b: 7/13/21, Swoyersville, Pa. BR/TR, 5'11", 206 lbs. Deb: 4/15/47 C																				
1947 Bos-A	7	8	.467	41	9	2	0	2	136	149	6	54	50	13.5	4.70	83	.283	.351	5	.143	-1	-15	-12	1	-1.3
1948 Bos-A	0	1	.000	9	0	0	0	0	14¹	18	1	6	6	15.1	5.65	78	.281	.343	1	.250	-0	-2	-2	-0	-0.1
1949 Bos-A	0	0	—	5	0	0	0	0	7²	7	1	1	5	9.4	2.35	186	.241	.267	0	—	0	2	2	0	0.0

YEAR TM/L	W	L	PCT	G	GS	CG	SH	SV	IP	H	HR	BB	SO	RAT	ERA	ERA+	OAV	OOB	BH	AVG	PB	PR	/A	PD	TPI
1950 StL-A	4	9	.308	29	13	4	0	0	109	162	13	36	36	17.1	6.44	77	.337	.394	5	.161	0	-23	-18	-1	-1.8
1951 Chi-A	5	6	.455	32	4	2	1	0	96²	101	6	31	29	12.3	3.54	114	.272	.328	8	.258	0	6	5	0	0.6
1952 Chi-A	8	4	.667	39	1	1	0	**11**	91	66	4	42	47	10.8	2.47	148	.208	.303	2	.091	-1	**12**	**12**	2	1.9
1953 Chi-A	10	6	.625	55	6	2	0	18	145²	140	9	52	69	12.2	3.40	118	.254	.325	7	.171	-2	10	10	2	1.3
1954 Chi-A	6	4	.600	37	6	2	1	6	109	88	9	29	48	9.7	2.72	137	.228	.284	3	.111	-2	12	12	-1	0.9
1955 Chi-A	2	0	1.000	13	0	0	0	1	17	16	0	9	6	13.2	1.59	249	.258	.352	1	.333	0	4	4	1	0.6
Bal-A	3	3	.500	35	1	0	0	6	65²	58	4	28	22	11.9	3.15	121	.238	.319	0	.000	-1	6	5	1	0.4
Yr	5	3	.625	48	1	0	0	7	82²	74	4	37	28	12.2	2.83	136	.242	.326	1	.077	-1	10	9	1	1.0
1956 Bal-A	0	0	—	13	0	0	0	0	19²	22	3	3	4	11.4	4.12	95	.297	.325	0	—	0	0	-0	1	0.1
Bos-A	0	2	.000	15	0	0	0	0	22²	23	1	10	11	13.1	3.57	129	.277	.355	0	—	0	1	3	1	0.3
Yr	0	2	.000	28	0	0	0	0	42¹	45	4	13	15	12.3	3.83	112	.283	.337	0	—	0	2	2	2	0.4
Total 10	45	43	.511	323	40	13	2	44	834¹	850	57	301	332	12.6	3.83	106	.267	.333	32	.157	-6	14	20	6	2.9

● **GUS DORNER**   Dorner, Augustus b: 8/18/1876, Chambersburg, Pa. d: 5/4/56, Chambersburg, Pa. BR/TR, 5'10", 176 lbs. Deb: 9/17/02

YEAR TM/L	W	L	PCT	G	GS	CG	SH	SV	IP	H	HR	BB	SO	RAT	ERA	ERA+	OAV	OOB	BH	AVG	PB	PR	/A	PD	TPI
1902 Cle-A	3	1	.750	4	4	4	1	0	36	33	1	13	5	11.8	1.25	275	.244	.315	5	.385	2	9	9	-0	1.2
1903 Cle-A	4	5	.444	12	8	4	2	0	73²	83	4	24	28	13.2	4.52	63	.283	.340	2	.080	-2	-13	-14	0	-1.6
1906 Cin-N	1	0	1.000	2	1	1	0	0	15	16	0	4	5	12.6	1.20	230	.276	.333	0	.000	-0	2	3	-0	0.1
Bos-N	8	25	.242	34	32	29	0	0	273¹	264	5	103	104	12.6	3.65	74	.260	.338	14	.140	-4	-31	-29	3	-3.5
Yr	8	26	.235	36	33	30	0	0	288¹	280	5	107	109	12.6	3.53	76	.261	.337	14	.133	-5	-29	-27	2	-3.4
1907 Bos-N	12	16	.429	36	31	24	2	0	271¹	253	4	92	85	11.9	3.12	82	.255	.327	12	.130	-3	-19	-17	-3	-2.4
1908 Bos-N	8	19	.296	38	28	14	3	0	216¹	176	8	77	41	11.1	3.54	68	.224	.305	12	.179	-1	-28	-27	2	-3.3
1909 Bos-N	1	2	.333	5	2	0	0	1	24²	17	1	17	7	13.1	2.55	110	.198	.343	1	.167	-0	0	1	-0	0.0
Total 6	36	69	.343	131	106	76	8	1	910¹	842	18	330	275	12.1	3.37	78	.250	.326	46	.149	-9	-80	-74	1	-9.5

● **BERT DORR**   Dorr, Charles Albert b: 2/2/1862, New York d: 6/16/14, Dickinson, N.Y. Deb: 8/24/1882

YEAR TM/L	W	L	PCT	G	GS	CG	SH	SV	IP	H	HR	BB	SO	RAT	ERA	ERA+	OAV	OOB	BH	AVG	PB	PR	/A	PD	TPI
1882 StL-a	2	6	.250	8	8	8	0	0	66	53	0	1	34	7.4	2.59	108	.205	.208	4	.154	-2	1	2	1	0.1

● **CAL DORSETT**   Dorsett, Calvin Leavelle "Preacher" b: 6/10/13, Lone Oak, Tex. d: 10/22/70, Elk City, Okla. BR/TR, 6', 180 lbs. Deb: 8/19/40

YEAR TM/L	W	L	PCT	G	GS	CG	SH	SV	IP	H	HR	BB	SO	RAT	ERA	ERA+	OAV	OOB	BH	AVG	PB	PR	/A	PD	TPI
1940 Cle-A	0	0	—	1	0	0	0	0	1	1	1	0	0	9.0	9.00	47	.250	.250	0	—	0	-1	-1	-0	0.0
1941 Cle-A	0	1	.000	5	2	0	0	0	11¹	21	0	10	0	24.6	10.32	38	.382	.477	0	.000	-0	-8	-8	-0	-0.6
1947 Cle-A	0	0	—	2	0	0	0	0	1¹	3	1	3	1	40.5	27.00	13	.500	.667	0	—	0	-3	-3	-0	0.0
Total 3	0	1	.000	8	2	0	0	0	13²	25	2	13	6	25.0	11.85	33	.385	.487	0	.000	-0	-12	-12	-0	-0.6

● **JIM DORSEY**   Dorsey, James Edward b: 8/2/55, Oak Park, Ill. BR/TR, 6'7", 190 lbs. Deb: 9/2/80

YEAR TM/L	W	L	PCT	G	GS	CG	SH	SV	IP	H	HR	BB	SO	RAT	ERA	ERA+	OAV	OOB	BH	AVG	PB	PR	/A	PD	TPI
1980 Cal-A	1	2	.333	4	4	0	0	0	15²	25	2	8	8	19.5	9.19	43	.368	.442	0	—	0	-9	-9	-0	-1.3
1984 Bos-A	0	0	—	2	0	0	0	0	2²	6	0	2	4	27.0	10.13	41	.462	.533	0	—	0	-2	-2	-0	0.0
1985 Bos-A	0	1	.000	2	1	0	0	0	5¹	12	2	10	2	37.1	20.25	21	.444	.595	0	—	0	-10	-9	-0	-1.2
Total 3	1	3	.250	8	5	0	0	0	23²	43	4	20	14	24.3	11.79	34	.398	.496	0	—	0	-20	-20	-0	-2.5

● **JERRY DORSEY**   Dorsey, Michael Jeremiah b: 1854, Canada d: 11/3/38, Auburn, N.Y. Deb: 7/9/1884 ♦

YEAR TM/L	W	L	PCT	G	GS	CG	SH	SV	IP	H	HR	BB	SO	RAT	ERA	ERA+	OAV	OOB	BH	AVG	PB	PR	/A	PD	TPI
1884 Bal-U	0	1	.000	1	1	0	0	0	4	7	1	0	3	15.8	9.00	30	.360	.360	0	.000	-1	-3	-3	0	-0.5

● **JACK DOSCHER**   Doscher, John Henry Jr. b: 7/27/1880, Troy, N.Y. d: 5/27/71, Park Ridge, N.J. BL/TL, 6'1", 205 lbs. Deb: 7/2/03 F

YEAR TM/L	W	L	PCT	G	GS	CG	SH	SV	IP	H	HR	BB	SO	RAT	ERA	ERA+	OAV	OOB	BH	AVG	PB	PR	/A	PD	TPI
1903 Chi-N	0	1	.000	1	1	0	0	0	3	6	0	2	5	27.0	12.00	26	.429	.529	0	.000	-0	-3	-3	-0	-0.6
Bro-N	0	0	—	3	0	0	0	0	7	8	1	9	4	23.1	7.71	41	.296	.486	0	.000	-0	-3	-4	-0	-0.1
Yr	0	1	.000	4	1	0	0	0	10	14	1	11	9	23.4	9.00	35	.333	.481	0	.000	-1	-6	-6	-0	-0.7
1904 Bro-N	0	0	—	2	0	0	0	0	6¹	1	0	1	2	2.8	0.00	—	.053	.100	1	.500	0	2	2	-0	0.2
1905 Bro-N	1	5	.167	12	7	6	0	0	71	60	1	30	33	11.8	3.17	91	.232	.318	2	.083	-2	-1	-2	-2	-0.5
1906 Bro-N	1	1	.500	2	1	0	0	0	14	12	0	4	10	10.3	1.29	196	.250	.308	0	.000	-1	2	2	-0	0.0
1908 Cin-N	1	3	.250	7	4	3	0	0	44¹	31	1	22	7	11.4	1.83	126	.196	.306	2	.133	-0	3	2	-0	0.2
Total 5	2	10	.167	27	13	10	0	0	145²	118	3	68	61	12.0	2.84	95	.225	.323	5	.100	-3	-1	-2	-3	-1.0

● **RICHARD DOTSON**   Dotson, Richard Elliott b: 1/10/59, Cincinnati, Ohio BR/TR, 6', 204 lbs. Deb: 9/4/79

YEAR TM/L	W	L	PCT	G	GS	CG	SH	SV	IP	H	HR	BB	SO	RAT	ERA	ERA+	OAV	OOB	BH	AVG	PB	PR	/A	PD	TPI
1979 Chi-A	2	0	1.000	5	5	1	1	0	24¹	28	0	6	13	12.6	3.70	115	.286	.327	0	—	0	1	1	0	0.1
1980 Chi-A	12	10	.545	33	32	8	1	0	198	185	20	87	109	12.6	4.27	94	.247	.331	0	—	0	-5	-5	1	-0.4
1981 Chi-A	9	8	.529	24	24	5	**4**	0	141	145	13	49	73	12.6	3.77	95	.270	.336	0	—	0	-2	-3	-0	-0.4
1982 Chi-A	11	15	.423	34	31	3	1	0	196²	219	24	73	109	13.6	3.84	105	.282	.348	0	—	0	5	4	-1	0.4
1983 *Chi-A	22	7	**.759**	35	35	8	1	0	240	209	19	106	137	12.1	3.23	130	.240	.328	0	—	0	22	26	4	3.4
1984 Chi-A★	14	15	.483	32	32	14	1	0	245²	216	24	103	120	11.9	3.59	116	.238	.321	0	—	0	11	15	-0	1.7
1985 Chi-A	3	4	.429	9	9	0	0	0	52¹	53	5	17	33	12.6	4.47	97	.261	.327	0	—	0	-2	-1	-0	-0.1
1986 Chi-A	10	17	.370	34	34	3	1	0	197	226	24	69	110	13.6	5.48	79	.289	.348	0	—	0	-29	-26	-1	-3.1
1987 Chi-A	11	12	.478	31	31	7	2	0	211¹	201	24	86	114	12.2	4.17	110	.249	.321	0	—	0	7	10	2	1.1
1988 NY-A	12	9	.571	32	29	4	0	0	171	178	27	72	77	13.4	5.00	79	.266	.341	0	—	0	-20	-20	-1	-2.3
1989 NY-A	2	5	.286	11	9	1	0	0	51²	69	8	17	14	15.2	5.57	69	.317	.369	0	—	0	-10	-10	-1	-1.2
Chi-A	3	7	.300	17	17	1	0	0	99²	112	8	41	55	13.8	3.88	98	.282	.349	0	—	0	-0	-1	-0	-0.1
Yr	5	12	.294	28	26	2	0	0	151¹	181	16	58	69	14.2	4.46	86	.293	.354	0	—	0	-10	-11	-1	-1.3
1990 KC-A	0	4	.000	8	7	0	0	0	28²	43	3	14	9	17.9	8.48	45	.355	.422	0	—	0	-15	-15	-0	-1.7
Total 12	111	113	.496	305	295	55	11	0	1857¹	1884	194	740	973	12.9	4.23	97	.264	.337	0	—	0	-35	-25	2	-2.6

● **GARY DOTTER**   Dotter, Gary Richard b: 8/7/42, St.Louis, Mo. BL/TL, 6'1", 180 lbs. Deb: 9/10/61

YEAR TM/L	W	L	PCT	G	GS	CG	SH	SV	IP	H	HR	BB	SO	RAT	ERA	ERA+	OAV	OOB	BH	AVG	PB	PR	/A	PD	TPI
1961 Min-A	0	0	—	2	0	0	0	0	6	6	0	4	2	15.0	9.00	47	.273	.385	0	.000	-0	-3	-3	0	0.0
1963 Min-A	0	0	—	2	0	0	0	0	2	0	0	2	0	0.0	0.00	—	.000	.000	0	—	0	1	1	0	0.0
1964 Min-A	0	0	—	3	0	0	0	0	4¹	3	1	3	6	12.5	2.08	172	.188	.316	0	—	0	1	1	-0	0.0
Total 3	0	0	—	7	0	0	0	0	12¹	9	1	7	10	11.7	5.11	76	.205	.314	0	.000	-0	-2	-2	0	0.0

● **BABE DOTY**   Doty, Elmer L. b: 12/17/1867, Genoa, Ohio d: 11/20/29, Toledo, Ohio BL/TR, 6', 160 lbs. Deb: 8/18/1890

YEAR TM/L	W	L	PCT	G	GS	CG	SH	SV	IP	H	HR	BB	SO	RAT	ERA	ERA+	OAV	OOB	BH	AVG	PB	PR	/A	PD	TPI
1890 Tol-a	1	0	1.000	1	1	1	0	0	9	9	0	4	4	10.0	1.00	395	.252	.273	0	.000	-0	3	3	-0	0.2

● **TOM DOUGHERTY**   Dougherty, Thomas James "Sugar Boy" b: 5/30/1881, Chicago, Ill. d: 11/6/53, Milwaukee, Wis. BL/TR, 195 lbs. Deb: 4/24/04

YEAR TM/L	W	L	PCT	G	GS	CG	SH	SV	IP	H	HR	BB	SO	RAT	ERA	ERA+	OAV	OOB	BH	AVG	PB	PR	/A	PD	TPI
1904 Chi-A	1	0	1.000	1	0	0	0	0	2	0	0	0	0	0.0	0.00	—	.000	.000	0	.000	-0	1	1	0	0.3

● **WHAMMY DOUGLAS**   Douglas, Charles William b: 2/17/35, Carrboro, N.C. BR/TR, 6'2", 185 lbs. Deb: 7/29/57

YEAR TM/L	W	L	PCT	G	GS	CG	SH	SV	IP	H	HR	BB	SO	RAT	ERA	ERA+	OAV	OOB	BH	AVG	PB	PR	/A	PD	TPI
1957 Pit-N	3	3	.500	11	8	0	0	0	47	48	5	30	28	15.5	3.26	116	.270	.384	1	.063	-1	3	3	-0	0.2

● **LARRY DOUGLAS**   Douglas, Lawrence Howard b: 6/5/1890, Jellico, Tenn. d: 11/4/49, Jellico, Tenn. 6'3", 175 lbs. Deb: 6/17/15

YEAR TM/L	W	L	PCT	G	GS	CG	SH	SV	IP	H	HR	BB	SO	RAT	ERA	ERA+	OAV	OOB	BH	AVG	PB	PR	/A	PD	TPI
1915 Bal-F	1	0	1.000	2	0	0	0	0	3	3	0	2	1	15.0	3.00	96	.273	.385	0	—	0	-0	-0	0	0.0

● **PHIL DOUGLAS**   Douglas, Phillip Brooks "Shufflin' Phil" b: 6/17/1890, Cedartown, Ga. d: 8/1/52, Sequatchie Valley, Tenn. BR/TR, 6'3", 190 lbs. Deb: 8/30/12

YEAR TM/L	W	L	PCT	G	GS	CG	SH	SV	IP	H	HR	BB	SO	RAT	ERA	ERA+	OAV	OOB	BH	AVG	PB	PR	/A	PD	TPI
1912 Chi-A	0	1	.000	3	1	0	0	0	12¹	21	0	6	7	19.7	7.30	44	.382	.443	0	.000	-0	-5	-6	0	-0.4
1914 Cin-N	11	18	.379	45	25	13	0	1	239¹	186	7	92	121	10.9	2.56	115	.223	.308	10	.137	-2	6	10	-2	0.7
1915 Cin-N	1	5	.167	8	7	0	1	0	46²	53	0	23	29	14.7	5.40	53	.299	.380	2	.118	-1	-14	-13	0	-1.6
Bro-N	5	5	.500	20	13	5	1	0	116²	104	1	17	63	9.7	2.62	106	.241	.278	6	.154	-1	2	2	0	0.1
Chi-N	1	1	.500	4	4	1	0	0	25	17	0	7	18	9.0	2.16	129	.187	.253	0	.000	-0	2	2	0	0.1
Yr	7	11	.389	32	24	7	2	0	188¹	174	1	47	110	10.6	3.25	86	.247	.295	8	.125	-3	-10	-9	1	-1.4
1917 Chi-N	14	20	.412	**51**	37	20	5	1	293¹	269	13	50	151	10.0	2.55	114	.250	.287	11	.126	-4	5	11	4	1.4
1918 *Chi-N	10	9	.526	25	19	11	2	2	156²	145	2	31	51	10.2	2.13	131	.246	.285	14	.255	1	11	11	3	1.9

YEAR	TM/L	W	L	PCT	G	GS	CG	SH	SV	IP	H	HR	BB	SO	RAT	ERA	ERA+	OAV	OOB	BH	AVG	PB	PR	/A	PD	TPI
1919	Chi-N	10	6	.625	25	19	8	4	0	161²	133	0	34	63	9.4	2.00	144	.230	.275	8	.157	-2	16	16	5	2.0
	NY-N	2	4	.333	8	6	4	0	0	51¹	53	0	6	21	10.5	2.10	133	.264	.288	0	.000	-2	5	4	0	0.2
	Yr	12	10	.545	33	25	12	4	0	213	186	0	40	84	9.6	2.03	141	.238	.276	8	.121	-4	21	20	5	2.2
1920	NY-N	14	10	.583	46	21	10	3	2	226	225	6	55	71	11.2	2.71	111	.263	.309	11	.151	-4	11	7	1	0.4
1921	*NY-N	15	10	.600	40	27	13	3	2	221²	266	17	55	55	13.1	4.22	87	.308	.351	16	.198	0	-11	-14	1	-1.3
1922	NY-N	11	4	.733	24	21	9	1	0	157²	154	6	35	33	**11.0**	**2.63**	**152**	**.257**	**.302**	12	.207	1	26	24	1	2.1
Total 9		94	93	.503	299	200	95	20	8	1708¹	1626	52	411	683	10.9	2.80	111	.256	.305	90	.161	-16	53	58	13	5.6

● **KIP DOWD**   Dowd, James Joseph   b: 2/16/1889, Holyoke, Mass.   d: 12/20/60, Holyoke, Mass.   BR/TR, 5'10.5", 160 lbs.   Deb: 7/5/10

| 1910 | Pit-N | 0 | 0 | — | 1 | 0 | 0 | 0 | 0 | 2 | 4 | 0 | 2 | 1 | 31.5 | 0.00 | — | .400 | .538 | 0 | — | 0 | 1 | 1 | -0 | 0.0 |

● **DAVE DOWLING**   Dowling, David Barclay   b: 8/23/42, Baton Rouge, La.   BR/TL, 6'2", 181 lbs.   Deb: 10/3/64

1964	StL-N	0	0	—	1	0	0	0	0	1	2	0	0	0	18.0	0.00	—	.400	.400	0	—	0	0	0	-0	0.0
1966	Chi-N	1	0	1.000	1	1	1	0	0	9	10	0	0	3	10.0	2.00	184	.270	.270	0	.000	-0	2	2	-0	0.1
Total 2		1	0	1.000	2	1	1	0	0	10	12	0	0	3	10.8	1.80	205	.286	.286	0	.000	-0	2	2	-0	0.1

● **PETE DOWLING**   Dowling, Henry Peter   b: St.Louis, Mo.   d: 6/30/05, Hot Lake, Ore.   TL, 5'11",   Deb: 7/17/1897

1897	Lou-N	1	2	.333	4	4	2	0	0	26	39	0	8	13	18.3	5.88	72	.343	.415	2	.200	-0	-5	-5	-0	-0.4
1898	Lou-N	13	20	.394	36	32	30	0	0	285²	284	7	120	84	13.4	4.16	86	.257	.342	21	.196	1	-17	-18	-1	-1.7
1899	Lou-N	13	17	.433	34	32	29	0	0	289²	321	4	93	88	13.4	3.11	124	.280	.343	27	.233	-1	24	24	-0	2.0
1901	Mil-A	1	4	.200	10	4	3	0	1	49²	71	1	14	25	16.1	5.62	64	.331	.383	4	.211	1	-11	-11	0	-0.8
	Cle-A	11	22	.333	33	30	28	2	0	256¹	269	1	104	99	13.6	3.86	92	.267	.344	16	.162	-4	-6	-9	-1	-1.2
	Yr	12	26	.316	43	34	31	2	1	306	340	2	118	124	13.9	4.15	86	.277	.348	20	.169	-3	-16	-20	-1	-2.0
Total 4		39	65	.375	117	102	92	2	1	907¹	984	13	339	299	13.8	3.87	95	.274	.348	70	.199	-3	-14	-19	-1	-2.1

● **AL DOWNING**   Downing, Alphonso Erwin   b: 6/28/41, Trenton, N.J.   BR/TL, 5'11", 177 lbs.   Deb: 7/19/61

1961	NY-A	0	1	.000	5	1	0	0	0	9	7	0	12	12	20.0	8.00	46	.212	.435	0	.000	-0	-4	-4	0	-0.4
1962	NY-A	0	0	—	1	0	0	0	0	1	0	0	1	1	0.0	0.00	—	.000	.000	0	—	0	0	0	0	0.0
1963	*NY-A	13	5	.722	24	22	10	4	0	175²	114	7	80	171	9.9	2.56	137	**.184**	.277	6	.103	-2	21	19	-1	1.5
1964	*NY-A	13	8	.619	37	35	11	1	2	244	201	18	120	**217**	11.8	3.47	104	.223	.314	15	.176	1	4	4	0	0.5
1965	NY-A	12	14	.462	35	32	8	2	0	212	185	16	105	179	12.4	3.40	100	.237	.329	8	.108	-1	1	0	0	0.0
1966	NY-A	10	11	.476	30	30	1	0	0	200	178	23	79	152	11.6	3.56	94	.235	.309	7	.100	-2	-3	-5	-4	-1.1
1967	NY-A★	14	10	.583	31	28	10	4	0	201²	158	13	61	171	10.0	2.63	119	.217	.283	8	.121	1	13	11	-1	1.3
1968	NY-A	3	3	.500	15	12	1	0	0	61¹	54	7	20	40	11.0	3.52	82	.237	.301	3	.176	0	-4	-4	-0	-0.4
1969	NY-A	7	5	.583	30	15	5	1	0	130²	117	12	49	85	11.4	3.38	103	.240	.309	6	.136	-1	4	1	-2	-0.1
1970	Oak-A	3	3	.500	10	6	1	0	0	41	39	5	22	26	13.6	3.95	90	.252	.348	2	.182	-0	-1	-2	2	-0.1
	Mil-A	2	10	.167	17	16	1	0	0	94¹	79	8	59	53	13.5	3.34	113	.232	.350	2	.083	-2	4	5	0	0.4
	Yr	5	13	.278	27	22	2	0	0	135¹	118	13	81	79	13.4	3.52	105	.237	.347	4	.114	-2	3	3	2	0.3
1971	LA-N	20	9	.690	37	36	12	**5**	0	262¹	245	16	84	136	11.4	2.68	121	.247	.308	16	.174	2	23	16	-1	1.9
1972	LA-N	9	9	.500	31	30	7	4	0	202²	196	13	67	117	12.0	2.98	112	.254	.319	8	.121	-1	11	8	5	1.1
1973	LA-N	9	9	.500	30	28	5	2	0	193	155	19	68	124	10.4	3.31	104	.219	.289	5	.088	-1	7	3	1	0.2
1974	*LA-N	5	6	.455	21	16	1	1	0	98¹	94	7	45	63	13.0	3.66	93	.255	.341	5	.172	-0	-0	-3	1	-0.2
1975	LA-N	2	1	.667	22	6	0	0	1	74²	59	6	28	39	10.7	2.89	118	.215	.293	0	.000	-1	6	4	1	0.2
1976	LA-N	1	2	.333	17	3	0	0	0	46²	43	3	18	30	11.8	3.86	88	.250	.321	0	.000	-1	-2	-2	0	-0.2
1977	LA-N	0	1	.000	12	1	0	0	0	20	22	4	16	23	17.1	6.75	57	.278	.400	0	.000	-0	-6	-7	-0	-0.3
Total 17		123	107	.535	405	317	73	24	3	2268¹	1946	177	933	1639	11.5	3.22	105	.232	.311	91	.127	-7	75	44	2	4.3

● **DAVE DOWNS**   Downs, David Ralph   b: 6/21/52, Logan, Utah   BR/TR, 6'5", 220 lbs.   Deb: 9/2/72   F

| 1972 | Phi-N | 1 | 1 | .500 | 4 | 4 | 1 | 1 | 0 | 23 | 25 | 1 | 3 | 5 | 11.3 | 2.74 | 131 | .294 | .326 | 2 | .250 | 0 | 2 | 2 | 0 | 0.2 |

● **KELLY DOWNS**   Downs, Kelly Robert   b: 10/25/60, Ogden, Utah   BR/TR, 6'4", 200 lbs.   Deb: 7/29/86   F

1986	SF-N	4	4	.500	14	14	1	0	0	88¹	78	5	30	64	11.3	2.75	128	.236	.305	5	.172	0	9	8	0	0.6
1987	*SF-N	12	9	.571	41	28	4	3	1	186	185	14	67	137	12.4	3.63	106	.258	.324	8	.143	-0	9	4	-4	0.0
1988	SF-N	13	9	.591	27	26	6	3	0	168	140	11	47	118	10.2	3.32	98	.225	.283	9	.167	2	-2	-1	0	0.1
1989	*SF-N	4	8	.333	18	15	0	0	0	82²	82	7	26	49	11.9	4.79	70	.261	.320	2	.091	-1	-12	-13	-1	-1.9
1990	SF-N	3	2	.600	13	9	0	0	0	63	56	2	20	31	11.0	3.43	106	.233	.298	0	.000	-1	3	2	1	0.1
1991	SF-N	10	4	.714	45	11	0	0	0	111²	99	12	53	62	12.5	4.19	85	.239	.329	2	.087	-1	-6	-8	1	-0.9
1992	SF-N	1	2	.333	19	7	0	0	0	62¹	65	4	24	33	13.3	3.47	99	.275	.350	0	.000	-1	2	0	-1	-0.0
	*Oak-A	5	5	.500	18	13	0	0	0	82	72	9	46	38	13.4	3.29	114	.237	.345	0	—	0	6	4	-1	0.6
1993	Oak-A	5	10	.333	42	12	0	0	0	119²	135	14	60	66	14.8	5.64	72	.287	.370	0	—	-0	-18	-21	-2	-2.3
Total 8		57	53	.518	237	135	11	6	1	963²	912	73	373	598	12.2	3.86	94	.250	.324	26	.123	-2	-6	-26	-7	-4.0

● **TOM DOWSE**   Dowse, Thomas Joseph   b: 8/12/1866, Ireland   d: 12/14/46, Riverside, Cal.   BR/TR, 5'11", 175 lbs.   Deb: 4/21/1890   ♦

| 1890 | Cle-N | 0 | 0 | — | 1 | 1 | 0 | 0 | 0 | 5 | 6 | 0 | 1 | 0 | 12.6 | 5.40 | 66 | .288 | .321 | 33 | .208 | -0 | -1 | -1 | 0 | 0.0 |

● **JESS DOYLE**   Doyle, Jesse Herbert   b: 4/14/1898, Knoxville, Tenn.   d: 4/15/61, Belleville, Ill.   BR/TR, 5'11", 175 lbs.   Deb: 4/14/25

1925	Det-A	4	7	.364	45	3	0	0	0	118¹	158	6	50	31	16.2	5.93	73	.340	.410	8	.242	3	-20	-21	-1	-1.7
1926	Det-A	0	0	—	2	0	0	0	1	4¹	6	0	1	2	14.5	4.15	98	.316	.350	1	1.000	0	-0	-0	-0	0.0
1927	Det-A	0	0	—	7	0	0	0	0	12¹	16	0	5	5	15.3	8.03	52	.314	.375	1	.333	1	-5	-5	-0	0.0
1931	StL-A	0	0	—	1	0	0	0	0	1	3	0	1	0	36.0	27.00	17	.500	.571	0	—	0	-3	-2	-0	0.0
Total 4		4	7	.364	55	3	0	0	9	136	183	6	57	38	16.2	6.22	69	.338	.406	10	.270	4	-28	-29	-1	-1.7

● **JOHN DOYLE**   Doyle, John Aloysius   b: 1858, Nova Scotia, Canada   d: 12/24/15, Providence, R.I.   Deb: 7/26/1882

| 1882 | StL-a | 0 | 3 | .000 | 3 | 3 | 3 | 0 | 0 | 24 | 41 | 0 | 3 | 5 | 16.5 | 2.63 | 107 | .355 | .371 | 2 | .182 | -0 | 0 | 0 | -1 | 0.0 |

● **SLOW JOE DOYLE**   Doyle, Judd Bruce   b: 9/15/1881, Clay Center, Kan.   d: 11/21/47, Tannersville, N.Y.   BR/TR, 5'8", 150 lbs.   Deb: 8/25/06

1906	NY-A	2	1	.667	9	6	3	2	0	45¹	34	1	13	28	9.5	2.38	124	.211	.275	3	.214	-0	2	3	0	0.2
1907	NY-A	11	11	.500	29	23	15	1	1	193²	169	2	67	94	11.2	2.65	106	.237	.308	8	.138	-1	-2	-3	-3	-0.1
1908	NY-A	1	1	.500	12	4	2	1	0	48	42	1	14	20	10.9	2.63	95	.235	.297	3	.214	0	-1	-1	-2	-0.1
1909	NY-A	8	6	.571	17	15	8	3	0	125²	103	3	37	57	10.2	2.58	98	.232	.294	7	.167	0	-1	-1	-4	-0.4
1910	NY-A	0	2	.000	3	2	1	0	0	12¹	19	0	5	6	18.2	8.03	33	.365	.431	1	.250	0	-8	-7	1	-0.9
	Cin-N	0	0	—	5	0	0	0	0	11¹	16	0	11	4	21.4	6.35	46	.327	.450	0	—	-0	-4	-4	-1	-0.1
Total 5		22	21	.512	75	50	29	7	1	436¹	383	7	147	209	11.2	2.85	95	.240	.308	22	.163	-1	-15	-7	-7	-1.4

● **PAUL DOYLE**   Doyle, Paul Sinnott   b: 10/2/39, Philadelphia, Pa.   BL/TL, 5'11", 172 lbs.   Deb: 5/28/69

1969	*Atl-N	2	0	1.000	36	0	0	0	6	39	31	4	16	25	10.8	2.08	174	.231	.313	0	.000	-0	7	7	1	0.5
1970	Cal-A	3	1	.750	40	0	0	0	5	42	43	7	21	34	13.9	5.14	70	.267	.355	0	.000	-0	-7	-7	1	-0.8
	SD-N	0	2	.000	9	0	0	0	0	9	11	0	9	6	19.3	6.43	62	.360	.484	0	.000	-0	-2	-2	-1	-0.5
1972	Cal-A	0	0	—	2	0	0	0	0	2¹	2	0	3	0	19.3	19.30	—	.250	.455	0	—	-0	1	0	0	0.0
Total 3		5	3	.625	87	0	0	0	11	90¹	85	11	46	65	13.2	3.79	96	.259	.352	0	.000	-1	-1	-2	3	-0.8

● **CARL DOYLE**   Doyle, William Carl   b: 7/30/12, Knoxville, Tenn.   d: 9/4/51, Knoxville, Tenn.   BR/TR, 6'1", 185 lbs.   Deb: 8/5/35

1935	Phi-A	2	7	.222	14	9	0	0	0	79²	86	3	72	34	18.1	5.99	76	.282	.422	4	.133	-2	-14	-13	1	-1.3
1936	Phi-A	0	3	.000	8	6	1	0	0	38²	66	4	29	12	23.3	10.94	47	.369	.469	4	.267	-1	-25	-25	-1	-1.4
1939	Bro-N	1	2	.333	5	1	1	1	1	17²	17	1	7	7	7.6	1.02	395	.136	.227	1	.167	0	6	6	0	1.1
1940	Bro-N	0	0	—	3	0	0	0	0	5²	18	3	6	4	44.5	27.00	15	.545	.651	1	1.000	1	-15	-14	0	-0.5

YEAR	TM/L	W	L	PCT	G	GS	CG	SH	SV	IP	H	HR	BB	SO	RAT	ERA	ERA+	OAV	OOB	BH	AVG	PB	PR	/A	PD	TPI
	StL-N	3	3	.500	21	5	1	0	0	81	99	7	41	44	16.2	5.89	68	.294	.380	6	.200	2	-18	-17	-0	-1.0
	Yr	3	3	.500	24	5	1	0	1	86²	117	10	47	48	17.7	7.27	55	.313	.398	7	.226	2	-33	-32	0	-1.5
Total	4	6	15	.286	51	21	6	1	2	222²	277	18	155	101	18.1	6.95	63	.303	.414	16	.195	1	-66	-63	-0	-3.1

● **TOM DOZIER**   Dozier, Thomas Dean b: 9/5/61, San Pablo, Cal.   BR/TR, 6'2", 190 lbs.   Deb: 5/17/86

YEAR	TM/L	W	L	PCT	G	GS	CG	SH	SV	IP	H	HR	BB	SO	RAT	ERA	ERA+	OAV	OOB	BH	AVG	PB	PR	/A	PD	TPI
1986	Oak-A	0	0	—	4	0	0	0	0	6¹	6	1	5	4	15.6	5.68	68	.261	.393	0	—	0	-1	-1	-0	0.6

● **BUZZ DOZIER**   Dozier, William Joseph b: 8/31/27, Waco, Tex.   BR/TR, 6'3", 185 lbs.   Deb: 9/12/47

YEAR	TM/L	W	L	PCT	G	GS	CG	SH	SV	IP	H	HR	BB	SO	RAT	ERA	ERA+	OAV	OOB	BH	AVG	PB	PR	/A	PD	TPI
1947	Was-A	0	0	—	2	0	0	0	0	4²	2	0	1	2	5.8	0.00	—	.133	.188	0	.000	-0	2	2	-0	0.0
1949	Was-A	0	0	—	2	0	0	0	0	6¹	12	0	6	1	25.6	11.37	37	.429	.529	0	.000	-0	-5	-5	-0	-0.1
Total	2	0	0	—	4	0	0	0	0	11	14	0	7	3	17.2	6.55	62	.326	.420	0	.000	-0	-3	-3	-0	-0.1

● **DOUG DRABEK**   Drabek, Douglas Dean b: 7/25/62, Victoria, Tex.   BR/TR, 6'1", 185 lbs.   Deb: 5/30/86

YEAR	TM/L	W	L	PCT	G	GS	CG	SH	SV	IP	H	HR	BB	SO	RAT	ERA	ERA+	OAV	OOB	BH	AVG	PB	PR	/A	PD	TPI
1986	NY-A	7	8	.467	27	21	0	0	0	131²	126	13	50	76	12.2	4.10	100	.251	.323	0	—	0	1	-0	-1	-0.1
1987	Pit-N	11	12	.478	29	28	1	1	0	176¹	165	22	46	120	10.8	3.88	106	.247	.296	7	.119	-1	4	4	1	0.5
1988	Pit-N	15	7	.682	33	32	3	1	0	219¹	194	21	50	127	10.3	3.08	111	.239	.288	13	.171	3	9	8	-1	1.0
1989	Pit-N	14	12	.538	35	34	8	5	0	244¹	215	21	69	123	10.6	2.80	120	.238	.295	8	.104	-2	19	15	-0	1.3
1990	*Pit-N	**22**	**6**	**.786**	33	33	9	3	0	231¹	190	15	56	131	9.7	2.76	131	.225	.275	18	.214	5	26	22	2	3.4
1991	*Pit-N	15	14	.517	35	35	5	2	0	234²	245	16	62	142	11.9	3.07	116	.274	.323	15	.179	1	16	13	2	1.9
1992	*Pit-N	15	11	.577	34	34	10	4	0	256²	218	17	54	177	9.7	2.77	124	.231	.277	14	.157	1	21	19	1	2.1
1993	Hou-N	9	18	.333	34	34	7	2	0	237²	242	18	60	157	11.5	3.79	102	.267	.315	6	.085	-2	7	2	0	0.1
1994	Hou-N★	12	6	.667	23	23	6	2	0	164²	132	14	45	121	9.8	2.84	143	.220	.277	14	.241	3	25	22	2	2.9
Total	9	120	94	.561	283	274	49	20	0	1896²	1727	157	492	1174	10.7	3.17	116	.244	.296	95	.159	9	128	106	5	13.1

● **MOE DRABOWSKY**   Drabowsky, Myron Walter b: 7/21/35, Ozanna, Poland   BR/TR, 6'2", 200 lbs.   Deb: 8/7/56   C

YEAR	TM/L	W	L	PCT	G	GS	CG	SH	SV	IP	H	HR	BB	SO	RAT	ERA	ERA+	OAV	OOB	BH	AVG	PB	PR	/A	PD	TPI
1956	Chi-N	2	4	.333	9	7	3	0	0	51	37	1	39	36	13.8	2.47	153	.207	.355	4	.250	0	7	7	-0	0.9
1957	Chi-N	13	15	.464	36	33	12	2	0	239²	214	22	94	170	11.9	3.53	110	.242	.321	15	.183	2	9	9	0	1.2
1958	Chi-N	9	11	.450	22	20	4	1	0	125²	118	19	73	77	14.0	4.51	87	.245	.350	7	.156	-1	-8	-8	-0	-1.3
1959	Chi-N	5	10	.333	31	23	3	1	0	141²	138	21	75	70	13.7	4.13	96	.251	.344	5	.111	-1	-3	-3	-0	-0.4
1960	Chi-N	3	1	.750	32	7	0	0	1	50¹	71	3	23	26	17.0	6.44	59	.338	.406	0	.000	-1	-15	-15	-1	-1.3
1961	Mil-N	0	2	.000	16	0	0	0	2	25¹	26	4	18	5	16.0	4.62	81	.277	.398	1	.250	0	-2	-2	-0	-0.2
1962	Cin-N	2	6	.250	23	10	1	0	1	83	84	13	31	56	13.1	4.99	81	.267	.344	1	.000	-2	-10	-9	-1	-1.0
	KC-A	1	1	.500	10	3	0	0	0	28	29	8	10	19	12.9	5.14	82	.266	.333	1	.167	-0	-4	-3	-0	-0.2
1963	KC-A	7	13	.350	26	22	9	2	0	174¹	135	16	64	109	10.7	3.05	128	.214	.295	10	.161	1	11	17	-2	1.8
1964	KC-A	5	13	.278	53	21	1	0	1	168²	176	24	72	119	13.7	5.29	72	.273	.353	1	.023	-4	-31	-28	1	-3.1
1965	KC-A	4	5	.167	14	5	0	0	0	38²	44	5	18	25	15.1	4.42	79	.291	.378	1	.091	-1	-4	-4	-0	-0.7
1966	*Bal-A	6	0	1.000	44	3	0	0	7	96	62	10	29	98	8.6	2.81	118	.181	.247	8	.364	4	7	6	-1	0.8
1967	Bal-A	7	5	.583	43	0	0	0	12	95¹	66	7	25	96	8.8	1.60	196	.194	.253	7	.350	2	17	16	0	3.0
1968	Bal-A	4	4	.500	45	0	0	0	7	61¹	35	3	25	46	9.4	1.91	153	.166	.267	2	.286	0	7	7	-0	1.2
1969	KC-A	11	9	.550	52	0	0	0	11	98	68	10	30	76	9.2	2.94	125	.190	.256	4	.235	1	7	8	1	2.0
1970	KC-A	1	2	.333	24	0	0	0	2	35²	28	3	12	38	10.6	3.28	114	.217	.294	1	.250	0	2	2	0	0.2
	*Bal-A	4	2	.667	21	0	0	0	1	33¹	30	7	15	21	12.4	3.78	96	.233	.317	0	.000	-1	-0	-0	-0	-0.2
	Yr	4	5	.556	45	0	0	0	3	69	58	10	27	59	11.2	3.52	105	.221	.296	1	.111	-0	1	1	-0	0.0
1971	StL-N	6	1	.857	51	0	0	0	8	60¹	45	3	33	49	11.9	3.43	105	.207	.317	1	.167	-0	0	1	-1	0.1
1972	StL-N	1	1	.500	30	0	0	0	2	27²	29	4	14	22	14.3	2.60	131	.259	.346	0	.000	-0	3	2	-1	0.1
	Chi-A	0	0	—	7	0	0	0	0	7¹	6	2	4	2	9.8	2.45	127	.240	.296	0	.000	-0	0	1	-0	0.0
Total	17	88	105	.456	589	154	33	6	55	1641	1441	182	702	1162	12.1	3.71	101	.236	.321	68	.162	-0	-5	4	-5	2.9

● **DICK DRAGO**   Drago, Richard Anthony b: 6/25/45, Toledo, Ohio   BR/TR, 6'1", 190 lbs.   Deb: 4/11/69

YEAR	TM/L	W	L	PCT	G	GS	CG	SH	SV	IP	H	HR	BB	SO	RAT	ERA	ERA+	OAV	OOB	BH	AVG	PB	PR	/A	PD	TPI
1969	KC-A	11	13	.458	41	26	10	2	1	200²	190	19	65	108	11.5	3.77	98	.248	.308	3	.058	-3	-3	-2	2	-0.3
1970	KC-A	9	15	.375	35	34	7	1	0	240	239	20	72	127	11.9	3.75	100	.266	.325	4	.053	-6	-1	-0	-1	-0.7
1971	KC-A	17	11	.607	35	34	15	4	0	241¹	251	14	46	109	11.4	2.98	115	.276	.318	10	.130	1	13	12	0	1.5
1972	KC-A	12	17	.414	34	33	11	2	0	239¹	230	22	51	135	10.8	3.01	101	.254	.298	4	.059	-2	1	1	-3	-0.5
1973	KC-A	12	14	.462	37	33	10	1	0	212²	252	16	76	98	14.2	4.23	97	.300	.363	0	—	0	-10	-3	-1	-0.2
1974	Bos-A	7	10	.412	33	18	8	0	3	175²	165	17	56	90	11.6	3.48	110	.251	.315	0	—	0	3	7	-2	0.7
1975	*Bos-A	2	2	.500	40	2	0	0	15	72²	66	3	31	43	12.4	3.84	106	.247	.323	0	—	0	-1	2	-0	-0.1
1976	Cal-A	7	8	.467	43	0	0	0	6	79¹	80	7	31	43	13.2	4.42	75	.264	.342	0	—	0	-8	-10	-2	-1.8
1977	Cal-A	0	1	.000	13	0	0	0	0	21	22	3	4	15	10.7	3.00	130	.272	.298	0	—	0	2	2	-0	0.1
	Bal-A	6	3	.667	36	0	0	0	3	39²	49	2	15	20	14.7	3.63	104	.308	.371	0	—	0	2	1	-0	0.5
	Yr	6	4	.600	49	0	0	0	3	60²	71	5	18	35	13.4	3.41	112	.293	.345	0	—	0	4	3	-1	0.8
1978	Bos-A	4	4	.500	37	1	0	0	7	77¹	71	6	32	42	12.5	3.03	136	.246	.329	0	—	0	6	9	-1	1.0
1979	Bos-A	10	6	.625	53	1	0	0	13	89	85	6	21	67	11.0	3.03	145	.254	.304	0	—	0	12	14	-0	2.6
1980	Bos-A	7	5	.583	43	7	1	0	3	132²	127	17	44	63	11.9	4.14	102	.251	.317	0	.000	0	-2	1	-1	0.0
1981	Sea-A	4	6	.400	39	0	0	0	3	53²	71	4	15	27	14.4	5.53	70	.324	.368	0	—	0	-11	-10	-0	-1.9
Total	13	108	117	.480	519	189	62	10	58	1875	1901	157	558	987	12.1	3.62	103	.266	.324	21	.077	-10	4	23	-5	0.5

● **BRIAN DRAHMAN**   Drahman, Brian Stacy b: 11/7/66, Kenton, Ky.   BR/TR, 6'3", 205 lbs.   Deb: 4/16/91

YEAR	TM/L	W	L	PCT	G	GS	CG	SH	SV	IP	H	HR	BB	SO	RAT	ERA	ERA+	OAV	OOB	BH	AVG	PB	PR	/A	PD	TPI
1991	Chi-A	3	2	.600	28	0	0	0	0	30²	21	4	13	18	10.0	3.23	123	.193	.279	0	—	0	3	3	-0	0.5
1992	Chi-A	0	0	—	5	0	0	0	0	7	6	0	2	1	10.3	2.57	150	.222	.276	0	—	0	1	1	-0	0.1
1993	Chi-A	0	0	—	5	0	0	0	1	5¹	7	0	2	3	15.2	0.00	—	.333	.391	0	—	0	3	2	0	0.1
1994	Fla-N	0	0	—	9	0	0	0	0	13	15	2	6	7	14.5	6.23	72	.300	.375	0	—	0	-3	-2	0	-0.1
Total	4	3	2	.600	47	0	0	0	1	56	49	6	23	29	11.6	3.54	116	.237	.313	0	—	0	4	4	-0	0.6

● **LOGAN DRAKE**   Drake, Logan Gaffney "L.G." b: 12/26/1900, Spartanburg, S.C.   d: 6/1/40, Columbia, S.C.   BR/TR, 5'10.5", 165 lbs.   Deb: 9/21/22

YEAR	TM/L	W	L	PCT	G	GS	CG	SH	SV	IP	H	HR	BB	SO	RAT	ERA	ERA+	OAV	OOB	BH	AVG	PB	PR	/A	PD	TPI
1922	Cle-A	0	0	—	1	0	0	0	0	3	4	0	2	1	18.0	3.00	134	.364	.462	0	.000	-0	0	0	-0	0.0
1923	Cle-A	0	0	—	4	0	0	0	0	4¹	2	0	4	1	14.5	4.15	95	.133	.350	0	—	-0	-0	-0	-0	0.0
1924	Cle-A	0	1	.000	5	1	0	0	0	11¹	18	0	10	8	23.0	10.32	41	.400	.518	0	.000	-0	-8	-8	-0	-0.6
Total	3	0	1	.000	10	1	0	0	0	18²	24	0	16	11	20.3	7.71	54	.338	.472	0	.000	-0	-7	-7	-1	-0.6

● **TOM DRAKE**   Drake, Thomas Kendall b: 8/7/14, Birmingham, Ala.   d: 7/2/88, Birmingham, Ala.   BR/TR, 6'1", 185 lbs.   Deb: 4/24/39

YEAR	TM/L	W	L	PCT	G	GS	CG	SH	SV	IP	H	HR	BB	SO	RAT	ERA	ERA+	OAV	OOB	BH	AVG	PB	PR	/A	PD	TPI
1939	Cle-A	0	1	.000	8	1	0	0	0	15	23	2	19	1	26.4	9.00	49	.377	.537	0	.000	-0	-7	-8	0	-0.4
1941	Bro-N	1	1	.500	10	2	0	0	0	24²	26	2	9	12	12.8	4.38	84	.280	.343	2	.400	0	-2	-2	-0	-0.1
Total	2	1	2	.333	18	3	0	0	0	39²	49	4	28	13	17.9	6.13	63	.318	.429	2	.286	0	-9	-10	0	-0.5

● **MIKE DRAPER**   Draper, Michael Anthony b: 9/14/66, Hagerstown, Md.   BR/TR, 6'2", 180 lbs.   Deb: 4/10/93

YEAR	TM/L	W	L	PCT	G	GS	CG	SH	SV	IP	H	HR	BB	SO	RAT	ERA	ERA+	OAV	OOB	BH	AVG	PB	PR	/A	PD	TPI
1993	NY-N	1	1	.500	29	1	0	0	0	42¹	52	3	14	16	14.2	4.25	94	.327	.381	2	.667	1	-1	-1	0	0.1

● **DAVE DRAVECKY**   Dravecky, David Francis b: 2/14/56, Youngstown, Ohio   BR/TL, 6'1", 195 lbs.   Deb: 6/15/82

YEAR	TM/L	W	L	PCT	G	GS	CG	SH	SV	IP	H	HR	BB	SO	RAT	ERA	ERA+	OAV	OOB	BH	AVG	PB	PR	/A	PD	TPI
1982	SD-N	5	3	.625	31	10	0	0	2	105	86	8	33	59	10.3	2.57	133	.225	.288	3	.130	-0	12	10	2	0.9
1983	SD-N★	14	10	.583	28	28	9	1	0	183²	181	18	44	74	11.2	3.58	97	.262	.309	6	.098	-1	1	-2	1	-0.3
1984	*SD-N	9	8	.529	50	14	3	2	8	156²	125	12	51	71	10.3	2.93	122	.222	.291	4	.098	-1	11	11	-2	1.0
1985	SD-N	13	11	.542	34	31	7	2	0	214²	200	16	57	105	11.1	2.93	120	.249	.300	8	.116	-0	16	14	-1	1.4
1986	SD-N	9	11	.450	26	26	3	1	0	161¹	149	16	54	87	11.4	3.07	119	.246	.309	7	.140	0	12	10	0	1.3
1987	SD-N	3	7	.300	30	10	1	1	0	79	71	10	31	60	12.0	3.76	105	.240	.318	3	.167	PB	2	/A	0	0.2
	*SF-N	7	5	.583	18	18	4	3	0	112¹	115	8	33	78	12.0	3.20	120	.272	.328	5	.132	0	11	8	1	0.9

YEAR TM/L	W	L	PCT	G	GS	CG	SH	SV	IP	H	HR	BB	SO	RAT	ERA	ERA+	OAV	OOB	BH	AVG	PB	PR	/A	PD	TPI
Yr	10	12	.455	48	28	5	3	0	191¹	186	18	64	138	11.9	3.43	113	.257	.319	8	.143	1	14	10	1	1.1
1988 SF-N	2	2	.500	7	7	1	0	0	37	33	4	8	19	10.0	3.16	103	.243	.285	1	.100	-0	1	0	0	0.0
1989 SF-N	2	0	1.000	2	2	0	0	0	8	2	4	5		9.0	3.46	97	.182	.265	1	.333	1	0	-0	0	0.1
Total 8	64	57	.529	226	146	28	9	10	1062²	968	97	315	558	11.0	3.13	115	.245	.304	38	.121	-2	67	54	1	5.5

● **TOM DREES**   Drees, Thomas Kent b: 6/17/63, Des Moines, Iowa   BB/TL, 6'6", 210 lbs.   Deb: 9/3/91

YEAR TM/L	W	L	PCT	G	GS	CG	SH	SV	IP	H	HR	BB	SO	RAT	ERA	ERA+	OAV	OOB	BH	AVG	PB	PR	/A	PD	TPI
1991 Chi-A	0	0	—	4	0	0	0	0	7¹	10	4	6	2	19.6	12.27	32	.345	.457	0		0	-7	-7	-0	0.1

● **DARREN DREIFORT**   Dreifort, Darren James b: 5/18/72, Wichita, Kan.   BR/TR, 6'2", 205 lbs.   Deb: 4/7/94

YEAR TM/L	W	L	PCT	G	GS	CG	SH	SV	IP	H	HR	BB	SO	RAT	ERA	ERA+	OAV	OOB	BH	AVG	PB	PR	/A	PD	TPI
1994 LA-N	0	5	.000	27	0	0	0	6	29	45	0	15	22	19.9	6.21	64	.357	.441	1	1.000	1	-6	-7	1	-1.3

● **CLEM DREISEWERD**   Dreisewerd, Clemens Johann "Steamboat" b: 1/24/16, Old Monroe, Mo.   BL/TL, 6'1.5", 195 lbs.   Deb: 8/29/44

YEAR TM/L	W	L	PCT	G	GS	CG	SH	SV	IP	H	HR	BB	SO	RAT	ERA	ERA+	OAV	OOB	BH	AVG	PB	PR	/A	PD	TPI
1944 Bos-A	2	4	.333	7	7	3	0	0	48²	52	2	9	9	11.3	4.07	84	.268	.300	3	.188	0	-3	-4	-1	-0.5
1945 Bos-A	0	1	.000	2	2	0	0	0	9²	13	0	2	3	14.9	4.66	73	.325	.372	0	.000	-0	-1	-1	-0	-0.2
1946 *Bos-A	4	1	.800	20	1	0	0	0	47¹	50	3	15	19	12.4	4.18	88	.276	.332	0	.000	-0	-4	-3	1	-0.3
1948 StL-A	0	2	.000	13	0	0	0	1	22¹	28	3	6	8	14.5	5.64	81	.318	.375	0	.000	-1	-3	-3	-0	-0.3
NY-N	0	0	—	4	0	0	0	1	12²	17	3	5	2	15.6	5.68	69	.321	.379	1	.250	1	-2	-2	-0	0.0
Total 4	6	8	.429	46	10	3	0	2	140²	160	14	39	39	12.8	4.54	82	.288	.336	4	.105	-1	-14	-13	-1	-1.3

● **KIRK DRESSENDORFER**   Dressendorfer, Kirk Richard b: 4/8/69, Houston, Tex.   BR/TR, 5'11", 190 lbs.   Deb: 4/13/91

YEAR TM/L	W	L	PCT	G	GS	CG	SH	SV	IP	H	HR	BB	SO	RAT	ERA	ERA+	OAV	OOB	BH	AVG	PB	PR	/A	PD	TPI
1991 Oak-A	3	3	.500	7	7	0	0	0	34²	33	5	21	17	14.0	5.45	70	.244	.346	0		0	-5	-6	-0	-0.7

● **BOB DRESSER**   Dresser, Robert Nicholson b: 10/4/1878, Newton, Mass. d: 7/27/24, Duxbury, Mass.   BL/TL,   Deb: 8/13/02

YEAR TM/L	W	L	PCT	G	GS	CG	SH	SV	IP	H	HR	BB	SO	RAT	ERA	ERA+	OAV	OOB	BH	AVG	PB	PR	/A	PD	TPI
1902 Bos-N	0	1	.000	1	1	1	0	0	9	12	0	0	8	12.0	3.00	94	.319	.319	1	.250	0	-0	-0	-0	0.0

● **ROB DRESSLER**   Dressler, Robert Anthony b: 2/2/54, Portland, Ore.   BR/TR, 6'3", 180 lbs.   Deb: 9/7/75

YEAR TM/L	W	L	PCT	G	GS	CG	SH	SV	IP	H	HR	BB	SO	RAT	ERA	ERA+	OAV	OOB	BH	AVG	PB	PR	/A	PD	TPI
1975 SF-N	1	0	1.000	3	2	1	0	0	16¹	17	0	4	6	11.6	1.10	345	.274	.318	0	.000	0	5	5	0	0.3
1976 SF-N	3	10	.231	25	19	0	0	0	107²	125	8	35	33	13.5	4.43	82	.291	.347	4	.129	-1	-11	-10	1	-1.1
1978 StL-N	0	1	.000	3	2	0	0	0	13	12	0	4	4	11.1	2.08	169	.267	.327	0	.000	-1	0	0	0	0.1
1979 Sea-A	3	2	.600	21	11	2	0	0	104	134	11	22	36	13.5	4.93	88	.312	.345	0	—	0	-8	-7	-0	-0.3
1980 Sea-A	4	10	.286	30	14	3	0	0	149¹	161	14	33	50	11.9	3.98	104	.280	.322	0	—	0	1	3	1	0.3
Total 5	11	23	.324	82	48	6	0	0	390¹	449	33	98	129	12.7	4.17	96	.291	.335	4	.105	-1	-12	-7	2	-0.7

● **DAVE DREW**   Drew, David   Deb: 5/14/1884 ♦

YEAR TM/L	W	L	PCT	G	GS	CG	SH	SV	IP	H	HR	BB	SO	RAT	ERA	ERA+	OAV	OOB	BH	AVG	PB	PR	/A	PD	TPI
1884 Phi-U	0	1	.000	1	0	0	0	0	7	7	0	0	2	9.0	3.86	60	.243	.243	4	.444	0	-1	-1	-0	-0.1

● **KARL DREWS**   Drews, Karl August b: 2/22/20, Staten Island, N.Y d: 8/15/63, Dania, Fla.   BR/TR, 6'4", 198 lbs.   Deb: 9/8/46

YEAR TM/L	W	L	PCT	G	GS	CG	SH	SV	IP	H	HR	BB	SO	RAT	ERA	ERA+	OAV	OOB	BH	AVG	PB	PR	/A	PD	TPI
1946 NY-A	0	1	.000	3	1	0	0	0	6¹	6	0	6	4	18.5	8.53	40	.250	.419	0	.000	-0	-4	-4	-0	-0.5
1947 *NY-A	6	6	.500	30	10	0	0	1	91²	92	6	55	45	14.9	4.91	72	.264	.373	1	.037	-2	-12	-14	1	-1.9
1948 NY-A	2	3	.400	19	2	0	0	1	38	35	3	31	11	15.6	3.79	108	.248	.384	0	.000	-1	2	1	1	0.2
StL-A	3	2	.600	20	2	0	0	2	38	43	3	38	11	19.2	8.05	57	.289	.433	0	.000	-0	-16	-15	0	-1.8
Yr	5	5	.500	39	4	0	0	3	76	78	6	69	22	17.4	5.92	73	.269	.409	0	.000	-1	-14	-14	1	-1.6
1949 StL-A	4	12	.250	31	23	3	1	0	139²	180	11	66	35	16.4	6.64	68	.317	.397	0	.000	-5	-38	-33	-1	-3.6
1951 Phi-N	1	0	1.000	5	3	1	0	0	23	29	2	7	13	15.7	6.26	61	.296	.367	2	.250	1	-6	-6	-0	-0.2
1952 Phi-N	14	15	.483	33	30	15	5	0	228²	213	13	52	96	10.6	2.72	135	.252	.298	9	.110	-2	26	24	0	2.8
1953 Phi-N	9	10	.474	47	27	6	0	3	185¹	218	26	72	72	13.5	4.52	93	.293	.346	7	.119	-2	-5	-6	2	-0.7
1954 Phi-N	1	0	1.000	8	0	0	0	0	16	18	2	8	6	14.6	5.63	72	.300	.382	0	.000	-1	-3	-3	-0	-0.2
Cin-N	4	4	.500	22	9	1	1	0	60	79	6	19	29	15.0	6.00	70	.326	.380	2	.167	1	-13	-12	-1	-1.3
Yr	5	4	.556	30	9	1	1	0	76	97	8	27	35	14.9	5.92	70	.320	.380	2	.125	1	-16	-15	0	-1.5
Total 8	44	53	.454	218	107	26	7	7	826²	913	72	332	322	13.9	4.76	84	.284	.357	21	.083	-12	-68	-68	3	-7.2

● **STEVE DREYER**   Dreyer, Steven William b: 11/19/69, Ames, Iowa   BR/TR, 6'3", 180 lbs.   Deb: 8/8/93

YEAR TM/L	W	L	PCT	G	GS	CG	SH	SV	IP	H	HR	BB	SO	RAT	ERA	ERA+	OAV	OOB	BH	AVG	PB	PR	/A	PD	TPI
1993 Tex-A	3	3	.500	10	6	0	0	0	41	48	7	20	23	15.1	5.71	73	.291	.371	0	—	0	-6	-7	-0	-0.9
1994 Tex-A	1	1	.500	5	3	0	0	0	17¹	19	1	8	11	14.5	5.71	79	.271	.354	0	—	0	-2	-2	0	0.1
Total 2	4	4	.500	15	9	0	0	0	58¹	67	8	28	34	15.0	5.71	75	.285	.366	0	—	0	-8	-9	-0	-0.8

● **DENNY DRISCOLL**   Driscoll, John F. b: 11/19/1855, Lowell, Mass. d: 7/11/1886, Lowell, Mass.   BL/TL, 5'10.5", 160 lbs.   Deb: 7/1/1880 ♦

YEAR TM/L	W	L	PCT	G	GS	CG	SH	SV	IP	H	HR	BB	SO	RAT	ERA	ERA+	OAV	OOB	BH	AVG	PB	PR	/A	PD	TPI
1880 Buf-N	1	3	.250	6	4	4	0	0	41²	48	1	9	17	12.3	3.89	63	.270	.305	10	.154	-1	-7	-7	0	-0.6
1882 Pit-a	13	9	.591	23	23	23	0	0	201	162	0	12	59	7.8	**1.21**	**216**	.206	.218	11	.138	-2	33	31	-4	2.4
1883 Pit-a	18	21	.462	41	40	35	1	0	336¹	427	3	39	79	12.5	3.99	81	.290	.309	27	.182	-5	-26	-29	6	-2.5
1884 Lou-a	6	6	.500	13	13	10	0	0	102	110	3	7	16	10.5	3.44	90	.252	.267	9	.188	-1	-2	-4	2	-0.3
Total 4	38	39	.494	83	80	72	1	0	681	747	6	67	171	10.8	3.08	97	.260	.277	60	.167	-9	-2	-8	4	-1.0

● **MICHAEL DRISCOLL**   Driscoll, Michael Columbus b: 10/19/1892, Rockland, Mass. d: 3/22/53, Foxboro, Mass.   BR/TR, 6'1", 160 lbs.   Deb: 7/6/16

YEAR TM/L	W	L	PCT	G	GS	CG	SH	SV	IP	H	HR	BB	SO	RAT	ERA	ERA+	OAV	OOB	BH	AVG	PB	PR	/A	PD	TPI
1916 Phi-A	0	1	.000	1	0	0	0	0	5	6	0	2	0	14.4	5.40	53	.273	.333	0	.000	-0	-1	-1	1	-0.2

● **TOM DROHAN**   Drohan, Thomas F b: 8/26/1887, Fall River, Mass. d: 9/17/26, Kewanee, Ill.   BR/TR, 5'10", 175 lbs.   Deb: 5/1/13

YEAR TM/L	W	L	PCT	G	GS	CG	SH	SV	IP	H	HR	BB	SO	RAT	ERA	ERA+	OAV	OOB	BH	AVG	PB	PR	/A	PD	TPI
1913 Was-A	0	0		2	0	0	0	0	2	5	1	0	2	22.5	9.00	33	.500	.500	0	—	0	-1	-1	0	0.0

● **DICK DROTT**   Drott, Richard Fred "Hummer" b: 7/1/36, Cincinnati, Ohio d: 8/16/85, Glendale Heights, Ill.   BR/TR, 6', 185 lbs.   Deb: 4/16/57

YEAR TM/L	W	L	PCT	G	GS	CG	SH	SV	IP	H	HR	BB	SO	RAT	ERA	ERA+	OAV	OOB	BH	AVG	PB	PR	/A	PD	TPI
1957 Chi-N	15	11	.577	38	32	7	3	0	229	200	22	129	170	13.2	3.58	108	.234	.340	8	.100	-5	8	8	-1	0.2
1958 Chi-N	7	11	.389	39	31	4	0	0	167¹	156	23	99	127	14.0	5.43	72	.245	.352	15	.273	3	-28	-28	1	-2.3
1959 Chi-N	1	2	.333	8	6	1	1	0	27¹	25	5	26	15	16.8	5.93	67	.245	.398	1	.125	-0	-6	-6	-0	-0.6
1960 Chi-N	0	6	.000	23	9	0	0	0	55¹	63	7	42	32	17.6	7.16	53	.296	.419	1	.100	-1	-21	-21	-0	-2.1
1961 Chi-N	1	4	.200	35	8	0	0	0	98	75	13	51	48	11.7	4.22	99	.215	.317	6	.273	1	-2	-0	-2	-0.1
1962 Hou-N	1	0	1.000	6	1	0	0	0	13	12	1	9	10	14.5	7.62	49	.240	.356	0	.000	-0	-5	-6	-0	-0.4
1963 Hou-N	2	12	.143	27	14	2	1	0	97²	95	13	49	58	13.8	4.98	63	.257	.353	3	.130	-1	-18	-20	-1	-2.8
Total 7	27	46	.370	176	101	14	5	0	687²	626	84	405	460	13.8	4.78	80	.243	.351	34	.168	-2	-72	-74	-5	-8.1

● **LOUIS DRUCKE**   Drucke, Louis Frank b: 12/3/1888, Waco, Tex. d: 9/22/55, Waco, Tex.   BR/TR, 6'1", 188 lbs.   Deb: 9/25/09

YEAR TM/L	W	L	PCT	G	GS	CG	SH	SV	IP	H	HR	BB	SO	RAT	ERA	ERA+	OAV	OOB	BH	AVG	PB	PR	/A	PD	TPI
1909 NY-N	2	1	.667	3	3	2	0	0	24	20	0	13	8	12.4	2.25	114	.227	.327	1	.125	-0	1	1	-0	0.0
1910 NY-N	12	11	.545	34	27	15	0	0	215¹	174	3	82	151	11.2	2.47	120	.228	.312	15	.214	4	14	12	2	1.7
1911 NY-N	4	4	.500	15	10	4	0	0	75²	83	1	41	42	15.7	4.04	83	.281	.384	2	.087	-1	-5	-6	1	-0.6
1912 NY-N	0	0	—	1	0	0	0	1	2	5	0	1	0	27.0	13.50	25	.417	.462	0	—	0	-2	-2	-0	-0.2
Total 4	18	15	.545	53	40	21	0	0	317	282	4	137	201	12.4	2.90	105	.243	.333	18	.178	2	7	5	2	0.9

● **CARL DRUHOT**   Druhot, Carl A. "Collie" b: 9/1/1882, Ohio d: 2/11/18, Portland, Ore.   BL/TL, 5'7", 150 lbs.   Deb: 4/18/06

YEAR TM/L	W	L	PCT	G	GS	CG	SH	SV	IP	H	HR	BB	SO	RAT	ERA	ERA+	OAV	OOB	BH	AVG	PB	PR	/A	PD	TPI
1906 Cin-N	2	2	.500	4	3	1	0	0	25	27	0	7	14	13.0	4.32	64	.270	.330	2	.222	-0	-5	-4	-1	-0.7
StL-N	6	7	.462	15	13	12	1	0	130¹	117	1	46	45	11.6	2.62	100	.238	.310	13	.232	1	0	1	0	0.2
Yr	8	9	.471	19	16	13	1	0	155¹	144	1	53	59	11.7	2.90	91	.243	.310	15	.231	1	-5	-4	-1	-0.5
1907 StL-N	0	1	.000	1	1	0	0	0	2¹	3	0	4	1	30.9	15.43	16	.600	.800	0	—	0	-3	-3	0	-0.9
Total 2	8	10	.444	20	17	13	1	0	157²	147	1	57	60	12.1	3.08	86	.247	.321	15	.231	1	-8	-8	-0	-1.4

● **TIM DRUMMOND**   Drummond, Timothy Darnell b: 12/24/64, LaPlata, Md.   BR/TR, 6'3", 170 lbs.   Deb: 9/12/87

YEAR TM/L	W	L	PCT	G	GS	CG	SH	SV	IP	H	HR	BB	SO	RAT	ERA	ERA+	OAV	OOB	BH	AVG	PB	PR	/A	PD	TPI
1987 Pit-N	0	0							6	5	0	3	5	12.0	4.50	91	.227	.320	0	.000	-0	-0	-0	-0	-0.0
1989 Min-A	0	0	—	8	0	0	0	1	16¹	16	0	8	9	14.3	3.86	107	.246	.347	0	—	0	0	1	-0	-0.5

YEAR TM/L	W	L	PCT	G	GS	CG	SH	SV	IP	H	HR	BB	SO	RAT	ERA	ERA+	OAV	OOB	BH	AVG	PB	PR	/A	PD	TPI
1990 Min-A	3	5	.375	35	4	0	0	1	91	104	8	36	49	13.9	4.35	95	.295	.362	0	—	0	-5	-2	-1	-0.6
Total 3	3	5	.375	49	4	0	0	2	113¹	125	8	47	63	13.9	4.29	97	.284	.357	0	.000	-0	-5	-2	-1	-1.1

● **DON DRYSDALE**   Drysdale, Donald Scott b: 7/23/36, Van Nuys, Cal. d: 7/3/93, Montreal, Que.   BR/TR, 6'6", 216 lbs. Deb: 4/17/56 H

YEAR TM/L	W	L	PCT	G	GS	CG	SH	SV	IP	H	HR	BB	SO	RAT	ERA	ERA+	OAV	OOB	BH	AVG	PB	PR	/A	PD	TPI
1956 *Bro-N	5	5	.500	25	12	2	0	0	99	95	9	31	55	11.7	2.64	150	.255	.317	5	.192	1	12	15	1	1.6
1957 Bro-N	17	9	.654	34	29	9	4	0	221	197	17	61	148	10.8	2.69	155	.236	.294	9	.123	-0	29	36	5	4.7
1958 LA-N	12	13	.480	44	29	6	1	0	211²	214	21	72	131	12.8	4.17	98	.263	.333	15	.227	8	-5	-2	3	1.0
1959 *LA-N★	17	13	.567	44	36	15	4	2	270²	237	26	93	242	11.6	3.46	122	.233	.308	15	.165	3	15	23	2	3.0
1960 LA-N	15	14	.517	41	36	15	5	2	269	214	27	72	246	9.9	2.84	140	.215	.275	13	.157	2	27	34	4	4.3
1961 LA-N☆	13	10	.565	40	37	10	3	0	244	236	29	83	182	12.5	3.69	118	.254	.329	16	.193	4	9	18	-1	1.8
1962 LA-N★	25	9	.735	43	41	19	2	1	314¹	272	21	78	232	10.3	2.83	128	.230	.283	22	.198	5	39	28	1	3.4
1963 *LA-N★	19	17	.528	42	42	17	3	0	315¹	287	25	57	251	10.1	2.63	115	.242	.283	16	.167	5	23	14	3	2.4
1964 LA-N★	18	16	.529	40	40	21	5	0	321¹	242	16	68	237	9.0	2.18	148	.207	.256	19	.173	4	48	38	2	4.7
1965 *LA-N★	23	12	.657	44	42	20	7	1	308¹	270	30	66	210	10.0	2.77	118	.232	.280	39	.300	22	26	17	0	4.4
1966 *LA-N	13	16	.448	40	40	11	3	0	273²	279	21	45	177	11.2	3.42	96	.265	.306	20	.189	4	6	-4	-1	-0.1
1967 LA-N★	13	16	.448	38	38	9	3	0	282	269	19	60	196	10.8	2.74	113	.251	.296	12	.129	-0	20	11	3	1.4
1968 LA-N★	14	12	.538	31	31	12	8	0	239	201	11	56	155	10.1	2.15	129	.231	.286	14	.177	1	22	16	2	2.4
1969 LA-N	5	4	.556	12	12	1	1	0	62²	71	9	13	24	12.4	4.45	75	.291	.332	3	.136	0	-6	-8	0	-1.0
Total 14	209	166	.557	518	465	167	49	6	3432	3084	280	855	2486	10.7	2.95	121	.239	.294	218	.186	60	266	230	25	34.0

● **MONK DUBIEL**   Dubiel, Walter John b: 2/12/18, Hartford, Conn. d: 10/23/69, Hartford, Conn.   BR/TR, 6', 190 lbs. Deb: 4/19/44

YEAR TM/L	W	L	PCT	G	GS	CG	SH	SV	IP	H	HR	BB	SO	RAT	ERA	ERA+	OAV	OOB	BH	AVG	PB	PR	/A	PD	TPI
1944 NY-A	13	13	.500	30	28	19	3	0	232	217	12	86	79	11.8	3.38	103	.248	.316	15	.181	-2	1	3	0	0.1
1945 NY-A	10	9	.526	26	20	9	1	0	151¹	157	9	62	45	13.0	4.64	75	.266	.335	16	.276	4	-21	-20	-2	-2.1
1948 Phi-N	8	10	.444	37	17	6	2	4	150¹	139	13	58	42	11.9	3.89	101	.248	.320	7	.167	0	1	1	-2	0.0
1949 Chi-N	6	9	.400	32	20	3	1	4	147²	142	16	54	52	12.0	4.14	97	.250	.317	10	.286	3	-2	-2	1	0.3
1950 Chi-N	6	10	.375	39	12	4	2	2	142²	152	12	67	51	13.9	4.16	101	.270	.348	9	.200	1	-0	1	2	0.3
1951 Chi-N	2	2	.500	22	0	0	0	1	54²	46	3	22	19	11.2	2.30	178	.232	.309	0	.000	-1	10	11	0	0.7
1952 Chi-N	0	0	—	1	0	0	0	0	0²	1	0	0	1	13.5	0.00	—	.333	.333	0	—	0	0	0	0	0.0
Total 7	45	53	.459	187	97	41	9	11	879¹	854	65	349	289	12.4	3.87	98	.254	.325	57	.207	5	-11	-6	-0	-0.7

● **BRIAN DuBOIS**   DuBois, Brian Andrew b: 4/18/67, Joliet, Ill.   BL/TL, 5'10", 195 lbs. Deb: 8/17/89

YEAR TM/L	W	L	PCT	G	GS	CG	SH	SV	IP	H	HR	BB	SO	RAT	ERA	ERA+	OAV	OOB	BH	AVG	PB	PR	/A	PD	TPI
1989 Det-A	0	4	.000	6	5	0	0	1	36	29	2	17	13	12.0	1.75	218	.218	.316	0	—	0	9	8	-0	1.2
1990 Det-A	3	5	.375	12	11	0	0	0	58¹	70	9	22	34	14.3	5.09	86	.310	.373	0	—	0	-8	-7	-1	-1.0
Total 2	3	9	.250	18	16	0	0	1	94¹	99	11	39	47	13.5	3.82	102	.276	.352	0	.000	0	1	1	-1	0.2

● **JEAN DUBUC**   Dubuc, Jean Joseph Octave Arthur "Chauncey" b: 9/15/1888, St.Johnsbury, Vt.   d: 8/28/58, Fort Myers, Fla.   BR/TR, 5'10.5", 185 lbs.   Deb: 6/25/08 C ◆

YEAR TM/L	W	L	PCT	G	GS	CG	SH	SV	IP	H	HR	BB	SO	RAT	ERA	ERA+	OAV	OOB	BH	AVG	PB	PR	/A	PD	TPI
1908 Cin-N	5	6	.455	15	9	7	1	0	85¹	62	2	41	32	11.4	2.74	84	.205	.309	4	.138	-1	-4	-7	0	-0.6
1909 Cin-N	2	5	.286	19	5	2	0	1	71¹	72	0	46	19	15.4	3.66	71	.269	.384	3	.167	0	-8	-8	0	-0.8
1912 Det-A	17	10	.630	37	26	23	2	3	250	217	2	109	97	12.0	2.77	118	.235	.321	29	.269	6	15	14	4	2.5
1913 Det-A	15	14	.517	36	28	22	1	0	242²	228	4	91	73	12.1	2.89	101	.252	.325	36	.267	5	1	1	8	1.9
1914 Det-A	13	14	.481	36	27	15	2	1	224	216	4	76	70	12.0	3.46	81	.257	.324	28	.226	7	-18	-16	3	-0.8
1915 Det-A	17	12	.586	39	33	22	5	2	258	231	6	88	74	11.5	3.21	94	.245	.316	23	.205	0	-8	-5	1	-0.4
1916 Det-A	10	10	.500	36	16	8	1	1	170¹	134	1	84	40	11.8	2.96	97	.233	.336	20	.256	5	-2	-2	1	0.8
1918 *Bos-A	0	1	.000	2	1	1	0	0	10²	11	1	5	1	13.5	4.22	64	.268	.348	1	.167	0	-2	-2	-0	-0.2
1919 NY-N	6	4	.600	36	5	1	0	3	132	119	4	37	32	10.8	2.66	105	.246	.303	6	.143	-1	4	2	2	0.2
Total 9	85	76	.528	256	150	101	12	13	1444¹	1290	20	577	438	11.9	3.04	96	.244	.324	150	.230	21	-22	-21	23	2.6

● **JIM DUCKWORTH**   Duckworth, James Raymond b: 5/24/39, National City, Cal.   BR/TR, 6'4", 194 lbs. Deb: 4/13/63

YEAR TM/L	W	L	PCT	G	GS	CG	SH	SV	IP	H	HR	BB	SO	RAT	ERA	ERA+	OAV	OOB	BH	AVG	PB	PR	/A	PD	TPI
1963 Was-A	4	12	.250	37	15	2	0	0	120²	131	13	67	66	15.5	6.04	61	.278	.379	0	.000	-3	-32	-31	-1	-4.1
1964 Was-A	1	6	.143	30	2	0	0	3	56	52	9	25	56	12.9	4.34	85	.244	.332	2	.222	0	-4	-4	0	-0.4
1965 Was-A	2	2	.500	17	8	0	0	0	64	45	11	36	74	11.7	3.94	88	.202	.318	0	.000	-2	-3	-3	-1	-0.5
1966 Was-A	0	3	.000	5	4	0	0	0	14¹	14	2	10	14	15.7	5.02	69	.259	.385	0	.000	-0	-3	-2	-0	-0.6
KC-A	0	2	.000	8	0	0	0	1	12	14	2	10	10	18.8	9.00	38	.292	.424	0	—	-0	-7	-7	-0	-1.3
Yr	0	5	.000	13	4	0	0	1	26¹	28	4	20	24	16.7	6.84	50	.269	.392	0	.000	-1	-10	-10	-1	-1.9
Total 4	7	25	.219	97	29	2	0	4	267	256	37	148	220	14.2	5.26	69	.253	.358	2	.034	-5	-50	-49	-2	-6.9

● **CLISE DUDLEY**   Dudley, Elzie Clise b: 8/8/03, Graham, N.C. d: 1/12/89, Moncks Corner, S.C   BL/TR, 6'1", 195 lbs. Deb: 4/18/29

YEAR TM/L	W	L	PCT	G	GS	CG	SH	SV	IP	H	HR	BB	SO	RAT	ERA	ERA+	OAV	OOB	BH	AVG	PB	PR	/A	PD	TPI
1929 Bro-N	6	14	.300	35	21	8	1	0	156²	202	9	64	33	15.9	5.69	81	.315	.385	5	.098	-1	-17	-19	2	-1.8
1930 Bro-N	4	4	.333	21	7	2	0	1	66²	103	3	27	18	17.8	6.35	77	.371	.430	5	.208	-0	-10	-11	1	-0.7
1931 Phi-N	8	14	.364	30	24	8	0	0	179	206	10	56	50	13.5	3.52	121	.287	.343	18	.214	-0	7	14	1	1.8
1932 Phi-N	1	1	.500	13	0	0	0	0	17²	23	3	8	6	15.8	7.13	62	.329	.397	4	.286	3	-6	-5	0	-0.3
1933 Pit-N	0	0	—	1	0	0	0	0	0¹	6	0	1	0	189.0	135.00	2	.857	.875	0	—	0	-5	-5	0	0.0
Total 5	17	33	.340	100	52	18	1	2	420¹	540	25	156	106	15.3	5.03	90	.315	.378	32	.185	1	-31	-24	4	-1.0

● **HAL DUES**   Dues, Hal Joseph b: 9/22/54, LaMarque, Tex.   BR/TR, 6'3", 180 lbs. Deb: 9/9/77

YEAR TM/L	W	L	PCT	G	GS	CG	SH	SV	IP	H	HR	BB	SO	RAT	ERA	ERA+	OAV	OOB	BH	AVG	PB	PR	/A	PD	TPI
1977 Mon-N	1	1	.500	6	4	0	0	0	23	26	2	9	9	14.0	4.30	88	.265	.327	0	.000	-1	-1	-1	0	-0.1
1978 Mon-N	5	6	.455	25	12	1	0	1	99	85	5	42	36	11.9	2.36	149	.240	.327	6	.194	0	13	13	-0	1.4
1980 Mon-N	0	1	.000	6	1	0	0	0	12¹	17	1	4	2	15.3	6.57	54	.333	.382	0	.000	-0	-4	-4	0	-0.3
Total 3	6	8	.429	37	17	1	0	1	134¹	128	8	55	47	12.5	3.08	116	.254	.333	6	.154	-1	8	7	0	1.0

● **LARRY DUFF**   Duff, Cecil Elba b: 11/30/1897, Radersburg, Mont. d: 11/10/69, Bend, Ore.   BL/TR, 6'1", 175 lbs. Deb: 9/5/22

YEAR TM/L	W	L	PCT	G	GS	CG	SH	SV	IP	H	HR	BB	SO	RAT	ERA	ERA+	OAV	OOB	BH	AVG	PB	PR	/A	PD	TPI
1922 Chi-A	1	1	.500	3	1	0	0	0	12²	16	1	3	7	13.5	4.97	82	.340	.380	2	.400	0	-1	-1	-0	-0.2

● **JIM DUFFALO**   Duffalo, James Francis b: 11/25/35, Helvetia, Pa.   BR/TR, 6'1", 175 lbs. Deb: 4/12/61

YEAR TM/L	W	L	PCT	G	GS	CG	SH	SV	IP	H	HR	BB	SO	RAT	ERA	ERA+	OAV	OOB	BH	AVG	PB	PR	/A	PD	TPI
1961 SF-N	5	1	.833	24	4	1	0	1	61²	59	9	32	37	13.6	4.23	90	.257	.352	5	.294	3	-1	-3	-1	0.0
1962 SF-N	1	2	.333	24	2	0	0	0	42	42	3	23	29	13.9	3.64	104	.256	.348	0	.000	-0	1	1	-1	0.0
1963 SF-N	4	2	.667	34	5	0	0	5	75¹	56	9	37	55	11.3	2.87	112	.209	.309	2	.111	-1	4	3	1	0.2
1964 SF-N	5	1	.833	35	3	1	0	3	74	57	9	31	55	10.9	2.92	122	.209	.294	1	.071	-1	5	5	-1	0.3
1965 SF-N	0	1	.000	2	0	0	0	0	0¹	4	0	2	0	81.0	27.00	13	.500	.750	0	—	-1	-1	-1	0	-1.6
Cin-N	0	1	.000	22	0	0	0	0	44¹	33	3	30	34	13.8	3.45	109	.212	.356	0	.000	-1	0	1	-1	0.0
Yr	0	2	.000	24	0	0	0	0	44²	34	3	32	34	14.3	3.63	103	.215	.364	0	.000	-1	-0	1	-1	-1.6
Total 5	15	8	.652	141	14	2	0	9	297²	248	27	155	210	12.5	3.39	106	.227	.329	8	.127	-1	8	7	-1	-1.1

● **JOHN DUFFIE**   Duffie, John Brown b: 10/4/45, Greenwood, S.C.   BR/TR, 6'7", 210 lbs. Deb: 9/18/67

YEAR TM/L	W	L	PCT	G	GS	CG	SH	SV	IP	H	HR	BB	SO	RAT	ERA	ERA+	OAV	OOB	BH	AVG	PB	PR	/A	PD	TPI
1967 LA-N	0	2	.000	2	2	0	0	0	9²	11	1	4	6	14.0	2.79	111	.282	.349	0	.000	-0	1	0	-0	0.0

● **BERNIE DUFFY**   Duffy, Bernard Allen b: 8/18/1893, Vinson, Okla. d: 2/9/62, Abilene, Tex.   BR/TR, 5'11", 180 lbs. Deb: 9/20/13

YEAR TM/L	W	L	PCT	G	GS	CG	SH	SV	IP	H	HR	BB	SO	RAT	ERA	ERA+	OAV	OOB	BH	AVG	PB	PR	/A	PD	TPI
1913 Pit-N	0	0	—	3	2	0	0	0	11¹	18	0	3	8	16.7	5.56	54	.360	.396	1	.250	0	-3	-3	0	0.0

● **DAN DUGAN**   Dugan, Daniel Phillip b: 2/22/07, Plainfield, N.J. d: 6/25/68, Green Brook, N.J.   BL/TL, 6'1.5", 187 lbs. Deb: 9/5/28

YEAR TM/L	W	L	PCT	G	GS	CG	SH	SV	IP	H	HR	BB	SO	RAT	ERA	ERA+	OAV	OOB	BH	AVG	PB	PR	/A	PD	TPI
1928 Chi-A	0	0	—	1	0	0	0	0	1²	0	0	0	0	0.0	.000	—	.000	.000	0	—	0	0	0	0	0.0
1929 Chi-A	1	4	.200	19	2	0	0	0	65	77	8	19	15	13.6	6.65	64	.300	.353	3	.150	-1	-17	-17	-2	-1.4
Total 2	1	4	.200	20	2	0	0	0	65¹	77	8	19	15	13.5	6.61	65	.298	.351	3	.150	-1	-17	-17	-2	-1.4

● **ED DUGAN**   Dugan, Edward John b: 1864, Brooklyn, N.Y.   Deb: 8/5/1884 F

YEAR TM/L	W	L	PCT	G	GS	CG	SH	SV	IP	H	HR	BB	SO	RAT	ERA	ERA+	OAV	OOB	BH	AVG	PB	PR	/A	PD	TPI
1884 Ric-a	5	14	.263	20	20	20	0	0	166¹	196	5	15	60	11.5	4.49	74	.267	.284	8	.114	-4	-23	-22	-2	-2.4

YEAR TM/L	W	L	PCT	G	GS	CG	SH	SV	IP	H	HR	BB	SO	RAT	ERA	ERA+	OAV	OOB	BH	AVG	PB	PR	/A	PD	TPI
● BILL DUGGLEBY Duggleby, William James "Frosty Bill" b: 3/16/1874, Utica, N.Y. d: 8/30/44, Redfield, N.Y. TR Deb: 4/21/1898																									
1898 Phi-N	3	3	.500	9	5	4	0	0	54	70	4	18	12	15.7	5.50	62	.311	.378	5	.238	2	-11	-12	1	-0.8
1901 Phi-N	19	12	.613	34	28	25	5	0	275²	294	9	40	94	11.2	2.87	118	.271	.303	19	.171	-3	14	16	5	1.8
1902 Phi-A	1	1	.500	2	2	2	0	0	17	19	0	4	4	12.2	3.18	116	.283	.323	0	.000	-0	1	1	1	0.1
Phi-N	11	17	.393	33	28	25	0	1	258²	282	2	57	60	12.2	3.38	83	.277	.323	17	.173	-1	-17	-16	2	-1.5
1903 Phi-N	13	16	.448	36	30	28	3	2	264¹	318	4	79	57	13.9	3.75	87	.303	.358	24	.231	2	-14	-14	1	-1.0
1904 Phi-N	12	13	.480	32	27	22	2	1	223²	265	3	53	55	13.2	3.78	71	.292	.338	14	.171	0	-26	-27	0	-2.7
1905 Phi-N	18	17	.514	38	36	27	1	0	289¹	270	10	83	75	11.4	2.46	116	.253	.315	11	.109	-2	18	15	-2	1.3
1906 Phi-N	13	19	.406	42	30	22	5	2	280¹	241	5	66	83	10.2	2.25	116	.227	.280	14	.141	-2	12	11	1	1.2
1907 Phi-N	0	2	.000	5	2	2	0	0	29	43	2	11	8	18.3	7.45	33	.371	.447	1	.111	0	-16	-16	1	-0.9
Pit-N	2	2	.500	9	3	1	1	0	40¹	34	0	12	4	10.5	2.68	91	.239	.308	2	.154	-0	-1	-1	1	0.0
Yr	2	4	.333	14	5	3	1	0	69¹	77	2	23	12	13.2	4.67	52	.293	.354	3	.136	0	-17	-17	2	-0.9
Total 8	92	102	.474	240	191	158	17	6	1732¹	1836	39	423	452	12.2	3.18	93	.272	.323	107	.166	-4	-41	-44	11	-2.5
● MARTIN DUKE Duke, Martin F. "Duck" (b: Martin F. Duck) b: 1867, Zanesville, Ohio d: 12/31/1898, Minneapolis, Minn. TL Deb: 8/24/1891																									
1891 Was-a	0	3	.000	4	3	2	0	0	23	36	0	19	5	21.5	7.43	50	.345	.446	1	.111	-1	-9	-9	-0	-0.9
● JAN DUKES Dukes, Noble Jan b: 8/16/45, Cheyenne, Wyo. BL/TL, 5'11", 175 lbs. Deb: 9/6/69																									
1969 Was-A	0	2	.000	8	0	0	0	0	11	8	0	4	3	9.8	2.45	141	.216	.293	0	.000	0	1	1	-0	0.2
1970 Was-A	0	0	—	5	0	0	0	0	6²	6	0	1	4	10.8	2.70	132	.240	.296	0	.000	-0	1	1	0	0.2
1972 Tex-A	0	0	—	3	0	0	0	0	2¹	1	0	5	0	23.1	3.86	78	.167	.545	0	—	0	-0	-0	0	0.0
Total 3	0	2	.000	16	0	0	0	0	20	15	0	10	7	11.7	2.70	128	.221	.329	0	—	0	2	2	-0	0.2
● TOM DUKES Dukes, Thomas Earl b: 8/31/42, Knoxville, Tenn. BR/TR, 6'2", 185 lbs. Deb: 8/15/67																									
1967 Hou-N	0	2	.000	17	0	0	0	0	23²	25	2	11	23	14.5	5.32	62	.275	.365	1	.500	0	-5	-5	-0	-0.5
1968 Hou-N	2	2	.500	43	0	0	0	4	52²	62	3	28	37	15.7	4.27	69	.291	.379	0	.000	-0	-8	-8	0	-0.7
1969 SD-N	1	0	1.000	13	0	0	0	1	22¹	26	2	10	15	14.5	7.25	49	.295	.367	0	.000	-0	-9	-9	0	-0.5
1970 SD-N	1	6	.143	53	0	0	0	10	69	62	7	25	56	11.6	4.04	98	.246	.319	0	.000	-1	0	-1	-0	-0.2
1971 *Bal-A	1	5	.167	28	0	0	0	1	38¹	40	4	8	30	11.5	3.52	95	.263	.304	1	.143	-0	-0	-1	-1	-0.2
1972 Cal-A	0	1	.000	7	0	0	0	5	11	11	1	0	8	9.8	1.64	178	.262	.279	0	—	0	2	2	-1	0.1
Total 6	5	16	.238	161	0	0	0	21	217	226	19	82	169	13.1	4.35	79	.270	.341	2	.095	-1	-20	-22	-2	-2.0
● BOB DULIBA Duliba, Robert John b: 1/9/35, Glen Lyon, Pa. BR/TR, 5'10", 185 lbs. Deb: 8/11/59																									
1959 StL-N	0	1	.000	11	0	0	0	1	22²	19	2	12	14	12.3	2.78	153	.237	.337	0	—	-0	3	4	1	0.2
1960 StL-N	4	4	.500	27	0	0	0	0	40²	49	6	16	23	14.4	4.20	97	.310	.374	1	.200	-0	-2	-0	-0	-0.1
1962 StL-N	2	0	1.000	28	0	0	0	2	39¹	31	3	17	22	11.4	2.06	207	.239	.323	0	.000	-0	8	10	0	0.5
1963 LA-A	1	1	.500	6	0	0	0	0	7²	3	0	6	4	10.6	1.17	292	.125	.300	0	.000	-0	2	2	-0	0.5
1964 LA-A	6	4	.600	58	0	0	0	9	72²	80	5	22	33	12.8	3.59	91	.287	.341	0	.000	-1	0	-2	1	-0.4
1965 Bos-A	4	2	.667	39	0	0	0	1	64¹	60	6	22	27	11.5	3.78	99	.248	.311	0	.000	-0	-2	-0	-0	-0.1
1967 KC-A	0	0	—	7	0	0	0	0	9²	14	3	1	6	13.0	6.52	49	.342	.359	0	—	-0	-4	-4	-0	0.0
Total 7	17	12	.586	176	0	0	0	14	257	257	25	96	129	12.4	3.47	108	.268	.335	1	.038	-2	6	8	1	0.6
● GEORGE DUMONT Dumont, George Henry "Pea Soup" b: 11/13/1895, Minneapolis, Minn. d: 10/13/56, Minneapolis, Minn. BR/TR, 5'11", 163 lbs. Deb: 9/14/15																									
1915 Was-A	2	1	.667	6	4	3	2	0	40	23	0	12	18	8.3	2.02	147	.169	.247	2	.167	-0	4	4	-1	0.2
1916 Was-A	2	3	.400	17	5	2	0	1	53	37	0	17	21	9.3	3.06	91	.194	.263	1	.071	-0	-1	-2	-1	-0.3
1917 Was-A	5	14	.263	37	23	8	2	2	204²	171	3	76	65	11.1	2.55	103	.227	.303	2	.034	-5	3	2	-3	-0.7
1918 Was-A	1	1	.500	4	1	1	0	0	14	18	0	6	12	15.4	5.14	58	.295	.358	1	.333	1	-4	-4	0	-0.4
1919 Bos-A	0	4	.000	13	2	0	0	0	35¹	45	1	19	12	16.6	4.33	70	.326	.411	0	.000	-0	-4	-5	-0	-0.5
Total 5	10	23	.303	77	35	14	4	3	347	294	4	130	128	11.3	2.85	96	.230	.306	6	.064	-5	-3	-4	-5	-1.7
● DAN DUMOULIN Dumoulin, Daniel Lynn b: 8/20/53, Kokomo, Ind. BR/TR, 6', 175 lbs. Deb: 9/5/77																									
1977 Cin-N	0	0	—	5	0	0	0	0	5¹	12	0	3	5	25.3	13.50	29	.462	.517	0	—	0	-6	-6	0	0.0
1978 Cin-N	1	0	1.000	3	0	0	0	0	5	7	0	3	2	19.8	1.80	197	.368	.478	0	—	0	1	1	0	0.2
Total 2	1	0	1.000	8	0	0	0	0	10¹	19	0	6	7	22.6	7.84	48	.422	.500	0	—	0	-5	-5	0	0.2
● NICK DUMOVICH Dumovich, Nicholas b: 1/2/02, Sacramento, Cal. d: 12/12/78, Laguna Hills, Cal. BL/TL, 6', 170 lbs. Deb: 4/20/23																									
1923 Chi-N	3	5	.375	28	8	1	0	1	94	118	4	45	23	15.9	4.60	87	.319	.397	7	.241	1	-6	-6	1	-0.2
● ED DUNDON Dundon, Edward Joseph "Dummy" b: 7/10/1859, Columbus, Ohio d: 8/18/1893, Columbus, Ohio TR Deb: 6/2/1883 ♦																									
1883 Col-a	3	16	.158	20	19	16	0	0	166²	213	7	38	31	13.6	4.48	69	.292	.327	15	.161	-3	-22	-26	0	-2.5
1884 Col-a	6	4	.600	11	9	7	0	0	81	85	9	15	37	11.1	3.78	80	.249	.281	12	.140	-1	-5	-7	1	-0.6
Total 2	9	20	.310	31	28	23	0	0	247²	298	16	53	68	12.8	4.25	72	.278	.312	27	.151	-4	-27	-33	1	-3.1
● JIM DUNEGAN Dunegan, James William b: 8/6/47, Burlington, Iowa BR/TR, 6'1", 205 lbs. Deb: 5/28/70																									
1970 Chi-N	0	2	.000	7	0	0	0	0	13¹	13	2	12	3	16.9	4.73	95	.277	.424	1	.250	-0	-1	-0	0	0.0
● WILEY DUNHAM Dunham, Henry Huston b: 1/30/1877, Piketown, Ohio d: 1/16/34, Cleveland, Ohio 6'1", 180 lbs. Deb: 5/24/02																									
1902 StL-N	2	3	.400	7	5	3	0	1	38	47	1	13	15	14.9	5.68	48	.303	.368	1	.083	-1	-12	-12	-0	-1.6
● DAVEY DUNKLE Dunkle, Edward Perks b: 8/30/1872, Philipsburg, Pa. d: 11/19/41, Lock Haven, Pa. BB/TR, 6'2", 220 lbs. Deb: 8/28/1897																									
1897 Phi-N	5	2	.714	7	7	7	0	0	62	72	0	23	9	13.9	3.48	121	.288	.288	4	.174	-1	6	5	-1	0.3
1898 Phi-N	1	4	.200	12	7	4	0	0	68¹	83	1	38	21	17.1	6.98	49	.297	.399	6	.214	-0	-26	-27	-1	-1.7
1899 Was-N	0	2	.000	4	2	2	0	0	26	46	3	14	9	21.1	10.04	39	.383	.452	3	.273	-0	-18	-18	-0	-1.0
1903 Chi-A	4	4	.500	12	7	6	0	1	82	96	1	31	26	14.3	4.06	69	.291	.357	10	.303	-2	-10	-11	-2	-1.0
Was-A	5	9	.357	14	13	10	0	0	108¹	111	4	33	51	12.3	4.24	74	.264	.324	4	.098	-4	-15	-13	-2	-2.0
Yr	9	13	.409	26	20	16	0	1	190¹	207	5	64	77	13.0	4.16	72	.275	.335	14	.189	-2	-25	-25	-4	-3.0
1904 Was-A	2	9	.182	12	11	7	0	0	74¹	95	1	23	23	14.7	4.96	54	.311	.365	4	.143	-2	-20	-19	-1	-2.7
Total 5	17	30	.362	61	47	36	0	1	421	503	10	162	139	14.7	5.02	65	.295	.364	31	.189	-4	-83	-83	-7	-8.1
● FRED DUNLAP Dunlap, Frederick C. "Sure Shot" b: 5/21/1859, Philadelphia, Pa. d: 12/1/02, Philadelphia, Pa. BR/TR, 5'8", 165 lbs. Deb: 5/1/1880 M♦																									
1884 StL-U	0	0	—	1	0	0	0	1	0²	2	0	0	1	27.0	13.50	18	.491	.491	185	.412	1	-1	-1	-0	-0.2
1887 *Det-N	0	0	—	1	0	0	0	0	2	4	0	0	1	18.0	4.50	90	.500	.500	72	.265	-0	0	-0	-0	0.0
Total 2	0	0	—	2	0	0	0	1	2²	6	0	0	2	20.3	6.75	54	.497	.497	1159	.292	1	-1	-1	-0	-0.2
● JACK DUNLEAVY Dunleavy, John Francis b: 9/14/1879, Harrison, N.J. d: 4/11/44, S.Norwalk, Conn. TL, 5'6", 167 lbs. Deb: 5/30/03 ♦																									
1903 StL-N	6	8	.429	14	13	9	0	0	102	101	2	57	51	14.6	4.06	80	.264	.371	48	.249	2	-9	-9	1	-0.8
1904 StL-N	1	4	.200	7	5	5	0	0	55	63	4	23	28	14.2	4.42	61	.275	.344	40	.233	2	-10	-11	1	-0.7
Total 2	7	12	.368	21	18	14	0	0	157	164	6	80	79	14.5	4.18	73	.268	.361	193	.241	4	-19	-20	1	-1.5
● JIM DUNN Dunn, James William "Bill" b: 2/25/31, Valdosta, Ga. BR/TR, 6'0.5", 185 lbs. Deb: 8/26/52																									
1952 Pit-N	0	0	—	3	0	0	0	0	5¹	4	0	3	2	11.8	3.38	118	.190	.292	0	.000	-0	0	0	0	0.0
● JACK DUNN Dunn, John Joseph b: 10/6/1872, Meadville, Pa. d: 10/22/28, Towson, Md. BR/TR, 5'9", . Deb: 5/6/1897 ♦																									
1897 Bro-N	14	9	.609	25	21	21	0	0	216²	251	6	66	26	13.5	4.57	90	.288	.344	29	.221	-2	-6	-11	1	-1.0
1898 Bro-N	16	21	.432	41	37	31	0	0	322²	352	10	82	66	12.5	3.60	100	.276	.327	41	.246	0	0	-0	-1	-0.1
1899 Bro-N	23	13	.639	41	34	29	2	2	299¹	323	8	86	48	12.8	3.70	106	.275	.334	30	.246	0	5	7	3	1.0

YEAR	TM/L	W	L	PCT	G	GS	CG	SH	SV	IP	H	HR	BB	SO	RAT	ERA	ERA+	OAV	OOB	BH	AVG	PB	PR	/A	PD	TPI
1900	Bro-N	3	4	.429	10	7	5	0	0	63	88	1	28	6	17.1	5.57	69	.329	.401	6	.231	-0	-13	-12	1	-1.0
	Phi-N	5	5	.500	10	9	9	1	0	80	87	2	29	12	13.6	4.84	75	.276	.347	10	.303	1	-10	-11	-1	-1.0
	Yr	8	9	.471	20	16	14	1	0	143	175	3	57	18	14.9	5.16	72	.299	.366	16	.271	1	-23	-23	1	-2.0
1901	Phi-N	0	1	.000	2	2	0	0	0	4²	11	0	7	1	38.6	21.21	16	.451	.599	1	1.000	1	-9	-9	-0	-1.2
	Bal-A	3	3	.500	9	6	6	0	0	59²	74	2	21	5	14.5	3.62	107	.301	.358	90	.249	0	-3	2	1	0.2
1902	NY-N	0	3	.000	3	2	2	0	0	26²	28	0	12	6	13.5	3.71	76	.270	.345	72	.211	0	-3	-3	1	-0.2
1904	NY-N	0	0	—	1	0	0	0	1	4	3	0	1	1	13.5	4.50	61	.167	.286	56	.309	0	-1	-0	0	0.0
Total	7	64	59	.520	142	118	103	3	3	1076²	1217	30	334	171	13.4	4.11	92	.283	.342	397	.245	1	-36	-38	5	-3.3

● **MIKE DUNNE**   Dunne, Michael Dennis b: 10/27/62, South Bend, Ind. BR/TR, 6'4", 190 lbs. Deb: 6/5/87

YEAR	TM/L	W	L	PCT	G	GS	CG	SH	SV	IP	H	HR	BB	SO	RAT	ERA	ERA+	OAV	OOB	BH	AVG	PB	PR	/A	PD	TPI
1987	Pit-N	13	6	.684	23	23	5	1	0	163¹	143	10	68	72	11.7	3.03	136	.240	.319	5	.094	-1	19	20	2	2.3
1988	Pit-N	7	11	.389	30	28	1	0	0	170	163	15	88	70	13.6	3.92	87	.255	.349	5	.109	-1	-9	-10	0	-1.0
1989	Pit-N	1	1	.500	3	3	0	0	0	14¹	17	1	9	4	19.5	7.53	45	.328	.419	1	.250	0	-6	-7	0	-0.7
	Sea-A	2	9	.182	15	15	1	0	0	85¹	104	7	37	38	15.1	5.27	76	.307	.378	0	—	0	-13	-12	-0	-1.3
1990	SD-N	0	3	.000	10	6	0	0	0	28²	28	4	17	15	14.1	5.65	68	.241	.338	0	.000	-1	-6	-6	1	-0.6
1992	Chi-A	2	0	1.000	4	1	0	0	0	12²	12	0	6	6	13.5	4.26	91	.255	.352	0	—	0	-0	-1	0	-0.1
Total	5	25	30	.455	85	76	7	1	0	474¹	471	37	225	205	13.4	4.08	93	.261	.347	11	.101	-1	-16	-15	3	-1.4

● **ANDY DUNNING**   Dunning, Andrew Jackson b: 8/12/1871, New York, N.Y. d: 6/21/52, New York, N.Y. BR/TR, 6', 175 lbs. Deb: 5/23/1889

YEAR	TM/L	W	L	PCT	G	GS	CG	SH	SV	IP	H	HR	BB	SO	RAT	ERA	ERA+	OAV	OOB	BH	AVG	PB	PR	/A	PD	TPI
1889	Pit-N	0	2	.000	2	2	2	0	0	18	20	1	16	4	18.0	7.00	54	.274	.403	0	.000	-1	-6	-7	0	-0.6
1891	NY-N	0	1	.000	1	1	0	0	0	2	3	1	3	2	27.0	4.50	71	.334	.501	0	—	0	-0	-0	-0	-0.1
Total	2	0	3	.000	3	3	2	0	0	20	23	2	19	6	18.9	6.75	55	.280	.415	0	.000	-1	-6	-7	0	-0.7

● **STEVE DUNNING**   Dunning, Steven John b: 5/15/49, Denver, Colo. BR/TR, 6'2", 205 lbs. Deb: 6/14/70

YEAR	TM/L	W	L	PCT	G	GS	CG	SH	SV	IP	H	HR	BB	SO	RAT	ERA	ERA+	OAV	OOB	BH	AVG	PB	PR	/A	PD	TPI
1970	Cle-A	4	9	.308	19	17	0	0	0	94¹	93	16	54	77	14.4	4.96	80	.261	.364	5	.161	-1	-13	-11	1	-1.2
1971	Cle-A	8	14	.364	31	29	3	1	1	184	173	25	109	132	14.0	4.50	85	.254	.361	10	.182	1	-21	-14	2	-1.2
1972	Cle-A	6	4	.600	16	16	1	0	0	105	98	16	43	52	12.1	3.26	99	.248	.322	9	.273	5	-2	-0	-1	0.5
1973	Cle-A	0	2	.000	4	3	0	0	0	18	17	2	13	10	15.0	6.50	60	.250	.370	0	—	0	-5	-5	-0	-0.5
	Tex-A	2	6	.250	23	12	2	0	0	94¹	101	11	52	38	14.7	5.34	70	.275	.367	0	—	0	-16	-17	-0	-1.3
	Yr	2	8	.200	27	15	2	0	0	112¹	118	13	65	48	14.7	5.53	68	.271	.367	0	—	0	-21	-22	-0	-1.8
1974	Tex-A	0	0	—	1	0	0	0	0	2¹	3	2	3	1	23.1	19.29	18	.333	.500	0	—	0	-4	-4	0	0.1
1976	Cal-A	0	0	—	4	0	0	0	0	6	9	2	6	4	22.5	7.50	44	.310	.429	0	—	0	-3	-3	-0	0.2
	Mon-N	2	6	.250	32	7	1	0	0	91¹	93	6	33	72	12.6	4.14	90	.274	.342	2	.133	-0	-6	-4	-0	-0.3
1977	Oak-A	1	0	1.000	6	0	0	0	0	18¹	17	2	10	4	13.3	3.93	102	.254	.351	0	—	0	0	0	0	0.1
Total	7	23	41	.359	136	84	7	1	1	613²	604	82	323	390	13.8	4.56	82	.261	.355	26	.194	6	-71	-58	3	-3.6

● **FRANK DUPEE**   Dupee, Frank Oliver b: 4/29/1877, Monkton, Vt. d: 8/14/56, Portland, Me. TL, 6'1", 200 lbs. Deb: 8/24/01

YEAR	TM/L	W	L	PCT	G	GS	CG	SH	SV	IP	H	HR	BB	SO	RAT	ERA	ERA+	OAV	OOB	BH	AVG	PB	PR	/A	PD	TPI
1901	Chi-A	0	1	.000	1	1	0	0	0	3	0	0	3	0	—	∞	0	—	1.000	0	—	0	-3	-3	0	-0.2

● **MIKE DUPREE**   Dupree, Michael Dennis b: 5/29/53, Kansas City, Kan. BR/TR, 6'1", 185 lbs. Deb: 4/13/76

YEAR	TM/L	W	L	PCT	G	GS	CG	SH	SV	IP	H	HR	BB	SO	RAT	ERA	ERA+	OAV	OOB	BH	AVG	PB	PR	/A	PD	TPI
1976	SD-N	0	0	—	12	0	0	0	0	15²	18	4	7	5	14.4	9.19	36	.286	.357	1	1.000	1	-10	-10	0	0.1

● **KID DURBIN**   Durbin, Blaine Alphonsus b: 9/10/1886, Kansas d: 9/11/43, Kirkwood, Mo. BL/TL, 5'8", 155 lbs. Deb: 4/24/07 ♦

YEAR	TM/L	W	L	PCT	G	GS	CG	SH	SV	IP	H	HR	BB	SO	RAT	ERA	ERA+	OAV	OOB	BH	AVG	PB	PR	/A	PD	TPI
1907	Chi-N	0	1	.000	5	1	1	0	1	16²	14	0	10	5	13.5	5.40	46	.233	.352	6	.333	1	-5	-5	0	-0.3

● **RYNE DUREN**   Duren, Rinold George b: 2/22/29, Cazenovia, Wis. BR/TR, 6'1", 195 lbs. Deb: 9/25/54

YEAR	TM/L	W	L	PCT	G	GS	CG	SH	SV	IP	H	HR	BB	SO	RAT	ERA	ERA+	OAV	OOB	BH	AVG	PB	PR	/A	PD	TPI
1954	Bal-A	0	0	—	1	0	0	0	0	2	3	0	1	2	18.0	9.00	40	.333	.400	0	—	0	-1	-1	-0	0.0
1957	KC-A	0	3	.000	14	6	0	0	0	42²	37	4	30	37	14.6	5.27	75	.236	.365	1	.071	-1	-7	-6	0	-0.5
1958	*NY-A☆	6	4	.600	44	1	0	0	20	75²	40	4	43	87	10.7	2.02	175	.157	.296	1	.077	-1	15	13	0	2.5
1959	NY-A★	3	6	.333	41	0	0	0	14	76²	49	6	43	96	11.2	1.88	194	.181	.301	0	.000	-1	17	15	-0	2.2
1960	*NY-A	3	4	.429	42	1	0	0	9	49	27	3	49	67	15.2	4.96	72	.160	.369	0	.000	-1	-6	-7	1	-1.3
1961	NY-A	0	1	.000	4	0	0	0	0	5	2	2	4	7	10.8	5.40	69	.125	.300	0	—	0	-1	-1	-0	0.0
	LA-A☆	6	12	.333	40	14	1	1	2	99	87	13	75	108	15.0	5.18	87	.233	.366	1	.040	-2	-13	-7	-1	-1.5
	Yr	6	13	.316	44	14	1	1	2	104	89	15	79	115	14.8	5.19	86	.229	.363	1	.040	-2	-14	-8	-2	-1.7
1962	LA-A	2	9	.182	42	3	0	0	2	71¹	53	1	57	74	14.6	4.42	87	.206	.363	1	.067	-1	-4	-1	-0	-0.9
1963	Phi-N	6	2	.750	33	7	1	0	2	87¹	65	6	52	84	12.6	3.30	98	.210	.332	3	.143	1	-0	-1	-1	-0.1
1964	Phi-N	0	0	—	2	0	0	0	0	3	5	0	1	5	21.0	6.00	58	.357	.438	0	—	0	-1	-1	-0	0.0
	Cin-N	0	2	.000	26	0	0	0	1	43²	41	9	15	39	12.2	2.89	125	.248	.322	0	.000	-0	3	2	-0	0.1
	Yr	0	2	.000	28	0	0	0	1	46²	46	1	16	44	12.5	3.09	117	.256	.327	0	.000	-0	2	3	-0	0.1
1965	Phi-N	0	0	—	6	0	0	0	0	11	10	0	4	6	12.3	3.27	106	.270	.357	0	—	0	-0	-0	-0	0.0
	Was-A	1	1	.500	16	0	0	0	0	23	24	0	18	18	17.6	6.65	52	.286	.429	0	—	0	-8	-8	-0	-0.7
Total	10	27	44	.380	311	32	2	1	57	589¹	443	40	392	630	13.4	3.83	98	.209	.344	7	.061	-5	-5	-6	-4	-0.4

● **DON DURHAM**   Durham, Donald Gary b: 3/21/49, Yosemite, Ky. BR/TR, 6', 170 lbs. Deb: 7/16/72

YEAR	TM/L	W	L	PCT	G	GS	CG	SH	SV	IP	H	HR	BB	SO	RAT	ERA	ERA+	OAV	OOB	BH	AVG	PB	PR	/A	PD	TPI
1972	StL-N	2	7	.222	10	8	1	0	0	47²	42	1	22	35	12.1	4.34	78	.240	.325	7	.500	4	-5	-5	-1	-0.5
1973	Tex-A	0	4	.000	15	4	0	0	1	40¹	49	7	23	23	16.3	7.59	49	.304	.395	0	—	0	-17	-17	-1	-1.6
Total	2	2	11	.154	25	12	1	0	1	88	91	8	45	58	14.0	5.83	61	.271	.359	7	.500	4	-22	-22	-1	-2.1

● **ED DURHAM**   Durham, Edward Fant "Bull" b: 8/17/08, Chester, S.C. d: 4/27/76, Chester, S.C. BL/TR, 5'11", 170 lbs. Deb: 4/19/29

YEAR	TM/L	W	L	PCT	G	GS	CG	SH	SV	IP	H	HR	BB	SO	RAT	ERA	ERA+	OAV	OOB	BH	AVG	PB	PR	/A	PD	TPI
1929	Bos-A	1	0	1.000	14	1	0	0	0	22¹	34	2	14	6	19.3	9.27	46	.374	.457	0	.000	-0	-12	-12	-0	-0.5
1930	Bos-A	4	15	.211	33	12	6	1	1	140	144	9	43	28	12.2	4.69	98	.270	.326	4	.098	-1	-1	-0	-0	-0.6
1931	Bos-A	8	10	.444	38	15	7	2	0	165¹	175	9	50	55	12.5	4.25	101	.266	.322	3	.056	-6	2	1	-2	-0.6
1932	Bos-A	6	13	.316	34	22	4	0	0	175¹	187	13	49	52	12.3	3.80	118	.274	.327	7	.123	-3	13	14	1	1.0
1933	Chi-A	10	6	.625	24	21	6	0	0	138²	137	12	46	65	12.2	4.48	95	.256	.320	10	.217	0	-3	-4	-1	-0.5
Total	5	29	44	.397	143	71	23	3	1	641²	677	45	202	204	12.5	4.45	99	.271	.329	24	.119	-14	-0	-3	-3	-1.2

● **JOHN DURHAM**   Durham, John Garfield b: 10/7/1881, Douglass, Kan. d: 5/7/49, Coffeyville, Kan. BR/TR, 6', 175 lbs. Deb: 9/15/02

YEAR	TM/L	W	L	PCT	G	GS	CG	SH	SV	IP	H	HR	BB	SO	RAT	ERA	ERA+	OAV	OOB	BH	AVG	PB	PR	/A	PD	TPI
1902	Chi-A	1	1	.500	3	3	3	0	0	20	21	0	16	3	16.6	5.85	58	.270	.395	1	.067	-1	-5	-5	0	-0.5

● **BULL DURHAM**   Durham, Louis Raphael (b: Louis Raphael Staub) b: 6/27/1877, New Oxford, Pa. d: 6/28/60, Bentley, Kan. BR/TR, 5'10", ? Deb: 9/15/04

YEAR	TM/L	W	L	PCT	G	GS	CG	SH	SV	IP	H	HR	BB	SO	RAT	ERA	ERA+	OAV	OOB	BH	AVG	PB	PR	/A	PD	TPI
1904	Bro-N	2	0	1.000	2	2	1	0	0	11	10	0	5	1	12.3	3.27	84	.250	.333	1	.250	0	-1	-1	-0	-0.1
1907	Was-A	0	0	—	2	0	0	0	0	5	10	0	4	1	27.0	12.60	19	.415	.516	0	.000	-0	-6	-6	-0	-0.2
1908	NY-N	0	0	—	1	0	0	0	0	2	2	0	1	2	13.5	9.00	27	.250	.333	0	—	0	-1	-1	-0	0.0
1909	NY-N	0	0	—	4	0	0	0	0	11	15	0	2	6	13.9	3.27	78	.326	.354	0	.000	-0	-1	-1	-0	-0.1
Total	4	2	0	1.000	9	2	1	0	0	29	37	0	12	6	15.5	5.28	49	.313	.381	1	.143	-0	-9	-9	-1	-0.2

● **RICH DURNING**   Durning, Richard Knott b: 10/10/1892, Louisville, Ky. d: 9/23/48, Castle Point, N.Y. BL/TL, 6'2", 178 lbs. Deb: 4/16/17

YEAR	TM/L	W	L	PCT	G	GS	CG	SH	SV	IP	H	HR	BB	SO	RAT	ERA	ERA+	OAV	OOB	BH	AVG	PB	PR	/A	PD	TPI
1917	Bro-N	0	0	—	1	0	0	0	0	1	0	0	0	0	0.00	0.00	—	.000	.000	0	—	0	0	0	-0	0.0
1918	Bro-N	0	0	—	1	0	0	0	0	2	3	0	4	0	31.5	13.50	21	.375	.583	0	—	0	-2	-2	0	0.0
Total	2	0	0	—	2	0	0	0	0	3	3	0	4	0	21.0	9.00	31	.273	.467	0	—	0	-2	-2	-0	0.0

● **JESSE DURYEA**   Duryea, James Newton "Cyclone Jim" b: 9/7/1859, Osage, Iowa d: 8/19/42, Algona, Iowa BR/TR, 5'10", 175 lbs. Deb: 4/20/1889

YEAR	TM/L	W	L	PCT	G	GS	CG	SH	SV	IP	H	HR	BB	SO	RAT	ERA	ERA+	OAV	OOB	BH	AVG	PB	PR	/A	PD	TPI
1889	Cin-a	32	19	.627	53	48	38	2	1	401	372	9	127	183	11.6	2.56	153	.238	.302	44	.272	6	**57**	**60**	0	6.7
1890	Cin-N	16	12	.571	33	32	29	2	0	274	270	11	60	108	11.1	2.92	122	.250	.294	15	.152	1	20	19	0	1.7
1891	Cin-N	1	9	.100	10	10	8	0	0	77	101	4	25	25	15.5	5.38	63	.305	.366	1	.031	-5	-17	-17	-0	-2.0
	StL-a	1	1	.500	3	3	2	0	0	24	19	0	10	13	10.9	3.38	125	.210	.289	4	.364	1	1	2	0	0.2

YEAR TM/L	W	L	PCT	G	GS	CG	SH	SV	IP	H	HR	BB	SO	RAT	ERA	ERA+	OAV	OOB	BH	AVG	PB	PR	/A	PD	TPI
1892 Cin-N	2	5	.286	9	7	5	0	0	68	55	3	26	21	11.1	3.57	91	.212	.292	3	.111	-1	-2	-2	1	-0.2
Was-N	3	11	.214	18	15	13	1	2	127	102	6	45	48	11.1	2.41	135	.211	.291	6	.120	-2	12	12	4	1.3
Yr	5	16	.238	27	22	18	1	2	195	157	9	71	69	10.9	2.82	116	.211	.287	9	.117	-3	10	10	4	1.1
1893 Was-N	4	10	.286	17	15	9	0	0	117	182	8	56	20	19.3	7.54	61	.345	.420	13	.277	-1	-37	-38	0	-2.9
Total 5	59	67	.468	143	130	104	5	3	1088	1101	41	349	416	12.5	3.45	109	.254	.318	86	.201	3	34	36	5	4.8

● ERV DUSAK
Dusak, Ervin Frank "Four Sack" b: 7/29/20, Chicago, Ill. BR/TR, 6'2", 185 lbs. Deb: 9/18/41 ◆

YEAR TM/L	W	L	PCT	G	GS	CG	SH	SV	IP	H	HR	BB	SO	RAT	ERA	ERA+	OAV	OOB	BH	AVG	PB	PR	/A	PD	TPI
1948 StL-N	0	0	—	1	0	0	0	0	1	0	0	1	0	9.0	0.00	—	.000	.250	65	.209	0	0	0	-0	0.0
1950 StL-N	0	2	.000	14	2	0	0	1	36¹	27	2	27	16	13.6	3.72	116	.211	.353	1	.083	-0	2	2	0	0.1
1951 StL-N	0	0	—	5	0	0	0	0	10	14	0	7	8	18.9	7.20	55	.333	.429	1	.500	1	-4	-4	0	0.2
Pit-N	0	1	.000	3	1	0	0	0	6²	10	2	9	2	27.0	12.15	35	.357	.526	12	.308	1	-6	-6	-0	-0.7
Yr	0	1	.000	8	1	0	0	0	16²	24	2	16	10	22.1	9.18	44	.343	.471	13	.317	1	-10	-9	-0	-0.5
Total 3	0	3	.000	23	3	0	0	1	54	51	4	44	26	16.2	5.33	79	.254	.393	251	.243	2	-8	-7	-0	-0.4

● CARL DUSER
Duser, Carl Robert b: 7/22/32, Hazleton, Pa. BL/TL, 6'1", 175 lbs. Deb: 9/15/56

YEAR TM/L	W	L	PCT	G	GS	CG	SH	SV	IP	H	HR	BB	SO	RAT	ERA	ERA+	OAV	OOB	BH	AVG	PB	PR	/A	PD	TPI
1956 KC-A	1	1	.500	2	2	0	0	0	6	14	0	2	5	24.0	9.00	48	.452	.485	0	.000	-0	-3	-3	0	-0.8
1958 KC-A	0	0	—	1	0	0	0	0	2	5	0	1	0	27.0	4.50	87	.500	.545	0	—	-0	-0	-0	0	0.0
Total 2	1	1	.500	3	2	0	0	0	8	19	0	3	5	24.8	7.88	54	.463	.500	0	.000	-0	-3	-3	0	-0.8

● BOB DUSTAL
Dustal, Robert Andrew b: 9/28/35, Sayreville, N.J. BR/TR, 6', 172 lbs. Deb: 4/9/63

YEAR TM/L	W	L	PCT	G	GS	CG	SH	SV	IP	H	HR	BB	SO	RAT	ERA	ERA+	OAV	OOB	BH	AVG	PB	PR	/A	PD	TPI
1963 Det-A	0	1	.000	7	0	0	0	0	6	10	1	6	5	22.5	9.00	42	.357	.455		0	—	-4	-4	1	-0.5

● BILL DUZEN
Duzen, William George b: 2/21/1870, Buffalo, N.Y. d: 3/11/44, Buffalo, N.Y. BR/TR, 5'11", 165 lbs. Deb: 9/21/1890

YEAR TM/L	W	L	PCT	G	GS	CG	SH	SV	IP	H	HR	BB	SO	RAT	ERA	ERA+	OAV	OOB	BH	AVG	PB	PR	/A	PD	TPI
1890 Buf-P	0	2	.000	2	2	2	0	0	13	20	2	14	5	23.5	13.85	30	.338	.465	1	.250	1	-14	-14	-0	-1.1

● FRANK DWYER
Dwyer, John Francis b: 3/25/1868, Lee, Mass. d: 2/4/43, Pittsfield, Mass. BR/TR, 5'8", 145 lbs. Deb: 9/20/1888 MC

YEAR TM/L	W	L	PCT	G	GS	CG	SH	SV	IP	H	HR	BB	SO	RAT	ERA	ERA+	OAV	OOB	BH	AVG	PB	PR	/A	PD	TPI
1888 Chi-N	4	1	.800	5	5	5	1	0	42	42	3	11	9	17	8.8	1.07	283	.198	.240	4	.190	-0	8	9	0	1.0
1889 Chi-N	16	13	.552	32	30	27	0	0	276	307	14	72	63	12.6	3.59	116	.273	.321	27	.200	-2	13	17	-2	1.1
1890 Chi-P	3	6	.333	12	6	6	0	1	69¹	98	4	25	17	16.0	6.23	70	.319	.371	14	.264	0	-15	-15	1	-1.3
1891 Cin-a	13	19	.406	35	31	29	1	0	289	332	10	124	101	14.5	4.52	91	.279	.351	40	.284	2	-25	-13	1	-0.8
Mil-a	6	4	.600	10	10	10	0	0	86	92	2	21	27	12.2	2.20	200	.264	.314	9	.225	-1	15	21	-0	1.9
Yr	19	23	.452	45	41	39	1	0	375	424	12	145	128	13.8	3.98	105	.274	.337	49	.271	1	-11	8	1	1.1
1892 StL-N	2	8	.200	10	10	6	0	0	64	90	1	24	16	16.3	5.63	57	.319	.377	2	.080	-1	-17	-17	1	-2.1
Cin-N	19	10	.655	33	27	24	3	1	259¹	251	5	49	45	11.2	2.33	141	.244	.282	21	.163	-4	28	27	-1	2.1
Yr	21	18	.538	43	37	30	3	1	323¹	341	6	73	61	11.7	2.98	109	.260	.301	23	.149	-5	11	10	-1	0.0
1893 Cin-N	18	15	.545	37	30	28	1	**2**	287¹	332	17	93	53	13.5	4.13	116	.281	.336	24	.200	-3	17	21	3	1.8
1894 Cin-N	19	22	.463	45	40	34	1	1	348	471	27	106	49	15.3	5.07	110	.320	.371	46	.267	1	10	19	1	1.7
1895 Cin-N	18	15	.545	37	31	23	2	0	280¹	355	10	74	46	14.2	4.24	117	.304	.353	30	.265	2	17	23	-0	2.1
1896 Cin-N	24	11	.686	36	34	30	3	1	288²	321	8	60	57	12.2	3.15	146	.279	.321	29	.264	4	39	47	-2	4.7
1897 Cin-N	18	13	.581	37	31	22	0	0	247¹	315	5	56	41	13.9	3.78	120	.307	.350	25	.266	0	15	21	-3	1.8
1898 Cin-N	16	10	.615	31	28	24	0	0	240	251	3	42	29	11.8	3.04	126	.272	.314	12	.141	-4	15	21	-2	1.4
1899 Cin-N	0	5	.000	5	5	2	0	0	32²	48	1	9	2	16.0	5.51	71	.341	.384	4	.364	1	-6	-6	-0	-0.6
Total 12	176	152	.537	365	318	270	12	6	2810	3301	109	764	563	13.3	3.85	115	.286	.336	287	.230	-7	113	177	-4	14.8

● BEN DYER
Dyer, Benjamin Franklin b: 2/13/1893, Chicago, Ill. d: 8/7/59, Kenosha, Wis. BR/TR, 5'10", 170 lbs. Deb: 5/23/14 ◆

YEAR TM/L	W	L	PCT	G	GS	CG	SH	SV	IP	H	HR	BB	SO	RAT	ERA	ERA+	OAV	OOB	BH	AVG	PB	PR	/A	PD	TPI
1918 Det-A	0	0	—	2	0	0	0	0	1²	1	0	1	0	5.00	0.00	—	.000	.000	5	.278	0	1	0	0	0.0

● EDDIE DYER
Dyer, Edwin Hawley b: 10/11/1900, Morgan City, La. d: 4/20/64, Houston, Tex. BL/TL, 5'11.5", 168 lbs. Deb: 7/8/22 M ◆

YEAR TM/L	W	L	PCT	G	GS	CG	SH	SV	IP	H	HR	BB	SO	RAT	ERA	ERA+	OAV	OOB	BH	AVG	PB	PR	/A	PD	TPI
1922 StL-N	0	0	—	2	0	0	0	0	3²	7	0	3	0	17.2	2.45	157	.412	.412	1	.333	1	1	1	0	0.1
1923 StL-N	2	1	.667	4	3	2	1	0	22	30	0	5	7	14.7	4.09	95	.333	.375	12	.267	0	-0	-0	-0	0.0
1924 StL-N	8	11	.421	29	15	7	1	0	136²	174	6	51	23	15.1	4.61	82	.331	.395	18	.237	1	-11	-13	1	-1.2
1925 StL-N	4	3	.571	27	5	1	0	3	82¹	93	4	24	15	13.6	4.15	104	.278	.340	3	.097	-2	1	2	-0	-0.1
1926 StL-N	1	0	1.000	6	0	0	0	0	9¹	7	0	14	4	21.2	11.57	34	.219	.468	1	.500	0	-8	-8	0	-0.7
1927 StL-N	0	0	—	2	0	0	0	0	2	5	1	2	1	31.5	18.00	22	.500	.583	0	—	0	-3	-3	-0	0.0
Total 6	15	15	.500	69	23	10	2	3	256	316	11	96	50	14.9	4.75	84	.313	.380	35	.223	1	-21	-22	1	-1.9

● MIKE DYER
Dyer, Michael Lawrence b: 9/8/66, Upland, Cal. BR/TR, 6'3", 195 lbs. Deb: 6/29/89

YEAR TM/L	W	L	PCT	G	GS	CG	SH	SV	IP	H	HR	BB	SO	RAT	ERA	ERA+	OAV	OOB	BH	AVG	PB	PR	/A	PD	TPI
1989 Min-A	4	7	.364	16	12	1	0	0	71	74	7	37	37	14.3	4.82	86	.273	.365	0	—	-0	-7	-5	-1	-1.0
1994 Pit-N	1	1	.500	14	0	0	0	4	15¹	15	1	12	13	17.6	5.87	72	.268	.423	0	.000	-0	-3	-3	-0	-0.5
Total 2	5	8	.385	30	12	1	0	4	86¹	89	3	49	50	14.9	5.00	83	.272	.375	0	.000	-0	-10	-8	-2	-1.5

● JIMMY DYGERT
Dygert, James Henry "Sunny Jim" b: 7/5/1884, Utica, N.Y. d: 2/8/36, New Orleans, La. BR/TR, 5'10", 185 lbs. Deb: 9/8/05

YEAR TM/L	W	L	PCT	G	GS	CG	SH	SV	IP	H	HR	BB	SO	RAT	ERA	ERA+	OAV	OOB	BH	AVG	PB	PR	/A	PD	TPI
1905 Phi-A	1	4	.200	6	3	2	0	0	35¹	41	2	11	24	13.8	4.33	62	.291	.351	4	.267	0	-7	-7	2	-0.7
1906 Phi-A	11	13	.458	35	25	15	4	0	213²	175	1	91	106	11.6	2.70	101	.227	.316	13	.176	-0	1	1	1	0.1
1907 Phi-A	21	8	.724	42	28	18	5	1	261²	200	2	85	151	10.4	2.34	112	**.214**	.292	12	.128	-4	6	8	-1	0.3
1908 Phi-A	11	15	.423	41	28	15	1	0	238²	184	4	97	164	11.0	2.87	89	.220	.309	6	.080	-6	-12	-8	3	-1.3
1909 Phi-A	9	5	.643	32	13	6	1	0	137¹	117	1	50	79	11.7	2.42	99	.242	.327	9	.214	1	-0	-2	-2	-0.2
1910 Phi-A	4	4	.500	19	8	6	1	0	99¹	81	0	49	59	12.1	2.54	94	.231	.331	3	.083	-2	-0	-2	-0	-0.6
Total 6	57	49	.538	175	105	62	16	2	986	798	9	383	583	11.3	2.65	97	.227	.312	47	.140	-11	-12	-8	-0	-2.4

● JIMMY DYKES
Dykes, James Joseph b: 11/10/1896, Philadelphia, Pa. d: 6/15/76, Philadelphia, Pa. BR/TR, 5'9", 185 lbs. Deb: 5/6/18 MC ◆

YEAR TM/L	W	L	PCT	G	GS	CG	SH	SV	IP	H	HR	BB	SO	RAT	ERA	ERA+	OAV	OOB	BH	AVG	PB	PR	/A	PD	TPI
1927 Phi-A	0	0	—	2	0	0	0	1	2	2	0	1	0	13.5	4.50	95	.333	.429	135	.324	1	-0	-0	-0	0.0

● ARNOLD EARLEY
Earley, Arnold Carl b: 6/4/33, Lincoln Park, Mich. BL/TL, 6'1", 200 lbs. Deb: 9/27/60

YEAR TM/L	W	L	PCT	G	GS	CG	SH	SV	IP	H	HR	BB	SO	RAT	ERA	ERA+	OAV	OOB	BH	AVG	PB	PR	/A	PD	TPI
1960 Bos-A	0	1	.000	2	0	0	0	0	4	9	1	4	5	29.3	15.75	26	.429	.520	0	.000	0	-5	-5	-0	-0.9
1961 Bos-A	2	4	.333	33	0	0	0	7	49²	42	3	34	44	13.8	3.99	105	.226	.345	0	.000	-1	1	0	0	0.1
1962 Bos-A	4	5	.444	38	3	0	0	5	68¹	76	8	46	59	16.2	5.80	71	.281	.388	2	.200	0	-14	-13	1	-1.6
1963 Bos-A	3	7	.300	53	4	0	0	1	115²	124	13	43	97	13.6	4.75	80	.270	.343	5	.278	1	-14	-12	1	-0.9
1964 Bos-A	1	1	.500	25	3	1	0	1	50¹	51	3	18	45	12.5	2.68	144	.266	.332	1	.111	0	5	7	1	0.4
1965 Bos-A	0	1	.000	57	0	0	0	0	74¹	79	5	29	47	13.4	3.63	103	.271	.344	0	.000	0	-1	0	-0	-0.1
1966 Chi-N	2	1	.667	13	0	0	0	0	17²	14	1	9	12	11.7	3.57	103	.226	.324	0	.000	0	-0	-1	-0	-0.1
1967 Hou-N	0	0	—	2	0	0	0	0	1¹	5	1	1	1	40.5	27.00	12	.625	.667	0	—	-0	-4	-4	-0	0.0
Total 8	12	20	.375	223	10	1	0	14	381¹	400	35	184	310	14.1	4.48	87	.269	.354	8	.157	0	-33	-25	1	-3.0

● TOM EARLEY
Earley, Thomas Francis Aloysius b: 2/19/17, Roxbury, Mass. d: 4/5/88, Nantucket, Mass. BR/TR, 6', 180 lbs. Deb: 9/27/38

YEAR TM/L	W	L	PCT	G	GS	CG	SH	SV	IP	H	HR	BB	SO	RAT	ERA	ERA+	OAV	OOB	BH	AVG	PB	PR	/A	PD	TPI
1938 Bos-N	1	0	1.000	2	1	1	0	0	11	8	2	1	4	8.2	3.27	105	.186	.222	0	.000	-1	1	0	-0	-0.1
1939 Bos-N	1	4	.200	14	2	0	0	0	40	49	1	19	14	15.7	4.72	78	.304	.385	3	.300	-1	-4	-5	1	-0.4
1940 Bos-N	2	0	1.000	4	1	1	0	0	16¹	16	1	3	5	11.6	3.86	96	.267	.323	2	.400	1	-0	-0	-0	0.1
1941 Bos-N	6	8	.429	33	13	6	1	3	138²	120	4	46	54	11.0	2.53	141	.233	.300	11	.234	1	17	16	-1	1.7
1942 Bos-N	6	11	.353	27	18	6	0	1	112²	120	10	55	28	14.1	4.71	71	.276	.359	4	.118	-1	-18	-17	0	-2.4
1945 Bos-N	2	1	.667	11	2	1	0	0	41	36	4	19	4	12.1	4.61	83	.235	.320	3	.214	1	-4	-4	0	-0.2
Total 6	18	24	.429	91	37	15	2	5	359²	349	27	143	104	12.5	3.78	94	.256	.330	23	.202	0	-7	-9	-0	-1.3

● BILL EARLEY
Earley, William Albert b: 1/30/56, Cincinnati, Ohio BR/TL, 6'4", 200 lbs. Deb: 9/22/86

YEAR TM/L	W	L	PCT	G	GS	CG	SH	SV	IP	H	HR	BB	SO	RAT	ERA	ERA+	OAV	OOB	BH	AVG	PB	PR	/A	PD	TPI
1986 StL-N	0	0	—	3	0	0	0	0	3	0	0	2	2	6.0	0.00	—	.000	.182	0	—	0	1	1	-0	0.0

YEAR TM/L	W	L	PCT	G	GS	CG	SH	SV	IP	H	HR	BB	SO	RAT	ERA	ERA+	OAV	OOB	BH	AVG	PB	PR	/A	PD	TPI

● **GEORGE EARNSHAW** Earnshaw, George Livingston "Moose" b: 2/15/1900, New York, N.Y. d: 12/1/76, Little Rock, Ark. BR/TR, 6'4", 210 lbs. Deb: 6/3/28 C

1928	Phi-A	7	7	.500	26	22	7	3	1	158¹	143	7	100	117	13.9	3.81	105	.240	.351	14	.246	1	4	4	-1	0.2
1929	*Phi-A	24	8	.750	44	33	13	1	9	254²	233	8	125	149	12.8	3.29	129	.241	.331	15	.172	-2	27	27	-3	2.4
1930	*Phi-A	22	13	.629	49	39	20	3	2	296	299	20	139	193	13.3	4.44	105	.266	.347	26	.228	1	7	8	-1	0.7
1931	*Phi-A	21	7	.750	43	30	23	3	6	281²	255	16	75	152	10.6	3.67	122	.236	.288	30	.263	6	22	26	0	2.9
1932	Phi-A	19	13	.594	36	33	21	1	0	245¹	262	28	94	109	13.2	4.77	95	.270	.336	26	.286	4	-8	-7	1	-0.3
1933	Phi-A	5	10	.333	21	18	4	0	0	117²	153	8	58	37	16.2	5.97	72	.311	.385	8	.182	-0	-22	-22	1	-2.2
1934	Chi-A	14	11	.560	33	30	16	2	0	227	242	28	104	97	13.9	4.52	105	.270	.349	16	.203	-0	-1	5	-1	0.5
1935	Chi-A	1	2	.333	3	3	0	0	0	18	26	2	11	8	18.5	9.00	51	.342	.425	2	.286	0	-9	-9	-0	-1.0
	Bro-N	8	12	.400	25	22	6	2	0	166	175	14	53	72	12.4	4.12	96	.270	.325	13	.217	1	-2	-3	0	-0.2
1936	Bro-N	4	9	.308	19	13	4	1	1	93	113	7	30	40	14.1	5.32	78	.297	.354	8	.242	-0	-13	-12	-0	-1.5
	StL-N	2	1	.667	20	6	1	0	1	57²	80	4	20	28	16.1	6.40	62	.333	.392	4	.222	1	-15	-16	1	-0.7
	Yr	6	10	.375	39	19	5	1	2	150²	193	11	50	68	14.7	5.73	71	.310	.364	12	.235	0	-29	-28	1	-2.2
Total	9	127	93	.577	319	249	115	18	12	1915¹	1949	142	809	1002	13.2	4.38	100	.265	.339	162	.230	9	-10	0	-2	0.8

● **LOGAN EASLEY** Easley, Kenneth Logan b: 11/4/61, Salt Lake City, Utah BR/TR, 6'1", 185 lbs. Deb: 4/9/87

1987	Pit-N	1	1	.500	17	0	0	0	1	26¹	23	5	17	21	14.0	5.47	75	.242	.363	0	.000	-0	-4	-4	1	-0.2
1989	Pit-N	1	0	1.000	10	0	0	0	1	12¹	8	1	7	6	11.7	4.38	77	.190	.320	0	.000	-0	-1	-1	-0	-0.2
Total	2	2	1	.667	27	0	0	0	2	38²	31	6	24	27	13.3	5.12	75	.226	.350	0	.000	-0	-5	-5	1	-0.4

● **MAL EASON** Eason, Malcolm Wayne "Kid" b: 3/13/1879, Brookville, Pa. d: 4/16/70, Douglas, Ariz. BR/TR, 6', 175 lbs. Deb: 10/1/00 U

1900	Chi-N	1	0	1.000	1	1	1	0	0	9	9	0	3	2	12.0	1.00	361	.260	.319	0	.000	-1	3	3	-0	0.2
1901	Chi-N	8	17	.320	27	25	23	1	0	220²	246	9	60	68	13.0	3.59	90	.280	.335	12	.138	-5	-7	-9	-2	-1.5
1902	Chi-N	1	1	.500	2	2	2	0	0	18	21	0	2	4	11.5	1.00	270	.291	.310	1	.200	-0	4	3	0	0.5
	Bos-N	9	11	.450	27	26	20	2	0	206¹	237	4	59	50	13.4	2.75	103	.288	.344	6	.083	-6	1	2	-1	-0.6
	Yr	10	12	.455	29	28	22	2	0	224¹	258	4	61	54	13.3	2.61	108	.288	.342	7	.091	-6	4	5	-0	-0.1
1903	Det-A	2	5	.286	7	6	6	1	0	56¹	60	1	19	21	13.1	3.36	87	.272	.338	2	.100	-2	-2	-3	1	-0.3
1905	Bro-N	5	21	.192	27	27	20	3	0	207	230	5	72	64	13.3	4.30	67	.292	.355	14	.173	-1	-30	-32	1	-3.5
1906	Bro-N	10	17	.370	34	26	18	3	1	227	212	4	74	64	11.7	3.25	78	.256	.323	8	.091	-4	-16	-18	1	-2.5
Total	6	36	72	.333	125	113	90	10	1	944¹	1015	20	289	273	12.8	3.39	85	.278	.338	43	.121	-19	-47	-54	2	-7.7

● **CARL EAST** East, Carlton William b: 8/27/1894, Marietta, Ga. d: 1/15/53, Whitesburg, Ga. BL/TR, 6'2", 178 lbs. Deb: 8/24/15 ◆

| 1915 | StL-A | 0 | 0 | — | 1 | 1 | 0 | 0 | 0 | 3¹ | 6 | 0 | 2 | 1 | 21.6 | 16.20 | 18 | .400 | .471 | 0 | .000 | -0 | -5 | -5 | -0 | 0.0 |

● **HUGH EAST** East, Gordon Hugh b: 7/7/19, Birmingham, Ala. d: 11/2/81, Charleston, S.C. BR/TR, 6'2", 185 lbs. Deb: 9/13/41

1941	NY-N	1	1	.500	2	2	1	0	0	15²	19	0	9	4	16.1	3.45	107	.297	.384	2	.222	0	0	0	-0	0.1
1942	NY-N	0	2	.000	4	1	0	0	0	7¹	15	1	7	2	27.0	9.82	34	.429	.524	1	.500	2	-5	-5	0	-1.0
1943	NY-N	1	3	.250	13	5	1	0	0	40¹	51	4	25	21	17.0	5.36	64	.298	.388	1	.077	-1	-9	-9	-1	-0.9
Total	3	2	6	.250	19	8	1	0	0	63¹	85	5	41	27	17.9	5.40	65	.315	.405	4	.167	1	-14	-13	-1	-1.8

● **JAMIE EASTERLY** Easterly, James Morris b: 2/17/53, Houston, Tex. BL/TL, 5'9", 180 lbs. Deb: 4/6/74

1974	Atl-N	0	0	—	3	0	0	0	0	2²	6	0	4	2	33.8	16.88	32	.400	.526	0	—	0	-4	-4	0	0.0
1975	Atl-N	2	9	.182	21	13	0	0	0	68²	73	5	42	34	15.3	4.98	76	.275	.379	1	.056	-2	-10	-9	-1	-1.5
1976	Atl-N	1	1	.500	4	4	0	0	0	22	23	0	13	11	14.7	4.91	77	.280	.379	1	.111	-0	-3	-3	0	-0.3
1977	Atl-N	2	4	.333	22	5	0	0	1	58²	72	5	30	37	16.1	6.14	72	.303	.387	4	.267	1	-15	-11	-1	-1.1
1978	Atl-N	3	6	.333	37	6	0	0	1	78	91	9	45	42	15.9	5.65	72	.299	.393	4	.211	0	-18	-14	0	-1.5
1979	Atl-N	0	0	—	4	0	0	0	0	2²	7	0	3	3	33.8	13.50	30	.467	.556	0	—	0	-3	-3	0	0.0
1981	*Mil-A	3	3	.500	44	0	0	0	4	62	46	0	34	31	11.6	3.19	107	.219	.328	0	—	0	3	2	0	0.2
1982	Mil-A	0	2	.000	28	0	0	0	2	30²	39	6	15	16	15.8	4.70	81	.312	.386	0	—	0	-2	-3	1	0.0
1983	Mil-A	0	1	.000	12	0	0	0	0	11²	14	0	10	6	20.1	3.86	97	.350	.500	0	.000	0	-0	-0	0	0.0
	Cle-A	4	2	.667	41	0	0	0	3	57	69	4	22	39	14.7	3.63	117	.309	.377	0	—	0	3	4	0	0.5
	Yr	4	3	.571	53	0	0	0	3	68²	83	4	32	45	15.3	3.67	113	.312	.390	0	.000	0	3	4	0	0.5
1984	Cle-A	3	1	.750	26	1	0	0	2	69¹	74	3	23	42	12.7	3.38	121	.273	.332	0	—	0	5	5	0	0.2
1985	Cle-A	4	1	.800	50	7	0	0	0	98²	96	9	53	58	14.0	3.92	105	.264	.363	0	—	0	3	2	-0	0.2
1986	Cle-A	0	2	.000	13	0	0	0	0	17²	27	3	12	9	19.9	7.64	54	.365	.453	0	—	0	-7	-7	-0	-0.6
1987	Cle-A	1	1	.500	9	0	0	0	0	31²	26	4	13	22	11.4	4.55	99	.218	.301	0	—	0	-0	-0	0	0.0
Total	13	23	33	.411	321	36	0	0	14	611¹	663	48	319	350	14.1	4.62	87	.283	.373	10	.161	-1	-49	-40	-2	-3.9

● **JACK EASTON** Easton, John S. b: 2/28/1867, Bridgeport, Ohio d: 11/28/03, Steubenville, Ohio Deb: 9/23/1889

1889	Col-a	1	0	1.000	4	1	1	0	1	18	13	0	21	7	18.5	3.50	104	.196	.410	0	.000	-1	1	0	-0	-0.1
1890	Col-a	15	14	.517	37	29	23	0	1	255²	213	4	125	147	12.6	3.52	102	.220	.321	19	.178	0	10	2	1	0.3
1891	Col-a	5	10	.333	18	16	13	0	0	135¹	145	3	59	52	14.6	4.52	77	.265	.352	15	.238	2	-12	-16	1	-1.1
	StL-a	3	2	.600	7	6	4	0	0	47²	48	3	23	22	14.2	5.10	83	.253	.346	5	.179	-1	-7	-5	-2	-0.6
	Col-a	0	2	.000	2	2	2	0	0	15	15	2	4	13	12.6	3.60	96	.252	.320	0	.000	-1	0	-0	-1	-0.1
	Yr	8	14	.364	27	24	19	0	0	198	208	8	86	87	13.5	4.59	79	.255	.327	20	.196	-0	-19	-21	-1	-1.8
1892	StL-N	2	0	1.000	5	2	0	0	0	31	38	2	26	4	19.5	6.39	50	.290	.419	3	.176	-0	-11	-11	0	-0.6
1894	Pit-N	0	1	.000	3	1	1	0	0	19²	26	0	4	1	15.1	4.12	127	.315	.368	0	.000	-1	3	2	-1	-0.1
Total	5	26	29	.473	76	57	46	0	2	522¹	498	14	262	246	14.0	4.12	89	.243	.343	42	.176	-2	-16	-27	-1	-2.3

● **RAWLY EASTWICK** Eastwick, Rawlins Jackson b: 10/24/50, Camden, N.J. BR/TR, 6'3", 180 lbs. Deb: 9/12/74

1974	Cin-N	0	0	—	8	0	0	0	2	17²	12	1	5	14	8.7	2.04	171	.188	.246	0	.000	-0	3	3	-0	0.0
1975	*Cin-N	5	3	.625	58	0	0	0	22	90	77	6	25	61	10.4	2.60	138	.229	.287	1	.067	-0	10	10	-1	1.1
1976	*Cin-N	11	5	.688	71	0	0	0	26	107²	93	3	27	70	10.2	2.09	168	.232	.284	0	.000	-2	17	17	-2	3.1
1977	Cin-N	2	2	.500	23	0	0	0	7	43¹	40	7	8	17	10.0	2.91	135	.244	.279	1	.167	-0	5	5	-1	0.5
	StL-N	3	7	.300	41	1	0	0	4	53²	74	6	21	30	15.9	4.70	82	.332	.389	2	.400	1	-5	-5	-0	-0.9
	Yr	5	9	.357	64	1	0	0	11	97	114	9	29	47	13.3	3.90	100	.295	.344	3	.273	1	0	-0	-2	-0.4
1978	NY-A	2	1	.667	8	0	0	0	0	24²	22	2	4	13	9.9	3.28	110	.232	.270	0	—	0	1	1	-0	0.2
	*Phi-N	2	1	.667	22	0	0	0	0	40¹	31	5	18	14	10.9	4.02	89	.209	.295	0	.000	-0	-2	-2	-1	-0.2
1979	Phi-N	3	6	.333	51	0	0	0	0	82²	90	8	25	47	12.6	4.90	78	.284	.338	0	—	-1	-11	-10	-2	-1.4
1980	KC-A	0	1	.000	14	0	0	0	0	22	37	2	8	6	19.2	5.32	76	.363	.420	0	—	0	-3	-3	1	-0.1
1981	Chi-N	0	1	.000	30	0	0	0	1	43¹	43	2	15	24	12.0	2.28	162	.264	.326	0	.000	-0	6	7	0	0.2
Total	8	28	27	.509	326	1	0	0	68	525¹	519	38	156	295	11.7	3.31	112	.258	.314	4	.071	-3	22	22	-7	2.5

● **CRAIG EATON** Eaton, Craig b: 9/7/54, Glendale, Ohio BR/TR, 5'11", 175 lbs. Deb: 9/5/79

| 1979 | KC-A | 0 | 0 | — | 5 | 0 | 0 | 0 | 0 | 10 | 8 | 0 | 3 | 4 | 9.9 | 2.70 | 158 | .222 | .282 | 0 | — | 0 | 2 | 2 | 0 | 0.0 |

● **ZEB EATON** Eaton, Zebulon Vance "Red" b: 2/2/20, Cooleemee, N.C. d: 12/17/89, W.Palm Beach, Fla. BR/TR, 5'10", 185 lbs. Deb: 4/18/44

1944	Det-A	0	0	—	6	0	0	0	0	15²	19	2	8	4	15.5	5.74	62	.322	.403	1	.100	-1	-4	-4	-0	-0.1
1945	*Det-A	4	2	.667	17	3	0	0	0	53¹	48	0	40	15	15.6	4.05	87	.247	.384	8	.250	2	-4	-3	0	-0.1
Total	2	4	2	.667	23	3	0	0	0	69	67	2	48	19	15.4	4.43	80	.265	.388	9	.214	2	-8	-7	-0	-0.2

● **GARY EAVE** Eave, Gary Louis b: 7/22/63, Monroe, La. BR/TR, 6'4", 200 lbs. Deb: 4/12/88

| 1988 | Atl-N | 0 | 0 | — | 5 | 0 | 0 | 0 | 0 | 5 | 7 | 0 | 3 | 0 | 18.0 | 9.00 | 41 | .333 | .417 | 0 | — | 0 | -3 | -3 | -0 | 0.0 |
| 1989 | Atl-N | 2 | 0 | 1.000 | 3 | 3 | 0 | 0 | 0 | 20² | 15 | 0 | 12 | 9 | 12.2 | 1.31 | 279 | .200 | .318 | 0 | .000 | -1 | 5 | 5 | -1 | 0.4 |

YEAR	TM/L	W	L	PCT	G	GS	CG	SH	SV	IP	H	HR	BB	SO	RAT	ERA	ERA+	OAV	OOB	BH	AVG	PB	PR	/A	PD	TPI
1990	Sea-A	0	3	.000	8	5	0	0	0	30	27	5	20	16	14.7	4.20	94	.241	.366	0	—	0	-1	-1	0	-0.1
Total	3	2	3	.400	16	8	0	0	0	55²	49	6	35	25	14.1	3.56	107	.236	.354	0	.000	-1	1	2	-1	0.3

● VALLIE EAVES
Eaves, Vallie Ennis "Chief" b: 9/6/11, Allen, Okla. d: 4/19/60, Norman, Okla. BR/TR, 6'2.5", 180 lbs. Deb: 9/12/35

YEAR	TM/L	W	L	PCT	G	GS	CG	SH	SV	IP	H	HR	BB	SO	RAT	ERA	ERA+	OAV	OOB	BH	AVG	PB	PR	/A	PD	TPI
1935	Phi-A	1	2	.333	3	3	1	0	0	14	12	0	15	6	17.4	5.14	88	.240	.415	0	.000	-1	-1	-1	-0	-0.2
1939	Chi-A	0	1	.000	2	1	1	0	0	11²	11	1	8	5	15.4	4.63	102	.250	.377	2	.333	0	-0	0	-0	0.0
1940	Chi-A	0	2	.000	5	3	0	0	0	18²	22	2	24	11	22.7	6.75	66	.301	.480	0	.000	-1	-5	-5	-1	-0.5
1941	Chi-A	3	3	.500	12	7	4	0	0	58²	56	4	21	24	12.3	3.53	99	.253	.327	2	.100	-1	1	-0	-1	-0.3
1942	Chi-N	0	0	—	2	0	0	0	0	3	4	0	2	0	21.0	9.00	36	.308	.438	0	—	0	-2	-2	-0	0.0
Total	5	4	8	.333	24	14	6	0	0	106	105	7	70	46	15.4	4.58	86	.262	.379	4	.114	-3	-7	-8	-3	-1.0

● EDDIE EAYRS
Eayrs, Edwin b: 11/10/1890, Blackstone, Mass. d: 11/30/69, Warwick, R.I. BL/TL, 5'7", 160 lbs. Deb: 6/30/13 ♦

YEAR	TM/L	W	L	PCT	G	GS	CG	SH	SV	IP	H	HR	BB	SO	RAT	ERA	ERA+	OAV	OOB	BH	AVG	PB	PR	/A	PD	TPI
1913	Pit-N	0	0	—	2	0	0	0	0	8	8	0	6	5	15.8	2.25	134	.267	.389	1	.167	-0	1	1	-0	0.0
1920	Bos-N	1	2	.333	7	3	0	0	0	26¹	36	1	12	7	17.1	5.47	56	.346	.424	80	.328	2	-7	-7	1	-0.5
1921	Bos-N	0	0	—	2	0	0	0	0	4²	9	0	9	1	34.7	17.36	21	.391	.563	2	1.067	-2	-7	-7	-0	-0.2
Total	3	1	2	.333	11	3	0	0	0	39	53	1	27	13	18.9	6.23	50	.338	.441	83	.306	0	-13	-14	0	-0.7

● HARRY ECCLES
Eccles, Harry Josiah "Bugs" b: 7/9/1893, Kennedy, N.Y. d: 6/2/55, Jamestown, N.Y. BL/TL, 6'2", 170 lbs. Deb: 9/13/15

YEAR	TM/L	W	L	PCT	G	GS	CG	SH	SV	IP	H	HR	BB	SO	RAT	ERA	ERA+	OAV	OOB	BH	AVG	PB	PR	/A	PD	TPI
1915	Phi-A	0	1	.000	5	1	0	0	1	21	18	2	6	13	10.3	4.71	62	.240	.296	1	.167	-0	-4	-4	-1	-0.3

● DENNIS ECKERSLEY
Eckersley, Dennis Lee b: 10/3/54, Oakland, Cal. BR/TR, 6'2", 190 lbs. Deb: 4/12/75

YEAR	TM/L	W	L	PCT	G	GS	CG	SH	SV	IP	H	HR	BB	SO	RAT	ERA	ERA+	OAV	OOB	BH	AVG	PB	PR	/A	PD	TPI
1975	Cle-A	13	7	.650	34	24	6	2	2	186²	147	16	90	152	11.8	2.60	145	.215	.312	0	—	0	24	24	-3	2.3
1976	Cle-A	13	12	.520	36	30	9	3	1	199¹	155	13	78	200	10.7	3.43	102	.214	.295	0	—	0	2	1	-0	0.1
1977	Cle-A★	14	13	.519	33	33	12	3	0	247¹	214	31	54	191	10.0	3.53	112	.231	**.278**	0	—	0	15	11	-3	0.9
1978	Bos-A	20	8	.714	35	35	16	3	0	268¹	258	30	71	162	11.3	2.99	138	.251	.304	0	—	0	23	34	-2	2.8
1979	Bos-A	17	10	.630	33	33	17	2	0	246²	234	29	59	150	10.9	2.99	**148**	.250	.298	0	—	♦	34	**39**	1	4.0
1980	Bos-A	12	14	.462	30	30	8	0	0	197²	188	25	44	121	10.1	4.28	99	.248	.291	0	—	0	-5	-1	-1	-0.4
1981	Bos-A	9	8	.529	23	23	8	2	0	154	160	9	35	79	11.6	4.27	91	.267	.310	0	—	0	-10	-7	-1	-0.8
1982	Bos-A★	13	13	.500	33	33	11	3	0	224¹	228	31	43	127	11.0	3.73	115	.261	.297	0	—	0	9	14	-1	1.2
1983	Bos-A	9	13	.409	28	28	2	0	0	176¹	223	27	39	77	13.7	5.61	77	.303	.343	0	—	0	-30	-25	-1	-2.7
1984	Bos-A	4	4	.500	9	9	2	0	0	64²	71	10	13	33	11.8	5.01	83	.284	.322	0	—	0	-7	-6	-1	-0.9
	*Chi-N	10	8	.556	24	24	2	0	0	160¹	152	11	36	81	10.8	3.03	129	.250	.296	6	.109	-3	10	16	1	1.5
1985	Chi-N	11	7	.611	25	25	6	2	0	169¹	145	15	19	117	8.9	3.08	129	.229	.255	7	.125	0	10	17	0	1.8
1986	Chi-N	6	11	.353	33	32	1	0	0	201	226	21	43	137	12.2	4.57	88	.285	.324	11	.159	-1	-19	-12	-0	-0.8
1987	Oak-A	6	8	.429	54	2	0	0	16	115²	99	11	17	113	9.3	3.03	136	.228	.262	0	—	0	18	14	1	2.0
1988	*Oak-A★	4	2	.667	60	0	0	0	45	72²	52	5	11	70	7.9	2.35	161	.198	.233	0	—	0	13	12	1	2.5
1989	Oak-A	4	0	1.000	51	0	0	0	33	57²	32	5	3	55	5.6	1.56	236	.162	.178	0	—	0	15	14	-0	2.8
1990	*Oak-A★	4	2	.667	63	0	0	0	48	73¹	41	2	4	73	5.5	0.61	605	.160	.172	0	—	0	27	25	-2	5.9
1991	Oak-A★	5	4	.556	67	0	0	0	43	76	60	11	9	87	8.3	2.96	129	.208	.235	0	—	0	10	7	0	1.8
1992	*Oak-A★	7	1	.875	69	0	0	0	51	80	62	5	11	93	8.3	1.91	196	.211	.242	0	—	0	18	16	1	4.2
1993	Oak-A	2	4	.333	64	0	0	0	36	67	67	7	13	80	11.0	4.16	98	.261	.301	0	—	0	-1	-1	-0	0.0
1994	Oak-A	5	4	.556	45	0	0	0	19	44¹	49	5	13	47	12.8	4.26	104	.275	.328	0	—	0	3	1	0	0.6
Total	20	188	153	.551	849	361	100	20	294	3082²	2863	319	705	2245	10.6	3.46	117	.244	.291	24	.133	-1	157	197	-13	28.8

● AL ECKERT
Eckert, Albert George "Obbie" b: 5/17/06, Milwaukee, Wis. d: 4/20/74, Milwaukee, Wis. BL/TL, 5'10", 174 lbs. Deb: 4/21/30

YEAR	TM/L	W	L	PCT	G	GS	CG	SH	SV	IP	H	HR	BB	SO	RAT	ERA	ERA+	OAV	OOB	BH	AVG	PB	PR	/A	PD	TPI
1930	Cin-N	0	1	.000	2	1	0	0	0	5	7	0	4	1	19.8	7.20	67	.304	.407	0	.000	-0	-1	-1	0	-0.2
1931	Cin-N	0	1	.000	14	1	0	0	0	18²	26	3	9	5	16.9	9.16	41	.325	.393	1	.333	0	-11	-11	-0	-0.5
1935	StL-N	0	0	—	2	0	0	0	0	3	7	0	1	1	24.0	12.00	34	.467	.500	0	—	0	-3	-3	-0	0.0
Total	3	0	2	.000	18	2	0	0	0	26²	40	3	14	7	18.2	9.11	44	.339	.409	1	.250	0	-15	-15	0	-0.7

● CHARLIE ECKERT
Eckert, Charles William "Buzz" b: 8/8/1897, Philadelphia, Pa. d: 8/22/86, Trevose, Pa. BR/TR, 5'10.5", 165 lbs. Deb: 9/18/19

YEAR	TM/L	W	L	PCT	G	GS	CG	SH	SV	IP	H	HR	BB	SO	RAT	ERA	ERA+	OAV	OOB	BH	AVG	PB	PR	/A	PD	TPI
1919	Phi-A	0	1	.000	2	1	1	0	0	16	17	1	3	6	11.3	3.94	87	.270	.303	1	.167	-0	-1	-1	0	-0.1
1920	Phi-A	0	0	—	2	0	0	0	0	5²	8	0	1	1	15.9	4.76	84	.421	.476	0	.000	-0	-1	-0	-0	-0.1
1922	Phi-A	0	2	.000	21	0	0	0	0	50	61	7	23	15	15.3	4.68	91	.319	.395	1	.091	-1	-4	-2	2	-0.1
Total	3	0	3	.000	25	1	1	0	0	71²	86	8	27	22	14.4	4.52	90	.315	.381	2	.111	-2	-5	-4	1	-0.3

● DON EDDY
Eddy, Donald Eugene b: 10/25/46, Mason City, Iowa BR/TL, 5'11", 170 lbs. Deb: 9/7/70

YEAR	TM/L	W	L	PCT	G	GS	CG	SH	SV	IP	H	HR	BB	SO	RAT	ERA	ERA+	OAV	OOB	BH	AVG	PB	PR	/A	PD	TPI
1970	Chi-A	0	0	—	7	0	0	0	0	11²	10	6	9	12	12.3	2.31	168	.244	.340	0	—	0	2	2	-0	0.0
1971	Chi-A	0	2	.000	22	0	0	0	0	22²	19	3	19	14	15.1	2.38	151	.232	.376	1	1.000	1	3	3	-1	0.3
Total	2	0	2	.000	29	0	0	0	0	34¹	29	9	25	23	14.2	2.36	157	.236	.365	1	1.000	1	5	5	-1	0.3

● STEVE EDDY
Eddy, Steven Allen b: 8/21/57, Sterling, Ill. BR/TR, 6'2", 185 lbs. Deb: 6/13/79

YEAR	TM/L	W	L	PCT	G	GS	CG	SH	SV	IP	H	HR	BB	SO	RAT	ERA	ERA+	OAV	OOB	BH	AVG	PB	PR	/A	PD	TPI
1979	Cal-A	1	1	.500	7	4	0	0	0	32¹	36	1	20	7	16.1	4.73	86	.290	.397	0	—	0	-2	-2	0	0.0

● JOE EDELEN
Edelen, Benny Joe b: 9/16/55, Durant, Okla. BR/TR, 6', 165 lbs. Deb: 4/18/81

YEAR	TM/L	W	L	PCT	G	GS	CG	SH	SV	IP	H	HR	BB	SO	RAT	ERA	ERA+	OAV	OOB	BH	AVG	PB	PR	/A	PD	TPI
1981	StL-N	1	0	1.000	13	0	0	0	0	17¹	29	2	3	10	17.1	9.35	38	.367	.398	1	.333	0	-11	-11	-0	-0.6
	Cin-N	1	0	1.000	5	0	0	0	0	12²	5	1	2	5	3.6	0.71	500	.128	.128	0	.000	-0	4	4	-1	0.2
	Yr	2	0	1.000	18	0	0	0	0	30	34	3	5	15	11.1	5.70	62	.283	.301	1	.200	-0	-7	-7	-1	-0.4
1982	Cin-N	0	0	—	9	0	0	0	0	15¹	22	2	8	11	17.6	8.80	42	.344	.417	1	.500	1	-9	-9	-0	-0.0
Total	2	2	0	1.000	27	0	0	0	0	45¹	56	5	11	26	13.5	6.75	53	.308	.351	2	.286	1	-16	-16	-1	-0.4

● ED EDELEN
Edelen, Edward Joseph "Doc" b: 3/16/12, Bryantown, Md. d: 2/1/82, LaPlata, Md. BR/TR, 6', 191 lbs. Deb: 8/20/32

YEAR	TM/L	W	L	PCT	G	GS	CG	SH	SV	IP	H	HR	BB	SO	RAT	ERA	ERA+	OAV	OOB	BH	AVG	PB	PR	/A	PD	TPI
1932	Was-A	0	0	—	2	0	0	0	0	1	0	0	6	0	54.0	27.00	16	.000	.600	0	—	0	-3	-3	-0	0.0

● JOHN EDELMAN
Edelman, John Rogers b: 7/27/35, Philadelphia, Pa. BR/TR, 6'3", 185 lbs. Deb: 6/2/55

YEAR	TM/L	W	L	PCT	G	GS	CG	SH	SV	IP	H	HR	BB	SO	RAT	ERA	ERA+	OAV	OOB	BH	AVG	PB	PR	/A	PD	TPI
1955	Mil-N	0	0	—	5	0	0	0	0	5²	7	0	8	3	23.8	11.12	34	.304	.484	0	—	0	-4	-5	0	0.0

● CHARLIE EDEN
Eden, Charles M. b: 1/18/1855, Lexington, Ky. d: 9/17/20, Cincinnati, Ohio BL/TL, 168 lbs. Deb: 8/17/1877 ♦

YEAR	TM/L	W	L	PCT	G	GS	CG	SH	SV	IP	H	HR	BB	SO	RAT	ERA	ERA+	OAV	OOB	BH	AVG	PB	PR	/A	PD	TPI
1884	Pit-a	0	1	.000	2	1	1	0	0	12	12	1	3	12	12.0	6.00	56	.255	.314	33	.270	1	-4	-4	-1	-0.2
1885	Pit-a	1	2	.333	4	1	0	0	0	15²	22	0	3	5	14.4	5.17	62	.314	.342	103	.254	1	-3	-3	-1	-0.5
Total	2	1	3	.250	6	2	1	0	0	27²	34	1	6	8	13.3	5.53	59	.291	.331	244	.261	-1	-7	-7	-1	-0.7

● TOM EDENS
Edens, Thomas Patrick b: 6/9/61, Ontario, Ore. BR/TR, 6'3", 185 lbs. Deb: 6/2/87

YEAR	TM/L	W	L	PCT	G	GS	CG	SH	SV	IP	H	HR	BB	SO	RAT	ERA	ERA+	OAV	OOB	BH	AVG	PB	PR	/A	PD	TPI
1987	NY-N	0	0	—	2	2	0	0	0	8	15	2	4	4	21.4	6.75	56	.417	.475	0	.000	-0	-2	-3	0	-0.2
1990	Mil-A	4	5	.444	35	6	0	0	2	89	89	8	33	40	12.7	4.45	87	.262	.334	0	—	0	-5	-6	-1	-0.6
1991	Min-A	2	2	.500	8	6	0	0	0	33	34	2	10	19	12.0	4.09	104	.256	.308	0	—	0	0	1	0	0.1
1992	Min-A	6	3	.667	52	0	0	0	3	76¹	65	1	36	57	12.1	2.83	143	.236	.329	0	—	0	9	10	-1	1.1
1993	Hou-N	1	1	.500	38	0	0	0	0	49	47	4	19	21	12.1	3.12	124	.263	.333	0	—	0	4	5	0	0.4
1994	Hou-N	4	1	.800	38	0	0	0	1	50	55	3	17	38	13.3	4.50	90	.289	.354	0	.000	-0	-2	-2	-1	-0.1
	Phi-N	1	0	1.000	7	0	0	0	0	4	4	0	1	1	11.3	2.25	183	.267	.313	0	—	0	1	1	0	0.2
	Yr	5	1	.833	45	0	0	0	1	54	59	3	18	39	13.1	4.33	94	.281	.338	0	.000	-0	-1	-1	-1	0.1
Total	6	18	12	.600	177	14	0	0	6	309¹	309	20	120	180	12.7	3.84	104	.265	.337	0	.000	-1	6	5	1	0.9

● BUTCH EDGE
Edge, Claude Lee b: 7/18/56, Houston, Tex. BR/TR, 6'3", 203 lbs. Deb: 8/13/79

YEAR	TM/L	W	L	PCT	G	GS	CG	SH	SV	IP	H	HR	BB	SO	RAT	ERA	ERA+	OAV	OOB	BH	AVG	PB	PR	/A	PD	TPI
1979	Tor-A	3	4	.429	9	9	1	0	0	51²	60	6	24	19	14.8	5.23	83	.283	.359	0	—	0	-6	-5	-0	-0.6

YEAR TM/L	W	L	PCT	G	GS	CG	SH	SV	IP	H	HR	BB	SO	RAT	ERA	ERA+	OAV	OOB	BH	AVG	PB	PR	/A	PD	TPI

● BILL EDGERTON
Edgerton, William Albert b: 8/16/41, South Bend, Ind. BL/TL, 6'2", 185 lbs. Deb: 9/3/66

YEAR TM/L	W	L	PCT	G	GS	CG	SH	SV	IP	H	HR	BB	SO	RAT	ERA	ERA+	OAV	OOB	BH	AVG	PB	PR	/A	PD	TPI
1966 KC-A	0	1	.000	6	1	0	0	0	8¹	10	0	7	3	18.4	3.24	105	.303	.425	0	—	0	0	0	0	0.0
1967 KC-A	1	0	1.000	7	0	0	0	0	8¹	11	1	3	6	16.2	2.16	147	.324	.395	0	—	0	1	1	0	0.1
1969 Sea-A	0	1	.000	4	0	0	0	0	4	10	1	0	2	24.8	13.50	27	.455	.478	0	—	0	-4	-4	0	-0.9
Total 3	1	2	.333	17	1	0	0	0	20²	31	2	10	11	18.7	4.79	70	.348	.426	0	—	0	-3	-3	1	-0.8

● GEORGE EDMONDSON
Edmondson, George Henderson "Big Ed" b: 5/18/1896, Waxahachie, Tex. d: 7/11/73, Waco, Tex. BR/TR, 6'1", 179 lbs. Deb: 8/15/22

YEAR TM/L	W	L	PCT	G	GS	CG	SH	SV	IP	H	HR	BB	SO	RAT	ERA	ERA+	OAV	OOB	BH	AVG	PB	PR	/A	PD	TPI
1922 Cle-A	0	0	—	2	0	0	0	0	2	4	0	0	0	18.0	9.00	45	.444	.444	0	—	0	-1	-1	0	0.0
1923 Cle-A	0	0	—	1	0	0	0	0	4	8	0	3	0	27.0	11.25	35	.444	.545	1	.000	-0	-3	-3	0	0.0
1924 Cle-A	0	0	—	5	1	0	0	0	8	10	1	5	3	16.9	9.00	47	.294	.385	1	.333	0	-4	-4	-0	0.0
Total 3	0	0	—	8	1	0	0	0	14	22	1	8	3	19.9	9.64	43	.361	.443	1	.250	-0	-9	-9	0	0.0

● PAUL EDMONDSON
Edmondson, Paul Michael b: 2/12/43, Kansas City, Kan. d: 2/13/70, Santa Barbara, Cal. BR/TR, 6'5", 195 lbs. Deb: 6/20/69

YEAR TM/L	W	L	PCT	G	GS	CG	SH	SV	IP	H	HR	BB	SO	RAT	ERA	ERA+	OAV	OOB	BH	AVG	PB	PR	/A	PD	TPI
1969 Chi-A	1	6	.143	14	13	1	0	0	87²	72	5	39	46	11.8	3.70	104	.227	.319	5	.172	-1	-1	2	3	0.4

● BOB EDMONDSON
Edmondson, Robert E. b: 4/30/1879, Paris, Ky. d: 8/14/31, Lawrence, Kan. BR/TR, 5'11", 185 lbs. Deb: 9/15/06 ◆

YEAR TM/L	W	L	PCT	G	GS	CG	SH	SV	IP	H	HR	BB	SO	RAT	ERA	ERA+	OAV	OOB	BH	AVG	PB	PR	/A	PD	TPI
1906 Was-A	0	1	.000	2	1	1	0	0	10	10	0	2	0	10.8	4.50	59	.263	.300	1	.333	0	-2	-2	0	-0.2

● SAM EDMONSTON
Edmonston, Samuel Sherwood "Big Sam" b: 8/30/1883, Washington, D.C. d: 4/12/79, Corpus Christi, Tex. BL/TL, 5'11.5", 185 lbs. Deb: 6/24/07

YEAR TM/L	W	L	PCT	G	GS	CG	SH	SV	IP	H	HR	BB	SO	RAT	ERA	ERA+	OAV	OOB	BH	AVG	PB	PR	/A	PD	TPI
1907 Was-A	0	0	—	1	0	0	0	0	3	8	0	1	0	27.0	9.00	27	.487	.516	0	.000	-0	-2	-2	0	0.0

● EDWARDS
Edwards Deb: 9/11/1875

YEAR TM/L	W	L	PCT	G	GS	CG	SH	SV	IP	H	HR	BB	SO	RAT	ERA	ERA+	OAV	OOB	BH	AVG	PB	PR	/A	PD	TPI
1875 Atl-n	0	1	.000	1	1	0	0	0	2	6	0	0	0	27.0	9.00	26	.429	.429	1	.200	0	-1	-1		-0.5

● FOSTER EDWARDS
Edwards, Foster Hamilton "Eddie" b: 9/1/03, Holstein, Iowa d: 1/4/80, Orleans, Mass. BR/TR, 6'3", 175 lbs. Deb: 7/2/25

YEAR TM/L	W	L	PCT	G	GS	CG	SH	SV	IP	H	HR	BB	SO	RAT	ERA	ERA+	OAV	OOB	BH	AVG	PB	PR	/A	PD	TPI
1925 Bos-N	0	0	—	1	0	0	0	0	2	6	0	1	1	31.5	9.00	45	.545	.583	0	—	0	-1	-1	-0	0.0
1926 Bos-N	2	0	1.000	3	3	1	0	0	25	20	0	13	6	11.9	0.72	492	.230	.330	0	.000	-2	9	8	0	0.4
1927 Bos-N	2	8	.200	29	11	1	0	0	92	95	2	45	37	14.0	4.99	74	.274	.362	1	.045	-2	-11	-13	-1	-1.5
1928 Bos-N	2	1	.667	21	3	2	0	0	49¹	67	4	23	17	16.8	5.66	69	.327	.400	1	.091	-1	-9	-10	-1	-0.6
1930 NY-A	0	0	—	2	0	0	0	0	1²	5	0	2	1	37.8	21.60	20	.500	.583	0	—	0	-3	-3	-0	0.0
Total 5	6	9	.400	56	17	4	0	0	170	193	4	84	60	14.9	4.76	79	.292	.377	2	.048	-5	-16	-19	-1	-1.7

● JIM JOE EDWARDS
Edwards, James Corbette "Little Joe" b: 12/14/1894, Banner, Miss. d: 1/19/65, Sarepta, Miss. BR/TR, 6'2", 185 lbs. Deb: 5/14/22

YEAR TM/L	W	L	PCT	G	GS	CG	SH	SV	IP	H	HR	BB	SO	RAT	ERA	ERA+	OAV	OOB	BH	AVG	PB	PR	/A	PD	TPI
1922 Cle-A	3	8	.273	25	7	0	0	0	92²	113	1	40	44	15.3	4.47	90	.313	.389	2	.087	-2	-4	-5	-1	-0.8
1923 Cle-A	10	10	.500	38	21	8	1	1	179¹	200	5	75	68	14.1	3.71	107	.286	.359	7	.119	-5	5	5	-1	-0.1
1924 Cle-A	4	3	.571	10	7	5	1	0	57	64	3	34	15	15.5	2.84	150	.305	.402	3	.150	-1	9	9	0	0.9
1925 Cle-A	0	3	.000	13	3	1	0	0	36	60	1	23	12	21.0	8.25	54	.382	.464	1	.111	-1	-15	-15	-1	-1.0
Chi-A	1	2	.333	9	4	1	0	0	45¹	46	4	23	20	13.9	3.97	105	.263	.352	3	.176	-1	2	1	1	0.0
Yr	1	5	.167	22	7	2	1	0	81¹	106	4	46	32	16.9	5.86	73	.318	.403	4	.154	-2	-13	-14	2	-1.0
1926 Chi-A	6	9	.400	32	16	3	3	1	142	140	4	63	41	12.9	4.18	92	.264	.343	5	.109	-3	-3	-5	-1	-0.9
1928 Cin-N	2	2	.500	18	1	0	0	2	32	43	1	20	11	17.7	7.59	52	.347	.438	4	.300	-1	-13	-13	-1	-1.6
Total 6	26	37	.413	145	59	23	6	4	584¹	666	18	278	211	14.7	4.37	92	.295	.376	24	.130	-13	-19	-23	-1	-3.5

● SHERMAN EDWARDS
Edwards, Sherman Stanley b: 7/25/09, Mt.Ida, Ark. d: 3/8/92, ElDorado, Ark. BR/TR, 6', 165 lbs. Deb: 9/21/34

YEAR TM/L	W	L	PCT	G	GS	CG	SH	SV	IP	H	HR	BB	SO	RAT	ERA	ERA+	OAV	OOB	BH	AVG	PB	PR	/A	PD	TPI
1934 Cin-N	0	0	—	1	0	0	0	0	3	4	0	1	1	15.0	3.00	136	.333	.385	0	.000	-0	0	0	0	0.0

● WAYNE EDWARDS
Edwards, Wayne Maurice b: 3/7/64, Burbank, Cal. BL/TL, 6'5", 185 lbs. Deb: 9/11/89

YEAR TM/L	W	L	PCT	G	GS	CG	SH	SV	IP	H	HR	BB	SO	RAT	ERA	ERA+	OAV	OOB	BH	AVG	PB	PR	/A	PD	TPI
1989 Chi-A	0	0	—	7	0	0	0	0	7¹	7	1	3	9	12.3	3.68	103	.269	.345	0	—	0	0	0	0	0.1
1990 Chi-A	5	3	.625	42	5	0	0	2	95	81	6	41	63	11.8	3.22	119	.234	.321	0	—	0	7	6	0	0.6
1991 Chi-A	0	2	.000	13	0	0	0	0	23¹	22	2	17	12	15.0	3.86	103	.259	.382	0	—	0	1	0	-0	0.0
Total 3	5	5	.500	62	5	0	0	2	125²	110	9	61	84	12.5	3.37	114	.241	.334	0	—	0	8	7	0	0.7

● HARRY EELLS
Eells, Harry Archibald "Slippery" b: 2/14/1881, Ida Grove, Iowa d: 10/15/40, Los Angeles, Cal. BR/TR, 6'1", 195 lbs. Deb: 4/22/06

YEAR TM/L	W	L	PCT	G	GS	CG	SH	SV	IP	H	HR	BB	SO	RAT	ERA	ERA+	OAV	OOB	BH	AVG	PB	PR	/A	PD	TPI
1906 Cle-A	4	5	.444	14	8	6	1	0	86¹	77	1	48	35	13.3	2.61	100	.242	.346	6	.188	1	1	0	1	0.1

● WISH EGAN
Egan, Aloysius Jerome b: 6/16/1881, Evart, Mich. d: 4/13/51, Detroit, Mich. BR/TR, 6'3", 185 lbs. Deb: 9/3/02

YEAR TM/L	W	L	PCT	G	GS	CG	SH	SV	IP	H	HR	BB	SO	RAT	ERA	ERA+	OAV	OOB	BH	AVG	PB	PR	/A	PD	TPI
1902 Det-A	0	2	.000	3	3	2	0	0	22	23	0	6	9	11.9	2.86	127	.269	.317	2	.250	-0	2	2	1	0.2
1905 StL-N	6	15	.286	23	19	18	0	0	171¹	189	2	39	29	12.4	3.57	83	.285	.333	6	.102	-3	-11	-11	5	-1.1
1906 StL-N	2	9	.182	16	12	7	0	0	86¹	97	3	27	14	13.1	4.59	57	.278	.333	2	.069	-2	-19	-19	1	-2.3
Total 3	8	26	.235	42	34	27	0	0	279²	309	5	72	52	12.6	3.83	76	.282	.332	10	.104	-5	-28	-28	6	-3.2

● JIM EGAN
Egan, James K. "Troy Terrier" b: 1858, Derby, Conn. d: 9/26/1884, New Haven, Conn. TL, Deb: 5/15/1882 ◆

YEAR TM/L	W	L	PCT	G	GS	CG	SH	SV	IP	H	HR	BB	SO	RAT	ERA	ERA+	OAV	OOB	BH	AVG	PB	PR	/A	PD	TPI
1882 Tro-N	4	6	.400	12	10	10	0	0	100	133	1	24	20	14.1	4.14	68	.315	.352	23	.200	-2	-14	-15	-2	-1.4

● RIP EGAN
Egan, John Joseph b: 7/9/1871, Philadelphia, Pa. d: 12/22/50, Cranston, R.I. TR, 5'11", 168 lbs. Deb: 4/30/1894 U

YEAR TM/L	W	L	PCT	G	GS	CG	SH	SV	IP	H	HR	BB	SO	RAT	ERA	ERA+	OAV	OOB	BH	AVG	PB	PR	/A	PD	TPI
1894 Was-N	0	0	—	1	0	0	0	0	5	8	1	2	2	18.0	10.80	49	.357	.410	0	.000	-0	-3	-3	0	0.0

● DICK EGAN
Egan, Richard Wallis b: 3/24/37, Berkeley, Cal. BL/TL, 6'4", 193 lbs. Deb: 4/9/63 C

YEAR TM/L	W	L	PCT	G	GS	CG	SH	SV	IP	H	HR	BB	SO	RAT	ERA	ERA+	OAV	OOB	BH	AVG	PB	PR	/A	PD	TPI
1963 Det-A	0	1	.000	20	0	0	0	0	21	25	4	3	16	12.0	5.14	73	.287	.311	0	—	0	-4	-3	0	-0.1
1964 Det-A	0	0	—	23	0	0	0	0	34¹	34	2	17	21	13.4	4.46	82	.246	.336	0	.000	-0	-3	-3	1	0.0
1966 Cal-A	0	0	—	11	0	0	0	0	14¹	17	2	6	11	14.4	4.40	76	.309	.377	0	.000	-0	-2	-2	-0	0.0
1967 LA-N	1	1	.500	20	0	0	0	0	31²	34	3	15	20	15.1	6.25	50	.272	.368	0	.000	-0	-10	-11	-1	-0.7
Total 4	1	2	.333	74	0	0	0	0	101¹	109	13	41	68	13.8	5.15	67	.272	.347	0	.000	-1	-18	-19	0	-0.8

● BRUCE EGLOFF
Egloff, Bruce Edward b: 4/10/65, Denver, Colo. BR/TR, 6'2", 215 lbs. Deb: 4/13/91

YEAR TM/L	W	L	PCT	G	GS	CG	SH	SV	IP	H	HR	BB	SO	RAT	ERA	ERA+	OAV	OOB	BH	AVG	PB	PR	/A	PD	TPI
1991 Cle-A	0	0	—	6	0	0	0	0	5²	8	0	4	8	19.1	4.76	87	.333	.429	0	—	0	-0	-0	0	0.0

● HOWARD EHMKE
Ehmke, Howard Jonathan "Bob" b: 4/24/1894, Silver Creek, N.Y. d: 3/17/59, Philadelphia, Pa. BR/TR, 6'3", 190 lbs. Deb: 4/12/15

YEAR TM/L	W	L	PCT	G	GS	CG	SH	SV	IP	H	HR	BB	SO	RAT	ERA	ERA+	OAV	OOB	BH	AVG	PB	PR	/A	PD	TPI
1915 Buf-F	0	2	.000	18	2	0	0	0	53²	69	2	25	18	16.6	5.53	51	.325	.409	0	.000	-2	-17	-16	2	-0.6
1916 Det-A	3	1	.750	5	4	4	0	0	37¹	34	0	15	15	11.8	3.13	91	.252	.327	2	.143	-1	-1	-1	1	-0.1
1917 Det-A	10	15	.400	35	25	13	4	2	206	174	3	88	90	11.7	2.97	89	.243	.330	17	.246	-2	-7	-7	2	-0.4
1919 Det-A	17	10	.630	33	31	20	2	0	248²	255	5	107	79	13.3	3.18	100	.274	.353	23	.253	3	1	0	4	0.7
1920 Det-A	15	18	.455	38	33	23	2	0	268¹	250	8	124	98	13.0	3.25	115	.253	.344	25	.238	2	16	14	6	2.4
1921 Det-A	13	14	.481	30	22	13	1	0	196¹	220	15	81	68	14.4	4.54	94	.286	.364	21	.284	2	-6	-1	-0	-0.4
1922 Det-A	17	17	.500	45	30	16	1	1	279²	299	12	101	108	13.6	4.22	92	.281	.356	16	.157	-4	-5	-10	2	-1.3
1923 Bos-A	20	17	.541	43	39	28	2	0	316²	318	12	119	121	13.0	3.78	109	.272	.349	25	.223	-2	7	12	5	1.6
1924 Bos-A	19	17	.528	45	36	26	4	4	315	324	9	81	119	11.9	3.46	126	.265	.316	28	.222	-2	27	32	3	3.3
1925 Bos-A	9	20	.310	34	31	22	0	0	260²	285	8	85	95	13.2	3.73	122	.285	.348	13	.148	-5	19	24	5	2.2
1926 Bos-A	3	10	.231	14	14	7	1	0	97¹	115	3	45	38	15.2	5.46	75	.303	.382	5	.147	-1	-16	-15	1	-1.6
Phi-A	12	4	.750	20	18	10	1	0	147¹	125	1	50	55	10.9	2.81	148	.232	.302	7	.152	-2	20	22	0	2.1
Yr	15	14	.517	34	32	17	2	0	244²	240	4	95	93	12.5	3.86	107	.260	.332	12	.150	-3	4	7	1	0.5
1927 Phi-A	12	10	.545	30	27	10	1	0	189²	200	13	60	68	13.0	4.22	101	.281	.349	14	.206	-1	-2	-1	3	0.2
1928 Phi-A	9	8	.529	38	18	5	1	0	139¹	135	6	44	34	11.8	3.62	111	.254	.316	11	.239	1	6	6	0	0.3
1929 *Phi-A	7	2	.778	11	8	2	0	0	54²	48	2	15	20	10.6	3.29	123	.233	.288	2	.105	0	5	5	0	0.4
1930 Phi-A	0	1	.000	3	1	0	0	0	10	22	4	2	4	24.3	11.70	40	.458	.509	1	.333	0	-8	-8	0	-0.5
Total 15	166	166	.500	427	339	199	20	14	2820²	2873	103	1042	1030	12.9	3.75	104	.271	.343	210	.208	-11	42	52	32	9.1

YEAR TM/L	W	L	PCT	G	GS	CG	SH	SV	IP	H	HR	BB	SO	RAT	ERA	ERA+	OAV	OOB	BH	AVG	PB	PR	/A	PD	TPI
● **RED EHRET**				Ehret, Philip Sydney			b: 8/31/1868, Louisville, Ky.		d: 7/28/40, Cincinnati, Ohio		BR/TR, 6′, 175 lbs.		Deb: 7/7/1888 ♦												
1888 KC-a	3	2	.600	7	6	5	0	0	52	58	1	22	12	14.4	3.98	86	.272	.348	12	.190	-1	-5	-3	1	-0.2
1889 Lou-a	10	29	.256	45	38	35	1	0	364	441	11	115	135	14.2	4.80	80	.290	.347	65	.252	2	-38	-38	3	-2.7
1890 *Lou-a	25	14	.641	43	38	35	4	2	359	351	5	79	174	11.2	2.53	152	.248	.296	31	.212	-3	53	53	-3	4.3
1891 Lou-a	13	13	.500	26	24	23	2	0	220²	225	4	70	76	12.5	3.47	105	.255	.318	22	.242	1	6	5	0	0.5
1892 Pit-N	16	20	.444	39	36	32	0	0	316	290	7	83	101	11.3	2.65	124	.234	.294	34	.258	3	22	23	-4	2.1
1893 Pit-N	18	18	.500	39	35	32	4	0	314¹	322	3	115	70	13.2	3.44	133	.257	.331	24	.176	-6	43	39	1	3.0
1894 Pit-N	19	21	.475	46	38	31	0	0	346²	441	12	128	102	15.0	5.14	102	.306	.367	23	.170	-11	7	4	-1	-0.6
1895 StL-N	6	19	.240	37	32	18	0	0	231²	360	11	88	55	17.8	6.02	80	.349	.405	21	.219	-3	-32	-30	0	-2.5
1896 Cin-N	18	14	.563	34	33	29	2	0	276²	298	5	74	60	12.4	3.42	135	.273	.324	20	.196	-3	29	37	1	3.1
1897 Cin-N	8	10	.444	34	19	11	0	2	184¹	256	3	47	43	15.4	4.78	95	.326	.374	13	.197	-3	-10	-5	-1	-0.7
1898 Lou-N	3	7	.300	12	10	9	0	0	89	130	3	20	20	15.5	5.76	62	.337	.375	9	.225	1	-21	-22	-1	-1.9
Total 11	139	167	.454	362	309	260	14	4	2754¹	3172	63	841	848	13.6	4.02	105	.282	.339	274	.217	-22	55	62	-4	4.4
● **RUBE EHRHARDT**				Ehrhardt, Welton Claude			b: 11/20/1894, Beecher, Ill.		d: 4/27/80, Chicago Heights, Ill.		BR/TR, 6′2″, 190 lbs.		Deb: 7/18/24												
1924 Bro-N	5	3	.625	15	9	6	2	0	83²	71	5	17	13	9.6	2.26	166	.232	.275	4	.138	-2	15	14	-2	0.8
1925 Bro-N	10	14	.417	36	24	12	0	1	207²	239	10	62	47	13.2	5.03	83	.293	.345	15	.211	2	-17	-20	4	-1.4
1926 Bro-N	2	5	.286	44	1	0	0	4	97	101	5	35	25	12.6	3.90	98	.275	.338	6	.250	-0	-1	-1	-2	-0.2
1927 Bro-N	3	7	.300	46	3	2	0	2	95²	90	3	37	22	12.2	3.57	111	.264	.341	6	.250	1	4	4	3	0.7
1928 Bro-N	1	3	.250	28	2	1	0	2	54	74	1	27	12	17.0	4.67	85	.352	.429	4	.286	-0	-4	-4	1	-0.2
1929 Cin-N	1	2	.333	24	1	1	1	1	49¹	58	2	22	9	14.8	4.74	96	.305	.380	2	.182	-0	-0	-1	1	0.0
Total 6	22	34	.393	193	40	22	3	10	587¹	633	26	200	128	12.9	4.15	97	.284	.345	37	.214	1	-4	-7	5	-0.3
● **HACK EIBEL**				Eibel, Henry Hack			b: 12/6/1893, Brooklyn, N.Y.		d: 10/16/45, Macon, Ga.		BL/TL, 5′11″, 220 lbs.		Deb: 6/13/12 ♦												
1920 Bos-A	0	0	—	3	0	0	0	0	10¹	10	0	3	5	11.3	3.48	105	.270	.325	8	.186	-0	0	0	-0	0.0
● **JUAN EICHELBERGER**				Eichelberger, Juan Tyrone			b: 10/21/53, St.Louis, Mo.		BR/TR, 6′3″, 205 lbs.		Deb: 9/7/78													
1978 SD-N	0	0	—	3	0	0	0	0	3¹	4	0	2	2	16.2	10.80	31	.267	.353	0	—	0	-3	-3	0	0.0
1979 SD-N	1	1	.500	3	3	1	0	0	21	15	1	11	12	11.1	3.43	103	.211	.317	2	.400	1	1	-0	-0	0.1
1980 SD-N	4	2	.667	15	13	0	0	0	88²	73	8	55	43	13.1	3.65	94	.233	.350	1	.111	-1	-1	-2	-1	-0.3
1981 SD-N	8	8	.500	25	24	3	1	0	141¹	136	6	74	87	13.6	3.50	93	.259	.353	4	.087	-3	-0	-4	1	-0.6
1982 SD-N	7	14	.333	31	24	8	0	0	177²	171	23	72	74	12.4	4.20	81	.251	.325	5	.091	-2	-12	-15	-1	-1.9
1983 Cle-A	4	11	.267	28	15	2	0	0	134	132	10	59	56	13.0	4.90	86	.259	.338	0	—	0	-13	-10	-1	-1.1
1988 Atl-N	2	0	1.000	20	0	0	0	0	37¹	44	2	10	13	13.0	3.86	95	.297	.342	0	.000	-0	-2	-1	0	0.0
Total 7	26	36	.419	125	79	14	1	0	603¹	575	50	283	281	12.9	4.10	87	.254	.339	14	.103	-4	-29	-35	-2	-3.8
● **MARK EICHHORN**				Eichhorn, Mark Anthony			b: 11/21/60, San Jose, Cal.		BR/TR, 6′4″, 200 lbs.		Deb: 8/30/82													
1982 Tor-A	0	3	.000	7	7	0	0	0	38	40	4	14	16	12.8	5.45	82	.260	.321	0	—	0	-6	-4	-1	-0.5
1986 Tor-A	14	6	.700	69	0	0	0	10	157	105	8	45	166	9.0	1.72	245	.191	.261	0	—	0	**43**	**44**	2	**5.8**
1987 Tor-A	10	6	.625	89	0	0	0	4	127²	110	14	52	96	11.8	3.17	142	.234	.318	0	—	0	18	19	2	2.3
1988 Tor-A	0	3	.000	37	0	0	0	0	66²	79	3	27	28	15.1	4.18	94	.304	.382	0	—	0	-2	-2	1	0.0
1989 Atl-N	5	5	.500	45	0	0	0	0	68¹	70	6	19	49	11.9	4.35	84	.275	.327	0	.000	-0	-6	-5	2	-0.5
1990 Cal-A	2	5	.286	60	0	0	0	13	84²	98	2	23	69	13.5	3.08	124	.289	.345	0	—	0	8	7	1	0.9
1991 Cal-A	3	3	.500	70	0	0	0	1	81²	63	3	13	49	8.6	1.98	207	.219	.257	0	—	0	19	19	2	1.5
1992 Cal-A	2	4	.333	42	0	0	0	2	56²	51	2	18	42	11.0	2.38	167	.238	.297	0	—	0	10	10	1	1.2
*Tor-A	2	0	1.000	23	0	0	0	0	31	35	1	7	19	12.8	4.35	94	.285	.333	0	—	0	-1	-1	1	-0.1
Yr	4	4	.500	65	0	0	0	2	87²	86	3	25	61	11.6	3.08	130	.253	.308	0	—	0	8	9	2	1.1
1993 *Tor-A	3	1	.750	54	0	0	0	0	72²	76	3	22	47	12.5	2.72	158	.272	.332	0	—	0	13	13	2	0.8
1994 Bal-A	6	5	.545	43	0	0	0	1	71	62	1	19	35	10.9	2.15	235	.240	.305	0	—	0	**21**	**23**	0	3.1
Total 10	47	41	.534	539	7	0	0	32	855¹	789	46	259	616	11.4	2.93	144	.247	.311	0	.000	-0	116	122	12	14.5
● **DAVE EILAND**				Eiland, David William			b: 7/5/66, Dade City, Fla.		BR/TR, 6′3″, 210 lbs.		Deb: 8/3/88													
1988 NY-A	0	0	—	3	3	0	0	0	12²	15	6	4	7	14.9	6.39	62	.294	.368	0	—	0	-3	-3	0	0.0
1989 NY-A	1	3	.250	6	6	0	0	0	34¹	44	5	13	11	15.5	5.77	67	.328	.396	0	—	0	-7	-7	-1	-0.8
1990 NY-A	2	1	.667	5	5	0	0	0	30¹	31	2	5	16	10.7	3.56	111	.254	.283	0	—	0	1	1	-0	0.1
1991 NY-A	2	5	.286	18	13	0	0	0	72²	87	10	23	18	14.0	5.33	78	.302	.360	0	—	0	-10	-12	-2	-1.0
1992 SD-N	0	2	.000	7	7	0	0	0	27	33	1	5	10	12.7	5.67	63	.287	.317	1	.111	1	-6	-6	0	-0.4
1993 SD-N	0	3	.000	10	9	0	0	0	48¹	58	5	17	14	14.2	5.21	79	.297	.357	1	.083	-1	-6	-6	-0	-0.4
Total 6	5	14	.263	49	43	0	0	0	225¹	268	29	67	76	13.7	5.23	76	.296	.350	2	.095	-0	-32	-31	-2	-2.5
● **DAVE EILERS**				Eilers, David Louis			b: 12/3/36, Oldenburg, Tex.		BR/TR, 5′11″, 188 lbs.		Deb: 7/27/64													
1964 Mil-N	0	0	—	6	0	0	0	0	7²	11	1	1	6	15.3	4.70	75	.333	.371	0	—	0	-1	-1	-0	0.0
1965 Mil-N	0	0	—	6	0	0	0	0	3²	8	1	0	1	19.6	12.27	29	.421	.421	0	—	0	-4	-4	-0	0.0
NY-N	1	1	.500	11	0	0	0	0	18	20	2	4	9	13.0	4.00	88	.274	.329	1	1.000	0	-1	-1	-0	-0.1
Yr	1	1	.500	17	0	0	0	0	21²	28	3	4	10	14.1	5.40	65	.304	.347	1	1.000	0	-4	-5	-0	-0.1
1966 NY-N	1	1	.500	23	0	0	0	2	34²	39	7	7	14	12.2	4.67	78	.287	.326	0	.000	-0	-4	-4	1	-0.2
1967 Hou-N	6	4	.600	35	0	0	0	1	59¹	68	3	17	22	13.3	3.94	84	.296	.352	0	.000	-1	-4	-4	-0	-0.8
Total 4	8	6	.571	81	0	0	0	3	123¹	146	14	29	52	13.3	4.45	78	.297	.345	1	.111	-0	-13	-14	-0	-1.1
● **JOEY EISCHEN**				Eischen, Joseph Raymond			b: 5/25/70, West Covina, Cal.		BL/TL, 6′1″, 190 lbs.		Deb: 6/19/94													
1994 Mon-N	0	0	—	1	0	0	0	0	0²	4	0	1	0	67.5	54.00	8	.667	.714	0	—	0	-4	-4	0	0.0
● **JAKE EISENHART**				Eisenhart, Jacob Henry			b: 10/3/22, Perkasie, Pa.		d: 12/20/87, Huntingdon, Pa.		BL/TL, 6′3.5″, 195 lbs.		Deb: 6/10/44												
1944 Cin-N	0	0	—	1	0	0	0	0	0¹	0	0	1	0	27.0	0.00	—	.000	.500	0	—	0	0	0	0	0.0
● **HARRY EISENSTAT**				Eisenstat, Harry			b: 10/10/15, Brooklyn, N.Y.		BL/TL, 5′11″, 185 lbs.		Deb: 5/19/35													
1935 Bro-N	0	1	.000	2	0	0	0	0	4²	9	2	4	2	21.2	13.50	29	.429	.478	0	.000	-0	-5	-5	1	-0.7
1936 Bro-N	1	2	.333	5	2	1	0	0	14¹	12	1	6	5	17.6	5.65	73	.344	.400	1	.333	-0	-3	-2	0	-0.4
1937 Bro-N	3	3	.500	13	4	0	0	0	47²	61	2	11	12	13.8	3.97	102	.308	.348	0	.000	-0	0	1	1	0.0
1938 Det-A	9	6	.600	32	9	5	0	4	125¹	131	7	29	37	11.6	3.73	134	.266	.308	5	.139	-1	15	18	1	1.8
1939 Det-A	2	2	.500	10	2	1	0	0	29²	39	3	9	6	14.6	6.98	70	.315	.361	3	.375	1	-8	-7	1	-0.6
Cle-A	6	7	.462	26	11	4	1	2	103²	109	8	23	38	11.5	3.30	133	.265	.304	8	.250	1	15	13	-1	1.4
Yr	8	9	.471	36	13	5	1	2	133¹	148	11	32	44	12.2	4.12	110	.277	.317	11	.275	1	7	6	0	0.8
1940 Cle-A	1	4	.200	27	3	0	0	4	71²	78	6	12	27	11.3	3.14	134	.282	.311	6	.273	-0	**10**	9	-0	0.7
1941 Cle-A	1	1	.500	21	0	0	0	0	34	43	2	16	11	16.1	4.24	93	.312	.391	2	.333	1	-0	-1	-1	-0.1
1942 Cle-A	2	1	.667	29	1	0	0	2	47²	58	1	6	19	12.1	2.45	140	.304	.325	1	.250	0	8	8	0	0.3
Total 8	25	27	.481	165	32	11	1	14	478²	550	30	114	157	12.6	3.84	114	.287	.328	26	.211	0	30	29	0	2.4
● **ED EITELJORGE**				Eiteljorge, Edward Henry			b: 10/14/1871, Berlin, Germany		d: 12/5/42, Greencastle, Ind.		BR/TR, 6′2″, 190 lbs.		Deb: 5/2/1890												
1890 Chi-N	0	1	.000	2	1	1	0	0	2	5	0	1	1	27.0	22.50	16	.458	.503	0	.000	-0	-4	-4	-0	-1.0
1891 Was-a	1	5	.167	8	7	6	0	0	61¹	79	3	41	23	18.9	6.16	61	.302	.414	5	.192	-1	-17	-17	2	-1.1
Total 2	1	6	.143	9	8	6	0	0	63¹	84	3	42	24	19.2	6.68	58	.308	.417	5	.185	-1	-21	-21	1	-2.1
● **HEINIE ELDER**				Elder, Henry Knox			b: 8/23/1890, Seattle, Wash.		d: 11/13/58, Long Beach, Cal.		BL/TL, 6′2″, 200 lbs.		Deb: 7/7/13												
1913 Det-A	0	0	—	1	0	0	0	0	3¹	4	0	5	0	24.3	8.10	36	.286	.474	0	.000	-0	-2	-2	-0	0.0

YEAR	TM/L	W	L	PCT	G	GS	CG	SH	SV	IP	H	HR	BB	SO	RAT	ERA	ERA+	OAV	OOB	BH	AVG	PB	PR	/A	PD	TPI

● CAL ELDRED Eldred, Calvin John b: 11/24/67, Cedar Rapids, Iowa BR/TR, 6'4", 215 lbs. Deb: 9/24/91

YEAR	TM/L	W	L	PCT	G	GS	CG	SH	SV	IP	H	HR	BB	SO	RAT	ERA	ERA+	OAV	OOB	BH	AVG	PB	PR	/A	PD	TPI
1991	Mil-A	2	0	1.000	3	3	0	0	0	16	20	2	6	10	14.6	4.50	88	.299	.356	0	—	0	-1	-1	-0	0.0
1992	Mil-A	11	2	.846	14	14	2	1	0	100¹	76	4	23	62	9.1	1.79	214	.207	.257	0	—	0	24	23	-0	3.1
1993	Mil-A	16	16	.500	36	36	8	1	0	**258**	232	32	91	180	11.6	4.01	106	.239	.311	0	—	0	9	7	-0	0.7
1994	Mil-A	11	11	.500	25	25	6	0	0	179	158	23	84	98	12.4	4.68	105	.236	.325	0	—	0	2	5	0	0.5
Total	4	40	29	.580	78	78	16	2	0	553¹	486	61	204	350	11.5	3.84	114	.234	.308	0	—	0	34	33	-1	4.3

● HOD ELLER Eller, Horace Owen b: 7/5/1894, Muncie, Ind. d: 7/18/61, Indianapolis, Ind BR/TR, 5'11.5", 185 lbs. Deb: 4/16/17

YEAR	TM/L	W	L	PCT	G	GS	CG	SH	SV	IP	H	HR	BB	SO	RAT	ERA	ERA+	OAV	OOB	BH	AVG	PB	PR	/A	PD	TPI
1917	Cin-N	10	5	.667	37	11	7	1	1	152¹	131	2	37	77	10.1	2.36	111	.239	.290	6	.133	-2	6	4	-2	0.0
1918	Cin-N	16	12	.571	37	22	14	0	1	217²	205	1	59	84	11.2	2.36	116	.253	.309	11	.157	-2	10	8	-4	0.3
1919	*Cin-N	19	9	.679	38	30	16	7	2	248¹	216	6	50	137	9.8	2.39	116	.238	.281	26	.280	7	14	11	-3	1.6
1920	Cin-N	13	12	.520	35	23	15	1	0	210¹	208	6	52	76	11.3	2.95	103	.266	.315	22	.253	1	4	2	-1	0.2
1921	Cin-N	2	2	.500	13	3	0	0	1	34¹	46	3	15	7	16.0	4.98	72	.322	.386	3	.231	0	-5	-5	-1	-0.7
Total	5	60	40	.600	160	89	52	9	5	863	806	18	213	381	10.8	2.62	108	.253	.303	68	.221	5	30	19	-11	1.4

● JOE ELLICK Ellick, Joseph J. b: 4/3/1854, Cincinnati, Ohio d: 4/21/23, Kansas City, Kan. 5'10", 162 lbs. Deb: 5/13/1875 MU♦

YEAR	TM/L	W	L	PCT	G	GS	CG	SH	SV	IP	H	HR	BB	SO	RAT	ERA	ERA+	OAV	OOB	BH	AVG	PB	PR	/A	PD	TPI
1878	Mil-N	0	1	.000	1	0	0	0	0	3	1	0	1	0	6.0	3.00	88	.100	.182	2	.154	-0	-0	-0	-0	-0.1

● BRUCE ELLINGSEN Ellingsen, Harold Bruce b: 4/26/49, Pocatello, Idaho BL/TL, 6', 180 lbs. Deb: 7/4/74

YEAR	TM/L	W	L	PCT	G	GS	CG	SH	SV	IP	H	HR	BB	SO	RAT	ERA	ERA+	OAV	OOB	BH	AVG	PB	PR	/A	PD	TPI
1974	Cle-A	1	1	.500	16	2	0	0	0	42	45	5	17	16	13.3	3.21	112	.278	.346	0	—	0	2	2	-0	0.1

● CLAUDE ELLIOTT Elliott, Claude Judson "Chaucer" or "Old Pardee" b: 11/17/1879, Pardeeville, Wis. d: 6/21/23, Pardeeville, Wis. BR/TR, 6', 190 lbs. Deb: 4/16/04

YEAR	TM/L	W	L	PCT	G	GS	CG	SH	SV	IP	H	HR	BB	SO	RAT	ERA	ERA+	OAV	OOB	BH	AVG	PB	PR	/A	PD	TPI
1904	Cin-N	3	1	.750	9	6	4	1	0	57²	53	1	23	19	12.5	2.97	99	.247	.331	5	.208	1	-1	-0	0	0.1
	NY-N	0	1	.000	3	1	0	0	0	15	21	2	3	8	14.4	3.00	91	.328	.358	1	.200	-0	-0	-1	-1	-0.1
	Yr	3	2	.600	12	7	5	1	0	72²	74	3	26	27	12.4	2.97	97	.261	.324	6	.207	1	-2	-1	-1	0.0
1905	NY-N	0	1	.000	10	2	2	0	**6**	38	41	3	12	20	12.8	4.03	73	.270	.327	3	.188	-0	-4	-5	1	-0.3
Total	2	3	3	.500	22	9	7	1	6	110²	115	6	38	47	12.8	3.33	87	.267	.333	9	.200	1	-6	-5	0	-0.3

● DONNIE ELLIOTT Elliott, Donald Glenn b: 9/20/68, Pasadena, Tex. BR/TR, 6'4", 190 lbs. Deb: 4/23/94

YEAR	TM/L	W	L	PCT	G	GS	CG	SH	SV	IP	H	HR	BB	SO	RAT	ERA	ERA+	OAV	OOB	BH	AVG	PB	PR	/A	PD	TPI
1994	SD-N	0	1	.000	30	1	0	0	0	33	31	3	21	24	14.5	3.27	128	.250	.363	0	.000	-0	3	3	-0	0.1

● HAL ELLIOTT Elliott, Harold William b: 5/29/1899, Mt.Clemens, Mich. d: 4/25/63, Honolulu, Hawaii BR/TR, 6'1.5", 170 lbs. Deb: 4/19/29

YEAR	TM/L	W	L	PCT	G	GS	CG	SH	SV	IP	H	HR	BB	SO	RAT	ERA	ERA+	OAV	OOB	BH	AVG	PB	PR	/A	PD	TPI
1929	Phi-N	3	7	.300	40	8	2	0	2	114¹	146	6	59	32	16.1	6.06	86	.313	.390	5	.167	-1	-17	-11	1	-0.8
1930	Phi-N	6	11	.353	**48**	11	2	0	0	117¹	191	7	58	37	19.2	7.67	71	.338	.447	3	.094	-3	-35	-29	2	-3.3
1931	Phi-N	0	2	.000	16	4	0	0	2	33	46	5	19	8	16.4	9.55	44	.338	.423	1	.111	-0	-21	-19	0	-1.3
1932	Phi-N	2	4	.333	16	7	0	0	0	57²	70	5	38	13	16.9	5.77	76	.297	.394	3	.167	-0	-12	-9	-1	-0.9
Total	4	11	24	.314	120	30	4	0	4	322¹	453	22	174	90	17.6	6.95	73	.338	.415	12	.135	-5	-85	-68	2	-6.3

● GLENN ELLIOTT Elliott, Herbert Glenn "Lefty" b: 11/11/19, Sapulpa, Okla d: 7/27/69, Portland, Ore. BB/TL, 5'10", 170 lbs. Deb: 4/17/47

YEAR	TM/L	W	L	PCT	G	GS	CG	SH	SV	IP	H	HR	BB	SO	RAT	ERA	ERA+	OAV	OOB	BH	AVG	PB	PR	/A	PD	TPI
1947	Bos-N	0	1	.000	11	0	0	0	1	19	18	4	11	8	13.7	4.74	82	.269	.372	1	.500	-0	-1	-2	0	0.0
1948	Bos-N	1	0	1.000	1	1	0	0	0	3	5	0	1	2	18.0	3.00	128	.357	.400	0	.000	-0	0	-0	-0	0.0
1949	Bos-N	3	4	.429	22	6	1	0	0	68¹	70	7	27	15	12.8	3.95	96	.269	.338	1	.059	-1	1	-1	1	-0.2
Total	3	4	5	.444	34	7	1	0	1	90¹	93	11	39	25	13.2	4.08	93	.273	.347	2	.095	-1	-0	-3	-1	-0.2

● JUMBO ELLIOTT Elliott, James Thomas b: 10/22/1900, St.Louis, Mo. d: 1/7/70, Terre Haute, Ind. BR/TL, 6'3", 235 lbs. Deb: 4/21/23

YEAR	TM/L	W	L	PCT	G	GS	CG	SH	SV	IP	H	HR	BB	SO	RAT	ERA	ERA+	OAV	OOB	BH	AVG	PB	PR	/A	PD	TPI
1923	StL-A	0	0	—	1	0	0	0	0	1	1	0	3	0	36.0	27.00	15	.333	.667	0	—	0	-3	-3	-0	-0.0
1925	Bro-N	0	2	.000	10	2	1	0	0	10²	17	0	9	3	22.8	8.44	50	.362	.474	0	.000	-1	-5	-5	-0	-0.8
1927	Bro-N	6	13	.316	30	21	12	2	3	188¹	188	5	60	99	11.9	3.30	120	.269	.327	9	.141	-1	13	14	-4	0.8
1928	Bro-N	9	14	.391	41	21	7	2	1	192	194	8	64	74	12.4	3.89	102	.268	.332	12	.176	2	2	2	-3	0.1
1929	Bro-N	1	2	.333	6	3	0	0	0	19	21	2	16	7	18.0	6.63	70	.280	.413	1	.250	-0	-4	-4	-0	-0.5
1930	Bro-N	10	7	.588	35	21	6	2	1	198¹	204	16	70	59	12.7	3.95	124	.271	.337	10	.147	-2	23	21	-3	1.1
1931	Phi-N	**19**	14	.576	**52**	30	12	2	5	249	288	15	83	99	13.6	4.27	100	.287	.344	11	.122	-6	-11	-1	-5	-1.2
1932	Phi-N	11	10	.524	39	22	9	0	0	166	210	14	47	62	14.0	5.42	81	.300	.346	12	.197	-1	-28	-19	-2	-2.3
1933	Phi-N	6	10	.375	35	21	6	0	2	161²	188	8	49	43	13.4	3.84	99	.295	.348	12	.231	-0	-9	-0	-4	-0.4
1934	Phi-N	0	1	.000	3	1	0	0	0	5¹	8	0	4	1	21.9	10.13	47	.333	.448	0	.000	-0	-4	-3	-0	-0.5
	Bos-N	1	1	.500	7	3	0	0	0	15¹	19	2	9	6	17.0	5.87	65	.284	.377	1	.250	-0	-3	-3	-0	-0.4
	Yr	1	2	.333	10	4	0	0	0	20²	27	2	13	7	17.9	6.97	58	.293	.387	1	.200	-0	-7	-7	-0	-0.9
Total	10	63	74	.460	252	144	51	8	12	1206²	1338	70	414	453	13.3	4.24	100	.283	.344	68	.163	-8	-29	2	-21	-4.1

● DOCK ELLIS Ellis, Dock Phillip b: 3/11/45, Los Angeles, Cal. BB/TR, 6'3", 210 lbs. Deb: 6/18/68

YEAR	TM/L	W	L	PCT	G	GS	CG	SH	SV	IP	H	HR	BB	SO	RAT	ERA	ERA+	OAV	OOB	BH	AVG	PB	PR	/A	PD	TPI
1968	Pit-N	6	5	.545	26	10	4	0	2	104	82	4	38	52	10.5	2.51	117	.213	.285	2	.069	-1	5	5	0	0.4
1969	Pit-N	11	17	.393	35	33	8	2	0	218²	206	14	76	173	11.8	3.58	97	.250	.316	6	.088	-3	0	-2	1	-0.5
1970	*Pit-N	13	10	.565	30	30	9	4	0	201²	194	9	87	128	13.0	3.21	121	.257	.342	7	.100	-3	19	15	2	1.5
1971	*Pit-N★	19	9	.679	31	31	11	2	0	226²	207	15	63	137	10.8	3.06	111	.239	.292	16	.203	-3	10	8	0	1.3
1972	*Pit-N	15	7	.682	25	25	4	1	0	163¹	156	6	33	96	10.6	2.70	123	.253	.294	9	.153	-1	14	11	-1	1.3
1973	Pit-N	12	14	.462	28	28	3	1	0	192	176	7	55	122	11.1	3.05	115	.240	.299	7	.108	-3	13	10	1	1.2
1974	*Pit-N	12	9	.571	26	26	9	0	0	176²	163	13	41	91	10.7	3.16	109	.242	.292	12	.214	3	9	6	-1	0.9
1975	*Pit-N	8	9	.471	27	24	5	2	0	140	163	9	45	69	13.4	3.79	93	.292	.345	4	.111	-0	-3	-4	-1	-0.5
1976	*NY-A	17	8	.680	32	32	8	1	0	211²	195	14	76	65	11.7	3.19	107	.247	.316	0	—	0	8	5	-3	0.3
1977	NY-A	1	1	.500	3	3	1	0	0	19²	18	1	8	5	11.9	1.83	215	.237	.310	0	—	0	5	5	-0	0.5
	Oak-A	1	5	.167	7	7	0	0	0	26	35	5	14	11	17.3	9.69	42	.315	.397	0	—	0	-16	-16	-0	-2.7
	Tex-A	10	6	.625	23	22	7	1	1	167¹	158	13	42	90	10.8	2.90	140	.254	.301	0	—	0	21	22	-2	1.8
	Yr	12	12	.500	33	32	8	1	1	213	211	19	64	106	11.6	3.63	112	.260	.314	0	—	0	10	10	-2	-0.4
1978	Tex-A	9	7	.563	24	24	3	0	0	141¹	131	15	46	45	11.4	4.20	89	.245	.307	0	—	0	-7	-7	-0	-0.7
1979	Tex-A	1	5	.167	10	9	0	0	0	46²	64	5	16	10	15.4	5.98	69	.323	.374	0	—	0	-9	-9	-0	-1.0
	NY-N	3	7	.300	17	14	1	0	0	85	110	9	34	41	15.4	6.04	60	.320	.383	2	.077	-1	-22	-23	0	-2.4
	Pit-N	0	0	—	3	1	0	0	0	6¹	7	1	2	1	14.1	2.57	151	.346	.393	0	.000	-0	1	1	-0	0.0
	Yr	4	7	.300	20	15	1	0	0	92	117	10	36	42	15.2	5.77	63	.316	.375	2	.074	-2	-21	-22	0	-2.4
Total	12	138	119	.537	345	317	71	14	1	2127²	2067	140	674	1136	11.8	3.46	103	.255	.315	65	.133	-7	49	26	-3	1.4

● JIM ELLIS Ellis, James Russell b: 3/25/45, Tulare, Cal. BR/TL, 6'2", 185 lbs. Deb: 8/11/67

YEAR	TM/L	W	L	PCT	G	GS	CG	SH	SV	IP	H	HR	BB	SO	RAT	ERA	ERA+	OAV	OOB	BH	AVG	PB	PR	/A	PD	TPI
1967	Chi-N	1	1	.500	8	1	0	0	0	16²	20	1	9	8	15.7	3.24	109	.313	.397	1	.200	0	0	1	-0	0.1
1969	StL-N	0	0	—	2	1	0	0	0	5¹	7	0	3	6	16.9	1.69	212	.318	.400	0	—	0	1	1	0	0.0
Total	2	1	1	.500	10	2	0	0	0	22	27	1	12	14	16.0	2.86	124	.314	.398	1	.200	0	1	1	0	0.1

● SAMMY ELLIS Ellis, Samuel Joseph b: 2/11/41, Youngstown, Ohio BL/TR, 6'1", 180 lbs. Deb: 4/14/62 C

YEAR	TM/L	W	L	PCT	G	GS	CG	SH	SV	IP	H	HR	BB	SO	RAT	ERA	ERA+	OAV	OOB	BH	AVG	PB	PR	/A	PD	TPI
1962	Cin-N	2	2	.500	8	4	0	0	0	28	29	6	29	27	19.0	6.75	60	.269	.428	2	.200	-0	-9	-8	-0	-1.0
1964	Cin-N	10	3	.769	52	5	2	0	14	122¹	101	9	28	125	9.6	2.57	140	.223	.270	2	.083	-0	13	14	0	1.9
1965	Cin-N☆	22	10	.688	44	39	15	2	0	263²	222	22	104	183	11.3	3.79	99	.226	.304	12	.125	-1	-7	-1	-3	-0.6
1966	Cin-N	12	19	.387	41	36	7	0	0	221	226	35	78	154	12.5	5.29	74	.264	.328	8	.114	-2	-41	-34	-3	-4.7
1967	Cin-N	8	11	.421	32	27	8	1	0	175²	197	18	67	80	13.7	3.84	98	.286	.353	4	.082	-2	-9	-2	-1	-1.0
1968	Cal-A	9	10	.474	42	24	8	0	0	164	150	24	56	93	11.6	3.95	74	.244	.313	2	.045	-3	-18	-19	-2	-2.8
1969	Chi-A	0	3	.000	10	5	0	0	0	29¹	42	6	16	15	18.1	5.83	66	.336	.415	1	.167	0	-7	-6	0	-0.5
Total	7	63	58	.521	229	140	35	3	18	1004	967	118	378	677	12.3	4.15	88	.253	.323	31	.104	-8	-78	-58	-9	-8.2

YEAR TM/L	W	L	PCT	G	GS	CG	SH	SV	IP	H	HR	BB	SO	RAT	ERA	ERA+	OAV	OOB	BH	AVG	PB	PR	/A	PD	TPI
● **GEORGE ELLISON**														Ellison, George Russell b: 1/24/1895, California d: 1/20/78, San Francisco, Cal. BR/TR, 6'3", 185 lbs. Deb: 8/21/20										
1920 Cle-A	0	0	—	1	0	0	0	0	1	0	0	2	1	18.0	0.00	—	.000	.400	0	—	0	0	0	0	0.0
● **DICK ELLSWORTH**														Ellsworth, Richard Clark b: 3/22/40, Lusk, Wyo. BL/TL, 6'4", 195 lbs. Deb: 6/22/58 F										
1958 Chi-N	0	1	.000	1	1	0	0	0	2¹	4	0	3	0	30.9	15.43	25	.364	.533	0	.000	-0	-3	-3	-0	-0.8
1960 Chi-N	7	13	.350	31	27	6	0	0	176²	170	12	72	94	12.4	3.72	102	.257	.332	2	.042	-3	1	1	-0	-0.2
1961 Chi-N	10	11	.476	37	31	7	1	0	186²	213	23	48	91	12.7	3.86	108	.292	.338	2	.036	-5	4	7	3	-0.5
1962 Chi-N	9	20	.310	37	33	6	0	1	208²	241	23	77	113	13.9	5.09	81	.291	.355	7	.113	1	-27	-22	0	-2.5
1963 Chi-N	22	10	.688	37	37	19	4	0	290²	223	14	75	185	9.3	2.11	**167**	.210	.263	9	.096	-2	38	**45**	2	**5.2**
1964 Chi-N☆	14	18	.438	37	36	16	1	0	256²	267	34	64	148	12.0	3.75	99	.266	.317	4	.046	-5	-6	-1	2	-0.5
1965 Chi-N	14	15	.483	36	34	8	0	1	222¹	227	22	57	130	11.7	3.81	97	.265	.313	7	.096	-2	-7	-3	2	-0.4
1966 Chi-N	8	22	.267	38	37	9	0	0	269¹	321	28	51	144	12.6	3.98	92	.294	.328	14	.156	-0	-11	-9	2	-0.8
1967 Phi-N	6	7	.462	32	21	3	1	0	125¹	152	6	36	45	13.9	4.38	78	.306	.359	4	.108	-1	-14	-14	2	-1.3
1968 Bos-A	16	7	.696	31	28	10	1	0	196	196	16	37	106	11.0	3.03	104	.266	.301	4	.056	-5	1	3	-0	-0.2
1969 Bos-A	0	0	—	2	2	0	0	0	12	16	1	4	4	15.0	3.75	101	.320	.370	0	.000	-0	-0	0	-0	-0.0
Cle-A	6	9	.400	34	22	3	1	0	135	162	10	40	48	13.8	4.13	91	.301	.354	6	.133	-1	-8	-6	0	-0.7
Yr	6	9	.400	36	24	3	1	0	147	178	11	44	52	13.9	4.10	92	.302	.356	6	.125	-2	-8	-5	0	-0.7
1970 Cle-A	3	3	.500	29	1	0	0	2	43²	49	4	14	13	13.2	4.53	87	.290	.358	0	.000	-0	-4	-3	1	-0.3
Mil-A	0	0	—	14	0	0	0	1	15²	11	0	3	9	8.6	1.72	220	.196	.250	0	—	-0	3	4	-0	0.1
Yr	3	3	.500	43	1	0	0	3	59¹	60	4	17	22	11.8	3.79	103	.269	.324	0	.000	-0	-1	1	1	-0.3
1971 Mil-A	0	1	.000	14	0	0	0	0	15²	11	0	9	10	18.4	4.91	71	.361	.435	0	—	-0	-2	-2	-0	-0.2
Total 13	115	137	.456	407	310	87	9	5	2155²	2274	194	595	1140	12.2	3.72	100	.272	.324	59	.088	-25	-37	-2	12	-2.2
● **STEVE ELLSWORTH**														Ellsworth, Steven Clark b: 7/30/60, Chicago, Ill. BR/TR, 6'8", 220 lbs. Deb: 4/7/88 F										
1988 Bos-A	1	6	.143	8	7	0	0	0	36	47	7	16	16	16.0	6.75	61	.315	.386	0	—	0	-11	-11	-0	-1.8
● **DON ELSTON**														Elston, Donald Ray b: 4/6/29, Campbellstown, Ohio d: 1/2/95, Evanston, Ill. BR/TR, 6', 170 lbs. Deb: 9/17/53										
1953 Chi-N	0	1	.000	2	1	0	0	0	5	11	1	0	2	19.8	14.40	31	.458	.458	0	.000	-0	-6	-6	-0	-0.8
1957 Bro-N	0	0	—	1	0	0	0	0	1	1	0	0	1	9.0	0.00	—	.250	.250	0	—	0	0	0	0	0.0
Chi-N	6	7	.462	39	14	2	0	8	144	139	15	55	102	12.4	3.56	109	.259	.334	4	.108	-2	5	5	0	0.3
Yr	6	7	.462	40	14	2	0	8	145	140	15	55	103	12.4	3.54	109	.259	.333	4	.108	-2	5	5	0	0.3
1958 Chi-N	9	8	.529	**69**	0	0	0	10	97	75	9	39	84	10.7	2.88	136	.214	.294	5	.357	-0	**12**	**11**	1	2.4
1959 Chi-N★	10	8	.556	**65**	0	0	0	13	97²	77	11	46	82	11.6	3.32	119	.218	.313	4	.211	-0	7	7	-0	1.3
1960 Chi-N	8	9	.471	60	0	0	0	11	127	109	17	55	85	11.9	3.40	111	.231	.316	3	.125	-1	5	5	-2	0.5
1961 Chi-N	6	7	.462	58	0	0	0	8	93¹	108	11	45	59	15.3	5.59	75	.297	.383	2	.182	-0	-16	-15	0	-2.1
1962 Chi-N	4	8	.333	57	0	0	0	8	66¹	57	6	32	37	12.2	2.44	170	.247	.341	0	.000	-1	11	13	1	2.5
1963 Chi-N	4	1	.800	51	0	0	0	6	70	57	6	21	41	10.3	2.83	124	.226	.291	0	.000	-0	4	5	-1	0.3
1964 Chi-N	2	5	.286	48	0	0	0	1	54¹	68	4	34	26	17.4	5.30	70	.330	.432	1	.167	-0	-11	-10	1	-1.1
Total 9	49	54	.476	450	15	2	0	63	755²	702	80	327	519	12.6	3.69	106	.251	.335	19	.153	-3	11	17	1	3.3
● **NARCISO ELVIRA**														Elvira, Narciso Chicho (Delgado) b: 10/29/67, Veracruz, Mex. BL/TL, 5'10", 160 lbs. Deb: 9/9/90										
1990 Mil-A	0	0	—	4	0	0	0	0	5	6	0	5	6	19.8	5.40	72	.300	.440	0	—	0	-1	-1	0	0.1
● **BONES ELY**														Ely, William Frederick b: 6/7/1863, N.Girard, Pa. d: 1/10/52, Berkeley, Cal. BR/TR, 6'1", 155 lbs. Deb: 6/19/1884 ◆										
1884 Buf-N	0	1	.000	1	1	0	0	0	5	17	1	5	4	39.6	14.40	22	.500	.564	0	.000	-1	-6	-6	-0	-0.7
1886 Lou-a	0	4	.000	6	4	4	0	**1**	44	53	0	26	28	16.2	5.32	68	.280	.367	5	.156	-1	-9	-8	0	-0.7
1890 Syr-a	0	0	—	1	0	0	0	0	2	7	0	0	0	31.5	22.50	16	.542	.542	130	.262	0	-4	-4	0	0.0
1894 StL-N	0	0	—	1	0	0	0	0	1	0	0	3	0	27.0	0.00	—	.000	.510	156	.306	-0	0	0	0	0.0
Total 4	0	5	.000	9	5	4	0	1	52	77	1	34	32	19.2	6.75	54	.322	.407	1331	.258	-1	-19	-18	0	-1.4
● **HARRY ELY**														Ely, Harry Deb: 9/24/1892										
1892 Bal-N	0	1	.000	1	1	0	0	0	7	14	0	7	0	29.6	7.71	44	.400	.523	0	.000	-0	-3	-3	-0	-0.4
● **ALAN EMBREE**														Embree, Alan Duane b: 1/23/70, Vancouver, Wash. BL/TL, 6'2", 185 lbs. Deb: 9/15/92										
1992 Cle-A	0	2	.000	4	4	0	0	0	18	19	3	8	12	14.0	7.00	56	.271	.354	0	—	0	-6	-6	-1	-0.6
● **RED EMBREE**														Embree, Charles Willard b: 8/30/17, ElMonte, Cal. BR/TR, 6', 165 lbs. Deb: 9/10/41										
1941 Cle-A	0	1	.000	1	1	0	0	0	4	7	0	3	4	24.8	6.75	58	.438	.550	0	.000	-1	-1	-1	-0	-0.3
1942 Cle-A	3	4	.429	19	6	2	0	0	63	58	0	31	44	13.0	3.86	89	.242	.333	2	.133	-1	-3	-0	-0.3	-0.3
1944 Cle-A	0	1	.000	3	1	0	0	0	3¹	2	0	5	4	18.9	13.50	24	.167	.412	0	—	-0	-4	-4	-0	-0.9
1945 Cle-A	4	4	.500	8	8	5	1	0	70	56	3	26	42	10.5	1.93	168	.215	.287	3	.143	-1	11	10	1	1.2
1946 Cle-A	8	12	.400	28	26	8	0	0	200	170	15	79	87	11.3	3.47	95	.227	.302	13	.186	-1	-3	-1	-0	-0.3
1947 Cle-A	8	10	.444	27	21	6	0	0	162²	137	13	67	56	11.3	3.15	110	.233	.313	9	.173	-1	10	6	1	0.5
1948 NY-A	5	3	.625	20	8	4	0	0	76²	77	6	30	25	12.7	3.76	101	.261	.331	4	.148	-1	5	3	-1	0.0
1949 StL-A	3	13	.188	35	19	4	0	1	127¹	146	13	89	24	16.8	5.37	84	.294	.405	6	.162	-0	-17	-12	-0	-1.4
Total 8	31	48	.392	141	90	29	1	1	707	653	50	330	286	12.6	3.72	98	.246	.331	37	.166	-2	4	-5	-2	-1.5
● **SLIM EMBREY**														Embrey, Charles Akin b: 8/17/01, Columbia, Tenn. d: 10/10/47, Nashville, Tenn. BR/TR, 6'2", 184 lbs. Deb: 10/1/23										
1923 Chi-A	0	0	—	1	0	0	0	0	2²	7	0	2	1	30.4	10.13	39	.500	.563	0	—	0	-2	-2	0	-0.3
● **CHARLIE EMIG**														Emig, Charles Henry b: 4/5/1875, Cincinnati, Ohio d: 10/2/75, Oklahoma City, Okla. TL, Deb: 9/4/1896										
1896 Lou-N	0	1	.000	1	1	1	0	0	7	12	1	9	2	24.8	7.88	55	.343	.489	0	.000	-1	-3	-3	1	-0.3
● **SLIM EMMERICH**														Emmerich, William Peter b: 9/29/19, Allentown, Pa. BR/TR, 6'1", 170 lbs. Deb: 5/14/45										
1945 NY-N	4	4	.500	31	7	1	0	0	100	111	8	33	27	13.1	4.86	80	.278	.334	3	.120	-2	-12	-11	-0	-0.9
1946 NY-N	0	0	—	2	0	0	0	0	4	6	1	0	1	13.5	4.50	76	.400	.400	0	—	0	-0	-0	-0	-0.0
Total 2	4	4	.500	33	7	1	0	0	104	117	9	33	28	13.1	4.85	80	.282	.336	3	.120	-2	-12	-11	-0	-0.9
● **BOB EMSLIE**														Emslie, Robert Daniel b: 1/27/1859, Guelph, Ont., Can. d: 4/26/43, St.Thomas, Ont., Canada BR/TR, 5'11", Deb: 7/25/1883 U										
1883 Bal-a	9	13	.409	24	23	21	1	0	201¹	188	3	41	62	10.2	3.17	110	.231	.268	16	.165	-3	3	7	2	0.5
1884 Bal-a	32	17	.653	50	50	50	4	0	455¹	419	5	88	264	10.3	2.75	126	.224	.264	37	.190	-5	25	36	-1	2.8
1885 Bal-a	3	10	.231	13	13	11	0	0	107	131	0	30	27	14.0	4.29	76	.298	.350	12	.235	-0	-12	-12	-1	-1.2
Phi-a	0	4	.000	4	4	3	0	0	28²	37	1	6	9	13.5	6.28	55	.291	.323	1	.083	-1	-10	-9	1	-1.0
Yr	3	14	.176	17	17	14	0	0	135²	168	1	36	36	13.5	4.71	70	.294	.336	13	.206	-1	-22	-21	-1	-2.2
Total 3	44	44	.500	91	90	85	5	0	792¹	775	9	165	362	10.9	3.19	108	.239	.279	66	.186	-9	6	22	1	1.1
● **LUIS ENCARNACION**														Encarnacion, Luis Martin Lora (b: Luis Martin Lora (Encarnacion)) b: 10/20/63, Santo Domingo, D.R. BR/TR, 5'10", 178 lbs. Deb: 7/27/90										
1990 KC-A	0	0	—	4	0	0	0	0	10¹	14	1	4	8	15.7	7.84	49	.311	.367	0	—	0	-5	-5	-0	0.1
● **JOE ENGEL**														Engel, Joseph William b: 3/12/1893, Washington, D.C. d: 6/12/69, Chattanooga, Tenn BR/TL, 6'1.5", 183 lbs. Deb: 5/30/12										
1912 Was-A	2	5	.286	17	10	2	0	1	75	70	2	50	29	14.9	3.96	84	.253	.375	1	.059	-1	-5	-5	1	-0.5
1913 Was-A	8	9	.471	36	24	6	2	0	164²	124	2	85	70	12.0	3.06	97	.207	.313	3	.061	-5	-2	-2	-0	-0.3
1914 Was-A	7	5	.583	35	15	1	0	3	124¹	108	2	75	41	13.6	2.97	95	.254	.372	3	.107	-1	-3	-2	-0	-0.2
1915 Was-A	0	3	.000	11	3	0	0	0	33²	30	1	19	9	13.9	3.21	93	.261	.380	0	.000	-0	-1	-1	-0	-0.1
1917 Cin-N	0	1	.000	1	1	1	0	0	8	12	0	6	2	20.3	5.63	47	.353	.450	0	.000	-0	-3	-3	-0	-0.3

YEAR	TM/L	W	L	PCT	G	GS	CG	SH	SV	IP	H	HR	BB	SO	RAT	ERA	ERA+	OAV	OOB	BH	AVG	PB	PR	/A	PD	TPI
1919	Cle-A	0	0	—		1	0	0	0	0	0	0	3	0		∞		—	1.000	0	—	0	-2	-2	-0	-0.2
1920	Was-A	0	0	—		1	0	0	0	1²	0	0	4	0	27.0	21.60	17	.000	.556	0	.000	-0	-3	-3	-0	0.0
Total	7	17	23	.425	102	53	10	2	4	407¹	344	6	242	151	13.5	3.38	88	.237	.355	7	.067	-6	-20	-18	-0	-2.1

● STEVE ENGEL Engel, Steven Michael b: 12/31/61, Cincinnati, Ohio BR/TL, 6'3", 216 lbs. Deb: 7/30/85

YEAR	TM/L	W	L	PCT	G	GS	CG	SH	SV	IP	H	HR	BB	SO	RAT	ERA	ERA+	OAV	OOB	BH	AVG	PB	PR	/A	PD	TPI
1985	Chi-N	1	5	.167	11	8	1	0	1	51²	61	10	26	29	15.2	5.57	72	.298	.377	3	.188	1	-11	-9	-0	-0.9

● RICK ENGLE Engle, Richard Douglas b: 4/7/57, Corbin, Ky. BR/TL, 5'11.5", 181 lbs. Deb: 9/2/81

YEAR	TM/L	W	L	PCT	G	GS	CG	SH	SV	IP	H	HR	BB	SO	RAT	ERA	ERA+	OAV	OOB	BH	AVG	PB	PR	/A	PD	TPI
1981	Mon-N	0	0	—		1	0	0	0	0	2	6	0	1	2	31.5	18.00	19	.500	.538	0	—	0	-3	-3	-0	0.0

● JACK ENRIGHT Enright, Jackson Percy b: 11/29/1895, Fort Worth, Tex. d: 8/18/75, Pompano Beach, Fla BR/TR, 5'11", 177 lbs. Deb: 9/26/17

YEAR	TM/L	W	L	PCT	G	GS	CG	SH	SV	IP	H	HR	BB	SO	RAT	ERA	ERA+	OAV	OOB	BH	AVG	PB	PR	/A	PD	TPI
1917	NY-A	0	1	.000	1	1	0	0	0	5	5	0	3	1	14.4	5.40	50	.294	.400	0	.000	-0	-2	-2	1	-0.2

● TERRY ENYART Enyart, Terry Gene b: 10/10/50, Ironton, Ohio BR/TL, 6'2", 190 lbs. Deb: 6/17/74

YEAR	TM/L	W	L	PCT	G	GS	CG	SH	SV	IP	H	HR	BB	SO	RAT	ERA	ERA+	OAV	OOB	BH	AVG	PB	PR	/A	PD	TPI
1974	Mon-N	0	0	—		2	0	0	0	0	1²	4	0	4	2	43.2	16.20	24	.444	.615	0	—	0	-2	-2	-0	0.0

● JOHNNY ENZMANN Enzmann, John "Gentleman John" b: 3/4/1890, Brooklyn, N.Y. d: 3/14/84, Riverhead, N.Y. BR/TR, 5'10", 165 lbs. Deb: 7/10/14

YEAR	TM/L	W	L	PCT	G	GS	CG	SH	SV	IP	H	HR	BB	SO	RAT	ERA	ERA+	OAV	OOB	BH	AVG	PB	PR	/A	PD	TPI
1914	Bro-N	1	0	1.000	7	1	0	0	0	19	21	1	8	5	15.2	4.74	60	.300	.395	0	.000	-1	-4	-4	1	-0.2
1918	Cle-A	5	7	.417	30	14	8	0	2	136²	130	4	29	38	10.8	2.37	127	.263	.310	7	.149	-5	6	10	0	0.6
1919	Cle-A	3	2	.600	14	4	2	0	0	55¹	67	0	8	13	12.5	2.28	147	.312	.342	2	.133	-0	6	7	-1	0.4
1920	Phi-N	2	3	.400	16	2	1	0	0	58²	79	1	16	35	15.3	3.84	89	.320	.373	4	.167	1	-5	-3	-0	-0.2
Total	4	11	12	.478	67	21	11	0	2	269²	297	6	61	91	12.4	2.84	111	.289	.338	13	.141	-3	3	10	-0	0.6

● AL EPPERLY Epperly, Albert Paul "Tub" or "Pard" b: 5/7/18, Glidden, Iowa BL/TR, 6'2", 194 lbs. Deb: 4/25/38

YEAR	TM/L	W	L	PCT	G	GS	CG	SH	SV	IP	H	HR	BB	SO	RAT	ERA	ERA+	OAV	OOB	BH	AVG	PB	PR	/A	PD	TPI
1938	Chi-N	2	0	1.000	9	4	1	0	0	27	28	1	15	10	14.3	3.67	104	.264	.355	2	.250	1	0	0	0	0.1
1950	Bro-N	0	0	—		5	0	0	0	0	9	14	1	5	3	19.0	5.00	82	.378	.452	0	—	0	-1	-1	-0	0.0
Total	2	2	0	1.000	14	4	1	0	0	36	42	2	20	13	15.5	4.00	97	.294	.380	2	.250	1	-0	-0	-0	0.1

● GREG ERARDI Erardi, Joseph Gregory b: 5/31/54, Syracuse, N.Y. BR/TR, 6'1", 190 lbs. Deb: 9/6/77

YEAR	TM/L	W	L	PCT	G	GS	CG	SH	SV	IP	H	HR	BB	SO	RAT	ERA	ERA+	OAV	OOB	BH	AVG	PB	PR	/A	PD	TPI
1977	Sea-A	0	1	.000	5	0	0	0	0	9	12	3	6	5	18.0	6.00	69	.300	.391	0	—	0	-2	-2	-0	-0.2

● EDDIE ERAUTT Erautt, Edward Lorenz Sebastian b: 9/26/24, Portland, Ore. BR/TR, 6', 186 lbs. Deb: 4/16/47 F

YEAR	TM/L	W	L	PCT	G	GS	CG	SH	SV	IP	H	HR	BB	SO	RAT	ERA	ERA+	OAV	OOB	BH	AVG	PB	PR	/A	PD	TPI
1947	Cin-N	4	9	.308	36	10	2	0	0	119	146	5	53	43	15.2	5.07	81	.307	.379	2	.069	-1	-13	-13	1	-1.3
1948	Cin-N	0	0	—		2	0	0	0	0	3	3	0	1	0	12.0	6.00	65	.250	.308	0	—	-1	-1	-1	-0	0.0
1949	Cin-N	4	11	.267	39	9	1	0	1	112²	99	6	61	43	13.0	3.36	125	.247	.351	4	.174	0	**9**	**10**	-1	1.2
1950	Cin-N	4	2	.667	33	2	1	0	1	65¹	82	9	22	35	15.2	5.65	75	.307	.373	2	.154	-2	-11	-10	1	-0.9
1951	Cin-N	0	0	—		30	0	0	0	0	39¹	50	4	23	20	17.4	5.72	71	.314	.411	0	.000	-0	-8	-7	1	-0.5
1953	Cin-N	0	0	—		4	0	0	0	0	4²	11	1	3	1	27.0	5.79	75	.500	.560	0	.000	-0	-1	-1	0	0.0
	StL-N	3	1	.750	20	1	0	0	0	35²	43	6	16	15	15.4	6.31	67	.299	.377	1	.167	-0	-8	-8	0	-0.8
	Yr	3	1	.750	24	1	0	0	0	40¹	54	7	19	16	16.7	6.25	68	.325	.401	1	.143	-0	-9	-9	0	-0.8
Total	6	15	23	.395	164	22	4	0	2	379²	434	34	179	157	14.9	4.86	86	.293	.376	9	.120	-2	-33	-29	0	-1.8

● DON ERICKSON Erickson, Don Lee b: 12/13/31, Springfield, Ill. BR/TR, 6', 175 lbs. Deb: 9/1/58

YEAR	TM/L	W	L	PCT	G	GS	CG	SH	SV	IP	H	HR	BB	SO	RAT	ERA	ERA+	OAV	OOB	BH	AVG	PB	PR	/A	PD	TPI
1958	Phi-N	0	1	.000	9	0	0	0	0	11²	11	3	9	5	15.4	4.63	86	.244	.370	0	.000	-0	-1	-1	-0	-0.1

● ERIC ERICKSON Erickson, Eric George Adolph b: 3/13/1895, Goteborg, Sweden d: 5/19/65, Jamestown, N.Y. BR/TR, 6'2", 190 lbs. Deb: 10/6/14

YEAR	TM/L	W	L	PCT	G	GS	CG	SH	SV	IP	H	HR	BB	SO	RAT	ERA	ERA+	OAV	OOB	BH	AVG	PB	PR	/A	PD	TPI
1914	NY-N	0	1	.000	1	1	0	0	0	5	8	0	3	3	19.8	0.00	—	.364	.440	0	.000	-1	2	1	-0	0.3
1916	Det-A	0	0	—		8	0	0	0	0	16	13	0	8	7	12.4	2.81	102	.220	.324	0	.000	-1	0	0	-1	-0.1
1918	Det-A	4	5	.444	12	9	8	0	1	94¹	81	4	29	48	10.8	2.48	107	.240	.306	4	.121	-3	3	2	-3	-0.4
1919	Det-A	0	2	.000	3	2	0	0	0	14²	17	0	10	4	17.2	6.75	47	.293	.406	1	.200	-0	-6	-6	-0	-0.7
	Was-A	6	11	.353	20	15	7	1	0	132	130	4	63	86	13.6	3.95	81	.254	.344	7	.146	-1	-11	-11	-3	-1.7
	Yr	6	13	.316	23	17	7	1	0	146²	147	7	73	90	13.9	4.23	76	.258	.349	8	.151	-2	-16	-17	-3	-2.4
1920	Was-A	12	16	.429	39	27	12	0	1	239¹	231	13	128	87	13.9	3.84	97	.264	.365	23	.277	4	-1	-3	-4	-0.3
1921	Was-A	8	10	.444	32	22	9	3	0	179	181	7	65	71	12.8	3.62	114	.269	.341	9	.150	-3	13	10	-3	0.2
1922	Was-A	4	12	.250	30	17	6	2	2	141²	144	8	73	61	14.0	4.96	78	.279	.372	6	.133	-2	-14	-17	-2	-2.1
Total	7	34	57	.374	145	93	42	6	4	822	805	37	379	367	13.3	3.85	93	.264	.352	50	.179	-6	-14	-23	-15	-4.8

● HAL ERICKSON Erickson, Harold James b: 7/17/19, Portland, Ore. BR/TR, 6'5", 230 lbs. Deb: 4/14/53

YEAR	TM/L	W	L	PCT	G	GS	CG	SH	SV	IP	H	HR	BB	SO	RAT	ERA	ERA+	OAV	OOB	BH	AVG	PB	PR	/A	PD	TPI
1953	Det-A	0	1	.000	18	0	0	0	1	32¹	43	4	10	19	15.3	4.73	86	.323	.379	0	.000	-1	-3	-3	-0	-0.2

● PAUL ERICKSON Erickson, Paul Walford "Li'L Abner" b: 12/14/15, Zion, Ill. BR/TR, 6'2", 200 lbs. Deb: 6/29/41

YEAR	TM/L	W	L	PCT	G	GS	CG	SH	SV	IP	H	HR	BB	SO	RAT	ERA	ERA+	OAV	OOB	BH	AVG	PB	PR	/A	PD	TPI
1941	Chi-N	5	7	.417	32	15	7	1	1	141	126	2	64	85	12.3	3.70	95	.234	.318	7	.152	0	-1	-3	-1	-0.3
1942	Chi-N	1	6	.143	18	7	1	0	0	63	70	4	41	26	15.9	5.43	59	.288	.391	3	.143	-1	-15	-16	0	-1.7
1943	Chi-N	1	3	.250	15	4	0	0	0	42²	47	4	22	24	15.0	6.12	55	.280	.370	3	.200	-1	-13	-13	0	-1.2
1944	Chi-N	5	9	.357	33	15	5	3	1	124¹	113	5	67	82	13.0	3.55	100	.243	.338	2	.056	-1	1	-0	2	0.0
1945	*Chi-N	7	4	.636	28	9	3	0	3	108¹	94	5	48	53	12.4	3.32	110	.233	.325	5	.156	0	6	4	-0	0.4
1946	Chi-N	9	7	.563	32	14	5	1	0	137	119	2	65	70	12.3	2.43	137	.232	.321	2	.050	-4	15	14	-1	1.0
1947	Chi-N	7	12	.368	40	20	6	0	1	174	179	17	93	82	14.3	4.34	91	.268	.362	15	.250	3	-6	-8	-1	-0.4
1948	Chi-N	0	0	—		3	0	0	0	0	5²	7	0	4	4	20.6	6.35	61	.292	.433	0	.000	-0	-2	-2	0	0.0
	Phi-N	2	0	1.000	4	2	0	0	0	17¹	19	2	17	5	18.7	5.19	76	.292	.439	1	.143	-0	-2	-2	-0	-0.2
	NY-N	0	0	—		2	0	0	0	0	1	0	0	2	1	18.0	0.00	—	.000	.400	0	—	0	0	0	-0	0.0
	Yr	2	0	1.000	9	2	0	0	0	24	26	2	25	10	19.1	5.25	76	.283	.436	1	.125	-0	-3	-3	-0	-0.2
Total	8	37	48	.435	207	86	27	5	6	814¹	774	41	425	432	13.5	3.86	93	.250	.345	38	.147	-2	-16	-26	-0	-2.4

● RALPH ERICKSON Erickson, Ralph Lief b: 6/25/02, Dubois, Idaho BL/TL, 6'1", 175 lbs. Deb: 9/11/29

YEAR	TM/L	W	L	PCT	G	GS	CG	SH	SV	IP	H	HR	BB	SO	RAT	ERA	ERA+	OAV	OOB	BH	AVG	PB	PR	/A	PD	TPI
1929	Pit-N	0	0	—		1	0	0	0	0	1	2	0	2	2	36.0	27.00	18	.500	.667	0	—	0	-2	-2	-0	0.0
1930	Pit-N	1	0	1.000	7	0	0	0	0	14	21	1	10	0	19.9	7.07	70	.375	.470	1	.250	-0	-4	-3	-0	-0.2
Total	2	1	0	1.000	8	0	0	0	0	15	23	1	12	2	21.0	8.40	59	.383	.486	1	.250	-0	-6	-6	-0	-0.2

● ROGER ERICKSON Erickson, Roger Farrell b: 8/30/56, Springfield, Ill. BR/TR, 6'3", 190 lbs. Deb: 4/6/78

YEAR	TM/L	W	L	PCT	G	GS	CG	SH	SV	IP	H	HR	BB	SO	RAT	ERA	ERA+	OAV	OOB	BH	AVG	PB	PR	/A	PD	TPI
1978	Min-A	14	13	.519	37	37	14	0	0	265²	268	19	79	121	12.0	3.96	96	.263	.321	0	—	0	-6	-4	0	-0.4
1979	Min-A	3	10	.231	24	21	0	0	0	123	154	17	48	47	14.9	5.63	78	.310	.372	0	—	0	-19	-17	-0	-1.7
1980	Min-A	7	13	.350	32	27	7	0	0	191²	198	13	56	97	12.1	3.25	134	.268	.322	0	—	0	17	24	-0	2.3
1981	Min-A	3	8	.273	14	14	1	0	0	91¹	93	7	31	44	12.2	3.84	103	.262	.321	0	—	0	-2	-1	-0	-0.1
1982	Min-A	4	3	.571	7	7	2	0	0	40²	56	4	12	12	15.3	4.87	87	.326	.373	0	—	0	-4	-3	1	-0.4
	NY-A	4	5	.444	16	11	0	0	0	70²	86	5	17	37	13.1	4.46	89	.301	.340	0	—	0	-4	-4	-1	-0.5
	Yr	8	8	.500	23	18	2	0	0	111¹	142	9	29	49	13.8	4.61	89	.308	.349	0	—	0	-7	-7	-1	-0.9
1983	NY-A	0	1	.000	5	0	0	0	0	16²	13	1	8	7	11.3	4.32	90	.213	.304	0	—	0	-0	-1	0	0.2
Total	6	35	53	.398	135	117	24	0	0	799¹	868	68	251	365	12.8	4.13	99	.277	.334	0	—	0	-18	-4	-1	-0.6

● SCOTT ERICKSON Erickson, Scott Gavin b: 2/2/68, Long Beach, Cal. BR/TR, 6'4", 220 lbs. Deb: 6/25/90

YEAR	TM/L	W	L	PCT	G	GS	CG	SH	SV	IP	H	HR	BB	SO	RAT	ERA	ERA+	OAV	OOB	BH	AVG	PB	PR	/A	PD	TPI
1990	Min-A	8	4	.667	19	17	1	1	0	113	108	9	51	53	13.1	2.87	145	.256	.343	0	—	0	13	16	-0	1.6
1991	*Min-A	**20**	8	.714	32	32	5	3	0	204	189	13	71	108	11.7	3.18	134	.248	.317	0	—	0	21	25	1	3.1
1992	Min-A	13	12	.520	32	32	5	3	0	212	197	18	83	101	12.2	3.40	119	.252	.330	0	—	0	13	15	2	1.8
1993	Min-A	8	19	.296	34	34	1	0	0	218²	266	17	71	116	14.3	5.19	84	.305	.364	0	—	0	-21	-20	1	-2.0

YEAR TM/L	W	L	PCT	G	GS	CG	SH	SV	IP	H	HR	BB	SO	RAT	ERA	ERA+	OAV	OOB	BH	AVG	PB	PR	/A	PD	TPI
1994 Min-A	8	11	.421	23	23	2	1	0	144	173	15	59	104	15.1	5.44	89	.299	.372	0	—	0	-10	-9	0	-1.0
Total 5	57	54	.514	140	138	14	7	0	891²	933	72	335	482	13.2	4.05	107	.273	.345	0	—	0	15	27	4	3.5

● **DICK ERRICKSON**   Errickson, Richard Merriwell "Lief"   b: 3/5/14, Vineland, N.J.   BL/TR, 6'1", 175 lbs.   Deb: 4/27/38

YEAR TM/L	W	L	PCT	G	GS	CG	SH	SV	IP	H	HR	BB	SO	RAT	ERA	ERA+	OAV	OOB	BH	AVG	PB	PR	/A	PD	TPI
1938 Bos-N	9	7	.563	34	10	6	1	6	122²	113	1	56	40	12.5	3.15	109	.246	.330	4	.114	-1	9	4	2	0.5
1939 Bos-N	6	9	.400	28	11	3	0	1	128¹	143	6	54	33	13.9	4.00	92	.293	.365	10	.227	-1	-1	-4	2	-0.2
1940 Bos-N	12	13	.480	34	29	17	3	4	236¹	241	8	90	34	12.6	3.16	118	.270	.338	13	.157	-2	18	15	1	1.4
1941 Bos-N	6	12	.333	38	23	5	2	1	165²	192	12	62	45	14.0	4.78	75	.287	.351	8	.178	-0	-21	-22	1	-2.2
1942 Bos-N	2	5	.286	21	4	0	0	1	59¹	76	8	20	15	14.6	5.01	67	.309	.361	2	.125	-1	-11	-11	-1	-1.4
Chi-N	1	1	.500	13	0	0	0	0	24	39	1	8	9	18.0	4.13	78	.411	.462	1	.000	-1	-2	-2	1	-0.2
Yr	3	6	.333	34	4	0	0	1	83¹	115	9	28	24	15.6	4.75	69	.337	.389	2	.095	-1	-13	-13	-0	-1.6
Total 5	36	47	.434	168	77	31	6	13	736¹	804	36	290	176	13.5	3.85	93	.282	.350	37	.162	-5	-9	-21	5	-2.1

● **CARL ERSKINE**   Erskine, Carl Daniel "Oisk"   b: 12/13/26, Anderson, Ind.   BR/TR, 5'10", 165 lbs.   Deb: 7/25/48

YEAR TM/L	W	L	PCT	G	GS	CG	SH	SV	IP	H	HR	BB	SO	RAT	ERA	ERA+	OAV	OOB	BH	AVG	PB	PR	/A	PD	TPI
1948 Bro-N	6	3	.667	17	9	3	0	0	64	51	5	35	29	12.2	3.23	124	.231	.339	2	.095	-2	5	5	-1	0.4
1949 *Bro-N	8	1	.889	22	3	2	0	0	79²	68	6	51	49	13.7	4.63	89	.235	.354	3	.115	-2	-5	-5	-0	-0.6
1950 Bro-N	7	6	.538	22	13	3	0	1	103	109	15	35	50	12.7	4.72	87	.273	.333	9	.243	-2	-7	-7	-1	-0.7
1951 Bro-N	16	12	.571	46	19	7	0	4	189²	206	23	78	95	13.6	4.46	88	.280	.351	8	.131	-2	-11	-11	-0	-1.8
1952 *Bro-N	14	6	.700	33	26	10	4	2	206²	167	17	71	131	10.5	2.70	135	.220	.289	10	.152	-0	24	22	2	2.3
1953 *Bro-N	20	6	.769	39	33	16	4	3	246²	213	26	95	187	11.3	3.54	120	.230	.304	20	.215	-0	20	20	-2	1.7
1954 Bro-N★	18	15	.545	38	37	12	2	1	260¹	239	31	92	166	11.6	4.15	98	.243	.311	14	.159	-1	-2	-2	-0	-0.4
1955 *Bro-N	11	8	.579	31	29	7	2	1	194²	185	29	64	84	11.5	3.79	107	.253	.313	15	.203	-0	5	6	-2	0.3
1956 *Bro-N	13	11	.542	31	28	8	1	0	186¹	189	25	57	95	11.9	4.25	93	.264	.320	8	.121	-3	-10	-6	1	-1.0
1957 Bro-N	5	3	.625	15	7	1	0	0	66	62	8	20	26	11.2	3.55	118	.248	.304	2	.091	-2	2	5	-1	0.2
1958 LA-N	4	4	.500	31	9	2	1	0	98¹	115	14	35	54	13.7	5.13	80	.297	.355	1	.037	-3	-13	-11	1	-1.0
1959 LA-N	0	3	.000	10	3	0	0	1	23	33	5	13	15	17.7	7.71	55	.320	.397	0	.000	-1	-10	-9	-0	-1.2
Total 12	122	78	.610	335	216	71	14	13	1718²	1637	199	646	981	12.0	4.00	101	.252	.321	92	.156	-13	-6	-4	-1.8

● **CHICO ESCARREGA**   Escarrega, Ernesto (Acosta)   b: 12/27/49, Los Mochis, Mex.   BR/TR, 5'11", 185 lbs.   Deb: 4/26/82

YEAR TM/L	W	L	PCT	G	GS	CG	SH	SV	IP	H	HR	BB	SO	RAT	ERA	ERA+	OAV	OOB	BH	AVG	PB	PR	/A	PD	TPI
1982 Chi-A	1	3	.250	38	2	0	0	1	73²	73	3	16	33	10.9	3.67	110	.263	.303	0	—	0	3	3	-1	0.1

● **DUKE ESPER**   Esper, Charles H.   b: 7/28/1868, Salem, N.J.   d: 8/31/10, Philadelphia, Pa.   TL, 5'11.5", 185 lbs.   Deb: 4/18/1890

YEAR TM/L	W	L	PCT	G	GS	CG	SH	SV	IP	H	HR	BB	SO	RAT	ERA	ERA+	OAV	OOB	BH	AVG	PB	PR	/A	PD	TPI
1890 Phi-a	8	9	.471	18	16	14	1	0	143²	176	1	67	61	15.5	4.89	78	.293	.368	18	.295	4	-16	-17	1	-1.1
Pit-N	0	2	.000	2	2	2	0	0	17	18	0	10	9	15.4	5.29	62	.263	.365	1	.143	-1	-3	-4	0	-0.3
Phi-N	5	0	1.000	5	5	4	0	0	41	40	1	16	18	12.3	3.07	119	.248	.316	3	.158	-1	2	3	0	0.2
Yr	5	2	.714	7	7	6	0	0	58	58	1	26	27	13.0	3.72	95	.251	.327	4	.154	-2	-1	-1	1	-0.1
1891 Phi-N	20	15	.571	39	36	25	1	1	296	302	8	121	108	13.1	3.56	96	.254	.327	27	.220	1	-7	-5	1	-0.4
1892 Phi-N	11	6	.647	21	18	14	0	1	160¹	171	2	58	45	12.9	3.42	95	.262	.324	17	.243	-2	-2	-3	-1	-0.2
Pit-N	2	0	1.000	3	3	1	0	0	18¹	18	0	12	5	14.7	5.40	61	.247	.353	0	.000	-1	-4	-4	-0	-0.5
Yr	13	6	.684	24	21	15	0	1	178²	189	2	70	50	13.0	3.63	90	.260	.325	17	.215	-3	-7	-7	-1	-0.7
1893 Was-N	12	28	.300	42	36	34	0	0	334¹	442	14	156	78	16.4	4.71	98	.309	.381	41	.287	7	-2	-3	1	0.4
1894 Was-N	5	10	.333	18	14	7	0	0	116	177	8	39	24	16.9	7.45	74	.346	.395	14	.259	1	-27	-28	0	-2.3
*Bal-N	10	2	.833	16	9	8	0	2	101	107	1	36	25	12.8	3.92	139	.269	.331	10	.222	-1	16	17	1	1.5
Yr	15	12	.556	34	23	15	0	2	217	284	9	75	49	14.9	5.81	92	.312	.365	24	.242	0	-12	-11	1	-0.8
1895 *Bal-N	10	12	.455	34	25	16	1	1	218¹	248	2	79	39	13.5	3.92	122	.282	.341	16	.178	-6	21	20	-2	0.8
1896 Bal-N	14	5	.737	20	18	14	1	0	155²	168	3	39	19	12.1	3.58	119	.273	.319	13	.197	-2	13	12	-2	0.7
1897 StL-N	1	6	.143	8	8	7	0	0	61¹	75	5	12	8	15.8	5.28	83	.350	.380	8	.320	1	-7	-6	1	-0.3
1898 StL-N	3	5	.375	10	8	6	0	0	64²	86	1	22	14	15.0	5.98	63	.317	.368	10	.370	2	-17	-16	0	-1.4
Total 9	101	100	.502	236	198	152	4	5	1727²	2048	46	667	453	14.3	4.39	96	.288	.351	178	.241	5	-33	-33	1	-2.9

● **NINO ESPINOSA**   Espinosa, Arnulfo Acevedo (b: Arnulfo Acevedo (Espinosa))
b: 8/15/53, Villa Altagracia, D.R.   d: 12/24/87, Villa Altagracia, D.R.   BR/TR, 6'1", 192 lbs.   Deb: 9/13/74

YEAR TM/L	W	L	PCT	G	GS	CG	SH	SV	IP	H	HR	BB	SO	RAT	ERA	ERA+	OAV	OOB	BH	AVG	PB	PR	/A	PD	TPI
1974 NY-N	0	0	—	2	1	0	0	0	9	12	1	0	2	12.0	5.00	71	.324	.324	1	.500	0	-1	-1	0	0.0
1975 NY-N	0	1	.000	2	0	0	0	0	3	8	0	1	2	27.0	18.00	19	.471	.500	0	—	0	-5	-5	-0	-1.1
1976 NY-N	4	4	.500	12	5	0	0	0	41²	41	3	13	30	11.7	3.67	90	.265	.321	0	.000	-1	-1	-2	-1	-0.5
1977 NY-N	10	13	.435	32	29	7	1	0	200	188	17	55	105	11.2	3.42	109	.249	.304	8	.129	-1	11	7	-0	0.6
1978 NY-N	11	15	.423	32	32	6	1	0	203²	230	24	75	76	13.6	4.73	74	.292	.355	14	.209	-2	-26	-28	2	-2.8
1979 Phi-N	14	12	.538	33	33	8	2	0	212	211	20	65	69	11.8	3.65	105	.262	.319	14	.194	-2	2	4	0	0.6
1980 Phi-N	3	5	.375	12	12	1	0	0	76¹	73	9	19	13	11.1	3.77	100	.250	.300	3	.115	-1	-1	-0	-1	-0.2
1981 Phi-N	2	5	.286	14	14	2	0	0	73²	98	11	24	22	15.0	6.11	59	.333	.386	4	.200	-0	-21	-20	-1	-1.8
Tor-A	0	0	—	1	0	0	0	0	1	4	0	0	0	36.0	9.00	44	.667	.667	0	—	0	-1	-1	-0	-0.2
Total 8	44	55	.444	140	126	24	5	0	820¹	865	85	252	338	12.4	4.17	88	.275	.331	44	.171	1	-44	-46	-2	-5.4

● **ALVARO ESPINOZA**   Espinoza, Alvaro Alberto   b: 2/19/62, Valencia, Venez.   BR/TR, 6', 170 lbs.   Deb: 9/14/84 ♦

YEAR TM/L	W	L	PCT	G	GS	CG	SH	SV	IP	H	HR	BB	SO	RAT	ERA	ERA+	OAV	OOB	BH	AVG	PB	PR	/A	PD	TPI
1991 NY-A	0	0	—	1	0	0	0	0	0²	0	0	0	0	0.0	0.00	—	.000	.000	123	.256	1	0	0	0	0.0

● **MARK ESSER**   Esser, Mark Gerald   b: 4/1/56, Erie, Pa.   BR/TL, 6'1", 190 lbs.   Deb: 4/22/79

YEAR TM/L	W	L	PCT	G	GS	CG	SH	SV	IP	H	HR	BB	SO	RAT	ERA	ERA+	OAV	OOB	BH	AVG	PB	PR	/A	PD	TPI
1979 Chi-A	0	0	—	2	0	0	0	0	1²	2	0	4	1	32.4	16.20	26	.286	.545	0	—	0	-2	-2	-0	0.0

● **BILL ESSICK**   Essick, William Earl "Vinegar Bill"   b: 12/18/1881, Grand Ridge, Ill.   d: 10/12/51, Los Angeles, Cal.   TR, 5'10", 175 lbs.   Deb: 9/12/06

YEAR TM/L	W	L	PCT	G	GS	CG	SH	SV	IP	H	HR	BB	SO	RAT	ERA	ERA+	OAV	OOB	BH	AVG	PB	PR	/A	PD	TPI
1906 Cin-N	2	2	.500	6	4	3	0	0	39¹	39	1	16	16	13.0	2.97	93	.273	.354	1	.077	-1	-1	-1	1	-0.3
1907 Cin-N	0	2	.000	3	2	2	0	0	21²	23	0	8	7	13.3	2.91	89	.274	.344	0	.000	-1	-1	-1	1	-0.1
Total 2	2	4	.333	9	6	5	0	0	61	62	1	24	23	13.1	2.95	91	.273	.350	1	.048	-2	-3	-2	-0	-0.4

● **DICK ESTELLE**   Estelle, Richard Henry   b: 1/18/42, Lakewood, N.J.   BB/TL, 6'2", 170 lbs.   Deb: 9/4/64

YEAR TM/L	W	L	PCT	G	GS	CG	SH	SV	IP	H	HR	BB	SO	RAT	ERA	ERA+	OAV	OOB	BH	AVG	PB	PR	/A	PD	TPI
1964 SF-N	1	2	.333	6	6	0	0	0	41²	39	3	23	23	13.4	3.02	118	.247	.343	1	.067	-1	2	3	-1	0.0
1965 SF-N	0	0	—	6	1	0	0	0	11¹	12	0	8	6	16.7	3.97	91	.261	.382	0	.000	0	-1	-0	0	0.0
Total 2	1	2	.333	12	7	0	0	0	53	51	3	31	29	14.1	3.23	111	.250	.352	1	.063	-1	2	2	-1	0.0

● **GEORGE ESTOCK**   Estock, George John   b: 11/2/24, Stirling, N.J.   BR/TR, 6', 185 lbs.   Deb: 4/21/51

YEAR TM/L	W	L	PCT	G	GS	CG	SH	SV	IP	H	HR	BB	SO	RAT	ERA	ERA+	OAV	OOB	BH	AVG	PB	PR	/A	PD	TPI
1951 Bos-N	0	1	.000	37	1	0	0	3	60¹	54	7	37	11	13.9	4.33	85	.258	.366	2	.286	1	-2	-4	0	0.0

● **CHUCK ESTRADA**   Estrada, Charles Leonard   b: 2/15/38, San Luis Obispo, Cal.   BR/TR, 6'1", 185 lbs.   Deb: 4/21/60 C

YEAR TM/L	W	L	PCT	G	GS	CG	SH	SV	IP	H	HR	BB	SO	RAT	ERA	ERA+	OAV	OOB	BH	AVG	PB	PR	/A	PD	TPI
1960 Bal-A★	18	11	.621	36	25	12	1	2	208²	162	18	101	144	11.6	3.58	106	.218	.323	9	.141	-0	7	5	-0	0.6
1961 Bal-A	15	9	.625	33	31	6	1	2	212	159	19	132	160	12.8	3.69	104	.207	.331	8	.114	-3	8	4	-2	-0.2
1962 Bal-A	9	17	.346	34	33	6	0	0	223¹	199	24	121	165	13.3	3.83	97	.240	.343	10	.152	-0	3	-3	-3	-0.6
1963 Bal-A	3	2	.600	9	9	1	0	0	31¹	26	2	19	16	13.2	4.60	76	.226	.341	1	.100	-1	-3	-4	-1	-0.7
1964 Bal-A	3	2	.600	17	6	0	0	0	54²	62	8	21	32	14.0	5.27	68	.282	.350	2	.143	-0	-10	-10	-1	-1.0
1966 Chi-N	1	1	.500	9	1	0	0	0	12¹	16	2	5	3	16.1	7.30	50	.314	.386	2	.000	-0	-5	-5	-0	-0.8
1967 NY-N	1	2	.333	9	2	0	0	0	21	28	5	17	15	18.8	9.41	36	.326	.442	0	—	-0	-15	-15	-0	-1.8
Total 7	50	44	.532	146	105	24	2	2	764¹	652	78	416	535	13.0	4.07	92	.232	.339	30	.129	-5	-15	-28	-8	-4.5

● **OSCAR ESTRADA**   Estrada, Oscar   b: 2/15/04, Havana, Cuba   d: 1/2/78, Havana, Cuba   BL/TL, 5'8", 160 lbs.   Deb: 4/21/29

YEAR TM/L	W	L	PCT	G	GS	CG	SH	SV	IP	H	HR	BB	SO	RAT	ERA	ERA+	OAV	OOB	BH	AVG	PB	PR	/A	PD	TPI
1929 StL-A	0	0	—	1	0	0	0	0	1	1	0	1	0	18.0	0.00	—	.250	.400	0	—	0	0	0	0	0.0

YEAR TM/L	W	L	PCT	G	GS	CG	SH	SV	IP	H	HR	BB	SO	RAT	ERA	ERA+	OAV	OOB	BH	AVG	PB	PR	/A	PD	TPI
● MARK ETTLES Ettles, Mark Edward b: 10/30/66, Perth, Australia BR/TR, 6', 178 lbs. Deb: 6/5/93																								
1993 SD-N	1	0	1.000	14	0	0	0	0	18	23	4	4	9	13.5	6.50	64	.307	.342	0	.000	-0	-5	-5	0	-0.2
● JOHN EUBANK Eubank, John Franklin "Honest John" b: 9/9/1872, Servia, Ind. d: 11/3/58, Bellevue, Mich. BR/TR, 6'2", 215 lbs. Deb: 9/19/05																								
1905 Det-A	1	0	1.000	3	2	0	0	0	17¹	13	0	3	1	8.8	2.08	132	.210	.258	5	.357	1	1	1	-0	0.2
1906 Det-A	4	10	.286	24	12	7	1	2	135	147	0	35	38	12.7	3.53	78	.280	.335	13	.206	0	-13	-12	1	-1.1
1907 Det-A	3	3	.500	15	8	4	1	0	81	88	0	20	17	12.0	2.67	98	.279	.321	4	.129	-1	-1	-0	1	-0.1
Total 3	8	13	.381	42	22	11	2	2	233¹	248	0	58	56	12.1	3.12	87	.275	.325	22	.204	-1	-13	-11	1	-1.0
● UEL EUBANKS Eubanks, Uel Melvin "Poss" b: 2/14/03, Quinlan, Tex. d: 11/21/54, Dallas, Tex. BR/TR, 6'3", 175 lbs. Deb: 7/20/22																								
1922 Chi-N	0	0	—	2	0	0	0	0	1²	5	0	4	1	48.6	27.00	16	.556	.692	1	1.000	1	-4	-4	0	0.1
● FRANK EUFEMIA Eufemia, Frank Anthony b: 12/23/59, Bronx, N.Y. BR/TR, 5'11", 185 lbs. Deb: 5/21/85																								
1985 Min-A	4	2	.667	39	0	0	0	2	61²	56	7	21	30	11.2	3.79	116	.250	.314	0	—	0	2	4	1	0.4
● CHICK EVANS Evans, Charles Franklin b: 10/15/1889, Arlington, Vt. d: 9/2/16, Schenectady, N.Y. BR/TR, Deb: 9/19/09																								
1909 Bos-N	0	3	.000	4	3	1	0	0	21²	25	0	14	11	16.2	4.57	62	.305	.406	0	.000	-1	-5	-4	-0	-0.7
1910 Bos-N	1	1	.500	13	1	0	0	2	31	28	1	27	12	16.8	5.23	64	.275	.439	1	.100	-1	-8	-7	0	-0.5
Total 2	1	4	.200	17	4	1	0	2	52²	53	1	41	23	16.6	4.96	63	.288	.425	1	.053	-2	-12	-11	0	-1.2
● ROY EVANS Evans, Roy b: 3/19/1874, Knoxville, Tenn. d: 8/15/15, Galveston, Tex. BR/TR, 6', 180 lbs. Deb: 5/15/1897																								
1897 StL-N	0	0	—	3	0	0	0	0	13	33	1	13	4	31.8	9.69	45	.469	.552	0	.000	0	-8	-8	-0	-0.1
Lou-N	5	4	.556	9	8	6	0	0	59¹	66	4	24	20	14.9	4.10	104	.279	.365	3	.130	-2	1	1	-1	-0.1
Yr	5	4	.556	12	8	6	0	0	72¹	99	5	37	24	17.9	5.10	84	.323	.410	3	.115	-2	-6	-7	-1	-0.1
1898 Was-N	3	3	.500	7	6	4	0	0	50²	50	0	25	11	14.6	3.38	109	.256	.361	1	.053	-2	1	2	-1	-0.1
1899 Was-N	3	4	.429	7	7	6	0	0	54	60	1	25	27	14.2	5.67	69	.281	.356	4	.200	-1	-11	-11	0	-1.1
1902 NY-N	8	13	.381	23	17	17	0	0	176	186	2	58	48	12.9	3.17	89	.271	.336	8	.148	-1	-8	-7	2	-0.7
Bro-N	5	6	.455	13	11	11	2	0	97¹	91	0	33	35	11.7	2.68	103	.247	.313	9	.265	2	1	1	-3	0.0
Yr	13	19	.406	36	28	28	2	0	273¹	277	2	91	83	12.2	3.00	93	.261	.320	17	.193	1	-7	-6	-2	-0.7
1903 Bro-N	5	9	.357	15	12	9	0	0	110	121	1	41	42	13.8	3.27	98	.297	.371	5	.172	0	-0	-1	-1	-0.2
StL-A	0	4	.000	7	4	4	0	0	54	66	1	14	24	13.8	4.17	70	.300	.350	2	.105	-1	-7	-8	0	-0.6
Total 5	29	43	.403	84	68	57	2	0	614¹	673	10	233	211	13.8	3.66	88	.281	.353	32	.159	-4	-30	-30	-5	-2.8
● RED EVANS Evans, Russell Edison b: 11/12/06, Chicago, Ill. d: 6/14/82, Lakeview, Ark. BR/TR, 5'11", 168 lbs. Deb: 4/24/36																								
1936 Chi-A	0	3	.000	17	0	0	0	1	47¹	70	4	22	19	17.5	7.61	68	.348	.402	2	.133	-1	-14	-13	1	-0.7
1939 Bro-N	1	8	.111	24	6	0	0	1	64¹	74	4	26	28	14.0	5.18	78	.284	.348	4	.308	1	-9	-8	1	-0.8
Total 2	1	11	.083	41	6	0	0	2	111²	144	8	48	47	15.5	6.21	73	.308	.372	6	.214	-0	-23	-21	3	-1.5
● JAKE EVANS Evans, Uriah L. P. "Bloody Jake" b: 9/1856, Baltimore, Md. d: 1/16/07, Baltimore, Md. TR, 5'8", 154 lbs. Deb: 5/1/1879 ♦																								
1880 Tro-N	0	0	—	1	0	0	0	0	4	11	0	0	0	24.8	13.50	19	.524	.524	46	.256	0	-5	-5	0	0.0
1882 Wor-N	0	1	.000	1	1	1	0	0	8	13	1	0	2	14.6	5.63	55	.317	.317	71	.213	-0	-2	-2	-0	-0.2
1883 Cle-N	0	0	—	1	0	0	0	0	3	0	0	1	0	0.0	0.00	—	.000	.000	79	.238	0	1	1	1	0.1
Total 3	0	1	.000	3	1	1	0	0	15	24	1	0	3	14.4	6.60	45	.338	.338	435	.238	-0	-6	-6	1	-0.1
● ART EVANS Evans, William Arthur b: 8/3/11, Elvins, Mo. d: 1/8/52, Wichita, Kan. BB/TL, 6'1.5", 181 lbs. Deb: 6/20/32																								
1932 Chi-A	0	0	—	7	0	0	0	0	18	19	1	10	6	14.5	3.00	144	.257	.345	0	.000	-0	3	3	0	0.0
● BILL EVANS Evans, William James b: 2/10/1894, Reidsville, N.C. d: 12/21/46, Burlington, N.C. BR/TR, 6', 175 lbs. Deb: 8/13/16																								
1916 Pit-N	2	5	.286	13	7	3	0	0	63	57	2	16	21	10.9	3.00	89	.249	.306	3	.150	-1	-3	-2	2	-0.1
1917 Pit-N	0	4	.000	8	2	1	0	0	26²	24	0	14	5	13.2	3.38	84	.231	.328	1	.111	-0	-2	-2	-0	-0.3
1919 Pit-N	0	4	.000	7	3	2	0	0	36²	41	1	18	15	14.5	5.65	54	.297	.378	0	.000	-1	-11	-11	1	-1.1
Total 3	2	13	.133	28	12	6	0	0	126¹	122	3	48	41	12.4	3.85	73	.259	.333	4	.100	-2	-16	-14	2	-1.5
● BILL EVANS Evans, William Lawrence b: 3/25/19, Quanah, Texas d: 11/30/83, Grand Junction, Colo. BR/TR, 6'2", 180 lbs. Deb: 4/21/49																								
1949 Chi-A	0	1	.000	4	0	0	0	0	6¹	6	0	8	1	19.9	7.11	59	.261	.452	0	—	-0	-2	-2	0	-0.3
1951 Bos-A	0	0	—	9	0	0	0	0	15¹	15	0	8	3	13.5	4.11	109	.268	.359	0	.000	-1	0	1	-0	-0.1
Total 2	0	1	.000	13	0	0	0	0	21²	21	0	16	4	15.4	4.98	88	.266	.389	0	.000	-1	-2	-1	-1	-0.4
● LEON EVERITT Everitt, Edward Leon b: 1/12/47, Marshall, Tex. BL/TR, 6'1.5", 195 lbs. Deb: 4/21/69																								
1969 SD-N	0	1	.000	5	0	0	0	0	15²	18	4	12	11	17.8	8.04	44	.300	.425	0	.000	-0	-8	-8	0	-0.4
● BRYAN EVERSGERD Eversgerd, Bryan David b: 2/11/69, Centralia, Ill. BR/TL, 6'1", 190 lbs. Deb: 4/30/94																								
1994 StL-N	2	3	.400	40	1	0	0	0	67²	75	8	20	47	12.9	4.52	90	.295	.351	0	.000	-1	-2	-3	1	-0.2
● BOB EWING Ewing, George Lemuel "Long Bob" b: 4/24/1873, New Hampshire, O. d: 6/20/47, Wapakoneta, Ohio BR/TR, 6'1.5", 170 lbs. Deb: 4/19/02																								
1902 Cin-N	5	6	.455	15	12	10	0	0	117²	126	1	47	44	13.5	2.98	100	.274	.345	12	.169	-1	-3	-0	-1	-0.2
1903 Cin-N	14	13	.519	29	28	27	1	1	246²	254	3	64	104	12.0	2.77	128	.265	.317	24	.253	4	14	22	4	2.9
1904 Cin-N	11	13	.458	26	24	22	0	0	212	198	3	58	99	11.0	2.46	119	.253	.308	25	.258	5	7	11	-1	1.6
1905 Cin-N	20	11	.645	40	34	30	4	0	311²	284	5	79	164	10.8	2.51	132	.246	.301	32	.262	4	17	27	-3	2.7
1906 Cin-N	13	14	.481	33	32	26	2	0	287²	248	4	60	145	9.7	2.38	116	.238	.281	14	.139	-3	8	12	1	0.8
1907 Cin-N	17	19	.472	41	37	31	2	0	332²	279	2	85	147	10.0	1.73	150	.231	.286	19	.154	-1	27	**32**	-6	2.9
1908 Cin-N	17	15	.531	37	32	23	4	3	293²	247	5	57	95	9.5	2.21	105	.241	.284	14	.149	-0	5	3	-3	-0.1
1909 Cin-N	11	12	.478	31	29	14	2	0	218¹	195	1	63	86	10.9	2.43	107	.238	.298	8	.110	-4	4	4	-4	-0.5
1910 Phi-N	16	14	.533	34	32	20	4	0	255¹	235	6	86	102	11.6	3.00	104	.251	.318	20	.222	2	1	4	-2	-0.2
1911 Phi-N	0	1	.000	4	3	1	0	0	24	29	2	14	12	16.1	7.88	44	.309	.398	2	.333	0	-12	-12	-0	-0.4
1912 StL-N	0	0	—	1	1	0	0	0	1	2	0	1	0	20.3	0.00	—	.333	.429	1	1.000	0	1	1	0	0.0
Total 11	124	118	.512	291	264	205	19	4	2301	2097	31	614	998	10.8	2.49	116	.247	.302	170	.195	7	69	102	-16	10.1
● JOHN EWING Ewing, John "Long John" b: 6/1/1863, Cincinnati, Ohio d: 4/23/1895, Denver, Colo. TR, Deb: 6/18/1883 F♦																								
1888 Lou-a	8	13	.381	21	21	21	2	0	191	175	3	34	87	10.2	2.83	109	.235	.276	16	.203	-2	5	5	0	0.4
1889 Lou-a	6	30	.167	40	39	37	1	0	331	407	6	147	155	15.4	4.87	79	.293	.367	23	.172	-6	-37	-37	2	-3.3
1890 NY-P	18	12	.600	35	31	27	1	2	267¹	293	6	104	145	13.9	4.24	107	.267	.339	24	.211	-3	-0	9	0	0.5
1891 NY-N	21	8	**.724**	33	30	28	5	0	269¹	237	2	105	138	11.8	**2.27**	141	.227	.305	23	.204	-2	32	28	0	2.3
Total 4	53	63	.457	129	121	113	9	2	1058²	1112	17	390	525	13.2	3.68	101	.260	.329	87	.192	-12	-1	3	3	-0.1
● BUCK EWING Ewing, William b: 10/17/1859, Hoagland, Ohio d: 10/20/06, Cincinnati, Ohio BR/TR, 5'10", 188 lbs. Deb: 9/9/1880 FMH♦																								
1882 Tro-N	0	0	—	1	0	0	0	0	1	2	0	1	0	27.0	9.00	31	.400	.500	89	.271	-1	-1	-1	0	0.0
1884 NY-N	0	1	.000	1	1	1	0	0	8	7	0	4	3	12.4	1.13	265	.241	.333	106	.277	0	2	2	-0	0.2
1885 NY-N	0	1	.000	1	1	0	0	0	2	4	0	3	0	31.5	4.50	59	.444	.583	104	.304	0	-1	-0	-0	-0.2
1888 *NY-N	0	0	—	2	0	0	0	0	7	8	1	4	6	16.7	2.57	107	.174	.255	127	.306	1	2	2	0	0.2
1889 *NY-N	2	0	1.000	3	2	1	0	0	20	23	0	6	12	13.9	4.05	97	.280	.344	133	.327	0	1	0	0	0.0
1890 NY-P	0	0	—	1	1	0	0	0	9	11	1	3	2	14.0	4.00	114	.289	.340	119	.338	0	1	0	0	0.1
Total 6	2	3	.400	9	5	2	0	0	47	55	2	23	23	15.1	3.45	105	.263	.339	1625	.303	4	1	1	-1	0.1
● GEORGE EYRICH Eyrich, George Lincoln b: 3/3/25, Reading, Pa. BR/TR, 5'11", 175 lbs. Deb: 6/13/43																								
1943 Phi-N	0	0	—	9	0	0	0	0	18²	27	1	9	5	17.4	3.38	100	.342	.409	0	.000	-0	0	-0	-0	0.0

● RED FABER
Faber, Urban Charles b: 9/6/1888, Cascade, Iowa d: 9/25/76, Chicago, Ill. BB/TR, 6'2", 180 lbs. Deb: 4/17/14 CH

YEAR TM/L	W	L	PCT	G	GS	CG	SH	SV	IP	H	HR	BB	SO	RAT	ERA	ERA+	OAV	OOB	BH	AVG	PB	PR	/A	PD	TPI
1914 Chi-A	10	9	.526	40	19	11	2	**4**	181¹	154	3	64	88	11.4	2.68	100	.239	.319	8	.145	2	1	0	2	0.3
1915 Chi-A	24	14	.632	**50**	32	21	2	2	299²	264	1	99	182	11.2	2.55	117	.240	.309	11	.131	2	13	14	-0	2.1
1916 Chi-A	17	9	.654	35	25	15	3	1	205¹	167	1	61	87	10.2	2.02	137	.228	.292	6	.095	-3	19	17	2	2.0
1917 *Chi-A	16	13	.552	41	29	16	3	3	248	224	1	85	84	11.6	1.92	138	.247	.319	4	.058	-4	20	20	2	2.2
1918 Chi-A	4	1	.800	11	9	5	1	1	80²	70	3	23	26	10.4	1.23	223	.245	.301	1	.042	-2	14	14	1	0.8
1919 Chi-A	11	9	.550	25	20	9	0	0	162¹	185	7	45	45	13.2	3.83	83	.287	.341	10	.185	-0	-11	-12	0	-1.3
1920 Chi-A	23	13	.639	40	39	28	2	1	319	332	6	88	108	12.0	2.99	126	.277	.328	11	.106	-4	29	28	-1	2.3
1921 Chi-A	25	15	.625	43	39	**32**	4	1	330²	293	10	87	124	**10.5**	**2.48**	**171**	**.242**	**.297**	16	.148	-4	**66**	**65**	1	**7.0**
1922 Chi-A	21	17	.553	43	38	**31**	4	2	**352**	334	10	83	148	**10.8**	2.81	145	.252	**.299**	25	.200	-4	**48**	**49**	1	4.9
1923 Chi-A	14	11	.560	32	31	15	2	0	232¹	233	6	62	91	11.7	3.41	116	.259	.311	15	.217	3	15	14	2	1.9
1924 Chi-A	9	11	.450	21	20	9	0	0	161¹	173	5	58	47	13.0	3.85	107	.282	.346	8	.148	-2	7	5	-2	0.6
1925 Chi-A	12	11	.522	34	32	16	1	0	238	266	8	59	71	12.4	3.78	110	.289	.333	8	.104	-4	16	10	1	0.6
1926 Chi-A	15	9	.625	27	25	13	1	0	184²	203	5	57	65	12.8	3.56	109	.281	.335	9	.150	-0	9	6	-3	0.4
1927 Chi-A	4	7	.364	18	15	6	0	0	110²	131	2	41	39	14.4	4.55	89	.312	.380	10	.270	2	-5	-6	-2	-0.2
1928 Chi-A	13	9	.591	27	27	16	2	0	201¹	223	11	68	43	13.2	3.75	108	.286	.347	8	.114	-3	6	7	1	0.6
1929 Chi-A	13	13	.500	31	31	15	1	0	234	241	10	61	68	12.0	3.88	110	.273	.327	10	.128	-3	9	10	2	0.9
1930 Chi-A	8	13	.381	29	26	10	0	1	169	188	7	49	62	12.9	4.21	110	.283	.337	5	.041	-8	8	8	2	0.6
1931 Chi-A	10	14	.417	44	19	5	1	1	184	210	11	57	49	13.2	3.82	112	.285	.339	4	.075	-8	12	9	-2	0.6
1932 Chi-A	2	11	.154	42	5	0	0	6	106	129	4	38	26	13.8	3.74	116	.290	.350	4	.222	3	**9**	7	-0	1.0
1933 Chi-A	3	4	.429	36	2	0	0	5	86¹	86	1	28	18	12.6	3.44	123	.275	.332	0	.000	-3	8	8	-1	0.3
Total 20	254	213	.544	669	483	273	29	28	4086²	4106	111	1213	1471	11.9	3.15	119	.266	.323	170	.134	-31	294	274	11	27.0

● ROY FACE
Face, Elroy Leon b: 2/20/28, Stephentown, N.Y. BR/TR, 5'8", 155 lbs. Deb: 4/16/53

YEAR TM/L	W	L	PCT	G	GS	CG	SH	SV	IP	H	HR	BB	SO	RAT	ERA	ERA+	OAV	OOB	BH	AVG	PB	PR	/A	PD	TPI
1953 Pit-N	6	8	.429	41	13	2	0	0	119	145	19	30	56	13.4	6.58	68	.297	.340	4	.133	-1	-30	-28	-1	-3.0
1955 Pit-N	5	7	.417	42	10	4	0	5	125²	128	10	40	84	12.0	3.58	115	.268	.325	3	.115	-1	6	7	-1	0.5
1956 Pit-N	12	13	.480	**68**	3	0	0	6	135¹	131	16	42	96	11.6	3.52	107	.256	.314	5	.192	-0	4	4	1	0.8
1957 Pit-N	4	6	.400	59	1	0	0	10	93²	97	9	24	53	11.7	3.07	123	.270	.318	2	.125	-1	8	7	-2	0.7
1958 Pit-N	5	2	.714	57	0	0	0	**20**	84	77	6	22	47	10.6	2.89	134	.244	.293	0	.000	-1	10	9	1	1.2
1959 Pit-N★	18	1	**.947**	57	0	0	0	10	93¹	91	5	25	69	11.3	2.70	143	.266	.318	3	.231	0	13	12	-0	2.6
1960 *Pit-N★	10	8	.556	**68**	0	0	0	24	114²	93	11	29	72	9.6	2.90	129	.226	.277	7	.412	2	11	11	1	2.5
1961 Pit-N★	6	12	.333	62	0	0	0	**17**	92	94	12	10	55	10.3	3.82	105	.267	.289	3	.273	0	2	2	2	0.6
1962 Pit-N	8	7	.533	63	0	0	0	**28**	91	74	7	18	45	9.2	1.88	209	.231	.274	1	.083	-1	**21**	**21**	-1	4.5
1963 Pit-N	3	9	.250	56	0	0	0	16	69²	75	6	19	41	12.5	3.23	102	.285	.340	2	.250	-0	0	1	1	0.3
1964 Pit-N	3	3	.500	55	0	0	0	4	79²	82	11	27	63	12.4	5.20	68	.269	.330	0	.000	-0	-15	-15	-0	-1.2
1965 Pit-N	5	2	.714	16	0	0	0	0	20¹	20	1	7	19	12.0	2.66	132	.263	.325	0	.000	-0	2	2	-1	0.6
1966 Pit-N	6	6	.500	54	0	0	0	18	70	68	9	24	67	12.0	2.70	132	.262	.326	0	.000	-1	7	7	1	1.5
1967 Pit-N	7	5	.583	61	0	0	0	17	74¹	62	5	22	41	10.2	2.42	139	.230	.288	0	.000	-1	8	8	-1	1.5
1968 Pit-N	2	4	.333	43	0	0	0	13	52	46	3	7	34	9.5	2.60	113	.238	.272	0	.000	-0	2	2	-0	0.3
Det-A	0	0	—	2	0	0	0	0	1	2	0	1	1	27.0	0.00	—	.500	.600	0	—	0	0	0	0	0.0
1969 Mon-N	4	2	.667	44	0	0	0	5	59¹	62	11	15	34	11.7	3.94	93	.263	.307	1	.500	0	-2	-2	-1	-0.2
Total 16	104	95	.523	848	27	6	0	193	1375	1347	141	362	877	11.3	3.48	109	.260	.310	31	.160	-4	48	48	0	13.2

● TONY FAETH
Faeth, Anthony Joseph b: 7/9/1893, Aberdeen, S.D. d: 12/22/82, St.Paul, Minn. BR/TR, 6', 180 lbs. Deb: 8/10/19

YEAR TM/L	W	L	PCT	G	GS	CG	SH	SV	IP	H	HR	BB	SO	RAT	ERA	ERA+	OAV	OOB	BH	AVG	PB	PR	/A	PD	TPI
1919 Cle-A	0	0	—	6	0	0	0	0	18¹	13	0	10	7	11.3	0.49	682	.224	.338	0	.000	-1	6	6	-0	-0.1
1920 Cle-A	0	0	—	13	0	0	0	0	25	31	0	20	14	18.7	4.32	88	.333	.456	0	.000	-1	-1	-1	-0	-0.1
Total 2	0	0	—	19	0	0	0	0	43¹	44	0	30	21	15.6	2.70	134	.291	.412	0	.000	-1	4	4	-0	-0.2

● EVERETT FAGAN
Fagan, Everett Joseph b: 1/13/18, Pottersville, N.J. d: 2/16/83, Morristown, N.J. BR/TR, 6', 195 lbs. Deb: 4/24/43

YEAR TM/L	W	L	PCT	G	GS	CG	SH	SV	IP	H	HR	BB	SO	RAT	ERA	ERA+	OAV	OOB	BH	AVG	PB	PR	/A	PD	TPI
1943 Phi-A	2	6	.250	18	2	0	0	3	37¹	41	4	14	9	13.7	6.27	54	.283	.354	0	.000	-0	-12	-12	0	-2.5
1946 Phi-A	0	1	.000	20	0	0	0	0	45	47	2	24	12	14.8	4.80	74	.264	.361	4	.286	1	-6	-6	-0	-0.1
Total 2	2	7	.222	38	2	0	0	3	82¹	88	6	38	21	14.3	5.47	64	.272	.358	4	.190	1	-19	-18	0	-2.6

● BILL FAGAN
Fagan, William A. "Clinkers" b: 2/15/1869, Troy, N.Y. d: 3/21/30, Troy, N.Y. TL, 5'11", 165 lbs. Deb: 9/15/1887

YEAR TM/L	W	L	PCT	G	GS	CG	SH	SV	IP	H	HR	BB	SO	RAT	ERA	ERA+	OAV	OOB	BH	AVG	PB	PR	/A	PD	TPI
1887 NY-a	1	4	.200	6	6	6	0	0	45	55	1	24	12	16.2	4.00	106	.306	.393	3	.143	-2	1	1	0	-0.1
1888 KC-a	5	11	.313	17	17	15	0	0	142¹	179	4	75	49	16.1	5.69	60	.296	.375	14	.215	-1	-42	-36	1	-3.0
Total 2	6	15	.286	23	23	21	0	0	187¹	234	5	99	61	16.1	5.28	69	.299	.379	17	.198	-3	-40	-34	1	-3.1

● FRANK FAHEY
Fahey, Francis Raymond b: 1/22/1896, Milford, Mass. d: 3/19/54, Boston, Mass. BB/TR, 6'1", 190 lbs. Deb: 4/25/18 ♦

YEAR TM/L	W	L	PCT	G	GS	CG	SH	SV	IP	H	HR	BB	SO	RAT	ERA	ERA+	OAV	OOB	BH	AVG	PB	PR	/A	PD	TPI
1918 Phi-A	0	0	—	3	0	0	0	0	9	5	0	14	1	20.0	6.00	49	.200	.500	3	.176	-0	-3	-3	-1	-0.1

● JERRY FAHR
Fahr, Gerald Warren b: 12/9/24, Marmaduke, Ark. BR/TR, 6'5", 185 lbs. Deb: 4/29/51

YEAR TM/L	W	L	PCT	G	GS	CG	SH	SV	IP	H	HR	BB	SO	RAT	ERA	ERA+	OAV	OOB	BH	AVG	PB	PR	/A	PD	TPI
1951 Cle-A	0	0	—	5	0	0	0	0	5²	11	1	2	0	20.6	4.76	80	.500	.542	0	—	0	-0	-1	-0	0.0

● PETE FAHRER
Fahrer, Clarence Willie b: 3/10/1890, Holgate, Ohio d: 6/10/67, Fremont, Mich. BL/TR, 6', 190 lbs. Deb: 8/17/14

YEAR TM/L	W	L	PCT	G	GS	CG	SH	SV	IP	H	HR	BB	SO	RAT	ERA	ERA+	OAV	OOB	BH	AVG	PB	PR	/A	PD	TPI
1914 Cin-N	0	0	—	5	0	0	0	0	8	8	0	4	2	13.5	1.13	260	.308	.400	0	.000	-0	1	2	0	0.0

● JIM FAIRBANK
Fairbank, James Lee "Lee" or "Smoky" b: 3/17/1881, Deansboro, N.Y. d: 12/27/55, Utica, N.Y. BR/TR, 5'10", 185 lbs. Deb: 9/18/03

YEAR TM/L	W	L	PCT	G	GS	CG	SH	SV	IP	H	HR	BB	SO	RAT	ERA	ERA+	OAV	OOB	BH	AVG	PB	PR	/A	PD	TPI
1903 Phi-A	1	1	.500	4	1	1	0	0	24	33	1	12	10	16.9	4.88	63	.325	.397	1	.100	-1	-5	-5	1	-0.3
1904 Phi-A	0	1	.000	3	1	1	0	0	17	19	0	13	6	18.0	6.35	42	.283	.414	0	—	0	-7	-7	1	-0.4
Total 2	1	2	.333	7	2	2	0	0	41	52	1	25	16	17.3	5.49	53	.309	.404	1	.063	-1	-12	-12	2	-0.7

● RAGS FAIRCLOTH
Faircloth, James Lamar b: 8/19/1892, Kenton, Tenn. d: 10/5/53, Tucson, Ariz. BR/TR, 5'11", 160 lbs. Deb: 5/6/19

YEAR TM/L	W	L	PCT	G	GS	CG	SH	SV	IP	H	HR	BB	SO	RAT	ERA	ERA+	OAV	OOB	BH	AVG	PB	PR	/A	PD	TPI
1919 Phi-N	0	0	—	2	0	0	0	0	2	5	0	4	0	22.5	9.00	36	.625	.625	0	—	0	-1	-1	0	0.0

● HECTOR FAJARDO
Fajardo, Hector (Nabarette) b: 11/16/70, Sahuayo, Mexico BR/TR, 6'4", 185 lbs. Deb: 8/10/91

YEAR TM/L	W	L	PCT	G	GS	CG	SH	SV	IP	H	HR	BB	SO	RAT	ERA	ERA+	OAV	OOB	BH	AVG	PB	PR	/A	PD	TPI
1991 Pit-N	0	0	—	2	2	0	0	0	6¹	10	0	7	8	24.2	9.95	36	.357	.486	0	.000	-0	-4	-4	0	0.0
Tex-A	0	2	.000	4	3	0	0	0	19	25	2	4	15	14.2	5.68	71	.329	.370		—	0	-3	-3	-0	-0.3
1993 Tex-A	0	0	—	1	0	0	0	0	0²	0	0	0	1	0.0	0.00	—	.000	.000		—	0	0	0	0	0.1
1994 Tex-A	5	7	.417	18	12	0	0	0	83¹	95	15	26	45	13.3	6.91	66	.284	.340		—	0	-20	-22	1	-2.4
Total 3	5	9	.357	25	17	0	0	0	109¹	130	17	37	69	14.0	6.83	64	.295	.354	0	.000	-0	-27	-30	-1	-2.6

● PETE FALCONE
Falcone, Peter Frank b: 10/1/53, Brooklyn, N.Y. BL/TL, 6'2", 185 lbs. Deb: 4/13/75

YEAR TM/L	W	L	PCT	G	GS	CG	SH	SV	IP	H	HR	BB	SO	RAT	ERA	ERA+	OAV	OOB	BH	AVG	PB	PR	/A	PD	TPI
1975 SF-N	12	11	.522	34	32	3	1	0	190	171	16	111	131	13.5	4.17	91	.244	.350	4	.062	-5	-12	-8	-1	-1.4
1976 StL-N	12	16	.429	32	32	9	2	0	212	173	12	93	138	11.4	3.23	110	.222	.306	8	.129	-1	6	7	-4	0.3
1977 StL-N	4	8	.333	27	22	1	1	1	124	130	19	61	75	14.1	5.44	71	.273	.359	10	.244	-2	-21	-22	-1	-1.8
1978 StL-N	2	7	.222	19	14	0	0	0	75	94	9	48	28	17.3	5.76	61	.319	.417	5	.238	1	-18	-19	-2	-2.1
1979 NY-N	6	14	.300	33	31	1	1	0	184	194	24	76	113	13.3	4.16	88	.276	.347	9	.173	0	-9	-11	-3	-1.3
1980 NY-N	7	10	.412	37	23	1	0	1	157¹	163	16	58	109	12.4	4.52	79	.269	.335	6	.146	-1	-16	-17	-3	-2.1
1981 NY-N	5	3	.625	35	9	1	1	1	95¹	84	3	36	56	11.3	2.55	137	.241	.312	4	.182	1	10	10	-2	0.8
1982 NY-N	8	10	.444	40	23	3	0	2	171	159	24	71	101	12.2	3.84	94	.252	.329	6	.113	-2	-5	-4	-3	-0.9
1983 Atl-N	9	4	.692	33	13	0	0	0	106²	102	14	60	59	13.8	3.63	107	.256	.335	1	.048	-1	-0	-3	-2	-0.4
1984 Atl-N	5	7	.417	35	16	2	1	2	120	115	9	57	55	12.9	4.13	93	.252	.335	7	.212	-1	-7	-4	-1	-0.4
Total 10	70	90	.438	325	217	25	7	7	1435¹	1385	152	671	865	13.0	4.07	90	.257	.341	62	.149	-6	-71	-63	-20	-8.9

YEAR TM/L	W	L	PCT	G	GS	CG	SH	SV	IP	H	HR	BB	SO	RAT	ERA	ERA+	OAV	OOB	BH	AVG	PB	PR	/A	PD	TPI

● CHET FALK   Falk, Chester Emanuel "Spot" b: 5/15/05, Austin, Tex. d: 1/7/82, Austin, Tex. BL/TL, 6'2", 170 lbs. Deb: 4/20/25 F

1925 StL-A	0	0	—	13	0	0	0	0	25	38	4	17	7	19.8	8.28	56	.362	.451	5	.625	2	-11	-10	0	0.3
1926 StL-A	4	4	.500	18	8	3	0	0	74	95	1	27	7	15.6	5.35	80	.338	.408	6	.194	-1	-11	-9	-1	-0.9
1927 StL-A	1	0	1.000	9	0	0	0	0	15²	25	1	10	2	20.1	5.74	76	.352	.432	1	.200	-0	-3	-2	0	-0.1
Total 3	5	4	.556	40	8	3	0	0	114²	158	4	54	16	17.1	6.04	73	.346	.422	12	.273	1	-25	-21	0	-0.7

● CY FALKENBERG   Falkenberg, Frederick Peter b: 12/17/1880, Chicago, Ill. d: 4/14/61, San Francisco, Cal BR/TR, 6'5", 180 lbs. Deb: 4/21/03

1903 Pit-N	1	5	.167	10	6	3	0	0	56	65	0	32	24	15.9	3.86	84	.295	.390	4	.190	-0	-4	-4	2	-0.2
1905 Was-A	7	2	.778	12	10	6	2	0	75¹	71	1	31	35	12.8	3.82	69	.250	.335	4	.125	-2	-10	-10	-1	-1.4
1906 Was-A	14	20	.412	40	36	30	2	1	298²	277	1	108	178	12.0	2.86	92	.249	.323	18	.170	1	-6	-8	1	-0.5
1907 Was-A	6	17	.261	32	24	17	1	1	233²	195	0	77	108	10.8	2.35	103	.229	.299	12	.140	-3	5	2	2	0.1
1908 Was-A	6	2	.750	17	8	5	1	0	82²	70	2	21	34	10.1	1.96	117	.236	.291	6	.222	0	4	3	1	0.4
Cle-A	2	4	.333	8	7	2	0	0	46¹	52	1	10	17	12.4	3.88	62	.284	.328	2	.118	-1	-8	-8	-1	-1.1
Yr	8	6	.571	25	15	7	1	0	129	122	3	31	51	10.8	2.65	88	.253	.301	8	.182	-1	-4	-5	-0	-0.7
1909 Cle-A	10	9	.526	24	18	13	2	0	165	135	0	50	82	10.4	2.40	107	.231	.297	9	.173	-1	1	3	3	0.5
1910 Cle-A	14	13	.519	37	29	18	3	1	256²	246	3	75	107	11.5	2.95	88	.261	.320	15	.183	-0	-12	-10	3	-0.8
1911 Cle-A	8	5	.615	15	13	7	0	1	106²	117	0	24	46	12.2	3.29	104	.282	.326	7	.175	-1	1	1	1	0.1
1913 Cle-A	23	10	.697	39	36	23	6	0	276	238	2	88	166	10.8	2.22	137	.235	.299	10	.119	-2	22	25	-2	2.5
1914 Ind-F	25	16	.610	**49**	43	33	**9**	3	377¹	332	5	89	**236**	10.2	2.22	141	.236	.284	21	.168	-4	28	38	3	3.8
1915 New-F	9	11	.450	25	21	14	0	1	172	175	4	47	76	12.1	3.24	79	.268	.326	3	.053	-7	-10	-13	1	-2.1
Bro-F	3	3	.500	7	7	5	1	0	48	31	1	12	20	8.3	1.50	181	.189	.249	1	.067	-2	7	7	-0	0.6
Yr	12	14	.462	32	28	19	1	1	220	206	5	59	96	10.9	2.86	91	.250	.301	4	.056	-9	-3	-7	1	-1.5
1917 Phi-A	2	6	.250	15	8	4	0	0	80²	86	1	26	35	12.5	3.35	82	.293	.350	5	.185	0	-6	-5	1	-0.3
Total 12	130	123	.514	330	266	180	27	8	2275	2090	23	690	1164	11.3	2.68	103	.248	.310	117	.152	-23	13	20	13	1.6

● ED FALLENSTEIN   Fallenstein, Edward Joseph "Jack" (b: Edward Joseph Valestin)
b: 12/22/08, Newark, N.J. d: 11/24/71, Orange, N.J. BR/TR, 6'3", 180 lbs. Deb: 4/16/31

1931 Phi-N	0	0	—	24	0	0	0	0	41²	56	2	26	15	17.7	7.13	60	.333	.423	1	.200	0	-15	-13	0	0.0
1933 Bos-N	2	1	.667	9	4	1	1	0	35	43	1	13	5	14.7	3.60	85	.305	.368	3	.375	1	-1	-2	-0	-0.1
Total 2	2	1	.667	33	4	1	1	0	76²	99	3	39	20	16.3	5.52	67	.320	.398	4	.308	1	-16	-16	-0	-0.1

● BOB FALLON   Fallon, Robert Joseph b: 2/18/60, Bronx, N.Y. BL/TL, 6'3", 200 lbs. Deb: 4/26/84

1984 Chi-A	0	0	—	3	3	0	0	0	14²	12	0	11	10	14.1	3.68	113	.235	.371	0	—	0	1	1	0	0.0
1985 Chi-A	0	0	—	10	0	0	0	0	16	25	5	9	17	19.1	6.19	70	.362	.436	0	—	0	-4	-3	1	-0.3
Total 2	0	0	—	13	3	0	0	0	30²	37	5	20	27	16.7	4.99	85	.308	.407	0	—	0	-3	-3	1	-0.3

● CLIFF FANNIN   Fannin, Clifford Bryson "Mule" b: 5/13/24, Louisa, Ky. d: 12/11/66, Sandusky, Ohio BL/TR, 6', 170 lbs. Deb: 9/2/45

1945 StL-A	0	0	—	5	0	0	0	0	10¹	8	0	5	6	11.3	2.61	135	.222	.317	0	.000	-0	1	1	-0	0.0
1946 StL-A	5	2	.714	27	7	4	1	2	86²	76	4	42	52	12.4	3.01	124	.236	.326	5	.161	-1	5	7	-0	0.5
1947 StL-A	6	8	.429	26	18	6	2	1	145²	134	10	77	77	13.1	3.58	108	.245	.340	9	.196	-0	2	5	-0	0.5
1948 StL-A	10	14	.417	34	29	10	3	1	213²	198	14	104	102	12.8	4.17	109	.245	.332	11	.169	-0	3	9	-2	0.7
1949 StL-A	8	14	.364	30	25	5	0	1	143	177	15	93	57	17.0	6.17	73	.308	.404	9	.164	-2	-31	-26	-3	-3.7
1950 StL-A	5	9	.357	25	16	3	0	1	102	116	18	58	42	15.4	6.53	76	.280	.369	6	.176	-2	-22	-18	-0	-2.2
1951 StL-A	0	2	.000	7	1	0	0	0	15¹	20	6	5	11	14.7	6.46	68	.317	.368	1	.250	-0	-4	-4	0	-0.4
1952 StL-A	0	2	.000	10	2	0	0	0	16¹	34	1	9	4	23.7	12.67	31	.453	.512	0	.000	0	-16	-16	-1	-1.7
Total 8	34	51	.400	164	98	28	6	6	733	763	72	393	352	14.2	4.85	89	.269	.358	41	.173	-5	-63	-42	-6	-6.3

● JACK FANNING   Fanning, John Jacob b: 1863, S.Orange, N.J. d: 6/10/17, Aberdeen, Wash. TR, 5'9", 163 lbs. Deb: 9/20/1889

1889 Ind-N	0	1	.000	1	1	0	0	0	1	3	0	2	0	45.0	18.00	23	.503	.628	0	.000	-0	-2	-2	0	-0.8
1894 Phi-N	1	3	.250	5	4	2	0	0	32¹	45	4	20	7	18.6	8.07	63	.326	.418	2	.154	-1	-10	-11	-0	-0.9
Total 2	1	4	.200	6	5	2	0	0	33¹	48	4	22	7	19.4	8.37	61	.333	.428	2	.143	-1	-11	-12	0	-1.7

● HARRY FANOK   Fanok, Harry Michael "The Flame Thrower" b: 5/11/40, Whippany, N.J. BB/TR, 6', 180 lbs. Deb: 4/16/63

1963 StL-N	2	1	.667	12	0	0	0	1	25²	24	3	21	25	16.1	5.26	67	.255	.397	2	.400	1	-6	-5	-0	-0.5
1964 StL-N	0	0	—	4	0	0	0	0	7²	5	0	3	10	9.4	5.87	65	.179	.258	0	.000	-0	-2	-2	-0	0.0
Total 2	2	1	.667	16	0	0	0	1	33¹	29	3	24	35	14.6	5.40	67	.238	.367	2	.333	1	-8	-7	-0	-0.5

● FRANK FANOVICH   Fanovich, Frank Joseph "Lefty" b: 1/11/22, New York, N.Y. BL/TL, 5'11", 180 lbs. Deb: 4/25/49

1949 Cin-N	0	2	.000	29	4	0	0	0	43¹	44	2	28	27	15.4	5.40	77	.257	.368	0	.000	-0	-7	-6	0	-0.2
1953 Phi-A	0	3	.000	26	3	0	0	0	61²	62	5	37	37	15.3	5.55	77	.273	.389	2	.182	-0	-11	-9	-1	-0.5
Total 2	0	5	.000	55	4	0	0	0	105	106	7	65	64	15.3	5.49	77	.266	.380	2	.133	-1	-17	-14	-0	-0.7

● STAN FANSLER   Fansler, Stanley Robert b: 2/12/65, Elkins, W.Va. BR/TR, 5'11", 180 lbs. Deb: 9/6/86

| 1986 Pit-N | 0 | 3 | .000 | 5 | 5 | 0 | 0 | 0 | 24 | 20 | 2 | 15 | 13 | 13.1 | 3.75 | 102 | .247 | .365 | 1 | .167 | -0 | -0 | 0 | -0 | 0.0 |

● HARRY FANWELL   Fanwell, Harry Clayton b: 10/16/1886, Patapsco, Md. d: 7/15/65, Baltimore, Md. BB/TR, 6', 175 lbs. Deb: 7/23/10

| 1910 Cle-A | 2 | 9 | .182 | 17 | 11 | 5 | 1 | 0 | 92 | 87 | 0 | 38 | 30 | 12.8 | 3.62 | 71 | .260 | .347 | 1 | .033 | -3 | -11 | -11 | 1 | -1.4 |

● ED FARMER   Farmer, Edward Joseph b: 10/18/49, Evergreen Park, Ill BR/TR, 6'5", 210 lbs. Deb: 6/9/71

1971 Cle-A	5	4	.556	43	4	0	0	0	78²	77	9	41	48	13.8	4.35	88	.263	.359	1	.071	-1	-8	-5	-0	-0.7
1972 Cle-A	2	5	.286	46	1	0	0	7	61¹	51	10	27	33	11.6	4.40	73	.231	.317	1	.143	-0	-9	-8	0	-1.1
1973 Cle-A	2	0	.000	16	0	0	0	1	17¹	25	4	5	10	15.6	4.67	84	.325	.366	0	—	0	-2	-1	-0	-0.2
Det-A	3	0	1.000	24	0	0	0	2	45	52	3	27	28	16.2	5.00	82	.292	.391	0	—	0	-6	-5	-1	-0.4
Yr	3	2	.600	40	0	0	0	3	62¹	77	7	32	38	16.0	4.91	82	.301	.383	0	—	0	-8	-6	-1	-0.6
1974 Phi-N	2	1	.667	14	3	0	0	0	31	41	5	27	20	19.7	8.42	45	.323	.442	1	.111	-1	-17	-16	-0	-1.5
1977 Bal-A	0	0	—	1	0	0	0	0	0	1	0	1	0	—	∞	—	1.000	1.000	0	—	0	-1	-1	0	0.3
1978 Mil-A	1	0	1.000	3	0	0	0	1	11	7	1	4	6	9.0	0.82	459	.175	.250	0	—	0	4	4	0	0.4
1979 Tex-A	2	0	1.000	11	2	0	0	0	33	30	2	19	25	13.9	4.36	95	.252	.364	0	—	0	-1	-1	-0	0.0
Chi-A	3	7	.300	42	3	0	0	14	81¹	66	2	34	48	11.2	2.43	175	.219	.301	0	—	0	16	16	0	2.5
Yr	5	7	.417	53	5	0	0	14	114¹	96	4	53	73	11.8	2.99	141	.226	.314	0	—	0	16	16	0	2.5
1980 Chi-A★	7	9	.438	64	0	0	0	30	99²	92	6	56	54	13.5	3.34	121	.244	.343	0	—	0	8	8	1	1.7
1981 Chi-A	3	3	.500	42	0	0	0	10	52²	53	5	34	42	15.0	4.61	78	.262	.371	0	—	0	-6	-6	1	-0.8
1982 Phi-N	2	6	.250	47	4	0	0	1	76	66	2	50	58	13.7	4.86	75	.234	.349	0	.000	-1	-11	-10	0	-1.3
1983 Phi-N	0	6	.000	12	3	0	0	0	26²	35	2	20	16	18.9	6.08	59	.307	.415	1	.167	-0	-7	-7	-0	-1.5
Oak-A	0	0	—	5	1	0	0	0	10¹	12	0	2	7	13.1	3.48	111	.366	.366	0	—	0	1	0	0	0.0
Total 11	30	43	.411	370	21	0	0	75	624	611	52	345	395	14.0	4.30	89	.257	.355	4	.085	-3	-38	-31	0	-2.6

● HOWARD FARMER   Farmer, Howard Earl b: 11/18/66, Gary, Ind. BR/TR, 6'3", 185 lbs. Deb: 7/2/90

| 1990 Mon-N | 0 | 3 | .000 | 6 | 4 | 0 | 0 | 0 | 23 | 26 | 9 | 10 | 14 | 14.1 | 7.04 | 52 | .302 | .375 | 2 | .400 | 1 | -8 | -9 | 1 | -0.8 |

● JIM FARR   Farr, James Alfred b: 5/18/56, Waverly, N.Y. BR/TR, 6'1", 195 lbs. Deb: 9/7/82

| 1982 Tex-A | 0 | 0 | — | 5 | 0 | 0 | 0 | 0 | 18 | 20 | 1 | 7 | 6 | 13.5 | 2.50 | 155 | .278 | .342 | 0 | — | 0 | 3 | 3 | -0 | 0.3 |

● STEVE FARR   Farr, Steven Michael b: 12/12/56, LaPlata, Md. BR/TR, 5'11", 198 lbs. Deb: 5/16/84

| 1984 Cle-A | 3 | 11 | .214 | 31 | 16 | 0 | 0 | 1 | 116 | 106 | 14 | 46 | 83 | 12.2 | 4.58 | 89 | .245 | .325 | 0 | — | 0 | -8 | -6 | 1 | -0.6 |
| 1985 *KC-A | 2 | 1 | .667 | 16 | 3 | 0 | 0 | 1 | 37² | 34 | 2 | 20 | 36 | 13.4 | 3.11 | 134 | .245 | .348 | 0 | — | 0 | 4 | 4 | 0 | 0.4 |

YEAR	TM/L	W	L	PCT	G	GS	CG	SH	SV	IP	H	HR	BB	SO	RAT	ERA	ERA+	OAV	OOB	BH	AVG	PB	PR	/A	PD	TPI
1986	KC-A	8	4	.667	56	0	0	0	8	109¹	90	10	39	83	10.9	3.13	136	.228	.304	0	—	0	13	14	1	1.5
1987	KC-A	4	3	.571	47	0	0	0	1	91	97	9	44	88	14.1	4.15	110	.270	.353	0	—	0	3	4	-1	0.0
1988	KC-A	5	4	.556	62	1	0	0	20	82²	74	5	30	72	11.5	2.50	159	.240	.312	0	—	0	13	14	-1	2.0
1989	KC-A	2	5	.286	51	2	0	0	18	63¹	75	5	22	56	13.9	4.12	93	.296	.355	0	—	0	-2	-2	-0	-0.3
1990	KC-A	13	7	.650	57	6	1	1	1	127	99	6	48	94	10.8	1.98	193	.220	.302	0	—	0	**27**	**26**	0	4.1
1991	NY-A	5	5	.500	60	0	0	0	23	70	57	4	20	60	10.5	2.19	189	.219	.288	0	—	0	15	15	1	3.3
1992	NY-A	2	2	.500	50	0	0	0	30	52	34	2	19	37	9.5	1.56	251	.186	.270	0	—	0	14	14	-1	2.8
1993	NY-A	2	2	.500	49	0	0	0	25	47	44	8	28	39	14.2	4.21	99	.253	.363	0	—	0	1	-0	1	0.2
1994	Cle-A	1	1	.500	19	0	0	0	4	15¹	17	3	15	12	20.0	5.28	93	.279	.436	0	—	0	-1	-1	0	-0.2
	Bos-A	1	0	1.000	11	0	0	0	0	13	24	2	3	8	18.7	6.23	83	.407	.435	0	—	0	-2	-2	-0	-0.2
	Yr	2	1	.667	30	0	0	0	4	28¹	41	5	18	20	18.7	5.72	88	.333	.418	0	—	0	-3	-2	0	-0.4
Total	11	48	45	.516	509	28	1	1	132	824¹	751	70	334	668	12.2	3.25	127	.244	.325	0	—	0	78	80	1	13.0

● **JOHN FARRELL**　　Farrell, John Edward b: 8/4/62, Monmouth Beach, N.J. BR/TR, 6'4", 210 lbs. Deb: 8/18/87

YEAR	TM/L	W	L	PCT	G	GS	CG	SH	SV	IP	H	HR	BB	SO	RAT	ERA	ERA+	OAV	OOB	BH	AVG	PB	PR	/A	PD	TPI
1987	Cle-A	5	1	.833	10	9	1	0	0	69	68	7	22	28	12.4	3.39	133	.256	.324	0	—	0	8	9	-0	0.6
1988	Cle-A	14	10	.583	31	30	4	0	0	210¹	216	15	67	92	12.5	4.24	97	.269	.332	0	—	0	-6	-3	-0	-0.5
1989	Cle-A	9	14	.391	31	31	7	2	0	208	196	14	71	132	11.3	3.63	109	.244	.311	0	—	0	6	8	-2	0.5
1990	Cle-A	4	5	.444	17	17	1	0	0	96²	108	10	33	44	13.2	4.28	91	.286	.345	0	—	0	-4	-4	-0	-0.3
1993	Cal-A	3	12	.200	21	17	0	0	0	90²	110	22	44	45	16.0	7.35	61	.301	.387	0	—	0	-30	-29	-0	-3.9
1994	Cal-A	1	2	.333	3	3	0	0	0	13	16	2	8	10	17.3	9.00	55	.308	.410	0	—	0	-6	-6	-0	-1.0
Total	6	36	44	.450	113	107	13	2	0	687²	714	70	245	351	12.9	4.48	93	.268	.336	0	—	0	-33	-25	-3	-4.6

● **KERBY FARRELL**　　Farrell, Major Kerby b: 9/3/13, Leapwood, Tenn. d: 12/17/75, Nashville, Tenn. BL/TL, 5'11", 172 lbs. Deb: 4/24/43 MC♦

YEAR	TM/L	W	L	PCT	G	GS	CG	SH	SV	IP	H	HR	BB	SO	RAT	ERA	ERA+	OAV	OOB	BH	AVG	PB	PR	/A	PD	TPI
1943	Bos-N	0	1	.000	5	0	0	0	0	23	24	1	9	4	12.9	4.30	79	.276	.344	75	.268		-2	-2	-0	0.0

● **TURK FARRELL**　　Farrell, Richard Joseph b: 4/8/34, Boston, Mass. d: 6/10/77, Great Yarmouth, England BR/TR, 6'4", 220 lbs. Deb: 9/21/56

YEAR	TM/L	W	L	PCT	G	GS	CG	SH	SV	IP	H	HR	BB	SO	RAT	ERA	ERA+	OAV	OOB	BH	AVG	PB	PR	/A	PD	TPI
1956	Phi-N	0	1	.000	1	1	0	0	0	4¹	6	0	3	0	20.8	12.46	30	.353	.476	0	.000	-0	-4	-4	0	-0.6
1957	Phi-N	10	2	.833	52	0	0	0	10	83¹	74	2	36	54	12.1	2.38	160	.242	.326	1	.111	0	**14**	13	0	2.2
1958	Phi-N★	8	9	.471	54	0	0	0	11	94	84	7	40	73	11.9	3.35	118	.244	.323	5	.208	0	6	6	-2	1.1
1959	Phi-N	1	6	.143	38	0	0	0	6	57	61	9	25	31	13.6	4.74	87	.288	.363	1	.167	-0	-5	-4	-0	-0.6
1960	Phi-N	10	6	.625	59	0	0	0	11	103¹	88	3	29	72	10.5	2.70	144	.239	.302	3	.200	1	12	14	-1	2.3
1961	Phi-N	2	1	.667	5	0	0	0	0	9²	10	3	6	10	15.8	6.52	63	.270	.386	1	.500	-0	-3	-3	-0	-0.7
	LA-N	6	6	.500	50	0	0	0	10	89	107	12	43	80	15.3	5.06	86	.296	.373	0	.000	-2	-10	-7	-2	-1.4
	Yr	8	7	.533	55	0	0	0	10	98²	117	15	49	90	15.2	5.20	83	.293	.372	1	.050	-2	-13	-10	-2	-2.1
1962	Hou-N★	10	20	.333	43	29	11	2	4	241²	210	21	55	203	10.1	3.02	124	.233	.280	14	.179	2	25	19	-2	2.3
1963	Hou-N	14	13	.519	34	26	12	0	1	202¹	161	12	35	141	8.8	3.02	104	.219	.256	9	.143	1	6	3	-2	0.4
1964	Hou-N★	11	10	.524	32	27	7	0	0	198¹	196	21	52	117	11.4	3.27	105	.261	.311	5	.072	-3	6	3	-1	-0.1
1965	Hou-N★	11	11	.500	33	29	8	3	1	208¹	202	18	35	122	10.4	3.50	96	.252	.286	10	.135	-1	1	-3	-2	-0.6
1966	Hou-N	6	10	.375	32	21	3	0	2	152²	167	23	28	101	11.5	4.60	74	.278	.310	7	.146	-0	-17	-20	-2	-2.2
1967	Hou-N	1	0	1.000	7	0	0	0	0	11²	11	0	7	10	14.7	4.63	72	.244	.358	0	.000	-0	-2	-2	-0	-0.2
	Phi-N	9	6	.600	50	1	0	0	12	92	76	6	15	68	9.0	2.05	166	.228	.263	2	.105	-1	14	14	-1	2.6
	Yr	10	6	.625	57	1	0	0	12	103²	87	6	22	78	9.5	2.34	145	.229	.273	2	.100	-1	12	12	-1	2.4
1968	Phi-N	4	6	.400	54	0	0	0	12	83	83	7	32	57	12.7	3.47	87	.271	.344	1	.167	-0	-4	-4	-0	-0.7
1969	Phi-N	3	4	.429	46	0	0	0	3	74¹	92	8	27	40	14.5	4.00	89	.307	.366	0	.000	-0	-3	-4	-2	-0.6
Total	14	106	111	.488	590	134	41	5	83	1705	1628	152	468	1177	11.2	3.45	103	.254	.307	59	.135	-3	35	21	-17	3.2

● **JEFF FASSERO**　　Fassero, Jeffrey Joseph b: 1/5/63, Springfield, Ill. BL/TL, 6'1", 180 lbs. Deb: 5/4/91

YEAR	TM/L	W	L	PCT	G	GS	CG	SH	SV	IP	H	HR	BB	SO	RAT	ERA	ERA+	OAV	OOB	BH	AVG	PB	PR	/A	PD	TPI
1991	Mon-N	2	5	.286	51	0	0	0	8	55¹	39	1	17	42	9.3	2.44	148	.196	.263	0	.000	0	8	7	1	1.2
1992	Mon-N	8	7	.533	70	0	0	0	1	85²	81	1	34	63	12.3	2.84	122	.249	.324	1	.143	0	6	6	0	1.1
1993	Mon-N	12	5	.706	56	15	1	0	1	149²	119	7	54	140	10.4	2.29	183	.216	.286	2	.063	-2	**29**	**31**	3	3.2
1994	Mon-N	8	6	.571	21	21	1	0	0	138²	119	13	40	119	10.4	2.99	142	.229	.286	3	.068	-2	19	19	3	1.9
Total	4	30	23	.566	198	36	2	0	10	429¹	358	22	145	364	10.6	2.64	151	.225	.291	6	.070	-4	62	64	4	7.4

● **FAST**　　Fast b: Milwaukee, Wis. Deb: 7/11/1887

YEAR	TM/L	W	L	PCT	G	GS	CG	SH	SV	IP	H	HR	BB	SO	RAT	ERA	ERA+	OAV	OOB	BH	AVG	PB	PR	/A	PD	TPI
1887	Ind-N	0	1	.000	4	2	1	0	**1**	15²	25	1	8	2	20.1	10.34	40	.347	.427	2	.182	-1	-11	-11	0	-0.6

● **DARCY FAST**　　Fast, Darcy Rae b: 3/10/47, Dallas, Ore. BL/TL, 6'3", 195 lbs. Deb: 6/15/68

YEAR	TM/L	W	L	PCT	G	GS	CG	SH	SV	IP	H	HR	BB	SO	RAT	ERA	ERA+	OAV	OOB	BH	AVG	PB	PR	/A	PD	TPI
1968	Chi-N	0	1	.000	8	0	0	0	0	10	8	1	8	10	14.4	5.40	59	.216	.356	0	.000	-0	-3	-2	0	-0.3

● **JACK FASZHOLZ**　　Faszholz, John Edward "Preacher" b: 4/11/27, St.Louis, Mo. BR/TR, 6'3", 205 lbs. Deb: 4/25/53

YEAR	TM/L	W	L	PCT	G	GS	CG	SH	SV	IP	H	HR	BB	SO	RAT	ERA	ERA+	OAV	OOB	BH	AVG	PB	PR	/A	PD	TPI
1953	StL-N	0	0	—	4	1	0	0	0	11²	16	3	1	7	13.9	6.94	61	.327	.353	0	.000	-0	-3	-3	-1	-0.1

● **BILL FAUL**　　Faul, William Alvan b: 4/21/40, Cincinnati, Ohio BR/TR, 5'10", 190 lbs. Deb: 9/19/62

YEAR	TM/L	W	L	PCT	G	GS	CG	SH	SV	IP	H	HR	BB	SO	RAT	ERA	ERA+	OAV	OOB	BH	AVG	PB	PR	/A	PD	TPI
1962	Det-A	0	0	—	1	0	0	0	0	1²	4	1	3	2	43.2	32.40	13	.444	.615	0	—	0	-5	-5	-0	0.0
1963	Det-A	5	6	.455	28	10	2	0	1	97	93	14	48	64	13.5	4.64	81	.251	.343	4	.148	-1	-11	-10	-2	-1.2
1964	Det-A	0	0	—	1	1	0	0	0	5	5	2	2	1	12.6	10.80	34	.250	.318	0	.000	-0	-4	-4	-0	-0.1
1965	Chi-N	6	6	.500	17	16	5	3	0	96²	83	12	18	59	9.7	3.54	104	.232	.275	3	.100	-1	0	2	-2	-0.1
1966	Chi-N	1	4	.200	17	6	1	0	0	51¹	47	12	18	32	12.1	5.08	72	.242	.319	0	.000	-2	-8	-8	-1	-0.9
1970	SF-N	0	0	—	7	0	0	0	0	9²	15	1	6	6	19.6	7.45	53	.357	.438	0	—	0	-4	-4	-0	-0.1
Total	6	12	16	.429	71	33	8	3	2	261¹	247	42	95	164	12.2	4.72	79	.249	.322	7	.097	-2	-32	-29	-5	-2.3

● **JIM FAULKNER**　　Faulkner, James Leroy "Lefty" b: 7/27/1899, Beatrice, Neb. d: 6/1/62, W.Palm Beach, Fla. BB/TL, 6'3", 190 lbs. Deb: 9/15/27

YEAR	TM/L	W	L	PCT	G	GS	CG	SH	SV	IP	H	HR	BB	SO	RAT	ERA	ERA+	OAV	OOB	BH	AVG	PB	PR	/A	PD	TPI
1927	NY-N	1	0	1.000	3	1	0	0	0	9²	13	0	5	2	17.7	3.72	104	.317	.404	1	.500	1	0	0	-0	0.1
1928	NY-N	9	8	.529	38	8	3	0	2	117¹	131	5	41	32	13.4	3.53	111	.289	.351	9	.231	1	6	5	1	0.8
1930	Bro-N	0	0	—	2	1	0	0	1	0¹	2	1	1	0	81.0	81.00	6	.667	.750	0	—	-0	-3	-3	-0	-1.2
Total	3	10	8	.556	43	10	3	0	3	127¹	146	6	47	34	13.9	3.75	104	.293	.359	10	.244	2	3	2	1	-0.3

● **BUCK FAUSETT**　　Fausett, Robert Shaw "Leaky" b: 4/8/08, Sheridan, Ark. d: 5/2/94, College Station, Tex. BL/TR, 5'10", 170 lbs. Deb: 4/18/44 ♦

YEAR	TM/L	W	L	PCT	G	GS	CG	SH	SV	IP	H	HR	BB	SO	RAT	ERA	ERA+	OAV	OOB	BH	AVG	PB	PR	/A	PD	TPI
1944	Cin-N	0	0	—	1	0	0	0	0	10²	13	0	7	3	18.6	5.91	59	.295	.415	3	.097	-0	-3	-3	0	0.0

● **CHARLIE FAUST**　　Faust, Charles Victor "Victory" b: 10/9/1880, Marion, Kan. d: 6/18/15, Fort Steilacoom, Wash. BR/TR, 6'2", Deb: 10/7/11

YEAR	TM/L	W	L	PCT	G	GS	CG	SH	SV	IP	H	HR	BB	SO	RAT	ERA	ERA+	OAV	OOB	BH	AVG	PB	PR	/A	PD	TPI
1911	NY-N	0	0	—	2	0	0	0	0	2	2	0	0	0	9.0	4.50	75	.250	.250	0	—	0	-0	-0	0	0.1

● **CLAY FAUVER**　　Fauver, Clayton King "Cayt" b: 8/1/1872, N.Eaton, Ohio d: 3/3/42, Chatsworth, Ga. BB/TR, 5'10", Deb: 9/7/1899

YEAR	TM/L	W	L	PCT	G	GS	CG	SH	SV	IP	H	HR	BB	SO	RAT	ERA	ERA+	OAV	OOB	BH	AVG	PB	PR	/A	PD	TPI
1899	Lou-N	1	0	1.000	1	1	1	0	0	9	11	0	2	1	13.0	0.00	—	.301	.337	0	.000	-1	4	4	-0	0.3

● **VERN FEAR**　　Fear, Luvern Carl b: 8/21/24, Everly, Iowa d: 9/6/76, Spencer, Iowa BB/TR, 6', 170 lbs. Deb: 8/3/52

YEAR	TM/L	W	L	PCT	G	GS	CG	SH	SV	IP	H	HR	BB	SO	RAT	ERA	ERA+	OAV	OOB	BH	AVG	PB	PR	/A	PD	TPI
1952	Chi-N	0	0	—	4	0	0	0	0	8	9	1	3	4	14.6	7.88	49	.290	.371	0	.000	-0	-4	-4	-0	0.0

● **JACK FEE**　　Fee, John b: 12/23/1867, Carbondale, Pa. d: 3/3/13, Carbondale, Pa. Deb: 9/14/1889

YEAR	TM/L	W	L	PCT	G	GS	CG	SH	SV	IP	H	HR	BB	SO	RAT	ERA	ERA+	OAV	OOB	BH	AVG	PB	PR	/A	PD	TPI
1889	Ind-N	2	2	.500	7	3	2	0	0	40	39	3	31	10	17.1	4.27	98	.248	.391	3	.143	-2	-1	-0	1	-0.1

● **HARRY FELDMAN**　　Feldman, Harry b: 11/10/19, New York, N.Y. d: 3/16/62, Fort Smith, Ark. BR/TR, 6', 175 lbs. Deb: 9/10/41

YEAR	TM/L	W	L	PCT	G	GS	CG	SH	SV	IP	H	HR	BB	SO	RAT	ERA	ERA+	OAV	OOB	BH	AVG	PB	PR	/A	PD	TPI
1941	NY-N	1	1	.500	3	3	1	1	0	20¹	21	0	6	9	12.0	3.98	93	.280	.333	1	.167	0	-1	-1	-0	-0.1
1942	NY-N	7	1	.875	31	6	2	1	0	114	100	5	73	49	13.7	3.16	106	.236	.350	11	.282	3	2	3	-0	0.5
1943	NY-N	4	5	.444	31	10	1	0	0	104²	114	7	58	49	15.1	4.30	80	.279	.374	4	.133	-1	-11	-10	0	-0.9

YEAR	TM/L	W	L	PCT	G	GS	CG	SH	SV	IP	H	HR	BB	SO	RAT	ERA	ERA+	OAV	OOB	BH	AVG	PB	PR	/A	PD	TPI
1944	NY-N	11	13	.458	40	27	8	1	2	205¹	214	18	91	70	13.5	4.16	88	.266	.342	15	.205	0	-13	-11	-2	-1.4
1945	NY-N	12	13	.480	35	30	10	3	1	217²	213	14	69	74	11.7	3.27	120	.251	.308	7	.097	-3	13	16	-2	1.1
1946	NY-N	0	2	.000	3	2	0	0	0	4	9	1	3	3	27.0	18.00	19	.474	.545	0	.000	-0	-6	-6	-0	-2.1
Total	6	35	35	.500	143	78	22	6	3	666	671	45	300	254	13.2	3.80	96	.260	.339	38	.172	-1	-16	-10	-5	-2.9

● HARRY FELIX

Felix, Harry b: 1870, Brooklyn, N.Y. d: 10/17/61, Miami, Fla. BR/TR, 5'7.5", 160 lbs. Deb: 10/5/01

YEAR	TM/L	W	L	PCT	G	GS	CG	SH	SV	IP	H	HR	BB	SO	RAT	ERA	ERA+	OAV	OOB	BH	AVG	PB	PR	/A	PD	TPI
1901	NY-N	0	0	—	1	0	0	0	0	2	3	0	0	0	13.5	0.00	—	.344	.344	0	.000	-0	1	1	-0	0.0
1902	Phi-N	1	3	.250	9	5	3	0	0	45	61	1	11	10	14.4	5.60	50	.323	.360	5	.135	-1	-14	-14	-1	-1.2
Total	2	1	3	.250	10	5	3	0	0	47	64	1	11	10	14.4	5.36	53	.324	.359	5	.132	-1	-13	-13	-1	-1.2

● BOB FELLER

Feller, Robert William Andrew (b: Robert William Feller) "Rapid Robert" b: 11/3/18, Van Meter, Iowa BR/TR, 6', 185 lbs. Deb: 7/19/36 H

YEAR	TM/L	W	L	PCT	G	GS	CG	SH	SV	IP	H	HR	BB	SO	RAT	ERA	ERA+	OAV	OOB	BH	AVG	PB	PR	/A	PD	TPI
1936	Cle-A	5	3	.625	14	8	5	0	1	62	52	1	47	76	15.0	3.34	151	.229	.371	3	.136	-2	12	12	-1	1.1
1937	Cle-A	9	7	.563	26	19	9	0	1	148²	116	4	106	150	13.6	3.39	136	.218	.351	9	.170	-1	20	20	1	1.9
1938	Cle-A☆	17	11	.607	39	36	20	2	1	277²	225	13	208	240	14.3	4.08	114	.220	.356	17	.181	-2	22	17	-2	1.4
1939	Cle-A★	24	9	.727	39	35	24	4	1	296²	227	13	142	246	11.3	2.85	154	.210	.303	21	.212	5	58	51	0	5.6
1940	Cle-A★	27	11	.711	43	37	31	4	2	320¹	245	13	118	261	10.3	2.61	161	.210	.285	18	.157	1	63	57	-4	6.1
1941	Cle-A★	25	13	.658	44	40	28	6	2	343	284	15	194	260	12.7	3.15	125	.226	.332	18	.150	-2	38	30	-1	3.2
1945	Cle-A	5	3	.625	9	9	7	1	0	72	50	1	35	59	10.9	2.50	130	.192	.293	4	.160	-0	7	6	-1	0.5
1946	Cle-A★	26	15	.634	48	42	36	10	4	371¹	277	11	153	348	10.5	2.18	152	.208	.291	16	.129	-2	55	46	-1	4.9
1947	Cle-A†	20	11	.645	42	37	20	5	3	299	230	17	127	196	10.9	2.68	130	.215	.300	18	.184	3	34	27	2	3.1
1948	*Cle-A†	19	15	.559	44	38	18	2	3	280¹	255	20	116	164	12.0	3.56	114	.241	.317	9	.095	-8	23	15	-1	0.7
1949	Cle-A	15	14	.517	36	28	15	0	0	211	198	18	84	108	12.1	3.75	106	.248	.320	17	.236	4	10	6	-4	0.7
1950	Cle-A★	16	11	.593	35	34	16	3	0	247	230	20	103	119	12.3	3.43	126	.247	.325	10	.122	-2	32	25	-4	1.7
1951	Cle-A	22	8	.733	33	32	16	4	0	249²	239	22	95	111	12.3	3.50	108	.253	.325	10	.123	-4	17	8	-3	0.1
1952	Cle-A	9	13	.409	30	30	11	0	0	191²	219	13	83	81	14.3	4.74	71	.288	.360	7	.117	1	-23	-30	-0	-3.0
1953	Cle-A	10	7	.588	25	25	10	1	0	175²	163	16	60	60	11.6	3.59	105	.251	.317	6	.107	-2	8	3	1	0.1
1954	Cle-A	13	3	.813	19	19	9	1	0	140	127	13	39	59	10.9	3.09	119	.239	.294	9	.188	1	10	9	-2	0.9
1955	Cle-A	4	4	.500	25	11	2	1	0	83	71	7	31	25	11.2	3.47	115	.235	.308	1	.048	-3	5	5	-1	0.1
1956	Cle-A	0	4	.000	19	4	2	0	1	58	63	7	23	18	13.3	4.97	85	.280	.347	0	.000	-2	-5	-5	-0	-0.6
Total	18	266	162	.621	570	484	279	44	21	3827	3271	224	1764	2581	12.0	3.25	122	.231	.319	193	.151	-7	385	301	-22	28.5

● TERRY FELTON

Felton, Terry Lane b: 10/29/57, Texarkana, Ark. BR/TR, 6'1", 180 lbs. Deb: 9/28/79

YEAR	TM/L	W	L	PCT	G	GS	CG	SH	SV	IP	H	HR	BB	SO	RAT	ERA	ERA+	OAV	OOB	BH	AVG	PB	PR	/A	PD	TPI
1979	Min-A	0	0	—	1	0	0	0	0	2	0	0	1	0	0.00	0.00	—	.000	.000	0	—	-0	1	1	-0	-0.2
1980	Min-A	0	3	.000	5	4	0	0	0	17²	20	2	9	14	15.3	7.13	61	.286	.375	0	—	-0	-6	-5	-0	-0.8
1981	Min-A	0	0	—	1	0	0	0	0	1¹	4	1	2	1	40.5	40.50	10	.500	.600	0	—	-0	-5	-5	-0	-0.1
1982	Min-A	0	13	.000	48	6	0	0	3	117¹	99	18	76	92	13.7	4.99	85	.230	.351	0	—	-0	-12	-10	-3	-1.2
Total	4	0	16	.000	55	10	0	0	3	138¹	123	21	87	108	14.0	5.53	77	.240	.355	0	—	-0	-22	-20	-3	-2.3

● HOD FENNER

Fenner, Horace Alfred b: 7/12/1897, Martin, Mich. d: 11/20/54, Detroit, Mich. BR/TR, 5'10.5", 165 lbs. Deb: 9/9/21

YEAR	TM/L	W	L	PCT	G	GS	CG	SH	SV	IP	H	HR	BB	SO	RAT	ERA	ERA+	OAV	OOB	BH	AVG	PB	PR	/A	PD	TPI
1921	Chi-A	0	0	—	2	1	0	0	0	7	14	0	3	1	21.9	7.71	55	.452	.500	1	.000	-0	-3	-3	-0	-0.1

● STAN FERENS

Ferens, Stanley "Lefty" b: 3/5/15, Wendel, Pa. BB/TL, 5'11", 170 lbs. Deb: 6/10/42

YEAR	TM/L	W	L	PCT	G	GS	CG	SH	SV	IP	H	HR	BB	SO	RAT	ERA	ERA+	OAV	OOB	BH	AVG	PB	PR	/A	PD	TPI
1942	StL-A	3	4	.429	19	3	1	0	0	69	76	2	21	23	12.7	3.78	98	.279	.331	3	.143	-1	-1	-1	-0	-0.1
1946	StL-A	2	9	.182	34	6	1	0	0	88	100	3	38	28	14.4	4.50	83	.293	.369	4	.167	-1	-10	-8	-1	-1.0
Total	2	5	13	.278	53	9	2	0	0	157	176	5	59	51	13.6	4.18	89	.287	.353	7	.156	-1	-11	-8	-1	-1.1

● CHARLIE FERGUSON

Ferguson, Charles Augustus b: 5/10/1875, Okemos, Mich. d: 5/17/31, Sault Ste. Marie, Mich. TR, 5'11", Deb: 9/20/01

YEAR	TM/L	W	L	PCT	G	GS	CG	SH	SV	IP	H	HR	BB	SO	RAT	ERA	ERA+	OAV	OOB	BH	AVG	PB	PR	/A	PD	TPI
1901	Chi-N	0	0	—	1	0	0	0	0	2	1	0	2	0	13.5	0.00	—	.149	.344	0	.000	-0	1	1	-0	0.0

● CHARLIE FERGUSON

Ferguson, Charles J. b: 4/17/1863, Charlottesville, Va. d: 4/29/1888, Philadelphia, Pa. BB/TR, 6', 165 lbs. Deb: 5/1/1884

YEAR	TM/L	W	L	PCT	G	GS	CG	SH	SV	IP	H	HR	BB	SO	RAT	ERA	ERA+	OAV	OOB	BH	AVG	PB	PR	/A	PD	TPI
1884	Phi-N	21	25	.457	50	47	46	2	1	416²	443	13	93	194	11.6	3.54	84	.253	.291	50	.246	7	-26	-26	-2	-1.7
1885	Phi-N	26	20	.565	48	45	45	5	0	405	345	5	81	197	9.5	2.22	126	.219	.257	72	.306	17	27	26	1	4.3
1886	Phi-N	30	9	.769	48	45	43	4	2	395²	317	11	69	212	8.8	1.98	167	.210	.244	66	.253	12	59	58	5	6.5
1887	Phi-N	22	10	.688	37	33	31	2	1	297¹	297	13	47	125	10.7	3.00	141	.254	.289	89	.337	14	36	41	3	4.7
Total	4	99	64	.607	183	170	165	13	4	1514²	1402	42	290	728	10.1	2.67	122	.233	.270	277	.288	49	95	97	6	13.8

● GEORGE FERGUSON

Ferguson, George Cecil "Cecil" b: 8/19/1886, Ellsworth, Ind. d: 9/5/43, Orlando, Fla. BR/TR, 5'10", 165 lbs. Deb: 4/19/06

YEAR	TM/L	W	L	PCT	G	GS	CG	SH	SV	IP	H	HR	BB	SO	RAT	ERA	ERA+	OAV	OOB	BH	AVG	PB	PR	/A	PD	TPI
1906	NY-N	2	0	1.000	22	1	1	1	7	52¹	43	1	24	32	11.9	2.58	101	.229	.322	5	.333	2	0	0	1	0.3
1907	NY-N	3	2	.600	15	5	4	0	1	64	63	2	20	37	12.4	2.11	118	.266	.336	1	.056	-1	3	3	-0	0.0
1908	Bos-N	11	11	.500	37	20	13	3	0	208	168	1	84	98	11.3	2.47	98	.230	.316	11	.169	1	-2	-1	-3	-0.4
1909	Bos-N	5	23	.179	36	30	19	3	0	226²	235	2	83	87	13.1	3.73	76	.282	.355	15	.205	1	-28	-23	-0	-2.5
1910	Bos-N	7	7	.500	26	14	10	1	0	123	110	3	58	40	12.8	3.80	87	.254	.351	7	.175	-1	-11	-7	-0	-0.8
1911	Bos-N	1	3	.250	6	3	0	0	0	24	40	3	12	4	19.5	9.75	39	.388	.452	2	.286	-1	-17	-16	-1	-1.9
Total	6	29	46	.387	142	73	47	8	8	698	659	12	281	298	12.6	3.34	83	.261	.343	41	.188	3	-55	-44	-2	-5.3

● ALEX FERGUSON

Ferguson, James Alexander b: 2/16/1897, Montclair, N.J. d: 4/26/76, Sepulveda, Cal. BR/TR, 6', 180 lbs. Deb: 8/16/18

YEAR	TM/L	W	L	PCT	G	GS	CG	SH	SV	IP	H	HR	BB	SO	RAT	ERA	ERA+	OAV	OOB	BH	AVG	PB	PR	/A	PD	TPI
1918	NY-A	0	0	—	1	0	0	0	0	1²	2	0	2	1	21.6	0.00	—	.333	.500	0	.000	-0	1	1	-0	0.0
1921	NY-A	3	1	.750	17	4	1	0	1	56¹	64	4	27	9	15.2	5.91	72	.296	.385	4	.211	-1	-10	-10	-0	-0.7
1922	Bos-A	9	16	.360	39	27	10	1	2	198¹	201	5	62	44	12.2	4.31	95	.265	.326	6	.092	-6	-6	-4	-1	-1.2
1923	Bos-A	9	13	.409	34	27	11	0	0	198¹	229	5	67	72	13.8	4.04	102	.297	.360	6	.097	-5	-1	2	-1	-0.5
1924	Bos-A	14	17	.452	41	32	15	0	2	237²	259	6	108	78	14.1	3.79	115	.286	.366	12	.140	-6	12	15	1	1.3
1925	Bos-A	0	2	.000	5	4	0	0	1	15²	22	6	5	6	16.1	10.91	42	.314	.368	0	.000	-0	-11	-11	-0	-1.2
	NY-A	4	2	.667	21	5	0	0	1	54¹	83	3	42	20	21.0	7.79	55	.358	.460	2	.133	-1	-20	-21	-1	-1.9
	*Was-A	5	1	.833	7	6	3	0	0	55¹	52	2	23	24	12.5	3.25	130	.256	.338	1	.050	-3	7	6	-0	0.2
	Yr	9	5	.643	33	15	3	0	2	125¹	157	11	70	49	16.4	6.18	69	.309	.395	3	.077	-4	-25	-26	-1	-2.9
1926	Was-A	3	4	.429	19	4	0	0	1	47²	69	4	18	16	17.0	7.74	50	.343	.405	2	.182	-0	-20	-21	-0	-2.5
1927	Phi-N	8	16	.333	31	31	16	0	0	227	280	15	65	73	13.9	4.84	85	.313	.363	7	.100	-5	-23	-18	-2	-2.0
1928	Phi-N	5	10	.333	34	19	8	0	2	134²	168	14	52	51	15.1	5.88	73	.314	.381	1	.026	-4	-28	-24	-2	-2.6
1929	Phi-N	1	2	.333	5	4	1	0	0	12²	19	2	10	3	20.6	12.08	43	.345	.446	0	.000	-1	-10	-10	-0	-1.6
	Bro-N	0	1	.000	3	3	0	0	0	2	7	2	1	1	36.0	22.50	21	.583	.615	1	1.000	-0	-4	-4	-0	-1.3
	Yr	1	3	.250	8	7	1	0	0	14²	26	4	11	4	22.7	13.50	38	.388	.474	1	.200	-1	-14	-14	-0	-2.9
Total	10	61	85	.418	257	166	62	2	10	1241²	1455	68	482	397	14.4	4.93	85	.299	.368	42	.106	-33	-115	-99	1	-14.0

● BOB FERGUSON

Ferguson, Robert Lester b: 4/18/19, Birmingham, Ala. BR/TR, 6'1.5", 180 lbs. Deb: 4/29/44

YEAR	TM/L	W	L	PCT	G	GS	CG	SH	SV	IP	H	HR	BB	SO	RAT	ERA	ERA+	OAV	OOB	BH	AVG	PB	PR	/A	PD	TPI
1944	Cin-N	0	3	.000	9	2	0	0	1	16	24	3	10	9	20.3	9.00	39	.358	.456	1	.333	0	-10	-10	-0	-1.6

● BOB FERGUSON

Ferguson, Robert Vavasour b: 1/31/1845, Brooklyn, N.Y. d: 5/3/1894, Brooklyn, N.Y. BB/TR, 5'9.5", 149 lbs. Deb: 5/18/1871 MU♦

YEAR	TM/L	W	L	PCT	G	GS	CG	SH	SV	IP	H	HR	BB	SO	RAT	ERA	ERA+	OAV	OOB	BH	AVG	PB	PR	/A	PD	TPI
1871	Mut-n	0	0	—	1	0	0	0	0	1	8	0	0	0	72.0	27.00	14	.571	.571	38	.241	-0	-3	-3		0.0
1873	Atl-n	0	1	.000	4	1	0	0	0	19¹	41	2	2	0	20.0	6.05	50	.380	.391	59	.259	-1	-6	-6		-0.2
1874	Atl-n	0	1	.000	1	1	1	0	0	9	12	0	3		15.0	4.00	70	.273	.319	63	.256	0	-1	-1		-0.1
1875	Har-n	0	0	—	2	0	0	0	0	2	9	1	0		40.5	13.50	19	.643	.652	88	.240	0	-2	-2		0.0
1877	Har-N	1	1	.500	3	2	1	0	0	25	38	0	2	1	14.4	3.96	61	.352	.364	65	.256	0	-3	-4	-0	-0.2
1883	Phi-N	0	0	—	1	0	0	0	0	1	0	0	0		18.0	9.00	34	.286	.286	85	.258	0	-1	-1		0.0
Total 4 n		0	2	.000	7	2	1	0	0	31¹	70	3	5	0	21.5	6.61	40	.389	.405	293	.252	1	-12	-13		-0.3
Total 2		1	1	.500	4	2	2	0	0	26	40	0	2	1	14.5	4.15	59	.348	.359	625	.271	1	-4	-5	-0	-0.2

YEAR TM/L	W	L	PCT	G	GS	CG	SH	SV	IP	H	HR	BB	SO	RAT	ERA	ERA+	OAV	OOB	BH	AVG	PB	PR	/A	PD	TPI

● **ALEX FERNANDEZ**   Fernandez, Alexander   b: 8/13/69, Miami Beach, Fla.   BR/TR, 6'2", 200 lbs.   Deb: 8/2/90

1990 Chi-A	5	5	.500	13	13	3	0	0	87²	89	6	34	61	12.9	3.80	101	.265	.338	0	—	0	1	0	-0	0.1
1991 Chi-A	9	13	.409	34	32	2	0	0	191²	186	16	88	145	13.0	4.51	88	.259	.341	0	—	0	-9	-11	1	-1.0
1992 Chi-A	8	11	.421	29	29	4	2	0	187²	199	21	50	95	12.3	4.27	90	.270	.324	0	—	0	-7	-9	2	-0.6
1993 *Chi-A	18	9	.667	34	34	3	1	0	247¹	221	27	67	169	10.7	3.13	133	.240	.296	0	—	0	33	29	2	3.2
1994 Chi-A	11	7	.611	24	24	4	3	0	170¹	163	25	50	122	11.3	3.86	122	.250	.305	0	—	0	18	16	0	1.5
Total 5	51	45	.531	134	132	16	6	0	884²	858	95	289	592	11.9	3.88	107	.255	.318	0	—	0	36	25	4	3.2

● **SID FERNANDEZ**   Fernandez, Charles Sidney   b: 10/12/62, Honolulu, Hawaii   BL/TL, 6'1", 220 lbs.   Deb: 9/20/83

1983 LA-N	0	1	.000	2	1	0	0	0	6	7	0	7	9	22.5	6.00	60	.280	.455	1	1.000	0	-2	-2	0	-0.2
1984 NY-N	6	6	.500	15	15	0	0	0	90	74	8	34	62	10.8	3.50	101	.226	.299	5	.179	-0	1	0	-2	-0.2
1985 NY-N	9	9	.500	26	26	3	0	0	170¹	108	14	80	180	10.0	2.80	123	**.181**	.280	11	.212	2	15	12	-0	1.4
1986 *NY-N★	16	6	.727	32	31	2	1	1	204¹	161	13	91	200	11.2	3.52	100	.216	.303	11	.162	1	4	0	-3	-0.1
1987 NY-N★	12	8	.600	28	27	3	1	0	156	130	16	67	134	11.8	3.81	99	.224	.313	7	.163	1	5	-1	-3	-0.2
1988 *NY-N	12	10	.545	31	31	1	1	0	187	127	15	70	189	9.8	3.03	106	**.191**	.274	14	.250	6	9	4	-3	0.7
1989 NY-N	14	5	.737	35	32	6	2	0	219¹	157	21	75	198	9.8	2.83	115	.198	.272	15	.211	4	16	11	-4	1.0
1990 NY-N	9	14	.391	30	30	2	1	0	179¹	130	18	67	181	10.1	3.46	108	**.200**	.280	11	.190	1	7	6	-2	0.5
1991 NY-N	1	3	.250	8	8	0	0	0	44	36	4	9	31	9.2	2.86	127	.222	.263	2	.154	0	4	4	1	0.4
1992 NY-N	14	11	.560	32	32	5	2	0	214²	162	12	67	193	9.8	2.73	127	.210	.277	15	.203	2	19	18	-2	2.1
1993 NY-N	5	6	.455	18	18	1	1	0	119²	82	17	36	81	9.1	2.93	137	.192	.260	3	.094	-1	15	14	-2	0.9
1994 Bal-A	6	6	.500	19	19	2	0	0	115¹	109	27	46	95	12.3	5.15	99	.248	.322	0	—	0	-4	-1	0	-0.4
Total 12	104	85	.550	276	270	25	9	1	1706	1283	165	649	1553	10.4	3.29	110	.208	.287	95	.192	17	88	65	-19	5.9

● **DON FERRARESE**   Ferrarese, Donald Hugh   b: 6/19/29, Oakland, Cal.   BR/TL, 5'9", 170 lbs.   Deb: 4/11/55

1955 Bal-A	0	0	—	6	0	0	0	0	9	8	0	11	5	19.0	3.00	127	.276	.475	0	.000	-0	1	1	-0	0.0
1956 Bal-A	4	10	.286	36	14	3	1	2	102	86	8	64	81	13.5	5.03	78	.229	.345	1	.036	-3	-10	-13	1	-1.8
1957 Bal-A	1	1	.500	8	2	0	0	0	19	14	1	12	13	12.3	4.74	76	.200	.317	0	.000	-0	-2	-2	0	-0.3
1958 Cle-A	3	4	.429	28	10	2	0	1	94²	91	6	46	62	13.1	3.71	98	.254	.341	3	.115	-1	1	-1	-1	-0.3
1959 Cle-A	5	3	.625	15	10	4	0	0	76	58	6	51	45	13.0	3.20	115	.219	.347	7	.259	2	6	4	0	0.6
1960 Chi-A	0	1	.000	5	0	0	0	0	4	8	2	9	4	38.3	18.00	21	.400	.586	1	.500	0	-6	-6	-0	-1.2
1961 Phi-N	5	12	.294	42	14	3	1	1	138²	120	14	68	89	12.3	3.76	108	.234	.325	6	.171	-1	4	5	-3	0.2
1962 Phi-N	0	1	.000	5	0	0	0	0	6²	9	1	3	6	16.2	8.10	48	.310	.375	1	.000	-0	-3	-3	0	-0.3
StL-N	1	4	.200	38	0	0	0	1	56²	55	2	31	45	13.8	2.70	158	.270	.369	1	.200	1	8	10	1	1.0
Yr	1	5	.167	43	0	0	0	1	63¹	64	3	34	51	14.1	3.27	129	.274	.368	2	.333	1	5	7	1	0.7
Total 8	19	36	.345	183	50	12	2	5	506²	449	39	295	350	13.3	4.00	98	.241	.347	20	.156	-2	-2	-5	-1	-2.1

● **BILL FERRAZZI**   Ferrazzi, William Joseph   b: 4/19/07, W.Quincy, Mass.   BR/TR, 6'2.5", 200 lbs.   Deb: 9/7/35

| 1935 Phi-A | 1 | 2 | .333 | 3 | 2 | 0 | 0 | 0 | 7 | 7 | 0 | 5 | 0 | 15.4 | 5.14 | 98 | .269 | .387 | 0 | — | 0 | -1 | -0 | 0 | -0.1 |

● **TONY FERREIRA**   Ferreira, Anthony Ross   b: 10/4/62, Riverside, Cal.   BL/TL, 6'1", 160 lbs.   Deb: 9/17/85

| 1985 KC-A | 0 | 0 | — | 2 | 0 | 0 | 0 | 0 | 5² | 6 | 0 | 2 | 5 | 12.7 | 7.94 | 52 | .273 | .333 | 0 | — | 0 | -2 | -2 | 0 | 0.0 |

● **WES FERRELL**   Ferrell, Wesley Cheek   b: 2/2/08, Greensboro, N.C.   d: 12/9/76, Sarasota, Fla.   BR/TR, 6'2", 195 lbs.   Deb: 9/9/27   F♦

1927 Cle-A	0	0	—	1	0	0	0	0	1	3	0	2	0	45.0	27.00	16	.600	.714	0	—	0	-3	-3	-0	0.0
1928 Cle-A	0	2	.000	2	2	1	0	0	16	15	0	5	4	11.3	2.25	184	.242	.299	1	.250	1	3	3	0	0.5
1929 Cle-A	21	10	.677	43	25	18	1	5	242²	256	7	109	100	13.6	3.60	124	.279	.358	22	.237	4	17	23	3	3.4
1930 Cle-A	25	13	.658	43	35	25	1	3	296²	299	14	106	143	12.3	3.31	146	.262	.325	35	.297	8	44	50	-3	6.2
1931 Cle-A	22	12	.647	40	35	**27**	2	3	276¹	276	9	130	123	13.3	3.75	123	.255	.336	37	.319	17	19	27	5	5.2
1932 Cle-A	23	13	.639	38	34	26	3	1	287²	299	17	104	105	12.6	3.66	130	.264	.326	31	.242	5	26	35	1	4.3
1933 Cle-A☆	11	12	.478	28	26	16	1	0	201	225	8	70	41	13.3	4.21	106	.282	.341	38	.271	7	2	5	1	1.6
1934 Bos-A	14	5	.737	26	23	17	3	1	181	205	4	49	67	12.6	3.63	132	.282	.327	22	.282	8	17	24	-2	2.8
1935 Bos-A	**25**	14	.641	41	38	**31**	3	0	**322¹**	336	16	108	110	12.5	3.52	135	.267	.326	52	.347	20	34	44	2	**7.2**
1936 Bos-A	20	15	.571	39	38	28	3	0	301	330	11	119	106	13.6	4.19	127	.274	.343	36	.267	11	28	38	-3	4.5
1937 Bos-A	3	6	.333	12	11	5	0	0	73¹	111	14	34	31	17.9	7.61	62	.348	.412	12	.364	6	-24	-23	2	-1.5
Was-A☆	11	13	.458	25	24	21	0	0	207²	214	11	88	92	13.2	3.94	112	.265	.339	27	.255	5	16	11	-1	1.5
Yr	14	19	.424	37	35	**26**	0	0	**281**	325	25	122	123	14.4	4.90	92	.288	.359	39	.281	11	-9	-12	1	0.0
1938 Was-A	13	8	.619	23	22	9	0	0	149	193	12	68	36	15.8	5.92	76	.311	.380	11	.224	7	-19	-23	1	-1.9
NY-A	2	2	.500	5	4	1	0	0	30	52	6	17	8	21.0	8.10	56	.388	.461	2	.167	-0	-11	-12	1	-1.1
Yr	15	10	.600	28	26	10	0	0	179	245	18	86	43	16.6	6.28	72	.324	.393	13	.213	7	-30	-35	2	-3.0
1939 NY-A	1	2	.333	3	3	1	0	0	19¹	14	2	17	6	14.4	4.66	94	.219	.383	1	.125	-0	-0	-1	0	-0.1
1940 Bro-N	0	0	—	1	0	0	0	0	4	4	0	4	4	20.3	6.75	59	.250	.429	0	.000	-0	-1	-1	0	-0.3
1941 Bos-N	2	1	.667	4	3	1	0	0	14	13	1	9	10	14.8	5.14	69	.241	.359	2	.500	2	-2	-4	-0	-0.3
Total 15	193	128	.601	374	323	227	17	13	2623	2845	132	1040	985	13.4	4.04	117	.275	.343	329	.280	100	147	195	6	32.3

● **TOM FERRICK**   Ferrick, Thomas Jerome   b: 1/6/15, New York, N.Y.   BR/TR, 6'2.5", 220 lbs.   Deb: 4/19/41   C

1941 Phi-A	8	10	.444	36	4	2	1	7	119¹	130	8	33	30	12.3	3.77	111	.275	.322	9	.205	1	5	6	3	1.2
1942 Cle-A	3	2	.600	31	2	2	0	3	81¹	76	3	32	28	9.7	1.99	173	.200	.282	4	.211	0	**15**	**13**	2	1.1
1946 Cle-A	0	0	—	9	0	0	0	1	18	25	3	4	9	14.5	5.00	66	.321	.354	2	.667	1	-3	-3	0	0.1
StL-A	4	1	.800	25	1	0	0	5	32¹	26	1	6	13	8.6	2.78	134	.224	.256	0	.000	-1	3	3	0	0.6
Yr	4	1	.800	34	1	0	0	6	50¹	51	4	9	22	10.7	3.58	100	.263	.296	2	.286	-1	-0	0	0	0.7
1947 Was-A	1	7	.125	31	0	0	0	9	60	57	1	20	23	11.6	3.15	118	.256	.317	1	.100	-1	4	4	2	0.2
1948 Was-A	2	5	.286	37	0	0	0	10	73²	75	3	38	34	13.8	4.15	105	.261	.348	1	.067	-1	1	2	1	0.2
1949 StL-A	6	4	.600	50	0	0	0	6	104¹	102	9	41	34	12.4	3.88	117	.258	.329	3	.143	-1	4	7	2	0.8
1950 StL-A	1	3	.250	16	0	0	0	2	24	24	2	7	6	11.6	4.13	120	.250	.324	1	.250	-1	1	1	0	0.4
*NY-A	8	4	.667	30	0	0	0	9	56²	49	5	22	20	11.3	3.65	118	.233	.306	2	.143	-0	6	4	1	1.0
Yr	9	7	.563	46	0	0	0	11	80²	73	7	29	26	11.4	3.79	118	.243	.310	3	.167	-0	7	6	1	1.4
1951 NY-A	1	1	.500	9	0	0	0	1	12	21	4	7	3	21.0	7.50	51	.389	.459	1	1.000	1	-5	-5	-0	-0.7
Was-A	2	0	1.000	22	0	0	0	2	41²	36	3	7	17	9.3	2.38	172	.234	.267	2	.286	0	8	8	0	0.5
Yr	3	1	.750	31	0	0	0	3	53²	57	7	14	20	11.9	3.52	115	.274	.320	3	.375	1	4	3	0	-0.2
1952 Was-A	4	3	.571	27	0	0	0	2	50²	53	7	11	28	11.4	3.02	118	.273	.312	1	.200	1	4	3	1	0.6
Total 9	40	40	.500	323	7	4	1	56	674	654	44	227	245	11.8	3.47	117	.256	.317	27	.184	-4	42	44	11	6.5

● **BOB FERRIS**   Ferris, Robert Eugene   b: 5/7/55, Arlington, Va.   BR/TR, 6'6", 225 lbs.   Deb: 9/12/79

1979 Cal-A	0	0	—	2	0	0	0	0	6	5	1	3	2	12.0	1.50	271	.217	.308	0	—	0	2	2	0	0.3
1980 Cal-A	0	2	.000	5	3	0	0	0	15¹	23	2	9	4	18.8	5.87	67	.354	.432	0	—	0	-3	-3	0	-0.4
Total 2	0	2	.000	7	3	0	0	0	21¹	28	3	12	6	16.9	4.64	86	.318	.400	0	—	0	-1	-2	0	-0.1

● **DAVE FERRISS**   Ferriss, David Meadow "Boo"   b: 12/5/21, Shaw, Miss.   BL/TR, 6'2", 208 lbs.   Deb: 4/29/45   C

1945 Bos-A†	21	10	.677	35	31	26	5	2	264²	263	6	85	94	12.1	2.96	115	.264	.327	32	.267	11	12	13	5	3.3
1946 *Bos-A☆	25	6	**.806**	40	35	26	6	3	274	274	14	71	106	11.4	3.25	113	.259	.308	24	.209	2	8	13	0	1.7
1947 Bos-A	12	11	.522	33	28	14	1	0	218¹	241	14	92	64	14.0	4.04	96	.287	.362	27	.273	7	-8	-4	-1	-0.7
1948 Bos-A	7	3	.700	31	9	1	0	3	115¹	127	7	61	30	15.2	5.23	84	.286	.381	9	.243	2	-12	-11	1	-0.7
1949 Bos-A	0	0	—	4	0	0	0	0	6²	7	1	4	1	16.2	4.05	108	.292	.414	1	1.000	1	0	0	-0	0.0

YEAR	TM/L	W	L	PCT	G	GS	CG	SH	SV	IP	H	HR	BB	SO	RAT	ERA	ERA+	OAV	OOB	BH	AVG	PB	PR	/A	PD	TPI
1950	Bos-A	0	0	—	1	0	0	0	0	1	2	0	1	1	27.0	18.00	27	.500	.600	0	—	0	-1	-1	0	0.0
Total	6	65	30	.684	144	103	67	12	8	880	914	42	314	296	12.8	3.64	103	.272	.338	93	.250	23	-2	10	5	4.6

● CY FERRY
Ferry, Alfred Joseph   b: 9/27/1878, Hudson, N.Y.   d: 9/27/38, Pittsfield, Mass.   BR/TR, 6'1", 170 lbs.   Deb: 5/12/04   F

YEAR	TM/L	W	L	PCT	G	GS	CG	SH	SV	IP	H	HR	BB	SO	RAT	ERA	ERA+	OAV	OOB	BH	AVG	PB	PR	/A	PD	TPI
1904	Det-A	0	1	.000	3	1	0	0	0	13	12	0	11	4	16.6	6.23	41	.246	.395	2	.333	1	-5	-5	0	-0.3
1905	Cle-A	0	0	—	1	1	0	0	0	2	3	1	0	0	22.5	13.50	20	.347	.470	0	.000	-0	-2	-2	0	0.0
Total	2	0	1	.000	4	2	1	0	0	15	15	1	11	6	17.4	7.20	36	.261	.406	2	.286	1	-8	-8	0	-0.3

● JACK FERRY
Ferry, John Francis   b: 4/7/1887, Pittsfield, Mass.   d: 8/29/54, Pittsfield, Mass.   BR/TR, 5'11", 175 lbs.   Deb: 9/4/10   F

YEAR	TM/L	W	L	PCT	G	GS	CG	SH	SV	IP	H	HR	BB	SO	RAT	ERA	ERA+	OAV	OOB	BH	AVG	PB	PR	/A	PD	TPI
1910	Pit-N	1	2	.333	6	3	2	0	0	31	26	0	8	12	10.2	2.32	133	.230	.287	3	.333	1	2	3	0	0.4
1911	Pit-N	6	4	.600	26	8	4	1	3	85²	83	3	27	32	11.8	3.15	109	.260	.322	9	.310	3	2	3	-2	0.4
1912	Pit-N	2	0	1.000	11	3	1	1	1	39	33	1	23	10	13.2	3.00	109	.234	.345	1	.077	-1	2	1	1	0.0
1913	Pit-N	1	0	1.000	4	0	0	0	0	5	4	0	2	2	10.8	5.40	56	.286	.375	0	—	0	-1	-1	0	-0.2
Total	4	10	6	.625	47	14	7	2	4	160²	146	4	60	56	11.8	3.02	110	.249	.323	13	.255	3	5	5	-1	0.6

● ALEX FERSON
Ferson, Alexander "Colonel"   b: 7/14/1866, Philadelphia, Pa.   d: 12/5/57, Boston, Mass.   BR/TR, 5'9", 165 lbs.   Deb: 5/4/1889

YEAR	TM/L	W	L	PCT	G	GS	CG	SH	SV	IP	H	HR	BB	SO	RAT	ERA	ERA+	OAV	OOB	BH	AVG	PB	PR	/A	PD	TPI
1889	Was-N	17	17	.500	36	34	28	1	0	288¹	319	9	105	85	13.6	3.90	101	.272	.338	13	.114	-5	4	1	-2	-0.5
1890	Buf-P	1	7	.125	10	10	7	0	0	71	88	5	40	13	16.4	5.45	75	.291	.376	7	.219	1	-10	-11	0	-0.7
1892	Bal-N	0	1	.000	2	1	1	0	0	9	17	1	6	8	23.0	11.00	31	.386	.460	0	.000	-1	-8	-8	-0	-0.7
Total	3	18	25	.419	48	45	36	1	0	368³	424	15	151	106	14.4	4.37	91	.279	.349	20	.133	-5	-14	-17	-3	-1.9

● LOU FETTE
Fette, Louis Henry William   b: 3/15/07, Alma, Mo.   d: 1/3/81, Warrensburg, Mo.   BR/TR, 6'1.5", 200 lbs.   Deb: 4/26/37

YEAR	TM/L	W	L	PCT	G	GS	CG	SH	SV	IP	H	HR	BB	SO	RAT	ERA	ERA+	OAV	OOB	BH	AVG	PB	PR	/A	PD	TPI
1937	Bos-N	20	10	.667	35	33	23	**5**	0	259	243	5	81	70	11.4	2.88	124	.251	.311	22	.239	3	30	20	0	2.5
1938	Bos-N	11	13	.458	33	32	17	3	1	239²	235	11	79	83	11.9	3.15	109	.258	.320	16	.188	0	17	7	2	0.9
1939	Bos-N★	10	10	.500	27	26	11	**6**	0	146	123	7	61	35	11.4	2.96	125	.229	.309	3	.061	-4	16	12	3	1.3
1940	Bos-N	0	5	.000	7	5	0	0	0	32¹	38	0	18	2	15.9	5.57	67	.302	.393	3	.375	1	-6	-7	-1	-0.8
	Bro-N	0	0	—	2	0	0	0	0	3	3	0	2	0	15.0	0.00	—	.300	.417	0	—	0	1	1	0	0.0
	Yr	0	5	.000	9	5	0	0	0	35¹	41	0	20	2	15.5	5.09	73	.299	.389	3	.375	1	-5	-5	-1	-0.8
1945	Bos-N	0	2	.000	5	1	0	0	0	11	16	1	7	4	19.6	5.73	67	.356	.453	0	.000	-0	-2	-2	0	-0.4
Total	5	41	40	.506	109	97	51	14	1	691	658	24	248	194	11.9	3.15	113	.253	.321	44	.186	-0	55	32	4	3.5

● MIKE FETTERS
Fetters, Michael Lee   b: 12/19/64, Van Nuys, Cal.   BR/TR, 6'4", 200 lbs.   Deb: 9/1/89

YEAR	TM/L	W	L	PCT	G	GS	CG	SH	SV	IP	H	HR	BB	SO	RAT	ERA	ERA+	OAV	OOB	BH	AVG	PB	PR	/A	PD	TPI
1989	Cal-A	0	0	—	1	0	0	0	0	3¹	5	1	4	4	16.2	8.10	47	.333	.375	0	—	0	-2	-2	0	0.2
1990	Cal-A	1	1	.500	26	2	0	0	1	67²	77	9	20	35	13.2	4.12	93	.287	.341	0	—	0	-2	-4	1	0.2
1991	Cal-A	2	5	.286	19	4	0	0	0	44²	53	4	28	24	16.9	4.84	85	.305	.410	0	—	0	-4	-4	-1	-0.6
1992	Mil-A	5	1	.833	50	0	0	0	2	62²	38	3	24	43	9.9	1.87	205	.185	.292	0	—	0	14	14	1	1.5
1993	Mil-A	3	3	.500	45	0	0	0	0	59¹	59	4	22	23	12.6	3.34	127	.278	.352	0	—	0	6	6	0	0.6
1994	Mil-A	1	4	.200	42	0	0	0	17	46	41	0	27	31	13.5	2.54	193	.243	.350	0	—	0	12	12	0	2.0
Total	6	12	14	.462	183	6	0	0	20	283²	273	21	122	160	13.0	3.36	123	.262	.347	0	—	0	26	24	1	3.9

● JOHN FICK
Fick, John Ralph   b: 5/18/21, Baltimore, Md.   d: 6/9/58, Somers Point, N.J.   BL/TL, 5'10", 150 lbs.   Deb: 7/29/44

YEAR	TM/L	W	L	PCT	G	GS	CG	SH	SV	IP	H	HR	BB	SO	RAT	ERA	ERA+	OAV	OOB	BH	AVG	PB	PR	/A	PD	TPI
1944	Phi-N	0	0	—	4	0	0	0	0	5¹	3	0	3	2	11.8	3.38	107	.150	.292	0	—	0	0	0	-0	0.0

● MARK FIDRYCH
Fidrych, Mark Steven "The Bird"   b: 8/14/54, Worcester, Mass.   BR/TR, 6'3", 175 lbs.   Deb: 4/20/76

YEAR	TM/L	W	L	PCT	G	GS	CG	SH	SV	IP	H	HR	BB	SO	RAT	ERA	ERA+	OAV	OOB	BH	AVG	PB	PR	/A	PD	TPI
1976	Det-A★	19	9	.679	31	29	**24**	4	0	250¹	217	12	53	97	9.8	**2.34**	159	.235	.279	0	—	0	33	**38**	5	**5.0**
1977	Det-A†	6	4	.600	11	11	7	1	0	81	82	2	12	42	10.6	2.89	148	.269	.299	0	—	0	11	13	-1	1.0
1978	Det-A	2	0	1.000	3	3	2	0	0	22	17	1	5	10	9.0	2.45	157	.213	.259	0	—	0	3	3	1	0.3
1979	Det-A	0	3	.000	4	4	0	0	0	14²	24	2	9	5	20.3	10.43	41	.371	.458	0	—	0	-10	-10	-0	-1.6
1980	Det-A	2	3	.400	9	9	1	0	0	44¹	58	5	20	16	16.0	5.68	72	.309	.378	0	—	0	-8	-8	1	-0.7
Total	5	29	19	.604	58	56	34	5	0	412¹	397	23	99	170	11.0	3.10	126	.255	.302	0	—	0	28	37	5	4.0

● CLARENCE FIEBER
Fieber, Clarence Thomas "Lefty"   b: 9/4/13, San Francisco, Cal   d: 8/20/85, Redwood City, Cal   BL/TL, 6'4", 187 lbs.   Deb: 5/18/32

YEAR	TM/L	W	L	PCT	G	GS	CG	SH	SV	IP	H	HR	BB	SO	RAT	ERA	ERA+	OAV	OOB	BH	AVG	PB	PR	/A	PD	TPI
1932	Chi-A	1	0	1.000	3	0	0	0	0	5¹	6	0	3	1	15.2	1.69	256	.273	.360	2	.222	0	2	2	0	0.3

● JIM FIELD
Field, James C.   b: 4/24/1863, Philadelphia, Pa.   d: 5/13/53, Atlantic City, N.J   6'1", 170 lbs.   Deb: 6/2/1883   ♦

YEAR	TM/L	W	L	PCT	G	GS	CG	SH	SV	IP	H	HR	BB	SO	RAT	ERA	ERA+	OAV	OOB	BH	AVG	PB	PR	/A	PD	TPI
1890	Roc-a	1	0	1.000	2	1	1	0	1	9²	7	0	4	2	11.2	2.79	128	.196	.295	38	.202	1	1	1	-0	0.1

● JOCKO FIELDS
Fields, John Joseph   b: 10/20/1864, Cork, Ireland   d: 10/14/50, Jersey City, N.J.   BR/TR, 5'10", 160 lbs.   Deb: 5/31/1887   ♦

YEAR	TM/L	W	L	PCT	G	GS	CG	SH	SV	IP	H	HR	BB	SO	RAT	ERA	ERA+	OAV	OOB	BH	AVG	PB	PR	/A	PD	TPI
1887	Pit-N	0	0	—	1	0	0	0	0	1	0	0	2	0	18.0	0.00	—	.000	.286	44	.268	0	0	0	-0	0.0

● LOU FIENE
Fiene, Louis Henry "Big Finn"   b: 12/29/1884, Ft.Dodge, Iowa   d: 12/22/64, Chicago, Ill.   BR/TR, 6', 175 lbs.   Deb: 5/7/06

YEAR	TM/L	W	L	PCT	G	GS	CG	SH	SV	IP	H	HR	BB	SO	RAT	ERA	ERA+	OAV	OOB	BH	AVG	PB	PR	/A	PD	TPI
1906	Chi-A	1	1	.500	6	2	1	0	0	31	35	0	9	12	13.9	2.90	87	.288	.356	2	.200	0	-1	-1	0	-0.1
1907	Chi-A	0	1	.000	6	1	1	0	1	26	30	0	7	15	13.5	4.15	58	.291	.348	2	.182	0	-5	-5	0	-0.3
1908	Chi-A	0	1	.000	1	1	1	0	0	9	9	0	1	3	10.0	4.00	58	.257	.278	0	.000	-0	-2	-2	0	-0.2
1909	Chi-A	2	5	.286	13	6	4	0	0	72	75	1	18	24	12.3	4.13	57	.284	.341	2	.069	-2	-13	-14	1	-1.4
Total	4	3	8	.273	26	10	7	0	1	138	149	1	35	54	12.7	3.85	62	.284	.342	6	.113	-2	-20	-22	2	-2.0

● DANNY FIFE
Fife, Danny Wayne   b: 10/5/49, Harrisburg, Ill.   BR/TR, 6'3", 175 lbs.   Deb: 8/18/73

YEAR	TM/L	W	L	PCT	G	GS	CG	SH	SV	IP	H	HR	BB	SO	RAT	ERA	ERA+	OAV	OOB	BH	AVG	PB	PR	/A	PD	TPI
1973	Min-A	3	2	.600	10	7	1	0	0	51²	54	2	29	18	15.0	4.35	91	.270	.371	0	—	0	-3	-2	-0	-0.2
1974	Min-A	0	0	—	4	0	0	0	0	4²	10	1	4	3	28.9	17.36	22	.417	.517	0	—	0	-7	-7	-0	-0.0
Total	2	3	2	.600	14	7	1	0	0	56¹	64	3	33	21	16.1	5.43	73	.286	.387	0	—	0	-10	-9	-0	-0.2

● JACK FIFIELD
Fifield, John Proctor   b: 10/5/1871, Enfield, N.H.   d: 11/27/39, Syracuse, N.Y.   BR/TR, 5'11", 160 lbs.   Deb: 4/28/1897

YEAR	TM/L	W	L	PCT	G	GS	CG	SH	SV	IP	H	HR	BB	SO	RAT	ERA	ERA+	OAV	OOB	BH	AVG	PB	PR	/A	PD	TPI
1897	Phi-N	5	18	.217	27	26	21	0	0	210²	263	8	80	38	15.0	5.51	76	.303	.368	18	.234	3	-28	-31	1	-2.2
1898	Phi-N	11	9	.550	21	21	18	2	0	171¹	170	2	60	31	13.0	3.31	104	.257	.335	7	.109	-4	6	2	-3	-0.4
1899	Phi-N	3	8	.273	14	11	9	1	1	92²	110	0	36	8	14.6	4.08	90	.294	.363	9	.257	1	-2	-4	1	-0.3
	Was-N	2	4	.333	6	6	6	0	0	47	73	1	17	12	17.6	6.13	64	.353	.408	4	.200	-0	-12	-12	-1	-1.2
	Yr	5	12	.294	20	17	15	1	1	139²	183	1	53	20	15.3	4.77	79	.313	.372	13	.236	1	-14	-16	-0	-1.5
Total	3	21	39	.350	68	64	54	3	1	521²	616	11	193	89	14.5	4.59	83	.292	.361	38	.194	-0	-36	-44	-2	-4.1

● FRANK FIGGEMEIER
Figgemeier, Frank Y.   b: 4/22/1874, St.Louis, Mo.   d: 4/15/15, St.Louis, Mo.   Deb: 9/25/1894

YEAR	TM/L	W	L	PCT	G	GS	CG	SH	SV	IP	H	HR	BB	SO	RAT	ERA	ERA+	OAV	OOB	BH	AVG	PB	PR	/A	PD	TPI
1894	Phi-N	0	1	.000	1	1	1	0	0	8	12	1	4	2	21.4	11.25	45	.342	.452	1	.333	0	-5	-5	0	-0.4

● ED FIGUEROA
Figueroa, Eduardo (Padilla)   b: 10/14/48, Ciales, P.R.   BR/TR, 6'1", 190 lbs.   Deb: 4/9/74

YEAR	TM/L	W	L	PCT	G	GS	CG	SH	SV	IP	H	HR	BB	SO	RAT	ERA	ERA+	OAV	OOB	BH	AVG	PB	PR	/A	PD	TPI
1974	Cal-A	2	8	.200	25	12	5	1	0	105¹	119	3	36	49	13.6	3.67	94	.294	.357	0	—	0	-1	-3	0	-0.2
1975	Cal-A	16	13	.552	33	32	16	2	0	244²	213	14	84	139	11.1	2.91	122	.233	.301	0	—	0	24	17	1	2.1
1976	*NY-A	19	10	.655	34	34	14	4	0	256²	237	13	94	119	11.7	3.02	113	.246	.315	0	—	0	14	11	-3	0.9
1977	*NY-A	16	11	.593	32	32	12	2	0	239¹	228	19	75	104	11.5	3.57	110	.252	.312	0	—	0	13	10	-2	0.9
1978	*NY-A	20	9	.690	35	35	12	2	0	253	233	22	77	92	11.1	2.99	121	.248	.301	0	—	0	22	18	-0	2.0
1979	NY-A	4	6	.400	16	16	4	0	0	104²	109	6	35	42	12.4	4.13	99	.275	.333	0	—	0	1	-1	0	0.1
1980	NY-A	3	3	.500	15	9	0	0	0	58	90	3	24	16	17.8	6.98	56	.363	.421	0	—	0	-19	-20	-1	-1.7
	Tex-A	0	7	.000	8	8	0	0	0	39²	62	3	12	9	16.8	5.90	66	.365	.407	0	—	0	-8	-9	1	-1.2
	Yr	3	10	.231	23	17	0	0	0	97²	152	6	36	25	17.3	6.54	60	.363	.410	0	—	0	-27	-29	1	-2.9
1981	Oak-A	0	0	—	2	1	0	0	0	8¹	8	1	6	1	15.1	5.40	64	.258	.378	0	—	0	-2	-2	0	-0.2
Total	8	80	67	.544	200	179	63	12	1	1309²	1299	90	443	571	12.1	3.51	104	.261	.324	0	—	0	44	23	-4	2.9

YEAR TM/L	W	L	PCT	G	GS	CG	SH	SV	IP	H	HR	BB	SO	RAT	ERA	ERA+	OAV	OOB	BH	AVG	PB	PR	/A	PD	TPI

● TOM FILER   Filer, Thomas Carson b: 12/1/56, Philadelphia, Pa.   BR/TR, 6'1", 198 lbs.   Deb: 6/8/82

1982 Chi-N	1	2	.333	8	8	0	0	0	40²	50	5	18	15	15.0	5.53	67	.301	.370	1	.083	-0	-9	-8	2	-0.4
1985 Tor-A	7	0	1.000	11	9	0	0	0	48²	38	6	18	24	10.4	3.88	108	.222	.296	0	—	0	1	2	-1	0.1
1988 Mil-A	5	8	.385	19	16	2	1	0	101²	108	8	33	39	12.6	4.43	90	.281	.339	0	—	0	-5	-5	3	-0.3
1989 Mil-A	7	3	.700	13	13	0	0	0	72¹	74	6	23	20	12.6	3.61	106	.271	.337	0	—	0	2	2	1	0.3
1990 Mil-A	2	3	.400	7	4	0	0	0	22	26	2	9	8	14.3	6.14	63	.289	.354	0	—	0	-5	-6	-1	-1.0
1992 NY-N	0	1	.000	9	1	0	0	0	22	18	2	6	9	9.8	2.05	170	.222	.276	0	.000	-0	4	3	0	0.1
Total 6	22	17	.564	67	51	2	1	0	307¹	314	29	107	115	12.5	4.25	92	.269	.333	1	.067	-1	-12	-12	5	-1.2

● EDDIE FILES   Files, Charles Edward b: 5/19/1883, Portland, Me.   d: 5/10/54, Cornish, Maine   BR/TR,   Deb: 10/3/08

| 1908 Phi-A | 0 | 0 | — | 2 | 0 | 0 | 0 | 0 | 9 | 8 | 0 | 3 | 6 | 13.0 | 6.00 | 43 | .286 | .394 | 0 | .000 | -0 | -4 | -3 | -0 | -0.1 |

● MARC FILLEY   Filley, Marcus Lucius b: 2/28/12, Troy, N.Y.   BR/TR, 5'11", 172 lbs.   Deb: 4/19/34

| 1934 Was-A | 0 | 0 | — | 1 | 0 | 0 | 0 | 0 | 0¹ | 2 | 0 | 0 | 0 | 54.0 | 27.00 | 16 | .667 | .667 | 0 | — | 0 | -1 | -1 | 0 | 0.0 |

● DANA FILLINGIM   Fillingim, Dana b: 11/6/1893, Columbus, Ga.   d: 2/3/61, Tuskegee, Ala.   BL/TR, 5'10", 175 lbs.   Deb: 8/2/15

1915 Phi-A	0	5	.000	8	4	1	0	0	39¹	42	0	32	17	17.2	3.43	85	.313	.449	2	.167	-0	-2	-2	-0	-0.3
1918 Bos-N	7	6	.538	14	13	10	4	0	113	99	0	28	29	10.5	2.23	120	.243	.300	9	.214	0	7	6	-0	0.7
1919 Bos-N	6	13	.316	32	18	9	0	2	186¹	185	2	39	50	10.9	3.38	85	.270	.312	16	.246	1	-10	-11	2	-0.7
1920 Bos-N	12	21	.364	37	31	22	2	0	272	292	6	66	66	12.4	3.11	98	.287	.340	16	.174	-2	1	-2	5	0.2
1921 Bos-N	15	10	.600	44	22	11	3	1	239²	249	10	56	54	11.5	3.45	106	.272	.316	21	.247	5	9	5	-1	0.8
1922 Bos-N	5	9	.357	25	12	5	1	2	117	143	6	37	25	13.9	4.54	88	.311	.363	6	.158	-2	-6	-7	-1	-0.9
1923 Bos-N	1	9	.100	35	12	1	0	0	100¹	141	6	36	27	16.0	5.20	77	.345	.399	7	.226	1	-13	-14	-0	-1.1
1925 Phi-N	1	0	1.000	5	1	0	0	0	8	19	0	6	2	26.0	10.38	46	.432	.500	0	.000	0	-6	-5	-0	-0.5
Total 8	47	73	.392	200	113	59	10	5	1076¹	1170	32	313	270	12.5	3.56	93	.287	.340	77	.209	4	-21	-30	5	-1.8

● PETE FILSON   Filson, William Peter b: 9/28/58, Darby, Pa.   BB/TL, 6'2", 195 lbs.   Deb: 5/15/82

1982 Min-A	0	2	.000	5	3	0	0	0	12¹	17	2	8	10	18.2	8.76	48	.321	.410	0	—	0	-6	-6	-0	-0.9
1983 Min-A	4	1	.800	26	8	0	0	1	90	87	9	29	49	11.7	3.40	125	.252	.312	0	—	0	7	8	-2	0.3
1984 Min-A	6	5	.545	55	7	0	0	1	118²	106	14	54	59	12.4	4.10	103	.238	.325	0	—	0	-1	1	-1	-0.1
1985 Min-A	4	5	.444	40	6	1	0	2	95²	93	13	30	42	11.6	3.67	120	.251	.307	0	—	0	5	8	-1	0.6
1986 Min-A	0	0	—	4	0	0	0	0	6¹	13	1	2	4	22.7	5.68	76	.406	.457	0	—	0	-1	-0	-0	-0.2
Chi-A	0	1	.000	3	1	0	0	0	11²	14	5	4	5	14.7	6.17	70	.286	.352	0	—	0	-3	-2	-0	-0.2
Yr	0	1	.000	7	1	0	0	0	18	27	5	7	8	17.0	6.00	72	.329	.382	0	—	0	-4	-3	-1	-0.2
1987 NY-A	1	0	1.000	7	2	0	0	0	22	26	2	9	10	14.7	3.27	134	.299	.371	0	—	0	3	3	1	0.2
1990 KC-A	0	4	.000	8	7	0	0	0	35	42	6	13	9	14.7	5.91	65	.282	.348	0	—	0	-8	-8	-1	-0.7
Total 7	15	18	.455	148	34	1	0	4	391²	398	51	150	187	12.8	4.18	102	.260	.329	0	—	0	-5	3	-4	-0.8

● JOEL FINCH   Finch, Joel D b: 8/20/56, South Bend, Ind.   BR/TR, 6'2", 175 lbs.   Deb: 6/12/79

| 1979 Bos-A | 0 | 3 | .000 | 15 | 7 | 0 | 0 | 0 | 57¹ | 65 | 5 | 25 | 25 | 14.3 | 4.87 | 91 | .289 | .363 | 0 | .000 | 0 | -4 | -3 | 1 | -0.1 |

● BILL FINCHER   Fincher, William Allen b: 5/26/1894, Atlanta, Ga.   d: 5/7/46, Shreveport, La.   BR/TR, 6'1", 180 lbs.   Deb: 4/23/16

| 1916 StL-A | 0 | 1 | .000 | 12 | 1 | 0 | 0 | 0 | 21 | 22 | 0 | 7 | 5 | 12.4 | 2.14 | 128 | .282 | .341 | 1 | .250 | 0 | 2 | 1 | 1 | 0.2 |

● TOMMY FINE   Fine, Thomas Morgan b: 10/10/14, Cleburne, Tex.   BB/TR, 6', 180 lbs.   Deb: 4/26/47

1947 Bos-A	1	2	.333	9	7	1	0	0	36	41	3	19	10	15.3	5.50	71	.285	.372	3	.333	1	-7	-6	2	-0.2
1950 StL-A	0	1	.000	14	0	0	0	0	36²	53	6	25	6	19.1	8.10	61	.342	.433	4	.333	1	-14	-13	-0	-0.2
Total 2	1	3	.250	23	7	1	0	0	72²	94	6	44	16	17.2	6.81	65	.314	.404	7	.333	2	-22	-19	1	-0.4

● ROLLIE FINGERS   Fingers, Roland Glen b: 8/25/46, Steubenville, Ohio   BR/TR, 6'4", 195 lbs.   Deb: 9/15/68   H

1968 Oak-A	0	0	—	1	0	0	0	0	1¹	4	1	0	0	40.5	27.00	10	.571	.667	0	—	0	-4	-4	-0	0.0
1969 Oak-A	6	7	.462	60	8	1	1	12	119	116	13	41	61	12.2	3.71	93	.257	.325	5	.200	0	-1	-4	2	-0.2
1970 Oak-A	7	9	.438	45	19	1	0	2	148	137	13	48	79	11.4	3.65	97	.250	.312	4	.103	-0	1	-2	1	-0.2
1971 *Oak-A	4	6	.400	48	8	2	1	17	129¹	94	14	30	98	9.2	2.99	111	.207	.268	7	.212	1	7	5	2	0.8
1972 *Oak-A	11	9	.550	65	0	0	0	21	111¹	85	8	32	113	9.5	2.51	113	.212	.272	6	.316	3	7	4	-0	1.2
1973 *Oak-A★	7	8	.467	62	2	0	0	22	126²	107	5	39	110	10.7	1.92	185	.226	.290	0	—	0	27	23	-1	3.4
1974 *Oak-A★	9	5	.643	76	0	0	0	18	119	104	5	29	95	10.1	2.65	125	.240	.289	0	—	0	13	9	2	1.6
1975 *Oak-A☆	10	6	.625	75	0	0	0	24	126²	95	13	33	115	9.5	2.98	122	.213	.276	0	.000	0	11	9	0	1.5
1976 Oak-A☆	13	11	.542	70	0	0	0	20	134²	118	3	40	113	11.0	2.47	136	.243	.310	0	—	0	16	13	2	3.0
1977 SD-N	8	9	.471	78	0	0	0	35	132¹	123	12	36	113	10.9	2.99	118	.248	.300	1	.050	-2	13	8	-0	1.2
1978 SD-N★	6	13	.316	67	0	0	0	37	107¹	84	4	29	72	9.6	2.52	132	.212	.267	2	.083	-1	13	10	0	2.5
1979 SD-N	9	9	.500	54	0	0	0	13	83²	91	7	37	65	13.9	4.52	78	.281	.356	1	.083	-1	-7	-9	-1	-2.3
1980 SD-N	11	9	.550	66	0	0	0	23	103	101	3	32	69	11.6	2.80	123	.263	.320	5	.278	3	9	7	-1	1.9
1981 *Mil-A★	6	3	.667	47	0	0	0	28	78	55	5	13	61	8.0	1.04	330	.198	.236	0	—	0	23	21	0	4.3
1982 Mil-A★	5	6	.455	50	0	0	0	29	79²	63	5	20	71	9.5	2.60	146	.220	.273	0	—	0	13	11	0	1.8
1984 Mil-A	1	2	.333	33	0	0	0	23	46	38	5	13	40	10.0	1.96	197	.213	.267	0	—	0	10	10	-0	1.8
1985 Mil-A	1	6	.143	47	0	0	0	17	55¹	59	7	19	24	12.7	5.04	83	.272	.331	0	—	0	-6	-5	-1	-0.9
Total 17	114	118	.491	944	37	4	2	341	1701¹	1474	123	492	1299	10.6	2.90	119	.235	.295	31	.172	3	145	105	6	21.8

● HERMAN FINK   Fink, Herman Adam b: 8/22/11, Concord, N.C.   d: 8/24/80, Salisbury, N.C.   BR/TR, 6'2", 198 lbs.   Deb: 9/16/35

1935 Phi-A	0	3	.000	5	3	0	0	0	15²	18	0	10	2	16.7	9.19	49	.290	.397	1	.200	-0	-8	-8	0	-1.2
1936 Phi-A	8	16	.333	34	24	9	0	3	188²	222	18	78	53	14.3	5.39	95	.294	.360	8	.125	-4	-7	-6	-2	-1.1
1937 Phi-A	2	1	.667	28	3	1	0	1	80	82	6	35	18	13.3	4.05	116	.263	.339	5	.208	-1	5	6	-0	0.1
Total 3	10	20	.333	67	30	10	0	4	284¹	322	24	123	73	14.1	5.22	95	.285	.356	14	.151	-5	-11	-12	-2	-2.2

● PEMBROKE FINLAYSON   Finlayson, Pembroke b: 7/31/1888, Cheraw, S.C.   d: 3/6/12, Brooklyn, N.Y.   BR/TR,   Deb: 6/6/08

1908 Bro-N	0	0	—	1	0	0	0	0	0¹	1	0	2	0	108.0	135.00	4	.000	.800	0	—	0	-5	-5	-0	-0.1
1909 Bro-N	0	0	—	1	0	0	0	0	7	7	0	4	2	14.1	5.14	50	.212	.297	0	.000	0	-2	-2	-0	-0.1
Total 2	0	0	—	2	0	0	0	0	7¹	7	0	8	2	18.4	11.05	23	.206	.357	0	.000	0	-7	-7	-0	-0.1

● CHUCK FINLEY   Finley, Charles Edward b: 11/26/62, Monroe, La.   BL/TL, 6'6", 220 lbs.   Deb: 5/29/86

1986 *Cal-A	3	1	.750	25	0	0	0	0	46¹	40	2	23	37	12.4	3.30	124	.235	.330	0	—	0	4	4	1	0.4
1987 Cal-A	2	7	.222	35	3	0	0	0	90²	102	7	43	63	14.7	4.67	92	.287	.369	0	—	0	-2	-4	-0	-0.3
1988 Cal-A	9	15	.375	31	31	2	0	0	194²	191	15	82	111	12.9	4.17	93	.263	.343	0	—	0	-4	-7	-1	-0.8
1989 Cal-A☆	16	9	.640	29	29	9	1	0	199²	171	13	82	156	11.5	2.57	148	.233	.312	0	—	0	29	28	-3	3.0
1990 Cal-A★	18	9	.667	32	32	7	2	0	236	210	17	81	177	11.2	2.40	159	.243	.309	0	—	0	39	37	-2	4.1
1991 Cal-A	18	9	.667	34	34	4	2	0	227¹	205	24	101	171	12.4	3.80	108	.244	.331	0	—	0	7	8	-0	0.6
1992 Cal-A	7	12	.368	31	31	4	1	0	204¹	212	24	98	124	13.8	3.96	100	.277	.362	0	—	0	-1	-0	-3	-0.3
1993 Cal-A	16	14	.533	35	35	13	2	0	251²	243	22	82	187	11.9	3.15	143	.253	.316	0	—	0	33	38	-2	3.7
1994 Cal-A	10	10	.500	25	25	7	0	0	183¹	178	21	71	148	12.2	4.32	115	.260	.332	0	—	0	10	14	0	1.1
Total 9	99	86	.535	277	220	46	10	0	1633¹	1552	144	663	1174	12.4	3.50	118	.255	.331	0	—	0	116	117	-13	11.5

● HAPPY FINNERAN   Finneran, Joseph Ignatius "Smokey Joe" b: 10/29/1891, E.Orange, N.J.   d: 2/3/42, Orange, N.J.   BR/TR, 5'10.5", 169 lbs.   Deb: 8/20/12

| 1912 Phi-N | 0 | 2 | .000 | 14 | 4 | 0 | 0 | 1 | 46¹ | 50 | 2 | 10 | 19 | 11.8 | 2.53 | 144 | .282 | .324 | 2 | .200 | 0 | 5 | 6 | -0 | 0.3 |
| 1913 Phi-N | 0 | 0 | — | 3 | 0 | 0 | 0 | 0 | 5 | 12 | 0 | 2 | 0 | 25.2 | 7.20 | 46 | .462 | .500 | 2 | .667 | 1 | -2 | -2 | -0 | 0.1 |

YEAR	TM/L	W	L	PCT	G	GS	CG	SH	SV	IP	H	HR	BB	SO	RAT	ERA	ERA+	OAV	OOB	BH	AVG	PB	PR	/A	PD	TPI
1914	Bro-F	12	11	.522	27	23	13	2	1	175¹	153	6	60	54	11.2	3.18	90	.237	.308	7	.127	-5	-6	-6	-1	-1.3
1915	Bro-F	10	12	.455	37	24	12	1	2	215¹	197	8	87	68	12.2	2.80	97	.249	.331	11	.149	-5	-2	-2	-1	-0.7
1918	Det-A	0	2	.000	5	2	0	0	1	13²	22	2	8	2	19.8	9.88	27	.393	.469	0	.000	-0	-11	-11	1	-1.5
	NY-A	3	6	.333	23	13	4	0	0	114¹	134	7	35	34	13.5	3.78	75	.305	.359	9	.231	1	-13	-12	-1	-0.9
	Yr	3	8	.273	28	15	4	0	1	128	156	7	43	36	14.1	4.43	63	.315	.372	9	.214	0	-23	-23	-0	-2.4
Total 5		25	33	.431	109	66	29	3	5	570	568	17	202	168	12.4	3.30	87	.266	.335	31	.168	-7	-29	-28	-2	-4.0

● **GAR FINNVOLD** Finnvold, Anders Gar b: 3/11/68, Boynton Beach, Fla. BR/TR, 6'5", 195 lbs. Deb: 5/10/94

YEAR	TM/L	W	L	PCT	G	GS	CG	SH	SV	IP	H	HR	BB	SO	RAT	ERA	ERA+	OAV	OOB	BH	AVG	PB	PR	/A	PD	TPI
1994	Bos-A	0	4	.000	8	8	0	0	0	36¹	45	4	15	17	15.6	5.94	86	.304	.380	0	—	0	-5	-3	0	-0.7

● **STEVE FIREOVID** Fireovid, Stephen John b: 6/6/57, Bryan, Ohio BB/TR, 6'2", 195 lbs. Deb: 9/6/81

YEAR	TM/L	W	L	PCT	G	GS	CG	SH	SV	IP	H	HR	BB	SO	RAT	ERA	ERA+	OAV	OOB	BH	AVG	PB	PR	/A	PD	TPI
1981	SD-N	0	1	.000	5	4	0	0	0	26¹	30	2	7	11	12.6	2.73	119	.294	.339	1	.143	-0	2	2	0	0.0
1983	SD-N	0	0	—	3	0	0	0	0	5	4	0	2	1	10.8	1.80	194	.235	.316	0	—	0	1	1	0	0.0
1984	Phi-N	0	0	—	6	0	0	0	0	5²	4	0	3	6	6.4	1.59	229	.200	.200	0	—	0	1	1	0	0.0
1985	Chi-A	0	0	—	4	0	0	0	0	7	17	0	2	7	24.4	5.14	84	.472	.500	0	—	0	-1	-1	-0	-0.1
1986	Sea-A	2	0	1.000	10	1	0	0	0	21	28	1	4	10	14.1	4.29	99	.333	.371	0	—	0	-0	-0	-0	0.0
1992	Tex-A	1	0	1.000	3	0	0	0	0	6²	10	0	4	0	18.9	4.05	94	.370	.452	0	—	0	-0	-0	-0	0.3
Total 6		3	1	.750	31	5	0	0	0	71²	93	3	19	27	14.2	3.39	110	.325	.369	1	.143	—	3	3	0	0.2

● **TED FIRTH** Firth, John E. b: 1856, Massachusetts d: 6/23/02, Tewksbury, Mass. Deb: 8/15/1884

YEAR	TM/L	W	L	PCT	G	GS	CG	SH	SV	IP	H	HR	BB	SO	RAT	ERA	ERA+	OAV	OOB	BH	AVG	PB	PR	/A	PD	TPI
1884	Ric-a	0	1	.000	1	1	0	0	0	9	14	0	5	0	19.0	8.00	41	.326	.396	1	.333	0	-5	-5	-0	-0.4

● **CARL FISCHER** Fischer, Charles William b: 11/5/05, Medina, N.Y. d: 12/10/63, Medina, N.Y. BR/TL, 6', 180 lbs. Deb: 7/19/30

YEAR	TM/L	W	L	PCT	G	GS	CG	SH	SV	IP	H	HR	BB	SO	RAT	ERA	ERA+	OAV	OOB	BH	AVG	PB	PR	/A	PD	TPI
1930	Was-A	1	1	.500	8	4	1	0	1	33¹	37	0	18	21	15.4	4.86	95	.285	.380	0	.000	-1	-1	-1	1	-0.1
1931	Was-A	13	9	.591	46	23	7	0	3	191	207	12	80	96	13.6	4.38	98	.273	.344	8	.121	-5	-0	-2	-4	-1.0
1932	Was-A	3	2	.600	12	7	1	1	1	50²	57	4	31	23	15.6	4.97	87	.282	.378	3	.200	1	-3	-4	-2	-0.4
	StL-A	3	7	.300	24	11	4	0	0	97	122	12	45	35	15.5	5.57	87	.310	.380	9	.265	0	-12	-8	-1	-0.7
	Yr	6	9	.400	36	18	5	1	1	147²	179	16	76	58	15.5	5.36	87	.300	.379	12	.245	1	-15	-11	-3	-1.1
1933	Det-A	11	15	.423	35	22	9	0	3	182²	176	5	84	93	13.0	3.55	122	.251	.334	9	.145	-3	15	15	-2	1.5
1934	Det-A	6	4	.600	20	15	4	1	1	95	107	5	38	39	13.8	4.36	101	.288	.356	2	.065	-3	1	0	-2	-0.4
1935	Det-A	0	1	.000	3	1	0	0	0	12	16	2	5	7	16.5	6.00	69	.320	.393	0	.000	-0	-2	-2	-0	-0.2
	Chi-A	5	5	.500	24	11	3	1	0	88²	102	7	39	31	14.5	6.19	75	.283	.356	4	.190	-0	-17	-15	-1	-1.6
	Yr	5	6	.455	27	12	3	1	0	100²	118	9	44	38	14.7	6.17	74	.286	.358	4	.174	-1	-19	-18	-1	-1.8
1937	Cle-A	0	1	.000	2	0	0	0	0	0²	2	0	1	0	40.5	27.00	17	.667	.750	0	—	-0	-2	-2	0	-1.4
	Was-A	4	5	.444	17	11	2	0	2	72	74	6	31	30	13.1	4.38	101	.270	.344	3	.136	-1	2	-0	-2	-0.2
	Yr	4	6	.400	19	11	2	0	2	72²	76	6	32	31	13.4	4.58	97	.274	.350	3	.136	-1	0	-1	-2	-1.6
Total 7		46	50	.479	191	105	31	3	11	823	900	53	372	376	14.0	4.63	96	.277	.354	38	.145	-12	-18	-18	-14	-4.5

● **HANK FISCHER** Fischer, Henry William "Bulldog" b: 1/11/40, Yonkers, N.Y. BR/TR, 6', 190 lbs. Deb: 4/16/62

YEAR	TM/L	W	L	PCT	G	GS	CG	SH	SV	IP	H	HR	BB	SO	RAT	ERA	ERA+	OAV	OOB	BH	AVG	PB	PR	/A	PD	TPI
1962	Mil-N	2	3	.400	29	0	0	0	4	37¹	43	4	20	29	15.2	5.30	72	.291	.375	0	.000	-0	-6	-6	-0	-0.9
1963	Mil-N	4	3	.571	31	6	1	0	0	74¹	74	8	28	72	13.0	4.96	65	.262	.340	2	.105	-1	-14	-14	-1	-1.4
1964	Mil-N	11	10	.524	37	28	9	5	2	168¹	177	17	39	99	11.7	4.01	88	.265	.309	8	.154	1	-9	-9	-1	-1.1
1965	Mil-N	8	9	.471	31	19	2	0	0	122²	126	18	39	79	12.3	3.89	91	.270	.331	4	.108	-1	-5	-5	-2	-1.0
1966	Atl-N	2	3	.400	14	8	0	0	0	48¹	55	3	14	22	13.0	3.91	93	.296	.348	0	.000	-2	-2	-1	-1	-0.4
	Cin-N	0	6	.000	11	9	0	0	0	38	53	3	15	24	16.8	6.63	59	.331	.399	1	.091	-1	-13	-12	-0	-1.7
	Yr	2	9	.182	25	17	0	0	0	86¹	108	6	29	46	14.6	5.11	73	.309	.366	1	.042	-2	-14	-13	-2	-2.1
	Bos-A	2	3	.400	6	5	1	0	0	31	35	4	11	26	13.6	2.90	131	.287	.351	2	.222	1	2	3	0	0.6
1967	Bos-A	1	2	.333	9	2	1	0	1	26²	24	3	8	18	11.1	2.36	148	.229	.289	1	.143	-0	3	3	-0	0.4
Total 6		30	39	.435	168	77	14	5	7	546²	587	60	174	369	12.8	4.23	84	.275	.334	18	.118	-3	-43	-41	-5	-5.5

● **JEFF FISCHER** Fischer, Jeffrey Thomas b: 8/17/63, W. Palm Beach, Fla. BR/TR, 6'3", 185 lbs. Deb: 6/19/87

YEAR	TM/L	W	L	PCT	G	GS	CG	SH	SV	IP	H	HR	BB	SO	RAT	ERA	ERA+	OAV	OOB	BH	AVG	PB	PR	/A	PD	TPI
1987	Mon-N	0	1	.000	4	2	0	0	0	13²	21	3	6	6	17.1	8.56	49	.362	.413	1	.200	0	-7	-7	-0	-0.4
1989	LA-N	0	0	—	2	0	0	0	0	3¹	7	1	0	2	18.9	13.50	25	.438	.438	0	—	0	-4	-4	-0	0.0
Total 2		0	1	.000	6	2	0	0	0	17	28	4	5	8	17.5	9.53	42	.378	.418	1	.200	0	-11	-10	-0	-0.4

● **RUBE FISCHER** Fischer, Reuben Walter b: 9/19/16, Carlock, S.D. BR/TR, 6'4", 190 lbs. Deb: 9/12/41

YEAR	TM/L	W	L	PCT	G	GS	CG	SH	SV	IP	H	HR	BB	SO	RAT	ERA	ERA+	OAV	OOB	BH	AVG	PB	PR	/A	PD	TPI
1941	NY-N	1	0	1.000	2	1	1	0	0	11	10	0	6	9	13.1	2.45	151	.238	.333	1	.333	0	1	2	-0	0.1
1943	NY-N	5	10	.333	22	17	4	1	1	130²	140	4	59	47	13.8	4.61	75	.281	.360	11	.256	3	-18	-17	-2	-1.7
1944	NY-N	6	14	.300	38	18	2	1	2	128²	128	7	87	39	15.5	5.18	71	.266	.384	5	.125	-2	-22	-22	-2	-3.4
1945	NY-N	3	8	.273	31	4	0	0	1	76²	90	6	49	27	16.4	5.63	69	.288	.387	4	.211	-2	-16	-15	-1	-1.8
1946	NY-N	1	2	.333	15	1	0	0	0	35²	48	3	21	14	17.4	6.31	55	.316	.399	1	.111	-1	-11	-11	-0	-0.9
Total 5		16	34	.320	108	41	7	1	4	382²	416	20	222	136	15.2	5.10	71	.280	.377	22	.193	2	-66	-63	-5	-7.7

● **TODD FISCHER** Fischer, Todd Richard b: 9/15/60, Columbus, Ohio BR/TR, 5'10", 170 lbs. Deb: 5/29/86

YEAR	TM/L	W	L	PCT	G	GS	CG	SH	SV	IP	H	HR	BB	SO	RAT	ERA	ERA+	OAV	OOB	BH	AVG	PB	PR	/A	PD	TPI
1986	Cal-A	0	0	—	9	0	0	0	0	17	18	4	8	7	13.8	4.24	97	.286	.366	0	—	0	-0	-0	-0	0.0

● **BILL FISCHER** Fischer, William Charles b: 10/11/30, Wausau, Wis. BR/TR, 6', 190 lbs. Deb: 4/21/56 C

YEAR	TM/L	W	L	PCT	G	GS	CG	SH	SV	IP	H	HR	BB	SO	RAT	ERA	ERA+	OAV	OOB	BH	AVG	PB	PR	/A	PD	TPI
1956	Chi-A	0	0	—	3	0	0	0	0	1²	6	0	1	2	37.8	21.60	19	.545	.583	0	.150	0	-3	-3	0	0.0
1957	Chi-A	7	8	.467	33	11	3	1	1	124	139	1	35	48	12.8	3.48	107	.291	.344	6	.150	-2	4	3	-1	0.1
1958	Chi-A	2	3	.400	17	3	0	0	0	36¹	43	6	13	16	13.9	6.69	54	.301	.359	1	.143	-0	-12	-12	-1	-1.4
	Det-A	2	4	.333	22	0	0	0	2	30²	46	4	9	16	17.3	7.63	53	.362	.421	0	.000	0	-13	-12	-0	-2.2
	Was-A	0	3	.000	3	3	0	0	0	21	24	1	5	10	12.9	3.86	99	.320	.370	1	.200	-0	-0	-0	-0	0.1
	Yr	4	10	.286	42	6	0	0	2	88	113	11	31	42	14.8	6.34	60	.325	.382	2	.154	-0	-25	-25	-3	-3.5
1959	Was-A	9	11	.450	34	29	6	1	0	187¹	211	16	43	62	12.4	4.28	92	.281	.324	7	.130	-2	-9	-8	4	-0.5
1960	Was-A	3	5	.375	20	7	1	0	0	77	85	7	17	31	11.9	4.91	79	.281	.320	3	.158	1	-9	-9	1	-0.6
	Det-A	5	3	.625	20	6	1	0	0	55	50	6	18	24	11.1	3.44	115	.244	.305	4	.364	2	3	3	0	0.7
	Yr	8	8	.500	40	13	2	0	0	132	135	13	35	55	11.6	4.30	91	.265	.313	7	.233	3	-6	-6	2	0.1
1961	Det-A	3	2	.600	26	1	0	0	3	46²	54	10	7	18	13.7	5.01	82	.292	.351	0	.000	-1	-5	-5	-0	-0.6
	KC-A	1	0	1.000	15	0	0	0	0	21	26	2	6	12	13.7	3.86	108	.321	.368	0	.000	-0	0	0	0	0.0
	Yr	4	2	.667	41	1	0	0	3	67²	80	12	13	30	13.7	4.66	89	.301	.356	0	.000	-1	-5	-4	-0	-0.6
1962	KC-A	4	12	.250	34	16	5	0	2	127²	150	16	8	38	11.2	3.95	107	.293	.305	4	.105	-2	0	4	-1	0.4
1963	KC-A	9	6	.600	45	2	0	0	3	95²	86	13	29	34	11.1	3.57	109	.242	.305	1	.067	-0	1	3	-1	0.4
1964	Min-A	0	1	.000	7	1	0	0	0	7¹	12	2	0	2	25.8	7.36	49	.471	.538	0	—	0	-3	-3	-0	-0.4
Total 9		45	58	.437	281	78	16	2	13	831¹	936	86	210	313	12.5	4.34	91	.287	.333	27	.136	-4	-46	-37	5	-4.2

● **LEO FISHEL** Fishel, Leo b: 12/13/1877, Babylon, N.Y. d: 5/19/60, Hempstead, N.Y. BR/TR, 6', 175 lbs. Deb: 5/3/1899

YEAR	TM/L	W	L	PCT	G	GS	CG	SH	SV	IP	H	HR	BB	SO	RAT	ERA	ERA+	OAV	OOB	BH	AVG	PB	PR	/A	PD	TPI
1899	NY-N	0	1	.000	1	1	1	0	0	9	9	0	6	6	17.0	6.00	63	.260	.399	1	.250	-0	-2	-2	0	-0.2

● **BRIAN FISHER** Fisher, Brian Kevin b: 3/18/62, Honolulu, Hawaii BR/TR, 6'4", 210 lbs. Deb: 5/7/85

YEAR	TM/L	W	L	PCT	G	GS	CG	SH	SV	IP	H	HR	BB	SO	RAT	ERA	ERA+	OAV	OOB	BH	AVG	PB	PR	/A	PD	TPI
1985	NY-A	4	4	.500	55	0	0	0	14	98¹	77	4	29	85	9.7	2.38	168	.216	.275	0	—	0	19	18	0	1.9
1986	NY-A	9	5	.643	62	0	0	0	6	96²	105	14	37	67	13.3	4.93	83	.277	.343	0	—	0	-8	-9	-1	-1.4
1987	Pit-N	11	9	.550	37	26	6	0	0	185¹	185	27	72	117	12.7	4.52	91	.262	.334	11	.190	5	-8	-8	-0	-0.6
1988	Pit-N	8	10	.444	33	22	1	1	1	146¹	157	13	57	66	13.5	4.61	74	.277	.348	2	.048	-2	-19	-20	-2	-2.7
1989	Pit-N	0	3	.000	9	0	0	0	0	17	25	3	10	8	18.5	7.94	42	.329	.407	0	.000	-1	-8	-9	-0	-1.5
1990	Hou-N	0	0	—	4	0	0	0	0	5	9	1	0	1	16.2	7.20	52	.409	.409	0	—	0	-2	-2	-0	0.0

YEAR TM/L	W	L	PCT	G	GS	CG	SH	SV	IP	H	HR	BB	SO	RAT	ERA	ERA+	OAV	OOB	BH	AVG	PB	PR	/A	PD	TPI
1992 Sea-A	4	3	.571	22	14	0	0	1	91¹	80	9	47	26	12.6	4.53	88	.234	.328	0	—	0	-6	-6	-0	-0.5
Total 7	36	34	.514	222	65	7	4	23	640	638	70	252	370	12.7	4.39	89	.261	.332	13	.124	2	-33	-36	-5	-4.8

● CHAUNCEY FISHER
Fisher, Chauncey Burr "Peach" or "Whoa Bill" b: 1/8/1872, Anderson, Ind. d: 4/27/39, Los Angeles, Cal. BR/TR, 5'11", 175 lbs. Deb: 9/20/1893 F

YEAR TM/L	W	L	PCT	G	GS	CG	SH	SV	IP	H	HR	BB	SO	RAT	ERA	ERA+	OAV	OOB	BH	AVG	PB	PR	/A	PD	TPI
1893 Cle-N	0	2	.000	2	2	2	0	0	18	26	0	9	9	17.5	5.50	89	.328	.397	2	.250	-0	-2	-1	0	-0.1
1894 Cle-N	0	2	.000	3	2	0	0	0	11	22	0	5	0	22.9	11.45	48	.410	.469	0	.000	-1	-7	-7	1	-0.8
Cin-N	2	8	.200	11	11	10	0	0	91	134	4	44	14	17.6	7.32	76	.338	.404	10	.233	-1	-20	-18	-1	-1.5
Yr	2	10	.167	14	13	10	0	0	102	156	4	49	14	18.1	7.76	71	.346	.410	10	.213	-2	-28	-25	-1	-2.3
1896 Cin-N	10	7	.588	27	15	13	2	2	159²	199	9	36	25	13.5	4.45	104	.303	.344	14	.246	-2	-3	3	-0	0.2
1897 Bro-N	9	7	.563	20	13	11	1	1	149	184	5	43	31	13.8	4.23	97	.301	.349	12	.203	-1	1	-2	-2	-0.4
1901 NY-N	0	0	—	1	1	0	0	0	4	11	0	2	1	29.3	15.75	21	.490	.531	0	.000	-0	-6	-6	-0	-0.1
StL-N	0	0	—	1	0	0	0	0	3	7	0	1	0	24.0	15.00	21	.449	.482	0	.000	-0	-4	-4	0	0.0
Yr	0	0	—	2	1	0	0	0	7	18	0	3	1	27.0	15.43	21	.473	.511	0	.000	-0	-9	-9	-0	-0.1
Total 5	21	26	.447	65	44	36	3	3	435²	583	18	140	80	15.1	5.37	86	.318	.368	38	.218	-3	-39	-35	-2	-2.7

● CLARENCE FISHER
Fisher, Clarence Henry b: 8/27/1898, Letart, W.Va. d: 11/2/65, Point Pleasant, W.Va. BR/TR, 6', 174 lbs. Deb: 9/14/19

YEAR TM/L	W	L	PCT	G	GS	CG	SH	SV	IP	H	HR	BB	SO	RAT	ERA	ERA+	OAV	OOB	BH	AVG	PB	PR	/A	PD	TPI
1919 Was-A	0	0	—	2	0	0	0	0	4	8	0	3	1	24.8	13.50	24	.421	.500	0	—	0	-5	-5	0	0.0
1920 Was-A	0	1	.000	2	0	0	0	0	3²	5	0	5	0	24.5	9.82	38	.714	.833	0	.000	-0	-2	-2	1	-0.5
Total 2	0	1	.000	4	0	0	0	0	7²	13	0	8	1	24.7	11.74	29	.500	.618	0	.000	-0	-7	-7	1	-0.5

● DON FISHER
Fisher, Donald Raymond b: 2/6/16, Cleveland, Ohio d: 7/29/73, Mayfield Heights, Ohio BR/TR, 6', 210 lbs. Deb: 8/25/45

YEAR TM/L	W	L	PCT	G	GS	CG	SH	SV	IP	H	HR	BB	SO	RAT	ERA	ERA+	OAV	OOB	BH	AVG	PB	PR	/A	PD	TPI
1945 NY-N	1	0	1.000	2	1	1	0	0	18	12	0	7	4	10.5	2.00	196	.190	.292	1	.143	-0	4	4	-0	0.2

● EDDIE FISHER
Fisher, Eddie Gene b: 7/16/36, Shreveport, La. BR/TR, 6'2.5", 200 lbs. Deb: 6/22/59

YEAR TM/L	W	L	PCT	G	GS	CG	SH	SV	IP	H	HR	BB	SO	RAT	ERA	ERA+	OAV	OOB	BH	AVG	PB	PR	/A	PD	TPI
1959 SF-N	2	6	.250	17	5	0	0	1	40	57	8	15	14.8		7.87	48	.339	.373	0	.000	-1	-17	-18	-1	-3.1
1960 SF-N	1	0	1.000	3	1	0	0	0	12²	11	2	7	9.2		3.55	98	.244	.277	3	.600	1	0	-0	0	0.1
1961 SF-N	0	2	.000	15	1	0	0	0	33²	36	7	9	16	12.0	5.35	71	.267	.313	1	.143	-0	-5	-6	-0	-0.3
1962 Chi-A	9	5	.643	57	12	2	1	5	182²	169	17	45	10.6		3.10	126	.245	.293	6	.130	-0	18	16	0	1.2
1963 Chi-A	9	8	.529	33	15	2	1	0	120²	114	14	28	67	10.7	3.95	89	.244	.290	5	.139	-1	-4	-6	1	-0.8
1964 Chi-A	6	3	.667	59	2	0	0	9	125	86	13	32	74	8.7	3.02	114	.192	.250	3	.167	-0	8	6	0	0.5
1965 Chi-A★	15	7	.682	82	0	0	0	24	165¹	118	13	43	90	8.9	2.40	133	.205	.262	4	.138	0	20	15	1	2.6
1966 Chi-A	1	3	.250	23	0	0	0	6	35¹	27	1	17	18	11.5	2.29	138	.214	.313	0	.000	-0	4	3	0	0.5
Bal-A	5	3	.625	44	0	0	0	13	71²	60	4	19	39	10.2	2.64	126	.226	.282	2	.154	-0	6	6	-0	0.8
Yr	6	6	.500	67	0	0	0	19	107	87	5	36	57	10.5	2.52	130	.221	.289	2	.133	-0	11	9	-0	1.3
1967 Bal-A	4	3	.571	46	0	0	0	1	89²	82	7	26	53	11.2	3.61	87	.245	.307	1	.200	-1	-4	-5	-1	-0.4
1968 Cle-A	4	2	.667	54	0	0	0	4	94²	87	8	17	42	10.1	2.85	104	.248	.286	0	.000	-1	1	1	1	0.1
1969 Cal-A	3	2	.600	52	1	0	0	2	96²	100	9	28	47	12.0	3.63	96	.272	.326	0	.000	-1	-0	-2	-0	-0.2
1970 Cal-A	4	4	.500	67	2	0	0	9	130¹	117	15	35	74	10.6	3.04	119	.239	.292	1	.091	-1	10	8	1	0.7
1971 Cal-A	10	8	.556	57	3	0	0	5	119	92	11	50	82	10.9	2.72	119	.211	.295	1	.063	-1	10	7	-0	0.9
1972 Cal-A	4	5	.444	43	1	0	0	4	81¹	73	6	31	32	11.5	3.76	77	.247	.319	2	.118	-1	-6	-8	-0	-1.1
Chi-A	0	1	.000	6	4	0	0	0	22¹	31	1	9	10	16.1	4.43	70	.348	.408	0	.000	-1	-3	-3	-0	-0.2
Yr	4	6	.400	49	5	0	0	4	103²	104	7	40	42	12.5	3.91	76	.267	.336	2	.083	-1	-10	-11	-0	-1.3
1973 Chi-A	6	7	.462	26	16	2	0	0	110²	135	12	38	57	14.3	4.88	81	.301	.360	0	—	0	-13	-11	0	-1.2
StL-N	2	1	.667	6	0	0	0	0	7	3	1	1	1	6.4	1.29	283	.125	.192	1	1.000	N	2	2	0	0.8
Total 15	85	70	.548	690	63	7	2	81	1538²	1398	149	438	812	10.9	3.41	101	.243	.299	30	.145	-5	26	5	3	0.9

● ED FISHER
Fisher, Edward Fredrick b: 10/31/1876, Wayne, Mich. d: 7/24/51, Spokane, Wash. BR/TR, 6'2", 200 lbs. Deb: 9/5/02

YEAR TM/L	W	L	PCT	G	GS	CG	SH	SV	IP	H	HR	BB	SO	RAT	ERA	ERA+	OAV	OOB	BH	AVG	PB	PR	/A	PD	TPI
1902 Det-A	0	0	—	1	0	0	0	0	4	4	0	1	0	11.3	0.00	—	.261	.306	0	—	-0	2	2	-0	-0.1

● FRITZ FISHER
Fisher, Frederick Brown b: 11/28/41, Adrian, Mich. BL/TL, 6'1", 180 lbs. Deb: 4/19/64

YEAR TM/L	W	L	PCT	G	GS	CG	SH	SV	IP	H	HR	BB	SO	RAT	ERA	ERA+	OAV	OOB	BH	AVG	PB	PR	/A	PD	TPI
1964 Det-A	0	0	—	1	0	0	0	0	0¹	2	0	2	1	108.0	108.00	3	.667	.800	0	—	0	-4	-4	0	0.0

● GEORGE FISHER
Fisher, George C. b: Wilmington, Del. BL, Deb: 7/17/1884 ♦

YEAR TM/L	W	L	PCT	G	GS	CG	SH	SV	IP	H	HR	BB	SO	RAT	ERA	ERA+	OAV	OOB	BH	AVG	PB	PR	/A	PD	TPI
1884 Phi-U	1	7	.125	8	8	8	0	0	70²	76	0	13	42	11.3	3.57	65	.257	.288	8	.222	-1	-9	-10	-1	-1.0
1885 Buf-N	0	1	.000	1	1	1	0	0	9	10	0	2	4	12.0	5.00	60	.256	.293	0	.000	-1	-2	-2	0	-0.2
Total 2	1	8	.111	9	9	9	0	0	79²	86	0	15	46	11.4	3.73	64	.257	.289	13	.140	-2	-11	-12	-1	-1.2

● HARRY FISHER
Fisher, Harry Devereux b: 1/3/26, Newbury, Ont., Can. d: 9/20/81, Waterloo, Ont., Canada BL/TR, 6', 180 lbs. Deb: 9/16/51 ♦

YEAR TM/L	W	L	PCT	G	GS	CG	SH	SV	IP	H	HR	BB	SO	RAT	ERA	ERA+	OAV	OOB	BH	AVG	PB	PR	/A	PD	TPI
1952 Pit-N	1	2	.333	8	3	0	0	0	18¹	17	4	13	5	15.7	6.87	58	.266	.405	5	.333	1	-6	-6	-1	-0.8

● JACK FISHER
Fisher, John Howard "Fat Jack" b: 3/4/39, Frostburg, Md. BR/TR, 6'2", 215 lbs. Deb: 4/14/59

YEAR TM/L	W	L	PCT	G	GS	CG	SH	SV	IP	H	HR	BB	SO	RAT	ERA	ERA+	OAV	OOB	BH	AVG	PB	PR	/A	PD	TPI
1959 Bal-A	1	6	.143	27	7	1	1	2	88²	76	7	38	52	11.7	3.05	124	.230	.311	3	.130	-1	8	7	-1	0.4
1960 Bal-A	12	11	.522	40	20	8	3	2	197²	174	13	78	99	11.6	3.41	111	.241	.317	11	.183	2	10	9	0	1.2
1961 Bal-A	10	13	.435	36	25	10	1	1	196	205	17	75	118	13.0	3.90	99	.270	.339	5	.089	-2	3	-1	-3	-0.6
1962 Bal-A	7	9	.438	32	25	4	0	1	152	173	23	56	81	13.7	5.09	73	.284	.346	5	.102	-1	-19	-24	-1	-2.3
1963 SF-N	6	10	.375	36	12	2	0	1	116	132	12	38	57	13.6	4.58	70	.284	.344	3	.103	-1	-17	-18	-0	-1.8
1964 NY-N	10	17	.370	40	34	8	1	0	227²	256	23	56	115	12.7	4.23	85	.283	.331	12	.158	-1	-18	-16	-1	-1.8
1965 NY-N	8	24	.250	43	36	10	0	0	253²	252	22	68	116	11.5	3.94	90	.259	.310	12	.154	0	-11	-12	2	-1.2
1966 NY-N	11	14	.440	38	33	10	0	0	230	229	26	54	127	11.4	3.68	99	.260	.309	6	.090	-2	-2	-1	3	0.0
1967 NY-N	9	18	.333	39	30	7	1	0	220¹	251	21	64	117	13.0	4.70	72	.287	.339	7	.100	-1	-32	-32	1	-3.7
1968 Chi-A	8	13	.381	35	28	2	0	0	180²	176	14	48	80	11.5	2.99	101	.257	.312	6	.113	-1	-0	1	-0	-0.1
1969 Cin-N	4	4	.500	34	15	0	0	1	113	137	15	30	55	13.7	5.50	68	.295	.345	4	.121	-1	-24	-22	-2	-1.8
Total 11	86	139	.382	400	265	62	9	9	1975²	2061	193	605	1017	12.4	4.06	88	.269	.326	74	.125	-6	-102	-108	-1	-12.2

● MAURICE FISHER
Fisher, Maurice Wayne b: 2/16/31, Uniondale, Ind. BR/TR, 6'5", 210 lbs. Deb: 4/16/55

YEAR TM/L	W	L	PCT	G	GS	CG	SH	SV	IP	H	HR	BB	SO	RAT	ERA	ERA+	OAV	OOB	BH	AVG	PB	PR	/A	PD	TPI
1955 Cin-N	0	0	—	1	0	0	0	0	2²	3	1	2	1	23.6	6.75	63	.385	.467	0	.000	-0	-1	-1	-0	0.0

● RAY FISHER
Fisher, Raymond Lyle "Chic" b: 10/4/1887, Middlebury, Vt. d: 11/3/82, Ann Arbor, Mich. BR/TR, 5'11.5", 180 lbs. Deb: 7/2/10

YEAR TM/L	W	L	PCT	G	GS	CG	SH	SV	IP	H	HR	BB	SO	RAT	ERA	ERA+	OAV	OOB	BH	AVG	PB	PR	/A	PD	TPI
1910 NY-A	5	3	.625	17	7	3	0	1	92¹	95	0	18	42	11.3	2.92	91	.274	.315	3	.103	-2	-4	-3	1	-0.3
1911 NY-A	10	11	.476	29	22	8	0	1	171²	178	3	55	99	12.5	3.25	111	.269	.330	7	.119	-3	2	7	4	0.8
1912 NY-A	2	8	.200	17	13	5	0	0	90¹	107	2	32	47	14.0	5.88	61	.312	.374	2	.065	-4	-26	-23	3	-2.2
1913 NY-A	12	16	.429	43	31	14	1	1	246¹	244	3	71	92	11.8	3.18	94	.261	.319	22	.278	3	-7	-5	2	0.0
1914 NY-A	10	12	.455	29	26	17	2	1	209	177	2	61	86	10.4	2.28	121	.241	.303	9	.138	-2	11	11	4	1.3
1915 NY-A	18	11	.621	30	28	20	4	0	247²	219	7	62	97	10.4	2.11	139	.243	.295	9	.108	-5	23	23	-0	2.1
1916 NY-A	11	8	.579	31	21	9	1	1	179	191	4	51	56	12.4	3.17	91	.285	.339	11	.177	-1	-7	-5	-1	-0.6
1917 NY-A	8	9	.471	23	18	12	3	0	144	126	3	43	64	10.7	2.19	123	.243	.304	9	.180	-0	8	8	1	1.1
1919 *Cin-N	14	5	.737	26	20	12	5	0	174¹	141	5	38	41	9.3	2.17	128	.226	.271	16	.271	3	14	12	3	2.1
1920 Cin-N	10	11	.476	33	21	10	1	0	201	189	5	50	56	11.1	2.73	111	.249	.302	17	.243	1	9	7	2	1.1
Total 10	100	94	.515	278	207	110	19	7	1755²	1667	34	481	680	11.2	2.82	106	.257	.312	105	.179	-8	23	30	19	5.4

● TOM FISHER
Fisher, Thomas Chalmers "Red" b: 11/1/1880, Anderson, Ind. d: 9/3/72, Anderson, Ind. BR/TR, 5'10.5", 185 lbs. Deb: 4/17/04 F

YEAR TM/L	W	L	PCT	G	GS	CG	SH	SV	IP	H	HR	BB	SO	RAT	ERA	ERA+	OAV	OOB	BH	AVG	PB	PR	/A	PD	TPI
1904 Bos-N	6	16	.273	31	21	19	2	0	214	257	5	82	84	14.7	4.25	65	.302	.370	21	.212	3	-36	-35	-5	-3.4

● TOM FISHER
Fisher, Thomas Gene b: 4/4/42, Cleveland, Ohio BR/TR, 6', 180 lbs. Deb: 9/20/67

YEAR TM/L	W	L	PCT	G	GS	CG	SH	SV	IP	H	HR	BB	SO	RAT	ERA	ERA+	OAV	OOB	BH	AVG	PB	PR	/A	PD	TPI
1967 Bal-A	0	0	—	2	0	0	0	0	3¹	2	0	2	1	10.8	0.00	—	.182	.308	0	—	0	1	1	-0	0.0

YEAR TM/L	W	L	PCT	G	GS	CG	SH	SV	IP	H	HR	BB	SO	RAT	ERA	ERA+	OAV	OOB	BH	AVG	PB	PR	/A	PD	TPI

● CHEROKEE FISHER   Fisher, William Charles b: 12/1845, Philadelphia, Pa. d: 9/26/12, New York, N.Y. BR/TR, 5'9", 164 lbs. Deb: 5/6/1871 ♦

1871 Rok-n	4	16	.200	24	24	22	1	0	213	295	3	31	15	13.8	4.35	94	.281	.302	28	.228	-3	-3	-6		-0.5
1872 Bal-n	10	1	.909	19	11	9	1	1	110¹	89	0	11	20	8.2	2.53	148	.189	.207	52	.230	-1	15	15		0.9
1873 Ath-n	3	4	.429	13	5	5	0	1	84¹	90	1	10	14	10.7	1.81	188	.227	.246	66	.261	1	13	15		0.8
1874 Har-n	14	23	.378	39	35	31	0	0	317	405	1	10		11.8	3.04	104	.275	.279	54	.223	-5	-1	4		0.0
1875 Phi-n	22	19	.537	41	41	36	2	0	356²	345	6	9		8.9	1.92	131	.232	.237	41	.232	-1	21	24		2.0
1876 Cin-N	4	20	.167	28	24	22	0	0	229¹	294	6	10	29	11.8	3.02	73	.285	.289	32	.248	-1	-18	-21	-2	-1.9
1878 Pro-N	0	1	.000	1	1	1	0	0	9	14	0	0	2	14.0	4.00	55	.304	.304	0	.000	-0	-2	-2	0	-0.2
Total 5 n	53	63	.457	136	116	103	4	2	1081¹	1224	11	71	49	10.8	2.78	116	.251	.262	241	.236	-10	45	53		3.2
Total 2	4	21	.160	29	25	23	0	0	238¹	308	6	6	31	11.9	3.06	72	.285	.289	32	.235	-10	-20	-23	-2	-2.1

● MAX FISKE   Fiske, Maximilian Patrick "Ski" b: 10/12/1888, Chicago, Ill. d: 5/15/28, Chicago, Ill. BR/TR, 5'11", 185 lbs. Deb: 4/19/14

| 1914 Chi-F | 12 | 12 | .500 | 38 | 22 | 7 | 0 | 0 | 198 | 161 | 7 | 59 | 87 | 10.3 | 3.14 | 85 | .231 | .298 | 16 | .235 | | -6 | -11 | -0 | -1.2 |

● PAUL FITTERY   Fittery, Paul Clarence b: 10/10/1887, Lebanon, Pa. d: 1/28/74, Cartersville, Ga. BB/TL, 5'8.5", 156 lbs. Deb: 9/5/14

1914 Cin-N	0	2	.000	8	4	2	0	0	43²	41	0	12	21	11.1	3.09	95	.246	.300	1	.059	-1	-1	-1	0	-0.2
1917 Phi-N	1	1	.500	17	2	1	0	0	55²	69	1	27	13	16.3	4.53	62	.317	.404	2	.091	-1	-11	-11	1	-0.3
Total 2	1	3	.250	25	6	3	0	0	99¹	110	1	39	34	14.0	3.90	73	.286	.360	3	.077	-2	-13	-11	2	-0.5

● JOHN FITZGERALD   Fitzgerald, John Francis b: 9/15/33, Brooklyn, N.Y. BL/TL, 6'3", 190 lbs. Deb: 9/28/58

| 1958 SF-N | 0 | 0 | — | 1 | 1 | 0 | 0 | 0 | 1 | 3 | 1 | 1 | 3 | 6.0 | 3.00 | 127 | .111 | .200 | 0 | .000 | -0 | 0 | 0 | 0 | 0.0 |

● JOHN FITZGERALD   Fitzgerald, John H. b: 5/30/1870, Natick, Mass. d: 3/31/21, Boston, Mass. Deb: 7/18/1891

| 1891 Bos-a | 1 | 1 | .500 | 6 | 3 | 2 | 0 | 1 | 32 | 49 | 2 | 11 | 16 | 17.4 | 5.63 | 62 | .340 | .394 | 1 | .071 | -2 | -7 | -8 | 0 | -0.5 |

● JOHN FITZGERALD   Fitzgerald, John J. Deb: 4/18/1890

| 1890 Roc-a | 3 | 8 | .273 | 11 | 11 | 8 | 1 | 0 | 78 | 77 | 0 | 45 | 35 | 14.8 | 4.04 | 88 | .250 | .357 | 6 | .194 | -0 | -1 | -4 | 1 | -0.4 |

● JOHN FITZGERALD   Fitzgerald, John T. b: Leadville, Col. Deb: 6/4/1891

1891 Lou-a	14	18	.438	33	32	29	3	0	276	280	6	95	111	12.7	3.59	102	.254	.321	19	.170	0	4	2	-4	-0.1
1892 Lou-N	1	3	.250	4	4	4	0	0	34	45	2	11	3	15.1	4.24	72	.306	.359	2	.133	-0	-4	-4	-1	-0.5
Total 2	15	21	.417	37	36	33	3	0	310	325	8	106	114	12.9	3.66	98	.260	.325	21	.165	-0	1	-2	-4	-0.6

● PAUL FITZKE   Fitzke, Paul Frederick Herman "Bob" b: 7/30/1900, LaCrosse, Wis. d: 6/30/50, Sacramento, Cal. BR/TR, 5'11.5", 185 lbs. Deb: 9/1/24

| 1924 Cle-A | 0 | 0 | — | 1 | 0 | 0 | 0 | 0 | 4 | 5 | 0 | 3 | 1 | 18.0 | 4.50 | 95 | .313 | .421 | 0 | .000 | -0 | -0 | -0 | | 0.0 |

● AL FITZMORRIS   Fitzmorris, Alan James b: 3/21/46, Buffalo, N.Y. BB/TR, 6'2", 190 lbs. Deb: 9/8/69

1969 KC-A	1	1	.500	7	0	0	0	2	10²	9	1	4	3	11.0	4.22	87	.237	.310	0	.000	-0	-1	-1	-0	-0.2
1970 KC-A	8	5	.615	43	11	2	0	1	117²	112	14	52	47	12.5	4.44	84	.254	.333	9	.290	4	-9	-9	1	-0.5
1971 KC-A	7	5	.583	36	15	2	1	0	127¹	112	6	55	53	11.9	4.17	82	.245	.327	3	.200	1	-10	-10	2	-0.6
1972 KC-A	2	5	.286	38	2	0	0	3	101	99	10	28	51	11.4	3.74	81	.252	.303	4	.174	1	-8	-8	2	-0.3
1973 KC-A	8	3	.727	15	13	3	1	0	89	88	5	25	26	11.4	2.83	145	.259	.310	0	—	0	10	13	2	1.1
1974 KC-A	13	6	.684	34	27	9	4	1	190	189	8	63	53	11.9	2.79	137	.260	.319	0	—	0	17	23	3	2.3
1975 KC-A	16	12	.571	35	35	11	3	0	242	239	16	76	78	11.9	3.57	108	.262	.322	0	—	0	6	7	1	0.8
1976 KC-A	15	11	.577	35	33	8	2	0	220¹	227	6	56	80	11.6	3.06	114	.273	.320	0	—	0	11	11	3	1.6
1977 Cle-A	6	10	.375	29	21	1	0	0	133	164	12	53	54	14.8	5.41	73	.306	.369	0	—	0	-20	-22	1	-2.0
1978 Cle-A	0	1	.000	7	0	0	0	0	14¹	14	2	5	4	17.0	6.28	59	.333	.415	0	—	0	-4	-4	-0	-0.2
Cal-A	1	0	1.000	9	2	0	0	0	31²	26	2	14	8	11.4	1.71	212	.236	.323	0	—	0	7	7	-0	0.5
Yr	1	1	.500	16	2	0	0	0	46	45	5	21	13	12.9	3.13	117	.268	.349	0	—	0	3	3	-0	0.3
Total 10	77	59	.566	288	159	36	11	7	1277	1284	83	433	458	12.2	3.65	101	.265	.327	24	.242	7	-1	5	12	2.5

● FREDDIE FITZSIMMONS   Fitzsimmons, Frederick Landis "Fat Freddie"
b: 7/28/01, Mishawaka, Ind. d: 11/18/79, Yucca Valley, Cal. BR/TR, 5'11", 185 lbs. Deb: 8/12/25 MC

1925 NY-N	6	3	.667	10	8	6	1	0	74²	70	4	18	17	10.6	2.65	152	.248	.293	9	.310	2	13	12	2	1.6
1926 NY-N	14	10	.583	37	26	12	0	0	219	224	7	58	48	11.8	2.88	130	.272	.322	11	.128	-6	23	21	3	1.8
1927 NY-N	17	10	.630	42	31	14	1	3	244²	260	15	67	78	12.2	3.72	104	.275	.325	18	.207	-0	6	4	2	0.6
1928 NY-N	20	9	.690	40	32	16	1	1	261¹	264	13	65	67	11.5	3.68	106	.268	.316	18	.191	1	9	7	2	0.9
1929 NY-N	15	11	.577	37	31	14	4	1	221²	242	14	66	55	12.6	4.10	112	.285	.338	15	.183	-2	15	12	4	1.4
1930 NY-N	19	7	.731	41	29	17	1	1	224¹	230	26	59	76	11.6	4.25	111	.266	.314	22	.265	5	18	12	7	2.2
1931 NY-N	18	11	.621	35	33	19	4	0	253²	242	16	62	78	10.8	3.05	121	.251	.296	21	.228	9	23	18	8	3.7
1932 NY-N	11	11	.500	35	31	11	0	0	237²	287	18	83	65	14.1	4.43	84	.299	.356	19	.221	4	-15	-19	7	-0.6
1933 *NY-N	16	11	.593	36	35	13	1	0	251²	243	14	72	65	11.3	2.90	111	.251	.305	19	.200	3	12	9	6	1.8
1934 NY-N	18	14	.563	38	37	14	3	1	263¹	266	12	51	73	10.9	3.04	127	.261	.297	22	.232	5	30	24	5	3.7
1935 NY-N	4	8	.333	18	15	6	4	0	94	104	7	22	23	12.2	4.02	96	.281	.323	8	.258	1	-0	-2	1	0.0
1936 *NY-N	10	7	.588	28	17	7	0	2	141	147	6	39	35	11.9	3.32	117	.274	.323	7	.149	-2	11	9	1	0.8
1937 NY-N	2	2	.500	6	4	1	0	0	27¹	28	3	8	13	11.9	4.61	84	.272	.324	3	.300	2	-2	-2	-0	-0.1
Bro-N	4	8	.333	13	13	4	0	0	90²	91	2	32	29	12.3	4.27	95	.263	.327	5	.167	-1	-4	-2	1	-0.3
Yr	6	10	.375	19	17	5	0	0	118	119	5	40	42	12.2	4.35	92	.265	.327	8	.200	1	-6	-5	1	-0.4
1938 Bro-N	11	8	.579	27	26	12	2	0	202²	205	8	43	38	11.1	3.02	129	.261	.302	12	.171	-1	17	20	6	2.3
1939 Bro-N	7	9	.438	27	20	5	0	0	151¹	178	8	28	44	12.4	3.87	104	.293	.327	11	.234	3	1	3	5	1.1
1940 Bro-N	16	2	.889	20	18	11	4	1	134¹	120	5	25	35	9.8	2.81	142	.233	.269	5	.106	-2	15	18	1	2.2
1941 *Bro-N	6	1	.857	13	12	3	1	0	82²	78	3	26	19	11.5	2.07	177	.245	.305	4	.143	-0	14	15	2	1.5
1942 Bro-N	0	0	—	1	1	0	0	0	3	6	1	1	0	21.0	15.00	22	.400	.438	1	.500	1	-4	-4	0	0.0
1943 Bro-N	3	4	.429	7	4	1	0	0	44²	50	5	6	21	12	14.5	5.44	62	.281	.360	1	.071	-1	-10	-10	-1	-1.5
Total 19	217	146	.598	513	426	186	29	13	3223²	3335	186	846	870	11.8	3.51	111	.268	.316	231	.200	21	174	144	60	23.1

● PATSY FLAHERTY   Flaherty, Patrick Joseph b: 6/29/1876, Mansfield, Pa. d: 1/23/68, Alexandria, La. BL/TL, 5'8", 165 lbs. Deb: 9/8/1899 ♦

1899 Lou-N	2	3	.400	5	4	4	0	0	39	41	0	5	10	10.8	2.31	167	.270	.298	5	.208	1	7	7	-1	0.7
1900 Pit-N	0	0	—	4	1	0	0	0	22	30	0	9	5	18.0	6.14	59	.324	.413	1	.111	-1	-6	-6	1	0.0
1903 Chi-A	11	25	.306	40	34	29	2	1	293²	338	9	50	65	12.3	3.74	75	.288	.324	14	.137	-3	-25	-30	3	-3.4
1904 Chi-A	1	2	.333	5	5	4	0	0	43	36	1	10	14	9.8	2.09	117	.228	.279	4	.333	2	2	1	0	0.5
Pit-N	19	9	.679	29	28	28	5	0	242	210	3	59	64	10.4	2.05	134	.232	.287	22	.212	5	19	19	5	3.4
1905 Pit-N	10	10	.500	27	20	15	0	1	187²	197	7	49	44	12.1	3.50	86	.272	.324	15	.197	2	-10	-10	2	-0.6
1907 Bos-N	12	15	.444	27	25	23	0	0	217	197	4	59	34	10.9	2.70	95	.248	.306	22	.191	2	-5	-3	2	0.1
1908 Bos-N	12	18	.400	31	31	21	0	0	244	221	6	81	50	11.4	3.25	74	.236	.303	12	.140	-0	-24	-23	2	-2.6
1910 Phi-N	0	0	—	1	0	0	0	0	0¹	1	0	1	0	54.0	0.00	—	.333	.500	1	.500	1	-0	0		0.0
1911 Bos-N	0	2	.000	4	2	1	0	0	14	21	0	8	0	20.6	7.07	54	.350	.451	27	.287	-1	-6	-5	-0	-0.6
Total 9	67	84	.444	173	150	125	7	2	1302²	1292	25	331	271	11.6	3.09	88	.259	.312	123	.197	10	-49	-50	14	-2.5

● MIKE FLANAGAN   Flanagan, Michael Kendall b: 12/16/51, Manchester, N.H. BL/TL, 6', 195 lbs. Deb: 9/5/75

1975 Bal-A	0	1	.000	2	1	0	0	0	9	7	1	6	7	14.0	2.79	126	.250	.357	0	—	0	1	1	0	0.3
1976 Bal-A	3	5	.375	20	10	4	0	0	85	83	7	33	56	12.3	4.13	79	.260	.330	0	—	0	-6	-8	0	-0.3
1977 Bal-A	15	10	.600	36	33	15	2	0	235	235	14	70	149	11.8	3.64	104	.266	.321	0	—	0	11	4	-0	0.8
1978 Bal-A☆	19	15	.559	40	40	17	2	0	281¹	271	22	87	167	11.5	4.03	87	.257	.315	0	—	0	-8	-17	-2	-1.5
1979 *Bal-A	23	9	.719	39	38	16	5	0	265²	245	23	70	190	10.8	3.08	130	.246	.297	0	—	0	33	27	-0	3.2

YEAR	TM/L	W	L	PCT	G	GS	CG	SH	SV	IP	H	HR	BB	SO	RAT	ERA	ERA+	OAV	OOB	BH	AVG	PB	PR	/A	PD	TPI
1980	Bal-A	16	13	.552	37	37	12	2	0	251¹	278	27	71	128	12.6	4.12	96	.287	.337	0	—	0	-2	-5	0	-0.5
1981	Bal-A	9	6	.600	20	20	3	2	0	116	108	11	37	72	11.4	4.19	87	.244	.305	0	—	0	-7	-7	1	-0.8
1982	Bal-A	15	11	.577	36	35	11	1	0	236	233	24	76	103	11.9	3.97	102	.259	.319	0	—	0	3	2	0	0.2
1983	*Bal-A	12	4	.750	20	20	3	1	0	125¹	135	10	31	50	12.1	3.30	120	.278	.324	0	—	0	11	9	-1	1.1
1984	Bal-A	13	13	.500	34	34	10	2	0	226²	213	24	81	115	11.7	3.53	110	.250	.316	0	—	0	11	8	-1	0.9
1985	Bal-A	4	5	.444	15	15	1	0	0	86	101	14	28	42	13.7	5.13	79	.297	.354	0	—	0	-9	-10	-0	-0.8
1986	Bal-A	7	11	.389	29	28	2	0	0	172	179	15	66	96	12.9	4.24	98	.270	.337	0	—	0	-1	-2	-2	-0.3
1987	Bal-A	3	6	.333	16	16	4	0	0	94²	102	9	36	50	13.1	4.94	89	.278	.342	0	—	0	-5	-6	-0	-0.3
	Tor-A	3	2	.600	7	7	0	0	0	49¹	46	3	15	43	11.1	2.37	189	.237	.292	0	—	0	11	12	-0	0.9
	Yr	6	8	.429	23	23	4	0	0	144	148	12	51	93	12.4	4.06	109	.263	.325	0	—	0	6	6	-1	0.6
1988	Tor-A	13	13	.500	34	34	2	1	0	211	220	23	80	99	13.1	4.18	94	.271	.341	0	—	0	-5	-6	1	-0.6
1989	*Tor-A	8	10	.444	30	30	1	1	0	171²	186	10	47	47	12.5	3.93	96	.283	.335	0	—	0	-1	-3	1	-0.1
1990	Tor-A	2	2	.500	5	5	0	0	0	20¹	28	3	8	5	15.9	5.31	74	.329	.387	0	—	0	-3	-3	0	-0.6
1991	Bal-A	2	7	.222	64	1	0	0	3	98¹	84	6	25	55	10.3	2.38	166	.236	.292	0	—	0	19	17	2	2.0
1992	Bal-A	0	0	—	42	0	0	0	0	34²	50	3	23	17	20.3	8.05	50	.338	.443	0	—	0	-16	-16	1	0.1
Total	18	167	143	.539	526	404	101	19	4	2770	2806	251	890	1491	12.1	3.90	100	.266	.325	0	—	0	36	-3	-1	3.7

● **RAY FLANIGAN** Flanigan, Raymond Arthur b: 1/8/23, Morgantown, W.Va. d: 3/28/93, Baltimore, Md. BR/TR, 6', 190 lbs. Deb: 9/20/46

1946	Cle-A	0	1	.000	3	1	0	0	0	9	11	1	8	2	19.0	11.00	30	.289	.413	1	.500	1	-7	-8	0	-0.6

● **TOM FLANIGAN** Flanigan, Thomas Anthony b: 9/6/34, Cincinnati, Ohio BR/TL, 6'3", 175 lbs. Deb: 4/14/54

1954	Chi-A	0	0	—	2	0	0	0	0	1²	1	0	1	0	10.8	0.00	—	.200	.333	0	—	0	1	1	0	0.0
1958	StL-N	0	0	—	1	0	0	0	0	1	2	1	1	0	27.0	9.00	46	.500	.600	0	—	0	-1	-1	-0	0.0
Total	2	0	0	—	3	0	0	0	0	2²	3	1	2	0	16.9	3.38	115	.333	.455	0	—	0	0	0	0	0.0

● **JACK FLATER** Flater, John William b: 9/22/1880, Sandymount, Md. d: 3/20/70, Westminster, Md. BR/TR, 5'10", 175 lbs. Deb: 9/18/08

1908	Phi-A	1	3	.250	5	3	3	0	0	39¹	35	0	12	8	11.2	2.06	125	.252	.320	2	.133	-0	1	2	2	0.4

● **JOHN FLAVIN** Flavin, John Thomas b: 5/7/42, Albany, Cal. BL/TL, 6'2", 208 lbs. Deb: 8/25/64

1964	Chi-N	0	1	.000	5	1	0	0	0	4²	11	0	3	5	27.0	13.50	28	.500	.560	0	.000	-0	-5	-5	-0	-1.0

● **FRANK FLEET** Fleet, Frank H. b: 1848, New York, N.Y. d: 6/13/1900, New York, N.Y. Deb: 10/18/1871 ◆

1871	Mut-n	0	1	.000	1	1	1	0	0	9	20	0	3	0	23.0	10.00	38	.370	.404	2	.333	0	-6	-6		-0.3
1873	Res-n	0	3	.000	3	3	2	0	0	24	57	0	0	1	21.4	5.63	60	.399	.399	23	.256	0	-6	-6		-0.4
1875	StL-n	2	1	.667	3	3	3	0	0	27	33	0	3		12.0	2.33	95	.277	.295	1	.063	-2	0	-0		-0.2
	Atl-n	0	1	.000	2	1	1	0	0	15¹	24	1	0		14.1	4.70	49	.312	.312	25	.223	-0	-4	-4		-0.2
	Yr	2	2	.500	5	4	4	0	0	42¹	57	1	3		12.8	3.19	71	.291	.302	26	.203	-2	-3	-4		-0.4
Total	3 n	2	6	.250	9	8	7	0	0	75¹	134	1	6	1	16.7	4.78	47	.341	.351	86	.231	-2	-19	-21		-1.1

● **DAVE FLEMING** Fleming, David Anthony b: 11/7/69, Jackson Heights, N.Y. BL/TL, 6'3", 200 lbs. Deb: 8/6/91

1991	Sea-A	1	0	1.000	9	3	0	0	0	17²	19	3	11	12.7	6.62	62	.284	.342	0	—	0	-5	-5	1	-0.1
1992	Sea-A	17	10	.630	33	33	7	4	0	228¹	225	13	60	112	11.4	3.39	117	.257	.307	0	—	0	14	15	-0	1.6
1993	Sea-A	12	5	.706	26	26	1	1	0	167¹	189	15	67	75	14.1	4.36	101	.290	.361	0	—	0	-1	1	1	0.1
1994	Sea-A	7	11	.389	23	23	0	0	0	117	152	17	65	65	16.8	6.46	76	.311	.394	0	—	0	-22	-20	0	-2.5
Total	4	37	26	.587	91	85	8	5	0	530¹	585	48	195	263	13.5	4.48	96	.281	.346	0	—	0	-13	-10	2	-0.9

● **BILL FLEMING** Fleming, Leslie Fletchard b: 7/31/13, Rowland, Cal. BR/TR, 6', 190 lbs. Deb: 8/21/40

1940	Bos-A	1	2	.333	10	6	1	0	0	46¹	53	4	20	24	14.6	4.86	93	.290	.366	0	.000	-2	-2	-2	-1	-0.3
1941	Bos-A	1	1	.500	16	1	0	0	1	41¹	32	4	24	20	12.2	3.92	106	.212	.320	2	.222	1	1	1	1	0.2
1942	Chi-N	5	6	.455	33	14	4	2	2	134¹	117	9	63	59	12.3	3.01	106	.230	.318	2	.051	-4	4	3	-1	-0.3
1943	Chi-N	0	1	1.000	11	0	0	0	0	32¹	41	2	12	12	15.6	6.40	52	.311	.381	0	.000	-1	-11	-11	1	-0.3
1944	Chi-N	9	10	.474	39	18	9	1	0	158¹	163	6	62	42	13.2	3.13	113	.269	.337	9	.170	-1	9	7	1	0.8
1946	Chi-N	0	1	.000	14	1	0	0	0	29¹	37	2	12	10	15.3	6.14	54	.301	.368	0	.000	-0	-9	-9	0	-0.3
Total	6	16	21	.432	123	40	14	3	3	442	443	27	193	167	13.2	3.79	94	.260	.339	13	.104	-7	-8	-11	1	-0.2

● **HUCK FLENER** Flener, Gregory Alan b: 2/25/69, Austin, Tex. BB/TL, 5'11", 185 lbs. Deb: 9/14/93

1993	Tor-A	0	0	—	6	0	0	0	0	6²	7	0	4	2	14.9	4.05	107	.269	.367	0	—	0	0	0	0	0.0

● **VAN FLETCHER** Fletcher, Alfred Vanoide b: 8/6/24, East Bend, N.C. BR/TR, 6'2", 185 lbs. Deb: 4/12/55

1955	Det-A	0	0	—	9	0	0	0	0	12	13	1	2	4	11.3	3.00	128	.260	.288	0	—	0	1	1	-0	0.0

● **PAUL FLETCHER** Fletcher, Edward Paul b: 1/14/67, Gallipolis, Ohio BR/TR, 6'1", 185 lbs. Deb: 7/11/93

1993	Phi-N	0	0	—	1	0	0	0	0	0¹	0	0	0	0	0.0	0.00	—	.000	.000	0	—	0	0	0	0	0.0

● **SAM FLETCHER** Fletcher, Samuel S. b: Altoona, Pa. TR, 6'2", 210 lbs. Deb: 10/6/09

1909	Bro-N	0	1	.000	1	1	1	0	0	9	13	0	2	5	15.0	8.00	32	.351	.385	0	.000	-0	-5	-5	-0	-0.5
1912	Cin-N	0	0	—	2	0	0	0	0	9²	15	1	11	3	24.2	12.10	28	.366	.500	2	.500	1	-9	-9	0	0.1
Total	2	0	1	.000	3	1	1	0	0	18²	28	1	13	8	19.8	10.13	30	.359	.451	2	.286	0	-15	-15	0	-0.4

● **TOM FLETCHER** Fletcher, Thomas Wayne b: 6/28/42, Elmira, N.Y. BB/TL, 6', 170 lbs. Deb: 9/12/62 F

1962	Det-A	0	0	—	1	0	0	0	0	2	2	0	2	1	18.0	0.00	—	.250	.400	0	—	0	1	1	0	0.0

● **JOHN FLINN** Flinn, John Richard b: 9/2/54, Merced, Cal. BR/TR, 6', 175 lbs. Deb: 5/6/78

1978	Bal-A	1	1	.500	13	0	0	0	0	15²	24	3	13	8	21.3	8.04	43	.348	.451	0	—	0	-7	-8	0	-0.5
1979	Bal-A	0	0	—	4	0	0	0	0	2²	2	0	1	0	10.1	0.00	—	.222	.300	0	—	0	1	1	0	0.1
1980	Mil-A	2	1	.667	20	1	0	0	0	37	31	3	20	15	12.4	3.89	99	.220	.317	0	—	0	1	-0	-0	0.0
1982	Bal-A	2	0	1.000	5	0	0	0	2	13²	13	1	3	13	10.5	1.32	306	.260	.302	0	—	0	4	4	0	0.6
Total	4	5	2	.714	42	1	0	0	2	69	70	7	37	36	14.0	4.17	92	.260	.350	0	—	0	-1	-3	-0	0.2

● **HILLY FLITCRAFT** Flitcraft, Hildreth Milton b: 8/21/23, Woodstown, N.J. BL/TL, 6'2", 180 lbs. Deb: 8/31/42

1942	Phi-N	0	0	—	3	0	0	0	0	3¹	6	0	2	1	21.6	8.10	41	.429	.500	0	—	0	-2	-2	0	0.0

● **MORT FLOHR** Flohr, Moritz Herman "Dutch" b: 8/15/11, Canisteo, N.Y. BL/TL, 6', 173 lbs. Deb: 6/8/34

1934	Phi-A	0	2	.000	14	3	0	0	0	30²	34	3	33	6	20.0	5.87	75	.296	.456	4	.333	1	-5	-5	1	-0.1

● **JESSE FLORES** Flores, Jesse (Sandoval) b: 11/2/14, Guadalajara, Mexico d: 12/17/91, Orange, Cal. BR/TR, 5'10", 175 lbs. Deb: 4/16/42

1942	Chi-N	0	1	.000	4	0	0	0	0	5¹	5	1	2	6	11.8	3.38	95	.227	.292	0	—	0	-0	-0	0	0.0
1943	Phi-A	12	14	.462	31	27	13	0	0	231¹	208	13	70	113	11.0	3.11	109	.240	.301	14	.175	-0	5	7	1	0.9
1944	Phi-A	9	11	.450	27	25	11	2	0	185²	172	8	49	65	10.9	3.39	103	.245	.298	11	.172	-0	2	-1	0	0.1
1945	Phi-A	7	10	.412	29	24	9	4	1	191¹	180	6	63	52	11.6	3.43	100	.250	.314	9	.148	-2	-1	-0	-3	-0.5
1946	Phi-A	9	7	.563	29	15	8	4	0	155	147	8	38	48	10.8	2.32	153	.249	.295	11	.250	3	20	21	-2	2.3
1947	Phi-A	4	13	.235	28	20	4	0	0	151¹	139	10	59	41	11.8	3.39	112	.244	.315	10	.227	1	5	7	-1	0.1
1950	Cle-A	3	3	.500	28	2	1	1	4	53	53	3	25	27	13.4	3.74	116	.261	.345	0	.000	-2	4	4	-2	0.1
Total	7	44	59	.427	176	113	46	11	6	973	904	49	306	352	11.3	3.18	112	.246	.307	55	.181	-0	35	41	-7	3.7

● **BRYCE FLORIE** Florie, Bryce Bettencourt b: 5/21/70, Charleston, S.C. BR/TR, 6', 185 lbs. Deb: 7/17/94

1994	SD-N	0	0	—	9	0	0	0	0	9¹	8	0	3	8	10.6	0.96	436	.242	.306	0	—	0	3	3	1	0.1

YEAR TM/L	W	L	PCT	G	GS	CG	SH	SV	IP	H	HR	BB	SO	RAT	ERA	ERA+	OAV	OOB	BH	AVG	PB	PR	/A	PD	TPI

● BEN FLOWERS Flowers, Bennett b: 6/15/27, Wilson, N.C. BR/TR, 6'4", 195 lbs. Deb: 9/29/51

1951 Bos-A	0	0	—	1	0	0	0	0	3	2	0	1	4	9.0	0.00	—	.200	.273	0	.000	-0	1	1	-0	0.0
1953 Bos-A	1	4	.200	32	6	1	1	3	79¹	87	6	24	36	12.7	3.86	109	.280	.333	3	.158	-0	1	3	1	0.2
1955 Det-A	0	0	—	4	0	0	0	0	6	5	1	2	2	10.5	6.00	64	.238	.304	0	.000	-0	-1	-1	0	0.0
StL-N	1	0	1.000	4	4	0	0	0	27¹	27	1	12	19	12.8	3.62	112	.255	.331	1	.100	-1	1	1	-0	-0.1
1956 StL-N	1	1	.500	3	3	0	0	0	11²	15	1	5	5	15.4	6.94	54	.341	.408	0	.000	-1	-4	-4	-0	-0.6
Phi-N	0	2	.000	32	0	0	0	0	41	54	9	10	22	14.3	5.71	65	.331	.374	0	.000	-0	-9	-9	1	-0.3
Yr	1	3	.250	35	3	0	0	0	52²	69	10	15	27	14.5	5.98	62	.330	.378	0	.000	-1	-13	-13	1	-0.8
Total 4	3	7	.300	76	13	1	1	3	168¹	190	18	54	86	13.2	4.49	90	.290	.346	4	.111	-2	-10	-9	1	-0.8

● DICKIE FLOWERS Flowers, Charles Richard b: 1850, Philadelphia, Pa. d: 10/5/1892, Philadelphia, Pa. Deb: 6/3/1871 ◆

| 1871 Tro-n | 0 | 0 | — | 1 | 0 | 0 | 0 | 0 | 1 | 1 | 0 | 0 | 0 | 9.0 | 0.00 | — | .333 | .333 | 33 | .314 | 0 | 0 | 0 | | 0.0 |

● WES FLOWERS Flowers, Charles Wesley b: 8/13/13, Vanndale, Ark. d: 12/31/88, Wynne, Ark. BL/TL, 6'1.5", 190 lbs. Deb: 8/8/40

1940 Bro-N	1	1	.500	5	2	0	0	0	21	23	2	10	8	15.4	3.43	117	.299	.400	1	.200	-0	1	1	0	0.1
1944 Bro-N	1	1	.500	9	1	0	0	0	17¹	26	3	13	3	20.8	7.79	46	.333	.435	3	.600	1	-8	-8	-0	-0.7
Total 2	2	2	.500	14	3	0	0	0	38¹	49	5	23	11	17.8	5.40	70	.316	.418	4	.400	1	-7	-7	-0	-0.6

● CARNEY FLYNN Flynn, Cornelius Francis Xavier b: 1/23/1875, Cincinnati, Ohio d: 2/10/47, Cincinnati, Ohio BL/TL, 5'11", 165 lbs. Deb: 7/17/1894

1894 Cin-N	0	2	.000	2	1	0	0	0	7²	16	4	10	4	31.7	17.61	32	.420	.550	0	.000	-1	-10	-10	-0	-1.4
1896 NY-N	0	1	.000	3	2	1	0	0	10²	18	0	8	4	26.2	11.81	36	.370	.503	2	.500	2	-9	-9	-0	-1.0
Was-N	0	1	.000	4	1	1	0	0	20	43	0	10	3	24.7	8.55	52	.428	.489	2	.250	-0	-9	-9	-1	-0.4
Yr	0	3	.000	7	3	2	0	0	30²	61	0	18	7	23.8	9.68	45	.396	.465	4	.333	1	-18	-18	-1	-1.4
Total 2	0	5	.000	9	4	2	0	0	38¹	77	4	28	11	26.5	11.27	41	.412	.506	4	.267	1	-29	-29	-1	-2.8

● JOCKO FLYNN Flynn, John A. b: 6/30/1864, Lawrence, Mass. d: 12/30/07, Lawrence, Mass. TR, 5'6.5", 143 lbs. Deb: 5/1/1886 ◆

| 1886 Chi-N | 23 | 6 | **.793** | 32 | 29 | 28 | 2 | 1 | 257 | 207 | 9 | 63 | 146 | 9.5 | 2.24 | 163 | .210 | .257 | 41 | .200 | 1 | 31 | 40 | 2 | 4.1 |

● STU FLYTHE Flythe, Stuart Mcguire b: 12/5/11, Conway, N.C. d: 10/18/63, Durham, N.C. BR/TR, 6'2", 175 lbs. Deb: 5/31/36

| 1936 Phi-A | 0 | 0 | — | 17 | 3 | 0 | 0 | 0 | 39¹ | 49 | 4 | 61 | 14 | 25.9 | 13.04 | 39 | .302 | .500 | 4 | .267 | 0 | -35 | -35 | -0 | 0.0 |

● GENE FODGE Fodge, Eugene Arlan "Suds" b: 7/9/31, South Bend, Ind. BR/TR, 6', 175 lbs. Deb: 4/20/58

| 1958 Chi-N | 1 | 1 | .500 | 16 | 4 | 1 | 0 | 0 | 39² | 47 | 5 | 11 | 15 | 13.2 | 4.76 | 82 | .296 | .341 | 0 | .000 | -1 | -4 | -4 | 0 | -0.2 |

● JIM FOGARTY Fogarty, James G. b: 2/12/1864, San Francisco, Cal d: 5/20/1891, Philadelphia, Pa. BR/TR, 5'10.5", 180 lbs. Deb: 5/1/1884 FM ◆

1884 Phi-N	0	0	—	1	0	0	0	0	1	2	0	1	0	18.0	0.00	—	.333	.333	80	.212	0	0	0	0	0.0
1886 Phi-N	0	1	.000	1	1	0	0	0	6	7	1	0	4	10.5	0.00	—	.250	.250	82	.293	0	2	2	0	0.4
1887 Phi-N	0	0	—	1	0	0	0	0	3	3	0	1	0	12.0	9.00	47	.200	.250	129	.261	0	-2	-2	-0	0.0
1889 Phi-N	0	0	—	4	0	0	0	0	4	4	0	2	1	13.5	9.00	48	.252	.336	129	.259	1	-2	-2	0	0.0
Total 4	0	1	.000	7	0	0	0	0	14	16	1	3	5	12.2	4.50	84	.247	.280	709	.246	2	-1	-1	0	0.4

● CURRY FOLEY Foley, Charles Joseph b: 1/14/1856, Milltown, Ireland d: 10/20/1898, Boston, Mass. TL, 5'10", 160 lbs. Deb: 5/13/1879 ◆

1879 Bos-N	9	9	.500	21	16	16	0	0	161²	175	1	15	57	10.6	2.51	99	.252	.268	46	.315	5	-0	-0	-2	0.2
1880 Bos-N	14	14	.500	36	28	21	1	0	238	264	3	40	68	11.5	3.89	58	.274	.292	8	-40	-43	1	-3.6		
1881 Buf-N	3	4	.429	10	6	2	0	0	41	70	1	5	2	16.5	5.27	53	.337	.352	96	.256	1	-11	-11	-0	-1.5
1882 Buf-N	0	0	—	1	0	0	0	0	1	2	0	0	0	18.0	18.00	16	.333	.333	104	.305	0	-2	-2	-0	0.0
1883 Buf-N	1	0	1.000	1	0	0	0	0	1	0	0	4	0	36.0	0.00	—	.000	.667	30	.270	0	0	0		0.3
Total 5	27	27	.500	69	50	39	2	0	442²	511	3	64	127	11.7	3.54	68	.273	.297	373	.286	14	-53	-56	-2	-4.6

● JOHN FOLEY Foley, John J b: Hannibal, Mo. TL, Deb: 9/18/1885

| 1885 Pro-N | 0 | 1 | .000 | 1 | 1 | 1 | 0 | 0 | 8 | 6 | 0 | 5 | 2 | 12.4 | 4.50 | 59 | .188 | .297 | 0 | .000 | 0 | -1 | -1 | 0 | -0.2 |

● TOM FOLEY Foley, Thomas Michael b: 9/9/59, Columbus, Ga. BL/TR, 6'1", 175 lbs. Deb: 4/9/83 ◆

| 1989 Mon-N | 0 | 0 | — | 1 | 0 | 0 | 0 | 0 | 0¹ | 1 | 1 | 0 | 0 | 27.0 | 27.00 | 13 | .500 | .500 | 86 | .229 | 0 | -1 | -1 | 0 | 0.0 |

● RICH FOLKERS Folkers, Richard Nevin b: 10/17/46, Waterloo, Iowa BL/TL, 6'2", 180 lbs. Deb: 6/10/70

1970 NY-N	0	2	.000	16	1	0	0	2	29¹	36	6	25	15	18.7	6.44	62	.313	.436	2	.333	0	-8	-8	1	-0.4
1972 StL-N	1	0	1.000	9	0	0	0	0	13¹	12	0	5	7	11.5	3.38	101	.240	.309	0	.000	-0	0	0	-0	0.0
1973 StL-N	4	4	.500	34	9	1	0	3	82¹	74	10	34	44	12.1	3.61	101	.239	.321	2	.100	-1	0	0	0	-0.1
1974 StL-N	6	2	.750	55	0	0	0	2	90	65	4	38	57	10.5	3.00	119	.207	.297	1	.100	-1	6	6	-1	0.3
1975 SD-N	6	11	.353	45	15	4	0	0	142	155	8	39	87	12.4	4.18	83	.278	.327	6	.167	1	-9	-11	-0	-1.1
1976 SD-N	2	3	.400	33	3	0	0	0	59²	67	10	26	26	14.2	5.28	62	.279	.352	0	.000	0	-12	-13	-0	-1.1
1977 Mil-A	0	1	.000	3	0	0	0	0	6¹	7	2	4	6	15.6	4.26	95	.269	.367	0	—	-0	-0	-0	0	0.0
Total 7	19	23	.452	195	28	5	0	7	423	416	40	170	242	12.6	4.11	86	.258	.332	11	.143	-1	-22	-27	-1	-2.4

● LEW FONSECA Fonseca, Lewis Albert b: 1/21/1899, Oakland, Cal. d: 11/26/89, Ely, Iowa BR/TR, 5'10.5", 180 lbs. Deb: 4/13/21 M ◆

| 1932 Chi-A | 0 | 0 | — | 1 | 0 | 0 | 0 | 0 | 1 | 1 | 0 | 0 | 0 | 0.0 | 0.00 | — | .000 | .000 | 5 | .135 | -0 | 0 | -0 | 0 | 0.0 |

● RAY FONTENOT Fontenot, Silton Ray b: 8/8/57, Lake Charles, La. BL/TL, 6', 175 lbs. Deb: 6/30/83

1983 NY-A	8	2	.800	15	15	3	1	0	97¹	101	3	25	27	11.7	3.33	117	.266	.314	0	—	0	8	6	1	0.8
1984 NY-A	8	9	.471	35	24	0	0	0	169¹	189	8	58	85	13.3	3.61	105	.290	.351	0	—	0	7	3	0	0.4
1985 Chi-N	6	10	.375	38	23	0	0	0	154²	177	23	45	70	12.9	4.36	91	.294	.343	2	.049	-3	-13	-6	2	-0.8
1986 Chi-N	3	5	.375	42	0	0	0	2	56	57	5	21	24	12.5	3.86	105	.266	.332	1	.167	-0	1	1	-1	0.1
Min-A	0	0	—	15	0	0	0	0	16¹	27	3	4	10	18.2	9.92	43	.360	.407	0	.000	0	-10	-10	0	0.0
Total 4	25	26	.490	145	62	3	1	2	493²	551	42	153	216	12.9	4.03	98	.287	.341	3	.063	-3	-10	-5	2	0.5

● JIM FOOR Foor, James Emerson b: 1/13/49, St.Louis, Mo. BL/TL, 6'2", 170 lbs. Deb: 4/9/71

1971 Det-A	0	0	—	3	0	0	0	0	1	2	0	4	2	54.0	18.00	20	.400	.667	0	—	0	-2	-2	0	0.0
1972 Det-A	1	0	1.000	7	0	0	0	0	3²	6	1	6	2	29.5	14.73	21	.353	.522	0	—	0	-5	-5	0	-1.2
1973 Pit-N	0	0	—	3	0	0	0	0	1¹	2	0	1	1	20.3	10.00	—	.286	.375	0	—	0	1	1	0	0.0
Total 3	1	0	1.000	13	0	0	0	0	6	10	1	11	5	31.5	12.00	28	.345	.525	0	—	0	-6	-6	0	-1.2

● DAVY FORCE Force, David W. "Wee Davy" or "Tom Thumb" b: 7/27/1849, New York, N.Y. d: 6/21/18, Englewood, N.J. BR/TR, 5'4", 130 lbs. Deb: 5/5/1871 ◆

1873 Bal-n	1	1	.500	3	1	1	0	0	18	23	0	0	0	11.5	3.50	93	.264	.264	86	.368	1	-0	-0		0.0
1874 Chi-n	0	0	—	1	0	0	0	0	7	22	4	0	0	28.3	12.86	24	.440	.440	93	.314	0	-8	-8		0.0
Total 2 n	1	1	.500	4	1	1	0	0	25	45	4	0	0	16.2	6.12	50	.328	.328	437	.335	2	-9	-9		0.0

● DAVE FORD Ford, David Alan b: 12/29/56, Cleveland, Ohio BR/TR, 6'4", 190 lbs. Deb: 9/2/78

1978 Bal-A	1	0	1.000	2	1	0	0	0	15	10	0	2	5	7.2	1.20	—	.196	.226	0	—	0	6	6	-0	1.1
1979 Bal-A	2	1	.667	9	2	0	0	2	30	23	2	7	9	9.0	2.10	191	.219	.268	0	—	0	7	6	0	1.0
1980 Bal-A	1	3	.250	25	3	0	0	0	69²	66	11	13	22	10.5	4.26	93	.251	.291	0	—	0	-2	-2	-1	-0.2
1981 Bal-A	1	2	.333	15	2	0	0	0	40	61	2	19	12	16.0	6.52	56	.359	.394	0	—	0	-13	-13	-0	-0.9
Total 4	5	6	.455	51	8	0	0	2	154²	160	15	41	48	11.3	4.02	96	.272	.311	0	—	0	-1	-1	-1	1.0

● WHITEY FORD Ford, Edward Charles "Chairman Of The Board" b: 10/21/28, New York, N.Y. BL/TL, 5'10", 181 lbs. Deb: 7/1/50 CH

| 1950 *NY-A | 9 | 1 | .900 | 20 | 12 | 7 | 2 | 1 | 112 | 87 | 7 | 52 | 59 | 11.3 | 2.81 | 153 | .216 | .309 | 7 | .194 | 0 | 22 | 18 | -0 | 1.5 |

YEAR TM/L	W	L	PCT	G	GS	CG	SH	SV	IP	H	HR	BB	SO	RAT	ERA	ERA+	OAV	OOB	BH	AVG	PB	PR	/A	PD	TPI
1953 *NY-A	18	6	.750	32	30	11	3	0	207	187	13	110	110	13.1	3.00	123	.245	.344	20	.267	6	23	16	0	2.3
1954 NY-A★	16	8	.667	34	28	11	3	1	210²	170	10	101	125	11.6	2.82	122	.227	.319	10	.161	2	21	14	1	1.8
1955 *NY-A★	**18**	7	.720	39	33	**18**	5	2	253²	188	20	113	137	10.7	2.63	143	.208	.297	14	.163	2	38	31	0	3.1
1956 *NY-A	19	6	**.760**	31	30	18	2	1	225²	187	13	84	141	11.0	**2.47**	156	.228	.303	17	.218	3	42	35	5	4.5
1957 *NY-A	11	5	.688	24	17	5	0	0	129¹	114	10	53	84	11.7	2.57	139	.237	.313	6	.143	-1	17	15	2	1.8
1958 *NY-A☆	14	7	.667	30	29	15	**7**	1	219¹	174	14	62	145	**9.8**	**2.01**	**176**	.217	**.276**	15	.205	-2	**43**	**37**	1	**3.9**
1959 NY-A★	16	10	.615	35	29	9	2	1	204	194	13	89	114	12.5	3.04	120	.250	.328	7	.231	7	19	14	4	2.8
1960 *NY-A★	12	9	.571	33	29	8	**4**	0	192²	168	15	65	85	10.9	3.08	116	.235	.299	8	.151	2	17	11	1	1.4
1961 *NY-A★	**25**	4	**.862**	39	39	11	3	0	**283**	242	23	92	209	10.7	3.21	116	.229	.292	17	.177	3	26	16	0	1.8
1962 *NY-A	17	8	.680	38	37	7	0	0	257²	243	22	69	160	11.0	2.90	129	.246	.298	10	.118	-1	31	24	4	2.6
1963 *NY-A	24	7	**.774**	38	37	13	3	1	269¹	240	26	56	189	10.0	2.74	128	.241	.283	13	.141	0	27	23	-0	2.5
1964 *NY-A☆	17	6	.739	39	36	12	8	1	244²	212	10	57	172	10.0	2.13	170	.230	.276	8	.119	1	41	40	2	4.2
1965 NY-A	16	13	.552	37	36	9	2	1	244¹	241	22	50	162	10.8	3.24	105	.258	.297	15	.183	2	6	4	2	0.9
1966 NY-A	2	5	.286	22	9	0	0	0	73	79	8	24	43	12.7	2.47	135	.277	.333	0	.000	-2	8	7	3	0.8
1967 NY-A	2	4	.333	7	7	2	1	0	44	40	2	9	21	10.0	1.64	191	.247	.287	2	.154	-0	8	7	2	1.3
Total 16	236	106	.690	498	438	156	45	10	3170¹	2766	228	1086	1956	11.0	2.75	133	.235	.301	177	.173	27	386	315	26	37.2

● **GENE FORD**　Ford, Eugene Matthew　b: 6/23/12, Ft.Dodge, Iowa　d: 9/7/70, Emmetsburg, Iowa　BR/TR, 6'2", 195 lbs.　Deb: 6/17/36

YEAR TM/L	W	L	PCT	G	GS	CG	SH	SV	IP	H	HR	BB	SO	RAT	ERA	ERA+	OAV	OOB	BH	AVG	PB	PR	/A	PD	TPI
1936 Bos-N	0	0	—	2	1	0	0	0	2	2	0	3	0	22.5	13.50	28	.250	.455	0	—	0	-2	-2	0	0.0
1938 Chi-A	0	0	—	4	0	0	0	0	14	21	1	12	2	21.2	10.29	48	.350	.458	1	.167	-0	-9	-8	0	0.0
Total 2	0	0	—	6	1	0	0	0	16	23	1	15	2	21.4	10.69	44	.338	.458	1	.167	-0	-11	-11	0	0.0

● **GENE FORD**　Ford, Eugene Wyman　b: 4/16/1881, Milton, N.S., Can.　d: 8/23/73, Dunedin, Fla.　BR/TR, 6', 170 lbs.　Deb: 5/5/05　F

YEAR TM/L	W	L	PCT	G	GS	CG	SH	SV	IP	H	HR	BB	SO	RAT	ERA	ERA+	OAV	OOB	BH	AVG	PB	PR	/A	PD	TPI
1905 Det-A	0	1	.000	7	1	1	0	0	35	51	0	14	20	17.2	5.66	48	.340	.404	0	.000	-1	-12	-11	0	-0.4

● **WENTY FORD**　Ford, Percival Edmund Wentworth　b: 11/25/46, Nassau, Bahamas　d: 7/8/80, Nassau, Bahamas　BR/TR, 5'11", 165 lbs.　Deb: 9/10/73

YEAR TM/L	W	L	PCT	G	GS	CG	SH	SV	IP	H	HR	BB	SO	RAT	ERA	ERA+	OAV	OOB	BH	AVG	PB	PR	/A	PD	TPI
1973 Atl-N	1	2	.333	4	2	1	0	0	16¹	17	3	8	4	14.3	5.51	71	.279	.371	2	.400	-0	-3	-3	0	-0.4

● **RUSS FORD**　Ford, Russell William　b: 4/25/1883, Brandon, Man., Can.　d: 1/24/60, Rockingham, N.C.　BR/TR, 5'11", 175 lbs.　Deb: 4/28/09　F

YEAR TM/L	W	L	PCT	G	GS	CG	SH	SV	IP	H	HR	BB	SO	RAT	ERA	ERA+	OAV	OOB	BH	AVG	PB	PR	/A	PD	TPI
1909 NY-A	0	0	—	1	0	0	0	0	3	4	0	4	0	33.0	9.00	28	.333	.579	0	.000	-0	-2	-2	0	0.0
1910 NY-A	26	6	.813	36	33	29	8	1	299²	194	4	70	209	8.2	1.65	161	.188	.245	20	.208	4	29	34	-3	4.0
1911 NY-A	22	11	.667	37	33	26	1	0	281¹	251	3	76	158	10.6	2.27	158	.237	.291	20	.196	-2	34	41	-1	4.3
1912 NY-A	13	21	.382	36	35	30	0	0	291²	317	10	79	112	12.4	3.55	101	.280	.329	32	.286	5	-7	1	1	0.9
1913 NY-A	12	18	.400	33	28	15	1	2	237	244	9	58	72	11.6	2.66	113	.275	.322	12	.162	0	7	9	-4	0.8
1914 Buf-F	21	6	**.778**	35	26	19	5	**6**	247¹	190	11	41	123	8.7	1.82	**163**	.214	.254	10	.128	-4	29	31	0	3.1
1915 Buf-F	5	9	.357	21	15	7	0	0	127¹	140	7	48	34	13.5	4.52	62	.285	.352	12	.279	-3	-25	-24	-0	-2.2
Total 7	99	71	.582	199	170	126	15	9	1487¹	1340	44	376	710	10.6	2.59	121	.243	.296	106	.209	5	64	89	-5	10.9

● **TOM FORD**　Ford, Thomas Walter　b: 1866, Chattanooga, Tenn.　d: 5/27/17, Chattanooga, Tenn.　5'10.5", 155 lbs.　Deb: 5/6/1890

YEAR TM/L	W	L	PCT	G	GS	CG	SH	SV	IP	H	HR	BB	SO	RAT	ERA	ERA+	OAV	OOB	BH	AVG	PB	PR	/A	PD	TPI
1890 Col-a	0	0	—	1	0	0	0	0	2	0	0	3	0	13.5	0.00	—	.000	.336	0	.000	-0	1	1	0	0.0
Bro-a	0	6	.000	7	6	6	0	0	49	70	2	32	12	18.7	5.14	76	.325	.413	1	.033	-3	-7	-7	0	-0.8
Yr	0	6	.000	8	6	6	0	0	51	70	2	35	12	18.7	4.94	79	.317	.410	1	.032	-3	-6	-6	1	-0.8

● **HAPPY FOREMAN**　Foreman, August　b: 7/20/1897, Memphis, Tenn.　d: 2/13/53, New York, N.Y.　BL/TL, 5'7", 160 lbs.　Deb: 9/3/24

YEAR TM/L	W	L	PCT	G	GS	CG	SH	SV	IP	H	HR	BB	SO	RAT	ERA	ERA+	OAV	OOB	BH	AVG	PB	PR	/A	PD	TPI
1924 Chi-A	0	0	—	3	0	0	0	0	4	7	0	4	1	24.8	2.25	183	.467	.579	0	.000	-0	1	1	-0	-0.1
1926 Bos-A	0	0	—	3	0	0	0	0	7¹	3	0	5	3	9.8	3.68	111	.130	.286	0	.000	-0	0	0	1	0.0
Total 2	0	0	—	6	0	0	0	0	11¹	10	0	9	4	15.1	3.18	129	.263	.404	0	.000	-1	1	1	0	-0.1

● **FRANK FOREMAN**　Foreman, Francis Isaiah "Monkey"　b: 5/1/1863, Baltimore, Md.　d: 11/19/57, Baltimore, Md.　BL/TL, 6', 160 lbs.　Deb: 5/15/1884　F♦

YEAR TM/L	W	L	PCT	G	GS	CG	SH	SV	IP	H	HR	BB	SO	RAT	ERA	ERA+	OAV	OOB	BH	AVG	PB	PR	/A	PD	TPI
1884 CP-U	1	2	.333	3	3	1	0	0	18	23	0	2	10	12.5	4.00	61	.291	.309	1	.091	-2	-3	-3	-0	-0.5
KC-U	0	1	.000	1	1	1	0	0	8	17	0	2	5	21.4	5.63	40	.406	.433	0	.000	-1	-3	-3	1	-0.3
Yr	1	3	.250	4	4	2	0	0	26	40	0	4	15	15.2	4.50	53	.331	.352	1	.071	-3	-6	-6	1	-0.8
1885 Bal-a	2	1	.667	3	3	2	0	0	27	33	0	9	11	14.3	6.00	54	.284	.341	4	.286	1	-8	-8	-0	-0.6
1889 Bal-a	23	21	.523	51	48	43	5	0	414	364	8	137	180	11.8	3.52	112	.229	.306	26	.144	-10	15	19	-2	0.5
1890 Cin-N	13	10	.565	25	24	20	0	0	198¹	201	6	89	90	14.1	3.95	90	.255	.345	10	.133	-0	-8	-9	-3	-1.1
1891 Was-a	18	20	.474	43	41	39	1	1	345¹	381	9	142	170	14.8	3.73	100	.271	.355	34	.222	9	-1	-1	-0	0.9
1892 Was-N	2	4	.333	11	7	4	0	0	60	53	3	37	16	14.3	3.30	99	.228	.345	13	.464	8	-0	-0	-1	0.6
Bal-N	0	3	.000	4	3	2	0	0	25	40	4	11	5	18.7	6.84	50	.348	.409	4	.174	0	-10	-9	-0	-0.8
Yr	2	7	.222	15	10	6	0	0	85	93	7	48	21	15.0	4.34	76	.263	.353	17	.333	8	-10	-10	-1	-0.2
1893 NY-N	0	1	.000	2	1	0	0	0	5²	19	1	10	0	47.6	27.00	17	.531	.641	0	.000	-1	-14	-14	-0	-1.4
1895 Cin-N	11	14	.440	32	27	19	0	1	219	253	11	92	55	14.8	4.11	121	.285	.362	29	.309	4	16	21	-3	1.9
1896 Cin-N	14	7	.667	27	22	17	0	1	185²	212	2	62	33	13.7	3.97	116	.285	.346	18	.243	-1	8	13	-1	1.0
1901 Bos-A	0	1	.000	1	1	1	0	0	8	8	1	2	1	13.5	9.00	39	.257	.342	0	.000	-1	-5	-5	-0	-0.5
Bal-A	12	6	.667	24	22	18	1	1	191¹	225	2	58	41	13.6	3.67	105	.290	.344	26	.325	5	-0	4	-3	0.5
Yr	12	7	.632	25	23	19	1	1	199¹	233	3	60	42	13.5	3.88	99	.288	.341	26	.310	4	-5	-1	-3	0.0
1902 Bal-A	0	2	.000	2	2	2	0	0	16¹	28	0	6	2	18.7	6.06	62	.377	.423	3	.429	1	-5	-4	1	-0.3
Total 11	96	93	.508	229	205	169	7	4	1721²	1857	47	659	586	13.9	3.97	100	.268	.344	169	.224	12	-17	1	-14	-0.1

● **BROWNIE FOREMAN**　Foreman, John Davis　b: 8/6/1875, Baltimore, Md.　d: 10/10/26, Baltimore, Md.　BL/TL, 5'8", 150 lbs.　Deb: 7/18/1895　F

YEAR TM/L	W	L	PCT	G	GS	CG	SH	SV	IP	H	HR	BB	SO	RAT	ERA	ERA+	OAV	OOB	BH	AVG	PB	PR	/A	PD	TPI
1895 Pit-N	8	6	.571	19	16	12	0	2	139²	131	0	64	54	13.8	3.22	140	**.244**	.346	3	.065	-6	24	20	2	1.3
1896 Pit-N	3	3	.500	9	9	5	0	0	61²	73	4	35	18	16.9	6.57	60	.292	.396	3	.150	0	-15	-16	1	-1.1
Cin-N	1	3	.250	4	4	3	1	0	23	41	2	16	9	23.1	11.35	41	.383	.472	2	.200	-0	-18	-17	0	-1.9
Yr	4	6	.400	13	13	8	1	0	84²	114	6	51	27	17.8	7.87	55	.312	.399	5	.167	-0	-33	-33	1	-3.0
Total 2	12	12	.500	32	29	20	1	2	224¹	245	6	115	81	15.6	4.97	89	.274	.375	8	.105	-6	-9	-13	3	-1.7

● **BILL FORMAN**　Forman, William Orange　b: 10/10/1886, Venango, Pa.　d: 10/3/58, Uniontown, Pa.　BB/TR, 5'11", 180 lbs.　Deb: 9/20/09

YEAR TM/L	W	L	PCT	G	GS	CG	SH	SV	IP	H	HR	BB	SO	RAT	ERA	ERA+	OAV	OOB	BH	AVG	PB	PR	/A	PD	TPI
1909 Was-A	0	2	.000	2	2	1	0	0	11	8	0	7	2	13.9	4.91	50	.211	.362	1	.333	0	-3	-3	1	-0.4
1910 Was-A	0	0	—	1	0	0	0	0	0²	1	0	0	0	13.5	13.50	18	.333	.333	0	—	0	-1	-1	-0	0.0
Total 2	0	2	.000	3	2	1	0	0	11²	9	0	7	2	13.9	5.40	45	.220	.360	1	.333	1	-4	-4	1	-0.4

● **MIKE FORNIELES**　Fornieles, Jose Miguel (Torres)　b: 1/18/32, Havana, Cuba　BR/TR, 5'11", 172 lbs.　Deb: 9/2/52

YEAR TM/L	W	L	PCT	G	GS	CG	SH	SV	IP	H	HR	BB	SO	RAT	ERA	ERA+	OAV	OOB	BH	AVG	PB	PR	/A	PD	TPI
1952 Was-A	2	2	.500	4	2	2	1	0	26¹	13	1	11	12	8.2	1.37	260	.143	.235	0	.000	-1	7	6	-0	0.8
1953 Chi-A	8	7	.533	39	16	5	0	3	153	160	8	61	72	13.1	3.59	112	.270	.340	4	.098	-3	7	7	2	0.6
1954 Chi-A	1	2	.333	15	6	0	0	0	42	41	4	14	18	11.8	4.29	87	.252	.311	3	.273	0	-3	-3	1	-0.1
1955 Chi-A	6	3	.667	26	9	2	0	2	86¹	84	12	29	23	12.0	3.86	102	.255	.319	3	.103	-2	1	1	-0	-0.1
1956 Chi-A	0	1	.000	6	0	0	0	0	15²	22	1	6	6	16.1	4.60	89	.306	.359	1	.200	0	-1	-1	-0	-0.1
Bal-A	4	7	.364	30	11	1	1	1	111	109	7	25	53	10.9	3.97	99	.266	.308	5	.167	-1	2	-1	2	0.1
Yr	4	8	.333	36	11	1	1	1	126²	131	8	31	59	11.5	4.05	97	.271	.315	6	.171	-1	2	-1	2	-0.1
1957 Bal-A	2	6	.250	15	4	1	0	0	57	57	4	17	11	11.7	4.26	84	.257	.310	1	.278	-1	-3	-4	1	-0.4
Bos-A	8	7	.533	25	18	7	1	2	125¹	136	7	38	64	12.7	3.52	113	.271	.327	6	.136	-2	4	7	1	0.4
Yr	10	13	.435	40	22	8	1	2	182¹	193	11	55	75	12.2	3.75	103	.267	.321	7	.177	-1	1	3	2	-0.1
1958 Bos-A	4	6	.400	37	7	1	0	1	110²	123	10	33	49	13.2	4.96	81	.284	.343	6	.207	-0	-15	-12	-0	-1.1
1959 Bos-A	5	3	.625	46	0	0	0	11	82	77	6	29	54	11.7	3.07	132	.254	.321	1	.158	-1	7	9	-0	1.0
1960 Bos-A	10	5	.667	**70**	0	0	0	**14**	109	86	6	49	64	11.6	2.64	153	.219	.315	2	.400	2	15	17	1	2.9
1961 Bos-A★	9	8	.529	57	2	1	0	15	119¹	121	18	54	70	13.3	4.68	89	.265	.345	5	.156	0	-9	-7	2	-0.9

YEAR	TM/L	W	L	PCT	G	GS	CG	SH	SV	IP	H	HR	BB	SO	RAT	ERA	ERA+	OAV	OOB	BH	AVG	PB	PR	/A	PD	TPI
1962	Bos-A	3	6	.333	42	1	0	0	5	82¹	96	14	37	36	15.4	5.36	77	.303	.390	3	.188	-0	-13	-11	-0	-1.3
1963	Bos-A	0	0	—	9	0	0	0	0	14	16	0	5	5	13.5	6.43	59	.286	.344	1	.333	1	-4	-4	-0	0.0
	Min-A	1	1	.500	11	0	0	0	0	22²	24	0	13	7	15.5	4.76	76	.273	.379	1	.167	-0	-3	-3	-1	-0.3
	Yr	1	1	.500	20	0	0	0	0	36²	40	0	18	12	14.7	5.40	68	.276	.364	2	.222	1	-7	-7	-1	-0.3
Total 12		63	64	.496	432	76	20	4	55	1156²	1165	98	421	576	12.6	3.96	100	.263	.332	52	.169	-6	-7	2	4	1.6

● KEN FORSCH

Forsch, Kenneth Roth: b: 9/8/46, Sacramento, Cal. BR/TR, 6'4", 210 lbs. Deb: 9/7/70 F

YEAR	TM/L	W	L	PCT	G	GS	CG	SH	SV	IP	H	HR	BB	SO	RAT	ERA	ERA+	OAV	OOB	BH	AVG	PB	PR	/A	PD	TPI
1970	Hou-N	1	2	.333	4	4	1	0	0	24	28	1	5	13	12.4	5.63	69	.298	.333	0	.000	-1	-4	-5	-0	-0.6
1971	Hou-N	8	8	.500	33	23	7	2	0	188¹	162	8	53	131	10.5	2.53	133	.230	.288	8	.136	-1	20	17	-2	1.1
1972	Hou-N	6	8	.429	30	24	1	0	0	156¹	163	19	62	113	13.0	3.91	86	.273	.341	6	.146	-1	-8	-10	-3	-1.1
1973	Hou-N	9	12	.429	46	26	5	0	4	201¹	197	18	74	149	12.3	4.20	86	.257	.325	4	.065	-4	-12	-13	-2	-1.9
1974	Hou-N	8	7	.533	70	0	0	0	10	103¹	98	3	37	48	12.1	2.79	124	.255	.326	0	.000	-1	10	8	-0	1.2
1975	Hou-N	4	8	.333	34	9	2	0	2	109	114	9	30	54	12.1	3.22	105	.277	.330	1	.045	-1	5	2	-0	0.1
1976	Hou-N★	4	3	.571	52	0	0	0	19	92	76	5	26	49	10.2	2.15	148	.226	.286	1	.091	-0	14	11	1	1.3
1977	Hou-N	5	8	.385	42	5	0	0	8	86	80	2	28	45	11.5	2.72	131	.246	.310	1	.077	-1	11	8	1	1.3
1978	Hou-N	10	6	.625	52	6	4	2	7	133¹	136	2	37	71	11.7	2.70	123	.268	.319	5	.185	0	13	9	1	1.2
1979	Hou-N	11	6	.647	26	24	10	2	0	177²	155	14	35	58	**9.6**	3.04	116	.236	**.275**	8	.138	0	14	9	2	1.1
1980	*Hou-N	12	13	.480	32	32	6	3	0	222¹	230	15	41	84	11.3	3.20	103		.304	18	.234	4	10	2	1	0.8
1981	Cal-A★	11	7	.611	20	20	10	**4**	0	153	143	7	55	10.2		2.88	126	.250	.289	0	—	0	13	13	1	1.6
1982	Cal-A	13	11	.542	37	35	12	4	0	228	225	25	57	73	11.6	3.87	105	.258	.311	0	—	0	5	5	-2	0.3
1983	Cal-A	11	12	.478	31	31	11	0	0	219¹	226	21	61	81	11.9	4.06	99	.266	.318	0	—	0	-0	-1	-1	-0.2
1984	Cal-A	1	1	.500	2	2	1	0	0	16¹	14	2	3	10	9.4	2.20	180	.237	.274	0	—	0	3	3	1	0.5
1986	Cal-A	0	1	.000	10	0	0	0	0	17	24	4	10	13	19.1	9.53	43	.343	.439	0	—	0	-10	-10	-0	-0.6
Total 16		114	113	.502	521	241	70	18	51	2127¹	2071	155	586	1047	11.4	3.37	106	.257	.311	52	.136	-5	83	48	-3	6.1

● BOB FORSCH

Forsch, Robert Herbert b: 1/13/50, Sacramento, Cal. BR/TL, 6'4", 200 lbs. Deb: 7/7/74 F

YEAR	TM/L	W	L	PCT	G	GS	CG	SH	SV	IP	H	HR	BB	SO	RAT	ERA	ERA+	OAV	OOB	BH	AVG	PB	PR	/A	PD	TPI
1974	StL-N	7	4	.636	19	14	5	2	0	100	84	5	34	39	10.7	2.97	120	.230	.298	7	.241	1	7	7	-0	0.9
1975	StL-N	15	10	.600	34	34	7	4	0	230	213	14	70	108	11.2	2.86	131	.244	.303	24	.308	9	20	23	2	3.7
1976	StL-N	8	10	.444	33	32	2	0	0	194	209	17	71	76	13.1	3.94	90	.277	.341	11	.177	1	-10	-9	1	-0.6
1977	StL-N	20	7	.741	35	35	8	2	0	217¹	210	20	69	95	11.7	3.48	111	.251	.311	12	.167	0	10	9	-1	0.9
1978	StL-N	11	17	.393	34	34	7	3	0	233²	205	15	97	114	11.8	3.70	95	.238	.318	15	.181	3	-3	-5	1	-0.1
1979	StL-N	11	11	.500	33	32	7	1	0	218²	215	16	52	92	11.1	3.83	98	.262	.309	8	.110	-0	-2	-2	1	-0.1
1980	StL-N	11	10	.524	31	31	8	0	0	214²	225	12	43	76	11.5	3.77	98	.273	.304	23	.295	9	-4	-2	2	1.0
1981	StL-N	10	5	.667	20	20	1	0	0	124¹	106	7	29	41	10.1	3.18	112	.232	.284	5	.122	-1	4	5	0	0.5
1982	*StL-N	15	9	.625	36	34	6	2	1	233	238	16	54	69	11.4	3.48	104	.268	.313	15	.205	3	3	4	-2	0.5
1983	StL-N	10	12	.455	34	30	6	2	0	187	190	23	54	56	11.9	4.28	85	.266	.320	13	.241	4	-14	-14	-0	-1.1
1984	StL-N	2	5	.286	16	11	1	0	0	52¹	64	6	19	21	14.3	6.02	58	.303	.361	4	.250	1	-14	-15	0	-1.6
1985	*StL-N	9	6	.600	34	19	3	1	2	136	132	11	47	48	12.0	3.90	91	.258	.323	11	.244	4	-5	-6	-0	-0.2
1986	StL-N	14	10	.583	33	33	3	0	0	230	211	19	68	104	11.0	3.25	112	.247	.304	13	.171	3	12	10	-1	1.3
1987	*StL-N	11	7	.611	33	30	2	1	0	179	189	15	45	89	12.0	4.32	96	.273	.321	17	.298	8	-5	-3	1	0.4
1988	StL-N	9	4	.692	30	12	1	1	0	108¹	111	8	38	40	12.4	3.73	93	.270	.333	7	.280	2	-3	-3	-2	-0.3
	Hou-N	1	4	.200	6	6	0	0	0	27²	42	4	6	14	16.3	6.51	51	.359	.400	1	.143	0	-9	-10	-0	-1.5
	Yr	10	8	.556	36	18	1	1	0	136¹	153	10	44	54	13.1	4.29	80	.287	.344	8	.250	2	-13	-13	-2	-1.8
1989	Hou-N	4	5	.444	37	15	0	0	0	107¹	133	10	46	40	15.0	5.32	64	.303	.370	4	.167	-0	-22	-23	-1	-1.9
Total 16		168	136	.553	498	422	67	19	3	2794²	2777	216	832	1133	11.8	3.76	97	.261	.318	190	.213	48	-35	-33	-3	1.8

● TERRY FORSTER

Forster, Terry Jay b: 1/14/52, Sioux Falls, S.D. BL/TL, 6'3", 210 lbs. Deb: 4/11/71

YEAR	TM/L	W	L	PCT	G	GS	CG	SH	SV	IP	H	HR	BB	SO	RAT	ERA	ERA+	OAV	OOB	BH	AVG	PB	PR	/A	PD	TPI
1971	Chi-A	2	3	.400	45	3	0	0	1	49²	46	5	23	48	12.7	3.99	90	.241	.326	2	.400	1	-3	-2	0	-0.1
1972	Chi-A	6	5	.545	62	0	0	0	29	100	75	0	44	104	11.0	2.25	139	.208	.300	10	.526	4	9	10	1	2.5
1973	Chi-A	6	11	.353	51	12	4	0	16	172²	174	7	78	120	13.1	3.23	122	.266	.344	0	.000	0	11	14	5	2.1
1974	Chi-A	7	8	.467	59	1	0	0	**24**	134¹	120	6	48	105	11.8	3.62	103	.245	.322	0	—	0	0	2	3	0.6
1975	Chi-A	3	3	.500	17	1	0	0	4	37	30	1	24	32	13.1	2.19	177	.236	.358	0	—	0	7	7	2	1.4
1976	Chi-A	2	12	.143	29	16	1	0	1	111¹	126	7	41	70	13.6	4.37	82	.288	.351	0	—	0	-10	-10	2	-1.0
1977	Pit-N	6	4	.600	33	6	0	0	1	87¹	90	7	32	58	12.8	4.43	90	.269	.337	9	.346	3	-5	-4	-0	-0.2
1978	*LA-N	5	4	.556	47	0	0	0	22	65¹	56	2	23	46	10.9	1.93	182	.233	.300	4	.500	2	12	11	-0	2.7
1979	LA-N	1	2	.333	17	0	0	0	2	16¹	18	0	11	8	16.0	5.51	66	.295	.403	0	—	0	-3	-3	1	-0.6
1980	LA-N	0	0	—	9	0	0	0	0	11²	10	0	4	2	10.8	3.09	113	.222	.286	0	—	0	1	1	0	0.0
1981	*LA-N	0	1	.000	21	0	0	0	1	30²	37	1	15	17	15.3	4.11	81	.308	.385	0	.000	-0	-2	-3	1	-0.5
1982	LA-N	5	6	.455	56	0	0	0	3	83	66	3	31	52	11.0	3.04	114	.221	.302	0	.000	-0	5	4	1	0.6
1983	Atl-N	3	2	.600	56	0	0	0	13	79¹	60	3	31	54	10.6	2.16	180	.217	.301	4	.500	2	13	15	1	1.7
1984	Atl-N	2	0	1.000	25	0	0	0	5	26²	30	1	7	10	12.5	2.70	143	.297	.343	2	.667	1	3	3	0	0.5
1985	Atl-N	2	3	.400	46	0	0	0	1	59¹	49	7	28	37	11.7	2.28	169	.222	.309	0	—	0	9	10	-1	0.8
1986	Cal-A	4	1	.800	41	0	0	0	5	41	47	2	17	28	14.7	3.51	117	.297	.376	0	—	0	3	3	1	0.5
Total 16		54	65	.454	614	39	5	0	127	1105²	1034	51	457	791	12.3	3.23	114	.251	.330	31	.397	11	48	57	16	11.5

● TIM FORTUGNO

Fortugno, Timothy Shawn b: 4/11/62, Clinton, Mass. BL/TL, 6'1", 195 lbs. Deb: 7/20/92

YEAR	TM/L	W	L	PCT	G	GS	CG	SH	SV	IP	H	HR	BB	SO	RAT	ERA	ERA+	OAV	OOB	BH	AVG	PB	PR	/A	PD	TPI
1992	Cal-A	1	1	.500	14	5	1	1	1	41²	32	5	19	31	12.1	5.18	77	.236	.318	0	—	0	-6	-6	-0	-0.3
1994	Cin-N	1	0	1.000	25	0	0	0	0	30	32	2	14	29	14.7	4.20	99	.288	.383	1	.333	0	-0	-1	1	0.1
Total 2		2	1	.667	39	5	1	1	1	71²	69	7	33	60	13.2	4.77	85	.257	.345	1	.333	0	-6	-6	0	-0.2

● GARY FORTUNE

Fortune, Garrett Reese b: 10/11/1894, High Point, N.C. d: 9/23/55, Washington, D.C. BB/TR, 5'11.5", 176 lbs. Deb: 10/5/16

YEAR	TM/L	W	L	PCT	G	GS	CG	SH	SV	IP	H	HR	BB	SO	RAT	ERA	ERA+	OAV	OOB	BH	AVG	PB	PR	/A	PD	TPI
1916	Phi-N	0	1	.000	1	1	0	0	0	5	2	0	4	3	10.8	3.60	74	.118	.286	0	.000	-0	-1	-1	-0	-0.2
1918	Phi-N	0	2	.000	5	2	1	0	0	31	41	2	19	10	17.7	8.13	37	.333	.427	2	.200	-0	-18	-18	-0	-1.0
1920	Bos-A	0	2	.000	14	3	1	0	0	41²	46	0	23	10	14.9	5.83	63	.282	.371	2	.167	-0	-9	-10	-1	-0.5
Total 3		0	5	.000	20	6	2	0	0	77²	89	2	46	23	15.8	6.61	51	.294	.389	4	.167	-0	-28	-28	-1	-1.7

● JERRY FOSNOW

Fosnow, Gerald Eugene b: 9/21/40, Deshler, Ohio BR/TL, 6'4", 195 lbs. Deb: 6/29/64

YEAR	TM/L	W	L	PCT	G	GS	CG	SH	SV	IP	H	HR	BB	SO	RAT	ERA	ERA+	OAV	OOB	BH	AVG	PB	PR	/A	PD	TPI
1964	Min-A	0	1	.000	7	0	0	0	0	10²	13	3	8	9	17.7	10.97	33	.302	.412	0	—	0	-9	-9	-0	-0.8
1965	Min-A	3	3	.500	29	0	0	0	2	46²	33	7	25	35	11.4	4.44	80	.193	.299	0	.000	-1	-5	-5	0	-0.6
Total 2		3	4	.429	36	0	0	0	2	57¹	46	10	33	44	12.6	5.65	63	.215	.323	0	.000	-1	-14	-13	-1	-1.4

● LARRY FOSS

Foss, Larry Curtis b: 4/18/36, Castleton, Kan. BR/TR, 6'2", 187 lbs. Deb: 9/18/61

YEAR	TM/L	W	L	PCT	G	GS	CG	SH	SV	IP	H	HR	BB	SO	RAT	ERA	ERA+	OAV	OOB	BH	AVG	PB	PR	/A	PD	TPI
1961	Pit-N	1	1	.500	3	3	0	0	0	15¹	15	3	11	9	16.4	5.87	68	.273	.412	1	.167	-0	-3	-3	-0	-0.4
1962	NY-N	0	1	.000	5	1	0	0	0	11²	17	2	7	3	19.3	4.63	90	.362	.455	0	.000	-0	-1	-1	-0	-0.1
Total 2		1	2	.333	8	4	0	0	0	27	32	5	18	12	17.7	5.33	76	.314	.431	1	.143	-0	-4	-4	-0	-0.5

● TONY FOSSAS

Fossas, Emilio Antonio (Morejon) b: 9/23/57, Havana, Cuba BL/TL, 6', 195 lbs. Deb: 5/15/88

YEAR	TM/L	W	L	PCT	G	GS	CG	SH	SV	IP	H	HR	BB	SO	RAT	ERA	ERA+	OAV	OOB	BH	AVG	PB	PR	/A	PD	TPI
1988	Tex-A	0	0	—	5	0	0	0	0	5²	11	2	2	0	20.6	4.76	86	.423	.464	0	—	0	-1	-0	0	-0.2
1989	Mil-A	2	2	.500	51	0	0	0	1	61	57	3	22	42	11.8	3.54	108	.256	.325	0	—	0	2	2	-0	0.0
1990	Mil-A	2	3	.400	32	0	0	0	1	29¹	44	5	10	24	16.6	6.44	60	.331	.378	0	—	0	-8	-8	-0	-1.3
1991	Bos-A	3	2	.600	64	0	0	0	1	57	49	3	28	29	12.6	3.47	124	.236	.335	0	—	0	4	5	1	0.5
1992	Bos-A	1	2	.333	60	0	0	0	2	29²	31	1	14	19	14.0	2.43	174	.279	.365	0	—	0	5	6	1	0.4
1993	Bos-A	1	1	.500	71	0	0	0	0	40	38	4	15	39	12.4	5.17	89	.242	.316	0	—	0	-5	-4	0	-0.3
1994	Bos-A	2	0	1.000	44	0	0	0	0	34	35	6	15	31	13.5	4.76	108	.263	.342	0	—	0	-1	-0	0	-0.1
Total 7		11	10	.524	327	0	0	0	5	256²	265	22	106	184	13.3	4.17	103	.267	.343	0	—	0	-1	3	2	-1.0

YEAR TM/L	W	L	PCT	G	GS	CG	SH	SV	IP	H	HR	BB	SO	RAT	ERA	ERA+	OAV	OOB	BH	AVG	PB	PR	/A	PD	TPI

● ALAN FOSTER Foster, Alan Benton b: 12/8/46, Pasadena, Cal. BR/TR, 6', 180 lbs. Deb: 4/25/67

1967 LA-N	0	1	.000	4	2	0	0	0	16²	10	4	3	15	7.0	2.16	143	.169	.210	0	.000	-0	2	2	0	0.1
1968 LA-N	1	1	.500	3	3	0	0	0	15²	11	1	2	10	7.5	1.72	160	.200	.228	1	.250	0	2	2	-0	0.3
1969 LA-N	3	9	.250	24	15	2	0	0	102²	119	11	29	59	13.3	4.38	76	.290	.342	2	.074	-1	-9	-12	-0	-1.4
1970 LA-N	10	13	.435	33	33	7	1	0	198²	200	22	81	83	12.8	4.26	90	.264	.337	7	.109	-2	-5	-9	-1	-1.2
1971 Cle-A	8	12	.400	36	26	3	0	0	181²	158	19	82	97	12.1	4.16	92	.232	.318	2	.039	-4	-14	-7	-4	-1.6
1972 Cal-A	0	1	.000	8	0	0	0	0	12²	12	3	6	11	14.2	4.97	59	.245	.351	0	—	-3	-3	-3	0	-0.2
1973 StL-N	13	9	.591	35	29	6	2	0	203²	195	17	63	106	11.6	3.14	116	.254	.315	13	.191	1	12	11	-2	1.1
1974 StL-N	7	10	.412	31	25	5	1	0	162¹	167	16	61	78	12.8	3.88	92	.268	.336	8	.167	-1	-5	-6	-1	-0.7
1975 SD-N	3	1	.750	17	4	1	0	0	44²	41	5	21	20	12.5	2.42	144	.244	.328	1	.091	-1	6	5	0	0.4
1976 SD-N	3	6	.333	26	11	2	0	0	86²	75	9	35	22	11.5	3.22	102	.235	.313	1	.056	-0	3	0	-1	-0.1
Total 10	48	63	.432	217	148	26	6	0	1025¹	988	99	383	501	12.2	3.74	96	.254	.324	35	.119	-8	-10	-15	-9	-3.3

● ED FOSTER Foster, Eddy Lee "Slim" b: Georgia d: 3/1/29, Montgomery, Ala. BR/TR, 6'1" Deb: 7/31/08

| 1908 Cle-A | 1 | 0 | 1.000 | 6 | 1 | 1 | 0 | 2 | 21 | 16 | 1 | 12 | 11 | 12.9 | 2.14 | 112 | .229 | .357 | 0 | .000 | -1 | 1 | 1 | -1 | -0.1 |

● RUBE FOSTER Foster, George b: 1/5/1888, Lehigh, Okla. d: 3/1/76, Bokoshe, Okla. BR/TR, 5'7.5", 170 lbs. Deb: 4/10/13

1913 Bos-A	3	4	.429	19	8	4	1	0	68¹	64	1	28	36	12.6	3.16	93	.249	.332	2	.095	-1	-2	-2	-0	-0.4
1914 Bos-A	14	8	.636	32	27	17	5	0	211²	164	2	52	89	9.5	1.70	158	.218	.274	11	.175	0	24	23	-0	2.6
1915 *Bos-A	19	8	.704	37	33	21	5	1	255¹	217	3	86	82	11.0	2.11	131	.237	.310	23	.277	7	23	19	1	2.8
1916 *Bos-A	14	7	.667	33	19	9	3	2	182¹	173	0	86	53	13.0	3.06	90	.263	.352	11	.177	0	-5	-6	2	-0.5
1917 Bos-A	8	7	.533	17	16	9	1	0	124²	108	1	53	34	11.9	2.53	102	.243	.329	11	.268	2	2	1	1	0.4
Total 5	58	34	.630	138	103	60	15	3	842¹	726	6	305	294	11.3	2.36	116	.240	.315	58	.215	9	43	35	2	4.9

● KEVIN FOSTER Foster, Kevin Christopher b: 1/13/69, Evanston, Ill. BR/TR, 6'1", 160 lbs. Deb: 9/12/93

1993 Phi-N	0	1	.000	2	1	0	0	0	6²	13	3	7	6	27.0	14.85	27	.394	.500	0	.000	-0	-8	-8	-0	-0.9
1994 Chi-N	3	4	.429	13	13	0	0	0	81	70	7	35	75	11.8	2.89	142	.234	.316	2	.074	-2	12	11	-1	0.6
Total 2	3	5	.375	15	14	0	0	0	87²	83	10	42	81	12.9	3.80	108	.250	.336	2	.069	-2	4	3	-1	-0.3

● LARRY FOSTER Foster, Larry Lynn b: 12/24/37, Lansing, Mich. BL/TR, 6', 185 lbs. Deb: 9/18/63

| 1963 Det-A | 0 | 0 | — | 1 | 0 | 0 | 0 | 0 | 2 | 4 | 0 | 1 | 1 | 22.5 | 13.50 | 28 | .364 | .417 | 0 | — | 0 | -2 | -2 | 0 | 0.0 |

● STEVE FOSTER Foster, Stephen Eugene b: 8/16/66, Dallas, Tex. BR/TR, 6', 180 lbs. Deb: 8/22/91

1991 Cin-N	0	0	—	11	0	0	0	0	14	7	1	4	11	7.1	1.93	197	.143	.208	0	—	0	3	3	-0	0.0
1992 Cin-N	1	1	.500	31	1	0	0	2	50	52	4	13	34	11.7	2.88	125	.275	.322	1	.200	0	3	4	1	0.3
1993 Cin-N	2	2	.500	17	0	0	0	0	25²	23	1	5	16	10.2	1.75	230	.235	.279	0	—	0	7	6	-1	0.9
Total 3	3	3	.500	59	1	0	0	2	89²	82	6	22	61	10.5	2.41	156	.244	.292	1	.200	0	13	13	0	1.2

● STEVE FOUCAULT Foucault, Steven Raymond b: 10/3/49, Duluth, Minn. BL/TR, 6', 205 lbs. Deb: 4/7/73

1973 Tex-A	2	4	.333	32	0	0	0	8	55²	54	6	31	28	14.2	3.88	96	.262	.367	0	—	0	-0	-1	1	0.2
1974 Tex-A	8	9	.471	69	0	0	0	12	144¹	123	8	40	106	10.5	2.24	159	.234	.295	0	—	0	22	21	1	2.9
1975 Tex-A	8	4	.667	59	0	0	0	10	107	96	10	55	56	13.0	4.12	91	.249	.349	0	—	0	-4	-4	-1	-0.6
1976 Tex-A	8	8	.500	46	0	0	0	5	75²	68	9	25	41	11.5	3.33	108	.249	.321	0	—	0	2	2	0	0.2
1977 Det-A	7	7	.500	44	0	0	0	13	74¹	64	7	17	58	9.8	3.15	136	.226	.270	0	—	0	8	9	-1	1.9
1978 Det-A	2	4	.333	24	0	0	0	4	37¹	48	1	21	18	16.9	3.13	123	.324	.412	0	—	0	3	3	-1	0.3
KC-A	0	0	—	3	0	0	0	0	2¹	5	0	1	0	23.1	3.86	99	.417	.462	0	—	0	-0	-0	0	-0.2
Yr	2	4	.333	27	0	0	0	4	39²	53	1	22	18	17.0	3.18	122	.323	.403	0	—	0	3	3	-1	0.1
Total 6	35	36	.493	277	0	0	0	52	496²	458	41	190	307	12.1	3.21	117	.250	.326	0	—	0	29	30	1	5.1

● JACK FOURNIER Fournier, John Frank b: 9/29/1892, AuSable, Mich. d: 9/5/73, Tacoma, Wash. BL/TR, 6', 195 lbs. Deb: 4/13/12 ♦

| 1922 StL-N | 0 | 0 | — | 1 | 0 | 0 | 0 | 0 | 1 | 0 | 0 | 0 | 0 | 0.0 | 0.00 | — | .000 | .000 | 119 | .295 | 0 | 0 | 0 | 0 | 0.0 |

● HENRY FOURNIER Fournier, Julius Henry "Frenchy" b: 8/8/1865, Syracuse, N.Y. d: 12/8/45, Detroit, Mich. TL, Deb: 8/22/1894

| 1894 Cin-N | 1 | 3 | .250 | 6 | 4 | 4 | 0 | 0 | 45 | 71 | 4 | 20 | 5 | 18.6 | 5.40 | 103 | .354 | .418 | 2 | .105 | -3 | -0 | 1 | 0 | -0.1 |

● DAVE FOUTZ Foutz, David Luther "Scissors" b: 9/7/1856, Carroll Co., Md. d: 3/5/1897, Waverly, Ind. BR/TR, 6'2", 161 lbs. Deb: 7/29/1884 FM♦

1884 StL-a	15	6	.714	25	25	19	2	0	206²	167	7	36	95	9.2	2.18	150	.212	.255	27	.227	1	25	25	3	2.5
1885 *StL-a	33	14	.702	47	46	46	2	0	407²	351	8	92	147	10.2	2.63	125	.227	.278	59	.248	5	28	29	7	3.8
1886 *StL-a	41	16	.719	59	57	55	11	1	504	418	5	144	283	10.2	2.11	163	.216	.274	116	.280	11	75	75	8	8.1
1887 *StL-a	25	12	.676	40	38	36	1	0	339¹	369	7	90	94	12.4	3.87	117	.258	.306	151	.357	15	16	25	0	3.1
1888 Bro-a	12	7	.632	23	19	19	0	0	176	146	3	35	73	9.5	2.51	119	.218	.262	156	.277	6	11	9	3	1.5
1889 *Bro-a	3	0	1.000	12	4	3	0	0	59²	70	2	19	21	13.4	4.37	85	.284	.335	152	.275	2	-3	-4	1	0.7
1890 *Bro-N	2	1	.667	5	2	2	0	2	29	29	0	6	4	11.2	1.86	185	.252	.295	154	.303	2	6	5	-1	0.6
1891 Bro-N	3	2	.600	6	5	5	0	0	52	51	1	16	14	11.8	3.29	100	.247	.304	134	.257	1	0	0	-0	0.1
1892 Bro-N	13	8	.619	27	20	17	5	0	203	210	3	63	56	12.3	3.41	93	.256	.313	41	.186	0	-3	-6	-3	-0.3
1893 Bro-N	0	0	—	6	0	0	0	0	18	28	2	8	3	18.0	7.50	59	.345	.403	137	.246	1	-6	-6	1	-0.1
1894 Bro-N	0	0	—	1	0	0	0	0	2	4	0	1	0	22.5	13.50	37	.410	.465	90	.307	0	-2	-2	0	0.0
Total 11	147	66	.690	251	216	202	16	4	1997¹	1843	38	510	790	10.9	2.84	124	.235	.286	1253	.276	45	147	148	18	19.6

● JESSE FOWLER Fowler, Jesse Peter "Pete" b: 10/30/1898, Spartanburg, S.C. d: 9/23/73, Columbia, S.C. BR/TL, 5'10.5", 158 lbs. Deb: 7/29/24 F

| 1924 StL-N | 1 | 1 | .500 | 13 | 1 | 0 | 0 | 0 | 32² | 28 | 0 | 18 | 5 | 13.2 | 4.41 | 86 | .226 | .333 | 2 | .222 | 0 | -2 | -2 | -1 | -0.2 |

● ART FOWLER Fowler, John Arthur b: 7/3/22, Converse, S.C. BR/TR, 5'11", 180 lbs. Deb: 4/17/54 FC

1954 Cin-N	12	10	.545	40	29	8	1	0	227²	256	20	85	93	13.6	3.83	109	.286	.351	6	.100	-1	6	9	-1	0.5
1955 Cin-N	11	10	.524	46	28	8	3	2	207²	198	20	63	94	11.4	3.90	109	.250	.306	12	.200	-0	3	8	-1	0.6
1956 Cin-N	11	11	.500	45	23	8	0	1	177²	191	15	35	86	11.4	4.05	98	.278	.313	7	.146	-0	-6	-1	1	-0.1
1957 Cin-N	3	0	1.000	33	7	1	0	0	87²	111	11	24	44	14.1	6.47	64	.310	.362	3	.176	-0	-25	-23	0	-0.7
1959 LA-N	3	4	.429	36	0	0	0	2	61	70	8	23	47	13.7	5.31	80	.294	.356	1	.083	-1	-9	-7	0	-0.9
1961 LA-A	5	8	.385	53	3	0	0	11	89	68	12	19	78	9.8	3.64	124	.209	.274	1	.077	-1	4	9	-1	1.1
1962 LA-A	4	3	.571	48	0	0	0	5	77	67	6	25	38	10.9	2.81	138	.234	.298	3	.273	1	10	9	0	0.9
1963 LA-A	5	3	.625	57	0	0	0	10	89¹	70	5	19	53	9.0	2.42	142	.219	.263	2	.222	-1	12	10	-1	1.0
1964 LA-A	0	2	.000	4	0	0	0	1	7	8	2	5	6	18.0	10.29	32	.296	.424	0	.000	-0	-5	-5	0	-1.3
Total 9	54	51	.514	362	90	25	4	32	1024	1039	99	308	539	11.9	4.03	102	.265	.320	35	.152	-2	-10	7	-3	1.1

● DICK FOWLER Fowler, Richard John b: 3/30/21, Toronto, Ont., Can. d: 5/22/72, Oneonta, N.Y. BR/TR, 6'4.5", 215 lbs. Deb: 9/13/41

1941 Phi-A	1	2	.333	4	3	1	0	0	24	26	4	8	8	12.8	3.38	124	.289	.347	0	.000	-1	2	2	-0	0.1
1942 Phi-A	6	11	.353	31	17	4	1	0	140	159	13	45	38	13.1	4.95	76	.287	.341	8	.160	-1	-20	-18	-2	-2.3
1945 Phi-A	1	2	.333	7	3	2	1	0	37¹	41	1	18	21	14.2	4.82	71	.283	.362	8	.444	3	-6	-6	-1	-0.1
1946 Phi-A	9	16	.360	32	28	14	3	0	205²	213	16	75	89	12.7	3.28	108	.263	.327	13	.183	-1	5	6	-1	0.5
1947 Phi-A	12	11	.522	36	31	16	4	0	227¹	210	12	85	75	11.8	2.81	136	.249	.319	14	.171	-3	23	25	-2	2.0
1948 Phi-A	15	8	.652	29	26	16	2	2	204²	221	15	76	50	13.2	3.78	113	.281	.348	14	.171	-1	9	9	1	0.7
1949 Phi-A	15	11	.577	31	28	15	4	1	213²	210	13	115	43	13.8	3.75	110	.262	.357	18	.234	3	11	9	1	1.3
1950 Phi-A	1	5	.167	11	9	2	0	0	66²	75	7	56	19	18.1	6.48	70	.300	.434	5	.192	-1	-14	-14	0	-1.1
1951 Phi-A	5	11	.313	22	22	8	0	0	125	141	11	72	29	15.4	5.62	76	.291	.384	8	.190	-0	-21	-19	-1	-2.1

YEAR TM/L	W	L	PCT	G	GS	CG	SH	SV	IP	H	HR	BB	SO	RAT	ERA	ERA+	OAV	OOB	BH	AVG	PB	PR	/A	PD	TPI
1952 Phi-A	1	2	.333	18	3	1	0	0	58²	71	4	28	14	15.8	6.44	61	.302	.386	0	.000	-2	-18	-16	1	-0.9
Total 10	66	79	.455	221	170	75	11	4	1303	1367	96	578	382	13.6	4.11	97	.273	.351	88	.186	-6	-27	-19	-6	-1.8

● **ALAN FOWLKES**   Fowlkes, Alan Kim b: 8/8/58, Brawley, Cal. BR/TR, 6'2", 190 lbs. Deb: 4/7/82

YEAR TM/L	W	L	PCT	G	GS	CG	SH	SV	IP	H	HR	BB	SO	RAT	ERA	ERA+	OAV	OOB	BH	AVG	PB	PR	/A	PD	TPI
1982 SF-N	4	2	.667	21	15	1	0	0	85	111	12	24	50	14.8	5.19	69	.321	.373	3	.115	-1	-15	-15	-0	-1.1
1985 Cal-A	0	0	—	2	0	0	0	0	7	8	4	4	5	15.4	9.00	46	.276	.364	0	—	0	-4	-4	0	0.0
Total 2	4	2	.667	23	15	1	0	0	92	119	16	28	55	14.9	5.48	66	.317	.373	3	.115	-1	-19	-19	-0	-1.1

● **HENRY FOX**   Fox, Henry (b: Henry Fuchs) b: 11/18/1874, Scranton, Pa. d: 6/6/27, Scranton, Pa. Deb: 9/4/02

YEAR TM/L	W	L	PCT	G	GS	CG	SH	SV	IP	H	HR	BB	SO	RAT	ERA	ERA+	OAV	OOB	BH	AVG	PB	PR	/A	PD	TPI
1902 Phi-N	0	0	—	1	0	0	0	1	1	1	2	0	1	27.0	18.00	16	.413	.513	0	—	0	-2	-2	0	-0.3

● **HOWIE FOX**   Fox, Howard Francis b: 3/1/21, Coburg, Ore. d: 10/9/55, San Antonio, Tex. BR/TR, 6'3", 210 lbs. Deb: 9/28/44

YEAR TM/L	W	L	PCT	G	GS	CG	SH	SV	IP	H	HR	BB	SO	RAT	ERA	ERA+	OAV	OOB	BH	AVG	PB	PR	/A	PD	TPI
1944 Cin-N	0	0	—	2	0	0	0	0	2¹	2	0	0	0	7.7	0.00	—	.222	.222	0	.000	-0	1	1	-0	0.0
1945 Cin-N	8	13	.381	45	15	7	0	0	164¹	169	6	77	54	13.8	4.93	76	.268	.353	13	.283	3	-21	-21	4	-1.7
1946 Cin-N	0	0	—	4	0	0	0	0	5	12	2	5	1	30.6	18.00	19	.462	.548	0	—	-0	-8	-8	0	0.0
1948 Cin-N	6	9	.400	34	24	5	0	0	171	185	11	62	63	13.1	4.53	86	.280	.343	12	.200	1	-11	-12	1	-0.7
1949 Cin-N	6	19	.240	38	30	9	0	0	215	221	13	77	60	12.6	3.98	105	.265	.330	17	.236	2	2	5	6	1.3
1950 Cin-N	11	8	.579	34	22	10	1	1	187	196	14	85	64	13.6	4.33	98	.269	.347	11	.175	-0	-4	-2	3	0.1
1951 Cin-N	9	14	.391	40	30	9	4	2	228	239	15	69	57	12.2	3.83	107	.272	.326	8	.114	-2	3	6	1	0.4
1952 Phi-N	2	7	.222	13	11	2	0	0	62	70	8	26	16	13.9	5.08	72	.287	.356	1	.048	-2	-9	-10	-1	-1.3
1954 Bal-A	1	2	.333	38	0	0	0	2	73²	80	2	34	27	14.2	3.67	98	.289	.371	4	.250	1	0	-1	1	0.2
Total 9	43	72	.374	248	132	42	5	6	1108¹	1174	71	435	342	13.2	4.33	92	.274	.343	66	.189	2	-46	-42	17	-1.7

● **JOHN FOX**   Fox, John Joseph b: 2/7/1859, Roxbury, Mass. d: 4/18/1893, Boston, Mass. Deb: 6/2/1881

YEAR TM/L	W	L	PCT	G	GS	CG	SH	SV	IP	H	HR	BB	SO	RAT	ERA	ERA+	OAV	OOB	BH	AVG	PB	PR	/A	PD	TPI
1881 Bos-N	6	8	.429	17	16	12	0	0	124¹	144	0	39	30	13.2	3.33	80	.279	.329	21	.178	-4	-8	-9	1	-1.1
1883 Bal-a	6	13	.316	20	19	18	0	0	165¹	209	4	32	49	13.1	4.03	86	.289	.320	14	.152	-4	-13	-10	-1	-1.3
1884 Pit-a	1	6	.143	7	7	7	0	0	59	76	2	16	22	14.5	5.64	60	.291	.339	6	.240	-4	-16	-15	1	-1.2
1886 Was-N	0	1	.000	1	1	1	0	0	8	11	0	11	3	24.8	9.00	37	.314	.478	1	.333	0	-5	-5	0	-0.4
Total 4	13	28	.317	45	43	38	0	0	356²	440	4	98	104	13.7	4.16	76	.287	.331	42	.176	-8	-42	-40	0	-4.0

● **TERRY FOX**   Fox, Terrence Edward b: 7/31/35, Chicago, Ill. BR/TR, 6', 175 lbs. Deb: 9/4/60

YEAR TM/L	W	L	PCT	G	GS	CG	SH	SV	IP	H	HR	BB	SO	RAT	ERA	ERA+	OAV	OOB	BH	AVG	PB	PR	/A	PD	TPI
1960 Mil-N	0	0	—	5	0	0	0	0	8¹	6	0	6	5	13.0	4.32	79	.200	.333	0	.000	-0	-1	-1	-0	0.0
1961 Det-A	5	2	.714	39	0	0	0	12	57¹	42	6	16	32	9.6	1.41	290	.200	.266	2	.167	-0	17	17	1	2.8
1962 Det-A	3	1	.750	44	0	0	0	16	58	48	2	16	29	10.1	1.71	238	.227	.285	2	.250	2	15	15	0	2.2
1963 Det-A	8	6	.571	46	0	0	0	11	80¹	81	9	20	35	11.5	3.59	104	.263	.312	1	.091	-0	0	1	0	0.3
1964 Det-A	4	3	.571	32	0	0	0	5	61	77	4	16	28	13.4	3.39	108	.316	.360	3	.250	1	2	2	1	0.4
1965 Det-A	6	4	.600	42	0	0	0	10	77²	59	7	31	34	10.8	2.78	125	.214	.300	0	.000	-1	6	6	2	1.0
1966 Det-A	0	1	.000	4	0	0	0	1	10	9	2	6	9	9.9	6.30	55	.243	.282	0	.000	-0	-3	-3	0	-0.4
Phi-N	3	2	.600	36	0	0	0	4	44¹	57	3	17	22	15.4	4.47	90	.322	.388	0	.000	-0	-4	-4	-0	-0.6
Total 7	29	19	.604	248	0	0	0	59	397	379	34	124	185	11.7	2.99	125	.254	.316	8	.123	1	31	33	4	5.7

● **BILL FOXEN**   Foxen, William Aloysius b: 5/31/1884, Tenafly, N.J. d: 4/17/37, Brooklyn, N.Y. BL/TL, 5'11.5", 165 lbs. Deb: 5/5/08

YEAR TM/L	W	L	PCT	G	GS	CG	SH	SV	IP	H	HR	BB	SO	RAT	ERA	ERA+	OAV	OOB	BH	AVG	PB	PR	/A	PD	TPI
1908 Phi-N	7	7	.500	22	16	10	2	0	147¹	126	2	53	52	11.4	1.95	124	.240	.319	5	.094	-3	7	8	2	0.6
1909 Phi-N	3	7	.300	18	7	5	1	0	83¹	65	0	32	37	10.9	3.35	78	.219	.303	5	.208	3	-7	-7	4	0.0
1910 Phi-N	5	5	.500	16	9	5	0	0	77²	73	2	40	33	13.4	2.55	123	.268	.368	4	.174	-1	4	5	2	0.7
Chi-N	0	0	—	2	0	0	0	0	5	7	0	3	2	18.0	9.00	32	.350	.435	0	.000	-0	-3	-3	-0	0.0
Yr	5	5	.500	18	9	5	0	0	82²	80	2	43	35	13.4	2.94	106	.271	.364	4	.160	-1	1	2	1	0.7
1911 Chi-N	1	1	.500	3	1	0	0	0	13	12	0	12	6	16.6	2.08	160	.255	.407	1	.250	1	2	2	1	0.4
Total 4	16	20	.444	61	33	20	3	0	326¹	283	4	140	130	12.1	2.56	105	.244	.333	15	.142	0	4	8	1	1.7

● **JIMMIE FOXX**   Foxx, James Emory "Beast" or "Double X" b: 10/22/07, Sudlersville, Md. d: 7/21/67, Miami, Fla. BR/TR, 6', 195 lbs. Deb: 5/1/25 CH♦

YEAR TM/L	W	L	PCT	G	GS	CG	SH	SV	IP	H	HR	BB	SO	RAT	ERA	ERA+	OAV	OOB	BH	AVG	PB	PR	/A	PD	TPI
1939 Bos-A☆	0	0	—	1	0	0	0	0	1	0	0	0	1	0.0	0.00	—	.000	.000	168	.360	1	1	0	-0	0.0
1945 Phi-N	1	0	1.000	9	2	0	0	0	22²	13	0	14	10	11.1	1.59	241	.171	.308	60	.268	2	6	6	-1	0.3
Total 2	1	0	1.000	10	2	0	0	0	23²	13	0	14	11	10.6	1.52	254	.165	.298	2646	.325	3	6	6	-1	0.3

● **PAUL FOYTACK**   Foytack, Paul Eugene b: 11/16/30, Scranton, Pa. BR/TR, 5'11", 180 lbs. Deb: 4/21/53

YEAR TM/L	W	L	PCT	G	GS	CG	SH	SV	IP	H	HR	BB	SO	RAT	ERA	ERA+	OAV	OOB	BH	AVG	PB	PR	/A	PD	TPI
1953 Det-A	0	0	—	6	0	0	0	0	9²	15	1	9	7	23.3	11.17	36	.375	.500	0	.000	-0	-8	-8	-0	0.0
1955 Det-A	0	1	.000	22	1	0	0	0	49²	48	4	36	38	15.2	5.26	73	.259	.380	1	.091	-7	-8	-0	-0.2
1956 Det-A	15	13	.536	43	33	16	1	1	256	211	24	142	184	12.5	3.59	115	.226	.330	11	.122	-6	16	15	-1	0.8
1957 Det-A	14	11	.560	38	27	8	1	1	212	175	19	104	118	12.0	3.14	123	.226	.321	14	.222	1	15	17	-2	1.7
1958 Det-A	15	13	.536	39	33	16	2	1	230	198	23	77	135	10.9	3.44	107	.233	.299	18	.240	2	8	15	-2	1.8
1959 Det-A	14	14	.500	39	37	11	2	1	240¹	239	34	64	110	11.4	4.64	87	.259	.308	9	.111	-4	-21	-16	-2	-2.1
1960 Det-A	2	11	.154	28	13	1	0	2	96²	108	11	49	38	14.6	6.14	64	.286	.369	7	.280	-4	-24	-23	-2	-2.8
1961 Det-A	11	10	.524	32	20	6	0	0	169²	152	27	56	89	11.1	3.93	104	.238	.301	12	.222	2	2	3	-3	0.2
1962 Det-A	10	7	.588	29	21	5	1	0	143²	145	18	86	63	14.9	4.39	93	.259	.359	6	.143	-1	-7	-5	-0	-0.6
1963 Det-A	0	1	.000	9	0	0	0	0	17²	18	4	8	7	13.2	8.66	43	.265	.342	0	.000	-0	-10	-10	-0	-0.7
LA-A	5	5	.500	25	8	0	0	0	70¹	68	9	29	37	12.4	3.71	92	.255	.328	4	.267	1	-1	-2	-1	-0.2
Yr	5	6	.455	34	8	0	0	1	88	86	13	37	44	12.6	4.70	74	.256	.330	4	.211	1	-11	-12	-1	-0.9
1964 LA-A	0	1	.000	2	0	0	0	0	2¹	4	2	2	1	23.1	15.43	21	.364	.462	0	—	-0	-3	-3	-0	-1.0
Total 11	86	87	.497	312	193	63	7	7	1498	1381	176	662	827	12.4	4.14	97	.246	.327	82	.178	-3	-39	-24	-13	-3.1

● **KEN FRAILING**   Frailing, Kenneth Douglas b: 1/19/48, Marion, Wis. BL/TL, 6', 190 lbs. Deb: 9/1/72

YEAR TM/L	W	L	PCT	G	GS	CG	SH	SV	IP	H	HR	BB	SO	RAT	ERA	ERA+	OAV	OOB	BH	AVG	PB	PR	/A	PD	TPI
1972 Chi-A	1	0	1.000	4	0	0	0	0	3	3	1	1	1	12.0	3.00	104	.250	.308	0	—	0	0	0	0	0.0
1973 Chi-A	0	0	—	10	0	0	0	0	18¹	18	1	7	15	12.8	1.96	202	.254	.329	0	—	0	4	4	-0	-0.2
1974 Chi-N	6	9	.400	55	16	1	0	0	125¹	150	11	43	71	13.9	3.88	98	.296	.353	8	.258	1	-4	-1	0	0.0
1975 Chi-N	2	5	.286	41	0	0	0	0	53	61	6	26	39	15.1	5.43	71	.293	.377	1	.143	1	-11	-9	2	-1.0
1976 Chi-N	1	2	.333	6	3	0	0	0	18²	20	0	5	10	12.1	2.41	160	.274	.321	0	.000	-0	2	3	0	0.4
Total 5	10	16	.385	116	19	1	0	0	218¹	252	19	82	136	13.9	3.96	97	.290	.354	9	.220	1	-8	-3	2	-0.8

● **OSSIE FRANCE**   France, Osman Beverly "O. B." b: 10/4/1858, Greensburg, Ohio d: 5/2/47, Akron, Ohio BL/TL, 5'8", 155 lbs. Deb: 7/14/1890

YEAR TM/L	W	L	PCT	G	GS	CG	SH	SV	IP	H	HR	BB	SO	RAT	ERA	ERA+	OAV	OOB	BH	AVG	PB	PR	/A	PD	TPI
1890 Chi-N	0	0	—	1	0	0	0	0	2	3	0	2	0	22.5	13.50	27	.336	.458	0	.000	-0	-2	-2	-0	0.0

● **EARL FRANCIS**   Francis, Earl Coleman b: 7/14/35, Slab Fork, W.Va. BR/TR, 6'2", 215 lbs. Deb: 6/30/60

YEAR TM/L	W	L	PCT	G	GS	CG	SH	SV	IP	H	HR	BB	SO	RAT	ERA	ERA+	OAV	OOB	BH	AVG	PB	PR	/A	PD	TPI
1960 Pit-N	1	0	1.000	7	0	0	0	0	18	14	0	4	9	9.5	2.00	188	.222	.279	0	.000	-1	4	4	-0	0.1
1961 Pit-N	2	8	.200	23	15	0	0	0	102²	110	4	47	53	13.9	4.21	95	.274	.351	3	.107	-1	-2	-3	-0	-0.2
1962 Pit-N	9	8	.529	36	23	5	1	0	176	153	8	83	121	12.2	3.07	128	.235	.323	10	.164	1	17	17	1	1.7
1963 Pit-N	4	6	.400	33	13	0	0	0	97¹	107	6	43	72	14.2	4.53	73	.284	.363	8	.308	3	-13	-13	-0	-1.0
1964 Pit-N	0	1	.000	2	0	0	0	0	6¹	7	2	1	6	12.8	4.26	81	.269	.321	0	.000	-0	-4	-4	-0	-0.5
1965 StL-N	0	0	—	2	0	0	0	0	5¹	7	1	3	2	16.9	5.06	76	.318	.400	0	.000	-0	-1	-1	-0	-0.1
Total 6	16	23	.410	103	52	5	1	0	405²	398	21	181	263	13.0	3.77	100	.258	.340	21	.172	2	1	0	1	0.1

● **RAY FRANCIS**   Francis, Ray James b: 3/8/1893, Sherman, Tex. d: 7/6/34, Atlanta, Ga. BL/TL, 6'1.5", 182 lbs. Deb: 4/18/22

YEAR TM/L	W	L	PCT	G	GS	CG	SH	SV	IP	H	HR	BB	SO	RAT	ERA	ERA+	OAV	OOB	BH	AVG	PB	PR	/A	PD	TPI
1922 Was-A	7	18	.280	39	26	15	2	2	225	265	7	66	64	13.5	4.28	90	.303	.356	13	.167	-2	-6	-10	-1	-1.3
1923 Det-A	5	8	.385	33	6	0	0	1	79¹	95	2	28	27	14.4	4.42	87	.308	.374	3	.143	-2	-4	-5	-0	-0.9
1925 NY-A	0	0	—	4	0	0	0	0	4²	5	0	3	1	17.4	7.71	55	.278	.409	0	—	0	-2	-2	-0	0.0
Bos-A	0	2	.000	6	4	0	0	0	28	44	3	13	4	18.6	7.71	59	.373	.439	1	.125	-0	-10	-10	0	-0.6

YEAR TM/L	W	L	PCT	G	GS	CG	SH	SV	IP	H	HR	BB	SO	RAT	ERA	ERA+	OAV	OOB	BH	AVG	PB	PR	/A	PD	TPI
Yr	0	2	.000	10	4	0	0	0	32²	49	3	16	5	18.2	7.71	58	.358	.429	1	.125	-0	-12	-12	-0	-0.6
Total 3	12	28	.300	82	36	15	2	3	337	409	12	110	96	14.2	4.65	84	.310	.368	17	.159	-4	-22	-27	-1	-2.8

● **JOHN FRANCO**   Franco, John Anthony   b: 9/17/60, Brooklyn, N.Y.   BL/TL, 5'10", 180 lbs.   Deb: 4/24/84

YEAR TM/L	W	L	PCT	G	GS	CG	SH	SV	IP	H	HR	BB	SO	RAT	ERA	ERA+	OAV	OOB	BH	AVG	PB	PR	/A	PD	TPI
1984 Cin-N	6	2	.750	54	0	0	0	4	79¹	74	3	36	55	12.7	2.61	145	.256	.343	0	.000	-0	9	10	1	1.2
1985 Cin-N	12	3	.800	67	0	0	0	12	99	83	5	40	61	11.3	2.18	173	.234	.314	2	.333	0	16	**18**	2	3.3
1986 Cin-N☆	6	6	.500	74	0	0	0	29	101	90	7	44	84	12.1	2.94	132	.242	.325	0	.000	-0	9	10	1	2.0
1987 Cin-N★	8	5	.615	68	0	0	0	32	82	76	6	27	61	11.3	2.52	168	.245	.306	0	.000	-0	14	16	-1	3.6
1988 Cin-N	6	6	.500	70	0	0	0	**39**	86	60	3	27	46	9.1	1.57	228	.198	.264	0	.000	-0	**18**	**19**	1	**5.0**
1989 Cin-N☆	4	8	.333	60	0	0	0	32	80²	77	3	36	60	12.6	3.12	115	.258	.337	1	.333	-0	3	4	1	1.2
1990 NY-N★	5	3	.625	55	0	0	0	**33**	67²	66	4	21	56	11.6	2.53	148	.252	.307	0	.000	-1	10	9	1	2.1
1991 NY-N	5	9	.357	52	0	0	0	30	55¹	61	2	18	45	13.0	2.93	124	.271	.328	0	.000	-0	5	4	1	1.7
1992 NY-N	6	2	.750	31	0	0	0	15	33	24	1	11	20	9.5	1.64	212	.209	.278	0	.000	-0	7	7	2	2.6
1993 NY-N	4	3	.571	35	0	0	0	10	36¹	46	6	19	29	16.3	5.20	77	.313	.395	0	.000	-0	-5	-5	1	-1.0
1994 NY-N	1	4	.200	47	0	0	0	**30**	50	47	2	19	42	12.1	2.70	158	.244	.315	0	.000	-0	8	9	0	2.0
Total 11	63	51	.553	613	0	0	0	266	770¹	704	42	298	559	11.8	2.63	145	.245	.318	3	.100	-2	93	102	9	23.7

● **TERRY FRANCONA**   Francona, Terry Jon   b: 4/22/59, Aberdeen, S.D.   BL/TL, 6'1", 190 lbs.   Deb: 8/19/81   F♦

YEAR TM/L	W	L	PCT	G	GS	CG	SH	SV	IP	H	HR	BB	SO	RAT	ERA	ERA+	OAV	OOB	BH	AVG	PB	PR	/A	PD	TPI
1989 Mil-A	0	0	—	1	0	0	0	0	1	0	0	0	1	0.0	0.00	—	.000	.000	54	.232	1	0	0	0	0.0

● **CHARLIE FRANK**   Frank, Charles   b: 5/30/1870, Mobile, Ala.   d: 5/24/22, Memphis, Tenn.   5'10", 170 lbs.   Deb: 8/18/1893   ♦

YEAR TM/L	W	L	PCT	G	GS	CG	SH	SV	IP	H	HR	BB	SO	RAT	ERA	ERA+	OAV	OOB	BH	AVG	PB	PR	/A	PD	TPI
1894 StL-N	0	0	—	2	0	0	0	0	3	6	1	7	1	39.0	15.00	36	.410	.601	89	.279	0	-3	-3	-0	0.0

● **FRED FRANKHOUSE**   Frankhouse, Frederick Meloy   b: 4/9/04, Port Royal, Pa.   d: 8/17/89, Port Royal, Pa.   BR/TR, 5'11", 175 lbs.   Deb: 9/11/27

YEAR TM/L	W	L	PCT	G	GS	CG	SH	SV	IP	H	HR	BB	SO	RAT	ERA	ERA+	OAV	OOB	BH	AVG	PB	PR	/A	PD	TPI
1927 StL-N	5	1	.833	6	6	5	1	0	50	41	2	16	20	10.4	2.70	146	.218	.283	5	.250	1	7	7	-1	0.7
1928 StL-N	3	2	.600	21	10	1	0	1	84	91	6	36	29	14.1	3.96	101	.277	.358	5	.185	1	0	0	1	0.2
1929 StL-N	7	2	.778	30	12	6	0	1	133¹	149	9	43	37	13.2	4.12	113	.289	.349	15	.288	4	9	8	3	1.0
1930 StL-N	2	3	.400	8	1	0	0	0	19²	31	1	11	4	19.2	7.32	69	.373	.447	0	.000	-1	-5	-5	0	-1.0
Bos-N	7	6	.538	27	11	3	1	0	110²	138	13	43	30	14.9	5.61	88	.313	.377	14	.359	4	-8	-8	-0	-0.4
Yr	9	9	.500	35	12	3	1	0	130¹	169	14	54	34	15.5	5.87	84	.323	.388	14	.318	3	-13	-13	-0	-1.4
1931 Bos-N	8	8	.500	26	15	6	1	0	127¹	125	4	43	50	12.1	4.03	94	.252	.315	6	.150	-0	-2	-3	1	-0.3
1932 Bos-N	4	6	.400	37	6	3	0	0	108²	113	7	45	35	13.3	3.56	106	.278	.355	3	.100	-1	4	2	3	0.4
1933 Bos-N	16	15	.516	43	30	14	2	2	244²	249	12	77	83	12.1	3.16	97	.267	.324	19	.237	4	5	3	4	0.5
1934 Bos-N★	17	9	.654	37	31	13	2	1	233²	239	10	77	78	12.3	3.20	120	.262	.322	17	.200	2	22	16	-0	1.8
1935 Bos-N	11	15	.423	40	29	10	1	0	230²	278	6	81	64	14.2	4.76	84	.293	.352	20	.263	6	-19	-25	3	-1.4
1936 Bro-N	13	10	.565	41	31	9	1	2	234¹	236	18	89	84	12.6	3.65	113	.257	.325	13	.143	-4	10	13	1	0.8
1937 Bro-N	10	13	.435	33	26	9	1	0	179¹	214	6	78	64	14.9	4.27	95	.297	.369	11	.190	-1	-7	-5	3	-0.3
1938 Bro-N	3	5	.375	30	8	2	1	0	93²	92	6	44	32	13.5	4.04	97	.256	.344	4	.154	-1	-3	-1	1	-0.1
1939 Bro-N	0	2	.000	38	3	1	0	4	38	37	3	18	12	13.3	2.61	142	.253	.339	0	.000	-1	6	5	-1	0.2
Total 13	106	97	.522	402	216	81	10	12	1888	2033	111	701	622	13.2	3.92	100	.275	.341	132	.208	12	18	-0	18	2.1

● **JACK FRANKLIN**   Franklin, Jack Wilford   b: 10/20/19, Paris, Ill.   d: 11/15/91, Panama City, Fla.   BR/TR, 5'11.5", 170 lbs.   Deb: 6/12/44

YEAR TM/L	W	L	PCT	G	GS	CG	SH	SV	IP	H	HR	BB	SO	RAT	ERA	ERA+	OAV	OOB	BH	AVG	PB	PR	/A	PD	TPI
1944 Bro-N	0	0	—	1	0	0	0	0	2	2	1	4	2	36.0	13.50	26	.250	.571	0	—	-0	-2	-2	-0	0.0

● **JAY FRANKLIN**   Franklin, John William   b: 3/16/53, Arlington, Va.   BR/TR, 6'2", 180 lbs.   Deb: 9/4/71

YEAR TM/L	W	L	PCT	G	GS	CG	SH	SV	IP	H	HR	BB	SO	RAT	ERA	ERA+	OAV	OOB	BH	AVG	PB	PR	/A	PD	TPI
1971 SD-N	0	1	.000	3	1	0	0	0	5²	5	3	4	4	14.3	6.35	52	.250	.375	0	.000	-0	-2	-2	0	-0.3

● **JOHN FRASCATORE**   Frascatore, John Vincent   b: 2/4/70, Ozone Park, N.Y.   BR/TR, 6'1", 200 lbs.   Deb: 7/21/94

YEAR TM/L	W	L	PCT	G	GS	CG	SH	SV	IP	H	HR	BB	SO	RAT	ERA	ERA+	OAV	OOB	BH	AVG	PB	PR	/A	PD	TPI
1994 StL-N	0	1	.000	1	1	0	0	0	3¹	7	2	2	2	24.3	16.20	25	.438	.500	0	.000	-0	-4	-4	0	-0.8

● **CHICK FRASER**   Fraser, Charles Carrolton   b: 3/17/1871, Chicago, Ill.   d: 5/8/40, Wendell, Idaho   BR/TR, 5'10.5", 188 lbs.   Deb: 4/19/1896   C

YEAR TM/L	W	L	PCT	G	GS	CG	SH	SV	IP	H	HR	BB	SO	RAT	ERA	ERA+	OAV	OOB	BH	AVG	PB	PR	/A	PD	TPI
1896 Lou-N	12	27	.308	43	38	36	0	1	349¹	396	9	166	91	15.2	4.87	89	.283	.371	22	.151	-9	-20	-21	3	-2.2
1897 Lou-N	15	19	.441	35	34	32	0	0	286¹	332	11	133	70	15.3	4.09	104	.288	.372	18	.161	-4	7	6	6	0.7
1898 Lou-N	7	17	.292	26	26	20	1	0	203	230	4	100	58	15.7	5.32	67	.283	.377	13	.167	-2	-39	-39	4	-3.5
Cle-N	2	3	.400	6	6	6	0	0	42	49	2	12	19	14.4	5.57	65	.289	.357	4	.250	-0	-9	-9	0	-0.8
Yr	9	20	.310	32	32	26	1	0	245	279	6	112	77	14.6	5.36	67	.278	.354	17	.181	-2	-48	-48	4	-4.3
1899 Phi-N	21	12	.636	35	33	29	4	0	270²	278	4	85	69	12.8	3.36	110	.265	.333	21	.179	-2	15	10	2	1.0
1900 Phi-N	15	9	.625	29	26	22	1	0	223¹	250	7	93	58	14.3	3.14	115	.282	.358	22	.259	4	14	12	3	1.7
1901 Phi-A	22	16	.579	40	37	35	2	0	331	344	6	132	110	13.8	3.81	99	.265	.347	26	.187	-3	-5	-1	2	-0.3
1902 Phi-N	12	13	.480	27	26	24	3	0	224	238	2	74	97	13.1	3.42	82	.272	.339	15	.174	0	-16	-15	-0	-1.5
1903 Phi-N	12	17	.414	31	29	26	1	1	250	260	8	97	104	13.4	4.50	73	.267	.344	19	.204	4	-34	-34	2	-2.7
1904 Phi-N	14	24	.368	42	36	32	2	1	302	287	5	100	127	11.9	3.25	82	.246	.311	17	.155	-1	-17	-19	2	-2.1
1905 Bos-N	14	21	.400	39	38	35	2	0	334¹	320	6	149	130	13.0	3.28	94	.254	.340	35	.224	3	-10	-7	-1	-0.3
1906 Cin-N	10	20	.333	31	28	25	2	0	236	221	1	80	115	11.8	2.67	103	.259	.329	14	.171	-1	-1	2	1	0.0
1907 Chi-N	8	5	.615	22	15	9	2	1	138¹	112	1	46	41	10.5	2.28	110	.229	.299	3	.067	-3	3	3	0	0.0
1908 Chi-N	11	9	.550	26	17	11	2	2	162²	141	4	61	66	11.5	2.27	104	.244	.323	6	.120	-2	2	2	4	0.4
1909 Chi-N	0	0	—	1	0	0	0	0	3	2	0	4	1	18.0	0.00	—	.222	.462	0	.000	-0	1	1	-0	0.0
Total 14	175	212	.452	433	389	342	22	6	3356	3460	69	1332	1098	13.4	3.68	92	.267	.345	235	.179	-15	-109	-108	29	-9.4

● **WILLIE FRASER**   Fraser, William Patrick   b: 5/26/64, New York, N.Y.   BR/TR, 6'1", 208 lbs.   Deb: 9/10/86

YEAR TM/L	W	L	PCT	G	GS	CG	SH	SV	IP	H	HR	BB	SO	RAT	ERA	ERA+	OAV	OOB	BH	AVG	PB	PR	/A	PD	TPI
1986 Cal-A	0	0	—	1	1	0	0	0	4¹	6	0	1	2	14.5	8.31	49	.353	.389		0	—	0	-2	-2	-0	0.1
1987 Cal-A	10	10	.500	36	23	5	1	1	176¹	160	26	63	106	11.7	3.92	110	.240	.312		0	—	0	10	7	-3	0.7
1988 Cal-A	12	13	.480	34	32	2	0	0	194²	203	33	80	86	13.5	5.41	71	.267	.344		0	—	0	-31	-34	-1	-3.7
1989 Cal-A	4	7	.364	44	0	0	0	0	91²	80	6	23	46	10.6	3.24	118	.235	.293		0	—	0	7	6	0	0.7
1990 Cal-A	5	4	.556	45	0	0	0	2	76	69	4	24	32	11.0	3.08	124	.241	.300		0	—	0	7	6	-1	0.6
1991 Tor-A	0	0	.000	13	1	0	0	0	26¹	33	4	11	12	16.1	6.15	68	.303	.382		0	—	0	-6	-6	-0	-0.7
StL-N	3	3	.500	35	0	0	0	0	49¹	44	9	21	25	12.4	4.93	75	.242	.330	0	.000	-0	-7	-7	-1	-0.9
1994 Fla-N	2	2	1.000	9	0	0	0	0	12¹	20	1	6	7	19.0	5.84	77	.370	.433		0	—	0	-2	-2	-0	-0.3
Total 7	36	39	.480	217	57	7	1	5	631¹	615	83	229	316	12.4	4.42	90	.255	.326		0	—	0	-24	-30	-6	-3.5

● **VIC FRASIER**   Frasier, Victor Patrick   b: 8/5/04, Ruston, La.   d: 1/10/77, Jacksonville, Tex.   BR/TR, 6', 182 lbs.   Deb: 4/18/31

YEAR TM/L	W	L	PCT	G	GS	CG	SH	SV	IP	H	HR	BB	SO	RAT	ERA	ERA+	OAV	OOB	BH	AVG	PB	PR	/A	PD	TPI
1931 Chi-A	13	15	.464	46	29	13	2	4	254	258	11	127	87	13.8	4.46	95	.259	.345	18	.209	1	-2	-6	-1	-0.6
1932 Chi-A	3	13	.188	29	21	4	0	0	146	180	14	70	33	15.7	6.23	69	.297	.374	4	.091	-3	-28	-31	2	-2.8
1933 Chi-A	1	1	.500	10	1	0	0	0	20¹	32	2	11	4	19.0	8.85	48	.368	.439	0	.000	-1	-10	-10	0	-0.8
Det-A	5	5	.500	20	14	4	0	0	104¹	129	9	59	26	16.3	6.64	65	.312	.399	7	.189	-0	-27	-27	2	-2.1
Yr	6	6	.500	30	15	4	0	0	124²	161	11	70	30	16.7	7.00	61	.321	.406	7	.171	-1	-38	-37	2	-2.9
1934 Det-A	1	3	.250	8	2	0	0	0	22²	30	0	12	11	17.1	5.96	74	.313	.394	2	.286	0	-4	-4	2	-0.4
1937 Bos-N	0	0	—	3	0	0	0	0	10	8	1	3	6	14.4	5.63	64	.364	.382	0	.000	-0	-2	-2	0	-0.2
1939 Chi-A	0	1	.000	10	1	0	0	0	23²	45	0	11	7	21.3	10.27	46	.405	.459	2	.286	-0	-15	-15	0	-0.5
Total 6	23	38	.377	126	68	21	2	4	579	686	37	291	170	15.4	5.77	75	.293	.373	33	.177	-3	-88	-94	4	-7.2

● **GEORGE FRAZIER**   Frazier, George Allen   b: 10/13/54, Oklahoma City, Okla   BR/TR, 6'5", 205 lbs.   Deb: 5/25/78

YEAR TM/L	W	L	PCT	G	GS	CG	SH	SV	IP	H	HR	BB	SO	RAT	ERA	ERA+	OAV	OOB	BH	AVG	PB	PR	/A	PD	TPI
1978 StL-N	0	3	.000	14	0	0	0	0	22	22	6	2	8	11.5	4.09	86	.250	.298	1	.333	0	-1	-1	0	-0.2
1979 StL-N	2	4	.333	25	0	0	0	2	32¹	35	3	12	14	13.4	4.45	84	.278	.345	0	.000	-0	-3	-2	-0	-0.4
1980 StL-N	1	4	.200	22	0	0	0	3	23	24	2	7	11	12.1	2.74	135	.273	.326	0	—	0	2	2	0	0.6

YEAR TM/L	W	L	PCT	G	GS	CG	SH	SV	IP	H	HR	BB	SO	RAT	ERA	ERA+	OAV	OOB	BH	AVG	PB	PR	/A	PD	TPI
1981 *NY-A	0	1	.000	16	0	0	0	3	27²	26	1	11	17	12.0	1.63	220	.245	.316	0	—	0	6	6	-0	0.4
1982 NY-A	4	4	.500	63	0	0	0	1	111²	103	7	39	69	11.8	3.47	115	.252	.325	0	—	0	8	6	-0	0.5
1983 NY-A	4	4	.500	61	0	0	0	8	115¹	94	5	45	78	11.1	3.43	113	.227	.307	0	—	0	8	6	-0	0.7
1984 Cle-A	3	2	.600	22	0	0	0	0	44¹	45	3	14	24	12.0	3.65	112	.259	.314	0	—	0	2	2	-1	0.0
*Chi-N	6	3	.667	37	0	0	0	3	63²	53	4	26	58	11.3	4.10	95	.221	.300	2	.286	0	-4	-1	-1	-0.3
1985 Chi-N	7	8	.467	51	0	0	0	2	76	88	11	52	46	16.9	6.39	62	.299	.410	0	.000	-1	-24	-20	-0	-3.9
1986 Chi-N	2	4	.333	35	0	0	0	0	51²	63	5	34	41	17.1	5.40	75	.310	.412	0	.000	-0	-10	-8	-1	-1.0
Min-A	1	1	.500	15	0	0	0	6	26²	23	2	16	25	13.2	4.39	98	.232	.339	0	—	0	-1	-0	-0	-0.2
1987 *Min-A	5	5	.500	54	0	0	0	2	81¹	77	9	51	58	14.4	4.98	93	.258	.369	0	—	0	-5	-3	-1	-0.7
Total 10	35	43	.449	415	0	0	0	29	675²	653	54	313	449	13.1	4.20	96	.257	.342	3	.143	-1	-20	-14	-4	-4.5

● **SCOTT FREDRICKSON**   Fredrickson, Scott Eric b: 8/19/67, Manchester, N.H. BR/TR, 6′3″, 215 lbs. Deb: 4/30/93

YEAR TM/L	W	L	PCT	G	GS	CG	SH	SV	IP	H	HR	BB	SO	RAT	ERA	ERA+	OAV	OOB	BH	AVG	PB	PR	/A	PD	TPI
1993 Col-N	0	1	.000	25	0	0	0	0	29	33	3	17	20	15.8	6.21	77	.287	.383	0	.000	-0	-7	-5	-0	-0.2

● **BUCK FREEMAN**   Freeman, Alexander Vernon b: 7/5/1893, Mart, Tex. d: 2/21/53, Fort Sam Houston, Tex. BB/TR, 5′10″, 167 lbs. Deb: 4/13/21

YEAR TM/L	W	L	PCT	G	GS	CG	SH	SV	IP	H	HR	BB	SO	RAT	ERA	ERA+	OAV	OOB	BH	AVG	PB	PR	/A	PD	TPI
1921 Chi-N	9	10	.474	38	20	6	0	3	177¹	189	12	70	42	13.6	4.11	93	.281	.356	11	.208	0	-6	-6	-1	-0.7
1922 Chi-N	0	1	.000	11	1	0	0	1	25²	47	0	10	10	20.7	8.77	48	.412	.468	1	.125	-1	-13	-13	1	-0.5
Total 2	9	11	.450	49	21	6	0	4	203	236	12	80	52	14.5	4.70	82	.300	.372	12	.197	-0	-20	-19	-0	-1.2

● **HARVEY FREEMAN**   Freeman, Harvey Bayard "Buck" b: 12/22/1897, Mottville, Mich. d: 1/10/70, Kalamazoo, Mich. BR/TR, 5′10″, 160 lbs. Deb: 7/10/21

YEAR TM/L	W	L	PCT	G	GS	CG	SH	SV	IP	H	HR	BB	SO	RAT	ERA	ERA+	OAV	OOB	BH	AVG	PB	PR	/A	PD	TPI
1921 Phi-A	1	4	.200	18	4	2	0	0	48	65	2	35	5	19.7	7.69	58	.346	.461	1	.083	-2	-18	-17	1	-1.5

● **HERSH FREEMAN**   Freeman, Hershell Baskin "Buster" b: 7/1/28, Gadsden, Ala. BR/TR, 6′3″, 220 lbs. Deb: 9/10/52

YEAR TM/L	W	L	PCT	G	GS	CG	SH	SV	IP	H	HR	BB	SO	RAT	ERA	ERA+	OAV	OOB	BH	AVG	PB	PR	/A	PD	TPI
1952 Bos-A	1	0	1.000	4	1	1	0	0	13²	13	1	5	5	12.5	3.29	120	.260	.339	2	.500	1	1	1	0	0.2
1953 Bos-A	1	4	.200	18	2	0	0	0	39	50	3	17	15	15.5	5.54	76	.316	.383	1	.091	-1	-7	-6	-0	-0.8
1955 Bos-A	0	0	—	2	0	0	0	0	1²	1	0	1	1	10.8	0.00	—	.200	.333	0	—	0	1	1	-0	0.1
Cin-N	7	4	.636	52	0	0	0	11	91²	94	3	30	37	12.4	2.16	196	.276	.338	3	.167	1	19	21	1	3.1
1956 Cin-N	14	5	.737	64	0	0	0	18	108²	112	2	34	50	12.2	3.40	117	.274	.331	1	.056	-1	5	7	-0	1.3
1957 Cin-N	7	2	.778	52	0	0	0	8	83²	90	14	14	36	11.5	4.52	91	.277	.313	2	.200	0	-6	-4	-1	-0.5
1958 Cin-N	0	0	—	3	0	0	0	0	7²	4	0	5	7	10.6	3.52	118	.154	.290	0	—	0	1	0	0	0.1
Chi-N	0	1	.000	9	0	0	0	0	13	23	3	3	7	18.0	8.31	47	.354	.382	0	.000	0	-6	-6	0	-0.4
Yr	0	1	.000	12	0	0	0	0	20²	27	3	8	14	15.2	6.53	61	.293	.350	0	.000	0	-6	-6	0	-0.4
Total 6	30	16	.652	204	3	1	0	37	359	387	25	109	158	12.6	3.74	110	.281	.336	9	.143	-0	6	15	1	2.9

● **JIMMY FREEMAN**   Freeman, Jimmy Lee b: 6/29/51, Carlsbad, N.Mex. BL/TL, 6′4″, 180 lbs. Deb: 9/1/72

YEAR TM/L	W	L	PCT	G	GS	CG	SH	SV	IP	H	HR	BB	SO	RAT	ERA	ERA+	OAV	OOB	BH	AVG	PB	PR	/A	PD	TPI
1972 Atl-N	2	2	.500	6	6	1	0	0	36	40	5	22	18	15.5	6.00	63	.278	.373	1	.077	-0	-10	-9	-1	-1.0
1973 Atl-N	0	2	.000	13	5	0	0	1	37¹	50	7	25	20	18.1	7.71	51	.327	.421	2	.154	-0	-17	-16	-1	-1.0
Total 2	2	4	.333	19	11	1	0	1	73¹	90	12	47	38	16.8	6.87	56	.303	.398	3	.115	-1	-27	-25	-2	-2.0

● **BUCK FREEMAN**   Freeman, John Frank b: 10/30/1871, Catasauqua, Pa. d: 6/25/49, Wilkes-Barre, Pa. BL/TL, 5′9″, 169 lbs. Deb: 6/27/1891 ♦

YEAR TM/L	W	L	PCT	G	GS	CG	SH	SV	IP	H	HR	BB	SO	RAT	ERA	ERA+	OAV	OOB	BH	AVG	PB	PR	/A	PD	TPI
1891 Was-a	3	2	.600	5	4	4	0	0	44	35	0	33	28	14.7	3.89	96	.211	.355	4	.222	0	-1	-1	-0	0.0
1899 Was-N	0	0	—	2	0	0	0	0	7	15	3	3	0	27.0	7.71	51	.430	.513	187	.318	1	-3	-3	-0	0.0
Total 2	3	2	.600	7	4	4	0	0	51	50	3	36	28	16.4	4.41	85	.249	.381	1235	.293	1	-4	-4	-0	0.0

● **JULIE FREEMAN**   Freeman, Julius Benjamin b: 11/7/1868, Missouri d: 6/10/21, St.Louis, Mo. BR, Deb: 10/10/1888

YEAR TM/L	W	L	PCT	G	GS	CG	SH	SV	IP	H	HR	BB	SO	RAT	ERA	ERA+	OAV	OOB	BH	AVG	PB	PR	/A	PD	TPI
1888 StL-a	0	1	.000	1	1	0	0	0	6¹	7	0	4	1	17.1	4.26	77	.270	.388	1	.333	1	-1	-1	-0	-0.1

● **MARK FREEMAN**   Freeman, Mark Price b: 12/7/30, Memphis, Tenn. BR/TR, 6′4″, 220 lbs. Deb: 4/18/59

YEAR TM/L	W	L	PCT	G	GS	CG	SH	SV	IP	H	HR	BB	SO	RAT	ERA	ERA+	OAV	OOB	BH	AVG	PB	PR	/A	PD	TPI
1959 KC-A	0	0	—	3	0	0	0	0	3²	6	0	3	1	22.1	9.82	41	.375	.474	0	—	-0	-2	-2	-0	0.0
NY-A	0	0	—	1	1	0	0	0	7	6	0	2	4	11.6	2.57	142	.240	.321	0	.000	-0	1	1	-0	0.0
Yr	0	0	—	4	1	0	0	0	10²	12	0	5	5	15.2	5.06	74	.286	.375	0	.000	-0	-1	-2	-0	0.0
1960 Chi-N	3	3	.500	30	8	1	0	1	76²	70	10	33	50	12.7	5.63	67	.240	.327	3	.150	-1	-16	-16	-2	-1.4
Total 2	3	3	.500	34	9	1	0	1	87¹	82	10	38	55	13.0	5.56	68	.246	.334	3	.136	-1	-17	-17	-2	-1.4

● **MARVIN FREEMAN**   Freeman, Marvin b: 4/10/63, Chicago, Ill. BR/TR, 6′7″, 200 lbs. Deb: 9/16/86

YEAR TM/L	W	L	PCT	G	GS	CG	SH	SV	IP	H	HR	BB	SO	RAT	ERA	ERA+	OAV	OOB	BH	AVG	PB	PR	/A	PD	TPI
1986 Phi-N	2	0	1.000	3	3	0	0	0	16	6	0	10	8	9.0	2.25	171	.120	.267	0	.000	-1	3	3	-0	0.2
1988 Phi-N	2	3	.400	11	11	0	0	0	51²	55	2	43	37	17.2	6.10	58	.276	.407	3	.214	0	-15	-15	0	-1.2
1989 Phi-N	0	0	—	1	1	0	0	0	3	2	1	5	3	21.0	6.00	59	.182	.438	0	—	-0	-1	-0	-0	0.0
1990 Phi-N	0	2	.000	16	3	0	0	0	32¹	34	5	14	26	14.2	5.57	69	.264	.349	0	.000	-1	-6	-6	-0	-0.5
Atl-N	1	0	1.000	9	0	0	0	0	15²	7	0	3	12	6.9	1.72	234	.130	.203	0	—	0	4	4	-0	0.2
Yr	1	2	.333	25	3	0	0	0	48	41	5	17	38	11.3	4.31	90	.220	.293	0	.000	-1	-3	-2	-0	-0.3
1991 Atl-N	1	0	1.000	34	0	0	0	1	48	37	2	13	34	9.8	3.00	130	.214	.277	0	.000	-0	4	5	-1	0.0
1992 *Atl-N	7	5	.583	58	0	0	0	3	64¹	61	7	29	41	12.7	3.22	114	.251	.333	2	.500	1	2	3	-1	0.6
1993 Atl-N	2	0	1.000	21	0	0	0	0	23²	24	1	10	25	13.3	6.08	66	.261	.340	1	—	0	-5	-5	-1	-0.5
1994 Col-N	10	2	.833	19	18	0	0	0	112²	113	10	23	67	11.3	2.80	178	.262	.307	4	.111	-0	18	27	1	2.8
Total 8	25	12	.676	172	36	0	0	5	367¹	339	27	150	250	12.3	3.77	109	.245	.326	9	.118	-2	2	14	-2	1.6

● **JAKE FREEZE**   Freeze, Carl Alexander b: 4/25/1900, Huntington, Ark. d: 4/9/83, San Angelo, Tex. BR/TR, 5′8″, 150 lbs. Deb: 7/1/25

YEAR TM/L	W	L	PCT	G	GS	CG	SH	SV	IP	H	HR	BB	SO	RAT	ERA	ERA+	OAV	OOB	BH	AVG	PB	PR	/A	PD	TPI
1925 Chi-A	0	0	—	2	0	0	0	0	3²	5	1	3	1	19.6	2.45	169	.333	.444	0	.000	-0	1	1	-0	0.0

● **DAVE FREISLEBEN**   Freisleben, David James b: 10/31/51, Coraopolis, Pa. BR/TR, 5′11″, 200 lbs. Deb: 4/26/74

YEAR TM/L	W	L	PCT	G	GS	CG	SH	SV	IP	H	HR	BB	SO	RAT	ERA	ERA+	OAV	OOB	BH	AVG	PB	PR	/A	PD	TPI
1974 SD-N	9	14	.391	33	31	6	2	0	211²	194	13	112	130	13.3	3.66	97	.241	.339	11	.172	2	-1	-2	-0	0.0
1975 SD-N	5	14	.263	36	27	4	1	0	181	206	11	82	77	14.7	4.28	81	.289	.368	4	.083	-1	-13	-16	0	-1.7
1976 SD-N	10	13	.435	34	24	6	3	1	172	163	10	66	81	12.2	3.51	93	.248	.321	7	.189	1	-0	-5	2	-0.2
1977 SD-N	7	9	.438	33	23	1	0	0	138²	140	21	71	72	13.8	4.61	77	.266	.356	5	.135	-0	-11	-16	-2	-1.9
1978 SD-N	0	3	.000	12	4	0	0	0	26²	41	3	15	16	18.9	6.08	55	.363	.438	0	.000	-1	-7	-8	-0	-0.9
Cle-A	1	4	.200	12	10	0	0	0	44¹	52	4	31	19	17.3	7.11	53	.299	.411	0	—	0	-16	-17	-0	-1.6
1979 Tor-A	2	3	.400	42	2	0	0	3	91	101	5	53	35	15.4	4.95	88	.294	.391	0	—	0	-7	-6	-1	-0.4
Total 6	34	60	.362	202	121	17	6	4	865¹	897	67	430	430	14.1	4.30	83	.269	.357	27	.141	2	-56	-71	-2	-6.7

● **TONY FREITAS**   Freitas, Antonio b: 5/5/08, Mill Valley, Cal. d: 3/13/94, Orangevale, Cal. BR/TL, 5′8″, 161 lbs. Deb: 5/31/32

YEAR TM/L	W	L	PCT	G	GS	CG	SH	SV	IP	H	HR	BB	SO	RAT	ERA	ERA+	OAV	OOB	BH	AVG	PB	PR	/A	PD	TPI
1932 Phi-A	12	5	.706	23	18	10	1	0	150¹	150	11	48	31	12.1	3.83	118	.263	.325	8	.148	-1	11	12	1	1.1
1933 Phi-A	2	4	.333	19	9	2	0	1	64¹	90	8	24	15	16.2	7.27	59	.337	.396	1	.063	-1	-21	-21	0	-1.8
1934 Cin-N	6	12	.333	30	18	5	0	1	152²	194	6	29	37	13.1	4.01	102	.311	.341	9	.191	0	1	1	2	0.4
1935 Cin-N	5	10	.333	31	15	8	0	0	143²	174	6	38	51	13.4	4.57	87	.295	.340	6	.130	-0	-9	-9	1	-0.3
1936 Cin-N	0	2	.000	4	3	0	0	0	7	6	0	2	1	10.3	1.29	297	.240	.296	0	.000	-0	2	2	0	0.5
Total 5	25	33	.431	107	63	22	1	4	518	614	31	137	135	13.2	4.48	94	.296	.343	24	.145	-2	-16	-16	4	-0.6

● **LARRY FRENCH**   French, Lawrence Herbert b: 11/1/07, Visalia, Cal. d: 2/9/87, San Diego, Cal. BR/TL, 6′1″, 195 lbs. Deb: 4/18/29

YEAR TM/L	W	L	PCT	G	GS	CG	SH	SV	IP	H	HR	BB	SO	RAT	ERA	ERA+	OAV	OOB	BH	AVG	PB	PR	/A	PD	TPI
1929 Pit-N	7	5	.583	30	13	6	0	0	123	130	10	62	49	14.3	4.90	97	.276	.364	8	.190	-1	-3	-2	1	-0.1
1930 Pit-N	17	18	.486	42	35	21	3	1	274²	325	20	89	90	13.8	4.36	114	.295	.351	22	.242	1	19	19	-1	1.9
1931 Pit-N	15	13	.536	39	33	20	1	1	275²	301	9	70	73	12.1	3.26	118	.278	.322	17	.179	-1	18	18	-1	1.5
1932 Pit-N	18	16	.529	47	33	19	3	4	274¹	297	12	60	72	11.9	3.02	126	.276	.316	19	.207	1	26	24	-4	2.5
1933 Pit-N	18	13	.581	47	35	21	5	1	291¹	299	9	55	88	10.8	2.72	122	.271	.294	15	.149	-2	20	19	-4	1.4
1934 Pit-N	12	18	.400	49	35	16	3	1	263²	299	8	59	103	12.3	3.58	115	.281	.321	16	.190	-0	14	16	-3	1.3
1935 *Chi-N	17	10	.630	42	30	16	4	2	246¹	279	10	44	90	11.9	2.96	133	.286	.318	12	.141	-4	29	27	1	2.4

YEAR	TM/L	W	L	PCT	G	GS	CG	SH	SV	IP	H	HR	BB	SO	RAT	ERA	ERA+	OAV	OOB	BH	AVG	PB	PR	/A	PD	TPI
1936	Chi-N	18	9	.667	43	28	16	**4**	3	252¹	262	16	54	104	11.5	3.39	118	.266	.308	18	.212	0	18	17	-3	1.3
1937	Chi-N	16	10	.615	42	28	11	4	0	208	229	17	65	100	12.8	3.98	100	.274	.327	9	.127	-4	-2	0	2	-0.2
1938	*Chi-N	10	19	.345	43	27	10	3	0	201¹	210	17	62	83	12.2	3.80	101	.271	.326	13	.210	2	-0	1	1	0.4
1939	Chi-N	15	8	.652	36	21	10	2	1	194	205	7	50	98	11.9	3.29	120	.269	.314	14	.192	1	13	14	2	1.8
1940	Chi-N★	14	14	.500	40	33	18	3	2	246	240	12	64	107	11.3	3.29	114	.256	.306	14	.165	1	15	12	2	1.7
1941	Chi-N	5	14	.263	26	18	6	1	0	138	161	10	43	60	13.4	4.63	76	.285	.338	9	.191	1	-15	-17	-1	-2.1
	*Bro-N	0	0	—	6	1	0	0	0	15²	16	1	4	8	12.1	3.45	106	.267	.323	1	.250	0	0	0	-0	0.0
	Yr	5	14	.263	32	19	6	1	0	153²	177	11	47	68	13.2	4.51	78	.282	.333	10	.196	1	-15	-17	-1	-2.1
1942	Bro-N	15	4	**.789**	38	14	8	4	0	147²	127	1	36	62	10.2	1.83	178	.233	.287	12	.300	4	24	24	-1	3.4
Total	14	197	171	.535	570	384	198	40	17	3152	3375	164	819	1187	12.1	3.44	114	.272	.320	199	.188	0	178	171	-7	17.2

● **BILL FRENCH**   French, William   b: Baltimore, Md.   Deb: 4/14/1873   ♦

YEAR	TM/L	W	L	PCT	G	GS	CG	SH	SV	IP	H	HR	BB	SO	RAT	ERA	ERA+	OAV	OOB	BH	AVG	PB	PR	/A	PD	TPI
1873	Mar-n	0	1	.000	1	1	1	0	0	9	30	1	0	0	30.0	12.00	27	.462	.462	4	.222	-0	-9	-9		-0.5

● **BENNY FREY**   Frey, Benjamin Rudolph   b: 4/6/06, Dexter, Mich.   d: 11/1/37, Jackson, Mich.   BR/TR, 5'10", 165 lbs.   Deb: 9/18/29

YEAR	TM/L	W	L	PCT	G	GS	CG	SH	SV	IP	H	HR	BB	SO	RAT	ERA	ERA+	OAV	OOB	BH	AVG	PB	PR	/A	PD	TPI
1929	Cin-N	1	2	.333	3	3	2	0	0	24	29	2	8	1	13.9	4.13	111	.302	.356	3	.375	1	2	1	1	0.3
1930	Cin-N	11	18	.379	44	28	14	2	1	245	295	15	62	43	13.2	4.70	103	.305	.349	25	.284	4	7	3	6	1.3
1931	Cin-N	8	12	.400	34	17	7	1	2	133²	166	2	36	19	13.7	4.92	76	.319	.365	14	.318	4	-16	-18	4	-1.6
1932	StL-N	0	2	.000	2	0	0	0	0	3	6	0	2	0	24.0	12.00	33	.600	.667	0	.000	-0	-3	-3	-0	-1.2
	Cin-N	4	10	.286	28	15	5	0	0	131¹	159	10	30	27	13.0	4.32	89	.299	.338	9	.205	-0	-6	-7	3	-0.4
	Yr	4	12	.250	30	15	5	0	0	134¹	165	10	32	27	13.3	4.49	86	.305	.345	9	.200	-0	-9	-9	2	-1.6
1933	Cin-N	6	4	.600	37	9	1	1	0	132	144	4	21	12	11.3	3.82	89	.281	.309	11	.262	3	-7	-6	2	0.1
1934	Cin-N	11	16	.407	39	30	12	2	2	245¹	288	10	42	33	12.2	3.52	116	.289	.319	14	.171	-0	15	15	4	1.9
1935	Cin-N	6	10	.375	38	13	3	1	3	114¹	164	6	32	24	15.7	6.85	58	.335	.381	11	.344	4	-36	-36	3	-3.9
1936	Cin-N	10	8	.556	31	12	5	0	0	131¹	164	5	30	20	13.3	4.25	90	.296	.332	11	.250	2	-3	-6	0	-0.5
Total	8	57	82	.410	256	127	49	7	8	1160	1415	54	263	179	13.1	4.50	90	.303	.341	98	.255	17	-47	-55	21	-4.0

● **STEVE FREY**   Frey, Steven Francis   b: 7/29/63, Meadowbrook, Pa.   BR/TL, 5'9", 170 lbs.   Deb: 5/10/89

YEAR	TM/L	W	L	PCT	G	GS	CG	SH	SV	IP	H	HR	BB	SO	RAT	ERA	ERA+	OAV	OOB	BH	AVG	PB	PR	/A	PD	TPI
1989	Mon-N	3	2	.600	20	0	0	0	0	21¹	29	4	11	15	17.3	5.48	64	.326	.406	0	—	-0	-5	-5	-0	-1.0
1990	Mon-N	8	2	.800	51	0	0	0	0	55²	44	4	29	29	12.0	2.10	174	.219	.320	0	.000	-0	10	10	-0	2.0
1991	Mon-N	0	1	.000	31	0	0	0	1	39²	43	3	23	21	15.2	4.99	72	.281	.379	0	.000	-0	-6	-6	-1	-0.2
1992	Cal-A	4	2	.667	51	0	0	0	4	45¹	39	6	22	24	12.5	3.57	111	.233	.335	0	—	0	2	2	0	0.3
1993	Cal-A	2	3	.400	55	0	0	0	13	48¹	41	1	26	22	13.0	2.98	151	.230	.338	0	—	0	7	8	0	1.0
1994	SF-N	1	0	1.000	44	0	0	0	9	31	37	6	15	20	15.7	4.94	82	.322	.409	0	—	-0	-2	-3	-0	-0.1
Total	6	18	10	.643	252	0	0	0	27	241¹	233	24	126	131	13.8	3.69	106	.259	.356	0	.000	0	7	6	-1	2.0

● **BERNIE FRIBERG**   Friberg, Bernard Albert (b: Gustaf Bernhard Friberg)
b: 8/18/1899, Manchester, N.H.   d: 12/8/58, Lynn, Mass.   BR/TR, 5'11", 178 lbs.   Deb: 8/20/19   ♦

YEAR	TM/L	W	L	PCT	G	GS	CG	SH	SV	IP	H	HR	BB	SO	RAT	ERA	ERA+	OAV	OOB	BH	AVG	PB	PR	/A	PD	TPI
1925	Phi-N	0	0	—	1	0	0	0	0	4	4	0	3	1	15.8	4.50	106	.286	.412	82	.270	0	-0	-0	-0	0.0

● **MARION FRICANO**   Fricano, Marion John   b: 7/15/23, Brant, N.Y.   d: 5/18/76, Tijuana, Mex.   BR/TR, 6', 170 lbs.   Deb: 9/6/52

YEAR	TM/L	W	L	PCT	G	GS	CG	SH	SV	IP	H	HR	BB	SO	RAT	ERA	ERA+	OAV	OOB	BH	AVG	PB	PR	/A	PD	TPI
1952	Phi-A	1	0	1.000	2	0	0	0	0	5	5	0	1	0	10.8	1.80	220	.238	.273	0	—	0	1	1	0	0.2
1953	Phi-A	9	12	.429	39	23	10	0	0	211	206	21	90	67	12.9	3.88	110	.257	.337	10	.145	-3	3	10	-2	0.4
1954	Phi-A	5	11	.313	37	20	4	0	1	151²	163	17	64	43	13.7	5.16	76	.275	.349	4	.098	-3	-24	-21	-2	-2.5
1955	KC-A	0	0	—	10	0	0	0	0	20	19	2	9	5	12.6	3.15	133	.253	.333	2	.667	1	2	2	0	0.1
Total	4	15	23	.395	88	43	14	0	1	387²	393	40	164	115	13.2	4.32	96	.264	.341	16	.142	-5	-19	-8	-3	-1.8

● **SKIPPER FRIDAY**   Friday, Grier William   b: 10/26/1897, Gastonia, N.C.   d: 8/25/62, Gastonia, N.C.   BR/TR, 5'11", 170 lbs.   Deb: 6/17/23

YEAR	TM/L	W	L	PCT	G	GS	CG	SH	SV	IP	H	HR	BB	SO	RAT	ERA	ERA+	OAV	OOB	BH	AVG	PB	PR	/A	PD	TPI
1923	Was-A	0	1	.000	7	2	1	0	0	30	35	2	22	9	17.7	6.90	55	.313	.434	2	.222	0	-10	-10	1	-0.2

● **CY FRIED**   Fried, Arthur Edwin   b: 7/23/1897, San Antonio, Tex.   d: 10/10/70, San Antonio, Tex.   BL/TL, 5'11.5", 150 lbs.   Deb: 9/17/20

YEAR	TM/L	W	L	PCT	G	GS	CG	SH	SV	IP	H	HR	BB	SO	RAT	ERA	ERA+	OAV	OOB	BH	AVG	PB	PR	/A	PD	TPI
1920	Det-A	0	0	—	2	0	0	0	0	1²	3	0	4	0	37.8	16.20	23	.500	.700	0	—	0	-2	-2	0	-0.2

● **BOB FRIEDRICHS**   Friedrichs, Robert George   b: 8/30/06, Cincinnati, Ohio   BR/TR, 5'11.5", 165 lbs.   Deb: 5/17/32

YEAR	TM/L	W	L	PCT	G	GS	CG	SH	SV	IP	H	HR	BB	SO	RAT	ERA	ERA+	OAV	OOB	BH	AVG	PB	PR	/A	PD	TPI
1932	Was-A	0	0	—	2	0	0	0	0	4	8	0	4	2	27.0	11.25	38	.250	.500	0	.000	-0	-3	-3	-0	0.0

● **BILL FRIEL**   Friel, William Edward   b: 4/1/1876, Renovo, Pa.   d: 12/24/59, St.Louis, Mo.   BL/TR, 5'10", 165 lbs.   Deb: 5/3/01   FU♦

YEAR	TM/L	W	L	PCT	G	GS	CG	SH	SV	IP	H	HR	BB	SO	RAT	ERA	ERA+	OAV	OOB	BH	AVG	PB	PR	/A	PD	TPI
1902	StL-A	0	0	—	1	0	0	0	0	4	4	0	1	0	9.0	4.50	78	.261	.261	64	.240	0	-0	-0	-0	0.0

● **DANNY FRIEND**   Friend, Daniel Sebastian   b: 4/18/1873, Cincinnati, Ohio   d: 6/1/42, Chillicothe, Ohio   TL, 5'9", 175 lbs.   Deb: 9/10/1895

YEAR	TM/L	W	L	PCT	G	GS	CG	SH	SV	IP	H	HR	BB	SO	RAT	ERA	ERA+	OAV	OOB	BH	AVG	PB	PR	/A	PD	TPI
1895	Chi-N	2	2	.500	5	5	5	0	0	41	50	5	14	10	14.7	5.27	97	.296	.360	4	.235	-1	-2	-1	0	-0.1
1896	Chi-N	18	14	.563	36	33	28	1	0	290²	298	11	139	86	14.7	4.74	96	.263	.363	30	.238	-1	-12	-6	-2	-0.8
1897	Chi-N	12	11	.522	24	24	23	0	0	203	244	5	86	58	15.4	4.52	99	.295	.373	25	.284	2	-5	-1	-2	-0.1
1898	Chi-N	0	2	.000	2	2	2	0	0	17	20	1	10	4	16.4	5.29	68	.291	.389	2	.286	-1	-3	-3	2	-0.1
Total	4	32	29	.525	67	64	58	1	0	551²	612	22	249	158	15.0	4.71	96	.279	.368	61	.256	0	-22	-12	-2	-1.1

● **BOB FRIEND**   Friend, Robert Bartmess "Warrior"   b: 11/24/30, Lafayette, Ind.   BR/TR, 6', 190 lbs.   Deb: 4/28/51

YEAR	TM/L	W	L	PCT	G	GS	CG	SH	SV	IP	H	HR	BB	SO	RAT	ERA	ERA+	OAV	OOB	BH	AVG	PB	PR	/A	PD	TPI
1951	Pit-N	6	10	.375	34	22	3	1	0	149²	173	12	68	41	14.5	4.27	99	.293	.366	4	.091	-2	-5	-1	0	-0.3
1952	Pit-N	7	17	.292	35	23	6	1	0	185	186	15	84	75	13.3	4.18	95	.258	.338	3	.058	-4	-9	-4	1	-0.8
1953	Pit-N	8	11	.421	32	24	8	0	0	170²	193	18	57	66	13.3	4.90	91	.286	.344	7	.135	-2	-12	-8	1	-0.9
1954	Pit-N	7	12	.368	35	20	4	2	2	170¹	204	16	58	70	13.9	5.07	83	.302	.358	14	.275	5	-19	-17	-1	-1.2
1955	Pit-N	14	9	.609	44	20	9	2	2	200¹	178	18	52	98	10.4	**2.83**	**145**	.242	.294	10	.164	-2	**27**	**29**	3	3.3
1956	Pit-N★	17	17	.500	49	42	19	4	3	314¹	310	25	85	166	11.4	3.46	109	.258	.308	16	.165	-1	11	11	-1	0.9
1957	Pit-N	14	18	.438	40	38	17	3	0	277	273	28	68	143	11.1	3.38	112	.257	.303	16	.184	1	15	13	-1	1.4
1958	Pit-N★	22	14	.611	38	38	16	1	0	274	299	25	61	135	12.0	3.68	105	.281	.322	10	.106	-4	8	6	-0	0.3
1959	Pit-N	8	19	.296	35	35	7	2	0	234²	267	19	52	104	12.5	4.03	96	.283	.325	12	.164	0	-2	-4	-0	-0.4
1960	*Pit-N★	18	12	.600	38	37	16	4	1	275²	266	16	45	183	10.5	3.00	125	.251	.281	6	.068	-5	23	23	0	1.9
1961	Pit-N	14	19	.424	41	35	10	1	1	236	271	15	45	108	12.2	3.85	104	.289	.324	11	.139	-3	5	4	-1	0.1
1962	Pit-N	18	14	.563	39	36	13	**5**	1	261²	280	23	53	144	11.5	3.06	129	.273	.310	11	.121	-3	26	25	0	2.5
1963	Pit-N	17	16	.515	39	38	12	4	0	268²	276	13	44	144	11.5	2.34	141	.233	.269	9	.105	-3	28	28	-1	3.1
1964	Pit-N	13	18	.419	35	35	13	3	0	240¹	253	10	50	128	11.5	3.33	105	.271	.310	5	.070	-3	5	5	2	0.4
1965	Pit-N	8	12	.400	34	34	8	2	0	222	221	17	47	74	11.2	3.24	108	.260	.305	3	.042	-5	7	7	0	0.0
1966	NY-A	4	2	.200	12	8	0	0	0	44²	50	7	16	22	14.1	4.84	69	.439	.361	0	—	-1	-7	-7	1	-0.8
	NY-N	5	8	.385	22	12	2	1	1	86	101	11	16	30	13.3	4.40	83	.289	.322	1	.034	-3	-8	-7	-2	-1.5
Total	16	197	230	.461	602	497	163	36	11	3611	3772	286	894	1734	11.7	3.58	107	.269	.315	138	.121	-36	94	100	2	8.0

● **PETE FRIES**   Fries, Peter Martin   b: 10/30/1857, Scranton, Pa.   d: 7/30/37, Chicago, Ill.   BL/TL, 5'8", 160 lbs.   Deb: 8/10/1883   ♦

YEAR	TM/L	W	L	PCT	G	GS	CG	SH	SV	IP	H	HR	BB	SO	RAT	ERA	ERA+	OAV	OOB	BH	AVG	PB	PR	/A	PD	TPI
1883	Col-a	0	3	.000	3	3	3	0	0	25	34	1	14	7	17.3	6.48	48	.305	.382	3	.300	1	-9	-9	0	-0.7

● **JOHN FRILL**   Frill, John Edmond   b: 4/3/1879, Reading, Pa.   d: 9/28/18, Westerly, R.I.   BR/TL, 5'10.5", 170 lbs.   Deb: 4/16/10

YEAR	TM/L	W	L	PCT	G	GS	CG	SH	SV	IP	H	HR	BB	SO	RAT	ERA	ERA+	OAV	OOB	BH	AVG	PB	PR	/A	PD	TPI
1910	NY-A	2	2	.500	10	5	3	1	1	48¹	55	1	5	27	11.4	4.47	59	.289	.311	2	.111	-1	-10	-10	0	-0.9
1912	StL-A	0	1	.000	3	3	0	0	0	4¹	16	1	1	2	37.4	20.77	16	.571	.600	1	.500	0	-8	-8	0	-1.3
	Cin-N	1	0	1.000	3	2	0	0	0	15	19	0	1	4	13.2	6.00	58	.345	.379	1	.250	0	-4	-4	0	-0.2
Total	2	3	3	.500	16	10	3	1	1	67²	90	2	7	33	13.4	5.85	49	.330	.356	4	.167	-1	-23	-22	0	-2.4

YEAR	TM/L	W	L	PCT	G	GS	CG	SH	SV	IP	H	HR	BB	SO	RAT	ERA	ERA+	OAV	OOB	BH	AVG	PB	PR	/A	PD	TPI
● **DANNY FRISELLA**				Frisella, Daniel Vincent "Bear"				b: 3/4/46, San Francisco, Cal.			d: 1/1/77, Phoenix, Ariz.			BL/TR, 6', 195 lbs.			Deb: 7/27/67								
1967	NY-N	1	6	.143	14	11	0	0	0	74	68	6	33	51	12.3	3.41	100	.249	.330	2	.087	-1	-0	-0	-0	-0.1
1968	NY-N	2	4	.333	19	4	0	0	2	50²	53	5	17	47	12.4	3.91	77	.270	.329	1	.083	-1	-5	-5	-0	-0.7
1969	NY-N	0	0	—	3	0	0	0	0	4²	8	1	3	5	21.2	7.71	47	.381	.458	0	.000	-0	-2	-2	-0	-0.0
1970	NY-N	8	3	.727	30	1	0	0	1	65²	49	4	34	54	11.4	3.02	133	.204	.303	4	.308	1	8	7	0	1.3
1971	NY-N	8	5	.615	53	0	0	0	12	90²	76	6	30	93	10.8	1.99	172	.227	.296	3	.231	1	15	14	1	2.6
1972	NY-N	5	8	.385	39	0	0	0	9	67¹	63	8	20	46	11.1	3.34	101	.243	.297	2	.286	0	1	0	1	0.2
1973	Atl-N	1	2	.333	42	0	0	0	8	45	40	5	23	27	12.8	4.20	94	.241	.337	1	.500	0	-3	-1	-0	-0.1
1974	Atl-N	3	4	.429	36	1	0	0	6	41²	37	4	28	27	14.0	5.18	73	.240	.357	0	.000	0	-7	-7	-0	-1.2
1975	SD-N	1	6	.143	65	0	0	0	9	97²	86	7	51	67	12.8	3.13	111	.242	.340	1	.200	0	5	4	-0	0.3
1976	StL-N	0	0	—	18	0	0	0	1	22²	19	3	13	11	12.7	3.97	89	.232	.337	0	.000	-0	-1	-1	-0	0.0
	Mil-A	5	2	.714	32	0	0	0	9	49¹	30	4	34	43	11.9	2.74	128	.175	.316	0	—	0	4	4	0	0.8
Total	10	34	40	.459	351	17	0	0	57	609²	529	53	286	471	12.1	3.32	106	.235	.323	14	.179	1	14	13	0	3.1
● **EMIL FRISK**				Frisk, John Emil		b: 10/15/1874, Kalkaska, Mich.			d: 1/27/22, Seattle, Wash.			BL/TR, 6'1", 190 lbs.			Deb: 9/2/1899 ♦										
1899	Cin-N	3	6	.333	9	9	9	0	0	68¹	81	1	17	17	13.7	3.95	99	.294	.349	7	.280	1	-1	-0	-0	0.1
1901	Det-A	5	4	.556	11	7	6	0	0	74²	94	1	26	22	14.7	4.34	89	.304	.361	15	.313	2	-6	-4	3	0.1
Total	2	8	10	.444	20	16	15	0	0	143	175	2	43	39	14.2	4.15	94	.299	.355	135	.267	3	-6	-4	2	0.2
● **CHARLIE FRITZ**				Fritz, Charles Cornelius		b: 6/18/1882, Mobile, Ala.			d: 7/30/43, Mobile, Ala.		TL,		Deb: 10/5/07											
1907	Phi-A	0	0	—	1	1	0	0	0	3	0	0	3	1	12.0	3.00	87	.000	.321	0	.000	-0	-0	-0	-0	0.0
● **BILL FROATS**				Froats, William John		b: 10/20/30, New York, N.Y.			BL/TL, 6', 180 lbs.		Deb: 4/22/55													
1955	Det-A	0	0	—	1	0	0	0	0	2	0	0	2	0	9.0	0.00	—	.000	.333	0	—	0	1	1	0	0.0
● **SAM FROCK**				Frock, Samuel William		b: 12/23/1882, Baltimore, Md.			d: 11/3/25, Baltimore, Md.			BR/TR, 6', 168 lbs.			Deb: 9/21/07									
1907	Bos-N	1	2	.333	5	3	3	1	0	33¹	28	1	12	11	11.1	2.97	86	.243	.320	1	.071	-1	-2	-2	-2	-0.4
1909	Pit-N	2	1	.667	8	4	3	0	1	36¹	44	0	4	11	12.6	2.48	110	.299	.331	2	.143	-1	1	1	0	0.0
1910	Pit-N	0	0	—	1	0	0	0	0	2	2	0	2	1	22.5	4.50	69	.400	.625	0	—	-0	-0	-0	0	0.0
	Bos-N	12	19	.387	45	29	13	2	2	255¹	245	8	91	170	12.0	3.21	104	.262	.330	16	.190	-3	-5	3	1	0.2
	Yr	12	19	.387	46	29	13	2	2	257¹	247	8	93	171	12.0	3.22	103	.263	.332	16	.190	-3	-5	3	2	0.2
1911	Bos-N	0	1	.000	4	1	1	0	0	16	29	0	5	8	19.7	5.63	68	.426	.473	1	.200	-0	-4	-3	0	-0.2
Total	4	15	23	.395	63	37	20	3	3	343	348	9	113	202	12.4	3.23	99	.274	.339	20	.171	-5	-11	-1	0	-0.4
● **TODD FROHWIRTH**				Frohwirth, Todd Gerard		b: 9/28/62, Milwaukee, Wis.			BR/TR, 6'4", 190 lbs.		Deb: 8/10/87													
1987	Phi-N	1	0	1.000	10	0	0	0	0	11	12	0	3	9	11.5	0.00	—	.293	.326	0	.000	-0	5	5	0	0.4
1988	Phi-N	1	2	.333	12	0	0	0	0	12	16	2	11	11	20.3	8.25	43	.327	.450	0	—	-0	-6	-6	1	-1.4
1989	Phi-N	1	0	1.000	45	0	0	0	0	62²	56	4	18	39	11.1	3.59	99	.240	.303	0	.000	-0	-1	-0	-0	0.0
1990	Phi-N	0	1	.000	5	0	0	0	0	1	3	0	6	1	81.0	18.00	21	.500	.750	0	—	-0	-2	-2	-0	-1.3
1991	Bal-A	7	3	.700	51	0	0	0	3	96¹	64	2	29	77	8.8	1.87	211	.190	.256	0	—	0	**24**	**22**	3	3.0
1992	Bal-A	4	3	.571	65	0	0	0	4	106	97	4	41	58	12.0	2.46	163	.247	.323	0	—	0	17	18	3	1.5
1993	Bal-A	6	7	.462	70	0	0	0	3	96¹	91	7	44	50	12.9	3.83	117	.256	.343	0	—	0	5	7	2	0.8
1994	Bos-A	0	3	.000	22	0	0	0	1	26²	40	3	17	13	19.9	10.80	48	.339	.431	0	—	0	-18	-17	-0	-2.0
Total	8	20	19	.513	280	0	0	0	11	412	379	22	168	258	12.2	3.50	117	.248	.327	0	.000	-0	25	28	8	1.0
● **ART FROMME**				Fromme, Arthur Henry		b: 9/3/1883, Quincy, Ill.			d: 8/24/56, Los Angeles, Cal.			BR/TR, 6', 178 lbs.			Deb: 9/14/06									
1906	StL-N	1	2	.333	3	3	3	1	0	25	19	0	10	11	10.8	1.44	183	.221	.309	2	.222	0	3	3	1	0.5
1907	StL-N	5	13	.278	23	16	13	2	0	145²	138	3	67	67	12.9	2.90	86	.256	.343	10	.182	1	-7	-6	0	-0.7
1908	StL-N	5	13	.278	20	14	9	2	0	116	102	1	50	62	11.9	2.72	87	.218	.296	5	.139	-1	-5	-5	-0	-0.9
1909	Cin-N	19	13	.594	37	34	22	4	2	279²	195	2	101	126	9.6	1.90	137	.201	.278	18	.191	2	22	22	2	3.1
1910	Cin-N	3	4	.429	11	5	1	0	0	49¹	44	2	39	10	15.3	2.92	100	.260	.402	2	.133	-1	1	-0	0	-0.1
1911	Cin-N	10	11	.476	38	26	11	1	0	208	190	8	79	107	12.3	3.46	96	.253	.331	14	.189	-1	-3	-1	0	-0.1
1912	Cin-N	16	18	.471	43	37	23	3	0	296	285	7	88	120	11.7	2.74	123	.260	.321	9	.087	-9	22	21	-0	1.2
1913	Cin-N	1	4	.200	9	7	2	0	0	56	55	1	21	24	12.7	4.18	78	.274	.351	3	.143	-0	-6	-6	-1	-0.6
	NY-N	11	6	.647	26	12	3	0	0	112¹	112	5	29	50	11.5	4.01	78	.260	.310	6	.171	-0	-10	-11	1	-1.4
	Yr	12	10	.545	35	19	5	0	0	168¹	167	6	50	74	11.7	4.06	78	.263	.329	9	.161	-1	-16	-17	1	-2.0
1914	NY-N	9	5	.643	38	12	3	1	2	138	142	7	44	57	12.6	3.20	83	.283	.349	7	.226	1	-6	-8	3	-0.4
1915	NY-N	0	1	.000	4	1	0	0	0	12¹	15	1	2	4	12.4	5.84	44	.306	.333	1	.333	1	-4	-4	0	-0.3
Total	10	80	90	.471	252	167	90	14	4	1438	1297	37	530	638	11.7	2.90	100	.246	.320	77	.162	-8	8	2	7	-0.0
● **DAVE FROST**				Frost, Carl David		b: 11/17/52, Long Beach, Cal.			BR/TR, 6'6", 235 lbs.		Deb: 9/11/77													
1977	Chi-A	1	1	.500	4	3	0	0	0	23²	30	0	3	15	12.9	3.04	134	.323	.351	0	—	0	3	3	-0	0.2
1978	Cal-A	5	4	.556	11	10	2	1	0	80¹	71	6	24	30	10.9	2.58	140	.240	.301	0	—	0	11	9	1	1.5
1979	*Cal-A	16	10	.615	36	33	12	2	1	239¹	226	17	77	107	11.6	3.57	114	.251	.314	0	—	0	17	13	-1	1.2
1980	Cal-A	4	8	.333	15	15	2	0	0	78¹	97	8	21	28	13.8	5.29	74	.308	.355	0	—	0	-11	-12	-1	-1.6
1981	Cal-A	1	8	.111	12	9	0	0	0	47¹	44	3	19	16	12.2	5.51	66	.250	.327	0	—	0	-10	-10	-1	-1.6
1982	KC-A	6	6	.500	21	14	0	0	0	81²	103	7	30	26	15.0	5.51	74	.313	.376	0	—	0	-13	-13	-1	-1.8
Total	6	33	37	.471	99	84	16	3	1	550²	571	41	174	222	12.4	4.10	96	.271	.330	0	—	0	-3	-9	-3	-2.1
● **JOHNSON FRY**				Fry, Johnson "Jay"		b: 11/21/01, Huntington, W.Va.			d: 4/7/59, Carmi, Ill.		BR/TR, 6'1", 150 lbs.		Deb: 8/24/23												
1923	Cle-A	0	0	—	1	0	0	0	0	3²	6	0	4	0	24.5	12.27	32	.353	.476	1	1.000	1	-3	-3	-0	0.1
● **CHARLIE FRYE**				Frye, Charles Andrew		b: 7/17/14, Hickory, N.C.			d: 5/25/45, Hickory, N.C.		BR/TR, 6'1", 175 lbs.		Deb: 7/28/40												
1940	Phi-N	0	6	.000	15	5	1	0	0	50¹	58	3	26	18	15.0	4.65	84	.291	.373	5	.263	1	-4	-4	-1	-0.4
● **WOODIE FRYMAN**				Fryman, Woodrow Thompson		b: 4/15/40, Ewing, Ky.			BR/TL, 6'2", 205 lbs.		Deb: 4/15/66													
1966	Pit-N	12	9	.571	36	28	9	3	1	181²	182	13	47	105	11.4	3.81	94	.261	.309	10	.159	-1	-4	-5	-2	-0.8
1967	Pit-N	3	8	.273	28	18	3	1	1	113¹	121	12	44	74	13.4	4.05	83	.276	.348	4	.118	-1	-9	-9	2	-0.7
1968	Phi-N☆	12	14	.462	34	32	10	5	0	213²	198	12	64	151	11.3	2.78	108	.246	.306	6	.085	-2	5	5	-1	0.2
1969	Phi-N	12	15	.444	36	35	10	1	0	228¹	243	15	89	150	13.5	4.41	80	.270	.343	9	.118	-2	-21	-22	-1	-2.6
1970	Phi-N	8	6	.571	27	20	4	3	0	127²	122	11	43	97	11.7	4.09	98	.254	.315	5	.128	-2	-1	-1	-0	-0.3
1971	Phi-N	10	7	.588	37	17	3	2	2	149¹	133	7	46	104	11.1	3.38	104	.242	.304	7	.189	0	1	2	2	0.6
1972	Phi-N	4	10	.286	23	17	3	2	1	119²	131	15	39	69	12.9	4.36	82	.279	.337	5	.152	1	-12	-10	1	-1.0
	*Det-A	10	3	.769	16	14	6	2	0	113²	93	6	31	72	10.4	2.06	153	.220	.285	5	.125	-2	13	14	-1	1.4
1973	Det-A	6	13	.316	34	29	1	0	0	169²	200	23	64	119	14.2	5.36	76	.294	.357	-0	—	0	-29	-24	-1	-2.2
1974	Det-A	6	9	.400	27	22	4	1	0	141²	120	16	67	92	12.1	4.32	88	.233	.326	0	—	0	-11	-8	-1	-1.0
1975	Mon-N	9	12	.429	38	20	7	3	3	157	141	10	68	118	12.3	3.32	115	.239	.323	10	.204	1	5	9	1	1.4
1976	Mon-N☆	13	13	.500	34	32	4	2	0	216¹	218	14	76	123	12.6	3.37	110	.263	.332	7	.109	-3	3	8	-0	0.6
1977	Cin-N	5	5	.500	17	12	0	0	0	75¹	83	13	45	57	15.5	5.38	73	.292	.393	7	.318	2	-12	-12	-1	-1.2
1978	Chi-N	2	4	.333	13	9	0	0	0	55²	64	6	37	28	16.3	5.17	78	.309	.414	1	.063	-1	-10	-7	-0	-0.7
	Mon-N	5	7	.417	19	17	4	1	0	94²	93	4	37	53	12.6	3.61	98	.260	.334	2	.059	-2	-0	-1	-0	-0.4
	Yr	7	11	.389	32	26	4	1	0	150¹	157	10	74	81	14.0	4.19	89	.276	.362	3	.060	-3	-10	-8	-1	-1.1
1979	Mon-N	3	6	.333	44	0	0	0	10	58	52	4	22	44	11.9	2.79	131	.248	.328	0	.000	-1	6	6	1	1.0
1980	Mon-N	7	4	.636	61	0	0	0	17	80	61	1	30	59	10.5	2.25	158	.209	.287	2	.167	-0	12	12	-1	2.1
1981	*Mon-N	5	3	.625	35	0	0	0	7	43	38	1	14	25	11.1	1.88	185	.247	.314	2	.667	1	8	8	0	1.9

YEAR	TM/L	W	L	PCT	G	GS	CG	SH	SV	IP	H	HR	BB	SO	RAT	ERA	ERA+	OAV	OOB	BH	AVG	PB	PR	/A	PD	TPI
1982	Mon-N	9	4	.692	60	0	0	0	12	69²	66	3	26	46	12.0	3.75	97	.259	.330	2	.222	0	-1	-1	1	0.0
1983	Mon-N	0	3	.000	6	0	0	0	1	3	8	1	1	1	27.0	21.00	17	.571	.600	0	—	0	-6	-6	0	-3.8
Total	18	141	155	.476	625	322	68	27	58	2411¹	2367	187	890	1587	12.4	3.77	96	.259	.329	84	.138	-12	-63	-43	4	-5.7

● **CHARLIE FUCHS**   Fuchs, Charles Thomas   b: 11/18/13, Union City, N.J.   d: 6/10/69, Weehawken, N.J.   BB/TR, 5'8", 168 lbs.   Deb: 4/17/42

YEAR	TM/L	W	L	PCT	G	GS	CG	SH	SV	IP	H	HR	BB	SO	RAT	ERA	ERA+	OAV	OOB	BH	AVG	PB	PR	/A	PD	TPI
1942	Det-A	3	3	.500	9	4	1	1	0	36²	43	5	19	15	15.5	6.63	60	.285	.368	1	.077	-1	-12	-11	1	-1.5
1943	Phi-N	2	7	.222	17	9	4	1	0	77²	76	4	34	12	13.1	4.29	79	.266	.350	2	.091	-2	-8	-8	-1	-1.1
	StL-A	0	0	—	13	0	0	0	0	35²	42	4	11	9	13.6	4.04	82	.294	.348	0	.000	-1	-3	-3	-0	-0.1
1944	Bro-N	1	0	1.000	8	0	0	0	0	15²	25	2	9	5	20.1	5.74	62	.347	.427	0	.000	0	-4	-4	1	-0.2
Total	3	6	10	.375	47	13	5	2	1	165²	186	15	73	41	14.4	4.89	72	.285	.363	3	.070	-4	-27	-25	-2	-2.9

● **MIGUEL FUENTES**   Fuentes, Miguel (Pinet)   b: 5/10/46, Loiza Aldea, P.R.   d: 1/29/70, Loiza Aldea, P.R.   BR/TR, 6', 160 lbs.   Deb: 9/1/69

YEAR	TM/L	W	L	PCT	G	GS	CG	SH	SV	IP	H	HR	BB	SO	RAT	ERA	ERA+	OAV	OOB	BH	AVG	PB	PR	/A	PD	TPI
1969	Sea-A	1	3	.250	8	4	1	0	0	26	29	1	16	14	15.6	5.19	70	.284	.381	2	.333	-1	-5	-5	-1	-0.6

● **OSCAR FUHR**   Fuhr, Oscar Lawrence   b: 8/22/1893, Defiance, Mo.   d: 3/27/75, Dallas, Tex.   BL/TL, 6'0.5", 176 lbs.   Deb: 4/19/21

YEAR	TM/L	W	L	PCT	G	GS	CG	SH	SV	IP	H	HR	BB	SO	RAT	ERA	ERA+	OAV	OOB	BH	AVG	PB	PR	/A	PD	TPI
1921	Chi-N	0	0	—	1	0	0	0	0	4	11	1	2	0	24.8	9.00	42	.500	.500	1	.000	-0	-2	-2	0	0.0
1924	Bos-A	3	6	.333	23	10	4	1	0	80¹	100	1	39	30	16.1	5.94	74	.310	.392	4	.182	-1	-15	-14	1	-1.3
1925	Bos-A	0	6	.000	39	6	0	0	0	91¹	138	7	30	27	16.9	6.60	69	.364	.415	5	.250	-1	-22	-21	1	-1.0
Total	3	3	12	.200	63	16	4	1	0	175²	249	9	69	59	16.7	6.35	70	.344	.407	9	.209	-1	-40	-37	2	-2.3

● **JOHN FULGHAM**   Fulgham, John Thomas   b: 6/9/56, St.Louis, Mo.   BR/TR, 6'2", 205 lbs.   Deb: 6/19/79

YEAR	TM/L	W	L	PCT	G	GS	CG	SH	SV	IP	H	HR	BB	SO	RAT	ERA	ERA+	OAV	OOB	BH	AVG	PB	PR	/A	PD	TPI
1979	StL-N	10	6	.625	20	19	10	2	0	146	123	10	26	75	9.4	2.53	149	.227	.267	6	.143	1	20	20	-2	2.0
1980	StL-N	4	6	.400	15	14	4	1	0	85¹	66	7	32	48	10.4	3.38	109	.219	.296	0	.000	-3	2	3	-0	0.0
Total	2	14	12	.538	35	33	14	3	0	231¹	189	17	58	123	9.8	2.84	132	.224	.277	6	.087	-2	22	23	-2	2.0

● **ED FULLER**   Fuller, Edward Ashton   b: 3/22/1868, Washington, D.C.   d: 3/16/35, Hyattsville, Md.   BR/TR, 6', 158 lbs.   Deb: 7/17/1886

YEAR	TM/L	W	L	PCT	G	GS	CG	SH	SV	IP	H	HR	BB	SO	RAT	ERA	ERA+	OAV	OOB	BH	AVG	PB	PR	/A	PD	TPI
1886	Was-N	0	1	.000	2	1	1	0	0	13	15	0	5	3	13.8	6.92	47	.375	.444	1	.143	-0	-5	-5	-0	-0.3

● **CURT FULLERTON**   Fullerton, Curtis Hooper   b: 9/13/1898, Ellsworth, Me.   d: 1/2/75, Winthrop, Mass.   BL/TR, 6', 162 lbs.   Deb: 4/14/21

YEAR	TM/L	W	L	PCT	G	GS	CG	SH	SV	IP	H	HR	BB	SO	RAT	ERA	ERA+	OAV	OOB	BH	AVG	PB	PR	/A	PD	TPI
1921	Bos-A	0	1	.000	4	1	1	0	0	15¹	22	3	10	4	19.4	8.80	48	.355	.452	0	.000	-0	-8	-8	-1	-0.5
1922	Bos-A	1	4	.200	31	3	0	0	0	64¹	70	4	35	17	15.4	5.46	75	.290	.391	2	.250	-1	-10	-10	1	-0.5
1923	Bos-A	2	15	.118	37	15	6	0	1	143¹	167	4	91	37	15.3	5.09	81	.300	.385	11	.297	2	-18	-16	-2	-1.6
1924	Bos-A	7	12	.368	33	20	9	0	2	152	166	1	73	33	14.5	4.32	101	.283	.368	3	.071	-3	-2	1	-0	-0.3
1925	Bos-A	0	3	.000	4	2	0	0	0	22²	22	1	9	3	13.1	3.18	143	.259	.344	2	.200	-0	3	3	1	0.4
1933	Bos-A	0	2	.000	6	2	0	0	0	25¹	36	6	13	10	17.8	8.53	51	.364	.442	2	.222	-0	-12	-12	-0	-0.7
Total	6	10	37	.213	115	43	18	0	3	423	483	19	211	104	15.2	5.11	83	.296	.384	20	.182	-1	-46	-40	-1	-3.1

● **CHICK FULMER**   Fulmer, Charles John   b: 2/12/1851, Philadelphia, Pa.   d: 2/15/40, Philadelphia, Pa.   BR/TR, 6', 158 lbs.   Deb: 8/23/1871   FU♦

YEAR	TM/L	W	L	PCT	G	GS	CG	SH	SV	IP	H	HR	BB	SO	RAT	ERA	ERA+	OAV	OOB	BH	AVG	PB	PR	/A	PD	TPI
1873	Phi-n	0	0	—	2	0	0	0	0	5	7	0	1	0	14.4	3.60	92	.304	.333	66	.280	-0	-0			0.0

● **CHRIS FULMER**   Fulmer, Christopher   b: 7/4/1858, Tamaqua, Pa.   d: 11/9/31, Tamaqua, Pa.   BR/TR, 5'8", 165 lbs.   Deb: 8/4/1884   ♦

YEAR	TM/L	W	L	PCT	G	GS	CG	SH	SV	IP	H	HR	BB	SO	RAT	ERA	ERA+	OAV	OOB	BH	AVG	PB	PR	/A	PD	TPI
1886	Bal-a	0	0	—	1	0	0	0	0	2	2	0	1	0	13.5	4.50	76	.250	.333	66	.244	0	-0	-0	-0	0.0

● **BILL FULTON**   Fulton, William David   b: 10/22/63, Pittsburgh, Pa.   BR/TR, 6'3", 195 lbs.   Deb: 9/12/87

YEAR	TM/L	W	L	PCT	G	GS	CG	SH	SV	IP	H	HR	BB	SO	RAT	ERA	ERA+	OAV	OOB	BH	AVG	PB	PR	/A	PD	TPI
1987	NY-A	1	0	1.000	3	0	0	0	0	4²	9	4	1	2	21.2	11.57	38	.409	.458	0	—	0	-4	-4	0	-0.6

● **FRANK FUNK**   Funk, Franklin Ray   b: 8/30/35, Washington, D.C.   BR/TR, 6', 175 lbs.   Deb: 9/3/60   C

YEAR	TM/L	W	L	PCT	G	GS	CG	SH	SV	IP	H	HR	BB	SO	RAT	ERA	ERA+	OAV	OOB	BH	AVG	PB	PR	/A	PD	TPI
1960	Cle-A	4	2	.667	9	0	0	0	1	31²	27	3	9	18	10.2	1.99	188	.248	.305	1	.111	-0	7	6	0	1.2
1961	Cle-A	11	11	.500	56	0	0	0	11	92¹	79	9	31	64	11.1	3.31	119	.234	.306	1	.059	-1	7	6	0	1.4
1962	Cle-A	2	1	.667	47	0	0	0	6	80²	62	11	32	49	10.9	3.24	120	.212	.298	1	.067	-1	6	6	0	0.1
1963	Mil-N	3	3	.500	25	0	0	0	0	43²	42	3	13	19	11.5	2.68	130	.258	.316	0	.000	-1	3	3	-1	0.2
Total	4	20	17	.541	137	0	0	0	18	248¹	210	26	85	150	11.0	3.01	125	.233	.305	3	.067	-3	23	21	-1	2.9

● **TOM FUNK**   Funk, Thomas James   b: 3/13/62, Kansas City, Mo.   BL/TL, 6'2", 210 lbs.   Deb: 7/24/86

YEAR	TM/L	W	L	PCT	G	GS	CG	SH	SV	IP	H	HR	BB	SO	RAT	ERA	ERA+	OAV	OOB	BH	AVG	PB	PR	/A	PD	TPI
1986	Hou-N	0	0	—	8	0	0	0	0	8¹	10	1	6	2	17.3	6.48	56	.286	.390	0	.000	-0	-3	-3	0	0.0

● **EDDIE FUSSELBACK**   Fusselback, Edward L.   b: 7/17/1856, Philadelphia, Pa.   d: 4/14/26, Philadelphia, Pa.   5'6", 156 lbs.   Deb: 5/3/1882   ♦

YEAR	TM/L	W	L	PCT	G	GS	CG	SH	SV	IP	H	HR	BB	SO	RAT	ERA	ERA+	OAV	OOB	BH	AVG	PB	PR	/A	PD	TPI
1882	StL-a	1	2	.333	4	2	2	0	1	23	34	2	3	3	14.1	4.70	60	.322	.335	31	.228	0	-5	-5	-1	-0.6

● **FRED FUSSELL**   Fussell, Frederick Morris "Moonlight Ace"   b: 10/7/1895, Sheridan, Mo.   d: 10/23/66, Syracuse, N.Y.   BL/TL, 5'10", 155 lbs.   Deb: 9/23/22

YEAR	TM/L	W	L	PCT	G	GS	CG	SH	SV	IP	H	HR	BB	SO	RAT	ERA	ERA+	OAV	OOB	BH	AVG	PB	PR	/A	PD	TPI
1922	Chi-N	1	1	.500	3	2	1	0	0	19	24	0	8	4	15.2	4.74	89	.333	.400	0	.000	-1	-1	-1	-0	-0.1
1923	Chi-N	3	5	.375	28	2	1	0	0	76¹	90	2	31	38	14.6	5.54	72	.298	.369	4	.200	-3	-13	-13	0	-1.2
1928	Pit-N	8	9	.471	28	20	9	2	1	159²	183	6	41	43	12.7	3.61	112	.295	.340	7	.121	-3	7	8	-3	0.2
1929	Pit-N	2	2	.500	21	3	0	0	1	39²	68	8	8	18	17.5	8.62	55	.389	.418	4	.250	2	-17	-17	-0	-1.3
Total	4	14	17	.452	80	27	11	2	5	294²	365	16	88	103	14.0	4.86	85	.312	.363	15	.150	-2	-25	-23	-2	-2.4

● **FRANK GABLER**   Gabler, Frank Harold "The Great Gabbo"   b: 11/6/11, E.Highlands, Cal.   d: 11/1/67, Long Beach, Cal.   BR/TR, 6'1", 175 lbs.   Deb: 4/19/35

YEAR	TM/L	W	L	PCT	G	GS	CG	SH	SV	IP	H	HR	BB	SO	RAT	ERA	ERA+	OAV	OOB	BH	AVG	PB	PR	/A	PD	TPI
1935	NY-N	2	1	.667	26	1	0	0	0	60	79	6	20	24	14.9	5.70	68	.315	.365	2	.125	-1	-12	-12	-0	-0.6
1936	*NY-N	9	8	.529	43	14	5	0	6	161²	170	11	34	46	11.5	3.12	125	.274	.315	10	.208	2	16	14	-1	1.5
1937	NY-N	0	0	—	6	0	0	0	0	9	20	1	2	3	22.0	10.00	39	.455	.478	0	—	0	-6	-6	0	0.0
	Bos-N	4	7	.364	19	9	2	1	2	76	84	7	16	19	11.8	5.09	70	.283	.319	4	.182	-0	-13	-13	-1	-1.6
	Yr	4	7	.364	25	9	2	1	2	85	104	8	18	22	12.9	5.61	64	.305	.340	4	.182	-0	-16	-19	-2	-1.6
1938	Bos-N	0	0	—	1	0	0	0	0	0¹	3	0	1	0	108.0	81.00	4	1.000	1.000	0	—	0	-3	-3	0	0.0
	Chi-A	1	7	.125	18	7	3	0	0	69¹	101	12	34	17	17.7	9.09	54	.348	.418	5	.238	0	-33	-32	-1	-2.9
Total	4	16	23	.410	113	31	10	1	8	376¹	457	37	107	109	13.6	5.26	76	.303	.351	21	.196	-2	-47	-53	-2	-3.6

● **GABE GABLER**   Gabler, John Richard   b: 10/2/30, Kansas City, Mo.   BB/TR, 6'2", 165 lbs.   Deb: 9/18/59

YEAR	TM/L	W	L	PCT	G	GS	CG	SH	SV	IP	H	HR	BB	SO	RAT	ERA	ERA+	OAV	OOB	BH	AVG	PB	PR	/A	PD	TPI
1959	NY-A	1	1	.500	3	1	0	0	0	19¹	21	1	10	11	14.9	2.79	130	.284	.376	0	.000	-1	2	2	0	0.1
1960	NY-A	3	3	.500	21	4	0	0	0	52	46	2	32	19	13.5	4.15	86	.242	.351	1	.091	-2	-3	-3	-0	-0.4
1961	Was-A	3	8	.273	29	9	0	0	4	92²	104	5	37	33	13.8	4.86	83	.283	.351	5	.200	1	-9	-9	1	-0.8
Total	3	7	12	.368	53	14	0	0	4	164	171	8	79	63	13.8	4.39	85	.271	.354	6	.143	-0	-8	-10	1	-1.1

● **KEN GABLES**   Gables, Kenneth Harlin "Coral"   b: 1/31/19, Walnut Grove, Mo.   d: 1/2/60, Walnut Grove, Mo.   BR/TR, 5'11", 210 lbs.   Deb: 4/18/45

YEAR	TM/L	W	L	PCT	G	GS	CG	SH	SV	IP	H	HR	BB	SO	RAT	ERA	ERA+	OAV	OOB	BH	AVG	PB	PR	/A	PD	TPI
1945	Pit-N	11	7	.611	29	16	6	0	1	138²	139	5	46	49	12.3	4.15	95	.256	.319	4	.103	-3	-5	-3	-2	-0.9
1946	Pit-N	2	4	.333	32	6	0	0	3	100²	113	4	52	39	14.8	5.27	67	.281	.365	6	.250	1	-21	-20	-2	-1.2
1947	Pit-N	0	0	—	1	0	0	0	0	0¹	3	0	0	0	81.0	54.00	8	.750	.750	0	—	0	-2	-2	0	0.0
Total	3	13	11	.542	62	23	6	0	4	239²	255	9	98	88	13.4	4.69	80	.269	.340	10	.159	-1	-28	-25	-4	-2.1

● **JOHN GADDY**   Gaddy, John Wilson "Sheriff"   b: 2/5/14, Wadesboro, N.C.   d: 5/3/66, Albemarle, N.C.   BR/TR, 6'0.5", 182 lbs.   Deb: 9/27/38

YEAR	TM/L	W	L	PCT	G	GS	CG	SH	SV	IP	H	HR	BB	SO	RAT	ERA	ERA+	OAV	OOB	BH	AVG	PB	PR	/A	PD	TPI
1938	Bro-N	2	0	1.000	2	2	1	0	0	13	13	0	4	3	12.5	0.69	564	.255	.321	0	.000	-1	4	5	-0	0.7

● **BRENT GAFF**   Gaff, Brent Allen   b: 10/5/58, Fort Wayne, Ind.   BR/TR, 6'2", 200 lbs.   Deb: 7/7/82

YEAR	TM/L	W	L	PCT	G	GS	CG	SH	SV	IP	H	HR	BB	SO	RAT	ERA	ERA+	OAV	OOB	BH	AVG	PB	PR	/A	PD	TPI
1982	NY-N	0	3	.000	7	5	0	0	0	31²	41	3	10	14	14.8	4.55	80	.323	.377	0	—	-3	-3	-3	-0	-0.3
1983	NY-N	1	0	1.000	4	0	0	0	0	10¹	18	0	1	4	16.5	6.10	59	.360	.373	0	—	-0	-3	-3	-0	-0.1
1984	NY-N	3	2	.600	47	0	0	0	1	84¹	77	4	36	42	12.2	3.63	97	.247	.327	0	—	-0	-1	-1	-0	-0.1
Total	3	4	5	.444	58	5	0	0	1	126¹	136	7	47	60	13.2	4.06	88	.278	.344	0	.000	-1	-7	-7	0	-0.7

YEAR	TM/L	W	L	PCT	G	GS	CG	SH	SV	IP	H	HR	BB	SO	RAT	ERA	ERA+	OAV	OOB	BH	AVG	PB	PR	/A	PD	TPI

● CHARLIE GAGUS Gagus, Charles Frederick (b: Charles Frederick Geggus) b: 3/25/1862, San Francisco, Cal d: 1/16/17, San Francisco, Cal Deb: 8/7/1884

| 1884 | Was-U | 10 | 9 | .526 | 23 | 21 | 19 | 0 | 0 | 177¹ | 143 | 2 | 38 | 156 | 9.2 | 2.54 | 95 | .206 | .247 | 38 | .247 | -3 | -2 | -3 | 1 | -0.4 |

● NEMO GAINES Gaines, Willard Roland b: 12/23/1897, Alexandria, Va. d: 1/26/79, Warrenton, Va. BL/TL, 6', 180 lbs. Deb: 6/26/21

| 1921 | Was-A | 0 | 0 | — | 4 | 0 | 0 | 0 | 0 | 4² | 5 | 0 | 2 | 1 | 13.5 | 0.00 | — | .294 | .368 | 0 | .000 | -0 | 2 | 2 | -0 | 0.0 |

● FRED GAISER Gaiser, Frederick Jacob b: 8/31/1885, Stuttgart, Germany d: 10/9/18, Trenton, N.J. Deb: 9/3/08

| 1908 | StL-N | 0 | 0 | — | 1 | 0 | 0 | 0 | 0 | 2¹ | 4 | 0 | 3 | 2 | 27.0 | 7.71 | 31 | .444 | .583 | 0 | .000 | -0 | -1 | -1 | 0 | 0.0 |

● DAN GAKELER Gakeler, Daniel Michael b: 5/1/64, Mt.Holly, N.J. BR/TR, 6'6", 215 lbs. Deb: 6/9/91

| 1991 | Det-A | 1 | 4 | .200 | 31 | 7 | 0 | 0 | 2 | 73² | 73 | 5 | 39 | 43 | 13.8 | 5.74 | 72 | .256 | .348 | 0 | — | 0 | -13 | -13 | 0 | -0.9 |

● BOB GALASSO Galasso, Robert Joseph b: 1/13/52, Connellsville, Pa. BL/TR, 6'1", 205 lbs. Deb: 7/24/77

1977	Sea-A	0	6	.000	11	7	0	0	0	35	57	8	8	21	17.5	9.00	46	.365	.407	0	—	0	-19	-19	-0	-2.5
1979	Mil-A	3	1	.750	31	0	0	0	3	51¹	64	5	26	28	15.8	4.38	95	.299	.375	0	—	0	-1	-1	-0	-0.1
1981	Sea-A	1	1	.500	13	1	0	0	1	31²	32	2	13	14	12.8	4.83	80	.264	.336	0	—	0	-4	-3	-0	-0.3
Total	3	4	8	.333	55	8	0	0	4	118	153	15	47	63	15.5	5.87	69	.312	.375	0	—	0	-24	-24	-1	-2.9

● MILT GALATZER Galatzer, Milton b: 5/4/07, Chicago, Ill. d: 1/29/76, San Francisco, Cal BL/TL, 5'10", 168 lbs. Deb: 6/25/33 ◆

| 1936 | Cle-A | 0 | 0 | — | 1 | 0 | 0 | 0 | 0 | 6 | 7 | 0 | 5 | 3 | 18.0 | 4.50 | 112 | .292 | .414 | 23 | .237 | 0 | 0 | 0 | 0 | 0.0 |

● RICH GALE Gale, Richard Blackwell b: 1/19/54, Littleton, N.H. BR/TR, 6'7", 225 lbs. Deb: 4/30/78 C

1978	KC-A	14	8	.636	31	30	9	3	0	192¹	171	10	100	88	12.8	3.09	124	.244	.340	0	—	0	14	16	-2	1.5
1979	KC-A	9	10	.474	34	31	2	1	0	181²	197	19	99	103	14.9	5.65	75	.278	.369	0	—	0	-29	-28	-1	-2.5
1980	*KC-A	13	9	.591	32	28	6	1	1	190²	169	16	78	97	11.8	3.92	103	.239	.316	0	—	0	2	3	-1	0.2
1981	KC-A	6	6	.500	19	15	2	0	0	101²	107	14	38	47	13.0	5.40	67	.270	.336	0	—	0	-20	-20	-2	-2.3
1982	SF-N	7	14	.333	33	29	2	0	0	170¹	193	9	81	102	14.7	4.23	85	.294	.376	6	.125	1	-12	-12	1	-1.2
1983	Cin-N	4	6	.400	33	7	0	0	1	89²	103	8	43	53	14.8	5.82	65	.286	.364	3	.150	1	-22	-20	-1	-2.1
1984	Bos-A	2	3	.400	13	4	0	0	0	43²	57	6	18	28	15.7	5.56	75	.315	.380	0	—	0	-8	-7	-0	-0.7
Total	7	55	56	.495	195	144	21	5	2	970	997	82	457	518	13.7	4.54	86	.269	.351	9	.132	2	-73	-69	-5	-7.1

● DENNY GALEHOUSE Galehouse, Dennis Ward b: 12/7/11, Marshallville, Ohio BR/TR, 6'1", 195 lbs. Deb: 4/30/34

1934	Cle-A	0	0	—	1	0	0	0	0	1	2	0	1	0	27.0	18.00	25	.500	.600	0	—	0	-2	-1	-0	0.0
1935	Cle-A	1	0	1.000	5	1	1	0	0	13	16	1	9	8	18.0	9.00	50	.314	.426	1	.250	-0	-7	-6	-0	-0.4
1936	Cle-A	8	7	.533	36	15	5	0	1	148¹	161	6	68	71	14.0	4.85	104	.280	.358	8	.170	-0	3	3	-2	0.0
1937	Cle-A	9	14	.391	36	29	7	0	3	200²	238	11	83	78	14.4	4.57	101	.302	.369	15	.208	-1	1	1	1	0.3
1938	Cle-A	7	8	.467	36	12	5	1	3	114	119	12	65	66	14.6	4.34	107	.275	.371	6	.154	-1	6	4	0	0.3
1939	Bos-A	9	10	.474	30	18	6	1	0	146²	160	6	52	68	13.1	4.54	104	.276	.337	3	.064	-3	1	3	0	0.1
1940	Bos-A	6	6	.500	25	20	5	0	0	120	155	10	41	53	14.7	5.18	87	.313	.366	3	.077	-4	-11	-9	1	-1.0
1941	StL-A	9	10	.474	30	24	11	2	0	190¹	183	10	68	61	12.1	3.64	118	.253	.320	13	.191	-0	11	14	1	1.3
1942	StL-A	12	12	.500	32	28	12	3	1	192¹	193	5	79	75	12.9	3.60	103	.262	.337	14	.194	1	12	13	1	0.4
1943	StL-A	11	11	.500	31	28	14	2	1	224	217	8	74	114	11.7	2.77	120	.255	.315	9	.125	-3	13	14	-3	0.7
1944	*StL-A	9	10	.474	24	19	6	2	0	153	162	6	44	80	12.2	3.12	115	.266	.316	3	.063	-4	5	8	-2	0.3
1946	StL-A	8	12	.400	30	24	11	2	0	180	194	9	52	90	12.3	3.65	102	.273	.322	5	.091	-3	-2	-2	-0	-0.4
1947	StL-A	1	3	.250	9	4	0	0	1	32¹	42	3	16	11	16.1	6.12	63	.311	.384	0	—	-1	-9	-8	-0	-1.0
	Bos-A	11	7	.611	21	21	11	3	0	149	150	7	34	38	11.1	3.32	117	.260	.301	5	.096	-4	6	9	-1	0.6
	Yr	12	10	.545	30	25	11	3	1	181¹	192	10	50	49	12.0	3.82	102	.269	.317	5	.083	-5	-2	1	-1	-0.4
1948	Bos-A	8	8	.500	27	15	6	1	3	137¹	152	10	46	38	13.1	4.00	110	.282	.341	7	.167	-0	4	6	-2	0.5
1949	Bos-A	0	0	—	2	0	0	0	0	2	4	1	3	0	31.5	13.50	32	.400	.538	0	—	0	-2	-2	0	0.0
Total	15	109	118	.480	375	258	100	17	13	2004	2148	104	735	851	13.0	3.97	105	.275	.338	92	.138	-25	20	40	-8	1.4

● DOUG GALLAGHER Gallagher, Douglas Eugene b: 2/21/40, Fremont, Ohio BR/TL, 6'3.5", 195 lbs. Deb: 4/9/62

| 1962 | Det-A | 0 | 4 | .000 | 9 | 2 | 0 | 0 | 1 | 25 | 31 | 2 | 15 | 14 | 16.6 | 4.68 | 87 | .290 | .377 | 2 | .333 | 1 | -2 | -2 | 0 | -0.1 |

● ED GALLAGHER Gallagher, Edward Michael "Lefty" b: 11/28/10, Dorchester, Mass. d: 12/22/81, Hyannis, Mass. BB/TL, 6'2", 197 lbs. Deb: 7/8/32

| 1932 | Bos-A | 0 | 3 | .000 | 9 | 3 | 0 | 0 | 0 | 23² | 30 | 3 | 28 | 6 | 22.1 | 12.55 | 36 | .323 | .479 | 0 | .000 | -1 | -21 | -21 | 0 | -2.1 |

● BILL GALLAGHER Gallagher, William John b: Philadelphia, Pa. TL, Deb: 5/2/1883 ◆

1883	Bal-a	0	5	.000	7	5	4	0	0	51²	79	0	6	19	14.8	5.40	64	.330	.346	10	.164	-1	-12	-11	-1	-0.9
1884	Phi-U	1	2	.333	3	3	3	0	0	25	32	3	4	12	13.0	3.24	66	.291	.316	1	.091	-2	-2	-3	0	-0.4
Total	2	1	7	.125	10	8	7	0	0	76²	111	3	10	31	14.2	4.70	66	.318	.337	11	.138	-3	-14	-14	-1	-1.3

● BERT GALLIA Gallia, Melvin Allys b: 10/14/1891, Beeville, Tex. d: 3/19/76, Devine, Tex. BR/TR, 6', 165 lbs. Deb: 9/4/12

1912	Was-A	0	0	—	2	0	0	0	0	2	0	0	3	0	13.5	—	.000	.333	0	—	0	1	1	-0	0.0
1913	Was-A	1	5	.167	31	4	0	0	3	96	85	2	46	46	12.9	4.13	72	.222	.317	2	.087	-2	-13	-12	2	-0.8
1914	Was-A	0	0	—	2	0	0	0	0	6	3	0	4	4	10.5	4.50	63	.120	.241	0	.000	-0	-1	-1	-0	-0.1
1915	Was-A	17	11	.607	43	29	14	3	1	259²	220	4	64	130	10.0	2.29	130	.234	.286	14	.165	-2	19	20	-2	1.7
1916	Was-A	17	12	.586	49	31	13	1	2	283²	278	3	99	120	12.2	2.76	101	.266	.334	18	.194	1	2	1	-3	-0.2
1917	Was-A	9	13	.409	42	23	9	1	1	207²	191	1	93	84	12.5	2.99	88	.258	.344	14	.209	2	-8	-8	-1	-0.8
1918	StL-A	8	6	.571	19	17	10	1	0	124	126	1	61	48	14.0	3.48	79	.268	.359	4	.130	-3	-10	-10	0	-1.4
1919	StL-A	12	14	.462	34	25	14	1	1	222¹	220	10	92	83	13.0	3.60	92	.264	.343	11	.153	-2	-9	-7	-2	-0.8
1920	StL-A	0	1	.000	2	1	0	0	0	3²	8	0	3	0	27.0	7.36	53	.400	.478	0	.000	-0	-1	-1	-0	-0.3
	Phi-N	2	6	.250	18	5	1	0	2	72	79	2	29	35	13.9	4.50	76	.287	.362	4	.174	-1	-11	-9	-1	-1.1
Total	9	66	68	.493	242	135	61	7	10	1277	1210	21	494	550	12.3	3.14	94	.256	.331	69	.167	-7	-31	-28	-3	-3.8

● PHIL GALLIVAN Gallivan, Philip Joseph b: 5/29/07, Seattle, Wash. d: 11/24/69, St.Paul, Minn. BR/TR, 6', 170 lbs. Deb: 4/21/31

1931	Bro-N	0	1	.000	6	1	0	0	0	15¹	12	3	7	1	17.6	5.28	72	.354	.417	0	.000	-0	-2	-3	1	-0.1
1932	Chi-A	1	3	.250	13	3	1	0	0	33¹	49	3	24	12	20.0	7.56	57	.338	.435	3	.375	1	-11	-12	-0	-1.1
1934	Chi-A	4	7	.364	35	7	3	0	1	126²	155	14	64	55	15.6	5.61	84	.295	.373	9	.225	1	-16	-12	1	-0.9
Total	3	5	11	.313	54	11	4	0	1	175¹	227	20	95	68	16.6	5.95	77	.309	.389	12	.235	2	-30	-27	1	-2.1

● BALVINO GALVEZ Galvez, Balvino (Jerez) b: 3/31/64, San Pedro De Macoris, D.R. BR/TR, 6', 170 lbs. Deb: 5/7/86

| 1986 | LA-N | 0 | 1 | .000 | 10 | 0 | 0 | 0 | 0 | 20² | 19 | 3 | 12 | 11 | 13.5 | 3.92 | 88 | .241 | .341 | 0 | .000 | -0 | -0 | -1 | 0 | -0.1 |

● JIM GALVIN Galvin, James Francis "Pud", "Gentle Jeems" or "The Little Steam Engine" b: 12/25/1856, St.Louis, Mo. d: 3/7/02, Pittsburgh, Pa. BR/TR, 5'8", 190 lbs. Deb: 5/22/1875 MUH

1875	StL-n	4	2	.667	8	7	7	1	1	62	53	0	1	9	7.8	2.18	102	.209	.213	6	.128	-1	2	0		-0.1
1879	Buf-N	37	27	.578	66	66	65	6	0	593	585	3	31	136	9.3	2.28	115	.243	.253	66	.249	5	14	22	3	2.8
1880	Buf-N	20	35	.364	58	54	46	5	0	458²	528	5	32	128	11.0	2.71	91	.273	.284	51	.212	-4	-17	-13	1	-1.5
1881	Buf-N	28	24	.538	56	53	48	5	0	474	546	4	46	136	11.2	2.37	117	.274	.291	50	.212	-1	21	21	7	2.6
1882	Buf-N	28	23	.549	52	51	48	3	0	445¹	476	8	40	162	10.4	3.17	93	.256	.272	44	.214	-5	-13	-12	1	-1.6
1883	Buf-N	46	29	.613	76	75	72	5	0	656¹	676	9	50	279	10.0	2.72	117	.251	.265	71	.220	-4	31	34	0	2.6
1884	Buf-N	46	22	.676	72	72	71	12	0	636¹	566	20	63	369	8.9	1.99	158	.227	.246	49	.179	-14	70	82	7	6.8
1885	Buf-N	13	19	.406	33	32	31	3	1	284	356	10	37	93	12.5	4.09	73	.292	.313	23	.189	-2	-40	-35	4	-3.0
	Pit-a	3	7	.300	11	11	9	0	0	88¹	97	6	7	27	10.6	3.67	88	.266	.280	4	.105	-4	-4	-4	-1	-0.7
1886	Pit-a	29	21	.580	50	49	2	0	0	434²	457	6	75	72	11.2	2.67	127	.263	.296	49	.253	2	38	35	3	3.6

YEAR TM/L	W	L	PCT	G	GS	CG	SH	SV	IP	H	HR	BB	SO	RAT	ERA	ERA+	OAV	OOB	BH	AVG	PB	PR	/A	PD	TPI
1887 Pit-N	28	21	.571	49	48	47	3	0	440²	490	12	67	76	11.6	3.29	118	.269	.299	41	.212	-2	38	29	8	3.0
1888 Pit-N	23	25	.479	50	50	49	6	0	437¹	446	9	53	107	10.4	2.63	101	.255	.280	25	.143	-6	10	2	-4	-0.1
1889 Pit-N	23	16	.590	41	40	38	4	0	341	392	19	78	77	12.7	4.17	90	.280	.322	28	.187	-1	-6	-16	1	-1.3
1890 Pit-P	12	13	.480	26	25	23	1	0	217	255	3	49	35	13.8	4.35	90	.290	.337	20	.206	-1	-3	-11	4	-0.7
1891 Pit-N	14	14	.500	33	31	23	2	0	246²	256	10	62	46	12.1	2.88	114	.258	.310	18	.165	-4	13	11	0	0.6
1892 Pit-N	5	6	.455	12	12	10	0	0	96	104	0	28	29	12.4	2.63	126	.265	.314	5	.122	-3	7	7	-0	0.4
StL-N	5	6	.455	12	12	10	0	0	92	102	4	26	27	12.8	3.23	99	.270	.322	2	.051	-5	1	-0	-2	-0.6
Yr	10	12	.455	24	24	20	0	0	188	206	4	54	56	12.6	2.92	111	.268	.318	7	.087	-7	8	7	-2	-0.2
Total 14	360	308	.539	697	682	639	57	1	5941¹	6352	122	744	1799	10.8	2.87	109	.261	.284	546	.202	-48	160	162	39	12.9

● **LOU GALVIN**　Galvin, Louis J.　b: 4/1862, St.Paul, Minn.　d: 6/17/1895,　Deb: 10/1/1884

YEAR TM/L	W	L	PCT	G	GS	CG	SH	SV	IP	H	HR	BB	SO	RAT	ERA	ERA+	OAV	OOB	BH	AVG	PB	PR	/A	PD	TPI
1884 StP-U	0	2	.000	3	3	3	0	0	25	21	0	10	17	11.2	2.88	46	.213	.285	2	.222	-1	-1	-4	-1	-0.4

● **BOB GAMBLE**　Gamble, Robert J.　b: 2/1867, Hazleton, Pa.　TR, 5'10", 155 lbs.　Deb: 5/2/1888

YEAR TM/L	W	L	PCT	G	GS	CG	SH	SV	IP	H	HR	BB	SO	RAT	ERA	ERA+	OAV	OOB	BH	AVG	PB	PR	/A	PD	TPI
1888 Phi-a	0	1	.000	1	1	1	0	0	9	10	0	3	2	13.0	8.00	37	.271	.326	1	.333	0	-5	-5	-0	-0.4

● **GUSSIE GANNON**　Gannon, James Edward　b: 11/26/1873, Erie, Pa.　d: 4/12/66, Erie, Pa.　BL/TL, 5'11", 154 lbs.　Deb: 6/15/1895

YEAR TM/L	W	L	PCT	G	GS	CG	SH	SV	IP	H	HR	BB	SO	RAT	ERA	ERA+	OAV	OOB	BH	AVG	PB	PR	/A	PD	TPI
1895 Pit-N	0	0	—	1	0	0	0	0	5	7	0	2	0	16.2	1.80	251	.326	.383	0	.000	-0	2	2	-0	-0.1

● **JOE GANNON**　Gannon, Joseph　b: St.Louis, Mo.　Deb: 8/28/1898

YEAR TM/L	W	L	PCT	G	GS	CG	SH	SV	IP	H	HR	BB	SO	RAT	ERA	ERA+	OAV	OOB	BH	AVG	PB	PR	/A	PD	TPI
1898 StL-N	0	1	.000	1	1	0	0	0	9	13	0	5	2	19.0	11.00	34	.335	.424	0	.000	-1	-7	-7	-0	-0.5

● **JIM GANTNER**　Gantner, James Elmer　b: 1/5/53, Fond Du Lac, Wis.　BL/TR, 6', 180 lbs.　Deb: 9/3/76 ♦

YEAR TM/L	W	L	PCT	G	GS	CG	SH	SV	IP	H	HR	BB	SO	RAT	ERA	ERA+	OAV	OOB	BH	AVG	PB	PR	/A	PD	TPI
1979 Mil-A	0	0	—	1	0	0	0	0	1	2	0	0	0	18.0		—	.400	.400	59	.284	1	0	0	0	0.0

● **KEITH GARAGOZZO**　Garagozzo, Keith John　b: 10/25/69, Camden, N.J.　BL/TL, 6', 170 lbs.　Deb: 4/5/94

YEAR TM/L	W	L	PCT	G	GS	CG	SH	SV	IP	H	HR	BB	SO	RAT	ERA	ERA+	OAV	OOB	BH	AVG	PB	PR	/A	PD	TPI
1994 Min-A	0	0	—	7	0	0	0	0	9¹	9	3	13	3	21.2	9.64	50	.273	.478	0	—	0	-5	-5	0	0.0

● **GENE GARBER**　Garber, Henry Eugene　b: 11/13/47, Lancaster, Pa.　BR/TR, 5'10", 175 lbs.　Deb: 6/17/69

YEAR TM/L	W	L	PCT	G	GS	CG	SH	SV	IP	H	HR	BB	SO	RAT	ERA	ERA+	OAV	OOB	BH	AVG	PB	PR	/A	PD	TPI
1969 Pit-N	0	0		2	1	0	0	0	5	6	3	1	3	12.6	5.40	65	.333	.368	0	.000	-0	-1	-1	-0	0.0
1970 Pit-N	0	3	.000	14	0	0	0	0	22¹	22	4	10	7	13.7	5.24	74	.275	.370	2	.667	1	-3	-3	1	-0.2
1972 Pit-N	0	0	—	4	0	0	0	0	6¹	7	3	3	4	14.2	7.11	47	.269	.345	0	.000	-0	-3	-3	0	0.0
1973 KC-A	9	9	.500	48	8	4	0	11	152²	164	14	49	60	12.7	4.24	97	.283	.341	0	—	0	-7	-2	1	-0.2
1974 KC-A	1	2	.333	17	0	0	0	1	28	35	3	13	14	15.8	4.82	79	.313	.389	0	—	0	-4	-3	-0	-0.7
Phi-N	4	0	1.000	34	0	0	0	4	48	39	1	31	27	13.3	2.06	183	.236	.360	0	—	0	8	9	0	0.9
1975 Phi-N	10	12	.455	71	0	0	0	14	110	104	13	27	69	10.9	3.60	104	.254	.304	2	.167	-0	3	3	0	0.3
1976 *Phi-N	9	3	.750	59	0	0	0	11	92²	78	4	30	92	10.9	2.82	126	.228	.298	2	.286	1	7	8	1	1.4
1977 *Phi-N	8	6	.571	64	0	0	0	19	103¹	82	6	23	78	9.3	2.35	170	.220	.270	0	.000	-1	18	19	2	3.3
1978 Phi-N	2	1	.667	22	0	0	0	3	38²	26	1	11	24	9.3	1.40	256	.191	.267	0	.000	-0	9	9	-0	0.8
Atl-N	4	4	.500	43	0	0	0	22	78¹	58	11	13	61	8.4	2.53	160	.204	.244	1	.091	-0	9	13	1	2.3
Yr	6	5	.545	65	0	0	0	25	117	84	12	24	85	8.5	2.15	181	.199	.245	1	.071	-1	18	23	1	3.1
1979 Atl-N	6	16	.273	68	0	0	0	25	106	121	10	24	56	12.7	4.33	94	.283	.328	3	.300	1	-7	-3	-1	-0.6
1980 Atl-N	5	5	.500	68	0	0	0	7	82¹	95	6	24	51	13.0	3.83	98	.288	.336	1	.500	0	-2	-1	2	0.1
1981 Atl-N	4	6	.400	35	0	0	0	2	58²	49	2	20	34	10.6	2.61	137	.214	.277	0	.000	-1	6	6	2	1.3
1982 *Atl-N	8	10	.444	69	0	0	0	30	119¹	100	4	32	68	10.1	2.34	160	.231	.288	2	.133	-0	17	18	2	4.1
1983 Atl-N	4	5	.444	43	0	0	0	9	60²	72	8	23	45	14.4	4.60	84	.300	.366	0	.000	-0	-7	-5	2	-0.6
1984 Atl-N	3	6	.333	62	0	0	0	11	106	103	7	24	55	11.0	3.06	126	.254	.299	2	.143	-0	6	9	1	1.0
1985 Atl-N	6	6	.500	59	0	0	0	1	97¹	98	8	25	68	11.6	3.61	107	.263	.313	1	.200	-0	0	3	1	0.4
1986 Atl-N	5	5	.500	61	0	0	0	24	78	76	3	20	56	11.2	2.54	157	.260	.310	1	.167	-0	10	12	1	2.6
1987 Atl-N	8	10	.444	49	0	0	0	10	69¹	87	7	28	48	15.1	4.41	98	.311	.375	0	.000	-0	-3	-1	-2	0.0
KC-A	0	0	—	13	0	0	0	8	14¹	13	1	1	3	9.4	2.51	181	.245	.273	0	—	0	3	3	0	0.3
1988 KC-A	0	4	.000	26	0	0	0	6	32²	29	4	13	20	12.1	3.58	111	.238	.321	0	—	0	1	1	0	0.2
Total 19	96	113	.459	931	9	4	0	218	1510	1464	123	445	940	11.6	3.34	116	.257	.314	17	.148	-0	59	92	20	16.7

● **BOB GARBER**　Garber, Robert Mitchell　b: 9/10/28, Hunker, Pa.　BR/TR, 6'1", 190 lbs.　Deb: 5/13/56

YEAR TM/L	W	L	PCT	G	GS	CG	SH	SV	IP	H	HR	BB	SO	RAT	ERA	ERA+	OAV	OOB	BH	AVG	PB	PR	/A	PD	TPI
1956 Pit-N	0	0	—	2	0	0	0	0	4	3	3	1	3	13.5	2.25	168	.200	.333	0	—	0	1	1	-0	0.0

● **RICH GARCES**　Garces, Richard Aron (Mendoza)　b: 5/18/71, Maracay, Venez.　BR/TR, 6', 187 lbs.　Deb: 9/18/90

YEAR TM/L	W	L	PCT	G	GS	CG	SH	SV	IP	H	HR	BB	SO	RAT	ERA	ERA+	OAV	OOB	BH	AVG	PB	PR	/A	PD	TPI
1990 Min-A	0	0	—	5	0	0	0	2	5²	4	0	4	1	12.7	1.59	261	.200	.333	0	—	0	1	2	0	-0.1
1993 Min-A	0	0	—	3	0	0	0	0	4	4	0	2	3	13.5	0.00	—	.250	.333	0	—	0	2	2	-0	0.0
Total 2	0	0	—	8	0	0	0	2	9²	8	0	6	4	13.0	0.93	456	.222	.333	0	—	0	3	4	-0	-0.1

● **MIKE GARCIA**　Garcia, Edward Miguel "The Big Bear"　b: 11/17/23, San Gabriel, Cal.　d: 1/13/86, Fairview Park, O.　BR/TR, 6'1", 200 lbs.　Deb: 10/3/48

YEAR TM/L	W	L	PCT	G	GS	CG	SH	SV	IP	H	HR	BB	SO	RAT	ERA	ERA+	OAV	OOB	BH	AVG	PB	PR	/A	PD	TPI
1948 Cle-A	0	0	—	1	0	0	0	0	2	3	0	0	1	13.5	0.00	—	.333	.333	0	—	0	1	1	0	0.0
1949 Cle-A	14	5	.737	41	20	8	5	2	175²	154	6	60	94	11.1	2.36	169	.241	.308	12	.235	3	36	32	1	3.6
1950 Cle-A	11	11	.500	33	29	11	0	0	184	191	15	74	76	13.0	3.86	112	.266	.334	13	.200	-1	15	10	2	1.1
1951 Cle-A	20	13	.606	47	30	15	1	6	254	239	10	82	118	11.5	3.15	120	.246	.307	18	.212	2	27	18	1	2.4
1952 Cle-A☆	22	11	.667	46	36	19	6	4	292¹	284	9	87	143	11.6	2.37	141	.253	.310	13	.137	-2	42	32	2	3.6
1953 Cle-A★	18	9	.667	38	35	21	3	0	271²	260	18	81	134	11.4	3.25	116	.250	.307	24	.250	-4	23	15	-0	1.7
1954 *Cle-A†	19	8	.704	45	34	13	5	5	258²	220	6	71	129	10.2	2.64	139	.229	.284	11	.136	-2	31	30	0	2.9
1955 Cle-A	11	13	.458	38	31	6	2	3	210²	230	17	56	100	12.3	4.02	99	.278	.327	15	.217	2	-1	-1	-1	0.6
1956 Cle-A	11	12	.478	35	30	8	4	0	197²	213	18	74	119	13.3	3.78	111	.272	.339	7	.115	-3	8	9	-0	0.6
1957 Cle-A	12	8	.600	38	27	9	1	0	211¹	221	14	73	110	12.8	3.75	99	.269	.333	12	.160	-1	1	-1	-2	-0.4
1958 Cle-A	1	0	1.000	6	1	0	0	0	8	15	2	7	2	25.9	9.00	41	.395	.500	0	.000	-0	-5	-5	0	-0.5
1959 Cle-A	3	6	.333	29	8	1	0	1	72	72	4	31	49	12.9	4.00	92	.265	.340	1	.071	-1	-1	-3	-0	-0.4
1960 Chi-A	0	0	—	15	0	0	0	2	17²	22	2	10	8	16.8	4.58	82	.338	.423	1	.333	0	-1	-2	0	-0.1
1961 Was-A	0	1	.000	16	0	0	0	0	19	23	1	13	14	17.5	4.74	85	.287	.394	0	—	0	-2	-2	-1	-0.1
Total 14	142	97	.594	428	281	111	27	23	2174²	2148	122	719	1117	12.0	3.27	117	.257	.319	127	.182	1	174	134	2	14.5

● **MIGUEL GARCIA**　Garcia, Miguel Angel (Silfontes)　b: 4/3/67, Caracas, Venez.　BL/TL, 5'11", 173 lbs.　Deb: 4/30/87

YEAR TM/L	W	L	PCT	G	GS	CG	SH	SV	IP	H	HR	BB	SO	RAT	ERA	ERA+	OAV	OOB	BH	AVG	PB	PR	/A	PD	TPI
1987 Cal-A	0	0	—	1	0	0	0	0	1²	3	0	3	0	32.4	16.20	27	.375	.545	0	—	0	-2	-2	0	0.1
Pit-N	0	0	—	1	0	0	0	0	0²	0	0	0	0	0.00	—	.000	.000	0	—	0	-0	-0	-0	0.0
1988 Pit-N	0	0	—	1	0	0	0	0	2	3	1	2	0	27.0	4.50	76	.375	.545	0	—	0	-0	-0	-0	0.0
1989 Pit-N	0	2	.000	11	0	0	0	0	16	25	2	9	11	19.8	8.44	40	.357	.416	1	1.000	0	-9	-9	0	-1.0
Total 3	0	2	.000	14	0	0	0	0	20¹	31	3	12	11	19.5	8.41	41	.352	.436	1	1.000	0	-11	-11	0	-0.9

● **RALPH GARCIA**　Garcia, Ralph　b: 12/14/48, Los Angeles, Cal.　BR/TR, 6', 195 lbs.　Deb: 9/26/72

YEAR TM/L	W	L	PCT	G	GS	CG	SH	SV	IP	H	HR	BB	SO	RAT	ERA	ERA+	OAV	OOB	BH	AVG	PB	PR	/A	PD	TPI
1972 SD-N	0	0	—	3	0	0	0	0	5	4	0	3	3	12.6	1.80	183	.211	.318	0	—	0	1	1	0	0.0
1974 SD-N	0	0	—	8	0	0	0	0	10¹	15	1	7	9	19.2	6.10	58	.357	.449	0	—	0	-3	-3	0	-0.2
Total 2	0	0	—	11	0	0	0	0	15¹	19	1	10	12	17.0	4.70	74	.311	.408	0	—	0	-2	-2	0	-0.2

● **RAMON GARCIA**　Garcia, Ramon (Garcia)　b: 3/5/24, LaEsperanza, Cuba　BR/TR, 5'10", 170 lbs.　Deb: 4/19/48

YEAR TM/L	W	L	PCT	G	GS	CG	SH	SV	IP	H	HR	BB	SO	RAT	ERA	ERA+	OAV	OOB	BH	AVG	PB	PR	/A	PD	TPI
1948 Was-A	0	0	—	4	0	0	0	0	3²	11	0	4	2	39.3	17.18	25	.524	.615	1	1.000	-0	-5	-5	0	0.1

● **RAMON GARCIA**　Garcia, Ramon Antonio (Fortunato)　b: 12/9/69, Guanare, Venez.　BR/TR, 6'2", 200 lbs.　Deb: 5/31/91

YEAR TM/L	W	L	PCT	G	GS	CG	SH	SV	IP	H	HR	BB	SO	RAT	ERA	ERA+	OAV	OOB	BH	AVG	PB	PR	/A	PD	TPI
1991 Chi-A	4	4	.500	16	15	0	0	0	78¹	79	13	31	40	12.9	5.40	74	.269	.343	0	—	0	-11	-12	1	-0.9

YEAR TM/L	W	L	PCT	G	GS	CG	SH	SV	IP	H	HR	BB	SO	RAT	ERA	ERA+	OAV	OOB	BH	AVG	PB	PR	/A	PD	TPI

● ART GARDNER   Gardner, Arthur Cecil   b: 12/26/1899, Brooklyn, N.Y.   d: 10/21/54, Copiague, N.Y.   BR/TR, Deb: 9/25/23

YEAR TM/L	W	L	PCT	G	GS	CG	SH	SV	IP	H	HR	BB	SO	RAT	ERA	ERA+	OAV	OOB	BH	AVG	PB	PR	/A	PD	TPI
1923 Phi-N	0	0	—	1	0	0	0	0	0	1	0	1	0		—	1.000	1.000		0	—	0	0	0	0	0.0

● MIKE GARDNER   Gardner, Michael James   b: 10/19/65, Sarnia, Ont., Can.   BB/TR, 6', 185 lbs.   Deb: 9/8/90

YEAR TM/L	W	L	PCT	G	GS	CG	SH	SV	IP	H	HR	BB	SO	RAT	ERA	ERA+	OAV	OOB	BH	AVG	PB	PR	/A	PD	TPI
1990 Sea-A	0	2	.000	5	3	0	0	0	12²	22	1	5	6	20.6	10.66	37	.379	.446	0	—	0	-10	-9	0	-1.2
1991 Bos-A	9	10	.474	22	22	0	0	0	130	140	18	47	91	12.9	4.85	89	.274	.335	0	—	0	-11	-8	-0	-1.3
1992 Bos-A	4	10	.286	28	18	0	0	0	130²	126	12	58	79	12.8	4.75	89	.253	.333	0	—	0	-12	-8	0	-0.9
1993 Mon-N	2	3	.400	24	2	0	0	0	38	40	3	19	21	14.2	5.21	80	.268	.355	0	.000	-0	-5	-4	0	-0.6
Det-A	0	0	—	10	0	0	0	0	11¹	12	0	7	4	15.1	3.97	108	.279	.380	0	—	0	0	0	0	0.0
1994 Det-A	2	2	.500	38	1	0	0	5	58²	53	10	23	31	11.7	4.14	115	.233	.304	0	—	0	4	4	0	0.3
Total 5	17	27	.386	127	46	0	0	5	381¹	393	44	159	232	13.1	4.91	88	.264	.338	0	.000	-0	-32	-25	-0	-3.7

● CHRIS GARDNER   Gardner, Christopher John   b: 3/30/69, Long Beach, Cal.   BR/TR, 6', 175 lbs.   Deb: 9/10/91

YEAR TM/L	W	L	PCT	G	GS	CG	SH	SV	IP	H	HR	BB	SO	RAT	ERA	ERA+	OAV	OOB	BH	AVG	PB	PR	/A	PD	TPI
1991 Hou-N	1	2	.333	5	4	0	0	0	24²	19	5	14	12	12.0	4.01	87	.218	.327	0	.000	-0	-1	-1	1	-0.1

● GID GARDNER   Gardner, Frank Washington   b: 6/9/1859, Attleboro, Mass.   d: 8/1/14, Cambridge, Mass.   165 lbs.   Deb: 8/23/1879 ◆

YEAR TM/L	W	L	PCT	G	GS	CG	SH	SV	IP	H	HR	BB	SO	RAT	ERA	ERA+	OAV	OOB	BH	AVG	PB	PR	/A	PD	TPI
1879 Tro-N	0	2	.000	2	2	2	0	0	14	27	0	3	3	17.4	5.79	43	.365	.365	1	.167	-0	-5	-5	-1	-0.6
1880 Cle-N	1	8	.111	9	9	9	0	0	77	80	2	20	21	11.7	2.57	91	.254	.299	6	.188	-0	-2	-2	-0	-0.2
1883 Bal-a	1	0	1.000	2	0	0	0	0	7	9	1	1	2	12.9	5.14	68	.293	.315	44	.273	1	-1	-1	-0	-0.1
1884 CP-U	0	1	.000	1	1	0	0	0	6	10	0	1	4	16.5	6.00	41	.349	.371	38	.255	-0	-2	-2	0	-0.2
1885 Bal-a	0	1	.000	1	1	1	0	0	9	16	2	6	3	23.0	10.00	33	.372	.460	37	.218	-0	-7	-7	0	-0.5
Total 5	2	12	.143	15	13	12	0	0	113	142	5	28	33	13.6	3.90	64	.289	.329	178	.233	-1	-17	-17	-1	-1.6

● HARRY GARDNER   Gardner, Harry Ray   b: 6/1/1887, Quincy, Mich.   d: 8/2/61, Canby, Ore.   BR/TR, 6'2", 180 lbs.   Deb: 4/17/11

YEAR TM/L	W	L	PCT	G	GS	CG	SH	SV	IP	H	HR	BB	SO	RAT	ERA	ERA+	OAV	OOB	BH	AVG	PB	PR	/A	PD	TPI
1911 Pit-N	1	1	.500	13	3	2	0	2	42	39	2	20	24	13.1	4.50	76	.244	.335	3	.214	0	-5	-5	-1	-0.3
1912 Pit-N	0	0	—	1	0	0	0	0	0¹	3	0	1	0	108.0	0.00	—	.500	.571	0	—	0	0	0	0	0.0
Total 2	1	1	.500	14	3	2	0	2	42¹	42	2	21	24	13.8	4.46	77	.253	.344	3	.214	0	-5	-5	-1	-0.3

● JIM GARDNER   Gardner, James Anderson   b: 10/4/1874, Pittsburgh, Pa.   d: 4/24/05, Pittsburgh, Pa.   TR,   Deb: 6/20/1895

YEAR TM/L	W	L	PCT	G	GS	CG	SH	SV	IP	H	HR	BB	SO	RAT	ERA	ERA+	OAV	OOB	BH	AVG	PB	PR	/A	PD	TPI
1895 Pit-N	8	2	.800	11	10	8	0	0	85¹	99	1	27	31	13.9	2.64	171	.286	.348	9	.265	1	20	18	-1	1.6
1897 Pit-N	5	5	.500	14	11	8	0	0	95¹	115	4	32	35	14.7	5.19	80	.296	.363	12	.158	-1	-9	-11	-0	-0.9
1898 Pit-N	10	13	.435	25	22	19	1	0	185¹	179	3	48	41	11.4	3.21	111	.252	.307	14	.154	-2	8	7	-2	0.4
1899 Pit-N	1	0	1.000	6	3	0	0	0	32¹	52	1	12	2	18.1	7.52	51	.361	.414	3	.231	-1	-13	-13	-2	-0.4
1902 Chi-N	1	2	.333	3	3	2	0	0	25	23	0	10	6	11.9	2.88	94	.244	.317	2	.200	-0	-0	-0	-0	0.0
Total 5	25	22	.532	59	49	37	1	0	423¹	468	9	130	115	13.2	3.85	100	.278	.338	40	.179	-1	6	1	-4	0.7

● MARK GARDNER   Gardner, Mark Allan   b: 3/1/62, Los Angeles, Cal.   BR/TR, 6'1", 190 lbs.   Deb: 5/16/89

YEAR TM/L	W	L	PCT	G	GS	CG	SH	SV	IP	H	HR	BB	SO	RAT	ERA	ERA+	OAV	OOB	BH	AVG	PB	PR	/A	PD	TPI
1989 Mon-N	0	3	.000	7	4	0	0	0	26¹	26	2	11	21	13.3	5.13	69	.250	.333	1	.167	-0	-5	-5	-0	-0.5
1990 Mon-N	7	9	.438	27	26	3	3	0	152²	129	13	61	135	11.7	3.42	107	.230	.315	5	.114	-1	6	4	2	0.5
1991 Mon-N	9	11	.450	27	27	0	0	0	168¹	139	17	75	107	11.7	3.85	94	.230	.319	5	.091	-2	-3	-4	-2	-0.9
1992 Mon-N	12	10	.545	33	30	0	0	0	179²	179	15	60	132	12.4	4.36	80	.259	.327	7	.140	1	-17	-18	-1	-2.1
1993 KC-A	4	6	.400	17	16	0	0	0	91²	92	17	36	54	13.0	6.19	74	.271	.348	0	—	0	-19	-16	-2	-1.9
1994 Fla-N	4	4	.500	20	14	0	0	0	92¹	97	14	30	57	12.5	4.87	92	.276	.335	1	.040	-2	-7	-4	-1	-0.6
Total 6	36	43	.456	131	117	3	3	0	711	662	78	273	506	12.2	4.37	87	.250	.327	19	.106	-5	-44	-44	-4	-5.5

● GLENN GARDNER   Gardner, Miles Glenn   b: 1/25/16, Burnsville, N.C.   d: 7/7/64, Rochester, N.Y.   BR/TR, 5'11", 180 lbs.   Deb: 7/21/45

YEAR TM/L	W	L	PCT	G	GS	CG	SH	SV	IP	H	HR	BB	SO	RAT	ERA	ERA+	OAV	OOB	BH	AVG	PB	PR	/A	PD	TPI
1945 StL-N	3	1	.750	17	4	2	1	1	54²	50	2	27	20	12.7	3.29	114	.242	.329	7	.333	2	3	3	-1	0.3

● ROB GARDNER   Gardner, Richard Frank   b: 12/19/44, Binghamton, N.Y.   BR/TL, 6'1", 176 lbs.   Deb: 9/1/65

YEAR TM/L	W	L	PCT	G	GS	CG	SH	SV	IP	H	HR	BB	SO	RAT	ERA	ERA+	OAV	OOB	BH	AVG	PB	PR	/A	PD	TPI
1965 NY-N	0	2	.000	5	4	0	0	0	28	23	4	7	19	9.6	3.21	110	.217	.265	0	.000	-1	1	1	0	0.0
1966 NY-N	4	8	.333	41	17	3	0	1	133²	147	15	64	74	14.4	5.12	71	.285	.367	7	.171	-0	-22	-22	0	-1.9
1967 Chi-N	0	2	.000	18	5	0	0	0	31²	33	2	6	16	11.1	3.98	89	.260	.293	0	.000	-0	-2	-2	0	-0.1
1968 Cle-A	0	0	—	5	0	0	0	0	2²	5	0	2	6	23.6	6.75	44	.417	.500	1	—	0	-1	-1	-0	0.0
1970 NY-A	1	0	1.000	1	1	0	0	0	7¹	8	2	4	6	14.7	4.91	72	.276	.364	1	.333	1	-1	-1	-0	-0.1
1971 Oak-A	0	0	—	4	1	0	0	0	7²	8	1	3	5	12.9	2.35	142	.267	.333	1	.500	0	1	1	0	0.1
NY-A	0	0	—	2	0	0	0	0	3	3	0	2	2	15.0	3.00	108	.273	.385	0	—	0	0	0	0	0.0
Yr	0	0	—	6	1	0	0	0	10²	11	1	5	7	13.5	2.53	131	.268	.348	1	.500	0	1	1	0	0.1
1972 NY-A	8	5	.615	20	14	0	0	0	97	91	9	28	58	11.0	3.06	96	.243	.296	3	.107	-1	-0	-0	-1	-0.4
1973 Oak-A	0	0	—	3	0	0	0	0	7¹	10	2	4	2	17.2	4.91	72	.370	.452	0	—	0	-1	-1	-0	0.4
Mil-A	1	1	.500	10	0	0	0	1	12²	17	0	13	5	21.3	9.95	38	.370	.470	0	—	0	-9	-9	0	-1.2
Yr	1	1	.500	13	0	0	0	1	20	27	2	17	7	20.2	8.10	45	.342	.464	0	—	0	-10	-10	0	-0.8
Total 8	14	18	.438	109	42	4	0	2	331	345	35	133	193	13.1	4.35	78	.269	.339	12	.138	-2	-34	-35	-0	-3.2

● WES GARDNER   Gardner, Wesley Brian   b: 4/29/61, Benton, Ark.   BR/TR, 6'4", 197 lbs.   Deb: 7/29/84

YEAR TM/L	W	L	PCT	G	GS	CG	SH	SV	IP	H	HR	BB	SO	RAT	ERA	ERA+	OAV	OOB	BH	AVG	PB	PR	/A	PD	TPI
1984 NY-N	1	1	.500	21	0	0	0	0	25¹	34	0	8	19	14.9	6.39	55	.321	.368	0	.000	-0	-8	-8	-0	-0.7
1985 NY-N	0	2	.000	9	0	0	0	0	12	18	1	8	11	19.5	5.25	66	.375	.464	0	—	0	-2	-2	-0	-0.3
1986 Bos-A	0	0	—	1	0	0	0	0	1	1	0	0	1	9.0	9.00	46	.333	.333	0	—	0	-1	-1	0	-0.1
1987 Bos-A	3	6	.333	49	1	0	0	10	89²	98	17	42	70	14.3	5.42	84	.279	.359	0	—	0	-10	-9	-1	-1.2
1988 *Bos-A	8	6	.571	36	18	1	0	2	149	119	16	106	106	11.2	3.50	117	.220	.305	0	—	0	8	10	0	0.8
1989 Bos-A	3	7	.300	22	16	0	0	0	86	97	10	47	81	15.2	5.97	69	.287	.376	0	—	0	-20	-18	-1	-2.2
1990 Bos-A	3	7	.300	34	9	0	0	0	77¹	77	6	35	58	13.3	4.89	83	.259	.341	0	—	0	-8	-7	-0	-1.0
1991 SD-N	0	1	.000	14	0	0	0	0	20¹	27	1	12	9	17.3	7.08	54	.310	.394	0	.000	-0	-8	-7	-0	-0.4
KC-A	0	0	—	3	0	0	0	0	5²	3	0	2	3	11.1	1.59	259	.208	.269	0	—	0	2	2	0	0.2
Total 8	18	30	.375	189	44	1	0	14	466¹	476	52	218	358	13.5	4.90	84	.265	.347	0	.000	-0	-47	-40	-2	-5.0

● BILL GARDNER   Gardner, William A.   b: 9/1868, Baltimore, Md.   Deb: 8/9/1887

YEAR TM/L	W	L	PCT	G	GS	CG	SH	SV	IP	H	HR	BB	SO	RAT	ERA	ERA+	OAV	OOB	BH	AVG	PB	PR	/A	PD	TPI
1887 Bal-a	0	1	.000	3	2	1	0	0	13	23	0	10	3	23.5	11.08	37	.426	.523	3	.273	0	-10	-10	-0	-0.5

● BILL GARFIELD   Garfield, William Milton   b: 10/26/1867, Sheffield, Ohio   d: 12/16/41, Danville, Ill.   BR/TR, 5'11.5", 160 lbs.   Deb: 7/10/1889

YEAR TM/L	W	L	PCT	G	GS	CG	SH	SV	IP	H	HR	BB	SO	RAT	ERA	ERA+	OAV	OOB	BH	AVG	PB	PR	/A	PD	TPI
1889 Pit-N	0	2	.000	4	2	2	0	0	29	45	2	17	4	19.6	7.76	48	.344	.423	0	.000	-2	-12	-13	-0	-0.8
1890 Cle-N	1	7	.125	9	8	7	0	0	70	91	3	35	16	17.2	4.89	73	.305	.393	4	.154	-1	-10	-10	-0	-1.0
Total 2	1	9	.100	13	10	9	0	0	99	136	5	52	20	17.9	5.73	63	.317	.402	4	.103	-3	-22	-23	-0	-1.8

● BOB GARIBALDI   Garibaldi, Robert Roy   b: 3/3/42, Stockton, Cal.   BL/TR, 6'4", 210 lbs.   Deb: 7/15/62

YEAR TM/L	W	L	PCT	G	GS	CG	SH	SV	IP	H	HR	BB	SO	RAT	ERA	ERA+	OAV	OOB	BH	AVG	PB	PR	/A	PD	TPI
1962 SF-N	0	0	—	9	0	0	0	1	12¹	13	1	5	9	13.1	5.11	74	.265	.333	0	.000	-0	-2	-2	0	0.0
1963 SF-N	0	1	.000	4	0	0	0	0	8	4	0	4	4	14.6	1.13	284	.276	.382	0	—	0	2	2	0	0.3
1966 SF-N	0	0	—	1	0	0	0	0	1	1	0	0	1	9.0	9.00	—	.250	.250	0	—	0	0	0	0	0.0
1969 SF-N	0	1	.000	1	1	0	0	0	5	6	0	2	1	14.4	1.80	194	.316	.381	0	.000	-0	1	1	0	0.2
Total 4	0	2	.000	15	1	0	0	1	26¹	28	1	11	15	13.1	3.08	116	.277	.354	0	.000	-0	1	1	0	0.5

● LOU GARLAND   Garland, Louis Lyman   b: 7/16/05, Archie, Mo.   d: 8/30/90, Idaho Falls, Idaho   BR/TR, 6'2.5", 200 lbs.   Deb: 8/31/31

YEAR TM/L	W	L	PCT	G	GS	CG	SH	SV	IP	H	HR	BB	SO	RAT	ERA	ERA+	OAV	OOB	BH	AVG	PB	PR	/A	PD	TPI
1931 Chi-A	0	2	.000	7	2	0	0	0	16²	30	2	14	4	24.3	10.26	41	.400	.500	0	.000	-0	-11	-11	1	-1.0

● WAYNE GARLAND   Garland, Marcus Wayne   b: 10/26/50, Nashville, Tenn.   BR/TR, 6', 195 lbs.   Deb: 9/13/73

YEAR TM/L	W	L	PCT	G	GS	CG	SH	SV	IP	H	HR	BB	SO	RAT	ERA	ERA+	OAV	OOB	BH	AVG	PB	PR	/A	PD	TPI
1973 Bal-A	0	1	.000	4	1	0	0	0	16	14	1	7	10	11.8	3.94	95	.233	.313	0	—	0	-0	-0	-0	0.0
1974 *Bal-A	5	5	.500	20	6	0	0	1	91	68	5	26	40	9.6	2.97	116	.211	.276	0	—	0	7	5	-1	0.6

YEAR TM/L	W	L	PCT	G	GS	CG	SH	SV	IP	H	HR	BB	SO	RAT	ERA	ERA+	OAV	OOB	BH	AVG	PB	PR	/A	PD	TPI
1975 Bal-A	2	5	.286	29	1	0	0	4	87¹	80	7	31	46	11.5	3.71	95	.252	.321	0	—	0	1	-2	-0	0.0
1976 Bal-A	20	7	.741	38	25	14	4	1	232¹	224	10	64	113	11.4	2.67	122	.255	.309	0	—	0	22	15	2	2.1
1977 Cle-A	13	19	.406	38	38	21	1	0	282²	281	25	88	118	11.8	3.60	110	.261	.318	0	—	0	14	11	-0	1.1
1978 Cle-A	2	3	.400	6	6	0	0	0	29²	43	6	16	13	18.2	7.89	47	.347	.426	0	—	0	-14	-14	0	-1.8
1979 Cle-A	4	10	.286	18	14	2	0	0	94²	120	11	34	40	14.9	5.23	81	.318	.379	0	—	0	-11	-10	-1	-1.4
1980 Cle-A	6	9	.400	25	20	4	1	0	150¹	163	18	48	55	13.0	4.61	88	.276	.337	0	—	0	-10	-9	-1	-0.9
1981 Cle-A	3	7	.300	12	10	2	1	0	56	89	8	14	15	16.6	5.79	63	.374	.409	0	—	0	-13	-13	-0	-2.0
Total 9	55	66	.455	190	121	43	7	6	1040	1082	89	328	450	12.4	3.89	96	.272	.330	0	—	0	-4	-18	-2	-2.3

● **MIKE GARMAN**   Garman, Michael Douglas b: 9/16/49, Caldwell, Idaho BR/TR, 6'3", 215 lbs. Deb: 9/22/69

YEAR TM/L	W	L	PCT	G	GS	CG	SH	SV	IP	H	HR	BB	SO	RAT	ERA	ERA+	OAV	OOB	BH	AVG	PB	PR	/A	PD	TPI
1969 Bos-A	1	0	1.000	2	2	0	0	0	12¹	13	0	10	10	16.8	4.38	87	.277	.404	2	.400	1	-1	-1	0	0.0
1971 Bos-A	1	1	.500	3	3	0	0	0	18²	15	3	9	6	12.1	3.86	96	.217	.316	2	.333	0	-1	-0	-1	-0.1
1972 Bos-A	0	1	.000	3	1	0	0	0	3¹	4	1	2	1	16.2	10.80	30	.286	.375	0	—	0	-3	-3	-0	-0.7
1973 Bos-A	0	0	—	12	0	0	0	0	22	32	1	15	9	19.2	5.32	76	.352	.443	0	—	0	-4	-3	-0	-0.4
1974 StL-N	7	2	.778	64	0	0	0	6	81²	66	4	27	45	10.5	2.64	135	.227	.297	1	.100	-1	9	8	0	1.0
1975 StL-N	3	8	.273	66	0	0	0	10	79	73	3	48	48	13.9	2.39	157	.245	.352	0	.000	0	11	12	-1	1.8
1976 Chi-N	2	4	.333	47	2	0	0	1	76¹	79	7	35	37	13.8	4.95	78	.273	.358	0	.000	-1	-12	-9	-0	-0.8
1977 *LA-N	4	4	.500	49	0	0	0	12	62²	60	7	22	29	12.1	2.73	140	.254	.323	0	.000	-1	8	8	-1	1.1
1978 LA-N	0	1	1.000	10	0	0	0	0	16¹	15	3	3	5	9.9	4.41	80	.259	.295	0	—	-2	-2	-0	-0.1
Mon-N	4	6	.400	47	0	0	0	13	61¹	54	5	31	23	12.5	4.40	80	.238	.329	0	—	0	-6	-6	-0	-1.3
Yr	4	7	.364	57	0	0	0	13	77²	69	8	34	28	11.9	4.40	80	.242	.323	0	.000	-1	-7	-8	-1	-1.4
Total 9	22	27	.449	303	8	0	0	42	433²	411	34	202	213	12.9	3.63	102	.254	.340	5	.119	-2	-0	4	-3	0.5

● **WILLIE GARONI**   Garoni, William b: 7/28/1877, Ft.Lee, N.J. d: 9/9/14, Ft.Lee, N.J. BR/TR, 6'1", 165 lbs. Deb: 9/7/1899

YEAR TM/L	W	L	PCT	G	GS	CG	SH	SV	IP	H	HR	BB	SO	RAT	ERA	ERA+	OAV	OOB	BH	AVG	PB	PR	/A	PD	TPI
1899 NY-N	0	1	.000	3	1	1	0	0	10	12	0	2	2	12.6	4.50	83	.297	.330	0	.000	-1	-1	-1	0	-0.1

● **SCOTT GARRELTS**   Garrelts, Scott William b: 10/30/61, Urbana, Ill. BR/TR, 6'4", 195 lbs. Deb: 10/2/82

YEAR TM/L	W	L	PCT	G	GS	CG	SH	SV	IP	H	HR	BB	SO	RAT	ERA	ERA+	OAV	OOB	BH	AVG	PB	PR	/A	PD	TPI
1982 SF-N	0	0	—	1	0	0	0	0	2	3	0	2	4	22.5	13.50	27	.333	.455	0	—	0	-2	-2	0	0.0
1983 SF-N	2	2	.500	5	5	1	1	0	35²	33	4	19	16	13.6	2.52	140	.254	.358	2	.222	0	4	4	0	0.5
1984 SF-N	2	3	.400	21	3	0	0	0	43	45	6	34	32	16.7	5.65	62	.274	.402	1	.100	-0	-10	-10	-1	-1.2
1985 SF-N☆	9	6	.600	74	0	0	0	13	105²	76	2	58	106	11.7	2.30	149	.198	.308	2	.222	1	15	13	2	2.5
1986 SF-N	13	9	.591	53	18	0	0	10	173²	144	17	74	125	11.4	3.11	113	.231	.314	8	.178	2	12	8	2	1.5
1987 *SF-N	11	7	.611	64	0	0	0	12	106¹	70	10	55	127	10.6	3.22	119	.192	.298	2	.200	1	10	7	-1	1.3
1988 SF-N	5	9	.357	65	0	0	0	13	98	80	3	46	86	11.8	3.58	91	.226	.318	1	.077	-1	-1	-3	-1	-0.7
1989 *SF-N	14	5	.737	30	29	2	1	0	193¹	149	11	46	119	**9.1**	**2.28**	**148**	.212	**.260**	9	.136	1	26	23	2	2.3
1990 SF-N	12	11	.522	31	31	4	2	0	182	190	16	70	80	13.0	4.15	88	.272	.341	4	.061	-3	-7	-10	-1	-1.6
1991 SF-N	1	1	.500	8	3	0	0	0	19²	25	5	9	8	15.6	6.41	56	.313	.382	0	.000	-1	-6	-6	-0	-0.6
Total 10	69	53	.566	352	89	9	4	48	959¹	815	74	413	703	11.6	3.29	107	.232	.315	29	.125	-1	41	24	1	4.0

● **CLARENCE GARRETT**   Garrett, Clarence Raymond "Laz" b: 3/6/1891, Reader, W.Va. d: 2/11/77, Moundsville, W.Va. BR/TR, 6'5.5", 185 lbs. Deb: 9/13/15

YEAR TM/L	W	L	PCT	G	GS	CG	SH	SV	IP	H	HR	BB	SO	RAT	ERA	ERA+	OAV	OOB	BH	AVG	PB	PR	/A	PD	TPI
1915 Cle-A	2	2	.500	4	4	2	0	0	23¹	19	1	6	5	10.0	2.31	132	.224	.283	0	.000	-0	2	2	1	0.4

● **GREG GARRETT**   Garrett, Gregory b: 3/12/48, Atascadero, Cal. BB/TL, 6', 200 lbs. Deb: 4/24/70

YEAR TM/L	W	L	PCT	G	GS	CG	SH	SV	IP	H	HR	BB	SO	RAT	ERA	ERA+	OAV	OOB	BH	AVG	PB	PR	/A	PD	TPI
1970 Cal-A	5	6	.455	32	7	0	0	0	74²	48	6	44	53	11.2	2.65	136	.190	.312	1	.067	-1	9	8	-0	1.0
1971 Cin-N	0	1	1.000	2	1	0	0	0	8²	7	0	10	2	11.7	1.04	323	.250	.447	1	.333	0	2	2	-0	0.3
Total 2	5	7	.417	34	8	0	0	0	83¹	55	6	54	55	11.9	2.48	144	.196	.327	2	.111	-1	11	10	-0	1.3

● **CLIFF GARRISON**   Garrison, Clifford William b: 8/13/06, Belmont, Okla. d: 8/25/94, Woodland, Cal. BR/TR, 6', 180 lbs. Deb: 4/16/28

YEAR TM/L	W	L	PCT	G	GS	CG	SH	SV	IP	H	HR	BB	SO	RAT	ERA	ERA+	OAV	OOB	BH	AVG	PB	PR	/A	PD	TPI
1928 Bos-A	0	0	—	6	0	0	0	0	16	22	2	6	6	15.8	7.88	52	.361	.418	0	.000	-0	-7	-7	1	0.0

● **JIM GARRY**   Garry, James Thomas b: 9/21/1869, Great Barrington, Mass. d: 1/15/17, Pittsfield, Mass. TL, Deb: 5/2/1893

YEAR TM/L	W	L	PCT	G	GS	CG	SH	SV	IP	H	HR	BB	SO	RAT	ERA	ERA+	OAV	OOB	BH	AVG	PB	PR	/A	PD	TPI
1893 Bos-N	0	1	.000	1	1	0	0	0	1	5	0	4	2	81.0	63.00	8	.628	.753	0	.000	-0	-6	-6	0	-2.1

● **NED GARVER**   Garver, Ned Franklin b: 12/25/25, Ney, Ohio BR/TR, 5'10.5", 180 lbs. Deb: 4/28/48

YEAR TM/L	W	L	PCT	G	GS	CG	SH	SV	IP	H	HR	BB	SO	RAT	ERA	ERA+	OAV	OOB	BH	AVG	PB	PR	/A	PD	TPI
1948 StL-A	7	11	.389	38	24	7	0	5	198	200	14	95	75	13.5	3.41	134	.268	.352	19	.288	4	19	25	1	2.7
1949 StL-A	12	17	.414	41	32	16	1	3	223²	245	14	102	70	14.1	3.98	114	.277	.354	14	.187	1	5	14	0	1.8
1950 StL-A	13	18	.419	37	31	**22**	2	0	260	264	18	108	85	13.0	3.39	**146**	.264	.338	26	.286	4	**34**	**45**	2	**5.7**
1951 StL-A★	20	12	.625	33	30	**24**	1	0	246	237	17	96	84	12.4	3.73	118	.255	.328	29	.305	7	11	18	1	3.1
1952 StL-A	7	10	.412	21	21	7	2	0	148²	130	14	55	60	11.4	3.69	106	.235	.309	9	.184	0	-0	4	-0	0.4
Det-A	1	0	1.000	1	1	1	0	0	9	9	1	3	3	12.0	2.00	190	.265	.324	0	.000	0	2	2	0	0.3
Yr	8	10	.444	22	22	8	2	0	157²	139	15	58	63	11.2	3.60	109	.235	.304	9	.176	0	1	5	0	0.7
1953 Det-A	11	11	.500	30	26	13	0	1	198¹	228	16	66	69	13.4	4.45	91	.290	.347	11	.153	-1	-10	-8	1	-0.8
1954 Det-A	14	11	.560	35	32	16	3	1	246¹	216	20	62	93	10.3	2.81	131	.236	.287	13	.165	-0	25	24	2	2.5
1955 Det-A	12	16	.429	33	32	16	1	0	230²	251	21	67	83	12.6	3.98	97	.279	.333	17	.224	5	-1	-4	0	0.1
1956 Det-A	0	2	.000	6	3	1	0	0	17²	15	2	13	6	14.8	4.08	101	.234	.372	0	.000	0	0	0	1	0.0
1957 KC-A	6	13	.316	24	23	6	1	0	145¹	120	13	55	61	11.1	3.84	103	.223	.301	8	.182	0	-1	2	-0	0.2
1958 KC-A	12	11	.522	31	28	10	3	1	201	192	24	66	72	11.6	4.03	97	.244	.304	12	.174	0	-6	-3	5	0.3
1959 KC-A	10	13	.435	32	30	9	2	1	201¹	214	22	42	61	11.6	3.71	108	.270	.309	20	.282	6	3	7	-0	1.3
1960 KC-A	4	9	.308	28	15	5	2	0	122¹	110	15	35	50	10.8	3.83	104	.240	.296	2	.074	-1	1	2	-0	0.1
1961 LA-A	0	3	.000	12	2	0	0	0	29	40	2	16	9	17.4	5.59	81	.348	.427	0	.000	-1	-5	-3	1	-0.3
Total 14	129	157	.451	402	330	153	18	12	2477¹	2471	213	881	881	12.3	3.73	112	.260	.325	180	.218	24	78	122	14	17.4

● **JERRY GARVIN**   Garvin, Theodore Jared b: 10/21/55, Oakland, Cal. BL/TL, 6'3", 195 lbs. Deb: 4/10/77

YEAR TM/L	W	L	PCT	G	GS	CG	SH	SV	IP	H	HR	BB	SO	RAT	ERA	ERA+	OAV	OOB	BH	AVG	PB	PR	/A	PD	TPI
1977 Tor-A	10	18	.357	34	34	12	1	0	244²	247	33	85	127	12.4	4.19	100	.264	.328	0	—	0	-4	0	5	0.4
1978 Tor-A	4	12	.250	26	22	3	0	0	144²	189	20	48	67	15.0	5.54	71	.319	.374	0	—	0	-29	-26	1	-2.5
1979 Tor-A	0	1	.000	8	1	0	0	0	22²	15	2	10	14	10.7	2.78	156	.197	.307	0	—	0	4	4	-0	0.1
1980 Tor-A	4	7	.364	61	0	0	0	8	82²	72	6	27	52	10.6	2.29	188	.233	.296	0	—	0	16	19	1	2.7
1981 Tor-A	1	2	.333	35	4	0	0	0	53	46	3	23	25	11.7	3.40	116	.240	.321	0	—	0	2	3	0	0.2
1982 Tor-A	1	1	.500	32	4	0	0	0	58¹	81	6	26	35	16.7	7.25	62	.335	.401	0	—	0	-21	-18	2	-1.0
Total 6	20	41	.328	196	65	15	1	8	606	648	74	219	320	13.0	4.43	94	.277	.342	0	—	0	-32	-18	9	-0.1

● **NED GARVIN**   Garvin, Virgil Lee b: 1/1/1874, Navasota, Tex. d: 6/16/08, Fresno, Cal. TR, 6'3.5", 160 lbs. Deb: 7/13/1896

YEAR TM/L	W	L	PCT	G	GS	CG	SH	SV	IP	H	HR	BB	SO	RAT	ERA	ERA+	OAV	OOB	BH	AVG	PB	PR	/A	PD	TPI
1896 Phi-N	0	1	.000	2	1	1	0	0	13	19	1	4	4	18.0	7.62	57	.337	.411	0	.000	-1	-5	-5	-0	-0.4
1899 Chi-N	9	13	.409	24	23	22	4	0	199	202	1	42	69	11.6	2.85	132	.263	.311	11	.155	-5	22	20	1	1.5
1900 Chi-N	10	18	.357	30	28	25	1	0	246¹	225	4	63	107	11.2	2.41	150	.243	.304	14	.154	-5	**35**	33	4	3.1
1901 Mil-A	7	20	.259	37	27	22	1	2	257¹	258	4	90	122	12.7	3.46	104	.258	.328	10	.108	-9	6	4	4	-0.2
1902 Chi-A	10	10	.500	23	19	16	2	0	175¹	169	3	43	55	11.3	2.21	153	.254	.307	9	.153	-2	27	23	3	2.4
Bro-N	1	1	.500	2	2	1	0	0	18	15	0	4	7	9.5	1.00	276	.227	.271	1	.143	0	4	4	0	0.4
1903 Bro-N	15	18	.455	38	34	30	2	0	298	277	6	84	154	11.3	3.08	104	.248	.308	8	.075	-8	6	4	8	0.2
1904 Bro-N	5	15	.250	23	22	16	0	0	181²	141	6	78	86	11.1	1.68	163	.218	.308	8	.127	-4	21	21	4	2.4
NY-A	1	1	.000	2	2	1	0	0	16	15	0	5	7	11.5	2.25	121	.292	.320	0	.000	-1	1	1	1	0.1
Total 7	57	97	.370	181	158	134	13	4	1400²	1320	20	413	612	11.6	2.72	125	.249	.312	61	.122	-35	117	104	24	9.5

● **HARRY GASPAR**   Gaspar, Harry Lambert b: 4/28/1883, Kingsley, Iowa d: 5/14/40, Orange, Cal. BR/TR, 6', 180 lbs. Deb: 4/21/09

YEAR TM/L	W	L	PCT	G	GS	CG	SH	SV	IP	H	HR	BB	SO	RAT	ERA	ERA+	OAV	OOB	BH	AVG	PB	PR	/A	PD	TPI
1909 Cin-N	19	11	.633	44	29	19	4	2	260	228	0	57	65	10.2	2.01	130	.242	.291	10	.122	-3	17	17	-5	1.1

YEAR TM/L	W	L	PCT	G	GS	CG	SH	SV	IP	H	HR	BB	SO	RAT	ERA	ERA+	OAV	OOB	BH	AVG	PB	PR	/A	PD	TPI
1910 Cin-N	15	17	.469	48	31	16	4	7	275	257	6	75	74	11.4	2.59	113	.255	.317	10	.115	-3	14	10	-2	0.6
1911 Cin-N	11	17	.393	44	32	11	2	4	253²	272	9	69	76	12.6	3.30	100	.283	.340	13	.153	-2	3	0	-1	-0.4
1912 Cin-N	1	3	.250	7	6	2	0	0	36²	38	0	16	13	13.5	4.17	81	.277	.357	3	.250	0	-3	-3	-0	-0.3
Total 4	46	48	.489	143	98	48	10	13	825¹	795	15	217	228	11.5	2.69	110	.261	.318	36	.135	-9	31	25	-8	1.0

● CHARLIE GASSAWAY

Gassaway, Charles Cason "Sheriff" b: 8/12/18, Gassaway, Ga. d: 1/15/92, Miami, Fla. BL/TL, 6'2.5", 210 lbs. Deb: 9/25/44

YEAR TM/L	W	L	PCT	G	GS	CG	SH	SV	IP	H	HR	BB	SO	RAT	ERA	ERA+	OAV	OOB	BH	AVG	PB	PR	/A	PD	TPI
1944 Chi-N	0	1	.000	2	2	0	0	0	11²	20	3	10	7	23.1	7.71	46	.385	.484	1	.250		-5	-5	-0	-0.4
1945 Phi-A	4	7	.364	24	11	4	0	0	118	114	4	55	50	13.0	3.74	92	.253	.336	6	.154	-2	-5	-4	-1	-0.7
1946 Cle-A	1	1	.500	13	6	0	0	0	50²	54	2	26	23	14.9	3.91	85	.273	.368	1	.067	-1	-2	-3	-0	-0.2
Total 3	5	9	.357	39	19	4	0	0	180¹	188	9	91	80	14.2	4.04	84	.268	.357	8	.138	-3	-12	-13	-2	-1.3

● MILT GASTON

Gaston, Nathaniel Milton b: 1/27/1896, Ridgefield Park, N.J. 6'1", 185 lbs. Deb: 4/20/24 F

YEAR TM/L	W	L	PCT	G	GS	CG	SH	SV	IP	H	HR	BB	SO	RAT	ERA	ERA+	OAV	OOB	BH	AVG	PB	PR	/A	PD	TPI
1924 NY-A	5	3	.625	29	2	0	0	1	86	92	3	44	24	14.9	4.50	92	.286	.382	6	.222	-1	-3	-3	-1	-0.5
1925 StL-A	15	14	.517	42	30	16	0	1	238²	284	8	101	84	14.7	4.41	106	.305	.376	21	.262	2	-0	7	-2	0.8
1926 StL-A	10	18	.357	32	28	14	1	0	214¹	227	13	101	39	13.9	4.33	99	.283	.366	13	.167	-2	-7	-1	-1	-0.3
1927 StL-A	13	17	.433	37	30	21	0	1	254	275	18	100	77	13.4	5.00	87	.281	.350	25	.260	5	-24	-18	1	-1.2
1928 Was-A	6	12	.333	28	22	8	3	0	148²	179	3	53	45	14.0	5.51	73	.302	.360	7	.143	-3	-24	-25	1	-2.7
1929 Bos-A	12	19	.387	39	29	20	1	2	243²	265	15	81	83	12.9	3.73	115	.289	.348	15	.192	0	14	15	-1	1.6
1930 Bos-A	13	20	.394	38	34	20	2	0	273	272	15	99	93	12.2	3.92	117	.259	.323	20	.204	-4	22	21	1	1.9
1931 Bos-A	2	13	.133	23	18	4	0	0	119	137	4	41	33	13.5	4.46	96	.291	.348	6	.158	-2	-1	-2	-0	-0.4
1932 Chi-A	7	17	.292	28	25	7	1	1	166²	183	10	73	44	13.9	4.00	108	.279	.352	14	.233	2	9	6	2	1.1
1933 Chi-A	8	12	.400	30	25	7	1	0	167	177	9	60	39	12.8	4.85	87	.272	.334	8	.154	-11	-11	-1	-1.2
1934 Chi-A	6	19	.240	29	28	10	1	0	194	247	16	84	48	15.4	5.85	81	.313	.379	10	.147	-5	-29	-24	3	-2.5
Total 11	97	164	.372	355	271	127	10	8	2105	2338	114	836	615	13.7	4.55	97	.287	.355	145	.200	-5	-54	-35	0	-3.4

● WELCOME GASTON

Gaston, Welcome Thornburg b: 12/19/1872, Guernsey Co., Ohio d: 12/13/44, Columbus, Ohio TL, Deb: 10/6/1898

YEAR TM/L	W	L	PCT	G	GS	CG	SH	SV	IP	H	HR	BB	SO	RAT	ERA	ERA+	OAV	OOB	BH	AVG	PB	PR	/A	PD	TPI
1898 Bro-N	1	1	.500	2	2	2	0	0	16	17	0	4	0	14.6	2.81	128	.270	.362	1	.125	-0	1	1	-0	0.1
1899 Bro-N	0	0	—	1	0	0	0	0	3	3	0	4	0	24.0	3.00	130	.260	.484	1	1.000	1	0	0	0	0.1
Total 2	1	1	.500	3	2	2	0	0	19	20	0	8	0	16.1	2.84	128	.269	.384	2	.222	1	2	2	-0	0.2

● HANK GASTRIGHT

Gastright, Henry Carl (b: Henry Carl Gastreich)
b: 3/29/1865, Covington, Ky. d: 10/9/37, Cold Springs, Ky. BR/TR, 6'2", 190 lbs. Deb: 4/19/1889

YEAR TM/L	W	L	PCT	G	GS	CG	SH	SV	IP	H	HR	BB	SO	RAT	ERA	ERA+	OAV	OOB	BH	AVG	PB	PR	/A	PD	TPI
1889 Col-a	10	16	.385	32	26	21	0	0	222²	255	8	104	115	14.7	4.57	79	.279	.355	17	.181	-4	-18	-23	-0	-2.4
1890 Col-a	30	14	.682	48	45	41	4	0	401¹	312	8	135	199	10.4	2.94	122	.208	.281	36	.213	3	42	29	-4	2.4
1891 Col-a	12	19	.387	35	33	28	1	0	283²	280	7	136	109	13.5	3.78	92	.249	.336	23	.197	2	-2	-10	1	-0.6
1892 Was-N	3	3	.500	11	7	6	0	0	79²	94	3	38	32	15.3	5.08	64	.282	.361	4	.138	-16	-14	-1	-1.1
1893 Pit-N	3	1	.750	9	5	3	0	0	59	74	5	39	12	17.7	6.25	73	.298	.399	1	.042	-4	-10	-11	1	-0.8
Bos-N	12	4	.750	19	18	16	0	0	156	179	7	76	27	15.2	5.13	96	.297	.364	13	.191	-8	-3	-2	-1.4
Yr	15	5	**.750**	28	23	19	0	0	215	253	12	115	39	15.8	5.44	89	.284	.371	14	.152	-6	-19	-15	-1	-1.4
1894 Bro-N	2	6	.250	16	8	6	1	2	93	135	1	55	20	19.0	6.39	77	.335	.423	7	.171	-3	-11	-15	-1	-1.2
1896 Cin-N	0	0	—	1	0	0	0	0	6	8	0	1	0	13.5	4.50	102	.317	.343	-0	.000	-0	-0	-0	0.0
Total 7	72	63	.533	171	142	121	6	2	1301¹	1337	39	584	514	13.7	4.20	92	.273	.358	101	.186	-8	-23	-51	-7	-4.3

● AUBREY GATEWOOD

Gatewood, Aubrey Lee b: 11/17/38, Little Rock, Ark. BR/TR, 6'1", 170 lbs. Deb: 9/11/63

YEAR TM/L	W	L	PCT	G	GS	CG	SH	SV	IP	H	HR	BB	SO	RAT	ERA	ERA+	OAV	OOB	BH	AVG	PB	PR	/A	PD	TPI
1963 LA-A	1	1	.500	4	3	1	0	0	24	12	0	16	13	10.5	1.50	228	.148	.289	0	.000	-1	6	5	-0	0.3
1964 LA-A	3	3	.500	15	7	1	0	0	60¹	59	4	12	25	10.7	2.24	147	.258	.298	2	.100	-1	9	7	-0	0.5
1965 Cal-A	4	5	.444	46	3	0	0	0	92	91	5	37	37	12.6	3.42	99	.266	.339	3	.214	1	0	-0	-1	0.0
1970 Atl-N	0	0	—	3	0	0	0	0	2	4	0	2	0	31.5	4.50	95	.364	.500	0	—	-0	-0	-0	0.0
Total 4	8	9	.471	68	13	1	0	0	178¹	166	9	67	75	11.9	2.78	122	.250	.322	5	.119	-1	15	12	-1	0.8

● CHIPPY GAW

Gaw, George Joseph b: 3/13/1892, W.Newton, Mass. d: 5/26/68, Boston, Mass. BR/TR, 5'11", 180 lbs. Deb: 4/20/20

YEAR TM/L	W	L	PCT	G	GS	CG	SH	SV	IP	H	HR	BB	SO	RAT	ERA	ERA+	OAV	OOB	BH	AVG	PB	PR	/A	PD	TPI
1920 Chi-N	1	1	.500	6	1	0	0	0	13	16	1	3	4	13.8	4.85	66	.320	.370	1	.250	-0	-2	-2	-0	-0.4

● DALE GEAR

Gear, Dale Dudley b: 2/2/1872, Lone Elm, Kan. d: 9/23/51, Topeka, Kan. BR/TR, 5'11", 165 lbs. Deb: 8/15/1896 ♦

YEAR TM/L	W	L	PCT	G	GS	CG	SH	SV	IP	H	HR	BB	SO	RAT	ERA	ERA+	OAV	OOB	BH	AVG	PB	PR	/A	PD	TPI
1896 Cle-N	0	2	.000	3	2	2	0	0	23	35	1	6	6	16.8	5.48	83	.346	.394	6	.400	2	-3	-2	-0	-0.1
1901 Was-A	4	11	.267	24	16	14	1	1	163	199	9	22	35	12.4	4.03	91	.297	.324	47	.236	0	-7	-7	2	-0.3
Total 2	4	13	.235	27	18	16	1	1	186	234	10	28	41	13.0	4.21	90	.304	.333	57	.239	2	-9	-9	2	-0.4

● DINTY GEARIN

Gearin, Dennis John b: 10/15/1897, Providence, R.I. d: 3/11/59, Providence, R.I. BL/TL, 5'4", 148 lbs. Deb: 8/6/23

YEAR TM/L	W	L	PCT	G	GS	CG	SH	SV	IP	H	HR	BB	SO	RAT	ERA	ERA+	OAV	OOB	BH	AVG	PB	PR	/A	PD	TPI
1923 *NY-N	1	1	.500	6	2	1	0	0	24	23	1	10	9	12.4	3.38	113	.264	.340	2	.286	2	1	-0	0.1
1924 NY-N	1	2	.333	6	3	2	0	0	29	30	3	16	9	14.3	2.48	148	.275	.368	3	.333	0	4	4	-0	0.4
Bos-N	0	1	.000	1	1	0	0	0	3	3	0	2	0	—	∞	—	1.000	1.000	0	—	-5	-5	0	-0.4
Yr	1	3	.250	7	4	2	0	0	29	33	3	18	9	15.8	4.03	91	.295	.392	3	.333	-1	-1	-0	0.0
Total 2	2	4	.333	13	6	3	0	0	53	56	4	28	18	14.3	3.74	100	.281	.370	5	.313	1	0	-1	0.1

● BOB GEARY

Geary, Robert Norton "Speed" b: 5/10/1891, Cincinnati, Ohio d: 1/3/80, Cincinnati, Ohio BR/TR, 5'11", 168 lbs. Deb: 4/25/18

YEAR TM/L	W	L	PCT	G	GS	CG	SH	SV	IP	H	HR	BB	SO	RAT	ERA	ERA+	OAV	OOB	BH	AVG	PB	PR	/A	PD	TPI
1918 Phi-A	2	5	.286	16	7	6	2	4	87	94	0	31	22	13.2	2.69	109	.289	.357	4	.148	-1	1	2	-1	0.1
1919 Phi-A	0	3	.000	9	2	1	0	0	32¹	32	1	18	9	13.9	4.73	72	.264	.360	5	.500	2	-5	-5	0	-0.2
1921 Cin-N	1	1	.500	10	1	0	0	0	29	38	1	2	10	12.4	4.34	82	.333	.345	2	.250	0	-2	-2	-0	-0.2
Total 3	3	9	.250	35	10	7	2	4	148¹	164	2	51	41	13.2	3.46	92	.293	.355	11	.244	1	-6	-5	-1	-0.3

● BOB GEBHARD

Gebhard, Robert Henry b: 1/3/43, Lamberton, Minn. BR/TR, 6'2", 210 lbs. Deb: 8/2/71 C

YEAR TM/L	W	L	PCT	G	GS	CG	SH	SV	IP	H	HR	BB	SO	RAT	ERA	ERA+	OAV	OOB	BH	AVG	PB	PR	/A	PD	TPI
1971 Min-A	1	2	.333	17	0	0	0	0	18	17	0	11	13	14.5	3.00	118	.254	.354	—	0	1	1	1	0.3
1972 Min-A	0	1	.000	13	0	0	0	1	21	36	3	13	13	21.9	8.57	37	.371	.455	—	0	-13	-13	1	-0.6
1974 Mon-N	0	0	—	1	0	0	0	0	2	5	1	0	0	22.5	4.50	85	.500	.500	—	0	-0	-0	0	0.0
Total 3	1	3	.250	31	0	0	0	1	41	58	4	24	26	18.7	5.93	57	.328	.417	—	0	-12	-12	1	-0.3

● PETE GEBRIAN

Gebrian, Peter "Gabe" b: 8/10/23, Bayonne, N.J. BR/TR, 6', 170 lbs. Deb: 5/6/47

YEAR TM/L	W	L	PCT	G	GS	CG	SH	SV	IP	H	HR	BB	SO	RAT	ERA	ERA+	OAV	OOB	BH	AVG	PB	PR	/A	PD	TPI
1947 Chi-A	2	3	.400	27	4	0	0	5	66¹	61	7	33	17	13.0	4.48	82	.247	.340	0	.000	-2	-6	-6	-1	-0.8

● JIM GEDDES

Geddes, James Lee b: 3/23/49, Columbus, Ohio BR/TR, 6'2", 200 lbs. Deb: 4/28/72

YEAR TM/L	W	L	PCT	G	GS	CG	SH	SV	IP	H	HR	BB	SO	RAT	ERA	ERA+	OAV	OOB	BH	AVG	PB	PR	/A	PD	TPI
1972 Chi-A	0	0	—	5	1	0	0	0	10¹	12	1	10	3	20.0	6.97	45	.293	.442	0	.000	-0	-4	-4	-0	0.0
1973 Chi-A	0	0	—	6	1	0	0	0	15²	14	0	14	7	17.8	2.87	138	.255	.431	0	.000	-0	2	2	0	0.0
Total 2	0	0	—	11	2	0	0	0	26	26	1	24	10	18.7	4.50	81	.271	.435	0	.000	-0	-3	-3	-0	0.0

● JOE GEDEON

Gedeon, Elmer Joseph b: 12/5/1893, Sacramento, Cal. d: 5/19/41, San Francisco, Cal BR/TR, 6', 167 lbs. Deb: 5/13/13 ♦

YEAR TM/L	W	L	PCT	G	GS	CG	SH	SV	IP	H	HR	BB	SO	RAT	ERA	ERA+	OAV	OOB	BH	AVG	PB	PR	/A	PD	TPI
1913 Was-A	0	0	—	1	0	0	0	0	0¹	1	0	0	0	0.00	—	.000	.000	13	.183	0	0	0	0	0.1

● COUNT GEDNEY

Gedney, Alfred W. b: 5/10/1849, Brooklyn, N.Y. d: 3/26/22, Hackensack, N.J. 5'9", 140 lbs. Deb: 4/27/1872 ♦

YEAR TM/L	W	L	PCT	G	GS	CG	SH	SV	IP	H	HR	BB	SO	RAT	ERA	ERA+	OAV	OOB	BH	AVG	PB	PR	/A	PD	TPI
1875 Mut-n	1	0	1.000	2	1	1	0	0	11	7	0	1		6.5	1.64	158	.179	.200	54	.203	-0	1	1		0.1

● JOHNNY GEE

Gee, John Alexander "Whiz" b: 12/7/15, Syracuse, N.Y. d: 1/23/88, Cortland, N.Y. BL/TL, 6'9", 225 lbs. Deb: 9/17/39

YEAR TM/L	W	L	PCT	G	GS	CG	SH	SV	IP	H	HR	BB	SO	RAT	ERA	ERA+	OAV	OOB	BH	AVG	PB	PR	/A	PD	TPI
1939 Pit-N	1	2	.333	3	3	1	0	0	19²	20	1	10	16	13.7	4.12	93	.253	.337	0	.000	-1	-0	-1	1	-0.1
1941 Pit-N	0	2	.000	3	2	0	0	0	7¹	10	0	5	2	18.4	6.14	59	.294	.385	1	.333	0	-2	-2	-0	-0.5
1943 Pit-N	4	4	.500	15	10	2	0	0	82	89	5	27	18	12.7	4.28	97	.280	.336	3	.115	-1	-8	-7	-3	-1.0
1944 Pit-N	0	0	—	4	0	0	0	0	11¹	20	0	6	3	19.9	7.15	52	.377	.431	1	.500	-1	-4	-4	0	0.0

YEAR	TM/L	W	L	PCT	G	GS	CG	SH	SV	IP	H	HR	BB	SO	RAT	ERA	ERA+	OAV	OOB	BH	AVG	PB	PR	/A	PD	TPI
	NY-N	0	0	—	4	0	0	0	0	4²	5	0	3	3	9.6	0.00	—	.263	.263	0	—	0	2	2	0	0.0
	Yr	0	0	—	8	0	0	0	0	16	25	0	5	6	16.9	5.06	73	.347	.390	1	.500	0	-3	-2	0	0.0
1945	NY-N	0	0	—	2	0	0	0	1	3	5	0	2	1	21.0	9.00	43	.385	.467	0	.000	-0	-2	-2	0	-0.1
1946	NY-N	2	4	.333	13	6	1	0	0	47¹	60	3	15	22	14.6	3.99	86	.308	.363	3	.231	0	-3	-3	-1	-0.4
Total 6		7	12	.368	44	21	4	0	1	175¹	209	8	64	65	14.1	4.41	80	.294	.354	8	.157	-1	-18	-17	-3	-2.1

● **BILLY GEER**   Geer, William Henry Harrison (b: George Harrison Geer)   b: 8/13/1849, Syracuse, N.Y.   TR, 5'8", 160 lbs.   Deb: 10/15/1874 ♦

YEAR	TM/L	W	L	PCT	G	GS	CG	SH	SV	IP	H	HR	BB	SO	RAT	ERA	ERA+	OAV	OOB	BH	AVG	PB	PR	/A	PD	TPI
1884	Bro-a	0	0	—	2	0	0	0	0	5	14	0	3	1	30.6	12.60	26	.609	.654	82	.210	0	-5	-5	-0	0.0

● **HENRY GEHRING**   Gehring, Henry   b: 1/24/1881, St.Paul, Minn.   d: 4/18/12, Kansas City, Mo.   BR/TR,   Deb: 7/16/07

YEAR	TM/L	W	L	PCT	G	GS	CG	SH	SV	IP	H	HR	BB	SO	RAT	ERA	ERA+	OAV	OOB	BH	AVG	PB	PR	/A	PD	TPI
1907	Was-A	3	7	.300	15	9	8	1	0	87	92	1	14	31	11.1	3.31	73	.273	.304	9	.205	3	-7	-9	-2	-0.8
1908	Was-A	0	1	.000	3	1	0	0	0	5	9	0	2	0	23.4	14.40	16	.450	.542	3	.600	2	-7	-7	0	-0.9
Total 2		3	8	.273	18	10	8	2	0	92	101	1	16	31	11.7	3.91	62	.283	.319	12	.245	5	-14	-15	-2	-1.7

● **PAUL GEHRMAN**   Gehrman, Paul Arthur "Dutch"   b: 5/3/12, Marquam, Ore.   d: 10/23/86, Bend, Ore.   BR/TR, 6', 195 lbs.   Deb: 9/15/37

YEAR	TM/L	W	L	PCT	G	GS	CG	SH	SV	IP	H	HR	BB	SO	RAT	ERA	ERA+	OAV	OOB	BH	AVG	PB	PR	/A	PD	TPI
1937	Cin-N	0	1	.000	2	1	0	0	0	9¹	11	0	5	1	15.4	2.89	129	.282	.364	0	.000	-0	1	1	0	0.1

● **GARY GEIGER**   Geiger, Gary Merle   b: 4/4/37, Sand Ridge, Ill.   BL/TR, 6', 168 lbs.   Deb: 4/15/58 ♦

YEAR	TM/L	W	L	PCT	G	GS	CG	SH	SV	IP	H	HR	BB	SO	RAT	ERA	ERA+	OAV	OOB	BH	AVG	PB	PR	/A	PD	TPI
1958	Cle-A	0	0	—	1	0	0	0	0	2	2	0	1	2	13.5	9.00	41	.286	.375	45	.231	-1	-1	-1	0	-0.1

● **EMIL GEIS**   Geis, Emil Michael   b: 3/1861, Villmar, Germany   BR/TR, 5'11", 170 lbs.   Deb: 7/19/1882

YEAR	TM/L	W	L	PCT	G	GS	CG	SH	SV	IP	H	HR	BB	SO	RAT	ERA	ERA+	OAV	OOB	BH	AVG	PB	PR	/A	PD	TPI
1882	Bal-a	4	9	.308	13	13	10	1	0	95²	84	2	22	10	10.0	4.80	57	.220	.263	6	.146	-2	-22	-22	-3	-2.5

● **BILL GEIS**   Geis, William J. (b: William J. Geiss)   b: 7/15/1858, Chicago, Ill.   d: 9/18/24, Chicago, Ill.   5'10", 164 lbs.   Deb: 5/1/1884 F♦

YEAR	TM/L	W	L	PCT	G	GS	CG	SH	SV	IP	H	HR	BB	SO	RAT	ERA	ERA+	OAV	OOB	BH	AVG	PB	PR	/A	PD	TPI
1884	Det-N	0	0	—	1	0	0	0	0	5	14	0	2	1	28.8	14.40	20	.424	.457	50	.177	-0	-6	-6	0	0.0

● **DAVE GEISEL**   Geisel, John David   b: 1/18/55, Windber, Pa.   BL/TL, 6'3", 210 lbs.   Deb: 6/13/78

YEAR	TM/L	W	L	PCT	G	GS	CG	SH	SV	IP	H	HR	BB	SO	RAT	ERA	ERA+	OAV	OOB	BH	AVG	PB	PR	/A	PD	TPI
1978	Chi-N	1	0	1.000	18	1	0	0	0	23¹	27	0	11	15	14.7	4.24	95	.278	.352	0	—	-0	-2	-1	-0	-0.1
1979	Chi-N	0	0	—	7	0	0	0	0	15	10	0	4	5	9.0	0.60	686	.189	.259	0	.000	-0	5	6	0	0.1
1981	Chi-N	2	0	1.000	11	2	0	0	0	16	11	0	10	7	11.8	0.56	657	.204	.328	0	.000	-0	5	6	-0	0.7
1982	Tor-A	1	1	.500	16	2	0	0	0	31²	32	6	17	22	14.5	3.98	113	.260	.359	0	—	0	0	2	-0	-0.3
1983	Tor-A	0	3	.000	47	0	0	0	5	52¹	47	4	31	50	13.8	4.64	93	.240	.349	0	—	-0	-3	-2	-1	-0.4
1984	Sea-A	1	1	.500	20	0	0	0	3	43¹	47	2	9	28	12.0	4.15	96	.273	.317	0	—	-0	-1	-1	-1	-0.1
1985	Sea-A	0	0	—	12	0	0	0	0	27	35	3	15	17	16.7	6.33	67	.310	.391	0	—	-0	-7	-6	-0	-0.1
Total 7		5	5	.500	131	6	0	0	8	208²	209	15	97	144	13.5	4.01	104	.259	.343	0	—	-1	-2	-4	-3	-0.3

● **VERN GEISHERT**   Geishert, Vernon William   b: 1/10/46, Madison, Wis.   BR/TR, 6'1", 215 lbs.   Deb: 8/26/69

YEAR	TM/L	W	L	PCT	G	GS	CG	SH	SV	IP	H	HR	BB	SO	RAT	ERA	ERA+	OAV	OOB	BH	AVG	PB	PR	/A	PD	TPI
1969	Cal-A	1	1	.500	11	3	0	0	1	31	32	4	7	18	11.6	4.65	75	.267	.313	0	—	-1	-4	-4	-0	-0.3

● **EMIL GEISS**   Geiss, Emil August   b: 3/20/1867, Chicago, Ill.   d: 10/4/11, Chicago, Ill.   BR/TR, 5'11", 170 lbs.   Deb: 5/18/1887 F♦

YEAR	TM/L	W	L	PCT	G	GS	CG	SH	SV	IP	H	HR	BB	SO	RAT	ERA	ERA+	OAV	OOB	BH	AVG	PB	PR	/A	PD	TPI
1887	Chi-N	0	1	.000	1	1	1	0	0	9	17	0	3	4	20.0	8.00	56	.395	.435	1	.083	-1	-4	-4	0	-0.3

● **CHARLIE GELBERT**   Gelbert, Charles Magnus   b: 1/26/06, Scranton, Pa.   d: 1/13/67, Easton, Pa.   BR/TR, 5'11", 170 lbs.   Deb: 4/16/29 ♦

YEAR	TM/L	W	L	PCT	G	GS	CG	SH	SV	IP	H	HR	BB	SO	RAT	ERA	ERA+	OAV	OOB	BH	AVG	PB	PR	/A	PD	TPI
1940	Was-A	0	0	—	2	0	0	0	0	4	5	2	1	0	18.0	9.00	46	.278	.381	20	.370	-1	-2	-2	0	0.0

● **JOHN GELNAR**   Gelnar, John Richard   b: 6/25/43, Granite, Okla   BR/TR, 6'1.5", 190 lbs.   Deb: 8/4/64

YEAR	TM/L	W	L	PCT	G	GS	CG	SH	SV	IP	H	HR	BB	SO	RAT	ERA	ERA+	OAV	OOB	BH	AVG	PB	PR	/A	PD	TPI
1964	Pit-N	0	0	—	7	0	0	0	0	9	11	2	1	4	12.0	5.00	70	.314	.333	0	—	-0	-1	-1	-0	-0.1
1967	Pit-N	0	1	.000	10	1	0	0	0	19	30	4	11	5	20.4	8.05	42	.375	.462	1	.167	0	-10	-10	-0	-0.5
1969	Sea-A	3	10	.231	39	10	0	0	3	108²	103	7	26	69	11.1	3.31	110	.250	.302	0	.053	-1	4	4	0	0.3
1970	Mil-A	4	3	.571	53	0	0	0	4	92¹	98	7	23	48	12.3	4.19	90	.277	.330	1	.083	-1	-5	-4	1	-0.2
1971	Mil-A	0	0	—	2	0	0	0	0	1¹	3	0	1	0	27.0	13.50	26	.429	.500	0	—	-0	-1	-1	0	-0.0
Total 5		7	14	.333	111	11	0	0	7	230¹	245	20	62	126	12.5	4.18	88	.276	.332	3	.081	-2	-14	-13	1	-0.4

● **JOE GENEWICH**   Genewich, Joseph Edward   b: 1/15/1897, Elmira, N.Y.   d: 12/21/85, Lockport, N.Y.   BR/TR, 6', 174 lbs.   Deb: 9/13/22

YEAR	TM/L	W	L	PCT	G	GS	CG	SH	SV	IP	H	HR	BB	SO	RAT	ERA	ERA+	OAV	OOB	BH	AVG	PB	PR	/A	PD	TPI
1922	Bos-N	0	2	.000	6	2	1	0	0	23	29	2	11	4	15.7	7.04	57	.319	.392	1	.167	-0	-8	-8	-0	-0.6
1923	Bos-N	13	14	.481	43	24	12	1	1	227¹	272	15	46	54	12.9	3.72	107	.303	.341	19	.247	2	7	7	2	1.1
1924	Bos-N	10	19	.345	34	27	11	2	1	200¹	258	4	65	43	14.9	5.21	73	.329	.386	10	.167	-2	-30	-31	-0	-4.0
1925	Bos-N	12	10	.545	34	21	10	0	0	169	185	4	41	34	12.4	3.99	100	.279	.327	15	.273	1	5	0	-1	0.1
1926	Bos-N	8	16	.333	37	26	12	2	0	216	239	6	63	59	12.8	3.88	92	.288	.342	11	.164	-1	-1	-4	-1	-0.8
1927	Bos-N	11	8	.579	40	19	7	0	1	181	199	7	54	38	12.7	3.83	97	.279	.332	11	.193	-1	2	2	-0	-0.3
1928	Bos-N	3	7	.300	13	11	4	0	0	80²	88	14	18	15	12.2	4.13	95	.280	.325	1	.038	-3	-1	-2	-1	-0.4
	NY-N	11	4	.733	26	18	10	2	3	158¹	136	10	54	37	10.9	3.18	123	.232	.298	13	.203	-1	14	13	1	1.1
	Yr	14	11	.560	39	29	14	2	3	239	224	24	72	52	11.2	3.50	112	.248	.304	14	.156	-4	13	11	2	0.7
1929	NY-N	3	7	.300	21	9	1	0	1	85	133	9	30	19	17.4	6.78	68	.359	.409	12	.375	3	-19	-21	0	-1.7
1930	NY-N	2	5	.286	18	9	3	0	3	61	71	6	20	13	13.6	5.61	84	.297	.354	3	.150	-1	-4	-6	2	-0.5
Total 9		73	92	.442	272	166	71	7	12	1401²	1610	77	402	316	13.1	4.29	91	.293	.345	96	.207	-4	-35	-58	5	-6.0

● **GARY GENTRY**   Gentry, Gary Edward   b: 10/6/46, Phoenix, Ariz.   BR/TR, 6', 183 lbs.   Deb: 4/10/69

YEAR	TM/L	W	L	PCT	G	GS	CG	SH	SV	IP	H	HR	BB	SO	RAT	ERA	ERA+	OAV	OOB	BH	AVG	PB	PR	/A	PD	TPI
1969	*NY-N	13	12	.520	35	35	6	3	0	233²	192	24	81	154	10.7	3.43	107	.222	.293	6	.081	-4	4	6	1	0.3
1970	NY-N	9	9	.500	32	29	5	2	1	188¹	155	19	86	134	11.9	3.68	109	.224	.318	4	.068	-2	8	7	-2	0.2
1971	NY-N	12	11	.522	32	31	8	3	0	203¹	167	16	82	155	11.3	3.23	105	.224	.305	5	.074	-5	5	4	-1	-0.2
1972	NY-N	7	10	.412	32	26	3	0	0	164	153	20	75	120	12.8	4.01	84	.250	.338	5	.104	-1	-10	-12	2	-1.1
1973	Atl-N	4	6	.400	16	14	3	0	1	86²	74	7	35	42	11.4	3.43	115	.231	.308	7	.233	1	2	5	-1	0.5
1974	Atl-N	0	0	—	3	1	0	0	0	6²	4	1	2	0	9.5	1.35	280	.167	.259	0	—	-0	2	2	-0	0.2
1975	Atl-N	1	1	.500	7	2	0	0	0	20	25	3	8	10	14.8	4.95	76	.313	.375	0	.000	-1	-3	-3	0	-0.3
Total 7		46	49	.484	157	138	25	8	2	902²	770	90	369	615	11.6	3.56	103	.231	.312	27	.095	-12	8	9	-1	-0.6

● **RUFE GENTRY**   Gentry, James Ruffus   b: 5/18/18, Daisy Station, N.C.   BR/TR, 6'1", 180 lbs.   Deb: 9/10/43 F

YEAR	TM/L	W	L	PCT	G	GS	CG	SH	SV	IP	H	HR	BB	SO	RAT	ERA	ERA+	OAV	OOB	BH	AVG	PB	PR	/A	PD	TPI
1943	Det-A	1	3	.250	4	4	2	0	0	29²	30	2	12	8	13.5	3.68	96	.268	.349	0	.000	-1	-1	-1	-0	-0.2
1944	Det-A	12	14	.462	37	30	10	3	0	203²	211	9	108	68	14.3	4.24	84	.273	.365	15	.197	-1	-18	-15	1	-1.8
1946	Det-A	0	0	—	2	0	0	0	0	3	4	0	7	1	33.0	15.00	24	.333	.579	0	—	-0	-4	-4	0	0.0
1947	Det-A	0	0	—	1	0	0	0	0	0¹	1	0	2	0	81.0	81.00	5	.500	.750	0	—	-0	-3	-3	0	0.0
1948	Det-A	0	0	—	4	0	0	0	0	6²	5	0	5	1	14.9	2.70	162	.208	.367	1	1.000	1	1	0	-0	0.0
Total 5		13	17	.433	48	34	12	3	0	243	251	11	134	78	14.5	4.37	82	.272	.368	16	.184	-1	-25	-21	0	-2.0

● **CHRIS GEORGE**   George, Christopher Sean   b: 9/24/66, Pittsburgh, Pa.   BR/TR, 6'2", 200 lbs.   Deb: 10/1/91

YEAR	TM/L	W	L	PCT	G	GS	CG	SH	SV	IP	H	HR	BB	SO	RAT	ERA	ERA+	OAV	OOB	BH	AVG	PB	PR	/A	PD	TPI
1991	Mil-A	0	0	—	2	1	0	0	0	6	8	0	2	2	12.0	3.00	132	.333	.333	0	—	0	1	1	-0	0.1

● **LEFTY GEORGE**   George, Thomas Edward   b: 8/13/1886, Pittsburgh, Pa.   d: 5/13/55, York, Pa.   BL/TL, 6', 155 lbs.   Deb: 4/14/11

YEAR	TM/L	W	L	PCT	G	GS	CG	SH	SV	IP	H	HR	BB	SO	RAT	ERA	ERA+	OAV	OOB	BH	AVG	PB	PR	/A	PD	TPI
1911	StL-A	4	9	.308	27	13	6	1	0	116¹	136	3	51	23	15.2	4.18	81	.256	.332	5	.114	-3	-11	-10	-1	-1.4
1912	Cle-A	0	5	.000	11	5	2	0	0	44¹	69	1	18	18	18.1	4.87	70	.373	.434	3	.214	1	-8	-7	0	-0.6
1915	Cin-N	2	2	.500	9	3	1	0	0	28	24	1	7	14	9.6	3.86	74	.242	.330	4	.333	-2	-3	-1	0	0.2
1918	Bos-N	1	5	.167	5	5	3	0	0	54¹	56	0	22	22	13.3	2.32	116	.281	.359	2	.091	-2	3	0	-2	0.3
Total 4		7	21	.250	52	26	14	2	0	243	285	5	98	77	14.9	3.85	82	.281	.355	14	.152	-2	-19	-19	-1	-1.9

● **BILL GEORGE**   George, William M.   b: 1/27/1865, Bellaire, Ohio   d: 8/23/16, Wheeling, W.Va.   BR/TL, 5'8", 165 lbs.   Deb: 5/11/1887 ♦

YEAR	TM/L	W	L	PCT	G	GS	CG	SH	SV	IP	H	HR	BB	SO	RAT	ERA	ERA+	OAV	OOB	BH	AVG	PB	PR	/A	PD	TPI
1887	NY-N	3	9	.250	13	13	11	0	0	108	126	4	89	49	19.1	5.25	72	.292	.428	9	.170	-4	-14	-18	2	-1.6

YEAR	TM/L	W	L	PCT	G	GS	CG	SH	SV	IP	H	HR	BB	SO	RAT	ERA	ERA+	OAV	OOB	BH	AVG	PB	PR	/A	PD	TPI
1888	*NY-N	2	1	.667	4	3	3	1	0	33²	18	0	11	26	8.0	1.34	205	.149	.226	9	.231	1	6	5	-0	0.5
1889	Col-a	0	0	—	2	0	0	0	0	8	11	1	3	3	15.8	7.88	46	.317	.371	4	.235	-0	-4	-4	0	-0.3
Total	3	5	10	.333	19	16	14	1	0	149²	155	2	103	78	16.4	4.51	78	.264	.387	26	.210	-3	-12	-16	2	-1.1

● OSCAR GEORGY
Georgy, Oscar John   b: 11/25/16, New Orleans, La.   BR/TR, 6'3.5", 180 lbs.   Deb: 6/4/38

YEAR	TM/L	W	L	PCT	G	GS	CG	SH	SV	IP	H	HR	BB	SO	RAT	ERA	ERA+	OAV	OOB	BH	AVG	PB	PR	/A	PD	TPI
1938	NY-N	0	0	—	1	0	0	0	0	1	2	0	1	0	27.0	18.00	21	.400	.500	0	—	0	-2	-2	-0	0.0

● DAVE GERARD
Gerard, David Frederick   b: 8/6/36, New York, N.Y.   BR/TR, 6'2", 205 lbs.   Deb: 4/10/62

YEAR	TM/L	W	L	PCT	G	GS	CG	SH	SV	IP	H	HR	BB	SO	RAT	ERA	ERA+	OAV	OOB	BH	AVG	PB	PR	/A	PD	TPI
1962	Chi-N	2	3	.400	39	0	0	0	3	58²	67	10	28	30	14.7	4.91	84	.289	.368	3	.375	1	-6	-5	-0	-0.4

● GEORGE GERBERMAN
Gerberman, George Alois   b: 3/8/42, ElCampo, Tex.   BR/TR, 6', 180 lbs.   Deb: 9/23/62

YEAR	TM/L	W	L	PCT	G	GS	CG	SH	SV	IP	H	HR	BB	SO	RAT	ERA	ERA+	OAV	OOB	BH	AVG	PB	PR	/A	PD	TPI
1962	Chi-N	0	0	—	1	1	0	0	0	5¹	3	1	5	1	13.5	1.69	246	.158	.333	0	.000	0	1	1	-0	0.0

● RUSTY GERHARDT
Gerhardt, Allen Russell   b: 8/13/50, Baltimore, Md.   BB/TL, 5'9", 175 lbs.   Deb: 7/27/74

YEAR	TM/L	W	L	PCT	G	GS	CG	SH	SV	IP	H	HR	BB	SO	RAT	ERA	ERA+	OAV	OOB	BH	AVG	PB	PR	/A	PD	TPI
1974	SD-N	2	1	.667	23	1	0	0	1	35²	44	1	17	22	15.9	7.07	50	.308	.389	1	.167	-0	-14	-14	-0	-1.2

● AL GERHEAUSER
Gerheauser, Albert "Lefty"   b: 6/24/17, St.Louis, Mo.   d: 5/28/72, Springfield, Mo.   BL/TL, 6'3", 190 lbs.   Deb: 4/24/43

YEAR	TM/L	W	L	PCT	G	GS	CG	SH	SV	IP	H	HR	BB	SO	RAT	ERA	ERA+	OAV	OOB	BH	AVG	PB	PR	/A	PD	TPI
1943	Phi-N	10	19	.345	38	31	11	2	0	215	222	10	70	92	12.3	3.60	94	.263	.321	8	.113	-3	-5	-5	-1	-1.1
1944	Phi-N	8	16	.333	30	29	10	2	0	182²	210	8	65	66	13.6	4.58	79	.285	.344	15	.231	3	-20	-20	-2	-2.1
1945	Pit-N	5	10	.333	32	14	5	0	1	140¹	170	5	54	55	14.4	3.91	101	.304	.366	12	.250	3	-2	1	2	0.5
1946	Pit-N	2	2	.500	35	3	1	0	0	81²	92	7	25	37	13.0	3.97	89	.286	.339	7	.333	2	-5	-4	1	0.1
1948	StL-A	0	3	.000	14	2	0	0	0	23¹	32	0	10	10	16.6	7.33	52	.317	.384	2	.333	1	-8	-7	-0	-0.8
Total	5	25	50	.333	149	79	27	4	1	643	726	30	224	255	13.4	4.13	88	.283	.342	44	.209	5	-40	-36	-0	-3.4

● STEVE GERKIN
Gerkin, Stephen Paul "Splinter"   b: 11/19/15, Grafton, W.Va.   d: 11/9/78, Bay Pines, Fla.   BR/TR, 6'1", 162 lbs.   Deb: 5/13/45

YEAR	TM/L	W	L	PCT	G	GS	CG	SH	SV	IP	H	HR	BB	SO	RAT	ERA	ERA+	OAV	OOB	BH	AVG	PB	PR	/A	PD	TPI
1945	Phi-A	0	12	.000	21	12	3	0	0	102	112	4	27	25	12.5	3.62	95	.285	.336	2	.059	-4	-3	-2	0	-0.6

● LES GERMAN
German, Lester Stanley   b: 6/1/1869, Baltimore, Md.   d: 6/10/34, Germantown, Md.   BR/TR, 5'8", 165 lbs.   Deb: 8/27/1890

YEAR	TM/L	W	L	PCT	G	GS	CG	SH	SV	IP	H	HR	BB	SO	RAT	ERA	ERA+	OAV	OOB	BH	AVG	PB	PR	/A	PD	TPI
1890	Bal-a	5	11	.313	17	16	15	0	0	132¹	147	2	54	37	14.6	4.83	84	.273	.353	6	.118	-2	-14	-11	-2	-1.4
1893	NY-N	8	8	.500	20	18	14	0	0	152	162	6	70	35	14.3	4.14	112	.265	.349	23	.311	2	9	9	-1	0.8
1894	NY-N	9	8	.529	23	15	10	0	1	134	178	7	66	17	17.1	5.78	91	.316	.397	17	.298	0	-7	-8	2	-0.5
1895	NY-N	7	11	.389	25	18	16	0	0	178¹	243	8	78	36	16.7	5.96	78	.320	.390	29	.261	3	-23	-26	-0	-1.7
1896	NY-N	0	0	—	1	0	0	0	0	2²	9	0	1	0	33.8	13.50	31	.540	.566	0	.000	0	-3	-3	0	0.0
	Was-N	2	20	.091	28	20	14	0	1	166²	240	6	74	20	17.2	6.32	70	.334	.400	16	.229	0	-36	-35	1	-3.3
	Yr	2	20	.091	29	20	14	0	1	169¹	249	6	75	20	17.5	6.43	68	.339	.404	16	.225	-0	-39	-38	1	-3.3
1897	Was-N	3	5	.375	15	5	4	0	0	83²	117	2	33	2	16.9	5.59	78	.328	.395	15	.341	2	-12	-12	-1	-0.7
Total	6	34	63	.351	129	92	73	0	2	849²	1096	30	376	147	16.2	5.49	83	.307	.382	106	.260	5	-86	-86	-0	-6.8

● ED GERNER
Gerner, Edwin Frederick "Lefty"   b: 7/22/1897, Philadelphia, Pa.   d: 5/15/70, Philadelphia, Pa.   BL/TL, 5'8.5", 175 lbs.   Deb: 5/14/19

YEAR	TM/L	W	L	PCT	G	GS	CG	SH	SV	IP	H	HR	BB	SO	RAT	ERA	ERA+	OAV	OOB	BH	AVG	PB	PR	/A	PD	TPI
1919	Cin-N	1	0	1.000	5	1	0	0	0	17	22	0	3	2	14.3	3.18	87	.333	.380	1	.167	0	-0	-1	0	-0.1

● LEFTY GERVAIS
Gervais, Lucien Edward   b: 7/6/1890, Grover, Wis.   d: 10/19/50, Los Angeles, Cal.   BL/TL, 5'10", 165 lbs.   Deb: 4/17/13

YEAR	TM/L	W	L	PCT	G	GS	CG	SH	SV	IP	H	HR	BB	SO	RAT	ERA	ERA+	OAV	OOB	BH	AVG	PB	PR	/A	PD	TPI
1913	Bos-N	0	1	.000	5	2	1	0	0	15²	18	0	4	1	12.6	5.74	57	.383	.431	0	.000	-0	-4	-4	-0	-0.3

● CHARLIE GESSNER
Gessner, Charles J.   b: Philadelphia, Pa.   Deb: 7/19/1886

YEAR	TM/L	W	L	PCT	G	GS	CG	SH	SV	IP	H	HR	BB	SO	RAT	ERA	ERA+	OAV	OOB	BH	AVG	PB	PR	/A	PD	TPI
1886	Phi-a	0	1	.000	1	1	1	0	0	8	13	0	5	0	22.5	9.00	39	.351	.455	1	.250	-0	-5	-5	-0	-0.4

● AL GETTEL
Gettel, Allen Jones   b: 9/17/17, Norfolk, Va.   BR/TR, 6'3.5", 200 lbs.   Deb: 4/20/45

YEAR	TM/L	W	L	PCT	G	GS	CG	SH	SV	IP	H	HR	BB	SO	RAT	ERA	ERA+	OAV	OOB	BH	AVG	PB	PR	/A	PD	TPI
1945	NY-A	9	8	.529	27	17	9	0	3	154²	141	11	53	67	11.7	3.90	89	.243	.314	16	.281	2	-9	-7	-1	-0.8
1946	NY-A	6	7	.462	26	11	5	2	0	103	89	6	40	54	11.4	2.97	116	.229	.305	4	.125	-2	6	5	0	0.5
1947	Cle-A	11	10	.524	31	21	9	0	0	149	122	12	62	64	11.3	3.20	109	.229	.313	15	.294	4	8	5	1	1.1
1948	Cle-A	0	1	.000	5	2	0	0	0	7²	15	2	10	4	30.5	17.61	23	.385	.520	0	.000	-0	-11	-12	-0	-1.2
	Chi-A	8	10	.444	22	19	7	0	1	148	154	7	60	49	13.3	4.01	106	.268	.342	13	.241	0	5	4	-1	0.4
	Yr	8	11	.421	27	21	7	0	1	155²	169	9	70	53	14.0	4.68	91	.275	.353	13	.228	-0	-7	-7	-1	-0.8
1949	Chi-A	2	5	.286	19	7	1	1	1	63	69	12	26	22	13.9	6.43	65	.283	.357	3	.167	-0	-16	-16	-1	-1.6
	Was-A	0	2	.000	16	1	0	0	1	34²	43	4	24	7	17.4	5.45	78	.314	.416	0	.000	-1	-5	-5	1	-0.3
	Yr	2	7	.222	35	8	1	1	2	97²	112	16	50	29	14.9	6.08	69	.292	.374	3	.115	-1	-20	-20	-0	-1.9
1951	NY-N	1	2	.333	30	1	0	0	0	57¹	52	12	25	36	12.1	4.87	80	.240	.318	1	.083	-1	-6	-6	1	-0.3
1955	StL-N	1	0	1.000	8	0	0	0	0	17	26	6	7	7	19.1	9.00	45	.361	.439	3	.500	1	-9	-9	-1	-0.4
Total	7	38	45	.458	184	79	31	5	6	734¹	711	72	310	310	12.7	4.28	88	.255	.334	55	.228	3	-37	-40	-1	-2.6

● CHARLIE GETTIG
Gettig, Charles Henry   b: 12/1870, Baltimore, Md.   d: 4/11/35, Baltimore, Md.   BR, 5'10", 172 lbs.   Deb: 8/5/1896   ◆

YEAR	TM/L	W	L	PCT	G	GS	CG	SH	SV	IP	H	HR	BB	SO	RAT	ERA	ERA+	OAV	OOB	BH	AVG	PB	PR	/A	PD	TPI
1896	NY-N	1	0	1.000	4	1	1	0	1	14	20	0	8	5	19.3	9.64	44	.332	.427	3	.333	1	-8	-8	0	-0.5
1897	NY-N	1	1	.500	3	2	2	0	0	19	23	0	9	7	16.1	5.21	80	.297	.384	15	.200	-0	-2	-2	0	-0.2
1898	NY-N	6	3	.667	17	8	7	0	0	115	141	1	39	14	14.7	3.83	91	.299	.363	49	.250	2	-3	-5	1	0.0
1899	NY-N	7	8	.467	18	15	12	0	0	128	161	3	54	25	15.4	4.43	85	.307	.376	24	.247	1	-8	-10	-1	-0.8
Total	4	15	12	.556	42	26	22	0	1	276	345	4	110	51	15.4	4.50	82	.304	.374	91	.241	4	-21	-25	1	-1.5

● TOM GETTINGER
Gettinger, Lewis Thomas Leyton (b: Lewis Thomas Leyton Gittinger)
b: 12/11/1868, Frederick, Md.   d: 7/26/43, Pensacola, Fla.   BL/TL, 5'10", 180 lbs.   Deb: 9/21/1889   ◆

YEAR	TM/L	W	L	PCT	G	GS	CG	SH	SV	IP	H	HR	BB	SO	RAT	ERA	ERA+	OAV	OOB	BH	AVG	PB	PR	/A	PD	TPI
1895	Lou-N	0	0	—	2	0	0	0	0	6¹	13	1	9	1	19.9	7.11	65	.415	.433	70	.269	0	-2	-2	0	0.0

● CHARLIE GETZIEN
Getzien, Charles H. "Pretzels"   b: 2/14/1864, Germany   d: 6/19/32, Chicago, Ill.   BR/TR, 5'10", 172 lbs.   Deb: 8/13/1884

YEAR	TM/L	W	L	PCT	G	GS	CG	SH	SV	IP	H	HR	BB	SO	RAT	ERA	ERA+	OAV	OOB	BH	AVG	PB	PR	/A	PD	TPI
1884	Det-N	5	12	.294	17	17	17	1	0	147¹	118	2	25	107	8.7	1.95	148	.204	.237	6	.109	-4	17	15	-2	1.0
1885	Det-N	12	25	.324	37	37	37	1	0	330	360	8	92	110	12.3	3.03	94	.264	.311	29	.212	-1	-8	-7	-2	-0.9
1886	Det-N	30	11	.732	43	43	42	1	0	386²	388	6	85	172	11.0	3.03	110	.250	.288	29	.176	-3	12	12	-2	0.4
1887	*Det-N	29	13	**.690**	43	42	41	2	0	366²	373	24	106	135	11.8	3.73	109	.254	.305	29	.186	-2	14	13	0	0.8
1888	Det-N	19	25	.432	46	46	45	3	0	404	411	13	54	202	10.5	3.05	91	.251	.279	41	.246	10	-9	-13	-2	-0.6
1889	Ind-N	18	22	.450	45	44	36	0	1	349	395	27	100	139	13.0	4.54	92	.277	.328	25	.180	2	-20	-14	-3	-1.3
1890	Bos-N	23	17	.575	40	40	39	4	0	350	342	5	82	140	11.0	3.19	118	.248	.292	34	.231	5	15	22	-2	2.2
1891	Bos-N	4	5	.444	11	9	7	0	0	89	112	4	23	29	13.7	3.84	95	.296	.337	7	.171	1	-5	-2	1	0.0
	Cle-N	0	1	.000	1	1	1	0	0	9	12	1	4	4	16.0	8.00	43	.308	.373	0	.000	-1	-5	-5	-1	-0.4
	Yr	4	6	.400	12	10	8	0	0	98	124	5	27	33	13.9	4.22	86	.297	.340	7	.156	0	-10	-6	0	-0.4
1892	StL-N	5	8	.385	13	13	12	0	0	108	159	5	31	32	16.3	5.67	56	.329	.377	9	.200	0	-29	-30	-1	-2.7
Total	9	145	139	.511	296	292	277	11	1	2539²	2670	95	602	1070	11.7	3.46	99	.259	.302	209	.198	8	-17	-9	-13	-1.5

● RUBE GEYER
Geyer, Jacob Bowman   b: 3/26/1884, Allegheny, Pa.   d: 10/12/62, Ford Township, Minn.   BR/TR, 5'10", 170 lbs.   Deb: 4/24/10

YEAR	TM/L	W	L	PCT	G	GS	CG	SH	SV	IP	H	HR	BB	SO	RAT	ERA	ERA+	OAV	OOB	BH	AVG	PB	PR	/A	PD	TPI
1910	StL-N	0	1	.000	4	0	0	0	0	4	5	0	3	5	18.0	4.50	66	.294	.400	0	.000	-0	-1	-1	-0	-0.2
1911	StL-N	9	6	.600	29	11	7	1	0	148²	141	7	56	46	12.3	3.27	103	.259	.335	13	.228	1	2	2	-0	0.1
1912	StL-N	7	14	.333	41	18	5	0	0	181	191	4	84	61	13.9	3.28	104	.288	.371	11	.208	-0	3	3	0	0.3
1913	StL-N	1	5	.167	30	4	2	0	1	78²	83	6	38	21	14.1	5.26	61	.282	.368	2	.091	-2	-18	-18	-1	-1.5
Total	4	17	26	.395	104	33	14	1	1	412¹	420	17	181	133	13.4	3.67	92	.276	.358	26	.195	-1	-14	-14	-2	-1.3

● TONY GHELFI
Ghelfi, Anthony Paul   b: 8/23/61, LaCrosse, Wis.   BR/TR, 6'3", 185 lbs.   Deb: 9/1/83

YEAR	TM/L	W	L	PCT	G	GS	CG	SH	SV	IP	H	HR	BB	SO	RAT	ERA	ERA+	OAV	OOB	BH	AVG	PB	PR	/A	PD	TPI
1983	Phi-N	1	1	.500	3	3	0	0	0	14¹	15	2	6	14	13.2	3.14	114	.268	.339	1	.250	0	1	1	1	0.2

YEAR	TM/L	W	L	PCT	G	GS	CG	SH	SV	IP	H	HR	BB	SO	RAT	ERA	ERA+	OAV	OOB	BH	AVG	PB	PR	/A	PD	TPI

● BOB GIALLOMBARDO   Giallombardo, Robert Paul b: 5/20/37, Brooklyn, N.Y. BL/TL, 6′, 175 lbs. Deb: 6/21/58

| 1958 | LA-N | 1 | 1 | .500 | 6 | 5 | 0 | 0 | 0 | 26¹ | 29 | 3 | 15 | 14 | 15.0 | 3.76 | 109 | .284 | .376 | 1 | .167 | -0 | 1 | 1 | 0 | 0.1 |

● JOE GIARD   Giard, Joseph Oscar "Peco" b: 10/7/1898, Ware, Mass. d: 7/10/56, Worcester, Mass. BL/TL, 5′10.5″, 170 lbs. Deb: 4/18/25

1925	StL-A	10	5	.667	30	21	9	4	0	160²	179	13	87	43	15.2	5.04	93	.295	.388	3	.057	-6	-12	-7	2	-0.9
1926	StL-A	3	10	.231	22	15	2	0	0	90	113	7	67	18	18.1	7.00	61	.318	.428	8	.276	0	-30	-27	-1	-3.2
1927	NY-A	0	0	—	16	0	0	0	0	27	38	1	19	10	19.0	8.00	48	.352	.449	2	.286	0	-12	-12	-0	0.0
Total	3	13	15	.464	68	36	11	4	0	277²	330	21	173	71	16.5	5.96	66	.309	.408	13	.146	-6	-53	-46	1	-4.1

● JOE GIBBON   Gibbon, Joseph Charles b: 4/10/35, Hickory, Miss. BR/TL, 6′4″, 210 lbs. Deb: 4/17/60

1960	*Pit-N	4	2	.667	27	9	0	0	0	80¹	87	5	31	60	13.2	4.03	93	.277	.342	4	.211	1	-2	-3	0	-0.1
1961	Pit-N	13	10	.565	30	29	7	3	0	195¹	185	16	57	145	11.3	3.32	120	.251	.309	8	.136	-2	16	15	-0	1.4
1962	Pit-N	3	4	.429	19	8	0	0	0	57	53	4	24	26	12.2	3.63	108	.250	.326	3	.176	-0	2	2	1	0.3
1963	Pit-N	5	12	.294	37	22	5	0	1	147¹	147	7	54	110	12.6	3.30	100	.258	.328	4	.093	-2	-0	-1	-1	-0.1
1964	Pit-N	10	7	.588	28	24	3	0	0	146²	145	10	54	97	12.6	3.68	95	.262	.334	12	.255	-2	-2	-3	1	0.1
1965	Pit-N	4	9	.308	31	15	1	0	1	105²	85	7	34	63	10.5	4.51	78	.221	.291	3	.115	-0	-11	-12	0	-1.4
1966	SF-N	4	6	.400	37	10	1	0	1	81	86	4	16	48	11.6	3.67	100	.275	.314	3	.200	-0	-1	0	1	0.2
1967	SF-N	6	2	.750	28	10	3	1	1	82	65	4	33	63	11.1	3.07	107	.220	.305	1	.042	-0	3	2	0	0.3
1968	SF-N	1	2	.333	29	0	0	0	1	40	33	3	19	22	12.1	1.57	187	.234	.333	0	.000	-0	6	6	0	0.5
1969	SF-N	1	3	.250	16	0	0	0	2	20	15	1	13	9	13.0	3.60	97	.211	.341	0	.000	-0	-0	-1	0	-0.2
	Pit-N	5	1	.833	35	0	0	0	9	51¹	38	5	17	35	10.0	1.93	181	.208	.282	0	.000	-1	9	9	1	1.4
	Yr	6	4	.600	51	0	0	0	11	71¹	53	6	30	44	10.7	2.40	146	.208	.296	0	.000	-1	9	9	2	1.4
1970	*Pit-N	0	1	.000	41	0	0	0	5	41	44	2	24	26	15.4	4.83	81	.280	.383	0	—	-0	-4	-4	0	-0.2
1971	Cin-N	5	6	.455	50	0	0	0	11	64¹	54	3	32	34	12.2	2.94	114	.239	.336	0	.000	-0	3	1	0	0.7
1972	Cin-N	0	0	—	2	0	0	0	0	0¹	3	1	1	1	108.0	54.00	6	.750	.800	0	—	-0	-2	-2	0	0.0
	Hou-N	0	0	—	9	0	0	0	0	7¹	13	2	5	4	23.3	9.82	34	.394	.487	0	—	-0	-5	-5	1	0.1
	Yr	0	0	—	11	0	0	0	0	7²	16	3	6	5	27.0	11.74	29	.432	.523	0	—	-0	-7	-7	1	0.1
Total	13	61	65	.484	419	127	20	4	32	1119²	1053	74	414	743	12.1	3.52	102	.251	.323	38	.144	-3	12	8	11	3.2

● NORWOOD GIBSON   Gibson, Norwood Ringold "Gibby" b: 3/11/1877, Peoria, Ill. d: 7/7/59, Peoria, Ill. BR/TR, 5′10″, 165 lbs. Deb: 4/29/03

1903	Bos-A	13	9	.591	24	21	17	2	0	183¹	166	2	65	76	11.7	3.19	95	.241	.313	17	.266	-5	-3	-0	2	0.1
1904	Bos-A	17	14	.548	33	32	29	1	0	273	216	8	81	112	9.9	2.21	121	.219	.280	6	.065	-6	12	14	-3	0.6
1905	Bos-A	4	7	.364	23	17	9	0	0	134	118	9	55	67	12.0	3.69	73	.238	.320	4	.095	-2	-15	-15	-2	-1.6
1906	Bos-A	0	2	.000	5	2	1	0	0	18²	25	2	7	3	15.4	5.30	52	.324	.380	1	.200	-0	-5	-5	-0	-0.5
Total	4	34	32	.515	85	72	56	3	0	609	525	21	208	258	11.1	2.93	95	.233	.303	28	.138	-4	-14	-9	-5	-1.4

● PAUL GIBSON   Gibson, Paul Marshall b: 1/4/60, Southampton, N.Y. BR/TL, 6′, 165 lbs. Deb: 4/8/88

1988	Det-A	4	2	.667	40	1	0	0	0	92	83	6	34	50	11.6	2.93	130	.240	.312	0	—	0	11	9	0	0.7
1989	Det-A	4	8	.333	45	13	0	0	0	132	129	11	57	77	13.1	4.64	82	.259	.342	0	—	0	-11	-12	-0	-1.0
1990	Det-A	5	4	.556	61	0	0	0	3	97¹	99	10	44	56	13.3	3.05	130	.269	.349	0	—	0	9	10	0	0.9
1991	Det-A	5	7	.417	68	0	0	0	8	96	112	10	48	52	15.3	4.59	90	.297	.381	0	—	0	-5	-5	-0	-0.7
1992	NY-N	0	1	.000	43	1	0	0	0	62	70	7	25	49	13.8	5.23	66	.287	.353	0	.000	-0	-12	-12	-1	-0.3
1993	NY-N	1	1	.500	8	0	0	0	0	8²	14	1	2	12	16.6	5.19	77	.350	.381	0	—	0	-1	-1	-0	-0.2
	NY-A	2	0	1.000	20	0	0	0	0	35¹	31	4	9	25	10.2	3.06	136	.238	.288	0	—	0	5	4	0	0.4
1994	NY-A	1	1	.500	30	0	0	0	0	29	26	5	17	21	13.7	4.97	89	.236	.344	0	—	0	-1	-2	0	0.2
Total	7	22	24	.478	315	15	0	0	11	552¹	564	54	236	342	13.2	4.06	97	.267	.344	0	.000	-0	-5	-8	-1	-0.0

● BOB GIBSON   Gibson, Robert (b: Pack Robert Gibson) b: 11/9/35, Omaha, Neb. BR/TR, 6′1.5″, 195 lbs. Deb: 4/15/59 CH

1959	StL-N	3	5	.375	13	9	2	1	0	75²	77	4	39	48	13.9	3.33	127	.273	.363	3	.115	-1	5	8	-0	0.7
1960	StL-N	3	6	.333	27	12	2	0	0	86²	97	7	48	69	15.2	5.61	73	.284	.374	5	.179	-0	-18	-15	1	-1.3
1961	StL-N	13	12	.520	35	27	10	2	1	211¹	186	13	119	166	13.2	3.24	136	.239	.344	13	.197	-2	19	27	1	3.3
1962	StL-N★	15	13	.536	32	30	15	**5**	1	233²	174	15	95	208	10.7	2.85	**150**	.204	.291	20	.263	6	28	37	1	**5.0**
1963	StL-N	18	9	.667	36	33	14	2	0	254²	224	19	96	204	11.8	3.39	105	.233	.311	18	.207	7	-3	4	-2	1.0
1964	*StL-N	19	12	.613	40	36	17	2	1	287¹	250	25	86	245	10.8	3.01	127	.232	.294	15	.156	1	17	26	-1	2.7
1965	StL-N★	20	12	.625	38	36	20	6	1	299	243	34	103	270	10.7	3.07	125	.222	.295	25	.240	8	16	26	-2	3.6
1966	StL-N†	21	12	.636	35	35	20	**5**	0	280¹	210	20	78	225	9.4	2.44	147	.207	.267	20	.200	8	36	36	-1	4.4
1967	*StL-N★	13	7	.650	24	24	10	2	0	175¹	151	10	40	147	10.0	2.98	130	.231	.278	8	.133	1	8	7	0	0.8
1968	*StL-N☆	22	9	.710	34	34	28	**13**	0	304²	198	11	62	**268**	**7.9**	**1.12**	**258**	**.184**	**.233**	16	.170	4	**63**	**60**	-3	**7.3**
1969	StL-N★	20	13	.606	35	35	**28**	4	0	314	251	12	95	269	10.2	2.18	164	.219	.285	29	.246	5	49	49	-2	**6.0**
1970	StL-N★	**23**	7	**.767**	34	34	23	3	0	294	262	13	88	274	10.8	3.12	132	.237	.296	33	.303	12	30	32	-1	4.2
1971	StL-N	16	13	.552	31	31	20	**5**	0	245²	215	14	76	185	10.9	3.04	118	.232	.296	15	.172	2	12	15	0	2.1
1972	StL-N★	19	11	.633	34	34	23	4	0	278	226	14	88	208	10.3	2.46	138	.224	.288	20	.194	7	31	29	2	4.2
1973	StL-N	12	10	.545	25	25	13	1	0	195	159	24	57	142	10.1	2.77	132	.224	.284	12	.185	2	19	19	-1	2.3
1974	StL-N	11	13	.458	33	33	9	1	0	240	236	24	104	129	12.9	3.83	93	.259	.338	17	.203	3	-6	-7	-1	-0.6
1975	StL-N	3	10	.231	22	14	1	0	2	109	120	10	62	60	15.4	5.04	75	.287	.384	5	.179	-0	-17	-16	-0	-1.7
Total	17	251	174	.591	528	482	255	56	6	3884²	3279	257	1336	3117	10.9	2.91	127	.228	.299	274	.206	65	290	335	-10	44.0

● BOB GIBSON   Gibson, Robert Louis b: 6/19/57, Philadelphia, Pa. BR/TR, 6′, 195 lbs. Deb: 4/13/83

1983	Mil-A	3	4	.429	27	7	0	0	0	80²	71	6	46	46	13.2	3.90	96	.237	.340	0	—	0	1	-2	-1	0.2
1984	Mil-A	2	5	.286	18	9	1	1	0	69	61	10	47	54	14.1	4.96	78	.236	.354	0	—	0	-7	-9	-0	-0.4
1985	Mil-A	6	7	.462	41	1	0	0	11	92¹	86	10	49	53	13.3	3.90	107	.260	.357	0	—	0	3	3	-0	0.4
1986	Mil-A	1	2	.333	11	1	0	0	0	26²	23	3	23	11	15.5	4.73	92	.232	.377	0	—	0	-2	-1	-0	-0.3
1987	NY-N	0	0	—	1	0	0	0	0	1	0	1	1	2	9.0	0.00	—	.000	.250	0	—	0	0	0	0	0.0
Total	5	12	18	.400	98	18	1	1	13	269²	241	29	166	166	13.7	4.24	94	.243	.353	0	—	0	-5	-8	-1	-0.1

● ROBERT GIBSON   Gibson, Robert Murray b: 8/20/1869, Duncansville, Pa. d: 12/19/49, Pittsburgh, Pa. BR/TR, 6′3″, 185 lbs. Deb: 6/4/1890

1890	Chi-N	1	0	1.000	1	1	1	0	0	9	6	0	2	1	8.0	8.00	—	.184	.231	0	.000	-0	4	4	0	0.4
	Pit-N	0	3	.000	3	3	2	0	0	12	24	0	23	3	37.5	17.25	19	.403	.584	3	.231	-0	-18	-19	-1	-2.5
	Yr	1	3	.250	4	4	3	0	0	21	30	0	25	4	24.9	9.86	35	.325	.483	3	.176	-1	-15	-15	-0	-2.1

● SAM GIBSON   Gibson, Samuel Braxton b: 8/5/1899, King, N.C. d: 1/31/83, High Point, N.C. BL/TR, 6′2″, 198 lbs. Deb: 4/19/26

1926	Det-A	12	9	.571	35	24	16	2	2	196¹	199	6	75	61	12.8	3.48	117	.269	.341	18	.250	2	12	13	0	1.4
1927	Det-A	11	12	.478	33	26	11	0	0	184²	201	9	86	76	14.4	3.80	111	.285	.369	14	.212	-1	-8	-8	-1	0.6
1928	Det-A	5	8	.385	20	18	5	1	0	119²	155	6	53	29	16.2	5.42	76	.322	.397	12	.286	2	-18	-17	-1	-1.5
1930	NY-A	0	1	.000	2	2	0	0	0	6	14	1	6	3	30.0	15.00	29	.424	.513	1	.333	0	-7	-7	-0	-0.8
1932	NY-N	4	8	.333	41	5	1	1	3	81²	107	7	30	39	15.3	4.85	77	.322	.382	5	.263	-0	-9	-10	-1	-1.4
Total	5	32	38	.457	131	75	33	4	5	588¹	676	27	250	208	14.5	4.28	95	.295	.370	50	.248	3	-15	-14	-3	-1.7

● GEORGE GICK   Gick, George Edward b: 10/18/15, Dunnington, Ind. BB/TR, 6′, 190 lbs. Deb: 10/3/37

1937	Chi-A	0	0	—	1	0	0	0	0	2	1	0	1	1	9.0	0.00	—	.000	.000	0	—	0	1	1	-0	0.1
1938	Chi-A	0	0	—	1	0	0	0	1	1	0	0	1	1	9.0	0.00	—	.000	.250	0	—	0	1	1	0	0.1
Total	2	0	0	—	2	0	0	0	1	3	1	0	2	2	9.0	0.00	—	.000	.100	0	—	0	2	2	-0	0.1

● BRETT GIDEON   Gideon, Byron Brett b: 8/8/63, Ozona, Tex. BR/TR, 6′2″, 200 lbs. Deb: 7/5/87

| 1987 | Pit-N | 1 | 5 | .167 | 29 | 0 | 0 | 0 | 3 | 36² | 34 | 6 | 10 | 31 | 11.0 | 4.66 | 88 | .243 | .298 | 1 | 1.000 | 1 | -2 | -2 | -0 | -0.3 |

YEAR	TM/L	W	L	PCT	G	GS	CG	SH	SV	IP	H	HR	BB	SO	RAT	ERA	ERA+	OAV	OOB	BH	AVG	PB	PR	/A	PD	TPI
1989	Mon-N	0	0	—	4	0	0	0	0	4²	5	1	5	2	19.3	1.93	183	.294	.455	0	—	0	1	1	-0	0.0
1990	Mon-N	0	0	—	1	0	0	0	0	1	2	0	4	0	54.0	9.00	41	.500	.750	0	—	0	-1	-1	0	0.0
Total	3	1	5	.167	34	0	0	0	3	42¹	41	7	19	33	13.0	4.46	90	.255	.337	1	1.000	1	-2	-2	-0	-0.3

● **JIM GIDEON**   Gideon, James Leslie   b: 9/26/53, Taylor, Tex.   BR/TR, 6'3", 190 lbs.   Deb: 9/14/75

YEAR	TM/L	W	L	PCT	G	GS	CG	SH	SV	IP	H	HR	BB	SO	RAT	ERA	ERA+	OAV	OOB	BH	AVG	PB	PR	/A	PD	TPI
1975	Tex-A	0	0	—	1	1	0	0	0	5²	7	1	5	2	19.1	7.94	47	.292	.414	0	—	0	-3	-3	-0	0.0

● **FLOYD GIEBELL**   Giebell, Floyd George   b: 12/10/09, Pennsboro, W.Va.   BL/TR, 6'2.5", 172 lbs.   Deb: 4/21/39

YEAR	TM/L	W	L	PCT	G	GS	CG	SH	SV	IP	H	HR	BB	SO	RAT	ERA	ERA+	OAV	OOB	BH	AVG	PB	PR	/A	PD	TPI
1939	Det-A	1	1	.500	9	0	0	0	0	15¹	19	1	12	9	18.2	2.93	167	.317	.431	0	.000	-0	3	3	-0	0.3
1940	Det-A	2	0	1.000	2	2	2	1	0	18	14	2	4	11	9.0	1.00	476	.206	.250	0	.000	-1	7	8	-0	0.7
1941	Det-A	0	0	—	17	2	0	0	0	34¹	45	3	26	10	18.6	6.03	75	.313	.418	2	.333	0	-7	-6	-0	0.0
Total	3	3	1	.750	28	4	2	2	0	67²	78	6	42	30	16.0	3.99	117	.287	.382	2	.143	-1	2	5	-1	1.0

● **PAUL GIEL**   Giel, Paul Robert   b: 2/29/32, Winona, Minn.   BR/TR, 5'11", 185 lbs.   Deb: 7/10/54

YEAR	TM/L	W	L	PCT	G	GS	CG	SH	SV	IP	H	HR	BB	SO	RAT	ERA	ERA+	OAV	OOB	BH	AVG	PB	PR	/A	PD	TPI
1954	NY-N	0	0	—	6	0	0	0	0	4¹	8	0	2	4	20.8	8.31	49	.421	.476	0	—	0	-2	-2	-0	0.0
1955	NY-N	4	4	.500	34	2	0	0	0	82¹	70	8	50	47	13.3	3.39	119	.233	.346	1	.053	-2	6	6	-1	0.3
1958	SF-N	4	5	.444	29	9	0	0	0	92	89	12	55	55	14.3	4.70	81	.259	.365	2	.074	-2	-8	-9	1	-0.8
1959	Pit-N	0	0	—	4	0	0	0	0	7²	17	0	6	3	27.0	14.09	27	.472	.548	0	—	0	-9	-9	0	0.0
1960	Pit-N	2	0	1.000	16	0	0	0	0	33	35	3	15	21	13.6	5.73	65	.276	.352	0	.000	-1	-7	-7	-1	-0.5
1961	Min-A	1	0	1.000	12	0	0	0	0	19¹	24	6	17	14	19.1	9.78	43	.289	.410	1	.500	0	-12	-12	0	-0.5
	KC-A	0	0	—	1	0	0	0	0	1²	6	1	3	1	48.6	37.80	11	.600	.692	0	—	0	-6	-6	0	0.0
	Yr	1	0	1.000	13	0	0	0	0	21	30	7	20	15	21.4	12.00	35	.319	.439	1	.500	0	-19	-18	-0	-0.5
Total	6	11	9	.550	102	11	0	0	0	240¹	249	30	148	145	15.0	5.39	73	.271	.374	4	.073	-4	-38	-39	-0	-1.5

● **BOB GIGGIE**   Giggie, Robert Thomas   b: 8/13/33, Dorchester, Mass.   BR/TR, 6'1", 200 lbs.   Deb: 4/18/59

YEAR	TM/L	W	L	PCT	G	GS	CG	SH	SV	IP	H	HR	BB	SO	RAT	ERA	ERA+	OAV	OOB	BH	AVG	PB	PR	/A	PD	TPI
1959	Mil-N	1	0	1.000	13	0	0	0	1	20	24	2	10	15	15.3	4.05	87	.316	.395	0	—	-0	-0	-1	1	0.0
1960	Mil-N	0	0	—	3	0	0	0	0	4¹	5	0	4	5	18.7	4.15	83	.278	.409	0	—	-0	-0	-0	-0	0.0
	KC-A	1	0	1.000	10	0	0	0	0	18²	24	1	15	8	18.8	5.79	69	.333	.448	0	.000	-0	-4	-4	0	-0.2
1962	KC-A	1	1	.500	4	2	0	0	0	14¹	17	5	3	4	13.2	6.28	67	.293	.339	0	.000	-0	-4	-3	-1	-0.5
Total	3	3	1	.750	30	2	0	0	1	57¹	70	8	32	32	16.2	5.18	74	.313	.401	0	.000	-1	-8	-8	0	-0.7

● **JOE GILBERT**   Gilbert, Joe Dennis   b: 4/20/52, Jasper, Tex.   BR/TL, 6'1", 167 lbs.   Deb: 4/30/72

YEAR	TM/L	W	L	PCT	G	GS	CG	SH	SV	IP	H	HR	BB	SO	RAT	ERA	ERA+	OAV	OOB	BH	AVG	PB	PR	/A	PD	TPI
1972	Mon-N	0	1	.000	22	0	0	0	0	33	41	3	18	25	16.1	8.45	42	.306	.388	0	.000	-0	-18	-18	-1	-0.6
1973	Mon-N	1	2	.333	21	0	0	0	1	29	30	1	19	17	15.2	4.97	77	.270	.377	0	.000	0	-4	-4	0	-0.4
Total	2	1	3	.250	43	0	0	0	1	62	71	4	37	42	15.7	6.82	54	.290	.383	0	.000	-0	-23	-22	-0	-1.0

● **BILL GILBERT**   Gilbert, Wilmer M.   b: 5/12/1870, Havre De Grace, Md   6', 180 lbs.   Deb: 9/15/1892

YEAR	TM/L	W	L	PCT	G	GS	CG	SH	SV	IP	H	HR	BB	SO	RAT	ERA	ERA+	OAV	OOB	BH	AVG	PB	PR	/A	PD	TPI
1892	Bal-N	0	1	.000	2	1	1	0	0	14	14	1	17	5	19.9	5.79	59	.250	.425	2	.333	1	-4	-4	-1	-0.2

● **BILL GILBRETH**   Gilbreth, William Freeman   b: 9/3/47, Abilene, Tex.   BL/TL, 6', 180 lbs.   Deb: 6/25/71

YEAR	TM/L	W	L	PCT	G	GS	CG	SH	SV	IP	H	HR	BB	SO	RAT	ERA	ERA+	OAV	OOB	BH	AVG	PB	PR	/A	PD	TPI
1971	Det-A	2	1	.667	9	5	2	0	0	30	28	4	21	14	15.3	4.80	75	.264	.395	2	.182	-0	-4	-4	0	-0.4
1972	Det-A	0	0	—	2	0	0	0	0	5	10	1	4	2	25.2	16.20	19	.476	.560	0	.000	-0	-7	-7	0	0.0
1974	Cal-A	0	0	—	3	0	0	0	0	1¹	2	0	1	0	20.3	13.50	25	.400	.500	0	—	0	-1	-1	0	0.0
Total	3	2	1	.667	14	5	2	0	0	36¹	40	5	26	16	16.8	6.69	53	.303	.425	2	.167	-0	-13	-13	-0	-0.4

● **BOB GILKS**   Gilks, Robert James   b: 7/2/1864, Cincinnati, Ohio   d: 8/21/44, Brunswick, Ga.   BR/TR, 5'8", 178 lbs.   Deb: 8/25/1887   ♦

YEAR	TM/L	W	L	PCT	G	GS	CG	SH	SV	IP	H	HR	BB	SO	RAT	ERA	ERA+	OAV	OOB	BH	AVG	PB	PR	/A	PD	TPI
1887	Cle-a	7	5	.583	13	13	12	1	0	108	104	1	42	28	12.9	3.08	141	.245	.326	26	.313	2	15	15	2	1.6
1888	Cle-a	0	2	.000	4	2	2	0	1	21	26	1	8	3	15.0	8.14	38	.293	.358	111	.229	-0	-12	-12	-0	-0.9
1890	Cle-N	2	2	.500	4	3	3	0	0	31²	34	0	9	5	13.4	4.26	84	.266	.334	116	.213	-0	-2	-2	-1	-0.3
Total	3	9	9	.500	21	18	17	1	1	160²	164	2	59	36	13.3	3.98	101	.256	.332	320	.231	2	0	1	1	0.4

● **ED GILL**   Gill, Edward James   b: 8/7/1895, Somerville, Mass.   BL/TL, 5'10", 165 lbs.   Deb: 7/5/19

YEAR	TM/L	W	L	PCT	G	GS	CG	SH	SV	IP	H	HR	BB	SO	RAT	ERA	ERA+	OAV	OOB	BH	AVG	PB	PR	/A	PD	TPI
1919	Was-A	1	1	.500	16	2	0	0	0	37¹	38	0	21	7	14.7	4.82	67	.260	.361	0	.000	-1	-7	-7	-1	-0.5

● **GEORGE GILL**   Gill, George Lloyd   b: 2/13/09, Catchings, Miss.   BR/TR, 6'1", 185 lbs.   Deb: 5/4/37

YEAR	TM/L	W	L	PCT	G	GS	CG	SH	SV	IP	H	HR	BB	SO	RAT	ERA	ERA+	OAV	OOB	BH	AVG	PB	PR	/A	PD	TPI
1937	Det-A	11	4	.733	31	10	4	1	1	127²	146	11	42	40	13.3	4.51	104	.285	.340	7	.140	-3	2	2	1	0.1
1938	Det-A	12	9	.571	24	23	13	1	0	164	195	15	50	30	13.6	4.12	121	.296	.348	6	.105	-4	12	16	-1	1.3
1939	Det-A	0	1	.000	3	1	0	0	0	8²	14	1	3	1	17.7	8.31	59	.368	.415	0	.000	-0	-4	-3	-0	-0.3
	StL-A	1	12	.077	27	11	5	0	0	95	139	10	34	24	16.7	7.11	68	.343	.398	4	.154	-2	-26	-24	1	-2.6
	Yr	1	13	.071	30	12	5	0	0	103²	153	11	37	25	16.8	7.21	68	.345	.400	4	.143	-2	-30	-27	1	-2.9
Total	3	24	26	.480	85	45	22	2	1	395¹	494	37	129	95	14.3	5.05	96	.306	.360	17	.126	-9	-16	-9	2	-1.5

● **HADDIE GILL**   Gill, Harold Edward   b: 1/23/1899, Brockton, Mass.   d: 8/1/32, Brockton, Mass.   BL/TL, 5'11", 165 lbs.   Deb: 8/16/23

YEAR	TM/L	W	L	PCT	G	GS	CG	SH	SV	IP	H	HR	BB	SO	RAT	ERA	ERA+	OAV	OOB	BH	AVG	PB	PR	/A	PD	TPI
1923	Cin-N	0	0	—	1	0	0	0	0	1	1	0	1	1	18.0	0.00	—	.333	.500	0	—	0	0	0	0	0.0

● **CLARAL GILLENWATER**   Gillenwater, Claral Lewis   b: 5/20/1900, Sims, Ind.   d: 2/26/78, Bradenton, Fla.   BR/TR, 6', 187 lbs.   Deb: 8/20/23

YEAR	TM/L	W	L	PCT	G	GS	CG	SH	SV	IP	H	HR	BB	SO	RAT	ERA	ERA+	OAV	OOB	BH	AVG	PB	PR	/A	PD	TPI
1923	Chi-A	1	3	.250	5	3	1	0	0	21¹	28	2	6	2	14.8	5.48	72	.337	.389	0	.000	-1	-4	-4	0	-0.6

● **TOM GILLES**   Gilles, Thomas Bradford   b: 7/2/62, Peoria, Ill.   BR/TR, 6'1", 185 lbs.   Deb: 6/7/90

YEAR	TM/L	W	L	PCT	G	GS	CG	SH	SV	IP	H	HR	BB	SO	RAT	ERA	ERA+	OAV	OOB	BH	AVG	PB	PR	/A	PD	TPI
1990	Tor-A	1	0	1.000	2	0	0	0	0	1¹	2	0	0	1	13.5	6.75	58	.333	.333	0	—	0	-0	-0	0	-0.3

● **JOHN GILLESPIE**   Gillespie, John Patrick "Silent John"   b: 2/25/1900, Oakland, Cal.   d: 2/15/54, Vallejo, Cal.   BR/TR, 5'11.5", 172 lbs.   Deb: 4/12/22

YEAR	TM/L	W	L	PCT	G	GS	CG	SH	SV	IP	H	HR	BB	SO	RAT	ERA	ERA+	OAV	OOB	BH	AVG	PB	PR	/A	PD	TPI
1922	Cin-N	3	3	.500	31	4	1	0	0	77²	84	2	29	21	13.6	4.52	88	.294	.367	2	.133	-1	-4	-5	1	-0.3

● **BOB GILLESPIE**   Gillespie, Robert William "Bunch"   b: 10/8/18, Columbus, Ohio   BR/TR, 6'4", 187 lbs.   Deb: 5/11/44

YEAR	TM/L	W	L	PCT	G	GS	CG	SH	SV	IP	H	HR	BB	SO	RAT	ERA	ERA+	OAV	OOB	BH	AVG	PB	PR	/A	PD	TPI
1944	Det-A	0	1	.000	7	0	0	0	0	11	9	0	12	4	15.5	6.55	54	.194	.396	0	.000	-0	-4	-4	0	-0.3
1947	Chi-A	5	8	.385	25	17	1	0	0	118	133	4	53	36	14.3	4.73	77	.291	.366	2	.061	-3	-13	-14	3	-1.4
1948	Chi-A	0	4	.000	25	6	1	0	0	72	81	3	33	19	14.0	5.13	83	.287	.364	0	.000	-2	-7	-7	-0	-0.6
1950	Bos-A	0	0	—	1	0	0	0	0	1¹	2	1	4	0	40.5	20.25	24	.333	.600	0	—	-2	-2	-2	0	0.0
Total	4	5	13	.278	58	23	2	0	0	202¹	223	8	102	59	14.5	5.07	76	.286	.369	2	.039	-5	-26	-27	3	-2.3

● **PAUL GILLIFORD**   Gilliford, Paul Gant "Gorilla"   b: 1/12/45, Bryn Mawr, Pa.   BR/TL, 5'11", 210 lbs.   Deb: 9/20/67

YEAR	TM/L	W	L	PCT	G	GS	CG	SH	SV	IP	H	HR	BB	SO	RAT	ERA	ERA+	OAV	OOB	BH	AVG	PB	PR	/A	PD	TPI
1967	Bal-A	0	0	—	2	0	0	0	0	3	6	1	1	2	21.0	12.00	26	.429	.467	0	—	0	-3	-3	0	0.0

● **JACK GILLIGAN**   Gilligan, John Patrick   b: 10/18/1884, Chicago, Ill.   d: 11/19/80, Modesto, Cal.   BB/TR, 6', 190 lbs.   Deb: 9/16/09

YEAR	TM/L	W	L	PCT	G	GS	CG	SH	SV	IP	H	HR	BB	SO	RAT	ERA	ERA+	OAV	OOB	BH	AVG	PB	PR	/A	PD	TPI
1909	StL-A	1	2	.333	3	3	3	0	0	23	28	1	9	4	15.3	5.48	44	.315	.390	1	.111	-1	-8	-8	-1	-1.0
1910	StL-A	0	3	.000	9	5	2	0	0	39¹	37	0	28	10	15.1	3.66	68	.253	.377	3	.200	-0	-5	-5	0	-0.4
Total	2	1	5	.167	12	8	5	0	0	62¹	65	1	37	14	15.2	4.31	57	.277	.382	4	.167	-1	-13	-13	-0	-1.4

● **GEORGE GILLPATRICK**   Gillpatrick, George F.   b: 2/28/1875, Holden, Mo.   d: 12/15/41, Kansas City, Mo.   Deb: 5/22/1898

YEAR	TM/L	W	L	PCT	G	GS	CG	SH	SV	IP	H	HR	BB	SO	RAT	ERA	ERA+	OAV	OOB	BH	AVG	PB	PR	/A	PD	TPI
1898	StL-N	0	2	.000	7	3	1	0	0	35	42	0	19	12	16.0	6.94	55	.295	.386	2	.125	-2	-13	-12	0	-0.8

● **FRANK GILMORE**   Gilmore, Frank T. "Shadow"   b: 4/27/1864, Webster, Mass.   d: 7/21/29, Hartford, Conn.   BR   Deb: 9/11/1886

YEAR	TM/L	W	L	PCT	G	GS	CG	SH	SV	IP	H	HR	BB	SO	RAT	ERA	ERA+	OAV	OOB	BH	AVG	PB	PR	/A	PD	TPI
1886	Was-N	4	4	.500	9	9	9	1	0	75	57	3	22	75	9.5	2.52	130	.200	.257	0	.000	-4	7	6	-1	0.1
1887	Was-N	7	20	.259	28	27	27	1	0	234²	247	7	92	114	13.5	3.87	105	.262	.336	6	.065	-11	5	5	-3	-0.8
1888	Was-N	1	9	.100	12	11	10	0	0	95²	131	4	29	23	15.7	6.59	43	.323	.378	1	.024	-5	-40	-40	-2	-3.7
Total	3	12	33	.267	49	47	46	2	0	405¹	435	14	143	212	13.3	4.26	85	.266	.333	7	.043	-20	-28	-29	-6	-4.4

YEAR TM/L	W	L	PCT	G	GS	CG	SH	SV	IP	H	HR	BB	SO	RAT	ERA	ERA+	OAV	OOB	BH	AVG	PB	PR	/A	PD	TPI
● **LEN GILMORE** Gilmore, Leonard Preston "Meow" b: 11/3/17, Fairview Park, Ind. BR/TR, 6'3", 175 lbs. Deb: 10/1/44																								
1944 Pit-N	0	1	.000	1	1	1	0	0	8	13	2	0	0	14.6	7.88	47	.361	.361	0	.000	-0	-4	-4	1	-0.3
● **JOHN GILROY** Gilroy, John M. b: 10/26/1869, Washington, D.C. d: 8/4/1897, Norfolk, Va. Deb: 8/30/1895																								
1895 Was-N	1	4	.200	8	4	2	0	0	41¹	63	3	24	2	19.8	6.53	73	.345	.432	7	.241	-1	-8	-8	1	-0.7
1896 Was-N	0	0	—	1	0	0	0	0	2	0	0	1	0	4.5		—	.000	.148	0	.000	-0	1	1	0	0.0
Total 2	1	4	.200	9	4	2	0	0	43¹	63	3	25	2	19.1	6.23	77	.334	.423	7	.233	-1	-7	-7	1	-0.7
● **HAL GILSON** Gilson, Harold "Lefty" b: 2/9/42, Los Angeles, Cal. BR/TL, 6'5", 195 lbs. Deb: 4/14/68																								
1968 StL-N	0	2	.000	13	0	0	0	2	21²	27	1	11	19	15.8	4.57	63	.310	.388	0	.000	-0	-4	-4	-1	-0.6
Hou-N	0	0	—	2	0	0	0	0	3²	7	0	1	1	22.1	7.36	40	.412	.474	0	—	0	-2	-2	0	0.0
Yr	0	2	.000	15	0	0	0	2	25¹	34	1	12	20	16.7	4.97	58	.327	.402	0	.000	-0	-6	-6	-1	-0.6
● **BILLY GING** Ging, William Joseph b: 11/7/1872, Elmira, N.Y. d: 9/14/50, Elmira, N.Y. BR/TR, 5'10", 170 lbs. Deb: 9/25/1899																								
1899 Bos-N	1	0	1.000	1	1	1	0	0	8	5	0	5	2	11.3	1.13	370	.180	.305	0	.000	-0	2	3	-0	0.2
● **JOE GINGRAS** Gingras, Joseph Elzead John b: 1/10/1894, New York, N.Y. d: 9/6/47, Jersey City, N.J. BR/TR, 6'2", 188 lbs. Deb: 6/18/15																								
1915 KC-F	0	0	—	2	0	0	0	0	4	6	0	1	2	15.8	6.75	39	.353	.389	0	.000	-0	-2	-2	-0	0.0
● **CHARLIE GIRARD** Girard, Charles August b: 12/16/1884, Brooklyn, N.Y. d: 8/6/36, Brooklyn, N.Y. BR/TR, 5'10", 175 lbs. Deb: 9/14/10																								
1910 Phi-N	1	2	.333	7	1	0	0	1	26²	33	2	12	11	15.9	6.41	49	.308	.388	1	.125	-0	-10	-10	-1	-1.2
● **DAVE GIUSTI** Giusti, David John b: 11/27/39, Seneca Falls, N.Y. BR/TR, 5'11", 195 lbs. Deb: 4/13/62																								
1962 Hou-N	2	3	.400	22	5	0	0	0	73²	82	7	30	43	13.7	5.62	66	.280	.347	7	.292	3	-14	-15	1	-0.6
1964 Hou-N	0	0	—	8	0	0	0	0	25²	24	1	8	16	11.2	3.16	108	.253	.311	2	.286	1	1	1	1	0.1
1965 Hou-N	8	7	.533	38	13	4	1	3	131¹	132	13	46	92	12.3	4.32	78	.259	.321	6	.171	2	-11	-14	1	-1.2
1966 Hou-N	15	14	.517	34	33	9	4	0	210	215	23	54	131	11.7	4.20	81	.260	.310	17	.230	5	-14	-18	-1	-1.9
1967 Hou-N	11	15	.423	37	33	8	1	1	221²	231	20	58	157	11.9	4.18	79	.265	.313	13	.155	3	-20	-21	-2	-2.2
1968 Hou-N	11	14	.440	37	34	12	2	1	251	226	15	67	186	10.6	3.19	93	.239	.293	15	.183	2	-6	-7	3	-0.1
1969 StL-N	3	7	.300	22	12	2	1	0	99²	96	7	37	62	12.1	3.61	99	.255	.323	5	.200	1	-0	-0	1	0.2
1970 *Pit-N	9	3	.750	66	1	0	0	26	103	98	7	39	85	12.0	3.06	128	.259	.328	3	.188	2	11	10	-0	1.7
1971 *Pit-N	5	6	.455	58	0	0	0	**30**	86	79	5	31	55	11.6	2.93	115	.241	.308	1	.059	-1	5	4	-1	0.7
1972 *Pit-N	7	4	.636	54	0	0	0	22	74²	59	3	20	54	9.5	1.93	172	.219	.273	0	.000	-1	13	12	1	2.5
1973 Pit-N★	9	2	.818	67	0	0	0	20	98²	89	9	37	64	11.5	2.37	148	.241	.310	4	.308	1	14	13	-2	1.9
1974 *Pit-N	7	5	.583	64	2	0	0	12	105¹	101	2	40	53	12.0	3.32	104	.258	.327	1	.111	-0	3	1	1	0.3
1975 *Pit-N	5	4	.556	61	0	0	0	17	91²	79	3	42	38	11.9	2.95	120	.237	.322	3	.300	1	7	6	0	0.9
1976 Pit-N	5	4	.556	40	0	0	0	6	58¹	59	5	27	24	13.3	4.32	81	.267	.347	0	.000	-0	-5	-5	0	-0.9
1977 Oak-A	3	3	.500	40	0	0	0	6	60¹	54	4	20	28	11.0	2.98	135	.245	.308	0	—	0	7	7	0	0.9
Chi-N	2	2	.000	20	0	0	0	0	25¹	30	2	14	15	15.6	6.04	73	.297	.383	0	.000	-0	-6	-5	-0	-0.4
Total 15	100	93	.518	668	133	35	9	145	1716²	1654	126	570	1103	11.7	3.60	95	.253	.315	77	.187	18	-14	-33	2	2.0
● **DAN GLADDEN** Gladden, Clinton Daniel b: 7/7/57, San Jose, Cal. BR/TR, 5'11", 180 lbs. Deb: 9/5/83 ◆																								
1988 Min-A	0	0	—	1	0	0	0	0	1	0	0	0	0			—	.000	.000	155	.269	1	0	0	0	0.0
1989 Min-A	0	0	—	1	0	0	0	0	1	2	0	1	0	27.0	9.00	46	.400	.500	136	.295	1	-1	-1	0	0.0
Total 2	0	0	—	2	0	0	0	0	2	2	0	1	0	13.5	4.50	97	.250	.333	1215	.270	2	-0	-0	0	0.0
● **FRED GLADDING** Gladding, Fred Earl b: 6/28/36, Flat Rock, Mich. BL/TR, 6', 225 lbs. Deb: 7/1/61 C																								
1961 Det-A	1	0	1.000	8	0	0	0	0	16¹	18	1	11	11	17.1	3.31	124	.286	.408	0	.000	-0	1	1	-0	0.0
1962 Det-A	0	0	—	6	0	0	0	0	5	3	0	2	4	9.0	0.00		.176	.263	0	—	0	2	2	0	0.0
1963 Det-A	1	1	.500	22	0	0	0	7	27¹	19	1	14	24	10.9	1.98	189	.198	.300	0	.000	-0	5	5	0	0.7
1964 Det-A	7	4	.636	42	0	0	0	7	67¹	57	7	27	59	11.5	3.07	119	.233	.314	0	.000	-1	4	4	1	0.8
1965 Det-A	6	2	.750	46	0	0	0	5	70	63	6	29	43	12.3	2.83	123	.239	.323	0	.000	-1	5	5	-1	0.5
1966 Det-A	5	0	1.000	51	0	0	0	2	74	62	6	29	57	11.2	3.28	106	.230	.307	0	.000	-0	1	2	-1	0.0
1967 Det-A	6	4	.600	42	1	0	0	12	77	62	6	19	64	9.9	1.99	164	.227	.287	0	.000	-2	11	11	-0	1.6
1968 Hou-N	0	0	—	7	0	0	0	2	4¹	8	0	4	3	24.9	14.54	20	.421	.522	0	—	0	-6	-6	-0	-0.8
1969 Hou-N	4	8	.333	57	0	0	0	**29**	72²	83	3	27	40	13.7	4.21	84	.289	.352	1	.100	-1	-5	-5	0	-1.4
1970 Hou-N	7	4	.636	63	0	0	0	18	71	84	4	24	60	14.1	4.06	96	.293	.354	0	.000	-0	-1	-1	0	-0.2
1971 Hou-N	5	4	.444	48	0	0	0	12	51¹	51	0	22	17	14.0	2.10	160	.268	.365	0	.000	-0	8	7	1	1.5
1972 Hou-N	5	6	.455	42	0	0	0	9	48²	38	1	12	18	9.6	2.77	121	.222	.281	0	.000	-1	4	3	1	0.8
1973 Hou-N	2	0	1.000	16	0	0	0	4	16	18	4	4	9	12.4	4.50	81	.290	.333	0	—	0	-1	-2	0	-0.2
Total 13	48	34	.585	450	1	0	0	109	601	566	38	223	394	12.2	3.13	113	.252	.327	1	.016	-6	29	28	-2	3.5
● **FRED GLADE** Glade, Frederick Monroe "Lucky" b: 1/25/1876, Dubuque, Iowa d: 11/21/34, Grand Island, Neb. BR/TR, 5'10", 175 lbs. Deb: 5/27/02																								
1902 Chi-N	0	1	.000	1	1	1	0	0	8	13	0	3	3	19.1	9.00	30	.364	.428	1	.333	1	-6	-6	0	-0.4
1904 StL-A	18	15	.545	35	34	30	6	1	289	248	6	58	156	9.9	2.27	109	.233	.281	19	.186	1	10	7	1	1.1
1905 StL-A	6	25	.194	32	32	28	2	0	275	257	3	58	127	10.7	2.81	91	.249	.296	9	.092	-6	-5	-8	4	-1.2
1906 StL-A	15	14	.517	35	32	28	4	1	266²	215	4	59	96	9.6	2.36	109	.224	.276	13	.137	-4	10	7	-3	0.0
1907 StL-A	13	9	.591	24	22	18	2	0	202	187	2	45	71	10.7	2.67	94	.248	.298	15	.205	2	-3	-3	-4	-0.6
1908 NY-A	0	4	.000	5	5	2	0	0	32	30	0	14	11	13.5	4.22	59	.275	.378	0	.000	-0	-6	-6	-1	-0.9
Total 6	52	68	.433	132	126	107	14	2	1072²	950	11	237	464	10.4	2.62	97	.240	.291	57	.150	-7	1	-10	-3	-2.0
● **JOHN GLAISER** Glaiser, John Burke "Bert" b: 7/28/1894, Yoakum, Tex. d: 3/7/59, Houston, Tex. BL/TR, 5'8", 165 lbs. Deb: 4/20/20																								
1920 Det-A	0	0	—	9	1	0	0	1	17	23	1	8	3	16.9	6.35	59	.354	.432	0	.000	-0	-5	-5	1	0.0
● **TOM GLASS** Glass, Thomas Joseph b: 4/29/1898, Greensboro, N.C. d: 12/15/81, Greensboro, N.C. BR/TR, 6'3", 170 lbs. Deb: 6/12/25																								
1925 Phi-A	1	0	1.000	2	0	0	0	0	5	9	0	2	0	16.2	5.40	86	.409	.409	0	.000	-0	-1	-0	-0	-0.1
● **JACK GLASSCOCK** Glasscock, John Wesley "Pebbly Jack" b: 7/22/1859, Wheeling, W.Va. d: 2/24/47, Wheeling, W.Va. BR/TR, 5'8", 160 lbs. Deb: 5/1/1879 M◆																								
1884 Cle-N	0	0	—	5	0	0	0	0	5	8	0	2	1	18.0	5.40	58	.333	.385	70	.249	0	-1	-1	1	0.1
1887 Ind-N	0	0	—	1	0	0	0	0	1	0	0	0	0	0.00		—	.000	.000	142	.294	0	0	0	0	0.0
1888 Ind-N	0	0	—	1	0	0	0	0	0¹	1	0	2	1	108.0	54.00	5	1.000	1.000	119	.269	0	-2	-2	0	0.0
1889 Ind-N	0	0	—	1	0	0	0	0	0²	3	0	3	0	81.0	0.00		—	.603	.752	205	.352	0	-0	-0	0	0.0
Total 4	0	0	—	5	0	0	0	0	7	12	0	7	3	25.7	6.43	53	.364	.488	2040	.290	0	-2	-1	1	0.1
● **LUKE GLAVENICH** Glavenich, Luke Frank b: 1/17/1893, Jackson, Cal. d: 5/22/35, Stockton, Cal. BR/TR, 5'9.5", 189 lbs. Deb: 4/12/13																								
1913 Cle-A	0	0	—	1	0	0	0	0	1	3	0	3	1	54.0	9.00	34	.500	.667	0	—	0	-1	-1	-0	0.0
● **TOM GLAVINE** Glavine, Thomas Michael b: 3/25/66, Concord, Mass. BL/TL, 6'1", 190 lbs. Deb: 8/17/87																								
1987 Atl-N	2	4	.333	9	9	0	0	0	50¹	55	5	33	20	16.3	5.54	78	.279	.391	2	.125	-0	-8	-7	1	-0.7
1988 Atl-N	7	17	.292	34	34	1	0	0	195¹	201	12	63	84	12.5	4.56	81	.270	.333	11	.183	1	-24	-19	2	-1.9
1989 Atl-N	14	8	.636	29	29	6	4	0	186	172	20	40	90	10.4	3.68	99	.243	.285	10	.149	0	-4	-1	1	0.1
1990 Atl-N	10	12	.455	33	33	1	0	0	214¹	232	18	78	129	13.1	4.28	94	.281	.343	7	.113	0	-12	-6	1	-0.4
1991 *Atl-N★	**20**	11	.645	34	34	**9**	1	0	246²	201	17	69	192	9.9	2.55	**152**	.222	.279	17	.230	4	31	37	3	5.5
1992 *Atl-N★	**20**	8	.714	33	33	7	**5**	0	225	197	6	70	129	10.8	2.76	133	.235	.295	19	.247	4	19	22	0	3.3
1993 *Atl-N☆	**22**	6	.786	36	36	4	2	0	239¹	236	16	90	120	12.3	3.20	126	.259	.327	14	.173	1	22	22	0	2.5

YEAR TM/L	W	L	PCT	G	GS	CG	SH	SV	IP	H	HR	BB	SO	RAT	ERA	ERA+	OAV	OOB	BH	AVG	PB	PR	/A	PD	TPI
1994 Atl-N	13	9	.591	25	25	2	0	0	165¹	173	10	70	140	13.3	3.97	104	.268	.341	10	.179	2	4	3	2	0.8
Total 8	108	75	.590	233	233	30	12	0	1522¹	1467	104	513	904	11.8	3.58	109	.254	.317	90	.183	12	29	52	10	9.2

● **RALPH GLAZE**   Glaze, Daniel Ralph b: 3/13/1882, Denver, Col. d: 10/31/68, Atascadero, Cal. BR/TR, 5'9", 165 lbs. Deb: 6/1/06

YEAR TM/L	W	L	PCT	G	GS	CG	SH	SV	IP	H	HR	BB	SO	RAT	ERA	ERA+	OAV	OOB	BH	AVG	PB	PR	/A	PD	TPI
1906 Bos-A	4	6	.400	19	10	7	0	0	123	110	4	32	56	10.8	3.59	77	.242	.299	10	.182	0	-12	-11	0	-0.8
1907 Bos-A	9	13	.409	32	21	11	1	0	182¹	150	4	48	68	10.0	2.32	111	.226	.282	11	.180	0	5	5	-4	0.2
1908 Bos-A	2	2	.500	10	3	2	0	0	34²	43	1	5	13	12.5	3.38	73	.253	.274	1	.077	-1	-4	-4	-1	-0.6
Total 3	15	21	.417	61	34	20	1	0	340	303	9	85	137	10.5	2.89	91	.235	.287	22	.171	-1	-11	-10	-4	-1.2

● **WHITEY GLAZNER**   Glazner, Charles Franklin b: 9/17/1893, Sycamore, Ala. d: 6/6/89, Orlando, Fla. BR/TR, 5'9", 165 lbs. Deb: 9/26/20

YEAR TM/L	W	L	PCT	G	GS	CG	SH	SV	IP	H	HR	BB	SO	RAT	ERA	ERA+	OAV	OOB	BH	AVG	PB	PR	/A	PD	TPI
1920 Pit-N	0	0	—	2	0	0	0	0	8²	9	0	2	1	11.4	3.12	103	.300	.344	0	.000	-0	0	0	-0	-0.1
1921 Pit-N	14	5	.737	36	25	15	0	1	234	214	5	58	88	10.9	2.77	139	**.250**	.306	10	.132	-3	26	28	-4	1.4
1922 Pit-N	11	12	.478	34	26	10	1	1	193	238	9	52	77	13.6	4.38	93	.309	.354	16	.246	3	-6	-7	-0	-0.4
1923 Pit-N	2	1	.667	7	4	1	1	1	30	29	5	11	8	12.0	3.30	122	.250	.315	4	.333	2	2	2	0	0.4
Phi-N	7	14	.333	28	23	12	2	1	161¹	195	11	63	51	14.7	4.69	98	.304	.371	9	.170	-1	-12	-1	-0	-0.3
Yr	9	15	.375	35	27	13	3	2	191¹	224	16	74	59	14.3	4.47	101	.296	.363	13	.200	1	-10	1	0	0.1
1924 Phi-N	7	16	.304	35	24	8	2	0	156²	210	14	63	41	15.9	5.92	75	.339	.403	8	.157	-4	-36	-25	1	-3.4
Total 5	41	48	.461	142	102	46	6	4	783²	895	44	249	266	13.4	4.21	99	.295	.353	47	.181	-3	-25	-3	-3	-2.4

● **JOE GLEASON**   Gleason, Joseph Paul b: 7/9/1895, Phelps, N.Y. d: 9/8/90, Phelps, N.Y. BR/TR, 5'10.5", 175 lbs. Deb: 9/11/20

YEAR TM/L	W	L	PCT	G	GS	CG	SH	SV	IP	H	HR	BB	SO	RAT	ERA	ERA+	OAV	OOB	BH	AVG	PB	PR	/A	PD	TPI
1920 Was-A	0	0	—	3	0	0	0	0	8	14	2	6	2	23.6	13.50	28	.326	.420	0	.000	1	-9	-9	0	0.1
1922 Was-A	2	2	.500	8	5	3	0	0	40²	53	3	18	12	15.9	4.65	83	.319	.389	2	.143	-0	-3	-4	-0	-0.3
Total 2	2	2	.500	11	5	3	0	0	48²	67	5	24	14	17.2	6.10	63	.321	.396	2	.125	0	-11	-12	0	-0.2

● **BILL GLEASON**   Gleason, William b: 1868, Cleveland, Ohio d: 12/2/1893, Cleveland, Ohio Deb: 4/24/1890

YEAR TM/L	W	L	PCT	G	GS	CG	SH	SV	IP	H	HR	BB	SO	RAT	ERA	ERA+	OAV	OOB	BH	AVG	PB	PR	/A	PD	TPI
1890 Cle-P	0	1	.000	1	1	0	0	0	4	14	1	6	0	45.0	27.00	15	.537	.624	0	.000	-0	-10	-10	-0	-1.2

● **KID GLEASON**   Gleason, William J. b: 10/26/1866, Camden, N.J. d: 1/2/33, Philadelphia, Pa. BB/TR, 5'7", 158 lbs. Deb: 4/20/1888 FMC ♦

YEAR TM/L	W	L	PCT	G	GS	CG	SH	SV	IP	H	HR	BB	SO	RAT	ERA	ERA+	OAV	OOB	BH	AVG	PB	PR	/A	PD	TPI
1888 Phi-N	7	16	.304	24	23	23	0	0	199²	199	11	53	89	11.9	2.84	105	.252	.309	17	.205	0	0	3	-3	0.0
1889 Phi-N	9	15	.375	29	21	15	0	1	205	242	8	97	64	15.3	5.58	78	.285	.364	25	.253	2	-36	-28	1	-2.3
1890 Phi-N	38	17	.691	60	55	54	6	**2**	506	479	8	167	222	11.8	2.63	139	.242	.306	47	.210	-6	53	58	-0	4.6
1891 Phi-N	24	22	.522	53	44	40	1	1	418	431	10	165	100	13.1	3.51	97	.256	.328	53	.248	6	-8	-5	-3	-0.2
1892 StL-N	20	24	.455	47	45	43	2	0	400	389	11	151	133	12.4	3.33	96	.245	.314	50	.215	8	-2	-6	5	0.7
1893 StL-N	21	22	.488	48	45	37	1	1	380¹	436	18	187	86	15.0	4.61	103	.279	.360	51	.256	4	2	5	1	0.8
1894 StL-N	2	6	.250	8	8	6	0	0	58	75	2	21	9	15.4	6.05	89	.310	.372	7	.250	-0	-5	-4	-1	-0.3
*Bal-N	15	5	.750	21	20	19	0	0	172	224	3	44	35	14.2	4.45	123	.311	.354	30	.349	4	17	19	-2	1.8
Yr	17	11	.607	29	28	25	0	0	230	299	5	65	44	14.4	4.85	112	.310	.356	37	.325	4	12	15	-0	1.5
1895 *Bal-N	2	4	.333	9	5	3	0	1	50¹	77	4	21	6	18.1	6.97	68	.345	.409	130	.309	2	-12	-12	-0	-1.0
Total 8	138	131	.513	299	266	240	10	6	2389¹	2552	75	906	744	13.3	3.79	103	.265	.333	1944	.261	20	10	29	-0	4.1

● **JERRY DON GLEATON**   Gleaton, Jerry Don b: 9/14/57, Brownwood, Tex. BL/TL, 6'3", 210 lbs. Deb: 7/11/79

YEAR TM/L	W	L	PCT	G	GS	CG	SH	SV	IP	H	HR	BB	SO	RAT	ERA	ERA+	OAV	OOB	BH	AVG	PB	PR	/A	PD	TPI
1979 Tex-A	0	1	.000	5	2	0	0	0	9²	15	0	2	2	16.8	6.52	64	.375	.419	0	—	0	-2	-3	0	-0.2
1980 Tex-A	0	0	—	5	0	0	0	0	7	5	0	2	2	11.6	2.57	151	.208	.321	0	—	0	1	1	0	0.1
1981 Sea-A	4	7	.364	20	13	1	0	0	85¹	88	10	38	31	13.5	4.75	81	.273	.354	0	—	0	-10	-8	-1	-1.2
1982 Sea-A	0	0	—	3	0	0	0	0	4²	7	3	2	1	19.3	13.50	31	.333	.417	0	—	0	-5	-5	-0	-0.4
1984 Chi-A	1	2	.333	11	1	0	0	2	18¹	20	2	6	4	13.3	3.44	121	.286	.351	0	—	0	1	1	-1	-0.1
1985 Chi-A	1	0	1.000	31	0	0	0	0	29²	37	3	13	22	15.2	5.76	75	.316	.385	0	—	0	-5	-5	-0	-0.2
1987 KC-A	4	4	.500	48	0	0	0	5	50²	38	4	28	44	11.7	4.26	107	.216	.324	0	—	0	1	2	1	0.2
1988 KC-A	0	4	.000	42	0	0	0	3	38	33	2	17	29	12.6	3.55	112	.232	.327	0	—	0	2	2	0	0.1
1989 KC-A	0	0	—	15	0	0	0	0	14¹	20	0	6	9	16.3	5.65	68	.345	.406	0	—	0	-3	-3	-0	-0.2
1990 Det-A	1	3	.250	57	0	0	0	13	82²	62	5	25	56	9.8	2.94	135	.213	.282	0	—	0	9	9	-0	0.7
1991 Det-A	3	2	.600	47	0	0	0	1	75¹	74	7	39	47	13.5	4.06	102	.269	.360	0	—	0	1	0	0	0.0
1992 Pit-N	1	0	1.000	23	0	0	0	0	31²	34	4	19	18	15.1	4.26	81	.283	.381	0	.000	0	-3	-3	-0	-0.1
Total 12	15	23	.395	307	16	1	0	26	447¹	433	40	199	265	12.9	4.25	95	.261	.345	0	.000	0	-14	-10	-0	-0.8

● **MARTIN GLENDON**   Glendon, Martin J. b: 2/8/1877, Milwaukee, Wis. d: 11/6/50, Norwood Park, Ill. 5'8", 165 lbs. Deb: 4/18/02

YEAR TM/L	W	L	PCT	G	GS	CG	SH	SV	IP	H	HR	BB	SO	RAT	ERA	ERA+	OAV	OOB	BH	AVG	PB	PR	/A	PD	TPI
1902 Cin-N	0	1	.000	1	1	0	0	0	3	5	0	4	0	27.0	12.00	25	.370	.513	0	.000	-0	-3	-3	-0	-0.7
1903 Cle-A	1	2	.333	3	3	3	0	0	27²	20	0	7	9	8.8	0.98	292	.202	.255	0	.000	-1	6	6	1	0.6
Total 2	1	3	.250	4	4	3	0	0	30²	25	0	11	9	10.6	2.05	140	.222	.292	0	.000	-1	3	3	1	-0.1

● **BOB GLENN**   Glenn, Burdette b: 6/16/1894, W.Sunbury, Pa. d: 6/3/77, Richmond, Cal. Deb: 7/27/20

YEAR TM/L	W	L	PCT	G	GS	CG	SH	SV	IP	H	HR	BB	SO	RAT	ERA	ERA+	OAV	OOB	BH	AVG	PB	PR	/A	PD	TPI
1920 StL-N	0	0	—	2	0	0	0	0	2	2	0	1	0	9.0	—		.222	.222	0		0	1	1	0	0.0

● **SAL GLIATTO**   Gliatto, Salvador Michael b: 5/7/02, Chicago, Ill. BB/TR, 5'8.5", 150 lbs. Deb: 4/19/30

YEAR TM/L	W	L	PCT	G	GS	CG	SH	SV	IP	H	HR	BB	SO	RAT	ERA	ERA+	OAV	OOB	BH	AVG	PB	PR	/A	PD	TPI
1930 Cle-A	0	0	—	8	0	0	0	0	15	21	1	9	7	19.2	6.60	73	.328	.427	0	—	0	-3	-3	-0	-0.2

● **GEORGE GLINATSIS**   Glinatsis, George b: 6/29/69, Youngstown, Ohio BR/TR, 6'4", 195 lbs. Deb: 7/18/94

YEAR TM/L	W	L	PCT	G	GS	CG	SH	SV	IP	H	HR	BB	SO	RAT	ERA	ERA+	OAV	OOB	BH	AVG	PB	PR	/A	PD	TPI
1994 Sea-A	0	1	.000	2	2	0	0	0	5¹	9	2	6	1	25.3	13.50	36	.429	.556	0	—	0	-5	-5	0	-0.7

● **ED GLYNN**   Glynn, Edward Paul b: 6/3/53, Flushing, N.Y. BR/TL, 6'2", 180 lbs. Deb: 9/19/75

YEAR TM/L	W	L	PCT	G	GS	CG	SH	SV	IP	H	HR	BB	SO	RAT	ERA	ERA+	OAV	OOB	BH	AVG	PB	PR	/A	PD	TPI
1975 Det-A	0	2	.000	3	1	0	0	0	14²	11	1	8	8	11.7	4.30	93	.220	.328	0	—	0	-1	-0	0	-0.1
1976 Det-A	1	3	.250	5	4	1	0	0	23²	22	3	20	17	16.0	6.08	61	.265	.408	0	—	0	-7	-6	-1	-1.0
1977 Det-A	2	1	.667	8	3	0	0	0	27¹	36	3	12	13	15.8	5.27	81	.316	.381	0	—	0	-4	-3	-0	-0.7
1978 Det-A	0	0	—	10	0	0	0	0	14²	11	3	4	9	9.2	3.07	126	.208	.263	0	—	0	1	1	1	0.1
1979 NY-N	1	4	.200	46	0	0	0	7	60	57	3	40	32	14.9	3.00	121	.259	.378	0	.000	0	5	4	-1	0.3
1980 NY-N	3	3	.500	38	0	0	0	1	52²	49	5	23	32	12.4	4.13	86	.246	.324	0	.000	0	-3	-3	1	-0.4
1981 Cle-A	0	0	—	4	0	0	0	0	7²	5	0	4	4	10.6	1.17	309	.192	.300	0	—	0	2	2	-0	0.0
1982 Cle-A	5	2	.714	47	0	0	0	4	49²	43	5	30	54	13.2	4.17	98	.232	.340	—		0	-1	-0	-0	-0.1
1983 Cle-A	0	2	.000	11	0	0	0	0	12¹	22	2	10	8	20.4	5.84	73	.373	.431	0	—	0	-2	-2	-0	-0.5
1985 Mon-N	0	0	—	4	0	0	0	0	2²	5	0	4	7	34.7	19.29	18	.455	.600	0	—	0	-4	-4	-0	-0.2
Total 10	12	17	.414	175	8	1	0	12	264²	261	26	151	184	14.1	4.25	90	.261	.359	0	.000	-1	-13	-12	-2	-2.4

● **JOT GOAR**   Goar, Joshua Mercer b: 1/31/1870, New Lisbon, Ind. d: 4/4/47, New Castle, Ind. BR/TR, 5'9", 160 lbs. Deb: 4/18/1896

YEAR TM/L	W	L	PCT	G	GS	CG	SH	SV	IP	H	HR	BB	SO	RAT	ERA	ERA+	OAV	OOB	BH	AVG	PB	PR	/A	PD	TPI
1896 Pit-N	0	1	.000	3	1	0	0	0	13¹	36	1	6	3	30.4	16.88	25	.485	.540	1	.167	-1	-19	-19	-1	-1.0
1898 Cin-N	0	0	—	1	0	0	0	0	2	4	0	1	0	22.5	9.00	43	.411	.466	0	—	0	-1	-1	0	0.0
Total 2	0	1	.000	4	1	0	0	0	15¹	40	1	9	3	29.3	15.85	26	.476	.532	1	.167	-1	-20	-20	-1	-1.0

● **GEORGE GOETZ**   Goetz, George Burt b: Greencastle, Pa. 6'2", 180 lbs. Deb: 6/17/1889

YEAR TM/L	W	L	PCT	G	GS	CG	SH	SV	IP	H	HR	BB	SO	RAT	ERA	ERA+	OAV	OOB	BH	AVG	PB	PR	/A	PD	TPI
1889 Bal-a	1	0	1.000	1	1	0	0	0	9	12	0	2	2	12.0	4.00	99	.310	.310	0	.000	-1	-0	-0	0	0.0

● **JOHN GOETZ**   Goetz, John Hardy b: 10/24/37, Goetzville, Mich. BR/TR, 6', 185 lbs. Deb: 4/16/60

YEAR TM/L	W	L	PCT	G	GS	CG	SH	SV	IP	H	HR	BB	SO	RAT	ERA	ERA+	OAV	OOB	BH	AVG	PB	PR	/A	PD	TPI
1960 Chi-N	0	0	—	4	0	0	0	0	6¹	10	2	4	6	19.9	12.79	30	.370	.452	0	.000	-0	-6	-6	0	0.0

● **BILL GOGOLEWSKI**   Gogolewski, William Joseph b: 10/26/47, Oshkosh, Wis. BL/TR, 6'4", 190 lbs. Deb: 9/3/70

YEAR TM/L	W	L	PCT	G	GS	CG	SH	SV	IP	H	HR	BB	SO	RAT	ERA	ERA+	OAV	OOB	BH	AVG	PB	PR	/A	PD	TPI
1970 Was-A	2	2	.500	8	5	0	0	0	33²	33	2	25	19	15.8	4.81	74	.260	.386	0	.000	-0	-4	-5	1	-0.5
1971 Was-A	6	5	.545	27	17	4	1	0	124¹	112	5	39	70	11.1	2.75	120	.241	.302	5	.156	0	10	8	-0	0.7

YEAR TM/L	W	L	PCT	G	GS	CG	SH	SV	IP	H	HR	BB	SO	RAT	ERA	ERA+	OAV	OOB	BH	AVG	PB	PR	/A	PD	TPI
1972 Tex-A	4	11	.267	36	21	2	1	2	150²	136	9	58	95	11.9	4.24	71	.239	.316	5	.125	-1	-20	-21	-0	-2.2
1973 Tex-A	3	6	.333	49	1	0	0	6	123²	139	10	48	77	13.7	4.22	88	.286	.351	0	—	0	-6	-7	2	-0.3
1974 Cle-A	0	0	—	5	0	0	0	0	13²	15	1	2	3	11.9	4.61	78	.283	.321	0	—	0	-2	-2	1	0.1
1975 Chi-A	0	0	—	19	0	0	0	2	55	61	5	28	37	14.7	5.24	74	.292	.378	0	—	0	-9	-8	1	0.0
Total 6	15	24	.385	144	44	6	2	10	501	496	32	200	301	12.7	4.02	85	.260	.334	10	.127	-1	-30	-34	5	-2.2

● **GREG GOHR** Gohr, Gregory James b: 10/29/67, Santa Clara, Cal. BR/TR, 6'3", 205 lbs. Deb: 4/7/93

YEAR TM/L	W	L	PCT	G	GS	CG	SH	SV	IP	H	HR	BB	SO	RAT	ERA	ERA+	OAV	OOB	BH	AVG	PB	PR	/A	PD	TPI
1993 Det-A	0	0	—	16	0	0	0	0	22²	26	1	14	23	16.7	5.96	72	.289	.396	0	—	0	-4	-4	-0	0.0
1994 Det-A	2	2	.500	8	6	0	0	0	34	36	3	21	21	15.1	4.50	106	.263	.361	0	—	0	1	1	0	0.1
Total 2	2	2	.500	24	6	0	0	0	56²	62	4	35	44	15.7	5.08	90	.273	.375	0	—	0	-3	-3	0	0.1

● **JIM GOLDEN** Golden, James Edward b: 3/20/36, Eldon, Mo. BL/TR, 6', 175 lbs. Deb: 9/30/60

YEAR TM/L	W	L	PCT	G	GS	CG	SH	SV	IP	H	HR	BB	SO	RAT	ERA	ERA+	OAV	OOB	BH	AVG	PB	PR	/A	PD	TPI
1960 LA-N	1	0	1.000	1	1	0	0	0	7	6	1	4	4	12.9	6.43	62	.240	.345	1	.333	0	-2	-2	-0	-0.2
1961 LA-N	1	1	.500	28	0	0	0	0	42	52	7	20	18	15.4	5.79	75	.306	.379	1	.000	-0	-8	-7	-0	-0.3
1962 Hou-N	7	11	.389	37	18	5	2	1	152²	163	13	50	88	12.6	4.07	92	.270	.326	12	.222	4	-2	-6	1	-0.2
1963 Hou-N	0	1	.000	3	1	0	0	0	6¹	12	0	2	5	19.9	5.68	55	.429	.467	0	—	0	-2	-2	0	-0.3
Total 4	9	13	.409	69	20	5	2	1	208	233	21	76	115	13.4	4.54	85	.282	.343	13	.217	4	-14	-16	0	-1.0

● **MIKE GOLDEN** Golden, Michael Henry b: 9/11/1851, Shirley, Mass. d: 1/11/29, Rockford, Ill. BR/TR, 5'8", 168 lbs. Deb: 5/5/1875 ◆

YEAR TM/L	W	L	PCT	G	GS	CG	SH	SV	IP	H	HR	BB	SO	RAT	ERA	ERA+	OAV	OOB	BH	AVG	PB	PR	/A	PD	TPI
1875 Wes-n	1	12	.077	13	13	13	0	0	112	110	0		14	10.0	2.81	96	.225	.247	6	.130	-4	-4	-1		-0.4
Chi-n	6	7	.462	14	14	12	1	0	119	129	0		11	10.6	2.87	87	.252	.268	40	.258	1	-5	-5		-0.3
Yr	7	19	.269	27	27	25	1	0	231	239	0		25	10.3	2.84	91	.239	.258	46	.249	-3	-10	-6		-0.7
1878 Mil-N	3	13	.188	22	18	15	0	0	161	217	1	33	52	14.0	4.14	63	.295	.325	44	.206	-2	-33	-27	0	-2.2

● **ROY GOLDEN** Golden, Roy Kramer b: 7/12/1888, Madisonville, O. d: 10/4/61, Norwood, Ohio BR/TR, 6'1", 195 lbs. Deb: 9/7/10

YEAR TM/L	W	L	PCT	G	GS	CG	SH	SV	IP	H	HR	BB	SO	RAT	ERA	ERA+	OAV	OOB	BH	AVG	PB	PR	/A	PD	TPI
1910 StL-N	2	3	.400	7	6	3	0	0	42²	44	3	33	31	16.7	4.43	67	.286	.418	4	.267	1	-7	-7	1	-0.6
1911 StL-N	4	9	.308	30	25	6	0	0	148²	127	6	129	81	15.8	5.02	67	.240	.394	5	.114	-1	-27	-27	-0	-2.2
Total 2	6	12	.333	37	31	9	0	0	191¹	171	9	162	112	16.0	4.89	67	.250	.399	9	.153	-1	-33	-34	1	-2.8

● **FRED GOLDSMITH** Goldsmith, Fred Ernest b: 5/15/1856, New Haven, Conn. d: 3/28/39, Berkley, Mich. BR/TR, 6'1", 195 lbs. Deb: 10/23/1875 U◆

YEAR TM/L	W	L	PCT	G	GS	CG	SH	SV	IP	H	HR	BB	SO	RAT	ERA	ERA+	OAV	OOB	BH	AVG	PB	PR	/A	PD	TPI
1879 Tro-N	2	4	.333	8	7	7	0	0	63	61	0	1	31	8.9	1.57	159	.237	.240	9	.237	0	6	6	-0	0.6
1880 Chi-N	21	3	.875	26	24	22	4	1	210¹	189	2	18	90	8.9	1.75	138	.231	.247	37	.261	2	14	16	2	1.9
1881 Chi-N	24	13	.649	39	39	37	5	0	330	328	4	44	76	10.1	2.59	106	.247	.271	38	.241	3	7	5	5	1.1
1882 Chi-N	28	17	.622	45	45	45	4	0	405	377	4	38	109	9.2	2.42	119	.236	.254	42	.230	-1	22	20	-2	1.4
1883 Chi-N	25	19	.568	46	45	40	2	0	383¹	346	14	39	82	11.6	3.15	101	.277	.294	52	.221	-0	-2	1	1	0.2
1884 Chi-N	9	11	.450	21	21	20	1	0	188	245	11	29	34	13.1	4.26	74	.298	.322	11	.136	-2	-27	-24	-3	-2.4
Bal-a	3	1	.750	4	4	3	0	0	30	29	0	2	11	9.6	2.70	128	.238	.256	2	.143	-0	2	3	1	0.3
Total 6	112	68	.622	189	185	174	16	1	1609²	1685	38	171	433	10.4	2.73	106	.256	.275	191	.224	-1	24	28	4	3.1

● **HAL GOLDSMITH** Goldsmith, Harold Eugene b: 8/18/1898, Peconic, N.Y. d: 10/20/85, Riverhead, N.Y. BR/TR, 6', 174 lbs. Deb: 6/23/26

YEAR TM/L	W	L	PCT	G	GS	CG	SH	SV	IP	H	HR	BB	SO	RAT	ERA	ERA+	OAV	OOB	BH	AVG	PB	PR	/A	PD	TPI
1926 Bos-N	5	7	.417	19	15	5	0	0	101	135	2	28	16	14.6	4.37	81	.333	.377	8	.211	0	-6	-9	1	-0.8
1927 Bos-N	1	3	.250	22	5	1	0	1	71²	83	4	26	13	13.5	3.52	106	.289	.348	5	.238	0	3	2	0	0.1
1928 Bos-N	0	0	—	4	0	0	0	0	8¹	14	2	1	1	16.2	3.24	121	.359	.375	0	.000	-0	1	1	0	0.0
1929 StL-N	0	0	—	2	0	0	0	0	4	3	1	1	0	9.0	6.75	69	.214	.267	0	.000	-0	-1	-1	-0	0.0
Total 4	6	10	.375	47	20	6	0	1	185	235	9	56	30	14.2	4.04	90	.315	.364	13	.210	0	-3	-8	1	-0.7

● **IZZY GOLDSTEIN** Goldstein, Isidore b: 6/6/08, Odessa, Russia d: 9/24/93, Delray Beach, Fla. BB/TR, 6', 160 lbs. Deb: 4/24/32

YEAR TM/L	W	L	PCT	G	GS	CG	SH	SV	IP	H	HR	BB	SO	RAT	ERA	ERA+	OAV	OOB	BH	AVG	PB	PR	/A	PD	TPI
1932 Det-A	3	2	.600	16	6	2	0	0	56¹	63	2	41	14	17.1	4.47	105	.276	.393	5	.294	1	0	1	0	0.2

● **DAVE GOLTZ** Goltz, David Allan b: 6/23/49, Pelican Rapids, Minn. BR/TR, 6'4", 215 lbs. Deb: 7/18/72

YEAR TM/L	W	L	PCT	G	GS	CG	SH	SV	IP	H	HR	BB	SO	RAT	ERA	ERA+	OAV	OOB	BH	AVG	PB	PR	/A	PD	TPI
1972 Min-A	3	3	.500	15	1	2	0	1	91	91	5	26	38	10.0	2.67	120	.224	.280	3	.103	-1	4	5	-0	0.3
1973 Min-A	6	4	.600	32	10	1	0	1	106¹	138	11	32	65	14.6	5.25	75	.318	.368	0	—	0	-17	-15	1	-1.3
1974 Min-A	10	10	.500	28	24	5	1	1	174¹	192	14	45	89	12.6	3.25	115	.282	.333	0	—	0	7	10	1	1.2
1975 Min-A	14	14	.500	32	32	15	1	0	243	235	18	72	128	11.6	3.67	105	.255	.313	0	—	0	3	5	1	0.6
1976 Min-A	14	14	.500	36	35	13	4	0	249¹	239	14	91	133	12.1	3.36	107	.254	.323	0	—	0	4	7	0	0.7
1977 Min-A	20	11	.645	39	39	19	2	0	303	284	21	91	186	11.2	3.36	119	.247	.304	0	—	0	24	21	-1	2.0
1978 Min-A	15	10	.600	29	29	13	2	0	220¹	209	12	67	116	11.3	2.49	153	.253	.309	0	—	0	31	32	0	3.7
1979 Min-A	14	13	.519	36	35	12	1	0	250²	282	22	69	132	12.6	4.16	105	.288	.336	0	—	0	1	6	-1	0.5
1980 LA-N	7	11	.389	35	27	2	2	1	171¹	198	12	59	91	13.5	4.31	81	.299	.356	6	.128	0	-13	-15	-0	-1.5
1981 *LA-N	2	7	.222	26	8	0	0	1	77	83	4	25	48	12.6	4.09	81	.288	.345	1	.059	-1	-5	-7	1	-0.8
1982 LA-N	0	1	.000	2	1	0	0	0	3²	6	0	3	2	14.7	4.91	71	.353	.353	0	.000	-0	-1	-1	0	-0.1
*Cal-A	8	5	.615	28	7	1	0	3	86	82	4	32	49	12.0	4.08	99	.252	.320	0	—	-2	-0	-0	-2	-0.2
1983 Cal-A	0	6	.000	15	6	0	0	0	63²	81	10	37	27	16.8	6.22	65	.315	.403	0	—	0	-15	-16	-0	-1.2
Total 12	113	109	.509	353	264	83	13	8	2039²	2104	149	646	1105	12.2	3.69	104	.269	.327	10	.106	-1	23	33	0	3.9

● **LUIS GOMEZ** Gomez, Luis (Sanchez) b: 8/19/51, Guadalajara, Mex. BR/TR, 5'9", 150 lbs. Deb: 4/28/74 ◆

YEAR TM/L	W	L	PCT	G	GS	CG	SH	SV	IP	H	HR	BB	SO	RAT	ERA	ERA+	OAV	OOB	BH	AVG	PB	PR	/A	PD	TPI
1981 Atl-N	0	0	—	1	0	0	0	0	1	3	0	2	0	45.0	27.00	13	.500	.625	7	.200	0	-3	-3	-0	0.0

● **PAT GOMEZ** Gomez, Patrick Alexander b: 3/17/68, Roseville, Cal. BL/TL, 5'11", 185 lbs. Deb: 4/6/93

YEAR TM/L	W	L	PCT	G	GS	CG	SH	SV	IP	H	HR	BB	SO	RAT	ERA	ERA+	OAV	OOB	BH	AVG	PB	PR	/A	PD	TPI
1993 SD-N	1	2	.333	27	1	0	0	0	31²	35	2	19	26	15.3	5.12	81	.292	.388	0	.000	0	-4	-3	-1	-0.4
1994 SF-N	0	1	.000	26	0	0	0	0	33¹	23	2	20	14	11.6	3.78	106	.211	.333	0	.000	-0	2	1	-1	-0.1
Total 2	1	3	.250	53	1	0	0	0	65	58	4	39	40	13.4	4.43	92	.253	.362	0	.000	-1	-2	-3	-1	-0.5

● **RUBEN GOMEZ** Gomez, Ruben (Colon) b: 7/13/27, Arroyo, P.R. BR/TR, 6', 175 lbs. Deb: 4/17/53

YEAR TM/L	W	L	PCT	G	GS	CG	SH	SV	IP	H	HR	BB	SO	RAT	ERA	ERA+	OAV	OOB	BH	AVG	PB	PR	/A	PD	TPI
1953 NY-N	13	11	.542	29	26	13	3	0	204	166	17	101	113	12.0	3.40	126	.218	.313	15	.208	-0	20	20	2	2.3
1954 *NY-N	17	9	.654	37	32	10	4	0	221²	202	20	109	106	12.9	2.88	140	.244	.337	14	.173	0	29	28	2	3.2
1955 NY-N	9	10	.474	33	31	9	3	1	185¹	207	20	63	79	13.5	4.56	88	.285	.348	18	.300	-4	-11	-11	3	-0.4
1956 NY-N	7	17	.292	40	31	4	2	0	196¹	191	19	77	76	12.7	4.58	83	.259	.337	11	.183	-0	-18	-17	2	-1.7
1957 NY-N	15	13	.536	38	36	16	1	0	238¹	233	26	71	124	11.7	3.78	104	.254	.311	16	.184	1	3	4	2	0.8
1958 SF-N	10	12	.455	42	30	8	1	1	207²	204	21	77	112	12.5	4.38	87	.261	.334	14	.200	1	-10	-13	2	-0.9
1959 Phi-N	3	8	.273	20	12	2	1	1	72¹	90	12	24	37	14.2	6.10	67	.300	.352	3	.176	-2	-17	-16	2	-2.0
1960 Phi-N	0	3	.000	22	1	0	0	0	52¹	68	7	9	24	13.4	5.33	73	.321	.351	1	.083	-1	-9	-8	-1	-0.6
1962 Cle-A	1	2	.333	15	4	1	0	0	45¹	50	5	25	21	15.3	4.37	89	.292	.389	3	.231	0	-2	-2	-1	-0.1
Min-A	1	1	.500	6	2	1	0	0	19¹	17	3	11	8	13.0	4.66	88	.254	.369	0	—	1	-1	1	0	-0.1
Yr	2	3	.400	21	6	1	0	0	64²	67	8	36	29	14.3	4.45	88	.276	.369	3	.167	-0	-3	-4	-1	-0.2
1967 Phi-N	0	0	—	7	0	0	0	0	11¹	8	2	7	9	11.9	3.97	86	.211	.333	0	—	0	-1	-1	1	0.1
Total 10	76	86	.469	289	205	63	15	5	1454	1436	154	574	677	12.7	4.09	97	.259	.334	95	.199	6	-17	-18	14	0.6

● **LEFTY GOMEZ** Gomez, Vernon Louis "Goofy" b: 11/26/08, Rodeo, Cal. d: 2/17/89, Greenbrae, Cal. BL/TL, 6'2", 173 lbs. Deb: 4/29/30 H

YEAR TM/L	W	L	PCT	G	GS	CG	SH	SV	IP	H	HR	BB	SO	RAT	ERA	ERA+	OAV	OOB	BH	AVG	PB	PR	/A	PD	TPI
1930 NY-A	2	5	.286	15	6	2	0	0	60	66	12	28	22	14.3	5.55	78	.280	.358	3	.150	-2	-6	-8	1	-0.8
1931 NY-A	21	9	.700	40	26	17	1	3	243	206	7	85	150	10.9	2.67	149	.226	.295	11	.133	-3	46	35	-1	3.5
1932 *NY-A★	24	7	.774	37	31	21	1	1	265¹	266	23	105	176	12.7	4.21	97	.259	.329	18	.173	-1	8	-4	-3	-0.8
1933 NY-A★	16	10	.615	35	30	14	4	2	234²	218	16	106	163	12.4	3.18	124	.240	.319	9	.112	-3	29	18	-4	1.1
1934 NY-A★	26	5	.839	38	33	25	6	1	281²	223	12	96	158	10.2	2.33	174	.215	.282	18	.131	-3	68	54	-2	4.8
1935 NY-A★	12	15	.444	34	30	15	2	1	246	223	18	86	138	11.4	3.18	127	.242	.309	10	.120	-6	35	24	1	1.6
1936 *NY-A☆	13	7	.650	31	30	10	0	1	188²	184	6	122	105	14.6	4.39	106	.254	.362	10	.145	-3	14	6	-1	0.1

YEAR	TM/L	W	L	PCT	G	GS	CG	SH	SV	IP	H	HR	BB	SO	RAT	ERA	ERA+	OAV	OOB	BH	AVG	PB	PR	/A	PD	TPI
1937	*NY-A★	21	11	.656	34	34	25	6	0	278¹	233	10	93	194	10.6	2.33	191	.223	.287	21	.200	-1	71	65	-3	6.5
1938	*NY-A★	18	12	.600	32	32	20	4	0	239	239	7	99	129	12.8	3.35	135	.260	.332	13	.151	-2	38	31	2	3.3
1939	*NY-A☆	12	8	.600	26	26	14	2	0	198	173	11	84	102	11.8	3.41	128	.235	.316	11	.151	-2	27	21	-1	1.5
1940	NY-A	3	3	.500	9	5	0	0	0	27¹	37	2	18	14	18.4	6.59	61	.325	.421	0	.000	-1	-7	-8	-1	-1.5
1941	NY-A	15	5	.750	23	23	8	2	0	156¹	151	10	103	76	14.7	3.74	105	.250	.360	9	.153	-1	7	3	-4	-0.1
1942	NY-A	6	4	.600	13	13	2	0	0	80	67	4	65	41	15.1	4.27	80	.237	.383	5	.152	-1	-5	-7	-2	-1.1
1943	Was-A	0	1	.000	1	1	0	0	0	4²	4	0	5	0	17.4	5.79	55	.250	.429	0	.000	-0	-1	-1	-1	-0.2
Total 14		189	102	.649	368	320	173	28	9	2503	2290	138	1095	1468	12.2	3.34	125	.242	.321	133	.147	-30	322	229	-15	17.9

● **JOE GONZALES**   Gonzales, Joe Madrid "Smokey" b: 3/19/15, San Francisco, Cal   BR/TR, 5'9", 175 lbs.   Deb: 8/28/37

YEAR	TM/L	W	L	PCT	G	GS	CG	SH	SV	IP	H	HR	BB	SO	RAT	ERA	ERA+	OAV	OOB	BH	AVG	PB	PR	/A	PD	TPI
1937	Bos-A	1	2	.333	8	2	0	0	0	31	37	1	11	11	13.9	4.35	109	.291	.348	0	.000	-2	1	1	0	0.0

● **RENE GONZALES**   Gonzales, Rene Adrian b: 9/3/60, Austin, Tex.   BR/TR, 6'3", 191 lbs.   Deb: 7/27/84 ♦

YEAR	TM/L	W	L	PCT	G	GS	CG	SH	SV	IP	H	HR	BB	SO	RAT	ERA	ERA+	OAV	OOB	BH	AVG	PB	PR	/A	PD	TPI
1993	Cal-A	0	0	—	1	0	0	0	0	1	0	0	0	0	0.0	0.00	—	.000	.000	84	.251	1	0	1	0	0.0

● **VINCE GONZALES**   Gonzales, Wenceslao (O'Reilly)
b: 9/28/25, Quivican, Cuba   d: 3/11/81, Ciudad Del Carmen Campeche, Mexico   BL/TL, 6'1", 165 lbs.   Deb: 4/13/55

YEAR	TM/L	W	L	PCT	G	GS	CG	SH	SV	IP	H	HR	BB	SO	RAT	ERA	ERA+	OAV	OOB	BH	AVG	PB	PR	/A	PD	TPI
1955	Was-A	0	0	—	1	0	0	0	0	2	6	0	3	1	40.5	27.00	14	.500	.600	0	—	0	-5	-5	-0	0.0

● **GERMAN GONZALEZ**   Gonzalez, German Jose (Caraballo) b: 3/7/62, Rio Caribe, Venez.   BR/TR, 6', 170 lbs.   Deb: 8/5/88

YEAR	TM/L	W	L	PCT	G	GS	CG	SH	SV	IP	H	HR	BB	SO	RAT	ERA	ERA+	OAV	OOB	BH	AVG	PB	PR	/A	PD	TPI
1988	Min-A	0	0	—	16	0	0	0	1	21¹	20	4	8	19	12.2	3.38	121	.244	.319	0	—	0	1	2	0	-0.1
1989	Min-A	3	2	.600	22	0	0	0	0	29	32	2	11	25	14.6	4.66	89	.274	.356	0	—	0	-2	-2	-0	-0.3
Total 2		3	2	.600	38	0	0	0	1	50¹	52	6	19	44	13.6	4.11	100	.261	.341	0	—	0	-1	-0	-0	-0.4

● **JULIO GONZALEZ**   Gonzalez, Julio Enrique (Herrera) b: 12/20/20, Banes, Cuba   d: 2/15/91, Banes, Cuba   BR/TR, 5'11", 150 lbs.   Deb: 8/9/49

YEAR	TM/L	W	L	PCT	G	GS	CG	SH	SV	IP	H	HR	BB	SO	RAT	ERA	ERA+	OAV	OOB	BH	AVG	PB	PR	/A	PD	TPI
1949	Was-A	0	0	—	13	0	0	0	0	34¹	33	3	27	5	16.0	4.72	90	.256	.389	1	.200	-0	-2	-2	-0	0.0

● **RALPH GOOD**   Good, Ralph Nelson "Holy" b: 4/25/1886, Monticello, Me.   d: 11/24/65, Waterville, Maine   BR/TR, 6', 165 lbs.   Deb: 7/1/10

YEAR	TM/L	W	L	PCT	G	GS	CG	SH	SV	IP	H	HR	BB	SO	RAT	ERA	ERA+	OAV	OOB	BH	AVG	PB	PR	/A	PD	TPI
1910	Bos-N	0	0	—	2	0	0	0	0	9	6	0	2	4	10.0	2.00	166	.188	.278	0	.000	-0	1	1	0	0.0

● **WILBUR GOOD**   Good, Wilbur David "Lefty" b: 9/28/1885, Punxsutawney, Pa.   d: 12/30/63, Brooksville, Fla.   BL/TL, 5'6", 165 lbs.   Deb: 8/18/05 ♦

YEAR	TM/L	W	L	PCT	G	GS	CG	SH	SV	IP	H	HR	BB	SO	RAT	ERA	ERA+	OAV	OOB	BH	AVG	PB	PR	/A	PD	TPI
1905	NY-A	0	2	.000	5	2	0	0	0	19	18	1	14	13	15.2	4.74	62	.251	.374	3	.375	-1	-4	-4	0	-0.3

● **HERB GOODALL**   Goodall, Herbert Frank b: 3/10/1870, Mansfield, Pa.   d: 1/20/38, Mansfield, Pa.   BR/TR, 5'9", 180 lbs.   Deb: 4/29/1890

YEAR	TM/L	W	L	PCT	G	GS	CG	SH	SV	IP	H	HR	BB	SO	RAT	ERA	ERA+	OAV	OOB	BH	AVG	PB	PR	/A	PD	TPI
1890	Lou-a	8	5	.615	18	13	8	1	4	109	94	2	51	46	12.8	3.39	114	.226	.324	19	.422	6	6	6	1	1.2

● **JOHN GOODELL**   Goodell, John Henry William "Lefty" b: 4/5/07, Muskogee, Okla.   BR/TL, 5'10", 165 lbs.   Deb: 4/19/28

YEAR	TM/L	W	L	PCT	G	GS	CG	SH	SV	IP	H	HR	BB	SO	RAT	ERA	ERA+	OAV	OOB	BH	AVG	PB	PR	/A	PD	TPI
1928	Chi-A	0	0	—	2	0	0	0	0	3	6	0	2	0	27.0	18.00	23	.500	.600	0	—	0	-5	-5	0	0.0

● **DWIGHT GOODEN**   Gooden, Dwight Eugene "Doc" b: 11/16/64, Tampa, Fla.   BR/TR, 6'3", 198 lbs.   Deb: 4/7/84

YEAR	TM/L	W	L	PCT	G	GS	CG	SH	SV	IP	H	HR	BB	SO	RAT	ERA	ERA+	OAV	OOB	BH	AVG	PB	PR	/A	PD	TPI
1984	NY-N★	17	9	.654	31	31	7	3	0	218	161	7	73	276	9.7	2.60	136	.202	.270	14	.200	1	24	23	1	2.9
1985	NY-N☆	24	4	.857	35	35	16	8	0	276²	198	13	69	268	8.8	1.53	226	.201	.254	21	.226	6	63	59	2	7.3
1986	*NY-N★	17	6	.739	33	33	12	2	0	250	197	17	80	200	10.1	2.84	124	.215	.280	7	.086	-3	24	19	2	1.7
1987	NY-N	15	7	.682	25	25	7	3	0	179²	162	11	53	148	10.9	3.21	118	.244	.301	14	.219	2	17	11	-0	1.5
1988	*NY-N★	18	9	.667	34	34	10	3	0	248¹	242	8	57	175	11.1	3.19	101	.256	.303	16	.178	3	7	1	5	0.9
1989	NY-N	9	4	.692	19	17	0	0	0	118¹	93	9	47	101	10.8	2.89	113	.211	.290	8	.200	2	8	5	0	0.7
1990	NY-N	19	7	.731	34	34	2	1	0	232²	229	10	70	223	11.8	3.83	98	.258	.317	14	.187	4	-1	-2	2	0.3
1991	NY-N	13	7	.650	27	27	3	1	0	190	185	12	56	150	11.6	3.60	101	.257	.313	15	.238	4	2	1	1	0.6
1992	NY-N	10	13	.435	31	31	3	0	0	206	197	11	70	145	11.8	3.67	95	.255	.319	19	.264	7	-4	-5	1	0.3
1993	NY-N	12	15	.444	29	29	7	2	0	208²	188	16	61	149	11.1	3.45	116	.242	.304	14	.200	4	14	13	-0	2.0
1994	NY-N	3	4	.429	7	7	0	0	0	41¹	46	9	15	40	13.5	6.31	68	.282	.346	2	.167	-0	-10	-9	1	-1.2
Total 11		157	85	.649	305	303	67	23	1	2169²	1898	123	651	1875	10.7	3.10	115	.235	.295	144	.197	29	145	116	14	17.0

● **ART GOODWIN**   Goodwin, Arthur Ingram b: 2/27/1877, Whiteley Twnshp., Pa.   d: 6/19/43, Franklin Township, Greene County, Pa.   TR, 5'8", 195 lbs.   Deb: 10/7/05

YEAR	TM/L	W	L	PCT	G	GS	CG	SH	SV	IP	H	HR	BB	SO	RAT	ERA	ERA+	OAV	OOB	BH	AVG	PB	PR	/A	PD	TPI
1905	NY-A	0	0	—	1	0	0	0	0	0¹	2	0	2	0	108.0	81.00	4	.680	.809	0	—	0	-3	-3	0	0.0

● **CLYDE GOODWIN**   Goodwin, Clyde Samuel b: 11/12/1886, Shade, Ohio   d: 10/12/63, Dayton, Ohio   BR/TR, 5'11", 145 lbs.   Deb: 9/18/06

YEAR	TM/L	W	L	PCT	G	GS	CG	SH	SV	IP	H	HR	BB	SO	RAT	ERA	ERA+	OAV	OOB	BH	AVG	PB	PR	/A	PD	TPI
1906	Was-A	0	2	.000	4	3	1	0	0	22¹	20	0	13	9	13.7	4.43	59	.243	.352	1	.200	-0	-4	-4	-1	-0.4

● **JIM GOODWIN**   Goodwin, James Patrick b: 8/15/26, St.Louis, Mo.   BL/TL, 6'1", 170 lbs.   Deb: 4/24/48

YEAR	TM/L	W	L	PCT	G	GS	CG	SH	SV	IP	H	HR	BB	SO	RAT	ERA	ERA+	OAV	OOB	BH	AVG	PB	PR	/A	PD	TPI
1948	Chi-A	0	0	—	8	1	0	0	1	10¹	9	0	12	3	19.2	8.71	49	.237	.431	1	.500	-0	-5	-5	0	-0.1

● **MARV GOODWIN**   Goodwin, Marvin Mardo b: 1/16/1891, Gordonsville, Va.   d: 10/21/25, Houston, Tex.   BR/TR, 5'11", 168 lbs.   Deb: 9/7/16

YEAR	TM/L	W	L	PCT	G	GS	CG	SH	SV	IP	H	HR	BB	SO	RAT	ERA	ERA+	OAV	OOB	BH	AVG	PB	PR	/A	PD	TPI
1916	Was-A	0	0	—	3	0	0	0	0	5²	5	0	3	1	12.7	3.18	88	.217	.308	0	—	-0	-0	-0	0	0.0
1917	StL-N	6	4	.600	14	12	6	3	0	85¹	70	1	19	38	9.4	2.21	122	.222	.266	4	.174	-0	5	5	2	0.7
1919	StL-N	11	9	.550	33	17	7	0	0	179	163	3	33	48	10.3	2.51	111	.245	.289	12	.200	1	8	6	-1	0.7
1920	StL-N	3	8	.273	32	12	3	0	1	116¹	153	1	28	23	14.4	4.95	60	.314	.357	7	.200	-0	-23	-25	-3	-2.5
1921	StL-N	1	2	.333	14	4	1	0	1	36¹	47	1	9	7	14.1	3.72	99	.315	.358	0	.000	-1	0	-0	0	0.0
1922	StL-N	0	0	—	2	0	0	0	0	4	3	0	3	0	13.5	2.25	172	.250	.400	2	—	0	1	1	0	0.0
1925	Cin-N	0	2	.000	4	3	2	0	0	20²	26	2	5	4	13.9	4.79	86	.317	.364	1	.250	-0	-1	-2	1	0.0
Total 7		21	25	.457	102	48	19	3	2	447¹	467	8	100	121	11.7	3.30	90	.269	.315	24	.186	0	-11	-17	0	-1.1

● **RAY GORDINIER**   Gordinier, Raymond Cornelius "Gordy" b: 4/11/1892, Rochester, N.Y.   d: 11/15/60, Rochester, N.Y.   BB/TR, 5'8.5", 170 lbs.   Deb: 9/17/21

YEAR	TM/L	W	L	PCT	G	GS	CG	SH	SV	IP	H	HR	BB	SO	RAT	ERA	ERA+	OAV	OOB	BH	AVG	PB	PR	/A	PD	TPI
1921	Bro-N	1	0	1.000	3	3	0	0	0	12	10	0	8	4	13.5	5.25	74	.227	.346	1	.250	-2	-2	-2	0	-0.1
1922	Bro-N	0	0	—	5	0	0	0	0	11¹	13	3	8	5	16.7	8.74	47	.289	.396	0	.000	-0	-6	-6	-0	-0.1
Total 2		1	0	1.000	8	3	0	0	0	23¹	23	3	16	9	15.0	6.94	57	.258	.371	1	.167	-0	-8	-8	0	-0.1

● **DON GORDON**   Gordon, Donald Thomas b: 10/10/59, New York, N.Y.   BR/TR, 6'1", 175 lbs.   Deb: 4/10/86

YEAR	TM/L	W	L	PCT	G	GS	CG	SH	SV	IP	H	HR	BB	SO	RAT	ERA	ERA+	OAV	OOB	BH	AVG	PB	PR	/A	PD	TPI
1986	Tor-A	0	1	.000	14	0	0	0	1	21²	28	1	8	13	15.4	7.06	60	.311	.374	0	—	0	-7	-7	-1	-0.4
1987	Tor-A	0	0	—	5	0	0	0	0	11	8	2	3	9	9.0	4.09	110	.200	.256	0	—	0	0	0	-0	0.0
	Cle-A	0	3	.000	21	0	0	0	0	39²	49	3	12	20	14.7	4.08	111	.295	.357	0	—	0	2	1	1	0.2
	Yr	0	3	.000	26	0	0	0	0	50²	57	5	15	29	13.5	4.09	111	.277	.338	0	—	0	2	1	1	0.2
1988	Cle-A	3	4	.429	38	0	0	0	0	59¹	65	5	19	20	13.2	4.40	93	.284	.347	0	—	0	-3	-2	1	-0.2
Total 3		3	8	.273	78	0	0	0	3	131²	150	11	42	56	13.7	4.72	91	.286	.348	0	—	0	-8	-6	1	-0.4

● **TOM GORDON**   Gordon, Thomas b: 11/18/67, Sebring, Fla.   BR/TR, 5'9", 160 lbs.   Deb: 9/8/88

YEAR	TM/L	W	L	PCT	G	GS	CG	SH	SV	IP	H	HR	BB	SO	RAT	ERA	ERA+	OAV	OOB	BH	AVG	PB	PR	/A	PD	TPI
1988	KC-A	0	2	.000	5	2	0	0	0	15²	16	1	7	18	13.2	5.17	77	.267	.343	0	—	0	-2	-2	-0	-0.2
1989	KC-A	17	9	.654	49	16	1	1	1	163	122	10	86	153	11.5	3.64	106	.210	.312	0	—	0	4	4	3	0.8
1990	KC-A	12	11	.522	32	32	6	1	0	195¹	192	17	99	175	13.5	3.73	103	.257	.347	0	—	0	4	2	0	0.3
1991	KC-A	9	14	.391	45	14	1	0	1	158	129	16	87	167	12.5	3.87	106	.221	.325	0	—	0	6	6	4	0.3
1992	KC-A	6	10	.375	40	11	0	0	0	117²	116	9	55	98	13.4	4.59	88	.258	.344	0	—	0	-9	-7	1	-1.0
1993	KC-A	12	6	.667	48	14	2	0	0	155²	125	11	77	143	11.7	3.58	128	.223	.318	0	—	0	13	17	1	1.5
1994	KC-A	11	7	.611	24	24	1	0	0	155¹	136	15	87	126	13.1	4.35	119	.237	.340	0	—	0	8	14	0	1.4
Total 7		67	59	.532	243	113	10	2	3	960²	836	79	498	880	12.6	3.94	107	.235	.332	0	—	0	22	31	6	3.4

● **CHARLIE GORIN**   Gorin, Charles Perry b: 2/6/28, Waco, Tex.   BL/TL, 5'10", 165 lbs.   Deb: 5/29/54

YEAR	TM/L	W	L	PCT	G	GS	CG	SH	SV	IP	H	HR	BB	SO	RAT	ERA	ERA+	OAV	OOB	BH	AVG	PB	PR	/A	PD	TPI
1954	Mil-N	0	1	.000	5	0	0	0	0	9²	5	0	6	12	10.2	1.86	200	.152	.282	0	.000	-0	2	2	-0	0.1

YEAR TM/L	W	L	PCT	G	GS	CG	SH	SV	IP	H	HR	BB	SO	RAT	ERA	ERA+	OAV	OOB	BH	AVG	PB	PR	/A	PD	TPI
1955 Mil-N	0	0	—	2	0	0	0	0	0¹	1	0	3	0	108.0	54.00	7	.500	.800	0	—	0	-2	-2	-0	0.0
Total 2	0	1	.000	7	0	0	0	0	10	6	0	9	12	13.5	3.60	103	.171	.341	0	.000	-0	1	0	-0	0.1

● **JACK GORMAN** Gorman, John F. "Stooping Jack" b: 1859, St.Louis, Mo. d: 9/9/1889, St.Louis, Mo. Deb: 7/1/1883 ♦

YEAR TM/L	W	L	PCT	G	GS	CG	SH	SV	IP	H	HR	BB	SO	RAT	ERA	ERA+	OAV	OOB	BH	AVG	PB	PR	/A	PD	TPI
1884 Pit-a	1	2	.333	3	3	3	0	0	25	22	0	5	10	10.1	4.68	72	.212	.255	4	.148	-0	-4	-4	0	-0.4

● **TOM GORMAN** Gorman, Thomas Aloysius b: 1/4/25, New York, N.Y. d: 12/26/92, Valley Stream, N.Y. BR/TR, 6'1", 190 lbs. Deb: 7/16/52

YEAR TM/L	W	L	PCT	G	GS	CG	SH	SV	IP	H	HR	BB	SO	RAT	ERA	ERA+	OAV	OOB	BH	AVG	PB	PR	/A	PD	TPI
1952 *NY-A	6	2	.750	12	6	1	1	1	60²	63	8	22	31	12.9	4.60	72	.272	.340	2	.087	-1	-6	-9	-0	-1.2
1953 *NY-A	4	5	.444	40	1	0	0	6	77	65	5	32	38	12.0	3.39	109	.226	.317	2	.133	-1	5	3	-0	0.2
1954 NY-A	0	0	—	23	0	0	0	2	36²	30	1	14	31	11.0	2.21	156	.222	.300	0	—	0	6	5	-0	0.0
1955 KC-A	7	6	.538	57	0	0	0	18	109	98	11	36	46	11.4	3.55	118	.246	.314	2	.083	-1	5	8	-1	0.9
1956 KC-A	9	10	.474	52	13	1	0	3	171¹	168	23	68	56	12.5	3.83	113	.258	.330	2	.051	-4	6	9	-0	0.6
1957 KC-A	5	9	.357	38	12	3	1	3	124²	125	18	33	66	11.5	3.83	103	.261	.310	4	.121	-2	-1	2	-0	0.0
1958 KC-A	4	4	.500	50	1	0	0	8	89²	86	8	20	44	10.9	3.51	111	.258	.306	2	.118	-1	3	4	-1	0.2
1959 KC-A	1	0	1.000	17	0	0	0	1	20¹	24	3	14	9	17.3	7.08	57	.293	.402	0	—	0	-7	-7	-1	-0.5
Total 8	36	36	.500	289	33	5	2	42	689¹	659	77	239	321	12.0	3.77	105	.254	.321	14	.090	-10	11	14	-4	0.2

● **TOM GORMAN** Gorman, Thomas David "Big Tom" b: 3/16/16, New York, N.Y. d: 8/11/86, Closter, N.J. BR/TL, 6'2", 200 lbs. Deb: 9/14/39 U

YEAR TM/L	W	L	PCT	G	GS	CG	SH	SV	IP	H	HR	BB	SO	RAT	ERA	ERA+	OAV	OOB	BH	AVG	PB	PR	/A	PD	TPI
1939 NY-N	0	0	—	4	0	0	0	0	5	7	0	1	2	14.4	7.20	55	.350	.381	0	.000	-0	-2	-2	0	0.0

● **TOM GORMAN** Gorman, Thomas Patrick b: 12/16/57, Portland, Ore. BL/TL, 6'4", 200 lbs. Deb: 9/2/81

YEAR TM/L	W	L	PCT	G	GS	CG	SH	SV	IP	H	HR	BB	SO	RAT	ERA	ERA+	OAV	OOB	BH	AVG	PB	PR	/A	PD	TPI
1981 Mon-N	0	0	—	9	0	0	0	0	15	12	0	6	13	11.4	4.20	83	.222	.311	0	—	0	-1	-1	1	0.1
1982 Mon-N	1	0	1.000	5	0	0	0	0	7	8	0	4	6	15.4	5.14	71	.286	.375	0	—	0	-1	-1	0	-0.1
NY-N	0	1	.000	3	1	0	0	0	9¹	8	0	0	7	7.7	0.96	376	.235	.235	0	.000	-0	3	3	0	0.3
Yr	1	1	.500	8	1	0	0	0	16¹	16	0	4	13	11.0	2.76	132	.254	.299	0	.000	-0	2	2	0	0.3
1983 NY-N	1	4	.200	25	4	0	0	0	49¹	45	3	15	30	10.9	4.93	74	.245	.302	1	.250	-0	-7	-7	-0	-0.7
1984 NY-N	6	0	1.000	36	0	0	0	0	57²	51	6	13	40	10.1	2.97	119	.238	.285	0	.000	-0	4	4	0	0.3
1985 NY-N	4	4	.500	34	2	0	0	0	52²	56	8	18	32	12.6	5.13	67	.277	.336	0	.000	-1	-9	-10	1	-1.3
1986 Phi-N	0	1	.000	8	0	0	0	0	11²	21	0	5	8	20.1	7.71	50	.382	.433	0	.000	-0	-5	-5	0	-0.4
1987 SD-N	0	0	—	6	0	0	0	0	11	11	1	5	8	13.1	4.09	97	.262	.340	0	—	0	-0	-0	-0	-0.0
Total 7	12	10	.545	126	7	0	0	0	213²	212	18	66	144	11.8	4.34	83	.261	.318	1	.071	-1	-17	-18	2	-1.8

● **JOE GORMLEY** Gormley, Joseph b: 12/20/1866, Summit Hill, Pa. d: 7/2/50, Summit Hill, Pa. BL/TL, Deb: 6/16/1891

YEAR TM/L	W	L	PCT	G	GS	CG	SH	SV	IP	H	HR	BB	SO	RAT	ERA	ERA+	OAV	OOB	BH	AVG	PB	PR	/A	PD	TPI
1891 Phi-N	0	1	.000	1	1	1	0	0	8	10	0	5	2	16.9	5.63	61	.295	.385	0	.000	-1	-2	-2	0	-0.2

● **HANK GORNICKI** Gornicki, Henry Frank b: 1/14/11, Niagara Falls, N.Y BR/TR, 6'1", 145 lbs. Deb: 4/17/41

YEAR TM/L	W	L	PCT	G	GS	CG	SH	SV	IP	H	HR	BB	SO	RAT	ERA	ERA+	OAV	OOB	BH	AVG	PB	PR	/A	PD	TPI
1941 StL-N	1	0	1.000	4	1	1	1	0	11¹	6	0	9	6	12.7	3.18	118	.158	.333	1	.250	0	1	1	-0	0.0
Chi-N	0	0	—	1	0	0	0	0	2	3	0	0	2	13.5	4.50	78	.375	.375	0	—	0	-0	-0	0	0.0
Yr	1	0	1.000	5	1	1	1	0	13¹	9	0	9	8	12.2	3.38	110	.191	.321	1	.250	0	1	0	0	0.0
1942 Pit-N	5	6	.455	25	14	7	2	2	112	89	2	40	48	10.4	2.57	132	.215	.286	4	.114	-1	9	10	-1	0.8
1943 Pit-N	9	13	.409	42	19	4	1	4	147	165	10	47	63	13.1	3.98	87	.286	.342	7	.175	-1	-10	-8	-1	-1.4
1946 Pit-N	0	0	—	7	0	0	0	0	12²	12	0	11	4	16.3	3.55	99	.255	.397	0	.000	-0	-0	-0	-0	-0.1
Total 4	15	19	.441	79	34	12	4	6	285	275	12	107	123	12.2	3.38	102	.254	.323	12	.146	-2	-0	2	-2	-0.7

● **JOHNNY GORSICA** Gorsica, John Joseph Perry (b: John Joseph Perry Gorczyca) b: 3/29/15, Bayonne, N.J. BR/TR, 6'2", 180 lbs. Deb: 4/22/40

YEAR TM/L	W	L	PCT	G	GS	CG	SH	SV	IP	H	HR	BB	SO	RAT	ERA	ERA+	OAV	OOB	BH	AVG	PB	PR	/A	PD	TPI
1940 *Det-A	7	7	.500	29	20	5	2	0	160	170	10	57	68	13.0	4.33	110	.272	.337	12	.194	-0	1	8	5	1.1
1941 Det-A	9	11	.450	33	21	8	1	2	171	193	14	55	59	13.2	4.47	102	.281	.336	17	.298	4	-6	1	4	0.9
1942 Det-A	3	2	.600	28	0	0	0	4	53	63	2	26	19	15.6	4.75	83	.310	.397	1	.100	-0	-6	-5	4	-0.1
1943 Det-A	4	5	.444	35	4	1	0	5	96¹	88	3	40	45	12.1	3.36	105	.247	.327	4	.174	-0	1	2	3	0.5
1944 Det-A	6	14	.300	34	19	8	1	4	162	192	5	32	47	12.7	4.11	87	.296	.333	7	.135	-1	-12	-10	3	-1.0
1946 Det-A	0	0	—	14	0	0	0	1	23²	28	5	11	14	14.8	4.56	80	.301	.375	2	.667	1	-3	-2	-0	0.0
1947 Det-A	2	0	1.000	31	0	0	0	1	57²	44	5	26	20	11.2	3.75	101	.208	.300	2	.200	-0	-0	0	1	0.2
Total 7	31	39	.443	204	64	22	4	17	723²	778	44	247	272	13.0	4.18	98	.276	.338	45	.207	4	-28	-7	20	1.6

● **RICH GOSSAGE** Gossage, Richard Michael "Goose" b: 7/5/51, Colorado Springs, Colo. BR/TR, 6'3", 217 lbs. Deb: 4/16/72

YEAR TM/L	W	L	PCT	G	GS	CG	SH	SV	IP	H	HR	BB	SO	RAT	ERA	ERA+	OAV	OOB	BH	AVG	PB	PR	/A	PD	TPI
1972 Chi-A	7	1	.875	36	1	0	0	2	80	72	2	44	57	13.5	4.27	73	.247	.353	0	.000	-2	-11	-10	-1	-1.3
1973 Chi-A	0	4	.000	20	4	1	0	0	49²	57	7	37	33	17.6	7.43	53	.311	.435	0	—	0	-20	-19	-0	-1.4
1974 Chi-A	4	6	.400	39	3	0	0	1	89¹	92	4	47	64	14.2	4.13	90	.272	.364	0	—	0	-5	-4	0	-0.5
1975 Chi-A★	9	8	.529	62	0	0	0	26	141²	99	3	70	130	11.1	1.84	210	.201	.306	0	—	0	30	32	-1	5.2
1976 Chi-A☆	9	17	.346	31	29	15	0	1	224	214	16	90	135	12.6	3.94	91	.254	.333	0	—	0	-10	-9	-1	-1.1
1977 Pit-N★	11	9	.550	72	0	0	0	26	133	78	9	49	151	8.7	1.62	245	.170	.253	5	.217	1	34	35	-1	6.6
1978 *NY-A★	10	11	.476	63	0	0	0	27	134¹	87	9	59	122	9.9	2.01	180	.187	.281	0	—	0	26	24	-1	4.7
1979 NY-A	5	3	.625	36	0	0	0	18	58¹	48	5	19	41	10.3	2.62	155	.227	.291	0	—	0	10	9	-1	1.8
1980 *NY-A★	6	2	.750	64	0	0	0	33	99	74	5	37	103	10.2	2.27	173	.211	.288	0	—	0	19	18	-1	2.7
1981 *NY-A†	3	2	.600	32	0	0	0	20	46²	22	2	14	48	7.1	0.77	463	.141	.216	0	—	0	15	15	0	3.2
1982 *NY-A☆	4	5	.444	56	0	0	0	30	93	63	5	28	102	8.8	2.23	179	.196	.261	0	—	0	19	18	-1	2.9
1983 NY-A	13	5	.722	57	0	0	0	22	87¹	82	5	25	90	11.1	2.27	172	.248	.303	0	—	0	17	16	-2	3.8
1984 *SD-N★	10	6	.625	62	0	0	0	25	102¹	75	6	36	84	9.9	2.90	123	.204	.277	4	.182	-1	8	8	-1	1.5
1985 SD-N★	5	3	.625	50	0	0	0	26	79	64	1	17	52	9.3	1.82	194	.226	.272	0	.000	-1	16	15	-1	2.5
1986 SD-N	5	7	.417	45	0	0	0	21	64²	69	8	20	63	12.7	4.45	82	.273	.331	0	.000	-0	-5	-6	-1	-1.6
1987 SD-N	5	4	.556	40	0	0	0	11	52	47	9	19	44	11.4	3.12	127	.244	.311	0	.000	-0	6	5	-0	0.9
1988 Chi-N	4	4	.500	46	0	0	0	13	43²	50	3	15	30	14.0	4.33	83	.291	.358	0	—	0	-4	-4	-0	-0.9
1989 SF-N	2	1	.667	31	0	0	0	4	43²	32	2	27	24	12.2	2.68	126	.212	.331	0	—	0	4	3	-1	0.2
NY-A	1	0	1.000	11	0	0	0	0	14¹	14	0	3	6	11.3	3.77	103	.275	.327	0	—	0	1	1	-0	0.2
1991 Tex-A	4	2	.667	44	0	0	0	1	40¹	33	4	16	28	11.6	3.57	113	.228	.317	0	—	0	2	2	-1	0.2
1992 Oak-A	0	2	.000	30	0	0	0	0	38	32	5	19	26	12.6	2.84	132	.230	.331	0	—	0	5	4	-0	0.6
1993 Oak-A	4	5	.444	39	0	0	0	1	47²	32	6	26	40	14.3	4.53	90	.266	.360	0	—	0	-2	-1	0	0.2
1994 Sea-A	3	0	1.000	36	0	0	0	1	47¹	44	6	15	29	11.8	4.18	117	.251	.321	0	—	0	3	4	0	0.2
Total 22	124	107	.537	1002	37	16	0	310	1809¹	1497	119	732	1502	11.3	3.01	125	.228	.310	9	.106	-3	158	154	-14	30.2

● **JIM GOTT** Gott, James William b: 8/3/59, Hollywood, Cal. BR/TR, 6'4", 220 lbs. Deb: 4/9/82

YEAR TM/L	W	L	PCT	G	GS	CG	SH	SV	IP	H	HR	BB	SO	RAT	ERA	ERA+	OAV	OOB	BH	AVG	PB	PR	/A	PD	TPI
1982 Tor-A	5	10	.333	30	23	1	1	0	136	134	15	66	82	13.4	4.43	101	.255	.341	0	—	0	-5	1	-0	0.0
1983 Tor-A	9	14	.391	34	30	6	1	0	176²	195	15	68	121	13.7	4.74	91	.280	.349	0	—	0	-13	-9	-1	-1.1
1984 Tor-A	7	6	.538	35	12	1	1	2	109²	93	7	49	73	11.9	4.02	102	.233	.322	0	—	0	-0	1	-0	-0.3
1985 SF-N	7	10	.412	26	26	2	0	0	148¹	144	10	51	78	11.9	3.88	89	.254	.317	10	.196	4	-5	-7	1	-0.3
1986 SF-N	0	0	—	9	2	0	0	0	13	16	0	13	9	20.1	7.62	46	.314	.453	0	.000	-0	-6	-6	-0	-0.1
1987 SF-N	1	0	1.000	30	3	0	0	0	56	53	4	32	63	14.0	4.50	85	.244	.347	1	.100	-1	-4	-0	-0	-0.8
Pit-N	0	2	.000	25	0	0	0	13	31	28	0	8	27	10.5	1.45	283	.233	.281	0	.000	-0	9	9	-0	1.4
Yr	1	2	.333	55	3	0	0	13	87	81	4	40	90	12.5	3.41	115	.238	.318	1	.091	-1	6	5	-0	1.4
1988 Pit-N	6	6	.500	67	0	0	0	34	77¹	68	6	22	76	10.7	3.49	97	.243	.303	0	—	0	6	6	-0	-0.3
1989 Pit-N	0	0	—	1	0	0	0	0	0²	1	0	1	0	27.0	0.00	—	.333	.500	0	—	0	-0	-0	0	0.0
1990 LA-N	3	5	.375	50	0	0	0	3	62	59	6	44	50	13.5	2.90	126	.257	.352	0	—	0	5	4	-0	0.6
1991 LA-N	4	3	.571	26	0	0	0	2	76	63	5	32	73	11.4	2.96	121	.223	.305	1	.500	-0	6	6	-0	0.6
1992 LA-N	3	3	.500	68	0	0	0	6	88	72	4	41	75	11.7	2.45	146	.223	.315	1	.500	2	10	10	-0	1.5
1993 LA-N	4	8	.333	62	0	0	0	25	77²	71	6	17	67	10.3	2.32	165	.248	.293	0	—	0	15	13	0	2.8

YEAR TM/L	W	L	PCT	G	GS	CG	SH	SV	IP	H	HR	BB	SO	RAT	ERA	ERA+	OAV	OOB	BH	AVG	PB	PR	/A	PD	TPI
1994 LA-N	5	3	.625	37	0	0	0	2	36¹	46	3	20	29	17.1	5.94	66	.322	.416			0	-7	-8	0	-1.6
Total 13	54	70	.435	529	96	10	3	88	1088²	1043	83	454	818	12.6	3.80	102	.253	.331	13	.181	5	7	9	0	2.7

● **TED GOULAIT**   Goulait, Theodore Lee b: 8/11/1889, St.Clair, Mich. d: 7/15/36, St.Clair, Mich.   BR/TR, 5'9.5", 172 lbs.   Deb: 9/28/12

YEAR TM/L	W	L	PCT	G	GS	CG	SH	SV	IP	H	HR	BB	SO	RAT	ERA	ERA+	OAV	OOB	BH	AVG	PB	PR	/A	PD	TPI
1912 NY-N	0	0	—	1	1	1	0	0	7	11	0	4	6	19.3	6.43	53	.367	.441	1	.500	0	-2	-2	0	0.0

● **AL GOULD**   Gould, Albert Frank "Pudgy" b: 1/20/1893, Muscatine, Iowa   d: 8/8/82, San Jose, Cal.   BR/TR, 5'6.5", 160 lbs.   Deb: 7/11/16

YEAR TM/L	W	L	PCT	G	GS	CG	SH	SV	IP	H	HR	BB	SO	RAT	ERA	ERA+	OAV	OOB	BH	AVG	PB	PR	/A	PD	TPI
1916 Cle-A	5	7	.417	30	9	6	1	1	106²	101	0	40	41	12.2	2.53	119	.256	.329	3	.103	-2	4	6	-1	0.4
1917 Cle-A	4	4	.500	27	7	1	0	0	94	95	1	52	24	14.4	3.64	78	.281	.382	5	.208	1	-10	-8	2	-0.5
Total 2	9	11	.450	57	16	7	1	1	200²	196	1	92	65	13.2	3.05	96	.267	.354	8	.151	-1	-7	-3	1	-0.1

● **CHARLIE GOULD**   Gould, Charles Harvey b: 8/21/1847, Cincinnati, Ohio d: 4/10/17, Flushing, N.Y.   BR/TR, 6', 172 lbs.   Deb: 5/5/1871   M♦

YEAR TM/L	W	L	PCT	G	GS	CG	SH	SV	IP	H	HR	BB	SO	RAT	ERA	ERA+	OAV	OOB	BH	AVG	PB	PR	/A	PD	TPI
1876 Cin-N	0	0	—	2	0	0	0	0	4¹	10	0	0	0	20.8	0.00	—	.400	.400	65	.252	0	1	1	-0	0.0

● **LARRY GOWELL**   Gowell, Lawrence Clyde b: 5/2/48, Lewiston, Me.   BR/TR, 6'2", 182 lbs.   Deb: 9/21/72

YEAR TM/L	W	L	PCT	G	GS	CG	SH	SV	IP	H	HR	BB	SO	RAT	ERA	ERA+	OAV	OOB	BH	AVG	PB	PR	/A	PD	TPI
1972 NY-A	0	1	.000	2	1	0	0	0	7	3	0	2	7	6.4	1.29	229	.143	.217	1	1.000	1	1	1	0	0.3

● **MAURO GOZZO**   Gozzo, Mauro Paul b: 3/7/66, New Britain, Conn.   BR/TR, 6'2", 210 lbs.   Deb: 8/8/89

YEAR TM/L	W	L	PCT	G	GS	CG	SH	SV	IP	H	HR	BB	SO	RAT	ERA	ERA+	OAV	OOB	BH	AVG	PB	PR	/A	PD	TPI
1989 Tor-A	4	1	.800	9	3	0	0	0	31²	35	1	9	10	12.8	4.83	78	.289	.344	0	—	0	-3	-4	-0	-0.5
1990 Cle-A	0	0	—	2	0	0	0	0	3	2	0	2	2	12.0	0.00	—	.182	.308	0	—	0	1	1	-0	0.0
1991 Cle-A	0	0	—	2	2	0	0	0	4²	9	0	7	3	30.9	19.29	22	.450	.593	0	—	0	-8	-8	-0	0.0
1992 Min-A	0	0	—	2	0	0	0	0	1²	7	2	0	1	37.8	27.00	15	.583	.583	0	—	0	-4	-4	-0	-0.2
1993 NY-N	0	1	.000	10	0	0	0	0	14	11	1	5	6	10.3	2.57	156	.212	.281	0	—	0	2	2	-1	0.1
1994 NY-N	3	5	.375	23	8	0	0	1	69	86	5	28	33	15.0	4.83	88	.304	.369	4	.250	1	-5	-4	-0	-0.4
Total 6	7	7	.500	48	13	0	0	1	124	150	9	51	55	14.7	5.30	77	.301	.368	4	.250	1	-17	-17	-2	-1.0

● **AL GRABOWSKI**   Grabowski, Alfons Francis b: 9/6/01, Syracuse, N.Y. d: 10/29/66, Memphis, N.Y.   BL/TL, 5'11.5", 175 lbs.   Deb: 9/11/29   F

YEAR TM/L	W	L	PCT	G	GS	CG	SH	SV	IP	H	HR	BB	SO	RAT	ERA	ERA+	OAV	OOB	BH	AVG	PB	PR	/A	PD	TPI
1929 StL-N	3	2	.600	6	6	4	2	0	50	44	0	8	22	9.4	2.52	185	.227	.257	4	.250	2	12	12	-0	1.2
1930 StL-N	6	4	.600	33	8	1	0	1	107	122	7	49	43	14.6	4.79	105	.295	.373	12	.364	3	2	3	-0	0.4
Total 2	9	6	.600	39	14	5	2	1	157	166	7	57	65	13.0	4.07	120	.273	.338	16	.327	4	14	15	-0	1.6

● **REGGIE GRABOWSKI**   Grabowski, Reginald John b: 7/16/07, Syracuse, N.Y. d: 4/2/55, Syracuse, N.Y.   BR/TR, 6'0.5", 185 lbs.   Deb: 4/15/32   F

YEAR TM/L	W	L	PCT	G	GS	CG	SH	SV	IP	H	HR	BB	SO	RAT	ERA	ERA+	OAV	OOB	BH	AVG	PB	PR	/A	PD	TPI
1932 Phi-N	2	2	.500	14	2	0	0	0	34¹	38	2	22	15	16.3	3.67	120	.273	.380	0	.000	-1	1	3	-1	0.2
1933 Phi-N	1	3	.250	10	5	4	1	0	48	38	4	10	9	9.2	2.44	157	.220	.266	2	.125	-1	5	7	-1	0.4
1934 Phi-N	1	3	.250	27	5	0	0	0	65¹	114	13	23	13	19.3	9.23	51	.384	.433	1	.056	-2	-38	-33	-1	-2.0
Total 3	4	8	.333	51	12	4	1	0	147²	190	19	55	37	15.3	5.73	81	.312	.375	3	.075	-3	-32	-23	-3	-1.4

● **JOHN GRAFF**   Graff, John F. b: Philadelphia, Pa.   Deb: 7/19/1893

YEAR TM/L	W	L	PCT	G	GS	CG	SH	SV	IP	H	HR	BB	SO	RAT	ERA	ERA+	OAV	OOB	BH	AVG	PB	PR	/A	PD	TPI
1893 Was-N	0	1	.000	2	1	1	0	0	12	21	1	13	4	26.3	11.25	41	.372	.496	1	.200	-0	-9	-9	-0	-0.5

● **PEACHES GRAHAM**   Graham, George Frederick b: 3/23/1877, Aledo, Ill.   d: 7/25/39, Long Beach, Cal.   BR/TR, 5'9", 180 lbs.   Deb: 9/14/02   F♦

YEAR TM/L	W	L	PCT	G	GS	CG	SH	SV	IP	H	HR	BB	SO	RAT	ERA	ERA+	OAV	OOB	BH	AVG	PB	PR	/A	PD	TPI
1903 Chi-N	0	1	.000	1	1	0	0	0	5	9	0	3	4	23.4	5.40	58	.429	.520	0	.000	-0	-1	-1	0	-0.2

● **SKINNY GRAHAM**   Graham, Kyle b: 8/14/1899, Oak Grove, Ala.   d: 12/1/73, Oak Grove, Ala.   BR/TR, 6'2", 172 lbs.   Deb: 9/3/24

YEAR TM/L	W	L	PCT	G	GS	CG	SH	SV	IP	H	HR	BB	SO	RAT	ERA	ERA+	OAV	OOB	BH	AVG	PB	PR	/A	PD	TPI
1924 Bos-N	0	4	.000	5	4	1	0	0	33	33	0	11	15	12.0	3.82	100	.287	.349	0	.000	-1	0	0	-0	-0.1
1925 Bos-N	7	12	.368	34	23	5	0	1	157	177	6	62	32	13.9	4.41	91	.296	.365	6	.136	-2	-3	-7	-2	-1.1
1926 Bos-N	3	3	.500	15	4	1	0	0	36¹	54	3	19	7	18.6	7.93	45	.370	.449	2	.167	-1	-17	-18	0	-2.4
1929 Det-A	1	3	.250	13	6	2	0	1	51²	70	2	33	7	18.5	5.57	77	.340	.438	2	.105	-1	-8	-7	-1	-0.7
Total 4	11	22	.333	67	37	9	0	2	278	334	11	125	61	15.1	5.02	79	.314	.390	10	.122	-5	-27	-32	-3	-4.3

● **OSCAR GRAHAM**   Graham, Oscar M. b: 7/20/1878, Plattsmouth, Neb.   d: 10/31/31, Moline, Ill.   BL/TL, 6'0.5",   Deb: 4/16/07

YEAR TM/L	W	L	PCT	G	GS	CG	SH	SV	IP	H	HR	BB	SO	RAT	ERA	ERA+	OAV	OOB	BH	AVG	PB	PR	/A	PD	TPI
1907 Was-A	4	9	.308	20	14	6	0	0	104	116	3	29	44	13.4	3.98	61	.284	.346	11	.229	3	-17	-18	-0	-1.7

● **BILL GRAHAM**   Graham, William James b: 7/22/1884, Owosso, Mich.   d: 2/15/36, Holt, Mich.   TL, 6',   Deb: 4/18/08

YEAR TM/L	W	L	PCT	G	GS	CG	SH	SV	IP	H	HR	BB	SO	RAT	ERA	ERA+	OAV	OOB	BH	AVG	PB	PR	/A	PD	TPI
1908 StL-A	6	7	.462	21	13	7	0	0	117¹	104	0	32	47	11.4	2.30	104	.240	.310	5	.119	-3	1	1	-0	-0.2
1909 StL-A	8	14	.364	34	21	13	3	1	187¹	171	3	60	82	11.3	3.12	77	.256	.322	10	.159	-0	-13	-15	1	-1.7
1910 StL-A	0	8	.000	9	6	1	0	0	43	46	2	13	12	13.2	3.56	70	.297	.366	2	.154	-0	-5	-5	-2	-1.1
Total 3	14	29	.326	64	40	21	3	1	347²	321	5	105	141	11.6	2.90	83	.256	.323	17	.144	-3	-17	-19	-1	-3.0

● **BILL GRAHAM**   Graham, William Albert b: 1/21/37, Flemingsburg, Ky.   BR/TR, 6'3", 217 lbs.   Deb: 10/2/66

YEAR TM/L	W	L	PCT	G	GS	CG	SH	SV	IP	H	HR	BB	SO	RAT	ERA	ERA+	OAV	OOB	BH	AVG	PB	PR	/A	PD	TPI
1966 Det-A	0	0	—	1	0	0	0	0	2	2	0	0	2	9.0	0.00	—	.250	.250	0	—	0	1	1	-0	0.0
1967 NY-N	1	2	.333	5	3	1	0	0	27¹	20	3	11	14	10.2	2.63	129	.200	.279	1	.125	-0	2	2	-1	0.1
Total 2	1	2	.333	6	3	1	0	0	29¹	22	3	11	16	10.1	2.45	138	.204	.277	1	.125	-0	3	3	-1	0.1

● **JOE GRAHE**   Grahe, Joseph Milton b: 8/14/67, W.Palm Beach, Fla.   BR/TR, 6'1", 196 lbs.   Deb: 8/4/90

YEAR TM/L	W	L	PCT	G	GS	CG	SH	SV	IP	H	HR	BB	SO	RAT	ERA	ERA+	OAV	OOB	BH	AVG	PB	PR	/A	PD	TPI
1990 Cal-A	3	4	.429	8	8	0	0	0	43¹	51	3	23	25	16.0	4.98	77	.293	.385	0	—	0	-5	-6	1	-0.7
1991 Cal-A	3	7	.300	18	10	1	0	0	73	84	2	33	40	14.8	4.81	85	.288	.366	0	—	0	-6	-6	0	-0.7
1992 Cal-A	5	6	.455	46	7	0	0	21	94²	85	5	39	39	12.4	3.52	113	.246	.332	0	—	0	4	5	0	0.8
1993 Cal-A	4	1	.800	45	0	0	0	11	56²	54	5	25	31	12.9	2.86	158	.251	.335	0	—	0	9	10	1	1.1
1994 Cal-A	2	5	.286	40	0	0	0	13	43¹	68	5	18	26	19.1	6.65	75	.362	.434	0	—	0	-9	-8	0	-1.5
Total 5	17	23	.425	157	25	1	0	45	311	342	20	138	161	14.5	4.34	97	.281	.364	0	—	0	-6	-6	3	-1.0

● **TOMMY GRAMLY**   Gramly, Bert Thomas b: 4/19/45, Dallas, Tex.   BR/TR, 6'3", 175 lbs.   Deb: 4/18/68

YEAR TM/L	W	L	PCT	G	GS	CG	SH	SV	IP	H	HR	BB	SO	RAT	ERA	ERA+	OAV	OOB	BH	AVG	PB	PR	/A	PD	TPI
1968 Cle-A	0	1	.000	3	0	0	0	0	3¹	3	0	2	1	13.5	2.70	110	.250	.357	0	—	0	0	0	-0	0.0

● **HANK GRAMPP**   Grampp, Henry Erchardt b: 9/28/03, New York, N.Y.   d: 3/24/86, New York, N.Y.   BR/TR, 6'1", 185 lbs.   Deb: 6/2/27

YEAR TM/L	W	L	PCT	G	GS	CG	SH	SV	IP	H	HR	BB	SO	RAT	ERA	ERA+	OAV	OOB	BH	AVG	PB	PR	/A	PD	TPI
1927 Chi-N	0	0	—	2	0	0	0	0	3	4	0	3	3	15.0	9.00	43	.333	.385		—	0	-2	-2	0	0.0
1929 Chi-N	0	1	.000	1	1	0	0	0	2	4	0	3	0	36.0	27.00	17	.500	.667	0	—	0	-5	-5	-0	-1.2
Total 2	0	1	.000	3	1	0	0	0	5	8	0	4	3	23.4	16.20	26	.400	.520	0	—	0	-7	-7	0	-1.2

● **JACK GRANEY**   Graney, John Gladstone b: 6/10/1886, St.Thomas, Ont., Can.   d: 4/20/78, Louisiana, Mo.   BL/TL, 5'9", 180 lbs.   Deb: 4/30/08   ♦

YEAR TM/L	W	L	PCT	G	GS	CG	SH	SV	IP	H	HR	BB	SO	RAT	ERA	ERA+	OAV	OOB	BH	AVG	PB	PR	/A	PD	TPI
1908 Cle-A	0	0	—	2	0	0	0	0	3¹	6	0	1	0	18.9	5.40	44	.400	.438	0	—	0	-1	-1	-0	0.0

● **JEFF GRANGER**   Granger, Jeffrey Adam b: 12/16/71, San Pedro, Cal.   BR/TL, 6'4", 200 lbs.   Deb: 9/16/93

YEAR TM/L	W	L	PCT	G	GS	CG	SH	SV	IP	H	HR	BB	SO	RAT	ERA	ERA+	OAV	OOB	BH	AVG	PB	PR	/A	PD	TPI
1993 KC-A	0	0	—	1	0	0	0	0	1	3	1	1	1	45.0	27.00	17	.500	.625	0	—	0	-3	-2	0	-0.3
1994 KC-A	0	1	.000	2	2	0	0	0	9¹	13	2	6	3	18.3	6.75	77	.325	.413	0	—	0	-2	-2	0	-0.1
Total 2	0	1	.000	3	2	0	0	0	10¹	16	3	7	4	20.9	8.71	59	.348	.444	0	—	0	-5	-4	0	-0.4

● **WAYNE GRANGER**   Granger, Wayne Allan b: 3/15/44, Springfield, Mass.   BR/TR, 6'2", 165 lbs.   Deb: 6/5/68

YEAR TM/L	W	L	PCT	G	GS	CG	SH	SV	IP	H	HR	BB	SO	RAT	ERA	ERA+	OAV	OOB	BH	AVG	PB	PR	/A	PD	TPI
1968 *StL-N	4	2	.667	34	0	0	0	4	44	40	2	12	27	11.0	2.25	129	.238	.297	1	.200	0	4	3	2	0.7
1969 Cin-N	9	6	.600	90	0	0	0	27	144²	143	10	40	68	11.8	2.80	134	.262	.320	2	.095	0	13	15	1	2.3
1970 *Cin-N	6	5	.545	67	0	0	0	35	84²	79	5	27	38	11.4	2.66	152	.252	.313	-1	.100	-1	13	13	2	2.9
1971 Cin-N	7	6	.538	70	0	0	0	11	100	94	8	28	51	11.1	3.33	101	.251	.304	1	.143	1	2	0	3	0.5
1972 Min-A	4	6	.400	38	0	0	0	19	89²	83	7	28	40	11.3	3.01	107	.243	.304	2	.200	0	4	4	0	0.5
1973 StL-N	4	3	.333	42	0	0	0	5	46²	50	5	21	14	14.1	4.24	98	.280	.367	0	—	-0	-3	-3	-0	-0.5
NY-A	0	1	.000	9	0	0	0	0	15¹	19	1	3	10	13.5	1.76	208	.279	.319	0	—	0	4	4	-1	0.2
1974 Chi-A	0	0	—	5	0	0	0	0	7²	16	1	3	4	22.3	8.22	45	.432	.475	0	—	0	-4	-4	0	0.0

YEAR TM/L	W	L	PCT	G	GS	CG	SH	SV	IP	H	HR	BB	SO	RAT	ERA	ERA+	OAV	OOB	BH	AVG	PB	PR	/A	PD	TPI
1975 Hou-N	2	5	.286	55	0	0	0	5	74	76	7	23	30	12.5	3.65	92	.264	.327	0	.000	-1	-0	-2	1	-0.2
1976 Mon-N	1	0	1.000	27	0	0	0	2	32	32	3	16	16	14.1	3.66	102	.264	.360	0	.000	-0	-1	0	0	-0.2
Total 9	35	35	.500	451	0	0	0	108	638²	632	47	201	303	12.0	3.14	113	.260	.322	7	.103	-1	27	28	8	6.2

● **GEORGE GRANT**   Grant, George Addison b: 1/6/03, E.Tallassee, Ala. d: 3/25/86, Montgomery, Ala. BR/TR, 5'11.5", 175 lbs. Deb: 9/17/23

YEAR TM/L	W	L	PCT	G	GS	CG	SH	SV	IP	H	HR	BB	SO	RAT	ERA	ERA+	OAV	OOB	BH	AVG	PB	PR	/A	PD	TPI
1923 StL-A	0	0	—	4	0	0	0	0	8²	15	0	3	2	18.7	5.19	80	.395	.439	0	.000	-0	-1	-1	0	0.0
1924 StL-A	1	2	.333	22	2	0	0	0	51¹	69	4	25	11	16.7	6.31	72	.325	.399	0	.000	-2	-12	-10	-1	-0.8
1925 StL-A	0	2	.000	12	0	0	0	0	16¹	26	2	8	7	18.7	6.06	77	.400	.466	1	.250	-0	-3	-3	0	-0.2
1927 Cle-A	4	6	.400	25	3	2	0	1	74²	85	1	40	19	15.1	4.46	94	.300	.387	2	.095	-2	-3	-3	0	-0.4
1928 Cle-A	10	8	.556	28	18	6	1	0	155¹	196	7	76	39	15.9	5.04	82	.319	.395	11	.183	-2	-17	-15	2	-1.5
1929 Cle-A	0	2	.000	12	0	0	0	0	24	41	2	23	5	24.0	10.50	42	.414	.525	0	.000	-0	-17	-16	0	-1.1
1931 Pit-N	0	0	—	11	0	0	0	0	17	28	0	7	6	19.1	7.41	52	.364	.424	0	.000	-0	-7	-7	0	-0.0
Total 7	15	20	.429	114	23	8	1	1	347¹	460	16	182	89	16.7	5.65	75	.331	.410	14	.135	-8	-59	-54	3	-4.0

● **JIM GRANT**   Grant, James Ronald b: 8/4/1894, Coalville, Iowa d: 11/30/85, Des Moines, Iowa BR/TL, 5'11", 180 lbs. Deb: 4/21/23

YEAR TM/L	W	L	PCT	G	GS	CG	SH	SV	IP	H	HR	BB	SO	RAT	ERA	ERA+	OAV	OOB	BH	AVG	PB	PR	/A	PD	TPI
1923 Phi-N	0	0	—	2	0	0	0	0	4	10	0	4	0	33.8	13.50	34	.588	.682	0	.000	-0	-4	-4	0	0.0

● **MUDCAT GRANT**   Grant, James Timothy "Jim" b: 8/13/35, Lacoochee, Fla. BR/TR, 6'1", 186 lbs. Deb: 4/17/58

YEAR TM/L	W	L	PCT	G	GS	CG	SH	SV	IP	H	HR	BB	SO	RAT	ERA	ERA+	OAV	OOB	BH	AVG	PB	PR	/A	PD	TPI
1958 Cle-A	10	11	.476	44	28	11	1	4	204	173	20	104	111	12.3	3.84	95	.228	.321	5	.076	-4	-2	-4	-2	-1.0
1959 Cle-A	10	7	.588	38	19	6	1	3	165¹	140	23	81	85	12.1	4.14	89	.232	.325	11	.200	1	-5	-8	-0	-0.7
1960 Cle-A	9	8	.529	33	19	5	0	0	159²	147	26	78	75	12.8	4.40	85	.243	.332	16	.281	4	-9	-12	-1	-0.9
1961 Cle-A	15	9	.625	35	35	11	3	0	244²	207	32	109	146	11.7	3.86	102	.227	.312	15	.170	1	4	2	1	0.4
1962 Cle-A	7	10	.412	26	23	6	1	0	149²	128	24	81	90	12.6	4.27	91	.233	.331	8	.151	-0	-5	-7	-0	-0.7
1963 Cle-A☆	13	14	.481	38	32	10	2	1	229¹	213	30	87	157	11.9	3.69	98	.243	.314	13	.188	3	-2	-2	-3	-0.2
1964 Cle-A	3	4	.429	13	9	1	0	0	62	82	11	25	43	15.7	5.95	60	.324	.387	6	.273	-0	-16	-16	-0	-1.2
Min-A	11	9	.550	26	23	10	1	1	166	162	21	36	75	10.7	2.82	127	.248	.288	10	.167	0	15	14	0	1.7
Yr	14	13	.519	39	32	11	1	1	228	244	32	61	118	12.0	3.67	98	.269	.315	16	.195	4	-1	-2	1	0.5
1965 *Min-A★	**21**	7	**.750**	41	39	14	**6**	0	270¹	252	34	61	142	10.4	3.30	108	.247	.289	15	.155	2	5	8	1	1.1
1966 Min-A	13	13	.500	35	35	10	3	0	249	248	23	49	110	11.0	3.25	111	.260	.300	15	.192	5	5	10	2	1.4
1967 Min-A	5	6	.455	27	14	2	0	0	95¹	121	10	17	50	13.1	4.72	73	.315	.346	5	.179	0	-16	-13	-2	-1.7
1968 LA-N	6	4	.600	37	4	1	0	3	94²	77	1	19	35	9.7	2.09	132	.226	.279	4	.129	0	9	7	1	0.9
1969 Mon-N	1	6	.143	11	10	1	0	0	50²	64	7	14	20	14.0	4.80	77	.299	.345	2	.125	-1	-7	-6	-0	-0.8
StL-N	7	5	.583	30	3	1	0	7	63¹	62	9	22	35	12.2	4.12	87	.252	.319	5	.294	1	-4	-4	-1	-0.7
Yr	8	11	.421	41	13	2	0	7	114	126	16	36	55	12.9	4.42	82	.273	.328	7	.212	1	-10	-10	-1	-1.5
1970 Oak-A	6	2	.750	72	0	0	0	24	123¹	104	8	30	54	10.0	1.82	194	.235	.288	2	.222	-0	**26**	**24**	1	2.8
Pit-N	2	1	.667	8	0	0	0	0	12	8	2	2	4	7.5	2.25	173	.190	.227	0	.000	-0	2	2	0	0.5
1971 Pit-N	5	3	.625	42	0	0	0	7	75	79	8	28	22	13.0	3.60	94	.274	.341	2	.250	1	-1	-2	1	-0.1
*Oak-A	1	0	1.000	15	0	0	0	3	27¹	25	3	6	13	10.2	1.98	169	.243	.284	1	.333	0	5	4	-0	0.2
Total 14	145	119	.549	571	293	89	18	53	2441²	2292	292	849	1267	11.7	3.63	100	.248	.313	135	.178	16	5	-3	-3	1.0

● **MARK GRANT**   Grant, Mark Andrew b: 10/24/63, Aurora, Ill. BR/TR, 6'2", 205 lbs. Deb: 4/27/84

YEAR TM/L	W	L	PCT	G	GS	CG	SH	SV	IP	H	HR	BB	SO	RAT	ERA	ERA+	OAV	OOB	BH	AVG	PB	PR	/A	PD	TPI
1984 SF-N	1	4	.200	11	10	0	0	0	53²	56	6	19	32	12.7	6.37	55	.272	.336	0	.000	-2	-17	-17	-0	-1.6
1986 SF-N	0	1	.000	4	1	0	0	0	10	6	0	5	5	9.9	3.60	98	.176	.282	0	.000	-0	0	-0	-0	0.0
1987 SF-N	1	2	.333	16	8	0	0	1	61	66	6	21	32	13.0	3.54	109	.282	.344	1	.083	-0	4	2	-1	0.0
SD-N	6	7	.462	17	17	2	1	0	102¹	104	16	52	58	13.7	4.66	85	.263	.348	3	.094	-1	-7	-8	-1	-1.0
Yr	7	9	.438	33	25	2	1	1	163¹	170	22	73	90	13.4	4.24	92	.269	.345	4	.091	-1	-3	-6	-1	-1.0
1988 SD-N	2	8	.200	33	11	0	0	0	97²	97	14	36	61	12.4	3.69	92	.268	.338	0	.000	-1	-3	-3	0	-0.4
1989 SD-N	8	2	.800	50	0	0	0	2	116¹	105	9	32	69	10.8	3.33	105	.248	.305	1	.050	-0	2	2	-0	0.1
1990 SD-N	1	1	.500	26	0	0	0	0	39	47	5	19	29	15.2	4.85	79	.305	.382	1	.500	1	-5	-4	1	-0.1
Atl-N	1	2	.333	33	0	0	0	3	52¹	61	4	18	40	13.8	4.64	87	.293	.352	1	.250	1	-5	-4	-0	-0.2
Yr	2	3	.400	59	0	0	0	3	91¹	108	9	37	69	14.4	4.73	83	.296	.362	2	.333	1	-10	-8	0	-0.3
1992 Sea-A	4	2	.333	23	10	0	0	0	81	100	6	22	42	13.6	3.89	102	.311	.358	0	—	0	0	1	-1	-0.1
1993 Hou-N	0	0	—	6	0	0	0	0	11	11	0	5	6	13.1	0.82	473	.275	.356	0	—	0	4	4	1	0.1
Col-N	0	1	1.000	14	0	0	0	1	14¹	23	4	6	8	18.2	12.56	38	.377	.433	0	—	0	-14	-12	-0	-0.9
Yr	0	1	1.000	20	0	0	0	1	25¹	34	4	11	14	16.0	7.46	59	.333	.398	0	—	0	-10	-9	1	-0.8
Total 8	22	32	.407	233	58	2	1	8	638²	676	72	235	382	13.0	4.31	87	.277	.343	7	.067	-3	-39	-40	-2	-4.1

● **RICK GRAPENTHIN**   Grapenthin, Richard Ray b: 4/16/58, Linn Grove, Iowa BR/TR, 6'2", 205 lbs. Deb: 5/3/83

YEAR TM/L	W	L	PCT	G	GS	CG	SH	SV	IP	H	HR	BB	SO	RAT	ERA	ERA+	OAV	OOB	BH	AVG	PB	PR	/A	PD	TPI
1983 Mon-N	0	1	.000	1	0	0	0	0	4	4	2	1	3	11.3	9.00	40	.267	.313	0	.000	-0	-2	-2	0	-0.4
1984 Mon-N	1	2	.333	13	1	0	0	2	23	19	3	7	9	10.2	3.52	97	.235	.295	1	.200	0	-0	-0	-0	0.0
1985 Mon-N	0	0	—	5	0	0	0	0	7	13	0	8	4	28.3	14.14	24	.394	.524	1	1.000	1	-8	-8	-0	-0.0
Total 3	1	3	.250	19	1	0	0	2	34	36	5	16	16	14.0	6.35	54	.279	.363	2	.286	1	-10	-11	0	-0.4

● **LOU GRASMICK**   Grasmick, Louis Junior b: 9/11/24, Baltimore, Md. BR/TR, 6', 195 lbs. Deb: 4/22/48

YEAR TM/L	W	L	PCT	G	GS	CG	SH	SV	IP	H	HR	BB	SO	RAT	ERA	ERA+	OAV	OOB	BH	AVG	PB	PR	/A	PD	TPI
1948 Phi-N	0	0	—	2	0	0	0	0	5	3	1	8	2	19.8	7.20	55	.176	.440	1	1.000	0	-2	-2	0	0.1

● **DON GRATE**   Grate, Donald "Buckeye" b: 8/27/23, Greenfield, Ohio BR/TR, 6'2.5", 180 lbs. Deb: 7/6/45

YEAR TM/L	W	L	PCT	G	GS	CG	SH	SV	IP	H	HR	BB	SO	RAT	ERA	ERA+	OAV	OOB	BH	AVG	PB	PR	/A	PD	TPI
1945 Phi-N	0	1	.000	4	0	0	0	0	8¹	18	0	12	6	32.4	17.28	22	.439	.566	0	.000	-0	-12	-12	-0	-1.2
1946 Phi-N	1	0	1.000	3	0	0	0	0	8	4	0	2	6	6.8	1.13	305	.160	.222	0	.000	0	2	2	-0	0.2
Total 2	1	1	.500	7	2	0	0	0	16¹	22	0	14	8	19.8	9.37	39	.333	.450	0	.000	-0	-10	-10	-1	-1.0

● **MARK GRATER**   Grater, Mark Anthony b: 1/19/64, Rochester, Pa. BR/TR, 5'10", 205 lbs. Deb: 6/12/91

YEAR TM/L	W	L	PCT	G	GS	CG	SH	SV	IP	H	HR	BB	SO	RAT	ERA	ERA+	OAV	OOB	BH	AVG	PB	PR	/A	PD	TPI
1991 StL-N	0	0	—	3	0	0	0	0	3	5	0	2	2	21.0	0.00	—	.385	.467	0	—	0	1	1	-0	0.0
1993 Det-A	0	0	—	6	0	0	0	0	5	6	0	4	2	18.0	5.40	79	.286	.400	0	—	0	-1	-1	-0	0.0
Total 2	0	0	—	9	0	0	0	0	8	11	0	6	4	19.1	3.38	121	.324	.425	0	—	0	1	1	-0	0.0

● **FRANK GRAVES**   Graves, Frank M. b: 11/2/1860, Cincinnati, Ohio 6', 163 lbs. Deb: 5/10/1886 ◆

YEAR TM/L	W	L	PCT	G	GS	CG	SH	SV	IP	H	HR	BB	SO	RAT	ERA	ERA+	OAV	OOB	BH	AVG	PB	PR	/A	PD	TPI
1886 StL-N	0	0	—	1	0	0	0	0	7	10	0	1	2	14.1	9.00	36	.323	.344	21	.152	-0	-4	-4	-0	0.0

● **CHARLIE GRAY**   Gray, Charles b: 1867, Indianapolis, Ind. Deb: 4/23/1890

YEAR TM/L	W	L	PCT	G	GS	CG	SH	SV	IP	H	HR	BB	SO	RAT	ERA	ERA+	OAV	OOB	BH	AVG	PB	PR	/A	PD	TPI
1890 Pit-N	1	4	.200	5	4	3	0	0	31	48	1	24	10	21.2	7.55	44	.343	.443	3	.200	-0	-14	-15	-1	-1.7

● **DAVE GRAY**   Gray, David Alexander b: 1/7/43, Ogden, Utah BR/TR, 6'1", 190 lbs. Deb: 6/14/64

YEAR TM/L	W	L	PCT	G	GS	CG	SH	SV	IP	H	HR	BB	SO	RAT	ERA	ERA+	OAV	OOB	BH	AVG	PB	PR	/A	PD	TPI
1964 Bos-A	0	0	—	9	1	0	0	0	13	18	3	20	17	26.3	9.00	43	.321	.500	1	1.000	0	-8	-7	0	0.1

● **CHUMMY GRAY**   Gray, George Edward b: 7/17/1873, Rockland, Me. d: 8/14/13, Rockland, Maine TR, 5'11.5", 163 lbs. Deb: 9/14/1899

YEAR TM/L	W	L	PCT	G	GS	CG	SH	SV	IP	H	HR	BB	SO	RAT	ERA	ERA+	OAV	OOB	BH	AVG	PB	PR	/A	PD	TPI
1899 Pit-N	3	3	.500	9	7	6	0	0	70²	85	1	24	9	14.4	3.44	111	.297	.360	1	.038	-3	3	3	2	0.1

● **JEFF GRAY**   Gray, Jeffrey Edward b: 4/10/63, Richmond, Va. BR/TR, 6'1", 175 lbs. Deb: 6/21/88

YEAR TM/L	W	L	PCT	G	GS	CG	SH	SV	IP	H	HR	BB	SO	RAT	ERA	ERA+	OAV	OOB	BH	AVG	PB	PR	/A	PD	TPI
1988 Cin-N	0	0	—	5	0	0	0	0	9¹	12	0	4	5	15.4	3.86	93	.333	.400	0	.000	-0	-0	-0	0	0.0
1990 *Bos-A	2	4	.333	41	0	0	0	9	50²	53	3	15	50	12.3	4.44	92	.268	.322	0	—	0	-1	-1	-0	-0.4
1991 Bos-A	2	3	.400	50	0	0	0	1	61²	39	7	10	41	7.3	2.34	184	.181	.220	0	—	0	12	13	1	1.1
Total 3	4	7	.364	96	0	0	0	10	121²	104	10	29	96	10.0	3.33	125	.231	.281	0	.000	-0	9	11	1	0.7

● **JOHNNY GRAY**   Gray, John Leonard b: 12/11/27, W.Palm Beach, Fla. BR/TR, 6'4", 226 lbs. Deb: 7/18/54

YEAR TM/L	W	L	PCT	G	GS	CG	SH	SV	IP	H	HR	BB	SO	RAT	ERA	ERA+	OAV	OOB	BH	AVG	PB	PR	/A	PD	TPI
1954 Phi-A	3	12	.200	18	16	5	0	0	105	111	10	91	51	17.3	6.51	60	.273	.406	1	.029	-4	-33	-30	0	-3.9

YEAR	TM/L	W	L	PCT	G	GS	CG	SH	SV	IP	H	HR	BB	SO	RAT	ERA	ERA+	OAV	OOB	BH	AVG	PB	PR	/A	PD	TPI
1955	KC-A	0	3	.000	8	5	0	0	0	26²	28	2	24	11	17.9	6.41	65	.277	.421	1	.125	-0	-7	-7	-1	-0.7
1957	Cle-A	1	3	.250	7	3	1	1	0	20	21	1	13	3	15.3	5.85	64	.288	.395	0	.000	-1	-5	-5	-0	-0.9
1958	Phi-N	0	0	—	15	0	0	0	0	17¹	12	3	14	10	13.5	4.15	95	.222	.382	0	.000	-0	-0	-0	-0	0.0
Total	4	4	18	.182	48	24	6	1	0	169	172	16	142	75	16.8	6.18	64	.271	.405	2	.043	-5	-45	-42	-1	-5.5

● **SAM GRAY**   Gray, Samuel David "Sad Sam"   b: 10/15/1897, Van Alstyne, Tex.   d: 4/16/53, McKinney, Tex.   BR/TR, 5'10", 175 lbs.   Deb: 4/19/24

YEAR	TM/L	W	L	PCT	G	GS	CG	SH	SV	IP	H	HR	BB	SO	RAT	ERA	ERA+	OAV	OOB	BH	AVG	PB	PR	/A	PD	TPI
1924	Phi-A	8	7	.533	34	19	8	2	2	151²	169	5	89	54	15.7	3.98	108	.284	.383	10	.175	-2	4	5	-1	0.2
1925	Phi-A	16	8	.667	32	28	14	4	3	203²	199	11	63	80	11.7	3.27	142	.260	.319	12	.179	-2	25	31	-3	2.8
1926	Phi-A	11	12	.478	38	18	5	0	0	150²	164	9	50	82	13.0	3.64	114	.279	.340	11	.216	1	6	9	-2	1.1
1927	Phi-A	9	6	.600	37	13	3	1	3	133¹	153	4	51	49	14.0	4.59	93	.295	.362	8	.190	-1	-7	-5	-0	-0.6
1928	StL-A	20	12	.625	35	31	21	2	3	262²	256	11	86	102	11.8	3.19	132	.260	.320	19	.188	-2	25	30	3	3.5
1929	StL-A	18	15	.545	43	37	23	**4**	1	**305**	336	18	96	109	12.8	3.72	119	.285	.340	19	.184	-2	18	24	-1	2.0
1930	StL-A	4	15	.211	27	24	7	0	0	167²	215	17	52	51	14.5	6.28	78	.316	.368	11	.204	-2	-30	-26	-1	-2.5
1931	StL-A	11	24	.314	43	37	13	0	2	258	323	20	54	88	13.3	5.09	91	.297	.332	14	.177	-1	-20	-13	-1	-1.7
1932	StL-A	7	12	.368	52	18	7	3	4	206²	250	6	53	79	13.2	4.53	107	.294	.336	13	.210	-0	-1	7	-1	0.5
1933	StL-A	7	4	.636	38	6	0	0	4	112	131	7	45	36	14.2	4.10	114	.301	.368	7	.219	1	2	7	-1	0.7
Total	10	111	115	.491	379	231	101	16	22	1951¹	2196	111	639	730	13.2	4.18	108	.286	.343	124	.191	-10	23	68	-7	6.0

● **TED GRAY**   Gray, Ted Glenn   b: 12/31/24, Detroit, Mich.   BB/TL, 5'11", 175 lbs.   Deb: 5/15/46

YEAR	TM/L	W	L	PCT	G	GS	CG	SH	SV	IP	H	HR	BB	SO	RAT	ERA	ERA+	OAV	OOB	BH	AVG	PB	PR	/A	PD	TPI
1946	Det-A	0	2	.000	3	2	0	0	1	11²	17	4	5	5	17.0	8.49	43	.340	.400	0	.000	-0	-6	-6	-0	-1.0
1948	Det-A	6	2	.750	26	11	3	1	0	85¹	73	2	72	60	15.6	4.22	104	.236	.385	7	.241	1	1	1	-0	0.1
1949	Det-A	10	10	.500	34	27	8	3	1	195	163	11	103	96	12.5	3.51	119	.227	.328	8	.127	-3	15	14	1	1.1
1950	Det-A★	10	7	.588	27	21	7	0	1	149¹	139	22	72	102	12.8	4.40	107	.248	.335	7	.140	-2	3	5	-2	0.1
1951	Det-A	7	14	.333	34	28	9	1	1	197¹	194	17	95	131	13.5	4.06	103	.256	.343	9	.143	-3	1	3	-1	-0.2
1952	Det-A	12	17	.414	35	32	13	2	0	224	212	21	101	138	12.7	4.14	92	.249	.331	13	.171	-2	-12	-8	1	-1.1
1953	Det-A	10	15	.400	30	28	8	0	0	176	166	25	76	115	12.7	4.60	88	.252	.336	14	.230	2	-12	-10	-1	-1.2
1954	Det-A	3	5	.375	19	10	2	0	0	72	70	8	56	29	16.0	5.38	69	.268	.401	1	.045	-2	-13	-13	-1	-1.7
1955	Chi-A	0	0	—	2	1	0	0	0	3	9	0	2	1	33.0	18.00	22	.500	.550	0	—	0	-5	-5	0	0.0
	Cle-A	0	0	—	2	0	0	0	0	2	5	1	2	1	31.5	18.00	22	.455	.538	0	—	0	-3	-3	0	0.0
	NY-A	0	0	—	1	1	0	0	0	3	3	0	0	1	9.0	3.00	125	.300	.300	0	.000	-0	0	-0	0	0.0
	Bal-A	1	2	.333	9	1	0	0	0	15¹	21	3	11	8	18.8	8.22	44	.344	.444	0	.000	-0	-7	-8	1	-1.2
	Yr	1	2	.333	14	3	0	0	0	23¹	38	4	15	11	20.4	9.64	40	.376	.457	0	.000	-0	-15	-15	1	-1.2
Total	9	59	74	.444	222	162	50	7	4	1134	1072	114	595	687	13.5	4.37	94	.251	.346	59	.159	-10	-38	-30	-4	-5.1

● **DOLLY GRAY**   Gray, William Denton   b: 12/4/1878, Ishpeming, Mich.   d: 4/4/56, Yuba City, Cal.   BL/TL, 6'2", 160 lbs.   Deb: 4/13/09

YEAR	TM/L	W	L	PCT	G	GS	CG	SH	SV	IP	H	HR	BB	SO	RAT	ERA	ERA+	OAV	OOB	BH	AVG	PB	PR	/A	PD	TPI
1909	Was-A	5	19	.208	36	26	19	0	1	218	210	1	77	87	12.2	3.59	68	.258	.329	13	.146	-1	-27	-28	-1	-3.2
1910	Was-A	8	19	.296	34	29	21	3	0	229	216	3	65	84	11.4	2.63	95	.249	.309	21	.247	4	-3	-4	2	0.2
1911	Was-A	2	13	.133	28	15	6	0	0	121	160	4	40	42	15.1	5.06	63	.331	.385	10	.227	-1	-23	-24	1	-2.3
Total	3	15	51	.227	98	70	46	3	0	568	586	8	182	213	12.5	3.52	75	.271	.333	44	.202	3	-53	-56	2	-5.3

● **ELI GRBA**   Grba, Eli   b: 8/9/34, Chicago, Ill.   BR/TR, 6'2", 207 lbs.   Deb: 7/10/59

YEAR	TM/L	W	L	PCT	G	GS	CG	SH	SV	IP	H	HR	BB	SO	RAT	ERA	ERA+	OAV	OOB	BH	AVG	PB	PR	/A	PD	TPI
1959	NY-A	2	5	.286	19	6	0	0	0	50¹	52	6	39	23	16.3	6.44	57	.269	.392	3	.214	1	-14	-16	-0	-1.8
1960	*NY-A	6	4	.600	24	9	1	0	1	80²	65	9	46	32	12.6	3.68	97	.226	.337	5	.238	2	2	-1	-1	0.1
1961	LA-A	11	13	.458	40	30	8	0	2	211²	197	26	114	105	13.5	4.25	106	.242	.340	15	.233	4	-5	6	-1	0.9
1962	LA-A	8	9	.471	40	29	8	0	0	176¹	185	19	75	90	13.4	4.54	85	.267	.340	12	.207	-3	-11	-13	-1	-0.8
1963	LA-A	1	2	.333	12	1	0	0	0	17¹	14	2	10	5	13.0	4.67	73	.222	.338	0	.000	-0	-2	-2	-0	-0.4
Total	5	28	33	.459	135	75	10	0	4	536¹	513	62	284	255	13.6	4.48	90	.250	.345	35	.219	10	-31	-27	-1	-2.0

● **BILL GREASON**   Greason, William Henry "Booster"   b: 9/3/24, Atlanta, Ga.   BR/TR, 5'10", 170 lbs.   Deb: 5/31/54

YEAR	TM/L	W	L	PCT	G	GS	CG	SH	SV	IP	H	HR	BB	SO	RAT	ERA	ERA+	OAV	OOB	BH	AVG	PB	PR	/A	PD	TPI
1954	StL-N	0	1	.000	3	2	0	0	0	4	8	4	4	2	27.0	13.50	30	.421	.522	0	.000	-0	-4	-4	0	-0.8

● **CHRIS GREEN**   Green, Christopher De Wayne   b: 9/5/60, Los Angeles, Cal.   BL/TL, 6'2", 214 lbs.   Deb: 4/17/84

YEAR	TM/L	W	L	PCT	G	GS	CG	SH	SV	IP	H	HR	BB	SO	RAT	ERA	ERA+	OAV	OOB	BH	AVG	PB	PR	/A	PD	TPI
1984	Pit-N	0	0	—	4	0	0	0	0	3	5	0	1	3	18.0	6.00	60	.417	.462	0	—	0	-1	-1	0	0.0

● **ED GREEN**   Green, Edward M.   b: 1850, Philadelphia, Pa.   Deb: 4/22/1890

YEAR	TM/L	W	L	PCT	G	GS	CG	SH	SV	IP	H	HR	BB	SO	RAT	ERA	ERA+	OAV	OOB	BH	AVG	PB	PR	/A	PD	TPI
1890	Phi-a	7	15	.318	25	22	20	1	1	191	267	4	94	56	17.3	5.80	66	.321	.393	15	.119	-4	-41	-42	3	-3.6

● **FRED GREEN**   Green, Fred Allen   b: 9/14/33, Titusville, N.J.   BR/TL, 6'4", 190 lbs.   Deb: 4/15/59   F

YEAR	TM/L	W	L	PCT	G	GS	CG	SH	SV	IP	H	HR	BB	SO	RAT	ERA	ERA+	OAV	OOB	BH	AVG	PB	PR	/A	PD	TPI
1959	Pit-N	1	2	.333	17	1	0	0	1	37¹	37	2	15	20	12.5	3.13	123	.259	.329	0	.000	-1	3	3	-0	0.2
1960	*Pit-N	8	4	.667	45	0	0	0	3	70	61	4	33	49	12.2	3.21	117	.243	.333	3	.375	3	4	4	-1	1.0
1961	Pit-N	0	0	—	13	0	0	0	0	20²	27	2	9	4	15.7	4.79	83	.321	.387	0	.000	-0	-2	-2	1	0.0
1962	Was-A	0	1	.000	5	0	0	0	0	7	7	3	6	2	16.7	6.43	63	.250	.382	0	—	0	-2	-2	0	-0.2
1964	Pit-N	0	0	—	8	0	0	0	0	7¹	10	1	0	2	12.3	1.23	286	.323	.323	0	—	0	2	2	0	0.0
Total	5	9	7	.563	88	1	0	0	4	142¹	142	12	63	77	13.0	3.48	110	.264	.343	3	.176	2	6	5	0	1.0

● **DALLAS GREEN**   Green, George Dallas   b: 8/4/34, Newport, Del.   BL/TR, 6'5", 210 lbs.   Deb: 6/18/60   M

YEAR	TM/L	W	L	PCT	G	GS	CG	SH	SV	IP	H	HR	BB	SO	RAT	ERA	ERA+	OAV	OOB	BH	AVG	PB	PR	/A	PD	TPI
1960	Phi-N	3	6	.333	23	10	5	1	0	108²	100	10	44	51	12.1	4.06	96	.248	.325	7	.206	0	-4	-2	-1	-0.1
1961	Phi-N	2	4	.333	42	10	1	1	1	128	160	8	47	51	14.7	4.85	84	.315	.375	5	.152	0	-12	-11	0	-0.4
1962	Phi-N	6	6	.500	37	10	2	0	1	129¹	145	10	43	58	13.4	3.83	101	.289	.352	2	.063	-1	2	1	2	0.2
1963	Phi-N	7	5	.583	40	14	4	0	2	120	134	10	38	68	13.1	3.23	100	.286	.342	3	.086	-1	1	1	0	0.1
1964	Phi-N	2	1	.667	25	0	0	0	0	42	63	8	14	21	16.9	5.79	60	.362	.416	0	.000	-0	-10	-11	-1	-0.8
1965	Was-A	0	0	—	6	2	0	0	0	14¹	14	0	3	6	10.7	3.14	111	.241	.279	0	—	0	1	1	0	0.0
1966	NY-N	0	0	—	4	0	0	0	0	5	6	2	1	1	14.4	5.40	67	.333	.400	0	—	0	-1	-1	0	0.0
1967	Phi-N	0	0	—	8	0	0	0	0	15	25	2	6	12	19.2	9.00	38	.362	.421	0	.000	-0	-9	-9	1	0.0
Total	8	20	22	.476	185	46	12	2	4	562¹	647	46	197	268	13.7	4.26	88	.294	.356	17	.120	-3	-33	-33	3	-1.1

● **HARVEY GREEN**   Green, Harvey George "Buck"   b: 2/9/15, Kenosha, Wis.   d: 7/24/70, Franklin, La.   BB/TR, 6'2.5", 185 lbs.   Deb: 9/12/35

YEAR	TM/L	W	L	PCT	G	GS	CG	SH	SV	IP	H	HR	BB	SO	RAT	ERA	ERA+	OAV	OOB	BH	AVG	PB	PR	/A	PD	TPI
1935	Bro-N	0	0	—	2	0	0	0	0	1	2	0	3	0	54.0	9.00	44	.400	.667	0	—	0	-1	-1	-0	0.0

● **TYLER GREEN**   Green, Tyler Scott   b: 2/18/70, Springfield, Ohio   BR/TR, 6'5", 185 lbs.   Deb: 4/9/93

YEAR	TM/L	W	L	PCT	G	GS	CG	SH	SV	IP	H	HR	BB	SO	RAT	ERA	ERA+	OAV	OOB	BH	AVG	PB	PR	/A	PD	TPI
1993	Phi-N	0	0	—	3	2	0	0	0	7¹	16	1	5	7	25.8	7.36	54	.444	.512	0	.000	-0	-3	-3	-0	-0.1

● **TOMMY GREENE**   Greene, Ira Thomas   b: 4/6/67, Lumberton, N.C.   BR/TR, 6'5", 225 lbs.   Deb: 9/10/89

YEAR	TM/L	W	L	PCT	G	GS	CG	SH	SV	IP	H	HR	BB	SO	RAT	ERA	ERA+	OAV	OOB	BH	AVG	PB	PR	/A	PD	TPI
1989	Atl-N	1	2	.333	4	4	1	1	0	26¹	22	5	6	9	9.6	4.10	89	.234	.280	1	.100	-1	-2	-1	-0	-0.2
1990	Atl-N	1	0	1.000	5	2	0	0	0	12¹	14	3	9	4	17.5	8.03	50	.286	.407	0	.000	-0	-6	-5	-0	-0.4
	Phi-N	2	3	.400	10	7	0	0	0	39	36	5	17	17	12.2	4.15	92	.247	.325	2	.182	0	-2	-1	-0	-0.2
	Yr	3	3	.500	15	9	0	0	0	51¹	50	8	26	21	13.3	5.08	76	.255	.342	2	.167	0	-7	-7	-1	-0.6
1991	Phi-N	13	7	.650	36	27	3	2	0	207²	177	19	66	154	10.7	3.38	108	.230	.294	19	.268	7	7	7	-3	1.1
1992	Phi-N	3	3	.500	13	12	0	0	0	64¹	75	7	34	39	15.2	5.32	66	.291	.373	3	.125	-1	-13	-13	-1	-1.3
1993	*Phi-N	16	4	.800	31	30	7	2	0	200	175	12	62	167	10.8	3.42	116	.233	.294	16	.222	6	14	12	-1	1.6
1994	Phi-N	2	0	1.000	7	7	0	0	0	35²	37	5	22	28	14.9	4.54	91	.273	.373	5	.385	2	-1	-2	-0	0.1
Total	6	38	19	.667	106	89	11	5	0	585¹	536	54	216	426	11.7	3.86	98	.243	.313	46	.228	14	-1	-4	-5	0.7

● **JUNE GREENE**   Greene, Julius Foust   b: 6/25/1899, Ramseur, N.C.   d: 3/19/74, Glendora, Cal.   BL/TR, 6'2.5", 185 lbs.   Deb: 4/20/28 ◆

YEAR	TM/L	W	L	PCT	G	GS	CG	SH	SV	IP	H	HR	BB	SO	RAT	ERA	ERA+	OAV	OOB	BH	AVG	PB	PR	/A	PD	TPI
1928	Phi-N	0	0	—	1	0	0	0	0	2	5	0	0	0	22.5	9.00	47	.556	.556	3	.500	2	-1	-1	0	0.2

YEAR TM/L	W	L	PCT	G	GS	CG	SH	SV	IP	H	HR	BB	SO	RAT	ERA	ERA+	OAV	OOB	BH	AVG	PB	PR	/A	PD	TPI
1929 Phi-N	0	0	—	5	0	0	0	0	13²	33	2	9	4	29.6	19.76	26	.465	.542	4	.211	0	-23	-22	0	0.0
Total 2	0	0	—	6	0	0	0	0	15²	38	2	9	4	28.7	18.38	28	.475	.543	7	.280	2	-24	-23	1	0.2

● **NELSON GREENE**   Greene, Nelson George "Lefty" b: 9/20/1900, Philadelphia, Pa. d: 4/6/83, Lebanon, Pa. BL/TL, 6′, 185 lbs. Deb: 4/28/24

YEAR TM/L	W	L	PCT	G	GS	CG	SH	SV	IP	H	HR	BB	SO	RAT	ERA	ERA+	OAV	OOB	BH	AVG	PB	PR	/A	PD	TPI
1924 Bro-N	0	1	.000	4	1	0	0	0	9	14	1	2	3	16.0	4.00	94	.350	.381	0	.000	-0	-0	-0	0	0.0
1925 Bro-N	2	0	1.000	11	0	0	0	1	22	45	4	7	4	21.3	10.64	39	.417	.452	2	.286	-0	-16	-16	0	-1.3
Total 2	2	1	.667	15	1	0	0	1	31	59	5	9	7	19.7	8.71	47	.399	.433	2	.250	-0	-16	-16	1	-1.3

● **KENT GREENFIELD**   Greenfield, Kent b: 7/1/02, Guthrie, Ky. d: 3/14/78, Guthrie, Ky. BR/TR, 6′1″, 180 lbs. Deb: 9/28/24

YEAR TM/L	W	L	PCT	G	GS	CG	SH	SV	IP	H	HR	BB	SO	RAT	ERA	ERA+	OAV	OOB	BH	AVG	PB	PR	/A	PD	TPI
1924 NY-N	0	1	.000	1	1	0	0	0	3	9	1	1	1	30.0	15.00	24	.500	.526	0	—	0	-4	-4	-0	-0.8
1925 NY-N	12	8	.600	29	21	12	0	0	171²	195	4	64	66	13.7	3.88	104	.288	.352	5	.081	-6	7	3	1	-0.2
1926 NY-N	13	12	.520	39	28	8	1	1	222²	206	17	82	74	11.8	3.96	95	.251	.322	6	.092	-5	-3	-5	-2	-1.2
1927 NY-N	2	2	.500	12	1	0	0	0	20	39	3	13	4	24.3	9.45	41	.411	.491	0	.000	-0	-12	-12	-0	-2.0
Bos-N	11	14	.440	27	26	11	1	0	190	203	3	59	59	12.6	3.84	97	.282	.341	11	.172	-2	2	-3	-0	-0.5
Yr	13	16	.448	39	27	11	1	0	210	242	6	72	63	13.7	4.37	85	.297	.357	11	.167	-2	-11	-15	-0	-2.5
1928 Bos-N	3	11	.214	32	23	5	0	0	143²	173	6	60	30	14.9	5.32	73	.307	.378	2	.053	-4	-21	-23	1	-2.2
1929 Bos-N	0	0	—	6	2	0	0	0	15²	33	1	15	7	28.7	10.91	43	.465	.568	0	.000	-1	-11	-11	1	0.0
Bro-N	0	0	—	6	0	0	0	0	8²	13	1	3	1	16.6	8.31	56	.382	.432	0	.000	-0	-3	-4	0	0.0
Yr	0	0	—	12	2	0	0	0	24¹	46	2	18	8	23.7	9.99	47	.430	.512	0	.000	-1	-14	-14	1	0.0
Total 6	41	48	.461	152	102	36	2	1	775¹	871	36	297	242	13.8	4.54	85	.290	.358	24	.101	-18	-46	-58	-0	-6.9

● **JOHN GREENING**   Greening, John A. (b: John A. Greenig) b: Philadelphia, Pa. Deb: 5/9/1888

YEAR TM/L	W	L	PCT	G	GS	CG	SH	SV	IP	H	HR	BB	SO	RAT	ERA	ERA+	OAV	OOB	BH	AVG	PB	PR	/A	PD	TPI
1888 Was-N	0	1	.000	1	1	1	0	0	9	17	2	4	2	21.0	11.00	25	.405	.457	0	.000	-0	-8	-8	-0	-0.6

● **BOB GREENWOOD**   Greenwood, Robert Chandler "Greenie" b: 3/13/28, Cananea, Mexico BR/TR, 6′5″, 200 lbs. Deb: 4/21/54

YEAR TM/L	W	L	PCT	G	GS	CG	SH	SV	IP	H	HR	BB	SO	RAT	ERA	ERA+	OAV	OOB	BH	AVG	PB	PR	/A	PD	TPI
1954 Phi-N	1	2	.333	11	4	0	0	0	36²	28	2	18	9	11.3	3.19	127	.209	.303	0	.000	-1	4	3	0	0.2
1955 Phi-N	0	0	—	1	0	0	0	0	2¹	7	1	0	0	27.0	15.43	26	.500	.500	0	.000	-0	-3	-3	-0	0.0
Total 2	1	2	.333	12	4	0	0	0	39	35	3	18	9	12.2	3.92	103	.236	.319	0	.000	-1	1	0	0	0.2

● **KENNY GREER**   Greer, Kenneth William b: 5/12/67, Boston, Mass. BR/TR, 6′2″, 210 lbs. Deb: 9/29/93

YEAR TM/L	W	L	PCT	G	GS	CG	SH	SV	IP	H	HR	BB	SO	RAT	ERA	ERA+	OAV	OOB	BH	AVG	PB	PR	/A	PD	TPI
1993 NY-N	1	0	1.000	1	0	0	0	0	1	0	0	0	2	0.0	0.00	—	.000	.000	0	—	0	0	0	0	0.5

● **DAVE GREGG**   Gregg, David Charles "Highpockets" b: 3/14/1891, Chehalis, Wash. d: 11/12/65, Clarkston, Wash. BR/TR, 6′1″, 185 lbs. Deb: 6/15/13 F

YEAR TM/L	W	L	PCT	G	GS	CG	SH	SV	IP	H	HR	BB	SO	RAT	ERA	ERA+	OAV	OOB	BH	AVG	PB	PR	/A	PD	TPI
1913 Cle-A	0	0	—	1	0	0	0	0	1	2	0	0	0	27.0	18.00	17	.400	.500	0	—	0	-2	-2	0	0.0

● **HAL GREGG**   Gregg, Harold Dana "Skeets" b: 7/11/21, Anaheim, Cal. d: 5/13/91, Bishop, Cal. BR/TR, 6′3.5″, 195 lbs. Deb: 8/18/43

YEAR TM/L	W	L	PCT	G	GS	CG	SH	SV	IP	H	HR	BB	SO	RAT	ERA	ERA+	OAV	OOB	BH	AVG	PB	PR	/A	PD	TPI
1943 Bro-N	0	3	.000	5	4	0	0	0	18²	21	2	21	7	20.3	9.64	35	.304	.467	0	.000	-0	-13	-13	-0	-1.6
1944 Bro-N	9	16	.360	39	31	6	0	2	197²	201	12	137	92	15.8	5.46	65	.258	.376	14	.206	-0	-41	-42	0	-4.7
1945 Bro-N†	18	13	.581	42	34	13	2	2	254¹	221	5	120	139	12.3	3.47	108	.232	.323	20	.220	3	9	8	-0	1.2
1946 Bro-N	6	4	.600	26	16	4	1	2	117¹	103	3	44	54	11.4	2.99	113	.236	.308	4	.125	-1	5	5	-2	0.1
1947 *Bro-N	4	5	.444	37	16	2	1	1	104¹	115	6	55	59	15.0	5.87	70	.272	.361	9	.265	2	-21	-20	-0	-1.4
1948 Pit-N	2	4	.333	22	8	1	0	1	74¹	72	3	34	25	13.2	4.60	88	.255	.342	6	.273	-2	-5	-4	-0	-0.2
1949 Pit-N	1	1	.500	8	1	0	0	0	18²	20	1	8	9	14.0	3.38	125	.303	.387	0	.000	-0	1	2	-0	0.1
1950 Pit-N	0	1	.000	5	1	0	0	0	5¹	10	2	7	3	30.4	13.50	32	.400	.545	0	.000	-0	-6	-5	-0	-0.8
1952 NY-N	0	1	.000	16	4	1	0	0	36¹	42	7	17	13	15.1	4.71	79	.286	.367	1	.125	-0	-4	-4	-1	-0.2
Total 9	40	48	.455	200	115	27	4	9	827	805	41	443	401	13.9	4.54	82	.253	.350	54	.205	4	-73	-74	-3	-7.5

● **VEAN GREGG**   Gregg, Sylveanus Augustus b: 4/13/1885, Chehalis, Wash. d: 7/29/64, Aberdeen, Was. BR/TR, 6′1″, 185 lbs. Deb: 4/12/11 F

YEAR TM/L	W	L	PCT	G	GS	CG	SH	SV	IP	H	HR	BB	SO	RAT	ERA	ERA+	OAV	OOB	BH	AVG	PB	PR	/A	PD	TPI
1911 Cle-A	23	7	.767	34	26	22	5	0	244²	172	2	86	125	9.9	**1.80**	189	**.205**	.286	14	.165	-4	42	44	0	4.7
1912 Cle-A	20	13	.606	37	34	26	1	2	271¹	242	4	90	184	11.3	2.59	132	.246	.316	17	.175	-3	22	25	-2	2.4
1913 Cle-A	20	13	.606	44	34	23	3	3	285²	258	2	124	166	12.4	2.24	136	.244	.318	13	.131	-4	22	25	-3	2.1
1914 Cle-A	9	3	.750	17	12	6	1	0	96²	88	0	48	56	12.9	3.07	94	.251	.347	6	.176	-1	-4	-2	-0	-0.3
Bos-A	3	4	.429	12	9	4	0	0	68¹	71	0	37	24	14.2	3.95	68	.283	.375	4	.211	0	-9	-10	-1	-1.0
Yr	12	7	.632	29	21	10	1	0	165	159	0	85	80	13.3	3.44	82	.263	.354	10	.189	1	-13	-12	-2	-1.3
1915 Bos-A	4	2	.667	18	9	3	1	0	75	71	2	32	43	13.0	3.36	83	.260	.348	7	.350	2	-4	-5	-0	-0.2
1916 Bos-A	2	5	.286	21	7	3	0	0	77²	71	0	30	41	12.1	3.01	92	.259	.339	1	.111	-2	-2	-2	-0	-0.3
1918 Phi-A	9	14	.391	30	25	17	3	2	199¹	180	4	67	63	11.4	3.12	94	.251	.320	12	.169	-1	-7	-4	-0	-0.9
1925 Was-A	2	2	.500	26	5	1	0	2	74¹	87	3	38	18	15.4	4.12	103	.318	.404	3	.214	0	2	1	-0	0.0
Total 8	92	63	.594	239	161	105	14	12	1393	1240	17	552	720	11.9	2.70	117	.248	.328	78	.171	-12	63	73	-8	6.5

● **FRANK GREGORY**   Gregory, Frank Ernst b: 7/25/1888, Spring Valley Township, Wis. d: 11/5/55, Beloit, Wis. BR/TR, 5′11″, 185 lbs. Deb: 9/5/12

YEAR TM/L	W	L	PCT	G	GS	CG	SH	SV	IP	H	HR	BB	SO	RAT	ERA	ERA+	OAV	OOB	BH	AVG	PB	PR	/A	PD	TPI
1912 Cin-N	2	0	1.000	4	2	1	0	0	15²	19	0	7	4	15.5	4.60	73	.297	.375	1	.200	-0	-2	-2	-1	-0.3

● **LEE GREGORY**   Gregory, Grover Leroy b: 6/2/38, Bakersfield, Cal. BL/TL, 6′1″, 180 lbs. Deb: 4/17/64

YEAR TM/L	W	L	PCT	G	GS	CG	SH	SV	IP	H	HR	BB	SO	RAT	ERA	ERA+	OAV	OOB	BH	AVG	PB	PR	/A	PD	TPI
1964 Chi-N	0	0	—	11	0	0	0	0	18	23	3	5	8	14.0	3.50	106	.333	.378	1	.077	0	0	0	0	0.0

● **HOWIE GREGORY**   Gregory, Howard Watterson b: 11/18/1886, Hannibal, Mo. d: 5/30/70, Tulsa, Okla. BL/TR, 6′, 175 lbs. Deb: 4/16/11

YEAR TM/L	W	L	PCT	G	GS	CG	SH	SV	IP	H	HR	BB	SO	RAT	ERA	ERA+	OAV	OOB	BH	AVG	PB	PR	/A	PD	TPI
1911 StL-A	0	1	.000	3	1	0	0	0	7	11	0	4	1	19.3	5.14	66	.393	.469	0	.000	-0	-1	-1	-0	-0.2

● **PAUL GREGORY**   Gregory, Paul Edwin "Pop" b: 6/9/08, Tomnolen, Miss. BR/TR, 6′2″, 180 lbs. Deb: 4/20/32

YEAR TM/L	W	L	PCT	G	GS	CG	SH	SV	IP	H	HR	BB	SO	RAT	ERA	ERA+	OAV	OOB	BH	AVG	PB	PR	/A	PD	TPI
1932 Chi-A	5	3	.625	33	9	2	0	0	117²	125	8	51	39	13.6	4.51	96	.273	.348	3	.079	-3	-0	-2	3	-0.1
1933 Chi-A	4	11	.267	23	17	5	0	0	103²	124	10	47	18	14.9	4.95	86	.296	.368	5	.143	-1	-8	-8	1	-1.0
Total 2	9	14	.391	56	26	8	0	0	221¹	249	18	98	57	14.2	4.72	91	.284	.358	8	.110	-4	-8	-11	4	-1.1

● **BILL GREIF**   Greif, William Briley b: 4/25/50, Ft.Stockton, Tex. BR/TR, 6′5″, 205 lbs. Deb: 7/19/71

YEAR TM/L	W	L	PCT	G	GS	CG	SH	SV	IP	H	HR	BB	SO	RAT	ERA	ERA+	OAV	OOB	BH	AVG	PB	PR	/A	PD	TPI
1971 Hou-N	1	1	.500	7	3	0	0	0	16	18	4	14	18	15.8	5.06	66	.290	.389	1	.333	0	-3	-3	-0	-0.3
1972 SD-N	5	16	.238	34	22	2	1	2	125¹	143	18	47	91	14.2	5.60	59	.287	.357	1	.030	-3	-30	-32	-2	-5.3
1973 SD-N	10	17	.370	36	31	9	3	1	199¹	181	20	62	120	11.2	3.21	108	.246	.309	6	.098	-2	10	6	-1	0.5
1974 SD-N	9	19	.321	43	35	7	1	1	226	244	16	95	137	14.1	4.66	76	.279	.359	4	.071	-2	-26	-28	-0	-3.2
1975 SD-N	4	6	.400	59	1	0	0	9	72	74	7	38	43	14.6	3.88	90	.269	.362	0	.000	-0	-2	-3	-2	-0.7
1976 SD-N	1	3	.250	5	5	0	0	0	22¹	27	2	11	9	15.3	8.06	41	.297	.373	0	.000	-1	-11	-12	-0	-1.7
StL-N	1	5	.167	47	1	0	0	6	54²	60	5	26	32	14.5	4.12	86	.290	.374	0	.000	-0	-4	-4	-0	-0.5
Yr	2	8	.200	52	6	0	0	6	77	87	7	37	41	14.5	5.26	66	.291	.373	0	.000	-1	-15	-15	-0	-2.2
Total 6	31	67	.316	231	97	18	5	19	715²	747	70	287	442	13.5	4.41	78	.272	.349	12	.072	-7	-66	-76	-5	-11.2

● **BILL GREVELL**   Grevell, William J. b: 3/5/1898, Williamstown, N.J. d: 6/21/23, Philadelphia, Pa. BR/TR, 5′11″, 170 lbs. Deb: 5/14/19

YEAR TM/L	W	L	PCT	G	GS	CG	SH	SV	IP	H	HR	BB	SO	RAT	ERA	ERA+	OAV	OOB	BH	AVG	PB	PR	/A	PD	TPI
1919 Phi-A	0	0	—	5	2	0	0	0	12	15	0	18	3	25.5	14.25	24	.306	.500	0	.000	-1	-15	-14	1	0.0

● **GREYSON**   Greyson TL Deb: 8/27/1873

YEAR TM/L	W	L	PCT	G	GS	CG	SH	SV	IP	H	HR	BB	SO	RAT	ERA	ERA+	OAV	OOB	BH	AVG	PB	PR	/A	PD	TPI
1873 Was-n	1	6	.143	7	7	7	0	0	63	112	3	7	3	17.0	5.43	62	.357	.371	4	.143	-2	-15	-15		-1.1

● **LEE GRIFFETH**   Griffeth, Leon Clifford b: 5/20/25, Carmel, N.Y. BB/TL, 5′11.5″, 180 lbs. Deb: 6/25/46

YEAR TM/L	W	L	PCT	G	GS	CG	SH	SV	IP	H	HR	BB	SO	RAT	ERA	ERA+	OAV	OOB	BH	AVG	PB	PR	/A	PD	TPI
1946 Phi-A	0	0	—	10	0	0	0	0	15¹	13	1	6	4	12.3	2.93	121	.232	.328	0	.000	-0	1	1	-0	0.0

● **HANK GRIFFIN**   Griffin, James Linton "Pepper" b: 7/11/1886, Whitehouse, Tex. d: 2/11/50, Terrell, Tex. BR/TR, 6′, 165 lbs. Deb: 5/5/11

YEAR TM/L	W	L	PCT	G	GS	CG	SH	SV	IP	H	HR	BB	SO	RAT	ERA	ERA+	OAV	OOB	BH	AVG	PB	PR	/A	PD	TPI
1911 Chi-N	0	0	—	1	1	0	0	0	1	1	1	3	1	36.0	18.00	18	.250	.571	0	—	0	-2	-2	0	0.0
Bos-N	0	6	.000	15	6	1	0	0	82²	96	3	34	30	14.8	5.23	73	.305	.383	7	.233	-0	-17	-13	0	-0.8

YEAR	TM/L	W	L	PCT	G	GS	CG	SH	SV	IP	H	HR	BB	SO	RAT	ERA	ERA+	OAV	OOB	BH	AVG	PB	PR	/A	PD	TPI
	Yr	0	6	.000	16	7	1	0	0	83²	97	4	37	31	15.1	5.38	71	.304	.387	7	.233	-0	-18	-14	0	-0.8
1912	Bos-N	0	0	—	3	0	0	0	0	1²	3	0	3	0	37.8	27.00	13	.750	.875	0	—	0	-4	-4	-0	0.0
Total	2	0	6	.000	19	7	1	0	0	85¹	100	4	40	31	15.5	5.80	66	.310	.397	7	.233	-0	-23	-19	0	-0.8

● **MARTY GRIFFIN** Griffin, Martin John b: 9/2/01, San Francisco, Cal d: 11/19/51, Los Angeles, Cal. BR/TR, 6'2", 200 lbs. Deb: 7/25/28

YEAR	TM/L	W	L	PCT	G	GS	CG	SH	SV	IP	H	HR	BB	SO	RAT	ERA	ERA+	OAV	OOB	BH	AVG	PB	PR	/A	PD	TPI
1928	Bos-A	0	3	.000	11	3	0	0	0	37²	42	0	17	9	14.1	5.02	82	.300	.376	4	.308	1	-4	-4	-0	-0.2

● **MIKE GRIFFIN** Griffin, Michael Leroy b: 6/26/57, Colusa, Cal. BR/TR, 6'5", 197 lbs. Deb: 9/17/79

YEAR	TM/L	W	L	PCT	G	GS	CG	SH	SV	IP	H	HR	BB	SO	RAT	ERA	ERA+	OAV	OOB	BH	AVG	PB	PR	/A	PD	TPI
1979	NY-A	0	0	—	3	0	0	0	1	4¹	5	0	2	5	14.5	4.15	98	.313	.389	0	—	0	-0	-0	-0	0.2
1980	NY-A	2	4	.333	13	9	0	0	0	54	64	6	23	24	14.7	4.83	81	.287	.356	0	—	0	-5	-5	-0	-0.4
1981	NY-A	0	0	—	2	0	0	0	0	4¹	5	0	0	4	10.4	2.08	172	.278	.278	0	—	0	1	1	0	0.1
	Chi-N	2	5	.286	16	9	0	0	1	52	64	4	9	20	12.6	4.50	82	.302	.330	2	.154	-0	-6	-5	0	-0.6
1982	SD-N	0	1	.000	7	0	0	0	0	10¹	9	0	3	4	10.5	3.48	98	.237	.293	0	.000	-0	0	-0	-0	0.0
1987	Bal-A	3	5	.375	23	6	1	0	0	74¹	78	9	33	42	13.8	4.36	101	.269	.350	0	—	-0	1	0	-1	0.2
1989	Cin-N	0	0	—	3	0	0	0	0	4¹	10	0	3	1	27.0	12.46	29	.500	.565	1	1.000	0	-4	-4	0	0.1
Total	6	7	15	.318	67	24	1	0	3	203²	235	19	73	101	13.8	4.60	87	.288	.349	3	.200	-0	-13	-13	-1	-0.4

● **PAT GRIFFIN** Griffin, Patrick Richard b: 5/6/1893, Niles, Ohio d: 6/7/27, Youngstown, Ohio BR/TR, 6'2", 180 lbs. Deb: 7/23/14

YEAR	TM/L	W	L	PCT	G	GS	CG	SH	SV	IP	H	HR	BB	SO	RAT	ERA	ERA+	OAV	OOB	BH	AVG	PB	PR	/A	PD	TPI
1914	Cin-N	0	0	—	1	0	0	0	0	1	3	0	2	0	45.0	9.00	33	.750	.833	0	—	0	-1	-1	0	0.0

● **TOM GRIFFIN** Griffin, Thomas James b: 2/22/48, Los Angeles, Cal. BR/TR, 6'3", 210 lbs. Deb: 4/10/69

YEAR	TM/L	W	L	PCT	G	GS	CG	SH	SV	IP	H	HR	BB	SO	RAT	ERA	ERA+	OAV	OOB	BH	AVG	PB	PR	/A	PD	TPI
1969	Hou-N	11	10	.524	31	31	6	3	0	188¹	156	19	93	200	12.2	3.54	100	.220	.317	9	.145	2	1	0	-2	0.1
1970	Hou-N	3	13	.188	23	20	7	0	0	111¹	118	9	72	72	15.6	5.74	68	.275	.383	2	.061	-2	-21	-23	-1	-3.1
1971	Hou-N	0	6	.000	10	6	0	0	0	37²	44	4	20	29	15.8	4.78	70	.288	.377	1	.111	-0	-5	-6	1	-0.8
1972	Hou-N	5	4	.556	39	5	1	1	3	94¹	92	7	38	83	12.7	3.24	104	.258	.334	7	.280	3	2	1	-1	0.4
1973	Hou-N	4	6	.400	25	12	4	0	0	99²	83	10	46	69	11.8	4.15	87	.229	.320	3	.107	-0	-5	-6	0	-0.5
1974	Hou-N	14	10	.583	34	34	8	3	0	211	202	14	89	110	12.6	3.54	98	.250	.328	20	.294	8	2	-2	1	0.7
1975	Hou-N	3	8	.273	17	13	3	1	0	79¹	89	11	46	56	15.5	5.33	63	.288	.384	3	.136	-0	-15	-17	1	-2.1
1976	Hou-N	5	3	.625	20	2	0	0	0	41²	44	4	37	33	17.7	6.05	53	.278	.418	0	.000	-0	-12	-13	0	-2.3
	SD-N	4	3	.571	11	11	2	0	0	70¹	56	0	42	36	12.7	2.94	111	.222	.336	2	.077	-2	4	3	-0	0.0
	Yr	9	6	.600	31	13	2	0	0	112	100	4	79	69	14.5	4.10	79	.242	.364	2	.065	-2	-7	-11	-0	-2.3
1977	SD-N	6	9	.400	38	20	0	0	0	151¹	144	17	88	89	14.1	4.46	79	.254	.359	6	.133	1	-9	-16	-2	-1.4
1978	Cal-A	3	4	.429	24	4	0	0	0	56	63	8	31	35	15.3	4.02	90	.279	.368	0	—	-0	-2	-3	1	-0.2
1979	SF-N	5	6	.455	59	3	0	0	2	94¹	83	9	46	82	12.7	3.91	89	.237	.333	1	.071	-1	-2	-4	2	-0.4
1980	SF-N	5	1	.833	42	4	0	0	0	107²	80	8	49	79	11.5	2.76	128	.212	.315	2	.111	0	10	9	0	0.5
1981	SF-N	8	8	.500	22	22	3	1	0	129¹	121	8	57	83	12.9	3.76	91	.249	.336	8	.195	2	-4	-5	-2	-0.2
1982	Pit-N	1	3	.250	6	4	0	0	0	22¹	32	5	15	8	19.3	8.87	42	.330	.425	2	.222	0	-13	-13	-0	-1.8
Total	14	77	94	.450	401	191	29	10	5	1494²	1407	133	769	1054	13.4	4.07	86	.249	.345	66	.163	12	-69	-94	1	-11.1

● **CLARK GRIFFITH** Griffith, Clark Calvin "The Old Fox" b: 11/20/1869, Clear Creek, Mo. d: 10/27/55, Washington, D.C. BR/TR, 5'6.5", 156 lbs. Deb: 4/11/1891 MH♦

YEAR	TM/L	W	L	PCT	G	GS	CG	SH	SV	IP	H	HR	BB	SO	RAT	ERA	ERA+	OAV	OOB	BH	AVG	PB	PR	/A	PD	TPI
1891	StL-a	11	8	.579	27	17	12	0	0	186¹	195	8	58	68	12.9	3.33	126	.260	.326	12	.156	-3	8	18	0	1.2
	Bos-a	3	1	.750	7	4	3	0	0	40	47	3	15	20	15.1	5.62	62	.283	.360	4	.174	2	-8	-9	-1	-0.6
	Yr	14	9	.609	34	21	15	0	0	226¹	242	11	73	88	12.7	3.74	109	.260	.317	16	.160	-1	-0	9	-1	0.6
1893	Chi-N	1	2	.333	4	2	2	0	0	19²	24	1	5	9	13.7	5.03	92	.292	.340	2	.182	-1	-1	-1	1	-0.1
1894	Chi-N	21	14	.600	36	30	28	0	0	261¹	328	12	85	71	14.7	4.92	114	.304	.362	33	.232	-0	12	20	1	1.9
1895	Chi-N	26	14	.650	42	41	39	0	0	353	434	11	91	79	13.9	3.93	130	.298	.348	46	.319	5	34	46	1	4.5
1896	Chi-N	23	11	.676	36	35	35	0	0	317²	370	3	70	81	12.8	3.54	128	.289	.331	36	.267	3	29	35	3	3.3
1897	Chi-N	21	18	.538	41	38	38	1	1	343²	410	3	86	102	13.4	3.72	120	.294	.342	38	.235	3	23	28	3	3.0
1898	Chi-N	24	10	.706	38	38	36	4	0	325²	305	1	64	97	10.8	**1.88**	**191**	.246	.294	20	.164	-2	63	62	5	5.8
1899	Chi-N	22	14	.611	38	38	35	0	0	319²	329	5	65	73	11.5	2.79	134	.266	.310	31	.258	6	38	34	6	4.5
1900	Chi-N	14	13	.519	30	30	27	4	0	248	245	6	51	61	11.3	3.05	118	.258	.306	24	.253	5	18	15	-1	1.8
1901	Chi-A	24	7	**.774**	35	30	26	5	1	266²	275	4	50	67	11.1	2.67	131	.263	.299	27	.303	14	30	24	0	3.7
1902	Chi-A	15	9	.625	28	24	20	3	0	213	247	11	47	51	13.1	4.18	81	.290	.339	20	.217	2	-14	-19	-1	-1.7
1903	NY-a	14	11	.560	25	24	22	2	0	213	201	3	33	69	10.1	2.70	116	.249	.283	11	.159	2	6	10	-3	1.0
1904	NY-A	7	5	.583	16	11	8	1	0	100¹	91	3	16	36	10.0	2.87	94	.243	.281	6	.143	-1	-3	-2	-1	-0.4
1905	NY-A	9	6	.600	25	7	4	2	1	101²	82	1	15	46	8.7	1.68	175	.222	.254	7	.219	1	11	14	-2	2.1
1906	NY-A	2	2	.500	17	2	1	0	2	59²	58	0	15	16	11.6	3.02	98	.258	.316	2	.111	-1	-2	-0	-1	0.0
1907	NY-A	0	0	—	4	0	0	0	0	8¹	15	0	6	5	22.7	8.64	32	.390	.472	0	.000	-0	-6	-5	0	0.0
1909	Cin-N	0	1	.000	1	1	0	0	0	6	11	0	2	3	19.5	6.00	43	.379	.419	0	.000	-0	-2	-2	1	-0.3
1912	Was-A	0	0	—	1	0	0	0	0	1	0	1	0	0	9.0	∞	—	1.000	1.000	0	.000	-0	-1	-1	0	-0.1
1913	Was-A	0	0	—	1	0	0	0	0	1	1	0	0	0	9.0	0.00	—	.250	.250	1	1.000	1	0	0	0	0.0
1914	Was-A	0	0	—	1	0	0	0	0	1	1	0	0	0	9.0	0.00	—	.250	.250	1	1.000	1	0	0	0	0.1
Total	20	237	146	.619	453	372	337	22	6	3385²	3670	76	774	955	12.3	3.31	121	.274	.322	321	.233	35	233	266	7	29.7

● **FRANK GRIFFITH** Griffith, Frank Wesley b: 11/18/1872, Gilman, Ill. d: 12/13/08, BL/TL, Deb: 8/13/1892

YEAR	TM/L	W	L	PCT	G	GS	CG	SH	SV	IP	H	HR	BB	SO	RAT	ERA	ERA+	OAV	OOB	BH	AVG	PB	PR	/A	PD	TPI
1892	Chi-N	0	1	.000	1	1	0	0	0	4	3	1	6	3	20.3	11.25	30	.200	.429	0	.000	-0	-4	-4	-0	-0.6
1894	Cle-N	1	2	.333	7	6	3	0	0	42¹	64	5	37	15	23.4	9.99	55	.344	.474	8	.333	2	-22	-21	-0	-0.9
Total	2	1	3	.250	8	7	3	0	0	46¹	67	6	43	18	23.1	10.10	52	.333	.471	8	.320	2	-25	-25	-0	-1.5

● **HAL GRIGGS** Griggs, Harold Lloyd b: 8/24/28, Shannon, Ga. BR/TR, 6', 170 lbs. Deb: 4/18/56

YEAR	TM/L	W	L	PCT	G	GS	CG	SH	SV	IP	H	HR	BB	SO	RAT	ERA	ERA+	OAV	OOB	BH	AVG	PB	PR	/A	PD	TPI
1956	Was-A	1	6	.143	34	12	1	0	1	98²	120	14	76	48	18.0	6.02	72	.307	.421	0	.000	-1	-20	-19	1	-1.2
1957	Was-A	0	1	.000	2	2	0	0	0	13²	11	1	7	11	11.9	3.29	118	.229	.327	1	.250	0	1	1	0	0.1
1958	Was-A	3	11	.214	32	21	3	0	0	137	138	20	74	69	14.1	5.52	69	.262	.355	5	.122	-2	-27	-26	-0	-2.6
1959	Was-A	2	8	.200	37	10	2	1	2	97²	103	8	52	43	14.4	5.25	75	.270	.359	1	.056	-2	-15	-15	-0	-1.6
Total	4	6	26	.188	105	45	6	1	3	347	372	43	209	172	15.2	5.50	73	.276	.375	7	.089	-5	-61	-58	1	-5.3

● **GUIDO GRILLI** Grilli, Guido John b: 1/9/39, Memphis, Tenn. BL/TL, 6', 188 lbs. Deb: 4/12/66

YEAR	TM/L	W	L	PCT	G	GS	CG	SH	SV	IP	H	HR	BB	SO	RAT	ERA	ERA+	OAV	OOB	BH	AVG	PB	PR	/A	PD	TPI
1966	Bos-A	0	1	.000	6	0	0	0	0	4²	5	1	9	4	27.0	7.71	49	.278	.519	1	.500	0	-2	-2	0	-0.4
	KC-A	0	1	.000	16	0	0	0	1	15²	19	0	11	8	19.0	6.89	49	.302	.429	0	—	0	-6	-6	-1	-0.5
	Yr	0	2	.000	22	0	0	0	1	20¹	24	1	20	12	20.8	7.08	49	.296	.452	1	.500	0	-8	-8	-1	-0.9

● **STEVE GRILLI** Grilli, Stephen Joseph b: 5/2/49, Brooklyn, N.Y. BR/TR, 6'2", 170 lbs. Deb: 9/19/75

YEAR	TM/L	W	L	PCT	G	GS	CG	SH	SV	IP	H	HR	BB	SO	RAT	ERA	ERA+	OAV	OOB	BH	AVG	PB	PR	/A	PD	TPI
1975	Det-A	0	0	—	3	0	0	0	0	6²	3	0	6	5	12.2	1.35	297	.136	.321	0	—	0	2	2	0	-0.2
1976	Det-A	3	1	.750	36	0	0	0	3	66	63	5	41	36	14.9	4.64	80	.258	.376	0	—	0	-8	-7	2	-0.3
1977	Det-A	1	2	.333	30	2	0	0	0	72²	71	8	49	49	15.2	4.83	89	.265	.384	0	—	0	-6	-4	-1	-0.3
1979	Tor-A	0	0	—	1	0	0	0	0	2¹	1	0	0	1	3.9	0.00	—	.143	.143	0	—	0	1	1	-0	-0.1
Total	4	4	3	.571	70	2	0	0	3	147²	138	13	96	91	14.7	4.51	89	.255	.375	0	—	0	-12	-8	1	-0.9

● **JOHN GRIM** Grim, John Helm b: 8/9/1867, Lebanon, Ky. d: 7/28/61, Indianapolis, Ind BR/TR, 6'2", 175 lbs. Deb: 9/29/1888 ♦

YEAR	TM/L	W	L	PCT	G	GS	CG	SH	SV	IP	H	HR	BB	SO	RAT	ERA	ERA+	OAV	OOB	BH	AVG	PB	PR	/A	PD	TPI
1890	Roc-a	0	0	—	1	0	0	0	0	3¹	3	0	4	3	18.9	0.00	—	.233	.415	51	.266	0	1	1	-0	0.0

● **BOB GRIM** Grim, Robert Anton b: 3/8/30, New York, N.Y. BR/TR, 6'1", 185 lbs. Deb: 4/18/54

YEAR	TM/L	W	L	PCT	G	GS	CG	SH	SV	IP	H	HR	BB	SO	RAT	ERA	ERA+	OAV	OOB	BH	AVG	PB	PR	/A	PD	TPI
1954	NY-A	20	6	.769	37	20	8	1	0	199	175	9	85	108	11.9	3.26	106	.244	.327	10	.143	-1	10	4	-1	0.2
1955	*NY-A	7	5	.583	26	11	1	1	4	92¹	81	9	42	63	12.3	4.19	89	.238	.326	3	.120	-1	-2	-5	0	-0.7

YEAR	TM/L	W	L	PCT	G	GS	CG	SH	SV	IP	H	HR	BB	SO	RAT	ERA	ERA+	OAV	OOB	BH	AVG	PB	PR	/A	PD	TPI
1956	NY-A	6	1	.857	26	6	1	0	5	74²	64	3	31	48	11.7	2.77	139	.235	.318	1	.063	-0	11	9	-1	0.8
1957	*NY-A★	12	8	.600	46	0	0	0	**19**	72	60	5	36	52	12.0	2.63	137	.239	.334	1	.111	-0	9	8	0	2.6
1958	NY-A	0	1	.000	11	0	0	0	0	16¹	12	3	10	11	12.7	5.51	64	.211	.338	0	.000	-0	-3	-4	-0	-0.2
	KC-A	7	6	.538	26	14	5	1	0	113²	118	7	41	54	12.8	3.56	110	.269	.336	6	.188	-0	3	4	-1	0.3
	Yr	7	7	.500	37	14	5	1	0	130	130	10	51	65	12.7	3.81	101	.262	.335	6	.182	-1	-1	1	-1	0.1
1959	KC-A	6	10	.375	40	9	3	1	4	125¹	124	10	57	65	13.2	4.09	98	.260	.343	3	.094	-1	-3	-1	-2	-0.4
1960	Cle-N	0	1	.000	3	0	0	0	0	2¹	6	0	1	2	27.0	11.57	32	.500	.538	0	—	0	-2	-2	0	-0.7
	Cin-N	2	2	.500	26	0	0	0	2	30¹	32	3	10	22	12.5	4.45	86	.274	.331	0	.000	-0	-2	-2	-0	-0.3
	StL-N	1	0	1.000	15	0	0	0	0	20²	22	1	9	15	13.5	3.05	134	.272	.344	0	.000	-0	2	2	0	0.1
	Yr	3	2	.600	41	0	0	0	2	51	54	4	19	37	12.9	3.88	101	.267	.330	0	.000	-0	-1	0	-0	-0.2
1962	KC-A	0	1	.000	12	0	0	0	3	13	14	0	8	3	15.2	6.23	68	.292	.393	0	.000	-0	-3	-3	1	-0.3
Total	8	61	41	.598	268	60	18	4	37	759²	708	50	330	443	12.5	3.61	104	.252	.334	24	.127	-4	19	11	-4	1.4

● **BURLEIGH GRIMES**   Grimes, Burleigh Arland "Ol' Stubblebeard"
b: 8/18/1893, Emerald, Wis.   d: 12/6/85, Clear Lake, Wis.   BR/TR, 5'10", 175 lbs.   Deb: 9/10/16   MCH

YEAR	TM/L	W	L	PCT	G	GS	CG	SH	SV	IP	H	HR	BB	SO	RAT	ERA	ERA+	OAV	OOB	BH	AVG	PB	PR	/A	PD	TPI
1916	Pit-N	2	3	.400	6	5	4	0	0	45²	40	1	10	20	9.9	2.36	114	.241	.284	3	.176	-0	1	2	1	0.2
1917	Pit-N	3	16	.158	37	17	8	1	0	194	186	5	70	72	12.2	3.53	81	.260	.331	16	.232	1	-18	-15	1	-1.1
1918	Bro-N	19	9	.679	**40**	30	19	7	1	269²	210	3	76	113	9.7	2.14	130	.216	.276	18	.200	0	19	19	4	2.6
1919	Bro-N	10	11	.476	25	21	13	1	0	181¹	179	2	60	82	12.2	3.47	86	.256	.321	17	.246	1	-11	-10	1	-0.9
1920	*Bro-N	23	11	**.676**	40	33	25	5	2	303²	271	4	67	131	10.1	2.22	144	.238	.282	34	.306	10	31	33	3	5.4
1921	Bro-N	**22**	13	.629	37	35	30	2	0	302¹	313	6	76	**136**	11.7	2.83	138	.274	.322	27	.237	2	32	**36**	4	**4.5**
1922	Bro-N	17	14	.548	36	34	18	1	1	259	324	17	84	99	14.4	4.76	85	.308	.363	22	.237	4	-19	-20	4	-1.2
1923	Bro-N	21	18	.538	39	38	**33**	2	0	327	356	9	100	119	12.9	3.58	108	.280	.338	30	.238	3	15	11	5	2.0
1924	Bro-N	22	13	.629	38	36	**30**	1	1	**310²**	351	15	91	135	13.0	3.82	98	.287	.339	37	.298	6	1	-3	5	0.9
1925	Bro-N	12	19	.387	33	31	19	0	0	246²	305	15	102	73	15.1	5.04	83	.309	.377	24	.250	5	-21	-23	8	-1.2
1926	Bro-N	12	13	.480	30	29	18	1	0	225¹	238	4	88	64	13.2	3.71	103	.276	.346	18	.222	1	3	3	3	0.6
1927	NY-N	19	8	.704	39	34	15	2	0	259²	274	12	87	102	12.7	3.54	109	.276	.337	18	.188	-0	11	9	5	1.3
1928	Pit-N	**25**	14	.641	**48**	37	**28**	**4**	3	**330¹**	311	11	77	97	10.8	2.99	136	.248	.297	42	.321	11	37	39	6	6.1
1929	Pit-N	17	7	.708	33	29	18	2	2	232²	245	11	70	62	12.3	3.13	**152**	.269	.324	26	.286	6	**41**	42	3	**4.7**
1930	Bos-N	3	5	.375	11	9	1	0	0	49	72	4	22	15	17.8	7.35	67	.353	.424	3	.188	-0	-13	-13	0	-1.6
	*StL-N	13	6	.684	22	19	10	1	0	152¹	174	5	43	58	13.1	3.01	166	.293	.345	15	.263	2	33	34	1	4.0
	Yr	16	11	.593	33	28	11	1	0	201¹	246	9	65	73	14.1	4.07	123	.307	.362	18	.247	2	20	21	2	2.4
1931	*StL-N	17	9	.654	29	28	17	3	0	212¹	240	11	59	67	13.1	3.65	108	.286	.340	14	.184	-2	5	7	3	0.8
1932	*Chi-N	6	11	.353	30	18	5	1	1	141¹	174	8	50	36	14.3	4.78	79	.297	.354	11	.250	-1	-14	-16	1	-1.5
1933	Chi-N	3	6	.333	17	7	3	1	3	69²	71	2	29	12	13.0	3.49	94	.277	.353	3	.150	-1	-1	-2	1	-0.2
	StL-N	0	1	.000	4	3	0	0	1	13²	15	1	8	4	15.8	5.27	66	.263	.364	1	.200	-0	-3	-3	-1	-0.3
	Yr	3	7	.300	21	10	3	1	4	83¹	86	3	37	16	13.4	3.78	87	.274	.352	4	.160	-0	-4	-4	-0	-0.5
1934	StL-N	2	1	.667	4	0	0	0	0	7²	5	1	2	1	8.2	3.52	120	.179	.233	0	—	0	0	1	0	0.2
	Pit-N	1	2	.333	8	4	0	0	0	27¹	36	0	10	9	15.5	7.24	57	.310	.370	1	.143	-0	-10	-10	1	-0.9
	Yr	3	3	.500	12	4	0	0	0	35	41	1	12	10	13.9	6.43	64	.285	.344	1	.143	-0	-9	-9	1	-0.7
	NY-A	1	2	.333	10	0	0	0	1	18	22	0	14	5	18.5	5.50	74	.319	.440	0	.000	-0	-2	-3	1	-0.4
Total	19	270	212	.560	616	497	314	35	18	4179²	4412	148	1295	1512	12.5	3.53	107	.273	.331	380	.248	52	118	121	58	24.0

● **JOHN GRIMES**   Grimes, John Thomas   b: 4/17/1869, Wooodstock, Md.   d: 1/17/64, San Francisco, Cal   BR/TR, 5'11", 160 lbs.   Deb: 7/28/1897

YEAR	TM/L	W	L	PCT	G	GS	CG	SH	SV	IP	H	HR	BB	SO	RAT	ERA	ERA+	OAV	OOB	BH	AVG	PB	PR	/A	PD	TPI
1897	StL-N	0	2	.000	3	1	1	0	0	19²	24	0	8	4	17.4	5.95	74	.298	.402	2	.286	1	-4	-3	1	-0.1

● **JASON GRIMSLEY**   Grimsley, Jason Alan   b: 8/7/67, Cleveland, Tex.   BR/TR, 6'3", 180 lbs.   Deb: 9/8/89

YEAR	TM/L	W	L	PCT	G	GS	CG	SH	SV	IP	H	HR	BB	SO	RAT	ERA	ERA+	OAV	OOB	BH	AVG	PB	PR	/A	PD	TPI
1989	Phi-N	1	3	.250	4	4	0	0	0	18¹	19	2	19	7	18.7	5.89	60	.268	.422	0	.000	-1	-5	-5	0	-0.9
1990	Phi-N	3	2	.600	11	11	0	0	0	57¹	47	1	43	41	14.4	3.30	116	.227	.365	3	.188	0	3	3	1	0.4
1991	Phi-N	1	7	.125	12	12	0	0	0	61	54	4	41	42	14.5	4.87	75	.242	.367	1	.059	-1	-8	-8	1	-0.9
1993	Cle-A	3	4	.429	10	6	0	0	0	42¹	52	3	20	27	15.5	5.31	81	.302	.378	0	—	0	-5	-5	-0	-0.7
1994	Cle-A	5	2	.714	14	13	1	0	0	82²	91	7	34	59	14.3	4.57	108	.283	.362	0	—	0	3	0	0	0.1
Total	5	13	18	.419	51	46	1	0	0	261²	263	17	157	176	14.9	4.57	92	.264	.371	4	.105	-1	-12	-11	2	-2.1

● **ROSS GRIMSLEY**   Grimsley, Ross Albert I   b: 6/4/22, Americus, Kan.   d: 2/6/94, Memphis, Tenn.   BL/TL, 6', 175 lbs.   Deb: 9/3/51   F

YEAR	TM/L	W	L	PCT	G	GS	CG	SH	SV	IP	H	HR	BB	SO	RAT	ERA	ERA+	OAV	OOB	BH	AVG	PB	PR	/A	PD	TPI
1951	Chi-A	0	0	—	7	0	0	0	0	14	12	1	10	8	14.1	3.86	105	.235	.361	0	.000	-0	0	0	-1	-0.1

● **ROSS GRIMSLEY**   Grimsley, Ross Albert Ii   b: 1/7/50, Topeka, Kan.   BL/TL, 6'3", 200 lbs.   Deb: 5/16/71   F

YEAR	TM/L	W	L	PCT	G	GS	CG	SH	SV	IP	H	HR	BB	SO	RAT	ERA	ERA+	OAV	OOB	BH	AVG	PB	PR	/A	PD	TPI
1971	Cin-N	10	7	.588	26	26	6	3	0	161¹	151	15	43	67	10.9	3.57	94	.250	.302	6	.118	-1	-2	-4	-1	-0.6
1972	*Cin-N	14	8	.636	30	28	4	1	1	197²	194	18	50	79	11.1	3.05	105	.260	.307	8	.121	-2	9	4	-0	0.1
1973	*Cin-N	13	10	.565	38	36	8	1	1	242¹	245	24	68	90	11.6	3.23	105	.266	.317	5	.061	-6	12	5	-2	0.4
1974	*Bal-A	18	13	.581	40	39	17	4	1	295²	267	26	76	158	10.5	3.07	112	.244	.295	0	—	0	18	12	0	1.4
1975	Bal-A	10	13	.435	35	32	8	1	0	197	210	29	47	89	11.8	4.07	86	.276	.319	0	—	0	-6	-12	0	-1.1
1976	Bal-A	8	7	.533	28	19	2	0	0	136²	143	8	35	41	11.8	3.95	83	.270	.317	0	—	0	-7	-10	-1	-1.1
1977	Bal-A	14	10	.583	34	34	11	2	0	218¹	230	24	74	53	12.6	3.96	96	.277	.337	0	—	0	-2	-4	2	-0.2
1978	Mon-N☆	20	11	.645	36	36	19	3	0	263	237	17	67	84	10.5	3.05	116	.243	.293	13	.144	-1	15	14	1	1.6
1979	Mon-N	10	9	.526	32	27	2	0	0	151¹	199	18	41	42	14.5	5.35	68	.322	.367	11	.200	1	-27	-28	-0	-3.1
1980	Mon-N	2	4	.333	11	7	0	0	0	41¹	61	5	12	11	16.1	6.31	56	.351	.396	2	.222	0	-12	-13	0	-1.6
	Cle-A	4	5	.444	14	11	2	0	0	74²	103	11	24	18	15.4	6.75	60	.331	.381	0	—	0	-23	-22	-1	-2.3
1982	Bal-A	1	2	.333	21	0	0	0	0	60	65	7	22	18	13.1	5.25	77	.283	.345	0	—	0	-8	-8	0	-0.3
Total	11	124	99	.556	345	295	79	15	3	2039¹	2105	202	559	750	11.8	3.81	92	.270	.320	45	.127	-10	-29	-67	-1	-7.6

● **DAN GRINER**   Griner, Donald Dexter "Rusty"   b: 3/7/1888, Centerville, Tenn.   d: 6/3/50, Bishopville, S.C.   BL/TR, 6'1.5", 200 lbs.   Deb: 8/17/12

YEAR	TM/L	W	L	PCT	G	GS	CG	SH	SV	IP	H	HR	BB	SO	RAT	ERA	ERA+	OAV	OOB	BH	AVG	PB	PR	/A	PD	TPI
1912	StL-N	3	4	.429	12	7	2	0	0	54	59	3	15	20	12.8	3.17	108	.278	.335	1	.077	-0	1	2	-1	0.0
1913	StL-N	10	22	.313	34	34	18	1	0	225	279	12	66	79	14.2	5.08	64	.312	.366	21	.259	-1	-47	-46	2	-5.0
1914	StL-N	9	13	.409	37	16	11	2	2	179	163	3	57	74	11.2	2.51	111	.254	.318	14	.255	4	5	6	-1	1.0
1915	StL-N	5	11	.313	37	18	9	3	3	150¹	137	4	46	46	11.4	2.81	99	.259	.328	14	.269	4	-1	-0	-2	0.2
1916	StL-N	0	0	—	4	0	0	1	0	11	15	0	3	3	15.5	4.09	65	.341	.396	1	.250	-2	-2	-2	0	-0.2
1918	Bro-N	1	5	.167	11	6	3	1	0	54¹	47	0	15	22	11.4	2.15	129	.267	.348	1	.071	-1	4	4	0	0.4
Total	6	28	55	.337	135	81	43	7	6	673²	700	22	202	244	12.5	3.49	86	.280	.342	52	.237	12	-39	-37	-2	-3.4

● **LEE GRISSOM**   Grissom, Lee Theo   b: 10/23/07, Sherman, Tex.   BB/TL, 6'3", 200 lbs.   Deb: 9/2/34   F

YEAR	TM/L	W	L	PCT	G	GS	CG	SH	SV	IP	H	HR	BB	SO	RAT	ERA	ERA+	OAV	OOB	BH	AVG	PB	PR	/A	PD	TPI
1934	Cin-N	0	1	.000	4	1	0	0	0	7	13	0	7	4	25.7	15.43	26	.382	.488	0	.000	-0	-9	-9	-0	-1.0
1935	Cin-N	1	1	.500	3	3	1	0	0	21	31	0	13	13	15.0	3.86	103	.333	.361	0	.000	-1	0	0	0	0.0
1936	Cin-N	1	1	.500	6	4	0	0	0	24¹	33	1	9	13	15.5	6.29	61	.320	.375	0	.000	-1	-6	-7	0	-0.6
1937	Cin-N★	12	17	.414	50	30	14	**5**	6	223²	193	7	93	149	11.7	3.26	114	.232	.313	7	.109	-3	16	12	-2	0.9
1938	Cin-N	2	3	.400	14	7	0	0	0	51	60	4	22	16	14.8	5.29	69	.300	.375	3	.188	-0	-9	-9	-0	-0.9
1939	*Cin-N	9	7	.563	33	21	3	0	0	153²	145	14	56	53	11.8	4.10	93	.249	.316	4	.085	-2	-3	-5	-2	-0.8
1940	NY-A	0	0	—	5	0	0	0	0	4²	4	0	7	2	11.6	0.00	—	.250	.333	0	—	0	2	2	0	0.1
	Bro-N	2	5	.286	14	10	3	1	0	73²	59	3	34	56	11.4	2.81	142	.215	.302	5	.217	0	9	10	1	0.8
1941	Bro-N	0	0	—	2	0	0	0	0	11¹	10	2	9	5	15.1	2.38	154	.238	.360	2	.250	-0	2	2	-0	0.3
	Phi-N	2	13	.133	29	18	2	0	0	131¹	120	4	69	74	13.2	3.97	93	.242	.338	6	.167	-5	-4	-4	-1	-0.5
	Yr	2	13	.133	33	19	2	0	1	142²	130	6	78	79	13.2	3.85	97	.242	.340	7	.184	-5	-3	-2	-1	-0.4
Total	8	29	48	.377	162	95	23	6	7	701²	668	35	305	384	12.6	3.89	97	.250	.329	26	.127	-8	-3	-8	-6	-2.0

YEAR TM/L	W	L	PCT	G	GS	CG	SH	SV	IP	H	HR	BB	SO	RAT	ERA	ERA+	OAV	OOB	BH	AVG	PB	PR	/A	PD	TPI

● **MARV GRISSOM** Grissom, Marvin Edward b: 3/31/18, Los Molinos, Cal. BR/TR, 6'3", 195 lbs. Deb: 9/10/46 FC

1946 NY-N	0	2	.000	4	3	0	0	0	18²	17	1	13	9	14.9	4.34	79	.254	.383	1	.200	-0	-2	-2	1	-0.1
1949 Det-A	2	4	.333	27	2	0	0	0	39¹	56	6	34	17	20.8	6.41	65	.335	.450	2	.222	1	-10	-10	0	-1.2
1952 Chi-A	12	10	.545	28	24	7	1	0	166	156	6	79	97	12.9	3.74	98	.250	.337	8	.151	-1	-1	-2	-2	-0.5
1953 Bos-A	2	6	.250	13	11	1	1	0	59¹	61	5	30	31	14.0	4.70	88	.266	.354	0	.000	-3	-5	-3	-1	-0.7
NY-N	4	2	.667	21	7	3	0	0	84¹	83	6	31	46	12.3	3.95	109	.255	.321	2	.074	-2	3	3	1	0.1
1954 *NY-N★	10	7	.588	56	3	1	1	19	122¹	100	13	50	64	11.6	2.35	171	.226	.314	2	.156	-1	23	23	-0	3.6
1955 NY-N	5	4	.556	55	0	0	0	8	89¹	76	6	41	49	12.4	2.92	138	.237	.334	2	.154	-1	11	11	0	1.2
1956 NY-N	1	1	.500	43	2	0	0	7	80²	71	3	16	49	9.8	1.56	242	.241	.282	1	.091	-0	**20**	**20**	-1	0.8
1957 NY-N	4	4	.500	55	0	0	0	14	82²	74	6	23	51	10.8	2.61	151	.243	.301	2	.167	0	12	12	1	1.7
1958 SF-N	7	5	.583	51	0	0	0	10	65¹	71	11	26	46	14.1	3.99	95	.287	.367	0	.000	-1	-0	-1	0	-0.3
1959 StL-N	0	0	—	3	0	0	0	0	2	6	2	4	0	27.0	22.50	19	.500	.500	0	—	0	-4	-4	0	0.0
Total 10	47	45	.511	356	52	12	3	58	810	771	65	343	459	12.7	3.41	115	.254	.335	23	.122	-7	47	47	-0	4.6

● **CONNIE GROB** Grob, Conrad George b: 11/9/32, Cross Plains, Wis. BL/TR, 6'0.5", 180 lbs. Deb: 4/22/56

| 1956 Was-A | 4 | 5 | .444 | 37 | 1 | 0 | 0 | 1 | 79¹ | 121 | 14 | 26 | 27 | 16.8 | 7.83 | 55 | .353 | .400 | 6 | .333 | 1 | -32 | -31 | 1 | -2.8 |

● **JOHNNY GRODZICKI** Grodzicki, John "Grod" b: 2/26/17, Nanticoke, Pa. BR/TR, 6'1.5", 200 lbs. Deb: 4/18/41 C

1941 StL-N	2	1	.667	5	1	0	0	0	13¹	9	0	11	10	11.5	1.35	279	.130	.298	0	.000	0	3	4	-0	0.8
1946 StL-N	0	0	—	3	0	0	0	0	4	4	1	4	2	18.0	9.00	38	.250	.400	0	—	0	-2	-2	0	0.0
1947 StL-N	0	1	.000	16	0	0	0	0	23¹	21	5	19	8	15.4	5.40	77	.253	.392	0	.000	-0	-3	-3	0	-0.1
Total 3	2	2	.500	24	1	0	0	0	40²	31	6	34	20	14.4	4.43	89	.214	.363	0	.000	0	-3	-2	0	0.7

● **STEVE GROMEK** Gromek, Stephen Joseph b: 1/15/20, Hamtramck, Mich. BB/TR, 6'2", 180 lbs. Deb: 8/18/41

1941 Cle-A	1	1	.500	9	2	1	0	2	23¹	25	0	11	19	13.9	4.24	93	.266	.343	1	.167	-0	-0	-1	-1	-0.2
1942 Cle-A	2	0	1.000	14	0	0	0	0	44¹	46	2	23	14	14.0	3.65	94	.267	.354	5	.333	3	0	-1	-1	0.2
1943 Cle-A	0	0	—	3	0	0	0	0	4	6	0	0	4	13.5	9.00	35	.353	.353	2	1.000	1	-3	-3	-0	0.1
1944 Cle-A	10	9	.526	35	21	12	2	1	203²	160	5	70	115	10.3	2.56	129	**.219**	.290	19	.260	5	20	17	-3	1.8
1945 Cle-A†	19	9	.679	33	30	21	3	1	251	229	6	66	101	10.7	2.55	128	.243	.295	21	.231	3	23	20	3	2.2
1946 Cle-A	5	15	.250	29	21	5	3	4	153²	159	20	47	75	12.2	4.33	76	.264	.321	11	.196	0	-14	-18	-1	-2.2
1947 Cle-A	3	5	.375	29	7	0	0	4	84¹	77	8	36	39	12.2	3.74	93	.240	.318	7	.318	2	-0	-2	-0	-0.1
1948 *Cle-A	9	3	.750	38	9	4	1	2	130	109	10	51	50	11.5	2.84	143	.226	.307	6	.146	-1	21	18	1	1.3
1949 Cle-A	4	6	.400	27	12	3	0	0	92	86	8	40	22	12.5	3.33	120	.250	.332	4	.167	-0	9	7	0	0.7
1950 Cle-A	10	7	.588	31	13	4	1	0	113¹	94	10	36	43	10.6	3.65	119	.226	.292	6	.158	-2	12	9	-0	0.9
1951 Cle-A	7	4	.636	27	8	4	0	1	107¹	98	6	29	40	11.0	2.77	137	.238	.295	8	.296	3	16	12	1	1.5
1952 Cle-A	7	7	.500	29	13	3	1	1	122²	109	14	28	65	10.2	3.67	91	.232	.278	3	.100	-0	0	-4	-3	-0.8
1953 Cle-A	1	1	.500	5	1	0	0	0	11	11	0	3	8	12.3	3.27	115	.268	.333	0	.000	-0	1	1	0	0.0
Det-A	6	8	.429	19	17	6	1	1	125²	138	17	36	59	13.0	4.51	90	.276	.335	3	.073	-4	-7	-6	-1	-1.1
Yr	7	9	.438	24	18	6	1	1	136²	149	17	39	67	12.9	4.41	92	.275	.333	3	.070	-4	-6	-6	-1	-1.1
1954 Det-A	18	16	.529	36	32	17	4	1	252²	236	26	57	102	10.9	2.74	135	.246	.297	15	.190	2	28	27	-3	3.4
1955 Det-A	13	10	.565	28	25	8	2	0	181	183	26	37	73	11.4	3.98	97	.261	.307	9	.167	4	-0	-3	-2	-0.1
1956 Det-A	8	6	.571	40	13	4	0	4	141	142	25	47	64	12.6	4.28	96	.263	.332	4	.148	2	-2	-3	-2	-0.3
1957 Det-A	0	1	.000	15	1	0	0	1	23²	32	3	13	11	17.5	6.08	63	.333	.418	0	.000	-0	-6	-6	-1	-0.4
Total 17	123	108	.532	447	225	92	17	23	2064²	1940	186	630	904	11.5	3.41	108	.247	.309	124	.197	15	96	63	-21	6.9

● **BOB GROOM** Groom, Robert b: 9/12/1884, Belleville, Ill. d: 2/19/48, Belleville, Ill. BR/TR, 6'2", 175 lbs. Deb: 4/13/09

1909 Was-A	7	26	.212	44	31	17	1	0	260²	218	2	105	131	11.6	2.87	85	.229	.314	8	.091	-6	-11	-13	4	-1.8
1910 Was-A	12	17	.414	34	30	22	3	0	257²	244	8	77	98	11.5	2.76	90	.260	.322	11	.120	-6	-7	-8	-2	-1.6
1911 Was-A	13	17	.433	37	32	20	2	2	254²	280	9	67	135	12.5	3.82	86	.282	.332	11	.134	-4	-13	-15	1	-1.9
1912 Was-A	24	13	.649	43	40	28	2	1	316	287	3	94	179	11.0	2.62	127	.246	.305	12	.117	-7	24	25	-2	1.9
1913 Was-A	16	16	.500	37	36	17	4	0	264¹	258	8	81	156	11.7	3.23	91	.254	.312	15	.163	1	-9	-8	2	-0.7
1914 StL-F	13	20	.394	42	34	23	1	1	280²	281	9	75	167	11.5	3.24	94	.262	.312	15	.160	-4	-11	-6	-0	-1.1
1915 StL-F	11	11	.500	37	26	11	4	2	209	200	6	73	111	11.8	3.27	88	.261	.327	10	.152	-3	-13	-9	0	-1.2
1916 StL-A	13	9	.591	41	26	8	1	4	217¹	174	1	98	92	11.4	2.57	107	.226	.315	7	.111	-2	6	4	2	0.4
1917 StL-A	8	19	.296	38	28	11	4	3	232²	193	3	95	82	11.3	2.94	88	.233	.315	8	.111	-4	-7	-9	-1	-1.6
1918 Cle-A	2	2	.500	14	5	0	0	0	43¹	70	0	18	8	18.5	7.06	43	.380	.438	1	.083	-0	-21	-20	0	-1.8
Total 10	119	150	.442	367	288	157	22	13	2336¹	2205	49	783	1159	11.7	3.10	93	.254	.319	98	.128	-35	-61	-58	2	-9.4

● **BUDDY GROOM** Groom, Wedsel Gary b: 7/10/65, Dallas, Tex. BL/TL, 6'2", 200 lbs. Deb: 6/20/92

1992 Det-A	0	5	.000	12	7	0	0	0	38²	48	4	22	15	16.3	5.82	68	.320	.407	0	—	0	-8	-8	-0	-1.0
1993 Det-A	0	2	.000	19	3	0	0	0	36²	48	4	13	15	15.5	6.14	70	.322	.384	0	—	0	-7	-8	0	-0.3
1994 Det-A	0	1	.000	40	0	0	0	1	32	31	4	13	27	12.9	3.94	121	.256	.338	0	—	0	3	3	0	0.1
Total 3	0	8	.000	71	10	0	0	1	107¹	127	12	48	57	15.0	5.37	80	.302	.379	0	—	0	-12	-13	0	-1.2

● **DON GROSS** Gross, Donald John b: 6/30/31, Weidman, Mich. BL/TL, 5'11", 186 lbs. Deb: 7/21/55

1955 Cin-N	4	5	.444	17	11	2	1	0	67¹	79	11	16	33	12.8	4.14	102	.298	.340	3	.158	-1	-1	1	0	0.0
1956 Cin-N	3	0	1.000	19	7	2	0	0	69¹	69	4	20	47	11.7	1.95	204	.257	.310	2	.105	-1	14	16	1	0.7
1957 Cin-N	7	9	.438	43	16	5	0	1	148¹	152	21	33	73	11.4	4.31	95	.264	.307	5	.109	-2	-7	-3	-0	-0.6
1958 Pit-N	5	7	.417	40	3	0	0	2	74²	67	9	38	59	12.8	3.98	97	.241	.334	1	.056	-0	-0	-1	1	-0.2
1959 Pit-N	1	0	.500	21	0	0	0	7	33	28	3	10	15	10.6	3.55	109	.228	.291	0	.000	-0	1	1	0	0.2
1960 Pit-N	0	1	.000	5	0	0	0	0	5¹	5	1	0	3	8.4	3.38	111	.238	.238	0	—	-0	-0	0	0	0.0
Total 6	20	22	.476	145	37	9	1	10	398	400	45	117	230	11.8	3.73	108	.261	.316	11	.106	-5	8	14	2	0.1

● **GREG GROSS** Gross, Gregory Eugene b: 8/1/52, York, Pa. BL/TL, 5'11", 175 lbs. Deb: 9/5/73 ◆

1986 Phi-N	0	0	—	1	0	0	0	0	0²	1	0	1	2	27.0	0.00	—	.333	.500	25	.248	0	0	0	0	0.0
1989 Hou-N	0	0	—	1	0	0	0	0	1	3	0	1	1	36.0	18.00	19	.500	.571	15	.200	0	-2	-2	0	0.0
Total 2	0	0	—	2	0	0	0	0	1²	4	0	2	3	32.4	10.80	33	.444	.545	1073	.287	0	-1	-1	0	0.0

● **KEVIN GROSS** Gross, Kevin Frank b: 6/8/61, Downey, Cal. BR/TR, 6'5", 215 lbs. Deb: 6/25/83

1983 Phi-N	4	6	.400	17	17	1	1	0	96	100	13	35	66	12.9	3.56	100	.265	.333	3	.091	-1	1	0	0	-0.1
1984 Phi-N	8	5	.615	44	14	1	0	1	129	140	8	44	84	13.2	4.12	88	.277	.341	2	.067	-2	-8	-7	1	-0.7
1985 Phi-N	15	13	.536	38	31	6	2	0	205²	194	11	81	151	12.3	3.41	108	.251	.328	9	.138	0	4	6	1	1.0
1986 Phi-N	12	12	.500	37	36	7	2	0	241²	240	28	94	154	12.7	4.02	96	.259	.333	15	.188	3	-8	-5	-1	-0.2
1987 Phi-N	9	16	.360	34	33	3	1	0	200²	205	26	87	110	13.5	4.35	97	.267	.350	12	.190	2	-6	-2	-2	-0.3
1988 Phi-N★	12	14	.462	33	33	5	1	0	231²	209	18	89	162	12.0	3.69	96	.239	.317	13	.173	1	-6	-3	-0	-0.3
1989 Mon-N	11	12	.478	31	31	4	3	0	201¹	188	20	88	158	12.6	4.38	81	.247	.330	9	.141	1	-20	-19	-0	-2.0
1990 Mon-N	9	12	.429	31	26	2	0	0	163¹	171	9	65	111	13.2	4.57	80	.272	.344	10	.200	4	-14	-17	-2	-1.8
1991 LA-N	10	11	.476	46	10	0	0	3	115²	123	10	50	95	13.6	3.58	100	.275	.351	7	.280	2	1	0	0	0.3
1992 LA-N	8	13	.381	34	30	4	3	0	204²	182	6	77	158	11.5	3.17	109	.241	.313	6	.095	-1	8	6	1	0.4
1993 LA-N	13	13	.500	33	32	3	0	0	202¹	224	23	74	150	13.5	4.14	92	.281	.346	13	.203	5	-2	-7	2	-0.1
1994 LA-N	9	7	.563	25	23	5	0	0	157¹	162	11	43	124	11.8	3.60	110	.263	.314	7	.149	0	11	6	2	0.2
Total 12	120	134	.472	403	316	37	14	5	2149¹	2138	180	827	1523	12.7	3.89	96	.261	.332	106	.161	14	-40	-41	1	-2.9

● **KIP GROSS** Gross, Kip Lee b: 8/24/64, Scottsbluff, Neb. BR/TR, 6'2", 195 lbs. Deb: 4/21/90

| 1990 Cin-N | 0 | 0 | — | 5 | 0 | 0 | 0 | 0 | 6¹ | 6 | 0 | 2 | 3 | 11.4 | 4.26 | 93 | .273 | .333 | 0 | — | 0 | -0 | -0 | -0 | 0.0 |

YEAR TM/L	W	L	PCT	G	GS	CG	SH	SV	IP	H	HR	BB	SO	RAT	ERA	ERA+	OAV	OOB	BH	AVG	PB	PR	/A	PD	TPI
1991 Cin-N	6	4	.600	29	9	1	0	0	85²	93	8	40	40	14.0	3.47	110	.279	.357	2	.091	-1	2	3	0	0.2
1992 LA-N	1	1	.500	16	1	0	0	0	23²	32	1	10	14	16.0	4.18	82	.323	.385	2	1.000	1	-2	-2	1	0.0
1993 LA-N	0	0	—	10	0	0	0	0	15	13	0	4	12	10.2	0.60	636	.236	.288	0	—	0	6	5	-0	0.0
Total 4	7	5	.583	60	10	1	0	0	130²	144	9	56	69	13.8	3.31	113	.283	.354	4	.167	-0	6	6	0	0.2

● **WAYNE GROSS**   Gross, Wayne Dale   b: 1/14/52, Riverside, Cal.   BL/TR, 6'2", 210 lbs.   Deb: 8/21/76 ♦

YEAR TM/L	W	L	PCT	G	GS	CG	SH	SV	IP	H	HR	BB	SO	RAT	ERA	ERA+	OAV	OOB	BH	AVG	PB	PR	/A	PD	TPI
1983 Oak-A	0	0	—	1	0	0	0	0	2¹	2	0	1	0	15.4	0.00	—	.222	.364	79	.233	1	1	1	-0	0.0

● **HARLEY GROSSMAN**   Grossman, Harley Joseph   b: 5/5/30, Evansville, Ind.   BR/TR, 6', 170 lbs.   Deb: 4/22/52

YEAR TM/L	W	L	PCT	G	GS	CG	SH	SV	IP	H	HR	BB	SO	RAT	ERA	ERA+	OAV	OOB	BH	AVG	PB	PR	/A	PD	TPI
1952 Was-A	0	0	—	1	0	0	0	0	0¹	2	1	0	0	54.0	54.00	7	.667	.667	0	—	0	-2	-2	0	0.0

● **ERNIE GROTH**   Groth, Ernest John "Dango"   b: 12/24/1884, Cedarburg, Wis.   d: 5/23/50, Milwaukee, Wis.   BR/TR, 5'11", 175 lbs.   Deb: 9/6/04

YEAR TM/L	W	L	PCT	G	GS	CG	SH	SV	IP	H	HR	BB	SO	RAT	ERA	ERA+	OAV	OOB	BH	AVG	PB	PR	/A	PD	TPI
1904 Chi-N	0	2	.000	3	2	2	0	1	16	22	1	6	9	16.3	5.63	47	.310	.372	0	—	-1	-5	-5	-0	-0.7

● **ERNEST GROTH**   Groth, Ernest William   b: 5/3/22, Beaver Falls, Pa.   BR/TR, 5'9", 185 lbs.   Deb: 9/11/47

YEAR TM/L	W	L	PCT	G	GS	CG	SH	SV	IP	H	HR	BB	SO	RAT	ERA	ERA+	OAV	OOB	BH	AVG	PB	PR	/A	PD	TPI
1947 Cle-A	0	0	—	2	0	0	0	0	1¹	0	0	1	1	6.8	0.00	—	.000	.250	0	—	0	1	1	0	0.0
1948 Cle-A	0	0	—	1	0	0	0	0	1	1	0	2	0	27.0	9.00	45	.250	.500	0	—	0	-1	-1	0	0.0
1949 Chi-A	0	1	.000	3	0	0	0	0	5	2	2	3	1	10.8	5.40	77	.125	.300	0	—	-1	-1	-1	-0	-0.1
Total 3	0	1	.000	6	0	0	0	0	7¹	3	2	6	2	12.3	4.91	82	.130	.333	0	—	-1	-1	-1	-0	-0.1

● **ORVAL GROVE**   Grove, Orval Leroy   b: 8/29/19, Mineral, Kan.   d: 4/20/92, Carmichael, Cal.   BR/TR, 6'3", 196 lbs.   Deb: 5/28/40

YEAR TM/L	W	L	PCT	G	GS	CG	SH	SV	IP	H	HR	BB	SO	RAT	ERA	ERA+	OAV	OOB	BH	AVG	PB	PR	/A	PD	TPI
1940 Chi-A	0	0	—	3	0	0	0	0	6	4	0	4	1	12.0	3.00	147	.182	.308	0	.000	-0	1	1	-0	0.0
1941 Chi-A	0	0	—	2	0	0	0	0	7	9	2	5	5	18.0	10.29	40	.321	.424	0	.000	-0	-5	-5	-0	0.0
1942 Chi-A	4	6	.400	12	8	2	0	0	66¹	77	1	33	21	15.1	5.16	70	.283	.363	5	.227	1	-11	-11	1	-1.3
1943 Chi-A	15	9	.625	32	25	18	3	2	216¹	192	9	72	76	11.1	2.75	122	.239	.304	12	.182	2	13	14	1	1.9
1944 Chi-A☆	14	15	.483	34	33	11	2	0	234²	237	11	71	105	12.1	3.72	92	.263	.322	8	.104	-3	-8	-8	4	-0.8
1945 Chi-A	14	12	.538	33	30	16	4	1	217	233	12	68	54	12.7	3.44	96	.273	.330	7	.099	-4	-2	-3	2	-0.6
1946 Chi-A	8	13	.381	33	26	10	1	0	205¹	213	10	78	60	12.9	3.02	113	.272	.340	7	.108	-2	11	9	2	0.8
1947 Chi-A	6	8	.429	25	19	6	1	0	135²	158	10	70	33	15.4	4.44	82	.296	.382	7	.146	-0	-11	-12	-1	-1.2
1948 Chi-A	2	10	.167	32	11	1	0	1	87²	110	6	42	18	15.9	6.16	69	.315	.393	2	.095	-2	-18	-19	2	-2.2
1949 Chi-A	0	0	—	1	0	0	0	0	2	4	1	1	1	81.0	54.00	8	.667	.750	0	—	0	-4	-4	0	0.0
Total 10	63	73	.463	207	152	66	11	4	1176²	1237	62	444	374	13.1	3.72	97	.272	.340	48	.129	-9	-33	-37	10	-3.4

● **LEFTY GROVE**   Grove, Robert Moses   b: 3/6/1900, Lonaconing, Md.   d: 5/22/75, Norwalk, Ohio   BL/TL, 6'3", 190 lbs.   Deb: 4/14/25   H

YEAR TM/L	W	L	PCT	G	GS	CG	SH	SV	IP	H	HR	BB	SO	RAT	ERA	ERA+	OAV	OOB	BH	AVG	PB	PR	/A	PD	TPI
1925 Phi-A	10	12	.455	45	18	5	0	1	197	207	11	131	**116**	15.7	4.75	98	.278	.390	8	.123	-6	-8	-2	2	-0.6
1926 Phi-A	13	13	.500	45	33	20	1	6	258	227	6	101	**194**	11.7	**2.51**	166	.244	.322	8	.099	-5	**43**	48	-1	4.0
1927 Phi-A	20	13	.606	51	28	14	1	9	262¹	251	6	79	**174**	11.4	3.19	134	.252	.309	10	.125	-3	28	31	-1	3.3
1928 Phi-A	**24**	8	**.750**	39	31	24	4	4	261²	228	10	64	**183**	10.1	2.58	156	.229	.277	15	.170	1	**43**	42	-3	**4.6**
1929 *Phi-A	20	6	**.769**	42	37	19	2	4	275²	278	8	81	**170**	11.8	**2.81**	151	.262	.316	22	.216	1	**44**	43	-3	3.5
1930 *Phi-A	**28**	5	**.848**	**50**	32	22	2	**9**	291	273	8	60	**209**	10.5	**2.54**	184	**.247**	**.288**	22	.200	0	**68**	69	0	**7.3**
1931 *Phi-A	**31**	4	**.886**	41	30	**27**	4	5	288²	249	10	62	**175**	**9.7**	**2.06**	218	.229	**.271**	23	.200	-2	**74**	78	-2	**8.7**
1932 Phi-A	25	10	.714	44	30	**27**	4	7	291²	269	13	79	188	10.8	**2.84**	159	.241	**.292**	18	.168	0	**53**	55	-2	**5.9**
1933 Phi-A★	**24**	8	**.750**	45	28	**21**	2	6	275¹	280	11	83	114	12.0	3.20	134	.261	.316	9	.086	-7	33	33	0	2.9
1934 Bos-A	8	8	.500	22	12	5	0	1	109¹	149	6	32	43	15.0	6.50	74	.320	.365	6	.162	-0	-24	-21	-1	-2.5
1935 Bos-A☆	20	12	.625	35	30	23	2	1	273	269	6	65	121	11.1	**2.70**	176	.257	.302	7	.079	-5	**53**	62	2	6.4
1936 Bos-A★	17	12	.586	35	30	22	**6**	2	253¹	237	14	65	130	10.9	**2.81**	189	.246	**.297**	11	.138	-3	**63**	71	0	**7.0**
1937 Bos-A☆	17	9	.654	32	32	21	3	0	262	269	14	83	153	12.1	3.02	157	.261	.317	13	.143	-3	46	50	-1	4.0
1938 Bos-A★	14	4	.778	24	21	12	1	1	163²	169	8	52	99	12.2	**3.08**	160	.263	.319	8	.148	-1	31	34	-0	3.1
1939 Bos-A☆	15	4	**.789**	23	23	17	2	0	191	180	8	58	81	11.3	**2.54**	186	.249	.305	9	.134	-1	44	46	-3	3.7
1940 Bos-A	7	6	.538	22	21	9	1	0	153¹	159	20	50	62	12.3	3.99	113	.269	.328	8	.151	-1	7	9	0	0.5
1941 Bos-A	7	7	.500	21	21	10	0	0	134	155	8	42	54	13.4	4.37	95	.287	.340	5	.111	-1	-3	-3	-2	-0.6
Total 17	300	141	.680	616	457	298	35	55	3940²	3849	162	1187	2266	11.6	3.06	148	.255	.311	202	.148	-37	595	643	-15	61.2

● **CHARLIE GROVER**   Grover, Charles Bert "Bugs" (Born Charles Byrd Grover)
b: 6/20/1890, Huntington Township, Ohio   d: 5/24/71, Emmett, Mich.   BL/TR, 6'1.5", 185 lbs.   Deb: 9/9/13

YEAR TM/L	W	L	PCT	G	GS	CG	SH	SV	IP	H	HR	BB	SO	RAT	ERA	ERA+	OAV	OOB	BH	AVG	PB	PR	/A	PD	TPI
1913 Det-A	0	0	—	2	1	0	0	0	10²	9	0	7	2	13.5	3.38	86	.265	.390	0	.000	-0	-1	-1	0	0.0

● **TOM GRUBBS**   Grubbs, Thomas Dillard "Judge"   b: 2/22/1894, Mt.Sterling, Ky.   d: 1/28/86, Lexington, Ky.   BR/TR, 6'2", 165 lbs.   Deb: 10/3/20

YEAR TM/L	W	L	PCT	G	GS	CG	SH	SV	IP	H	HR	BB	SO	RAT	ERA	ERA+	OAV	OOB	BH	AVG	PB	PR	/A	PD	TPI
1920 NY-N	0	1	.000	1	1	0	0	0	5	9	0	4	0	16.2	7.20	42	.409	.409	0	.000	-0	-2	-2	-0	-0.4

● **HENRY GRUBER**   Gruber, Henry John   b: 12/14/1863, Hamden, Conn.   d: 9/26/32, New Haven, Conn.   BR/TR, 5'9", 155 lbs.   Deb: 7/28/1887

YEAR TM/L	W	L	PCT	G	GS	CG	SH	SV	IP	H	HR	BB	SO	RAT	ERA	ERA+	OAV	OOB	BH	AVG	PB	PR	/A	PD	TPI
1887 Det-N	4	3	.571	7	7	7	0	0	62¹	63	3	21	12	12.1	2.74	148	.262	.322	4	.167	-1	9	9	-1	0.7
1888 Det-N	11	14	.440	27	25	25	3	0	240	196	8	41	71	9.0	2.29	121	.213	.249	13	.141	-1	15	13	1	1.1
1889 Cle-N	7	16	.304	25	23	23	0	1	205	198	6	94	74	13.2	3.64	111	.246	.331	7	.101	-1	8	9	-0	0.7
1890 Cle-P	22	23	.489	48	44	39	1	0	383¹	464	15	204	110	16.0	4.27	93	.287	.372	36	.221	6	-2	-13	1	-0.5
1891 Cle-N	17	22	.436	44	40	35	1	0	348²	407	10	119	79	13.8	4.13	84	.281	.338	23	.163	1	-30	-26	2	-2.0
Total 5	61	78	.439	151	139	129	5	1	1239¹	1328	42	479	346	13.4	3.67	99	.264	.332	83	.170	5	1	-7	3	0.0

● **AL GRUNWALD**   Grunwald, Alfred Henry "Stretch"   b: 2/13/30, Los Angeles, Cal.   BL/TL, 6'4", 210 lbs.   Deb: 4/18/55

YEAR TM/L	W	L	PCT	G	GS	CG	SH	SV	IP	H	HR	BB	SO	RAT	ERA	ERA+	OAV	OOB	BH	AVG	PB	PR	/A	PD	TPI
1955 Pit-N	0	0	—	3	0	0	0	0	7²	7	1	7	2	16.4	4.70	88	.241	.389	2	.500	-1	-1	-0	-0	0.1
1959 KC-A	0	1	.000	6	1	0	0	1	11¹	18	1	11	9	23.0	7.94	50	.360	.475	0	.000	-1	-5	-5	-0	-0.5
Total 2	0	1	.000	9	1	0	0	1	19	25	2	18	11	20.4	6.63	61	.316	.443	2	.250	0	-6	-5	-0	-0.4

● **JOE GRZENDA**   Grzenda, Joseph Charles   b: 6/8/37, Scranton, Pa.   BR/TL, 6'2", 180 lbs.   Deb: 4/26/61

YEAR TM/L	W	L	PCT	G	GS	CG	SH	SV	IP	H	HR	BB	SO	RAT	ERA	ERA+	OAV	OOB	BH	AVG	PB	PR	/A	PD	TPI
1961 Det-A	1	0	1.000	4	0	0	0	0	5²	9	2	2	2	17.5	7.94	52	.375	.423	1	1.000	0	-2	-2	0	-0.3
1964 KC-A	0	2	.000	20	0	0	0	0	25	34	2	13	17	17.3	5.40	71	.324	.403	0	.000	-0	-5	-4	1	-0.2
1966 KC-A	0	2	.000	21	0	0	0	0	22	28	1	12	14	16.4	3.27	104	.337	.421	0	.000	-0	0	1	1	0.1
1967 NY-N	0	0	—	11	0	0	0	0	16²	14	0	8	12	12.4	2.16	157	.237	.338	0	.000	-0	2	2	-1	-0.1
1969 *Min-A	4	1	.800	38	0	0	0	3	48²	52	4	17	24	12.9	3.88	94	.281	.345	0	.000	-1	-1	-1	1	0.0
1970 Was-A	3	6	.333	49	3	0	0	6	84²	84	3	34	38	13.1	5.00	71	.267	.343	0	.000	-1	-12	-14	0	-1.6
1971 Was-A	5	2	.714	46	0	0	0	5	70¹	54	2	17	56	9.2	1.92	172	.217	.270	1	.143	-0	12	11	-0	1.2
1972 StL-N	1	0	1.000	30	0	0	0	0	35	46	2	17	15	17.0	5.66	60	.326	.410	0	.000	-0	-9	-9	0	-0.2
Total 8	14	13	.519	219	3	0	0	14	308	323	20	120	173	13.2	4.00	88	.277	.349	2	.067	-2	-15	-17	3	-1.1

● **CECILIO GUANTE**   Guante, Cecilio (Magallana)   b: 2/1/60, Villa Mella, D.R.   BR/TR, 6'3", 205 lbs.   Deb: 5/1/82

YEAR TM/L	W	L	PCT	G	GS	CG	SH	SV	IP	H	HR	BB	SO	RAT	ERA	ERA+	OAV	OOB	BH	AVG	PB	PR	/A	PD	TPI
1982 Pit-N	0	0	—	10	0	0	0	0	27	28	1	5	26	11.7	3.33	111	.264	.310	0	.000	-1	1	1	-0	-0.1
1983 Pit-N	2	6	.250	49	0	0	0	9	100¹	90	5	46	82	12.4	3.32	112	.241	.327	2	.091	-1	3	4	-1	0.2
1984 Pit-N	2	3	.400	27	0	0	0	0	41¹	30	3	16	30	10.9	2.61	138	.224	.311	0	.000	-0	4	5	-1	0.5
1985 Pit-N	4	6	.400	63	0	0	0	4	109	84	5	40	92	10.7	2.72	131	.214	.295	1	.059	-1	10	10	-1	0.8
1986 Pit-N	5	2	.714	52	0	0	0	4	78	65	11	29	63	11.3	3.35	115	.225	.302	0	.000	-0	3	4	-2	0.2
1987 NY-A	3	2	.600	23	0	0	0	1	44	42	8	20	46	12.9	5.73	77	.247	.330	0	—	0	-6	-7	-1	-0.7
1988 NY-A	5	6	.455	56	0	0	0	11	75	59	6	22	60	10.3	2.88	137	.213	.283	0	.000	0	9	9	-2	1.4
Tex-A	0	0	—	7	0	0	0	0	4²	8	1	4	4	23.1	1.93	212	.400	.500	0	—	0	1	1	-0	-0.1
Yr	5	6	.455	63	0	0	0	11	79²	67	7	26	65	10.5	2.82	140	.220	.283	0	—	0	10	10	-2	1.3
1989 Tex-A	6	6	.500	50	0	0	0	2	69	66	7	36	69	13.8	3.91	101	.249	.348	0	—	0	-0	-1	-0	-0.1

YEAR	TM/L	W	L	PCT	G	GS	CG	SH	SV	IP	H	HR	BB	SO	RAT	ERA	ERA+	OAV	OOB	BH	AVG	PB	PR	/A	PD	TPI
1990	Cle-A	2	3	.400	26	1	0	0	0	46²	38	10	18	30	11.4	5.01	78	.220	.304	0	—	0	-6	-6	0	-0.5
Total	9	29	34	.460	363	1	0	0	35	595	512	61	236	503	11.7	3.48	110	.232	.313	3	.061	-3	20	23	-8	1.6

● EDDIE GUARDADO
Guardado, Edward Adrain   b: 10/2/70, Stockton, Cal.   BR/TL, 6′, 190 lbs.   Deb: 6/13/93

YEAR	TM/L	W	L	PCT	G	GS	CG	SH	SV	IP	H	HR	BB	SO	RAT	ERA	ERA+	OAV	OOB	BH	AVG	PB	PR	/A	PD	TPI
1993	Min-A	3	8	.273	19	16	0	0	0	94²	123	13	36	46	15.2	6.18	70	.319	.379	0	—	0	-20	-19	-1	-1.9
1994	Min-A	0	2	.000	4	4	0	0	0	17	26	3	4	8	15.9	8.47	57	.351	.385	0	—	0	-7	-7	0	-0.6
Total	2	3	10	.231	23	20	0	0	0	111²	149	16	40	54	15.3	6.53	68	.325	.380	0	—	0	-26	-26	-1	-2.5

● MARK GUBICZA
Gubicza, Mark Steven   b: 8/14/62, Philadelphia, Pa.   BR/TR, 6′6″, 215 lbs.   Deb: 4/6/84

YEAR	TM/L	W	L	PCT	G	GS	CG	SH	SV	IP	H	HR	BB	SO	RAT	ERA	ERA+	OAV	OOB	BH	AVG	PB	PR	/A	PD	TPI
1984	KC-A	10	14	.417	29	29	4	2	0	189	172	13	75	111	12.0	4.05	99	.243	.320	0	—	0	-1	-0	2	0.1
1985	*KC-A	14	10	.583	29	28	0	0	0	177¹	160	14	77	99	12.3	4.06	102	.238	.321	0	—	0	2	2	2	0.4
1986	KC-A	12	6	.667	35	24	3	2	0	180²	155	8	84	118	12.2	3.64	117	.233	.324	0	—	0	11	12	3	1.3
1987	KC-A	13	18	.419	35	35	10	2	0	241²	231	18	120	166	13.3	3.98	114	.259	.350	0	—	0	13	15	4	2.0
1988	KC-A★	20	8	.714	35	35	8	4	0	269²	237	11	83	183	10.9	2.70	147	.234	.296	0	—	0	38	38	3	4.2
1989	KC-A★	15	11	.577	36	36	8	2	0	255	252	10	63	173	11.3	3.04	127	.259	.307	0	—	0	24	23	2	2.5
1990	KC-A	4	7	.364	16	16	2	0	0	94	101	5	38	71	13.7	4.50	85	.283	.358	0	—	0	-6	-7	-0	-0.6
1991	KC-A	9	12	.429	26	26	0	0	0	133	168	10	42	89	14.6	5.68	72	.308	.364	0	—	0	-23	-23	-2	-2.9
1992	KC-A	7	6	.538	18	18	2	1	0	111¹	110	8	36	81	11.9	3.72	109	.259	.318	0	—	0	3	4	0	0.3
1993	KC-A	5	8	.385	49	6	0	0	2	104¹	128	2	43	80	14.9	4.66	98	.307	.374	0	—	0	-4	-1	-1	-0.2
1994	KC-A	7	9	.438	22	22	0	0	0	130	158	11	26	59	12.7	4.50	115	.301	.334	0	—	0	4	10	0	0.5
Total	11	116	109	.516	330	275	37	13	2	1886	1872	110	687	1230	12.4	3.86	109	.260	.329	0	—	0	59	72	18	7.6

● MARV GUDAT
Gudat, Marvin John   b: 8/27/05, Goliad, Tex.   d: 3/1/54, Los Angeles, Cal.   BL/TL, 5′11″, 162 lbs.   Deb: 5/21/29 ◆

YEAR	TM/L	W	L	PCT	G	GS	CG	SH	SV	IP	H	HR	BB	SO	RAT	ERA	ERA+	OAV	OOB	BH	AVG	PB	PR	/A	PD	TPI
1929	Cin-N	1	1	.500	7	2	2	0	0	26²	29	4	4	0	11.1	3.38	135	.282	.308	2	.200	-0	4	4	-1	0.1
1932	*Chi-N	0	0	—	1	0	0	0	0	1	1	0	0	2	9.0	0.00	—	.250	.250	24	.255	0	0	0	0	0.0
Total	2	1	1	.500	8	2	2	0	0	27²	30	4	4	2	11.1	3.25	139	.280	.306	26	.250	-0	4	4	-1	0.1

● LEE GUETTERMAN
Guetterman, Arthur Lee   b: 11/22/58, Chattanooga, Tenn.   BL/TL, 6′8″, 225 lbs.   Deb: 9/12/84

YEAR	TM/L	W	L	PCT	G	GS	CG	SH	SV	IP	H	HR	BB	SO	RAT	ERA	ERA+	OAV	OOB	BH	AVG	PB	PR	/A	PD	TPI
1984	Sea-A	0	0	—	3	0	0	0	0	4¹	9	0	2	2	22.8	4.15	96	.450	.500	0	—	0	-0	-0	0	0.0
1986	Sea-A	0	4	.000	41	4	1	0	0	76	108	4	30	38	16.8	7.34	58	.347	.412	0	—	0	-27	-26	0	-1.2
1987	Sea-A	11	4	.733	25	17	2	1	0	113¹	117	13	35	42	12.2	3.81	124	.267	.324	0	—	0	8	11	1	1.2
1988	NY-A	1	2	.333	20	2	0	0	0	40²	49	2	14	15	14.2	4.65	85	.306	.366	0	—	0	-3	-3	-0	-0.2
1989	NY-A	5	5	.500	70	0	0	0	13	103	98	6	26	51	10.8	2.45	158	.258	.305	0	—	0	16	16	2	2.2
1990	NY-A	11	7	.611	64	0	0	0	2	93	80	6	26	48	10.3	3.39	117	.236	.290	0	—	0	5	6	1	1.2
1991	NY-A	3	4	.429	64	0	0	0	6	88	91	6	25	35	12.2	3.68	112	.268	.323	0	—	0	4	4	0	0.4
1992	NY-A	1	1	.500	15	0	0	0	0	22²	35	5	13	5	19.1	9.53	41	.354	.429	0	—	0	-14	-14	-0	-1.0
	NY-N	3	4	.429	43	0	0	0	2	43¹	57	5	14	15	15.0	5.82	60	.324	.377	0	.000	-0	-11	-11	-1	-1.9
1993	StL-N	3	3	.500	40	0	0	0	1	46	41	1	16	19	11.5	2.93	135	.240	.312	1	.500	1	6	5	-1	0.6
Total	9	38	34	.528	385	23	3	1	24	630¹	685	51	201	270	12.8	4.27	96	.281	.339	1	.250	0	-16	-12	3	1.3

● WHITEY GUESE
Guese, Theodore   b: 1/24/1872, New Bremen, Ohio   d: 4/8/51, Wapakoneta, Ohio   BR/TR, 6′0.5″, 200 lbs.   Deb: 7/13/01

YEAR	TM/L	W	L	PCT	G	GS	CG	SH	SV	IP	H	HR	BB	SO	RAT	ERA	ERA+	OAV	OOB	BH	AVG	PB	PR	/A	PD	TPI
1901	Cin-N	1	4	.200	6	5	4	0	0	44¹	62	5	14	11	16.0	6.09	53	.328	.383	3	.200	1	-14	-14	-2	-1.3

● RON GUIDRY
Guidry, Ronald Ames   b: 8/28/50, Lafayette, La.   BL/TL, 5′11″, 162 lbs.   Deb: 7/27/75

YEAR	TM/L	W	L	PCT	G	GS	CG	SH	SV	IP	H	HR	BB	SO	RAT	ERA	ERA+	OAV	OOB	BH	AVG	PB	PR	/A	PD	TPI
1975	NY-A	0	1	.000	10	1	0	0	0	15²	15	0	9	15	14.4	3.45	106	.259	.368	0	—	0	1	0	-1	0.1
1976	*NY-A	0	0	—	7	0	0	0	0	16	20	1	4	12	13.5	5.63	61	.294	.333	0	—	0	-4	-4	0	0.1
1977	*NY-A	16	7	.696	31	25	9	5	1	210²	174	12	65	176	10.2	2.82	140	.224	.284	0	—	0	29	26	-1	2.6
1978	NY-A★	**25**	3	**.893**	35	35	16	**9**	0	273²	187	13	72	248	**8.6**	**1.74**	**208**	**.193**	**.250**	0	—	0	**61**	**57**	2	**6.2**
1979	NY-A★	18	8	.692	33	30	15	2	0	236¹	203	20	71	201	10.4	**2.78**	146	.236	.294	0	—	0	38	34	-0	3.5
1980	*NY-A	17	10	.630	37	29	5	3	1	219²	215	19	80	166	12.1	3.56	110	.260	.326	0	—	0	11	9	2	1.5
1981	*NY-A	11	5	.688	23	21	0	0	0	127	100	12	26	104	**9.0**	2.76	129	.214	**.257**	0	—	0	13	11	1	1.5
1982	NY-A☆	14	8	.636	34	33	6	1	0	222	216	22	69	162	11.6	3.81	105	.254	.311	0	—	0	6	4	-2	0.2
1983	NY-A†	21	9	.700	31	31	**21**	3	0	250¹	232	26	60	156	10.6	3.42	114	.244	.291	0	—	0	18	13	-0	1.4
1984	NY-A	10	11	.476	29	28	5	1	0	195²	223	24	44	127	12.4	4.51	84	.287	.327	0	—	0	-11	-16	-0	-1.5
1985	NY-A	**22**	6	.786	34	33	11	2	0	259	243	28	42	143	9.9	3.27	122	.248	.279	0	—	0	25	21	-1	2.0
1986	NY-A	9	12	.429	30	30	5	0	0	192¹	202	28	38	140	11.3	3.98	103	.265	.301	0	—	0	4	2	-1	0.1
1987	NY-A	5	8	.385	22	17	2	0	0	117²	111	14	30	96	11.5	3.67	119	.248	.308	0	—	0	10	9	-0	0.9
1988	NY-A	2	3	.400	12	10	0	0	0	56	57	7	15	32	11.9	4.18	94	.259	.312	0	—	0	-1	-1	-1	-0.1
Total	14	170	91	.651	368	323	95	26	4	2392	2198	226	633	1778	10.7	3.29	119	.244	.294	0	—	0	201	167	-3	18.3

● SKIP GUINN
Guinn, Drannon Eugene   b: 10/25/44, St.Charles, Mo.   BR/TL, 5′10″, 180 lbs.   Deb: 5/7/68

YEAR	TM/L	W	L	PCT	G	GS	CG	SH	SV	IP	H	HR	BB	SO	RAT	ERA	ERA+	OAV	OOB	BH	AVG	PB	PR	/A	PD	TPI
1968	Atl-N	0	0	—	3	0	0	0	0	5	3	0	3	4	10.8	3.60	83	.167	.286	0	—	0	-0	-0	-0	-0.0
1969	Hou-N	1	2	.333	28	0	0	0	0	27	34	3	21	33	18.7	6.67	53	.304	.418	0	.000	0	-9	-9	-0	-1.0
1971	Hou-N	0	0	—	4	0	0	0	1	4²	1	0	3	3	7.7	0.00	—	.067	.222	0	—	0	2	2	0	0.1
Total	3	1	2	.333	35	0	0	0	1	36²	38	3	27	40	16.2	5.40	64	.262	.382	0	.000	-0	-8	-8	-0	-0.9

● LEFTY GUISE
Guise, Witt Orison   b: 9/18/09, Driggs, Ark.   d: 8/13/68, Little Rock, Ark.   BL/TL, 6′2″, 172 lbs.   Deb: 9/13/40

YEAR	TM/L	W	L	PCT	G	GS	CG	SH	SV	IP	H	HR	BB	SO	RAT	ERA	ERA+	OAV	OOB	BH	AVG	PB	PR	/A	PD	TPI
1940	Cin-N	0	0	—	2	0	0	0	0	7²	8	0	5	1	16.4	1.17	323	.296	.424	1	.333	0	2	2	0	0.0

● DON GULLETT
Gullett, Donald Edward   b: 1/6/51, Lynn, Ky.   BR/TL, 6′, 190 lbs.   Deb: 4/10/70   C

YEAR	TM/L	W	L	PCT	G	GS	CG	SH	SV	IP	H	HR	BB	SO	RAT	ERA	ERA+	OAV	OOB	BH	AVG	PB	PR	/A	PD	TPI
1970	*Cin-N	5	2	.714	44	2	0	0	6	77²	54	4	44	76	11.4	2.43	166	.196	.306	4	.211	1	14	14	-1	1.4
1971	*Cin-N	16	6	**.727**	35	31	4	3	0	217²	196	14	64	107	10.3	2.65	127	.242	.299	9	.120	-2	20	17	-2	1.2
1972	*Cin-N	9	10	.474	31	16	2	0	2	134²	127	15	43	96	11.4	3.94	81	.250	.309	8	.211	2	-7	-11	-2	-1.5
1973	Cin-N	18	8	.692	45	30	7	4	2	228¹	198	24	69	153	10.6	3.51	97	.232	.292	12	.188	3	4	-3	-0	0.0
1974	Cin-N	17	11	.607	36	35	10	3	0	243	201	22	88	183	10.8	3.04	115	.222	.292	19	.237	4	16	12	-0	1.7
1975	*Cin-N	15	4	**.789**	22	22	8	3	0	159²	127	11	56	98	10.4	2.42	148	.218	.289	14	.226	3	21	21	-1	2.6
1976	*Cin-N	11	3	.786	23	20	4	0	0	126	119	8	48	64	11.9	3.00	117	.253	.322	8	.182	-0	7	7	-0	0.8
1977	*NY-A	14	4	.778	22	22	7	1	0	158¹	137	14	69	116	11.8	3.58	110	.232	.314	0	—	0	8	6	-2	0.5
1978	NY-A	4	2	.667	8	8	0	0	0	44²	46	3	20	28	13.5	3.63	100	.269	.349	0	—	0	1	-0	-0	0.0
Total	9	109	50	.686	266	186	44	14	11	1390	1205	115	501	921	11.1	3.11	113	.233	.302	74	.194	10	83	63	-8	6.7

● BILL GULLICKSON
Gullickson, William Lee   b: 2/20/59, Marshall, Minn.   BR/TR, 6′3″, 215 lbs.   Deb: 9/26/79

YEAR	TM/L	W	L	PCT	G	GS	CG	SH	SV	IP	H	HR	BB	SO	RAT	ERA	ERA+	OAV	OOB	BH	AVG	PB	PR	/A	PD	TPI
1979	Mon-N	0	0	—	1	0	0	0	0	1	0	0	0	0	18.0	0.00	—	.500	.500	0	—	0	0	0	0	0.0
1980	Mon-N	10	5	.667	24	19	5	2	0	141	127	6	50	120	11.4	3.00	119	.238	.305	7	.175	0	9	9	0	1.0
1981	*Mon-N	7	9	.438	22	22	3	2	0	157¹	142	3	34	115	10.3	2.80	125	.239	.284	7	.152	0	12	12	-1	1.1
1982	Mon-N	12	14	.462	34	34	6	0	0	236²	231	25	61	155	11.3	3.57	102	.254	.304	10	.122	-2	-1	2	-4	-0.4
1983	Mon-N	17	12	.586	34	34	10	1	0	242¹	230	19	59	120	10.9	3.75	96	.251	.299	11	.134	1	-3	-4	-1	-0.5
1984	Mon-N	12	9	.571	32	32	3	0	0	226²	230	27	37	100	10.6	3.61	95	.265	.295	8	.110	-2	-1	-5	-4	-1.1
1985	Mon-N	14	12	.538	29	29	4	1	0	181¹	187	8	47	68	11.7	3.52	96	.271	.318	12	.188	2	1	-0	-3	-0.3
1986	Cin-N	15	12	.556	37	37	6	0	0	244²	245	24	60	121	11.3	3.38	114	.264	.310	6	.076	-4	9	13	-2	0.7
1987	Cin-N	10	11	.476	27	27	3	1	0	165	172	33	39	89	11.6	4.85	87	.267	.310	11	.208	2	-14	-11	-2	-1.2
	NY-A	4	2	.667	8	8	1	0	0	48	46	7	9	30	10.5	4.88	90	.253	.299	0	—	0	-3	-3	-0	-0.4
1990	Hou-N	10	14	.417	32	32	2	1	0	193¹	221	21	61	73	13.2	3.82	97	.287	.341	9	.158	2	-1	-2	-3	-0.4
1991	Det-A	**20**	9	.690	35	35	4	2	0	226¹	256	22	44	91	12.1	3.90	107	.288	.324	0	—	0	5	6	-3	0.5
1992	Det-A	14	13	.519	34	34	4	1	0	221²	228	35	50	64	11.3	4.34	91	.267	.308	0	—	0	-10	-10	-0	-1.1

YEAR TM/L	W	L	PCT	G	GS	CG	SH	SV	IP	H	HR	BB	SO	RAT	ERA	ERA+	OAV	OOB	BH	AVG	PB	PR	/A	PD	TPI
1993 Det-A	13	9	.591	28	28	2	0	0	159^1	186	28	44	70	13.2	5.37	80	.291	.340	0	—	0	-19	-19	0	-2.1
1994 Det-A	4	5	.444	21	19	1	0	0	115^1	156	24	25	65	14.4	5.93	80	.322	.361	0	—	0	-14	-15	0	-0.9
Total 14	162	136	.544	398	390	54	11	0	2560	2659	282	622	1279	11.7	3.93	97	.268	.314	81	.141	-1	-26	-30	-20	-4.9

● AD GUMBERT
Gumbert, Addison Courtney   b: 10/10/1868, Pittsburgh, Pa.   d: 4/23/25, Pittsburgh, Pa.   BR/TR, 5'10", 200 lbs.   Deb: 9/15/1888   F

YEAR TM/L	W	L	PCT	G	GS	CG	SH	SV	IP	H	HR	BB	SO	RAT	ERA	ERA+	OAV	OOB	BH	AVG	PB	PR	/A	PD	TPI
1888 Chi-N	3	3	.500	6	6	5	0	0	48^2	44	0	10	16	10.9	3.14	96	.234	.291	2	.333	-1	-2	-1	-1	0.0
1889 Chi-N	16	13	.552	31	28	25	2	0	246^1	258	16	76	91	12.7	3.62	115	.261	.323	44	.288	11	11	15	-1	2.2
1890 Bos-P	23	12	.657	39	33	27	1	0	277^1	338	18	86	81	14.1	3.96	111	.288	.342	35	.241	5	8	14	2	1.7
1891 Chi-N	17	11	.607	32	31	24	1	0	256^1	282	5	90	73	13.4	3.58	93	.269	.333	32	.305	12	-7	-7	1	0.6
1892 Chi-N	22	19	.537	46	45	39	0	0	382^2	399	11	107	118	12.2	3.41	97	.258	.312	42	.236	4	-5	-4	1	0.1
1893 Pit-N	11	7	.611	22	20	16	2	0	162^2	207	5	78	40	16.0	5.15	88	.301	.376	21	.293	1	-9	-11	-2	-0.9
1894 Pit-N	15	14	.517	37	31	26	0	0	269	372	13	84	65	15.5	6.02	87	.324	.374	33	.292	5	-21	-23	1	-1.3
1895 Bro-N	11	16	.407	33	26	20	0	1	234	288	11	69	45	14.2	5.08	87	.298	.352	35	.361	11	-8	-18	-1	-0.7
1896 Bro-N	0	4	.000	5	4	2	0	0	31	34	2	11	3	13.1	3.77	109	.276	.336	2	.182	-0	2	1	1	0.2
Phi-N	5	3	.625	11	10	7	1	0	77^1	99	0	23	14	14.7	4.54	95	.308	.362	9	.265	1	-2	-2	-1	-0.1
Yr	5	7	.417	16	14	9	1	0	108^1	133	2	34	17	14.2	4.32	99	.300	.355	11	.244	1	1	-1	0	0.1
Total 9	123	102	.547	262	234	191	7	1	1985^1	2321	81	634	546	13.8	4.27	97	.283	.341	261	.273	52	-31	-33	1	1.8

● HARRY GUMBERT
Gumbert, Harry Edward "Gunboat"   b: 11/5/09, Elizabeth, Pa.   BR/TR, 6'2", 185 lbs.   Deb: 9/12/35

YEAR TM/L	W	L	PCT	G	GS	CG	SH	SV	IP	H	HR	BB	SO	RAT	ERA	ERA+	OAV	OOB	BH	AVG	PB	PR	/A	PD	TPI
1935 NY-N	1	2	.333	6	3	1	0	0	23^2	35	1	10	11	17.1	6.08	63	.330	.388	0	.000	-1	-5	-6	-0	-0.7
1936 *NY-N	11	3	.786	39	15	3	0	0	140^2	157	7	54	52	13.6	3.90	100	.281	.346	11	.250	2	2	-0	3	0.5
1937 *NY-N	10	11	.476	34	24	10	1	1	200^1	194	11	62	65	11.7	3.68	106	.257	.317	13	.181	-1	5	5	8	1.1
1938 NY-N	15	13	.536	38	33	14	1	0	235^2	238	13	84	84	12.6	4.01	94	.261	.328	13	.155	-3	-6	-6	8	-0.2
1939 NY-N	18	11	.621	36	34	14	2	0	243^2	257	21	81	81	12.5	4.32	91	.271	.329	18	.200	-0	-11	-11	6	-0.5
1940 NY-N	12	14	.462	35	30	14	2	2	237	230	17	81	77	11.9	3.76	103	.252	.316	17	.195	2	2	3	4	0.9
1941 NY-N	1	1	.500	5	5	1	0	0	32^1	34	3	18	9	14.5	4.45	83	.266	.356	2	.167	-0	-3	-3	1	-0.1
StL-N	11	5	.688	33	17	8	3	1	144^1	139	7	30	53	10.6	2.74	137	.251	.291	17	.321	6	14	16	4	2.7
Yr	12	6	.667	38	22	9	3	1	176^2	173	10	48	62	11.3	3.06	123	.254	.304	19	.292	5	11	14	4	2.6
1942 *StL-N	9	5	.643	38	19	5	0	5	163	156	1	59	52	11.9	3.26	105	.250	.315	6	.111	-2	1	3	5	0.5
1943 StL-N	10	5	.667	21	19	7	3	0	133	115	4	32	40	9.9	2.84	118	.237	.284	7	.156	-2	8	8	2	0.8
1944 StL-N	4	2	.667	10	7	3	0	1	61^1	60	1	19	16	11.6	2.49	141	.258	.313	4	.190	-0	8	7	1	0.8
Cin-N	10	8	.556	24	19	11	2	2	155^1	157	7	40	40	11.5	3.30	106	.262	.310	5	.096	-2	5	3	2	0.4
Yr	14	10	.583	34	26	14	2	3	216^2	217	8	59	56	11.5	3.07	114	.261	.311	9	.123	-2	13	10	3	1.2
1946 Cin-N	6	8	.429	36	10	5	0	4	119	112	8	42	44	11.7	3.25	103	.248	.314	8	.250	1	2	1	1	0.4
1947 Cin-N	10	10	.500	46	0	0	0	10	90^1	88	3	47	43	13.5	3.89	106	.260	.351	6	.273	1	2	2	0	0.6
1948 Cin-N	10	8	.556	61	0	0	0	17	106^1	123	5	34	25	13.3	3.47	113	.291	.344	1	.040	-1	6	5	4	1.2
1949 Cin-N	4	3	.571	29	0	0	0	2	40^2	58	5	12	14	14.8	5.53	76	.341	.374	0	.000	-0	-7	-6	1	-0.9
Pit-N	1	4	.200	16	0	0	0	3	27^2	30	5	18	5	15.6	5.86	72	.270	.372	1	.250	-0	-6	-5	1	-0.8
Yr	5	7	.417	45	0	0	0	5	68^1	88	10	26	17	15.0	5.66	74	.312	.370	1	.167	-0	-12	-11	2	-1.7
1950 Pit-N	0	0	—	1	0	0	0	0	1^2	3	0	2	0	27.0	5.40	81	.333	.455	1	1.000	-0	-0	-0	0	0.1
Total 15	143	113	.559	508	235	96	14	48	2156	2186	121	721	709	12.2	3.68	102	.263	.323	130	.184	-2	18	17	50	6.8

● BILLY GUMBERT
Gumbert, William Skeen   b: 8/8/1865, Pittsburgh, Pa.   d: 4/13/46, Pittsburgh, Pa.   BR/TR, 6'1.5", 200 lbs.   Deb: 6/19/1890   F

YEAR TM/L	W	L	PCT	G	GS	CG	SH	SV	IP	H	HR	BB	SO	RAT	ERA	ERA+	OAV	OOB	BH	AVG	PB	PR	/A	PD	TPI
1890 Pit-N	4	6	.400	10	10	8	0	0	79^1	96	0	31	18	15.3	5.22	63	.290	.365	9	.243	3	-15	-17	-1	-1.3
1892 Pit-N	3	2	.600	6	3	2	0	0	39^2	30	0	23	2	12.3	1.36	242	.201	.312	2	.111	-1	8	9	-1	0.8
1893 Lou-N	0	0	—	1	1	0	0	0	0^2	2	0	5	0	94.5	27.00	16	.503	.780	1	1.000	1	-2	-2	-0	0.1
Total 3	7	8	.467	17	14	10	0	0	119^2	128	0	59	21	14.7	4.06	81	.264	.355	12	.214	3	-8	-10	-1	-0.4

● DAVE GUMPERT
Gumpert, David Lawrence   b: 5/5/58, South Haven, Mich.   BR/TR, 6'1", 190 lbs.   Deb: 7/25/82

YEAR TM/L	W	L	PCT	G	GS	CG	SH	SV	IP	H	HR	BB	SO	RAT	ERA	ERA+	OAV	OOB	BH	AVG	PB	PR	/A	PD	TPI
1982 Det-A	0	0	—	5	1	0	0	1	2	7	1	2	0	40.5	27.00	15	.700	.750	0	—	-0	-5	-5	-0	-0.6
1983 Det-A	0	2	.000	26	0	0	0	0	44^1	43	1	7	14	10.2	2.64	148	.257	.287	0	—	0	7	6	-1	0.3
1985 Chi-N	1	0	1.000	9	0	0	0	0	10^1	12	0	7	4	16.5	3.48	115	.279	.380	0	.000	-0	0	1	-0	0.0
1986 Chi-N	2	0	1.000	38	0	0	0	2	59^2	60	4	28	45	13.4	4.37	92	.267	.350	0	.000	-1	-4	-2	-1	-0.2
1987 KC-A	0	0	—	8	0	0	0	0	19^1	27	3	6	13	15.4	6.05	75	.333	.379	0	—	-0	-3	-3	-0	-0.1
Total 5	3	2	.600	86	1	0	0	5	135^2	149	9	50	76	13.3	4.31	95	.283	.347	0	.000	-2	-6	-4	-2	-0.6

● RANDY GUMPERT
Gumpert, Randall Pennington   b: 1/23/18, Monocacy, Pa.   BR/TR, 6'3", 205 lbs.   Deb: 6/13/36

YEAR TM/L	W	L	PCT	G	GS	CG	SH	SV	IP	H	HR	BB	SO	RAT	ERA	ERA+	OAV	OOB	BH	AVG	PB	PR	/A	PD	TPI
1936 Phi-A	1	2	.333	22	3	2	0	2	62^1	74	2	32	9	15.3	4.76	107	.295	.375	6	.273	0	2	**2**	-1	0.1
1937 Phi-A	0	0	—	10	1	0	0	0	12	16	1	15	5	24.0	12.00	39	.333	.500	1	.333	0	-10	-10	0	0.0
1938 Phi-A	0	2	.000	4	2	0	0	0	12^1	14	1	10	1	24.8	10.95	44	.393	.479	1	.250	-0	-8	-8	1	-0.9
1946 NY-A	11	3	.786	33	12	4	0	1	132^2	113	8	32	63	9.8	2.31	150	.229	.276	6	.128	-2	18	17	-1	1.4
1947 NY-A	4	1	.800	24	6	2	0	0	56^1	71	4	28	25	15.8	5.43	65	.311	.387	1	.071	-1	-11	-12	0	-1.1
1948 NY-A	1	0	1.000	15	0	0	0	0	25	27	0	6	12	12.2	2.88	142	.267	.315	0	—	0	4	3	0	0.1
Chi-A	2	6	.250	16	11	6	1	0	97^1	103	6	13	31	10.9	3.79	112	.275	.303	4	.138	-2	5	5	-1	0.1
Yr	3	6	.333	31	11	6	1	0	122^1	130	6	19	43	11.1	3.60	117	.273	.303	4	.138	-2	9	8	-1	0.2
1949 Chi-A	13	16	.448	34	32	18	3	1	234	223	22	83	78	11.8	3.81	110	.253	.318	16	.190	-1	10	9	1	1.0
1950 Chi-A	5	12	.294	40	17	6	1	0	155^1	165	15	58	48	13.2	4.75	94	.273	.343	3	.071	-4	-3	-5	-0	-0.8
1951 Chi-A☆	9	8	.529	33	16	7	1	2	141^2	156	20	34	45	12.1	4.32	93	.272	.314	15	.333	3	-3	-4	-3	-0.5
1952 Bos-A	1	0	1.000	10	1	0	0	0	19^2	15	1	6	6	9.6	4.12	96	.205	.266	0	.000	-1	-1	-0	-0	-0.1
Was-A	4	9	.308	20	12	2	0	0	104	112	12	30	29	12.7	4.24	84	.273	.318	7	.206	-0	-7	-8	-1	-0.9
Yr	5	9	.357	30	13	2	0	0	123^2	127	13	35	35	12.2	4.22	86	.262	.318	7	.179	-0	-8	-8	-1	-1.0
Total 10	51	59	.464	261	113	47	6	7	1052^2	1099	92	346	352	12.5	4.17	98	.268	.328	60	.182	-8	-4	-10	-5	-1.6

● ERIC GUNDERSON
Gunderson, Eric Andrew   b: 3/29/66, Portland, Ore.   BR/TL, 6', 175 lbs.   Deb: 4/11/90

YEAR TM/L	W	L	PCT	G	GS	CG	SH	SV	IP	H	HR	BB	SO	RAT	ERA	ERA+	OAV	OOB	BH	AVG	PB	PR	/A	PD	TPI
1990 SF-N	1	2	.333	7	4	0	0	0	19^2	24	2	11	14	16.0	5.49	66	.293	.376	0	.000	-1	-4	-4	-0	-0.6
1991 SF-N	0	0	—	2	0	0	0	1	3^1	6	1	2	2	18.9	5.40	66	.353	.389	0	—	-0	-1	-1	0	0.0
1992 Sea-A	2	1	.667	9	0	0	0	0	9^1	12	1	5	2	17.4	8.68	46	.324	.419	0	—	-0	-5	-5	-0	-1.3
1994 NY-N	0	0	—	14	0	0	0	0	9	5	0	4	4	9.0	0.00	—	.185	.290	0	—	0	4	4	0	0.0
Total 4	3	3	.500	32	4	0	0	1	41^1	47	3	21	22	15.0	5.01	77	.288	.373	0	.000	-1	-5	-5	-0	-1.9

● RED GUNKEL
Gunkel, Woodward William   b: 4/15/1894, Sheffield, Ill.   d: 4/19/54, Chicago, Ill.   BB/TR, 5'8", 158 lbs.   Deb: 6/18/16

YEAR TM/L	W	L	PCT	G	GS	CG	SH	SV	IP	H	HR	BB	SO	RAT	ERA	ERA+	OAV	OOB	BH	AVG	PB	PR	/A	PD	TPI
1916 Cle-A	0	0	—	1	0	0	0	0	1	0	0	1	1	18.0	0.00	—	.000	.500	0	—	0	0	0	-0	0.0

● LARRY GURA
Gura, Lawrence Cyril   b: 11/26/47, Joliet, Ill.   BB/TL, 6'1", 185 lbs.   Deb: 4/30/70

YEAR TM/L	W	L	PCT	G	GS	CG	SH	SV	IP	H	HR	BB	SO	RAT	ERA	ERA+	OAV	OOB	BH	AVG	PB	PR	/A	PD	TPI
1970 Chi-N	1	3	.250	20	3	1	0	1	38	35	6	23	21	14.0	3.79	119	.254	.364	0	.000	-1	1	3	0	0.2
1971 Chi-N	0	0	—	6	0	0	0	1	3	6	1	0	3	21.0	6.00	66	.400	.438	0	.000	-0	-1	-1	-0	-0.1
1972 Chi-N	0	0	—	7	0	0	0	0	12^1	11	3	3	13	10.2	3.65	104	.250	.298	0	.000	-0	-0	0	-0	0.0
1973 Chi-N	2	4	.333	21	7	1	0	0	64^2	79	10	11	43	12.7	4.87	81	.296	.326	3	.200	-2	-9	-7	-1	-0.4
1974 NY-A	5	1	.833	8	8	4	2	0	56	54	2	12	17	10.6	2.41	145	.248	.287	0	—	0	8	7	-0	0.8
1975 NY-A	7	8	.467	26	20	5	0	0	151^1	173	13	41	65	12.9	3.51	104	.295	.344	0	—	0	-0	1	1	0.1
1976 *KC-A	4	0	1.000	20	2	1	1	1	62^2	47	4	20	22	9.8	2.30	152	.213	.281	0	—	0	9	8	1	0.6
1977 *KC-A	8	5	.615	52	6	1	1	10	106^1	108	8	28	46	11.6	3.13	129	.265	.314	0	—	0	11	11	0	1.4
1978 *KC-A	16	4	.800	35	26	10	3	0	221^2	183	13	60	81	10.0	2.72	141	.229	.286	0	—	0	26	27	2	2.6
1979 KC-A	13	12	.520	39	33	7	1	0	233^2	226	29	73	85	11.8	4.47	95	.253	.315	0	—	0	-7	-5	1	-0.5
1980 *KC-A☆	18	10	.643	36	36	16	4	0	283^1	272	20	76	113	11.2	2.95	137	.255	.307	0	—	0	34	35	1	3.3

YEAR	TM/L	W	L	PCT	G	GS	CG	SH	SV	IP	H	HR	BB	SO	RAT	ERA	ERA+	OAV	OOB	BH	AVG	PB	PR	/A	PD	TPI
1981	*KC-A	11	8	.579	23	23	12	2	0	172¹	139	11	35	61	9.3	2.72	133	.223	.269	0	—	0	18	17	0	1.9
1982	KC-A	18	12	.600	37	37	8	3	0	248	251	31	64	98	11.6	4.03	101	.261	.311	0	—	0	1	1	2	0.4
1983	KC-A	11	18	.379	34	31	5	0	0	200¹	220	23	76	57	13.7	4.90	83	.284	.354	0	—	0	-19	-18	3	-2.0
1984	KC-A	12	9	.571	31	25	3	0	0	168²	175	26	67	68	13.1	5.18	78	.269	.341	0	—	0	-22	-22	1	-2.3
1985	KC-A	0	0	—	3	0	0	0	1	4¹	7	1	4	2	22.8	12.46	33	.368	.478	0	—	0	-4	-4	0	-0.2
	Chi-N	0	3	.000	9	0	0	0	0	20¹	24	6	6	7	18.1	8.41	47	.370	.414	0	.000	-0	-11	-10	0	-1.2
Total	16	126	97	.565	403	261	71	16	14	2047	2020	204	600	801	11.7	3.76	105	.260	.317	3	.091	-2	39	45	11	4.8

● CHARLIE GUTH
Guth, Charles J.   b: 1856, Chicago, Ill.   d: 7/5/1883, Cambridge, Mass.   Deb: 9/30/1880

YEAR	TM/L	W	L	PCT	G	GS	CG	SH	SV	IP	H	HR	BB	SO	RAT	ERA	ERA+	OAV	OOB	BH	AVG	PB	PR	/A	PD	TPI
1880	Chi-N	1	0	1.000	1	1	1	0	0	9	12	0	1	7	13.0	5.00	48	.293	.310	1	.250	0	-3	-3	-0	-0.2

● MARK GUTHRIE
Guthrie, Mark Andrew   b: 9/22/65, Buffalo, N.Y.   BB/TR, 6'4", 195 lbs.   Deb: 7/25/89

YEAR	TM/L	W	L	PCT	G	GS	CG	SH	SV	IP	H	HR	BB	SO	RAT	ERA	ERA+	OAV	OOB	BH	AVG	PB	PR	/A	PD	TPI
1989	Min-A	2	4	.333	13	8	0	0	0	57¹	66	7	21	38	13.8	4.55	91	.292	.355	0	—	0	-4	-3	-0	-0.7
1990	Min-A	7	9	.438	24	21	3	1	0	144²	154	8	39	101	12.1	3.79	109	.276	.325	0	—	0	2	6	1	0.2
1991	*Min-A	7	5	.583	41	12	0	0	2	98	116	11	41	72	14.5	4.32	99	.303	.372	0	—	0	-2	-1	-1	-0.1
1992	Min-A	2	3	.400	54	0	0	0	5	75	59	7	23	76	9.8	2.88	141	.215	.276	0	—	0	9	10	-0	0.7
1993	Min-A	2	1	.667	22	0	0	0	0	21	20	2	16	15	15.4	4.71	92	.267	.396	0	—	0	-1	-1	-0	-0.1
1994	Min-A	4	2	.667	50	2	0	0	1	51¹	65	8	18	38	14.9	6.14	79	.316	.376	0	—	0	-8	-7	-0	-0.7
Total	6	24	24	.500	204	43	3	1	8	447¹	480	43	158	340	12.9	4.16	102	.279	.341	0	—	0	-5	4	-0	-0.7

● JOSE GUZMAN
Guzman, Jose Alberto (Mirabal)   b: 4/9/63, Santa Isabel, P.R.   BR/TR, 6'2", 195 lbs.   Deb: 9/10/85

YEAR	TM/L	W	L	PCT	G	GS	CG	SH	SV	IP	H	HR	BB	SO	RAT	ERA	ERA+	OAV	OOB	BH	AVG	PB	PR	/A	PD	TPI
1985	Tex-A	3	2	.600	5	5	0	0	0	32²	27	3	14	24	11.3	2.76	153	.214	.293	0	—	0	5	5	0	0.7
1986	Tex-A	9	15	.375	29	29	2	0	0	172¹	199	23	60	87	13.8	4.54	95	.293	.355	0	—	0	-7	-5	0	-0.6
1987	Tex-A	14	14	.500	37	30	6	0	0	208¹	196	30	82	143	12.1	4.67	96	.251	.324	0	—	0	-5	-4	1	-0.4
1988	Tex-A	11	13	.458	30	30	6	2	0	206²	180	20	82	157	11.6	3.70	110	.231	.308	0	—	0	6	9	-0	0.7
1991	Tex-A	13	7	.650	25	25	5	1	0	169²	152	10	84	125	12.7	3.08	131	.239	.331	0	—	0	19	18	2	2.2
1992	Tex-A	16	11	.593	33	33	5	0	0	224	229	17	73	179	12.3	3.66	104	.268	.329	0	—	0	7	3	-0	0.4
1993	Chi-N	12	10	.545	30	30	2	1	0	191	188	25	74	163	12.5	4.34	92	.258	.329	7	.111	-3	-6	-7	0	-1.0
1994	Chi-N	2	2	.500	4	4	0	0	0	19²	22	1	13	11	16.5	9.15	45	.289	.400	0	.000	-1	-11	-11	-0	-1.7
Total	8	80	74	.519	193	186	26	4	0	1224¹	1193	129	482	889	12.5	4.05	101	.256	.329	7	.099	-3	8	8	3	0.3

● JUAN GUZMAN
Guzman, Juan Andres (Correa)   b: 10/28/66, Santo Domingo, D.R.   BR/TR, 5'11", 190 lbs.   Deb: 6/7/91

YEAR	TM/L	W	L	PCT	G	GS	CG	SH	SV	IP	H	HR	BB	SO	RAT	ERA	ERA+	OAV	OOB	BH	AVG	PB	PR	/A	PD	TPI
1991	*Tor-A	10	3	.769	23	23	1	0	0	138²	98	6	66	123	10.9	2.99	141	.197	.296	0	—	0	17	19	-2	1.4
1992	*Tor-A★	16	5	.762	28	28	1	0	0	180²	135	6	72	165	10.4	2.64	155	.207	.287	0	—	0	26	29	-2	3.1
1993	*Tor-A	14	3	.824	33	33	2	1	0	221	211	17	110	194	13.2	3.99	108	.252	.341	0	—	0	8	8	-2	0.3
1994	Tor-A	12	11	.522	25	25	2	0	0	147¹	165	20	76	124	14.9	5.68	85	.282	.367	0	—	0	-14	-14	0	-1.8
Total	4	52	22	.703	109	109	6	1	0	687²	609	49	324	606	12.4	3.80	114	.237	.325	0	—	0	37	42	-6	3.0

● JOHNNY GUZMAN
Guzman, Ramon Dionny (Estrella)   b: 1/21/71, Hatillo Palma, D.R.   BR/TL, 5'10", 155 lbs.   Deb: 6/8/91

YEAR	TM/L	W	L	PCT	G	GS	CG	SH	SV	IP	H	HR	BB	SO	RAT	ERA	ERA+	OAV	OOB	BH	AVG	PB	PR	/A	PD	TPI
1991	Oak-A	1	0	1.000	5	0	0	0	0	5	11	0	2	3	23.4	9.00	43	.500	.542	0	—	0	-3	-3	0	-0.5
1992	Oak-A	0	0	—	2	0	0	0	0	3	8	0	0	0	27.0	12.00	31	.471	.500	0	—	0	-3	-3	-0	0.0
Total	2	1	0	1.000	7	0	0	0	0	8	19	0	2	3	24.8	10.13	38	.487	.524	0	—	0	-5	-6	0	-0.5

● SANTIAGO GUZMAN
Guzman, Santiago Donovan (b: Santiago Donovan (Guzman))   b: 7/25/49, San Pedro De Macoris, D.R.   BR/TR, 6'2", 180 lbs.   Deb: 9/30/69

YEAR	TM/L	W	L	PCT	G	GS	CG	SH	SV	IP	H	HR	BB	SO	RAT	ERA	ERA+	OAV	OOB	BH	AVG	PB	PR	/A	PD	TPI
1969	StL-N	0	1	.000	1	1	0	0	0	7¹	9	2	3	7	14.7	4.91	73	.321	.387	1	.333	0	-1	-1	-0	-0.1
1970	StL-N	1	1	.500	8	3	1	0	0	13²	14	1	13	9	17.8	7.24	57	.275	.422	1	.200	0	-5	-5	-0	-0.6
1971	StL-N	0	0	—	2	1	0	0	0	10	6	0	2	13	7.2	0.00	—	.162	.205	0	.000	-0	4	4	-0	0.0
1972	StL-N	0	0	—	1	0	0	0	0	1	1	0	0	0	9.0	9.00	38	.250	.250	0	—	0	-1	-1	-0	0.0
Total	4	1	2	.333	12	5	1	0	0	32	30	4	18	29	13.5	4.50	85	.250	.348	2	.222	0	-3	-2	-1	-0.7

● BRUNO HAAS
Haas, Bruno Philip "Boon"   b: 5/5/1891, Worcester, Mass.   d: 6/5/52, Sarasota, Fla.   BB/TL, 5'10", 180 lbs.   Deb: 6/23/15   ♦

YEAR	TM/L	W	L	PCT	G	GS	CG	SH	SV	IP	H	HR	BB	SO	RAT	ERA	ERA+	OAV	OOB	BH	AVG	PB	PR	/A	PD	TPI
1915	Phi-A	0	1	.000	6	2	1	0	0	14¹	23	0	28	7	32.0	11.93	25	.404	.600	1	.056	-1	-14	-14	0	-0.9

● MOOSE HAAS
Haas, Bryan Edmund   b: 4/22/56, Baltimore, Md.   BR/TR, 6', 180 lbs.   Deb: 9/8/76

YEAR	TM/L	W	L	PCT	G	GS	CG	SH	SV	IP	H	HR	BB	SO	RAT	ERA	ERA+	OAV	OOB	BH	AVG	PB	PR	/A	PD	TPI
1976	Mil-A	0	1	.000	5	2	0	0	0	16	12	0	12	9	13.5	3.94	89	.207	.343	0	—	0	-1	-1	1	0.1
1977	Mil-A	10	12	.455	32	32	6	0	0	197²	195	21	84	113	12.8	4.33	94	.261	.338	0	—	0	-6	-6	-2	-0.8
1978	Mil-A	2	3	.400	7	6	2	0	0	30²	33	4	8	32	12.0	6.16	61	.273	.318	0	—	0	-8	-8	-0	-1.2
1979	Mil-A	11	11	.500	29	28	8	1	0	184²	198	26	59	95	12.5	4.78	87	.275	.330	0	—	0	-12	-13	-1	-1.4
1980	Mil-A	16	15	.516	33	33	14	3	0	252²	246	25	56	146	10.8	3.10	125	.258	.300	0	—	0	26	21	0	2.4
1981	*Mil-A	11	7	.611	24	22	5	0	0	137¹	146	10	40	64	12.3	4.46	77	.275	.327	0	—	0	-12	-16	-1	-1.9
1982	*Mil-A	11	8	.579	32	27	3	0	1	193¹	232	15	39	104	12.8	4.47	85	.302	.339	0	—	0	-8	-15	-2	-1.3
1983	Mil-A	13	3	.813	25	25	7	3	0	179	170	17	42	75	10.7	3.27	114	.251	.296	0	—	0	16	9	-1	0.7
1984	Mil-A	9	11	.450	31	30	4	0	0	189²	205	15	43	84	11.8	3.99	96	.279	.318	0	—	0	-0	-3	0	0.2
1985	Mil-A	8	8	.500	27	26	6	1	0	161²	165	21	25	78	10.6	3.84	108	.260	.289	0	—	0	5	6	-1	0.4
1986	Oak-A	7	2	.778	12	12	1	0	0	72¹	58	4	19	40	9.7	2.74	141	.218	.273	0	—	0	12	9	-0	1.2
1987	Oak-A	2	2	.500	9	9	0	0	0	40²	57	7	9	13	14.6	5.75	72	.335	.369	0	—	0	-6	-7	-0	-0.6
Total	12	100	83	.546	266	252	56	8	2	1655	1717	162	436	853	11.8	4.01	97	.269	.317	0	—	0	6	-23	-5	-2.2

● DAVE HAAS
Haas, Robert David   b: 10/19/65, Independence, Mo.   BR/TR, 6'1", 200 lbs.   Deb: 9/8/91

YEAR	TM/L	W	L	PCT	G	GS	CG	SH	SV	IP	H	HR	BB	SO	RAT	ERA	ERA+	OAV	OOB	BH	AVG	PB	PR	/A	PD	TPI
1991	Det-A	1	0	1.000	11	0	0	0	0	10²	8	1	12	6	17.7	6.75	62	.242	.457	0	—	0	-3	-3	-0	-0.3
1992	Det-A	5	3	.625	12	11	1	1	0	61²	68	8	16	29	12.4	3.94	100	.276	.323	0	—	0	-0	-0	-0	0.0
1993	Det-A	1	2	.333	20	0	0	0	0	28	45	9	8	17	17.0	6.11	70	.375	.414	0	—	0	-6	-6	-0	-0.5
Total	3	7	5	.583	43	11	1	1	0	100¹	121	18	36	52	14.3	4.84	84	.303	.364	0	—	0	-9	-9	-0	-0.8

● BOB HABENICHT
Habenicht, Robert Julius "Hobby"   b: 2/13/26, St.Louis, Mo.   d: 12/24/80, Richmond, Va.   BR/TR, 6'2", 185 lbs.   Deb: 4/17/51

YEAR	TM/L	W	L	PCT	G	GS	CG	SH	SV	IP	H	HR	BB	SO	RAT	ERA	ERA+	OAV	OOB	BH	AVG	PB	PR	/A	PD	TPI
1951	StL-N	0	0	—	3	0	0	0	0	5	5	0	9	1	25.2	7.20	55	.278	.519	0	.000	0	-2	-2	0	0.0
1953	StL-A	0	0	—	1	0	0	0	0	1²	1	0	1	1	16.2	5.40	78	.167	.375	0	—	0	-0	-0	-0	0.0
Total	2	0	0	—	4	0	0	0	0	6²	6	0	10	2	23.0	6.75	60	.250	.486	0	.000	0	-2	-2	0	0.0

● JOHN HABYAN
Habyan, John Gabriel   b: 1/29/64, Bay Shore, N.Y.   BR/TR, 6'1", 195 lbs.   Deb: 9/29/85

YEAR	TM/L	W	L	PCT	G	GS	CG	SH	SV	IP	H	HR	BB	SO	RAT	ERA	ERA+	OAV	OOB	BH	AVG	PB	PR	/A	PD	TPI
1985	Bal-A	1	0	1.000	2	0	0	0	0	2²	3	0	0	2	10.1	0.00	—	.250	.250	0	—	0	1	1	0	0.6
1986	Bal-A	1	3	.250	6	5	0	0	0	26¹	24	3	18	14	14.4	4.44	93	.250	.368	0	—	0	-1	-1	-0	-0.1
1987	Bal-A	6	7	.462	27	13	0	0	0	116¹	110	20	40	64	11.8	4.80	92	.248	.313	0	—	0	-4	-5	1	-0.4
1988	Bal-A	1	0	1.000	7	0	0	0	0	14²	24	2	4	4	16.0	4.30	91	.355	.394	0	—	0	-1	-1	-0	0.2
1990	NY-A	0	0	—	6	0	0	0	0	8²	10	0	4	4	13.5	2.08	191	.294	.351	0	—	0	2	2	-0	0.2
1991	NY-A	4	2	.667	66	0	0	0	2	90	73	2	20	70	9.5	2.30	180	.225	.275	0	—	0	18	18	0	1.2
1992	NY-A	5	6	.455	56	0	0	0	7	72²	84	6	21	44	13.3	3.84	102	.295	.347	0	—	0	1	1	-0	0.0
1993	NY-A	2	1	.667	36	0	0	0	0	42¹	45	5	16	29	13.0	4.04	103	.276	.341	0	—	0	-0	-0	-0	-0.2
	KC-A	0	0	—	12	0	0	0	0	14	14	1	4	10	11.6	4.50	102	.259	.310	0	—	0	-0	-0	-0	-0.2
	Yr	2	1	.667	48	0	0	0	0	56¹	59	6	20	39	12.6	4.15	103	.269	.331	0	—	0	-0	-0	-0	-0.3
1994	StL-N	0	0	—	52	0	0	0	1	47¹	59	2	20	46	13.3	3.23	126	.305	.387	0	—	0	5	4	1	0.2
Total	9	21	19	.525	270	18	0	0	12	435	435	41	145	287	12.1	3.74	111	.263	.325	0	—	0	22	20	3	1.9

● WARREN HACKER
Hacker, Warren Louis   b: 11/21/24, Marissa, Ill.   BR/TR, 6'1", 185 lbs.   Deb: 9/24/48

YEAR	TM/L	W	L	PCT	G	GS	CG	SH	SV	IP	H	HR	BB	SO	RAT	ERA	ERA+	OAV	OOB	BH	AVG	PB	PR	/A	PD	TPI
1948	Chi-N	0	1	.000	3	1	0	0	0	3	7	0	3	0	30.0	21.00	19	.438	.526	0	—	0	-6	-6	0	-1.3
1949	Chi-N	5	8	.385	30	12	3	0	0	125²	141	7	53	40	14.2	4.23	95	.283	.356	7	.184	-1	-3	-3	1	-0.3

YEAR	TM/L	W	L	PCT	G	GS	CG	SH	SV	IP	H	HR	BB	SO	RAT	ERA	ERA+	OAV	OOB	BH	AVG	PB	PR	/A	PD	TPI
1950	Chi-N	0	1	.000	5	3	1	0	1	15^1	20	3	8	5	16.4	5.28	80	.313	.389	0	.000	-1	-2	-2	1	-0.1
1951	Chi-N	0	0	—	2	0	0	0	1	1^1	3	0	0	2	27.0	13.50	30	.500	.571	0	—	0	-1	-1	0	0.0
1952	Chi-N	15	9	.625	33	20	12	5	1	185	144	17	31	84	**8.6**	2.58	149	**.212**	**.247**	7	.121	-2	24	26	-4	2.8
1953	Chi-N	12	19	.387	39	32	9	0	2	221^2	225	35	54	106	11.4	4.38	101	.254	.299	17	.218	0	2	2	-3	0.0
1954	Chi-N	6	13	.316	39	18	4	1	2	158^2	157	28	37	80	11.2	4.25	99	.257	.304	13	.236	1	-3	-1	-1	-0.1
1955	Chi-N	11	15	.423	35	30	13	0	3	213	202	38	43	80	10.4	4.27	96	.245	.285	18	.250	2	-5	-4	-4	-0.6
1956	Chi-N	3	13	.188	34	24	4	0	0	168	190	28	44	65	12.6	4.66	81	.285	.330	8	.148	-2	-17	-17	-3	-1.9
1957	Cin-N	3	2	.600	15	6	0	0	0	43^1	50	5	13	18	13.7	5.19	79	.294	.355	1	.125	-0	-6	-5	-0	-0.6
	Phi-N	4	4	.500	20	10	1	0	0	74	72	10	18	33	11.1	4.50	85	.257	.304	6	.261	1	-5	-6	-1	-0.5
	Yr	7	6	.538	35	16	1	0	0	117^1	122	15	31	51	11.8	4.76	82	.267	.315	7	.226	1	-11	-11	-1	-1.1
1958	Phi-N	0	1	.000	9	1	0	0	0	17	24	2	8	4	16.9	7.41	53	.329	.395	0	.000	-0	-7	-7	-0	-0.4
1961	Chi-A	3	3	.500	42	0	0	0	8	57^1	62	8	8	40	11.1	3.77	104	.272	.300	1	.111	-1	2	1	-1	-0.1
Total 12		62	89	.411	306	157	47	6	17	1283^1	1297	181	320	557	11.5	4.21	96	.259	.307	78	.195	-2	-32	-22	-15	-3.1

● **JIM HACKETT**   Hackett, James Joseph "Sunny Jim" b: 10/1/1877, Jacksonville, Ill. d: 3/28/61, Douglas, Mich. BR/TR, 6'2", 185 lbs. Deb: 9/14/02 ♦

YEAR	TM/L	W	L	PCT	G	GS	CG	SH	SV	IP	H	HR	BB	SO	RAT	ERA	ERA+	OAV	OOB	BH	AVG	PB	PR	/A	PD	TPI
1902	StL-N	0	3	.000	4	3	3	0	0	30^1	46	0	16	7	18.7	6.23	44	.348	.422	6	.286	1	-12	-12	-0	-0.9
1903	StL-N	1	3	.250	7	6	5	0	1	48^1	47	0	18	21	12.7	3.72	88	.249	.324	80	.228	1	-2	-2	-0	-0.1
Total 2		1	6	.143	11	9	8	0	1	78^2	93	0	34	28	15.0	4.69	65	.290	.365	86	.231	2	-14	-14	-0	-1.0

● **HARVEY HADDIX**   Haddix, Harvey "The Kitten" b: 9/18/25, Medway, Ohio d: 1/8/94, Springfield, Ohio BL/TL, 5'9.5", 170 lbs. Deb: 8/20/52 C

YEAR	TM/L	W	L	PCT	G	GS	CG	SH	SV	IP	H	HR	BB	SO	RAT	ERA	ERA+	OAV	OOB	BH	AVG	PB	PR	/A	PD	TPI
1952	StL-N	2	2	.500	7	6	3	0	0	42	31	4	10	31	9.2	2.79	133	.201	.259	3	.214	-0	4	4	-1	0.4
1953	StL-N☆	20	9	.690	36	33	19	**6**	1	253	220	24	69	163	10.4	3.06	139	.232	.287	28	.289	10	35	34	1	4.7
1954	StL-N†	18	13	.581	43	35	13	3	4	259^2	247	26	77	184	11.3	3.57	115	.249	.305	18	.194	3	14	16	-0	2.0
1955	StL-N★	12	16	.429	37	30	9	2	1	208	216	27	62	150	12.2	4.46	91	.249	.325	12	.164	0	-10	-9	-1	-0.9
1956	StL-N	1	0	1.000	4	4	1	1	0	23^2	28	3	10	16	14.5	5.32	71	.298	.365	2	.222	1	-4	-4	-0	-0.1
	Phi-N	12	8	.600	31	26	11	2	2	206^2	196	23	55	154	11.2	3.48	107	.247	.301	22	.237	4	7	5	-1	0.9
	Yr	13	8	.619	35	30	12	3	2	230^1	224	26	65	170	11.5	3.67	102	.253	.308	24	.235	5	3	1	-1	0.8
1957	Phi-N	10	13	.435	27	25	8	1	0	170^2	176	18	39	136	11.4	4.06	94	.264	.306	21	.309	7	-3	-5	-2	-0.1
1958	Cin-N	8	7	.533	29	26	8	1	0	184	191	28	43	110	11.8	3.52	118	.268	.315	11	.180	3	9	13	-1	1.2
1959	Pit-N	12	12	.500	31	29	14	2	0	224^1	189	26	49	149	**9.6**	3.13	124	.228	**.273**	12	.145	-0	20	18	-0	1.8
1960	*Pit-N	11	10	.524	29	28	4	0	1	172^1	189	13	38	101	11.9	3.97	94	.277	.316	17	.254	4	-4	-3	3	0.3
1961	Pit-N	10	6	.625	29	22	5	2	0	156	159	15	41	99	11.7	4.10	97	.266	.316	8	.143	1	-1	-2	0	-0.1
1962	Pit-N	9	6	.600	28	20	4	0	0	141^1	146	17	42	101	12.1	4.20	96	.264	.319	13	.250	4	-4	-4	-0	0.0
1963	Pit-N	3	4	.429	49	1	0	0	1	70	67	7	20	70	11.7	3.34	99	.256	.319	2	.182	1	-0	-0	-0	0.0
1964	Bal-A	5	5	.500	49	0	0	0	10	89^2	68	5	23	90	9.3	2.31	155	.211	.268	0	.000	-2	13	13	1	1.5
1965	Bal-A	3	2	.600	24	0	0	0	1	33^2	31	5	23	21	15.0	3.48	100	.248	.373	0	.000	-0	-0	-0	-0	-0.0
Total 14		136	113	.546	453	285	99	20	21	2235	2154	240	601	1575	11.3	3.63	108	.252	.305	169	.212	35	75	74	1	11.6

● **GEORGE HADDOCK**   Haddock, George Silas "Gentleman George" b: 12/25/1866, Portsmouth, N.H. d: 4/18/26, Boston, Mass. BR/TR, 5'11", 155 lbs. Deb: 9/27/1888

YEAR	TM/L	W	L	PCT	G	GS	CG	SH	SV	IP	H	HR	BB	SO	RAT	ERA	ERA+	OAV	OOB	BH	AVG	PB	PR	/A	PD	TPI
1888	Was-N	0	2	.000	2	2	2	0	0	16	9	0	2	3	6.8	2.25	125	.148	.188	1	.200	-1	1	1	1	0.2
1889	Was-N	11	19	.367	33	31	30	0	0	276^1	299	10	123	106	14.0	4.20	94	.268	.345	25	.223	7	-6	-8	0	0.3
1890	Buf-P	9	26	.257	35	34	31	0	0	290^2	366	15	149	123	16.4	5.76	71	.295	.376	36	.247	7	-49	-54	4	-3.4
1891	Bos-a	34	11	.756	51	47	37	**5**	1	379^2	330	8	137	169	11.4	2.49	140	.226	.299	45	.243	9	**52**	42	6	5.3
1892	Bro-N	29	13	.690	46	44	39	3	1	381^1	340	11	163	132	12.2	3.14	101	.229	.311	28	.177	1	6	1	2	2.4
1893	Bro-N	8	9	.471	23	20	12	0	0	151	193	10	89	37	17.2	5.60	79	.302	.393	24	.282	4	-16	-20	-3	-1.5
1894	Phi-N	4	3	.571	10	7	5	0	0	56	63	0	34	7	15.8	5.79	88	.281	.378	5	.172	-1	-3	-4	-1	-0.4
	Was-N	0	4	.000	4	4	4	0	0	29	50	2	17	1	21.1	8.69	61	.375	.449	3	.188	-1	-11	-11	-0	-1.0
	Yr	4	7	.364	14	11	9	0	0	85	113	2	51	8	17.5	6.78	76	.315	.402	8	.178	-1	-14	-15	1	-1.4
Total 7		95	87	.522	204	189	160	8	2	1580	1650	56	714	599	13.8	4.07	93	.259	.340	167	.227	25	-25	-53	11	-0.6

● **BUMP HADLEY**   Hadley, Irving Darius b: 7/5/04, Lynn, Mass. d: 2/15/63, Lynn, Mass. BR/TR, 5'11", 190 lbs. Deb: 4/20/26

YEAR	TM/L	W	L	PCT	G	GS	CG	SH	SV	IP	H	HR	BB	SO	RAT	ERA	ERA+	OAV	OOB	BH	AVG	PB	PR	/A	PD	TPI
1926	Was-A	0	0	—	1	0	0	0	0	3	6	0	2	0	24.0	12.00	32	.429	.500	0	—	0	-3	-3	-0	0.0
1927	Was-A	14	6	.700	30	27	13	0	0	198^2	177	2	86	60	12.3	2.85	142	.244	.332	19	.271	2	28	27	0	2.6
1928	Was-A	12	13	.480	33	31	16	3	0	231^2	236	4	100	80	13.4	3.54	113	.268	.348	17	.210	1	13	12	-0	1.3
1929	Was-A	6	16	.273	37	27	7	1	0	195^1	196	10	85	98	13.2	5.62	75	.263	.342	6	.097	-4	-30	-30	1	-3.1
1930	Was-A	15	11	.577	42	34	15	1	2	260^1	242	6	105	162	12.2	3.73	123	.247	.323	21	.226	1	27	25	2	2.2
1931	Was-A	11	10	.524	**55**	11	2	1	8	179^2	145	4	92	124	11.9	3.06	140	**.218**	.314	9	.167	-1	26	25	2	2.7
1932	Chi-A	1	1	.500	3	2	1	0	0	18^2	17	2	8	13	12.1	3.86	112	.262	.342	1	.167	-0	1	1	0	0.1
	StL-A	13	20	.394	40	33	12	1	1	229^2	244	21	163	132	16.3	5.53	88	.274	.391	22	.282	4	-27	-17	-3	-1.9
	Yr	14	21	.400	43	35	13	1	1	248^1	261	23	171	145	15.9	5.40	89	.273	.388	23	.274	4	-25	-16	-3	-1.8
1933	StL-A	15	20	.429	45	36	19	2	3	316^1	309	17	141	149	12.9	3.92	119	.256	.335	17	.156	-4	13	26	-3	1.9
1934	StL-A	10	16	.385	39	32	7	2	1	213	212	14	127	79	14.6	4.35	115	.257	.361	17	.203	-1	3	15	-0	1.5
1935	Was-A	10	15	.400	35	32	13	0	0	230^1	268	18	102	77	14.6	4.92	88	.292	.366	15	.195	1	-12	-15	-1	-1.2
1936	*NY-A	14	4	.778	31	17	8	1	1	173^2	194	12	89	74	14.7	4.35	107	.283	.366	16	.235	2	13	6	1	0.7
1937	*NY-A	11	8	.579	29	25	6	0	0	178^1	199	16	83	70	14.3	5.30	84	.281	.358	11	.169	1	-13	-17	1	-1.4
1938	NY-A	9	8	.529	29	17	4	0	1	167^1	165	13	66	61	12.6	3.60	126	.254	.325	5	.093	-1	22	17	3	1.6
1939	*NY-A	12	6	.667	26	18	7	1	2	154	132	10	85	65	12.9	2.98	146	.237	.342	11	.177	-1	28	24	2	2.6
1940	NY-A	3	5	.375	25	2	0	0	2	80	88	4	52	37	14.6	5.74	70	.276	.379	3	.111	-2	-12	-15	0	-1.4
1941	NY-N	1	0	1.000	3	2	0	0	0	13	19	1	9	4	19.4	6.23	59	.345	.438	0	.000	-0	-4	-4	-0	-0.3
	Phi-A	4	6	.400	25	9	0	0	3	102^1	131	13	47	31	15.8	5.01	84	.310	.381	4	.129	-1	-10	-9	-1	-0.9
Total 16		161	165	.494	528	355	135	14	25	2945^2	2980	167	1442	1318	13.7	4.24	105	.263	.350	190	.189	-1	65	69	2	7.0

● **MICKEY HAEFNER**   Haefner, Milton Arnold b: 10/9/12, Lenzburg, Ill. d: 1/3/95, New Athens, Ill. BL/TL, 5'8", 160 lbs. Deb: 4/22/43

YEAR	TM/L	W	L	PCT	G	GS	CG	SH	SV	IP	H	HR	BB	SO	RAT	ERA	ERA+	OAV	OOB	BH	AVG	PB	PR	/A	PD	TPI
1943	Was-A	11	5	.688	36	13	8	1	6	165^1	126	4	60	65	10.3	2.29	140	.208	.283	6	.133	0	19	17	-0	1.8
1944	Was-A	12	15	.444	31	28	18	3	1	228	221	7	71	86	11.7	3.04	107	.251	.310	11	.157	-1	10	5	1	0.6
1945	Was-A	16	14	.533	37	28	19	1	3	238^1	226	10	69	83	11.4	3.47	89	.247	.305	20	.244	4	-3	-10	-1	-0.7
1946	Was-A	14	11	.560	33	27	17	2	1	227^2	220	10	80	85	12.1	2.85	118	.251	.317	15	.203	4	17	13	-1	1.7
1947	Was-A	10	14	.417	34	28	14	4	1	193	195	8	85	77	13.2	3.64	102	.264	.343	8	.136	-1	1	2	-1	0.0
1948	Was-A	5	13	.278	28	20	4	0	0	147^2	151	7	61	45	13.3	4.02	108	.265	.342	7	.163	-1	4	5	-2	0.7
1949	Was-A	5	5	.500	19	12	4	1	1	91^2	85	7	53	23	13.7	4.42	96	.249	.353	5	.200	1	-2	-1	1	0.1
	Chi-A	4	6	.400	14	12	4	1	1	80^1	84	9	41	17	14.6	4.37	95	.251	.370	6	.261	2	-2	-0	-0	0.0
	Yr	9	11	.450	33	24	8	2	1	172	169	16	94	40	14.0	4.40	96	.260	.358	11	.229	2	-4	-2	1	0.1
1950	Chi-A	1	6	.143	24	9	2	0	1	70^2	83	11	52	17	16.6	5.73	78	.299	.400	4	.200	-0	-9	-10	-1	-0.8
	Bos-N	0	2	.000	8	2	1	0	0	24	23	3	12	10	13.1	5.63	68	.247	.333	2	.286	1	-4	-5	-0	-0.3
Total 8		78	91	.462	261	179	91	13	13	1466^2	1414	76	577	508	12.5	3.50	102	.252	.326	84	.188	8	31	13	1	3.0

● **BUD HAFEY**   Hafey, Daniel Albert b: 8/6/12, Berkeley, Cal. d: 7/27/86, Sacramento, Cal. BR/TR, 6', 185 lbs. Deb: 4/21/35 F♦

YEAR	TM/L	W	L	PCT	G	GS	CG	SH	SV	IP	H	HR	BB	SO	RAT	ERA	ERA+	OAV	OOB	BH	AVG	PB	PR	/A	PD	TPI
1939	Phi-N	0	0	—	2	0	0	0	0	1^1	7	0	1	0	54.0	33.75	12	.700	.727	9	.176	-0	-4	-4	0	0.0

● **LEO HAFFORD**   Hafford, Leo Edgar b: 9/17/1883, Somerville, Mass. d: 10/2/11, Willimantic, Conn. TR, 6', 170 lbs. Deb: 4/15/06

YEAR	TM/L	W	L	PCT	G	GS	CG	SH	SV	IP	H	HR	BB	SO	RAT	ERA	ERA+	OAV	OOB	BH	AVG	PB	PR	/A	PD	TPI
1906	Cin-N	1	1	.500	3	1	0	0	0	13	13	0	11	5	11.8	0.95	291	.191	.313	2	.222	-0	4	4	-1	0.3

● **FRANK HAFNER**   Hafner, Francis R. b: 8/14/1867, Hannibal, Mo. d: 3/2/57, Hannibal, Mo. TR, Deb: 5/5/1888

YEAR	TM/L	W	L	PCT	G	GS	CG	SH	SV	IP	H	HR	BB	SO	RAT	ERA	ERA+	OAV	OOB	BH	AVG	PB	PR	/A	PD	TPI
1888	KC-a	0	2	.000	2	2	2	0	0	18	24	2	16	5	20.5	7.00	49	.309	.433	0	.000	-1	-8	-7	-0	-0.6

YEAR TM/L	W	L	PCT	G	GS	CG	SH	SV	IP	H	HR	BB	SO	RAT	ERA	ERA+	OAV	OOB	BH	AVG	PB	PR	/A	PD	TPI

● ART HAGAN Hagan, Arthur Charles b: 3/17/1863, Providence, R.I. d: 3/25/36, Providence, R.I. TR , Deb: 6/30/1883

YEAR TM/L	W	L	PCT	G	GS	CG	SH	SV	IP	H	HR	BB	SO	RAT	ERA	ERA+	OAV	OOB	BH	AVG	PB	PR	/A	PD	TPI
1883 Phi-N	1	14	.067	17	16	15	0	0	137	207	2	33	39	15.8	5.45	57	.342	.376	6	.102	-5	-35	-36	-1	-3.3
Buf-N	0	2	.000	2	2	1	0	0	15	17	0	6	7	13.8	3.60	88	.270	.333	0	.000	-1	-1	-1	0	-0.2
Yr	1	16	.059	19	18	16	0	0	152	224	2	39	46	15.6	5.27	59	.335	.371	6	.091	-7	-36	-37	-1	-3.5
1884 Buf-N	1	2	.333	3	3	3	0	0	26	53	1	4	4	19.7	5.88	54	.384	.401	4	.308	-1	-8	-8	-1	-0.7
Total 2	2	18	.100	22	21	19	0	0	178	277	3	43	50	16.2	5.36	58	.343	.376	10	.127	-6	-44	-45	-2	-4.2

● CASEY HAGEMAN Hageman, Kurt Moritz b: 5/12/1887, Mt.Oliver, Pa. d: 4/1/64, New Bedford, Pa. BR/TR, 5'10.5", 186 lbs. Deb: 9/18/11

YEAR TM/L	W	L	PCT	G	GS	CG	SH	SV	IP	H	HR	BB	SO	RAT	ERA	ERA+	OAV	OOB	BH	AVG	PB	PR	/A	PD	TPI
1911 Bos-A	0	2	.000	2	2	1	0	0	17	16	2	5	8	11.6	2.12	155	.262	.328	0	.000	-0	2	2	-1	0.1
1912 Bos-A	0	0	—	2	1	0	0	0	1¹	5	0	3	1	54.0	27.00	13	.500	.615	0	—	0	-4	-3	-0	0.0
1914 StL-N	2	4	.333	12	7	2	0	0	55¹	43	0	20	21	11.1	2.44	155	.215	.302	2	.125	-1	2	2	1	0.3
Chi-N	1	1	.500	16	1	0	0	1	46²	44	0	12	17	11.4	3.47	80	.254	.314	7	.467	3	-4	-4	-1	0.0
Yr	3	5	.375	28	8	2	0	1	102	87	0	32	38	10.8	2.91	96	.230	.295	9	.290	2	-1	-1	-0	0.3
Total 3	3	7	.300	32	11	4	0	1	120¹	108	2	40	47	11.7	3.07	93	.243	.318	9	.257	2	-3	-3	-1	0.4

● KEVIN HAGEN Hagen, Kevin Eugene b: 3/8/60, Renton, Wash. BR/TR, 6'2", 185 lbs. Deb: 6/4/83

YEAR TM/L	W	L	PCT	G	GS	CG	SH	SV	IP	H	HR	BB	SO	RAT	ERA	ERA+	OAV	OOB	BH	AVG	PB	PR	/A	PD	TPI
1983 StL-N	2	2	.500	9	4	0	0	0	22¹	34	0	7	7	16.5	4.84	75	.362	.406	0	.000	-1	-3	-3	0	-0.5
1984 StL-N	1	0	1.000	4	0	0	0	0	7¹	9	0	1	2	12.3	2.45	141	.300	.323	0	—	0	1	1	0	0.1
Total 2	3	2	.600	13	4	0	0	0	29²	43	0	8	9	15.5	4.25	84	.347	.386	0	.000	-1	-2	-2	-0	-0.4

● RIP HAGERMAN Hagerman, Zeriah Zequiel b: 6/20/1888, Linden, Kan. d: 1/30/30, Albuquerque, N.Mex BR/TR, 6'2", 200 lbs. Deb: 4/16/09

YEAR TM/L	W	L	PCT	G	GS	CG	SH	SV	IP	H	HR	BB	SO	RAT	ERA	ERA+	OAV	OOB	BH	AVG	PB	PR	/A	PD	TPI
1909 Chi-N	4	4	.500	13	7	4	1	0	79	64	0	28	33	10.7	1.82	140	.225	.298	3	.130	-0	7	6	-0	0.5
1914 Cle-A	9	15	.375	37	26	12	3	0	198	189	3	118	112	14.2	3.09	93	.265	.374	1	.016	-5	-8	-4	-3	-1.4
1915 Cle-A	6	14	.300	29	22	7	0	0	151	156	4	77	69	14.2	3.52	87	.277	.370	4	.105	-2	-10	-8	-3	-1.5
1916 Cle-A	0	0	—	2	0	0	0	0	3²	5	1	2	1	22.1	12.27	25	.333	.474	0	.000	-0	-4	-4	-0	0.0
Total 4	19	33	.365	81	55	23	4	0	431²	414	8	225	214	13.6	3.09	93	.263	.360	8	.065	-9	-14	-10	-6	-2.4

● NOODLES HAHN Hahn, Frank George b: 4/29/1879, Nashville, Tenn. d: 2/6/60, Candler, N.C. BL/TL, 5'9", 160 lbs. Deb: 4/18/1899

YEAR TM/L	W	L	PCT	G	GS	CG	SH	SV	IP	H	HR	BB	SO	RAT	ERA	ERA+	OAV	OOB	BH	AVG	PB	PR	/A	PD	TPI
1899 Cin-N	23	8	.742	38	34	32	4	0	309	280	3	68	**145**	10.4	2.68	146	.242	.289	16	.147	-4	40	43	-4	2.8
1900 Cin-N	16	20	.444	39	37	29	**4**	0	311¹	306	4	89	**132**	11.6	3.27	112	.257	.312	24	.209	0	15	14	-0	1.4
1901 Cin-N	22	19	.537	42	42	**41**	2	0	**375¹**	370	12	69	**239**	10.7	2.71	118	.256	.294	24	.170	-1	26	20	-0	1.9
1902 Cin-N	23	12	.657	36	36	35	6	0	321	282	2	58	142	9.7	1.77	170	.236	.275	22	.185	0	36	44	-2	4.6
1903 Cin-N	22	12	.647	34	34	34	5	0	296	297	3	47	127	10.7	2.52	141	.262	.297	18	.161	-2	25	34	-1	3.2
1904 Cin-N	16	18	.471	35	34	33	2	0	297²	258	3	35	98	9.1	2.06	143	.234	.262	17	.172	1	23	29	-0	3.3
1905 Cin-N	5	3	.625	13	8	5	1	0	77	85	0	9	17	11.2	2.81	118	.272	.297	4	.167	-1	2	4	-2	0.1
1906 NY-A	3	2	.600	6	6	3	1	0	42	38	0	6	17	10.1	3.86	77	.244	.286	4	.333	1	-5	-4	-1	-0.4
Total 8	130	94	.580	243	231	212	25	0	2029¹	1916	27	381	917	10.4	2.55	133	.249	.289	129	.176	-5	161	187	-11	16.9

● FRED HAHN Hahn, Frederick Aloys b: 2/16/29, Nyack, N.Y. d: 8/16/84, Valhalla, N.Y. BR/TL, 6'3", 174 lbs. Deb: 4/19/52

YEAR TM/L	W	L	PCT	G	GS	CG	SH	SV	IP	H	HR	BB	SO	RAT	ERA	ERA+	OAV	OOB	BH	AVG	PB	PR	/A	PD	TPI
1952 StL-N	0	0	—	1	0	0	0	0	2	2	0	1	0	13.5	0.00	—	.250	.333	0	—	0	1	1	0	0.0

● HAL HAID Haid, Harold Augustine b: 12/21/1897, Barberton, Ohio d: 8/13/52, Los Angeles, Cal. BR/TR, 5'10.5", 150 lbs. Deb: 9/5/19

YEAR TM/L	W	L	PCT	G	GS	CG	SH	SV	IP	H	HR	BB	SO	RAT	ERA	ERA+	OAV	OOB	BH	AVG	PB	PR	/A	PD	TPI
1919 StL-A	0	0	—	1	0	0	0	0	2	5	0	3	1	36.0	18.00	18	.556	.667			0	-3	-3	0	0.0
1928 StL-N	2	2	.500	27	0	0	0	**5**	47	39	1	11	20	9.8	2.30	174	.218	.267	3	.375	1	9	9	0	1.0
1929 StL-N	9	9	.500	38	12	8	0	4	154²	171	8	66	41	14.1	4.07	115	.284	.360	4	.082	-4	11	10	-1	0.6
1930 StL-N	3	2	.600	20	0	0	0	2	33	38	1	14	13	15.0	4.09	123	.297	.379	0	.000	-0	3	3	1	0.5
1931 Bos-N	0	2	.000	27	0	0	0	1	56	59	3	16	20	12.5	4.50	84	.263	.321	1	.125	-1	-4	-4	2	0.0
1933 Chi-A	0	0	—	6	0	0	0	0	14²	18	2	13	7	20.3	7.98	53	.310	.452	1	.250	0	-6	-6	0	0.0
Total 6	14	15	.483	119	12	8	0	12	307¹	330	15	123	103	13.7	4.16	106	.275	.349	9	.125	-3	10	9	2	2.1

● JESSE HAINES Haines, Jesse Joseph "Pop" b: 7/22/1893, Clayton, Ohio d: 8/5/78, Dayton, Ohio BR/TR, 6', 190 lbs. Deb: 7/20/18 CH

YEAR TM/L	W	L	PCT	G	GS	CG	SH	SV	IP	H	HR	BB	SO	RAT	ERA	ERA+	OAV	OOB	BH	AVG	PB	PR	/A	PD	TPI
1918 Cin-N	0	0	—	1	0	0	0	0	5	5	0	1	2	10.8	1.80	148	.294	.333	1	1.000	0	1	0	0	0.1
1920 StL-N	13	20	.394	**47**	37	19	4	2	301²	303	9	80	120	11.7	2.98	100	.270	.324	19	.176	-1	5	0	-5	-0.7
1921 StL-N	18	12	.600	37	29	13	**3**	0	244¹	261	15	56	84	12.0	3.50	105	.286	.333	17	.181	-3	8	5	2	0.4
1922 StL-N	11	9	.550	29	26	11	2	0	183	207	10	45	62	12.6	3.84	101	.286	.329	12	.167	-2	5	1	1	0.0
1923 StL-N	20	13	.606	37	36	23	1	0	266	283	7	75	73	12.3	3.11	125	.275	.328	20	.202	-2	26	23	0	2.4
1924 StL-N	8	19	.296	35	31	16	1	0	222²	275	14	66	69	14.0	4.41	86	.309	.360	14	.189	-2	-13	-15	-1	-1.9
1925 StL-N	13	14	.481	29	25	15	0	0	207	234	11	52	63	12.5	4.57	95	.290	.334	13	.176	-2	-7	-6	-1	-0.4
1926 *StL-N	13	4	.765	33	21	14	3	1	183	186	10	48	46	11.6	3.25	120	.265	.314	13	.213	-1	12	13	-3	0.7
1927 StL-N	24	10	.706	38	36	**25**	**6**	1	300²	273	11	77	89	10.6	2.72	145	.245	.297	23	.202	-1	40	41	1	4.3
1928 *StL-N	20	8	.714	33	28	20	1	0	240¹	238	14	72	77	11.8	3.18	126	.266	.324	16	.184	-1	22	22	-3	1.9
1929 StL-N	13	10	.565	28	25	12	0	0	179²	230	21	73	59	15.3	5.71	82	.313	.376	11	.159	-3	-20	-21	-4	-2.7
1930 *StL-N	13	8	.619	29	24	14	1	0	182	215	15	54	68	13.4	4.30	117	.298	.348	16	.246	1	14	14	-3	1.2
1931 StL-N	12	3	.800	19	17	8	2	0	122¹	134	2	28	27	11.9	3.02	131	.278	.318	6	.133	-2	12	13	-1	1.0
1932 StL-N	3	5	.375	20	10	4	1	0	85¹	116	4	16	27	14.0	4.75	83	.326	.357	5	.185	0	-8	-8	-1	-0.7
1933 StL-N	9	6	.600	32	10	5	0	1	115¹	113	3	37	37	11.8	2.50	139	.252	.311	2	.067	-2	11	13	-2	1.2
1934 *StL-N	4	4	.500	37	6	0	0	1	90	86	6	19	17	10.9	3.50	121	.262	.311	3	.158	-1	**6**	**7**	2	0.7
1935 StL-N	6	5	.545	30	12	3	0	2	115¹	110	4	28	24	10.8	3.59	114	.252	.299	9	.273	1	6	7	-0	0.5
1936 StL-N	7	5	.583	25	9	4	0	1	99¹	110	4	21	19	12.0	3.90	101	.284	.323	5	.167	-1	1	1	-0	0.0
1937 StL-N	3	3	.500	16	6	2	0	0	65²	81	5	23	18	14.4	4.52	88	.303	.361	4	.182	-0	-1	-1	-0	-0.5
Total 19	210	158	.571	555	388	208	24	10	3208²	3460	165	871	981	12.3	3.64	108	.280	.330	209	.186	-22	114	104	-21	7.0

● JIM HAISLIP Haislip, James Clifton "Slim" b: 8/4/1891, Farmersville, Tex. d: 1/22/70, Dallas, Tex. BR/TR, 6'1", 186 lbs. Deb: 8/27/13

YEAR TM/L	W	L	PCT	G	GS	CG	SH	SV	IP	H	HR	BB	SO	RAT	ERA	ERA+	OAV	OOB	BH	AVG	PB	PR	/A	PD	TPI
1913 Phi-N	0	0	—	1	0	0	0	0	3	4	0	3	0	21.0	6.00	56	.400	.538	0	.000	-0	-1	-1	0	0.0

● ED HALBRITER Halbriter, Edward L. b: 2/2/1860, Auburn, N.Y. d: 8/9/36, Los Angeles, Cal. Deb: 5/23/1882

YEAR TM/L	W	L	PCT	G	GS	CG	SH	SV	IP	H	HR	BB	SO	RAT	ERA	ERA+	OAV	OOB	BH	AVG	PB	PR	/A	PD	TPI
1882 Phi-a	0	1	.000	1	1	1	0	0	8	17	1	4	4	23.6	7.88	38	.406	.458	0	.000	-1	-5	-4	-0	-0.4

● DAD HALE Hale, Ray Luther b: 2/18/1879, Allegan, Mich. d: 2/1/46, Allegan, Mich. BR/TR, 5'10", 180 lbs. Deb: 4/21/02

YEAR TM/L	W	L	PCT	G	GS	CG	SH	SV	IP	H	HR	BB	SO	RAT	ERA	ERA+	OAV	OOB	BH	AVG	PB	PR	/A	PD	TPI
1902 Bos-N	1	4	.200	8	6	3	0	0	47	69	1	18	12	16.9	6.32	45	.341	.397	0	.000	-1	-18	-18	-0	-1.8
Bal-A	0	1	.000	3	2	1	0	0	14	21	0	6	6	18.0	4.50	84	.346	.414	0	.000	-1	-1	-1	-1	-0.2
Total 1	1	5	.167	11	8	4	0	0	61	90	1	24	18	17.1	5.90	51	.342	.401	0	.000	-2	-20	-19	-1	-2.0

● ED HALICKI Halicki, Edward Louis b: 10/4/50, Newark, N.J. BR/TR, 6'7", 220 lbs. Deb: 7/8/74

YEAR TM/L	W	L	PCT	G	GS	CG	SH	SV	IP	H	HR	BB	SO	RAT	ERA	ERA+	OAV	OOB	BH	AVG	PB	PR	/A	PD	TPI
1974 SF-N	1	8	.111	16	11	2	0	0	74¹	84	6	31	40	14.2	4.24	90	.275	.345	6	.240	-1	-5	-4	-1	-0.3
1975 SF-N	9	13	.409	24	23	7	2	0	159²	143	6	59	153	11.6	3.49	109	.240	.312	6	.113	-2	2	5	-1	0.5
1976 SF-N	12	14	.462	32	31	8	4	0	186¹	171	10	61	130	11.3	3.62	100	.246	.309	9	.170	1	-3	0	-0	0.1
1977 SF-N	16	12	.571	37	37	7	2	0	257²	241	27	70	168	11.1	3.32	118	.244	.298	15	.176	3	17	17	-3	1.7
1978 SF-N	9	10	.474	29	28	9	4	0	199	166	11	45	105	9.9	2.85	121	.221	**.271**	9	.136	-2	16	13	-2	0.8
1979 SF-N	5	8	.385	33	19	3	1	0	125²	134	12	47	81	13.2	4.58	76	.266	.333	1	.206	1	-12	-15	-1	-1.3
1980 SF-N	0	0	—	11	2	0	0	0	25	29	5	10	14	14.0	5.40	65	.293	.358	1	.167	-0	-5	-5	0	0.0
Cal-A	3	1	.750	10	6	0	0	0	35¹	39	5	11	16	12.7	4.84	81	.279	.331	0	—	0	-3	-4	-1	-0.4
Total 7	55	66	.455	192	157	36	13	1	1063	1007	82	334	707	11.6	3.62	102	.247	.308	53	.165	3	8	8	-7	1.1

YEAR TM/L	W	L	PCT	G	GS	CG	SH	SV	IP	H	HR	BB	SO	RAT	ERA	ERA+	OAV	OOB	BH	AVG	PB	PR	/A	PD	TPI

● DREW HALL
Hall, Andrew Clark b: 3/27/63, Louisville, Ky. BL/TL, 6'4", 205 lbs. Deb: 9/14/86

YEAR TM/L	W	L	PCT	G	GS	CG	SH	SV	IP	H	HR	BB	SO	RAT	ERA	ERA+	OAV	OOB	BH	AVG	PB	PR	/A	PD	TPI
1986 Chi-N	1	2	.333	5	4	1	0	1	23^2	24	3	10	21	12.9	4.56	89	.267	.340	1	.143	0	-2	-1	-0	-0.2
1987 Chi-N	1	1	.500	21	0	0	0	0	32^2	40	4	14	20	14.9	6.89	62	.308	.375	0	.000	-0	-10	-9	-0	-0.6
1988 Chi-N	1	1	.500	19	0	0	0	1	22^1	26	4	9	22	14.5	7.66	47	.295	.367	0	.000	-0	-10	-10	-0	-0.9
1989 Tex-A	2	1	.667	38	0	0	0	0	58^1	42	3	33	45	12.0	3.70	107	.207	.326	0	—	0	1	2	0	0.1
1990 Mon-N	4	7	.364	42	0	0	0	3	58^1	52	6	29	40	12.5	5.09	72	.242	.332	0	.000	-0	-8	-9	1	-1.7
Total 5	9	12	.429	125	4	1	0	5	195^1	184	20	95	148	13.0	5.21	75	.253	.343	1	.063	-1	-30	-29	-0	-3.3

● CHARLEY HALL
Hall, Charles Louis "Sea Lion" (b: Carlos Clolo) b: 7/27/1885, Ventura, Cal. d: 12/6/43, Ventura, Cal. BR/TR, 6'1", 187 lbs. Deb: 7/12/06

YEAR TM/L	W	L	PCT	G	GS	CG	SH	SV	IP	H	HR	BB	SO	RAT	ERA	ERA+	OAV	OOB	BH	AVG	PB	PR	/A	PD	TPI
1906 Cin-N	4	8	.333	14	9	9	1	1	95	86	1	50	49	13.6	3.32	83	.258	.368	6	.128	-1	-7	-6	-0	-0.9
1907 Cin-N	4	2	.667	11	8	5	0	0	68	51	0	43	25	13.0	2.51	103	.226	.359	7	.269	-1	-0	-1	-1	0.1
1909 Bos-A	6	4	.600	11	7	3	0	0	59^2	59	0	17	27	11.9	2.56	98	.271	.332	3	.158	-1	-1	-0	-0	-0.2
1910 Bos-A	12	9	.571	35	16	13	0	2	188^2	142	6	73	95	10.7	1.91	134	.207	.292	17	.207	3	13	14	0	2.0
1911 Bos-A	8	7	.533	32	10	6	0	4	146^1	149	3	72	83	13.9	3.75	87	.279	.370	4	.141	-1	-7	-8	-2	-1.0
1912 *Bos-A	15	8	.652	34	20	9	2	2	191	178	3	70	83	11.9	3.02	113	.257	.329	20	.267	5	6	8	1	1.6
1913 Bos-A	5	4	.556	35	4	2	0	2	105	97	1	46	48	12.7	3.43	86	.235	.319	9	.214	1	-6	-6	-1	-0.5
1916 StL-N	0	4	.000	10	5	2	0	1	42^2	45	1	14	15	12.4	5.48	48	.280	.337	2	.143	-1	-14	-13	-0	-1.3
1918 Det-A	0	1	.000	6	1	0	0	0	13^1	14	1	6	2	13.5	6.75	39	.269	.345	0	.000	-0	-6	-6	-1	-0.5
Total 9	54	47	.535	188	80	49	3	12	909^2	821	16	391	427	12.4	3.09	95	.248	.334	73	.197	7	-21	-17	-2	-0.7

● BERT HALL
Hall, Herbert Ernest b: 10/15/1888, Portland, Ore. d: 7/18/48, Seattle, Wash. BR/TR, 5'10", 178 lbs. Deb: 8/21/11

YEAR TM/L	W	L	PCT	G	GS	CG	SH	SV	IP	H	HR	BB	SO	RAT	ERA	ERA+	OAV	OOB	BH	AVG	PB	PR	/A	PD	TPI
1911 Phi-N	0	1	.000	7	1	0	0	0	18	19	0	13	8	16.5	4.00	86	.297	.423	1	.333	0	-1	-1	-1	-0.1

● HERB HALL
Hall, Herbert Silas "Iron Duke" b: 6/5/1893, Steelville, Ill. d: 7/1/70, Fresno, Cal. BB/TR, 6'4", 220 lbs. Deb: 4/28/18

YEAR TM/L	W	L	PCT	G	GS	CG	SH	SV	IP	H	HR	BB	SO	RAT	ERA	ERA+	OAV	OOB	BH	AVG	PB	PR	/A	PD	TPI
1918 Det-A	0	0	—	3	0	0	0	0	6	12	0	7	1	31.5	15.00	18	.500	.636	0	.000	-0	-8	-8	0	0.0

● JOHN HALL
Hall, John Sylvester b: 1/9/24, Muskogee, Okla. BR/TR, 6'2.5", 170 lbs. Deb: 4/21/48

YEAR TM/L	W	L	PCT	G	GS	CG	SH	SV	IP	H	HR	BB	SO	RAT	ERA	ERA+	OAV	OOB	BH	AVG	PB	PR	/A	PD	TPI
1948 Bro-N	0	0	—	3	0	0	0	0	4^1	4	1	2	2	12.5	6.23	64	.267	.353	0	—	0	-1	-1	0	0.0

● MARC HALL
Hall, Marcus b: 8/12/1887, Joplin, Mo. d: 2/24/15, Joplin, Mo. BR/TR, 6'1.5", 190 lbs. Deb: 8/20/10

YEAR TM/L	W	L	PCT	G	GS	CG	SH	SV	IP	H	HR	BB	SO	RAT	ERA	ERA+	OAV	OOB	BH	AVG	PB	PR	/A	PD	TPI
1910 StL-A	1	7	.125	8	7	5	0	0	46^1	50	0	31	25	16.3	4.27	58	.289	.406	1	.067	-2	-9	-9	1	-1.5
1913 Det-A	10	12	.455	30	21	8	1	0	165	154	1	79	69	12.8	3.27	89	.255	.344	4	.089	-3	-6	-6	0	-1.1
1914 Det-A	4	6	.400	25	8	1	0	0	90^1	88	1	27	18	11.5	2.69	104	.267	.322	1	.043	-2	1	1	0	-0.1
Total 3	15	25	.375	63	36	14	1	0	301^2	292	2	137	112	12.9	3.25	87	.264	.348	6	.072	-7	-15	-15	1	-2.7

● DARREN HALL
Hall, Michael Darren b: 7/14/64, Marysville, Ohio BR/TR, 6'3", 205 lbs. Deb: 4/30/94

YEAR TM/L	W	L	PCT	G	GS	CG	SH	SV	IP	H	HR	BB	SO	RAT	ERA	ERA+	OAV	OOB	BH	AVG	PB	PR	/A	PD	TPI
1994 Tor-A	2	3	.400	30	0	0	0	17	31^2	26	3	14	28	11.7	3.41	141	.226	.315	0	—	0	5	5	0	1.2

● DICK HALL
Hall, Richard Wallace b: 9/27/30, St.Louis, Mo. BR/TR, 6'6", 200 lbs. Deb: 4/15/52 ♦

YEAR TM/L	W	L	PCT	G	GS	CG	SH	SV	IP	H	HR	BB	SO	RAT	ERA	ERA+	OAV	OOB	BH	AVG	PB	PR	/A	PD	TPI
1955 Pit-N	6	6	.500	15	13	4	0	1	94^1	92	8	28	46	11.6	3.91	105	.253	.310	7	.175	1	1	2	-2	0.2
1956 Pit-N	0	7	.000	19	9	1	0	1	62^1	64	8	21	27	12.3	4.76	87	.270	.329	10	.345	2	-7	-7	-1	-0.5
1957 Pit-N	0	0	—	8	0	0	0	0	10	17	4	5	7	20.7	10.80	35	.362	.434	0	.000	-0	-8	-8	-0	-0.1
1959 Pit-N	0	0	—	2	1	0	0	0	8^2	12	1	1	3	13.5	3.12	124	.333	.351	0	.000	-0	1	1	-0	0.0
1960 KC-A	8	13	.381	29	28	9	1	0	182^1	183	28	38	79	11.1	4.05	98	.261	.301	6	.107	-2	-4	-1	-1	-0.4
1961 Bal-A	7	5	.583	43	6	1	2	4	122^1	102	10	30	92	9.7	3.09	124	.227	.275	5	.139	-1	13	10	1	1.1
1962 Bal-A	6	6	.500	43	6	1	0	6	118^1	102	9	19	71	9.2	2.28	162	.230	.262	4	.167	1	22	19	-0	2.1
1963 Bal-A	5	5	.500	47	3	0	0	12	111^2	91	12	16	74	8.9	2.98	116	.224	.260	13	.464	6	8	6	1	1.4
1964 Bal-A	9	1	.900	45	0	0	0	7	87^2	58	8	16	52	7.6	1.85	193	.188	.228	2	.125	-0	17	17	-0	2.1
1965 Bal-A	11	8	.579	48	0	0	0	12	93^2	84	8	11	79	9.1	3.07	113	.243	.266	5	.333	3	4	4	-1	1.1
1966 Bal-A	6	2	.750	32	0	0	0	7	66	59	8	8	44	9.5	3.95	84	.233	.265	2	.167	-0	-4	-5	-0	-0.6
1967 Phi-N	10	8	.556	48	1	1	0	0	86	83	5	12	49	10.2	2.20	155	.255	.286	1	.071	-1	11	12	1	2.7
1968 Phi-N	4	1	.800	32	0	0	0	0	46	53	5	5	31	11.5	4.89	61	.296	.319	1	.333	-0	-10	-10	-1	-1.1
1969 *Bal-A	5	2	.714	39	0	0	0	6	65^2	49	3	9	31	8.1	1.92	186	.213	.246	2	.286	1	12	12	1	1.5
1970 *Bal-A	10	5	.667	32	0	0	0	3	61^1	51	8	6	30	8.4	3.08	118	.229	.249	1	.083	-1	4	4	-1	0.7
1971 *Bal-A	6	6	.500	27	0	0	0	1	43^1	51	4	11	26	13.3	4.98	67	.302	.348	2	.400	1	-7	-8	-1	-2.1
Total 16	93	75	.554	495	74	20	3	68	1259^2	1152	130	236	741	10.0	3.32	110	.244	.283	150	.210	10	55	48	-7	8.1

● BOB HALL
Hall, Robert Lewis b: 12/22/23, Swissvale, Pa. d: 3/12/83, St.Petersburg, Fla BR/TR, 6'2", 195 lbs. Deb: 4/23/49

YEAR TM/L	W	L	PCT	G	GS	CG	SH	SV	IP	H	HR	BB	SO	RAT	ERA	ERA+	OAV	OOB	BH	AVG	PB	PR	/A	PD	TPI
1949 Bos-N	6	4	.600	31	6	2	0	0	74^1	77	7	41	43	14.4	4.36	87	.272	.366	8	.364	3	-3	-5	-2	-0.5
1950 Bos-N	0	2	.000	21	4	0	0	0	50^1	58	8	33	22	16.6	6.97	55	.293	.399	1	.083	-1	-16	-17	-0	-0.7
1953 Pit-N	3	12	.200	37	17	6	1	1	152	172	17	72	68	14.5	5.39	83	.286	.364	6	.158	0	-19	-15	-1	-1.4
Total 3	9	18	.333	89	27	8	1	1	276^2	307	32	146	133	14.6	5.40	77	.284	.371	15	.208	2	-37	-38	-3	-2.6

● TOM HALL
Hall, Tom Edward b: 11/23/47, Thomasville, N.C. BL/TL, 6', 155 lbs. Deb: 6/9/68

YEAR TM/L	W	L	PCT	G	GS	CG	SH	SV	IP	H	HR	BB	SO	RAT	ERA	ERA+	OAV	OOB	BH	AVG	PB	PR	/A	PD	TPI
1968 Min-A	2	1	.667	8	4	0	0	0	29^2	27	1	12	18	12.1	2.43	127	.239	.317	0	.000	-1	2	2	-0	0.1
1969 *Min-A	8	7	.533	31	18	5	2	0	140^2	129	12	50	92	11.5	3.33	110	.243	.308	8	.186	1	5	5	-2	0.4
1970 *Min-A	11	6	.647	52	11	1	0	4	155^1	94	11	66	184	9.4	2.55	146	.173	.265	8	.182	-0	20	20	-2	1.9
1971 Min-A	4	7	.364	48	11	0	0	9	129^2	104	13	58	137	11.2	3.33	107	.216	.300	9	.265	2	2	3	1	0.6
1972 *Cin-N	10	1	.909	47	7	1	1	8	124^1	77	13	56	134	9.8	2.61	123	.173	.269	3	.100	-1	12	8	-2	0.6
1973 *Cin-N	8	5	.615	54	7	0	0	8	103^2	74	13	48	96	10.6	3.47	98	.202	.295	1	.045	-2	2	-1	-2	-0.5
1974 Cin-N	3	1	.750	40	1	0	0	1	64	54	9	30	48	11.8	4.08	86	.232	.319	0	.000	-0	-3	-4	-0	-0.3
1975 Cin-N	0	0	—	2	0	0	0	0	2	2	0	3	2	18.0	0.00	—	.250	.400	0	—	1	1	1	0	0.0
NY-N	4	3	.571	34	4	0	0	1	60^2	58	10	31	48	13.6	4.75	73	.254	.351	2	.400	1	-8	-9	-0	-0.9
Yr	4	3	.571	36	4	0	0	1	62^2	60	10	33	51	13.8	4.60	74	.254	.353	2	.400	1	-7	-8	-0	-0.9
1976 NY-N	1	1	.500	5	0	0	0	0	4^2	5	2	5	4	19.3	5.79	57	.250	.400	0	—	0	-3	-1	-0	-0.5
*KC-A	1	1	.500	31	0	0	0	1	30^1	28	4	18	25	13.6	4.45	79	.246	.348	0	—	0	-3	-3	1	-0.2
1977 KC-A	0	0	—	6	0	0	0	0	7^2	4	2	6	10	11.7	3.52	115	.154	.313	0	—	0	0	0	-0	0.0
Total 10	52	33	.612	358	63	7	3	32	852^2	656	88	382	797	11.0	3.27	107	.211	.299	31	.161	-1	28	22	-8	1.2

● BILL HALL
Hall, William Bernard "Beanie" b: 2/22/1894, Charleston, W.Va. d: 8/15/47, Newport, Ky. BR/TR, 6'2", 250 lbs. Deb: 7/4/13

YEAR TM/L	W	L	PCT	G	GS	CG	SH	SV	IP	H	HR	BB	SO	RAT	ERA	ERA+	OAV	OOB	BH	AVG	PB	PR	/A	PD	TPI
1913 Bro-N	0	0	—	3	0	0	0	0	4^2	4	0	5	3	19.3	5.79	57	.267	.476	0	.000	-0	-1	-1	0	0.0

● JOHN HALLA
Halla, John Arthur b: 5/13/1884, St.Louis, Mo. d: 9/30/47, ElSegundo, Cal. BL/TL, 5'11", 175 lbs. Deb: 8/18/05

YEAR TM/L	W	L	PCT	G	GS	CG	SH	SV	IP	H	HR	BB	SO	RAT	ERA	ERA+	OAV	OOB	BH	AVG	PB	PR	/A	PD	TPI
1905 Cle-A	0	0	—	3	0	0	0	0	12^2	12	0	4	4	9.2	2.84	93	.251	.267	1	.200	-0	-0	-0	0	0.0

● BILL HALLAHAN
Hallahan, William Anthony "Wild Bill" b: 8/4/02, Binghamton, N.Y. d: 7/8/81, Binghamton, N.Y. BR/TL, 5'10.5", 170 lbs. Deb: 4/16/25

YEAR TM/L	W	L	PCT	G	GS	CG	SH	SV	IP	H	HR	BB	SO	RAT	ERA	ERA+	OAV	OOB	BH	AVG	PB	PR	/A	PD	TPI
1925 StL-N	1	0	1.000	6	0	0	0	0	15^1	14	0	11	8	14.7	3.52	123	.259	.385	1	.333	0	1	1	0	0.1
1926 *StL-N	1	4	.200	19	3	0	0	0	56^2	45	1	32	28	12.4	3.65	107	.260	.379	1	.250	0	1	2	-1	0.1
1929 *StL-N	4	4	.500	20	12	5	0	0	93^2	94	6	60	52	14.8	4.42	106	.269	.376	4	.154	-1	3	3	1	0.2
1930 *StL-N	15	9	.625	35	32	13	2	2	237^1	233	15	126	177	13.6	4.66	108	.260	.351	10	.123	-6	8	9	0	0.2
1931 *StL-N	19	9	.679	37	30	16	3	4	248^2	242	10	112	159	12.8	3.29	120	.254	.339	8	.119	-2	16	18	-2	1.2
1932 *StL-N	12	7	.632	25	22	13	1	0	176^1	169	10	69	108	12.1	3.11	126	.253	.323	12	.214	-2	15	16	-1	1.7
1933 StL-N★	16	13	.552	36	32	16	2	0	244^1	245	11	93	98	12.6	3.50	99	.260	.330	12	.150	-4	-4	-1	-3	-0.5
1934 *StL-N	8	12	.400	32	26	10	2	0	162^1	195	7	66	70	14.4	4.26	99	.294	.358	16	.182	-0	-4	-1	-0	-0.2
1935 StL-N	15	8	.652	40	23	8	2	1	181^1	196	7	57	73	12.6	3.42	120	.275	.329	8	.143	-2	12	14	-1	1.3

YEAR	TM/L	W	L	PCT	G	GS	CG	SH	SV	IP	H	HR	BB	SO	RAT	ERA	ERA+	OAV	OOB	BH	AVG	PB	PR	/A	PD	TPI
1936	StL-N	2	2	.500	9	6	1	0	0	37	58	4	17	16	18.2	6.32	62	.360	.421	5	.556	3	-9	-10	0	-0.6
	Cin-N	5	9	.357	23	19	5	2	0	135	150	3	57	32	13.9	4.33	88	.287	.359	9	.191	1	-5	-8	1	-0.5
	Yr	7	11	.389	32	25	6	2	0	172	208	7	74	48	14.8	4.76	81	.305	.373	14	.250	3	-14	-17	1	-1.1
1937	Cin-N	3	9	.250	21	9	2	0	0	63	90	3	29	18	17.3	6.14	61	.345	.414	2	.095	-1	-16	-17	0	-2.7
1938	Phi-N	1	8	.111	21	10	1	0	0	89	107	4	45	22	15.6	5.46	71	.295	.376	5	.192	-0	-17	-16	-0	-1.4
Total	12	102	94	.520	324	224	90	14	8	1740¹	1838	71	779	856	13.6	4.03	102	.274	.351	90	.162	-9	2	12	-6	-1.1

● **JACK HALLETT** Hallett, Jack Price b: 11/13/14, Toledo, Ohio d: 6/11/82, Toledo, Ohio BR/TR, 6'4", 215 lbs. Deb: 9/13/40

YEAR	TM/L	W	L	PCT	G	GS	CG	SH	SV	IP	H	HR	BB	SO	RAT	ERA	ERA+	OAV	OOB	BH	AVG	PB	PR	/A	PD	TPI
1940	Chi-A	1	1	.500	2	2	1	0	0	14	15	1	6	9	14.1	6.43	69	.273	.355	2	.400	0	-3	-3	0	-0.3
1941	Chi-A	5	5	.500	22	6	3	0	0	74²	96	7	38	25	16.5	6.03	68	.306	.386	4	.154	0	-16	-16	0	-1.8
1942	Pit-N	0	1	.000	3	3	2	0	0	22¹	23	0	8	16	12.5	4.84	70	.274	.337	3	.375	2	-4	-4	0	0.0
1943	Pit-N	1	2	.333	9	4	2	1	0	47²	36	0	11	11	9.1	1.70	205	.212	.264	4	.286	2	9	9	-1	0.7
1946	Pit-N	5	7	.417	35	9	3	1	0	115	107	0	39	64	11.4	3.29	107	.267	.332	6	.231	0	2	3	0	0.4
1948	NY-N	0	0	—	2	0	0	0	0	4	3	0	4	3	15.8	4.50	87	.214	.389	0	.000	-0	-0	-0	-0	0.0
Total	6	12	16	.429	73	24	11	2	0	277²	280	8	106	128	12.7	4.05	92	.270	.340	19	.237	4	-12	-10	-1	-1.0

● **BILL HALLMAN** Hallman, William Wilson b: 3/31/1867, Pittsburgh, Pa. d: 9/11/20, Philadelphia, Pa. BR/TR, 5'8", 160 lbs. Deb: 4/23/1888 M♦

YEAR	TM/L	W	L	PCT	G	GS	CG	SH	SV	IP	H	HR	BB	SO	RAT	ERA	ERA+	OAV	OOB	BH	AVG	PB	PR	/A	PD	TPI
1896	Phi-N	0	0	—	1	0	0	0	0	2	4	0	2	0	27.0	18.00	24	.411	.511	150	.320	0	-3	-3	-0	0.0

● **CHARLIE HALLSTROM** Hallstrom, Charles E. "Swedish Wonder" b: 1/22/1864, Jonkoping, Sweden d: 5/6/49, Chicago, Ill. Deb: 9/23/1885

YEAR	TM/L	W	L	PCT	G	GS	CG	SH	SV	IP	H	HR	BB	SO	RAT	ERA	ERA+	OAV	OOB	BH	AVG	PB	PR	/A	PD	TPI
1885	Pro-N	0	1	.000	1	1	1	0	0	9	18	3	6	2	24.0	11.00	24	.409	.480	0	.000	-1	-8	-8	-0	-0.6

● **DOC HAMANN** Hamann, Elmer Joseph b: 12/21/1900, New Ulm, Minn. d: 1/11/73, Milwaukee, Wis. BR/TR, 6'1", 180 lbs. Deb: 9/21/22

YEAR	TM/L	W	L	PCT	G	GS	CG	SH	SV	IP	H	HR	BB	SO	RAT	ERA	ERA+	OAV	OOB	BH	AVG	PB	PR	/A	PD	TPI
1922	Cle-A	0	0	—	1	0	0	0	0	0	3	0	3	0	—	∞	—	1.000	1.000	0	—	0	-6	-6	0	-0.5

● **ROGER HAMBRIGHT** Hambright, Roger Dee b: 3/26/49, Sunnyside, Wash. BR/TR, 5'10", 180 lbs. Deb: 7/19/71

YEAR	TM/L	W	L	PCT	G	GS	CG	SH	SV	IP	H	HR	BB	SO	RAT	ERA	ERA+	OAV	OOB	BH	AVG	PB	PR	/A	PD	TPI
1971	NY-A	3	1	.750	18	0	0	0	2	26²	22	5	10	14	10.8	4.39	74	.224	.296	1	.500	0	-3	-3	0	-0.5

● **JOHN HAMILL** Hamill, John Alexander Charles b: 12/18/1860, New York, N.Y. d: 12/6/11, Bristol, R.I. BR/TR, 5'8", 158 lbs. Deb: 5/1/1884

YEAR	TM/L	W	L	PCT	G	GS	CG	SH	SV	IP	H	HR	BB	SO	RAT	ERA	ERA+	OAV	OOB	BH	AVG	PB	PR	/A	PD	TPI
1884	Was-a	2	17	.105	19	19	18	1	0	156²	197	8	43	50	14.1	4.48	68	.287	.333	7	.099	-3	-21	-25	-1	-2.6

● **DAVE HAMILTON** Hamilton, David Edward b: 12/13/47, Seattle, Wash. BL/TL, 6', 190 lbs. Deb: 5/29/72

YEAR	TM/L	W	L	PCT	G	GS	CG	SH	SV	IP	H	HR	BB	SO	RAT	ERA	ERA+	OAV	OOB	BH	AVG	PB	PR	/A	PD	TPI
1972	*Oak-A	6	6	.500	25	14	1	0	0	101¹	94	7	31	55	11.2	2.93	97	.249	.307	4	.154	2	1	-1	-0	0.1
1973	Oak-A	6	4	.600	16	11	1	0	0	69²	74	8	24	34	12.8	4.39	81	.274	.336	0	—	0	-4	-7	-1	-0.8
1974	Oak-A	7	4	.636	29	18	1	1	0	117	104	10	48	69	12.1	3.15	105	.241	.324	0	—	0	6	2	-0	0.2
1975	Oak-A	1	2	.333	11	4	0	0	0	35²	42	4	18	20	15.1	4.04	90	.290	.368	0	—	0	-1	-2	-0	-0.1
	Chi-A	6	5	.545	30	1	0	0	6	69²	63	4	29	51	11.9	2.84	136	.246	.323	0	—	0	7	8	0	1.3
	Yr	7	7	.500	41	5	0	0	6	105¹	105	8	47	71	13.0	3.25	117	.261	.339	0	—	0	6	6	0	1.2
1976	Chi-A	6	6	.500	45	1	0	0	10	90¹	81	4	45	62	13.0	3.59	99	.243	.340	0	—	0	-1	-0	-1	-0.1
1977	Chi-A	4	5	.444	55	0	0	0	9	67¹	71	6	33	45	13.9	3.61	113	.270	.351	0	—	0	3	4	0	0.5
1978	StL-N	0	0	—	13	0	0	0	0	14	16	5	6	8	14.1	6.43	55	.296	.367	0	.000	-0	-4	-5	-0	0.0
	Pit-N	0	0	.000	16	0	0	0	1	26¹	23	2	12	15	12.0	3.42	108	.221	.302	0	.000	-1	0	1	-0	0.0
	Yr	0	0	.000	29	0	0	0	1	40¹	39	7	18	23	12.7	4.46	81	.247	.324	0	.000	-1	-4	-4	-0	0.0
1979	Oak-A	4	4	.429	40	7	1	0	5	82²	80	5	43	52	13.5	3.70	109	.261	.353	0	—	0	5	3	1	0.4
1980	Oak-A	0	3	.000	21	0	0	0	0	30	44	4	28	22	22.5	11.40	33	.344	.472	0	—	0	-25	-25	-0	-2.2
Total	9	39	41	.488	301	57	4	1	31	704	692	61	317	434	13.1	3.85	93	.259	.341	4	.121	1	-12	-22	-2	-0.7

● **EARL HAMILTON** Hamilton, Earl Andrew b: 7/19/1891, Gibson City, Ill. d: 11/17/68, Anaheim, Cal. BL/TL, 5'8", 160 lbs. Deb: 4/14/11

YEAR	TM/L	W	L	PCT	G	GS	CG	SH	SV	IP	H	HR	BB	SO	RAT	ERA	ERA+	OAV	OOB	BH	AVG	PB	PR	/A	PD	TPI
1911	StL-A	5	12	.294	32	17	10	1	0	177	191	4	69	55	13.4	3.97	85	.284	.354	6	.107	-1	-12	-12	1	-1.0
1912	StL-A	11	14	.440	41	26	17	1	2	249²	228	2	86	139	11.6	3.24	102	.248	.319	13	.178	-0	2	2	-2	0.1
1913	StL-A	13	12	.520	31	24	19	3	1	217¹	197	3	83	101	12.0	2.57	114	.241	.318	10	.135	-2	9	9	-1	0.7
1914	StL-A	17	18	.486	44	35	20	5	1	302¹	265	6	100	111	11.2	2.50	108	.239	.307	15	.176	4	8	7	-4	0.8
1915	StL-A	9	17	.346	35	27	13	1	0	204	203	4	69	63	12.5	2.87	100	.274	.346	7	.113	-2	2	-0	-2	-0.4
1916	StL-A	0	0	—	1	0	0	0	0	4	4	0	4	0	18.0	9.00	31	.250	.400	0	—	-0	-3	-3	-0	0.0
	Det-A	1	2	.333	5	5	3	0	0	37¹	34	0	22	7	14.5	2.65	108	.254	.375	1	.077	-1	1	1	1	0.1
	StL-A	5	7	.417	22	12	3	0	0	91¹	97	2	26	25	12.3	3.05	90	.284	.339	0	.000	-1	-2	-3	-1	-0.7
	Yr	6	9	.400	28	17	6	0	0	132²	135	2	52	32	12.8	3.12	89	.273	.344	1	.027	-2	-4	-5	-1	-0.6
1917	StL-A	0	0	—	27	8	2	1	0	83	86	1	41	19	14.0	3.14	83	.274	.361	7	.368	3	-4	-5	-1	-0.3
1918	Pit-N	6	0	1.000	6	6	6	1	0	54	47	0	13	20	10.0	0.83	345	.242	.290	2	.286	1	12	12	-0	1.7
1919	Pit-N	8	11	.421	28	19	9	1	1	160¹	167	3	49	39	12.4	3.31	91	.280	.340	7	.135	-2	-7	-5	2	-0.7
1920	Pit-N	10	13	.435	39	23	12	0	3	230²	223	2	69	74	11.5	3.24	99	.258	.314	10	.149	-3	-3	-1	-0	-0.4
1921	Pit-N	13	15	.464	35	30	12	2	1	225	237	5	58	59	12.1	3.36	114	.272	.323	12	.160	-0	11	12	4	1.6
1922	Pit-N	11	7	.611	33	14	9	1	2	160	183	6	40	34	12.6	3.99	102	.296	.339	9	.155	-2	2	1	-1	-0.1
1923	Pit-N	7	9	.438	28	15	5	0	1	141	148	6	42	42	12.2	3.77	106	.271	.324	9	.173	-2	4	4	2	0.5
1924	Phi-N	0	1	.000	3	0	0	0	0	6	9	0	2	2	18.0	10.50	42	.391	.462	0	.000	-0	-4	-4	0	-0.6
Total	14	116	147	.441	410	261	140	16	13	2342²	2319	43	773	790	12.1	3.16	102	.264	.329	112	.153	-9	13	15	-4	1.3

● **JACK HAMILTON** Hamilton, Jack Edwin b: 12/25/38, Burlington, Iowa BR/TR, 6', 200 lbs. Deb: 4/13/62

YEAR	TM/L	W	L	PCT	G	GS	CG	SH	SV	IP	H	HR	BB	SO	RAT	ERA	ERA+	OAV	OOB	BH	AVG	PB	PR	/A	PD	TPI
1962	Phi-N	9	12	.429	41	26	4	1	2	182	185	18	107	101	14.7	5.09	76	.268	.370	3	.056	-4	-23	-25	2	-2.7
1963	Phi-N	2	1	.667	19	1	0	0	1	30	22	3	17	23	11.7	5.40	60	.200	.307	0	.000	-0	-7	-7	1	-0.7
1964	Det-A	1	0	1.000	5	1	0	0	0	15	24	2	8	5	19.8	8.40	44	.364	.440	0	.000	-0	-8	-8	-1	-0.5
1965	Det-A	1	1	.500	4	1	0	0	0	4¹	6	1	4	3	20.8	14.54	24	.316	.435	0	—	0	-5	-5	0	-1.8
1966	NY-N	6	13	.316	57	13	3	1	13	148²	138	13	88	93	14.0	3.93	92	.248	.356	5	.132	-1	-5	-5	1	-0.7
1967	NY-N	2	0	1.000	17	1	0	0	1	31¹	31	2	16	22	11.8	3.73	91	.205	.306	1	.200	1	-1	-1	-0	0.0
	Cal-A	9	6	.600	26	20	6	0	1	119¹	104	6	63	74	12.7	3.24	97	.239	.337	6	.158	-0	-0	-1	-0	-0.2
1968	Cal-A	3	1	.750	21	2	1	0	2	38	34	0	15	18	11.6	3.32	88	.246	.320	1	.143	-0	-1	-2	-0	-0.2
1969	Cle-A	0	0	.000	20	0	0	0	1	30²	37	7	23	13	17.6	4.40	86	.316	.429	0	.000	-0	-3	-2	-0	-0.2
	Chi-A	0	3	.000	8	0	0	0	0	12¹	13	1	7	5	21.9	11.68	31	.333	.411	0	—	-0	-11	-11	-0	-2.1
	Yr	0	3	.000	28	0	0	0	1	43	60	3	30	18	18.8	6.49	58	.345	.441	0	.000	-0	-14	-13	-0	-2.3
Total	8	32	40	.444	218	65	8	2	20	611²	597	48	348	357	14.1	4.53	78	.259	.359	16	.107	-6	-66	-67	4	-9.1

● **JEFF HAMILTON** Hamilton, Jeffrey Robert b: 3/19/64, Flint, Mich. BR/TR, 6'3", 207 lbs. Deb: 6/28/86 ♦

YEAR	TM/L	W	L	PCT	G	GS	CG	SH	SV	IP	H	HR	BB	SO	RAT	ERA	ERA+	OAV	OOB	BH	AVG	PB	PR	/A	PD	TPI
1989	LA-N	0	1	.000	1	0	0	0	0	1	2	0	1	2	16.2	5.40	63	.286	.375	134	.245	0	-0	-0	0	-0.2

● **JOEY HAMILTON** Hamilton, Johns Joseph b: 9/9/70, Statesboro, Ga. BR/TR, 6'4", 220 lbs. Deb: 5/24/94

YEAR	TM/L	W	L	PCT	G	GS	CG	SH	SV	IP	H	HR	BB	SO	RAT	ERA	ERA+	OAV	OOB	BH	AVG	PB	PR	/A	PD	TPI
1994	SD-N	9	6	.600	16	16	1	1	0	108²	98	7	29	61	11.0	2.98	141	.241	.302	0	.000	-4	15	15	0	1.5

● **STEVE HAMILTON** Hamilton, Steve Absher b: 11/30/35, Columbia, Ky. BL/TL, 6'7", 195 lbs. Deb: 4/23/61 C

YEAR	TM/L	W	L	PCT	G	GS	CG	SH	SV	IP	H	HR	BB	SO	RAT	ERA	ERA+	OAV	OOB	BH	AVG	PB	PR	/A	PD	TPI
1961	Cle-A	0	0	—	2	0	0	0	0	3	2	0	3	4	15.0	3.00	131	.200	.385	1	1.000	0	0	0	0	0.1
1962	Was-A	3	8	.273	41	10	1	0	2	107¹	103	10	39	83	12.2	3.77	107	.248	.317	2	.077	-1	2	3	0	0.3
1963	Was-A	0	1	.000	3	0	0	0	0	6	5	0	5	3	31.5	13.50	27	.556	.636	0	—	-0	-2	-2	0	-0.9
	*NY-A	5	1	.833	34	0	0	0	5	62¹	49	3	24	63	10.7	2.60	135	.220	.298	4	.286	1	7	6	1	0.9
	Yr	5	2	.714	37	0	0	0	5	64¹	54	3	26	64	11.3	2.94	120	.232	.312	4	.286	1	5	4	1	0.0
1964	*NY-A	2	2	.778	30	3	1	0	3	60¹	55	6	15	49	10.4	3.28	110	.246	.293	4	.200	1	4	2	2	0.4
1965	NY-A	3	1	.750	46	1	0	0	5	58¹	47	8	16	51	9.7	1.39	245	.214	.267	1	.167	0	13	13	-2	1.0
1966	NY-A	8	3	.727	44	3	1	1	3	90	69	8	22	57	9.4	3.00	111	.218	.276	1	.053	-2	4	3	-1	0.1

YEAR	TM/L	W	L	PCT	G	GS	CG	SH	SV	IP	H	HR	BB	SO	RAT	ERA	ERA+	OAV	OOB	BH	AVG	PB	PR	/A	PD	TPI
1967	NY-A	2	4	.333	44	0	0	0	4	62	57	7	23	55	11.8	3.48	90	.250	.321	1	.111	-0	-2	-2	0	-0.3
1968	NY-A	2	2	.500	40	0	0	0	11	50²	37	0	13	42	9.1	2.13	136	.211	.270	0	.000	0	5	4	0	0.7
1969	NY-A	3	4	.429	38	0	0	0	2	57	39	7	21	39	9.5	3.32	105	.194	.270	0	.000	-1	2	1	-1	-0.1
1970	NY-A	4	3	.571	35	0	0	0	2	45¹	36	3	16	33	10.5	2.78	126	.222	.296	0	.000	-1	5	4	0	0.6
	Chi-A	0	0	—	3	0	0	0	0	3	4	0	1	3	15.0	6.00	65	.333	.385	0	—	0	-1	-1	0	0.0
	Yr	4	3	.571	38	0	0	0	3	48¹	40	3	17	36	10.6	2.98	119	.227	.295	0	.000	-1	4	3	1	0.6
1971	*SF-N	2	2	.500	39	0	0	0	4	44²	29	4	11	38	8.3	3.02	112	.186	.244	0	.000	-0	2	2	-0	0.1
1972	Chi-N	1	0	1.000	22	0	0	0	0	17	24	1	8	13	17.5	4.76	80	.333	.407	0	.000	-0	-2	-2	-0	-0.1
Total	12	40	31	.563	421	17	3	1	42	663	556	51	214	531	10.6	3.05	114	.229	.295	14	.125	-2	36	32	-1	2.8

● LUKE HAMLIN
Hamlin, Luke Daniel "Hot Potato"   b: 7/3/04, Ferris Center, Mich.   d: 2/18/78, Clare, Mich.   BL/TR, 6'2", 168 lbs.   Deb: 9/18/33

YEAR	TM/L	W	L	PCT	G	GS	CG	SH	SV	IP	H	HR	BB	SO	RAT	ERA	ERA+	OAV	OOB	BH	AVG	PB	PR	/A	PD	TPI
1933	Det-A	1	0	1.000	3	3	0	0	0	16²	20	3	10	10	16.2	4.86	89	.294	.385	2	.400	1	-1	-1	-1	0.0
1934	Det-A	2	3	.400	20	5	1	0	1	75¹	87	11	44	30	15.7	5.38	82	.289	.380	6	.231	-0	-7	-8	-0	-0.5
1937	Bro-N	11	13	.458	39	25	11	1	1	185²	183	4	48	93	11.2	3.59	113	.252	.298	11	.186	-1	7	9	-3	0.7
1938	Bro-N	12	15	.444	44	30	10	3	6	237¹	243	14	65	97	11.8	3.68	106	.263	.313	11	.141	-3	3	6	-4	0.0
1939	Bro-N	20	13	.606	40	36	19	2	0	269²	255	27	54	88	10.3	3.64	111	.248	.285	13	.126	-5	8	12	-5	0.4
1940	Bro-N	9	8	.529	33	25	9	2	0	182¹	183	17	34	91	10.8	3.06	131	.256	.292	5	.086	-4	16	19	-4	0.8
1941	Bro-N	8	8	.500	30	20	5	1	1	136	139	14	41	58	12.0	4.24	87	.261	.316	6	.146	-1	-9	-9	-2	-1.2
1942	Pit-N	4	4	.500	23	14	6	1	0	112	128	3	19	44	11.8	3.94	86	.281	.312	9	.243	1	-8	-7	-2	-0.6
1944	Phi-A	6	12	.333	29	23	9	2	0	190	204	13	38	58	11.6	3.74	93	.271	.309	13	.232	-3	-7	-6	-5	-0.7
Total	9	73	76	.490	261	181	70	12	9	1405	1442	106	353	563	11.6	3.77	103	.262	.308	76	.164	-8	2	16	-25	-1.1

● PETE HAMM
Hamm, Peter Whitfield   b: 9/20/47, Buffalo, N.Y.   BR/TR, 6'5", 210 lbs.   Deb: 7/29/70

YEAR	TM/L	W	L	PCT	G	GS	CG	SH	SV	IP	H	HR	BB	SO	RAT	ERA	ERA+	OAV	OOB	BH	AVG	PB	PR	/A	PD	TPI
1970	Min-A	0	2	.000	10	0	0	0	0	16¹	17	3	7	13	13.2	5.51	68	.262	.333	0	.000	-0	-3	-3	-1	-0.4
1971	Min-A	2	4	.333	13	8	1	0	0	44	55	7	18	16	15.1	6.75	53	.309	.376	3	.273	1	-16	-16	0	-1.8
Total	2	2	6	.250	23	8	1	0	0	60¹	72	10	25	19	14.6	6.41	56	.296	.364	3	.250	1	-19	-19	-0	-2.2

● ATLEE HAMMAKER
Hammaker, Charlton Atlee   b: 1/24/58, Carmel, Cal.   BB/TL, 6'3", 200 lbs.   Deb: 8/13/81

YEAR	TM/L	W	L	PCT	G	GS	CG	SH	SV	IP	H	HR	BB	SO	RAT	ERA	ERA+	OAV	OOB	BH	AVG	PB	PR	/A	PD	TPI
1981	KC-A	1	3	.250	10	6	0	0	0	39	44	2	12	11	12.9	5.54	65	.286	.337	0	—	0	-8	-8	-1	-0.8
1982	SF-N	12	8	.600	29	27	4	1	0	175	189	16	28	102	11.3	4.11	87	.278	.309	4	.068	-4	-10	-10	1	-1.4
1983	SF-N★	10	9	.526	23	23	8	3	0	172¹	147	9	32	127	9.5	2.25	157	.228	.267	6	.102	-1	26	25	1	2.7
1984	SF-N	2	0	1.000	6	6	0	0	0	33	32	3	9	24	11.2	2.18	161	.256	.306	2	.182	1	5	5	0	0.4
1985	SF-N	5	12	.294	29	29	1	1	0	170²	161	14	47	100	11.0	3.74	92	.247	.298	4	.085	-3	-3	-6	1	-0.7
1987	*SF-N	10	10	.500	31	27	2	0	0	168¹	159	26	57	107	11.7	3.58	107	.248	.313	7	.123	-1	9	5	-1	0.3
1988	SF-N	9	9	.500	43	17	3	1	5	144²	136	11	41	65	11.2	3.73	87	.248	.304	4	.121	-0	-5	-4	-0	-0.8
1989	*SF-N	6	6	.500	28	9	0	0	0	76²	78	5	23	30	12.0	3.76	90	.271	.327	7	.368	1	-2	-3	-1	-0.3
1990	SF-N	4	5	.444	25	6	0	0	0	67¹	69	7	21	28	12.0	4.28	85	.273	.328	1	.059	-1	-4	-5	-1	-0.7
	SD-N	0	4	.000	9	1	0	0	0	19¹	16	1	6	16	10.2	4.66	82	.213	.272	1	.500	-0	-2	-2	-0	-0.3
	Yr	4	9	.308	34	7	0	0	0	86²	85	8	27	44	11.6	4.36	84	.256	.312	2	.105	-0	-5	-7	-1	-1.0
1991	SD-N	0	1	.000	1	1	0	0	0	4²	8	0	3	1	21.2	5.79	66	.364	.440	0	.000	-0	-1	-1	0	-0.2
1994	Chi-A	0	0	—	2	0	0	0	0	1¹	1	0	0	1	6.8	0.00	—	.200	.200	0	—	0	1	1	0	0.0
Total	11	59	67	.468	236	152	18	6	5	1072¹	1040	92	279	612	11.2	3.61	98	.254	.304	36	.118	-7	7	-8	1	-1.8

● CHRIS HAMMOND
Hammond, Christopher Andrew   b: 1/21/66, Atlanta, Ga.   BL/TL, 6'1", 190 lbs.   Deb: 7/16/90   F

YEAR	TM/L	W	L	PCT	G	GS	CG	SH	SV	IP	H	HR	BB	SO	RAT	ERA	ERA+	OAV	OOB	BH	AVG	PB	PR	/A	PD	TPI
1990	Cin-N	0	2	.000	3	3	0	0	0	11¹	13	2	12	4	19.9	6.35	62	.302	.455	0	.000	-0	-3	-3	0	-0.5
1991	Cin-N	7	7	.500	20	18	0	0	0	99²	92	4	48	50	12.8	4.06	94	.250	.340	12	.353	5	-4	-3	0	0.1
1992	Cin-N	7	10	.412	28	26	0	0	0	147¹	149	13	55	79	12.6	4.21	85	.266	.334	6	.136	2	-12	-10	-0	-0.9
1993	Fla-N	11	12	.478	32	32	1	0	0	191	207	18	66	108	12.9	4.66	93	.277	.337	12	.190	4	-13	-7	-3	-0.3
1994	Fla-N	4	4	.500	13	13	1	1	0	73¹	74	5	23	40	12.6	3.07	147	.281	.338	3	.136	-0	9	12	-2	1.0
Total	5	29	35	.453	96	92	2	1	0	522²	540	42	204	281	12.9	4.24	95	.270	.340	33	.199	11	-23	-12	-1	-0.6

● GRANNY HAMNER
Hamner, Granville Wilbur   b: 4/26/27, Richmond, Va.   d: 9/12/93, Philadelphia, Pa.   BR/TR, 5'10", 163 lbs.   Deb: 9/14/44   F♦

YEAR	TM/L	W	L	PCT	G	GS	CG	SH	SV	IP	H	HR	BB	SO	RAT	ERA	ERA+	OAV	OOB	BH	AVG	PB	PR	/A	PD	TPI
1956	Phi-N	0	1	.000	3	1	0	0	0	8¹	10	0	2	4	13.0	4.32	86	.294	.333	90	.224	1	-1	-1	-0	0.0
1957	Phi-N	0	0	—	1	0	0	0	0	1	1	0	0	1	9.0	0.00	—	.250	.250	114	.227	0	0	0	0	0.0
1962	KC-A	0	1	.000	3	0	0	0	0	4	10	0	6	3	36.0	9.00	47	.476	.593	0	—	0	-2	-2	-0	-0.4
Total	3	0	2	.000	7	1	0	0	0	13¹	21	0	8	8	19.6	5.40	72	.356	.433	1529	.262	1	-3	-3	-0	-0.4

● RALPH HAMNER
Hamner, Ralph Conant "Bruz"   b: 9/12/16, Gibsland, La.   BR/TR, 6'3", 165 lbs.   Deb: 4/28/46

YEAR	TM/L	W	L	PCT	G	GS	CG	SH	SV	IP	H	HR	BB	SO	RAT	ERA	ERA+	OAV	OOB	BH	AVG	PB	PR	/A	PD	TPI
1946	Chi-A	2	7	.222	25	7	1	0	1	71¹	80	2	39	29	15.6	4.42	77	.276	.371	3	.167	1	-7	-8	-1	-1.0
1947	Chi-N	1	2	.333	3	3	2	0	0	25	24	1	0	16	14	14.4	2.52	157	.267	.377	1	.125	-0	4	4	-1	0.4
1948	Chi-N	5	9	.357	27	17	5	0	0	111¹	110	12	69	53	14.9	4.69	83	.259	.369	6	.182	1	-9	-10	2	-0.8
1949	Chi-N	0	2	.000	6	1	0	0	0	12¹	22	1	8	3	22.6	8.76	46	.407	.492	0	.000	-0	-6	-6	1	-0.8
Total	4	8	20	.286	61	28	8	0	1	220	236	15	132	99	15.5	4.58	82	.275	.378	10	.164	0	-18	-20	1	-2.2

● MIKE HAMPTON
Hampton, Michael William   b: 9/9/72, Brooksville, Fla.   BR/TL, 5'10", 180 lbs.   Deb: 4/17/93

YEAR	TM/L	W	L	PCT	G	GS	CG	SH	SV	IP	H	HR	BB	SO	RAT	ERA	ERA+	OAV	OOB	BH	AVG	PB	PR	/A	PD	TPI
1993	Sea-A	1	3	.250	13	3	0	0	1	17	28	3	17	8	23.8	9.53	46	.368	.484	0	.000	-0	-10	-10	-0	-2.0
1994	Hou-N	2	1	.667	44	0	0	0	0	41¹	46	4	16	24	13.9	3.70	110	.282	.354	0	.000	-0	2	2	2	0.2
Total	2	3	4	.429	57	3	0	0	1	58¹	74	7	33	32	16.8	5.40	77	.310	.398	0	.000	-0	-7	-8	1	-1.8

● GARRY HANCOCK
Hancock, Ronald Garry   b: 1/23/54, Tampa, Fla.   BL/TL, 6', 175 lbs.   Deb: 7/16/78   ♦

YEAR	TM/L	W	L	PCT	G	GS	CG	SH	SV	IP	H	HR	BB	SO	RAT	ERA	ERA+	OAV	OOB	BH	AVG	PB	PR	/A	PD	TPI
1984	Oak-A	0	0	—	1	0	0	0	0	1¹	0	0	0	0	0.0	0.00	—	.000	.000	13	.217	0	1	1	0	0.0

● RICH HAND
Hand, Richard Allen   b: 7/10/48, Bellevue, Wash.   BR/TR, 6'1", 195 lbs.   Deb: 4/9/70

YEAR	TM/L	W	L	PCT	G	GS	CG	SH	SV	IP	H	HR	BB	SO	RAT	ERA	ERA+	OAV	OOB	BH	AVG	PB	PR	/A	PD	TPI
1970	Cle-A	6	13	.316	35	25	3	1	3	159²	132	27	69	110	11.6	3.83	103	.228	.314	6	.146	-1	-2	2	0	0.1
1971	Cle-A	2	6	.250	15	12	0	0	0	60²	74	6	38	20	17.2	5.79	66	.311	.414	2	.125	-0	-16	-13	-1	-1.7
1972	Tex-A	10	14	.417	30	28	2	1	0	170²	139	12	103	109	12.9	3.32	91	.226	.340	8	.154	1	-5	-6	-0	-0.7
1973	Tex-A	2	3	.400	8	7	1	0	0	41²	46	2	19	14	15.1	5.40	69	.290	.368	0	—	0	-7	-8	-1	-0.8
	Cal-A	4	3	.571	16	6	0	0	0	54²	58	5	21	19	13.2	3.62	98	.274	.342	0	—	0	1	0	1	0.2
	Yr	6	6	.500	24	13	1	0	0	96¹	107	7	40	33	13.8	4.39	82	.277	.347	0	—	0	-6	-8	0	-0.6
Total	4	24	39	.381	104	78	6	2	3	487¹	452	52	250	278	13.2	4.01	88	.249	.345	16	.147	-1	-29	-25	-1	-2.9

● JIM HANDIBOE
Handiboe, James Edward "Nick"   b: 7/17/1866, Columbus, Ohio   d: 11/8/42, Columbus, Ohio   BR/TR, 5'11", 160 lbs.   Deb: 5/28/1886

YEAR	TM/L	W	L	PCT	G	GS	CG	SH	SV	IP	H	HR	BB	SO	RAT	ERA	ERA+	OAV	OOB	BH	AVG	PB	PR	/A	PD	TPI
1886	Pit-a	7	7	.500	14	14	12	1	0	114	82	1	33	83	10.0	3.32	102	.195	.273	5	.114	-2	2	1	-0	-0.2

● VERN HANDRAHAN
Handrahan, James Vernon   b: 11/27/38, Charlottetown, P.E.I., Canada   BL/TR, 6'2", 185 lbs.   Deb: 4/14/64

YEAR	TM/L	W	L	PCT	G	GS	CG	SH	SV	IP	H	HR	BB	SO	RAT	ERA	ERA+	OAV	OOB	BH	AVG	PB	PR	/A	PD	TPI
1964	KC-A	0	1	.000	18	1	0	0	0	35²	33	9	25	18	15.1	6.06	63	.252	.380	2	.222	0	-10	-9	0	-0.2
1966	KC-A	0	1	.000	16	1	0	0	0	25¹	20	5	15	18	12.8	4.26	80	.227	.346	0	.000	-0	-2	-2	-0	-0.1
Total	2	0	2	.000	34	2	0	0	1	61	53	14	40	36	14.2	5.31	69	.242	.366	2	.167	-0	-12	-11	0	-0.3

● BILL HANDS
Hands, William Alfred   b: 5/6/40, Hackensack, N.J.   BR/TR, 6'2", 185 lbs.   Deb: 6/3/65

YEAR	TM/L	W	L	PCT	G	GS	CG	SH	SV	IP	H	HR	BB	SO	RAT	ERA	ERA+	OAV	OOB	BH	AVG	PB	PR	/A	PD	TPI
1965	SF-N	0	2	.000	4	2	0	0	0	6	13	0	6	5	28.5	16.50	22	.433	.528	0	.000	-0	-9	-9	0	-2.0
1966	Chi-N	8	13	.381	41	26	0	0	2	159	168	17	59	93	13.1	4.58	80	.272	.340	2	.041	-3	-17	-16	1	-2.2
1967	Chi-N	7	8	.467	49	11	3	1	6	150	134	9	48	84	11.0	2.46	144	.239	.301	4	.105	-1	15	18	-0	1.9
1968	Chi-N	16	10	.615	38	34	11	4	0	258²	221	26	36	148	9.2	2.89	109	.231	.264	5	.061	-5	3	8	-0	0.2
1969	Chi-N	20	14	.588	41	41	18	3	0	300	268	21	73	181	10.4	2.49	162	.237	.287	9	.092	-5	37	51	1	5.5
1970	Chi-N	18	15	.545	39	38	12	2	1	265	278	20	76	170	12.2	3.70	122	.269	.322	10	.133	1	10	24	1	3.0

YEAR	TM/L	W	L	PCT	G	GS	CG	SH	SV	IP	H	HR	BB	SO	RAT	ERA	ERA+	OAV	OOB	BH	AVG	PB	PR	/A	PD	TPI
1971	Chi-N	12	18	.400	36	35	14	1	0	242¹	248	27	50	128	11.1	3.42	115	.260	.298	6	.083	-3	1	14	-0	1.3
1972	Chi-N	11	8	.579	32	28	6	3	0	189	168	12	47	96	10.3	3.00	127	.237	.286	1	.018	-4	10	17	-2	1.0
1973	Min-A	7	10	.412	39	15	3	1	2	142	138	14	41	78	11.5	3.49	114	.252	.307	0	—	0	5	7	-1	0.7
1974	Min-A	4	5	.444	35	10	0	0	3	115¹	130	9	25	74	12.4	4.45	84	.284	.327	0	—	0	-11	-9	-1	-0.8
	Tex-A	2	0	1.000	2	2	1	1	0	14	11	0	3	4	9.0	1.93	185	.208	.250	0	—	0	3	3	0	0.4
	Yr	6	5	.545	37	12	1	1	3	129¹	141	9	28	78	11.8	4.18	89	.274	.311	0	—	0	-8	-6	-1	-0.4
1975	Tex-A	6	7	.462	18	18	4	1	0	109²	118	12	28	67	12.2	4.02	93	.271	.319	0	—	0	-3	-3	-0	-0.3
Total	11	111	110	.502	374	260	72	17	14	1951	1895	167	492	1128	11.2	3.35	114	.253	.302	37	.078	-20	44	104	-0	8.7

● CHRIS HANEY
Haney, Christopher Deane b: 11/16/68, Baltimore, Md. BL/TL, 6'3", 185 lbs. Deb: 6/21/91 F

YEAR	TM/L	W	L	PCT	G	GS	CG	SH	SV	IP	H	HR	BB	SO	RAT	ERA	ERA+	OAV	OOB	BH	AVG	PB	PR	/A	PD	TPI
1991	Mon-N	3	7	.300	16	16	0	0	0	84²	94	6	43	51	14.7	4.04	90	.280	.363	2	.074	-2	-3	-4	1	-0.5
1992	Mon-N	2	3	.400	9	6	1	1	0	38	40	6	10	27	12.8	5.45	64	.270	.333	2	.222	0	-8	-8	-0	-1.0
	KC-A	2	3	.400	7	7	1	1	0	42	35	5	16	27	10.9	3.86	105	.226	.298	0	—	0	1	1	-1	0.2
1993	KC-A	9	9	.500	23	23	1	1	0	124	141	13	53	65	14.3	6.02	76	.286	.359	0	—	0	-23	-20	-0	-2.4
1994	KC-A	2	2	.500	6	6	0	0	0	28¹	36	2	11	18	15.2	7.31	71	.333	.400	0	—	0	-8	-7	0	-1.0
Total	4	18	24	.429	61	58	3	3	0	317	346	32	133	188	13.9	5.25	79	.279	.353	4	.111	-1	-43	-39	0	-5.1

● DON HANKINS
Hankins, Donald Wayne b: 2/9/02, Pendleton, Ind. d: 5/16/63, Winston-Salem, N.C BR/TR, 6'3", 183 lbs. Deb: 4/23/27

YEAR	TM/L	W	L	PCT	G	GS	CG	SH	SV	IP	H	HR	BB	SO	RAT	ERA	ERA+	OAV	OOB	BH	AVG	PB	PR	/A	PD	TPI
1927	Det-A	2	1	.667	20	1	0	0	2	42²	67	1	13	10	16.9	6.33	67	.383	.426	1	.143	-1	-10	-10	-0	-0.7

● FRANK HANKINSON
Hankinson, Frank Edward b: 4/29/1856, New York, N.Y. d: 4/5/11, Palisades Park, N.J BR/TR, 5'11", 168 lbs. Deb: 5/1/1878 ◆

YEAR	TM/L	W	L	PCT	G	GS	CG	SH	SV	IP	H	HR	BB	SO	RAT	ERA	ERA+	OAV	OOB	BH	AVG	PB	PR	/A	PD	TPI
1878	Chi-N	0	1	.000	1	1	1	0	0	9	11	0	0	4	11.0	6.00	40	.282	.282	64	.267	-0	-4	-4	-0	-0.3
1879	Chi-N	15	10	.600	26	25	25	2	0	230²	248	0	27	69	10.7	2.50	103	.255	.275	31	.181	-4	0	2	4	0.2
1880	Cle-N	1	1	.500	4	2	2	0	1	25	20	0	3	8	8.3	1.08	218	.215	.240	55	.209	-0	4	4	1	0.4
1885	NY-a	0	0	—	1	0	0	0	0	2	2	1	1	0	13.5	4.50	66	.500	.600	81	.224	0	-0	-0	-0	0.0
Total	4	16	12	.571	32	28	28	2	1	266²	281	1	31	81	10.5	2.50	102	.253	.274	747	.228	-4	-0	1	5	0.3

● JIM HANLEY
Hanley, James Patrick b: 10/13/1885, Providence, R.I. d: 5/1/61, Elmhurst, N.Y. BR/TL, 5'11", 165 lbs. Deb: 7/3/13

YEAR	TM/L	W	L	PCT	G	GS	CG	SH	SV	IP	H	HR	BB	SO	RAT	ERA	ERA+	OAV	OOB	BH	AVG	PB	PR	/A	PD	TPI
1913	NY-A	0	0	—	1	0	0	0	0	4	4	0	4	3	20.3	6.75	42	.313	.450	0	.000	-0	-2	-2	0	0.0

● PRESTON HANNA
Hanna, Preston Lee b: 9/10/54, Pensacola, Fla. BR/TR, 6'1", 195 lbs. Deb: 9/13/75

YEAR	TM/L	W	L	PCT	G	GS	CG	SH	SV	IP	H	HR	BB	SO	RAT	ERA	ERA+	OAV	OOB	BH	AVG	PB	PR	/A	PD	TPI
1975	Atl-N	0	0	—	4	0	0	0	0	5²	7	0	5	2	22.2	1.59	238	.304	.467	0	—	0	1	1	-0	0.0
1976	Atl-N	0	0	—	5	0	0	0	0	8	11	0	4	3	16.9	4.50	84	.333	.405	0	.000	-0	-1	-1	-0	0.0
1977	Atl-N	2	6	.250	17	9	1	0	0	60	69	6	34	37	15.8	4.95	90	.285	.378	1	.071	-0	-7	-3	1	-0.3
1978	Atl-N	7	13	.350	29	28	0	0	0	140¹	132	10	93	90	14.6	5.13	79	.251	.367	9	.184	-1	-24	-17	-0	-2.1
1979	Atl-N	1	1	.500	6	4	0	0	0	24¹	27	1	15	15	15.5	2.96	137	.284	.382	0	.000	-1	2	3	1	0.3
1980	Atl-N	2	0	1.000	32	2	0	0	0	79¹	63	3	44	35	12.5	3.18	118	.224	.335	2	.143	0	4	5	-1	0.3
1981	Atl-N	2	1	.667	20	1	0	0	0	35¹	45	2	23	22	17.3	6.37	56	.341	.439	1	.250	0	-11	-11	2	-0.7
1982	Atl-N	3	0	1.000	20	1	0	0	0	36	36	2	28	17	16.0	3.75	99	.277	.405	2	.400	1	-1	-0	-1	-0.0
	Oak-A	0	4	.000	23	2	1	0	0	48¹	54	3	33	32	16.4	5.59	70	.287	.396	0	—	0	-8	-9	-0	-0.7
Total	8	17	25	.405	156	47	2	0	0	437¹	444	28	279	253	15.1	4.61	86	.269	.378	15	.161	1	-45	-31	1	-3.5

● GERRY HANNAHS
Hannahs, Gerald Ellis b: 3/6/53, Binghamton, N.Y. BL/TL, 6'3", 210 lbs. Deb: 9/8/76

YEAR	TM/L	W	L	PCT	G	GS	CG	SH	SV	IP	H	HR	BB	SO	RAT	ERA	ERA+	OAV	OOB	BH	AVG	PB	PR	/A	PD	TPI
1976	Mon-N	2	0	1.000	3	3	0	0	0	16	20	2	12	10	18.0	6.75	55	.323	.432	3	.375	1	-6	-5	-0	-0.5
1977	Mon-N	1	5	.167	8	7	0	0	0	37	43	7	17	21	14.6	4.86	78	.291	.364	0	.000	-0	-4	-4	-0	-0.7
1978	LA-N	0	0	—	1	0	0	0	0	2	3	0	1	0	13.5	9.00	39	.333	.333	0	—	0	-1	-1	0	-0.1
1979	LA-N	0	2	.000	4	2	0	0	1	16	10	2	13	6	12.9	3.38	108	.175	.329	1	.250	0	1	0	0	0.1
Total	4	3	7	.300	16	12	0	0	1	71	76	11	42	42	15.0	5.07	74	.275	.371	4	.211	1	-10	-10	-1	-1.1

● JIM HANNAN
Hannan, James John b: 1/7/40, Jersey City, N.J. BR/TR, 6'3", 205 lbs. Deb: 4/17/62

YEAR	TM/L	W	L	PCT	G	GS	CG	SH	SV	IP	H	HR	BB	SO	RAT	ERA	ERA+	OAV	OOB	BH	AVG	PB	PR	/A	PD	TPI
1962	Was-A	2	4	.333	42	3	0	0	4	68	56	6	49	39	13.9	3.31	122	.230	.360	1	.091	-1	5	5	0	0.5
1963	Was-A	2	2	.500	13	2	0	0	0	27²	23	2	17	14	13.0	4.88	76	.228	.339	0	.000	-0	-4	-4	0	-0.5
1964	Was-A	4	7	.364	49	7	0	0	3	106	108	13	45	67	13.0	4.16	89	.266	.339	3	.150	-1	-6	-5	-1	-0.7
1965	Was-A	1	1	.500	4	1	1	1	0	14²	18	0	6	5	15.3	4.91	71	.340	.417	0	.000	-0	-2	-2	-1	-0.4
1966	Was-A	3	9	.250	30	18	2	0	0	114	125	9	59	68	14.8	4.26	81	.288	.377	2	.067	-2	-10	-10	-0	-1.2
1967	Was-A	1	1	.500	8	2	0	0	0	21²	28	3	7	14	15.0	5.40	59	.315	.371	0	.000	-0	-5	-5	-0	-0.5
1968	Was-A	10	6	.625	25	22	4	1	0	140¹	147	6	50	75	12.9	3.01	97	.272	.338	3	.064	-2	-1	-2	-0	-0.5
1969	Was-A	7	6	.538	35	28	1	1	0	158¹	138	17	91	72	13.1	3.64	95	.238	.343	6	.115	-2	-0	-3	-1	-0.5
1970	Was-A	9	11	.450	42	17	1	1	0	128	119	17	54	61	12.2	4.01	89	.250	.328	4	.129	-0	-4	-6	1	-0.9
1971	Det-A	1	0	1.000	7	0	0	0	0	11	7	1	7	6	12.3	3.27	110	.189	.333	0	.000	-0	0	0	1	0.1
	Mil-A	1	1	.500	21	1	0	0	0	32¹	38	7	21	17	16.7	5.01	69	.295	.397	0	.000	-0	-6	-6	-0	-0.4
	Yr	2	1	.667	28	1	0	0	0	43¹	45	8	28	23	15.4	4.57	77	.269	.378	0	.000	-1	-5	-5	0	-0.3
Total	10	41	48	.461	276	101	9	4	7	822	807	79	406	438	13.4	3.88	89	.261	.350	19	.091	-9	-34	-38	-1	-5.0

● LOY HANNING
Hanning, Loy Vernon b: 10/18/17, Bunker, Mo. d: 6/24/86, Anaconda, Mo. BR/TR, 6'2", 175 lbs. Deb: 9/20/39

YEAR	TM/L	W	L	PCT	G	GS	CG	SH	SV	IP	H	HR	BB	SO	RAT	ERA	ERA+	OAV	OOB	BH	AVG	PB	PR	/A	PD	TPI
1939	StL-A	0	1	.000	4	1	0	0	0	10	6	1	4	8	9.0	3.60	135	.158	.238	0	.000	-0	1	1	-0	0.1
1942	StL-A	1	1	.500	11	0	0	0	0	17¹	26	2	12	9	20.3	7.79	48	.356	.453	1	.250	-0	-8	-8	1	-0.7
Total	2	1	2	.333	15	1	0	0	0	27¹	32	3	16	17	16.1	6.26	66	.288	.383	1	.200	-0	-7	-6	1	-0.6

● ANDY HANSEN
Hansen, Andrew Viggo "Swede" b: 11/24/24, Lake Worth, Fla. BR/TR, 6'3", 190 lbs. Deb: 6/30/44

YEAR	TM/L	W	L	PCT	G	GS	CG	SH	SV	IP	H	HR	BB	SO	RAT	ERA	ERA+	OAV	OOB	BH	AVG	PB	PR	/A	PD	TPI
1944	NY-N	3	3	.500	23	4	0	0	1	52²	63	3	32	15	16.7	6.49	56	.301	.402	2	.167	0	-17	-17	1	-1.6
1945	NY-N	4	3	.571	23	13	4	0	3	92²	98	7	28	37	12.4	4.66	84	.273	.329	2	.000	-3	-9	-8	2	-0.7
1947	NY-N	1	5	.167	27	9	1	0	0	82¹	78	8	38	18	12.7	4.37	93	.248	.330	4	.190	-0	-3	-3	1	-0.1
1948	NY-N	5	3	.625	36	9	3	0	1	100	96	4	36	27	11.9	2.97	133	.255	.320	1	.050	-0	11	11	-1	0.7
1949	NY-N	2	6	.250	33	2	0	0	1	66¹	58	7	28	26	11.7	4.61	86	.234	.312	0	.000	-0	-4	-5	-0	-0.5
1950	NY-N	0	1	.000	31	1	0	0	3	57	64	8	26	19	14.4	5.53	74	.279	.355	0	.000	-0	-9	-9	-0	-0.4
1951	Phi-N	3	1	.750	24	1	0	0	0	39	34	4	11	11	9.7	2.54	152	.228	.268	1	.333	1	6	6	1	0.7
1952	Phi-N	5	6	.455	43	2	0	0	4	77¹	76	6	27	18	12.3	3.26	112	.259	.328	2	.182	1	3	1	1	0.1
1953	Phi-N	0	2	.000	30	1	0	0	3	51¹	60	6	24	17	14.9	4.03	104	.296	.373	2	.286	0	1	1	1	0.1
Total	9	23	30	.434	270	39	8	0	16	618²	627	53	246	188	12.9	4.22	93	.263	.335	12	.102	-3	-19	-20	5	-1.1

● SNIPE HANSEN
Hansen, Roy Emil Frederick b: 2/21/07, Chicago, Ill. d: 9/11/78, Chicago, Ill. BB/TL, 6'3", 195 lbs. Deb: 7/5/30

YEAR	TM/L	W	L	PCT	G	GS	CG	SH	SV	IP	H	HR	BB	SO	RAT	ERA	ERA+	OAV	OOB	BH	AVG	PB	PR	/A	PD	TPI
1930	Phi-N	0	7	.000	22	6	1	0	0	84¹	123	8	38	25	17.4	6.72	81	.364	.431	3	.111	-2	-16	-12	-1	-1.0
1932	Phi-N	10	10	.500	39	23	5	0	2	191	215	13	51	56	12.8	3.72	118	.278	.328	8	.127	-4	3	15	-2	0.9
1933	Phi-N	6	14	.300	32	22	8	0	0	168¹	199	12	30	47	12.5	4.44	86	.294	.328	9	.155	-3	-21	-12	-1	-1.7
1934	Phi-N	6	12	.333	50	16	5	2	3	151	194	15	61	40	15.4	5.42	87	.307	.371	10	.233	-0	-23	-12	-1	-1.1
1935	Phi-N	0	1	.000	2	1	0	0	0	4¹	8	0	5	0	27.0	12.46	36	.421	.542	0	.000	-0	-4	-4	0	-0.7
	StL-A	0	1	.000	10	3	0	0	1	26²	44	2	9	8	18.2	8.78	55	.364	.412	1	.143	-1	-13	-12	-1	-0.5
Total	5	22	45	.328	155	71	19	2	6	625²	783	50	194	176	14.3	5.01	90	.306	.358	31	.155	-10	-73	-36	-3	-4.1

● ROY HANSEN
Hansen, Roy Inglof "Ing" b: 3/6/1898, Beloit, Wis. d: 2/9/77, Beloit, Wis. BR/TR, 6', 165 lbs. Deb: 5/28/18

YEAR	TM/L	W	L	PCT	G	GS	CG	SH	SV	IP	H	HR	BB	SO	RAT	ERA	ERA+	OAV	OOB	BH	AVG	PB	PR	/A	PD	TPI
1918	Was-A	1	0	1.000	8	0	0	0	0	9	10	0	3	2	14.0	3.00	91	.278	.350	0	—	0	-0	-0	0	0.0

● F. C. HANSFORD
Hansford, F. C. TL, 6', 180 lbs. Deb: 6/9/1898

YEAR	TM/L	W	L	PCT	G	GS	CG	SH	SV	IP	H	HR	BB	SO	RAT	ERA	ERA+	OAV	OOB	BH	AVG	PB	PR	/A	PD	TPI
1898	Bro-N	0	0	—	1	0	0	0	0	7	10	0	5	0	19.3	3.86	93	.332	.428	0	.000	-1	-0	-0	-0	-0.1

YEAR TM/L	W	L	PCT	G	GS	CG	SH	SV	IP	H	HR	BB	SO	RAT	ERA	ERA+	OAV	OOB	BH	AVG	PB	PR	/A	PD	TPI

● **DON HANSKI** Hanski, Donald Thomas (b: Donald Thomas Hanyzewski) b: 2/27/16, LaPorte, Ind. d: 9/2/57, Worth, Ill. BL/TL, 5'11", 180 lbs. Deb: 5/6/43 ◆

1943 Chi-A	0	0	—	1	0	0	0	0	1	1	0	1	0	18.0	0.00	—	.333	.500	5	.238	-0	0	0	-0	0.0
1944 Chi-A	0	0	—	2	0	0	0	0	3	5	0	2	0	21.0	12.00	29	.357	.438	0	.000	-0	-3	-3	-0	0.0
Total 2	0	0	—	3	0	0	0	0	4	6	0	3	0	20.3	9.00	38	.353	.450	5	.227	-0	-2	-2	-0	0.0

● **OLLIE HANSON** Hanson, Earl Sylvester b: 1/19/1896, Holbrook, Mass. d: 8/19/51, Clifton, N.J. BR/TR, 5'11", 178 lbs. Deb: 4/27/21

| 1921 Chi-N | 0 | 2 | .000 | 2 | 2 | 1 | 0 | 0 | 9 | 9 | 0 | 6 | 2 | 16.0 | 7.00 | 55 | .265 | .390 | 0 | .000 | -0 | -3 | -3 | 0 | -0.6 |

● **ERIK HANSON** Hanson, Erik Brian b: 5/18/65, Kinnelon, N.J. BR/TR, 6'6", 210 lbs. Deb: 9/5/88

1988 Sea-A	2	3	.400	6	6	0	0	0	41²	35	4	12	36	10.4	3.24	128	.230	.291	0	—	0	3	4	-0	0.4
1989 Sea-A	9	5	.643	17	17	1	0	0	113¹	103	7	32	75	11.1	3.18	127	.243	.304	0	—	0	9	11	0	1.1
1990 Sea-A	18	9	.667	33	33	5	1	0	236	205	15	68	211	10.5	3.24	122	.232	.289	0	—	0	17	19	-0	2.0
1991 Sea-A	8	8	.500	27	27	2	1	0	174²	182	16	56	143	12.4	3.81	108	.269	.327	0	—	0	5	6	-1	0.4
1992 Sea-A	8	17	.320	31	30	6	1	0	186²	209	14	57	112	13.2	4.82	82	.287	.345	0	—	0	-18	-18	0	-2.1
1993 Sea-A	11	12	.478	31	30	7	0	0	215	215	17	60	163	11.7	3.47	127	.263	.317	0	—	0	20	22	1	2.2
1994 Cin-N	5	5	.500	22	21	0	0	0	122²	137	10	23	101	12.0	4.11	101	.283	.320	6	.154	-1	1	1	-0	0.0
Total 7	61	59	.508	167	164	21	3	0	1090	1086	83	308	841	11.7	3.74	110	.261	.315	6	.154	-1	38	45	-0	4.0

● **ED HANYZEWSKI** Hanyzewski, Edward Michael b: 9/18/20, Union Mills, Ind. d: 10/8/91, Fargo, N.D. BR/TR, 6'1", 200 lbs. Deb: 5/12/42

1942 Chi-N	1	1	.500	6	1	0	0	0	19	17	2	8	6	11.8	3.79	84	.254	.333	1	.200	-0	-1	-1	0	-0.1
1943 Chi-N	8	7	.533	33	16	3	0	0	130	120	8	45	55	11.6	2.56	130	.243	.309	1	.049	-4	12	11	2	1.0
1944 Chi-N	2	5	.286	14	7	3	0	0	58¹	61	6	20	19	12.7	4.47	79	.261	.322	1	.059	-1	-6	-6	3	-0.4
1945 Chi-N	0	0	—	2	1	0	0	0	4²	7	1	1	0	15.4	5.79	63	.350	.381	0	.000	-0	-1	-1	0	-0.1
1946 Chi-N	1	0	1.000	3	0	0	0	0	6	8	0	5	1	21.0	4.50	74	.348	.483	0	.000	-0	-1	-1	0	-0.1
Total 5	12	13	.480	58	25	6	0	0	218	213	11	79	81	12.2	3.30	102	.254	.321	4	.062	-5	4	2	5	0.4

● **MEL HARDER** Harder, Melvin Leroy "Chief" b: 10/15/09, Beemer, Neb. BR/TR, 6'1", 195 lbs. Deb: 4/24/28 MC

1928 Cle-A	0	2	.000	23	1	0	0	1	49	64	4	32	15	17.6	6.61	63	.335	.430	0	.000	-1	-14	-13	-1	-0.7
1929 Cle-A	1	0	1.000	11	0	0	0	0	17²	24	2	5	4	16.3	5.60	79	.333	.400	0	.000	-0	-3	-2	-0	-0.2
1930 Cle-A	11	10	.524	36	19	7	0	2	175¹	205	9	68	44	14.2	4.21	115	.295	.361	9	.143	-4	9	12	-1	0.8
1931 Cle-A	13	14	.481	40	24	9	0	1	194	229	8	72	63	14.2	4.36	106	.289	.352	19	.253	1	0	6	0	0.8
1932 Cle-A	15	13	.536	39	32	17	1	0	254²	277	9	68	90	12.3	3.75	127	.272	.319	17	.181	-0	21	28	3	2.9
1933 Cle-A	15	17	.469	43	31	14	2	4	253	254	10	67	81	11.5	**2.95**	151	.259	.309	16	.190	-1	**37**	**42**	8	**5.7**
1934 Cle-A★	20	12	.625	44	29	17	**6**	4	255¹	246	6	81	91	11.8	2.61	**174**	.254	.316	14	.161	-1	**54**	**55**	2	**6.4**
1935 Cle-A★	22	11	.667	42	35	17	4	2	287¹	313	6	53	95	11.5	3.29	137	.275	.307	21	.206	-1	37	39	5	4.4
1936 Cle-A★	15	15	.500	36	30	13	0	1	224²	294	13	71	84	14.9	5.17	97	.313	.365	11	.138	-4	-3	-3	0	-0.7
1937 Cle-A★	15	12	.556	38	30	13	0	2	233²	269	9	86	95	13.8	4.28	108	.288	.350	15	.174	-1	9	9	2	0.9
1938 Cle-A	17	10	.630	38	29	15	2	4	240	257	16	62	102	12.2	3.83	121	.271	.319	10	.114	-5	26	22	2	1.8
1939 Cle-A	15	9	.625	29	26	12	1	1	208	213	15	64	67	12.1	3.50	121	.269	.326	10	.139	-2	26	21	-2	1.8
1940 Cle-A	12	11	.522	31	25	5	0	0	186¹	200	16	59	76	12.8	4.06	104	.278	.337	11	.177	-1	7	3	1	-0.4
1941 Cle-A	5	4	.556	15	10	1	0	1	68²	76	8	37	21	15.1	5.24	75	.279	.370	2	.080	-2	-8	-10	-1	-1.2
1942 Cle-A	13	14	.481	29	29	13	4	0	198²	179	8	82	74	12.0	3.44	100	.240	.317	8	.119	-3	5	0	1	-0.2
1943 Cle-A	8	7	.533	19	18	6	1	0	135¹	126	7	61	40	12.5	3.06	102	.254	.337	10	.213	-2	4	1	0	0.2
1944 Cle-A	12	10	.545	30	27	12	2	0	196¹	211	5	69	64	13.0	3.71	89	.278	.341	16	.216	-1	-6	-9	-1	-0.9
1945 Cle-A	3	7	.300	11	11	7	0	0	76	93	4	23	16	13.7	3.67	88	.303	.352	2	.080	-2	-3	-4	1	-0.6
1946 Cle-A	5	4	.556	13	12	4	1	0	92¹	85	4	31	21	11.3	3.41	97	.249	.311	3	.086	-2	1	-1	-2	-0.5
1947 Cle-A	6	4	.600	14	9	1	0	0	17	93	4	17	30	17.4	4.50	77	.289	.347	5	.179	0	-7	-9	-1	-1.1
Total 20	223	186	.545	582	433	181	25	23	3426¹	3706	161	1118	1160	12.8	3.80	113	.276	.334	199	.165	-27	190	182	18	20.0

● **JIM HARDIN** Hardin, James Warren b: 8/6/43, Morris Chapel, Tenn. d: 3/9/91, Key West, Fla. BR/TR, 6', 175 lbs. Deb: 6/23/67

1967 Bal-A	8	3	.727	19	14	5	2	0	111	85	9	27	64	9.3	2.27	139	.211	.266	5	.135	-0	12	11	-1	1.0
1968 Bal-A	18	13	.581	35	35	16	2	0	244	188	20	70	160	9.9	2.51	117	.212	.277	7	.085	-3	13	11	-0	1.1
1969 Bal-A	6	7	.462	30	20	3	1	1	137²	128	18	43	64	11.6	3.60	99	.248	.313	7	.156	2	-0	-1	-1	0.0
1970 Bal-A	6	5	.545	36	19	3	2	1	145¹	150	13	26	78	11.0	3.53	103	.267	.301	3	.067	-1	3	2	-2	-0.2
1971 Bal-A	0	0	—	6	0	0	0	0	5²	12	0	3	2	23.8	4.76	70	.480	.536	0	—	-0	-1	-1	0	-0.5
NY-A	0	2	.000	12	3	0	0	0	28¹	35	3	9	14	14.3	5.08	64	.313	.369	0	.000	-0	-5	-6	-0	-0.5
Yr	0	2	.000	18	3	0	0	0	34	47	3	12	17	15.9	5.03	65	.343	.400	0	.000	-0	-6	-7	-0	-0.5
1972 Atl-N	5	2	.714	26	9	1	0	2	79²	93	11	24	25	13.4	4.41	86	.287	.340	2	.095	-1	-8	-5	-5	0.9
Total 6	43	32	.573	164	100	28	7	4	751²	691	70	202	408	11.0	3.18	104	.244	.300	24	.103	-3	14	11	-5	0.9

● **CHARLIE HARDING** Harding, Charles Harold "Slim" b: 1/3/1891, Nashville, Tenn. d: 10/30/71, Bold Springs, Tenn BR/TR, 6'2.5", 172 lbs. Deb: 9/18/13

| 1913 Det-A | 0 | 0 | — | 1 | 0 | 0 | 0 | 0 | 2 | 3 | 0 | 1 | 0 | 18.0 | 4.50 | 65 | .375 | .444 | 0 | — | -0 | -0 | -0 | 0 | 0.0 |

● **ALEX HARDY** Hardy, David Alexander "Dooney" b: 1877, Toronto, Ont., Canada d: 4/22/40, Toronto, Ont., Can. TL, Deb: 9/4/02

1902 Chi-N	2	2	.500	4	4	4	0	0	35	29	0	12	12	10.5	3.60	75	.226	.292	3	.214	0	-3	-3	-1	-0.4
1903 Chi-N	1	1	.500	3	3	1	0	0	12²	21	0	7	4	20.6	6.39	49	.375	.453	1	.167	0	-4	-5	0	-0.5
Total 2	3	3	.500	7	7	5	1	0	47²	50	0	19	16	13.2	4.34	65	.271	.342	4	.200	0	-8	-8	-0	-0.9

● **RED HARDY** Hardy, Francis Joseph b: 1/6/23, Marmarth, N.Dak. BR/TR, 5'11", 175 lbs. Deb: 6/20/51

| 1951 NY-N | 0 | 0 | — | 2 | 0 | 0 | 0 | 0 | 1¹ | 4 | 0 | 1 | 0 | 40.5 | 6.75 | 58 | .571 | .667 | 0 | — | -0 | -0 | -0 | 0 | 0.0 |

● **HARRY HARDY** Hardy, Harry b: 11/5/1875, Steubenville, Ohio d: 9/4/43, Steubenville, Ohio BL/TL, 5'6", 155 lbs. Deb: 9/26/05

1905 Was-A	1	1	.500	3	2	2	0	0	24	20	0	6	10	9.8	1.88	141	.228	.277	1	.111	-1	2	2	-1	-0.1
1906 Was-A	0	3	.000	5	3	2	0	0	20	35	0	12	4	21.1	9.00	29	.385	.457	0	.000	-1	-14	-14	1	-1.7
Total 2	1	4	.200	8	5	4	0	0	44	55	0	18	14	14.9	5.11	52	.308	.371	1	.067	-2	-12	-12	-0	-1.8

● **LARRY HARDY** Hardy, Howard Lawrence b: 1/10/48, Goose Creek, Tex. BR/TR, 5'10", 180 lbs. Deb: 4/28/74

1974 SD-N	9	4	.692	76	1	0	0	2	101²	129	9	44	57	15.3	4.69	76	.317	.384	0	.000	-1	-12	-13	1	-1.5
1975 SD-N	0	0	—	3	0	0	0	0	2²	8	2	3	2	33.8	13.50	26	.500	.556	0	—	-0	-3	-3	-0	-0.0
1976 Hou-N	0	0	—	15	0	0	0	3	21²	34	2	10	10	18.3	7.06	45	.362	.423	0	.000	-0	-9	-9	0	-0.3
Total 3	9	4	.692	94	1	0	0	5	126	171	14	56	70	16.2	5.29	66	.331	.396	0	.000	-1	-24	-25	1	-1.8

● **JACK HARDY** Hardy, John Graydon b: 10/8/59, St.Petersburg, Fla. BR/TR, 6'2", 175 lbs. Deb: 5/23/89

| 1989 Chi-A | 0 | 0 | — | 5 | 0 | 0 | 0 | 0 | 12¹ | 14 | 1 | 5 | 4 | 14.6 | 6.57 | 58 | .286 | .364 | 0 | — | 0 | -4 | -4 | 0 | 0.2 |

● **STEVE HARGAN** Hargan, Steven Lowell b: 9/8/42, Ft.Wayne, Ind. BR/TR, 6'3", 180 lbs. Deb: 8/3/65

1965 Cle-A	4	3	.571	17	8	1	0	2	60¹	55	2	28	37	12.5	3.43	101	.246	.332	1	.053	-1	0	0	0	-0.1
1966 Cle-A	13	10	.565	38	21	7	3	0	192	173	9	45	132	10.3	2.48	138	.241	.286	7	.121	-2	20	20	0	2.3
1967 Cle-A☆	14	13	.519	30	29	15	**6**	0	223	180	9	72	141	10.3	2.62	125	.224	.290	11	.164	-1	15	16	1	2.3
1968 Cle-A	8	15	.348	32	27	4	2	0	158¹	139	11	81	78	12.8	4.15	71	.241	.340	9	.176	1	-21	-21	-2	-3.1
1969 Cle-A	5	14	.263	32	23	1	1	0	143²	145	11	76	74	14.3	5.70	66	.265	.363	7	.159	-1	-33	-31	2	-3.6
1970 Cle-A	11	3	.786	23	19	8	1	0	142²	101	14	53	72	9.9	2.90	136	.201	.281	5	.111	3	13	17	1	1.5
1971 Cle-A	1	13	.071	37	16	1	0	0	113¹	138	14	56	52	15.9	6.19	62	.304	.388	1	.063	-1	-34	-30	-2	-3.8
1972 Cle-A	0	1	.000	12	1	0	0	0	20	23	1	6	10	17.1	5.85	55	.291	.404	0	.000	-0	-6	-6	1	-0.8
1974 Tex-A	12	9	.571	37	27	8	2	0	186²	202	15	48	98	12.3	3.95	90	.275	.324	0		-0	-7	-8	2	-0.7

YEAR	TM/L	W	L	PCT	G	GS	CG	SH	SV	IP	H	HR	BB	SO	RAT	ERA	ERA+	OAV	OOB	BH	AVG	PB	PR	/A	PD	TPI
1975	Tex-A	9	10	.474	33	26	8	1	0	189¹	203	17	62	93	12.9	3.80	99	.275	.336	0	—	0	-1	-1	2	0.1
1976	Tex-A	8	8	.500	35	8	2	1	1	124¹	127	8	38	63	12.2	3.62	99	.261	.318	0	—	0	-1	-0	-0	-0.1
1977	Tor-A	1	3	.250	6	5	1	0	0	29¹	36	2	14	11	15.3	5.22	80	.308	.382	0	—	0	-4	-3	0	-0.4
	Tex-A	1	0	1.000	6	0	0	0	0	12¹	22	2	5	10	19.7	8.76	47	.393	.443	0	—	0	-6	-6	-0	-0.5
	Yr	2	3	.400	12	5	1	0	0	41²	58	4	19	21	16.6	6.26	66	.335	.401	0	—	0	-10	-10	-0	-0.9
	Atl-N	0	3	.000	16	5	0	0	0	36²	49	3	16	18	16.0	6.87	65	.325	.389	0	.000	-1	-12	-10	1	-0.7
Total	12	87	107	.448	354	215	56	17	4	1632	1593	125	614	891	12.4	3.92	91	.257	.328	42	.129	-7	-77	-64	6	-7.6

● ALAN HARGESHEIMER
Hargesheimer, Alan Robert b: 11/21/56, Chicago, Ill. BR/TR, 6'3", 195 lbs. Deb: 7/14/80

YEAR	TM/L	W	L	PCT	G	GS	CG	SH	SV	IP	H	HR	BB	SO	RAT	ERA	ERA+	OAV	OOB	BH	AVG	PB	PR	/A	PD	TPI
1980	SF-N	4	6	.400	15	13	0	0	0	75	82	3	32	40	13.7	4.32	82	.285	.356	4	.182	1	-6	-7	-1	-0.8
1981	SF-N	1	2	.333	6	3	0	0	0	18²	20	1	9	6	14.5	4.34	79	.299	.390	1	.200	0	-2	-2	0	-0.2
1983	Chi-N	0	0	—	5	0	0	0	0	4	6	0	2	5	18.0	9.00	42	.375	.444	0	—	0	-2	-2	-0	0.0
1986	KC-A	0	1	.000	5	1	0	0	0	13	18	1	7	4	18.0	6.23	68	.340	.426	0	—	0	-3	-3	-0	-0.3
Total	4	5	9	.357	31	17	0	0	0	110²	126	5	50	55	14.5	4.72	77	.297	.374	5	.185	1	-13	-14	-1	-1.3

● MIKE HARKEY
Harkey, Michael Anthony b: 10/25/66, San Diego, Cal. BR/TR, 6'5", 220 lbs. Deb: 9/5/88

YEAR	TM/L	W	L	PCT	G	GS	CG	SH	SV	IP	H	HR	BB	SO	RAT	ERA	ERA+	OAV	OOB	BH	AVG	PB	PR	/A	PD	TPI
1988	Chi-N	0	3	.000	5	5	0	0	0	34²	33	0	15	18	13.0	2.60	139	.248	.333	1	.091	-1	3	4	-1	0.2
1990	Chi-N	12	6	.667	27	27	2	1	0	173²	153	14	59	94	11.3	3.26	125	.234	.305	14	.250	3	10	16	-1	1.8
1991	Chi-N	0	2	.000	4	4	0	0	0	18²	21	3	6	15	13.0	5.30	73	.273	.325	2	.400	1	-3	-3	0	-0.2
1992	Chi-N	4	0	1.000	7	7	0	0	0	38	34	4	15	21	11.8	1.89	190	.243	.321	4	.267	1	7	7	-0	0.9
1993	Chi-N	10	10	.500	28	28	1	0	0	157¹	187	17	43	67	13.3	5.26	76	.305	.353	5	.093	-2	-21	-22	-1	-2.8
1994	Col-N	1	6	.143	24	13	0	0	0	91²	125	10	35	39	15.8	5.79	86	.336	.395	4	.182	-1	-16	-8	1	-0.5
Total	6	27	27	.500	95	84	3	1	0	514	553	48	173	254	13.0	4.25	97	.278	.340	30	.184	1	-21	-7	-2	-0.6

● JOHN HARKINS
Harkins, John Joseph "Pa" b: 4/12/1859, New Brunswick, N.J. d: 11/20/40, New Brunswick, N.J. BR/TR, 6'1", 205 lbs. Deb: 5/2/1884

YEAR	TM/L	W	L	PCT	G	GS	CG	SH	SV	IP	H	HR	BB	SO	RAT	ERA	ERA+	OAV	OOB	BH	AVG	PB	PR	/A	PD	TPI
1884	Cle-N	12	32	.273	46	45	42	3	0	391	399	7	108	192	11.7	3.68	86	.249	.297	47	.205	-4	-30	-23	-1	-2.4
1885	Bro-a	14	20	.412	34	34	33	1	0	293	303	7	56	141	11.2	3.75	88	.250	.287	42	.264	5	-16	-15	4	-0.5
1886	Bro-a	15	16	.484	34	33	33	0	0	292¹	286	6	114	118	12.5	3.60	97	.244	.313	32	.225	3	-5	-4	2	0.2
1887	Bro-a	10	14	.417	24	24	22	0	0	199	262	6	77	36	15.6	6.02	72	.309	.369	23	.235	-0	-38	-38	-1	-3.2
1888	Bal-a	0	1	.000	1	1	1	0	0	8	12	0	3	2	16.9	6.75	44	.335	.386	0	.000	-0	-3	-3	-1	-0.2
Total	5	51	83	.381	139	137	131	4	0	1183¹	1262	26	358	489	12.5	4.09	85	.259	.312	144	.228	4	-93	-81	5	-6.2

● SPEC HARKNESS
Harkness, Frederick Harvey b: 12/13/1887, Los Angeles, Cal. d: 5/16/52, Compton, Cal. BR/TR, 5'11", 180 lbs. Deb: 6/13/10

YEAR	TM/L	W	L	PCT	G	GS	CG	SH	SV	IP	H	HR	BB	SO	RAT	ERA	ERA+	OAV	OOB	BH	AVG	PB	PR	/A	PD	TPI
1910	Cle-A	10	7	.588	26	16	6	1	1	136¹	132	2	55	60	12.5	3.04	85	.268	.345	7	.140	-1	-8	-7	-1	-1.1
1911	Cle-A	2	2	.500	12	6	3	0	0	53¹	62	1	21	25	14.0	4.22	81	.310	.376	6	.316	1	-5	-5	-2	-0.4
Total	2	12	9	.571	38	22	9	1	1	189²	194	3	76	85	13.0	3.37	84	.280	.354	13	.188	-0	-13	-12	-3	-1.5

● DICK HARLEY
Harley, Henry Risk b: 8/18/1874, Springfield, Ohio d: 5/16/61, Springfield, Ohio BR/TR, Deb: 4/15/05

YEAR	TM/L	W	L	PCT	G	GS	CG	SH	SV	IP	H	HR	BB	SO	RAT	ERA	ERA+	OAV	OOB	BH	AVG	PB	PR	/A	PD	TPI
1905	Bos-N	2	5	.286	9	4	4	1	0	65²	72	5	19	19	12.6	4.66	67	.286	.338	1	.045	-2	-12	-11	2	-1.1

● LARRY HARLOW
Harlow, Larry Duane b: 11/13/51, Colorado Springs, Colo. BL/TL, 6'2", 185 lbs. Deb: 9/20/75 ♦

YEAR	TM/L	W	L	PCT	G	GS	CG	SH	SV	IP	H	HR	BB	SO	RAT	ERA	ERA+	OAV	OOB	BH	AVG	PB	PR	/A	PD	TPI
1978	Bal-A	0	0	—	1	0	0	0	0	0²	2	1	4	1	81.0	67.50	5	.500	.750	112	.243	1	-5	-5	0	0.0

● BILL HARMAN
Harman, William Bell b: 1/2/19, Bridgewater, Va. BR/TR, 6'4", 200 lbs. Deb: 6/17/41 ♦

YEAR	TM/L	W	L	PCT	G	GS	CG	SH	SV	IP	H	HR	BB	SO	RAT	ERA	ERA+	OAV	OOB	BH	AVG	PB	PR	/A	PD	TPI
1941	Phi-N	0	0	—	5	0	0	0	0	13	15	0	8	3	15.9	4.85	76	.319	.418	1	.071	-0	-2	-2	-0	-0.1

● BOB HARMON
Harmon, Robert Green "Hickory Bob" b: 10/15/1887, Liberal, Mo. d: 11/27/61, Monroe, La. BB/TR, 6', 187 lbs. Deb: 6/23/09

YEAR	TM/L	W	L	PCT	G	GS	CG	SH	SV	IP	H	HR	BB	SO	RAT	ERA	ERA+	OAV	OOB	BH	AVG	PB	PR	/A	PD	TPI
1909	StL-N	6	11	.353	21	17	10	0	0	159	155	6	65	48	12.7	3.68	69	.265	.342	13	.255	4	-19	-20	-0	-1.7
1910	StL-N	13	15	.464	43	33	15	0	2	236	227	1	133	87	14.0	4.46	67	.258	.360	14	.184	2	-37	-39	2	-3.8
1911	StL-N	23	16	.590	51	41	28	2	4	348	290	10	181	144	12.4	3.13	108	.235	.336	17	.153	0	11	10	1	1.1
1912	StL-N	18	18	.500	43	34	15	3	0	268	284	4	116	73	13.5	3.93	87	.281	.357	23	.232	1	-15	-15	4	-1.3
1913	StL-N	8	21	.276	42	27	16	1	2	273¹	291	6	99	66	13.0	3.92	83	.286	.353	24	.261	5	-22	-21	2	-1.4
1914	Pit-N	13	17	.433	37	30	19	2	3	245	226	3	55	61	10.6	2.53	105	.252	.300	12	.140	-1	7	3	-1	0.1
1915	Pit-N	16	17	.485	37	32	25	5	1	269²	242	6	62	86	10.2	2.50	109	.247	.294	14	.147	1	7	7	4	1.4
1916	Pit-N	8	11	.421	31	17	10	2	0	172²	175	4	39	62	11.2	2.81	95	.267	.309	6	.109	-3	-4	-3	2	-0.2
1918	Pit-N	2	7	.222	16	9	5	0	0	82¹	76	3	12	7	9.6	2.62	110	.254	.283	4	.148	-1	1	2	0	0.2
Total	9	107	133	.446	321	240	143	15	12	2054	1966	43	762	634	12.1	3.33	90	.260	.331	127	.184	7	-71	-76	14	-5.6

● PETE HARNISCH
Harnisch, Peter Thomas b: 9/23/66, Commack, N.Y. BB/TR, 6'1", 195 lbs. Deb: 9/13/88

YEAR	TM/L	W	L	PCT	G	GS	CG	SH	SV	IP	H	HR	BB	SO	RAT	ERA	ERA+	OAV	OOB	BH	AVG	PB	PR	/A	PD	TPI
1988	Bal-A	0	2	.000	2	2	0	0	0	13	13	1	9	10	15.2	5.54	70	.260	.373	0	—	0	-2	-2	0	-0.3
1989	Bal-A	5	9	.357	18	17	2	0	0	103¹	97	10	64	70	14.5	4.62	82	.249	.362	0	—	0	-8	-9	-1	-1.1
1990	Bal-A	11	11	.500	31	31	3	0	0	188²	189	17	86	122	13.2	4.34	87	.261	.341	0	—	0	-9	-11	-2	-1.4
1991	Hou-N★	12	9	.571	33	33	4	2	0	216²	169	14	83	172	10.7	2.70	130	**.212**	.291	6	.097	-1	24	19	-3	1.3
1992	Hou-N	9	10	.474	34	34	0	0	0	206²	182	18	64	164	10.9	3.70	91	.233	.296	11	.164	2	-5	-8	-3	-0.8
1993	Hou-N	16	9	.640	33	33	5	**4**	0	217²	171	20	79	185	10.6	2.98	130	**.214**	.290	7	.104	-1	26	22	-4	1.8
1994	Hou-N	8	5	.615	17	17	1	0	0	95	100	13	39	62	13.5	5.40	75	.269	.343	6	.171	1	-13	-14	-1	-1.6
Total	7	61	55	.526	168	167	15	6	0	1041	921	93	424	785	11.8	3.73	99	.236	.314	30	.130	0	13	-4	-13	-2.1

● JACK HARPER
Harper, Charles William b: 4/2/1878, Galloway, Pa. d: 9/30/50, Jamestown, N.Y. BR/TR, 6', 178 lbs. Deb: 9/18/1899

YEAR	TM/L	W	L	PCT	G	GS	CG	SH	SV	IP	H	HR	BB	SO	RAT	ERA	ERA+	OAV	OOB	BH	AVG	PB	PR	/A	PD	TPI
1899	Cle-N	1	4	.200	5	5	5	0	0	37	44	3	12	14	14.4	3.89	95	.295	.359	2	.182	1	-0	-1	-0	0.0
1900	StL-N	0	1	.000	1	1	0	0	0	4	2	0	2	0	18.0	12.00	30	.319	.410	0	.000	-0	-3	-3	-0	-0.6
1901	StL-N	23	13	.639	39	37	28	1	0	308²	294	7	99	128	11.9	3.62	88	.249	.316	20	.172	1	-10	-15	1	-1.3
1902	StL-A	15	11	.577	29	26	20	2	0	222¹	224	8	81	74	12.7	4.13	85	.262	.332	17	.205	-0	-14	-15	1	-1.4
1903	Cin-N	8	9	.471	17	15	13	0	0	135	143	2	70	45	14.9	4.33	82	.271	.367	14	.250	2	-16	-12	1	-1.0
1904	Cin-N	23	9	.719	35	35	31	6	0	293²	262	2	85	125	10.9	2.30	128	.234	.293	18	.159	-2	14	21	-5	1.4
1905	Cin-N	9	13	.409	26	23	15	1	1	179¹	189	2	69	70	13.3	3.86	86	.271	.344	10	.167	1	-17	-11	-0	-1.3
1906	Cin-N	1	4	.200	5	5	3	0	0	36²	38	1	20	10	14.7	4.17	66	.286	.387	3	.273	1	-6	-6	-1	-0.7
	Chi-N	0	0	—	1	1	0	0	0	1	0	0	0	0	0.00	—	.000	.000	0	—	0	0	0	0	0.0
	Yr	1	4	.200	6	6	3	0	0	37²	38	1	20	10	13.9	4.06	68	.275	.367	3	.273	1	-6	-5	-1	-0.7
Total	8	80	64	.556	158	148	115	10	1	1216²	1198	25	438	466	12.5	3.55	92	.256	.327	84	.186	3	-51	-39	-3	-4.9

● GEORGE HARPER
Harper, George B. b: 8/17/1866, Milwaukee, Wis. d: 12/11/31, Stockton, Cal. BR/TR, 5'10", 165 lbs. Deb: 7/11/1894

YEAR	TM/L	W	L	PCT	G	GS	CG	SH	SV	IP	H	HR	BB	SO	RAT	ERA	ERA+	OAV	OOB	BH	AVG	PB	PR	/A	PD	TPI
1894	Phi-N	6	6	.500	12	9	7	0	0	86¹	128	3	49	24	18.7	5.32	96	.340	.419	6	.150	-4	0	-2	-1	-0.5
1896	Bro-N	4	8	.333	16	11	7	0	0	86	106	4	39	22	15.5	5.55	74	.300	.375	6	.162	-0	-11	-14	1	-1.3
Total	2	10	14	.417	28	20	14	0	0	172¹	234	7	88	46	17.1	5.43	85	.321	.398	12	.156	-4	-11	-16	0	-1.8

● HARRY HARPER
Harper, Harry Clayton b: 4/24/1895, Hackensack, N.J. d: 4/23/63, New York, N.Y. BL/TL, 6'2", 165 lbs. Deb: 6/27/13

YEAR	TM/L	W	L	PCT	G	GS	CG	SH	SV	IP	H	HR	BB	SO	RAT	ERA	ERA+	OAV	OOB	BH	AVG	PB	PR	/A	PD	TPI
1913	Was-A	0	0	—	4	0	0	0	0	12²	10	1	5	9	11.4	3.55	83	.204	.291	1	.250	0	-1	-1	0	0.0
1914	Was-A	2	1	.667	23	3	1	0	2	57	45	1	35	50	13.4	3.47	81	.211	.336	3	.250	0	-5	-4	-1	-0.4
1915	Was-A	4	4	.500	19	10	5	2	1	86¹	66	1	40	54	11.2	1.77	168	.222	.317	0	.000	-4	11	11	-2	0.5
1916	Was-A	14	10	.583	36	34	13	2	0	249²	209	4	101	149	11.5	2.45	114	.235	.319	18	.207	1	10	9	-4	0.5
1917	Was-A	11	12	.478	31	31	10	4	0	179¹	145	4	106	99	12.8	3.01	87	.230	.345	7	.117	-3	-7	-8	-3	-1.6
1918	Was-A	11	10	.524	35	32	14	3	1	244	216	1	104	78	10.8	2.18	125	.212	.303	11	.134	-4	16	15	-5	0.3
1919	Was-A	5	21	.222	35	31	8	0	0	208	220	3	97	87	14.1	3.72	86	.284	.370	11	.169	-2	-11	-12	-1	-1.8
1920	Bos-A	5	14	.263	27	22	11	0	0	162²	163	6	66	71	12.8	3.04	120	.275	.349	6	.120	-3	14	11	-3	0.0
1921	*NY-A	4	3	.571	8	7	4	0	0	52²	52	3	25	22	13.5	3.76	113	.263	.351	2	.125	-1	3	3	-2	0.0

YEAR TM/L	W	L	PCT	G	GS	CG	SH	SV	IP	H	HR	BB	SO	RAT	ERA	ERA+	OAV	OOB	BH	AVG	PB	PR	/A	PD	TPI
1923 Bro-N	0	1	.000	1	1	0	0	0	3²	8	2	3	4	27.0	14.73	26	.421	.500	0	.000	-0	-4	-4	-0	-0.7
Total 10	57	76	.429	219	171	66	12	5	1256	1100	26	582	623	12.3	2.87	105	.243	.335	59	.147	-16	26	21	-21	-2.7

● **JACK HARPER**   Harper, John Wesley b: 8/5/1893, Hendricks, W.Va. d: 6/18/27, Halstead, Kan. BR/TR, 5'11", 180 lbs. Deb: 4/17/15

YEAR TM/L	W	L	PCT	G	GS	CG	SH	SV	IP	H	HR	BB	SO	RAT	ERA	ERA+	OAV	OOB	BH	AVG	PB	PR	/A	PD	TPI
1915 Phi-A	0	0	—	3	0	0	0	0	8²	5	0	1	3	6.2	3.12	94	.161	.188	0	.000	-0	-0	-0	0	0.0

● **BILL HARPER**   Harper, William Homer "Blue Sleeve" b: 6/14/1889, Bertrand, Mo. d: 6/17/51, Somerville, Tenn. BB/TR, 6'1", 180 lbs. Deb: 6/10/11

1911 StL-A	0	0	—	2	0	0	0	0	8	9	0	4	6	15.8	6.75	50	.300	.400	0	.000	-0	-3	-3	0	0.0

● **SLIM HARRELL**   Harrell, Oscar Martin b: 7/31/1890, Grandview, Tex. d: 4/30/71, Hillsboro, Tex. BR/TR, 6'3", 180 lbs. Deb: 6/21/12

1912 Phi-A	0	0	—	1	0	0	0	0	3	4	0	4	1	12.0	0.00	—	.364	.364	0	.000	-0	1	1	-0	0.0

● **RAY HARRELL**   Harrell, Raymond James "Cowboy" b: 2/16/12, Petrolia, Tex. d: 1/28/84, Alexandria, La. BR/TR, 6'1", 185 lbs. Deb: 4/16/35

YEAR TM/L	W	L	PCT	G	GS	CG	SH	SV	IP	H	HR	BB	SO	RAT	ERA	ERA+	OAV	OOB	BH	AVG	PB	PR	/A	PD	TPI
1935 StL-N	1	1	.500	11	1	0	0	0	29²	39	4	11	13	15.2	6.67	61	.320	.376	0	.000	-1	-9	-8	-0	-0.6
1937 StL-N	3	7	.300	35	15	1	1	1	96²	99	7	59	41	14.9	5.87	68	.263	.366	1	.045	-2	-21	-20	-1	-2.1
1938 StL-N	2	3	.400	32	3	1	0	0	63	78	6	29	32	15.7	4.86	81	.308	.386	0	.000	-1	-7	-6	-0	-0.6
1939 Chi-N	0	2	.000	4	2	0	0	0	17¹	29	2	6	5	18.2	8.31	47	.387	.432	0	.000	-1	-8	-8	-0	-0.8
Phi-N	3	7	.300	22	10	4	0	0	94²	101	6	56	35	15.3	5.42	74	.270	.371	3	.115	-1	-16	-15	-3	-1.7
Yr	3	9	.250	26	12	4	0	0	112	130	8	62	40	15.8	5.87	68	.290	.381	3	.097	-2	-24	-23	-3	-2.5
1940 Pit-N	0	0	—	3	0	0	0	0	3¹	5	0	2	3	18.9	8.10	47	.333	.412	0	—	0	-2	-2	-0	-0.1
1945 NY-N	0	0	—	12	0	0	0	0	25¹	34	1	14	7	17.4	4.97	79	.343	.430	1	.200	1	-3	-3	0	0.1
Total 6	9	20	.310	119	31	6	1	3	330	385	26	177	136	15.6	5.70	70	.293	.381	5	.069	-5	-66	-63	-3	-5.7

● **BILL HARRELSON**   Harrelson, William Charles b: 11/17/45, Tahlequah, Okla. BB/TR, 6'5", 215 lbs. Deb: 7/31/68

1968 Cal-A	1	6	.143	10	5	1	0	0	33²	28	4	26	22	14.7	5.08	57	.226	.364	1	.100	-0	-8	-8	-0	-1.7

● **ANDY HARRINGTON**   Harrington, Andrew Francis b: 11/13/1888, Wakefield, Mass. d: 11/12/38, Malden, Mass. BR/TR, 6', 193 lbs. Deb: 9/8/13

1913 Cin-N	0	0	—	1	0	0	0	0	4	6	0	1	1	15.8	9.00	36	.353	.389	1	.500	0	-3	-3	-0	0.0

● **BILL HARRINGTON**   Harrington, William Womble b: 10/3/27, Sanford, N.C. BR/TR, 5'11", 160 lbs. Deb: 4/16/53

YEAR TM/L	W	L	PCT	G	GS	CG	SH	SV	IP	H	HR	BB	SO	RAT	ERA	ERA+	OAV	OOB	BH	AVG	PB	PR	/A	PD	TPI
1953 Phi-A	0	0	—	1	0	0	0	0	2	5	0	0	2	22.5	13.50	32	.500	.500	0	—	0	-2	-2	-0	0.0
1955 KC-A	3	3	.500	34	1	0	0	2	76²	69	6	41	26	13.1	4.11	102	.246	.347	2	.118	-1	-1	1	-1	-0.1
1956 KC-A	2	2	.500	23	1	0	0	1	37²	40	3	26	14	15.8	6.45	67	.274	.384	0	.000	-1	-10	-9	-0	-0.9
Total 3	5	5	.500	58	2	0	0	3	116¹	114	9	67	40	14.2	5.03	84	.261	.362	2	.083	-1	-13	-10	-1	-1.0

● **BEN HARRIS**   Harris, Ben Franklin b: 12/17/1889, Donelson, Tenn. d: 4/29/27, St.Louis, Mo. BR/TR, 6', 220 lbs. Deb: 4/19/14

1914 KC-F	7	7	.500	31	14	5	0	1	154	179	7	41	40	13.2	4.09	68	.303	.354	9	.200	1	-21	-22	1	-1.7
1915 KC-F	0	0	—	1	0	0	0	0	2	1	0	0	0	4.5	0.00	—	.143	.143	0	—	0	1	1	0	0.0
Total 2	7	7	.500	32	14	5	0	1	156	180	7	41	40	13.1	4.04	69	.301	.352	9	.200	1	-20	-22	1	-1.7

● **LUM HARRIS**   Harris, Chalmer Luman b: 1/17/15, New Castle, Ala. BR/TR, 6'1", 180 lbs. Deb: 4/19/41 MC

YEAR TM/L	W	L	PCT	G	GS	CG	SH	SV	IP	H	HR	BB	SO	RAT	ERA	ERA+	OAV	OOB	BH	AVG	PB	PR	/A	PD	TPI
1941 Phi-A	4	4	.500	33	10	5	0	2	131²	134	16	51	49	12.8	4.78	88	.260	.329	11	.275	2	-9	-9	-1	-0.4
1942 Phi-A	11	15	.423	26	20	10	1	0	166	146	14	70	60	11.8	3.74	101	.234	.313	10	.161	-2	-2	-1	-1	-0.1
1943 Phi-A	7	21	.250	32	27	15	1	1	216²	241	17	63	55	12.8	4.20	81	.279	.330	12	.171	-1	-22	-19	-0	-2.4
1944 Phi-A	10	9	.526	23	22	12	2	0	174¹	193	8	26	33	11.3	3.30	105	.281	.308	10	.169	-1	2	3	-1	0.2
1946 Phi-A	3	14	.176	34	12	4	0	0	125¹	153	11	49	33	14.4	5.24	68	.308	.369	8	.222	1	-24	-24	3	-2.4
1947 Was-A	0	0	—	3	0	0	0	0	6¹	7	0	7	2	19.9	2.84	131	.318	.483	0	.000	-0	1	1	0	0.1
Total 6	35	63	.357	151	91	46	4	3	820	874	66	265	232	12.6	4.16	88	.273	.329	51	.190	-0	-54	-47	1	-5.1

● **BUBBA HARRIS**   Harris, Charles b: 2/15/26, Sulligent, Ala. BR/TR, 6'4", 204 lbs. Deb: 4/29/48

1948 Phi-A	5	2	.714	45	0	0	0	5	93²	89	2	35	32	12.0	4.13	104	.249	.317	3	.125	-1	2	2	-0	0.0
1949 Phi-A	1	1	.500	37	0	0	0	3	84¹	92	12	42	18	14.4	5.44	75	.286	.370	3	.125	-2	-12	-12	2	-0.3
1951 Phi-A	0	0	—	3	0	0	0	0	4	4	0	5	2	22.5	9.00	48	.250	.455	0	—	0	-2	-2	-0	0.0
Cle-A	0	0	—	2	0	0	0	0	4	5	0	4	1	20.3	4.50	84	.333	.474	0	—	0	-0	-0	-0	0.0
Yr	0	0	—	5	0	0	0	0	8	9	0	9	3	20.3	6.75	60	.281	.439	0	—	0	-2	-2	-0	0.0
Total 3	6	3	.667	87	0	0	0	8	186	190	14	86	53	13.5	4.84	87	.267	.349	6	.125	-3	-12	-13	2	-0.3

● **GREG HARRIS**   Harris, Greg Allen b: 11/2/55, Lynwood, Cal. BB/TR, 6', 175 lbs. Deb: 5/20/81

YEAR TM/L	W	L	PCT	G	GS	CG	SH	SV	IP	H	HR	BB	SO	RAT	ERA	ERA+	OAV	OOB	BH	AVG	PB	PR	/A	PD	TPI
1981 NY-N	3	5	.375	16	14	0	0	1	68²	65	8	28	54	12.5	4.46	78	.245	.322	4	.182	-0	-7	-7	-1	-0.9
1982 Cin-N	2	6	.250	34	10	1	0	1	91¹	96	12	37	67	13.3	4.83	77	.274	.346	3	.167	-0	-12	-11	0	-0.9
1983 Cin-N	0	0	—	1	0	0	0	0	1	2	0	3	1	54.0	27.00	14	.500	.750	0	.000	-0	-3	-3	0	0.0
1984 Mon-N	0	1	.000	15	0	0	0	2	17²	10	0	7	15	9.7	2.04	168	.172	.284	0	.000	0	3	3	0	0.2
*SD-N	2	1	.667	19	1	0	0	1	36²	28	3	18	30	11.8	2.70	132	.209	.312	3	.375	1	4	4	-0	0.4
Yr	2	2	.500	34	1	0	0	3	54¹	38	3	25	45	10.8	2.48	142	.196	.294	3	.333	1	7	6	-0	0.6
1985 Tex-A	5	4	.556	58	0	0	0	11	113	74	7	43	111	9.7	2.47	171	.186	.274	0	—	0	21	22	1	2.1
1986 Tex-A	10	8	.556	73	0	0	0	20	111¹	103	12	42	95	11.8	2.83	152	.251	.322	0	—	0	17	18	1	3.4
1987 Tex-A	5	10	.333	42	19	0	0	0	140²	157	18	56	106	13.9	4.86	92	.281	.351	0	—	0	-6	-6	-0	-0.5
1988 Phi-N	4	6	.400	66	1	0	0	0	107	80	7	52	71	11.4	2.36	151	.209	.311	3	.333	1	13	14	-0	1.5
1989 Phi-N	2	2	.500	44	0	0	0	0	75¹	64	7	43	51	13.0	3.58	99	.234	.342	1	.167	1	-1	-0	1	0.1
Bos-A	2	2	.500	15	0	0	0	0	28	21	1	15	26	11.6	2.57	159	.208	.310	0	—	0	3	3	0	0.3
1990 *Bos-A	13	9	.591	34	30	1	0	0	184¹	186	13	77	117	13.1	4.00	102	.265	.342	0	—	0	-2	1	3	0.3
1991 Bos-A	11	12	.478	53	21	0	0	2	173	157	13	69	127	12.0	3.85	112	.243	.321	0	—	0	5	9	2	1.3
1992 Bos-A	4	9	.308	70	2	0	1	4	107²	82	6	60	73	12.2	2.51	168	.215	.327	0	—	0	17	20	0	2.5
1993 Bos-A	6	7	.462	**80**	0	0	0	8	112²	95	7	60	103	13.2	3.77	123	.232	.344	0	—	0	7	11	-0	1.2
1994 Bos-A	3	4	.429	35	0	0	0	2	45²	60	8	23	44	16.6	8.28	62	.321	.398	0	—	0	-18	-16	-0	-2.3
NY-A	0	1	.000	3	0	0	0	0	5	4	1	3	4	16.2	5.40	82	.222	.391	0	—	0	-0	-1	0	0.1
Yr	3	5	.375	38	0	0	0	2	50²	64	9	26	48	16.3	7.99	63	.309	.391	0	—	0	-18	-16	-0	-2.2
Total 14	72	87	.453	658	98	4	0	54	1418²	1284	123	636	1094	12.5	3.72	111	.243	.331	14	.215	3	41	62	8	8.7

● **GREG HARRIS**   Harris, Gregory Wade b: 12/1/63, Greensboro, N.C. BR/TR, 6'3", 190 lbs. Deb: 9/14/88

YEAR TM/L	W	L	PCT	G	GS	CG	SH	SV	IP	H	HR	BB	SO	RAT	ERA	ERA+	OAV	OOB	BH	AVG	PB	PR	/A	PD	TPI
1988 SD-N	2	0	1.000	3	1	1	0	0	18	13	0	3	15	8.0	1.50	226	.200	.235	0	.000	-1	4	4	-0	0.3
1989 SD-N	8	9	.471	56	8	0	0	6	135	106	8	52	106	10.7	2.60	134	.215	.293	1	.053	-1	13	13	1	1.8
1990 SD-N	8	8	.500	73	0	0	0	9	117½	92	6	49	97	11.1	2.30	166	.220	.307	1	.083	-0	19	20	0	3.0
1991 SD-N	9	5	.643	20	20	3	2	0	133	116	16	27	95	9.7	2.23	170	.233	.274	3	.083	-1	21	23	-1	2.2
1992 SD-N	4	8	.333	20	20	0	0	0	118	113	13	35	66	11.4	4.12	87	.252	.309	4	.129	-1	-8	-7	0	-0.6
1993 SD-N	10	9	.526	22	22	4	0	0	152	151	18	39	83	11.4	3.67	113	.257	.307	9	.170	-1	6	8	1	1.1
Col-N	1	8	.111	13	13	0	0	0	73¹	88	15	30	40	15.0	6.50	73	.299	.372	1	.050	-2	-20	-14	0	-1.6
Yr	11	17	.393	35	35	4	0	0	225¹	239	33	69	123	12.5	4.59	94	.270	.325	10	.137	-0	-14	-6	1	-0.5
1994 Col-N	3	12	.200	29	19	1	0	1	130	154	22	52	82	14.6	6.65	75	.300	.370	7	.175	-0	-35	-24	1	-2.4
Total 7	45	59	.433	236	103	8	2	16	876²	833	98	287	584	11.7	3.80	106	.251	.315	26	.119	-3	1	21	2	3.8

● **HERB HARRIS**   Harris, Herbert Benjamin "Hub" or "Lefty" b: 4/24/13, Chicago, Ill. BL/TL, 6'1", 175 lbs. Deb: 7/21/36

1936 Phi-N	0	0	—	4	0	0	0	0	7	14	0	5	0	25.7	10.29	44	.438	.526	0	.000	-0	-5	-4	0	0.0

● **JOE HARRIS**   Harris, Joseph White b: 2/1/1882, Melrose, Mass. d: 4/12/66, Melrose, Mass. BR/TR, 6'1", 198 lbs. Deb: 9/22/05

1905 Bos-A	1	2	.333	3	3	3	0	0	23	16	0	8	14	9.4	2.35	115	.198	.270	1	.111	-1	1	1	-0	0.0

YEAR	TM/L	W	L	PCT	G	GS	CG	SH	SV	IP	H	HR	BB	SO	RAT	ERA	ERA+	OAV	OOB	BH	AVG	PB	PR	/A	PD	TPI
1906	Bos-A	2	21	.087	30	24	20	1	2	235	211	5	67	99	10.9	3.52	78	.243	.302	13	.160	-2	-22	-20	6	-1.5
1907	Bos-A	0	7	.000	12	5	3	0	0	59	57	0	13	24	10.8	3.05	85	.256	.300	4	.190	-0	-3	-3	0	-0.4
Total	3	3	30	.091	45	32	26	1	2	317	284	5	88	137	10.8	3.35	81	.242	.300	18	.162	-3	-24	-22	6	-1.9

● **MICKEY HARRIS**   Harris, Maurice Charles   b: 1/30/17, New York, N.Y.   d: 4/15/71, Farmington, Mich.   BL/TL, 6′, 195 lbs.   Deb: 4/23/40

YEAR	TM/L	W	L	PCT	G	GS	CG	SH	SV	IP	H	HR	BB	SO	RAT	ERA	ERA+	OAV	OOB	BH	AVG	PB	PR	/A	PD	TPI
1940	Bos-A	4	2	.667	13	9	3	0	0	68¹	83	8	26	36	14.6	5.00	90	.292	.356	6	.273	2	-5	-4	0	-0.1
1941	Bos-A	8	14	.364	35	22	11	1	1	194	189	6	86	111	12.9	3.25	128	.250	.328	6	.109	2	19	20	-1	2.2
1946	*Bos-A☆	17	9	.654	34	30	15	0	0	222²	236	18	76	131	12.7	3.64	101	.268	.329	18	.231	4	-3	1	-1	0.3
1947	Bos-A	5	4	.556	15	6	1	0	0	51²	42	3	23	35	11.3	2.44	159	.225	.310	5	.417	3	7	8	0	1.7
1948	Bos-A	7	10	.412	20	17	6	1	0	113²	120	10	59	42	14.3	5.30	83	.273	.360	2	.063	-1	-13	-12	-2	-1.7
1949	Bos-A	2	3	.400	7	6	2	0	0	37²	53	3	20	14	17.7	5.02	87	.323	.400	1	.083	-1	-3	-3	0	-0.4
	Was-A	2	12	.143	23	19	4	0	1	129	151	8	55	54	14.4	5.16	82	.292	.360	8	.205	1	-14	-13	-2	-1.2
	Yr	4	15	.211	30	25	6	0	1	166²	204	11	75	68	15.1	5.13	83	.299	.368	9	.176	1	-17	-16	-2	-1.6
1950	Was-A	5	9	.357	53	0	0	0	15	98	93	10	46	41	12.9	4.78	94	.247	.330	4	.235	1	-2	-3	-1	-0.5
1951	Was-A	6	8	.429	41	0	0	0	4	87¹	87	6	43	47	13.5	3.81	107	.260	.347	3	.188	0	3	3	-1	0.4
1952	Was-A	0	0	—	1	0	0	0	0	1	1	1	0	0	9.0	9.00	40	.250	.250	0	—	0	-1	-1	-0	0.0
	Cle-A	3	0	1.000	29	0	0	0	1	46²	42	6	21	23	12.3	4.63	72	.249	.335	1	.200	-0	-5	-7	0	-0.4
	Yr	3	0	1.000	30	0	0	0	1	47²	43	7	21	23	12.3	4.72	71	.249	.333	1	.200	-0	-6	-7	-0	-0.4
Total	9	59	71	.454	271	109	42	2	21	1050	1097	79	455	534	13.4	4.18	98	.267	.342	54	.188	11	-16	-9	-7	0.3

● **REGGIE HARRIS**   Harris, Reginald Allen   b: 8/12/68, Waynesboro, Va.   BR/TR, 6′1″, 180 lbs.   Deb: 7/4/90

YEAR	TM/L	W	L	PCT	G	GS	CG	SH	SV	IP	H	HR	BB	SO	RAT	ERA	ERA+	OAV	OOB	BH	AVG	PB	PR	/A	PD	TPI
1990	Oak-A	1	0	1.000	16	1	0	0	0	41¹	25	5	21	31	10.5	3.48	107	.176	.291	0	—	0	2	1	0	0.2
1991	Oak-A	0	0	—	2	0	0	0	0	3	5	0	3	2	24.0	12.00	32	.455	.571	0	—	0	-3	-3	0	0.0
Total	2	1	0	1.000	18	1	0	0	0	44¹	30	5	24	33	11.4	4.06	92	.196	.313	0	—	0	-1	-2	-1	0.2

● **BOB HARRIS**   Harris, Robert Arthur   b: 5/1/17, Gillette, Wyo.   d: 8/8/89, North Platte, Neb.   BR/TR, 6′, 185 lbs.   Deb: 9/19/38

YEAR	TM/L	W	L	PCT	G	GS	CG	SH	SV	IP	H	HR	BB	SO	RAT	ERA	ERA+	OAV	OOB	BH	AVG	PB	PR	/A	PD	TPI
1938	Det-A	1	0	1.000	3	1	1	0	0	10	14	0	4	7	16.2	7.20	69	.318	.375	1	.333	0	-3	-2	0	-0.1
1939	Det-A	1	1	.500	5	1	0	0	0	18	18	4	8	9	13.0	4.00	122	.269	.347	2	.400	0	1	2	0	0.2
	StL-A	3	12	.200	28	16	6	0	0	126	162	5	71	48	16.5	5.71	85	.321	.405	7	.189	-0	-15	-12	3	-0.9
	Yr	4	13	.235	33	17	6	0	0	144	180	9	79	57	16.2	5.50	89	.315	.398	9	.214	-0	-14	-10	3	-0.7
1940	StL-A	11	15	.423	35	28	8	1	1	193²	225	24	85	49	14.5	4.93	93	.290	.362	15	.250	3	-12	-7	-0	-0.6
1941	StL-A	12	14	.462	34	29	9	2	1	186²	237	18	85	57	15.6	5.21	83	.312	.383	7	.115	-3	-22	-19	-2	-2.6
1942	StL-A	1	5	.167	16	6	0	0	0	33²	37	2	17	9	14.4	5.61	66	.268	.348	0	.000	-1	-7	-7	-1	-1.2
	Phi-A	1	5	.167	16	8	2	1	0	78	77	5	24	26	11.7	2.88	131	.253	.308	7	.269	-0	7	8	2	0.9
	Yr	2	10	.167	22	14	2	1	0	111²	114	7	41	35	12.5	3.71	101	.258	.321	7	.194	-0	-1	1	2	-0.3
Total	5	30	52	.366	127	89	26	4	2	646	770	58	294	205	14.9	4.96	89	.297	.370	39	.193	1	-51	-38	3	-4.3

● **GENE HARRIS**   Harris, Tyrone Eugene   b: 12/5/64, Sebring, Fla.   BR/TR, 5′11″, 190 lbs.   Deb: 4/5/89

YEAR	TM/L	W	L	PCT	G	GS	CG	SH	SV	IP	H	HR	BB	SO	RAT	ERA	ERA+	OAV	OOB	BH	AVG	PB	PR	/A	PD	TPI
1989	Mon-N	1	1	.500	11	0	0	0	0	20	16	1	10	11	11.7	4.95	71	.242	.342	0	.000	—	-3	-3	2	-0.2
	Sea-A	1	4	.200	10	6	0	0	0	33¹	47	3	15	14	17.0	6.48	62	.353	.423	0	—	0	-10	-9	-1	-1.4
1990	Sea-A	1	2	.333	25	0	0	0	0	38	31	5	30	43	14.7	4.74	84	.217	.356	0	—	0	-4	-3	-0	-0.3
1991	Sea-A	0	0	—	8	0	0	0	1	13¹	15	1	10	6	16.9	4.05	102	.273	.385	0	—	0	0	0	0	0.0
1992	Sea-A	0	0	—	8	0	0	0	0	9	8	3	3	6	14.0	7.00	57	.235	.350	0	—	0	-3	-3	-0	0.0
	SD-N	0	2	.000	14	1	0	0	0	21¹	15	0	9	19	10.5	2.95	121	.195	.287	1	.333	0	1	1	0	0.2
1993	SD-N	6	6	.500	59	0	0	0	23	59¹	57	3	37	39	14.4	3.03	136	.254	.363	0	.000	-0	7	7	1	2.0
1994	SD-N	1	1	.500	13	0	0	0	0	12¹	21	2	8	9	21.2	8.03	52	.389	.468	0	.000	-0	-5	-5	-0	-0.8
	Det-A	0	0	—	11	0	0	0	1	11¹	13	1	4	10	14.3	7.15	67	.271	.340	0	—	0	-3	-3	0	0.0
Total	6	10	16	.385	159	7	0	0	26	218	223	19	129	157	14.7	4.75	84	.267	.369	1	.167	-0	-20	-18	1	-0.5

● **BUDDY HARRIS**   Harris, Walter Francis   b: 12/5/48, Philadelphia, Pa.   BR/TR, 6′7″, 245 lbs.   Deb: 9/10/70

YEAR	TM/L	W	L	PCT	G	GS	CG	SH	SV	IP	H	HR	BB	SO	RAT	ERA	ERA+	OAV	OOB	BH	AVG	PB	PR	/A	PD	TPI
1970	Hou-N	0	0	—	2	0	0	0	0	6¹	6	3	0	2	8.5	5.68	68	.240	.240	0	.000	-0	-1	-1	-0	0.0
1971	Hou-N	1	1	.500	20	0	0	0	0	30²	33	3	16	21	14.4	6.46	52	.275	.360	0	.000	-0	-10	-11	-1	-0.7
Total	2	1	1	.500	22	0	0	0	0	37	39	6	16	23	13.4	6.32	55	.269	.342	0	.000	-0	-11	-12	-1	-0.7

● **BILL HARRIS**   Harris, William Milton   b: 6/23/1900, Wylie, Tex.   d: 8/21/65, Indian Trail, N.C.   BR/TR, 6′1″, 180 lbs.   Deb: 4/22/23

YEAR	TM/L	W	L	PCT	G	GS	CG	SH	SV	IP	H	HR	BB	SO	RAT	ERA	ERA+	OAV	OOB	BH	AVG	PB	PR	/A	PD	TPI
1923	Cin-N	3	2	.600	22	3	1	0	0	69²	79	3	18	18	12.9	5.17	75	.292	.342	6	.353	1	-9	-10	0	-0.5
1924	Cin-N	0	0	—	3	0	0	0	0	7	10	2	0	5	15.4	9.00	42	.323	.364	1	1.000	0	-4	-4	0	0.1
1931	Pit-N	2	2	.500	4	4	3	1	0	31	21	0	8	10	8.7	0.87	442	.194	.256	1	.091	-1	10	10	0	1.3
1932	Pit-N	10	9	.526	37	17	4	0	2	168	178	6	38	63	11.9	3.64	105	.271	.317	10	.182	-1	4	3	-2	0.1
1933	Pit-N	4	4	.500	31	0	0	0	0	58²	68	1	14	19	12.7	3.22	103	.289	.332	0	.000	-1	1	1	-1	-0.1
1934	Pit-N	0	0	—	11	2	0	0	0	19	28	2	7	8	17.1	6.63	62	.350	.409	1	.500	0	-5	-5	0	0.1
1938	Bos-A	5	5	.500	13	11	5	1	1	80¹	83	5	21	26	11.8	4.03	122	.268	.316	6	.214	-0	7	8	-0	0.8
Total	7	24	22	.522	121	37	13	2	3	433²	467	17	109	149	12.2	3.92	101	.276	.324	25	.203	-1	4	2	-2	1.8

● **BILL HARRIS**   Harris, William Thomas   b: 12/3/31, Duguayville, N.B., Canada   BL/TR, 5′8″, 187 lbs.   Deb: 9/27/57

YEAR	TM/L	W	L	PCT	G	GS	CG	SH	SV	IP	H	HR	BB	SO	RAT	ERA	ERA+	OAV	OOB	BH	AVG	PB	PR	/A	PD	TPI
1957	Bro-N	0	1	.000	1	1	0	0	0	7	9	1	1	3	12.9	3.86	108	.321	.345	1	.500	1	0	0	0	0.1
1959	LA-N	0	0	—	1	0	0	0	0	1²	0	0	3	1	16.2	0.00	—	.000	.375	0	—	0	1	1	0	0.0
Total	2	0	1	.000	2	1	0	0	0	8²	9	1	4	3	13.5	3.12	134	.273	.351	1	.500	0	1	1	0	0.1

● **BOB HARRISON**   Harrison, Robert Lee   b: 9/22/30, St.Louis, Mo.   BL/TR, 5′11″, 178 lbs.   Deb: 9/23/55

YEAR	TM/L	W	L	PCT	G	GS	CG	SH	SV	IP	H	HR	BB	SO	RAT	ERA	ERA+	OAV	OOB	BH	AVG	PB	PR	/A	PD	TPI
1955	Bal-A	0	0	—	1	0	0	0	0	2	3	0	4	0	31.5	9.00	42	.500	.700	0	—	0	-1	-1	-0	0.0
1956	Bal-A	0	0	—	1	1	0	0	0	1²	3	0	5	0	43.2	16.20	24	.375	.615	0	—	0	-2	-2	-0	0.0
Total	2	0	0	—	2	1	0	0	0	3²	6	0	9	0	36.8	12.27	31	.429	.652	0	—	0	-3	-3	-0	0.0

● **RORIC HARRISON**   Harrison, Roric Edward   b: 9/20/46, Los Angeles, Cal.   BR/TR, 6′3″, 195 lbs.   Deb: 4/18/72

YEAR	TM/L	W	L	PCT	G	GS	CG	SH	SV	IP	H	HR	BB	SO	RAT	ERA	ERA+	OAV	OOB	BH	AVG	PB	PR	/A	PD	TPI
1972	Bal-A	3	4	.429	39	2	0	0	4	94	68	2	34	62	10.1	2.30	134	.209	.292	2	.118	1	8	8	-1	0.7
1973	Atl-N	11	8	.579	38	22	3	0	5	177¹	161	15	98	130	13.3	4.16	94	.242	.342	3	.056	-2	-10	-5	-1	-0.8
1974	Atl-N	6	11	.353	20	20	3	0	0	126	148	12	49	46	14.3	4.71	80	.294	.360	7	.184	-2	-15	-13	-2	-1.6
1975	Atl-N	3	4	.429	15	7	2	0	1	54²	58	7	19	22	12.7	4.77	79	.266	.325	3	.200	1	-7	-6	0	-0.7
	Cle-A	7	7	.500	19	19	4	0	0	126	137	6	46	52	13.4	4.79	79	.275	.341	0	—	0	-14	-14	-1	-1.5
1978	Min-A	0	1	.000	9	0	0	0	0	12	18	0	11	7	21.8	7.50	50	.346	.460	0	—	0	-5	-5	-0	-0.5
Total	5	30	35	.462	140	70	12	0	10	590	590	45	257	319	13.1	4.24	87	.261	.340	15	.121	2	-43	-35	-5	-4.4

● **TOM HARRISON**   Harrison, Thomas James   b: 1/18/45, Trail, B.C., Canada   BR/TR, 6′3″, 200 lbs.   Deb: 5/7/65   ◆

YEAR	TM/L	W	L	PCT	G	GS	CG	SH	SV	IP	H	HR	BB	SO	RAT	ERA	ERA+	OAV	OOB	BH	AVG	PB	PR	/A	PD	TPI
1965	KC-A	0	0	—	1	0	0	0	0	1	2	0	1	0	27.0	9.00	39	.667	.750	0	—	0	-1	-1	-0	0.0

● **SLIM HARRISS**   Harriss, William Jennings Bryan   b: 12/11/1896, Brownwood, Tex.   d: 9/19/63, Temple, Tex.   BR/TR, 6′6″, 180 lbs.   Deb: 4/19/20

YEAR	TM/L	W	L	PCT	G	GS	CG	SH	SV	IP	H	HR	BB	SO	RAT	ERA	ERA+	OAV	OOB	BH	AVG	PB	PR	/A	PD	TPI
1920	Phi-A	9	14	.391	31	25	11	1	0	192	226	5	57	60	13.5	4.08	99	.305	.359	7	.106	-7	-6	-1	3	-0.5
1921	Phi-A	11	16	.407	39	28	14	0	2	227²	258	16	73	92	13.4	4.27	104	.290	.350	12	.148	-7	0	5	-1	-0.2
1922	Phi-A	9	20	.310	47	32	13	0	3	229²	262	19	94	102	14.1	5.02	85	.290	.359	13	.176	-4	-25	-19	1	-2.5
1923	Phi-A	10	16	.385	46	28	9	0	2	209¹	221	9	95	89	13.7	4.00	103	.280	.359	4	.066	-3	-0	3	5	-0.3
1924	Phi-A	6	10	.375	36	12	4	1	2	123	138	6	62	45	14.9	4.68	92	.291	.377	7	.167	-3	-6	-5	4	-0.5
1925	Phi-A	19	12	.613	46	33	15	2	1	252²	263	16	82	95	13.0	3.49	133	.268	.336	18	.205	-3	25	33	4	3.6
1926	Phi-A	3	5	.375	12	10	8	0	0	57	66	6	22	13	13.9	4.11	102	.289	.352	1	.059	-2	-1	0	0	-0.1
	Bos-A	6	10	.375	21	18	6	1	0	113	135	0	33	34	13.5	4.46	91	.311	.362	7	.206	-0	-6	-5	1	-0.5

YEAR	TM/L	W	L	PCT	G	GS	CG	SH	SV	IP	H	HR	BB	SO	RAT	ERA	ERA+	OAV	OOB	BH	AVG	PB	PR	/A	PD	TPI
	Yr	9	15	.375	33	28	8	1	0	170	201	0	55	47	13.7	4.34	95	.304	.359	8	.157	-2	-6	-4	1	-0.6
1927	Bos-A	14	21	.400	44	27	11	1	1	217²	253	8	66	77	13.6	4.18	101	.298	.355	8	.121	-5	-1	1	1	-0.2
1928	Bos-A	8	11	.421	27	15	4	1	1	128¹	141	5	33	37	12.3	4.63	89	.287	.335	5	.139	-3	-8	-7	-2	-1.3
Total	9	95	135	.413	349	228	89	7	16	1750¹	1963	75	630	644	13.5	4.25	100	.290	.354	82	.145	-40	-27	3	15	-2.2

● EARL HARRIST
Harrist, Earl "Irish" b: 8/20/19, Dubach, La. BR/TR, 6', 178 lbs. Deb: 8/18/45

YEAR	TM/L	W	L	PCT	G	GS	CG	SH	SV	IP	H	HR	BB	SO	RAT	ERA	ERA+	OAV	OOB	BH	AVG	PB	PR	/A	PD	TPI
1945	Cin-N	2	4	.333	14	5	1	0	0	62¹	60	2	27	15	12.7	3.61	104	.249	.327	0	.000	-2	1	1	-1	-0.2
1947	Chi-A	3	8	.273	33	4	0	0	5	93²	85	3	49	55	13.2	3.56	103	.248	.347	5	.208	-0	2	1	1	0.2
1948	Chi-A	1	3	.250	11	1	0	0	0	23	23	4	13	14	15.3	5.87	73	.267	.382	0	.000	-1	-4	-4	0	-0.7
	Was-A	3	3	.500	23	4	0	0	0	60²	70	1	37	21	16.3	4.60	94	.293	.394	3	.167	-1	-2	-2	-1	-0.3
	Yr	4	6	.400	34	5	0	0	0	83²	93	5	50	35	15.7	4.95	87	.284	.383	3	.136	-2	-6	-6	-1	-1.0
1952	StL-A	2	8	.200	36	9	1	0	5	116²	119	7	47	49	13.6	4.01	98	.269	.352	3	.097	-2	-4	-1	1	-0.3
1953	Chi-A	1	0	1.000	7	0	0	0	0	8¹	9	1	5	1	15.1	7.56	53	.290	.389	0	.000	-0	-3	-3	-0	-0.4
	Det-A	0	2	.000	8	1	0	0	0	18²	25	2	15	7	19.3	8.68	47	.333	.444	0	.000	-0	-10	-10	1	-0.8
	Yr	1	2	.333	15	1	0	0	0	27	34	3	20	8	18.0	8.33	49	.321	.429	0	.000	-0	-13	-13	1	-1.2
Total	5	12	28	.300	132	24	2	0	10	383¹	391	20	193	162	14.2	4.34	90	.268	.361	11	.115	-7	-21	-18	0	-2.5

● JACK HARSHMAN
Harshman, John Elvin b: 7/12/27, San Diego, Cal. BL/TL, 6'2", 185 lbs. Deb: 9/16/48 ♦

YEAR	TM/L	W	L	PCT	G	GS	CG	SH	SV	IP	H	HR	BB	SO	RAT	ERA	ERA+	OAV	OOB	BH	AVG	PB	PR	/A	PD	TPI
1952	NY-N	0	2	.000	2	2	0	0	0	6¹	12	2	6	6	25.6	14.21	26	.429	.529	0	.000	-0	-7	-7	0	-1.5
1954	Chi-A	14	8	.636	35	21	9	4	1	177	157	7	96	134	13.1	2.95	127	.238	.339	8	.143	-3	15	15	-1	2.1
1955	Chi-A	11	7	.611	32	23	9	0	0	179¹	144	16	97	116	12.3	3.36	117	.224	.330	11	.183	4	12	12	-0	1.4
1956	Chi-A	15	11	.577	34	30	15	4	0	226²	183	14	102	143	11.4	3.10	132	.221	.308	12	.169	6	27	25	-2	3.0
1957	Chi-A	8	8	.500	30	26	6	0	1	151¹	142	16	82	83	13.6	4.10	91	.250	.349	10	.222	5	-5	-6	-3	-0.3
1958	Bal-A	12	15	.444	34	29	17	3	4	236¹	204	20	75	161	10.7	2.89	124	.231	.294	16	.195	8	23	18	1	3.4
1959	Bal-A	0	6	.000	14	8	0	0	0	47¹	58	6	28	24	16.7	6.85	55	.319	.415	1	.200	1	-16	-16	-1	-1.5
	Bos-A	2	3	.400	8	8	0	0	0	24²	29	3	10	14	14.2	6.57	62	.284	.348	1	.143	0	-7	-7	-1	-1.2
	Cle-A	5	1	.833	13	6	5	1	1	66	46	6	13	35	8.0	2.59	142	.179	.219	7	.206	2	9	8	-0	0.9
	Yr	7	10	.412	35	16	5	1	1	138	133	14	51	73	12.0	4.76	79	.244	.308	10	.196	5	-14	-15	-1	-1.8
1960	Cle-A	2	4	.333	15	8	0	0	0	54¹	50	7	30	25	13.3	3.98	94	.243	.339	3	.176	-0	-1	-1	-1	-0.2
Total	8	69	65	.515	217	155	61	12	7	1169¹	1025	96	539	741	12.2	3.50	109	.235	.323	76	.179	29	50	41	-5	6.1

● OSCAR HARSTAD
Harstad, Oscar Theander b: 5/24/1892, Parkland, Wash. d: 11/14/67, Corvallis, Ore. BR/TR, 6', 174 lbs. Deb: 4/23/15

YEAR	TM/L	W	L	PCT	G	GS	CG	SH	SV	IP	H	HR	BB	SO	RAT	ERA	ERA+	OAV	OOB	BH	AVG	PB	PR	/A	PD	TPI
1915	Cle-A	3	5	.375	32	7	4	0	1	82	81	1	35	35	12.8	3.40	90	.270	.348	2	.125	-1	-4	-3	2	-0.2

● BILLY HART
Hart, Robert Lee b: 5/16/1866, Palmyra, Mo. d: 5/14/44, Hannibal, Mo. 5'8", Deb: 7/13/1890

YEAR	TM/L	W	L	PCT	G	GS	CG	SH	SV	IP	H	HR	BB	SO	RAT	ERA	ERA+	OAV	OOB	BH	AVG	PB	PR	/A	PD	TPI
1890	StL-a	12	8	.600	26	24	20	0	0	201¹	188	6	66	95	12.1	3.67	118	.240	.312	15	.192	-1	5	15	-3	0.8

● BILL HART
Hart, William Franklin b: 7/19/1865, Louisville, Ky. d: 9/19/36, Cincinnati, Ohio TR, 5'10", 163 lbs. Deb: 7/26/1886 U

YEAR	TM/L	W	L	PCT	G	GS	CG	SH	SV	IP	H	HR	BB	SO	RAT	ERA	ERA+	OAV	OOB	BH	AVG	PB	PR	/A	PD	TPI
1886	Phi-a	9	13	.409	22	22	22	2	0	186	183	7	66	78	12.4	3.19	110	.234	.299	10	.137	-5	5	6	1	0.3
1887	Phi-a	1	2	.333	3	3	3	0	0	26	28	1	17	14	15.9	4.50	95	.272	.380	2	.077	-2	-1	-1	0	-0.2
1892	Bro-N	9	12	.429	28	23	16	2	1	195	188	3	96	65	13.4	3.28	97	.243	.332	24	.192	3	0	-2	3	0.3
1895	Pit-N	14	17	.452	36	29	24	0	1	261²	293	4	135	85	15.2	4.75	95	.279	.369	25	.236	-2	1	-7	6	-0.3
1896	StL-N	12	29	.293	42	41	37	0	0	336	411	11	141	65	15.2	5.12	85	.299	.399	30	.186	-5	-28	-29	6	-2.5
1897	StL-N	9	27	.250	39	38	31	0	0	294²	395	10	148	67	17.1	6.26	70	.318	.398	39	.250	-1	-64	-61	3	-5.2
1898	Pit-N	5	9	.357	16	15	13	1	1	125	141	4	44	19	13.8	4.82	74	.282	.349	12	.240	0	-17	-18	0	-1.6
1901	Cle-A	7	11	.389	20	19	16	0	0	157²	180	3	57	48	14.1	3.77	94	.283	.352	14	.219	-2	-2	-4	2	-0.3
Total	8	66	120	.355	206	190	162	5	3	1582	1819	43	704	431	14.8	4.65	86	.282	.359	155	.207	-14	-105	-114	22	-9.5

● CHUCK HARTENSTEIN
Hartenstein, Charles Oscar "Twiggy" b: 5/26/42, Seguin, Tex. BR/TR, 5'11", 165 lbs. Deb: 9/11/65 C♦

YEAR	TM/L	W	L	PCT	G	GS	CG	SH	SV	IP	H	HR	BB	SO	RAT	ERA	ERA+	OAV	OOB	BH	AVG	PB	PR	/A	PD	TPI
1966	Chi-N	0	0	—	5	0	0	0	0	9¹	11	0	3	4	11.6	1.93	191	.222	.300	0	—	0	2	2	0	0.2
1967	Chi-N	9	5	.643	45	0	0	0	10	73	74	4	17	20	11.3	3.08	115	.278	.324	1	.063	-1	2	4	-0	0.7
1968	Chi-N	2	4	.333	28	0	0	0	1	35²	41	3	11	17	13.4	4.54	70	.291	.346	0	.000	-0	-6	-5	-0	-1.0
1969	Pit-N	5	4	.556	56	0	0	0	10	95²	94	9	27	44	10.8	3.95	88	.241	.303	1	.071	-4	-5	-1	0	-0.5
1970	Pit-N	1	1	.500	17	0	0	0	1	23²	25	3	8	14	12.5	4.56	85	.278	.337	0	.000	-0	-1	-2	1	-0.1
	StL-N	0	0	—	6	0	0	0	0	13¹	24	1	5	9	19.6	8.78	47	.375	.420	0	.000	-0	-7	-7	0	0.0
	Yr	1	1	.500	23	0	0	0	1	37	49	4	13	23	15.1	6.08	65	.316	.369	0	.000	-0	-8	-9	1	-0.1
	Bos-A	0	3	.000	17	0	0	0	1	19	21	6	9	11	16.1	8.05	49	.288	.395	0	.000	-0	-9	-9	-1	-1.4
1977	Tor-A	0	2	.000	13	0	0	0	0	27¹	40	8	6	15	15.5	6.59	64	.348	.385	0	—	-0	-8	-7	0	-0.5
Total	6	17	19	.472	187	0	0	0	23	297	317	34	89	135	12.6	4.52	80	.280	.337	2	.054	-2	-31	-29	2	-2.8

● FRANK HARTER
Harter, Franklin Pierce "Chief" b: 9/19/1886, Keyesport, Ill. d: 4/14/59, Breese, Ill. BR/TR, 5'11", 165 lbs. Deb: 8/31/12

YEAR	TM/L	W	L	PCT	G	GS	CG	SH	SV	IP	H	HR	BB	SO	RAT	ERA	ERA+	OAV	OOB	BH	AVG	PB	PR	/A	PD	TPI
1912	Cin-N	1	2	.333	6	3	1	0	0	29¹	25	1	11	12	11.0	3.07	110	.234	.305	1	.091	-1	1	1	-1	-0.1
1913	Cin-N	1	1	.500	17	2	0	0	0	46²	47	3	19	10	12.7	3.86	84	.272	.344	2	.143	-1	-3	-3	-1	-0.3
1914	Ind-F	1	2	.333	6	1	1	0	0	24²	33	0	7	8	14.6	4.01	78	.330	.374	0	.000	-1	-3	-2	0	-0.4
Total	3	3	5	.375	29	6	2	0	0	100²	105	4	37	30	12.7	3.67	89	.276	.341	3	.091	-3	-5	-5	-2	-0.8

● MIKE HARTLEY
Hartley, Michael Edward b: 8/31/61, Hawthorne, Cal. BR/TR, 6'1", 192 lbs. Deb: 9/10/89

YEAR	TM/L	W	L	PCT	G	GS	CG	SH	SV	IP	H	HR	BB	SO	RAT	ERA	ERA+	OAV	OOB	BH	AVG	PB	PR	/A	PD	TPI
1989	LA-N	0	1	.000	5	0	0	0	0	6	2	0	0	4	3.0	1.50	228	.100	.100	0	.000	-0	1	1	0	0.2
1990	LA-N	6	3	.667	32	6	1	1	1	79¹	58	7	30	76	10.2	2.95	124	.200	.280	1	.077	-1	7	6	-0	0.6
1991	LA-N	2	0	1.000	40	0	0	0	0	57	53	7	37	44	14.7	4.42	81	.245	.363	0	.000	-0	-5	-5	0	-0.1
	Phi-N	2	1	.667	18	0	0	0	0	26¹	21	4	10	19	11.6	3.76	98	.219	.312	0	.000	-0	-0	-1	-0	-0.1
	Yr	4	1	.800	58	0	0	0	0	83¹	74	11	47	63	13.4	4.21	86	.234	.339	0	.000	-0	-5	-6	-1	-0.3
1992	Phi-N	7	6	.538	46	0	0	0	0	55	54	5	23	53	12.9	3.44	102	.255	.333	0	.000	-0	3	3	-2	0.0
1993	Min-A	1	2	.333	53	0	0	0	0	81	86	4	36	57	14.3	4.00	109	.281	.370	0	—	-1	3	3	-2	0.0
Total	5	18	13	.581	194	6	1	1	4	304²	274	27	136	253	12.6	3.63	104	.240	.330	1	.043	-2	7	5	-3	0.5

● CHARLIE HARTMAN
Hartman, Charles Otto b: 8/10/1888, Los Angeles, Cal. d: 10/22/60, Los Angeles, Cal. Deb: 6/24/08

YEAR	TM/L	W	L	PCT	G	GS	CG	SH	SV	IP	H	HR	BB	SO	RAT	ERA	ERA+	OAV	OOB	BH	AVG	PB	PR	/A	PD	TPI
1908	Bos-A	0	0	—	1	0	0	0	0	2	1	0	2	1	13.5	4.50	55	.143	.333	0	—	-0	-0	-0	0	0.0

● BOB HARTMAN
Hartman, Robert Louis b: 8/28/37, Kenosha, Wis. BR/TL, 5'11", 185 lbs. Deb: 4/26/59

YEAR	TM/L	W	L	PCT	G	GS	CG	SH	SV	IP	H	HR	BB	SO	RAT	ERA	ERA+	OAV	OOB	BH	AVG	PB	PR	/A	PD	TPI
1959	Mil-N	0	0	—	3	0	0	0	0	1²	6	0	2	1	43.2	27.00	13	.545	.615	0	—	-0	-4	-4	-0	0.0
1962	Cle-A	0	1	.000	8	2	0	0	0	17¹	14	1	8	11	11.4	3.12	124	.209	.293	0	.000	-1	2	1	-0	0.0
Total	2	0	1	.000	11	2	0	0	0	19	20	1	10	12	14.2	5.21	74	.256	.341	0	.000	-1	-3	-3	-0	0.0

● RAY HARTRANFT
Hartranft, Raymond Joseph b: 9/19/1890, Quakertown, Pa. d: 2/10/55, Spring City, Pa. BL/TL, 6'1", 195 lbs. Deb: 6/16/13

YEAR	TM/L	W	L	PCT	G	GS	CG	SH	SV	IP	H	HR	BB	SO	RAT	ERA	ERA+	OAV	OOB	BH	AVG	PB	PR	/A	PD	TPI
1913	Phi-N	0	0	—	1	0	0	0	0	1	3	0	1	0	36.0	9.00	37	.500	.571	0	—	-0	-1	-1	0	0.0

● JEFF HARTSOCK
Hartsock, Jeffrey Roger b: 11/19/66, Fairfield, Ohio BR/TR, 6', 190 lbs. Deb: 9/12/92

YEAR	TM/L	W	L	PCT	G	GS	CG	SH	SV	IP	H	HR	BB	SO	RAT	ERA	ERA+	OAV	OOB	BH	AVG	PB	PR	/A	PD	TPI
1992	Chi-N	0	0	—	4	0	0	0	0	9¹	15	2	4	6	18.3	6.75	53	.375	.432	0	.000	-0	-3	-3	0	0.0

● CLINT HARTUNG
Hartung, Clinton Clarence "Floppy" or "The Hondo Hurricane" b: 8/10/22, Hondo, Tex. BR/TR, 6'4", 215 lbs. Deb: 4/15/47 ♦

YEAR	TM/L	W	L	PCT	G	GS	CG	SH	SV	IP	H	HR	BB	SO	RAT	ERA	ERA+	OAV	OOB	BH	AVG	PB	PR	/A	PD	TPI
1947	NY-N	9	7	.563	23	20	8	1	0	138	140	15	69	54	13.8	4.57	89	.263	.350	29	.309	9	-8	-8	-1	0.1
1948	NY-N	8	8	.500	36	19	6	2	1	153¹	146	15	72	42	13.1	4.75	83	.258	.347	10	.179	2	-14	-14	-0	-1.2
1949	NY-N	9	11	.450	33	25	8	0	0	154²	156	16	86	48	14.3	5.00	80	.261	.361	12	.190	4	-17	-18	2	-0.8
1950	NY-N	3	3	.500	20	8	1	0	0	65¹	87	10	44	23	18.3	6.61	62	.326	.425	13	.302	4	-18	-18	2	-0.8
Total	4	29	29	.500	112	72	23	3	1	511¹	529	56	271	167	14.3	5.02	80	.269	.361	90	.238	19	-56	-57	3	-3.4

YEAR TM/L	W	L	PCT	G	GS	CG	SH	SV	IP	H	HR	BB	SO	RAT	ERA	ERA+	OAV	OOB	BH	AVG	PB	PR	/A	PD	TPI
● PAUL HARTZELL				Hartzell, Paul Franklin b: 11/2/53, Bloomsburg, Pa. BR/TR, 6'5", 200 lbs. Deb: 4/10/76																				
1976 Cal-A	7	4	.636	37	15	7	2	2	166	166	6	43	51	11.9	2.77	120	.266	.323	0	—	0	14	10	1	1.3
1977 Cal-A	8	12	.400	41	23	6	0	4	189¹	200	14	38	79	11.5	3.57	110	.274	.313	0	—	0	10	7	1	0.8
1978 Cal-A	6	10	.375	54	12	5	0	6	157	168	8	41	55	12.3	3.44	105	.278	.329	0	—	0	6	3	1	0.7
1979 Min-A	6	10	.375	28	26	4	0	0	163	193	18	44	44	13.3	5.36	82	.301	.350	0	—	0	-21	-18	1	-1.4
1980 Bal-A	0	2	.000	6	0	0	0	0	17²	22	3	9	5	15.8	6.62	60	.310	.387	0	—	0	-5	-5	-1	-0.6
1984 Mil-A	0	1	.000	4	1	0	0	0	10¹	17	0	6	3	20.0	7.84	49	.370	.442	0	—	0	-4	-5	0	-0.4
Total 6	27	39	.409	170	77	22	2	12	703¹	766	49	181	237	12.4	3.90	98	.282	.332	0	—	0	-0	-7	3	0.4
● BRYAN HARVEY				Harvey, Bryan Stanley b: 6/2/63, Chattanooga, Tenn. BR/TR, 6'2", 215 lbs. Deb: 5/16/87																				
1987 Cal-A	0	0	—	3	0	0	0	0	5	6	0	2	3	14.4	0.00	—	.300	.364	0	—	0	2	2	-0	0.0
1988 Cal-A	7	5	.583	50	0	0	0	17	76	59	4	20	67	9.5	2.13	181	.214	.269	0	—	0	15	15	-2	2.8
1989 Cal-A	3	3	.500	51	0	0	0	25	55	36	6	41	78	12.6	3.44	111	.183	.324	0	—	0	3	2	0	0.6
1990 Cal-A	4	4	.500	54	0	0	0	25	64¹	45	4	35	82	11.2	3.22	119	.201	.309	0	—	0	5	4	-0	1.0
1991 Cal-A☆	2	4	.333	67	0	0	0	**46**	78²	51	6	17	101	7.9	1.60	256	.178	.227	0	—	0	22	22	-0	4.5
1992 Cal-A	0	4	.000	25	0	0	0	13	28²	22	4	11	34	10.4	2.83	141	.208	.282	0	—	0	4	4	-1	0.8
1993 Fla-N★	1	5	.167	59	0	0	0	45	69	45	4	13	73	7.6	1.70	255	.186	.227	0	—	0	18	20	-1	4.6
1994 Fla-N	0	0	—	12	0	0	0	6	10¹	12	1	4	10	13.9	5.23	86	.279	.340	0	—	0	-1	-1	-0	-0.1
Total 8	17	25	.405	321	0	0	0	177	387	276	29	143	448	9.8	2.42	166	.198	.274	0	—	0	68	68	-3	14.2
● ERWIN HARVEY				Harvey, Ervin King "Zaza" b: 1/5/1879, Saratoga, Cal. d: 6/3/54, Santa Monica, Cal. BL/TL, 6', 190 lbs. Deb: 5/3/00 ♦																				
1900 Chi-N	0	0	—	1	0	0	0	0	4	3	0	1	0	9.0	0.00	—	.208	.260	-1	—	2	2	2	-0	-0.1
1901 Chi-A	3	6	.333	16	9	5	0	1	92	91	2	34	27	12.7	3.62	96	.255	.329	10	.250	2	0	-1	2	0.3
Total 2	3	6	.333	17	9	5	0	1	96	94	2	35	27	12.6	3.47	101	.253	.326	86	.332	2	2	0	2	0.2
● HERB HASH				Hash, Herbert Howard b: 2/13/11, Woolwine, Va. BR/TR, 6'1", 180 lbs. Deb: 4/19/40																				
1940 Bos-A	7	7	.500	34	12	3	1	3	120	123	11	84	36	15.9	4.95	91	.266	.385	7	.175	-0	-8	-6	1	-0.6
1941 Bos-A	1	0	1.000	4	0	0	0	1	8¹	7	1	7	3	15.1	5.40	77	.226	.368	-0	.000	-0	-1	-1	0	-0.2
Total 2	8	7	.533	38	12	3	1	4	128¹	130	12	91	39	15.8	4.98	90	.264	.384	7	.167	-1	-9	-7	1	-0.8
● ANDY HASSLER				Hassler, Andrew Earl b: 10/18/51, Texas City, Tex. BL/TL, 6'5", 220 lbs. Deb: 5/30/71																				
1971 Cal-A	0	3	.000	6	4	0	0	0	18²	25	0	15	13	19.8	3.86	84	.333	.451	0	.000	-1	-1	-1	0	-0.2
1973 Cal-A	0	4	.000	7	4	1	0	0	31²	33	0	19	16	15.6	3.69	96	.262	.372	0	—	-0	-1	-0	0	0.3
1974 Cal-A	7	11	.389	23	22	10	2	0	162	132	6	79	76	12.2	2.61	132	.225	.326	0	—	0	18	15	0	1.7
1975 Cal-A	3	12	.200	30	18	6	1	0	133¹	158	12	53	82	14.6	5.94	60	.303	.373	0	—	0	-32	-35	1	-2.9
1976 Cal-A	0	6	.000	14	4	0	0	0	47¹	50	3	17	16	12.7	5.13	65	.284	.347	0	—	0	-8	-10	-0	-0.7
*KC-A	5	6	.455	19	14	4	1	0	99²	89	2	39	45	11.6	2.89	121	.242	.314	0	—	0	7	7	1	0.7
Yr	5	12	.294	33	18	4	1	0	147	139	5	56	61	11.9	3.61	95	.254	.323	0	—	0	-2	-3	1	0.0
1977 *KC-A	9	6	.600	29	27	3	1	0	156¹	166	7	75	83	14.2	4.20	96	.270	.354	0	—	0	-2	-3	0	-0.2
1978 KC-A	4	2	.200	11	9	1	0	0	58¹	76	1	24	26	15.7	4.32	88	.317	.383	0	—	0	-4	-1	-0	-0.3
Bos-A	2	1	.667	13	2	0	0	1	30	38	0	13	23	15.3	3.00	137	.302	.367	0	—	0	3	4	-0	0.3
Yr	3	5	.375	24	11	1	0	1	88¹	114	1	37	49	15.4	3.87	101	.308	.371	0	—	0	-1	-0	-1	0.0
1979 Bos-A	1	2	.333	8	0	0	0	0	15¹	23	0	7	7	18.2	8.80	50	.365	.437	0	—	0	-8	-7	-0	-1.4
NY-N	4	5	.444	29	8	1	0	4	80¹	74	5	42	53	13.0	3.70	98	.252	.345	0	.000	-2	0	-1	1	-0.2
1980 Pit-N	0	0	—	6	0	0	0	0	11²	9	2	4	4	10.0	3.86	94	.243	.317	0	.000	-0	-0	-0	1	0.0
Cal-A	5	1	.833	41	0	0	0	10	83	67	8	27	75	11.4	2.49	158	.214	.299	0	—	0	14	13	-1	1.3
1981 Cal-A	4	3	.571	42	0	0	0	5	75²	72	8	33	44	12.5	3.21	114	.262	.341	0	—	0	4	4	1	0.4
1982 *Cal-A	2	1	.667	54	0	0	0	4	71¹	58	5	40	33	12.9	2.78	146	.232	.347	0	—	0	10	10	2	0.7
1983 Cal-A	0	5	.000	42	0	0	0	4	36¹	42	2	17	20	14.6	5.45	74	.302	.378	0	—	0	-6	-6	1	-0.7
1984 StL-N	1	0	1.000	8	0	0	0	0	2¹	4	2	1	2	23.1	11.57	30	.364	.462	0	—	0	-2	-2	0	-0.7
1985 StL-N	1	0	1.000	10	0	0	0	0	10	9	1	4	5	11.7	1.80	196	.225	.295	0	—	0	2	2	-0	0.2
Total 14	44	71	.383	387	112	26	5	29	1123¹	1125	67	520	630	13.4	3.83	97	.264	.349	0	.000	-3	-5	-15	4	-1.7
● CHARLIE HASTINGS				Hastings, Charles Morton b: 11/11/1870, Ironton, Ohio d: 8/3/34, Parkersburg, W.Va. 5'11", 179 lbs. Deb: 5/3/1893																				
1893 Cle-N	4	5	.444	15	9	6	0	1	92	128	5	33	14	16.2	4.70	104	.320	.379	7	.179	-0	-0	2	-2	0.0
1896 Pit-N	5	10	.333	17	13	9	0	1	104	126	1	49	19	15.3	5.88	71	.297	.372	8	.216	-0	-18	-19	1	-2.0
1897 Pit-N	5	4	.556	16	10	9	0	0	118	138	3	47	42	14.6	4.58	91	.289	.362	10	.233	3	-3	-5	-1	-0.1
1898 Pit-N	4	10	.286	19	13	12	0	0	137¹	142	2	52	40	13.4	3.41	104	.265	.341	10	.233	2	3	2	1	0.5
Total 4	18	29	.383	67	45	36	0	2	451¹	534	11	176	115	14.7	4.55	91	.291	.362	35	.216	5	-18	-21	-1	-1.6
● BOB HASTY				Hasty, Robert Keller b: 5/3/1896, Canton, Ga. d: 5/28/72, Dallas, Ga. BR/TR, 6'3", 210 lbs. Deb: 9/11/19																				
1919 Phi-A	0	2	.000	2	2	1	0	0	12	15	1	4	5	14.3	5.25	65	.306	.358	1	.333	0	-3	-2	-1	-0.4
1920 Phi-A	1	3	.250	19	4	1	0	0	71²	91	5	28	12	14.9	5.02	80	.323	.384	6	.250	0	-10	-8	2	-0.2
1921 Phi-A	5	16	.238	35	22	9	0	0	179¹	238	8	40	46	14.1	4.87	92	.331	.368	20	.294	-2	-12	-8	-0	-0.5
1922 Phi-A	9	14	.391	28	26	14	1	0	192¹	225	20	41	33	12.6	4.26	100	.293	.336	15	.200	-2	-0	-2	-0	-0.4
1923 Phi-A	13	15	.464	44	36	10	1	1	243¹	274	11	72	56	13.1	4.44	93	.291	.347	17	.193	-3	-12	-9	-1	-1.2
1924 Phi-A	1	3	.250	18	4	0	0	0	52²	57	4	30	15	15.0	5.64	76	.282	.378	1	.077	-1	-8	-8	2	-0.5
Total 6	29	53	.354	146	94	35	2	1	751¹	900	49	215	167	13.5	4.65	91	.305	.355	60	.221	-3	-49	-35	-4	-3.2
● MICKEY HATCHER				Hatcher, Michael Vaughn b: 3/15/55, Cleveland, Ohio BR/TR, 6'2", 200 lbs. Deb: 8/3/79 C♦																				
1989 LA-N	0	0	—	1	0	0	0	0	1	0	0	3	0	36.0	9.00	38	—	.667	66	.295	0	-1	-1	0	0.0
● GIL HATFIELD				Hatfield, Gilbert "Colonel" b: 1/27/1855, Hoboken, N.J. d: 5/27/21, Hoboken, N.J. TR , 5'9.5", 168 lbs. Deb: 9/24/1885 F♦																				
1889 NY-N	2	4	.333	6	5	0	0	1	52	53	2	25	28	13.7	3.98	99	.256	.339	23	.184	-0	0	-0	0	-0.1
1890 NY-P	1	1	.500	3	0	0	0	0	7²	8	1	4	3	15.3	3.52	129	.257	.360	80	.279	0	1	1	-0	0.2
1891 Was-a	0	0	—	4	0	0	0	0	18	29	1	14	3	21.5	11.00	34	.351	.445	128	.256	1	-15	-15	-0	0.0
Total 3	3	5	.375	13	5	0	0	1	77²	90	4	43	34	15.6	5.56	71	.281	.369	295	.248	1	-14	-14	-0	0.2
● JOHN HATFIELD				Hatfield, John Van Buskirk b: 7/20/1847, New Jersey d: 2/20/09, Long Island City, N.Y. 5'10", 165 lbs. Deb: 5/18/1871 FM♦																				
1874 Mut-n	0	1	.000	3	0	0	0	0	8	11	0	1	2	13.5	2.25	137	.324	.343	68	.235	-0	1	1		0.1
● HILLY HATHAWAY				Hathaway, Hillary Houston b: 9/12/69, Jacksonville, Fla. BL/TL, 6'4", 195 lbs. Deb: 9/8/92																				
1992 Cal-A	0	0	—	2	1	0	0	0	5²	8	0	3	1	17.5	7.94	50	.333	.407	0	—	0	-3	-2	-0	0.0
1993 Cal-A	4	3	.571	11	11	0	0	0	57¹	71	6	26	11	16.0	5.02	90	.326	.410	0	—	0	-4	-3	1	-0.5
Total 2	4	3	.571	13	12	0	0	0	63	79	7	29	12	16.1	5.29	84	.326	.409	0	—	0	-7	-6	0	-0.5
● RAY HATHAWAY				Hathaway, Ray Wilson b: 10/13/16, Greenville, Ohio BR/TR, 6', 165 lbs. Deb: 4/20/45																				
1945 Bro-N	0	1	.000	4	1	0	0	0	9	11	1	6	3	17.0	4.00	94	.297	.395	0	.000	-0	-0	-0	0	0.0
● JOE HATTEN				Hatten, Joseph Hilarian b: 11/17/16, Bancroft, Iowa d: 12/16/88, Redding, Cal. BR/TL, 6', 176 lbs. Deb: 4/21/46																				
1946 Bro-N	14	11	.560	42	30	13	1	2	222	207	10	110	85	13.1	2.84	119	.253	.347	6	.076	-6	14	13	-2	0.6
1947 *Bro-N	17	8	.680	42	30	11	0	1	225¹	211	9	105	76	12.8	3.63	114	.205	.339	17	.205	0	11	12	3	1.5
1948 Bro-N	13	10	.565	42	30	11	1	0	208²	228	14	94	73	14.0	3.58	112	.283	.360	13	.206	1	9	10	4	1.5
1949 *Bro-N	12	8	.600	37	29	11	2	2	187¹	194	15	69	58	12.7	4.18	98	.271	.337	12	.179	-1	-3	-2	-0	-0.3
1950 Bro-N	2	2	.500	23	8	2	1	0	68²	82	10	31	29	14.8	4.59	89	.294	.365	2	.111	-1	-3	-4	-1	-0.4

YEAR	TM/L	W	L	PCT	G	GS	CG	SH	SV	IP	H	HR	BB	SO	RAT	ERA	ERA+	OAV	OOB	BH	AVG	PB	PR	/A	PD	TPI
1951	Bro-N	1	0	1.000	11	6	0	0	0	49¹	55	3	21	22	13.9	4.56	86	.281	.350	2	.133	-1	-3	-3	1	-0.1
	Chi-N	2	6	.250	23	6	1	0	0	75¹	82	8	37	23	14.3	5.14	80	.281	.364	4	.235	-0	-10	-9	-0	-0.8
	Yr	3	6	.333	34	12	1	0	0	124²	137	11	58	45	14.1	4.91	82	.281	.358	6	.188	-1	-13	-12	1	-0.9
1952	Chi-N	4	4	.500	13	8	2	0	0	50¹	65	6	25	15	16.3	6.08	63	.314	.391	1	.067	-1	-13	-12	1	-1.7
Total	7	65	49	.570	233	149	51	8	4	1087	1124	70	492	381	13.5	3.87	101	.271	.351	57	.160	-8	1	5	6	0.3

● **CLYDE HATTER**   Hatter, Clyde Melno b: 8/7/08, Poplar Hills, Ky. d: 10/16/37, Yosemite, Ky. BR/TL, 5'11", 170 lbs. Deb: 4/23/35

YEAR	TM/L	W	L	PCT	G	GS	CG	SH	SV	IP	H	HR	BB	SO	RAT	ERA	ERA+	OAV	OOB	BH	AVG	PB	PR	/A	PD	TPI
1935	Det-A	0	0	—	8	2	0	0	0	33¹	44	2	30	15	20.3	7.56	55	.319	.444	3	.300	0	-12	-13	-1	-0.1
1937	Det-A	1	0	1.000	3	0	0	0	0	9¹	17	0	11	4	28.0	11.57	40	.415	.547	0	.000	-0	-7	-7	-0	-0.6
Total	2	1	0	1.000	11	2	0	0	0	42²	61	2	41	19	21.9	8.44	51	.341	.468	3	.231	0	-19	-20	-1	-0.7

● **CHRIS HAUGHEY**   Haughey, Christopher Francis "Bud" b: 10/3/25, Astoria, N.Y. BR/TR, 6'1", 180 lbs. Deb: 10/3/43

YEAR	TM/L	W	L	PCT	G	GS	CG	SH	SV	IP	H	HR	BB	SO	RAT	ERA	ERA+	OAV	OOB	BH	AVG	PB	PR	/A	PD	TPI
1943	Bro-N	0	1	.000	1	0	0	0	0	7	5	0	10	0	19.3	3.86	87	.238	.484	0	.000	-0	-0	-0	-0	-0.1

● **PHIL HAUGSTAD**   Haugstad, Philip Donald b: 2/23/24, Black River Falls, Wis. BR/TR, 6'2", 165 lbs. Deb: 9/1/47

YEAR	TM/L	W	L	PCT	G	GS	CG	SH	SV	IP	H	HR	BB	SO	RAT	ERA	ERA+	OAV	OOB	BH	AVG	PB	PR	/A	PD	TPI
1947	Bro-N	1	0	1.000	6	1	0	0	0	12²	14	1	4	4	12.8	2.84	145	.298	.353	0	.000	-0	2	2	-0	0.1
1948	Bro-N	0	0	—	1	0	0	0	0	1	1	0	1	0	9.0	0.00	—	.333	.333	0	—	-0	0	0	0	0.0
1951	Bro-N	0	1	.000	21	1	0	0	0	30²	28	4	24	22	16.1	6.46	61	.233	.374	0	.000	-0	-9	-9	0	-0.2
1952	Cin-N	0	0	—	9	0	0	0	0	12	8	1	12	2	15.0	6.75	56	.190	.393	0	.000	-0	-4	-4	0	0.0
Total	4	1	1	.500	37	2	0	0	0	56¹	51	6	41	28	15.3	5.59	70	.241	.374	0	.000	-0	-10	-10	1	-0.1

● **TOM HAUSMAN**   Hausman, Thomas Matthew b: 3/31/53, Mobridge, S.D. BR/TR, 6'5", 200 lbs. Deb: 4/26/75

YEAR	TM/L	W	L	PCT	G	GS	CG	SH	SV	IP	H	HR	BB	SO	RAT	ERA	ERA+	OAV	OOB	BH	AVG	PB	PR	/A	PD	TPI
1975	Mil-A	3	6	.333	29	9	1	0	0	112	110	7	47	46	13.1	4.10	93	.258	.340	0	—	0	-4	-3	1	-0.2
1976	Mil-A	0	0	—	3	0	0	0	0	3¹	3	0	3	1	16.2	5.40	65	.250	.400	0	—	0	-1	-1	0	0.2
1978	NY-N	3	3	.500	10	10	0	0	0	51²	58	6	9	16	11.8	4.70	74	.287	.321	3	.176	1	-6	-7	0	-0.7
1979	NY-N	2	6	.250	19	10	1	0	2	78²	84	9	19	33	10.1	2.75	133	.226	.284	3	.115	-1	9	8	0	0.7
1980	NY-N	6	5	.545	55	4	0	0	1	122	125	12	26	53	11.4	3.98	89	.266	.309	1	.063	-1	-5	-6	1	-0.5
1981	NY-N	0	1	.000	20	0	0	0	0	33	28	2	7	13	9.5	2.18	160	.235	.278	0	.000	-0	5	5	0	0.2
1982	NY-N	1	2	.333	21	0	0	0	0	36²	44	4	6	16	12.8	4.42	82	.295	.331	0	.000	-0	-3	-3	-1	-0.3
	Atl-N	0	0	—	3	0	0	0	0	3²	6	0	4	2	24.5	4.91	76	.500	.625	0	—	0	-1	-0	0	0.0
	Yr	1	2	.333	24	0	0	0	0	40¹	50	4	10	18	13.4	4.46	82	.299	.339	0	.000	-0	-4	-4	-0	-0.3
Total	7	15	23	.395	160	33	2	0	3	441	439	37	121	180	11.8	3.80	96	.262	.317	7	.111	-2	-7	-8	2	-0.6

● **CLEM HAUSMANN**   Hausmann, Clemens Raymond b: 8/17/19, Houston, Tex. d: 8/29/72, Baytown, Tex. BR/TR, 5'9", 165 lbs. Deb: 4/28/44

YEAR	TM/L	W	L	PCT	G	GS	CG	SH	SV	IP	H	HR	BB	SO	RAT	ERA	ERA+	OAV	OOB	BH	AVG	PB	PR	/A	PD	TPI
1944	Bos-A	4	7	.364	32	12	3	0	2	137	139	6	69	43	13.9	3.42	99	.266	.355	3	.079	-3	0	-0	-0	-0.3
1945	Bos-A	5	7	.417	31	13	4	2	2	125	131	5	60	30	13.9	5.04	68	.270	.352	4	.103	-3	-23	-23	2	-2.2
1949	Phi-A	0	0	—	1	0	0	0	0	1	0	0	2	0	18.0	9.00	46	.000	.500	0	—	0	-1	-1	0	0.0
Total	3	9	14	.391	64	25	7	2	4	263	270	11	131	73	13.9	4.21	81	.267	.354	7	.091	-5	-24	-23	2	-2.5

● **BRAD HAVENS**   Havens, Bradley David b: 11/17/59, Highland Park, Mich BL/TL, 6'1", 196 lbs. Deb: 6/5/81

YEAR	TM/L	W	L	PCT	G	GS	CG	SH	SV	IP	H	HR	BB	SO	RAT	ERA	ERA+	OAV	OOB	BH	AVG	PB	PR	/A	PD	TPI
1981	Min-A	3	6	.333	14	12	1	1	0	78	76	6	24	43	11.7	3.58	110	.257	.315	0	—	0	1	3	-1	0.0
1982	Min-A	10	14	.417	33	32	4	1	0	208²	201	32	80	129	12.1	4.31	98	.250	.318	0	—	0	-6	-2	-3	-0.5
1983	Min-A	5	8	.385	16	14	1	0	0	80¹	110	11	38	40	16.6	8.18	52	.333	.402	0	—	0	-37	-35	-2	-4.7
1985	Bal-A	0	1	.000	8	1	0	0	0	14¹	20	4	10	19	18.8	8.79	46	.333	.429	0	—	0	-7	-8	-0	-0.3
1986	Bal-A	3	3	.500	46	0	0	0	1	71	64	7	29	57	11.6	4.56	91	.248	.324	0	—	0	-3	-3	1	-0.1
1987	LA-N	0	0	—	31	1	0	0	1	35¹	30	2	23	23	13.8	4.33	92	.227	.346	0	.000	-0	-1	-1	-1	-0.1
1988	LA-N	0	0	—	9	0	0	0	0	9²	15	1	4	8	17.7	4.66	72	.357	.413	0	.000	-0	-1	-1	1	0.1
	Cle-A	2	3	.400	28	0	0	0	0	57¹	62	6	17	50	12.4	3.14	131	.273	.324	0	—	0	5	6	-0	0.4
1989	Cle-A	0	0	—	7	0	0	0	0	13¹	18	3	7	6	16.9	4.05	98	.353	.431	0	—	0	-0	-1	1	0.0
	Det-A	1	2	.333	13	1	0	0	0	22²	28	3	14	15	17.9	5.56	69	.308	.417	0	—	0	-4	-4	0	-0.4
	Yr	1	2	.333	20	1	0	0	0	36	46	6	21	21	17.5	5.00	77	.319	.417	0	—	0	-4	-5	1	-0.4
Total	8	24	37	.393	205	61	6	2	3	590²	624	76	246	370	13.3	4.81	86	.272	.344	0	.000	-0	-54	-46	-4	-5.6

● **ED HAWK**   Hawk, Edward b: 5/11/1890, Neosho, Mo. d: 3/26/36, Neosho, Mo. BL/TR, 5'11", 175 lbs. Deb: 9/7/11

YEAR	TM/L	W	L	PCT	G	GS	CG	SH	SV	IP	H	HR	BB	SO	RAT	ERA	ERA+	OAV	OOB	BH	AVG	PB	PR	/A	PD	TPI
1911	StL-A	0	4	.000	5	4	4	0	0	37²	38	1	8	14	11.9	3.35	101	.253	.309	2	.154	-1	-0	0	0	-0.1

● **BILL HAWKE**   Hawke, William Victor "Dick" b: 4/28/1870, Elsmere, Del. d: 12/11/02, Wilmington, Del. BR/TR, 5'8.5", 169 lbs. Deb: 7/28/1892

YEAR	TM/L	W	L	PCT	G	GS	CG	SH	SV	IP	H	HR	BB	SO	RAT	ERA	ERA+	OAV	OOB	BH	AVG	PB	PR	/A	PD	TPI
1892	StL-N	5	5	.500	14	11	10	1	0	97¹	108	2	45	55	14.9	3.70	86	.270	.355	4	.089	-4	-4	-5	0	-0.9
1893	StL-N	0	1	.000	1	1	0	0	0	5¹	9	0	3	1	20.3	5.06	93	.363	.432	1	.333	-0	-0	-0	-0	-0.0
	Bal-N	11	16	.407	29	29	22	1	0	225	248	8	108	69	14.6	4.76	100	.271	.354	16	.172	-4	-2	-1	0	-0.4
	Yr	11	17	.393	30	30	22	1	0	230¹	257	8	111	70	14.7	4.77	100	.274	.356	17	.177	-4	-3	-1	0	-0.4
1894	*Bal-N	16	9	.640	32	25	17	0	3	206	264	9	78	68	16.5	5.81	94	.308	.374	28	.304	-2	-11	-8	1	-0.5
Total	3	32	31	.508	76	66	49	2	3	533²	629	19	234	193	15.0	4.98	95	.286	.363	49	.210	-7	-18	-15	1	-1.8

● **ANDY HAWKINS**   Hawkins, Melton Andrew b: 1/21/60, Waco, Tex. BR/TR, 6'3", 223 lbs. Deb: 7/17/82

YEAR	TM/L	W	L	PCT	G	GS	CG	SH	SV	IP	H	HR	BB	SO	RAT	ERA	ERA+	OAV	OOB	BH	AVG	PB	PR	/A	PD	TPI
1982	SD-N	2	5	.286	15	10	1	0	0	63²	66	4	27	25	13.4	4.10	84	.274	.352	0	.000	-2	-4	-5	-1	-0.7
1983	SD-N	5	7	.417	21	19	4	1	0	119²	106	8	48	59	12.0	2.93	119	.244	.326	2	.065	-1	9	7	1	0.7
1984	*SD-N	8	9	.471	36	22	2	1	0	146	143	13	72	77	13.4	4.68	76	.254	.341	8	.195	1	-18	-18	-1	-2.0
1985	SD-N	18	8	.692	33	33	5	2	0	228²	229	16	65	69	11.7	3.15	112	.267	.321	6	.078	-4	11	10	-1	0.6
1986	SD-N	10	8	.556	37	35	3	1	0	209¹	218	24	75	117	12.8	4.30	85	.268	.334	10	.149	-1	-14	-15	-2	-1.4
1987	SD-N	3	10	.231	24	20	0	0	0	117²	131	16	49	51	13.9	5.05	78	.287	.358	5	.156	-1	-13	-14	0	-1.4
1988	SD-N	14	11	.560	33	33	4	2	0	217²	196	16	76	91	11.5	3.35	101	.244	.314	7	.113	-2	2	1	-3	-0.2
1989	NY-A	15	15	.500	34	34	5	2	0	208	238	23	76	98	13.8	4.80	81	.290	.355	0	—	0	-21	-21	-3	-2.9
1990	NY-A	5	12	.294	28	26	2	1	0	157²	156	20	82	74	13.7	5.37	74	.260	.351	0	—	0	-26	-24	-2	-2.5
1991	NY-A	0	2	.000	4	3	0	0	0	12²	23	5	6	5	20.6	9.95	42	.383	.439	0	—	0	-8	-8	1	-0.9
	Oak-A	4	4	.500	15	14	1	0	0	77	68	5	36	40	12.7	4.79	80	.237	.332	0	—	0	-6	-8	0	-0.7
	Yr	4	6	.400	19	17	1	0	0	89²	91	10	42	45	13.9	5.52	70	.262	.350	0	—	0	-14	-16	1	-1.6
Total	10	84	91	.480	280	249	27	10	0	1558¹	1574	152	612	706	12.9	4.22	87	.265	.338	38	.117	-8	-86	-96	-11	-11.5

● **WYNN HAWKINS**   Hawkins, Wynn Firth "Hawk" b: 2/20/36, E.Palestine, Ohio BR/TR, 6'3", 195 lbs. Deb: 4/22/60

YEAR	TM/L	W	L	PCT	G	GS	CG	SH	SV	IP	H	HR	BB	SO	RAT	ERA	ERA+	OAV	OOB	BH	AVG	PB	PR	/A	PD	TPI
1960	Cle-A	4	4	.500	15	9	1	0	0	66	68	10	39	39	14.7	4.23	88	.269	.369	2	.100	-1	-3	-4	1	-0.4
1961	Cle-A	7	9	.438	30	21	3	1	1	133	139	16	59	51	13.5	4.06	97	.270	.347	4	.108	-2	-1	-2	-1	-0.5
1962	Cle-A	1	0	1.000	3	0	0	0	0	3²	9	1	1	0	24.5	7.36	53	.429	.455	0	—	0	-1	-1	-0	-0.3
Total	3	12	13	.480	48	30	4	1	1	202²	216	27	99	90	14.1	4.17	93	.274	.357	6	.105	-3	-5	-7	1	-1.2

● **PINK HAWLEY**   Hawley, Emerson P. b: 12/5/1872, Beaver Dam, Wis. d: 9/19/38, Beaver Dam, Wis. BL/TR, 5'10", 185 lbs. Deb: 8/13/1892

YEAR	TM/L	W	L	PCT	G	GS	CG	SH	SV	IP	H	HR	BB	SO	RAT	ERA	ERA+	OAV	OOB	BH	AVG	PB	PR	/A	PD	TPI
1892	StL-N	6	14	.300	20	20	18	0	0	166¹	160	4	63	63	12.7	3.19	100	.243	.319	12	.169	-2	2	0	-2	-0.4
1893	StL-N	5	17	.227	31	24	21	0	1	227	249	6	103	73	14.7	4.60	103	.270	.356	26	.286	7	2	3	2	0.6
1894	StL-N	19	27	.413	53	41	36	0	0	392²	481	14	149	120	14.9	4.90	110	.298	.365	43	.264	2	18	22	2	2.1
1895	Pit-N	31	22	.585	**56**	50	44	**4**	1	**444**¹	449	7	122	142	12.2	3.18	142	.258	.319	57	.308	14	**79**	66	2	**7.4**
1896	Pit-N	22	21	.512	49	43	37	2	0	378	382	2	157	137	13.5	3.57	118	.260	.343	39	.239	2	33	26	3	2.8
1897	Pit-N	18	18	.500	40	39	33	0	0	311¹	362	7	94	88	13.9	4.80	87	.288	.350	30	.231	-2	-17	-22	0	-2.0
1898	Cin-N	27	11	.711	43	37	32	0	0	331	357	5	91	66	12.8	3.37	114	.273	.331	24	.185	-4	9	17	-5	0.7
1899	Cin-N	14	17	.452	34	29	25	0	1	250¹	289	7	65	46	13.4	4.24	99	.289	.344	22	.218	-1	-11	-9	-2	-1.2
1900	NY-N	18	18	.500	41	38	**34**	2	0	329¹	377	7	89	80	13.3	3.53	103	.287	.341	25	.203	-2	6	3	4	0.5

YEAR	TM/L	W	L	PCT	G	GS	CG	SH	SV	IP	H	HR	BB	SO	RAT	ERA	ERA+	OAV	OOB	BH	AVG	PB	PR	/A	PD	TPI
1901	Mil-A	7	14	.333	26	23	17	0	0	182¹	228	3	41	50	13.7	4.59	78	.302	.346	19	.260	2	-19	-20	1	-1.5
Total	10	167	179	.483	393	344	297	11	3	3012²	3334	62	974	868	13.5	3.96	107	.277	.342	297	.241	15	103	89	-0	9.0

● **SCOTT HAWLEY**   Hawley, Marvin Hiram b: Painesville, Ohio d: 4/28/04, Alliance, Ohio   Deb: 9/22/1894

YEAR	TM/L	W	L	PCT	G	GS	CG	SH	SV	IP	H	HR	BB	SO	RAT	ERA	ERA+	OAV	OOB	BH	AVG	PB	PR	/A	PD	TPI
1894	Bos-N	0	1	.000	1	1	1	0	0	7	10	0	7	1	24.4	7.71	74	.332	.485	0	.000	-1	-2	-2	0	-0.2

● **HAL HAYDEL**   Haydel, John Harold b: 7/9/44, Houma, La. BR/TR, 6', 190 lbs. Deb: 9/7/70

YEAR	TM/L	W	L	PCT	G	GS	CG	SH	SV	IP	H	HR	BB	SO	RAT	ERA	ERA+	OAV	OOB	BH	AVG	PB	PR	/A	PD	TPI
1970	Min-A	2	0	1.000	4	0	0	0	0	9	7	2	4	4	11.0	3.00	124	.226	.314	2	.667	2	1	1	-0	0.4
1971	Min-A	4	2	.667	31	0	0	0	1	40	33	3	20	29	12.1	4.27	83	.243	.348	1	.333	0	-4	-3	0	-0.5
Total	2	6	2	.750	35	0	0	0	1	49	40	5	24	33	12.1	4.04	89	.240	.342	3	.500	2	-3	-2	-0	-0.1

● **LEFTY HAYDEN**   Hayden, Eugene Franklin b: 4/14/35, San Francisco, Cal BL/TL, 6'2", 175 lbs. Deb: 6/26/58

YEAR	TM/L	W	L	PCT	G	GS	CG	SH	SV	IP	H	HR	BB	SO	RAT	ERA	ERA+	OAV	OOB	BH	AVG	PB	PR	/A	PD	TPI
1958	Cin-N	0	0	—	3	0	0	0	0	3²	5	0	1	3	14.7	4.91	84	.313	.353	0	—	-0	-0	-0	-1	0.0

● **BEN HAYES**   Hayes, Ben Joseph b: 8/4/57, Niagara Falls, N.Y. BR/TR, 6'1", 180 lbs. Deb: 6/25/82

YEAR	TM/L	W	L	PCT	G	GS	CG	SH	SV	IP	H	HR	BB	SO	RAT	ERA	ERA+	OAV	OOB	BH	AVG	PB	PR	/A	PD	TPI
1982	Cin-N	2	0	1.000	26	0	0	0	0	45²	37	3	22	38	11.6	1.97	188	.219	.309	0	.000	-0	8	9	-1	0.3
1983	Cin-N	4	6	.400	60	0	0	0	7	69¹	82	8	37	44	15.6	6.49	59	.301	.387	0	.000	-1	-22	-21	0	-3.2
Total	2	6	6	.500	86	0	0	0	9	115	119	11	59	82	14.0	4.70	80	.270	.357	0	.000	-1	-14	-12	-1	-2.9

● **JIM HAYES**   Hayes, James Millard "Whitey" b: 2/25/12, Montevallo, Ala. d: 11/27/93, Decatur, Ga. BL/TR, 6'1", 168 lbs. Deb: 7/13/35

YEAR	TM/L	W	L	PCT	G	GS	CG	SH	SV	IP	H	HR	BB	SO	RAT	ERA	ERA+	OAV	OOB	BH	AVG	PB	PR	/A	PD	TPI
1935	Was-A	2	4	.333	7	4	1	0	0	28	38	0	23	9	19.6	8.36	52	.322	.433	2	.250	-0	-12	-13	-1	-2.0

● **HEATH HAYNES**   Haynes, Heath Burnett b: 11/30/68, Wheeling, W.Va. BR/TR, 6', 175 lbs. Deb: 6/1/94

YEAR	TM/L	W	L	PCT	G	GS	CG	SH	SV	IP	H	HR	BB	SO	RAT	ERA	ERA+	OAV	OOB	BH	AVG	PB	PR	/A	PD	TPI
1994	Mon-N	0	0	—	4	0	0	0	0	3²	3	0	3	1	14.7	0.00	—	.231	.375	0	—	0	2	2	-0	0.0

● **JOE HAYNES**   Haynes, Joseph Walton b: 9/21/17, Lincolnton, Ga. d: 1/6/67, Hopkins, Minn. BR/TR, 6'2.5", 190 lbs. Deb: 4/24/39 C

YEAR	TM/L	W	L	PCT	G	GS	CG	SH	SV	IP	H	HR	BB	SO	RAT	ERA	ERA+	OAV	OOB	BH	AVG	PB	PR	/A	PD	TPI
1939	Was-A	8	12	.400	27	20	10	1	0	173	186	10	78	64	13.8	5.36	81	.276	.352	14	.209	0	-14	-19	-1	-1.9
1940	Was-A	3	6	.333	22	7	1	0	0	63¹	85	4	34	23	17.1	6.54	64	.327	.407	2	.105	-2	-15	-17	-1	-2.1
1941	Chi-A	0	0	—	8	0	0	0	0	28	30	0	11	18	13.2	3.86	106	.280	.347	3	.273	0	1	1	-0	0.0
1942	Chi-A	8	5	.615	40	1	1	0	6	103	88	6	47	35	12.1	2.62	137	.234	.324	5	.179	0	12	11	0	1.5
1943	Chi-A	7	2	.778	35	2	1	0	3	109¹	114	2	32	37	12.2	2.96	113	.263	.316	9	.265	2	4	5	-1	0.5
1944	Chi-A	5	6	.455	33	12	8	0	2	154¹	148	5	43	44	11.1	2.57	134	.254	.306	10	.200	1	15	15	0	1.3
1945	Chi-A	5	5	.500	14	13	6	1	1	104	92	5	29	34	10.6	3.55	94	.237	.291	7	.175	-2	-2	-3	-1	-0.4
1946	Chi-A	7	9	.438	32	23	9	0	2	177¹	203	14	60	61	13.6	3.76	91	.289	.349	14	.246	3	-5	-7	-1	-0.2
1947	Chi-A	14	6	.700	29	22	7	2	0	182	174	6	61	50	11.7	**2.42**	**151**	.250	.312	17	.262	2	26	25	0	2.9
1948	Chi-A☆	9	10	.474	27	22	8	0	0	149²	167	13	52	40	13.3	3.97	107	.284	.344	8	.160	-1	5	5	-2	0.2
1949	Was-A	2	9	.182	37	10	0	0	2	96¹	106	6	55	19	15.3	6.26	68	.283	.380	6	.240	1	-22	-21	1	-2.0
1950	Was-A	7	5	.583	27	10	1	1	0	101²	124	14	46	15	15.5	5.84	77	.305	.382	7	.200	1	-14	-15	-1	-1.3
1951	Was-A	1	4	.200	26	3	1	0	2	73	85	9	37	18	15.2	4.56	90	.290	.372	7	.333	2	-4	-4	-1	-0.1
1952	Was-A	0	3	.000	22	2	0	0	3	66	70	2	35	18	14.5	4.50	79	.275	.364	2	.105	-1	-6	-7	-1	-0.5
Total	14	76	82	.481	379	147	53	5	21	1581	1672	95	620	475	13.2	4.01	96	.272	.342	111	.213	7	-20	-31	-2	-2.1

● **RAY HAYWARD**   Hayward, Raymond Alton b: 4/27/61, Enid, Okla. BL/TL, 6'1", 190 lbs. Deb: 9/20/86

YEAR	TM/L	W	L	PCT	G	GS	CG	SH	SV	IP	H	HR	BB	SO	RAT	ERA	ERA+	OAV	OOB	BH	AVG	PB	PR	/A	PD	TPI
1986	SD-N	0	2	.000	3	3	0	0	0	10	16	1	4	6	18.0	9.00	41	.340	.392	0	.000	-0	-6	-6	-0	-1.0
1987	SD-N	0	0	—	4	0	0	0	0	6	12	3	3	2	22.5	16.50	24	.444	.500	0	.000	-0	-8	-8	1	0.0
1988	Tex-A	4	6	.400	12	12	1	1	0	62²	63	6	35	37	14.1	5.46	75	.276	.373	0	—	0	-10	-10	1	-1.3
Total	3	4	8	.333	19	15	1	1	0	78²	91	10	42	45	15.2	6.75	60	.301	.387	0	.000	-1	-25	-24	1	-2.3

● **BILL HAYWOOD**   Haywood, William Kiernan b: 4/21/37, Colon, Panama BR/TR, 6'3", 205 lbs. Deb: 7/28/68

YEAR	TM/L	W	L	PCT	G	GS	CG	SH	SV	IP	H	HR	BB	SO	RAT	ERA	ERA+	OAV	OOB	BH	AVG	PB	PR	/A	PD	TPI
1968	Was-A	0	0	—	14	0	0	0	0	23	27	1	12	10	16.0	4.70	62	.314	.410	0	—	0	-4	-5	-0	0.0

● **ED HEAD**   Head, Edward Marvin b: 1/25/18, Selma, La. d: 1/31/80, Bastrop, La. BR/TR, 6'1", 175 lbs. Deb: 7/27/40

YEAR	TM/L	W	L	PCT	G	GS	CG	SH	SV	IP	H	HR	BB	SO	RAT	ERA	ERA+	OAV	OOB	BH	AVG	PB	PR	/A	PD	TPI
1940	Bro-N	1	2	.333	13	5	2	0	0	39¹	40	0	18	13	13.3	4.12	97	.260	.337	2	.182	-0	-1	-1	-1	-0.2
1942	Bro-N	10	6	.625	36	15	5	1	4	136²	118	11	47	78	11.1	3.56	92	.231	.300	13	.333	4	-4	-4	0	-0.1
1943	Bro-N	9	10	.474	47	18	7	3	6	169²	166	8	66	83	12.3	3.66	92	.250	.318	7	.152	-2	-5	-6	1	-0.7
1944	Bro-N	4	3	.571	9	8	5	1	0	63¹	54	2	19	17	10.4	2.70	132	.232	.290	5	.263	1	6	6	-1	0.6
1946	Bro-N	3	2	.600	13	7	3	1	1	56	56	3	24	17	12.9	3.21	105	.267	.342	5	.313	1	1	1	-0	0.2
Total	5	27	23	.540	118	53	22	6	11	465	434	24	174	208	11.8	3.48	98	.245	.314	32	.244	5	-2	-4	-0	-0.2

● **RALPH HEAD**   Head, Ralph b: 8/30/1893, Tallapoosa, Ga. d: 10/8/62, Muscadine, Ala. BR/TR, 5'10", 175 lbs. Deb: 4/18/23

YEAR	TM/L	W	L	PCT	G	GS	CG	SH	SV	IP	H	HR	BB	SO	RAT	ERA	ERA+	OAV	OOB	BH	AVG	PB	PR	/A	PD	TPI
1923	Phi-N	2	9	.182	35	13	5	0	0	132¹	185	13	57	24	16.5	6.66	69	.341	.404	3	.071	-5	-39	-30	-1	-2.6

● **TOM HEALEY**   Healey, Thomas F. b: 1853, Cranston, R.I. d: 2/6/1891, Lewiston, Maine TR , Deb: 6/13/1878

YEAR	TM/L	W	L	PCT	G	GS	CG	SH	SV	IP	H	HR	BB	SO	RAT	ERA	ERA+	OAV	OOB	BH	AVG	PB	PR	/A	PD	TPI
1878	Pro-N	0	3	.000	3	3	3	0	0	24	27	1	2	7	12.8	3.00	74	.278	.327	2	.222	0	-2	-2	-0	-0.2
	Ind-N	6	4	.600	11	10	9	0	1	89	98	1	13	18	11.2	2.22	91	.270	.295	8	.178	-1	1	2	-1	-0.3
	Yr	6	7	.462	14	13	12	0	1	113	125	2	20	20	11.5	2.39	87	.272	.302	10	.185	-1	-1	-4	-0	-0.5

● **JOHN HEALY**   Healy, John J. "Egyptian" or "Long John" b: 10/27/1866, Cairo, Ill. d: 3/16/1899, St.Louis, Mo. BR/TR, 6'2", 158 lbs. Deb: 9/11/1885

YEAR	TM/L	W	L	PCT	G	GS	CG	SH	SV	IP	H	HR	BB	SO	RAT	ERA	ERA+	OAV	OOB	BH	AVG	PB	PR	/A	PD	TPI
1885	StL-N	1	7	.125	8	8	8	0	0	66	54	0	20	32	10.1	3.00	92	.210	.267	1	.042	-3	-1	-2	1	-0.4
1886	StL-N	17	23	.425	43	41	39	3	0	353²	315	5	118	213	11.0	2.88	112	.230	.291	14	.097	-12	17	14	-2	0.0
1887	Ind-N	12	29	.293	41	41	40	3	0	341	415	24	108	75	14.2	5.17	80	.294	.350	24	.174	-4	-42	-39	-4	-4.0
1888	Ind-N	12	24	.333	37	37	36	1	0	321¹	347	13	87	124	12.6	3.89	76	.267	.330	30	.229	4	-37	-33	1	-2.8
1889	Was-N	1	11	.083	13	12	10	0	0	101	139	2	38	49	16.2	6.24	63	.317	.378	10	.222	1	-25	-26	2	-2.0
	Chi-N	1	4	.200	5	5	5	0	0	46	48	4	18	22	13.7	4.50	92	.261	.339	2	.100	-2	-2	-2	-0	-0.3
	Yr	2	15	.118	18	17	15	0	0	147	187	6	56	71	15.1	5.69	70	.298	.359	12	.185	-1	-27	-27	1	-2.3
1890	Tol-a	22	21	.512	46	46	44	2	0	389	326	5	127	225	11.0	2.89	137	.221	.293	34	.218	7	42	46	-2	4.7
1891	Bal-a	8	10	.444	23	22	19	0	0	170¹	179	6	57	54	12.7	3.75	100	.261	.322	9	.141	-2	-1	-0	-5	-0.6
1892	Bal-N	3	6	.333	9	8	5	0	0	68¹	82	4	21	24	13.8	4.74	72	.286	.339	6	.222	0	-11	-10	-0	-1.0
	Lou-N	1	1	.500	2	2	2	0	0	18¹	15	0	7	4	9.8	1.96	156	.214	.286	2	.286	1	3	2	-1	0.3
	Yr	4	7	.364	11	10	7	0	0	86²	97	4	28	28	12.8	4.15	81	.270	.320	8	.235	1	-8	-8	-1	-0.7
Total	8	78	136	.364	227	222	208	9	0	1875	1920	63	599	822	12.4	3.84	94	.257	.318	132	.174	-9	-57	-50	-10	-6.1

● **CHARLIE HEARD**   Heard, Charles b: 1/30/1872, Philadelphia, Pa. d: 2/20/45, Philadelphia, Pa. BR/TR, 6'2", 190 lbs. Deb: 7/14/1890 ♦

YEAR	TM/L	W	L	PCT	G	GS	CG	SH	SV	IP	H	HR	BB	SO	RAT	ERA	ERA+	OAV	OOB	BH	AVG	PB	PR	/A	PD	TPI
1890	Pit-N	0	6	.000	6	6	5	0	0	44	75	5	32	13	22.3	8.39	39	.365	.455	8	.186	-1	-24	-25	-1	-2.3

● **JAY HEARD**   Heard, Jehosie b: 1/17/20, Atlanta, Ga. BL/TL, 5'7", 155 lbs. Deb: 4/24/54

YEAR	TM/L	W	L	PCT	G	GS	CG	SH	SV	IP	H	HR	BB	SO	RAT	ERA	ERA+	OAV	OOB	BH	AVG	PB	PR	/A	PD	TPI
1954	Bal-A	0	0	—	2	0	0	0	0	3¹	6	1	3	2	24.3	13.50	27	.375	.474	0	—	0	-4	-4	0	0.0

● **BUNNY HEARN**   Hearn, Bunn b: 5/21/1891, Chapel Hill, N.C. d: 10/10/59, Wilson, N.C. BL/TL, 5'11", 190 lbs. Deb: 9/17/10

YEAR	TM/L	W	L	PCT	G	GS	CG	SH	SV	IP	H	HR	BB	SO	RAT	ERA	ERA+	OAV	OOB	BH	AVG	PB	PR	/A	PD	TPI
1910	StL-N	1	3	.250	5	5	4	0	0	39	49	2	16	14	15.2	5.08	59	.322	.391	2	.133	-0	-9	-9	-1	-0.9
1911	StL-N	0	0	—	2	0	0	0	0	2²	7	1	0	1	23.6	13.50	25	.538	.538	0	.000	-0	-3	-3	-0	0.0
1913	NY-N	1	1	.500	2	2	1	0	0	13	13	0	7	8	13.8	2.77	113	.277	.370	2	.400	1	1	1	0	0.1
1915	Pit-F	6	11	.353	29	17	8	1	0	175²	187	6	49	77	11.6	3.38	80	.285	.326	10	.189	-0	-13	-13	-1	-1.3
1918	Bos-N	5	6	.455	17	12	9	1	0	126¹	119	2	29	30	10.5	2.49	108	.256	.300	8	.178	-1	4	3	1	0.2
1920	Bos-N	0	3	.000	11	4	2	0	0	43	54	3	11	9	13.8	5.65	54	.329	.375	2	.143	-0	-12	-12	0	-0.9
Total	6	13	24	.351	66	40	24	2	0	399²	429	14	100	111	12.0	3.56	78	.287	.333	24	.180	-2	-32	-34	-1	-2.8

YEAR TM/L	W	L	PCT	G	GS	CG	SH	SV	IP	H	HR	BB	SO	RAT	ERA	ERA+	OAV	OOB	BH	AVG	PB	PR	/A	PD	TPI

● **BUNNY HEARN**   Hearn, Elmer Lafayette b: 1/13/04, Brooklyn, N.Y. d: 3/31/74, Venice, Fla.   BL/TL, 5'8", 160 lbs. Deb: 4/13/26

1926 Bos-N	4	9	.308	34	12	3	0	2	117¹	121	4	56	40	13.6	4.22	84	.276	.358	3	.100	-2	-5	-9	2	-0.9
1927 Bos-N	0	2	.000	8	0	0	0	0	12²	16	0	9	5	17.8	4.26	87	.327	.431	2	.400	1	-0	-1	0	0.0
1928 Bos-N	1	0	1.000	7	0	0	0	0	10	6	0	8	8	13.5	6.30	62	.167	.333	0	.000	-0	-3	-3	-0	-0.3
1929 Bos-N	2	0	1.000	10	1	0	0	0	18¹	18	2	9	12	13.3	4.42	106	.277	.365	0	.000	-0	1	1	1	0.1
Total 4	7	11	.389	59	13	3	0	2	158¹	161	4	82	65	13.9	4.38	85	.273	.363	5	.132	-2	-8	-12	2	-1.1

● **JIM HEARN**   Hearn, James Tolbert b: 4/11/21, Atlanta, Ga.   BR/TR, 6'3", 205 lbs. Deb: 4/17/47

1947 StL-N	12	7	.632	37	21	4	1	1	162	151	9	63	57	11.9	3.22	128	.248	.319	8	.145	-1	15	16	-1	1.5
1948 StL-N	8	6	.571	34	13	3	0	1	89²	92	9	35	27	12.9	4.22	97	.271	.342	5	.200	-3	-3	-1	-2	-0.4
1949 StL-N	1	3	.250	17	4	0	0	0	42	48	3	23	18	15.6	5.14	81	.294	.388	1	.100	-0	-5	-5	-0	-0.4
1950 StL-N	0	1	.000	6	0	0	0	0	9	12	1	6	4	18.0	10.00	43	.333	.429	1	1.000	-0	-6	-6	-0	-0.5
NY-N	11	3	.786	16	16	11	5	0	125	72	8	38	54	7.9	1.94	211	.169	.237	6	.136	-0	31	30	3	3.3
Yr	11	4	.733	22	16	11	**5**	0	134	84	9	44	58	8.6	2.49	165	.182	.253	7	.156	-0	25	24	0	2.8
1951 *NY-N	17	9	.654	34	34	11	0	0	211¹	204	21	82	66	12.3	3.62	108	.251	.321	12	.162	-0	8	7	5	1.3
1952 NY-N☆	14	7	.667	37	34	11	1	1	223²	208	16	97	89	12.5	3.78	98	.245	.326	14	.182	4	-1	-2	4	0.6
1953 NY-N	9	12	.429	36	32	11	0	0	196²	206	22	84	77	13.4	4.53	95	.266	.341	9	.136	0	-5	-5	2	-0.3
1954 NY-N	8	8	.500	29	18	3	2	1	130	137	10	66	45	14.2	4.15	97	.272	.359	1	.111	-1	-1	-2	1	-0.1
1955 NY-N	14	16	.467	39	33	11	1	0	226²	225	27	66	86	11.7	3.73	108	.260	.314	12	.156	1	8	7	2	1.2
1956 NY-N	5	11	.313	30	19	2	0	1	129¹	124	7	44	66	11.9	3.97	95	.254	.319	4	.098	-3	-3	-3	-0	-0.6
1957 Phi-N	5	1	.833	36	4	1	0	3	74	79	6	18	46	12.0	3.65	104	.274	.321	0	.000	-2	2	1	1	0.0
1958 Phi-N	5	3	.625	39	1	0	0	0	73¹	88	6	27	33	14.1	4.17	95	.292	.351	0	.000	-1	-2	-2	-1	-0.4
1959 Phi-N	0	2	.000	6	0	0	0	0	11	15	2	6	1	17.2	5.73	72	.333	.412	0	.000	-0	-2	-2	-0	-0.3
Total 13	109	89	.551	396	229	63	10	8	1703²	1661	157	655	669	12.4	3.81	105	.255	.326	77	.141	-3	35	35	11	4.9

● **SPENCER HEATH**   Heath, Spencer Paul b: 11/5/1894, Chicago, Ill. d: 1/25/30, Chicago, Ill.   BB/TR, 6', 170 lbs. Deb: 5/4/20

| 1920 Chi-A | 0 | 0 | — | 4 | 0 | 0 | 0 | 0 | 7 | 19 | 1 | 2 | 0 | 27.0 | 15.43 | 24 | .475 | .500 | 0 | .000 | -1 | -9 | -9 | -0 | -0.1 |

● **JEFF HEATHCOCK**   Heathcock, Ronald Jeffrey b: 11/18/59, Covina, Cal.   BR/TR, 6'4", 205 lbs. Deb: 9/3/83

1983 Hou-N	2	1	.667	6	3	0	0	1	28	19	1	4	12	7.7	3.21	106	.181	.218	0	.000	-1	1	1	0	0.0
1985 Hou-N	3	1	.750	14	7	1	0	1	56¹	50	9	13	25	10.2	3.36	103	.239	.287	1	.063	0	1	1	0	0.1
1987 Hou-N	4	2	.667	19	2	0	0	1	42²	44	4	9	15	11.4	3.16	124	.277	.320	0	.000	-1	4	4	0	0.4
1988 Hou-N	0	5	.000	17	1	0	0	0	31	33	2	16	12	14.5	5.81	57	.275	.365	0	—	-8	-9	0	-1.3
Total 4	9	9	.500	56	13	1	0	3	158	146	16	42	64	10.9	3.76	94	.246	.300	1	.029	-2	-1	-4	0	-0.8

● **NEAL HEATON**   Heaton, Neal b: 3/3/60, Holtsville, N.Y.   BL/TL, 6'1", 205 lbs. Deb: 9/3/82

1982 Cle-A	0	2	.000	8	4	0	0	0	31	32	1	6	14	13.9	5.23	78	.260	.345	0	—	0	-4	-4	-0	-0.2
1983 Cle-A	11	7	.611	39	16	4	3	7	149¹	157	11	44	75	12.2	4.16	102	.269	.321	0	—	0	-2	1	-2	-0.2
1984 Cle-A	12	15	.444	38	34	4	1	0	198²	231	21	75	75	13.9	5.21	78	.293	.354	0	—	0	-27	-25	-3	-3.3
1985 Cle-A	9	17	.346	36	33	5	1	0	207²	244	19	80	82	14.3	4.90	84	.298	.365	0	—	0	-17	-18	-3	-2.1
1986 Cle-A	3	6	.333	12	12	2	0	0	74¹	73	8	34	24	13.1	4.24	98	.254	.335	0	—	0	-0	-1	0	-0.1
Min-A	4	9	.308	21	17	3	0	1	124¹	128	18	47	66	12.7	3.98	108	.273	.340	0	—	0	3	4	-1	0.3
Yr	7	15	.318	33	29	5	0	1	198²	201	26	81	90	12.8	4.08	104	.266	.337	0	—	0	3	3	-1	0.2
1987 Mon-N	13	10	.565	32	32	3	1	0	193¹	207	25	37	105	11.5	4.52	93	.273	.310	14	.209	-2	-9	-7	-1	-0.7
1988 Mon-N	3	10	.231	32	11	0	0	2	97¹	98	14	43	43	13.3	4.99	72	.271	.354	-0	.143	-0	-17	-15	-0	-2.0
1989 Pit-N	6	7	.462	42	18	1	0	0	147¹	127	12	55	67	11.5	3.05	110	.233	.311	9	.214	1	7	5	1	0.5
1990 Pit-N☆	12	9	.571	30	24	0	0	0	146	143	17	38	68	11.3	3.45	105	.263	.314	2	.047	-3	6	3	-0	0.1
1991 Pit-N	3	3	.500	42	1	0	0	0	68²	72	6	21	34	12.7	4.33	83	.275	.338	4	.286	1	-5	-6	-1	-0.4
1992 KC-A	3	1	.750	31	0	0	0	0	41	43	5	22	29	14.5	4.17	97	.274	.367	0	—	0	-1	-1	-0	-0.2
Mil-A	0	0	—	1	0	0	0	0	1	0	0	1	2	9.0	0.00	—	.000	.250	0	—	0	0	0	0	0.1
Yr	3	1	.750	32	0	0	0	0	42	43	5	23	31	14.1	4.07	99	.262	.353	0	—	0	-1	-0	-0	-0.1
1993 NY-A	1	0	1.000	18	0	0	0	0	27	34	6	11	15	16.0	6.00	69	.301	.378	0	—	0	-5	-6	0	0.1
Total 12	80	96	.455	382	202	22	6	10	1507	1589	163	524	699	12.8	4.37	91	.273	.337	32	.171	2	-72	-68	-11	-8.1

● **DAVE HEAVERLO**   Heaverlo, David Wallace b: 8/25/50, Ellensburg, Wash.   BR/TR, 6'1", 210 lbs. Deb: 4/14/75

1975 SF-N	3	1	.750	42	0	0	0	1	64	62	2	31	35	13.2	2.39	159	.262	.349	2	.500	1	9	10	1	0.7
1976 SF-N	4	4	.500	61	0	0	0	1	75	85	2	15	40	12.2	4.44	82	.289	.328	1	.333	0	-8	-7	1	-0.6
1977 SF-N	5	1	.833	56	0	0	0	1	98²	92	10	21	58	10.6	2.55	153	.251	.297	0	.000	-0	15	15	2	1.0
1978 Oak-A	3	6	.333	69	0	0	0	10	130	141	11	41	71	12.8	3.25	112	.281	.339	0	—	0	7	6	3	0.8
1979 Oak-A	4	11	.267	62	0	0	0	9	85²	97	7	42	40	15.0	4.20	96	.294	.380	0	—	0	-0	-2	0	-0.2
1980 Sea-A	6	3	.667	60	0	0	0	4	78²	75	9	35	42	13.2	3.89	106	.253	.342	0	—	0	1	2	-2	0.1
1981 Oak-A	1	0	1.000	6	0	0	0	0	5²	7	0	3	2	15.9	1.59	219	.292	.370	0	—	0	1	1	0	0.4
Total 7	26	26	.500	356	0	0	0	26	537²	559	41	188	288	12.8	3.41	113	.273	.339	3	.231	1	26	26	4	2.2

● **WALLY HEBERT**   Hebert, Wallace Andrew "Preacher" b: 8/21/07, Lake Charles, La.   BL/TL, 6'1", 195 lbs. Deb: 5/1/31

1931 StL-A	6	7	.462	23	13	5	0	0	103	128	11	43	26	15.2	5.07	91	.306	.375	9	.209	-1	-8	-5	-2	-0.8
1932 StL-A	1	12	.077	35	15	2	0	1	108¹	145	6	45	29	16.0	6.48	75	.322	.386	12	.353	2	-24	-20	0	-1.7
1933 StL-A	4	6	.400	33	10	3	0	1	88¹	114	4	35	19	15.3	5.30	84	.308	.369	9	.391	4	-10	-6	1	-1.6
1943 Pit-N	10	11	.476	34	23	12	1	0	184	197	3	45	41	11.9	2.98	117	.272	.316	13	.220	1	8	10	1	1.4
Total 4	21	36	.368	125	61	22	1	1	483²	584	24	168	115	14.1	4.63	91	.298	.355	43	.270	5	-34	-21	-1	-1.5

● **GUY HECKER**   Hecker, Guy Jackson b: 4/3/1856, Youngsville, Pa. d: 12/3/38, Wooster, Ohio   BR/TR, 6', 190 lbs. Deb: 5/2/1882 MU♦

1882 Lou-a	6	6	.500	13	11	10	0	0	104	75	0	5	33	**6.9**	1.30	191	**.188**	**.198**	94	.276	4	16	14	3	2.1
1883 Lou-a	26	23	.531	51	50	49	3	0	451	509	4	72	153	11.6	3.33	90	.267	.293	88	.273	12	-1	-17	3	-0.2
1884 Lou-a	**52**	20	.722	**75**	73	**72**	6	0	**670²**	526	4	56	**385**	**8.0**	**1.80**	172	.204	**.226**	94	.297	28	108	**96**	7	**12.6**
1885 Lou-a	30	23	.566	53	53	51	2	0	480	454	6	54	209	9.9	2.18	148	.237	.265	81	.273	9	57	56	5	**6.6**
1886 Lou-a	26	23	.531	49	48	45	2	0	420²	390	6	118	133	11.1	2.87	127	.231	.285	117	.341	18	27	36	1	5.2
1887 Lou-a	18	12	.600	34	32	32	2	0	285¹	299	9	50	58	12.1	4.16	105	.272	.307	118	.319	11	4	7	1	1.8
1888 Lou-a	8	17	.320	26	25	25	0	0	223¹	251	6	43	63	12.3	3.39	91	.274	.313	48	.227	2	-8	-8	1	-0.4
1889 Lou-a	5	13	.278	19	16	15	0	0	151¹	215	7	47	33	15.9	5.59	69	.324	.373	93	.284	4	-29	-29	1	-2.2
1890 Pit-N	2	9	.182	14	12	11	0	0	119²	160	9	41	32	16.6	5.11	64	.311	.369	77	.226	2	-21	-24	-1	-1.6
Total 9	173	146	.542	334	320	310	15	1	2906	2905	50	489	1099	10.7	2.92	114	.247	.281	810	.283	90	154	128	24	23.9

● **HARRY HEDGPETH**   Hedgpeth, Harry Malcolm b: 9/4/1888, Fayetteville, N.C. d: 7/30/66, Richmond, Va.   BL/TL, 6'1.5", 194 lbs. Deb: 10/3/13

| 1913 Was-A | 0 | 0 | — | 1 | 0 | 0 | 0 | 1 | 1 | 1 | 0 | 0 | 0 | 9.0 | 0.00 | — | .250 | .250 | 0 | — | 0 | 0 | 0 | 0 | 0.1 |

● **MIKE HEDLUND**   Hedlund, Michael David "Red" b: 8/11/46, Dallas, Tex.   BR/TR, 6'1", 190 lbs. Deb: 5/8/65

1965 Cle-A	0	0	—	6	0	0	0	0	5¹	6	0	5	4	18.6	5.06	69	.286	.423	0	.000	-0	-1	-1	-0	0.0
1968 Cle-A	0	0	—	3	0	0	0	0	1²	6	0	2	0	48.6	10.80	27	.545	.643	0	—	0	-1	-1	0	0.0
1969 KC-A	3	6	.333	34	16	3	0	2	125	123	8	40	74	11.8	3.24	114	.259	.318	5	.152	-1	5	3	2	0.3
1970 KC-A	2	3	.400	9	7	0	0	0	15	18	6	7	5	15.0	7.20	52	.300	.373	0	.000	-0	-6	-6	-0	-1.7
1971 KC-A	15	8	.652	32	30	9	1	0	205²	168	19	72	66	10.5	2.71	126	.227	.296	6	.088	-0	17	16	3	1.8
1972 KC-A	5	7	.417	29	16	1	0	2	113	119	10	41	52	13.1	4.78	63	.275	.343	6	.188	-0	-22	-22	1	-2.2
Total 6	25	24	.510	113	62	13	1	4	465²	440	39	167	211	11.9	3.56	96	.253	.321	17	.123	-5	-7	-8	5	-1.5

YEAR TM/L	W	L	PCT	G	GS	CG	SH	SV	IP	H	HR	BB	SO	RAT	ERA	ERA+	OAV	OOB	BH	AVG	PB	PR	/A	PD	TPI
● **DANNY HEEP** Heep, Daniel William b: 7/3/57, San Antonio, Tex. BL/TL, 5'11", 185 lbs. Deb: 8/31/79 ♦																									
1988 *LA-N	0	0	—	1	0	0	0	0	2	2	1	0	0	9.0	9.00	37	.222	.222	36	.242	0	-1	-1	-0	0.0
1990 *Bos-A	0	0	—	1	0	0	0	0	1	4	0	0	0	36.0	9.00	45	.667	.667	12	.174	0	-1	-1	-0	0.0
Total 2	0	0	—	2	0	0	0	0	3	6	1	0	0	18.0	9.00	40	.400	.400	503	.257	1	-2	-2	-0	0.0
● **BOB HEFFNER** Heffner, Robert Frederic b: 9/13/38, Allentown, Pa. BR/TR, 6'4", 205 lbs. Deb: 6/19/63																									
1963 Bos-A	4	9	.308	20	19	3	1	0	124²	131	15	36	77	12.2	4.26	89	.267	.319	5	.116	-1	-9	-7	-0	-0.8
1964 Bos-A	7	9	.438	55	10	1	1	6	158²	152	20	44	112	11.3	4.08	94	.251	.305	7	.159	0	-8	-4	-1	-0.5
1965 Bos-A	0	2	.000	27	1	0	0	0	49	59	9	18	42	14.3	7.16	52	.304	.366	0	.000	-1	-20	-19	-1	-0.9
1966 Cle-A	0	1	.000	5	1	0	0	0	13	12	1	3	7	10.4	3.46	99	.240	.283	0	.000	0	-0	-0	-1	0.0
1968 Cal-A	0	0	—	7	0	0	0	0	8	6	0	6	3	13.5	2.25	129	.240	.387	0	—	0	1	1	-0	0.0
Total 5	11	21	.344	114	31	4	2	6	353¹	360	45	107	241	12.0	4.51	84	.264	.320	12	.128	-1	-36	-29	-2	-2.2
● **RANDY HEFLIN** Heflin, Randolph Rutherford b: 9/11/18, Fredericksburg, Va. BL/TL, 6', 185 lbs. Deb: 6/9/45																									
1945 Bos-A	4	10	.286	20	14	6	2	0	102	102	3	61	39	14.7	4.06	84	.272	.380	3	.086	-3	-8	-7	1	-1.1
1946 Bos-A	0	1	.000	5	1	0	0	0	14²	16	0	12	6	17.8	2.45	149	.296	.433	2	.667	1	2	2	1	0.3
Total 2	4	11	.267	25	15	6	2	0	116²	118	3	73	45	15.1	3.86	89	.275	.387	5	.132	-2	-6	-5	2	-0.8
● **JAKE HEHL** Hehl, Herman Jacob b: 12/8/1899, Brooklyn, N.Y. d: 7/4/61, Brooklyn, N.Y. BR/TR, 5'11", 180 lbs. Deb: 6/20/18																									
1918 Bro-N	0	0	—	1	0	0	0	0	1	0	0	0	0	9.0	0.00	—	.000	.250	0	—	0	0	0	0	0.0
● **EMMETT HEIDRICK** Heidrick, John Emmett "Snags" b: 7/9/1876, Queenstown, Pa. d: 1/20/16, Clarion, Pa. BL/TR, 6', 185 lbs. Deb: 9/14/1898 ♦																									
1902 StL-A	0	0	—	1	0	0	0	0	1	0	0	0	0	0.0	0.00	—	.000	.000	129	.289	0	0	0	-0	0.0
● **FRANK HEIFER** Heifer, Franklin "Heck" b: 1/18/1854, Reading, Pa. d: 8/29/1893, Reading, Pa. 5'10.5", 175 lbs. Deb: 6/4/1875 ♦																									
1875 Bos-n	0	0	—	2	0	0	0	1	2¹	7	0	0		27.0	7.71	31	.500	.500	14	.275	1	-1	-1		-0.1
● **FRED HEIMACH** Heimach, Frederick Amos "Lefty" b: 1/27/01, Camden, N.J. d: 6/1/73, Ft.Myers, Fla. BL/TL, 6', 175 lbs. Deb: 10/1/20																									
1920 Phi-A	0	1	.000	1	1	0	0	0	5	13	0	1	0	25.2	14.40	28	.542	.560	0	.000	-0	-6	-6	1	-0.7
1921 Phi-A	1	0	1.000	1	1	1	1	0	9	7	0	1	0	8.0	8.00	49	.226	.250	1	.250	-0	4	4	1	0.6
1922 Phi-A	7	11	.389	37	19	7	0	1	171²	220	18	63	47	15.0	5.03	85	.316	.375	15	.250	2	-19	-15	1	-1.0
1923 Phi-A	6	12	.333	40	19	10	0	0	208¹	238	14	69	63	13.5	4.32	95	.292	.352	30	.254	2	-8	-5	0	-0.1
1924 Phi-A	14	12	.538	40	26	10	0	0	198	243	2	60	60	14.0	4.73	91	.306	.357	29	.322	6	-11	-10	2	-0.3
1925 Phi-A	0	1	.000	10	0	0	0	0	20¹	24	2	9	6	15.0	3.98	117	.312	.391	1	.167	1	2	0	0	0.1
1926 Phi-A	1	0	1.000	13	1	0	0	0	31²	28	1	5	8	9.4	2.84	147	.239	.270	1	.100	-1	4	5	2	0.2
Bos-A	2	9	.182	20	13	6	0	0	102	119	5	42	17	14.2	5.65	72	.303	.370	13	.295	2	-18	-18	3	-1.1
Yr	3	9	.250	33	14	6	0	0	133²	147	6	47	25	13.1	4.98	82	.288	.348	14	.259	1	-14	-13	5	-0.9
1928 NY-A	2	3	.400	13	9	5	0	0	68	66	3	16	25	11.0	3.31	114	.250	.295	5	.167	1	6	3	0	0.1
1929 NY-A	11	6	.647	35	10	3	3	4	134²	141	4	29	26	11.6	4.01	96	.272	.314	9	.184	1	4	-2	0	-0.1
1930 Bro-N	0	2	.000	9	0	0	1	0	7¹	14	0	3	1	20.9	4.91	100	.424	.472	1	.250	-0	0	0	0	0.0
1931 Bro-N	9	7	.563	31	10	7	1	1	135¹	145	6	23	43	11.2	3.46	110	.274	.306	12	.197	1	6	5	4	1.0
1932 Bro-N	9	4	.692	36	15	7	0	0	167²	203	7	28	30	12.7	3.97	96	.299	.333	9	.164	1	-2	-3	1	0.0
1933 Bro-N	0	0	—	10	3	0	0	0	29²	49	2	11	7	18.8	10.01	32	.374	.431	2	.200	-0	-22	-22	-0	-0.7
Total 13	62	69	.473	296	127	56	5	7	1288²	1510	64	360	334	13.2	4.46	90	.296	.346	128	.236	12	-61	-61	16	-2.0
● **GORMAN HEIMUELLER** Heimueller, Gorman John b: 9/24/55, Los Angeles, Cal. BL/TL, 6'4", 195 lbs. Deb: 7/12/83																									
1983 Oak-A	3	5	.375	16	14	2	1	0	83²	93	8	29	31	13.2	4.41	87	.286	.346	0	—	0	-3	-5	2	0.2
1984 Oak-A	0	1	.000	6	0	0	0	0	14²	21	2	7	3	17.2	6.14	61	.344	.412	0	—	0	-3	-4	0	0.2
Total 2	3	6	.333	22	14	2	1	0	98¹	114	10	36	34	13.8	4.67	82	.295	.357	0	—	0	-7	-9	3	0.2
● **DON HEINKEL** Heinkel, Donald Elliott b: 10/20/59, Racine, Wis. BL/TR, 6', 185 lbs. Deb: 4/7/88																									
1988 Det-A	0	0	—	21	0	0	0	1	36¹	30	4	12	30	10.7	3.96	96	.219	.287	0	—	0	0	-1	-0	0.1
1989 StL-N	1	1	.500	7	5	0	0	0	26¹	40	2	7	16	16.1	5.81	62	.348	.385	0	.000	0	-7	-6	0	-0.4
Total 2	1	1	.500	28	5	0	0	1	62²	70	6	19	46	12.9	4.74	79	.278	.331	0	.000	0	-7	-7	0	-0.3
● **KEN HEINTZELMAN** Heintzelman, Kenneth Alphonse b: 10/14/15, Peruque, Mo. BR/TL, 5'11.5", 185 lbs. Deb: 10/3/37 F																									
1937 Pit-N	1	0	1.000	1	1	1	0	0	9	6	0	3	4	10.0	2.00	193	.207	.303	0	.000	-1	2	2	-1	0.1
1938 Pit-N	0	0	—	3	0	0	0	0	2	1	0	3	1	18.0	9.00	42	.167	.444	0	—	0	-1	-0	0	0.0
1939 Pit-N	1	1	.500	17	2	1	1	0	35²	35	2	18	13	13.4	5.05	76	.250	.335	2	.222	0	-4	-5	-0	-0.2
1940 Pit-N	8	8	.500	39	16	5	2	3	165	193	7	65	71	14.3	4.47	85	.292	.359	9	.167	-1	-11	-12	3	-1.0
1941 Pit-N	11	11	.500	35	24	13	2	0	196	206	8	83	81	13.3	3.44	105	.272	.345	8	.127	-2	4	4	1	0.3
1942 Pit-N	8	11	.421	27	18	5	3	0	130	143	6	39	63	14.3	4.57	74	.281	.361	3	.086	-2	-18	-17	-2	-2.6
1946 Pit-N	8	12	.400	32	24	6	2	1	157²	165	7	86	57	14.3	3.77	94	.271	.362	6	.136	-1	-6	-4	2	-0.4
1947 Pit-N	0	0	—	2	1	0	0	0	4	9	2	6	2	33.8	20.25	21	.409	.536	0	—	0	-7	-7	0	-0.5
Phi-N	7	10	.412	24	19	8	0	1	136	144	12	46	55	12.7	4.04	99	.277	.338	5	.116	-2	0	-0	-3	-0.5
Yr	7	10	.412	26	20	8	0	1	140	153	14	52	57	13.3	4.50	89	.282	.347	5	.116	-2	-8	-8	-3	-0.8
1948 Phi-N	6	11	.353	27	16	5	2	2	130	117	10	45	57	11.3	4.29	92	.241	.307	6	.135	-1	-5	-5	-1	-0.8
1949 Phi-N	17	10	.630	33	32	15	**5**	0	250²	239	19	93	65	12.0	3.02	130	.255	.323	13	.157	-1	28	26	-3	2.2
1950 *Phi-N	3	9	.250	23	19	4	1	0	125¹	122	10	54	39	12.6	4.09	99	.250	.325	1	.053	-3	-1	-2	-0	-0.6
1951 Phi-N	6	12	.333	35	12	3	0	0	118¹	119	13	53	55	13.4	4.18	92	.267	.350	3	.107	-1	-3	-4	-1	-0.9
1952 Phi-N	1	3	.250	23	1	0	0	0	42²	41	1	12	20	11.2	3.16	115	.266	.319	0	.000	-0	3	2	-1	0.1
Total 13	77	98	.440	319	183	66	18	10	1501²	1540	100	630	564	13.1	3.93	96	.267	.341	56	.127	-16	-18	-23	-7	-4.2
● **CLARENCE HEISE** Heise, Clarence Edward "Lefty" b: 8/7/07, Topeka, Kan. BL/TL, 5'10", 172 lbs. Deb: 4/22/34																									
1934 StL-N	0	0	—	1	0	0	0	0	2	3	1	0	1	13.5	4.50	94	.300	.300	0	—	0	-0	-0	-0	0.0
● **JIM HEISE** Heise, James Edward b: 10/2/32, Scottdale, Pa. BR/TR, 6'1", 185 lbs. Deb: 6/29/57																									
1957 Was-A	0	3	.000	8	2	0	0	0	19	25	2	16	8	19.4	8.05	48	.329	.446	0	.000	-0	-9	-9	-0	-1.2
● **ROY HEISER** Heiser, Le Roy Barton b: 6/22/42, Baltimore, Md. BR/TR, 6'4", 190 lbs. Deb: 9/2/61																									
1961 Was-A	0	0	—	3	0	0	0	0	5²	6	1	9	1	25.4	6.35	63	.261	.485	0	.000	-0	-1	-1	-0	-0.1
● **CRESE HEISMANN** Heismann, Christian Ernest b: 4/16/1880, Cincinnati, Ohio d: 11/19/51, Cincinnati, Ohio BR/TL, 6'2", 175 lbs. Deb: 9/25/01																									
1901 Cin-N	0	1	.000	3	2	1	0	0	13²	18	1	6	6	17.8	5.93	54	.315	.408	2	.400	1	-4	-4	-1	-0.2
1902 Cin-N	2	1	.667	5	3	2	1	0	33	33	1	10	15	13.1	2.45	122	.260	.338	3	.214	0	1	2	0	0.2
Bal-A	0	3	.000	3	3	0	0	0	16	20	1	12	2	19.1	8.44	45	.306	.428	1	.143	-1	-9	-8	-0	-1.2
Total 2	2	5	.286	11	8	5	2	0	62²	71	3	28	23	15.7	4.74	69	.285	.379	6	.231	1	-11	-10	-1	-1.2
● **HARRY HEITMANN** Heitmann, Henry Anton b: 10/6/1896, Albany, N.Y. d: 12/15/58, Brooklyn, N.Y. BR/TR, 6', 175 lbs. Deb: 7/27/18																									
1918 Bro-N	0	1	.000	1	1	0	0	0	0¹	4	0	0	0	108.0	108.00	3	1.000	1.000	0	—	0	-4	-4	0	-3.0
● **MEL HELD** Held, Melvin Nicholas "Country" b: 4/12/29, Edon, Ohio BR/TR, 6'1", 178 lbs. Deb: 4/27/56																									
1956 Bal-A	0	0	—	4	0	0	0	0	7	7	1	3	4	12.9	5.14	76	.318	.400	0	—	0	-1	-1	0	0.0
● **RICK HELLING** Helling, Ricky Allen b: 12/15/70, Devils Lake, N.D. BR/TR, 6'3", 215 lbs. Deb: 4/10/94																									
1994 Tex-A	3	2	.600	9	9	1	1	0	52	62	14	18	25	13.8	5.88	77	.295	.351	0	—	0	-6	-8	0	-0.6

YEAR TM/L	W	L	PCT	G	GS	CG	SH	SV	IP	H	HR	BB	SO	RAT	ERA	ERA+	OAV	OOB	BH	AVG	PB	PR	/A	PD	TPI

● HORACE HELMBOLD   Helmbold, Horace b: Philadelphia, Pa. Deb: 10/11/1890

| 1890 Phi-a | 0 | 1 | .000 | 1 | 1 | 1 | 0 | 0 | 7 | 17 | 0 | 6 | 3 | 29.6 | 14.14 | 27 | .451 | .526 | 0 | .000 | -1 | -8 | -8 | 0 | -0.7 |

● RUSS HEMAN   Heman, Russell Fredrick b: 2/10/33, Olive, Cal. BR/TR, 6'4", 200 lbs. Deb: 4/20/61

1961 Cle-A	0	0	—	6	0	0	0	1	10	8	0	8	4	15.3	3.60	109	.216	.370	0	.000	-0	0	0	0	0.0
LA-A	0	0	—	6	0	0	0	0	10	4	1	2	2	6.3	1.80	251	.125	.200	0	.000	-0	2	3	0	0.0
Yr	0	0	—	12	0	0	0	1	20	12	1	10	6	10.3	2.70	156	.171	.284	0	.000	-0	3	3	0	0.0

● GEORGE HEMMING   Hemming, George Earl "Old Wax Figger"
b: 12/15/1868, Carrollton, Ohio d: 6/3/30, Springfield, Mass. BR/TR, 5'11", 170 lbs. Deb: 4/21/1890

1890 Cle-P	0	1	.000	3	1	1	0	0	21	25	1	19	3	19.7	6.86	58	.283	.421	2	.182	-1	-6	-7	1	-0.2
Bro-P	8	4	.667	19	11	11	0	3	123	117	3	59	32	13.1	3.80	117	.240	.326	9	.158	-4	6	9	0	0.3
Yr	8	5	.615	22	12	12	0	3	144	142	4	78	35	13.9	4.25	103	.246	.338	11	.162	-5	-0	2	1	0.1
1891 Bro-N	8	15	.348	27	22	19	1	0	199²	231	11	84	83	14.7	4.96	67	.279	.353	13	.159	-1	-36	-37	1	-3.3
1892 Cin-N	0	1	.000	1	0	0	0	0	6	10	1	2	0	18.0	7.50	44	.357	.400	1	.333	0	-3	-3	0	-0.3
Lou-N	2	2	.500	4	4	4	0	0	35	36	1	17	12	13.6	4.63	66	.255	.335	1	.077	-1	-5	-6	0	-0.6
Yr	2	3	.400	5	4	4	0	0	41	46	2	19	12	14.3	5.05	61	.272	.346	2	.125	-1	-8	-9	0	-0.9
1893 Lou-N	18	17	.514	41	32	32	1	1	332	369	7	176	79	15.2	5.10	86	.273	.363	32	.203	-2	-16	-26	2	-2.0
1894 Lou-N	13	19	.406	35	32	32	1	1	294¹	358	7	133	66	15.3	4.37	117	.297	.371	33	.252	-1	31	24	-1	1.9
*Bal-N	4	0	1.000	6	6	4	0	0	45¹	48	0	26	4	15.1	3.57	153	.269	.368	6	.286	-1	9	9	0	0.7
Yr	17	19	.472	41	38	36	1	1	339²	406	7	159	70	15.0	4.27	121	.291	.365	39	.257	-3	40	33	-1	2.6
1895 Bal-N	20	13	.606	34	31	26	1	0	262²	288	10	96	43	13.4	4.05	118	.275	.339	33	.282	-3	21	21	-3	1.9
1896 Bal-N	15	6	.714	25	21	20	3	0	202	233	9	54	33	12.9	4.19	102	.287	.333	25	.258	-4	2	-3	0	0.2
1897 Lou-N	3	4	.429	9	8	7	0	0	67	80	5	25	7	14.2	5.10	83	.294	.355	5	.179	-1	-6	-6	1	-0.5
Total 8	91	82	.526	204	168	156	7	6	1587²	1795	55	691	362	14.4	4.53	98	.279	.353	160	.223	-0	-1	-19	-2	-1.9

● BERNIE HENDERSON   Henderson, Bernard "Barnyard" b: 4/12/1899, Douglassville, Tex d: 6/6/66, Linden, Tex. BR/TR, 5'9", 175 lbs. Deb: 9/5/21

| 1921 Cle-A | 0 | 1 | .000 | 2 | 1 | 0 | 0 | 0 | 3 | 5 | 0 | 0 | 1 | 15.0 | 9.00 | 47 | .333 | .333 | 0 | .000 | -0 | -2 | -2 | -0 | -0.4 |

● ED HENDERSON   Henderson, Edward J. (b: Eugene J. Ball) b: 12/25/1884, Newark, N.J. d: 1/15/64, New York, N.Y. BL/TL, 5'9", 168 lbs. Deb: 5/15/14

1914 Pit-F	0	1	.000	6	1	1	0	0	16	14	2	8	4	12.4	3.94	73	.241	.333	0	.000	-0	-2	-2	-1	-0.2
Ind-F	1	0	1.000	2	1	1	0	0	10	8	0	4	1	13.5	4.50	69	.229	.357	0	.000	-1	-2	-2	-0	-0.2
Yr	1	1	.500	8	2	2	0	0	26	22	2	12	5	12.8	4.15	71	.237	.343	0	.000	-1	-4	-3	-1	-0.4

● HARDIE HENDERSON   Henderson, James Harding b: 10/31/1862, Philadelphia, Pa. d: 2/6/03, Philadelphia, Pa. BR/TR, Deb: 5/2/1883 U

1883 Phi-N	0	1	.000	1	1	1	0	0	9	26	0	2	2	28.0	19.00	16	.481	.500	2	.250	-1	-16	-16	-0	-0.9
Bal-a	10	32	.238	45	42	38	0	0	358¹	383	4	87	145	11.8	4.02	87	.256	.297	31	.162	-6	-28	-21	-2	-2.6
1884 Bal-a	27	23	.540	52	52	50	4	0	439¹	382	9	116	346	10.5	2.62	132	.216	.271	46	.227	2	31	41	1	4.4
1885 Bal-a	25	35	.417	61	61	59	0	0	539¹	530	7	117	263	11.3	3.19	102	.253	.298	51	.223	3	4	4	-0	0.7
1886 Bal-a	3	15	.167	19	19	19	0	0	171¹	188	0	66	88	13.8	4.62	74	.252	.320	16	.235	2	-22	-23	2	-1.4
Bro-a	10	4	.714	14	14	14	0	0	124	112	2	51	49	11.8	2.90	120	.232	.306	9	.180	-1	8	8	0	0.6
Yr	13	19	.406	33	33	33	0	0	295¹	300	2	117	137	12.7	3.90	88	.242	.308	25	.212	1	-15	-15	2	-0.8
1887 Bro-a	5	8	.385	13	12	12	0	0	111²	127	3	63	28	15.7	3.95	109	.281	.375	5	.122	-3	4	4	1	0.2
1888 Pit-N	1	3	.250	5	5	4	0	0	35¹	43	0	20	9	16.6	5.35	50	.289	.380	5	.278	1	-10	-11	0	-0.9
Total 6	81	121	.401	210	206	197	4	0	1788¹	1800	25	522	930	11.9	3.50	98	.247	.302	165	.204	-2	-30	-13	2	0.1

● JOE HENDERSON   Henderson, Joseph Lee b: 7/4/46, Lake Cormorant, Miss. BL/TR, 6'2", 195 lbs. Deb: 6/7/74

1974 Chi-A	1	0	1.000	5	3	0	0	0	15	21	2	11	12	19.2	8.40	44	.328	.427	0	.000	-0	-8	-8	0	-0.5
1976 Cin-N	2	0	1.000	4	0	0	0	0	11	9	0	8	7	13.9	0.00	—	.225	.354	0	—	-0	4	4	0	0.9
1977 Cin-N	0	2	.000	7	0	0	0	0	9	17	2	6	8	23.0	12.00	33	.386	.460	0	.000	-0	-8	-8	-0	-1.5
Total 3	3	2	.600	16	3	0	0	0	35	47	4	25	27	18.5	6.69	55	.318	.416	0	.000	0	-12	-12	-0	-1.1

● ROD HENDERSON   Henderson, Rodney Wood b: 3/11/71, Greensburg, Ky. BR/TR, 6'4", 195 lbs. Deb: 4/19/94

| 1994 Mon-N | 0 | 1 | .000 | 3 | 2 | 0 | 0 | 0 | 6² | 9 | 1 | 7 | 3 | 21.6 | 9.45 | 45 | .333 | .471 | 0 | .000 | -0 | -4 | -4 | 0 | -0.5 |

● BILL HENDERSON   Henderson, William Maxwell b: 11/4/01, Pensacola, Fla. d: 10/6/66, Pensacola, Fla. BR/TR, 6', 190 lbs. Deb: 6/20/30

| 1930 NY-A | 0 | 0 | — | 3 | 0 | 0 | 0 | 0 | 8 | 7 | 1 | 4 | 2 | 12.4 | 4.50 | 96 | .250 | .344 | 1 | .500 | 0 | 0 | -0 | 0 | 0.0 |

● BOB HENDLEY   Hendley, Charles Robert b: 4/30/39, Macon, Ga. BR/TL, 6'2", 190 lbs. Deb: 6/23/61

1961 Mil-N	5	7	.417	19	13	3	0	0	97	96	8	39	44	12.5	3.90	96	.262	.333	1	.032	-3	1	-2	1	-0.4
1962 Mil-N	11	13	.458	35	29	7	2	1	200	188	17	59	112	11.1	3.60	105	.247	.301	7	.119	1	8	4	1	0.6
1963 Mil-N	9	9	.500	41	24	7	3	3	169¹	153	16	64	105	11.6	3.93	82	.244	.315	5	.106	-1	-12	-13	1	-1.4
1964 SF-N	10	11	.476	30	29	4	1	0	163¹	161	18	59	104	12.2	3.64	98	.258	.325	5	.106	-1	-2	-1	-2	-0.5
1965 SF-N	4	0	—	8	2	0	0	0	15	27	6	13	8	24.6	12.60	29	.397	.500	0	.000	-0	-15	-15	0	0.0
Chi-N	4	4	.500	18	10	2	0	0	62	59	9	25	38	12.3	4.35	85	.244	.317	0	.000	-1	-6	-5	1	-0.7
Yr	4	4	.500	26	12	2	0	0	77	86	15	38	46	14.6	5.96	62	.277	.357	0	.000	-2	-21	-20	1	-0.7
1966 Chi-N	4	5	.444	43	6	0	0	7	89²	98	10	39	65	13.8	3.91	94	.285	.358	3	.167	1	-3	-2	1	-0.1
1967 Chi-N	2	0	1.000	7	0	0	0	0	12¹	17	4	3	10	14.6	6.57	54	.315	.351	0	.000	-0	-4	-4	-0	-0.8
NY-N	3	3	.500	15	13	2	0	0	70²	65	11	28	36	12.0	3.44	99	.241	.314	2	.111	-0	-1	-0	-2	-0.2
Yr	5	3	.625	22	13	2	0	0	83	82	15	31	46	12.4	3.90	87	.253	.320	2	.083	-1	-5	-5	-2	-1.0
Total 7	48	52	.480	216	126	25	6	12	879¹	864	99	329	522	12.3	3.97	90	.257	.325	23	.095	-6	-34	-38	0	-3.5

● ED HENDRICKS   Hendricks, Edward "Big Ed" b: 6/20/1886, Zeeland, Mich. d: 11/28/30, Jackson, Mich. BL/TL, 6'3", 200 lbs. Deb: 9/15/10

| 1910 NY-N | 0 | 1 | .000 | 4 | 1 | 1 | 0 | 1 | 12 | 12 | 0 | 4 | 2 | 12.0 | 3.75 | 79 | .261 | .320 | 0 | .000 | -1 | -1 | -1 | -1 | -0.2 |

● ELLIE HENDRICKS   Hendricks, Elrod Jerome b: 12/22/40, Charlotte Amalie, V.I. BL/TR, 6'1", 175 lbs. Deb: 4/13/68 C♦

| 1978 Bal-A | 0 | 0 | — | 1 | 0 | 0 | 0 | 0 | 2¹ | 1 | 0 | 1 | 0 | 7.7 | 0.00 | — | .125 | .222 | 6 | .333 | 1 | 1 | 1 | -0 | 0.0 |

● DON HENDRICKSON   Hendrickson, Donald William b: 7/14/15, Kewanna, Ind. d: 1/19/77, Norfolk, Va. BR/TR, 6'2", 204 lbs. Deb: 7/4/45

1945 Bos-N	4	8	.333	37	2	1	0	5	73¹	74	8	39	14	14.0	4.91	78	.261	.353	3	.167	-0	-9	-9	-1	-1.5
1946 Bos-N	0	1	.000	2	0	0	0	0	2	4	0	2	2	27.0	4.50	78	.364	.462	0	.000	-0	-0	-0	-0	-0.1
Total 2	4	9	.308	39	2	1	0	5	75¹	78	8	41	16	14.3	4.90	78	.265	.357	3	.158	-0	-9	-9	-1	-1.6

● CLAUDE HENDRIX   Hendrix, Claude Raymond b: 4/13/1889, Olathe, Kan. d: 3/22/44, Allentown, Pa. BR/TR, 6', 195 lbs. Deb: 6/7/11

1911 Pit-N	4	6	.400	22	12	6	1	1	118²	85	1	53	57	10.5	2.73	126	.204	.295	4	.098	-1	9	9	4	1.0
1912 Pit-N	24	9	**.727**	39	32	25	4	1	288²	256	6	105	176	11.5	2.59	126	.246	.320	39	.322	16	26	22	5	4.3
1913 Pit-N	14	15	.483	42	25	17	2	3	241	216	3	89	138	11.6	2.84	106	.248	.321	27	.273	10	10	5	2	1.7
1914 Chi-F	**29**	10	.744	**49**	37	**34**	6	5	362	262	6	77	189	**8.6**	**1.69**	157	**.203**	**.251**	30	.231	4	**48**	39	6	**5.4**
1915 Chi-F	16	15	.516	40	31	26	5	4	285	256	7	84	107	10.8	3.00	84	.241	.298	30	.265	11	-9	-15	-4	-1.0
1916 Chi-N	8	16	.333	36	24	15	3	2	218	193	4	67	117	11.0	2.68	108	.242	.306	16	.200	-2	2	-2	1	1.1
1917 Chi-N	10	12	.455	40	21	13	1	1	215	202	8	72	81	11.6	2.60	112	.257	.322	22	.256	3	7	-2	1	1.1
1918 *Chi-N	20	7	**.741**	32	27	21	3	0	233	229	2	54	86	11.0	2.78	100	.259	.305	24	.264	-0	0	1	1	1.1
1919 Chi-N	10	14	.417	32	25	12	0	0	206¹	208	3	57	70	11.6	2.62	110	.266	.311	15	.192	-0	7	6	1	10.8
1920 Chi-N	9	12	.429	27	23	12	0	0	203²	216	6	54	72	12.1	3.58	90	.273	.322	15	.181	-2	-0	-5	0	-0.1
Total 10	144	116	.554	360	257	184	27	17	2371¹	2123	41	697	1092	10.9	2.65	110	.243	.303	222	.241	50	82	71	14	14.4

YEAR	TM/L	W	L	PCT	G	GS	CG	SH	SV	IP	H	HR	BB	SO	RAT	ERA	ERA+	OAV	OOB	BH	AVG	PB	PR	/A	PD	TPI
● LAFAYETTE HENION	Henion, Lafayette Marion b: 6/7/1899, Eureka, Cal. d: 7/22/55, San Luis Obispo, Cal. BR/TR, 5'11", 154 lbs. Deb: 9/10/19																									
1919	Bro-N	0	0	—	1	0	0	0	0	3	2	0	2	2	12.0	6.00	50	.200	.333	0	.000	-0	-1	-1	-0	0.0
● TOM HENKE	Henke, Thomas Anthony b: 12/21/57, Kansas City, Mo. BR/TR, 6'5", 215 lbs. Deb: 9/10/82																									
1982	Tex-A	1	0	1.000	8	0	0	0	0	15²	14	0	8	9	13.2	1.15	337	.246	.348	0	—	0	5	5	0	0.7
1983	Tex-A	1	0	1.000	8	0	0	0	1	16	16	1	4	17	11.3	3.38	119	.262	.308	0	—	0	1	1	0	0.2
1984	Tex-A	1	1	.500	25	0	0	0	2	28¹	36	0	20	25	18.1	6.35	65	.313	.419	0	—	0	-7	-7	-0	-0.7
1985	*Tor-A	3	3	.500	28	0	0	0	13	40	29	4	8	42	8.3	2.02	208	.206	.248	0	—	0	9	10	-0	2.0
1986	Tor-A	9	5	.643	63	0	0	0	27	91¹	63	6	32	118	9.5	3.35	126	.191	.265	0	—	0	8	9	-2	1.6
1987	Tor-A★	0	6	.000	72	0	0	0	34	94	62	10	25	128	8.3	2.49	180	.188	.245	0	—	0	21	21	1	2.9
1988	Tor-A	4	4	.500	52	0	0	0	25	68	60	6	24	66	11.4	2.91	135	.237	.308	0	—	0	8	8	0	1.5
1989	*Tor-A	8	3	.727	64	0	0	0	20	89	66	5	25	116	9.4	1.92	196	.205	.266	0	—	0	19	18	0	3.1
1990	Tor-A	2	4	.333	61	0	0	0	32	74²	58	8	19	75	9.4	2.17	182	.213	.267	0	—	0	14	15	-1	2.4
1991	*Tor-A	0	2	.000	49	0	0	0	32	50¹	33	4	11	53	7.9	2.32	181	.184	.232	0	—	0	10	11	-1	1.6
1992	*Tor-A	3	2	.600	57	0	0	0	34	55²	40	5	22	46	10.0	2.26	180	.197	.276	0	—	0	10	11	-1	2.2
1993	Tex-A	5	5	.500	66	0	0	0	40	74¹	55	7	27	79	10.0	2.91	143	.205	.280	0	—	0	12	10	1	2.6
1994	Tex-A	3	6	.333	37	0	0	0	15	38	33	6	12	39	10.7	3.79	120	.232	.292	0	—	0	4	3	0	1.2
Total	13	40	41	.494	590	0	0	0	275	735¹	565	62	237	813	9.9	2.73	151	.211	.278	0	—	0	115	114	-3	21.3
● WELDON HENLEY	Henley, Weldon b: 10/25/1880, Jasper, Ga. d: 11/16/60, Palatka, Fla. BR/TR, 6', 175 lbs. Deb: 4/23/03																									
1903	Phi-A	12	10	.545	29	21	13	1	0	186¹	186	3	67	86	12.8	3.91	78	.259	.333	9	.132	-3	-20	-18	-1	-2.3
1904	Phi-A	15	17	.469	36	34	31	5	0	295²	245	3	76	130	10.3	2.53	106	.227	.289	24	.222	2	2	5	4	1.2
1905	Phi-A	4	11	.267	25	19	13	1	0	183²	155	4	67	82	11.3	2.60	103	.230	.308	11	.169	-1	1	1	4	0.4
1907	Bro-N	1	5	.167	7	7	5	0	0	56	54	2	21	11	12.2	3.05	77	.273	.345	4	.200	1	-4	-4	2	-0.2
Total	4	32	43	.427	97	81	62	7	0	721²	640	12	231	309	11.4	2.94	93	.240	.310	48	.184	-2	-20	-16	9	-0.9
● MIKE HENNEMAN	Henneman, Michael Alan b: 12/11/61, St.Charles, Mo. BR/TR, 6'4", 205 lbs. Deb: 5/11/87																									
1987	*Det-A	11	3	.786	55	0	0	0	7	96²	86	8	30	75	11.1	2.98	142	.238	.301	0	.000	—	16	13	0	1.9
1988	Det-A	9	6	.600	65	0	0	0	22	91¹	72	7	24	58	9.7	1.87	204	.218	.275	0	—	0	21	20	-1	4.1
1989	Det-A☆	11	4	.733	60	0	0	0	8	90	84	4	51	69	14.0	3.70	103	.251	.358	0	—	0	2	1	0	0.2
1990	Det-A	8	6	.571	69	0	0	0	22	94¹	90	4	33	50	12.0	3.05	130	.253	.321	0	—	0	9	9	1	0.8
1991	Det-A	10	2	.833	60	0	0	0	21	84¹	81	2	34	61	12.3	2.88	144	.258	.330	0	—	0	11	12	-0	2.1
1992	Det-A	2	6	.250	60	0	0	0	24	77¹	75	6	20	58	11.1	3.96	100	.256	.304	0	—	0	-0	-0	1	0.0
1993	Det-A	5	3	.625	63	0	0	0	24	71²	69	4	32	58	12.2	2.64	162	.251	.333	0	—	0	13	13	-1	2.2
1994	Det-A	1	3	.250	30	0	0	0	8	34²	43	5	17	27	16.1	5.19	92	.297	.378	0	—	0	-2	-2	-0	-0.2
Total	8	57	33	.633	462	0	0	0	136	640¹	600	40	241	456	12.1	3.12	130	.249	.321	0	.000	—	71	67	-0	12.1
● GEORGE HENNESSEY	Hennessey, George "Three Star" b: 10/28/07, Slatington, Pa. d: 1/15/88, Princeton, N.J. BR/TR, 5'10", 168 lbs. Deb: 9/2/37																									
1937	StL-A	0	1	.000	5	0	0	0	0	7	15	2	6	4	27.0	10.29	47	.500	.583	0	—	0	-4	-4	0	-0.5
1942	Phi-N	1	1	.500	5	1	0	0	0	17	11	1	10	2	11.1	2.65	125	.180	.296	0	.000	-1	1	1	-0	0.0
1945	Chi-N	0	0	—	2	0	0	0	0	3²	7	0	1	2	19.6	7.36	50	.438	.471	0	—	0	-1	-2	-0	-0.1
Total	3	1	2	.333	12	1	0	0	0	27²	33	3	17	8	16.3	5.20	72	.308	.403	0	.000	-1	-5	-5	-0	-0.5
● PHIL HENNIGAN	Hennigan, Phillip Winston b: 4/10/46, Jasper, Tex. BR/TR, 5'11.5", 185 lbs. Deb: 9/2/69																									
1969	Cle-A	2	1	.667	9	0	0	0	0	16¹	14	0	4	10	10.5	3.31	114	.241	.302	0	.000	-0	1	1	-1	0.1
1970	Cle-A	6	3	.667	42	1	0	0	3	71²	69	7	44	43	14.7	4.02	99	.263	.371	1	.143	1	-2	-0	1	0.1
1971	Cle-A	4	3	.571	57	0	0	0	14	82	80	13	51	69	14.7	4.94	77	.261	.371	0	.000	-0	-13	-10	-1	-1.3
1972	Cle-A	5	3	.625	38	1	0	0	5	67¹	54	8	18	44	9.9	2.67	120	.226	.286	1	.083	-0	3	4	0	0.4
1973	NY-N	0	4	.000	30	0	0	0	3	43¹	50	6	16	22	13.9	6.23	58	.289	.353	1	.333	-0	-12	-13	-1	-1.3
Total	5	17	14	.548	176	2	0	0	25	280²	267	34	133	188	13.2	4.26	86	.257	.347	3	.100	1	-25	-18	-2	-2.0
● PETE HENNING	Henning, Ernest Herman b: 12/28/1887, Crown Point, Ind. d: 11/4/39, Dyer, Ind. BR/TR, 5'11", 185 lbs. Deb: 4/17/14																									
1914	KC-F	5	10	.333	28	14	7	0	2	138	153	5	58	45	14.2	4.83	58	.291	.369	8	.182	-0	-30	-31	0	-3.1
1915	KC-F	9	15	.375	40	20	15	1	2	207	181	5	76	73	11.3	3.17	83	.235	.307	14	.206	-1	-10	-13	4	-1.2
Total	2	14	25	.359	68	34	22	1	4	345	334	10	134	118	12.5	3.83	70	.258	.332	22	.196	-1	-40	-44	4	-4.3
● RICK HENNINGER	Henninger, Richard Lee b: 1/11/48, Hastings, Neb. BR/TR, 6'6", 225 lbs. Deb: 9/3/73																									
1973	Tex-A	1	0	1.000	6	2	0	0	0	23	23	1	11	6	13.3	2.74	136	.261	.343	0	—	0	3	3	-1	0.1
● RANDY HENNIS	Hennis, Randall Philip b: 12/16/65, Clearlake, Cal. BR/TR, 6'6", 220 lbs. Deb: 9/17/90																									
1990	Hou-N	0	0	—	3	1	0	0	0	9²	1	0	3	4	4.7	0.00	—	.033	.147	0	.000	-0	4	4	-0	0.0
● DWAYNE HENRY	Henry, Dwayne Allen b: 2/16/62, Elkton, Md. BR/TR, 6'3", 205 lbs. Deb: 9/7/84																									
1984	Tex-A	0	1	.000	3	0	0	0	0	4¹	5	0	7	2	24.9	8.31	50	.294	.500	0	—	0	-2	-2	-0	-0.5
1985	Tex-A	2	2	.500	16	0	0	0	3	21	16	0	7	20	9.9	2.57	164	.211	.277	0	—	0	4	4	-0	0.8
1986	Tex-A	1	0	1.000	19	0	0	0	1	19¹	14	1	22	17	17.2	4.66	92	.209	.411	0	—	0	-1	-1	-0	-0.1
1987	Tex-A	0	0	—	5	0	0	0	0	10	12	2	9	7	18.9	9.00	50	.293	.420	0	—	0	-5	-5	-0	-0.6
1988	Tex-A	0	1	.000	11	0	0	0	1	10¹	15	1	9	10	23.5	8.71	47	.326	.466	0	—	0	-5	-5	-0	-0.6
1989	Atl-N	0	2	.000	12	0	0	0	1	12²	12	2	5	16	12.1	4.26	86	.250	.321	0	—	0	-1	-1	-0	-0.2
1990	Atl-N	2	2	.500	34	0	0	0	0	38¹	41	3	25	34	15.5	5.63	72	.273	.377	0	—	0	-8	-7	-1	-0.7
1991	Hou-N	3	2	.600	52	0	0	0	0	67²	51	7	39	51	12.2	3.19	110	.219	.336	0	.000	-0	4	2	-1	0.1
1992	Cin-N	3	3	.500	60	0	0	0	0	83²	59	4	44	72	11.2	3.33	108	.194	.304	1	.250	0	2	0	-0	0.2
1993	Cin-N	0	1	.000	3	0	0	0	0	4²	6	0	4	2	19.3	3.86	104	.273	.385	0	.000	0	-0	0	-0	0.0
	Sea-A	2	1	.667	31	0	0	0	2	54	56	6	35	35	15.5	6.67	66	.273	.384	0	—	0	-14	-14	-2	-0.9
Total	10	13	15	.464	246	0	0	0	9	326	287	26	206	266	13.9	4.61	85	.239	.354	1	.167	-0	-28	-26	-3	-1.8
● EARL HENRY	Henry, Earl Clifford "Hook" b: 6/10/17, Roseville, Ohio BL/TL, 5'11", 172 lbs. Deb: 9/23/44																									
1944	Cle-A	1	1	.500	2	2	1	0	0	17²	18	0	3	5	10.7	4.58	72	.269	.300	0	.000	-0	-2	-3	-0	-0.3
1945	Cle-A	0	3	.000	15	1	0	0	0	21²	20	0	20	10	17.0	5.40	60	.253	.410	2	.500	1	-5	-5	1	-0.4
Total	2	1	4	.200	17	3	1	0	0	39¹	38	0	23	15	14.2	5.03	65	.260	.365	2	.222	1	-7	-8	1	-0.8
● BUTCH HENRY	Henry, Floyd Bluford b: 10/7/68, ElPaso, Tex. BL/TL, 6'1", 195 lbs. Deb: 4/9/92																									
1992	Hou-N	6	9	.400	28	28	2	1	0	165²	185	16	41	96	12.3	4.02	84	.285	.329	8	.148	1	-10	-12	1	-0.9
1993	Col-N	2	8	.200	20	15	1	0	0	84²	117	14	24	39	15.1	6.59	72	.331	.375	2	.091	-1	-24	-17	-0	-1.9
	Mon-N	1	1	.500	10	1	0	0	0	18¹	18	1	4	8	10.8	3.93	106	.250	.289	0	.000	-0	0	-1	-0	0.0
	Yr	3	9	.250	30	16	1	0	0	103	135	15	28	47	14.2	6.12	76	.313	.354	2	.083	-2	-24	-17	-1	-1.9
1994	Mon-N	8	3	.727	24	15	0	0	1	107¹	97	10	20	70	10.0	2.43	174	.241	.280	9	.290	3	21	22	-0	2.4
Total	3	17	21	.447	82	59	3	1	1	376	417	41	89	213	12.2	4.14	95	.282	.325	19	.174	2	-12	-8	0	-0.4
● DUTCH HENRY	Henry, Frank John b: 5/12/02, Cleveland, Ohio d: 8/23/68, Cleveland, Ohio BL/TL, 6'1", 175 lbs. Deb: 9/16/21																									
1921	StL-A	0	0	—	1	0	0	0	0	2	2	0	1	0	13.5	4.50	100	.250	.250	1	1.000	0	-0	-0	-0	0.0
1922	StL-A	0	0	—	4	0	0	0	2	5	7	0	5	3	21.6	5.40	77	.280	.400	0	—	0	-1	-1	0	-0.1
1923	Bro-N	4	6	.400	17	9	5	2	0	94¹	105	1	28	28	12.9	3.91	99	.281	.334	8	.229	1	1	-0	4	0.0
1924	Bro-N	1	2	.333	16	4	0	0	0	46	69	0	15	11	16.4	5.67	66	.352	.398	5	.250	-0	-9	-10	0	-0.5
1927	NY-N	11	6	.647	45	15	0	0	2	163²	186	6	31	40	11.8	4.23	91	.278	.311	13	.236	1	-6	-7	-2	-0.7

YEAR TM/L	W	L	PCT	G	GS	CG	SH	SV	IP	H	HR	BB	SO	RAT	ERA	ERA+	OAV	OOB	BH	AVG	PB	PR	/A	PD	TPI
1928 NY-N	3	6	.333	17	8	4	0	1	64	82	7	25	23	15.2	3.80	103	.325	.388	3	.158	-1	1	1	1	0.1
1929 NY-N	5	6	.455	27	9	4	0	1	101¹	129	10	31	27	14.3	3.82	120	.316	.366	7	.250	2	10	9	-1	0.8
Chi-A	1	0	1.000	2	1	1	0	0	15	20	1	7	2	16.2	6.00	71	.308	.375	1	.143	0	-3	-3	-1	-0.2
1930 Chi-A	2	17	.105	35	16	4	0	0	155	211	12	48	35	15.3	4.88	95	.331	.381	12	.235	1	-4	-4	3	-0.1
Total 8	27	43	.386	164	62	25	3	6	646¹	809	42	190	170	14.0	4.39	95	.308	.356	50	.231	6	-10	-16	0	-0.6

● **JIM HENRY**   Henry, James Francis   b: 6/26/10, Danville, Pa.   d: 8/15/76, Memphis, Tenn.   BR/TR, 6'2", 175 lbs.   Deb: 4/23/36

YEAR TM/L	W	L	PCT	G	GS	CG	SH	SV	IP	H	HR	BB	SO	RAT	ERA	ERA+	OAV	OOB	BH	AVG	PB	PR	/A	PD	TPI
1936 Bos-A	5	1	.833	21	8	4	0	0	76¹	75	10	40	36	13.8	4.60	116	.255	.348	3	.115	-1	4	6	0	0.3
1937 Bos-A	1	0	1.000	3	2	1	0	0	15¹	15	2	11	8	15.3	5.28	90	.263	.382	0	.000	-0	-1	-1	-0	-0.1
1939 Phi-N	0	1	.000	9	1	0	0	1	23	24	3	8	7	12.9	5.09	79	.276	.344	0	.000	-1	-3	-3	-1	-0.3
Total 3	6	2	.750	33	11	3	0	1	114²	114	15	59	51	13.8	4.79	104	.260	.352	3	.083	-2	-0	2	-1	-0.1

● **JOHN HENRY**   Henry, John Michael   b: 9/2/1863, Springfield, Mass.   d: 6/11/39, Hartford, Conn.   TL,   Deb: 8/13/1884 ♦

YEAR TM/L	W	L	PCT	G	GS	CG	SH	SV	IP	H	HR	BB	SO	RAT	ERA	ERA+	OAV	OOB	BH	AVG	PB	PR	/A	PD	TPI
1884 Cle-N	1	4	.200	5	5	5	1	0	42	46	4	26	23	15.4	3.64	87	.257	.351	4	.154	-1	-3	-2	1	-0.3
1885 Bal-a	2	7	.222	9	9	9	0	0	71	71	0	13	31	10.9	4.31	76	.247	.284	9	.265	1	-8	-8	2	-0.5
1886 Was-N	1	3	.250	4	4	4	0	0	27²	35	1	15	19	16.3	4.23	78	.285	.362	5	.357	1	-3	-3	-0	-0.3
Total 3	4	14	.222	18	18	18	1	0	140²	152	5	54	73	13.3	4.09	79	.258	.322	53	.243	1	-14	-13	2	-1.1

● **DOUG HENRY**   Henry, Richard Douglas   b: 12/10/63, Sacramento, Cal.   BR/TR, 6'4", 185 lbs.   Deb: 7/15/91

YEAR TM/L	W	L	PCT	G	GS	CG	SH	SV	IP	H	HR	BB	SO	RAT	ERA	ERA+	OAV	OOB	BH	AVG	PB	PR	/A	PD	TPI
1991 Mil-A	2	1	.667	32	0	0	0	15	36	16	1	14	28	7.5	1.00	397	.133	.224	0	—	0	12	12	-1	2.2
1992 Mil-A	1	4	.200	68	0	0	0	29	65	64	6	24	52	12.2	4.02	96	.256	.321	0	—	0	-1	-1	0	-0.1
1993 Mil-A	4	4	.500	54	0	0	0	17	55	67	7	25	38	15.5	5.56	76	.300	.378	0	—	0	-8	-8	0	-1.5
1994 Mil-A	2	3	.400	25	0	0	0	2	31¹	31	1	7	23	16.1	4.60	107	.271	.394	0	.000	0	1	1	0	0.1
Total 4	9	12	.429	179	0	0	0	61	187¹	179	21	86	138	12.9	3.99	104	.252	.336	0	.000	0	5	4	-0	0.7

● **BILL HENRY**   Henry, William Francis   b: 2/15/42, Long Beach, Cal.   BL/TL, 6'3", 195 lbs.   Deb: 9/13/66

YEAR TM/L	W	L	PCT	G	GS	CG	SH	SV	IP	H	HR	BB	SO	RAT	ERA	ERA+	OAV	OOB	BH	AVG	PB	PR	/A	PD	TPI
1966 NY-A	0	0	—	2	0	0	0	0	3	0	0	2	3	6.0	—	.000	.200	0	—	0	1	1	0	0.0

● **BILL HENRY**   Henry, William Rodman   b: 10/15/27, Alice, Tex.   BL/TL, 6'2", 180 lbs.   Deb: 4/17/52

YEAR TM/L	W	L	PCT	G	GS	CG	SH	SV	IP	H	HR	BB	SO	RAT	ERA	ERA+	OAV	OOB	BH	AVG	PB	PR	/A	PD	TPI
1952 Bos-A	5	4	.556	13	10	5	0	0	76²	75	7	36	23	13.3	3.87	102	.254	.339	8	.258	2	-2	1	-1	0.1
1953 Bos-A	5	5	.500	21	12	4	1	1	85²	86	4	33	56	12.9	3.26	129	.260	.334	6	.188	-0	7	9	-1	0.9
1954 Bos-A	3	7	.300	24	13	3	1	0	95²	104	9	49	38	14.5	4.52	91	.270	.354	4	.118	-1	-8	-4	-1	-0.7
1955 Bos-A	2	4	.333	17	7	0	0	0	59²	56	7	21	23	11.6	3.32	129	.247	.310	2	.105	-1	4	6	0	0.5
1958 Chi-N	5	4	.556	44	0	0	0	6	81¹	63	8	17	58	9.0	2.88	136	.214	.259	4	.235	-1	10	9	-1	1.1
1959 Chi-N	9	8	.529	**65**	0	0	0	12	134¹	111	19	26	115	9.2	2.68	147	.227	.267	6	.194	-0	19	**19**	-1	2.5
1960 Cin-N★	1	5	.167	51	0	0	0	17	67²	62	8	20	58	11.4	3.19	120	.247	.313	0	.000	-1	4	5	1	0.6
1961 *Cin-N	2	1	.667	47	0	0	0	16	53¹	50	8	15	53	11.0	2.19	185	.244	.295	0	.000	-1	11	11	0	1.2
1962 Cin-N	4	2	.667	40	0	0	0	11	37¹	40	2	20	35	14.7	4.58	88	.280	.372	1	.333	-1	-3	-2	-1	-0.5
1963 Cin-N	1	3	.250	47	0	0	0	14	52	55	4	11	45	11.6	4.15	81	.279	.321	1	.167	-1	-5	-5	-0	-0.7
1964 Cin-N	2	2	.500	37	0	0	0	6	52	31	2	12	28	8.0	0.87	418	.170	.234	3	.500	1	15	16	-0	1.7
1965 Cin-N	2	0	1.000	3	0	0	0	0	5	3	0	1	5	7.2	0.00	—	.176	.222	0	—	0	2	2	-0	0.9
SF-N	2	2	.500	35	0	0	0	4	42	40	2	8	35	10.5	3.64	99	.248	.288	1	.200	-0	-0	-0	-1	-0.1
Yr	4	2	.667	38	0	0	0	4	47	43	2	9	40	10.1	3.26	111	.242	.282	1	.200	-0	1	2	-1	0.8
1966 SF-N	1	1	.500	35	0	0	0	4	22	15	3	10	15	10.6	2.45	149	.190	.289	0	.000	-0	3	3	0	0.2
1967 SF-N	2	0	1.000	28	1	0	0	2	21²	16	1	9	23	11.2	2.08	158	.198	.293	0	.000	-0	3	3	0	0.3
1968 SF-N	0	2	.000	7	1	0	0	0	5	4	0	3	0	14.4	5.40	55	.250	.400	0	—	-1	-1	-1	0	-0.5
Pit-N	0	0	—	10	0	0	0	0	16²	29	2	3	9	18.4	8.10	36	.382	.420	0	.000	-0	-9	-10	-1	-0.1
Yr	0	2	.000	17	1	0	0	0	21²	33	2	6	9	17.0	7.48	39	.355	.406	0	.000	-0	-11	-11	-1	-0.6
1969 Hou-N	0	0	—	3	0	0	0	0	5	2	0	2	2	7.2	0.00	—	.111	.200	0	—	0	2	2	0	0.0
Total 16	46	50	.479	527	44	12	2	90	913	842	89	296	621	11.5	3.26	119	.244	.308	36	.177	-0	51	63	-6	7.4

● **ROY HENSHAW**   Henshaw, Roy Knikelbine   b: 7/29/11, Chicago, Ill.   d: 6/8/93, LaGrange, Ill.   BR/TL, 5'8", 155 lbs.   Deb: 4/15/33

YEAR TM/L	W	L	PCT	G	GS	CG	SH	SV	IP	H	HR	BB	SO	RAT	ERA	ERA+	OAV	OOB	BH	AVG	PB	PR	/A	PD	TPI
1933 Chi-N	2	1	.667	21	0	0	0	0	38²	32	0	20	16	12.6	4.19	78	.230	.335	2	.200	-0	-4	-4	-1	-0.4
1935 *Chi-N	13	5	.722	31	18	7	3	1	142²	135	6	68	53	13.1	3.28	120	.249	.337	13	.255	2	12	10	-3	1.0
1936 Chi-N	6	5	.545	39	14	6	2	1	129¹	152	5	69	69	14.8	3.97	100	.296	.370	6	.136	-2	1	0	-2	-0.4
1937 Bro-N	5	12	.294	42	16	5	0	2	156¹	176	14	69	98	14.3	5.07	80	.278	.352	8	.167	-2	-20	-18	0	-1.9
1938 StL-N	5	11	.313	27	15	4	0	0	130	132	7	48	34	12.5	4.02	99	.266	.347	9	.220	-1	-3	-1	0	-0.3
1942 Det-A	2	4	.333	23	2	0	0	0	61²	63	7	27	24	13.3	4.09	97	.269	.347	1	.083	-1	-3	-1	-1	-0.2
1943 Det-A	0	2	.000	26	3	0	0	0	71¹	75	2	33	33	14.0	3.76	93	.276	.360	1	.111	-1	-4	-2	0	-0.2
1944 Det-A	0	0	—	7	1	0	0	0	12¹	17	0	6	10	16.8	8.76	41	.315	.383	0	.000	-1	-7	-7	0	0.0
Total 8	33	40	.452	216	69	22	5	7	742¹	782	40	327	337	13.7	4.16	94	.271	.349	41	.179	-5	-29	-22	-8	-2.3

● **PHIL HENSIEK**   Hensiek, Philip Frank "Sid"   b: 10/13/01, St.Louis, Mo.   d: 2/21/72, St.Louis, Mo.   BR/TR, 6', 160 lbs.   Deb: 8/15/35

YEAR TM/L	W	L	PCT	G	GS	CG	SH	SV	IP	H	HR	BB	SO	RAT	ERA	ERA+	OAV	OOB	BH	AVG	PB	PR	/A	PD	TPI
1935 Was-A	0	3	.000	6	1	0	0	1	13	21	2	9	6	20.8	9.69	45	.356	.441	2	.667	1	-8	-8	-0	-1.4

● **CHUCK HENSLEY**   Hensley, Charles Floyd   b: 3/11/59, Tulare, Cal.   BL/TL, 6'3", 190 lbs.   Deb: 5/10/86

YEAR TM/L	W	L	PCT	G	GS	CG	SH	SV	IP	H	HR	BB	SO	RAT	ERA	ERA+	OAV	OOB	BH	AVG	PB	PR	/A	PD	TPI
1986 SF-N	0	0	—	11	0	0	0	1	7¹	5	2	2	6	8.6	2.45	143	.179	.233	0	—	0	1	1	0	0.0

● **PAT HENTGEN**   Hentgen, Patrick George   b: 11/13/68, Detroit, Mich.   BR/TR, 6'2", 200 lbs.   Deb: 9/3/91

YEAR TM/L	W	L	PCT	G	GS	CG	SH	SV	IP	H	HR	BB	SO	RAT	ERA	ERA+	OAV	OOB	BH	AVG	PB	PR	/A	PD	TPI
1991 Tor-A	0	0	—	3	1	0	0	0	7¹	5	1	3	3	12.3	2.45	171	.208	.345	0	—	0	1	1	0	-0.2
1992 Tor-A	5	2	.714	28	2	0	0	0	50¹	49	7	32	39	14.5	5.36	76	.254	.360	0	—	0	-8	-7	-1	-1.2
1993 *Tor-A☆	19	9	.679	34	32	3	0	0	216¹	215	27	74	122	12.3	3.87	112	.258	.323	0	—	0	11	11	-2	1.1
1994 Tor-A★	13	8	.619	24	24	6	3	0	174²	158	21	59	147	11.3	3.40	142	.240	.306	0	—	0	27	28	0	2.9
Total 4	37	19	.661	89	59	9	3	0	448²	427	56	168	311	12.2	3.83	117	.250	.322	0	—	0	31	33	-2	2.6

● **BILL HEPLER**   Hepler, William Lewis   b: 9/25/45, Covington, Va.   BL/TL, 6', 160 lbs.   Deb: 4/23/66

YEAR TM/L	W	L	PCT	G	GS	CG	SH	SV	IP	H	HR	BB	SO	RAT	ERA	ERA+	OAV	OOB	BH	AVG	PB	PR	/A	PD	TPI
1966 NY-N	3	3	.500	37	3	0	0	0	69	71	3	51	25	16.3	3.52	103	.274	.399	3	.214	0	1	1	-1	0.0

● **RON HERBEL**   Herbel, Ronald Samuel   b: 1/16/38, Denver, Colo.   BR/TR, 6'1", 195 lbs.   Deb: 9/10/63

YEAR TM/L	W	L	PCT	G	GS	CG	SH	SV	IP	H	HR	BB	SO	RAT	ERA	ERA+	OAV	OOB	BH	AVG	PB	PR	/A	PD	TPI
1963 SF-N	0	0	—	2	0	0	0	0	1¹	1	0	1	1	13.5	6.75	47	.200	.333	0	—	0	-1	-1	0	0.0
1964 SF-N	9	9	.500	40	22	7	2	1	161	162	7	61	98	12.6	3.07	116	.259	.328	4	.000	-4	8	9	2	0.7
1965 SF-N	12	9	.571	47	21	6	1	0	170²	172	16	47	106	11.7	3.85	94	.261	.313	1	.020	-4	-6	-5	2	-0.8
1966 SF-N	4	5	.444	32	18	0	0	0	129²	149	15	39	55	13.2	4.16	88	.291	.344	1	.026	-4	-8	-7	-1	-0.9
1967 SF-N	4	5	.444	42	11	1	1	1	125²	125	10	35	52	11.6	3.08	107	.268	.322	3	.107	-1	4	3	4	0.6
1968 SF-N	0	0	—	28	2	0	0	0	42²	55	5	15	18	15.0	3.38	87	.309	.366	0	.000	-1	0	-1	0	-0.1
1969 SF-N	4	1	.800	39	4	2	0	1	87¹	92	7	23	34	12.0	4.02	87	.275	.323	0	.000	-2	-4	-5	0	-0.4
1970 SD-N	7	5	.583	64	0	0	0	9	111	114	14	39	53	12.7	4.95	80	.266	.333	0	.000	-1	-11	-12	-0	-1.5
NY-N	2	2	.500	12	0	0	0	1	13	14	1	2	8	11.1	1.38	291	.275	.302	0	—	-1	4	4	0	1.1
Yr	9	7	.563	**76**	1	0	0	10	124	128	15	41	61	12.3	4.57	87	.262	.319	0	.000	-1	-7	-8	-0	-0.4
1971 Atl-N	0	1	.000	25	0	0	0	0	51²	61	6	23	22	15.3	5.23	71	.300	.383	1	.091	-1	-10	-9	0	-0.3
Total 9	42	37	.532	331	79	11	3	16	894	945	81	285	447	12.6	3.83	94	.273	.332	6	.029	-15	-25	-25	7	-1.5

◉ **ERNIE HERBERT**   Herbert, Ernie Albert "Tex"   b: 1/30/1887, Hale, Mo.   d: 1/13/68, Dallas, Tex.   BR/TR, 5'10", 165 lbs.   Deb: 7/27/13

YEAR TM/L	W	L	PCT	G	GS	CG	SH	SV	IP	H	HR	BB	SO	RAT	ERA	ERA+	OAV	OOB	BH	AVG	PB	PR	/A	PD	TPI
1913 Cin-N	0	0	—	6	0	0	0	1	17¹	12	0	5	5	9.3	2.08	156	.179	.247	1	.250	-1	2	2	-1	-0.1
1914 StL-F	1	1	.500	18	2	0	0	1	50¹	56	2	27	24	15.6	3.75	81	.293	.392	7	.538	2	-5	-4	-2	-0.2

YEAR	TM/L	W	L	PCT	G	GS	CG	SH	SV	IP	H	HR	BB	SO	RAT	ERA	ERA+	OAV	OOB	BH	AVG	PB	PR	/A	PD	TPI
1915	StL-F	1	0	1.000	11	1	1	0	0	48	48	1	18	23	12.9	3.38	85	.253	.327	5	.278	1	-3	-3	-1	0.0
Total 3		2	1	.667	35	3	1	0	1	115²	116	3	50	52	13.5	3.35	90	.259	.344	13	.371	3	-6	-4	-4	-0.3

● **FRED HERBERT** Herbert, Frederick (b: Herbert Frederick Kemman) b: 3/4/1887, LaGrange, Ill. d: 5/29/63, Tice, Fla. BR/TR, 6', 185 lbs. Deb: 9/25/15

YEAR	TM/L	W	L	PCT	G	GS	CG	SH	SV	IP	H	HR	BB	SO	RAT	ERA	ERA+	OAV	OOB	BH	AVG	PB	PR	/A	PD	TPI
1915	NY-N	1	1	.500	2	2	1	0	0	17	12	0	4	6	8.5	1.06	242	.197	.246	1	.167	-0	3	3	0	0.4

● **RAY HERBERT** Herbert, Raymond Ernest b: 12/15/29, Detroit, Mich. BR/TR, 5'11", 185 lbs. Deb: 8/27/50

YEAR	TM/L	W	L	PCT	G	GS	CG	SH	SV	IP	H	HR	BB	SO	RAT	ERA	ERA+	OAV	OOB	BH	AVG	PB	PR	/A	PD	TPI
1950	Det-A	1	2	.333	8	3	1	0	1	22¹	20	1	12	5	12.9	3.63	129	.244	.340	2	.286	0	2	3	1	0.4
1951	Det-A	4	0	1.000	5	0	0	0	0	12²	8	0	9	9	12.1	1.42	294	.190	.333	0	.000	-0	4	4	-0	1.1
1953	Det-A	4	6	.400	43	3	0	0	6	87²	109	5	46	37	15.9	5.24	78	.308	.387	3	.158	-0	-12	-11	3	-1.0
1954	Det-A	3	6	.333	42	4	0	0	0	84¹	114	6	50	44	17.7	5.87	63	.334	.422	3	.176	2	-20	-20	2	-1.6
1955	KC-A	1	8	.111	23	11	2	0	0	87²	99	10	40	30	14.4	6.26	67	.292	.368	4	.190	-0	-22	-20	-2	-1.6
1958	KC-A	8	8	.500	42	16	5	0	3	175	161	20	55	108	11.3	3.50	112	.248	.311	10	.192	1	5	8	2	1.1
1959	KC-A	11	11	.500	37	26	10	2	1	183²	196	24	62	99	12.7	4.85	83	.275	.334	12	.211	2	-20	-17	-1	-1.8
1960	KC-A	14	15	.483	37	33	14	0	1	252²	256	17	72	122	11.9	3.28	121	.267	.323	13	.171	1	17	20	3	2.5
1961	KC-A	3	6	.333	13	12	1	0	0	83²	103	10	30	34	14.5	5.38	78	.303	.363	3	.107	-1	-13	-11	-0	-1.1
	Chi-A	9	6	.600	21	20	4	0	0	137²	142	15	36	50	11.6	4.05	97	.265	.311	12	.226	4	-0	-2	1	0.3
	Yr	12	12	.500	34	32	5	0	0	221¹	245	25	66	84	12.6	4.55	88	.278	.328	15	.185	3	-13	-13	1	-0.8
1962	Chi-A★	20	9	.690	35	35	12	2	0	236²	228	13	74	115	11.5	3.27	119	.255	.312	16	.195	5	18	17	3	2.8
1963	Chi-A	13	10	.565	33	33	14	7	0	224²	230	12	35	105	10.7	3.24	108	.265	.295	14	.222	6	10	7	2	1.5
1964	Chi-A	6	7	.462	20	19	1	1	0	111²	117	14	17	40	11.0	3.47	100	.275	.306	5	.139	-1	2	-0	-1	-0.2
1965	Phi-N	5	8	.385	25	19	4	1	1	130²	162	13	19	51	12.5	3.86	90	.309	.334	11	.268	3	-5	-6	0	-0.2
1966	Phi-N	2	5	.286	23	2	0	0	2	50¹	57	5	14	15	12.5	4.29	84	.293	.345	1	.077	-1	-4	-4	-0	-0.6
Total 14		104	107	.493	407	236	68	13	15	1881¹	2000	167	571	864	12.4	4.01	96	.276	.331	109	.192	20	-38	-35	18	1.6

● **GIL HEREDIA** Heredia, Gilbert b: 10/26/65, Nogales, Ariz. BR/TR, 6'1", 190 lbs. Deb: 9/1/91

YEAR	TM/L	W	L	PCT	G	GS	CG	SH	SV	IP	H	HR	BB	SO	RAT	ERA	ERA+	OAV	OOB	BH	AVG	PB	PR	/A	PD	TPI
1991	SF-N	0	2	.000	7	4	0	0	0	33	27	4	7	13	9.3	3.82	94	.233	.276	3	.429	1	-0	-1	0	0.0
1992	SF-N	2	3	.400	13	4	0	0	0	30	32	3	16	15	14.7	5.40	61	.278	.371	1	.167	0	-6	-7	-1	-1.2
	Mon-N	0	0	—	7	1	0	0	0	14²	12	1	4	7	9.8	1.84	188	.250	.308	0	.000	-0	3	3	0	0.0
	Yr	2	3	.400	20	5	0	0	0	44²	44	4	20	22	12.9	4.23	79	.268	.348	1	.111	-0	-4	-4	-1	-1.2
1993	Mon-N	4	2	.667	20	9	1	0	2	57¹	66	4	14	40	12.9	3.92	106	.293	.340	2	.154	-0	1	2	1	0.2
1994	Mon-N	6	3	.667	39	3	0	0	0	75¹	85	7	13	62	11.9	3.46	122	.281	.314	5	.313	1	6	7	0	0.8
Total 4		12	10	.545	86	21	1	0	2	210¹	222	19	54	137	12.0	3.81	103	.275	.324	11	.244	2	3	-0	0	-0.2

● **UBALDO HEREDIA** Heredia, Ubaldo Jose (Martinez) b: 5/4/56, Ciudad Bolivar, Ven. BR/TR, 6'2", 180 lbs. Deb: 5/12/87

YEAR	TM/L	W	L	PCT	G	GS	CG	SH	SV	IP	H	HR	BB	SO	RAT	ERA	ERA+	OAV	OOB	BH	AVG	PB	PR	/A	PD	TPI
1987	Mon-N	0	1	.000	2	2	0	0	0	10	10	2	3	6	12.6	5.40	78	.263	.333	0	.000	-0	-1	-1	0	-0.1

● **ART HERMAN** Herman, Arthur b: 5/11/1871, Louisville, Ky. d: 9/20/55, Los Angeles, Cal. Deb: 6/29/1896

YEAR	TM/L	W	L	PCT	G	GS	CG	SH	SV	IP	H	HR	BB	SO	RAT	ERA	ERA+	OAV	OOB	BH	AVG	PB	PR	/A	PD	TPI
1896	Lou-N	4	6	.400	14	12	9	0	0	94¹	122	4	36	13	15.3	5.63	77	.311	.371	5	.139	-4	-13	-14	-1	-1.5
1897	Lou-N	0	1	.000	3	2	1	0	0	18	23	1	5	4	14.0	4.00	107	.308	.351	2	.333	1	1	1	0	0.2
Total 2		4	7	.364	17	14	10	0	0	112¹	145	5	41	17	15.1	5.37	80	.310	.368	7	.167	-2	-13	-13	-1	-1.3

● **JESUS HERNAIZ** Hernaiz, Jesus Rafael (Rodriguez) b: 1/8/45, Santurce, P.R. BR/TR, 6'2", 175 lbs. Deb: 6/14/74

YEAR	TM/L	W	L	PCT	G	GS	CG	SH	SV	IP	H	HR	BB	SO	RAT	ERA	ERA+	OAV	OOB	BH	AVG	PB	PR	/A	PD	TPI
1974	Phi-N	2	3	.400	27	0	0	0	1	41¹	53	6	25	16	17.0	5.88	64	.323	.413	0	.000	-0	-10	-10	-0	-1.2

● **XAVIER HERNANDEZ** Hernandez, Francis Xavier b: 8/16/65, Port Arthur, Tex. BL/TR, 6'2", 185 lbs. Deb: 6/4/89

YEAR	TM/L	W	L	PCT	G	GS	CG	SH	SV	IP	H	HR	BB	SO	RAT	ERA	ERA+	OAV	OOB	BH	AVG	PB	PR	/A	PD	TPI
1989	Tor-A	1	0	1.000	7	0	0	0	0	22²	25	2	8	7	13.5	4.76	79	.278	.343	0	—	0	-2	-3	-1	-0.1
1990	Hou-N	2	1	.667	34	0	0	0	0	62¹	60	8	24	24	12.7	4.62	80	.256	.336	1	.333	0	-6	-6	-1	-0.4
1991	Hou-N	2	7	.222	32	6	0	0	3	63	66	6	32	55	14.0	4.71	74	.263	.346	0	.000	-0	-7	-8	0	-0.4
1992	Hou-N	9	1	.900	77	0	0	0	7	111	81	5	42	96	10.2	2.11	159	.200	.281	0	.000	-1	17	15	-2	1.3
1993	Hou-N	4	5	.444	72	0	0	0	9	96²	75	6	28	101	9.7	2.61	149	.212	.272	0	.000	-1	15	14	-1	1.3
1994	NY-A	4	4	.500	31	0	0	0	6	40	48	7	21	37	16.0	5.85	76	.300	.388	0	—	0	-6	-6	-0	-1.2
Total 6		22	18	.550	253	7	0	0	25	395²	355	34	155	320	11.9	3.57	104	.238	.314	1	.037	-2	13	6	-4	-0.3

● **EVELIO HERNANDEZ** Hernandez, Gregorio Evelio (Lopez) b: 12/24/30, Guanabacoa, Havana, Cuba BR/TR, 6'1", 195 lbs. Deb: 9/12/56

YEAR	TM/L	W	L	PCT	G	GS	CG	SH	SV	IP	H	HR	BB	SO	RAT	ERA	ERA+	OAV	OOB	BH	AVG	PB	PR	/A	PD	TPI
1956	Was-A	1	1	.500	4	4	1	0	0	22²	24	2	8	9	12.7	4.76	91	.276	.337	2	.182	-0	-2	-1	-0	-0.1
1957	Was-A	0	0	—	14	2	0	0	0	36	38	2	20	15	14.5	4.25	92	.268	.358	0	.000	-1	-2	-1	-1	-0.1
Total 2		1	1	.500	18	6	1	0	0	58²	62	4	28	24	13.8	4.45	91	.271	.350	2	.118	-1	-3	-3	-1	-0.2

● **WILLIE HERNANDEZ** Hernandez, Guillermo (Villanueva) b: 11/14/54, Aguada, P.R. BL/TL, 6'3", 180 lbs. Deb: 4/9/77

YEAR	TM/L	W	L	PCT	G	GS	CG	SH	SV	IP	H	HR	BB	SO	RAT	ERA	ERA+	OAV	OOB	BH	AVG	PB	PR	/A	PD	TPI
1977	Chi-N	8	7	.533	67	1	0	0	4	110	94	11	28	78	10.1	3.03	145	.234	.285	1	.063	-1	11	17	3	2.4
1978	Chi-N	8	2	.800	54	0	0	0	4	59²	57	6	35	38	14.0	3.77	107	.263	.368	0	.000	-0	-1	2	1	0.3
1979	Chi-N	4	4	.500	51	2	0	0	0	79	85	8	39	53	14.6	5.01	82	.281	.370	2	.250	-0	-11	-8	-0	-0.7
1980	Chi-N	1	9	.100	53	7	0	0	0	108¹	115	8	45	75	13.5	4.40	89	.276	.349	4	.211	-0	-10	-6	2	-0.3
1981	Chi-N	0	0	—	12	0	0	0	2	13²	14	0	8	13	14.5	3.95	94	.280	.379	0	—	-0	-0	0	0	0.0
1982	Chi-N	4	6	.400	75	0	0	0	10	75	74	6	24	54	11.9	3.00	124	.268	.329	0	.000	-0	5	6	2	1.2
1983	Chi-N	1	0	1.000	11	1	0	0	1	19²	16	0	6	18	10.1	3.20	118	.222	.282	1	.500	1	1	1	0	0.2
	*Phi-N	8	4	.667	63	0	0	0	7	95²	93	9	26	75	11.3	3.29	108	.254	.305	5	.385	2	3	3	-0	0.6
	Yr	9	4	.692	74	1	0	0	8	115¹	109	9	32	93	11.1	3.28	110	.249	.301	6	.400	2	4	4	0	0.8
1984	*Det-A★	9	3	.750	80	0	0	0	32	140¹	96	6	36	112	8.7	1.92	204	.194	.254	0	—	0	32	31	-1	4.1
1985	Det-A★	8	10	.444	74	0	0	0	31	106²	82	13	14	76	8.2	2.70	151	.210	.239	0	.000	-0	17	16	-2	3.4
1986	Det-A☆	8	7	.533	64	0	0	0	24	88²	87	13	21	77	11.5	3.55	116	.251	.304	0	—	-0	6	6	1	1.2
1987	*Det-A	3	4	.429	45	0	0	0	8	49	53	8	20	30	13.4	3.67	115	.276	.344	0	—	-0	4	3	-1	0.4
1988	Det-A	6	5	.545	63	0	0	0	10	67²	50	8	31	59	11.3	3.06	125	.208	.309	0	—	-0	7	6	1	1.2
1989	Det-A	2	2	.500	32	0	0	0	15	31¹	36	4	15	30	15.2	5.74	66	.293	.379	0	—	-0	-6	-7	0	-1.5
Total 13		70	63	.526	744	11	0	0	147	1044²	952	97	349	788	11.4	3.38	118	.245	.311	13	.206	1	57	70	6	12.5

● **JEREMY HERNANDEZ** Hernandez, Jeremy Stuart b: 7/6/66, Burbank, Cal. BR/TR, 6'5", 195 lbs. Deb: 9/2/91

YEAR	TM/L	W	L	PCT	G	GS	CG	SH	SV	IP	H	HR	BB	SO	RAT	ERA	ERA+	OAV	OOB	BH	AVG	PB	PR	/A	PD	TPI
1991	SD-N	0	0	—	9	0	0	0	2	14¹	8	0	5	9	8.2	0.00	—	.157	.232	0	.000	6	6	6	0	0.2
1992	SD-N	1	4	.200	26	0	0	0	1	36²	39	4	11	25	12.5	4.17	86	.291	.349	0	.000	-0	-3	-2	0	-0.3
1993	SD-N	0	2	.000	21	0	0	0	0	34¹	42	7	7	26	12.6	4.72	88	.301	.336	0	.000	-0	-2	-2	0	-0.1
	Cle-A	6	5	.545	49	0	0	0	8	77¹	75	12	27	44	11.9	3.14	138	.261	.325	0	—	-0	10	10	-0	1.5
1994	Fla-N	3	3	.500	21	0	0	0	9	23¹	16	0	14	13	12.3	2.70	167	.205	.340	0	.000	-0	4	5	0	1.5
Total 4		10	14	.417	126	0	0	0	20	186	179	18	64	117	11.9	3.34	124	.261	.327	0	.000	-1	15	16	0	2.8

● **MANNY HERNANDEZ** Hernandez, Manuel Antonio (Montas) b: 5/7/61, LaRomana, D.R. BR/TR, 6', 150 lbs. Deb: 6/5/86

YEAR	TM/L	W	L	PCT	G	GS	CG	SH	SV	IP	H	HR	BB	SO	RAT	ERA	ERA+	OAV	OOB	BH	AVG	PB	PR	/A	PD	TPI
1986	Hou-N	2	3	.400	9	4	0	0	0	27²	33	2	12	9	14.6	3.90	92	.306	.375	0	.000	-1	-1	-1	-0	-0.2
1987	Hou-N	0	4	.000	6	3	0	0	0	21²	25	1	5	12	12.9	5.40	73	.301	.348	0	.000	-0	-3	-4	-0	-0.6
1989	NY-N	0	0	—	1	0	0	0	0	1	0	0	0	1	0.0	0.00	—	.000	.000	0	—	-0	1	1	0	0.0
Total 3		2	7	.222	16	7	0	0	0	50¹	58	3	17	22	13.6	4.47	83	.299	.358	0	.000	-1	-3	-4	-0	-0.8

● **RAMON HERNANDEZ** Hernandez, Ramon (Gonzalez) b: 8/31/40, Carolina, P.R. BB/TL, 5'9", 170 lbs. Deb: 4/11/67

YEAR	TM/L	W	L	PCT	G	GS	CG	SH	SV	IP	H	HR	BB	SO	RAT	ERA	ERA+	OAV	OOB	BH	AVG	PB	PR	/A	PD	TPI
1967	Atl-N	0	2	.000	46	0	0	0	5	51²	60	5	14	28	13.2	4.18	79	.296	.347	0	.000	-0	-5	-5	1	-0.3
1968	Chi-N	0	1	.000	9	0	0	0	0	9	14	1	3	9	15.0	9.00	35	.350	.366	0	—	-0	-6	-6	0	0.0
1971	Pit-N	0	1	.000	10	0	0	0	0	12¹	5	0	2	7	5.1	0.73	463	.122	.163	1	.500	-0	4	4	0	0.6
1972	*Pit-N	5	0	1.000	53	0	0	0	14	70	50	3	22	47	9.6	1.67	199	.194	.265	2	.167	0	14	13	0	1.6

YEAR TM/L	W	L	PCT	G	GS	CG	SH	SV	IP	H	HR	BB	SO	RAT	ERA	ERA+	OAV	OOB	BH	AVG	PB	PR	/A	PD	TPI
1973 Pit-N	4	5	.444	59	0	0	0	11	89²	71	5	25	64	10.0	2.41	146	.218	.282	1	.125	0	12	11	1	1.5
1974 *Pit-N	5	2	.714	58	0	0	0	2	68²	68	3	18	33	11.5	2.75	125	.258	.310	1	.250	1	7	5	-1	0.6
1975 *Pit-N	7	2	.778	46	0	0	0	5	64	62	0	28	43	12.7	2.95	120	.252	.328	0	.000	-0	5	4	1	0.7
1976 Pit-N	2	2	.500	37	0	0	0	3	43	42	3	16	17	12.3	3.56	98	.262	.333	0	.000	-0	-0	-1	-0	-0.1
Chi-N	0	0	—	2	0	0	0	0	1²	2	0	0	1	10.8	0.00	—	.333	.333	0	—	0	1	1	0	0.0
Yr	2	2	.500	39	0	0	0	3	44²	44	3	16	18	12.1	3.43	102	.257	.321	0	.000	0	0	0	-0	-0.1
1977 Chi-N	0	0	—	6	0	0	0	1	7²	11	1	3	4	16.4	8.22	53	.306	.359	0	.000	-0	-4	-3	0	-0.1
Bos-A	0	1	.000	12	0	0	0	1	12²	12	2	6	8	15.6	5.68	79	.280	.337	0	—	0	-2	-2	-0	-0.2
Total 9	23	15	.605	337	0	0	0	46	430¹	399	23	135	255	11.5	3.03	115	.245	.308	5	.125	1	25	22	1	4.3

● ROBERTO HERNANDEZ
Hernandez, Roberto Manuel (Rodriguez)   b: 11/11/64, Santurce, P.R.   BR/TR, 6'4", 220 lbs.   Deb: 9/2/91

YEAR TM/L	W	L	PCT	G	GS	CG	SH	SV	IP	H	HR	BB	SO	RAT	ERA	ERA+	OAV	OOB	BH	AVG	PB	PR	/A	PD	TPI
1991 Chi-A	1	0	1.000	9	3	0	0	0	15	18	1	7	6	15.0	7.80	51	.290	.362	0	—	0	-6	-6	-0	-0.4
1992 Chi-A	7	3	.700	43	0	0	0	12	71	45	4	20	68	8.7	1.65	234	.180	.252	0	—	0	18	17	-0	3.0
1993 *Chi-A	3	4	.429	70	0	0	0	38	78²	66	6	20	71	9.8	2.29	183	.228	.277	0	—	0	18	17	-0	3.2
1994 Chi-A	4	4	.500	45	0	0	0	14	47²	44	5	19	50	12.1	4.91	96	.238	.312	0	—	0	-1	-1	-0	-0.1
Total 4	15	11	.577	167	3	0	0	64	212¹	173	16	66	195	10.3	3.05	137	.220	.284	0	—	0	29	26	-1	5.6

● RUDY HERNANDEZ
Hernandez, Rudolph Albert (Fuentes)   b: 12/10/31, Santiago, D.R.   BR/TR, 6'3", 185 lbs.   Deb: 7/3/60

YEAR TM/L	W	L	PCT	G	GS	CG	SH	SV	IP	H	HR	BB	SO	RAT	ERA	ERA+	OAV	OOB	BH	AVG	PB	PR	/A	PD	TPI
1960 Was-A	4	1	.800	21	0	0	0	0	34²	34	2	21	22	14.5	4.41	88	.262	.368	1	.167	-0	-2	-2	-0	-0.3
1961 Was-A	0	1	.000	7	0	0	0	0	9	8	0	3	4	11.0	3.00	134	.250	.314	0	—	0	1	1	0	0.1
Total 2	4	2	.667	28	0	0	0	0	43²	42	2	24	26	13.8	4.12	95	.259	.358	1	.167	-0	-1	-1	-0	-0.2

● WALT HERRELL
Herrell, Walter William "Reds"   b: 2/19/1889, Rockville, Md.   d: 1/23/49, Front Royal, Va.   Deb: 6/10/11

YEAR TM/L	W	L	PCT	G	GS	CG	SH	SV	IP	H	HR	BB	SO	RAT	ERA	ERA+	OAV	OOB	BH	AVG	PB	PR	/A	PD	TPI
1911 Was-A	0	0	—	1	0	0	0	0	2	3	0	4	0	31.5	18.00	18	.556	.636	0	.000	-0	-3	-3	-0	0.0

● BOBBY HERRERA
Herrera, Procopio Rodriguez "Tito" (b: Procopio Rodriguez (Herrera))   b: 7/26/26, Nuevo Laredo, Mex   BR/TR, 6', 184 lbs.   Deb: 4/19/51

YEAR TM/L	W	L	PCT	G	GS	CG	SH	SV	IP	H	HR	BB	SO	RAT	ERA	ERA+	OAV	OOB	BH	AVG	PB	PR	/A	PD	TPI
1951 StL-A	0	0	—	3	0	0	0	0	2	6	2	4	1	42.4	27.00	16	.462	.611	0	—	0	-6	-6	-0	0.0

● TROY HERRIAGE
Herriage, William Troy "Dutch"   b: 12/20/30, Tipton, Okla.   BR/TR, 6'1", 170 lbs.   Deb: 4/25/56

YEAR TM/L	W	L	PCT	G	GS	CG	SH	SV	IP	H	HR	BB	SO	RAT	ERA	ERA+	OAV	OOB	BH	AVG	PB	PR	/A	PD	TPI
1956 KC-A	1	13	.071	31	16	1	0	0	103	135	16	64	59	17.9	6.64	65	.321	.418	3	.120	-1	-28	-26	-2	-3.3

● TOM HERRIN
Herrin, Thomas Edward   b: 9/12/29, Shreveport, La.   BR/TR, 6'3", 190 lbs.   Deb: 4/13/54

YEAR TM/L	W	L	PCT	G	GS	CG	SH	SV	IP	H	HR	BB	SO	RAT	ERA	ERA+	OAV	OOB	BH	AVG	PB	PR	/A	PD	TPI
1954 Bos-A	1	2	.333	14	1	0	0	0	28¹	34	3	22	8	17.8	7.31	56	.315	.431	1	.125	-0	-11	-10	1	-0.9

● ART HERRING
Herring, Arthur L "Red" or "Sandy"   b: 3/10/07, Altus, Okla.   BR/TR, 5'7", 168 lbs.   Deb: 9/12/29

YEAR TM/L	W	L	PCT	G	GS	CG	SH	SV	IP	H	HR	BB	SO	RAT	ERA	ERA+	OAV	OOB	BH	AVG	PB	PR	/A	PD	TPI
1929 Det-A	2	1	.667	4	4	0	0	0	32	38	0	19	15	16.3	4.78	90	.302	.397	3	.214	1	-2	-2	-0	0.0
1930 Det-A	3	3	.500	23	6	1	0	0	77²	97	2	36	16	15.8	5.33	90	.315	.392	3	.130	-2	-6	-5	-0	-0.5
1931 Det-A	7	13	.350	35	16	9	0	1	165	186	8	67	64	14.2	4.31	106	.281	.355	11	.200	-1	1	5	2	0.6
1932 Det-A	1	2	.333	12	0	0	0	0	22¹	25	2	15	12	16.5	5.24	90	.284	.394	0	.000	-0	-2	-1	-0	-0.2
1933 Det-A	1	2	.333	24	3	1	0	0	61	61	6	20	20	12.1	3.84	112	.264	.325	1	.077	-1	3	3	-1	0.0
1934 Bro-N	2	4	.333	14	4	2	0	0	49¹	63	2	29	15	16.8	6.20	63	.307	.393	2	.143	1	-12	-13	-0	-1.3
1939 Chi-N	0	0	—	7	0	0	0	0	14¹	13	2	5	8	11.9	5.65	84	.250	.328	0	.000	-0	-1	-1	-0	-0.2
1944 Bro-N	3	4	.429	12	6	3	1	1	55¹	59	3	17	19	12.5	3.42	104	.277	.333	3	.200	0	1	1	-0	0.2
1945 Bro-N	7	4	.636	22	15	7	2	2	124	103	11	43	34	10.8	3.48	108	.222	.292	4	.095	-2	4	4	1	0.2
1946 Bro-N	7	2	.778	35	2	0	0	5	86	91	2	29	34	12.7	3.35	101	.277	.338	4	.182	0	1	0	2	0.2
1947 Pit-N	1	3	.250	11	0	0	0	2	10²	18	3	4	6	18.6	8.44	50	.360	.407	0	.000	-0	-5	-5	-0	-1.8
Total 11	34	38	.472	199	56	25	3	13	697²	754	41	284	243	13.6	4.32	96	.276	.349	31	.149	-4	-18	-14	4	-2.6

● HERB HERRING
Herring, Herbert Lee   b: 7/22/1891, Danville, Ark.   d: 4/22/64, Tucson, Ariz.   BR/TR, 5'11", 178 lbs.   Deb: 9/4/12

YEAR TM/L	W	L	PCT	G	GS	CG	SH	SV	IP	H	HR	BB	SO	RAT	ERA	ERA+	OAV	OOB	BH	AVG	PB	PR	/A	PD	TPI
1912 Was-A	0	0	—	1	0	0	0	0	1	1	0	0	0	18.0	0.00	—	.250	.400	0	—	0	0	0	-0	0.0

● LEFTY HERRING
Herring, Silas Clarke   b: 3/4/1880, Philadelphia, Pa.   d: 2/11/65, Massapequa, N.Y.   BL/TL, 5'11", 160 lbs.   Deb: 5/16/1899 ◆

YEAR TM/L	W	L	PCT	G	GS	CG	SH	SV	IP	H	HR	BB	SO	RAT	ERA	ERA+	OAV	OOB	BH	AVG	PB	PR	/A	PD	TPI
1899 Was-N	0	0	—	2	0	0	0	0	2	2	0	2	0	9.0	0.00	—	.000	.260	1	1.000	1	1	1	0	0.1

● BILL HERRING
Herring, William Francis "Smoke"   b: 10/31/1893, New York, N.Y.   d: 9/10/62, Honesdale, Pa.   BR/TR, 6'3", 185 lbs.   Deb: 6/26/15

YEAR TM/L	W	L	PCT	G	GS	CG	SH	SV	IP	H	HR	BB	SO	RAT	ERA	ERA+	OAV	OOB	BH	AVG	PB	PR	/A	PD	TPI
1915 Bro-F	0	0	—	3	0	0	0	0	3	5	1	2	3	24.0	15.00	18	.385	.500	0	—	0	-4	-4	-0	0.0

● LEROY HERRMANN
Herrmann, Leroy George   b: 2/27/06, Steward, Ill.   d: 7/3/72, Livermore, Cal.   BR/TR, 5'10", 185 lbs.   Deb: 7/30/32

YEAR TM/L	W	L	PCT	G	GS	CG	SH	SV	IP	H	HR	BB	SO	RAT	ERA	ERA+	OAV	OOB	BH	AVG	PB	PR	/A	PD	TPI
1932 Chi-N	2	1	.667	7	0	0	0	0	12²	18	0	9	5	19.2	6.39	59	.346	.443	1	.500	0	-4	-4	-0	-0.7
1933 Chi-N	0	1	.000	9	0	0	0	1	21	26	3	8	4	16.3	5.57	59	.299	.384	1	.167	-0	-5	-5	-1	-0.4
1935 Cin-N	3	5	.375	29	8	2	0	0	108	124	9	31	30	13.6	3.58	111	.297	.357	8	.267	1	5	5	-0	0.4
Total 3	5	7	.417	45	9	2	0	1	141²	168	12	48	39	14.5	4.13	93	.302	.370	10	.263	1	-4	-4	-1	-0.7

● MARTY HERRMANN
Herrmann, Martin John "Lefty"   b: 1/10/1893, Oldenburg, Ind.   d: 9/11/56, Cincinnati, Ohio   BL/TL, 5'10", 150 lbs.   Deb: 7/10/18   F

YEAR TM/L	W	L	PCT	G	GS	CG	SH	SV	IP	H	HR	BB	SO	RAT	ERA	ERA+	OAV	OOB	BH	AVG	PB	PR	/A	PD	TPI
1918 Bro-N	0	0	—	1	0	0	0	0	1	0	0	1	0	9.0	0.00	—	.000	.250	0	—	0	0	0	-0	0.0

● FRANK HERSHEY
Hershey, Frank   b: 12/13/1877, Gorham, N.Y.   d: 12/15/49, Canandaigua, N.Y.   TR , 175 lbs.   Deb: 4/20/05

YEAR TM/L	W	L	PCT	G	GS	CG	SH	SV	IP	H	HR	BB	SO	RAT	ERA	ERA+	OAV	OOB	BH	AVG	PB	PR	/A	PD	TPI
1905 Bos-N	0	1	.000	1	1	0	0	0	4	5	0	2	1	15.8	6.75	46	.313	.389	0	.000	-0	-2	-2	-0	-0.3

● OREL HERSHISER
Hershiser, Orel Leonard Quinton   b: 9/16/58, Buffalo, N.Y.   BR/TR, 6'3", 192 lbs.   Deb: 9/1/83

YEAR TM/L	W	L	PCT	G	GS	CG	SH	SV	IP	H	HR	BB	SO	RAT	ERA	ERA+	OAV	OOB	BH	AVG	PB	PR	/A	PD	TPI
1983 LA-N	0	0	—	8	0	0	0	1	8	7	1	6	5	14.6	3.38	106	.233	.361	0	—	0	0	0	0	0.0
1984 LA-N	11	8	.579	45	20	8	4	2	189²	160	9	50	150	10.2	2.66	133	.225	.279	10	.200	2	20	18	1	2.1
1985 *LA-N	19	3	.864	36	34	9	5	0	239²	179	8	68	157	9.5	2.03	171	.206	.268	15	.197	3	42	39	2	4.2
1986 LA-N	14	14	.500	35	35	8	1	0	231²	213	13	86	153	11.8	3.85	90	.243	.314	17	.239	4	-3	-10	1	-0.6
1987 LA-N★	16	16	.500	37	35	10	1	1	264²	247	17	74	190	11.2	3.06	130	.247	.305	19	.211	4	30	27	1	3.6
1988 *LA-N★	23	8	.742	35	34	15	8	1	267	208	18	73	178	9.6	2.26	147	.213	.271	11	.129	-0	35	32	6	4.5
1989 LA-N☆	15	15	.500	35	33	8	4	0	256²	226	9	77	178	10.7	2.31	148	.240	.299	14	.182	3	34	31	4	4.6
1990 LA-N	1	1	.500	4	4	0	0	0	25¹	26	1	4	16	11.0	4.26	86	.260	.295	0	.000	-1	-1	-1	-0	-0.2
1991 LA-N	7	2	.778	21	21	0	0	0	112	112	3	32	73	12.0	3.46	104	.259	.317	8	.258	3	3	2	1	0.6
1992 LA-N	10	15	.400	33	33	1	0	0	210²	209	15	69	130	12.2	3.67	94	.257	.322	15	.221	4	-4	-5	3	0.2
1993 LA-N	12	14	.462	33	33	5	1	0	215²	201	17	72	141	11.7	3.59	104	.246	.312	26	.356	10	11	5	3	1.9
1994 LA-N	6	6	.500	21	21	1	0	0	135¹	146	15	42	72	12.6	3.79	104	.279	.335	9	.205	2	6	2	1	0.6
Total 12	134	102	.568	343	303	65	24	5	2156	1934	126	653	1443	11.0	3.00	119	.239	.300	144	.214	34	172	140	24	21.5

● JOE HESKETH
Hesketh, Joseph Thomas   b: 2/15/59, Lackawanna, N.Y.   BR/TR, 6'2", 170 lbs.   Deb: 8/7/84

YEAR TM/L	W	L	PCT	G	GS	CG	SH	SV	IP	H	HR	BB	SO	RAT	ERA	ERA+	OAV	OOB	BH	AVG	PB	PR	/A	PD	TPI
1984 Mon-N	2	2	.500	11	5	1	1	1	45	38	2	15	32	10.6	1.80	190	.233	.298	1	.100	0	9	8	-0	0.8
1985 Mon-N	10	5	.667	25	25	2	1	1	155¹	125	10	45	113	9.8	2.49	136	.222	.280	4	.091	-1	19	16	-1	1.3
1986 Mon-N	6	5	.545	15	15	0	0	0	82²	92	11	31	67	13.6	5.01	74	.283	.349	0	.000	-2	-12	-12	-1	-1.7
1987 Mon-N	0	0	—	18	0	0	0	1	28²	23	2	15	31	12.6	3.14	134	.211	.317	0	.000	-0	3	3	-1	-0.1
1988 Mon-N	4	3	.571	60	0	0	0	9	72²	63	7	35	64	12.4	2.85	126	.242	.332	0	.000	0	5	6	1	0.4
1989 Mon-N	6	4	.600	43	0	0	0	3	48¹	54	5	26	44	14.9	5.77	61	.292	.379	1	.500	-0	-12	-12	-1	-2.4
1990 Mon-N	1	0	1.000	2	0	0	0	0	3	2	0	2	3	12.0	0.00	—	.200	.333	0	—	0	1	1	0	0.4
Atl-N	0	2	.000	31	0	0	0	0	31	30	5	23	21	15.7	5.81	69	.248	.373	0	—	0	-6	-6	-0	-0.2
Yr	1	2	.333	33	0	0	0	0	34	32	5	25	24	15.2	5.29	76	.244	.322	0	—	0	-6	-5	-0	0.1
Bos-A	0	4	.000	12	6	0	0	0	25²	37	2	11	26	16.8	3.51	116	.333	.393	0	—	0	1	2	-0	0.1
1991 Bos-A	12	4	.750	39	17	0	0	0	153¹	142	19	53	104	11.4	3.29	131	.250	.314	0	—	0	14	17	0	1.6

YEAR	TM/L	W	L	PCT	G	GS	CG	SH	SV	IP	H	HR	BB	SO	RAT	ERA	ERA+	OAV	OOB	BH	AVG	PB	PR	/A	PD	TPI
1992	Bos-A	8	9	.471	30	25	1	0	1	148²	162	15	58	104	13.4	4.36	97	.276	.343	0	—	0	-7	-2	0	-0.2
1993	Bos-A	3	4	.429	28	5	0	0	1	53¹	62	4	29	34	15.4	5.06	91	.294	.379	0	—	0	-4	-3	-0	-0.5
1994	Bos-A	8	5	.615	25	20	0	0	0	114	117	9	46	83	13.0	4.26	121	.267	.340	0	—	0	7	11	0	1.1
Total	11	60	47	.561	339	114	4	2	21	961²	947	85	378	726	12.5	3.78	107	.259	.330	6	.070	-2	16	28	-1	0.7

● OTTO HESS
Hess, Otto C. b: 10/10/1878, Bern, Switzerland d: 2/25/26, Tucson, Ariz. BL/TL, 6'1", 170 lbs. Deb: 8/3/02 ♦

YEAR	TM/L	W	L	PCT	G	GS	CG	SH	SV	IP	H	HR	BB	SO	RAT	ERA	ERA+	OAV	OOB	BH	AVG	PB	PR	/A	PD	TPI
1902	Cle-A	2	4	.333	7	4	4	0	0	43²	67	0	23	13	18.8	5.98	58	.351	.424	1	.071	-1	-12	-12	1	-1.3
1904	Cle-A	8	7	.533	21	16	15	4	0	151¹	134	2	31	64	10.1	1.67	152	.238	.284	12	.120	-3	16	15	-0	1.1
1905	Cle-A	10	15	.400	26	25	22	4	0	213²	179	1	72	109	11.0	3.16	83	.229	.301	44	.254	5	-12	-12	1	-0.9
1906	Cle-A	20	17	.541	43	36	33	7	3	333²	274	4	85	167	10.3	1.83	143	.227	.291	31	.201	1	32	29	-2	3.3
1907	Cle-A	6	6	.500	17	14	7	0	1	93¹	84	1	37	36	12.8	2.89	87	.242	.336	4	.133	0	-4	-4	-1	-0.6
1908	Cle-A	0	0	—	4	0	0	0	0	7	11	0	4	2	15.4	5.14	47	.407	.429	0	.000	-1	-2	-2	0	0.0
1912	Bos-N	12	17	.414	33	31	21	0	0	254	270	3	90	80	13.3	3.76	95	.283	.354	23	.245	3	-10	-5	-4	-0.6
1913	Bos-N	7	17	.292	29	27	19	2	0	218¹	231	12	70	80	12.7	3.83	86	.279	.340	26	.313	8	-15	-13	1	-0.5
1914	Bos-N	5	6	.455	14	11	7	1	1	89	89	2	33	24	12.8	3.03	91	.271	.347	11	.234	1	-2	-3	2	-0.1
1915	Bos-N	0	1	.000	4	1	1	0	0	14	16	0	6	5	15.4	3.86	67	.286	.375	2	.400	1	-2	-2	-0	-0.1
Total	10	70	90	.438	198	165	129	18	5	1418	1355	25	448	580	12.0	2.98	98	.257	.324	154	.216	14	-11	-11	-2	0.4

● GEORGE HESSELBACHER
Hesselbacher, George Edward b: 1/18/1895, Philadelphia, Pa. d: 2/18/80, Rydal, Pa. BR/TR, 6'2", 175 lbs. Deb: 6/29/16

YEAR	TM/L	W	L	PCT	G	GS	CG	SH	SV	IP	H	HR	BB	SO	RAT	ERA	ERA+	OAV	OOB	BH	AVG	PB	PR	/A	PD	TPI
1916	Phi-A	0	4	.000	6	4	2	0	0	26	37	3	22	6	20.4	7.27	39	.349	.461	1	.125	-0	-13	-13	1	-1.6

● LARRY HESTERFER
Hesterfer, Lawrence b: 6/9/1878, Newark, N.J. d: 9/22/43, Cedar Grove, N.J. BR/TL, 5'8", 145 lbs. Deb: 9/5/01

YEAR	TM/L	W	L	PCT	G	GS	CG	SH	SV	IP	H	HR	BB	SO	RAT	ERA	ERA+	OAV	OOB	BH	AVG	PB	PR	/A	PD	TPI
1901	NY-N	0	1	.000	1	1	1	0	0	6	15	0	3	2	27.0	7.50	44	.466	.511	0	.000	0	-3	-3	-0	-0.3

● JOHNNY HETKI
Hetki, John Edward b: 5/12/22, Leavenworth, Kan. BR/TR, 6'1", 205 lbs. Deb: 9/14/45

YEAR	TM/L	W	L	PCT	G	GS	CG	SH	SV	IP	H	HR	BB	SO	RAT	ERA	ERA+	OAV	OOB	BH	AVG	PB	PR	/A	PD	TPI
1945	Cin-N	1	2	.333	5	2	2	0	0	32²	28	1	11	9	10.7	3.58	105	.235	.300	1	.091	-1	1	1	1	0.0
1946	Cin-N	6	6	.500	32	11	4	0	1	126¹	121	3	31	41	10.9	2.99	112	.253	.300	11	.333	3	6	5	-1	0.7
1947	Cin-N	3	4	.429	37	5	2	0	0	96	110	7	48	33	14.9	5.81	71	.287	.368	6	.222	1	-19	-18	0	-1.1
1948	Cin-N	1	0	1.000	3	0	0	0	0	6²	8	0	3	3	14.9	9.45	41	.286	.355	0	.000	0	-4	-4	-0	-0.5
1950	Cin-N	1	2	.333	22	1	0	0	0	53	53	9	27	21	14.1	5.09	83	.265	.361	2	.222	0	-6	-5	-0	-0.3
1952	StL-A	0	1	.000	3	1	0	0	0	9¹	15	2	2	4	16.4	3.86	101	.357	.386	0	.000	0	-0	-0	-0	0.0
1953	Pit-N	3	6	.333	54	0	0	0	6	118¹	120	9	33	37	11.7	3.95	113	.266	.318	5	.208	1	4	7	0	0.7
1954	Pit-N	4	4	.500	58	1	0	0	9	83	102	11	30	27	14.3	4.99	84	.297	.353	2	.222	-0	-8	-7	-1	-0.9
Total	8	18	26	.409	214	23	8	0	13	525¹	557	41	185	175	12.8	4.39	91	.272	.335	27	.235	5	-26	-23	-2	-1.4

● ERIC HETZEL
Hetzel, Eric Paul b: 9/25/63, Crowley, La. BR/TR, 6'3", 175 lbs. Deb: 7/1/89

YEAR	TM/L	W	L	PCT	G	GS	CG	SH	SV	IP	H	HR	BB	SO	RAT	ERA	ERA+	OAV	OOB	BH	AVG	PB	PR	/A	PD	TPI
1989	Bos-A	2	3	.400	12	11	0	0	0	50¹	61	7	28	33	16.3	6.26	66	.296	.386	0	—	0	-13	-12	-1	-1.2
1990	Bos-A	1	4	.200	9	8	0	0	0	35	39	3	21	20	15.7	5.91	69	.281	.379	0	—	0	-8	-7	-0	-1.0
Total	2	3	7	.300	21	19	0	0	0	85¹	100	10	49	53	16.0	6.12	67	.290	.383	0	—	0	-21	-19	-2	-2.2

● ED HEUSSER
Heusser, Edward Burlton "The Wild Elk Of The Wasatch" b: 5/7/09, Mill Creek, Utah d: 3/1/56, Aurora, Cal. BB/TR, 6'0.5", 187 lbs. Deb: 4/25/35

YEAR	TM/L	W	L	PCT	G	GS	CG	SH	SV	IP	H	HR	BB	SO	RAT	ERA	ERA+	OAV	OOB	BH	AVG	PB	PR	/A	PD	TPI
1935	StL-N	5	5	.500	33	11	2	0	2	123¹	125	5	27	39	11.2	2.92	140	.263	.305	4	.118	-1	15	16	-1	1.0
1936	StL-N	7	3	.700	42	3	0	0	3	104¹	130	6	38	26	14.8	5.43	73	.310	.373	7	.269	-3	-16	-17	-0	-1.3
1938	Phi-N	0	0	—	1	0	0	0	0	1	2	1	1	0	27.0	27.00	14	.400	.500	0	—	0	-3	-3	-0	0.0
1940	Phi-A	6	13	.316	41	6	2	0	5	110	144	11	42	39	15.4	4.99	89	.308	.368	5	.167	1	-7	-7	-1	-0.9
1943	Cin-N	4	3	.571	26	10	2	1	0	91	97	4	23	28	11.9	3.46	96	.275	.319	5	.185	-1	-1	-1	-1	-0.3
1944	Cin-N	13	11	.542	30	23	17	4	2	192²	165	9	42	42	9.7	**2.38**	146	.231	.275	15	.217	1	26	24	-1	2.9
1945	Cin-N	11	16	.407	31	30	18	4	1	223	248	10	60	56	12.6	3.71	101	.280	.328	19	.247	4	2	1	0	0.6
1946	Cin-N	7	14	.333	29	21	9	1	2	167²	167	11	39	47	11.1	3.22	104	.260	.304	11	.208	2	4	2	-2	0.2
1948	Phi-N	3	2	.600	33	0	0	0	3	74	89	9	28	22	14.2	4.99	79	.299	.359	4	.158	-1	-8	-9	-0	-0.6
Total	9	56	67	.455	266	104	50	10	18	1087	1167	66	300	299	12.3	3.69	101	.274	.324	69	.206	8	11	6	-5	1.6

● JOE HEVING
Heving, Joseph William b: 9/2/1900, Covington, Ky. d: 4/11/70, Covington, Ky. BR/TR, 6'1", 185 lbs. Deb: 4/29/30 F

YEAR	TM/L	W	L	PCT	G	GS	CG	SH	SV	IP	H	HR	BB	SO	RAT	ERA	ERA+	OAV	OOB	BH	AVG	PB	PR	/A	PD	TPI
1930	NY-N	7	5	.583	41	2	0	0	6	89²	109	7	27	37	13.8	5.22	91	.309	.360	5	.227	-0	-2	-5	4	-0.3
1931	NY-N	1	6	.143	22	0	0	0	3	42¹	48	4	11	26	13.0	4.89	76	.277	.328	1	.125	-0	-5	-6	1	-0.9
1933	Chi-A	7	5	.583	40	6	3	1	6	118	113	6	27	47	10.8	2.67	159	.249	.295	8	.211	0	21	21	0	2.1
1934	Chi-A	1	7	.125	33	2	0	0	4	88	133	12	44	40	18.8	7.26	65	.343	.419	5	.185	1	-27	-25	1	-1.9
1937	Cle-A	8	4	.667	40	0	0	0	6	72²	92	6	30	35	15.4	4.83	95	.311	.378	2	.263	0	-2	-2	1	-0.1
1938	Cle-A	1	1	.500	3	0	0	0	0	6	10	0	5	0	22.5	9.00	52	.370	.469	0	.000	-0	-3	-3	-0	-0.7
	Bos-A	8	1	.889	16	11	7	1	2	82	94	5	22	34	12.8	3.73	132	.283	.330	4	.133	-1	10	11	2	1.1
	Yr	9	2	.818	19	11	7	1	2	88	104	5	27	34	13.5	4.09	120	.290	.341	4	.129	-2	7	8	2	0.4
1939	Bos-A	11	3	.786	46	5	1	0	7	107	124	8	34	43	13.5	3.70	128	.295	.350	6	.188	-1	**11**	**12**	0	1.4
1940	Bos-A	12	7	.632	39	7	4	0	3	119	129	7	42	55	13.2	4.01	112	.272	.335	8	.200	0	6	9	3	0.9
1941	Cle-A	5	2	.714	27	3	2	1	5	70²	63	2	31	18	12.1	2.29	172	.240	.323	0	.000	-1	15	13	2	1.5
1942	Cle-A	5	3	.625	27	2	0	0	3	46¹	52	5	25	13	15.3	4.86	71	.278	.369	0	.000	-1	-6	-7	0	-1.3
1943	Cle-A	1	1	.500	30	1	0	0	5	72	58	1	34	34	11.8	2.75	113	.230	.326	1	.071	-0	4	3	2	0.3
1944	Cle-A	8	3	.727	**63**	1	0	0	10	119²	106	2	41	46	11.2	1.96	169	.239	.307	4	.182	-1	**20**	18	1	2.0
1945	Bos-N	1	0	1.000	3	0	0	0	0	5¹	5	0	3	1	15.2	3.38	114	.294	.429	0	.000	-0	0	0	1	0.1
Total	13	76	48	.613	430	40	17	3	63	1038²	1136	64	380	429	13.3	3.90	108	.279	.344	47	.170	-4	40	36	14	4.2

● JAKE HEWITT
Hewitt, Charles Jacob b: 6/6/1870, Maidsville, W.Va. d: 5/18/59, Morgantown, W.Va. BL/TL, 5'7", 150 lbs. Deb: 8/6/1895

YEAR	TM/L	W	L	PCT	G	GS	CG	SH	SV	IP	H	HR	BB	SO	RAT	ERA	ERA+	OAV	OOB	BH	AVG	PB	PR	/A	PD	TPI
1895	Pit-N	1	0	1.000	4	2	1	0	2	13	13	0	2	4	11.1	4.15	109	.256	.298	1	.167	-1	1	1	-0	0.0

● GREG HEYDEMAN
Heydeman, Gregory George b: 1/2/52, Carmel, Cal. BR/TR, 6', 180 lbs. Deb: 9/2/73

YEAR	TM/L	W	L	PCT	G	GS	CG	SH	SV	IP	H	HR	BB	SO	RAT	ERA	ERA+	OAV	OOB	BH	AVG	PB	PR	/A	PD	TPI
1973	LA-N	0	0	—	1	0	0	0	0	2	2	0	1	1	18.0	4.50	76	.222	.364	0	—	0	-0	-0	-0	0.0

● JOHN HEYNER
Heyner, John b: Hyde Park, Ill. Deb: 8/19/1890

YEAR	TM/L	W	L	PCT	G	GS	CG	SH	SV	IP	H	HR	BB	SO	RAT	ERA	ERA+	OAV	OOB	BH	AVG	PB	PR	/A	PD	TPI
1890	Pit-N	0	0	—	1	0	0	0	0	4	7	2	5	1	27.0	13.50	24	.371	.503	0	.000	-0	-4	-5	0	0.0

● GREG HIBBARD
Hibbard, James Gregory b: 9/13/64, New Orleans, La. BL/TL, 6', 180 lbs. Deb: 5/31/89

YEAR	TM/L	W	L	PCT	G	GS	CG	SH	SV	IP	H	HR	BB	SO	RAT	ERA	ERA+	OAV	OOB	BH	AVG	PB	PR	/A	PD	TPI
1989	Chi-A	6	7	.462	23	23	2	0	0	137¹	142	16	41	55	12.1	3.21	118	.268	.323	0	—	0	10	9	1	0.9
1990	Chi-A	14	9	.609	33	33	3	0	0	211	202	15	55	92	11.2	3.16	121	.255	.308	0	—	0	18	16	-1	1.6
1991	Chi-A	11	11	.500	32	29	5	0	0	194	196	23	57	71	11.8	4.31	92	.266	.320	0	—	0	-5	-7	-1	-0.8
1992	Chi-A	10	7	.588	31	28	0	0	0	176	187	17	57	69	12.8	4.40	88	.277	.340	0	—	0	-9	-11	2	-0.7
1993	Chi-N	15	11	.577	31	31	1	0	0	191	209	19	47	82	12.2	3.96	101	.286	.332	6	.092	-3	2	1	0	-0.2
1994	Sea-A	1	5	.167	15	14	0	0	0	80²	115	11	31	39	16.5	6.69	73	.328	.385	0	—	0	-17	-16	0	-1.0
Total	6	57	50	.533	165	158	11	1	0	990	1051	86	288	408	12.4	4.05	98	.275	.330	6	.092	-3	-1	-9	0	-0.3

● JOHN HIBBARD
Hibbard, John Denison b: 12/2/1864, Chicago, Ill. d: 11/17/37, Hollywood, Cal. TL, Deb: 7/31/1884

YEAR	TM/L	W	L	PCT	G	GS	CG	SH	SV	IP	H	HR	BB	SO	RAT	ERA	ERA+	OAV	OOB	BH	AVG	PB	PR	/A	PD	TPI
1884	Chi-N	1	1	.500	2	2	2	1	0	17	18	1	9	4	14.3	2.65	118	.300	.391	0	.000	-1	1	1	-0	0.0

● BRYAN HICKERSON
Hickerson, Bryan David b: 10/13/63, Bemidji, Minn. BL/TL, 6'2", 195 lbs. Deb: 7/25/91

YEAR	TM/L	W	L	PCT	G	GS	CG	SH	SV	IP	H	HR	BB	SO	RAT	ERA	ERA+	OAV	OOB	BH	AVG	PB	PR	/A	PD	TPI
1991	SF-N	2	2	.500	17	6	0	0	0	50	53	5	17	43	12.6	3.60	99	.275	.333	0	.000	1	-0	-0	-1	-0.3
1992	SF-N	5	3	.625	61	6	0	0	0	87¹	74	7	21	68	9.9	3.09	107	.234	.286	0	.000	0	4	2	-2	-0.1
1993	SF-N	7	5	.583	47	15	0	0	0	120¹	137	14	39	69	13.2	4.26	92	.291	.347	4	.143	-0	-3	-5	-2	-0.6

YEAR TM/L	W	L	PCT	G	GS	CG	SH	SV	IP	H	HR	BB	SO	RAT	ERA	ERA+	OAV	OOB	BH	AVG	PB	PR	/A	PD	TPI
1994 SF-N	4	8	.333	28	14	0	0	1	98¹	118	20	38	59	14.4	5.40	74	.301	.364	5	.185	1	-13	-15	-2	-1.7
Total 4	18	18	.500	153	36	0	0	1	356	382	44	115	239	12.6	4.20	89	.279	.336	9	.127	-1	-11	-18	-6	-2.7

● JIM HICKEY
Hickey, James Robert "Sid" b: 10/22/20, N.Abington, Mass. BR/TR, 6'1", 204 lbs. Deb: 4/25/42

YEAR TM/L	W	L	PCT	G	GS	CG	SH	SV	IP	H	HR	BB	SO	RAT	ERA	ERA+	OAV	OOB	BH	AVG	PB	PR	/A	PD	TPI
1942 Bos-N	0	1	.000	1	1	0	0	0	1¹	4	1	2	0	40.5	20.25	16	.500	.600	0	.000	-0	-3	-3	-0	-1.0
1944 Bos-N	0	0	.—	8	0	0	0	0	9¹	15	0	5	3	20.3	4.82	79	.366	.447	0	.000	-0	-1	-1	0	0.0
Total 2	0	1	.000	9	1	0	0	0	10²	19	1	7	3	22.8	6.75	56	.388	.474	0	.000	-0	-4	-4	-0	-1.0

● JOHN HICKEY
Hickey, John William b: 11/3/1881, Minneapolis, Minn. d: 12/28/41, Seattle, Wash. BR/TL, 5'10", 170 lbs. Deb: 4/16/04

YEAR TM/L	W	L	PCT	G	GS	CG	SH	SV	IP	H	HR	BB	SO	RAT	ERA	ERA+	OAV	OOB	BH	AVG	PB	PR	/A	PD	TPI
1904 Cle-A	0	1	.000	2	2	1	0	0	12¹	14	0	11	5	18.2	7.30	35	.286	.417	0	.000	-1	-6	-7	0	-0.5

● KEVIN HICKEY
Hickey, Kevin John b: 2/25/57, Chicago, Ill. BL/TL, 6'1", 200 lbs. Deb: 4/14/81

YEAR TM/L	W	L	PCT	G	GS	CG	SH	SV	IP	H	HR	BB	SO	RAT	ERA	ERA+	OAV	OOB	BH	AVG	PB	PR	/A	PD	TPI
1981 Chi-A	0	2	.000	41	0	0	0	3	44¹	38	3	18	17	11.6	3.65	98	.232	.311	0	—	0	0	-0	1	0.2
1982 Chi-A	4	4	.500	60	0	0	0	6	78	73	4	30	38	12.1	3.00	134	.256	.331	0	—	0	9	9	2	1.2
1983 Chi-A	1	2	.333	23	0	0	0	5	20²	23	5	11	8	14.8	5.23	80	.264	.347	0	—	0	-3	-2	-0	-0.7
1989 Bal-A	2	3	.400	51	0	0	0	2	49¹	38	3	23	28	11.3	2.92	130	.220	.315	0	—	0	5	5	-0	0.5
1990 Bal-A	1	3	.250	37	0	0	0	0	26¹	26	3	13	17	13.3	5.13	74	.265	.351	0	—	0	-4	-4	-0	-0.5
1991 Bal-A	1	0	1.000	19	0	0	0	0	14	15	3	6	10	13.5	9.00	44	.278	.350	0	—	0	-8	-8	-0	-0.5
Total 6	9	14	.391	231	0	0	0	17	232²	213	21	101	118	12.3	3.91	99	.247	.329	0	—	0	1	-1	2	0.2

● CHARLIE HICKMAN
Hickman, Charles Taylor "Cheerful Charlie" or "Piano Legs"
b: 3/4/1876, Taylortown, Dunkard Township, Pa. d: 4/19/34, Morgantown, W.Va. BR/TR, 5'11.5", 215 lbs. Deb: 9/8/1897 ♦

YEAR TM/L	W	L	PCT	G	GS	CG	SH	SV	IP	H	HR	BB	SO	RAT	ERA	ERA+	OAV	OOB	BH	AVG	PB	PR	/A	PD	TPI
1897 *Bos-N	0	0	.—	2	0	0	1	0	7²	10	0	5	0	17.6	5.87	76	.312	.405	2	.667	2	-1	-1	0	0.1
1898 Bos-N	1	2	.333	6	3	3	1	2	33	22	0	13	9	9.5	2.18	169	.189	.270	15	.259	2	5	6	-1	0.4
1899 Bos-N	6	0	1.000	11	9	5	2	1	66¹	52	3	40	14	13.6	4.48	93	.216	.346	25	.397	6	-5	-2	-1	0.2
1901 NY-N	3	5	.375	9	9	6	0	0	65	76	1	26	11	14.5	4.57	72	.290	.360	113	.278	2	-9	-9	1	-0.7
1902 Cle-A	0	1	.000	1	1	1	0	0	8	11	0	5	1	19.1	7.88	44	.327	.428	161	.378	1	-4	-4	-0	-0.3
1907 Was-A	0	0	.—	1	0	0	0	0	5	4	0	2	5	16.2	3.60	67	.221	.390	55	.278	0	-1	-1	1	0.1
Total 6	10	8	.556	30	22	15	3	4	185	175	4	94	37	13.7	4.28	86	.249	.347	1176	.295	11	-14	-12	-1	-0.2

● ERNIE HICKMAN
Hickman, Ernest P. b: 1856, E.St.Louis, Ill. d: 11/19/1891, E.St.Louis, Ill Deb: 6/7/1884

YEAR TM/L	W	L	PCT	G	GS	CG	SH	SV	IP	H	HR	BB	SO	RAT	ERA	ERA+	OAV	OOB	BH	AVG	PB	PR	/A	PD	TPI
1884 KC-U	4	13	.235	17	17	15	0	0	137¹	172	5	36	68	13.6	4.52	49	.287	.327	12	.167	-7	-32	-35	-1	-3.6

● JIM HICKMAN
Hickman, James Lucius b: 5/10/37, Henning, Tenn. BR/TR, 6'4", 205 lbs. Deb: 4/14/62 ♦

YEAR TM/L	W	L	PCT	G	GS	CG	SH	SV	IP	H	HR	BB	SO	RAT	ERA	ERA+	OAV	OOB	BH	AVG	PB	PR	/A	PD	TPI
1967 LA-N	0	0	.—	1	0	0	0	0	2	2	1	1	2	9.0	4.50	96	.286	.286	16	.163	-0	-0	-0	-0	-0.1

● JESSE HICKMAN
Hickman, Jesse Owens b: 2/18/39, Lecompte, La. BR/TR, 6'2", 186 lbs. Deb: 6/5/65

YEAR TM/L	W	L	PCT	G	GS	CG	SH	SV	IP	H	HR	BB	SO	RAT	ERA	ERA+	OAV	OOB	BH	AVG	PB	PR	/A	PD	TPI
1965 KC-A	0	1	.000	12	0	0	0	0	15¹	9	3	8	16	10.0	5.87	59	.184	.298	0	—	0	-4	-4	-0	-0.3
1966 KC-A	0	0	.—	1	0	0	0	0	1	1	0	1	0	9.0	0.00	—	.000	.333	0	—	0	0	0	-0	0.0
Total 2	0	1	.000	13	0	0	0	0	16¹	9	3	9	16	9.9	5.51	63	.176	.300	0	—	0	-4	-4	-0	-0.3

● KIRBY HIGBE
Higbe, Walter Kirby b: 4/8/15, Columbia, S.C. d: 5/6/85, Columbia, S.C. BR/TR, 5'11", 190 lbs. Deb: 10/3/37

YEAR TM/L	W	L	PCT	G	GS	CG	SH	SV	IP	H	HR	BB	SO	RAT	ERA	ERA+	OAV	OOB	BH	AVG	PB	PR	/A	PD	TPI
1937 Chi-N	1	0	1.000	1	0	0	0	0	5	4	1	5	2	9.0	5.40	74	.182	.217	0	.000	-0	-1	-1	-0	-0.2
1938 Chi-N	0	0	.—	2	2	0	0	0	10	10	1	6	4	14.4	5.40	71	.263	.364	0	.000	-0	-2	-2	1	0.0
1939 Chi-N	2	1	.667	9	2	0	0	0	22²	12	0	22	16	13.5	3.18	124	.158	.347	2	.286	1	2	2	-0	0.3
Phi-N	10	14	.417	34	26	14	1	2	187¹	208	10	101	79	15.3	4.85	83	.283	.378	11	.167	-2	-19	-18	-4	-2.6
Yr	12	15	.444	43	28	14	1	2	210	220	10	123	95	15.1	4.67	86	.272	.374	13	.178	-2	-18	-16	-4	-2.3
1940 Phi-N☆	14	19	.424	41	36	20	1	1	283	242	12	121	**137**	11.6	3.72	105	.232	.313	17	.165	-2	4	6	-1	0.4
1941 *Bro-N	**22**	9	.710	**48**	39	19	2	3	298	244	16	132	121	11.5	3.14	117	.220	.306	21	.188	1	16	17	-5	1.3
1942 Bro-N	16	11	.593	38	32	13	2	0	221²	180	17	106	115	11.7	3.25	100	.223	.315	8	.104	-4	2	0	-1	-0.6
1943 Bro-N	13	10	.565	35	27	8	1	0	185	189	4	95	108	14.1	3.70	91	.264	.354	9	.138	-2	-6	-7	-1	-1.1
1946 Bro-N★	17	8	.680	42	29	11	3	1	210²	178	6	107	134	12.2	3.03	111	.229	.323	10	.130	-4	9	8	1	0.6
1947 Bro-N	2	0	1.000	4	3	0	0	0	15²	18	0	12	10	17.8	5.17	80	.295	.419	1	.200	0	-2	-2	-0	-0.2
Pit-N	11	17	.393	46	30	10	1	5	225	204	22	110	99	12.7	3.72	113	.240	.329	10	.139	-1	8	13	-4	0.9
Yr	13	17	.433	50	33	10	1	5	240²	222	22	122	109	13.0	3.81	111	.243	.334	11	.143	-1	7	11	-4	0.7
1948 Pit-N	8	7	.533	56	8	3	0	10	158	140	11	83	86	12.9	3.36	121	.240	.337	10	.208	1	10	12	-1	1.2
1949 Pit-N	0	2	.000	7	1	0	0	0	15¹	25	2	12	5	21.7	13.50	31	.379	.474	0	.000	-0	-16	-16	-0	-1.6
NY-N	2	0	1.000	37	2	0	0	2	80¹	72	12	41	38	12.8	3.47	115	.242	.335	1	.067	-0	5	5	-1	1.0
Yr	2	2	.500	44	3	0	0	2	95²	97	14	53	43	14.2	5.08	79	.266	.361	1	.056	-1	-11	-11	-1	-1.0
1950 NY-N	0	3	.000	18	1	0	0	0	34²	37	2	30	17	17.4	4.93	83	.285	.419	1	.250	0	-3	-3	1	-0.1
Total 12	118	101	.539	418	238	98	11	24	1952¹	1763	117	979	971	12.8	3.69	102	.241	.333	101	.153	-14	7	14	-16	-1.7

● IRV HIGGINBOTHAM
Higginbotham, Irving Clinton b: 4/26/1882, Homer, Neb. d: 6/12/59, Seattle, Wash. BR/TR, 6'1", 196 lbs. Deb: 8/11/06

YEAR TM/L	W	L	PCT	G	GS	CG	SH	SV	IP	H	HR	BB	SO	RAT	ERA	ERA+	OAV	OOB	BH	AVG	PB	PR	/A	PD	TPI
1906 StL-N	1	4	.200	7	6	4	0	0	47¹	50	1	11	14	11.8	3.23	81	.266	.310	4	.222	0	-3	-3	1	-0.2
1908 StL-N	3	8	.273	19	11	7	1	0	107	113	0	33	38	12.5	3.20	74	.270	.328	5	.132	-1	-10	-10	-1	-1.3
1909 StL-N	1	0	1.000	3	1	1	0	0	11¹	5	0	2	5	5.6	1.59	159	.143	.189	0	.000	-0	1	1	-1	0.2
Chi-N	5	2	.714	19	6	4	0	1	78	64	0	20	32	10.0	2.19	116	.213	.269	6	.231	1	4	3	-1	0.2
Yr	6	2	.750	22	7	5	0	1	89¹	69	0	22	34	9.5	2.12	120	.205	.260	6	.207	0	5	4	-2	0.2
Total 3	10	14	.417	48	24	16	1	1	243²	232	1	66	86	11.3	2.81	88	.246	.300	15	.176	-1	-8	-9	-1	-1.3

● DENNIS HIGGINS
Higgins, Dennis Dean b: 8/4/39, Jefferson City, Mo. BR/TR, 6'4", 190 lbs. Deb: 4/12/66

YEAR TM/L	W	L	PCT	G	GS	CG	SH	SV	IP	H	HR	BB	SO	RAT	ERA	ERA+	OAV	OOB	BH	AVG	PB	PR	/A	PD	TPI
1966 Chi-A	1	0	1.000	42	0	0	0	5	93	66	9	33	86	10.1	2.52	126	.202	.286	3	.176	0	9	7	1	0.2
1967 Chi-A	1	2	.333	9	0	0	0	0	12¹	13	0	10	8	19.0	5.84	53	.271	.426	0	.000	-0	-4	-4	0	-0.9
1968 Was-A	4	4	.500	59	0	0	0	13	99²	81	9	46	66	11.7	3.25	90	.226	.319	2	.133	-0	-3	-4	-1	-0.6
1969 Was-A	10	9	.526	55	0	0	0	16	85¹	79	7	56	71	14.6	3.48	100	.252	.371	1	.091	-1	1	-0	1	-0.1
1970 Cle-A	4	6	.400	58	0	0	0	11	90¹	82	8	54	82	13.7	3.99	99	.248	.358	3	.250	1	-3	-4	-1	0.1
1971 StL-N	1	0	1.000	3	0	0	0	0	7	6	0	2	6	10.3	3.86	93	.240	.296	0	.000	-0	-0	-0	-0	0.0
1972 StL-N	1	2	.333	15	1	0	0	0	22²	19	0	22	20	16.3	3.97	86	.226	.387	0	.000	-0	-1	-1	-0	-0.2
Total 7	22	23	.489	241	2	0	0	46	410¹	346	32	223	339	12.8	3.42	98	.233	.340	9	.155	-0	0	-3	-1	-1.6

● EDDIE HIGGINS
Higgins, Thomas Edward "Doc" or "Irish" b: 3/18/1888, Nevada, Ill. d: 2/14/59, Elgin, Ill. BR/TR, 6'0.5", 174 lbs. Deb: 5/14/09

YEAR TM/L	W	L	PCT	G	GS	CG	SH	SV	IP	H	HR	BB	SO	RAT	ERA	ERA+	OAV	OOB	BH	AVG	PB	PR	/A	PD	TPI
1909 StL-N	3	3	.500	16	5	5	0	0	66	68	4	15	17	11.7	4.50	56	.273	.322	4	.190	-1	-14	-14	0	-1.2
1910 StL-N	0	1	.000	2	0	0	0	0	10¹	15	0	7	1	19.2	4.35	68	.349	.440	2	.400	1	-2	-2	1	0.0
Total 2	3	4	.429	18	5	5	0	0	76¹	83	4	24	18	12.7	4.48	58	.284	.341	6	.231	-1	-15	-16	1	-1.2

● ED HIGH
High, Edward T. "Lefty" b: 12/26/1876, Baltimore, Md. d: 2/10/26, Baltimore, Md. TL, Deb: 7/4/01

YEAR TM/L	W	L	PCT	G	GS	CG	SH	SV	IP	H	HR	BB	SO	RAT	ERA	ERA+	OAV	OOB	BH	AVG	PB	PR	/A	PD	TPI
1901 Det-A	0	1	1.000	3	1	1	0	0	18	21	0	6	4	14.0	3.50	101	.288	.350	0	.000	-1	0	1	0	0.0

● TEDDY HIGUERA
Higuera, Teodoro Valenzuela (Valenzuela) b: 11/9/58, Los Mochis, Mexico BB/TL, 5'10", 178 lbs. Deb: 4/23/85

YEAR TM/L	W	L	PCT	G	GS	CG	SH	SV	IP	H	HR	BB	SO	RAT	ERA	ERA+	OAV	OOB	BH	AVG	PB	PR	/A	PD	TPI
1985 Mil-A	15	8	.652	32	30	7	0	0	212¹	186	22	63	127	10.7	3.90	107	.235	.293	0	—	0	6	6	-3	0.4
1986 Mil-A★	20	11	.645	34	34	15	4	0	248¹	226	26	74	207	11.0	2.79	155	.241	.299	0	—	0	38	42	-1	4.8
1987 Mil-A	18	10	.643	35	35	14	3	0	261²	236	24	87	240	11.2	3.85	119	.241	.304	0	—	0	18	21	-2	1.6
1988 Mil-A	16	9	.640	31	31	8	1	2	227¹	168	15	59	192	**9.2**	2.45	162	.207	**.265**	0	—	0	**38**	38	1	4.3
1989 Mil-A	9	6	.600	22	22	2	1	0	135¹	125	9	48	91	11.6	3.46	111	.248	.318	0	—	0	4	4	0	0.4
1990 Mil-A	11	10	.524	27	27	6	0	0	170	167	16	50	129	11.6	3.76	103	.255	.312	0	—	0	2	3	-1	0.4
1991 Mil-A	3	2	.600	7	6	0	0	0	36¹	37	2	10	33	11.9	4.46	89	.262	.316	0	—	0	-1	-2	-0	-0.2

YEAR	TM/L	W	L	PCT	G	GS	CG	SH	SV	IP	H	HR	BB	SO	RAT	ERA	ERA+	OAV	OOB	BH	AVG	PB	PR	/A	PD	TPI
1993	Mil-A	1	3	.250	8	8	0	0	0	30	43	4	16	27	18.0	7.20	59	.333	.411	0	—		-10	-10	-1	-1.1
1994	Mil-A	1	5	.167	17	12	0	0	0	58²	74	13	36	35	17.2	7.06	70	.311	.406	0	—	0	-15	-14	0	-1.1
Total 9		94	64	.595	213	205	50	12	0	1380	1262	131	443	1081	11.3	3.61	116	.243	.306	0	—	0	83	90	-9	9.3

● **WHITEY HILCHER**   Hilcher, Walter Frank b: 2/28/09, Chicago, Ill. d: 11/21/62, Minneapolis, Minn.   BR/TR, 6', 174 lbs.   Deb: 9/17/31

YEAR	TM/L	W	L	PCT	G	GS	CG	SH	SV	IP	H	HR	BB	SO	RAT	ERA	ERA+	OAV	OOB	BH	AVG	PB	PR	/A	PD	TPI
1931	Cin-N	0	1	.000	2	1	0	0	0	12	16	0	4	5	15.8	3.00	125	.320	.382	0	.000	-1	1	1	-0	0.0
1932	Cin-N	0	3	.000	11	2	0	0	0	18²	24	3	10	4	16.4	7.71	50	.316	.395	1	.333	-1	-8	-8	0	-1.0
1935	Cin-N	2	0	1.000	4	2	1	1	0	19¹	19	0	5	9	11.2	2.79	142	.264	.312	1	.167	-0	3	3	1	0.3
1936	Cin-N	1	2	.333	14	1	0	0	0	35	44	3	14	10	15.2	6.17	62	.299	.364	0	.000	-1	-8	-9	-1	-0.8
Total 4		3	6	.333	31	6	1	1	0	85	103	6	33	28	14.6	5.29	73	.299	.363	2	.095	-2	-13	-14	-0	-1.5

● **ORAL HILDEBRAND**   Hildebrand, Oral Clyde b: 4/7/07, Indianapolis, Ind. d: 9/8/77, Southport, Ind.   BR/TR, 6'3", 175 lbs.   Deb: 9/8/31

YEAR	TM/L	W	L	PCT	G	GS	CG	SH	SV	IP	H	HR	BB	SO	RAT	ERA	ERA+	OAV	OOB	BH	AVG	PB	PR	/A	PD	TPI
1931	Cle-A	2	1	.667	5	2	2	0	0	26²	25	0	13	6	13.8	4.39	105	.243	.345	2	.182	-1	0	1	-0	0.0
1932	Cle-A	8	6	.571	27	15	7	0	0	129¹	124	7	62	49	12.9	3.69	129	.249	.333	7	.146	-3	11	15	-2	0.9
1933	Cle-A☆	16	11	.593	36	31	15	**6**	0	220¹	205	8	88	90	12.0	3.76	118	.245	.318	16	.190	-1	13	17	-0	1.6
1934	Cle-A	11	9	.550	33	28	10	1	1	198	225	14	99	72	14.9	4.50	101	.282	.364	13	.171	-1	-0	1	1	0.0
1935	Cle-A	9	8	.529	34	20	8	0	5	171¹	171	12	63	49	12.4	3.94	114	.263	.331	9	.164	-2	10	11	-0	0.8
1936	Cle-A	10	11	.476	36	21	9	0	4	174²	197	10	83	65	14.6	4.90	103	.283	.362	12	.190	-0	3	3	-1	0.2
1937	StL-A	8	17	.320	30	27	12	1	1	201¹	228	18	87	75	14.2	5.14	94	.284	.356	14	.200	-1	-12	-7	-1	-0.8
1938	StL-A	8	10	.444	23	23	10	0	0	163	194	18	73	66	14.9	5.69	87	.297	.370	15	.254	-1	-16	-13	-3	-1.3
1939	*NY-A	10	4	.714	21	15	7	1	2	126²	102	11	41	50	10.2	3.06	143	.219	.284	8	.182	-1	22	18	-1	1.6
1940	NY-A	1	1	.500	13	0	0	0	0	19¹	19	1	14	5	15.8	1.86	217	.268	.395	0	.000	-0	5	5	-0	0.4
Total 10		83	78	.516	258	182	80	9	13	1430²	1490	99	623	527	13.4	4.35	107	.267	.343	96	.187	-9	36	50	-8	3.4

● **TOM HILGENDORF**   Hilgendorf, Thomas Eugene b: 3/10/42, Clinton, Iowa   BB/TL, 6'1", 190 lbs.   Deb: 8/15/69

YEAR	TM/L	W	L	PCT	G	GS	CG	SH	SV	IP	H	HR	BB	SO	RAT	ERA	ERA+	OAV	OOB	BH	AVG	PB	PR	/A	PD	TPI
1969	StL-N	0	0	—	6	0	0	0	2	6¹	3	0	2	2	7.1	1.42	251	.150	.227	1	1.000	1	2	2	-0	0.2
1970	StL-N	0	4	.000	20	0	0	0	3	20²	22	0	13	13	15.2	3.92	105	.272	.372	0	.000	-0	0	0	0	0.1
1972	Cle-A	3	1	.750	19	5	1	0	0	47	51	4	21	25	14.2	2.68	120	.283	.365	1	.077	-1	2	3	0	0.2
1973	Cle-A	5	3	.625	48	1	1	0	6	94²	87	9	36	58	12.0	3.14	125	.242	.316	0	—	0	7	8	1	0.8
1974	Cle-A	4	3	.571	35	0	0	0	1	48¹	58	6	17	23	14.2	4.84	75	.302	.362	0	—	0	-7	-7	0	-0.9
1975	Phi-N	7	3	.700	53	0	0	0	0	96²	81	6	38	52	11.2	2.14	174	.230	.307	3	.250	1	16	17	1	1.9
Total 6		19	14	.576	184	6	2	0	14	313²	302	25	127	173	12.5	3.04	122	.255	.331	5	.185	1	20	24	2	2.3

● **CARMEN HILL**   Hill, Carmen Proctor "Specs" or "Bunker" b: 10/1/1895, Royalton, Minn. d: 1/1/90, Indianapolis, Ind.   BR/TR, 6'1", 180 lbs.   Deb: 8/24/15

YEAR	TM/L	W	L	PCT	G	GS	CG	SH	SV	IP	H	HR	BB	SO	RAT	ERA	ERA+	OAV	OOB	BH	AVG	PB	PR	/A	PD	TPI
1915	Pit-N	2	1	.667	8	3	2	1	0	47	42	0	13	24	10.9	1.15	238	.255	.317	2	.154	0	8	8	1	0.7
1916	Pit-N	0	0	—	2	0	0	0	0	6¹	11	0	5	5	24.2	8.53	31	.611	.708	0	—	0	-4	-4	-0	0.0
1918	Pit-N	2	3	.400	6	4	3	0	0	43²	24	0	17	15	8.5	1.24	232	.160	.246	2	.167	0	7	8	0	1.1
1919	Pit-N	0	0	—	4	0	0	0	0	5	12	0	1	1	23.4	9.00	34	.480	.500	0	—	0	-3	-3	0	0.0
1922	NY-N	2	1	.667	8	4	0	0	0	28¹	33	0	5	6	12.1	4.76	84	.295	.325	2	.182	-0	-2	-2	1	-0.2
1926	Pit-N	3	3	.500	6	6	4	1	0	39²	42	2	9	8	12.0	3.40	116	.288	.338	3	.176	-1	2	2	1	0.4
1927	*Pit-N	22	11	.667	43	31	22	3	2	277²	260	12	80	95	11.2	3.24	127	.249	.305	22	.212	2	21	27	1	3.2
1928	Pit-N	16	10	.615	36	31	16	1	2	237	229	16	81	73	11.9	3.53	115	.259	.324	20	.233	2	12	14	-3	1.3
1929	Pit-N	2	3	.400	27	3	0	0	3	79	94	4	35	28	14.7	3.99	120	.297	.366	1	.036	-3	6	7	0	0.1
	StL-N	0	0	—	3	1	0	0	0	8²	10	2	8	1	19.7	8.31	56	.303	.452	0	.000	-0	-3	-4	0	0.0
	Yr	2	3	.400	30	4	0	0	3	87²	104	6	43	29	15.2	4.41	108	.297	.376	1	.032	-4	**3**	**3**	0	0.1
1930	StL-N	0	1	.000	4	2	0	0	0	14²	12	0	13	8	15.3	7.36	68	.240	.397	1	.333	0	-4	-4	-0	-0.2
Total 10		49	33	.598	147	85	47	5	8	787	769	38	267	264	12.0	3.44	116	.261	.326	53	.191	-0	40	49	1	6.4

● **RED HILL**   Hill, Clifford Joseph b: 1/20/1893, Marshall, Tex. d: 8/11/38, ElPaso, Tex.   BB/TL,   Deb: 4/21/17

YEAR	TM/L	W	L	PCT	G	GS	CG	SH	SV	IP	H	HR	BB	SO	RAT	ERA	ERA+	OAV	OOB	BH	AVG	PB	PR	/A	PD	TPI
1917	Phi-A	0	0	—	1	0	0	0	0	2²	5	0	1	0	20.3	6.75	41	.385	.429	0		0	-1	-1	0	0.0

● **DAVE HILL**   Hill, David Burnham b: 11/11/37, New Orleans, La.   BR/TL, 6'2", 170 lbs.   Deb: 8/22/57

YEAR	TM/L	W	L	PCT	G	GS	CG	SH	SV	IP	H	HR	BB	SO	RAT	ERA	ERA+	OAV	OOB	BH	AVG	PB	PR	/A	PD	TPI
1957	KC-A	0	0	—	2	0	0	0	0	2¹	6	3	3	1	34.7	27.00	15	.462	.563	0		0	-6	-6	-0	0.0

● **DONNIE HILL**   Hill, Donald Earl b: 11/12/60, Pomona, Cal.   BB/TR, 5'10", 160 lbs.   Deb: 7/25/83 ◆

YEAR	TM/L	W	L	PCT	G	GS	CG	SH	SV	IP	H	HR	BB	SO	RAT	ERA	ERA+	OAV	OOB	BH	AVG	PB	PR	/A	PD	TPI
1990	Cal-A	0	0	—	1	0	0	0	0	1	0	0	1	1	9.0	0.00	—	.000	.250	93	.264		1	0	0	0.0

● **GARRY HILL**   Hill, Garry Alton b: 11/3/46, Rutherfordton, N.C.   BR/TR, 6'2", 195 lbs.   Deb: 6/12/69

YEAR	TM/L	W	L	PCT	G	GS	CG	SH	SV	IP	H	HR	BB	SO	RAT	ERA	ERA+	OAV	OOB	BH	AVG	PB	PR	/A	PD	TPI
1969	Atl-N	0	1	.000	1	1	0	0	0	2¹	6	1	1	2	27.0	15.43	23	.462	.500	0		0	-3	-3	0	-0.8

● **HERBERT HILL**   Hill, Herbert Lee b: 8/19/1891, Hutchins, Tex. d: 9/2/70, Farmers Branch, Tex.   BR/TR, 5'11.5", 175 lbs.   Deb: 7/17/15

YEAR	TM/L	W	L	PCT	G	GS	CG	SH	SV	IP	H	HR	BB	SO	RAT	ERA	ERA+	OAV	OOB	BH	AVG	PB	PR	/A	PD	TPI
1915	Cle-A	0	0	—	1	0	0	0	0	2	2	0	1	0	13.5	0.00		.250	.500	0			1	1	-0	0.0

● **KEN HILL**   Hill, Kenneth Wade b: 12/14/65, Lynn, Mass.   BR/TR, 6'2", 175 lbs.   Deb: 9/3/88

YEAR	TM/L	W	L	PCT	G	GS	CG	SH	SV	IP	H	HR	BB	SO	RAT	ERA	ERA+	OAV	OOB	BH	AVG	PB	PR	/A	PD	TPI
1988	StL-N	0	1	.000	4	1	0	0	0	14	16	0	6	6	14.1	5.14	68	.286	.355	0	.000	-0	-3	-3	0	-0.2
1989	StL-N	7	15	.318	33	33	2	1	0	196²	186	9	99	112	13.3	3.80	96	.252	.344	9	.153	-0	-7	-4	0	-0.4
1990	StL-N	5	6	.455	17	14	1	0	0	78²	79	7	33	58	12.9	5.49	69	.264	.339	4	.211	1	-15	-15	-1	-1.7
1991	StL-N	11	10	.524	30	30	0	0	0	181¹	147	15	67	121	10.9	3.57	104	.224	.302	5	.100	-1	2	3	0	0.2
1992	Mon-N	16	9	.640	33	33	3	3	0	218	187	13	75	150	10.9	2.68	129	.230	.298	11	.177	5	20	19	1	3.0
1993	Mon-N	9	7	.563	28	28	2	0	0	183²	163	7	74	90	11.9	3.23	129	.238	.318	6	.115	-1	16	19	3	1.8
1994	Mon-N★	**16**	5	.762	23	23	2	1	0	154²	145	12	44	85	11.3	3.32	128	.248	.307	7	.146	-0	15	16	2	2.2
Total 7		64	53	.547	168	162	10	5	0	1027	923	63	398	622	11.6	3.50	109	.241	.317	42	.143	4	30	36	8	4.9

● **MILT HILL**   Hill, Milton Giles b: 8/22/65, Atlanta, Ga.   BR/TR, 6', 180 lbs.   Deb: 8/1/91

YEAR	TM/L	W	L	PCT	G	GS	CG	SH	SV	IP	H	HR	BB	SO	RAT	ERA	ERA+	OAV	OOB	BH	AVG	PB	PR	/A	PD	TPI
1991	Cin-N	1	1	.500	22	0	0	0	0	33¹	36	1	8	20	11.9	3.78	101	.295	.338	0	—	-0	-0	0	-1	-0.1
1992	Cin-N	0	0	—	14	0	0	0	1	20	15	1	5	10	9.4	3.15	114	.211	.273	0		0	1	1	-0	0.1
1993	Cin-N	3	0	1.000	19	0	0	0	0	28²	34	5	9	23	13.5	5.65	71	.301	.352	0	.000	-0	-5	-5	-1	-0.6
1994	Atl-N	0	0	—	10	0	0	0	0	11¹	18	3	6	10	19.1	7.94	52	.367	.436	0		-0	-5	-5	-0	-0.1
	Sea-A	1	0	1.000	13	0	0	0	0	23²	30	4	11	16	15.6	6.46	76	.306	.376	0		0	-4	-4	-0	-0.1
Total 4		5	1	.833	78	0	0	0	1	117	133	14	39	79	13.3	5.08	80	.294	.351	0	.000	-0	-14	-13	-1	-0.8

● **BILL HILL**   Hill, William Cicero "Still Bill" b: 8/2/1874, Chattanooga, Tenn. d: 1/28/38, Cincinnati, Ohio   BL/TL, 6'1", 201 lbs.   Deb: 4/18/1896 F

YEAR	TM/L	W	L	PCT	G	GS	CG	SH	SV	IP	H	HR	BB	SO	RAT	ERA	ERA+	OAV	OOB	BH	AVG	PB	PR	/A	PD	TPI
1896	Lou-N	9	28	.243	43	39	32	0	2	319²	353	14	155	104	14.8	4.31	100	.278	.364	24	.207	-5	2	1	4	-0.1
1897	Lou-N	7	26	.292	27	26	20	1	0	199	209	6	91	55	13.3	3.62	118	.268	.341	15	.095	-8	15	14	2	0.8
1898	Cin-N	13	14	.481	33	32	26	0	0	262	261	3	119	75	13.6	3.98	96	.258	.346	13	.133	-7	-11	-4	1	-0.9
1899	Cle-N	3	6	.333	11	10	7	0	0	72¹	96	1	39	26	17.3	6.97	53	.318	.403	4	.129	-2	-25	-26	1	-2.6
	Bal-N	3	4	.429	7	7	6	0	0	61	64	1	18	17	12.5	3.25	122	.269	.329	7	.292	1	4	5	1	0.6
	Bro-N	1	0	1.000	2	1	1	0	0	11	11	0	6	3	13.9	0.82	478	.262	.352	3	.600	2	4	4	0	0.6
	Yr	7	10	.412	21	18	14	0	0	144¹	171	1	63	46	14.6	4.93	78	.291	.359	14	.233	1	-17	-18	1	-1.4
Total 4		36	69	.343	124	115	92	3	3	925	994	24	406	280	14.2	4.16	99	.273	.355	58	.167	-20	-11	-6	7	-1.6

● **HOMER HILLEBRAND**   Hillebrand, Homer Hiller Henry "Doc" b: 10/10/1879, Freeport, Ill. d: 1/20/74, Elsinore, Cal.   BR/TL, 5'8", 165 lbs.   Deb: 4/24/05 ◆

YEAR	TM/L	W	L	PCT	G	GS	CG	SH	SV	IP	H	HR	BB	SO	RAT	ERA	ERA+	OAV	OOB	BH	AVG	PB	PR	/A	PD	TPI
1905	Pit-N	5	2	.714	10	6	4	0	1	60²	43	0	19	37	9.5	2.82	107	.198	.269	26	.236	1	1	1	-1	0.2
1906	Pit-N	3	2	.600	7	5	4	1	0	53	42	1	21	32	10.9	2.21	121	.220	.300	5	.238	1	3	3	1	0.5
1908	Pit-N	0	0	—	1	0	0	0	0	1	1	0	0	1	9.0	0.00	—	.333	.333	0		-0	-0	-0	-0	0.0
Total 3		8	4	.667	18	11	8	1	1	114²	86	1	40	70	10.1	2.51	113	.209	.284	31	.237	2	4	4	1	0.7

YEAR TM/L	W	L	PCT	G	GS	CG	SH	SV	IP	H	HR	BB	SO	RAT	ERA	ERA+	OAV	OOB	BH	AVG	PB	PR	/A	PD	TPI

● **SHAWN HILLEGAS**   Hillegas, Shawn Patrick   b: 8/21/64, Dos Palos, Cal.   BR/TR, 6'2", 208 lbs.   Deb: 8/9/87

YEAR TM/L	W	L	PCT	G	GS	CG	SH	SV	IP	H	HR	BB	SO	RAT	ERA	ERA+	OAV	OOB	BH	AVG	PB	PR	/A	PD	TPI
1987 LA-N	4	3	.571	12	10	0	0	0	58	52	5	31	51	12.9	3.57	111	.241	.336	0	.000	-1	3	3	-1	0.1
1988 LA-N	3	4	.429	11	10	0	0	0	56²	54	5	17	30	11.8	4.13	81	.250	.314	2	.133	0	-4	-5	-1	-0.7
Chi-A	3	2	.600	6	6	0	0	0	40	30	4	18	26	11.0	3.15	126	.207	.299	0	—	0	4	4	-0	0.4
1989 Chi-A	7	11	.389	50	13	0	0	3	119²	132	12	51	76	14.0	4.74	80	.279	.353	0	—	0	-11	-12	-1	-1.8
1990 Chi-A	0	0	—	7	0	0	0	0	11¹	4	0	5	5	7.1	0.79	481	.111	.220	0	—	0	4	4	-0	0.1
1991 Cle-A	3	4	.429	51	3	0	0	7	83	67	7	46	66	12.5	4.34	96	.223	.330	0	—	0	-2	-2	-0	-0.2
1992 NY-A	1	8	.111	21	9	1	1	0	78¹	96	12	33	46	14.8	5.51	71	.306	.372	0	—	0	-14	-14	-1	-1.5
Oak-A	0	0	—	5	0	0	0	0	7²	8	1	4	3	14.1	2.35	159	.276	.364	0	—	0	1	1	-0	0.2
Yr	1	8	.111	26	9	1	1	0	86	104	13	37	49	14.8	5.23	75	.301	.368	0	—	0	-12	-13	-1	-1.3
1993 Oak-A	3	6	.333	18	11	0	0	0	60²	78	8	33	29	17.1	6.97	58	.317	.406	0	—	0	-18	-20	-1	-2.3
Total 7	24	38	.387	181	62	1	1	10	515¹	521	54	238	332	13.5	4.61	84	.264	.347	2	.069	-1	-37	-41	-6	-5.7

● **FRANK HILLER**   Hiller, Frank Walter "Dutch"   b: 7/13/20, Newark, N.J.   d: 1/8/87, West Chester, Pa.   BR/TR, 6', 200 lbs.   Deb: 5/25/46

YEAR TM/L	W	L	PCT	G	GS	CG	SH	SV	IP	H	HR	BB	SO	RAT	ERA	ERA+	OAV	OOB	BH	AVG	PB	PR	/A	PD	TPI
1946 NY-A	0	2	.000	3	1	0	0	0	11¹	13	2	6	4	15.1	4.76	72	.295	.380	1	.250	0	-2	-2	-0	-0.3
1948 NY-A	5	2	.714	22	5	1	0	0	62¹	59	8	30	25	13.0	4.04	101	.244	.330	6	.375	2	2	0	0	0.2
1949 NY-A	0	2	.000	4	0	0	0	1	7²	9	0	7	3	18.8	5.87	69	.290	.421	1	.500	0	-1	-2	-0	-0.4
1950 Chi-N	12	5	.706	38	17	9	2	1	153	153	16	32	55	11.1	3.53	119	.258	.300	5	.114	0	10	11	1	1.0
1951 Chi-N	6	12	.333	24	21	6	2	1	141¹	147	17	31	50	11.9	4.84	85	.268	.317	6	.125	-2	-14	-12	1	-1.4
1952 Cin-N	5	8	.385	28	15	6	1	1	124¹	129	14	37	50	12.5	4.63	81	.271	.331	5	.167	1	-12	-12	0	-1.1
1953 NY-N	2	1	.667	19	1	0	0	0	33²	43	6	15	10	16.6	6.15	70	.303	.385	2	.500	1	-7	-7	1	-0.4
Total 7	30	32	.484	138	60	22	5	4	533²	553	56	158	197	12.4	4.42	92	.266	.325	26	.176	-1	-24	-22	3	-2.4

● **JOHN HILLER**   Hiller, John Frederick   b: 4/8/43, Toronto, Ont., Canada   BR/TL, 6', 195 lbs.   Deb: 9/6/65

YEAR TM/L	W	L	PCT	G	GS	CG	SH	SV	IP	H	HR	BB	SO	RAT	ERA	ERA+	OAV	OOB	BH	AVG	PB	PR	/A	PD	TPI
1965 Det-A	0	0	—	5	0	0	0	1	6	5	0	1	4	9.0	0.00	—	.227	.261	0	—	0	2	2	-0	0.1
1966 Det-A	0	0	—	1	0	0	0	0	2	2	0	2	1	18.0	9.00	39	.286	.444	0	—	0	-1	-1	-0	0.0
1967 Det-A	4	3	.571	23	6	2	2	3	65	57	4	9	49	9.1	2.63	124	.233	.260	2	.133	-0	4	5	-0	0.5
1968 *Det-A	9	6	.600	39	12	4	1	2	128	92	9	51	78	10.1	2.39	126	.200	.280	3	.081	-2	8	9	-0	0.8
1969 Det-A	4	4	.500	40	8	1	1	4	99¹	97	13	44	74	12.9	3.99	94	.257	.336	6	.286	-1	-4	-3	-1	-0.2
1970 Det-A	6	6	.500	47	5	1	1	3	104	82	12	46	89	11.3	3.03	123	.219	.307	0	.000	-2	8	8	-1	0.6
1972 *Det-A	1	2	.333	24	3	1	0	3	44¹	39	4	13	26	11.2	2.03	155	.232	.299	0	.000	-0	5	5	-1	0.5
1973 Det-A	10	5	.667	**65**	0	0	0	**38**	125¹	89	7	39	124	9.2	1.44	285	.198	.262	0	—	0	**33**	**37**	0	**6.7**
1974 Det-A☆	17	14	.548	59	0	0	0	13	150	127	9	62	134	11.5	2.64	144	.231	.312	0	—	0	16	19	-2	3.9
1975 Det-A	2	3	.400	36	0	0	0	14	70²	52	6	36	87	11.2	2.17	185	.205	.303	0	—	0	13	15	-0	1.5
1976 Det-A	12	8	.600	56	1	1	1	13	121	93	7	67	117	12.0	2.38	156	.219	.329	0	.000	0	15	**18**	-1	3.3
1977 Det-A	8	14	.364	45	8	3	0	7	124	120	16	61	115	13.2	3.56	121	.258	.345	0	—	0	7	10	-1	1.6
1978 Det-A	9	4	.692	51	0	0	0	15	92¹	64	6	35	74	9.6	2.34	165	.202	.281	0	—	0	15	16	-1	2.6
1979 Det-A	4	7	.364	43	0	0	0	9	79¹	83	14	55	46	15.7	5.22	83	.274	.385	0	—	0	-9	-8	-0	-1.2
1980 Det-A	1	0	1.000	11	0	0	0	0	30²	38	3	14	18	15.3	4.40	93	.309	.380	0	—	0	-1	-1	-0	-0.1
Total 15	87	76	.534	545	43	13	6	125	1242	1040	110	535	1036	11.5	2.83	133	.229	.312	11	.109	-3	112	130	-8	20.6

● **DAVE HILLMAN**   Hillman, Darius Dutton   b: 9/14/27, Dungannon, Va.   BR/TR, 5'11", 168 lbs.   Deb: 4/30/55

YEAR TM/L	W	L	PCT	G	GS	CG	SH	SV	IP	H	HR	BB	SO	RAT	ERA	ERA+	OAV	OOB	BH	AVG	PB	PR	/A	PD	TPI
1955 Chi-N	0	0	—	25	3	0	0	0	57²	63	10	25	23	13.9	5.31	77	.283	.357	1	.100	0	-8	-8	0	0.0
1956 Chi-N	0	2	.000	2	2	0	0	0	12¹	11	0	5	6	11.7	2.19	172	.216	.286	0	.000	-1	2	2	0	0.3
1957 Chi-N	6	11	.353	32	14	1	0	1	103¹	115	13	37	53	13.2	4.35	89	.280	.340	0	.000	-2	-5	-6	-0	-1.1
1958 Chi-N	4	8	.333	31	16	3	0	1	125²	132	13	31	65	11.7	3.15	124	.265	.308	6	.146	-1	11	11	-0	0.8
1959 Chi-N	8	11	.421	39	24	4	1	0	191	178	16	43	88	10.5	3.53	112	.248	.292	9	.150	1	9	9	1	1.0
1960 Bos-A	0	3	.000	16	3	0	0	0	36²	41	6	12	14	13.0	5.65	72	.281	.335	0	.000	-0	-7	-7	0	-0.5
1961 Bos-A	3	2	.600	28	1	0	0	0	78	70	8	23	39	10.7	2.77	151	.242	.298	0	.000	-2	11	12	0	0.5
1962 Cin-N	0	0	—	2	0	0	0	0	3²	8	0	1	0	22.1	9.82	41	.421	.450	0	—	0	-2	-2	-0	-0.1
NY-N	0	0	—	13	1	0	0	1	15²	21	5	3	8	17.2	6.32	66	.333	.417	0	.000	-0	-4	-4	0	-0.1
Yr	0	0	—	15	1	0	0	1	19¹	29	5	4	8	18.2	6.98	59	.354	.424	0	.000	-0	-7	-6	-0	-0.1
Total 8	21	37	.362	188	64	8	1	3	624	639	71	185	296	11.9	3.87	103	.264	.317	16	.098	-5	6	8	1	0.9

● **ERIC HILLMAN**   Hillman, John Eric   b: 4/27/66, Gary, Ind.   BL/TL, 6'10", 225 lbs.   Deb: 5/18/92

YEAR TM/L	W	L	PCT	G	GS	CG	SH	SV	IP	H	HR	BB	SO	RAT	ERA	ERA+	OAV	OOB	BH	AVG	PB	PR	/A	PD	TPI
1992 NY-N	2	2	.500	11	8	0	0	0	52¹	67	6	9	16	13.6	5.33	65	.318	.354	1	.077	-1	-11	-11	-1	-0.9
1993 NY-N	2	9	.182	27	22	3	1	0	145	173	12	24	60	12.5	3.97	101	.299	.331	7	.159	-0	1	1	-1	0.0
1994 NY-N	0	3	.000	11	6	0	0	0	34²	45	9	11	20	15.1	7.79	55	.321	.379	0	.000	-1	-14	-14	-0	-1.1
Total 3	4	14	.222	49	36	3	1	0	232	285	30	45	96	13.1	4.85	81	.306	.344	8	.123	-2	-23	-24	-1	-2.0

● **CHARLIE HILSEY**   Hilsey, Charles T.   b: 3/23/1864, Philadelphia, Pa.   d: 10/31/18, Philadelphia, Pa.   5'7", 180 lbs.   Deb: 9/27/1883 ◆

YEAR TM/L	W	L	PCT	G	GS	CG	SH	SV	IP	H	HR	BB	SO	RAT	ERA	ERA+	OAV	OOB	BH	AVG	PB	PR	/A	PD	TPI
1883 Phi-N	0	3	.000	3	3	3	0	0	26	36	1	4	8	13.8	5.54	56	.305	.328	1	.100	-1	-7	-7	-0	-0.7
1884 Phi-a	2	1	.667	3	3	3	0	0	27	29	0	5	10	11.3	4.67	73	.257	.288	5	.208	0	-4	-4	1	-0.3
Total 2	2	4	.333	6	6	6	0	0	53	65	1	9	18	12.6	5.09	64	.281	.308	6	.176	-1	-11	-11	0	-1.0

● **HOWARD HILTON**   Hilton, Howard James   b: 1/3/64, Oxnard, Cal.   BR/TR, 6'3", 230 lbs.   Deb: 4/9/90

YEAR TM/L	W	L	PCT	G	GS	CG	SH	SV	IP	H	HR	BB	SO	RAT	ERA	ERA+	OAV	OOB	BH	AVG	PB	PR	/A	PD	TPI
1990 StL-N	0	0	—	2	0	0	0	0	3	2	0	3	2	15.0	0.00	—	.182	.357	0	—	0	1	1	-0	0.0

● **SAM HINDS**   Hinds, Samuel Russell   b: 7/11/53, Frederick, Md.   BR/TR, 6'6", 215 lbs.   Deb: 5/21/77

YEAR TM/L	W	L	PCT	G	GS	CG	SH	SV	IP	H	HR	BB	SO	RAT	ERA	ERA+	OAV	OOB	BH	AVG	PB	PR	/A	PD	TPI
1977 Mil-A	0	3	.000	29	1	0	0	2	72¹	72	5	40	46	14.2	4.73	86	.266	.364	0	—	0	-5	-5	-0	-0.3

● **PAUL HINES**   Hines, Paul A.   b: 3/1/1852, Washington, D.C.   d: 7/10/35, Hyattsville, Md.   BR/TR, 5'9.5", 173 lbs.   Deb: 4/20/1872 ◆

YEAR TM/L	W	L	PCT	G	GS	CG	SH	SV	IP	H	HR	BB	SO	RAT	ERA	ERA+	OAV	OOB	BH	AVG	PB	PR	/A	PD	TPI
1884 *Pro-N	0	0	—	1	0	0	0	0	1	3	0	0	0	27.0	0.00	—	.500	.500	148	.302	0	0	0	-0	0.0

● **PAUL HINRICHS**   Hinrichs, Paul Edwin "Herky"   b: 8/31/25, Marengo, Iowa   BR/TR, 6', 180 lbs.   Deb: 5/16/51

YEAR TM/L	W	L	PCT	G	GS	CG	SH	SV	IP	H	HR	BB	SO	RAT	ERA	ERA+	OAV	OOB	BH	AVG	PB	PR	/A	PD	TPI
1951 Bos-A	0	0	—	4	0	0	0	0	3¹	7	1	4	1	29.7	21.60	21	.412	.524	0	—	0	-6	-6	0	0.0

● **DUTCH HINRICHS**   Hinrichs, William Louis   b: 4/27/1889, Orange, Cal.   d: 8/18/72, Kingsburg, Cal.   BR/TR, 6'3", 195 lbs.   Deb: 6/25/10

YEAR TM/L	W	L	PCT	G	GS	CG	SH	SV	IP	H	HR	BB	SO	RAT	ERA	ERA+	OAV	OOB	BH	AVG	PB	PR	/A	PD	TPI
1910 Was-A	0	1	.000	3	0	0	0	1	7	10	0	3	5	16.7	2.57	97	.357	.419	0	.000	-1	-0	-0	-1	-0.1

● **JERRY HINSLEY**   Hinsley, Jerry Dean   b: 4/9/44, Hugo, Okla.   BR/TR, 5'11", 165 lbs.   Deb: 4/18/64

YEAR TM/L	W	L	PCT	G	GS	CG	SH	SV	IP	H	HR	BB	SO	RAT	ERA	ERA+	OAV	OOB	BH	AVG	PB	PR	/A	PD	TPI
1964 NY-N	0	2	.000	9	2	0	0	0	15¹	21	0	7	11	16.4	8.22	44	.313	.378	0	.000	-1	-8	-8	-1	-1.0
1967 NY-N	0	0	—	2	0	0	0	0	5	6	0	4	3	18.0	3.60	94	.316	.435	0	—	0	-0	-0	-0	0.0
Total 2	0	2	.000	11	2	0	0	0	20¹	27	0	11	14	16.8	7.08	50	.314	.392	0	.000	-1	-8	-8	-1	-1.0

● **RICH HINTON**   Hinton, Richard Michael   b: 5/22/47, Tucson, Ariz.   BL/TL, 6'2", 185 lbs.   Deb: 7/17/71

YEAR TM/L	W	L	PCT	G	GS	CG	SH	SV	IP	H	HR	BB	SO	RAT	ERA	ERA+	OAV	OOB	BH	AVG	PB	PR	/A	PD	TPI
1971 Chi-A	3	4	.429	18	2	0	0	0	24¹	27	1	6	15	12.6	4.44	81	.310	.362	0	.000	-0	-3	-2	1	-0.5
1972 NY-A	1	0	1.000	7	3	0	0	0	16²	20	2	8	13	15.1	4.86	61	.299	.373	0	.000	-0	-3	-4	-0	-0.3
Tex-A	0	1	.000	5	0	0	0	0	11¹	7	1	10	4	13.5	2.38	126	.171	.333	1	.500	1	1	1	0	0.2
Yr	1	1	.500	12	3	0	0	0	28	27	3	18	17	14.5	3.86	77	.245	.352	1	.200	1	-2	-3	-0	-0.1
1975 Chi-A	1	0	1.000	15	0	0	0	0	37¹	41	3	15	30	13.5	4.82	80	.270	.335	0	—	0	-4	-4	1	0.0
1976 Cin-N	1	2	.333	14	0	0	0	0	17²	30	4	7	8	20.9	7.64	46	.380	.456	0	.000	-0	-9	-8	0	-1.3
1978 Chi-A	2	6	.250	29	4	2	0	1	80²	78	5	28	48	12.0	4.02	95	.261	.348	0	—	0	-2	-2	-0	-0.3
1979 Chi-A	1	2	.333	16	2	0	0	2	41²	57	4	13	27	14.5	6.05	73	.322	.368	0	—	0	-8	-8	-0	-0.6
Sea-A	0	2	.000	14	1	0	0	0	20	23	4	5	7	13.5	5.40	81	.284	.341	0	—	0	-3	-2	-0	-0.2

YEAR TM/L	W	L	PCT	G	GS	CG	SH	SV	IP	H	HR	BB	SO	RAT	ERA	ERA+	OAV	OOB	BH	AVG	PB	PR	/A	PD	TPI
Yr	1	4	.200	30	3	0	0	2	61²	80	8	13	34	13.9	5.84	73	.310	.348	0	—	0	-11	-11	0	-0.8
Total 6	9	17	.346	116	13	2	0	3	249²	283	24	91	152	13.7	4.87	78	.289	.354	1	.143	0	-31	-30	0	-3.0

● **HERB HIPPAUF**   Hippauf, Herbert August b: 5/9/40, New York, N.Y. BR/TL, 6', 180 lbs. Deb: 4/27/66

YEAR TM/L	W	L	PCT	G	GS	CG	SH	SV	IP	H	HR	BB	SO	RAT	ERA	ERA+	OAV	OOB	BH	AVG	PB	PR	/A	PD	TPI
1966 Atl-N	0	1	.000	3	0	0	0	0	2²	6	0	1	1	23.6	13.50	27	.462	.500	0	—	0	-3	-3	-0	-0.9

● **HARLEY HISNER**   Hisner, Harley Parnell b: 11/6/26, Naples, Ind. BR/TR, 6'1", 185 lbs. Deb: 9/30/51

| 1951 Bos-A | 0 | 1 | .000 | 1 | 1 | 0 | 0 | 0 | 6 | 7 | 0 | 4 | 3 | 16.5 | 4.50 | 99 | .292 | .393 | 1 | .500 | 0 | -0 | -0 | 0 | 0.0 |

● **STERLING HITCHCOCK**   Hitchcock, Sterling Alex b: 4/29/71, Fayetteville, N.C. BL/TL, 6'1", 200 lbs. Deb: 9/11/92

1992 NY-A	0	2	.000	3	3	0	0	0	13	23	2	6	6	20.8	8.31	47	.377	.441	0	—	0	-6	-6	0	-0.7
1993 NY-A	1	2	.333	6	6	0	0	0	31	32	4	14	26	13.6	4.65	89	.271	.353	0	—	0	-1	-2	-0	-0.1
1994 NY-A	4	1	.800	23	5	1	0	2	49¹	48	3	29	37	14.0	4.20	106	.265	.367	0	—	0	3	1	0	0.1
Total 3	5	5	.500	32	14	1	0	2	93¹	103	9	49	69	14.9	4.92	87	.286	.375	0	—	0	-4	-7	-0	-0.7

● **BRUCE HITT**   Hitt, Bruce Smith b: 3/14/1897, Comanche, Tex. d: 11/10/73, Portland, Ore. BR/TR, 6'1", 190 lbs. Deb: 9/23/17

| 1917 StL-N | 0 | 0 | — | 2 | 0 | 0 | 0 | 0 | 4 | 7 | 1 | 1 | 1 | 18.0 | 9.00 | 30 | .368 | .400 | 1 | .000 | -0 | -3 | -3 | -0 | 0.0 |

● **ROY HITT**   Hitt, Roy Wesley "Rhino" b: 6/22/1887, Carleton, Neb. d: 2/8/56, Pomona, Cal. BL/TL, 5'10", 200 lbs. Deb: 4/27/07

| 1907 Cin-N | 6 | 10 | .375 | 21 | 18 | 14 | 2 | 0 | 153¹ | 143 | 2 | 56 | 63 | 12.4 | 3.40 | 76 | .258 | .339 | 10 | .179 | -0 | -16 | -14 | -1 | -1.5 |

● **LLOYD HITTLE**   Hittle, Lloyd Eldon "Red" b: 2/21/24, Lodi, Cal. BR/TL, 5'10.5", 164 lbs. Deb: 6/12/49

1949 Was-A	5	7	.417	36	9	3	2	0	109	123	2	57	32	14.9	4.21	101	.285	.369	4	.143	-2	-0	1	-1	-0.2
1950 Was-A	2	4	.333	11	4	1	0	0	43¹	60	1	17	9	16.0	4.98	90	.326	.383	1	.077	-1	-2	-2	1	-0.3
Total 2	7	11	.389	47	13	4	2	0	152¹	183	3	74	41	15.2	4.43	98	.298	.373	5	.122	-3	-2	-2	0	-0.5

● **MYRIL HOAG**   Hoag, Myril Oliver b: 3/9/08, Davis, Cal. d: 7/28/71, High Springs, Fla BR/TR, 5'11", 180 lbs. Deb: 4/15/31 ◆

1939 StL-A★	0	0	—	1	0	0	0	0	1	0	0	0	0	0.0	0.00	—	.000	.000	142	.295	0	1	1	0	0.0
1945 Cle-A	0	0	—	2	0	0	0	0	3	3	0	1	0	12.0	0.00	—	.300	.364	27	.211	0	1	1	0	0.0
Total 2	0	0	—	3	0	0	0	0	4	3	0	1	0	9.0	0.00	—	.214	.267	854	.271	1	2	2	0	0.0

● **ED HOBAUGH**   Hobaugh, Edward Russell b: 6/27/34, Kittanning, Pa. BR/TR, 6', 176 lbs. Deb: 4/19/61

1961 Was-A	7	9	.438	26	18	3	0	0	126¹	142	12	64	67	14.7	4.42	91	.281	.363	4	.098	-2	-6	-6	0	-0.8
1962 Was-A	2	1	.667	26	2	0	0	1	69¹	66	9	25	37	11.8	3.76	107	.258	.324	2	.167	0	2	2	-1	0.0
1963 Was-A	0	0	—	9	1	0	0	0	16	20	3	6	11	15.8	6.19	60	.308	.384	1	.500	-2	-5	-4	0	0.2
Total 3	9	10	.474	61	21	3	0	1	211²	228	24	95	115	13.9	4.34	92	.276	.352	7	.127	-1	-8	-8	-0	-0.6

● **GLEN HOBBIE**   Hobbie, Glen Frederick b: 4/24/36, Witt, Ill. BR/TR, 6'2", 195 lbs. Deb: 9/20/57

1957 Chi-N	0	0	—	2	0	0	0	0	4¹	6	0	5	3	22.8	10.38	37	.333	.478	0	.000	-0	-3	-3	0	0.0
1958 Chi-N	10	6	.625	55	16	2	1	2	168¹	163	13	93	91	14.1	3.74	105	.252	.353	7	.146	-2	4	3	4	0.5
1959 Chi-N	16	13	.552	46	33	10	3	0	234	204	15	106	138	12.2	3.69	107	.236	.324	9	.114	-3	7	7	1	0.5
1960 Chi-N	16	20	.444	46	36	16	4	1	258²	253	27	101	134	12.6	3.97	95	.256	.330	13	.151	1	-6	-5	4	-0.2
1961 Chi-N	7	13	.350	36	29	7	2	2	198²	207	26	54	103	12.1	4.26	98	.268	.321	11	.167	2	-5	-2	3	0.4
1962 Chi-N	5	14	.263	42	23	5	0	0	162	198	19	62	87	14.6	5.22	79	.304	.367	6	.122	-1	-23	-19	1	-2.1
1963 Chi-N	7	10	.412	36	24	4	1	0	165¹	172	17	49	94	12.3	3.92	90	.270	.328	4	.080	-2	-12	-8	-1	-1.1
1964 Chi-N	0	3	.000	8	4	0	0	0	27¹	39	4	10	14	16.5	7.90	47	.325	.382	0	.000	-0	-13	-13	0	-1.2
StL-N	1	2	.333	13	5	1	0	1	44¹	41	4	15	18	11.6	4.26	89	.241	.306	2	.154	1	-4	-2	1	0.0
Yr	1	5	.167	21	9	1	0	1	71²	80	8	25	32	13.3	5.65	67	.275	.334	2	.111	1	-17	-15	1	-1.2
Total 8	62	81	.434	284	170	45	11	6	1263	1283	125	495	682	12.9	4.20	93	.264	.337	52	.131	-5	-55	-42	13	-3.2

● **JOHN HOBBS**   Hobbs, John Douglas b: 11/11/56, Philadelphia, Pa. BR/TR, 6'3", 190 lbs. Deb: 8/31/81

| 1981 Min-A | 0 | 0 | — | 4 | 0 | 0 | 0 | 0 | 5² | 5 | 0 | 6 | 1 | 20.6 | 3.18 | 124 | .238 | .448 | 0 | — | 0 | 0 | -0 | -0 | -0.1 |

● **HARRY HOCH**   Hoch, Harry Keller b: 1/9/1887, Woodside, Del. d: 10/26/81, Lewes, Del. BR/TR, 5'10.5", 165 lbs. Deb: 4/16/08

1908 Phi-N	2	1	.667	3	3	2	0	0	26	20	0	13	4	12.1	2.77	88	.211	.318	1	.200	1	-1	-1	0	0.0
1914 StL-A	0	2	.000	15	2	1	0	0	54	55	1	27	13	14.0	3.00	90	.284	.377	1	.056	-2	-2	-2	2	-0.1
1915 StL-A	0	4	.000	12	3	1	0	0	40	52	2	26	9	18.2	7.20	40	.311	.413	2	.200	0	-19	-19	-0	-1.7
Total 3	2	7	.222	30	8	4	0	0	120	127	3	66	26	15.0	4.35	62	.279	.378	4	.121	-1	-22	-22	2	-1.8

● **CHUCK HOCKENBERY**   Hockenbery, Charles Marion b: 12/15/50, LaCrosse, Wis. BB/TR, 6'1", 195 lbs. Deb: 7/4/75

| 1975 Cal-A | 0 | 5 | .000 | 16 | 6 | 0 | 0 | 1 | 41 | 48 | 3 | 19 | 15 | 15.4 | 5.27 | 67 | .296 | .380 | 0 | — | 0 | -7 | -8 | -0 | -0.9 |

● **GEORGE HOCKETTE**   Hockette, George Edward "Lefty" b: 4/7/08, Perth, Miss. d: 1/20/74, Plantation, Fla. BL/TL, 6', 174 lbs. Deb: 9/17/34

1934 Bos-A	2	1	.667	3	3	3	2	0	27¹	22	3	6	14	9.2	1.65	292	.218	.262	3	.273	0	9	10	-0	1.1
1935 Bos-A	2	3	.400	23	4	0	0	0	61	83	6	12	11	14.2	5.16	92	.329	.362	2	.143	-1	-5	-3	3	0.0
Total 2	4	4	.500	26	7	3	2	0	88¹	105	9	18	25	12.6	4.08	117	.297	.333	5	.200	-0	4	7	3	1.1

● **SHOVEL HODGE**   Hodge, Clarence Clemet b: 7/6/1893, Mount Andrew, Ala. d: 12/31/67, Ft.Walton Beach, Fla. BL/TR, 6'4", 190 lbs. Deb: 9/6/20

1920 Chi-A	1	1	.500	4	2	1	0	0	19²	15	0	12	5	12.4	2.29	165	.224	.342	0	—	-1	3	3	-1	0.1
1921 Chi-A	6	8	.429	36	10	5	0	2	142²	191	7	54	25	15.8	6.56	65	.335	.397	17	.327	3	-36	-37	3	-2.5
1922 Chi-A	7	6	.538	35	8	2	0	1	139	154	3	65	37	14.3	4.14	98	.300	.381	12	.207	-1	-2	-1	2	-0.1
Total 3	14	15	.483	75	20	8	0	3	301¹	360	10	131	67	14.9	5.17	80	.313	.387	29	.250	1	-34	-35	4	-2.5

● **ED HODGE**   Hodge, Ed Oliver b: 4/19/58, Bellflower, Cal. BL/TL, 6'2", 192 lbs. Deb: 5/1/84

| 1984 Min-A | 4 | 3 | .571 | 25 | 15 | 0 | 0 | 0 | 100 | 116 | 13 | 29 | 59 | 13.1 | 4.77 | 88 | .291 | .340 | 0 | — | 0 | -9 | -6 | -2 | -0.7 |

● **ELI HODKEY**   Hodkey, Aloysius Joseph b: 11/3/17, Lorain, Ohio BL/TL, 6'4", 185 lbs. Deb: 9/12/46

| 1946 Phi-N | 0 | 1 | .000 | 2 | 1 | 0 | 0 | 0 | 4¹ | 9 | 0 | 5 | 0 | 29.1 | 12.46 | 28 | .391 | .500 | 0 | .000 | -0 | -4 | -4 | -0 | -0.8 |

● **CHARLIE HODNETT**   Hodnett, Charles b: 1861, Iowa Deb: 5/3/1883

1883 StL-a	2	2	.500	4	4	3	0	0	32	28	1	6	11	9.8	1.41	248	.220	.261	2	.182	-0	7	7	0	0.8
1884 StL-U	12	2	.857	14	14	12	1	0	121	121	0	16	41	10.2	2.01	119	.243	.267	12	.207	-1	6	5	-2	0.1
Total 2	14	4	.778	18	18	15	1	0	153	149	1	23	47	10.1	1.88	139	.238	.266	14	.203	-2	13	12	-2	0.9

● **GEORGE HODSON**   Hodson, George S. b: 6/1870, Pennsylvania Deb: 8/9/1894

1894 Bos-N	4	4	.500	12	11	8	0	0	74	103	4	35	12	17.4	5.84	97	.326	.402	3	.100	-4	-4	-1	-1	-0.5
1895 Phi-N	1	2	.333	4	2	1	0	0	17	27	4	9	6	19.1	9.53	50	.354	.422	0	.000	-1	-9	-9	-1	-1.1
Total 2	5	6	.455	16	13	9	0	0	91	130	8	44	18	17.7	6.53	84	.331	.406	3	.086	-5	-13	-10	-2	-1.6

● **BILLY HOEFT**   Hoeft, William Frederick b: 5/17/32, Oshkosh, Wis. BL/TL, 6'3", 205 lbs. Deb: 4/18/52

1952 Det-A	2	7	.222	34	10	1	0	4	125	123	14	63	67	13.8	4.32	88	.260	.353	6	.150	-1	-9	-7	1	-0.8
1953 Det-A	9	14	.391	29	27	9	0	2	197²	223	24	58	90	13.0	4.83	84	.283	.335	11	.172	0	-18	-17	-2	-1.8
1954 Det-A	7	15	.318	34	25	10	4	1	175	180	22	59	114	12.5	4.58	81	.266	.328	10	.192	4	-17	-17	-2	-1.7
1955 Det-A☆	16	7	.696	32	29	17	**7**	0	220	187	15	75	133	11.0	2.99	129	.229	.298	17	.202	9	24	21	-3	2.1
1956 Det-A	20	14	.588	38	34	18	4	0	248	276	22	104	172	14.0	4.06	101	.287	.360	20	.250	6	3	1	-3	0.5
1957 Det-A	9	11	.450	34	28	10	1	0	207	188	15	69	111	11.4	3.48	111	.244	.310	10	.149	5	7	9	-3	0.8
1958 Det-A	10	9	.526	36	21	6	0	3	143	148	15	49	94	12.5	4.15	97	.268	.328	12	.273	3	-6	-2	-2	-0.1

YEAR TM/L	W	L	PCT	G	GS	CG	SH	SV	IP	H	HR	BB	SO	RAT	ERA	ERA+	OAV	OOB	BH	AVG	PB	PR	/A	PD	TPI
1959 Det-A	1	1	.500	2	2	0	0	0	9	6	0	4	2	11.0	5.00	81	.188	.297	1	.333	0	-1	-1	0	-0.2
Bos-A	0	3	.000	5	3	0	0	0	17²	22	1	8	8	15.8	5.60	72	.319	.397	0	.000	-0	-3	-3	0	-0.5
Bal-A	1	1	.500	16	3	0	0	0	41	50	6	19	30	15.1	5.71	66	.307	.379	3	.250	1	-8	-9	-0	-0.3
Yr	2	5	.286	23	8	0	0	0	67²	78	7	31	40	14.5	5.59	70	.290	.363	4	.222	0	-13	-13	-0	-1.0
1960 Bal-A	2	1	.667	19	0	0	0	0	18²	18	2	14	14	15.4	4.34	88	.240	.360	0	.000	-0	-1	-1	0	-0.1
1961 Bal-A	7	4	.636	35	12	3	1	3	138	106	7	55	100	10.6	2.02	190	.216	.296	7	.179	1	31	28	1	2.4
1962 Bal-A	4	8	.333	57	4	0	0	7	113²	103	7	43	73	11.6	4.59	81	.243	.315	3	.158	3	-8	-11	-0	-1.0
1963 SF-N	2	0	1.000	23	0	0	0	4	24¹	26	5	10	8	13.3	4.44	72	.271	.340	1	1.000	0	-3	-3	-0	-0.4
1964 Mil-N	4	0	1.000	42	0	0	0	4	73¹	76	9	18	47	11.7	3.80	93	.271	.318	2	.222	1	-2	-2	0	0.0
1965 Chi-N	2	2	.500	29	2	1	0	1	51¹	41	3	20	44	10.7	2.81	131	.215	.289	3	.273	1	4	5	-1	0.4
1966 Chi-N	1	2	.333	36	0	0	0	3	41	43	4	14	30	12.7	4.61	80	.264	.326	1	.250	0	-5	-4	1	-0.3
SF-N	0	2	.000	4	0	0	0	0	3²	4	0	3	3	17.2	7.36	50	.250	.368	0	—	0	-2	-2	-0	-0.7
Yr	1	4	.200	40	0	0	0	3	44²	47	4	17	33	13.1	4.84	76	.261	.325	1	.250	0	-6	-6	-0	-1.0
Total 15	97	101	.490	505	200	75	17	33	1847¹	1820	173	685	1140	12.4	3.94	98	.259	.327	107	.202	24	-15	-15	-11	-1.4

● **ART HOELSKOETTER**   Hoelskoetter, Arthur "Holley" or "Hoss" (a.k.a. Arthur H. Hostetter)
b: 9/30/1882, St.Louis, Mo. d: 8/3/54, St.Louis, Mo. BR/TR, 6'2", Deb: 9/10/05 ♦

YEAR TM/L	W	L	PCT	G	GS	CG	SH	SV	IP	H	HR	BB	SO	RAT	ERA	ERA+	OAV	OOB	BH	AVG	PB	PR	/A	PD	TPI
1905 StL-N	0	1	.000	1	1	1	0	0	6	6	1	5	4	16.5	1.50	199	.273	.407	20	.241	0	1	1	0	0.2
1906 StL-N	1	4	.200	12	3	2	0	0	58¹	53	1	34	20	13.6	4.63	57	.240	.344	71	.224	1	-13	-13	-1	-1.1
1907 StL-N	0	0	—	2	0	0	0	0	11	9	0	10	8	17.2	5.73	44	.209	.382	98	.247	0	-4	-4	-1	0.0
Total 3	1	5	.167	15	4	3	0	0	75¹	68	2	49	32	14.3	4.54	58	.238	.355	225	.236	1	-16	-16	-1	-0.9

● **JOE HOERNER**   Hoerner, Joseph Walter b: 11/12/36, Dubuque, Iowa BR/TL, 6'1", 200 lbs. Deb: 9/27/63

YEAR TM/L	W	L	PCT	G	GS	CG	SH	SV	IP	H	HR	BB	SO	RAT	ERA	ERA+	OAV	OOB	BH	AVG	PB	PR	/A	PD	TPI
1963 Hou-N	0	0	—	1	0	0	0	0	3	2	0	0	2	6.0	0.00	—	.182	.182	0	.000	-0	1	1	0	0.0
1964 Hou-N	0	0	—	7	0	0	0	0	11	13	3	6	4	15.5	4.91	70	.310	.396	0	.000	-0	-2	-2	0	-0.1
1966 StL-N	5	1	.833	57	0	0	0	13	76	57	5	21	63	9.7	1.54	233	.212	.279	1	.125	1	17	17	-1	2.0
1967 *StL-N	4	4	.500	57	0	0	0	15	66	52	5	20	50	10.0	2.59	127	.225	.290	2	.182	0	6	5	-0	0.9
1968 *StL-N	8	2	.800	47	0	0	0	17	48²	34	2	12	42	8.5	1.48	196	.192	.243	0	.000	-1	8	8	-0	2.3
1969 StL-N	2	3	.400	45	0	0	0	15	53¹	54	5	9	35	11.5	2.87	125	.230	.269	0	.000	-1	4	4	0	0.6
1970 Phi-N☆	9	5	.643	44	0	0	0	9	57²	53	5	20	39	11.5	2.65	150	.247	.314	2	.200	1	9	9	-2	2.1
1971 Phi-N	4	5	.444	49	0	0	0	9	73	57	6	21	57	9.7	1.97	179	.215	.275	1	.100	-1	12	13	-0	1.8
1972 Phi-N	0	2	.000	15	0	0	0	3	21²	21	2	5	12	11.2	2.08	173	.259	.310	0	.000	-0	3	4	-1	0.4
Atl-N	1	3	.250	25	0	0	0	2	23¹	34	4	8	19	16.6	6.56	53	.351	.406	0	.000	-0	-8	-7	-1	-1.4
Yr	1	5	.167	40	0	0	0	5	45	55	6	13	31	13.8	4.40	84	.301	.350	0	.000	-1	-5	-4	-1	-1.0
1973 Atl-N	2	2	.500	20	0	0	0	2	12²	17	1	4	10	14.9	6.39	61	.333	.382	0	—	0	-4	-3	-0	-1.2
KC-A	2	0	1.000	22	0	0	0	4	19¹	28	0	13	15	19.1	5.12	80	.329	.418	0	—	0	-3	-2	-0	-0.9
1974 KC-A	2	3	.400	30	0	0	0	1	35¹	32	3	12	24	12.2	3.82	100	.244	.327	0	—	0	-1	-0	-1	-0.5
1975 Phi-N	0	0	—	25	0	0	0	0	21	25	3	8	20	14.6	2.57	145	.298	.366	0	.000	-0	2	3	-1	-0.1
1976 Tex-A	0	4	.000	41	0	0	0	8	35	41	3	19	15	15.4	5.14	70	.315	.403	0	—	0	-6	-6	-1	-1.1
1977 Cin-N	0	0	—	8	0	0	0	0	5²	9	3	3	5	23.8	12.71	31	.375	.500	0	—	0	-6	-6	-0	0.0
Total 14	39	34	.534	493	0	0	0	99	562²	519	50	181	412	11.5	2.99	119	.249	.314	6	.102	-1	35	36	-7	4.9

● **LEFTY HOERST**   Hoerst, Frank Joseph b: 8/11/17, Philadelphia, Pa. BL/TL, 6'3", 192 lbs. Deb: 4/26/40

YEAR TM/L	W	L	PCT	G	GS	CG	SH	SV	IP	H	HR	BB	SO	RAT	ERA	ERA+	OAV	OOB	BH	AVG	PB	PR	/A	PD	TPI
1940 Phi-N	1	0	1.000	6	0	0	0	0	12	12	1	8	3	15.0	5.25	74	.250	.357	0	.000	-0	-2	-2	1	-0.1
1941 Phi-N	3	10	.231	37	11	1	0	0	105²	111	7	50	33	13.8	5.20	71	.275	.357	4	.182	0	-18	-18	2	-1.7
1942 Phi-N	4	16	.200	33	22	5	0	1	150¹	162	11	78	52	14.4	5.20	64	.271	.357	7	.152	-0	-32	-32	2	-3.7
1946 Phi-N	1	6	.143	18	7	2	0	0	68¹	77	4	36	17	15.0	4.61	74	.288	.375	1	.059	-1	-9	-9	-1	-1.1
1947 Phi-N	1	1	.500	4	1	0	0	0	11¹	19	1	3	0	17.5	7.94	50	.358	.393	2	.500	1	-5	-5	-0	-0.6
Total 5	10	33	.233	98	41	8	0	1	348	381	24	175	105	14.5	5.17	68	.279	.362	14	.154	-1	-66	-65	4	-7.2

● **RED HOFF**   Hoff, Chester Cornelius b: 5/8/1891, Ossining, N.Y. BL/TL, 5'9", 162 lbs. Deb: 9/6/11

YEAR TM/L	W	L	PCT	G	GS	CG	SH	SV	IP	H	HR	BB	SO	RAT	ERA	ERA+	OAV	OOB	BH	AVG	PB	PR	/A	PD	TPI
1911 NY-A	0	1	.000	5	1	0	0	0	20²	21	0	7	10	12.2	2.18	165	.262	.322	2	.286	-0	3	3	1	0.2
1912 NY-A	0	1	.000	5	1	0	0	0	15²	20	0	6	14	14.9	6.89	52	.303	.361	1	.200	-0	-6	-6	-0	-0.3
1913 NY-A	0	0	—	2	0	0	0	0	3	0	0	1	2	3.0	0.00	—	.000	.111	0	—	-0	1	1	-0	0.1
1915 StL-A	2	2	.500	11	3	2	0	0	43²	26	0	24	23	10.5	1.24	232	.169	.285	3	.176	-1	8	8	1	0.7
Total 4	2	4	.333	23	5	2	0	0	83	67	0	38	49	11.5	2.49	127	.218	.305	6	.200	-1	6	6	1	0.6

● **BILL HOFFER**   Hoffer, William Leopold "Chick" or "Wizard"
b: 11/8/1870, Cedar Rapids, Iowa d: 7/21/59, Cedar Rapids, Ia. BR/TR, 5'9", 155 lbs. Deb: 4/26/1895

YEAR TM/L	W	L	PCT	G	GS	CG	SH	SV	IP	H	HR	BB	SO	RAT	ERA	ERA+	OAV	OOB	BH	AVG	PB	PR	/A	PD	TPI
1895 *Bal-N	31	6	**.838**	41	38	32	**4**	0	314	296	9	124	80	12.6	3.21	148	.245	.325	27	.214	-3	55	54	-2	4.3
1896 *Bal-N	25	7	**.781**	35	35	32	3	0	309	317	1	95	93	12.3	3.38	127	.263	.323	38	.304	11	34	31	2	3.6
1897 *Bal-N	22	11	.667	38	33	29	1	0	303¹	350	5	104	62	14.0	4.30	97	.287	.351	33	.237	2	0	-4	-0	-0.3
1898 Bal-N	0	4	.000	4	4	4	0	0	34¹	62	0	16	5	20.7	7.34	49	.386	.445	5	.208	-0	-14	-14	-0	-1.2
Pit-N	3	0	1.000	4	3	3	0	0	31	26	0	15	11	11.9	1.74	204	.226	.316	1	.091	-1	6	6	-0	0.5
Yr	3	4	.429	8	7	7	0	0	65¹	88	0	31	16	16.4	4.68	76	.318	.387	6	.171	-0	-8	-8	-0	-0.7
1899 Pit-N	8	10	.444	23	19	15	2	0	163²	169	5	64	44	13.4	3.63	105	.266	.343	18	.198	-1	4	3	-0	0.2
1901 Cle-A	3	8	.273	16	10	10	0	**3**	99	113	2	35	19	13.5	4.55	78	.283	.343	6	.136	-1	-10	-11	-0	-1.1
Total 6	92	46	.667	161	142	125	10	3	1254¹	1333	22	453	314	13.2	3.75	112	.270	.339	128	.229	6	76	65	-1	6.0

● **DANNY HOFFMAN**   Hoffman, Daniel John b: 3/2/1880, Canaan, Conn. d: 3/14/22, Manchester, Conn. BL/TL, 5'9", 175 lbs. Deb: 4/20/03 ♦

YEAR TM/L	W	L	PCT	G	GS	CG	SH	SV	IP	H	HR	BB	SO	RAT	ERA	ERA+	OAV	OOB	BH	AVG	PB	PR	/A	PD	TPI
1903 Phi-A	0	0	—	1	0	0	0	0	3	2	0	2	0	12.0	3.00	102	.189	.319	61	.246	0	-0	0	-0	0.0

● **FRANK HOFFMAN**   Hoffman, Frank J. "The Texas Wonder" b: Houston, Tex. TR, Deb: 8/13/1888

YEAR TM/L	W	L	PCT	G	GS	CG	SH	SV	IP	H	HR	BB	SO	RAT	ERA	ERA+	OAV	OOB	BH	AVG	PB	PR	/A	PD	TPI
1888 KC-a	3	9	.250	12	12	12	0	0	104	102	3	42	38	13.0	2.77	124	.247	.326	6	.154	-1	3	8	0	0.7

● **GUY HOFFMAN**   Hoffman, Guy Alan b: 7/9/56, Ottawa, Ill. BL/TL, 5'9", 185 lbs. Deb: 7/4/79

YEAR TM/L	W	L	PCT	G	GS	CG	SH	SV	IP	H	HR	BB	SO	RAT	ERA	ERA+	OAV	OOB	BH	AVG	PB	PR	/A	PD	TPI
1979 Chi-A	0	5	.000	24	0	0	0	2	30¹	30	0	23	18	16.0	5.34	80	.261	.388	0	—	0	-4	-4	0	-0.6
1980 Chi-A	1	0	1.000	23	1	0	0	1	37²	34	1	17	24	13.1	2.63	153	.268	.346	0	—	0	6	6	-1	0.1
1983 Chi-A	1	0	1.000	11	0	0	0	0	6	14	1	2	2	24.0	7.50	56	.483	.516	0	—	0	-2	-2	-0	-0.6
1986 Chi-N	6	2	.750	32	8	1	0	0	84	92	6	29	47	13.2	3.86	105	.288	.351	1	.067	-1	-1	2	-1	-0.1
1987 Cin-N	9	10	.474	36	22	0	0	0	158²	160	20	49	87	12.1	4.37	97	.265	.325	5	.111	-2	-5	-3	-2	-0.6
1988 Tex-A	0	0	—	11	0	0	0	0	22¹	22	5	8	9	12.5	5.24	78	.247	.316	0	—	0	-3	-1	-0	-0.1
Total 6	17	17	.500	137	31	1	0	3	339	356	33	128	187	13.1	4.25	98	.274	.343	6	.100	-2	-10	-3	-4	-1.9

● **TREVOR HOFFMAN**   Hoffman, Trevor William b: 10/13/67, Bellflower, Cal. BR/TR, 6'1", 200 lbs. Deb: 4/6/93 F

YEAR TM/L	W	L	PCT	G	GS	CG	SH	SV	IP	H	HR	BB	SO	RAT	ERA	ERA+	OAV	OOB	BH	AVG	PB	PR	/A	PD	TPI
1993 Fla-N	2	2	.500	28	0	0	0	2	35²	24	5	19	26	10.9	3.28	132	.185	.289	0	.000	-0	3	4	0	0.5
SD-N	2	4	.333	39	0	0	0	3	54¹	56	5	20	53	12.8	4.31	96	.264	.330	1	.200	0	-2	-1	-0	-0.2
Yr	4	6	.400	67	0	0	0	5	90	80	10	39	79	12.0	3.90	108	.233	.313	1	.143	-0	1	3	0	0.3
1994 SD-N	4	4	.500	47	0	0	0	20	56	39	4	20	68	9.5	2.57	163	.193	.266	0	.000	-0	10	10	0	2.1
Total 2	8	10	.444	114	0	0	0	25	146	119	14	59	147	11.0	3.39	124	.219	.296	1	.100	-1	12	13	0	2.4

● **BILL HOFFMAN**   Hoffman, William Joseph b: 3/3/18, Philadelphia, Pa. BL/TL, 5'9", 170 lbs. Deb: 8/13/39

YEAR TM/L	W	L	PCT	G	GS	CG	SH	SV	IP	H	HR	BB	SO	RAT	ERA	ERA+	OAV	OOB	BH	AVG	PB	PR	/A	PD	TPI
1939 Phi-N	0	0	—	3	0	0	0	0	6	8	2	7	1	27.0	13.50	30	.333	.529	0	.000	-0	-6	-6	-0	0.0

● **JOHN HOFFORD**   Hofford, John William b: 5/25/1863, Philadelphia, Pa. d: 12/16/15, Philadelphia, Pa. Deb: 9/26/1885

YEAR TM/L	W	L	PCT	G	GS	CG	SH	SV	IP	H	HR	BB	SO	RAT	ERA	ERA+	OAV	OOB	BH	AVG	PB	PR	/A	PD	TPI
1885 Pit-a	0	3	.000	3	3	3	0	0	25	28	1	9	21	13.3	3.60	89	.275	.333	1	.125	-1	-1	-1	0	-0.1

YEAR TM/L	W	L	PCT	G	GS	CG	SH	SV	IP	H	HR	BB	SO	RAT	ERA	ERA+	OAV	OOB	BH	AVG	PB	PR	/A	PD	TPI
1886 Pit-a	3	6	.333	9	9	9	0	0	81	88	1	40	25	14.4	4.33	78	.261	.343	10	.294	3	-8	-9	1	-0.4
Total 2	3	9	.250	12	12	12	0	0	106	116	2	49	46	14.2	4.16	80	.264	.341	11	.262	2	-9	-10	1	-0.5

● **GEORGE HOGAN**   Hogan, George A. b: 9/25/1885, Marion, Ohio d: 2/22/22, Bartlesville, Okla   BR/TR, 6′, 160 lbs. Deb: 4/18/14 F

YEAR TM/L	W	L	PCT	G	GS	CG	SH	SV	IP	H	HR	BB	SO	RAT	ERA	ERA+	OAV	OOB	BH	AVG	PB	PR	/A	PD	TPI
1914 KC-F	0	1	.000	4	1	0	0	0	13	12	1	7	7	13.8	4.15	67	.255	.364	0	.000	-1	-2	-2	0	-0.2

● **EDDIE HOGAN**   Hogan, Robert Edward b: 4/1860, St.Louis, Mo.   BR, 5′7″, 153 lbs. Deb: 7/5/1882 ♦

YEAR TM/L	W	L	PCT	G	GS	CG	SH	SV	IP	H	HR	BB	SO	RAT	ERA	ERA+	OAV	OOB	BH	AVG	PB	PR	/A	PD	TPI
1882 StL-a	0	1	.000	1	1	1	0	0	8	10	0	0	4	11.3	1.13	249	.287	.287	1	.333	0	1	1	-1	0.1

● **BRAD HOGG**   Hogg, Carter Bradley b: 3/26/1888, Buena Vista, Ga. d: 4/2/35, Buena Vista, Ga.   BR/TR, 6′, 185 lbs. Deb: 9/1/11

YEAR TM/L	W	L	PCT	G	GS	CG	SH	SV	IP	H	HR	BB	SO	RAT	ERA	ERA+	OAV	OOB	BH	AVG	PB	PR	/A	PD	TPI
1911 Bos-N	0	3	.000	8	3	2	0	1	25²	33	0	14	8	16.8	6.66	57	.337	.425	4	.444	1	-9	-8	0	-0.7
1912 Bos-N	1	1	.500	10	1	0	0	1	31	37	2	16	12	16.0	6.97	51	.308	.389	1	.091	-1	-12	-12	-1	-0.8
1915 Chi-N	1	0	1.000	2	2	1	1	0	13	12	1	6	10	13.2	2.08	134	.245	.339	0	.000	-0	1	1	0	0.1
1918 Phi-N	13	13	.500	29	25	17	3	1	228	201	3	61	81	10.6	2.53	119	.245	.302	18	.228	3	6	12	2	2.0
1919 Phi-N	5	12	.294	22	19	13	0	0	150¹	163	7	55	48	13.4	4.43	73	.292	.360	17	.283	1	-25	-20	-2	-2.1
Total 5	20	29	.408	71	50	33	4	3	448	446	13	152	149	12.3	3.70	85	.271	.338	40	.247	5	-40	-27	-1	-1.5

● **BILL HOGG**   Hogg, William Johnston "Buffalo Bill" b: 9/11/1881, Port Huron, Mich. d: 12/8/09, New Orleans, La.   BR/TR, 6′, 200 lbs. Deb: 4/25/05

YEAR TM/L	W	L	PCT	G	GS	CG	SH	SV	IP	H	HR	BB	SO	RAT	ERA	ERA+	OAV	OOB	BH	AVG	PB	PR	/A	PD	TPI
1905 NY-A	9	13	.409	39	22	9	3	1	205	178	1	101	125	12.8	3.20	92	.235	.335	4	.060	-6	-12	-6	-5	-1.8
1906 NY-A	14	13	.519	28	25	15	3	0	206	171	5	72	107	11.1	2.93	101	.229	.307	9	.125	-5	-5	1	-5	-0.9
1907 NY-A	10	8	.556	25	21	13	0	0	166²	173	3	83	64	14.1	3.08	91	.269	.358	11	.183	-1	-10	-5	-1	-0.7
1908 NY-A	4	16	.200	24	21	6	0	0	152¹	155	4	63	72	13.1	3.01	82	.262	.337	4	.093	-3	-10	-9	-2	-1.7
Total 4	37	50	.425	116	89	43	6	1	730	677	13	319	368	12.7	3.06	92	.247	.334	28	.116	-14	-38	-20	-12	-5.1

● **CHIEF HOGSETT**   Hogsett, Elon Chester b: 11/2/03, Brownell, Kan.   BL/TL, 6′, 190 lbs. Deb: 9/18/29

YEAR TM/L	W	L	PCT	G	GS	CG	SH	SV	IP	H	HR	BB	SO	RAT	ERA	ERA+	OAV	OOB	BH	AVG	PB	PR	/A	PD	TPI
1929 Det-A	1	2	.333	4	4	2	1	0	28²	34	0	9	9	13.8	2.83	152	.312	.370	2	.200	-0	5	5	0	0.4
1930 Det-A	9	8	.529	33	17	4	0	1	146	174	9	63	54	15.2	5.42	88	.300	.377	17	.293	3	-13	-10	2	-0.6
1931 Det-A	3	9	.250	22	12	5	0	2	112¹	150	8	33	47	15.1	5.93	77	.324	.375	11	.234	0	-19	-17	0	-1.5
1932 Det-A	11	9	.550	47	15	7	0	7	178	201	8	66	56	13.8	3.54	133	.286	.351	14	.246	1	19	23	2	2.9
1933 Det-A	6	10	.375	45	2	0	0	9	116	137	7	56	39	15.3	4.50	96	.296	.377	8	.211	-0	-3	-2	1	-0.3
1934 *Det-A	3	2	.600	26	0	0	0	3	50¹	61	4	19	23	14.5	4.29	102	.303	.367	3	.231	-0	1	1	1	0.1
1935 *Det-A	6	6	.500	40	0	0	0	5	96²	109	4	49	39	15.2	3.54	118	.288	.377	6	.261	2	10	7	3	1.2
1936 Det-A	0	1	.000	3	0	0	0	0	4	8	1	1	1	20.3	9.00	55	.400	.429	0	—	-0	-2	-2	0	-0.3
StL-A	13	15	.464	39	29	10	1	0	215¹	278	15	90	67	16.0	5.52	97	.310	.383	10	.143	-2	-11	-3	-1	-0.5
Yr	13	16	.448	42	29	10	1	0	219¹	286	16	91	68	16.1	5.58	96	.312	.384	10	.143	-2	-13	-5	-1	-0.8
1937 StL-A	6	19	.240	37	26	8	1	2	177¹	245	19	75	68	16.5	6.29	77	.328	.393	13	.210	-0	-33	-29	-1	-3.3
1938 Was-A	5	6	.455	31	9	1	0	3	91	107	12	36	33	14.9	6.03	75	.292	.368	7	.304	3	-13	-15	0	-1.3
1944 Det-A	0	0	—	3	0	0	0	0	6¹	7	1	4	1	18.5	0.00	—	.250	.382	0	.000	-0	2	3	-0	0.0
Total 11	63	87	.420	330	114	37	2	33	1222	1511	85	501	441	15.3	5.02	94	.305	.376	91	.226	8	-57	-42	9	-3.2

● **CAL HOGUE**   Hogue, Calvin Grey b: 10/24/27, Dayton, Ohio BR/TR, 6′, 185 lbs. Deb: 7/15/52

YEAR TM/L	W	L	PCT	G	GS	CG	SH	SV	IP	H	HR	BB	SO	RAT	ERA	ERA+	OAV	OOB	BH	AVG	PB	PR	/A	PD	TPI
1952 Pit-N	1	8	.111	19	12	3	0	0	83²	79	4	68	34	16.2	4.84	82	.258	.399	6	.250	1	-10	-8	-2	-0.8
1953 Pit-N	1	1	.500	3	2	2	0	0	19	19	4	16	10	17.1	5.21	86	.250	.387	0	.000	-1	-2	-2	0	-0.2
1954 Pit-N	0	1	.000	3	2	0	0	0	11	11	4	12	7	18.8	4.91	85	.282	.451	0	.000	-0	-1	-1	0	-0.1
Total 3	2	10	.167	25	16	5	0	0	113²	109	12	96	51	16.6	4.91	83	.259	.402	6	.188	0	-13	-10	-1	-1.1

● **BOBBY HOGUE**   Hogue, Robert Clinton b: 4/5/21, Miami, Fla. d: 12/22/87, Miami, Fla.   BR/TR, 5′10″, 195 lbs. Deb: 4/24/48

YEAR TM/L	W	L	PCT	G	GS	CG	SH	SV	IP	H	HR	BB	SO	RAT	ERA	ERA+	OAV	OOB	BH	AVG	PB	PR	/A	PD	TPI
1948 Bos-N	8	2	.800	40	1	0	0	2	86¹	88	4	19	43	11.4	3.23	119	.265	.309	2	.095	-1	7	6	1	0.4
1949 Bos-N	2	2	.500	33	0	0	0	3	72	78	4	25	23	13.1	3.13	121	.280	.343	6	.286	1	7	5	2	0.6
1950 Bos-N	3	5	.375	36	1	0	0	7	62²	69	8	31	15	14.9	5.03	77	.280	.370	3	.231	1	-6	-8	1	-1.0
1951 Bos-N	0	0	—	3	0	0	0	0	5	4	1	3	0	12.6	5.40	68	.235	.350	1	.500	0	-1	-1	-0	0.0
StL-A	1	1	.500	18	0	0	0	1	29²	31	1	23	11	16.4	5.16	85	.279	.403	2	.667	-1	-3	-3	1	0.0
*NY-A	1	0	1.000	7	0	0	0	0	7¹	4	0	3	2	8.6	0.00	—	.174	.269	0	—	0	3	3	0	0.4
Yr	2	1	.667	25	0	0	0	1	37	35	1	26	13	14.8	4.14	104	.261	.381	2	.667	1	-0	1	1	0.4
1952 NY-A	3	5	.375	27	0	0	0	4	47¹	52	8	25	12	14.8	5.32	62	.294	.384	3	.273	0	-9	-11	-1	-1.9
StL-A	0	1	.000	8	1	0	0	0	16¹	10	1	13	2	12.7	2.76	142	.179	.333	0	.000	-0	2	2	0	0.1
Yr	3	6	.333	35	1	0	0	4	63²	62	7	38	14	14.1	4.66	74	.265	.368	3	.231	0	-7	-8	-1	-1.8
Total 5	18	16	.529	172	3	0	0	17	326²	336	25	142	108	13.4	3.97	96	.271	.350	17	.233	3	0	-6	1	-1.4

● **WALLY HOLBOROW**   Holborow, Walter Albert b: 11/30/13, New York, N.Y. d: 7/14/86, Ft.Lauderdale, Fla.   BR/TR, 5′11″, 187 lbs. Deb: 9/27/44

YEAR TM/L	W	L	PCT	G	GS	CG	SH	SV	IP	H	HR	BB	SO	RAT	ERA	ERA+	OAV	OOB	BH	AVG	PB	PR	/A	PD	TPI
1944 Was-A	0	0	—	1	0	0	0	0	3	0	0	2	1	6.0	0.00	—	.000	.182	0	—	1	1	0	0	0.0
1945 Was-A	1	1	.500	15	1	1	1	0	31¹	20	0	16	14	10.3	2.30	135	.189	.295	0	.000	-0	4	3	-1	0.1
1948 Phi-A	1	2	.333	5	1	0	0	0	17¹	32	1	7	3	20.3	5.71	75	.421	.470	2	.500	1	-3	-3	1	-0.2
Total 3	2	3	.400	21	2	2	1	0	51²	52	1	25	18	13.4	3.31	106	.272	.356	2	.333	1	2	1	-0	-0.1

● **KEN HOLCOMBE**   Holcombe, Kenneth Edward b: 8/23/18, Burnsville, N.C.   BR/TR, 5′11.5″, 169 lbs. Deb: 4/27/45

YEAR TM/L	W	L	PCT	G	GS	CG	SH	SV	IP	H	HR	BB	SO	RAT	ERA	ERA+	OAV	OOB	BH	AVG	PB	PR	/A	PD	TPI
1945 NY-A	3	3	.500	23	6	2	0	0	55¹	43	2	27	20	11.4	1.79	194	.226	.323	2	.133	-1	10	10	-0	1.0
1948 Cin-N	0	0	—	2	0	0	0	0	2¹	3	0	2	1	15.7	7.71	51	.300	.300	0	—	-1	-1	-0	0	0.0
1950 Chi-A	3	10	.231	24	15	5	0	1	96	122	10	45	37	15.7	4.59	98	.307	.378	5	.156	-2	-0	-1	-0	-0.3
1951 Chi-A	11	12	.478	28	23	12	2	0	159¹	142	9	69	39	11.9	3.78	107	.241	.321	11	.250	1	6	4	2	0.9
1952 Chi-A	0	5	.000	7	7	1	0	0	35	38	3	18	12	14.9	6.17	59	.286	.379	0	.000	-1	-10	-10	-1	-1.3
StL-A	0	2	.000	12	1	0	0	0	21	20	1	9	7	12.4	3.86	101	.263	.341	1	.333	-0	-0	-0	1	0.1
Yr	0	7	.000	19	8	1	0	0	56	58	4	27	19	13.7	5.30	71	.275	.357	1	.077	-1	-10	-10	1	-1.2
1953 Bos-A	1	0	1.000	3	0	0	0	0	6	9	0	2	2	18.0	6.00	70	.333	.400	0	.000	-0	-1	-1	0	-0.2
Total 6	18	32	.360	99	48	18	2	2	375	377	25	170	118	13.2	3.98	101	.265	.345	19	.179	-3	3	3	3	0.2

● **FRED HOLDSWORTH**   Holdsworth, Fredrick William b: 5/29/52, Detroit, Mich.   BR/TR, 6′1″, 190 lbs. Deb: 7/27/72

YEAR TM/L	W	L	PCT	G	GS	CG	SH	SV	IP	H	HR	BB	SO	RAT	ERA	ERA+	OAV	OOB	BH	AVG	PB	PR	/A	PD	TPI
1972 Det-A	0	1	.000	2	2	0	0	0	7	7	3	2	5	19.3	12.86	24	.419	.455	1	.333	0	-8	-8	-0	-0.8
1973 Det-A	0	0	—	5	2	0	0	0	14²	13	5	9	7	11.7	6.75	61	.236	.311	0	—	0	-5	-4	-0	-0.7
1974 Det-A	0	3	.000	8	5	0	0	0	35²	40	4	14	16	13.9	4.29	89	.286	.355	0	—	-0	-3	-4	-1	-0.5
1976 Bal-A	4	1	.800	16	0	0	0	2	39²	24	0	13	24	8.4	2.04	160	.179	.252	0	—	0	7	5	-0	0.9
1977 Bal-A	0	1	.000	12	0	0	0	0	14¹	17	0	16	9	21.3	6.28	60	.333	.500	0	—	-0	-4	-4	-0	-0.2
Mon-N	3	3	.500	14	6	0	0	0	42¹	35	6	18	21	11.3	3.19	119	.230	.312	0	.000	-1	3	3	0	0.3
1978 Mon-N	0	0	—	6	0	0	0	0	8²	16	3	8	3	24.9	7.27	48	.381	.480	0	—	-0	-4	-4	0	-0.2
1980 Mil-A	0	0	—	9	0	0	0	0	19²	24	2	9	9	15.1	4.58	85	.286	.355	0	—	0	-2	-2	0	-0.2
Total 7	7	10	.412	72	15	0	0	4	182	182	18	86	94	13.4	4.40	84	.264	.347	1	.077	-1	-13	-15	-2	-0.4

● **WALTER HOLKE**   Holke, Walter Henry "Union Man" b: 12/25/1892, St.Louis, Mo. d: 10/12/54, St.Louis, Mo.   BB/TL, 6′1.5″, 185 lbs. Deb: 10/6/14 C♦

YEAR TM/L	W	L	PCT	G	GS	CG	SH	SV	IP	H	HR	BB	SO	RAT	ERA	ERA+	OAV	OOB	BH	AVG	PB	PR	/A	PD	TPI
1923 Phi-N	0	0	—	1	0	0	0	0	0¹	1	0	0	0	27.0	0.00	—	.500	.500	175	.311	0	0	0	0	0.0

● **AL HOLLAND**   Holland, Alfred Willis b: 8/16/52, Roanoke, Va.   BR/TL, 5′11″, 207 lbs. Deb: 9/5/77

YEAR TM/L	W	L	PCT	G	GS	CG	SH	SV	IP	H	HR	BB	SO	RAT	ERA	ERA+	OAV	OOB	BH	AVG	PB	PR	/A	PD	TPI
1977 Pit-N	0	0	—	2	0	0	0	0	2¹	4	0	0	1	15.4	7.71	52	.400	.400	0	—	0	-1	-1	0	0.0
1979 SF-N	0	0	—	3	0	0	0	0	7	3	0	5	9	10.3	0.00	—	.125	.276	0	—	0	3	3	-0	0.0
1980 SF-N	5	3	.625	54	0	0	0	7	82¹	71	2	34	65	11.6	1.75	202	.233	.312	1	.200	1	17	16	0	2.1
1981 SF-N	7	5	.583	47	0	0	0	7	100²	87	4	44	78	11.9	2.41	142	.233	.317	1	.063	-1	12	11	-1	1.4
1982 SF-N	7	3	.700	58	7	0	0	5	129²	115	12	40	97	10.8	3.33	108	.231	.289	2	.059	-3	4	4	0	0.0

YEAR TM/L	W	L	PCT	G	GS	CG	SH	SV	IP	H	HR	BB	SO	RAT	ERA	ERA+	OAV	OOB	BH	AVG	PB	PR	/A	PD	TPI
1983 *Phi-N	8	4	.667	68	0	0	0	25	91²	63	8	30	100	9.1	2.26	158	.188	.255	0	.000	-1	14	13	-2	2.3
1984 Phi-N☆	5	10	.333	68	0	0	0	29	98¹	82	14	30	61	10.3	3.39	107	.225	.286	0	.000	-1	2	3	-2	0.3
1985 Phi-N	0	1	.000	3	0	0	0	1	4	5	0	4	1	20.3	4.50	82	.333	.474	0	—	0	-0	-0	-0	-0.1
Pit-N	1	3	.250	38	0	0	0	4	58²	48	5	17	47	10.0	3.38	106	.227	.285	2	.400	2	1	1	-1	0.2
Yr	1	4	.200	41	0	0	0	5	62²	53	5	21	48	10.6	3.45	104	.233	.298	2	.400	2	1	1	-1	0.1
Cal-A	1	0	1.000	15	0	0	0	0	24¹	17	4	10	14	10.0	1.48	278	.193	.276	0	—	0	7	7	-0	0.3
1986 NY-A	1	0	1.000	25	1	0	0	0	40²	44	5	9	37	11.7	5.09	80	.268	.306	0	—	0	-4	-5	-1	-0.2
1987 NY-A	0	0	—	3	0	0	0	0	6¹	9	1	9	5	25.6	14.21	31	.321	.486	0	—	0	-7	-7	-0	0.0
Total 10	34	30	.531	384	11	0	0	78	646	548	55	232	513	10.9	2.98	121	.227	.296	6	.083	-2	48	46	-6	6.3

● **MUL HOLLAND** Holland, Howard Arthur b: 1/6/03, Franklin, Va. d: 2/16/69, Winchester, Va. BR/TR, 6'4", 185 lbs. Deb: 5/25/26

YEAR TM/L	W	L	PCT	G	GS	CG	SH	SV	IP	H	HR	BB	SO	RAT	ERA	ERA+	OAV	OOB	BH	AVG	PB	PR	/A	PD	TPI
1926 Cin-N	0	0	—	3	0	0	0	0	6²	3	0	5	0	10.8	1.35	273	.136	.296	1	.500	0	2	2	1	0.1
1927 NY-N	1	0	1.000	2	0	0	0	0	2	0	0	3	0	13.5	0.00	—	.000	.333	0	—	0	1	1	-0	0.4
1929 StL-N	0	1	.000	8	0	0	0	0	14¹	13	3	7	5	13.2	9.42	50	.232	.328	1	.250	0	-7	-8	-0	-0.4
Total 3	1	1	.500	13	0	0	0	0	23	16	3	15	5	12.5	6.26	69	.190	.320	2	.333	1	-5	-5	0	0.1

● **BILL HOLLAND** Holland, William David "Dutch" b: 6/4/15, Varina, N.C. BL/TL, 6'1", 190 lbs. Deb: 9/17/39

YEAR TM/L	W	L	PCT	G	GS	CG	SH	SV	IP	H	HR	BB	SO	RAT	ERA	ERA+	OAV	OOB	BH	AVG	PB	PR	/A	PD	TPI
1939 Was-A	0	1	.000	3	0	0	0	0	4	6	1	5	2	24.8	11.25	39	.400	.550	0	—	0	-3	-3	0	-0.6

● **ED HOLLEY** Holley, Edward Edgar b: 7/23/1899, Benton, Ky. d: 10/26/86, Paducah, Ky. BR/TR, 6'1.5", 195 lbs. Deb: 5/24/28

YEAR TM/L	W	L	PCT	G	GS	CG	SH	SV	IP	H	HR	BB	SO	RAT	ERA	ERA+	OAV	OOB	BH	AVG	PB	PR	/A	PD	TPI
1928 Chi-N	0	0	—	13	1	0	0	0	31	31	1	16	10	14.2	3.77	102	.265	.363	0	.000	-0	1	0	-1	-0.1
1932 Phi-N	11	14	.440	34	30	16	2	0	228	247	15	55	87	12.2	3.95	102	.273	.319	12	.132	-6	-2	12	-2	0.4
1933 Phi-N	13	15	.464	30	28	12	3	0	206²	219	18	62	56	12.8	3.53	108	.273	.335	12	.162	-2	-4	7	-3	0.4
1934 Phi-N	1	8	.111	15	13	2	0	0	72²	85	10	31	14	14.9	7.18	66	.294	.370	5	.208	-1	-25	-20	-1	-2.2
Pit-N	0	3	.000	5	4	0	0	0	9¹	20	1	6	2	27.0	15.43	27	.426	.509	2	1.000	2	-12	-12	0	-2.4
Yr	1	11	.083	20	17	2	0	0	82	105	11	37	16	15.8	8.12	57	.309	.380	7	.269	1	-37	-32	-1	-4.6
Total 4	25	40	.385	97	76	30	5	0	547²	602	45	170	169	13.1	4.40	95	.279	.339	31	.158	-8	-42	-13	-6	-3.9

● **BUG HOLLIDAY** Holliday, James Wear b: 2/8/1867, St.Louis, Mo. d: 2/15/10, Cincinnati, Ohio BR/TR, 5'11", 151 lbs. Deb: 4/17/1889 U♦

YEAR TM/L	W	L	PCT	G	GS	CG	SH	SV	IP	H	HR	BB	SO	RAT	ERA	ERA+	OAV	OOB	BH	AVG	PB	PR	/A	PD	TPI
1892 Cin-N	0	0	—	1	0	0	0	0	4	13	1	0	0	31.5	11.25	29	.520	.539	176	.292	0	-4	-4	0	0.0
1896 Cin-N	0	0	—	1	0	0	0	0	1	4	0	2	0	63.0	0.00	—	.582	.709	27	.321	0	0	1	-0	0.0
Total 2	0	0	—	2	0	0	0	0	5	17	0	3	0	37.8	9.00	39	.533	.585	1134	.311	1	-3	-3	-0	0.0

● **CARL HOLLING** Holling, Carl b: 7/9/1896, Dana, Cal. d: 7/18/62, Santa Rosa, Cal. BR/TR, 6'1", 172 lbs. Deb: 4/19/21

YEAR TM/L	W	L	PCT	G	GS	CG	SH	SV	IP	H	HR	BB	SO	RAT	ERA	ERA+	OAV	OOB	BH	AVG	PB	PR	/A	PD	TPI
1921 Det-A	3	7	.300	35	11	4	0	4	136	162	8	58	38	14.8	4.30	99	.305	.378	13	.271	1	-0	-2	2	0.2
1922 Det-A	1	1	.500	5	1	0	0	0	9¹	21	1	5	2	27.0	15.43	55	.525	.596	0	.000	-0	-12	-10	-1	-1.9
Total 2	4	8	.333	40	12	4	0	4	145¹	183	9	63	40	15.6	5.02	85	.320	.394	13	.260	1	-12	-12	2	-1.7

● **AL HOLLINGSWORTH** Hollingsworth, Albert Wayne "Boots" b: 2/25/08, St.Louis, Mo. BL/TL, 6', 174 lbs. Deb: 4/16/35 C

YEAR TM/L	W	L	PCT	G	GS	CG	SH	SV	IP	H	HR	BB	SO	RAT	ERA	ERA+	OAV	OOB	BH	AVG	PB	PR	/A	PD	TPI
1935 Cin-N	6	13	.316	38	22	8	0	0	173¹	165	5	76	89	12.6	3.89	102	.243	.321	8	.148	-2	2	2	1	0.0
1936 Cin-N	9	10	.474	29	25	9	0	0	184	204	4	66	76	13.5	4.16	92	.281	.345	23	.315	7	-3	-7	-2	-0.1
1937 Cin-N	9	15	.375	43	24	11	1	5	202¹	224	8	73	74	13.3	3.91	95	.278	.339	19	.250	3	0	-4	1	-0.1
1938 Cin-N	2	2	.500	9	4	1	0	1	34	43	2	12	13	14.6	7.15	51	.307	.362	1	.250	1	-13	-13	0	-1.2
Phi-N	5	16	.238	24	21	11	1	0	174¹	177	4	77	80	13.1	3.82	102	.264	.340	15	.224	-0	-1	1	-2	-0.1
Yr	7	18	.280	33	25	12	1	0	208¹	220	6	89	93	13.3	4.36	88	.272	.344	18	.228	1	-13	-12	-2	-1.3
1939 Phi-N	1	9	.100	15	10	3	0	0	60	78	2	27	24	15.8	5.85	69	.317	.385	2	.100	-1	-13	-12	1	-1.9
Bro-N	1	2	.333	8	5	1	0	0	27¹	33	1	11	11	14.8	5.27	76	.311	.381	1	.125	-1	-4	-4	1	-0.3
Yr	2	11	.154	23	15	4	0	0	87¹	111	3	38	35	15.5	5.67	71	.315	.384	3	.107	-2	-17	-16	1	-2.2
1940 Was-A	1	0	1.000	3	2	0	0	0	18	18	0	11	7	14.5	5.50	76	.261	.363	1	.167	0	-2	-3	1	0.0
1942 StL-A	10	6	.625	33	18	7	1	4	161	173	4	52	60	12.7	2.96	125	.272	.329	10	.179	0	12	13	0	1.4
1943 StL-A	6	13	.316	35	20	9	1	3	154	169	7	51	63	13.0	4.21	79	.281	.339	7	.140	-1	-16	-15	-1	-2.0
1944 *StL-A	5	7	.417	26	10	3	2	1	92²	108	3	37	22	14.2	4.47	81	.291	.357	2	.071	-2	-11	-9	-1	-1.4
1945 StL-A	12	9	.571	26	22	15	1	1	173¹	164	4	68	64	12.0	2.70	130	.251	.322	12	.197	1	13	16	2	2.2
1946 StL-A	0	0	—	5	0	0	0	0	11	23	1	4	9	22.1	6.55	57	.411	.450	0	.000	-0	-4	-3	-1	-0.1
Chi-A	3	2	.600	21	2	0	0	0	55	63	2	22	22	13.0	4.58	74	.288	.353	0	.000	-1	-7	-7	-0	-0.8
Yr	3	2	.600	26	2	0	0	0	66	86	3	26	31	15.3	4.91	71	.313	.372	0	.000	-1	-10	-11	-1	-0.9
Total 11	70	104	.402	315	185	78	7	15	1520¹	1642	47	587	608	13.3	3.99	93	.275	.341	103	.196	3	-44	-44	-2	-4.4

● **BONNIE HOLLINGSWORTH** Hollingsworth, John Burnette b: 12/26/1895, Jacksboro, Tenn. d: 1/4/90, Knoxville, Tenn. BR/TR, 5'10", 170 lbs. Deb: 5/30/22

YEAR TM/L	W	L	PCT	G	GS	CG	SH	SV	IP	H	HR	BB	SO	RAT	ERA	ERA+	OAV	OOB	BH	AVG	PB	PR	/A	PD	TPI
1922 Pit-N	0	0	—	9	0	0	0	0	13²	17	0	8	7	17.1	7.90	52	.315	.413	0	—	0	-6	-6	-0	0.0
1923 Was-A	3	7	.300	17	8	1	0	0	72²	72	3	50	26	15.5	4.09	92	.272	.393	2	.091	-1	-1	-3	-1	-0.5
1924 Bro-N	1	0	1.000	3	1	1	0	0	8²	8	0	10	2	18.7	6.23	60	.267	.450	0	.000	-1	-2	-2	0	-0.3
1928 Bos-N	0	2	.000	7	2	0	0	0	22¹	30	2	13	10	17.3	5.24	75	.341	.426	1	.167	-0	-3	-3	0	-0.2
Total 4	4	9	.308	36	11	2	0	0	117¹	127	5	81	50	16.3	4.91	78	.291	.406	3	.097	-2	-12	-14	-1	-1.0

● **JESSIE HOLLINS** Hollins, Jessie Edward b: 1/27/70, Conroe, Tex. BR/TR, 6'3", 190 lbs. Deb: 9/19/92

YEAR TM/L	W	L	PCT	G	GS	CG	SH	SV	IP	H	HR	BB	SO	RAT	ERA	ERA+	OAV	OOB	BH	AVG	PB	PR	/A	PD	TPI
1992 Chi-N	0	0	—	4	0	0	0	0	4²	8	1	5	0	25.1	13.50	27	.400	.520	0	—	0	-5	-5	-0	0.0

● **JOHN HOLLISON** Hollison, John Henry "Swede" b: 5/3/1870, Chicago, Ill. d: 8/19/69, Chicago, Ill. BR/TL, 5'8", 162 lbs. Deb: 8/13/1892

YEAR TM/L	W	L	PCT	G	GS	CG	SH	SV	IP	H	HR	BB	SO	RAT	ERA	ERA+	OAV	OOB	BH	AVG	PB	PR	/A	PD	TPI
1892 Chi-N	0	0	—	1	0	0	0	0	4	1	1	0	2		2.25	148	.077	.077	0	.000	-0	0	0	-0	0.0

● **BOBO HOLLOMAN** Holloman, Alva Lee b: 3/7/25, Thomaston, Ga. d: 5/1/87, Athens, Ga. BR/TR, 6'2", 207 lbs. Deb: 4/18/53

YEAR TM/L	W	L	PCT	G	GS	CG	SH	SV	IP	H	HR	BB	SO	RAT	ERA	ERA+	OAV	OOB	BH	AVG	PB	PR	/A	PD	TPI
1953 StL-A	3	7	.300	22	10	1	1	0	65¹	69	2	50	25	16.5	5.23	80	.275	.397	2	.105	-2	-9	-8	-0	-1.2

● **JIM HOLLOWAY** Holloway, James Madison b: 9/22/08, Plaquemine, La. BR/TR, 6'1", 165 lbs. Deb: 5/17/29

YEAR TM/L	W	L	PCT	G	GS	CG	SH	SV	IP	H	HR	BB	SO	RAT	ERA	ERA+	OAV	OOB	BH	AVG	PB	PR	/A	PD	TPI
1929 Phi-N	0	0	—	3	0	0	0	0	4²	7	1	2	1	28.9	13.50	38	.455	.556	1	1.000	0	-5	-4	-0	0.0

● **KEN HOLLOWAY** Holloway, Kenneth Eugene (b: Kenneth Eugene Hollaway) b: 8/8/1897, Thomas County, Ga. d: 9/25/68, Thomasville, Ga. BR/TR, 6', 185 lbs. Deb: 8/27/22

YEAR TM/L	W	L	PCT	G	GS	CG	SH	SV	IP	H	HR	BB	SO	RAT	ERA	ERA+	OAV	OOB	BH	AVG	PB	PR	/A	PD	TPI
1922 Det-A	0	0	—	1	0	0	0	0	1	1	0	0	1	9.0	0.00	—	.250	.250	0	—	0	0	0	0	0.0
1923 Det-A	11	6	.524	42	24	7	1	1	194	232	12	75	55	14.7	4.45	87	.302	.372	8	.123	-5	-10	-13	1	-1.5
1924 Det-A	14	6	.700	49	14	5	0	3	181²	209	6	61	46	13.7	4.07	101	.299	.361	11	.190	-1	3	1	-2	0.2
1925 Det-A	13	4	.765	38	14	6	0	2	157²	170	8	67	29	13.6	4.62	93	.282	.356	11	.229	-1	-4	-6	-2	-0.8
1926 Det-A	4	6	.400	36	12	3	0	2	139	192	2	42	43	15.7	5.12	79	.343	.397	11	.239	-2	-17	-16	-1	-1.0
1927 Det-A	11	12	.478	36	23	11	1	6	183¹	210	10	61	36	13.5	4.07	103	.299	.359	8	.129	-5	1	3	2	0.0
1928 Det-A	4	8	.333	30	11	5	0	2	120¹	137	8	32	32	13.0	4.34	95	.291	.343	4	.121	-2	-4	-3	1	-0.4
1929 Cle-A	6	5	.545	25	11	6	2	0	119	118	2	37	32	11.9	3.03	147	.264	.323	7	.171	-2	16	19	-2	1.2
1930 Cle-A	1	1	.500	12	2	0	0	0	30	49	5	14	8	18.9	8.40	57	.374	.434	0	.000	-2	-13	-12	1	-0.9
NY-A	0	0	—	16	0	0	0	0	34¹	52	3	8	11	15.7	5.24	82	.374	.408	3	.231	-0	-2	-3	-0	0.0
Yr	1	1	.500	28	2	0	0	0	64¹	101	8	22	19	17.2	6.72	68	.374	.421	3	.120	-3	-15	-16	1	-0.9
Total 9	64	52	.552	285	111	43	4	18	1160	1370	50	397	293	14.0	4.40	95	.303	.364	63	.167	-18	-29	-30	4	-3.2

● **JEFF HOLLY** Holly, Jeffrey Owen b: 3/1/53, San Pedro, Cal. BL/TL, 6'5", 210 lbs. Deb: 5/1/77

YEAR TM/L	W	L	PCT	G	GS	CG	SH	SV	IP	H	HR	BB	SO	RAT	ERA	ERA+	OAV	OOB	BH	AVG	PB	PR	/A	PD	TPI
1977 Min-A	2	3	.400	18	5	0	0	0	48¹	57	8	12	32	13.0	6.89	58	.300	.345	0	—	0	-15	-16	-1	-1.3
1978 Min-A	1	1	.500	15	1	0	0	0	35¹	28	1	18	12	11.7	3.57	107	.222	.319	0	—	1	1	1	0	0.0

YEAR TM/L	W	L	PCT	G	GS	CG	SH	SV	IP	H	HR	BB	SO	RAT	ERA	ERA+	OAV	OOB	BH	AVG	PB	PR	/A	PD	TPI
1979 Min-A	0	0	—	6	0	0	0	0	6^1	10	0	3	5	18.5	7.11	62	.385	.448	0	—	0	-2	-2	0	0.0
Total 3	3	4	.429	39	6	0	0	0	90	95	9	33	49	12.9	5.60	70	.278	.343	0	—	0	-16	-17	-0	-1.3

● **BRAD HOLMAN** — Holman, Bradley Thomas b: 2/9/68, Kansas City, Mo. BR/TR, 6'5", 200 lbs. Deb: 7/4/93 F

YEAR TM/L	W	L	PCT	G	GS	CG	SH	SV	IP	H	HR	BB	SO	RAT	ERA	ERA+	OAV	OOB	BH	AVG	PB	PR	/A	PD	TPI
1993 Sea-A	1	3	.250	19	0	0	0	3	36^1	27	1	16	17	11.9	3.72	118	.208	.318	0	—	0	2	3	-1	0.2

● **BRIAN HOLMAN** — Holman, Brian Scott b: 1/25/65, Denver, Colo. BR/TR, 6'4", 185 lbs. Deb: 6/25/88 F

YEAR TM/L	W	L	PCT	G	GS	CG	SH	SV	IP	H	HR	BB	SO	RAT	ERA	ERA+	OAV	OOB	BH	AVG	PB	PR	/A	PD	TPI
1988 Mon-N	4	8	.333	18	16	1	1	0	100^1	101	3	34	58	12.1	3.23	111	.264	.324	3	.107	-1	2	4	-1	0.2
1989 Mon-N	1	2	.333	10	3	0	0	0	31^2	34	2	15	23	14.2	4.83	73	.270	.352	1	.125	-0	-5	-5	-0	-0.5
Sea-A	8	10	.444	23	22	6	2	0	159^2	160	9	62	82	12.9	3.44	117	.261	.335	0	—	0	8	10	1	1.2
1990 Sea-A	11	11	.500	28	28	3	0	0	189^2	188	17	66	121	12.3	4.03	98	.260	.327	0	.000	0	-3	-2	-1	-0.3
1991 Sea-A	13	14	.481	30	30	5	3	0	195^1	199	16	77	108	13.2	3.69	112	.268	.345	0	—	0	9	9	2	1.4
Total 4	37	45	.451	109	99	15	6	0	676^2	682	47	254	392	12.8	3.71	106	.263	.335	4	.108	-1	12	18	-0	2.0

● **SCOTT HOLMAN** — Holman, Randy Scott b: 9/18/58, Santa Paula, Cal. BR/TR, 6'1", 190 lbs. Deb: 9/20/80

YEAR TM/L	W	L	PCT	G	GS	CG	SH	SV	IP	H	HR	BB	SO	RAT	ERA	ERA+	OAV	OOB	BH	AVG	PB	PR	/A	PD	TPI
1980 NY-N	0	0	—	4	0	0	0	0	7	6	0	1	3	9.0	1.29	276	.250	.280	0	—	0	2	2	-0	0.0
1982 NY-N	2	1	.667	4	4	1	0	0	26^2	23	2	7	11	10.1	2.36	154	.232	.283	2	.222	0	4	4	1	0.5
1983 NY-N	1	7	.125	35	10	0	0	0	101	90	7	52	44	12.7	3.74	97	.242	.336	5	.217	0	-1	-1	2	0.2
Total 3	3	8	.273	43	14	1	0	0	134^2	119	9	60	58	12.0	3.34	108	.240	.324	7	.219	0	4	4	2	0.7

● **SHAWN HOLMAN** — Holman, Shawn Leroy b: 11/10/64, Sewickley, Pa. BR/TR, 6'2", 185 lbs. Deb: 9/5/89

YEAR TM/L	W	L	PCT	G	GS	CG	SH	SV	IP	H	HR	BB	SO	RAT	ERA	ERA+	OAV	OOB	BH	AVG	PB	PR	/A	PD	TPI
1989 Det-A	0	0	—	5	0	0	0	0	10	8	0	11	9	17.1	1.80	212	.211	.388	0	—	0	2	2	-0	0.0

● **DARREN HOLMES** — Holmes, Darren Lee b: 4/25/66, Asheville, N.C. BR/TR, 6', 199 lbs. Deb: 9/1/90

YEAR TM/L	W	L	PCT	G	GS	CG	SH	SV	IP	H	HR	BB	SO	RAT	ERA	ERA+	OAV	OOB	BH	AVG	PB	PR	/A	PD	TPI
1990 LA-N	0	1	.000	14	0	0	0	0	17^1	15	1	11	19	13.5	5.19	70	.238	.351	0	—	0	-3	-3	-0	-0.2
1991 Mil-A	1	4	.200	40	0	0	0	3	76^1	90	6	27	59	13.9	4.72	84	.295	.354	0	—	0	-5	-6	1	-0.2
1992 Mil-A	4	4	.500	41	0	0	0	6	42^1	35	1	11	31	10.2	2.55	150	.224	.284	0	—	0	7	6	0	1.4
1993 Col-N	3	3	.500	62	0	0	0	25	66^2	56	6	20	60	10.5	4.05	118	.224	.285	0	—	0	-5	-0	0	0.9
1994 Col-N	0	3	.000	29	0	0	0	3	28^1	35	5	24	33	19.1	6.35	78	.313	.438	0	.000	-0	-7	-4	0	-0.5
Total 5	8	15	.348	186	0	0	0	37	231	231	19	93	202	12.9	4.36	98	.260	.334	0	.000	-0	-8	-2	0	1.4

● **CHICK HOLMES** — Holmes, Elwood Marter b: 3/22/1896, Beverly, N.J. d: 4/15/54, Camden, N.J. TR, Deb: 6/27/18

YEAR TM/L	W	L	PCT	G	GS	CG	SH	SV	IP	H	HR	BB	SO	RAT	ERA	ERA+	OAV	OOB	BH	AVG	PB	PR	/A	PD	TPI
1918 Phi-A	0	0	—	2	0	0	0	0	2	4	0	1	0	27.0	13.50	22	.400	.500	0	—	0	-2	-2	-0	0.0

● **JIM HOLMES** — Holmes, James Scott b: 8/2/1882, Lawrenceburg, Ky. d: 3/10/60, Jacksonville, Fla. Deb: 9/8/06

YEAR TM/L	W	L	PCT	G	GS	CG	SH	SV	IP	H	HR	BB	SO	RAT	ERA	ERA+	OAV	OOB	BH	AVG	PB	PR	/A	PD	TPI
1906 Phi-A	0	1	.000	3	1	0	0	0	9	10	0	8	1	19.0	4.00	68	.284	.430	3	.600	1	-1	-1	0	0.0
1908 Bro-N	1	4	.200	13	1	1	0	0	40	37	0	20	10	13.5	3.37	69	.270	.375	1	.077	-1	-4	-5	-2	-0.9
Total 2	1	5	.167	16	2	1	0	0	49	47	0	28	11	14.5	3.49	69	.273	.387	4	.222	0	-6	-6	-2	-0.9

● **DUCKY HOLMES** — Holmes, James William b: 1/28/1869, Des Moines, Iowa d: 8/6/32, Truro, Iowa BL/TR, 5'6", 170 lbs. Deb: 8/8/1895 ♦

YEAR TM/L	W	L	PCT	G	GS	CG	SH	SV	IP	H	HR	BB	SO	RAT	ERA	ERA+	OAV	OOB	BH	AVG	PB	PR	/A	PD	TPI
1895 Lou-N	1	0	1.000	2	1	1	0	0	14	16	1	4	0	13.5	5.79	80	.283	.341	60	.373	1	-2	-2	-0	-0.2
1896 Lou-N	0	1	.000	2	1	0	0	0	12	26	0	8	3	25.5	7.50	58	.430	.497	38	.270	0	-4	-4	0	-0.2
Total 2	1	1	.500	4	2	1	0	0	26	42	1	12	3	19.0	6.58	68	.359	.423	1014	.282	1	-6	-6	0	-0.2

● **HERM HOLSHOUSER** — Holshouser, Herman Alexander b: 1/20/07, Rockwell, N.C. BR/TR, 6', 170 lbs. Deb: 4/15/30

YEAR TM/L	W	L	PCT	G	GS	CG	SH	SV	IP	H	HR	BB	SO	RAT	ERA	ERA+	OAV	OOB	BH	AVG	PB	PR	/A	PD	TPI
1930 StL-A	0	1	.000	25	1	0	0	1	62^1	103	8	28	37	19.3	7.80	63	.376	.439	2	.125	-1	-22	-20	-0	-0.4

● **VERN HOLTGRAVE** — Holtgrave, Lavern George "Woody" b: 10/18/42, Aviston, Ill. BR/TR, 6'1", 183 lbs. Deb: 9/26/65

YEAR TM/L	W	L	PCT	G	GS	CG	SH	SV	IP	H	HR	BB	SO	RAT	ERA	ERA+	OAV	OOB	BH	AVG	PB	PR	/A	PD	TPI
1965 Det-A	0	0	—	1	0	0	0	0	3	4	0	2	2	18.0	6.00	58	.308	.400	0	—	0	-1	-1	-0	0.0

● **BRIAN HOLTON** — Holton, Brian John b: 11/29/59, McKeesport, Pa. BR/TR, 6', 193 lbs. Deb: 9/9/85

YEAR TM/L	W	L	PCT	G	GS	CG	SH	SV	IP	H	HR	BB	SO	RAT	ERA	ERA+	OAV	OOB	BH	AVG	PB	PR	/A	PD	TPI
1985 LA-N	1	1	.500	3	0	0	0	0	4	9	0	1	1	22.5	9.00	39	.450	.476	0	—	0	-2	-2	-0	-1.0
1986 LA-N	2	3	.400	12	3	0	0	0	24^1	28	1	6	24	12.9	4.44	78	.292	.340	0	.000	-1	-2	-3	-0	-0.5
1987 LA-N	3	2	.600	53	1	0	0	2	83^1	87	11	32	58	12.9	3.89	102	.269	.335	1	.200	0	2	1	1	0.1
1988 *LA-N	7	3	.700	45	0	0	0	1	84^2	69	1	26	49	10.2	1.70	196	.228	.292	0	.000	-1	16	15	-0	1.7
1989 Bal-A	5	7	.417	39	12	0	0	0	116^1	140	11	39	51	13.9	4.02	94	.300	.355	0	—	-1	-2	-3	-0	-0.3
1990 Bal-A	2	3	.400	33	0	0	0	0	58	69	7	21	27	13.8	4.50	84	.292	.350	0	—	0	-4	-5	1	-0.3
Total 6	20	19	.513	185	16	0	0	3	370^2	401	31	125	210	12.8	3.62	102	.278	.337	1	.050	-1	8	3	1	-0.3

● **KEN HOLTZMAN** — Holtzman, Kenneth Dale b: 11/3/45, St.Louis, Mo. BR/TL, 6'2", 175 lbs. Deb: 9/4/65

YEAR TM/L	W	L	PCT	G	GS	CG	SH	SV	IP	H	HR	BB	SO	RAT	ERA	ERA+	OAV	OOB	BH	AVG	PB	PR	/A	PD	TPI
1965 Chi-N	0	0	—	3	0	0	0	0	4	2	1	3	3	11.3	2.25	164	.143	.294	0	—	0	1	1	0	0.0
1966 Chi-N	11	16	.407	34	33	9	0	0	220^2	194	27	68	171	10.8	3.79	97	.235	.296	9	.123	-3	-5	-3	-2	-0.8
1967 Chi-N	9	0	1.000	12	12	3	0	0	92^2	76	11	44	62	11.8	2.53	140	.222	.314	7	.200	1	9	10	0	1.1
1968 Chi-N	11	14	.440	34	32	6	3	1	215	201	17	76	151	11.8	3.35	94	.248	.317	10	.125	-2	-9	-4	1	-0.7
1969 Chi-N	17	13	.567	39	39	12	6	0	261^1	248	18	93	176	11.9	3.58	112	.247	.314	15	.150	-1	0	13	-1	1.2
1970 Chi-N	17	11	.607	39	38	15	1	0	287^2	271	30	94	202	11.5	3.38	133	.258	.309	21	.200	1	21	36	0	3.4
1971 Chi-N	9	15	.375	30	29	9	3	0	195	213	18	64	143	12.9	4.48	88	.276	.333	9	.130	-1	-22	-12	-1	-1.5
1972 *Oak-A☆	19	11	.633	39	37	16	4	0	265^1	232	23	52	134	9.8	2.51	113	.236	.278	16	.178	2	16	10	0	1.4
1973 *Oak-A★	21	13	.618	40	40	16	4	0	297^1	275	22	66	157	10.4	2.97	120	.243	.287	0	—	0	28	19	-1	2.0
1974 *Oak-A	19	17	.528	39	38	9	3	0	255^1	273	14	51	117	11.5	3.07	108	.272	.309	0	—	0	16	7	0	1.0
1975 *Oak-A	18	14	.563	39	38	13	2	0	266^1	217	16	108	122	11.2	3.14	115	.222	.303	0	.000	-0	19	14	3	1.9
1976 Bal-A	5	4	.556	13	13	6	1	0	97^2	100	4	35	25	12.5	2.86	115	.271	.336	0	—	0	7	5	1	0.5
NY-A	9	7	.563	21	21	10	2	0	149	165	14	35	41	12.1	4.17	82	.283	.323	0	—	0	-11	-12	-1	-1.3
Yr	14	11	.560	34	34	16	3	0	246^2	265	18	70	66	12.2	3.65	92	.277	.326	0	—	0	-4	-8	1	-0.8
1977 NY-A	2	3	.400	18	11	0	0	0	71^2	105	7	24	14	16.3	5.78	68	.362	.413	0	—	0	-14	-15	2	-0.6
1978 NY-A	1	0	1.000	5	3	0	0	0	17^2	21	3	9	2	15.3	4.08	89	.313	.395	0	—	0	-1	-1	1	0.2
Chi-N	0	3	.000	23	6	0	0	0	53	61	10	35	36	16.5	6.11	66	.286	.390	2	.200	-1	-15	-12	-0	-0.8
1979 Chi-N	6	9	.400	23	20	3	2	0	117^2	133	15	53	44	14.7	4.59	90	.287	.368	10	.233	2	-11	-6	-2	-0.7
Total 15	174	150	.537	451	410	127	31	3	2867^1	2787	249	910	1601	11.8	3.49	104	.255	.315	99	.163	-1	31	48	1	6.3

● **MARK HOLZEMER** — Holzemer, Mark Harold b: 8/20/69, Littleton, Colo. BL/TL, 6', 165 lbs. Deb: 8/21/93

YEAR TM/L	W	L	PCT	G	GS	CG	SH	SV	IP	H	HR	BB	SO	RAT	ERA	ERA+	OAV	OOB	BH	AVG	PB	PR	/A	PD	TPI
1993 Cal-A	0	3	.000	5	4	0	0	0	23^1	34	2	13	10	19.3	8.87	51	.340	.431	0	—	0	-12	-11	0	-1.3

● **RICK HONEYCUTT** — Honeycutt, Frederick Wayne b: 6/29/52, Chattanooga, Tenn. BL/TL, 5'11", 190 lbs. Deb: 8/24/77

YEAR TM/L	W	L	PCT	G	GS	CG	SH	SV	IP	H	HR	BB	SO	RAT	ERA	ERA+	OAV	OOB	BH	AVG	PB	PR	/A	PD	TPI
1977 Sea-A	0	1	.000	10	3	0	0	0	29	26	7	11	17	12.4	4.34	95	.239	.325	0	—	0	-1	-1	-1	0.0
1978 Sea-A	5	11	.313	26	24	4	1	0	134^1	150	12	49	50	13.5	4.89	78	.285	.349	0	—	0	-17	-16	1	-1.5
1979 Sea-A	11	12	.478	33	28	8	1	0	194	201	22	67	83	12.7	4.04	108	.268	.333	0	—	0	4	7	-1	0.6
1980 Sea-A☆	10	17	.370	30	30	9	1	0	203^1	221	22	60	79	12.6	3.94	105	.280	.333	0	—	0	2	4	-0	0.5
1981 Tex-A	11	6	.647	20	20	8	2	0	127^2	120	12	17	40	9.7	3.31	105	.246	.272	0	—	0	5	2	1	0.5
1982 Tex-A	5	17	.227	30	26	4	1	0	164	201	20	54	64	14.2	5.27	73	.305	.360	0	—	0	-22	-25	1	-2.5
1983 Tex-A★	14	8	.636	25	25	5	2	0	174^2	168	9	37	56	10.9	**2.42**	**165**	.262	.308	0	—	0	**32**	31	3	4.3
*LA-N	2	3	.400	9	7	1	0	0	39	46	3	18	14	14.1	5.77	62	.297	.359	1	.083	-1	-9	-9	2	-1.0
1984 LA-N	10	9	.526	29	28	2	0	0	183^2	180	11	51	75	11.4	2.84	124	.258	.310	8	.145	2	15	14	2	1.6
1985 *LA-N	8	12	.400	31	25	1	0	1	142	141	9	49	67	12.1	3.42	102	.261	.323	5	.132	0	3	1	3	0.4
1986 LA-N	11	9	.550	32	28	0	0	0	171	164	9	45	100	11.2	3.32	104	.249	.300	3	.070	0	8	3	2	0.5
1987 LA-N	2	12	.143	27	20	1	0	0	115^2	133	10	45	92	14.0	4.59	86	.278	.343	7	.233	2	-7	-8	-0	-0.7

YEAR TM/L	W	L	PCT	G	GS	CG	SH	SV	IP	H	HR	BB	SO	RAT	ERA	ERA+	OAV	OOB	BH	AVG	PB	PR	/A	PD	TPI
Oak-A	1	4	.200	7	4	0	0	0	23^2	25	3	9	10	13.7	5.32	77	.275	.353	0	—	0	-2	-3	-0	-0.5
1988 *Oak-A	3	2	.600	55	0	0	0	7	79^2	74	6	25	47	11.5	3.50	108	.253	.318	0	—	0	4	2	1	0.4
1989 *Oak-A	2	5	.500	64	0	0	0	12	76^2	56	5	26	52	9.7	2.35	157	.207	.279	0	—	0	13	11	1	1.1
1990 *Oak-A	2	2	.500	63	0	0	0	7	63^1	46	2	22	38	9.8	2.70	138	.204	.278	0	.000	0	8	7	1	0.7
1991 Oak-A	2	4	.333	43	0	0	0	0	37^2	37	3	20	26	14.1	3.58	107	.261	.360	0	—	0	2	1	0	0.4
1992 *Oak-A	1	4	.200	54	0	0	0	3	39	41	2	10	32	12.5	3.69	101	.272	.329	0	—	0	1	0	-1	0.2
1993 Oak-A	1	4	.200	52	0	0	0	1	41^2	30	7	20	21	11.0	2.81	145	.211	.313	0	—	0	7	6	-0	1.0
1994 Tex-A	1	2	.333	42	0	0	0	1	25	37	4	9	18	17.3	7.20	63	.349	.410	0	—	0	-7	-7	0	-0.5
Total 18	102	141	.420	682	268	47	11	32	2065	2097	176	639	985	12.1	3.75	102	.265	.324	24	.133	2	40	19	14	5.5

● DON HOOD
Hood, Donald Harris b: 10/16/49, Florence, S.C. BL/TL, 6'2", 180 lbs. Deb: 7/16/73

YEAR TM/L	W	L	PCT	G	GS	CG	SH	SV	IP	H	HR	BB	SO	RAT	ERA	ERA+	OAV	OOB	BH	AVG	PB	PR	/A	PD	TPI
1973 Bal-A	3	2	.600	8	4	1	1	1	32^1	31	1	6	18	10.6	3.90	96	.256	.297	0	—	0	-0	-1	-1	-0.1
1974 Bal-A	1	1	.500	20	2	0	0	1	57^1	47	1	20	26	10.5	3.45	100	.223	.290	0	—	0	1	-0	-0	0.0
1975 Cle-A	6	10	.375	29	19	2	0	0	135^1	136	16	57	51	12.8	4.39	86	.268	.342	0	—	0	-9	-9	-2	-1.1
1976 Cle-A	3	5	.375	33	6	0	0	1	77^2	89	5	41	32	15.5	4.87	72	.296	.387	0	—	0	-12	-12	0	-1.1
1977 Cle-A	2	1	.667	41	5	1	0	0	105	87	3	49	62	12.0	3.00	131	.224	.317	0	—	0	12	11	-2	0.4
1978 Cle-A	5	6	.455	36	19	1	0	0	154^2	166	13	77	73	14.2	4.48	83	.278	.361	0	—	0	-12	-13	0	-0.7
1979 Cle-A	1	0	1.000	13	0	0	0	1	22	13	1	14	7	11.5	3.68	116	.169	.304	0	—	0	1	1	0	0.1
NY-A	3	1	.750	27	6	0	0	1	67^1	62	3	30	22	12.6	3.07	132	.252	.338	0	—	0	9	7	1	0.5
Yr	4	1	.800	40	6	0	0	2	89^1	75	4	44	29	12.2	3.22	128	.231	.327	0	—	0	10	9	1	0.6
1980 StL-N	4	6	.400	33	4	0	0	0	82^1	90	2	34	35	13.8	3.39	109	.288	.362	4	.200	-0	2	3	1	0.4
1982 KC-A	4	0	1.000	30	3	0	0	1	66^2	71	7	22	31	12.8	3.51	116	.276	.338	0	—	0	4	4	0	0.3
1983 KC-A	2	3	.400	27	0	0	0	0	47^2	48	5	14	17	12.1	2.27	180	.273	.333	0	—	0	10	10	1	1.1
Total 10	34	35	.493	297	72	6	1	6	848^1	840	57	364	374	13.0	3.79	101	.263	.342	4	.200	-0	5	2	-0	-0.2

● WALLY HOOD
Hood, Wallace James Jr. b: 9/24/25, Los Angeles, Cal. BR/TR, 6'1", 190 lbs. Deb: 9/23/49 F

YEAR TM/L	W	L	PCT	G	GS	CG	SH	SV	IP	H	HR	BB	SO	RAT	ERA	ERA+	OAV	OOB	BH	AVG	PB	PR	/A	PD	TPI
1949 NY-A	0	0	—	2	0	0	0	0	2^1	0	0	1	2	3.9	0.00	—	.000	.143	0	—	0	1	1	-0	0.0

● JAY HOOK
Hook, James Wesley b: 11/18/36, Waukegan, Ill. BL/TR, 6'2", 182 lbs. Deb: 9/3/57

YEAR TM/L	W	L	PCT	G	GS	CG	SH	SV	IP	H	HR	BB	SO	RAT	ERA	ERA+	OAV	OOB	BH	AVG	PB	PR	/A	PD	TPI
1957 Cin-N	0	1	.000	3	2	0	0	0	10	6	0	8	6	12.6	4.50	91	.176	.333	0	.000	-0	-1	-0	0	-0.1
1958 Cin-N	0	1	.000	1	1	0	0	0	3	3	2	2	5	15.0	12.00	35	.250	.357	0	.000	-0	-3	-3	-0	-0.6
1959 Cin-N	5	5	.500	17	15	4	0	0	79	79	11	39	37	13.8	5.13	79	.266	.357	1	.125	-1	-10	-9	-1	-1.2
1960 Cin-N	11	18	.379	36	33	10	2	0	222	222	31	73	103	12.2	4.50	85	.263	.325	6	.083	-3	-18	-17	-1	-2.4
1961 Cin-N	1	3	.250	22	5	0	0	0	62^2	83	14	22	36	15.8	7.76	52	.273	.386	2	.133	-1	-26	-26	-1	-1.6
1962 NY-N	8	19	.296	37	34	13	0	0	213^2	230	31	71	113	13.0	4.84	86	.273	.335	14	.203	2	-21	-16	-0	-1.5
1963 NY-N	4	14	.222	41	20	3	0	1	152^2	168	21	53	89	13.6	5.48	64	.281	.348	9	.237	-2	-37	-34	-1	-3.7
1964 NY-N	0	1	.000	3	2	0	0	0	9^2	17	2	7	5	22.3	9.31	38	.395	.480	0	.000	-0	-6	-6	0	-0.5
Total 8	29	62	.319	160	112	30	2	1	752^2	808	112	275	394	13.3	5.23	75	.276	.344	34	.151	-2	-123	-110	-4	-11.6

● BUCK HOOKER
Hooker, William Edward b: 8/28/1880, Richmond, Va. d: 7/2/29, Richmond, Va. TR, 5'6", Deb: 9/5/02

YEAR TM/L	W	L	PCT	G	GS	CG	SH	SV	IP	H	HR	BB	SO	RAT	ERA	ERA+	OAV	OOB	BH	AVG	PB	PR	/A	PD	TPI
1902 Cin-N	0	1	.000	1	1	1	0	0	8	11	1	0	0	12.4	4.50	67	.326	.326	0	.000	-0	-2	-1	-0	-0.2
1903 Cin-N	0	0	—	1	0	0	0	0	2^1	2	0	1	0	15.4	0.00	—	.250	.400	0	.000	-0	1	1	-0	0.0
Total 2	0	1	.000	2	1	1	0	0	10^1	13	1	2	0	13.1	3.48	90	.311	.343	0	.000	-1	-1	-0	-1	-0.2

● HARRY HOOPER
Hooper, Harry Bartholomew b: 8/24/1887, Bell Station, Cal. d: 12/18/74, Santa Cruz, Cal. BL/TR, 5'10", 168 lbs. Deb: 4/16/09 H♦

YEAR TM/L	W	L	PCT	G	GS	CG	SH	SV	IP	H	HR	BB	SO	RAT	ERA	ERA+	OAV	OOB	BH	AVG	PB	PR	/A	PD	TPI
1913 Bos-A	0	0	—	1	0	0	0	0	2	2	0	1	0	13.5	0.00	—	.333	.429	169	.288	—	1	1	-0	0.0

● BOB HOOPER
Hooper, Robert Nelson b: 5/30/22, Leamington, Ont., Canada d: 3/17/80, New Brunswick, N.J BR/TR, 5'11", 195 lbs. Deb: 4/19/50

YEAR TM/L	W	L	PCT	G	GS	CG	SH	SV	IP	H	HR	BB	SO	RAT	ERA	ERA+	OAV	OOB	BH	AVG	PB	PR	/A	PD	TPI
1950 Phi-A	15	10	.600	45	20	3	0	5	170^1	181	15	91	58	14.4	5.02	91	.272	.361	7	.125	-2	-8	-9	3	-1.0
1951 Phi-A	12	10	.545	38	23	9	0	5	189	192	13	61	64	12.2	4.38	98	.267	.327	15	.208	-1	-5	-2	1	-0.2
1952 Phi-A	8	15	.348	43	14	4	0	6	144^1	158	13	68	40	14.3	5.18	76	.279	.361	8	.195	1	-24	-20	3	-2.6
1953 Cle-A	5	4	.556	43	0	0	0	7	69^1	50	4	38	16	11.7	4.02	93	.206	.318	1	.083	-1	-0	-2	1	-0.3
1954 Cle-A	0	0	—	17	0	0	0	2	34^2	39	3	16	12	14.5	4.93	74	.289	.368	0	.000	-1	-5	-5	-0	-0.1
1955 Cin-N	0	2	.000	8	0	0	0	0	13	20	2	6	6	18.0	7.62	56	.357	.419	0	.000	-0	-5	-5	0	-0.6
Total 6	40	41	.494	194	57	16	0	25	620^2	640	50	280	196	13.5	4.80	87	.268	.348	31	.166	-4	-48	-42	8	-4.8

● LEON HOOTEN
Hooten, Michael Leon b: 4/4/48, Downey, Cal. BR/TR, 5'11", 180 lbs. Deb: 4/13/74

YEAR TM/L	W	L	PCT	G	GS	CG	SH	SV	IP	H	HR	BB	SO	RAT	ERA	ERA+	OAV	OOB	BH	AVG	PB	PR	/A	PD	TPI
1974 Oak-A	0	0	—	6	0	0	0	0	8^1	6	1	4	1	11.9	3.24	102	.207	.324							

● BURT HOOTON
Hooton, Burt Carlton b: 2/7/50, Greenville, Tex. BR/TR, 6'1", 210 lbs. Deb: 6/17/71

YEAR TM/L	W	L	PCT	G	GS	CG	SH	SV	IP	H	HR	BB	SO	RAT	ERA	ERA+	OAV	OOB	BH	AVG	PB	PR	/A	PD	TPI
1971 Chi-N	2	0	1.000	3	3	2	1	0	21^1	8	2	10	22	7.6	2.11	186	.111	.220	0	.000	-1	3	4	-0	0.3
1972 Chi-N	11	14	.440	33	31	9	3	0	218^1	201	13	81	132	11.7	2.80	136	.246	.315	9	.125	-1	16	24	1	2.8
1973 Chi-N	14	17	.452	42	34	9	2	0	239^2	248	12	73	134	12.2	3.68	107	.270	.327	9	.129	-0	-1	7	-1	0.7
1974 Chi-N	7	11	.389	48	21	3	1	1	176^1	214	16	51	94	13.7	4.80	79	.299	.384	3	.060	-4	-23	-19	3	-1.9
1975 Chi-N	0	2	.000	3	3	0	0	0	11	18	2	4	5	18.0	8.18	47	.383	.431	0	.000	-0	-6	-5	1	-0.7
LA-N	18	7	.720	31	30	12	4	0	223^2	172	16	64	148	9.5	2.82	121	.210	.267	9	.129	1	20	14	-2	1.4
Yr	18	9	.667	34	33	12	4	0	234^2	190	18	68	153	9.9	3.07	111	.219	.276	9	.123	0	14	9	-1	0.7
1976 LA-N	11	15	.423	33	33	8	4	0	226^2	203	16	60	116	10.5	3.26	104	.241	.292	6	.097	-2	8	3	-2	0.0
1977 *LA-N	12	7	.632	32	31	6	2	1	223^1	184	14	60	153	10.0	2.62	146	.225	.281	11	.164	-0	32	30	0	2.4
1978 *LA-N	19	10	.655	32	32	10	3	0	236	196	17	61	104	9.8	2.71	130	.226	.277	10	.149	1	23	21	-1	2.6
1979 LA-N	11	10	.524	29	29	12	1	0	212	191	11	63	129	10.9	2.97	122	.241	.302	11	.147	1	18	16	-0	1.4
1980 LA-N	14	8	.636	34	33	4	2	1	206^2	194	22	64	118	11.2	3.66	96	.249	.306	4	.063	-3	-1	-4	-0	-0.7
1981 *LA-N★	11	6	.647	23	23	5	4	0	142^1	124	3	33	74	10.1	2.28	146	.237	.285	8	.190	2	19	16	-1	2.1
1982 LA-N	4	7	.364	21	21	2	2	0	120^2	130	5	33	51	12.3	4.03	86	.275	.325	3	.086	-1	-6	-8	0	-0.7
1983 LA-N	9	8	.529	33	27	2	0	0	160	156	21	59	87	12.2	4.22	85	.254	.321	8	.160	1	-11	-11	-0	-1.1
1984 LA-N	3	6	.333	54	0	0	0	4	110	109	5	43	62	12.4	3.44	103	.263	.333	1	.071	-1	2	1	-0	0.0
1985 Tex-A	3	8	.385	29	20	2	0	0	124	149	18	40	62	13.7	5.23	81	.297	.349	0	—	0	-15	-14	-1	-1.4
Total 15	151	136	.526	480	377	86	29	7	2652	2497	193	799	1491	11.3	3.38	108	.250	.306	92	.123	-9	77	77	-4	7.2

● JOHN HOOVER
Hoover, John Nicklaus b: 11/22/62, Fresno, Cal. BR/TR, 6'2", 190 lbs. Deb: 5/23/90

YEAR TM/L	W	L	PCT	G	GS	CG	SH	SV	IP	H	HR	BB	SO	RAT	ERA	ERA+	OAV	OOB	BH	AVG	PB	PR	/A	PD	TPI
1990 Tex-A	0	0	—	2	0	0	0	0	4^2	8	0	3	2	21.2	11.57	34	.364	.440	0	—	0	-4	-4	-0	0.0

● DICK HOOVER
Hoover, Richard Lloyd b: 12/11/25, Columbus, Ohio d: 4/12/81, Lake Placid, Fla. BL/TL, 6', 170 lbs. Deb: 4/16/52

YEAR TM/L	W	L	PCT	G	GS	CG	SH	SV	IP	H	HR	BB	SO	RAT	ERA	ERA+	OAV	OOB	BH	AVG	PB	PR	/A	PD	TPI
1952 Bos-N	0	0	—	2	0	0	0	0	4^2	8	0	2	0	21.2	7.71	47	.348	.423	0	—	0	-2	-2	-0	0.0

● JOHN HOPE
Hope, John Alan b: 12/21/70, Ft.Lauderdale, Fla. BR/TR, 6'3", 195 lbs. Deb: 8/29/93

YEAR TM/L	W	L	PCT	G	GS	CG	SH	SV	IP	H	HR	BB	SO	RAT	ERA	ERA+	OAV	OOB	BH	AVG	PB	PR	/A	PD	TPI
1993 Pit-N	0	2	.000	7	7	0	0	0	38	47	2	8	13	13.5	4.03	101	.313	.356	1	.077	-1	0	0	-0	0.0
1994 Pit-N	0	0	—	9	0	0	0	0	14	18	1	4	6	15.4	5.79	73	.310	.375	1	.333	0	-2	-2	-0	0.0
Total 2	0	2	.000	16	7	0	0	0	52	65	3	12	14	14.0	4.50	91	.313	.362	2	.125	-1	-2	-1	1	0.0

● SAM HOPE
Hope, Samuel b: 12/4/1878, Brooklyn, N.Y. d: 6/30/46, Greenport, N.Y. BR/TR, 5'10", Deb: 8/5/07

YEAR TM/L	W	L	PCT	G	GS	CG	SH	SV	IP	H	HR	BB	SO	RAT	ERA	ERA+	OAV	OOB	BH	AVG	PB	PR	/A	PD	TPI
1907 Phi-A	0	0	—	1	0	0	0	0	0^1	3	0	0	0	81.0	0.00	—	.762	.762	0	—	0	0	0	0	0.0

● PAUL HOPKINS
Hopkins, Paul Henry b: 9/25/04, Chester, Conn. BR/TR, 6', 175 lbs. Deb: 9/29/27

YEAR TM/L	W	L	PCT	G	GS	CG	SH	SV	IP	H	HR	BB	SO	RAT	ERA	ERA+	OAV	OOB	BH	AVG	PB	PR	/A	PD	TPI
1927 Was-A	1	0	1.000	2	1	0	0	0	9	13	1	4	5	17.0	5.00	81	.361	.425	2	.667	1	-1	-1	0	0.0
1929 Was-A	0	1	.000	7	0	0	0	0	16^1	15	1	9	5	13.2	2.20	192	.250	.348	0	.000	-1	4	4	-0	0.1

YEAR TM/L	W	L	PCT	G	GS	CG	SH	SV	IP	H	HR	BB	SO	RAT	ERA	ERA+	OAV	OOB	BH	AVG	PB	PR	/A	PD	TPI
StL-A	0	0	—	2	0	0	0	0	2	0	0	2	1	9.0	0.00	—	.000	.286	0	—	0	1	1	-0	0.0
Yr	0	1	.000	9	0	0	0	0	18¹	15	1	11	6	12.8	1.96	217	.231	.342	0	.000	-1	5	5	-0	0.1
Total 2	1	1	.500	11	1	0	0	0	27¹	28	2	15	11	14.2	2.96	142	.277	.371	2	.333	1	4	4	-0	0.1

● LEFTY HOPPER
Hopper, Clarence F. b: 5/27/1874, Jersey City, N.J. TL, Deb: 10/10/1898

YEAR TM/L	W	L	PCT	G	GS	CG	SH	SV	IP	H	HR	BB	SO	RAT	ERA	ERA+	OAV	OOB	BH	AVG	PB	PR	/A	PD	TPI
1898 Bro-N	0	2	.000	2	2	0	0	0	11	14	0	5	1	15.5	4.91	73	.307	.376	0	.000	-1	-2	-2	-0	-0.3

● JIM HOPPER
Hopper, James McDaniel b: 9/1/19, Charlotte, N.C. d: 1/23/82, Charlotte, N.C. BR/TR, 6'1", 175 lbs. Deb: 4/21/46

YEAR TM/L	W	L	PCT	G	GS	CG	SH	SV	IP	H	HR	BB	SO	RAT	ERA	ERA+	OAV	OOB	BH	AVG	PB	PR	/A	PD	TPI
1946 Pit-N	0	1	.000	2	1	0	0	0	4	6	1	3	1	20.3	11.25	31	.316	.409	0	—	0	-3	-3	-0	-0.7

● BILL HOPPER
Hopper, William Booth "Bird Dog" b: 10/26/1890, Jackson, Tenn. d: 1/14/65, Allen Park, Mich. BR/TR, 6', 175 lbs. Deb: 9/11/13

YEAR TM/L	W	L	PCT	G	GS	CG	SH	SV	IP	H	HR	BB	SO	RAT	ERA	ERA+	OAV	OOB	BH	AVG	PB	PR	/A	PD	TPI
1913 StL-N	0	3	.000	3	3	2	0	0	24	20	2	8	3	11.6	3.75	86	.230	.316	3	.375	1	-1	-1	-0	0.0
1914 StL-N	0	0	—	3	0	0	0	0	5	6	0	5	1	19.8	3.60	78	.286	.423	—	—	0	-0	-0	-0	0.0
1915 Was-A	0	1	.000	13	0	0	0	1	31¹	39	0	16	8	16.1	4.60	65	.348	.434	1	.200	0	-6	-6	1	-0.1
Total 3	0	4	.000	19	3	2	0	1	60¹	65	2	29	12	14.6	4.18	73	.295	.387	4	.308	1	-8	-7	1	-0.1

● JOHN HORAN
Horan, Patrick J. b: 1863, Ireland 5'10.5", 160 lbs. Deb: 5/17/1884

YEAR TM/L	W	L	PCT	G	GS	CG	SH	SV	IP	H	HR	BB	SO	RAT	ERA	ERA+	OAV	OOB	BH	AVG	PB	PR	/A	PD	TPI
1884 CP-U	3	6	.333	13	10	9	0	0	98	94	0	24	55	10.8	3.49	70	.236	.279	6	.088	-8	-11	-11	-1	-1.4

● JOE HORLEN
Horlen, Joel Edward b: 8/14/37, San Antonio, Tex. BR/TR, 6', 175 lbs. Deb: 9/4/61

YEAR TM/L	W	L	PCT	G	GS	CG	SH	SV	IP	H	HR	BB	SO	RAT	ERA	ERA+	OAV	OOB	BH	AVG	PB	PR	/A	PD	TPI
1961 Chi-A	1	3	.250	5	4	0	0	0	17²	25	2	13	11	19.4	6.62	59	.338	.437	0	.000	-1	-5	-5	0	-1.0
1962 Chi-A	7	6	.538	20	19	5	1	0	108²	108	11	43	63	12.7	4.89	80	.262	.335	2	.053	-3	-11	-12	2	-1.3
1963 Chi-A	11	7	.611	33	21	3	0	0	124	122	10	55	61	13.0	3.27	107	.261	.341	9	.225	1	5	3	1	0.7
1964 Chi-A	13	9	.591	32	28	9	2	0	210²	142	11	55	138	**8.6**	1.88	184	**.190**	**.250**	11	.159	-1	41	37	3	4.2
1965 Chi-A	13	13	.500	34	34	7	4	0	219	203	16	39	125	10.1	2.88	111	.245	.281	9	.132	0	14	8	-0	0.9
1966 Chi-A	10	13	.435	37	29	4	2	1	211	185	14	53	124	10.4	2.43	130	.233	.286	4	.067	-4	24	17	6	2.2
1967 Chi-A☆	19	7	**.731**	35	35	13	**6**	0	258	185	18	58	103	**8.7**	2.06	151	.203	**.253**	14	.169	1	**34**	**30**	3	3.5
1968 Chi-A	12	14	.462	35	35	4	1	0	223²	197	16	70	102	11.3	2.37	127	.238	.308	7	.104	-1	15	16	2	2.1
1969 Chi-A	13	16	.448	36	35	7	2	0	235²	237	20	77	121	12.2	3.78	102	.261	.323	14	.182	-1	-4	-2	-1	0.0
1970 Chi-A	6	16	.273	28	26	4	0	0	172¹	198	18	41	77	12.7	4.86	80	.287	.331	6	.115	-2	-22	-18	4	-1.9
1971 Chi-A	8	9	.471	34	18	3	0	2	137¹	150	12	30	82	12.1	4.26	84	.284	.329	4	.100	-2	-12	-10	1	-1.4
1972 *Oak-A	3	4	.429	32	6	0	0	1	84	74	3	20	58	10.5	3.00	95	.236	.291	-0	.176	-0	1	-1	-0	-0.1
Total 12	116	117	.498	361	290	59	18	4	2002	1829	145	554	1065	11.0	3.11	109	.243	.300	83	.134	-12	78	66	22	7.9

● TRADER HORNE
Horne, Berlyn Dale "Sonny" b: 4/12/1899, Bachman, Ohio d: 2/3/83, Franklin, Ohio BB/TR, 5'9", 155 lbs. Deb: 4/24/29

YEAR TM/L	W	L	PCT	G	GS	CG	SH	SV	IP	H	HR	BB	SO	RAT	ERA	ERA+	OAV	OOB	BH	AVG	PB	PR	/A	PD	TPI
1929 Chi-N	1	1	.500	11	1	0	0	0	23	24	3	21	6	17.6	5.09	91	.273	.413	2	.400	1	-1	-1	0	0.0

● JACK HORNER
Horner, William Frank b: 9/21/1863, Baltimore, Md. d: 7/14/10, New Orleans, La. BR, Deb: 5/7/1894

YEAR TM/L	W	L	PCT	G	GS	CG	SH	SV	IP	H	HR	BB	SO	RAT	ERA	ERA+	OAV	OOB	BH	AVG	PB	PR	/A	PD	TPI
1894 Bal-N	0	1	.000	2	1	0	1	0	11	15	0	7	2	18.8	9.00	61	.321	.421	1	.167	-0	-4	-4	0	-0.3

● JOE HORNUNG
Hornung, Michael Joseph "Ubbo Ubbo" b: 6/12/1857, Carthage, N.Y. d: 10/30/31, Howard Beach, N.Y. BR/TR, 5'8.5", 164 lbs. Deb: 5/1/1879 U♦

YEAR TM/L	W	L	PCT	G	GS	CG	SH	SV	IP	H	HR	BB	SO	RAT	ERA	ERA+	OAV	OOB	BH	AVG	PB	PR	/A	PD	TPI
1880 Buf-N	0	0	—	1	0	0	0	0	3	2	0	1	0	9.0	6.00	41	.167	.231	91	.266	0	-1	-1	-0	0.0

● HANSON HORSEY
Horsey, Hanson b: 11/26/1889, Galena, Md. d: 12/1/49, Millington, Md. BR/TR, 5'11", 165 lbs. Deb: 4/27/12

YEAR TM/L	W	L	PCT	G	GS	CG	SH	SV	IP	H	HR	BB	SO	RAT	ERA	ERA+	OAV	OOB	BH	AVG	PB	PR	/A	PD	TPI
1912 Cin-N	0	0	—	1	1	0	0	0	4	14	0	3	0	38.3	22.50	15	.609	.654	0	.000	-0	-8	-9	-0	-0.1

● VINCE HORSMAN
Horsman, Vincent Stanley Joseph b: 3/9/67, Halifax, N.S., Can. BR/TL, 6'2", 175 lbs. Deb: 9/5/91

YEAR TM/L	W	L	PCT	G	GS	CG	SH	SV	IP	H	HR	BB	SO	RAT	ERA	ERA+	OAV	OOB	BH	AVG	PB	PR	/A	PD	TPI
1991 Tor-A	0	0	—	4	0	0	0	0	4	2	0	3	2	11.3	0.00	—	.167	.333	0	—	0	2	2	-0	-0.2
1992 Oak-A	2	1	.667	58	0	0	0	1	43¹	39	3	21	18	12.5	2.49	150	.252	.341	0	—	0	7	6	-0	0.5
1993 Oak-A	2	0	1.000	40	0	0	0	0	25	25	2	15	17	15.5	5.40	75	.255	.371	0	—	0	-3	-4	-0	-0.3
1994 Oak-A	0	1	.000	33	0	0	0	0	29¹	29	2	11	20	12.6	4.91	91	.266	.339	0	—	0	-0	-2	0	0.4
Total 4	4	2	.667	135	0	0	0	1	101²	95	7	50	57	13.2	3.81	106	.254	.348	0	—	0	5	3	-1	0.4

● OSCAR HORSTMANN
Horstmann, Oscar Theodore b: 6/2/1891, Alma, Mo. d: 5/11/77, Salina, Kan. BR/TR, 5'11", 165 lbs. Deb: 4/18/17

YEAR TM/L	W	L	PCT	G	GS	CG	SH	SV	IP	H	HR	BB	SO	RAT	ERA	ERA+	OAV	OOB	BH	AVG	PB	PR	/A	PD	TPI
1917 StL-N	9	4	.692	35	11	4	1	1	138²	111	5	54	50	11.0	3.44	78	.225	.307	9	.196	1	-11	-12	-0	-1.1
1918 StL-N	0	2	.000	9	2	0	0	0	23	29	0	14	6	16.8	5.48	49	.349	.443	0	.000	-0	-7	-7	1	-0.5
1919 StL-N	0	1	.000	6	2	0	0	0	15	14	0	12	5	15.6	3.00	93	.264	.400	1	.500	1	-0	-0	-0	0.0
Total 3	9	7	.563	50	15	4	1	1	176²	154	5	80	61	12.1	3.67	74	.245	.334	10	.192	1	-18	-19	1	-1.6

● ELMER HORTON
Horton, Elmer E. "Herky Jerky" b: 9/4/1869, Hamilton, Ohio d: 8/12/20, Vienna, N.Y. Deb: 9/24/1896

YEAR TM/L	W	L	PCT	G	GS	CG	SH	SV	IP	H	HR	BB	SO	RAT	ERA	ERA+	OAV	OOB	BH	AVG	PB	PR	/A	PD	TPI
1896 Pit-N	0	2	.000	2	2	0	0	0	15	22	0	9	3	19.2	9.60	44	.338	.426	0	.000	-1	-9	-9	-1	-0.9
1898 Bro-N	0	1	.000	1	1	0	0	0	9	16	0	6	0	22.0	10.00	36	.383	.460	1	.250	-0	-6	-6	-0	-0.5
Total 2	0	3	.000	3	3	0	0	0	24	38	0	15	3	20.3	9.75	41	.356	.439	1	.091	-1	-15	-15	-1	-1.4

● RICKY HORTON
Horton, Ricky Neal b: 7/30/59, Poughkeepsie, N.Y. BL/TL, 6'2", 195 lbs. Deb: 4/7/84

YEAR TM/L	W	L	PCT	G	GS	CG	SH	SV	IP	H	HR	BB	SO	RAT	ERA	ERA+	OAV	OOB	BH	AVG	PB	PR	/A	PD	TPI
1984 StL-N	9	4	.692	37	18	1	1	1	125²	140	14	39	76	12.9	3.44	101	.285	.339	2	.065	-2	2	0	3	0.2
1985 *StL-N	3	2	.600	49	3	0	0	1	89²	84	5	34	59	12.1	2.91	121	.251	.326	1	.063	-0	7	6	2	0.5
1986 StL-N	4	3	.571	42	9	1	0	3	100¹	77	7	26	49	9.3	2.24	162	.218	.273	1	.056	-0	16	16	2	1.3
1987 *StL-N	8	3	.727	67	6	0	0	7	125	127	15	42	55	12.2	3.82	109	.263	.323	5	.172	0	4	5	2	0.7
1988 Chi-A	6	10	.375	52	9	0	0	2	109¹	120	6	36	28	13.3	4.86	82	.291	.355	—	—	0	-11	-11	1	-1.3
*LA-N	1	1	.500	12	0	0	0	0	9	11	2	2	8	13.0	5.00	67	.306	.342	0	—	0	-2	-2	1	-0.3
1989 StL-N	0	0	—	23	0	0	0	0	26²	35	1	11	12	15.9	5.06	67	.343	.412	0	.000	-0	-5	-5	-0	0.0
StL-N	0	3	.000	11	8	0	0	0	45²	50	2	10	14	12.4	4.73	77	.282	.332	3	.273	1	-6	-6	-0	-0.2
Yr	0	3	.000	34	8	0	0	0	72¹	85	3	21	26	13.6	4.85	73	.301	.356	3	.250	1	-11	-10	-0	-0.2
1990 StL-N	1	1	.500	32	0	0	0	0	32	32	1	22	18	16.1	4.93	77	.315	.399	0	.000	-0	-5	-5	2	-0.1
Total 7	32	27	.542	325	53	3	1	15	673¹	696	55	222	319	12.5	3.76	100	.273	.334	12	.109	-1	0	-2	12	0.8

● DAVE HOSKINS
Hoskins, David Taylor b: 8/3/25, Greenwood, Miss. d: 4/2/70, Flint, Mich. BL/TR, 6'1", 180 lbs. Deb: 4/18/53

YEAR TM/L	W	L	PCT	G	GS	CG	SH	SV	IP	H	HR	BB	SO	RAT	ERA	ERA+	OAV	OOB	BH	AVG	PB	PR	/A	PD	TPI
1953 Cle-A	9	3	.750	26	7	3	0	1	112²	102	9	38	55	11.5	3.99	94	.243	.312	15	.259	4	0	-3	0	0.1
1954 Cle-A	0	1	.000	14	1	0	0	0	26²	29	3	10	9	13.2	3.04	121	.284	.348	-1	.000	-1	2	2	-0	0.1
Total 2	9	4	.692	40	8	3	0	1	139¹	131	12	48	64	11.8	3.81	98	.251	.319	15	.227	3	2	-1	0	0.1

● GENE HOST
Host, Eugene Earl "Twinkles" or "Slick" b: 1/1/33, Leeper, Pa. BB/TL, 5'11", 190 lbs. Deb: 9/16/56

YEAR TM/L	W	L	PCT	G	GS	CG	SH	SV	IP	H	HR	BB	SO	RAT	ERA	ERA+	OAV	OOB	BH	AVG	PB	PR	/A	PD	TPI
1956 Det-A	0	0	—	1	1	0	0	0	4²	9	2	4	5	21.2	7.71	53	.409	.458	0	.000	-0	-2	-2	-0	0.0
1957 KC-A	0	2	.000	11	2	0	0	0	23²	29	5	12	9	16.4	7.23	55	.315	.406	0	.000	-1	-9	-9	-0	-0.7
Total 2	0	2	.000	12	3	0	0	0	28¹	38	7	16	14	17.2	7.31	55	.333	.415	0	.000	-1	-11	-10	0	-0.7

● BYRON HOUCK
Houck, Byron Simon "Duke" b: 8/28/1891, Prosper, Minn. d: 6/17/69, Santa Cruz, Cal. BR/TR, 6', 175 lbs. Deb: 5/15/12

YEAR TM/L	W	L	PCT	G	GS	CG	SH	SV	IP	H	HR	BB	SO	RAT	ERA	ERA+	OAV	OOB	BH	AVG	PB	PR	/A	PD	TPI
1912 Phi-A	8	8	.500	30	17	10	0	1	180²	148	9	74	77	11.7	2.94	105	.234	.326	4	.065	-7	8	3	-1	-0.5
1913 Phi-A	14	6	.700	41	19	4	1	0	176	147	3	122	71	14.1	4.14	67	.214	.337	5	.083	-4	-24	-27	-2	-3.4
1914 Phi-A	2	0	—	3	3	0	0	0	11	14	0	16	4	16.4	3.27	80	.318	.400	1	.333	—	-1	-0	1	-0.0
Bro-F	2	6	.250	17	9	3	0	0	92	95	4	43	45	13.7	3.13	92	.272	.355	7	.233	2	-2	-3	-3	-0.3
1918 StL-A	2	4	.333	27	2	0	0	0	71²	58	0	29	29	10.9	2.39	115	.225	.303	3	.150	-1	**3**	**3**	-1	0.1
Total 4	26	24	.520	118	50	17	1	1	531¹	462	16	274	224	12.8	3.30	87	.234	.334	20	.114	-9	-16	-24	-6	-4.1

● CHARLIE HOUGH
Hough, Charles Oliver b: 1/5/48, Honolulu, Hawaii BR/TR, 6'2", 190 lbs. Deb: 8/12/70

YEAR TM/L	W	L	PCT	G	GS	CG	SH	SV	IP	H	HR	BB	SO	RAT	ERA	ERA+	OAV	OOB	BH	AVG	PB	PR	/A	PD	TPI
1970 LA-N	0	0	—	8	0	0	0	2	17	18	7	11	8	15.4	5.29	72	.265	.367	1	.333	0	-2	-3	0	0.0

YEAR TM/L	W	L	PCT	G	GS	CG	SH	SV	IP	H	HR	BB	SO	RAT	ERA	ERA+	OAV	OOB	BH	AVG	PB	PR	/A	PD	TPI
1971 LA-N	0	0	—	4	0	0	0	0	4¹	3	1	3	4	12.5	4.15	78	.200	.333	0	—	0	-0	-0	0	0.0
1972 LA-N	0	0	—	2	0	0	0	0	2²	2	0	2	4	16.9	3.38	99	.200	.385	0	—	0	0	-0	0	0.0
1973 LA-N	4	2	.667	37	0	0	0	5	71²	52	3	45	70	12.9	2.76	124	.207	.341	3	.214	0	7	5	0	0.6
1974 *LA-N	9	4	.692	49	0	0	0	0	96	65	12	40	63	10.2	3.75	91	.196	.291	0	.000	-1	-1	-4	-0	-0.6
1975 LA-N	3	7	.300	38	0	0	0	4	61	43	3	34	34	12.5	2.95	115	.195	.323	2	.333	1	5	3	-1	0.5
1976 LA-N	12	8	.600	77	0	0	0	18	142²	102	6	77	81	11.8	2.21	153	.200	.314	6	.286	2	20	19	-1	3.3
1977 *LA-N	6	12	.333	70	1	0	0	22	127¹	98	10	70	105	12.4	3.32	115	.213	.326	4	.182	1	8	7	-1	1.2
1978 *LA-N	5	5	.500	55	0	0	0	7	93¹	69	6	48	66	11.8	3.28	107	.205	.313	4	.333	1	3	2	-0	0.4
1979 LA-N	7	5	.583	42	14	0	0	0	151¹	152	16	66	76	13.4	4.76	76	.264	.348	6	.158	-0	-17	-19	0	-1.4
1980 LA-N	1	3	.250	19	1	0	0	1	32¹	37	4	21	25	16.7	5.57	63	.291	.400	1	.500	0	-7	-7	-1	-0.9
Tex-A	2	2	.500	16	2	2	1	0	61¹	54	2	37	47	13.8	3.96	98	.240	.355	0	—	0	-0	-0	-0	0.1
1981 Tex-A	4	1	.800	21	5	2	0	1	82	61	4	31	69	10.4	2.96	117	.207	.290	0	—	0	6	5	-1	0.2
1982 Tex-A	16	13	.552	34	34	12	2	0	228	217	21	72	128	11.7	3.95	98	.251	.314	0	—	0	3	-2	1	0.2
1983 Tex-A	15	13	.536	34	33	11	3	0	252	219	22	95	152	11.3	3.18	126	.238	.311	0	—	0	25	23	4	2.9
1984 Tex-A	16	14	.533	36	36	**17**	1	0	266	260	26	94	164	12.3	3.76	110	.255	.324	0	—	0	7	12	3	1.5
1985 Tex-A	14	16	.467	34	34	14	1	0	250¹	198	23	83	141	10.4	3.31	128	.215	.285	0	—	0	23	26	1	2.9
1986 Tex-A★	17	10	.630	33	33	7	2	0	230¹	188	32	89	146	11.2	3.79	113	.221	.302	0	—	0	10	13	1	1.5
1987 Tex-A	18	13	.581	40	40	13	0	0	**285**¹	238	36	124	223	12.0	3.79	118	.223	.314	0	—	0	21	22	3	2.4
1988 Tex-A	15	16	.484	34	34	10	0	0	252	202	20	126	174	12.1	3.32	123	.221	.324	0	—	0	18	21	4	2.9
1989 Tex-A	10	13	.435	30	30	5	1	0	182	168	28	95	94	13.3	4.35	91	.245	.342	0	—	0	-9	-8	-2	-1.0
1990 Tex-A	12	12	.500	32	32	5	0	0	218²	190	24	119	114	13.2	4.07	96	.235	.342	0	—	0	-4	-4	-0	-0.4
1991 Chi-A	9	10	.474	31	29	4	1	0	199¹	167	21	94	107	12.3	4.02	99	.229	.326	0	—	0	2	-1	0	0.1
1992 Chi-A	7	12	.368	27	27	4	0	0	176¹	160	19	66	76	11.9	3.93	98	.239	.314	0	—	0	0	-1	-1	-0.2
1993 Fla-N	9	16	.360	34	34	0	0	0	204¹	202	20	71	126	12.4	4.27	101	.259	.328	2	.032	-5	-5	1	2	-0.2
1994 Fla-N	5	9	.357	21	21	1	1	0	113²	118	17	52	65	14.3	5.15	87	.274	.366	4	.121	-1	-12	-8	-0	-1.0
Total 25	216	216	.500	858	440	107	13	61	3801¹	3283	383	1665	2362	12.1	3.75	106	.233	.322	33	.146	-2	101	99	13	15.0

● **PAT HOUSE**   House, Patrick Lory b: 9/1/40, Boise, Idaho BL/TL, 6'3", 185 lbs. Deb: 9/6/67

YEAR TM/L	W	L	PCT	G	GS	CG	SH	SV	IP	H	HR	BB	SO	RAT	ERA	ERA+	OAV	OOB	BH	AVG	PB	PR	/A	PD	TPI
1967 Hou-N	1	0	1.000	6	0	0	0	0	4	3	0	0	2	9.0	4.50	74	.214	.267	0	—	0	-1	-1	0	-0.1
1968 Hou-N	1	1	.500	18	0	0	0	1	16¹	21	0	6	6	16.0	7.71	38	.323	.397	0	—	0	-9	-9	-0	-1.1
Total 2	2	1	.667	24	0	0	0	1	20¹	24	0	6	8	14.6	7.08	43	.304	.375	0	—	0	-9	-9	-0	-1.2

● **TOM HOUSE**   House, Thomas Ross b: 4/29/47, Seattle, Wash. BL/TL, 5'11", 190 lbs. Deb: 6/23/71 C

YEAR TM/L	W	L	PCT	G	GS	CG	SH	SV	IP	H	HR	BB	SO	RAT	ERA	ERA+	OAV	OOB	BH	AVG	PB	PR	/A	PD	TPI
1971 Atl-N	1	0	1.000	11	1	0	0	0	20²	20	2	3	11	10.5	3.05	122	.263	.300	2	.400	1	1	2	0	0.1
1972 Atl-N	0	0	—	8	0	0	0	2	9¹	7	1	6	7	13.5	2.89	131	.226	.368	0	.000	-0	1	1	0	0.0
1973 Atl-N	4	2	.667	52	0	0	0	4	67¹	58	13	31	42	12.2	4.68	84	.243	.335	2	.200	0	-8	-6	-0	-0.5
1974 Atl-N	6	2	.750	56	0	0	0	11	102²	74	5	27	64	9.1	1.93	196	.203	.264	4	.400	1	19	21	1	2.4
1975 Atl-N	7	7	.500	58	0	0	0	11	79¹	79	2	36	36	13.3	3.18	119	.262	.344	1	.111	-0	4	5	1	1.1
1976 Bos-A	1	3	.250	36	0	0	0	4	43²	39	4	19	27	12.4	4.33	90	.241	.328	0	—	0	-4	-2	1	-0.2
1977 Bos-A	1	0	1.000	8	0	0	0	0	7²	15	0	6	2	24.7	12.91	35	.405	.488	0	—	0	-8	-7	-0	-0.9
Sea-A	4	5	.444	26	11	1	0	1	89¹	94	12	19	39	11.8	3.93	105	.268	.313	0	—	0	1	2	-1	0.1
Yr	5	5	.500	34	11	1	0	1	97	109	12	25	45	12.8	4.64	89	.281	.331	0	—	0	-6	-5	-1	-0.8
1978 Sea-A	5	4	.556	34	9	3	0	2	116	130	10	35	29	13.2	4.66	82	.289	.347	0	—	0	-12	-11	-0	-0.8
Total 8	29	23	.558	289	21	4	0	33	536	516	49	182	261	12.1	3.79	102	.256	.324	9	.257	1	-5	5	1	1.3

● **FRED HOUSE**   House, Willard Edwin b: 10/3/1890, Cabool, Mo. d: 11/16/23, Kansas City, Mo. BR/TR, 6'3", 190 lbs. Deb: 4/22/13

YEAR TM/L	W	L	PCT	G	GS	CG	SH	SV	IP	H	HR	BB	SO	RAT	ERA	ERA+	OAV	OOB	BH	AVG	PB	PR	/A	PD	TPI
1913 Det-A	1	2	.333	19	2	0	0	0	53²	64	1	17	16	13.9	5.20	56	.325	.384	0	.000	-1	-14	-14	1	-0.7

● **CHARLIE HOUSEHOLDER**   Householder, Charles F. b: 1856, Harrisburg, Pa. BR/TR, 5'7", 150 lbs. Deb: 4/20/1884 ♦

YEAR TM/L	W	L	PCT	G	GS	CG	SH	SV	IP	H	HR	BB	SO	RAT	ERA	ERA+	OAV	OOB	BH	AVG	PB	PR	/A	PD	TPI
1884 CP-U	0	0	—	2	0	0	0	0	3	4	0	0	3	12.0	3.00	81	.300	.300	74	.239	-0	-0	-0	-0	0.0

● **FRANK HOUSEMAN**   Houseman, Frank b: Holland Deb: 9/2/1886

YEAR TM/L	W	L	PCT	G	GS	CG	SH	SV	IP	H	HR	BB	SO	RAT	ERA	ERA+	OAV	OOB	BH	AVG	PB	PR	/A	PD	TPI
1886 Bal-a	0	1	.000	1	1	1	0	0	8	6	0	1	5	9.0	3.38	101	.182	.229	1	.250	-0	0	0	0	0.0

● **JOE HOUSER**   Houser, Joseph William b: 7/3/1891, Steubenville, Ohio d: 1/3/53, Orlando, Fla. BL/TL, 5'9.5", 160 lbs. Deb: 4/24/14

YEAR TM/L	W	L	PCT	G	GS	CG	SH	SV	IP	H	HR	BB	SO	RAT	ERA	ERA+	OAV	OOB	BH	AVG	PB	PR	/A	PD	TPI
1914 Buf-F	0	1	.000	7	2	0	0	0	23	21	1	20	6	16.0	5.48	54	.250	.394	1	.143	-0	-7	-6	1	-0.2

● **ART HOUTTEMAN**   Houtteman, Arthur Joseph b: 8/7/27, Detroit, Mich. BR/TR, 6'2", 188 lbs. Deb: 4/29/45

YEAR TM/L	W	L	PCT	G	GS	CG	SH	SV	IP	H	HR	BB	SO	RAT	ERA	ERA+	OAV	OOB	BH	AVG	PB	PR	/A	PD	TPI
1945 Det-A	0	2	.000	13	0	0	0	0	25¹	27	1	11	9	13.9	5.33	66	.270	.348	0	.000	-1	-6	-5	1	-0.4
1946 Det-A	0	1	.000	1	1	0	0	0	8	15	1	0	2	16.9	9.00	41	.385	.385	1	.500	0	-5	-5	-0	-0.4
1947 Det-A	7	2	.778	23	9	7	2	0	110²	106	6	36	58	11.6	3.42	110	.247	.306	12	.300	2	4	4	-0	0.5
1948 Det-A	2	16	.111	43	20	4	0	10	164¹	186	11	52	74	13.1	4.66	94	.287	.342	11	.196	-2	-7	-5	4	-0.4
1949 Det-A	15	10	.600	34	25	13	2	0	203²	227	19	59	85	12.9	3.71	112	.282	.335	19	.244	1	11	10	5	1.7
1950 Det-A★	19	12	.613	41	34	21	**4**	4	274²	257	29	99	88	11.9	3.54	132	.251	.322	14	.151	-3	32	35	3	3.5
1952 Det-A	8	20	.286	35	28	10	2	1	221	218	19	65	109	11.7	4.36	87	.253	.309	7	.101	-4	-17	-14	1	-1.9
1953 Det-A	2	6	.250	16	9	3	1	0	68²	87	11	29	28	15.7	5.90	69	.309	.381	3	.158	0	-15	-14	-0	-1.4
Cle-A	7	7	.500	22	13	6	1	3	109	113	4	25	40	11.8	3.80	99	.269	.318	5	.147	-1	2	-1	0	-0.2
Yr	9	13	.409	38	22	9	2	4	177²	200	15	54	68	13.1	4.61	84	.283	.339	8	.151	-1	-12	-15	-0	-1.6
1954 *Cle-A	15	7	.682	32	25	11	1	0	188	198	14	59	68	12.3	3.35	110	.277	.330	18	.277	8	7	2	1	1.4
1955 Cle-A	10	6	.625	35	12	3	1	0	124¹	126	15	44	53	12.5	3.98	100	.265	.330	6	.158	-1	-0	0	2	0.2
1956 Cle-A	2	2	.500	22	4	0	0	0	46²	60	5	31	19	18.3	6.56	64	.317	.424	2	.167	-0	-12	-12	0	-1.0
1957 Cle-A	0	0	—	3	0	0	0	0	4	6	1	3	3	20.3	6.75	55	.353	.450	0	—	0	-1	-1	0	0.0
Bal-A	0	0	—	5	1	0	0	0	6²	20	0	3	3	31.1	17.55	20	.513	.548	1	.500	0	-10	-10	0	-0.1
Yr	0	0	—	8	1	0	0	0	10²	26	1	6	6	27.0	13.50	27	.464	.516	1	.500	0	-12	-12	0	0.1
Total 12	87	91	.489	325	181	78	14	20	1555	1646	136	516	639	12.7	4.14	99	.272	.333	99	.193	-4	-16	-11	17	1.7

● **ED HOVLIK**   Hovlik, Edward Charles b: 8/20/1891, Cleveland, Ohio d: 3/19/55, Painesville, Ohio BR/TR, 6', 180 lbs. Deb: 7/14/18 F

YEAR TM/L	W	L	PCT	G	GS	CG	SH	SV	IP	H	HR	BB	SO	RAT	ERA	ERA+	OAV	OOB	BH	AVG	PB	PR	/A	PD	TPI
1918 Was-A	2	1	.667	8	2	1	0	0	28	25	0	10	10	11.3	1.29	212	.272	.343	1	.125	-1	5	4	-1	0.4
1919 Was-A	0	0	—	3	0	0	0	0	5²	12	0	9	3	33.4	12.71	25	.480	.618	0	.000	-0	-6	-6	0	0.0
Total 2	2	1	.667	11	2	1	0	0	33²	37	0	19	13	15.0	3.21	88	.316	.412	1	.100	-1	-1	-1	0	0.4

● **JOE HOVLIK**   Hovlik, Joseph b: 8/16/1884, Czechoslovakia d: 11/3/51, Oxford Junction, Ia BR/TR, 5'10.5", 194 lbs. Deb: 7/10/09 F

YEAR TM/L	W	L	PCT	G	GS	CG	SH	SV	IP	H	HR	BB	SO	RAT	ERA	ERA+	OAV	OOB	BH	AVG	PB	PR	/A	PD	TPI
1909 Was-A	0	0	—	3	0	0	0	0	6	13	0	3	1	25.5	4.50	54	.419	.486	0	.000	0	-1	-1	0	0.1
1910 Was-A	0	0	—	1	0	0	0	0	1²	6	0	0	0	37.8	16.20	15	.500	.538	0	—	0	-3	-3	0	0.0
1911 Chi-A	2	0	1.000	12	3	1	1	0	47	47	1	20	24	12.8	3.06	105	.257	.330	1	.077	-0	1	1	0	0.1
Total 3	2	0	1.000	16	3	1	1	0	54²	66	1	23	25	15.0	3.62	86	.292	.363	1	.067	-0	-2	-3	1	0.2

● **BRUCE HOWARD**   Howard, Bruce Ernest b: 3/23/43, Salisbury, Md. BB/TR, 6'2", 180 lbs. Deb: 9/4/63 F

YEAR TM/L	W	L	PCT	G	GS	CG	SH	SV	IP	H	HR	BB	SO	RAT	ERA	ERA+	OAV	OOB	BH	AVG	PB	PR	/A	PD	TPI
1963 Chi-A	2	1	.667	7	0	0	0	0	17	12	0	14	9	13.8	2.65	132	.207	.361	1	.250	0	2	2	-0	0.3
1964 Chi-A	2	1	.667	3	3	1	1	0	22¹	10	0	8	17	7.7	0.81	429	.139	.235	0	.000	-1	7	7	-0	0.9
1965 Chi-A	9	8	.529	30	22	1	1	0	148	123	13	72	120	11.9	3.47	92	.224	.316	6	.146	0	-0	-4	-1	-0.4
1966 Chi-A	9	5	.643	27	21	4	2	0	149	110	14	44	85	9.4	2.30	138	.202	.263	3	.073	0	19	14	0	1.3
1967 Chi-A	3	10	.231	30	17	0	0	0	112²	102	9	52	76	12.5	3.43	90	.240	.327	5	.179	1	-3	-4	1	-0.3
1968 Bal-A	0	2	.000	10	5	0	0	0	31	26	2	26	19	16.8	3.77	78	.268	.414	2	.286	2	-3	-3	-0	0.1
Was-A	1	4	.200	13	7	0	0	0	48²	62	7	23	23	15.7	5.36	54	.330	.403	0	.000	-2	-13	-13	1	-1.4

YEAR	TM/L	W	L	PCT	G	GS	CG	SH	SV	IP	H	HR	BB	SO	RAT	ERA	ERA+	OAV	OOB	BH	AVG	PB	PR	/A	PD	TPI
	Yr	1	6	.143	23	12	0	0	0	79²	92	9	49	42	15.9	4.74	62	.302	.398	2	.087	0	-16	-16	1	-1.3
Total 6		26	31	.456	120	75	7	4	1	528²	449	45	239	349	11.8	3.18	99	.231	.317	17	.116	2	9	-2	1	0.5

● **CHRIS HOWARD**   Howard, Christian b: 11/18/65, Lynn, Mass. BR/TL, 6', 185 lbs. Deb: 9/21/93

YEAR	TM/L	W	L	PCT	G	GS	CG	SH	SV	IP	H	HR	BB	SO	RAT	ERA	ERA+	OAV	OOB	BH	AVG	PB	PR	/A	PD	TPI
1993	Chi-A	1	0	1.000	3	0	0	0	0	2¹	2	0	3	1	19.3	0.00	—	.286	.500	0	—	0	1	1	-0	0.4
1994	Bos-A	1	0	1.000	37	0	0	0	1	39²	35	5	12	22	10.7	3.63	142	.233	.290	0	—	0	5	7	0	-0.1
Total 2		2	0	1.000	40	0	0	0	1	42	37	5	15	23	11.1	3.43	148	.236	.302	0	—	0	6	8	-0	0.3

● **DAVID HOWARD**   Howard, David Wayne b: 2/26/67, Sarasota, Fla. BB/TR, 6', 165 lbs. Deb: 4/14/91 F♦

YEAR	TM/L	W	L	PCT	G	GS	CG	SH	SV	IP	H	HR	BB	SO	RAT	ERA	ERA+	OAV	OOB	BH	AVG	PB	PR	/A	PD	TPI
1994	KC-A	0	0	—	1	0	0	0	0	2	2	0	5	0	31.5	4.50	115	.286	.583	19	.229	0	0	0	0	0.0

● **EARL HOWARD**   Howard, Earl Nycum b: 6/25/1893, Everett, Pa. d: 4/4/37, Everett, Pa. BR/TR, 6'1", 160 lbs. Deb: 4/18/18

YEAR	TM/L	W	L	PCT	G	GS	CG	SH	SV	IP	H	HR	BB	SO	RAT	ERA	ERA+	OAV	OOB	BH	AVG	PB	PR	/A	PD	TPI
1918	StL-N	0	0	—	1	0	0	0	0	2	0	0	2	0	9.0	0.00	—	.000	.286	0	—	0	1	1	1	0.1

● **FRED HOWARD**   Howard, Fred Irving b: 9/2/56, Portland, Maine BR/TR, 6'3", 190 lbs. Deb: 5/26/79

YEAR	TM/L	W	L	PCT	G	GS	CG	SH	SV	IP	H	HR	BB	SO	RAT	ERA	ERA+	OAV	OOB	BH	AVG	PB	PR	/A	PD	TPI
1979	Chi-A	1	5	.167	28	6	0	0	0	68	73	5	32	36	14.0	3.57	119	.283	.364	0	—	0	5	5	-1	0.3

● **DEL HOWARD**   Howard, George Elmer b: 12/24/1877, Kenney, Ill. d: 12/24/56, Seattle, Wash. BL/TR, 6', 180 lbs. Deb: 4/15/05 F♦

YEAR	TM/L	W	L	PCT	G	GS	CG	SH	SV	IP	H	HR	BB	SO	RAT	ERA	ERA+	OAV	OOB	BH	AVG	PB	PR	/A	PD	TPI
1905	Pit-N	0	0	—	1	0	0	0	0	6	4	1	0	0	9.0	0.00	—	.200	.273	127	.292	0	2	2	0	0.0

● **LEE HOWARD**   Howard, Lee Vincent b: 11/11/23, Staten Island, N.Y. BL/TL, 6'2", 175 lbs. Deb: 9/22/46

YEAR	TM/L	W	L	PCT	G	GS	CG	SH	SV	IP	H	HR	BB	SO	RAT	ERA	ERA+	OAV	OOB	BH	AVG	PB	PR	/A	PD	TPI
1946	Pit-N	0	1	.000	3	2	1	0	0	13¹	14	0	9	6	15.5	2.03	174	.286	.397	0	.000	-1	2	2	-0	0.1
1947	Pit-N	0	0	—	2	0	0	0	0	2²	4	1	0	2	13.5	3.38	125	.333	.333	0	—	0	0	0	-0	0.0
Total 2		0	1	.000	5	2	1	0	0	16	18	1	9	8	15.2	2.25	162	.295	.386	0	.000	-1	2	2	-0	0.1

● **CAL HOWE**   Howe, Calvin Earl b: 11/27/24, Rock Falls, Ill. BL/TL, 6'3", 205 lbs. Deb: 9/26/52

YEAR	TM/L	W	L	PCT	G	GS	CG	SH	SV	IP	H	HR	BB	SO	RAT	ERA	ERA+	OAV	OOB	BH	AVG	PB	PR	/A	PD	TPI
1952	Chi-N	0	0	—	1	0	0	0	0	2	0	1	2	4	4.5	0.00	—	.000	.143	0	—	0	1	1	0	0.0

● **LES HOWE**   Howe, Lester Curtis "Lucky" b: 8/24/1895, Brooklyn, N.Y. d: 7/16/76, Woodmere, N.Y. BR/TR, 5'11.5", 170 lbs. Deb: 8/18/23

YEAR	TM/L	W	L	PCT	G	GS	CG	SH	SV	IP	H	HR	BB	SO	RAT	ERA	ERA+	OAV	OOB	BH	AVG	PB	PR	/A	PD	TPI
1923	Bos-A	1	0	1.000	12	2	0	0	0	30	23	0	7	7	9.3	2.40	171	.211	.265	0	.000	-1	5	6	0	0.1
1924	Bos-A	1	0	1.000	4	0	0	0	0	7¹	11	1	2	3	17.2	7.36	59	.423	.483	1	.500	0	-3	-2	0	-0.2
Total 2		2	0	1.000	16	2	0	0	0	37¹	34	1	9	10	10.8	3.38	123	.252	.308	1	.125	-1	3	3	0	-0.1

● **STEVE HOWE**   Howe, Steven Roy b: 3/10/58, Pontiac, Mich. BL/TL, 6'1", 180 lbs. Deb: 4/11/80

YEAR	TM/L	W	L	PCT	G	GS	CG	SH	SV	IP	H	HR	BB	SO	RAT	ERA	ERA+	OAV	OOB	BH	AVG	PB	PR	/A	PD	TPI
1980	LA-N	7	9	.438	59	0	0	0	17	84²	83	4	22	39	11.4	2.66	132	.256	.307	1	.091	-1	9	8	1	1.9
1981	*LA-N	5	3	.625	41	0	0	0	8	54	51	2	18	32	11.5	2.50	133	.254	.315	0	.000	0	6	5	-1	0.8
1982	LA-N★	7	5	.583	66	0	0	0	13	99¹	87	3	17	49	9.4	2.08	166	.240	.274	0	—	-1	17	15	-0	2.1
1983	LA-N	4	7	.364	46	0	0	0	18	68²	55	2	12	52	8.9	1.44	249	.217	.256	1	.125	0	17	16	1	3.8
1985	LA-N	1	1	.500	19	0	0	0	3	22	30	2	5	11	14.7	4.91	71	.319	.360	0	—	0	-3	-4	0	-0.4
	Min-A	2	3	.400	13	0	0	0	0	19	28	1	7	10	16.6	6.16	72	.333	.385	0	—	0	-4	-4	-0	-1.1
1987	Tex-A	3	3	.500	24	0	0	0	1	31¹	33	2	8	19	12.6	4.31	104	.280	.341	0	—	0	1	1	0	0.1
1991	NY-A	3	1	.750	37	0	0	0	3	48¹	39	1	7	34	9.1	1.68	247	.222	.263	0	—	0	13	13	0	1.2
1992	NY-A	3	0	1.000	20	0	0	0	6	22	9	1	3	12	4.9	2.45	160	.122	.156	0	—	0	4	4	1	0.8
1993	NY-A	3	5	.375	51	0	0	0	4	50²	58	7	10	19	12.6	4.97	83	.297	.341	0	—	0	-4	-5	1	-0.6
1994	NY-A	3	0	1.000	40	0	0	0	15	40	28	2	7	18	7.9	1.80	246	.194	.232	0	—	0	13	12	0	1.8
Total 10		41	37	.526	416	0	0	0	88	540	501	24	116	295	10.5	2.75	137	.247	.292	2	.074	-1	68	62	3	10.4

● **HARRY HOWELL**   Howell, Henry Harry b: 11/14/1876, New Jersey d: 5/22/56, Spokane, Wash. BR/TR, 5'9", Deb: 10/10/1898 U♦

YEAR	TM/L	W	L	PCT	G	GS	CG	SH	SV	IP	H	HR	BB	SO	RAT	ERA	ERA+	OAV	OOB	BH	AVG	PB	PR	/A	PD	TPI
1898	Bro-N	2	0	1.000	2	2	2	2	0	18	15	0	11	2	13.5	5.00	72	.225	.343	2	.250		-3	-3	0	-0.2
1899	Bal-N	13	8	.619	28	25	21	0	1	209¹	248	5	69	58	14.1	3.91	101	.294	.355	12	.146	-3	-1	1	1	-0.2
1900	*Bro-N	6	5	.545	21	10	7	2	0	110¹	131	4	36	26	13.9	3.75	102	.294	.351	12	.286	4	-1	1	1	0.5
1901	Bal-A	14	21	.400	37	34	32	1	0	294²	333	5	79	93	12.8	3.67	106	.281	.330	41	.218	1	0	7	-1	0.6
1902	Bal-A	9	15	.375	26	23	19	1	0	199	243	5	48	33	13.5	4.12	92	.301	.346	93	.268	5	-12	-8	4	0.1
1903	NY-A	9	6	.600	25	15	13	0	0	155²	140	4	44	62	11.0	3.53	89	.240	.300	23	.217	2	-10	-7	3	-0.1
1904	StL-A	13	21	.382	34	33	32	2	0	299²	254	1	60	122	9.8	2.19	113	.231	.278	25	.221	5	14	10	9	2.9
1905	StL-A	15	22	.405	38	37	**35**	4	0	323	252	2	101	198	10.2	1.98	129	.216	.286	26	.193	3	25	20	18	**4.9**
1906	StL-A	15	14	.517	35	33	30	6	1	276²	233	1	61	140	9.9	2.11	122	.231	.282	13	.126	-3	18	14	7	2.1
1907	StL-A	16	15	.516	42	35	26	2	3	316¹	258	0	88	118	10.1	1.93	130	.225	.285	27	.237	6	22	21	8	3.7
1908	StL-A	18	18	.500	41	32	27	2	1	324¹	279	1	70	117	10.2	1.89	127	.240	.293	22	.183	1	18	18	0	2.3
1909	StL-A	1	1	.500	10	3	0	0	0	37¹	42	0	8	16	12.8	3.13	77	.294	.344	6	.176	0	-3	-3	-0	-0.2
1910	StL-A	0	0	—	1	0	0	0	0	3¹	7	0	2	1	24.3	10.80	23	.467	.529	0	—	-0	-3	-3	0	0.0
Total 13		131	146	.473	340	282	244	20	6	2567²	2435	27	677	986	11.2	2.74	108	.252	.307	302	.217	21	64	64	51	16.4

● **JAY HOWELL**   Howell, Jay Canfield b: 11/26/55, Miami, Fla. BR/TR, 6'3", 205 lbs. Deb: 8/10/80

YEAR	TM/L	W	L	PCT	G	GS	CG	SH	SV	IP	H	HR	BB	SO	RAT	ERA	ERA+	OAV	OOB	BH	AVG	PB	PR	/A	PD	TPI
1980	Cin-N	0	0	—	5	0	0	0	0	3¹	8	0	0	1	24.3	13.50	26	.471	.500	0	—	0	-4	-4	-0	0.0
1981	Chi-N	2	0	1.000	10	2	0	0	0	22¹	23	3	10	10	14.1	4.84	76	.277	.368	0	.000	0	-3	-3	1	-0.1
1982	NY-A	2	3	.400	6	6	0	0	0	28	42	1	13	21	17.7	7.71	52	.341	.404	0	—	0	-11	-12	-0	-1.6
1983	NY-A	1	5	.167	19	12	2	0	0	82	89	7	35	61	13.9	5.38	72	.275	.351	0	—	0	-12	-14	-0	-0.7
1984	NY-A	9	4	.692	61	1	0	0	7	103²	86	5	34	109	10.4	2.69	141	.223	.286	0	—	0	15	13	2	1.9
1985	Oak-A☆	8	8	.529	63	0	0	0	29	98	98	5	31	68	11.9	2.85	135	.261	.319	0	—	0	14	11	0	2.6
1986	Oak-A	3	6	.333	38	0	0	0	16	53¹	53	3	23	42	13.0	3.38	115	.262	.341	0	—	0	5	3	-0	0.8
1987	Oak-A★	3	4	.429	36	0	0	0	16	44¹	48	6	21	35	14.2	5.89	70	.277	.359	0	—	0	-7	-9	-0	-1.4
1988	*LA-N	5	3	.625	50	0	0	0	21	65	44	1	21	70	9.1	2.08	160	.188	.258	0	.000	-0	10	9	-0	1.8
1989	LA-N★	5	3	.625	56	0	0	0	28	79²	60	3	22	55	9.3	1.58	216	.211	.268	0	—	0	17	16	-0	3.0
1990	LA-N	5	5	.500	45	0	0	0	16	66	59	5	20	59	11.6	2.18	168	.242	.315	0	.000	-0	12	11	-0	2.2
1991	LA-N	6	5	.545	44	0	0	0	16	51	39	3	11	40	9.0	3.18	113	.213	.262	0	—	0	3	2	0	0.7
1992	LA-N	1	3	.250	41	0	0	0	4	46²	41	2	18	36	11.6	1.54	223	.230	.305	0	—	0	10	10	-0	1.1
1993	Atl-N	3	3	.500	54	0	0	0	0	58¹	48	3	16	37	9.9	2.31	173	.229	.283	0	—	0	11	11	-0	1.0
1994	Tex-A	4	1	.800	40	0	0	0	2	43	44	10	16	22	12.8	5.44	83	.262	.330	0	—	0	-3	-4	0	-0.4
Total 15		58	53	.523	568	21	2	0	155	844²	782	57	291	666	11.6	3.34	113	.246	.313	0	.000	-1	56	42	2	10.9

● **KEN HOWELL**   Howell, Kenneth b: 11/28/60, Detroit, Mich. BR/TR, 6'3", 228 lbs. Deb: 6/25/84

YEAR	TM/L	W	L	PCT	G	GS	CG	SH	SV	IP	H	HR	BB	SO	RAT	ERA	ERA+	OAV	OOB	BH	AVG	PB	PR	/A	PD	TPI
1984	LA-N	5	5	.500	32	1	0	0	6	51¹	49		9	54	10.7	3.33	106	.267	.303	0	.000	-1	1	1	0	0.2
1985	*LA-N	4	7	.364	56	0	0	0	12	86	66	8	35	85	10.6	3.77	92	.208	.287	0	.000	-0	-2	-3	0	-0.5
1986	LA-N	6	12	.333	62	0	0	0	12	97²	86	7	63	104	14.0	3.87	89	.239	.357	0	.000	-1	-2	-5	-1	-1.1
1987	LA-N	3	4	.429	40	2	0	0	1	55	54	7	29	60	13.6	4.91	81	.265	.356	1	.250	0	-5	-6	-0	-0.7
1988	LA-N	0	1	.000	4	1	0	0	0	12²	14	2	5	12	14.2	6.39	72	.320	.370	0	—	-0	-4	-4	-0	-0.3
1989	Phi-N	12	12	.500	33	32	1	1	0	204	155	11	86	164	10.7	3.44	103	.215	.300	6	.092	-2	1	2	-1	-0.1
1990	Phi-N	8	7	.533	18	18	2	0	0	106²	106	12	49	70	13.3	4.64	82	.260	.343	1	.067	-1	-10	-10	-1	-1.4
Total 7		38	48	.442	245	54	3	1	31	613¹	534	46	275	549	12.0	3.95	91	.237	.323	9	.079	-5	-20	-24	-3	-3.9

● **DIXIE HOWELL**   Howell, Millard b: 1/7/20, Bowman, Ky. d: 3/18/60, Hollywood, Fla. BL/TR, 6'2", 210 lbs. Deb: 9/14/40

YEAR	TM/L	W	L	PCT	G	GS	CG	SH	SV	IP	H	HR	BB	SO	RAT	ERA	ERA+	OAV	OOB	BH	AVG	PB	PR	/A	PD	TPI
1940	Cle-A	0	0	—	2	0	0	0	0	4	3	0	2	2	10.8	1.80	234	.143	.333	0	—	0	1	1	0	0.0
1949	Cin-N	0	1	.000	5	1	0	0	0	13¹	21	3	8	7	19.6	8.10	52	.362	.439	1	.111	-0	-6	-6	0	-0.4
1955	Chi-A	8	3	.727	35	0	0	0	4	73²	70	1	25	25	11.6	2.93	135	.250	.311	8	.381	2	8	8	1	1.7
1956	Chi-A	5	6	.455	34	1	0	0	4	64¹	79	3	36	28	16.4	4.62	89	.309	.398	4	.235	2	-3	-4	0	-0.4

YEAR TM/L	W	L	PCT	G	GS	CG	SH	SV	IP	H	HR	BB	SO	RAT	ERA	ERA+	OAV	OOB	BH	AVG	PB	PR	/A	PD	TPI
1957 Chi-A	6	5	.545	37	0	0	0	6	68¹	64	6	30	37	12.4	3.29	113	.255	.335	5	.185	4	4	3	1	1.0
1958 Chi-A	0	0	—	1	0	0	0	0	1²	5	0	5	0	54.0	0.00	—	.000	.000	0	—	0	1	1	0	0.0
Total 6	19	15	.559	115	2	0	0	19	226¹	236	13	103	99	13.6	3.78	104	.273	.352	18	.243	8	5	4	2	1.9

● **ROLAND HOWELL**   Howell, Roland Boatner "Billiken" · b: 1/3/1892, Napoleonville, La. · d: 3/31/73, Baton Rouge, La. · BR/TR, 6'4", 210 lbs. · Deb: 6/14/12

YEAR TM/L	W	L	PCT	G	GS	CG	SH	SV	IP	H	HR	BB	SO	RAT	ERA	ERA+	OAV	OOB	BH	AVG	PB	PR	/A	PD	TPI
1912 StL-N	0	0	—	3	0	0	0	0	1²	5	0	5	0	54.0	27.00	13	.556	.714	0	—	0	-4	-4	-0	0.0

● **PETER HOY**   Hoy, Peter Alexander · b: 6/29/66, Brockville, Ont., Canada · BL/TR, 6'7", 220 lbs. · Deb: 4/11/92

YEAR TM/L	W	L	PCT	G	GS	CG	SH	SV	IP	H	HR	BB	SO	RAT	ERA	ERA+	OAV	OOB	BH	AVG	PB	PR	/A	PD	TPI
1992 Bos-A	0	0	—	5	0	0	0	0	3²	8	0	2	2	24.5	7.36	57	.471	.526	0	—	0	-1	-1	0	0.0

● **TEX HOYLE**   Hoyle, Roland Edison · b: 7/17/21, Carbondale, Pa. · d: 7/4/94, Carbondale, Pa. · BR/TR, 6'4", 170 lbs. · Deb: 4/18/52

YEAR TM/L	W	L	PCT	G	GS	CG	SH	SV	IP	H	HR	BB	SO	RAT	ERA	ERA+	OAV	OOB	BH	AVG	PB	PR	/A	PD	TPI
1952 Phi-A	0	0	—	3	0	0	0	0	2¹	9	2	1	1	38.6	27.00	15	.563	.588	0	—	0	-6	-6	0	0.0

● **LA MARR HOYT**   Hoyt, Dewey La Marr · b: 1/1/55, Columbia, S.C. · BR/TR, 6'1", 222 lbs. · Deb: 9/14/79

YEAR TM/L	W	L	PCT	G	GS	CG	SH	SV	IP	H	HR	BB	SO	RAT	ERA	ERA+	OAV	OOB	BH	AVG	PB	PR	/A	PD	TPI
1979 Chi-A	0	0	—	2	0	0	0	0	3	2	0	0	6	6.0	0.00	—	.200	.200	0	—	0	1	1	-0	0.0
1980 Chi-A	9	3	.750	24	13	3	1	0	112¹	123	8	41	55	13.3	4.57	88	.281	.345	0	—	0	-7	-7	-2	-0.8
1981 Chi-A	9	3	.750	43	1	0	0	10	90²	80	10	28	60	11.0	3.57	100	.240	.305	0	—	0	1	0	-1	0.0
1982 Chi-A	19	15	.559	39	32	14	2	0	239²	248	17	48	124	11.2	3.53	114	.266	.303	0	—	0	14	13	-1	1.6
1983 *Chi-A	24	10	.706	36	36	11	1	0	260²	236	27	31	148	**9.3**	3.66	114	.238	**.262**	0	—	0	12	15	5	2.3
1984 Chi-A	13	18	.419	34	34	11	1	0	235²	244	31	43	126	11.2	4.47	93	.266	.302	0	—	0	-13	-8	1	-0.9
1985 SD-N★	16	8	.667	31	31	8	3	0	210¹	210	20	20	83	9.9	3.47	102	.261	.281	4	.063	-4	3	2	1	-0.1
1986 SD-N	8	11	.421	35	25	1	0	0	159	170	27	68	85	13.6	5.15	71	.276	.351	6	.130	-1	-25	-26	-2	-3.1
Total 8	98	68	.590	244	172	48	8	10	1311¹	1313	140	279	681	11.0	3.99	98	.260	.302	10	.091	-5	-13	-10	1	-1.0

● **WAITE HOYT**   Hoyt, Waite Charles "Schoolboy" · b: 9/9/1899, Brooklyn, N.Y. · d: 8/25/84, Cincinnati, Ohio · BR/TR, 6', 180 lbs. · Deb: 7/24/18 · H

YEAR TM/L	W	L	PCT	G	GS	CG	SH	SV	IP	H	HR	BB	SO	RAT	ERA	ERA+	OAV	OOB	BH	AVG	PB	PR	/A	PD	TPI
1918 NY-N	0	0	—	1	0	0	0	0	1	0	0	0	2	0.0	0.00	—	.000	.000	0	.000	-0	0	0	0	0.0
1919 Bos-A	4	6	.400	13	11	6	1	0	105¹	99	1	22	28	10.3	3.25	93	.262	.303	5	.132	-3	-0	-3	1	-0.4
1920 Bos-A	6	6	.500	22	11	6	2	1	121¹	123	2	47	45	12.7	4.38	83	.270	.339	5	.116	-3	-8	-10	1	-1.1
1921 *NY-A	19	13	.594	43	32	21	1	3	282¹	301	3	81	102	12.3	3.09	137	.276	.329	22	.222	-2	37	36	-1	3.3
1922 *NY-A	19	12	.613	37	31	17	3	0	265	271	13	76	95	12.1	3.43	117	.269	.326	20	.217	1	18	17	-2	1.7
1923 *NY-A	17	9	.654	37	28	19	1	1	238²	227	9	66	60	11.2	3.02	131	.253	.307	16	.190	-2	26	24	-1	2.1
1924 NY-A	18	13	.581	46	32	14	2	4	247	295	8	76	71	13.6	3.79	110	.300	.352	10	.133	-5	12	10	-0	0.6
1925 NY-A	11	14	.440	46	30	17	1	6	243	283	14	78	66	13.4	4.00	107	.292	.346	24	.304	6	11	7	3	1.3
1926 *NY-A	16	12	.571	40	28	12	1	4	217²	224	4	62	79	11.9	3.85	100	.264	.316	16	.211	0	-0	-3	-0	-0.3
1927 *NY-A	22	7	**.759**	36	32	23	3	1	256¹	242	10	54	86	10.5	2.63	146	.251	.294	22	.222	-3	43	35	-0	3.5
1928 *NY-A	23	7	.767	42	31	19	3	**8**	273	279	16	60	67	11.2	3.36	112	.272	.313	28	.257	2	21	12	-1	1.2
1929 NY-A	10	9	.526	30	25	12	0	1	201²	219	9	69	57	13.0	4.24	91	.279	.339	17	.224	1	0	-9	-2	-0.7
1930 NY-A	2	2	.500	8	7	2	0	0	47²	64	7	9	10	13.8	4.53	90	.317	.346	1	.063	-2	1	-1	-0	-0.3
Det-A	9	8	.529	26	20	8	1	4	135²	176	7	47	25	14.9	4.78	100	.313	.368	9	.196	-2	-2	-0	-3	-0.5
Yr	11	10	.524	34	27	10	1	4	183¹	240	14	56	35	14.6	4.71	99	.314	.363	10	.161	-4	-1	-1	-3	-0.8
1931 Det-A	3	8	.273	16	12	5	0	0	92	124	2	32	10	15.5	5.87	78	.319	.374	4	.133	-2	-15	-13	-0	-1.5
*Phi-A	10	5	.667	16	14	9	2	0	111	130	9	37	30	13.5	4.22	107	.298	.353	13	.302	3	2	3	1	0.7
Yr	13	13	.500	32	26	14	2	0	203	254	11	69	40	14.3	4.97	91	.307	.360	17	.233	0	-13	-10	0	-0.8
1932 Bro-N	1	3	.250	8	4	0	0	1	26²	38	3	12	7	16.9	7.76	49	.342	.407	0	.000	-1	-12	-12	1	-1.5
NY-N	5	7	.417	18	12	3	0	0	97¹	103	6	25	29	12.3	3.42	109	.275	.328	3	.097	-2	5	3	1	0.2
Yr	6	10	.375	26	16	3	0	1	124	141	9	37	36	13.3	4.35	86	.290	.347	3	.081	-3	-7	-9	2	-1.3
1933 Pit-N	5	7	.417	36	8	4	1	4	117	118	3	19	44	10.6	2.92	114	.262	.293	5	.156	-1	5	5	1	0.5
1934 Pit-N	15	6	.714	48	15	8	3	5	190²	184	6	43	105	10.8	2.93	141	.252	.296	10	.179	-1	24	25	-1	2.5
1935 Pit-N	7	11	.389	39	11	5	0	6	164	187	8	27	63	11.8	3.40	121	.285	.315	14	.259	2	11	13	-0	1.5
1936 Pit-N	7	5	.583	22	9	6	0	1	116²	115	5	20	37	10.6	2.70	150	.255	.291	6	.154	1	17	18	1	1.6
1937 Pit-N	1	2	.333	11	0	0	0	2	28	31	3	6	11	11.9	4.50	86	.270	.306	1	.083	-1	-2	-2	-1	-0.4
Bro-N	7	7	.500	27	19	10	1	0	167	180	5	30	44	11.3	3.23	125	.270	.301	4	.083	-2	13	15	-1	0.8
Yr	8	9	.471	38	19	10	1	2	195	211	8	36	65	11.4	3.42	117	.270	.302	5	.083	-3	11	13	-2	0.4
1938 Bro-N	0	3	.000	6	1	0	0	0	16¹	24	1	5	3	16.0	4.96	79	.333	.377	0	.000	-0	-2	-2	-0	-0.4
Total 21	237	182	.566	674	423	226	26	52	3762¹	4037	154	1003	1206	12.2	3.59	112	.276	.325	255	.198	-17	210	173	-7	14.4

● **AL HRABOSKY**   Hrabosky, Alan Thomas · b: 7/21/49, Oakland, Cal. · BR/TL, 5'11", 185 lbs. · Deb: 6/16/70

YEAR TM/L	W	L	PCT	G	GS	CG	SH	SV	IP	H	HR	BB	SO	RAT	ERA	ERA+	OAV	OOB	BH	AVG	PB	PR	/A	PD	TPI
1970 StL-N	2	1	.667	16	1	0	0	0	19	22	2	7	12	13.7	4.74	87	.286	.345	0	.000	-0	-1	-1	-1	-0.3
1971 StL-N	0	0	—	1	0	0	0	0	2	2	0	2	2	18.0	—	.250	.250	0	—	-0	1	1	-0	0.0
1972 StL-N	1	0	1.000	5	0	0	0	0	7	2	0	3	9	6.4	0.00	—	.087	.192	0	.000	-0	3	3	-0	0.3
1973 StL-N	2	4	.333	44	0	0	0	5	56	45	2	21	57	10.9	2.09	174	.220	.298	0	.000	-0	10	10	-1	1.1
1974 StL-N	8	1	.889	65	0	0	0	9	88¹	71	3	38	82	11.2	2.95	121	.221	.306	4	.308	1	6	7	-1	0.7
1975 StL-N	13	3	.813	65	0	0	0	**22**	97¹	72	3	33	82	9.8	1.66	226	.205	.275	3	.200	1	**21**	**23**	-2	4.8
1976 StL-N	8	6	.571	68	0	0	0	13	95¹	89	5	39	73	12.5	3.30	107	.252	.333	0	.000	-0	2	2	-0	0.4
1977 StL-N	6	5	.545	65	0	0	0	10	86¹	82	12	41	68	13.1	4.38	88	.256	.346	0	.000	-1	-5	-5	-1	-0.9
1978 *KC-A	8	7	.533	58	0	0	0	20	75	52	6	35	60	10.6	2.88	133	.200	.297	0	—	0	3	4	-2	1.8
1979 KC-A	9	4	.692	58	0	0	0	11	65	67	3	41	39	15.1	3.74	114	.272	.378	0	—	0	3	4	-2	0.5
1980 Atl-N	4	2	.667	45	0	0	0	9	59²	58	8	31	31	12.2	3.62	103	.223	.318	0	.000	-0	-0	1	-2	-0.1
1981 Atl-N	1	1	.500	24	0	0	0	1	33²	24	1	9	18	8.8	1.07	335	.207	.264	0	.000	-0	9	9	-1	0.5
1982 Atl-N	2	1	.667	31	0	0	0	3	37¹	41	5	17	20	14.0	5.54	67	.285	.360	1	.333	-1	-8	-8	-1	-0.8
Total 13	64	35	.646	545	0	0	0	97	722	619	50	315	548	11.8	3.10	121	.234	.318	8	.143	-0	49	52	-11	8.0

● **CARL HUBBELL**   Hubbell, Carl Owen "King Carl" or "The Mealticket" · b: 6/22/03, Carthage, Mo. · d: 11/21/88, Scottsdale, Ariz. · BR/TL, 6', 170 lbs. · Deb: 7/26/28 · H

YEAR TM/L	W	L	PCT	G	GS	CG	SH	SV	IP	H	HR	BB	SO	RAT	ERA	ERA+	OAV	OOB	BH	AVG	PB	PR	/A	PD	TPI
1928 NY-N	10	6	.625	20	14	8	1	1	124	117	7	21	37	10.2	2.83	138	.248	.284	5	.106	-3	16	15	2	1.7
1929 NY-N	18	11	.621	39	35	19	1	1	268	273	11	67	106	11.6	3.69	124	.265	.313	12	.129	-6	30	26	5	2.3
1930 NY-N	17	12	.586	37	32	17	3	2	241²	263	11	58	117	12.4	3.87	122	.278	.327	13	.151	-5	29	23	-1	1.7
1931 NY-N	14	12	.538	36	30	21	4	3	248	211	14	67	155	**10.2**	2.65	139	**.227**	**.282**	20	.241	4	34	29	-2	3.1
1932 NY-N	18	11	.621	40	32	22	0	2	284	260	20	40	137	**9.6**	2.50	148	.238	**.268**	26	.241	4	43	38	6	**4.8**
1933 *NY-N★	23	12	.657	45	33	22	**10**	5	**308²**	256	6	47	156	**8.9**	1.66	193	**.227**	**.260**	20	.183	1	**58**	**53**	7	**7.5**
1934 NY-N★	21	12	.636	49	34	25	5	8	313	286	17	37	118	9.3	2.30	168	.239	**.263**	23	.197	-1	**61**	**54**	4	6.0
1935 NY-N☆	23	12	.657	42	35	24	1	0	302²	314	27	49	150	10.9	3.27	118	.263	.294	26	.239	4	25	20	4	2.9
1936 *NY-N★	26	6	**.813**	42	34	25	3	3	304	265	7	57	123	9.7	2.31	169	.236	**.276**	25	.227	1	**58**	**54**	1	**5.5**
1937 *NY-N★	22	8	**.733**	39	32	18	4	4	261²	261	18	55	**159**	11.0	3.20	122	.257	.298	21	.216	1	21	20	1	2.1
1938 NY-N☆	13	10	.565	24	22	13	1	1	179	171	16	33	104	**10.4**	3.07	123	.249	**.285**	9	.155	-2	14	14	1	1.3
1939 NY-N	11	9	.550	29	18	10	0	2	154	150	11	24	62	**10.3**	2.75	143	.249	**.280**	8	.151	-1	20	20	1	2.5
1940 NY-N★	11	12	.478	31	27	11	2	0	214¹	220	22	59	86	11.8	3.65	106	.259	.309	15	.185	-0	5	5	-0	0.6
1941 NY-N	11	9	.550	26	22	11	1	1	164	169	10	53	75	12.3	3.57	104	.266	.325	8	.140	-2	1	2	-3	-0.2
1942 NY-N☆	11	8	.579	24	20	11	0	0	157¹	158	17	34	61	11.0	3.95	85	.259	.299	11	.200	-0	-1	-0	-1	-0.3
1943 NY-N	4	4	.500	12	11	3	0	0	66	87	4	7	24	15.1	4.91	70	.322	.378	4	.200	-0	-11	-11	-1	-1.3
Total 16	253	154	.622	535	431	260	36	33	3590¹	3461	227	725	1677	10.6	2.98	130	.251	.291	246	.191	-5	393	355	22	39.2

● **BILL HUBBELL**   Hubbell, Wilbert William · b: 6/17/1897, San Francisco, Cal. · d: 8/3/80, Lakewood, Colo. · BR/TR, 6'1.5", 195 lbs. · Deb: 9/24/19

YEAR TM/L	W	L	PCT	G	GS	CG	SH	SV	IP	H	HR	BB	SO	RAT	ERA	ERA+	OAV	OOB	BH	AVG	PB	PR	/A	PD	TPI
1919 NY-N	1	1	.500	2	2	0	0	0	18¹	19	0	4	3	11.3	1.96	143	.260	.299	1	.125	-1	2	2	-0	0.1
1920 NY-N	0	1	.000	14	0	0	0	2	30	26	2	15	8	12.6	2.10	143	.239	.336	1	.200	-0	3	3	1	0.2

YEAR	TM/L	W	L	PCT	G	GS	CG	SH	SV	IP	H	HR	BB	SO	RAT	ERA	ERA+	OAV	OOB	BH	AVG	PB	PR	/A	PD	TPI
	Phi-N	9	9	.500	24	18	9	1	2	150	176	3	42	26	13.3	3.84	89	.301	.352	7	.132	-3	-12	-7	-2	-1.3
	Yr	9	10	.474	38	18	9	1	4	180	202	5	57	34	13.1	3.55	94	.291	.348	8	.138	-3	-8	-4	-1	-1.1
1921	Phi-N	9	16	.360	36	30	15	1	2	220¹	269	18	38	43	12.7	4.33	98	.306	.337	12	.160	-2	-13	-2	-1	-0.4
1922	Phi-N	7	15	.318	35	24	11	1	1	189	257	14	41	33	14.4	5.00	93	.317	.353	12	.171	-2	-19	-7	-0	-0.8
1923	Phi-N	1	6	.143	22	5	1	0	0	55	102	13	17	8	19.8	8.35	55	.394	.435	4	.235	0	-27	-23	0	-2.3
1924	Phi-N	10	9	.526	36	22	9	2	2	179	233	6	45	30	14.1	4.83	92	.324	.365	13	.220	-1	-19	-7	0	-0.7
1925	Phi-N	0	0	—	2	0	0	0	0	2²	5	0	1	0	20.3	0.00	—	.385	.429	0	.000	-0	1	1	1	0.0
	Bro-N	3	6	.333	33	5	3	0	1	86²	120	8	24	16	15.2	5.30	79	.337	.382	3	.150	0	-10	-11	1	-0.8
	Yr	3	6	.333	35	5	3	0	1	89¹	125	8	25	16	15.3	5.14	82	.339	.384	3	.143	0	-9	-9	2	-0.8
Total 7		40	63	.388	204	106	50	5	10	931	1207	67	225	167	14.0	4.68	89	.317	.359	53	.172	-8	-93	-52	0	-6.0

● **EARL HUCKLEBERRY** Huckleberry, Earl Eugene b: 5/23/10, Konawa, Okla. BR/TR, 5'11", 165 lbs. Deb: 9/13/35

YEAR	TM/L	W	L	PCT	G	GS	CG	SH	SV	IP	H	HR	BB	SO	RAT	ERA	ERA+	OAV	OOB	BH	AVG	PB	PR	/A	PD	TPI
1935	Phi-A	1	0	1.000	1	1	0	0	0	6²	8	1	4	2	16.2	9.45	48	.296	.387	0	.000	-0	-4	-4	-0	-0.4

● **JOHN HUDEK** Hudek, John Raymond b: 8/8/66, Tampa, Fla. BB/TR, 6'1", 200 lbs. Deb: 4/23/94

YEAR	TM/L	W	L	PCT	G	GS	CG	SH	SV	IP	H	HR	BB	SO	RAT	ERA	ERA+	OAV	OOB	BH	AVG	PB	PR	/A	PD	TPI
1994	Hou-N★	0	2	.000	42	0	0	0	16	39¹	24	5	18	39	9.8	2.97	137	.174	.274	0	—	0	5	5	-0	0.6

● **WILLIS HUDLIN** Hudlin, George Willis "Ace" b: 5/23/06, Wagoner, Okla. BR/TR, 6', 190 lbs. Deb: 8/15/26 C

YEAR	TM/L	W	L	PCT	G	GS	CG	SH	SV	IP	H	HR	BB	SO	RAT	ERA	ERA+	OAV	OOB	BH	AVG	PB	PR	/A	PD	TPI
1926	Cle-A	1	3	.250	8	2	1	0	0	32¹	25	1	13	6	11.1	2.78	146	.227	.320	1	.125	0	4	5	2	0.7
1927	Cle-A	18	12	.600	43	30	18	1	0	264²	291	5	83	65	13.1	4.01	105	.283	.343	24	.250	2	4	6	3	1.1
1928	Cle-A	14	14	.500	42	26	10	0	7	220¹	231	7	90	62	13.4	4.04	103	.279	.355	14	.194	-0	0	2	2	0.5
1929	Cle-A	17	15	.531	40	33	22	2	1	280¹	299	7	73	60	12.0	3.34	133	.272	.318	19	.196	-3	28	34	7	**3.9**
1930	Cle-A	13	16	.448	37	33	13	1	1	216²	255	12	76	60	13.8	4.57	106	.293	.351	16	.219	-1	2	6	5	1.0
1931	Cle-A	15	14	.517	44	34	15	1	4	254¹	313	14	88	83	14.2	4.60	100	.301	.356	20	.200	1	-6	1	4	0.5
1932	Cle-A	12	8	.600	33	21	12	0	2	181²	204	10	59	65	13.1	4.71	101	.278	.332	13	.203	1	-5	1	1	0.2
1933	Cle-A	5	13	.278	34	17	6	0	1	147¹	161	7	61	44	13.7	3.97	112	.275	.346	6	.146	-1	5	8	4	1.1
1934	Cle-A	15	10	.600	36	26	15	1	4	195	210	8	65	58	12.9	4.75	96	.277	.338	14	.206	3	-6	-4	5	0.2
1935	Cle-A	15	11	.577	36	29	14	3	5	231²	252	8	61	45	12.3	3.69	122	.277	.324	24	.279	6	20	21	0	2.7
1936	Cle-A	1	5	.167	27	7	1	0	0	64	112	11	31	20	20.4	9.00	56	.397	.460	2	.111	-1	-28	-28	1	-2.0
1937	Cle-A	12	11	.522	35	23	10	2	2	175²	213	16	43	31	13.2	4.10	112	.295	.337	10	.169	-1	10	10	3	1.3
1938	Cle-A	8	8	.500	29	15	8	0	1	127	158	13	45	27	14.5	4.89	95	.303	.361	5	.116	-2	-1	-4	1	-0.5
1939	Cle-A	9	10	.474	27	20	7	0	3	143	175	6	42	28	13.7	4.91	90	.303	.352	9	.188	1	-5	-8	5	-0.4
1940	Cle-A	2	1	.667	4	4	2	0	0	23²	31	3	2	8	12.5	4.94	85	.316	.330	1	.125	-0	-1	-2	-0	-0.2
	Was-A	1	2	.333	8	6	1	0	0	37¹	50	9	5	9	13.7	6.51	64	.314	.343	1	.100	-1	-9	-10	0	-0.7
	StL-A	0	1	.000	6	1	0	0	0	11¹	19	0	8	4	21.4	11.12	41	.358	.443	1	.500	-1	-8	-8	0	-0.6
	Yr	3	4	.429	18	11	3	0	0	72¹	100	12	15	21	14.3	6.72	63	.321	.352	3	.150	-1	-19	-20	1	-1.5
	NY-N	0	1	.000	1	1	0	0	0	5	9	1	1	5	18.0	10.80	36	.409	.435	0	.000	-0	-4	-4	0	-0.5
1944	StL-A	0	1	.000	1	0	0	0	0	2	3	0	0	1	13.5	4.50	80	.300	.300	0	—	0	-0	-0	-0	-0.1
Total 16		158	156	.503	491	328	155	11	31	2613¹	3011	118	846	677	13.4	4.41	102	.289	.345	180	.201	4	-0	26	42	8.2

● **CHARLIE HUDSON** Hudson, Charles b: 8/18/49, Ada, Okla. BL/TL, 6'3", 185 lbs. Deb: 5/21/72

YEAR	TM/L	W	L	PCT	G	GS	CG	SH	SV	IP	H	HR	BB	SO	RAT	ERA	ERA+	OAV	OOB	BH	AVG	PB	PR	/A	PD	TPI
1972	StL-N	1	0	1.000	12	0	0	0	0	12¹	10	1	0	7	13.1	5.11	67	.233	.353	0	—	0	-2	-2	0	-0.2
1973	Tex-A	4	2	.667	25	4	1	1	1	62¹	59	3	31	34	13.0	4.62	81	.254	.342	0	—	0	-6	-6	0	-0.5
1975	Cal-A	0	1	.000	3	1	0	0	0	5²	7	0	4	0	17.5	9.53	37	.304	.407	0	—	0	-4	-4	0	-0.2
Total 3		5	3	.625	40	5	1	1	1	80¹	76	3	42	38	13.3	5.04	73	.255	.349	0	—	0	-11	-12	0	-0.9

● **CHARLES HUDSON** Hudson, Charles Lynn b: 3/16/59, Ennis, Tex. BB/TR, 6'3", 185 lbs. Deb: 5/31/83

YEAR	TM/L	W	L	PCT	G	GS	CG	SH	SV	IP	H	HR	BB	SO	RAT	ERA	ERA+	OAV	OOB	BH	AVG	PB	PR	/A	PD	TPI
1983	*Phi-N	8	8	.500	26	26	3	0	0	169¹	158	13	53	101	11.2	3.35	106	.248	.305	5	.093	-2	5	4	-1	0.1
1984	Phi-N	9	11	.450	30	30	1	1	0	173²	181	12	52	94	12.2	4.04	90	.265	.319	5	.089	-2	-9	-8	-2	-1.3
1985	Phi-N	8	13	.381	38	26	0	0	0	193	188	23	74	122	12.3	3.78	97	.252	.320	8	.140	-1	-4	-2	-1	-0.5
1986	Phi-N	7	10	.412	33	23	0	0	0	144	165	20	58	82	13.9	4.94	78	.291	.357	2	.047	-3	-20	-17	-0	-2.2
1987	NY-A	11	7	.611	35	16	6	2	0	154²	137	19	57	100	11.5	3.61	122	.239	.311	0	—	0	15	13	-2	1.3
1988	NY-A	6	6	.500	28	12	1	0	2	106¹	99	9	36	58	11.3	4.49	88	.235	.306	0	—	0	-6	-6	-0	-0.7
1989	Det-A	1	5	.167	18	7	0	0	0	66²	75	14	31	23	14.6	6.35	60	.288	.369	0	—	0	-18	-19	-1	-1.5
Total 7		50	60	.455	208	140	14	3	2	1007²	997	110	361	580	12.2	4.14	92	.258	.324	20	.095	-8	-37	-35	-8	-4.8

● **HAL HUDSON** Hudson, Hal Campbell "Bud" or "Lefty" b: 5/4/27, Grosse Pointe, Mich. BL/TL, 5'10", 175 lbs. Deb: 4/20/52

YEAR	TM/L	W	L	PCT	G	GS	CG	SH	SV	IP	H	HR	BB	SO	RAT	ERA	ERA+	OAV	OOB	BH	AVG	PB	PR	/A	PD	TPI
1952	StL-A	0	0	—	3	0	0	0	0	5²	9	0	6	0	23.8	12.71	31	.360	.484	0	.000	-0	-6	-6	-0	0.0
	Chi-A	0	0	—	2	0	0	0	0	4	7	0	1	4	18.0	2.25	162	.389	.421	0	—	0	1	1	-0	0.0
	Yr	0	0	—	5	0	0	0	0	9²	16	0	7	4	21.4	8.38	45	.372	.460	0	.000	-0	-5	-5	-0	0.0
1953	Chi-A	0	0	—	1	0	0	0	0	0²	0	0	0	0		0.00	—	.000	.000	0	—	0	0	0	-0	0.0
Total 2		0	0	—	6	0	0	0	0	10¹	16	0	7	4	20.0	7.84	49	.364	.451	0	.000	-0	-5	-5	-0	0.0

● **JESSE HUDSON** Hudson, Jesse James b: 7/22/48, Mansfield, La. BL/TL, 6'2", 165 lbs. Deb: 9/19/69

YEAR	TM/L	W	L	PCT	G	GS	CG	SH	SV	IP	H	HR	BB	SO	RAT	ERA	ERA+	OAV	OOB	BH	AVG	PB	PR	/A	PD	TPI
1969	NY-N	0	0	—	1	0	0	0	0	2	2	0	1	3	18.0	4.50	81	.250	.400	0	—	0	-0	-0	0	0.0

● **NAT HUDSON** Hudson, Nathaniel P. b: 1/12/1859, Chicago, Ill. d: 3/14/28, Chicago, Ill. BR/TR, Deb: 4/18/1886

YEAR	TM/L	W	L	PCT	G	GS	CG	SH	SV	IP	H	HR	BB	SO	RAT	ERA	ERA+	OAV	OOB	BH	AVG	PB	PR	/A	PD	TPI
1886	*StL-a	16	10	.615	29	27	25	0	1	234¹	224	3	62	100	11.1	3.03	113	.243	.293	35	.233	1	11	11	-1	0.9
1887	StL-a	4	4	.500	9	9	7	0	0	67	91	2	20	15	15.4	4.97	91	.305	.357	12	.250	0	-5	-3	-2	-0.4
1888	StL-a	25	10	.714	39	37	36	5	0	333	283	8	59	130	9.6	2.54	128	.222	.264	50	.255	5	19	27	-1	2.7
1889	StL-a	3	2	.600	9	5	4	0	0	60	71	2	15	13	13.5	4.20	101	.285	.336	13	.250	0	-2	-0	-1	0.0
Total 4		48	26	.649	86	78	72	5	1	694¹	669	15	156	258	11.0	3.08	114	.244	.291	110	.247	6	23	34	-1	3.2

● **REX HUDSON** Hudson, Rex Haughton b: 8/11/53, Tulsa, Okla. BB/TR, 5'11", 165 lbs. Deb: 7/27/74

YEAR	TM/L	W	L	PCT	G	GS	CG	SH	SV	IP	H	HR	BB	SO	RAT	ERA	ERA+	OAV	OOB	BH	AVG	PB	PR	/A	PD	TPI
1974	LA-N	0	0	—	1	0	0	0	0	2	6	2	0	0	27.0	22.50	15	.500	.500	0	—	0	-4	-4	-0	0.0

● **SID HUDSON** Hudson, Sidney Charles b: 1/3/15, Coalfield, Tenn. BR/TR, 6'4", 180 lbs. Deb: 4/18/40 C

YEAR	TM/L	W	L	PCT	G	GS	CG	SH	SV	IP	H	HR	BB	SO	RAT	ERA	ERA+	OAV	OOB	BH	AVG	PB	PR	/A	PD	TPI
1940	Was-A	17	16	.515	38	31	19	3	1	252	272	20	81	96	12.7	4.57	91	.274	.330	22	.237	2	-5	-11	1	-1.0
1941	Was-A★	13	14	.481	33	33	17	3	0	249²	242	12	97	108	12.3	3.46	117	.253	.322	16	.186	-0	19	16	2	1.8
1942	Was-A☆	10	17	.370	35	31	19	1	2	239¹	266	9	70	72	12.8	4.36	84	.276	.328	19	.213	1	-19	-19	3	-1.5
1946	Was-A	8	11	.421	31	15	6	1	1	142¹	160	9	37	35	12.7	3.60	93	.280	.328	12	.279	3	-2	-4	2	0.0
1947	Was-A	6	9	.400	20	17	5	1	0	106	113	8	58	37	14.6	5.60	66	.272	.363	12	.308	2	-22	-22	1	-2.4
1948	Was-A	4	16	.200	39	29	4	0	1	182	217	11	107	53	16.3	5.88	74	.299	.394	14	.237	2	-32	-31	3	-2.4
1949	Was-A	8	17	.320	38	27	11	2	1	209	234	16	91	54	14.2	4.22	101	.283	.357	16	.239	2	-1	-1	4	0.6
1950	Was-A	14	14	.500	30	30	17	0	0	237²	226	17	98	75	13.8	4.09	110	.284	.356	20	.215	-1	13	11	3	0.6
1951	Was-A	5	12	.294	23	19	8	0	0	138²	168	8	52	43	14.5	5.13	80	.302	.365	12	.273	-2	-15	-16	3	-1.3
1952	Was-A	3	4	.429	7	7	6	0	0	62²	59	7	29	24	12.6	2.73	130	.257	.340	4	.167	-0	7	6	2	0.8
	Bos-A	7	9	.438	21	18	7	0	0	134¹	145	9	36	50	12.6	3.62	109	.276	.330	8	.174	-1	1	5	4	0.8
	Yr	10	13	.435	28	25	13	0	0	197	204	16	65	74	12.6	3.34	114	.270	.333	12	.171	-1	7	11	6	1.6
1953	Bos-A	6	9	.400	30	17	4	0	2	156	164	13	49	60	12.5	3.52	120	.269	.327	7	.140	-2	8	12	1	0.9
1954	Bos-A	3	4	.429	33	5	0	0	5	71¹	83	5	37	38	14.5	4.42	98	.278	.369	2	.154	-1	-5	-9	2	-0.3
Total 12		104	152	.406	380	279	123	11	13	2181	2384	136	835	734	13.5	4.28	95	.278	.345	164	.220	1	-54	-55	28	-2.7

● **AL HUENKE** Huenke, Albert A. b: 6/26/1891, New Bremen, Ohio d: 9/20/74, St.Marys, Ohio BR/TR, 6', 175 lbs. Deb: 10/6/14

YEAR	TM/L	W	L	PCT	G	GS	CG	SH	SV	IP	H	HR	BB	SO	RAT	ERA	ERA+	OAV	OOB	BH	AVG	PB	PR	/A	PD	TPI
1914	NY-N	0	0	—	1	0	0	0	0	2	2	0	0	2	9.0	4.50	59	.250	.250	0	.000	-0	-0	-0	-0	0.0

YEAR TM/L	W	L	PCT	G	GS	CG	SH	SV	IP	H	HR	BB	SO	RAT	ERA	ERA+	OAV	OOB	BH	AVG	PB	PR	/A	PD	TPI
● **PHIL HUFFMAN** Huffman, Phillip Lee b: 6/20/58, Freeport, Tex. BR/TR, 6'2", 180 lbs. Deb: 4/10/79																									
1979 Tor-A	6	18	.250	31	31	2	1	0	173	220	25	68	56	15.0	5.77	75	.304	.364	0	—	0	-30	-28	0	-3.2
1985 Bal-A	0	0	—	2	1	0	0	0	4²	7	1	5	2	23.1	15.43	26	.350	.480	0	—	0	-6	-6	0	0.0
Total 2	6	18	.250	33	32	2	1	0	177²	227	26	73	58	15.2	6.03	72	.305	.367	0	—	0	-36	-33	0	-3.2
● **ED HUGHES** Hughes, Edward J. b: 10/5/1880, Chicago, Ill. d: 10/11/27, McHenry, Ill. BR/TR, 6'1", 180 lbs. Deb: 8/29/02 F♦																									
1905 Bos-A	3	2	.600	6	4	2	0	0	33¹	38	0	9	8	13.0	4.59	59	.288	.338	3	.214	-0	-7	-7	-2	-1.1
1906 Bos-A	0	0	—	2	0	0	0	0	10	15	0	3	3	16.2	5.40	51	.349	.392	0	.000	-0	-3	-3	-0	-0.1
Total 2	3	2	.600	8	4	2	0	0	43¹	53	0	12	11	13.7	4.78	57	.303	.351	4	.190	-1	-10	-10	-2	-1.2
● **JIM HUGHES** Hughes, James Jay "Jay" b: 1/22/1874, Sacramento, Cal. d: 6/2/24, Sacramento, Cal. BR/TR, Deb: 4/18/1898 F																									
1898 Bal-N	23	12	.657	38	35	31	5	0	300²	268	4	100	81	11.6	3.20	112	.237	.309	37	.226	4	14	13	2	1.9
1899 Bro-N	**28**	6	**.824**	35	35	30	3	0	291²	250	6	119	99	11.8	2.68	146	.232	.316	27	.252	5	38	40	2	4.7
1901 Bro-N	17	12	.586	31	29	24	0	0	250²	265	3	102	96	13.6	3.27	103	.269	.345	16	.176	-1	2	2	1	0.2
1902 Bro-N	15	11	.577	31	30	27	0	0	254	228	3	55	94	10.3	2.87	96	.240	.288	20	.213	5	-3	-3	2	0.4
Total 4	83	41	.669	135	129	112	8	0	1097	1011	16	376	370	11.8	3.00	114	.244	.315	100	.219	13	51	52	8	7.2
● **JIM HUGHES** Hughes, James Michael b: 7/2/51, Los Angeles, Cal. BR/TR, 6'3", 190 lbs. Deb: 9/14/74																									
1974 Min-A	0	2	.000	2	2	1	0	0	10¹	8	2	4	8	10.5	5.23	72	.216	.293	0	—	0	-2	-2	0	-0.3
1975 Min-A	16	14	.533	37	34	12	2	0	249²	241	17	127	130	13.7	3.82	101	.255	.351	0	—	0	-1	-1	1	0.1
1976 Min-A	9	14	.391	37	26	3	0	0	177	190	17	73	87	13.8	4.98	72	.281	.358	0	—	0	-29	-27	-1	-3.5
1977 Min-A	0	0	—	2	0	0	0	0	4¹	4	0	1	1	10.4	2.08	192	.250	.294	0	—	0	1	1	-0	0.1
Total 4	25	30	.455	78	62	16	2	0	441¹	443	36	205	226	13.6	4.30	87	.265	.352	0	—	0	-31	-27	-1	-3.6
● **JIM HUGHES** Hughes, James Robert b: 3/21/23, Chicago, Ill. BR/TR, 6'1", 200 lbs. Deb: 9/13/52																									
1952 Bro-N	2	1	.667	6	0	0	0	0	18²	16	0	11	8	13.0	1.45	252	.235	.342	0	.000	-0	5	5	-1	0.6
1953 *Bro-N	4	3	.571	48	0	0	0	0	85²	80	6	41	49	12.8	3.47	123	.245	.332	4	.286	1	8	8	-1	0.7
1954 Bro-N	8	4	.667	**60**	0	0	0	24	86²	76	7	44	58	12.5	3.22	127	.239	.331	3	.188	-0	8	8	-1	1.4
1955 Bro-N	0	2	.000	24	0	0	0	6	42²	41	16	19	20	12.7	4.22	96	.256	.335	0	.000	-2	-1	-1	0	-0.2
1956 Bro-N			—	5	0	0	0	0	12	10	3	4	8	10.5	5.25	76	.233	.298	0	.000	-2	-2	-2	-0	-0.1
Chi-N	1	3	.250	25	1	0	0	0	45¹	43	4	30	20	15.3	5.16	73	.259	.385	2	.286	1	-7	-7	-1	-0.5
Yr	1	3	.250	30	1	0	0	0	57¹	53	7	34	28	14.3	5.18	74	.254	.368	2	.222	0	-9	-9	-1	-0.6
1957 Chi-A	0	0	—	4	0	0	0	0	5	12	0	3	2	27.0	10.80	35	.462	.517	0	—	0	-4	-4	0	0.0
Total 6	15	13	.536	172	1	0	0	39	296	278	30	152	165	13.2	3.83	106	.251	.344	9	.170	-1	7	7	-3	1.9
● **MICKEY HUGHES** Hughes, Michael J. b: 10/25/1866, New York, N.Y. d: 4/10/31, Jersey City, N.J. TR, 5'6", 165 lbs. Deb: 4/22/1888 F																									
1888 Bro-a	25	13	.658	40	40	40	2	0	363	281	5	98	159	9.5	2.13	140	.206	.262	19	.137	-7	38	34	-1	2.4
1889 *Bro-a	9	8	.529	20	17	13	0	0	153	172	6	86	54	15.6	4.35	86	.275	.369	12	.176	-3	-9	-11	-0	-1.2
1890 Bro-N	4	4	.500	9	8	6	0	0	66¹	77	1	30	22	15.1	5.16	67	.282	.361	1	.038	-4	-12	-13	0	-1.4
Phi-a	1	3	.250	6	5	4	0	0	41¹	64	0	21	15	19.6	5.44	70	.343	.424	2	.125	-1	-7	-7	-1	-0.7
Total 3	39	28	.582	75	70	63	2	0	623²	594	12	235	250	12.3	3.22	102	.242	.314	34	.137	-14	10	4	-1	-0.9
● **DICK HUGHES** Hughes, Richard Henry b: 2/13/38, Stephens, Ark. BR/TR, 6'3", 195 lbs. Deb: 9/11/66																									
1966 StL-N	2	1	.667	6	2	1	1	0	21	12	0	7	20	9.0	1.71	209	.162	.253	2	.400	1	4	4	0	0.8
1967 *StL-N	16	6	**.727**	37	27	12	3	3	222¹	164	22	48	161	**8.8**	2.67	123	**.203**	**.252**	10	.128	-1	17	15	-2	1.2
1968 *StL-N	2	2	.500	25	5	0	0	4	64	45	7	21	49	9.3	3.52	82	.202	.270	0	.000	-1	-4	-4	1	-0.4
Total 3	20	9	.690	68	34	13	4	8	307¹	221	29	76	230	8.9	2.78	116	.200	.256	12	.122	-1	18	15	-1	1.6
● **TOM HUGHES** Hughes, Thomas Edward b: 9/13/34, Ancon, C.Z. BL/TR, 6'2", 180 lbs. Deb: 9/13/59																									
1959 StL-N	0	2	.000	2	2	0	0	0	4	9	2	2	2	24.8	15.75	27	.409	.458	0	.000	-0	-5	-5	-0	-1.5
● **TOM HUGHES** Hughes, Thomas James "Long Tom" b: 11/29/1878, Chicago, Ill. d: 2/8/56, Chicago, Ill. BR/TR, 6'1", 175 lbs. Deb: 9/7/00 F																									
1900 Chi-N	1	1	.500	3	3	3	0	0	21	31	0	7	12	16.7	5.14	70	.341	.395	0	.000	-0	-3	-4	0	-0.3
1901 Chi-N	10	23	.303	37	35	32	1	0	308¹	309	4	115	225	12.9	3.24	100	.259	.333	14	.119	-8	3	-0	-2	-1.0
1902 Bal-A	7	5	.583	13	13	12	1	0	108¹	120	2	32	45	12.8	3.90	97	.281	.334	6	.140	-2	-4	-2	1	-0.3
Bos-A	3	3	.500	9	8	4	0	0	49¹	51	0	24	15	13.9	3.28	109	.267	.352	11	.367	2	2	2	-0	0.4
Yr	10	8	.556	22	21	16	1	0	157²	171	2	56	60	13.0	3.71	100	.276	.337	17	.233	0	-2	0	1	0.1
1903 *Bos-A	20	7	.741	33	31	25	5	0	244²	232	4	60	112	11.1	2.57	118	.250	.301	26	.280	7	11	13	-4	1.5
1904 NY-A	7	11	.389	19	18	12	1	0	136¹	141	3	48	75	12.8	3.70	73	.268	.335	13	.241	1	-17	-15	-3	-2.0
Was-A	2	13	.133	16	14	14	0	1	124¹	133	4	34	48	12.5	3.47	77	.274	.330	13	.228	3	-12	-11	-1	-1.1
Yr	9	24	.273	35	32	26	1	1	260²	274	7	82	123	12.5	3.59	75	.270	.328	26	.234	4	-29	-26	-3	-3.1
1905 Was-A	17	20	.459	39	35	26	6	0	291¹	239	3	79	149	10.1	2.35	133	.225	.285	22	.212	4	10	10	-4	1.3
1906 Was-A	7	17	.292	30	24	18	1	0	204	230	6	81	90	13.9	3.62	73	.287	.355	14	.212	3	-21	-22	-4	-2.6
1907 Was-A	7	14	.333	34	23	18	2	**4**	211	206	4	47	102	11.3	3.11	78	.258	.309	19	.237	3	-13	-16	-1	-1.3
1908 Was-A	18	15	.545	43	31	24	3	4	276¹	224	7	77	165	10.0	2.21	103	.227	.287	17	.195	2	6	2	1	0.6
1909 Was-A	4	7	.364	22	13	7	0	0	120¹	113	1	33	77	11.3	2.69	90	.246	.303	2	.083	-0	-3	-3	-0	-0.5
1911 Was-A	11	17	.393	34	27	17	2	0	223	251	7	77	86	13.4	3.47	95	.288	.348	15	.185	-1	-3	-5	-2	-0.9
1912 Was-A	13	10	.565	31	26	11	1	0	196	201	8	78	108	13.1	2.94	113	.270	.344	13	.194	1	8	9	0	1.0
1913 Was-A	4	12	.250	36	12	4	0	0	129²	129	6	61	59	14.2	4.30	98	.253	.350	4	.111	-1	-20	-19	-1	-2.4
Total 13	131	175	.428	399	313	227	25	16	2644	2610	51	853	1368	12.1	3.09	93	.259	.323	190	.198	12	-57	-64	-18	-7.6
● **TOM HUGHES** Hughes, Thomas L. "Salida Tom" b: 1/28/1884, Coal Creek, Colo. d: 11/1/61, Los Angeles, Cal. BR/TR, 6'2", 175 lbs. Deb: 9/18/06																									
1906 NY-A	1	0	1.000	3	1	1	0	0	15	11	2	1	5	7.2	4.20	71	.208	.222	1	.200	-0	-3	-2	-1	-0.2
1907 NY-A	2	0	1.000	4	3	2	0	0	27	16	0	11	10	9.7	2.67	105	.174	.276	1	.143	-0	-0	0	-1	-0.1
1909 NY-A	7	8	.467	24	15	9	2	2	118²	109	3	37	69	11.4	2.65	95	.249	.313	5	.128	0	-2	-2	-1	-0.2
1910 NY-A	7	9	.438	23	15	11	0	1	151²	153	2	37	64	11.5	3.50	76	.271	.320	9	.164	-1	-17	-14	1	-1.4
1914 Bos-N	2	0	1.000	2	2	1	0	0	17	14	0	4	11	9.5	2.65	104	.226	.273	0	.000	-1	0	0	1	0.0
1915 Bos-N	16	14	.533	**50**	25	17	4	**9**	280¹	208	4	58	171	8.9	2.12	122	.213	.265	9	.100	-3	20	15	-2	1.1
1916 Bos-N	16	3	**.842**	40	18	7	1	5	161	121	2	51	97	10.1	2.35	106	.215	.290	10	.192	2	5	2	-1	0.4
1917 Bos-N	5	3	.625	11	8	6	2	0	74	54	1	30	40	10.6	1.95	131	.216	.307	0	.000	-3	6	5	-0	0.4
1918 Bos-N	0	2	.000	3	3	1	0	0	18¹	17	0	6	9	11.3	3.44	78	.250	.311	2	.333	1	-1	-2	0	0.0
Total 9	56	39	.589	160	85	55	9	17	863	703	14	235	476	10.1	2.56	102	.229	.291	37	.130	-4	8	4	-4	-0.2
● **TOMMY HUGHES** Hughes, Thomas Owen b: 10/7/19, Wilkes-Barre, Pa. d: 11/28/90, Wilkes-Barre, Pa. BR/TR, 6'1", 190 lbs. Deb: 4/19/41																									
1941 Phi-N	9	14	.391	34	24	9	2	0	170	187	12	82	59	14.5	4.45	83	.280	.362	11	.200	0	-15	-14	1	-1.6
1942 Phi-N	12	18	.400	40	31	19	0	1	253	224	8	99	77	11.5	3.06	108	.238	.310	8	.100	-5	7	7	3	0.5
1946 Phi-N	6	9	.400	29	13	3	2	1	111	123	5	44	34	13.6	4.38	78	.281	.349	3	.097	-1	-12	-12	-1	-1.7
1947 Phi-N	4	11	.267	29	15	4	1	1	127	121	5	59	44	12.8	3.47	115	.265	.350	2	.050	-4	8	8	0	0.5
1948 Cin-N	0	4	.000	12	4	0	0	0	27	43	3	24	7	22.3	9.00	48	.364	.472	1	.143	-0	-15	-15	-0	-1.9
Total 5	31	56	.356	144	87	31	5	3	688	698	33	308	221	13.2	3.92	91	.266	.344	25	.117	-10	-27	-26	2	-4.2
● **VERN HUGHES** Hughes, Vernon Alexander "Lefty" b: 4/15/1893, Etna, Pa. d: 9/26/61, Sewickley, Pa. BL/TL, 5'10", 155 lbs. Deb: 7/6/14																									
1914 Bal-F	0	0	—	3	0	0	0	0	5²	5	0	3	3	12.7	3.18	95	.250	.348	0	.000	-0	-0	-0	-0	0.0

YEAR TM/L	W	L	PCT	G	GS	CG	SH	SV	IP	H	HR	BB	SO	RAT	ERA	ERA+	OAV	OOB	BH	AVG	PB	PR	/A	PD	TPI
● **BILL HUGHES** Hughes, William Nesbert b: 11/18/1896, Philadelphia, Pa. d: 2/25/63, Birmingham, Ala. BR/TR, 5'10.5", 155 lbs. Deb: 9/15/21																									
1921 Pit-N	0	0	—	1	0	0	0	0	2	3	0	1	2	22.5	4.50	85	.375	.500	0	—	0	-0	-0	0	0.0
● **BILL HUGHES** Hughes, William R. b: 11/25/1866, Blandensville, Ill. d: 8/25/43, Santa Ana, Cal. BL/TL, Deb: 9/28/1884 ♦																									
1885 Phi-a	0	2	.000	2	2	2	0	0	16²	18	0	10	4	16.2	4.86	71	.269	.380	3	.188	0	-3	-3	-0	-0.2
● **JIM HUGHEY** Hughey, James Ulysses "Coldwater Jim" b: 3/8/1869, Wakeshma, Mich. d: 3/29/45, Coldwater, Mich. TR, 6', Deb: 9/29/1891																									
1891 Mil-a	1	0	1.000	2	1	1	0	0	15	18	0	3	9	12.6	3.00	146	.287	.320	1	.143	-1	1	2	0	0.1
1893 Chi-N	0	1	.000	2	2	1	0	0	9	14	0	3	4	18.0	11.00	42	.345	.403	0	.000	0	-6	-6	0	-0.4
1896 Pit-N	6	8	.429	25	14	11	0	0	155	171	3	67	48	14.2	4.99	84	.278	.355	14	.215	-1	-11	-14	-3	-1.3
1897 Pit-N	6	10	.375	25	17	13	0	1	149¹	193	3	45	38	14.8	5.06	82	.310	.364	8	.127	-5	-12	-15	-2	-1.7
1898 StL-N	7	24	.226	35	33	31	0	0	283²	325	2	71	74	12.9	3.93	96	.285	.333	11	.113	-5	-10	-5	-1	-1.0
1899 Cle-N	4	30	.118	36	34	32	0	0	283	403	9	88	54	16.3	5.41	68	.334	.389	18	.162	-6	-49	-54	-4	-5.7
1900 StL-N	5	7	.417	20	12	11	0	0	112²	147	4	40	23	15.4	5.19	70	.314	.376	7	.171	0	-19	-19	-2	-1.8
Total 7	29	80	.266	145	113	100	0	1	1007²	1271	21	317	250	14.7	4.87	80	.306	.363	59	.153	-17	-106	-110	-11	-11.8
● **TEX HUGHSON** Hughson, Cecil Carlton b: 2/9/16, Buda, Tex. d: 8/6/93, Austin, Tex. BR/TR, 6'3", 198 lbs. Deb: 4/16/41																									
1941 Bos-A	5	3	.625	12	8	4	0	0	61	70	3	13	22	12.4	4.13	101	.289	.328	1	.059	-1	0	0	0	-0.1
1942 Bos-A☆	**22**	6	.786	38	30	**22**	4	4	**281**	258	10	75	**113**	10.7	2.59	144	.245	.296	18	.176	1	33	**35**	1	3.8
1943 Bos-A★	12	15	.444	35	32	**20**	4	2	266	242	23	73	114	10.7	2.64	126	.247	.300	9	.105	-4	19	20	1	1.7
1944 Bos-A★	18	5	**.783**	28	23	19	2	5	203¹	172	4	41	112	**9.5**	2.26	151	.225	**.267**	10	.152	-1	26	26	-0	3.0
1946 *Bos-A	20	11	.645	39	35	21	6	3	278	252	15	51	172	9.9	2.75	133	.238	.274	12	.132	-2	23	28	-2	2.7
1947 Bos-A	12	11	.522	29	26	13	3	0	189¹	173	17	71	119	11.7	3.33	117	.244	.314	2	.033	-6	8	12	-0	0.7
1948 Bos-A	3	1	.750	15	0	0	0	0	19¹	21	0	7	6	13.0	5.12	86	.276	.337	0	.000	-0	-2	-2	-1	-0.4
1949 Bos-A	4	2	.667	29	2	0	0	3	77²	82	5	41	35	14.4	5.33	82	.268	.356	1	.045	-3	-10	-8	-2	-1.0
Total 8	96	54	.640	225	156	99	19	17	1375²	1270	77	372	693	10.8	2.94	125	.245	.297	53	.119	-15	99	111	-3	10.4
● **MARK HUISMANN** Huismann, Mark Lawrence b: 5/11/58, Littleton, Colo. BR/TR, 6'3", 195 lbs. Deb: 8/16/83																									
1983 KC-A	2	1	.667	13	0	0	0	0	30²	29	1	17	20	13.5	5.58	73	.250	.346	0	—	0	-5	-5	-1	-0.5
1984 *KC-A	3	3	.500	38	0	0	0	3	75	84	7	21	54	12.7	4.20	96	.286	.335	0	—	0	-2	-1	-0	-0.1
1985 KC-A	1	0	1.000	9	0	0	0	0	18²	14	1	3	9	8.2	1.93	216	.219	.254	0	—	0	5	5	0	0.4
1986 KC-A	0	1	.000	10	0	0	0	1	17¹	18	1	6	13	12.5	4.15	102	.269	.329	0	—	0	0	0	0	0.0
Sea-A	3	3	.500	36	1	0	0	4	80	80	18	19	59	11.2	3.71	114	.256	.301	0	—	0	4	5	0	0.4
Yr	3	4	.429	46	1	0	0	5	97¹	98	19	25	72	11.5	3.79	112	.258	.305	0	—	0	4	5	0	0.4
1987 Sea-A	0	0	—	6	0	0	0	0	14²	10	1	4	15	9.8	4.91	96	.196	.281	0	—	0	-1	-0	0	0.0
Cle-A	2	3	.400	20	0	0	0	2	35¹	38	6	8	23	11.7	5.09	89	.271	.311	0	—	0	-3	-2	-0	-0.3
Yr	2	3	.400	26	0	0	0	2	50	48	7	12	38	10.8	5.04	91	.247	.291	0	—	0	-3	-3	-0	-0.3
1988 Det-A	1	0	1.000	5	0	0	0	0	5¹	6	0	2	6	13.5	5.06	75	.286	.348	0	—	0	-1	-1	0	0.0
1989 Bal-A	0	0	—	8	0	0	0	1	11¹	13	0	0	13	10.3	6.35	60	.277	.277	0	—	0	-3	-3	1	0.1
1990 Pit-N	1	0	1.000	2	0	0	0	0	3	6	2	1	2	24.0	9.00	40	.462	.533	0	—	0	-2	-2	-0	-0.5
1991 Pit-N	0	0	—	5	0	0	0	0	5	7	0	2	5	16.2	7.20	50	.304	.360	0	—	0	-2	-2	0	0.0
Total 9	13	11	.542	152	1	0	0	11	296¹	305	37	83	219	11.9	4.40	95	.266	.318	0	—	0	-9	-7	1	-0.7
● **HARRY HULIHAN** Hulihan, Harry Joseph b: 4/18/1899, Rutland, Vt. d: 9/11/80, Rutland, Vt. BR/TL, 5'11", 170 lbs. Deb: 8/16/22																									
1922 Bos-N	2	3	.400	7	6	2	0	0	40	40	0	26	16	15.7	3.15	127	.274	.398	2	.154	-0	4	4	-1	0.3
● **HANK HULVEY** Hulvey, James Hensel b: 7/18/1897, Mt.Sidney, Va. d: 4/9/82, Mount Sydney, Va. BB/TR, 6', 180 lbs. Deb: 9/5/23																									
1923 Phi-A	0	1	.000	1	1	0	0	0	7	10	1	2	2	15.4	7.71	53	.357	.400	1	.500	0	-3	-3	0	-0.3
● **TOM HUME** Hume, Thomas Hubert b: 3/29/53, Cincinnati, Ohio BR/TR, 6'1", 185 lbs. Deb: 5/25/77																									
1977 Cin-N	3	3	.500	14	5	0	0	0	43	54	5	17	22	14.9	7.12	55	.305	.366	2	.200	1	-15	-15	-0	-1.7
1978 Cin-N	8	11	.421	42	23	3	0	1	174	198	12	50	90	13.0	4.14	86	.289	.341	3	.067	-3	-11	-11	0	-1.4
1979 *Cin-N	10	9	.526	57	12	2	0	17	163	162	10	33	80	10.8	2.76	**135**	.262	.300	8	.174	0	18	18	0	2.4
1980 Cin-N	9	10	.474	78	0	0	0	25	137	121	6	38	68	10.6	2.56	140	.240	.297	3	.188	1	16	15	3	3.1
1981 Cin-N	9	4	.692	51	0	0	0	13	67²	63	7	31	27	12.6	3.46	103	.259	.345	0	.000	0	0	1	-0	0.1
1982 Cin-N★	2	6	.250	46	0	0	0	17	63²	72	7	21	22	11.2	3.11	119	.245	.310	0	.000	-1	3	4	-1	0.6
1983 Cin-N	3	5	.375	48	0	0	0	9	66	66	8	41	34	15.0	4.77	80	.264	.374	0	.000	-1	-8	-7	1	-1.0
1984 Cin-N	4	13	.235	54	0	0	0	3	113¹	142	14	41	59	14.6	5.64	67	.309	.367	3	.136	0	-26	-23	-2	-3.3
1985 Cin-N	3	5	.375	56	0	0	0	3	80	65	7	35	50	11.6	3.26	116	.224	.314	0	.000	-1	3	5	-0	0.4
1986 Phi-N	4	1	.800	48	1	0	0	4	94¹	89	5	34	51	12.0	2.77	139	.252	.323	0	.000	1	10	11	1	1.7
1987 Phi-N	1	4	.200	38	6	0	0	0	70²	75	10	41	29	15.3	5.60	76	.277	.380	3	.200	-0	-12	-11	0	-0.6
Cin-N	1	0	1.000	11	0	0	0	0	13¹	14	0	2	4	11.5	4.05	105	.292	.333	0	.000	0	0	0	-0	0.0
Yr	2	4	.333	49	6	0	0	0	84	89	10	43	33	14.3	5.36	79	.274	.360	3	.200	-0	-12	-10	0	-0.6
Total 11	57	71	.445	543	55	5	0	92	1086	1106	88	384	536	12.5	3.85	97	.268	.334	22	.120	-5	-22	-14	5	-0.7
● **BILL HUMPHREY** Humphrey, Byron William b: 6/17/11, Vienna, Mo. d: 2/13/92, Springfield, Mo. BR/TR, 6', 180 lbs. Deb: 4/24/38																									
1938 Bos-A	0	0	—	2	0	0	0	0	2	5	0	1	0	27.0	9.00	55	.500	.545	0	—	0	-1	-1	-0	0.0
● **BOB HUMPHREYS** Humphreys, Robert William b: 8/18/35, Covington, Va. BR/TR, 5'11", 170 lbs. Deb: 9/8/62																									
1962 Det-A	0	1	.000	4	0	0	0	1	5	8	3	2	3	18.0	7.20	57	.381	.435	0	—	0	-2	-2	0	-0.4
1963 StL-N	0	1	.000	9	0	0	0	0	10²	11	4	7	8	16.0	5.06	70	.282	.404	0	—	0	-2	-2	0	-0.2
1964 *StL-N	2	0	1.000	28	0	0	0	0	42²	32	3	15	36	10.1	2.53	150	.213	.289	1	.250	1	5	6	-0	0.4
1965 Chi-N	2	0	1.000	41	0	0	0	0	65²	59	6	27	38	12.1	3.15	117	.244	.325	0	.000	-0	3	4	-1	0.0
1966 Was-A	7	3	.700	58	1	0	0	3	111²	91	6	28	88	9.9	2.82	123	.229	.287	2	.167	1	8	8	-0	0.8
1967 Was-A	6	2	.750	48	2	0	0	4	105²	93	13	41	54	11.6	4.17	76	.238	.314	2	.133	1	-11	-12	-1	-1.1
1968 Was-A	5	7	.417	56	0	0	0	2	92²	78	13	30	56	10.5	3.69	79	.233	.296	2	.400	1	-7	-8	1	-0.9
1969 Was-A	3	3	.500	47	0	0	0	5	79²	69	9	38	43	12.2	3.05	114	.233	.322	1	.077	-1	5	4	0	0.3
1970 Was-A	0	0	—	5	0	0	0	0	6²	4	0	9	6	17.6	1.35	263	.200	.448	0	—	0	2	2	-0	0.4
Mil-A	2	4	.333	23	1	0	0	0	45²	37	3	22	32	12.0	3.15	120	.222	.319	0	.000	-1	3	3	-0	0.4
Yr	2	4	.333	28	1	0	0	0	52¹	41	3	31	38	12.7	2.92	129	.219	.336	0	.000	-1	5	5	-0	0.4
Total 9	27	21	.563	319	4	0	0	20	566	482	55	219	364	11.4	3.36	101	.234	.312	8	.131	1	3	3	-2	-0.7
● **BERT HUMPHRIES** Humphries, Albert b: 9/26/1880, California, Pa. d: 9/21/45, Orlando, Fla. BR/TR, 5'11.5", 182 lbs. Deb: 4/16/10																									
1910 Phi-N	0	0	—	5	0	0	0	0	9²	13	4	2	3	15.8	4.66	67	.317	.378	0	.000	0	-2	-2	0	0.0
1911 Phi-N	3	1	.750	11	5	2	0	0	41	56	1	10	13	15.8	4.17	83	.339	.398	5	.333	3	-4	-3	-1	-0.1
Cin-N	4	3	.571	14	7	3	0	0	65	62	3	18	16	11.9	2.35	141	.266	.335	1	.063	-1	8	7	0	0.6
Yr	7	4	.636	25	12	5	0	0	106	118	4	28	29	12.9	3.06	110	.292	.347	6	.194	2	4	4	-0	0.5
1912 Cin-N	9	11	.450	30	15	9	2	1	158²	162	8	36	58	11.7	3.23	104	.270	.319	7	.137	-2	3	3	-1	-0.1
1913 Chi-N	16	4	**.800**	28	20	13	4	1	181	169	10	24	61	9.7	2.69	118	.250	.277	12	.194	-1	10	10	-2	0.9
1914 Chi-N	10	11	.476	34	22	8	2	0	171	162	5	37	62	10.6	2.68	104	.250	.293	13	.236	2	2	2	-0	0.6
1915 Chi-N	8	13	.381	31	22	10	4	3	171²	183	1	23	45	11.1	2.31	120	.280	.309	8	.174	0	8	9	-2	0.9
Total 6	50	43	.538	153	91	45	10	9	798	807	31	151	258	11.1	2.79	110	.267	.309	46	.186	3	26	25	-3	2.8
● **JOHNNY HUMPHRIES** Humphries, John William b: 6/23/15, Clifton Forge, Va d: 6/24/65, New Orleans, La. BR/TR, 6'1", 185 lbs. Deb: 5/8/38																									
1938 Cle-A	9	8	.529	**45**	6	1	0	6	103¹	105	6	63	56	14.7	5.23	89	.264	.367	3	.103	-1	-5	-7	-1	-1.1

YEAR TM/L	W	L	PCT	G	GS	CG	SH	SV	IP	H	HR	BB	SO	RAT	ERA	ERA+	OAV	OOB	BH	AVG	PB	PR	/A	PD	TPI
1939 Cle-A	2	4	.333	15	1	0	0	2	28¹	30	0	32	12	20.0	8.26	53	.294	.467	0	.000	-1	-11	-12	-0	-2.2
1940 Cle-A	0	2	.000	19	1	1	0	1	33²	35	5	29	17	17.6	8.29	51	.269	.410	0	.000	-1	-15	-15	-1	-1.0
1941 Chi-A	4	2	.667	14	6	4	4	1	73¹	63	2	22	25	10.6	1.84	223	.230	.290	2	.087	-1	19	18	-1	1.2
1942 Chi-A	12	12	.500	28	28	17	2	0	228¹	227	9	59	71	11.5	2.68	134	.257	.309	18	.225	5	25	23	-2	2.7
1943 Chi-A	11	11	.500	28	27	8	2	0	188¹	198	7	54	51	12.3	3.30	101	.268	.322	20	.290	5	-0	1	-2	0.6
1944 Chi-A	8	10	.444	30	20	8	0	1	169	170	9	57	42	12.3	3.67	93	.267	.331	10	.189	0	-5	-5	-3	-0.8
1945 Chi-A	6	14	.300	22	21	10	1	1	153	172	11	48	33	13.1	4.24	78	.282	.337	8	.148	-3	-15	-16	-4	-2.5
1946 Phi-N	0	0	—	10	1	0	0	0	24²	24	1	9	10	12.4	4.01	85	.258	.330	2	.250	0	-2	-2	-1	-0.1
Total 9	52	63	.452	211	111	49	9	12	1002	1024	50	373	317	12.8	3.78	97	.265	.334	63	.191	4	-9	-13	-14	-3.2

● **BEN HUNT**   Hunt, Benjamin Franklin "High Pockets"   b: 11/10/1888, Eufaula, Okla.   d: 9/27/27, Greybull, Wyo.   BL/TL, 6'5", 190 lbs.   Deb: 8/24/10

YEAR TM/L	W	L	PCT	G	GS	CG	SH	SV	IP	H	HR	BB	SO	RAT	ERA	ERA+	OAV	OOB	BH	AVG	PB	PR	/A	PD	TPI
1910 Bos-A	2	3	.400	7	7	3	0	0	46²	45	4	20	19	12.5	4.05	63	.266	.344	1	.056	-2	-8	-8	-1	-1.0
1913 StL-N	0	1	.000	2	1	0	0	0	8	6	0	9	6	18.0	3.38	96	.240	.457	0	.000	-0	-0	-0	1	0.0
Total 2	2	4	.333	9	8	3	0	0	54²	51	4	29	25	13.3	3.95	67	.263	.362	1	.050	-2	-8	-8	-0	-1.0

● **KEN HUNT**   Hunt, Kenneth Raymond   b: 12/14/38, Ogden, Utah   BR/TR, 6'4", 200 lbs.   Deb: 4/16/61

YEAR TM/L	W	L	PCT	G	GS	CG	SH	SV	IP	H	HR	BB	SO	RAT	ERA	ERA+	OAV	OOB	BH	AVG	PB	PR	/A	PD	TPI
1961 *Cin-N	9	10	.474	29	22	4	0	0	136¹	130	13	66	75	13.3	3.96	103	.257	.349	7	.179	0	1	2	-1	0.1

● **GEORGE HUNTER**   Hunter, George Henry   b: 7/8/1887, Buffalo, N.Y.   d: 1/11/68, Harrisburg, Pa.   BB/TL, 5'8.5", 165 lbs.   Deb: 5/4/09   F♦

YEAR TM/L	W	L	PCT	G	GS	CG	SH	SV	IP	H	HR	BB	SO	RAT	ERA	ERA+	OAV	OOB	BH	AVG	PB	PR	/A	PD	TPI
1909 Bro-N	4	10	.286	16	13	10	0	0	113¹	104	2	38	43	11.5	2.46	105	.254	.322	28	.228	2	2	2	0	0.5

● **CATFISH HUNTER**   Hunter, James Augustus "Jim"   b: 4/8/46, Hertford, N.C.   BR/TR, 6', 195 lbs.   Deb: 5/13/65   H

YEAR TM/L	W	L	PCT	G	GS	CG	SH	SV	IP	H	HR	BB	SO	RAT	ERA	ERA+	OAV	OOB	BH	AVG	PB	PR	/A	PD	TPI
1965 KC-A	8	8	.500	32	20	3	2	0	133	124	21	46	82	11.6	4.26	82	.246	.311	6	.150	-1	-12	-11	-2	-1.5
1966 KC-A☆	9	11	.450	30	25	4	0	0	176²	158	17	64	103	11.4	4.02	84	.239	.308	9	.153	1	-12	-12	-3	-1.5
1967 KC-A★	13	17	.433	35	35	13	5	0	259²	209	16	84	196	10.2	2.81	113	.219	.284	18	.196	4	12	11	-5	1.2
1968 Oak-A	13	13	.500	36	34	11	2	1	234	210	29	69	172	10.9	3.35	84	.238	.296	19	.232	5	-10	-14	-3	-1.3
1969 Oak-A	12	15	.444	38	35	10	3	0	247	210	34	85	150	10.9	3.35	103	.234	.304	19	.224	4	7	2	-1	0.6
1970 Oak-A	18	14	.563	40	40	9	1	0	262¹	253	32	74	178	11.5	3.81	93	.250	.307	18	.200	4	-3	-8	-2	-0.7
1971 *Oak-A	21	11	.656	37	37	16	4	0	273²	225	27	80	181	10.2	2.96	113	.223	.282	36	.350	13	15	11	-4	2.4
1972 *Oak-A☆	21	7	**.750**	38	37	16	5	0	295¹	200	21	70	191	8.3	2.04	139	.189	.242	23	.219	3	33	26	-3	2.7
1973 *Oak-A★	21	5	**.808**	36	36	11	3	0	256¹	222	39	69	124	10.3	3.34	106	.232	.284	1	1.000	1	14	6	-4	0.2
1974 *Oak-A★	**25**	12	.676	41	41	23	6	0	318¹	268	25	46	143	**9.0**	**2.49**	133	.229	**.260**	0	—	0	**40**	29	-4	3.0
1975 NY-A★	**23**	14	.622	39	39	**30**	7	0	**328**	248	25	83	177	9.2	2.58	141	**.208**	.263	0	—	0	44	39	-4	3.8
1976 *NY-A★	17	15	.531	36	36	21	2	0	298²	268	28	68	173	10.2	3.53	97	.241	.286	0	.000	0	-0	-4	-2	-0.6
1977 *NY-A	9	9	.500	22	22	8	1	0	143¹	137	29	47	52	11.7	4.71	84	.250	.313	0	—	0	-10	-12	-3	-1.6
1978 *NY-A	12	6	.667	21	20	5	1	0	118	98	16	35	56	10.2	3.58	101	.226	.286	0	—	0	2	0	-1	0.0
1979 NY-A	2	9	.182	19	19	1	0	0	105	128	15	34	34	14.0	5.31	77	.312	.366	0	—	0	-13	-14	-1	-1.4
Total 15	224	166	.574	500	476	181	42	1	3449¹	2958	374	954	2012	10.3	3.26	104	.231	.287	149	.226	33	109	50	-40	5.3

● **JIM HUNTER**   Hunter, James Mac Gregor   b: 6/22/64, Jersey City, N.J.   BR/TR, 6'3", 205 lbs.   Deb: 5/17/91

YEAR TM/L	W	L	PCT	G	GS	CG	SH	SV	IP	H	HR	BB	SO	RAT	ERA	ERA+	OAV	OOB	BH	AVG	PB	PR	/A	PD	TPI
1991 Mil-A	0	5	.000	8	6	0	0	0	31	45	3	17	14	19.2	7.26	55	.349	.440	0	—	0	-11	-11	1	-1.4

● **LEM HUNTER**   Hunter, Robert Lemuel   b: 1/16/1863, Warren, Ohio   d: 11/9/56, W.Lafayette, Ohio   Deb: 9/1/1883   ♦

YEAR TM/L	W	L	PCT	G	GS	CG	SH	SV	IP	H	HR	BB	SO	RAT	ERA	ERA+	OAV	OOB	BH	AVG	PB	PR	/A	PD	TPI
1883 Cle-N	0	0	—	1	1	0	0	0	6¹	10	0	2	4	17.1	1.42	222	.370	.414	1	.250	-0	1	1	0	0.0

● **WILLARD HUNTER**   Hunter, Willard Mitchell   b: 3/8/34, Newark, N.J.   BR/TL, 6'2", 180 lbs.   Deb: 4/16/62

YEAR TM/L	W	L	PCT	G	GS	CG	SH	SV	IP	H	HR	BB	SO	RAT	ERA	ERA+	OAV	OOB	BH	AVG	PB	PR	/A	PD	TPI
1962 LA-N	0	0	—	1	0	0	0	0	2	6	1	4	1	45.0	40.50	9	.545	.667	0	—	0	-8	-8	0	0.0
NY-N	1	6	.143	27	6	1	0	0	63	67	9	34	40	14.6	5.57	75	.270	.360	3	.231	0	-11	-10	-1	-1.0
Yr	1	6	.143	28	6	1	0	0	65	73	10	38	41	15.5	6.65	63	.281	.375	3	.231	0	-20	-18	-1	-1.0
1964 NY-N	3	3	.500	41	0	0	0	5	49	54	4	9	22	11.9	4.41	81	.284	.323	1	1.000	0	-5	-5	-0	-0.6
Total 2	4	9	.308	69	6	1	0	5	114	127	14	47	63	14.0	5.68	69	.283	.355	4	.286	1	-24	-22	-1	-1.6

● **WALT HUNTZINGER**   Huntzinger, Walter Henry "Shakes"   b: 2/6/1899, Pottsville, Pa.   d: 8/11/81, Upper Darby, Pa.   BR/TR, 6', 150 lbs.   Deb: 9/29/23

YEAR TM/L	W	L	PCT	G	GS	CG	SH	SV	IP	H	HR	BB	SO	RAT	ERA	ERA+	OAV	OOB	BH	AVG	PB	PR	/A	PD	TPI
1923 NY-N	0	1	.000	2	1	0	0	0	8	9	0	1	2	11.3	7.88	49	.290	.313	0	.000	-0	-3	-4	-0	-0.4
1924 NY-N	1	1	.500	12	2	0	0	1	32¹	41	3	9	6	13.9	4.45	82	.318	.362	4	.500	1	-2	-3	-0	-0.1
1925 NY-N	5	1	.833	26	1	0	0	0	64¹	68	3	17	19	11.9	3.50	115	.281	.328	1	.091	-1	**6**	4	-1	0.1
1926 StL-N	0	4	.000	9	4	2	0	0	34	35	4	14	9	13.0	4.24	92	.267	.338	1	—	0	-2	-1	-1	-0.2
Chi-N	1	1	.500	11	0	0	0	2	28²	26	0	8	4	11.6	0.94	408	.260	.333	1	.143	-1	9	9	0	0.5
Yr	1	5	.167	20	4	2	0	2	62²	61	4	22	13	12.4	2.73	142	.264	.336	2	.067	-2	8	8	1	0.5
Total 4	7	8	.467	60	8	2	0	3	167¹	179	10	49	40	12.4	3.60	108	.283	.337	6	.167	-1	8	6	-1	0.1

● **TOM HURD**   Hurd, Thomas Carr "Whitey"   b: 5/27/24, Danville, Va.   d: 9/5/82, Waterloo, Iowa   BR/TR, 5'9", 155 lbs.   Deb: 7/30/54

YEAR TM/L	W	L	PCT	G	GS	CG	SH	SV	IP	H	HR	BB	SO	RAT	ERA	ERA+	OAV	OOB	BH	AVG	PB	PR	/A	PD	TPI
1954 Bos-A	2	0	1.000	16	0	0	0	1	29²	21	2	12	14	10.0	3.03	135	.198	.280	1	.333	0	2	4	0	0.3
1955 Bos-A	8	6	.571	43	0	0	0	5	80²	72	7	38	48	12.4	3.01	142	.242	.330	1	.071	-1	8	11	-0	1.9
1956 Bos-A	3	4	.429	40	0	0	0	5	76	84	5	47	34	15.9	5.33	87	.289	.393	6	.500	2	-10	-6	-1	-0.5
Total 3	13	10	.565	99	0	0	0	11	186¹	177	14	97	96	13.4	3.96	111	.255	.350	8	.276	1	1	9	-1	1.7

● **BRUCE HURST**   Hurst, Bruce Vee   b: 3/24/58, St.George, Utah   BL/TL, 6'3", 215 lbs.   Deb: 4/12/80

YEAR TM/L	W	L	PCT	G	GS	CG	SH	SV	IP	H	HR	BB	SO	RAT	ERA	ERA+	OAV	OOB	BH	AVG	PB	PR	/A	PD	TPI
1980 Bos-A	2	2	.500	12	7	0	0	0	30²	39	4	16	16	16.7	9.10	46	.307	.393	0	—	0	-17	-17	-0	-2.0
1981 Bos-A	2	0	1.000	5	5	0	0	0	23	23	1	12	11	14.1	4.30	90	.258	.353	0	—	0	-2	-1	-0	-0.2
1982 Bos-A	3	7	.300	28	19	0	0	0	117	161	16	40	53	15.7	5.77	75	.333	.388	0	—	0	-22	-19	-1	-1.7
1983 Bos-A	12	12	.500	33	32	6	2	0	211¹	241	22	62	115	13.5	4.09	106	.290	.342	—		0	-1	6	0	0.7
1984 Bos-A	12	12	.500	33	33	9	2	0	218	232	25	88	136	13.3	3.92	106	.271	.343	—		0	2	6	0	0.6
1985 Bos-A	11	13	.458	35	31	6	1	0	229¹	243	16	70	189	12.4	4.51	95	.273	.328	—		0	-9	-6	-0	-0.5
1986 *Bos-A	13	8	.619	25	25	11	4	0	174¹	169	18	50	167	11.5	2.99	139	.256	.311	—		0	23	23	-1	2.5
1987 Bos-A☆	15	13	.536	33	33	15	3	0	238²	239	35	76	190	11.9	4.41	103	.262	.320	—		0	1	3	0	0.3
1988 *Bos-A	18	6	.750	33	33	7	2	0	216²	222	21	65	166	12.0	3.66	113	.264	.318	—		0	7	11	0	1.1
1989 SD-N	15	11	.577	33	33	**10**	2	0	244²	214	16	66	179	10.3	2.69	130	.237	.289	5	.071	-1	22	22	1	2.3
1990 SD-N	11	9	.550	33	33	9	**4**	0	223²	188	21	59	162	10.1	3.14	122	.228	.284	6	.090	-2	16	17	0	1.2
1991 SD-N	15	8	.652	31	31	4	0	0	221²	201	17	59	141	10.7	3.29	115	.241	.293	9	.134	-0	10	13	-1	1.1
1992 SD-N	14	9	.609	32	32	6	4	0	217¹	223	22	51	131	11.3	3.85	93	.265	.309	11	.159	1	-8	-7	-1	-0.6
1993 SD-N	0	1	.000	2	2	0	0	0	4¹	9	0	3	2	24.9	12.46	33	.409	.480	0	—	0	-4	-4	0	-0.7
Col-N	0	1	.000	3	3	0	0	0	8²	6	1	3	6	9.3	5.19	92	.194	.265	0	.000	-0	-1	-0	0	-0.0
Yr	0	2	.000	5	5	0	0	0	13	15	1	6	8	14.5	7.62	60	.283	.356	0	—	0	-5	-5	0	-0.7
1994 Tex-A	2	1	.667	8	8	0	0	0	38	53	9	16	24	16.3	7.11	64	.342	.404	0	—	0	-10	-11	0	-0.4
Total 15	145	113	.562	379	359	83	23	0	2417¹	2463	258	740	1689	12.0	3.92	103	.265	.321	31	.113	-3	7	36	2	3.7

● **JAMES HURST**   Hurst, James Lavon   b: 6/1/67, Plantation, Fla.   BL/TL, 6', 160 lbs.   Deb: 4/4/94

YEAR TM/L	W	L	PCT	G	GS	CG	SH	SV	IP	H	HR	BB	SO	RAT	ERA	ERA+	OAV	OOB	BH	AVG	PB	PR	/A	PD	TPI
1994 Tex-A	0	0	—	8	0	0	0	0	10²	17	1	8	5	21.1	10.13	45	.362	.455	0	—	0	-6	-7	0	0.3

● **JONATHAN HURST**   Hurst, Jonathan   b: 10/20/66, New York, N.Y.   BR/TR, 6'3", 175 lbs.   Deb: 6/9/92

YEAR TM/L	W	L	PCT	G	GS	CG	SH	SV	IP	H	HR	BB	SO	RAT	ERA	ERA+	OAV	OOB	BH	AVG	PB	PR	/A	PD	TPI
1992 Mon-N	1	1	.500	3	3	0	0	0	16¹	18	1	7	4	14.3	5.51	63	.281	.361	0	.000	-0	-4	-4	0	-0.5
1994 NY-N	0	1	.000	7	0	0	0	0	10	15	5	5	6	18.0	12.60	34	.341	.408	0	—	0	-9	-9	-0	-0.8
Total 2	1	2	.333	10	3	0	0	0	26¹	33	6	12	10	15.7	8.20	47	.306	.380	0	—	0	-13	-13	0	-1.3

YEAR	TM/L	W	L	PCT	G	GS	CG	SH	SV	IP	H	HR	BB	SO	RAT	ERA	ERA+	OAV	OOB	BH	AVG	PB	PR	/A	PD	TPI

● **BILL HUSTED** Husted, William J. b: 10/11/1866, Gloucester, N.J. d: 5/17/41, Gloucester, N.J. Deb: 4/29/1890

| 1890 | Phi-P | 5 | 10 | .333 | 18 | 17 | 12 | 0 | 0 | 129 | 148 | 2 | 67 | 33 | 15.3 | 4.88 | 88 | .276 | .361 | 6 | .107 | -6 | -9 | -9 | -2 | -1.3 |

● **BERT HUSTING** Husting, Berthold Juneau "Pete" b: 3/6/1878, Fond Du Lac, Wis. d: 9/3/48, Milwaukee, Wis. BR/TR, Deb: 8/16/00

1900	Pit-N	0	0	—	2	0	0	0	0	8	10	2	5	7	18.0	5.63	65	.305	.413	0	.000	-1	-2	-2	1	0.0
1901	Mil-A	10	15	.400	34	26	19	0	1	217¹	234	4	95	67	14.2	4.27	84	.272	.353	19	.202	-1	-14	-16	5	-1.2
1902	Bos-A	0	1	.000	1	1	0	0	0	8	15	0	8	4	25.9	9.00	40	.398	.504	1	.250	1	-5	-5	0	-0.4
	Phi-A	14	5	.737	32	27	17	1	0	204	240	7	91	44	15.0	3.79	97	.293	.370	13	.159	-3	-5	-3	2	-0.3
	Yr	14	6	.700	33	28	18	1	0	212	255	7	99	48	15.4	3.99	92	.298	.377	14	.163	-3	-10	-8	3	-0.7
Total	3	24	21	.533	69	54	37	1	1	437¹	499	14	199	122	14.8	4.16	87	.285	.366	33	.180	-4	-26	-26	8	-1.9

● **JOHNNY HUTCHINGS** Hutchings, John Richard Joseph b: 4/14/16, Chicago, Ill. d: 4/27/63, Indianapolis, Ind. BB/TR, 6'2", 250 lbs. Deb: 4/26/40

1940	*Cin-N	2	1	.667	19	4	0	0	0	54	53	3	18	18	12.0	3.50	108	.260	.323	2	.154	0	2	2	-1	0.0
1941	Cin-N	0	0	—	8	0	0	0	0	11	12	0	4	5	13.1	4.09	88	.279	.340	0	—	-1	-1	-1	0	0.0
	Bos-N	1	6	.143	36	7	1	1	2	95²	110	6	22	36	12.8	4.14	86	.287	.333	4	.148	0	-5	-6	0	-0.4
	Yr	1	6	.143	44	7	1	1	2	106²	122	6	26	41	12.8	4.13	86	.286	.333	4	.148	0	-6	-7	0	-0.4
1942	Bos-N	1	0	1.000	20	3	0	0	0	65²	66	2	34	27	14.0	4.39	76	.260	.352	1	.050	-2	-8	-8	-1	-0.4
1944	Bos-N	1	4	.200	14	7	1	0	0	56²	55	3	26	26	13.0	3.97	96	.252	.335	1	.067	-1	-2	-1	-1	-0.2
1945	Bos-N	7	6	.538	57	12	3	2	3	185	173	6	75	99	12.3	3.75	102	.244	.320	13	.241	2	1	2	0	0.3
1946	Bos-N	0	1	.000	1	1	0	0	0	3	5	1	1	1	18.0	9.00	38	.357	.400	0	.000	0	-2	-2	-0	-0.5
Total	6	12	18	.400	155	34	5	3	6	471	474	36	180	212	12.7	3.96	93	.260	.330	21	.162	-1	-15	-14	-2	-1.2

● **FRED HUTCHINSON** Hutchinson, Frederick Charles b: 8/12/19, Seattle, Wash. d: 11/12/64, Bradenton, Fla. BL/TR, 6'2", 200 lbs. Deb: 5/2/39 M♦

1939	Det-A	3	6	.333	13	12	3	0	0	84²	95	9	51	22	15.5	5.21	94	.287	.382	13	.382	3	-6	-3	-0	0.0
1940	*Det-A	3	7	.300	17	10	1	0	0	76	85	6	26	32	13.4	5.68	84	.281	.342	8	.267	0	-11	-8	0	-0.8
1946	Det-A	14	11	.560	28	26	16	3	2	207	184	14	66	138	10.9	3.09	118	.236	.295	28	.315	8	10	13	3	2.8
1947	Det-A	18	10	.643	33	25	18	3	2	219²	211	14	61	113	11.2	3.03	124	.251	.304	32	.302	11	16	18	2	3.7
1948	Det-A	13	11	.542	33	28	15	0	2	221	223	32	48	92	**11.1**	4.32	101	.258	**.297**	23	.205	4	-1	1	3	0.9
1949	Det-A	15	7	.682	33	21	9	4	1	188²	167	18	52	54	**10.5**	2.96	141	.237	**.290**	18	.247	4	26	25	2	3.4
1950	Det-A	17	8	.680	39	26	10	1	0	231²	269	18	48	71	12.5	3.96	118	.290	.329	31	.326	10	16	19	2	2.9
1951	Det-A★	10	10	.500	31	20	9	2	2	188¹	204	11	27	53	11.1	3.68	113	.275	.302	16	.188	-2	9	10	1	1.0
1952	Det-A	2	1	.667	12	1	0	0	0	37¹	40	4	9	12	12.1	3.38	113	.276	.323	1	.056	-1	1	2	2	0.2
1953	Det-A	0	0	—	3	0	0	0	0	9²	9	0	4	2	8.4	2.79	146	.243	.243	1	.167	0	1	1	-0	0.0
Total	10	95	71	.572	242	169	81	13	7	1464	1487	126	388	591	11.6	3.73	113	.262	.311	171	.263	39	62	79	15	14.1

● **IRA HUTCHINSON** Hutchinson, Ira Kendall b: 8/31/10, Chicago, Ill. d: 8/21/73, Chicago, Ill. BR/TR, 5'10.5", 180 lbs. Deb: 9/24/33

1933	Chi-A	0	0	—	1	1	0	0	0	4	7	1	3	2	22.5	13.50	31	.368	.455	1	.500	0	-4	-4	-0	-0.1
1937	Bos-N	4	6	.400	31	8	1	0	0	91²	99	4	35	29	13.3	3.73	96	.286	.353	3	.115	-1	2	-1	1	-0.2
1938	Bos-N	9	8	.529	36	12	4	1	4	151	150	3	61	38	12.8	2.74	125	.258	.332	9	.173	-1	18	12	1	1.3
1939	Bro-N	5	2	.714	41	1	0	0	1	105³	103	9	51	46	13.2	4.34	93	.265	.352	1	.037	-3	-5	-4	1	-0.4
1940	StL-N	4	2	.667	20	2	1	0	1	63¹	68	3	19	19	12.4	3.13	128	.271	.322	4	.222	0	5	6	0	0.6
1941	StL-N	1	5	.167	29	0	0	0	5	46²	32	3	19	19	10.2	3.86	98	.196	.288	2	.250	0	-1	-0	0	-0.1
1944	Bos-N	9	7	.563	40	8	1	1	1	119²	136	8	53	22	14.4	4.21	91	.296	.373	4	.138	-1	-8	-5	1	-0.7
1945	Bos-N	3	4	.400	11	0	0	0	1	28²	33	2	8	4	13.2	5.02	76	.277	.328	0	.000	-1	-4	-4	1	-0.7
Total	8	34	33	.507	209	32	7	2	13	610²	628	33	249	179	13.1	3.76	100	.270	.344	24	.140	-7	2	-1	5	-0.1

● **BILL HUTCHISON** Hutchison, William Forrest "Wild Bill" b: 12/17/1859, New Haven, Conn. d: 3/19/26, Kansas City, Mo. BR/TR, 5'9", 175 lbs. Deb: 6/10/1884

1884	KC-U	1	1	.500	2	2	2	0	0	17	14	0	1	5	7.9	2.65	84	.209	.221	2	.250	-0	-0	-1	2	0.0
1889	Chi-N	16	17	.485	37	36	33	3	0	318	306	11	117	136	12.2	3.54	118	.245	.314	21	.158	-5	17	22	5	1.8
1890	Chi-N	**42**	25	.627	**71**	66	**65**	5	**2**	**603**	505	20	199	289	10.7	2.70	135	.220	.286	53	.203	-4	58	64	5	5.9
1891	Chi-N	**44**	19	.698	**66**	58	**56**	4	1	**561**	508	26	178	261	11.1	2.81	119	.232	.292	45	.185	-1	34	33	-2	2.7
1892	Chi-N	37	36	.507	**75**	71	**67**	5	0	**627**	572	11	187	**316**	11.1	2.74	121	.233	.291	57	.217	3	38	41	4	4.8
1893	Chi-N	16	24	.400	44	40	38	2	0	348¹	420	9	156	80	15.2	4.75	97	.289	.364	41	.253	1	-3	-5	-3	-0.5
1894	Chi-N	14	16	.467	36	34	28	0	0	277²	373	9	140	59	17.2	6.06	93	.318	.399	42	.309	5	-23	-14	-2	-0.7
1895	Chi-N	13	21	.382	38	35	30	2	0	291	371	13	129	85	15.9	4.73	108	.305	.378	25	.198	-7	2	12	-0	0.4
1897	StL-N	1	4	.200	6	5	2	0	0	49	55	5	22	5	17.8	6.07	73	.324	.408	5	.278	1	-8	-7	-1	-0.7
Total	9	184	163	.530	375	347	321	21	3	3083	3124	104	1129	1236	12.7	3.58	111	.255	.322	291	.216	-8	114	141	8	13.7

● **HERB HUTSON** Hutson, George Herbert b: 7/17/49, Savannah, Ga. BR/TR, 6'2", 205 lbs. Deb: 4/10/74

| 1974 | Chi-N | 0 | 2 | .000 | 20 | 0 | 0 | 0 | 0 | 28² | 24 | 3 | 15 | 22 | 12.6 | 3.45 | 110 | .233 | .336 | 0 | .000 | -1 | 1 | 1 | -1 | 0.2 |

● **MARK HUTTON** Hutton, Mark Steven b: 2/6/70, South Adelaide, Australia BR/TR, 6'6", 240 lbs. Deb: 7/23/93

1993	NY-A	1	1	.500	7	4	0	0	0	22	24	2	17	12	17.2	5.73	72	.293	.420	0	—	0	-3	-4	0	-0.3
1994	NY-A	0	0	—	2	0	0	0	0	3²	4	0	1	1	9.8	4.91	90	.250	.250	0	—	0	-0	-0	0	0.3
Total	2	1	1	.500	9	4	0	0	0	25²	28	2	17	13	16.1	5.61	75	.286	.397	0	—	0	-3	-4	-0	0.0

● **TOM HUTTON** Hutton, Thomas George b: 4/20/46, Los Angeles, Cal. BL/TL, 5'11", 180 lbs. Deb: 9/16/66 ♦

| 1980 | Mon-N | 0 | 0 | — | 1 | 0 | 0 | 0 | 0 | 1 | 3 | 1 | 1 | 1 | 36.0 | 27.00 | 13 | .500 | .571 | 12 | .218 | 0 | -3 | -3 | 0 | 0.0 |

● **DICK HYDE** Hyde, Richard Elde b: 8/3/28, Hindsboro, Ill. BR/TR, 5'11", 170 lbs. Deb: 4/23/55

1955	Was-A	0	0	—	3	0	0	0	0	2	0	1	4	1	13.5	4.50	85	.286	.375	0	—	-0	-0	-0	-0	0.0
1957	Was-A	4	3	.571	52	0	0	0	1	109¹	104	4	56	46	13.7	4.12	95	.261	.361	3	.167	-0	-4	-3	1	-0.1
1958	Was-A	10	3	.769	53	0	0	0	18	103	82	1	35	49	10.4	1.75	218	.220	.291	0	.000	-2	**23**	**24**	2	3.9
1959	Was-A	2	5	.286	37	0	0	0	4	54¹	56	5	27	29	14.1	4.97	79	.269	.359	0	.000	-1	-7	-6	-2	-0.7
1960	Was-A	0	1	.000	9	0	0	0	0	8²	11	2	5	4	17.7	4.15	94	.355	.459	0	—	-0	-0	-0	-0	0.0
1961	Bal-A	1	2	.333	15	0	0	0	0	21	18	1	13	15	13.7	5.57	69	.228	.344	1	1.000	0	-4	-4	1	-0.3
Total	6	17	14	.548	169	2	0	0	23	298¹	273	13	137	144	12.8	3.56	109	.249	.339	4	.093	-2	8	10	6	2.8

● **JIM HYNDMAN** Hyndman, James William b: 7/1865, Ontario, Canada Deb: 7/23/1886 ♦

| 1886 | Phi-a | 0 | 1 | .000 | 1 | 1 | 0 | 0 | 0 | 2 | 5 | 1 | 5 | 1 | 49.5 | 27.00 | 13 | .455 | .647 | 0 | .000 | -1 | -5 | -5 | 0 | -1.2 |

● **PAT HYNES** Hynes, Patrick J. b: 3/12/1884, St.Louis, Mo. d: 3/12/07, St.Louis, Mo. TL, Deb: 9/27/03 ♦

1903	StL-N	0	1	.000	1	1	1	0	0	9	10	1	6	1	16.0	4.00	82	.294	.400	0	.000	-0	-1	-1	-1	-0.2
1904	StL-A	1	0	1.000	5	2	1	0	0	26	35	1	7	6	14.5	6.23	40	.322	.363	60	.236	0	-10	-11	-1	-0.5
Total	2	1	1	.500	6	3	2	0	0	35	45	1	13	7	14.9	5.66	47	.316	.373	60	.233	0	-12	-12	-2	-0.7

● **HAM IBURG** Iburg, Herman Edward b: 10/29/1877, San Francisco, Cal d: 2/11/45, San Francisco, Cal BR/TR, 5'11", 165 lbs. Deb: 4/17/02

| 1902 | Phi-N | 11 | 18 | .379 | 30 | 30 | 20 | 1 | 0 | 236 | 286 | 1 | 62 | 106 | 13.7 | 3.89 | 72 | .299 | .349 | 12 | .138 | -5 | -29 | -28 | 0 | -3.5 |

● **GARY IGNASIAK** Ignasiak, Gary Raymond b: 9/1/49, Anchorville, Mich. BR/TL, 5'11", 185 lbs. Deb: 9/20/73 F

| 1973 | Det-A | 0 | 0 | — | 3 | 0 | 0 | 0 | 0 | 4² | 5 | 0 | 3 | 4 | 15.4 | 3.86 | 106 | .278 | .381 | 0 | — | 0 | -0 | 0 | 0 | 0.0 |

● **MIKE IGNASIAK** Ignasiak, Michael James b: 3/12/66, Mt.Clemens, Mich. BB/TR, 5'11", 175 lbs. Deb: 8/22/91 F

| 1991 | Mil-A | 2 | 1 | .667 | 4 | 1 | 0 | 0 | 0 | 12² | 7 | 2 | 8 | 10 | 10.7 | 5.68 | 70 | .163 | .294 | 0 | — | 0 | -2 | -2 | -0 | -0.4 |
| 1993 | Mil-A | 1 | 1 | .500 | 27 | 0 | 0 | 0 | 0 | 37 | 32 | 2 | 21 | 28 | 13.4 | 3.65 | 116 | .241 | .353 | 0 | — | 0 | 3 | 2 | -1 | 0.1 |

YEAR TM/L	W	L	PCT	G	GS	CG	SH	SV	IP	H	HR	BB	SO	RAT	ERA	ERA+	OAV	OOB	BH	AVG	PB	PR	/A	PD	TPI
1994 Mil-A	3	1	.750	23	5	0	0	0	47²	51	5	13	24	12.3	4.53	109	.276	.327	0	—	0	1	2	0	0.1
Total 3	6	3	.667	54	6	0	0	0	97¹	90	9	42	62	12.5	4.35	104	.249	.333	0	—	0	2	2	-1	-0.2

● **BLAISE ILSLEY**   Ilsley, Blaise Francis b: 4/9/64, Alpena, Mich. BL/TL, 6'1", 195 lbs. Deb: 4/4/94

YEAR TM/L	W	L	PCT	G	GS	CG	SH	SV	IP	H	HR	BB	SO	RAT	ERA	ERA+	OAV	OOB	BH	AVG	PB	PR	/A	PD	TPI
1994 Chi-N	0	0	—	10	0	0	0	0	15	25	2	9	9	20.4	7.80	53	.385	.459	0	.000	-0	-6	-6	0	0.0

● **DOC IMLAY**   Imlay, Harry Miller b: 1/12/1889, Allentown, N.J. d: 10/7/48, Bordentown, N.J. BR/TR, 5'11", 168 lbs. Deb: 7/7/13

YEAR TM/L	W	L	PCT	G	GS	CG	SH	SV	IP	H	HR	BB	SO	RAT	ERA	ERA+	OAV	OOB	BH	AVG	PB	PR	/A	PD	TPI
1913 Phi-N	0	0	—	9	0	0	0	0	13²	19	1	7	7	17.1	7.24	46	.358	.433	0	.000	-0	-6	-6	0	0.0

● **BOB INGERSOLL**   Ingersoll, Robert Randolph b: 1/8/1883, Rapid City, S.D. d: 1/13/27, Minneapolis, Minn. BR/TR, 5'11.5", 175 lbs. Deb: 4/23/14

YEAR TM/L	W	L	PCT	G	GS	CG	SH	SV	IP	H	HR	BB	SO	RAT	ERA	ERA+	OAV	OOB	BH	AVG	PB	PR	/A	PD	TPI
1914 Cin-N	0	0	—	4	0	0	0	0	6	5	0	5	2	16.5	3.00	98	.250	.423	1	1.000	0	-0	-0	-0	0.0

● **BERT INKS**   Inks, Albert Preston (b: Albert Preston Inkstein) b: 1/27/1871, Ligonier, Ind. d: 10/3/41, Ligonier, Ind. BL/TL, 6'3", 175 lbs. Deb: 9/2/1891

YEAR TM/L	W	L	PCT	G	GS	CG	SH	SV	IP	H	HR	BB	SO	RAT	ERA	ERA+	OAV	OOB	BH	AVG	PB	PR	/A	PD	TPI
1891 Bro-N	3	10	.231	13	13	11	1	0	96¹	99	2	43	47	13.8	4.02	82	.256	.339	10	.286	2	-7	-8	-0	-0.7
1892 Bro-N	4	2	.667	9	8	4	1	0	58	48	0	33	25	13.2	3.88	82	.216	.328	10	.400	3	-4	-5	-0	-0.1
Was-N	1	2	.333	3	3	3	0	0	21	29	0	10	11	17.6	5.14	63	.315	.394	3	.300	1	-4	-4	-0	-0.4
Yr	5	4	.556	12	11	7	1	0	79	77	0	43	36	13.9	4.22	76	.242	.336	13	.371	4	-8	-9	-0	-0.5
1894 Bal-N	9	4	.692	22	14	10	0	1	133	181	4	54	30	16.6	5.55	98	.321	.391	18	.316	2	-3	-1	-1	-0.1
Lou-N	2	6	.250	8	8	8	0	0	59²	87	2	34	8	18.4	6.49	79	.336	.415	12	.444	3	-8	-9	-0	-0.6
Yr	11	10	.524	30	22	18	0	1	192²	268	6	88	38	16.7	5.84	92	.321	.387	30	.357	5	-11	-11	-1	-0.7
1895 Lou-N	7	20	.259	28	27	21	0	0	205¹	294	5	78	42	17.0	6.40	72	.331	.394	21	.250	-0	-37	-40	1	-3.6
1896 Phi-N	0	1	.000	3	1	0	0	0	10¹	21	1	5	2	23.5	7.84	55	.415	.477	1	.200	-0	-4	-4	-1	-0.4
Cin-N	1	1	.500	3	3	2	0	0	20	21	0	9	2	13.9	4.50	102	.268	.351	0	.000	-1	-0	-0	-1	-0.1
Yr	1	2	.333	6	4	2	0	0	30¹	42	1	14	4	16.9	5.64	80	.323	.393	1	.083	-1	-4	-4	-1	-0.5
Total 5	27	46	.370	89	77	59	2	1	603²	780	12	266	167	16.2	5.52	81	.307	.382	75	.300	9	-68	-72	-2	-6.0

● **JEFF INNIS**   Innis, Jeffrey David b: 7/5/62, Decatur, Ill. BR/TR, 6'1", 170 lbs. Deb: 5/16/87

YEAR TM/L	W	L	PCT	G	GS	CG	SH	SV	IP	H	HR	BB	SO	RAT	ERA	ERA+	OAV	OOB	BH	AVG	PB	PR	/A	PD	TPI
1987 NY-N	0	1	.000	17	1	0	0	0	25²	29	5	4	28	11.9	3.16	120	.279	.312	0	.000	-0	3	2	-0	0.0
1988 NY-N	1	1	.500	12	0	0	0	0	19	19	0	2	14	9.9	1.89	170	.250	.269	0	—	0	3	3	-1	0.2
1989 NY-N	0	1	.000	29	0	0	0	0	39²	38	2	8	16	10.7	3.18	103	.255	.297	0	.000	-0	1	0	1	0.1
1990 NY-N	1	3	.250	18	0	0	0	1	26¹	19	4	10	12	10.3	2.39	156	.209	.294	0	—	0	4	4	0	0.6
1991 NY-N	0	2	.000	69	0	0	0	0	84²	66	2	23	47	9.5	2.66	137	.219	.274	0	.000	-0	10	9	3	0.5
1992 NY-N	6	9	.400	76	0	0	0	1	88	85	4	36	39	13.0	2.86	121	.266	.351	0	.000	-0	6	6	2	1.2
1993 NY-N	2	3	.400	67	0	0	0	3	76²	81	5	38	36	14.7	4.11	98	.278	.373	0	—	-1	-1	-1	0	0.0
Total 7	10	20	.333	288	1	0	0	5	360	337	22	121	192	11.8	3.05	119	.253	.322	0	—	-1	27	23	6	2.6

● **DANE IORG**   Iorg, Dane Charles b: 5/11/50, Eureka, Cal. BL/TR, 6', 180 lbs. Deb: 4/9/77 F◆

YEAR TM/L	W	L	PCT	G	GS	CG	SH	SV	IP	H	HR	BB	SO	RAT	ERA	ERA+	OAV	OOB	BH	AVG	PB	PR	/A	PD	TPI
1986 SD-N	0	0	—	2	0	0	0	0	3	5	2	1	2	18.0	12.00	30	.357	.400	24	.226	4	-3	-3	-0	0.0

● **HOOKS IOTT**   Iott, Clarence Eugene b: 12/3/19, Mountain Grove, Mo. d: 8/17/80, St.Petersburg, Fla BB/TL, 6'2", 200 lbs. Deb: 9/6/41

YEAR TM/L	W	L	PCT	G	GS	CG	SH	SV	IP	H	HR	BB	SO	RAT	ERA	ERA+	OAV	OOB	BH	AVG	PB	PR	/A	PD	TPI
1941 StL-A	0	0	—	2	0	0	0	0	2	2	0	1	1	13.5	9.00	48	.250	.333	0	—	-0	-1	-1	0	0.0
1947 StL-A	0	1	.000	4	0	0	0	0	8¹	15	4	14	6	31.3	16.20	24	.375	.537	0	.000	-0	-12	-11	0	-1.1
NY-N	3	8	.273	20	9	2	1	0	71¹	67	3	52	46	15.1	5.93	69	.251	.375	3	.143	1	-15	-15	-0	-1.9
Total 2	3	9	.250	26	9	2	1	0	81²	84	7	67	53	16.8	7.05	58	.267	.397	3	.130	1	-27	-27	0	-3.0

● **DARYL IRVINE**   Irvine, Daryl Keith b: 11/15/64, Harrisonburg, Va. BR/TR, 6'3", 195 lbs. Deb: 4/28/90

YEAR TM/L	W	L	PCT	G	GS	CG	SH	SV	IP	H	HR	BB	SO	RAT	ERA	ERA+	OAV	OOB	BH	AVG	PB	PR	/A	PD	TPI
1990 Bos-A	1	1	.500	11	0	0	0	0	17¹	15	0	9	9	13.0	4.67	87	.246	.352	0	—	0	-1	-1	-0	-0.4
1991 Bos-A	0	0	—	9	0	0	0	0	18	25	2	9	8	18.0	6.00	72	.321	.404	0	—	0	-4	-3	-0	-0.2
1992 Bos-A	3	4	.429	21	0	0	0	0	28	31	1	14	10	15.1	6.11	69	.287	.379	0	—	0	-7	-6	-1	-1.5
Total 3	4	5	.444	41	0	0	0	0	63¹	71	3	33	27	15.3	5.68	74	.287	.380	0	—	0	-12	-10	1	-2.1

● **ARTHUR IRWIN**   Irwin, Arthur Albert "Doc" or "Sandy" b: 2/14/1858, Toronto, Ont., Can. d: 7/16/21, Atlantic Ocean BL/TR, 5'8.5", 158 lbs. Deb: 5/1/1880 FMU◆

YEAR TM/L	W	L	PCT	G	GS	CG	SH	SV	IP	H	HR	BB	SO	RAT	ERA	ERA+	OAV	OOB	BH	AVG	PB	PR	/A	PD	TPI
1884 *Pro-N	0	0	—	1	0	0	0	0	3	5	0	1	0	18.0	3.00	94	.357	.400	97	.240	-0	0	0	0	0.0
1889 Was-N	0	0	—	1	0	0	0	0	1	1	0	0	0	9.0	0.00	—	.252	.252	73	.233	-0	0	0	0	0.0
Total 2	0	0	—	2	0	0	0	0	4	6	0	1	0	15.8	2.25	138	.334	.369	934	.241	0	0	0	0	0.0

● **BILL IRWIN**   Irwin, William Franklin "Phil" b: 9/16/1859, Neville, Ohio d: 8/7/33, Ft.Thomas, Ky. BR/TR, 6', 195 lbs. Deb: 8/30/1886

YEAR TM/L	W	L	PCT	G	GS	CG	SH	SV	IP	H	HR	BB	SO	RAT	ERA	ERA+	OAV	OOB	BH	AVG	PB	PR	/A	PD	TPI
1886 Cin-a	0	2	.000	2	2	2	0	0	17	18	2	6	6	13.8	5.82	60	.247	.321	0	.000	-0	-4	-4	0	-0.4

● **FRANK ISBELL**   Isbell, William Frank "Bald Eagle" b: 8/21/1875, Delevan, N.Y. d: 7/15/41, Wichita, Kan. BL/TR, 5'11", 190 lbs. Deb: 5/1/1898 ◆

YEAR TM/L	W	L	PCT	G	GS	CG	SH	SV	IP	H	HR	BB	SO	RAT	ERA	ERA+	OAV	OOB	BH	AVG	PB	PR	/A	PD	TPI
1898 Chi-N	4	7	.364	13	9	7	0	0	81	86	0	42	16	15.0	3.56	101	.270	.367	37	.233	0	0	-0	0	0.0
1901 Chi-A	0	0	—	1	0	0	0	0	1	2	0	0	0	18.0	9.00	39	.409	.409	143	.257	0	-1	-1	0	0.0
1902 Chi-A	0	0	—	1	1	0	0	0	1	3	0	1	1	36.0	9.00	38	.514	.585	130	.252	0	-1	-1	1	0.1
1906 *Chi-A	0	0	—	1	0	0	0	0	2	1	0	0	2	4.5	0.00	—	.152	.152	153	.279	0	1	1	-0	0.1
1907 Chi-A	0	0	—	1	0	0	0	0	0¹	0	0	0	0	0.0	0.00	—	.000	.000	118	.243	0	0	0	0	0.1
Total 5	4	7	.364	17	10	7	0	0	85¹	92	0	43	19	15.0	3.59	99	.273	.367	1056	.250	1	-0	-0	1	0.2

● **AL JACKSON**   Jackson, Alvin Neil b: 12/25/35, Waco, Tex. BL/TL, 5'10", 169 lbs. Deb: 6/1/59 C

YEAR TM/L	W	L	PCT	G	GS	CG	SH	SV	IP	H	HR	BB	SO	RAT	ERA	ERA+	OAV	OOB	BH	AVG	PB	PR	/A	PD	TPI
1959 Pit-N	0	0	—	8	3	0	0	0	18	30	1	8	13	19.0	6.50	60	.405	.463	1	.200	-0	-5	-5	-0	-0.1
1961 Pit-N	1	0	1.000	3	2	1	0	0	23²	20	2	4	15	9.1	3.42	117	.233	.267	0	.000	-1	2	1	1	0.1
1962 NY-N	8	20	.286	36	33	12	4	0	231¹	244	16	78	118	12.7	4.40	95	.273	.335	5	.068	-5	-12	-5	4	-0.6
1963 NY-N	13	17	.433	37	34	11	0	0	227	237	25	84	142	13.2	3.96	88	.267	.338	16	.203	2	-17	-12	2	-1.2
1964 NY-N	11	16	.407	40	31	11	3	1	213¹	229	18	60	112	12.4	4.26	84	.272	.323	11	.153	2	-17	-16	-0	-1.6
1965 NY-N	8	20	.286	37	31	11	3	0	205¹	217	17	61	120	12.5	4.34	81	.271	.329	7	.117	-1	-18	-18	-2	-2.2
1966 StL-N	13	15	.464	36	30	11	3	0	232²	222	18	45	90	10.4	2.51	143	.250	.288	13	.176	2	28	28	4	4.2
1967 StL-N	9	4	.692	38	11	1	1	1	107	117	7	29	42	12.4	3.95	83	.279	.327	8	.258	2	-7	-8	-0	-0.4
1968 NY-N	3	7	.300	25	9	0	0	0	92²	88	5	17	59	10.4	3.69	82	.249	.287	7	.250	1	-7	-7	1	-0.6
1969 NY-N	0	0	—	9	0	0	0	0	11	18	1	4	10	18.8	10.64	34	.353	.411	0	.000	-0	-9	-9	-0	-0.3
Cin-N	1	0	1.000	33	0	0	0	3	27¹	27	5	17	16	15.5	5.27	71	.260	.379	1	.250	-0	-5	-5	-0	-0.3
Yr	1	0	1.000	42	0	0	0	3	38¹	45	6	21	26	16.2	6.81	55	.285	.379	1	.200	-0	-14	-13	-0	-0.3
Total 10	67	99	.404	302	184	54	14	10	1389¹	1449	115	407	738	12.3	3.98	91	.268	.324	69	.159	3	-67	-56	16	-2.6

● **CHARLIE JACKSON**   Jackson, Charles Bernard b: 8/4/1876, Versailles, Ohio d: 11/23/57, Scottsbluff, Neb. TR, Deb: 8/11/05

YEAR TM/L	W	L	PCT	G	GS	CG	SH	SV	IP	H	HR	BB	SO	RAT	ERA	ERA+	OAV	OOB	BH	AVG	PB	PR	/A	PD	TPI
1905 Det-A	0	2	.000	2	2	1	0	0	11	14	1	7	3	17.2	5.73	48	.311	.403	1	.250	0	-4	-4	-0	-0.6

● **DANNY JACKSON**   Jackson, Danny Lynn b: 1/5/62, San Antonio, Tex. BR/TL, 6', 205 lbs. Deb: 9/11/83

YEAR TM/L	W	L	PCT	G	GS	CG	SH	SV	IP	H	HR	BB	SO	RAT	ERA	ERA+	OAV	OOB	BH	AVG	PB	PR	/A	PD	TPI
1983 KC-A	1	1	.500	4	3	0	0	0	19	26	1	6	9	15.2	5.21	78	.325	.372	0	—	0	-2	-2	0	-0.2
1984 KC-A	2	6	.250	15	11	0	0	0	76	84	4	35	40	14.7	4.26	94	.285	.370	0	—	0	-2	-2	-0	-0.3
1985 *KC-A	14	12	.538	32	32	4	3	0	208	209	7	76	114	12.6	3.42	122	.261	.329	0	—	0	17	17	-1	1.8
1986 KC-A	11	12	.478	32	27	4	1	0	185²	177	13	79	115	12.6	3.20	133	.256	.335	0	—	0	20	22	-1	2.3
1987 KC-A	9	18	.333	36	34	11	2	0	224	219	11	109	152	13.5	4.02	113	.258	.347	0	—	0	11	13	-2	1.2
1988 Cin-N☆	23	8	.742	35	35	15	6	0	260²	206	13	71	161	10.0	2.73	131	.218	.275	13	.144	-0	21	25	2	3.2
1989 Cin-N	6	11	.353	22	20	2	1	0	115²	122	16	57	70	14.0	5.60	64	.271	.354	8	.222	-1	-27	-26	-1	-3.3
1990 *Cin-N	6	6	.500	22	21	0	0	0	117¹	119	11	40	76	12.3	3.61	109	.266	.329	2	.054	-2	2	4	-1	0.1
1991 Chi-N	1	5	.167	17	14	0	0	0	70²	89	4	48	31	17.6	6.75	58	.309	.409	2	.087	-1	-24	-23	-1	-1.9
1992 Chi-N	4	9	.308	19	19	0	0	0	113	117	5	48	51	13.4	4.22	85	.270	.346	3	.083	-2	-9	-8	-1	-1.2

YEAR	TM/L	W	L	PCT	G	GS	CG	SH	SV	IP	H	HR	BB	SO	RAT	ERA	ERA+	OAV	OOB	BH	AVG	PB	PR	/A	PD	TPI
	*Pit-N	4	4	.500	15	15	0	0	0	88¹	94	1	29	46	12.6	3.36	102	.276	.334	2	.083	-1	1	1	0	0.0
	Yr	8	13	.381	34	34	0	0	0	201¹	211	6	77	97	12.9	3.84	92	.269	.336	5	.083	-3	-8	-7	-1	-1.2
1993	Phi-N	12	11	.522	32	32	2	1	0	210¹	214	12	80	120	12.8	3.77	105	.263	.332	5	.077	-2	6	5	-2	0.0
1994	Phi-N★	14	6	.700	25	25	4	1	0	179¹	183	13	46	129	11.6	3.26	126	.266	.314	9	.158	1	19	17	1	2.0
Total	12	107	109	.495	304	288	42	14	1	1868	1859	109	724	1114	12.6	3.77	106	.261	.332	44	.120	-7	33	44	-6	3.7

● DARRELL JACKSON
Jackson, Darrell Preston   b: 4/3/56, Los Angeles, Cal.   BB/TL, 5′10″, 150 lbs.   Deb: 6/16/78

YEAR	TM/L	W	L	PCT	G	GS	CG	SH	SV	IP	H	HR	BB	SO	RAT	ERA	ERA+	OAV	OOB	BH	AVG	PB	PR	/A	PD	TPI
1978	Min-A	4	6	.400	19	15	1	1	0	92¹	89	9	48	54	13.5	4.48	85	.256	.350	0	—	0	-7	-7	-1	-0.8
1979	Min-A	4	4	.500	24	8	1	0	0	69¹	89	5	26	43	15.1	4.28	102	.319	.379	0	—	0	-1	1	1	0.0
1980	Min-A	9	9	.500	32	25	1	0	1	172	161	15	69	90	12.1	3.87	113	.250	.325	0	—	0	3	9	-0	0.9
1981	Min-A	3	3	.500	14	5	0	0	0	32²	35	1	19	26	15.2	4.41	90	.282	.382	0	—	0	-3	-2	-1	-0.4
1982	Min-A	0	5	.000	13	7	0	0	0	44²	51	6	24	16	15.3	6.25	68	.297	.386	0	—	0	-11	-10	-0	-1.1
Total	5	20	27	.426	102	60	3	1	1	411	425	36	186	229	13.5	4.38	96	.272	.352	0	—	0	-18	-8	-2	-1.4

● DARRIN JACKSON
Jackson, Darrin Jay   b: 8/22/62, Los Angeles, Cal.   BR/TR, 6′1″, 170 lbs.   Deb: 6/17/85   ♦

YEAR	TM/L	W	L	PCT	G	GS	CG	SH	SV	IP	H	HR	BB	SO	RAT	ERA	ERA+	OAV	OOB	BH	AVG	PB	PR	/A	PD	TPI
1991	SD-N	0	0	—	1	0	0	0	0	3	2	0	2	2	22.5	9.00	42	.375	.500	94	.262	0	-1	-1	-0	0.0

● GRANT JACKSON
Jackson, Grant Dwight "Buck"   b: 9/28/42, Fostoria, Ohio   BB/TL, 6′, 190 lbs.   Deb: 9/3/65   C

YEAR	TM/L	W	L	PCT	G	GS	CG	SH	SV	IP	H	HR	BB	SO	RAT	ERA	ERA+	OAV	OOB	BH	AVG	PB	PR	/A	PD	TPI
1965	Phi-N	1	1	.500	6	2	0	0	0	13²	17	4	5	15	14.5	7.24	48	.304	.361	0	.000	-0	-6	-6	0	-0.8
1966	Phi-N	0	0	—	2	0	0	0	0	1²	0	0	3	0	27.0	5.40	67	.333	.556	0	—	-0	-0	-0	0	0.0
1967	Phi-N	2	3	.400	43	4	0	0	1	84¹	86	3	43	83	14.0	3.84	89	.267	.357	2	.133	-0	-4	-4	-2	-0.4
1968	Phi-N	1	6	.143	33	6	1	0	1	61	59	4	20	49	11.7	2.95	102	.248	.306	3	.300	1	0	0	0	0.2
1969	Phi-N☆	14	18	.438	38	35	13	4	1	253	237	16	92	180	11.9	3.34	106	.249	.318	12	.140	-1	7	6	-2	0.5
1970	Phi-N	5	15	.250	32	23	1	0	0	149²	170	17	61	104	14.0	5.29	75	.288	.356	4	.091	-2	-21	-22	0	-2.7
1971	*Bal-A	4	3	.571	29	9	0	0	0	77²	72	7	20	51	10.9	3.13	107	.249	.302	2	.091	-0	3	2	-0	0.2
1972	*Bal-A	1	1	.500	32	0	0	0	8	41	33	1	9	34	9.2	2.63	117	.217	.261	0	.000	-0	2	2	0	0.2
1973	*Bal-A	8	0	1.000	45	0	0	0	9	80¹	54	5	24	47	8.7	1.90	196	.198	.263	0	—	-0	17	16	-0	2.0
1974	*Bal-A	6	4	.600	49	0	0	0	12	66²	48	7	22	56	9.6	2.57	135	.198	.268	0	—	-0	8	7	-1	1.1
1975	Bal-A	4	3	.571	41	0	0	0	7	48¹	42	3	21	39	11.9	3.35	105	.241	.327	0	—	-0	2	1	-0	0.1
1976	Bal-A	1	1	.500	13	0	0	0	3	19¹	19	1	9	14	14.0	5.12	64	.268	.366	0	—	-0	-3	-4	-0	-0.5
	*NY-A	6	0	1.000	21	2	1	1	1	58²	38	1	16	25	8.4	1.69	202	.186	.249	0	—	-0	12	11	-1	1.0
	Yr	7	1	.875	34	2	1	1	4	78	57	2	25	39	9.6	2.54	133	.205	.273	0	—	-0	8	7	-2	0.5
1977	Pit-N	5	3	.625	49	2	0	0	4	91	81	11	39	41	12.0	3.86	103	.240	.321	6	.333	2	1	1	-1	0.2
1978	Pit-N	7	5	.583	60	0	0	0	5	77¹	89	7	32	45	14.2	3.26	114	.298	.367	3	.250	1	3	4	0	0.7
1979	*Pit-N	8	5	.615	72	0	0	0	14	82	67	9	35	39	11.4	2.96	131	.230	.317	0	.000	-1	7	8	-1	1.4
1980	Pit-N	8	4	.667	61	0	0	0	9	71	71	4	20	31	11.5	2.92	125	.275	.327	0	.000	-0	5	6	-0	1.0
1981	Pit-N	1	2	.333	35	0	0	0	4	32¹	30	1	10	17	11.1	2.51	143	.248	.305	0	.000	-0	4	4	-1	0.4
	Mon-N	1	0	1.000	10	0	0	0	0	10²	14	2	9	4	19.4	7.59	46	.333	.451	0	—	-0	-5	-5	-0	-0.4
	Yr	2	2	.500	45	0	0	0	4	43	44	3	19	21	13.2	3.77	95	.267	.342	0	.000	-0	-1	-1	-1	0.0
1982	KC-A	3	1	.750	20	0	0	0	0	38¹	42	7	21	15	15.3	5.17	79	.271	.365	0	—	-0	-5	-5	-0	-0.5
	Pit-N	0	0	—	1	0	0	0	0	0²	1	1	0	0	13.5	13.50	27	.333	.333	0	—	-0	-1	-1	-0	0.0
Total	18	86	75	.534	692	83	16	5	79	1358²	1272	109	511	889	11.9	3.46	104	.251	.322	32	.136	-2	26	22	-9	3.7

● JOHN JACKSON
Jackson, John Lewis   b: 7/15/09, Wynnefield, Pa.   d: 10/22/56, Somers Point, N.J.   BR/TR, 6′2″, 180 lbs.   Deb: 6/20/33

YEAR	TM/L	W	L	PCT	G	GS	CG	SH	SV	IP	H	HR	BB	SO	RAT	ERA	ERA+	OAV	OOB	BH	AVG	PB	PR	/A	PD	TPI
1933	Phi-N	2	2	.500	10	7	1	0	0	54	74	3	35	11	19.0	6.00	64	.329	.430	3	.143	-1	-16	-13	-2	-1.2

● LARRY JACKSON
Jackson, Lawrence Curtis   b: 6/2/31, Nampa, Idaho   d: 8/28/90, Boise, Idaho   BR/TR, 6′2″, 190 lbs.   Deb: 4/17/55

YEAR	TM/L	W	L	PCT	G	GS	CG	SH	SV	IP	H	HR	BB	SO	RAT	ERA	ERA+	OAV	OOB	BH	AVG	PB	PR	/A	PD	TPI
1955	StL-N	9	14	.391	37	25	4	1	2	177¹	189	25	72	88	13.7	4.31	94	.277	.353	3	.053	-6	-5	-5	0	-1.1
1956	StL-N	2	2	.500	51	1	0	0	9	85¹	75	5	45	50	12.8	4.11	92	.240	.337	1	.091	-0	-3	-3	2	-0.1
1957	StL-N★	15	9	.625	41	22	6	2	1	210¹	196	21	57	96	11.0	3.47	114	.248	.302	13	.181	-0	10	12	4	1.7
1958	StL-N★	13	13	.500	49	23	11	1	8	198	211	21	51	124	12.4	3.68	112	.272	.325	9	.150	-2	6	10	-2	0.8
1959	StL-N	14	13	.519	40	37	12	3	0	256	271	13	64	145	11.9	3.30	128	.270	.316	9	.112	-3	18	27	-0	2.2
1960	StL-N★	18	13	.581	43	38	14	3	0	282	277	22	70	171	11.2	3.48	118	.257	.304	20	.211	2	9	19	-2	2.0
1961	StL-N	14	11	.560	33	28	12	3	0	211	203	20	56	113	11.2	3.75	117	.252	.303	13	.176	0	7	15	2	1.8
1962	StL-N	16	11	.593	36	35	11	2	0	252¹	267	25	44	112	12.0	3.75	114	.269	.318	15	.169	2	6	15	1	1.7
1963	Chi-N★	14	18	.438	37	37	13	4	0	275	256	11	54	153	10.3	2.55	137	.245	.286	17	.195	2	22	29	2	4.1
1964	Chi-N	24	11	.686	40	38	19	3	0	297²	265	17	58	148	9.8	3.14	118	.235	.273	20	.175	1	13	19	7	3.0
1965	Chi-N	14	21	.400	39	39	11	4	0	257¹	268	28	57	131	11.5	3.85	96	.267	.310	11	.128	1	-9	-5	3	-0.2
1966	Chi-N	0	2	.000	3	2	0	0	0	8	14	3	4	2	20.3	13.50	27	.368	.429	0	.000	-0	-9	-9	-0	-1.5
	Phi-N	15	13	.536	35	33	12	5	0	247	243	22	58	107	11.1	2.99	120	.259	.306	13	.146	-0	17	17	1	2.0
	Yr	15	15	.500	38	35	12	5	0	255	257	25	62	112	11.4	3.32	108	.264	.311	13	.141	-1	8	8	2	0.5
1967	Phi-N	13	15	.464	40	37	11	4	0	261²	242	17	54	139	10.4	3.10	110	.241	.284	14	.161	0	8	9	4	1.5
1968	Phi-N	13	17	.433	34	34	12	2	0	229	229	16	60	127	10.8	2.77	109	.248	.297	12	.141	-0	6	6	2	0.9
Total	14	194	183	.515	558	429	149	37	20	3262²	3206	259	824	1709	11.3	3.40	113	.256	.306	170	.156	-5	95	155	25	18.8

● MIKE JACKSON
Jackson, Michael Ray   b: 12/22/64, Houston, Tex.   BR/TR, 6′1″, 185 lbs.   Deb: 8/11/86

YEAR	TM/L	W	L	PCT	G	GS	CG	SH	SV	IP	H	HR	BB	SO	RAT	ERA	ERA+	OAV	OOB	BH	AVG	PB	PR	/A	PD	TPI
1986	Phi-N	0	0	—	9	0	0	0	0	13¹	12	2	4	3	12.2	3.38	114	.250	.333	0	—	-0	1	1	-0	0.0
1987	Phi-N	3	10	.231	55	7	0	0	1	109¹	88	16	56	93	12.1	4.20	101	.219	.319	2	.118	-0	-1	0	-1	-0.1
1988	Sea-A	6	5	.545	62	0	0	0	4	99¹	74	10	43	76	10.8	2.63	158	.209	.298	0	—	-0	15	17	-0	1.8
1989	Sea-A	4	6	.400	65	0	0	0	7	99¹	81	8	54	94	12.8	3.17	127	.223	.333	0	—	-0	8	9	-1	1.0
1990	Sea-A	5	7	.417	63	0	0	0	3	77¹	64	8	44	69	12.8	4.54	87	.229	.338	0	—	-0	-5	-5	1	-0.7
1991	Sea-A	7	7	.500	72	0	0	0	14	88²	64	5	34	74	10.6	3.25	127	.201	.290	0	—	-0	8	9	-1	1.4
1992	SF-N	6	6	.500	67	0	0	0	2	82	76	7	33	80	12.4	3.73	89	.252	.333	0	.000	-0	-2	-4	-0	-0.6
1993	SF-N	6	6	.500	81	0	0	0	1	77¹	58	7	24	70	9.9	3.03	129	.204	.273	2	.667	2	9	8	0	1.3
1994	SF-N	3	2	.600	36	0	0	0	4	42¹	23	4	11	51	7.7	1.49	270	.164	.235	0	.000	-0	13	12	0	1.6
Total	9	40	49	.449	510	7	0	0	36	689	540	67	303	610	11.4	3.37	118	.217	.309	4	.174	1	44	47	-2	5.7

● MIKE JACKSON
Jackson, Michael Warren   b: 3/27/46, Paterson, N.J.   BL/TL, 6′3″, 190 lbs.   Deb: 5/10/70

YEAR	TM/L	W	L	PCT	G	GS	CG	SH	SV	IP	H	HR	BB	SO	RAT	ERA	ERA+	OAV	OOB	BH	AVG	PB	PR	/A	PD	TPI
1970	Phi-N	1	1	.500	5	0	0	0	0	6¹	4	0	4	4	14.2	1.42	281	.286	.400	1	1.000	0	2	2	0	0.6
1971	StL-N	0	0	—	1	0	0	0	0	0²	1	0	1	0	27.0	0.00	—	.333	.500	0	—	-0	0	0	0	0.0
1972	KC-A	1	2	.333	7	3	0	0	0	19²	24	0	14	15	17.4	6.41	47	.320	.427	0	.000	-1	-7	-7	1	-1.0
1973	KC-A	0	0	—	9	0	0	0	0	22¹	25	3	20	13	18.5	6.85	60	.301	.442	0	—	-0	-8	-7	-0	0.0
	Cle-A	0	0	—	1	0	0	0	0	0²	1	0	1	0	13.5	0.00	—	.333	.333	0	—	-0	0	0	-0	0.0
	Yr	0	0	—	10	0	0	0	0	23	26	3	21	13	18.0	6.65	62	.295	.426	0	—	-0	-7	-7	-0	0.0
Total	4	2	3	.400	23	3	0	0	0	49²	57	3	39	33	17.6	5.80	63	.308	.431	1	.143	-0	-12	-12	1	-0.4

● ROY LEE JACKSON
Jackson, Roy Lee   b: 5/1/54, Opelika, Ala.   BR/TR, 6′2″, 194 lbs.   Deb: 9/13/77

YEAR	TM/L	W	L	PCT	G	GS	CG	SH	SV	IP	H	HR	BB	SO	RAT	ERA	ERA+	OAV	OOB	BH	AVG	PB	PR	/A	PD	TPI
1977	NY-N	0	2	.000	4	4	0	0	0	24	25	2	15	13	16.1	6.00	62	.263	.381	0	.000	-1	-6	-6	-1	-0.6
1978	NY-N	0	0	—	4	2	0	0	0	9	12	1	6	4	20.6	9.24	38	.429	.509	1	.667	1	-8	-8	0	0.1
1979	NY-N	1	0	1.000	8	0	0	0	0	16¹	11	1	5	10	9.4	2.20	165	.200	.279	1	1.000	1	3	3	0	0.2
1980	NY-N	1	7	.125	24	8	1	0	0	70²	78	4	20	58	12.5	4.20	84	.287	.336	3	.188	1	-5	-5	-1	-0.6
1981	Tor-A	1	2	.333	39	0	0	0	7	82	65	6	25	50	10.2	2.61	151	.275	.347	0	—	-0	9	10	0	0.6
1982	Tor-A	8	8	.500	48	2	0	0	6	97	77	7	31	71	10.2	3.06	146	.218	.284	0	—	-0	11	15	0	2.4
1983	Tor-A	8	3	.727	49	0	0	0	7	92	92	6	41	48	13.3	4.50	96	.267	.351	0	—	-0	-4	-2	0	0.0
1984	Tor-A	7	8	.467	54	0	0	0	10	86	73	12	31	58	11.0	3.56	115	.230	.301	0	—	-0	4	5	0	0.9

YEAR	TM/L	W	L	PCT	G	GS	CG	SH	SV	IP	H	HR	BB	SO	RAT	ERA	ERA+	OAV	OOB	BH	AVG	PB	PR	/A	PD	TPI
1985	SD-N	2	3	.400	22	2	0	0	2	40	32	4	13	28	10.3	2.70	131	.224	.293	0	.000	-1	4	4	0	0.4
1986	Min-A	0	1	.000	28	0	0	0	1	58¹	57	7	16	32	11.7	3.86	112	.256	.314	0	—	0	2	3	-1	-0.1
Total	10	28	34	.452	280	18	1	0	34	559	531	50	203	351	12.1	3.77	107	.254	.325	6	.194	1	8	17	-1	2.8

● TONY JACOBS
Jacobs, Anthony Robert b: 8/5/25, Dixmoor, Ill. d: 12/21/80, Nashville, Tenn. BB/TR, 5'9", 150 lbs. Deb: 9/19/48

YEAR	TM/L	W	L	PCT	G	GS	CG	SH	SV	IP	H	HR	BB	SO	RAT	ERA	ERA+	OAV	OOB	BH	AVG	PB	PR	/A	PD	TPI
1948	Chi-N	0	0	—	1	0	0	0	0	2	3	1	0	2	13.5	4.50	87	.333	.333	0	—	0	-0	-0	0	0.0
1955	StL-N	0	0	—	1	0	0	0	0	2	6	1	1	1	31.5	18.00	23	.500	.538	0	.000	-0	-3	-3	0	0.0
Total	2	0	0	—	2	0	0	0	0	4	9	2	1	3	22.5	11.25	35	.429	.455	0	.000	-0	-3	-3	0	0.0

● ART JACOBS
Jacobs, Arthur Edward b: 8/28/02, Luckey, Ohio d: 6/8/67, Inglewood, Cal. BL/TL, 5'10", 170 lbs. Deb: 6/18/39

YEAR	TM/L	W	L	PCT	G	GS	CG	SH	SV	IP	H	HR	BB	SO	RAT	ERA	ERA+	OAV	OOB	BH	AVG	PB	PR	/A	PD	TPI
1939	Cin-N	0	0	—	1	0	0	0	1	1	2	0	1	0	27.0	9.00	43	.400	.500	0	—	0	-1	-1	-0	-0.1

● BUCKY JACOBS
Jacobs, Newton Smith b: 3/21/13, Altavista, Va. d: 6/15/90, Richmond, Va. BR/TR, 5'11", 155 lbs. Deb: 6/27/37

YEAR	TM/L	W	L	PCT	G	GS	CG	SH	SV	IP	H	HR	BB	SO	RAT	ERA	ERA+	OAV	OOB	BH	AVG	PB	PR	/A	PD	TPI
1937	Was-A	1	1	.500	11	1	0	0	0	22¹	26	0	11	8	14.9	4.84	92	.295	.374	0	.000	-1	-1	-1	0	-0.1
1939	Was-A	0	0	—	2	0	0	0	0	3	1	0	0	1	3.0	0.00	—	.100	.100	0	—	0	2	1	-0	0.1
1940	Was-A	0	1	.000	9	0	0	0	0	15	16	1	9	6	16.2	6.00	69	.271	.386	0	.000	-0	-3	-3	1	-0.1
Total	3	1	2	.333	22	1	0	0	0	40¹	43	1	20	15	14.5	4.91	88	.274	.363	0	.000	-1	-2	-3	2	-0.2

● ELMER JACOBS
Jacobs, William Elmer b: 8/10/1892, Salem, Mo. d: 2/10/58, Salem, Mo. BR/TR, 6', 165 lbs. Deb: 4/23/14

YEAR	TM/L	W	L	PCT	G	GS	CG	SH	SV	IP	H	HR	BB	SO	RAT	ERA	ERA+	OAV	OOB	BH	AVG	PB	PR	/A	PD	TPI
1914	Phi-N	1	3	.250	14	7	1	0	0	50²	65	2	20	17	15.6	4.80	61	.342	.413	0	.000	-2	-11	-10	0	-0.9
1916	Pit-N	6	10	.375	34	17	8	0	0	153	151	2	38	46	11.4	2.94	91	.258	.308	3	.075	-2	-5	-4	-2	-0.8
1917	Pit-N	6	19	.240	38	25	10	1	2	227¹	214	3	76	58	11.7	2.81	101	.262	.329	12	.179	-1	-2	1	2	0.1
1918	Pit-N	0	1	.000	8	4	0	0	0	23¹	31	0	14	2	17.4	5.79	50	.344	.433	2	.286	0	-8	-8	1	-0.2
	Phi-N	9	5	.643	18	14	12	4	1	123	91	3	42	33	10.0	2.41	124	.210	.285	6	.158	-1	5	8	-2	0.6
	Yr	9	6	.600	26	18	12	4	1	146¹	122	3	56	35	11.2	2.95	101	.233	.312	8	.178	-1	-3	0	-1	0.4
1919	Phi-N	6	10	.375	17	15	13	0	0	128²	150	5	44	37	14.0	3.85	84	.304	.368	8	.178	-1	-13	-9	1	-1.1
	StL-N	3	6	.333	17	8	4	1	1	85¹	81	2	25	31	11.7	2.53	110	.264	.329	8	.348	3	4	2	-0	0.6
	Yr	9	16	.360	34	23	17	1	1	214	231	7	69	68	12.8	3.32	92	.287	.347	16	.235	2	-10	-6	1	-0.5
1920	StL-N	4	8	.333	23	9	1	0	1	77²	91	2	33	21	14.9	5.21	57	.296	.374	5	.192	-0	-18	-19	1	-2.7
1924	Chi-N	11	12	.478	38	22	13	1	1	190¹	181	9	72	50	12.1	3.74	104	.258	.329	6	.111	-4	3	4	1	0.1
1925	Chi-N	2	3	.400	18	4	1	1	1	55²	63	6	22	19	13.9	5.17	84	.274	.340	3	.231	-0	-6	-5	0	-0.4
1927	Chi-A	2	4	.333	25	8	2	1	0	74¹	105	3	37	22	17.7	4.60	88	.354	.432	3	.150	-1	-4	-5	2	-0.3
Total	9	50	81	.382	250	133	65	9	7	1189¹	1223	40	423	336	12.8	3.55	91	.275	.343	56	.161	-8	-57	-44	5	-5.0

● BEANY JACOBSON
Jacobson, Albert L. (b: Albin L. Jacobson) b: 6/5/1881, Port Washington, Wis. d: 1/31/33, Decatur, Ill. BL/TL, 6', 170 lbs. Deb: 4/30/04

YEAR	TM/L	W	L	PCT	G	GS	CG	SH	SV	IP	H	HR	BB	SO	RAT	ERA	ERA+	OAV	OOB	BH	AVG	PB	PR	/A	PD	TPI
1904	Was-A	6	23	.207	33	30	23	1	0	253²	276	6	57	75	11.9	3.55	75	.278	.319	8	.091	-6	-27	-25	2	-3.1
1905	Was-A	7	8	.467	22	17	12	0	0	144¹	139	1	35	50	11.2	3.30	80	.254	.305	7	.159	1	-10	-10	-2	-1.1
1906	StL-A	9	9	.500	24	15	12	0	0	155	146	3	27	53	10.3	2.50	103	.252	.290	5	.091	-4	3	1	0	-0.2
1907	StL-A	1	6	.143	7	7	6	0	0	57¹	55	1	26	16	12.7	2.98	84	.254	.334	4	.222	-0	-3	-3	-0	-0.4
	Bos-A	0	0	—	2	1	0	0	0	2	2	0	3	1	22.5	9.00	29	.262	.470	-	—	-0	-1	-1	0	0.0
	Yr	1	6	.143	9	8	6	0	0	59¹	57	1	29	17	13.0	3.19	79	.255	.340	4	.222	-0	-4	-4	-0	-0.4
Total	4	23	46	.333	88	70	53	1	0	612¹	618	11	148	195	11.4	3.19	82	.264	.311	24	.117	-9	-38	-38	-0	-4.8

● LARRY JACOBUS
Jacobus, Stuart Louis b: 12/18/1893, Cincinnati, Ohio d: 8/19/65, N.College Hill, O. BB/TR, 6'2", 186 lbs. Deb: 7/15/18

YEAR	TM/L	W	L	PCT	G	GS	CG	SH	SV	IP	H	HR	BB	SO	RAT	ERA	ERA+	OAV	OOB	BH	AVG	PB	PR	/A	PD	TPI
1918	Cin-N	0	1	.000	5	0	0	0	0	17¹	25	0	1	8	13.5	5.71	47	.368	.377	0	.000	-1	-6	-6	-0	-0.4

● JASON JACOME
Jacome, Jason James b: 11/24/70, Tulsa, Okla. BL/TL, 6'1", 155 lbs. Deb: 7/2/94

YEAR	TM/L	W	L	PCT	G	GS	CG	SH	SV	IP	H	HR	BB	SO	RAT	ERA	ERA+	OAV	OOB	BH	AVG	PB	PR	/A	PD	TPI
1994	NY-N	4	3	.571	8	8	1	1	0	54	54	3	17	30	11.8	2.67	160	.269	.326	1	.063	-1	9	10	1	1.1

● PAT JACQUEZ
Jacquez, Patrick Thomas b: 4/23/47, Stockton, Cal. BR/TR, 6', 200 lbs. Deb: 4/18/71

YEAR	TM/L	W	L	PCT	G	GS	CG	SH	SV	IP	H	HR	BB	SO	RAT	ERA	ERA+	OAV	OOB	BH	AVG	PB	PR	/A	PD	TPI
1971	Chi-A	0	0	—	2	0	0	0	0	2	4	0	2	1	27.0	4.50	80	.444	.545	0	.000	-0	-0	-0	0	0.0

● JAKE JAECKEL
Jaeckel, Paul Henry b: 4/1/42, E.Los Angeles, Cal. BR/TR, 5'10", 170 lbs. Deb: 9/19/64

YEAR	TM/L	W	L	PCT	G	GS	CG	SH	SV	IP	H	HR	BB	SO	RAT	ERA	ERA+	OAV	OOB	BH	AVG	PB	PR	/A	PD	TPI
1964	Chi-N	1	0	1.000	4	0	0	0	1	8	4	0	3	2	7.9	0.00	—	.160	.250	0	.000	-0	3	3	-0	0.5

● CHARLIE JAEGER
Jaeger, Charles Thomas b: 4/17/1875, Ottawa, Ill. d: 9/27/42, Ottawa, Ill. BR/TR, Deb: 9/9/04

YEAR	TM/L	W	L	PCT	G	GS	CG	SH	SV	IP	H	HR	BB	SO	RAT	ERA	ERA+	OAV	OOB	BH	AVG	PB	PR	/A	PD	TPI
1904	Det-A	3	3	.500	8	6	5	0	0	49	49	0	15	13	12.9	2.57	99	.261	.335	1	.059	-0	-0	-1	-0	-0.3

● JOE JAEGER
Jaeger, Joseph Peter "Zip" b: 3/3/1895, St.Cloud, Minn. d: 12/13/63, Hampton, Iowa BR/TR, 6'1", 190 lbs. Deb: 7/28/20

YEAR	TM/L	W	L	PCT	G	GS	CG	SH	SV	IP	H	HR	BB	SO	RAT	ERA	ERA+	OAV	OOB	BH	AVG	PB	PR	/A	PD	TPI
1920	Chi-N	0	0	—	2	0	0	0	0	3	6	0	4	0	30.0	12.00	27	.500	.625	0	.000	-0	-3	-3	0	0.0

● SIG JAKUCKI
Jakucki, Sigmund "Jack" b: 8/20/09, Camden, N.J. d: 5/28/79, Galveston, Tex. BR/TR, 6'2.5", 198 lbs. Deb: 8/30/36

YEAR	TM/L	W	L	PCT	G	GS	CG	SH	SV	IP	H	HR	BB	SO	RAT	ERA	ERA+	OAV	OOB	BH	AVG	PB	PR	/A	PD	TPI
1936	StL-A	0	3	.000	7	2	0	0	0	20²	32	2	12	9	19.6	8.71	62	.348	.429	0	.000	-1	-8	-8	0	-0.9
1944	*StL-A	13	9	.591	35	24	12	4	3	198	211	17	54	67	12.2	3.55	101	.268	.318	11	.151	-2	-3	1	0	0.1
1945	StL-A	12	10	.545	30	24	15	1	2	192¹	188	9	65	55	11.9	3.51	100	.257	.318	13	.186	0	-3	-0	1	-0.0
Total	3	25	22	.532	72	50	27	5	5	411	431	28	131	131	12.4	3.79	96	.268	.325	24	.161	-2	-14	-6	1	-0.7

● LEFTY JAMERSON
Jamerson, Charles Dewey "Charlie" b: 1/26/1900, Enfield, Ill. d: 8/4/80, Mocksville, N.C. BL/TL, 6'1", 195 lbs. Deb: 8/16/24

YEAR	TM/L	W	L	PCT	G	GS	CG	SH	SV	IP	H	HR	BB	SO	RAT	ERA	ERA+	OAV	OOB	BH	AVG	PB	PR	/A	PD	TPI
1924	Bos-A	0	0	—	1	0	0	0	0	1	1	0	3	0	36.0	18.00	24	.250	.571	0	—	0	-2	-2	-0	0.0

● JEFF JAMES
James, Jeffrey Lynn "Jesse" b: 9/29/41, Indianapolis, Ind. BR/TR, 6'3", 195 lbs. Deb: 4/13/68

YEAR	TM/L	W	L	PCT	G	GS	CG	SH	SV	IP	H	HR	BB	SO	RAT	ERA	ERA+	OAV	OOB	BH	AVG	PB	PR	/A	PD	TPI
1968	Phi-N	4	4	.500	29	13	1	1	0	116	112	8	46	83	12.6	4.27	70	.256	.332	4	.121	-1	-17	-16	0	-1.2
1969	Phi-N	2	2	.500	6	5	1	0	0	31²	36	5	14	21	14.2	5.40	66	.288	.360	2	.182	-0	-6	-7	-0	-0.8
Total	2	6	6	.500	35	18	2	1	0	147²	148	13	60	104	12.9	4.51	69	.263	.338	6	.136	-1	-23	-23	-0	-2.0

● JOHNNY JAMES
James, John Phillip b: 7/23/33, Bonners Ferry, Idaho BL/TR, 5'10", 160 lbs. Deb: 9/6/58

YEAR	TM/L	W	L	PCT	G	GS	CG	SH	SV	IP	H	HR	BB	SO	RAT	ERA	ERA+	OAV	OOB	BH	AVG	PB	PR	/A	PD	TPI
1958	NY-A	0	0	—	1	0	0	0	0	3	2	0	4	4	18.0	0.00	—	.250	.500	0	.000	-0	1	1	0	0.0
1960	NY-A	5	1	.833	28	0	0	0	2	43¹	38	3	26	29	13.9	4.36	82	.248	.368	0	.000	-0	-2	-4	0	-0.5
1961	NY-A	0	0	—	1	0	0	0	0	1¹	1	0	0	2	6.8	6.8	0	—	.250	.250	0	—	0	1	1	0	0.0
	LA-A	0	2	.000	36	3	0	0	0	71¹	66	12	54	41	15.4	5.30	85	.246	.377	0	.000	-1	-10	-6	0	-0.3
	Yr	0	2	.000	37	3	0	0	0	72²	67	12	54	43	15.2	5.20	86	.246	.375	0	.000	-1	-10	-6	0	-0.3
Total	3	5	3	.625	66	3	0	0	2	119	107	15	84	73	14.8	4.76	87	.247	.375	0	.000	-1	-11	-8	0	-0.8

● RICK JAMES
James, Richard Lee b: 10/11/47, Sheffield, Ala. BR/TR, 6'2.5", 205 lbs. Deb: 9/20/67

YEAR	TM/L	W	L	PCT	G	GS	CG	SH	SV	IP	H	HR	BB	SO	RAT	ERA	ERA+	OAV	OOB	BH	AVG	PB	PR	/A	PD	TPI
1967	Chi-N	0	1	.000	3	1	0	0	0	4²	9	1	2	2	21.2	13.50	26	.529	.579	0	.000	-0	-5	-5	-0	-0.9

● BOB JAMES
James, Robert Harvey b: 8/15/58, Glendale, Cal. BR/TR, 6'4", 230 lbs. Deb: 9/7/78

YEAR	TM/L	W	L	PCT	G	GS	CG	SH	SV	IP	H	HR	BB	SO	RAT	ERA	ERA+	OAV	OOB	BH	AVG	PB	PR	/A	PD	TPI
1978	Mon-N	0	1	.000	4	1	0	0	0	4	4	1	4	3	18.0	9.00	39	.267	.421	0	—	0	-2	-2	0	-0.5
1979	Mon-N	0	0	—	2	0	0	0	0	2	2	1	2	0	22.5	13.50	27	.250	.455	0	—	0	-2	-2	0	0.0
1982	Mon-N	0	0	—	7	0	0	0	0	9	10	0	8	11	18.0	6.00	61	.294	.429	0	—	0	-2	-2	0	0.0
	Det-A	0	2	.000	12	1	0	0	0	19²	22	4	8	20	13.7	5.03	81	.278	.345	0	—	0	-2	-2	0	-0.2
1983	Det-A	0	0	—	4	0	0	0	0	4	9	0	4	5	29.2	11.25	35	.313	.421	0	—	0	-3	-3	-0	0.0
	Mon-N	1	0	1.000	27	0	0	0	7	50	37	3	23	56	11.3	2.88	125	.210	.312	2	.286	0	4	4	1	0.4
1984	Mon-N	6	6	.500	62	0	0	0	10	96	92	6	45	91	13.2	3.66	94	.251	.339	2	.143	0	-1	-2	-1	-0.5
1985	Chi-A	8	7	.533	69	0	0	0	32	110	90	5	23	88	9.4	2.13	203	.226	.271	0	—	0	25	27	-1	5.1
1986	Chi-A	5	4	.556	49	0	0	0	14	58¹	61	8	23	32	13.6	5.25	82	.268	.345	0	—	0	-7	-6	-1	-1.4

YEAR	TM/L	W	L	PCT	G	GS	CG	SH	SV	IP	H	HR	BB	SO	RAT	ERA	ERA+	OAV	OOB	BH	AVG	PB	PR	/A	PD	TPI
1987	Chi-A	4	6	.400	43	0	0	0	10	54	54	10	17	34	12.5	4.67	98	.256	.323	0	—	0	-1	-1	0	-0.3
Total	8	24	26	.480	279	2	0	0	73	407	377	39	157	340	12.2	3.80	105	.246	.323	4	.190	0	8	9	-2	2.6

● **LEFTY JAMES**   James, William A. b: 7/1/1889, Glen Roy, Ohio d: 5/3/33, Glen Roy, Ohio BL/TL, 5'11.5", 175 lbs. Deb: 4/13/12

YEAR	TM/L	W	L	PCT	G	GS	CG	SH	SV	IP	H	HR	BB	SO	RAT	ERA	ERA+	OAV	OOB	BH	AVG	PB	PR	/A	PD	TPI
1912	Cle-A	0	1	.000	3	1	0	0	1	6	8	0	4	2	21.0	7.50	45	.348	.483	0	.000	-0	-3	-3	-0	-0.5
1913	Cle-A	2	2	.500	11	4	3	0	0	39	42	0	9	18	12.5	3.00	101	.273	.325	3	.231	-0	0	-1	-1	-0.1
1914	Cle-A	0	3	.000	17	6	1	0	0	50²	44	0	32	16	13.9	3.20	90	.251	.373	0	.000	-1	-3	-2	1	-0.1
Total	3	2	6	.250	31	11	4	0	1	95²	94	0	45	36	13.7	3.39	88	.267	.361	3	.107	-1	-6	-4	0	-0.7

● **BILL JAMES**   James, William Henry "Big Bill" b: 1/20/1887, Detroit, Mich. d: 5/24/42, Venice, Cal. BB/TR, 6'4", 195 lbs. Deb: 6/12/11

YEAR	TM/L	W	L	PCT	G	GS	CG	SH	SV	IP	H	HR	BB	SO	RAT	ERA	ERA+	OAV	OOB	BH	AVG	PB	PR	/A	PD	TPI
1911	Cle-A	2	4	.333	8	6	4	0	0	51²	58	1	32	21	16.0	4.88	70	.284	.387	1	.059	-1	-9	-8	-1	-1.0
1912	Cle-A	0	0	—	3	0	0	0	0	13²	15	0	9	5	15.8	4.61	74	.288	.393	0	.000	-2	-2	-2	-1	-0.1
1914	StL-A	15	14	.517	44	35	20	3	1	284	269	4	109	109	12.2	2.85	95	.257	.330	10	.112	-3	-5	-5	5	-0.4
1915	StL-A	7	10	.412	34	23	8	0	1	170¹	155	2	92	58	13.4	3.59	80	.255	.359	8	.190	1	-12	-14	2	-1.1
	Det-A	7	3	.700	11	9	3	1	0	67	57	1	33	24	12.1	2.42	125	.243	.336	6	.286	2	4	5	1	1.0
	Yr	14	13	.519	45	32	11	1	1	237¹	212	3	125	82	12.8	3.26	89	.249	.345	14	.222	2	-9	-9	3	-0.1
1916	Det-A	8	12	.400	30	20	8	0	1	151²	141	1	79	61	13.7	3.68	78	.255	.360	3	.068	-3	-14	-14	-0	-2.1
1917	Det-A	13	10	.565	34	23	10	2	1	198	163	2	96	62	12.3	2.09	127	.229	.330	12	.211	2	13	12	-0	1.7
1918	Det-A	6	11	.353	19	18	8	1	0	122	127	3	68	42	14.8	3.76	71	.279	.379	5	.109	-3	-13	-15	2	-2.1
1919	Det-A	1	0	1.000	2	1	0	0	0	9¹	11	0	7	3	18.3	5.79	55	.324	.432	1	.250	-0	-3	-3	-0	-0.3
	Bos-A	3	5	.375	13	7	4	0	0	72²	74	2	39	12	14.4	4.09	74	.280	.379	3	.143	-1	-7	-9	-0	-0.9
	*Chi-A	3	2	.600	5	5	3	2	0	39¹	39	0	14	11	12.6	2.52	126	.281	.355	2	.143	-1	3	3	-1	0.2
	Yr	7	7	.500	20	13	7	2	0	121¹	125	2	60	26	13.9	3.71	83	.282	.370	6	.154	-2	-6	-8	-0	-1.0
Total	8	65	71	.478	203	147	68	9	4	1179²	1110	16	578	408	13.2	3.20	88	.258	.352	51	.142	-8	-44	-49	8	-5.1

● **BILL JAMES**   James, William Lawrence "Seattle Bill" b: 3/12/1892, Iowa Hill, Cal. d: 3/10/71, Oroville, Cal. BR/TR, 6'3", 196 lbs. Deb: 4/17/13

YEAR	TM/L	W	L	PCT	G	GS	CG	SH	SV	IP	H	HR	BB	SO	RAT	ERA	ERA+	OAV	OOB	BH	AVG	PB	PR	/A	PD	TPI
1913	Bos-N	6	10	.375	24	14	10	1	0	135²	134	4	57	73	13.1	2.79	118	.264	.347	12	.255	1	6	8	0	1.0
1914	*Bos-N	26	7	**.788**	46	37	30	4	2	332¹	261	7	118	156	10.6	1.90	145	.225	.304	33	.256	4	**33**	**32**	-1	**3.6**
1915	Bos-N	5	4	.556	13	10	4	0	0	68¹	68	3	22	23	12.1	3.03	86	.269	.332	1	.048	-2	-2	-3	1	-0.5
1919	Bos-N	0	0	—	1	0	0	0	0	5¹	6	0	2	1	13.5	3.38	85	.273	.333	0	.000	-0	-0	-0	0	0.0
Total	4	37	21	.638	84	61	44	5	2	541²	469	14	199	253	11.5	2.28	126	.242	.319	46	.231	4	37	35	1	4.1

● **CHARLIE JAMIESON**   Jamieson, Charles Devine "Cuckoo" b: 2/7/1893, Paterson, N.J. d: 10/27/69, Paterson, N.J. BL/TL, 5'8.5", 165 lbs. Deb: 9/20/15 ◆

YEAR	TM/L	W	L	PCT	G	GS	CG	SH	SV	IP	H	HR	BB	SO	RAT	ERA	ERA+	OAV	OOB	BH	AVG	PB	PR	/A	PD	TPI
1916	Was-A	0	0	—	1	0	0	0	0	4	2	0	3	2	11.3	4.50	62	.143	.294	36	.248	0	-1	-1	-0	0.0
1917	Was-A	0	0	—	1	0	0	0	0	2¹	10	0	2	1	46.3	38.57	7	.625	.667	6	.171	0	-9	-9	-0	0.0
1918	Phi-A	2	1	.667	5	2	1	0	0	23	24	0	13	2	15.3	4.30	68	.261	.364	84	.202	0	-4	-4	-0	-0.5
1919	Cle-A	0	0	—	4	1	0	0	0	13	12	0	8	0	13.8	5.54	60	.250	.357	6	.353	0	-3	-3	-0	0.1
1922	Cle-A	0	0	—	2	0	0	0	0	5²	7	0	4	2	17.5	3.18	126	.318	.423	183	.323	1	1	1	-0	0.0
Total	5	2	1	.667	13	3	1	0	0	48	55	0	30	7	16.3	6.19	51	.286	.388	1990	.303	2	-17	-16	-1	-0.4

● **JERRY JANESKI**   Janeski, Gerard Joseph b: 4/18/46, Pasadena, Cal. BR/TR, 6'4", 205 lbs. Deb: 4/10/70

YEAR	TM/L	W	L	PCT	G	GS	CG	SH	SV	IP	H	HR	BB	SO	RAT	ERA	ERA+	OAV	OOB	BH	AVG	PB	PR	/A	PD	TPI
1970	Chi-A	10	17	.370	35	35	4	1	0	205²	247	22	63	79	13.8	4.77	82	.300	.353	5	.074	-4	-24	-20	1	-2.6
1971	Was-A	1	5	.167	23	10	0	0	1	61²	72	5	34	19	15.9	4.96	67	.304	.398	3	.214	1	-10	-11	1	-1.0
1972	Tex-A	0	1	.000	4	1	0	0	0	12²	11	0	7	7	12.8	2.84	106	.229	.327	0	.000	-0	0	0	0	0.0
Total	3	11	23	.324	62	46	4	1	1	280	330	27	104	105	14.2	4.72	79	.298	.362	8	.098	-4	-34	-31	2	-3.6

● **LARRY JANSEN**   Jansen, Lawrence Joseph b: 7/16/20, Verboort, Ore. BR/TR, 6'2", 190 lbs. Deb: 4/17/47 C

YEAR	TM/L	W	L	PCT	G	GS	CG	SH	SV	IP	H	HR	BB	SO	RAT	ERA	ERA+	OAV	OOB	BH	AVG	PB	PR	/A	PD	TPI
1947	NY-N	21	5	**.808**	42	30	20	1	1	248	241	23	57	104	10.9	3.16	129	.262	.306	16	.186	-0	25	25	-0	2.4
1948	NY-N	18	12	.600	42	36	15	4	2	277	283	25	54	126	11.0	3.61	109	.265	.303	13	.137	-2	11	10	2	1.0
1949	NY-N	15	16	.484	37	35	17	3	0	259²	271	36	62	113	11.6	3.85	104	.263	.306	16	.165	-0	6	4	3	0.6
1950	NY-N★	19	13	.594	40	35	21	**5**	3	275	238	31	55	161	**9.6**	3.01	136	.232	**.271**	16	.167	-0	35	33	2	3.8
1951	*NY-N☆	**23**	11	.676	39	34	18	3	0	278²	254	26	56	145	10.1	3.04	129	.239	.279	9	.094	-5	29	27	3	2.9
1952	NY-N	11	11	.500	34	27	8	1	2	167¹	183	16	47	74	12.7	4.09	91	.281	.335	8	.178	3	-7	-7	2	-0.4
1953	NY-N	11	16	.407	36	26	6	0	1	184²	185	24	55	88	11.8	4.14	104	.256	.311	8	.133	-1	3	3	-1	0.2
1954	NY-N	2	2	.500	13	7	0	0	0	40²	57	5	15	15	16.2	5.98	67	.337	.395	4	.286	1	-9	-9	1	-0.5
1956	Cin-N	2	3	.400	8	7	2	0	1	34²	53	5	16	12	16.7	5.19	77	.281	.329	1	.100	1	-5	-5	-0	-0.8
Total	9	122	89	.578	291	237	107	17	10	1765²	1751	191	410	842	11.1	3.58	112	.258	.302	90	.150	-6	87	82	11	9.2

● **KEVIN JARVIS**   Jarvis, Kevin Thomas b: 8/1/69, Lexington, Ky. BL/TR, 6'2", 200 lbs. Deb: 4/6/94

YEAR	TM/L	W	L	PCT	G	GS	CG	SH	SV	IP	H	HR	BB	SO	RAT	ERA	ERA+	OAV	OOB	BH	AVG	PB	PR	/A	PD	TPI
1994	Cin-N	1	1	.500	6	3	0	0	0	17²	22	4	5	10	13.8	7.13	58	.301	.346	1	.250	0	-6	-6	0	-0.5

● **RAY JARVIS**   Jarvis, Raymond Arnold b: 5/10/46, Providence, R.I. BR/TR, 6'2", 198 lbs. Deb: 4/15/69

YEAR	TM/L	W	L	PCT	G	GS	CG	SH	SV	IP	H	HR	BB	SO	RAT	ERA	ERA+	OAV	OOB	BH	AVG	PB	PR	/A	PD	TPI
1969	Bos-A	5	6	.455	29	12	2	0	1	100¹	105	8	43	36	13.5	4.75	80	.274	.352	2	.069	-2	-13	-11	1	-1.2
1970	Bos-A	0	1	.000	15	0	0	0	0	16	17	1	14	8	18.6	3.94	101	.274	.423	0	—	0	-0	0	0	0.0
Total	2	5	7	.417	44	12	2	0	1	116¹	122	9	57	44	14.2	4.64	82	.274	.363	2	.069	-2	-13	-11	1	-1.2

● **PAT JARVIS**   Jarvis, Robert Patrick b: 3/18/41, Carlyle, Ill. BR/TR, 5'10.5", 180 lbs. Deb: 8/4/66

YEAR	TM/L	W	L	PCT	G	GS	CG	SH	SV	IP	H	HR	BB	SO	RAT	ERA	ERA+	OAV	OOB	BH	AVG	PB	PR	/A	PD	TPI
1966	Atl-N	6	2	.750	10	9	3	1	0	62¹	46	1	12	41	8.5	2.31	157	.206	.250	0	.000	-2	9	9	-1	0.8
1967	Atl-N	15	10	.600	32	30	7	1	0	194	195	15	62	118	12.1	3.66	91	.260	.320	6	.085	-3	-6	-7	-2	-1.4
1968	Atl-N	16	12	.571	34	34	14	1	0	256	202	15	50	157	8.9	2.60	115	.214	.255	12	.141	0	11	11	-3	1.0
1969	*Atl-N	13	11	.542	37	33	4	1	0	217¹	204	25	73	123	11.5	4.43	91	.246	.308	8	.113	-2	-20	-20	-0	-2.3
1970	Atl-N	16	16	.500	36	34	11	1	0	254	240	21	72	173	11.1	3.61	119	.247	.299	15	.183	-0	12	19	2	2.4
1971	Atl-N	6	14	.300	35	23	3	3	1	162¹	162	16	51	68	12.0	4.10	90	.261	.320	5	.106	-2	-12	-7	1	-1.0
1972	Atl-N	11	7	.611	37	6	0	0	2	98²	94	7	44	56	12.6	4.10	92	.260	.341	3	.125	-0	-7	-3	1	-0.5
1973	Mon-N	2	1	.667	28	0	0	0	0	39¹	37	6	16	19	12.4	3.20	119	.250	.327	0	.000	-0	2	3	-0	0.1
Total	8	85	73	.538	249	169	42	8	3	1284	1180	106	380	755	11.0	3.58	101	.243	.300	49	.121	-10	-11	-3	-0	-0.9

● **HI JASPER**   Jasper, Henry W. b: 11/15/1880, St.Louis, Mo. d: 5/22/37, St.Louis, Mo. BR/TR, 5'11", 180 lbs. Deb: 4/19/14

YEAR	TM/L	W	L	PCT	G	GS	CG	SH	SV	IP	H	HR	BB	SO	RAT	ERA	ERA+	OAV	OOB	BH	AVG	PB	PR	/A	PD	TPI
1914	Chi-A	1	0	1.000	16	0	0	0	0	32¹	22	0	20	19	12.0	3.34	80	.210	.341	0	.000	-1	-2	-2	1	0.0
1915	Chi-A	0	1	.000	3	2	1	0	0	15²	8	2	9	15	9.8	4.60	65	.157	.283	2	.286	0	-3	-3	1	0.0
1916	StL-N	5	6	.455	21	9	5	0	0	107	97	0	42	37	12.3	3.28	81	.254	.339	7	.212	1	-8	-8	2	-0.5
1919	Cle-A	4	5	.444	12	10	5	0	0	82²	83	1	28	25	12.1	3.59	93	.269	.330	3	.103	-2	-3	-2	1	-0.4
Total	4	10	12	.455	52	21	8	0	0	237²	210	3	99	96	12.0	3.48	84	.248	.333	12	.162	-2	-16	-15	5	-0.9

● **LARRY JASTER**   Jaster, Larry Edward b: 1/13/44, Midland, Mich. BL/TL, 6'3.5", 205 lbs. Deb: 9/17/65

YEAR	TM/L	W	L	PCT	G	GS	CG	SH	SV	IP	H	HR	BB	SO	RAT	ERA	ERA+	OAV	OOB	BH	AVG	PB	PR	/A	PD	TPI
1965	StL-N	3	0	1.000	4	3	3	0	0	28	21	1	7	10	9.0	1.61	239	.206	.257	2	.200	0	6	7	-1	0.7
1966	StL-N	11	5	.688	26	21	6	**5**	0	151²	124	17	45	92	10.3	3.26	110	.227	.291	8	.178	1	6	5	-0	0.6
1967	*StL-N	9	7	.563	34	23	2	1	3	152¹	141	12	44	87	11.0	3.01	109	.244	.300	5	.100	-1	6	5	-2	0.1
1968	*StL-N	9	13	.409	31	21	3	1	0	154²	153	13	38	70	11.5	3.50	83	.262	.313	6	.140	0	-9	-10	-2	-1.6
1969	Mon-N	1	6	.143	24	11	0	0	0	77	95	17	28	39	14.6	5.49	67	.302	.362	8	.421	3	-16	-16	-2	-1.2
1970	Atl-N	1	1	.500	14	0	0	0	0	22¹	33	5	8	19	16.5	6.85	60	.359	.410	0	.000	-0	-7	-6	1	-0.5
1972	Atl-N	1	1	.500	5	1	1	0	0	12¹	12	4	3	6	14.6	5.11	74	.267	.377	0	.000	-0	-2	-2	-0	-0.3
Total	7	35	33	.515	138	80	15	7	3	598	579	69	173	323	11.6	3.64	93	.256	.314	29	.170	3	-16	-17	-7	-2.2

● **AL JAVERY**   Javery, Alva William "Beartracks" b: 6/5/18, Worcester, Mass. d: 9/13/77, Woodstock, Conn. BR/TR, 6'3", 183 lbs. Deb: 4/23/40

YEAR	TM/L	W	L	PCT	G	GS	CG	SH	SV	IP	H	HR	BB	SO	RAT	ERA	ERA+	OAV	OOB	BH	AVG	PB	PR	/A	PD	TPI
1940	Bos-N	2	4	.333	29	4	1	0	1	83¹	99	2	36	42	14.8	5.51	68	.293	.364	2	.087	-1	-15	-17	-2	-1.4

YEAR	TM/L	W	L	PCT	G	GS	CG	SH	SV	IP	H	HR	BB	SO	RAT	ERA	ERA+	OAV	OOB	BH	AVG	PB	PR	/A	PD	TPI
1941	Bos-N	10	11	.476	34	23	9	1	1	160²	181	5	65	54	14.1	4.31	83	.283	.355	6	.103	-4	-12	-13	1	-1.8
1942	Bos-N	12	16	.429	42	37	19	5	0	261	251	8	78	85	11.4	3.03	110	.251	.307	9	.105	-5	8	9	2	0.6
1943	Bos-N★	17	16	.515	41	35	19	5	0	303	288	13	99	134	11.6	3.21	106	.248	.309	17	.163	-3	6	7	2	0.7
1944	Bos-N☆	10	19	.345	40	33	11	3	3	254	248	12	118	137	13.0	3.54	108	.262	.345	12	.152	-3	2	8	-2	0.3
1945	Bos-N	2	7	.222	17	14	2	1	0	77¹	92	4	51	18	16.6	6.28	61	.295	.394	6	.207	-0	-21	-21	1	-2.0
1946	Bos-N	0	1	.000	2	1	0	0	0	3¹	5	0	5	0	27.0	13.50	25	.417	.588	0	.000	-0	-4	-4	-0	-0.9
Total	7	53	74	.417	205	147	61	15	5	1142²	1164	44	452	470	12.9	3.80	94	.264	.335	52	.137	-15	-37	-31	2	-4.5

● **JOEY JAY**   Jay, Joseph Richard   b: 8/15/35, Middletown, Conn.   BB/TR, 6'4", 228 lbs.   Deb: 7/21/53

YEAR	TM/L	W	L	PCT	G	GS	CG	SH	SV	IP	H	HR	BB	SO	RAT	ERA	ERA+	OAV	OOB	BH	AVG	PB	PR	/A	PD	TPI
1953	Mil-N	1	0	1.000	3	1	1	1	0	10	6	0	5	4	9.9	0.00		.188	.297	0	.000	-0	5	4	-0	0.3
1954	Mil-N	1	0	1.000	15	1	0	0	0	18	21	3	16	13	19.0	6.50	57	.304	.442	0	—	0	-5	-6	-0	-0.3
1955	Mil-N	0	0	—	12	1	0	0	0	19	23	2	13	3	17.1	4.74	79	.324	.429	2	.667	1	-1	-2	-1	-0.2
1957	Mil-N	0	0	—	1	0	0	0	0	0²	0	0	0	0	0.0	0.00		.000	.000	—	—	0	0	0	-0	0.1
1958	Mil-N	7	5	.583	18	12	6	3	0	96²	60	8	43	74	9.7	2.14	164	.177	.272	3	.094	-1	19	15	0	1.7
1959	Mil-N	6	11	.353	34	19	4	1	0	136¹	130	11	64	88	13.1	4.09	87	.248	.336	3	.086	-1	-2	-8	2	-0.9
1960	Mil-N	9	8	.529	32	11	3	0	1	133¹	128	10	59	90	13.0	3.24	106	.254	.339	7	.156	-0	8	3	-0	0.3
1961	*Cin-N☆	21	10	.677	34	34	14	**4**	0	247¹	217	25	92	157	11.4	3.53	115	.236	.309	8	.090	-5	14	15	-1	1.0
1962	Cin-N	21	14	.600	39	37	16	4	0	273	269	26	100	155	12.3	3.76	107	.260	.327	15	.167	5	6	8	-2	1.0
1963	Cin-N	7	18	.280	30	22	4	1	1	170	172	19	73	116	13.1	4.29	78	.266	.343	8	.160	-3	-19	-18	-0	-2.5
1964	Cin-N	11	11	.500	34	23	10	0	2	183	167	17	36	134	10.1	3.39	107	.245	.285	2	.057	-3	3	5	2	0.0
1965	Cin-N	9	8	.529	37	24	4	1	1	155²	150	11	63	102	12.5	4.22	89	.252	.328	2	.041	-3	-12	-8	-0	-1.2
1966	Cin-N	6	2	.750	12	10	1	1	0	73²	78	8	23	44	12.7	3.91	100	.275	.335	3	.115	-1	-2	-0	-1	-0.2
	Atl-N	0	4	.000	9	8	0	0	1	29²	39	4	20	19	18.2	7.89	46	.315	.414	1	.125	-0	-14	-14	-0	-1.7
	Yr	6	6	.500	21	18	1	1	1	103¹	117	12	43	63	14.0	5.05	76	.285	.354	4	.118	-1	-17	-14	-1	-1.9
Total	13	99	91	.521	310	203	63	16	7	1546¹	1460	153	607	999	12.2	3.77	99	.251	.325	55	.114	-10	-5	-6	-2	-2.4

● **DOMINGO JEAN**   Jean, Domingo (Luisa)   b: 1/9/69, San Pedro De Macoris, D.R.   BR/TR, 6'2", 175 lbs.   Deb: 8/8/93

YEAR	TM/L	W	L	PCT	G	GS	CG	SH	SV	IP	H	HR	BB	SO	RAT	ERA	ERA+	OAV	OOB	BH	AVG	PB	PR	/A	PD	TPI
1993	NY-A	1	1	.500	10	6	0	0	0	40¹	37	7	19	20	12.5	4.46	93	.237	.320	0	—	0	-1	-1	-0	0.0

● **TEX JEANES**   Jeanes, Ernest Lee   b: 12/19/1900, Maypearl, Tex.   d: 4/5/73, Longview, Tex.   BR/TR, 6', 176 lbs.   Deb: 4/20/21 ◆

YEAR	TM/L	W	L	PCT	G	GS	CG	SH	SV	IP	H	HR	BB	SO	RAT	ERA	ERA+	OAV	OOB	BH	AVG	PB	PR	/A	PD	TPI
1922	Cle-A	0	0	—	1	0	0	0	0	0	0	0	1	0	—	—		—	1.000	0	.000	0	0	0	-0	0.0
1927	NY-N	0	0	—	1	0	0	0	0	1	2	0	2	0	36.0	9.00	43	.400	.571	6	.300	0	-1	-1	-0	0.0
Total	2	0	0	—	2	0	0	0	0	1	2	0	3	0	45.0	9.00	43	.400	.625	20	.274	0	-1	-1	-0	0.0

● **GEORGE JEFFCOAT**   Jeffcoat, George Edward   b: 12/24/13, New Brookland, S.C   d: 10/13/78, Leesville, S.C.   BR/TR, 5'11.5", 175 lbs.   Deb: 4/20/36   F

YEAR	TM/L	W	L	PCT	G	GS	CG	SH	SV	IP	H	HR	BB	SO	RAT	ERA	ERA+	OAV	OOB	BH	AVG	PB	PR	/A	PD	TPI
1936	Bro-N	5	6	.455	40	5	3	0	3	95²	84	7	63	46	14.6	4.52	92	.239	.366	3	.130	-1	-5	-4	-1	-0.6
1937	Bro-N	1	3	.250	21	3	1	1	0	54¹	58	4	27	29	14.2	5.13	79	.274	.358	0	.000	-2	-7	-7	-0	-0.6
1939	Bro-N	0	0	—	1	0	0	0	0	2	2	0	0	1	9.0	0.00	—	.286	.286	0	—	0	1	1	-0	0.0
1943	Bos-N	1	2	.333	8	1	0	0	0	17²	15	1	10	10	12.7	3.06	112	.217	.316	2	.500	1	1	1	-0	0.2
Total	4	7	11	.389	70	9	4	1	3	169²	159	12	100	86	14.1	4.51	89	.248	.358	5	.128	-2	-11	-9	-1	-1.0

● **HAL JEFFCOAT**   Jeffcoat, Harold Bentley   b: 9/6/24, W.Columbia, S.C.   BR/TR, 5'10.5", 185 lbs.   Deb: 4/20/48   F◆

YEAR	TM/L	W	L	PCT	G	GS	CG	SH	SV	IP	H	HR	BB	SO	RAT	ERA	ERA+	OAV	OOB	BH	AVG	PB	PR	/A	PD	TPI
1954	Chi-N	5	6	.455	43	3	1	0	7	104	110	12	58	35	14.9	5.19	81	.276	.373	8	.258	2	-13	-11	1	-0.8
1955	Chi-N	8	6	.571	50	1	0	0	6	100²	107	5	53	32	14.7	2.95	139	.276	.369	4	.174	1	12	13	1	1.9
1956	Cin-N	8	2	.800	38	16	2	0	1	171	189	12	55	55	13.1	3.84	104	.281	.340	8	.148	-1	-1	3	3	0.3
1957	Cin-N	12	13	.480	37	31	10	1	0	207	236	29	46	63	12.6	4.52	91	.294	.338	14	.203	6	-15	-9	-1	-0.6
1958	Cin-N	6	8	.429	49	0	0	0	9	75	76	8	26	35	12.5	3.72	111	.268	.333	5	.556	2	2	4	1	1.1
1959	Cin-N	0	1	.000	17	0	0	0	0	21²	21	3	10	12	12.9	3.32	122	.253	.333	1	1.000	1	2	2	0	0.2
	StL-N	0	1	.000	11	0	0	0	1	17²	33	4	9	7	21.4	9.17	46	.402	.462	0	.000	-0	-10	-10	-0	-0.5
	Yr	0	2	.000	28	0	0	0	1	39¹	54	7	19	19	16.7	5.95	70	.327	.397	1	.250	1	-9	-8	-0	-0.3
Total	6	39	37	.513	245	51	13	1	25	697	772	73	257	239	13.6	4.22	97	.285	.352	487	.248	10	-24	-10	5	1.6

● **MIKE JEFFCOAT**   Jeffcoat, James Michael   b: 8/3/59, Pine Bluff, Ark.   BL/TL, 6'2", 187 lbs.   Deb: 8/21/83

YEAR	TM/L	W	L	PCT	G	GS	CG	SH	SV	IP	H	HR	BB	SO	RAT	ERA	ERA+	OAV	OOB	BH	AVG	PB	PR	/A	PD	TPI
1983	Cle-A	1	3	.250	11	2	0	0	0	32²	32	-1	13	9	12.7	3.31	128	.256	.331	0	—	0	3	3	-0	0.3
1984	Cle-A	5	2	.714	63	1	0	0	1	75¹	82	7	24	41	12.8	2.99	137	.281	.338	0	—	0	8	9	1	0.9
1985	Cle-A	0	0	—	9	0	0	0	0	9²	8	1	6	4	13.0	2.79	148	.235	.350	0	—	0	1	1	1	0.1
	SF-N	0	2	.000	19	1	0	0	0	22	27	4	6	10	14.3	5.32	65	.307	.365	0	.000	0	-4	-5	1	-0.3
1987	Tex-A	0	1	.000	2	2	0	0	0	7	11	4	4	1	19.3	12.86	35	.355	.429	0	—	0	-7	-7	0	-0.7
1988	Tex-A	0	0	—	5	2	0	0	0	10	19	1	5	5	23.4	11.70	35	.432	.510	0	—	0	-9	-8	0	-1.4
1989	Tex-A	9	6	.600	22	22	2	2	0	130²	139	7	33	64	12.1	3.58	111	.270	.319	0	—	0	4	6	0	0.5
1990	Tex-A	5	6	.455	44	12	1	0	5	110²	122	12	28	58	12.4	4.47	88	.283	.330	0	—	0	-7	-7	-1	-0.8
1991	Tex-A	5	3	.625	70	0	0	0	1	79²	104	8	25	43	15.0	4.63	87	.320	.376	1	1.000	1	-5	-5	0	-0.4
1992	Tex-A	0	1	.000	6	3	0	0	0	19²	28	2	5	6	15.1	7.32	52	.350	.388	0	—	0	-7	-8	0	-0.3
1994	Fla-N	0	0	—	4	0	0	0	0	2²	4	2	0	1	13.5	10.13	44	.364	.364	0	—	0	-2	-2	0	-0.3
Total	10	25	26	.490	255	45	3	2	7	500	576	49	149	242	13.3	4.37	91	.292	.346	1	.500	1	-23	-22	0	-2.1

● **JESSE JEFFERSON**   Jefferson, Jesse Harrison   b: 3/3/49, Midlothian, Va.   BR/TR, 6'3", 195 lbs.   Deb: 6/23/73

YEAR	TM/L	W	L	PCT	G	GS	CG	SH	SV	IP	H	HR	BB	SO	RAT	ERA	ERA+	OAV	OOB	BH	AVG	PB	PR	/A	PD	TPI
1973	Bal-A	6	5	.545	18	15	3	0	0	100²	104	15	46	52	13.4	4.11	91	.267	.345	0	—	0	-3	-4	1	-0.3
1974	Bal-A	1	0	1.000	20	2	0	0	0	57¹	55	2	38	31	14.6	4.40	79	.261	.373	0	—	0	-5	-6	0	0.1
1975	Bal-A	0	2	.000	4	0	0	0	0	7²	9	0	8	4	15.3	2.35	149	.227	.433	0	—	0	1	1	0	0.3
	Chi-A	5	9	.357	22	21	1	0	0	107²	100	10	94	67	16.4	5.10	76	.249	.394	0	—	0	-16	-15	1	-1.7
	Yr	5	11	.313	26	21	1	0	0	115¹	105	10	102	71	16.3	4.92	78	.248	.397	0	—	0	-15	-14	1	-1.4
1976	Chi-A	2	5	.286	19	9	0	0	0	62¹	86	3	42	39	18.8	8.52	42	.339	.436	0	—	0	-35	-34	-1	-3.3
1977	Tor-A	9	17	.346	33	33	8	0	0	217	224	23	83	114	12.8	4.31	97	.269	.336	0	—	0	-6	-3	0	-0.3
1978	Tor-A	7	16	.304	31	30	9	2	0	211²	214	28	86	97	12.9	4.38	90	.267	.340	0	—	0	-15	-11	0	-1.2
1979	Tor-A	2	10	.167	34	10	2	0	0	116	150	19	43	45	15.3	5.51	79	.328	.390	0	—	0	-17	-15	1	-1.4
1980	Tor-A	4	13	.235	29	18	2	2	0	121²	130	12	52	53	13.6	5.47	79	.281	.357	0	—	0	-19	-16	1	-2.1
	Pit-N	1	0	1.000	1	1	0	0	0	6²	3	0	2	4	6.8	1.35	270	.143	.217	0	.000	-0	2	2	0	0.3
1981	Cal-A	2	4	.333	26	5	0	0	0	77	80	4	24	27	12.4	3.62	101	.269	.328	0	—	0	0	-1	0	-0.1
Total	9	39	81	.325	237	144	25	4	1	1085²	1151	116	520	522	14.0	4.81	83	.277	.360	0	.000	-0	-112	-101	3	-9.7

● **FERGIE JENKINS**   Jenkins, Ferguson Arthur   b: 12/13/43, Chatham, Ont., Can.   BR/TR, 6'5", 210 lbs.   Deb: 9/10/65   H

YEAR	TM/L	W	L	PCT	G	GS	CG	SH	SV	IP	H	HR	BB	SO	RAT	ERA	ERA+	OAV	OOB	BH	AVG	PB	PR	/A	PD	TPI
1965	Phi-N	2	1	.667	7	0	0	0	1	12¹	7	2	2	10	6.6	2.19	158	.159	.196	0	.000	-0	2	2	-0	0.4
1966	Phi-N	0	0	—	2	0	0	0	0	2¹	3	0	1	2	15.4	3.86	93	.273	.333	0	—	0	-0	-0	-0	-0.0
	Chi-N	6	8	.429	60	12	2	1	5	182	147	24	51	148	9.9	3.31	111	.219	.277	7	.137	1	6	7	-2	0.5
	Yr	6	8	.429	61	12	2	1	5	184¹	150	24	52	150	10.0	3.32	111	.220	.280	7	.137	1	6	7	-2	0.5
1967	Chi-N★	20	13	.606	38	38	**20**	3	0	289²	230	30	83	236	9.9	2.80	127	.217	.277	14	.151	1	19	24	2	3.1
1968	Chi-N	20	15	.571	40	40	20	3	0	308	255	26	65	260	9.4	2.63	120	.222	.266	16	.160	2	12	18	-1	2.3
1969	Chi-N	21	15	.583	43	42	23	7	1	311¹	284	27	71	**273**	10.5	3.21	125	.242	.290	15	.139	-1	13	28	0	3.2
1970	Chi-N	22	16	.579	40	39	**24**	3	0	313	265	30	60	274	**9.5**	3.39	133	.224	**.265**	23	.124	-3	23	39	-1	4.0
1971	Chi-N★	**24**	13	.649	39	39	**30**	3	0	**325**	304	29	37	263	9.6	2.77	142	.246	.271	28	.243	10	25	42	2	6.4
1972	Chi-N☆	20	12	.625	36	36	23	5	0	289¹	253	26	62	184	10.0	3.20	119	.234	.280	20	.183	5	8	19	3	2.7
1973	Chi-N	14	16	.467	38	38	7	1	0	271	267	35	57	170	10.9	3.89	101	.259	.301	10	.124	3	-3	3	0	0.0
1974	Tex-A	**25**	12	.676	41	41	**29**	6	0	328¹	286	27	45	225	9.3	2.82	122	.232	.264	1	.500	1	29	27	-0	3.0
1975	Tex-A	17	18	.486	37	37	22	4	0	270	261	37	56	157	10.9	3.93	95	.251	.295	0	—	0	-5	-5	1	-0.6

YEAR	TM/L	W	L	PCT	G	GS	CG	SH	SV	IP	H	HR	BB	SO	RAT	ERA	ERA+	OAV	OOB	BH	AVG	PB	PR	/A	PD	TPI
1976	Bos-A	12	11	.522	30	29	12	2	0	209	201	20	43	142	10.7	3.27	119	.253	.296	0	—	0	6	15	-1	0.9
1977	Bos-A	10	10	.500	28	28	11	1	0	193	190	30	36	105	10.5	3.68	122	.257	.291	0	—	0	8	17	1	1.3
1978	Tex-A	18	8	.692	34	30	16	4	0	249	228	21	41	157	9.8	3.04	123	.245	.279	0	—	0	20	20	2	2.2
1979	Tex-A	16	14	.533	37	37	10	3	0	259	252	40	81	164	11.7	4.07	102	.256	.314	0	—	0	4	2	4	0.7
1980	Tex-A	12	12	.500	29	29	12	0	0	198	190	22	52	129	11.2	3.77	103	.250	.301	0	—	0	6	3	1	0.5
1981	Tex-A	5	8	.385	19	16	1	0	0	106	122	14	40	63	13.8	4.50	77	.290	.351	0	—	0	-10	-12	2	-1.1
1982	Chi-N	14	15	.483	34	34	4	1	0	217¹	221	19	68	134	12.2	3.15	119	.264	.323	10	.149	-1	11	14	-0	1.6
1983	Chi-N	6	9	.400	33	29	3	1	0	167¹	176	19	46	96	12.3	4.30	88	.275	.329	13	.245	3	-13	-10	-1	-0.6
Total	19	284	226	.557	664	594	267	49	7	4500²	4142	484	997	3192	10.4	3.34	115	.243	.289	148	.165	13	157	254	14	30.9

● JACK JENKINS
Jenkins, Warren Washington b: 12/22/42, Covington, Va. BR/TR, 6'2", 195 lbs. Deb: 9/13/62

YEAR	TM/L	W	L	PCT	G	GS	CG	SH	SV	IP	H	HR	BB	SO	RAT	ERA	ERA+	OAV	OOB	BH	AVG	PB	PR	/A	PD	TPI
1962	Was-A	0	1	.000	3	1	1	0	0	13¹	12	4	7	10	12.8	4.05	100	.245	.339	0	.000	-0	-0	-0	-0	-0.1
1963	Was-A	0	2	.000	4	2	0	0	0	12¹	16	2	12	5	20.4	5.84	64	.340	.475	1	.333	0	-3	-3	0	-0.4
1969	LA-N	0	0	—	1	0	0	0	0	1	0	0	0	1	0.0	0.00	—	.000	.000	0	—	0	0	0	0	0.0
Total	3	0	3	.000	8	3	1	0	0	26²	28	6	19	16	15.9	4.73	82	.283	.398	1	.143	-0	-3	-3	0	-0.5

● WILLIE JENSEN
Jensen, William Christian b: 11/17/1889, Philadelphia, Pa. d: 3/27/17, Philadelphia, Pa. BL/TR, 5'11.5", 170 lbs. Deb: 9/10/12

YEAR	TM/L	W	L	PCT	G	GS	CG	SH	SV	IP	H	HR	BB	SO	RAT	ERA	ERA+	OAV	OOB	BH	AVG	PB	PR	/A	PD	TPI
1912	Det-A	1	2	.333	5	4	1	0	0	33	43	1	18	8	17.2	4.91	66	.339	.429	0	.000	-2	-6	-6	-0	-0.7
1914	Phi-A	0	1	.000	1	1	1	0	0	9	7	1	2	9	9.0	2.00	131	.226	.273	0	.000	0	1	1	0	0.1
Total	2	1	3	.250	6	5	2	0	0	42	50	2	20	9	15.4	4.29	73	.316	.400	0	.000	-2	-5	-5	-0	-0.6

● VIRGIL JESTER
Jester, Virgil Milton b: 7/23/27, Denver, Colo. BR/TR, 5'11", 188 lbs. Deb: 6/18/52

YEAR	TM/L	W	L	PCT	G	GS	CG	SH	SV	IP	H	HR	BB	SO	RAT	ERA	ERA+	OAV	OOB	BH	AVG	PB	PR	/A	PD	TPI
1952	Bos-N	3	5	.375	19	8	4	1	0	73	80	5	23	25	12.8	3.33	108	.283	.339	4	.211	1	3	2	-1	0.2
1953	Mil-N	0	0	—	2	0	0	0	0	2	4	1	4	0	36.0	22.50	17	.400	.571	0	—	0	-4	-4	0	0.0
Total	2	3	5	.375	21	8	4	1	0	75	84	6	27	25	13.4	3.84	94	.287	.349	4	.211	1	-1	-2	-1	0.2

● GERMAN JIMENEZ
Jimenez, German (Camarena) b: 12/5/62, Santiago, Mex. BL/TL, 5'11", 200 lbs. Deb: 6/28/88

YEAR	TM/L	W	L	PCT	G	GS	CG	SH	SV	IP	H	HR	BB	SO	RAT	ERA	ERA+	OAV	OOB	BH	AVG	PB	PR	/A	PD	TPI
1988	Atl-N	1	6	.143	15	9	0	0	0	55²	65	4	12	26	12.6	5.01	73	.294	.333	1	.059	-1	-10	-8	-1	-1.2

● JUAN JIMENEZ
Jimenez, Juan Antonio (Martes) b: 3/8/49, LaTorre, La Vega, D.R. BR/TR, 6'1", 165 lbs. Deb: 9/9/74

YEAR	TM/L	W	L	PCT	G	GS	CG	SH	SV	IP	H	HR	BB	SO	RAT	ERA	ERA+	OAV	OOB	BH	AVG	PB	PR	/A	PD	TPI
1974	Pit-N	0	0	—	4	0	0	0	0	4	6	0	2	2	18.0	6.75	51	.353	.421	0	—	0	-1	-1	-0	0.0

● MIGUEL JIMENEZ
Jimenez, Miguel Anthony b: 8/19/69, New York, N.Y. BR/TR, 6'2", 205 lbs. Deb: 9/12/93

YEAR	TM/L	W	L	PCT	G	GS	CG	SH	SV	IP	H	HR	BB	SO	RAT	ERA	ERA+	OAV	OOB	BH	AVG	PB	PR	/A	PD	TPI
1993	Oak-A	1	0	1.000	5	4	0	0	0	27	27	5	16	13	14.7	4.00	102	.262	.367	0	—	0	1	0	-1	0.2
1994	Oak-A	1	4	.200	8	7	0	0	0	34	38	9	32	22	18.8	7.41	60	.275	.415	0	—	0	-10	-11	-0	-1.1
Total	2	2	4	.333	13	11	0	0	0	61	65	14	48	35	17.0	5.90	73	.270	.395	0	—	0	-9	-11	-1	-0.9

● TOMMY JOHN
John, Thomas Edward b: 5/22/43, Terre Haute, Ind. BR/TL, 6'3", 185 lbs. Deb: 9/6/63

YEAR	TM/L	W	L	PCT	G	GS	CG	SH	SV	IP	H	HR	BB	SO	RAT	ERA	ERA+	OAV	OOB	BH	AVG	PB	PR	/A	PD	TPI
1963	Cle-A	0	2	.000	6	3	0	0	0	20¹	23	1	6	9	12.8	2.21	164	.284	.333	0	.000	-1	3	3	-0	0.2
1964	Cle-A	2	9	.182	25	14	2	1	0	94¹	97	10	35	65	12.6	3.91	92	.262	.326	5	.208	0	-3	-3	1	-0.3
1965	Chi-A	14	7	.667	39	27	6	1	3	183²	162	12	58	126	10.9	3.09	103	.237	.298	10	.169	2	8	2	3	0.8
1966	Chi-A	14	11	.560	34	33	10	5	0	223	195	12	57	138	10.5	2.62	121	.235	.290	10	.145	2	20	14	1	1.8
1967	Chi-A	10	13	.435	31	29	9	6	0	178¹	143	12	47	110	9.8	2.47	126	.219	.277	8	.157	-0	15	13	6	2.3
1968	Chi-A★	10	5	.667	25	25	5	1	0	177¹	135	10	49	117	9.9	1.98	153	.212	.280	12	.194	-2	20	21	6	2.9
1969	Chi-A	9	11	.450	33	33	6	2	0	232¹	230	16	90	128	12.4	3.25	119	.261	.330	9	.114	-2	9	16	7	1.9
1970	Chi-A	12	17	.414	37	37	10	2	0	269¹	253	19	101	138	12.1	3.27	119	.251	.324	17	.202	1	13	19	4	2.5
1971	Chi-A	13	16	.448	38	35	10	3	0	229¹	244	17	58	131	12.0	3.61	99	.274	.321	10	.145	-1	-4	-1	-1	-0.3
1972	LA-N	11	5	.688	29	29	4	1	0	186²	172	14	40	117	10.4	2.89	115	.244	.287	10	.159	-1	12	9	4	1.1
1973	LA-N	16	7	.696	36	31	4	2	0	218	202	16	50	116	10.6	3.10	111	.246	.293	15	.203	-2	14	8	7	1.8
1974	LA-N	13	3	.813	22	22	5	3	0	153	133	4	42	78	10.4	2.59	131	.235	.289	6	.118	-1	18	14	2	1.5
1976	LA-N	10	10	.500	31	31	6	2	0	207	207	7	61	91	11.7	3.09	110	.261	.314	7	.109	-2	10	7	-1	0.3
1977	*LA-N	20	7	.741	31	31	11	3	0	220¹	225	12	50	123	11.4	2.78	138	.267	.311	11	.177	1	28	26	2	3.4
1978	*LA-N☆	17	10	.630	33	30	7	0	1	213	230	11	53	124	12.2	3.30	106	.271	.318	8	.121	-1	7	5	2	0.7
1979	NY-A☆	21	9	.700	37	36	17	3	0	276¹	268	9	65	111	11.0	2.96	137	.260	.306	0	—	0	**38**	34	2	3.8
1980	*NY-A★	22	9	.710	36	36	16	6	0	265¹	270	13	56	78	11.3	3.43	114	.268	.311	0	—	0	18	15	1	1.7
1981	*NY-A	9	8	.529	20	20	7	0	0	140¹	135	10	39	50	11.4	2.63	136	.254	.311	0	—	0	16	15	1	1.9
1982	NY-A	10	10	.500	30	26	9	2	0	186²	190	11	34	54	10.9	3.66	109	.266	.302	0	—	0	8	7	2	0.8
	*Cal-A	4	2	.667	7	7	1	0	0	35	49	4	5	14	13.9	3.86	105	.336	.358	0	—	0	1	1	0	0.2
	Yr	14	12	.538	37	33	10	2	0	221²	239	15	39	68	11.3	3.69	108	.274	.305	0	—	0	9	7	2	1.0
1983	Cal-A	11	13	.458	34	34	9	0	0	234²	287	20	49	65	13.0	4.33	93	.304	.340	0	—	0	-7	-8	1	-0.7
1984	Cal-A	7	13	.350	32	29	4	1	0	181¹	223	15	56	47	14.0	4.52	88	.306	.359	0	—	0	-11	-11	0	-1.0
1985	Cal-A	2	4	.333	12	6	0	0	0	38¹	51	3	15	17	15.7	4.70	87	.329	.392	0	—	0	-2	-3	-1	-0.2
	Oak-A	2	6	.250	11	11	0	0	0	48	66	6	13	8	15.0	6.19	62	.332	.376	0	—	0	-11	-12	1	-1.6
	Yr	4	10	.286	23	17	0	0	0	86¹	117	9	28	25	15.2	5.53	72	.328	.378	0	—	0	-13	-15	2	-1.8
1986	NY-A	5	3	.625	13	10	1	0	0	70²	73	6	15	28	11.5	2.93	140	.275	.319	0	—	0	10	9	1	1.0
1987	NY-A	13	6	.684	33	33	3	1	0	187²	212	12	47	63	12.7	4.03	109	.288	.336	0	—	0	9	7	-1	0.6
1988	NY-A	9	8	.529	35	32	0	0	0	176¹	221	11	46	81	13.9	4.49	88	.308	.355	0	—	0	-10	-11	-2	-0.7
1989	NY-A	2	7	.222	10	10	0	0	0	63²	87	6	22	18	15.8	5.80	67	.336	.394	0	—	0	-14	-14	2	-1.4
Total	26	288	231	.555	760	700	162	46	4	4710¹	4783	302	1259	2245	11.7	3.34	110	.265	.316	141	.157	1	214	179	55	25.0

● AUGIE JOHNS
Johns, Augustus Francis "Lefty" b: 9/10/1899, St.Louis, Mo. d: 9/12/75, San Antonio, Tex. BL/TL, 5'8.5", 170 lbs. Deb: 4/16/26

YEAR	TM/L	W	L	PCT	G	GS	CG	SH	SV	IP	H	HR	BB	SO	RAT	ERA	ERA+	OAV	OOB	BH	AVG	PB	PR	/A	PD	TPI
1926	Det-A	6	4	.600	35	14	3	1	1	112²	117	6	69	40	15.3	5.35	76	.271	.377	4	.143	-1	-17	-16	-2	-1.6
1927	Det-A	0	0	—	1	0	0	0	0	1	1	0	1	1	18.0	9.00	47	.333	.500	0	—	0	-1	-1	0	0.0
Total	2	6	4	.600	36	14	3	1	1	113²	118	6	70	41	15.3	5.38	75	.271	.378	4	.143	-1	-17	-17	-2	-1.6

● OLLIE JOHNS
Johns, Oliver Tracy b: 8/21/1879, Trenton, Ohio d: 6/17/61, Hamilton, Ohio BL/TL, Deb: 9/24/05

YEAR	TM/L	W	L	PCT	G	GS	CG	SH	SV	IP	H	HR	BB	SO	RAT	ERA	ERA+	OAV	OOB	BH	AVG	PB	PR	/A	PD	TPI
1905	Cin-N	1	0	1.000	4	1	1	0	0	18	31	1	4	8	17.5	3.50	94	.369	.398	1	.200	-0	-1	-0	-0	-0.1

● ABE JOHNSON
Johnson, Abraham b: Chicago, Ill. Deb: 7/16/1893

YEAR	TM/L	W	L	PCT	G	GS	CG	SH	SV	IP	H	HR	BB	SO	RAT	ERA	ERA+	OAV	OOB	BH	AVG	PB	PR	/A	PD	TPI
1893	Chi-N	0	0	—	1	0	0	0	0	1	2	0	2	0	45.0	36.00	13	.403	.628	0	—	0	-3	-3	-0	-0.5

● RANKIN JOHNSON
Johnson, Adam Rankin Jr. b: 3/1/17, Hayden, Ariz. BR/TR, 6'3", 177 lbs. Deb: 4/17/41 F

YEAR	TM/L	W	L	PCT	G	GS	CG	SH	SV	IP	H	HR	BB	SO	RAT	ERA	ERA+	OAV	OOB	BH	AVG	PB	PR	/A	PD	TPI
1941	Phi-A	1	0	1.000	7	0	0	0	0	10	14	0	3	0	15.3	3.60	116	.326	.370	0	.000	-0	1	1	0	0.1

● RANKIN JOHNSON
Johnson, Adam Rankin Sr. "Tex" b: 2/4/1888, Burnet, Tex. d: 7/2/72, Williamsport, Pa. BR/TR, 6'1.5", 185 lbs. Deb: 4/20/14 F

YEAR	TM/L	W	L	PCT	G	GS	CG	SH	SV	IP	H	HR	BB	SO	RAT	ERA	ERA+	OAV	OOB	BH	AVG	PB	PR	/A	PD	TPI
1914	Bos-A	4	9	.308	16	13	4	2	0	99¹	92	2	34	24	11.7	3.08	87	.265	.336	4	.133	-1	-4	-4	-2	-0.8
	Chi-F	5	3	.643	16	14	12	2	0	120	88	5	29	60	9.1	1.58	169	.209	.267	4	.108	-3	17	14	-1	1.1
1915	Chi-F	2	4	.333	11	6	3	0	0	57	58	2	23	19	12.9	4.42	57	.270	.343	1	.045	-1	-11	-12	-2	-1.7
	Bal-F	7	11	.389	23	19	12	2	0	150²	143	3	58	62	12.1	3.35	86	.255	.326	8	.157	-2	-10	-8	-3	-1.4
	Yr	9	15	.375	34	25	15	2	0	207²	201	5	81	81	12.3	3.64	76	.259	.330	9	.123	-5	-21	-20	-5	-3.1
1918	StL-N	1	1	.500	6	2	1	0	0	23	20	0	7	8	10.6	2.74	99	.263	.325	1	.250	-0	-1	-1	0	0.1
Total	3	23	30	.434	72	53	31	6	2	450	401	12	151	169	11.2	2.92	93	.248	.315	18	.125	-9	-7	-10	-7	-2.7

● ART JOHNSON
Johnson, Arthur Gilbert b: 2/15/1897, Warren, Pa. d: 6/7/82, Sarasota, Fla. BB/TL, 6'1", 167 lbs. Deb: 9/18/27

YEAR	TM/L	W	L	PCT	G	GS	CG	SH	SV	IP	H	HR	BB	SO	RAT	ERA	ERA+	OAV	OOB	BH	AVG	PB	PR	/A	PD	TPI
1927	NY-N	0	0	—	1	0	0	0	0	3	1	0	1	0	6.0	0.00	—	.125	.222	0	—	0	1	1	-0	0.0

YEAR TM/L	W	L	PCT	G	GS	CG	SH	SV	IP	H	HR	BB	SO	RAT	ERA	ERA+	OAV	OOB	BH	AVG	PB	PR	/A	PD	TPI
● **ART JOHNSON**		Johnson, Arthur Henry "Lefty"			b: 7/16/16, Winchester, Mass.			BL/TL, 6'2", 185 lbs.			Deb: 9/22/40														
1940 Bos-N	0	1	.000	2	1	0	0	0	6	10	0	3	1	21.0	10.50	35	.345	.424	0	.000	-0	-4	-5	0	-0.6
1941 Bos-N	7	15	.318	43	18	6	0	1	183¹	189	7	71	70	13.0	3.53	101	.270	.342	8	.145	-2	2	1	-0	-0.1
1942 Bos-N	0	0	—	4	0	0	0	0	6¹	4	0	5	0	14.2	1.42	235	.190	.370	0	.000	-0	1	1	-0	0.0
Total 3	7	16	.304	49	19	6	0	1	195²	203	7	79	71	13.3	3.68	97	.271	.346	8	.140	-2	-1	-2	1	-0.7
● **BEN JOHNSON**		Johnson, Benjamin Franklin			b: 5/16/31, Greenwood, S.C.			BR/TR, 6'2", 190 lbs.			Deb: 9/6/59														
1959 Chi-N	0	0	—	4	2	0	0	1	16²	17	1	4	6	11.3	2.16	183	.262	.304	0	.000	-0	3	3	-0	-0.1
1960 Chi-N	2	1	.667	17	0	0	0	1	29¹	39	3	11	9	15.6	4.91	77	.355	.418	0	.000	-0	-4	-4	1	-0.3
Total 2	2	1	.667	21	2	0	0	1	46	56	4	15	15	14.1	3.91	98	.320	.377	0	.000	-1	-0	-0	0	-0.4
● **CHET JOHNSON**		Johnson, Chester Lillis "Chesty Chet"			b: 8/1/17, Redmond, Wash.		d: 4/10/83, Seattle, Wash.	BL/TL, 6', 175 lbs.			Deb: 9/12/46 F														
1946 StL-A	0	0	—	5	3	0	0	0	18	20	0	13	8	16.5	5.00	75	.286	.398	0	.000	-1	-3	-3	-1	-0.2
● **BART JOHNSON**		Johnson, Clair Barth			b: 1/3/50, Torrance, Cal.			BR/TR, 6'5", 215 lbs.			Deb: 9/8/69														
1969 Chi-A	1	3	.250	4	3	0	0	0	22¹	22	2	6	18	11.3	3.22	120	.259	.308	1	.167	-0	1	2	-0	0.3
1970 Chi-A	4	7	.364	18	15	2	1	0	89²	92	11	46	71	14.1	4.82	81	.268	.358	8	.276	2	-11	-9	-0	-0.8
1971 Chi-A	12	10	.545	53	16	4	0	14	178	148	9	111	153	13.4	2.93	122	.227	.345	11	.193	0	10	13	-1	1.7
1972 Chi-A	0	3	.000	9	0	0	0	1	13²	18	2	13	9	21.1	9.22	34	.327	.464	0	.000	-0	-9	-9	-0	-2.0
1973 Chi-A	3	3	.500	22	9	0	0	0	80²	76	6	40	56	13.2	4.13	96	.252	.343	0	—	0	-3	-2	-0	-0.4
1974 Chi-A	10	4	.714	18	18	8	2	0	121²	105	6	32	76	10.2	2.74	136	.229	.281	0	—	0	12	13	-2	1.3
1976 Chi-A	9	16	.360	32	32	8	3	0	211¹	231	20	62	91	12.5	4.73	75	.282	.334	0	—	0	-28	-27	0	-2.9
1977 Chi-A	4	5	.444	29	4	0	0	2	92	114	5	38	46	15.1	4.01	102	.302	.369	0	—	0	0	1	-0	0.1
Total 8	43	51	.457	185	97	22	6	17	809¹	806	61	348	520	13.0	3.94	95	.261	.339	20	.215	3	-28	-19	-4	-2.7
● **CONNIE JOHNSON**		Johnson, Clifford			b: 12/27/22, Stone Mountain, Ga			BR/TR, 6'4", 200 lbs.			Deb: 4/17/53														
1953 Chi-A	4	4	.500	14	10	2	1	0	60²	55	4	38	44	14.1	3.56	113	.238	.351	1	.050	-2	3	3	-1	0.1
1955 Chi-A	7	4	.636	17	16	5	2	0	99	95	5	52	72	13.5	3.45	114	.251	.343	5	.152	-1	6	5	-1	0.3
1956 Chi-A	0	1	.000	5	2	0	0	0	12¹	11	1	7	6	13.1	3.65	114	.234	.333	0	.000	-0	1	1	0	0.0
Bal-A	9	10	.474	26	25	9	2	0	183²	165	12	62	130	11.2	3.43	114	.239	.303	15	.259	3	15	10	-3	1.0
Yr	9	11	.450	31	27	9	2	0	196	176	13	69	136	11.3	3.44	114	.239	.305	15	.246	3	16	11	-3	1.0
1957 Bal-A	14	11	.560	35	30	14	3	0	242	212	17	66	177	10.5	3.20	112	.235	.289	12	.135	-4	16	11	-4	0.2
1958 Bal-A	6	9	.400	26	17	4	0	1	118¹	116	13	32	68	11.3	3.88	93	.260	.310	7	.206	1	-1	-4	-2	-0.5
Total 5	40	39	.506	123	100	34	8	1	716	654	52	257	497	11.5	3.44	109	.243	.310	40	.169	-3	38	26	-10	1.1
● **DANE JOHNSON**		Johnson, Dane Edward			b: 2/10/63, Coral Gables, Fla.			BR/TR, 6'5", 205 lbs.			Deb: 5/30/94														
1994 Chi-A	2	1	.667	15	0	0	0	0	12¹	16	2	11	9	19.7	6.57	71	.327	.450	0	—	0	-2	-3	0	-0.5
● **DAVE JOHNSON**		Johnson, David Charles			b: 10/4/48, Abilene, Tex.			BR/TR, 6'1", 183 lbs.			Deb: 7/2/74														
1974 Bal-A	2	2	.500	11	0	0	0	2	15¹	17	1	5	6	12.9	2.93	118	.274	.328	0	—	0	1	1	-0	0.2
1975 Bal-A	0	1	.000	6	0	0	0	0	8²	8	0	7	4	15.6	4.15	84	.250	.385	0	—	0	-0	-1	0	0.0
1977 Min-A	2	5	.286	30	6	0	0	0	72²	86	7	23	33	14.1	4.58	87	.299	.361	0	—	0	-4	-5	-0	-0.4
1978 Min-A	2	2	.000	6	1	0	0	0	12	15	1	9	7	18.0	7.50	51	.313	.421	0	—	0	-5	-5	-0	-0.7
Total 4	4	10	.286	53	7	0	0	2	108²	126	9	44	50	14.5	4.64	83	.293	.365	0	—	0	-8	-10	-0	-0.9
● **DAVE JOHNSON**		Johnson, David Wayne			b: 10/24/59, Baltimore, Md.			BR/TR, 5'10", 180 lbs.			Deb: 5/29/87														
1987 Pit-N	0	0	—	5	0	0	0	0	6¹	13	1	2	4	21.3	9.95	41	.448	.484	0	—	0	-4	-4	0	0.0
1989 Bal-A	4	7	.364	14	14	4	0	0	89¹	90	11	28	26	12.3	4.23	90	.265	.328	0	—	0	-3	-4	-2	-0.7
1990 Bal-A	13	9	.591	30	29	3	0	0	180	196	30	43	68	12.1	4.10	93	.280	.324	0	—	0	-4	-6	-3	-0.9
1991 Bal-A	4	8	.333	22	14	0	0	0	84	127	18	24	38	16.6	7.07	56	.349	.395	0	—	0	-28	-29	-1	-3.5
1993 Det-A	1	1	.500	6	0	0	0	0	8¹	13	3	5	7	21.6	12.96	33	.342	.444	0	—	0	-8	-8	-0	-1.5
Total 5	22	25	.468	77	57	7	0	0	368	439	63	102	143	13.5	5.11	75	.298	.349	0	—	0	-47	-52	-6	-6.6
● **DON JOHNSON**		Johnson, Donald Roy			b: 11/12/26, Portland, Ore.			BR/TR, 6'3", 200 lbs.			Deb: 4/20/47														
1947 NY-A	4	3	.571	15	8	2	0	0	54¹	57	2	23	16	13.4	3.64	97	.270	.345	0	.000	-2	0	-1	-1	-0.3
1950 NY-A	1	0	1.000	8	0	0	0	0	18	35	2	12	9	23.5	10.00	43	.398	.470	0	.000	-0	-11	-11	-0	-0.6
StL-A	5	6	.455	25	12	4	1	0	96	126	14	55	31	17.1	6.09	81	.325	.410	2	.069	-3	-16	-12	-1	-1.5
Yr	6	6	.500	33	12	4	1	0	114	161	16	67	40	18.1	6.71	72	.338	.421	2	.063	-4	-27	-24	-1	-2.1
1951 StL-A	0	1	.000	6	3	0	0	0	15	27	4	18	8	27.6	12.60	35	.391	.523	1	.333	-14	-14	-14	0	-0.7
Was-A	7	11	.389	21	20	8	1	0	143²	138	9	58	52	12.4	3.95	104	.255	.329	4	.085	-5	3	2	-0	-0.3
Yr	7	12	.368	27	23	8	1	0	158²	165	13	76	60	13.8	4.76	87	.270	.352	5	.100	-5	-11	-11	-0	-1.0
1952 Was-A	0	5	.000	29	6	0	0	2	69	80	4	33	37	15.3	4.43	80	.287	.370	1	.077	-1	-6	-7	-0	-0.6
1954 Chi-A	8	7	.533	46	16	3	3	7	144	129	14	43	68	10.8	3.13	119	.243	.300	1	.029	-3	10	10	0	0.7
1955 Bal-A	2	4	.333	31	5	0	0	1	68	89	4	35	27	16.4	5.82	65	.333	.411	0	.000	-1	-14	-15	0	-1.3
1958 SF-N	0	0	—	17	0	0	0	1	23	31	2	14	16	16.0	6.26	61	.323	.387	0	.000	-0	-6	-6	-0	-0.3
Total 7	27	38	.415	198	70	17	5	12	631	712	55	285	262	14.4	4.78	84	.288	.364	9	.058	-16	-54	-55	-2	-4.9
● **EARL JOHNSON**		Johnson, Earl Douglas "Lefty"			b: 4/2/19, Redmond, Was.			BL/TL, 6'3", 190 lbs.			Deb: 7/20/40 F														
1940 Bos-A	6	2	.750	17	10	2	0	0	70¹	69	0	39	26	14.1	4.09	110	.260	.359	2	.074	-3	2	3	1	0.1
1941 Bos-A	4	5	.444	17	12	4	0	0	93²	90	4	51	46	13.8	4.52	92	.247	.344	10	.294	2	-4	-4	2	0.1
1946 *Bos-A	5	4	.556	29	5	0	0	3	80	78	5	39	40	13.4	3.71	99	.250	.337	5	.227	2	-2	-0	-0	0.1
1947 Bos-A	12	11	.522	45	17	6	3	8	142¹	129	7	62	65	12.2	2.97	131	.246	.328	12	.273	1	12	14	2	2.8
1948 Bos-A	10	4	.714	35	3	1	0	0	91¹	98	7	42	45	13.8	4.53	97	.276	.353	3	.097	-3	-2	-1	2	-0.3
1949 Bos-A	3	6	.333	19	3	0	0	0	49¹	65	1	29	20	17.9	7.48	58	.327	.422	0	.000	-1	-18	-17	-1	-2.7
1950 Bos-A	0	0	—	11	0	0	0	0	13²	18	0	8	6	17.8	7.24	68	.333	.429	0	.000	-0	-4	-4	1	0.0
1951 Det-A	0	0	—	6	0	0	0	0	5²	9	0	2	2	17.5	6.35	66	.375	.423	0	—	0	-1	-1	0	0.0
Total 8	40	32	.556	179	50	13	3	17	546¹	556	24	272	250	13.9	4.30	96	.265	.353	32	.187	-2	-18	-10	7	0.1
● **WALT JOHNSON**		Johnson, Ellis Walter			b: 12/8/1892, Minneapolis, Minn.		d: 1/4/65, Minneapolis, Minn.	BR/TR, 6'0.5", 180 lbs.			Deb: 7/6/12														
1912 Chi-A	0	0	—	3	0	0	0	0	11²	11	0	7	7	14.7	3.86	83	.262	.380	0	.000	-0	-1	-1	-0	0.0
1915 Chi-A	0	0	—	1	0	0	0	0	2	3	0	3	3	13.5	9.00	33	.333	.333	—	—	0	-1	-1	-0	0.0
1917 Phi-A	0	2	.000	4	2	0	0	0	13²	15	0	5	8	13.2	7.24	48	.294	.357	0	.000	-0	-7	-7	-0	-0.8
Total 3	0	2	.000	8	2	0	0	0	27¹	29	0	12	18	13.8	5.93	50	.284	.365	0	.000	-0	-9	-9	-0	-0.8
● **ERNIE JOHNSON**		Johnson, Ernest Thorwald			b: 6/16/24, Brattleboro, Vt.			BR/TR, 6'4", 195 lbs.			Deb: 4/28/50														
1950 Bos-N	2	0	1.000	16	0	0	0	0	20²	37	1	13	16	21.8	6.97	55	.394	.467	1	.500	0	-6	-7	-1	-0.4
1952 Bos-N	6	3	.667	29	10	2	1	1	92	100	7	31	45	13.0	4.11	88	.270	.329	2	.091	-0	-4	-5	-1	-0.4
1953 Mil-N	4	3	.571	36	1	0	0	0	81	79	4	22	36	11.6	2.67	147	.263	.320	1	.071	-1	15	11	-0	0.7
1954 Mil-N	5	2	.714	40	4	1	0	2	99¹	77	11	34	68	10.1	2.81	133	.219	.290	3	.231	0	14	10	1	0.8
1955 Mil-N	5	7	.417	40	2	0	0	4	92	81	5	55	43	13.5	3.42	110	.240	.349	2	.100	-1	6	3	-0	0.3
1956 Mil-N	4	3	.571	36	0	0	0	1	51	54	9	21	36	13.4	3.71	93	.270	.343	1	.250	0	-0	-1	-1	-0.1
1957 *Mil-N	7	3	.700	30	0	0	0	4	65	59	9	26	44	13.0	3.88	90	.265	.336	6	.353	-0	-3	1	0	-0.0
1958 Mil-N	3	1	.750	15	0	0	0	0	23¹	35	4	10	13	17.7	8.10	43	.357	.422	0	.000	-0	-11	-12	-1	-1.8
1959 Bal-A	4	1	.800	31	0	0	0	1	50¹	57	6	19	29	14.1	4.11	92	.286	.357	2	.333	1	-1	-2	1	-0.1
Total 9	40	23	.635	273	19	4	1	19	574²	587	56	231	319	13.0	3.77	98	.266	.340	18	.180	2	13	-5	5	-1.1

YEAR TM/L	W	L	PCT	G	GS	CG	SH	SV	IP	H	HR	BB	SO	RAT	ERA	ERA+	OAV	OOB	BH	AVG	PB	PR	/A	PD	TPI
● **FRED JOHNSON** Johnson, Frederick Edward "Deacon" or "Cactus" b: 3/10/1894, Tolar, Tex. d: 6/14/73, Kerrville, Tex. BR/TR, 6', 185 lbs. Deb: 9/27/22																									
1922 NY-N	0	2	.000	2	2	1	0	0	18	20	3	1	8	10.5	4.00	100	.294	.304	0	.000	-1	0	0	-0	-0.1
1923 NY-N	2	0	1.000	3	2	1	0	0	17	11	2	7	5	9.5	4.24	90	.177	.261	0	.000	-1	-0	-1	1	-0.1
1938 StL-A	3	7	.300	17	6	3	0	3	69	91	7	27	24	15.5	5.61	89	.316	.377	6	.240	-0	-6	-5	-2	-0.8
1939 StL-A	0	1	.000	5	2	1	0	0	14	23	0	9	2	20.6	6.43	76	.383	.464	0	.000	-1	-3	-2	1	-0.1
Total 4	5	10	.333	27	12	6	0	3	118	145	12	44	39	14.5	5.26	88	.303	.363	6	.154	-2	-9	-8	0	-1.1
● **CHIEF JOHNSON** Johnson, George Howard "Murphy" or "Big Murph" b: 3/30/1886, Winnebago, Neb. d: 6/11/22, Des Moines, Iowa BR/TR, 5'11.5", 190 lbs. Deb: 4/16/13																									
1913 Cin-N	14	16	.467	44	31	13	3	0	269	251	8	86	107	11.5	3.01	108	.256	.320	10	.114	-3	6	7	0	0.5
1914 Cin-N	0	0	—	1	1	0	0	0	4	6	0	2	1	18.0	6.75	43	.333	.400	0	—	0	-2	-2	-0	0.0
KC-F	9	10	.474	20	19	12	2	0	134	157	2	33	78	13.0	3.16	88	.298	.345	6	.122	-2	-4	-6	-3	-1.2
1915 KC-F	17	17	.500	46	34	19	4	2	281¹	253	5	71	118	10.6	2.75	96	.242	.295	11	.126	-4	-1	-4	2	-0.6
Total 3	40	43	.482	111	85	44	9	2	688¹	667	15	192	304	11.5	2.95	98	.259	.315	27	.121	-9	-1	-4	-1	-1.3
● **HANK JOHNSON** Johnson, Henry Ward b: 5/21/06, Bradenton, Fla. d: 8/20/82, Bradenton, Fla. BR/TR, 5'11.5", 175 lbs. Deb: 4/17/25																									
1925 NY-A	1	3	.250	24	4	2	1	0	67	88	3	37	25	17.9	6.85	62	.319	.414	1	.059	-1	-18	-19	1	-1.0
1926 NY-A	0	0	—	1	0	0	0	1	1	2	0	2	0	36.0	18.00	21	.400	.571	0	—	0	-2	-2	-0	-0.3
1928 NY-A	14	9	.609	31	22	10	1	0	199	188	16	104	110	13.7	4.30	88	.250	.351	19	.241	2	-6	-12	0	-1.1
1929 NY-A	3	3	.500	12	8	2	0	0	42²	37	5	39	24	16.0	5.06	76	.237	.390	1	.071	-1	-4	-6	-1	-0.9
1930 NY-A	14	11	.560	44	15	7	1	2	175¹	177	12	104	115	14.5	4.67	92	.265	.366	17	.266	5	-0	-7	2	-0.9
1931 NY-A	13	8	.619	40	23	8	0	4	196¹	176	13	102	106	12.8	4.72	84	.234	.326	15	.195	2	-7	-16	-3	-1.7
1932 NY-A	2	2	.500	5	4	2	0	0	31¹	34	7	15	27	14.1	4.88	83	.266	.343	3	.231	0	-1	-3	-0	-0.3
1933 Bos-A	8	6	.571	25	21	7	0	1	155¹	156	13	74	65	13.5	4.06	108	.263	.348	12	.231	1	3	4	-2	0.2
1934 Bos-A	6	8	.429	31	14	7	1	1	124¹	162	12	53	66	15.9	5.36	90	.316	.385	10	.233	1	-12	-8	-1	-0.8
1935 Bos-A	2	1	.667	13	2	0	0	1	31	41	3	14	14	16.0	5.52	86	.331	.399	0	.000	-1	-4	-3	-1	-0.4
1936 Phi-A	0	2	.000	3	3	0	0	0	11²	16	4	10	6	20.8	7.71	66	.296	.415	1	.250	-0	-3	-3	-0	-0.4
1939 Cin-N	0	3	.000	20	0	0	0	1	31¹	30	1	13	10	12.4	2.01	191	.268	.344	2	.400	1	7	6	-1	0.5
Total 12	63	56	.529	249	116	45	4	11	1066¹	1107	89	567	568	14.4	4.75	88	.268	.361	81	.215	9	-47	-67	-6	-6.1
● **JIM JOHNSON** Johnson, James Brian b: 11/3/45, Muskegon, Mich. BL/TL, 5'11", 175 lbs. Deb: 4/13/70																									
1970 SF-N	1	0	1.000	3	0	0	0	0	6²	8	0	5	2	17.6	8.10	49	.320	.433	0	.000	0	-3	-3	0	-0.4
● **JERRY JOHNSON** Johnson, Jerry Michael b: 12/3/43, Miami, Fla. BR/TR, 6'3", 200 lbs. Deb: 7/17/68																									
1968 Phi-N	4	4	.500	16	11	2	0	0	80²	82	5	29	40	12.6	3.24	93	.264	.330	2	.080	-0	-2	-2	1	-0.2
1969 Phi-N	6	13	.316	33	21	4	2	1	147¹	151	18	57	82	12.9	4.28	83	.268	.338	9	.209	2	-11	-12	-1	-1.4
1970 StL-N	2	0	1.000	7	0	0	0	0	11¹	6	1	3	5	7.1	3.18	130	.146	.205	0	.000	0	1	1	0	0.2
SF-N	3	4	.429	33	1	0	0	3	65¹	67	5	38	44	14.6	4.27	93	.266	.364	1	.067	-1	-2	-2	-0	-0.4
Yr	5	4	.556	40	1	0	0	4	76²	73	6	41	49	13.5	4.11	97	.249	.343	1	.063	-1	-1	-1	-1	-0.2
1971 *SF-N	12	9	.571	67	0	0	0	18	109	93	9	48	85	11.7	2.97	114	.230	.313	2	.154	-0	6	5	-0	1.2
1972 SF-N	8	6	.571	48	0	0	0	8	73¹	73	4	40	57	13.9	4.42	79	.261	.353	0	.000	-1	-8	-8	0	-1.6
1973 Cle-A	5	6	.455	39	1	0	0	5	59²	70	7	39	45	16.4	6.18	63	.299	.399	0	—	0	-16	-15	0	-2.8
1974 Hou-N	2	1	.667	34	0	0	0	6	45	47	2	24	32	14.2	4.80	72	.276	.366	0	.000	-0	-6	-7	0	-0.8
1975 SD-N	3	1	.750	21	4	0	0	0	54	60	3	31	18	15.2	5.17	67	.282	.373	1	.083	-0	-9	-10	-1	-0.9
1976 SD-N	1	3	.250	24	1	0	0	0	39	39	0	26	27	15.0	5.31	62	.260	.369	0	.000	-0	-8	-9	-0	-0.9
1977 Tor-A	2	4	.333	43	0	0	0	5	86	91	9	54	54	15.2	4.60	91	.279	.382	0	—	0	-5	-4	0	-0.4
Total 10	48	51	.485	365	39	6	2	41	770²	779	63	389	489	13.7	4.31	83	.265	.352	15	.123	-2	-60	-62	-1	-7.5
● **JOHNNY JOHNSON** Johnson, John Clifford "Swede" b: 9/29/14, Belmore, Ohio d: 6/26/91, Iron Mountain, Mich. BL/TL, 6', 182 lbs. Deb: 4/19/44																									
1944 NY-A	0	2	.000	22	1	0	0	3	26²	25	0	24	11	16.9	4.05	86	.243	.391	3	.500	1	-2	-2	-1	-0.1
1945 Chi-A	3	0	1.000	29	0	0	0	4	69²	85	2	35	38	15.6	4.26	78	.306	.385	4	.286	2	-7	-7	-1	-0.3
Total 2	3	2	.600	51	1	0	0	7	96¹	110	2	59	49	16.0	4.20	80	.289	.387	7	.350	3	-9	-9	-2	-0.4
● **YOUNGY JOHNSON** Johnson, John Godfred b: 7/22/1877, San Francisco, Cal. d: 8/28/36, Berkeley, Cal. TR, Deb: 4/29/1897																									
1897 Phi-N	1	2	.333	5	2	1	0	0	29	39	0	12	7	16.4	4.66	90	.319	.389	1	.077	-2	-1	-1	-0	-0.3
1899 NY-N	0	0	—	1	0	0	0	0	2	0	0	2	1	9.0	0.00	—	.000	.260	0	.000	-0	1	1	0	0.0
Total 2	1	2	.333	6	2	1	0	0	31	39	0	14	8	16.0	4.35	96	.305	.382	1	.071	-2	-0	-1	-0	-0.3
● **JOHN HENRY JOHNSON** Johnson, John Henry b: 8/21/56, Houston, Tex. BL/TL, 6'2", 190 lbs. Deb: 4/10/78																									
1978 Oak-A	11	10	.524	33	30	7	2	0	186	164	18	82	91	11.9	3.39	107	.238	.319	0	—	0	8	5	-3	0.4
1979 Oak-A	2	8	.200	14	13	1	0	0	84²	89	13	36	50	13.4	4.36	93	.269	.342	0	—	0	-1	-3	-1	-0.2
Tex-A	2	6	.250	17	12	1	0	0	82¹	79	12	36	46	12.7	4.92	84	.255	.334	0	—	0	-6	-7	-1	-0.6
Yr	4	14	.222	31	25	2	0	0	167	168	25	72	96	13.0	4.63	88	.261	.336	0	—	0	-8	-10	-1	-0.8
1980 Tex-A	2	2	.500	33	0	0	0	4	38²	27	2	15	44	10.0	2.33	167	.199	.283	0	—	0	7	7	0	0.7
1981 Tex-A	3	1	.750	24	0	0	0	2	23²	19	2	6	9	9.9	2.66	130	.232	.292	0	—	0	3	2	1	0.6
1983 Bos-A	3	2	.600	34	1	0	0	1	53¹	58	3	20	51	13.3	3.71	117	.283	.350	0	—	0	3	4	-0	0.2
1984 Bos-A	1	2	.333	30	3	0	0	0	63²	64	7	27	57	12.9	3.53	118	.260	.333	0	—	0	3	4	0	0.3
1986 Mil-A	2	1	.667	19	0	0	0	1	44	43	2	10	42	10.8	2.66	163	.251	.293	0	—	0	7	8	0	0.3
1987 Mil-A	0	1	.000	10	0	0	0	0	12	18	1	18	20	20.5	9.57	48	.365	.451	0	—	0	-15	-15	0	-0.5
Total 8	26	33	.441	214	61	9	2	9	602²	585	60	250	407	12.5	3.90	102	.256	.331	0	—	0	6	6	-5	1.1
● **JOHN JOHNSON** Johnson, John Louis (b: John Louis Mercer) b: 11/18/1869, Pekin, Ill. d: 1/28/41, Kansas City, Mo. TL, 5'10", 165 lbs. Deb: 9/11/1894																									
1894 Phi-N	1	1	.500	4	3	2	0	0	32²	44	3	15	10	16.5	6.06	84	.319	.389	3	.188	-1	-3	-3	0	-0.2
● **JOE JOHNSON** Johnson, Joseph Richard b: 10/30/61, Brookline, Mass. BR/TR, 6'2", 195 lbs. Deb: 7/25/85																									
1985 Atl-N	4	4	.500	15	14	1	0	0	85²	95	9	24	34	12.8	4.10	94	.285	.339	1	.043	-1	-5	-2	-2	-0.5
1986 Atl-N	6	7	.462	17	15	2	0	0	87	101	8	35	49	14.3	4.97	80	.289	.358	3	.115	-1	-12	-10	2	-1.2
Tor-A	7	2	.778	16	15	0	0	0	88	94	3	22	39	12.2	3.89	109	.281	.331	0	—	0	3	3	-1	0.1
1987 Tor-A	3	5	.375	14	14	0	0	0	66²	77	10	18	27	13.1	5.13	88	.289	.339	0	—	0	-5	-5	-0	-0.5
Total 3	20	18	.526	62	58	3	0	0	327¹	367	30	99	149	13.1	4.48	92	.286	.342	4	.082	-2	-19	-13	-2	-2.1
● **KEN JOHNSON** Johnson, Kenneth Travis b: 6/16/33, W.Palm Beach, Fla. BR/TR, 6'4", 210 lbs. Deb: 9/13/58																									
1958 KC-A	0	0	—	2	0	0	0	0	2¹	6	1	3	1	34.7	27.00	14	.429	.529	0	—	0	-6	-6	0	0.0
1959 KC-A	1	1	.500	2	2	0	0	0	11	11	2	5	8	13.1	4.09	98	.268	.348	0	.000	-0	-0	-0	0	0.0
1960 KC-A	5	10	.333	42	6	2	0	0	120¹	120	16	45	83	12.9	4.26	93	.263	.338	5	.167	-1	-5	-4	2	-0.3
1961 KC-A	0	4	.000	6	1	0	0	0	9¹	11	2	7	4	17.4	10.61	39	.297	.409	0	.000	-0	-7	-7	1	-2.1
*Cin-N	6	2	.750	15	11	3	1	1	83	71	11	22	42	10.3	3.25	125	.229	.284	6	.240	1	7	7	1	0.9
1962 Hou-N	7	16	.304	33	31	5	1	0	197	195	18	46	178	11.3	3.84	97	.257	.305	4	.077	-3	-2	-2	1	-0.4
1963 Hou-N	11	17	.393	37	32	6	1	0	224	204	12	50	148	10.5	2.65	119	.242	.291	5	.068	-4	16	12	2	1.4
1964 Hou-N	11	16	.407	35	35	7	1	0	218	209	15	44	117	10.7	3.63	94	.250	.293	6	.079	-2	-2	-5	1	-0.6
1965 Hou-N	3	2	.600	8	8	2	0	0	51²	52	4	11	28	11.7	4.18	80	.267	.319	2	.111	-0	-4	-5	1	-0.3
Mil-N	13	8	.619	29	26	8	1	2	179²	165	15	37	123	10.1	3.21	110	.240	.282	7	.115	-2	7	6	-3	0.2
Yr	16	10	.615	37	34	10	1	2	231¹	217	19	48	151	10.4	3.42	102	.244	.285	9	.114	-2	3	2	-2	-0.1
1966 Atl-N	14	8	.636	32	31	6	3	0	215²	213	24	46	105	10.8	3.30	110	.262	.301	10	.143	-0	7	8	0	0.8
1967 Atl-N	13	9	.591	29	29	6	0	0	210¹	191	19	38	85	10.1	2.74	121	.244	.285	9	.127	-0	15	14	-2	1.2

YEAR	TM/L	W	L	PCT	G	GS	CG	SH	SV	IP	H	HR	BB	SO	RAT	ERA	ERA+	OAV	OOB	BH	AVG	PB	PR	/A	PD	TPI
1968	Atl-N	5	8	.385	31	16	1	0	0	135	145	10	25	57	11.9	3.47	86	.279	.324	7	.175	-0	-7	-7	-1	-0.8
1969	Atl-N	0	1	.000	9	2	0	0	1	29	32	4	9	20	12.7	4.97	73	.283	.336	0	.000	-0	-4	-4	0	-0.2
	NY-A	1	2	.333	12	0	0	0	0	26	19	1	11	21	10.4	3.46	100	.202	.286	0	.000	-0	0	0	1	0.1
	Chi-N	1	2	.333	9	1	0	0	1	19	17	2	13	14	14.2	2.84	142	.230	.345	0	.000	-0	2	2	0	0.3
1970	Mon-N	0	0	—	3	0	0	0	0	6	9	1	1	4	18.0	7.50	55	.321	.387	0	—	-0	-2	-2	0	0.0
Total	13	91	106	.462	334	231	50	7	9	1737[1]	1670	157	413	1042	11.1	3.46	101	.253	.302	61	.114	-12	18	8	5	0.2

● KEN JOHNSON
Johnson, Kenneth Wandersee "Hook" b: 1/14/23, Topeka, Kan. BL/TL, 6'1", 185 lbs. Deb: 9/18/47

YEAR	TM/L	W	L	PCT	G	GS	CG	SH	SV	IP	H	HR	BB	SO	RAT	ERA	ERA+	OAV	OOB	BH	AVG	PB	PR	/A	PD	TPI
1947	StL-N	1	0	1.000	2	1	1	0	0	10	2	0	5	8	7.2	0.00	—	.063	.211	2	.500	1	5	5	0	0.5
1948	StL-N	2	4	.333	13	4	0	0	0	45[1]	43	1	30	20	14.7	4.76	86	.262	.379	6	.300	-0	-4	-3	-0	-0.3
1949	StL-N	1	0	1.000	14	2	0	0	0	33[2]	29	1	35	18	17.9	6.42	65	.250	.435	2	.250	0	-9	-8	1	-0.1
1950	StL-N	0	0	—	2	0	0	0	0	2	1	0	3	1	18.0	0.00	—	.167	.444	0	—	0	1	1	0	0.0
	*Phi-N	4	1	.800	14	8	3	1	0	60[2]	61	3	43	32	15.6	4.01	101	.260	.376	3	.158	-0	1	0	-0	0.0
	Yr	4	1	.800	16	8	3	1	0	62[2]	62	3	46	33	15.7	3.88	105	.257	.378	3	.158	-0	2	1	0	0.0
1951	Phi-N	5	8	.385	20	18	4	3	0	106[1]	103	8	68	58	14.7	4.57	84	.259	.371	5	.143	-1	-7	-9	-0	-1.0
1952	Det-A	0	0	—	9	1	0	0	0	11[1]	12	1	11	10	18.3	6.35	60	.273	.418	1	.333	0	-3	-3	0	0.0
Total	6	12	14	.462	74	34	8	4	0	269[1]	251	14	195	147	15.2	4.58	87	.252	.379	19	.213	-1	-17	-18	1	-0.9

● LLOYD JOHNSON
Johnson, Lloyd William "Eppa" b: 12/24/10, Santa Rosa, Cal. d: 10/8/80, Stockton, Cal. BL/TL, 6'4", 204 lbs. Deb: 4/21/34

YEAR	TM/L	W	L	PCT	G	GS	CG	SH	SV	IP	H	HR	BB	SO	RAT	ERA	ERA+	OAV	OOB	BH	AVG	PB	PR	/A	PD	TPI
1934	Pit-N	0	0	—	1	0	0	0	0	1	1	0	0	0	9.0	0.00	—	.333	.333	0	—	0	0	0	-0	0.0

● MIKE JOHNSON
Johnson, Michael Norton b: 3/2/51, Slayton, Minn. BR/TR, 6'1", 185 lbs. Deb: 7/25/74

YEAR	TM/L	W	L	PCT	G	GS	CG	SH	SV	IP	H	HR	BB	SO	RAT	ERA	ERA+	OAV	OOB	BH	AVG	PB	PR	/A	PD	TPI
1974	SD-N	0	2	.000	18	0	0	0	0	21[1]	29	1	15	15	19.0	4.64	77	.326	.429	0	—	0	-2	-3	-0	-0.2

● RANDY JOHNSON
Johnson, Randall David b: 9/10/63, Walnut Creek, Cal. BR/TL, 6'10", 225 lbs. Deb: 9/15/88

YEAR	TM/L	W	L	PCT	G	GS	CG	SH	SV	IP	H	HR	BB	SO	RAT	ERA	ERA+	OAV	OOB	BH	AVG	PB	PR	/A	PD	TPI
1988	Mon-N	3	0	1.000	4	4	1	0	0	26	23	3	7	25	10.4	2.42	148	.225	.275	1	.111	-0	3	3	-1	0.3
1989	Mon-N	0	4	.000	7	6	0	0	0	29[2]	29	2	26	26	16.7	6.67	53	.264	.404	1	.143	-0	-10	-10	-0	-1.2
	Sea-A	7	9	.438	22	22	2	0	0	131	118	11	70	104	13.1	4.40	92	.244	.344	0	—	0	-7	-5	0	-0.6
1990	Sea-A☆	14	11	.560	33	33	5	2	0	219[2]	174	26	120	194	12.3	3.65	109	.216	.321	0	—	0	6	8	-1	0.6
1991	Sea-A	13	10	.565	33	33	2	1	0	201[1]	151	15	152	228	14.1	3.98	104	.213	.361	0	—	0	3	3	-1	0.2
1992	Sea-A	12	14	.462	31	31	6	2	0	210[1]	154	13	144	**241**	13.5	3.77	105	**.206**	.347	0	—	0	4	5	-1	0.4
1993	Sea-A★	19	8	.704	35	34	10	3	1	255[1]	185	22	99	**308**	10.6	3.24	109	**.203**	.292	0	—	0	31	33	1	3.1
1994	Sea-A★	13	6	.684	23	23	9	4	0	172	132	14	72	**204**	11.0	3.19	154	.216	.304	0	—	0	31	33	0	3.1
Total	7	81	62	.566	188	186	35	12	1	1245[1]	966	106	690	1330	12.4	3.70	113	.215	.328	2	.125	-1	59	69	-3	5.9

● BOB JOHNSON
Johnson, Robert Dale b: 4/25/43, Aurora, Ill. BL/TR, 6'4", 220 lbs. Deb: 9/19/69

YEAR	TM/L	W	L	PCT	G	GS	CG	SH	SV	IP	H	HR	BB	SO	RAT	ERA	ERA+	OAV	OOB	BH	AVG	PB	PR	/A	PD	TPI
1969	NY-N	0	0	—	2	0	0	0	0	1[2]	1	0	1	1	10.8	0.00	—	.167	.286	0	—	0	1	1	-0	0.1
1970	KC-A	8	13	.381	40	26	10	1	4	214	178	18	82	206	11.4	3.07	122	.228	.310	6	.105	-1	15	16	-1	1.3
1971	*Pit-N	9	10	.474	31	27	7	1	0	174[2]	170	19	55	101	12.0	3.45	98	.259	.323	3	.063	-1	0	-1	-3	-0.4
1972	*Pit-N	4	4	.500	31	11	1	0	3	115[2]	98	14	46	79	11.5	2.96	112	.231	.312	5	.143	-0	6	5	-2	0.1
1973	Pit-N	4	2	.667	50	2	0	0	0	92	98	12	34	68	13.4	3.62	97	.276	.348	0	.000	-1	0	-1	-2	-0.4
1974	Cle-A	3	4	.429	14	10	0	0	0	72	75	12	37	36	14.4	4.38	83	.273	.365	0	—	0	-6	-6	-0	-0.6
1977	Atl-N	0	1	.000	15	0	0	0	0	22[1]	24	7	14	16	16.1	7.25	61	.270	.381	1	.333	-0	-8	-7	-1	-0.3
Total	7	28	34	.452	183	76	18	2	12	692[1]	644	82	269	507	12.3	3.48	102	.249	.327	15	.096	-4	9	6	-7	-0.2

● ROY JOHNSON
Johnson, Roy J "Hardrock" b: 10/1/1895, Madill, Okla. d: 1/10/86, Scottsdale, Ariz. BR/TR, 6', 185 lbs. Deb: 8/7/18 MC

YEAR	TM/L	W	L	PCT	G	GS	CG	SH	SV	IP	H	HR	BB	SO	RAT	ERA	ERA+	OAV	OOB	BH	AVG	PB	PR	/A	PD	TPI
1918	Phi-A	1	5	.167	10	8	3	0	0	50	47	0	34	12	14.9	3.42	86	.254	.376	1	.067	-2	-4	-3	-0	-0.5

● JING JOHNSON
Johnson, Russell Conwell b: 10/9/1894, Parker Ford, Pa. d: 12/6/50, Pottstown, Pa. BR/TR, 5'9", 172 lbs. Deb: 6/27/16

YEAR	TM/L	W	L	PCT	G	GS	CG	SH	SV	IP	H	HR	BB	SO	RAT	ERA	ERA+	OAV	OOB	BH	AVG	PB	PR	/A	PD	TPI
1916	Phi-A	2	8	.200	12	12	8	0	0	84[1]	90	3	39	25	13.8	3.74	76	.288	.368	2	.074	-1	-8	-8	3	-0.7
1917	Phi-A	9	12	.429	34	23	13	0	0	191	184	8	56	55	11.5	2.78	99	.260	.319	12	.203	2	-2	-1	2	0.4
1919	Phi-A	9	15	.375	34	25	12	0	0	202	222	8	62	67	12.8	3.61	95	.291	.346	14	.194	-0	-9	-4	5	0.1
1927	Phi-A	4	2	.667	17	3	2	0	0	51[2]	42	1	16	16	10.8	3.48	122	.235	.312	2	.167	-0	4	4	1	0.5
1928	Phi-A	0	0	—	3	0	0	0	0	10[2]	13	1	5	3	15.2	5.06	79	.310	.383	2	.500	1	-1	-1	0	0.1
Total	5	24	37	.393	100	63	35	0	0	539[2]	551	17	178	166	12.4	3.35	95	.275	.338	32	.184	-1	-17	-10	10	0.4

● SI JOHNSON
Johnson, Silas Kenneth b: 10/5/06, Danway, Ill. d: 5/12/94, Sheridan, Ill. BR/TR, 5'11.5", 185 lbs. Deb: 5/2/28

YEAR	TM/L	W	L	PCT	G	GS	CG	SH	SV	IP	H	HR	BB	SO	RAT	ERA	ERA+	OAV	OOB	BH	AVG	PB	PR	/A	PD	TPI
1928	Cin-N	0	0	—	3	0	0	0	0	10[1]	9	0	5	1	12.2	4.35	91	.250	.341	1	.250	0	-0	-0	-0	0.0
1929	Cin-N	0	0	—	1	0	0	0	0	2	2	0	1	0	13.5	4.50	101	.250	.333	0	—	0	-0	-0	-0	0.0
1930	Cin-N	3	1	.750	35	3	0	0	0	78[1]	86	5	31	47	13.9	4.94	98	.286	.360	4	.235	-0	0	-1	-0	-0.1
1931	Cin-N	11	19	.367	42	33	14	0	0	262[1]	273	5	74	95	12.1	3.77	99	.269	.323	13	.149	-3	3	-1	-5	-0.9
1932	Cin-N	13	15	.464	42	27	14	2	2	245	246	8	57	94	11.2	3.27	118	.259	.302	10	.125	-4	17	16	-0	1.3
1933	Cin-N	7	18	.280	34	28	14	4	1	211[1]	212	7	54	51	11.5	3.49	97	.263	.312	5	.042	-7	-4	-2	-1	-1.1
1934	Cin-N	7	22	.241	46	31	9	0	3	215[2]	264	15	84	89	14.8	5.22	78	.297	.362	10	.139	-3	-28	-27	-3	-3.7
1935	Cin-N	5	11	.313	30	20	4	1	0	130	155	14	59	40	15.0	6.23	64	.293	.367	1	.024	-4	-32	-33	-1	-3.7
1936	Cin-N	0	0	—	2	0	0	0	0	4	7	1	0	2	15.8	13.50	28	.368	.368	0	—	0	-4	-4	-0	-0.4
	StL-N	5	3	.625	12	9	3	1	0	61[2]	82	4	11	21	13.7	4.38	90	.314	.344	4	.190	-0	-2	-3	-1	-0.5
	Yr	5	3	.625	14	9	3	1	0	65[2]	89	5	11	23	13.8	4.93	80	.318	.346	4	.190	-0	-7	-7	-1	-0.5
1937	StL-N	12	12	.500	38	21	12	1	0	192[1]	222	14	43	64	12.4	3.32	120	.292	.330	9	.138	-3	13	14	-2	1.2
1938	StL-N	0	3	.000	6	3	0	0	0	15[2]	21	0	6	4	19.0	7.47	53	.380	.429	0	.000	-0	-6	-6	-0	-1.0
1940	Phi-N	5	14	.263	37	14	5	0	1	138[1]	145	13	42	58	12.3	4.88	80	.268	.323	6	.140	-2	-16	-15	-2	-2.3
1941	Phi-N	5	12	.294	39	21	6	1	0	163[1]	207	8	54	80	14.4	4.52	82	.309	.362	7	.149	-2	-16	-15	-1	-1.7
1942	Phi-N	8	19	.296	39	26	10	1	0	195[1]	198	6	72	78	12.5	3.69	90	.266	.332	6	.103	-4	-8	-8	-3	-1.7
1943	Phi-N	8	3	.727	21	14	9	1	2	113	110	4	25	46	10.8	3.27	103	.252	.292	6	.182	-0	1	1	-0	0.1
1946	Phi-N	0	0	—	1	0	0	0	0	3	7	1	4	2	21.0	3.00	114	.538	.538	1	1.000	0	0	0	-0	0.0
	Bos-N	6	5	.545	28	12	5	1	1	127	134	8	35	41	12.3	2.76	124	.272	.325	5	.135	-2	9	9	-1	0.5
	Yr	6	5	.545	29	12	5	1	1	130	141	9	39	43	12.5	2.77	124	.279	.330	6	.158	-1	9	10	-1	0.5
1947	Bos-N	6	8	.429	36	10	3	0	0	112[2]	124	7	34	27	12.7	4.23	92	.275	.327	1	.033	-3	-2	-4	3	-0.5
Total	17	101	165	.380	492	272	108	13	15	2281[2]	2510	120	687	840	12.8	4.09	92	.279	.333	87	.123	-37	-76	-79	-17	-14.1

● SYL JOHNSON
Johnson, Sylvester W (Born Sylvester Johnson) b: 12/31/1900, Portland, Ore. d: 2/20/85, Portland, Ore. BR/TR, 5'11", 180 lbs. Deb: 4/24/22 C

YEAR	TM/L	W	L	PCT	G	GS	CG	SH	SV	IP	H	HR	BB	SO	RAT	ERA	ERA+	OAV	OOB	BH	AVG	PB	PR	/A	PD	TPI
1922	Det-A	7	3	.700	29	8	3	0	1	97	99	7	30	29	12.3	3.71	105	.273	.336	7	.222	-0	4	2	-2	0.0
1923	Det-A	12	7	.632	37	18	7	0	1	176[1]	181	12	47	93	11.8	3.98	97	.274	.325	10	.161	-1	0	-2	-3	-0.8
1924	Det-A	5	4	.556	29	9	2	0	3	104	117	6	42	55	14.2	4.93	83	.287	.360	7	.206	-0	-8	-9	-1	-0.9
1925	Det-A	0	2	.000	6	0	0	0	0	13	11	1	10	6	14.5	3.46	124	.250	.389	0	.000	-0	1	1	0	0.1
1926	StL-N	0	3	.000	19	6	1	0	0	49	54	3	15	10	13.0	4.22	92	.297	.357	0	.000	-1	-2	-2	-0	-0.4
1927	StL-N	0	0	—	2	0	0	0	0	3	3	1	0	2	9.0	6.00	66	.250	.250	0	—	-1	-1	-1	-0	-0.1
1928	*StL-N	8	4	.667	34	6	2	0	8	120	117	6	33	66	11.6	3.90	103	.259	.315	6	.158	-0	0	0	0	0.0
1929	StL-N	13	7	.650	42	19	12	0	3	182[1]	186	16	50	80	12.2	3.60	129	.265	.325	7	.117	-2	23	21	-4	1.4
1930	*StL-N	12	10	.545	32	24	8	0	2	187[2]	215	13	38	92	13.3	4.65	108	.293	.332	15	.214	-1	7	8	-3	0.4
1931	StL-N	11	9	.550	32	23	7	1	0	186	186	9	29	82	10.5	3.00	131	.255	.286	14	.233	-1	18	19	-3	1.8
1932	StL-N	5	14	.263	32	22	7	0	0	164[2]	199	14	35	70	13.0	4.92	80	.299	.333	10	.196	-1	-19	-18	-1	-2.0
1933	StL-N	3	3	.500	35	1	0	0	0	84	89	7	16	28	11.6	4.29	81	.271	.311	5	.238	-2	5	5	-2	-0.7
1934	Cin-N	0	0	—	2	0	0	0	0	6[2]	9	2	0	2	12.2	2.70	151	.310	.310	1	.500	1	1	1	-0	0.1
	Phi-N	5	9	.357	42	10	4	3	3	133[2]	122	14	24	54	9.9	3.50	135	.242	.277	8	.195	-1	8	18	-4	1.4

YEAR TM/L	W	L	PCT	G	GS	CG	SH	SV	IP	H	HR	BB	SO	RAT	ERA	ERA+	OAV	OOB	BH	AVG	PB	PR	/A	PD	TPI
Yr	5	9	.357	44	10	4	3	3	140¹	131	16	24	54	10.0	3.46	136	.245	.279	9	.209	1	9	19	-4	1.5
1935 Phi-N	10	8	.556	37	18	8	1	6	174²	182	15	31	89	11.1	3.56	128	.265	.299	14	.241	1	9	19	-3	1.7
1936 Phi-N	5	7	.417	39	8	1	0	7	111	129	10	29	48	13.1	4.30	106	.288	.335	9	.250	-0	-3	3	-2	0.1
1937 Phi-N	4	10	.286	32	15	4	0	3	138	155	20	22	46	11.7	5.02	86	.288	.318	7	.146	-3	-17	-11	-1	-1.3
1938 Phi-N	2	7	.222	22	6	2	0	0	83	87	4	11	21	10.6	4.23	92	.267	.291	1	.034	-3	-4	-3	-2	-0.8
1939 Phi-N	8	8	.500	22	14	6	0	2	111	112	10	15	37	10.4	3.81	105	.264	.291	5	.152	-1	1	2	-1	0.1
1940 Phi-N	2	2	.500	17	2	2	0	2	40²	37	6	5	13	9.3	4.20	93	.236	.259	0	.000	-1	-2	-1	-0	-0.3
Total 19	112	117	.489	542	210	82	11	43	2165²	2290	173	488	920	11.7	4.06	104	.273	.316	127	.181	-10	8	43	-36	-0.1

● **TOM JOHNSON**   Johnson, Thomas Raymond b: 4/2/51, St.Paul, Minn.   BR/TR, 6'1", 185 lbs.   Deb: 9/10/74

YEAR TM/L	W	L	PCT	G	GS	CG	SH	SV	IP	H	HR	BB	SO	RAT	ERA	ERA+	OAV	OOB	BH	AVG	PB	PR	/A	PD	TPI
1974 Min-A	2	0	1.000	4	0	0	0	1	7	4	0	0	4	5.1	0.00	—	.167	.167	0	—	0	3	3	-0	1.0
1975 Min-A	1	2	.333	18	0	0	0	3	38²	40	4	21	17	14.7	4.19	92	.263	.360	0	—	0	-2	-1	0	-0.1
1976 Min-A	3	1	.750	18	1	0	0	0	48¹	44	2	8	37	9.7	2.61	138	.243	.275	0	—	0	5	5	0	0.3
1977 Min-A	16	7	.696	71	0	0	0	15	146²	152	11	47	87	12.5	3.13	127	.272	.334	0	—	0	15	14	1	2.4
1978 Min-A	1	4	.200	18	0	0	0	3	32²	42	2	17	21	16.8	5.51	69	.318	.404	0	—	0	-6	-6	0	-1.0
Total 5	23	14	.622	129	1	0	0	22	273¹	282	19	93	166	12.6	3.39	114	.269	.334	0	—	0	15	15	1	2.6

● **VIC JOHNSON**   Johnson, Victor Oscar b: 8/3/20, Eau Claire, Wis.   BR/TL, 6', 160 lbs.   Deb: 5/3/44

YEAR TM/L	W	L	PCT	G	GS	CG	SH	SV	IP	H	HR	BB	SO	RAT	ERA	ERA+	OAV	OOB	BH	AVG	PB	PR	/A	PD	TPI
1944 Bos-A	0	3	.000	7	5	0	0	0	27¹	42	0	15	7	18.8	6.26	54	.362	.435	0	.000	-1	-9	-9	1	-0.9
1945 Bos-A	6	4	.600	26	9	4	1	2	85¹	90	4	46	21	14.6	4.01	85	.276	.369	5	.167	-1	-6	-6	1	-0.7
1946 Cle-A	0	1	.000	9	1	0	0	0	13²	20	1	8	3	18.4	9.22	36	.357	.438	0	.000	-0	-9	-9	0	-0.6
Total 3	6	8	.429	42	15	4	1	2	126¹	152	5	69	31	15.9	5.06	67	.305	.392	5	.119	-3	-23	-23	2	-2.2

● **WALTER JOHNSON**   Johnson, Walter Perry "Barney" or "The Big Train"
b: 11/6/1887, Humboldt, Kan.   d: 12/10/46, Washington, D.C.   BR/TR, 6'1", 200 lbs.   Deb: 8/2/07   MH♦

YEAR TM/L	W	L	PCT	G	GS	CG	SH	SV	IP	H	HR	BB	SO	RAT	ERA	ERA+	OAV	OOB	BH	AVG	PB	PR	/A	PD	TPI
1907 Was-A	5	9	.357	14	12	11	2	0	110¹	100	1	20	71	10.0	1.88	129	.244	.282	4	.111	-2	8	7	-2	0.4
1908 Was-A	14	14	.500	36	30	23	6	1	256¹	194	0	53	160	9.1	1.65	139	.211	.262	13	.165	3	21	18	-4	2.0
1909 Was-A	13	25	.342	40	36	27	4	1	296¹	247	1	84	164	10.5	2.22	110	.221	.284	13	.129	-3	9	7	-2	0.4
1910 Was-A	25	17	.595	45	42	38	8	1	370	262	1	76	313	8.5	1.36	183	.205	.257	24	.175	1	48	46	-1	5.8
1911 Was-A	25	13	.658	40	37	36	6	1	322¹	292	8	70	207	10.5	1.90	173	.238	.283	30	.234	3	52	50	4	6.4
1912 Was-A	33	12	.733	50	37	34	7	2	369	259	2	76	303	8.6	1.39	240	.196	.248	38	.264	9	79	80	1	11.2
1913 Was-A	36	7	.837	48	36	29	11	2	346	232	9	38	243	7.3	1.14	258	.187	.217	35	.261	10	69	70	0	10.9
1914 Was-A	28	18	.609	51	40	33	9	1	371²	287	3	74	225	9.0	1.72	164	.217	.265	30	.221	8	42	45	2	7.3
1915 Was-A	27	13	.675	47	39	35	7	4	336¹	258	1	56	203	8.9	1.55	192	.214	.260	34	.231	6	52	53	2	7.7
1916 Was-A	25	20	.556	48	38	36	3	1	369²	290	0	82	228	9.3	1.90	147	.220	.270	32	.225	8	38	37	-5	5.1
1917 Was-A	23	16	.590	47	34	30	8	3	326	248	3	68	188	9.1	2.21	119	.211	.263	33	.254	10	16	15	-1	3.0
1918 Was-A	23	13	.639	39	29	29	8	3	326	241	2	70	162	8.8	1.27	215	.210	.260	40	.267	6	55	53	-3	7.6
1919 Was-A	20	14	.588	39	29	27	7	2	290¹	235	0	51	147	9.1	1.49	216	.219	.259	24	.192	2	56	56	0	7.2
1920 Was-A	8	10	.444	21	15	12	4	3	143²	135	5	27	78	10.5	3.13	119	.245	.286	17	.266	4	11	10	-1	1.4
1921 Was-A	17	14	.548	35	32	25	1	1	264	265	7	92	143	12.2	3.51	117	.263	.326	30	.270	4	23	18	-3	2.0
1922 Was-A	15	16	.484	41	31	23	4	4	280	283	8	99	105	12.5	2.99	129	.267	.334	22	.204	-1	33	27	1	2.8
1923 Was-A	17	12	.586	42	34	18	3	4	261¹	263	9	73	130	12.3	3.48	108	.269	.333	18	.194	1	15	8	-2	0.7
1924 *Was-A	23	7	.767	38	38	20	6	0	277²	233	10	77	158	10.4	2.72	148	.224	.284	32	.283	7	47	41	-1	4.5
1925 *Was-A	20	7	.741	30	29	16	3	0	229	217	7	78	108	11.9	3.07	138	.250	.317	42	.433	17	34	30	-4	4.3
1926 Was-A	15	16	.484	33	33	22	2	0	260²	259	13	73	125	11.6	3.63	107	.263	.317	20	.194	1	11	7	-5	0.7
1927 Was-A	5	6	.455	18	15	7	1	0	107²	113	7	26	48	12.2	5.10	80	.278	.332	16	.348	6	-11	-12	0	-0.5
Total 21	417	279	.599	802	666	531	110	34	5914²	4913	97	1363	3509	9.9	2.17	147	.227	.279	547	.235	99	706	668	-23	90.5

● **BILL JOHNSON**   Johnson, William Charles b: 10/6/60, Wilmington, Del.   BR/TR, 6'5", 205 lbs.   Deb: 9/6/83

YEAR TM/L	W	L	PCT	G	GS	CG	SH	SV	IP	H	HR	BB	SO	RAT	ERA	ERA+	OAV	OOB	BH	AVG	PB	PR	/A	PD	TPI
1983 Chi-N	1	0	1.000	10	0	0	0	0	12¹	17	0	3	4	14.6	4.38	87	.347	.385	0	—	0	-1	-1	0	0.0
1984 Chi-N	0	0	—	4	0	0	0	0	5¹	4	0	1	3	8.4	1.69	232	.235	.278	0	—	0	1	1	0	0.0
Total 2	1	0	1.000	14	0	0	0	0	17²	21	0	4	7	12.7	3.57	107	.318	.357	0	—	0	0	1	1	0.0

● **JEFF JOHNSON**   Johnson, William Jeffrey b: 8/4/66, Durham, N.C.   BR/TL, 6'3", 200 lbs.   Deb: 6/5/91

YEAR TM/L	W	L	PCT	G	GS	CG	SH	SV	IP	H	HR	BB	SO	RAT	ERA	ERA+	OAV	OOB	BH	AVG	PB	PR	/A	PD	TPI
1991 NY-A	6	11	.353	23	23	0	0	0	127	156	15	33	62	13.8	5.95	70	.305	.354	0	—	0	-26	-26	1	-2.8
1992 NY-A	2	3	.400	13	8	0	0	0	52²	71	4	23	14	16.4	6.66	59	.340	.398	0	—	0	-16	-16	-0	-1.3
1993 NY-A	0	2	.000	2	2	0	0	0	2²	12	1	2	0	47.3	30.38	14	.600	.636	0	—	0	-8	-8	0	-2.6
Total 3	8	16	.333	38	33	0	0	0	182¹	239	20	58	76	15.1	6.52	63	.320	.375	0	—	0	-50	-49	1	-6.7

● **JOEL JOHNSTON**   Johnston, Joel Raymond b: 3/8/67, West Chester, Pa.   BR/TR, 6'4", 220 lbs.   Deb: 9/5/91

YEAR TM/L	W	L	PCT	G	GS	CG	SH	SV	IP	H	HR	BB	SO	RAT	ERA	ERA+	OAV	OOB	BH	AVG	PB	PR	/A	PD	TPI
1991 KC-A	1	0	1.000	13	0	0	0	0	22¹	9	0	9	21	7.3	0.40	1022	.120	.214	0	—	0	9	9	-0	0.3
1992 KC-A	0	0	—	5	0	0	0	0	2²	3	2	2	0	16.9	13.50	30	.273	.385	0	—	0	-3	-3	-0	-0.2
1993 Pit-N	2	4	.333	33	0	0	0	2	53¹	38	7	19	31	9.6	3.38	120	.203	.277	2	.333	1	4	4	-1	0.5
1994 Pit-N	0	0	—	4	0	0	0	0	3¹	14	0	4	5	54.0	29.70	14	.583	.667	0	—	0	-9	-9	-0	-0.2
Total 4	3	4	.429	55	0	0	0	2	81²	64	9	34	57	11.0	3.97	103	.215	.300	2	.333	1	1	1	-1	0.6

● **JOHN JOHNSTONE**   Johnstone, John William b: 11/25/68, Liverpool, N.Y.   BR/TR, 6'3", 195 lbs.   Deb: 9/3/93

YEAR TM/L	W	L	PCT	G	GS	CG	SH	SV	IP	H	HR	BB	SO	RAT	ERA	ERA+	OAV	OOB	BH	AVG	PB	PR	/A	PD	TPI
1993 Fla-N	0	2	.000	7	0	0	0	0	10²	16	1	7	5	19.4	5.91	73	.340	.426	0	—	0	-2	-2	-0	-0.3
1994 Fla-N	1	2	.333	17	0	0	0	0	21¹	23	4	16	23	16.9	5.91	76	.264	.385	0	—	0	-4	-3	-0	-0.4
Total 2	1	4	.200	24	0	0	0	0	32	39	5	23	28	17.7	5.91	75	.291	.399	0	—	0	-6	-5	-0	-0.7

● **ROY JOINER**   Joiner, Roy Merrill "Pop" b: 10/30/06, Red Bluff, Cal.   d: 12/26/89, Red Bluff, Cal.   BL/TL, 6', 170 lbs.   Deb: 4/30/34

YEAR TM/L	W	L	PCT	G	GS	CG	SH	SV	IP	H	HR	BB	SO	RAT	ERA	ERA+	OAV	OOB	BH	AVG	PB	PR	/A	PD	TPI
1934 Chi-N	0	1	.000	20	2	0	0	0	34	61	3	8	9	18.3	8.21	46	.391	.421	2	.200	-0	-16	-16	-0	-0.5
1935 Chi-N	0	0	—	2	0	0	0	0	3¹	6	0	2	0	21.6	5.40	73	.429	.500	0	.000	-0	-1	-1	0	0.0
1940 NY-N	3	2	.600	30	2	0	0	1	53	66	8	17	25	14.9	3.40	114	.308	.373	3	.273	1	3	3	0	0.3
Total 3	3	3	.500	52	4	0	0	1	90¹	133	11	27	34	16.4	5.28	74	.346	.397	5	.227	0	-13	-14	0	-0.2

● **DAVE JOLLY**   Jolly, David "Gabby" b: 10/14/24, Stony Point, N.C.   d: 5/27/63, Durham, N.C.   BR/TR, 6', 165 lbs.   Deb: 5/9/53

YEAR TM/L	W	L	PCT	G	GS	CG	SH	SV	IP	H	HR	BB	SO	RAT	ERA	ERA+	OAV	OOB	BH	AVG	PB	PR	/A	PD	TPI
1953 Mil-N	0	1	.000	24	0	0	0	0	38¹	34	4	27	23	14.6	3.52	111	.239	.365	1	.500	1	3	2	0	0.1
1954 Mil-N	11	6	.647	47	1	0	0	10	111¹	87	6	64	62	12.4	2.43	154	.215	.326	9	.290	3	20	16	0	3.0
1955 Mil-N	3	3	.400	36	0	0	0	6	58¹	58	6	51	23	17.0	5.71	66	.258	.397	1	.167	0	-11	-13	1	-0.9
1956 Mil-N	2	3	.400	29	0	0	0	2	45²	39	7	35	20	14.6	3.74	92	.228	.359	0	.000	-0	-1	-1	1	-0.2
1957 Mil-N	1	1	.500	23	0	0	0	1	37²	37	4	21	27	14.6	5.02	70	.264	.372	3	.600	1	-5	-6	0	-0.2
Total 5	16	14	.533	159	1	0	0	19	291¹	255	27	198	155	14.2	3.77	98	.236	.357	14	.292	5	8	-3	0	1.7

● **COWBOY JONES**   Jones, Albert Edward "Bronco" b: 8/23/1874, Golden, Colo.   d: 2/9/58, Inglewood, Cal.   BL/TL, 5'11", 160 lbs.   Deb: 6/24/1898

YEAR TM/L	W	L	PCT	G	GS	CG	SH	SV	IP	H	HR	BB	SO	RAT	ERA	ERA+	OAV	OOB	BH	AVG	PB	PR	/A	PD	TPI
1898 Cle-N	4	4	.500	9	9	7	0	0	72	76	0	29	26	13.6	3.00	121	.269	.345	2	.071	-3	5	5	-2	0.0
1899 StL-N	6	5	.545	12	12	9	0	0	85¹	111	1	22	28	14.7	3.59	111	.314	.364	5	.172	0	3	4	2	0.6
1900 StL-N	13	19	.406	39	36	29	3	0	292²	334	10	82	68	13.4	3.57	102	.286	.343	21	.179	-3	4	2	5	0.4
1901 StL-N	2	6	.250	10	9	7	0	0	76¹	97	4	22	25	14.4	4.48	71	.307	.358	4	.148	0	-10	-11	2	-0.8
Total 4	25	34	.424	70	66	52	3	0	526¹	618	15	155	147	13.8	3.63	100	.292	.349	32	.159	-5	2	-0	6	0.2

● **ALEX JONES**   Jones, Alexander b: 12/25/1869, Pittsburgh, Pa.   d: 4/4/41, Woodville, Pa.   BL/TL, 5'6", 135 lbs.   Deb: 9/25/1889

YEAR TM/L	W	L	PCT	G	GS	CG	SH	SV	IP	H	HR	BB	SO	RAT	ERA	ERA+	OAV	OOB	BH	AVG	PB	PR	/A	PD	TPI
1889 Pit-N	1	0	1.000	1	1	1	0	0	9	7	0	1	10	8.0	3.00	125	.208	.231	1	.200	0	1	1	0	0.1
1892 Lou-N	5	11	.313	18	16	13	1	0	146²	130	3	56	44	12.0	3.31	93	.228	.307	8	.145	-1	-0	-4	2	-0.3

YEAR TM/L	W	L	PCT	G	GS	CG	SH	SV	IP	H	HR	BB	SO	RAT	ERA	ERA+	OAV	OOB	BH	AVG	PB	PR	/A	PD	TPI
Was-N	0	3	.000	4	4	3	0	0	27	33	0	14	7	16.3	4.00	81	.290	.377	3	.273	0	-2	-2	-1	-0.2
Yr	5	14	.263	22	20	16	1	0	173^2	163	3	70	51	12.2	3.42	91	.235	.307	11	.167	-1	-3	-6	1	-0.5
1894 Phi-N	1	0	1.000	1	1	1	0	0	9	10	0	0	2	10.0	2.00	255	.278	.278	1	.250	-0	3	3	0	0.2
1903 Det-A	0	1	.000	2	2	0	0	0	8^2	19	0	6	2	26.0	12.46	23	.435	.503	0	.000	-1	-9	-9	-0	-0.8
Total 4	7	15	.318	26	24	18	1	0	200^1	199	3	77	65	12.9	3.73	86	.250	.324	13	.165	-1	-7	-12	1	-1.0

● AL JONES
Jones, Alfornia b: 2/10/59, Charleston, Miss. BR/TR, 6'4", 210 lbs. Deb: 8/6/83

YEAR TM/L	W	L	PCT	G	GS	CG	SH	SV	IP	H	HR	BB	SO	RAT	ERA	ERA+	OAV	OOB	BH	AVG	PB	PR	/A	PD	TPI
1983 Chi-A	0	0	—	2	0	0	0	0	2^1	3	0	2	0	19.3	3.86	109	.375	.500	0	—	0	0	0	-0	0.0
1984 Chi-A	1	1	.500	20	0	0	0	5	20^1	23	3	11	15	15.5	4.43	94	.299	.393	0	—	0	-1	-1	0	-0.3
1985 Chi-A	1	0	1.000	5	0	0	0	0	6	3	0	3	4	15.0	1.50	288	.167	.286	0	—	0	2	2	0	0.3
Total 3	2	1	.667	27	0	0	0	5	28^2	29	3	16	19	14.4	3.77	111	.282	.383	0	—	0	1	1	0	0.3

● ART JONES
Jones, Arthur Lennox b: 2/7/06, Kershaw, S.C. d: 11/25/80, Columbia, S.C. BR/TR, 6', 165 lbs. Deb: 4/23/32

YEAR TM/L	W	L	PCT	G	GS	CG	SH	SV	IP	H	HR	BB	SO	RAT	ERA	ERA+	OAV	OOB	BH	AVG	PB	PR	/A	PD	TPI
1932 Bro-N	0	0	—	1	0	0	0	0	1	2	0	1	0	27.0	18.00	21	.667	.750	0	—	0	-2	-2	-0	0.0

● BARRY JONES
Jones, Barry Louis b: 2/15/63, Centerville, Ind. BR/TR, 6'4", 225 lbs. Deb: 7/18/86

YEAR TM/L	W	L	PCT	G	GS	CG	SH	SV	IP	H	HR	BB	SO	RAT	ERA	ERA+	OAV	OOB	BH	AVG	PB	PR	/A	PD	TPI
1986 Pit-N	3	4	.429	26	0	0	0	3	37^1	29	3	21	29	12.1	2.89	132	.215	.321	1	.200	0	3	4	1	0.8
1987 Pit-N	2	4	.333	32	0	0	0	1	43^1	55	6	23	28	16.2	5.61	73	.314	.394	0	.000	-0	-7	-7	0	-0.9
1988 Pit-N	1	1	.500	42	0	0	0	2	56^1	57	3	21	31	12.6	3.04	112	.271	.341	0	.000	-0	3	2	0	0.0
Chi-A	2	2	.500	17	0	0	0	0	26	15	3	17	17	11.1	2.42	164	.170	.305	0	—	0	4	4	0	0.7
1989 Chi-A	3	2	.600	22	0	0	0	1	30^1	22	2	8	17	9.2	2.37	160	.208	.270	0	—	0	5	5	1	0.9
1990 Chi-A	11	4	.733	65	0	0	0	1	74	62	3	33	45	11.7	2.31	160	.235	.322	0	—	0	13	12	2	2.7
1991 Mon-N	4	9	.308	**77**	0	0	0	13	88^2	76	8	33	46	11.2	3.35	108	.246	.321	0	.000	-0	3	3	1	0.5
1992 Phi-N	5	6	.455	44	0	0	0	0	54^1	65	3	24	19	15.1	4.64	75	.305	.381	0	.000	-0	-7	-7	1	-1.3
NY-N	2	0	1.000	17	0	0	0	0	15^1	20	0	11	11	18.2	9.39	37	.317	.419	0	—	0	-10	-10	0	-1.4
Yr	7	6	.538	61	0	0	0	1	69^2	85	3	35	30	15.5	5.68	61	.304	.381	0	.000	-0	-17	-17	1	-2.7
1993 Chi-A	0	1	.000	6	0	0	0	0	7^1	14	2	3	7	20.9	8.59	49	.412	.459	0	—	0	-3	-4	-0	-0.3
Total 8	33	33	.500	348	0	0	0	23	433	415	32	194	250	12.8	3.66	102	.260	.342	1	.063	-1	4	5	1	1.7

● CALVIN JONES
Jones, Calvin Douglas b: 9/26/63, Compton, Cal. BR/TR, 6'3", 185 lbs. Deb: 6/14/91

YEAR TM/L	W	L	PCT	G	GS	CG	SH	SV	IP	H	HR	BB	SO	RAT	ERA	ERA+	OAV	OOB	BH	AVG	PB	PR	/A	PD	TPI
1991 Sea-A	2	2	.500	27	0	0	0	2	46^1	33	0	29	42	12.2	2.53	163	.209	.335	0	—	0	8	8	0	0.8
1992 Sea-A	3	5	.375	38	1	0	0	0	61^2	50	8	47	49	14.4	5.69	70	.226	.367	0	—	0	-12	-12	-0	-1.4
Total 2	5	7	.417	65	1	0	0	2	108	83	8	76	91	13.5	4.33	93	.219	.354	0	—	0	-4	-4	0	-0.6

● DEACON JONES
Jones, Carroll Elmer b: 12/20/1892, Arcadia, Kan. d: 12/28/52, Pittsburg, Kan. BR/TR, 6'1", 174 lbs. Deb: 9/23/16

YEAR TM/L	W	L	PCT	G	GS	CG	SH	SV	IP	H	HR	BB	SO	RAT	ERA	ERA+	OAV	OOB	BH	AVG	PB	PR	/A	PD	TPI
1916 Det-A	0	0	—	1	0	0	0	0	7	7	0	5	2	15.4	2.57	111	.269	.387	0	.000	—	0	0	-0	0.0
1917 Det-A	4	4	.500	24	6	2	0	0	77	69	0	26	28	11.8	2.92	91	.256	.334	0	.000	-1	-2	-2	1	-0.2
1918 Det-A	3	1	.750	21	4	1	0	0	67	60	0	38	15	13.3	3.09	86	.244	.347	5	.185	-1	-2	-3	1	-0.1
Total 3	7	5	.583	46	10	3	0	0	151	136	0	69	45	12.6	2.98	89	.251	.343	5	.114	-2	-4	-5	2	-0.3

● BUMPUS JONES
Jones, Charles Leander b: 1/1/1870, Cedarville, Ohio d: 6/25/38, Xenia, Ohio BR/TR, Deb: 10/15/1892

YEAR TM/L	W	L	PCT	G	GS	CG	SH	SV	IP	H	HR	BB	SO	RAT	ERA	ERA+	OAV	OOB	BH	AVG	PB	PR	/A	PD	TPI
1892 Cin-N	1	0	1.000	1	1	1	0	0	9	0	0	4	3	4.0	0.00	—	.000	.129	0	.000	-0	3	3	-1	0.3
1893 Cin-N	1	3	.250	6	5	2	0	0	28^2	37	1	23	6	20.4	10.05	48	.304	.434	4	.250	1	-17	-17	-1	-1.5
NY-N	0	1	.000	1	1	0	0	0	4	5	0	10	1	36.0	11.25	41	.297	.575	0	—	0	-3	-3	1	-0.4
Yr	1	4	.200	7	6	2	0	0	32^2	42	1	33	7	20.9	10.19	47	.292	.428	4	.250	1	-20	-20	-0	-1.9
Total 2	2	4	.333	8	7	3	0	0	41^2	42	1	37	10	18.4	7.99	56	.254	.407	4	.222	1	-17	-16	-1	-1.6

● CHARLEY JONES
Jones, Charles Wesley "Baby" (b: Benjamin Wesley Rippay) b: 4/30/1850, Alamance Co., N.C. BR/TR, 5'11.5", 202 lbs. Deb: 5/4/1875 U♦

YEAR TM/L	W	L	PCT	G	GS	CG	SH	SV	IP	H	HR	BB	SO	RAT	ERA	ERA+	OAV	OOB	BH	AVG	PB	PR	/A	PD	TPI
1887 NY-a	0	0	—	2	0	0	0	0	2	2	0	0	0	9.0	3.00	142	.286	.545	63	.255	0	0	-0	-1	0.0

● DALE JONES
Jones, Dale Eldon "Nubs" b: 12/17/18, Marquette, Neb. d: 11/8/80, Orlando, Fla. BR/TR, 6'1", 172 lbs. Deb: 9/7/41

YEAR TM/L	W	L	PCT	G	GS	CG	SH	SV	IP	H	HR	BB	SO	RAT	ERA	ERA+	OAV	OOB	BH	AVG	PB	PR	/A	PD	TPI
1941 Phi-N	0	1	.000	7	0	0	0	0	8^1	13	0	6	2	20.5	7.56	49	.342	.432	1	.333	0	-4	-4	0	-0.4

● JACK JONES
Jones, Daniel Albion "Jumping Jack" b: 10/23/1860, Litchfield, Conn. d: 10/19/36, Wallingford, Conn. TR, Deb: 7/9/1883

YEAR TM/L	W	L	PCT	G	GS	CG	SH	SV	IP	H	HR	BB	SO	RAT	ERA	ERA+	OAV	OOB	BH	AVG	PB	PR	/A	PD	TPI
1883 Det-N	6	5	.545	12	12	9	1	0	92^2	103	0	19	33	11.8	3.50	89	.259	.293	8	.190	-2	-4	-4	-2	-0.6
Phi-a	5	2	.714	7	7	7	0	0	65	58	1	6	28	8.9	2.63	132	.223	.241	6	.240	0	5	6	-0	0.5
Total 1	11	7	.611	19	19	16	1	0	157^2	161	1	25	61	10.6	3.14	104	.245	.273	14	.209	-1	1	2	-1	-0.1

● DICK JONES
Jones, Decatur Poindexter b: 5/22/02, Meadville, Miss. BL/TR, 6', 184 lbs. Deb: 9/11/26

YEAR TM/L	W	L	PCT	G	GS	CG	SH	SV	IP	H	HR	BB	SO	RAT	ERA	ERA+	OAV	OOB	BH	AVG	PB	PR	/A	PD	TPI
1926 Was-A	2	1	.667	4	3	1	0	0	21	20	0	11	3	13.3	4.29	90	.263	.356	2	.200	0	-1	-1	0	-0.1
1927 Was-A	0	0	—	2	0	0	0	0	3^1	8	0	5	1	35.1	21.60	19	.444	.565	0	—	0	-6	-6	-0	0.0
Total 2	2	1	.667	6	3	1	0	0	24^1	28	0	16	4	16.3	6.66	58	.298	.400	2	.200	-0	-7	-7	-0	-0.1

● DOUG JONES
Jones, Douglas Reid b: 6/24/57, Lebanon, Ind. BR/TR, 6'3", 195 lbs. Deb: 4/9/82

YEAR TM/L	W	L	PCT	G	GS	CG	SH	SV	IP	H	HR	BB	SO	RAT	ERA	ERA+	OAV	OOB	BH	AVG	PB	PR	/A	PD	TPI
1982 Mil-A	0	0	—	4	0	0	0	0	2^2	5	1	1	1	20.3	10.13	37	.385	.429	0	—	0	-2	-2	0	0.0
1986 Cle-A	1	0	1.000	11	0	0	0	1	18	18	0	6	12	12.5	2.50	166	.257	.325	0	—	0	3	3	0	0.3
1987 Cle-A	6	5	.545	49	0	0	0	8	91^1	101	4	24	87	12.9	3.15	143	.281	.336	0	—	0	13	14	1	1.8
1988 Cle-A★	3	4	.429	51	0	0	0	37	83^1	69	1	16	72	9.4	2.27	181	.218	.260	0	—	0	16	17	0	3.1
1989 Cle-A★	7	10	.412	59	0	0	0	32	80^2	76	4	13	65	10.0	2.34	169	.251	.284	0	—	0	14	14	1	4.3
1990 Cle-A☆	5	5	.500	66	0	0	0	43	84^1	66	5	22	55	9.6	2.56	153	.218	.275	0	—	0	13	13	1	2.9
1991 Cle-A	4	8	.333	36	4	0	0	7	63^1	87	7	17	48	14.8	5.54	75	.320	.360	0	—	0	-10	-10	1	-1.8
1992 Hou-N★	11	8	.579	80	0	0	0	36	111^2	96	5	17	93	9.5	1.85	181	.235	.274	0	.000	0	20	19	1	4.5
1993 Hou-N	4	10	.286	71	0	0	0	26	85^1	102	7	21	66	13.5	4.54	85	.298	.348	0	—	0	-5	-6	-0	-1.4
1994 Phi-N★	2	4	.333	47	0	0	0	27	54	55	2	6	38	10.2	2.17	190	.255	.275	1	1.000	0	12	12	0	2.6
Total 10	43	54	.443	474	4	0	0	217	674^2	675	36	143	537	11.2	2.99	133	.259	.303	1	.200	0	75	74	0	16.3

● EARL JONES
Jones, Earl Leslie "Lefty" b: 6/11/19, Fresno, Cal. d: 1/24/89, Fresno, Cal. BL/TL, 5'10.5", 190 lbs. Deb: 7/6/45

YEAR TM/L	W	L	PCT	G	GS	CG	SH	SV	IP	H	HR	BB	SO	RAT	ERA	ERA+	OAV	OOB	BH	AVG	PB	PR	/A	PD	TPI
1945 StL-A	0	0	—	10	0	0	0	1	28^1	18	0	18	13	11.4	2.54	139	.184	.310	2	.200	1	3	3	-1	0.1

● ELIJAH JONES
Jones, Elijah Albert "Bumpus" b: 1/27/1882, Oxford, Mich. d: 4/29/43, Pontiac, Mich. BR/TR, 5'11.5", Deb: 4/13/07

YEAR TM/L	W	L	PCT	G	GS	CG	SH	SV	IP	H	HR	BB	SO	RAT	ERA	ERA+	OAV	OOB	BH	AVG	PB	PR	/A	PD	TPI
1907 Det-A	0	1	.000	4	1	0	0	1	16	23	0	9	4	15.8	5.06	52	.338	.383	0	.000	-1	-4	-4	-0	-0.4
1909 Det-A	1	1	.500	2	2	0	0	0	10	10	0	2	7	9.0	2.70	93	.278	.278	1	.250	0	-0	-0	-0	-0.1
Total 2	1	2	.333	6	3	1	0	1	26	33	0	11	4	13.2	4.15	62	.317	.349	1	.125	-0	-5	-5	-1	-0.5

● GARY JONES
Jones, Gareth Howell b: 6/12/45, Huntington Park, Cal. BL/TL, 6', 191 lbs. Deb: 9/25/70 F

YEAR TM/L	W	L	PCT	G	GS	CG	SH	SV	IP	H	HR	BB	SO	RAT	ERA	ERA+	OAV	OOB	BH	AVG	PB	PR	/A	PD	TPI
1970 NY-A	0	0	—	2	0	0	0	0	2	3	0	1	2	18.0	0.00	—	.375	.444	0	—	0	1	1	-0	0.0
1971 NY-A	0	0	—	12	0	0	0	0	14	19	1	7	10	16.7	9.00	36	.317	.388	0	.000	0	-9	-9	-0	0.0
Total 2	0	0	—	14	0	0	0	0	16	22	1	8	12	16.9	7.88	41	.324	.395	0	.000	0	-8	-8	-0	0.0

● GORDON JONES
Jones, Gordon Bassett b: 4/2/30, Portland, Ore. d: 4/25/94, Lodi, Cal. BR/TR, 6', 190 lbs. Deb: 8/6/54 C

YEAR TM/L	W	L	PCT	G	GS	CG	SH	SV	IP	H	HR	BB	SO	RAT	ERA	ERA+	OAV	OOB	BH	AVG	PB	PR	/A	PD	TPI
1954 StL-N	4	4	.500	11	10	4	2	0	81	78	3	19	48	10.9	2.00	206	.248	.293	3	.125	-1	19	19	-0	1.7
1955 StL-N	1	4	.200	15	9	4	0	0	57	66	9	14	35	15.0	5.84	70	.286	.365	1	.071	-1	-11	-11	-1	-1.1
1956 StL-N	0	2	.000	5	1	0	0	0	11^1	14	2	5	6	15.1	5.56	68	.311	.380	1	.500	-0	-3	-3	-1	-0.2
1957 NY-N	0	1	.000	5	1	0	0	0	11^2	16	1	4	7	15.4	6.17	64	.320	.370	1	.500	0	-3	-3	-1	-0.2
1958 SF-N	3	1	.750	11	0	0	0	1	30^1	33	2	5	8	11.6	2.37	161	.284	.320	0	.000	-1	5	5	1	0.6
1959 SF-N	3	2	.600	31	0	0	0	2	43^2	45	6	19	29	13.4	4.33	88	.280	.359	0	.000	0	-2	-3	-0	-0.4

YEAR	TM/L	W	L	PCT	G	GS	CG	SH	SV	IP	H	HR	BB	SO	RAT	ERA	ERA+	OAV	OOB	BH	AVG	PB	PR	/A	PD	TPI
1960	Bal-A	1	1	.500	29	0	0	0	2	55	59	9	13	30	11.9	4.42	86	.281	.326	2	.400	1	-3	-4	0	-0.1
1961	Bal-A	0	0	—	3	0	0	0	0	5	5	3	0	4	9.0	5.40	71	.250	.250	0	—	0	-1	-1	-0	0.0
1962	KC-A	3	2	.600	21	0	0	0	6	32²	31	10	14	28	12.4	6.34	67	.252	.328	0	.000	-1	-9	-8	-0	-1.4
1964	Hou-N	0	1	.000	34	0	0	0	0	50	58	3	14	28	13.0	4.14	83	.290	.336	1	.250	0	-3	-4	-0	-0.1
1965	Hou-N	0	0	—	1	0	0	0	0	1	0	0	0	0	0.0	0.00	—	.000	.000	0	—	0	0	0	-0	0.0
Total 11		15	18	.455	171	21	4	2	12	378²	405	49	120	232	12.6	4.16	94	.275	.332	8	.119	-3	-10	-11	-2	-1.4

● **HENRY JONES**   Jones, Henry b: Pittsburgh, Pa. Deb: 4/22/1890

1890	Pit-N	2	1	.667	5	4	2	0	0	31	35	1	14	13	14.2	3.48	95	.276	.348	2	.222	-0	0	-1	-1	-0.1

● **JIMMY JONES**   Jones, James Condia b: 4/20/64, Dallas, Tex. BR/TR, 6'2", 190 lbs. Deb: 9/21/86

1986	SD-N	2	0	1.000	3	3	1	1	0	18	10	1	3	15	6.5	2.50	146	.164	.203	1	.167	-0	2	2	-0	0.2
1987	SD-N	9	7	.563	30	22	2	1	0	145²	154	14	54	51	13.2	4.14	96	.270	.339	1	-1	-3	1	0		0.0
1988	SD-N	9	14	.391	29	29	3	0	0	179	192	14	44	82	12.0	4.12	82	.277	.323	9	.164	1	-13	-14	-1	-1.4
1989	NY-A	2	1	.667	11	6	0	0	0	48	56	7	16	25	13.9	5.25	74	.293	.354	0	—	0	-7	-7	1	-0.3
1990	NY-A	1	2	.333	17	7	0	0	0	50	72	8	23	25	17.3	6.30	63	.344	.412	0	—	0	-13	-13	-1	-0.8
1991	Hou-N	6	8	.429	26	22	1	1	0	135¹	143	9	51	88	13.1	4.39	80	.270	.337	7	.184	2	-11	-13	-1	-1.0
1992	Hou-N	10	6	.625	25	23	0	0	0	139¹	135	13	39	69	11.6	4.07	83	.258	.315	6	.167	2	-9	-11	-1	-1.1
1993	Mon-N	4	1	.800	12	6	0	0	0	39²	47	6	9	21	12.7	6.35	66	.285	.322	1	.111	0	-10	-10	-0	-1.0
Total 8		43	39	.524	153	118	7	3	0	755	809	72	239	376	12.7	4.46	81	.275	.333	32	.166	7	-62	-69	3	-5.4

● **JIM JONES**   Jones, James Tilford "Sheriff" b: 12/25/1876, London, Ky. d: 5/6/53, London, Ky. BR/TR, 5'10", 162 lbs. Deb: 6/29/1897 ◆

1897	Lou-N	0	0	—	1	0	0	0	0	6²	19	1	5	0	35.1	18.90	23	.498	.576	1	.250	1	-11	-11	-0	-0.0
1901	NY-N	0	1	.000	1	1	1	0	0	5	6	0	2	3	14.4	10.80	31	.295	.358	19	.209	-0	-4	-4	-0	-0.5
Total 2		0	1	.000	2	1	1	0	0	11²	25	1	7	3	26.2	15.43	25	.428	.504	79	.230	1	-15	-15	-0	-0.5

● **JEFF JONES**   Jones, Jeffrey Allen b: 7/29/56, Detroit, Mich. BR/TR, 6'3", 210 lbs. Deb: 4/10/80

1980	Oak-A	1	3	.250	35	0	0	0	5	44¹	32	2	26	34	12.0	2.84	133	.204	.321	0	—	0	6	5	1	0.6
1981	*Oak-A	4	1	.800	33	0	0	0	3	61	51	7	40	43	13.9	3.39	102	.233	.359	0	—	0	2	1	-0	0.0
1982	Oak-A	3	1	.750	18	2	0	0	0	37	44	6	26	18	17.3	5.11	76	.306	.415	0	—	0	-4	-5	-0	-0.5
1983	Oak-A	1	1	.500	13	1	0	0	0	29²	43	7	8	14	16.1	5.76	67	.339	.387	0	—	0	-6	-6	-0	-0.4
1984	Oak-A	0	3	.000	13	0	0	0	0	33	31	4	12	19	11.7	3.55	106	.258	.326	0	—	0	2	1	-0	0.4
Total 5		9	9	.500	112	3	0	0	8	205	201	26	112	128	14.0	3.95	94	.262	.361	0	—	0	0	-3	0	0.1

● **BROADWAY JONES**   Jones, Jesse Frank b: 11/15/1898, Millsboro, Del. d: 9/7/77, Lewes, Del. BR/TR, 5'9", 154 lbs. Deb: 7/4/23

1923	Phi-N	0	0	—	3	0	0	0	0	8	5	0	7	1	13.5	9.00	51	.185	.353	1	.500	0	-4	-4	-0	0.0

● **JOHNNY JONES**   Jones, John Paul "Admiral" b: 8/25/1892, Arcadia, La. d: 6/5/80, Ruston, La. BR/TR, 6'1", 151 lbs. Deb: 4/24/19

1919	NY-N	0	0	—	2	0	0	0	1	6²	9	0	3	2	17.6	5.40	52	.310	.394	-0	-2	-2	0			-0.1
1920	Bos-N	1	0	1.000	3	1	0	0	0	9²	16	1	5	6	19.6	6.52	47	.372	.438	1	.250	1	-4	-4	0	-0.3
Total 2		1	0	1.000	5	1	0	0	1	16¹	25	1	8	9	18.7	6.06	49	.347	.420	1	.143	0	-5	-6	0	-0.4

● **STACY JONES**   Jones, Joseph Stacy b: 5/26/67, Gadsden, Ala. BR/TR, 6'6", 225 lbs. Deb: 7/30/91

1991	Bal-A	0	0		4	1	0	0	0	11	11	1	5	10	13.1	4.09	97	.256	.333	0	—	0	0	-0	0	0.3

● **KEN JONES**   Jones, Kenneth Frederick "Broadway" b: 4/13/03, Dover, N.J. d: 5/15/91, Hartford, Conn. BR/TR, 6'3", 193 lbs. Deb: 5/19/24

1924	Det-A	0	0	—	1	0	0	0	0	2	1	0	1	0	9.0	0.00	—	.143	.250	0	—	0	1	1	-0	0.0
1930	Bos-N	0	1	.000	8	1	0	0	0	19²	28	1	4	4	14.6	5.95	83	.359	.390	1	.200	-0	-2	-2	-0	-0.1
Total 2		0	1	.000	9	1	0	0	0	21²	29	1	5	4	14.1	5.40	90	.341	.378	1	.200	-0	-1	-1	-0	-0.1

● **MIKE JONES**   Jones, Michael b: 7/6/1865, Hamilton, Ont., Canada d: 3/24/1894, Hamilton, Ont., Canada BL/TL, 5'11.5", 168 lbs. Deb: 8/12/1890

1890	Lou-a	2	0	1.000	3	3	3	0	0	22	21	2	9	6	12.3	3.27	118	.244	.315	4	.444	2	1	1	-0	0.2

● **MIKE JONES**   Jones, Michael Carl b: 7/30/59, Penfield, N.Y. BL/TL, 6'6", 215 lbs. Deb: 9/6/80

1980	KC-A	0	1	.000	3	1	0	0	0	4²	6	0	5	2	21.2	11.57	35	.333	.478	0	—	0	-4	-4	-0	-0.7
1981	*KC-A	6	3	.667	12	11	0	0	0	75²	74	7	28	29	12.4	3.21	112	.256	.326	0	—	0	4	3	0	0.4
1984	*KC-A	2	3	.400	23	12	0	0	0	81	86	10	36	43	13.7	4.89	82	.270	.346	0	—	0	-8	-8	-1	-0.5
1985	KC-A	3	3	.500	33	1	0	0	0	64	62	6	39	32	14.2	4.78	87	.257	.361	0	—	0	-5	-4	-0	-0.4
Total 4		11	10	.524	71	25	0	0	0	225¹	228	23	108	106	13.5	4.43	88	.263	.347	0	—	0	-13	-13	-1	-1.2

● **ODELL JONES**   Jones, Odell b: 1/13/53, Tulare, Cal. BR/TR, 6'3", 175 lbs. Deb: 9/11/75

1975	Pit-N	0	0	—						3	1	0	2	2	3.0	0.00	—	.100	.100	0		0	1	1	0	0.0
1977	Pit-N	3	7	.300	34	15	1	0	0	108	118	14	31	66	12.7	5.08	78	.278	.332	4	.143	-1	-14	-13	-2	-1.4
1978	Pit-N	1	0	1.000	3	1	0	0	0	9	7	0	4	10	11.0	2.00	185	.206	.289	0	.000	0	2	2	-0	0.4
1979	Sea-A	3	11	.214	25	19	3	0	0	118²	151	16	58	72	16.1	6.07	72	.317	.395	0	—	0	-24	-23	-2	-2.4
1981	Pit-N	4	5	.444	13	8	0	0	0	54¹	51	3	30	30	12.3	3.31	108	.250	.326	2	.200	-0	1	2	0	0.3
1983	Tex-A	6	3	.333	42	0	0	0	10	67	56	4	22	50	10.7	3.09	130	.223	.291	0	—	0	7	7	-1	1.0
1984	Tex-A	2	4	.333	33	0	0	0	0	59¹	62	7	23	28	13.2	3.64	114	.281	.354	0	—	0	2	3	1	0.4
1986	Bal-A	2	2	.500	21	0	0	0	2	49¹	58	4	23	32	14.8	3.83	108	.305	.380	0	—	0	2	2	-0	0.1
1988	Mil-A	5	0	1.000	28	2	0	0	1	80²	75	8	29	48	11.7	4.35	91	.251	.319	0	—	0	-3	-3	-1	-0.3
Total 9		24	35	.407	201	45	4	0	13	549¹	579	56	213	338	13.2	4.42	92	.275	.344	6	.154	-1	-27	-23	-5	-1.9

● **OSCAR JONES**   Jones, Oscar Winfield "Flip Flap" b: 1/21/1879, London Grove, Pa. d: 10/8/46, Perkasie, Pa. BR/TR, 5'7", 163 lbs. Deb: 4/20/03

1903	Bro-N	19	14	.576	38	36	31	4	0	324¹	320	4	77	95	11.5	2.94	109	.260	.313	32	.256	1	12	9	-3	0.7
1904	Bro-N	17	25	.405	46	41	38	0	0	377	387	7	92	96	11.8	2.75	100	.270	.321	24	.175	-1	-0	0	-7	-0.8
1905	Bro-N	8	15	.348	29	20	14	0	1	174	197	6	56	66	13.6	4.66	62	.285	.347	13	.200	-0	-32	-34	-4	-4.3
Total 3		44	54	.449	113	97	83	4	1	875¹	904	17	225	257	12.1	3.20	90	.269	.324	69	.211	2	-20	-25	-14	-4.4

● **PERCY JONES**   Jones, Percy Lee b: 10/28/1899, Harwood, Tex. d: 3/18/79, Dallas, Tex. BR/TL, 5'11.5", 175 lbs. Deb: 8/6/20

1920	Chi-N	0	0	—	4	0	0	0	0	7	15	1	3	0	24.4	11.57	28	.455	.514	0	.000	-0	-7	-7	-0	-0.6
1921	Chi-N	3	5	.375	32	5	1	0	0	98²	116	2	39	46	14.5	4.56	84	.295	.365	6	.222	-0	-9	-8	-2	-0.8
1922	Chi-N	8	9	.471	44	26	7	1	0	162	197	10	68	45	15.0	4.78	88	.310	.381	4	.085	-4	-12	-10	0	-1.3
1925	Chi-N	6	6	.500	28	13	6	0	0	124	123	12	71	60	14.4	4.65	93	.263	.366	6	.154	-3	-5	-4	-2	-0.4
1926	Chi-N	12	7	.632	30	20	10	2	2	160²	151	9	90	80	13.8	3.09	125	.256	.359	13	.260	-3	13	13	-1	1.6
1927	Chi-N	7	8	.467	30	11	5	0	0	112²	123	7	72	37	16.1	4.07	95	.285	.394	14	.350	3	-2	-3	2	0.1
1928	Chi-N	10	6	.625	39	18	9	1	3	154	167	4	56	41	13.4	4.03	95	.288	.358	11	.196	0	-1	-3	0	-0.4
1929	Bos-N	7	15	.318	35	22	11	1	0	188¹	219	15	84	69	14.7	4.64	101	.298	.373	9	.148	-3	2	1	-1	-0.1
1930	Pit-N	0	1	.000	9	2	0	0	0	19	26	3	11	3	18.9	6.63	75	.329	.430	0	.000	-0	-4	-3	-1	-0.2
Total 9		53	57	.482	251	117	49	8	6	1026	1137	53	494	381	14.7	4.34	95	.288	.373	63	.194	-5	-24	-24	1	-1.5

● **RANDY JONES**   Jones, Randall Leo b: 1/12/50, Fullerton, Cal. BR/TL, 6', 178 lbs. Deb: 6/16/73

1973	SD-N	7	6	.538	20	19	6	1	0	139²	129	13	37	77	10.8	3.16	110	.241	.291	8	.167	0	8	5	0	0.4
1974	SD-N	8	22	.267	40	34	4	1	2	208¹	217	16	78	124	13.6	4.46	70	.270	.339	11	.159	-1	-19	-21	-2	-2.6
1975	SD-N★	20	12	.625	37	36	18	6	0	285	242	16	56	103	**9.4**	**2.24**	155	.232	.271	11	.133	-1	44	39	5	**4.9**
1976	SD-N★	**22**	14	.611	40	40	**25**	5	0	**315¹**	274	15	50	93	**9.4**	2.74	119	.234	**.267**	6	.058	-6	27	19	8	2.3
1977	SD-N	6	12	.333	27	25	1	0	0	147¹	173	12	36	44	12.8	4.58	77	.291	.332	5	.116	-1	-11	-17	4	-1.6

YEAR TM/L	W	L	PCT	G	GS	CG	SH	SV	IP	H	HR	BB	SO	RAT	ERA	ERA+	OAV	OOB	BH	AVG	PB	PR	/A	PD	TPI
1978 SD-N	13	14	.481	37	36	7	2	0	253	263	6	64	71	11.6	2.88	115	.272	.317	15	.183	1	20	12	2	1.6
1979 SD-N	11	12	.478	39	39	6	0	0	263	257	17	64	112	11.1	3.63	97	.259	.306	15	.174	0	3	-3	4	0.2
1980 SD-N	5	13	.278	24	24	4	3	0	154²	165	14	29	53	11.3	3.91	88	.275	.310	3	.067	-3	-5	-8	3	-0.9
1981 NY-N	1	8	.111	13	12	0	0	0	59¹	65	8	38	14	15.8	4.85	72	.274	.377	2	.118	-1	-9	-9	2	-1.2
1982 NY-N	7	10	.412	28	20	2	1	0	107²	130	11	51	44	15.5	4.60	79	.304	.384	4	.148	0	-12	-12	3	-1.4
Total 10	100	123	.448	305	285	73	19	2	1933	1915	129	503	735	11.3	3.42	101	.260	.309	79	.132	-12	44	6	32	1.7

● **BOBBY JONES** Jones, Robert Joseph b: 2/10/70, Fresno, Cal. BR/TR, 6'4", 210 lbs. Deb: 8/14/93

YEAR TM/L	W	L	PCT	G	GS	CG	SH	SV	IP	H	HR	BB	SO	RAT	ERA	ERA+	OAV	OOB	BH	AVG	PB	PR	/A	PD	TPI
1993 NY-N	2	4	.333	9	9	0	0	0	61²	61	6	22	35	12.4	3.65	110	.262	.331	1	.050	-2	3	2	-0	0.0
1994 NY-N	12	7	.632	24	24	1	1	0	160	157	10	56	80	12.2	3.15	135	.257	.324	5	.109	-2	19	20	2	2.2
Total 2	14	11	.560	33	33	1	1	0	221²	218	16	78	115	12.3	3.29	127	.259	.326	6	.091	-4	22	22	2	2.2

● **SAM JONES** Jones, Samuel "Toothpick Sam" b: 12/14/25, Stewartsville, Ohio d: 11/5/71, Morgantown, W.Va. BR/TR, 6'4", 200 lbs. Deb: 9/22/51

YEAR TM/L	W	L	PCT	G	GS	CG	SH	SV	IP	H	HR	BB	SO	RAT	ERA	ERA+	OAV	OOB	BH	AVG	PB	PR	/A	PD	TPI
1951 Cle-A	0	1	.000	2	1	0	0	0	8²	4	0	5	4	9.3	2.08	182	.143	.273	0	.000	-0	2	1	-0	0.1
1952 Cle-A	2	3	.400	14	4	0	0	1	36	38	6	37	28	19.8	7.25	46	.270	.434	1	.100	-1	-14	-16	-1	-2.1
1955 Chi-N★	14	20	.412	36	34	12	4	0	241²	175	22	185	**198**	13.9	4.10	100	**.206**	.357	14	.182	-2	-2	-0	-0	-0.2
1956 Chi-N	9	14	.391	33	28	8	2	0	188²	155	21	115	**176**	13.3	3.91	96	.221	.338	10	.175	0	-3	-3	-1	-0.4
1957 StL-N	12	9	.571	28	27	10	2	0	182²	164	17	71	154	11.9	3.60	110	.239	.316	10	.159	-1	6	7	0	0.7
1958 StL-N	14	13	.519	35	35	14	2	0	250	204	23	107	**225**	11.4	2.88	143	.223	.309	9	.100	-6	30	**35**	-0	2.9
1959 SF-N★	**21**	15	.583	50	35	16	**4**	4	270²	232	18	109	209	11.6	**2.83**	135	**.228**	.307	11	.129	-2	**34**	30	-2	3.4
1960 SF-N	18	14	.563	39	35	13	3	0	234	200	18	91	190	11.3	3.19	109	.230	.306	16	.200	1	15	7	-2	0.9
1961 SF-N	8	8	.500	37	17	2	0	1	128¹	134	12	57	105	14.0	4.49	85	.264	.348	5	.139	-1	-7	-10	-2	-1.3
1962 Det-A	2	4	.333	30	6	1	0	1	81¹	77	13	35	73	12.6	3.65	111	.254	.335	2	.095	-1	3	4	-0	0.2
1963 StL-N	2	0	1.000	11	0	0	0	2	11	15	0	5	8	16.4	9.00	39	.319	.385	0	—	0	-7	-7	-0	-1.4
1964 Bal-A	0	0	—	7	0	0	0	0	10¹	5	1	6	6	8.7	2.61	137	.152	.263	0	—	0	1	1	-0	0.0
Total 12	102	101	.502	322	222	76	17	9	1643¹	1403	151	822	1376	12.5	3.59	108	.230	.328	78	.149	-11	58	50	-8	2.8

● **SAM JONES** Jones, Samuel Pond "Sad Sam" b: 7/26/1892, Woodsfield, Ohio d: 7/6/66, Barnesville, Ohio BR/TR, 6', 170 lbs. Deb: 6/13/14

YEAR TM/L	W	L	PCT	G	GS	CG	SH	SV	IP	H	HR	BB	SO	RAT	ERA	ERA+	OAV	OOB	BH	AVG	PB	PR	/A	PD	TPI
1914 Cle-A	0	0	—	1	0	0	0	0	3¹	2	0	2	0	10.8	2.70	107	.200	.333	1	.500	0	0	0	0	0.0
1915 Cle-A	4	9	.308	48	9	2	0	4	145²	131	0	63	42	12.0	3.65	84	.252	.334	5	.156	-0	-11	-10	-0	-0.9
1916 Bos-A	0	1	.000	12	0	0	0	1	27	25	0	10	7	11.7	3.67	76	.272	.343	2	.333	1	-3	-3	0	-0.1
1917 Bos-A	0	1	.000	9	1	0	0	1	16¹	15	1	6	5	11.6	4.41	59	.259	.328	0	.000	-1	-3	-3	1	-0.3
1918 *Bos-A	16	5	**.762**	24	21	16	5	0	184	151	1	70	44	11.2	2.25	119	.230	.312	10	.175	2	11	9	-1	1.1
1919 Bos-A	12	20	.375	35	31	21	5	1	245	258	4	95	67	13.2	3.75	81	.278	.350	11	.136	-0	-14	-20	3	-2.2
1920 Bos-A	13	16	.448	37	33	21	3	0	274	302	9	79	86	12.6	3.94	93	.288	.340	20	.217	1	-4	-9	-1	-0.8
1921 Bos-A	23	16	.590	40	38	25	**5**	1	298²	318	11	78	98	12.1	3.22	131	.279	.329	24	.240	5	35	33	-3	4.0
1922 *NY-A	13	13	.500	45	28	20	0	**8**	260	270	16	76	81	12.1	3.67	109	.275	.329	23	.284	8	11	10	-1	1.6
1923 *NY-A	21	8	.724	39	27	18	3	4	243	239	11	69	68	11.6	3.63	109	.257	.312	19	.224	1	10	8	1	1.1
1924 NY-A	9	6	.600	36	21	8	3	3	178²	187	6	76	53	13.3	3.66	115	.276	.350	9	.176	-0	12	11	-1	0.7
1925 NY-A	15	21	.417	43	31	14	1	2	246²	267	14	104	92	13.6	4.63	92	.281	.354	13	.162	-3	-7	-10	-0	-1.5
1926 *NY-A	9	8	.529	39	23	6	1	5	161	186	6	80	69	15.1	4.98	77	.298	.381	10	.204	1	-17	-20	-1	-2.0
1927 StL-A	8	14	.364	30	26	11	0	0	189²	211	13	102	72	15.0	4.32	101	.282	.371	6	.109	-2	-4	1	-2	-0.3
1928 Was-A	17	7	.708	30	27	19	4	0	224²	209	5	78	63	11.6	2.84	141	.253	.319	20	.253	6	30	29	1	3.5
1929 Was-A	9	9	.500	24	24	8	1	0	153²	156	5	49	36	12.2	3.92	108	.264	.324	8	.157	0	5	5	-1	0.4
1930 Was-A	15	7	.682	25	25	14	1	0	183¹	195	4	61	60	12.7	4.07	113	.277	.337	9	.148	-1	12	11	-1	0.8
1931 Was-A	9	10	.474	25	24	8	1	1	148	185	10	47	58	14.4	4.32	99	.304	.358	15	.313	4	1	-0	-0	0.3
1932 Chi-A	10	15	.400	30	28	10	0	0	200¹	217	9	75	64	13.3	4.22	102	.270	.335	11	.193	2	6	2	3	0.7
1933 Chi-A	10	12	.455	27	25	11	2	0	176²	181	13	65	60	12.7	3.36	126	.265	.333	9	.155	-0	18	17	-1	1.8
1934 Chi-A	8	12	.400	27	26	11	0	0	183¹	217	16	60	60	13.7	5.11	93	.289	.343	12	.200	2	-12	-8	-2	-0.7
1935 Chi-A	8	7	.533	21	19	7	0	0	140	162	9	55	31	13.8	4.05	114	.284	.343	8	.167	0	6	9	0	0.9
Total 22	229	217	.513	647	487	250	36	31	3883	4084	152	1396	1223	12.9	3.84	104	.274	.339	245	.197	25	81	61	-8	8.1

● **SHELDON JONES** Jones, Sheldon Leslie "Available" b: 2/2/22, Tecumseh, Neb. d: 4/18/91, Greenville, N.C. BR/TR, 6', 180 lbs. Deb: 9/9/46

YEAR TM/L	W	L	PCT	G	GS	CG	SH	SV	IP	H	HR	BB	SO	RAT	ERA	ERA+	OAV	OOB	BH	AVG	PB	PR	/A	PD	TPI
1946 NY-N	1	2	.333	6	4	1	0	0	28	21	4	17	24	12.5	3.21	107	.208	.328	2	.250	0	1	1	-0	0.1
1947 NY-N	2	2	.500	15	6	1	0	0	55²	51	2	29	24	13.4	3.88	105	.250	.352	2	.125	-1	1	1	-1	-0.1
1948 NY-N	16	8	.667	55	21	8	1	5	201¹	204	16	90	82	13.4	3.35	117	.263	.344	13	.203	1	14	13	0	1.6
1949 NY-N	15	12	.556	42	27	11	1	0	207¹	198	19	88	79	12.8	3.34	119	.248	.331	8	.121	-3	16	15	-0	1.4
1950 NY-N	13	16	.448	40	28	11	2	2	199	188	26	90	97	12.9	4.61	89	.249	.335	6	.105	-2	-10	-11	-2	-1.9
1951 *NY-N	6	11	.353	41	12	2	0	4	120¹	119	12	52	58	13.1	4.26	92	.260	.340	3	.097	-1	-4	-5	-2	-0.7
1952 Bos-N	1	4	.200	39	1	0	0	1	70	81	8	31	40	14.5	4.76	76	.286	.359	1	.125	-0	-8	-9	-0	-0.6
1953 Chi-N	0	2	.000	22	2	0	0	0	38¹	47	3	16	9	16.0	5.40	82	.299	.382	0	.000	-1	-5	-4	0	-0.3
Total 8	54	57	.486	260	101	33	4	12	920	909	90	413	413	13.3	3.96	100	.258	.342	35	.136	-7	4	1	-3	-0.5

● **SHERMAN JONES** Jones, Sherman Jarvis "Roadblock" b: 2/10/35, Winton, N.C. BL/TR, 6'4", 205 lbs. Deb: 8/2/60

YEAR TM/L	W	L	PCT	G	GS	CG	SH	SV	IP	H	HR	BB	SO	RAT	ERA	ERA+	OAV	OOB	BH	AVG	PB	PR	/A	PD	TPI
1960 SF-N	1	1	.500	16	0	0	0	0	32	37	3	11	10	13.8	3.09	112	.291	.353	2	.286	0	2	1	-1	0.1
1961 *Cin-N	1	1	.500	24	2	0	0	0	55	51	6	27	32	13.1	4.42	92	.256	.351	2	.182	0	-2	-2	-0	-0.1
1962 NY-N	0	4	.000	8	3	0	0	3	23¹	31	3	8	11	15.8	7.71	54	.326	.390	3	.429	1	-10	-9	-0	-1.2
Total 3	2	6	.250	48	5	0	0	3	110¹	119	12	46	53	13.9	4.73	83	.283	.360	7	.280	1	-10	-10	-1	-1.2

● **STEVE JONES** Jones, Steven Howell b: 4/22/41, Huntington Park, Cal. BL/TL, 5'10", 175 lbs. Deb: 8/15/67 F

YEAR TM/L	W	L	PCT	G	GS	CG	SH	SV	IP	H	HR	BB	SO	RAT	ERA	ERA+	OAV	OOB	BH	AVG	PB	PR	/A	PD	TPI
1967 Chi-A	2	2	.500	11	0	0	0	0	25²	21	1	12	17	11.6	4.21	74	.223	.311	1	.250	0	-3	-3	-0	-0.5
1968 Was-A	1	2	.333	7	0	0	0	0	10²	8	3	7	11	12.7	5.91	49	.205	.326	0	.000	-0	-3	-4	-0	-1.0
1969 KC-A	2	3	.400	20	4	0	0	0	44²	45	3	24	31	14.5	4.23	87	.260	.360	1	.125	0	-3	-3	-0	-0.2
Total 3	5	7	.417	38	7	0	0	0	81	74	7	43	59	13.3	4.44	76	.242	.341	2	.154	1	-9	-9	-1	-1.7

● **RICK JONES** Jones, Thomas Fredrick b: 4/16/55, Jacksonville, Fla. BL/TL, 6'5", 190 lbs. Deb: 4/18/76

YEAR TM/L	W	L	PCT	G	GS	CG	SH	SV	IP	H	HR	BB	SO	RAT	ERA	ERA+	OAV	OOB	BH	AVG	PB	PR	/A	PD	TPI
1976 Bos-A	5	3	.625	24	14	1	0	0	104¹	133	6	26	45	13.8	3.36	116	.311	.352	0	—	0	2	6	-0	0.4
1977 Sea-A	1	4	.200	10	10	1	0	0	42¹	47	10	37	16	17.9	5.10	81	.283	.414	0	—	0	-5	-5	-0	-0.4
1978 Sea-A	0	2	.000	3	2	0	0	0	12¹	17	1	7	11	17.5	5.84	65	.315	.393	0	—	0	-3	-3	-0	-0.4
Total 3	6	9	.400	37	26	1	0	0	159	197	17	70	72	15.2	4.02	99	.304	.373	0	—	0	-6	-1	-0	-0.4

● **TIM JONES** Jones, Timmothy Byron b: 1/24/54, Sacramento, Cal. BB/TR, 6'5", 220 lbs. Deb: 9/4/77

YEAR TM/L	W	L	PCT	G	GS	CG	SH	SV	IP	H	HR	BB	SO	RAT	ERA	ERA+	OAV	OOB	BH	AVG	PB	PR	/A	PD	TPI
1977 Pit-N	1	0	1.000	10	0	0	0	0	10	4	0	3	6	6.3	0.90	—	.118	.189	0	.000	-0	4	4	-0	0.4

● **TODD JONES** Jones, Todd Barton Givin b: 4/24/68, Marietta, Ga. BL/TR, 6'3", 200 lbs. Deb: 7/7/93

YEAR TM/L	W	L	PCT	G	GS	CG	SH	SV	IP	H	HR	BB	SO	RAT	ERA	ERA+	OAV	OOB	BH	AVG	PB	PR	/A	PD	TPI
1993 Hou-N	1	2	.333	27	0	0	0	2	37¹	28	4	15	25	10.6	3.13	124	.214	.299	0	—	0	4	3	-0	0.2
1994 Hou-N	5	2	.714	48	0	0	0	5	72²	52	3	26	63	9.8	2.72	149	.202	.278	2	.400	1	12	11	-1	1.0
Total 2	6	4	.600	75	0	0	0	7	110	80	7	41	88	10.1	2.86	140	.206	.285	2	.400	1	16	14	-2	1.2

● **TIM JONES** Jones, William Timothy b: 12/1/62, Sumter, S.C. BL/TR, 5'10", 172 lbs. Deb: 7/26/88 ♦

YEAR TM/L	W	L	PCT	G	GS	CG	SH	SV	IP	H	HR	BB	SO	RAT	ERA	ERA+	OAV	OOB	BH	AVG	PB	PR	/A	PD	TPI
1990 StL-N	0	0	—	1	0	0	0	0	1¹	1	0	2	0	20.3	6.75	57	.167	.375	28	.219	0	-0	-0	0	0.0

● **CLAUDE JONNARD** Jonnard, Claude Alfred b: 11/23/1897, Nashville, Tenn. d: 8/27/59, Nashville, Tenn. BR/TR, 6'1", 165 lbs. Deb: 10/1/21 F

YEAR TM/L	W	L	PCT	G	GS	CG	SH	SV	IP	H	HR	BB	SO	RAT	ERA	ERA+	OAV	OOB	BH	AVG	PB	PR	/A	PD	TPI
1921 NY-N	0	0	—	1	0	0	0	1	4	4	0	0	7	9.0	0.00	—	.267	.267	0	.000	-0	2	2	-0	0.1
1922 NY-N	6	1	.857	33	0	0	0	**5**	96	96	7	28	44	11.9	3.84	104	.272	.331	1	.042	-3	3	2	-2	-0.3

YEAR TM/L	W	L	PCT	G	GS	CG	SH	SV	IP	H	HR	BB	SO	RAT	ERA	ERA+	OAV	OOB	BH	AVG	PB	PR	/A	PD	TPI
1923 *NY-N	4	3	.571	**45**	1	1	0	**5**	96	105	6	35	45	13.1	3.28	116	.279	.340	1	.038	-3	8	6	-1	0.1
1924 *NY-N	4	5	.444	34	3	1	0	5	89²	80	2	24	40	10.6	2.41	152	.229	.282	1	.045	-3	**15**	**13**	-0	1.0
1926 StL-A	0	2	.000	12	3	0	0	1	36	46	1	24	13	17.5	6.00	71	.313	.409	0	.000	-1	-8	-7	1	-0.3
1929 Chi-N	0	1	.000	12	2	0	0	0	27²	41	4	11	11	17.2	7.48	62	.320	.379	2	.200	-1	-9	-9	0	-0.2
Total 6	14	12	.538	137	9	2	0	17	349¹	372	20	122	160	12.9	3.79	104	.272	.334	5	.056	-9	10	6	-1	0.4

● **CHARLIE JORDAN**   Jordan, Charles T. "Kid" b: 10/4/1871, Baltimore, Md. d: 6/1/28, Hazleton, Pa. Deb: 7/31/1896

YEAR TM/L	W	L	PCT	G	GS	CG	SH	SV	IP	H	HR	BB	SO	RAT	ERA	ERA+	OAV	OOB	BH	AVG	PB	PR	/A	PD	TPI
1896 Phi-N	0	0	—	2	0	0	0	0	4²	9	0	2	3	21.2	7.71	56	.402	.451	1	.500	0	-2	-2	0	0.0

● **HARRY JORDAN**   Jordan, Harry J. b: 2/14/1873, Pittsburgh, Pa. d: 3/1/20, Pittsburgh, Pa. Deb: 9/25/1894

YEAR TM/L	W	L	PCT	G	GS	CG	SH	SV	IP	H	HR	BB	SO	RAT	ERA	ERA+	OAV	OOB	BH	AVG	PB	PR	/A	PD	TPI
1894 Pit-N	1	0	1.000	1	1	1	0	0	9	10	0	2	1	13.0	4.00	131	.278	.334	0	.000	-0	1	1	-0	0.1
1895 Pit-N	0	2	.000	2	2	2	0	0	17	24	0	4	4	16.4	4.24	107	.327	.386	2	.286	-0	1	1	-0	0.1
Total 2	1	2	.333	3	3	3	0	0	26	34	0	6	5	15.2	4.15	115	.311	.369	2	.200	-0	1	1	-1	0.1

● **MILT JORDAN**   Jordan, Milton Mignot b: 5/24/27, Mineral Springs, Pa. d: 5/13/93, Ithaca, N.Y. BR/TR, 6'2.5", 207 lbs. Deb: 4/16/53

YEAR TM/L	W	L	PCT	G	GS	CG	SH	SV	IP	H	HR	BB	SO	RAT	ERA	ERA+	OAV	OOB	BH	AVG	PB	PR	/A	PD	TPI
1953 Det-A	0	1	.000	8	1	0	0	0	17	26	3	5	6	16.4	5.82	70	.366	.408	1	.500	0	-3	-3	0	-0.1

● **NILES JORDAN**   Jordan, Niles Chapman b: 12/1/25, Lyman, Wash. BL/TL, 5'11", 180 lbs. Deb: 8/26/51

YEAR TM/L	W	L	PCT	G	GS	CG	SH	SV	IP	H	HR	BB	SO	RAT	ERA	ERA+	OAV	OOB	BH	AVG	PB	PR	/A	PD	TPI
1951 Phi-N	2	3	.400	5	5	2	1	0	36²	35	4	8	11	10.6	3.19	121	.250	.291	1	.077	-1	3	3	-1	0.2
1952 Cin-N	0	1	.000	3	1	0	0	0	6¹	14	1	3	2	24.2	9.95	38	.452	.500	0	.000	-0	-4	-4	0	-0.6
Total 2	2	4	.333	8	6	2	1	0	43	49	5	11	13	12.6	4.19	92	.287	.330	1	.071	-1	-1	-2	-1	-0.4

● **RIP JORDAN**   Jordan, Raymond Willis "Lanky" b: 9/28/1889, Portland, Me. d: 6/5/60, Meriden, Conn. BL/TR, 6', 172 lbs. Deb: 6/25/12

YEAR TM/L	W	L	PCT	G	GS	CG	SH	SV	IP	H	HR	BB	SO	RAT	ERA	ERA+	OAV	OOB	BH	AVG	PB	PR	/A	PD	TPI
1912 Chi-A	0	0	—	4	0	0	0	0	12¹	13	2	3	1	12.4	5.11	63	.289	.347	0	.000	-1	-2	-3	-0	-0.1
1919 Was-A	0	0	—	1	1	0	0	0	4	6	1	2	2	18.0	11.25	29	.353	.421	0	.000	-0	-4	-4	-0	0.0
Total 2	0	0	—	5	1	0	0	0	16¹	19	3	5	3	13.8	6.61	48	.306	.368	0	.000	-1	-6	-6	-1	-0.1

● **ORVILLE JORGENS**   Jorgens, Orville Edward b: 6/4/08, Rockford, Ill. d: 1/11/92, Colorado Springs, Colo. BR/TR, 6'1", 180 lbs. Deb: 4/19/35 F

YEAR TM/L	W	L	PCT	G	GS	CG	SH	SV	IP	H	HR	BB	SO	RAT	ERA	ERA+	OAV	OOB	BH	AVG	PB	PR	/A	PD	TPI
1935 Phi-N	10	15	.400	**53**	24	6	0	2	188¹	216	12	96	57	15.3	4.83	94	.283	.370	6	.097	-5	-17	-6	3	-0.9
1936 Phi-N	8	8	.500	39	21	4	0	0	167¹	196	16	69	58	14.6	4.79	95	.290	.361	12	.200	-1	-14	-5	1	-0.4
1937 Phi-N	3	4	.429	52	11	1	0	3	140²	159	12	68	34	14.8	4.41	98	.298	.383	5	.143	-1	-8	-1	2	0.0
Total 3	21	27	.438	144	56	11	0	5	496¹	571	40	233	149	14.9	4.70	95	.290	.370	23	.146	-7	-39	-12	5	-1.3

● **ADDIE JOSS**   Joss, Adrian b: 4/12/1880, Woodland, Wis. d: 4/14/11, Toledo, Ohio BR/TR, 6'3", 185 lbs. Deb: 4/26/02 H

YEAR TM/L	W	L	PCT	G	GS	CG	SH	SV	IP	H	HR	BB	SO	RAT	ERA	ERA+	OAV	OOB	BH	AVG	PB	PR	/A	PD	TPI
1902 Cle-A	17	13	.567	32	29	28	**5**	0	269¹	225	2	75	106	10.5	2.77	124	.228	.291	12	.117	-5	24	20	6	2.0
1903 Cle-A	18	13	.581	32	31	31	3	0	283²	232	3	37	120	**8.8**	2.19	130	.223	**.256**	22	.193	0	24	21	4	2.7
1904 Cle-A	14	10	.583	25	24	20	5	0	192¹	160	0	30	83	9.2	**1.59**	159	.227	.266	10	.132	-4	22	20	0	2.2
1905 Cle-A	20	12	.625	33	32	31	3	0	286	246	4	46	132	9.5	2.01	131	.233	.273	13	.134	-0	21	20	5	2.7
1906 Cle-A	21	9	.700	34	31	28	9	1	282	220	3	43	106	8.5	1.72	152	.218	.252	21	.210	2	30	28	2	3.7
1907 Cle-A	**27**	11	.711	42	38	34	6	2	338²	279	3	54	127	9.0	1.83	137	.226	.263	13	.114	-5	27	26	9	3.4
1908 Cle-A	24	11	.686	42	35	29	9	2	325	232	2	30	130	**7.3**	**1.16**	**206**	**.197**	**.218**	15	.155	2	45	44	2	5.9
1909 Cle-A	14	13	.519	33	28	24	4	0	242²	198	0	31	67	8.6	1.71	150	.226	.255	8	.100	-3	21	23	0	2.4
1910 Cle-A	5	5	.500	13	12	9	1	0	107¹	96	2	18	49	9.7	2.26	114	.245	.282	4	.111	-1	3	4	2	0.4
Total 9	160	97	.623	286	260	234	45	5	2327	1888	19	364	920	8.9	1.89	142	.223	.260	118	.144	-14	216	207	30	25.4

● **MIKE JOYCE**   Joyce, Michael Lewis b: 2/12/41, Detroit, Mich. BR/TR, 6'2", 193 lbs. Deb: 7/2/62

YEAR TM/L	W	L	PCT	G	GS	CG	SH	SV	IP	H	HR	BB	SO	RAT	ERA	ERA+	OAV	OOB	BH	AVG	PB	PR	/A	PD	TPI
1962 Chi-A	2	1	.667	25	1	0	0	2	43¹	40	2	14	9	11.2	3.32	118	.247	.307	3	.429	1	3	3	0	0.3
1963 Chi-A	0	0	—	6	0	0	0	0	10²	13	1	8	7	17.7	8.44	42	.289	.396	0	—	-0	-6	-6	-0	0.0
Total 2	2	1	.667	31	1	0	0	2	54	53	3	22	16	12.5	4.33	88	.256	.328	3	.429	1	-3	-3	0	0.3

● **DICK JOYCE**   Joyce, Richard Edward b: 11/18/43, Portland, Me. BL/TL, 6'5", 225 lbs. Deb: 9/3/65

YEAR TM/L	W	L	PCT	G	GS	CG	SH	SV	IP	H	HR	BB	SO	RAT	ERA	ERA+	OAV	OOB	BH	AVG	PB	PR	/A	PD	TPI
1965 KC-A	0	1	.000	5	3	0	0	0	13	12	0	4	7	11.1	2.77	126	.240	.296	0	.000	-0	1	1	-0	0.0

● **BOB JOYCE**   Joyce, Robert Emmett b: 1/14/15, Stockton, Cal. d: 12/10/81, San Francisco, Cal BR/TR, 6'1", 180 lbs. Deb: 5/4/39

YEAR TM/L	W	L	PCT	G	GS	CG	SH	SV	IP	H	HR	BB	SO	RAT	ERA	ERA+	OAV	OOB	BH	AVG	PB	PR	/A	PD	TPI
1939 Phi-A	3	5	.375	30	6	1	0	0	107²	156	13	37	25	16.2	6.69	70	.337	.387	3	.086	-3	-25	-24	1	-1.6
1946 NY-N	3	4	.429	14	7	2	0	0	60²	79	3	20	24	14.7	5.34	64	.315	.365	3	.158	0	-13	-13	1	-1.2
Total 2	6	9	.400	44	13	3	0	0	168¹	235	16	57	49	15.7	6.20	69	.329	.380	6	.111	-3	-38	-37	2	-2.8

● **RALPH JUDD**   Judd, Ralph Wesley b: 12/7/01, Perrysburg, Ohio d: 5/6/57, Lapeer, Mich. BL/TL, 5'10", 170 lbs. Deb: 10/2/27

YEAR TM/L	W	L	PCT	G	GS	CG	SH	SV	IP	H	HR	BB	SO	RAT	ERA	ERA+	OAV	OOB	BH	AVG	PB	PR	/A	PD	TPI
1927 Was-A	0	0	—	1	0	0	0	1	4	8	0	2	2	22.5	6.75	60	.400	.455	0	.000	-0	-1	-1	-0	-0.1
1929 NY-N	3	0	1.000	18	0	0	0	0	50²	49	4	11	21	10.7	2.66	172	.261	.302	0	.000	-2	12	11	0	0.4
1930 NY-N	0	0	—	2	0	0	0	0	7²	13	0	3	0	18.8	5.87	81	.390	.441	0	.000	-1	-1	-1	-0	-0.1
Total 3	3	0	1.000	21	0	0	0	1	62¹	70	4	16	23	12.4	3.32	138	.290	.334	0	.000	-3	10	9	0	0.2

● **OSCAR JUDD**   Judd, Thomas William Oscar "Ossie" b: 2/14/08, London, Ont., Can. BL/TL, 6'0.5", 180 lbs. Deb: 4/16/41

YEAR TM/L	W	L	PCT	G	GS	CG	SH	SV	IP	H	HR	BB	SO	RAT	ERA	ERA+	OAV	OOB	BH	AVG	PB	PR	/A	PD	TPI
1941 Bos-A	0	0	—	7	0	0	0	1	12¹	15	1	10	5	18.2	8.76	48	.300	.417	2	.500	2	-6	-6	-0	0.1
1942 Bos-A	8	10	.444	31	19	11	0	2	150¹	135	3	90	70	13.6	3.89	96	.239	.346	18	.269	6	-4	-3	-0	0.3
1943 Bos-A☆	11	6	.647	23	20	8	1	0	155¹	131	2	69	53	11.8	2.90	114	.230	.317	14	.259	4	7	7	2	1.4
1944 Bos-A	1	1	.500	9	6	1	0	0	30	30	1	15	9	13.5	3.60	94	.261	.346	2	.182	1	-1	-1	-0	0.0
1945 Bos-A	0	1	.000	2	1	0	0	0	6¹	14	1	3	5	18.5	8.53	40	.333	.394	1	.500	0	-4	-4	-0	-0.4
Phi-N	5	4	.556	23	9	3	1	2	82²	80	3	40	30	13.2	3.81	101	.254	.340	8	.267	3	-0	0	1	0.4
1946 Phi-N	11	12	.478	30	24	12	1	2	173¹	169	6	90	65	13.5	3.53	97	.260	.350	25	.316	8	-2	-2	4	1.1
1947 Phi-N	4	15	.211	32	19	8	1	0	146²	155	6	69	54	13.9	4.60	87	.279	.361	12	.188	2	-9	-10	1	-0.7
1948 Phi-N	0	2	.000	4	1	0	0	0	14¹	19	1	11	7	18.8	6.91	57	.317	.423	1	.167	0	-5	-5	-0	-0.5
Total 8	40	51	.440	161	99	43	4	7	771¹	744	24	397	304	13.4	3.90	93	.256	.347	83	.262	26	-23	-22	8	1.7

● **JEFF JUDEN**   Juden, Jeffrey Daniel b: 1/19/71, Salem, Mass. BR/TR, 6'7", 245 lbs. Deb: 9/15/91

YEAR TM/L	W	L	PCT	G	GS	CG	SH	SV	IP	H	HR	BB	SO	RAT	ERA	ERA+	OAV	OOB	BH	AVG	PB	PR	/A	PD	TPI
1991 Hou-N	0	2	.000	4	3	0	0	0	18	19	3	7	11	13.0	6.00	58	.275	.342	0	.000	-1	-5	-5	-1	-0.6
1993 Hou-N	0	1	.000	2	0	0	0	0	5	4	1	4	7	14.4	5.40	72	.222	.364	0	—	0	-1	-1	-0	-0.2
1994 Phi-N	1	4	.200	6	5	0	0	0	27²	29	4	12	22	13.7	6.18	67	.276	.356	1	.111	-0	-6	-6	-0	-1.0
Total 3	1	7	.125	12	8	0	0	0	50²	52	8	23	40	13.5	6.04	64	.271	.352	1	.071	-1	-11	-12	-1	-1.8

● **HOWIE JUDSON**   Judson, Howard Kolls b: 2/16/26, Hebron, Ill. BR/TR, 6'1", 195 lbs. Deb: 4/22/48

YEAR TM/L	W	L	PCT	G	GS	CG	SH	SV	IP	H	HR	BB	SO	RAT	ERA	ERA+	OAV	OOB	BH	AVG	PB	PR	/A	PD	TPI
1948 Chi-A	4	5	.444	40	5	0	0	1	107¹	102	7	56	38	13.5	4.78	89	.255	.351	3	.103	-2	-6	-6	0	-0.7
1949 Chi-A	1	14	.067	26	12	3	0	1	108	114	6	70	63	15.4	4.58	91	.274	.380	2	.065	-3	-5	-5	0	-0.8
1950 Chi-A	2	3	.400	46	3	1	0	1	112	105	10	63	34	13.7	3.94	114	.252	.353	2	.100	-1	**8**	**7**	-2	0.1
1951 Chi-A	5	6	.455	27	14	3	0	0	121²	124	5	55	43	13.4	3.77	107	.264	.343	4	.121	-2	5	4	0	0.1
1952 Chi-A	0	1	.000	21	0	0	0	0	34	30	4	22	15	13.8	4.24	86	.244	.359	0	.000	-0	-2	-2	-0	-0.1
1953 Cin-N	0	1	.000	10	6	0	0	0	38²	58	8	11	11	16.1	5.59	78	.341	.381	1	.111	-1	-6	-5	0	-0.2
1954 Cin-N	5	7	.417	37	8	0	0	0	93¹	86	9	42	27	12.6	3.95	106	.251	.338	2	.083	-2	1	-2	2	-0.1
Total 7	17	37	.315	207	48	8	0	14	615	619	60	319	204	13.9	4.29	98	.265	.356	14	.093	-9	-4	-6	-3	-1.4

● **KEN JUNGELS**   Jungels, Kenneth Peter "Curly" b: 6/23/16, Aurora, Ill. d: 9/9/75, West Bend, Wis. BR/TR, 6'1", 180 lbs. Deb: 9/15/37

YEAR TM/L	W	L	PCT	G	GS	CG	SH	SV	IP	H	HR	BB	SO	RAT	ERA	ERA+	OAV	OOB	BH	AVG	PB	PR	/A	PD	TPI
1937 Cle-A	0	0	—	3	0	0	0	0	3	3	0	1	0	12.0	0.00	—	.273	.333	0	—	0	2	2	0	0.0
1938 Cle-A	1	0	1.000	9	0	0	0	0	15¹	21	1	18	7	24.1	8.80	53	.339	.500	0	.000	-1	-7	-7	-0	-0.4
1940 Cle-A	0	0	—	2	0	0	0	0	3¹	3	0	1	1	10.8	2.70	156	.273	.333	0	.000	-0	1	1	0	0.0

YEAR	TM/L	W	L	PCT	G	GS	CG	SH	SV	IP	H	HR	BB	SO	RAT	ERA	ERA+	OAV	OOB	BH	AVG	PB	PR	/A	PD	TPI
1941	Cle-A	0	0	—	6	0	0	0	0	13²	17	4	8	6	17.1	7.24	54	.293	.388	0	.000	-0	-5	-5	-0	-0.1
1942	Pit-N	0	0	—	6	0	0	0	0	13²	12	0	4	7	10.5	6.59	51	.235	.291	1	.500	0	-5	-5	-0	0.0
Total	5	1	0	1.000	25	0	0	0	0	49	56	5	32	21	16.7	6.80	60	.290	.399	1	.100	-1	-14	-15	-0	-0.5

● **MIKE JUREWICZ**   Jurewicz, Michael Allen   b: 9/20/45, Buffalo, N.Y.   BB/TL, 6'3", 205 lbs.   Deb: 9/7/65

| 1965 | NY-A | 0 | 0 | — | 2 | 0 | 0 | 0 | 0 | 2¹ | 5 | 0 | 1 | 2 | 23.1 | 7.71 | 44 | .417 | .462 | 0 | | 0 | -1 | -1 | -0 | 0.0 |

● **AL JURISICH**   Jurisich, Alvin Joseph   b: 8/25/21, New Orleans, La.   d: 11/3/81, New Orleans, La.   BR/TR, 6'2", 193 lbs.   Deb: 4/26/44

1944	*StL-N	7	9	.438	30	14	5	2	1	130	102	7	65	53	11.9	3.39	104	.221	.323	8	.178	-1	3	2	-1	0.0
1945	StL-N	3	3	.500	27	6	1	0	0	71²	61	7	41	42	12.9	5.15	73	.232	.338	2	.087	-2	-11	-11	-1	-1.1
1946	Phi-N	4	3	.571	13	10	2	1	1	68¹	71	9	31	34	13.6	3.69	93	.263	.341	3	.130	-0	-2	-2	-1	-0.4
1947	Phi-N	1	7	.125	34	12	5	0	3	118¹	110	15	52	48	12.4	4.94	81	.258	.340	1	.032	-3	-12	-12	-2	-1.2
Total	4	15	22	.405	104	42	13	3	5	388¹	344	38	189	177	12.5	4.24	87	.242	.334	14	.115	-6	-21	-24	-5	-2.7

● **WALT JUSTIS**   Justis, Walter Newton "Smoke"   b: 8/17/1883, Moores Hill, Ind.   d: 10/4/41, Lawrenceburg, Ind.   BR/TR, 5'11.5", 195 lbs.   Deb: 8/1/05

| 1905 | Det-A | 0 | 0 | — | 2 | 0 | 0 | 0 | 0 | 3¹ | 4 | 0 | 6 | 0 | 29.7 | 8.10 | 34 | .298 | .539 | 0 | | 0 | -2 | -2 | -0 | 0.0 |

● **HEROLD JUUL**   Juul, Earl Herold   b: 5/21/1893, Chicago, Ill.   d: 1/4/42, Chicago, Ill.   BR/TR, 5'9.5", 150 lbs.   Deb: 4/24/14

| 1914 | Bro-F | 0 | 3 | .000 | 9 | 3 | 0 | 0 | 0 | 29 | 26 | 0 | 31 | 16 | 18.0 | 6.21 | 46 | .248 | .423 | 2 | .222 | -0 | -11 | -11 | -0 | -1.0 |

● **HERB JUUL**   Juul, Herbert Victor   b: 2/2/1886, Chicago, Ill.   d: 11/14/28, Chicago, Ill.   BL/TL, 5'11", 150 lbs.   Deb: 7/11/11 ♦

| 1911 | Cin-N | 0 | 0 | — | 1 | 0 | 0 | 0 | 0 | 4 | 3 | 0 | 4 | 2 | 15.8 | 4.50 | 74 | .231 | .412 | 0 | .000 | -0 | -0 | -1 | -0 | 0.0 |

● **JIM KAAT**   Kaat, James Lee   b: 11/7/38, Zeeland, Mich.   BL/TL, 6'4", 217 lbs.   Deb: 8/2/59   C♦

1959	Was-A	0	2	.000	3	2	0	0	0	5	7	1	4	2	23.4	12.60	31	.350	.500	-0	.000	-0	-5	-5	-0	-1.4
1960	Was-A	1	5	.167	13	9	0	0	0	50	48	8	31	25	15.1	5.58	70	.255	.375	2	.143	-1	-9	-9	0	-1.0
1961	Min-A	9	17	.346	36	29	8	1	0	200²	188	12	82	122	12.6	3.90	109	.248	.331	15	.238	3	3	8	3	1.6
1962	Min-A☆	18	14	.563	39	35	16	**5**	1	269	243	23	75	173	11.2	3.14	130	.243	.307	18	.180	3	25	28	6	**4.2**
1963	Min-A	10	10	.500	31	27	7	1	1	178¹	195	24	38	105	12.2	4.19	87	.274	.319	8	.131	-0	-11	-11	4	-0.7
1964	Min-A	17	11	.607	36	34	13	0	1	243	231	23	60	171	11.1	3.22	111	.251	.304	14	.169	5	11	10	3	1.9
1965	*Min-A★	18	11	.621	45	42	7	2	2	264¹	267	25	63	154	11.4	2.83	126	.258	.304	23	.247	6	19	21	3	3.5
1966	Min-A★	**25**	13	.658	41	41	**19**	3	0	304²	271	29	55	205	9.7	2.75	131	.235	.271	23	.195	4	23	**29**	0	**4.1**
1967	Min-A	16	13	.552	42	38	13	2	0	263¹	269	21	42	211	10.9	3.04	114	.260	.295	17	.172	5	6	12	1	1.8
1968	Min-A	14	12	.538	30	29	9	2	0	208	192	16	40	130	10.2	2.94	105	.243	.282	12	.156	0	1	3	-0	0.4
1969	Min-A	14	13	.519	40	32	10	0	1	242¹	252	23	75	139	12.5	3.49	105	.265	.325	18	.207	4	4	-3	0	0.9
1970	*Min-A	14	10	.583	45	34	4	1	0	230¹	244	26	58	120	11.9	3.56	105	.273	.319	15	.197	3	4	2	2	0.9
1971	Min-A	13	14	.481	39	38	15	4	0	260¹	275	16	47	137	11.3	3.32	107	.268	.304	15	.161	-0	4	7	-0	0.7
1972	Min-A	10	2	.833	15	15	5	0	0	113¹	94	9	20	64	9.1	2.06	155	.227	.263	13	.289	5	13	14	-0	2.3
1973	Min-A	11	12	.478	29	28	7	2	0	181¹	206	26	39	93	12.3	4.41	90	.282	.322	0		0	-12	-9	-1	-1.2
	Chi-A	4	1	.800	7	7	3	1	0	42²	44	4	4	16	10.1	4.22	94	.260	.277	0		0	-2	-1	-1	-0.2
	Yr	15	13	.536	36	35	10	3	0	224¹	250	30	43	109	11.8	4.37	90	.276	.309	0		0	-14	-10	-2	-1.4
1974	Chi-A	21	13	.618	42	39	15	3	0	277¹	263	18	63	142	10.8	2.92	128	.250	.296	0	.000	0	21	25	-2	2.8
1975	Chi-A★	20	14	.588	43	41	12	1	0	303²	321	20	77	142	12.1	3.11	124	.274	.324	0		0	22	26	-2	2.5
1976	*Phi-N	12	14	.462	38	35	7	1	0	227²	241	21	32	83	10.8	3.48	102	.274	.300	14	.177	2	1	2	-3	0.1
1977	Phi-N	6	11	.353	35	27	2	0	0	160¹	211	20	40	55	14.2	5.39	74	.320	.361	10	.189	1	-26	-25	-2	-2.4
1978	Phi-N	8	5	.615	26	24	1	0	0	140¹	150	9	32	48	12.0	4.10	87	.280	.326	7	.146	-1	-8	-8	-2	-1.0
1979	Phi-N	1	0	1.000	3	1	0	0	0	8¹	9	1	5	2	15.1	4.32	89	.281	.378	0	.000	0	-1	-0	-0	0.0
	NY-A	2	3	.400	40	1	0	0	2	58¹	64	4	14	23	12.3	3.86	106	.287	.335	0		0	2	1	-1	0.0
1980	NY-A	0	1	.000	4	0	0	0	0	5	8	0	4	1	21.6	7.20	54	.381	.480	0		0	-2	-2	1	-0.3
	StL-N	8	7	.533	49	14	0	0	4	129²	140	6	33	36	12.0	3.82	97	.281	.325	5	.143	-1	-3	-2	-2	-0.3
1981	StL-N	6	6	.500	41	1	0	0	4	53	60	2	17	8	13.1	3.40	105	.299	.353	3	.375	1	1	1	1	0.4
1982	*StL-N	5	3	.625	62	2	0	0	2	75	79	6	23	35	12.5	4.08	89	.276	.334	0	.000	-1	-4	-4	1	-0.5
1983	StL-N	0	0	—	24	0	0	0	0	34²	48	5	10	15	15.6	3.89	93	.327	.369	0	.000	-0	-1	-1	0	0.0
Total	25	283	237	.544	898	625	180	31	18	4530¹	4620	395	1083	2461	11.6	3.45	107	.264	.311	232	.185	41	74	119	6	19.0

● **GEORGE KAHLER**   Kahler, George Runnells "Krum"   b: 9/6/1889, Athens, Ohio   d: 2/7/24, Battle Creek, Va.   BR/TR, 6', 183 lbs.   Deb: 8/13/10

1910	Cle-A	6	4	.600	12	12	8	2	0	95¹	80	0	46	38	12.3	1.60	161	.237	.335	5	.143	-2	10	10	-1	0.8
1911	Cle-A	9	8	.529	30	17	10	0	1	154¹	153	1	66	97	13.5	3.27	104	.270	.360	9	.167	-2	1	3	-1	-0.1
1912	Cle-A	12	19	.387	41	32	17	3	1	246¹	263	1	121	104	14.4	3.69	92	.291	.382	9	.112	-5	-10	-8	-4	-1.7
1913	Cle-A	5	11	.313	24	15	5	0	0	117²	118	1	32	43	11.8	3.14	97	.266	.322	2	.061	-3	-3	-1	-4	-0.9
1914	Cle-A	0	1	.000	2	1	1	0	0	14	17	0	7	3	15.4	3.86	75	.309	.387	0	.000	-0	-2	-2	-0	-0.2
Total	5	32	43	.427	109	77	41	5	2	627²	631	3	272	285	13.4	3.17	101	.274	.358	25	.121	-13	-4	2	-9	-2.1

● **DON KAINER**   Kainer, Donald Wayne   b: 9/3/55, Houston, Tex.   BR/TR, 6'3", 205 lbs.   Deb: 9/6/80

| 1980 | Tex-A | 0 | 0 | — | 4 | 3 | 0 | 0 | 0 | 19² | 22 | 0 | 9 | 10 | 15.6 | 1.83 | 213 | .289 | .386 | 0 | — | 0 | 5 | 5 | 1 | 0.1 |

● **DON KAISER**   Kaiser, Clyde Donald "Tiger"   b: 2/3/35, Byng, Okla.   BR/TR, 6'5", 195 lbs.   Deb: 7/20/55

1955	Chi-N	0	0	—	11	0	0	0	0	18¹	20	2	5	11	12.8	5.40	76	.274	.329	0	.000	-0	-3	-3	-0	-0.1
1956	Chi-N	4	9	.308	27	22	5	1	0	150¹	144	15	52	74	11.8	3.59	105	.247	.310	2	.043	-5	3	3	-0	-0.3
1957	Chi-N	2	6	.250	20	13	1	0	0	72	91	4	28	23	14.9	5.00	77	.316	.377	2	.105	-1	-9	-9	2	-0.8
Total	3	6	15	.286	58	35	6	1	0	240²	255	21	85	108	12.8	4.15	92	.270	.332	4	.059	-6	-9	-9	1	-1.2

● **JEFF KAISER**   Kaiser, Jeffrey Patrick   b: 7/24/60, Wyandotte, Mich.   BR/TL, 6'3", 195 lbs.   Deb: 4/11/85

1985	Oak-A	0	0	—	15	0	0	0	0	16²	25	6	20	10	24.8	14.58	26	.342	.489	0	—	0	-19	-20	1	0.1
1987	Cle-A	0	0	—	2	0	0	0	0	3¹	4	1	3	2	21.6	16.20	28	.286	.444	0	—	0	-4	-4	0	0.0
1988	Cle-A	0	0	—	3	0	0	0	0	2²	2	0	1	6	10.1	0.00	—	.286	.375	0	—	0	1	1	0	0.0
1989	Cle-A	0	1	.000	6	0	0	0	0	3²	5	1	5	4	24.5	7.36	54	.313	.476	0	—	0	-1	-1	-0	-0.5
1990	Cle-A	0	0	—	5	0	0	0	0	12²	16	2	7	9	16.3	3.55	110	.308	.390	0	—	0	0	0	0	0.0
1991	Det-A	0	1	.000	10	0	0	0	2	11	9	1	8	4	19.8	9.00	46	.286	.423	0	—	0	-3	-3	0	-0.8
1993	Cin-N	0	0	—	6	0	0	0	0	3¹	4	0	2	4	16.2	2.70	149	.286	.375	0	—	0	0	-0	-0	0.0
	NY-N	0	0	—	6	0	0	0	0	4²	6	1	3	5	17.4	11.57	35	.353	.450	0	—	0	-4	-4	0	0.0
	Yr	0	0	—	9	0	0	0	0	8	10	1	5	9	16.9	7.88	51	.323	.417	0	—	0	-3	-3	0	0.0
Total	7	0	2	.000	50	0	0	0	2	52	68	12	46	38	20.1	9.17	43	.318	.443	0	—	0	-30	-30	1	-1.2

● **BOB KAISER**   Kaiser, Robert Thomas   b: 4/29/50, Cincinnati, Ohio   BB/TL, 5'10", 175 lbs.   Deb: 9/3/71

| 1971 | Cle-A | 0 | 0 | — | 5 | 0 | 0 | 0 | 0 | 8 | 5 | 3 | 4 | 4 | 19.5 | 4.50 | 85 | .333 | .448 | 0 | — | 0 | -1 | -0 | 0 | -0.1 |

● **GEORGE KAISERLING**   Kaiserling, George   b: 5/12/1893, Steubenville, Ohio   d: 3/2/18, Steubenville, Ohio   BR/TR, 6', 175 lbs.   Deb: 4/20/14

1914	Ind-F	17	10	.630	37	33	20	1	0	275¹	288	8	72	75	12.3	3.11	100	.274	.330	11	.112	-7	-7	0	-3	-1.0
1915	New-F	15	15	.500	41	29	16	5	2	261¹	246	1	73	75	11.3	2.24	114	.257	.316	12	.152	-3	14	9	-1	0.6
Total	2	32	25	.561	78	62	36	6	2	536²	534	9	145	150	11.8	2.68	106	.266	.323	23	.130	-10	8	9	-5	-0.4

● **BILL KALFASS**   Kalfass, William Philip "Lefty"   b: 3/3/16, New York, N.Y.   d: 9/8/68, Brooklyn, N.Y.   BR/TL, 6'3.5", 190 lbs.   Deb: 9/15/37

| 1937 | Phi-A | 1 | 0 | 1.000 | 3 | 1 | 1 | 0 | 0 | 12 | 10 | 0 | 10 | 9 | 15.0 | 3.00 | 157 | .233 | .377 | 0 | .000 | -1 | 2 | 2 | -0 | 0.1 |

YEAR TM/L	W	L	PCT	G	GS	CG	SH	SV	IP	H	HR	BB	SO	RAT	ERA	ERA+	OAV	OOB	BH	AVG	PB	PR	/A	PD	TPI

● RUDY KALLIO   Kallio, Rudolph b: 12/14/1892, Portland, Ore.   d: 4/6/79, Newport, Ore.   BR/TR, 5'10", 160 lbs.   Deb: 4/25/18

1918 Det-A	8	14	.364	30	22	10	2	0	181¹	178	4	76	70	12.7	3.62	73	.261	.336	9	.161	-1	-17	-19	-0	-2.4
1919 Det-A	0	0	—	12	1	0	0	1	22¹	28	0	8	3	14.9	5.64	57	.326	.389	0	.000	-1	-6	-6	-0	-0.2
1925 Bos-A	1	4	.200	7	4	0	0	0	18²	28	0	9	2	18.3	7.71	59	.364	.437	2	.333	0	-7	-7	-0	-1.3
Total 3	9	18	.333	49	27	10	2	1	222¹	234	4	93	75	13.4	4.17	69	.277	.351	11	.167	-1	-30	-32	-1	-3.9

● SCOTT KAMIENIECKI   Kamieniecki, Scott Andrew b: 4/19/64, Mt.Clemens, Mich.   BR/TR, 6', 195 lbs.   Deb: 6/18/91

1991 NY-A	4	4	.500	9	9	0	0	0	55¹	54	8	22	34	12.8	3.90	106	.256	.335	0	—	0	1	1	1	0.2
1992 NY-A	6	14	.300	28	28	4	0	0	188	193	13	74	88	13.0	4.36	90	.269	.342	0	—	0	-9	-9	-1	-0.9
1993 NY-A	10	7	.588	30	20	2	0	1	154¹	163	17	59	72	13.1	4.08	102	.277	.346	0	—	0	4	1	1	0.4
1994 NY-A	8	6	.571	22	16	1	0	0	117¹	115	13	59	71	13.6	3.76	118	.261	.353	0	—	0	14	9	0	1.2
Total 4	28	31	.475	89	73	7	0	1	515	525	51	214	265	13.2	4.09	101	.268	.345	0	—	0	10	3	1	0.9

● BOB KAMMEYER   Kammeyer, Robert Lynn b: 12/2/50, Kansas City, Kan.   BR/TR, 6'4", 210 lbs.   Deb: 7/3/78

1978 NY-A	0	0	—	7	0	0	0	0	21²	24	1	6	11	13.3	5.82	62	.276	.337	0	—	0	-5	-5	1	0.1
1979 NY-A	0	0	—	1	0	0	0	0	0	7	2	0	0	—	∞	—	1.000	1.000	0	—	0	-8	-8	0	-0.6
Total 2	0	0	—	8	0	0	0	0	21²	31	3	6	11	16.6	9.14	40	.330	.388	0	—	0	-13	-13	1	-0.5

● IKE KAMP   Kamp, Alphonse Francis b: 9/5/1900, Roxbury, Mass.   d: 2/25/55, Boston, Mass.   BB/TL, 6', 170 lbs.   Deb: 9/16/24

1924 Bos-N	0	1	.000	1	1	0	0	0	7	9	0	5	4	18.0	5.14	74	.360	.467	0	.000	-0	-1	-1	0	-0.1
1925 Bos-N	2	4	.333	24	4	1	0	0	58¹	68	0	35	20	15.9	5.09	79	.301	.395	2	.167	-0	-5	-7	0	-0.6
Total 2	2	5	.286	25	5	1	0	0	65¹	77	0	40	24	16.1	5.10	78	.307	.402	2	.154	-0	-6	-8	1	-0.7

● HARRY KANE   Kane, Harry "Klondike" (b: Harry Cohen) b: 7/27/1883, Hamburg, Ark.   d: 9/15/32, Portland, Ore.   BL/TL,   Deb: 8/8/02

1902 StL-A	0	1	.000	4	1	0	0	0	23	34	2	16	7	19.6	5.48	64	.343	.434	1	.111	-1	-5	-5	-0	-0.3
1903 Det-A	0	2	.000	3	3	2	0	0	18	26	0	8	10	17.5	8.50	34	.336	.405	1	.143	-0	-11	-11	-1	-1.0
1905 Phi-N	1	1	.500	2	2	1	0	0	17	12	0	8	12	10.6	1.59	184	.203	.299	1	.167	-0	3	3	-0	0.2
1906 Phi-N	1	3	.250	6	3	4	0	0	28	28	0	18	14	15.8	3.86	68	.255	.374	0	.000	-1	-4	-4	0	-0.6
Total 4	2	7	.222	15	9	7	1	0	86	100	2	50	43	16.1	4.81	62	.289	.385	3	.100	-2	-17	-17	-1	-1.7

● ERV KANTLEHNER   Kantlehner, Erving Leslie "Peanuts" b: 7/31/1892, San Jose, Cal.   d: 2/3/90, Santa Barbara, Cal.   BL/TL, 6', 190 lbs.   Deb: 4/17/14

1914 Pit-N	3	2	.600	21	5	3	2	0	67	51	0	39	26	12.5	3.09	86	.218	.337	1	.067	-0	-2	-3	-0	-0.3
1915 Pit-N	5	12	.294	29	18	10	1	3	163	135	1	58	64	10.9	2.26	121	.230	.304	15	.288	3	9	8	1	1.4
1916 Pit-N	5	15	.250	34	21	7	0	2	165	151	1	57	49	11.6	3.16	85	.249	.317	8	.174	-0	-10	-9	1	-1.0
Phi-N	0	0	—	3	0	0	0	0	4	7	0	3	2	22.5	9.00	29	.500	.588	0	—	0	-3	-3	0	-0.0
Yr	5	15	.250	37	21	7	2	2	169	158	1	60	51	11.6	3.30	81	.253	.318	8	.174	-0	-13	-12	1	-1.0
Total 3	13	29	.310	87	44	20	5	5	399	344	2	157	141	11.5	2.84	95	.239	.318	24	.212	2	-6	-6	2	0.1

● PAUL KARDOW   Kardow, Paul Otto "Tex" b: 9/19/15, Humble, Tex.   d: 4/27/68, San Antonio, Tex.   BR/TR, 6'6", 210 lbs.   Deb: 7/1/36

| 1936 Cle-A | 0 | 0 | — | 2 | 0 | 0 | 0 | 0 | 2 | 1 | 0 | 2 | 0 | 13.5 | 4.50 | 112 | .167 | .375 | 0 | — | 0 | 0 | 0 | 0 | 0.0 |

● ED KARGER   Karger, Edwin "Loose" b: 5/6/1883, San Angelo, Tex.   d: 9/9/57, Delta, Colo.   BR/TL, 5'11", 185 lbs.   Deb: 4/15/06

1906 Pit-N	2	3	.400	6	2	0	0	0	28	21	0	9	8	10.3	1.93	139	.204	.281	1	.091	-1	2	2	1	0.5
StL-N	5	16	.238	25	20	17	0	1	191²	193	0	43	73	11.4	2.72	97	.271	.319	17	.233	4	-2	-2	3	0.6
Yr	7	19	.269	31	22	17	0	1	219²	214	0	52	81	11.2	2.62	100	.262	.312	18	.214	3	0	0	4	1.1
1907 StL-N	15	19	.441	39	32	29	6	1	314	257	2	65	137	9.5	2.04	123	.223	.270	20	.179	1	15	16	4	2.6
1908 StL-N	4	9	.308	22	15	9	1	0	141¹	148	1	50	34	12.7	3.06	77	.260	.322	13	.241	0	-11	-11	-1	-0.8
1909 Cin-N	1	3	.250	9	5	1	0	0	34¹	26	0	30	8	15.2	4.46	58	.217	.382	3	.273	2	-7	-7	-0	-0.6
Bos-A	5	2	.714	12	6	3	0	0	68	71	0	22	17	12.7	3.18	79	.271	.337	3	.125	-0	-5	-5	-0	-0.4
1910 Bos-A	11	7	.611	27	25	16	1	1	183¹	162	5	53	81	10.8	3.19	80	.230	.289	20	.294	6	-14	-13	-2	-0.9
1911 Bos-A	5	8	.385	25	18	6	1	0	131	134	4	42	57	12.4	3.37	97	.272	.334	11	.234	3	-0	-1	-0	0.2
Total 6	48	67	.417	165	123	81	9	3	1091²	1012	12	314	415	11.2	2.79	94	.246	.305	88	.220	18	-22	-20	5	1.0

● ANDY KARL   Karl, Anton Andrew b: 4/8/14, Mt.Vernon, N.Y.   d: 4/8/89, LaJolla, Cal.   BR/TR, 6'1.5", 175 lbs.   Deb: 4/24/43

1943 Bos-A	1	1	.500	11	0	0	0	1	26	31	0	13	6	15.2	3.46	96	.310	.389	2	.286	0	-0	-0	1	0.1
Phi-N	1	2	.333	9	2	0	0	0	26²	44	0	11	4	18.6	7.09	48	.383	.437	2	.250	1	-11	-11	-0	-1.0
1944 Phi-N	3	2	.600	38	0	0	0	2	89	76	1	21	26	9.9	2.33	155	.237	.287	3	.200	1	13	13	1	0.9
1945 Phi-N	8	8	.500	67	2	1	0	15	180²	175	7	50	51	11.4	2.99	128	.253	.306	7	.143	-2	16	17	1	1.6
1946 Phi-N	3	7	.300	40	0	0	0	5	65¹	84	6	22	15	14.7	4.96	69	.321	.375	1	.100	-0	-11	-11	-1	-1.8
1947 Bos-N	2	3	.400	27	0	0	0	3	35	41	2	13	5	13.9	3.86	101	.318	.380	1	.167	-0	1	0	2	0.2
Total 5	18	23	.439	191	4	1	0	26	422²	451	16	130	107	12.5	3.51	104	.279	.334	16	.168	-0	7	7	6	0.2

● BILL KARNS   Karns, William Arthur b: 12/28/1875, Richmond, Iowa   d: 11/15/41, Seattle, Wash.   BL/TL,   Deb: 8/1/01

| 1901 Bal-A | 1 | 0 | 1.000 | 3 | 1 | 1 | 0 | 0 | 17 | 30 | 0 | 9 | 5 | 20.6 | 6.35 | 61 | .379 | .443 | 1 | .143 | -1 | -5 | -5 | -0 | -0.3 |

● HERB KARPEL   Karpel, Herbert "Lefty" b: 12/27/17, Brooklyn, N.Y.   BL/TL, 5'9.5", 180 lbs.   Deb: 4/19/46

| 1946 NY-A | 0 | 0 | — | 2 | 0 | 0 | 0 | 0 | 1² | 4 | 0 | 0 | 2 | 21.6 | 10.80 | 32 | .500 | .500 | 0 | — | 0 | -1 | -1 | -0 | 0.0 |

● BENN KARR   Karr, Benjamin Joyce "Baldy" b: 11/28/1893, Mt.Pleasant, Miss.   d: 12/8/68, Memphis, Tenn.   BL/TR, 6', 175 lbs.   Deb: 4/20/20

1920 Bos-A	3	8	.273	26	6	3	0	0	91²	109	3	24	21	13.2	4.81	76	.304	.349	21	.280	6	-10	-12	-1	-0.8
1921 Bos-A	8	7	.533	26	7	5	0	0	117²	123	8	38	37	12.4	3.67	115	.283	.342	16	.258	1	8	7	-0	0.9
1922 Bos-A	5	12	.294	41	13	7	0	1	183¹	212	10	45	41	12.9	4.47	92	.302	.348	21	.214	-1	-9	-7	-1	-0.7
1925 Cle-A	11	12	.478	32	24	12	1	0	197²	248	8	80	41	15.2	4.78	92	.317	.385	24	.261	4	-8	-8	2	-0.8
1926 Cle-A	5	6	.455	30	7	4	0	0	113¹	137	9	41	23	14.6	5.00	81	.291	.355	10	.222	2	-12	-12	1	-0.8
1927 Cle-A	3	3	.500	22	5	1	0	2	76²	92	5	32	17	14.7	5.05	83	.315	.385	4	.200	1	-8	-7	2	-0.3
Total 6	35	48	.422	177	58	29	1	5	780¹	921	43	260	180	13.5	4.60	90	.303	.362	96	.245	12	-40	-39	2	-1.9

● STEVE KARSAY   Karsay, Stefan Andrew b: 3/24/72, Flushing, N.Y.   BR/TR, 6'3", 210 lbs.   Deb: 8/17/93

1993 Oak-A	3	3	.500	8	8	0	0	0	49	49	4	16	33	12.3	4.04	101	.258	.322	0	—	0	2	0	-1	0.3
1994 Oak-A	1	1	.500	4	4	1	0	0	28	26	1	8	15	11.3	2.57	173	.252	.313	0	—	0	7	6	0	0.6
Total 2	4	4	.500	12	12	1	0	0	77	75	5	24	48	11.9	3.51	120	.256	.319	0	—	0	8	6	-1	0.9

● JACK KATOLL   Katoll, John "Big Jack" b: 6/24/1872, Germany   d: 6/18/55, Hartland, Ill.   BR/TR, 5'11", 195 lbs.   Deb: 9/9/1898

1898 Chi-N	0	1	.000	2	1	1	0	0	11	8	0	1	9	7.4	0.82	438	.202	.222	0	.000	-1	3	3	-0	0.2
1899 Chi-N	1	1	.500	2	2	2	0	0	18	17	0	4	1	11.0	6.00	62	.249	.301	0	.000	-1	-4	-5	-0	-0.4
1901 Chi-A	11	10	.524	27	25	19	0	0	208	231	3	53	59	12.8	2.81	124	.278	.330	10	.125	-4	20	15	2	1.1
1902 Chi-A	0	0	—	1	0	0	0	0	1	1	0	2	0	9.0	0.00	—	.261	.261	0	.000	-0	0	0	0	0.0
Bal-A	5	10	.333	15	13	13	0	0	123	175	5	32	25	15.5	4.02	94	.334	.374	10	.175	-0	-6	-3	4	0.0
Yr	5	10	.333	16	13	13	0	0	124	176	5	34	25	15.2	3.99	94	.334	.374	10	.172	-0	-6	-3	4	0.0
Total 4	17	22	.436	47	41	35	0	0	361	432	8	90	90	13.4	3.32	109	.295	.341	20	.134	-6	13	11	6	0.9

● BOB KATZ   Katz, Robert Clyde b: 1/30/11, Lancaster, Pa.   d: 12/14/62, St.Joseph, Mich.   BR/TR, 5'11.5", 190 lbs.   Deb: 5/12/44

| 1944 Cin-N | 0 | 1 | .000 | 6 | 2 | 0 | 0 | 0 | 18¹ | 17 | 0 | 7 | 4 | 11.8 | 3.93 | 89 | .254 | .324 | 0 | .000 | -1 | -1 | -1 | 1 | 0.0 |

● CURT KAUFMAN   Kaufman, Curt Gerrard b: 7/19/57, Omaha, Neb.   BR/TR, 6'2", 175 lbs.   Deb: 9/10/82

| 1982 NY-A | 1 | 0 | 1.000 | 7 | 0 | 0 | 0 | 0 | 8² | 9 | 2 | 6 | 1 | 15.6 | 5.19 | 77 | .265 | .375 | 0 | — | 0 | -1 | -1 | -0 | -0.1 |

YEAR	TM/L	W	L	PCT	G	GS	CG	SH	SV	IP	H	HR	BB	SO	RAT	ERA	ERA+	OAV	OOB	BH	AVG	PB	PR	/A	PD	TPI
1983	NY-A	0	0	—	4	0	0	0	0	8²	10	0	4	8	14.5	3.12	125	.303	.378	0	—	0	1	1	-0	0.1
1984	Cal-A	2	3	.400	29	1	0	0	1	69	68	13	20	41	11.5	4.57	87	.254	.306	0	—	0	-4	-5	0	-0.3
Total 3		3	3	.500	40	1	0	0	1	86¹	87	15	30	50	12.2	4.48	88	.260	.321	0	—	0	-5	-5	0	-0.3

● TONY KAUFMANN

Kaufmann, Anthony Charles   b: 12/16/1900, Chicago, Ill.   d: 6/4/82, Elgin, Ill.   BR/TR, 5'11", 165 lbs.   Deb: 9/23/21 C♦

YEAR	TM/L	W	L	PCT	G	GS	CG	SH	SV	IP	H	HR	BB	SO	RAT	ERA	ERA+	OAV	OOB	BH	AVG	PB	PR	/A	PD	TPI
1921	Chi-N	1	0	1.000	2	1	1	0	1	13	12	0	3	6	10.4	4.15	92	.240	.283	2	.400	1	-1	-0	-1	0.0
1922	Chi-N	7	13	.350	37	9	4	1	3	153	161	15	57	45	13.1	4.06	103	.273	.343	9	.200	1	1	2	-1	0.3
1923	Chi-N	14	10	.583	33	24	18	2	3	206¹	209	14	67	72	12.5	3.10	129	.264	.330	16	.216	3	21	21	-1	2.4
1924	Chi-N	16	11	.593	34	26	16	3	0	208¹	218	21	66	79	12.4	4.02	97	.272	.330	24	.316	6	-3	-3	-1	0.1
1925	Chi-N	13	13	.500	31	23	14	2	2	196	221	9	77	49	14.0	4.50	96	.292	.363	15	.192	1	-5	-4	-0	-0.3
1926	Chi-N	9	7	.563	26	21	14	1	2	169²	169	6	44	52	11.6	3.02	127	.262	.316	15	.250	2	15	15	-2	1.4
1927	Chi-N	3	3	.500	9	6	3	0	0	53¹	75	8	19	21	16.5	6.41	60	.338	.400	5	.313	1	-15	-15	-2	-1.0
	Phi-N	0	3	.000	5	5	1	0	0	18²	37	2	8	4	21.7	10.61	39	.425	.474	1	.143	0	-14	-13	-0	-1.6
	StL-N	0	0	—	1	0	0	0	0	0¹	4	0	1	0	135.0	81.00	5	1.000	1.000	0	—	0	-3	-3	0	0.0
	Yr	3	6	.333	15	11	4	0	0	72¹	116	10	28	25	17.9	7.84	50	.366	.417	6	.261	3	-32	-31	1	-2.6
1928	StL-N	0	0	—	4	1	0	0	0	4²	8	1	4	2	25.1	9.64	41	.444	.565	0	—	0	-3	-3	-0	-0.2
1930	StL-N	1	0	1.000	2	1	0	0	0	10¹	15	2	4	2	16.5	7.84	64	.357	.413	1	.333	1	-3	-3	-0	-0.2
1931	StL-N	1	1	.500	15	1	0	0	1	49	65	3	17	13	15.2	6.06	65	.319	.374	2	.111	-1	-12	-12	-0	-0.6
1935	StL-N	0	0	—	3	0	0	0	0	3²	4	0	1	0	12.3	2.45	167	.286	.333	0	—	0	1	1	0	0.0
Total 11		64	62	.508	202	118	71	9	12	1086¹	1198	81	368	345	13.3	4.18	97	.284	.347	91	.220	17	-22	-17	-5	0.5

● STEVE KEALEY

Kealey, Steven William   b: 5/13/47, Torrance, Cal.   BR/TR, 6', 185 lbs.   Deb: 9/9/68

YEAR	TM/L	W	L	PCT	G	GS	CG	SH	SV	IP	H	HR	BB	SO	RAT	ERA	ERA+	OAV	OOB	BH	AVG	PB	PR	/A	PD	TPI
1968	Cal-A	0	1	.000	6	0	0	0	0	10	10	0	5	4	13.5	2.70	108	.256	.341	0	—	0	0	0	-1	0.0
1969	Cal-A	2	0	1.000	15	3	1	1	0	36²	48	4	13	17	15.2	3.93	89	.322	.380	0	.000	-1	-2	-1	-1	-0.3
1970	Cal-A	1	0	1.000	17	0	0	0	1	21²	19	2	6	14	10.4	4.15	87	.260	.316	1	.250	1	-1	-1	-1	-0.1
1971	Chi-A	2	2	.500	54	1	0	0	6	77¹	69	10	26	50	11.1	3.84	93	.239	.302	2	.200	1	-3	-2	-0	-0.1
1972	Chi-A	3	2	.600	40	0	0	0	4	57¹	50	4	12	37	9.7	3.30	95	.234	.274	0	.000	-0	-2	-1	-1	-0.2
1973	Chi-A	0	0	—	7	0	0	0	0	11¹	23	2	7	4	23.8	15.09	26	.418	.484	0	—	-0	-14	-14	-0	-0.0
Total 6		8	5	.615	139	4	1	1	11	214¹	219	22	69	126	12.1	4.28	80	.267	.325	3	.115	-0	-21	-20	-3	-0.7

● ED KEAS

Keas, Edward James   b: 2/2/1863, Dubuque, Iowa   d: 1/12/40, Dubuque, Iowa   Deb: 8/25/1888

YEAR	TM/L	W	L	PCT	G	GS	CG	SH	SV	IP	H	HR	BB	SO	RAT	ERA	ERA+	OAV	OOB	BH	AVG	PB	PR	/A	PD	TPI
1888	Cle-a	3	3	.500	6	6	6	0	0	51	53	1	12	18	11.6	2.29	135	.258	.302	2	.087	-2	4	5	1	0.3

● RAY KEATING

Keating, Raymond Herbert   b: 7/21/1891, Bridgeport, Conn.   d: 12/28/63, Sacramento, Cal.   BR/TR, 5'11", 185 lbs.   Deb: 9/12/12

YEAR	TM/L	W	L	PCT	G	GS	CG	SH	SV	IP	H	HR	BB	SO	RAT	ERA	ERA+	OAV	OOB	BH	AVG	PB	PR	/A	PD	TPI
1912	NY-A	0	3	.000	6	5	3	0	0	35²	36	0	18	24	13.9	5.80	62	.265	.355	6	.375	1	-10	-9	0	-0.5
1913	NY-A	6	12	.333	28	21	9	2	0	151¹	147	3	51	83	11.9	3.21	93	.253	.316	3	.070	-3	-5	-4	-2	-0.9
1914	NY-A	7	11	.389	34	25	14	0	1	210	198	1	67	109	11.6	2.96	93	.253	.316	12	.169	-0	-5	-5	2	-0.1
1915	NY-A	3	6	.333	11	10	8	1	0	79¹	66	3	45	37	12.9	3.63	81	.228	.337	4	.154	-1	-6	-6	1	-0.6
1916	NY-A	5	6	.455	14	11	6	0	0	91	91	4	37	35	12.9	3.07	94	.272	.349	7	.241	1	-2	-2	2	0.1
1918	NY-A	2	2	.500	15	6	1	0	0	48¹	39	0	30	16	13.2	3.91	72	.238	.362	3	.188	1	-6	-6	0	-0.5
1919	Bos-N	7	11	.389	22	14	9	1	0	136	129	2	45	48	11.6	2.98	96	.261	.325	7	.152	-1	-3	-3	0	-0.2
Total 7		30	51	.370	130	92	50	4	1	751²	706	13	293	349	12.2	3.29	88	.254	.329	42	.170	-2	-35	-33	5	-2.7

● BOB KEATING

Keating, Robert M.   b: 9/22/1862, Springfield, Mass.   d: 1/19/22, Springfield, Mass.   BL/TL, 6'4", 190 lbs.   Deb: 8/27/1887

YEAR	TM/L	W	L	PCT	G	GS	CG	SH	SV	IP	H	HR	BB	SO	RAT	ERA	ERA+	OAV	OOB	BH	AVG	PB	PR	/A	PD	TPI
1887	Bal-a	0	1	.000	1	1	1	0	0	9	16	0	6	0	22.0	11.00	37	.372	.449	1	.250	-0	-7	-7	0	-0.4

● CACTUS KECK

Keck, Frank Joseph   b: 1/13/1899, St.Louis, Mo.   d: 2/6/81, Kirkwood, Mo.   BR/TR, 5'11", 170 lbs.   Deb: 5/26/22

YEAR	TM/L	W	L	PCT	G	GS	CG	SH	SV	IP	H	HR	BB	SO	RAT	ERA	ERA+	OAV	OOB	BH	AVG	PB	PR	/A	PD	TPI
1922	Cin-N	7	6	.538	27	15	5	1	1	131	138	4	29	27	11.8	3.37	119	.276	.322	7	.159	-1	11	9	-3	0.3
1923	Cin-N	3	6	.333	35	6	1	0	2	87	84	5	32	16	12.3	3.72	104	.254	.325	1	.059	-1	3	1	1	0.1
Total 2		10	12	.455	62	21	6	1	3	218	222	9	61	43	12.0	3.51	112	.267	.323	8	.131	-2	13	10	-3	0.4

● DAVE KEEFE

Keefe, David Edwin   b: 1/9/1897, Williston, Vt.   d: 2/4/78, Kansas City, Mo.   BL/TR, 5'9", 165 lbs.   Deb: 4/21/17 C

YEAR	TM/L	W	L	PCT	G	GS	CG	SH	SV	IP	H	HR	BB	SO	RAT	ERA	ERA+	OAV	OOB	BH	AVG	PB	PR	/A	PD	TPI
1917	Phi-A	1	0	1.000	3	0	0	0	0	5	5	0	4	1	16.2	1.80	153	.278	.409	0	.000	-0	1	1	0	0.1
1919	Phi-A	0	1	.000	1	1	1	0	0	9	8	0	3	5	11.0	4.00	86	.242	.306	0	.000	-0	-1	-1	0	-0.1
1920	Phi-A	6	7	.462	31	13	7	1	0	130¹	129	2	30	41	11.4	2.97	136	.262	.313	10	.250	-0	12	15	1	1.5
1921	Phi-A	2	9	.182	44	12	4	0	1	173	214	19	64	68	14.7	4.68	95	.311	.374	10	.175	-3	-8	-4	-2	-0.7
1922	Cle-A	0	0	—	18	1	0	0	0	36¹	47	2	12	11	14.6	6.19	65	.333	.386	2	.333	1	-9	-9	-0	-0.2
Total 5		9	17	.346	97	27	12	1	1	353²	403	23	113	126	13.4	4.15	101	.294	.352	22	.206	-3	-5	2	-1	0.8

● GEORGE KEEFE

Keefe, George W.   b: 1/7/1867, Washington, D.C.   d: 8/24/35, Washington, D.C.   BL/TL, 5'9", 168 lbs.   Deb: 7/30/1886

YEAR	TM/L	W	L	PCT	G	GS	CG	SH	SV	IP	H	HR	BB	SO	RAT	ERA	ERA+	OAV	OOB	BH	AVG	PB	PR	/A	PD	TPI
1886	Was-N	0	3	.000	4	4	4	0	0	31¹	28	0	15	5	12.4	5.17	64	.233	.319	0	.000	-2	-6	-7	-1	-0.7
1887	Was-N	0	1	1.000	1	1	1	0	0	8	16	1	4	0	24.8	9.00	45	.364	.440	0	.000	-1	-4	-4	-0	-0.4
1888	Was-N	6	7	.462	13	13	13	1	0	114	87	3	43	52	10.6	2.84	99	.206	.286	9	.214	1	0	-0	1	0.2
1889	Was-N	8	18	.308	30	27	24	0	0	230	266	6	143	90	16.2	5.13	77	.281	.377	16	.163	-2	-28	-30	-2	-2.8
1890	Buf-P	6	16	.273	25	22	22	0	0	196	280	11	138	55	19.4	6.52	63	.322	.417	16	.203	-2	-50	-53	-1	-3.9
1891	Was-a	0	3	.000	5	4	4	0	0	37	44	0	17	11	15.1	2.68	140	.286	.360	2	.143	-0	4	4	1	0.3
Total 6		20	48	.294	78	71	68	1	1	616¹	721	20	360	213	16.0	5.05	74	.282	.374	43	.172	-3	-85	-90	-4	-7.3

● JOHN KEEFE

Keefe, John Thomas   b: 5/5/1867, Fitchburg, Mass.   d: 8/9/37, Fitchburg, Mass.   TL ,   Deb: 4/28/1890

YEAR	TM/L	W	L	PCT	G	GS	CG	SH	SV	IP	H	HR	BB	SO	RAT	ERA	ERA+	OAV	OOB	BH	AVG	PB	PR	/A	PD	TPI
1890	Syr-a	17	24	.415	43	41	36	2	0	352¹	355	9	148	120	13.5	4.32	82	.254	.336	30	.191	-5	-17	-31	0	-3.1

● BOBBY KEEFE

Keefe, Robert Francis   b: 6/16/1882, Folsom, Cal.   d: 12/7/64, Sacramento, Cal.   BR/TR, 5'11", 155 lbs.   Deb: 4/15/07

YEAR	TM/L	W	L	PCT	G	GS	CG	SH	SV	IP	H	HR	BB	SO	RAT	ERA	ERA+	OAV	OOB	BH	AVG	PB	PR	/A	PD	TPI
1907	NY-A	3	5	.375	19	3	0	0	3	57²	60	1	20	20	12.6	2.50	112	.270	.333	1	.053	-2	0	2	0	0.1
1911	Cin-N	12	13	.480	39	26	15	0	3	234¹	196	7	76	105	10.6	2.69	123	.229	.294	6	.086	-2	19	16	-5	0.8
1912	Cin-N	1	3	.250	17	6	0	0	2	68²	78	0	33	29	15.1	5.24	64	.289	.375	3	.167	-1	-14	-14	-0	-0.9
Total 3		16	21	.432	75	35	15	0	8	360²	334	8	129	154	11.8	3.14	103	.248	.317	10	.093	-5	5	4	-5	0.0

● TIM KEEFE

Keefe, Timothy John "Smiling Tim" or "Sir Timothy"
b: 1/1/1857, Cambridge, Mass.   d: 4/23/33, Cambridge, Mass.   BR/TR, 5'10.5", 185 lbs.   Deb: 8/6/1880   UH

YEAR	TM/L	W	L	PCT	G	GS	CG	SH	SV	IP	H	HR	BB	SO	RAT	ERA	ERA+	OAV	OOB	BH	AVG	PB	PR	/A	PD	TPI
1880	Tro-N	6	6	.500	12	12	12	0	0	105	71	0	17	43	7.5	**0.86**	294	**.187**	.222	10	.233	-0	18	19	1	2.2
1881	Tro-N	18	27	.400	45	45	45	4	0	402	442	4	81	103	11.7	3.25	91	.274	.309	35	.230	4	-21	-13	-0	-0.9
1882	Tro-N	17	26	.395	43	42	41	1	0	375	368	4	81	116	10.8	2.50	113	.244	.283	43	.228	5	17	14	5	2.2
1883	NY-a	41	27	.603	**68**	68	**68**	5	0	**619**	488	6	108	**359**	8.7	2.41	138	**.203**	.237	57	.220	4	61	64	6	6.6
1884	*NY-a	37	17	.685	57	57	56	4	0	482²	378	5	75	317	8.7	2.26	138	**.203**	.240	50	.238	12	53	46	-0	5.5
1885	NY-N	32	13	.711	46	46	45	7	0	400	300	6	102	227	9.0	**1.58**	169	.203	.255	27	.163	-1	55	49	0	4.7
1886	NY-N	**42**	20	.677	**64**	64	62	2	0	535	479	9	102	297	9.8	2.56	126	.231	.267	35	.171	1	45	39	1	3.7
1887	NY-N	35	19	.648	56	56	54	2	0	476²	428	11	108	189	10.3	3.12	121	**.230**	**.276**	42	.220	8	51	35	3	3.8
1888	*NY-N	**35**	12	**.745**	51	51	48	**8**	0	434¹	317	5	90	**335**	8.7	**1.74**	157	**.196**	.243	23	.127	-6	**54**	48	1	4.2
1889	*NY-N	28	13	.683	47	45	39	1	0	364	319	9	151	225	12.1	3.31	119	**.228**	.312	23	.154	-8	28	25	2	2.1
1890	NY-P	17	11	.607	30	29	23	1	0	229	228	6	85	88	12.6	3.38	134	.248	.317	10	.109	-5	22	30	1	2.4
1891	NY-N	2	5	.286	11	9	4	0	0	55	71	1	27	29	16.7	5.24	61	.302	.383	2	.095	-1	-12	-12	-0	-1.2
	Phi-N	3	6	.333	11	10	9	0	0	78¹	84	2	28	35	13.3	3.91	87	.264	.331	5	.172	0	-5	-5	0	-0.4
	Yr	5	11	.313	19	17	13	0	0	133¹	155	3	55	64	14.4	4.45	75	.278	.347	7	.140	-1	-16	-17	-1	-1.6
1892	Phi-N	19	16	.543	39	38	31	2	0	313¹	264	4	100	127	10.8	2.36	138	.219	.286	10	.085	-7	32	31	-1	2.2

YEAR	TM/L	W	L	PCT	G	GS	CG	SH	SV	IP	H	HR	BB	SO	RAT	ERA	ERA+	OAV	OOB	BH	AVG	PB	PR	/A	PD	TPI
1893	Phi-N	10	7	.588	22	22	17	0	0	178	202	3	79	53	14.9	4.40	104	.277	.358	18	.228	0	5	4	-2	0.1
Total	14	342	225	.603	599	593	554	39	2	5047¹	4439	75	1234	2543	10.3	2.62	125	.227	.276	390	.187	11	404	375	18	37.2

● ED KEEGAN
Keegan, Edward Charles   b: 7/8/39, Camden, N.J.   BR/TR, 6'3", 165 lbs.   Deb: 8/24/59

YEAR	TM/L	W	L	PCT	G	GS	CG	SH	SV	IP	H	HR	BB	SO	RAT	ERA	ERA+	OAV	OOB	BH	AVG	PB	PR	/A	PD	TPI
1959	Phi-N	0	3	.000	3	3	0	0	0	9	19	2	13	3	33.0	18.00	23	.432	.569	0	.000	-0	-14	-14	-0	-2.6
1961	KC-A	0	0	—	6	0	0	0	1	6	6	0	5	3	16.5	4.50	93	.261	.393	0	—	0	-0	-0	-0	0.0
1962	Phi-N	0	0	—	4	0	0	0	0	8	6	1	5	5	13.5	2.25	172	.214	.353	0	—	0	2	1	-0	0.0
Total	3	0	3	.000	13	3	0	0	1	23	31	3	23	11	21.9	9.00	45	.326	.467	0	.000	-0	-13	-13	-1	-2.6

● BOB KEEGAN
Keegan, Robert Charles "Smiley"   b: 8/4/20, Rochester, N.Y.   BR/TR, 6'2.5", 207 lbs.   Deb: 5/24/53

YEAR	TM/L	W	L	PCT	G	GS	CG	SH	SV	IP	H	HR	BB	SO	RAT	ERA	ERA+	OAV	OOB	BH	AVG	PB	PR	/A	PD	TPI
1953	Chi-A	7	5	.583	22	11	4	2	1	98²	84	4	33	32	10.5	2.74	147	.223	.293	9	.321	2	14	14	1	1.9
1954	Chi-A★	16	9	.640	31	27	14	2	2	209²	211	16	82	61	12.6	3.09	121	.266	.336	9	.120	-2	15	15	-1	1.4
1955	Chi-A	2	5	.286	18	11	1	0	0	58²	83	4	28	29	17.2	5.83	68	.336	.406	6	.333	2	-12	-12	0	-1.1
1956	Chi-A	5	7	.417	20	16	4	0	0	101²	119	15	35	32	13.3	3.93	104	.286	.344	4	.125	-1	3	2	-0	0.1
1957	Chi-A	10	8	.556	30	20	6	2	2	142²	131	22	37	36	10.7	3.53	106	.243	.294	4	.103	-1	4	3	-1	0.1
1958	Chi-A	0	2	.000	14	2	0	0	0	29²	44	9	18	8	18.8	6.07	60	.358	.440	0	.000	-1	-8	-8	1	-0.5
Total	6	40	36	.526	135	87	29	6	5	644²	668	70	233	198	12.7	3.66	105	.270	.335	32	.163	-2	16	14	-1	1.9

● BURT KEELEY
Keeley, Burton Elwood "Speed"   b: 11/2/1879, Wilmington, Ill.   d: 5/3/52, Ely, Minn.   BR/TR, 5'9", 170 lbs.   Deb: 4/18/08

YEAR	TM/L	W	L	PCT	G	GS	CG	SH	SV	IP	H	HR	BB	SO	RAT	ERA	ERA+	OAV	OOB	BH	AVG	PB	PR	/A	PD	TPI
1908	Was-A	6	11	.353	28	15	12	1	1	169²	173	3	48	68	11.9	2.97	77	.259	.313	5	.102	-3	-11	-13	2	-1.5
1909	Was-A	0	0	—	2	0	0	0	0	7	12	0	1	0	18.0	11.57	21	.364	.400	1	.500	-0	-7	-7	1	0.1
Total	2	6	11	.353	30	15	12	1	1	176²	185	3	49	68	12.2	3.31	69	.264	.317	6	.118	-3	-18	-20	2	-1.4

● VIC KEEN
Keen, Howard Victor   b: 3/16/1899, Bel Air, Md.   d: 12/10/76, Salisbury, Md.   BR/TR, 5'9", 165 lbs.   Deb: 8/13/18

YEAR	TM/L	W	L	PCT	G	GS	CG	SH	SV	IP	H	HR	BB	SO	RAT	ERA	ERA+	OAV	OOB	BH	AVG	PB	PR	/A	PD	TPI
1918	Phi-A	0	1	.000	1	1	0	0	0	8	9	1	1	1	11.3	3.38	87	.300	.323	0	.000	-0	-1	-0	-1	-0.1
1921	Chi-N	0	3	.000	5	4	1	0	0	25	29	0	9	9	14.0	4.68	82	.319	.386	0	.000	-0	-2	-2	0	-0.3
1922	Chi-N	1	2	.333	7	3	2	0	1	34²	36	4	10	11	12.2	3.89	108	.275	.331	4	.333	-1	1	1	-0	0.2
1923	Chi-N	12	8	.600	35	17	10	1	0	177	169	8	57	46	11.7	3.00	133	.255	.319	8	.151	-3	20	20	-2	1.6
1924	Chi-N	15	14	.517	40	28	15	0	3	234²	242	17	80	75	12.5	3.80	103	.272	.335	12	.156	-4	2	3	-3	-0.5
1925	Chi-N	2	6	.250	30	8	1	0	1	83¹	125	8	41	19	17.9	6.26	69	.359	.427	6	.240	0	-18	-18	1	-1.4
1926	*StL-N	10	9	.526	26	21	12	1	0	152	179	15	42	29	13.1	4.56	86	.295	.342	3	.057	-6	-12	-11	2	-2.0
1927	StL-N	2	1	.667	21	0	0	0	0	33²	39	3	8	12	13.1	4.81	82	.293	.343	1	.250	0	-3	-3	0	-0.2
Total	8	42	44	.488	165	82	41	1	6	748¹	828	56	248	202	13.1	4.11	97	.287	.346	34	.148	-12	-15	-11	-6	-2.7

● KID KEENAN
Keenan, Harry Leon   b: 1875, Louisville, Ky.   d: 6/11/03, Covington, Ky.   TR,   Deb: 8/11/1891

YEAR	TM/L	W	L	PCT	G	GS	CG	SH	SV	IP	H	HR	BB	SO	RAT	ERA	ERA+	OAV	OOB	BH	AVG	PB	PR	/A	PD	TPI
1891	Cin-a	0	1	.000	1	1	1	0	0	8	6	0	4	5	12.4	0.00	—	.201	.316	2	.500	0	3	4	-0	0.5

● JIM KEENAN
Keenan, James William   b: 2/10/1858, New Haven, Conn.   d: 9/21/26, Cincinnati, Ohio   BR/TR, 5'10", 186 lbs.   Deb: 5/17/1875   ♦

YEAR	TM/L	W	L	PCT	G	GS	CG	SH	SV	IP	H	HR	BB	SO	RAT	ERA	ERA+	OAV	OOB	BH	AVG	PB	PR	/A	PD	TPI
1884	Ind-a	0	0	—	1	0	0	0	0	3	2	0	0	0	6.0	3.00	110	.182	.182	73	.293	0	0	0	-0	0.0
1885	Cin-a	0	0	—	1	0	0	0	0	8	7	0	1	0	9.0	1.13	290	.233	.258	35	.265	0	2	2	0	0.0
1886	Cin-a	0	1	.000	2	0	0	0	0	8	8	0	3	2	12.4	3.38	104	.258	.324	40	.270	0	0	0	-0	0.0
Total	3	0	1	.000	4	0	0	0	0	19	17	0	4	2	9.9	2.37	142	.236	.276	452	.241	1	2	2	0	0.0

● JIMMIE KEENAN
Keenan, James William "Sparkplug"   b: 5/25/1898, Avon, N.Y.   d: 6/5/80, Seminole, Fla.   BL/TL, 5'7", 155 lbs.   Deb: 9/9/20

YEAR	TM/L	W	L	PCT	G	GS	CG	SH	SV	IP	H	HR	BB	SO	RAT	ERA	ERA+	OAV	OOB	BH	AVG	PB	PR	/A	PD	TPI
1920	Phi-N	0	0	—	1	0	0	0	0	3	3	0	1	2	12.0	3.00	114	.333	.400	0	.000	-0	0	0	0	0.0
1921	Phi-N	1	2	.333	15	2	0	0	0	32¹	48	3	15	7	17.8	6.68	63	.364	.432	0	.000	-1	-10	-9	-1	-0.9
Total	2	1	2	.333	16	2	0	0	0	35¹	51	3	16	9	17.3	6.37	65	.362	.430	0	.000	-2	-10	-9	-0	-0.9

● JEFF KEENER
Keener, Jeffrey Bruce   b: 1/14/59, Pana, Ill.   BL/TR, 6', 170 lbs.   Deb: 6/8/82

YEAR	TM/L	W	L	PCT	G	GS	CG	SH	SV	IP	H	HR	BB	SO	RAT	ERA	ERA+	OAV	OOB	BH	AVG	PB	PR	/A	PD	TPI
1982	StL-N	1	1	.500	19	0	0	0	0	22¹	19	1	19	25	15.3	1.61	224	.235	.380	0	—	0	5	5	0	0.4
1983	StL-N	0	0	—	4	0	0	0	0	4¹	6	0	1	4	16.6	8.31	44	.333	.400	0	—	0	-2	-2	0	-0.0
Total	2	1	1	.500	23	0	0	0	0	26²	25	1	20	29	15.5	2.70	134	.253	.383	0	—	0	3	3	0	0.4

● JOE KEENER
Keener, Joseph Donald   b: 4/21/53, San Pedro, Cal.   BR/TR, 6'4", 200 lbs.   Deb: 9/18/76

YEAR	TM/L	W	L	PCT	G	GS	CG	SH	SV	IP	H	HR	BB	SO	RAT	ERA	ERA+	OAV	OOB	BH	AVG	PB	PR	/A	PD	TPI
1976	Mon-N	0	1	.000	2	2	0	0	0	4¹	7	0	8	1	33.2	10.38	36	.389	.593	0	.000	-0	-3	-3	0	-0.6

● HARRY KEENER
Keener, Joshua Harry "Beans"   b: 9/1869, Easton, Pa.   d: 3/5/12, Easton, Pa.   TR,   Deb: 6/27/1896

YEAR	TM/L	W	L	PCT	G	GS	CG	SH	SV	IP	H	HR	BB	SO	RAT	ERA	ERA+	OAV	OOB	BH	AVG	PB	PR	/A	PD	TPI
1896	Phi-N	3	11	.214	16	13	11	0	0	113¹	144	5	39	28	15.2	5.88	73	.307	.371	16	.314	2	-19	-20	0	-1.6

● RICKEY KEETON
Keeton, Rickey   b: 3/18/57, Cincinnati, Ohio   BR/TR, 6'2", 190 lbs.   Deb: 5/27/80

YEAR	TM/L	W	L	PCT	G	GS	CG	SH	SV	IP	H	HR	BB	SO	RAT	ERA	ERA+	OAV	OOB	BH	AVG	PB	PR	/A	PD	TPI
1980	Mil-A	2	2	.500	5	5	0	0	0	28¹	34	4	9	8	14.0	4.76	81	.307	.358	0	—	0	-2	-3	0	-0.3
1981	Mil-A	1	0	1.000	17	0	0	0	0	35¹	47	4	11	9	14.8	5.09	67	.329	.377	0	—	0	-6	-7	0	-0.2
Total	2	3	2	.600	22	5	0	0	0	63²	82	8	20	17	14.4	4.95	73	.319	.368	0	—	0	-8	-9	0	-0.5

● FRANK KEFFER
Keffer, Frank   b: Harrisburg, Pa.   Deb: 4/19/1890

YEAR	TM/L	W	L	PCT	G	GS	CG	SH	SV	IP	H	HR	BB	SO	RAT	ERA	ERA+	OAV	OOB	BH	AVG	PB	PR	/A	PD	TPI
1890	Syr-a	1	1	.500	2	1	1	0	0	16	15	0	9	4	13.5	5.63	63	.240	.336	1	.143	-1	-3	-4	0	-0.4

● CHET KEHN
Kehn, Chester Lawrence   b: 10/30/21, San Diego, Cal.   d: 4/5/84, San Diego, Cal.   BR/TR, 5'11", 168 lbs.   Deb: 4/30/42

YEAR	TM/L	W	L	PCT	G	GS	CG	SH	SV	IP	H	HR	BB	SO	RAT	ERA	ERA+	OAV	OOB	BH	AVG	PB	PR	/A	PD	TPI
1942	Bro-N	0	0	—	3	1	0	0	0	7²	8	2	4	3	14.1	7.04	46	.267	.353	2	1.000	1	-3	-3	0	0.2

● KATSY KEIFER
Keifer, Sherman Carl   b: 9/3/1891, California, Pa.   d: 2/19/27, Outwood, Ken.   BB/TL,   Deb: 10/8/14

YEAR	TM/L	W	L	PCT	G	GS	CG	SH	SV	IP	H	HR	BB	SO	RAT	ERA	ERA+	OAV	OOB	BH	AVG	PB	PR	/A	PD	TPI
1914	Ind-F	1	0	1.000	1	1	1	0	0	9	6	0	2	2	8.0	2.00	156	.194	.242	1	.333	0	1	1	0	0.2

● MIKE KEKICH
Kekich, Michael Dennis   b: 4/2/45, San Diego, Cal.   BR/TL, 6'1", 200 lbs.   Deb: 6/9/65

YEAR	TM/L	W	L	PCT	G	GS	CG	SH	SV	IP	H	HR	BB	SO	RAT	ERA	ERA+	OAV	OOB	BH	AVG	PB	PR	/A	PD	TPI
1965	LA-N	0	1	.000	5	1	0	0	0	10¹	10	2	13	9	20.0	9.58	34	.263	.451	0	.000	-0	-7	-7	-0	-0.7
1968	LA-N	2	10	.167	25	20	1	1	0	115	116	9	46	84	12.8	3.91	71	.267	.339	3	.081	-2	-12	-15	-1	-1.8
1969	NY-A	4	6	.400	28	13	1	0	1	105	91	11	49	66	12.2	4.54	77	.236	.325	3	.111	-1	-11	-12	-1	-1.3
1970	NY-A	6	3	.667	26	14	1	0	0	98²	103	12	55	63	14.5	4.83	73	.267	.360	3	.094	-1	-12	-14	-1	-1.4
1971	NY-A	10	9	.526	37	24	3	0	0	170¹	167	13	82	93	13.4	4.07	79	.257	.344	8	.154	-1	-11	-16	1	-1.5
1972	NY-A	10	13	.435	29	28	2	0	0	175¹	172	13	76	78	12.9	3.70	80	.263	.344	8	.136	-1	-12	-15	-1	-2.1
1973	NY-A	1	1	.500	5	4	0	0	0	14²	20	1	14	4	22.1	9.20	40	.351	.493	0	—	0	-9	-9	-0	-1.0
	Cle-A	1	4	.200	16	6	0	0	0	50	73	6	35	26	19.4	7.02	56	.349	.443	0	—	0	-18	-17	-1	-1.6
	Yr	2	5	.286	21	10	0	0	0	64²	93	7	49	30	19.8	7.52	51	.346	.447	0	—	0	-27	-26	-2	-2.6
1975	Tex-A	0	0	—	23	0	0	0	0	31¹	33	2	21	19	15.5	3.73	101	.282	.391	0	—	0	0	0	0	0.1
1977	Sea-A	5	4	.556	41	2	0	0	3	90	90	11	51	55	14.4	5.60	73	.265	.365	0	—	0	-15	-15	-0	-1.4
Total	9	39	51	.433	235	112	8	1	6	860²	875	80	442	497	13.9	4.59	72	.268	.358	25	.120	-5	-108	-121	-4	-12.7

● GEORGE KELB
Kelb, George Francis "Pugger" or "Lefty"   b: 7/17/1870, Toledo, Ohio   d: 10/20/36, Toledo, Ohio   BL/TL,   Deb: 4/17/1898

YEAR	TM/L	W	L	PCT	G	GS	CG	SH	SV	IP	H	HR	BB	SO	RAT	ERA	ERA+	OAV	OOB	BH	AVG	PB	PR	/A	PD	TPI
1898	Cle-N	0	1	.000	3	1	1	0	0	16¹	23	1	0	8	15.4	4.41	82	.329	.374	1	.200	-0	-1	-1	0	-0.1

● HAL KELLEHER
Kelleher, Harold Joseph   b: 6/24/13, Philadelphia, Pa.   d: 8/27/89, Cape May Court House, N.J.   BR/TR, 6', 165 lbs.   Deb: 9/17/35

YEAR	TM/L	W	L	PCT	G	GS	CG	SH	SV	IP	H	HR	BB	SO	RAT	ERA	ERA+	OAV	OOB	BH	AVG	PB	PR	/A	PD	TPI
1935	Phi-N	2	0	1.000	3	3	2	1	0	25	26	0	12	12	14.0	1.80	252	.260	.345	3	.375	1	6	8	0	0.7
1936	Phi-N	0	5	.000	14	4	1	0	0	44	60	2	29	13	18.8	5.32	85	.331	.432	2	.167	-0	-6	-4	0	-0.4
1937	Phi-N	2	4	.333	27	2	1	0	0	58¹	72	3	31	20	17.0	6.63	65	.308	.404	3	.176	-0	-18	-15	-0	-1.4
1938	Phi-N	0	0	—	6	0	0	0	0	7¹	16	0	9	4	30.7	18.41	21	.432	.543	1	.500	-0	-12	-12	0	0.1
Total	4	4	9	.308	50	9	4	1	0	134²	174	5	81	49	17.8	5.95	74	.315	.413	9	.231	0	-30	-23	0	-1.0

YEAR	TM/L	W	L	PCT	G	GS	CG	SH	SV	IP	H	HR	BB	SO	RAT	ERA	ERA+	OAV	OOB	BH	AVG	PB	PR	/A	PD	TPI

● RON KELLER　Keller, Ronald Lee　b: 6/3/43, Indianapolis, Ind.　BR/TR, 6′2″, 200 lbs.　Deb: 7/9/66

1966	Min-A	0	0	—	2	0	0	0	0	5¹	7	1	1	1	13.5	5.06	71	.318	.348	0	.000	-0	-1	-1	0	0.0
1968	Min-A	0	1	.000	7	1	0	0	0	16	18	2	4	11	12.9	2.81	110	.305	.359	0	—	-0	0	0	0	0.0
Total	2	0	1	.000	9	1	0	0	0	21¹	25	3	5	12	13.1	3.38	95	.309	.356	0	.000	-0	-1	-0	0	0.0

● AL KELLETT　Kellett, Alfred Henry　b: 10/30/01, Red Bank, N.J.　d: 7/14/60, New York, N.Y.　BR/TR, 6′3″, 200 lbs.　Deb: 7/1/23

1923	Phi-A	0	1	.000	5	0	0	0	0	10	11	0	8	1	17.1	6.30	65	.282	.404	1	.333	0	-3	-2	1	-0.1
1924	Bos-A	0	0	—	1	0	0	0	0	0	0	0	2	0	—	∞	—	—	1.000	0	—	0	-2	-2	0	-0.2
Total	2	0	1	.000	6	0	0	0	0	10	11	0	10	1	18.9	8.10	51	.282	.429	1	.333	0	-5	-4	1	-0.3

● HARRY KELLEY　Kelley, Harry Leroy　b: 2/13/06, Parkin, Ark.　d: 3/23/58, Parkin, Ark.　BR/TR, 5′9.5″, 170 lbs.　Deb: 4/16/25

1925	Was-A	1	1	.500	6	1	0	0	0	16	30	0	12	7	23.6	9.00	47	.405	.488	0	.000	-1	-8	-8	1	-0.8
1926	Was-A	0	0	—	7	1	0	0	0	10	17	0	8	6	23.4	8.10	48	.405	.510	0	—	-0	-5	-5	-0	0.0
1936	Phi-A	15	12	.556	35	27	20	1	3	235¹	250	21	75	82	12.5	3.86	132	.275	.332	18	.198	-1	31	32	-2	2.9
1937	Phi-A	13	21	.382	41	29	14	0	0	205	267	16	79	68	15.3	5.36	88	.306	.365	16	.225	1	-17	-15	-1	-1.9
1938	Phi-A	0	2	.000	4	3	0	0	0	8	17	0	10	3	30.4	16.88	29	.436	.551	0	.000	-0	-11	-11	-0	-1.8
	Was-A	9	8	.529	38	14	7	2	1	148¹	162	12	46	44	12.7	4.49	100	.276	.330	12	.250	1	5	0	0	0.2
	Yr	9	10	.474	42	17	7	2	1	156¹	179	12	56	47	13.6	5.12	88	.286	.346	12	.240	1	-6	-10	0	-1.6
1939	Was-A	4	3	.571	15	3	2	0	1	53²	69	2	14	20	14.4	4.70	93	.314	.363	4	.267	1	-0	-2	0	-0.2
Total	6	42	47	.472	146	78	43	3	5	676¹	812	51	244	230	14.2	4.86	98	.296	.356	50	.216	0	-5	-4	-2	-1.6

● DICK KELLEY　Kelley, Richard Anthony　b: 1/8/40, Boston, Mass.　d: 12/12/91, Northridge, Cal.　BR/TL, 6′, 175 lbs.　Deb: 4/15/64

1964	Mil-N	0	0	—	2	0	0	0	0	2	2	0	3	2	22.5	18.00	20	.250	.455	0	—	0	-3	-3	-0	0.0
1965	Mil-N	1	1	.500	21	4	0	0	0	45	37	5	20	31	11.4	3.00	117	.226	.310	0	.000	-1	3	3	-0	0.1
1966	Atl-N	7	5	.583	20	13	2	2	0	81	75	6	21	50	11.0	3.22	113	.247	.302	1	.036	-3	3	4	-2	0.1
1967	Atl-N	2	9	.182	39	9	1	1	2	98	88	8	42	75	12.0	3.77	88	.247	.328	4	.250	1	-4	-5	1	-0.3
1968	Atl-N	2	4	.333	31	11	1	0	1	98	86	4	45	73	12.1	2.76	109	.238	.324	1	.043	-1	3	3	1	0.2
1969	SD-N	4	8	.333	27	23	1	1	0	136	113	11	61	96	11.8	3.57	99	.230	.321	5	.106	-2	0	-1	2	-0.1
1971	SD-N	2	3	.400	48	1	0	0	2	59²	52	5	23	42	11.9	3.47	95	.232	.315	1	.333	0	-0	-1	-0	-0.1
Total	7	18	30	.375	188	61	5	5	5	519²	453	39	215	369	11.8	3.39	100	.237	.319	12	.096	-5	1	-1	2	-0.2

● TOM KELLEY　Kelley, Thomas Henry　b: 1/5/44, Manchester, Conn.　BR/TR, 6′, 191 lbs.　Deb: 5/5/64

1964	Cle-A	0	0	—	6	0	0	0	0	9²	7	1	9	7	17.7	5.59	64	.237	.396	0	—	0	-2	-2	-0	0.0
1965	Cle-A	2	1	.667	4	4	1	0	0	30	19	3	13	31	9.6	2.40	145	.186	.278	2	.222	0	4	4	-0	0.4
1966	Cle-A	4	8	.333	31	7	1	0	0	95¹	97	14	42	64	13.1	4.34	79	.264	.340	4	.143	-1	-10	-10	-1	-1.4
1967	Cle-A	0	0	—	1	0	0	0	0	1	0	0	2	1	18.0	0.00	—	.000	.500	0	—	0	0	0	0	0.0
1971	Atl-N	9	5	.643	28	20	5	0	0	143	140	8	69	68	13.2	2.96	125	.262	.347	2	.047	-4	8	12	-1	0.7
1972	Atl-N	5	7	.417	27	14	2	1	0	116¹	122	12	65	59	14.5	4.56	83	.272	.364	3	.088	-2	-14	-10	-3	-1.4
1973	Atl-N	0	1	.000	7	0	0	0	0	12²	15	0	7	5	14.2	2.84	138	.289	.385	0	.000	-0	1	2	-0	0.1
Total	7	20	22	.476	104	45	9	1	0	408	400	38	207	234	13.4	3.75	97	.270	.349	11	.095	-6	-13	-4	-5	-1.6

● ALEX KELLNER　Kellner, Alexander Raymond　b: 8/26/24, Tucson, Ariz.　BR/TL, 6′, 200 lbs.　Deb: 4/29/48　F

1948	Phi-A	0	0	—	13	1	0	0	0	23	21	0	16	14	15.3	7.83	55	.239	.368	0	.000	-1	-9	-9	-0	-0.1
1949	Phi-A☆	20	12	.625	38	27	19	0	1	245	243	18	129	94	13.7	3.75	110	.261	.352	20	.217	1	12	10	-0	1.3
1950	Phi-A	8	20	.286	36	29	15	0	2	225¹	253	28	112	85	14.7	5.47	83	.282	.363	16	.200	-1	-22	-23	-2	-2.7
1951	Phi-A	11	14	.440	33	29	11	1	2	209²	218	20	93	94	13.5	4.46	96	.272	.350	18	.228	-1	-8	-4	-1	-0.6
1952	Phi-A	12	14	.462	34	33	14	2	0	231¹	223	21	86	105	12.2	4.36	91	.252	.321	17	.207	0	-18	-10	-2	-1.2
1953	Phi-A	11	12	.478	25	25	14	2	0	201²	210	8	51	81	11.8	3.93	109	.269	.317	15	.217	1	2	8	-2	0.8
1954	Phi-A	6	17	.261	27	27	8	1	0	173²	204	16	88	69	15.4	5.39	72	.301	.387	10	.182	-0	-32	-29	0	-3.3
1955	KC-A	11	8	.579	30	24	6	3	0	162²	164	18	60	75	12.7	4.20	99	.265	.335	12	.214	2	-4	-1	-0	0.2
1956	KC-A	7	4	.636	20	17	5	0	0	91²	103	15	33	44	13.5	4.32	100	.289	.353	6	.200	-2	-7	-5	0	0.1
1957	KC-A	6	5	.545	28	21	3	0	0	132²	141	18	41	72	12.5	4.27	93	.278	.335	11	.234	4	-7	-5	0	0.1
1958	KC-A	0	0	—	7	6	0	0	0	33²	40	5	8	22	12.8	5.88	66	.315	.356	1	.091	-0	-8	-7	-0	-0.4
	Cin-N	7	3	.700	18	7	4	0	0	82	74	8	20	42	10.6	2.30	180	.243	.296	3	.357	3	15	17	-2	2.1
1959	StL-N	2	1	.667	12	4	0	0	0	37	31	9	10	19	10.2	3.16	134	.220	.276	2	.222	0	3	4	0	0.3
Total	12	101	112	.474	321	250	99	9	5	1849¹	1925	184	747	816	13.2	4.41	95	.270	.343	138	.215	7	-78	-47	-8	-3.5

● WALT KELLNER　Kellner, Walter Joseph　b: 4/26/29, Tucson, Ariz.　BR/TR, 6′, 200 lbs.　Deb: 9/6/52　F

1952	Phi-A	0	0	—	1	0	0	0	1	4	4	0	3	2	15.8	6.75	59	.250	.368	0	.000	-0	-1	-1	-0	-0.1
1953	Phi-A	0	0	—	2	0	0	0	0	3	1	0	4	4	18.0	6.00	71	.111	.429	0	—	-0	-1	-1	-0	0.0
Total	2	0	0	—	3	0	0	0	1	7	5	0	7	6	16.7	6.43	64	.200	.394	0	.000	-0	-2	-2	0	-0.1

● AL KELLOGG　Kellogg, Albert C.　b: 9/9/1886, Providence, R.I.　d: 7/21/53, Portland, Ore.　TL, 6′3″, 208 lbs.　Deb: 9/25/08

| 1908 | Phi-A | 0 | 2 | .000 | 3 | 3 | 2 | 0 | 0 | 17 | 20 | 1 | 9 | 8 | 15.9 | 5.82 | 44 | .294 | .385 | 1 | .125 | -0 | -6 | -6 | 0 | -0.7 |

● WIN KELLUM　Kellum, Winford Ansley　b: 4/11/1876, Waterford, Ont., Canada　d: 8/10/51, Big Rapids, Mich.　BB/TL, 5′10″, 190 lbs.　Deb: 4/26/01

1901	Bos-A	2	3	.400	6	6	5	0	0	48	61	3	7	8	13.3	6.38	55	.306	.339	3	.167	-1	-14	-15	1	-1.2
1904	Cin-N	15	10	.600	31	24	22	1	2	224²	206	1	46	70	10.5	2.60	113	.244	.291	13	.159	2	3	8	1	1.1
1905	StL-N	3	3	.500	11	7	5	1	0	74	70	1	10	19	11.0	2.92	102	.255	.283	5	.200	1	0	1	0	0.2
Total	3	20	16	.556	48	37	32	2	2	346²	337	5	63	97	10.7	3.19	95	.256	.297	21	.168	2	-10	-6	3	0.1

● BRYAN KELLY　Kelly, Bryan Keith　b: 2/24/59, Silver Spring, Md.　BR/TR, 6′2″, 195 lbs.　Deb: 9/2/86

1986	Det-A	1	2	.333	6	4	0	0	0	20	21	4	10	18	13.9	4.50	92	.269	.352	0	—	0	-1	-1	-0	-0.1
1987	Det-A	0	1	.000	5	0	0	0	0	10²	12	2	7	10	16.0	5.06	83	.286	.388	0	—	0	-1	-1	-0	-0.1
Total	2	1	3	.250	11	4	0	0	0	30²	33	6	17	28	14.7	4.70	89	.275	.365	0	—	0	-1	-2	-0	-0.2

● ED KELLY　Kelly, Edward Leo　b: 12/10/1888, Pawtucket, R.I.　d: 11/4/28, Red Lodge, Mont.　BR/TR, 5′11.5″, 173 lbs.　Deb: 4/14/14

| 1914 | Bos-A | 0 | 0 | — | 3 | 0 | 0 | 0 | 0 | 2¹ | 1 | 0 | 1 | 4 | 7.7 | 0.00 | — | .100 | .182 | 0 | — | -0 | 1 | 1 | 0 | 0.0 |

● GEORGE KELLY　Kelly, George Lange "Highpockets"　b: 9/10/1895, San Francisco, Cal.　d: 10/13/84, Burlingame, Cal.　BR/TR, 6′4″, 190 lbs.　Deb: 8/18/15　FCH♦

| 1917 | NY-N | 1 | 0 | 1.000 | 1 | 0 | 0 | 0 | 0 | 5 | 4 | 0 | 1 | 2 | 9.0 | 0.00 | — | .211 | .250 | 0 | .000 | -0 | 2 | 1 | -0 | 0.3 |

● HERB KELLY　Kelly, Herbert Barrett "Moke"　b: 6/4/1892, Mobile, Ala.　d: 5/18/73, Torrance, Cal.　BL/TL, 5′9″, 160 lbs.　Deb: 9/25/14

1914	Pit-N	0	2	.000	5	2	2	0	0	25²	24	1	7	6	10.9	2.45	108	.253	.304	2	.222	0	1	1	0	0.0
1915	Pit-N	1	1	.500	5	1	0	0	0	11	10	0	4	6	12.3	4.09	67	.250	.333	1	.500	1	-2	-2	1	-0.1
Total	2	1	3	.250	10	3	2	0	0	36²	34	1	11	12	11.3	2.95	91	.252	.313	3	.273	1	-1	-1	1	-0.1

● MIKE KELLY　Kelly, Michael J.　b: 11/9/02, St.Louis, Mo.　BR/TR, 6′1″, 178 lbs.　Deb: 9/3/26

| 1926 | Phi-N | 0 | 0 | — | 4 | 0 | 0 | 0 | 0 | 6² | 9 | 0 | 4 | 2 | 18.9 | 9.45 | 44 | .346 | .452 | 0 | .000 | -0 | -4 | -4 | -0 | -0.1 |

● KING KELLY　Kelly, Michael Joseph　b: 12/31/1857, Troy, N.Y.　d: 11/8/1894, Boston, Mass.　BR/TR, 5′10″, 170 lbs.　Deb: 5/1/1878　MH♦

1880	Chi-N	0	0	—	1	0	0	0	0	3	3	0	1	1	12.0	0.00	—	.250	.308	100	.291	0	1	1	-0	0.0
1883	Chi-N	0	0	—	1	0	0	0	0	1	0	0	1	0	9.0	0.00	—	.333	.333	109	.255	0	0	0	-0	0.0
1884	Chi-N	0	1	.000	2	0	0	0	0	5¹	12	2	2	1	23.6	8.44	37	.400	.438	160	.354	0	-3	-3	-0	-0.4
1887	Bos-N	1	0	1.000	3	0	0	0	0	13	17	1	14	3	21.5	3.46	117	.298	.437	156	.322	1	1	1	-0	0.1
1890	Bos-P	1	0	1.000	1	0	0	0	0	2	1	0	2	2	13.5	4.50	98	.142	.332	111	.326	1	-0	-0	-0	0.0

YEAR TM/L	W	L	PCT	G	GS	CG	SH	SV	IP	H	HR	BB	SO	RAT	ERA	ERA+	OAV	OOB	BH	AVG	PB	PR	/A	PD	TPI
1891 Cin-a	0	1	.000	3	0	0	0	0	15¹	21	2	7	0	17.0	5.28	78	.315	.389	84	.297	1	-3	-2	0	0.0
1892 *Bos-N	0	0	—	1	0	0	0	0	6	8	0	4	0	22.5	1.50	234	.308	.455	53	.189	0	1	1	-0	0.0
Total 7	2	2	.500	12	0	0	0	0	45²	63	5	30	4	19.1	4.14	92	.312	.412	1813	.308	4	-3	-2	-0	-0.3

● **REN KELLY**　Kelly, Reynolds Joseph　b: 11/18/1899, San Francisco, Cal　d: 8/24/63, Millbrae, Cal.　BR/TR, 6', 183 lbs.　Deb: 9/18/23　F

1923 Phi-A	0	0	—	1	0	0	0	0	7	7	0	4	1	14.1	2.57	160	.259	.355	0	.000	-0	1	1	-0	-0.1

● **BOB KELLY**　Kelly, Robert Edward　b: 10/4/27, Cleveland, Ohio　BR/TR, 6', 180 lbs.　Deb: 5/4/51

1951 Chi-N	7	4	.636	35	11	4	0	0	123²	130	8	55	48	13.5	4.66	88	.275	.352	5	.161	-1	-10	-8	-0	-0.7
1952 Chi-N	4	9	.308	31	15	3	2	0	125¹	114	7	46	50	11.7	3.59	107	.236	.306	8	.216	0	2	4	1	0.5
1953 Chi-N	0	1	.000	14	0	0	0	0	17	27	1	9	6	19.6	9.53	47	.375	.451	0	.000	-0	-10	-10	-0	-0.5
Cin-N	1	2	.333	28	5	0	0	2	66¹	71	7	26	29	13.2	4.34	100	.276	.343	2	.118	-1	-0	0	-0	-0.1
Yr	1	3	.250	42	5	0	0	2	83¹	98	9	35	35	14.4	5.40	81	.297	.364	2	.111	-1	-10	-9	-0	-0.6
1958 Cin-N	0	0	—	2	1	0	0	0	2	3	0	3	1	27.0	4.50	92	.500	.667	0	—	0	-0	-0	0	0.0
Cle-A	0	2	.000	13	3	0	0	0	27²	29	4	13	12	14.0	5.20	70	.282	.368	1	.250	-0	-4	-5	-0	-0.3
Total 4	12	18	.400	123	35	7	2	2	362	374	28	152	146	13.2	4.50	90	.268	.343	16	.178	-1	-22	-18	1	-1.1

● **BILL KELSO**　Kelso, William Eugene　b: 2/19/40, Kansas City, Mo.　BR/TR, 6'4", 215 lbs.　Deb: 7/31/64

1964 LA-A	2	0	1.000	10	1	1	1	0	23²	19	3	9	21	11.0	2.28	144	.218	.299	0	.000	-0	4	3	0	0.2
1966 Cal-A	1	1	.500	5	0	0	0	0	11¹	11	1	6	11	14.3	2.38	141	.244	.346	0	.000	-0	1	1	-0	0.2
1967 Cal-A	5	3	.625	69	0	0	0	11	112	85	6	63	91	12.2	2.97	106	.219	.333	2	.105	-1	3	2	1	0.2
1968 Cin-N	4	1	.800	35	0	0	0	1	54	56	6	15	39	12.3	4.00	79	.277	.336	0	.000	-1	-6	-5	-1	-0.7
Total 4	12	5	.706	119	2	1	1	12	201	171	16	93	162	12.2	3.13	102	.237	.331	2	.059	-2	2	1	-0	-0.1

● **RUSS KEMMERER**　Kemmerer, Russell Paul "Rusty" or "Dutch"　b: 11/1/31, Pittsburgh, Pa.　BR/TR, 6'3", 200 lbs.　Deb: 6/27/54

1954 Bos-A	5	3	.625	19	9	2	1	0	75¹	71	4	41	37	13.6	3.82	108	.257	.357	3	.143	-0	-1	2	0	0.2
1955 Bos-A	1	1	.500	7	2	0	0	0	17¹	18	3	15	13	17.1	7.27	59	.269	.402	0	.000	-0	-6	-6	-0	-0.6
1957 Bos-A	0	0	—	1	0	0	0	0	4	5	0	2	1	15.8	4.50	89	.333	.412	0	.000	-0	-0	-0	-0	-0.0
Was-A	7	11	.389	39	26	6	0	0	172¹	214	20	71	81	15.0	4.96	79	.309	.375	3	.067	-1	-22	-20	-3	-2.3
Yr	7	11	.389	40	26	6	0	0	176¹	219	20	73	82	15.0	4.95	79	.309	.375	3	.065	-1	-23	-21	-3	-2.3
1958 Was-A	6	15	.286	40	30	6	0	0	224¹	234	25	74	111	12.5	4.61	83	.276	.330	11	.159	-2	-21	-20	-0	-1.9
1959 Was-A	8	17	.320	37	28	8	0	0	206	221	20	71	89	12.9	4.50	87	.276	.338	8	.133	-1	-15	-13	0	-1.5
1960 Was-A	0	2	.000	3	3	0	0	0	17¹	18	2	10	10	15.1	7.79	50	.269	.372	0	.000	-0	-8	-8	1	-0.6
Chi-A	6	3	.667	36	7	2	1	2	120²	111	9	45	76	11.7	2.98	127	.248	.318	0	.000	-3	12	11	0	0.5
Yr	6	5	.545	39	10	2	1	2	138	129	7	55	86	12.1	3.59	106	.250	.323	0	.000	-3	4	3	1	-0.1
1961 Chi-A	3	3	.500	47	2	0	0	2	96²	102	10	26	35	11.9	4.38	89	.278	.326	3	.200	-1	-4	-5	1	-0.1
1962 Chi-A	2	1	.667	20	0	0	0	0	28	30	3	11	17	13.2	3.86	101	.270	.336	1	.500	1	0	0	1	0.2
Hou-N	5	3	.625	36	2	0	0	0	68	72	10	15	23	11.9	4.10	91	.272	.318	3	.333	1	-3	-0	1	-0.2
1963 Hou-N	0	0	—	17	0	0	0	1	36²	48	1	8	12	13.7	5.65	56	.320	.354	2	.286	0	-10	-10	1	-0.2
Total 9	43	59	.422	302	109	24	2	8	1066²	1144	103	389	505	13.1	4.46	86	.277	.342	34	.128	-5	-76	-72	1	-6.3

● **DUTCH KEMNER**　Kemner, Herman John　b: 3/4/1899, Quincy, Ill.　d: 1/16/88, Quincy, Ill.　BR/TR, 5'10.5", 175 lbs.　Deb: 4/19/29

1929 Cin-N	0	0	—	9	0	0	0	1	15¹	19	0	8	10	15.8	7.63	60	.328	.409	1	.250	-0	-5	-5	0	-0.1

● **ED KENNA**　Kenna, Edward Benninghaus "The Pitching Poet"　b: 10/17/1877, Charleston, W.Va.　d: 3/22/12, Grant, Fla.　TR, 6', 180 lbs.　Deb: 5/5/02

1902 Phi-A	1	1	.500	2	2	1	0	0	17	19	1	11	5	16.4	5.29	69	.283	.391	1	.125	-0	-3	-3	0	-0.3

● **VERN KENNEDY**　Kennedy, Lloyd Vernon　b: 3/20/07, Kansas City, Mo.　d: 1/28/93, Mendon, Mo.　BL/TR, 6', 175 lbs.　Deb: 9/18/34

1934 Chi-A	0	2	.000	3	3	1	0	0	19¹	21	1	9	7	14.0	3.72	127	.300	.380	2	.286	0	2	2	1	0.3
1935 Chi-A	11	11	.500	31	25	16	2	1	211²	211	17	95	65	13.2	3.91	118	.262	.343	18	.247	1	13	17	2	1.8
1936 Chi-A☆	21	9	.700	35	34	20	1	0	274¹	282	13	147	99	14.2	4.63	112	.268	.360	32	.283	5	13	17	1	2.0
1937 Chi-A	14	13	.519	32	30	15	1	0	221	238	16	124	114	14.9	5.09	90	.273	.366	20	.230	-1	-12	-12	0	-1.0
1938 Det-A☆	12	9	.571	33	26	11	0	2	190¹	215	13	113	53	15.6	5.06	99	.287	.381	23	.291	3	-6	-1	2	0.3
1939 Det-A	0	3	.000	4	4	1	0	0	21	25	4	9	9	15.0	6.43	76	.301	.376	2	.286	-0	-4	-4	1	-0.3
StL-A	9	17	.346	33	27	12	1	0	191²	229	18	115	55	16.2	5.73	85	.297	.389	10	.149	-2	-24	-18	-1	-2.3
Yr	9	20	.310	37	31	13	1	0	212²	254	22	124	64	16.0	5.80	84	.297	.387	12	.162	-2	-28	-22	0	-2.6
1940 StL-A	12	17	.414	34	32	18	0	0	222¹	263	18	122	70	15.7	5.59	82	.298	.385	25	.298	6	-30	-25	2	-1.8
1941 StL-A	2	4	.333	6	6	2	0	0	45	44	5	27	6	14.2	4.40	98	.259	.360	6	.400	2	-1	-0	0	0.2
Was-A	1	7	.125	17	7	2	0	0	66¹	77	5	39	22	16.0	5.70	71	.297	.393	3	.143	-1	-11	-12	-1	-1.3
Yr	3	11	.214	23	13	4	0	0	111¹	121	10	66	28	15.3	5.17	80	.282	.380	9	.250	2	-13	-13	-1	-1.1
1942 Cle-A	4	8	.333	28	12	4	0	1	108	99	1	50	37	12.5	4.08	84	.244	.328	6	.200	1	-5	-8	0	-0.6
1943 Cle-A	10	7	.588	28	17	8	1	0	146²	130	4	59	63	11.7	2.45	127	.242	.319	12	.231	1	14	11	1	1.5
1944 Cle-A	2	5	.286	12	10	2	0	0	59	66	0	37	17	15.7	5.03	66	.289	.389	2	.087	-2	-11	-11	1	-1.3
Phi-N	1	5	.167	12	7	3	0	0	55¹	60	7	20	23	13.0	4.23	85	.269	.329	6	.286	1	-4	-4	0	-0.3
1945 Phi-N	0	3	.000	12	3	0	0	0	36	43	2	14	13	14.3	5.50	70	.301	.358	2	.182	-0	-7	-7	-1	-0.4
Cin-N	5	12	.294	24	20	11	1	1	157²	170	10	69	38	13.8	4.00	94	.280	.356	12	.226	2	-3	-4	1	-0.1
Yr	5	15	.250	36	23	11	1	1	193²	213	12	83	51	13.9	4.28	88	.283	.356	14	.219	2	-10	-11	2	-0.5
Total 12	104	132	.441	344	263	126	7	5	2025²	2173	130	1049	691	14.4	4.67	94	.277	.363	181	.244	19	-77	-63	13	-3.3

● **MONTE KENNEDY**　Kennedy, Montia Calvin　b: 5/11/22, Amelia, Va.　BR/TL, 6'2", 185 lbs.　Deb: 4/18/46

1946 NY-N	9	10	.474	38	27	10	1	1	186²	153	14	116	71	13.2	3.42	101	.224	.340	15	.234	2	-0	0	-0	0.2
1947 NY-N	9	12	.429	34	24	9	0	0	148¹	158	8	88	60	15.2	4.85	84	.272	.372	8	.167	-1	-13	-13	-0	-1.6
1948 NY-N	3	9	.250	25	16	7	1	0	114¹	118	10	57	63	14.0	4.01	98	.264	.351	4	.129	-1	-1	-1	-1	-0.3
1949 NY-N	12	14	.462	38	32	14	4	1	223¹	208	13	100	95	12.5	3.43	116	.242	.323	12	.145	-1	15	14	-2	1.1
1950 NY-N	5	4	.556	36	17	5	0	2	114¹	120	14	53	41	13.9	4.72	87	.269	.351	2	.056	-3	-7	-8	-0	-0.9
1951 *NY-N	1	2	.333	29	5	1	0	0	68	68	0	31	22	13.1	2.25	174	.270	.350	3	.200	1	13	13	0	0.5
1952 NY-N	3	4	.429	31	6	2	1	0	83¹	73	6	31	48	11.4	3.02	122	.230	.303	2	.091	-1	7	6	1	0.4
1953 NY-N	0	0	—	18	0	0	0	0	22²	30	2	19	11	19.9	7.15	60	.337	.459	0	—	-0	-7	-7	0	-0.0
Total 8	42	55	.433	249	127	48	7	4	961	928	67	495	411	13.5	3.84	101	.253	.344	46	.153	-5	6	4	-4	-0.6

● **TED KENNEDY**　Kennedy, Theodore A.　b: 2/1865, Henry, Ill.　d: 10/31/07, St.Louis, Mo.　BL　Deb: 6/12/1885

1885 Chi-N	7	2	.778	9	9	8	0	0	78²	91	5	28	36	13.6	3.43	88	.288	.346	3	.083	-4	-5	-3	-0	-0.7
1886 Phi-a	5	15	.250	20	19	19	0	0	172²	196	4	65	68	14.0	4.53	77	.271	.338	3	.044	-9	-21	-20	1	-2.4
Lou-a	0	4	.000	4	4	4	0	0	32	53	1	16	14	19.7	5.34	68	.351	.417	1	.077	-1	-7	-6	-1	-0.7
Yr	5	19	.208	24	23	23	0	0	204²	249	5	81	82	14.6	4.66	76	.282	.343	4	.049	-10	-28	-26	0	-3.1
Total 2	12	21	.364	33	32	31	0	0	283¹	340	10	109	118	14.5	4.32	79	.286	.350	7	.060	-14	-33	-29	-0	-3.8

● **BILL KENNEDY**　Kennedy, William Aulton "Lefty"　b: 3/14/21, Carnesville, Ga.　d: 4/9/83, Seattle, Wash.　BL/TL, 6'2", 195 lbs.　Deb: 4/26/48

1948 Cle-A	1	0	1.000	6	0	0	0	0	11¹	16	0	13	12	23.0	11.12	37	.333	.475	2	.667	1	-9	-9	0	-0.5
StL-A	7	8	.467	26	20	3	0	0	132	132	10	104	77	16.4	4.70	97	.259	.389	11	.250	-1	-6	-2	-1	-0.2
Yr	8	8	.500	32	23	3	0	0	143¹	148	10	117	89	17.0	5.21	87	.265	.397	13	.277	2	-15	-11	-1	-0.5
1949 StL-A	4	11	.267	48	16	2	0	1	153²	172	13	93	69	14.5	4.69	97	.285	.365	6	.150	-2	-8	-3	-2	-0.5
1950 StL-A	0	0	—	1	0	0	0	0	2	1	0	2	1	13.5	0.00	—	.143	.333	0	—	-0	1	1	0	0.0
1951 StL-A	1	5	.167	19	5	1	0	0	56	76	4	37	29	18.3	5.79	76	.332	.427	2	.125	-2	-10	-9	1	-0.8
1952 Chi-A	2	2	.500	47	1	0	0	5	70²	54	4	38	46	11.8	2.80	130	.213	.318	3	.231	0	7	7	1	0.4

YEAR TM/L	W	L	PCT	G	GS	CG	SH	SV	IP	H	HR	BB	SO	RAT	ERA	ERA+	OAV	OOB	BH	AVG	PB	PR	/A	PD	TPI
1953 Bos-A	0	0	—	16	0	0	0	2	24¹	24	2	17	14	15.5	3.70	114	.255	.375	1	.500	0	1	1	-0	0.0
1956 Cin-N	0	0	—	1	0	0	0	0	2	6	1	0	0	27.0	18.00	22	.667	.667	0	—	0	-3	-3	-0	0.0
1957 Cin-N	0	2	.000	8	0	0	0	0	12²	16	1	5	8	15.6	6.39	64	.314	.386	0	.000	0	-4	-3	0	-0.6
Total 8	15	28	.349	172	45	6	0	11	464²	497	34	289	256	15.5	4.73	92	.275	.379	25	.208	-1	-31	-20	-2	-2.2

● BILL KENNEDY
Kennedy, William Gorman   b: 12/22/18, Alexandria, Va.   BL/TL, 6'1", 175 lbs.   Deb: 5/1/42

YEAR TM/L	W	L	PCT	G	GS	CG	SH	SV	IP	H	HR	BB	SO	RAT	ERA	ERA+	OAV	OOB	BH	AVG	PB	PR	/A	PD	TPI
1942 Was-A	0	1	.000	8	2	1	0	2	18	21	1	10	4	15.5	8.00	46	.296	.383	0	.000	-1	-9	-9	1	-0.6
1946 Was-A	1	2	.333	21	2	0	0	3	39	40	1	29	18	15.9	6.00	56	.270	.390	1	.125	-0	-11	-11	-0	-1.1
1947 Was-A	0	0	—	2	0	0	0	0	6²	10	1	5	1	20.3	8.10	46	.370	.469	0	.000	-0	-3	-3	0	0.0
Total 3	1	3	.250	31	4	1	0	5	63²	71	3	44	23	16.3	6.79	51	.289	.397	1	.071	-1	-23	-23	0	-1.7

● BRICKYARD KENNEDY
Kennedy, William P.   b: 10/7/1867, Bellaire, Ohio   d: 9/23/15, Bellaire, Ohio   BR/TR, 5'11", 160 lbs.   Deb: 4/26/1892

YEAR TM/L	W	L	PCT	G	GS	CG	SH	SV	IP	H	HR	BB	SO	RAT	ERA	ERA+	OAV	OOB	BH	AVG	PB	PR	/A	PD	TPI
1892 Bro-N	13	8	.619	26	21	18	0	1	191	189	3	95	108	13.6	3.86	82	.248	.335	14	.165	-1	-12	-15	-0	-1.5
1893 Bro-N	25	20	.556	46	44	40	2	1	382²	376	15	168	107	13.0	3.72	119	.249	.327	39	.248	2	40	30	5	3.2
1894 Bro-N	24	20	.545	48	41	34	0	2	360²	445	15	149	107	15.1	4.92	101	.300	.368	49	.304	4	16	1	3	0.6
1895 Bro-N	19	12	.613	39	33	26	2	1	279²	335	13	93	39	14.0	5.12	86	.292	.349	39	.307	4	-10	-22	-1	-1.6
1896 Bro-N	17	20	.459	42	38	28	1	1	305²	334	12	130	76	14.0	4.42	93	.276	.352	23	.189	-7	-2	-10	3	-1.3
1897 Bro-N	18	20	.474	44	40	36	2	1	343¹	370	6	149	81	13.8	3.91	105	.273	.348	40	.272	4	16	8	2	1.2
1898 Bro-N	16	22	.421	40	39	38	0	0	339¹	360	12	123	73	12.9	3.37	107	.270	.334	34	.252	3	9	8	6	1.6
1899 Bro-N	22	9	.710	40	33	27	2	2	277¹	297	11	86	55	13.3	2.79	140	.274	.329	27	.248	4	33	35	0	3.7
1900 Bro-N	20	13	.606	42	35	26	2	0	292	316	5	111	75	13.4	3.91	98	.275	.343	37	.301	7	-7	-2	1	0.5
1901 Bro-N	3	5	.375	14	8	6	0	0	85¹	80	1	24	28	11.1	3.06	110	.246	.300	6	.167	-1	3	3	-0	0.0
1902 NY-A	4	4	.200	6	6	4	1	0	38²	44	0	16	9	14.0	3.96	71	.286	.353	4	.267	1	-5	-5	-1	-0.6
1903 *Pit-N	9	6	.600	18	15	10	1	0	125¹	130	6	57	39	13.6	3.45	94	.277	.357	21	.362	8	-2	-3	-1	0.3
Total 12	187	159	.540	405	353	293	13	9	3021	3276	93	1201	797	13.5	3.96	102	.273	.343	333	.261	27	78	33	15	6.1

● ART KENNEY
Kenney, Arthur Joseph   b: 4/29/16, Milford, Mass.   BL/TL, 6', 175 lbs.   Deb: 7/1/38

YEAR TM/L	W	L	PCT	G	GS	CG	SH	SV	IP	H	HR	BB	SO	RAT	ERA	ERA+	OAV	OOB	BH	AVG	PB	PR	/A	PD	TPI
1938 Bos-N	0	0	—	2	0	0	0	0	2¹	3	0	8	2	42.4	15.43	22	.300	.611	0	—	0	-3	-3	0	0.0

● ED KENT
Kent, Edward C.   b: 1859, New York   TL, 5'6.5", 152 lbs.   Deb: 8/14/1884

YEAR TM/L	W	L	PCT	G	GS	CG	SH	SV	IP	H	HR	BB	SO	RAT	ERA	ERA+	OAV	OOB	BH	AVG	PB	PR	/A	PD	TPI
1884 Tol-a	0	1	.000	1	1	1	0	0	9	14	0	3	4	18.0	6.00	57	.298	.353	0	.000	-1	-3	-3	-0	-0.2

● MAURY KENT
Kent, Maurice Allen   b: 9/17/1885, Marshalltown, Ia.   d: 4/19/66, Iowa City, Iowa   BR/TR, 6', 168 lbs.   Deb: 4/15/12

YEAR TM/L	W	L	PCT	G	GS	CG	SH	SV	IP	H	HR	BB	SO	RAT	ERA	ERA+	OAV	OOB	BH	AVG	PB	PR	/A	PD	TPI
1912 Bro-N	5	5	.500	20	9	2	1	0	93	107	3	46	24	14.9	4.84	69	.296	.377	8	.229	1	-15	-15	1	-1.3
1913 Bro-N	0	0	—	3	0	0	0	0	7¹	5	0	3	1	9.8	2.45	134	.192	.276	0	.000	-0	1	1	-0	-0.1
Total 2	5	5	.500	23	9	2	1	0	100¹	112	3	49	25	14.5	4.66	72	.289	.371	8	.211	1	-14	-15	1	-1.4

● MATT KEOUGH
Keough, Matthew Lon   b: 7/3/55, Pomona, Cal.   BR/TR, 6'3", 190 lbs.   Deb: 9/3/77   F

YEAR TM/L	W	L	PCT	G	GS	CG	SH	SV	IP	H	HR	BB	SO	RAT	ERA	ERA+	OAV	OOB	BH	AVG	PB	PR	/A	PD	TPI
1977 Oak-A	1	3	.250	7	6	0	0	0	42²	39	4	22	23	13.1	4.85	83	.247	.343	0	—	0	-4	-4	-1	-0.3
1978 Oak-A★	8	15	.348	32	32	6	0	0	197¹	178	9	85	108	12.2	3.24	112	.241	.323	0	—	0	11	9	2	1.1
1979 Oak-A	2	17	.105	30	28	7	1	0	176²	220	18	78	95	15.5	5.04	80	.315	.389	0	—	0	-16	-20	2	-1.3
1980 Oak-A	16	13	.552	34	32	20	2	0	250	218	24	94	121	11.4	2.92	129	.236	.310	0	—	0	31	24	-1	3.0
1981 *Oak-A	10	6	.625	19	19	10	2	0	140¹	125	11	45	60	10.9	3.40	102	.239	.299	0	—	0	4	1	-2	0.2
1982 Oak-A	11	18	.379	34	34	10	2	0	209¹	233	38	101	75	14.6	5.72	68	.284	.366	0	—	0	-38	-42	-3	-4.8
1983 Oak-A	2	3	.400	14	4	0	0	0	44	50	7	31	28	16.6	6.52	70	.284	.391	0	—	0	-7	-8	-1	-0.6
NY-A	3	4	.429	12	12	0	0	0	55²	59	12	20	26	13.1	5.17	75	.266	.332	0	—	0	-7	-8	-0	-0.7
Yr	5	7	.417	26	16	0	0	0	99²	109	19	51	54	14.6	5.33	73	.273	.358	0	—	0	-14	-16	-1	-1.3
1985 StL-N	0	1	.000	4	1	0	0	0	10	10	0	4	3	13.5	4.50	79	.278	.366	0	.000	-0	-1	-1	0	-0.1
1986 Chi-N	2	2	.500	19	2	0	0	0	29	36	4	12	19	15.2	4.97	81	.316	.386	2	.400	1	-4	-3	-0	-0.3
Hou-N	3	2	.600	10	5	0	0	0	35	22	5	18	25	10.5	3.09	117	.180	.291	4	.364	1	2	2	-1	0.4
Yr	5	4	.556	29	7	0	0	0	64	58	9	30	44	12.5	3.94	96	.245	.332	6	.375	2	-2	-1	-1	0.1
Total 9	58	84	.408	215	175	53	7	0	1190	1190	132	510	590	13.1	4.17	91	.262	.341	6	.333	2	-28	-50	-5	-3.4

● KURT KEPSHIRE
Kepshire, Kurt David   b: 7/3/59, Bridgeport, Conn.   BL/TR, 6'1", 180 lbs.   Deb: 7/4/84

YEAR TM/L	W	L	PCT	G	GS	CG	SH	SV	IP	H	HR	BB	SO	RAT	ERA	ERA+	OAV	OOB	BH	AVG	PB	PR	/A	PD	TPI
1984 StL-N	6	5	.545	17	16	2	2	0	109	100	7	44	71	11.9	3.30	105	.249	.323	2	.056	-2	3	2	-2	-0.2
1985 StL-N	10	9	.526	32	29	1	0	0	153¹	155	16	71	67	13.3	4.75	74	.264	.343	6	.118	-1	-20	-21	-2	-2.6
1986 StL-N	0	1	.000	2	1	0	0	0	8	8	2	4	6	13.5	4.50	81	.258	.343	0	.000	-0	-1	-1	0	-0.1
Total 3	16	15	.516	51	46	3	2	0	270¹	263	25	119	144	12.7	4.16	88	.258	.335	8	.091	-3	-17	-20	-3	-2.9

● CHARLIE KERFELD
Kerfeld, Charles Patrick   b: 9/28/63, Knob Knoster, Mo.   BR/TR, 6'6", 225 lbs.   Deb: 7/27/85

YEAR TM/L	W	L	PCT	G	GS	CG	SH	SV	IP	H	HR	BB	SO	RAT	ERA	ERA+	OAV	OOB	BH	AVG	PB	PR	/A	PD	TPI
1985 Hou-N	4	2	.667	11	6	0	0	0	44¹	44	2	25	30	14.0	4.06	85	.268	.365	0	.000	-1	-2	-2	-0	-0.6
1986 *Hou-N	11	2	.846	61	0	0	0	7	93²	71	5	42	77	11.0	2.59	139	.213	.305	1	.111	-0	12	10	-1	1.5
1987 Hou-N	0	2	.000	21	0	0	0	0	29²	34	3	21	17	17.0	6.67	59	.309	.424	0	.000	-0	-9	-9	-0	-0.6
1990 Hou-N	0	2	.000	5	0	0	0	0	3¹	9	1	6	4	40.5	16.20	23	.529	.652	0	—	0	-5	-5	-0	-2.1
Atl-N	3	1	.750	25	0	0	0	2	30²	31	2	23	27	15.8	5.58	72	.270	.391	0	—	0	-6	-5	-1	-0.8
Yr	3	3	.500	30	0	0	0	2	34	40	3	29	31	18.3	6.62	60	.303	.429	0	—	0	-11	-10	-1	-2.9
Total 4	18	9	.667	123	6	0	0	9	201²	189	12	117	155	13.8	4.20	88	.256	.360	1	.038	-2	-10	-11	-2	-2.6

● GUS KERIAZAKOS
Keriazakos, Constantine Nicholas   b: 7/28/31, W.Orange, N.J.   BR/TR, 6'3", 187 lbs.   Deb: 10/1/50

YEAR TM/L	W	L	PCT	G	GS	CG	SH	SV	IP	H	HR	BB	SO	RAT	ERA	ERA+	OAV	OOB	BH	AVG	PB	PR	/A	PD	TPI
1950 Chi-A	0	1	.000	1	1	0	0	0	2¹	7	0	5	1	46.3	19.29	23	.500	.632	1	1.000	0	-4	-4	-0	-0.9
1954 Was-A	2	3	.400	22	3	2	0	0	59²	59	4	30	33	13.4	3.77	94	.262	.349	1	.067	-1	-0	-1	-0	-0.2
1955 KC-A	0	1	.000	5	1	0	0	0	11²	15	4	7	8	17.0	12.34	34	.333	.423	0	.000	-0	-11	-11	-0	-0.8
Total 3	2	5	.286	28	5	2	0	0	73²	81	8	42	42	15.0	5.62	65	.285	.377	2	.105	-1	-15	-16	-0	-1.9

● BILL KERKSIECK
Kerksieck, Wayman William   b: 12/6/13, Ulm, Ark.   d: 3/11/70, Stuttgart, Ark.   BR/TR, 6'1", 183 lbs.   Deb: 6/21/39

YEAR TM/L	W	L	PCT	G	GS	CG	SH	SV	IP	H	HR	BB	SO	RAT	ERA	ERA+	OAV	OOB	BH	AVG	PB	PR	/A	PD	TPI
1939 Phi-N	0	2	.000	23	2	1	0	0	62²	81	13	32	13	16.2	7.18	56	.328	.405	1	.083	-0	-23	-22	-1	-0.7

● JIM KERN
Kern, James Lester   b: 3/15/49, Gladwin, Mich.   BR/TR, 6'5", 205 lbs.   Deb: 9/6/74

YEAR TM/L	W	L	PCT	G	GS	CG	SH	SV	IP	H	HR	BB	SO	RAT	ERA	ERA+	OAV	OOB	BH	AVG	PB	PR	/A	PD	TPI
1974 Cle-A	0	1	.000	4	1	0	0	0	15¹	16	1	14	11	17.6	4.70	77	.262	.400	0	—	0	-2	-2	-0	-0.1
1975 Cle-A	1	2	.333	13	7	0	0	0	71²	60	5	45	55	13.8	3.77	100	.233	.357	0	—	0	0	0	0	0.0
1976 Cle-A	10	7	.588	50	2	0	0	15	117²	91	2	50	111	11.2	2.37	147	.222	.314	0	—	0	15	15	0	2.6
1977 Cle-A★	8	10	.444	60	0	0	0	18	92	85	3	47	91	13.5	3.42	115	.260	.363	0	—	0	6	5	0	1.3
1978 Cle-A★	10	10	.500	58	0	0	0	13	99¹	77	4	58	95	12.5	3.08	121	.224	.342	0	.000	0	8	7	1	1.7
1979 Tex-A★	13	5	.722	71	0	0	0	29	143	99	5	62	136	10.3	1.57	204	.199	.290	0	—	0	42	41	-1	6.7
1980 Tex-A	3	11	.214	38	1	0	0	2	63¹	65	4	45	40	15.9	4.83	81	.279	.400	0	—	0	-6	-7	0	-1.1
1981 Tex-A	1	2	.333	23	0	0	0	6	30	21	0	22	20	13.2	2.70	128	.204	.349	0	—	0	3	3	-0	0.6
1982 Cin-N	3	5	.375	50	0	0	0	6	76	51	4	48	43	13.1	2.84	130	.222	.342	0	.000	0	8	7	1	0.8
Chi-A	2	1	.667	13	1	0	0	3	28	20	3	12	23	10.3	5.14	78	.204	.291	0	—	0	-3	-3	0	-0.4
1983 Chi-A	0	0	—	1	0	0	0	0	0²	1	0	0	0	13.5	0.00	—	.333	.333	0	—	0	1	1	-0	0.0
1984 Phi-N	0	1	.000	8	0	0	0	0	13¹	20	3	10	8	20.3	10.13	36	.339	.435	0	.000	-0	-10	-10	-0	-0.7
Mil-A	1	0	1.000	6	0	0	0	0	4²	4	1	4	4	17.4	0.00	—	.300	.391	0	—	0	3	3	-0	0.5
1985 Mil-A	0	1	.000	5	0	0	0	0	11	14	1	5	6	15.5	6.55	64	.318	.388	0	—	0	-3	-3	1	-0.2
1986 Cle-A	1	1	.500	27¹	0	0	0	0	27¹	34	1	23	16	19.8	7.90	52	.298	.429	0	—	0	-11	-11	-0	-0.6
Total 13	53	57	.482	416	14	0	0	88	793¹	670	35	444	651	13.0	3.32	115	.235	.344	0	.000	-0	48	45	1	11.0

YEAR TM/L	W	L	PCT	G	GS	CG	SH	SV	IP	H	HR	BB	SO	RAT	ERA	ERA+	OAV	OOB	BH	AVG	PB	PR	/A	PD	TPI

● **DICKIE KERR** Kerr, Richard Henry b: 7/3/1893, St.Louis, Mo. d: 5/4/63, Houston, Tex. BL/TL, 5'7", 155 lbs. Deb: 4/25/19

1919 *Chi-A	13	7	.650	39	17	10	1	0	212¹	208	2	64	79	11.6	2.88	110	.259	.316	17	.250	5	8	7	1	1.2
1920 Chi-A	21	9	.700	45	27	19	3	5	253²	266	7	72	72	12.1	3.37	112	.278	.331	14	.156	-4	12	11	3	1.1
1921 Chi-A	19	17	.528	44	37	25	3	1	308²	357	12	96	80	13.5	4.72	90	.295	.352	25	.238	5	-15	-17	-0	-1.2
1925 Chi-A	0	1	.000	12	2	0	0	0	36²	45	3	18	4	15.7	5.15	81	.304	.383	4	.333	1	-3	-4	0	0.0
Total 4	53	34	.609	140	83	54	7	6	811¹	876	24	250	235	12.7	3.84	99	.281	.338	60	.218	7	2	-2	4	1.1

● **JOE KERRIGAN** Kerrigan, Joseph Thomas b: 11/30/54, Philadelphia, Pa. BR/TR, 6'5", 205 lbs. Deb: 7/9/76 C

1976 Mon-N	2	6	.250	38	0	0	0	1	56²	63	3	23	22	14.0	3.81	98	.289	.362	0	.000	-0	-2	-1	1	-0.1
1977 Mon-N	3	5	.375	66	0	0	0	11	89¹	94	4	33	43	11.7	3.22	118	.241	.315	0	.000	-1	7	6	1	0.6
1978 Bal-A	3	1	.750	26	2	0	0	3	71²	75	10	36	41	14.2	4.77	73	.273	.361	0	—	-0	-8	-10	2	-0.5
1980 Bal-A	0	0	—	1	0	0	0	0	2¹	3	0	0	1	11.6	3.86	103	.273	.273	0	—	0	0	0	0	0.1
Total 4	8	12	.400	131	2	0	0	15	220	221	17	92	107	13.1	3.89	95	.264	.342	0	.000	-1	-3	-5	3	0.1

● **RICK KESTER** Kester, Richard Lee b: 7/7/46, Iola, Kan. BR/TR, 6', 190 lbs. Deb: 8/18/68

1968 Atl-N	0	0	—	5	0	0	0	0	6¹	8	0	3	9	15.6	5.68	53	.308	.379	0	—	0	-2	-2	-0	0.0
1969 Atl-N	0	0	—	1	0	0	0	0	2	5	1	0	2	22.5	13.50	27	.455	.455	0	—	0	-2	-2	-0	0.0
1970 Atl-N	0	0	—	15	0	0	0	0	32¹	36	3	19	20	15.3	5.57	77	.283	.377	0	.000	-1	-5	-5	-1	-0.2
Total 3	0	0	—	21	0	0	0	0	40²	49	4	22	31	15.7	5.98	68	.299	.382	0	.000	-1	-10	-9	-1	-0.2

● **GUS KETCHUM** Ketchum, Augustus Franklin b: 3/21/1897, Royse City, Tex. d: 9/6/80, Oklahoma City, Okla. BR/TR, 5'9.5", 170 lbs. Deb: 8/7/22

| 1922 Phi-A | 0 | 1 | .000 | 6 | 0 | 0 | 0 | 0 | 16 | 19 | 2 | 8 | 4 | 15.8 | 5.63 | 76 | .302 | .389 | 0 | .000 | -1 | -3 | -2 | -1 | -0.3 |

● **HENRY KEUPPER** Keupper, Henry J. b: 6/24/1887, Staunton, Ill. d: 8/14/60, Marion, Ill. BL/TL, 6'1", 185 lbs. Deb: 4/19/14

| 1914 StL-F | 8 | 20 | .286 | 42 | 25 | 12 | 1 | 0 | 213 | 256 | 3 | 49 | 70 | 13.1 | 4.27 | 71 | .291 | .332 | 17 | .250 | 1 | -33 | -29 | 2 | -3.1 |

● **JIMMY KEY** Key, James Edward b: 4/22/61, Huntsville, Ala. BR/TL, 6'1", 190 lbs. Deb: 4/6/84

1984 Tor-A	4	5	.444	63	0	0	0	10	62	70	8	32	44	15.0	4.65	88	.286	.371	0	—	0	-5	-4	1	-0.7
1985 *Tor-A★	14	6	.700	35	32	3	0	0	212²	188	22	50	85	10.2	3.00	140	.237	.284	0	—	0	27	28	4	2.9
1986 Tor-A	14	11	.560	36	35	4	2	0	232	222	24	74	141	11.6	3.57	118	.256	.317	0	—	0	16	17	3	1.8
1987 Tor-A	17	8	.680	36	36	8	1	0	261	210	24	66	161	**9.6**	**2.76**	**163**	**.221**	**.273**	0	—	0	**49**	**50**	2	4.4
1988 Tor-A	12	5	.706	21	21	2	2	0	131¹	127	13	30	65	11.1	3.29	119	.250	.298	0	—	0	10	9	-0	1.1
1989 *Tor-A	13	14	.481	33	33	5	0	0	216	226	18	27	118	10.7	3.88	97	.270	.295	0	—	0	-3	-2	0	0.0
1990 Tor-A	13	7	.650	27	27	0	0	0	154²	169	20	22	88	11.2	4.25	93	.281	.307	0	—	0	-6	-5	0	-0.7
1991 *Tor-A★	16	12	.571	33	33	2	2	0	209¹	207	12	44	125	10.9	3.05	138	.254	.295	0	—	0	24	27	3	3.5
1992 *Tor-A	13	13	.500	33	33	4	2	0	216²	205	24	59	117	11.1	3.53	116	.254	.301	0	—	0	10	13	0	1.4
1993 NY-A★	18	6	**.750**	34	34	4	2	0	236²	219	26	43	173	10.0	3.00	138	.246	.282	0	—	0	35	30	3	3.0
1994 NY-A★	**17**	4	.810	25	25	1	0	0	168	177	10	52	97	12.4	3.27	136	.273	.330	0	—	0	29	22	2	2.7
Total 11	151	91	.624	376	309	33	12	10	2100¹	2020	201	499	1214	10.9	3.36	124	.253	.299	0	—	0	189	186	15	19.4

● **DANA KIECKER** Kiecker, Dana Ervin b: 2/25/61, Sleepy Eye, Minn. BR/TR, 6'3", 180 lbs. Deb: 4/12/90

1990 *Bos-A	8	9	.471	32	25	0	0	0	152	145	7	54	93	12.3	3.97	103	.253	.328	0	—	0	-1	2	2	0.0
1991 Bos-A	2	3	.400	18	5	0	0	0	40¹	56	6	23	21	18.1	7.36	58	.344	.431	0	—	0	-15	-14	1	-1.6
Total 2	10	12	.455	50	30	0	0	0	192¹	201	13	77	114	13.5	4.68	88	.273	.351	0	—	0	-16	-12	3	-1.6

● **JOE KIEFER** Kiefer, Joseph William "Harlem Joe" or "Smoke" b: 7/19/1899, W.Leyden, N.Y. d: 7/5/75, Utica, N.Y. BR/TR, 5'11", 190 lbs. Deb: 10/1/20

1920 Chi-A	0	1	.000	2	1	0	0	0	4²	7	0	4	1	25.1	15.43	24	.333	.481	0	.000	-0	-6	-6	-0	-0.9
1925 Bos-A	0	2	.000	2	2	0	0	0	15	20	0	9	4	18.0	6.00	76	.351	.448	0	.000	-1	-3	-2	1	-0.3
1926 Bos-A	0	2	.000	11	1	0	0	0	30	29	2	16	4	14.1	4.80	85	.266	.370	1	.143	-0	-3	-2	0	-0.1
Total 3	0	5	.000	15	4	0	0	0	49²	56	2	30	9	16.3	6.16	68	.299	.407	1	.077	-1	-11	-11	1	-1.3

● **MARK KIEFER** Kiefer, Mark Andrew b: 11/13/68, Orange, Cal. BR/TR, 6'4", 175 lbs. Deb: 9/20/93 F

1993 Mil-A	0	0	—	6	0	0	0	1	9¹	3	0	5	7	8.7	0.00	—	.097	.243	0	—	0	4	4	0	0.2
1994 Mil-A	1	0	1.000	7	0	0	0	0	10²	15	4	8	14	19.4	8.44	58	.357	.460	0	—	0	-4	-4	0	-0.4
Total 2	1	0	1.000	13	0	0	0	1	20	18	4	13	21	14.4	4.50	102	.247	.368	0	—	0	0	0	0	-0.2

● **JOHN KIELY** Kiely, John Francis b: 10/4/64, Boston, Mass. BR/TR, 6'3", 210 lbs. Deb: 7/26/91

1991 Det-A	0	1	.000	7	0	0	0	0	6²	13	0	9	1	31.1	14.85	28	.448	.590	0	—	0	-8	-8	-0	-1.1
1992 Det-A	4	2	.667	39	0	0	0	0	55	44	2	28	18	11.8	2.13	186	.224	.321	0	—	0	11	11	2	1.4
1993 Det-A	0	2	.000	8	0	0	0	0	11²	13	2	13	5	20.8	7.71	56	.295	.466	0	—	0	-4	-4	1	-0.5
Total 3	4	5	.444	54	0	0	0	0	73¹	70	4	50	24	15.0	4.17	96	.260	.380	0	—	0	-1	-1	3	-0.2

● **LEO KIELY** Kiely, Leo Patrick "Kiki" b: 11/30/29, Hoboken, N.J. d: 1/18/84, Montclair, N.J. BL/TL, 6'2", 180 lbs. Deb: 6/27/51

1951 Bos-A	7	7	.500	17	16	4	0	0	113¹	106	9	39	46	11.7	3.34	134	.251	.317	5	.143	-1	10	14	1	1.7
1954 Bos-A	5	8	.385	28	19	4	1	0	131	153	12	58	59	14.6	3.50	117	.295	.367	9	.180	-3	3	9	-1	0.7
1955 Bos-A	3	3	.500	33	4	0	0	6	90	91	5	37	36	12.8	2.80	153	.269	.341	5	.192	-0	12	15	1	1.3
1956 Bos-A	2	2	.500	23	0	0	0	3	31¹	47	1	14	9	18.1	5.17	89	.362	.432	1	.167	-0	-4	-2	0	-0.3
1958 Bos-A	5	2	.714	47	0	0	0	12	81	73	3	18	26	10.8	3.00	134	.254	.300	0	.000	-2	7	9	1	1.0
1959 Bos-A	3	3	.500	41	0	0	0	7	55²	67	8	18	30	13.9	4.20	97	.299	.354	0	.000	-1	-2	-1	0	-0.1
1960 KC-A	1	2	.333	20	0	0	0	1	20²	21	1	5	16	11.8	1.74	229	.266	.318	0	.000	-0	5	5	1	0.9
Total 7	26	27	.491	209	39	8	1	29	523	562	39	189	212	13.1	3.37	125	.279	.343	20	.144	-4	31	49	5	5.2

● **DARRYL KILE** Kile, Darryl Andrew b: 12/2/68, Garden Grove, Cal. BR/TR, 6'5", 185 lbs. Deb: 4/8/91

1991 Hou-N	7	11	.389	37	22	0	0	0	153²	144	16	84	100	13.7	3.69	95	.246	.347	0	—	-3	-3	-2	-0	-0.8
1992 Hou-N	5	10	.333	22	22	2	0	0	125¹	124	8	63	90	13.7	3.95	85	.261	.352	5	.156	1	-6	-8	-2	-1.1
1993 Hou-N☆	15	8	.652	32	26	4	2	0	171²	152	12	69	141	12.4	3.51	110	.239	.327	5	.094	-1	10	7	-2	0.6
1994 Hou-N	9	6	.600	24	24	0	0	0	147²	153	13	82	105	14.9	4.57	89	.275	.377	7	.149	1	-6	-8	-1	-0.7
Total 4	36	35	.507	115	94	6	2	0	598¹	573	49	298	436	13.6	3.91	95	.254	.350	17	.100	-2	-2	-13	-6	-2.0

● **JOHN KILEY** Kiley, John Frederick b: 7/1/1859, Dedham, Mass. d: 12/18/40, Norwood, Mass. BL/TL, 5'7", 147 lbs. Deb: 5/1/1884 ♦

| 1891 Bos-N | 0 | 1 | .000 | 1 | 1 | 1 | 0 | 0 | 8 | 13 | 3 | 5 | 2 | 20.3 | 6.75 | 54 | .352 | .429 | 0 | .000 | 0 | -3 | -0 | 0 | -0.2 |

● **PAUL KILGUS** Kilgus, Paul Nelson b: 2/2/62, Bowling Green, Ky. BL/TL, 6'1", 185 lbs. Deb: 6/7/87

1987 Tex-A	2	7	.222	25	12	0	0	0	89¹	95	14	31	42	12.9	4.13	108	.271	.334	0	—	0	3	3	-1	0.2
1988 Tex-A	12	15	.444	32	32	5	3	0	203¹	190	18	71	88	12.0	4.16	98	.243	.314	0	—	0	-4	-2	1	-0.1
1989 *Chi-N	6	10	.375	35	23	0	0	0	145¹	164	9	49	61	13.5	4.39	86	.283	.344	3	.073	-3	-14	-10	0	-1.3
1990 Tor-A	0	0	—	11	0	0	0	0	16¹	19	2	7	7	14.9	6.06	65	.306	.386	0	—	0	-5	-4	0	-0.1
1991 Bal-A	0	2	.000	38	0	0	0	0	62	60	8	24	32	12.6	5.08	78	.259	.333	0	—	0	-7	-8	2	-0.5
1993 StL-N	1	0	1.000	22	1	0	0	0	28²	18	1	8	21	8.5	0.63	631	.180	.248	1	.200	-0	11	11	0	0.4
Total 6	21	34	.382	163	68	5	3	4	545¹	546	52	190	251	12.5	4.19	96	.259	.327	4	.087	-2	-15	-9	2	-0.7

● **MIKE KILKENNY** Kilkenny, Michael David b: 4/11/45, Bradford, Ont., Can. BR/TR, 6'3.5", 175 lbs. Deb: 4/11/69

1969 Det-A	8	6	.571	39	15	6	4	2	128¹	99	13	63	97	11.6	3.37	111	.211	.310	2	.054	-2	4	5	-0	0.4
1970 Det-A	7	6	.538	36	21	3	0	0	129	141	10	70	105	14.9	5.16	72	.279	.369	3	.077	-3	-21	-21	0	-2.1
1971 Det-A	4	5	.444	30	11	2	0	1	86¹	83	8	44	47	13.4	5.00	82	.247	.338	2	.083	-2	-15	-14	-0	-1.6
1972 Det-A	0	0	—	1	0	0	0	0	1	1	1	0	0	9.0	9.00	35	.250	.250	0	—	0	-1	-1	0	0.0

YEAR	TM/L	W	L	PCT	G	GS	CG	SH	SV	IP	H	HR	BB	SO	RAT	ERA	ERA+	OAV	OOB	BH	AVG	PB	PR	/A	PD	TPI
	Oak-A	0	0	—	1	0	0	0	0	1	0	0	0	0	0.0	0.00	—	.000	.000	0	—	0	-2	-0	-0	0.0
	SD-N	0	0	—	5	0	0	0	0	4¹	7	1	3	5	20.8	8.31	40	.350	.435	0	—	0	-2	-2	0	0.0
	Cle-A	4	1	.800	22	7	1	0	1	58	51	5	39	44	14.0	3.41	94	.237	.354	1	.071	-1	-2	-1	1	-0.2
	Yr	4	1	.800	24	7	1	0	1	60	52	6	39	44	13.6	3.45	95	.234	.349	1	.071	-1	-3	-2	1	-0.3
1973	Cle-A	0	0	—	5	0	0	0	0	2	5	1	5	3	49.5	22.50	17	.455	.647	0	—	0	-4	-4	0	0.0
Total	5	23	18	.561	139	54	12	4	4	410	387	39	224	301	13.6	4.43	82	.248	.345	8	.070	-8	-41	-37	1	-3.6

● **EVANS KILLEEN**   Killeen, Evans Henry b: 2/27/36, Brooklyn, N.Y. BR/TR, 6′, 190 lbs. Deb: 9/7/59

YEAR	TM/L	W	L	PCT	G	GS	CG	SH	SV	IP	H	HR	BB	SO	RAT	ERA	ERA+	OAV	OOB	BH	AVG	PB	PR	/A	PD	TPI
1959	KC-A	0	0	—	4	0	0	0	0	5²	4	0	4	1	12.7	4.76	84	.211	.348	0	—	0	-1	-0	-0	0.0

● **HENRY KILLEEN**   Killeen, Henry b: 1871, Troy, N.Y. 5′9″, 150 lbs. Deb: 9/11/1891

YEAR	TM/L	W	L	PCT	G	GS	CG	SH	SV	IP	H	HR	BB	SO	RAT	ERA	ERA+	OAV	OOB	BH	AVG	PB	PR	/A	PD	TPI
1891	Cle-N	0	1	.000	1	1	1	0	0	8²	11	1	8	3	19.7	6.23	56	.298	.423	0	.000	-0	-3	-3	0	-0.2

● **FRANK KILLEN**   Killen, Frank Bissell "Lefty" b: 11/30/1870, Pittsburgh, Pa. d: 12/3/39, Pittsburgh, Pa. BL/TL, 6′1″, 200 lbs. Deb: 8/27/1891

YEAR	TM/L	W	L	PCT	G	GS	CG	SH	SV	IP	H	HR	BB	SO	RAT	ERA	ERA+	OAV	OOB	BH	AVG	PB	PR	/A	PD	TPI
1891	Mil-a	7	4	.636	11	11	11	2	0	96²	79	1	51	38	11.8	1.68	262	.202	.306	8	.229	1	22	29	-0	3.0
1892	Was-N	29	26	.527	60	52	46	2	0	459²	448	15	182	147	12.7	3.31	98	.245	.320	37	.199	10	-1	-3	3	1.0
1893	Pit-N	**36**	14	.720	55	48	38	2	0	415	401	12	140	99	12.1	3.64	125	.246	.312	47	.275	14	47	42	1	5.2
1894	Pit-N	14	11	.560	28	28	20	1	0	204	261	3	86	62	15.5	4.50	116	.308	.375	21	.262	0	19	17	1	1.5
1895	Pit-N	5	5	.500	13	11	6	0	0	95	113	2	57	25	16.2	5.49	82	.291	.383	13	.342	4	-8	-10	1	-0.4
1896	Pit-N	**30**	18	.625	**52**	50	**44**	5	0	432¹	476	7	119	134	12.7	3.41	123	.277	.329	40	.231	9	46	38	2	4.2
1897	Pit-N	17	23	.425	42	41	**38**	1	0	337¹	417	4	76	99	13.4	4.46	94	.301	.341	32	.248	4	-5	-10	-1	-0.6
1898	Pit-N	10	11	.476	23	23	17	0	0	177²	201	3	41	48	12.8	3.75	95	.283	.332	17	.262	2	-3	-4	-0	-0.2
	Was-N	6	9	.400	17	16	15	0	0	128¹	149	4	29	43	12.6	3.58	102	.283	.288	15	.273	3	0	1	-0	0.5
	Yr	16	20	.444	40	39	32	0	0	306	350	7	70	91	12.4	3.68	98	.283	.322	32	.267	5	-2	-3	-1	0.3
1899	Was-N	0	2	.000	2	2	1	0	0	12	18	0	4	3	17.3	6.00	65	.345	.403	1	.200	-0	-3	-3	-1	-0.4
	Bos-N	7	5	.583	12	12	11	0	0	99¹	108	3	26	23	12.4	4.26	98	.277	.327	7	.171	-2	-4	-1	-0	-0.3
	Yr	7	7	.500	14	14	12	0	0	111¹	126	3	30	26	12.9	4.45	93	.284	.334	8	.174	-3	-7	-4	-1	-0.7
1900	Chi-N	3	3	.500	6	6	6	0	0	54	65	1	11	4	13.0	4.67	77	.297	.337	3	.150	-1	-6	-6	-0	-0.6
Total	10	164	131	.556	321	300	253	13	0	2511¹	2730	55	822	725	13.0	3.78	109	.272	.332	241	.241	44	104	92	5	12.9

● **ED KILLIAN**   Killian, Edwin Henry "Twilight Ed" b: 11/12/1876, Racine, Wis. d: 7/18/28, Detroit, Mich. BL/TL, 5′11″, 170 lbs. Deb: 8/25/03

YEAR	TM/L	W	L	PCT	G	GS	CG	SH	SV	IP	H	HR	BB	SO	RAT	ERA	ERA+	OAV	OOB	BH	AVG	PB	PR	/A	PD	TPI
1903	Cle-A	3	4	.429	9	8	7	3	0	61²	61	1	13	18	11.4	2.48	115	.258	.307	5	.179	1	3	3	-0	0.2
1904	Det-A	14	20	.412	40	34	32	4	1	331²	293	0	93	124	10.9	2.44	104	.238	.300	18	.143	-3	6	4	-5	-0.5
1905	Det-A	23	14	.622	39	37	33	**8**	0	313¹	263	0	102	110	10.9	2.27	121	.229	.299	32	.271	6	14	16	-4	2.2
1906	Det-A	10	6	.625	21	16	14	0	2	149²	165	1	54	47	13.5	3.43	81	.283	.349	9	.170	-1	-12	-11	-2	-1.5
1907	*Det-A	25	13	.658	41	34	29	3	1	314	286	2	91	96	11.1	1.78	147	.244	.305	39	.320	10	27	29	-2	4.7
1908	*Det-A	12	9	.571	27	23	15	0	1	180²	170	3	53	47	11.5	2.99	81	.252	.314	10	.137	-3	-12	-11	3	-1.4
1909	Det-A	11	9	.550	25	19	14	3	1	173¹	150	1	49	54	10.6	1.71	147	.236	.297	10	.161	-1	15	15	-1	1.6
1910	Det-A	4	3	.571	11	9	5	1	0	74	75	2	27	20	13.1	3.04	87	.268	.345	4	.148	-1	-4	-3	-1	-0.5
Total	8	102	78	.567	213	180	149	22	6	1598¹	1463	9	482	516	11.3	2.38	110	.245	.309	127	.209	6	36	42	-12	4.8

● **JACK KILLILAY**   Killilay, John William b: 5/24/1887, Leavenworth, Kan. d: 10/21/68, Tulsa, Okla. BR/TR, 5′11″, 165 lbs. Deb: 5/13/11

YEAR	TM/L	W	L	PCT	G	GS	CG	SH	SV	IP	H	HR	BB	SO	RAT	ERA	ERA+	OAV	OOB	BH	AVG	PB	PR	/A	PD	TPI
1911	Bos-A	4	2	.667	14	7	1	0	0	61	65	0	36	28	16.4	3.54	93	.302	.425	1	.042	-2	-1	-2	0	-0.4

● **MATT KILROY**   Kilroy, Matthew Aloysius "Matches" b: 6/21/1866, Philadelphia, Pa. d: 3/2/40, Philadelphia, Pa. BL/TL, 5′9″, 175 lbs. Deb: 4/17/1886 F

YEAR	TM/L	W	L	PCT	G	GS	CG	SH	SV	IP	H	HR	BB	SO	RAT	ERA	ERA+	OAV	OOB	BH	AVG	PB	PR	/A	PD	TPI
1886	Bal-a	29	34	.460	**68**	68	**66**	5	0	583	476	10	182	**513**	10.5	3.37	102	.210	.274	38	.174	-5	5	4	6	0.4
1887	Bal-a	**46**	19	.708	69	69	66	6	0	589¹	585	9	157	217	11.6	3.07	134	.253	.306	59	.247	9	**80**	67	10	**7.3**
1888	Bal-a	17	21	.447	40	40	35	2	0	321	347	5	79	135	12.6	4.04	74	.266	.319	26	.179	-0	-35	-38	-1	-3.7
1889	Bal-a	29	25	.537	59	56	**55**	5	0	480²	476	8	142	217	12.1	2.85	139	.250	.312	57	.274	10	54	59	8	**6.9**
1890	Bos-P	9	15	.375	30	27	18	0	0	217²	268	14	87	48	15.3	4.26	103	.290	.361	20	.215	-0	-1	3	1	0.3
1891	Cin-a	1	4	.200	7	6	4	0	0	45¹	51	1	19	6	15.5	2.98	138	.274	.366	3	.150	-1	4	6	0	0.5
1892	Was-N	1	1	.500	4	3	2	0	0	26¹	20	0	15	1	12.6	2.39	136	.202	.319	2	.200	-1	3	3	2	0.5
1893	Lou-N	3	2	.600	5	5	1	0	0	35	57	2	23	4	21.6	9.00	49	.355	.448	7	.438	3	-17	-18	1	-1.4
1894	Lou-N	0	5	.000	8	7	3	0	0	37	46	2	20	11	16.5	3.89	131	.302	.390	2	.118	-2	6	5	1	0.4
1898	Chi-N	6	7	.462	13	11	10	0	0	100¹	119	2	30	18	14.4	4.31	83	.293	.357	22	.229	2	-8	-8	1	-0.6
Total	10	141	133	.515	303	292	264	19	0	2435²	2445	53	754	1170	12.3	3.47	109	.252	.314	236	.222	15	92	83	28	10.4

● **MIKE KILROY**   Kilroy, Michael Joseph b: 11/4/1872, Philadelphia, Pa. d: 10/2/60, Philadelphia, Pa. BR/TR, Deb: 9/1/1888 F

YEAR	TM/L	W	L	PCT	G	GS	CG	SH	SV	IP	H	HR	BB	SO	RAT	ERA	ERA+	OAV	OOB	BH	AVG	PB	PR	/A	PD	TPI
1888	Bal-a	0	1	.000	1	1	1	0	0	9	12	1	5	1	17.0	8.00	37	.309	.388	0	.000	-0	-5	-5	-0	-0.4
1891	Phi-N	0	2	.000	3	1	0	0	0	10	15	1	4	3	18.9	9.90	34	.334	.413	2	.400	1	-7	-7	-0	-0.9
Total	2	0	3	.000	4	2	1	0	0	19	27	2	9	4	18.0	9.00	36	.322	.401	2	.222	0	-12	-12	-0	-1.3

● **NEWT KIMBALL**   Kimball, Newell W. b: 3/27/15, Logan, Utah BR/TR, 6′2.5″, 190 lbs. Deb: 5/7/37

YEAR	TM/L	W	L	PCT	G	GS	CG	SH	SV	IP	H	HR	BB	SO	RAT	ERA	ERA+	OAV	OOB	BH	AVG	PB	PR	/A	PD	TPI
1937	Chi-N	0	0	—	2	0	0	0	0	5	12	1	1	0	23.4	10.80	37	.444	.464	0	.000	-0	-4	-4	0	0.0
1938	Chi-N	0	0	—	1	0	0	0	0	1	3	0	1	2	27.0	9.00	43	.500	.500	0	—	0	-1	-1	0	0.0
1940	Bro-N	3	1	.750	21	0	0	0	1	33²	29	2	15	21	11.8	3.21	125	.238	.321	0	.000	-1	2	3	-0	0.2
	StL-N	1	0	1.000	2	1	0	0	0	14	11	1	6	6	10.9	2.57	155	.208	.288	2	.333	1	2	2	-0	0.2
	Yr	4	1	.800	23	1	0	0	1	47²	40	3	21	27	11.5	3.02	132	.229	.311	2	.182	0	4	5	-1	0.4
1941	Bro-N	3	1	.750	15	5	1	0	0	52	43	0	29	17	12.5	3.63	101	.225	.327	1	.250	-0	0	1	-0	0.2
1942	Bro-N	2	0	1.000	14	1	0	0	0	29¹	27	0	9	8	14.4	3.68	89	.265	.385	1	.200	—	-1	-1	-2	-0.2
1943	Bro-N	1	1	.500	5	0	0	0	0	11	9	0	5	2	11.5	1.64	205	.214	.298	0	.000	-0	2	2	0	0.4
	Phi-N	1	6	.143	34	6	2	0	2	89²	85	4	42	33	12.8	4.12	82	.253	.338	3	.188	1	-7	-7	-2	-0.7
	Yr	2	7	.222	39	6	2	0	3	100²	94	4	47	35	12.7	3.84	88	.249	.333	3	.158	1	-5	-5	-2	-0.3
Total	6	11	9	.550	94	13	4	0	5	235²	219	8	117	88	12.9	3.78	94	.249	.339	9	.180	1	-6	-6	-4	-0.1

● **SAM KIMBER**   Kimber, Samuel Jackson b: 10/29/1852, Philadelphia, Pa. d: 11/7/25, Philadelphia, Pa. BR/TR, 5′10.5″, 165 lbs. Deb: 5/1/1884

YEAR	TM/L	W	L	PCT	G	GS	CG	SH	SV	IP	H	HR	BB	SO	RAT	ERA	ERA+	OAV	OOB	BH	AVG	PB	PR	/A	PD	TPI
1884	Bro-a	18	20	.474	41	41	41	4	0	361¹	364	6	72	122	11.2	3.81	87	.247	.289	21	.148	-5	-23	-20	-1	-2.2
1885	Pro-N	0	1	.000	1	1	1	0	0	8	15	1	5	4	22.5	11.25	24	.405	.476	0	.000	-0	-7	-8	0	-0.6
Total	2	18	21	.462	42	42	42	4	0	369¹	379	7	77	126	11.5	3.97	83	.251	.294	21	.145	-6	-30	-27	-1	-2.8

● **HARRY KIMBERLIN**   Kimberlin, Harry Lydle "Murphy" or "Mule Trader" b: 3/13/09, Sullivan, Mo. BR/TR, 6′3″, 175 lbs. Deb: 7/11/36

YEAR	TM/L	W	L	PCT	G	GS	CG	SH	SV	IP	H	HR	BB	SO	RAT	ERA	ERA+	OAV	OOB	BH	AVG	PB	PR	/A	PD	TPI
1936	StL-A	0	0	—	13	0	0	0	0	20	24	3	16	4	18.0	5.40	100	.296	.412			-0	-1	-0	-0	-0.1
1937	StL-A	0	2	.000	3	2	1	0	0	15¹	16	2	9	5	14.7	2.35	206	.254	.347	1	.200	0	4	4	-0	0.5
1938	StL-A	0	0	—	1	1	0	0	0	8	8	1	7	2	12.4	3.38	147	.286	.355	0	.000	-0	1	-0	-0	0.0
1939	StL-A	1	2	.333	17	3	0	0	0	41	59	6	19	11	17.6	5.49	89	.326	.396	3	.333	0	-4	-3	-0	-0.1
Total	4	1	4	.200	34	6	2	0	0	84¹	107	12	47	21	16.6	4.70	106	.303	.388	4	.250	0	3	1	-0	0.3

● **HAL KIME**   Kime, Harold Lee "Lefty" b: 3/15/1899, W.Salem, Ohio d: 5/16/39, Columbus, Ohio BL/TL, 5′9″, 160 lbs. Deb: 6/19/20

YEAR	TM/L	W	L	PCT	G	GS	CG	SH	SV	IP	H	HR	BB	SO	RAT	ERA	ERA+	OAV	OOB	BH	AVG	PB	PR	/A	PD	TPI
1920	StL-N	0	0	—	4	0	0	0	0	7	9	0	4	2	15.4	2.57	116	.333	.400	0	.000	-0	0	0	0	0.0

● **CHAD KIMSEY**   Kimsey, Clyde Elias b: 8/6/06, Copperhill, Tenn. d: 12/3/42, Pryor, Okla. BL/TR, 6′2″, 200 lbs. Deb: 4/21/29

YEAR	TM/L	W	L	PCT	G	GS	CG	SH	SV	IP	H	HR	BB	SO	RAT	ERA	ERA+	OAV	OOB	BH	AVG	PB	PR	/A	PD	TPI
1929	StL-A	3	6	.333	24	3	1	0	1	64¹	83	2	19	13	14.3	5.04	88	.340	.388	8	.267	3	-6	-4	3	0.0
1930	StL-A	6	10	.375	42	4	1	0	0	113¹	139	8	45	32	14.8	6.35	77	.312	.377	24	.343	-7	-21	-19	1	-1.3
1931	StL-A	4	6	.400	42	1	0	0	0	94¹	121	7	27	27	14.3	4.39	106	.332	.360	10	.270	5	0	**3**	2	1.0
1932	StL-A	4	2	.667	33	0	0	0	3	78¹	85	3	33	13	13.6	4.02	121	.281	.352	6	.333	1	4	7	1	0.5
	Chi-A	1	1	.500	7	0	0	0	2	11	8	0	5	6	11.5	2.45	176	.211	.318	0	.000	-0	2	1	0	0.5

YEAR	TM/L	W	L	PCT	G	GS	CG	SH	SV	IP	H	HR	BB	SO	RAT	ERA	ERA+	OAV	OOB	BH	AVG	PB	PR	/A	PD	TPI
	Yr	5	3	.625	40	0	0	0	5	89¹	93	3	38	19	13.3	3.83	125	.274	.348	6	.300	1	6	**10**	2	1.2
1933	Chi-A	4	1	.800	28	2	0	0	0	96	124	7	36	19	15.4	5.53	77	.318	.381	5	.152	-2	-13	-14	1	-0.7
1936	Det-A	2	3	.400	22	0	0	0	3	52	58	2	29	11	15.2	4.85	102	.284	.376	5	.313	2	1	1	2	0.4
Total	6	24	29	.453	227	10	2	0	17	509¹	618	23	194	121	14.5	5.07	92	.307	.371	58	.282	16	-33	-24	11	0.6

● ELLIS KINDER   Kinder, Ellis Raymond "Old Folks"   b: 7/26/14, Atkins, Ark.   d: 10/16/68, Jackson, Tenn.   BR/TR, 6', 195 lbs.   Deb: 4/30/46

YEAR	TM/L	W	L	PCT	G	GS	CG	SH	SV	IP	H	HR	BB	SO	RAT	ERA	ERA+	OAV	OOB	BH	AVG	PB	PR	/A	PD	TPI
1946	StL-A	3	3	.500	33	7	1	0	1	86²	78	8	36	59	11.8	3.32	112	.241	.318	1	.053	-	2	4	-1	0.1
1947	StL-A	8	15	.348	34	26	10	2	1	194¹	201	11	82	110	13.1	4.49	86	.264	.336	8	.129	-4	-17	-13	-3	-2.1
1948	Bos-A	10	7	.588	28	22	10	1	0	178	183	10	63	53	12.5	3.74	117	.266	.330	6	.097	-4	11	13	-3	0.4
1949	Bos-A	23	6	**.793**	43	30	19	**6**	4	252	251	21	99	138	12.6	3.36	130	.260	.330	12	.130	-4	24	28	-4	2.1
1950	Bos-A	14	12	.538	48	23	11	1	9	207	212	23	78	95	12.7	4.26	115	.263	.328	13	.183	-1	7	15	-2	1.4
1951	Bos-A	11	2	.846	**63**	2	1	0	**14**	127	108	9	46	84	10.9	2.55	175	.230	.298	4	.118	-3	**22**	**27**	-2	2.7
1952	Bos-A	5	6	.455	23	10	4	0	4	97²	85	11	28	50	10.5	2.58	153	.234	.290	0	.000	-4	12	15	-0	1.3
1953	Bos-A	10	6	.625	**69**	0	0	0	**27**	107	84	8	38	39	10.4	1.85	227	.215	.288	11	.379	3	**26**	**28**	0	5.9
1954	Bos-A	8	8	.500	48	2	0	0	15	107	106	7	36	67	11.9	3.62	114	.260	.321	5	.185	0	1	6	-2	0.9
1955	Bos-A	5	5	.500	43	0	0	0	18	66²	57	5	15	31	9.9	2.84	151	.229	.275	3	.250	0	8	11	-1	2.1
1956	StL-N	0	1	.000	22	0	0	0	6	25²	23	3	9	4	11.2	3.51	108	.245	.311	0	.000	-0	1	1	-1	0.0
	Chi-A	3	1	.750	29	0	0	0	3	29²	33	2	8	19	12.4	2.73	150	.277	.323	0	.000	-0	5	5	-1	0.6
1957	Chi-A	0	0	—	1	0	0	0	0	1	0	0	1	0	9.0	0.00	—	.000	.250	0		0	0	0	-0	0.0
Total	12	102	71	.590	484	122	56	10	102	1479¹	1421	118	539	749	12.0	3.43	125	.252	.318	63	.142	-19	101	139	-17	15.4

● SILVER KING   King, Charles Frederick (b: Charles Frederick Koenig)   b: 1/11/1868, St.Louis, Mo.   d: 5/21/38, St.Louis, Mo.   BR/TR, 6', 170 lbs.   Deb: 9/28/1886

YEAR	TM/L	W	L	PCT	G	GS	CG	SH	SV	IP	H	HR	BB	SO	RAT	ERA	ERA+	OAV	OOB	BH	AVG	PB	PR	/A	PD	TPI
1886	KC-N	1	3	.250	5	5	5	0	0	39	43	1	9	23	12.0	4.85	78	.243	.280	1	.045	-2	-7	-5	1	-0.5
1887	*StL-a	32	12	.727	46	44	43	2	1	390	401	4	109	128	12.2	3.78	120	.260	.316	46	.207	-4	22	33	-3	2.0
1888	*StL-a	45	21	.682	**66**	65	**64**	**6**	0	**585²**	437	6	76	258	**8.3**	**1.64**	**198**	**.200**	**.237**	43	.208	9	**92**	105	-1	**11.4**
1889	StL-a	35	16	.686	56	53	47	2	1	458	462	15	125	188	11.9	3.14	134	.254	.309	43	.228	1	36	55	-3	4.5
1890	Chi-P	30	22	.577	56	56	48	**4**	0	461	420	5	163	185	11.7	**2.69**	**161**	**.232**	.301	31	.168	-6	**79**	**84**	6	**7.1**
1891	Pit-N	14	29	.326	48	44	40	3	1	384¹	382	7	144	160	12.7	3.11	105	.249	.321	25	.169	-1	10	7	-2	0.4
1892	NY-N	23	24	.489	52	47	46	1	0	419¹	397	15	174	177	12.7	3.24	99	.240	.320	35	.210	6	2	-1	-1	0.4
1893	NY-N	3	4	.429	7	7	4	0	0	49	69	4	26	13	17.8	8.63	54	.322	.401	3	.176	1	-22	-22	-0	-2.0
	Cin-N	5	6	.455	17	15	8	1	1	105	119	2	56	30	15.6	4.89	98	.277	.369	6	.162	-0	-3	-1	-0	-0.1
	Yr	8	10	.444	24	22	12	1	1	154	188	6	82	43	16.2	6.08	78	.291	.377	9	.167	1	-24	-23	-0	-2.1
1896	Was-N	10	7	.588	22	16	12	0	1	145¹	179	7	43	35	14.0	4.09	108	.300	.351	16	.276	3	4	5	-3	0.5
1897	Was-N	6	9	.400	23	19	12	0	1	154	196	7	45	32	14.7	4.79	91	.307	.363	11	.193	-0	-8	-8	1	-0.5
Total	10	204	153	.571	398	371	329	19	6	3190²	3105	69	970	1229	11.9	3.18	122	.247	.308	260	.199	7	207	253	-6	23.2

● CLYDE KING   King, Clyde Edward   b: 5/23/25, Goldsboro, N.C.   BB/TR, 6'1", 175 lbs.   Deb: 6/21/44   MC

YEAR	TM/L	W	L	PCT	G	GS	CG	SH	SV	IP	H	HR	BB	SO	RAT	ERA	ERA+	OAV	OOB	BH	AVG	PB	PR	/A	PD	TPI
1944	Bro-N	2	1	.667	14	3	1	0	0	43²	42	1	12	14	11.3	3.09	115	.256	.311	2	.200	-0	3	2	-1	0.0
1945	Bro-N	5	5	.500	42	2	0	0	3	112¹	131	8	48	29	14.3	4.09	92	.295	.364	4	.125	-2	-4	-4	1	-0.5
1947	Bro-N	6	5	.545	29	9	2	0	0	87²	85	11	29	31	11.7	2.77	149	.252	.311	3	.115	-1	13	13	-1	1.3
1948	Bro-N	1	0	1.000	9	0	0	0	0	12¹	14	3	6	5	15.3	8.03	50	.286	.375	0	.000	-0	-6	-6	0	-0.4
1951	Bro-N	14	7	.667	48	3	1	0	6	121¹	118	15	50	33	12.7	4.15	94	.263	.341	4	.138	-0	-3	-3	0	-0.5
1952	Bro-N	2	0	1.000	23	0	0	0	2	42²	56	5	12	17	14.6	5.06	72	.318	.365	0	.000	-1	-6	-7	1	-0.3
1953	Cin-N	3	6	.333	35	4	0	0	2	76	78	15	32	21	13.3	5.21	84	.271	.348	0	.000	-1	-8	-7	-0	-0.9
Total	7	32	25	.561	200	21	4	0	11	496	524	58	189	150	13.1	4.14	95	.275	.343	13	.114	-4	-11	-11	-0	-1.3

● ERIC KING   King, Eric Steven   b: 4/10/64, Oxnard, Cal.   BR/TR, 6'2", 215 lbs.   Deb: 5/15/86

YEAR	TM/L	W	L	PCT	G	GS	CG	SH	SV	IP	H	HR	BB	SO	RAT	ERA	ERA+	OAV	OOB	BH	AVG	PB	PR	/A	PD	TPI
1986	Det-A	11	4	.733	33	16	3	1	3	138¹	108	11	63	79	11.6	3.51	117	.216	.313	0	—	0	10	9	0	1.0
1987	*Det-A	6	9	.400	55	4	0	0	9	116	111	15	60	89	13.6	4.89	86	.251	.345	0	—	0	-6	-9	2	-0.8
1988	Det-A	4	1	.800	23	5	0	0	3	68²	60	5	34	45	13.0	3.41	112	.233	.334	0	—	0	3	3	-1	0.2
1989	Chi-A	9	10	.474	25	25	1	1	0	159¹	144	13	64	72	12.0	3.39	112	.244	.322	0	—	0	9	7	-0	0.8
1990	Chi-A	12	4	.750	25	25	2	2	0	151	135	10	40	70	10.8	3.28	117	.237	.294	0	—	0	11	9	-1	0.9
1991	Cle-A	6	11	.353	25	24	2	1	0	150²	166	7	44	59	12.7	4.60	90	.279	.332	0	—	0	-8	-7	-2	-1.0
1992	Det-A	4	6	.400	17	14	0	0	1	79¹	90	12	28	45	13.5	5.22	76	.285	.345	0	—	0	-11	-11	-1	-1.4
Total	7	52	45	.536	203	113	8	5	16	863¹	814	73	333	459	12.3	3.97	100	.249	.324	0	—	0	8	2	-3	-0.3

● KEVIN KING   King, Kevin Ray   b: 2/11/69, Atwater, Cal.   BL/TL, 6'4", 170 lbs.   Deb: 9/2/93

YEAR	TM/L	W	L	PCT	G	GS	CG	SH	SV	IP	H	HR	BB	SO	RAT	ERA	ERA+	OAV	OOB	BH	AVG	PB	PR	/A	PD	TPI
1993	Sea-A	0	1	.000	13	0	0	0	0	11²	9	3	4	8	10.8	6.17	71	.231	.318	0	—	0	-2	-2	-0	-0.3
1994	Sea-A	0	2	.000	19	0	0	0	0	15¹	21	0	17	6	22.9	7.04	70	.333	.481	0	—	0	-4	-4	0	-0.5
Total	2	0	3	.000	32	0	0	0	0	27	30	3	21	14	17.7	6.67	70	.294	.424	0	—	0	-6	-6	-0	-0.8

● NELLIE KING   King, Nelson Joseph   b: 3/15/28, Shenandoah, Pa.   BR/TR, 6'6", 185 lbs.   Deb: 4/15/54

YEAR	TM/L	W	L	PCT	G	GS	CG	SH	SV	IP	H	HR	BB	SO	RAT	ERA	ERA+	OAV	OOB	BH	AVG	PB	PR	/A	PD	TPI
1954	Pit-N	0	0	—	4	0	0	0	0	7	10	0	1	3	14.1	5.14	81	.400	.423	0	—	-1	-1	-0	0	0.0
1955	Pit-N	1	3	.250	17	4	0	0	0	54¹	60	2	14	21	12.6	2.98	138	.286	.336	0	.000	-2	6	7	-0	0.3
1956	Pit-N	4	1	.800	38	0	0	0	5	60	54	8	19	25	11.1	3.15	120	.241	.303	0	.000	-1	4	4	-1	0.2
1957	Pit-N	2	1	.667	36	0	0	0	1	52	69	7	16	23	15.1	4.50	84	.337	.390	0	.000	-1	-4	-4	-0	-0.3
Total	4	7	5	.583	95	4	0	0	6	173¹	193	17	50	72	12.9	3.58	109	.291	.345	0	.000	-3	6	6	-1	0.2

● BRIAN KINGMAN   Kingman, Brian Paul   b: 7/27/54, Los Angeles, Cal.   BR/TR, 6'2", 200 lbs.   Deb: 6/28/79

YEAR	TM/L	W	L	PCT	G	GS	CG	SH	SV	IP	H	HR	BB	SO	RAT	ERA	ERA+	OAV	OOB	BH	AVG	PB	PR	/A	PD	TPI
1979	Oak-A	8	7	.533	18	17	5	1	0	112²	113	10	33	58	11.9	4.31	94	.258	.314	0	—	0	-1	-3	-2	-0.5
1980	Oak-A	8	20	.286	32	30	10	1	0	211¹	209	21	82	116	12.6	3.83	98	.256	.326	0	—	0	5	-2	-2	-0.2
1981	*Oak-A	3	6	.333	18	15	3	1	0	100¹	112	10	32	52	13.3	3.95	88	.286	.347	0	—	0	-3	-5	-2	-0.4
1982	Oak-A	4	12	.250	23	20	3	0	1	122²	131	11	57	46	14.3	4.48	87	.279	.365	0	—	0	-5	-8	-3	-0.8
1983	SF-N	0	0	—	3	0	0	0	0	4²	10	1	1	1	21.2	7.71	46	.417	.440	0	—	0	-2	-2	-0	0.0
Total	5	23	45	.338	94	82	21	3	1	551²	575	52	205	273	13.0	4.13	92	.269	.338	0	—	0	-7	-20	-9	-1.9

● DAVE KINGMAN   Kingman, David Arthur   b: 12/21/48, Pendleton, Ore.   BR/TR, 6'6", 210 lbs.   Deb: 7/30/71   ♦

YEAR	TM/L	W	L	PCT	G	GS	CG	SH	SV	IP	H	HR	BB	SO	RAT	ERA	ERA+	OAV	OOB	BH	AVG	PB	PR	/A	PD	TPI
1973	SF-N	0	0	—	2	0	0	0	0	4	3	0	6	4	20.3	9.00	42	.200	.429	62	.203	1	-2	-2	-0	0.0

● DENNIS KINNEY   Kinney, Dennis Paul   b: 2/26/52, Toledo, Ohio   BL/TL, 6'1", 190 lbs.   Deb: 4/9/78

YEAR	TM/L	W	L	PCT	G	GS	CG	SH	SV	IP	H	HR	BB	SO	RAT	ERA	ERA+	OAV	OOB	BH	AVG	PB	PR	/A	PD	TPI
1978	Cle-A	0	2	.000	18	0	0	0	5	38²	37	3	14	19	12.1	4.42	84	.259	.329	0	—	0	-3	-3	-0	-0.2
	SD-N	0	1	.000	7	0	0	0	0	7	6	3	4	2	12.9	6.43	52	.222	.323	0	.000	-0	-2	-2	-0	-0.4
1979	SD-N	0	0	—	13	0	0	0	0	18	17	2	8	11	13.0	3.50	101	.250	.338	0	.000	-0	0	0	-0	0.0
1980	SD-N	4	6	.400	50	0	0	0	0	82²	79	4	37	40	12.7	4.25	81	.252	.333	1	.083	-0	-6	-7	-1	-1.0
1981	Det-A	0	0	—	6	0	0	0	0	3²	5	0	4	3	22.1	9.82	38	.313	.450	0	—	0	-3	-2	-0	-0.2
1982	Oak-A	0	0	—	3	0	0	0	0	4	9	1	4	0	27.0	8.31	47	.474	.565	0	—	0	-2	-2	0	0.4
Total	5	4	9	.308	97	0	0	0	6	154¹	153	12	71	75	13.2	4.55	78	.261	.344	1	.071	-1	-15	-17	-1	-1.4

● WALT KINNEY   Kinney, Walter William   b: 9/9/1893, Denison, Tex.   d: 7/1/71, Escondido, Cal.   BL/TL, 6'2", 186 lbs.   Deb: 7/26/18

YEAR	TM/L	W	L	PCT	G	GS	CG	SH	SV	IP	H	HR	BB	SO	RAT	ERA	ERA+	OAV	OOB	BH	AVG	PB	PR	/A	PD	TPI
1918	Bos-A	0	0	—	5	0	0	0	0	15	5	0	8	4	9.0	1.80	149	.106	.263	0	.000	-1	2	1	-0	-0.1
1919	Phi-A	9	15	.375	43	21	13	0	2	202²	199	7	91	97	13.2	3.64	94	.262	.347	25	.284	5	-9	-5	3	0.5
1920	Phi-A	2	4	.333	12	8	5	1	0	61	59	3	28	19	13.3	3.10	130	.261	.345	9	.346	2	5	6	0	0.8
1923	Phi-A	0	1	.000	5	1	0	0	0	12	11	0	9	9	15.0	7.50	55	.229	.351	1	.167	1	-5	-5	-0	-0.3
Total	4	11	20	.355	63	30	18	1	2	290²	274	10	136	129	13.0	3.59	99	.254	.343	35	.280	7	-8	-2	2	0.9

YEAR	TM/L	W	L	PCT	G	GS	CG	SH	SV	IP	H	HR	BB	SO	RAT	ERA	ERA+	OAV	OOB	BH	AVG	PB	PR	/A	PD	TPI

● **MIKE KINNUNEN**   Kinnunen, Michael John   b: 4/1/58, Seattle, Wash.   BL/TL, 6'1", 185 lbs.   Deb: 6/12/80

1980	Min-A	0	0	—	21	0	0	0	0	24²	29	1	9	8	14.2	5.11	85	.290	.355	0	—	0	-3	-2	0	-0.2
1986	Bal-A	0	0	—	9	0	0	0	0	7	8	1	5	1	16.7	6.43	64	.308	.419	0	—	0	-2	-2	0	0.1
1987	Bal-A	0	0	—	18	0	0	0	0	20	27	3	16	14	19.3	4.95	89	.338	.448	0	—	0	-1	-1	-0	0.1
Total	3	0	0	—	48	0	0	0	0	51²	64	5	30	23	16.5	5.23	83	.311	.401	0	—	0	-6	-5	0	0.0

● **ED KINSELLA**   Kinsella, Edward William "Rube"   b: 1/15/1882, Lexington, Ill.   d: 1/17/76, Bloomington, Ill.   BR/TR, 6'1.5", 175 lbs.   Deb: 9/16/05

1905	Pit-N	0	1	.000	3	2	2	0	0	17	19	0	3	11	12.2	2.65	113	.292	.333	0	.000	-0	1	1	-1	-0.1
1910	StL-A	1	3	.250	10	5	2	0	0	50	62	0	16	10	14.4	3.78	65	.321	.379	3	.250	2	-7	-7	1	-0.3
Total	2	1	4	.200	13	7	4	0	0	67	81	0	19	21	13.8	3.49	75	.314	.368	3	.200	2	-6	-7	0	-0.4

● **MATT KINZER**   Kinzer, Matthew Roy   b: 6/17/63, Indianapolis, Ind.   BR/TR, 6'2", 210 lbs.   Deb: 5/18/89

1989	StL-N	0	2	.000	8	1	0	0	0	13¹	25	3	4	8	19.6	12.83	28	.403	.439	0	.000	-0	-14	-14	-0	-1.8
1990	Det-A	0	0	—	1	0	0	0	0	1²	3	0	3	1	32.4	16.20	24	.375	.545	0	—	-0	-2	-2	0	-0.1
Total	2	0	2	.000	9	1	0	0	0	15	28	3	7	9	21.0	13.20	28	.400	.455	0	.000	-0	-16	-16	-1	-1.9

● **HARRY KINZY**   Kinzy, Henry Hershel "Slim"   b: 7/19/10, Hallsville, Tex.   BR/TR, 6'4", 185 lbs.   Deb: 6/8/34

| 1934 | Chi-A | 0 | 1 | .000 | 13 | 2 | 1 | 0 | 0 | 34¹ | 38 | 1 | 31 | 12 | 19.1 | 4.98 | 95 | .290 | .440 | 3 | .300 | 1 | -2 | -1 | -0 | 0.0 |

● **FRED KIPP**   Kipp, Fred Leo   b: 10/1/31, Piqua, Kan.   BL/TL, 6'4", 200 lbs.   Deb: 9/10/57

1957	Bro-N	0	0	—	1	0	0	0	0	4	6	2	0	3	13.5	9.00	46	.333	.333	0	.000	-0	-2	-2	0	0.0
1958	LA-N	6	6	.500	40	9	0	0	0	102¹	107	16	45	58	13.5	5.01	82	.273	.349	9	.250	1	-12	-10	1	-0.9
1959	LA-N	0	0	—	2	0	0	0	0	2²	2	0	3	1	16.9	0.00	—	.222	.417	0	—	0	1	1	0	0.0
1960	NY-A	0	1	.000	4	0	0	0	0	4¹	4	0	0	2	8.3	6.23	57	.250	.250	0	—	0	-1	-1	0	-0.3
Total	4	6	7	.462	47	9	0	0	0	113¹	119	18	48	64	13.3	5.08	80	.274	.347	9	.243	1	-14	-13	1	-1.2

● **BOB KIPPER**   Kipper, Robert Wayne   b: 7/8/64, Aurora, Ill.   BR/TL, 6'2", 200 lbs.   Deb: 4/12/85

1985	Cal-A	0	1	.000	2	1	0	0	0	3¹	7	1	3	0	27.0	21.60	19	.467	.556	0	—	0	-6	-6	0	-1.2
	Pit-N	1	2	.333	5	4	0	0	0	24²	21	4	7	13	10.2	5.11	70	.221	.275	2	.250	0	-4	-4	0	-0.4
1986	Pit-N	6	8	.429	20	19	0	0	0	114	123	17	34	81	12.6	4.03	95	.271	.324	1	.030	-3	-4	-2	-1	-0.7
1987	Pit-N	5	9	.357	24	20	1	1	0	110²	117	25	52	83	13.9	5.94	69	.271	.352	8	.242	2	-23	-22	-0	-2.3
1988	Pit-N	2	6	.250	50	0	0	0	0	65	54	7	26	39	11.4	3.74	91	.234	.317	0	.000	-0	-2	-1	-0	-0.2
1989	Pit-N	3	4	.429	52	0	0	0	4	83	55	5	33	58	9.5	2.93	115	.188	.270	1	.111	-0	5	4	-1	0.5
1990	Pit-N	5	2	.714	41	1	0	0	3	62²	44	6	25	35	10.5	3.02	120	.195	.286	1	.143	0	5	4	-0	0.5
1991	*Pit-N	2	2	.500	52	0	0	0	4	60	66	7	22	38	13.2	4.65	77	.276	.337	0	.000	-1	-6	-7	-0	-0.7
1992	Min-A	3	3	.500	25	0	0	0	0	38²	40	8	14	22	13.3	4.42	92	.268	.343	0	—	0	-2	-2	0	-0.2
Total	8	27	37	.422	271	45	1	1	11	562	527	81	217	369	12.1	4.34	86	.247	.320	13	.137	-1	-37	-39	-2	-4.9

● **THORNTON KIPPER**   Kipper, Thornton John   b: 9/27/28, Bagley, Wis.   BR/TR, 6'3", 190 lbs.   Deb: 6/7/53

1953	Phi-N	3	3	.500	20	3	0	0	0	45²	59	8	12	15	14.0	4.73	89	.319	.360	1	.091	-1	-2	-3	-0	-0.4
1954	Phi-N	0	0	—	11	0	0	0	1	13²	22	0	12	5	23.0	7.90	51	.379	.493	0	.000	-0	-6	-6	0	-0.1
1955	Phi-N	0	1	.000	24	0	0	0	0	39²	47	4	22	15	15.9	4.99	80	.301	.391	1	.333	1	-4	-5	-1	-0.1
Total	3	3	4	.429	55	3	0	0	1	99	128	12	46	35	16.0	5.27	78	.321	.394	2	.125	-1	-12	-13	-1	-0.6

● **CLAY KIRBY**   Kirby, Clayton Laws   b: 6/25/48, Washington, D.C.   d: 10/11/91, Arlington, Va.   BR/TR, 6'3", 185 lbs.   Deb: 4/11/69

1969	SD-N	7	20	.259	35	35	2	0	0	215²	204	18	100	113	12.9	3.80	93	.252	.339	4	.061	-2	-5	-6	-2	-1.1
1970	SD-N	10	16	.385	36	34	6	1	0	214²	198	29	120	154	13.7	4.53	88	.248	.352	11	.149	-0	-11	-13	-2	-1.6
1971	SD-N	15	13	.536	38	36	13	2	0	267¹	213	20	103	231	10.7	2.83	117	.216	.292	8	.093	-3	19	14	-0	1.1
1972	SD-N	12	14	.462	34	34	9	2	0	238²	197	21	116	175	11.9	3.13	105	.226	.318	5	.068	-4	9	4	-1	0.4
1973	SD-N	8	18	.308	34	31	4	2	0	191²	214	30	66	129	13.2	4.79	72	.282	.341	5	.093	-3	-24	-28	-2	-3.8
1974	Cin-N	12	9	.571	36	35	7	1	0	230²	210	15	91	160	11.8	3.28	106	.242	.316	7	.095	-3	9	5	-2	-0.1
1975	Cin-N	10	6	.625	26	19	1	0	0	110²	113	13	54	48	14.0	4.72	76	.263	.352	6	.188	1	-13	-14	-2	-1.9
1976	Mon-N	1	8	.111	22	15	0	0	0	78²	81	10	63	51	16.7	5.72	65	.273	.403	1	.056	-1	-19	-18	-1	-2.0
Total	8	75	104	.419	261	239	42	8	0	1548	1430	156	713	1061	12.6	3.84	92	.246	.331	47	.098	-15	-37	-56	-13	-9.5

● **JOHN KIRBY**   Kirby, John F.   b: 1/13/1865, St.Louis, Mo.   d: 10/6/31, St.Louis, Mo.   TR, 5'8", 172 lbs.   Deb: 8/1/1884

1884	KC-U	0	1	.000	2	2	1	0	0	11	13	0	2	1	12.3	4.09	55	.275	.305	1	.143	-1	-2	-2	1	-0.2
1885	StL-N	5	8	.385	14	14	14	0	0	129¹	118	0	44	46	11.3	3.55	77	.241	.303	3	.060	-6	-10	-12	-2	-1.6
1886	StL-N	11	26	.297	41	41	38	1	0	325	329	9	134	129	12.8	3.30	98	.252	.322	15	.110	-9	-1	-3	-2	-1.2
1887	Ind-N	1	6	.143	8	8	5	0	0	62	70	3	43	7	16.7	6.10	68	.272	.381	4	.138	-2	-14	-13	-1	-1.3
	Cle-a	0	5	.000	5	5	5	0	0	41	62	1	28	6	20.2	9.00	48	.339	.432	3	.167	-1	-21	-21	-0	-1.7
1888	KC-a	1	4	.200	5	5	5	0	0	43	48	0	7	11	11.7	4.19	82	.272	.304	1	.063	-2	-5	-4	-0	-0.5
Total	5	18	50	.265	75	75	68	1	0	611¹	640	13	258	200	13.4	4.09	80	.260	.332	27	.105	-21	-53	-55	-3	-6.5

● **LA RUE KIRBY**   Kirby, La Rue   b: 12/30/1889, Eureka, Mich.   d: 6/10/61, Lansing, Mich.   BB/TR, 6', 185 lbs.   Deb: 8/7/12 ◆

1912	NY-N	1	0	1.000	3	1	0	0	0	11	13	1	6	2	16.4	5.73	59	.295	.392	1	.200	-0	-3	-3	0	-0.2
1915	StL-F	0	0	—	1	0	0	0	0	7	7	1	2	7	11.6	5.14	56	.269	.321	38	.213	-0	-2	-2	-0	0.0
Total	2	1	0	1.000	4	1	0	0	0	18	20	2	8	9	14.5	5.50	58	.286	.367	87	.230	-0	-5	-5	-0	-0.2

● **MIKE KIRCHER**   Kircher, Michael Andrew (b: Wolfgang Andrew Kerscher)
    b: 9/30/1897, Rochester, N.Y.   d: 6/26/72, Rochester, N.Y.   BB/TR, 6', 180 lbs.   Deb: 8/8/19

1919	Phi-A	0	0	—	8	0	0	0	0	8	15	0	3	2	20.3	7.88	44	.429	.474	0	.000	-0	-4	-4	-1	-0.1
1920	StL-N	2	1	.667	9	3	1	0	0	36²	50	0	5	5	14.0	5.40	55	.333	.363	3	.273	0	-9	-10	-1	-0.9
1921	StL-N	0	1	.000	3	0	0	0	0	3¹	4	0	1	2	16.2	8.10	45	.364	.462	0	—	0	-2	-2	0	-0.4
Total	3	2	2	.500	14	3	1	0	0	48	69	0	9	9	15.2	6.00	52	.352	.389	3	.214	-0	-15	-15	-2	-1.4

● **BILL KIRK**   Kirk, William Partlemore   b: 7/19/35, Coatesville, Pa.   BL/TL, 6', 165 lbs.   Deb: 9/23/61

| 1961 | KC-A | 0 | 0 | — | 1 | 1 | 0 | 0 | 0 | 3 | 6 | 2 | 1 | 3 | 21.0 | 12.00 | 35 | .375 | .412 | 0 | — | 0 | -3 | -3 | -0 | 0.0 |

● **DON KIRKWOOD**   Kirkwood, Donald Paul   b: 9/24/49, Pontiac, Mich.   BR/TR, 6'3", 188 lbs.   Deb: 9/13/74

1974	Cal-A	0	0	—	3	0	0	0	0	7¹	12	0	6	4	22.1	8.59	40	.375	.474	0	—	0	-4	-4	-0	0.2
1975	Cal-A	6	5	.545	44	2	0	0	7	84	85	6	28	49	12.1	3.11	114	.270	.329	0	—	0	6	4	-0	0.8
1976	Cal-A	6	12	.333	28	26	4	0	0	157²	167	12	57	78	12.8	4.62	72	.278	.341	0	—	0	-19	-23	1	-2.1
1977	Cal-A	1	0	1.000	13	0	0	0	1	17²	20	3	9	10	14.8	5.09	77	.290	.372	0	—	0	-2	-2	1	-0.2
	Chi-A	1	1	.500	16	0	0	0	0	40	49	3	10	24	13.5	5.17	79	.310	.355	0	—	0	-5	-5	-0	-0.2
	Yr	2	1	.667	29	0	0	0	1	57²	69	6	19	34	13.9	5.15	78	.304	.360	0	—	0	-7	-7	1	-0.2
1978	Tor-A	4	5	.444	16	9	3	0	0	68	76	6	25	29	13.4	4.24	93	.284	.351	0	—	0	-4	-2	0	-0.4
Total	5	18	23	.439	120	37	7	0	8	374²	409	30	135	194	13.1	4.37	82	.284	.347	0	—	0	-28	-33	2	-1.7

● **HARRY KIRSCH**   Kirsch, Harry Louis "Casey"   b: 10/17/1887, Pittsburgh, Pa.   d: 12/25/25, Overbrook, Pa.   BR/TR, 5'11", 170 lbs.   Deb: 4/16/10

| 1910 | Cle-A | 0 | 0 | — | 2 | 0 | 0 | 0 | 0 | 3 | 5 | 0 | 1 | 5 | 18.0 | 6.00 | 43 | .385 | .429 | 0 | — | 0 | -1 | -1 | -0 | 0.0 |

● **GARLAND KISER**   Kiser, Garland Routhard   b: 7/8/68, Charlotte, N.C.   BL/TL, 6'3", 190 lbs.   Deb: 9/9/91

| 1991 | Cle-A | 0 | 0 | — | 7 | 0 | 0 | 0 | 0 | 4² | 7 | 0 | 4 | 3 | 23.1 | 9.64 | 43 | .368 | .500 | 0 | — | 0 | -3 | -3 | -0 | 0.0 |

● RUBE KISINGER
Kisinger, Charles Samuel b: 12/13/1876, Adrian, Mich. d: 7/14/41, Huron, Ohio BR/TR, 6', 190 lbs. Deb: 9/10/02

YEAR TM/L	W	L	PCT	G	GS	CG	SH	SV	IP	H	HR	BB	SO	RAT	ERA	ERA+	OAV	OOB	BH	AVG	PB	PR	/A	PD	TPI
1902 Det-A	2	3	.400	5	5	5	0	0	43¹	48	0	14	7	13.5	3.12	117	.281	.346	3	.158	-1	2	3	-0	0.2
1903 Det-A	7	9	.438	16	14	13	2	0	118²	118	0	27	33	11.1	2.96	98	.259	.303	6	.128	-3	0	-1	1	-0.3
Total 2	9	12	.429	21	19	18	2	0	162	166	0	41	40	11.7	3.00	103	.265	.315	9	.136	-4	2	2	1	-0.1

● BRUCE KISON
Kison, Bruce Eugene b: 2/18/50, Pasco, Wash. BR/TR, 6'4", 178 lbs. Deb: 7/4/71 C

YEAR TM/L	W	L	PCT	G	GS	CG	SH	SV	IP	H	HR	BB	SO	RAT	ERA	ERA+	OAV	OOB	BH	AVG	PB	PR	/A	PD	TPI
1971 *Pit-N	6	5	.545	18	13	2	1	0	95¹	93	6	36	60	12.7	3.40	100	.259	.337	2	.065	-1	1	-0	1	0.0
1972 *Pit-N	9	7	.563	32	18	6	1	3	152	123	11	69	102	11.9	3.26	102	.220	.316	10	.189	2	3	1	-1	0.2
1973 Pit-N	3	0	1.000	7	7	0	0	0	43²	36	4	24	26	12.6	3.09	114	.232	.339	1	.083	0	3	2	0	0.2
1974 *Pit-N	9	8	.529	40	16	1	0	2	129	123	8	57	71	13.3	3.49	99	.247	.338	4	.108	-0	2	-1	1	0.0
1975 *Pit-N	12	11	.522	33	29	6	0	0	192	160	10	92	89	12.0	3.23	109	.227	.320	7	.119	-2	8	7	2	0.8
1976 Pit-N	14	9	.609	31	29	6	1	1	193	180	10	52	98	11.0	3.08	113	.246	.299	12	.203	4	9	9	1	1.5
1977 Pit-N	9	10	.474	33	32	3	1	0	193	209	25	55	122	12.6	4.90	81	.278	.333	18	.261	5	-21	-20	1	-1.3
1978 Pit-N	6	6	.500	28	11	0	0	0	96	81	9	39	62	11.7	3.19	116	.229	.314	4	.138	1	4	5	1	0.8
1979 *Pit-N	13	7	.650	33	25	3	1	0	172¹	157	13	45	105	10.8	3.19	122	.246	.300	8	.145	0	10	13	1	1.6
1980 Cal-A	3	6	.333	13	13	2	1	0	73¹	73	5	32	28	13.3	4.91	80	.264	.346	0	—	0	-7	-8	-1	-0.8
1981 Cal-A	1	1	.500	11	4	0	0	0	44	40	8	14	19	11.0	3.48	105	.241	.300	0	—	0	1	1	1	0.1
1982 *Cal-A	10	5	.667	33	16	3	1	1	142	120	15	44	86	10.7	3.17	128	.226	.292	0	—	0	14	14	2	1.6
1983 Cal-A	11	5	.688	26	17	4	1	2	126²	128	13	43	83	12.4	4.05	99	.264	.330	0	—	0	0	-1	1	0.1
1984 Cal-A	4	5	.444	20	7	0	0	2	65¹	72	10	28	66	14.6	5.37	74	.280	.364	0	—	0	-10	-10	-1	-1.3
1985 Bos-A	5	3	.625	22	9	0	0	1	92	98	9	32	56	12.8	4.11	104	.274	.335	0	—	0	0	2	2	0.0
Total 15	115	88	.567	380	246	36	8	12	1809²	1693	150	662	1073	12.1	3.66	102	.248	.321	66	.163	8	18	14	11	3.5

● BILL KISSINGER
Kissinger, William Francis "Shang" b: 8/15/1871, Dayton, Ky. d: 4/20/29, Cincinnati, Ohio BR/TR, 185 lbs. Deb: 5/30/1895 ♦

YEAR TM/L	W	L	PCT	G	GS	CG	SH	SV	IP	H	HR	BB	SO	RAT	ERA	ERA+	OAV	OOB	BH	AVG	PB	PR	/A	PD	TPI
1895 Bal-N	1	0	1.000	2	2	1	0	0	11¹	18	1	2	3	15.9	3.97	120	.354	.378	1	.200	-0	1	1	-0	0.0
StL-N	4	12	.250	24	14	9	0	0	140²	222	8	51	31	18.0	6.72	72	.352	.408	24	.247	-2	-30	-29	0	-2.4
Yr	5	12	.294	26	16	10	0	0	152	240	8	53	34	17.8	6.51	74	.353	.406	25	.245	-2	-29	-28	0	-2.4
1896 StL-N	2	9	.182	20	12	11	0	1	136	209	5	55	22	18.0	6.49	67	.349	.411	22	.301	1	-32	-32	2	-1.7
1897 StL-N	0	4	.000	7	4	2	0	0	31¹	51	1	15	5	21.3	11.49	38	.362	.451	13	.333	2	-25	-25	0	-2.0
Total 3	7	25	.219	53	32	23	0	1	319¹	500	15	123	61	18.2	6.99	66	.352	.413	60	.280	1	-86	-85	2	-6.1

● FRANK KITSON
Kitson, Frank L. b: 4/11/1872, Hopkins, Mich. d: 4/14/30, Allegan, Mich. BL/TR, 5'11", 165 lbs. Deb: 5/19/1898

YEAR TM/L	W	L	PCT	G	GS	CG	SH	SV	IP	H	HR	BB	SO	RAT	ERA	ERA+	OAV	OOB	BH	AVG	PB	PR	/A	PD	TPI
1898 Bal-N	8	5	.615	17	13	13	1	0	119¹	123	0	35	32	12.5	3.24	110	.264	.327	4	.314	4	5	4	0	0.8
1899 Bal-N	22	16	.579	40	37	34	2	0	327²	329	6	65	75	11.2	2.77	143	.261	.303	27	.201	-2	39	43	-2	3.9
1900 *Bro-N	15	13	.536	40	30	21	2	4	253¹	283	12	56	55	12.4	4.19	92	.282	.325	32	.294	5	-14	-10	-5	-0.9
1901 Bro-N	19	11	.633	38	32	26	5	2	280²	312	9	67	127	12.5	2.98	112	.279	.326	35	.263	5	11	12	-3	1.5
1902 Bro-N	19	12	.613	31	30	28	3	0	259²	251	4	48	107	10.6	2.84	97	.254	.293	8	.274	8	-2	-2	1	0.6
1903 Det-A	15	16	.484	31	28	28	2	0	257²	277	8	38	102	11.2	2.58	113	.274	.303	21	.181	-1	11	9	-2	0.7
1904 Det-A	8	13	.381	26	24	19	0	1	199²	211	6	38	69	11.5	3.07	83	.272	.312	15	.208	1	-10	-11	-0	-1.1
1905 Det-A	12	14	.462	33	27	21	3	1	225²	230	3	57	78	11.9	3.47	72	.265	.319	16	.184	-1	-20	-18	-2	-2.4
1906 Was-A	6	14	.300	30	21	15	1	0	197	196	2	57	59	11.8	3.65	72	.262	.320	22	.244	8	-21	-22	-0	-1.3
1907 Was-A	0	3	.000	5	3	2	0	0	32	41	1	9	11	14.6	3.94	62	.313	.366	1	.100	-0	-5	-5	-1	-0.6
NY-A	4	0	1.000	12	4	3	0	0	61	75	0	17	14	14.2	3.10	90	.304	.359	7	.280	1	-4	-2	-2	-0.2
Yr	4	3	.571	17	7	5	0	0	93	116	1	26	25	14.1	3.39	79	.306	.356	8	.229	0	-9	-7	-2	-0.8
Total 10	128	117	.522	303	249	210	19	8	2213²	2328	52	487	729	11.8	3.18	99	.270	.315	234	.240	27	-10	-4	-16	1.0

● MALACHI KITTRIDGE
Kittridge, Malachi Jeddidah "Jeddidah" b: 10/12/1869, Clinton, Mass. d: 6/23/28, Gary, Ind. BR/TR, 5'7", 170 lbs. Deb: 4/19/1890 M♦

YEAR TM/L	W	L	PCT	G	GS	CG	SH	SV	IP	H	HR	BB	SO	RAT	ERA	ERA+	OAV	OOB	BH	AVG	PB	PR	/A	PD	TPI
1896 Chi-N	0	0	—	1	0	0	0	0	1²	2	0	1	0	16.2	5.40	84	.295	.385	48	.223	-0	0	0	0	0.0

● HUGO KLAERNER
Klaerner, Hugo Emil "Dutch" b: 10/15/08, Fredericksburg, Tex. d: 2/3/82, Fredericksburg, Tex. BR/TR, 5'11", 190 lbs. Deb: 9/10/34

YEAR TM/L	W	L	PCT	G	GS	CG	SH	SV	IP	H	HR	BB	SO	RAT	ERA	ERA+	OAV	OOB	BH	AVG	PB	PR	/A	PD	TPI
1934 Chi-A	0	2	.000	3	3	1	0	0	17¹	24	4	16	9	20.8	10.90	43	.329	.449	2	.333	1	-12	-12	1	-0.8

● FRED KLAGES
Klages, Frederick Albert Antony b: 10/31/43, Ambridge, Pa. BR/TR, 6'2", 185 lbs. Deb: 9/11/66

YEAR TM/L	W	L	PCT	G	GS	CG	SH	SV	IP	H	HR	BB	SO	RAT	ERA	ERA+	OAV	OOB	BH	AVG	PB	PR	/A	PD	TPI
1966 Chi-A	1	0	1.000	3	3	0	0	0	15²	9	0	7	6	9.2	1.72	184	.167	.262	3	.500	1	3	3	0	0.3
1967 Chi-A	4	4	.500	11	9	0	0	0	44²	43	6	16	17	12.1	3.83	81	.255	.324	0	.000	-1	-3	-4	-1	-0.8
Total 2	5	4	.556	14	12	0	0	0	60¹	52	6	23	23	11.3	3.28	95	.234	.309	3	.167	-0	-1	-1	-1	-0.5

● AL KLAWITTER
Klawitter, Albert "Dutch" b: 4/12/1888, Wilkes-Barre, Pa. d: 5/2/50, Milwaukee, Wis. BR/TR, 5'11.5", 187 lbs. Deb: 9/20/09

YEAR TM/L	W	L	PCT	G	GS	CG	SH	SV	IP	H	HR	BB	SO	RAT	ERA	ERA+	OAV	OOB	BH	AVG	PB	PR	/A	PD	TPI
1909 NY-N	1	1	.500	6	3	2	0	1	27	24	1	13	6	12.3	2.00	128	.247	.336	3	.333	1	2	1	1	0.4
1910 NY-N	0	0	—	1	0	0	0	0	1	2	0	2	0	36.0	9.00	33	.400	.571	0	—	0	-1	-1	-0	0.0
1913 Det-A	1	2	.333	8	3	1	0	0	32	39	0	15	10	15.2	5.91	49	.305	.378	0	.000	-2	-11	-11	0	-1.0
Total 3	2	3	.400	15	6	3	0	1	60	65	1	30	16	14.3	4.20	66	.283	.365	3	.150	-0	-9	-10	1	-0.6

● TOM KLAWITTER
Klawitter, Thomas Carl b: 6/24/58, LaCrosse, Wis. BR/TL, 6'2", 190 lbs. Deb: 4/14/85

YEAR TM/L	W	L	PCT	G	GS	CG	SH	SV	IP	H	HR	BB	SO	RAT	ERA	ERA+	OAV	OOB	BH	AVG	PB	PR	/A	PD	TPI
1985 Min-A	0	0	—	7	2	0	0	0	9¹	7	2	13	5	19.3	6.75	65	.226	.455	0	—	0	-3	-2	0	-0.3

● HAL KLEINE
Kleine, Harold John b: 6/8/23, St.Louis, Mo. d: 12/10/57, St.Louis, Mo. BL/TR, 6'2", 193 lbs. Deb: 4/26/44

YEAR TM/L	W	L	PCT	G	GS	CG	SH	SV	IP	H	HR	BB	SO	RAT	ERA	ERA+	OAV	OOB	BH	AVG	PB	PR	/A	PD	TPI
1944 Cle-A	1	2	.333	11	6	1	0	0	40²	38	0	36	13	16.4	5.75	127	.248	.392	2	.143	-1	-11	-11	-1	-0.9
1945 Cle-A	0	0	—	3	0	0	0	0	7	8	0	7	5	19.3	3.86	84	.286	.429	1	.333	1	-0	-0	-0	0.0
Total 2	1	2	.333	14	6	1	0	0	47²	46	0	43	18	16.8	5.48	60	.254	.397	3	.176	-0	-11	-12	-1	-0.9

● TED KLEINHANS
Kleinhans, Theodore Otto b: 4/8/1899, Deer Park, Wis. d: 7/24/85, Redington Beach, Fla. BR/TL, 6', 170 lbs. Deb: 4/20/34

YEAR TM/L	W	L	PCT	G	GS	CG	SH	SV	IP	H	HR	BB	SO	RAT	ERA	ERA+	OAV	OOB	BH	AVG	PB	PR	/A	PD	TPI
1934 Phi-N	0	0	—	5	0	0	0	0	6	11	1	3	2	21.0	9.00	52	.379	.438	0	.000	-0	-3	-3	0	0.0
Cin-N	2	6	.250	24	9	0	0	0	80	107	2	38	23	16.4	5.74	71	.321	.392	3	.130	-1	-15	-15	1	-1.2
Yr	2	6	.250	29	9	0	0	0	86	118	3	41	25	16.7	5.97	69	.326	.396	3	.125	-1	-18	-18	2	-1.2
1936 NY-A	1	1	.500	19	0	0	0	1	29¹	36	4	23	10	18.1	5.83	80	.300	.413	1	.167	-0	-3	-4	-0	-0.3
1937 Cin-N	1	2	.333	7	3	1	0	0	27¹	29	1	12	13	13.8	2.30	162	.271	.350	2	.250	1	5	4	-1	0.4
1938 Cin-N	0	0	—	1	0	0	0	0	1	2	0	2	0	18.0	9.00	41	.400	.400	0	—	0	-1	-1	-0	0.0
Total 4	4	9	.308	56	12	1	0	1	143²	185	4	76	48	16.5	5.26	79	.311	.391	6	.158	-1	-16	-17	1	-1.1

● NUB KLEINKE
Kleinke, Norbert George b: 5/19/11, Fond Du Lac, Wis. d: 3/16/50, Off Marin Coast, Cal. BR/TR, 6'1", 170 lbs. Deb: 4/25/35

YEAR TM/L	W	L	PCT	G	GS	CG	SH	SV	IP	H	HR	BB	SO	RAT	ERA	ERA+	OAV	OOB	BH	AVG	PB	PR	/A	PD	TPI
1935 StL-N	0	0	—	4	2	0	0	0	12²	19	1	9	5	15.6	4.97	82	.358	.393	0	.000	-0	-1	-1	-0	0.0
1937 StL-N	1	1	.500	5	2	1	0	0	20²	25	0	7	9	13.9	4.79	83	.321	.376	0	.000	-1	-2	-2	0	-0.2
Total 2	1	1	.500	9	4	1	0	0	33¹	44	1	16	14	14.6	4.86	83	.336	.383	0	.000	-1	-3	-3	0	-0.2

● ED KLEPFER
Klepfer, Edward Lloyd "Big Ed" b: 3/17/1888, Summerville, Pa. d: 8/9/50, Tulsa, Okla. BR/TR, 6', 185 lbs. Deb: 7/4/11

YEAR TM/L	W	L	PCT	G	GS	CG	SH	SV	IP	H	HR	BB	SO	RAT	ERA	ERA+	OAV	OOB	BH	AVG	PB	PR	/A	PD	TPI
1911 NY-A	0	0	—	2	0	0	0	0	4	5	0	2	4	15.8	6.75	50	.250	.318	0	.000	-0	-2	-1	0	0.0
1913 NY-A	0	1	.000	8	1	0	0	0	24²	38	2	12	10	19.0	7.66	39	.373	.448	1	.167	0	-13	-13	0	-0.4
1915 Chi-A	1	0	1.000	3	2	1	0	0	12²	11	0	5	3	11.4	2.84	105	.234	.308	0	.000	-0	0	-0	0	0.0
Cle-A	1	6	.143	8	7	2	0	0	43	47	0	11	13	12.1	2.09	146	.283	.328	2	.167	-0	4	5	1	0.8
Yr	2	6	.250	11	9	3	0	0	55²	58	0	16	16	12.0	2.26	134	.272	.323	2	.133	-0	4	5	0	0.8
1916 Cle-A	6	6	.500	31	13	4	1	2	143	136	6	46	62	11.7	2.52	119	.262	.327	1	.025	-4	5	8	-0	0.2
1917 Cle-A	14	4	.778	41	27	9	0	1	213	208	6	55	66	11.1	2.37	120	.264	.312	2	.032	-6	7	11	-2	0.1
1919 Cle-A	0	0	—	5	0	0	0	0	7¹	12	1	6	7	22.1	7.36	45	.375	.474	0	.000	-0	-3	-3	0	0.0
Total 6	22	17	.564	98	50	16	1	3	447²	457	3	137	165	12.1	2.81	104	.273	.330	6	.048	-11	-2	6	-1	0.7

YEAR TM/L	W	L	PCT	G	GS	CG	SH	SV	IP	H	HR	BB	SO	RAT	ERA	ERA+	OAV	OOB	BH	AVG	PB	PR	/A	PD	TPI

● **ED KLIEMAN** Klieman, Edward Frederick "Specs" or "Babe" b: 3/21/18, Norwood, Ohio d: 11/15/79, Homosassa, Fla. BR/TR, 6'1", 190 lbs. Deb: 9/24/43

YEAR TM/L	W	L	PCT	G	GS	CG	SH	SV	IP	H	HR	BB	SO	RAT	ERA	ERA+	OAV	OOB	BH	AVG	PB	PR	/A	PD	TPI
1943 Cle-A	0	1	.000	1	1	1	0	0	9	8	0	5	2	13.0	1.00	311	.286	.394	0	.000	-0	2	2	-0	0.2
1944 Cle-A	11	13	.458	47	19	5	1	5	178¹	185	4	70	44	13.2	3.38	98	.274	.348	6	.105	-3	1	-2	1	-0.5
1945 Cle-A	5	8	.385	38	12	4	1	4	126¹	123	3	49	33	12.5	3.85	84	.261	.336	8	.200	-1	-7	-8	3	-0.5
1946 Cle-A	0	0	—	9	0	0	0	0	15	18	0	10	2	16.8	6.60	50	.290	.389	0	.000	-0	-5	-5	-1	-0.1
1947 Cle-A	5	4	.556	**58**	0	0	0	**17**	92	78	5	39	21	11.6	3.03	115	.231	.315	2	.105	-1	7	5	2	0.7
1948 *Cle-A	3	2	.600	44	0	0	0	4	79²	62	3	46	18	12.4	2.60	156	.229	.345	2	.143	-0	**15**	**13**	1	0.9
1949 Was-A	0	0	—	2	0	0	0	0	3	8	0	3	1	33.0	18.00	24	.500	.579	1	1.000	-0	-5	-5	-0	0.0
Chi-A	2	0	1.000	18	0	0	0	3	33	33	2	15	9	13.1	3.00	139	.273	.353	2	.250	0	4	4	1	0.4
Yr	2	0	1.000	20	0	0	0	3	36	41	2	18	10	14.8	4.25	98	.299	.381	3	.333	1	-0	-1	1	0.4
1950 Phi-A	0	0	—	5	0	0	0	0	5²	10	0	2	0	22.2	9.53	48	.357	.438	0	.000	-0	-3	-3	-0	-0.1
Total 8	26	28	.481	222	32	10	2	33	542	525	17	239	130	13.0	3.49	100	.261	.345	21	.146	-3	10	1	6	1.1

● **RON KLIMKOWSKI** Klimkowski, Ronald Bernard b: 3/1/44, Jersey City, N.J. BR/TR, 6'2", 190 lbs. Deb: 9/15/69

YEAR TM/L	W	L	PCT	G	GS	CG	SH	SV	IP	H	HR	BB	SO	RAT	ERA	ERA+	OAV	OOB	BH	AVG	PB	PR	/A	PD	TPI
1969 NY-A	0	0	—	3	1	0	0	0	14	6	0	5	3	7.1	0.64	541	.130	.216	0	.000	-0	5	4	-0	-0.1
1970 NY-A	6	7	.462	45	3	1	1	0	98¹	80	7	33	40	10.6	2.65	132	.223	.294	1	.053	-2	12	9	0	1.1
1971 Oak-A	2	2	.500	26	0	0	0	0	45¹	37	3	23	25	12.1	3.38	99	.220	.318	2	.400	1	0	-0	1	0.2
1972 NY-A	0	3	.000	16	2	0	0	1	31¹	32	3	15	11	13.8	4.02	73	.271	.358	0	.000	-1	-3	-4	0	-0.5
Total 4	8	12	.400	90	6	1	1	4	189	155	13	76	79	11.2	2.90	116	.224	.306	3	.091	-2	13	10	1	0.7

● **BOBBY KLINE** Kline, John Robert b: 1/27/29, St.Petersburg, Fla BR/TR, 6', 179 lbs. Deb: 4/11/55 ♦

YEAR TM/L	W	L	PCT	G	GS	CG	SH	SV	IP	H	HR	BB	SO	RAT	ERA	ERA+	OAV	OOB	BH	AVG	PB	PR	/A	PD	TPI
1955 Was-A	0	0	—	1	0	0	0	0	1	4	1	1	0	45.0	27.00	14	.667	.714	31	.221	0	-3	-3	0	0.0

● **BOB KLINE** Kline, Robert George "Junior" b: 12/9/09, Enterprise, Ohio d: 3/16/87, Westerville, Ohio BR/TR, 6'3", 200 lbs. Deb: 9/17/30

YEAR TM/L	W	L	PCT	G	GS	CG	SH	SV	IP	H	HR	BB	SO	RAT	ERA	ERA+	OAV	OOB	BH	AVG	PB	PR	/A	PD	TPI
1930 Bos-A	0	0	—	1	0	0	0	0	1	1	0	0	0	9.0	0.00	—	.333	.333	0	—	0	1	1	-0	0.0
1931 Bos-A	5	5	.500	28	10	3	0	0	98	110	4	35	25	13.6	4.41	98	.298	.364	9	.333	-0	-1	-2	3	0.3
1932 Bos-A	11	13	.458	47	19	4	1	2	172	203	10	76	31	14.7	5.28	85	.294	.365	7	.130	-3	-15	-15	3	-1.8
1933 Bos-A	7	8	.467	46	8	1	0	4	127	127	5	67	16	14.2	4.54	97	.265	.362	6	.176	-1	-4	-2	3	0.0
1934 Phi-A	6	2	.750	20	0	0	0	1	39²	50	6	13	14	14.3	6.35	69	.314	.366	3	.333	-1	-8	-9	1	-1.3
Was-A	1	0	1.000	6	0	0	0	0	4	10	0	4	1	33.8	15.75	27	.500	.600	0	—	0	-5	-5	-0	-1.0
Yr	7	2	.778	26	0	0	0	1	43²	60	6	17	15	16.1	7.21	61	.335	.396	3	.333	1	-13	-14	2	-2.3
Total 5	30	28	.517	148	37	8	1	7	441²	501	24	195	87	14.4	5.05	87	.291	.367	25	.202	-1	-32	-32	9	-3.8

● **RON KLINE** Kline, Ronald Lee b: 3/9/32, Callery, Pa. BR/TR, 6'3", 205 lbs. Deb: 4/21/52

YEAR TM/L	W	L	PCT	G	GS	CG	SH	SV	IP	H	HR	BB	SO	RAT	ERA	ERA+	OAV	OOB	BH	AVG	PB	PR	/A	PD	TPI
1952 Pit-N	0	7	.000	27	11	0	0	0	78²	74	3	66	27	16.7	5.49	73	.253	.401	0	.000	-2	-15	-13	-1	-1.4
1955 Pit-N	6	13	.316	36	19	3	1	2	136²	161	13	53	48	14.4	4.15	99	.298	.366	5	.132	-2	-2	-1	2	0.0
1956 Pit-N	14	18	.438	44	39	9	2	2	264	263	26	81	125	11.9	3.38	112	.263	.321	10	.127	-3	12	12	-0	1.1
1957 Pit-N	9	16	.360	40	31	11	2	0	205	214	28	61	88	12.1	4.04	94	.268	.321	4	.061	-6	-4	-6	-1	-1.3
1958 Pit-N	13	16	.448	32	32	11	2	0	237¹	220	25	92	109	11.8	3.53	110	.252	.323	2	.027	-6	11	9	1	0.4
1959 Pit-N	11	13	.458	33	29	7	0	0	186	186	23	70	91	12.5	4.26	91	.263	.331	8	.136	-2	-6	-8	-1	-1.1
1960 StL-N	4	9	.308	34	17	1	0	1	117²	133	11	43	54	13.5	6.04	68	.284	.344	5	.143	-2	-30	-25	1	-2.6
1961 LA-A	3	6	.333	26	12	0	0	0	104²	119	16	44	70	14.1	4.90	92	.288	.358	2	.097	-2	-10	-5	1	-0.5
Det-A	5	3	.625	10	8	3	1	0	56¹	53	3	17	27	11.2	2.72	151	.245	.300	3	.167	-0	8	9	-1	1.1
Yr	8	9	.471	36	20	3	1	1	161	172	19	61	97	13.0	4.14	106	.272	.336	6	.122	-2	-2	4	0	0.6
1962 Det-A	3	6	.333	36	4	0	0	2	77¹	88	9	28	47	13.7	4.31	94	.284	.347	2	.125	-1	-3	-2	1	-0.3
1963 Was-A	3	8	.273	62	1	0	0	17	93²	85	3	30	49	11.3	2.79	133	.249	.316	1	.091	-0	9	10	-1	1.4
1964 Was-A	10	7	.588	61	0	0	0	14	81¹	81	7	21	40	11.5	2.32	159	.262	.313	1	.167	-0	12	12	-0	3.0
1965 Was-A	7	6	.538	74	0	0	0	**29**	99¹	106	7	32	52	12.7	2.63	132	.275	.333	0	.000	-1	9	9	-1	1.7
1966 Was-A	4	6	.400	63	0	0	0	23	90¹	79	12	17	46	9.6	2.39	145	.237	.274	1	.167	-0	10	11	-2	1.7
1967 Min-A	7	1	.875	54	0	0	0	7	71²	71	10	15	36	10.9	3.77	92	.261	.302	0	.000	-1	-4	-2	-1	-0.4
1968 Pit-N	12	5	.706	56	0	0	0	7	112²	94	3	31	48	10.1	1.68	174	.234	.293	0	.000	-1	**16**	**16**	-1	2.4
1969 Pit-N	1	3	.250	20	0	0	0	3	31	37	3	5	15	12.5	5.81	60	.296	.328	0	.000	-0	-8	-8	-0	-1.2
SF-N	0	2	.000	7	0	0	0	0	11	16	1	6	7	18.0	4.09	86	.364	.440	0	—	0	-1	-1	-0	-0.1
Yr	1	5	.167	27	0	0	0	3	42	53	4	11	22	13.7	5.36	65	.310	.352	0	—	-0	-8	-9	-1	-1.3
Bos-A	0	1	.000	16	0	0	0	1	17	24	4	17	7	21.7	4.76	80	.329	.456	0	—	0	-2	-2	-0	-0.1
1970 Atl-N	0	0	—	5	0	0	0	0	6¹	9	4	2	3	15.6	7.11	60	.321	.367	0	—	-0	-2	-2	-0	-0.1
Total 17	114	144	.442	736	203	44	8	108	2078	2113	218	731	989	12.5	3.75	101	.266	.331	45	.092	-28	1	13	-5	3.7

● **STEVE KLINE** Kline, Steven Jack b: 10/6/47, Wenatchee, Wash. BR/TR, 6'3", 205 lbs. Deb: 7/10/70

YEAR TM/L	W	L	PCT	G	GS	CG	SH	SV	IP	H	HR	BB	SO	RAT	ERA	ERA+	OAV	OOB	BH	AVG	PB	PR	/A	PD	TPI
1970 NY-A	6	6	.500	16	15	5	0	0	100¹	99	8	24	49	11.0	3.41	103	.254	.298	5	.179	2	3	1	1	0.4
1971 NY-A	12	13	.480	31	30	15	1	0	222¹	206	21	37	81	9.8	2.96	109	.244	.276	9	.136	-0	13	7	3	1.1
1972 NY-A	16	9	.640	32	32	11	4	0	236¹	210	11	44	58	10.1	2.40	123	.237	.281	7	.092	-3	17	14	2	1.5
1973 NY-A	4	7	.364	14	13	2	1	0	74	76	5	31	19	13.1	4.01	91	.270	.344	0	—	0	-2	-3	-0	-0.2
1974 NY-A	2	2	.500	4	4	0	0	0	26	26	3	5	6	11.1	3.46	101	.263	.305	0	—	0	0	-0	0	0.1
Cle-A	3	8	.273	16	11	1	0	0	71	70	9	31	17	13.3	5.07	71	.266	.352	0	—	0	-11	-11	1	-1.5
Yr	5	10	.333	20	15	1	0	0	97	96	12	36	23	12.6	4.64	77	.264	.337	0	—	0	-11	-11	1	-1.4
1977 Atl-N	0	0	—	16	0	0	0	1	20¹	21	4	12	10	14.6	6.64	67	.259	.355	0	—	0	-6	-5	-0	-0.1
Total 6	43	45	.489	129	105	34	6	1	750¹	708	61	184	240	10.9	3.26	101	.249	.298	21	.124	-1	14	3	5	1.3

● **BILL KLING** Kling, William b: 1/14/1867, Kansas City, Mo. d: 8/26/34, Kansas City, Mo. BL/TR, 6', 190 lbs. Deb: 8/13/1891 F

YEAR TM/L	W	L	PCT	G	GS	CG	SH	SV	IP	H	HR	BB	SO	RAT	ERA	ERA+	OAV	OOB	BH	AVG	PB	PR	/A	PD	TPI
1891 Phi-N	4	2	.667	12	7	4	0	0	75	90	2	32	26	14.9	4.32	79	.286	.356	6	.194	1	-8	-8	-1	-0.5
1892 Bal-N	0	2	.000	2	2	0	0	0	11	17	1	7	7	21.3	11.45	30	.340	.441	1	.250	1	-10	-10	-0	-1.1
1895 Lou-N	0	0	—	1	0	0	0	0	1	0	0	1	0	9.0	0.00	—	.000	.256	0	.000	-0	1	1	-0	0.0
Total 3	4	4	.500	15	9	4	0	0	87	107	3	40	33	15.6	5.17	66	.291	.367	7	.194	1	-18	-17	-1	-1.6

● **SCOTT KLINGENBECK** Klingenbeck, Scott Edward b: 2/3/71, Cincinnati, Ohio BR/TR, 6'2", 205 lbs. Deb: 6/2/94

YEAR TM/L	W	L	PCT	G	GS	CG	SH	SV	IP	H	HR	BB	SO	RAT	ERA	ERA+	OAV	OOB	BH	AVG	PB	PR	/A	PD	TPI
1994 Bal-A	1	0	1.000	1	1	0	0	0	7	6	1	4	5	14.1	3.86	132	.240	.367	0	—	0	1	1	0	0.0

● **BOB KLINGER** Klinger, Robert Harold b: 6/4/08, Allenton, Mo. d: 8/19/77, Villa Ridge, Mo. BR/TR, 6', 180 lbs. Deb: 4/19/38

YEAR TM/L	W	L	PCT	G	GS	CG	SH	SV	IP	H	HR	BB	SO	RAT	ERA	ERA+	OAV	OOB	BH	AVG	PB	PR	/A	PD	TPI
1938 Pit-N	12	5	.706	28	21	10	1	1	159¹	152	9	42	58	11.3	2.99	127	.253	.308	10	.167	-2	14	14	0	1.3
1939 Pit-N	14	17	.452	37	33	10	2	0	225	251	11	81	64	13.4	4.36	88	.284	.346	17	.202	0	-11	-13	3	-1.3
1940 Pit-N	8	13	.381	39	22	3	0	3	142	196	5	53	48	16.1	5.39	71	.329	.388	6	.143	-2	-24	-25	1	-3.4
1941 Pit-N	9	4	.692	35	9	3	0	4	116²	127	5	30	36	12.2	3.93	92	.276	.322	8	.250	-2	-4	-4	0	-0.3
1942 Pit-N	8	11	.421	37	19	8	1	1	152²	151	6	46	58	11.7	3.24	104	.252	.307	8	.200	1	1	1	2	0.5
1943 Pit-N	8	5	.579	33	25	14	3	0	195	185	6	58	65	11.2	2.72	128	.252	.307	16	.246	3	14	16	0	1.9
1946 *Bos-A	3	2	.600	28	1	0	0	**9**	57	49	1	25	16	11.8	2.37	155	.238	.323	5	.313	1	7	8	0	1.1
1947 Bos-A	1	1	.500	28	0	0	0	5	42	42	5	24	12	14.4	3.86	101	.253	.351	1	.111	-1	-1	-0	-0	-0.1
Total 8	66	61	.520	265	130	48	7	23	1089²	1153	46	358	357	12.6	3.68	100	.271	.331	71	.204	-3	-3	-0	5	-0.3

● **JOE KLINK** Klink, Joseph Charles b: 2/3/62, Johnstown, Pa. BL/TL, 5'11", 170 lbs. Deb: 4/9/87

YEAR TM/L	W	L	PCT	G	GS	CG	SH	SV	IP	H	HR	BB	SO	RAT	ERA	ERA+	OAV	OOB	BH	AVG	PB	PR	/A	PD	TPI
1987 Min-A	0	1	.000	12	0	0	0	0	23	24	4	11	17	18.8	6.65	69	.359	.421	0	—	0	-6	-5	-0	-0.3
1990 *Oak-A	0	0	—	40	0	0	0	0	39²	34	1	18	19	11.8	2.04	182	.233	.317	0	—	0	8	7	-1	0.9
1991 Oak-A	10	3	.769	62	0	0	0	2	62	60	4	21	34	12.5	4.35	88	.259	.333	0	—	0	-2	-4	-0	-0.7
1993 Fla-N	0	2	.000	59	0	0	0	1	37²	37	0	24	22	14.6	5.02	86	.266	.374	0	.000	-0	-4	-4	-1	-0.2
Total 4	10	6	.625	173	0	0	0	3	162¹	168	9	74	92	13.7	4.27	94	.271	.353	0	.000	-0	-3	-4	-2	-1.2

YEAR	TM/L	W	L	PCT	G	GS	CG	SH	SV	IP	H	HR	BB	SO	RAT	ERA	ERA+	OAV	OOB	BH	AVG	PB	PR	/A	PD	TPI

● JOHNNY KLIPPSTEIN   Klippstein, John Calvin   b: 10/17/27, Washington, D.C.   BR/TR, 6'1", 185 lbs.   Deb: 5/3/50

YEAR	TM/L	W	L	PCT	G	GS	CG	SH	SV	IP	H	HR	BB	SO	RAT	ERA	ERA+	OAV	OOB	BH	AVG	PB	PR	/A	PD	TPI
1950	Chi-N	2	9	.182	33	11	3	0	1	104²	112	9	64	51	15.5	5.25	80	.279	.383	11	.333	4	-13	-12	-1	-0.8
1951	Chi-N	6	6	.500	35	11	1	1	2	123²	125	10	53	56	13.4	4.29	95	.263	.344	4	.108	-2	-5	-3	-0	-0.4
1952	Chi-N	9	14	.391	41	25	7	2	3	202²	208	17	89	110	13.5	4.44	87	.265	.344	11	.175	1	-16	-13	1	-1.2
1953	Chi-N	10	11	.476	48	19	5	0	6	167²	169	15	107	113	15.2	4.83	92	.258	.369	9	.155	-1	-10	-7	-2	-1.0
1954	Chi-N	4	11	.267	36	21	4	0	1	148	155	13	96	69	15.5	5.29	79	.272	.381	6	.133	-2	-20	-18	-1	-1.7
1955	Cin-N	9	10	.474	39	14	3	2	0	138	120	13	60	68	12.0	3.39	125	.233	.318	2	.065	-2	10	13	-0	1.4
1956	Cin-N	12	11	.522	37	29	11	0	1	211	219	26	82	86	13.3	4.09	97	.275	.350	7	.099	-4	-8	-3	1	-0.6
1957	Cin-N	8	11	.421	46	18	3	1	3	146	146	17	68	99	13.4	5.05	81	.261	.344	3	.073	-3	-19	-15	-1	-2.3
1958	Cin-N	3	2	.600	12	4	0	0	1	33	37	5	14	22	14.2	4.91	84	.285	.359	1	.125	-0	-4	-3	-1	-0.5
	LA-N	3	5	.375	45	0	0	0	9	90	81	12	44	73	12.7	3.80	108	.248	.341	1	.050	-2	2	3	-0	0.1
	Yr	6	7	.462	57	4	0	0	10	123	118	17	58	95	13.0	4.10	100	.258	.344	2	.071	-2	-2	0	-0	-0.4
1959	*LA-N	4	0	1.000	28	0	0	0	2	45²	48	8	33	30	16.4	5.91	72	.276	.397	1	.143	-0	-10	-9	-0	-0.8
1960	Cle-A	5	5	.500	49	0	0	0	14	74¹	53	8	35	64	10.8	2.91	129	.205	.303	2	.143	-0	8	7	0	1.2
1961	Was-A	2	2	.500	42	1	0	0	0	71²	83	13	43	41	16.3	6.78	59	.297	.399	1	.143	-0	-22	-22	1	-1.1
1962	Cin-N	7	6	.538	40	7	0	0	4	108²	113	13	64	67	15.0	4.47	90	.278	.381	3	.125	-0	-6	-5	0	-0.5
1963	Phi-N	5	6	.455	49	1	0	0	8	112	80	3	46	86	10.4	1.93	168	.204	.293	1	.038	-2	17	16	-1	1.6
1964	Phi-N	2	1	.667	11	0	0	0	1	22¹	22	6	8	13	12.9	4.03	86	.250	.327	0	.000	-0	-1	-1	1	-0.2
	Min-A	0	4	.000	33	0	0	0	2	45²	44	7	20	39	12.8	1.97	181	.260	.342	0	.000	-0	8	8	1	0.9
1965	*Min-A	9	3	.750	56	0	0	0	5	76¹	59	8	31	59	11.0	2.24	159	.217	.304	0	.000	-1	10	11	-1	1.7
1966	Min-A	1	1	.500	26	0	0	0	3	39²	35	2	20	26	12.9	3.40	106	.238	.337	0	.000	-0	1	1	-0	0.0
1967	Det-A	0	0	—	5	0	0	0	0	6²	6	1	1	1	9.5	5.40	60	.250	.280	0	—	0	-2	-2	-0	0.0
Total	18	101	118	.461	711	161	37	6	66	1967²	1915	203	978	1158	13.6	4.24	94	.258	.350	63	.125	-14	-80	-54	-0	-4.2

● FRED KLOBEDANZ   Klobedanz, Frederick Augustus "Duke"   b: 6/13/1871, Waterbury, Conn.   d: 4/12/40, Waterbury, Conn.   BL/TL, 5'11", 190 lbs.   Deb: 8/20/1896

YEAR	TM/L	W	L	PCT	G	GS	CG	SH	SV	IP	H	HR	BB	SO	RAT	ERA	ERA+	OAV	OOB	BH	AVG	PB	PR	/A	PD	TPI
1896	Bos-N	6	4	.600	10	9	9	0	0	80²	69	5	31	26	11.9	3.01	151	.230	.316	13	.317	2	12	14	-1	1.5
1897	*Bos-N	26	7	.788	38	37	30	2	0	309¹	344	13	125	92	14.3	4.60	97	.279	.357	48	.324	9	-10	-4	-4	0.1
1898	Bos-N	19	10	.655	35	33	25	0	0	270²	281	13	99	51	13.0	3.89	95	.266	.335	27	.213	0	-8	-6	-1	-0.6
1899	Bos-N	1	4	.200	5	5	4	0	0	33¹	39	2	9	8	13.5	4.86	86	.291	.345	2	.182	1	-4	-3	1	-0.2
1902	Bos-N	1	0	1.000	1	1	1	0	0	8	9	0	2	4	13.5	1.13	251	.284	.345	1	.500	1	1	2	-0	0.3
Total	5	53	25	.679	89	85	69	2	0	702	742	33	266	181	13.5	4.12	101	.269	.343	91	.277	13	-8	2	-6	1.1

● STAN KLOPP   Klopp, Stanley Harold "Betz"   b: 12/22/10, Womelsdorf, Pa.   d: 3/11/80, Robesonia, Pa.   BR/TR, 6'1.5", 180 lbs.   Deb: 4/30/44

YEAR	TM/L	W	L	PCT	G	GS	CG	SH	SV	IP	H	HR	BB	SO	RAT	ERA	ERA+	OAV	OOB	BH	AVG	PB	PR	/A	PD	TPI
1944	Bos-N	1	2	.333	24	0	0	0	0	46¹	47	1	33	17	15.5	4.27	89	.272	.388	2	.286	1	-3	-2	-1	-0.2

● BRENT KNACKERT   Knackert, Brent Bradley   b: 8/1/69, Los Angeles, Cal.   BR/TR, 6'3", 185 lbs.   Deb: 4/10/90

YEAR	TM/L	W	L	PCT	G	GS	CG	SH	SV	IP	H	HR	BB	SO	RAT	ERA	ERA+	OAV	OOB	BH	AVG	PB	PR	/A	PD	TPI
1990	Sea-A	1	1	.500	24	2	0	0	0	37¹	50	5	21	28	17.6	6.51	61	.313	.399	0	—	0	-11	-11	-0	-0.5

● CHRIS KNAPP   Knapp, Robert Christian   b: 9/16/53, Cherry Point, N.C.   BR/TR, 6'5", 195 lbs.   Deb: 9/4/75

YEAR	TM/L	W	L	PCT	G	GS	CG	SH	SV	IP	H	HR	BB	SO	RAT	ERA	ERA+	OAV	OOB	BH	AVG	PB	PR	/A	PD	TPI
1975	Chi-A	0	0	—	2	0	0	0	0	2	2	0	4	3	27.0	4.50	86	.250	.500	0	—	0	-0	-0	0	-0.1
1976	Chi-A	3	1	.750	11	6	1	0	0	52¹	54	5	32	41	15.0	4.82	74	.273	.377	0	—	0	-8	-7	-0	-0.6
1977	Chi-A	12	7	.632	27	26	4	0	0	146¹	166	16	61	103	14.4	4.80	85	.283	.357	0	—	0	-12	-12	-1	-1.4
1978	Cal-A	14	8	.636	30	29	6	0	0	188¹	178	25	67	126	11.8	4.21	86	.250	.317	0	—	0	-9	-13	-2	-1.5
1979	*Cal-A	5	5	.500	20	18	3	0	0	98	109	8	35	36	13.4	5.51	74	.275	.337	0	—	0	-14	-16	-0	-1.3
1980	Cal-A	2	11	.154	32	20	1	0	1	117¹	133	18	51	46	14.7	6.14	64	.289	.369	0	—	0	-27	-29	-1	-2.9
Total	6	36	32	.529	122	99	15	0	1	604¹	642	72	250	355	13.6	4.99	77	.272	.347	0	—	0	-70	-76	-5	-7.8

● FRANK KNAUSS   Knauss, Frank H.   b: 1868, Cleveland, Ohio   BL/TL, 170 lbs.   Deb: 6/25/1890

YEAR	TM/L	W	L	PCT	G	GS	CG	SH	SV	IP	H	HR	BB	SO	RAT	ERA	ERA+	OAV	OOB	BH	AVG	PB	PR	/A	PD	TPI
1890	Col-a	17	12	.586	37	34	28	3	2	275²	206	3	106	148	10.9	2.81	128	.201	.290	24	.226	5	33	24	-1	2.5
1891	Cle-N	3	3	.000	3	3	1	0	0	15	23	2	6	9	21.0	7.20	48	.339	.438	1	.167	-0	-6	-6	0	-0.9
1892	Cin-N	0	0	—	1	0	0	0	0	8	13	0	5	2	20.3	3.38	97	.351	.429	1	.333	0	-0	-0	-1	0.1
1894	Cle-N	0	1	.000	2	2	1	0	0	11	7	0	14	2	19.6	5.73	95	.181	.431	0	.000	-1	-0	-0	1	0.0
1895	NY-N	0	0	—	1	1	0	0	0	3²	9	0	2	1	27.0	17.18	27	.458	.509	0	.000	-0	-5	-5	-0	0.0
Total	5	17	16	.515	44	40	30	3	2	313¹	258	5	135	159	12.1	3.30	111	.218	.312	26	.217	4	20	12	-0	1.7

● RUDY KNEISCH   Kneisch, Rudolph Frank   b: 4/10/1899, Baltimore, Md.   d: 4/6/65, Baltimore, Md.   BR/TL, 5'10.5", 175 lbs.   Deb: 9/21/26

YEAR	TM/L	W	L	PCT	G	GS	CG	SH	SV	IP	H	HR	BB	SO	RAT	ERA	ERA+	OAV	OOB	BH	AVG	PB	PR	/A	PD	TPI
1926	Det-A	0	1	.000	2	2	1	0	0	17	18	2	6	4	13.8	2.65	153	.273	.351	0	.000	-1	3	3	0	0.1

● PHIL KNELL   Knell, Philip Louis   b: 3/12/1865, San Francisco, Cal   d: 6/5/44, Santa Monica, Cal.   BR/TL, 5'7.5", 154 lbs.   Deb: 7/6/1888

YEAR	TM/L	W	L	PCT	G	GS	CG	SH	SV	IP	H	HR	BB	SO	RAT	ERA	ERA+	OAV	OOB	BH	AVG	PB	PR	/A	PD	TPI
1888	Pit-N	1	2	.333	3	3	3	0	0	26¹	20	1	18	15	14.7	3.76	71	.217	.374	1	.091	-1	-3	-3	-0	-0.4
1890	Phi-P	22	11	.667	35	31	30	2	0	286²	287	10	166	99	15.1	3.83	112	.249	.358	29	.220	-1	13	14	0	1.1
1891	Col-a	28	27	.509	58	52	47	5	0	462	363	4	226	228	12.5	2.92	118	.209	.319	34	.158	-9	41	28	5	2.2
1892	Was-N	9	13	.409	22	21	17	1	0	170	156	4	76	74	12.9	3.65	89	.234	.323	8	.118	-5	-7	-8	-0	-1.2
	Phi-N	5	5	.500	11	9	7	0	0	80	87	0	35	43	15.0	4.05	80	.266	.357	3	.088	-3	-7	-7	-2	-1.1
	Yr	14	18	.438	33	30	24	1	0	250	243	4	111	117	13.1	3.78	86	.242	.324	11	.108	-7	-14	-15	-2	-2.3
1894	Pit-N	0	0	—	1	0	0	0	0	7	11	0	6	0	23.1	11.57	45	.353	.472	0	.000	-1	-5	-5	1	0.0
	Lou-N	7	21	.250	32	28	25	0	0	247	330	9	104	67	16.3	5.32	96	.317	.386	31	.274	0	0	-6	-2	-0.6
	Yr	7	21	.250	33	28	25	0	0	254	341	9	110	67	16.3	5.49	93	.318	.388	31	.267	-0	-5	-11	-2	-0.6
1895	Lou-N	0	6	.000	10	6	3	0	0	56²	75	3	21	19	16.2	6.51	71	.313	.383	6	.231	0	-11	-12	1	-0.8
	Cle-N	7	5	.583	20	13	9	0	0	116²	149	7	53	30	16.0	5.40	92	.306	.381	11	.200	-3	-8	-5	0	-0.6
	Yr	7	11	.389	30	19	12	0	0	173¹	224	10	74	49	15.8	5.76	85	.306	.374	17	.210	-3	-19	-17	1	-1.4
Total	6	79	90	.467	192	163	141	8	0	1452¹	1478	38	705	575	14.4	4.05	99	.256	.351	123	.187	-21	14	-5	2	-1.4

● CHARLIE KNEPPER   Knepper, Charles   b: 2/18/1871, Anderson, Ind.   d: 2/6/46, Muncie, Ind.   BR/TL, 6'4", 190 lbs.   Deb: 5/26/1899

YEAR	TM/L	W	L	PCT	G	GS	CG	SH	SV	IP	H	HR	BB	SO	RAT	ERA	ERA+	OAV	OOB	BH	AVG	PB	PR	/A	PD	TPI
1899	Cle-N	4	22	.154	27	26	26	0	0	219²	307	11	77	43	16.3	5.78	64	.329	.390	12	.135	-5	-47	-51	-1	-5.0

● BOB KNEPPER   Knepper, Robert Wesley   b: 5/25/54, Akron, Ohio   BL/TL, 6'2", 200 lbs.   Deb: 9/10/76

YEAR	TM/L	W	L	PCT	G	GS	CG	SH	SV	IP	H	HR	BB	SO	RAT	ERA	ERA+	OAV	OOB	BH	AVG	PB	PR	/A	PD	TPI
1976	SF-N	1	2	.333	4	4	0	0	0	25	26	0	11	11	11.9	3.24	112	.277	.327	1	.111	-0	1	1	0	0.1
1977	SF-N	11	9	.550	27	27	6	2	0	166	151	14	72	100	12.3	3.36	116	.242	.323	10	.182	1	10	10	-1	1.2
1978	SF-N	17	11	.607	36	35	16	6	0	260	218	10	85	147	10.6	2.63	131	.229	.295	5	.063	-3	27	24	-2	1.9
1979	SF-N	9	12	.429	34	34	6	2	0	207¹	241	30	77	123	13.9	4.64	75	.289	.352	12	.182	3	-21	-27	-1	-2.2
1980	SF-N	9	16	.360	35	33	8	1	0	215	242	15	61	103	13.0	4.10	86	.281	.335	10	.152	0	-12	-13	2	-1.3
1981	*Hou-N★	9	5	.643	22	22	6	5	0	156²	128	5	38	75	9.8	2.18	151	.226	.280	7	.149	1	23	19	-1	1.8
1982	Hou-N	5	15	.250	33	29	4	1	0	180	193	14	60	108	12.8	4.45	75	.278	.338	3	.058	-2	-17	-23	-2	-2.5
1983	Hou-N	6	13	.316	35	29	4	0	0	203	202	12	71	125	12.3	3.19	107	.261	.326	12	.182	-3	10	5	1	0.9
1984	Hou-N	15	10	.600	35	34	11	3	0	233²	223	26	55	140	10.7	3.20	104	.251	.296	13	.171	4	10	3	-4	0.6
1985	Hou-N	15	13	.536	37	37	4	0	0	241	253	16	54	131	11.6	3.55	98	.271	.313	11	.141	0	1	-2	-3	-0.5
1986	*Hou-N	17	12	.586	40	38	8	5	0	258	232	19	62	143	10.4	3.14	115	.242	.290	9	.099	-3	17	13	2	1.3
1987	Hou-N	8	17	.320	33	31	1	0	0	177²	226	26	54	76	14.4	5.27	74	.313	.364	5	.098	-1	-23	-27	-2	-3.2
1988	Hou-N★	14	5	.737	27	27	3	1	0	175	156	13	67	103	11.6	3.14	106	.243	.316	6	.125	-1	6	4	2	0.5
1989	Hou-N	4	10	.286	22	20	1	0	0	113	135	12	60	45	15.7	5.89	57	.303	.388	7	.226	5	-30	-31	1	-2.9
	SF-N	3	2	.600	13	6	1	1	0	52	55	4	15	19	12.3	3.46	97	.270	.323	1	.083	1	-0	-1	-0	-0.1
	Yr	7	12	.368	35	26	2	1	0	165	190	16	75	64	14.5	5.13	66	.290	.364	8	.186	6	-30	-32	1	-3.0
1990	SF-N	3	3	.500	12	7	0	0	0	44¹	56	7	19	24	15.4	5.68	64	.311	.380	3	.231	1	-9	-10	0	-1.1
Total	15	146	155	.485	445	413	78	30	0	2708	2737	228	857	1473	12.1	3.68	95	.264	.323	115	.137	7	-8	-55	1	-5.5

YEAR TM/L	W	L	PCT	G	GS	CG	SH	SV	IP	H	HR	BB	SO	RAT	ERA	ERA+	OAV	OOB	BH	AVG	PB	PR	/A	PD	TPI
● **LOU KNERR**			Knerr, Wallace Luther b: 8/21/21, Strasburg, Pa. d: 3/23/80, Denver, Pa. BR/TR, 6'1", 210 lbs. Deb: 4/17/45																					
1945 Phi-A	5	11	.313	27	17	5	0	0	130	142	6	74	41	15.0	4.22	81	.283	.376	9	.191	-1	-12	-11	0	-1.4
1946 Phi-A	3	16	.158	30	22	6	0	0	148¹	171	13	67	58	14.5	5.40	66	.288	.361	9	.180	0	-31	-31	-0	-3.5
1947 Was-A	0	0	—	6	0	0	0	0	9	17	1	8	5	25.0	11.00	34	.405	.500	1	1.000	0	-7	-7	0	0.1
Total 3	8	27	.229	63	39	11	0	0	287¹	330	20	149	104	15.1	5.04	69	.290	.373	19	.194	-1	-51	-49	0	-4.8
● **ELMER KNETZER**			Knetzer, Elmer Ellsworth "Baron" b: 7/22/1885, Carrick, Pa. d: 10/3/75, Pittsburgh, Pa. BR/TR, 5'10", 180 lbs. Deb: 9/11/09																					
1909 Bro-N	1	3	.250	5	4	3	0	0	35²	33	2	22	7	13.9	3.03	86	.252	.359	0	.000	-2	-2	-2	1	-0.3
1910 Bro-N	7	5	.583	20	15	10	3	0	132²	122	1	60	56	12.4	3.19	95	.255	.339	2	.053	-3	-2	-2	-2	-0.6
1911 Bro-N	11	12	.478	35	20	11	3	0	204	202	1	93	66	13.1	3.49	96	.277	.359	6	.097	-4	-2	-3	-1	-0.8
1912 Bro-N	7	9	.438	33	16	4	1	0	140¹	135	6	70	61	13.4	4.55	74	.254	.345	5	.135	-1	-18	-19	-0	-2.0
1914 Pit-F	20	12	.625	37	30	20	3	1	272	257	9	88	146	11.5	2.88	99	.254	.315	9	.099	-9	0	0	2	-0.8
1915 Pit-F	18	14	.563	41	33	22	3	3	279	256	5	89	120	11.2	2.58	105	.251	.311	12	.132	-7	5	4	-0	-0.3
1916 Bos-N	0	2	.000	2	0	0	0	0	5	11	0	2	2	23.4	7.20	35	.524	.565	0	—	-0	-3	-3	1	-0.8
Cin-N	5	12	.294	36	16	12	0	1	171¹	161	6	48	70	11.1	2.89	90	.252	.307	8	.154	-1	-5	-6	3	-0.4
Yr	5	14	.263	38	16	12	0	1	176¹	172	6	50	72	11.5	3.01	86	.261	.316	8	.154	-1	-8	-8	3	-1.2
1917 Cin-N	0	0	—	11	0	0	0	0	27¹	29	0	12	7	14.2	2.96	88	.282	.368	0	.000	-0	-1	-1	0	0.0
Total 8	69	69	.500	220	134	82	13	6	1267¹	1206	30	484	535	12.1	3.15	93	.258	.330	42	.109	-25	-27	-32	2	-6.0
● **LON KNIGHT**			Knight, Alonzo P. b: 6/16/1853, Philadelphia, Pa. d: 4/23/32, Philadelphia, Pa. BR/TR, 5'11.5", 165 lbs. Deb: 9/4/1875 MU♦																					
1875 Ath-n	6	5	.545	13	13	12	0	0	107	114	0	12		10.6	2.44	108	.259	.279	6	.128	-3	0	2		-0.1
1876 Phi-N	10	22	.313	34	32	27	0	0	282	383	0	34	12	13.3	2.62	93	.297	.315	60	.250	-1	-10	-6	-1	-0.6
1884 Phi-a	0	1	.000	2	1	1	0	0	14	24	1	4	0	18.6	9.00	38	.348	.392	131	.271	0	-9	-9	0	-0.4
1885 Phi-a	0	0	—	1	0	0	0	0	4	1	0	1	1	10.8	1.80	191	.103	.146	25	.210	-0	1	1	0	0.0
Pro-N	0	0	—	1	0	0	0	0	4	4	1	4	1	18.0	6.75	39	.235	.381	13	.160	-0	-2	-2	-0	0.0
Total 3	10	23	.303	38	33	28	0	0	305	415	1	44	16	13.6	2.95	84	.293	.315	549	.245	-1	-20	-16	-1	-1.0
● **JACK KNIGHT**			Knight, Elma Russell b: 1/12/1895, Pittsboro, Miss. d: 7/30/76, San Antonio, Tex. BL/TR, 6', 175 lbs. Deb: 9/20/22																					
1922 StL-N	0	0	—	1	1	0	0	0	4	9	0	3	1	27.0	9.00	43	.474	.545	1	.500	0	-2	-2	0	0.0
1925 Phi-N	7	6	.538	33	11	4	0	3	105¹	161	14	36	19	16.9	6.84	70	.354	.402	9	.205	-1	-30	-24	-1	-2.7
1926 Phi-N	3	12	.200	35	15	5	0	2	142²	206	14	48	29	16.0	6.62	63	.347	.396	12	.214	-0	-44	-39	5	-3.1
1927 Bos-N	0	0	—	3	0	0	0	0	3	6	0	2	0	24.0	15.00	25	.429	.500	0	—	0	-4	-4	1	0.1
Total 4	10	18	.357	72	27	9	0	5	255	382	28	89	49	16.7	6.85	64	.353	.403	22	.216	0	-80	-70	6	-5.7
● **GEORGE KNIGHT**			Knight, George Henry b: 11/24/1855, Lakeville, Conn. d: 10/4/12, Lakeville, Conn. Deb: 9/28/1875																					
1875 NH-n	1	0	1.000	1	1	1	0	0	9	12	0	0		12.0	2.00	115	.293	.293	0	.000	-1	0	0		0.0
● **JOE KNIGHT**			Knight, Joseph William "Quiet Joe" b: 9/28/1859, Port Stanley, Ont., Canada d: 10/16/38, Lynhurst, Ont., Canada BL/TL, 5'11", 185 lbs. Deb: 5/16/1884 ♦																					
1884 Phi-N	2	4	.333	6	6	6	0	0	51	66	2	21	8	15.4	5.47	55	.293	.364	6	.250	1	-14	-14	-0	-1.2
● **HUB KNOLLS**			Knolls, Oscar Edward b: 12/18/1883, Valparaiso, Ind. d: 7/1/46, Chicago, Ill. TR, 6'2", 190 lbs. Deb: 5/1/06																					
1906 Bro-N	0	0	—	2	0	0	0	0	6²	13	0	2	3	20.3	4.05	62	.382	.417	1	1.000	1	-1	-1	-1	0.0
● **JACK KNOTT**			Knott, John Henry b: 3/2/07, Dallas, Tex. d: 10/13/81, Brownwood, Tex. BR/TR, 6'2.5", 200 lbs. Deb: 4/13/33																					
1933 StL-A	1	8	.111	20	9	0	0	0	82²	88	11	33	19	13.4	5.01	93	.269	.340	7	.304	1	-7	-3	-1	-0.3
1934 StL-A	10	3	.769	45	10	2	0	4	138	149	17	67	56	14.2	4.96	101	.278	.359	4	.133	-1	-7	1	1	0.0
1935 StL-A	11	8	.579	48	19	7	2	7	187²	219	8	78	45	14.3	4.60	104	.287	.353	7	.115	-5	-3	4	1	0.0
1936 StL-A	9	17	.346	47	23	9	0	6	192²	272	15	93	60	17.2	7.29	74	.330	.401	4	.070	-5	-48	-41	-1	-4.9
1937 StL-A	8	18	.308	38	22	8	0	2	191¹	220	25	91	74	14.9	4.89	99	.291	.362	6	.140	-4	-6	-1	-2	-0.7
1938 StL-A	1	2	.333	7	4	0	0	0	30	35	3	15	8	15.0	4.80	104	.285	.362	1	.100	-1	-0	1	-0	-0.1
Chi-A	5	10	.333	20	18	9	0	0	131	135	8	54	35	13.0	4.05	121	.271	.342	5	.125	-2	11	12	1	1.0
Yr	6	12	.333	27	22	9	0	0	161	170	11	69	43	13.4	4.19	117	.273	.346	6	.120	-3	11	13	1	0.9
1939 Chi-A	11	6	.647	25	23	8	0	0	149²	157	13	41	56	12.0	4.15	114	.269	.318	8	.151	-3	8	10	-1	0.6
1940 Chi-A	11	9	.550	25	23	4	0	0	158	166	12	54	35	12.5	4.56	97	.265	.324	5	.088	-4	-3	-2	-1	-0.7
1941 Phi-A	13	11	.542	27	26	11	0	0	194¹	212	20	81	54	13.7	4.40	95	.279	.350	5	.077	-5	-5	-3	-1	-1.0
1942 Phi-A	2	10	.167	20	14	4	0	0	95¹	127	7	36	31	15.5	5.57	68	.310	.367	4	.138	-1	-20	-19	1	-2.0
1946 Phi-A	0	1	.000	3	1	0	0	0	6¹	7	1	1	2	12.8	5.68	68	.280	.333	0	—	-0	-2	-2	0	-0.2
Total 11	82	103	.443	325	192	62	4	19	1557	1787	140	642	484	14.2	4.97	95	.287	.355	58	.120	-29	-83	-46	-5	-8.3
● **ED KNOUFF**			Knouff, Edward "Fred" b: 6/1868, Philadelphia, Pa. d: 9/14/1900, Philadelphia, Pa. BR/TR, 210 lbs. Deb: 7/1/1885 ♦																					
1885 Phi-a	7	6	.538	14	13	12	0	0	106	103	0	44	43	13.2	3.65	94	.228	.309	9	.188	-1	-5	-4	1	-0.3
1886 Bal-a	0	1	.000	1	1	1	0	0	9	2	0	5	8	10.0	2.00	171	.067	.263	0	.000	-0	1	1	0	0.2
1887 Bal-a	2	6	.250	9	9	6	0	0	63	79	0	41	27	19.0	7.57	54	.295	.413	9	.290	0	-23	-24	0	-2.0
StL-a	4	2	.667	6	6	6	1	0	50	40	0	36	18	14.2	4.50	101	.225	.364	10	.179	-1	-1	-0	-0	-0.1
Yr	6	8	.429	15	15	12	1	0	113	119	0	77	45	15.8	6.21	69	.259	.369	19	.218	-1	-24	-24	0	-2.1
1888 StL-a	5	4	.556	9	9	9	0	0	81	66	0	37	25	12.3	2.67	122	.214	.315	3	.097	-2	4	5	-2	0.1
Cle-a	0	1	.000	2	2	1	0	0	9	8	0	2	2	12.0	1.00	309	.230	.309	1	.167	0	2	2	1	0.3
Yr	5	5	.500	11	11	10	0	0	90	74	0	39	27	11.5	2.50	130	.211	.294	4	.108	-2	6	7	-1	0.4
1889 Phi-a	2	0	1.000	3	3	2	0	0	25	37	2	9	5	16.9	3.96	96	.333	.388	3	.250	-0	-0	-0	-0	0.0
Total 5	20	20	.500	44	43	37	1	0	343	335	2	175	128	14.4	4.17	89	.242	.344	35	.187	-4	-22	-18	0	-1.8
● **DAROLD KNOWLES**			Knowles, Darold Duane b: 12/9/41, Brunswick, Mo. BL/TL, 6', 190 lbs. Deb: 4/18/65 C																					
1965 Bal-A	0	1	.000	5	1	0	0	0	14²	14	5	10	12	16.6	9.20	36	.250	.391	0	.000	-0	-9	-9	0	-0.6
1966 Phi-N	6	5	.545	69	0	0	0	13	100¹	98	4	46	88	13.5	3.05	118	.260	.351	4	.250	0	6	6	2	1.1
1967 Was-A	6	8	.429	61	1	0	0	14	113¹	91	5	52	85	11.7	2.70	117	.228	.322	1	.063	-1	7	6	2	1.0
1968 Was-A	1	1	.500	32	0	0	0	4	41¹	38	0	12	37	11.1	2.18	134	.241	.298	1	.250	0	4	3	0	0.4
1969 Was-A★	9	2	.818	53	0	0	0	13	84¹	73	8	31	59	11.5	2.24	155	.236	.314	1	.077	-0	13	11	0	1.9
1970 Was-A	2	14	.125	71	0	0	0	27	119¹	100	4	58	71	12.2	2.04	175	.231	.328	1	.050	-1	22	20	2	**3.7**
1971 Was-A	2	2	.500	12	0	0	0	2	15¹	17	2	6	16	13.5	3.52	94	.266	.329	0	—	-0	-0	-0	-0	-0.0
*Oak-A	5	2	.714	43	0	0	0	7	52²	40	3	16	40	10.1	3.59	93	.221	.295	1	.125	-0	-1	-1	-0	-0.2
Yr	7	4	.636	55	0	0	0	9	68	57	5	22	56	10.9	3.57	93	.233	.304	1	.100	-1	-1	-2	-1	-0.3
1972 Oak-A	5	1	.833	54	0	0	0	11	65²	49	1	37	36	11.8	1.37	207	.212	.321	3	.250	-0	12	11	3	1.9
1973 *Oak-A	6	8	.429	52	1	1	9	99	87	7	49	46	12.6	3.09	115	.246	.343	5	—	0	8	5	2	0.9
1974 Oak-A	3	3	.500	45	1	0	0	0	53¹	61	6	35	18	16.5	4.22	79	.296	.403	0	—	-0	-4	-5	1	-0.3
1975 Chi-N	6	9	.400	58	0	0	0	15	88¹	107	3	36	63	14.9	5.81	66	.298	.367	1	.067	-1	-21	-19	3	-3.5
1976 Chi-N	5	7	.417	58	0	0	0	0	71²	61	9	22	39	10.7	2.89	134	.242	.318	2	.143	-1	5	8	2	1.8
1977 Tex-A	5	2	.714	42	0	0	0	4	50¹	50	3	23	14	13.4	3.22	127	.272	.359	0	—	0	5	5	0	0.8
1978 Mon-N	3	3	.500	60	0	0	0	6	72	63	3	30	34	11.6	2.38	148	.250	.330	1	.167	-0	10	9	2	1.1
1979 StL-N	2	5	.286	48	0	0	0	6	48²	54	5	17	22	13.1	4.07	92	.277	.335	0	—	0	-1	-1	-0	-0.6
1980 StL-N	0	1	.000						1²	3	1	0	1	16.2	10.80	34	.375	.375	0	—	0	-1	-1	-0	-0.6
Total 16	66	74	.471	765	8	1	1	143	1092	1006	65	480	681	12.6	3.12	112	.250	.336	15	.120	-2	53	45	20	8.9
● **TOM KNOWLSON**			Knowlson, Thomas Herbert "Doc" b: 4/23/1895, Pittsburgh, Pa. d: 4/11/43, Miami Shores, Fla. BB/TR, 5'11", 178 lbs. Deb: 7/3/15																					
1915 Phi-A	4	6	.400	18	9	8	0	0	100²	99	1	60	24	14.8	3.49	84	.273	.386	3	.083	-3	-6	-6	-0	-0.9

YEAR	TM/L	W	L	PCT	G	GS	CG	SH	SV	IP	H	HR	BB	SO	RAT	ERA	ERA+	OAV	OOB	BH	AVG	PB	PR	/A	PD	TPI

● BILL KNOWLTON   Knowlton, William Young   b: 8/18/1892, Philadelphia, Pa.   d: 2/25/44, Philadelphia, Pa.   BR/TR,   Deb: 9/3/20

| 1920 | Phi-A | 0 | 1 | .000 | 1 | 1 | 0 | 0 | 0 | 5² | 9 | 0 | 3 | 5 | 23.8 | 4.76 | 84 | .346 | .469 | 0 | .000 | -0 | -1 | -0 | 0 | -0.1 |

● KURT KNUDSEN   Knudsen, Kurt David   b: 2/20/67, Arlington Heights, Ill.   BR/TR, 6'3", 200 lbs.   Deb: 5/16/92

1992	Det-A	2	3	.400	48	1	0	0	5	70²	70	9	41	51	14.3	4.58	86	.264	.365	0	—	0	-5	-5	0	-0.4
1993	Det-A	3	2	.600	30	0	0	0	2	37²	41	9	16	29	14.6	4.78	90	.281	.367	0	—	0	-2	-2	-0	-0.3
1994	Det-A	1	0	1.000	4	0	0	0	0	5¹	7	2	11	1	30.4	13.50	35	.304	.529	0	—	0	-5	-5	-0	-0.7
Total	3	6	5	.545	82	1	0	0	7	113²	118	20	68	81	15.1	5.07	81	.272	.377	0	—	0	-12	-12	-0	-1.4

● MARK KNUDSON   Knudson, Mark Richard   b: 10/28/60, Denver, Colo.   BR/TR, 6'5", 215 lbs.   Deb: 7/8/85

1985	Hou-N	0	2	.000	2	2	0	0	0	11	21	0	3	4	19.6	9.00	38	.429	.462	0	.000	0	-7	-7	-0	-0.9
1986	Hou-N	1	5	.167	9	7	0	0	0	42²	48	5	15	20	13.5	4.22	85	.279	.340	0	.000	-1	-2	-3	-1	-0.5
	Mil-A	0	1	.000	4	1	0	0	0	17²	22	7	5	9	13.8	7.64	57	.286	.329	0	—	0	-7	-7	-0	-0.4
1987	Mil-A	4	4	.500	15	8	1	0	0	62	88	7	14	26	14.8	5.37	85	.331	.364	0	—	0	-6	-6	-1	-0.9
1988	Mil-A	0	0	—	5	0	0	0	0	16	17	1	2	7	10.7	1.13	354	.279	.302	0	—	0	5	5	0	0.5
1989	Mil-A	8	5	.615	40	7	1	0	0	123²	110	15	29	47	10.3	3.35	115	.237	.286	0	—	0	7	7	-1	0.5
1990	Mil-A	10	9	.526	30	27	4	2	0	168¹	187	14	40	56	12.3	4.12	94	.282	.325	0	—	0	-4	-5	-2	-0.6
1991	Mil-A	1	3	.250	12	7	0	0	0	35	54	8	15	23	18.0	7.97	50	.355	.417	0	—	0	-15	-16	-1	-1.5
1993	Col-N	0	0	—	4	0	0	0	0	5²	16	4	5	3	33.4	22.24	21	.471	.538	0	.000	-0	-11	-11	-0	0.0
Total	8	24	29	.453	121	59	6	2	0	482	563	61	128	195	13.1	4.72	84	.290	.337	0	.000	-1	-40	-41	-5	-4.3

● KEVIN KOBEL   Kobel, Kevin Richard   b: 10/2/53, Buffalo, N.Y.   BR/TL, 6'1", 195 lbs.   Deb: 9/8/73

1973	Mil-A	0	1	.000	2	1	0	0	0	8¹	9	2	8	4	18.4	8.64	44	.273	.415	0	—	0	-4	-5	-0	-0.4
1974	Mil-A	6	14	.300	34	24	3	2	0	169¹	166	16	54	74	11.8	3.99	91	.258	.317	0	—	0	-7	-7	1	-0.7
1976	Mil-A	0	1	.000	3	0	0	0	0	4	6	3	3	1	22.5	11.25	31	.375	.500	0	—	0	-3	-3	0	-0.7
1978	NY-N	5	6	.455	32	11	1	0	0	108¹	95	9	30	51	10.6	2.91	120	.239	.295	4	.160	0	8	7	-1	0.6
1979	NY-N	6	8	.429	30	27	1	1	0	161²	169	14	46	67	12.1	3.51	104	.274	.328	9	.196	0	4	2	0	0.3
1980	NY-N	1	4	.200	14	1	0	0	0	24¹	36	5	11	8	17.4	7.03	51	.353	.416	0	.000	-0	-9	-9	-0	-1.7
Total	6	18	34	.346	115	64	5	3	0	476	481	49	152	205	12.1	3.88	93	.266	.326	13	.178	0	-12	-15	0	-2.6

● ALAN KOCH   Koch, Alan Goodman   b: 3/25/38, Decatur, Ala.   BR/TR, 6'4", 195 lbs.   Deb: 7/26/63

1963	Det-A	1	1	.500	7	1	0	0	0	10	21	3	9	5	27.9	10.80	35	.467	.564	2	.667	1	-8	-8	0	-1.2
1964	Det-A	0	0	—	3	0	0	0	0	4	6	1	3	1	20.3	6.75	54	.375	.474	0	—	0	-1	-1	-0	0.0
	Was-A	3	10	.231	32	14	1	0	0	114	110	18	43	67	12.3	4.89	76	.253	.325	8	.250	2	-16	-15	-2	-1.6
	Yr	3	10	.231	35	14	1	0	0	118	116	19	46	68	12.6	4.96	75	.258	.331	8	.250	2	-17	-17	-2	-1.6
Total	2	4	11	.267	42	15	1	0	0	128	137	22	55	73	13.8	5.41	68	.277	.354	10	.286	3	-25	-24	-2	-2.8

● DICK KOECHER   Koecher, Richard Finlay "Highpockets"   b: 3/30/26, Philadelphia, Pa.   BL/TL, 6'5", 196 lbs.   Deb: 9/29/46

1946	Phi-N	0	1	.000	1	1	0	0	0	2²	7	0	1	2	27.0	10.13	34	.467	.500	0	.000	-0	-2	-2	-0	-0.5
1947	Phi-N	0	2	.000	3	2	1	0	0	17	20	1	10	4	16.4	4.76	84	.299	.397	0	.000	-1	-1	-1	-0	-0.2
1948	Phi-N	0	1	.000	3	0	0	0	0	6	4	0	3	2	10.5	3.00	132	.235	.350	0	—	0	1	1	-0	0.1
Total	3	0	4	.000	7	3	1	0	0	25²	31	1	14	8	16.1	4.91	80	.313	.404	0	.000	-1	-3	-3	0	-0.6

● MARK KOENIG   Koenig, Mark Anthony   b: 7/19/04, San Francisco, Cal.   d: 4/22/93, Willows, Cal.   BB/TR, 6', 180 lbs.   Deb: 9/8/25   ♦

1930	Det-A	0	1	.000	2	1	0	0	0	9	11	0	8	6	20.0	10.00	48	.314	.455	64	.240	0	-5	-5	-0	-0.4
1931	Det-A	0	0	—	3	0	0	0	0	7	7	0	11	3	23.1	6.43	71	.280	.500	92	.253	0	-2	-1	0	0.0
Total	2	0	1	.000	5	1	0	0	0	16	18	0	19	9	21.4	8.44	56	.300	.475	1190	.279	0	-7	-7	-0	-0.4

● WILL KOENIGSMARK   Koenigsmark, William Thomas   b: 2/27/1896, Waterloo, Ill.   d: 7/1/72, Waterloo, Ill.   BR/TR, 6'4", 180 lbs.   Deb: 9/10/19

| 1919 | StL-N | 0 | 0 | — | 1 | 0 | 0 | 0 | 0 | 2 | 2 | 0 | 1 | 0 | — | ∞ | — | 1.000 | 1.000 | 0 | — | 0 | -2 | -2 | 0 | -0.2 |

● ELMER KOESTNER   Koestner, Elmer Joseph "Bob"   b: 11/30/1885, Piper City, Ill.   d: 10/27/59, Fairbury, Ill.   BR/TR, 6'1.5", 175 lbs.   Deb: 4/23/10

1910	Cle-A	5	10	.333	27	13	8	1	2	145	145	6	63	44	13.3	3.04	85	.282	.367	15	.313	2	-8	-7	-2	-0.7
1914	Chi-N	0	0	—	4	0	0	0	0	6¹	6	0	4	6	14.2	2.84	98	.261	.370	0	.000	-0	-0	-0	-0	0.0
	Cin-N	0	0	—	5	1	0	0	0	18¹	18	0	9	6	13.3	4.42	66	.265	.351	2	.400	1	-3	-3	0	0.1
	Yr	0	0	—	9	1	0	0	0	24²	24	0	13	12	13.5	4.01	72	.264	.356	2	.333	1	-3	-3	-0	0.1
Total	2	5	10	.333	36	14	8	1	2	169²	169	6	76	56	13.3	3.18	83	.279	.365	17	.315	3	-12	-10	-2	-0.6

● JOE KOHLMAN   Kohlman, Joseph James "Blackie"   b: 1/28/13, Philadelphia, Pa.   d: 3/16/74, Philadelphia, Pa.   BR/TR, 6', 160 lbs.   Deb: 9/26/37

1937	Was-A	1	0	1.000	2	2	1	0	0	13	15	0	3	3	12.5	4.15	107	.283	.321	1	.200	0	1	0	-0	0.0
1938	Was-A	0	0	—	7	0	0	0	0	14¹	12	1	11	5	14.4	6.28	72	.240	.377	0	.000	-0	-2	-3	0	0.0
Total	2	1	0	1.000	9	2	1	0	0	27¹	27	1	14	8	13.5	5.27	85	.262	.350	1	.125	-1	-2	-2	0	0.0

● EDDIE KOLB   Kolb, Edward William   b: 7/20/1880, Cincinnati, Ohio   BR/TR,   Deb: 10/15/1899

| 1899 | Cle-N | 0 | 1 | .000 | 1 | 1 | 1 | 0 | 0 | 8 | 18 | 0 | 5 | 1 | 27.0 | 10.13 | 36 | .442 | .513 | 1 | .250 | -0 | -6 | -6 | -1 | -0.5 |

● RAY KOLP   Kolp, Raymond Carl "Jockey"   b: 10/1/1894, New Berlin, Ohio   d: 7/29/67, New Orleans, La.   BR/TR, 5'10.5", 187 lbs.   Deb: 4/16/21

1921	StL-A	8	7	.533	37	18	5	1	0	166²	208	12	51	43	14.0	4.97	90	.314	.363	7	.127	-5	-13	-9	1	-1.1
1922	StL-A	14	4	.778	32	18	9	1	0	169²	199	10	36	54	12.7	3.93	106	.292	.332	17	.298	5	2	4	-4	0.4
1923	StL-A	5	12	.294	34	17	11	1	1	171¹	178	11	54	44	12.5	3.89	107	.273	.335	6	.111	-4	2	5	-2	-0.1
1924	StL-A	5	7	.417	25	12	5	1	0	96²	131	4	25	29	14.6	5.68	79	.329	.375	6	.200	-0	-16	-13	-1	-1.4
1927	Cin-N	3	3	.500	24	5	2	1	3	82¹	86	5	29	28	12.7	3.06	124	.278	.342	6	.200	-0	8	7	0	0.5
1928	Cin-N	13	10	.565	44	24	12	1	3	209	219	9	55	61	12.0	3.19	124	.280	.330	15	.214	3	19	18	1	2.2
1929	Cin-N	8	10	.444	30	16	1	0	0	145¹	173	8	39	27	11.8	4.03	113	.283	.328	8	.163	-2	11	9	1	0.8
1930	Cin-N	7	12	.368	37	19	5	2	3	168²	180	10	34	40	11.4	4.22	114	.278	.314	12	.245	1	14	11	-1	1.1
1931	Cin-N	4	9	.308	30	10	2	0	1	107	144	8	39	24	15.7	4.96	75	.332	.392	4	.125	-1	-13	-15	-1	-1.8
1932	Cin-N	6	10	.375	32	19	7	2	1	159²	176	13	27	42	11.6	3.89	99	.280	.313	9	.184	-1	-0	-1	-2	-0.4
1933	Cin-N	9	6	.400	30	14	4	0	3	150¹	168	7	23	28	11.5	3.53	96	.290	.318	7	.156	-1	-3	-2	1	-0.2
1934	Cin-N	0	2	.000	28	2	0	0	3	61²	78	1	12	19	13.4	4.52	90	.312	.348	1	.083	-1	-3	-3	2	-0.1
Total	12	79	95	.454	383	174	66	11	18	1688	1918	98	424	439	12.7	4.08	102	.292	.338	98	.184	-7	8	13	-6	-0.1

● HAL KOLSTAD   Kolstad, Harold Everette   b: 6/1/35, Rice Lake, Wis.   BR/TR, 5'9", 190 lbs.   Deb: 4/22/62

1962	Bos-A	0	2	.000	27	2	0	0	2	61¹	65	11	35	36	15.0	5.43	76	.269	.366	1	.056	-2	-10	-9	0	-0.5
1963	Bos-A	0	2	.000	7	0	0	0	0	11	16	4	6	6	18.0	13.09	39	.340	.436	0	.000	-0	-12	-11	-0	-1.7
Total	2	0	4	.000	34	2	0	0	2	72¹	81	15	41	42	15.7	6.59	62	.280	.377	1	.053	-2	-22	-20	0	-2.2

● ED KONETCHY   Konetchy, Edward Joseph "Big Ed"   b: 9/3/1885, LaCrosse, Wis.   d: 5/27/47, Ft. Worth, Tex.   BR/TR, 6'2.5", 195 lbs.   Deb: 6/29/07   ♦

1910	StL-N	0	0	—	1	0	0	0	0	4	4	0	1	0	11.3	4.50	66	.267	.313	157	.302	0	-1	-1	-0	0.0
1913	StL-N	1	0	1.000	1	0	0	0	0	4²	1	0	4	3	9.6	0.00	—	.071	.278	139	.276	0	2	2	-0	0.4
1918	Bos-N	0	1	.000	1	1	0	0	0	8	14	1	2	3	18.0	6.75	40	.378	.410	103	.236	0	-4	-4	-0	-0.4
Total	3	1	1	.500	3	1	0	0	0	16²	19	1	7	6	14.0	4.32	67	.288	.356	2150	.281	0	-3	-3	-1	0.0

● DOUG KONIECZNY   Konieczny, Douglas James   b: 9/27/51, Detroit, Mich.   BR/TR, 6'4", 220 lbs.   Deb: 9/11/73

1973	Hou-N	0	0	—	2	2	0	0	0	13	12	4	6	11	11.1	5.54	66	.279	.340	0	.000	-0	-3	-3	-0	-0.2
1974	Hou-N	0	3	.000	6	3	0	0	0	16	18	0	12	6	18.0	7.88	44	.290	.421	0	.000	-1	-8	-8	-0	-1.3
1975	Hou-N	6	13	.316	32	29	6	0	0	171	184	15	87	89	14.3	4.47	75	.280	.365	8	.160	1	-16	-21	-2	-2.2

YEAR	TM/L	W	L	PCT	G	GS	CG	SH	SV	IP	H	HR	BB	SO	RAT	ERA	ERA+	OAV	OOB	BH	AVG	PB	PR	/A	PD	TPI
1977	Hou-N	1	1	.500	4	4	0	0	0	21	26	1	8	7	15.0	6.00	59	.302	.368	1	.143	-0	-5	-6	0	-0.5
Total	4	7	18	.280	44	38	4	1	0	221	240	16	111	110	14.5	4.93	69	.283	.368	9	.138	-0	-31	-37	-2	-4.2

● **ALEX KONIKOWSKI** Konikowski, Alexander James "Whitey" b: 6/8/28, Throop, Pa. BR/TR, 6'1", 187 lbs. Deb: 6/16/48

YEAR	TM/L	W	L	PCT	G	GS	CG	SH	SV	IP	H	HR	BB	SO	RAT	ERA	ERA+	OAV	OOB	BH	AVG	PB	PR	/A	PD	TPI
1948	NY-N	2	3	.400	22	1	0	0	1	33¹	46	7	17	9	17.0	7.56	52	.346	.420	0	.000	0	-13	-13	1	-1.7
1951	*NY-N	0	0	—	3	0	0	0	0	4	2	0	0	5	4.5	0.00	—	.154	.154	0	—	0	2	2	0	0.0
1954	NY-N	0	0	—	10	0	0	0	0	12	10	1	12	6	16.5	7.50	54	.244	.415	0	—	-0	-5	-5	-0	0.0
Total	3	2	3	.400	35	1	0	0	1	49¹	58	8	29	20	15.9	6.93	57	.310	.403	0	.000	0	-16	-16	0	-1.7

● **JIM KONSTANTY** Konstanty, Casimir James b: 3/2/17, Strykersville, N.Y. d: 6/11/76, Oneonta, N.Y. BR/TR, 6'1.5", 202 lbs. Deb: 6/18/44

YEAR	TM/L	W	L	PCT	G	GS	CG	SH	SV	IP	H	HR	BB	SO	RAT	ERA	ERA+	OAV	OOB	BH	AVG	PB	PR	/A	PD	TPI
1944	Cin-N	6	4	.600	20	12	5	1	0	112²	113	11	33	19	11.7	2.80	125	.266	.320	10	.294	2	10	9	1	1.0
1946	Bos-N	0	1	.000	10	1	0	0	0	15¹	17	2	7	9	14.1	5.28	65	.283	.358	0	.000	-0	-3	-3	1	-0.1
1948	Phi-N	1	0	1.000	6	0	0	0	2	9²	7	0	2	7	8.4	0.93	424	.233	.281	0	.000	-0	3	3	-0	0.4
1949	Phi-N	9	5	.643	53	0	0	0	7	97	98	9	29	43	11.9	3.25	121	.280	.337	3	.176	-0	9	8	1	1.2
1950	*Phi-N★	16	7	.696	74	0	0	0	22	152	108	11	50	56	9.4	2.66	152	.205	.274	4	.108	-2	25	23	-1	3.6
1951	Phi-N	4	11	.267	58	1	0	0	9	115²	127	9	31	27	12.3	4.05	95	.282	.328	3	.158	-0	-1	-3	1	-0.2
1952	Phi-N	5	3	.625	42	2	2	1	6	80	87	9	21	16	12.1	3.94	93	.274	.319	1	.071	-0	-2	-3	-0	-0.3
1953	Phi-N	14	10	.583	48	19	7	0	5	170²	198	18	42	45	12.8	4.43	95	.290	.334	11	.220	-0	-3	-4	0	-0.5
1954	Phi-N	2	3	.400	33	1	0	0	3	50¹	62	7	12	11	13.2	3.75	108	.316	.356	0	.000	-2	2	2	0	0.0
	NY-A	1	1	.500	9	0	0	0	2	18¹	11	0	6	3	8.3	0.98	350	.183	.258	0	.000	-0	6	5	0	0.6
1955	NY-A	7	2	.778	45	0	0	0	11	73²	68	5	24	19	11.2	2.32	161	.247	.308	1	.125	-0	13	12	-0	1.7
1956	NY-A	0	0	—	8	0	0	0	2	11	15	3	6	6	17.2	4.91	79	.319	.396	0	.000	-0	-1	-1	0	-0.1
	StL-N	1	1	.500	27	0	0	0	5	39¹	46	4	7	11	13.0	4.58	83	.301	.327	0	—	-0	-4	-3	-1	-0.3
Total	11	66	48	.579	433	36	14	2	74	945²	957	88	269	268	11.7	3.46	112	.268	.320	33	.163	-5	54	44	2	7.0

● **ERNIE KOOB** Koob, Ernest Gerald b: 9/11/1893, Keeler, Mich. d: 11/12/41, Lemay, Mo. BL/TL, 5'10", 160 lbs. Deb: 6/23/15

YEAR	TM/L	W	L	PCT	G	GS	CG	SH	SV	IP	H	HR	BB	SO	RAT	ERA	ERA+	OAV	OOB	BH	AVG	PB	PR	/A	PD	TPI
1915	StL-A	4	5	.444	28	13	6	0	1	133²	119	2	50	37	12.1	2.36	122	.254	.339	5	.135	-1	9	8	-2	0.2
1916	StL-A	11	8	.579	33	20	10	2	2	166²	153	1	56	26	11.6	2.54	108	.252	.321	0	.000	-1	5	4	-4	0.0
1917	StL-A	6	14	.300	39	18	3	1	1	133²	139	1	57	47	13.6	3.91	67	.280	.361	4	.114	-1	-18	-19	1	-2.9
1919	StL-A	2	3	.400	25	4	0	0	0	66	77	3	23	11	13.9	4.64	72	.296	.358	0	.000	-2	-10	-10	0	-0.9
Total	4	23	30	.434	125	55	19	3	4	500	488	7	186	121	12.6	3.13	90	.266	.342	9	.070	-5	-15	-18	-4	-3.6

● **CAL KOONCE** Koonce, Calvin Lee b: 11/18/40, Fayetteville, N.C. d: 10/28/93, Winston-Salem, N.C. BR/TR, 6'1", 185 lbs. Deb: 4/14/62

YEAR	TM/L	W	L	PCT	G	GS	CG	SH	SV	IP	H	HR	BB	SO	RAT	ERA	ERA+	OAV	OOB	BH	AVG	PB	PR	/A	PD	TPI
1962	Chi-N	10	10	.500	35	30	3	1	0	190²	200	17	86	84	13.8	3.97	105	.271	.353	6	.094	-4	0	4	-1	-0.1
1963	Chi-N	2	6	.250	21	13	0	0	0	72²	75	9	32	44	13.5	4.58	77	.273	.353	2	.105	-0	-10	-9	1	-0.8
1964	Chi-N	3	0	1.000	6	2	0	0	0	31	30	1	7	17	10.7	2.03	183	.254	.296	0	.000	-1	5	6	2	0.6
1965	Chi-N	7	9	.438	38	23	3	1	0	173	181	17	52	88	12.4	3.69	100	.271	.329	5	.102	-0	-3	-0	-0	0.0
1966	Chi-N	5	5	.500	45	5	0	0	2	108²	113	13	35	65	12.3	3.81	97	.268	.325	3	.130	0	-2	-2	1	0.0
1967	Chi-N	2	2	.500	34	0	0	0	2	51	52	2	21	24	13.1	4.59	77	.268	.343	0	.000	-1	-7	-6	1	-0.5
	NY-N	3	3	.500	11	6	2	1	0	45	45	2	7	24	10.4	2.80	121	.259	.287	2	.154	-1	3	3	1	0.5
	Yr	5	5	.500	45	6	2	1	2	96	97	4	28	52	11.7	3.75	93	.262	.314	2	.100	-1	-4	-3	2	0.0
1968	NY-N	6	4	.600	55	2	0	0	11	97	80	4	32	50	10.5	2.41	125	.235	.303	0	.000	-1	6	7	-1	0.8
1969	NY-N	6	3	.667	40	0	0	0	7	83	85	8	42	48	14.1	4.99	73	.269	.360	4	.235	-0	-13	-12	1	-1.3
1970	NY-N	0	2	.000	13	0	0	0	0	22	25	2	14	10	16.4	3.27	123	.301	.408	0	—	-2	2	2	0	0.2
	Bos-A	3	4	.429	23	8	1	0	0	76¹	64	9	29	37	11.3	3.54	112	.231	.311	2	.095	-0	2	4	2	0.5
1971	Bos-A	1	0	1.000	13	1	0	0	0	21	22	3	9	4	14.1	5.57	66	.278	.367	0	.000	-0	-5	-4	1	-0.1
Total	10	47	49	.490	334	90	9	3	24	971¹	972	85	368	504	12.6	3.78	98	.264	.335	24	.100	-6	-22	-9	9	-0.2

● **JERRY KOOSMAN** Koosman, Jerome Martin b: 12/23/42, Appleton, Minn. BR/TL, 6'2", 208 lbs. Deb: 4/14/67

YEAR	TM/L	W	L	PCT	G	GS	CG	SH	SV	IP	H	HR	BB	SO	RAT	ERA	ERA+	OAV	OOB	BH	AVG	PB	PR	/A	PD	TPI
1967	NY-N	0	2	.000	9	3	0	0	0	22¹	22	3	19	11	16.5	6.04	56	.259	.394	0	.000	0	-7	-7	0	-0.5
1968	NY-N★	19	12	.613	35	34	17	7	0	263²	221	16	69	178	10.2	2.08	145	.228	.285	7	.077	-3	26	27	-1	3.0
1969	*NY-N★	17	9	.654	32	32	16	6	0	241	187	14	68	180	9.7	2.28	160	.216	.277	4	.048	-7	35	37	-1	3.1
1970	NY-N	12	7	.632	30	29	5	1	0	212	189	22	71	118	11.1	3.14	128	.237	.300	6	.086	-2	21	21	-3	1.2
1971	NY-N	6	11	.353	26	24	4	0	0	165²	160	12	51	96	11.5	3.04	112	.256	.313	6	.160	-0	8	7	1	0.6
1972	NY-N	11	12	.478	34	24	4	1	1	163	155	14	52	147	11.8	4.14	81	.250	.314	4	.085	-0	-12	-14	2	-2.2
1973	*NY-N	14	15	.483	35	35	12	3	0	263	234	18	76	156	10.7	2.84	127	.242	.300	4	.103	-3	24	23	-1	2.0
1974	NY-N	15	11	.577	35	35	13	0	0	265	258	16	85	188	11.9	3.36	106	.257	.320	16	.186	2	8	6	-0	0.8
1975	NY-N	14	13	.519	36	34	11	4	2	239²	234	19	98	173	12.6	3.42	101	.261	.337	14	.179	1	5	1	-1	0.3
1976	NY-N	21	10	.677	34	32	17	3	0	247¹	205	19	66	200	9.9	2.69	122	.226	.279	17	.215	3	22	17	0	2.4
1977	NY-N	8	20	.286	32	32	6	1	0	226²	195	17	81	192	11.1	3.49	107	.232	.302	8	.111	-3	10	6	2	0.2
1978	NY-N	3	15	.167	38	32	3	0	2	235¹	221	17	84	160	12.0	3.75	93	.255	.327	6	.086	-3	-4	-7	2	-0.7
1979	Min-A	20	13	.606	37	36	10	2	0	263²	268	19	83	157	12.1	3.38	130	.268	.326	0	—	0	24	29	2	3.6
1980	Min-A	16	13	.552	38	34	8	0	0	243¹	252	24	69	149	12.1	4.03	108	.272	.326	0	—	0	0	9	1	0.8
1981	Min-A	3	9	.250	19	13	2	1	5	94¹	98	8	34	55	12.6	4.20	94	.272	.335	0	—	0	-6	-3	0	-0.4
	Chi-A	1	4	.200	8	3	1	0	0	27	27	2	7	21	11.3	3.33	107	.260	.306	0	—	0	1	1	-0	0.1
	Yr	4	13	.235	27	16	3	1	5	121¹	125	10	41	76	12.3	4.01	96	.267	.325	0	—	0	-5	-2	-0	-0.3
1982	Chi-A	11	7	.611	42	19	3	1	2	173¹	194	9	38	88	12.1	3.84	105	.287	.327	0	—	0	4	4	0	0.4
1983	*Chi-A	11	7	.611	37	24	2	1	2	169²	176	19	53	90	12.5	4.77	88	.266	.326	0	—	0	-13	-11	0	-1.1
1984	Phi-N	14	15	.483	36	34	3	1	0	224	232	16	67	137	11.9	3.25	112	.267	.317	8	.108	-3	8	9	-1	0.8
1985	Phi-N	6	4	.600	19	18	3	1	0	99¹	107	14	34	60	13.0	4.62	80	.276	.340	3	.088	-2	-11	-10	-0	-1.2
Total	19	222	209	.515	612	527	140	33	17	3839¹	3635	290	1198	2556	11.5	3.36	110	.252	.313	109	.119	-22	145	143	-6	13.1

● **HOWIE KOPLITZ** Koplitz, Howard Dean b: 5/4/38, Oshkosh, Wis. BR/TR, 5'11", 195 lbs. Deb: 9/8/61

YEAR	TM/L	W	L	PCT	G	GS	CG	SH	SV	IP	H	HR	BB	SO	RAT	ERA	ERA+	OAV	OOB	BH	AVG	PB	PR	/A	PD	TPI
1961	Det-A	2	0	1.000	4	1	1	0	0	12	16	0	4	9	18.0	2.25	182	.327	.421	0	.000	-1	2	2	-0	0.3
1962	Det-A	3	0	1.000	10	6	1	0	0	37²	54	5	10	10	15.3	5.26	77	.342	.381	3	.231	1	-5	-5	0	-0.3
1964	Was-A	0	0	—	6	1	0	0	0	17	20	3	13	9	17.5	4.76	78	.290	.402	0	.000	-2	-2	-2	0	0.0
1965	Was-A	4	7	.364	33	11	0	0	1	106²	97	11	48	59	12.5	4.05	86	.249	.336	3	.100	-1	-7	-7	1	-0.7
1966	Was-A	0	0	—	1	0	0	0	0	2	0	0	1	0	4.5	0.00	—	.000	.200	0	—	0	1	1	0	0.0
Total	5	9	7	.563	54	19	2	0	1	175¹	187	19	80	87	13.9	4.21	87	.280	.359	6	.118	-1	-11	-11	1	-0.7

● **GEORGE KORINCE** Korince, George Eugene "Moose" b: 1/10/46, Ottawa, Ont., Canada BR/TR, 6'3", 210 lbs. Deb: 9/10/66

YEAR	TM/L	W	L	PCT	G	GS	CG	SH	SV	IP	H	HR	BB	SO	RAT	ERA	ERA+	OAV	OOB	BH	AVG	PB	PR	/A	PD	TPI
1966	Det-A	0	0	—	2	0	0	0	0	3	1	0	3	2	15.0	0.00	—	.091	.333	0	—	0	1	1	-0	0.0
1967	Det-A	1	0	1.000	9	0	0	0	0	14	10	1	11	11	13.5	5.14	63	.204	.350	0	.000	-0	-3	-3	-0	-0.2
Total	2	1	0	1.000	11	0	0	0	0	17	11	1	14	13	13.8	4.24	78	.183	.347	0	.000	-0	-2	-2	-0	-0.2

● **JIM KORWAN** Korwan, James "Long Jim" b: 3/4/1874, Brooklyn, N.Y. d: 7/24/1899, Brooklyn, N.Y. BR/TR, 6'1", 181 lbs. Deb: 4/24/1894

YEAR	TM/L	W	L	PCT	G	GS	CG	SH	SV	IP	H	HR	BB	SO	RAT	ERA	ERA+	OAV	OOB	BH	AVG	PB	PR	/A	PD	TPI
1894	Bro-N	0	0	—	1	0	0	0	0	5	9	1	5	2	25.2	14.40	34	.385	.493	0	—	0	-5	-5	-0	0.0
1897	Chi-N	1	2	.333	5	4	3	0	0	34	47	1	28	12	20.1	5.82	77	.325	.438	0	.000	-2	-6	-5	2	-0.4
Total	2	1	2	.333	6	4	3	0	0	39	56	2	33	14	20.8	6.92	66	.333	.446	0	.000	-2	-11	-10	2	-0.4

● **BILL KOSKI** Koski, William John "T-Bone" b: 2/6/32, Madera, Cal. BR/TR, 6'4", 185 lbs. Deb: 4/28/51

YEAR	TM/L	W	L	PCT	G	GS	CG	SH	SV	IP	H	HR	BB	SO	RAT	ERA	ERA+	OAV	OOB	BH	AVG	PB	PR	/A	PD	TPI
1951	Pit-N	0	1	.000	13	1	0	0	0	27	26	2	28	6	18.0	6.67	63	.257	.419	0	—	-1	-8	-7	-1	-0.4

● **DAVE KOSLO** Koslo, George Bernard (b: George Bernard Koslowski) b: 3/31/20, Menasha, Wis. d: 12/1/75, Menasha, Wis. BL/TL, 5'11", 180 lbs. Deb: 9/12/41

YEAR	TM/L	W	L	PCT	G	GS	CG	SH	SV	IP	H	HR	BB	SO	RAT	ERA	ERA+	OAV	OOB	BH	AVG	PB	PR	/A	PD	TPI
1941	NY-N	1	2	.333	4	3	2	0	0	23²	17	0	10	12	10.3	1.90	194	.202	.287	1	.111	-1	5	5	-1	0.5

YEAR	TM/L	W	L	PCT	G	GS	CG	SH	SV	IP	H	HR	BB	SO	RAT	ERA	ERA+	OAV	OOB	BH	AVG	PB	PR	/A	PD	TPI
1942	NY-N	3	6	.333	19	11	3	1	0	78	79	7	32	42	12.9	5.08	66	.261	.333	3	.120	-0	-15	-15	-1	-1.7
1946	NY-N	14	19	.424	40	35	17	3	1	265¹	251	15	101	121	12.1	3.63	95	.249	.320	11	.125	-3	-6	-6	2	-0.8
1947	NY-N	15	10	.600	39	31	10	3	0	217¹	223	23	82	86	12.8	4.39	93	.259	.326	10	.128	-1	-8	-8	-1	-1.0
1948	NY-N	8	10	.444	35	18	5	3	3	149	168	7	62	58	14.0	3.87	102	.290	.359	5	.114	-1	2	1	-1	-0.1
1949	NY-N	11	14	.440	38	23	15	0	4	212	193	13	43	64	10.0	2.50	159	.239	.278	10	.145	1	36	35	0	4.2
1950	NY-N	13	15	.464	40	22	7	1	3	186²	190	18	68	68	12.7	3.91	105	.268	.337	8	.123	-1	5	4	-0	0.4
1951	*NY-N	10	9	.526	39	16	5	2	3	149²	153	18	45	54	12.0	3.31	118	.258	.313	5	.100	-1	11	10	2	1.3
1952	NY-N	10	7	.588	41	17	8	2	5	166¹	154	10	47	67	11.0	3.19	116	.242	.296	2	.037	-4	10	9	1	0.7
1953	NY-N	6	12	.333	37	12	2	0	2	111²	135	8	36	36	13.9	4.76	90	.296	.349	1	.033	-3	-6	-6	-1	-1.1
1954	Bal-A	0	1	.000	3	1	0	0	0	14¹	20	1	3	3	14.4	3.14	133	.333	.365	0	.000	-0	1	1	-0	0.0
	Mil-N	1	1	.500	12	0	0	0	1	17¹	13	0	9	7	11.4	3.12	120	.228	.333	0	.000	-0	2	1	-1	0.1
1955	Mil-N	0	1	.000	1	0	0	0	0	0	1	1	0	0	—	∞	—	1.000	1.000	-	—	0	1	-1	-1	-0.1
Total	12	92	107	.462	348	189	74	15	22	1591¹	1597	121	538	606	12.2	3.68	105	.260	.321	56	.109	-15	34	32	2	2.4

● **JOE KOSTAL**   Kostal, Joseph William "Cudgey" b: 3/17/1876, Chicago, Ill. d: 10/17/33, Guelph, Ont., Can. BR/TR, 5'6", 130 lbs. Deb: 7/14/1896

YEAR	TM/L	W	L	PCT	G	GS	CG	SH	SV	IP	H	HR	BB	SO	RAT	ERA	ERA+	OAV	OOB	BH	AVG	PB	PR	/A	PD	TPI
1896	Lou-N	0	0	—	2	0	0	0	0	2	4	0	0	0	18.0	0.00	—	.411	.411	0	—	0	1	1	-0	0.1

● **SANDY KOUFAX**   Koufax, Sanford (b: Sanford Braun) b: 12/30/35, Brooklyn, N.Y. BR/TL, 6'2", 210 lbs. Deb: 6/24/55 H

YEAR	TM/L	W	L	PCT	G	GS	CG	SH	SV	IP	H	HR	BB	SO	RAT	ERA	ERA+	OAV	OOB	BH	AVG	PB	PR	/A	PD	TPI
1955	Bro-N	2	2	.500	12	5	2	2	0	41²	33	2	28	30	13.4	3.02	134	.216	.341	0	.000	-2	5	5	-0	0.2
1956	Bro-N	2	4	.333	16	10	0	0	0	58²	66	10	29	30	14.6	4.91	81	.286	.365	2	.118	-0	-7	-6	-1	-0.7
1957	Bro-N	5	4	.556	34	13	2	0	0	104¹	83	14	51	122	11.7	3.88	107	.216	.311	0	.000	-3	-0	3	-2	-0.3
1958	LA-N	11	11	.500	40	26	5	0	1	158²	132	19	105	131	13.5	4.48	91	.220	.337	6	.122	-2	-9	-7	-0	-1.1
1959	*LA-N	8	6	.571	35	23	6	1	2	153¹	136	23	92	173	13.4	4.05	104	.235	.340	6	.111	-1	-2	-3	-1	-0.2
1960	LA-N	8	13	.381	37	26	7	2	1	175	133	20	100	197	12.0	3.91	102	.207	.315	7	.123	-2	-3	1	-1	-0.2
1961	LA-N★	18	13	.581	42	35	15	2	1	255²	212	27	96	269	10.9	3.52	123	.222	.295	5	.065	-5	15	23	-3	1.8
1962	LA-N☆	14	7	.667	28	26	11	2	1	184¹	134	13	57	216	9.4	2.54	143	.197	.261	6	.087	-3	29	22	-2	1.9
1963	*LA-N☆	25	5	.833	40	40	20	11	0	311	214	18	58	306	8.0	1.88	161	.189	.230	7	.064	-4	49	39	-4	3.0
1964	LA-N☆	19	5	.792	29	28	15	7	1	223	154	13	53	223	8.4	1.74	187	.191	.241	7	.095	-2	45	37	-4	3.5
1965	*LA-N★	26	8	.765	43	41	27	8	2	335²	216	26	71	382	7.8	2.04	160	.179	.228	20	.177	5	56	46	-2	5.0
1966	*LA-N★	27	9	.750	41	41	27	5	0	323	241	19	77	317	8.9	1.73	191	.205	.253	9	.076	-5	67	56	-4	5.4
Total	12	165	87	.655	397	314	137	40	9	2324¹	1754	204	817	2396	10.0	2.76	131	.205	.276	75	.097	-25	243	221	-25	18.5

● **JOE KOUKALIK**   Koukalik, Joseph b: 3/3/1880, Chicago, Ill. d: 12/27/45, Chicago, Ill. 5'8", 160 lbs. Deb: 9/1/04

YEAR	TM/L	W	L	PCT	G	GS	CG	SH	SV	IP	H	HR	BB	SO	RAT	ERA	ERA+	OAV	OOB	BH	AVG	PB	PR	/A	PD	TPI
1904	Bro-N	0	1	.000	1	1	1	0	0	8	10	0	4	1	15.8	1.13	244	.333	.412	0	.000	-0	1	1	-0	0.1

● **LOU KOUPAL**   Koupal, Louis Laddie b: 12/19/1898, Tabor, S.D. d: 12/8/61, San Gabriel, Cal. BR/TR, 5'11", 175 lbs. Deb: 4/17/25

YEAR	TM/L	W	L	PCT	G	GS	CG	SH	SV	IP	H	HR	BB	SO	RAT	ERA	ERA+	OAV	OOB	BH	AVG	PB	PR	/A	PD	TPI
1925	Pit-N	0	0	—	6	0	0	0	0	9	14	1	7	0	21.0	9.00	50	.378	.477	0	.000	-0	-5	-5	0	0.0
1926	Pit-N	0	2	.000	6	2	1	0	0	19²	22	0	8	7	14.2	3.20	123	.289	.365	1	.250	0	1	2	-0	0.2
1928	Bro-N	1	0	1.000	17	1	1	0	1	37¹	43	0	15	10	14.2	2.41	165	.303	.373	1	.111	-1	7	6	1	0.2
1929	Bro-N	0	1	.000	18	3	0	0	4	40¹	49	3	25	17	16.5	5.36	86	.308	.402	1	.071	-2	-3	-3	-1	-0.3
	Phi-N	5	5	.500	15	12	3	0	2	86²	106	5	29	18	14.2	4.78	109	.305	.362	4	.125	-2	-1	4	-1	0.1
	Yr	5	6	.455	33	15	3	0	6	127	155	8	54	35	15.0	4.96	101	.306	.375	5	.109	-4	-3	1	-1	-0.2
1930	Phi-N	0	4	.000	13	4	1	0	0	36²	54	2	17	11	17.2	8.59	64	.344	.414	1	.083	-1	-15	-13	-1	-1.3
1937	StL-A	4	9	.308	26	13	6	0	0	105²	150	10	55	24	17.5	6.56	74	.339	.412	3	.094	-3	-23	-20	-0	-2.3
Total	6	10	21	.323	101	35	12	0	7	335¹	436	23	156	87	16.0	5.58	86	.322	.394	11	.106	-9	-38	-29	-2	-3.4

● **FABIAN KOWALIK**   Kowalik, Fabian Lorenz b: 4/22/08, Falls City, Tex. d: 8/14/54, Karnes City, Tex. BR/TR, 5'11", 185 lbs. Deb: 9/4/32

YEAR	TM/L	W	L	PCT	G	GS	CG	SH	SV	IP	H	HR	BB	SO	RAT	ERA	ERA+	OAV	OOB	BH	AVG	PB	PR	/A	PD	TPI
1932	Chi-A	0	1	.000	2	1	0	0	0	10¹	16	2	4	2	18.3	6.97	62	.340	.404	5	.385	1	-3	-3	-0	-0.1
1935	*Chi-N	2	2	.500	20	2	1	0	1	55	60	2	19	20	12.9	4.42	89	.280	.339	3	.200	-0	-2	-3	1	-0.2
1936	Chi-N	0	2	.000	6	0	0	0	0	16	24	1	7	1	17.4	6.75	59	.358	.419	0	.000	-1	-5	-5	-0	-0.6
	Phi-N	1	5	.167	22	8	2	0	0	77	100	5	31	19	15.5	5.38	84	.308	.372	13	.228	-0	-12	-7	-2	-0.7
	Bos-N	0	1	.000	1	1	1	0	0	9	18	0	2	0	20.0	8.00	48	.419	.444	2	.400	1	-4	-4	-0	-0.3
	Yr	1	8	.111	29	9	3	0	0	102	142	6	40	20	16.1	5.82	75	.325	.382	15	.224	-0	-20	-16	-1	-1.6
Total	3	3	11	.214	51	12	4	0	2	167¹	218	10	63	42	15.3	5.43	78	.313	.373	23	.242	-0	-26	-22	-1	-1.9

● **JOE KRAEMER**   Kraemer, Joseph Wayne b: 9/10/64, Olympia, Wash. BL/TL, 6'2", 185 lbs. Deb: 8/22/89

YEAR	TM/L	W	L	PCT	G	GS	CG	SH	SV	IP	H	HR	BB	SO	RAT	ERA	ERA+	OAV	OOB	BH	AVG	PB	PR	/A	PD	TPI
1989	Chi-N	0	1	.000	1	1	0	0	0	3²	7	0	2	5	22.1	4.91	77	.368	.429	0	.000	-0	-1	-0	-0	-0.1
1990	Chi-N	0	0	—	18	0	0	0	0	25	31	2	14	16	16.9	7.20	57	.310	.405	0	—	0	-9	-9	0	0.0
Total	2	0	1	.000	19	1	0	0	0	28²	38	2	16	21	17.6	6.91	58	.319	.409	0	.000	-0	-10	-9	0	-0.1

● **JOE KRAKAUSKAS**   Krakauskas, Joseph Victor Lawrence b: 3/28/15, Montreal, Que., Can d: 7/8/60, Hamilton, Ont., Can. BL/TL, 6'1", 203 lbs. Deb: 9/9/37

YEAR	TM/L	W	L	PCT	G	GS	CG	SH	SV	IP	H	HR	BB	SO	RAT	ERA	ERA+	OAV	OOB	BH	AVG	PB	PR	/A	PD	TPI
1937	Was-A	4	1	.800	5	4	3	0	0	40	33	0	22	18	12.4	2.70	164	.226	.327	2	.125	-0	9	8	-1	0.7
1938	Was-A	7	5	.583	29	10	5	1	0	121¹	99	4	88	104	14.1	3.12	145	.220	.352	6	.182	-1	23	19	-1	1.6
1939	Was-A	11	17	.393	39	29	12	0	1	217¹	230	13	114	110	14.3	4.60	95	.276	.364	16	.208	3	1	-6	-2	-0.6
1940	Was-A	1	6	.143	32	10	2	0	2	109	137	7	73	68	17.3	6.44	65	.309	.406	8	.250	-1	-25	-28	1	-1.4
1941	Cle-A	1	2	.333	12	5	0	0	0	41²	39	3	29	25	14.7	4.10	96	.245	.362	1	.077	-1	-0	-1	-1	-0.1
1942	Cle-A	0	0	—	3	0	0	0	0	7	7	1	4	2	14.1	3.86	89	.259	.355	0	.000	-0	-0	-0	-1	0.0
1946	Cle-A	2	5	.286	29	5	0	0	1	47¹	60	5	25	20	16.2	5.51	60	.314	.394	0	.000	-1	-11	-12	1	-1.7
Total	7	26	36	.419	149	63	22	1	4	583²	605	30	355	347	14.9	4.53	93	.269	.369	33	.180	-0	-4	-20	-1	-1.5

● **JACK KRALICK**   Kralick, John Francis b: 6/1/35, Youngstown, Ohio BL/TL, 6'2", 180 lbs. Deb: 4/15/59

YEAR	TM/L	W	L	PCT	G	GS	CG	SH	SV	IP	H	HR	BB	SO	RAT	ERA	ERA+	OAV	OOB	BH	AVG	PB	PR	/A	PD	TPI
1959	Was-A	0	0	—	6	0	0	0	0	12¹	13	5	6	7	13.9	6.57	60	.289	.373	0	.000	-0	-4	-4	1	0.1
1960	Was-A	8	6	.571	35	18	7	2	0	151	139	12	45	71	11.2	3.04	128	.245	.305	5	.122	-1	14	14	-1	1.1
1961	Min-A	13	11	.542	33	33	11	2	0	242	257	21	64	137	12.0	3.61	118	.274	.323	13	.151	-2	11	17	2	1.5
1962	Min-A	12	11	.522	39	37	7	1	0	242²	239	30	61	139	11.2	3.86	106	.258	.305	18	.202	1	3	6	1	0.9
1963	Min-A	1	4	.200	5	5	1	1	0	25²	28	2	8	13	13.0	3.86	94	.280	.339	1	.167	1	-1	-1	0	0.0
	Cle-A	13	9	.591	28	27	10	3	0	197¹	187	19	41	116	10.4	2.92	124	.249	.288	11	.183	1	16	15	-1	1.7
	Yr	14	13	.519	33	32	11	4	0	223	215	21	49	129	10.7	3.03	120	.252	.293	12	.182	1	15	15	-1	1.7
1964	Cle-A☆	12	7	.632	30	29	8	3	0	190²	196	17	51	119	12.1	3.21	112	.267	.322	10	.156	-1	9	8	0	0.7
1965	Cle-A	5	11	.313	30	16	1	0	0	86	106	9	21	34	13.5	4.92	71	.298	.340	3	.143	-1	-14	-14	-1	-2.5
1966	Cle-A	3	4	.429	27	4	0	0	0	68¹	69	9	20	31	11.9	3.82	90	.268	.324	1	.077	-1	-3	-3	1	-0.3
1967	Cle-A	0	2	.000	2	0	0	0	0	2	4	0	1	1	22.5	9.00	36	.444	.500	-	—	0	-1	-1	1	-0.9
Total	9	67	65	.508	235	169	45	12	1	1218	1238	124	318	668	11.7	3.56	108	.264	.314	62	.162	-0	30	38	1	2.3

● **STEVE KRALY**   Kraly, Steve Charles "Lefty" b: 4/18/29, Whiting, Ind. BL/TL, 5'10", 152 lbs. Deb: 8/9/53

YEAR	TM/L	W	L	PCT	G	GS	CG	SH	SV	IP	H	HR	BB	SO	RAT	ERA	ERA+	OAV	OOB	BH	AVG	PB	PR	/A	PD	TPI
1953	NY-A	0	2	.000	5	3	0	0	0	25	19	2	16	8	13.3	3.24	114	.209	.339	0	.000	-1	2	1	0	0.0

● **JACK KRAMER**   Kramer, John Henry b: 1/5/18, New Orleans, La. BR/TR, 6'2", 190 lbs. Deb: 4/25/39

YEAR	TM/L	W	L	PCT	G	GS	CG	SH	SV	IP	H	HR	BB	SO	RAT	ERA	ERA+	OAV	OOB	BH	AVG	PB	PR	/A	PD	TPI
1939	StL-A	9	16	.360	40	31	10	2	0	211²	269	18	127	68	17.0	5.83	84	.318	.409	9	.136	-1	-28	-23	-1	-2.3
1940	StL-A	3	7	.300	16	9	1	0	0	64²	86	4	26	12	15.6	6.26	73	.327	.388	1	.050	-1	-14	-12	0	-1.6
1941	StL-A	4	3	.571	29	3	0	0	0	59¹	69	5	40	20	16.5	5.16	83	.289	.391	0	.000	-1	-7	-6	-0	-0.5
1943	StL-A	0	0	—	3	0	0	0	0	3	7	0	2	1	21.0	8.00	42	.297	.435	1	.500	1	-5	-5	-0	0.1
1944	*StL-A	17	13	.567	33	31	18	1	0	257	233	9	75	124	10.8	2.49	145	.241	.297	14	.165	1	27	32	3	4.3
1945	StL-A†	10	15	.400	29	25	15	3	2	193	190	13	73	99	12.3	3.36	105	.254	.320	9	.148	-0	0	4	1	0.5
1946	StL-A★	13	11	.542	31	28	13	3	0	194²	190	6	68	69	11.9	3.19	117	.257	.319	8	.136	-1	7	12	-0	1.2

YEAR	TM/L	W	L	PCT	G	GS	CG	SH	SV	IP	H	HR	BB	SO	RAT	ERA	ERA+	OAV	OOB	BH	AVG	PB	PR	/A	PD	TPI
1947	StL-A☆	11	16	.407	33	28	9	1	1	199¹	206	16	89	77	13.4	4.97	78	.270	.348	7	.113	-2	-28	-24	1	-3.0
1948	Bos-A	18	5	**.783**	29	29	14	2	0	205	233	12	64	72	13.0	4.35	101	.284	.336	11	.151	-1	-1	1	-3	-0.2
1949	Bos-A	6	8	.429	21	18	7	2	1	111²	126	8	49	24	14.2	5.16	85	.286	.358	9	.257	3	-12	-10	-1	-0.9
1950	NY-N	3	6	.333	35	9	1	0	1	86²	91	6	39	27	13.7	3.53	116	.268	.346	2	.100	1	6	5	0	0.6
1951	NY-N	0	0	—	4	1	0	0	0	4²	11	0	3	2	27.0	15.43	25	.524	.583	0	—	0	-6	-6	0	0.0
	NY-A	1	3	.250	19	3	0	0	0	40²	46	1	21	15	14.8	4.65	82	.280	.362	1	.100	-0	-2	-4	-1	-0.5
Total	12	95	103	.480	322	215	88	14	7	1637¹	1761	92	682	613	13.5	4.24	96	.276	.347	72	.144	0	-63	-35	0	-2.3

● RANDY KRAMER

Kramer, Randall John b: 9/20/60, Palo Alto, Cal. BR/TR, 6'2", 170 lbs. Deb: 9/11/88

YEAR	TM/L	W	L	PCT	G	GS	CG	SH	SV	IP	H	HR	BB	SO	RAT	ERA	ERA+	OAV	OOB	BH	AVG	PB	PR	/A	PD	TPI
1988	Pit-N	1	2	.333	5	1	0	0	0	10	12	1	1	7	12.6	5.40	63	.316	.350	0	.000	-0	-2	-2	-0	-0.6
1989	Pit-N	5	9	.357	35	15	1	1	2	111¹	90	10	61	52	12.8	3.96	85	.224	.337	5	.152	-0	-6	-7	-1	-1.0
1990	Pit-N	0	1	.000	12	2	0	0	0	25²	27	3	9	15	13.3	4.91	74	.273	.345	0	.000	-1	-3	-4	1	-0.1
	Chi-N	0	2	.000	10	2	0	0	0	20¹	20	3	12	12	14.6	3.98	102	.253	.359	0	.000	-0	-0	-0	-0	0.0
	Yr	0	3	.000	22	4	0	0	0	46	47	6	21	27	13.5	4.50	85	.261	.342	0	.000	-1	-4	-3	0	-0.1
1992	Sea-A	0	1	.000	4	4	0	0	0	16¹	30	2	6	6	20.9	7.71	51	.400	.458	0	—	0	-7	-7	-0	-0.4
Total	4	6	15	.286	66	24	1	1	2	183²	179	19	90	92	13.8	4.51	78	.259	.354	5	.122	-1	-18	-20	-2	-2.1

● TOM KRAMER

Kramer, Thomas Joseph b: 1/9/68, Cincinnati, Ohio BB/TR, 6', 185 lbs. Deb: 9/12/91

YEAR	TM/L	W	L	PCT	G	GS	CG	SH	SV	IP	H	HR	BB	SO	RAT	ERA	ERA+	OAV	OOB	BH	AVG	PB	PR	/A	PD	TPI
1991	Cle-A	0	0	—	4	0	0	0	0	4²	10	1	6	4	30.9	17.36	24	.476	.593	0		0	-7	-7	-0	0.0
1993	Cle-A	7	3	.700	39	16	1	0	0	121	126	19	59	71	13.9	4.02	108	.269	.353	0		0	4	4	-1	0.2
Total	2	7	3	.700	43	16	1	0	0	125²	136	20	65	75	14.5	4.51	96	.278	.364	0		0	-3	-3	-1	0.2

● GENE KRAPP

Krapp, Eugene Hamlet "Rubber Arm" b: 5/12/1887, Rochester, N.Y. d: 4/13/23, Detroit, Mich. BR/TR, 5'5", 165 lbs. Deb: 4/14/11

YEAR	TM/L	W	L	PCT	G	GS	CG	SH	SV	IP	H	HR	BB	SO	RAT	ERA	ERA+	OAV	OOB	BH	AVG	PB	PR	/A	PD	TPI
1911	Cle-A	13	9	.591	35	26	14	1	1	222	188	1	138	132	13.7	3.41	100	.232	.353	17	.230	4	-1	0	4	0.8
1912	Cle-A	2	5	.286	9	7	4	0	0	58²	57	0	42	22	15.8	4.60	74	.273	.404	7	.318	1	-8	-8	2	-0.5
1914	Buf-F	16	14	.533	36	29	18	1	0	252²	198	4	115	106	11.6	2.49	119	.210	.304	11	.143	-2	11	13	5	1.8
1915	Buf-F	9	19	.321	38	30	14	1	0	231	188	6	123	93	12.3	3.51	80	.230	.333	9	.129	-3	-20	-18	7	-1.7
Total	4	40	47	.460	118	92	50	3	1	764¹	631	11	418	353	12.7	3.23	95	.227	.335	44	.181	-1	-19	-13	19	0.4

● JACK KRAUS

Kraus, John William "Tex" or "Texas Jack" b: 4/26/18, San Antonio, Tex. d: 1/2/76, San Antonio, Tex. BR/TL, 6'4", 190 lbs. Deb: 4/25/43

YEAR	TM/L	W	L	PCT	G	GS	CG	SH	SV	IP	H	HR	BB	SO	RAT	ERA	ERA+	OAV	OOB	BH	AVG	PB	PR	/A	PD	TPI
1943	Phi-N	9	15	.375	34	25	10	1	2	199²	197	7	78	48	12.4	3.16	107	.259	.328	4	.067	-5	5	5	1	0.2
1945	Phi-N	4	9	.308	19	13	0	0	0	81²	96	3	40	28	15.4	5.40	71	.293	.376	3	.120	-1	-15	-14	0	-2.0
1946	NY-N	2	1	.667	17	1	0	0	0	25	25	4	15	7	14.8	6.12	56	.260	.366	0	.000	-0	-8	-7	1	-0.8
Total	3	15	25	.375	70	39	10	1	2	306¹	318	14	133	83	13.4	4.00	88	.268	.345	7	.080	-6	-17	-17	2	-2.6

● HARRY KRAUSE

Krause, Harry William "Hal" b: 7/12/1887, San Francisco, Cal. d: 10/23/40, San Francisco, Cal BB/TL, 5'10", 165 lbs. Deb: 4/20/08

YEAR	TM/L	W	L	PCT	G	GS	CG	SH	SV	IP	H	HR	BB	SO	RAT	ERA	ERA+	OAV	OOB	BH	AVG	PB	PR	/A	PD	TPI
1908	Phi-A	1	1	.500	4	2	2	0	0	21	20	0	4	10	11.6	2.57	100	.247	.307	0	.000	-1	-0	-0	-1	-0.2
1909	Phi-A	18	8	.692	32	21	16	7	0	213	151	2	49	139	9.0	**1.39**	**173**	.204	.266	12	.156	-1	26	24	-3	2.6
1910	Phi-A	6	6	.500	16	11	9	2	0	112¹	99	4	42	60	11.9	2.88	82	.254	.339	8	.211	-1	-5	-6	-2	-0.8
1911	Phi-A	11	8	.579	27	19	12	1	2	169	155	2	47	85	11.2	3.04	104	.251	.313	15	.254	2	-6	-3	-2	0.1
1912	Phi-A	0	2	.000	4	2	0	0	0	5¹	10	1	2	1	21.9	13.50	23	.435	.500	1	.250	0	-6	-6	0	-1.6
	Cle-A	0	1	.000	2	2	0	0	0	4²	11	0	2	1	25.1	11.57	29	.500	.542	0		0	-4	-4	-0	-0.7
	Yr	0	3	.000	6	4	0	0	0	10	21	1	4	2	22.5	12.60	26	.457	.500	1	.250	0	-10	-10	-0	-2.3
Total	5	36	26	.581	85	57	39	10	2	525¹	446	8	146	298	10.7	2.50	107	.238	.305	36	.195	1	16	10	-6	-0.6

● LEW KRAUSSE

Krausse, Lewis Bernard Jr. b: 4/25/43, Media, Pa. BR/TR, 5'11", 186 lbs. Deb: 6/16/61 F

YEAR	TM/L	W	L	PCT	G	GS	CG	SH	SV	IP	H	HR	BB	SO	RAT	ERA	ERA+	OAV	OOB	BH	AVG	PB	PR	/A	PD	TPI
1961	KC-A	2	5	.286	12	8	2	1	0	55²	49	3	46	32	15.5	4.85	86	.243	.386	2	.118	-1	-5	-4	-1	-0.6
1964	KC-A	0	2	.000	5	4	0	0	0	14²	21	1	9	9	20.3	7.36	52	.349	.446	0	.000	-0	-6	-6	-0	-0.7
1965	KC-A	2	4	.333	7	5	0	0	0	25	29	1	8	22	13.3	5.04	69	.284	.336	0	.000	-1	-4	-4	-1	-1.0
1966	KC-A	14	9	.609	36	22	4	1	3	177²	144	8	63	87	10.8	2.99	114	.222	.297	8	.154	0	9	8	-3	0.8
1967	KC-A	7	17	.292	48	19	0	0	6	160	140	17	67	96	11.9	4.27	75	.236	.317	6	.146	1	-19	-19	-0	-2.9
1968	Oak-A	10	11	.476	36	25	2	0	4	185	147	16	62	105	10.3	3.11	91	.217	.286	9	.161	3	-3	-6	-2	-0.6
1969	Oak-A	7	7	.500	43	16	4	2	7	140	134	23	48	85	12.0	4.44	77	.256	.325	8	.167	4	-13	-16	-1	-1.3
1970	Mil-A	13	18	.419	37	35	8	1	0	216	235	33	67	130	12.8	4.75	80	.275	.330	9	.138	1	-25	-23	-0	-3.0
1971	Mil-A	8	12	.400	43	22	1	0	0	180¹	164	23	62	92	11.5	2.94	118	.239	.307	1	.023	-3	10	11	-0	0.7
1972	Bos-A	1	3	.250	24	7	0	0	0	60²	74	9	28	54	15.6	6.38	50	.308	.387	2	.125	-0	-22	-21	1	-1.5
1973	StL-N	0	0	—	1	0	0	0	0	2	2	0	1	1	13.5	0.00	—	.250	.333	0		0	1	1	0	0.0
1974	Atl-N	4	3	.571	29	4	0	0	0	66²	95	5	32	27	13.4	4.18	90	.258	.346	2	.333	2	-4	-3	-1	-0.2
Total	12	68	91	.428	321	167	21	5	21	1283²	1205	137	493	721	12.2	4.00	85	.248	.322	47	.133	6	-81	-84	-9	-10.3

● LEW KRAUSSE

Krausse, Lewis Bernard Sr. b: 6/8/12, Media, Pa. d: 9/6/88, Sarasota, Fla. BR/TR, 6'0.5", 167 lbs. Deb: 6/11/31 F

YEAR	TM/L	W	L	PCT	G	GS	CG	SH	SV	IP	H	HR	BB	SO	RAT	ERA	ERA+	OAV	OOB	BH	AVG	PB	PR	/A	PD	TPI
1931	Phi-A	1	0	1.000	3	1	1	0	0	11	6	2	9	6	9.8	4.09	110	.150	.261	0	.000	0	0	0	0	0.1
1932	Phi-A	4	1	.800	20	3	2	1	0	57	64	3	24	16	13.9	4.58	99	.281	.349	2	.133	-0	-1	-0	1	0.1
Total	2	5	1	.833	23	4	3	1	0	68	70	5	30	17	13.2	4.50	100	.261	.336	2	.118	0	-0	-0	1	0.1

● KEN KRAVEC

Kravec, Kenneth Peter b: 7/29/51, Cleveland, Ohio BL/TL, 6'2", 185 lbs. Deb: 9/4/75

YEAR	TM/L	W	L	PCT	G	GS	CG	SH	SV	IP	H	HR	BB	SO	RAT	ERA	ERA+	OAV	OOB	BH	AVG	PB	PR	/A	PD	TPI
1975	Chi-A	0	1	.000	2	1	0	0	0	4¹	1	0	8	1	18.7	6.23	60	.071	.409	0	—	0	-1	-1	1	-0.2
1976	Chi-A	1	5	.167	9	8	1	0	0	49²	49	3	32	38	14.9	4.89	72	.257	.366	0	—	0	-8	-7	-0	-0.8
1977	Chi-A	11	8	.579	26	25	6	1	0	166²	161	12	57	125	12.1	4.10	99	.250	.317	0	—	0	-1	-0	0	-0.8
1978	Chi-A	11	16	.407	30	30	7	2	0	203	188	22	95	154	13.0	4.08	93	.245	.336	0	—	0	-7	-6	-0	-0.8
1979	Chi-A	15	13	.536	36	35	10	3	1	250	208	20	111	132	12.0	3.74	113	.233	.327	0	—	0	13	14	-1	1.3
1980	Chi-A	3	6	.333	20	15	0	0	0	81²	100	13	44	37	16.4	6.94	58	.298	.387	0	—	0	-26	-26	0	-2.4
1981	Chi-N	1	6	.143	24	12	0	0	0	78¹	80	5	39	50	14.1	5.06	73	.268	.361	0	.000	-1	-14	-12	1	-1.1
1982	Chi-N	1	1	.500	13	2	0	0	0	25	27	3	18	20	16.2	6.12	61	.267	.378	0	.000	-0	-7	-7	-0	-0.5
Total	8	43	56	.434	160	128	24	6	1	858²	814	78	404	557	13.2	4.47	89	.251	.341	0	.000	-1	-51	-46	-0	-4.5

● RAY KRAWCZYK

Krawczyk, Raymond Allen b: 10/9/59, Pittsburgh, Pa. BR/TR, 6'1", 186 lbs. Deb: 6/29/84

YEAR	TM/L	W	L	PCT	G	GS	CG	SH	SV	IP	H	HR	BB	SO	RAT	ERA	ERA+	OAV	OOB	BH	AVG	PB	PR	/A	PD	TPI
1984	Pit-N	0	0	—	5	0	0	0	0	5¹	7	0	4	3	18.6	3.38	107	.350	.458	0		0	0	0	-0	0.0
1985	Pit-N	0	2	.000	8	0	0	0	0	8¹	20	1	6	9	29.2	14.04	25	.455	.529	0		0	-10	-10	0	-1.9
1986	Pit-N	0	1	.000	12	0	0	0	0	12¹	17	3	10	7	19.7	7.30	53	.321	.429	0		0	-5	-5	-0	-0.4
1988	Cal-A	0	1	.000	14	1	0	0	0	24¹	29	2	8	17	14.4	4.81	80	.299	.364	0		0	-2	-2	-0	0.0
1989	Mil-A	0	0	—	1	0	0	0	0	2	4	0	1	6	22.5	13.50	28	.400	.455	0		0	-2	-2	0	0.0
Total	5	0	4	.000	39	1	0	0	1	52¹	77	6	29	42	18.7	7.05	54	.344	.426	0		0	-19	-19	-0	-2.3

● RAY KREMER

Kremer, Remy Peter "Wiz" b: 3/23/1893, Oakland, Cal. d: 2/8/65, Pinole, Cal. BR/TR, 6'1", 190 lbs. Deb: 4/18/24

YEAR	TM/L	W	L	PCT	G	GS	CG	SH	SV	IP	H	HR	BB	SO	RAT	ERA	ERA+	OAV	OOB	BH	AVG	PB	PR	/A	PD	TPI
1924	Pit-N	18	10	.643	41	30	17	**4**	1	259¹	262	7	51	64	11.0	3.19	120	.265	.304	13	.151	-4	19	19	-2	1.3
1925	*Pit-N	17	8	.680	40	27	14	0	2	214²	232	19	47	62	12.1	3.69	121	.281	.323	14	.197	1	14	15	-0	1.2
1926	Pit-N	20	6	**.769**	37	26	18	3	5	231¹	221	9	51	74	10.7	**2.61**	**151**	.252	.296	21	.253	2	**31**	**34**	-3	**3.7**
1927	*Pit-N	19	8	.704	35	28	18	3	2	226	205	9	53	63	10.3	**2.47**	**166**	.244	.289	14	.169	-1	36	41	3	4.3
1928	Pit-N	15	13	.536	34	31	16	1	0	219	245	15	68	61	13.4	4.64	87	.297	.352	14	.179	0	-16	-14	-4	-1.9
1929	Pit-N	18	10	.643	34	27	14	0	0	221²	226	21	60	66	11.7	4.26	112	.271	.323	14	.198	1	11	13	-3	0.8
1930	Pit-N	**20**	12	.625	39	38	18	1	0	**276**	366	29	63	58	14.0	5.02	99	.322	.359	16	.157	-0	-2	-1	-0	-0.9
1931	Pit-N	11	15	.423	30	30	15	1	0	230	246	6	58	58	12.4	3.33	116	.271	.323	17	.227	4	14	13	-6	1.2
1932	Pit-N	4	3	.571	11	10	3	1	0	56²	61	5	20	12	14.4	4.29	89	.270	.321	2	.105	-1	-3	-3	-2	-0.6

YEAR	TM/L	W	L	PCT	G	GS	CG	SH	SV	IP	H	HR	BB	SO	RAT	ERA	ERA+	OAV	OOB	BH	AVG	PB	PR	/A	PD	TPI
1933	Pit-N	1	0	1.000	7	0	0	0	0	20	36	2	9	4	20.2	10.35	32	.387	.441	0	.000	-1	-16	-16	1	-0.7
Total	10	143	85	.627	308	247	134	14	10	1954²	2108	122	483	516	12.1	3.76	113	.278	.323	122	.178	-7	90	104	-27	8.8

● **JIM KREMMEL**   Kremmel, James Louis b: 2/28/48, Belleville, Ill.   BL/TL, 6', 175 lbs.   Deb: 7/4/73

YEAR	TM/L	W	L	PCT	G	GS	CG	SH	SV	IP	H	HR	BB	SO	RAT	ERA	ERA+	OAV	OOB	BH	AVG	PB	PR	/A	PD	TPI
1973	Tex-A	0	2	.000	4	2	0	0	0	9	15	1	6	6	23.0	9.00	41	.366	.469	0	—	0	-5	-5	-0	-0.9
1974	Chi-N	0	2	.000	23	2	0	0	0	31	37	3	18	22	16.3	5.23	73	.303	.397	0	.000	-0	-6	-5	-0	-0.3
Total	2	0	4	.000	27	4	0	0	0	40	52	4	24	28	17.8	6.07	62	.319	.416	0	.000	-0	-11	-10	-0	-1.2

● **RED KRESS**   Kress, Ralph b: 1/2/07, Columbia, Cal.   d: 11/29/62, Los Angeles, Cal.   BR/TR, 5'11.5", 165 lbs.   Deb: 9/24/27 C ◆

YEAR	TM/L	W	L	PCT	G	GS	CG	SH	SV	IP	H	HR	BB	SO	RAT	ERA	ERA+	OAV	OOB	BH	AVG	PB	PR	/A	PD	TPI
1935	Was-A	0	0	—	3	0	0	0	0	5²	8	0	5	5	20.6	12.71	34	.333	.448	75	.298	1	-5	-5	0	0.1
1946	NY-N	0	0	—	1	0	0	0	0	3²	5	1	1	1	17.2	12.27	28	.333	.412	0	.000	0	-4	-4	1	0.1
Total	2	0	0	—	4	0	0	0	0	9¹	13	1	6	6	19.3	12.54	32	.333	.435	1454	.286	1	-9	-9	1	0.2

● **LOU KRETLOW**   Kretlow, Louis Henry "Lena" b: 6/27/21, Apache, Okla.   BR/TR, 6'2", 185 lbs.   Deb: 9/26/46

YEAR	TM/L	W	L	PCT	G	GS	CG	SH	SV	IP	H	HR	BB	SO	RAT	ERA	ERA+	OAV	OOB	BH	AVG	PB	PR	/A	PD	TPI
1946	Det-A	1	0	1.000	1	1	1	0	0	9	7	2	4	9	9.0	3.00	122	.206	.250	2	.500	1	1	1	-0	0.2
1948	Det-A	2	1	.667	5	2	1	0	0	23¹	21	1	11	9	12.3	4.63	94	.233	.317	4	.500	1	-1	-1	0	0.0
1949	Det-A	3	2	.600	25	10	1	0	0	76	85	5	69	40	18.4	6.16	68	.290	.427	0	.000	-4	-17	-17	2	-1.1
1950	StL-A	0	2	.000	9	2	0	0	0	14¹	25	2	18	10	28.3	11.93	41	.403	.549	0	.000	-0	-12	-11	-0	-1.3
	Chi-A	0	0	—	11	1	0	0	0	21¹	17	1	27	14	18.6	3.80	118	.221	.423	0	.000	-1	2	2	-1	-0.1
	Yr	0	2	.000	20	3	0	0	0	35²	42	3	45	24	22.0	7.07	66	.298	.468	0	.000	-1	-10	-9	-1	-1.4
1951	Chi-A	6	9	.400	26	18	7	1	0	137	129	6	74	89	13.5	4.20	96	.250	.347	4	.083	-5	-1	-3	-0	-0.8
1952	Chi-A	4	4	.500	19	11	4	2	1	79	52	5	56	63	12.4	2.96	123	.186	.323	1	.050	-0	6	6	-1	0.4
1953	Chi-A	0	0	—	9	3	0	0	0	20²	12	2	30	15	18.7	3.48	116	.171	.426	0	.000	-0	1	1	1	0.1
	StL-A	1	5	.167	22	11	0	0	0	81	93	5	52	37	16.1	5.11	82	.286	.385	5	.200	-1	-10	-8	-2	-0.8
	Yr	1	5	.167	31	14	0	0	0	101²	105	7	82	52	16.6	4.78	87	.265	.391	5	.172	-1	-9	-7	-1	-0.7
1954	Bal-A	6	11	.353	32	20	5	0	0	166²	169	12	82	82	13.6	4.37	82	.269	.354	8	.157	-0	-12	-15	-0	-1.3
1955	Bal-A	0	4	.000	15	5	0	0	0	38¹	50	3	27	26	18.3	8.22	46	.316	.419	1	.091	-1	-18	-19	1	-1.6
1956	KC-A	4	9	.308	25	20	3	0	0	118²	121	17	74	61	14.8	5.31	82	.262	.364	2	.061	-3	-15	-13	-1	-1.5
Total	10	27	47	.365	199	104	22	3	1	785¹	781	62	522	450	15.0	4.87	82	.261	.372	27	.114	-13	-76	-77	-1	-7.8

● **RICK KREUGER**   Kreuger, Richard Allen b: 11/3/48, Grand Rapids, Mich.   BR/TL, 6'2", 185 lbs.   Deb: 9/6/75

YEAR	TM/L	W	L	PCT	G	GS	CG	SH	SV	IP	H	HR	BB	SO	RAT	ERA	ERA+	OAV	OOB	BH	AVG	PB	PR	/A	PD	TPI
1975	Bos-A	0	0	—	2	0	0	0	0	4	3	0	1	1	9.0	4.50	90	.200	.250	0	—	0	-0	-0	0	-0.1
1976	Bos-A	2	1	.667	8	4	1	0	0	31	31	3	16	12	13.6	4.06	96	.272	.362	0	—	0	-2	-1	1	0.0
1977	Bos-A	0	1	1.000	1	0	0	0	0	0	2	0	0	0	—	∞	—	1.000	1.000	0	—	0	-2	-2	0	-0.2
1978	Cle-A	0	0	—	6	0	0	0	0	9¹	6	1	3	7	8.7	3.86	97	.194	.265	0	—	0	-0	-0	0	0.0
Total	4	2	2	.500	17	4	1	0	0	44¹	42	4	20	20	12.6	4.47	87	.259	.341	0	—	0	-4	-3	1	-0.3

● **FRANK KREUTZER**   Kreutzer, Franklin James b: 2/7/39, Buffalo, N.Y.   BR/TL, 6'1", 190 lbs.   Deb: 9/20/62

YEAR	TM/L	W	L	PCT	G	GS	CG	SH	SV	IP	H	HR	BB	SO	RAT	ERA	ERA+	OAV	OOB	BH	AVG	PB	PR	/A	PD	TPI
1962	Chi-A	0	0	—	1	0	0	0	0	1¹	0	0	1	1	6.8	0.00	—	.000	.200	0	—	0	1	1	0	0.0
1963	Chi-A	1	0	1.000	1	1	0	0	0	5	3	1	1	0	7.2	1.80	195	.188	.235	0	.000	-0	1	1	0	0.2
1964	Chi-A	3	1	.750	17	2	0	0	1	40¹	37	1	18	32	12.3	3.35	103	.239	.318	1	.125	0	1	0	1	0.1
	Was-A	2	6	.250	13	9	0	0	0	45¹	48	6	23	27	14.3	4.76	78	.267	.353	0	.000	-1	-6	-5	0	-1.0
	Yr	5	7	.417	30	11	0	0	1	85²	85	7	41	59	13.3	4.10	87	.253	.336	1	.053	-1	-5	-5	1	-0.9
1965	Was-A	2	6	.250	33	14	2	1	0	85¹	73	7	54	65	13.6	4.32	80	.232	.348	1	.045	-1	-8	-8	-2	-1.0
1966	Was-A	0	5	.000	9	6	0	0	0	31¹	30	9	10	24	11.8	6.03	57	.236	.297	2	.250	-0	-9	-9	0	-1.2
1969	Was-A	0	0	—	4	0	0	0	0	2	3	0	2	2	22.5	4.50	77	.333	.455	0	—	0	-0	-0	0	0.0
Total	6	8	18	.308	78	32	2	1	1	210²	194	24	109	151	13.1	4.40	80	.241	.334	4	.078	-2	-20	-21	-1	-2.9

● **KRIEGER**   Krieger   Deb: 7/28/1884 ◆

YEAR	TM/L	W	L	PCT	G	GS	CG	SH	SV	IP	H	HR	BB	SO	RAT	ERA	ERA+	OAV	OOB	BH	AVG	PB	PR	/A	PD	TPI
1884	KC-U	0	1	.000	1	1	0	0	0	7	9	0	5	3	18.0	0.00	—	.292	.391	0	.000	-1	2	2	0	0.1

● **KURT KRIEGER**   Krieger, Kurt Ferdinand "Dutch" b: 9/16/26, Traisen, Austria   d: 8/16/70, St.Louis, Mo.   BR/TR, 6'3", 212 lbs.   Deb: 4/21/49

YEAR	TM/L	W	L	PCT	G	GS	CG	SH	SV	IP	H	HR	BB	SO	RAT	ERA	ERA+	OAV	OOB	BH	AVG	PB	PR	/A	PD	TPI
1949	StL-N	0	0	—	1	0	0	0	0	1	0	1	0	0	9.0	0.00	—	.000	.250	0	—	0	0	0	-0	0.0
1951	StL-N	0	0	—	2	0	0	0	0	4	6	1	6	3	24.8	15.75	25	.353	.500	0	—	0	-5	-5	0	0.0
Total	2	0	0	—	3	0	0	0	0	5	6	1	6	3	21.6	12.60	32	.300	.462	0	—	0	-5	-5	0	0.0

● **HOWIE KRIST**   Krist, Howard Wilbur "Spud" b: 2/28/16, W.Henrietta, N.Y.   d: 4/23/89, Buffalo, N.Y.   BL/TR, 6'1", 175 lbs.   Deb: 9/12/37

YEAR	TM/L	W	L	PCT	G	GS	CG	SH	SV	IP	H	HR	BB	SO	RAT	ERA	ERA+	OAV	OOB	BH	AVG	PB	PR	/A	PD	TPI
1937	StL-N	3	1	.750	6	4	1	0	0	27²	34	0	10	6	14.3	4.23	94	.304	.361	0	.000	-1	-1	-1	-1	-0.3
1938	StL-N	0	0	—	2	0	0	0	0	1¹	1	0	1	0	6.8	0.00	—	.250	.250	0	—	0	1	1	0	0.0
1941	StL-N	10	0	1.000	37	8	2	0	2	114	107	10	35	36	11.3	4.03	93	.246	.304	9	.237	-1	-5	-3	-1	-0.3
1942	StL-N	13	3	.813	34	8	3	0	1	118¹	103	2	43	47	11.3	2.51	136	.233	.304	6	.143	-1	11	12	-2	1.2
1943	*StL-N	11	5	.688	34	17	9	2	3	164¹	141	5	62	57	11.3	2.90	116	.233	.309	10	.167	-2	9	8	-5	0.1
1946	StL-N	0	2	.000	15	0	0	0	0	18²	22	3	8	3	14.9	6.75	51	.306	.383	0	—	0	-7	-7	0	-0.7
Total	6	37	11	.771	128	37	15	2	6	444¹	408	20	158	150	11.6	3.32	106	.244	.313	25	.168	-3	7	10	-9	0.1

● **GUS KROCK**   Krock, August H. b: 5/9/1866, Milwaukee, Wis.   d: 3/22/05, Pasadena, Cal.   TL, 6', 196 lbs.   Deb: 4/24/1888

YEAR	TM/L	W	L	PCT	G	GS	CG	SH	SV	IP	H	HR	BB	SO	RAT	ERA	ERA+	OAV	OOB	BH	AVG	PB	PR	/A	PD	TPI
1888	Chi-N	25	14	.641	39	39	39	4	0	339²	295	20	45	161	9.2	2.44	124	.227	.258	22	.164	-3	16	22	-3	1.6
1889	Chi-N	3	3	.500	7	7	5	0	0	60²	86	10	14	16	15.1	4.90	85	.324	.362	4	.167	-1	-6	-5	0	-0.5
	Ind-N	2	2	.500	4	4	3	0	0	32	48	2	14	10	17.4	7.31	57	.336	.396	5	.357	1	-12	-11	-1	-0.9
	Was-N	2	4	.333	6	6	6	0	0	48	65	1	22	17	16.5	5.25	73	.314	.382	2	.087	-2	-7	-7	-0	-0.8
	Yr	7	9	.438	17	17	14	0	0	140²	199	13	50	43	16.0	5.57	73	.322	.374	11	.180	-2	-24	-23	-1	-2.2
1890	Buf-P	0	3	.000	4	3	3	0	0	25	43	1	15	5	20.9	6.12	67	.363	.435	1	.083	-1	-5	-6	0	-0.5
Total	3	32	26	.552	60	59	56	4	0	505¹	537	34	110	209	11.7	3.49	97	.264	.306	34	.164	-7	-14	-6	-4	-1.1

● **RUBE KROH**   Kroh, Floyd Myron b: 8/25/1886, Friendship, N.Y.   d: 3/17/44, New Orleans, La.   BL/TL, 6'2", 186 lbs.   Deb: 9/30/06

YEAR	TM/L	W	L	PCT	G	GS	CG	SH	SV	IP	H	HR	BB	SO	RAT	ERA	ERA+	OAV	OOB	BH	AVG	PB	PR	/A	PD	TPI
1906	Bos-A	1	0	1.000	1	1	1	1	0	9	2	0	4	6	6.0	0.00	—	.074	.192	0	.000	-0	3	3	0	0.4
1907	Bos-A	1	4	.200	7	5	1	0	0	34¹	33	0	8	11	11.3	2.62	98	.255	.308	3	.273	-0	-0	-0	-0	0.0
1908	Chi-N	0	0	—	2	1	0	0	0	12	9	0	4	11	9.8	1.50	157	.200	.265	0	.000	-0	1	1	0	0.0
1909	Chi-N	9	4	.692	17	13	10	2	0	120¹	97	2	30	51	9.6	1.65	155	.224	.276	6	.150	-0	13	12	1	1.4
1910	Chi-N	3	1	.750	6	4	1	0	0	34¹	33	1	15	16	13.1	4.46	65	.254	.340	1	.250	-0	-5	-6	-1	-0.6
1912	Bos-N	0	0	—	3	1	0	0	0	6¹	8	1	6	1	19.9	5.68	63	.364	.500	1	.500	-0	-2	-1	0	0.1
Total	6	14	9	.609	36	25	13	3	0	216¹	182	4	67	92	10.6	2.29	115	.231	.296	13	.181	-0	9	8	2	1.3

● **GARY KROLL**   Kroll, Gary Melvin b: 7/8/41, Culver City, Cal.   BR/TR, 6'6", 220 lbs.   Deb: 7/26/64

YEAR	TM/L	W	L	PCT	G	GS	CG	SH	SV	IP	H	HR	BB	SO	RAT	ERA	ERA+	OAV	OOB	BH	AVG	PB	PR	/A	PD	TPI
1964	Phi-N	0	0	—	2	0	0	0	0	3	3	0	2	2	15.0	3.00	116	.250	.357	0	—	0	0	0	-0	0.0
	NY-N	0	1	.000	8	2	0	0	0	21²	19	1	15	24	14.5	4.15	86	.241	.368	1	.333	-0	-1	-1	1	0.1
	Yr	0	1	.000	10	2	0	0	0	24²	22	1	17	26	14.6	4.01	89	.242	.367	1	.333	-0	-1	-1	0	0.1
1965	NY-N	6	6	.500	32	11	1	0	0	87	83	12	41	62	13.4	4.45	79	.249	.342	3	.115	-1	-9	-9	-0	-1.2
1966	Hou-N	0	0	—	10	0	0	0	0	23²	26	2	11	22	14.1	3.80	90	.280	.356	0	.000	-0	-1	-0	-0	0.0
1969	Cle-A	0	0	—	19	0	0	0	1	24	16	3	22	28	14.3	4.13	91	.188	.355	0	—	0	-1	-0	-0	0.0
Total	4	6	7	.462	71	13	1	0	1	159¹	147	18	91	138	13.8	4.24	84	.245	.350	4	.125	-1	-12	-12	-1	-1.1

● **BILL KRUEGER**   Krueger, William Culp b: 4/24/58, Waukegan, Ill.   BL/TL, 6'5", 210 lbs.   Deb: 4/10/83

YEAR	TM/L	W	L	PCT	G	GS	CG	SH	SV	IP	H	HR	BB	SO	RAT	ERA	ERA+	OAV	OOB	BH	AVG	PB	PR	/A	PD	TPI
1983	Oak-A	7	6	.538	17	16	2	0	0	109²	104	7	53	58	13.0	3.61	107	.252	.340	0	—	0	5	3	-2	0.2
1984	Oak-A	10	10	.500	26	24	1	0	0	142	156	9	85	61	15.4	4.75	79	.285	.383	0	—	0	-12	-16	-2	-1.7
1985	Oak-A	9	10	.474	32	23	2	0	0	151¹	165	13	69	56	14.0	4.52	85	.276	.353	0	—	0	-6	-11	-1	-1.0

YEAR TM/L	W	L	PCT	G	GS	CG	SH	SV	IP	H	HR	BB	SO	RAT	ERA	ERA+	OAV	OOB	BH	AVG	PB	PR	/A	PD	TPI
1986 Oak-A	1	2	.333	11	3	0	0	1	34¹	40	4	13	10	13.9	6.03	64	.301	.363	0	—	0	-7	-8	1	-0.5
1987 Oak-A	0	3	.000	9	0	0	0	0	5²	9	0	8	2	27.0	9.53	43	.360	.515	0	—	0	-3	-3	-0	-1.4
LA-N	0	0	—	2	0	0	0	0	2¹	3	0	1	2	15.4	0.00	—	.250	.308	0	—	0	1	1	-0	0.0
1988 LA-N	0	0	—	1	1	0	0	0	2¹	4	0	2	1	27.0	11.57	29	.364	.500	0	—	0	-2	-2	0	0.0
1989 Mil-A	3	2	.600	34	5	0	0	3	93²	96	9	33	72	12.4	3.84	100	.264	.325	0	—	0	0	-0	-0	0.0
1990 Mil-A	6	8	.429	30	17	0	0	0	129	137	10	54	64	13.5	3.98	97	.276	.351	0	—	0	-1	-2	-1	-0.2
1991 Sea-A	11	8	.579	35	25	1	0	0	175	194	15	60	91	13.3	3.60	114	.289	.351	0	—	0	10	10	1	1.1
1992 Min-A	10	6	.625	27	27	2	2	0	161¹	166	18	46	86	12.0	4.30	94	.263	.317	0	—	0	-6	-4	-3	-0.8
Mon-N	0	2	.000	9	2	0	0	0	17¹	23	7	0	13	16.1	6.75	51	.315	.383	0	.000	-0	-6	-6	-0	-0.7
1993 Det-A	6	4	.600	32	7	0	0	0	82	90	6	30	60	13.6	3.40	126	.285	.354	0	—	0	8	8	0	0.9
1994 Det-A	0	2	.000	16	2	0	0	0	19²	26	3	17	17	20.1	9.61	50	.321	.444	0	—	0	-11	-11	-0	-0.9
SD-N	3	2	.600	8	7	1	0	0	41	42	5	7	30	11.0	4.83	87	.259	.294	6	.500	3	-3	-3	0	0.1
Total 12	66	65	.504	289	159	9	2	4	1166²	1255	99	485	623	13.6	4.30	92	.277	.350	6	.400	2	-33	-44	-8	-5.1

● **ABE KRUGER**　Kruger, Abraham　b: 2/14/1885, Morris Run, Pa.　d: 7/4/62, Elmira, N.Y.　BR/TR, 6'2", 190 lbs.　Deb: 10/6/08

YEAR TM/L	W	L	PCT	G	GS	CG	SH	SV	IP	H	HR	BB	SO	RAT	ERA	ERA+	OAV	OOB	BH	AVG	PB	PR	/A	PD	TPI
1908 Bro-N	0	1	.000	2	1	0	0	0	6¹	5	0	3	2	15.6	4.26	55	.238	.407	0	.000	-0	-1	-1	1	-0.1

● **MIKE KRUKOW**　Krukow, Michael Edward　b: 1/21/52, Long Beach, Cal.　BR/TR, 6'5", 205 lbs.　Deb: 9/6/76

YEAR TM/L	W	L	PCT	G	GS	CG	SH	SV	IP	H	HR	BB	SO	RAT	ERA	ERA+	OAV	OOB	BH	AVG	PB	PR	/A	PD	TPI
1976 Chi-N	0	0	—	2	0	0	0	0	4¹	6	0	2	1	16.6	8.31	46	.333	.400	0	.000	-0	-2	-2	-0	0.0
1977 Chi-N	8	14	.364	34	33	1	1	0	172	195	16	61	106	13.6	4.40	100	.281	.341	11	.200	-0	-9	-0	1	0.0
1978 Chi-N	9	3	.750	27	20	3	1	0	138	125	11	53	81	11.9	3.91	103	.243	.320	11	.244	3	-5	2	-0	0.4
1979 Chi-N	9	9	.500	28	28	0	0	0	164²	172	13	81	119	14.0	4.21	98	.275	.361	16	.314	5	-9	-2	-2	0.1
1980 Chi-N	10	15	.400	34	34	3	0	0	205	200	13	80	130	12.6	4.39	89	.258	.334	16	.246	2	-18	-11	-3	-1.3
1981 Chi-N	9	9	.500	25	25	2	1	0	144¹	146	11	55	101	12.7	3.68	100	.264	.333	9	.180	-0	3	0	0	0.1
1982 Phi-N	13	11	.542	33	33	7	2	0	208	211	8	82	138	12.8	3.12	118	.268	.339	13	.181	-0	11	13	2	1.5
1983 SF-N	11	11	.500	31	31	2	1	0	184¹	189	17	76	136	13.1	3.95	89	.261	.333	16	.254	5	-7	-9	-2	-0.6
1984 SF-N	11	12	.478	35	33	3	1	1	199¹	234	22	78	141	14.3	4.56	77	.290	.356	10	.139	-1	-22	-23	-2	-2.7
1985 SF-N	8	11	.421	28	28	6	1	0	194²	176	19	49	150	10.5	3.38	102	.238	.288	12	.218	5	5	1	-0	0.6
1986 SF-N★	20	9	.690	34	34	10	2	0	245	204	24	55	178	9.7	3.05	115	.223	.271	12	.146	-0	18	13	-1	1.4
1987 *SF-N	5	6	.455	30	28	3	0	0	163	182	24	46	104	12.7	4.80	80	.288	.338	9	.167	1	-13	-17	1	-0.8
1988 SF-N	7	4	.636	20	20	1	0	0	124²	111	13	31	75	10.6	3.54	92	.236	.291	3	.073	-0	-1	-4	-0	-0.4
1989 SF-N	4	3	.571	8	8	0	0	0	43	37	5	18	18	11.7	3.98	85	.236	.318	1	.063	-1	-2	-3	0	-0.5
Total 14	124	117	.515	369	355	41	10	1	2190¹	2188	196	767	1478	12.3	3.90	96	.260	.325	139	.193	17	-57	-42	-5	-2.2

● **AL KRUMM**　Krumm, Albert　b: 1/1865, Pennsylvania　TR,　Deb: 5/17/1889

YEAR TM/L	W	L	PCT	G	GS	CG	SH	SV	IP	H	HR	BB	SO	RAT	ERA	ERA+	OAV	OOB	BH	AVG	PB	PR	/A	PD	TPI
1889 Pit-N	0	1	.000	1	1	1	0	0	9	8	0	10	4	18.0	10.00	37	.231	.403	0	.000	-1	-6	-6	-0	-0.5

● **JOHNNY KUCAB**　Kucab, John Albert　b: 12/17/19, Olyphant, Pa.　d: 5/26/77, Youngstown, Ohio　BR/TR, 6'2", 185 lbs.　Deb: 9/14/50

YEAR TM/L	W	L	PCT	G	GS	CG	SH	SV	IP	H	HR	BB	SO	RAT	ERA	ERA+	OAV	OOB	BH	AVG	PB	PR	/A	PD	TPI
1950 Phi-A	1	1	.500	4	2	2	0	0	26	29	4	8	12	12.8	3.46	131	.282	.333	1	.111	-0	3	3	-1	0.1
1951 Phi-A	4	3	.571	30	1	0	0	4	74²	76	9	23	23	12.1	4.22	101	.265	.322	0	.000	-2	-1	0	-2	-0.3
1952 Phi-A	0	1	.000	25	0	0	0	2	51¹	64	5	20	17	14.9	5.26	75	.312	.376	2	.200	-0	-9	-7	-0	-0.2
Total 3	5	5	.500	59	3	2	0	6	152	169	18	51	48	13.1	4.44	95	.284	.343	3	.086	-2	-7	-4	-2	-0.4

● **JACK KUCEK**　Kucek, John Andrew Charles　b: 6/8/53, Warren, Ohio　BR/TR, 6'2", 200 lbs.　Deb: 8/8/74

YEAR TM/L	W	L	PCT	G	GS	CG	SH	SV	IP	H	HR	BB	SO	RAT	ERA	ERA+	OAV	OOB	BH	AVG	PB	PR	/A	PD	TPI
1974 Chi-A	1	4	.200	9	7	0	0	0	37²	48	3	21	25	16.7	5.26	71	.320	.407	0	—	0	-7	-6	1	-0.8
1975 Chi-A	0	0	—	2	0	0	0	0	3²	9	0	4	2	31.9	4.91	79	.500	.591	0	—	0	-0	-0	-0	0.0
1976 Chi-A	0	0	—	2	0	0	0	0	4²	9	2	4	2	25.1	9.64	37	.429	.520	0	—	0	-3	-3	-0	0.0
1977 Chi-A	0	1	.000	8	3	0	0	0	34¹	35	4	10	25	12.2	3.63	112	.267	.329	0	—	0	2	2	1	0.1
1978 Chi-A	2	3	.400	10	5	3	0	0	52	42	5	27	30	11.9	3.29	116	.220	.317	0	—	0	3	3	-0	0.2
1979 Chi-A	0	0	—	1	0	0	0	0	0²	0	0	3	0	40.5	0.00	—	.000	.500	0	—	0	0	0	0	0.0
Phi-N	1	0	1.000	4	0	0	0	0	4¹	6	2	1	2	14.5	8.31	46	.333	.368	0	—	0	-2	-2	-0	-0.4
1980 Tor-A	3	8	.273	23	12	0	0	1	68	83	9	41	35	16.5	6.75	64	.300	.392	0	—	0	-21	-19	-1	-2.7
Total 7	7	16	.304	59	27	3	0	2	205²	232	25	111	121	15.2	5.12	78	.287	.376	0	—	0	-29	-26	0	-3.6

● **JOHNNY KUCKS**　Kucks, John Charles　b: 7/27/33, Hoboken, N.J.　BR/TR, 6'3", 184 lbs.　Deb: 4/17/55

YEAR TM/L	W	L	PCT	G	GS	CG	SH	SV	IP	H	HR	BB	SO	RAT	ERA	ERA+	OAV	OOB	BH	AVG	PB	PR	/A	PD	TPI
1955 *NY-A	8	7	.533	29	13	3	1	0	126²	122	8	44	49	11.9	3.41	110	.252	.317	2	.050	-4	8	5	-0	0.1
1956 *NY-A☆	18	9	.667	34	31	12	3	0	224¹	223	19	72	67	12.2	3.85	100	.261	.326	11	.143	-2	8	0	-0	-0.1
1957 *NY-A	8	10	.444	37	23	4	1	2	179¹	169	13	59	78	11.8	3.56	101	.251	.319	6	.109	-2	4	0	3	0.2
1958 *NY-A	8	8	.500	34	15	4	1	4	126	132	14	39	46	12.6	3.93	90	.269	.331	5	.125	-1	-2	-6	1	-0.7
1959 NY-A	0	1	.000	9	1	0	0	0	16²	21	5	9	9	16.2	8.64	42	.323	.405	0	.000	-0	-9	-9	-0	-0.5
KC-A	8	11	.421	33	23	6	1	1	151¹	163	10	42	51	12.9	3.87	104	.278	.339	4	.085	-3	-0	2	2	0.2
Yr	8	12	.400	42	24	6	1	1	168	184	15	51	60	13.2	4.34	91	.282	.345	4	.082	-3	-9	-7	2	-0.4
1960 KC-A	4	10	.286	31	17	1	0	0	114	140	22	43	38	14.5	6.00	66	.306	.367	4	.133	-1	-27	-26	-0	-2.8
Total 6	54	56	.491	207	123	30	7	7	938¹	970	91	308	338	12.6	4.10	92	.269	.333	32	.110	-12	-18	-32	5	-3.7

● **BERT KUCZYNSKI**　Kuczynski, Bernard Carl　b: 1/8/20, Philadelphia, Pa.　BR/TR, 6', 195 lbs.　Deb: 6/2/43

YEAR TM/L	W	L	PCT	G	GS	CG	SH	SV	IP	H	HR	BB	SO	RAT	ERA	ERA+	OAV	OOB	BH	AVG	PB	PR	/A	PD	TPI
1943 Phi-A	1	1	.000	6	1	0	0	0	24²	36	2	9	8	17.1	4.01	85	.336	.398	0	—	-0	-2	-2	-0	-0.1

● **FRED KUHAULUA**　Kuhaulua, Fred Mahele　b: 2/23/53, Honolulu, Hawaii　BL/TL, 5'11", 175 lbs.　Deb: 8/2/77

YEAR TM/L	W	L	PCT	G	GS	CG	SH	SV	IP	H	HR	BB	SO	RAT	ERA	ERA+	OAV	OOB	BH	AVG	PB	PR	/A	PD	TPI
1977 Cal-A	0	0	—	3	1	0	0	0	6¹	15	1	7	3	31.3	15.63	25	.455	.550	0	—	0	-8	-8	0	0.0
1981 SD-N	1	0	1.000	5	4	0	0	0	29¹	28	1	9	16	11.4	2.45	133	.257	.314	1	.111	-0	3	3	-1	-0.1
Total 2	1	0	1.000	8	5	0	0	0	35²	43	2	16	19	14.9	4.79	70	.303	.373	1	.111	-0	-5	-6	-1	-0.1

● **BUB KUHN**　Kuhn, Bernard Daniel　b: 10/12/1899, Vicksburg, Mich.　d: 11/20/56, Detroit, Mich.　BL/TR, 6'1.5", 182 lbs.　Deb: 9/1/24

YEAR TM/L	W	L	PCT	G	GS	CG	SH	SV	IP	H	HR	BB	SO	RAT	ERA	ERA+	OAV	OOB	BH	AVG	PB	PR	/A	PD	TPI
1924 Cle-A	0	1	.000	1	0	0	0	0	1	4	1	0	0	36.0	27.00	16	.667	.667	0	—	0	-3	-3	0	-1.2

● **JOHN KULL**　Kull, John A.　b: 6/24/1882, Shenandoah, Pa.　d: 3/30/36, Schuylkill, Pa.　BL/TL, 6'2", 190 lbs.　Deb: 10/2/09

YEAR TM/L	W	L	PCT	G	GS	CG	SH	SV	IP	H	HR	BB	SO	RAT	ERA	ERA+	OAV	OOB	BH	AVG	PB	PR	/A	PD	TPI
1909 Phi-A	1	0	1.000	1	0	0	0	0	3	3	0	5	4	27.0	3.00	80	.250	.500	1	1.000	0	-0	-0	0	0.0

● **MIKE KUME**　Kume, John Michael　b: 5/19/26, Premier, W.Va.　BR/TR, 6'1", 195 lbs.　Deb: 8/26/55

YEAR TM/L	W	L	PCT	G	GS	CG	SH	SV	IP	H	HR	BB	SO	RAT	ERA	ERA+	OAV	OOB	BH	AVG	PB	PR	/A	PD	TPI
1955 KC-A	0	2	.000	6	4	0	0	0	23²	35	1	15	7	20.2	7.99	52	.354	.453	1	.125	-0	-11	-10	-0	-0.8

● **JEFF KUNKEL**　Kunkel, Jeffrey William　b: 3/25/62, W.Palm Beach, Fla.　BR/TR, 6'2", 180 lbs.　Deb: 7/23/84　F♦

YEAR TM/L	W	L	PCT	G	GS	CG	SH	SV	IP	H	HR	BB	SO	RAT	ERA	ERA+	OAV	OOB	BH	AVG	PB	PR	/A	PD	TPI
1988 Tex-A	0	0	—	1	0	0	0	0	1	0	0	0	0	0.0	0.00	—	.000	.000	35	.227	0	0	0	0	0.0
1989 Tex-A	0	0	—	1	0	0	0	0	1²	4	1	3	1	37.8	21.60	18	.444	.583	79	.270	1	-3	-3	0	0.0
Total 2	0	0	—	2	0	0	0	0	2²	4	1	3	1	23.6	13.50	30	.333	.467	192	.221	2	-3	-3	0	0.0

● **BILL KUNKEL**　Kunkel, William Gustave James　b: 7/7/36, Hoboken, N.J.　d: 5/4/85, Red Bank, N.J.　BR/TR, 6'1", 187 lbs.　Deb: 4/15/61　FU

YEAR TM/L	W	L	PCT	G	GS	CG	SH	SV	IP	H	HR	BB	SO	RAT	ERA	ERA+	OAV	OOB	BH	AVG	PB	PR	/A	PD	TPI
1961 KC-A	3	4	.429	58	2	0	0	4	88²	103	11	32	46	13.7	5.18	81	.289	.348	1	.125	-0	-11	-10	-0	-0.8
1962 KC-A	0	0	—	9	0	0	0	0	7²	8	3	4	6	14.1	3.52	120	.258	.343	0	—	0	1	1	0	0.0
1963 NY-A	3	2	.600	22	0	0	0	0	46¹	42	3	13	31	10.7	2.72	129	.239	.291	2	.333	1	5	4	-1	0.4
Total 3	6	6	.500	89	2	0	0	4	142²	153	17	49	83	12.7	4.29	92	.272	.330	3	.214	1	-6	-5	-1	-0.4

● **EARL KUNZ**　Kunz, Earl Dewey "Pinches"　b: 12/25/1899, Sacramento, Cal.　d: 4/14/63, Sacramento, Cal.　BR/TR, 5'10", 170 lbs.　Deb: 4/19/23

YEAR TM/L	W	L	PCT	G	GS	CG	SH	SV	IP	H	HR	BB	SO	RAT	ERA	ERA+	OAV	OOB	BH	AVG	PB	PR	/A	PD	TPI
1923 Pit-N	1	2	.333	21	2	1	0	1	45²	48	2	24	12	14.2	5.52	73	.293	.383	1	.083	-1	-8	-8	-1	-0.7

YEAR TM/L	W	L	PCT	G	GS	CG	SH	SV	IP	H	HR	BB	SO	RAT	ERA	ERA+	OAV	OOB	BH	AVG	PB	PR	/A	PD	TPI

● RYAN KUROSAKI   Kurosaki, Ryan Yoshitomo b: 7/3/52, Honolulu, Hawaii   BR/TR, 5′10″, 160 lbs.   Deb: 5/20/75

| 1975 StL-N | 0 | 0 | — | 7 | 0 | 0 | 0 | 0 | 13 | 15 | 3 | 7 | 6 | 15.2 | 7.62 | 49 | .283 | .367 | 0 | .000 | -0 | -6 | -6 | -0 | 0.0 |

● HAL KURTZ   Kurtz, Harold James "Bud" b: 8/20/43, Washington, D.C.   BR/TR, 6′3″, 205 lbs.   Deb: 4/18/68

| 1968 Cle-A | 1 | 0 | 1.000 | 28 | 0 | 0 | 0 | 1 | 38 | 37 | 2 | 15 | 16 | 13.5 | 5.21 | 57 | .255 | .345 | 0 | .000 | -0 | -9 | -10 | -1 | -0.4 |

● ED KUSEL   Kusel, Edward D. b: 2/15/1886, Cleveland, Ohio   d: 10/20/48, Cleveland, Ohio   TR , 6′, 165 lbs.   Deb: 9/18/09

| 1909 StL-A | 0 | 3 | .000 | 3 | 3 | 3 | 0 | 0 | 24 | 43 | 1 | 1 | 2 | 16.5 | 7.13 | 34 | .384 | .389 | 3 | .300 | 1 | -12 | -13 | -1 | -1.2 |

● EMIL KUSH   Kush, Emil Benedict b: 11/4/16, Chicago, Ill.   d: 11/26/69, River Grove, Ill.   BR/TR, 5′11″, 185 lbs.   Deb: 9/21/41

1941 Chi-N	0	0	—	2	0	0	0	0	4	2	0	2	0	4.5	2.25	156	.143	.143	0	.000	-0	1	1	-0	0.0
1942 Chi-N	0	0	—	1	0	0	0	0	2	1	0	1	1	9.0	0.00	—	.167	.286	0	.000	-0	1	1	0	0.0
1946 Chi-N	9	2	.818	40	6	1	1	2	129²	120	4	43	50	11.5	3.05	109	.253	.319	8	.211	0	5	4	2	0.6
1947 Chi-N	8	3	.727	47	1	1	0	5	91	80	8	53	44	13.5	3.36	117	.247	.358	5	.250	1	7	6	1	0.9
1948 Chi-N	1	4	.200	34	1	0	0	3	72	70	5	37	31	13.6	4.38	89	.253	.345	2	.154	-0	-3	-4	1	-0.2
1949 Chi-N	3	3	.500	26	0	0	0	2	47²	51	7	24	22	14.5	3.78	107	.283	.374	3	.333	1	1	1	1	0.4
Total 6	21	12	.636	150	8	2	1	12	346¹	324	24	158	150	12.8	3.48	106	.254	.341	18	.220	2	12	9	5	1.7

● CRAIG KUSICK   Kusick, Craig Robert b: 9/30/48, Milwaukee, Wis.   BR/TR, 6′3″, 232 lbs.   Deb: 9/8/73 ♦

| 1979 Tor-A | 0 | 0 | — | 1 | 0 | 0 | 0 | 0 | 3² | 3 | 1 | 0 | 0 | 7.4 | 4.91 | 88 | .214 | .214 | 11 | .204 | 1 | -0 | -0 | -0 | 0.0 |

● MARTY KUTYNA   Kutyna, Marion John b: 11/14/32, Philadelphia, Pa.   BR/TR, 6′, 190 lbs.   Deb: 9/19/59

1959 KC-A	0	0	—	4	0	0	0	1	7¹	7	0	1	1	9.8	0.00	—	.250	.276	0	—	0	3	3	0	0.1
1960 KC-A	3	2	.600	51	0	0	0	4	61²	64	7	32	20	14.0	3.94	101	.274	.361	1	.200	-0	-0	-0	0	0.0
1961 Was-A	6	8	.429	50	6	0	0	3	143	147	12	48	64	12.4	3.97	101	.271	.332	7	.206	-0	1	1	3	0.4
1962 Was-A	5	6	.455	54	0	0	0	0	78	83	9	27	25	12.7	4.04	100	.275	.334	1	.125	-0	-1	-0	1	0.1
Total 4	14	16	.467	159	6	0	0	8	290	301	28	108	110	12.8	3.88	103	.272	.338	9	.191	-0	3	4	4	0.6

● JERRY KUTZLER   Kutzler, Jerry Scott b: 3/25/65, Waukegan, Ill.   BL/TR, 6′1″, 175 lbs.   Deb: 4/28/90

| 1990 Chi-A | 2 | 1 | .667 | 7 | 7 | 0 | 0 | 0 | 31¹ | 38 | 2 | 14 | 21 | 14.9 | 6.03 | 63 | .304 | .374 | 0 | — | 0 | -7 | -8 | -0 | -0.7 |

● BOB KUZAVA   Kuzava, Robert Leroy "Sarge" b: 5/28/23, Wyandotte, Mich.   BB/TL, 6′2″, 204 lbs.   Deb: 9/21/46

1946 Cle-A	1	0	1.000	2	2	0	0	0	12	9	0	11	4	15.8	3.00	110	.191	.356	1	.200	-0	1	0	0	0.1
1947 Cle-A	1	1	.500	4	4	1	1	0	21²	22	1	9	11	13.3	4.15	84	.265	.344	1	.111	-1	-1	-2	1	-0.1
1949 Chi-A	10	6	.625	29	18	9	1	0	156²	139	6	91	83	13.3	4.02	104	.240	.344	2	.036	-6	3	3	-2	-0.6
1950 Chi-A	1	3	.250	10	7	1	0	0	44¹	43	5	27	21	14.2	5.68	79	.257	.361	1	.083	-0	-5	-6	-0	-0.5
Was-A	8	7	.533	22	22	8	1	0	155	156	8	75	84	13.5	3.95	114	.263	.346	5	.100	-2	11	9	-1	0.5
Yr	9	10	.474	32	29	9	1	0	199¹	199	13	102	105	13.6	4.33	104	.261	.350	6	.097	-2	5	3	-1	0.0
1951 Was-A	3	3	.500	8	8	3	0	0	52¹	57	5	28	22	15.0	5.50	74	.284	.377	3	.176	-0	-8	-8	0	-0.8
*NY-A	8	4	.667	23	8	4	1	5	82¹	76	5	27	50	11.4	2.40	159	.241	.303	3	.136	-0	16	13	-1	1.8
Yr	11	7	.611	31	16	7	1	5	134²	133	10	55	72	12.6	3.61	109	.257	.329	6	.154	-0	8	5	-1	1.0
1952 *NY-A	8	8	.500	28	12	6	1	3	133	115	7	63	67	12.1	3.45	96	.240	.329	4	.093	-1	3	-2	-2	-0.5
1953 *NY-A	6	5	.545	33	6	2	2	4	92¹	92	9	34	48	12.3	3.31	111	.264	.330	1	.048	-1	7	4	-2	0.2
1954 NY-A	1	3	.250	20	3	0	0	0	39²	46	3	18	22	14.5	5.45	63	.297	.370	0	.000	-1	-8	-9	-1	-1.0
Bal-A	1	3	.250	4	4	0	0	0	23²	30	0	11	15	15.6	4.18	86	.323	.394	0	.000	-1	-1	-2	-1	-0.4
Yr	2	6	.250	24	7	0	0	1	63¹	76	3	29	37	14.9	4.97	70	.304	.376	0	.000	-1	-9	-10	-1	-1.4
1955 Bal-A	0	1	.000	6	1	0	0	0	12¹	10	2	6	5	10.2	3.65	105	.227	.286	0	—	0	-1	-0	0	0.0
Phi-N	1	0	1.000	17	4	0	0	0	32¹	47	5	12	13	16.4	7.24	55	.333	.386	1	.143	-0	-11	-12	-0	-0.3
1957 Pit-N	0	0	—	4	0	0	0	0	2	3	0	3	1	27.0	9.00	42	.333	.500	0	—	0	-1	-1	-0	0.0
StL-N	0	0	—	3	0	0	0	0	2¹	4	0	2	2	23.1	3.86	103	.364	.462	0	—	0	0	0	0	0.0
Yr	0	0	—	7	0	0	0	0	4¹	7	0	5	3	24.9	6.23	62	.350	.480	0	—	0	-1	-1	0	0.0
Total 10	49	44	.527	213	99	34	7	13	862	849	54	415	446	13.3	4.05	97	.260	.345	22	.086	-14	5	-12	-8	-1.6

● CLEM LABINE   Labine, Clement Walter b: 8/6/26, Lincoln, R.I.   BR/TR, 6′, 180 lbs.   Deb: 4/18/50

1950 Bro-N	0	0	—	1	0	0	0	0	2	2	0	1	0	13.5	4.50	91	.286	.375	0	—	0	-0	-0	-0	0.0
1951 Bro-N	5	1	.833	14	6	5	2	0	65¹	51	4	20	39	9.9	2.20	178	.223	.285	3	.143	-1	13	12	-1	0.9
1952 Bro-N	8	4	.667	25	9	0	0	0	77	76	3	47	43	14.5	5.14	71	.259	.364	1	.045	-2	-12	-13	1	-1.9
1953 *Bro-N	11	6	.647	37	7	0	0	7	110¹	92	9	30	44	10.0	2.77	154	.225	.278	2	.071	-1	19	18	0	2.7
1954 Bro-N	7	6	.538	47	2	0	0	5	108¹	101	7	56	43	13.1	4.15	98	.247	.339	1	.033	-2	-1	-1	1	-0.2
1955 *Bro-N	13	5	.722	60	8	1	0	11	144¹	121	12	55	67	11.0	3.24	125	.229	.301	3	.087	-1	13	13	3	2.1
1956 *Bro-N☆	10	6	.625	62	3	1	0	19	115²	111	11	39	75	11.9	3.35	119	.253	.318	2	.100	-1	5	8	1	1.3
1957 Bro-N★	5	7	.417	58	0	0	0	17	104²	104	8	27	67	11.4	3.44	121	.259	.307	2	.100	-1	5	8	2	1.3
1958 LA-N	6	6	.500	52	2	0	0	14	104	112	8	33	43	12.6	4.15	99	.283	.340	1	.056	-1	-2	-1	0	-0.2
1959 *LA-N	5	10	.333	56	0	0	0	9	84²	91	11	25	37	12.4	3.93	108	.282	.335	0	—	0	3	1	5	0.5
1960 LA-N	0	1	.000	13	0	0	0	0	17	26	1	8	15	18.0	5.82	68	.356	.420	1	.500	1	-4	-4	-0	-0.2
Det-A	0	3	.000	14	0	0	0	0	19¹	19	2	12	6	14.4	5.12	77	.257	.360	0	.000	-0	-3	-4	1	-0.4
*Pit-N	3	0	1.000	15	0	0	0	3	30¹	29	0	11	21	12.2	1.48	253	.254	.325	0	—	0	8	8	0	0.9
1961 Pit-N	4	1	.800	56	1	0	0	8	92²	102	4	31	49	13.1	3.69	108	.284	.344	1	.100	-0	4	3	-1	0.1
1962 NY-N	0	0	—	3	0	0	0	0	4	5	1	1	2	13.5	11.25	37	.278	.316	0	—	0	-3	-3	0	0.0
Total 13	77	56	.579	513	38	7	2	96	1079²	1043	81	396	551	12.1	3.63	112	.256	.323	17	.075	-11	41	50	8	6.9

● BOB LACEY   Lacey, Robert Joseph b: 8/25/53, Fredericksburg, Va.   BR/TL, 6′5″, 210 lbs.   Deb: 5/13/77

1977 Oak-A	6	8	.429	64	0	0	0	7	121²	100	13	43	69	10.6	3.03	133	.234	.304	0	—	0	14	13	3	2.0
1978 Oak-A	8	9	.471	74	0	0	0	5	119²	126	10	35	60	12.2	3.01	121	.270	.323	0	—	0	10	8	2	1.4
1979 Oak-A	1	5	.167	42	0	0	0	4	47²	66	7	24	33	17.2	5.85	69	.327	.401	0	—	0	-9	-10	0	-1.2
1980 Oak-A	3	2	.600	47	1	1	1	6	79²	68	7	21	45	10.2	2.94	128	.234	.288	0	—	0	10	7	-0	0.6
1981 Cle-A	0	0	—	14	0	0	0	0	21¹	36	1	3	11	16.5	7.59	48	.371	.390	0	—	0	-9	-9	-0	0.0
Tex-A	0	0	—	1	0	0	0	0	1	1	1	0	0	9.0	9.00	39	.250	.250	0	—	0	-1	-1	0	0.0
Yr	0	0	—	15	0	0	0	0	22¹	37	1	3	11	16.1	7.66	47	.356	.374	0	—	0	-10	-10	0	0.0
1983 Cal-A	1	2	.333	8	0	0	0	0	8²	12	1	7	2	12.5	5.19	77	.343	.343	0	—	0	-1	-1	-0	-0.3
1984 SF-N	1	3	.250	34	0	0	0	0	51	55	5	13	26	12.0	3.88	90	.276	.321	2	.333	1	-2	-2	0	-0.1
Total 7	20	29	.408	284	2	1	1	22	450²	464	49	139	251	12.1	3.67	103	.269	.325	2	.333	1	12	6	5	2.4

● MARCEL LACHEMANN   Lachemann, Marcel Ernest b: 6/13/41, Los Angeles, Cal.   BR/TR, 6′, 185 lbs.   Deb: 6/4/69   FMC

1969 Oak-A	4	1	.800	28	0	0	0	3	43¹	43	1	19	16	13.3	3.95	87	.261	.344	0	.000	-0	-2	-2	1	-0.3
1970 Oak-A	3	3	.500	41	0	0	0	2	58²	58	6	18	39	12.0	2.78	127	.266	.328	0	.000	-1	6	5	1	0.6
1971 Oak-A	0	0	—	1	0	0	0	0	0¹	2	1	1	0	81.0	54.00	6	1.000	1.000	0	.000	-0	-2	-2	0	0.0
Total 3	7	4	.636	70	0	0	0	5	102	103	7	38	55	12.8	3.44	102	.268	.340	0	.000	-1	3	1	2	0.3

● AL LACHOWICZ   Lachowicz, Allen Robert b: 9/6/60, Pittsburgh, Pa.   BR/TR, 6′3″, 198 lbs.   Deb: 9/13/83

| 1983 Tex-A | 0 | 1 | .000 | 2 | 1 | 0 | 0 | 0 | 8 | 9 | 0 | 2 | 8 | 12.4 | 2.25 | 178 | .281 | .324 | 0 | — | 0 | 2 | 2 | 0 | 0.2 |

● LACKEY   Lackey, b: Columbus, Ohio   Deb: 10/2/1890

| 1890 Phi-a | 0 | 0 | — | 1 | 0 | 0 | 0 | 0 | 2 | 1 | 0 | 3 | 1 | 18.0 | 9.00 | 43 | .144 | .403 | 0 | .000 | -0 | -1 | -1 | -0 | 0.0 |

● GEORGE LaCLAIRE — LaClaire, George Lewis "Frenchy" b: 10/18/1886, Milton, Vt. d: 10/10/18, Farnham, Que., Can. BR/TR, 5'9", 170 lbs. Deb: 6/5/14

YEAR TM/L	W	L	PCT	G	GS	CG	SH	SV	IP	H	HR	BB	SO	RAT	ERA	ERA+	OAV	OOB	BH	AVG	PB	PR	/A	PD	TPI
1914 Pit-F	5	2	.714	22	7	5	1	0	103¹	99	0	25	49	10.9	4.01	71	.262	.309	5	.147	-2	-13	-13	0	-1.0
1915 Pit-F	1	2	.333	14	3	1	0	1	45²	43	1	13	10	11.0	3.35	81	.253	.306	2	.154	-1	-3	-3	1	-0.3
Buf-F	0	0	—	1	0	0	0	0	3	4	0	1	2	15.0	6.00	47	.333	.385	0	—	-0	-1	-1	-0	0.0
Bal-F	1	8	.111	18	9	6	1	1	84	76	2	22	30	10.5	2.46	116	.246	.296	2	.083	-2	2	4	0	0.2
Yr	2	10	.167	33	12	7	1	2	132²	123	3	36	42	10.8	2.85	99	.251	.302	4	.108	-3	-2	-1	0	-0.1
Total 2	7	12	.368	55	19	12	2	2	236	222	3	61	91	10.8	3.36	85	.255	.305	9	.127	-5	-15	-14	1	-1.1

● FRANK LaCORTE — LaCorte, Frank Joseph b: 10/13/51, San Jose, Cal. BR/TR, 6'1", 180 lbs. Deb: 9/8/75

YEAR TM/L	W	L	PCT	G	GS	CG	SH	SV	IP	H	HR	BB	SO	RAT	ERA	ERA+	OAV	OOB	BH	AVG	PB	PR	/A	PD	TPI
1975 Atl-N	0	3	.000	3	2	0	0	0	13²	13	1	6	10	12.5	5.27	72	.245	.322	0	.000	-1	-3	-2	0	-0.5
1976 Atl-N	3	12	.200	19	17	0	0	0	105¹	97	6	53	79	13.3	4.70	81	.249	.348	3	.091	-2	-14	-11	-0	-1.6
1977 Atl-N	1	8	.111	14	7	0	0	0	37	67	10	29	28	23.8	11.68	38	.394	.488	2	.200	-0	-32	-30	-0	-5.3
1978 Atl-N	0	1	.000	2	2	0	0	0	14²	9	0	4	7	8.0	3.68	110	.180	.241	0	.000	-0	-0	1	-0	0.0
1979 Atl-N	0	0	—	6	0	0	0	0	8¹	9	2	5	6	15.1	7.56	54	.273	.368	0	.000	-0	-4	-3	-0	0.0
Hou-N	1	2	.333	12	3	0	0	0	27	21	3	10	24	10.3	5.00	70	.208	.279	0	.000	-0	-4	*-4	-1	-0.5
Yr	1	2	.333	18	3	0	0	0	35¹	30	5	15	30	11.5	5.60	65	.224	.302	0	.000	-0	-7	-8	-1	-0.5
1980 *Hou-N	8	5	.615	55	0	0	0	11	83	61	4	43	66	11.3	2.82	117	.210	.311	1	.167	0	7	4	-2	0.6
1981 *Hou-N	4	2	.667	37	0	0	0	5	42	41	1	21	40	13.3	3.64	90	.258	.344	1	.333	-1	-0	-3	-0	-0.3
1982 Hou-N	1	5	.167	55	0	0	0	7	76¹	71	6	46	51	13.8	4.48	74	.247	.350	0	.000	-1	-7	-10	-2	-1.2
1983 Hou-N	4	4	.500	37	0	0	0	3	53¹	35	8	28	44	11.0	5.06	67	.190	.304	1	.200	0	-9	-10	-0	-1.5
1984 Cal-A	1	2	.333	13	1	0	0	0	29¹	33	9	13	13	14.1	7.06	56	.282	.354	0	—	-0	-10	-10	-0	-0.9
Total 10	23	44	.343	253	32	1	0	26	490	457	49	258	372	13.2	5.01	72	.249	.345	8	.104	-4	-75	-77	-7	-11.2

● MIKE LaCOSS — LaCoss, Michael James b: 5/30/56, Glendale, Cal. BR/TR, 6'4", 190 lbs. Deb: 7/18/78

YEAR TM/L	W	L	PCT	G	GS	CG	SH	SV	IP	H	HR	BB	SO	RAT	ERA	ERA+	OAV	OOB	BH	AVG	PB	PR	/A	PD	TPI
1978 Cin-N	4	8	.333	16	15	2	1	0	96	104	5	46	31	14.2	4.50	79	.288	.370	2	.067	-2	-10	-10	-1	-1.4
1979 *Cin-N★	14	8	.636	35	32	6	1	0	205²	202	13	79	73	12.4	3.50	107	.263	.333	9	.129	-1	5	5	1	0.5
1980 Cin-N	10	12	.455	34	29	4	2	0	169¹	207	9	68	59	14.7	4.62	77	.303	.367	5	.091	-3	-19	-20	-1	-2.5
1981 Cin-N	4	7	.364	20	13	1	1	0	78	102	9	30	22	15.3	6.12	58	.325	.386	0	.000	-2	-23	-22	0	-3.0
1982 Hou-N	6	6	.500	41	8	0	0	0	115	107	3	54	51	12.9	2.90	115	.252	.342	6	.250	2	9	5	-1	0.7
1983 Hou-N	5	7	.417	38	17	2	0	1	138	142	10	56	53	13.0	4.43	77	.273	.346	3	.086	-2	-12	-16	1	-1.4
1984 Hou-N	7	5	.583	39	18	2	1	3	132	132	3	55	86	12.8	4.02	83	.261	.334	4	.129	-1	-6	-10	-0	-1.0
1985 KC-A	1	1	.500	21	0	0	0	1	40²	49	2	29	26	17.3	5.09	82	.304	.411	0	—	0	-4	-4	0	-0.2
1986 SF-N	10	13	.435	37	31	4	1	0	204¹	179	17	70	86	11.2	3.57	99	.240	.310	14	.230	6	3	-1	1	0.5
1987 *SF-N	13	10	.565	39	26	2	1	0	171	184	16	63	79	13.1	3.68	104	.283	.348	3	.060	-2	8	3	4	0.5
1988 SF-N	7	7	.500	19	19	1	0	0	114¹	99	5	47	70	11.6	3.62	90	.234	.312	8	.242	3	-2	-5	3	0.1
1989 *SF-N	10	10	.500	45	18	0	0	6	150¹	143	3	65	78	12.9	3.17	106	.255	.340	3	.073	-1	5	3	-1	0.3
1990 SF-N	6	4	.600	13	12	1	0	0	77²	75	9	39	39	13.2	3.94	92	.259	.347	1	.043	-1	-1	-3	-1	-0.5
1991 SF-N	1	5	.167	18	5	0	0	0	47¹	61	4	24	30	16.5	7.23	50	.314	.395	2	.222	-1	-19	-19	-0	-2.1
Total 14	98	103	.488	415	243	26	9	12	1739²	1786	99	725	783	13.1	4.02	88	.270	.345	60	.125	-4	-66	-93	8	-9.5

● PETE LADD — Ladd, Peter Linwood b: 7/17/56, Portland, Maine BR/TR, 6'3", 240 lbs. Deb: 8/17/79

YEAR TM/L	W	L	PCT	G	GS	CG	SH	SV	IP	H	HR	BB	SO	RAT	ERA	ERA+	OAV	OOB	BH	AVG	PB	PR	/A	PD	TPI
1979 Hou-N	1	1	.500	10	0	0	0	0	12¹	8	1	8	6	13.1	2.92	120	.178	.327	0	.000	-0	1	1	0	0.1
1982 *Mil-A	1	3	.250	16	0	0	0	3	18	16	5	6	12	11.0	4.00	95	.239	.301	0	—	0	0	-0	-1	-0.1
1983 Mil-A	3	4	.429	44	0	0	0	25	49¹	30	3	16	41	8.6	2.55	146	.172	.246	0	—	0	8	6	-0	1.7
1984 Mil-A	4	9	.308	54	1	0	0	3	91	94	16	38	75	13.2	5.24	73	.266	.339	0	—	0	-13	-14	-2	-2.0
1985 Mil-A	0	0	—	29	0	0	0	2	45²	58	5	10	22	13.8	4.53	92	.315	.357	0	—	0	-2	-2	-0	-0.2
1986 Sea-A	8	6	.571	52	0	0	0	6	70²	69	10	18	53	11.5	3.82	111	.258	.313	0	—	0	3	3	-1	0.5
Total 6	17	23	.425	205	1	0	0	39	287	275	40	96	209	11.9	4.14	96	.252	.318	0	.000	-0	-2	-6	-4	0.2

● DOYLE LADE — Lade, Doyle Marion "Porky" b: 2/17/21, Fairbury, Neb. BR/TR, 5'10", 183 lbs. Deb: 9/18/46

YEAR TM/L	W	L	PCT	G	GS	CG	SH	SV	IP	H	HR	BB	SO	RAT	ERA	ERA+	OAV	OOB	BH	AVG	PB	PR	/A	PD	TPI
1946 Chi-N	0	2	.000	3	2	0	0	0	15¹	15	0	3	8	11.2	4.11	81	.238	.284	1	.200	-0	-1	-1	-0	-0.2
1947 Chi-N	11	10	.524	34	25	7	1	0	187¹	202	15	79	62	13.5	3.94	100	.276	.347	13	.217	2	2	0	2	0.5
1948 Chi-N	5	6	.455	19	12	6	0	0	87¹	99	4	31	29	13.5	4.02	97	.283	.343	5	.156	-1	-1	-1	1	-0.1
1949 Chi-N	4	5	.444	36	13	5	1	1	129²	141	14	58	43	14.0	5.00	81	.274	.350	7	.219	-2	-14	-14	0	-0.7
1950 Chi-N	5	6	.455	34	12	2	0	2	117²	126	14	50	36	13.6	4.74	89	.275	.349	10	.286	3	-8	-7	3	-0.0
Total 5	25	29	.463	126	64	20	2	3	537¹	583	47	221	178	13.6	4.39	91	.275	.346	36	.220	6	-21	-23	7	-0.5

● STEVE LADEW — Ladew, Stephen b: St.Louis, Mo. Deb: 9/27/1889 ♦

YEAR TM/L	W	L	PCT	G	GS	CG	SH	SV	IP	H	HR	BB	SO	RAT	ERA	ERA+	OAV	OOB	BH	AVG	PB	PR	/A	PD	TPI
1889 KC-a	0	0	—	1	0	0	0	0	2	1	0	3	0	18.0	4.50	93	.144	.403	0	.000	-0	-0	-0	0	0.0

● FLIP LAFFERTY — Lafferty, Frank Bernard b: 5/4/1854, Scranton, Pa. d: 2/8/10, Wilmington, Del. TR, Deb: 9/15/1876 ♦

YEAR TM/L	W	L	PCT	G	GS	CG	SH	SV	IP	H	HR	BB	SO	RAT	ERA	ERA+	OAV	OOB	BH	AVG	PB	PR	/A	PD	TPI
1876 Phi-N	0	1	.000	1	1	1	0	0	9	5	0	0	0	5.0	0.00	—	.152	.152	0	.000	-1	2	2	0	0.2

● ED LAFITTE — Lafitte, Edward Francis "Doc" b: 4/7/1886, New Orleans, La. d: 4/12/71, Jenkintown, Pa. BR/TR, 6'2", 188 lbs. Deb: 4/16/09

YEAR TM/L	W	L	PCT	G	GS	CG	SH	SV	IP	H	HR	BB	SO	RAT	ERA	ERA+	OAV	OOB	BH	AVG	PB	PR	/A	PD	TPI
1909 Det-A	0	1	.000	3	1	1	0	1	14	22	2	2	11	16.1	3.86	65	.344	.373	1	.250	0	-2	-2	0	-0.2
1911 Det-A	11	8	.579	29	20	15	0	1	172¹	205	2	52	63	13.7	3.92	88	.302	.356	11	.157	-2	-11	-9	-2	-1.3
1912 Det-A	0	0	—	1	0	0	0	0	1²	2	0	2	0	21.6	16.20	20	.333	.500	0	—	0	-2	-2	-0	0.0
1914 Bro-F	18	15	.545	42	33	23	0	2	290²	260	7	127	137	12.5	2.63	109	.248	.338	26	.257	3	8	8	3	1.5
1915 Bro-F	6	9	.400	17	16	7	0	0	117²	134	5	57	34	14.1	3.98	88	.288	.371	14	.264	2	-16	-16	-2	-1.9
Buf-F	2	2	.500	14	5	1	1	1	50¹	53	1	22	17	13.8	3.40	82	.286	.368	2	.118	-1	-4	-3	-0	-0.4
Yr	8	11	.421	31	21	8	1	1	168	179	7	79	51	13.9	3.80	72	.287	.369	16	.229	1	-20	-20	-2	-2.3
Total 5	37	35	.514	106	75	47	1	5	646²	668	18	262	262	13.3	3.34	89	.276	.353	54	.220	1	-27	-25	-0	-2.3

● ED LAGGER — Lagger, Edwin Joseph b: 7/14/12, Joliet, Ill. d: 11/10/81, Joliet, Ill. BR/TR, 6'3", 200 lbs. Deb: 6/15/34

YEAR TM/L	W	L	PCT	G	GS	CG	SH	SV	IP	H	HR	BB	SO	RAT	ERA	ERA+	OAV	OOB	BH	AVG	PB	PR	/A	PD	TPI
1934 Phi-A	0	0	—	8	0	0	0	0	18	27	1	14	2	21.0	11.00	40	.342	.447	0	.000	-1	-13	-13	1	0.0

● LERRIN LaGROW — LaGrow, Lerrin Harris b: 7/8/48, Phoenix, Ariz. BR/TR, 6'5", 220 lbs. Deb: 7/28/70

YEAR TM/L	W	L	PCT	G	GS	CG	SH	SV	IP	H	HR	BB	SO	RAT	ERA	ERA+	OAV	OOB	BH	AVG	PB	PR	/A	PD	TPI
1970 Det-A	0	1	.000	10	0	0	0	0	12¹	16	2	6	7	16.1	7.30	51	.308	.379	0	.000	-0	-5	-5	-0	-0.4
1972 *Det-A	1	1	.000	16	0	0	0	0	27¹	22	0	6	9	9.2	1.32	239	.222	.267	0	—	0	5	6	-0	0.3
1973 Det-A	1	5	.167	21	3	0	0	3	54	54	8	23	33	13.0	4.33	94	.263	.341	0	—	0	-3	-1	1	-0.2
1974 Det-A	8	19	.296	37	34	11	0	0	216¹	245	21	80	85	13.6	4.66	82	.287	.350	0	—	0	-25	-21	3	-2.2
1975 Det-A	7	14	.333	32	26	7	2	0	164¹	183	15	66	75	13.7	4.38	92	.280	.348	0	—	0	-11	-7	-2	-1.1
1976 StL-N	0	1	.000	8	2	1	0	0	24¹	21	0	7	10	10.7	1.48	239	.241	.305	0	—	-1	5	6	0	0.2
1977 Chi-A	7	3	.700	66	0	0	0	25	98²	81	10	35	63	10.7	2.46	166	.230	.302	0	—	0	17	18	1	2.7
1978 Chi-A	6	5	.545	52	0	0	0	16	88	85	9	38	41	12.9	4.40	86	.260	.342	0	—	0	-6	-6	2	-0.8
1979 Chi-A	0	3	.000	11	2	0	0	1	17²	27	2	16	9	22.4	9.17	46	.346	.463	0	—	0	-10	-10	-0	-1.5
LA-N	5	1	.833	31	0	0	0	4	37	38	2	18	21	13.6	3.41	107	.270	.352	1	.333	0	1	1	-0	0.1
1980 Phi-N	0	2	.000	25	0	0	0	3	39	42	5	17	21	13.6	4.15	91	.276	.349	1	.250	0	-2	-2	-0	-0.1
Total 10	34	55	.382	309	67	19	2	54	779	814	74	312	375	13.1	4.11	94	.271	.342	2	.154	-0	-33	-21	2	-2.9

● JEFF LAHTI — Lahti, Jeffrey Allen b: 10/8/56, Oregon City, Ore. BR/TR, 6', 180 lbs. Deb: 6/27/82

YEAR TM/L	W	L	PCT	G	GS	CG	SH	SV	IP	H	HR	BB	SO	RAT	ERA	ERA+	OAV	OOB	BH	AVG	PB	PR	/A	PD	TPI
1982 *StL-N	5	4	.556	59	0	0	0	0	56²	52	3	21	22	12.1	3.81	95	.245	.318	1	.077	-1	-1	-1	2	-0.2
1983 StL-N	3	3	.500	53	0	0	0	0	74	64	2	29	26	11.4	3.16	114	.240	.316	0	.000	-1	4	4	1	0.3
1984 StL-N	4	2	.667	63	0	0	0	0	84²	69	6	34	45	11.2	3.72	93	.225	.306	1	.167	-0	-1	-2	0	-0.1
1985 *StL-N	5	2	.714	52	0	0	0	19	68¹	63	3	26	41	11.7	1.84	192	.251	.321	0	.000	-1	13	13	-0	2.0

YEAR	TM/L	W	L	PCT	G	GS	CG	SH	SV	IP	H	HR	BB	SO	RAT	ERA	ERA+	OAV	OOB	BH	AVG	PB	PR	/A	PD	TPI
1986	StL-N	0	0	—	4	0	0	0	0	2¹	3	0	1	3	15.4	0.00	—	.333	.400	0	—	0	1	1	0	0.0
Total	5	17	11	.607	205	1	0	0	20	286	252	14	111	137	11.6	3.12	114	.240	.316	2	.053	-3	15	14	2	2.0

● EDDIE LAKE Lake, Edward Erving "Sparky" b: 3/18/16, Antioch, Cal. BR/TR, 5'7", 160 lbs. Deb: 9/26/39 ♦

YEAR	TM/L	W	L	PCT	G	GS	CG	SH	SV	IP	H	HR	BB	SO	RAT	ERA	ERA+	OAV	OOB	BH	AVG	PB	PR	/A	PD	TPI
1944	Bos-A	0	0	—	6	0	0	0	0	19¹	20	2	11	7	15.8	4.19	81	.278	.395	26	.206	1	-2	-2	0	0.1

● JOE LAKE Lake, Joseph Henry b: 1/6/1881, Brooklyn, N.Y. d: 6/30/50, Brooklyn, N.Y. BR/TR, 6', 185 lbs. Deb: 4/21/08

YEAR	TM/L	W	L	PCT	G	GS	CG	SH	SV	IP	H	HR	BB	SO	RAT	ERA	ERA+	OAV	OOB	BH	AVG	PB	PR	/A	PD	TPI
1908	NY-A	9	22	.290	38	27	19	2	0	269¹	252	6	77	118	11.2	3.17	78	.242	.298	21	.188	0	-23	-21	-4	-2.8
1909	NY-A	14	11	.560	31	26	17	3	1	215¹	180	2	59	117	10.2	1.88	135	.225	.283	14	.173	1	14	16	5	2.7
1910	StL-A	11	17	.393	35	29	24	1	2	261¹	243	2	77	141	11.1	2.20	112	.248	.304	21	.231	2	9	8	1	1.2
1911	StL-A	10	15	.400	30	25	14	2	0	215¹	245	3	40	69	12.1	3.30	102	.282	.316	21	.262	2	1	2	6	1.0
1912	StL-A	1	7	.125	11	6	4	0	0	57	70	0	16	28	13.7	4.42	75	.314	.363	3	.150	-1	-7	-7	2	-0.8
	Det-A	9	11	.450	26	14	11	0	1	162²	190	3	39	86	12.8	3.10	105	.296	.340	9	.145	-3	4	3	0	0.1
	Yr	10	18	.357	37	20	15	0	1	219²	260	3	55	114	13.0	3.44	95	.301	.345	12	.146	-5	-3	-4	2	-0.7
1913	Det-A	8	7	.533	28	12	6	0	1	137	149	3	24	35	11.4	3.28	89	.278	.309	12	.267	4	-5	-6	3	0.2
Total	6	62	90	.408	199	139	95	8	5	1318	1329	19	332	594	11.5	2.85	99	.261	.309	101	.206	4	-7	-5	12	1.6

● AL LAKEMAN Lakeman, Albert Wesley "Moose" b: 12/31/18, Cincinnati, Ohio d: 5/25/76, Spartanburg, S.C. BR/TR, 6'2", 195 lbs. Deb: 4/19/42 C♦

YEAR	TM/L	W	L	PCT	G	GS	CG	SH	SV	IP	H	HR	BB	SO	RAT	ERA	ERA+	OAV	OOB	BH	AVG	PB	PR	/A	PD	TPI
1948	Phi-N	0	0	—	1	0	0	0	0	0²	1	0	1	0	13.5	13.50	29	.333	.333	11	.162	0	-1	-1	-0	0.0

● JACK LAMABE Lamabe, John Alexander b: 10/3/36, Farmingdale, N.Y. BR/TR, 6'1", 198 lbs. Deb: 4/17/62

YEAR	TM/L	W	L	PCT	G	GS	CG	SH	SV	IP	H	HR	BB	SO	RAT	ERA	ERA+	OAV	OOB	BH	AVG	PB	PR	/A	PD	TPI
1962	Pit-N	3	1	.750	46	0	0	0	2	78	74	0	40	56	12.7	2.88	134	.238	.329	0	.000	-1	9	9	1	0.5
1963	Bos-A	7	4	.636	65	0	0	0	2	151¹	139	8	46	93	11.2	3.15	120	.247	.308	3	.094	-1	8	11	1	0.8
1964	Bos-A	9	13	.409	39	25	3	0	1	177¹	235	25	57	109	14.9	5.89	65	.318	.369	6	.115	-1	-45	-40	-0	-4.6
1965	Bos-A	0	3	.000	14	0	0	0	0	25¹	34	5	14	17	18.1	8.17	46	.340	.436	0	.000	-0	-13	-13	-0	-1.4
	Hou-N	0	2	.000	3	2	0	0	0	12²	17	3	3	6	14.2	4.26	79	.315	.351	1	.250	-0	-1	-1	-0	-0.2
1966	Chi-A	7	9	.438	34	17	3	2	0	121¹	116	9	35	67	11.3	3.93	81	.251	.305	2	.057	-2	-7	-10	-0	-1.5
1967	Chi-A	1	0	1.000	3	0	0	0	0	5	7	0	1	3	14.4	1.80	172	.318	.348	0	—	0	1	1	0	0.1
	NY-N	0	3	.000	16	2	0	0	1	31²	24	4	8	23	9.1	3.98	85	.200	.250	0	.000	-0	-2	-2	-0	-0.2
	*StL-N	3	4	.429	23	1	1	1	4	47²	43	2	10	30	10.0	2.83	116	.244	.285	2	.200	-0	3	2	0	0.4
	Yr	3	7	.300	39	3	1	1	5	79¹	67	6	18	53	9.6	3.29	101	.226	.270	2	.133	-0	1	0	0	0.2
1968	Chi-N	3	2	.600	42	0	0	0	1	61¹	68	7	24	30	13.6	4.26	74	.289	.358	1	.200	-0	-9	-7	-1	-0.6
Total	7	33	41	.446	285	49	7	3	15	711²	753	67	238	434	12.7	4.24	85	.272	.333	15	.096	-6	-55	-51	-0	-6.7

● AL LaMACCHIA LaMacchia, Alfred Anthony b: 7/22/21, St.Louis, Mo. BR/TR, 5'10.5", 190 lbs. Deb: 9/27/43

YEAR	TM/L	W	L	PCT	G	GS	CG	SH	SV	IP	H	HR	BB	SO	RAT	ERA	ERA+	OAV	OOB	BH	AVG	PB	PR	/A	PD	TPI
1943	StL-A	0	1	.000	1	1	0	0	0	4	9	0	2	2	24.8	11.25	30	.450	.500	0	.000	-0	-4	-4	-0	-0.6
1945	StL-A	2	0	1.000	5	0	0	0	0	9	6	0	3	2	9.0	2.00	176	.207	.281	0	.000	-0	1	2	0	0.3
1946	StL-A	0	0	—	8	0	0	0	0	15	17	2	7	3	14.4	6.00	62	.279	.353	0	.000	-0	-4	-4	-0	0.0
	Was-A	0	1	.000	2	0	0	0	0	2²	6	1	2	0	27.0	16.88	20	.462	.533	0	—	0	-4	-4	-0	-1.1
	Yr	0	1	.000	10	0	0	0	0	17²	23	3	9	3	16.3	7.64	48	.311	.386	0	.000	-0	-8	-8	-0	-1.1
Total	3	2	2	.500	16	1	0	0	0	30²	38	3	14	7	15.3	6.46	55	.309	.380	0	.000	-1	-10	-10	-1	-1.4

● FRANK LAMANNA Lamanna, Frank "Hank" b: 8/22/19, Watertown, Pa. d: 9/1/80, Syracuse, N.Y. BR/TR, 6'2.5", 195 lbs. Deb: 4/16/40

YEAR	TM/L	W	L	PCT	G	GS	CG	SH	SV	IP	H	HR	BB	SO	RAT	ERA	ERA+	OAV	OOB	BH	AVG	PB	PR	/A	PD	TPI
1940	Bos-N	1	0	1.000	5	1	0	0	0	13¹	13	1	8	3	14.2	4.73	79	.271	.375	1	.200	-0	-1	-1	0	-0.1
1941	Bos-N	5	4	.556	35	4	0	0	1	72²	77	5	56	23	16.6	5.33	67	.285	.410	9	.281	1	-14	-14	1	-1.4
1942	Bos-N	0	1	.000	5	0	0	0	0	6²	5	1	3	2	10.8	5.40	62	.208	.296	0	.000	-0	-2	-2	-0	-0.3
Total	3	6	5	.545	45	5	0	0	1	92²	95	7	67	28	15.8	5.24	68	.278	.398	10	.256	1	-17	-17	1	-1.8

● FRANK LAMANSKE Lamanske, Frank James "Lefty" b: 9/30/06, Oglesby, Ill. d: 8/4/71, Olney, Ill. BL/TL, 5'11", 170 lbs. Deb: 4/27/35

YEAR	TM/L	W	L	PCT	G	GS	CG	SH	SV	IP	H	HR	BB	SO	RAT	ERA	ERA+	OAV	OOB	BH	AVG	PB	PR	/A	PD	TPI
1935	Bro-N	0	0	—	2	0	0	0	0	3²	5	0	1	1	14.7	7.36	54	.313	.353	0	.000	-0	-1	-1	0	0.0

● WAYNE LaMASTER LaMaster, Noble Wayne b: 2/13/07, Speed, Ind. d: 8/4/89, New Albany, Ind. BL/TL, 5'8", 170 lbs. Deb: 4/19/37

YEAR	TM/L	W	L	PCT	G	GS	CG	SH	SV	IP	H	HR	BB	SO	RAT	ERA	ERA+	OAV	OOB	BH	AVG	PB	PR	/A	PD	TPI
1937	Phi-N	15	19	.441	50	30	10	1	4	220¹	255	24	82	135	13.8	5.31	82	.290	.352	15	.190	-2	-34	-24	-4	-3.9
1938	Phi-N	4	7	.364	18	12	1	0	0	63²	80	8	31	35	16.1	7.77	50	.301	.380	9	.409	4	-28	-27	1	-3.4
	Bro-N	0	1	.000	3	0	0	0	0	11¹	17	0	3	3	15.9	4.76	82	.340	.377	1	.167	-0	-1	-1	-0	-0.1
	Yr	4	8	.333	21	12	1	0	0	75	97	8	34	38	15.7	7.32	53	.304	.371	10	.357	4	-29	-29	1	-3.5
Total	2	19	27	.413	71	42	11	2	4	295¹	352	32	116	173	14.4	5.82	72	.295	.360	25	.234	1	-64	-53	-4	-7.4

● JOHN LAMB Lamb, John Andrew b: 7/20/46, Sharon, Conn. BR/TR, 6'3", 180 lbs. Deb: 8/12/70

YEAR	TM/L	W	L	PCT	G	GS	CG	SH	SV	IP	H	HR	BB	SO	RAT	ERA	ERA+	OAV	OOB	BH	AVG	PB	PR	/A	PD	TPI
1970	Pit-N	0	1	.000	23	0	0	0	3	32¹	23	2	13	24	10.6	2.78	140	.209	.304	0	.000	-0	5	4	-1	0.1
1971	Pit-N	0	0	—	2	0	0	0	0	4¹	3	0	1	1	8.3	0.00	—	.188	.235	0	.000	-0	2	2	0	0.0
1973	Pit-N	0	1	.000	22	0	0	0	2	29²	37	3	10	11	14.3	6.07	58	.308	.362	0	.000	-0	-8	-8	-0	-0.4
Total	3	0	2	.000	47	0	0	0	5	66¹	63	5	24	36	12.1	4.07	91	.256	.327	0	.000	-1	-2	-3	-1	-0.3

● RAY LAMB Lamb, Raymond Richard b: 12/28/44, Glendale, Cal. BR/TR, 6'1", 175 lbs. Deb: 8/1/69

YEAR	TM/L	W	L	PCT	G	GS	CG	SH	SV	IP	H	HR	BB	SO	RAT	ERA	ERA+	OAV	OOB	BH	AVG	PB	PR	/A	PD	TPI
1969	LA-N	0	1	.000	10	0	0	0	0	15	12	2	7	11	11.4	1.80	185	.235	.328	0	.000	-0	3	3	0	0.2
1970	LA-N	6	1	.857	35	0	0	0	0	57	59	4	27	32	14.2	3.79	101	.277	.369	0	.000	-0	2	0	-1	-0.1
1971	Cle-A	6	12	.333	43	21	3	1	1	158¹	147	11	69	91	12.3	3.35	114	.247	.326	4	.093	-2	2	8	-2	0.5
1972	Cle-A	5	6	.455	34	9	0	0	1	107²	101	5	29	64	11.0	3.09	104	.248	.299	0	.000	-1	-0	1	-1	-0.1
1973	Cle-A	3	3	.500	32	1	0	0	2	86	98	7	42	60	14.9	4.60	85	.291	.373	—	—	0	-8	-7	-0	-0.5
Total	5	20	23	.465	154	31	3	1	4	424	417	29	174	258	12.7	3.54	104	.260	.335	4	.058	-4	-1	7	-4	-0.3

● CLAYTON LAMBERT Lambert, Clayton Patrick b: 3/26/17, Summitt, Ill. d: 4/3/81, Ogden, Utah BR/TR, 6'2", 185 lbs. Deb: 4/22/46

YEAR	TM/L	W	L	PCT	G	GS	CG	SH	SV	IP	H	HR	BB	SO	RAT	ERA	ERA+	OAV	OOB	BH	AVG	PB	PR	/A	PD	TPI
1946	Cin-N	2	2	.500	23	4	2	0	1	52²	48	3	20	20	11.8	4.27	78	.251	.325	2	.154	-1	-5	-5	-1	-0.6
1947	Cin-N	0	0	—	3	0	0	0	0	5²	12	3	6	1	28.6	15.88	26	.444	.545	0	—	0	-7	-7	-0	0.0
Total	2	2	2	.500	26	4	2	0	1	58¹	60	6	26	21	13.4	5.40	63	.275	.355	2	.143	-1	-12	-13	-1	-0.6

● GENE LAMBERT Lambert, Eugene Marion b: 4/26/21, Crenshaw, Miss. BR/TR, 5'11", 175 lbs. Deb: 9/14/41

YEAR	TM/L	W	L	PCT	G	GS	CG	SH	SV	IP	H	HR	BB	SO	RAT	ERA	ERA+	OAV	OOB	BH	AVG	PB	PR	/A	PD	TPI
1941	Phi-N	0	1	.000	2	1	0	0	0	9	4	0	3	0	13.0	2.00	185	.297	.333	0	.000	-0	2	2	-0	0.1
1942	Phi-N	0	0	—	1	0	0	0	0	1	3	0	0	1	27.0	9.00	37	.500	.500	0	—	0	-1	-1	0	0.0
Total	2	0	1	.000	3	1	0	0	0	10	14	0	2	4	14.4	2.70	138	.326	.356	0	.000	-0	1	1	0	0.1

● OTIS LAMBETH Lambeth, Otis Samuel b: 5/13/1890, Berlin, Kan. d: 6/5/76, Moran, Kan. BR/TR, 6', 175 lbs. Deb: 7/16/16

YEAR	TM/L	W	L	PCT	G	GS	CG	SH	SV	IP	H	HR	BB	SO	RAT	ERA	ERA+	OAV	OOB	BH	AVG	PB	PR	/A	PD	TPI
1916	Cle-A	4	3	.571	15	5	3	0	1	74	69	1	38	28	13.4	2.92	103	.256	.354	3	.111	-1	-1	1	-2	-0.3
1917	Cle-A	7	6	.538	26	10	2	0	2	97¹	97	2	30	27	12.8	3.14	90	.274	.349	6	.188	-0	-5	-3	-1	-0.6
1918	Cle-A	0	0	—	2	0	0	0	0	7	10	0	6	3	20.6	6.43	47	.370	.485	1	1.000	0	-3	-3	-0	0.0
Total	3	11	9	.550	43	15	5	0	3	178¹	176	3	74	58	13.3	3.18	92	.270	.357	10	.167	-1	-9	-5	-3	-0.9

● FRED LAMLINE Lamline, Frederick Arthur "Dutch" (b: Frederick Arthur Lamlein)
b: 8/14/1887, Port Huron, Mich. d: 9/20/70, Port Huron, Mich. BR/TR, 5'11", 171 lbs. Deb: 9/18/12

YEAR	TM/L	W	L	PCT	G	GS	CG	SH	SV	IP	H	HR	BB	SO	RAT	ERA	ERA+	OAV	OOB	BH	AVG	PB	PR	/A	PD	TPI
1912	Chi-A	0	0	—	1	0	0	0	0	2	7	0	2	0	40.5	31.50	10	.583	.643	0	—	0	-6	-6	0	0.0
1915	StL-N	0	0	—	4	0	0	0	0	19	21	0	3	11	12.3	1.42	196	.300	.347	1	.125	-0	3	3	0	0.0
Total	2	0	0	—	5	0	0	0	0	21	28	0	5	11	15.0	4.29	66	.341	.393	1	.125	-0	-3	-3	0	0.0

● DENNIS LAMP Lamp, Dennis Patrick b: 9/23/52, Los Angeles, Cal. BR/TR, 6'3", 210 lbs. Deb: 8/21/77

YEAR	TM/L	W	L	PCT	G	GS	CG	SH	SV	IP	H	HR	BB	SO	RAT	ERA	ERA+	OAV	OOB	BH	AVG	PB	PR	/A	PD	TPI
1977	Chi-N	0	2	.000	11	3	0	0	0	30	43	3	8	12	15.9	6.30	70	.344	.393	3	.375	1	-8	-6	0	-0.3

YEAR TM/L	W	L	PCT	G	GS	CG	SH	SV	IP	H	HR	BB	SO	RAT	ERA	ERA+	OAV	OOB	BH	AVG	PB	PR	/A	PD	TPI
1978 Chi-N	7	15	.318	37	36	6	3	0	223²	221	16	56	73	11.3	3.30	122	.258	.307	15	.205	0	7	18	3	2.1
1979 Chi-N	11	10	.524	38	32	6	1	0	200¹	223	14	46	86	12.3	3.50	117	.287	.331	9	.155	-1	5	14	4	1.6
1980 Chi-N	10	14	.417	41	37	2	1	0	202²	259	16	82	83	15.2	5.20	75	.317	.380	6	.098	-3	-36	-29	2	-3.2
1981 Chi-A	7	6	.538	27	10	3	0	0	127	103	4	43	71	10.4	2.41	148	.222	.289	0	—	0	18	16	1	1.7
1982 Chi-A	11	8	.579	44	27	3	2	5	189²	206	9	59	78	12.9	3.99	101	.279	.337	0	—	0	2	1	2	0.2
1983 *Chi-A	7	7	.500	49	5	1	0	15	116¹	123	6	29	44	12.1	3.71	113	.275	.325	0	—	0	5	6	0	0.9
1984 Tor-A	8	8	.500	56	4	0	0	9	85	97	9	38	45	14.4	4.55	90	.285	.359	0	—	0	-5	-4	1	-0.7
1985 *Tor-A	11	0	1.000	53	1	0	0	2	105²	96	7	27	68	10.5	3.32	127	.247	.296	0	—	0	10	10	2	1.2
1986 Tor-A	2	6	.250	40	2	0	0	2	73	93	5	23	30	14.3	5.05	83	.309	.358	0	—	0	-7	-7	0	-0.7
1987 Oak-A	1	3	.250	36	5	0	0	0	56²	76	5	22	36	15.6	5.08	81	.326	.387	0	—	0	-4	-6	-0	-0.1
1988 Bos-A	7	6	.538	46	0	0	0	0	82²	92	3	19	49	12.3	3.48	118	.284	.328	0	—	0	4	6	1	1.0
1989 Bos-A	4	2	.667	42	0	0	0	2	112¹	96	4	27	61	9.9	2.32	176	.235	.283	0	—	0	19	22	2	1.2
1990 *Bos-A	3	5	.375	47	1	0	0	0	105²	114	10	30	49	12.5	4.68	87	.279	.333	0	—	0	-9	-7	-0	-0.5
1991 Bos-A	6	3	.667	51	0	0	0	0	92	100	8	31	57	13.1	4.70	92	.275	.337	0	—	0	-6	-4	-0	-0.4
1992 Pit-N	1	1	.500	21	0	0	0	0	28	33	3	9	15	14.1	5.14	67	.292	.355	0	.000	-0	-5	-5	0	-0.4
Total 16	96	96	.500	639	163	21	7	35	1830²	1975	122	549	857	12.6	3.93	103	.278	.333	33	.164	-3	-11	26	18	3.6

● **HENRY LAMPE**   Lampe, Henry Joseph   b: 9/19/1872, Boston, Mass.   d: 9/16/36, Dorchester, Mass.   BR/TL, 5'11.5", 175 lbs.   Deb: 5/14/1894

YEAR TM/L	W	L	PCT	G	GS	CG	SH	SV	IP	H	HR	BB	SO	RAT	ERA	ERA+	OAV	OOB	BH	AVG	PB	PR	/A	PD	TPI
1894 Bos-N	0	1	.000	2	1	0	0	0	5¹	17	5	7	1	40.5	11.81	48	.525	.610	0	.000	-0	-4	-4	0	-0.4
1895 Phi-N	0	2	.000	7	3	2	0	0	44	68	3	33	18	20.9	7.57	63	.348	.444	2	.125	-1	-14	-14	-0	-0.5
Total 2	0	3	.000	9	4	2	0	0	49¹	85	8	40	19	23.0	8.03	61	.373	.469	2	.111	-1	-17	-17	0	-0.9

● **DICK LANAHAN**   Lanahan, Richard Anthony   b: 9/27/11, Washington, D.C.   d: 3/12/75, Rochester, Minn.   BL/TL, 6', 186 lbs.   Deb: 9/15/35

YEAR TM/L	W	L	PCT	G	GS	CG	SH	SV	IP	H	HR	BB	SO	RAT	ERA	ERA+	OAV	OOB	BH	AVG	PB	PR	/A	PD	TPI
1935 Was-A	0	3	.000	3	3	0	0	0	20²	27	2	17	10	20.0	5.66	76	.314	.438	1	.167	-0	-3	-3	-0	-0.4
1937 Was-A	0	1	.000	6	2	0	0	0	11¹	16	2	13	2	23.8	12.71	35	.320	.469	0	.000	0	-10	-10	0	-0.6
1940 Pit-N	6	8	.429	40	8	4	0	2	108	121	8	42	45	13.7	4.25	90	.279	.345	4	.118	-2	-5	-5	-0	-0.8
1941 Pit-N	0	1	.000	7	0	0	0	0	12	13	1	3	5	13.5	5.25	69	.283	.353	0	.000	-0	-2	-2	-0	-0.2
Total 4	6	13	.316	56	13	4	0	2	152	177	13	75	62	15.3	5.15	76	.288	.371	5	.119	-2	-20	-21	0	-2.0

● **LES LANCASTER**   Lancaster, Lester Wayne   b: 4/21/62, Dallas, Tex.   BR/TR, 6'2", 205 lbs.   Deb: 4/7/87

YEAR TM/L	W	L	PCT	G	GS	CG	SH	SV	IP	H	HR	BB	SO	RAT	ERA	ERA+	OAV	OOB	BH	AVG	PB	PR	/A	PD	TPI
1987 Chi-N	8	3	.727	27	18	0	0	0	132¹	138	14	51	78	12.9	4.90	87	.268	.335	4	.082	-2	-12	-9	-1	-1.0
1988 Chi-N	4	6	.400	44	3	1	0	5	85²	89	4	34	36	13.0	3.78	95	.273	.343	1	.050	-1	-3	-2	1	-0.3
1989 *Chi-N	4	2	.667	42	0	0	0	8	72²	60	7	15	56	9.3	1.36	276	.226	.267	2	.182	0	17	**19**	-1	2.1
1990 Chi-N	9	5	.643	55	6	1	1	6	109	121	11	40	65	13.4	4.62	88	.283	.346	1	.050	-1	-10	-7	-1	-0.8
1991 Chi-N	9	7	.563	64	11	0	0	3	156	150	13	49	102	11.7	3.52	110	.256	.317	5	.179	0	3	6	-1	0.5
1992 Det-A	3	4	.429	41	1	0	0	0	86²	101	11	51	35	16.1	6.33	62	.294	.389	0	—	0	-23	-23	-1	-1.7
1993 StL-N	4	1	.800	50	0	0	0	0	61¹	56	5	21	36	11.4	2.93	135	.242	.308	0	—	-0	8	7	-1	0.4
Total 7	41	28	.594	323	39	3	1	22	703²	715	60	261	408	12.6	4.05	98	.265	.333	13	.098	-4	-21	-7	-2	-0.8

● **GARY LANCE**   Lance, Gary Dean   b: 9/21/48, Greenville, S.C.   BB/TR, 6'3", 195 lbs.   Deb: 9/28/77

YEAR TM/L	W	L	PCT	G	GS	CG	SH	SV	IP	H	HR	BB	SO	RAT	ERA	ERA+	OAV	OOB	BH	AVG	PB	PR	/A	PD	TPI
1977 KC-A	0	1	.000	1	0	0	0	0	2	2	0	2	0	18.0	4.50	90	.286	.444	0	—	0	-0	-0	-0	-0.1

● **DOC LANDIS**   Landis, Samuel H.   b: 8/16/1854, Philadelphia, Pa.   BR , 5'11", 172 lbs.   Deb: 5/2/1882

YEAR TM/L	W	L	PCT	G	GS	CG	SH	SV	IP	H	HR	BB	SO	RAT	ERA	ERA+	OAV	OOB	BH	AVG	PB	PR	/A	PD	TPI
1882 Phi-a	1	1	.500	2	2	2	0	0	17	16	1	0	13	9.0	3.18	94	.232	.243	2	.167	-0	-1	-0	-0	-0.1
Bal-a	11	27	.289	42	39	35	0	0	341	409	7	46	62	12.0	3.33	83	.278	.300	29	.166	-6	-24	-22	-2	-2.6
Yr	12	28	.300	44	41	37	0	0	358	425	8	47	75	11.9	3.32	83	.276	.298	31	.166	-7	-25	-22	-3	-2.7

● **BILL LANDIS**   Landis, William Henry   b: 10/8/42, Hanford, Cal.   BL/TL, 6'2", 178 lbs.   Deb: 9/28/63

YEAR TM/L	W	L	PCT	G	GS	CG	SH	SV	IP	H	HR	BB	SO	RAT	ERA	ERA+	OAV	OOB	BH	AVG	PB	PR	/A	PD	TPI
1963 KC-A	0	0	—	1	0	0	0	0	1²	1	0	1	3	5.4	0.00	—	.000	.167	0	—	0	1	1	-0	0.0
1967 Bos-A	1	0	1.000	18	1	0	0	0	25²	24	6	11	23	12.3	5.26	66	.253	.330	0	.000	-0	-6	-5	-1	-0.3
1968 Bos-A	3	3	.500	38	1	0	0	3	60	48	4	30	59	12.0	3.15	100	.223	.324	0	.000	-1	-1	0	-1	-0.2
1969 Bos-A	5	5	.500	45	5	0	0	1	82¹	82	7	49	50	14.6	5.25	72	.269	.375	0	.000	-0	-15	-13	-0	-1.5
Total 4	9	8	.529	102	7	0	0	4	169²	154	17	91	135	13.3	4.46	79	.248	.349	0	.000	-1	-21	-17	-2	-2.0

● **LARRY LANDRETH**   Landreth, Larry Robert   b: 3/11/55, Stratford, Ont., Can   BR/TR, 6'1", 175 lbs.   Deb: 9/16/76

YEAR TM/L	W	L	PCT	G	GS	CG	SH	SV	IP	H	HR	BB	SO	RAT	ERA	ERA+	OAV	OOB	BH	AVG	PB	PR	/A	PD	TPI
1976 Mon-N	1	2	.333	3	3	0	0	0	11	13	1	10	7	18.8	4.09	91	.310	.442	0	.000	-0	-1	-1	-0	-0.2
1977 Mon-N	0	2	.000	4	1	0	0	0	9¹	16	0	8	5	23.1	9.64	39	.381	.480	0	.000	-0	-6	-6	-0	-1.1
Total 2	1	4	.200	7	4	0	0	0	20¹	29	1	18	12	20.8	6.64	57	.345	.461	0	.000	-1	-7	-6	-1	-1.3

● **JOE LANDRUM**   Landrum, Joseph Butler   b: 12/13/28, Columbia, S.C.   BR/TR, 5'11", 180 lbs.   Deb: 7/13/50   F

YEAR TM/L	W	L	PCT	G	GS	CG	SH	SV	IP	H	HR	BB	SO	RAT	ERA	ERA+	OAV	OOB	BH	AVG	PB	PR	/A	PD	TPI
1950 Bro-N	0	0	—	7	0	0	0	1	6²	12	2	1	5	18.9	8.10	51	.414	.452	0	—	0	-3	-3	0	-0.1
1952 Bro-N	1	3	.250	9	5	2	0	0	38	46	3	10	17	13.5	5.21	70	.301	.348	1	.125	-0	-6	-7	0	-0.7
Total 2	1	3	.250	16	5	2	0	1	44²	58	5	11	22	14.3	5.64	66	.319	.364	1	.125	-0	-9	-10	0	-0.8

● **BILL LANDRUM**   Landrum, Thomas William   b: 8/17/57, Columbia, S.C.   BR/TR, 6'2", 200 lbs.   Deb: 8/31/86   F

YEAR TM/L	W	L	PCT	G	GS	CG	SH	SV	IP	H	HR	BB	SO	RAT	ERA	ERA+	OAV	OOB	BH	AVG	PB	PR	/A	PD	TPI
1986 Cin-N	0	0	—	10	0	0	0	0	13¹	23	0	4	14	18.2	6.75	57	.390	.429	0	.000	-0	-4	-4	-0	0.0
1987 Cin-N	3	2	.600	44	2	0	0	2	65	68	3	34	42	14.1	4.71	90	.292	.382	1	.200	-0	-5	-3	1	-0.2
1988 Chi-N	1	0	1.000	7	0	0	0	0	12¹	19	1	3	6	16.1	5.84	62	.365	.400	0	.000	-0	-3	-3	-0	-0.3
1989 Pit-N	2	3	.400	56	0	0	0	26	81	60	2	28	51	9.8	1.67	201	.205	.275	0	.000	-0	16	15	-0	2.1
1990 *Pit-N	7	3	.700	54	0	0	0	13	71²	69	4	21	39	11.3	2.13	169	.262	.317	1	.111	-0	13	12	-0	2.0
1991 *Pit-N	4	4	.500	61	0	0	0	17	76¹	76	4	19	45	11.2	3.18	112	.252	.297	0	.000	-0	4	3	-1	0.4
1992 Mon-N	1	1	.500	18	0	0	0	0	20	27	3	9	7	17.1	7.20	48	.325	.404	0	—	0	-8	-8	-0	-0.8
1993 Cin-N	0	2	.000	18	0	0	0	0	21²	18	1	6	14	10.0	3.74	108	.231	.286	0	—	0	1	1	1	0.1
Total 8	18	15	.545	268	2	0	0	58	361¹	360	18	124	218	12.1	3.39	109	.265	.327	2	.080	-1	14	12	-0	3.3

● **JERRY LANE**   Lane, Jerald Hal   b: 2/7/26, Ashland, N.Y.   d: 7/24/88, Chattanooga, Tenn   BR/TR, 6'0.5", 205 lbs.   Deb: 7/7/53

YEAR TM/L	W	L	PCT	G	GS	CG	SH	SV	IP	H	HR	BB	SO	RAT	ERA	ERA+	OAV	OOB	BH	AVG	PB	PR	/A	PD	TPI
1953 Was-A	1	4	.200	20	2	0	0	0	56²	64	3	16	26	12.9	4.92	79	.288	.339	1	.111	0	-6	-6	-0	-0.5
1954 Cin-N	1	0	1.000	3	0	0	0	0	10²	9	0	3	2	10.1	1.69	248	.237	.293	0	.000	-0	3	3	-1	0.2
1955 Cin-N	0	2	.000	8	0	0	0	0	11	11	2	6	5	13.9	4.91	86	.289	.386	0	—	0	-1	-1	-0	-0.1
Total 3	2	6	.250	31	2	0	0	0	78¹	84	5	25	33	12.6	4.48	89	.282	.340	1	.077	-0	-4	-4	-1	-0.4

● **SAM LANFORD**   Lanford, Lewis Grover   b: 1/8/1886, Woodruff, S.C.   d: 9/14/70, Woodruff, S.C.   BR/TR, 5'9", 155 lbs.   Deb: 8/19/07

YEAR TM/L	W	L	PCT	G	GS	CG	SH	SV	IP	H	HR	BB	SO	RAT	ERA	ERA+	OAV	OOB	BH	AVG	PB	PR	/A	PD	TPI
1907 Was-A	0	1	.000	2	1	0	0	0	7	10	1	5	2	23.1	5.14	47	.337	.477	1	.333	0	-2	-2	-0	-0.3

● **WALT LANFRANCONI**   Lanfranconi, Walter Oswald   b: 11/9/16, Barre, Vt.   d: 8/18/86, Barre, Vt.   BR/TR, 5'7.5", 155 lbs.   Deb: 9/12/41

YEAR TM/L	W	L	PCT	G	GS	CG	SH	SV	IP	H	HR	BB	SO	RAT	ERA	ERA+	OAV	OOB	BH	AVG	PB	PR	/A	PD	TPI
1941 Chi-N	0	1	.000	2	1	0	0	0	6	7	0	2	1	13.5	3.00	117	.280	.333	0	.000	-0	0	0	-0	0.0
1947 Bos-N	4	4	.500	36	4	1	0	1	64	65	2	27	18	12.9	2.95	132	.272	.346	0	.000	-1	**8**	**7**	1	0.8
Total 2	4	5	.444	38	5	1	0	1	70	72	2	29	19	13.0	2.96	131	.273	.345	0	.000	-1	8	7	1	0.8

● **MARTY LANG**   Lang, Martin John   b: 9/27/05, Hooper, Neb.   d: 1/13/68, Lakewood, Colo.   BR/TL, 5'11", 160 lbs.   Deb: 7/4/30

YEAR TM/L	W	L	PCT	G	GS	CG	SH	SV	IP	H	HR	BB	SO	RAT	ERA	ERA+	OAV	OOB	BH	AVG	PB	PR	/A	PD	TPI
1930 Pit-N	0	0	—	2	0	0	0	0	1²	9	2	3	2	64.8	54.00	9	.692	.750	0	—	0	-9	-9	-0	0.0

● **CHIP LANG**   Lang, Robert David   b: 8/21/52, Pittsburgh, Pa.   BR/TR, 6'4", 205 lbs.   Deb: 9/8/75

YEAR TM/L	W	L	PCT	G	GS	CG	SH	SV	IP	H	HR	BB	SO	RAT	ERA	ERA+	OAV	OOB	BH	AVG	PB	PR	/A	PD	TPI
1975 Mon-N	0	0	—	1	1	0	0	0	1²	2	0	3	2	27.0	10.80	35	.333	.556	0	—	0	-1	-1	-0	0.0
1976 Mon-N	1	3	.250	29	2	0	0	0	62¹	56	3	34	30	13.4	4.19	89	.242	.347	1	.167	-0	-5	-4	0	-0.2
Total 2	1	3	.250	30	3	0	0	0	64	58	3	37	32	13.8	4.36	85	.245	.354	1	.167	-0	-6	-5	0	-0.2

YEAR TM/L	W	L	PCT	G	GS	CG	SH	SV	IP	H	HR	BB	SO	RAT	ERA	ERA+	OAV	OOB	BH	AVG	PB	PR	/A	PD	TPI

● FRANK LANGE   Lange, Frank Herman "Seagan"   b: 10/28/1883, Columbia, Wis.   d: 12/26/45, Madison, Wis.   BR/TR, 5'11", 180 lbs.   Deb: 5/16/10

YEAR TM/L	W	L	PCT	G	GS	CG	SH	SV	IP	H	HR	BB	SO	RAT	ERA	ERA+	OAV	OOB	BH	AVG	PB	PR	/A	PD	TPI
1910 Chi-A	9	4	.692	23	15	6	1	0	130²	93	2	54	98	10.7	1.65	145	.204	.301	13	.255	3	13	11	-2	1.2
1911 Chi-A	8	8	.500	29	22	8	1	0	161²	151	3	77	104	12.9	3.23	100	.251	.339	22	.289	8	2	-0	-1	0.7
1912 Chi-A	10	10	.500	31	20	11	2	3	165¹	165	4	68	96	12.9	3.27	98	.270	.347	14	.215	2	1	-1	-1	0.0
1913 Chi-A	1	3	.250	12	3	0	0	0	40²	46	0	20	20	14.8	4.87	60	.295	.379	3	.167	1	-9	-9	1	-0.6
Total 4	28	25	.528	95	60	25	4	3	498¹	455	9	219	318	12.5	2.96	100	.249	.335	52	.248	14	7	1	-2	1.3

● ERV LANGE   Lange, Erwin Henry   b: 8/12/1887, Forest Park, Ill.   d: 4/24/71, Maywood, Ill.   BR/TR, 5'10", 170 lbs.   Deb: 4/19/14

YEAR TM/L	W	L	PCT	G	GS	CG	SH	SV	IP	H	HR	BB	SO	RAT	ERA	ERA+	OAV	OOB	BH	AVG	PB	PR	/A	PD	TPI
1914 Chi-F	12	11	.522	36	22	10	2	2	190	162	3	55	87	10.4	2.23	119	.224	.282	9	.176	2	14	9	-3	0.9

● DICK LANGE   Lange, Richard Otto   b: 9/1/48, Harbor Beach, Mich.   BR/TR, 5'10", 185 lbs.   Deb: 9/9/72

YEAR TM/L	W	L	PCT	G	GS	CG	SH	SV	IP	H	HR	BB	SO	RAT	ERA	ERA+	OAV	OOB	BH	AVG	PB	PR	/A	PD	TPI
1972 Cal-A	0	0	—	2	1	0	0	0	7²	7	0	2	8	10.6	4.70	62	.233	.281	0	.000	-0	-1	-2	0	0.0
1973 Cal-A	2	1	.667	17	4	1	0	0	52²	61	9	21	27	14.2	4.44	80	.292	.359	0	—	0	-4	-5	0	-0.3
1974 Cal-A	3	8	.273	21	18	1	0	0	113²	111	10	47	57	12.8	3.80	90	.248	.325	0	—	0	-2	-5	-1	-0.5
1975 Cal-A	4	6	.400	30	8	1	0	1	102	119	12	53	45	15.3	5.21	68	.292	.374	0	—	0	-16	-19	-0	-1.7
Total 4	9	15	.375	70	31	3	0	1	276	298	31	123	137	13.9	4.47	78	.272	.349	0	.000	-0	-24	-30	-1	-2.5

● RICK LANGFORD   Langford, James Rick   b: 3/20/52, Farmville, Va.   BR/TR, 6', 180 lbs.   Deb: 6/13/76

YEAR TM/L	W	L	PCT	G	GS	CG	SH	SV	IP	H	HR	BB	SO	RAT	ERA	ERA+	OAV	OOB	BH	AVG	PB	PR	/A	PD	TPI
1976 Pit-N	0	1	.000	12	1	0	0	0	23	27	2	14	17	16.0	6.26	56	.307	.402	1	.200	0	-7	-7	0	-0.2
1977 Oak-A	8	19	.296	37	31	6	1	0	208¹	223	18	73	141	12.9	4.02	100	.273	.334	0	—	0	1	0	1	0.1
1978 Oak-A	7	13	.350	37	24	4	2	0	175²	169	15	56	92	11.7	3.43	106	.253	.314	0	—	0	6	4	1	0.6
1979 Oak-A	12	16	.429	34	29	14	1	0	218²	233	22	57	101	12.1	4.28	94	.273	.322	0	—	0	-2	-6	2	0.0
1980 Oak-A	19	12	.613	35	33	**28**	2	0	**290**	276	29	64	102	10.6	3.26	116	.255	.297	0	—	0	25	16	1	2.2
1981 *Oak-A	12	10	.545	24	24	**18**	2	0	195¹	190	14	58	84	11.6	2.99	116	.255	.311	0	—	0	14	10	-2	1.0
1982 Oak-A	11	16	.407	32	31	15	2	0	237¹	265	33	49	79	12.0	4.21	93	.281	.318	0	.000	0	-4	-8	1	-0.8
1983 Oak-A	0	4	.000	7	7	0	0	0	20	43	4	10	2	24.7	12.15	32	.448	.509	0	—	0	-18	-18	-0	-2.7
1984 Oak-A	0	0	—	3	2	0	0	0	8²	15	2	2	2	17.7	8.31	46	.366	.395	0	—	0	-4	-4	-0	-0.3
1985 Oak-A	3	5	.375	23	3	0	0	0	59	60	8	15	21	11.4	3.51	110	.261	.306	0	—	0	4	2	-0	0.3
1986 Oak-A	1	10	.091	16	11	0	0	0	55	69	13	18	30	14.4	7.36	53	.300	.353	0	—	0	-19	-21	-1	-3.5
Total 11	73	106	.408	260	196	85	10	0	1491	1570	160	416	671	12.1	4.01	95	.271	.322	1	.167	0	-3	-32	3	-3.0

● MARK LANGSTON   Langston, Mark Edward   b: 8/20/60, San Diego, Cal.   BR/TL, 6'2", 190 lbs.   Deb: 4/7/84

YEAR TM/L	W	L	PCT	G	GS	CG	SH	SV	IP	H	HR	BB	SO	RAT	ERA	ERA+	OAV	OOB	BH	AVG	PB	PR	/A	PD	TPI
1984 Sea-A	17	10	.630	35	33	5	2	0	225	188	16	118	**204**	12.6	3.40	117	.230	.332	0	—	0	15	15	1	1.8
1985 Sea-A	7	14	.333	24	24	2	0	0	126²	122	16	91	72	15.3	5.47	77	.255	.376	0	—	0	-19	-18	2	-2.3
1986 Sea-A	12	14	.462	37	36	9	0	0	239¹	234	30	123	**245**	13.6	4.85	87	.255	.346	0	—	0	-18	-16	-1	-1.6
1987 Sea-A★	19	13	.594	35	35	14	3	0	272	242	30	114	**262**	11.9	3.84	123	.238	.318	0	—	0	19	27	1	2.7
1988 Sea-A	15	11	.577	35	35	9	3	0	261¹	222	32	110	235	11.5	3.34	125	.233	.314	0	—	0	18	24	3	2.5
1989 Sea-A	4	5	.444	10	10	2	1	0	73¹	60	3	19	60	10.2	3.56	113	.221	.282	0	—	0	3	4	0	0.3
Mon-N	12	9	.571	24	24	6	4	0	176²	138	13	93	175	11.8	2.39	147	.218	.318	11	.172	0	22	22	-0	2.7
1990 Cal-A	10	17	.370	33	33	5	1	0	223	215	13	104	195	13.1	4.40	87	.259	.345	0	—	0	-12	-14	2	-1.3
1991 Cal-A☆	19	8	.704	34	34	7	0	0	246¹	190	30	96	183	10.5	3.00	137	.215	.293	0	—	0	30	30	1	3.2
1992 Cal-A★	13	14	.481	32	32	9	2	0	229	206	14	74	174	11.2	3.66	109	.242	.307	0	.000	0	7	8	2	1.1
1993 Cal-A★	16	11	.593	35	35	7	0	0	256¹	220	22	85	196	10.7	3.20	141	.234	.298	0	—	0	32	37	3	3.9
1994 Cal-A	7	8	.467	18	18	2	1	0	119¹	121	19	54	109	13.2	4.68	107	.268	.346	0	—	0	2	4	0	0.3
Total 11	151	134	.530	352	349	77	17	0	2448¹	2158	244	1081	2110	12.1	3.74	112	.239	.322	11	.167	0	98	122	13	13.4

● MAX LANIER   Lanier, Hubert Max   b: 8/18/15, Denton, N.C.   BR/TL, 5'10", 187 lbs.   Deb: 4/20/38   F

YEAR TM/L	W	L	PCT	G	GS	CG	SH	SV	IP	H	HR	BB	SO	RAT	ERA	ERA+	OAV	OOB	BH	AVG	PB	PR	/A	PD	TPI
1938 StL-N	0	3	.000	18	3	1	0	0	45	57	1	28	14	17.4	4.20	94	.317	.414	1	.100	-0	-2	-1	-0	-0.1
1939 StL-N	2	1	.667	7	6	2	0	0	37²	29	0	13	14	10.3	2.39	172	.220	.295	4	.286	1	6	7	-0	0.6
1940 StL-N	9	6	.600	35	11	4	2	3	105	113	1	38	49	13.0	3.34	119	.276	.339	6	.200	-0	6	8	1	1.1
1941 StL-N	10	8	.556	35	18	8	4	0	153	126	4	59	93	10.9	2.82	133	.225	.300	10	.192	-1	14	16	2	2.0
1942 *StL-N	13	8	.619	34	20	8	2	2	161	137	4	60	93	11.1	2.96	116	.234	.308	12	.255	2	6	8	2	1.4
1943 *StL-N☆	15	7	.682	32	25	14	2	3	213¹	195	3	75	123	11.5	**1.90**	**177**	.246	.312	12	.164	-2	**35**	**35**	0	3.5
1944 *StL-N†	17	12	.586	33	30	16	5	0	224¹	192	5	71	141	10.7	2.65	133	.234	.297	14	.182	-0	24	22	-0	2.6
1945 StL-N	2	2	.500	4	3	3	0	0	26	22	0	8	16	10.4	1.73	216	.222	.280	2	.182	0	6	6	-0	0.8
1946 StL-N	6	0	1.000	6	6	3	1	0	56	45	1	19	36	10.4	1.93	179	.228	.300	5	.200	1	9	9	-0	1.0
1949 StL-N	5	4	.556	15	15	4	1	0	92	92	5	35	37	12.4	3.82	109	.261	.328	2	.074	-2	4	4	0	0.6
1950 StL-N	11	9	.550	27	27	10	2	0	181¹	173	13	68	89	12.0	3.13	137	.249	.317	11	.162	-1	20	24	0	2.3
1951 StL-N	11	9	.550	31	23	8	2	1	160	149	14	50	59	11.2	3.26	122	.248	.306	8	.151	-2	12	12	0	1.3
1952 NY-N	7	12	.368	37	16	4	1	5	137	124	11	65	47	12.6	3.94	94	.244	.333	11	.268	3	-3	-4	3	0.0
1953 NY-N	0	0	—	3	0	0	0	0	5¹	6	1	2	3	18.6	6.75	64	.381	.458	0	.000	0	-1	-1	0	-0.0
StL-A	0	1	.000	10	1	0	0	0	22¹	28	2	19	8	18.9	7.25	58	.322	.443	1	.167	-0	-8	-8	-0	-0.3
Total 14	108	82	.568	327	204	91	21	17	1619¹	1490	65	611	821	11.8	3.01	125	.247	.318	99	.185	-3	127	136	5	16.3

● JOHNNY LANNING   Lanning, John Young "Tobacco Chewin' Johnny"   b: 9/6/10, Asheville, N.C.   d: 11/8/89, Asheville, N.C.   BR/TR, 6'1", 185 lbs.   Deb: 4/17/36   F

YEAR TM/L	W	L	PCT	G	GS	CG	SH	SV	IP	H	HR	BB	SO	RAT	ERA	ERA+	OAV	OOB	BH	AVG	PB	PR	/A	PD	TPI
1936 Bos-N	7	11	.389	28	20	3	1	0	153	154	9	55	33	12.3	3.65	105	.263	.326	7	.135	-2	6	3	-2	0.0
1937 Bos-N	5	7	.417	32	11	4	1	2	116²	107	10	40	37	11.4	3.93	91	.236	.300	4	.121	-1	-0	-5	-0	-0.5
1938 Bos-N	8	7	.533	32	18	4	1	0	138	146	5	52	39	13.0	3.72	92	.267	.332	9	.188	-1	1	-4	-1	-0.6
1939 Bos-N	5	6	.455	37	6	3	0	4	129	120	6	53	45	12.2	3.42	108	.252	.329	6	.143	-1	7	4	0	0.2
1940 Pit-N	8	4	.667	38	7	2	0	2	115²	119	8	39	42	12.3	4.05	94	.268	.327	7	.200	1	-3	-3	-0	-0.2
1941 Pit-N	11	11	.500	34	23	9	0	1	175²	175	6	47	41	11.4	3.13	116	.256	.304	6	.107	-2	10	9	1	1.1
1942 Pit-N	6	8	.429	34	8	2	1	1	119¹	125	7	26	31	11.5	3.32	102	.274	.314	4	.138	1	-0	-1	0	0.0
1943 Pit-N	4	1	.800	12	0	0	0	0	27	23	0	9	11	10.7	2.33	149	.223	.286	1	.167	0	3	3	-1	0.6
1945 Pit-N	0	0	—	1	0	0	0	0	2	8	1	0	0	36.0	36.00	11	.571	.571	0	—	0	-7	-7	0	0.0
1946 Pit-N	4	5	.444	27	9	3	0	1	91	97	3	31	16	12.8	3.07	115	.269	.329	3	.143	-0	3	5	1	0.5
1947 Bos-N	0	0	—	3	0	0	0	0	3²	4	0	6	0	24.5	9.82	40	.400	.625	0	—	0	-2	-2	0	0.0
Total 11	58	60	.492	278	104	30	4	13	1071	1078	55	358	295	12.1	3.58	101	.261	.321	47	.146	-7	19	5	-1	1.1

● RED LANNING   Lanning, Lester Alfred   b: 5/13/1895, Harvard, Ill.   d: 6/13/62, Bristol, Conn.   BL/TL, 5'9", 165 lbs.   Deb: 6/20/16   ◆

YEAR TM/L	W	L	PCT	G	GS	CG	SH	SV	IP	H	HR	BB	SO	RAT	ERA	ERA+	OAV	OOB	BH	AVG	PB	PR	/A	PD	TPI
1916 Phi-A	0	3	.000	6	3	1	0	0	24¹	38	1	17	9	21.1	8.14	35	.362	.460	6	.182	1	-14	-14	0	-1.4

● TOM LANNING   Lanning, Thomas Newton   b: 4/22/07, Asheville, N.C.   d: 11/4/67, Marietta, Ga.   BL/TL, 6'1", 165 lbs.   Deb: 9/14/38   F

YEAR TM/L	W	L	PCT	G	GS	CG	SH	SV	IP	H	HR	BB	SO	RAT	ERA	ERA+	OAV	OOB	BH	AVG	PB	PR	/A	PD	TPI
1938 Phi-N	0	1	.000	3	1	0	0	0	7	9	0	2	2	14.1	6.43	60	.300	.344	1	1.000	0	-2	-2	-0	-0.2

● GENE LANSING   Lansing, Eugene Hewitt "Jigger"   b: 1/11/1898, Albany, N.Y.   d: 1/18/45, Rensselaer, N.Y.   BR/TR, 6'1", 185 lbs.   Deb: 4/27/22

YEAR TM/L	W	L	PCT	G	GS	CG	SH	SV	IP	H	HR	BB	SO	RAT	ERA	ERA+	OAV	OOB	BH	AVG	PB	PR	/A	PD	TPI
1922 Bos-N	0	1	.000	15	1	0	0	0	40²	46	1	22	14	15.0	5.98	67	.301	.389	0	.000	-1	-8	-9	-0	-0.3

● PAUL LaPALME   LaPalme, Paul Edmore "Lefty"   b: 12/14/23, Springfield, Mass.   BL/TL, 5'10", 184 lbs.   Deb: 5/28/51

YEAR TM/L	W	L	PCT	G	GS	CG	SH	SV	IP	H	HR	BB	SO	RAT	ERA	ERA+	OAV	OOB	BH	AVG	PB	PR	/A	PD	TPI
1951 Pit-N	1	5	.167	22	8	1	0	0	54¹	79	6	31	24	18.4	6.29	67	.333	.413	1	.100	-0	-14	-12	-1	-1.3
1952 Pit-N	1	2	.333	31	2	0	0	0	59²	56	6	37	25	14.2	3.92	102	.253	.363	1	.100	-0	-1	0	1	0.0
1953 Pit-N	8	16	.333	35	24	7	1	2	176¹	191	20	64	86	13.0	4.59	97	.272	.333	5	.085	-5	-6	-2	-2	-0.9
1954 Pit-N	4	10	.286	33	15	2	0	0	120²	147	15	54	57	15.0	5.52	76	.302	.372	5	.143	-0	-19	-18	-1	-1.1
1955 StL-N	3	4	.571	36	7	1	0	5	91²	76	10	34	39	10.9	2.75	148	.228	.301	4	.211	0	13	13	1	1.1
1956 StL-N	0	0	—	1	0	0	0	0	0²	4	0	2	0	81.0	81.00	5	.667	.750	0	—	-0	-6	-6	-0	0.0
Cin-N	2	4	.333	11	2	0	0	0	27	26	7	4	4	10.0	4.67	85	.257	.286	2	.500	-0	-3	-2	-0	-0.3

YEAR	TM/L	W	L	PCT	G	GS	CG	SH	SV	IP	H	HR	BB	SO	RAT	ERA	ERA+	OAV	OOB	BH	AVG	PB	PR	/A	PD	TPI
	Yr	2	4	.333	12	2	0	0	0	27²	30	7	6	4	11.7	6.51	61	.280	.319	2	.500	1	-8	-8	-0	-0.3
	Chi-A	3	1	.750	29	0	0	0	2	45²	31	2	27	23	11.4	2.36	173	.195	.312	0	.000	-1	9	9	1	0.7
1957	Chi-A	1	4	.200	35	0	0	0	7	40¹	35	5	19	19	12.3	3.35	112	.235	.325	2	.500	1	2	2	1	0.5
Total 7		24	45	.348	253	51	10	2	14	616¹	645	71	272	277	13.4	4.42	95	.269	.345	20	.136	-4	-25	-16	-0	-2.0

● ANDY LAPIHUSKA
Lapihuska, Andrew "Apples" b: 11/1/22, Delmont, N.J. BL/TR, 5'10.5", 175 lbs. Deb: 9/12/42

YEAR	TM/L	W	L	PCT	G	GS	CG	SH	SV	IP	H	HR	BB	SO	RAT	ERA	ERA+	OAV	OOB	BH	AVG	PB	PR	/A	PD	TPI
1942	Phi-N	0	2	.000	3	2	0	0	0	20²	17	0	13	8	13.9	5.23	63	.221	.348	2	.286	0	-4	-4	-0	-0.3
1943	Phi-N	0	0	—	1	0	0	0	0	2¹	5	1	3	0	30.9	23.14	15	.417	.533	0	.000	-0	-5	-5	-0	-0.0
Total 2		0	2	.000	4	2	0	0	0	23	22	1	16	8	15.7	7.04	47	.247	.374	2	.222	0	-10	-10	0	-0.3

● DAVE LaPOINT
LaPoint, David Jeffrey b: 7/29/59, Glens Falls, N.Y. BL/TL, 6'3", 215 lbs. Deb: 9/10/80

YEAR	TM/L	W	L	PCT	G	GS	CG	SH	SV	IP	H	HR	BB	SO	RAT	ERA	ERA+	OAV	OOB	BH	AVG	PB	PR	/A	PD	TPI
1980	Mil-A	1	0	1.000	5	3	0	0	0	15	17	2	13	5	18.0	6.00	64	.293	.423	0	—	0	-3	-4	-1	-0.1
1981	StL-N	1	0	1.000	3	2	0	0	0	10²	12	1	2	4	12.7	4.22	84	.293	.341	0	.000	-1	-1	-1	-0	-0.1
1982	*StL-N	9	3	.750	42	21	0	0	0	152²	170	8	52	81	13.3	3.42	106	.290	.350	2	.053	-3	3	3	-3	-0.4
1983	StL-N	12	9	.571	37	29	1	0	0	191¹	191	12	84	113	13.1	3.95	92	.267	.347	9	.153	1	-7	-7	-1	-0.7
1984	StL-N	12	10	.545	33	33	2	1	0	193	205	9	77	130	13.2	3.96	88	.278	.347	4	.068	-3	-8	-11	-2	-1.6
1985	SF-N	7	17	.292	31	31	2	1	0	206²	215	18	74	122	12.6	3.57	96	.269	.331	10	.167	2	0	-3	-2	-0.4
1986	Det-A	3	6	.333	16	8	0	0	0	67²	85	11	32	36	15.6	5.72	72	.307	.379	0	—	0	-12	-12	-1	-1.4
	SD-N	1	4	.200	24	4	0	0	0	61¹	67	8	24	41	13.5	4.26	86	.276	.343	0	.000	-1	-4	-4	-0	-0.4
1987	StL-N	1	1	.500	6	2	0	0	0	16	24	5	4	11	15.2	6.75	62	.351	.392	0	.000	0	-5	-5	-0	-0.5
	Chi-A	6	3	.667	14	12	2	1	0	82²	69	7	31	43	11.0	2.94	156	.224	.297	0	—	0	14	15	2	1.5
1988	Chi-A	10	11	.476	25	25	1	1	0	161¹	151	10	47	79	11.2	3.40	117	.245	.300	0	—	0	10	10	-2	1.0
	Pit-N	4	2	.667	8	8	1	0	0	52	54	4	10	19	11.1	2.77	123	.271	.306	1	.063	-1	4	4	0	0.3
1989	NY-A	6	9	.400	20	20	0	0	0	113²	146	12	45	51	15.3	5.62	69	.310	.373	0	—	0	-22	-22	-2	-2.6
1990	NY-A	7	10	.412	28	27	2	0	0	157²	180	11	57	67	13.6	4.11	97	.292	.353	0	—	0	-4	-2	-0	-0.3
1991	Phi-N	0	1	.000	2	2	0	0	0	5	10	1	6	3	30.6	16.20	23	.435	.567	0	.000	-0	-7	-7	0	-1.0
Total 12		80	86	.482	294	227	11	4	1	1486²	1598	117	559	802	13.2	4.02	93	.277	.343	26	.104	-6	-40	-46	-12	-6.7

● TERRY LARKIN
Larkin, Frank S. d: 9/16/1894, Brooklyn, N.Y. BR/TR, Deb: 5/20/1876 ♦

YEAR	TM/L	W	L	PCT	G	GS	CG	SH	SV	IP	H	HR	BB	SO	RAT	ERA	ERA+	OAV	OOB	BH	AVG	PB	PR	/A	PD	TPI
1876	NY-N	0	1	.000	1	1	1	0	0	9	9	0	0	0	9.0	3.00	71	.231	.231	0	.000	-1	-1	-1	-0	-0.1
1877	Har-N	29	25	.537	56	56	55	0	0	501	510	2	53	96	10.1	2.14	114	**.245**	.264	52	.228	6	37	16	-1	1.8
1878	Chi-N	29	26	.527	56	56	56	1	0	506	511	4	31	163	9.6	2.24	108	.246	.257	65	.288	13	4	10	-4	1.8
1879	Chi-N	31	23	.574	58	58	57	4	0	513¹	514	6	30	142	9.5	2.44	105	.240	**.250**	50	.219	1	3	7	-7	0.1
1880	Tro-N	0	5	.000	5	5	3	0	0	38	83	1	10	5	22.0	8.76	29	.421	.449	3	.150	-2	-27	-26	-0	-2.4
Total 5		89	80	.527	176	176	172	9	0	1567¹	1627	12	124	406	10.1	2.43	102	.249	.263	215	.235	19	17	9	-12	1.2

● PAT LARKIN
Larkin, Patrick Clibborn b: 6/14/60, Arcadia, Cal. BL/TL, 6', 180 lbs. Deb: 7/16/83

YEAR	TM/L	W	L	PCT	G	GS	CG	SH	SV	IP	H	HR	BB	SO	RAT	ERA	ERA+	OAV	OOB	BH	AVG	PB	PR	/A	PD	TPI
1983	SF-N	0	0	—	5	0	0	0	0	10¹	13	1	3	6	15.7	4.35	81	.317	.391	0	.000	-0	-1	-1	-0	0.0

● STEVE LARKIN
Larkin, Stephen Patrick b: 12/9/10, Cincinnati, Ohio d: 5/2/69, Norristown, Pa. BR/TR, 6'1", 195 lbs. Deb: 5/6/34

YEAR	TM/L	W	L	PCT	G	GS	CG	SH	SV	IP	H	HR	BB	SO	RAT	ERA	ERA+	OAV	OOB	BH	AVG	PB	PR	/A	PD	TPI
1934	Det-A	0	0	—	2	1	0	0	0	6	8	0	5	0	19.5	1.50	293	.296	.406	1	.333	1	2	2	0	0.1

● DAVE LaROCHE
LaRoche, David Eugene b: 5/14/48, Colorado Springs, Colo. BL/TL, 6'2", 200 lbs. Deb: 5/11/70 C

YEAR	TM/L	W	L	PCT	G	GS	CG	SH	SV	IP	H	HR	BB	SO	RAT	ERA	ERA+	OAV	OOB	BH	AVG	PB	PR	/A	PD	TPI
1970	Cal-A	4	1	.800	38	0	0	0	4	49²	41	6	21	44	12.0	3.44	105	.224	.317	2	.250	1	1	1	0	0.2
1971	Cal-A	5	1	.833	56	0	0	0	9	72	55	3	27	63	10.4	2.50	129	.212	.289	1	.091	-0	8	6	-1	0.5
1972	Min-A	5	7	.417	62	0	0	0	10	95¹	72	9	39	79	11.0	2.83	113	.209	.300	1	.091	-0	2	4	0	0.7
1973	Chi-N	4	1	.800	45	0	0	0	5	54¹	55	7	29	34	14.1	5.80	68	.274	.368	2	.500	1	-13	-11	1	-0.9
1974	Chi-N	5	6	.455	49	4	0	0	5	92	103	9	47	49	15.0	4.79	80	.286	.373	9	.333	3	-12	-10	-0	-1.0
1975	Cle-A	5	3	.625	61	0	0	0	17	82¹	61	5	57	94	13.1	2.19	173	.210	.344	0	—	0	15	15	1	2.1
1976	Cle-A☆	1	4	.200	61	0	0	0	21	96¹	57	2	49	104	10.0	2.24	156	.175	.285	0	—	0	14	13	-1	1.3
1977	Cle-A	2	2	.500	13	0	0	0	0	18²	15	3	7	18	10.6	5.30	74	.234	.310	0	—	0	-3	-3	-0	-0.6
	Cal-A★	6	5	.545	46	0	0	0	13	81¹	64	8	37	61	11.4	3.10	126	.218	.310	0	—	0	9	7	0	1.2
	Yr	8	7	.533	59	0	0	0	17	100	79	11	44	79	11.3	3.51	112	.220	.309	0	—	0	6	4	-0	0.6
1978	Cal-A	10	9	.526	59	0	0	0	25	95²	73	7	48	70	11.6	2.82	128	.215	.316	0	—	0	10	8	-0	2.3
1979	*Cal-A	7	11	.389	53	1	0	0	10	85²	107	13	32	59	14.8	5.57	73	.314	.376	0	—	0	-13	-14	-2	-2.5
1980	Cal-A	5	3	.375	52	9	1	0	4	128	122	14	39	89	11.5	4.08	96	.256	.317	0	—	0	-1	-2	-1	-0.2
1981	*NY-A	4	1	.800	26	1	0	0	6	47	38	3	16	24	10.5	2.49	144	.229	.301	0	—	0	6	6	-1	0.6
1982	NY-A	4	2	.667	25	0	0	0	4	50	54	4	11	31	11.9	3.42	117	.273	.314	0	—	0	1	0	-0	0.2
1983	NY-A	0	0	—	1	0	0	0	0	1	2	1	0	0	18.0	18.00	22	.400	.400	0	—	0	-2	-2	-0	0.2
Total 14		65	58	.528	647	15	1	0	126	1049¹	919	94	459	819	12.1	3.53	105	.239	.325	15	.246	4	26	21	-1	4.2

● JOHN LaROSE
LaRose, Henry John b: 10/25/51, Pawtucket, R.I. BL/TL, 6'1", 185 lbs. Deb: 9/20/78

YEAR	TM/L	W	L	PCT	G	GS	CG	SH	SV	IP	H	HR	BB	SO	RAT	ERA	ERA+	OAV	OOB	BH	AVG	PB	PR	/A	PD	TPI
1978	Bos-A	0	0	—	1	0	0	0	0	2	3	1	3	0	27.0	22.50	18	.375	.545	0	—	0	-4	-4	0	-0.5

● DON LARSEN
Larsen, Don James b: 8/7/29, Michigan City, Ind. BR/TR, 6'4", 227 lbs. Deb: 4/18/53

YEAR	TM/L	W	L	PCT	G	GS	CG	SH	SV	IP	H	HR	BB	SO	RAT	ERA	ERA+	OAV	OOB	BH	AVG	PB	PR	/A	PD	TPI
1953	StL-A	7	12	.368	38	22	7	2	2	192²	201	11	64	96	12.6	4.16	101	.267	.328	23	.284	5	-3	1	-1	0.8
1954	Bal-A	3	21	.125	29	28	12	1	0	201²	213	18	89	80	13.5	4.37	82	.274	.349	22	.250	8	-15	-18	0	-1.0
1955	*NY-A	9	2	.818	19	13	5	1	2	97	81	8	51	44	12.4	3.06	122	.229	.329	6	.146	2	10	7	-1	0.9
1956	*NY-A	11	5	.688	38	20	6	1	1	179²	133	19	96	107	11.6	3.26	119	.204	.313	19	.241	6	18	12	-1	1.5
1957	*NY-A	10	4	.714	27	20	4	1	0	139²	113	17	87	81	12.9	3.74	96	.220	.333	14	.250	5	1	-2	-0	0.1
1958	*NY-A	9	6	.600	19	19	5	3	0	114¹	100	4	52	55	12.3	3.07	115	.233	.322	15	.306	9	9	6	-1	1.4
1959	NY-A	6	7	.462	25	18	3	1	3	124²	122	14	76	69	14.4	4.33	84	.260	.365	12	.255	4	-7	-10	-0	-0.6
1960	KC-A	1	10	.091	22	15	0	0	0	83²	97	11	42	43	15.0	5.38	74	.293	.373	6	.207	0	-14	-13	-0	-1.6
1961	KC-A	1	0	1.000	8	1	0	0	0	15	21	2	11	13	19.8	4.20	100	.344	.452	1	.300	1	-0	-0	-0	0.2
	Chi-A	7	2	.778	25	3	0	0	2	74¹	64	5	29	53	11.4	4.12	95	.231	.306	8	.320	3	-1	-2	0	0.1
	Yr	8	2	.800	33	4	0	0	2	89¹	85	7	40	66	12.7	4.13	96	.251	.332	14	.311	4	-1	-2	1	0.3
1962	*SF-N	5	4	.556	49	0	0	0	11	86¹	83	9	47	58	13.8	4.38	87	.256	.354	5	.200	1	-4	-6	0	-0.6
1963	SF-N	7	7	.500	46	6	0	0	3	62	46	8	30	44	11.0	3.05	105	.203	.296	2	.182	0	2	1	0	0.3
1964	SF-N	0	1	.000	6	0	0	0	0	10¹	10	0	6	4	13.9	4.35	82	.256	.356	0	—	-0	-1	-1	-0	-0.1
	Hou-N	4	8	.333	30	10	2	1	1	103¹	92	4	20	58	9.8	2.26	151	.233	.272	3	.097	0	15	13	0	1.6
	Yr	4	9	.308	36	10	2	1	1	113²	102	4	26	64	10.2	2.45	140	.235	.280	3	.094	0	14	12	0	1.5
1965	Hou-N	0	0	—	1	1	0	0	0	5¹	8	0	3	1	18.6	5.06	66	.348	.423	0	.000	-0	-1	-1	0	0.0
	Bal-A	1	2	.333	27	1	0	0	1	54	53	4	20	40	12.3	2.67	130	.255	.323	1	.273	1	5	3	-0	0.6
1967	Chi-N	0	0	—	3	0	0	0	0	4	5	1	2	2	15.8	9.00	39	.333	.412	0	—	0	-3	-3	0	-0.0
Total 14		81	91	.471	412	171	44	11	26	1548	1442	130	725	849	12.8	3.78	99	.247	.332	144	.242	46	10	-9	-1	3.5

● DAN LARSON
Larson, Daniel James b: 7/4/54, Los Angeles, Cal. BR/TR, 6', 180 lbs. Deb: 7/18/76

YEAR	TM/L	W	L	PCT	G	GS	CG	SH	SV	IP	H	HR	BB	SO	RAT	ERA	ERA+	OAV	OOB	BH	AVG	PB	PR	/A	PD	TPI
1976	Hou-N	5	8	.385	13	13	5	0	0	92¹	81	3	28	42	10.7	3.02	106	.236	.296	9	.290	4	5	2	0	0.7
1977	Hou-N	1	7	.125	32	10	1	0	1	97²	108	13	45	44	14.3	5.81	61	.280	.358	6	.214	1	-21	-24	-0	-1.7
1978	Phi-N	0	0	—	1	0	0	0	0	1	1	1	1	2	18.0	9.00	40	.250	.400	0	—	-0	-1	-1	-0	-0.1
1979	Phi-N	1	1	.500	3	3	0	0	0	19	17	1	9	12	12.8	4.26	90	.250	.346	0	.000	-1	-1	-1	0	-0.1
1980	Phi-N	0	5	.000	12	7	0	0	0	45²	46	4	24	17	13.8	3.15	120	.271	.361	2	.154	0	3	3	-1	0.3
1981	Phi-N	3	0	1.000	5	4	1	0	0	26	27	4	15	13	15.6	4.15	88	.262	.353	1	.111	0	-1	-0	-0	-0.2
1982	Chi-N	0	4	.000	12	6	0	0	0	39²	51	4	18	22	16.1	5.67	66	.327	.403	3	.273	4	-9	-9	1	-0.6
Total 7		10	25	.286	78	43	7	0	1	323¹	331	30	140	151	13.3	4.40	80	.269	.346	21	.216	4	-26	-31	1	-1.6

YEAR TM/L	W	L	PCT	G	GS	CG	SH	SV	IP	H	HR	BB	SO	RAT	ERA	ERA+	OAV	OOB	BH	AVG	PB	PR	/A	PD	TPI

● AL LARY   Lary, Alfred Allen b: 9/26/29, Northport, Ala.   BR/TR, 6'3", 185 lbs.   Deb: 9/6/54   F♦

1954 Chi-N	0	0	—	1	1	0	0	0	6	3	0	7	4	15.0	3.00	140	.150	.370	1	.500	0	1	1	0	0.0
1962 Chi-N	0	1	.000	15	3	0	0	0	34	42	5	15	18	15.1	7.15	58	.311	.380	1	.167	0	-12	-11	-0	-0.3
Total 2	0	1	.000	16	4	0	0	0	40	45	5	22	22	15.1	6.52	64	.290	.379	2	.250	1	-11	-11	-0	-0.3

● FRANK LARY   Lary, Frank Strong "Mule" or "The Yankee Killer" b: 4/10/30, Northport, Ala.   BR/TR, 5'11", 180 lbs.   Deb: 9/14/54   F

1954 Det-A	0	0	—	3	0	0	0	0	3²	4	0	3	5	17.2	2.45	150	.286	.412	0	—	0	1	1	0	0.0
1955 Det-A	14	15	.483	36	31	16	2	1	235	232	10	89	98	12.5	3.10	124	.262	.334	16	.195	1	22	19	1	2.5
1956 Det-A	**21**	13	.618	41	38	20	3	1	**294**	289	20	116	165	12.8	3.15	131	.257	.333	19	.184	0	33	31	-0	3.4
1957 Det-A	11	16	.407	40	35	12	2	3	237²	250	23	72	107	12.6	3.98	97	.276	.337	9	.123	-3	-5	-3	0	-0.6
1958 Det-A	16	15	.516	39	34	**19**	3	1	260¹	249	20	68	131	11.4	2.90	130	.251	.307	15	.170	-1	25	33	-0	3.6
1959 Det-A	17	10	.630	32	32	11	3	0	223	225	23	46	137	11.4	3.55	114	.261	.307	10	.125	4	8	13	-0	1.2
1960 Det-A★	15	15	.500	38	36	**15**	2	1	**274¹**	262	25	62	149	11.3	3.51	113	.249	.302	17	.183	4	11	14	-2	1.6
1961 Det-A★	23	9	.719	36	36	**22**	4	0	275¹	252	24	66	146	10.6	3.24	127	.243	.293	25	.231	4	24	26	4	3.7
1962 Det-A	2	6	.250	17	14	2	1	0	80	98	17	21	41	13.8	5.74	71	.297	.346	4	.167	1	-16	-15	-1	-1.3
1963 Det-A	4	9	.308	16	14	6	0	0	107¹	90	15	26	46	10.1	3.27	114	.226	.281	8	.229	1	4	6	1	0.9
1964 Det-A	0	2	.000	6	4	0	0	0	18	24	3	10	6	18.5	7.00	52	.316	.416	0	.000	-1	-7	-7	-1	-0.8
NY-N	2	3	.400	13	8	3	1	1	57¹	62	7	14	27	12.6	4.55	79	.279	.333	2	.118	1	-6	-6	-0	-0.5
Mil-N	1	0	1.000	5	2	0	0	0	12¹	15	4	0	4	10.9	4.38	80	.306	.306	0	.000	-0	-1	-1	0	-0.0
Yr	3	3	.500	18	10	3	1	1	69²	77	11	14	31	11.8	4.52	79	.279	.314	2	.100	1	-8	-7	-0	-0.5
1965 NY-N	1	3	.250	14	7	0	0	1	57¹	48	4	16	23	10.2	2.98	118	.233	.291	4	.211	0	4	3	0	0.3
Chi-N	1	0	1.000	14	1	0	0	2	26²	23	4	7	14	10.8	4.05	79	.230	.294	1	.500	-0	-2	-3	-0	-0.1
Total 12	128	116	.525	350	292	126	21	11	2162¹	2123	197	616	1099	11.8	3.49	113	.257	.316	130	.177	5	95	112	3	13.9

● FRED LASHER   Lasher, Frederick Walter b: 8/19/41, Poughkeepsie, N.Y.   BR/TR, 6'4", 210 lbs.   Deb: 4/12/63

1963 Min-A	0	0	—	11	0	0	0	0	11¹	12	1	11	10	18.3	4.76	76	.286	.434	0	.000	-0	-1	-1	0	0.0
1967 Det-A	2	1	.667	17	0	0	0	9	30	25	1	11	28	11.1	3.90	84	.221	.296	1	.111	-0	-2	-2	-0	-0.4
1968 *Det-A	5	1	.833	34	0	0	0	5	48²	37	5	22	32	10.9	3.33	90	.215	.304	1	.111	-0	-2	-1	1	-0.2
1969 Det-A	2	1	.667	32	0	0	0	0	44	34	5	22	26	11.9	3.07	122	.224	.330	0	.000	-0	3	3	0	0.2
1970 Det-A	1	3	.250	12	0	0	0	3	9	10	1	12	8	23.0	5.00	75	.278	.469	0	.000	-0	-1	-1	0	-0.6
Cle-A	1	7	.125	43	1	0	0	5	57²	57	6	30	44	14.0	4.06	98	.264	.361	0	.000	-1	-2	-1	-1	-0.3
Yr	2	10	.167	55	1	0	0	8	66²	67	6	42	52	15.1	4.18	94	.264	.375	0	.000	-1	-3	-2	-1	-0.9
1971 Cal-A	0	0	—	2	0	0	0	0	1¹	4	0	2	0	40.5	27.00	12	.667	.750	0	—	-0	-3	-4	-0	-0.1
Total 6	11	13	.458	151	1	0	0	22	202	179	18	110	148	13.2	3.88	91	.243	.347	2	.063	-2	-10	-8	-0	-1.3

● BILL LASKEY   Laskey, William Alan b: 12/20/57, Toledo, Ohio   BR/TR, 6'5", 190 lbs.   Deb: 4/23/82

1982 SF-N	13	12	.520	32	31	7	1	0	189¹	186	14	43	88	11.0	3.14	115	.261	.304	8	.129	-2	10	10	0	1.0
1983 SF-N	13	10	.565	25	25	1	0	0	148¹	151	18	45	81	12.1	4.19	84	.266	.323	5	.106	-0	-9	-11	-1	-1.6
1984 SF-N	9	14	.391	35	34	2	0	0	207²	222	20	50	71	12.0	4.33	81	.273	.320	4	.063	-0	-17	-19	-3	-2.5
1985 SF-N	5	11	.313	19	19	0	0	0	114	110	10	39	42	11.8	3.55	97	.255	.317	4	.133	1	0	-1	0	-0.1
Mon-N	0	5	.000	11	7	0	0	0	34¹	55	9	14	18	18.6	9.44	36	.362	.423	1	.143	-0	-22	-23	1	-2.7
Yr	5	16	.238	30	26	0	0	0	148¹	165	19	53	60	13.3	4.91	70	.281	.343	5	.135	0	-22	-25	1	-2.8
1986 SF-N	1	1	.500	20	0	0	0	1	27¹	28	5	13	8	13.5	4.28	82	.275	.357	0	.000	-0	-2	-2	0	-0.2
1988 Cle-A	1	0	1.000	17	0	0	0	1	24¹	32	0	6	17	14.1	5.18	79	.320	.358	0	—	0	-3	-3	-0	-0.3
Total 6	42	53	.442	159	116	10	1	2	745¹	784	76	210	325	12.2	4.14	85	.272	.325	22	.105	-4	-44	-50	-2	-6.4

● BILL LASLEY   Lasley, Willard Almond b: 7/13/02, Gallipolis, Ohio   d: 8/21/90, Seattle, Wash.   BB/TR, 6', 175 lbs.   Deb: 9/19/24

| 1924 StL-A | 0 | 0 | — | 2 | 0 | 0 | 0 | 0 | 4 | 7 | 0 | 2 | 0 | 20.3 | 6.75 | 67 | .412 | .474 | 0 | .000 | -0 | -1 | -1 | -0 | 0.0 |

● TOM LASORDA   Lasorda, Thomas Charles b: 9/22/27, Norristown, Pa.   BL/TL, 5'10", 175 lbs.   Deb: 8/5/54   MC

1954 Bro-N	0	0	—	4	0	0	0	0	9	8	2	5	5	13.0	5.00	82	.242	.342	0	.000	-1	-1	-1	0	0.0
1955 Bro-N	0	0	—	4	1	0	0	0	4	5	1	6	4	27.0	13.50	30	.313	.522	0	—	0	-4	-4	-0	0.0
1956 KC-A	0	4	.000	18	5	0	0	1	45¹	40	6	45	28	17.5	6.15	70	.240	.409	1	.077	-1	-10	-9	0	-0.8
Total 3	0	4	.000	26	6	0	0	1	58¹	53	9	56	37	17.4	6.48	66	.245	.409	1	.071	-2	-15	-14	0	-0.8

● BILL LATHAM   Latham, William Carol b: 8/29/60, Birmingham, Ala.   BL/TL, 6'2", 190 lbs.   Deb: 4/15/85

1985 NY-N	1	3	.250	7	3	0	0	0	22²	21	1	7	10	11.1	3.97	87	.250	.308	1	.333	1	-1	-1	0	-0.1
1986 Min-A	0	1	.000	7	2	0	0	0	16	24	1	6	8	17.4	7.31	59	.358	.419	0	—	0	-6	-5	-1	-0.5
Total 2	1	4	.200	14	5	0	0	0	38²	45	2	13	18	13.7	5.35	71	.298	.358	1	.333	1	-7	-7	0	-0.6

● BILL LATHROP   Lathrop, William George b: 8/12/1891, Hanover, Wis.   d: 11/20/58, Janesville, Wis.   BR/TR, 6'2.5", 184 lbs.   Deb: 7/29/13

1913 Chi-A	0	1	.000	6	0	0	0	0	17	16	0	12	9	15.4	4.24	69	.262	.392	0	.000	-1	-2	-2	0	-0.2
1914 Chi-A	1	2	.333	19	1	0	0	0	47²	41	0	19	7	11.7	2.64	102	.241	.325	0	.000	-1	1	0	1	-0.1
Total 2	1	3	.250	25	1	0	0	0	64²	57	0	31	16	12.7	3.06	90	.247	.343	0	.000	-2	-2	-2	1	-0.3

● BARRY LATMAN   Latman, Arnold Barry b: 5/21/36, Los Angeles, Cal.   BR/TR, 6'3", 210 lbs.   Deb: 9/10/57

1957 Chi-A	1	2	.333	7	2	0	1	0	12¹	12	2	13	9	19.0	8.03	47	.267	.441	0	.000	-0	-6	-6	0	-1.3
1958 Chi-A	3	0	1.000	13	3	1	1	0	47²	27	1	17	28	8.5	0.76	481	.162	.243	1	.083	-0	16	15	-1	0.8
1959 Chi-A	8	5	.615	37	21	5	2	0	156	138	15	72	97	12.3	3.75	100	.235	.323	6	.128	-1	2	0	-3	-0.4
1960 Cle-A	7	7	.500	31	20	4	0	0	147¹	146	19	72	94	13.7	4.03	93	.258	.348	9	.225	1	-3	-5	-1	-0.4
1961 Cle-A☆	13	5	.722	45	18	4	2	5	176²	163	23	54	108	11.3	4.02	98	.244	.306	4	.073	-3	-0	-3	-2	-0.8
1962 Cle-A	8	13	.381	45	21	7	1	5	179¹	179	23	72	117	12.8	4.17	93	.261	.336	10	.189	2	-4	-6	-1	-0.5
1963 Cle-A	7	12	.368	38	21	4	2	2	149¹	146	23	52	133	12.3	4.94	73	.257	.325	8	.182	2	-22	-22	3	-2.1
1964 LA-A	6	10	.375	45	18	2	0	1	138	128	15	52	81	12.2	3.85	85	.244	.321	5	.125	-1	-3	-9	-1	-1.2
1965 Cal-A	1	1	.500	18	0	0	0	0	31²	30	3	16	18	13.1	2.84	120	.254	.343	0	.000	-0	2	2	-1	0.1
1966 Hou-N	2	7	.222	31	9	0	0	1	103	88	5	35	74	11.4	2.71	126	.233	.310	4	.154	0	10	8	-0	0.7
1967 Hou-N	3	6	.333	39	1	0	0	0	77²	73	13	34	70	13.1	4.52	73	.253	.342	1	.091	-1	-10	-10	0	-1.2
Total 11	59	68	.465	344	134	28	10	16	1219	1130	142	489	829	12.3	3.91	94	.246	.325	48	.145	-1	-17	-34	-8	-6.4

● BILL LATTIMORE   Lattimore, William Hershel "Slothful Bill"
b: 5/25/1884, Roxton, Tex.   d: 10/30/19, Colorado Springs, Colo.   BL/TL, 5'9", 165 lbs.   Deb: 4/17/08

| 1908 Cle-A | 1 | 2 | .333 | 4 | 4 | 1 | 1 | 0 | 24 | 24 | 0 | 7 | 5 | 11.6 | 4.50 | 53 | .247 | .298 | 4 | .444 | 1 | -6 | -6 | -1 | -0.6 |

● CHUCK LAUER   Lauer, John Charles b: 1865, Pittsburgh, Pa.   TR,   Deb: 7/17/1884   ♦

| 1884 Pit-a | 0 | 2 | .000 | 3 | 3 | 2 | 0 | 0 | 19 | 23 | 0 | 9 | 8 | 16.6 | 7.58 | 44 | .277 | .368 | 5 | .114 | -1 | -9 | -9 | -1 | -0.8 |

● GEORGE LAUZERIQUE   Lauzerique, George Albert b: 7/22/47, Havana, Cuba   BR/TR, 6'1", 180 lbs.   Deb: 9/17/67

1967 KC-A	0	2	.000	3	2	0	0	0	16	11	2	6	10	10.1	2.25	142	.193	.281	0	.000	-0	2	2	0	0.2
1968 Oak-A	0	0	—	1	0	0	0	0	3	0	0	1	0	0.00	—	.000	.333	0	—	-0	0	0	-0	0.0
1969 Oak-A	3	4	.429	19	8	1	0	0	61¹	58	14	27	39	12.8	4.70	73	.250	.333	2	.100	-0	-7	-9	1	-0.9
1970 Mil-A	1	2	.333	11	4	0	0	0	35	41	7	14	24	14.4	6.94	55	.295	.364	2	.200	1	-13	-12	0	-0.9
Total 4	4	8	.333	34	14	2	0	0	113¹	110	23	48	73	12.9	5.00	70	.256	.336	4	.121	-0	-18	-19	1	-1.6

● GARY LAVELLE   Lavelle, Gary Robert b: 1/3/49, Scranton, Pa.   BB/TL, 6'1", 200 lbs.   Deb: 9/10/74

| 1974 SF-N | 0 | 3 | .000 | 10 | 0 | 0 | 0 | 0 | 16² | 14 | 1 | 10 | 12 | 13.0 | 2.16 | 176 | .222 | .329 | 0 | .000 | -0 | 3 | 3 | -0 | 0.5 |

YEAR	TM/L	W	L	PCT	G	GS	CG	SH	SV	IP	H	HR	BB	SO	RAT	ERA	ERA+	OAV	OOB	BH	AVG	PB	PR	/A	PD	TPI
1975	SF-N	6	3	.667	65	0	0	0	8	82¹	80	3	48	51	14.3	2.95	129	.260	.365	1	.111	-0	6	8	0	1.0
1976	SF-N	10	6	.625	65	0	0	0	12	110¹	102	6	52	71	12.7	2.69	135	.246	.333	1	.077	-1	10	11	-2	1.7
1977	SF-N★	7	7	.500	73	0	0	0	20	118¹	106	4	37	93	10.9	2.05	190	.239	.298	0	.000	-2	24	24	1	3.6
1978	SF-N	13	10	.565	67	0	0	0	14	97²	96	3	44	63	13.1	3.32	104	.263	.345	1	.067	-1	3	1	0	0.3
1979	SF-N	7	9	.438	70	0	0	0	20	96²	86	5	42	80	12.1	2.51	139	.247	.332	1	.250	0	13	11	0	2.2
1980	SF-N	6	8	.429	62	0	0	0	9	100	106	4	36	66	12.8	3.42	103	.275	.336	0	.000	-1	2	1	0	0.1
1981	SF-N	2	6	.250	34	3	0	0	4	65²	58	3	23	45	11.4	3.84	89	.244	.316	3	.273	1	-3	-3	1	-0.2
1982	SF-N	10	7	.588	68	0	0	0	8	104²	97	6	29	76	10.9	2.67	135	.247	.300	2	.154	1	11	11	2	2.1
1983	SF-N☆	7	4	.636	56	0	0	0	20	87	73	4	19	68	9.5	2.59	137	.229	.272	0	.000	-2	10	9	2	1.6
1984	SF-N	5	4	.556	77	0	0	0	12	101	92	5	42	71	12.0	2.76	127	.246	.324	0	.000	0	9	8	-1	0.8
1985	*Tor-A	5	7	.417	69	0	0	0	8	72²	54	5	36	50	11.1	3.10	136	.214	.313	0	—	0	8	9	-0	1.5
1987	Tor-A	2	3	.400	23	0	0	0	1	27²	36	2	19	17	17.9	5.53	81	.313	.410	0	—	0	-3	-3	-0	-0.5
	Oak-A	0	0	—	6	0	0	0	0	4¹	4	0	3	6	14.5	8.31	50	.267	.389	0	—	0	-2	-2	-0	0.3
	Yr	2	3	.400	29	0	0	0	1	32	40	2	22	23	17.4	5.91	75	.305	.405	0	—	0	-5	-5	-0	-0.2
Total	13	80	77	.510	745	3	0	0	136	1085	1004	51	440	769	12.1	2.93	125	.249	.325	9	.081	-6	92	89	4	15.0

● **JIMMY LAVENDER** Lavender, James Sanford b: 3/25/1884, Barnesville, Ga. d: 1/12/60, Cartersville, Ga. BR/TR, 5'11", 165 lbs. Deb: 4/23/12

YEAR	TM/L	W	L	PCT	G	GS	CG	SH	SV	IP	H	HR	BB	SO	RAT	ERA	ERA+	OAV	OOB	BH	AVG	PB	PR	/A	PD	TPI
1912	Chi-N	16	13	.552	42	31	15	3	3	251²	240	8	89	109	12.1	3.04	110	.257	.328	13	.149	-3	10	8	1	0.6
1913	Chi-N	10	14	.417	40	20	10	0	2	204	206	6	98	91	14.0	3.66	87	.267	.359	8	.118	-4	-10	-11	-2	-1.8
1914	Chi-N	11	11	.500	37	28	11	2	0	214¹	191	11	87	87	12.1	3.07	91	.247	.331	11	.175	-2	-7	-7	3	-0.1
1915	Chi-N	10	16	.385	41	24	13	1	4	220	178	5	67	117	10.4	2.58	108	.228	.298	9	.134	-2	4	5	3	0.7
1916	Chi-N	10	14	.417	36	25	9	4	2	188	163	3	62	91	11.2	2.82	103	.240	.312	8	.151	-2	-4	-2	-1	-0.1
1917	Phi-N	6	8	.429	28	14	7	0	1	129¹	119	5	44	52	11.6	3.55	79	.250	.317	5	.139	-1	-12	-11	-2	-1.5
Total	6	63	76	.453	224	142	65	10	12	1207¹	1097	38	447	547	11.9	3.09	97	.249	.325	54	.144	-9	-19	-12	2	-2.2

● **RON LAW** Law, Ronald David b: 3/14/46, Hamilton, Ont., Can. BR/TR, 6'2", 165 lbs. Deb: 6/29/69

YEAR	TM/L	W	L	PCT	G	GS	CG	SH	SV	IP	H	HR	BB	SO	RAT	ERA	ERA+	OAV	OOB	BH	AVG	PB	PR	/A	PD	TPI
1969	Cle-A	3	4	.429	35	1	0	0	1	52¹	68	2	34	29	17.9	4.99	76	.325	.424	1	.143	-0	-8	-7	0	-0.9

● **VANCE LAW** Law, Vance Aaron b: 10/1/56, Boise, Idaho BR/TR, 6'2", 190 lbs. Deb: 6/1/80 F♦

YEAR	TM/L	W	L	PCT	G	GS	CG	SH	SV	IP	H	HR	BB	SO	RAT	ERA	ERA+	OAV	OOB	BH	AVG	PB	PR	/A	PD	TPI
1986	Mon-N	0	0	—	3	0	0	0	0	4	3	0	2	0	11.3	2.25	164	.214	.313	81	.225	1	1	1	0	0.0
1987	Mon-N	0	0	—	3	0	0	0	0	3¹	5	0	2	2	13.5	5.40	78	.333	.333	119	.273	1	-0	-0	0	0.0
1991	Oak-A	0	0	—	1	0	0	0	0	0²	1	0	1	0	27.0	0.00	—	.333	.500	28	.209	1	0	0	0	0.0
Total	3	0	0	—	7	0	0	0	0	8	9	0	3	2	13.5	3.38	116	.281	.343	972	.256	3	0	0	0	0.0

● **VERN LAW** Law, Vernon Sanders "Deacon" b: 3/12/30, Meridian, Idaho BR/TR, 6'2", 195 lbs. Deb: 6/11/50 FC

YEAR	TM/L	W	L	PCT	G	GS	CG	SH	SV	IP	H	HR	BB	SO	RAT	ERA	ERA+	OAV	OOB	BH	AVG	PB	PR	/A	PD	TPI
1950	Pit-N	7	9	.438	27	17	5	1	0	128	137	11	49	57	13.4	4.92	89	.272	.341	3	.073	-2	-11	-8	-2	-1.2
1951	Pit-N	6	9	.400	28	14	2	1	2	114	109	9	51	41	13.1	4.50	94	.253	.341	11	.344	5	-3	-3	-1	0.0
1954	Pit-N	9	13	.409	39	18	7	0	3	161²	201	20	56	57	14.5	5.51	76	.311	.368	12	.231	-3	-26	-24	-1	-2.5
1955	Pit-N	10	10	.500	43	24	8	1	1	200²	221	19	61	82	12.7	3.81	108	.280	.333	16	.254	3	5	7	0	1.0
1956	Pit-N	8	16	.333	39	32	6	0	2	195²	218	24	49	60	12.6	4.32	87	.281	.329	10	.175	-1	-12	-12	-1	-1.3
1957	Pit-N	10	8	.556	31	25	9	3	1	172²	172	18	32	55	10.7	2.87	132	.256	.291	12	.190	1	19	18	-2	1.7
1958	Pit-N	14	12	.538	35	29	6	1	3	202¹	235	16	39	56	12.2	3.96	98	.297	.331	12	.194	6	-0	-2	-0	0.3
1959	Pit-N	18	9	.667	34	33	20	2	1	266	245	25	53	110	10.2	2.98	130	.243	.282	16	.167	1	29	26	1	2.8
1960	*Pit-N★	20	9	.690	35	35	**18**	3	0	271²	266	25	40	120	10.3	3.08	122	.257	.287	17	.181	3	21	20	1	2.6
1961	Pit-N	3	4	.429	11	10	1	0	0	59¹	72	10	18	20	13.8	4.70	85	.305	.357	5	.263	1	-4	-5	-1	-0.3
1962	Pit-N	10	7	.588	23	20	7	2	0	139¹	156	21	27	78	11.9	3.94	100	.276	.310	14	.311	5	0	-0	1	0.6
1963	Pit-N	4	5	.444	18	12	1	1	0	76²	91	11	13	31	12.2	4.93	67	.296	.325	5	.217	1	-14	-14	-1	-1.3
1964	Pit-N	12	13	.480	35	29	7	5	0	192	203	18	32	94	11.1	3.61	97	.270	.300	19	.311	8	-2	-2	-1	0.6
1965	Pit-N	17	9	.654	29	28	13	4	0	217¹	182	17	35	101	9.1	2.15	163	.229	.264	20	.244	4	33	33	1	4.6
1966	Pit-N	12	8	.600	31	28	8	4	0	177²	203	19	24	88	11.7	4.05	88	.292	.320	16	.242	5	-9	-9	2	-0.4
1967	Pit-N	2	6	.250	25	10	1	0	0	97	122	8	18	43	13.1	4.18	81	.308	.340	3	.111	-0	-9	-0	-0	-0.7
Total	16	162	147	.524	483	364	119	28	13	2672	2833	268	597	1092	11.7	3.77	101	.272	.314	191	.216	45	14	15	2	6.5

● **BROOKS LAWRENCE** Lawrence, Brooks Ulysses "Bull" b: 1/30/25, Springfield, Ohio BR/TR, 6', 205 lbs. Deb: 6/24/54

YEAR	TM/L	W	L	PCT	G	GS	CG	SH	SV	IP	H	HR	BB	SO	RAT	ERA	ERA+	OAV	OOB	BH	AVG	PB	PR	/A	PD	TPI
1954	StL-N	15	6	.714	35	18	8	0	1	158²	141	17	72	72	12.5	3.74	110	.243	.335	10	.189	0	6	6	0	0.8
1955	StL-N	3	8	.273	46	10	2	1	1	96	102	11	58	52	15.7	6.56	62	.278	.387	2	.095	-2	-27	-27	1	-2.8
1956	Cin-N☆	19	10	.655	49	30	11	1	1	218²	210	26	71	96	11.6	3.99	100	.256	.317	11	.157	-1	-5	-0	3	0.2
1957	Cin-N	16	13	.552	49	32	12	1	4	250¹	234	26	76	121	11.4	3.52	117	.247	.309	14	.171	-0	10	16	-0	1.8
1958	Cin-N	8	13	.381	46	23	6	2	5	181	194	12	55	74	12.6	4.13	96	.275	.331	6	.113	-2	-4	-4	-0	-0.2
1959	Cin-N	7	12	.368	43	14	3	0	10	128¹	144	17	45	64	13.5	4.77	85	.281	.344	6	.150	-1	-12	-10	-1	-1.6
1960	Cin-N	1	0	1.000	7	0	0	0	1	7²	9	1	8	2	20.0	10.57	36	.310	.459	0	—	0	-6	-6	0	-0.8
Total	7	69	62	.527	275	127	42	5	22	1040²	1034	110	385	481	12.6	4.25	96	.261	.332	49	.154	-5	-38	-20	4	-2.6

● **BOB LAWRENCE** Lawrence, Robert Andrew "Larry" b: 12/14/1899, Brooklyn, N.Y. d: 11/6/83, Jamaica, N.Y. BR/TR, 5'11", 180 lbs. Deb: 7/19/24

YEAR	TM/L	W	L	PCT	G	GS	CG	SH	SV	IP	H	HR	BB	SO	RAT	ERA	ERA+	OAV	OOB	BH	AVG	PB	PR	/A	PD	TPI
1924	Chi-A	0	0	—	1	0	0	0	0	1	1	0	1	1	18.0	9.00	46	.250	.400	0	—	0	-1	-1	0	0.0

● **AL LAWSON** Lawson, Alfred William b: 3/24/1869, London, England d: 11/29/54, San Antonio, Tex. BR/TR, 5'11", 161 lbs. Deb: 5/13/1890

YEAR	TM/L	W	L	PCT	G	GS	CG	SH	SV	IP	H	HR	BB	SO	RAT	ERA	ERA+	OAV	OOB	BH	AVG	PB	PR	/A	PD	TPI
1890	Bos-N	0	1	.000	1	1	1	0	0	9	12	1	4	1	16.0	4.00	94	.310	.375	0	.000	-0	-0	-0	0	0.0
	Pit-N	0	2	.000	2	2	1	0	0	10	15	0	10	2	22.5	9.00	37	.336	.458	0	.000	-1	-6	-6	0	-0.9
	Yr	0	3	.000	3	3	2	0	0	19	27	0	14	3	19.4	6.63	53	.324	.421	0	.000	-1	-6	-7	0	-0.9

● **ROXIE LAWSON** Lawson, Alfred Voyle b: 4/13/06, Donnellson, Iowa d: 4/9/77, Stockport, Iowa BR/TR, 6', 170 lbs. Deb: 8/3/30

YEAR	TM/L	W	L	PCT	G	GS	CG	SH	SV	IP	H	HR	BB	SO	RAT	ERA	ERA+	OAV	OOB	BH	AVG	PB	PR	/A	PD	TPI
1930	Cle-A	1	2	.333	7	4	2	0	0	33²	46	1	23	10	18.4	6.15	79	.324	.418	1	.091	-1	-6	-5	-0	-0.4
1931	Cle-A	0	2	.000	17	3	0	0	0	55²	72	5	36	20	17.5	7.60	61	.304	.396	2	.143	-0	-20	-18	-1	-0.6
1933	Det-A	0	1	.000	4	2	0	0	0	16	17	2	17	6	19.1	7.31	59	.270	.425	0	.000	-1	-5	-5	0	-0.3
1935	Det-A	3	1	.750	7	4	4	2	2	40	34	3	24	16	13.0	1.57	265	.233	.341	4	.308	1	13	12	-1	1.2
1936	Det-A	8	6	.571	41	8	3	0	3	128	139	13	71	34	15.0	5.48	90	.281	.376	10	.222	1	-6	-8	-1	-0.6
1937	Det-A	18	7	.720	37	29	15	0	1	217¹	236	17	115	68	14.6	5.26	89	.271	.357	21	.259	3	-15	-14	-1	-1.2
1938	Det-A	8	9	.471	27	16	5	0	1	127	154	13	82	39	16.7	5.46	92	.299	.395	2	.044	-1	-9	-6	-1	-1.1
1939	Det-A	1	1	.500	2	1	0	0	0	11¹	17	1	7	4	11.1	4.76	103	.167	.286	0	.000	-1	-0	-0	0	0.0
	StL-A	3	7	.300	36	14	5	0	0	150²	181	10	83	43	15.9	5.32	92	.307	.394	8	.186	-1	-12	-8	-1	-0.5
	Yr	4	8	.333	38	15	5	0	0	162	188	11	90	47	15.6	5.28	92	.297	.387	8	.170	-2	-12	-7	-0	-0.5
1940	StL-A	5	3	.625	30	2	0	0	4	72	72	5	36	18	16.4	5.13	89	.278	.396	1	.045	-6	-4	-0	-0	-0.7
Total	9	47	39	.547	208	83	34	2	11	851²	963	70	512	258	15.7	5.37	89	.285	.380	49	.173	-6	-67	-57	-2	-4.2

● **BOB LAWSON** Lawson, Robert Baker b: 8/23/1876, Brookneal, Va. d: 10/28/52, Chapel Hill, N.C. BR/TR, 5'10", 170 lbs. Deb: 5/7/01

YEAR	TM/L	W	L	PCT	G	GS	CG	SH	SV	IP	H	HR	BB	SO	RAT	ERA	ERA+	OAV	OOB	BH	AVG	PB	PR	/A	PD	TPI
1901	Bos-N	2	2	.500	6	4	4	0	0	46	45	0	28	12	14.9	3.33	109	.254	.366	4	.148	-0	-0	1	1	0.2
1902	Bal-A	0	2	.000	3	2	1	0	0	13	21	0	3	5	18.0	4.85	78	.363	.414	1	.167	-0	-2	-2	0	-0.2
Total	2	2	4	.333	9	6	5	0	0	59	66	0	31	17	15.6	3.66	100	.281	.377	5	.152	-1	-2	-0	1	0.0

● **STEVE LAWSON** Lawson, Steven George b: 12/28/50, Oakland, Cal. BR/TL, 6'1", 175 lbs. Deb: 8/3/72

YEAR	TM/L	W	L	PCT	G	GS	CG	SH	SV	IP	H	HR	BB	SO	RAT	ERA	ERA+	OAV	OOB	BH	AVG	PB	PR	/A	PD	TPI
1972	Tex-A	0	0	—	13	0	0	0	0	16	13	1	10	13	12.9	2.81	107	.213	.324	1	1.000	0	0	0	-0	0.0

● **BILL LAXTON** Laxton, William Harry b: 1/5/48, Camden, N.J. BL/TL, 6'1", 190 lbs. Deb: 9/15/70

YEAR	TM/L	W	L	PCT	G	GS	CG	SH	SV	IP	H	HR	BB	SO	RAT	ERA	ERA+	OAV	OOB	BH	AVG	PB	PR	/A	PD	TPI
1970	Phi-N	0	0	—	2	0	0	0	0	2	2	2	2	2	22.5	13.50	30	.250	.455	0	—	0	-2	-2	-0	0.0

YEAR TM/L	W	L	PCT	G	GS	CG	SH	SV	IP	H	HR	BB	SO	RAT	ERA	ERA+	OAV	OOB	BH	AVG	PB	PR	/A	PD	TPI
1971 SD-N	0	2	.000	18	0	0	0	0	27²	32	4	26	23	19.2	6.83	48	.305	.447	0	—	0	-10	-11	-0	-0.7
1974 SD-N	0	1	.000	30	1	0	0	0	44²	37	5	38	40	15.7	4.03	88	.226	.380	1	.200	0	-2	-2	-0	-0.1
1976 Det-A	0	5	.000	26	3	0	0	2	94²	77	13	51	74	12.7	4.09	91	.221	.331	0	—	0	-6	-4	-2	-0.4
1977 Sea-A	3	2	.600	43	0	0	0	3	72²	62	10	39	49	13.0	4.95	83	.233	.340	0	—	0	-7	-7	-1	-0.6
Cle-A	0	0	—	2	0	0	0	0	1²	2	0	2	1	21.6	5.40	73	.286	.444	0	—	0	-0	-0	-0	0.0
Yr	3	2	.600	45	0	0	0	3	74¹	64	10	41	50	12.7	4.96	83	.228	.326	0	—	0	-7	-7	-1	-0.6
Total 5	3	10	.231	121	4	0	0	5	243¹	212	34	158	189	14.2	4.73	79	.236	.359	1	.200	0	-28	-26	-3	-1.8

● **TIM LAYANA**   Layana, Timothy Joseph b: 3/2/64, Inglewood, Cal.   BR/TR, 6'2", 195 lbs.   Deb: 4/9/90

YEAR TM/L	W	L	PCT	G	GS	CG	SH	SV	IP	H	HR	BB	SO	RAT	ERA	ERA+	OAV	OOB	BH	AVG	PB	PR	/A	PD	TPI
1990 Cin-N	5	3	.625	55	0	0	0	2	80	71	7	44	53	13.2	3.49	113	.244	.347	0	.000	-1	3	4	0	0.4
1991 Cin-N	0	2	.000	22	0	0	0	0	20²	23	1	11	14	14.8	6.97	55	.277	.362	0	.000	-0	-8	-7	-0	-0.6
1993 SF-N	0	0	—	1	0	0	0	0	2	7	1	1	1	36.0	22.50	17	.538	.571	0	—	0	-4	-4	0	-0.1
Total 3	5	5	.500	78	0	0	0	2	102²	101	9	56	68	13.9	4.56	86	.261	.357	0	.000	-1	-9	-7	1	-0.2

● **DANNY LAZAR**   Lazar, John Daniel b: 11/14/43, East Chicago, Ind.   BL/TL, 6'1", 190 lbs.   Deb: 6/21/68

YEAR TM/L	W	L	PCT	G	GS	CG	SH	SV	IP	H	HR	BB	SO	RAT	ERA	ERA+	OAV	OOB	BH	AVG	PB	PR	/A	PD	TPI
1968 Chi-A	0	1	.000	8	1	0	0	0	13¹	14	1	4	11	12.2	4.05	75	.269	.321	0	.000	0	-2	-2	0	-0.1
1969 Chi-A	0	0	—	9	3	0	0	0	20²	21	5	11	9	14.4	6.53	59	.280	.379	0	.000	-0	-7	-6	-0	-0.1
Total 2	0	1	.000	17	4	0	0	0	34	35	6	15	20	13.5	5.56	63	.276	.357	0	.000	-0	-8	-8	-0	-0.2

● **JACK LAZORKO**   Lazorko, Jack Thomas b: 3/30/56, Hoboken, N.J.   BR/TR, 5'11", 200 lbs.   Deb: 6/4/84

YEAR TM/L	W	L	PCT	G	GS	CG	SH	SV	IP	H	HR	BB	SO	RAT	ERA	ERA+	OAV	OOB	BH	AVG	PB	PR	/A	PD	TPI
1984 Mil-A	0	1	.000	15	1	0	0	1	39²	37	7	22	24	13.6	4.31	89	.245	.345	0	—	0	-1	-2	0	0.2
1985 Sea-A	0	0	—	15	0	0	0	1	20¹	23	1	8	7	15.0	3.54	119	.291	.378	0	—	0	1	2	1	0.0
1986 Det-A	0	0	—	3	0	0	0	0	6²	8	0	4	3	16.2	4.05	102	.296	.387	0	—	0	0	0	0	0.0
1987 Cal-A	5	6	.455	26	11	2	0	0	117²	108	20	44	55	11.8	4.59	94	.248	.320	0	—	0	-2	-4	2	0.0
1988 Cal-A	0	1	.000	10	3	0	0	0	37²	37	5	16	19	12.9	3.35	115	.255	.333	0	—	0	3	2	0	0.2
Total 5	5	8	.385	69	15	2	0	2	222	213	33	94	108	12.7	4.22	98	.254	.334	0	—	0	1	-2	3	0.4

● **CHARLIE LEA**   Lea, Charles William b: 12/25/56, Orleans, France   BR/TR, 6'4", 197 lbs.   Deb: 6/12/80

YEAR TM/L	W	L	PCT	G	GS	CG	SH	SV	IP	H	HR	BB	SO	RAT	ERA	ERA+	OAV	OOB	BH	AVG	PB	PR	/A	PD	TPI
1980 Mon-N	7	5	.583	21	19	0	0	0	104	103	5	55	56	13.8	3.72	96	.262	.356	3	.081	-2	-1	-2	-1	-0.5
1981 Mon-N	5	4	.556	16	11	2	2	0	64¹	63	4	26	31	12.6	4.62	76	.268	.344	2	.133	-0	-8	-8	-0	-1.1
1982 Mon-N	12	10	.545	27	27	4	2	0	177²	145	16	56	115	10.2	3.24	112	.222	.283	8	.123	-1	7	8	-1	0.7
1983 Mon-N	16	11	.593	33	33	8	4	0	222	195	15	84	137	11.4	3.12	115	.238	.309	8	.114	-2	12	11	-1	1.0
1984 Mon-N★	15	10	.600	30	30	8	0	0	224¹	198	19	68	123	10.8	2.89	119	.239	.309	8	.111	-3	17	13	0	1.2
1987 Mon-N	0	1	.000	1	1	0	0	0	1	4	1	2	1	54.0	36.00	12	.571	.667	0	—	0	-4	-4	-0	-1.3
1988 Min-A	7	7	.500	24	23	0	0	0	130	156	19	50	72	14.6	4.85	84	.301	.368	0	—	0	-13	-11	-1	-1.3
Total 7	62	48	.564	152	144	22	8	0	923¹	864	79	341	535	11.9	3.54	102	.250	.320	29	.112	-7	11	8	-4	-1.5

● **RICK LEACH**   Leach, Richard Max b: 5/4/57, Ann Arbor, Mich.   BL/TL, 6', 195 lbs.   Deb: 4/30/81 ♦

YEAR TM/L	W	L	PCT	G	GS	CG	SH	SV	IP	H	HR	BB	SO	RAT	ERA	ERA+	OAV	OOB	BH	AVG	PB	PR	/A	PD	TPI
1984 Tor-A	0	0	—	1	0	0	0	0	1	2	1	2	0	36.0	27.00	15	.400	.571	23	.261	0	-3	-3	0	0.0

● **TERRY LEACH**   Leach, Terry Hester b: 3/13/54, Selma, Ala.   BR/TR, 6', 215 lbs.   Deb: 8/12/81

YEAR TM/L	W	L	PCT	G	GS	CG	SH	SV	IP	H	HR	BB	SO	RAT	ERA	ERA+	OAV	OOB	BH	AVG	PB	PR	/A	PD	TPI
1981 NY-N	1	1	.500	21	1	0	0	0	35¹	26	2	12	16	9.7	2.55	137	.205	.273	0	.000	1	4	4	1	0.3
1982 NY-N	2	1	.667	21	1	1	1	3	45¹	46	2	18	30	12.7	4.17	87	.271	.340	1	.125	-0	-3	-3	-0	-0.3
1985 NY-N	3	4	.429	22	4	1	1	1	55²	48	3	14	30	10.2	2.91	119	.235	.288	2	.167	1	4	3	1	0.6
1986 NY-N	0	0	—	6	0	0	0	0	6²	6	0	3	4	12.2	2.70	131	.222	.300	0	—	0	1	1	0	0.0
1987 NY-N	11	1	.917	44	12	1	1	0	131¹	132	14	29	61	11.1	3.22	117	.262	.304	2	.061	-2	13	8	1	0.6
1988 *NY-N	7	2	.778	52	0	0	0	3	92	95	5	24	51	11.9	2.54	127	.268	.320	2	.143	-0	9	7	2	0.9
1989 NY-N	0	0	—	10	0	0	0	0	21¹	19	1	4	2	10.1	4.22	77	.244	.289	0	.000	-0	-2	-1	0	0.0
KC-A	5	6	.455	30	0	0	0	2	73²	78	4	36	34	14.0	4.15	93	.278	.362	0	—	0	-2	-3	1	-0.2
1990 Min-A	2	5	.286	55	0	0	0	2	81²	84	2	21	46	11.7	3.20	130	.268	.316	0	—	0	6	9	1	0.8
1991 *Min-A	1	2	.333	50	0	0	0	0	67¹	82	3	14	32	12.8	3.61	118	.299	.333	0	—	0	4	5	1	0.2
1992 Chi-A	6	5	.545	51	0	0	0	0	73²	57	2	20	22	9.9	1.95	197	.215	.280	0	—	0	16	16	1	2.3
1993 Chi-A	0	0	—	14	0	0	0	1	16	16	2	3	9	10.1	2.81	149	.250	.286	0	—	0	3	2	-0	0.0
Total 11	38	27	.585	376	21	3	3	10	700	688	38	197	331	11.5	3.15	119	.259	.313	7	.097	-1	53	47	8	5.2

● **LUIS LEAL**   Leal, Luis Enrique (Alvarado) b: 3/21/57, Barquisimeto, Venz.   BR/TR, 6'3", 205 lbs.   Deb: 5/25/80

YEAR TM/L	W	L	PCT	G	GS	CG	SH	SV	IP	H	HR	BB	SO	RAT	ERA	ERA+	OAV	OOB	BH	AVG	PB	PR	/A	PD	TPI
1980 Tor-A	3	4	.429	13	10	1	0	0	59²	72	6	31	26	15.7	4.53	95	.314	.398	0	—	0	-3	-1	-1	-0.2
1981 Tor-A	7	13	.350	29	19	3	0	1	129²	127	8	44	71	12.2	3.68	107	.254	.321	0	—	0	-0	4	-1	0.4
1982 Tor-A	12	15	.444	38	38	10	0	0	249²	250	24	79	111	12.0	3.93	114	.262	.320	0	—	0	4	15	-1	1.2
1983 Tor-A	13	12	.520	35	35	7	1	0	217¹	216	23	65	116	11.9	4.31	100	.257	.315	0	—	0	-6	-0	-1	-0.3
1984 Tor-A	13	8	.619	35	35	6	2	0	222¹	221	27	77	134	12.4	3.89	105	.258	.323	0	—	0	3	5	0	0.4
1985 Tor-A	3	6	.333	15	14	0	0	0	67¹	82	13	24	33	14.6	5.75	73	.303	.366	0	—	0	-12	-12	0	-1.3
Total 6	51	58	.468	165	151	27	3	1	946	968	101	320	491	12.5	4.14	103	.265	.328	0	—	0	-15	11	-2	0.2

● **KING LEAR**   Lear, Charles Bernard b: 1/23/1891, Greencastle, Pa.   d: 10/31/76, Greencastle, Pa.   BR/TR, 6', 175 lbs.   Deb: 5/2/14

YEAR TM/L	W	L	PCT	G	GS	CG	SH	SV	IP	H	HR	BB	SO	RAT	ERA	ERA+	OAV	OOB	BH	AVG	PB	PR	/A	PD	TPI
1914 Cin-N	1	2	.333	17	4	3	1	1	55²	55	3	19	20	12.3	3.07	95	.271	.339	3	.188	-1	-2	-1	-0	-0.0
1915 Cin-N	6	10	.375	40	15	9	0	0	167²	169	5	45	46	11.8	3.01	95	.270	.324	8	.170	-1	-5	-3	-4	-0.8
Total 2	7	12	.368	57	19	12	1	1	223¹	224	10	64	66	11.9	3.02	95	.270	.328	11	.175	-0	-6	-4	-4	-0.8

● **FRANK LEARY**   Leary, Francis Patrick b: 2/26/1881, Wayland, Mass.   d: 10/4/07, Natick, Mass.   TR,   Deb: 4/30/07

YEAR TM/L	W	L	PCT	G	GS	CG	SH	SV	IP	H	HR	BB	SO	RAT	ERA	ERA+	OAV	OOB	BH	AVG	PB	PR	/A	PD	TPI
1907 Cin-N	0	1	.000	2	1	0	0	0	8	7	0	6	4	14.6	1.13	231	.269	.406	0	.000	-0	1	1	0	0.2

● **JACK LEARY**   Leary, John J. b: 1858, New Haven, Conn.   TL, 5'11", 186 lbs.   Deb: 8/21/1880 ♦

YEAR TM/L	W	L	PCT	G	GS	CG	SH	SV	IP	H	HR	BB	SO	RAT	ERA	ERA+	OAV	OOB	BH	AVG	PB	PR	/A	PD	TPI
1880 Bos-N	0	1	.000	1	1	0	0	0	3	8	0	0	1	24.0	15.00	15	.727	.727	0	.000	-0	-4	-4	0	-0.8
1881 Det-N	0	2	.000	2	2	1	0	0	13	13	0	2	2	10.4	4.15	70	.255	.283	3	.273	1	-2	-2	-0	-0.2
1882 Pit-a	1	0	1.000	3	3	1	0	0	18²	28	1	3	5	14.9	6.27	42	.325	.348	75	.292	1	-7	-8	-0	-0.2
Bal-a	2	1	.667	3	3	3	0	0	26	29	1	8	2	12.8	1.38	199	.264	.314	4	.222	1	4	2	0	0.4
Yr	3	1	.750	6	6	4	0	0	44²	57	2	11	7	13.7	3.43	79	.291	.329	79	.287	1	-4	-4	-0	0.2
1884 Alt-U	0	3	.000	3	3	2	0	0	24	31	0	2	7	12.4	5.25	51	.306	.306	3	.091	-2	-7	-0	-0	-0.7
CP-U	0	2	.000	2	1	1	0	0	10	14	0	5	6	17.1	5.40	45	.310	.379	7	.175	-1	-3	-3	-0	-0.5
Yr	0	5	.000	5	4	3	0	0	34	45	0	7	13	13.8	5.29	49	.298	.330	10	.137	-3	-11	-10	-0	-1.2
Total 4	3	9	.250	14	12	8	0	0	94²	123	1	20	23	13.6	4.56	59	.301	.334	125	.232	-2	-21	-20	-0	-2.0

● **TIM LEARY**   Leary, Timothy James b: 12/23/58, Santa Monica, Cal.   BR/TR, 6'3", 205 lbs.   Deb: 4/12/81

YEAR TM/L	W	L	PCT	G	GS	CG	SH	SV	IP	H	HR	BB	SO	RAT	ERA	ERA+	OAV	OOB	BH	AVG	PB	PR	/A	PD	TPI
1981 NY-N	0	0	—	1	1	0	0	0	2	0	0	1	3	4.5	0.00	—	.000	.143	0	.000	0	1	1	0	0.0
1983 NY-N	1	1	.500	2	2	1	0	0	10²	15	0	4	9	16.0	3.38	107	.319	.373	1	.333	0	1	1	0	0.1
1984 NY-N	3	3	.500	20	7	0	0	0	53²	61	2	18	29	13.6	4.02	88	.285	.346	3	.300	2	-3	-3	-1	-0.2
1985 Mil-A	1	4	.200	5	5	0	0	0	33¹	40	5	13	29	13.2	4.05	103	.296	.340	0	—	0	0	0	1	0.1
1986 Mil-A	12	12	.500	33	30	3	2	0	188¹	216	20	53	110	13.2	4.21	103	.289	.342	0	—	0	-3	-1	0	-0.2
1987 LA-N	3	11	.214	39	12	0	0	1	107²	121	15	36	61	13.3	4.76	83	.285	.344	7	.304	2	-8	-10	-1	-0.9
1988 *LA-N	17	11	.607	35	34	9	6	0	228²	201	13	56	180	10.4	2.91	114	.234	.285	18	.269	6	14	11	2	2.0
1989 LA-N	6	7	.462	19	14	2	0	0	117¹	121	8	37	59	12.3	3.38	101	.274	.309	2	.061	-2	1	1	-1	-0.1
Cin-N	2	7	.222	14	14	0	0	0	89²	84	9	31	64	13.2	3.71	97	.278	.342	5	.192	-2	-2	-1	0	0.0
Yr	8	14	.364	33	31	2	0	0	207	205	17	68	123	12.0	3.52	99	.259	.320	7	.119	-1	-1	-1	-0	0.0
1990 NY-A	9	19	.321	31	31	6	1	0	208	202	18	78	138	12.4	4.11	97	.257	.330	0	—	0	-5	-3	2	-0.2

YEAR TM/L	W	L	PCT	G	GS	CG	SH	SV	IP	H	HR	BB	SO	RAT	ERA	ERA+	OAV	OOB	BH	AVG	PB	PR	/A	PD	TPI
1991 NY-A	4	10	.286	28	18	1	0	0	120²	150	20	57	83	15.7	6.49	64	.312	.389	0	—	0	-32	-31	-0	-3.1
1992 NY-A	5	6	.455	18	15	2	0	0	97	84	9	57	34	13.5	5.57	70	.245	.359	0	—	0	-18	-18	-1	-1.8
Sea-A	3	4	.429	8	8	1	0	0	44	47	3	30	12	16.8	4.91	81	.280	.404	0	—	0	-5	-5	1	-0.6
Yr	8	10	.444	26	23	3	0	0	141	131	12	87	46	14.2	5.36	73	.251	.364	0	—	0	-22	-22	-0	-2.4
1993 Sea-A	11	9	.550	33	27	0	0	0	169¹	202	21	58	68	14.2	5.05	87	.300	.362	0	—	0	-14	-12	1	-1.1
1994 Tex-A	1	1	.500	6	3	0	0	0	21	26	4	11	9	16.3	8.14	56	.306	.392	0	—	0	-8	-8	-0	-0.5
Total 13	78	105	.426	292	224	25	9	1	1491¹	1570	147	535	888	13.0	4.36	89	.273	.340	36	.221	9	-78	-77	6	-5.9

● **RAZOR LEDBETTER**   Ledbetter, Ralph Overton   b: 12/8/1894, Rutherford College, N.C.   d: 2/1/69, W.Palm Beach, Fla.   BR/TR, 6'3", 190 lbs.   Deb: 4/16/15

YEAR TM/L	W	L	PCT	G	GS	CG	SH	SV	IP	H	HR	BB	SO	RAT	ERA	ERA+	OAV	OOB	BH	AVG	PB	PR	/A	PD	TPI
1915 Det-A	0	0	—	1	0	0	0	0	1	1	0	0	0	9.0	0.00	—	.333	.333	0	—	0	0	0	0	0.0

● **DON LEE**   Lee, Donald Edward   b: 2/26/34, Globe, Ariz.   BR/TR, 6'4", 210 lbs.   Deb: 4/23/57   F

YEAR TM/L	W	L	PCT	G	GS	CG	SH	SV	IP	H	HR	BB	SO	RAT	ERA	ERA+	OAV	OOB	BH	AVG	PB	PR	/A	PD	TPI
1957 Det-A	1	3	.250	11	6	0	0	0	38²	48	6	18	19	15.6	4.66	83	.308	.383	2	.167	-0	-4	-3	-0	-0.4
1958 Det-A	0	0	—	1	0	0	0	0	2	1	1	1	0	13.5	9.00	45	.143	.333	0	—	0	-1	-1	-0	0.0
1960 Was-A	8	7	.533	44	20	1	0	3	165	160	16	64	88	12.4	3.44	113	.258	.330	5	.116	-0	8	8	1	0.8
1961 Min-A	3	6	.333	37	10	4	0	3	115	93	12	35	65	10.3	3.52	120	.221	.288	2	.067	-3	6	9	2	0.6
1962 Min-A	3	3	.500	9	9	0	0	0	52	51	8	24	28	14.2	4.50	91	.256	.357	4	.211	-0	-3	-2	-0	-0.2
LA-A	8	8	.500	27	22	4	2	2	153¹	153	12	39	74	11.4	3.11	124	.256	.305	9	.184	-0	15	13	-2	1.1
Yr	11	11	.500	36	31	5	2	2	205¹	204	20	63	102	11.8	3.46	113	.254	.310	13	.191	-0	12	10	-2	0.9
1963 LA-A	8	11	.421	40	22	3	2	1	154	148	9	51	89	12.2	3.68	93	.251	.320	7	.156	-1	-1	-4	-1	-0.7
1964 LA-A	5	4	.556	33	8	0	0	2	89¹	99	6	25	73	12.6	2.72	121	.279	.328	6	.261	2	9	6	-1	0.7
1965 Cal-A	0	1	.000	10	0	0	0	0	14	21	4	5	12	17.4	6.43	53	.350	.409	1	.333	1	-5	-5	-0	-0.3
Hou-N	0	0	—	7	0	0	0	0	8	8	0	3	3	13.5	3.38	99	.267	.353	0	.000	-0	0	0	0	0.0
1966 Hou-N	2	0	1.000	9	0	0	0	0	18	17	1	4	9	10.5	2.50	137	.250	.292	1	1.000	1	2	2	1	0.3
Chi-N	2	1	.667	16	0	0	0	0	19	28	3	12	7	18.9	7.11	52	.346	.430	0	—	0	-7	-7	-0	-1.0
Yr	4	1	.800	25	0	0	0	0	37	45	4	16	16	14.4	4.86	73	.302	.370	1	1.000	1	-5	-5	1	-0.7
Total 9	40	44	.476	244	97	13	4	11	828¹	827	81	281	467	12.4	3.61	104	.260	.326	37	.164	-1	20	14	1	0.9

● **MARK LEE**   Lee, Mark Linden   b: 6/14/53, Inglewood, Cal.   BR/TR, 6'4", 225 lbs.   Deb: 4/23/78

YEAR TM/L	W	L	PCT	G	GS	CG	SH	SV	IP	H	HR	BB	SO	RAT	ERA	ERA+	OAV	OOB	BH	AVG	PB	PR	/A	PD	TPI
1978 SD-N	5	1	.833	56	0	0	0	6	85	74	4	36	31	11.9	3.28	101	.240	.324	0	.000	-1	3	0	2	0.1
1979 SD-N	2	4	.333	46	1	0	0	5	65	88	3	25	25	15.9	4.29	82	.332	.394	2	.333	1	-4	-6	1	-0.4
1980 Pit-N	0	1	.000	4	0	0	0	0	5²	5	0	3	2	12.7	4.76	76	.227	.320	0	—	0	-1	-1	0	0.0
1981 Pit-N	0	2	.000	12	0	0	0	0	19²	17	1	5	5	10.1	2.75	131	.233	.282	1	.500	1	2	1	1	0.4
Total 4	7	8	.467	118	1	0	0	9	175¹	184	6	69	63	13.2	3.64	94	.275	.347	3	.231	1	-0	-4	4	0.1

● **MARK LEE**   Lee, Mark Owen   b: 7/20/64, Williston, N.Dak.   BL/TL, 6'3", 198 lbs.   Deb: 9/8/88

YEAR TM/L	W	L	PCT	G	GS	CG	SH	SV	IP	H	HR	BB	SO	RAT	ERA	ERA+	OAV	OOB	BH	AVG	PB	PR	/A	PD	TPI
1988 KC-A	0	0	—	4	0	0	0	0	6	6	1	0	1	12.6	3.60	111	.300	.333	0	—	0	0	0	0	0.0
1990 Mil-A	1	0	1.000	11	0	0	0	0	21¹	20	1	4	14	10.1	2.11	184	.256	.293	0	—	0	4	4	-0	0.2
1991 Mil-A	2	5	.286	62	0	0	0	1	67²	72	10	31	43	13.8	3.86	103	.283	.364	0	—	0	2	1	1	0.3
Total 3	3	5	.375	77	0	0	0	1	94	98	11	36	57	12.9	3.45	115	.278	.347	0	—	0	6	5	0	0.5

● **MIKE LEE**   Lee, Michael Randall   b: 5/19/41, Bell, Cal.   BL/TL, 6'5", 220 lbs.   Deb: 5/6/60

YEAR TM/L	W	L	PCT	G	GS	CG	SH	SV	IP	H	HR	BB	SO	RAT	ERA	ERA+	OAV	OOB	BH	AVG	PB	PR	/A	PD	TPI
1960 Cle-A	0	0	—	7	0	0	0	0	9	6	1	11	6	18.0	2.00	187	.207	.439	0	—	0	2	2	-0	0.0
1963 LA-A	1	1	.500	6	4	0	0	0	26	30	3	14	11	15.6	3.81	90	.300	.391	0	.000	-1	-1	-1	1	-0.1
Total 2	1	1	.500	13	4	0	0	0	35	36	4	25	17	16.2	3.34	105	.279	.404	0	.000	-1	1	1	1	-0.1

● **BOB LEE**   Lee, Robert Dean "Moose" or "Horse"   b: 11/26/37, Ottumwa, Iowa   BR/TR, 6'3", 230 lbs.   Deb: 4/15/64

YEAR TM/L	W	L	PCT	G	GS	CG	SH	SV	IP	H	HR	BB	SO	RAT	ERA	ERA+	OAV	OOB	BH	AVG	PB	PR	/A	PD	TPI
1964 LA-A	6	5	.545	64	5	0	0	19	137	87	6	58	111	9.6	1.51	217	.182	.272	0	.000	-2	**32**	27	-2	2.6
1965 Cal-A☆	9	7	.563	69	0	0	0	23	131¹	95	11	42	89	9.5	1.92	217	.205	.272	3	.143	1	22	22	-1	3.5
1966 Cal-A	5	4	.556	61	0	0	0	16	101²	90	8	31	46	10.8	2.74	122	.237	.297	0	.000	-0	8	7	-1	0.8
1967 LA-N	0	0	—	4	0	0	0	0	6²	9	2	3	2	13.5	5.40	57	.222	.323	0	—	0	-2	-2	-0	0.0
Cin-N	3	3	.500	27	1	0	0	2	50²	51	0	25	33	13.5	4.44	84	.262	.345	3	.375	1	-6	-4	-1	-0.5
Yr	3	3	.500	31	1	0	0	2	57¹	57	2	28	35	13.3	4.55	81	.254	.337	3	.375	1	-8	-6	-1	-0.5
1968 Cin-N	2	4	.333	44	1	0	0	3	65¹	73	4	37	34	15.3	5.10	62	.302	.396	1	.200	0	-15	-14	-1	-1.6
Total 5	25	23	.521	269	7	0	0	63	492²	402	31	196	315	11.0	2.70	125	.225	.304	7	.104	-1	40	36	-6	4.8

● **ROY LEE**   Lee, Roy Edwin   b: 9/28/17, Elmira, N.Y.   d: 11/11/85, St.Louis, Mo.   BL/TL, 5'11.5", 175 lbs.   Deb: 9/23/45

YEAR TM/L	W	L	PCT	G	GS	CG	SH	SV	IP	H	HR	BB	SO	RAT	ERA	ERA+	OAV	OOB	BH	AVG	PB	PR	/A	PD	TPI
1945 NY-N	0	2	.000	3	1	0	0	0	7	8	3	3	4	14.1	11.57	34	.267	.333	0	.000	-0	-6	-7	-1	-1.3

● **TOM LEE**   Lee, Thomas Frank   b: 6/8/1862, Philadelphia, Pa.   d: 3/4/1886, Milwaukee, Wis.   Deb: 6/14/1884

YEAR TM/L	W	L	PCT	G	GS	CG	SH	SV	IP	H	HR	BB	SO	RAT	ERA	ERA+	OAV	OOB	BH	AVG	PB	PR	/A	PD	TPI
1884 Chi-N	1	4	.200	5	5	5	0	0	45¹	55	12	15	14	13.9	3.77	83	.272	.323	3	.125	-2	-4	-3	-0	-0.4
Bal-U	5	8	.385	15	14	12	0	0	122	121	1	29	81	11.1	3.39	79	.242	.283	23	.280	-2	-13	-10	0	-0.9
Total 1	6	12	.333	20	19	17	0	0	167¹	176	13	44	95	11.8	3.50	80	.251	.295	26	.245	-4	-17	-13	0	-1.3

● **THORNTON LEE**   Lee, Thornton Starr "Lefty"   b: 9/13/06, Sonoma, Cal.   BL/TL, 6'3", 205 lbs.   Deb: 9/19/33   F

YEAR TM/L	W	L	PCT	G	GS	CG	SH	SV	IP	H	HR	BB	SO	RAT	ERA	ERA+	OAV	OOB	BH	AVG	PB	PR	/A	PD	TPI
1933 Cle-A	1	1	.500	3	2	2	0	0	17¹	13	1	11	7	12.5	4.15	107	.203	.320	3	.375	1	0	1	-0	0.2
1934 Cle-A	1	1	.500	24	6	0	0	0	85²	105	8	44	41	16.0	5.04	90	.308	.392	2	.095	-1	-5	-5	0	-0.2
1935 Cle-A	7	10	.412	32	20	8	1	1	180²	179	6	71	81	12.7	4.04	112	.259	.331	12	.197	-1	8	9	2	0.8
1936 Cle-A	3	5	.375	43	8	2	0	3	127	138	2	67	49	14.7	4.89	103	.271	.358	5	.122	-2	**2**	2	2	0.1
1937 Chi-A	12	10	.545	30	25	13	2	0	204²	209	17	60	80	11.9	3.52	131	.260	.312	15	.211	-0	25	25	-1	2.2
1938 Chi-A	13	12	.520	33	30	18	1	1	245¹	252	12	94	77	12.8	3.49	140	.263	.331	26	.258	-6	36	**38**	-2	3.8
1939 Chi-A	15	11	.577	33	29	15	2	3	235	260	14	70	81	12.8	4.21	112	.285	.338	15	.165	-3	11	14	0	1.1
1940 Chi-A	12	13	.480	28	27	24	1	0	228	223	13	56	87	11.1	3.47	127	.254	.300	23	.274	4	23	24	-3	2.4
1941 Chi-A★	22	11	.667	35	34	**30**	3	1	300¹	258	18	92	130	**10.6**	2.37	173	.232	**.293**	29	.254	5	**59**	58	-2	**6.6**
1942 Chi-A	2	6	.250	11	8	4	1	0	76	82	4	31	25	13.6	3.32	109	.278	.351	6	.200	1	3	2	0	0.1
1943 Chi-A	5	9	.357	19	19	7	1	0	127	129	8	50	35	13.0	4.18	80	.266	.340	3	.071	-4	-12	-12	-3	-1.9
1944 Chi-A	3	9	.250	15	14	6	0	0	113¹	105	3	25	39	10.4	3.02	114	.246	.290	4	.095	-3	5	5	2	0.4
1945 Chi-A†	15	12	.556	29	28	19	1	0	228¹	208	6	76	108	11.6	2.44	136	.245	.314	14	.175	-1	23	22	-1	2.4
1946 Chi-A	2	4	.333	7	7	2	0	0	43¹	39	1	23	23	13.1	3.53	97	.244	.342	4	.267	-1	-0	-1	-0	-0.1
1947 Chi-A	3	7	.300	21	11	2	1	0	86²	86	5	56	57	15.0	4.47	82	.261	.372	6	.207	0	-7	-8	-0	-0.8
1948 NY-N	1	3	.250	11	4	1	0	0	32¹	43	3	12	17	14.9	4.41	89	.304	.365	1	.091	-1	-2	-2	0	-0.2
Total 16	117	124	.485	374	272	155	14	10	2331¹	2327	121	838	937	12.4	3.56	119	.260	.326	167	.200	1	169	172	-7	16.9

● **BILL LEE**   Lee, William Crutcher "Big Bill"   b: 10/21/09, Plaquemine, La.   d: 6/15/77, Plaquemine, La.   BR/TR, 6'3", 195 lbs.   Deb: 4/29/34

YEAR TM/L	W	L	PCT	G	GS	CG	SH	SV	IP	H	HR	BB	SO	RAT	ERA	ERA+	OAV	OOB	BH	AVG	PB	PR	/A	PD	TPI
1934 Chi-N	13	14	.481	35	29	16	4	1	214¹	218	9	74	104	12.3	3.40	114	.263	.325	10	.132	-2	16	11	2	1.2
1935 *Chi-N	20	6	**.769**	39	32	18	3	1	252	241	11	84	100	11.8	2.96	133	.251	.314	24	.235	2	30	27	-0	2.7
1936 Chi-N	18	11	.621	43	33	20	**4**	1	258²	238	14	93	102	11.6	3.31	121	.246	.314	12	.138	-3	21	19	1	1.7
1937 Chi-N	14	15	.483	42	33	17	2	1	272¹	289	14	73	108	12.0	3.54	113	.273	.320	15	.172	-1	13	13	3	1.5
1938 *Chi-N★	22	9	.710	44	37	19	**9**	2	291	281	18	74	121	11.0	2.66	144	.252	.299	20	.198	1	37	38	1	4.0
1939 Chi-N★	19	15	.559	37	36	20	1	0	282¹	295	18	85	105	12.1	3.44	114	.272	.325	13	.126	-4	15	16	5	1.7
1940 Chi-N	9	17	.346	37	30	19	0	0	211¹	246	12	70	75	13.5	5.03	75	.295	.350	11	.180	-5	-28	-30	1	-3.5
1941 Chi-N	8	14	.364	28	22	12	0	1	167¹	179	6	43	62	12.0	3.76	93	.270	.316	11	.186	1	-2	-5	-1	-0.3
1942 Chi-N	13	13	.500	32	30	18	4	0	219²	221	6	67	75	11.8	3.85	83	.258	.312	11	.159	1	-13	-16	-1	-1.5
1943 Chi-N	3	7	.300	13	12	4	0	0	78¹	83	4	27	18	12.6	3.56	94	.273	.332	7	.269	1	-2	-2	-1	-0.2
Phi-N	1	5	.167	13	7	2	0	3	60²	70	4	21	17	13.6	4.60	73	.298	.358	1	.059	-2	-8	-8	-1	-1.1

YEAR	TM/L	W	L	PCT	G	GS	CG	SH	SV	IP	H	HR	BB	SO	RAT	ERA	ERA+	OAV	OOB	BH	AVG	PB	PR	/A	PD	TPI
	Yr	4	12	.250	26	19	6	0	3	139	153	8	48	35	13.1	4.01	84	.284	.344	8	.186	-0	-10	-10	-2	-1.3
1944	Phi-N	10	11	.476	31	28	11	3	1	208¹	199	9	57	50	11.2	3.15	115	.248	.300	14	.194	-0	11	11	2	1.2
1945	Phi-N	3	6	.333	13	13	2	0	0	77¹	107	0	30	13	15.9	4.66	82	.318	.374	4	.167	-1	-7	-7	0	-0.7
	Bos-N	6	3	.667	16	13	6	1	0	106¹	112	6	36	12	12.5	2.79	137	.279	.338	4	.129	-1	12	12	1	1.0
	Yr	9	9	.500	29	26	8	1	0	183²	219	6	66	25	14.0	3.58	107	.297	.354	8	.145	-1	5	5	1	0.3
1946	Bos-N	10	9	.526	25	21	8	0	0	140	148	7	45	32	12.5	4.18	82	.273	.330	8	.170	-1	-12	-12	1	-1.4
1947	Chi-N	0	2	.000	14	2	0	0	0	24	26	2	14	9	15.4	4.50	88	.268	.366	1	.333	-0	-1	-1	0	-0.1
Total	14	169	157	.518	462	378	182	29	13	2864	2953	138	893	998	12.2	3.54	106	.266	.322	165	.168	-10	78	66	14	6.2

● BILL LEE   Lee, William Francis "Spaceman" b: 12/28/46, Burbank, Cal. BL/TL, 6'3", 210 lbs. Deb: 6/25/69

YEAR	TM/L	W	L	PCT	G	GS	CG	SH	SV	IP	H	HR	BB	SO	RAT	ERA	ERA+	OAV	OOB	BH	AVG	PB	PR	/A	PD	TPI
1969	Bos-A	1	3	.250	20	1	0	0	0	52	56	9	28	45	14.9	4.50	84	.281	.376	0	.000	-1	-5	-4	-0	-0.4
1970	Bos-A	2	2	.500	11	5	0	0	1	37	48	3	14	19	15.1	4.62	86	.320	.378	0	.000	-1	-4	-3	1	-0.3
1971	Bos-A	9	2	.818	47	3	0	0	2	102	102	7	46	73	13.1	2.74	135	.256	.335	5	.217	0	8	11	0	1.3
1972	Bos-A	7	4	.636	47	0	0	0	5	84¹	75	5	32	43	11.5	3.20	100	.248	.322	3	.188	1	-1	0	3	0.5
1973	Bos-A☆	17	11	.607	38	33	18	1	1	284²	275	20	76	120	11.3	2.75	146	.257	.309	0	—	0	34	40	1	4.0
1974	Bos-A	17	15	.531	38	37	16	1	0	282¹	320	25	67	95	12.5	3.51	110	.290	.333	0	—	0	3	11	4	1.3
1975	*Bos-A	17	9	.654	41	34	17	4	0	260	274	20	69	78	12.0	3.95	103	.273	.322	0	—	0	-5	4	2	0.5
1976	Bos-A	5	7	.417	24	14	1	0	3	96	124	13	28	29	14.5	5.63	70	.307	.356	0	—	0	-22	-18	1	-2.1
1977	Bos-A	9	5	.643	27	16	4	0	1	128	155	14	29	31	12.9	4.43	101	.306	.344	0	—	0	-5	1	2	0.1
1978	Bos-A	10	10	.500	28	24	8	1	0	177	198	20	46	44	13.2	3.46	119	.285	.343	0	—	0	6	13	0	0.8
1979	Mon-N	16	10	.615	33	33	6	3	0	222	230	20	46	59	11.2	3.04	121	.265	.303	16	.216	2	17	15	1	2.0
1980	Mon-N	4	6	.400	24	18	2	0	0	118	156	13	22	34	13.8	4.96	72	.319	.352	9	.220	1	-18	-18	-0	-1.4
1981	*Mon-N	5	6	.455	31	7	0	0	6	88²	90	6	14	34	10.8	2.94	119	.265	.298	8	.364	1	5	5	3	1.4
1982	Mon-N	0	0	—	7	0	0	0	0	12¹	19	1	1	1	14.6	4.38	83	.352	.364	0	—	0	-1	-0	0	0.0
Total	14	119	90	.569	416	225	72	10	19	1944¹	2122	176	531	713	12.4	3.62	107	.280	.329	41	.208	5	12	55	16	7.7

● WATTY LEE   Lee, Wyatt Arnold b: 8/12/1879, Lynch Station, Va. d: 3/6/36, Washington, D.C. BL/TL, 5'10.5", 171 lbs. Deb: 4/30/01 ◆

YEAR	TM/L	W	L	PCT	G	GS	CG	SH	SV	IP	H	HR	BB	SO	RAT	ERA	ERA+	OAV	OOB	BH	AVG	PB	PR	/A	PD	TPI
1901	Was-A	16	16	.500	36	33	25	2	0	262	328	14	45	63	13.2	4.40	83	.303	.337	33	.256	4	-21	-21	2	-1.5
1902	Was-A	5	7	.417	13	10	10	0	0	98	118	5	20	24	13.4	5.05	73	.298	.345	100	.256	3	-16	-15	1	-1.2
1903	Was-A	8	12	.400	22	20	15	2	0	166²	169	5	40	70	11.7	3.08	102	.262	.312	48	.208	1	-2	-1	3	0.6
1904	Pit-N	1	2	.333	5	3	1	0	0	22²	34	0	9	5	18.3	8.74	31	.337	.407	4	.333	1	-15	-15	0	-1.5
Total	4	30	37	.448	76	66	51	4	0	549¹	649	24	114	162	13.0	4.29	83	.292	.334	185	.242	10	-55	-50	5	-3.6

● SAM LEEVER   Leever, Samuel "Deacon" or "The Goshen Schoolmaster"
b: 12/23/1871, Goshen, Ohio d: 5/19/53, Goshen, Ohio BR/TR, 5'10.5", 175 lbs. Deb: 5/26/1898

YEAR	TM/L	W	L	PCT	G	GS	CG	SH	SV	IP	H	HR	BB	SO	RAT	ERA	ERA+	OAV	OOB	BH	AVG	PB	PR	/A	PD	TPI
1898	Pit-N	1	0	1.000	5	3	2	0	0	33	26	0	5	15	8.7	2.45	145	.215	.253	3	.250	0	4	4	-0	0.1
1899	Pit-N	21	23	.477	51	39	35	4	3	379	353	7	122	121	11.5	3.18	120	.247	.311	33	.226	3	28	27	1	3.0
1900	*Pit-N	15	13	.536	30	29	25	3	0	232²	236	2	48	84	11.3	2.71	134	.263	.306	18	.205	0	26	24	-1	2.4
1901	Pit-N	14	5	.737	21	20	18	2	0	176	182	2	39	82	11.7	2.86	114	.265	.311	13	.183	-0	9	8	2	0.8
1902	Pit-N	15	7	.682	28	26	23	4	2	222	203	2	31	86	9.8	2.39	114	.243	.277	16	.178	-0	10	9	-4	0.3
1903	*Pit-N	25	7	.781	36	34	30	7	1	284¹	255	2	60	90	10.1	2.06	157	.238	.282	19	.165	-4	38	37	-0	3.4
1904	Pit-N	18	11	.621	34	32	26	1	0	253¹	224	5	54	63	10.1	2.17	127	.237	.282	26	.263	7	16	16	-1	2.4
1905	Pit-N	20	5	.800	33	29	20	3	1	229²	199	5	54	81	10.4	2.70	115	.231	.286	9	.102	-4	8	8	0	0.4
1906	Pit-N	22	7	.759	36	31	25	6	0	260¹	232	3	48	76	9.9	2.32	115	.243	.284	20	.211	2	9	10	-5	0.7
1907	Pit-N	14	9	.609	31	24	17	5	0	216²	182	3	46	65	9.8	1.66	147	.229	.278	11	.151	-1	20	19	-5	1.3
1908	Pit-N	15	7	.682	38	20	14	4	2	192²	179	1	41	28	10.6	2.10	110	.249	.295	9	.148	0	6	4	-4	0.1
1909	Pit-N	8	1	.889	19	4	2	0	2	70	74	0	14	23	11.8	2.83	96	.276	.322	4	.167	0	-2	-1	-0	-0.1
1910	Pit-N	6	5	.545	26	8	4	0	2	111	104	3	25	33	10.9	2.76	112	.259	.313	2	.065	-3	3	4	1	0.2
Total	13	194	100	.660	388	299	241	39	13	2660²	2449	29	587	847	10.6	2.47	123	.245	.293	183	.184	1	175	169	-15	15.0

● BILL LEFEBVRE   Lefebvre, Wilfred Henry "Lefty" b: 11/11/15, Natick, R.I. BL/TL, 5'11.5", 180 lbs. Deb: 6/10/38 ◆

YEAR	TM/L	W	L	PCT	G	GS	CG	SH	SV	IP	H	HR	BB	SO	RAT	ERA	ERA+	OAV	OOB	BH	AVG	PB	PR	/A	PD	TPI
1938	Bos-A	0	0	—	1	0	0	0	0	4	8	2	0	0	20.3	13.50	37	.400	.429	1	1.000	1	-4	-4	-0	0.1
1939	Bos-A	1	1	.500	5	3	0	0	0	26¹	35	2	14	8	16.7	5.81	81	.333	.412	3	.300	1	-3	-3	-1	-0.2
1943	Was-A	2	0	1.000	6	3	1	0	0	32¹	33	3	16	10	13.6	4.45	72	.268	.353	4	.286	2	-4	-4	-0	-0.1
1944	Was-A	2	4	.333	24	4	2	0	3	69²	86	3	21	18	14.0	4.52	72	.305	.355	16	.258	3	-8	-10	-0	-0.3
Total	4	5	5	.500	36	10	3	0	3	132¹	162	10	51	36	14.6	5.03	71	.306	.369	24	.276	7	-20	-21	-1	-0.5

● CRAIG LEFFERTS   Lefferts, Craig Lindsay b: 9/29/57, Munich, W.Germany BL/TL, 6'1", 210 lbs. Deb: 4/7/83

YEAR	TM/L	W	L	PCT	G	GS	CG	SH	SV	IP	H	HR	BB	SO	RAT	ERA	ERA+	OAV	OOB	BH	AVG	PB	PR	/A	PD	TPI
1983	Chi-N	3	4	.429	56	5	0	0	1	89	80	13	29	60	11.2	3.13	121	.243	.308	2	.111	-1	5	6	0	0.5
1984	*SD-N	3	4	.429	62	0	0	0	10	105²	88	4	24	56	9.6	2.13	167	.229	.276	5	.294	1	17	17	-1	1.5
1985	SD-N	7	6	.538	60	0	0	0	2	83¹	75	7	30	48	11.3	3.35	106	.244	.312	1	.250	0	2	2	-0	0.2
1986	SD-N	9	8	.529	83	0	0	0	4	107²	98	7	44	72	12.0	3.09	118	.253	.331	1	.125	1	7	7	2	1.3
1987	SD-N	2	2	.500	33	0	0	0	2	51¹	56	9	15	39	12.8	4.38	90	.272	.327	1	.333	-0	-2	-2	-1	-0.2
	*SF-N	3	3	.500	44	0	0	0	4	47¹	36	4	18	18	10.3	3.23	119	.216	.292	1	.250	1	4	3	-1	0.4
	Yr	5	5	.500	77	0	0	0	6	98²	92	13	33	57	11.4	3.83	102	.245	.306	2	.286	1	3	1	-1	0.2
1988	SF-N	3	8	.273	64	0	0	0	11	92¹	74	7	23	58	9.6	2.92	112	.225	.278	0	.000	-1	5	3	-1	0.3
1989	*SF-N	2	4	.333	70	0	0	0	20	107	93	11	22	71	9.8	2.69	125	.233	.275	0	.000	-1	10	8	-1	0.6
1990	SD-N	7	5	.583	56	0	0	0	23	78²	68	10	22	60	10.4	2.52	152	.228	.283	1	.250	0	11	11	0	2.5
1991	SD-N	1	6	.143	54	0	0	0	23	69	74	5	14	48	11.6	3.91	97	.285	.324	0	.000	-1	-2	-1	0	-0.2
1992	SD-N	13	9	.591	27	27	0	0	0	163¹	180	16	35	81	11.8	3.69	97	.285	.322	4	.077	-3	-2	-2	-1	-0.6
	Bal-A	1	3	.250	25	5	1	0	0	33	34	3	6	23	10.9	4.09	98	.268	.301	0	—	0	-1	0	-1	-0.1
1993	Tex-A	3	9	.250	52	6	0	0	0	83¹	102	17	28	58	14.1	6.05	69	.304	.360	0	—	0	-16	-18	0	-2.0
1994	Cal-A	1	1	.500	30	0	0	0	0	34²	50	4	12	27	16.1	4.67	107	.350	.400	0	—	0	0	1	0	-0.1
Total	12	58	72	.446	696	45	2	0	101	1145²	1108	120	322	719	11.3	3.43	108	.257	.311	16	.121	-3	39	36	-3	4.0

● PHIL LEFTWICH   Leftwich, Philip Dale b: 5/19/69, Lynchburg, Va. BR/TR, 6'5", 205 lbs. Deb: 7/29/93

YEAR	TM/L	W	L	PCT	G	GS	CG	SH	SV	IP	H	HR	BB	SO	RAT	ERA	ERA+	OAV	OOB	BH	AVG	PB	PR	/A	PD	TPI
1993	Cal-A	4	6	.400	12	12	1	0	0	▸80²	72	7	31	31	12.4	3.79	119	.262	.327	0	—	0	5	6	0	0.6
1994	Cal-A	5	10	.333	20	20	1	0	0	114	127	16	42	67	13.6	5.68	88	.283	.349	0	—	0	-11	-9	0	-1.1
Total	2	9	16	.360	32	32	2	0	0	194²	208	21	69	98	13.1	4.90	98	.275	.340	0	—	0	-6	-2	0	-0.5

● REGIS LEHENY   Leheny, Regis Francis b: 1/5/08, Pittsburgh, Pa. d: 11/2/76, Pittsburgh, Pa. BL/TL, 6'0.5", 180 lbs. Deb: 5/21/32

YEAR	TM/L	W	L	PCT	G	GS	CG	SH	SV	IP	H	HR	BB	SO	RAT	ERA	ERA+	OAV	OOB	BH	AVG	PB	PR	/A	PD	TPI
1932	Bos-A	0	0	—	2	0	0	0	0	2²	5	0	3	1	27.0	16.88	27	.417	.533	0	.000	-0	-4	-4	0	0.0

● JIM LEHEW   Lehew, James Anthony b: 8/19/37, Baltimore, Md. BR/TR, 6', 185 lbs. Deb: 9/13/61

YEAR	TM/L	W	L	PCT	G	GS	CG	SH	SV	IP	H	HR	BB	SO	RAT	ERA	ERA+	OAV	OOB	BH	AVG	PB	PR	/A	PD	TPI
1961	Bal-A	0	0	—	2	0	0	0	0	2	1	0	0	0	4.5	0.00	—	.167	.167	0	—	0	1	1	0	0.0
1962	Bal-A	0	0	—	6	0	0	0	0	9²	10	0	3	2	12.1	1.86	199	.303	.361	0	.000	-0	2	2	0	0.0
Total	2	0	0	—	8	0	0	0	0	11²	11	0	3	2	10.8	1.54	241	.282	.333	0	.000	-0	3	3	0	0.0

● KEN LEHMAN   Lehman, Kenneth Karl b: 6/10/28, Seattle, Wash. BL/TL, 6', 186 lbs. Deb: 9/5/52

YEAR	TM/L	W	L	PCT	G	GS	CG	SH	SV	IP	H	HR	BB	SO	RAT	ERA	ERA+	OAV	OOB	BH	AVG	PB	PR	/A	PD	TPI
1952	*Bro-N	1	2	.333	4	3	0	0	0	15¹	19	1	6	7	14.7	5.28	69	.297	.357	0	.000	0	-3	-3	0	-0.4
1956	Bro-N	2	3	.400	25	4	0	0	0	49¹	65	11	23	29	16.1	5.66	70	.325	.395	3	.300	1	-10	-9	1	-0.7
1957	Bro-N	0	0	—	7	0	0	0	0	7	9	1	3	3	10.3	0.00	—	.259	.286	0	—	0	2	2	0	0.3
	Bal-A	8	3	.727	30	3	1	0	6	68	57	7	12	22	10.5	2.78	129	.232	.295	4	.200	0	8	6	-1	1.2
1958	Bal-A	2	1	.667	31	1	1	0	0	62	64	5	18	36	12.2	3.48	103	.276	.333	1	.071	-1	2	1	0	-0.1

YEAR TM/L	W	L	PCT	G	GS	CG	SH	SV	IP	H	HR	BB	SO	RAT	ERA	ERA+	OAV	OOB	BH	AVG	PB	PR	/A	PD	TPI
1961 Phi-N	1	1	.500	41	2	0	0	1	63¹	61	6	25	27	12.4	4.26	96	.260	.333	0	.000	-1	-2	-1	1	0.0
Total 5	14	10	.583	134	13	2	0	7	265	273	24	95	134	12.6	3.91	97	.272	.337	9	.161	1	-2	-3	2	0.0

● **NORM LEHR**   Lehr, Norman Carl Michael "King"   b: 5/28/01, Rochester, N.Y.   d: 7/17/68, Livonia, N.Y.   BR/TR, 6', 168 lbs.   Deb: 5/20/26

YEAR TM/L	W	L	PCT	G	GS	CG	SH	SV	IP	H	HR	BB	SO	RAT	ERA	ERA+	OAV	OOB	BH	AVG	PB	PR	/A	PD	TPI
1926 Cle-A	0	0	—	4	0	0	0	0	14²	11	0	4	4	9.2	3.07	132	.216	.273	0	.000	-1	2	2	1	0.0

● **HANK LEIBER**   Leiber, Henry Edward   b: 1/17/11, Phoenix, Ariz.   d: 11/8/93, Tucson, Ariz.   BR/TR, 6'1.5", 205 lbs.   Deb: 4/16/33 ♦

YEAR TM/L	W	L	PCT	G	GS	CG	SH	SV	IP	H	HR	BB	SO	RAT	ERA	ERA+	OAV	OOB	BH	AVG	PB	PR	/A	PD	TPI
1942 NY-N	0	1	.000	1	1	1	0	0	9	9	0	5	5	15.0	6.00	56	.290	.405	32	.218	0	-3	-3	0	-0.2

● **CHARLIE LEIBRANDT**   Leibrandt, Charles Louis   b: 10/4/56, Chicago, Ill.   BR/TL, 6'3", 200 lbs.   Deb: 9/17/79

YEAR TM/L	W	L	PCT	G	GS	CG	SH	SV	IP	H	HR	BB	SO	RAT	ERA	ERA+	OAV	OOB	BH	AVG	PB	PR	/A	PD	TPI
1979 *Cin-N	0	0	—	3	0	0	0	0	4¹	2	0	2	1	8.3	0.00	—	.154	.267	0	—	0	2	2	0	0.0
1980 Cin-N	10	9	.526	36	27	5	2	0	173²	200	15	54	62	13.3	4.25	84	.292	.346	11	.196	1	-13	-13	1	-1.1
1981 Cin-N	1	1	.500	7	4	1	1	0	30	28	0	15	9	12.9	3.60	99	.262	.352	0	.000	-0	-0	-0	0	0.0
1982 Cin-N	5	7	.417	36	11	0	0	2	107²	130	4	48	34	15.0	5.10	73	.308	.381	2	.080	-1	-18	-17	-0	-2.0
1984 *KC-A	11	7	.611	23	23	0	0	0	143²	158	11	38	53	12.5	3.63	111	.277	.326	0	—	0	6	6	-2	0.6
1985 *KC-A	17	9	.654	33	33	8	3	0	237²	223	17	68	108	11.1	2.69	155	.248	.302	0	—	0	38	39	4	4.5
1986 KC-A	14	11	.560	35	34	8	1	0	231¹	238	18	63	108	11.9	4.09	104	.268	.319	0	—	0	2	4	2	0.6
1987 KC-A	16	11	.593	35	35	8	3	0	240¹	235	23	74	151	11.6	3.41	134	.253	.308	0	—	0	28	31	4	3.5
1988 KC-A	13	12	.520	35	35	7	2	0	243	244	20	62	125	11.5	3.19	125	.264	.313	0	—	0	21	22	2	2.3
1989 KC-A	5	11	.313	33	27	3	1	0	161	196	13	54	73	14.1	5.14	75	.304	.360	0	—	0	-23	-23	-0	-2.1
1990 Atl-N	9	11	.450	24	24	5	2	0	162¹	164	9	35	76	11.3	3.16	128	.261	.304	9	.180	1	11	16	1	2.1
1991 *Atl-N	15	13	.536	36	36	1	1	0	229²	212	18	56	128	10.7	3.49	111	.245	.294	3	.043	-4	5	10	4	1.2
1992 *Atl-N	15	7	.682	32	31	5	2	0	193	191	9	42	104	11.1	3.36	109	.258	.302	7	.121	-1	3	6	3	0.9
1993 Tex-A	9	10	.474	26	26	1	0	0	150¹	169	15	45	89	13.1	4.55	91	.284	.339	0	—	0	-4	-7	5	-0.1
Total 14	140	119	.541	394	346	52	18	2	2308	2390	172	656	1121	12.0	3.71	108	.268	.321	32	.120	-5	60	77	25	10.4

● **LEFTY LEIFIELD**   Leifield, Albert Peter   b: 9/5/1883, Trenton, Ill.   d: 10/10/70, Alexandria, Va.   BL/TL, 6'1", 165 lbs.   Deb: 9/3/05   C

YEAR TM/L	W	L	PCT	G	GS	CG	SH	SV	IP	H	HR	BB	SO	RAT	ERA	ERA+	OAV	OOB	BH	AVG	PB	PR	/A	PD	TPI
1905 Pit-N	5	2	.714	8	7	6	1	0	56	52	0	14	10	11.3	2.89	104	.248	.307	7	.350	3	1	1	1	0.5
1906 Pit-N	18	13	.581	37	31	24	8	1	255²	214	3	68	111	10.4	1.87	143	.231	.294	11	.125	-3	22	23	1	2.7
1907 Pit-N	20	16	.556	40	33	24	6	1	286	270	1	100	112	12.0	2.33	105	.256	.328	15	.147	0	5	3	4	0.8
1908 Pit-N	15	14	.517	34	26	18	5	2	218²	168	1	86	87	10.9	2.10	110	.212	.299	17	.227	3	6	5	-0	1.0
1909 *Pit-N	19	8	.704	32	27	13	3	0	201²	172	4	54	43	10.4	2.37	115	.229	.286	14	.192	2	5	8	-2	1.0
1910 Pit-N	15	13	.536	40	30	13	3	0	218²	197	6	67	64	11.3	2.64	117	.253	.320	11	.183	0	10	11	3	1.7
1911 Pit-N	16	16	.500	42	37	26	2	1	318	301	7	82	111	11.3	2.63	130	.260	.318	24	.235	6	27	28	-1	3.2
1912 Pit-N	1	2	.333	6	1	1	1	0	23²	29	1	10	8	15.6	4.18	78	.302	.380	1	.143	0	-2	-2	1	-0.1
Chi-N	7	2	.778	13	9	4	1	0	70²	68	0	21	23	11.7	2.42	138	.258	.319	3	.115	-1	8	7	1	0.8
Yr	8	4	.667	19	10	5	2	0	94¹	97	1	31	31	12.5	2.86	116	.268	.331	4	.121	-1	6	5	2	0.7
1913 Chi-N	0	1	.000	6	1	0	0	0	21¹	28	0	5	4	13.9	5.48	58	.329	.367	0	.000	-1	-5	-5	1	-0.3
1918 StL-A	2	6	.250	15	6	3	1	0	67	61	1	19	22	11.0	2.55	107	.252	.312	1	.053	-2	3	1	1	0.1
1919 StL-A	6	4	.600	19	9	6	2	0	92	96	4	25	18	12.2	2.93	113	.270	.325	3	.100	-2	3	4	1	0.2
1920 StL-A	0	0	—	4	0	0	0	0	9	17	0	3	3	20.0	7.00	56	.405	.444	0	.000	-0	-3	-3	-0	-0.1
Total 12	124	97	.561	296	217	138	33	7	1838	1673	27	554	616	11.3	2.47	116	.248	.313	107	.175	6	77	81	10	11.5

● **DAVE LEIPER**   Leiper, David Paul   b: 6/18/62, Whittier, Cal.   BL/TL, 6'1", 160 lbs.   Deb: 9/2/84

YEAR TM/L	W	L	PCT	G	GS	CG	SH	SV	IP	H	HR	BB	SO	RAT	ERA	ERA+	OAV	OOB	BH	AVG	PB	PR	/A	PD	TPI
1984 Oak-A	1	0	1.000	8	0	0	0	0	7	12	5	3	5	21.9	9.00	42	.353	.436	0	—	0	-4	-4	0	-0.5
1986 Oak-A	2	2	.500	33	0	0	0	1	31²	28	3	18	15	13.6	4.83	80	.252	.366	0	—	0	-2	-3	0	-0.3
1987 Oak-A	2	1	.667	45	0	0	0	1	52¹	49	6	18	33	11.7	3.78	109	.246	.312	0	—	0	4	2	1	0.3
SD-N	1	0	1.000	12	0	0	0	1	16	16	2	5	10	11.8	4.50	88	.267	.323	0	—	0	-1	-1	-0	-0.1
1988 SD-N	3	0	1.000	35	0	0	0	1	54	45	1	14	33	9.8	2.17	157	.231	.282	1	.500	0	8	7	0	0.5
1989 SD-N	0	1	.000	22	0	0	0	0	28²	40	4	20	7	19.5	5.02	70	.333	.437	0	.000	-0	-5	-5	1	-0.1
1994 Oak-A	0	0	—	26	0	0	0	1	18²	13	0	6	14	9.6	1.93	230	.206	.286	0	—	0	6	5	0	0.4
Total 6	9	4	.692	181	0	0	0	5	208¹	203	16	86	115	12.7	3.76	102	.260	.338	1	.333	0	6	2	2	0.2

● **JACK LEIPER**   Leiper, John Henry Thomas   b: 12/23/1867, Chester, Pa.   d: 8/23/60, West Goshen, Pa.   BL/TL, 5'11",   Deb: 9/4/1891

YEAR TM/L	W	L	PCT	G	GS	CG	SH	SV	IP	H	HR	BB	SO	RAT	ERA	ERA+	OAV	OOB	BH	AVG	PB	PR	/A	PD	TPI
1891 Col-a	2	2	.500	6	5	4	0	0	45	41	3	39	19	16.8	5.40	64	.234	.386	3	.143	-2	-8	-10	-1	-0.8

● **JOHN LEISTER**   Leister, John William   b: 1/3/61, San Antonio, Tex.   BR/TR, 6'2", 200 lbs.   Deb: 5/28/87

YEAR TM/L	W	L	PCT	G	GS	CG	SH	SV	IP	H	HR	BB	SO	RAT	ERA	ERA+	OAV	OOB	BH	AVG	PB	PR	/A	PD	TPI
1987 Bos-A	0	2	.000	8	6	0	0	0	30¹	49	9	12	16	18.1	9.20	49	.368	.421	0	—	0	-16	-16	-1	-0.9
1990 Bos-A	0	0	—	2	1	0	0	0	5²	7	0	4	3	17.5	4.76	86	.304	.407	0	—	0	-1	-0	-0	-0.2
Total 2	0	2	.000	10	7	0	0	0	36	56	9	16	19	18.0	8.50	53	.359	.419	0	—	0	-17	-16	-1	-1.1

● **AL LEITER**   Leiter, Alois Terry   b: 10/23/65, Toms River, N.J.   BL/TL, 6'3", 210 lbs.   Deb: 9/15/87   F

YEAR TM/L	W	L	PCT	G	GS	CG	SH	SV	IP	H	HR	BB	SO	RAT	ERA	ERA+	OAV	OOB	BH	AVG	PB	PR	/A	PD	TPI
1987 NY-A	2	2	.500	4	4	0	0	0	22²	24	2	15	28	15.5	6.35	69	.273	.379	—	0	-5	-5	-0	-0.7
1988 NY-A	4	4	.500	14	14	0	0	0	57¹	49	7	33	60	13.7	3.92	100	.231	.348	—	0	0	0	1	0.1
1989 NY-A	1	2	.333	4	4	0	0	0	26²	23	1	21	22	15.5	6.08	64	.235	.380	—	0	-6	-7	-0	-0.6
Tor-A	0	0	—	1	1	0	0	0	6²	9	1	2	4	14.9	4.05	93	.310	.355	—	0	-0	-0	-0	-0.0
Yr	1	2	.333	5	5	0	0	0	33¹	32	2	23	26	14.9	5.67	68	.246	.359	—	0	-7	-7	-1	-0.6
1990 Tor-A	0	0	—	4	0	0	0	0	6¹	1	0	2	5	4.3	0.00	—	.050	.136	—	0	3	3	0	-0.1
1991 Tor-A	0	0	—	3	0	0	0	0	1²	3	0	5	1	43.2	27.00	16	.429	.667	—	0	-4	-4	0	-0.2
1992 Tor-A	0	0	—	1	0	0	0	0	1	1	0	2	0	27.0	9.00	45	.200	.429	—	0	-1	-1	0	-0.2
1993 *Tor-A	9	6	.600	34	12	1	1	2	105	93	8	56	66	13.1	4.11	105	.240	.342	—	0	2	2	-1	0.2
1994 Tor-A	6	7	.462	20	20	1	0	0	111²	125	6	65	100	15.5	5.08	95	.285	.380	—	0	-3	-3	0	-0.3
Total 8	22	21	.512	85	55	2	1	2	339	328	25	201	286	14.4	4.75	92	.255	.362	—	0	-14	-14	-1	-1.8

● **MARK LEITER**   Leiter, Mark Edward   b: 4/13/63, Joliet, Ill.   BR/TR, 6'3", 200 lbs.   Deb: 7/24/90   F

YEAR TM/L	W	L	PCT	G	GS	CG	SH	SV	IP	H	HR	BB	SO	RAT	ERA	ERA+	OAV	OOB	BH	AVG	PB	PR	/A	PD	TPI
1990 NY-A	1	1	.500	8	3	0	0	0	26¹	33	5	9	21	15.0	6.84	58	.314	.379	—	0	-9	-8	1	-0.5
1991 Det-A	9	7	.563	38	15	1	0	1	134²	125	16	50	103	12.1	4.21	99	.245	.319	—	0	-2	-1	-1	-0.2
1992 Det-A	8	5	.615	35	14	1	0	0	112	116	9	43	75	13.0	4.18	95	.277	.348	—	0	-3	-3	-0	-0.3
1993 Det-A	6	6	.500	27	13	1	0	0	106²	111	17	44	70	13.3	4.73	91	.267	.341	—	0	-5	-5	-1	-0.6
1994 Cal-A	4	7	.364	40	7	0	0	3	95¹	99	13	35	71	13.5	4.72	106	.265	.343	—	0	1	0	0	0.2
Total 5	28	26	.519	148	52	3	0	3	475	484	60	181	340	13.0	4.57	94	.265	.339	—	0	-17	-15	-0	-1.4

● **BILL LEITH**   Leith, William "Shady Bill"   b: 5/31/1873, Matteawan, N.Y.   d: 7/16/40, Beacon, N.Y.   TL,   Deb: 9/25/1899

YEAR TM/L	W	L	PCT	G	GS	CG	SH	SV	IP	H	HR	BB	SO	RAT	ERA	ERA+	OAV	OOB	BH	AVG	PB	PR	/A	PD	TPI
1899 Was-N	0	0	—	1	0	0	0	0	2	4	0	2	1	31.5	18.00	22	.413	.552	0	.000	-0	-3	-3	-0	0.0

● **DOC LEITNER**   Leitner, George Aloysius   b: 9/14/1865, Piermont, N.Y.   d: 5/18/37, New York, N.Y.   BR/TR, 5'11.5", 185 lbs.   Deb: 8/10/1887

YEAR TM/L	W	L	PCT	G	GS	CG	SH	SV	IP	H	HR	BB	SO	RAT	ERA	ERA+	OAV	OOB	BH	AVG	PB	PR	/A	PD	TPI
1887 Ind-N	2	6	.250	8	8	8	0	0	65	69	6	41	27	15.2	5.68	73	.259	.358	4	.148	-3	-12	-11	-2	-1.3

● **DUMMY LEITNER**   Leitner, George Michael   b: 6/19/1871, Parkton, Md.   d: 2/20/60, Baltimore, Md.   BL/TR, 5'7", 120 lbs.   Deb: 6/29/01

YEAR TM/L	W	L	PCT	G	GS	CG	SH	SV	IP	H	HR	BB	SO	RAT	ERA	ERA+	OAV	OOB	BH	AVG	PB	PR	/A	PD	TPI
1901 Phi-A	0	0	—	1	0	0	0	0	2	1	0	1	2	9.0	—	.148	.257	0	.000	-0	1	1	-0	0.0
NY-N	0	2	.000	2	2	2	0	0	18	27	0	4	3	16.0	4.50	73	.344	.383	1	.143	-0	-2	-2	-0	-0.3
1902 Cle-A	0	0	—	1	1	0	0	0	8	11	0	1	0	13.5	4.50	77	.327	.346	1	.250	-0	-1	-1	0	0.0
Chi-A	0	0	—	1	0	0	0	0	4	9	0	2	0	29.3	13.50	25	.443	.534	0	.000	-0	-4	-4	0	-0.0
Yr	0	0	—	2	1	0	0	0	12	20	0	3	0	18.8	7.50	46	.370	.424	1	.143	-0	-5	-5	1	0.0
Total 2	0	2	.000	5	3	2	0	0	32	48	0	8	4	16.6	5.34	63	.344	.392	2	.133	-1	-7	-7	0	-0.3

YEAR	TM/L	W	L	PCT	G	GS	CG	SH	SV	IP	H	HR	BB	SO	RAT	ERA	ERA+	OAV	OOB	BH	AVG	PB	PR	/A	PD	TPI

● BILL LELIVELT   Lelivelt, William John b: 10/21/1884, Chicago, Ill.   d: 2/14/68, Chicago, Ill.   BR/TR, 6′, 195 lbs.   Deb: 7/19/09   F

YEAR	TM/L	W	L	PCT	G	GS	CG	SH	SV	IP	H	HR	BB	SO	RAT	ERA	ERA+	OAV	OOB	BH	AVG	PB	PR	/A	PD	TPI
1909	Det-A	0	1	.000	4	2	1	0	1	20	27	0	4	4	13.0	4.50	56	.325	.341	2	.333	1	-4	-4	0	-0.2
1910	Det-A	0	1	.000	1	1	1	0	0	9	6	0	3	2	9.0	1.00	263	.207	.281	1	.500	1	2	2	0	0.3
Total	2	0	2	.000	5	3	2	0	1	29	33	0	5	6	11.8	3.41	75	.295	.325	3	.375	2	-3	-3	0	0.1

● DAVE LEMANCZYK   Lemanczyk, David Lawrence b: 8/17/50, Syracuse, N.Y.   BR/TR, 6′4″, 235 lbs.   Deb: 4/15/73

YEAR	TM/L	W	L	PCT	G	GS	CG	SH	SV	IP	H	HR	BB	SO	RAT	ERA	ERA+	OAV	OOB	BH	AVG	PB	PR	/A	PD	TPI
1973	Det-A	0	0	—	1	0	0	0	0	2¹	4	0	0	0	15.4	11.57	35	.364	.364	0	—	0	-2	-2	-0	-0.1
1974	Det-A	2	1	.667	22	3	0	0	0	78²	79	12	44	52	14.3	4.00	95	.261	.358	0	—	0	-3	-2	1	-0.1
1975	Det-A	2	7	.222	26	6	4	0	0	109	120	8	46	67	14.0	4.46	90	.281	.355	0	—	0	-8	-5	0	-0.7
1976	Det-A	4	6	.400	20	10	1	0	0	81¹	86	7	34	51	13.3	5.09	73	.271	.342	0	—	0	-14	-12	1	-1.6
1977	Tor-A	13	16	.448	34	34	11	0	0	252	278	20	87	105	13.2	4.25	99	.282	.343	0	—	0	-5	-1	0	-0.2
1978	Tor-A	4	14	.222	29	20	3	0	0	136²	170	16	65	62	15.7	6.26	63	.313	.389	0	—	0	-38	-35	-1	-4.2
1979	Tor-A☆	8	10	.444	22	20	11	3	0	143	137	12	45	63	11.8	3.71	117	.258	.324	0	—	0	8	10	0	1.0
1980	Tor-A	2	5	.286	10	8	0	0	0	43¹	57	4	15	10	15.0	5.40	82	.322	.375	0	—	0	-7	-5	1	-0.8
	Cal-A	2	4	.333	21	2	0	0	0	66²	81	8	27	19	14.9	4.32	91	.301	.369	0	—	0	-2	-3	-2	-0.3
	Yr	4	9	.308	31	10	0	0	0	110	138	12	42	29	14.9	4.75	86	.308	.370	0	—	0	-9	-8	-1	-1.1
Total	8	37	63	.370	185	103	30	3	0	913	1012	87	363	429	13.8	4.62	88	.284	.354	0	—	0	-72	-56	0	-7.0

● DENNY LEMASTER   Lemaster, Denver Clayton b: 2/25/39, Corona, Cal.   BR/TL, 6′1″, 185 lbs.   Deb: 7/15/62

YEAR	TM/L	W	L	PCT	G	GS	CG	SH	SV	IP	H	HR	BB	SO	RAT	ERA	ERA+	OAV	OOB	BH	AVG	PB	PR	/A	PD	TPI
1962	Mil-N	3	4	.429	17	12	4	1	0	86²	75	11	32	69	11.4	3.01	126	.233	.308	4	.121	-1	9	8	-2	0.3
1963	Mil-N	11	14	.440	46	31	10	1	1	237	199	30	85	190	10.8	3.04	106	.227	.296	14	.189	3	7	5	-3	0.5
1964	Mil-N	17	11	.607	39	35	9	3	1	221	216	27	75	185	12.0	4.15	85	.252	.315	9	.134	0	-15	-15	0	-1.8
1965	Mil-N	7	13	.350	32	23	4	1	0	146¹	140	12	58	111	12.4	4.43	80	.251	.325	4	.089	-1	-14	-15	-0	-2.0
1966	Atl-N	11	8	.579	27	27	10	3	0	171	170	25	41	139	11.2	3.74	97	.258	.303	7	.119	-1	-2	-2	-0	-0.5
1967	Atl-N†	9	9	.500	31	31	8	2	0	215¹	184	20	72	148	10.8	3.34	99	.229	.295	7	.104	-2	1	-1	-1	-0.3
1968	Hou-N	10	15	.400	33	32	7	2	0	224	231	11	72	146	12.3	2.81	105	.262	.321	2	.031	-3	4	4	-3	-0.3
1969	Hou-N	13	17	.433	38	37	11	1	1	244²	232	20	72	173	11.2	3.16	112	.246	.300	15	.170	3	12	10	-1	1.4
1970	Hou-N	7	12	.368	39	21	3	0	3	162	169	22	65	103	13.1	4.56	85	.268	.338	8	.178	2	-9	-12	-2	-1.2
1971	Hou-N	0	2	.000	42	0	0	0	0	60	59	6	22	28	12.3	3.45	98	.262	.331	1	.167	-0	0	-1	-0	-0.2
1972	Mon-N	2	0	1.000	13	0	0	0	0	19²	28	2	6	13	16.0	7.78	46	.329	.380	1	.333	1	-9	-9	-1	-0.9
Total	11	90	105	.462	357	249	66	14	8	1787²	1703	184	600	1305	11.7	3.58	96	.249	.312	72	.130	1	-18	-28	-13	-4.8

● DICK LeMAY   LeMay, Richard Paul b: 8/28/38, Cincinnati, Ohio   BL/TL, 6′3″, 190 lbs.   Deb: 6/13/61

YEAR	TM/L	W	L	PCT	G	GS	CG	SH	SV	IP	H	HR	BB	SO	RAT	ERA	ERA+	OAV	OOB	BH	AVG	PB	PR	/A	PD	TPI
1961	SF-N	3	6	.333	27	5	1	0	3	83¹	65	11	36	54	11.3	3.56	107	.217	.309	2	.077	-2	4	4	-0	0.1
1962	SF-N	0	1	.000	9	0	0	1	0	9¹	9	2	9	5	17.4	7.71	49	.265	.419	—	—	0	-4	-4	0	-0.4
1963	Chi-N	0	1	.000	9	1	0	0	0	15¹	26	1	4	10	17.6	5.28	66	.394	.429	0	.000	-0	-3	-3	-0	-0.2
Total	3	3	8	.273	45	6	1	0	4	108	100	14	49	69	12.8	4.17	91	.250	.338	2	.071	-1	-3	-5	-0	-0.5

● BOB LEMON   Lemon, Robert Granville b: 9/22/20, San Bernardino, Cal.   BL/TR, 6′, 185 lbs.   Deb: 9/9/41   MCH♦

YEAR	TM/L	W	L	PCT	G	GS	CG	SH	SV	IP	H	HR	BB	SO	RAT	ERA	ERA+	OAV	OOB	BH	AVG	PB	PR	/A	PD	TPI
1946	Cle-A	4	5	.444	32	5	1	0	1	94	77	1	68	39	13.9	2.49	133	.229	.359	16	.180	2	11	9	4	1.3
1947	Cle-A	11	5	.688	37	15	6	1	3	167¹	150	7	97	65	13.5	3.44	101	.242	.348	18	.321	9	5	1	4	1.6
1948	*Cle-A☆	20	14	.588	43	37	**20**	10	2	293²	231	12	129	147	11.1	2.82	144	.216	.302	34	.286	14	**48**	40	8	**6.8**
1949	Cle-A☆	22	10	.688	37	33	22	2	1	279²	211	19	137	138	11.4	2.99	133	.211	.309	29	.269	16	37	31	6	**5.7**
1950	Cle-A★	**23**	11	.676	44	37	**22**	3	0	288	281	28	146	**170**	13.4	3.84	113	.257	.345	37	.272	17	23	16	5	3.7
1951	Cle-A★	17	14	.548	42	34	17	1	2	263¹	244	19	124	132	12.6	3.52	108	.244	.328	21	.206	5	18	4	7	1.7
1952	Cle-A★	22	11	.667	42	36	**28**	5	4	309²	236	15	105	131	10.1	2.50	134	**.208**	.279	28	.226	7	40	29	7	4.6
1953	Cle-A☆	21	15	.583	41	36	23	5	1	286²	283	16	110	98	12.7	3.36	112	.262	.336	26	.232	8	20	13	8	3.2
1954	*Cle-A★	**23**	7	.767	36	33	**21**	2	0	258¹	228	16	92	110	11.3	2.72	135	.237	.307	21	.214	6	29	27	4	**4.1**
1955	Cle-A★	**18**	10	.643	35	31	5	0	2	211¹	218	17	74	100	12.6	3.88	103	.266	.330	19	.244	6	2	3	2	1.1
1956	Cle-A★	20	14	.588	39	35	**21**	2	3	255¹	230	23	89	94	11.5	3.03	139	.257	.307	18	.194	5	32	33	4	**5.2**
1957	Cle-A	6	11	.353	21	17	2	0	0	117¹	129	6	44	45	15.3	4.60	81	.287	.385	3	.065	-3	-11	-12	-3	-1.5
1958	Cle-A	0	1	.000	11	0	0	0	0	25¹	41	3	16	8	20.6	5.33	68	.376	.460	3	.231	0	-4	-5	-1	-0.1
Total	13	207	128	.618	460	350	188	31	22	2850	2559	181	1251	1277	12.2	3.23	119	.241	.324	274	.232	90	251	193	60	37.4

● DAVE LEMONDS   Lemonds, David Lee b: 7/5/48, Charlotte, N.C.   BL/TL, 6′1.5″, 180 lbs.   Deb: 6/30/69

YEAR	TM/L	W	L	PCT	G	GS	CG	SH	SV	IP	H	HR	BB	SO	RAT	ERA	ERA+	OAV	OOB	BH	AVG	PB	PR	/A	PD	TPI
1969	Chi-N	0	1	.000	2	1	0	0	0	4²	7	0	5	0	19.3	3.86	104	.313	.476	0	.000	-0	-0	0	0	0.0
1972	Chi-A	4	7	.364	31	18	0	0	0	94²	87	6	38	69	12.0	2.95	106	.244	.322	3	.120	-1	1	2	-0	0.1
Total	2	4	8	.333	33	19	0	0	0	99¹	92	6	43	69	12.3	2.99	106	.250	.330	3	.115	-2	1	1	1	0.1

● MARK LEMONGELLO   Lemongello, Mark b: 7/21/55, Jersey City, N.J.   BR/TR, 6′1″, 180 lbs.   Deb: 9/14/76

YEAR	TM/L	W	L	PCT	G	GS	CG	SH	SV	IP	H	HR	BB	SO	RAT	ERA	ERA+	OAV	OOB	BH	AVG	PB	PR	/A	PD	TPI
1976	Hou-N	3	1	.750	4	4	1	0	0	29	26	2	7	9	10.2	2.79	114	.236	.282	0	.000	-1	2	1	1	0.2
1977	Hou-N	9	14	.391	34	30	5	0	0	214²	237	20	52	83	12.2	3.48	102	.281	.325	6	.087	-4	10	2	-1	-0.2
1978	Hou-N	9	14	.391	33	30	9	1	1	210¹	204	20	66	77	11.9	3.94	84	.259	.323	11	.172	1	-8	-15	-0	-1.4
1979	Tor-A	1	9	.100	18	10	2	0	0	83	97	14	34	40	14.5	6.29	69	.299	.371	0	—	0	-19	-18	1	-1.8
Total	4	22	38	.367	89	74	17	1	1	537	564	56	159	209	12.4	4.06	88	.273	.329	17	.121	-3	-15	-30	1	-3.2

● ED LENNON   Lennon, Edward Francis b: 8/17/1897, Philadelphia, Pa.   d: 9/13/47, Philadelphia, Pa.   BR/TR, 5′11″, 170 lbs.   Deb: 6/30/28

YEAR	TM/L	W	L	PCT	G	GS	CG	SH	SV	IP	H	HR	BB	SO	RAT	ERA	ERA+	OAV	OOB	BH	AVG	PB	PR	/A	PD	TPI
1928	Phi-N	0	0	—	5	0	0	0	0	12¹	19	0	10	6	21.2	8.76	49	.373	.475	0	.000	-1	-7	-6	-0	-0.1

● DANILO LEON   Leon, Danilo Enrique (Lineco) b: 4/3/67, LaConcepcion, Venez.   BR/TR, 6′1″, 170 lbs.   Deb: 6/6/92

YEAR	TM/L	W	L	PCT	G	GS	CG	SH	SV	IP	H	HR	BB	SO	RAT	ERA	ERA+	OAV	OOB	BH	AVG	PB	PR	/A	PD	TPI
1992	Tex-A	1	1	.500	15	0	0	0	0	18¹	18	5	10	15	15.2	5.89	64	.254	.369	0	—	0	-4	-4	0	-0.4

● IZZY LEON   Leon, Isidoro (Becerra) b: 1/4/11, Cruces, Las Villas, Cuba   BR/TR, 5′10″, 160 lbs.   Deb: 6/21/45

YEAR	TM/L	W	L	PCT	G	GS	CG	SH	SV	IP	H	HR	BB	SO	RAT	ERA	ERA+	OAV	OOB	BH	AVG	PB	PR	/A	PD	TPI
1945	Phi-N	0	4	.000	14	4	0	0	0	38²	49	3	19	11	15.8	5.35	72	.312	.386	1	.111	-0	-7	-7	0	-0.6

● MAX LEON   Leon, Maximino (Molino) b: 2/4/50, Pozo Hondo, Aculo, Mexico   BR/TR, 6′, 170 lbs.   Deb: 7/18/73

YEAR	TM/L	W	L	PCT	G	GS	CG	SH	SV	IP	H	HR	BB	SO	RAT	ERA	ERA+	OAV	OOB	BH	AVG	PB	PR	/A	PD	TPI
1973	Atl-N	2	2	.500	12	1	1	0	0	27	30	6	9	18	14.0	5.33	74	.278	.350	2	.286	0	-5	-4	-0	-0.6
1974	Atl-N	4	7	.364	34	2	1	1	3	75	68	5	14	38	10.0	2.64	143	.244	.280	2	.133	-1	8	9	1	1.4
1975	Atl-N	2	1	.667	50	1	0	0	6	85	90	5	33	53	13.8	4.13	91	.274	.352	3	.333	1	-5	-3	1	-0.3
1976	Atl-N	2	4	.333	30	0	0	0	0	36	32	2	15	16	12.3	2.75	138	.234	.318	0	.000	-0	3	4	-1	0.7
1977	Atl-N	4	4	.500	31	9	0	0	1	81²	89	9	25	44	13.6	3.97	112	.280	.349	6	.316	1	-1	4	0	0.5
1978	Atl-N	0	0	—	5	0	0	0	0	5²	6	1	4	1	17.5	6.35	64	.273	.407	—	—	-2	-1	-0	0	-0.1
Total	6	14	18	.438	162	13	2	1	13	310¹	315	28	100	170	12.7	3.71	107	.264	.332	13	.250	-1	1	9	1	2.0

● DENNIS LEONARD   Leonard, Dennis Patrick b: 5/8/51, Brooklyn, N.Y.   BR/TR, 6′1″, 190 lbs.   Deb: 9/4/74

YEAR	TM/L	W	L	PCT	G	GS	CG	SH	SV	IP	H	HR	BB	SO	RAT	ERA	ERA+	OAV	OOB	BH	AVG	PB	PR	/A	PD	TPI
1974	KC-A	0	4	.000	5	4	0	0	0	22	28	0	12	8	17.6	5.32	72	.329	.430	0	—	0	-4	-4	1	-0.5
1975	KC-A	15	7	.682	32	30	8	0	0	212¹	212	18	90	146	13.2	3.77	102	.263	.344	0	—	0	0	2	0	0.2
1976	*KC-A	17	10	.630	35	34	16	2	0	259	247	16	70	150	11.4	3.51	100	.255	.313	0	—	0	-0	-4	-0	-0.5
1977	*KC-A	**20**	12	.625	38	37	21	5	1	292²	246	18	79	244	10.2	3.04	133	.227	.285	0	—	0	33	32	-2	3.1
1978	*KC-A	21	17	.553	40	40	20	4	0	294²	283	27	78	183	11.3	3.33	115	.254	.308	0	—	0	14	16	0	1.9
1979	KC-A	14	12	.538	32	32	12	**5**	0	236	226	33	56	126	10.8	4.08	104	.253	.299	0	—	0	4	5	0	0.3
1980	*KC-A	20	11	.645	38	38	8	3	0	280	271	30	80	155	11.3	3.79	107	.255	.306	0	—	0	5	5	1	0.5
1981	*KC-A	13	11	.542	26	26	9	2	0	**201²**	202	15	40	107	11.0	2.99	121	.258	.298	0	—	0	15	14	1	1.7
1982	KC-A	10	6	.625	21	21	3	0	0	130²	145	20	46	58	13.3	5.10	80	.279	.340	0	—	0	-15	/-15	1	-1.5
1983	KC-A	6	3	.667	10	10	1	0	0	63	69	3	19	31	12.6	3.71	110	.277	.328	0	—	0	2	3	0	0.3

YEAR TM/L	W	L	PCT	G	GS	CG	SH	SV	IP	H	HR	BB	SO	RAT	ERA	ERA+	OAV	OOB	BH	AVG	PB	PR	/A	PD	TPI
1985 KC-A	0	0	—	2	0	0	0	0	2	1	0	0	1	4.5	0.00	—	.143	.143	0	—	0	1	1	-0	0.0
1986 KC-A	8	13	.381	33	30	5	2	0	192²	207	22	51	114	12.2	4.44	96	.275	.324	0	—	0	-6	-4	0	-0.4
Total 12	144	106	.576	312	302	103	23	1	2187	2137	202	622	1323	11.6	3.70	106	.257	.312	0	—	0	52	58	-3	5.4

● **ELMER LEONARD** Leonard, Elmer Ellsworth "Tiny" b: 11/12/1888, Napa, Cal. d: 5/27/81, Napa, Cal. BR/TR, 6'3.5", 210 lbs. Deb: 6/22/11

YEAR TM/L	W	L	PCT	G	GS	CG	SH	SV	IP	H	HR	BB	SO	RAT	ERA	ERA+	OAV	OOB	BH	AVG	PB	PR	/A	PD	TPI
1911 Phi-A	2	2	.500	5	1	1	0	0	19	26	0	10	10	18.0	2.84	111	.329	.418	2	.286	1	1	1	-1	0.1

● **DUTCH LEONARD** Leonard, Emil John b: 3/25/09, Auburn, Ill. d: 4/17/83, Springfield, Ill. BR/TR, 6', 175 lbs. Deb: 8/31/33 C

YEAR TM/L	W	L	PCT	G	GS	CG	SH	SV	IP	H	HR	BB	SO	RAT	ERA	ERA+	OAV	OOB	BH	AVG	PB	PR	/A	PD	TPI
1933 Bro-N	2	3	.400	10	3	2	0	0	40	42	0	10	6	11.7	2.93	110	.261	.304	0	.000	-1	2	1	0	0.0
1934 Bro-N	14	11	.560	44	20	11	2	5	183²	210	12	33	58	12.1	3.28	113	.286	.320	12	.179	-1	16	13	1	1.7
1935 Bro-N	2	9	.182	43	11	4	0	8	137²	152	11	29	41	11.9	3.92	101	.280	.318	1	.026	-4	1	1	-1	-0.5
1936 Bro-N	0	0	—	16	0	0	0	1	32	34	2	5	8	11.0	3.66	113	.262	.289	2	.400	0	1	2	1	0.1
1938 Was-A	12	15	.444	33	31	15	3	0	223¹	221	11	53	68	**11.3**	3.43	132	.256	.305	19	.232	3	34	27	0	3.1
1939 Was-A	20	8	.714	34	34	21	2	0	269¹	273	16	59	88	11.3	3.54	123	.262	.305	21	.221	0	32	24	2	2.4
1940 Was-A☆	14	19	.424	35	35	23	2	0	289	328	19	78	124	12.7	3.49	120	.286	.332	16	.158	-5	29	22	5	2.2
1941 Was-A	18	13	.581	34	33	19	4	0	256	271	6	54	91	11.5	3.45	117	.270	.309	9	.102	-5	20	17	-1	1.2
1942 Was-A	2	2	.500	6	5	1	1	0	35	28	1	5	15	8.5	4.11	89	.214	.243	1	.100	-1	-2	-2	-0	-0.2
1943 Was-A★	11	13	.458	31	30	15	2	1	219²	218	9	46	51	11.0	3.28	98	.257	.298	7	.104	-4	0	-2	-2	-0.5
1944 Was-A☆	14	14	.500	32	31	17	3	0	229¹	222	8	37	62	10.3	3.06	106	.252	.284	18	.228	2	9	5	1	0.9
1945 Was-A†	17	7	.708	31	29	12	4	1	216	208	9	35	96	10.2	2.13	146	.248	.279	18	.231	1	30	23	0	2.8
1946 Was-A	10	10	.500	26	23	7	2	0	161²	182	9	36	62	12.4	3.56	94	.281	.323	9	.170	-1	-1	-4	3	-0.2
1947 Phi-N	17	12	.586	32	29	19	3	0	235	224	14	57	103	10.8	2.68	149	.258	.306	14	.175	-1	36	35	3	4.3
1948 Phi-N	12	17	.414	34	31	16	1	0	225²	226	9	54	92	11.3	2.51	157	.265	.312	12	.145	-3	36	36	4	4.6
1949 Chi-N	7	16	.304	33	28	10	1	0	180	198	4	43	83	12.4	4.15	97	.272	.319	12	.203	0	-2	-2	-1	-0.1
1950 Chi-N	5	1	.833	35	1	0	0	6	74	70	7	27	28	12.0	3.77	111	.248	.318	1	.063	-2	3	4	0	0.2
1951 Chi-N☆	10	6	.625	41	1	0	0	3	81²	69	3	28	30	10.9	2.64	155	.234	.305	0	.000	-3	12	13	2	2.4
1952 Chi-N	2	2	.500	45	0	0	0	11	66²	56	3	24	37	11.2	2.16	178	.235	.313	2	.200	0	12	13	2	1.4
1953 Chi-N	2	3	.400	45	0	0	0	6	62²	72	9	24	27	13.9	4.60	97	.289	.354	3	.300	1	-2	-1	-0	0.0
Total 20	191	181	.513	640	375	192	30	44	3218¹	3304	158	737	1170	11.5	3.25	119	.265	.309	177	.168	-21	267	224	24	25.8

● **DUTCH LEONARD** Leonard, Hubert Benjamin b: 4/16/1892, Birmingham, Ohio d: 7/11/52, Fresno, Cal. BL/TL, 5'10.5", 185 lbs. Deb: 4/12/13

YEAR TM/L	W	L	PCT	G	GS	CG	SH	SV	IP	H	HR	BB	SO	RAT	ERA	ERA+	OAV	OOB	BH	AVG	PB	PR	/A	PD	TPI
1913 Bos-A	14	16	.467	42	28	14	3	1	259¹	245	0	94	144	11.9	2.39	123	.253	.321	15	.181	1	16	16	-2	1.7
1914 Bos-A	19	5	.792	36	25	17	7	3	224²	139	3	60	176	**8.3**	**0.96**	**280**	**.180**	**.246**	10	.147	-1	**44**	43	-3	4.6
1915 *Bos-A	15	7	.682	32	21	10	2	0	183¹	130	3	67	116	10.4	2.36	118	**.208**	.299	14	.264	5	12	9	-4	1.1
1916 *Bos-A	18	12	.600	48	34	17	6	6	274	244	6	66	144	10.4	2.36	117	.247	.300	17	.200	2	14	12	-6	0.9
1917 Bos-A	16	17	.485	37	36	26	4	1	294¹	257	4	72	144	10.2	2.17	119	.236	.286	9	.087	-6	16	13	-5	0.3
1918 Bos-A	8	6	.571	16	16	12	3	0	125¹	119	0	53	47	12.5	2.72	99	.254	.332	8	.186	0	1	1	-2	-0.2
1919 Det-A	14	13	.519	29	28	18	4	0	217¹	212	7	65	102	11.8	2.77	115	.254	.313	11	.155	-3	11	10	-4	0.5
1920 Det-A	10	17	.370	28	27	10	3	0	191¹	192	8	63	76	12.4	4.33	86	.271	.338	12	.211	2	-11	-13	-1	-1.5
1921 Det-A	11	13	.458	36	32	16	1	1	245	273	16	63	120	12.7	3.75	114	.286	.336	14	.171	-4	15	14	-3	0.6
1924 Det-A	3	2	.600	9	7	3	0	1	51¹	68	1	18	26	15.3	4.56	90	.327	.383	4	.211	-0	-2	-3	-0	-0.3
1925 Det-A	11	4	.733	18	18	9	0	0	125²	143	7	43	65	13.4	4.51	95	.289	.347	10	.200	-1	-2	-3	-2	-0.6
Total 11	139	112	.554	331	272	152	33	13	2192	2022	54	664	1160	11.3	2.76	115	.249	.311	124	.173	-5	114	98	-32	7.1

● **DAVE LEONHARD** Leonhard, David Paul b: 1/22/41, Arlington, Va. BR/TR, 5'11", 165 lbs. Deb: 9/21/67

YEAR TM/L	W	L	PCT	G	GS	CG	SH	SV	IP	H	HR	BB	SO	RAT	ERA	ERA+	OAV	OOB	BH	AVG	PB	PR	/A	PD	TPI
1967 Bal-A	0	0	—	3	2	0	0	1	14¹	11	1	6	9	11.3	3.14	100	.200	.290	0	.000	-1	0	0	0	0.0
1968 Bal-A	7	7	.500	28	18	5	2	1	126¹	95	10	57	61	11.0	3.13	93	.216	.309	4	.129	-1	-2	-3	-1	-0.3
1969 *Bal-A	7	4	.636	37	3	1	1	1	94	78	8	38	37	11.1	2.49	143	.228	.305	2	.095	-0	12	11	-1	1.2
1970 Bal-A	0	0	—	23	0	0	0	0	28¹	32	5	18	14	15.9	5.08	72	.294	.394	0	.000	-0	-4	-5	-1	0.1
1971 *Bal-A	2	3	.400	12	6	1	1	1	54	51	5	19	18	11.8	2.83	118	.252	.320	5	.278	1	4	3	1	0.5
1972 Bal-A	0	0	—	14	0	0	0	0	20	20	3	12	7	14.4	4.50	68	.260	.360	1	1.000	1	-3	-3	0	0.1
Total 6	16	14	.533	117	29	7	4	5	337	287	32	150	146	11.8	3.15	103	.234	.320	12	.156	1	6	4	3	1.6

● **RUDY LEOPOLD** Leopold, Rudolph Matas b: 7/27/05, Grand Cane, La. d: 9/3/65, Baton Rouge, La. BL/TL, 6', 160 lbs. Deb: 7/4/28

YEAR TM/L	W	L	PCT	G	GS	CG	SH	SV	IP	H	HR	BB	SO	RAT	ERA	ERA+	OAV	OOB	BH	AVG	PB	PR	/A	PD	TPI
1928 Chi-A	0	0	—	2	0	0	0	0	2¹	3	0	0	0	11.6	3.86	105	.273	.273	0	.000	-0	0	0	-0	0.0

● **RANDY LERCH** Lerch, Randy Louis b: 10/9/54, Sacramento, Cal. BL/TL, 6'5", 190 lbs. Deb: 9/14/75

YEAR TM/L	W	L	PCT	G	GS	CG	SH	SV	IP	H	HR	BB	SO	RAT	ERA	ERA+	OAV	OOB	BH	AVG	PB	PR	/A	PD	TPI
1975 Phi-N	0	0	—	3	0	0	0	0	7	6	1	1	8	9.0	6.43	58	.231	.259	0	—	0	-2	-2	-0	0.0
1976 Phi-N	0	0	—	1	0	0	0	1	3	3	0	0	0	9.0	3.00	118	.250	.250	1	1.000	1	0	0	-0	0.1
1977 Phi-N	10	6	.625	32	28	4	1	0	168²	207	20	75	81	15.1	5.07	79	.312	.383	9	.167	-0	-22	-20	2	-1.5
1978 *Phi-N	11	8	.579	33	28	5	0	0	184	183	15	70	96	12.4	3.96	90	.263	.332	15	.250	7	-8	-8	1	0.0
1979 Phi-N	10	13	.435	37	35	6	1	0	214	228	20	60	92	12.2	3.74	102	.281	.333	11	.153	1	-0	2	2	0.4
1980 Phi-N	4	14	.222	30	22	2	0	0	150	178	15	59	57	14.0	5.16	73	.302	.362	12	.267	3	-26	-23	1	-2.1
1981 *Mil-A	7	9	.438	23	18	1	0	0	110²	134	8	43	53	14.4	4.31	79	.303	.365	0	—	0	-8	-11	0	-1.2
1982 Mil-A	8	7	.533	21	20	1	0	0	108²	123	12	51	33	14.7	4.97	76	.286	.366	0	—	0	-11	-14	-1	-1.5
Mon-N	2	0	1.000	6	4	0	0	0	23²	26	0	8	12	12.9	3.42	106	.289	.347	2	.250	1	0	0	-0	0.1
1983 Mon-N	1	3	.250	19	5	0	0	0	38²	45	6	18	24	14.9	6.75	53	.292	.370	2	.222	1	-13	-14	-0	-1.2
SF-N	1	0	1.000	7	0	0	0	0	10²	9	1	8	6	14.3	3.38	105	.231	.362	0	—	0	0	0	-0	0.0
Yr	2	3	.400	26	5	0	0	0	49¹	54	7	26	30	14.6	6.02	59	.277	.362	2	.222	1	-13	-13	-0	-1.2
1984 SF-N	5	3	.625	37	4	0	0	2	72¹	80	3	36	48	14.6	4.23	83	.287	.370	1	.133	1	-5	-6	1	-0.5
1986 Phi-N	1	1	.500	4	0	0	0	0	8	10	0	7	5	19.1	7.88	49	.286	.405	1	.333	1	-4	-4	-0	-0.7
Total 11	60	64	.484	253	164	18	2	3	1099¹	1232	101	432	507	13.7	4.53	82	.289	.356	55	.206	15	-98	-98	4	-8.1

● **LOUIS LeROY** LeRoy, Louis Paul "Chief" b: 2/18/1879, Omro, Wis. d: 10/10/44, Shawano, Wis. BR/TR, 5'10", 180 lbs. Deb: 9/22/05

YEAR TM/L	W	L	PCT	G	GS	CG	SH	SV	IP	H	HR	BB	SO	RAT	ERA	ERA+	OAV	OOB	BH	AVG	PB	PR	/A	PD	TPI
1905 NY-A	1	1	.500	3	3	2	0	0	24	26	1	6	10	10.5	3.75	78	.277	.292	1	.125	-0	-3	-2	-0	-0.2
1906 NY-A	2	0	1.000	11	2	1	0	1	44²	33	0	12	28	9.5	2.22	134	.209	.273	2	.143	-1	2	4	1	0.2
1910 Bos-A	0	0	—	1	0	0	0	0	4	7	0	3	1	22.5	11.25	23	.389	.450	0	.000	-0	-4	-4	0	0.0
Total 3	3	1	.750	15	5	3	0	1	72²	66	1	15	39	10.4	3.22	91	.245	.292	3	.130	-1	-4	-1	1	0.0

● **BARRY LERSCH** Lersch, Barry Lee b: 9/7/44, Denver, Colo. BB/TR, 6', 180 lbs. Deb: 4/8/69

YEAR TM/L	W	L	PCT	G	GS	CG	SH	SV	IP	H	HR	BB	SO	RAT	ERA	ERA+	OAV	OOB	BH	AVG	PB	PR	/A	PD	TPI
1969 Phi-N	0	3	.000	10	4	0	0	0	17²	20	6	10	13	15.8	7.13	50	.286	.383	0	.000	-0	-7	-7	1	-1.2
1970 Phi-N	6	3	.667	42	11	3	0	3	138	119	17	47	92	10.9	3.26	122	.232	.297	2	.065	-2	12	11	-1	0.5
1971 Phi-N	5	14	.263	38	30	3	0	0	214¹	203	28	50	113	10.7	3.78	93	.252	.298	10	.169	-2	-7	-6	-1	-0.4
1972 Phi-N	4	6	.400	36	8	3	0	0	100²	86	8	33	48	10.9	3.04	118	.231	.299	0	.000	-2	5	6	-0	0.3
1973 Phi-N	3	6	.333	42	4	0	0	0	98¹	105	10	27	51	12.3	4.39	86	.279	.330	3	.176	0	-8	-7	-0	-0.6
1974 StL-N	0	0	—	1	1	0	0	0	1¹	3	1	5	0	54.0	40.50	9	.429	.667	0	—	0	-5	-5	0	0.0
Total 6	18	32	.360	169	53	9	1	6	570¹	536	70	172	317	11.3	3.97	97	.250	.308	15	.113	-3	-11	-8	-1	-1.4

● **DON LESHNOCK** Leshnock, Donald Lee b: 11/25/46, Youngstown, Ohio BR/TL, 6'3", 195 lbs. Deb: 6/7/72

YEAR TM/L	W	L	PCT	G	GS	CG	SH	SV	IP	H	HR	BB	SO	RAT	ERA	ERA+	OAV	OOB	BH	AVG	PB	PR	/A	PD	TPI
1972 Det-A	0	0	—	1	0	0	0	0	1	2	0	0	0	18.0	0.00	—	.400	.400	0	—	0	0	0	0	0.0

● **CURT LESKANIC** Leskanic, Curtis John b: 4/2/68, Homestead, Pa. BR/TR, 6', 180 lbs. Deb: 6/27/93

YEAR TM/L	W	L	PCT	G	GS	CG	SH	SV	IP	H	HR	BB	SO	RAT	ERA	ERA+	OAV	OOB	BH	AVG	PB	PR	/A	PD	TPI
1993 Col-N	1	5	.167	18	8	0	0	0	57	59	7	27	30	13.9	5.37	89	.266	.351	2	.154	0	-8	-4	0	-0.4
1994 Col-N	1	1	.500	8	3	0	0	0	22¹	27	2	10	17	14.9	5.64	88	.314	.385	1	.167	0	-4	-2	-0	-0.1
Total 2	2	6	.250	26	11	0	0	0	79¹	86	9	37	47	14.2	5.45	89	.279	.360	3	.158	0	-12	-5	-1	-0.5

YEAR	TM/L	W	L	PCT	G	GS	CG	SH	SV	IP	H	HR	BB	SO	RAT	ERA	ERA+	OAV	OOB	BH	AVG	PB	PR	/A	PD	TPI
● **BRAD LESLEY**				Lesley, Bradley Jay b: 9/11/58, Turlock, Cal. BR/TR, 6'6", 230 lbs. Deb: 7/31/82																					
1982	Cin-N	0	2	.000	28	0	0	0	4	38¹	27	1	13	29	9.4	2.58	143	.197	.267	0	.000	-0	4	5	-0	0.3
1983	Cin-N	0	0	—	5	0	0	0	0	8¹	9	1	0	5	9.7	2.16	176	.290	.290	0	—	0	1	2	-0	0.1
1984	Cin-N	0	1	.000	16	0	0	0	2	19¹	17	3	14	7	14.4	5.12	74	.246	.373	1	.500	0	-3	-3	0	-0.2
1985	Mil-A	1	0	1.000	5	0	0	0	0	6¹	8	2	2	5	14.2	9.95	42	.296	.345	0	—	0	-4	-4	-0	-0.5
Total	4	1	3	.250	54	0	0	0	6	72¹	61	7	29	46	11.2	3.86	98	.231	.307	1	.333	-0	-2	-1	-0	-0.4
● **WALT LEVERENZ**				Leverenz, Walter Fred "Tiny" b: 7/21/1887, Chicago, Ill. d: 3/19/73, Atascadero, Cal. BL/TL, 5'10", 175 lbs. Deb: 4/18/13																					
1913	StL-A	6	17	.261	30	27	13	2	1	202²	159	3	89	87	11.5	2.58	114	.222	.318	12	.176	-1	8	8	-1	0.6
1914	StL-A	1	12	.077	27	16	5	0	0	111¹	107	5	63	41	14.1	3.80	71	.264	.368	6	.182	-1	-13	-14	-1	-1.7
1915	StL-A	0	2	.000	5	1	0	0	1	9	11	0	8	3	20.0	8.00	36	.333	.476	0	.000	-0	-5	-5	0	-1.1
Total	3	7	31	.184	62	44	18	2	2	323	277	8	160	131	12.7	3.15	91	.240	.341	18	.176	-1	-10	-11	-3	-2.2
● **DIXIE LEVERETT**				Leverett, Gorham Vance b: 3/29/1894, Georgetown, Tex. d: 2/20/57, Beaverton, Ore. BR/TR, 5'11", 190 lbs. Deb: 5/6/22																					
1922	Chi-A	13	10	.565	33	27	16	4	2	223²	224	11	79	60	12.3	3.34	122	.264	.329	21	.253	3	18	18	-1	1.9
1923	Chi-A	10	13	.435	38	24	9	0	3	192²	212	6	64	64	13.2	4.06	97	.280	.341	16	.267	4	-2	-2	-1	0.1
1924	Chi-A	2	3	.400	21	11	4	0	0	99	123	2	41	29	15.2	5.82	71	.314	.383	6	.188	-1	-17	-19	0	-0.8
1926	Chi-A	1	1	.500	6	3	1	0	0	24	31	1	7	12	14.3	6.00	64	.316	.362	1	.143	-0	-5	-6	-0	-0.4
1929	Bos-N	3	7	.300	24	12	3	0	1	97²	135	5	30	28	15.7	6.36	74	.339	.393	6	.188	-1	-18	-18	-0	-1.6
Total	5	29	34	.460	122	77	33	4	6	637	725	25	221	193	13.6	4.51	92	.291	.353	50	.234	6	-25	-27	-1	-0.8
● **HOD LEVERETTE**				Leverette, Horace Wilbur "Levy" b: 2/4/1889, Shreveport, La. d: 4/10/58, St.Petersburg, Fla BR/TR, 6', 180 lbs. Deb: 4/22/20																					
1920	StL-A	0	2	.000	3	2	0	0	0	10¹	9	1	12	0	18.3	5.23	75	.250	.438	0	.000	-0	-2	-1	1	-0.2
● **DUTCH LEVSEN**				Levsen, Emil Henry b: 4/29/1898, Wyoming, Iowa d: 3/12/72, St.Louis Park, Minn. BR/TR, 6', 180 lbs. Deb: 9/28/23																					
1923	Cle-A	0	0	—	3	0	0	0	0	4¹	4	0	1	0	8.3	0.00	—	.267	.267	0	.000	-0	2	2	1	0.1
1924	Cle-A	1	1	.500	4	1	1	0	0	16¹	22	0	3	4	14.3	4.41	97	.333	.371	0	.000	-1	-0	-0	0	-0.1
1925	Cle-A	1	2	.333	4	3	2	0	0	24¹	30	1	16	9	17.4	5.55	80	.313	.416	2	.250	-0	-3	-3	-1	-0.3
1926	Cle-A	16	13	.552	33	31	18	2	0	237¹	235	11	85	53	12.4	3.41	119	.261	.330	17	.205	-0	16	17	-1	1.8
1927	Cle-A	3	7	.300	25	13	2	1	0	80¹	96	1	37	15	15.1	5.49	77	.303	.379	5	.200	-1	-12	-11	1	-1.2
1928	Cle-A	0	3	.000	11	3	0	0	0	41¹	39	4	31	7	15.7	5.44	76	.258	.391	0	.000	-2	-6	-6	-0	-0.6
Total	6	21	26	.447	80	51	23	3	0	404	426	17	173	88	13.6	4.17	99	.276	.354	24	.178	-4	-4	-2	-1	-0.3
● **DENNIS LEWALLYN**				Lewallyn, Dennis Dale b: 8/11/53, Pensacola, Fla. BR/TR, 6'4", 200 lbs. Deb: 9/21/75																					
1975	LA-N	0	0	—	2	0	0	0	0	3	1	0	0	3	3.0	0.00	—	.100	.100	0	—	0	1	1	0	0.0
1976	LA-N	1	1	.500	4	2	0	0	0	16²	12	1	6	4	9.7	2.16	157	.207	.281	0	.000	-1	2	2	0	0.2
1977	LA-N	3	1	.750	5	1	0	0	0	17	22	1	4	8	13.8	4.24	90	.306	.342	0	—	-1	-1	-0	-3	-0.3
1978	LA-N	0	0	—	1	0	0	0	0	2	2	0	0	0	9.0	0.00	—	.250	.250	0	—	0	1	1	0	0.0
1979	LA-N	0	1	.000	7	0	0	0	0	12¹	19	0	5	1	18.2	5.11	71	.358	.424	1	.500	0	-2	-2	0	-0.1
1980	Tex-A	0	0	—	4	0	0	0	0	5²	7	0	4	1	17.5	7.94	49	.304	.407	0	—	0	-2	-3	0	0.1
1981	Cle-A	0	0	—	7	0	0	0	0	13¹	16	1	2	11	12.2	5.40	67	.296	.321	0	—	0	-3	-3	-0	-0.3
1982	Cle-A	0	1	.000	4	0	0	0	0	10¹	13	3	1	3	12.2	6.97	59	.310	.326	0	—	0	-3	-3	-0	-0.3
Total	8	4	4	.500	34	3	0	0	1	80¹	92	6	22	28	12.9	4.48	82	.287	.335	1	.077	-1	-6	-7	0	-0.4
● **DAN LEWANDOWSKI**				Lewandowski, Daniel William b: 1/6/28, Buffalo, N.Y. BR/TR, 6', 180 lbs. Deb: 9/22/51																					
1951	StL-N	0	1	.000	2	0	0	0	0	1	3	0	1	1	36.0	9.00	44	.500	.571	0	—	0	-1	-1	0	-0.4
● **LEWIS**				Lewis b: Brooklyn, N.Y. Deb: 7/12/1890 ♦																					
1890	Buf-P	0	1	.000	1	1	0	0	0	3	13	3	7	1	60.0	60.00	7	.590	.689	1	.200	-0	-19	-19	1	-2.0
● **TED LEWIS**				Lewis, Edward Morgan "Parson" b: 12/25/1872, Machynlleth, Wales d: 5/24/36, Durham, N.H. BR/TR, 5'10.5", 158 lbs. Deb: 7/6/1896																					
1896	Bos-N	1	4	.200	6	5	4	0	0	41²	37	2	27	12	13.8	3.24	140	.236	.349	2	.111	-2	5	6	1	0.4
1897	*Bos-N	21	12	.636	38	34	30	2	1	290	316	11	125	65	14.0	3.85	116	.275	.351	28	.248	-2	15	20	-5	1.2
1898	Bos-N	26	8	**.765**	41	33	29	1	2	313¹	267	9	109	72	11.1	2.90	127	.229	.300	37	.282	4	25	28	-1	2.9
1899	Bos-N	17	11	.607	29	25	23	2	0	234²	245	10	73	60	12.5	3.49	119	.269	.328	25	.260	0	10	17	-4	1.4
1900	Bos-N	13	12	.520	30	22	19	1	0	209	215	10	86	66	13.1	4.13	100	.265	.339	10	.138	-4	-10	-0	-3	-0.6
1901	Bos-A	16	17	.485	39	34	31	1	1	316¹	299	14	91	103	11.3	3.53	100	.247	.304	21	.174	-2	5	0	-0	-0.1
Total	6	94	64	.595	183	153	136	7	4	1405	1379	57	511	378	12.4	3.53	113	.255	.324	123	.223	-5	49	71	-13	4.9
● **DUFFY LEWIS**				Lewis, George Edward b: 4/18/1888, San Francisco, Cal d: 6/17/79, Salem, N.H. BL/TL, 5'10.5", 165 lbs. Deb: 4/16/10 C♦																					
1913	Bos-A	0	0	—	1	0	0	0	0	1	3	0	1	0	27.0	18.00	16	.500	.500	164	.298		-2	-2	-0	0.0
● **JIM LEWIS**				Lewis, James Martin b: 10/12/55, Miami, Fla. BR/TR, 6'3", 190 lbs. Deb: 9/12/79																					
1979	Sea-A	0	0	—	2	0	0	0	0	2¹	10	1	1	0	42.4	15.43	28	.625	.647	0	—	0	-3	-3	-0	-0.1
1982	NY-A	0	0	—	1	0	0	0	0	0²	3	0	3	0	81.0	54.00	7	.500	.667	0	—	0	-4	-4	-0	0.1
1983	Min-A	0	0	—	6	0	0	0	0	18	24	5	7	8	16.0	6.50	65	.324	.390	0	—	0	-5	-5	0	-0.2
1985	Sea-A	0	1	.000	2	1	0	0	0	4²	8	1	1	1	21.2	7.71	54	.421	.500	0	—	0	-2	-2	-0	-0.4
Total	4	0	1	.000	11	1	0	0	0	25²	45	7	12	9	21.0	8.77	48	.391	.462	0	—	0	-13	-13	-0	-0.6
● **JIM LEWIS**				Lewis, James Steven b: 7/20/64, Jackson, Mich. BR/TR, 6'2", 200 lbs. Deb: 8/9/91																					
1991	SD-N	0	0	—	12	0	0	0	0	13	14	2	11	10	17.3	4.15	91	.275	.403	0	.000	-0	-1	-1	1	0.0
● **RICHIE LEWIS**				Lewis, Richie Todd b: 1/25/66, Muncie, Ind. BR/TR, 5'10", 170 lbs. Deb: 7/31/92																					
1992	Bal-A	1	1	.500	2	2	0	0	0	6²	13	1	7	4	27.0	10.80	37	.406	.513	0	—	0	-5	-5	0	-1.1
1993	Fla-N	6	3	.667	57	0	0	0	0	77¹	68	7	43	65	13.0	3.26	133	.239	.340	1	.500	0	7	9	1	1.0
1994	Fla-N	1	4	.200	45	0	0	0	0	54	62	7	38	45	16.8	5.67	79	.284	.393	0	.000	0	-9	-7	-0	-0.6
Total	3	8	8	.500	104	2	0	0	0	138	143	15	88	114	15.2	4.57	96	.267	.373	1	.143	0	-7	-3	-0	-0.7
● **SCOTT LEWIS**				Lewis, Scott Allen b: 12/5/65, Grants Pass, Ore. BR/TR, 6'3", 190 lbs. Deb: 9/25/90																					
1990	Cal-A	1	1	.500	2	2	1	0	0	16¹	10	2	2	9	6.6	2.20	173	.172	.200	0	—	0	3	3	-0	0.3
1991	Cal-A	3	5	.375	16	11	0	0	0	60¹	81	3	21	37	15.5	6.27	65	.316	.373	0	—	0	-15	-14	-0	-1.6
1992	Cal-A	4	0	1.000	21	2	0	0	0	38¹	36	3	14	18	12.2	3.99	100	.255	.331	0	—	0	-0	1	0	0.1
1993	Cal-A	1	2	.333	15	4	0	0	0	32	37	3	12	10	14.3	4.22	107	.311	.383	0	—	0	0	1	-1	0.0
1994	Cal-A	0	1	.000	20	0	0	0	0	31	46	5	10	10	16.8	6.10	82	.359	.414	0	—	0	-4	-4	0	-0.1
Total	5	9	9	.500	74	19	1	0	0	178	210	16	59	84	14.0	5.01	85	.299	.360	0	—	0	-16	-15	-0	-1.3
● **BERT LEWIS**				Lewis, William Burton b: 10/3/1895, Tonawanda, N.Y. d: 3/24/50, Tonawanda, N.Y. BR/TR, 6'2", 176 lbs. Deb: 4/19/24																					
1924	Phi-N	0	0	—	12	0	0	0	0	18	23	1	7	3	15.5	6.00	74	.315	.383	0	.000	-1	-4	-3	0	-0.1
● **TERRY LEY**				Ley, Terrence Richard b: 2/21/47, Portland, Ore. BL/TL, 6', 190 lbs. Deb: 8/20/71																					
1971	NY-A	0	0	—	6	0	0	0	0	9	9	1	9	7	20.0	5.00	65	.257	.435	0	—	0	-2	-2	0	0.0
● **AL LIBKE**				Libke, Albert Walter b: 9/12/18, Tacoma, Wash. BL/TR, 6'4", 215 lbs. Deb: 4/19/45 ♦																					
1945	Cin-N	0	0	—	4	0	0	0	0	4¹	3	0	3	2	12.5	0.00	—	.200	.333	127	.283	1	2	2	0	0.0
1946	Cin-N	0	0	—	1	1	0	0	0	5	4	0	3	2	12.6	3.60	93	.235	.350	109	.253	0	-0	-0	-0	0.0
Total	2	0	0	—	5	1	0	0	0	9¹	7	0	6	4	12.5	1.93	183	.219	.342	236	.268	2	2	2	0	0.0

● DON LIDDLE — Liddle, Donald Eugene b: 5/25/25, Mt.Carmel, Ill. BL/TL, 5'10", 165 lbs. Deb: 4/17/53

YEAR TM/L	W	L	PCT	G	GS	CG	SH	SV	IP	H	HR	BB	SO	RAT	ERA	ERA+	OAV	OOB	BH	AVG	PB	PR	/A	PD	TPI
1953 Mil-N	7	6	.538	31	15	4	0	2	128^2	119	6	55	63	12.3	3.08	127	.248	.328	3	.088	-2	17	12	-1	0.9
1954 *NY-N	9	4	.692	28	19	4	3	0	126^2	100	5	55	44	11.2	3.06	132	.223	.312	7	.189	2	14	14	-1	1.4
1955 NY-N	10	4	.714	33	13	4	0	1	106^1	97	18	61	56	13.7	4.23	95	.246	.353	5	.185	1	-2	-2	-1	-0.2
1956 NY-N	1	2	.333	11	5	1	0	1	41^1	45	5	14	21	13.1	3.92	97	.278	.339	2	.167	-0	-1	-1	0	0.0
StL-N	1	2	.333	14	2	0	0	0	24^2	36	8	18	14	19.7	8.39	45	.353	.450	0	.000	-0	-13	-13	-0	-1.4
Yr	2	4	.333	25	7	1	0	1	66	81	13	32	35	15.4	5.59	68	.302	.377	2	.143	-0	-13	-13	-0	-1.4
Total 4	28	18	.609	117	54	13	3	4	427^2	397	42	203	198	12.8	3.75	106	.250	.339	17	.152	1	16	10	-2	0.7

● DUTCH LIEBER — Lieber, Charles Edwin b: 2/1/10, Alameda, Cal. d: 12/31/61, Sawtelle, Cal. BR/TR, 6'0.5", 180 lbs. Deb: 4/18/35

YEAR TM/L	W	L	PCT	G	GS	CG	SH	SV	IP	H	HR	BB	SO	RAT	ERA	ERA+	OAV	OOB	BH	AVG	PB	PR	/A	PD	TPI
1935 Phi-A	1	1	.500	18	1	0	0	2	46^2	45	1	19	14	12.5	3.09	147	.263	.340	2	.143	-1	7	8	0	0.3
1936 Phi-A	0	1	.000	3	0	0	0	0	11^2	17	0	6	1	17.7	7.71	66	.362	.434	0	.000	-0	-3	-3	1	-0.2
Total 2	1	2	.333	21	1	0	0	2	58^1	62	1	25	15	13.6	4.01	116	.284	.361	2	.118	-2	4	4	1	0.1

● JON LIEBER — Lieber, Jonathan Ray b: 4/2/70, Council Bluffs, Iowa BL/TR, 6'3", 220 lbs. Deb: 5/15/94

YEAR TM/L	W	L	PCT	G	GS	CG	SH	SV	IP	H	HR	BB	SO	RAT	ERA	ERA+	OAV	OOB	BH	AVG	PB	PR	/A	PD	TPI
1994 Pit-N	6	7	.462	17	17	1	0	0	108^2	116	12	25	71	11.8	3.73	114	.271	.313	4	.103	-1	6	6	-1	0.4

● GLENN LIEBHARDT — Liebhardt, Glenn Ignatius "Sandy" b: 7/31/10, Cleveland, Ohio d: 3/14/92, Winston-Salem, N.C. BR/TR, 5'10.5", 170 lbs. Deb: 4/22/30 F

YEAR TM/L	W	L	PCT	G	GS	CG	SH	SV	IP	H	HR	BB	SO	RAT	ERA	ERA+	OAV	OOB	BH	AVG	PB	PR	/A	PD	TPI
1930 Phi-A	0	1	.000	5	0	0	0	0	9	14	2	8	2	22.0	11.00	42	.359	.468	0	.000	-0	-6	-6	-0	-0.6
1936 StL-A	0	0	—	24	0	0	0	0	55^1	98	4	27	20	20.7	8.78	61	.375	.438	0	.000	-2	-23	-21	-2	-0.3
1938 StL-A	0	0	—	2	0	0	0	0	3	4	1	0	1	12.0	6.00	83	.308	.308	0	.000	-0	-0	-0	0	-0.0
Total 3	0	1	.000	31	0	0	0	0	67^1	116	7	35	23	20.5	8.96	59	.371	.437	0	.000	-2	-30	-28	-2	-0.9

● GLENN LIEBHARDT — Liebhardt, Glenn John b: 3/10/1883, Milton, Ind. d: 7/13/56, Cleveland, Ohio BR/TR, 5'10", 175 lbs. Deb: 10/2/06 F

YEAR TM/L	W	L	PCT	G	GS	CG	SH	SV	IP	H	HR	BB	SO	RAT	ERA	ERA+	OAV	OOB	BH	AVG	PB	PR	/A	PD	TPI
1906 Cle-A	2	0	1.000	2	2	2	2	0	18	13	0	1	9	7.0	1.50	175	.205	.218	0	.000	-1	2	2	0	0.2
1907 Cle-A	18	14	.563	38	34	27	4	1	280^1	254	1	85	110	11.2	2.05	122	.244	.307	14	.161	-1	15	14	1	1.6
1908 Cle-A	15	16	.484	38	26	19	3	0	262	222	2	81	146	10.5	2.20	109	.235	.297	14	.175	0	6	6	1	0.7
1909 Cle-A	1	5	.167	12	4	1	0	1	52^1	54	0	16	15	12.2	2.92	87	.314	.376	0	.000	-2	-3	-2	-2	-0.6
Total 4	36	35	.507	90	66	49	7	2	612^2	543	3	183	280	10.9	2.17	114	.244	.306	28	.147	-4	21	20	0	1.9

● GENE LILLARD — Lillard, Robert Eugene b: 11/12/13, Santa Barbara, Cal d: 4/12/91, Goleta, Cal. BR/TR, 5'10.5", 178 lbs. Deb: 5/8/36 F♦

YEAR TM/L	W	L	PCT	G	GS	CG	SH	SV	IP	H	HR	BB	SO	RAT	ERA	ERA+	OAV	OOB	BH	AVG	PB	PR	/A	PD	TPI
1939 Chi-N	3	5	.375	20	7	2	0	0	55	68	2	36	31	17.5	6.55	60	.309	.413	1	.100	-1	-16	-16	0	-1.9
1940 StL-N	0	1	.000	2	1	0	0	0	4^2	8	1	4	2	25.1	13.50	30	.364	.481	0	—	0	-5	-5	0	-0.8
Total 2	3	6	.333	22	8	2	0	0	59^2	76	3	40	33	18.1	7.09	56	.314	.420	8	.182	-1	-21	-21	0	-2.7

● JIM LILLIE — Lillie, James J. "Grasshopper" (b: James J. Lilly) b: 7/27/1861, New Haven, Conn. d: 11/9/1890, Kansas City, Mo. Deb: 5/17/1883 ♦

YEAR TM/L	W	L	PCT	G	GS	CG	SH	SV	IP	H	HR	BB	SO	RAT	ERA	ERA+	OAV	OOB	BH	AVG	PB	PR	/A	PD	TPI
1883 Buf-N	0	1	.000	3	0	0	0	0	12	16	0	2	4	13.5	3.00	106	.302	.327	47	.234	0	0	0	0	0.0
1884 Buf-N	0	1	.000	2	1	0	0	0	13	22	0	5	4	18.7	6.23	51	.324	.370	105	.223	-0	-5	-4	0	-0.2
1886 KC-N	0	0	—	1	0	0	0	0	6	8	0	1	0	13.5	4.50	84	.348	.375	73	.175	-0	-1	-0	0	0.0
Total 3	0	2	.000	6	1	0	0	0	31	46	0	8	8	15.7	4.65	71	.319	.355	332	.219	-0	-5	-5	1	-0.2

● DEREK LILLIQUIST — Lilliquist, Derek Jansen b: 2/20/66, Winter Park, Fla. BL/TL, 6', 200 lbs. Deb: 4/13/89

YEAR TM/L	W	L	PCT	G	GS	CG	SH	SV	IP	H	HR	BB	SO	RAT	ERA	ERA+	OAV	OOB	BH	AVG	PB	PR	/A	PD	TPI
1989 Atl-N	8	10	.444	32	30	0	0	0	165^2	202	16	34	79	12.9	3.97	92	.301	.337	12	.190	0	-9	-6	-1	-0.7
1990 Atl-N	2	8	.200	12	11	0	0	0	61^2	75	10	19	34	13.9	6.28	64	.301	.353	8	.348	4	-17	-15	-1	-1.9
SD-N	3	3	.500	16	7	1	0	0	60^1	61	6	23	29	12.8	4.33	88	.266	.339	3	.150	-0	-4	-3	-2	-0.5
Yr	5	11	.313	28	18	1	0	0	122	136	16	42	63	13.3	5.31	74	.282	.342	11	.256	4	-21	-19	-3	-2.4
1991 SD-N	0	2	.000	6	2	0	0	0	14^1	25	3	4	7	18.2	8.79	43	.379	.414	0	.000	-0	-8	-8	0	-0.9
1992 Cle-A	5	3	.625	71	0	0	0	6	61^2	39	5	18	47	8.6	1.75	223	.186	.257	0	—	0	15	15	0	2.2
1993 Cle-A	4	4	.500	56	2	0	0	10	64	64	5	19	40	11.8	2.25	192	.263	.319	0	—	0	15	15	-0	2.1
1994 Cle-A	1	3	.250	36	0	0	0	0	29^1	34	6	8	15	13.2	4.91	101	.304	.355	0	—	-0	0	0	0	-0.1
Total 6	23	33	.411	229	52	1	1	17	457	500	51	125	251	12.5	4.00	99	.281	.331	23	.213	4	-8	-3	-4	0.2

● JOSE LIMA — Lima, Jose Desiderio Rodriguez (b: Jose Desiderio Rodriguez (Lima)) b: 9/30/72, Santiago, D.R. BR/TR, 6'2", 170 lbs. Deb: 4/20/94

YEAR TM/L	W	L	PCT	G	GS	CG	SH	SV	IP	H	HR	BB	SO	RAT	ERA	ERA+	OAV	OOB	BH	AVG	PB	PR	/A	PD	TPI
1994 Det-A	0	1	.000	3	1	0	0	0	6^2	11	2	3	7	18.9	13.50	35	.355	.412	0	—	0	-6	-6	0	-0.7

● EZRA LINCOLN — Lincoln, Ezra Perry b: 11/17/1868, Raynham, Mass. d: 5/7/51, Taunton, Mass. BL/TL, 5'11", 160 lbs. Deb: 5/2/1890

YEAR TM/L	W	L	PCT	G	GS	CG	SH	SV	IP	H	HR	BB	SO	RAT	ERA	ERA+	OAV	OOB	BH	AVG	PB	PR	/A	PD	TPI
1890 Cle-N	3	11	.214	15	15	13	0	0	118	157	1	53	22	16.1	4.42	81	.310	.376	8	.157	-3	-11	-11	0	-1.2
Syr-a	0	3	.000	3	3	2	0	0	20	33	1	4	6	17.1	10.35	34	.358	.391	0	.000	-1	-14	-15	-0	-1.5
Total 1	3	14	.176	18	18	15	0	0	138	190	2	57	28	16.2	5.28	68	.317	.379	8	.136	-4	-26	-26	0	-2.7

● VIVE LINDAMAN — Lindaman, Vivan Alexander b: 10/28/1877, Charles City, Iowa d: 2/13/27, Charles City, Iowa BR/TR, 6'1", 200 lbs. Deb: 4/14/06

YEAR TM/L	W	L	PCT	G	GS	CG	SH	SV	IP	H	HR	BB	SO	RAT	ERA	ERA+	OAV	OOB	BH	AVG	PB	PR	/A	PD	TPI
1906 Bos-N	12	23	.343	39	37	32	2	0	307^1	303	4	90	115	11.8	2.43	111	.264	.324	14	.132	-2	7	9	-2	0.7
1907 Bos-N	11	15	.423	34	28	24	2	1	260	252	10	108	90	13.0	3.63	70	.265	.349	11	.122	-2	-34	-31	-2	-3.5
1908 Bos-N	12	16	.429	43	30	21	0	1	270^2	246	7	70	68	10.8	2.36	102	.249	.306	15	.176	0	0	-3	-3	-0.2
1909 Bos-N	1	6	.143	15	6	6	1	0	66	75	3	28	13	14.2	4.64	61	.299	.371	6	.273	1	-15	-13	-1	-1.4
Total 4	36	60	.375	131	101	83	7	2	904	876	22	296	286	12.0	2.92	88	.263	.329	46	.152	-3	-41	-34	-8	-4.4

● PAUL LINDBLAD — Lindblad, Paul Aaron b: 8/9/41, Chanute, Kan. BL/TL, 6'1", 195 lbs. Deb: 9/15/65

YEAR TM/L	W	L	PCT	G	GS	CG	SH	SV	IP	H	HR	BB	SO	RAT	ERA	ERA+	OAV	OOB	BH	AVG	PB	PR	/A	PD	TPI
1965 KC-A	0	1	.000	4	0	0	0	0	7^1	12	3	0	12	16.0	11.05	32	.353	.371	0	.000	-0	-6	-6	0	-0.7
1966 KC-A	5	10	.333	38	14	0	0	1	121	138	14	37	69	13.2	4.17	82	.292	.348	5	.147	-0	-10	-10	-0	-1.2
1967 KC-A	5	8	.385	46	10	1	1	6	115^2	106	15	35	83	11.4	3.58	89	.241	.306	7	.206	2	-4	-5	-0	-0.5
1968 Oak-A	4	3	.571	47	1	0	0	1	56^1	51	6	14	42	10.4	2.40	118	.237	.284	3	.375	1	4	3	0	0.6
1969 Oak-A	9	6	.600	60	0	0	0	9	78^1	72	8	33	64	12.3	4.14	83	.240	.319	4	.333	1	-4	-6	-0	-1.1
1970 Oak-A	8	2	.800	62	0	0	0	9	63^1	52	7	28	42	11.4	2.70	131	.222	.305	0	.000	-1	7	6	-0	0.9
1971 Oak-A	1	0	1.000	16	0	0	0	0	16	18	1	2	4	11.8	3.94	85	.295	.328	1	.333	0	-1	-1	0	0.0
Was-A	6	4	.600	43	0	0	0	8	83^2	58	6	29	50	9.6	2.58	128	.196	.272	3	.158	0	8	7	1	1.1
Yr	7	4	.636	51	0	0	0	8	99^2	76	7	31	54	9.8	2.80	118	.212	.279	4	.182	1	7	6	1	1.1
1972 Tex-A	5	8	.385	**66**	0	0	0	7	99^2	95	7	29	51	11.2	2.62	115	.257	.311	3	.200	0	5	4	-1	0.6
1973 *Oak-A	1	5	.167	36	3	0	0	0	78	89	8	28	43	13.8	3.69	96	.292	.357	0	—	0	1	-1	-1	-0.2
1974 Oak-A	4	4	.500	45	2	0	0	6	100^2	85	4	30	46	10.5	2.06	161	.231	.292	0	—	0	17	14	0	1.3
1975 *Oak-A	9	1	.900	68	0	0	0	7	122^1	105	6	43	58	10.0	2.72	133	.237	.305	0	—	0	14	12	1	1.2
1976 Oak-A	6	5	.545	65	0	0	0	5	114^2	111	6	24	37	10.8	3.06	110	.253	.296	0	.000	-0	6	4	1	0.7
1977 Tex-A	4	5	.444	42	1	0	0	4	98^2	103	16	29	46	12.1	4.20	97	.270	.324	0	—	0	-2	-0	-0	-0.2
1978 Tex-A	1	1	.500	18	0	0	0	2	39^2	42	1	15	26	13.2	3.63	103	.279	.354	0	—	0	1	0	-0	0.0
*NY-A	0	0	—	7	1	0	0	0	18^1	21	4	8	9	14.2	4.42	82	.284	.354				-1	-2	0	-0.2
Yr	1	1	.500	25	1	0	0	2	58	62	6	23	34	13.2	3.88	95	.276	.343				-1	-1	0	-0.2
Total 14	68	63	.519	655	32	1	1	64	1213^2	1157	112	384	671	11.6	3.29	104	.253	.314	26	.195	5	35	17	2	2.7

● LYMAN LINDE — Linde, Lyman Gilbert b: 9/20/20, Beaver Dam, Wis. BR/TR, 5'11", 185 lbs. Deb: 9/11/47

YEAR TM/L	W	L	PCT	G	GS	CG	SH	SV	IP	H	HR	BB	SO	RAT	ERA	ERA+	OAV	OOB	BH	AVG	PB	PR	/A	PD	TPI
1947 Cle-A	0	0	—	1	0	0	0	0	0^2	3	0	1	0	54.0	27.00	18	.600	.667	0	—	0	-2	-2	-0	-0.0
1948 Cle-A	0	0	—	3	0	0	0	0	10	9	1	4	1	11.7	5.40	75	.243	.317	0	.000	-0	-1	-1	-0	-0.1
Total 2	0	0	—	4	0	0	0	0	10^2	12	1	5	1	14.3	6.75	60	.286	.362	0	.000	-0	-3	-3	-0	-0.1

● JOHNNY LINDELL — Lindell, John Harlan b: 8/30/16, Greeley, Colo. d: 8/27/85, Newport Beach, Cal. BR/TR, 6'4.5", 217 lbs. Deb: 4/18/41 ♦

YEAR TM/L	W	L	PCT	G	GS	CG	SH	SV	IP	H	HR	BB	SO	RAT	ERA	ERA+	OAV	OOB	BH	AVG	PB	PR	/A	PD	TPI
1942 NY-A	2	1	.667	23	2	0	0	1	52^2	52	3	22	28	12.8	3.76	92	.254	.329	6	.250	1	-1	-2	-0	0.0

YEAR	TM/L	W	L	PCT	G	GS	CG	SH	SV	IP	H	HR	BB	SO	RAT	ERA	ERA+	OAV	OOB	BH	AVG	PB	PR	/A	PD	TPI
1953	Pit-N	5	16	.238	27	23	13	1	0	175²	173	17	116	102	15.1	4.71	95	.262	.377	26	.286	6	-8	-5	3	1.1
	Phi-N	1	1	.500	5	3	2	0	0	23¹	22	0	23	16	17.4	4.24	99	.259	.417	7	.389	2	0	-0	-0	0.2
	Yr	6	17	.261	32	26	15	1	0	199	195	17	139	118	15.1	4.66	95	.259	.375	33	.303	8	-8	-5	2	1.3
Total	2	8	18	.308	55	28	15	1	1	251²	247	20	161	146	14.8	4.47	95	.260	.371	762	.273	9	-9	-7	2	1.3

● ERNIE LINDEMANN
Lindemann, Ernest. b: 6/10/1883, New York, N.Y. d: 12/27/51, Brooklyn, N.Y. BR/TR, Deb: 6/28/07

YEAR	TM/L	W	L	PCT	G	GS	CG	SH	SV	IP	H	HR	BB	SO	RAT	ERA	ERA+	OAV	OOB	BH	AVG	PB	PR	/A	PD	TPI
1907	Bos-N	0	0	—	1	1	0	0	0	6¹	6	0	4	3	14.2	5.68	45	.286	.400	1	.500	0	-2	-2	0	0.1

● CARL LINDQUIST
Lindquist, Carl Emil b: 5/9/19, Morris Run, Pa. BR/TR, 6'2", 185 lbs. Deb: 9/27/43

YEAR	TM/L	W	L	PCT	G	GS	CG	SH	SV	IP	H	HR	BB	SO	RAT	ERA	ERA+	OAV	OOB	BH	AVG	PB	PR	/A	PD	TPI
1943	Bos-N	0	2	.000	2	2	0	0	0	13	17	3	4	1	14.5	6.23	55	.315	.362	0	.000	-1	-4	-4	0	-0.5
1944	Bos-N	0	0	—	5	0	0	0	0	8²	8	1	2	4	10.4	3.12	123	.222	.263	0	.000	-0	0	1	-0	0.0
Total	2	0	2	.000	7	2	0	0	0	21²	25	4	6	5	12.9	4.98	72	.278	.323	0	.000	-1	-4	-3	-0	-0.5

● JIM LINDSEY
Lindsey, James Kendrick b: 1/24/1898, Greensburg, La. d: 10/25/63, Jackson, La. BR/TR, 6'1", 175 lbs. Deb: 5/1/22

YEAR	TM/L	W	L	PCT	G	GS	CG	SH	SV	IP	H	HR	BB	SO	RAT	ERA	ERA+	OAV	OOB	BH	AVG	PB	PR	/A	PD	TPI
1922	Cle-A	4	5	.444	29	5	0	0	1	83²	105	4	24	29	14.2	6.02	67	.324	.376	4	.167	-1	-18	-19	-1	-1.9
1924	Cle-A	0	0	—	3	0	0	0	0	3	8	0	3	4	33.0	21.00	20	.500	.579	0	.000	-1	-6	-6	-0	-0.7
1929	StL-N	1	1	.500	2	2	1	0	0	16¹	20	1	2	8	12.7	5.51	85	.290	.319	1	.200	-0	-1	-2	-0	-0.2
1930	*StL-N	7	5	.583	39	6	3	0	5	105²	131	6	46	50	15.4	4.43	113	.312	.385	8	.286	1	6	7	-3	0.5
1931	*StL-N	6	4	.600	35	2	1	1	7	74²	77	2	45	32	14.7	2.77	142	.270	.370	1	.111	-1	9	10	-1	1.3
1932	StL-N	3	3	.500	33	5	2	0	3	89¹	96	6	38	31	13.7	4.94	80	.279	.354	3	.143	-1	-10	-10	-1	-0.9
1933	StL-N	0	0	—	2	0	0	0	0	2	2	0	1	1	13.5	4.50	77	.286	.375	0	—	-0	-0	-0	-0	0.0
1934	Cin-N	0	0	—	4	0	0	0	0	4	4	0	2	2	15.8	4.50	91	.286	.412	0	—	-0	-0	-0	-0	0.0
	StL-N	0	1	.000	11	0	0	0	1	14	21	2	3	7	15.4	6.43	66	.328	.358	0	.000	-0	-4	-3	-0	-0.3
	Yr	0	1	.000	15	0	0	0	1	18	25	2	5	9	15.0	6.00	70	.316	.357	0	.000	-0	-4	-4	-0	-0.3
1937	Bro-N	0	1	.000	20	0	0	0	2	38¹	43	4	12	15	13.1	3.52	115	.295	.352	1	.167	-2	2	2	-1	0.0
Total	9	21	20	.512	177	20	5	1	19	431	507	25	176	175	14.5	4.70	91	.300	.370	18	.186	-3	-23	-21	-6	-1.5

● AXEL LINDSTROM
Lindstrom, Axel Olaf b: 8/26/1895, Gustavsberg, Sweden d: 6/24/40, Asheville, N.C. BR/TR, 5'10", 180 lbs. Deb: 10/3/16

YEAR	TM/L	W	L	PCT	G	GS	CG	SH	SV	IP	H	HR	BB	SO	RAT	ERA	ERA+	OAV	OOB	BH	AVG	PB	PR	/A	PD	TPI
1916	Phi-A	0	0	—	1	0	0	0	1	4	2	0	1	1	6.8	4.50	63	.182	.250	1	.500	0	-1	-1	-0	0.0

● DICK LINES
Lines, Richard George b: 8/17/38, Montreal, Que., Can. BR/TL, 6'1", 175 lbs. Deb: 4/16/66

YEAR	TM/L	W	L	PCT	G	GS	CG	SH	SV	IP	H	HR	BB	SO	RAT	ERA	ERA+	OAV	OOB	BH	AVG	PB	PR	/A	PD	TPI
1966	Was-A	5	2	.714	53	0	0	0	2	83	63	4	24	49	9.5	2.28	152	.213	.274	0	.000	-1	11	11	2	1.1
1967	Was-A	2	5	.286	54	0	0	0	4	85²	83	6	24	54	11.2	3.36	94	.245	.295	1	.111	1	-1	-2	0	-0.1
Total	2	7	7	.500	107	0	0	0	6	168²	146	10	48	103	10.4	2.83	117	.230	.285	1	.053	-1	9	9	2	1.0

● FRED LINK
Link, Edward Theodore "Laddie" b: 3/11/1886, Columbus, Ohio d: 5/22/39, Houston, Tex. BL/TL, 6', 170 lbs. Deb: 4/15/10

YEAR	TM/L	W	L	PCT	G	GS	CG	SH	SV	IP	H	HR	BB	SO	RAT	ERA	ERA+	OAV	OOB	BH	AVG	PB	PR	/A	PD	TPI
1910	Cle-A	5	6	.455	22	13	6	1	1	127²	121	0	50	55	12.5	3.17	82	.259	.340	7	.167	-1	-9	-8	-1	-1.0
	StL-A	0	1	.000	3	3	0	0	0	17	24	0	13	5	20.1	4.24	58	.375	.487	1	.167	-0	-3	-3	-0	-0.2
	Yr	5	7	.417	25	16	6	1	1	144²	145	0	63	60	13.0	3.30	78	.270	.347	8	.167	-1	-12	-12	-2	-1.2

● ED LINKE
Linke, Edward Karl "Babe" b: 11/9/11, Chicago, Ill. d: 6/21/88, Chicago, Ill. BR/TR, 5'11", 180 lbs. Deb: 4/27/33

YEAR	TM/L	W	L	PCT	G	GS	CG	SH	SV	IP	H	HR	BB	SO	RAT	ERA	ERA+	OAV	OOB	BH	AVG	PB	PR	/A	PD	TPI
1933	Was-A	1	0	1.000	3	2	0	0	0	16	15	0	11	6	14.6	5.06	83	.250	.366	1	.167	0	-1	-2	-0	-0.1
1934	Was-A	2	2	.500	7	4	2	0	0	34²	38	1	9	9	12.2	4.15	104	.277	.322	2	.182	0	1	1	0	0.1
1935	Was-A	11	7	.611	40	22	10	1	3	178	211	6	80	51	14.8	5.01	86	.296	.367	20	.294	6	-11	-14	-1	-0.8
1936	Was-A	1	5	.167	13	6	1	0	0	52	73	4	14	11	15.1	7.10	67	.330	.370	6	.400	5	-12	-13	1	-0.7
1937	Was-A	6	1	.857	36	7	0	0	3	128²	158	11	59	61	15.5	5.60	79	.304	.379	10	.217	1	-14	-17	-0	-0.8
1938	StL-A	1	7	.125	21	2	0	0	0	39²	60	6	33	18	21.1	7.94	63	.337	.463	2	.200	-0	-14	-13	1	-2.0
Total	6	22	22	.500	120	43	13	1	6	449	555	28	206	156	15.4	5.61	79	.305	.377	41	.263	12	-51	-58	-0	-4.3

● ROYCE LINT
Lint, Royce James b: 1/1/21, Birmingham, Ala. BL/TL, 6'1", 165 lbs. Deb: 4/13/54

YEAR	TM/L	W	L	PCT	G	GS	CG	SH	SV	IP	H	HR	BB	SO	RAT	ERA	ERA+	OAV	OOB	BH	AVG	PB	PR	/A	PD	TPI
1954	StL-N	2	3	.400	30	4	1	1	0	70¹	75	9	30	36	13.4	4.86	85	.273	.344	1	.100	1	-6	-6	1	-0.2

● DOUG LINTON
Linton, Douglas Warren b: 2/9/65, Santa Ana, Cal. BR/TR, 6'1", 185 lbs. Deb: 8/3/92

YEAR	TM/L	W	L	PCT	G	GS	CG	SH	SV	IP	H	HR	BB	SO	RAT	ERA	ERA+	OAV	OOB	BH	AVG	PB	PR	/A	PD	TPI
1992	Tor-A	1	3	.250	8	3	0	0	0	24	31	5	17	16	18.0	8.63	47	.323	.425	0	—	0	-12	-12	-0	-1.7
1993	Tor-A	0	1	.000	4	1	0	0	0	11	11	0	9	4	17.2	6.55	66	.256	.396	0	—	0	-3	-3	-0	-0.2
	Cal-A	2	0	1.000	19	0	0	0	0	25²	35	4	14	19	17.2	7.71	58	.324	.402	0	—	0	-10	-9	-0	-0.6
	Yr	2	1	.667	23	1	0	0	0	36²	46	4	23	23	16.9	7.36	60	.299	.390	0	—	0	-12	-12	-0	-0.8
1994	NY-N	6	2	.750	32	3	0	0	0	50¹	74	4	20	29	16.8	4.47	95	.341	.397	0	.000	-1	-1	-1	-1	-0.3
Total	3	9	6	.600	63	7	0	0	0	111	151	17	60	68	17.2	6.32	68	.325	.404	0	.000	-1	-26	-25	-2	-2.8

● FRANK LINZY
Linzy, Frank Alfred b: 9/15/40, Ft.Gibson, Okla BR/TR, 6'1", 190 lbs. Deb: 8/14/63

YEAR	TM/L	W	L	PCT	G	GS	CG	SH	SV	IP	H	HR	BB	SO	RAT	ERA	ERA+	OAV	OOB	BH	AVG	PB	PR	/A	PD	TPI
1963	SF-N	0	0	—	8	1	0	0	0	16²	22	0	10	14	17.8	4.86	66	.324	.418	0	.000	-0	-3	-3	0	-0.0
1965	SF-N	9	3	.750	57	0	0	0	21	81²	76	2	23	35	11.2	1.43	251	.250	.309	4	.222	1	19	20	5	4.9
1966	SF-N	7	11	.389	51	0	0	0	16	100¹	107	4	34	57	12.8	2.96	124	.273	.334	3	.150	0	7	8	1	1.7
1967	SF-N	7	7	.500	57	0	0	0	17	95²	67	4	34	38	9.5	1.51	218	.203	.277	0	.000	-2	20	19	3	3.9
1968	SF-N	9	8	.529	57	0	0	0	12	94²	76	1	27	36	9.9	2.09	141	.218	.277	0	.000	-1	9	9	4	2.3
1969	SF-N	14	9	.609	58	0	0	0	11	116¹	129	6	38	62	13.2	3.64	96	.283	.342	8	.267	3	-1	-2	3	0.3
1970	SF-N	2	1	.667	20	0	0	0	1	25²	33	2	11	16	15.8	7.01	57	.327	.398	0	.000	-0	-8	-9	0	-1.0
	StL-N	3	5	.375	47	0	0	0	2	61¹	66	2	23	19	13.1	3.67	112	.282	.346	0	.000	-0	3	3	1	0.4
	Yr	5	6	.455	67	0	0	0	3	87	99	5	34	35	14.6	4.66	88	.293	.358	0	.000	-0	-6	-6	1	-0.6
1971	StL-N	4	3	.571	50	0	0	0	6	59¹	49	2	27	24	11.5	2.12	170	.226	.311	2	.500	1	9	10	1	1.5
1972	Mil-A	2	2	.500	47	0	0	0	12	77¹	70	4	27	24	11.5	3.03	100	.248	.318	1	.111	0	1	1	0	0.1
1973	Mil-A	2	6	.250	42	1	0	0	13	63	68	7	21	21	12.9	3.57	105	.282	.342	0	—	0	1	1	0	0.3
1974	Phi-N	0	2	.000	22	0	0	0	0	24²	27	1	7	12	12.4	3.28	115	.284	.333	0	—	1	1	1	0	0.3
Total	11	62	57	.521	516	2	0	0	111	816²	790	35	282	358	12.0	2.85	122	.257	.323	18	.149	0	58	57	20	14.6

● ANGELO LiPETRI
LiPetri, Michael Angelo b: 7/6/30, Brooklyn, N.Y. BR/TR, 6'1.5", 180 lbs. Deb: 4/25/56

YEAR	TM/L	W	L	PCT	G	GS	CG	SH	SV	IP	H	HR	BB	SO	RAT	ERA	ERA+	OAV	OOB	BH	AVG	PB	PR	/A	PD	TPI
1956	Phi-N	0	0	—	6	0	0	0	0	11	7	2	3	6	9.0	3.27	114	.175	.250	0	.000	-0	1	1	0	0.0
1958	Phi-N	0	0	—	4	0	0	0	0	4	6	1	0	1	15.8	11.25	35	.353	.389	0	—	0	-3	-3	0	0.0
Total	2	0	0	—	10	0	0	0	0	15	13	3	3	7	10.8	5.40	70	.228	.290	0	.000	-0	-3	-3	0	0.0

● TOM LIPP
Lipp, Thomas C. (b: Thomas C. Lieb) b: 6/4/1870, Baltimore, Md. d: 5/30/32, Baltimore, Md. 5'11.5", 170 lbs. Deb: 9/18/1897

YEAR	TM/L	W	L	PCT	G	GS	CG	SH	SV	IP	H	HR	BB	SO	RAT	ERA	ERA+	OAV	OOB	BH	AVG	PB	PR	/A	PD	TPI
1897	Phi-N	0	1	.000	1	1	0	0	0	3	8	0	2	1	30.0	15.00	28	.482	.537	1	1.000	0	-4	-4	-0	-0.7

● NIG LIPSCOMB
Lipscomb, Gerard b: 2/24/11, Rutherfordton, N.C d: 2/27/78, Huntersville, N.C. BR/TR, 6', 175 lbs. Deb: 4/23/37 ♦

YEAR	TM/L	W	L	PCT	G	GS	CG	SH	SV	IP	H	HR	BB	SO	RAT	ERA	ERA+	OAV	OOB	BH	AVG	PB	PR	/A	PD	TPI
1937	StL-A	0	0	—	3	0	0	0	0	9²	14	1	2	3	16.8	6.52	74	.333	.409	31	.323	1	-2	-2	-0	0.0

● HOD LISENBEE
Lisenbee, Horace Milton b: 9/23/1898, Clarksville, Tenn d: 11/14/87, Clarksville, Tenn. BR/TR, 5'11", 170 lbs. Deb: 4/23/27

YEAR	TM/L	W	L	PCT	G	GS	CG	SH	SV	IP	H	HR	BB	SO	RAT	ERA	ERA+	OAV	OOB	BH	AVG	PB	PR	/A	PD	TPI
1927	Was-A	18	9	.667	39	34	17	4	0	242	221	6	78	105	11.2	3.57	114	.245	.307	11	.133	-5	15	13	-2	0.6
1928	Was-A	2	6	.250	16	9	3	0	0	77	102	4	32	13	16.2	6.08	66	.326	.397	4	.174	-0	-17	-18	-1	-1.6
1929	Bos-A	0	0	—	5	0	0	0	0	8²	10	1	4	2	14.5	5.19	82	.294	.368	0	—	-0	-1	-1	0	0.0
1930	Bos-A	10	17	.370	37	31	15	0	0	237¹	254	20	86	99	13.1	4.40	105	.280	.346	20	.267	1	-6	-4	-3	0.3
1931	Bos-A	5	12	.294	41	17	6	0	0	164²	190	13	69	42	13.2	5.19	83	.281	.332	12	.226	-2	-15	-16	-2	-1.5
1932	Bos-A	0	4	.000	19	6	3	0	0	73¹	87	9	25	13	13.9	5.65	80	.296	.353	1	.048	-2	-10	-9	-1	-0.7
1936	Phi-A	1	7	.125	19	7	4	0	0	85²	115	4	24	17	14.6	6.20	82	.322	.365	3	.120	-1	-11	-10	-1	-0.9

YEAR TM/L	W	L	PCT	G	GS	CG	SH	SV	IP	H	HR	BB	SO	RAT	ERA	ERA+	OAV	OOB	BH	AVG	PB	PR	/A	PD	TPI
1945 Cin-N	1	3	.250	31	3	0	0	1	80¹	97	12	16	14	12.9	5.49	68	.294	.330	0	.000	-3	-15	-15	-1	-1.1
Total 8	37	58	.389	207	107	48	4	1	969	1076	74	314	253	13.1	4.81	90	.282	.340	51	.169	-10	-47	-51	-11	-4.9

● AD LISKA
Liska, Adolph James b: 7/10/06, Dwight, Neb. BR/TR, 5'11.5", 160 lbs. Deb: 4/17/29

YEAR TM/L	W	L	PCT	G	GS	CG	SH	SV	IP	H	HR	BB	SO	RAT	ERA	ERA+	OAV	OOB	BH	AVG	PB	PR	/A	PD	TPI
1929 Was-A	3	9	.250	24	10	4	0	0	94¹	87	1	42	33	12.6	4.77	89	.249	.335	5	.172	-1	-6	-6	3	-0.4
1930 Was-A	9	7	.563	32	16	7	1	1	150²	140	6	71	40	12.9	3.29	140	.250	.340	5	.096	-4	23	22	6	2.2
1931 Was-A	0	1	.000	2	1	0	0	0	4	9	0	1	2	22.5	6.75	64	.450	.476	0	.000	-0	-1	-1	0	-0.2
1932 Phi-N	2	0	1.000	8	0	0	0	1	26²	22	0	10	6	11.1	1.69	261	.239	.320	0	.000	-1	6	8	1	0.7
1933 Phi-N	3	1	.750	45	1	0	0	1	75²	96	5	26	23	14.5	4.52	84	.310	.363	1	.071	-1	-10	-6	4	-0.1
Total 5	17	18	.486	111	28	11	1	3	351¹	354	12	150	104	13.1	3.87	112	.266	.344	11	.107	-7	13	19	14	2.2

● MARK LITTELL
Littell, Mark Alan b: 1/17/53, Cape Girardeau, Mo. BL/TR, 6'3", 210 lbs. Deb: 6/14/73

YEAR TM/L	W	L	PCT	G	GS	CG	SH	SV	IP	H	HR	BB	SO	RAT	ERA	ERA+	OAV	OOB	BH	AVG	PB	PR	/A	PD	TPI
1973 KC-A	1	3	.250	8	7	1	0	0	38	44	5	23	16	15.9	5.68	72	.288	.381	0	—	0	-8	-7	-0	-0.9
1975 KC-A	1	2	.333	7	3	1	0	0	24¹	19	1	15	19	12.6	3.70	104	.229	.347	0	—	0	0	0	1	0.1
1976 *KC-A	8	4	.667	60	1	0	0	16	104	68	1	60	92	11.1	2.08	169	.188	.304	0	.000	0	17	16	-1	2.4
1977 *KC-A	8	4	.667	48	5	0	0	12	104²	73	6	55	106	11.1	3.61	112	.198	.304	0	.000	-0	5	5	-1	0.5
1978 StL-N	4	8	.333	72	2	0	0	11	106¹	80	8	59	130	12.1	2.79	126	.213	.326	0	.000	-0	9	9	-1	1.0
1979 StL-N	9	4	.692	63	0	0	0	13	82¹	60	2	39	67	10.8	2.19	172	.203	.296	0	.000	-1	14	14	-1	2.5
1980 StL-N	0	2	.000	14	0	0	0	2	10²	14	2	7	7	17.7	9.28	40	.304	.412	0	.000	-0	-7	-7	-0	-1.4
1981 StL-N	1	3	.250	28	1	0	0	2	41	36	2	31	22	14.7	4.39	81	.237	.366	2	.250	-0	-4	-4	-1	-0.4
1982 StL-N	0	1	.000	16	0	0	0	0	20²	22	1	15	7	16.1	5.23	69	.272	.385	0	.000	-0	-4	-4	-1	-0.2
Total 9	32	31	.508	316	19	2	0	56	532	416	28	304	466	12.3	3.32	112	.217	.326	2	.059	-2	23	24	-4	3.6

● JEFF LITTLE
Little, Donald Jeffrey b: 12/25/54, Fremont, Ohio BR/TL, 6'6", 220 lbs. Deb: 9/6/80

YEAR TM/L	W	L	PCT	G	GS	CG	SH	SV	IP	H	HR	BB	SO	RAT	ERA	ERA+	OAV	OOB	BH	AVG	PB	PR	/A	PD	TPI
1980 StL-N	1	1	.500	7	2	0	0	0	18²	18	0	9	17	13.0	3.86	96	.250	.333	1	.167	-0	-1	-0	-0	-0.1
1982 Min-A	2	0	1.000	33	0	0	0	0	36¹	33	6	27	26	14.9	4.21	101	.244	.370	0	—	0	-1	-0	-1	-0.2
Total 2	3	1	.750	40	2	0	0	0	55	51	6	36	43	14.2	4.09	99	.246	.358	1	.167	-0	-1	-0	-1	-0.3

● JOHN LITTLEFIELD
Littlefield, John Andrew b: 1/5/54, Covina, Cal. BR/TR, 6'2", 200 lbs. Deb: 6/8/80

YEAR TM/L	W	L	PCT	G	GS	CG	SH	SV	IP	H	HR	BB	SO	RAT	ERA	ERA+	OAV	OOB	BH	AVG	PB	PR	/A	PD	TPI
1980 StL-N	5	5	.500	52	0	0	0	9	66	71	2	20	22	12.5	3.14	118	.282	.337	0	.000	-1	3	4	0	0.6
1981 SD-N	2	3	.400	42	0	0	0	2	64	53	5	28	21	11.5	3.66	89	.235	.322	0	.000	-0	-1	-3	-0	-0.3
Total 2	7	8	.467	94	0	0	0	11	130	124	7	48	43	12.0	3.39	102	.259	.330	0	.000	-1	2	1	-0	0.3

● DICK LITTLEFIELD
Littlefield, Richard Bernard b: 3/18/26, Detroit, Mich. BL/TL, 6', 180 lbs. Deb: 7/7/50

YEAR TM/L	W	L	PCT	G	GS	CG	SH	SV	IP	H	HR	BB	SO	RAT	ERA	ERA+	OAV	OOB	BH	AVG	PB	PR	/A	PD	TPI
1950 Bos-A	2	2	.500	15	2	0	0	1	23¹	27	6	24	13	20.1	9.26	53	.297	.448	0	—	-1	-12	-11	1	-1.6
1951 Chi-A	1	1	.500	4	2	0	0	1	9²	9	1	17	7	24.2	8.38	48	.243	.481	0	.000	0	-5	-5	-0	-0.7
1952 Det-A	0	3	.000	28	1	0	0	1	47²	46	4	25	32	13.4	4.34	88	.257	.348	1	.143	-0	-4	-3	-1	-0.3
StL-A	2	3	.400	7	5	3	0	0	46¹	35	4	17	34	10.1	2.72	144	.205	.277	1	.063	-2	5	6	-1	0.3
Yr	2	6	.250	35	6	3	0	1	94	81	8	42	66	11.8	3.54	109	.231	.314	2	.087	-2	1	3	-2	0.0
1953 StL-A	7	12	.368	36	22	6	0	1	152¹	153	17	84	104	14.2	5.08	83	.264	.361	8	.190	-1	-18	-15	-1	-1.8
1954 Bal-A	0	0	—	3	0	0	0	0	6	8	0	6	5	22.5	10.50	34	.333	.484	0	.000	-0	-5	-5	-0	0.0
Pit-N	10	11	.476	23	21	7	1	0	155	140	14	80	85	12.9	3.60	116	.239	.337	8	.163	0	8	10	-3	1.0
1955 Pit-N	5	12	.294	35	17	4	1	0	130	148	6	68	70	15.1	5.12	80	.290	.375	8	.176	-1	-16	-15	-2	-1.8
1956 Pit-N	0	0	—	6	2	0	0	0	12²	14	2	6	10	14.2	4.26	88	.286	.364	0	.000	-0	-1	-1	-0	-0.1
StL-N	0	2	.000	3	2	0	0	0	9²	9	2	4	5	12.1	7.45	51	.237	.310	0	.000	-0	-4	-4	-0	-0.7
NY-N	4	4	.500	31	7	0	0	2	97	78	16	39	65	10.9	4.08	93	.231	.310	2	.083	-2	-3	-3	-0	-0.4
Yr	4	6	.400	40	11	0	0	2	119¹	101	20	49	80	11.3	4.37	86	.238	.316	2	.071	-2	-8	-8	-1	-1.2
1957 Chi-N	2	3	.400	48	2	0	0	4	65²	76	12	37	51	15.6	5.35	72	.295	.385	2	.182	-0	-11	-11	-1	-1.0
1958 Mil-N	0	1	.000	4	0	0	0	1	6¹	7	2	1	7	12.8	4.26	83	.280	.333	0	—	-0	-0	-1	-0	-0.1
Total 9	33	54	.379	243	83	16	2	9	761²	750	91	413	495	13.9	4.71	86	.260	.355	28	.145	-5	-65	-56	-9	-7.2

● CARLISLE LITTLEJOHN
Littlejohn, Charles Carlisle b: 10/6/01, Irene, Tex. d: 10/27/77, Kansas City, Mo. BR/TR, 5'10", 175 lbs. Deb: 5/11/27

YEAR TM/L	W	L	PCT	G	GS	CG	SH	SV	IP	H	HR	BB	SO	RAT	ERA	ERA+	OAV	OOB	BH	AVG	PB	PR	/A	PD	TPI
1927 StL-N	3	1	.750	14	2	1	0	0	42	47	4	14	16	13.1	4.50	88	.292	.349	5	.417	-1	-3	-3	-1	-0.2
1928 StL-N	2	1	.667	12	2	1	0	0	32	36	2	14	6	14.1	3.66	109	.286	.357	0	.000	-2	1	1	-0	-0.1
Total 2	5	2	.714	26	4	2	0	0	74	83	6	28	22	13.5	4.14	96	.289	.352	5	.217	-0	-2	-1	-1	-0.3

● GREG LITTON
Litton, Jon Gregory b: 7/13/64, New Orleans, La. BR/TR, 6', 175 lbs. Deb: 5/2/89 ◆

YEAR TM/L	W	L	PCT	G	GS	CG	SH	SV	IP	H	HR	BB	SO	RAT	ERA	ERA+	OAV	OOB	BH	AVG	PB	PR	/A	PD	TPI
1991 SF-N	0	0	—	1	0	0	0	0	1	0	3	0	0	36.0	9.00	40	.250	.571	23	.181	-1	-1	-0	-0	0.0

● BUDDY LIVELY
Lively, Everett Adrian "Red" b: 2/14/25, Birmingham, Ala. BR/TR, 6'0.5", 200 lbs. Deb: 4/17/47 F

YEAR TM/L	W	L	PCT	G	GS	CG	SH	SV	IP	H	HR	BB	SO	RAT	ERA	ERA+	OAV	OOB	BH	AVG	PB	PR	/A	PD	TPI
1947 Cin-N	4	7	.364	38	17	3	1	0	123	126	16	63	52	13.8	4.68	88	.265	.351	6	.188	2	-9	-8	-0	-0.5
1948 Cin-N	0	0	—	10	0	0	0	0	22²	13	0	11	12	9.9	2.38	164	.165	.275	0	.000	-0	4	4	-1	-0.1
1949 Cin-N	4	6	.400	31	10	3	1	1	103¹	91	11	53	30	12.5	3.92	107	.245	.339	4	.154	0	1	3	-1	0.2
Total 3	8	13	.381	79	27	6	2	1	249	230	27	127	94	12.9	4.16	99	.248	.339	10	.167	1	-3	-1	-2	-0.4

● JACK LIVELY
Lively, Henry Everett b: 5/29/1885, Joppa, Ala. d: 12/5/67, Arab, Ala. BR/TR, 5'9", 185 lbs. Deb: 4/16/11 F

YEAR TM/L	W	L	PCT	G	GS	CG	SH	SV	IP	H	HR	BB	SO	RAT	ERA	ERA+	OAV	OOB	BH	AVG	PB	PR	/A	PD	TPI
1911 Det-A	7	5	.583	18	14	10	0	0	113²	143	1	34	45	14.6	4.59	75	.313	.369	11	.256	3	-16	-14	-1	-1.1

● WES LIVENGOOD
Livengood, Wesley Amos b: 7/18/10, Salisbury, N.C. BR/TR, 6'2", 172 lbs. Deb: 5/30/39

YEAR TM/L	W	L	PCT	G	GS	CG	SH	SV	IP	H	HR	BB	SO	RAT	ERA	ERA+	OAV	OOB	BH	AVG	PB	PR	/A	PD	TPI
1939 Cin-N	0	0	—	5	0	0	0	0	5²	9	0	4	3	19.1	9.53	40	.360	.429				-4	-4	-0	0.0

● JAKE LIVINGSTONE
Livingstone, Jacob M. b: 1/1/1880, St.Petersburg, Russia d: 3/22/49, Wassaic, N.Y. Deb: 9/6/01

YEAR TM/L	W	L	PCT	G	GS	CG	SH	SV	IP	H	HR	BB	SO	RAT	ERA	ERA+	OAV	OOB	BH	AVG	PB	PR	/A	PD	TPI
1901 NY-N	0	0	—	2	0	0	0	0	12	26	0	7	6	27.0	9.00	37	.430	.511	1	.167	-0	-8	-8	-0	0.0

● CLEM LLEWELLYN
Llewellyn, Clement Manley "Lew" b: 8/1/1895, Dobson, N.C. d: 11/26/69, Concord, N.C. BL/TR, 6'2", 195 lbs. Deb: 6/18/22

YEAR TM/L	W	L	PCT	G	GS	CG	SH	SV	IP	H	HR	BB	SO	RAT	ERA	ERA+	OAV	OOB	BH	AVG	PB	PR	/A	PD	TPI
1922 NY-A	0	0	—	1	0	0	0	0	1	1	0	0	0	9.0	—		.250	.250	0	—	0	0	0	-0	0.0

● GRAEME LLOYD
Lloyd, Graeme John b: 4/9/67, Victoria, Australia BL/TL, 6'7", 215 lbs. Deb: 4/11/93

YEAR TM/L	W	L	PCT	G	GS	CG	SH	SV	IP	H	HR	BB	SO	RAT	ERA	ERA+	OAV	OOB	BH	AVG	PB	PR	/A	PD	TPI
1993 Mil-A	3	4	.429	55	0	0	0	0	63²	64	5	13	31	11.3	2.83	150	.256	.301	0	—	0	11	10	1	1.1
1994 Mil-A	2	3	.400	43	0	0	0	3	47	49	4	15	31	12.8	5.17	95	.269	.335	0	—	0	-2	-1	0	-0.1
Total 2	5	7	.417	98	0	0	0	3	110²	113	9	28	62	12.0	3.82	118	.262	.315	0	—	0	9	9	1	1.0

● HARRY LOCHHEAD
Lochhead, Robert Henry b: 3/29/1876, Stockton, Cal. d: 8/22/09, Stockton, Cal. BR/TR, 5'11", 172 lbs. Deb: 4/16/1899 ◆

YEAR TM/L	W	L	PCT	G	GS	CG	SH	SV	IP	H	HR	BB	SO	RAT	ERA	ERA+	OAV	OOB	BH	AVG	PB	PR	/A	PD	TPI
1899 Cle-N	0	0	—	1	0	0	0	0	3²	4	0	2	0	14.7	0.00	—	.277	.365	129	.238	0	2	2	-0	0.0

● CHUCK LOCKE
Locke, Charles Edward b: 5/5/32, Malden, Mo. BR/TR, 5'11", 185 lbs. Deb: 9/16/55

YEAR TM/L	W	L	PCT	G	GS	CG	SH	SV	IP	H	HR	BB	SO	RAT	ERA	ERA+	OAV	OOB	BH	AVG	PB	PR	/A	PD	TPI
1955 Bal-A	0	0	—	2	0	0	0	0	3	0	0	1	1	3.0	0.00	—	.000	.100	0	—	0	1	1	-0	0.0

● BOBBY LOCKE
Locke, Lawrence Donald b: 3/3/34, Rowes Run, Pa. BR/TR, 5'11", 185 lbs. Deb: 6/18/59

YEAR TM/L	W	L	PCT	G	GS	CG	SH	SV	IP	H	HR	BB	SO	RAT	ERA	ERA+	OAV	OOB	BH	AVG	PB	PR	/A	PD	TPI
1959 Cle-A	3	2	.600	24	7	0	0	2	77²	66	6	41	40	12.7	3.13	118	.233	.336	8	.333	3	6	5	0	0.7
1960 Cle-A	3	5	.375	32	11	0	0	2	123	121	10	37	53	11.7	3.37	111	.255	.311	9	.237	3	7	5	0	0.8
1961 Cle-A	4	4	.500	37	4	0	0	2	95¹	112	12	40	37	14.5	4.53	87	.300	.371	4	.211	0	-5	-6	1	-0.4
1962 StL-N	0	0	—	2	0	0	0	0	2	1	0	2	1	13.5	0.00	—	.143	.333	1	1.000	1	1	1	0	0.0
Phi-N	1	0	1.000	6	0	0	0	0	15²	16	4	10	9	14.9	5.74	67	.262	.366	2	.286	1	-3	-3	-1	-0.1
Yr	1	0	1.000	8	0	0	0	0	17²	17	4	12	10	14.8	5.09	77	.250	.363	2	.286	-0	-2	-2	-1	-0.1
1963 Phi-N	0	0	—	9	0	0	0	0	10²	10	0	5	7	12.7	5.91	55	.244	.326	0	.000	-0	-3	-3	-0	-0.1

YEAR	TM/L	W	L	PCT	G	GS	CG	SH	SV	IP	H	HR	BB	SO	RAT	ERA	ERA+	OAV	OOB	BH	AVG	PB	PR	/A	PD	TPI
1964	Phi-N	0	0	—	8	0	0	0	0	19^1	21	2	6	11	12.6	2.79	124	.276	.329	0	.000	-0	2	1	0	0.0
1965	Cin-N	0	1	.000	11	0	0	0	0	17^1	20	2	8	8	14.5	5.71	66	.299	.373	0	.000	0	-4	-4	1	-0.1
1967	Cal-A	3	0	1.000	9	1	0	0	0	19^1	14	1	3	7	8.4	2.33	135	.203	.247	2	.667	1	2	2	0	0.5
1968	Cal-A	2	3	.400	29	0	0	0	2	36^1	51	3	13	21	16.1	6.44	45	.331	.387	0	.000	-0	-14	-14	-1	-2.2
Total	9	16	15	.516	165	23	2	2	10	416^2	432	40	165	194	13.1	4.02	91	.269	.340	25	.255	8	-12	-17	4	-0.8

● RON LOCKE
Locke, Ronald Thomas b: 4/4/42, Wakefield, R.I. BR/TL, 5'11", 168 lbs. Deb: 4/23/64

YEAR	TM/L	W	L	PCT	G	GS	CG	SH	SV	IP	H	HR	BB	SO	RAT	ERA	ERA+	OAV	OOB	BH	AVG	PB	PR	/A	PD	TPI
1964	NY-N	1	2	.333	25	3	0	0	0	41^1	46	3	22	17	15.0	3.48	103	.289	.379	0	.000	-0	0	0	-0	0.0

● BOB LOCKER
Locker, Robert Awtry b: 3/15/38, George, Iowa BB/TR, 6'3", 200 lbs. Deb: 4/14/65

YEAR	TM/L	W	L	PCT	G	GS	CG	SH	SV	IP	H	HR	BB	SO	RAT	ERA	ERA+	OAV	OOB	BH	AVG	PB	PR	/A	PD	TPI
1965	Chi-A	5	2	.714	51	0	0	0	2	91^1	71	6	30	69	10.1	3.15	101	.216	.285	0	.000	-2	3	0	3	0.2
1966	Chi-A	9	8	.529	56	0	0	0	12	95	73	2	23	70	9.6	2.46	129	.206	.264	4	.250	1	10	7	3	2.0
1967	Chi-A	7	5	.583	**77**	0	0	0	20	124^2	102	5	23	80	9.7	2.09	148	.222	.274	0	.000	-1	16	14	5	2.4
1968	Chi-A	5	4	.556	70	0	0	0	10	90^1	78	4	27	62	10.6	2.29	132	.234	.293	0	.000	-1	7	7	2	1.2
1969	Chi-A	2	3	.400	17	0	0	0	4	22	26	6	6	15	13.1	6.55	59	.292	.337	0	.000	-0	-7	-7	0	-1.6
	Sea-A	3	3	.500	51	0	0	0	6	78^1	69	3	26	46	11.3	2.18	166	.234	.302	1	.083	-0	13	13	2	1.3
	Yr	5	6	.455	68	0	0	0	10	100^1	95	9	32	61	11.7	3.14	117	.247	.310	1	.077	-1	5	6	2	-0.3
1970	Mil-A	0	1	.000	28	0	0	0	3	31^2	37	1	10	19	14.8	3.41	111	.306	.382	0	.000	-0	1	1	-0	0.0
	Oak-A	3	3	.500	38	0	0	0	4	56^1	49	1	19	33	11.0	2.88	123	.232	.299	1	.167	-0	5	4	1	0.5
	Yr	3	4	.429	66	0	0	0	7	88	86	2	29	52	11.9	3.07	118	.254	.315	1	.143	-0	6	5	0	0.5
1971	*Oak-A	7	2	.778	47	0	0	0	6	72^1	63	3	19	46	10.9	2.86	116	.249	.300	0	.000	-0	5	4	1	0.6
1972	*Oak-A	6	1	.857	56	0	0	0	10	78	69	1	16	47	10.0	2.65	107	.235	.280	0	.000	-0	4	2	-1	0.2
1973	Chi-N	10	6	.625	63	0	0	0	18	106^1	96	6	42	76	12.0	2.54	155	.244	.323	1	.067	-1	13	17	2	3.2
1975	Chi-N	0	1	.000	22	0	0	0	0	32^2	38	3	16	14	15.4	4.96	77	.306	.394	0	—	0	-5	-4	1	-0.1
Total	10	57	39	.594	576	0	0	0	95	879	776	41	257	577	10.9	2.75	122	.237	.300	7	.074	-4	64	58	18	9.9

● SKIP LOCKWOOD
Lockwood, Claude Edward b: 8/17/46, Boston, Mass. BR/TR, 6', 190 lbs. Deb: 4/23/65 ♦

YEAR	TM/L	W	L	PCT	G	GS	CG	SH	SV	IP	H	HR	BB	SO	RAT	ERA	ERA+	OAV	OOB	BH	AVG	PB	PR	/A	PD	TPI
1969	Sea-A	0	1	.000	6	3	0	0	0	23	24	3	6	10	11.7	3.52	103	.279	.326	0	.000	-1	0	0	0	0.0
1970	Mil-A	5	12	.294	27	26	3	1	0	173^2	173	22	79	93	13.4	4.30	88	.266	.351	12	.226	2	-11	-10	-1	-0.8
1971	Mil-A	10	15	.400	33	32	5	1	0	208	191	18	91	115	12.4	3.33	104	.246	.329	5	.081	-1	3	3	-3	-0.1
1972	Mil-A	8	15	.348	29	27	5	3	0	170	148	11	71	106	11.8	3.60	84	.232	.313	7	.132	-1	-10	-11	-3	-1.8
1973	Mil-A	5	12	.294	37	15	3	0	0	154^2	164	10	59	87	13.3	3.90	96	.280	.352	0	—	0	-1	-2	-0	-0.2
1974	Cal-A	2	5	.286	37	2	0	0	1	81^1	87	8	32	39	13.1	4.32	80	.264	.343	0	—	0	-6	-8	-0	-0.7
1975	NY-N	1	3	.250	24	0	0	0	2	48^1	28	3	25	61	10.1	1.49	232	.174	.289	1	.167	-0	11	11	-1	0.9
1976	NY-N	10	7	.588	56	0	0	0	19	94^1	62	6	34	108	9.3	2.67	123	.186	.266	6	.333	3	9	7	-0	1.7
1977	NY-N	4	8	.333	63	0	0	0	20	104	87	5	31	84	10.6	3.38	111	.227	.291	2	.200	-0	6	4	-2	0.4
1978	NY-N	7	13	.350	57	0	0	0	15	90^2	78	10	31	73	10.8	3.57	98	.236	.302	2	.182	1	-0	-1	-2	-0.3
1979	NY-N	2	5	.286	27	0	0	0	9	42^1	33	3	14	42	10.0	1.49	245	.224	.292	0	.000	-0	11	10	-1	2.1
1980	Bos-A	3	1	.750	24	1	0	0	0	45^2	61	4	17	11	15.4	5.32	79	.321	.377	0	—	-0	-7	-6	-1	-0.6
Total	12	57	97	.370	420	106	16	5	68	1236	1130	98	490	829	12.0	3.55	99	.246	.323	40	.154	3	4	-3	-13	0.6

● MILO LOCKWOOD
Lockwood, Milo Hathaway b: 4/7/1858, Solon, Ohio d: 10/9/1897, Economy, Pa. 5'10", 160 lbs. Deb: 4/17/1884 ♦

YEAR	TM/L	W	L	PCT	G	GS	CG	SH	SV	IP	H	HR	BB	SO	RAT	ERA	ERA+	OAV	OOB	BH	AVG	PB	PR	/A	PD	TPI
1884	Was-U	1	9	.100	11	10	6	0	0	67^2	99	4	15	48	15.2	7.45	32	.320	.351	14	.209	-2	-38	-38	1	-3.8

● BILLY LOES
Loes, William b: 12/13/29, Long Island City, N.Y. BR/TR, 6'1", 170 lbs. Deb: 5/18/50

YEAR	TM/L	W	L	PCT	G	GS	CG	SH	SV	IP	H	HR	BB	SO	RAT	ERA	ERA+	OAV	OOB	BH	AVG	PB	PR	/A	PD	TPI
1950	Bro-N	0	0	—	10	0	0	0	0	12^2	16	5	5	2	14.9	7.82	52	.314	.375	0	.000	0	-5	-5	-0	0.0
1952	*Bro-N	13	8	.619	39	21	8	4	1	187^1	154	12	71	115	11.0	2.69	135	.224	.299	5	.093	-3	22	20	-0	1.8
1953	*Bro-N	14	8	.636	32	25	9	1	0	162^2	165	21	53	75	12.2	4.54	94	.261	.322	7	.125	-2	-5	-5	3	-0.5
1954	Bro-N	13	5	.722	28	21	6	0	0	147^2	154	14	60	97	13.1	4.14	99	.269	.339	4	.118	-2	-1	-1	-1	-0.4
1955	*Bro-N	10	4	.714	22	19	6	0	0	128	116	16	46	85	11.5	3.59	113	.240	.308	4	.091	-3	6	7	-0	0.4
1956	Bro-N	0	1	.000	1	1	0	0	0	1^1	5	1	1	2	40.5	40.50	10	.556	.600	0	—	0	-5	-5	0	-1.6
	Bal-A	2	7	.222	21	6	1	0	3	56^2	65	4	23	22	14.3	4.76	82	.291	.363	4	.176	-1	-4	-5	1	-0.8
1957	Bal-A★	12	7	.632	31	18	8	3	4	155^1	142	8	37	86	10.6	3.24	111	.245	.295	4	.080	-3	9	6	2	0.6
1958	Bal-A	3	9	.250	32	10	1	0	5	114	106	10	44	44	12.5	3.63	99	.252	.334	2	.067	-2	2	-0	0	-0.3
1959	Bal-A	4	7	.364	37	0	0	0	14	64^1	58	5	25	34	12.0	4.06	93	.239	.317	1	.125	-0	-1	-2	1	-0.3
1960	SF-N	2	3	.600	37	0	0	0	5	45^2	40	9	17	28	12.0	4.93	71	.247	.333	1	.250	-0	-6	-7	1	-0.8
1961	SF-N	6	5	.545	26	18	3	1	0	114^2	114	13	39	55	12.4	4.24	90	.258	.325	5	.156	-0	-3	-5	0	-0.5
Total	11	80	63	.559	316	139	42	9	32	1190^1	1135	118	421	645	12.0	3.89	99	.252	.321	38	.110	-17	9	-5	6	-2.4

● FRANK LOFTUS
Loftus, Francis Patrick b: 3/10/1898, Scranton, Pa. d: 10/27/80, Belchertown, Mass. BR/TR, 5'9", 190 lbs. Deb: 9/26/26

YEAR	TM/L	W	L	PCT	G	GS	CG	SH	SV	IP	H	HR	BB	SO	RAT	ERA	ERA+	OAV	OOB	BH	AVG	PB	PR	/A	PD	TPI
1926	Was-A	0	0	—	1	0	0	0	0	1	3	0	2	0	45.0	9.00	43	.600	.714	0	—	0	-1	-1	-0	0.0

● BOB LOGAN
Logan, Robert Dean "Lefty" b: 2/10/10, Thompson, Neb. d: 5/20/78, Indianapolis, Ind. BR/TL, 5'10", 170 lbs. Deb: 4/18/35

YEAR	TM/L	W	L	PCT	G	GS	CG	SH	SV	IP	H	HR	BB	SO	RAT	ERA	ERA+	OAV	OOB	BH	AVG	PB	PR	/A	PD	TPI
1935	Bro-N	0	1	.000	2	0	0	0	0	2^2	2	0	1	1	10.1	3.38	118	.182	.250	0	—	0	0	0	0	0.1
1937	Det-A	0	0	—	1	0	0	0	0	2	0	1	0	1	27.0	0.00	—	.333	.500	0	—	0	0	0	0	0.0
	Chi-N	0	0	—	4	0	0	0	0	6^1	6	0	4	2	14.2	1.42	280	.261	.370	0	.000	-0	2	2	-0	0.1
1938	Chi-N	0	2	.000	14	0	0	0	2	22^2	18	0	17	10	14.3	2.78	138	.222	.364	0	.000	-0	3	3	-0	0.2
1941	Cin-N	0	1	.000	2	0	0	0	0	3^1	5	0	5	0	27.0	8.10	44	.333	.500	0	—	0	-2	-2	0	-0.4
1945	Bos-N	7	11	.389	34	25	5	1	1	187	213	9	53	53	12.9	3.18	121	.283	.331	13	.213	1	13	14	0	1.4
Total	5	7	15	.318	57	25	5	1	4	222^2	245	9	81	67	13.3	3.15	122	.277	.339	13	.200	1	16	17	0	1.3

● BILL LOHRMAN
Lohrman, William Le Roy b: 5/22/13, Brooklyn, N.Y. BR/TR, 6'1", 185 lbs. Deb: 6/19/34

YEAR	TM/L	W	L	PCT	G	GS	CG	SH	SV	IP	H	HR	BB	SO	RAT	ERA	ERA+	OAV	OOB	BH	AVG	PB	PR	/A	PD	TPI
1934	Phi-N	0	1	.000	4	0	0	0	1	6	5	0	1	2	9.0	4.50	105	.217	.250	1	.500	0	-0	0	0	0.1
1937	NY-N	1	0	1.000	2	1	1	0	1	10	5	0	2	3	6.3	0.90	432	.152	.200	0	.000	-0	3	3	0	0.4
1938	NY-N	9	6	.600	31	14	3	0	0	152	152	9	33	52	11.1	3.32	114	.253	.294	4	.082	-4	8	8	2	0.5
1939	NY-N	12	13	.480	38	24	9	1	1	185^2	200	15	45	70	12.0	4.07	96	.282	.327	14	.233	4	-3	-3	-0	0.2
1940	NY-N	10	15	.400	31	28	11	4	1	195	200	19	43	73	11.4	3.78	103	.264	.306	8	.123	-2	1	2	2	0.2
1941	NY-N	9	10	.474	33	20	6	2	1	159	184	7	40	61	12.7	4.02	92	.286	.327	11	.229	4	-7	-6	0	-0.3
1942	StL-N	1	1	.500	5	0	0	0	0	12^2	11	0	2	6	9.2	1.42	241	.244	.277	2	.667	1	3	3	0	0.5
	NY-N	13	4	.765	26	19	12	2	0	158	143	11	33	41	10.1	2.56	131	.240	.282	7	.121	-3	13	14	-1	1.1
	Yr	14	5	.737	31	19	12	2	0	170^2	154	11	35	47	10.1	2.48	136	.240	.281	9	.148	-2	16	17	-1	1.6
1943	NY-N	5	6	.455	17	12	3	0	1	80^1	110	7	25	16	15.3	5.15	67	.324	.374	1	.037	-3	-16	-15	-1	-2.3
	Bro-N	0	2	.000	6	2	2	0	0	27^2	29	2	10	5	13.0	3.58	94	.274	.342	1	.143	-0	-1	-1	-0	0.0
	Yr	5	8	.385	23	14	5	0	1	108	139	9	35	21	14.6	4.75	72	.311	.362	2	.059	-3	-16	-16	-1	-2.3
1944	Bro-N	0	0	—	3	0	0	0	0	2^2	4	0	4	1	27.0	0.00	—	.500	.667	0	—	0	1	1	-0	0.0
	Cin-N	0	1	.000	2	1	0	0	0	1^2	3	0	1	0	37.8	27.00	13	.500	.583	0	—	0	-4	-4	-0	-1.6
	Yr	0	1	.000	5	1	0	0	0	4^1	9	0	6	1	31.2	10.38	34	.500	.625	0	—	0	-3	-3	-0	-1.6
Total	9	60	59	.504	198	121	47	9	8	990^2	1048	70	240	330	11.8	3.69	101	.271	.315	49	.153	-3	-1	2	3	-1.4

● MICKEY LOLICH
Lolich, Michael Stephen b: 9/12/40, Portland, Ore. BB/TL, 6', 210 lbs. Deb: 5/12/63

YEAR	TM/L	W	L	PCT	G	GS	CG	SH	SV	IP	H	HR	BB	SO	RAT	ERA	ERA+	OAV	OOB	BH	AVG	PB	PR	/A	PD	TPI
1963	Det-A	5	9	.357	33	18	4	0	0	144^1	145	13	56	103	12.8	3.55	105	.265	.338	2	.056	-1	1	3	-1	0.2
1964	Det-A	18	9	.667	44	33	12	6	2	232	196	26	64	192	10.3	3.26	112	.225	.282	7	.109	1	9	10	-2	1.0
1965	Det-A	15	9	.625	43	37	7	3	3	243^2	216	23	72	226	11.1	3.44	101	.236	.301	5	.058	-6	1	1	-2	-0.7
1966	Det-A	14	14	.500	40	33	5	1	3	203^2	204	24	83	173	12.9	4.77	73	.257	.331	9	.141	1	-30	-29	-3	-4.0
1967	Det-A	14	13	.519	31	30	11	**6**	0	204	165	14	56	174	10.1	3.04	107	.221	.282	12	.197	3	4	5	-2	0.7

YEAR TM/L	W	L	PCT	G	GS	CG	SH	SV	IP	H	HR	BB	SO	RAT	ERA	ERA+	OAV	OOB	BH	AVG	PB	PR	/A	PD	TPI
1968 *Det-A	17	9	.654	39	32	8	4	1	220	178	23	65	197	10.4	3.19	94	.219	.286	8	.114	0	-5	-4	-2	-0.8
1969 Det-A☆	19	11	.633	37	36	15	1	1	280²	214	22	122	271	11.2	3.14	119	.210	.304	8	.088	-3	15	18	-0	1.6
1970 Det-A	14	19	.424	40	39	13	3	0	272²	272	27	109	230	12.7	3.80	98	.260	.333	11	.134	1	-2	0	-1	0.0
1971 Det-A★	**25**	14	.641	45	45	**29**	4	0	**376**	336	36	92	**308**	10.4	2.92	123	.237	.287	15	.130	1	23	28	-4	2.6
1972 *Det-A★	22	14	.611	41	41	23	4	0	327¹	282	29	74	250	10.1	2.50	126	.234	.284	6	.067	-0	20	23	-4	2.2
1973 Det-A	16	15	.516	42	42	17	3	0	308²	315	35	79	214	11.6	3.82	107	.266	.315	0	—	0	-0	9	-1	0.7
1974 Det-A	16	21	.432	41	41	27	3	0	308	310	35	78	202	11.4	4.15	92	.268	.316	0	—	0	-18	-12	-4	-1.7
1975 Det-A	12	18	.400	32	32	19	1	0	240²	260	19	64	139	12.1	3.78	106	.279	.325	0	—	0	-0	6	-2	0.5
1976 NY-N	8	13	.381	31	30	5	2	0	192²	184	14	52	120	11.0	3.22	102	.252	.302	7	.130	0	6	2	-1	0.1
1978 SD-N	2	1	.667	20	2	0	0	1	34²	30	0	11	13	10.9	1.56	214	.240	.307	0	.000	0	8	7	-0	0.6
1979 SD-N	0	2	.000	27	5	0	0	0	49¹	59	4	22	20	14.8	4.74	74	.304	.375	0	.000	0	-6	-7	0	-0.3
Total 16	217	191	.532	586	496	195	41	11	3638¹	3366	347	1099	2832	11.3	3.44	104	.246	.306	90	.110	-4	25	58	-25	2.7

● **TIM LOLLAR** Lollar, William Timothy b: 3/17/56, Poplar Bluff, Mo. BL/TL, 6'3", 200 lbs. Deb: 6/28/80

YEAR TM/L	W	L	PCT	G	GS	CG	SH	SV	IP	H	HR	BB	SO	RAT	ERA	ERA+	OAV	OOB	BH	AVG	PB	PR	/A	PD	TPI
1980 NY-A	1	0	1.000	14	1	0	0	2	32¹	33	3	20	13	14.8	3.34	117	.280	.384	0	—	0	2	2	0	0.1
1981 SD-N	2	8	.200	24	11	0	0	0	76²	87	4	51	38	16.6	6.10	53	.293	.402	3	.167	1	-22	-22	2	-2.6
1982 SD-N	16	9	.640	34	34	4	2	0	232²	192	20	87	150	10.9	3.13	109	.224	.298	21	.247	9	12	8	0	1.8
1983 SD-N	7	12	.368	30	30	1	0	0	175²	170	21	85	135	13.3	4.61	76	.258	.347	14	.241	6	-19	-22	-2	-1.8
1984 *SD-N	11	13	.458	31	31	3	2	0	195²	168	18	105	131	12.6	3.91	91	.234	.333	15	.221	7	-7	-7	-2	-0.4
1985 Chi-A	3	5	.375	18	13	0	0	0	83	83	10	58	61	15.4	4.66	93	.266	.383	0	—	0	-5	-3	-0	-0.3
Bos-A	5	5	.500	16	10	1	0	1	67	57	9	40	44	13.2	4.57	94	.230	.339	0	.000	0	-3	-2	-1	-0.4
Yr	8	10	.444	34	23	1	0	1	150	140	19	98	105	14.3	4.62	93	.248	.360	0	.000	0	-8	-5	-1	-0.7
1986 Bos-A	2	0	1.000	32	1	0	0	0	43	51	7	34	28	18.4	6.91	60	.300	.429	1	1.000	0	-13	-13	1	-0.4
Total 7	47	52	.475	199	131	9	4	4	906	841	93	480	600	13.3	4.27	85	.249	.345	54	.234	24	-55	-63	-3	-4.0

● **VIC LOMBARDI** Lombardi, Victor Alvin b: 9/20/22, Reedley, Cal. BL/TL, 5'7", 158 lbs. Deb: 4/18/45

YEAR TM/L	W	L	PCT	G	GS	CG	SH	SV	IP	H	HR	BB	SO	RAT	ERA	ERA+	OAV	OOB	BH	AVG	PB	PR	/A	PD	TPI
1945 Bro-N	10	11	.476	38	24	9	0	4	203²	195	11	86	64	12.6	3.31	113	.252	.331	13	.183	-1	11	10	-1	0.9
1946 Bro-N	13	10	.565	41	25	13	2	3	193	170	10	84	60	11.9	2.89	117	.235	.316	14	.230	2	11	10	0	1.4
1947 *Bro-N	12	11	.522	33	20	7	3	3	174²	156	12	65	72	11.5	2.99	138	.241	.312	16	.242	2	21	22	1	3.0
1948 Pit-N	10	9	.526	38	17	9	0	4	163	156	9	67	54	12.4	3.70	110	.255	.330	10	.208	1	5	7	1	0.9
1949 Pit-N	5	5	.500	34	12	4	0	1	134	149	14	68	64	14.8	4.57	92	.286	.372	17	.347	5	-8	-5	1	0.3
1950 Pit-N	0	5	.000	39	2	0	0	1	76¹	93	14	48	26	16.9	6.60	66	.310	.409	4	.250	1	-21	-19	0	-1.0
Total 6	50	51	.495	223	100	42	5	16	944²	919	70	418	340	12.9	3.68	106	.257	.337	74	.238	10	19	25	3	5.5

● **LOU LOMBARDO** Lombardo, Louis b: 11/18/28, Carlstadt, N.J. BL/TL, 6'2", 210 lbs. Deb: 9/22/48

YEAR TM/L	W	L	PCT	G	GS	CG	SH	SV	IP	H	HR	BB	SO	RAT	ERA	ERA+	OAV	OOB	BH	AVG	PB	PR	/A	PD	TPI
1948 NY-N	0	0	—	2	0	0	0	0	5¹	5	1	5	0	18.6	6.75	58	.250	.423	0	.000	-0	-2	-2	0	0.0

● **JIM LONBORG** Lonborg, James Reynold b: 4/16/42, Santa Maria, Cal. BR/TR, 6'5", 210 lbs. Deb: 4/23/65

YEAR TM/L	W	L	PCT	G	GS	CG	SH	SV	IP	H	HR	BB	SO	RAT	ERA	ERA+	OAV	OOB	BH	AVG	PB	PR	/A	PD	TPI
1965 Bos-A	9	17	.346	32	31	7	1	0	185¹	193	20	65	113	12.7	4.47	85	.262	.324	8	.136	0	-21	-15	-2	-2.1
1966 Bos-A	10	10	.500	45	23	3	1	2	181²	173	18	55	131	11.6	3.86	98	.249	.310	5	.093	-2	-9	-1	-1	-0.4
1967 *Bos-A☆	22	9	.710	39	39	15	2	0	273¹	228	23	83	**246**	10.9	3.16	110	.225	.296	14	.141	-1	2	10	-2	0.7
1968 Bos-A	6	10	.375	23	17	4	1	0	113¹	89	11	59	73	12.6	4.29	74	.216	.330	11	.282	3	-16	-14	-2	-1.8
1969 Bos-A	7	11	.389	29	23	4	0	0	143²	148	15	65	100	13.8	4.51	84	.270	.355	4	.098	-1	-14	-11	-0	-1.4
1970 Bos-A	4	1	.800	9	4	0	0	0	34	33	3	9	21	11.1	3.18	125	.260	.309	4	.444	1	2	3	0	0.7
1971 Bos-A	10	7	.588	27	26	5	1	0	167²	167	15	67	100	13.4	4.13	89	.259	.342	9	.170	0	-13	-8	1	-0.7
1972 Mil-A	14	12	.538	33	30	11	2	1	223	197	17	76	143	11.5	2.83	107	.238	.311	10	.145	-1	6	5	-2	0.3
1973 Phi-N	13	16	.448	38	30	6	0	0	199¹	218	25	80	106	13.9	4.88	78	.279	.353	8	.136	0	-27	-24	-1	-3.2
1974 Phi-N	17	13	.567	39	39	16	3	0	283	280	22	70	121	11.3	3.21	118	.261	.310	9	.096	-4	13	18	-4	1.0
1975 Phi-N	8	6	.571	27	26	6	2	0	159¹	161	12	45	72	11.9	4.12	90	.257	.312	1	.023	-3	-9	-7	-0	-0.8
1976 *Phi-N	18	10	.643	33	32	8	1	0	222	210	18	50	118	10.7	3.08	115	.249	.294	11	.164	1	10	11	-3	1.2
1977 *Phi-N	11	4	.733	25	25	4	1	0	157²	157	16	50	100	12.1	4.11	97	.261	.323	5	.104	-2	-4	-2	-1	-0.5
1978 Phi-N	8	10	.444	22	22	1	0	0	113²	132	16	45	48	14.2	5.23	68	.293	.359	6	.176	1	-21	-21	-0	-2.9
1979 Phi-N	0	1	.000	4	1	0	0	0	7¹	14	3	4	7	23.3	11.05	35	.389	.463	0	.000	-0	-6	-6	-0	-0.7
Total 15	157	137	.534	425	368	90	15	4	2464¹	2400	233	823	1475	12.2	3.86	94	.255	.322	105	.136	-5	-106	-63	-18	-10.6

● **LEP LONG** Long, Lester b: 7/12/1888, Summit, N.J. d: 10/21/58, Birmingham, Ala. BR/TR, 5'10", 153 lbs. Deb: 6/29/11

YEAR TM/L	W	L	PCT	G	GS	CG	SH	SV	IP	H	HR	BB	SO	RAT	ERA	ERA+	OAV	OOB	BH	AVG	PB	PR	/A	PD	TPI
1911 Phi-A	0	0	—	4	0	0	0	0	8	15	0	5	4	22.5	4.50	70	.405	.476	0	.000	-0	-1	-1	0	0.0

● **RED LONG** Long, Nelson b: 9/28/1876, Burlington, Ont., Canada d: 8/11/29, Hamilton, Ont., Can BR/TR, 6'1", 190 lbs. Deb: 9/11/02

YEAR TM/L	W	L	PCT	G	GS	CG	SH	SV	IP	H	HR	BB	SO	RAT	ERA	ERA+	OAV	OOB	BH	AVG	PB	PR	/A	PD	TPI
1902 Bos-N	0	0	—	1	1	1	0	0	8	4	0	3	5	9.0	1.13	251	.150	.260	0	.000	-0	1	2	-0	0.0

● **BOB LONG** Long, Robert Earl b: 11/11/54, Jasper, Tenn. BR/TR, 6'3", 178 lbs. Deb: 9/2/81

YEAR TM/L	W	L	PCT	G	GS	CG	SH	SV	IP	H	HR	BB	SO	RAT	ERA	ERA+	OAV	OOB	BH	AVG	PB	PR	/A	PD	TPI
1981 Pit-N	1	2	.333	5	3	0	0	0	19²	23	2	10	8	15.1	5.95	60	.299	.379	0	.000	-0	-5	-5	-1	-0.8
1985 Sea-A	0	0	—	28	0	0	0	0	38¹	30	7	17	29	11.5	3.76	112	.210	.302	0	—	0	2	2	-0	0.0
Total 2	1	2	.333	33	3	0	0	0	58	53	9	27	37	12.7	4.50	89	.241	.329	0	.000	-0	-3	-3	-1	-0.8

● **TOM LONG** Long, Thomas Francis "Little Hawk" b: 4/22/1898, Memphis, Tenn. d: 9/16/73, Louisville, Ky. BL/TL, 5'9", 154 lbs. Deb: 4/26/24

YEAR TM/L	W	L	PCT	G	GS	CG	SH	SV	IP	H	HR	BB	SO	RAT	ERA	ERA+	OAV	OOB	BH	AVG	PB	PR	/A	PD	TPI
1924 Bro-N	0	0	—	1	0	0	0	0	2	2	0	2	0	18.0	9.00	42	.333	.500	0	—	0	-1	-1	-0	0.0

● **BILL LONG** Long, William Douglas b: 2/29/60, Cincinnati, Ohio BR/TR, 6', 185 lbs. Deb: 7/21/85

YEAR TM/L	W	L	PCT	G	GS	CG	SH	SV	IP	H	HR	BB	SO	RAT	ERA	ERA+	OAV	OOB	BH	AVG	PB	PR	/A	PD	TPI
1985 Chi-A	0	1	.000	4	3	0	0	0	14	25	4	5	13	19.3	10.29	42	.391	.435	0	—	0	-10	-9	-0	-0.5
1987 Chi-A	8	8	.500	29	23	5	2	1	169	179	20	28	72	11.2	4.37	105	.272	.304	0	—	0	2	4	0	0.2
1988 Chi-A	8	11	.421	47	18	3	0	2	174	187	21	43	77	12.1	4.03	98	.280	.327	0	—	0	-1	-1	-0	-0.2
1989 Chi-A	5	5	.500	30	8	0	0	0	98²	101	8	37	51	13.0	3.92	97	.265	.336	0	—	0	-0	-1	0	-0.2
1990 Chi-A	0	1	.000	4	0	0	0	0	5²	6	2	2	2	12.7	6.35	60	.261	.320	0	—	0	-2	-2	-0	-0.2
Chi-N	6	1	.857	42	0	0	0	5	55²	66	8	21	32	14.2	4.37	93	.301	.365	0	.000	-0	-4	-2	-0	-0.2
1991 Mon-N	0	0	—	3	0	0	0	0	1²	4	0	4	2	43.2	10.80	33	.500	.667	0	—	0	-1	-1	0	0.0
Total 6	27	27	.500	159	52	8	2	9	518²	568	63	140	247	12.5	4.37	95	.281	.331	0	—	0	-16	-13	1	-0.9

● **BRIAN LOONEY** Looney, Brian James b: 9/26/69, New Haven, Conn. BL/TL, 5'10", 180 lbs. Deb: 9/26/93

YEAR TM/L	W	L	PCT	G	GS	CG	SH	SV	IP	H	HR	BB	SO	RAT	ERA	ERA+	OAV	OOB	BH	AVG	PB	PR	/A	PD	TPI
1993 Mon-N	0	0	—	3	1	0	0	0	6	8	0	2	7	15.0	3.00	139	.308	.357	0	.000	-0	-0	-0	0	0.0
1994 Mon-N	0	0	—	1	0	0	0	0	2	4	1	0	2	22.5	22.50	19	.400	.455	0	—	0	-4	-4	-0	0.0
Total 2	0	0	—	4	1	0	0	0	8	12	1	2	9	16.9	7.88	53	.333	.385	0	.000	-0	-3	-3	-0	0.0

● **PETE LOOS** Loos, Ivan b: 3/23/1878, Philadelphia, Pa. d: 2/23/56, Darby, Pa. TR, Deb: 5/2/01

YEAR TM/L	W	L	PCT	G	GS	CG	SH	SV	IP	H	HR	BB	SO	RAT	ERA	ERA+	OAV	OOB	BH	AVG	PB	PR	/A	PD	TPI
1901 Phi-A	0	1	.000	1	1	0	0	0	2	8	0	4	0	54.0	27.00	14	.409	.675	0	—	0	-3	-3	0	-1.2

● **ED LOPAT** Lopat, Edmund Walter (b: Edmund Walter Lopatynski) b: 6/21/18, New York, N.Y. d: 6/15/92, Darien, Conn. BL/TL, 5'10", 185 lbs. Deb: 4/30/44 MC

YEAR TM/L	W	L	PCT	G	GS	CG	SH	SV	IP	H	HR	BB	SO	RAT	ERA	ERA+	OAV	OOB	BH	AVG	PB	PR	/A	PD	TPI
1944 Chi-A	11	10	.524	27	25	13	1	0	210	207	12	59	75	11.9	3.26	105	.265	.316	25	.309	6	4	4	1	1.2
1945 Chi-A	10	13	.435	26	24	17	1	1	199¹	226	8	56	74	13.0	4.11	81	.285	.336	24	.293	5	-16	-17	-1	-1.4
1946 Chi-A	13	13	.500	29	29	20	2	0	231	216	18	48	89	10.3	2.73	125	.248	.288	22	.253	6	20	18	1	2.8
1947 Chi-A	16	13	.552	31	31	22	3	0	252²	241	11	73	109	11.3	2.81	130	.253	.307	19	.198	0	25	24	-1	2.6
1948 NY-A	17	11	.607	31	30	14	3	0	226²	246	16	64	83	12.5	3.65	112	.284	.336	14	.173	-1	16	11	2	1.2
1949 *NY-A	15	10	.600	31	30	14	4	1	215¹	222	19	69	70	12.4	3.26	124	.269	.330	20	.263	7	22	19	0	2.7
1950 *NY-A	18	8	.692	35	32	15	3	1	236¹	244	19	65	72	11.9	3.47	124	.266	.317	19	.232	8	29	22	1	2.9
1951 *NY-A★	21	9	.700	31	31	20	4	0	234²	209	12	71	93	10.9	2.91	131	.239	**.298**	15	.179	1	31	24	2	3.0

YEAR	TM/L	W	L	PCT	G	GS	CG	SH	SV	IP	H	HR	BB	SO	RAT	ERA	ERA+	OAV	OOB	BH	AVG	PB	PR	/A	PD	TPI
1952	*NY-A	10	5	.667	20	19	10	2	0	149¹	127	11	53	56	11.1	2.53	131	.234	.307	9	.173	1	19	13	0	1.4
1953	*NY-A	16	4	**.800**	25	24	9	3	0	178¹	169	13	32	50	10.3	**2.42**	**152**	.250	.288	12	.190	1	31	25	1	2.9
1954	NY-A	12	4	.750	26	23	7	0	0	170	189	14	33	54	12.1	3.55	97	.288	.328	1	.018	-5	3	-2	-1	-0.8
1955	NY-A	4	8	.333	16	12	3	1	0	86²	101	12	16	24	12.3	3.74	100	.294	.328	4	.138	-1	2	0	-1	-0.2
	Bal-A	3	4	.429	10	7	1	0	0	49	57	8	9	10	12.7	4.22	90	.294	.335	3	.176	0	-1	-2	1	-0.2
	Yr	7	12	.368	26	19	4	1	0	135²	158	20	25	34	12.3	3.91	96	.293	.328	7	.152	-1	1	-2	-0	-0.4
Total 12		166	112	.597	340	318	164	27	3	2439¹	2464	179	650	859	11.6	3.21	116	.264	.315	187	.211	29	186	138	4	18.1

● **ART LOPATKA**   Lopatka, Arthur Joseph b: 5/28/19, Chicago, Ill. BB/TL, 5'10", 170 lbs. Deb: 9/12/45

YEAR	TM/L	W	L	PCT	G	GS	CG	SH	SV	IP	H	HR	BB	SO	RAT	ERA	ERA+	OAV	OOB	BH	AVG	PB	PR	/A	PD	TPI
1945	StL-N	1	0	1.000	4	1	1	0	0	11²	7	0	3	5	8.5	1.54	243	.159	.229	1	.250	0	3	3	0	0.2
1946	Phi-N	0	1	.000	4	1	0	0	0	5¹	13	1	4	4	28.7	16.88	20	.448	.515	0	—	0	-8	-8	0	-1.2
Total 2		1	1	.500	8	2	1	0	0	17	20	1	7	9	14.8	6.35	57	.274	.346	1	.250	0	-5	-5	-0	-1.0

● **ALBIE LOPEZ**   Lopez, Albert Anthony b: 8/18/71, Mesa, Ariz. BR/TR, 6'1", 205 lbs. Deb: 7/6/93

YEAR	TM/L	W	L	PCT	G	GS	CG	SH	SV	IP	H	HR	BB	SO	RAT	ERA	ERA+	OAV	OOB	BH	AVG	PB	PR	/A	PD	TPI
1993	Cle-A	3	1	.750	9	9	0	0	0	49²	49	7	32	25	14.9	5.98	72	.262	.373	0	—	0	-9	-9	-0	-0.6
1994	Cle-A	1	2	.333	4	4	1	1	0	17	20	3	6	18	14.3	4.24	117	.290	.355	0	—	0	1	1	0	-0.1
Total 2		4	3	.571	13	13	1	1	0	66²	69	10	38	43	14.7	5.54	81	.270	.368	0	—	0	-8	-8	-0	-0.7

● **AURELIO LOPEZ**   Lopez, Aurelio Alejandro (Rios) b: 9/21/48, Tecamachalco, Mexico d: 9/22/92, Matehuala, Mex. BR/TR, 6', 220 lbs. Deb: 9/1/74

YEAR	TM/L	W	L	PCT	G	GS	CG	SH	SV	IP	H	HR	BB	SO	RAT	ERA	ERA+	OAV	OOB	BH	AVG	PB	PR	/A	PD	TPI
1974	KC-A	0	0	—	8	0	0	0	0	16	21	0	10	5	17.4	5.63	68	.344	.437	0	—	0	-4	-3	0	0.0
1978	StL-N	4	2	.667	25	4	0	0	0	65	52	4	32	46	11.8	4.29	82	.218	.313	3	.214	0	-5	-6	-1	-0.6
1979	Det-A	10	5	.667	61	0	0	0	21	127	95	12	51	106	10.6	2.41	179	.210	.294	0	—	0	25	27	-0	3.7
1980	Det-A	13	6	.684	67	1	0	0	21	124	125	15	45	97	12.6	3.77	109	.263	.330	0	—	0	4	5	-1	0.7
1981	Det-A	5	2	.714	29	3	0	0	3	81²	70	8	31	53	11.4	3.64	104	.233	.309	0	—	0	1	0	-0	0.1
1982	Det-A	3	1	.750	19	0	0	0	3	41	41	8	21	26	13.2	5.27	77	.268	.349	0	—	0	-5	-5	0	-0.6
1983	Det-A☆	9	8	.529	57	0	0	0	18	115¹	87	12	49	90	10.7	2.81	139	.210	.295	0	—	0	16	14	-1	2.5
1984	*Det-A	10	1	.909	71	0	0	0	14	137²	109	16	52	94	10.7	2.94	133	.221	.298	0	—	0	16	15	-2	1.3
1985	Det-A	3	7	.300	51	0	0	0	5	86¹	82	15	41	53	12.9	4.80	85	.250	.335	0	—	0	-6	-7	-0	-0.8
1986	*Hou-N	3	3	.500	45	0	0	0	7	78	64	6	25	44	10.3	3.46	104	.221	.283	0	.000	-1	2	1	-2	-0.2
1987	Hou-N	2	1	.667	26	0	0	0	1	38	39	6	12	21	12.6	4.50	87	.273	.338	0	.000	-0	-2	-2	-0	-0.2
Total 11		62	36	.633	459	9	0	0	93	910	785	102	367	635	11.5	3.56	111	.234	.313	3	.125	-1	41	39	-8	5.9

● **RAMON LOPEZ**   Lopez, Jose Ramon (Hevia) b: 5/26/33, Las Villas, Cuba d: 9/4/82, Miami, Fla. BR/TR, 6', 175 lbs. Deb: 8/21/66

YEAR	TM/L	W	L	PCT	G	GS	CG	SH	SV	IP	H	HR	BB	SO	RAT	ERA	ERA+	OAV	OOB	BH	AVG	PB	PR	/A	PD	TPI
1966	Cal-A	0	1	.000	4	1	0	0	0	7	4	1	4	2	10.3	5.14	65	.154	.267	0	—	0	-1	-1	-0	-0.2

● **MARCELINO LOPEZ**   Lopez, Marcelino Pons b: 9/23/43, Havana, Cuba BR/TL, 6'3", 210 lbs. Deb: 4/14/63

YEAR	TM/L	W	L	PCT	G	GS	CG	SH	SV	IP	H	HR	BB	SO	RAT	ERA	ERA+	OAV	OOB	BH	AVG	PB	PR	/A	PD	TPI
1963	Phi-N	1	0	1.000	4	2	0	0	0	6	8	0	7	2	22.5	6.00	54	.333	.484	0	.000	-0	-2	-2	0	-0.3
1965	Cal-A	14	13	.519	35	32	8	1	1	215¹	185	12	82	122	11.3	2.93	116	.230	.305	14	.203	3	13	11	4	2.3
1966	Cal-A	7	14	.333	37	32	6	2	1	199	188	20	68	132	12.0	3.93	85	.251	.321	11	.190	2	-11	-13	2	-1.0
1967	Cal-A	0	2	.000	4	3	0	0	0	9	11	1	9	6	20.0	9.00	35	.324	.465	1	.500	0	-6	-6	-0	-1.1
	Bal-A	1	0	1.000	4	4	0	0	0	17²	15	1	10	15	12.7	2.55	124	.227	.329	0	.000	-0	1	1	-1	0.0
	Yr	1	2	.333	8	7	0	0	0	26²	26	2	19	21	15.2	4.73	67	.257	.375	1	.143	0	-4	-5	-1	-1.1
1969	*Bal-A	5	3	.625	27	4	0	0	0	69¹	65	3	34	57	13.1	4.41	81	.252	.344	3	.214	1	-6	-7	-1	-0.7
1970	*Bal-A	1	1	.500	25	3	0	0	0	60²	47	2	37	49	12.5	2.08	176	.217	.331	1	.077	-1	11	11	-1	0.2
1971	Mil-A	2	7	.222	31	11	0	0	0	67²	64	5	60	42	16.5	4.66	75	.251	.394	1	.059	-1	-9	-9	-1	-1.2
1972	Cle-A	0	0	—	4	2	0	0	0	8¹	8	0	10	1	19.4	5.40	60	.276	.462	0	.000	-0	-2	-2	0	-0.2
Total 8		31	40	.437	171	93	14	3	2	653	591	44	317	426	12.7	3.62	94	.243	.334	31	.171	4	-11	-15	4	-1.8

● **BRIS LORD**   Lord, Bristol Robotham "The Human Eyeball" b: 9/21/1883, Upland, Pa. d: 11/13/64, Annapolis, Md. BR/TR, 5'9", 185 lbs. Deb: 4/21/05 ♦

YEAR	TM/L	W	L	PCT	G	GS	CG	SH	SV	IP	H	HR	BB	SO	RAT	ERA	ERA+	OAV	OOB	BH	AVG	PB	PR	/A	PD	TPI
1907	Phi-A	0	0	—	1	0	0	0	0	3	3	0	0	0	27.0	9.00	29	.516	.516	31	.182	0	-1	-1	-0	0.0

● **LEFTY LORENZEN**   Lorenzen, Adolph Andreas b: 1/12/1893, Davenport, Iowa d: 3/5/63, Davenport, Iowa BL/TL, 5'10", 164 lbs. Deb: 9/12/13

YEAR	TM/L	W	L	PCT	G	GS	CG	SH	SV	IP	H	HR	BB	SO	RAT	ERA	ERA+	OAV	OOB	BH	AVG	PB	PR	/A	PD	TPI
1913	Det-A	0	0	—	1	0	0	0	0	2	4	0	3	0	31.5	18.00	16	.667	.778	1	.500	0	-3	-3	1	0.1

● **ANDREW LORRAINE**   Lorraine, Andrew Jason b: 8/11/72, Los Angeles, Cal. BL/TL, 6'3", 195 lbs. Deb: 7/17/94

YEAR	TM/L	W	L	PCT	G	GS	CG	SH	SV	IP	H	HR	BB	SO	RAT	ERA	ERA+	OAV	OOB	BH	AVG	PB	PR	/A	PD	TPI
1994	Cal-A	0	2	.000	4	3	0	0	0	18²	30	7	11	10	19.8	10.61	47	.366	.441	0	—	0	-12	-12	0	-1.1

● **JOE LOTZ**   Lotz, Joseph Peter "Smokey" b: 1/2/1891, Remsen, Iowa d: 1/1/71, Castro Valley, Cal. BR/TR, 5'8.5", 175 lbs. Deb: 7/15/16

YEAR	TM/L	W	L	PCT	G	GS	CG	SH	SV	IP	H	HR	BB	SO	RAT	ERA	ERA+	OAV	OOB	BH	AVG	PB	PR	/A	PD	TPI
1916	StL-N	0	3	.000	12	3	1	0	0	40	31	1	17	18	11.0	4.27	62	.225	.314	4	.333	1	-7	-7	-1	-0.5

● **ART LOUDELL**   Loudell, Arthur (b: Arthur Laudel) b: 4/10/1882, Latham, Mo. d: 2/19/61, Kansas City, Mo. BR/TR, 5'11", 173 lbs. Deb: 8/13/10

YEAR	TM/L	W	L	PCT	G	GS	CG	SH	SV	IP	H	HR	BB	SO	RAT	ERA	ERA+	OAV	OOB	BH	AVG	PB	PR	/A	PD	TPI
1910	Det-A	1	1	.500	5	2	1	0	0	21¹	23	0	14	12	15.6	3.38	78	.284	.389	1	.143	-0	-2	-2	-1	-0.3

● **LARRY LOUGHLIN**   Loughlin, Larry John b: 8/16/41, Tacoma, Wash. BL/TL, 6'1", 190 lbs. Deb: 5/27/67

YEAR	TM/L	W	L	PCT	G	GS	CG	SH	SV	IP	H	HR	BB	SO	RAT	ERA	ERA+	OAV	OOB	BH	AVG	PB	PR	/A	PD	TPI
1967	Phi-N	0	0	—	3	0	0	0	0	5¹	9	1	4	5	21.9	15.19	22	.375	.464	1	1.000	1	-7	-7	-0	0.1

● **DON LOUN**   Loun, Donald Nelson b: 11/9/40, Frederick, Md. BR/TL, 6'2", 185 lbs. Deb: 9/23/64

YEAR	TM/L	W	L	PCT	G	GS	CG	SH	SV	IP	H	HR	BB	SO	RAT	ERA	ERA+	OAV	OOB	BH	AVG	PB	PR	/A	PD	TPI
1964	Was-A	1	1	.500	2	2	1	0	0	13	13	0	3	3	11.1	2.08	178	.250	.291	0	.000	-0	2	2	0	0.4

● **SLIM LOVE**   Love, Edward Haughton b: 8/1/1890, Love, Miss. d: 11/30/42, Memphis, Tenn. BL/TL, 6'7", 195 lbs. Deb: 9/8/13

YEAR	TM/L	W	L	PCT	G	GS	CG	SH	SV	IP	H	HR	BB	SO	RAT	ERA	ERA+	OAV	OOB	BH	AVG	PB	PR	/A	PD	TPI
1913	Was-A	1	0	1.000	5	1	0	0	0	16²	14	0	6	6	10.8	1.62	182	.226	.294	1	.200	0	2	2	-1	0.1
1916	NY-A	2	0	1.000	20	1	0	0	0	47²	46	2	23	21	13.0	4.91	59	.274	.361	0	.000	-2	-11	-11	-0	-0.6
1917	NY-A	6	5	.545	33	9	2	0	0	130¹	115	0	57	82	11.9	2.35	114	.251	.335	6	.167	-1	5	5	-2	0.1
1918	NY-A	13	12	.520	38	29	13	1	1	228²	207	3	116	95	13.1	3.07	92	.253	.353	17	.230	2	-7	-6	-5	-0.9
1919	Det-A	6	4	.600	22	8	4	0	1	89²	92	3	40	46	13.9	3.01	106	.275	.363	6	.222	0	2	2	-2	0.0
1920	Det-A	0	0	—	1	0	0	0	0	4¹	6	0	4	2	20.8	8.31	45	.375	.500	0	—	0	-2	-2	0	-0.2
Total 6		28	21	.571	119	48	19	1	4	517¹	480	8	246	251	12.9	3.04	94	.259	.351	30	.192	-0	-11	-10	-9	-1.3

● **VANCE LOVELACE**   Lovelace, Vance Odell b: 8/9/63, Tampa, Fla. BL/TL, 6'5", 205 lbs. Deb: 9/10/88

YEAR	TM/L	W	L	PCT	G	GS	CG	SH	SV	IP	H	HR	BB	SO	RAT	ERA	ERA+	OAV	OOB	BH	AVG	PB	PR	/A	PD	TPI
1988	Cal-A	0	0	—	3	0	0	0	0	1¹	2	1	3	0	33.8	13.50	29	.400	.625	0	—	0	-1	-1	0	0.1
1989	Cal-A	0	0	—	1	0	0	0	0	1	0	0	1	1	9.0	0.00	—	.000	.250	0	—	0	0	0	0	0.1
1990	Sea-A	0	0	—	2¹	0	0	0	0	2¹	3	0	6	1	38.6	3.86	103	.300	.588	0	—	0	0	0	-0	0.1
Total 3		0	0	—	9	0	0	0	0	4²	5	1	10	2	30.9	5.79	67	.278	.552	0	—	0	-1	-1	0	0.1

● **LYNN LOVENGUTH**   Lovenguth, Lynn Richard b: 11/29/22, Camden, N.Y. BL/TR, 5'10.5", 170 lbs. Deb: 4/18/55

YEAR	TM/L	W	L	PCT	G	GS	CG	SH	SV	IP	H	HR	BB	SO	RAT	ERA	ERA+	OAV	OOB	BH	AVG	PB	PR	/A	PD	TPI
1955	Phi-N	0	1	.000	14	0	0	0	0	18	17	1	10	14	14.5	4.50	88	.258	.372	0	.000	-0	-1	-1	-0	-0.1
1957	StL-N	0	1	.000	2	1	0	0	0	9	6	0	6	6	12.0	2.00	198	.182	.308	0	.000	-0	2	2	-0	0.1
Total 2		0	2	.000	16	1	0	0	0	27	23	1	16	20	13.7	3.67	108	.232	.350	0	.000	-0	1	1	-0	0.0

● **JOHN LOVETT**   Lovett, John b: 5/6/1877, Monday, Ohio d: 12/5/37, Murray City, Ohio Deb: 5/22/03

YEAR	TM/L	W	L	PCT	G	GS	CG	SH	SV	IP	H	HR	BB	SO	RAT	ERA	ERA+	OAV	OOB	BH	AVG	PB	PR	/A	PD	TPI
1903	StL-N	0	0	—	3	1	0	0	0	5	6	0	5	3	21.6	5.40	60	.300	.462	1	.333	0	-1	-1	-0	0.0

● **LEN LOVETT**   Lovett, Leonard Walker b: 7/17/1852, Lancaster Co., Pa d: 11/18/22, Newark, Del. BR/TR, Deb: 8/4/1873 ♦

YEAR	TM/L	W	L	PCT	G	GS	CG	SH	SV	IP	H	HR	BB	SO	RAT	ERA	ERA+	OAV	OOB	BH	AVG	PB	PR	/A	PD	TPI
1873	Res-n	0	1	.000	1	1	1	0	0	9	22	0	1	1	23.0	7.00	48	.400	.411	2	.400	0	-4	-4		-0.2

● **TOM LOVETT**   Lovett, Thomas Joseph b: 12/7/1863, Providence, R.I. d: 3/19/28, Providence, R.I. BR, 5'8", 162 lbs. Deb: 6/4/1885

YEAR	TM/L	W	L	PCT	G	GS	CG	SH	SV	IP	H	HR	BB	SO	RAT	ERA	ERA+	OAV	OOB	BH	AVG	PB	PR	/A	PD	TPI
1885	Phi-a	7	8	.467	16	16	15	1	0	138²	130	3	38	56	11.2	3.70	93	.236	.291	13	.224	-0	-7	-4	-1	-0.5

YEAR TM/L	W	L	PCT	G	GS	CG	SH	SV	IP	H	HR	BB	SO	RAT	ERA	ERA+	OAV	OOB	BH	AVG	PB	PR	/A	PD	TPI
1889 *Bro-a	17	10	.630	29	28	23	1	0	229	234	3	65	92	12.1	4.32	86	.256	.311	19	.190	-1	-12	-15	-0	-1.5
1890 *Bro-N	30	11	.732	44	41	39	4	0	372	327	14	141	124	11.7	2.78	124	.229	.306	33	.201	-1	33	27	-0	2.3
1891 Bro-N	23	19	.548	44	43	39	1	0	365²	361	14	129	129	12.6	3.69	90	.248	.318	25	.163	-5	-14	-16	-2	-2.0
1893 Bro-N	3	5	.375	14	8	6	0	1	96	134	2	35	15	16.4	6.56	67	.321	.381	9	.180	-2	-20	-23	-1	-1.6
1894 Bos-N	8	6	.571	15	13	10	0	0	104	155	12	36	23	16.8	5.97	95	.341	.393	7	.143	-5	-7	-3	-1	-0.8
Total 6	88	59	.599	162	149	132	9	1	1305¹	1341	48	444	439	12.7	3.94	94	.257	.322	106	.185	-13	-28	-34	-5	-4.1

● **PETE LOVRICH**   Lovrich, Peter b: 10/16/42, Blue Island, Ill. BR/TR, 6'4", 200 lbs. Deb: 4/26/63

YEAR TM/L	W	L	PCT	G	GS	CG	SH	SV	IP	H	HR	BB	SO	RAT	ERA	ERA+	OAV	OOB	BH	AVG	PB	PR	/A	PD	TPI
1963 KC-A	1	1	.500	20	1	0	0	0	20²	25	5	10	16	15.7	7.84	50	.291	.371	0	—	0	-10	-9	-1	-0.9

● **GROVER LOWDERMILK**   Lowdermilk, Grover Cleveland "Slim" b: 1/15/1885, Sandborn, Ind. d: 3/31/68, Odin, Ill. BR/TR, 6'4", 190 lbs. Deb: 7/3/09 F

YEAR TM/L	W	L	PCT	G	GS	CG	SH	SV	IP	H	HR	BB	SO	RAT	ERA	ERA+	OAV	OOB	BH	AVG	PB	PR	/A	PD	TPI
1909 StL-N	0	2	.000	7	3	1	0	0	29	28	0	30	14	18.9	6.21	41	.292	.473	1	.100	-1	-12	-12	-0	-0.8
1911 StL-N	0	1	.000	11	2	1	1	0	33¹	37	1	33	15	19.4	7.29	46	.301	.456	1	.111	-1	-14	-14	-0	-0.4
1912 Chi-N	0	1	.000	2	1	1	0	0	13	17	1	14	8	21.5	9.69	34	.304	.443	0	.000	-1	-9	-9	-0	-0.6
1915 StL-A	9	17	.346	38	29	14	1	0	222¹	183	1	133	130	13.4	3.12	92	.234	.357	9	.125	-3	-4	-6	0	-1.0
Det-A	4	1	.800	7	5	0	0	0	28	17	0	24	18	13.5	4.18	73	.185	.359	1	.125	-0	-4	-4	0	-0.6
Yr	13	18	.419	45	34	14	1	0	250¹	200	1	157	148	12.9	3.24	89	.225	.342	10	.125	-3	-8	-10	-1	-1.6
1916 Det-A	0	0	—	1	0	0	0	0	0¹	3	0	3	0	81.0	0.00	—	.000	.750	0	—	0	0	0	0	0.0
Cle-A	1	5	.167	10	9	2	0	0	51¹	52	0	45	28	17.5	3.16	95	.277	.424	3	.167	-1	-2	-1	0	-0.1
Yr	1	5	.167	11	9	2	0	0	51²	52	0	48	28	17.9	3.14	96	.275	.429	3	.167	-1	-2	-1	0	-0.1
1917 StL-A	2	1	.667	3	2	1	0	0	19	16	0	4	9	9.5	1.42	183	.225	.267	0	.000	-1	3	2	0	0.3
1918 StL-A	2	6	.250	13	11	4	0	0	80	74	1	38	25	12.9	3.15	87	.255	.347	7	.250	1	-3	-4	2	0.1
1919 StL-A	0	0	—	7	0	0	0	0	12	6	0	4	6	11.3	0.75	442	.176	.349	0	.000	-1	3	3	-0	0.0
*Chi-A	5	5	.500	20	11	5	0	0	96²	95	0	43	43	13.2	2.79	114	.268	.353	3	.088	-3	5	4	1	0.2
Yr	5	5	.500	27	11	5	0	0	108²	101	0	47	49	12.6	2.57	125	.256	.342	3	.086	-4	8	8	1	0.2
1920 Chi-A	0	0	—	3	0	0	0	0	5¹	9	0	5	0	23.6	6.75	56	.409	.519	0	—	0	-2	-1	0	0.0
Total 9	23	39	.371	122	73	30	3	0	590¹	534	4	376	296	14.4	3.58	82	.253	.375	25	.131	-8	-40	-41	5	-2.9

● **LOU LOWDERMILK**   Lowdermilk, Louis Bailey b: 2/23/1887, Sandborn, Ind. d: 12/27/75, Centralia, Ill. BR/TL, 6'1", 180 lbs. Deb: 4/20/11 F

YEAR TM/L	W	L	PCT	G	GS	CG	SH	SV	IP	H	HR	BB	SO	RAT	ERA	ERA+	OAV	OOB	BH	AVG	PB	PR	/A	PD	TPI
1911 StL-N	3	4	.429	16	3	3	0	0	65	72	0	29	20	14.7	3.46	98	.304	.391	2	.111	-1	-0	-1	-2	-0.3
1912 StL-N	1	1	.500	4	1	1	0	1	15	14	0	9	2	13.8	3.00	114	.246	.348	1	.250	0	1	1	0	0.1
Total 2	4	5	.444	20	4	4	0	1	80	86	0	38	22	14.5	3.37	100	.293	.383	3	.136	-1	0	0	-2	-0.2

● **GEORGE LOWE**   Lowe, George Wesley "Doc" b: 4/25/1895, Ridgefield Park, N.J. d: 9/2/81, Somers Point, N.J. BR/TR, 6'2", 180 lbs. Deb: 7/28/20

YEAR TM/L	W	L	PCT	G	GS	CG	SH	SV	IP	H	HR	BB	SO	RAT	ERA	ERA+	OAV	OOB	BH	AVG	PB	PR	/A	PD	TPI
1920 Cin-N	0	0	—	1	0	0	0	0	2	1	0	1	0	9.0	0.00	—	.167	.286	0	—	0	1	1	0	0.0

● **BOBBY LOWE**   Lowe, Robert Lincoln "Link" b: 7/10/1868, Pittsburgh, Pa. d: 12/8/51, Detroit, Mich. BR/TR, 5'10", 150 lbs. Deb: 4/19/1890 M♦

YEAR TM/L	W	L	PCT	G	GS	CG	SH	SV	IP	H	HR	BB	SO	RAT	ERA	ERA+	OAV	OOB	BH	AVG	PB	PR	/A	PD	TPI
1891 Bos-N	0	0	—	1	0	0	0	0	3	1	0	4	0	36.0	9.00	41	.501	.572	129	.260	0	-1	-1	-0	0.0

● **TURK LOWN**   Lown, Omar Joseph b: 5/30/24, Brooklyn, N.Y. BR/TR, 6'1", 185 lbs. Deb: 4/24/51

YEAR TM/L	W	L	PCT	G	GS	CG	SH	SV	IP	H	HR	BB	SO	RAT	ERA	ERA+	OAV	OOB	BH	AVG	PB	PR	/A	PD	TPI
1951 Chi-N	4	9	.308	31	18	3	1	0	127	125	14	90	39	15.3	5.46	75	.260	.378	8	.205	1	-21	-19	0	-1.6
1952 Chi-N	4	11	.267	33	19	5	0	0	156²	154	13	93	73	14.4	4.37	88	.257	.359	7	.140	-0	-11	-9	1	-0.7
1953 Chi-N	8	7	.533	49	12	2	0	3	148¹	166	20	84	76	15.3	5.16	86	.282	.373	6	.125	-2	-14	-12	2	-1.0
1954 Chi-N	0	2	.000	15	0	0	0	0	22	27	1	15	16	15.5	6.14	68	.261	.369	0	—	0	-5	-5	1	-0.3
1956 Chi-N	9	8	.529	61	0	0	0	13	110²	95	10	78	74	14.2	3.58	105	.240	.366	5	.217	2	2	2	-1	0.6
1957 Chi-N	5	7	.417	67	0	0	0	12	93	74	10	51	51	12.1	3.77	103	.221	.324	2	.200	1	1	1	2	0.3
1958 Chi-N	0	0	—	4	0	0	0	0	4	2	0	4	3	11.3	4.50	87	.154	.313	0	—	0	-0	-0	0	0.0
Cin-N	0	2	.000	11	0	0	0	0	11²	12	2	12	9	18.5	5.40	77	.273	.429	0	.000	0	-2	-2	-0	-0.3
Yr	0	2	.000	15	0	0	0	0	15²	14	2	16	12	16.7	5.17	79	.246	.403	0	.000	0	-2	-2	-0	-0.3
1959 *Chi-A	9	2	.818	60	0	0	0	15	93¹	73	12	42	63	11.3	2.89	130	.215	.305	1	.250	1	10	9	1	1.4
1960 Chi-A	2	3	.400	45	0	0	0	0	67¹	60	6	34	39	12.6	3.88	98	.239	.330	1	.200	1	-0	-1	0	0.0
1961 Chi-A	7	5	.583	59	0	0	0	11	101	87	13	35	50	10.9	2.76	142	.238	.304	0	.000	-2	14	13	-1	1.5
1962 Chi-A	4	2	.667	42	0	0	0	6	56¹	58	3	25	40	13.4	3.04	129	.269	.347	0	.000	1	6	5	1	0.8
Total 11	55	61	.474	504	49	10	1	73	1032	978	105	590	574	13.8	4.12	96	.252	.352	35	.164	1	-21	-18	7	0.7

● **SAM LOWRY**   Lowry, Samuel Joseph b: 3/25/20, Philadelphia, Pa. d: 12/1/92, Philadelphia, Pa. BR/TR, 5'11", 170 lbs. Deb: 9/19/42

YEAR TM/L	W	L	PCT	G	GS	CG	SH	SV	IP	H	HR	BB	SO	RAT	ERA	ERA+	OAV	OOB	BH	AVG	PB	PR	/A	PD	TPI
1942 Phi-A	0	0	—	1	0	0	0	0	3	3	0	1	0	12.0	6.00	63	.250	.308	0	—	0	-1	-1	-0	0.0
1943 Phi-A	0	0	—	5	0	0	0	0	18	18	1	9	3	13.5	5.00	68	.269	.355	1	.167	0	-3	-3	0	0.0
Total 2	0	0	—	6	0	0	0	0	21	21	1	10	3	13.3	5.14	67	.266	.348	1	.143	0	-4	-4	0	0.0

● **MIKE LOYND**   Loynd, Michael Wallace b: 3/26/64, St.Louis, Mo. BR/TR, 6'4", 210 lbs. Deb: 7/24/86

YEAR TM/L	W	L	PCT	G	GS	CG	SH	SV	IP	H	HR	BB	SO	RAT	ERA	ERA+	OAV	OOB	BH	AVG	PB	PR	/A	PD	TPI
1986 Tex-A	2	2	.500	9	8	0	0	1	42	49	4	19	33	15.0	5.36	80	.290	.368	0	—	0	-6	-5	0	-0.5
1987 Tex-A	1	5	.167	26	8	0	0	1	69¹	82	14	38	48	15.7	6.10	73	.287	.372	0	—	0	-13	-13	-1	-1.0
Total 2	3	7	.300	35	16	0	0	2	111¹	131	18	57	81	15.4	5.82	76	.288	.371	0	—	0	-18	-17	-1	-1.5

● **PAT LUBY**   Luby, John Perkins b: 6/1869, Charleston, S.C. d: 4/24/1899, Charleston, S.C. TR, 6', 185 lbs. Deb: 6/16/1890

YEAR TM/L	W	L	PCT	G	GS	CG	SH	SV	IP	H	HR	BB	SO	RAT	ERA	ERA+	OAV	OOB	BH	AVG	PB	PR	/A	PD	TPI
1890 Chi-N	20	9	.690	34	31	26	0	1	267²	226	6	95	85	11.3	3.19	115	.222	.298	31	.267	8	11	14	-2	1.7
1891 Chi-N	8	11	.421	30	24	18	0	1	206	221	11	94	52	14.6	4.76	70	.264	.352	24	.245	7	-32	-33	-0	-1.8
1892 Chi-N	10	16	.385	31	26	24	1	1	247¹	247	10	106	64	13.2	3.13	106	.250	.329	31	.190	-1	4	5	1	0.6
1895 Lou-N	1	5	.167	11	6	5	0	0	71¹	115	5	19	12	17.8	6.81	68	.357	.405	15	.283	3	-16	-17	1	-0.7
Total 4	39	41	.488	106	87	73	1	3	792¹	809	32	314	213	13.3	3.91	91	.255	.332	101	.235	18	-33	-31	-0	-0.2

● **RED LUCAS**   Lucas, Charles Frederick "The Nashville Narcissus" b: 4/28/02, Columbia, Tenn. d: 7/9/86, Nashville, Tenn. BL/TR, 5'9.5", 170 lbs. Deb: 4/19/23 ♦

YEAR TM/L	W	L	PCT	G	GS	CG	SH	SV	IP	H	HR	BB	SO	RAT	ERA	ERA+	OAV	OOB	BH	AVG	PB	PR	/A	PD	TPI
1923 NY-N	0	0	—	3	0	0	0	0	5¹	9	0	4	3	21.9	—	—	.346	.433	0	.000	-0	2	2	1	0.1
1924 Bos-N	1	4	.200	27	4	1	0	0	83²	112	5	18	30	14.6	5.16	74	.332	.377	11	.333	2	-12	-12	1	-0.4
1926 Cin-N	8	5	.615	39	11	7	1	2	154	161	8	30	34	11.3	3.68	100	.277	.314	23	.303	6	2	0	-1	0.9
1927 Cin-N	18	11	.621	37	23	19	4	2	239²	231	6	39	51	10.1	3.38	112	.256	.287	47	.313	7	14	11	-1	2.3
1928 Cin-N	13	9	.591	27	19	13	4	1	167¹	164	9	42	35	11.1	3.39	117	.258	.304	23	.315	6	11	11	-0	1.9
1929 Cin-N	19	12	.613	32	32	28	2	0	270	267	14	58	72	10.9	3.60	127	.257	.297	41	.293	11	33	29	0	4.0
1930 Cin-N	14	16	.467	33	28	18	1	1	210²	270	15	44	53	13.5	5.38	90	.315	.349	38	.336	15	-10	-13	-3	-2.0
1931 Cin-N	14	13	.519	29	29	24	3	0	238	261	10	39	56	11.3	3.59	104	.280	.309	43	.281	11	7	4	1	1.6
1932 Cin-N	13	17	.433	31	31	28	0	0	269¹	261	10	35	62	9.9	2.94	131	.249	.274	48	.287	13	28	27	-0	4.4
1933 Cin-N	10	16	.385	29	29	21	3	0	219²	248	16	18	40	11.0	3.40	100	.289	.305	35	.287	12	-2	-0	0	1.4
1934 Pit-N	10	9	.526	29	21	12	1	0	172²	198	14	40	44	12.5	4.38	94	.283	.324	23	.219	-3	-6	-5	-3	-0.5
1935 Pit-N	8	6	.571	20	19	8	2	0	125²	136	10	23	29	11.5	3.44	119	.272	.307	21	.318	8	9	8	1	1.6
1936 Pit-N	15	4	.789	27	22	12	0	0	175²	178	7	26	53	10.6	3.18	128	.257	.287	26	.241	5	16	17	-1	2.0
1937 Pit-N	8	10	.444	20	20	9	1	0	126¹	150	12	21	40	12.4	4.27	90	.290	.322	22	.268	5	-5	-6	-2	-0.4
1938 Pit-N	6	3	.667	13	13	4	0	0	84	90	5	16	19	11.5	3.54	107	.283	.319	5	.109	-2	2	2	0	-0.1
Total 15	157	135	.538	396	301	204	22	7	2542	2736	136	455	602	11.4	3.72	107	.275	.308	404	.281	98	92	77	-9	18.5

● **GARY LUCAS**   Lucas, Gary Paul b: 11/8/54, Riverside, Cal. BL/TL, 6'5", 200 lbs. Deb: 4/16/80

YEAR TM/L	W	L	PCT	G	GS	CG	SH	SV	IP	H	HR	BB	SO	RAT	ERA	ERA+	OAV	OOB	BH	AVG	PB	PR	/A	PD	TPI
1980 SD-N	5	8	.385	46	18	0	0	3	150	138	8	43	85	10.9	3.24	106	.250	.306	6	.171	-0	6	3	1	0.3
1981 SD-N	7	7	.500	57	0	0	0	13	90	78	1	36	53	11.7	2.00	163	.247	.330	1	.100	-1	15	13	0	2.3
1982 SD-N	1	10	.091	65	0	0	0	16	97¹	89	5	29	64	11.0	3.24	106	.245	.303	0	.000	-1	4	2	1	0.3

YEAR	TM/L	W	L	PCT	G	GS	CG	SH	SV	IP	H	HR	BB	SO	RAT	ERA	ERA+	OAV	OOB	BH	AVG	PB	PR	/A	PD	TPI
1983	SD-N	5	8	.385	62	0	0	0	17	91	85	9	34	60	11.8	2.87	122	.245	.312	0	.000	-1	8	6	-1	0.9
1984	Mon-N	0	3	.000	55	0	0	0	8	53	54	4	20	42	12.6	2.72	126	.267	.333	0	.000	-0	5	4	2	0.5
1985	Mon-N	6	2	.750	49	0	0	0	1	67²	63	6	24	31	11.6	3.19	106	.251	.316	0	.000	-1	3	1	-0	0.1
1986	*Cal-A	4	1	.800	27	0	0	0	2	45²	45	1	6	31	10.1	3.15	130	.253	.277	0	—	0	5	5	1	0.6
1987	Cal-A	1	5	.167	48	0	0	0	3	74¹	66	7	35	44	12.5	3.63	118	.241	.331	0	—	0	7	6	1	0.5
Total 8		29	44	.397	409	18	0	0	63	669	618	41	227	410	11.5	3.01	118	.249	.314	7	.087	-4	53	40	4	5.5

● **RAY LUCAS** Lucas, Ray Wesley "Luke" b: 10/2/08, Springfield, Ohio d: 10/9/69, Harrison, Mich. BR/TR, 6'2", 175 lbs. Deb: 9/28/29

YEAR	TM/L	W	L	PCT	G	GS	CG	SH	SV	IP	H	HR	BB	SO	RAT	ERA	ERA+	OAV	OOB	BH	AVG	PB	PR	/A	PD	TPI
1929	NY-N	0	0	—	3	0	0	0	1	8	3	0	3	1	6.8	0.00	—	.111	.200	1	.500	0	4	4	0	0.2
1930	NY-N	0	0	—	6	0	0	0	0	10¹	9	2	10	1	17.4	6.97	68	.265	.444	0	.000	-0	-2	-3	1	0.0
1931	NY-N	0	0	—	1	0	0	0	0	2	1	1	1	0	9.0	4.50	82	.143	.250	0	—	0	-0	-0	-0	0.0
1933	Bro-N	0	0	—	2	0	0	0	0	5	6	0	4	0	19.8	7.20	45	.316	.458	0	—	0	-2	-2	0	0.0
1934	Bro-N	1	1	.500	10	2	0	0	0	30²	39	2	14	3	16.4	6.75	58	.328	.412	2	.333	1	-9	-10	1	-0.3
Total 5		1	1	.500	22	2	0	0	1	56	58	5	32	5	15.3	5.79	71	.282	.391	3	.333	1	-10	-11	2	-0.1

● **JOE LUCEY** Lucey, Joseph Earl "Scootch" b: 3/27/1897, Holyoke, Mass. d: 7/30/80, Holyoke, Mass. BR/TR, 6', 168 lbs. Deb: 7/6/20 ♦

YEAR	TM/L	W	L	PCT	G	GS	CG	SH	SV	IP	H	HR	BB	SO	RAT	ERA	ERA+	OAV	OOB	BH	AVG	PB	PR	/A	PD	TPI
1925	Bos-A	0	1	.000	7	2	0	0	0	11	18	0	14	2	26.2	9.00	50	.360	.500	2	.133	-1	-6	-5	1	-0.4

● **CON LUCID** Lucid, Cornelius Cecil b: 2/24/1874, Dublin, Ireland d: 6/25/31, Houston, Tex. 5'7", 170 lbs. Deb: 5/1/1893

YEAR	TM/L	W	L	PCT	G	GS	CG	SH	SV	IP	H	HR	BB	SO	RAT	ERA	ERA+	OAV	OOB	BH	AVG	PB	PR	/A	PD	TPI
1893	Lou-N	0	1	.000	2	1	0	0	0	6	10	0	10	0	31.5	15.00	29	.360	.542	1	.333	0	-7	-7	-0	-0.7
1894	Bro-N	5	3	.625	10	9	7	0	0	71¹	87	6	44	15	17.7	6.56	75	.298	.405	7	.212	-2	-10	-13	-2	-1.3
1895	Bro-N	10	7	.588	21	19	12	2	0	137	164	6	72	24	16.0	5.52	80	.292	.380	13	.245	-2	-11	-17	-1	-1.4
	Phi-N	6	3	.667	10	10	7	1	0	69²	80	3	35	19	16.0	5.94	81	.284	.380	10	.345	4	-9	-9	-2	-0.7
	Yr	16	10	.615	31	29	19	3	0	206²	244	7	107	43	15.7	5.66	80	.287	.373	23	.280	6	-20	-26	-2	-2.1
1896	Phi-N	1	4	.200	5	5	5	0	0	42	75	2	17	3	20.1	8.36	52	.384	.438	2	.125	-2	-19	-19	-1	-1.7
1897	StL-N	1	5	.167	6	6	5	0	0	49	66	0	26	4	16.9	3.67	120	.319	.395	3	.176	-0	3	4	1	0.4
Total 5		23	23	.500	54	50	36	3	0	375	482	15	204	65	17.1	6.02	76	.308	.397	36	.238	2	-52	-60	-5	-5.4

● **LOU LUCIER** Lucier, Louis Joseph b: 3/23/18, Northbridge, Mass. BR/TR, 5'8", 160 lbs. Deb: 4/23/43

YEAR	TM/L	W	L	PCT	G	GS	CG	SH	SV	IP	H	HR	BB	SO	RAT	ERA	ERA+	OAV	OOB	BH	AVG	PB	PR	/A	PD	TPI
1943	Bos-A	3	4	.429	16	9	3	0	0	74	94	1	33	23	15.7	3.89	85	.322	.394	4	.200	-0	-5	-5	3	-0.1
1944	Bos-A	0	0	—	3	0	0	0	0	5¹	7	0	7	2	23.6	5.06	67	.292	.452	0	.000	-0	-1	-1	-0	0.0
	Phi-N	0	0	—	1	0	0	0	0	2	3	0	2	1	22.5	13.50	27	.333	.455	0	—	0	-2	-2	-0	0.0
1945	Phi-N	0	1	.000	13	0	0	0	1	20¹	14	1	5	5	8.4	2.21	173	.194	.247	1	.250	-0	4	4	1	0.3
Total 3		3	5	.375	33	9	3	0	1	101²	118	2	47	31	14.8	3.81	90	.297	.374	5	.200	-0	-4	-4	4	0.2

● **WILLIE LUDOLPH** Ludolph, William Francis "Wee Willie" b: 1/21/1900, San Francisco, Cal d: 4/8/52, Oakland, Cal. BR/TR, 6'1.5", 170 lbs. Deb: 5/28/24

YEAR	TM/L	W	L	PCT	G	GS	CG	SH	SV	IP	H	HR	BB	SO	RAT	ERA	ERA+	OAV	OOB	BH	AVG	PB	PR	/A	PD	TPI
1924	Det-A	0	0	—	3	0	0	0	0	5²	5	0	2	1	12.7	4.76	86	.250	.348	0	.000	-0	-0	-0	0	0.0

● **STEVE LUEBBER** Luebber, Stephen Lee b: 7/9/49, Clinton, Mo. BR/TR, 6'3", 195 lbs. Deb: 6/27/71

YEAR	TM/L	W	L	PCT	G	GS	CG	SH	SV	IP	H	HR	BB	SO	RAT	ERA	ERA+	OAV	OOB	BH	AVG	PB	PR	/A	PD	TPI
1971	Min-A	2	5	.286	18	12	0	0	1	68	73	7	37	35	15.1	5.03	71	.278	.375	1	.053	-2	-12	-11	0	-1.3
1972	Min-A	0	0	—	2	0	0	0	0	2¹	1	0	2	1	19.3	0.00	—	.333	.455	0		0	1	1	0	0.0
1976	Min-A	4	5	.444	38	12	2	1	2	119¹	109	9	62	45	13.0	4.00	90	.248	.342	0		0	-6	-5	-1	-0.6
1979	Tor-A	0	0	—	1	0	0	0	0	0	2	0	1	0	—	∞	—	1.000	1.000	0		0	-1	-1	0	-0.1
1981	Bal-A	0	0	—	7	0	0	0	0	16²	24	3	4	12	16.7	7.56	48	.366	.408	0		0	-7	-7	0	0.0
Total 5		6	10	.375	66	24	2	1	3	206¹	213	19	106	93	14.2	4.62	77	.271	.362	1	.053	-2	-26	-24	-1	-2.0

● **LARRY LUEBBERS** Luebbers, Larry Christopher b: 10/11/69, Cincinnati, Ohio BR/TR, 6'6", 190 lbs. Deb: 7/3/93

YEAR	TM/L	W	L	PCT	G	GS	CG	SH	SV	IP	H	HR	BB	SO	RAT	ERA	ERA+	OAV	OOB	BH	AVG	PB	PR	/A	PD	TPI
1993	Cin-N	2	5	.286	14	14	0	0	0	77¹	74	7	38	38	13.2	4.54	89	.261	.350	6	.250	1	-4	-4	-1	-0.3

● **DICK LUEBKE** Luebke, Richard Raymond b: 4/8/35, Chicago, Ill. d: 12/4/74, San Diego, Cal. BR/TL, 6'4", 200 lbs. Deb: 8/11/62

YEAR	TM/L	W	L	PCT	G	GS	CG	SH	SV	IP	H	HR	BB	SO	RAT	ERA	ERA+	OAV	OOB	BH	AVG	PB	PR	/A	PD	TPI
1962	Bal-A	0	1	.000	10	0	0	0	0	13¹	12	0	6	7	12.2	2.70	137	.250	.333	0		0	2	1	-0	0.1

● **RICK LUECKEN** Luecken, Richard Fred b: 11/15/60, McAllen, Tex. BR/TR, 6'6", 210 lbs. Deb: 6/6/89

YEAR	TM/L	W	L	PCT	G	GS	CG	SH	SV	IP	H	HR	BB	SO	RAT	ERA	ERA+	OAV	OOB	BH	AVG	PB	PR	/A	PD	TPI
1989	KC-A	2	1	.667	19	0	0	0	0	23²	23	3	13	16	13.7	3.42	112	.258	.353	0		0	1	1	-0	0.1
1990	Atl-N	1	4	.200	36	0	0	0	1	53	73	5	30	35	18.0	5.77	70	.336	.424	1	.333	1	-12	-10	0	-0.9
	Tor-A	0	0	—	1	0	0	0	0	1	2	1	1	0	27.0	9.00	44	.500	.600	0		0	-1	-1	0	0.0
Total 2		3	5	.375	56	0	0	0	2	77²	98	9	44	51	16.8	5.10	78	.316	.406	1	.333	1	-11	-10	-0	-0.8

● **HENRY LUFF** Luff, Henry T. b: 9/14/1856, Philadelphia, Pa. d: 10/11/16, Philadelphia, Pa. 5'11", 175 lbs. Deb: 4/21/1875 ♦

YEAR	TM/L	W	L	PCT	G	GS	CG	SH	SV	IP	H	HR	BB	SO	RAT	ERA	ERA+	OAV	OOB	BH	AVG	PB	PR	/A	PD	TPI
1875	NH-n	1	6	.143	10	7	5	0	0	69²	100	2	3		13.3	4.78	48	.297	.303	46	.279	3	-18	-19	-1	-1.2

● **URBANO LUGO** Lugo, Rafael Urbano (Colina) b: 8/12/62, Punto Fijo, Venez. BR/TR, 6', 190 lbs. Deb: 4/28/85

YEAR	TM/L	W	L	PCT	G	GS	CG	SH	SV	IP	H	HR	BB	SO	RAT	ERA	ERA+	OAV	OOB	BH	AVG	PB	PR	/A	PD	TPI
1985	Cal-A	3	4	.429	20	10	1	0	0	83	86	10	29	42	12.9	3.69	111	.274	.343	0		0	4	4	0	0.3
1986	Cal-A	1	1	.500	6	3	0	0	0	21¹	21	4	6	9	11.4	3.80	108	.266	.318	0		0	1	1	-0	0.1
1987	Cal-A	0	2	.000	7	5	0	0	0	28	42	8	18	24	19.3	9.32	46	.339	.423	0		0	-15	-16	-0	-0.9
1988	Cal-A	0	0	—	1	0	0	0	0	2	2	1	1	1	13.5	9.00	40	.250	.333	0		0	-1	-1	0	0.0
1989	Mon-N	0	0	—	3	0	0	0	0	4	4	1	0	2	9.0	6.75	52	.250	.250	0		0	-1	-1	0	0.0
1990	Det-A	2	0	1.000	13	1	0	0	0	24¹	30	9	13	12	17.0	7.03	56	.313	.411	0		0	-8	-8	-0	-0.6
Total 6		6	7	.462	50	19	1	0	0	162²	185	33	67	91	14.3	5.31	77	.290	.364	0		0	-21	-22	-0	-1.1

● **WILD BILL LUHRSEN** Luhrsen, William Ferdinand b: 4/14/1884, Buckley, Ill. d: 8/15/73, Little Rock, Ark. BR/TR, 5'9", 165 lbs. Deb: 8/23/13

YEAR	TM/L	W	L	PCT	G	GS	CG	SH	SV	IP	H	HR	BB	SO	RAT	ERA	ERA+	OAV	OOB	BH	AVG	PB	PR	/A	PD	TPI
1913	Pit-N	3	1	.750	5	3	2	0	0	29	25	3	16	11	13.3	2.48	121	.248	.361	0	.000	-1	2	2	1	0.2

● **AL LUKENS** Lukens, Albert P. b: 11/1868, Pennsylvania 5'9", 168 lbs. Deb: 6/23/1894

YEAR	TM/L	W	L	PCT	G	GS	CG	SH	SV	IP	H	HR	BB	SO	RAT	ERA	ERA+	OAV	OOB	BH	AVG	PB	PR	/A	PD	TPI
1894	Phi-N	0	1	.000	3	2	1	0	0	15	26	0	10	2	23.4	10.20	50	.376	.474	0		-2	-8	-8	-0	-0.5

● **RALPH LUMENTI** Lumenti, Raphael Anthony b: 12/21/36, Milford, Mass. BL/TL, 6'3", 185 lbs. Deb: 9/7/57

YEAR	TM/L	W	L	PCT	G	GS	CG	SH	SV	IP	H	HR	BB	SO	RAT	ERA	ERA+	OAV	OOB	BH	AVG	PB	PR	/A	PD	TPI
1957	Was-A	0	0	1.000	3	2	0	0	0	9¹	9	1	5	8	14.5	6.75	58	.250	.357	0	.000	-0	-3	-3	0	-0.3
1958	Was-A	1	2	.333	8	4	0	0	0	21	21	2	36	20	24.9	8.57	44	.266	.500	2	.250	0	-11	-11	0	-1.3
1959	Was-A	0	0	—	2	0	0	0	0	3	2	0	1	2	9.0	0.00	—	.200	.273	0		0	1	1	-0	0.0
Total 3		1	3	.250	13	6	0	0	0	33¹	32	3	42	30	20.5	7.29	53	.256	.450	2	.200	0	-13	-13	0	-1.6

● **MEMO LUNA** Luna, Guillermo Romero b: 6/25/30, Tacubaya, Mexico BL/TL, 6', 168 lbs. Deb: 4/20/54

YEAR	TM/L	W	L	PCT	G	GS	CG	SH	SV	IP	H	HR	BB	SO	RAT	ERA	ERA+	OAV	OOB	BH	AVG	PB	PR	/A	PD	TPI
1954	StL-N	0	1	.000	1	1	0	0	0	0²	2	0	2	0	54.0	27.00	15	.667	.800	0	—		-2	-2	-0	-1.2

● **JACK LUNDBOM** Lundbom, John Frederick b: 3/10/1877, Manistee, Mich. d: 10/31/49, Manistee, Mich. BR/TR, 6'2", 187 lbs. Deb: 5/9/02

YEAR	TM/L	W	L	PCT	G	GS	CG	SH	SV	IP	H	HR	BB	SO	RAT	ERA	ERA+	OAV	OOB	BH	AVG	PB	PR	/A	PD	TPI
1902	Cle-A	1	1	.500	8	3	1	0	0	34	48	1	16	7	17.2	6.62	52	.332	.403	4	.267	-0	-11	-12	-0	-0.6

● **CARL LUNDGREN** Lundgren, Carl Leonard b: 2/16/1880, Marengo, Ill. d: 8/21/34, Marengo, Ill. BR/TR, 5'11", 175 lbs. Deb: 6/19/02

YEAR	TM/L	W	L	PCT	G	GS	CG	SH	SV	IP	H	HR	BB	SO	RAT	ERA	ERA+	OAV	OOB	BH	AVG	PB	PR	/A	PD	TPI
1902	Chi-N	9	9	.500	18	18	17	1	0	160	158	2	45	68	11.8	1.97	137	.258	.315	7	.106	-4	14	13	-3	0.7
1903	Chi-N	11	9	.550	27	20	16	0	**3**	193	191	1	60	77	12.0	2.94	107	.262	.323	7	.115	-1	7	4	-2	0.0
1904	Chi-N	17	9	.654	31	27	25	2	1	242	203	2	77	106	10.6	2.60	102	.226	.290	20	.222	4	4	2	-1	0.4
1905	Chi-N	13	5	.722	29	19	16	3	0	169¹	132	1	65	95	10.3	2.23	134	.220	.293	11	.180	1	15	14	1	1.6
1906	Chi-N	17	6	.739	27	24	21	5	2	207²	160	2	89	103	11.1	2.21	119	.221	.313	12	.179	2	10	10	-1	1.2
1907	Chi-N	18	7	.720	28	25	21	7	0	207	130	6	92	84	9.7	1.17	212	**.185**	.282	7	.106	-3	**30**	30	-0	3.6
1908	Chi-N	6	9	.400	23	15	9	1	0	138²	149	5	56	38	13.3	4.22	56	.284	.353	7	.149	-1	-29	-29	-2	-3.3

YEAR TM/L	W	L	PCT	G	GS	CG	SH	SV	IP	H	HR	BB	SO	RAT	ERA	ERA+	OAV	OOB	BH	AVG	PB	PR	/A	PD	TPI
1909 Chi-N	0	1	.000	2	1	0	0	0	4¹	6	0	4	0	20.8	4.15	61	.353	.476	1	.500	0	-1	-1	-0	-0.2
Total 8	91	55	.623	179	149	125	19	6	1322	1129	16	476	535	11.2	2.42	113	.235	.308	72	.157	-2	50	44	-8	4.0

● DEL LUNDGREN
Lundgren, Ebin Delmar b: 9/21/1899, Lindsborg, Kan. d: 10/19/84, Lindsborg, Kan. BR/TR, 5'8", 160 lbs. Deb: 4/27/24

YEAR TM/L	W	L	PCT	G	GS	CG	SH	SV	IP	H	HR	BB	SO	RAT	ERA	ERA+	OAV	OOB	BH	AVG	PB	PR	/A	PD	TPI
1924 Pit-N	0	1	.000	8	1	0	0	0	16²	25	0	3	4	15.7	6.48	59	.403	.439	0	.000	-1	-5	-5	0	-0.3
1926 Bos-A	0	2	.000	18	1	0	0	0	31	35	2	28	11	19.2	7.55	54	.307	.455	0	.000	-0	-12	-12	0	-0.7
1927 Bos-A	5	12	.294	30	17	5	2	0	136¹	160	7	87	39	16.6	6.27	67	.302	.405	7	.159	-2	-32	-31	-2	-3.5
Total 3	5	15	.250	56	19	5	2	0	184	220	9	118	54	16.9	6.51	64	.312	.416	7	.137	-3	-49	-48	-2	-4.5

● DOLF LUQUE
Luque, Adolfo Domingo De Guzman "The Pride Of Havana" b: 8/4/1890, Havana, Cuba d: 7/3/57, Havana, Cuba BR/TR, 5'7", 160 lbs. Deb: 5/20/14 C

YEAR TM/L	W	L	PCT	G	GS	CG	SH	SV	IP	H	HR	BB	SO	RAT	ERA	ERA+	OAV	OOB	BH	AVG	PB	PR	/A	PD	TPI
1914 Bos-N	0	1	.000	2	1	1	0	0	8²	5	0	4	1	9.3	4.15	66	.167	.265	0	.000	-0	-1	-1	-1	-0.2
1915 Bos-N	0	0	—	2	1	0	0	0	5	6	0	4	3	18.0	3.60	72	.286	.400	0	.000	-0	-0	-1	0	0.0
1918 Cin-N	6	3	.667	12	10	9	1	0	83	84	1	32	26	12.7	3.80	70	.277	.348	9	.321	5	-10	-10	-0	-0.6
1919 *Cin-N	10	3	.769	30	9	6	2	3	106	89	2	36	40	10.8	2.63	105	.237	.308	4	.125	-0	3	2	1	0.3
1920 Cin-N	13	9	.591	37	23	10	1	1	207²	168	5	60	72	10.1	2.51	121	**.225**	.286	17	.266	4	14	12	-2	1.5
1921 Cin-N	17	19	.472	41	36	25	3	3	304	318	13	64	102	11.3	3.38	106	.273	.312	30	.270	6	14	7	1	1.3
1922 Cin-N	13	23	.361	39	32	18	0	0	261	266	7	72	79	11.7	3.31	121	.268	.318	18	.209	2	23	20	0	2.6
1923 Cin-N	**27**	8	**.771**	41	37	28	**6**	2	322	279	2	88	151	10.4	**1.93**	**200**	**.235**	.291	21	.202	2	74	69	1	7.4
1924 Cin-N	10	15	.400	31	28	13	2	0	219¹	229	5	63	86	11.7	3.16	119	.271	.316	11	.178	-1	17	15	1	1.6
1925 Cin-N	16	18	.471	36	36	22	**4**	0	291	263	7	78	140	10.6	**2.63**	**156**	**.239**	.291	26	.255	5	53	48	4	6.1
1926 Cin-N	13	16	.448	34	30	16	1	0	233²	231	4	77	83	11.9	3.43	108	.260	.321	27	.346	8	10	7	2	1.8
1927 Cin-N	13	12	.520	29	27	17	2	0	230¹	225	10	56	76	11.0	3.20	111	.260	.305	18	.217	2	18	15	4	2.1
1928 Cin-N	11	10	.524	33	29	11	1	1	234¹	254	12	84	72	13.1	3.57	117	.284	.347	8	.119	-1	11	10	-2	0.5
1929 Cin-N	5	16	.238	32	22	8	0	0	176	213	7	56	43	13.9	4.50	101	.310	.364	15	.278	4	4	1	0	0.5
1930 Bro-N	14	8	.636	31	24	16	2	2	199	221	18	58	62	12.6	4.30	114	.287	.337	18	.240	1	15	14	1	1.5
1931 Bro-N	7	6	.538	19	15	5	0	0	102²	122	6	27	25	13.1	4.56	84	.297	.342	4	.133	-1	-8	-9	-1	-1.0
1932 NY-N	6	7	.462	38	5	1	0	5	110	128	4	32	32	13.1	4.01	93	.290	.338	1	.040	-2	-2	-4	-1	-0.5
1933 *NY-N	8	2	.800	35	0	0	0	4	80¹	75	4	19	23	10.5	2.69	119	.251	.296	5	.263	1	6	5	0	0.7
1934 NY-N	4	3	.571	26	0	0	0	7	42¹	54	3	17	12	15.3	3.83	101	.316	.381	2	.286	1	1	1	0	0.2
1935 NY-N	1	0	1.000	2	0	0	0	0	3²	1	0	1	2	4.9	0.00		.077	.143	1	1.000	0	2	2	-0	0.5
Total 20	194	179	.520	550	365	206	26	28	3220¹	3231	113	918	1130	11.7	3.24	117	.265	.318	237	.227	37	245	200	13	26.3

● JOHNNY LUSH
Lush, John Charles b: 10/8/1885, Williamsport, Pa. d: 11/18/46, Beverly Hills, Cal BL/TL, 5'9.5", 165 lbs. Deb: 4/22/04 ◆

YEAR TM/L	W	L	PCT	G	GS	CG	SH	SV	IP	H	HR	BB	SO	RAT	ERA	ERA+	OAV	OOB	BH	AVG	PB	PR	/A	PD	TPI
1904 Phi-N	0	6	.000	7	6	3	0	0	42²	52	1	27	27	18.1	3.59	75	.301	.415	102	.276	4	-4	-4	1	-0.3
1905 Phi-N	2	0	1.000	2	1	1	0	0	17	12	0	8	8	11.1	1.59	184	.194	.296	5	.313	1	3	3	0	0.4
1906 Phi-N	18	15	.545	37	35	24	5	0	281	254	2	119	151	12.5	2.37	110	.236	.321	56	.264	7	8	8	3	2.1
1907 Phi-N	3	5	.375	8	8	5	2	0	57¹	48	0	21	20	11.3	2.98	81	.227	.306	8	.200	1	-3	-4	1	-0.4
StL-N	7	10	.412	20	19	15	3	0	144	132	2	42	71	11.4	2.50	100	.246	.311	23	.280	5	-0	-0	-0	0.8
Yr	10	15	.400	28	27	20	5	0	201¹	180	2	63	91	11.2	2.64	94	.240	.306	31	.254	6	-4	-4	0	0.4
1908 StL-N	11	18	.379	38	32	23	3	1	250²	221	6	57	93	10.4	2.12	111	.231	.283	15	.169	1	7	7	0	1.0
1909 StL-N	11	18	.379	34	28	21	2	0	221¹	215	1	69	66	12.0	3.13	81	.260	.324	22	.239	4	-13	-15	-1	-1.4
1910 StL-N	14	13	.519	36	24	13	1	1	225¹	235	6	70	54	12.5	3.20	93	.276	.336	21	.226	4	-4	-5	-2	-0.4
Total 7	66	85	.437	182	154	105	16	2	1239¹	1169	17	413	490	11.9	2.68	97	.249	.318	252	.254	24	-7	-11	1	1.8

● SPARKY LYLE
Lyle, Albert Walter b: 7/22/44, DuBois, Pa. BL/TL, 6'1", 192 lbs. Deb: 7/4/67

YEAR TM/L	W	L	PCT	G	GS	CG	SH	SV	IP	H	HR	BB	SO	RAT	ERA	ERA+	OAV	OOB	BH	AVG	PB	PR	/A	PD	TPI
1967 Bos-A	1	2	.333	27	0	0	0	5	43¹	33	3	14	42	10.2	2.28	153	.213	.287	2	.250	1	5	6	-0	0.6
1968 Bos-A	6	1	.857	49	0	0	0	11	65²	67	6	14	52	11.1	2.74	115	.261	.299	1	.125	-0	2	3	-1	0.3
1969 Bos-A	8	3	.727	71	0	0	0	17	102²	91	8	48	93	12.3	2.54	150	.240	.327	2	.118	-1	12	14	1	2.1
1970 Bos-A	1	7	.125	63	0	0	0	20	67¹	62	5	34	51	13.0	3.88	102	.244	.336	0	.000	-1	-1	-1	1	-0.1
1971 Bos-A	6	4	.600	50	0	0	0	16	52¹	41	5	23	37	11.0	2.75	134	.228	.315	3	1.000	1	4	5	0	1.6
1972 NY-A	9	5	.643	59	0	0	0	**35**	107²	84	3	29	75	9.4	1.92	153	.216	.271	4	.190	1	**14**	**12**	-1	2.7
1973 NY-A★	5	9	.357	51	0	0	0	27	82¹	66	4	18	63	9.2	2.51	146	.216	.259	0			12	11	0	2.6
1974 NY-A	9	3	.750	66	0	0	0	15	114	93	6	43	89	10.8	1.66	210	.226	.300	0	.000	-1	**25**	23	-1	3.0
1975 NY-A	5	7	.417	49	0	0	0	6	89¹	94	1	36	65	13.3	3.12	117	.275	.347	0			6	5	0	0.8
1976 *NY-A☆	7	8	.467	64	0	0	0	**23**	103²	82	7	42	61	10.8	2.26	151	.225	.305	0			15	13	1	2.5
1977 *NY-A★	13	5	.722	**72**	0	0	0	26	137	131	7	33	68	10.9	2.17	182	.257	.305	0			**29**	**27**	-1	**4.4**
1978 *NY-A	9	3	.750	59	0	0	0	9	111²	116	6	33	33	12.3	3.47	104	.278	.337	0			4	2	0	0.3
1979 Tex-A	5	8	.385	67	0	0	0	13	95	78	9	28	48	10.0	3.13	133	.226	.284	0			11	11	1	1.6
1980 Tex-A	3	2	.600	49	0	0	0	8	80²	97	4	28	43	13.9	4.69	83	.306	.362	0			-6	-7	-0	-0.5
Phi-N	0	0	—	10	0	0	0	2	14	11	0	6	6	10.9	1.93	196	.220	.304	0			3	3	-1	0.2
1981 *Phi-N	9	6	.600	48	0	0	0	9	75	85	4	33	29	14.3	4.44	82	.301	.377	2	.400	1	-8	-7	1	-1.1
1982 Phi-N	3	3	.500	34	0	0	0	2	36²	50	3	12	12	15.2	5.15	71	.327	.376	1	.500	1	-6	-6	1	-0.9
Chi-A	0	0	—	10	0	0	0	1	6	6	1	1	6	13.5	3.00	134	.262	.367	0			1	1	1	0.2
Total 16	99	76	.566	899	0	0	0	238	1390¹	1292	84	481	873	11.6	2.88	127	.251	.316	15	.192	2	121	119	-4	19.9

● JIM LYLE
Lyle, James Charles b: 7/24/1900, Lake, Miss. d: 10/10/77, Williamsport, Pa. BR/TR, 6'1", 180 lbs. Deb: 10/2/25

YEAR TM/L	W	L	PCT	G	GS	CG	SH	SV	IP	H	HR	BB	SO	RAT	ERA	ERA+	OAV	OOB	BH	AVG	PB	PR	/A	PD	TPI
1925 Was-A	0	0	—	1	0	0	0	0	3	5	0	1	3	18.0	6.00	70	.333	.375	0	—	0	-1	-1	-0	-0.1

● ADRIAN LYNCH
Lynch, Adrian Ryan b: 2/9/1897, Laurens, Iowa d: 3/16/34, Davenport, Iowa BB/TR, 6'1.5", 185 lbs. Deb: 8/4/20

YEAR TM/L	W	L	PCT	G	GS	CG	SH	SV	IP	H	HR	BB	SO	RAT	ERA	ERA+	OAV	OOB	BH	AVG	PB	PR	/A	PD	TPI
1920 StL-A	2	0	1.000	5	3	1	0	0	22¹	23	1	17	8	16.5	5.24	75	.277	.406	2	.222	0	-4	-3	-1	-0.3

● ED LYNCH
Lynch, Edward Francis b: 2/25/56, Brooklyn, N.Y. BR/TR, 6'6", 230 lbs. Deb: 8/31/80

YEAR TM/L	W	L	PCT	G	GS	CG	SH	SV	IP	H	HR	BB	SO	RAT	ERA	ERA+	OAV	OOB	BH	AVG	PB	PR	/A	PD	TPI
1980 NY-N	1	1	.500	5	4	0	0	0	19¹	24	0	6	9	14.0	5.12	69	.304	.353	2	.333	0	-3	-3	0	-0.3
1981 NY-N	4	5	.444	17	13	0	0	0	80¹	79	6	21	27	11.3	2.91	120	.254	.303	3	.143	1	5	5	-1	0.6
1982 NY-N	4	8	.333	43	12	0	0	2	139¹	145	6	40	51	12.0	3.55	102	.273	.325	0	.000	-3	1	1	-1	-0.4
1983 NY-N	10	10	.500	30	27	1	0	0	174²	208	17	41	44	13.0	4.28	85	.302	.344	8	.154	-1	-13	-13	-1	-1.5
1984 NY-N	9	8	.529	40	13	0	0	0	124	169	14	24	62	14.3	4.50	79	.324	.359	6	.222	1	-13	-13	-1	-1.8
1985 NY-N	10	8	.556	31	29	1	0	0	191	188	19	27	65	10.2	3.44	100	.256	.283	4	.077	-2	3	0	-4	-0.6
1986 NY-N	0	0	—	1	0	0	0	0	1²	2	0	0	1	10.8	0.00	—	.286	.286	0	—	0	1	1	0	0.0
Chi-N	7	5	.583	23	13	1	0	0	99²	105	10	23	57	11.6	3.79	107	.279	.322	1	.033	-2	-1	-1	-4	0.0
Yr	7	5	.583	24	13	1	0	0	101¹	107	10	23	58	11.6	3.73	108	.279	.321	1	.033	-2	-0	-3	-4	0.0
1987 Chi-N	2	9	.182	23	16	0	0	0	110¹	130	17	48	80	14.7	5.38	79	.295	.367	3	.188	-0	-16	-14	1	-1.2
Total 8	47	54	.465	248	119	8	2	8	940¹	1050	89	229	396	12.4	4.00	92	.284	.324	27	.114	-6	-35	-33	-8	-5.2

● JACK LYNCH
Lynch, John H. b: 2/5/1857, New York, N.Y. d: 4/20/23, Bronx, N.Y. BR/TR, 5'8", 185 lbs. Deb: 5/2/1881

YEAR TM/L	W	L	PCT	G	GS	CG	SH	SV	IP	H	HR	BB	SO	RAT	ERA	ERA+	OAV	OOB	BH	AVG	PB	PR	/A	PD	TPI
1881 Buf-N	10	9	.526	20	19	17	0	0	165²	203	2	29	32	12.6	3.59	77	.297	.325	13	.167	-3	-15	-15	1	-1.5
1883 NY-a	13	15	.464	29	29	29	1	0	255	263	6	25	119	10.2	4.09	82	.249	.267	20	.187	-3	-22	-21	-1	-2.1
1884 NY-a	37	15	.712	55	54	54	5	0	496	420	10	42	292	8.6	2.67	117	.215	.236	30	.152	-7	32	25	-5	1.0
1885 NY-a	23	21	.523	44	43	43	1	0	379	410	17	42	177	10.8	3.61	82	.263	.283	30	.196	2	-15	-27	-3	-2.3
1886 NY-a	20	30	.400	51	50	50	1	0	432²	485	10	116	193	12.8	3.95	86	.271	.320	27	.160	-6	-24	-26	-3	-3.1
1887 NY-a	7	14	.333	21	21	21	0	0	187	245	8	36	45	13.7	5.10	83	.305	.338	14	.169	-4	-17	-18	2	-1.5
1890 Bro-a	0	1	.000	1	1	1	0	0	9	22	1	5	1	27.0	12.00	32	.452	.503	3	.750	2	-8	-8	1	-0.4
Total 7	110	105	.512	221	217	215	8	0	1924¹	2048	54	295	859	11.1	3.69	89	.260	.289	137	.173	-18	-69	-91	-10	-10.4

YEAR	TM/L	W	L	PCT	G	GS	CG	SH	SV	IP	H	HR	BB	SO	RAT	ERA	ERA+	OAV	OOB	BH	AVG	PB	PR	/A	PD	TPI

● MIKE LYNCH   Lynch, Michael Joseph b: 6/28/1880, Holyoke, Mass. d: 4/2/27, Garrison, N.Y.   BR/TR, 6'2", 170 lbs.   Deb: 6/21/04

YEAR	TM/L	W	L	PCT	G	GS	CG	SH	SV	IP	H	HR	BB	SO	RAT	ERA	ERA+	OAV	OOB	BH	AVG	PB	PR	/A	PD	TPI
1904	Pit-N	15	11	.577	27	24	24	1	0	222²	200	1	91	95	12.4	2.71	101	.243	.330	20	.230	4	1	1	-2	0.2
1905	Pit-N	17	8	.680	33	22	13	0	2	206¹	191	3	107	106	13.2	3.79	79	.254	.351	11	.136	-1	-18	-18	0	-2.2
1906	Pit-N	6	5	.545	18	12	7	0	0	119	101	2	31	48	10.6	2.42	110	.232	.295	8	.205	-0	3	3	-1	0.2
1907	Pit-N	2	2	.500	7	4	2	0	0	36	37	0	22	9	15.0	2.25	108	.282	.390	3	.250	1	1	1	0	0.3
	NY-N	3	6	.333	12	10	7	0	1	72	68	3	30	34	12.3	3.38	73	.249	.323	8	.296	2	-7	-7	0	-0.6
	Yr	5	8	.385	19	14	9	0	1	108	105	3	52	43	13.1	3.00	82	.259	.344	11	.282	3	-6	-6	2	-0.3
Total	4	43	32	.573	97	72	53	1	3	656	597	9	281	292	12.4	3.05	91	.248	.333	50	.203	5	-21	-20	-1	-2.1

● TOM LYNCH   Lynch, Thomas S. b: 1863, Peru, Ill. d: 5/13/03, Peru, Ill.   BL, 5'11", 175 lbs.   Deb: 8/5/1884

YEAR	TM/L	W	L	PCT	G	GS	CG	SH	SV	IP	H	HR	BB	SO	RAT	ERA	ERA+	OAV	OOB	BH	AVG	PB	PR	/A	PD	TPI
1884	Chi-N	0	0	—	1	1	0	0	0	7	7	1	3	2	12.9	2.57	122	.241	.313	0	.000	-1	0	0	0	0.0

● RED LYNN   Lynn, Japhet Monroe b: 12/27/13, Kenney, Tex. d: 10/27/77, Bellville, Tex.   BR/TR, 6', 162 lbs.   Deb: 4/25/39

YEAR	TM/L	W	L	PCT	G	GS	CG	SH	SV	IP	H	HR	BB	SO	RAT	ERA	ERA+	OAV	OOB	BH	AVG	PB	PR	/A	PD	TPI
1939	Det-A	0	1	.000	4	0	0	0	0	8¹	11	2	3	3	16.2	8.64	57	.324	.395	0	.000	-0	-4	-3	0	-0.4
	NY-N	1	0	1.000	26	0	0	0	1	49²	44	3	21	22	12.1	3.08	127	.240	.325	0	.000	-1	5	5	-1	-0.1
1940	NY-N	4	3	.571	33	0	0	0	3	42¹	40	3	24	25	13.8	3.83	101	.247	.348	0	.000	-1	0	0	-1	-0.1
1944	Chi-N	5	4	.556	22	7	4	1	1	84¹	80	4	37	35	12.6	4.06	87	.251	.331	6	.207	-0	-4	-5	1	-0.3
Total	3	10	8	.556	85	7	4	1	5	184²	175	12	85	85	12.9	3.95	96	.251	.336	6	.146	-1	-3	-4	-1	-0.9

● AL LYONS   Lyons, Albert Harold b: 7/18/18, St.Joseph, Mo. d: 12/20/65, Inglewood, Cal.   BR/TR, 6'2", 195 lbs.   Deb: 4/19/44

YEAR	TM/L	W	L	PCT	G	GS	CG	SH	SV	IP	H	HR	BB	SO	RAT	ERA	ERA+	OAV	OOB	BH	AVG	PB	PR	/A	PD	TPI
1944	NY-A	0	0	—	11	0	0	0	0	39²	43	2	24	14	15.7	4.54	77	.291	.397	9	.346	2	-5	-5	-1	0.2
1946	NY-A	0	1	.000	2	1	0	0	0	8¹	11	0	6	4	19.4	5.40	64	.314	.429	0	.000	-1	-2	-2	0	-0.2
1947	NY-A	1	0	1.000	6	0	0	0	0	11	8	2	9	7	22.1	9.00	39	.367	.466	4	.667	2	-6	-7	0	-0.3
	Pit-N	1	2	.333	13	0	0	0	0	28¹	36	4	12	16	15.6	7.31	58	.300	.368	2	.200	1	-10	-10	1	-0.7
1948	Bos-N	1	0	1.000	7	0	0	0	0	12²	17	1	8	5	17.8	7.82	49	.309	.397	2	.167	0	-5	-6	1	-0.2
Total	4	3	3	.500	39	1	0	0	0	100	125	9	59	46	16.9	6.30	59	.307	.400	17	.293	5	-29	-28	2	-1.2

● GEORGE LYONS   Lyons, George Tony "Smooth" b: 1/25/1891, Bible Grove, Ill. d: 8/12/81, Nevada, Mo.   BR/TR, 5'11", 180 lbs.   Deb: 9/6/20

YEAR	TM/L	W	L	PCT	G	GS	CG	SH	SV	IP	H	HR	BB	SO	RAT	ERA	ERA+	OAV	OOB	BH	AVG	PB	PR	/A	PD	TPI
1920	StL-N	2	1	.667	7	2	1	0	0	23¹	21	2	9	5	12.0	3.09	97	.262	.344	1	.143	-0	0	0	1	0.0
1924	StL-A	3	2	.600	26	6	2	0	0	77²	97	2	45	25	17.0	5.21	87	.323	.420	5	.250	-0	-8	-6	1	-0.2
Total	2	5	3	.625	33	8	3	0	0	101	118	4	54	30	15.9	4.72	88	.311	.405	6	.222	-0	-8	-7	2	-0.2

● HARRY LYONS   Lyons, Harry P. b: 3/25/1866, Chester, Pa. d: 6/30/12, Mauricetown, N.J.   BR/TR, 5'10.5", 157 lbs.   Deb: 8/29/1887 ◆

YEAR	TM/L	W	L	PCT	G	GS	CG	SH	SV	IP	H	HR	BB	SO	RAT	ERA	ERA+	OAV	OOB	BH	AVG	PB	PR	/A	PD	TPI
1890	Roc-a	0	0	—	1	0	0	0	0	3²	8	0	1	2	22.1	12.27	29	.424	.453	152	.260	-1	-3	-4	1	0.0

● HERSH LYONS   Lyons, Herschel Englebert b: 7/23/15, Fresno, Cal.   BR/TR, 5'11", 195 lbs.   Deb: 4/17/41

YEAR	TM/L	W	L	PCT	G	GS	CG	SH	SV	IP	H	HR	BB	SO	RAT	ERA	ERA+	OAV	OOB	BH	AVG	PB	PR	/A	PD	TPI
1941	StL-N	0	0	—	1	0	0	0	0	1¹	1	0	3	1	27.0	0.00	—	.200	.500	0	—	0	1	1	0	0.0

● STEVE LYONS   Lyons, Stephen John b: 6/3/60, Tacoma, Wash.   BL/TR, 6'3", 192 lbs.   Deb: 4/15/85 ◆

YEAR	TM/L	W	L	PCT	G	GS	CG	SH	SV	IP	H	HR	BB	SO	RAT	ERA	ERA+	OAV	OOB	BH	AVG	PB	PR	/A	PD	TPI
1990	Chi-A	0	0	—	1	0	0	0	0	2	2	0	4	1	27.0	4.50	85	.250	.500	28	.192	0	-0	-0	0	0.0
1991	Bos-A	0	0	—	1	0	0	0	0	1	2	0	0	1	18.0	0.00	—	.400	.400	51	.241	0	0	0	0	0.0
Total	2	0	0	—	2	0	0	0	0	3	4	0	4	2	24.0	3.00	133	.308	.471	545	.252	0	0	0	0	0.0

● TED LYONS   Lyons, Theodore Amar b: 12/28/1900, Lake Charles, La. d: 7/25/86, Sulphur, La.   BB/TR, 5'11", 200 lbs.   Deb: 7/2/23   MCH ◆

YEAR	TM/L	W	L	PCT	G	GS	CG	SH	SV	IP	H	HR	BB	SO	RAT	ERA	ERA+	OAV	OOB	BH	AVG	PB	PR	/A	PD	TPI
1923	Chi-A	2	1	.667	9	1	0	0	0	22²	30	2	15	6	18.3	6.35	62	.323	.422	1	.200	-0	-6	-6	1	-0.6
1924	Chi-A	12	11	.522	41	22	12	0	3	216¹	279	10	72	52	14.7	4.87	85	.322	.375	17	.221	0	-15	-18	-3	-1.9
1925	Chi-A	**21**	11	.656	43	32	19	**5**	3	262²	274	7	83	45	12.3	3.26	128	.278	.335	18	.186	-3	33	26	2	2.7
1926	Chi-A	18	16	.529	39	31	24	3	2	283²	268	6	106	51	11.9	3.01	128	.252	.320	22	.212	-0	32	27	4	3.3
1927	Chi-A	**22**	14	.611	39	34	**30**	2	2	307²	291	6	67	71	10.5	2.84	143	.251	.292	28	.255	5	**45**	41	0	**5.1**
1928	Chi-A	15	14	.517	39	27	21	0	6	240	276	11	68	60	13.0	3.98	102	.295	.344	23	.253	1	2	2	2	0.5
1929	Chi-A	14	20	.412	37	31	21	1	2	259¹	276	11	76	57	12.3	4.10	105	.278	.331	20	.220	1	4	5	3	1.0
1930	Chi-A	22	15	.595	42	36	**29**	1	1	297²	331	12	57	69	11.8	3.78	122	.285	.319	38	.311	8	29	28	3	4.1
1931	Chi-A	4	6	.400	22	12	7	0	0	101	117	6	33	16	13.4	4.01	106	.296	.350	5	.152	-1	4	3	-1	0.0
1932	Chi-A	10	15	.400	33	26	19	1	2	230²	243	10	71	58	12.4	3.28	132	.272	.327	19	.260	5	31	27	-1	3.0
1933	Chi-A	10	21	.323	36	27	14	2	1	228	260	10	74	74	13.2	4.38	97	.280	.333	26	.286	6	-3	-4	0	0.2
1934	Chi-A	11	13	.458	30	24	21	0	1	205	249	15	66	53	13.9	4.87	97	.293	.345	20	.206	-1	-8	-3	2	0.0
1935	Chi-A	15	8	.652	23	22	19	3	0	190²	194	15	56	54	11.9	3.02	153	.262	.317	18	.220	-0	30	34	-1	3.6
1936	Chi-A	10	13	.435	26	24	15	1	0	182	227	21	45	48	13.6	5.14	101	.305	.347	11	.157	-3	-2	1	1	0.4
1937	Chi-A	12	7	.632	22	22	11	0	0	169¹	182	21	45	45	12.1	4.15	111	.278	.326	12	.211	1	9	9	0	1.0
1938	Chi-A	9	11	.450	23	23	17	1	0	194²	238	13	52	54	13.4	3.70	132	.299	.342	14	.194	-1	24	26	2	2.3
1939	Chi-A☆	14	6	.700	21	21	16	0	0	172²	162	7	26	65	**9.9**	2.76	171	.247	**.276**	18	.295	4	36	38	-1	4.3
1940	Chi-A	12	8	.600	22	22	17	**4**	0	186¹	188	17	37	72	10.9	3.24	137	.252	.287	8	.240	2	24	25	-2	2.3
1941	Chi-A	12	10	.545	22	22	19	2	0	187¹	199	9	37	63	11.5	3.70	111	.269	.308	20	.270	4	9	8	1	1.3
1942	Chi-A	14	6	.700	20	20	20	1	0	180¹	167	11	26	50	9.7	**2.10**	172	.245	.275	16	.239	4	31	30	1	**4.0**
1946	Chi-A	1	4	.200	5	5	5	0	0	42²	43	2	9	10	9.9	2.32	147	.235	.275	0	.000	-1	6	5	0	0.5
Total	21	260	230	.531	594	484	356	27	23	4161	4489	223	1121	1073	12.2	3.67	118	.276	.324	364	.233	32	313	302	12	36.7

● TOBY LYONS   Lyons, Thomas A. b: 3/27/1869, Cambridge, Mass. d: 8/27/20, Boston, Mass.   Deb: 4/18/1890

YEAR	TM/L	W	L	PCT	G	GS	CG	SH	SV	IP	H	HR	BB	SO	RAT	ERA	ERA+	OAV	OOB	BH	AVG	PB	PR	/A	PD	TPI
1890	Syr-a	0	2	.000	3	3	2	0	0	22¹	40	1	26	6	25.0	10.48	34	.377	.484	4	.333	1	-16	-17	0	-1.0

● RICK LYSANDER   Lysander, Richard Eugene b: 2/21/53, Huntington Park, Cal.   BR/TR, 6'2", 190 lbs.   Deb: 4/12/80

YEAR	TM/L	W	L	PCT	G	GS	CG	SH	SV	IP	H	HR	BB	SO	RAT	ERA	ERA+	OAV	OOB	BH	AVG	PB	PR	/A	PD	TPI
1980	Oak-A	0	0	—	5	0	0	0	0	13²	24	3	4	5	18.4	7.90	48	.381	.418	0	—	0	-6	-6	0	0.4
1983	Min-A	5	12	.294	61	4	1	1	3	125	132	8	43	58	12.7	3.38	126	.275	.337	0	—	0	9	12	1	1.4
1984	Min-A	4	3	.571	36	0	0	0	5	56²	62	4	27	22	14.1	3.49	120	.283	.362	0	—	0	3	4	0	0.3
1985	Min-A	0	2	.000	35	1	0	0	3	61	72	3	22	26	13.9	6.05	73	.305	.364	0	—	0	-13	-11	-1	-0.8
Total	4	9	17	.346	137	5	1	1	11	256¹	290	16	96	111	13.6	4.28	99	.291	.354	0	—	0	-6	-1	0	1.3

● BILL LYSTON   Lyston, William Edward b: 1863, Near Baltimore, Md. d: 8/4/44, Baltimore, Md.   TR,   Deb: 8/29/1891

YEAR	TM/L	W	L	PCT	G	GS	CG	SH	SV	IP	H	HR	BB	SO	RAT	ERA	ERA+	OAV	OOB	BH	AVG	PB	PR	/A	PD	TPI
1891	Col-a	0	1	.000	1	1	1	0	0	6	10	1	4	1	25.5	10.50	33	.359	.488	0	.000	-0	-5	-5	-0	-0.5
1894	Cle-N	0	0	—	1	1	0	0	0	3²	5	1	4	0	22.1	9.82	56	.321	.460	0	.000	-0	-2	-2	-0	0.0
Total	2	0	1	.000	2	2	1	0	0	9²	15	1	10	1	24.2	10.24	41	.346	.478	0	.000	-0	-6	-7	-0	-0.5

● DUKE MAAS   Maas, Duane Fredrick b: 1/31/29, Utica, Mich. d: 12/7/76, Mt.Clemens, Mich.   BR/TR, 5'10", 170 lbs.   Deb: 4/21/55

YEAR	TM/L	W	L	PCT	G	GS	CG	SH	SV	IP	H	HR	BB	SO	RAT	ERA	ERA+	OAV	OOB	BH	AVG	PB	PR	/A	PD	TPI
1955	Det-A	5	6	.455	18	16	5	2	0	86²	94	9	32	42	14.0	4.88	79	.271	.369	5	.167	0	-9	-10	0	-1.1
1956	Det-A	0	7	.000	26	7	0	0	0	63¹	81	9	32	34	16.9	6.54	63	.313	.401	3	.188	0	-17	-17	0	-1.7
1957	Det-A	10	14	.417	45	26	8	2	6	219¹	210	23	65	116	11.4	3.28	118	.252	.309	6	.085	-4	12	14	0	1.2
1958	KC-A	4	5	.444	10	7	3	1	1	55¹	49	3	13	19	10.2	3.90	100	.241	.290	3	.176	0	-1	0	0	0.1
	*NY-A	7	3	.700	22	13	2	1	0	101¹	93	9	36	50	11.6	3.82	92	.242	.310	3	.088	-2	-1	-3	-1	-0.6
	Yr	11	8	.579	32	20	5	2	1	156²	142	12	49	69	11.1	3.85	95	.241	.302	6	.118	-1	-3	-3	-1	-0.5
1959	NY-A	14	8	.636	38	21	3	1	4	138	149	14	53	67	13.3	4.43	82	.278	.345	5	.125	-1	-9	-12	1	-1.9
1960	*NY-A	5	1	.833	35	1	0	0	7	70¹	70	6	35	28	13.6	4.09	87	.265	.353	0	.000	-1	-2	-1	0	-0.4
1961	NY-A	0	0	—	1	0	0	0	0	0¹	1	0	0	0	54.0	54.00	7	1.000	1.000	0	—	0	-2	-2	0	0.0
Total	7	45	44	.506	195	91	21	7	15	734²	745	71	284	356	12.8	4.19	90	.264	.336	25	.117	-7	-27	-34	0	-4.4

YEAR TM/L	W	L	PCT	G	GS	CG	SH	SV	IP	H	HR	BB	SO	RAT	ERA	ERA+	OAV	OOB	BH	AVG	PB	PR	/A	PD	TPI

● BOB MABE   Mabe, Robert Lee b: 10/8/29, Danville, Va. BR/TR, 5'11", 165 lbs. Deb: 4/18/58

1958 StL-N	3	9	.250	31	13	4	0	0	111²	113	11	41	74	12.7	4.51	91	.260	.330	1	.042	-2	-7	-5	0	-0.6
1959 Cin-N	4	2	.667	18	1	0	0	3	29²	29	6	19	8	14.6	5.46	74	.254	.361	0	.000	-1	-5	-5	-0	-1.0
1960 Bal-A	0	0	—	2	0	0	0	0	0²	4	0	1	0	67.5	27.00	14	.571	.625	0	—	0	-2	-2	-0	0.0
Total 3	7	11	.389	51	14	4	0	3	142	146	17	61	82	13.4	4.82	85	.263	.340	1	.032	-3	-14	-11	0	-1.6

● MAC MacARTHUR   MacArthur, Malcolm b: 1/19/1862, Glasgow, Scotland d: 10/18/32, Detroit, Mich. TR. Deb: 5/2/1884

| 1884 Ind-a | 1 | 5 | .167 | 6 | 6 | 6 | 0 | 0 | 52 | 57 | 1 | 21 | 19 | 13.8 | 5.02 | 66 | .263 | .333 | 2 | .095 | -2 | -10 | -10 | -0 | -1.0 |

● FRANK MacCORMACK   MacCormack, Frank Louis b: 9/21/54, Jersey City, N.J. BR/TR, 6'4", 210 lbs. Deb: 6/14/76

1976 Det-A	0	5	.000	9	8	0	0	0	32²	35	1	34	14	19.3	5.79	64	.294	.455	0	.000	0	-8	-8	-0	-1.1
1977 Sea-A	0	0	—	3	3	0	0	0	7	4	0	12	4	24.4	3.86	107	.174	.500	0	—	0	0	0	0	0.1
Total 2	0	5	.000	12	11	0	0	0	39²	39	1	46	18	20.2	5.45	69	.275	.464	0	.000	0	-8	-7	-0	-1.0

● ROB MacDONALD   MacDonald, Robert Joseph b: 4/27/65, East Orange, N.J. BL/TL, 6'3", 200 lbs. Deb: 8/14/90

1990 Tor-A	0	0	—	4	0	0	0	0	2¹	0	0	2	0	7.7	0.00	—	.000	.250	0	—	0	1	1	-0	-0.1
1991 *Tor-A	3	3	.500	45	0	0	0	0	53²	51	5	25	24	12.7	2.85	148	.252	.335	0	—	0	7	8	-1	0.5
1992 Tor-A	1	0	1.000	27	0	0	0	0	47¹	50	4	16	26	12.7	4.37	93	.270	.332	0	—	0	-2	-2	-1	-0.3
1993 Det-A	3	3	.500	68	0	0	0	3	65²	64	8	33	39	13.8	5.35	80	.268	.356	0	—	0	-7	-8	1	-0.6
Total 4	7	6	.538	144	0	0	0	3	169	168	17	76	89	13.1	4.21	100	.261	.341	0	—	0	-1	-0	-1	-0.5

● BILL MACDONALD   Macdonald, William Paul b: 3/28/29, Alameda, Cal. d: 5/4/91, Shasta Lake, Cal. BR/TR, 5'10", 170 lbs. Deb: 5/6/50

1950 Pit-N	8	10	.444	32	20	6	2	1	153	138	17	88	60	13.4	4.29	102	.243	.346	6	.122	-2	-3	2	-3	-0.3
1953 Pit-N	0	1	.000	4	1	0	0	0	7¹	12	0	8	4	25.8	12.27	36	.400	.538	0	—	0	-7	-6	-0	-0.7
Total 2	8	11	.421	36	21	6	2	1	160¹	150	17	96	64	13.9	4.66	94	.251	.356	6	.122	-2	-9	-5	-3	-1.0

● JIMMY MACE   Mace, Harry L. b: Washington, D.C. 5'11", 185 lbs. Deb: 5/5/1891

| 1891 Was-a | 0 | 1 | .000 | 3 | 1 | 1 | 0 | 0 | 16 | 18 | 0 | 8 | 3 | 15.2 | 7.31 | 51 | .274 | .362 | 0 | .000 | -1 | -6 | -6 | -0 | -0.4 |

● DANNY MacFAYDEN   MacFayden, Daniel Knowles "Deacon Danny" b: 6/10/05, N.Truro, Mass. d: 8/26/72, Brunswick, Me. BR/TR, 5'11", 170 lbs. Deb: 8/25/26

1926 Bos-A	0	1	.000	3	1	1	0	0	13	10	0	7	1	11.8	4.85	84	.217	.321	1	.333	0	-1	-1	1	0.0
1927 Bos-A	5	8	.385	34	16	6	1	2	160¹	176	9	59	42	13.5	4.27	99	.294	.363	13	.283	-4	-2	-1	-2	0.2
1928 Bos-A	9	15	.375	33	28	9	0	0	195	215	12	78	61	13.8	4.75	87	.289	.361	9	.143	-1	-15	-14	-1	-1.6
1929 Bos-A	10	18	.357	32	26	14	4	0	221	225	8	81	61	12.7	3.62	118	.271	.340	13	.176	-3	15	16	2	1.7
1930 Bos-A	11	14	.440	36	33	18	1	2	269²	293	9	93	76	13.1	4.21	109	.281	.343	14	.141	-4	13	12	2	0.7
1931 Bos-A	16	12	.571	35	32	17	2	0	230²	263	4	79	74	13.6	4.02	107	.281	.341	10	.123	-5	9	7	2	0.5
1932 Bos-A	1	10	.091	12	11	6	0	0	77²	91	3	33	29	14.5	5.10	88	.289	.358	3	.120	-2	-5	-5	0	-0.7
NY-A	7	5	.583	17	15	9	0	1	121¹	137	11	37	33	13.1	3.93	104	.281	.334	5	.102	-3	7	2	-2	-0.3
Yr	8	15	.348	29	26	15	0	1	199	228	14	70	62	13.6	4.39	97	.284	.342	8	.108	-4	2	-3	-1	-1.0
1933 NY-A	3	2	.600	25	6	2	0	0	90¹	120	8	37	28	15.8	5.88	66	.319	.383	1	.029	-4	-16	-20	-1	-1.3
1934 NY-A	4	3	.571	22	11	4	0	0	96	110	5	31	41	13.4	4.50	90	.288	.345	4	.103	-2	-0	-5	-1	-0.5
1935 Cin-N	1	2	.333	7	4	1	0	0	36	39	1	13	13	13.0	4.75	84	.281	.342	1	.091	-1	-3	-3	1	-0.2
Bos-N	5	13	.278	28	20	7	1	0	151²	200	8	34	46	14.2	5.10	74	.314	.354	8	.157	-1	-18	-22	2	-2.1
Yr	6	15	.286	35	24	8	1	0	187²	239	9	47	59	14.0	5.04	76	.308	.352	9	.145	-2	-21	-25	3	-2.3
1936 Bos-N	17	13	.567	37	31	21	2	0	266²	268	5	66	86	11.4	2.87	134	.259	.307	8	.096	-5	34	29	3	2.7
1937 Bos-N	14	14	.500	32	32	16	2	0	246	250	5	60	70	11.4	2.93	123	.268	.313	13	.157	-2	27	18	1	1.8
1938 Bos-N	14	9	.609	29	29	19	5	0	219²	208	6	64	58	11.3	2.95	116	.247	.304	9	.117	-4	20	12	-1	0.6
1939 Bos-N	8	14	.364	33	28	8	0	2	191²	221	11	59	46	13.3	3.90	95	.291	.345	12	.179	-1	0	-4	1	-0.4
1940 Pit-N	4	5	.444	35	8	0	0	2	91¹	112	5	27	24	14.1	3.55	107	.302	.356	5	.179	-0	3	3	1	0.3
1941 Was-A	0	1	.000	5	0	0	0	0	7	12	1	5	3	21.9	10.29	39	.375	.459	0	—	0	-5	-5	-0	-0.5
1943 Bos-N	2	1	.667	10	1	0	0	0	21¹	31	1	9	5	17.3	5.91	58	.344	.410	1	.250	0	-6	-6	-0	-0.8
Total 17	132	159	.454	465	332	158	18	9	2706	2981	112	872	797	13.0	3.96	101	.281	.340	129	.142	-34	58	11	10	0.1

● JULIO MACHADO   Machado, Julio Segundo (Rondon) b: 12/1/65, Zulia, Venezuela BR/TR, 5'9", 165 lbs. Deb: 9/7/89

1989 NY-N	0	1	.000	10	0	0	0	0	11	9	0	3	14	9.8	3.27	100	.214	.267	0	—	0	-0	-0	-0	0.0
1990 NY-N	4	1	.800	27	0	0	0	0	34¹	32	4	17	27	13.4	3.15	119	.248	.345	0	—	0	2	2	0	0.3
Mil-A	0	0	—	10	0	0	0	3	13	9	0	8	12	11.8	0.69	559	.191	.309	0	—	0	5	5	-0	0.3
1991 Mil-A	3	3	.500	54	0	0	0	3	88²	65	12	55	98	12.5	3.45	115	.211	.336	0	—	0	6	5	-1	0.4
Total 3	7	5	.583	101	0	0	0	6	147	115	16	83	151	12.4	3.12	123	.219	.331	0	—	0	14	12	-1	1.0

● CHUCK MACHEMEHL   Machemehl, Charles Walter b: 4/20/47, Brenham, Tex. BR/TR, 6'4", 200 lbs. Deb: 4/6/71

| 1971 Cle-A | 0 | 2 | .000 | 14 | 0 | 0 | 0 | 3 | 18¹ | 16 | 2 | 15 | 9 | 15.2 | 6.38 | 60 | .246 | .387 | 1 | .500 | 0 | -6 | -5 | 0 | -0.7 |

● DENNY MACK   Mack, Dennis Joseph (b: Dennis Joseph McGee) b: 1851, Easton, Pa. d: 4/10/1888, Wilkes-Barre, Pa. BR/TR, 5'7", 164 lbs. Deb: 5/6/1871 MU♦

| 1871 Rok-n | 0 | 1 | .000 | 3 | 1 | 1 | 0 | 0 | 13 | 20 | 0 | 3 | 4 | 15.9 | 3.46 | 118 | .299 | .329 | 30 | .246 | -0 | 1 | 1 | | 0.0 |

● FRANK MACK   Mack, Frank George "Stubby" b: 2/2/1900, Oklahoma City, Okla. d: 7/2/71, Clearwater, Fla. BR/TR, 6'1.5", 180 lbs. Deb: 8/16/22

1922 Chi-A	2	2	.500	8	4	1	1	0	34¹	36	2	16	11	13.6	3.67	111	.281	.361	3	.250	1	2	-1	0	-0.1
1923 Chi-A	0	1	.000	11	0	0	0	0	23¹	23	0	11	6	13.1	4.24	93	.284	.370	0	.000	-1	-1	-1	0	-0.1
1925 Chi-A	0	0	—	8	0	0	0	0	13¹	24	1	13	6	25.0	9.45	44	.444	.552	1	.333	0	-7	-8	0	0.0
Total 3	2	3	.400	27	4	1	1	0	71	83	3	40	23	15.6	4.94	82	.316	.406	4	.190	0	-7	-7	-1	0.0

● TONY MACK   Mack, Tony Lynn b: 4/30/61, Lexington, Ky. BR/TR, 5'10", 177 lbs. Deb: 7/27/85

| 1985 Cal-A | 0 | 1 | .000 | 1 | 1 | 0 | 0 | 0 | 2¹ | 8 | 0 | 4 | 0 | 30.9 | 15.43 | 27 | .571 | .571 | 0 | — | 0 | -3 | -3 | -0 | -0.7 |

● BILL MACK   Mack, William Francis b: 2/12/1885, Elmira, N.Y. d: 9/30/71, Elmira, N.Y. BL/TL, 6'1", 155 lbs. Deb: 7/14/08

| 1908 Chi-N | 0 | 0 | — | 2 | 0 | 0 | 0 | 0 | 6 | 5 | 1 | 1 | 2 | 10.5 | 3.00 | 78 | .263 | .333 | 2 | .667 | 1 | -0 | -0 | -0 | 0.2 |

● KEN MacKENZIE   MacKenzie, Kenneth Purvis b: 3/10/34, Gore Bay, Ont., Can. BR/TL, 6', 185 lbs. Deb: 5/2/60

1960 Mil-N	0	1	.000	9	0	0	0	0	8¹	9	2	3	9	13.0	6.48	53	.281	.343	0	.000	-0	-3	-3	0	-0.3
1961 Mil-N	0	1	.000	5	0	0	0	0	7	8	1	2	4	14.1	5.14	73	.296	.367	0	.000	-0	-1	-1	0	-0.1
1962 NY-N	5	4	.556	42	1	0	0	1	80	87	10	34	51	13.9	4.95	84	.280	.356	1	.083	-1	-9	-7	1	-0.7
1963 NY-N	3	1	.750	34	0	0	0	3	58	63	11	12	41	11.9	4.97	70	.267	.308	0	.000	-0	-11	-10	-1	-0.9
StL-N	0	0	—	8	0	0	0	0	9	9	1	3	7	12.0	4.00	89	.250	.308	0	—	0	-1	-0	0	0.0
Yr	3	1	.750	42	0	0	0	3	67	72	12	15	48	11.7	4.84	72	.262	.308	0	.000	-0	-12	-10	-0	-0.9
1964 SF-N	0	0	—	10	0	0	0	0	9	9	1	3	3	12.0	5.00	71	.265	.324	0	—	0	-1	-1	0	0.0
1965 Hou-N	0	3	.000	21	0	0	0	0	37	46	7	6	26	12.6	3.89	86	.299	.325	3	.273	1	-2	-2	-0	-0.1
Total 6	8	10	.444	129	1	0	0	5	208	231	33	63	142	13.0	4.80	78	.278	.334	4	.111	-2	-27	-24	-1	-2.1

● JOHN MACKINSON   Mackinson, John Joseph b: 10/29/23, Orange, N.J. d: 10/17/89, Reseda, Cal. BR/TR, 5'10.5", 160 lbs. Deb: 4/16/53

1953 Phi-A	0	0	—	1	0	0	0	0	1¹	1	0	2	0	20.3	0.00	—	.200	.429	0	—	0	1	1	0	0.0
1955 StL-N	0	1	.000	8	1	0	0	0	20²	24	3	10	8	15.2	7.84	52	.296	.380	0	.000	-0	-9	-9	-0	-0.4
Total 2	0	1	.000	9	1	0	0	0	22	25	3	12	8	15.5	7.36	55	.291	.384	0	.000	-0	-8	-8	-0	-0.4

● BILLY MacLEOD   MacLeod, William Daniel b: 5/13/42, Gloucester, Mass. BL/TL, 6'2", 190 lbs. Deb: 9/13/62

| 1962 Bos-A | 0 | 1 | .000 | 2 | 0 | 0 | 0 | 0 | 1² | 4 | 0 | 1 | 2 | 27.0 | 5.40 | 76 | .444 | .500 | 0 | — | 0 | -0 | -0 | -0 | -0.1 |

YEAR TM/L	W	L	PCT	G	GS	CG	SH	SV	IP	H	HR	BB	SO	RAT	ERA	ERA+	OAV	OOB	BH	AVG	PB	PR	/A	PD	TPI

● **MAX MACON**   Macon, Max Cullen b: 10/14/15, Pensacola, Fla. d: 8/5/89, Jupiter, Fla. BL/TL, 6'3", 175 lbs. Deb: 4/21/38 ♦

1938 StL-N	4	11	.267	38	12	5	1	2	129¹	133	9	61	39	13.8	4.11	96	.268	.352	11	.306	2	-5	-2	1	0.0
1940 Bro-N	1	0	1.000	2	0	0	0	0	2	5	2	0	1	22.5	22.50	18	.455	.455	1	1.000	0	-4	-4	-0	-1.3
1942 Bro-N	5	3	.625	14	8	4	1	1	84	67	3	33	27	10.9	1.93	169	.220	.300	12	.279	4	13	12	-0	1.6
1943 Bro-N	7	5	.583	25	9	0	0	0	77	91	4	32	21	14.8	5.96	56	.291	.364	9	.164	-1	-22	-22	1	-3.2
1944 Bos-N	0	0	—	1	0	0	0	0	3	10	2	1	1	33.0	21.00	18	.556	.579	100	.273		-6	-6	0	0.0
1947 Bos-N	0	0	—	1	0	0	0	0	2	1	0	1	1	9.0	0.00	—	.167	.286	0	—	0	1	1	0	0.0
Total 6	17	19	.472	81	29	9	2	3	297¹	307	20	128	90	13.5	4.24	85	.267	.345	133	.265	5	-23	-21	1	-2.9

● **HARRY MacPHERSON**   MacPherson, Harry William b: 7/10/26, N.Andover, Mass. BR/TR, 5'10", 150 lbs. Deb: 8/14/44

| 1944 Bos-N | 0 | 0 | — | 1 | 0 | 0 | 0 | 0 | 1 | 0 | 0 | 1 | 0 | 9.0 | — | .000 | .250 | 0 | — | 0 | 0 | 0 | 0 | 0.0 |

● **JIMMY MACULLAR**   Macullar, James F. "Little Mac" b: 1/16/1855, Boston, Mass. d: 4/8/24, Baltimore, Md. BR/TL, 5'6", 155 lbs. Deb: 5/5/1879 MU♦

1885 Bal-a	0	0	—	1	0	0	0	0	1	0	0	0	0	0.0	0.00	—	.000	.000	61	.191	0	0	0	-0	0.0
1886 Bal-a	0	0	—	1	0	0	0	0	2	4	0	0	1	18.0	9.00	38	.400	.400	55	.205	0	-1	-1	-0	0.0
Total 2	0	0	—	2	0	0	0	0	3	4	0	0	1	12.0	6.00	56	.308	.308	319	.207	0	-1	-1	-0	0.0

● **KEITH MacWHORTER**   MacWhorter, Keith b: 12/30/55, Worcester, Mass. BR/TR, 6'4", 190 lbs. Deb: 5/10/80

| 1980 Bos-A | 0 | 3 | .000 | 14 | 2 | 0 | 0 | 0 | 42¹ | 46 | 3 | 18 | 21 | 14.0 | 5.53 | 76 | .280 | .359 | 0 | — | 0 | -7 | -6 | 0 | -0.5 |

● **LEN MADDEN**   Madden, Leonard Joseph "Lefty" b: 7/2/1890, Toledo, Ohio d: 9/9/49, Toledo, Ohio BL/TL, 6'2", 165 lbs. Deb: 8/31/12

| 1912 Chi-N | 0 | 1 | .000 | 6 | 2 | 0 | 0 | 0 | 12¹ | 16 | 1 | 9 | 5 | 19.0 | 2.92 | 114 | .302 | .413 | 1 | .250 | 0 | 1 | 1 | 0 | 0.0 |

● **MIKE MADDEN**   Madden, Michael Anthony b: 1/13/58, Denver, Colo. BL/TL, 6'1", 190 lbs. Deb: 4/5/83

1983 Hou-N	9	5	.643	28	13	0	0	0	94²	76	4	45	44	11.6	3.14	108	.231	.325	1	.045	-1	5	3	0	0.3
1984 Hou-N	2	3	.400	17	7	0	0	0	40²	46	1	35	29	17.9	5.53	60	.297	.426	2	.333	1	-9	-10	-1	-1.1
1985 Hou-N	0	0	—	13	0	0	0	0	19	29	1	11	16	18.9	4.26	81	.363	.440	0	—	0	-1	-2	-0	0.0
1986 Hou-N	1	2	.333	13	6	0	0	0	39²	47	3	22	30	15.7	4.08	88	.297	.383	0	.000	-0	-2	-2	-0	-0.2
Total 4	12	10	.545	71	26	0	0	0	194	198	9	113	119	14.5	3.94	87	.274	.373	3	.081	-1	-7	-11	-1	-1.0

● **KID MADDEN**   Madden, Michael Joseph b: 10/22/1866, Portland, Me. d: 3/16/1896, Portland, Maine TL, 5'7.5", 130 lbs. Deb: 5/6/1887

1887 Bos-N	21	14	.600	37	37	36	3	0	321	317	20	122	81	12.9	3.79	107	.251	.327	32	.242	4	10	10	-2	0.9
1888 Bos-N	7	11	.389	20	18	17	1	0	165	142	6	24	53	9.9	2.95	97	.228	.273	11	.164	-2	-2	-2	1	-0.3
1889 Bos-N	10	10	.500	22	19	18	1	1	178	194	7	64	64	14.2	4.40	95	.269	.348	25	.291	2	-8	-5	0	-0.2
1890 Bos-P	2	3	.600	10	7	5	1	0	62	85	2	25	24	17.1	4.79	92	.313	.387	7	.184	-1	-4	-3	0	-0.2
1891 Bos-a	0	1	.000	1	1	1	0	0	8	10	2	6	6	21.4	6.75	52	.296	.444	2	.667	1	-3	-3	0	-0.1
Bal-a	13	12	.520	32	27	20	1	1	224	239	4	88	56	14.1	4.10	91	.264	.345	29	.271	5	-9	-9	4	-0.1
Yr	13	13	.500	33	28	21	1	1	232	249	6	94	62	14.2	4.19	89	.264	.346	31	.282	6	-12	-12	4	-0.3
Total 5	54	50	.519	122	109	97	7	2	958	987	41	336	284	13.2	3.92	97	.259	.332	106	.245	10	-15	-11	4	-0.1

● **MORRIS MADDEN**   Madden, Morris De Wayne b: 8/31/60, Laurens, S.C. BL/TL, 6' ", 155 lbs. Deb: 6/11/87

1987 Det-A	0	0	—	2	0	0	0	0	1²	4	0	3	0	37.8	16.20	26	.444	.583	0	—	0	-2	-2	-0	0.0
1988 Pit-N	0	0	—	5	0	0	0	0	5²	5	0	7	3	19.1	0.00	—	.294	.500	0	—	0	2	2	0	0.0
1989 Pit-N	2	2	.500	9	3	0	0	0	14	17	0	13	6	19.3	7.07	47	.327	.462	0	.000	-0	-6	-6	-1	-1.5
Total 3	2	2	.500	16	3	0	0	0	21¹	26	0	23	9	20.7	5.91	58	.333	.485	0	.000	-0	-6	-6	-1	-1.5

● **NICK MADDOX**   Maddox, Nicholas b: 11/9/1886, Govans, Md. d: 11/27/54, Pittsburgh, Pa. BL/TR, 6', 175 lbs. Deb: 9/13/07

1907 Pit-N	5	1	.833	6	6	6	1	0	54	32	0	13	38	8.2	0.83	292	.178	.249	5	.250	2	10	10	-0	1.5
1908 Pit-N	23	8	.742	36	32	22	4	1	260²	209	5	90	70	10.7	2.28	101	.223	.298	25	.266	8	2	1	-1	0.9
1909 *Pit-N	13	8	.619	31	27	17	4	0	203¹	173	2	39	56	10.0	2.21	123	.232	.283	15	.224	4	9	12	-1	1.4
1910 Pit-N	2	3	.400	20	7	2	0	0	87¹	73	0	28	29	10.9	3.40	91	.246	.321	6	.214	1	-4	-3	-0	-0.1
Total 4	43	20	.683	93	72	47	9	1	605¹	487	7	170	193	10.3	2.29	112	.225	.292	51	.244	15	17	19	-2	3.7

● **GREG MADDUX**   Maddux, Gregory Alan b: 4/14/66, San Angelo, Tex. BR/TR, 6', 150 lbs. Deb: 9/3/86 F

1986 Chi-N	2	4	.333	6	5	1	0	0	31	44	3	11	20	16.3	5.52	73	.336	.392	4	.333	1	-6	-5	0	-0.8
1987 Chi-N	6	14	.300	30	27	1	1	0	155²	181	17	74	101	15.0	5.61	76	.294	.374	5	.119	-2	-26	-23	6	-2.2
1988 Chi-N☆	18	8	.692	34	34	9	3	0	249	230	13	81	140	11.6	3.18	113	.244	.309	19	.198	2	7	12	3	1.7
1989 *Chi-N	19	12	.613	35	35	7	1	0	238¹	222	13	82	135	11.7	2.95	128	.249	.317	17	.210	2	15	21	3	3.4
1990 Chi-N	15	15	.500	35	35	8	2	0	237	242	11	71	144	12.0	3.46	118	.265	.321	12	.145	-2	9	16	8	2.6
1991 Chi-N	15	11	.577	37	37	7	2	0	263	232	18	66	198	10.4	3.35	116	.237	.289	18	.205	3	10	15	6	2.4
1992 Chi-N★	20	11	.645	35	35	9	4	0	268	201	7	70	199	9.6	2.18	165	.210	.273	15	.170	2	39	42	6	6.2
1993 *Atl-N	20	10	.667	36	36	8	1	0	267	228	14	52	197	9.6	2.36	170	.232	.274	15	.165	-1	50	49	7	6.1
1994 Atl-N★	16	6	.727	25	25	10	3	0	202	150	4	31	156	8.3	1.56	266	.207	.245	14	.222	2	60	58	3	7.1
Total 9	131	91	.590	273	269	60	17	0	1911	1730	100	538	1290	10.9	3.02	129	.242	.300	119	.185	7	157	187	40	26.5

● **MIKE MADDUX**   Maddux, Michael Ausley b: 8/27/61, Dayton, Ohio BL/TR, 6'2", 180 lbs. Deb: 6/3/86 F

1986 Phi-N	3	7	.300	16	16	0	0	0	78	88	6	34	44	14.4	5.42	71	.286	.362	1	.045	-1	-15	-14	-1	-1.7
1987 Phi-N	2	0	1.000	7	2	0	0	0	17	17	0	5	15	11.6	2.65	160	.254	.306	0	.000	-0	3	3	-0	0.3
1988 Phi-N	4	3	.571	25	11	0	0	0	88²	91	6	34	59	13.2	3.76	95	.275	.351	3	.130	-0	-3	-2	1	0.0
1989 Phi-N	1	3	.250	16	4	2	1	0	43²	52	3	14	26	14.0	5.15	69	.304	.364	0	.000	-1	-8	-8	2	-0.6
1990 LA-N	0	1	.000	11	2	0	0	0	20²	24	3	4	11	12.6	6.53	56	.293	.333	0	.000	-0	-6	-7	-0	-0.3
1991 SD-N	7	2	.778	64	1	0	0	5	98²	78	4	27	57	9.7	2.46	154	.221	.278	1	.077	-0	13	15	1	1.5
1992 SD-N	2	2	.500	50	1	0	0	5	79²	71	2	24	60	10.7	2.37	151	.236	.292	1	.111	-0	10	11	2	0.9
1993 NY-N	3	8	.273	58	0	0	0	5	75	67	5	27	57	11.8	3.60	111	.243	.319	0	.000	-0	4	3	1	0.6
1994 NY-N	2	1	.667	27	0	0	0	2	44	45	7	13	32	11.9	5.11	83	.263	.315	0	.000	-0	-4	-4	1	-0.2
Total 9	24	27	.471	274	37	2	1	18	545¹	533	34	182	361	12.1	3.83	99	.259	.324	6	.068	-4	-7	-2	6	0.5

● **TONY MADIGAN**   Madigan, William J. "Tice" b: 7/1868, Washington, D.C. d: 12/4/54, Washington, D.C. TR, 5'5.5", 126 lbs. Deb: 7/10/1886

| 1886 Was-N | 1 | 13 | .071 | 14 | 14 | 13 | 0 | 0 | 115² | 159 | 3 | 44 | 29 | 15.8 | 5.06 | 65 | .320 | .375 | 4 | .083 | -4 | -22 | -23 | 0 | -2.4 |

● **DAVE MADISON**   Madison, David Pledger b: 2/1/21, Brooksville, Miss. d: 12/8/85, Macon, Miss. BR/TR, 6'3", 190 lbs. Deb: 9/26/50

1950 NY-A	0	0	—	1	0	0	0	0	3	3	1	4	1	12.0	6.00	72	.273	.333	0	—	0	-0	-1	-0	0.0
1952 StL-A	4	2	.667	31	4	0	0	0	78	78	7	48	35	15.0	4.38	89	.264	.374	2	.118	-1	-6	-4	-0	-0.4
Det-A	1	1	.500	10	1	0	0	0	15	16	1	10	7	16.2	7.80	48	.291	.409	0	.000	-0	-7	-7	-0	-0.8
Yr	5	3	.625	41	5	0	0	0	93	94	8	58	42	14.8	4.94	79	.265	.370	2	.105	-1	-13	-11	-0	-1.2
1953 Det-A	3	4	.429	32	1	0	0	0	62	76	7	44	27	17.9	6.82	60	.303	.413	1	.091	-1	-19	-19	-1	-1.9
Total 3	8	7	.533	74	6	0	0	0	158	173	16	103	70	16.2	5.70	70	.282	.392	3	.100	-2	-33	-30	-1	-3.1

● **ALEX MADRID**   Madrid, Alexander b: 4/18/63, Springerville, Ariz BR/TR, 6'3", 200 lbs. Deb: 7/20/87

1987 Mil-A	0	0	—	3	0	0	0	0	5¹	11	1	1	1	20.3	15.19	30	.440	.462	0	—	0	-6	-6	-0	-0.1
1988 Phi-N	1	1	.500	5	2	1	0	0	16¹	15	0	6	8	11.6	2.76	129	.246	.313	0	.000	-0	1	1	-0	0.1
1989 Phi-N	1	2	.333	6	3	0	0	0	24²	32	3	14	13	17.1	5.47	65	.314	.402	0	.000	-0	-5	-5	-1	-0.7
Total 3	2	3	.400	14	5	1	0	0	46¹	58	4	21	16	15.5	5.63	65	.309	.381	0	.000	-0	-11	-10	-1	-0.7

● **HECTOR MAESTRI**   Maestri, Hector Anibal (Garcia) b: 4/19/35, Havana, Cuba BR/TR, 5'10", 158 lbs. Deb: 9/24/60

| 1960 Was-A | 0 | 0 | — | 1 | 0 | 0 | 0 | 0 | 2 | 1 | 0 | 1 | 1 | 9.0 | 0.00 | — | .167 | .286 | 0 | — | 0 | 1 | 1 | -0 | 0.0 |

YEAR TM/L	W	L	PCT	G	GS	CG	SH	SV	IP	H	HR	BB	SO	RAT	ERA	ERA+	OAV	OOB	BH	AVG	PB	PR	/A	PD	TPI
1961 Was-A	0	1	.000	1	1	0	0	0	6	6	1	2	2	12.0	1.50	268	.250	.308	0	.000	-0	2	2	-0	0.3
Total 2	0	1	.000	2	1	0	0	0	8	7	1	3	3	11.3	1.13	354	.233	.303	0	.000	-0	3	3	-0	0.3

● BILL MAGEE   Magee, William J.   b: 1875, Canada   BR/TR, 5'10", 154 lbs.   Deb: 5/18/1897

YEAR TM/L	W	L	PCT	G	GS	CG	SH	SV	IP	H	HR	BB	SO	RAT	ERA	ERA+	OAV	OOB	BH	AVG	PB	PR	/A	PD	TPI
1897 Lou-N	4	12	.250	22	16	13	1	0	155¹	186	6	99	44	17.1	5.39	79	.294	.398	13	.210	-2	-19	-19	1	-1.6
1898 Lou-N	16	15	.516	38	33	29	3	0	295¹	294	8	129	55	13.5	4.05	88	.258	.343	14	.126	-9	-15	-16	-2	-2.3
1899 Lou-N	3	7	.300	12	10	6	1	0	71	91	1	28	13	16.2	5.20	74	.311	.388	3	.111	-2	-11	-11	1	-1.2
Phi-N	3	5	.375	9	9	7	0	0	70	82	0	32	4	15.6	5.66	65	.292	.378	5	.161	-2	-14	-15	-1	-1.5
Was-N	1	4	.200	8	7	4	0	0	42	54	3	28	11	19.1	8.57	46	.311	.427	5	.333	1	-22	-22	1	-1.7
Yr	7	16	.304	29	26	17	1	0	183	227	4	88	28	15.8	6.15	62	.297	.375	13	.178	-4	-47	-48	1	-4.4
1901 StL-N	0	0	—	1	1	0	0	0	8	8	0	4	3	13.5	4.50	71	.259	.344	2	.500	1	-1	-1	-0	0.1
NY-N	0	4	.000	6	5	4	0	0	42¹	56	4	11	14	15.1	5.95	56	.316	.369	2	.143	-1	-12	-12	0	-1.0
Yr	0	4	.000	7	6	4	0	0	50¹	64	4	15	17	14.8	5.72	57	.307	.365	4	.222	1	-13	-14	-0	-0.9
1902 NY-N	0	0	—	2	1	0	0	0	5	5	0	1	2	10.8	3.60	78	.260	.297	0	.000	-0	-0	-0	-0	-0.0
Phi-N	2	4	.333	8	6	6	0	0	53²	61	1	18	15	13.8	3.69	76	.286	.350	4	.211	-0	-5	-5	-0	-0.6
Yr	2	4	.333	10	7	6	0	0	58²	66	1	19	17	13.5	3.68	76	.284	.345	4	.200	-1	-6	-6	-0	-0.6
Total 5	29	51	.363	106	88	69	5	0	742²	837	23	350	161	15.1	4.93	75	.283	.370	48	.169	-13	-99	-102	-0	-9.8

● SAL MAGLIE   Maglie, Salvatore Anthony "The Barber"   b: 4/26/17, Niagara Falls, N.Y   d: 12/28/92, Niagara Falls, N.Y.   BR/TR, 6'2", 180 lbs.   Deb: 8/9/45 C

YEAR TM/L	W	L	PCT	G	GS	CG	SH	SV	IP	H	HR	BB	SO	RAT	ERA	ERA+	OAV	OOB	BH	AVG	PB	PR	/A	PD	TPI
1945 NY-N	5	4	.556	13	10	7	3	0	84¹	72	2	22	32	10.2	2.35	167	.231	.286	5	.167	-1	14	15	0	1.4
1950 NY-N	18	4	.818	47	16	12	5	1	206	169	14	86	96	11.6	2.71	151	.226	.314	8	.121	-1	33	32	3	3.3
1951 *NY-N★	23	6	.793	42	37	22	3	4	298	254	27	86	146	10.4	2.93	134	.230	.289	17	.152	-3	34	33	1	2.9
1952 NY-N☆	18	8	.692	35	31	12	5	1	216	199	16	75	112	11.7	2.92	127	.244	.312	5	.072	-3	20	19	1	1.9
1953 NY-N	8	9	.471	27	24	9	3	0	145¹	158	19	47	80	12.8	4.15	103	.278	.334	13	.271	2	2	-2	0	0.3
1954 *NY-N	14	6	.700	34	32	9	1	2	218¹	222	21	70	117	12.2	3.26	124	.262	.320	8	.127	-2	20	19	0	1.4
1955 NY-N	9	5	.643	23	21	6	0	0	129²	142	18	48	71	13.4	3.75	107	.278	.344	5	.125	-2	4	4	-2	0.0
Cle-A	0	2	.000	10	2	0	0	2	25²	26	0	7	11	11.9	3.86	103	.252	.306	0	.000	-0	0	0	-1	-0.1
1956 Cle-A	0	0	—	2	0	0	0	0	5	6	1	2	2	14.4	3.60	117	.300	.364	0	—	-0	0	0	0	0.0
*Bro-N	13	5	.722	28	26	9	3	0	191	154	21	52	108	9.9	2.87	138	.222	.281	9	.129	-3	19	23	-2	1.5
1957 Bro-N	6	6	.500	19	17	4	1	1	101¹	94	12	26	50	11.0	2.93	142	.245	.300	1	.034	-3	11	14	-1	1.2
NY-A	2	0	1.000	6	3	1	1	3	26	22	1	7	9	10.4	1.73	207	.227	.286	2	.250	0	6	5	-0	0.6
1958 NY-A	1	1	.500	7	3	0	0	0	23¹	27	3	9	7	13.9	4.63	76	.300	.364	1	.143	1	-2	-3	0	-0.1
StL-N	2	6	.250	10	10	2	0	0	53	46	7	14	25	12.4	4.75	87	.232	.324	2	.125	-1	-5	-4	-1	-0.6
Total 10	119	62	.657	303	232	93	25	14	1723	1591	169	562	862	11.5	3.15	127	.245	.309	76	.135	-16	156	160	-2	13.7

● MIKE MAGNANTE   Magnante, Michael Anthony   b: 6/17/65, Glendale, Cal.   BL/TL, 6'1", 180 lbs.   Deb: 4/22/91

YEAR TM/L	W	L	PCT	G	GS	CG	SH	SV	IP	H	HR	BB	SO	RAT	ERA	ERA+	OAV	OOB	BH	AVG	PB	PR	/A	PD	TPI
1991 KC-A	0	1	.000	38	0	0	0	0	55	55	3	23	42	12.5	2.45	168	.262	.335	0	—	0	10	10	-0	0.1
1992 KC-A	4	9	.308	44	12	0	0	0	89¹	115	5	35	31	15.3	4.94	82	.325	.389	0	—	0	-10	-9	2	-1.2
1993 KC-A	1	2	.333	7	6	0	0	0	35¹	37	3	11	16	12.5	4.08	112	.282	.343	0	—	0	1	2	0	0.0
1994 KC-A	2	3	.400	36	1	0	0	0	47	55	5	16	21	13.6	4.60	113	.289	.345	0	—	0	1	3	0	-0.1
Total 4	7	15	.318	125	19	0	0	0	226²	262	16	85	110	13.9	4.13	106	.296	.360	0	—	0	2	6	2	-1.2

● JIM MAGNUSON   Magnuson, James Robert   b: 8/18/46, Marinette, Wis.   d: 5/30/91, Green Bay, Wis.   BR/TL, 6'2", 190 lbs.   Deb: 6/28/70

YEAR TM/L	W	L	PCT	G	GS	CG	SH	SV	IP	H	HR	BB	SO	RAT	ERA	ERA+	OAV	OOB	BH	AVG	PB	PR	/A	PD	TPI
1970 Chi-A	1	5	.167	13	6	0	0	0	44²	45	7	16	20	12.5	4.84	81	.263	.330	0	.000	-1	-6	-5	-0	-0.7
1971 Chi-A	1	1	.500	15	4	0	0	0	30	30	0	16	11	14.4	4.50	80	.265	.366	0	.000	-0	-3	-3	-0	-0.3
1973 NY-A	0	1	.000	8	0	0	0	0	27¹	38	2	9	9	15.5	4.28	86	.342	.392	0	—	0	-1	-2	0	0.0
Total 3	2	7	.222	36	10	0	0	0	102	113	9	41	40	13.9	4.59	82	.286	.358	0	.000	-2	-10	-10	0	-1.0

● JOE MAGRANE   Magrane, Joseph David   b: 7/2/64, Des Moines, Iowa   BR/TL, 6'6", 225 lbs.   Deb: 4/25/87

YEAR TM/L	W	L	PCT	G	GS	CG	SH	SV	IP	H	HR	BB	SO	RAT	ERA	ERA+	OAV	OOB	BH	AVG	PB	PR	/A	PD	TPI
1987 *StL-N	9	7	.563	27	26	4	2	0	170¹	157	9	60	101	12.0	3.54	117	.245	.320	7	.135	1	10	12	-0	1.1
1988 StL-N	5	9	.357	24	24	4	3	0	165¹	133	6	51	100	10.1	2.18	160	.217	.280	8	.167	1	23	24	2	2.5
1989 StL-N	18	9	.667	34	33	9	3	0	234²	219	5	72	127	11.4	2.91	124	.251	.316	11	.138	1	15	19	-1	2.1
1990 StL-N	10	17	.370	31	31	3	2	0	203¹	204	10	59	100	12.2	3.59	106	.264	.322	7	.127	0	5	5	1	0.8
1992 StL-N	1	2	.333	5	5	0	0	0	31¹	34	2	15	20	14.6	4.02	84	.279	.367	2	.200	1	-2	-2	-0	-0.1
1993 StL-N	8	10	.444	22	20	0	0	0	116	127	15	37	38	13.1	4.97	80	.286	.348	4	.114	-1	-12	-13	-1	-1.8
Cal-A	3	2	.600	8	8	0	0	0	48	48	4	21	24	12.9	3.94	114	.265	.342	0	—	0	2	3	2	0.4
1994 Cal-A	2	6	.250	20	11	1	0	0	74	89	18	51	33	17.8	7.30	61	.300	.412	0	—	0	-21	-19	0	-1.8
Total 7	56	62	.475	171	158	21	10	0	1043	1011	69	366	543	12.2	3.65	107	.257	.326	39	.139	3	21	28	4	3.2

● PETE MAGRINI   Magrini, Peter Alexander   b: 6/8/42, San Francisco, Cal.   BR/TR, 6', 195 lbs.   Deb: 4/13/66

YEAR TM/L	W	L	PCT	G	GS	CG	SH	SV	IP	H	HR	BB	SO	RAT	ERA	ERA+	OAV	OOB	BH	AVG	PB	PR	/A	PD	TPI
1966 Bos-A	0	1	.000	3	1	0	0	0	7¹	8	0	8	3	20.9	9.82	39	.308	.486	0	.000	-0	-5	-5	-0	-0.6

● ART MAHAFFEY   Mahaffey, Arthur   b: 6/4/38, Cincinnati, Ohio   BR/TR, 6'2", 200 lbs.   Deb: 7/30/60

YEAR TM/L	W	L	PCT	G	GS	CG	SH	SV	IP	H	HR	BB	SO	RAT	ERA	ERA+	OAV	OOB	BH	AVG	PB	PR	/A	PD	TPI
1960 Phi-N	7	3	.700	14	12	5	1	0	93¹	78	9	34	56	10.9	2.31	168	.229	.301	3	.100	-2	15	16	-1	1.5
1961 Phi-N★	11	19	.367	36	32	12	3	0	219¹	205	27	70	158	11.6	4.10	99	.249	.314	8	.127	-2	-2	-1	-2	-0.4
1962 Phi-N★	19	14	.576	41	39	20	2	0	274	253	36	81	177	11.4	3.94	98	.246	.309	13	.141	1	0	-2	-4	-0.6
1963 Phi-N	7	10	.412	26	22	6	1	0	149	143	18	48	97	11.8	3.99	81	.255	.319	10	.200	2	-12	-12	-1	-1.2
1964 Phi-N	12	9	.571	34	29	2	2	0	157¹	161	17	82	80	14.2	4.52	77	.269	.362	6	.120	0	-17	-18	-2	-2.4
1965 Phi-N	2	5	.286	22	9	1	0	0	71	82	11	32	52	15.3	6.21	56	.294	.381	2	.095	-1	-21	-22	-1	-2.1
1966 StL-N	1	4	.200	12	5	0	0	1	35	37	7	21	19	15.2	6.43	56	.276	.378	0	.000	-1	-11	-11	-1	-1.6
Total 7	59	64	.480	185	148	46	9	1	999	959	125	368	639	12.3	4.17	89	.255	.328	42	.134	-2	-47	-50	-11	-6.8

● ROY MAHAFFEY   Mahaffey, Lee Roy "Popeye"   b: 2/9/03, Belton, S.C.   d: 7/23/69, Anderson, S.C.   BR/TR, 6', 180 lbs.   Deb: 8/31/26

YEAR TM/L	W	L	PCT	G	GS	CG	SH	SV	IP	H	HR	BB	SO	RAT	ERA	ERA+	OAV	OOB	BH	AVG	PB	PR	/A	PD	TPI
1926 Pit-N	0	0	—	4	0	0	0	0	4²	5	0	1	3	13.5	0.00	—	.294	.368	0	.000	-0	2	2	-0	-0.1
1927 Pit-N	1	0	1.000	2	1	0	0	0	9¹	9	0	9	4	20.3	7.71	53	.300	.500	2	.400	0	-4	-4	-0	-0.3
1930 Phi-A	9	5	.643	33	16	6	0	0	152²	186	16	53	38	14.3	5.01	93	.298	.357	7	.119	-5	-6	-6	-1	-1.0
1931 *Phi-A	15	4	.789	30	20	8	0	2	162¹	161	9	82	59	13.6	4.21	107	.258	.347	12	.190	1	3	5	-3	0.3
1932 Phi-A	13	13	.500	37	28	13	0	0	222²	245	27	96	106	14.0	5.09	89	.274	.348	15	.172	-1	-15	-14	-2	-1.6
1933 Phi-A	13	10	.565	33	23	9	0	0	179¹	198	5	74	66	13.9	5.17	83	.275	.346	14	.215	-0	-18	-18	-2	-2.0
1934 Phi-A	6	7	.462	37	14	3	0	2	129	142	10	56	37	13.8	5.37	82	.276	.347	13	.271	2	-13	-14	-2	-1.1
1935 Phi-A	8	4	.667	27	17	5	0	0	136	153	11	42	39	13.2	3.90	116	.283	.341	9	.176	-2	8	10	0	0.4
1936 StL-A	2	6	.250	21	9	1	0	1	60	82	6	40	13	18.5	8.10	66	.315	.409	1	.063	-1	-20	-18	-2	-2.2
Total 9	67	49	.578	224	128	45	0	5	1056	1181	84	452	365	14.1	5.01	90	.280	.353	73	.184	-7	-63	-57	-13	-7.6

● LOU MAHAFFEY   Mahaffey, Louis Wood   b: 1/3/1874, Kentucky   d: 10/26/49, Torrance, Cal.   BR, 5'9", 170 lbs.   Deb: 4/26/1898

YEAR TM/L	W	L	PCT	G	GS	CG	SH	SV	IP	H	HR	BB	SO	RAT	ERA	ERA+	OAV	OOB	BH	AVG	PB	PR	/A	PD	TPI
1898 Lou-N	0	1	.000	1	1	1	0	0	9	10	0	5	1	15.0	3.00	119	.279	.367	0	.000	-0	1	1	-0	0.0

● ART MAHAN   Mahan, Arthur Leo   b: 6/8/13, Somerville, Mass.   BL/TL, 5'11", 178 lbs.   Deb: 4/30/40 ◆

YEAR TM/L	W	L	PCT	G	GS	CG	SH	SV	IP	H	HR	BB	SO	RAT	ERA	ERA+	OAV	OOB	BH	AVG	PB	PR	/A	PD	TPI
1940 Phi-N	0	0	—	1	0	0	0	0	1	1	0	0	1	18.0	0.00	—	.333	.333	133	.244	0	0	0	0	0.0

● MICKEY MAHLER   Mahler, Michael James   b: 7/30/52, Montgomery, Ala.   BB/TL, 6'3", 189 lbs.   Deb: 9/13/77 F

YEAR TM/L	W	L	PCT	G	GS	CG	SH	SV	IP	H	HR	BB	SO	RAT	ERA	ERA+	OAV	OOB	BH	AVG	PB	PR	/A	PD	TPI
1977 Atl-N	1	2	.333	5	5	0	0	0	23	31	4	9	14	16.0	6.26	71	.326	.390	3	.500	2	-6	-5	-0	-0.4
1978 Atl-N	4	11	.267	34	21	1	0	0	134²	130	16	66	92	13.6	4.68	87	.255	.349	4	.098	-1	-16	-9	-1	-1.3
1979 Atl-N	5	11	.313	26	18	1	0	0	100	123	11	47	71	15.6	5.85	69	.304	.381	3	.111	-1	-24	-20	-1	-2.9
1980 Pit-N	0	0	—	2	0	0	0	0	1	4	1	3	1	63.0	63.00	6	.571	.700	0	—	0	-7	-7	0	0.0

YEAR TM/L	W	L	PCT	G	GS	CG	SH	SV	IP	H	HR	BB	SO	RAT	ERA	ERA+	OAV	OOB	BH	AVG	PB	PR	/A	PD	TPI
1981 Cal-A	0	0	—	6	0	0	0	0	6¹	1	0	2	5	4.3	0.00	—	.056	.150	0	—	0	3	3	0	0.0
1982 Cal-A	2	0	1.000	6	0	0	0	0	8	9	0	6	5	16.9	1.13	360	.300	.417	0	—	0	3	3	-0	0.6
1985 Mon-N	1	4	.200	9	7	1	1	1	48¹	40	3	24	32	12.1	3.54	96	.229	.325	3	.188	1	0	-1	-1	-0.1
Det-A	1	2	.333	3	2	0	0	0	20²	19	2	4	14	10.0	1.74	234	.241	.277	0	—	0	6	5	-0	0.8
1986 Tex-A	0	2	.000	29	5	0	0	3	63	71	3	29	28	14.7	4.14	104	.295	.377	0	—	0	-0	1	-0	0.0
Tor-A	0	0	—	2	0	0	0	0	1	1	0	0	0	18.0	0.00	—	.200	.333	0	—	0	1	1	0	0.0
Yr	0	2	.000	31	5	0	0	3	64	72	3	29	28	14.3	4.08	105	.285	.360	0	—	0	1	2	0	0.0
Total 8	14	32	.304	122	58	3	1	4	406	429	40	190	262	14.1	4.68	86	.274	.359	13	.144	-1	-41	-29	-3	-3.3

● RICK MAHLER   Mahler, Richard Keith   b: 8/5/53, Austin, Tex.   BR/TR, 6'1", 202 lbs.   Deb: 4/20/79   F

YEAR TM/L	W	L	PCT	G	GS	CG	SH	SV	IP	H	HR	BB	SO	RAT	ERA	ERA+	OAV	OOB	BH	AVG	PB	PR	/A	PD	TPI
1979 Atl-N	0	0	—	15	0	0	0	0	22	28	4	11	12	16.0	6.14	66	.311	.386	1	.500	0	-6	-5	-0	0.0
1980 Atl-N	0	0	—	9	0	0	0	0	3²	2	0	0	1	4.9	2.45	152	.154	.154	0	—	0	1	0	0	0.0
1981 Atl-N	8	6	.571	34	14	1	0	2	112¹	109	5	43	54	12.3	2.80	128	.258	.328	4	.148	-1	9	10	1	1.2
1982 *Atl-N	9	10	.474	39	33	5	2	0	205¹	213	18	62	105	12.1	4.21	89	.272	.327	11	.190	2	-14	-11	2	-0.6
1983 Atl-N	0	0	—	10	0	0	0	0	14¹	16	0	9	7	15.7	5.02	77	.296	.397	0	.000	-0	-2	-2	-0	0.0
1984 Atl-N	13	10	.565	38	29	9	1	0	222	209	13	62	106	11.1	3.12	123	.251	.305	21	.296	5	12	18	2	2.6
1985 Atl-N	17	15	.531	39	39	6	1	0	266²	272	24	79	107	11.9	3.48	111	.268	.322	14	.156	-1	3	11	1	1.3
1986 Atl-N	14	18	.438	39	39	7	1	0	237²	283	25	95	137	14.4	4.88	81	.301	.367	16	.193	2	-31	-24	2	-2.6
1987 Atl-N	8	13	.381	39	28	3	1	0	197	212	24	95	95	13.7	4.98	87	.283	.357	11	.169	1	-20	-14	2	-1.0
1988 Atl-N	9	16	.360	39	34	5	0	0	249	279	17	42	131	11.9	3.69	100	.282	.317	9	.125	-2	-7	-0	1	-0.1
1989 Cin-N	9	13	.409	40	31	5	2	0	220²	242	15	51	102	12.4	3.83	94	.282	.329	11	.177	2	-8	-6	-0	-0.4
1990 *Cin-N	7	6	.538	35	16	2	1	4	134²	134	16	39	68	11.8	4.28	92	.261	.317	4	.114	-1	-7	-5	-0	-0.6
1991 Mon-N	1	3	.250	10	6	0	0	0	37¹	37	2	15	17	12.5	3.62	100	.268	.340	1	.111	-0	0	1	0	0.0
Atl-N	1	1	.500	13	2	0	0	0	28²	33	2	13	10	15.1	5.65	69	.282	.364	1	.200	-0	-6	-6	-0	-0.3
Yr	2	4	.333	23	8	0	0	0	66	70	4	28	27	13.6	4.50	83	.273	.350	2	.143	-0	-6	-6	-1	-0.3
Total 13	96	111	.464	392	271	43	9	6	1951¹	2069	165	606	952	12.5	3.99	96	.275	.332	104	.179	7	-77	-33	10	-0.5

● PAT MAHOMES   Mahomes, Patrick Lavon   b: 8/9/70, Bryan, Tex.   BR/TR, 6'1", 175 lbs.   Deb: 4/12/92

YEAR TM/L	W	L	PCT	G	GS	CG	SH	SV	IP	H	HR	BB	SO	RAT	ERA	ERA+	OAV	OOB	BH	AVG	PB	PR	/A	PD	TPI
1992 Min-A	3	4	.429	14	13	0	0	0	69²	73	5	37	44	14.2	5.04	80	.279	.368	0	—	0	-9	-8	-1	-1.0
1993 Min-A	1	5	.167	12	5	0	0	0	37¹	47	8	16	23	15.4	7.71	56	.309	.379	0	—	0	-14	-14	0	-1.8
1994 Min-A	9	5	.643	21	21	0	0	0	120	121	22	62	53	13.8	4.72	103	.269	.359	0	—	0	1	2	0	0.2
Total 3	13	14	.481	47	39	0	0	0	227	241	35	115	120	14.2	5.31	85	.279	.365	0	—	0	-22	-20	-1	-2.6

● AL MAHON   Mahon, Alfred Gwinn "Lefty"   b: 9/23/09, Albion, Neb.   d: 12/26/77, New Haven, Conn.   BL/TL, 5'11", 160 lbs.   Deb: 4/22/30

YEAR TM/L	W	L	PCT	G	GS	CG	SH	SV	IP	H	HR	BB	SO	RAT	ERA	ERA+	OAV	OOB	BH	AVG	PB	PR	/A	PD	TPI
1930 Phi-A	0	0	—	3	0	0	0	0	4¹	11	0	7	0	37.4	22.85	20	.579	.692	0	.000	0	-9	-9	-0	-1.0

● CHRIS MAHONEY   Mahoney, Christopher John   b: 6/11/1885, Milton, Mass.   d: 7/15/54, Visalia, Cal.   BR/TR, 5'9", 160 lbs.   Deb: 7/12/10

YEAR TM/L	W	L	PCT	G	GS	CG	SH	SV	IP	H	HR	BB	SO	RAT	ERA	ERA+	OAV	OOB	BH	AVG	PB	PR	/A	PD	TPI
1910 Bos-A	0	1	.000	2	1	0	0	1	11	16	1	5	6	17.2	3.27	78	.327	.389	1	.143	-0	-1	-1	1	-0.1

● MIKE MAHONEY   Mahoney, George W. "Big Mike"   b: 12/5/1873, Boston, Mass.   d: 1/3/40, Boston, Mass.   BR, 6'4", 220 lbs.   Deb: 5/18/1897   ♦

YEAR TM/L	W	L	PCT	G	GS	CG	SH	SV	IP	H	HR	BB	SO	RAT	ERA	ERA+	OAV	OOB	BH	AVG	PB	PR	/A	PD	TPI
1897 Bos-N	0	0	—	1	0	0	0	0	1	3	0	1	1	36.0	18.00	25	.511	.582	1	.500	0	-2	-2	0	0.0

● BOB MAHONEY   Mahoney, Robert Paul   b: 6/20/28, LeRoy, Minn.   BR/TR, 6'1", 185 lbs.   Deb: 5/3/51

YEAR TM/L	W	L	PCT	G	GS	CG	SH	SV	IP	H	HR	BB	SO	RAT	ERA	ERA+	OAV	OOB	BH	AVG	PB	PR	/A	PD	TPI
1951 Chi-A	0	0	—	3	0	0	0	0	6²	5	1	5	3	13.5	5.40	75	.208	.345	0	—	0	-1	-1	-0	0.0
StL-A	2	5	.286	30	4	0	0	0	81	86	7	41	30	14.1	4.44	99	.274	.358	4	.222	-0	-3	-0	-1	-0.1
Yr	2	5	.286	33	4	0	0	0	87²	91	8	46	33	14.1	4.52	97	.269	.357	4	.222	-0	-4	-1	-1	-0.1
1952 StL-A	0	0	—	3	0	0	0	0	3	8	0	4	1	36.0	18.00	22	.500	.600	0	—	0	-5	-5	-0	0.0
Total 2	2	5	.286	36	4	0	0	0	90²	99	8	50	34	14.8	4.96	88	.280	.369	4	.222	-0	-9	-6	-1	-0.1

● DUSTER MAILS   Mails, John Walter "Walter" or "The Great"   b: 10/1/1894, San Quentin, Cal.   d: 7/5/74, San Francisco, Cal   BL/TL, 6', 195 lbs.   Deb: 9/28/15

YEAR TM/L	W	L	PCT	G	GS	CG	SH	SV	IP	H	HR	BB	SO	RAT	ERA	ERA+	OAV	OOB	BH	AVG	PB	PR	/A	PD	TPI
1915 Bro-N	0	1	.000	2	0	0	0	0	5	6	2	5	3	19.8	3.60	77	.333	.478	-0	-0	-0	-0	-0	0	-0.1
1916 Bro-N	0	1	.000	11	0	0	0	0	17¹	15	1	9	13	12.5	3.63	74	.242	.338	1	.250	0	-2	-2	-0	-0.1
1920 *Cle-A	7	0	1.000	9	8	6	2	0	63¹	54	1	18	25	10.2	1.85	206	.230	.285	4	.200	0	14	14	-1	1.3
1921 Cle-A	14	8	.636	34	24	10	2	2	194¹	210	4	89	87	13.9	3.94	108	.283	.361	6	.094	-4	8	7	-3	0.0
1922 Cle-A	4	7	.364	26	13	4	0	1	104	122	8	40	54	14.4	5.28	76	.291	.359	5	.161	-0	-14	-15	-1	-1.3
1925 StL-N	7	7	.500	21	14	9	0	0	131	145	11	58	49	14.4	4.60	94	.279	.360	6	.133	-2	-5	-4	-1	-0.7
1926 StL-N	0	1	.000	1	0	0	0	0	1	2	0	1	1	27.0	9.00	—	.400	.500	0	—	0	0	0	0	0.5
Total 7	32	25	.561	104	59	29	5	2	516	554	27	220	232	13.7	4.10	100	.277	.352	22	.133	-7	0	0	-5	0.0

● WOODY MAIN   Main, Forrest Harry   b: 2/12/22, Delano, Cal.   d: 6/27/92, Whittier, Cal.   BR/TR, 6'3.5", 195 lbs.   Deb: 4/21/48

YEAR TM/L	W	L	PCT	G	GS	CG	SH	SV	IP	H	HR	BB	SO	RAT	ERA	ERA+	OAV	OOB	BH	AVG	PB	PR	/A	PD	TPI
1948 Pit-N	1	1	.500	17	0	0	0	0	27	35	4	19	12	18.0	8.33	49	.324	.425	0	.000	-0	-13	-13	0	-0.8
1950 Pit-N	1	0	1.000	12	0	0	0	1	20¹	21	2	11	12	14.6	4.87	90	.256	.351	2	.400	0	-2	-1	0	0.0
1952 Pit-N	2	12	.143	48	11	2	0	2	153¹	149	14	52	79	11.8	4.46	90	.253	.314	2	.054	-3	-12	-8	-3	-1.3
1953 Pit-N	0	0	—	2	0	0	0	0	4	5	1	2	4	15.8	11.25	40	.294	.368	0	—	0	-3	-3	-0	0.0
Total 4	4	13	.235	79	11	2	0	3	204²	210	21	84	107	13.0	5.14	79	.264	.335	4	.091	-3	-30	-25	-3	-2.1

● ALEX MAIN   Main, Miles Grant   b: 5/13/1884, Montrose, Mich.   d: 12/29/65, Royal Oak, Mich.   BL/TR, 6'5", 195 lbs.   Deb: 4/18/14

YEAR TM/L	W	L	PCT	G	GS	CG	SH	SV	IP	H	HR	BB	SO	RAT	ERA	ERA+	OAV	OOB	BH	AVG	PB	PR	/A	PD	TPI
1914 Det-A	6	6	.500	32	12	5	1	3	138¹	131	2	59	55	12.6	2.67	105	.259	.340	4	.100	-2	1	2	4	0.4
1915 KC-F	13	14	.481	35	28	18	2	3	230	181	4	75	91	10.2	2.54	103	.222	.291	15	.197	-0	5	2	3	0.6
1918 Phi-N	2	2	.500	8	4	1	1	0	35	30	1	16	14	13.1	4.63	65	.240	.349	1	.091	-1	-7	-6	-0	-0.8
Total 3	21	22	.488	75	44	24	4	6	403¹	342	7	150	160	11.3	2.77	98	.236	.313	20	.157	-3	-1	-2	7	0.2

● JIM MAINS   Mains, James Royal   b: 6/12/22, Bridgton, Maine   d: 3/17/69, Bridgton, Maine   BR/TR, 6'2", 190 lbs.   Deb: 8/22/43

YEAR TM/L	W	L	PCT	G	GS	CG	SH	SV	IP	H	HR	BB	SO	RAT	ERA	ERA+	OAV	OOB	BH	AVG	PB	PR	/A	PD	TPI
1943 Phi-A	0	1	.000	1	1	1	0	0	8	9	0	3	4	13.5	5.63	60	.281	.343	0	.000	0	-2	-2	-0	-0.2

● WILLARD MAINS   Mains, Willard Eben "Grasshopper"   b: 7/7/1868, N.Windham, Maine   d: 5/23/23, Bridgton, Maine   TR, 6'2", 190 lbs.   Deb: 8/3/1888

YEAR TM/L	W	L	PCT	G	GS	CG	SH	SV	IP	H	HR	BB	SO	RAT	ERA	ERA+	OAV	OOB	BH	AVG	PB	PR	/A	PD	TPI
1888 Chi-N	1	1	.500	2	2	1	0	0	11	8	0	6	5	12.3	4.91	62	.211	.333	1	.143	-0	-3	-2	-0	-0.4
1891 Cin-a	12	12	.500	30	23	19	0	0	204	196	3	107	76	13.9	2.69	153	.244	.342	22	.244	1	23	32	3	3.5
Mil-a	0	2	.000	2	2	1	0	0	10	14	1	10	2	21.6	10.80	41	.320	.447	3	.600	1	-8	-7	-0	-0.9
Yr	12	14	.462	32	25	20	0	0	214	210	4	117	78	13.8	3.07	135	.245	.335	25	.263	2	16	25	3	2.6
1896 Bos-N	3	2	.600	8	5	3	0	1	42²	43	1	31	13	16.0	5.48	83	.260	.383	6	.273	-0	-5	-4	-0	-0.4
Total 3	16	17	.485	42	32	24	0	1	267²	261	5	154	96	14.5	3.53	118	.249	.353	32	.258	1	8	19	3	1.8

● FRANK MAKOSKY   Makosky, Frank   b: 1/20/10, Boonton, N.J.   d: 1/10/87, Stroudsburg, Pa.   BR/TR, 6'1", 185 lbs.   Deb: 4/30/37

YEAR TM/L	W	L	PCT	G	GS	CG	SH	SV	IP	H	HR	BB	SO	RAT	ERA	ERA+	OAV	OOB	BH	AVG	PB	PR	/A	PD	TPI
1937 NY-A	5	2	.714	26	1	1	0	3	58	64	6	24	27	13.7	4.97	90	.277	.345	5	.313	1	-2	-3	2	-0.1

● TOM MAKOWSKI   Makowski, Thomas Anthony   b: 12/22/50, Buffalo, N.Y.   BR/TL, 5'11", 185 lbs.   Deb: 5/1/75

YEAR TM/L	W	L	PCT	G	GS	CG	SH	SV	IP	H	HR	BB	SO	RAT	ERA	ERA+	OAV	OOB	BH	AVG	PB	PR	/A	PD	TPI
1975 Det-A	0	0	—	3	0	0	0	0	9¹	10	2	9	3	18.3	4.82	83	.278	.422	0	—	0	-1	-1	0	-0.1

● JOHN MALARKEY   Malarkey, John S. "Liz"   b: 5/4/1872, Springfield, Ohio   d: 10/29/49, Cincinnati, Ohio   TR, 5'11", 155 lbs.   Deb: 9/21/1894

YEAR TM/L	W	L	PCT	G	GS	CG	SH	SV	IP	H	HR	BB	SO	RAT	ERA	ERA+	OAV	OOB	BH	AVG	PB	PR	/A	PD	TPI
1894 Was-N	2	1	.667	3	3	3	0	0	26	42	1	5	3	16.3	4.15	127	.359	.386	1	.071	-2	3	3	-1	0.0
1895 Was-N	0	8	.000	22	8	5	0	2	100²	129	6	50	32	18.1	5.99	80	.316	.410	5	.135	-4	-14	-13	-1	-1.2
1896 Was-N	1	0	1.000	1	1	0	0	0	7	9	0	2	0	15.4	1.29	343	.309	.374	1	.500	1	2	2	0	0.4
1899 Chi-N	0	1	.000	1	1	0	0	0	9	19	0	5	7	25.0	13.00	29	.426	.494	1	.200	0	-9	-9	0	-0.6
1902 Bos-N	8	10	.444	21	19	17	1	1	170¹	158	0	58	39	11.4	2.59	109	.246	.308	13	.210	-0	4	4	2	0.9

YEAR TM/L	W	L	PCT	G	GS	CG	SH	SV	IP	H	HR	BB	SO	RAT	ERA	ERA+	OAV	OOB	BH	AVG	PB	PR	/A	PD	TPI
1903 Bos-N	11	16	.407	32	27	25	2	0	253	266	5	96	98	13.3	3.09	104	.272	.344	14	.161	1	5	3	2	0.6
Total 6	21	37	.362	80	59	51	3	3	566	629	10	227	179	13.9	3.64	96	.281	.353	35	.169	-2	-8	-9	2	0.1

● **BILL MALARKEY**   Malarkey, William John b: 11/26/1878, Port Byron, Ill. d: 12/12/56, Phoenix, Ariz. BR/TR, 5'10", 185 lbs. Deb: 4/16/08

YEAR TM/L	W	L	PCT	G	GS	CG	SH	SV	IP	H	HR	BB	SO	RAT	ERA	ERA+	OAV	OOB	BH	AVG	PB	PR	/A	PD	TPI
1908 NY-N	0	2	.000	15	0	0	0	2	35	31	1	10	12	10.8	2.57	94	.242	.302	0	.000	-1	-1	-1	-0	-0.2

● **CARLOS MALDONADO**   Maldonado, Carlos Cesar (Delgado) b: 10/18/66, Chepo, Panama BB/TR, 6'2", 210 lbs. Deb: 9/16/90

YEAR TM/L	W	L	PCT	G	GS	CG	SH	SV	IP	H	HR	BB	SO	RAT	ERA	ERA+	OAV	OOB	BH	AVG	PB	PR	/A	PD	TPI
1990 KC-A	0	0	—	4	0	0	0	0	6	9	0	4	9	19.5	9.00	43	.346	.433	0	—	0	-3	-3	-0	0.1
1991 KC-A	0	0	—	5	0	0	0	0	7²	11	0	9	1	23.5	8.22	50	.333	.476	0	—	0	-4	-3	-0	-0.1
1993 Mil-A	2	2	.500	29	0	0	0	1	37¹	40	2	17	18	13.7	4.58	93	.282	.358	0	—	0	-1	-1	0	-0.1
Total 3	2	2	.500	38	0	0	0	1	51	60	2	30	28	15.9	5.65	74	.299	.390	0	—	0	-8	-8	-1	-0.1

● **CY MALIS**   Malis, Cyrus Sol b: 2/26/07, Philadelphia, Pa. d: 1/12/71, N.Hollywood, Cal. BR/TR, 5'11", 175 lbs. Deb: 8/17/34

YEAR TM/L	W	L	PCT	G	GS	CG	SH	SV	IP	H	HR	BB	SO	RAT	ERA	ERA+	OAV	OOB	BH	AVG	PB	PR	/A	PD	TPI
1934 Phi-N	0	0	—	1	0	0	0	0	3²	4	0	2	1	14.7	4.91	96	.267	.353	0	—	0	-0	-0	-0	0.0

● **MAL MALLETTE**   Mallette, Malcolm Francis b: 1/30/22, Syracuse, N.Y. BL/TL, 6'2", 200 lbs. Deb: 9/25/50

YEAR TM/L	W	L	PCT	G	GS	CG	SH	SV	IP	H	HR	BB	SO	RAT	ERA	ERA+	OAV	OOB	BH	AVG	PB	PR	/A	PD	TPI
1950 Bro-N	0	0	—	2	0	0	0	0	1¹	2	0	1	2	20.3	0.00	—	.333	.429	0	—	0	1	1	0	0.0

● **ROB MALLICOAT**   Mallicoat, Robbin Dale b: 11/16/64, St.Helens, Ore. BL/TL, 6'3", 180 lbs. Deb: 9/11/87

YEAR TM/L	W	L	PCT	G	GS	CG	SH	SV	IP	H	HR	BB	SO	RAT	ERA	ERA+	OAV	OOB	BH	AVG	PB	PR	/A	PD	TPI
1987 Hou-N	0	0	—	4	1	0	0	0	6²	8	0	6	4	18.9	6.75	58	.320	.452	0	—	0	-2	-2	0	0.0
1991 Hou-N	0	2	.000	24	0	0	0	1	23¹	22	2	13	18	14.3	3.86	91	.259	.370	0	.000	-0	-1	-1	-1	-0.2
1992 Hou-N	0	0	—	23	0	0	0	0	23²	26	2	19	20	19.0	7.23	47	.283	.431	0	.000	-0	-10	-10	-0	-0.2
Total 3	0	2	.000	51	1	0	0	1	53²	56	4	38	42	16.9	5.70	61	.277	.409	0	.000	-0	-12	-13	-1	-0.2

● **ALEX MALLOY**   Malloy, Archibald Alexander "Lick" b: 10/31/1886, Laurinburg, N.C. d: 3/1/61, Ferris, Tex. BR/TR, 6'2", 180 lbs. Deb: 9/10/10

YEAR TM/L	W	L	PCT	G	GS	CG	SH	SV	IP	H	HR	BB	SO	RAT	ERA	ERA+	OAV	OOB	BH	AVG	PB	PR	/A	PD	TPI
1910 StL-A	0	6	.000	7	6	4	0	0	52²	47	0	17	27	11.3	2.56	97	.261	.332	1	.063	-1	-0	-1	0	-0.2

● **HERM MALLOY**   Malloy, Herman "Tug" b: 6/1/1885, Massillon, Ohio d: 5/9/42, Nimishillen, Ohio BR/TR, 6', Deb: 10/6/07

YEAR TM/L	W	L	PCT	G	GS	CG	SH	SV	IP	H	HR	BB	SO	RAT	ERA	ERA+	OAV	OOB	BH	AVG	PB	PR	/A	PD	TPI
1907 Det-A	0	1	.000	1	1	1	0	0	8	13	1	5	6	20.3	5.63	46	.366	.444	1	.250	0	-3	-3	-0	-0.3
1908 Det-A	0	2	.000	3	2	2	0	0	17	20	1	4	8	13.8	3.71	65	.278	.333	3	.333	1	-2	-2	1	-0.1
Total 2	0	3	.000	4	3	3	0	0	25	33	2	9	14	15.8	4.32	57	.307	.371	4	.308	1	-5	-5	1	-0.4

● **BOB MALLOY**   Malloy, Robert Paul b: 5/28/18, Canonsburg, Pa. BR/TR, 5'11", 185 lbs. Deb: 5/4/43

YEAR TM/L	W	L	PCT	G	GS	CG	SH	SV	IP	H	HR	BB	SO	RAT	ERA	ERA+	OAV	OOB	BH	AVG	PB	PR	/A	PD	TPI
1943 Cin-N	0	0	—	6	0	0	0	0	10	14	1	8	4	19.8	6.30	53	.778	.846	2	.667	1	-3	-3	-0	0.1
1944 Cin-N	1	1	.500	9	0	0	0	0	23¹	22	0	11	4	12.7	3.09	113	.265	.351	0	.000	-1	1	1	0	0.2
1946 Cin-N	2	5	.286	27	3	1	0	2	72	71	2	26	24	12.4	2.75	122	.265	.334	5	.278	1	5	5	-1	0.5
1947 Cin-N	0	0	—	1	0	0	0	0	1	3	1	0	1	27.0	18.00	18	.600	.600	0	—	0	-2	-2	0	0.0
1949 StL-A	1	1	.500	5	0	0	0	0	9²	6	0	7	2	12.1	2.79	162	.200	.351	0	.000	-0	2	2	0	0.3
Total 5	4	7	.364	48	3	1	0	2	116	116	4	52	35	13.2	3.26	106	.287	.371	7	.226	1	3	3	-1	0.9

● **BOB MALLOY**   Malloy, Robert William b: 11/24/64, Arlington, Va. BR/TR, 6'5", 200 lbs. Deb: 5/26/87

YEAR TM/L	W	L	PCT	G	GS	CG	SH	SV	IP	H	HR	BB	SO	RAT	ERA	ERA+	OAV	OOB	BH	AVG	PB	PR	/A	PD	TPI
1987 Tex-A	0	0	—	2	2	0	0	0	11	13	6	3	8	13.1	6.55	68	.271	.314	0	—	0	-3	-3	-0	0.0
1990 Mon-N	0	0	—	1	0	0	0	0	2	1	0	1	1	9.0	0.00	—	.143	.250	0	—	0	1	1	-0	0.0
Total 2	0	0	—	3	2	0	0	0	13	14	6	4	9	12.5	5.54	78	.255	.305	0	—	0	-2	-2	-0	0.0

● **MALONE**   Malone Deb: 6/20/1872

YEAR TM/L	W	L	PCT	G	GS	CG	SH	SV	IP	H	HR	BB	SO	RAT	ERA	ERA+	OAV	OOB	BH	AVG	PB	PR	/A	PD	TPI
1872 Eck-n	0	3	.000	3	3	3	0	0	27	98	1	0	0	32.7	11.33	31	.516	.516	5	.313	1	-23	-24		-1.3

● **CHUCK MALONE**   Malone, Charles Ray b: 7/8/65, Harrisburg, Ark. BR/TR, 6'7", 250 lbs. Deb: 9/6/90

YEAR TM/L	W	L	PCT	G	GS	CG	SH	SV	IP	H	HR	BB	SO	RAT	ERA	ERA+	OAV	OOB	BH	AVG	PB	PR	/A	PD	TPI
1990 Phi-N	1	0	1.000	7	0	0	0	0	7¹	3	1	11	7	17.2	3.68	104	.130	.412	0	—	0	0	0	-0	0.0

● **PAT MALONE**   Malone, Perce Leigh b: 9/25/02, Altoona, Pa. d: 5/13/43, Altoona, Pa. BL/TR, 6', 200 lbs. Deb: 4/12/28

YEAR TM/L	W	L	PCT	G	GS	CG	SH	SV	IP	H	HR	BB	SO	RAT	ERA	ERA+	OAV	OOB	BH	AVG	PB	PR	/A	PD	TPI
1928 Chi-N	18	13	.581	42	25	16	2	2	250²	218	15	99	155	11.6	2.84	136	.236	.314	18	.189	1	32	28	0	3.3
1929 *Chi-N	**22**	10	.688	40	30	19	**5**	2	267	283	12	102	**166**	13.2	3.57	129	.276	.345	22	.210	2	34	31	-3	3.0
1930 Chi-N	20	9	.690	45	35	**22**	1	4	271²	290	14	96	142	13.0	3.94	124	.271	.334	26	.248	5	31	28	-2	2.8
1931 Chi-N	16	9	.640	39	30	12	2	0	228²	229	9	88	112	12.7	3.90	99	.258	.328	17	.215	2	-1	-1	0	0.0
1932 *Chi-N	15	17	.469	37	33	17	2	0	237	222	13	78	120	11.6	3.38	111	.244	.308	14	.179	1	13	10	-3	0.9
1933 Chi-N	10	14	.417	31	26	13	2	0	186¹	186	10	59	72	12.1	3.91	84	.258	.318	10	.159	-2	-12	-13	-1	-1.9
1934 Chi-N	14	7	.667	34	21	8	1	0	191	200	14	55	111	12.2	3.53	110	.270	.322	11	.172	-2	11	7	-1	0.4
1935 NY-A	3	5	.375	29	2	0	0	3	56¹	53	7	33	25	13.9	5.43	75	.252	.357	0	.000	-3	-6	-9	-1	-1.4
1936 *NY-A	12	4	.750	35	9	5	0	**9**	134²	144	4	60	72	13.9	3.81	122	.273	.352	10	.196	-1	18	13	-2	1.2
1937 NY-A	4	4	.500	28	9	3	0	0	92	109	5	35	49	14.5	5.48	81	.291	.357	1	.030	-5	-9	-11	-2	-1.5
Total 10	134	92	.593	357	220	115	15	26	1915	1934	103	705	1024	12.6	3.74	111	.262	.330	129	.188	-14	112	85	-14	6.8

● **CHARLIE MALONEY**   Maloney, Charles Michael b: 5/22/1886, Cambridge, Mass. d: 1/17/67, Arlington, Mass. BR/TR, 5'8", 155 lbs. Deb: 8/10/08

YEAR TM/L	W	L	PCT	G	GS	CG	SH	SV	IP	H	HR	BB	SO	RAT	ERA	ERA+	OAV	OOB	BH	AVG	PB	PR	/A	PD	TPI
1908 Bos-N	0	0	—	1	0	0	0	0	2	3	0	1	0	18.0	4.50	54	.429	.500	0	—	0	-0	-0	-0	0.0

● **JIM MALONEY**   Maloney, James William b: 6/2/40, Fresno, Cal. BL/TR, 6'2", 207 lbs. Deb: 7/27/60

YEAR TM/L	W	L	PCT	G	GS	CG	SH	SV	IP	H	HR	BB	SO	RAT	ERA	ERA+	OAV	OOB	BH	AVG	PB	PR	/A	PD	TPI
1960 Cin-N	2	6	.250	11	10	2	1	0	63²	61	5	37	48	14.1	4.66	82	.255	.360	2	.111	-0	-6	-6	-0	-0.7
1961 *Cin-N	6	7	.462	27	11	1	0	2	94²	86	16	59	57	13.9	4.37	93	.242	.352	11	.379	4	-4	-3	-1	-0.1
1962 Cin-N	9	7	.563	22	17	3	0	1	115¹	90	11	66	105	12.3	3.51	115	.214	.323	8	.186	0	6	7	-1	0.7
1963 Cin-N	23	7	.767	33	33	13	6	0	250¹	183	17	88	265	10.6	2.77	121	.202	.276	15	.169	1	14	16	-2	1.8
1964 Cin-N	15	10	.600	31	31	11	2	0	216	175	16	83	214	10.8	2.71	133	.222	.297	11	.151	1	20	22	-2	2.4
1965 Cin-N★	20	9	.690	33	33	14	5	0	255¹	189	13	110	244	10.7	2.54	148	.206	.295	20	.225	7	28	34	-1	4.6
1966 Cin-N	16	8	.667	32	32	10	**5**	0	224²	174	18	90	216	11.0	2.80	139	.214	.300	18	.222	3	20	27	-0	3.2
1967 Cin-N	15	11	.577	30	29	6	3	0	196¹	181	8	72	153	11.7	3.25	115	.247	.317	11	.159	-0	3	11	-1	1.3
1968 Cin-N	16	10	.615	33	32	8	5	0	207	183	17	80	181	11.5	3.61	88	.239	.313	18	.243	6	-14	-10	-2	-0.8
1969 Cin-N	12	5	.706	30	27	6	3	0	178²	135	11	86	102	11.2	2.77	136	.208	.302	11	.200	6	16	20	-1	2.4
1970 Cin-N	0	1	.000	7	3	0	0	0	16²	26	3	15	7	23.2	11.34	36	.366	.489	0	—	0	-14	-14	-0	-0.9
1971 Cal-A	0	3	.000	13	4	0	0	0	30¹	35	3	24	14	17.8	5.04	64	.294	.417	1	.200	-0	-5	-6	-0	-0.6
Total 12	134	84	.615	302	262	74	30	4	1849	1518	138	810	1605	11.5	3.19	115	.224	.310	126	.201	26	64	98	-10	13.3

● **PAUL MALOY**   Maloy, Paul Augustus "Biff" b: 6/4/1892, Bascom, Ohio d: 3/18/76, Sandusky, Ohio BR/TR, 5'11", 185 lbs. Deb: 7/11/13

YEAR TM/L	W	L	PCT	G	GS	CG	SH	SV	IP	H	HR	BB	SO	RAT	ERA	ERA+	OAV	OOB	BH	AVG	PB	PR	/A	PD	TPI
1913 Bos-A	0	0	—	2	0	0	0	0	2	2	0	1	0	22.5	9.00	33	.286	.500	0	—	0	-1	-1	-0	0.0

● **GORDON MALTZBERGER**   Maltzberger, Gordon Ralph "Maltzy" b: 9/4/12, Utopia, Tex. d: 12/11/74, Rialto, Cal. BR/TR, 6', 170 lbs. Deb: 4/27/43 C

YEAR TM/L	W	L	PCT	G	GS	CG	SH	SV	IP	H	HR	BB	SO	RAT	ERA	ERA+	OAV	OOB	BH	AVG	PB	PR	/A	PD	TPI
1943 Chi-A	7	4	.636	37	0	0	0	**14**	98²	86	8	24	48	10.2	2.46	136	.236	.287	3	.120	0	9	10	0	1.5
1944 Chi-A	10	5	.667	46	0	0	0	**12**	91¹	81	2	19	49	10.0	2.96	116	.235	.277	3	.136	-1	5	5	-1	0.8
1946 Chi-A	2	0	1.000	19	0	0	0	5	39²	30	1	6	17	8.4	1.59	215	.205	.242	0	.000	-0	8	8	-1	0.4
1947 Chi-A	1	4	.200	33	0	0	0	5	63²	61	6	25	22	12.3	3.39	108	.257	.331	1	.143	0	2	1	0	0.3
Total 4	20	13	.606	135	0	0	0	33	293¹	258	17	74	136	10.3	2.70	128	.236	.288	7	.117	0	25	24	0	3.0

● **AL MAMAUX**   Mamaux, Albert Leon b: 5/30/1894, Pittsburgh, Pa. d: 1/2/63, Santa Monica, Cal. BR/TR, 6'0.5", 168 lbs. Deb: 9/23/13

YEAR TM/L	W	L	PCT	G	GS	CG	SH	SV	IP	H	HR	BB	SO	RAT	ERA	ERA+	OAV	OOB	BH	AVG	PB	PR	/A	PD	TPI
1913 Pit-N	0	0	—	2	0	0	0	0	3	2	0	2	2	12.0	3.00	100	.167	.286	0	—	-0	0	0	0	0.0
1914 Pit-N	5	2	.714	13	6	4	2	0	63	41	1	24	30	9.6	1.71	155	.186	.272	5	.250	1	8	7	1	1.0
1915 Pit-N	21	8	.724	38	31	17	8	0	251²	182	3	96	152	10.3	2.04	134	.208	.293	15	.163	-2	20	19	-3	1.5
1916 Pit-N	21	15	.583	45	37	26	6	1	310	264	3	136	163	11.9	2.53	106	.239	.327	21	.191	1	3	5	0	0.9

YEAR	TM/L	W	L	PCT	G	GS	CG	SH	SV	IP	H	HR	BB	SO	RAT	ERA	ERA+	OAV	OOB	BH	AVG	PB	PR	/A	PD	TPI
1917	Pit-N	2	11	.154	16	13	5	0	0	85²	92	1	50	22	15.2	5.25	54	.278	.378	7	.226	0	-24	-23	-1	-3.2
1918	Bro-N	0	1	.000	2	1	0	0	0	8	14	0	2	2	18.0	6.75	41	.438	.471	0	.000	-0	-4	-4	1	-0.4
1919	Bro-N	10	12	.455	30	22	16	2	0	199¹	174	2	66	80	11.0	2.66	112	.245	.312	11	.175	0	6	7	-1	0.7
1920	*Bro-N	12	8	.600	41	17	9	2	4	190²	172	6	63	101	11.3	2.69	119	.255	.322	10	.167	-0	9	11	-1	1.0
1921	Bro-N	3	3	.500	12	1	0	0	1	43	36	1	13	21	10.5	3.14	124	.240	.305	2	.182	-0	3	4	1	0.5
1922	Bro-N	1	4	.200	37	7	1	0	3	87²	97	7	33	35	13.6	3.70	110	.290	.358	4	.235	3	4	4	0	0.5
1923	Bro-N	0	2	.000	5	1	0	0	0	13	20	0	6	5	18.0	8.31	47	.385	.448	1	.500	0	-6	-6	0	-0.8
1924	NY-A	1	1	.500	14	2	0	0	0	38	44	2	20	12	15.4	5.68	73	.308	.396	1	.077	-1	-6	-6	-1	-0.5
Total	12	76	67	.531	254	138	78	15	10	1293	1138	22	511	625	11.7	2.90	104	.245	.325	77	.182	2	13	17	-3	1.2

● HAL MANDERS   Manders, Harold Carl b: 6/14/17, Waukee, Iowa BR/TR, 6', 187 lbs. Deb: 8/12/41

YEAR	TM/L	W	L	PCT	G	GS	CG	SH	SV	IP	H	HR	BB	SO	RAT	ERA	ERA+	OAV	OOB	BH	AVG	PB	PR	/A	PD	TPI
1941	Det-A	1	0	1.000	8	0	0	0	0	15¹	13	0	8	7	12.9	2.35	194	.236	.344	0	.000	-1	3	4	-0	0.1
1942	Det-A	2	0	1.000	18	0	0	0	0	33	39	4	15	14	15.0	4.09	97	.307	.385	1	.250	0	-2	-1	0	0.0
1946	Det-A	0	0	—	2	0	0	0	0	6	8	1	2	3	16.5	10.50	35	.364	.440	1	.500	0	-5	-5	-0	0.0
	Chi-N	0	1	.000	2	1	0	0	0	6	11	1	3	4	22.5	9.00	37	.423	.500	0	.000	-0	-4	-4	-0	-0.6
Total	3	3	1	.750	30	1	0	0	0	60¹	71	6	28	28	15.4	4.77	84	.309	.393	2	.167	-0	-7	-5	-1	-0.5

● LEO MANGUM   Mangum, Leo Allan "Blackie" b: 5/24/1896, Durham, N.C. d: 7/9/74, Lima, Ohio BR/TR, 6'1", 187 lbs. Deb: 7/11/24

YEAR	TM/L	W	L	PCT	G	GS	CG	SH	SV	IP	H	HR	BB	SO	RAT	ERA	ERA+	OAV	OOB	BH	AVG	PB	PR	/A	PD	TPI
1924	Chi-A	1	4	.200	13	7	1	0	0	47	69	3	25	12	18.2	7.09	58	.359	.436	1	.071	-1	-15	-15	0	-1.4
1925	Chi-A	1	0	1.000	7	0	0	0	0	15	25	0	6	6	18.6	7.80	53	.373	.425	2	.500	-1	-6	-6	-0	-0.3
1928	NY-N	0	0	—	1	1	0	0	0	3	6	0	5	1	33.0	15.00	26	.500	.647	1	1.000	0	-4	-4	1	0.1
1932	Bos-N	0	0	—	7	0	0	0	0	10¹	17	1	0	3	14.8	5.23	72	.333	.333	0	.000	-0	-2	-2	1	0.1
1933	Bos-N	4	3	.571	25	5	2	1	0	84	93	2	11	28	11.1	3.32	92	.280	.303	2	.091	-2	0	-2	2	-0.2
1934	Bos-N	5	3	.625	29	3	1	0	1	94¹	127	9	23	28	14.3	5.72	67	.315	.352	9	.281	2	-17	-20	1	-1.2
1935	Bos-N	0	0	—	3	0	0	0	0	4²	6	0	2	0	15.4	3.86	98	.300	.364	0	—	-0	0	-0	0	0.0
Total	7	11	10	.524	85	16	4	1	1	258¹	343	15	72	78	14.5	5.37	68	.318	.362	15	.200	-0	-43	-49	4	-2.9

● ERNIE MANNING   Manning, Ernest Devon "Ed" b: 10/9/1890, Florala, Ala. d: 4/28/73, Pensacola, Fla. BL/TR, 6', 175 lbs. Deb: 5/3/14

YEAR	TM/L	W	L	PCT	G	GS	CG	SH	SV	IP	H	HR	BB	SO	RAT	ERA	ERA+	OAV	OOB	BH	AVG	PB	PR	/A	PD	TPI
1914	StL-A	0	0	—	4	0	0	0	0	10	11	0	3	3	12.6	3.60	75	.297	.350	0	.000	-0	-1	-1	0	0.0

● JIM MANNING   Manning, James Benjamin b: 7/21/43, L'Anse, Mich. BR/TR, 6'1", 185 lbs. Deb: 4/15/62

YEAR	TM/L	W	L	PCT	G	GS	CG	SH	SV	IP	H	HR	BB	SO	RAT	ERA	ERA+	OAV	OOB	BH	AVG	PB	PR	/A	PD	TPI
1962	Min-A	0	0	—	5	1	0	0	0	7	14	0	1	3	20.6	5.14	79	.389	.421	0	—	-0	-1	-1	0	0.0

● JACK MANNING   Manning, John E. b: 12/20/1853, Braintree, Mass. d: 8/15/29, Boston, Mass. BR/TR, 5'8.5", 158 lbs. Deb: 4/23/1873 M♦

YEAR	TM/L	W	L	PCT	G	GS	CG	SH	SV	IP	H	HR	BB	SO	RAT	ERA	ERA+	OAV	OOB	BH	AVG	PB	PR	/A	PD	TPI
1874	Bal-n	4	16	.200	22	20	18	0	0	179²	221	3	10		12.1	3.41	89	.272	.281	59	.351	7	-8	-7		-0.1
1875	Bos-n	15	2	.882	27	17	8	1	7	139¹	153	1	14		10.8	2.19	108	.258	.258	94	.274	4	4	3		0.4
1876	Bos-N	18	5	.783	34	20	13	0	5	197¹	213	1	32	24	11.2	2.14	105	.252	.279	76	.264	3	4	2	0	0.4
1877	Cin-N	0	4	.000	10	4	2	0	1	44	83	1	7	6	18.4	6.95	38	.379	.398	4	-20	-21	0		-1.3
1878	Bos-N	1	0	1.000	3	1	1	0	0	11¹	24	1	5	2	23.0	14.29	17	.393	.439	63	.254	0	-15	-15	0	-0.9
Total 2 n	19	18	.514	49	37	26	1	7	319¹	384	4	24		11.5	2.87	95	.266	.278	197	.292	11	-4	-5		0.3
Total 3	19	9	.679	47	25	16	0	6	252²	320	3	44	32	13.0	3.53	66	.284	.311	725	.257	11	-32	-34	1	-1.8

● RUBE MANNING   Manning, Walter S. b: 4/29/1883, Chambersburg, Pa. d: 4/23/30, Williamsport, Pa. BR/TR, 6', 180 lbs. Deb: 9/25/07

YEAR	TM/L	W	L	PCT	G	GS	CG	SH	SV	IP	H	HR	BB	SO	RAT	ERA	ERA+	OAV	OOB	BH	AVG	PB	PR	/A	PD	TPI
1907	NY-A	0	1	.000	1	1	1	0	0	9	8	0	3	3	12.0	3.00	93	.240	.321	0	.000	-0	-0	-0	-0	-0.1
1908	NY-A	13	16	.448	41	26	19	2	1	245	228	4	86	113	12.2	2.94	84	.256	.334	17	.187	0	-15	-12	-1	-1.6
1909	NY-A	7	11	.389	26	21	11	2	1	173	167	2	48	71	11.7	3.17	80	.265	.326	11	.183	0	-13	-12	-1	-1.4
1910	NY-A	2	4	.333	16	9	4	0	0	75	80	4	25	25	13.1	3.72	71	.283	.349	5	.192	0	-10	-9	-1	-0.7
Total	4	22	32	.407	84	57	35	4	2	502	483	10	162	212	12.1	3.14	81	.263	.333	33	.183	0	-39	-34	-3	-3.8

● RAMON MANON   Manon, Ramon (Reyes) b: 1/20/68, Santo Domingo, D.R. BR/TR, 6', 150 lbs. Deb: 4/19/90

YEAR	TM/L	W	L	PCT	G	GS	CG	SH	SV	IP	H	HR	BB	SO	RAT	ERA	ERA+	OAV	OOB	BH	AVG	PB	PR	/A	PD	TPI
1990	Tex-A	0	0	—	1	0	0	0	0	2	3	0	3	0	27.0	13.50	29	.333	.500		—	0	-2	-2	0	-0.1

● TOM MANSELL   Mansell, Thomas E. "Brick" b: 1/1/1855, Auburn, N.Y. d: 10/6/34, Auburn, N.Y. BL/TL, 5'8", 160 lbs. Deb: 5/1/1879 F♦

YEAR	TM/L	W	L	PCT	G	GS	CG	SH	SV	IP	H	HR	BB	SO	RAT	ERA	ERA+	OAV	OOB	BH	AVG	PB	PR	/A	PD	TPI
1883	Det-N	0	0	—	1	0	0	0	0	6²	21	2	5	3	35.1	18.90	16	.553	.605	29	.221	0	-12	-12	-0	0.0

● LOU MANSKE   Manske, Louis Hugo b: 7/4/1884, Milwaukee, Wis. d: 4/27/63, Milwaukee, Wis. BL/TL, 6', Deb: 8/31/06

YEAR	TM/L	W	L	PCT	G	GS	CG	SH	SV	IP	H	HR	BB	SO	RAT	ERA	ERA+	OAV	OOB	BH	AVG	PB	PR	/A	PD	TPI
1906	Pit-N	0	0	—	2	1	0	0	0	8	12	0	5	6	19.1	5.63	48	.387	.472	0	.000	-1	-3	-3	-0	-0.1

● BARRY MANUEL   Manuel, Barry Paul b: 8/12/65, Mamou, La. BR/TR, 5'11", 180 lbs. Deb: 9/6/91

YEAR	TM/L	W	L	PCT	G	GS	CG	SH	SV	IP	H	HR	BB	SO	RAT	ERA	ERA+	OAV	OOB	BH	AVG	PB	PR	/A	PD	TPI
1991	Tex-A	1	0	1.000	8	0	0	0	0	16	7	0	6	5	7.3	1.13	358	.143	.236	0	—	0	5	5	1	0.4
1992	Tex-A	1	0	1.000	3	0	0	0	0	5²	6	2	1	9	12.7	4.76	80	.261	.320	0	—	0	-1	-1	-0	0.1
Total 2	2	0	1.000	11	0	0	0	0	21²	13	2	7	14	8.7	2.08	191	.181	.262	0	—	0	5	5	0	0.5

● MOXIE MANUEL   Manuel, Mark Garfield b: 10/16/1881, Metropolis, Ill. d: 4/26/24, Memphis, Tenn. BR/TB, 5'11", 170 lbs. Deb: 9/25/05

YEAR	TM/L	W	L	PCT	G	GS	CG	SH	SV	IP	H	HR	BB	SO	RAT	ERA	ERA+	OAV	OOB	BH	AVG	PB	PR	/A	PD	TPI
1905	Was-A	0	0	—	3	1	1	0	0	10	9	0	3	3	11.7	5.40	49	.242	.315	1	.250	0	-3	-3	0	0.0
1908	Chi-A	3	4	.429	18	6	3	0	1	60¹	52	0	25	25	11.8	3.28	71	.251	.338	1	.063	-1	-6	-6	0	-0.9
Total 2	3	4	.429	21	7	4	0	1	70¹	61	0	28	28	11.8	3.58	66	.250	.334	2	.100	-1	-9	-10	0	-0.9

● DICK MANVILLE   Manville, Richard Wesley b: 12/25/26, Des Moines, Iowa BR/TR, 6'4", 192 lbs. Deb: 4/30/50

YEAR	TM/L	W	L	PCT	G	GS	CG	SH	SV	IP	H	HR	BB	SO	RAT	ERA	ERA+	OAV	OOB	BH	AVG	PB	PR	/A	PD	TPI
1950	Bos-N	0	0	—	1	0	0	0	0	2	0	0	3	0	13.5	0.00	—	.000	.300	0	—	0	1	1	-0	0.0
1952	Chi-N	0	0	—	11	0	0	0	0	17	25	2	12	6	19.6	7.94	48	.362	.457	1	.500	0	-8	-8	0	0.1
Total 2	0	0	—	12	0	0	0	0	19	25	2	15	6	18.9	7.11	54	.329	.440	1	.500	0	-7	-7	0	0.1

● JOSIAS MANZANILLO   Manzanillo, Josias (Adams) b: 10/16/67, San Pedro De Macoris, D.R. BR/TR, 6', 190 lbs. Deb: 10/5/91 F

YEAR	TM/L	W	L	PCT	G	GS	CG	SH	SV	IP	H	HR	BB	SO	RAT	ERA	ERA+	OAV	OOB	BH	AVG	PB	PR	/A	PD	TPI
1991	Bos-A	0	0	—	1	0	0	0	0	1	2	0	3	0	45.0	18.00	24	.400	.625	0	—	0	-2	-2	-0	-0.1
1993	Mil-A	1	1	.500	10	1	0	0	0	17	22	1	10	10	18.0	9.53	45	.314	.415	0	—	0	-10	-10	1	-1.0
	NY-N	0	0	—	6	0	0	0	0	12	8	0	9	11	12.8	3.00	134	.186	.327	0	.000	-0	1	1	-0	0.1
1994	NY-N	3	2	.600	37	0	0	0	2	47¹	34	4	13	48	9.5	2.66	160	.200	.269	0	.000	-0	8	8	-0	0.8
Total 3	4	3	.571	54	1	0	0	2	77¹	66	6	35	70	12.3	4.42	95	.229	.323	0	.000	-1	-2	-2	0	-0.3

● RAVELO MANZANILLO   Manzanillo, Ravelo (Adams) b: 10/17/63, San Pedro De Macoris, D.R. BL/TL, 6', 210 lbs. Deb: 9/25/88 F

YEAR	TM/L	W	L	PCT	G	GS	CG	SH	SV	IP	H	HR	BB	SO	RAT	ERA	ERA+	OAV	OOB	BH	AVG	PB	PR	/A	PD	TPI
1988	Chi-A	0	1	.000	2	2	0	0	0	9¹	7	1	12	10	19.3	5.79	69	.212	.435	0	—	0	-2	-2	0	-0.2
1994	Pit-N	4	2	.667	46	0	0	0	1	50	45	4	42	39	16.2	4.14	103	.245	.393	2	.667	1	0	1	0	0.2
Total 2	4	3	.571	48	2	0	0	1	59¹	52	5	54	49	16.7	4.40	96	.240	.400	2	.667	1	-1	-1	0	0.0

● ROLLA MAPEL   Mapel, Rolla Hamilton "Lefty" b: 3/9/1890, Lees Summit, Mo. d: 4/6/66, San Diego, Cal. BL/TL, 5'11.5", 165 lbs. Deb: 8/31/19

YEAR	TM/L	W	L	PCT	G	GS	CG	SH	SV	IP	H	HR	BB	SO	RAT	ERA	ERA+	OAV	OOB	BH	AVG	PB	PR	/A	PD	TPI
1919	StL-A	0	3	.000	4	3	2	0	0	20	17	0	17	2	16.6	4.50	74	.262	.435	1	.167	-0	-3	-3	1	-0.3

● PAUL MARAK   Marak, Paul Patrick b: 8/2/65, Lakenheath, England BR/TR, 6'2", 175 lbs. Deb: 9/1/90

YEAR	TM/L	W	L	PCT	G	GS	CG	SH	SV	IP	H	HR	BB	SO	RAT	ERA	ERA+	OAV	OOB	BH	AVG	PB	PR	/A	PD	TPI
1990	Atl-N	1	2	.333	7	7	1	1	0	39	39	2	19	15	14.1	3.69	109	.267	.363	1	.091	-0	0	1	1	0.2

● GEORGES MARANDA   Maranda, Georges Henri b: 1/15/32, Levis, Que., Can. BR/TR, 6'2", 195 lbs. Deb: 4/26/60

YEAR	TM/L	W	L	PCT	G	GS	CG	SH	SV	IP	H	HR	BB	SO	RAT	ERA	ERA+	OAV	OOB	BH	AVG	PB	PR	/A	PD	TPI
1960	SF-N	1	4	.200	17	4	0	0	0	50²	50	6	30	28	14.2	4.62	75	.254	.352	2	.167	-0	-5	-6	2	-0.4
1962	Min-A	1	3	.250	32	4	0	0	0	72²	69	11	35	36	13.4	4.46	92	.252	.345	4	.250	1	-4	-3	1	0.0
Total 2	2	7	.222	49	8	0	0	0	123¹	119	17	65	64	13.7	4.52	85	.253	.348	6	.214	1	-9	-10	2	-0.4

YEAR TM/L	W	L	PCT	G	GS	CG	SH	SV	IP	H	HR	BB	SO	RAT	ERA	ERA+	OAV	OOB	BH	AVG	PB	PR	/A	PD	TPI

● FIRPO MARBERRY
Marberry, Fredrick b: 11/30/1898, Streetman, Tex. d: 6/30/76, Mexia, Tex. BR/TR, 6'1", 190 lbs. Deb: 8/11/23 U

YEAR TM/L	W	L	PCT	G	GS	CG	SH	SV	IP	H	HR	BB	SO	RAT	ERA	ERA+	OAV	OOB	BH	AVG	PB	PR	/A	PD	TPI
1923 Was-A	4	0	1.000	11	4	2	0	0	44²	42	1	17	18	12.5	2.82	133	.258	.339	2	.143	-1	6	5	-0	0.3
1924 *Was-A	11	12	.478	50	15	6	0	15	195¹	190	3	70	68	12.4	3.09	131	.262	.335	8	.136	-4	25	21	-1	2.0
1925 *Was-A	9	5	.643	55	0	0	0	15	93¹	84	4	45	53	12.8	3.47	122	.246	.341	5	.263	1	10	8	1	1.5
1926 Was-A	12	7	.632	64	5	3	0	22	138	120	4	66	43	12.3	3.00	129	.243	.336	6	.176	-1	16	13	-1	1.9
1927 Was-A	10	7	.588	56	10	2	0	9	155¹	177	4	68	74	14.4	4.64	88	.296	.371	5	.122	-3	-9	-10	-1	-1.5
1928 Was-A	13	13	.500	48	11	7	1	3	161¹	160	4	42	76	11.4	3.85	104	.268	.319	5	.109	-4	3	3	-1	-0.1
1929 Was-A	19	12	.613	49	26	16	0	11	250¹	233	6	69	121	11.1	3.06	139	.252	.308	19	.235	2	33	33	-2	3.8
1930 Was-A	15	5	.750	33	22	9	2	1	185	190	15	53	56	11.8	4.09	113	.270	.321	24	.329	5	12	11	-1	1.3
1931 Was-A	16	4	.800	45	25	11	1	7	219	211	13	63	88	11.4	3.45	124	.252	.307	19	.232	1	23	20	-2	1.7
1932 Was-A	8	4	.667	54	15	8	1	13	197²	202	13	72	66	12.6	4.01	108	.268	.333	11	.167	-2	10	7	1	0.4
1933 Det-A	16	11	.593	37	32	15	1	2	238¹	232	13	61	84	11.1	3.29	131	.254	.302	11	.122	-5	26	27	-3	2.0
1934 *Det-A	15	5	.750	38	19	6	1	3	155²	174	12	48	64	12.8	4.57	96	.276	.327	12	.218	-2	-1	-3	-2	-0.3
1935 Det-A	0	1	.000	5	2	1	0	0	19	22	2	9	7	14.7	4.26	98	.289	.365	1	.200	0	0	-0	-0	0.1
1936 NY-N	0	0	—	1	0	0	0	0	0¹	1	0	0	0	27.0	0.00	—	.500	.500	0	.000	-0	0	0	-0	0.0
Was-A	0	2	.000	5	1	0	0	0	14	11	2	3	4	9.6	3.86	124	.208	.263	0	.000	-0	2	1	-0	0.1
Total 14	148	88	.627	551	187	86	7	101	2067¹	2049	96	686	822	12.1	3.63	116	.262	.325	128	.192	-8	156	136	-12	13.1

● WALT MARBET
Marbet, Walter William b: 9/13/1890, Plymouth Co., Ia. d: 9/24/56, Hohenwald, Tenn. BR/TR, 6'1", 175 lbs. Deb: 6/17/13

YEAR TM/L	W	L	PCT	G	GS	CG	SH	SV	IP	H	HR	BB	SO	RAT	ERA	ERA+	OAV	OOB	BH	AVG	PB	PR	/A	PD	TPI
1913 StL-N	0	1	.000	3	1	0	0	0	3¹	9	0	4	1	35.1	16.20	20	.500	.591	0	—	0	-5	-5	-0	-1.1

● PHIL MARCHILDON
Marchildon, Philip Joseph "Babe" b: 10/25/13, Penetanguishene, Ont., Canada BR/TR, 5'11", 175 lbs. Deb: 9/22/40

YEAR TM/L	W	L	PCT	G	GS	CG	SH	SV	IP	H	HR	BB	SO	RAT	ERA	ERA+	OAV	OOB	BH	AVG	PB	PR	/A	PD	TPI
1940 Phi-A	0	2	.000	2	2	1	0	0	10	12	1	8	4	18.0	7.20	62	.286	.400	0	.000	-1	-3	-3	0	-0.5
1941 Phi-A	10	15	.400	30	27	14	1	0	204¹	188	15	118	74	13.6	3.57	117	.245	.348	11	.167	1	13	14	-3	1.3
1942 Phi-A	17	14	.548	38	31	18	1	1	244	215	14	140	110	13.2	4.20	90	.235	.339	20	.238	3	-15	-12	-3	-1.3
1945 Phi-A	0	1	.000	3	2	0	0	0	9	5	0	11	2	16.0	4.00	86	.179	.410	1	.500	1	-1	-1	0	0.0
1946 Phi-A	13	16	.448	36	29	16	1	1	226²	197	14	114	95	12.5	3.49	101	.237	.332	5	.067	-6	0	1	-2	-0.6
1947 Phi-A	19	9	.679	35	35	21	2	0	276²	228	15	141	128	12.2	3.22	118	.224	.323	15	.153	-2	15	18	-3	1.3
1948 Phi-A	9	15	.375	33	30	12	1	0	226¹	214	19	131	66	13.9	4.53	95	.251	.353	5	.069	-5	-6	-6	-1	-1.2
1949 Phi-A	0	3	.000	7	6	0	0	0	16	24	3	19	2	24.8	11.81	35	.358	.506	1	.167	-0	-14	-14	-0	-2.0
1950 Bos-A	0	0	—	1	0	0	0	0	1¹	1	0	2	0	20.3	6.75	73	.200	.429	0	—	0	-0	-0	-0	0.0
Total 9	68	75	.476	185	162	82	6	2	1214¹	1084	81	684	481	13.3	3.93	100	.240	.342	58	.143	-10	-10	-1	-11	-3.0

● JOHNNY MARCUM
Marcum, John Alfred "Footsie" b: 9/9/09, Campbellsburg, Ky. d: 9/10/84, Louisville, Ky. BL/TR, 5'11", 197 lbs. Deb: 9/7/33 ♦

YEAR TM/L	W	L	PCT	G	GS	CG	SH	SV	IP	H	HR	BB	SO	RAT	ERA	ERA+	OAV	OOB	BH	AVG	PB	PR	/A	PD	TPI
1933 Phi-A	3	2	.600	5	5	4	2	0	37	28	0	20	14	11.7	1.95	220	.200	.300	2	.167	0	10	10	0	1.3
1934 Phi-A	14	11	.560	37	31	17	2	0	232	257	13	88	92	13.5	4.50	97	.280	.346	30	.268	6	-0	-3	-0	0.2
1935 Phi-A	17	12	.586	39	27	19	2	3	242²	256	9	83	99	12.6	4.08	111	.268	.328	37	.311	9	10	13	-3	1.9
1936 Bos-A	8	13	.381	31	23	9	1	1	174	194	14	52	57	12.7	4.81	100	.281	.332	18	.205	1	4	10	0	1.0
1937 Bos-A	13	11	.542	37	23	9	1	3	183²	230	17	47	59	13.7	4.85	98	.306	.348	23	.267	5	-5	-2	1	0.3
1938 Bos-A	5	6	.455	15	11	7	0	0	92¹	113	11	25	25	13.5	4.09	120	.298	.342	5	.135	-1	7	9	-1	0.7
1939 StL-A	2	5	.286	12	6	2	0	0	47²	66	12	10	14	14.5	7.74	63	.332	.367	10	.455	3	-17	-15	-0	-1.5
Chi-A	3	3	.500	19	6	2	0	0	90	125	15	19	32	14.4	6.00	79	.326	.357	16	.281	2	-14	-13	-1	-0.5
Yr	5	8	.385	31	12	4	0	0	137²	191	27	29	46	14.4	6.60	72	.327	.359	26	.329	6	-30	-28	-1	-2.0
Total 7	65	63	.508	195	132	69	8	7	1099¹	1269	91	344	392	13.3	4.66	101	.287	.340	141	.265	25	-4	7	-4	3.4

● LEO MARENTETTE
Marentette, Leo John b: 2/18/41, Detroit, Mich. BR/TR, 6'2", 200 lbs. Deb: 9/26/65

YEAR TM/L	W	L	PCT	G	GS	CG	SH	SV	IP	H	HR	BB	SO	RAT	ERA	ERA+	OAV	OOB	BH	AVG	PB	PR	/A	PD	TPI
1965 Det-A	0	0	—	2	0	0	0	0	3	1	0	1	3	6.0	0.00	—	.111	.200	0	—	0	1	1	0	0.0
1969 Mon-N	0	0	—	3	0	0	0	0	5¹	9	1	1	4	16.9	6.75	54	.391	.417	0	.000	-0	-2	-2	0	0.0
Total 2	0	0	—	5	0	0	0	0	8¹	10	1	2	7	13.0	4.32	83	.313	.353	0	.000	-0	-1	-1	0	0.0

● JOE MARGONERI
Margoneri, Joseph Emanuel b: 1/13/30, Somerset, Pa. BL/TL, 6', 185 lbs. Deb: 4/25/56

YEAR TM/L	W	L	PCT	G	GS	CG	SH	SV	IP	H	HR	BB	SO	RAT	ERA	ERA+	OAV	OOB	BH	AVG	PB	PR	/A	PD	TPI
1956 NY-N	6	6	.500	23	13	2	0	0	91²	88	12	49	49	13.5	3.93	96	.254	.346	3	.103	-1	-2	-1	-0	-0.3
1957 NY-N	1	1	.500	13	2	1	0	0	34¹	44	1	21	18	17.3	5.24	75	.314	.407	0	.000	-1	-5	-5	-0	-0.4
Total 2	7	7	.500	36	15	3	0	0	126	132	13	70	67	14.5	4.29	89	.271	.364	3	.081	-2	-7	-6	-1	-0.7

● JUAN MARICHAL
Marichal, Juan Antonio (Sanchez) "Manito" b: 10/20/37, Laguna Verde, D.R. BR/TR, 6', 185 lbs. Deb: 7/19/60 H

YEAR TM/L	W	L	PCT	G	GS	CG	SH	SV	IP	H	HR	BB	SO	RAT	ERA	ERA+	OAV	OOB	BH	AVG	PB	PR	/A	PD	TPI
1960 SF-N	6	2	.750	11	11	6	1	0	81¹	59	5	28	58	9.6	2.66	131	.200	.269	4	.129	0	10	7	0	0.7
1961 SF-N	13	10	.565	29	27	9	3	0	185	183	24	48	124	11.3	3.89	98	.257	.306	7	.119	-2	3	-2	-1	-0.5
1962 *SF-N★	18	11	.621	37	36	18	3	1	262²	233	34	90	153	11.2	3.36	113	.234	.300	21	.236	4	17	13	-1	1.6
1963 SF-N☆	25	8	.758	41	40	18	5	0	321¹	259	27	61	248	9.0	2.41	133	.216	.256	20	.179	3	31	28	-3	2.8
1964 SF-N★	21	8	.724	33	33	22	4	0	269	241	18	52	206	9.8	2.48	144	.236	.273	14	.144	-1	32	33	1	3.4
1965 SF-N★	22	13	.629	39	37	24	10	1	295¹	224	27	46	240	8.3	2.13	169	.205	.240	17	.173	1	46	48	-0	6.0
1966 SF-N★	25	6	.806	37	36	25	4	0	307¹	228	32	36	222	7.9	2.23	165	.202	.230	28	.250	6	47	49	0	5.8
1967 SF-N★	14	10	.583	26	26	18	2	0	202¹	195	20	42	166	10.6	2.76	119	.249	.288	14	.177	3	14	12	-2	1.5
1968 SF-N★	26	9	.743	38	38	30	5	0	326	295	21	46	218	9.6	2.43	121	.238	.269	20	.163	1	20	19	3	2.7
1969 SF-N☆	21	11	.656	37	36	27	8	0	299²	244	15	54	205	9.1	2.10	167	.222	.263	15	.138	-1	50	47	4	5.4
1970 SF-N	12	10	.545	34	33	14	1	0	242²	269	28	48	123	11.8	4.12	97	.277	.312	5	.059	-6	-2	-4	2	-0.7
1971 *SF-N★	18	11	.621	37	37	18	4	0	279	244	27	56	159	9.8	2.94	116	.233	.274	14	.133	0	16	14	3	1.8
1972 SF-N	6	16	.273	25	24	6	0	0	165	176	16	46	72	12.3	3.71	94	.277	.329	10	.196	1	-5	-4	0	-0.4
1973 SF-N	11	15	.423	34	32	9	2	0	207¹	231	22	37	87	11.7	3.82	100	.277	.309	13	.188	-1	-4	-0	4	0.5
1974 Bos-A	5	1	.833	11	9	0	0	0	57¹	61	3	14	21	12.1	4.87	79	.270	.318	0	—	-0	-8	-7	-0	-0.9
1975 LA-N	0	1	.000	2	2	0	0	0	6	11	2	5	1	24.0	13.50	25	.407	.500	0	.000	-0	-7	-7	0	-0.8
Total 16	243	142	.631	471	457	244	52	2	3507¹	3153	320	709	2303	10.0	2.89	122	.237	.278	202	.165	10	262	247	9	28.9

● DAN MARION
Marion, Donald G. "Rube" b: 7/31/1890, Cleveland, Ohio d: 1/18/33, Milwaukee, Wis. BR/TR, 6'1", 187 lbs. Deb: 4/23/14

YEAR TM/L	W	L	PCT	G	GS	CG	SH	SV	IP	H	HR	BB	SO	RAT	ERA	ERA+	OAV	OOB	BH	AVG	PB	PR	/A	PD	TPI
1914 Bro-F	3	2	.600	17	9	4	0	0	89¹	97	1	38	41	14.2	3.93	73	.281	.362	7	.194	-2	-10	-10	-1	-0.8
1915 Bro-F	12	9	.571	35	25	15	2	0	208¹	193	1	64	46	11.2	3.20	85	.248	.308	13	.176	-2	-11	-11	-1	-1.3
Total 2	15	11	.577	52	34	19	2	0	297²	290	2	102	87	12.1	3.42	81	.258	.325	20	.182	-3	-21	-22	-2	-2.1

● DUKE MARKELL
Markell, Harry Duquesne (b: Harry Duquesne Makowsky)
b: 8/17/23, Paris, France d: 6/14/84, Ft.Lauderdale, Fla. BR/TR, 6'1.5", 209 lbs. Deb: 9/6/51

YEAR TM/L	W	L	PCT	G	GS	CG	SH	SV	IP	H	HR	BB	SO	RAT	ERA	ERA+	OAV	OOB	BH	AVG	PB	PR	/A	PD	TPI
1951 StL-A	1	1	.500	5	2	1	0	0	27	25	3	20	10	19.0	6.33	69	.298	.433	1	.167	-0	-5	-5	-1	-0.4

● CLIFF MARKLE
Markle, Clifford Monroe b: 5/3/1894, Dravosburg, Pa. d: 5/24/74, Temple City, Cal. BR/TR, 5'9", 163 lbs. Deb: 9/18/15

YEAR TM/L	W	L	PCT	G	GS	CG	SH	SV	IP	H	HR	BB	SO	RAT	ERA	ERA+	OAV	OOB	BH	AVG	PB	PR	/A	PD	TPI
1915 NY-A	2	0	1.000	5	2	2	0	0	23	15	1	6	12	8.2	0.39	750	.185	.241	0	.000	0	7	6	-1	0.5
1916 NY-A	3	5	.571	11	7	3	1	0	45²	46	4	31	14	15.0	4.53	64	.256	.390	0	.000	-1	-9	-8	-0	-1.4
1921 Cin-N	2	6	.250	10	6	5	0	0	67	75	0	20	23	12.8	3.76	95	.291	.342	3	.125	-2	0	-1	-0	-0.4
1922 Cin-N	4	5	.444	25	3	2	0	0	75²	75	4	33	34	12.8	3.81	105	.268	.345	3	.150	-2	0	-1	-2	0.1
1924 NY-A	0	3	.000	7	3	0	0	0	23¹	29	1	20	7	18.9	8.87	47	.333	.458	0	.000	-1	-12	-12	-0	-1.4
Total 5	12	17	.414	56	21	12	1	0	234²	235	4	9	110	90	13.4	4.10	87	.271	.356	6	.087	-5	-12	-14	-3	-2.6

● DICK MARLOWE
Marlowe, Richard Burton b: 6/27/29, Hickory, N.C. d: 12/30/68, Toledo, Ohio BR/TR, 6'2", 170 lbs. Deb: 9/19/51

YEAR TM/L	W	L	PCT	G	GS	CG	SH	SV	IP	H	HR	BB	SO	RAT	ERA	ERA+	OAV	OOB	BH	AVG	PB	PR	/A	PD	TPI
1951 Det-A	0	0	—	2	1	0	0	0	1	2	0	2	1	37.8	32.40	13	.500	.583	0	—	-0	-5	-5	-0	-1.8
1952 Det-A	0	2	.000	4	1	0	0	0	11	21	1	3	3	19.6	7.36	52	.420	.453	0	.000	-0	-5	-4	-0	-0.7
1953 Det-A	6	7	.462	42	11	2	0	0	119²	152	13	42	52	14.7	5.26	77	.319	.377	7	.219	-0	-17	-16	-1	-1.6

YEAR	TM/L	W	L	PCT	G	GS	CG	SH	SV	IP	H	HR	BB	SO	RAT	ERA	ERA+	OAV	OOB	BH	AVG	PB	PR	/A	PD	TPI
1954	Det-A	5	4	.556	38	2	0	0	2	84	76	11	40	39	12.4	4.18	88	.244	.330	3	.167	0	-4	-5	-1	-0.5
1955	Det-A	1	0	1.000	4	1	1	0	1	15	12	1	4	9	9.6	1.80	213	.218	.271	0	.000	-0	4	3	-0	0.2
1956	Det-A	1	1	.500	7	1	0	0	0	11	12	1	9	4	17.2	5.73	72	.279	.404	0	.000	-0	-2	-2	-0	-0.3
	Chi-A	0	0	—	1	0	0	0	0	1	2	1	1	0	27.0	9.00	46	.500	.600	0	—	0	-1	-1	-0	0.0
	Yr	1	1	.500	8	1	0	0	0	12	14	2	10	4	18.0	6.00	69	.298	.421	0	.000	-0	-2	-3	-0	-0.3
Total 6		13	15	.464	98	17	3	0	3	243¹	280	28	101	108	14.2	4.99	78	.295	.364	10	.175	-1	-30	-29	-2	-4.7

● **LOU MARONE**   Marone, Louis Stephen b: 12/3/45, San Diego, Cal. BR/TL, 5'11", 185 lbs. Deb: 5/30/69

YEAR	TM/L	W	L	PCT	G	GS	CG	SH	SV	IP	H	HR	BB	SO	RAT	ERA	ERA+	OAV	OOB	BH	AVG	PB	PR	/A	PD	TPI
1969	Pit-N	1	1	.500	29	0	0	0	0	35¹	24	2	13	25	9.9	2.55	137	.195	.283	0	—	0	4	4	-1	0.1
1970	Pit-N	0	0	—	1	0	0	0	0	2¹	2	1	0	0	7.7	3.86	101	.222	.222	0	—	0	0	0	-0	0.0
Total 2		1	1	.500	30	0	0	0	0	37²	26	3	13	25	9.8	2.63	134	.197	.279	0	—	0	4	4	-1	0.1

● **RUBE MARQUARD**   Marquard, Richard William b: 10/9/1889, Cleveland, Ohio d: 6/1/80, Baltimore, Md. BB/TL, 6'3", 180 lbs. Deb: 9/25/08 H

YEAR	TM/L	W	L	PCT	G	GS	CG	SH	SV	IP	H	HR	BB	SO	RAT	ERA	ERA+	OAV	OOB	BH	AVG	PB	PR	/A	PD	TPI
1908	NY-N	0	1	.000	1	1	0	0	0	5	6	0	2	2	16.2	3.60	67	.316	.409	0	.000	-0	-1	-1	-0	-0.2
1909	NY-N	5	13	.278	29	21	8	0	1	173	155	6	73	109	12.3	2.60	98	.248	.335	8	.148	-1	-0	-1	-0	-0.3
1910	NY-N	4	4	.500	13	8	2	0	0	70²	65	2	40	52	13.9	4.46	67	.254	.363	3	.111	-2	-11	-12	-0	-1.4
1911	*NY-N	24	7	.774	45	33	22	5	3	277²	221	9	106	237	10.7	2.50	135	.219	.296	17	.163	-1	28	27	-4	2.3
1912	*NY-N	26	11	.703	43	38	22	1	1	294²	286	9	80	175	11.3	2.57	132	.255	.306	21	.219	2	28	27	-3	2.9
1913	*NY-N	23	10	.697	42	33	20	4	3	288	248	10	49	151	9.4	2.50	125	.237	.273	23	.219	2	23	20	-6	1.8
1914	NY-N	12	22	.353	39	33	15	4	2	268	261	9	47	92	10.4	3.06	87	.262	.297	15	.179	-1	-8	-12	1	-1.6
1915	NY-N	9	8	.529	27	20	10	2	2	169	178	8	33	79	11.3	3.73	69	.272	.308	6	.109	-3	-18	-22	-0	-2.4
	Bro-N	2	2	.500	6	3	0	0	1	24²	29	0	5	13	12.4	6.20	45	.276	.309	1	.125	-0	-9	-9	-0	-1.5
	Yr	11	10	.524	33	23	10	2	3	193²	207	8	38	92	11.4	4.04	64	.272	.307	7	.111	-3	-28	-31	-0	-3.9
1916	*Bro-N	13	6	.684	36	21	15	2	5	205	169	2	38	107	9.1	1.58	170	.229	.267	9	.143	-1	24	25	-4	2.1
1917	Bro-N	19	12	.613	37	29	14	2	0	232²	200	6	60	117	10.1	2.55	110	.232	.282	15	.200	0	4	6	-4	0.4
1918	Bro-N	9	18	.333	34	29	19	4	1	239	231	7	59	89	11.0	2.64	106	.260	.307	13	.171	-2	3	4	-2	0.0
1919	Bro-N	3	3	.500	8	7	3	0	0	59	54	1	10	29	9.8	2.29	130	.244	.277	6	.261	1	4	4	-1	0.4
1920	*Bro-N	10	7	.588	28	26	10	1	0	189²	181	5	35	89	10.3	3.23	99	.251	.287	10	.169	-1	-2	-0	-4	-0.6
1921	Cin-N	17	14	.548	39	35	18	2	0	265²	291	8	50	88	11.8	3.39	106	.285	.323	19	.200	-1	12	6	-3	0.1
1922	Bos-N	11	15	.423	39	24	7	0	1	198	255	12	66	57	14.6	5.09	79	.322	.374	14	.222	-1	-22	-24	1	-2.6
1923	Bos-N	11	14	.440	38	29	11	3	0	239	265	10	65	78	12.5	3.73	107	.288	.337	12	.140	-6	7	7	0	0.0
1924	Bos-N	1	2	.333	6	6	1	0	0	36	33	3	13	10	11.8	3.00	127	.254	.326	3	.273	0	3	3	-0	0.3
1925	Bos-N	2	8	.200	26	8	0	0	0	72	105	5	27	19	16.5	5.75	70	.341	.394	3	.136	-1	-12	-14	-2	-1.9
Total 18		201	177	.532	536	404	197	30	19	3306²	3233	107	858	1593	11.2	3.08	103	.260	.310	198	.179	-17	53	36	-31	-2.2

● **JIM MARQUIS**   Marquis, James Milburn b: 11/18/1900, Yoakum, Tex. d: 8/5/92, Jackson, Cal. BR/TR, 5'11", 174 lbs. Deb: 8/8/25

YEAR	TM/L	W	L	PCT	G	GS	CG	SH	SV	IP	H	HR	BB	SO	RAT	ERA	ERA+	OAV	OOB	BH	AVG	PB	PR	/A	PD	TPI
1925	NY-A	0	0	—	2	0	0	0	0	7¹	12	1	6	0	22.1	9.82	43	.414	.514	0	.000	-0	-4	-5	0	0.0

● **CONNIE MARRERO**   Marrero, Conrado Eugenio (Ramos) b: 4/25/11, Las Villas, Cuba BR/TR, 5'7", 158 lbs. Deb: 4/21/50

YEAR	TM/L	W	L	PCT	G	GS	CG	SH	SV	IP	H	HR	BB	SO	RAT	ERA	ERA+	OAV	OOB	BH	AVG	PB	PR	/A	PD	TPI
1950	Was-A	6	10	.375	27	19	8	1	1	152	159	17	55	63	12.9	4.50	100	.269	.335	6	.122	-1	1	-0	-3	-0.4
1951	Was-A☆	11	9	.550	25	25	16	2	0	187	198	8	71	66	13.1	3.90	105	.268	.335	10	.164	-2	5	4	-2	0.1
1952	Was-A	11	8	.579	22	22	16	2	0	184¹	175	9	53	77	11.3	2.88	123	.249	.305	5	.079	-5	16	14	-3	0.5
1953	Was-A	8	7	.533	22	20	10	2	2	145²	130	14	48	65	11.3	3.03	129	.241	.309	6	.125	-2	16	14	-1	1.1
1954	Was-A	3	6	.333	22	8	1	0	0	66¹	74	12	22	26	13.0	4.75	75	.287	.343	0	—	0	-8	-9	-1	-1.3
Total 5		39	40	.494	118	94	51	7	3	735¹	736	60	249	297	12.3	3.67	108	.260	.323	27	.114	-11	30	23	-10	0.0

● **BUCK MARROW**   Marrow, Charles Kennon b: 8/29/09, Tarboro, N.C. d: 11/21/82, Newport News, Va. BR/TR, 6'4", 200 lbs. Deb: 7/3/32

YEAR	TM/L	W	L	PCT	G	GS	CG	SH	SV	IP	H	HR	BB	SO	RAT	ERA	ERA+	OAV	OOB	BH	AVG	PB	PR	/A	PD	TPI
1932	Det-A	2	5	.286	18	7	2	0	1	63²	70	6	29	31	14.8	4.81	98	.278	.366	3	.158	-0	-2	-1	1	0.0
1937	Bro-N	1	2	.333	6	3	1	0	0	16¹	19	2	9	2	15.4	6.61	61	.284	.368	0	.000	-1	-5	-5	0	-0.8
1938	Bro-N	0	1	.000	15	0	0	0	0	19²	23	1	11	6	16.9	4.58	85	.291	.398	0	.000	-0	-2	-1	0	-0.1
Total 3		3	8	.273	39	10	3	0	1	99²	112	9	49	39	15.4	5.06	88	.281	.373	3	.120	-1	-9	-7	1	-0.9

● **ED MARS**   Mars, Edward M. b: 12/4/1866, Chicago, Ill. d: 12/9/41, Chicago, Ill. 5'9", 166 lbs. Deb: 8/12/1890

YEAR	TM/L	W	L	PCT	G	GS	CG	SH	SV	IP	H	HR	BB	SO	RAT	ERA	ERA+	OAV	OOB	BH	AVG	PB	PR	/A	PD	TPI
1890	Syr-a	9	5	.643	16	14	14	0	0	121¹	132	2	49	76	14.0	4.67	76	.269	.341	14	.275	4	-11	-15	1	-1.0

● **CUDDLES MARSHALL**   Marshall, Clarence Westly b: 4/28/25, Bellingham, Wash. BR/TR, 6'3", 200 lbs. Deb: 4/24/46

YEAR	TM/L	W	L	PCT	G	GS	CG	SH	SV	IP	H	HR	BB	SO	RAT	ERA	ERA+	OAV	OOB	BH	AVG	PB	PR	/A	PD	TPI
1946	NY-A	3	4	.429	23	11	1	0	0	81	96	4	56	32	16.9	5.33	65	.308	.413	4	.143	-1	-16	-17	1	-1.3
1948	NY-A	0	0	—	1	0	0	0	0	1	0	0	3	0	27.0	0.00	—	.000	.500	0	—	0	0	-0	-0	-0.0
1949	NY-A	3	0	1.000	21	2	0	0	3	49¹	48	3	48	13	17.9	5.11	79	.259	.417	1	.111	-0	-5	-6	1	-0.4
1950	StL-A	1	3	.250	28	2	0	0	1	53²	72	1	51	24	20.8	7.88	63	.321	.449	4	.333	1	-20	-17	-1	-1.2
Total 4		7	7	.500	73	15	1	0	4	185	216	8	158	69	18.3	5.98	67	.298	.426	9	.184	-1	-41	-40	1	-2.9

● **MIKE MARSHALL**   Marshall, Michael Grant b: 1/15/43, Adrian, Mich. BR/TR, 5'10", 180 lbs. Deb: 5/31/67

YEAR	TM/L	W	L	PCT	G	GS	CG	SH	SV	IP	H	HR	BB	SO	RAT	ERA	ERA+	OAV	OOB	BH	AVG	PB	PR	/A	PD	TPI
1967	Det-A	1	3	.250	37	0	0	0	10	59	51	6	20	41	11.1	1.98	165	.233	.303	2	.222	0	8	8	1	1.0
1969	Sea-A	3	10	.231	20	14	3	1	0	87²	99	8	35	47	14.0	5.13	71	.281	.350	7	.259	3	-15	-15	3	-1.4
1970	Hou-N	0	1	.000	4	0	0	0	0	5¹	8	0	4	5	21.9	8.44	46	.400	.520	0	—	0	-3	-3	1	-0.4
	Mon-N	3	7	.300	24	5	0	0	3	64²	56	4	29	38	11.8	3.48	118	.225	.306	1	.091	0	4	5	2	0.9
	Yr	3	8	.273	28	5	0	0	3	70	64	4	33	43	12.5	3.86	106	.237	.320	1	.091	0	1	2	2	0.5
1971	Mon-N	5	8	.385	66	0	0	0	23	111¹	100	9	50	85	12.4	4.28	82	.247	.336	3	.188	0	-10	-9	3	-1.1
1972	Mon-N	14	8	.636	65	0	0	0	18	116	82	3	47	95	10.2	1.78	199	.202	.289	3	.136	0	22	23	2	5.3
1973	Mon-N	14	11	.560	92	0	0	0	31	179	163	10	75	124	12.2	2.66	143	.252	.333	8	.242	1	20	23	3	4.5
1974	*LA-N★	15	12	.556	106	0	0	0	21	208¹	191	9	56	143	10.7	2.42	141	.247	.299	8	.235	1	28	23	1	3.5
1975	LA-N☆	9	14	.391	57	0	0	0	13	109¹	98	8	39	64	11.6	3.29	103	.242	.315	1	.067	-1	4	1	2	0.4
1976	LA-N	4	3	.571	30	0	0	0	8	62²	64	2	25	39	12.9	4.45	76	.270	.342	0	.000	0	-7	-7	2	-0.8
	Atl-N	2	1	.667	24	0	0	0	6	36²	35	4	14	17	12.3	3.19	119	.259	.333	1	.167	0	1	2	0	0.4
	Yr	6	4	.600	54	0	0	0	14	99¹	99	6	39	56	12.6	3.99	89	.264	.335	1	.091	0	-5	-5	2	-0.4
1977	Atl-N	1	0	1.000	4	0	0	0	0	6	12	1	2	6	21.0	9.00	49	.400	.438	1	1.000	0	-3	-3	-0	-0.4
	Tex-A	2	2	.500	12	4	0	0	1	35²	42	0	13	18	14.4	4.04	101	.304	.373	0	—	0	0	0	0	0.0
1978	Min-A	10	12	.455	54	0	0	0	21	99	80	3	37	56	10.7	2.45	156	.225	.300	0	—	0	14	15	1	4.0
1979	Min-A	10	15	.400	90	1	0	0	32	142²	132	8	48	81	11.6	2.65	165	.254	.322	0	—	0	25	27	3	5.7
1980	Min-A	1	3	.250	18	0	0	0	1	32¹	42	4	12	13	15.6	6.12	71	.323	.389	0	—	0	-6	-6	1	-1.1
1981	NY-N	3	2	.600	20	0	0	0	2	31	26	2	8	9	9.9	2.61	133	.224	.274	0	—	0	3	3	-0	0.5
Total 14		97	112	.464	723	24	3	1	188	1386²	1281	79	514	880	11.9	3.14	118	.249	.321	35	.196	6	84	87	20	21.0

● **RUBE MARSHALL**   Marshall, Roy De Verne "Cy" b: 1/19/1890, Salineville, Ohio d: 6/11/80, Dover, Ohio BR/TR, 5'11", 170 lbs. Deb: 9/28/12

YEAR	TM/L	W	L	PCT	G	GS	CG	SH	SV	IP	H	HR	BB	SO	RAT	ERA	ERA+	OAV	OOB	BH	AVG	PB	PR	/A	PD	TPI
1912	Phi-N	0	1	.000	2	1	0	0	0	3	12	0	1	2	39.0	21.00	17	.632	.650	0	—	0	-6	-6	0	-1.2
1913	Phi-N	0	1	.000	14	1	0	0	0	45¹	54	2	22	18	15.3	4.57	73	.297	.376	1	.091	-1	-7	-6	0	-0.2
1914	Phi-N	6	7	.462	27	19	7	0	1	134¹	144	2	50	49	13.3	3.75	78	.279	.349	6	.140	-2	-14	-12	1	-1.3
1915	Buf-F	2	1	.667	21	4	1	0	0	59¹	62	1	33	21	14.7	3.94	71	.281	.379	5	.294	1	-8	-8	-1	-0.4
Total 4		8	10	.444	64	25	9	0	1	242	272	5	106	90	14.4	4.17	72	.290	.367	12	.169	-2	-35	-32	-0	-3.1

● **PHONNEY MARTIN**   Martin, Alphonse Case b: 8/4/1845, New York, N.Y. d: 5/24/33, Hollis, N.Y. 5'7", 148 lbs. Deb: 4/26/1872 ◆

YEAR	TM/L	W	L	PCT	G	GS	CG	SH	SV	IP	H	HR	BB	SO	RAT	ERA	ERA+	OAV	OOB	BH	AVG	PB	PR	/A	PD	TPI
1872	Tro-n	1	2	.333	8	3	0	0	0	37¹	73	0	2	1	18.1	5.79	64	.365	.372	0	—	0	-4	-4	0	-0.4
	Eck-n	2	7	.222	10	9	9	0	0	85	142	1	4	2	15.5	4.45	78	.318	.324	14	.177	-3	-7	-9	0	-0.7
	Yr	3	9	.250	18	12	9	0	0	122¹	215	1	6	3	16.3	4.86	73	.332	.338	48	.241	-2	-15	-18	-1	-1.1

YEAR	TM/L	W	L	PCT	G	GS	CG	SH	SV	IP	H	HR	BB	SO	RAT	ERA	ERA+	OAV	OOB	BH	AVG	PB	PR	/A	PD	TPI
1873	Mut-n	0	1	.000	6	1	1	0	0	34	50	0	7	1	15.1	3.44	92	.294	.322	30	.216	-1	-1	-1		0.0
Total	2 n	3	10	.231	24	13	10	0	0	156¹	265	1	13	4	16.0	4.55	70	.324	.335	78	.231	-3	-23	-24		-1.1

● **BARNEY MARTIN**   Martin, Barnes Robertson   b: 3/3/23, Columbia, S.C.   BR/TR, 5'11", 170 lbs.   Deb: 4/22/53   F

YEAR	TM/L	W	L	PCT	G	GS	CG	SH	SV	IP	H	HR	BB	SO	RAT	ERA	ERA+	OAV	OOB	BH	AVG	PB	PR	/A	PD	TPI
1953	Cin-N	0	0	—	1	0	0	0	0	2	3	0	1	1	18.0	9.00	48	.333	.400	0	—	0	-1	-1	-0	0.0

● **RENIE MARTIN**   Martin, Donald Renie   b: 8/30/55, Dover, Del.   BR/TR, 6'4", 190 lbs.   Deb: 5/9/79

YEAR	TM/L	W	L	PCT	G	GS	CG	SH	SV	IP	H	HR	BB	SO	RAT	ERA	ERA+	OAV	OOB	BH	AVG	PB	PR	/A	PD	TPI
1979	KC-A	0	3	.000	25	0	0	0	5	34²	32	1	14	25	12.2	5.19	82	.248	.326	0	—	0	-4	-4	1	-0.4
1980	*KC-A	10	10	.500	32	20	2	0	2	137¹	133	18	70	68	13.4	4.39	92	.255	.345	0	—	0	-5	-5	-0	-0.8
1981	*KC-A	4	5	.444	29	0	0	0	4	61²	55	2	29	25	12.3	2.77	130	.244	.331	0	—	0	6	6	1	1.0
1982	SF-N	7	10	.412	29	25	1	0	0	141¹	148	14	64	63	13.5	4.65	77	.274	.350	13	.265	3	-16	-17	1	-1.4
1983	SF-N	2	4	.333	37	6	0	0	1	94¹	95	11	51	43	14.2	4.20	84	.268	.365	9	.346	4	-6	-7	1	0.2
1984	SF-N	1	1	.500	12	0	0	0	0	23¹	29	2	16	8	17.4	3.86	91	.305	.405	3	.500	1	-1	-1	1	0.1
	Phi-N	0	2	.000	9	0	0	0	0	15²	17	2	12	5	16.7	4.60	79	.274	.392	0	—	-0	-2	-2	1	-0.1
	Yr	1	3	.250	21	0	0	0	0	39	46	4	28	13	17.1	4.15	86	.293	.400	3	.375	1	-2	-3	2	0.0
Total	6	24	35	.407	173	51	3	0	12	508¹	509	50	256	237	13.6	4.27	88	.264	.352	25	.301	8	-28	-29	5	-1.4

● **SPEED MARTIN**   Martin, Elwood Good   b: 9/15/1893, Wawawai, Wash.   d: 6/14/83, Lemon Grove, Cal.   BR/TR, 6', 165 lbs.   Deb: 7/5/17

YEAR	TM/L	W	L	PCT	G	GS	CG	SH	SV	IP	H	HR	BB	SO	RAT	ERA	ERA+	OAV	OOB	BH	AVG	PB	PR	/A	PD	TPI
1917	StL-A	0	2	.000	9	2	0	0	0	15²	20	0	5	5	14.4	5.74	45	.339	.391	0	.000	-0	-5	-5	1	-0.6
1918	Chi-N	5	2	.714	9	5	4	1	1	53²	47	0	14	16	10.4	1.84	151	.246	.301	3	.188	-0	5	6	1	0.9
1919	Chi-N	8	8	.500	35	14	7	2	2	163²	158	2	52	54	11.8	2.47	116	.259	.321	8	.182	-1	8	7	2	0.8
1920	Chi-N	4	15	.211	35	13	6	0	2	136	165	2	50	44	14.3	4.83	66	.305	.365	7	.159	-0	-26	-25	1	-3.1
1921	Chi-N	11	15	.423	37	28	13	1	1	217¹	245	12	68	86	13.0	4.35	88	.298	.353	17	.233	1	-14	-13	2	-1.0
1922	Chi-N	1	0	1.000	1	1	0	0	0	6	10	0	2	2	18.0	7.50	56	.385	.429	0	.000	-0	-2	-2	-0	-0.3
Total	6	29	42	.408	126	63	30	4	6	592¹	645	16	191	207	12.8	3.78	87	.287	.344	35	.194	-0	-33	-32	7	-3.3

● **FRED MARTIN**   Martin, Fred Turner   b: 6/27/15, Williams, Okla.   d: 6/11/79, Chicago, Ill.   BR/TR, 6'1", 185 lbs.   Deb: 4/21/46   C

YEAR	TM/L	W	L	PCT	G	GS	CG	SH	SV	IP	H	HR	BB	SO	RAT	ERA	ERA+	OAV	OOB	BH	AVG	PB	PR	/A	PD	TPI
1946	StL-N	2	1	.667	6	3	2	0	0	28²	29	0	8	19	11.6	4.08	85	.254	.303	3	.273	0	-2	-2	0	-0.1
1949	StL-N	6	0	1.000	21	5	3	0	0	70	65	3	20	30	10.9	2.44	170	.243	.295	6	.300	1	12	13	0	1.1
1950	StL-N	4	2	.667	30	2	0	0	0	63¹	87	4	30	19	16.8	5.12	84	.331	.401	4	.267	1	-7	-6	1	-0.3
Total	3	12	3	.800	57	10	5	0	0	162	181	7	58	68	13.3	3.78	108	.281	.341	13	.283	2	3	6	1	0.7

● **DOC MARTIN**   Martin, Harold Winthrop   b: 9/23/1887, Roxbury, Mass.   d: 4/14/35, Milton, Mass.   BR/TR, 5'11", 165 lbs.   Deb: 10/7/08

YEAR	TM/L	W	L	PCT	G	GS	CG	SH	SV	IP	H	HR	BB	SO	RAT	ERA	ERA+	OAV	OOB	BH	AVG	PB	PR	/A	PD	TPI
1908	Phi-A	0	1	.000	1	0	0	0	0	2	2	0	3	2	27.0	13.50	19	.286	.545	0	.000	-0	-2	-2	-0	-0.8
1911	Phi-A	1	1	.500	11	3	1	0	0	38	40	1	17	21	14.7	4.50	70	.272	.367	3	.214	0	-5	-6	0	-0.2
1912	Phi-A	0	0	—	2	0	0	0	0	4¹	5	0	5	4	22.8	10.38	30	.333	.524	0	.000	-1	-3	-4	0	0.0
Total	3	1	2	.333	14	4	1	0	0	44¹	47	1	25	27	16.0	5.48	57	.278	.393	3	.167	-0	-11	-12	1	-1.0

● **PEPPER MARTIN**   Martin, John Leonard Roosevelt "The Wild Horse Of The Osage"   b: 2/29/04, Temple, Okla.   d: 3/5/65, McAlester, Okla.   BR/TR, 5'8", 170 lbs.   Deb: 4/16/28   C◆

YEAR	TM/L	W	L	PCT	G	GS	CG	SH	SV	IP	H	HR	BB	SO	RAT	ERA	ERA+	OAV	OOB	BH	AVG	PB	PR	/A	PD	TPI
1934	*StL-N★	0	0	—	1	0	0	0	0	2	1	0	0	0	4.5	4.50	94	.167	.167	131	.289	0	-0	-0	0	0.0
1936	StL-N	0	0	—	1	0	0	0	0	2	1	0	2	0	13.5	0.00	—	.200	.429	177	.309	1	1	1	-0	0.0
Total	2	0	0	—	2	0	0	0	0	4	2	0	2	0	9.0	2.25	181	.182	.308	1227	.298	1	1	1	0	0.0

● **JOHN MARTIN**   Martin, John Robert   b: 4/11/56, Wyandotte, Mich.   BB/TL, 6', 190 lbs.   Deb: 8/27/80

YEAR	TM/L	W	L	PCT	G	GS	CG	SH	SV	IP	H	HR	BB	SO	RAT	ERA	ERA+	OAV	OOB	BH	AVG	PB	PR	/A	PD	TPI
1980	StL-N	2	3	.400	9	5	1	0	0	42	39	1	9	23	10.3	4.29	86	.247	.287	3	.273	1	-3	-3	-1	-0.3
1981	StL-N	8	5	.615	17	15	4	0	0	102²	85	10	26	36	9.9	3.42	104	.228	.283	7	.212	2	1	2	0	0.4
1982	StL-N	4	5	.444	24	6	0	0	0	66	56	6	30	21	11.7	4.23	86	.230	.314	1	.091	-0	-5	-4	-1	-0.7
1983	StL-N	3	1	.750	26	5	0	0	0	66¹	60	6	26	29	11.9	3.53	103	.242	.319	4	.222	-1	1	1	1	0.2
	Det-A	0	0	—	15	0	0	0	1	13¹	15	2	4	11	12.8	7.43	53	.294	.345	0	—	0	-5	-5	-0	-0.1
Total	4	17	14	.548	91	32	5	0	1	290¹	255	25	95	120	11.0	3.94	92	.238	.302	15	.205	3	-11	-10	-1	-0.5

● **MORRIE MARTIN**   Martin, Morris Webster "Lefty"   b: 9/3/22, Dixon, Mo.   BL/TL, 6', 180 lbs.   Deb: 4/25/49

YEAR	TM/L	W	L	PCT	G	GS	CG	SH	SV	IP	H	HR	BB	SO	RAT	ERA	ERA+	OAV	OOB	BH	AVG	PB	PR	/A	PD	TPI
1949	Bro-N	1	3	.250	10	4	0	0	0	30²	39	5	15	15	16.4	7.04	58	.320	.403	2	.200	-0	-10	-10	-1	-1.1
1951	Phi-A	11	4	.733	35	13	3	1	0	138	139	13	63	35	13.5	3.78	113	.259	.343	11	.220	-1	5	8	2	0.8
1952	Phi-A	0	2	.000	5	5	0	0	0	25¹	32	1	15	13	17.4	6.39	62	.302	.398	1	.111	-1	-8	-7	0	-0.6
1953	Phi-A	10	12	.455	58	11	2	0	7	156¹	158	12	64	64	13.0	4.43	97	.262	.336	4	.095	-4	-8	-3	0	-0.7
1954	Phi-A	2	4	.333	13	6	2	0	0	52²	57	9	19	24	13.3	5.47	71	.278	.345	4	.235	0	-10	-9	-0	-0.9
	Chi-A	5	4	.556	35	2	1	0	5	70	52	5	24	31	9.9	2.06	182	.210	.282	2	.133	-0	13	13	-1	1.7
	Yr	7	8	.467	48	8	3	0	5	122²	109	14	43	55	11.2	3.52	108	.237	.304	6	.188	-0	3	4	-1	0.8
1955	Chi-A	2	3	.400	37	0	0	0	2	52	50	4	20	22	12.5	3.63	109	.259	.335	3	.300	-1	2	1	0	0.3
1956	Chi-A	1	0	1.000	10	0	0	0	0	18¹	21	1	7	9	13.7	4.91	84	.292	.354	1	.200	-0	-2	-2	0	-0.1
	Bal-A	1	1	.500	9	0	0	0	0	5	10	1	2	3	23.4	10.80	36	.400	.464	0	—	-0	-4	-4	0	-1.3
	Yr	2	1	.667	19	0	0	0	0	23¹	31	2	9	12	15.8	6.17	66	.316	.380	1	.200	-0	-5	-5	0	-1.4
1957	StL-N	0	0	—	4	1	0	0	0	10²	5	0	4	7	8.4	2.53	157	.143	.250	0	.000	-0	2	2	0	0.0
1958	StL-N	3	1	.750	17	0	0	0	0	24²	19	3	12	16	12.0	4.74	87	.211	.317	0	.000	-1	-2	-2	0	-0.3
	Cle-A	2	0	1.000	14	0	0	0	1	18²	20	0	8	5	13.5	2.41	151	.294	.368	0	—	0	3	3	0	0.3
1959	Chi-N	0	0	—	3	0	0	0	0	2¹	5	2	1	1	27.0	19.29	20	.455	.538	0	—	-0	-4	-4	0	0.0
Total	10	38	34	.528	250	42	8	1	15	604²	607	56	249	245	13.1	4.29	95	.262	.341	28	.170	-6	-23	-13	2	-1.9

● **PAT MARTIN**   Martin, Patrick Francis   b: 4/13/1892, Brooklyn, N.Y.   d: 2/4/49, Brooklyn, N.Y.   BL/TL, 5'11.5", 170 lbs.   Deb: 9/20/19

YEAR	TM/L	W	L	PCT	G	GS	CG	SH	SV	IP	H	HR	BB	SO	RAT	ERA	ERA+	OAV	OOB	BH	AVG	PB	PR	/A	PD	TPI
1919	Phi-A	0	2	.000	2	2	1	0	0	11	11	0	8	6	15.5	4.09	84	.256	.373	0	—	-0	-1	-1	-0	-0.2
1920	Phi-A	1	4	.200	8	5	2	0	0	32¹	48	2	25	14	21.4	6.12	66	.364	.478	4	.400	1	-8	-8	-1	-0.9
Total	2	1	6	.143	10	7	3	0	0	43¹	59	2	33	20	19.9	5.61	69	.337	.453	4	.308	1	-9	-8	-1	-1.1

● **PAUL MARTIN**   Martin, Paul Charles   b: 3/10/32, Brownstone, Pa.   BR/TR, 6'6", 235 lbs.   Deb: 7/2/55

YEAR	TM/L	W	L	PCT	G	GS	CG	SH	SV	IP	H	HR	BB	SO	RAT	ERA	ERA+	OAV	OOB	BH	AVG	PB	PR	/A	PD	TPI
1955	Pit-N	0	1	.000	7	1	0	0	0	7	13	0	17	3	39.9	14.14	29	.464	.674	0	—	0	-8	-8	-0	-0.9

● **RAY MARTIN**   Martin, Raymond Joseph   b: 3/13/25, Norwood, Mass.   BR/TR, 6'2", 177 lbs.   Deb: 8/15/43

YEAR	TM/L	W	L	PCT	G	GS	CG	SH	SV	IP	H	HR	BB	SO	RAT	ERA	ERA+	OAV	OOB	BH	AVG	PB	PR	/A	PD	TPI
1943	Bos-N	0	0	—	2	0	0	0	0	3¹	3	0	1	1	10.8	8.10	42	.231	.286	0	.000	-0	-2	-2	0	0.0
1947	Bos-N	1	0	1.000	1	1	1	0	0	9	7	0	4	2	11.0	1.00	389	.212	.297	0	.000	-0	3	3	0	0.4
1948	Bos-N	0	0	—	2	0	0	0	0	2¹	0	0	1	0	3.9	0.00	—	.000	.125	0	—	0	1	1	-0	0.0
Total	3	1	0	1.000	5	1	1	0	0	14²	10	0	6	3	9.8	2.45	154	.189	.271	0	.000	0	2	2	1	0.4

● **JOE MARTINA**   Martina, Joseph John "Oyster Joe"   b: 7/8/1889, New Orleans, La.   d: 3/22/62, New Orleans, La.   BR/TR, 6', 183 lbs.   Deb: 4/19/24

YEAR	TM/L	W	L	PCT	G	GS	CG	SH	SV	IP	H	HR	BB	SO	RAT	ERA	ERA+	OAV	OOB	BH	AVG	PB	PR	/A	PD	TPI
1924	*Was-A	6	8	.429	24	13	6	2	0	125¹	129	7	56	57	13.7	4.67	86	.271	.355	14	.326	3	-6	-9	-2	-0.7

● **ALFREDO MARTINEZ**   Martinez, Alfredo   b: 3/15/57, Los Angeles, Cal.   BR/TR, 6'3", 185 lbs.   Deb: 4/20/80

YEAR	TM/L	W	L	PCT	G	GS	CG	SH	SV	IP	H	HR	BB	SO	RAT	ERA	ERA+	OAV	OOB	BH	AVG	PB	PR	/A	PD	TPI
1980	Cal-A	7	9	.438	30	23	4	1	0	149¹	150	14	59	57	12.7	4.52	87	.259	.328	0	—	0	-8	-10	-2	-1.0
1981	Cal-A	0	0	—	2	0	0	0	0	6	5	1	3	4	12.0	3.00	122	.227	.320	0	—	0	0	-0	0	0.0
Total	2	7	9	.438	32	23	4	1	0	155¹	155	15	62	61	12.6	4.46	88	.257	.328	0	—	0	-8	-9	-2	-1.0

● **DAVE MARTINEZ**   Martinez, David   b: 9/26/64, New York, N.Y.   BL/TL, 5'10", 150 lbs.   Deb: 6/15/86   ◆

YEAR	TM/L	W	L	PCT	G	GS	CG	SH	SV	IP	H	HR	BB	SO	RAT	ERA	ERA+	OAV	OOB	BH	AVG	PB	PR	/A	PD	TPI
1990	Mon-N	0	0	—	1	0	0	0	0	2	2	0	2	0	108.0	54.00	7	.667	.800	109	.279	0	-2	-2	0	-0.9

YEAR TM/L	W	L	PCT	G	GS	CG	SH	SV	IP	H	HR	BB	SO	RAT	ERA	ERA+	OAV	OOB	BH	AVG	PB	PR	/A	PD	TPI
● **TIPPY MARTINEZ** Martinez, Felix Anthony b: 5/31/50, LaJunta, Colo. BL/TL, 5'10", 180 lbs. Deb: 8/9/74																								
1974 NY-A	0	0	—	10	0	0	0	0	12²	14	0	9	10	17.1	4.26	82	.286	.407	0	—	0	-1	-1	-0	0.1
1975 NY-A	1	2	.333	23	2	0	0	8	37	27	6	32	20	14.6	2.68	136	.208	.368	0	—	0	5	4	-1	0.4
1976 NY-A	2	0	1.000	11	0	0	0	2	28	18	1	14	14	10.3	1.93	177	.191	.296	0	—	0	5	5	1	0.5
Bal-A	3	1	.750	28	0	0	0	8	41²	32	0	28	31	13.2	2.59	126	.222	.353	0	—	0	4	3	1	0.6
Yr	5	1	.833	39	0	0	0	10	69²	50	1	42	45	12.9	2.33	143	.210	.333	0	—	0	9	8	2	1.1
1977 Bal-A	5	1	.833	41	0	0	0	9	50	46	7	27	29	13.3	2.70	140	.266	.363	0	—	0	8	6	1	1.2
1978 Bal-A	3	3	.500	42	0	0	0	5	69	77	4	40	57	15.4	4.83	72	.281	.375	0	—	0	-8	-10	-1	-0.4
1979 *Bal-A	10	3	.769	39	0	0	0	3	78	59	0	31	61	10.5	2.88	139	.210	.291	0	—	0	12	10	1	1.9
1980 Bal-A	4	4	.500	53	0	0	0	10	80²	69	5	34	68	11.6	3.01	131	.240	.322	0	—	0	9	8	2	1.2
1981 Bal-A	3	3	.500	37	0	0	0	11	59	48	4	30	50	12.2	2.90	125	.231	.333	0	—	0	5	5	1	0.7
1982 Bal-A	8	8	.500	76	0	0	0	16	95	81	6	37	78	11.3	3.41	118	.240	.317	0	—	0	7	7	-0	1.3
1983 *Bal-A☆	9	3	.750	65	0	0	0	21	103¹	76	10	37	81	9.8	2.35	168	.211	.284	0	—	0	20	18	2	3.1
1984 Bal-A	4	9	.308	55	0	0	0	17	89²	88	9	51	72	14.0	3.91	99	.260	.356	0	—	0	1	-0	0	-0.1
1985 Bal-A	3	3	.500	49	0	0	0	4	70	70	8	37	47	13.8	5.40	75	.261	.351	0	—	0	-10	-11	1	-0.8
1986 Bal-A	0	2	.000	14	0	0	0	0	16	18	1	12	11	16.9	5.63	73	.295	.411	0	—	0	-3	-3	-0	-0.3
1988 Min-A	0	0	—	3	0	0	0	0	4	8	1	4	3	29.3	18.00	23	.471	.591	0	—	0	-6	-6	-0	-0.6
Total 14	55	42	.567	546	2	0	0	115	834	732	53	425	632	12.6	3.45	111	.242	.337	0	—	0	47	34	9	9.4
● **BUCK MARTINEZ** Martinez, John Albert b: 11/7/48, Redding, Cal. BR/TR, 5'10", 190 lbs. Deb: 6/18/69 ♦																								
1979 Mil-A	0	0	—	1	0	0	0	0	1	1	0	1	0	18.0	9.00	46	.250	.400	53	.270	1	-1	-1	0	0.0
● **DENNIS MARTINEZ** Martinez, Jose Dennis (Emilia) b: 5/14/55, Granada, Nicaragua BR/TR, 6'1", 185 lbs. Deb: 9/14/76																								
1976 Bal-A	1	2	.333	4	2	1	0	0	27²	23	1	8	18	10.1	2.60	126	.237	.295	0	—	0	3	2	0	0.5
1977 Bal-A	14	7	.667	42	13	5	0	4	166²	157	10	64	107	12.4	4.10	92	.253	.330	0	—	0	-1	-6	0	-0.6
1978 Bal-A	16	11	.593	40	38	15	2	0	276¹	257	20	93	142	11.5	3.52	99	.250	.314	0	—	0	8	-1	4	0.5
1979 *Bal-A	15	16	.484	40	39	**18**	3	0	**292¹**	279	28	78	132	11.0	3.66	109	.253	.303	0	—	0	18	11	3	1.5
1980 Bal-A	6	4	.600	25	12	2	0	1	99²	103	12	44	42	13.5	3.97	100	.272	.351	0	—	0	1	-0	0	0.0
1981 Bal-A	**14**	5	.737	25	24	9	2	0	179	173	10	62	88	11.9	3.32	109	.254	.318	0	—	0	7	6	4	1.1
1982 Bal-A	16	12	.571	40	39	10	2	0	252	262	30	87	111	12.7	4.21	96	.267	.331	0	—	0	-4	-5	0	-0.5
1983 Bal-A	7	16	.304	32	25	4	0	0	153	209	21	45	71	15.1	5.53	71	.330	.376	0	—	0	-25	-27	5	-2.9
1984 Bal-A	6	9	.400	34	20	2	0	0	141²	145	26	37	77	11.9	5.02	77	.263	.315	0	—	0	-16	-18	1	-1.5
1985 Bal-A	13	11	.542	33	31	3	1	0	180	203	29	63	68	13.8	5.15	78	.288	.353	0	—	0	-20	-22	0	-2.5
1986 Bal-A	0	0	—	4	0	0	0	0	6²	11	0	2	2	17.6	6.75	61	.367	.406	0	—	0	-2	-2	0	0.1
Mon-N	3	6	.333	19	15	1	1	0	98	103	11	28	63	12.3	4.59	80	.274	.329	3	.100	-0	-10	-10	1	-0.8
1987 Mon-N	11	4	.733	22	22	3	1	0	144²	133	9	40	84	11.1	3.30	127	.244	.302	3	.065	-2	13	15	0	1.2
1988 Mon-N	15	13	.536	34	34	9	2	0	235¹	215	21	55	120	10.6	2.72	132	.239	.287	15	.192	2	19	23	0	3.0
1989 Mon-N	16	7	.696	34	33	5	2	0	232	227	21	49	142	11.0	3.18	111	.257	.301	9	.125	-1	8	9	3	1.1
1990 Mon-N★	10	11	.476	32	32	7	2	0	226	191	16	49	156	9.8	2.95	124	.228	.275	7	.103	-2	21	18	1	1.5
1991 Mon-N★	14	11	.560	31	31	**9**	**5**	0	222	187	9	62	123	10.3	**2.39**	151	.226	.283	11	.153	1	**32**	30	4	3.9
1992 Mon-N★	16	11	.593	32	32	6	0	0	226¹	172	12	60	147	9.6	2.47	141	.211	.273	14	.189	1	26	25	3	3.5
1993 Mon-N	15	9	.625	35	34	2	0	1	224²	211	27	64	138	11.5	3.85	108	.246	.307	11	.159	-0	5	8	3	1.1
1994 Cle-A	11	6	.647	24	24	7	3	0	176²	166	14	44	92	11.1	3.52	141	.247	.301	0	—	0	25	28	0	2.1
Total 19	219	171	.562	582	500	117	26	6	3560²	3427	327	1034	1923	11.5	3.63	106	.253	.311	73	.143	-3	107	84	34	12.3
● **JOSE MARTINEZ** Martinez, Jose Miguel (Martinez) b: 4/1/71, Guayubin, D.R. BR/TR, 6'2", 180 lbs. Deb: 5/10/94																								
1994 SD-N	0	2	.000	4	1	0	0	0	12	18	2	5	7	17.3	6.75	62	.375	.434	0	.000	-0	-3	-3	0	-0.5
● **MARTY MARTINEZ** Martinez, Orlando (Oliva) b: 8/23/41, Havana, Cuba BB/TR, 6'1", 175 lbs. Deb: 5/2/62 MC♦																								
1969 Hou-N	0	0	—	1	0	0	0	0	0²	1	1	0	0	13.5	13.50	26	.333	.333	61	.308	0	-1	-1	-0	0.0
● **PEDRO MARTINEZ** Martinez, Pedro (Aquino) b: 11/29/68, Villa Mella, D.R. BL/TL, 6'2", 155 lbs. Deb: 6/29/93																								
1993 SD-N	3	1	.750	32	0	0	0	0	37	23	4	13	32	9.0	2.43	170	.172	.250	0	.000	-0	7	7	-0	0.6
1994 SD-N	3	2	.600	48	1	0	0	3	68¹	52	4	49	52	13.4	2.90	145	.210	.342	0	.000	-1	10	10	1	0.8
Total 2	6	3	.667	80	1	0	0	3	105¹	75	8	62	84	11.9	2.73	153	.196	.312	0	.000	-1	17	17	1	1.4
● **PEDRO MARTINEZ** Martinez, Pedro Jaime (b: Pedro Jaime (Martinez)) b: 7/25/71, Manoguayabo, D.R. BR/TR, 5'11", 150 lbs. Deb: 9/24/92 F																								
1992 LA-N	0	1	.000	2	1	0	0	0	8	6	0	1	8	7.9	2.25	153	.200	.226	0	.000	-0	1	1	-0	0.1
1993 LA-N	10	5	.667	65	2	0	0	2	107	76	5	57	119	11.5	2.61	146	.201	.312	0	.000	-0	17	14	-2	1.7
1994 Mon-N	11	5	.688	24	23	1	1	0	144²	115	11	45	142	10.6	3.42	124	.220	.295	4	.091	-1	13	13	-1	1.1
Total 3	21	11	.656	91	26	1	1	2	259²	197	16	103	269	10.9	3.05	132	.212	.300	4	.080	-2	31	29	-3	2.9
● **RAMON MARTINEZ** Martinez, Ramon Jaime (b: Ramon Jaime (Martinez)) b: 3/22/68, Santo Domingo, D.R. BR/TR, 6'4", 165 lbs. Deb: 8/13/88 F																								
1988 LA-N	1	3	.250	9	6	0	0	0	35²	27	0	22	23	12.4	3.79	88	.216	.333	0	.000	-1	-2	-0	-1	-0.3
1989 LA-N	6	4	.600	15	15	2	2	0	98²	79	11	41	89	11.4	3.19	107	.219	.308	6	.162	-0	3	2	1	0.4
1990 LA-N★	20	6	.769	33	33	**12**	3	0	234¹	191	22	67	223	10.1	2.92	125	.220	.279	10	.125	-2	23	19	0	1.9
1991 LA-N	17	13	.567	33	33	6	4	0	220¹	190	18	69	150	10.9	3.27	110	.229	.294	9	.117	-1	10	8	-1	0.8
1992 LA-N	8	11	.421	25	25	1	1	0	150²	141	11	69	101	12.8	4.00	86	.245	.331	6	.120	-1	-8	-9	-1	-1.4
1993 LA-N	10	12	.455	32	32	4	3	0	211²	202	15	104	127	13.2	3.44	111	.255	.344	9	.129	-2	14	9	2	0.8
1994 LA-N	12	7	.632	24	24	4	**3**	0	170	160	18	56	119	11.8	3.97	100	.249	.315	18	.273	5	5	-0	-1	0.3
Total 7	74	56	.569	171	168	29	16	0	1121¹	990	95	428	832	11.6	3.44	106	.236	.312	58	.150	-1	45	27	-0	2.5
● **ROGELIO MARTINEZ** Martinez, Rogelio (Ulloa) "Limonar" b: 11/5/18, Cidra, Cuba BR/TR, 6', 180 lbs. Deb: 7/13/50																								
1950 Was-A	0	1	.000	2	1	0	0	0	1¹	4	0	2	0	40.5	27.00	17	.500	.600	0	—	0	-3	-3	-0	-1.5
● **SILVIO MARTINEZ** Martinez, Silvio Ramon (Cabrera) b: 8/19/55, Santiago, D.R. BR/TR, 5'10", 170 lbs. Deb: 4/9/77																								
1977 Chi-A	0	1	.000	10	0	0	0	1	21	28	4	12	10	17.1	5.57	73	.337	.421	0	—	0	-4	-3	0	-0.2
1978 StL-N	9	8	.529	22	22	5	2	0	138¹	114	11	71	45	12.2	3.64	96	.228	.326	8	.170	0	-1	-2	-1	-0.4
1979 StL-N	15	8	.652	32	29	8	2	0	206²	204	14	67	102	11.8	3.27	115	.259	.317	8	.129	-2	11	11	-3	0.7
1980 StL-N	5	10	.333	25	20	2	0	0	119²	127	8	48	39	13.3	4.81	77	.273	.343	3	.086	-2	-16	-15	-2	-2.1
1981 StL-N	2	5	.286	18	16	0	0	0	97	95	4	39	34	12.5	3.99	89	.260	.333	7	.200	1	-5	-5	-1	-0.3
Total 5	31	32	.492	107	87	14	4	1	582²	568	41	237	230	12.5	3.88	95	.258	.331	26	.145	-3	-15	-14	-7	-2.3
● **WEDO MARTINI** Martini, Guido Joe "Southern" b: 7/1/13, Birmingham, Ala. d: 10/28/70, Philadelphia, Pa. BR/TR, 5'10", 165 lbs. Deb: 7/28/35																								
1935 Phi-A	0	2	.000	3	2	0	0	0	6¹	8	0	11	1	27.0	17.05	27	.333	.543	0	.000	-0	-9	-9	1	-1.7
● **JOE MARTY** Marty, Joseph Anton b: 9/1/13, Sacramento, Cal. d: 10/4/84, Sacramento, Cal. BR/TR, 6', 182 lbs. Deb: 4/22/37 ♦																								
1939 Phi-N	0	0	—	1	0	0	0	0	4	2	0	3	1	11.3	4.50	89	.154	.313	76	.254	0	-0	-0	-0	0.0
● **RANDY MARTZ** Martz, Randy Carl b: 5/28/56, Harrisburg, Pa. BL/TR, 6'4", 210 lbs. Deb: 9/6/80																								
1980 Chi-N	1	2	.333	6	6	0	0	0	30¹	28	1	11	5	11.6	2.08	188	.241	.307	1	.111	-1	5	6	1	0.6
1981 Chi-N	5	7	.417	26	16	3	0	0	107²	101	9	32	12.8	3.68	100	.256	.338	6	.214	1	-2	-0	1	-0.8
1982 Chi-N	11	10	.524	28	24	1	0	1	147²	157	17	36	40	11.9	4.21	89	.272	.318	6	.143	1	-10	-8	1	-0.8
1983 Chi-A	0	0	—	1	1	0	0	0	5	4	0	1	1	14.4	3.60	116	.211	.348	0	—	0	0	0	-0	-0.1
Total 4	17	19	.472	68	45	2	0	7	290²	292	24	100	78	12.3	3.78	99	.262	.325	13	.165	1	-7	-1	1	-0.2

YEAR TM/L	W	L	PCT	G	GS	CG	SH	SV	IP	H	HR	BB	SO	RAT	ERA	ERA+	OAV	OOB	BH	AVG	PB	PR	/A	PD	TPI
● **DEL MASON** Mason, Adelbert William b: 10/29/1883, Newfane, N.Y. d: 12/31/62, Winter Park, Fla. BR/TR, 6′, 160 lbs. Deb: 4/23/04																									
1904 Was-A	0	3	.000	5	3	2	0	0	33	45	1	13	16	16.4	6.00	44	.325	.391	0	.000	-2	-12	-12	-1	-1.2
1906 Cin-N	0	1	.000	2	1	1	0	0	12	10	1	6	4	12.8	4.50	61	.250	.362	0	.000	-1	-2	-2	-0	-0.3
1907 Cin-N	5	12	.294	25	17	13	1	0	146	144	2	55	45	12.6	3.14	83	.277	.353	8	.182	-0	-11	-9	1	-1.0
Total 3	5	16	.238	32	21	16	1	0	191	199	4	74	65	13.3	3.72	70	.285	.361	8	.125	-3	-26	-23	-0	-2.5
● **CHARLIE MASON** Mason, Charles E. b: 6/25/1853, New Orleans, La. d: 10/21/36, Philadelphia, Pa. BR/TR, 175 lbs. Deb: 4/26/1875 M♦																									
1875 Was-n	0	0	—	1	0	0	0	0	2	3	0	1		18.0	4.50	58	.300	.364	3	.088	-0	-0			0.0
● **ERNIE MASON** Mason, Ernest b: New Orleans, La. d: 7/30/04, Covington, La. Deb: 7/17/1894																									
1894 StL-N	0	3	.000	4	2	2	0	0	22²	34	1	10	3	17.5	7.15	76	.342	.403	3	.250	-0	-5	-4	-1	-0.4
● **HANK MASON** Mason, Henry b: 6/19/31, Marshall, Mo. BR/TR, 6′, 185 lbs. Deb: 9/12/58																									
1958 Phi-N	0	0	—	1	0	0	0	0	5	7	0	2	3	18.0	10.80	37	.368	.455	0	.000	-0	-4	-4	-0	0.0
1960 Phi-N	0	0	—	3	0	0	0	0	5²	9	1	5	3	22.2	9.53	41	.375	.483	0	.000	-0	-4	-4	-0	0.0
Total 2	0	0	—	4	0	0	0	0	10²	16	1	7	6	20.3	10.13	39	.372	.471	0	.000	-0	-7	-7	-0	0.0
● **MIKE MASON** Mason, Michael Paul b: 11/21/58, Faribault, Minn. BL/TL, 6′2″, 205 lbs. Deb: 9/13/82																									
1982 Tex-A	1	2	.333	4	4	0	0	0	23	23	3	9	8	11.7	5.09	76	.244	.316	0	—	0	-3	-3	0	-0.2
1983 Tex-A	0	2	.000	5	0	0	0	0	10²	10	0	6	9	14.3	5.91	68	.244	.354	0	—	0	-2	-2	0	-0.3
1984 Tex-A	9	13	.409	36	24	4	0	0	184¹	159	18	51	113	10.4	3.61	115	.233	.288	0	—	0	8	11	-1	1.0
1985 Tex-A	8	15	.348	38	30	1	1	0	179	212	22	73	92	14.5	4.83	88	.299	.366	0	—	0	-14	-12	-1	-1.4
1986 Tex-A	7	3	.700	27	22	2	1	0	135	135	11	56	85	12.7	4.33	99	.257	.329	0	—	0	-4	-4	-0	-0.1
1987 Tex-A	0	2	.000	8	6	0	0	0	29	37	6	22	21	19.6	5.59	80	.322	.447	0	—	0	-4	-4	-0	-0.2
Chi-N	4	1	.800	17	4	0	0	0	38	43	4	23	28	15.9	5.68	75	.303	.404	2	.222	0	-7	-6	-0	-0.7
1988 Min-A	0	1	.000	5	0	0	0	0	6²	9	1	9	7	23.0	10.80	38	.286	.459	0	—	0	-5	-5	-0	-0.7
Total 7	29	39	.426	140	90	7	2	0	605²	625	65	249	363	13.2	4.53	93	.268	.342	2	.222	0	-28	-21	-1	-2.6
● **ROGER MASON** Mason, Roger Le Roy b: 9/18/58, Bellaire, Mich. BR/TR, 6′6″, 215 lbs. Deb: 9/4/84																									
1984 Det-A	1	1	.500	5	2	0	0	1	22	23	1	10	15	13.5	4.50	87	.271	.347	0	—	0	-1	-1	0	-0.1
1985 SF-N	1	3	.250	5	5	1	1	0	29²	28	1	11	26	11.8	2.12	162	.243	.310	1	.091	-0	5	4	-0	0.5
1986 SF-N	3	4	.429	11	11	0	0	0	60	56	5	30	43	13.4	4.80	73	.250	.346	1	.048	-2	-7	-9	-1	-1.1
1987 SF-N	1	1	.500	5	5	0	0	0	26	30	4	10	18	13.8	4.50	85	.303	.367	1	.125	0	-1	-2	-0	-0.1
1989 Hou-N	0	0	—	2	0	0	0	0	1¹	2	0	1	3	27.0	20.25	17	.333	.500	0	—	0	-2	-2	-0	-0.2
1991 *Pit-N	3	2	.600	24	0	0	0	0	29²	21	2	6	21	8.5	3.03	118	.200	.250	0	—	0	2	2	0	0.4
1992 *Pit-N	5	7	.417	65	0	0	0	8	88	80	11	33	56	12.0	4.09	84	.246	.323	0	.000	-1	-6	-6	-1	-1.2
1993 SD-N	0	7	.000	34	0	0	0	0	50	43	1	18	39	11.3	3.24	128	.242	.318	0	.000	-0	4	5	-0	0.6
*Phi-N	5	5	.500	34	0	0	0	0	49²	47	9	16	32	11.4	4.89	81	.246	.304	1	.333	-0	-5	-5	-1	-1.0
Yr	5	12	.294	68	0	0	0	0	99²	90	10	34	71	11.2	4.06	100	.241	.304	1	.167	-0	-0	-0	-2	-0.4
1994 Phi-N	1	1	.500	6	0	0	0	0	8²	11	2	5	7	16.6	5.19	79	.306	.390	0	—	0	-1	-1	-0	-0.2
NY-N	2	4	.333	41	0	0	0	1	51¹	44	6	20	26	11.6	3.51	122	.232	.311	0	—	0	4	4	-1	0.4
Yr	3	5	.375	47	0	0	0	1	60	55	8	25	33	12.3	3.75	113	.243	.324	0	—	0	3	3	-1	0.2
Total 9	22	35	.386	232	23	2	1	13	416¹	385	42	161	286	12.1	4.02	94	.248	.323	4	.071	-2	-8	-12	-5	-1.8
● **WALT MASTERS** Masters, Walter Thomas b: 3/28/07, Pen Argyl, Pa. d: 7/10/92, Ottawa, Ont., Can. BR/TR, 5′10.5″, 180 lbs. Deb: 7/9/31																									
1931 Was-A	0	0	—	3	0	0	0	1	9	7	0	4	1	11.0	2.00	215	.226	.314	0	.000	-0	2	2	1	0.1
1937 Phi-A	0	0	—	1	0	0	0	0	1	5	0	1	0	54.0	36.00	12	.714	.750	0	—	0	-4	-4	-0	0.0
1939 Phi-A	0	0	—	4	0	0	0	0	11	15	0	8	2	18.8	6.55	72	.306	.404	0	.000	-0	-2	-2	0	0.0
Total 3	0	0	—	8	0	0	0	1	21	27	0	13	3	17.1	6.00	75	.310	.400	0	.000	-1	-3	-3	1	0.1
● **PAUL MASTERSON** Masterson, Paul Nickalis "Lefty" b: 10/16/15, Chicago, Ill. BL/TL, 5′11″, 165 lbs. Deb: 9/15/40																									
1940 Phi-N	0	0	—	2	0	0	0	0	5	5	0	2	3	12.6	7.20	54	.263	.333	0	.000	-1	-2	-2	0	0.0
1941 Phi-N	1	0	1.000	2	1	1	0	0	11¹	11	0	6	8	13.5	4.76	78	.250	.340	0	.000	-1	-1	-1	0	-0.2
1942 Phi-N	0	0	—	4	0	0	0	0	8¹	10	1	5	3	16.2	6.48	51	.303	.395	0	—	0	-3	-3	0	-0.2
Total 3	1	0	1.000	8	1	1	0	0	24²	26	1	13	14	14.2	5.84	62	.271	.358	0	.000	-1	-6	-6	0	-0.2
● **WALT MASTERSON** Masterson, Walter Edward b: 6/22/20, Philadelphia, Pa. BR/TR, 6′2″, 189 lbs. Deb: 5/8/39																									
1939 Was-A	2	2	.500	24	5	1	0	0	58¹	66	2	48	12	17.9	5.55	78	.293	.422	2	.154	-0	-6	-8	-1	-0.5
1940 Was-A	3	13	.188	31	19	3	0	2	130¹	128	6	88	68	15.1	4.90	85	.257	.371	7	.184	-0	-8	-11	-1	-1.2
1941 Was-A	4	3	.571	34	6	1	0	3	78¹	101	3	53	40	17.8	5.97	68	.321	.420	2	.105	-1	-16	-17	-1	-1.5
1942 Was-A	5	9	.357	25	15	8	4	2	142²	138	6	54	63	12.2	3.34	109	.251	.321	7	.156	-0	5	5	-2	0.2
1945 Was-A	1	2	.333	4	2	1	1	0	25	21	1	10	14	11.2	1.08	287	.228	.304	1	.111	-1	6	6	0	0.6
1946 Was-A	5	6	.455	29	9	2	1	0	91¹	105	8	67	61	17.2	6.01	56	.295	.411	2	.080	-1	-25	-27	0	-3.1
1947 Was-A★	12	16	.429	35	31	14	4	1	253	215	11	97	135	11.2	3.13	119	.234	.309	11	.133	-3	16	17	3	1.8
1948 Was-A★	8	15	.348	33	27	9	2	2	188	171	12	122	72	14.2	3.83	113	.247	.363	11	.193	-0	10	11	-2	1.0
1949 Was-A	3	2	.600	10	7	3	0	0	53	42	4	21	17	11.2	3.23	132	.216	.303	1	.056	-1	6	6	1	0.5
Bos-A	3	4	.429	18	5	1	0	4	55	58	2	35	19	15.2	4.25	102	.283	.387	2	.118	-1	0	1	-1	-0.1
Yr	6	6	.500	28	12	4	0	4	108	100	6	56	36	13.0	3.75	115	.249	.341	3	.086	-2	5	7	-0	0.4
1950 Bos-A	8	6	.571	33	15	6	0	1	129¹	145	15	82	94	15.6	5.64	87	.287	.387	6	.136	-3	-15	-11	-1	-1.1
1951 Bos-A	3	0	1.000	30	1	0	0	2	59¹	53	1	32	39	12.9	3.34	134	.228	.341	2	.182	-1	5	7	0	0.3
1952 Bos-A	1	1	.500	5	1	0	0	0	9¹	18	1	11	3	28.0	11.57	34	.400	.518	0	.000	-0	-8	-8	0	-1.4
Was-A	9	8	.529	24	21	11	0	2	160²	153	11	72	89	12.8	3.70	96	.253	.336	6	.120	-1	-0	-2	1	-0.3
Yr	10	9	.526	29	22	11	0	2	170	171	12	83	92	13.4	4.13	87	.263	.350	6	.115	-1	-9	-10	1	-1.7
1953 Was-A	10	12	.455	29	20	10	4	0	166¹	145	16	62	95	11.4	3.63	107	.232	.304	7	.137	-1	7	5	0	0.5
1956 Det-A	1	1	.500	35	0	0	0	0	49²	54	4	32	28	15.8	4.17	99	.289	.395	1	.250	0	-0	-0	-0	-0.1
Total 14	78	100	.438	399	184	70	15	20	1649²	1613	101	886	815	13.8	4.15	96	.258	.353	68	.140	-14	-24	-27	0	-4.4
● **LEN MATARAZZO** Matarazzo, Leonard b: 9/12/28, New Castle, Pa. BR/TL, 6′4″, 195 lbs. Deb: 9/6/52																									
1952 Phi-A	0	0	—	1	0	0	0	0	1	1	0	1	0	18.0	0.00	—	.250	.400	0	—	0	0	-0	-0	0.0
● **GREG MATHEWS** Mathews, Gregory Inman b: 5/17/62, Harbor City, Cal. BR/TL, 6′2″, 180 lbs. Deb: 6/3/86																									
1986 StL-N	11	8	.579	23	22	1	0	0	145¹	139	15	44	67	11.5	3.65	100	.259	.317	2	.047	-3	1	-0	-2	-0.5
1987 *StL-N	11	11	.500	32	32	2	1	0	197²	184	17	71	108	11.6	3.73	111	.249	.314	13	.191	1	8	9	-1	0.9
1988 StL-N	4	6	.400	13	13	1	0	0	68	61	4	33	31	12.7	4.24	82	.247	.340	4	.174	0	-6	-6	-0	-0.8
1990 StL-N	0	5	.000	11	10	0	0	0	50²	53	2	30	18	15.1	5.33	72	.277	.381	3	.214	-1	-9	-9	-1	-0.5
1992 Phi-N	2	3	.400	14	7	0	0	0	52¹	54	7	24	27	13.6	5.16	68	.270	.351	0	.000	-1	-10	-10	-1	-1.0
Total 5	28	33	.459	93	84	4	1	0	514	491	45	202	251	12.3	4.08	94	.256	.330	22	.136	-1	-16	-15	-3	-1.9
● **BOBBY MATHEWS** Mathews, Robert T. b: 11/21/1851, Baltimore, Md. d: 4/17/1898, Baltimore, Md. BR/TR, 5′5.5″, 140 lbs. Deb: 5/4/1871 U♦																									
1871 Kek-n	6	11	.353	19	19	19	**1**	0	169	261	5	21	17	15.0	5.17	88	.305	.322	24	.270	-3	-18	-11		-0.8
1872 Bal-n	25	18	.581	49	47	39	0	0	405¹	477	3	52	**55**	11.7	3.15	119	.256	.277	50	.226	-7	25	27		1.2
1873 Mut-n	29	23	.558	52	52	47	2	0	443	489	5	62	**75**	11.2	2.56	124	.251	.273	43	.193	-2	34	30		2.0
1874 Mut-n	42	22	.656	65	65	62	**4**	0	578	647	6	39		10.7	**2.30**	**133**	.258	.270	70	.236	-3	**44**	**49**		3.6
1875 Mut-n	29	38	.433	70	70	**69**	3	0	**626²**	709	6	23		10.5	2.41	107	.259	.265	47	.175	-12	3	12		-0.1
1876 NY-N	21	34	.382	56	56	55	2	0	516	693	8	24	37	12.5	2.86	75	.301	.308	40	.183	-10	-32	-41	-3	-4.3

YEAR TM/L	W	L	PCT	G	GS	CG	SH	SV	IP	H	HR	BB	SO	RAT	ERA	ERA+	OAV	OOB	BH	AVG	PB	PR	/A	PD	TPI
1877 Cin-N	3	12	.200	15	15	13	0	0	129¹	208	0	17	9	15.7	4.04	66	.339	.357	10	.169	-3	-18	-20	-1	-2.1
1879 Pro-N	12	6	.667	27	25	15	1	1	189	194	4	26	90	10.5	2.29	103	.258	.282	35	.202	-0	4	1	0	0.1
1881 Pro-N	4	8	.333	14	14	10	1	0	102¹	121	2	21	28	12.5	3.17	84	.268	.300	11	.193	-2	-4	-6	-1	-0.7
Bos-N	1	0	1.000	5	1	1	0	2	23	22	0	11	5	12.9	2.35	113	.239	.320	12	.169	-1	1	1	-0	0.0
Yr	5	8	.385	19	15	11	1	2	125¹	143	2	32	33	12.6	3.02	88	.263	.304	23	.180	-3	-3	-5	-2	-0.7
1882 Bos-N	19	15	.559	34	32	31	0	0	285	278	5	22	153	9.5	2.87	100	.232	.246	38	.225	-2	1	-0	-4	-0.6
1883 Phi-a	30	13	.698	44	44	41	1	0	381	396	11	31	203	10.1	2.46	141	.251	.265	31	.186	-7	36	43	-1	3.2
1884 Phi-a	30	18	.625	49	49	48	3	0	430²	401	10	49	286	9.7	3.32	102	.232	.258	34	.185	-5	-4	3	-2	-0.4
1885 Phi-a	30	17	.638	48	48	46	2	0	422¹	394	3	57	286	10.0	2.43	142	.233	.267	30	.168	-7	38	47	2	3.8
1886 Phi-a	13	9	.591	24	24	22	0	0	197²	226	3	53	93	13.3	3.96	88	.267	.320	21	.239	-0	-11	-10	0	-0.9
1887 Phi-a	3	4	.429	7	7	7	0	0	58	75	4	25	9	16.0	6.67	64	.298	.368	5	.200	-0	-15	-15	0	-1.3
Total 5 n	131	112	.539	255	253	236	9	0	2222	2583	19	197	147	11.3	2.76	116	.261	.275	234	.213	-27	89	107		5.9
Total 10	166	136	.550	323	315	289	10	3	2734¹	3008	50	336	1199	11.2	3.00	100	.261	.285	267	.192	-27	-3	-3	-11	-3.2

● TERRY MATHEWS
Mathews, Terry Alan b: 10/5/64, Alexandria, La. BL/TR, 6'2", 200 lbs. Deb: 6/21/91

YEAR TM/L	W	L	PCT	G	GS	CG	SH	SV	IP	H	HR	BB	SO	RAT	ERA	ERA+	OAV	OOB	BH	AVG	PB	PR	/A	PD	TPI
1991 Tex-A	4	0	1.000	34	2	0	0	1	57¹	54	5	18	51	11.5	3.61	112	.251	.312	0	—	0	3	3	0	0.2
1992 Tex-A	2	4	.333	40	0	0	0	0	42¹	48	4	31	26	17.0	5.95	64	.294	.410	0	—	-0	-9	-10	0	-1.3
1994 Fla-N	2	1	.667	24	2	0	0	0	43	45	4	9	21	11.5	3.35	134	.268	.309	3	.500	1	4	6	0	0.5
Total 3	8	5	.615	98	4	0	0	1	142²	147	13	58	98	13.1	4.23	97	.269	.343	3	.500	1	-2	-2	0	-0.6

● CHRISTY MATHEWSON
Mathewson, Christopher "Matty" or "Big Six"
b: 8/12/1880, Factoryville, Pa. d: 10/7/25, Saranac Lake, N.Y. BR/TR, 6'1.5", 195 lbs. Deb: 7/17/00 FMCH

YEAR TM/L	W	L	PCT	G	GS	CG	SH	SV	IP	H	HR	BB	SO	RAT	ERA	ERA+	OAV	OOB	BH	AVG	PB	PR	/A	PD	TPI
1900 NY-N	0	3	.000	6	1	1	0	0	33²	37	1	20	15	16.3	5.08	71	.278	.389	2	.182	0	-5	-5	0	-0.3
1901 NY-N	20	17	.541	40	38	36	5	0	336	288	3	97	221	10.7	2.41	137	.230	.292	28	.215	-1	34	33	8	4.1
1902 NY-N	14	17	.452	34	32	29	8	0	276²	241	3	73	159	10.5	2.11	133	.235	.292	26	.205	2	20	21	4	3.0
1903 NY-N	30	13	.698	45	42	37	3	2	366¹	321	4	100	267	10.6	2.26	134	.231	.287	28	.226	3	41	44	2	5.3
1904 NY-N	33	12	.733	48	46	33	4	1	367²	306	7	78	212	9.5	2.03	134	.226	.270	30	.226	6	29	28	6	4.7
1905 *NY-N	31	9	.775	43	37	32	8	2	338²	252	4	64	206	8.4	1.28	230	.205	.245	30	.236	10	65	62	6	9.6
1906 NY-N	22	12	.647	38	35	22	6	1	266²	262	3	77	128	11.5	2.97	88	.259	.313	24	.264	7	-10	-11	4	-0.2
1907 NY-N	24	12	.667	41	36	31	8	2	315	250	6	53	178	8.7	2.00	124	.212	.247	20	.187	3	17	17	1	2.5
1908 NY-N	37	11	.771	56	44	34	11	5	390²	285	5	42	259	7.6	1.43	169	.200	.225	20	.155	1	41	43	10	7.3
1909 NY-N	25	6	.806	37	33	26	8	2	275¹	192	2	36	149	7.5	1.14	224	.200	.228	25	.263	7	45	43	6	7.0
1910 NY-N	27	9	.750	38	35	27	2	0	318¹	292	5	60	184	10.0	1.89	157	.248	.286	25	.234	7	40	38	7	6.0
1911 *NY-N	26	13	.667	45	37	29	5	3	307	303	5	38	141	10.0	1.99	169	.259	.283	22	.196	0	48	47	7	6.7
1912 *NY-N	23	12	.657	43	34	27	0	4	310	311	6	34	134	10.1	2.12	159	.260	.281	29	.264	5	44	43	5	5.2
1913 *NY-N	25	11	.694	40	35	25	4	2	306	291	8	21	93	9.2	2.06	152	.252	.266	19	.184	-0	39	36	4	4.6
1914 NY-N	24	13	.649	41	35	29	5	2	312	314	16	23	80	9.8	3.00	88	.263	.278	23	.219	6	-7	-12	2	-0.6
1915 NY-N	8	14	.364	27	24	11	1	0	186	199	9	20	57	10.6	3.58	72	.277	.298	8	.157	3	-17	-21	1	-2.1
1916 NY-N	3	4	.429	12	6	4	1	2	65²	59	3	7	16	9.0	2.33	104	.243	.264	0	.000	-1	2	1	2	0.2
Cin-N	1	0	1.000	1	1	1	0	0	9	15	1	1	3	16.0	8.00	32	.366	.381	3	.600	-1	-5	-5	0	-0.3
Yr	4	4	.500	13	7	5	1	2	74²	74	4	8	19	9.9	3.01	81	.261	.281	3	.136	-1	-3	-5	2	-0.1
Total 17	373	188	.665	635	551	434	79	28	4780²	4218	91	844	2502	9.6	2.13	136	.236	.273	362	.215	59	420	403	68	62.7

● HENRY MATHEWSON
Mathewson, Henry b: 12/24/1886, Factoryville, Pa. d: 7/1/17, Factoryville, Pa. BR/TR, 6'3", 175 lbs. Deb: 9/28/06 F

YEAR TM/L	W	L	PCT	G	GS	CG	SH	SV	IP	H	HR	BB	SO	RAT	ERA	ERA+	OAV	OOB	BH	AVG	PB	PR	/A	PD	TPI
1906 NY-N	0	1	.000	2	1	1	0	1	10	7	0	14	2	19.8	5.40	48	.194	.431	0	.000	-0	-3	-3	0	-0.3
1907 NY-N	0	0	—	1	0	0	0	1	1	1	0	0	0	9.0	0.00	—	.250	.250	0	—	0	0	-0	0	0.1
Total 2	0	1	.000	3	1	1	0	2	11	8	0	14	2	18.8	4.91	53	.200	.418	0	.000	-0	-3	-3	0	-0.2

● CARL MATHIAS
Mathias, Carl Lynwood "Stubby" b: 6/13/36, Bechtelsville, Pa BB/TL, 5'11", 195 lbs. Deb: 7/31/60

YEAR TM/L	W	L	PCT	G	GS	CG	SH	SV	IP	H	HR	BB	SO	RAT	ERA	ERA+	OAV	OOB	BH	AVG	PB	PR	/A	PD	TPI
1960 Cle-A	0	1	.000	7	0	0	0	0	15¹	14	2	8	13	12.9	3.52	106	.233	.324	—	-0	1	0	-0	0	0.0
1961 Was-A	0	1	.000	4	3	0	0	0	13²	22	3	4	7	17.8	11.20	36	.361	.409	1	.200	-0	-11	-11	0	-0.7
Total 2	0	2	.000	11	3	0	0	0	29	36	5	12	20	15.2	7.14	54	.298	.366	1	.167	-0	-10	-11	0	-0.7

● RON MATHIS
Mathis, Ronald Vance b: 9/25/58, Kansas City, Mo. BR/TR, 6', 175 lbs. Deb: 4/13/85

YEAR TM/L	W	L	PCT	G	GS	CG	SH	SV	IP	H	HR	BB	SO	RAT	ERA	ERA+	OAV	OOB	BH	AVG	PB	PR	/A	PD	TPI
1985 Hou-N	3	5	.375	23	8	0	0	1	70	83	7	27	34	14.3	6.04	57	.293	.357	1	.071	-1	-19	-20	-0	-2.2
1987 Hou-N	0	1	.000	8	0	0	0	0	12	10	2	11	8	15.8	5.25	75	.233	.389	0	.000	-0	-2	-2	0	-0.1
Total 2	3	6	.333	31	8	0	0	1	82	93	9	38	42	14.5	5.93	60	.285	.362	1	.063	-1	-21	-22	-0	-2.3

● JON MATLACK
Matlack, Jonathan Trumpbour b: 1/19/50, West Chester, Pa. BL/TL, 6'3", 205 lbs. Deb: 7/11/71

YEAR TM/L	W	L	PCT	G	GS	CG	SH	SV	IP	H	HR	BB	SO	RAT	ERA	ERA+	OAV	OOB	BH	AVG	PB	PR	/A	PD	TPI
1971 NY-N	0	3	.000	7	6	0	0	0	37	31	2	15	24	11.2	4.14	82	.228	.305	3	.273	1	-3	-3	-1	-0.2
1972 NY-N	15	10	.600	34	32	8	4	0	244	215	14	71	169	10.6	2.32	145	.234	.291	10	.128	1	31	28	-1	2.9
1973 *NY-N	14	16	.467	34	34	14	3	0	242	210	16	99	205	11.6	3.20	113	.236	.314	9	.138	2	12	11	1	1.6
1974 NY-N★	13	15	.464	34	34	14	7	0	265¹	221	8	76	195	10.2	2.41	148	.226	.285	8	.101	-4	36	34	-0	3.1
1975 NY-N★	16	12	.571	33	32	8	3	0	228²	224	15	58	154	11.1	3.38	102	.254	.300	7	.100	0	6	2	-2	0.0
1976 NY-N☆	17	10	.630	35	35	16	6	0	262	236	18	57	153	10.2	2.95	112	.242	.286	17	.193	4	16	10	-1	1.3
1977 NY-N	7	15	.318	26	26	5	3	0	169	175	19	43	123	11.7	4.21	89	.273	.321	3	.060	-2	-6	-9	-0	-1.2
1978 Tex-A	15	13	.536	35	33	18	2	1	270	252	14	51	157	10.2	2.27	166	.245	.284	0	—	0	45	44	0	4.7
1979 Tex-A	5	4	.556	13	13	2	0	0	85	98	9	19	35	12.1	4.13	100	.293	.325	0	—	0	1	0	0	0.1
1980 Tex-A	10	10	.500	35	34	8	1	1	234²	265	17	48	142	12.0	3.68	106	.287	.323	0	—	0	9	6	-3	0.1
1981 Tex-A	4	7	.364	17	16	1	1	0	104¹	101	8	41	43	12.3	4.14	84	.258	.330	0	—	-0	-6	-6	0	-0.7
1982 Tex-A	7	7	.500	33	14	1	0	1	147²	158	14	37	78	12.0	3.53	109	.275	.321	0	—	0	9	6	0	0.0
1983 Tex-A	2	4	.333	25	9	0	0	0	73¹	90	7	27	38	14.7	4.66	86	.307	.372	0	—	-0	-5	-5	1	-0.3
Total 13	125	126	.498	361	318	97	30	3	2363	2276	161	638	1516	11.2	3.18	114	.254	.305	57	.129	2	145	115	-5	12.1

● AL MATTERN
Mattern, Alonzo Albert b: 6/16/1883, W.Rush, N.Y. d: 11/6/58, West Rush, N.Y. BL/TR, 5'10", 165 lbs. Deb: 9/16/08

YEAR TM/L	W	L	PCT	G	GS	CG	SH	SV	IP	H	HR	BB	SO	RAT	ERA	ERA+	OAV	OOB	BH	AVG	PB	PR	/A	PD	TPI
1908 Bos-N	1	2	.333	5	3	1	1	0	30¹	30	0	6	8	10.7	2.08	116	.265	.303	1	.125	-0	1	1	-0	0.0
1909 Bos-N	15	21	.417	47	32	24	2	3	316¹	322	4	108	98	12.3	2.85	99	.268	.330	17	.168	-1	-9	-1	3	0.1
1910 Bos-N	16	19	.457	51	37	17	6	1	305	288	5	121	94	12.2	2.98	112	.257	.332	16	.163	-4	2	12	1	0.9
1911 Bos-N	4	15	.211	33	21	11	0	0	186¹	228	13	63	51	14.1	4.97	77	.320	.376	11	.175	-2	-33	-24	2	-2.1
1912 Bos-N	0	1	.000	2	1	0	0	0	6¹	10	0	1	3	15.6	7.11	50	.313	.333	0	.000	-0	-3	-2	-0	-0.3
Total 5	36	58	.383	138	94	53	9	4	844¹	878	22	299	254	12.7	3.37	95	.276	.340	45	.165	-8	-41	-15	5	-1.4

● C. V. MATTERSON
Matterson, C. V. b: Ohio Deb: 6/13/1884 ♦

YEAR TM/L	W	L	PCT	G	GS	CG	SH	SV	IP	H	HR	BB	SO	RAT	ERA	ERA+	OAV	OOB	BH	AVG	PB	PR	/A	PD	TPI
1884 StL-U	1	0	1.000	1	1	1	0	0	6	9	1	3	3	18.0	9.00	27	.325	.391	0	.000	-1	-4	-4	-0	-0.5

● EDDIE MATTESON
Matteson, Henry Edson "Matty" b: 9/7/1884, Guys Mills, Pa. d: 9/1/43, Westfield, N.Y. BR/TR, 5'10.5", 160 lbs. Deb: 5/30/14

YEAR TM/L	W	L	PCT	G	GS	CG	SH	SV	IP	H	HR	BB	SO	RAT	ERA	ERA+	OAV	OOB	BH	AVG	PB	PR	/A	PD	TPI
1914 Phi-N	3	2	.600	15	3	2	0	0	58	58	1	23	28	12.7	3.10	95	.278	.352	4	.182	-0	-2	-1	-2	-0.3
1918 Was-A	5	3	.625	14	6	2	0	0	67²	57	2	15	17	9.7	1.73	158	.238	.286	2	.105	-2	8	8	-1	0.6
Total 2	8	5	.615	29	9	4	0	0	125²	115	3	38	45	11.1	2.36	120	.257	.318	6	.146	-2	6	6	-3	0.3

● JOE MATTHEWS
Matthews, John Joseph "Lefty" b: 9/29/1898, Baltimore, Md. d: 2/8/68, Hagerstown, Md. BB/TL, 6', 170 lbs. Deb: 9/18/22

YEAR TM/L	W	L	PCT	G	GS	CG	SH	SV	IP	H	HR	BB	SO	RAT	ERA	ERA+	OAV	OOB	BH	AVG	PB	PR	/A	PD	TPI
1922 Bos-N	0	1	.000	3	1	0	0	0	10	5	1	6	2	10.8	3.60	111	.143	.286	0	.000	-0	1	0	-0	0.0

● WILLIAM MATTHEWS
Matthews, William Calvin b: 1/12/1878, Mahanoy City, Pa. d: 1/23/46, Mahanoy City, Pa. TR Deb: 8/28/09

YEAR TM/L	W	L	PCT	G	GS	CG	SH	SV	IP	H	HR	BB	SO	RAT	ERA	ERA+	OAV	OOB	BH	AVG	PB	PR	/A	PD	TPI
1909 Bos-A	0	0	—	5	1	0	0	0	16²	16	1	10	6	14.0	3.24	77	.271	.377	0	.000	-1	-1	-1	-0	-0.2

YEAR TM/L	W	L	PCT	G	GS	CG	SH	SV	IP	H	HR	BB	SO	RAT	ERA	ERA+	OAV	OOB	BH	AVG	PB	PR	/A	PD	TPI
● DALE MATTHEWSON Matthewson, Dale Wesley b: 5/15/23, Catasauqua, Pa. d: 2/20/84, Blairsville, Ga. BR/TR, 5'11.5", 145 lbs. Deb: 7/3/43																									
1943 Phi-N	0	3	.000	11	1	0	0	0	26	26	1	8	8	11.8	4.85	70	.271	.327	0	.000	-0	-4	-4	-0	-0.5
1944 Phi-N	0	0	—	17	1	0	0	0	32	27	1	16	8	12.1	3.94	92	.237	.331	1	.333	0	-1	-1	-0	0.0
Total 2	0	3	.000	28	2	0	0	0	58	53	2	24	16	11.9	4.34	81	.252	.329	1	.200	-0	-5	-5	-0	-0.5
● MIKE MATTIMORE Mattimore, Michael Joseph b: 1859, Renovo, Pa. d: 4/28/31, Butte, Mont. BL/TL, 5'8.5", 160 lbs. Deb: 5/3/1887 ♦																									
1887 NY-N	3	3	.500	7	7	6	1	0	57¹	47	2	28	12	12.4	2.35	160	.218	.319	8	.250	-0	11	9	-1	0.6
1888 Phi-a	15	10	.600	26	24	24	4	0	221	221	6	65	80	12.2	3.38	88	.251	.312	38	.268	7	-8	-10	4	0.2
1889 Phi-a	2	1	.667	5	1	1	0	1	31	43	0	13	6	16.5	5.81	65	.319	.383	17	.233	1	-7	-7	-0	-0.5
KC-a	0	0	—	1	0	0	0	0	3	3	1	2	1	15.0	3.00	139	.252	.360	12	.160	-0	0	0	-0	-0.0
Yr	2	1	.667	6	1	1	0	1	34	46	1	15	7	16.1	5.56	69	.311	.375	29	.196	1	-6	-7	-0	-0.5
1890 Bro-a	6	13	.316	19	19	19	0	0	178¹	201	3	76	33	14.6	4.54	86	.276	.354	17	.132	-3	-13	-13	-0	-1.3
Total 4	26	27	.491	58	51	50	5	1	490²	515	12	184	132	13.4	3.83	90	.261	.334	92	.204	5	-17	-20	2	-1.2
● EARL MATTINGLY Mattingly, Laurence Earl b: 11/4/04, Brookville, Md. d: 9/8/93, Olney, Mnd. BR/TR, 5'10.5", 164 lbs. Deb: 4/15/31																									
1931 Bro-N	0	1	.000	8	0	0	0	0	14¹	15	0	10	6	17.0	2.51	152	.268	.397	0	.000	-0	2	2	1	0.1
● RICK MATULA Matula, Richard Carlton b: 11/22/53, Wharton, Tex. BR/TR, 6', 190 lbs. Deb: 4/8/79																									
1979 Atl-N	8	10	.444	28	28	1	0	0	171¹	193	14	64	67	13.7	4.15	98	.286	.350	5	.094	-3	-8	-2	1	-0.4
1980 Atl-N	11	13	.458	33	30	3	1	0	176²	195	17	60	62	13.0	4.58	82	.286	.343	6	.105	-3	-19	-17	1	-2.2
1981 Atl-N	0	0	—	5	0	0	0	0	7	8	1	2	0	12.9	6.43	56	.000	.333	0	.000	-0	-2	-2	0	-0.0
Total 3	19	23	.452	66	58	4	1	0	355	396	32	126	129	13.3	4.41	88	.286	.347	11	.099	-6	-30	-21	2	-2.6
● HARRY MATUZAK Matuzak, Harry George "Matty" b: 1/27/10, Omer, Mich. d: 11/16/78, Fairhope, Ala. BR/TR, 5'11.5", 185 lbs. Deb: 4/19/34																									
1934 Phi-A	0	3	.000	11	0	0	0	0	24	28	2	10	9	14.6	4.88	90	.292	.364	1	.167	-0	-1	-1	0	-0.1
1936 Phi-A	0	1	.000	6	1	0	0	0	15	21	0	4	8	15.0	7.20	71	.318	.357	-0	.000	-0	-4	-3	-0	-0.2
Total 2	0	4	.000	17	1	0	0	0	39	49	2	14	17	14.8	5.77	81	.302	.362	1	.111	-0	-5	-4	0	-0.3
● HAL MAUCK Mauck, Alfred Maris b: 3/6/1869, Princeton, Ind. d: 4/27/21, Princeton, Ind. BR/TR, 5'11", 185 lbs. Deb: 4/29/1893																									
1893 Chi-N	8	10	.444	23	18	12	1	0	143	168	2	60	23	14.9	4.41	105	.284	.359	9	.148	-5	4	4	-1	-0.2
● AL MAUL Maul, Albert Joseph "Smiling Al" b: 10/9/1865, Philadelphia, Pa. d: 5/3/58, Philadelphia, Pa. BR/TR, 6', 175 lbs. Deb: 6/20/1884 ♦																									
1884 Phi-U	0	1	.000	1	1	1	0	0	8	10	1	4	7	12.4	4.50	52	.287	.306	0	.000	-1	-2	-2	-0	-0.3
1887 Phi-N	4	2	.667	7	5	4	0	0	50¹	72	2	15	18	15.9	5.54	76	.326	.374	17	.304	3	-8	-7	0	-0.5
1888 Pit-N	0	2	.000	3	1	1	0	0	26	20	0	5	12	16.4	6.35	42	.342	.383	54	.208	1	-7	-7	-0	-0.6
1889 Pit-N	1	4	.200	6	4	4	0	0	42	64	3	28	11	19.9	9.86	38	.340	.428	71	.276	2	-27	-29	1	-1.0
1890 Pit-P	16	12	.571	30	28	26	2	0	246²	258	13	104	81	13.6	3.79	103	.258	.335	42	.259	7	12	3	5	1.2
1891 Pit-N	1	2	.333	8	3	3	0	1	39	44	0	16	13	14.5	2.31	142	.274	.351	28	.188	1	5	4	-0	0.3
1893 Was-N	12	21	.364	37	33	29	1	0	297	355	17	144	72	15.7	5.30	87	.288	.370	34	.254	10	-21	-22	0	-1.0
1894 Was-N	11	15	.423	29	27	21	0	0	204²	275	12	73	34	15.7	5.94	89	.318	.378	30	.240	2	-14	-15	2	-1.0
1895 Was-N	10	5	.667	16	16	14	0	0	135²	136	5	37	34	11.7	**2.45**	196	.257	.309	18	.250	1	35	35	1	3.3
1896 Was-N	5	2	.714	8	8	7	0	0	62	75	0	20	18	14.4	3.63	121	.296	.357	8	.286	2	5	5	-1	0.5
1897 Was-N	0	1	.000	1	1	0	0	0	2	4	1	0	2	22.5	9.00	48	.411	.465	0	.000	-0	-1	-1	-0	-0.3
Bal-N	0	0	—	2	2	0	0	0	7²	9	0	8	2	24.7	7.04	59	.290	.488	1	.333	0	-2	-2	-0	-0.0
Yr	0	1	.000	3	3	0	0	0	9²	13	1	8	2	24.2	7.45	56	.319	.484	1	.250	-0	-3	-3	-0	-0.3
1898 Bal-N	20	7	.741	28	26	21	6	0	239²	207	3	49	31	9.8	2.10	170	.231	.274	19	.204	4	40	39	-5	3.9
1899 Bro-N	2	0	1.000	4	4	2	0	0	26	35	1	6	2	14.9	4.50	87	.321	.368	3	.273	-0	-2	-2	-0	-0.1
1900 Phi-N	2	3	.400	5	4	3	0	0	38	53	2	3	6	13.7	6.16	59	.329	.349	5	.200	-1	-10	-11	0	-1.0
1901 NY-N	2	3	.000	5	3	2	0	0	39	58	1	8	5	23.2	11.37	29	.417	.474	3	.375	-1	-17	-17	-0	-1.7
Total 15	84	80	.512	188	168	143	4	1	1434²	1662	59	518	346	14.1	4.43	96	.284	.349	331	.240	32	-15	-28	4	0.7
● ERNIE MAUN Maun, Ernest Gerald b: 2/3/01, Clearwater, Kan. d: 1/1/87, Corpus Christi, Tex. BR/TR, 6', 165 lbs. Deb: 5/16/24																									
1924 NY-N	1	1	.500	22	0	0	0	1	35	46	2	10	5	14.7	5.91	62	.326	.375	2	.667	1	-8	-9	-1	-0.5
1926 Phi-N	1	4	.200	14	5	0	0	0	37²	57	4	18	9	18.2	6.45	64	.339	.406	3	.250	-0	-11	-10	-0	-1.1
Total 2	2	5	.286	36	5	0	0	1	72²	103	6	28	14	16.5	6.19	63	.333	.392	5	.333	1	-19	-18	-1	-1.6
● DICK MAUNEY Mauney, Richard b: 1/26/20, Concord, N.C. d: 2/6/70, Albemarle, N.C. BR/TR, 5'11.5", 164 lbs. Deb: 6/13/45																									
1945 Phi-N	6	10	.375	20	16	6	2	1	122²	127	7	27	35	11.4	3.08	124	.268	.310	6	.146	-0	10	10	1	1.3
1946 Phi-N	6	4	.600	24	7	3	1	2	90	98	4	18	31	11.9	2.70	127	.279	.320	4	.167	-1	7	7	0	0.8
1947 Phi-N	0	0	—	9	1	0	0	1	16¹	15	1	7	6	12.7	3.86	104	.288	.383	0	.000	-0	0	0	1	0.1
Total 3	12	14	.462	53	24	9	3	4	229	240	12	52	72	11.7	2.99	123	.274	.319	10	.149	-1	17	18	2	2.2
● HARRY MAUPIN Maupin, Harry Carr b: 7/11/1872, Wellsville, Mo. d: 8/25/52, Parsons, Kan. 5'7", 150 lbs. Deb: 10/5/1898																									
1898 StL-N	0	2	.000	2	2	1	0	0	18	22	0	3	3	14.0	5.50	69	.299	.352	3	.429	1	-4	-3	-1	-0.3
1899 Cle-N	0	3	.000	5	3	2	0	0	25	55	0	7	6	22.7	12.60	29	.436	.470	0	.000	-2	-24	-25	-1	-2.2
Total 2	0	5	.000	7	5	4	0	0	43	77	0	10	6	19.0	9.63	39	.385	.426	3	.176	-1	-28	-28	-2	-2.5
● RALPH MAURIELLO Mauriello, Ralph "Tami" b: 8/25/34, Brooklyn, N.Y. BR/TR, 6'3", 195 lbs. Deb: 9/13/58																									
1958 LA-N	1	1	.500	3	2	0	0	0	11²	10	1	8	11	13.9	4.63	89	.238	.360	0	.000	-1	-1	-1	-0	-0.2
● TIM MAUSER Mauser, Timothy Edward b: 10/4/66, Fort Worth, Tex. BR/TR, 6', 185 lbs. Deb: 7/7/91																									
1991 Phi-N	0	0	—	3	0	0	0	0	10²	18	3	3	6	17.7	7.59	48	.367	.404	0	.000	-0	-5	-5	-0	-0.1
1993 Phi-N	0	0	—	8	0	0	0	0	16¹	15	1	7	14	12.7	4.96	80	.238	.324	0	.000	-0	-2	-2	1	0.0
SD-N	0	1	.000	28	0	0	0	0	37²	36	5	17	32	12.7	3.58	115	.248	.327	0	.000	-0	2	2	1	0.1
Yr	0	1	.000	36	0	0	0	0	54	51	6	24	46	12.5	4.00	102	.244	.322	0	.000	-0	0	0	1	0.1
1994 SD-N	2	4	.333	35	0	0	0	2	49	50	3	19	32	12.9	3.49	120	.269	.340	1	.250	-0	4	4	-0	0.5
Total 3	2	5	.286	74	0	0	0	2	113²	119	12	46	84	13.2	4.12	99	.269	.340	1	.077	-0	-0	-1	0	0.5
● LARRY MAXIE Maxie, Larry Hans b: 10/10/40, Upland, Cal. BR/TR, 6'4", 220 lbs. Deb: 8/30/69																									
1969 Atl-N	0	0	—	2	0	0	0	0	3	1	0	1	1	9.0	3.00	120	.111	.273	0	—	-0	0	0	0	0.0
● BERT MAXWELL Maxwell, James Albert b: 10/17/1886, Texarkana, Ark. d: 12/10/61, Brady, Tex. BB/TR, 6', 180 lbs. Deb: 9/12/06																									
1906 Pit-N	0	1	.000	1	1	0	0	0	8	8	0	2	1	11.3	5.63	48	.286	.333	0	.000	-0	-3	-3	0	-0.3
1908 Phi-A	0	0	—	4	0	0	0	0	13	23	0	9	7	23.5	11.08	23	.348	.442	0	.000	-1	-13	-12	-0	-0.1
1911 NY-N	1	2	.333	4	3	3	0	0	31	37	3	0	7	13.4	2.90	116	.311	.359	1	.111	-0	2	2	1	0.2
1914 Bro-F	3	4	.429	12	8	6	1	0	71¹	76	3	26	19	12.7	3.28	88	.276	.337	2	.087	-2	-3	-3	1	-0.5
Total 4	4	7	.364	21	12	9	1	0	123¹	144	6	42	35	13.9	4.16	71	.295	.357	3	.075	-3	-17	-16	1	-0.7
● JAKIE MAY May, Frank Spruiell b: 11/25/1895, Youngville, N.C. d: 6/3/70, Wendell, N.C. BR/TL, 5'8", 178 lbs. Deb: 6/26/17																									
1917 StL-N	0	0	—	15	1	0	0	0	29¹	29	0	11	18	13.2	3.38	80	.302	.391	0	.000	-1	-2	-2	2	0.1
1918 StL-N	5	6	.455	29	15	6	0	0	152²	149	2	69	61	13.6	3.83	71	.264	.358	3	.067	-1	-18	-19	-2	-1.7
1919 StL-N	3	12	.200	28	19	8	1	0	125²	99	1	87	58	14.3	3.22	87	.230	.377	6	.162	-1	-4	-6	-1	-1.0
1920 StL-N	1	4	.200	16	5	3	0	0	70²	65	0	37	33	13.9	3.06	98	.251	.360	5	.227	-1	-2	-1	0	-0.1
1921 StL-N	1	3	.250	7	1	0	0	0	21	19	1	12	6	14.5	4.71	78	.333	.414	2	.333	-1	-2	-1	-0	-0.4
1924 Cin-N	3	3	.500	38	4	2	0	**6**	99	104	3	29	59	12.6	3.00	126	.276	.337	3	.111	-2	10	9	-0	1.0
1925 Cin-N	8	9	.471	36	12	7	1	2	137¹	146	3	45	74	13.0	3.87	106	.272	.337	8	.186	-0	6	4	0	0.4

YEAR	TM/L	W	L	PCT	G	GS	CG	SH	SV	IP	H	HR	BB	SO	RAT	ERA	ERA+	OAV	OOB	BH	AVG	PB	PR	/A	PD	TPI
1926	Cin-N	13	9	.591	45	15	9	1	3	167²	175	4	44	103	12.1	3.22	115	.276	.329	7	.146	-1	11	9	-1	0.8
1927	Cin-N	15	12	.556	44	28	17	2	1	235²	242	4	70	121	12.4	3.51	108	.274	.337	14	.184	0	11	7	1	0.8
1928	Cin-N	3	5	.375	21	11	1	1	1	79¹	99	1	35	39	15.3	4.42	89	.315	.386	8	.296	1	-4	-4	-1	-0.4
1929	Cin-N	10	14	.417	41	24	10	0	3	199	219	5	75	92	13.5	4.61	99	.285	.352	13	.203	-1	2	1	-0	-0.2
1930	Cin-N	3	11	.214	26	18	5	1	0	112¹	147	6	41	44	15.5	5.77	84	.320	.383	5	.128	-1	-10	-12	-1	-1.2
1931	Chi-N	5	5	.500	31	4	1	0	2	79	81	2	43	38	14.5	3.87	100	.275	.372	5	.227	1	-0	-0	0	0.1
1932	*Chi-N	2	2	.500	35	0	0	0	1	53²	61	3	19	20	13.8	4.36	86	.281	.345	1	.125	-0	-3	-4	-0	-0.3
Total	14	72	95	.431	410	161	70	7	19	1562¹	1645	35	617	765	13.5	3.88	97	.278	.355	80	.171	-4	-3	-23	-6	-2.7

● RUDY MAY
May, Rudolph b: 7/18/44, Coffeyville, Kan. BL/TL, 6'3", 207 lbs. Deb: 4/18/65

YEAR	TM/L	W	L	PCT	G	GS	CG	SH	SV	IP	H	HR	BB	SO	RAT	ERA	ERA+	OAV	OOB	BH	AVG	PB	PR	/A	PD	TPI
1965	Cal-A	4	9	.308	30	19	2	1	0	124	111	7	78	76	14.0	3.92	87	.245	.361	6	.200	3	-6	-7	-2	-0.6
1969	Cal-A	10	13	.435	43	25	4	0	2	180¹	142	20	66	133	10.5	3.44	101	.220	.296	4	.082	-2	4	1	-1	-0.1
1970	Cal-A	7	13	.350	38	34	2	2	0	208²	190	20	81	164	11.8	4.01	90	.245	.319	6	.087	-2	-7	-9	0	-1.1
1971	Cal-A	11	12	.478	32	31	7	2	0	208¹	160	12	87	156	11.5	3.02	107	.213	.297	10	.147	0	10	5	-1	0.5
1972	Cal-A	12	11	.522	35	30	10	3	1	205¹	162	15	82	169	10.7	2.94	99	.215	.293	7	.113	-1	3	-1	-2	-0.4
1973	Cal-A	7	17	.292	34	28	10	4	0	185	177	20	80	134	12.6	4.38	81	.254	.333	0	—	0	-12	-17	2	-1.8
1974	Cal-A	0	1	.000	18	3	0	0	2	27	29	2	10	12	13.3	7.00	49	.274	.342	0	—	0	-10	-11	1	-0.1
	NY-A	8	4	.667	17	15	8	2	0	114¹	75	5	48	90	10.0	2.28	153	.188	.282	0	—	0	17	15	-2	1.6
	Yr	8	5	.615	35	18	8	2	2	141¹	104	7	58	102	10.6	3.18	109	.204	.291	0	—	0	7	5	-0	1.5
1975	Cal-A	14	12	.538	32	31	13	1	0	212	179	9	99	145	11.9	3.06	119	.231	.320	0	—	0	17	14	-1	1.7
1976	NY-A	4	3	.571	11	11	2	1	0	68	49	5	28	38	10.3	3.57	96	.206	.292	0	—	0	-0	-1	-0	-0.1
	Bal-A	11	7	.611	24	21	5	1	0	152¹	156	11	42	71	11.7	3.78	87	.267	.316	0	—	0	-4	-9	-1	-1.0
	Yr	15	10	.600	35	32	7	2	0	220¹	205	16	70	109	11.2	3.72	89	.249	.308	0	—	0	-5	-10	-1	-1.1
1977	Bal-A	18	14	.563	37	37	11	4	0	251²	243	25	78	105	11.7	3.61	105	.255	.315	0	—	0	13	5	-3	0.6
1978	Mon-N	8	10	.444	27	23	4	1	0	144	141	15	42	87	11.8	3.88	91	.255	.315	6	.143	-0	-5	-6	-2	-0.8
1979	Mon-N	10	3	.769	33	7	2	1	0	93²	88	4	31	67	11.8	2.31	159	.255	.324	3	.143	-0	15	14	1	1.9
1980	*NY-A	15	5	.750	41	17	3	1	3	175¹	144	14	39	133	**9.4**	**2.46**	**159**	.224	**.268**	0	—	0	31	28	0	3.2
1981	*NY-A	6	11	.353	27	22	4	0	1	147²	137	10	41	79	11.0	4.14	86	.246	.300	0	—	0	-8	-9	1	-0.9
1982	NY-A	6	6	.500	41	6	0	0	3	106	109	4	14	85	10.5	2.89	138	.267	.292	0	—	0	14	13	1	1.5
1983	NY-A	1	5	.167	15	0	0	0	0	18¹	22	1	12	16	17.2	6.87	57	.293	.398	0	—	0	-6	-6	0	-1.6
Total	16	152	156	.494	535	360	87	24	12	2622	2314	199	958	1760	11.4	3.46	102	.238	.310	42	.123	-2	64	20	-7	2.5

● SCOTT MAY
May, Scott Francis b: 11/11/61, West Bend, Wis. BR/TR, 6'1", 185 lbs. Deb: 9/2/88

YEAR	TM/L	W	L	PCT	G	GS	CG	SH	SV	IP	H	HR	BB	SO	RAT	ERA	ERA+	OAV	OOB	BH	AVG	PB	PR	/A	PD	TPI
1988	Tex-A	0	0	—	3	1	0	0	0	7¹	8	3	4	4	14.7	8.59	48	.296	.387	0	—	0	-4	-4	0	-0.2
1991	Chi-N	0	0	—	2	0	0	0	0	2	6	0	1	1	31.5	18.00	22	.545	.583	0	—	0	-3	-3	-0	0.0
Total	2	0	0	—	5	1	0	0	0	9¹	14	3	5	5	18.3	10.61	38	.368	.442	0	—	0	-7	-7	-0	-0.2

● BUCKSHOT MAY
May, William Herbert b: 12/13/1899, Bakersfield, Cal. d: 3/15/84, Bakersfield, Cal. BR/TR, 6'2", 169 lbs. Deb: 5/9/24

YEAR	TM/L	W	L	PCT	G	GS	CG	SH	SV	IP	H	HR	BB	SO	RAT	ERA	ERA+	OAV	OOB	BH	AVG	PB	PR	/A	PD	TPI
1924	Pit-N	0	0	—	1	0	0	0	0	1	2	0	0	1	18.0	0.00	—	.500	.500	0	—	0	0	0	0	0.0

● ED MAYER
Mayer, Edwin David b: 11/30/31, San Francisco, Cal BL/TL, 6'2", 185 lbs. Deb: 9/15/57

YEAR	TM/L	W	L	PCT	G	GS	CG	SH	SV	IP	H	HR	BB	SO	RAT	ERA	ERA+	OAV	OOB	BH	AVG	PB	PR	/A	PD	TPI
1957	Chi-N	0	0	—	3	1	0	0	0	7²	8	2	2	3	12.9	5.87	66	.258	.324	1	.500	0	-2	-2	0	0.1
1958	Chi-N	2	2	.500	19	0	0	0	1	23²	15	0	16	14	12.9	3.80	103	.190	.347	1	.200	-0	-0	-0	-0	0.0
Total	2	2	2	.500	22	1	0	0	1	31¹	23	2	18	17	12.9	4.31	91	.209	.341	2	.286	-0	-1	-1	0	0.1

● ERSKINE MAYER
Mayer, Erskine John (b: James Erskine) b: 1/16/1889, Atlanta, Ga. d: 3/10/57, Los Angeles, Cal. BR/TR, 6', 168 lbs. Deb: 9/4/12 F

YEAR	TM/L	W	L	PCT	G	GS	CG	SH	SV	IP	H	HR	BB	SO	RAT	ERA	ERA+	OAV	OOB	BH	AVG	PB	PR	/A	PD	TPI
1912	Phi-N	0	1	.000	7	1	0	0	0	21¹	27	1	7	5	14.8	6.33	57	.318	.376	0	.000	-0	-7	-6	0	-0.3
1913	Phi-N	9	9	.500	39	19	7	2	1	170²	172	6	46	51	12.0	3.11	107	.272	.330	6	.120	-2	2	4	0	0.2
1914	Phi-N	21	19	.525	48	39	24	4	2	321	308	8	91	116	11.6	2.58	114	.256	.315	21	.194	2	8	13	4	2.3
1915	*Phi-N	21	15	.583	43	33	20	2	2	274²	240	9	59	114	10.3	2.36	116	.243	.295	21	.239	5	12	12	1	2.2
1916	Phi-N	7	7	.500	28	16	7	2	0	140	148	7	33	62	11.9	3.15	84	.281	.328	5	.132	-1	-8	-8	3	-0.5
1917	Phi-N	11	6	.647	28	18	11	1	0	160	160	6	33	64	11.1	2.76	102	.268	.310	10	.196	-0	-1	1	-0	0.0
1918	Phi-N	7	4	.636	13	13	7	0	0	104	108	2	26	16	11.9	3.12	96	.274	.328	8	.216	1	-4	-1	-0	-0.1
	Pit-N	9	3	.750	15	14	11	1	0	123¹	122	1	27	25	11.2	2.26	127	.268	.314	7	.167	2	7	8	-2	0.8
	Yr	16	7	.696	28	27	18	1	0	227¹	230	3	53	41	11.4	2.65	110	.270	.316	15	.190	3	3	7	-2	0.7
1919	Pit-N	5	3	.625	18	10	6	0	1	88¹	100	2	12	20	11.6	4.48	67	.287	.294	6	.207	0	-15	-14	-1	-1.4
	*Chi-A	1	3	.250	6	2	0	0	0	23²	30	1	11	9	15.6	8.37	38	.316	.387	0	.000	-0	-14	-14	-0	-1.9
Total	8	91	70	.565	245	165	93	12	6	1427	1415	43	345	482	11.4	2.96	99	.264	.316	84	.185	5	-21	-5	4	1.3

● SAM MAYER
Mayer, Samuel Frankel (b: Samuel Frankel Erskine) b: 2/28/1893, Atlanta, Ga. d: 7/1/62, Atlanta, Ga. BR/TL, 5'10", 164 lbs. Deb: 9/14/15 F♦

YEAR	TM/L	W	L	PCT	G	GS	CG	SH	SV	IP	H	HR	BB	SO	RAT	ERA	ERA+	OAV	OOB	BH	AVG	PB	PR	/A	PD	TPI
1915	Was-A	0	0	—	1	0	0	0	0	0	0	0	2	0	—	—	—	—	1.000	7	.241	0	0	0	0	0.0

● AL MAYS
Mays, Albert C. b: 5/17/1865, Canal Dover, Ohio d: 5/7/05, Parkersburg, W.Va. BR , Deb: 5/10/1885

YEAR	TM/L	W	L	PCT	G	GS	CG	SH	SV	IP	H	HR	BB	SO	RAT	ERA	ERA+	OAV	OOB	BH	AVG	PB	PR	/A	PD	TPI
1885	Lou-a	6	11	.353	17	17	17	0	0	150	129	3	43	61	10.8	2.76	117	.219	.282	13	.213	0	8	8	-0	0.7
1886	NY-a	11	28	.282	41	41	39	1	0	350	330	7	140	163	12.4	3.39	101	.240	.317	16	.119	-9	2	1	-1	-0.8
1887	NY-a	17	34	.333	52	52	50	0	0	441¹	551	11	136	124	14.4	4.73	90	.298	.353	45	.204	-1	-21	-24	6	-1.5
1888	Bro-a	9	9	.500	18	18	17	1	0	160²	150	1	32	67	10.8	2.80	107	.238	.287	5	.079	-4	5	3	2	0.1
1889	Col-a	10	7	.588	21	19	13	1	0	140	167	4	56	52	14.6	4.82	75	.287	.354	7	.130	-1	-15	-19	1	-1.7
1890	Col-a	0	1	.000	1	1	1	0	0	9	14	0	8	2	23.0	8.00	45	.350	.463	0	.000	-0	-4	-4	-1	-0.4
Total	6	53	90	.371	150	148	137	3	0	1251	1341	26	415	469	13.1	3.91	94	.265	.328	86	.160	-16	-26	-35	7	-3.6

● CARL MAYS
Mays, Carl William "Sub" b: 11/12/1891, Liberty, Ky. d: 4/4/71, El Cajon, Cal. BL/TR, 5'11.5", 195 lbs. Deb: 4/15/15

YEAR	TM/L	W	L	PCT	G	GS	CG	SH	SV	IP	H	HR	BB	SO	RAT	ERA	ERA+	OAV	OOB	BH	AVG	PB	PR	/A	PD	TPI
1915	Bos-A	6	5	.545	38	6	2	0	**7**	131²	119	0	21	65	9.9	2.60	107	.244	.282	9	.237	2	5	3	2	0.6
1916	*Bos-A	18	13	.581	44	24	14	2	3	245	208	3	74	76	10.7	2.39	116	.234	.299	18	.234	7	12	10	9	3.2
1917	Bos-A	22	9	.710	35	33	27	2	0	289	230	1	74	91	9.9	1.74	148	.221	.282	27	.252	6	30	27	8	4.8
1918	*Bos-A	21	13	.618	35	33	**30**	**8**	0	293¹	230	2	81	114	9.9	2.21	121	.221	.284	30	.288	10	19	15	9	4.1
1919	Bos-A	5	11	.313	21	16	14	2	2	146	131	3	40	53	10.8	2.47	123	.247	.306	8	.151	-2	12	9	3	1.1
	NY-A	9	3	.750	13	13	12	1	0	120	96	2	37	54	10.4	1.65	193	.216	.283	14	.311	3	21	21	1	2.7
	Yr	14	14	.500	34	29	26	3	2	266	227	5	77	107	10.5	2.10	148	.231	.291	22	.224	1	33	30	4	3.8
1920	NY-A	26	11	.703	45	37	26	**6**	2	312	310	13	84	92	11.6	3.06	125	.263	.316	26	.239	2	26	26	6	3.7
1921	*NY-A	**27**	9	**.750**	**49**	38	30	1	**7**	336²	332	11	76	70	11.1	3.05	139	.257	.303	49	.343	12	46	44	3	5.8
1922	*NY-A	12	14	.462	34	29	21	1	2	240	257	12	50	41	11.8	3.60	111	.285	.327	23	.250	1	12	11	6	1.7
1923	NY-A	5	2	.714	23	7	2	0	0	81¹	119	8	32	16	17.2	6.20	64	.357	.420	4	.148	1	-20	-20	3	-1.2
1924	Cin-N	20	9	.690	37	27	15	2	0	226	238	3	36	63	11.4	3.15	120	.270	.302	24	.289	7	18	16	8	3.4
1925	Cin-N	3	5	.375	12	5	3	0	2	51²	60	5	13	10	13.1	3.31	124	.294	.342	6	.250	1	6	5	1	0.8
1926	Cin-N	19	12	.613	39	33	**24**	3	1	281	286	3	53	58	11.0	3.14	118	.269	.306	22	.224	2	21	17	10	3.1
1927	Cin-N	3	7	.300	14	9	6	0	0	82	90	1	10	17	11.0	3.51	108	.276	.300	13	.406	5	4	2	1	1.3
1928	Cin-N	4	1	.800	14	7	4	0	0	62²	67	3	22	10	12.8	3.88	102	.275	.335	8	.296	1	1	-0	1	0.2
1929	NY-N	7	2	.778	14	9	3	0	1	64	81	3	31	32	12.7	4.32	106	.287	.333	12	.353	4	5	4	2	0.8
Total	15	207	126	.622	490	325	231	29	31	3021¹	2912	73	734	862	11.1	2.92	119	.257	.307	291	.268	64	217	189	74	36.1

● MATT MAYSEY
Maysey, Matthew Samuel b: 1/8/67, Hamilton, Ont., Canada BR/TR, 6'4", 225 lbs. Deb: 7/8/92

YEAR	TM/L	W	L	PCT	G	GS	CG	SH	SV	IP	H	HR	BB	SO	RAT	ERA	ERA+	OAV	OOB	BH	AVG	PB	PR	/A	PD	TPI
1992	Mon-N	0	0	—	2	0	0	0	0	2¹	4	1	0	1	19.3	3.86	90	.364	.417	0	—	0	-0	-0	-0	0.0
1993	Mil-A	1	2	.333	23	0	0	0	0	22	28	4	13	10	17.2	5.73	74	.322	.416	1	1.000	0	-3	-4	-1	-0.5
Total	2	1	2	.333	25	0	0	0	0	24¹	32	5	13	11	17.4	5.55	75	.327	.416	1	1.000	0	-4	-4	-1	-0.5

YEAR	TM/L	W	L	PCT	G	GS	CG	SH	SV	IP	H	HR	BB	SO	RAT	ERA	ERA+	OAV	OOB	BH	AVG	PB	PR	/A	PD	TPI
● **JACK McADAMS**	McAdams, George D. b: 12/17/1886, Benton, Ark. d: 5/21/37, San Francisco, Cal BR/TR, 6'1.5", 170 lbs. Deb: 7/22/11																									
1911	StL-N	0	0	—	6	0	0	0	0	9²	7	0	5	4	13.0	3.72	91	.226	.368	0	.000	-0	-0	-0	0	0.0
● **BILL McAFEE**	McAfee, William Fort b: 9/7/07, Smithville, Ga. d: 7/8/58, Culpeper, Va. BR/TR, 6'2", 186 lbs. Deb: 5/12/30																									
1930	Chi-N	0	0		2	0	0	0	0	1	3	0	2	0	45.0	0.00	—	.375	.500	0	—	0	1	1	-0	0.0
1931	Bos-N	0	1	.000	18	1	0	0	0	29²	39	2	10	9	14.9	6.37	59	.333	.386	0	.000	-0	-8	-9	-0	-0.3
1932	Was-A	6	1	.857	8	5	2	0	0	41¹	47	3	22	10	15.0	3.92	110	.287	.371	2	.111	-2	3	2	1	0.2
1933	Was-A	3	2	.600	27	1	0	0	5	53	64	3	21	14	14.6	6.62	63	.296	.361	4	.267	2	-14	-14	-0	-1.2
1934	StL-A	1	0	1.000	28	0	0	0	0	61²	84	4	26	11	16.5	5.84	86	.332	.401	3	.188	-0	-9	-6	-1	-0.2
Total 5		10	4	.714	83	7	2	0	5	186²	237	12	81	44	15.5	5.69	78	.313	.382	9	.173	-0	-28	-26	1	-1.5
● **JIMMY McALEER**	McAleer, James Robert "Loafer" b: 7/10/1864, Youngstown, Ohio d: 4/29/31, Youngstown, Ohio BR/TR, 6', 175 lbs. Deb: 4/24/1889 M ◆																									
1901	Cle-A	0	0	—	1	0	0	0	0	0¹	2	0	3	0	135.0	0.00	—	.675	.839	1	.143	-0	0	0	0	0.0
● **JACK McALEESE**	McAleese, John James b: 1877, Sharon, Pa. d: 11/15/50, New York, N.Y. BR/TR, 5'8", Deb: 8/10/01 ◆																									
1901	Chi-A	0	0	—	1	0	0	0	0	3	7	0	1	1	24.0	9.00	39	.447	.480	0	.000	-2	-2	-2	0	0.0
● **SPORT McALLISTER**	McAllister, Lewis William b: 7/23/1874, Austin, Miss. d: 7/17/62, Wyandotte, Mich. BB/TR, 5'11", 180 lbs. Deb: 8/7/1896 ◆																									
1896	Cle-N	0	0	—	1	0	0	0	0	4	9	0	2	0	24.8	6.75	67	.439	.489	6	.222	-0	-1	-0	0	0.0
1897	Cle-N	1	2	.333	4	3	3	0	0	28	29	3	9	10	12.2	4.50	100	.265	.321	30	.219	-0	-1	-0	1	0.0
1898	Cle-N	3	4	.429	9	7	6	0	0	65¹	73	2	23	9	13.6	4.55	80	.280	.346	13	.228	1	-7	-7	-1	-0.6
1899	Cle-N	0	1	.000	3	1	1	0	0	16	29	0	10	2	24.2	9.56	38	.389	.486	99	.237	0	-10	-10	-0	-0.5
Total 4		4	7	.364	17	11	10	0	0	113¹	140	5	44	21	15.2	5.32	73	.301	.370	358	.247	1	-19	-18	-0	-1.1
● **ERNIE McANALLY**	McAnally, Ernest Lee b: 8/15/46, Pittsburg, Tex. BR/TR, 6'1", 190 lbs. Deb: 4/11/71																									
1971	Mon-N	11	12	.478	31	25	8	2	0	177²	150	9	87	98	12.4	3.90	90	.228	.326	7	.117	-2	-9	-7	0	-1.1
1972	Mon-N	6	15	.286	29	27	4	2	0	170	165	13	71	102	12.7	3.81	93	.259	.337	6	.113	-2	-7	-5	3	-0.5
1973	Mon-N	7	9	.438	27	24	4	0	0	147	158	13	54	72	13.2	4.04	94	.274	.340	9	.184	-1	-6	-4	-0	-0.5
1974	Mon-N	6	13	.316	25	21	5	2	0	128²	126	10	56	79	13.0	4.48	86	.256	.336	5	.119	-2	-12	-9	1	-1.4
Total 4		30	49	.380	112	97	21	6	0	623¹	599	45	268	351	12.8	4.03	91	.253	.334	27	.132	-6	-34	-25	3	-3.5
● **JIM McANDREW**	McAndrew, James Clement b: 1/11/44, Lost Nation, Iowa BR/TR, 6'2", 185 lbs. Deb: 7/21/68																									
1968	NY-N	4	7	.364	12	12	2	1	0	79	66	5	17	46	9.9	2.28	133	.230	.282	1	.045	-1	6	7	-1	0.8
1969	NY-N	6	7	.462	27	21	4	2	0	135	112	12	44	90	10.5	3.47	105	.225	.291	5	.135	-1	2	3	-1	0.1
1970	NY-N	10	14	.417	32	27	9	3	2	184¹	166	18	38	111	10.1	3.56	113	.239	.281	8	.148	1	10	9	-2	1.0
1971	NY-N	2	5	.286	24	10	0	0	0	90¹	78	10	32	42	11.1	4.38	78	.227	.294	1	.043	-1	-9	-10	1	-0.8
1972	NY-N	11	8	.579	28	23	4	0	1	160²	133	12	38	81	9.9	2.80	120	.225	.278	2	.047	-2	12	10	-1	0.8
1973	NY-N	3	8	.273	23	12	0	0	1	80¹	109	7	31	38	16.0	5.38	67	.330	.393	2	.133	2	-15	-16	-1	-1.9
1974	SD-N	1	4	.200	15	5	1	0	0	41²	47	7	13	16	13.2	5.62	63	.284	.335	1	.143	-0	-9	-10	-1	-1.1
Total 7		37	53	.411	161	110	20	6	4	771¹	712	73	213	424	11.0	3.65	98	.245	.300	20	.100	-3	-4	-6	-6	-1.1
● **DIXIE McARTHUR**	McArthur, Oland Alexander b: 2/1/1892, Vernon, Ala. d: 5/31/86, West Point, Miss. BR/TR, 6'1", 185 lbs. Deb: 7/10/14																									
1914	Pit-N	0	0	—	1	0	0	0	0	1	1	0	1	0	9.0	0.00	—	.250	.250	0	—	0	0	0	0	0.0
● **WICKEY McAVOY**	McAvoy, James Eugene b: 10/22/1894, Rochester, N.Y. d: 7/6/73, Rochester, N.Y. BR/TR, 5'11", 172 lbs. Deb: 9/29/13 ◆																									
1918	Phi-A	0	0	—	1	0	0	0	0	0²	1	1	0	0	13.5	13.50	22	.500	.500	66	.244	-0	-1	-1	0	0.0
● **TOM McAVOY**	McAvoy, Thomas John b: 8/12/36, Brooklyn, N.Y. BL/TL, 6'3", 200 lbs. Deb: 9/27/59																									
1959	Was-A	0	0	—	1	0	0	0	0	2²	1	0	2	0	10.1	0.00	—	.125	.300	0	.000	-0	1	1	0	0.0
● **AL McBEAN**	McBean, Alvin O'Neal b: 5/15/38, Charlotte Amalie, V.I. BR/TR, 6', 180 lbs. Deb: 7/2/61																									
1961	Pit-N	3	2	.600	27	2	0	0	0	74¹	72	4	42	49	14.3	3.75	106	.263	.369	4	.267	1	2	2	2	0.5
1962	Pit-N	15	10	.600	33	29	6	2	0	189²	212	11	65	119	13.5	3.70	106	.285	.348	14	.209	2	5	5	0	0.8
1963	Pit-N	13	3	.813	55	7	2	1	11	122¹	100	5	39	74	10.4	2.57	128	.222	.287	6	.194	2	10	10	2	1.8
1964	Pit-N	8	3	.727	58	0	0	0	22	89²	76	4	17	41	9.7	1.91	184	.234	.280	-1	.083	-1	**16**	**16**	4	3.3
1965	Pit-N	6	6	.500	62	1	0	0	18	114	111	6	40	54	12.3	2.29	153	.260	.331	6	.222	-1	16	15	1	2.4
1966	Pit-N	4	3	.571	47	0	0	0	3	86²	95	9	24	54	12.6	3.22	111	.280	.332	1	.100	-1	4	3	1	0.3
1967	Pit-N	7	4	.636	51	8	5	0	4	131	118	6	43	54	11.1	2.54	132	.248	.312	6	.207	2	12	12	0	1.4
1968	Pit-N	9	12	.429	36	28	3	2	0	198¹	204	10	63	100	12.3	3.58	82	.269	.330	13	.194	3	-13	-15	4	-0.9
1969	SD-N	0	1	.000	1	1	0	0	0	7	10	1	2	1	15.4	5.14	69	.345	.387	1	.500	-0	-1	-1	-0	-0.1
	LA-N	2	6	.250	31	0	0	0	4	48¹	46	6	21	26	12.8	3.91	85	.258	.343	0	.000	-0	-2	-3	-1	-0.7
	Yr	2	7	.222	32	1	0	0	4	55¹	56	7	23	27	13.2	4.07	82	.271	.349	1	.200	-0	-3	-4	-1	-0.8
1970	LA-N	0	0	—	1	0	0	0	0	1	1	0	0	0	9.0	0.00	—	.333	.333	0	—	0	0	0	0	0.0
	Pit-N	0	0	—	7	0	0	0	1	10	13	2	7	3	18.0	8.10	48	.317	.417	0	.000	-0	-5	-5	-0	-0.1
	Yr	0	0	—	8	0	0	0	1	11	14	2	7	3	17.2	7.36	53	.318	.412	0	.000	-0	-4	-4	-0	-0.1
Total 10		67	50	.573	409	76	22	5	63	1072¹	1058	63	365	575	12.2	3.13	111	.262	.327	52	.197	9	45	40	13	8.7
● **PRYOR McBEE**	McBee, Pryor Edward "Lefty" b: 6/20/01, Blanco, Okla. d: 4/19/63, Roseville, Cal. BR/TL, 6'1", 190 lbs. Deb: 5/22/26																									
1926	Chi-A	0	0	—	1	0	0	0	0	1¹	1	0	3	0	27.0	6.75	57	.250	.571	0	—	0	-0	-0	0	0.0
● **DICK McBRIDE**	McBride, James Dickson b: 1845, Philadelphia, Pa. d: 10/10/16, Philadelphia, Pa. TR, 5'9", 150 lbs. Deb: 5/20/1871 M																									
1871	Ath-n	18	5	**.783**	25	25	25	0	0	222	285	3	40	15	13.2	4.58	88	.280	.307	31	.235	-4	-9	-14		-1.1
1872	Ath-n	30	14	.682	47	47	47	1	0	419	513	3	26	44	11.6	3.01	121	.268	.278	73	.281	3	33	29		2.1
1873	Ath-n	24	19	.558	46	46	38	**3**	0	382²	453	3	47	25	11.8	3.32	103	.263	.282	71	.281	3	3	4		0.4
1874	Ath-n	33	22	.600	55	55	55	0	0	487	514	5	29		**10.0**	2.55	124	**.241**	**.251**	57	.216	-8	24	33		1.9
1875	Ath-n	44	14	.759	60	60	59	6	0	538	602	4	25		10.5	1.97	134	.266	.274	73	.271	4	29	40		3.6
1876	Bos-N	0	0	.000	4	4	0	0	0	33	53	1	5	2	15.8	2.73	83	.353	.374	-1	.188	-1	-2	-2	-0	-0.3
Total 5 n		149	74	.668	233	233	224	10	0	2048²	2367	18	167	84	11.1	2.86	115	.261	.275	305	.259	-4	75	98		6.9
● **KEN McBRIDE**	McBride, Kenneth Faye b: 8/12/35, Huntsville, Ala. BR/TR, 6', 195 lbs. Deb: 8/4/59 C																									
1959	Chi-A	0	1	.000	11	0	0	0	1	22²	20	1	17	12	14.7	3.18	118	.230	.356	1	.167	-0	2	1	1	0.1
1960	Chi-A☆	0	1	.000	5	0	0	0	0	4²	6	0	3	4	19.3	3.86	98	.333	.455	0	—	0	0	-0	-0	0.0
1961	LA-A☆	12	15	.444	38	36	11	1	1	241²	229	28	102	180	12.6	3.65	124	.252	.332	7	.084	-5	10	23	4	2.3
1962	LA-A†	11	5	.688	24	23	6	0	0	149¹	136	9	70	83	13.0	3.50	110	.249	.344	9	.164	0	8	6	5	1.1
1963	LA-A★	13	12	.520	36	36	11	2	0	251	198	20	82	147	10.5	3.26	105	.218	.293	15	.172	2	10	5	3	0.9
1964	LA-A	4	13	.235	29	21	0	0	0	116¹	104	14	75	66	15.1	5.26	62	.239	.370	6	.214	3	-21	-26	3	-2.8
1965	Cal-A	0	3	.000	8	6	0	0	0	22	24	1	14	11	16.4	6.14	55	.270	.381	0	—	0	-7	-0	-0	-0.9
Total 7		40	50	.444	151	122	28	7	3	807²	717	75	363	503	12.6	3.79	101	.240	.332	38	.144	-0	2	15		0.7
● **PETE McBRIDE**	McBride, Peter William b: 7/9/1875, Adams, Mass. d: 7/3/44, N.Adams, Mass. BR/TR, 5'10", 170 lbs. Deb: 9/20/1898																									
1898	Cle-N	0	1	.000	1	1	1	0	0	7	9	0	4	6	18.0	6.43	56	.309	.411	2	1.000	2	-2	-2	-0	-0.1
1899	StL-N	2	4	.333	11	6	4	0	0	64	65	4	40	26	15.3	4.08	98	.263	.375	5	.185	-0	-2	-1	-1	-0.1
Total 2		2	5	.286	12	7	5	0	0	71	74	4	44	32	15.6	4.31	92	.268	.378	7	.241	-2	-4	-3	-1	-0.2
● **RALPH McCABE**	McCabe, Ralph Herbert "Mack" b: 10/21/18, Napanee, Ont., Can. d: 5/3/74, Windsor, Ont., Can. BR/TR, 6'4", 195 lbs. Deb: 9/18/46																									
1946	Cle-A	0	1	.000	1	1	0	0	0	4	5	3	2	3	18.0	11.25	29	.313	.421	0	.000	-0	-3	-4	0	-0.6

YEAR TM/L	W	L	PCT	G	GS	CG	SH	SV	IP	H	HR	BB	SO	RAT	ERA	ERA+	OAV	OOB	BH	AVG	PB	PR	/A	PD	TPI

● DICK McCABE   McCabe, Richard James b: 2/21/1896, Mamaroneck, N.Y. d: 4/11/50, Buffalo, N.Y. BR/TR, 5'10.5", 159 lbs. Deb: 5/30/18

1918 Bos-A	0	1	.000	3	1	0	0	0	9²	13	0	2	3	14.0	2.79	96	.351	.385	0	.000	-0	-0	-0	-0	0.0
1922 Chi-A	1	0	1.000	3	0	0	0	0	3¹	4	0	0	1	10.8	5.40	75	.308	.308	0	—	0	-1	-0	-0	-0.1
Total 2	1	1	.500	6	1	0	0	0	13	17	0	2	4	13.2	3.46	88	.340	.365	0	.000	-0	-1	-1	-0	-0.1

● TIM McCABE   McCabe, Timothy J. b: 10/19/1894, Ironton, Mo. d: 4/12/77, Ironton, Mo. BR/TR, 6', 190 lbs. Deb: 8/16/15

1915 StL-A	3	1	.750	7	4	4	1	0	41²	25	1	9	17	7.6	1.30	221	.177	.232	1	.067	-1	8	7	-1	0.5
1916 StL-A	2	0	1.000	13	0	0	0	0	25²	29	0	7	7	13.3	3.16	87	.282	.339	0	.000	-0	-1	-1	1	0.0
1917 StL-A	0	0	—	1	0	0	0	0	2¹	4	1	4	2	30.9	23.14	11	.400	.571	0	—	0	-5	-5	0	0.0
1918 StL-A	0	0	—	1	0	0	0	0	1¹	2	0	1	0	20.3	13.50	20	.333	.429	0	—	0	-2	-2	0	0.0
Total 4	5	1	.833	22	4	4	1	0	71	60	2	21	26	10.6	2.92	96	.231	.296	1	.053	-1	-0	-1	1	0.5

● HARRY McCAFFERY   McCaffery, Harry Charles b: 11/25/1858, St.Louis, Mo. d: 4/19/28, St.Louis, Mo. BR/TR, 5'10.5", 185 lbs. Deb: 6/15/1882 U♦

| 1885 Cin-a | 1 | 0 | 1.000 | 1 | 1 | 0 | 0 | 0 | 9 | 13 | 1 | 2 | 2 | 17.0 | 6.00 | 54 | .342 | .405 | 0 | .000 | -0 | -3 | -3 | -0 | -0.3 |

● BILL McCAHAN   McCahan, William Glenn b: 6/7/21, Philadelphia, Pa. d: 7/3/86, Fort Worth, Tex. BR/TR, 5'11", 200 lbs. Deb: 9/15/46

1946 Phi-A	1	1	.500	4	2	2	1	0	18	16	0	9	6	12.5	1.00	355	.246	.338	2	.400	1	5	5	0	0.7
1947 Phi-A	10	5	.667	29	19	10	1	0	165¹	160	7	62	47	12.1	3.32	115	.252	.318	9	.164	-1	7	9	1	0.8
1948 Phi-A	4	7	.364	17	15	5	0	0	86²	98	8	65	20	16.9	5.71	75	.284	.398	8	.258	1	-14	-14	-1	-1.5
1949 Phi-A	1	1	.500	7	4	0	0	0	20²	23	0	9	3	13.1	2.61	157	.291	.364	1	.200	-0	4	3	-0	0.2
Total 4	16	14	.533	57	40	17	2	0	290²	297	15	145	76	13.7	3.84	103	.264	.348	20	.208	1	2	4	-1	0.2

● WINDY McCALL   McCall, John William b: 7/18/25, San Francisco, Cal. BL/TL, 6', 180 lbs. Deb: 4/25/48

1948 Bos-A	0	1	.000	1	1	0	0	0	1¹	6	1	1	0	47.3	20.25	22	.600	.636	0	—	0	-2	-2	0	-0.9
1949 Bos-A	0	0	—	5	0	0	0	0	9¹	13	2	10	8	22.2	11.57	38	.333	.469	2	.667	1	-8	-7	-0	0.0
1950 Pit-N	0	0	—	2	0	0	0	0	6²	12	2	4	5	21.6	9.45	46	.387	.457	0	.000	-0	-4	-4	0	0.0
1954 NY-N	2	5	.286	33	4	0	0	2	61	50	5	29	38	12.1	3.25	124	.219	.315	0	.000	-1	6	5	-1	0.3
1955 NY-N	6	5	.545	42	6	4	0	3	95	86	8	37	50	12.2	3.69	109	.244	.326	2	.118	-1	4	3	1	0.4
1956 NY-N	3	4	.429	46	4	0	0	7	77¹	74	7	20	41	11.1	3.61	105	.252	.302	3	.200	-1	1	1	-2	0.3
1957 NY-N	0	0	—	5	0	0	0	0	3	8	1	2	2	33.0	15.00	26	.533	.611	0	—	0	-4	-4	-0	0.0
Total 7	11	15	.423	134	15	4	0	12	253²	249	26	103	144	12.9	4.22	94	.257	.335	7	.146	-1	-7	-7	-3	-0.2

● LARRY McCALL   McCall, Larry Stephen b: 9/8/52, Asheville, N.C. BL/TR, 6'2", 195 lbs. Deb: 9/10/77

1977 NY-A	0	1	.000	2	0	0	0	0	6	12	1	0	1	19.5	7.50	53	.375	.394	0	—	0	-2	-2	-0	-0.3
1978 NY-A	1	1	.500	5	1	0	0	0	16	20	2	6	7	15.2	5.63	64	.323	.391	0	—	0	-3	-4	0	-0.2
1979 Tex-A	1	0	1.000	2	1	0	0	0	8¹	7	0	3	3	10.8	2.16	192	.226	.294	0	—	0	2	2	0	0.3
Total 3	2	2	.500	9	2	0	0	0	30¹	39	3	10	10	14.8	5.04	76	.312	.368	0	—	0	-4	-4	-0	-0.2

● DUTCH McCALL   McCall, Robert Leonard b: 12/27/20, Columbia, Tenn. BL/TL, 6'1", 184 lbs. Deb: 4/27/48

| 1948 Chi-N | 4 | 13 | .235 | 30 | 20 | 5 | 0 | 0 | 151¹ | 158 | 14 | 85 | 89 | 14.5 | 4.82 | 81 | .268 | .361 | 9 | .170 | 1 | -14 | -15 | 1 | -1.3 |

● RANDY McCAMENT   McCament, Larry Randall b: 7/29/62, Albuquerque, N.Mex. BR/TR, 6'3", 195 lbs. Deb: 6/28/89

1989 SF-N	1	1	.500	25	0	0	0	0	36²	32	4	23	12	13.7	3.93	86	.241	.357	1	.333	-0	-2	-2	-0	0.0
1990 SF-N	0	0	—	3	0	0	0	0	6	8	0	5	5	19.5	3.00	121	.333	.448	0	.000	-0	1	0	-0	0.0
Total 2	1	1	.500	28	0	0	0	0	42²	40	4	28	17	14.6	3.80	90	.255	.371	1	.250	-0	-1	-2	0	0.0

● GENE McCANN   McCann, Henry Eugene "Mike" b: 6/13/1876, Baltimore, Md. d: 4/26/43, New York, N.Y. TR, 5'10", Deb: 4/19/01

1901 Bro-N	2	3	.400	6	5	3	0	0	34	34	1	16	9	14.3	3.44	97	.259	.357	0	.000	-1	-0	-0	-1	-0.1
1902 Bro-N	1	2	.333	3	3	3	0	0	30	32	0	12	9	13.2	2.40	115	.273	.340	1	.083	-1	1	1	1	0.1
Total 2	3	5	.375	9	8	6	0	0	64	66	1	28	18	13.8	2.95	104	.265	.349	1	.045	-2	1	1	1	0.1

● ARCH McCARTHY   McCarthy, Archibald Joseph b: Ypsilanti, Mich. TR, 6', 160 lbs. Deb: 8/14/02

| 1902 Det-A | 2 | 7 | .222 | 10 | 8 | 8 | 0 | 0 | 72 | 90 | 2 | 31 | 10 | 15.6 | 6.13 | 60 | .306 | .380 | 2 | .071 | -3 | -20 | -20 | -2 | -2.3 |

● JOHNNY McCARTHY   McCarthy, John Joseph b: 1/7/10, Chicago, Ill. d: 9/13/73, Mundelein, Ill. BL/TL, 6'1.5", 185 lbs. Deb: 9/2/34 ♦

| 1939 NY-N | 0 | 0 | — | 1 | 0 | 0 | 0 | 0 | 5 | 8 | 1 | 2 | 0 | 18.0 | 7.20 | 55 | .364 | .417 | 21 | .262 | 0 | -2 | -2 | 0 | 0.0 |

● TOMMY McCARTHY   McCarthy, Thomas Francis Michael b: 7/24/1863, Boston, Mass. d: 8/5/22, Boston, Mass. BR/TR, 5'7", 170 lbs. Deb: 7/10/1884 MH♦

1884 Bos-U	0	7	.000	7	6	5	0	0	56	73	2	14	18	14.0	4.82	49	.295	.333	45	.215	-2	-15	-15	1	-1.4
1886 Phi-N	0	0	—	1	0	0	0	0	1	0	0	1	1	9.00	0.00	—	.000	.250	5	.185	0	0	0	0	0.0
1888 *StL-a	0	0	—	2	0	0	0	0	4¹	3	1	2	1	10.4	4.15	79	.188	.279	140	.274	-0	-1	-0	-0	0.0
1889 StL-a	0	0	—	1	0	0	0	0	5	4	0	6	1	18.0	7.20	59	.213	.403	176	.291	-2	-2	-2	0	0.0
1891 StL-a	0	0	—	1	0	0	0	0	1²	2	0	0	0	18.0	9.00	47	.402	.402	179	.310	-1	-1	-0	0	0.0
1894 Bos-N	0	0	—	1	0	0	0	0	2	1	0	3	0	18.0	4.50	126	.280	.410	188	.349	0	0	0	0	0.0
Total 6	0	7	.000	13	6	5	0	0	69¹	83	3	26	21	14.1	4.93	54	.280	.338	1496	.292	-1	-17	-17	1	-1.4

● TOM McCARTHY   McCarthy, Thomas Michael b: 6/18/61, Lundstahl, W.Ger. BR/TR, 6', 180 lbs. Deb: 7/5/85

1985 Bos-A	0	0	—	3	0	0	0	0	5	7	1	4	2	19.8	10.80	40	.350	.458	0	—	0	-4	-4	-0	-0.1
1988 Chi-A	2	0	1.000	6	0	0	0	1	13	9	0	2	5	9.0	1.38	287	.191	.255	0	—	0	4	4	0	0.7
1989 Chi-A	1	2	.333	31	0	0	0	0	66²	72	8	20	27	12.7	3.51	108	.280	.337	0	—	0	3	2	1	0.2
Total 3	3	2	.600	40	0	0	0	1	84²	88	9	26	34	12.5	3.61	107	.272	.333	0	—	0	3	1	0	0.8

● TOM McCARTHY   McCarthy, Thomas Patrick b: 5/22/1884, Ft.Wayne, Ind. d: 3/28/33, Mishawaka, Ind. TR, 5'7", 170 lbs. Deb: 5/10/08

1908 Cin-N	0	1	.000	1	1	0	0	0	3²	6	0	3	3	22.1	9.82	23	.300	.391	0	.000	-0	-3	-3	0	-0.6
Pit-N	0	0	—	2	1	0	0	0	6	3	0	6	1	13.5	0.00	—	.176	.391	0	.000	-0	2	2	1	0.4
Bos-N	7	3	.700	14	11	7	2	0	94	77	0	28	27	10.1	1.63	148	.235	.298	6	.171	-0	8	8	0	1.0
Yr	7	4	.636	17	13	7	2	0	103²	86	0	37	31	10.8	1.82	132	.236	.308	6	.146	-1	6	7	1	0.4
1909 Bos-N	0	5	.000	8	7	3	0	0	46¹	47	3	28	11	15.0	3.50	81	.272	.379	2	.125	-0	-5	-3	-0	-0.4
Total 2	7	9	.438	25	20	10	2	0	150	133	3	65	42	12.1	2.34	108	.248	.332	8	.140	-1	2	3	-0	-0.0

● BILL McCARTHY   McCarthy, William Thomas b: 4/11/1882, Ashland, Mass. d: 5/29/39, Boston, Mass. BR/TR, 5'11", 180 lbs. Deb: 4/21/06

| 1906 Bos-N | 0 | 0 | — | 1 | 0 | 0 | 0 | 0 | 2 | 2 | 0 | 3 | 0 | 22.5 | 9.00 | 30 | .182 | .357 | 0 | .000 | -0 | -1 | -1 | -0 | 0.0 |

● JOHN McCARTY   McCarty, John A. b: St.Louis, Mo. TR, Deb: 4/18/1889

| 1889 KC-a | 8 | 6 | .571 | 15 | 14 | 13 | 0 | 0 | 119² | 147 | 4 | 61 | 36 | 16.1 | 3.91 | 107 | .293 | .376 | 18 | .228 | -2 | -1 | 4 | -0 | 0.2 |

● KIRK McCASKILL   McCaskill, Kirk Edward b: 4/9/61, Kapuskasing, Ont., Canada BR/TR, 6'1", 200 lbs. Deb: 5/1/85

1985 Cal-A	12	12	.500	30	29	6	1	0	189²	189	23	64	102	12.2	4.70	87	.258	.321	0	—	0	-12	-12	-0	-1.4
1986 *Cal-A	17	10	.630	34	33	10	2	0	246¹	207	19	92	202	11.1	3.36	122	.230	.303	0	—	0	22	20	-0	2.2
1987 Cal-A	4	6	.400	14	13	1	1	0	74²	84	14	34	56	14.5	5.67	76	.286	.364	0	—	0	-10	-11	1	-1.2
1988 Cal-A	8	6	.571	23	23	4	2	0	146¹	155	9	61	98	13.3	4.31	90	.274	.346	0	—	0	-6	-7	0	-0.4
1989 Cal-A	15	10	.600	32	32	6	4	0	212	202	16	59	107	11.2	2.93	130	.254	.308	0	—	0	22	21	2	2.6
1990 Cal-A	12	11	.522	29	29	2	0	0	174¹	161	9	72	78	12.1	3.25	117	.244	.320	0	—	0	13	11	2	1.5
1991 Cal-A	10	19	.345	30	30	1	0	0	177²	193	16	66	71	13.3	4.26	96	.283	.349	0	—	0	-3	-3	1	-0.4
1992 Chi-A	12	13	.480	34	34	0	0	0	209	193	11	95	109	12.7	4.18	96	.242	.328	0	—	0	-6	-7	2	-0.6
1993 *Chi-A	4	8	.333	30	14	0	0	0	113²	144	12	36	65	14.3	5.23	80	.313	.364	0	—	0	-11	-13	2	-1.0

YEAR TM/L	W	L	PCT	G	GS	CG	SH	SV	IP	H	HR	BB	SO	RAT	ERA	ERA+	OAV	OOB	BH	AVG	PB	PR	/A	PD	TPI
1994 Chi-A	1	4	.200	40	0	0	0	3	52²	51	6	22	37	12.5	3.42	137	.252	.326	0	—	0	8	7	0	0.7
Total 10	95	99	.490	296	237	30	11	5	1596¹	1579	138	601	925	12.4	3.99	101	.259	.328	0	—	0	18	5	8	2.0

● STEVE McCATTY McCatty, Steven Earl b: 3/20/54, Detroit, Mich. BR/TR, 6'3", 205 lbs. Deb: 9/17/77

YEAR TM/L	W	L	PCT	G	GS	CG	SH	SV	IP	H	HR	BB	SO	RAT	ERA	ERA+	OAV	OOB	BH	AVG	PB	PR	/A	PD	TPI
1977 Oak-A	0	0	—	4	2	0	0	0	14¹	16	1	7	9	15.1	5.02	80	.276	.364	0	—	0	-2	-2	-1	0.0
1978 Oak-A	0	0	—	9	0	0	0	0	20	26	1	9	10	15.7	4.50	81	.310	.376	0	—	0	-2	-2	-0	0.3
1979 Oak-A	11	12	.478	31	23	8	0	0	185²	207	17	80	87	14.4	4.22	96	.284	.363	0	—	0	-0	-4	-2	-0.2
1980 Oak-A	14	14	.500	33	31	11	1	0	221²	202	27	99	114	12.5	3.86	98	.240	.325	0	—	0	4	-2	-1	0.1
1981 *Oak-A	**14**	7	.667	22	22	16	**4**	0	185²	140	12	61	91	9.8	2.33	149	.211	.279	0	—	0	**27**	24	-1	2.8
1982 Oak-A	6	3	.667	21	20	2	0	0	128²	124	16	70	66	13.8	3.99	98	.255	.354	0	—	0	1	-1	-1	-0.1
1983 Oak-A	6	9	.400	38	24	3	2	5	167	156	16	82	65	12.9	3.99	97	.247	.334	0	—	0	1	-2	-2	-0.4
1984 Oak-A	8	14	.364	33	30	4	0	0	179²	206	24	71	63	13.9	4.76	79	.289	.355	0	—	0	-15	-20	-2	-1.9
1985 Oak-A	4	4	.500	30	9	1	0	0	82²	95	10	41	36	14.7	5.57	69	.286	.371	0	—	0	-14	-16	-0	-1.2
Total 9	63	63	.500	221	161	45	7	5	1188¹	1172	124	520	541	13.0	3.99	95	.258	.339	0	—	0	2	-26	-9	-0.6

● AL McCAULEY McCauley, Allen A. b: 3/4/1863, Indianapolis, Ind. d: 8/24/17, Wayne Twnshp., Ind BL/TL, 6', 180 lbs. Deb: 6/21/1884 ♦

YEAR TM/L	W	L	PCT	G	GS	CG	SH	SV	IP	H	HR	BB	SO	RAT	ERA	ERA+	OAV	OOB	BH	AVG	PB	PR	/A	PD	TPI
1884 Ind-a	2	7	.222	10	9	9	0	0	76	87	2	25	34	13.3	5.09	65	.261	.313	10	.189	2	-16	-15	2	-1.1

● JOE McCLAIN McClain, Joseph Fred b: 5/5/33, Johnson City, Tenn. BR/TR, 6', 183 lbs. Deb: 4/14/61

YEAR TM/L	W	L	PCT	G	GS	CG	SH	SV	IP	H	HR	BB	SO	RAT	ERA	ERA+	OAV	OOB	BH	AVG	PB	PR	/A	PD	TPI
1961 Was-A	8	18	.308	33	29	7	2	1	212	221	22	48	76	11.6	3.86	104	.270	.313	14	.206	1	4	4	-3	0.3
1962 Was-A	0	4	.000	10	4	0	0	0	24	33	8	11	6	17.3	9.38	43	.327	.404	1	.143	-0	-14	-14	0	-1.9
Total 2	8	22	.267	43	33	7	2	1	236	254	30	59	82	12.2	4.42	91	.276	.324	15	.200	1	-11	-11	-3	-1.6

● PAUL McCLELLAN McClellan, Paul William b: 2/3/66, San Mateo, Cal. BR/TR, 6'2", 180 lbs. Deb: 9/2/90

YEAR TM/L	W	L	PCT	G	GS	CG	SH	SV	IP	H	HR	BB	SO	RAT	ERA	ERA+	OAV	OOB	BH	AVG	PB	PR	/A	PD	TPI
1990 SF-N	0	1	.000	4	1	0	0	0	7²	14	3	6	2	24.7	11.74	31	.389	.488	1	.500	0	-7	-7	-0	-0.7
1991 SF-N	3	6	.333	13	12	1	0	0	71	68	12	25	44	11.9	4.56	78	.252	.318	3	.143	-0	-7	-8	-1	-1.0
Total 2	3	7	.300	17	13	1	0	0	78²	82	15	31	46	13.2	5.26	68	.268	.339	4	.174	0	-14	-15	-1	-1.7

● JIM McCLOSKEY McCloskey, James Ellwood "Irish" b: 5/26/10, Danville, Pa. d: 8/18/71, Jersey City, N.J. BL/TL, 5'9.5", 180 lbs. Deb: 4/21/36

YEAR TM/L	W	L	PCT	G	GS	CG	SH	SV	IP	H	HR	BB	SO	RAT	ERA	ERA+	OAV	OOB	BH	AVG	PB	PR	/A	PD	TPI
1936 Bos-N	0	0	—	4	1	0	0	0	8	14	1	3	2	19.1	11.25	34	.378	.439	0	.000	-0	-6	-7	0	0.0

● JOHN McCLOSKEY McCloskey, James John b: 8/20/1882, Wyoming, Pa. d: 6/5/19, Wilkes-Barre, Pa. Deb: 5/3/06

YEAR TM/L	W	L	PCT	G	GS	CG	SH	SV	IP	H	HR	BB	SO	RAT	ERA	ERA+	OAV	OOB	BH	AVG	PB	PR	/A	PD	TPI
1906 Phi-N	3	2	.600	9	4	3	0	0	41	46	2	9	6	12.3	2.85	92	.280	.322	3	.200	0	-1	-1	-1	-0.2
1907 Phi-N	0	0	—	3	0	0	0	0	9	15	0	6	3	22.0	7.00	35	.417	.512	0	.000	0	-5	-5	0	-0.1
Total 2	3	2	.600	12	4	3	0	0	50	61	2	15	9	14.0	3.60	72	.305	.359	3	.158	0	-6	-6	-1	-0.2

● BOB McCLURE McClure, Robert Craig b: 4/29/52, Oakland, Cal. BR/TL, 5'11", 170 lbs. Deb: 8/13/75 C

YEAR TM/L	W	L	PCT	G	GS	CG	SH	SV	IP	H	HR	BB	SO	RAT	ERA	ERA+	OAV	OOB	BH	AVG	PB	PR	/A	PD	TPI
1975 KC-A	1	0	1.000	12	0	0	0	1	15¹	4	0	14	15	10.6	0.00	—	.077	.273	0	—	0	6	7	0	0.5
1976 KC-A	0	0	—	8	0	0	0	0	4	3	0	8	3	24.8	9.00	39	.214	.500	0	—	0	-2	-2	-0	-0.1
1977 Mil-A	2	1	.667	68	0	0	0	6	71¹	64	2	34	57	12.5	2.52	161	.249	.339	0	—	0	12	12	2	0.9
1978 Mil-A	2	6	.250	44	0	0	0	9	65	53	8	30	47	12.3	3.74	101	.223	.325	0	—	0	0	0	-1	0.0
1979 Mil-A	5	2	.714	36	0	0	0	5	51	53	6	24	37	14.1	3.88	107	.269	.357	0	—	0	2	2	-0	0.2
1980 Mil-A	5	8	.385	52	5	2	1	10	90²	83	6	37	47	12.1	3.08	126	.241	.318	0	—	0	10	8	-1	1.4
1981 *Mil-A	0	0	—	4	0	0	0	0	7²	7	1	4	6	12.9	3.52	97	.233	.324	0	—	0	0	-0	-0	0.2
1982 *Mil-A	12	7	.632	34	26	3	0	0	172²	160	21	74	99	12.4	4.22	90	.248	.329	0	—	0	-3	-8	-1	-0.8
1983 Mil-A	9	9	.500	24	23	4	0	0	142	152	11	68	68	14.3	4.50	83	.277	.362	0	—	0	-7	-12	-1	-1.4
1984 Mil-A	4	8	.333	39	18	1	0	1	139²	154	9	52	68	13.4	4.38	88	.282	.347	0	—	0	-6	-8	-0	-0.4
1985 Mil-A	4	1	.800	38	1	0	0	3	85²	91	10	30	57	13.0	4.31	97	.274	.340	0	—	0	-2	-1	-0	-0.1
1986 Mil-A	2	1	.667	13	0	0	0	0	16¹	18	2	10	11	15.4	3.86	112	.286	.384	0	—	0	1	1	-0	-0.2
Mon-N	2	5	.286	52	0	0	0	6	62²	53	2	23	42	11.1	3.02	122	.232	.306	1	.250	0	5	5	0	0.6
1987 Mon-N	6	1	.857	52	0	0	0	5	52¹	47	8	20	33	11.5	3.44	122	.241	.312	0	.000	0	4	4	0	0.6
1988 Mon-N	1	3	.250	19	0	0	0	2	19	23	3	6	12	14.2	6.16	58	.307	.366	0	.000	0	-6	-5	-0	-1.2
NY-N	1	0	1.000	14	0	0	0	0	11	12	1	2	7	12.3	4.09	79	.279	.326	0	—	0	-1	-1	-0	-0.1
Yr	2	3	.400	33	0	0	0	2	30	35	4	8	19	13.2	5.40	64	.289	.338	0	.000	-0	-7	-6	-0	-1.3
1989 Cal-A	6	1	.857	48	0	0	0	3	52¹	39	2	15	36	9.5	1.55	246	.212	.275	0	—	0	14	13	-1	1.8
1990 Cal-A	2	0	1.000	11	0	0	0	0	7	7	0	3	6	12.9	6.43	59	.269	.345	0	—	0	-2	-2	-0	-0.5
1991 Cal-A	0	0	—	13	0	0	0	0	9²	13	3	5	7	17.7	9.31	44	.317	.404	0	—	0	-6	-6	-0	-1.1
StL-N	1	1	.500	32	0	0	0	0	23	24	1	8	15	12.9	3.13	119	.282	.351	1	1.000	0	1	1	-0	0.2
1992 StL-N	2	2	.500	71	0	0	0	0	54	52	6	25	24	13.2	3.17	107	.261	.350	0	.000	0	1	0	-0	0.1
1993 Fla-N	1	1	.500	14	0	0	0	0	6¹	13	1	5	6	25.6	7.11	61	.419	.500	0	—	0	-2	-2	-0	-0.5
Total 19	68	57	.544	698	73	12	1	52	1158²	1125	104	497	701	12.9	3.81	101	.257	.338	2	.222	0	21	6	-4	1.2

● HARRY McCLUSKEY McCluskey, Harry Robert b: 3/29/1892, Clay Center, Ohio d: 6/7/62, Toledo, Ohio BL/TL, 5'11.5", 173 lbs. Deb: 7/29/15

YEAR TM/L	W	L	PCT	G	GS	CG	SH	SV	IP	H	HR	BB	SO	RAT	ERA	ERA+	OAV	OOB	BH	AVG	PB	PR	/A	PD	TPI
1915 Cin-N	0	0	—	3	0	0	0	0	5	4	0	2	2	7.2	5.40	53	.182	.182	0	.000	-0	-1	-1	-0	-0.1

● ALEX McCOLL McColl, Alexander Boyd "Red" b: 3/29/1894, Eagleville, Ohio d: 2/6/91, Kingsville, Ohio BB/TR, 6'1", 178 lbs. Deb: 8/27/33

YEAR TM/L	W	L	PCT	G	GS	CG	SH	SV	IP	H	HR	BB	SO	RAT	ERA	ERA+	OAV	OOB	BH	AVG	PB	PR	/A	PD	TPI
1933 *Was-A	1	0	1.000	4	1	1	0	0	17	13	0	7	5	10.6	2.65	158	.210	.290	2	.333	1	3	3	-0	0.2
1934 Was-A	3	4	.429	42	2	1	0	1	112	129	6	36	29	13.3	3.86	112	.291	.345	3	.097	-2	8	6	2	0.3
Total 2	4	4	.500	46	3	2	0	1	129	142	6	43	34	13.0	3.70	116	.281	.338	5	.135	-1	11	9	2	0.5

● RALPH McCONNAUGHEY McConnaughey, Ralph James b: 8/5/1889, Vandergrift, Pa. d: 6/4/66, Detroit, Mich. BR/TR, 5'8.5", 166 lbs. Deb: 7/8/14

YEAR TM/L	W	L	PCT	G	GS	CG	SH	SV	IP	H	HR	BB	SO	RAT	ERA	ERA+	OAV	OOB	BH	AVG	PB	PR	/A	PD	TPI
1914 Ind-F	0	2	.000	7	2	1	0	0	26	23	3	16	7	13.8	4.85	64	.245	.360	1	.125	-0	-6	-5	-0	-0.4

● GEORGE McCONNELL McConnell, George Neely "Slats" b: 9/16/1877, Shelbyville, Tenn d: 5/10/64, Chattanooga, Tenn. BR/TR, 6'3", 190 lbs. Deb: 4/13/09 ♦

YEAR TM/L	W	L	PCT	G	GS	CG	SH	SV	IP	H	HR	BB	SO	RAT	ERA	ERA+	OAV	OOB	BH	AVG	PB	PR	/A	PD	TPI
1909 NY-A	0	1	.000	2	1	0	0	0	4	3	0	4	3	13.5	2.25	112	.231	.375	9	.209	0	0	0	1	0.1
1912 NY-A	8	12	.400	23	20	19	0	0	176²	172	3	52	91	11.6	2.75	131	.269	.328	27	.297	3	11	17	5	2.9
1913 NY-A	4	15	.211	35	20	8	0	3	180	162	2	60	72	11.4	3.20	94	.245	.314	12	.179	-1	-5	-4	5	-0.1
1914 Chi-N	0	1	.000	1	1	0	0	0	7	3	0	3	3	7.7	1.29	216	.125	.222	0	.000	-0	1	1	0	0.2
1915 Chi-F	**25**	10	**.714**	44	35	23	4	1	303	262	6	89	151	10.7	2.20	114	.232	.292	31	.248	4	18	11	3	2.0
1916 Chi-N	4	12	.250	28	21	8	1	0	171¹	137	8	35	82	9.3	2.57	113	.223	.271	9	.158	-2	1	6	2	0.6
Total 6	41	51	.446	133	98	58	5	4	842	739	21	242	403	10.7	2.60	112	.240	.300	88	.229	4	26	30	15	5.7

● BILLY McCOOL McCool, William John b: 7/14/44, Batesville, Ind. BR/TL, 6'2", 203 lbs. Deb: 4/24/64

YEAR TM/L	W	L	PCT	G	GS	CG	SH	SV	IP	H	HR	BB	SO	RAT	ERA	ERA+	OAV	OOB	BH	AVG	PB	PR	/A	PD	TPI
1964 Cin-N	6	5	.545	40	3	0	0	7	89¹	66	3	29	87	9.7	2.42	150	.206	.274	0	.000	-2	11	12	-2	1.3
1965 Cin-N	9	10	.474	62	2	0	0	21	105¹	93	9	47	120	12.3	4.27	88	.237	.324	1	.037	-2	-9	-6	-0	-1.5
1966 Cin-N☆	8	8	.500	57	0	0	0	18	105¹	76	5	41	104	10.3	2.48	157	.205	.290	3	.167	-0	13	17	2	3.4
1967 Cin-N	3	7	.300	31	11	0	0	7	97¹	92	8	56	83	14.1	3.42	110	.246	.352	2	.077	-1	-1	-4	-1	0.2
1968 Cin-N	3	4	.429	30	4	0	0	9	50²	59	4	41	30	17.8	4.97	64	.294	.413	1	.125	-0	-11	-10	-1	-1.6
1969 SD-N	3	5	.375	54	0	0	0	7	58²	59	7	42	35	16.4	4.30	82	.266	.396	0	.000	-0	-5	-5	-0	-0.8
1970 StL-N	0	3	.000	18	0	0	0	1	21²	20	0	16	12	15.0	6.23	56	.250	.375	0	.000	-0	-5	-5	-0	-0.7
Total 7	32	42	.432	292	20	0	0	58	528¹	465	31	272	471	12.9	3.59	103	.237	.336	7	.069	-6	-6	6	-1	0.3

● JIM McCORMICK McCormick, James b: 1856, Glasgow, Scotland d: 3/10/18, Paterson, N.J. BR/TR, 5'10.5", 215 lbs. Deb: 5/20/1878 M

YEAR TM/L	W	L	PCT	G	GS	CG	SH	SV	IP	H	HR	BB	SO	RAT	ERA	ERA+	OAV	OOB	BH	AVG	PB	PR	/A	PD	TPI
1878 Ind-N	5	8	.385	14	14	12	1	0	117	128	0	15	36	11.0	1.69	120	.269	.292	8	.143	-3	8	4	2	0.3
1879 Cle-N	20	40	.333	62	60	59	3	0	546¹	582	4	74	197	10.8	2.42	103	.259	.282	62	.220	-1	4	5	4	0.7
1880 Cle-N	45	28	.616	**74**	74	**72**	7	0	**657²**	585	2	75	260	9.0	1.85	127	.226	.247	71	.246	1	38	**37**	1	**4.0**

YEAR	TM/L	W	L	PCT	G	GS	CG	SH	SV	IP	H	HR	BB	SO	RAT	ERA	ERA+	OAV	OOB	BH	AVG	PB	PR	/A	PD	TPI
1881	Cle-N	26	30	.464	59	58	57	2	0	526	484	4	84	178	9.7	2.45	107	.235	.265	79	.256	6	19	10	-3	1.2
1882	Cle-N	**36**	30	.545	**68**	67	**65**	4	0	**595²**	550	14	103	200	9.9	2.37	118	.238	.271	57	.218	-4	35	28	-2	2.0
1883	Cle-N	28	12	**.700**	43	41	36	1	1	342	316	1	65	145	10.0	**1.84**	**171**	.233	.268	37	.236	-1	49	50	7	5.4
1884	Cle-N	19	22	.463	42	41	39	3	0	359	357	17	75	182	10.8	2.43	110	.247	.285	50	.263	2	5	12	0	1.3
	Cin-U	21	3	**.875**	24	24	24	**7**	0	210	151	3	14	161	**7.1**	**1.54**	**166**	**.188**	**.202**	27	.245	-6	21	**24**	2	1.8
1885	Pro-N	1	3	.250	4	4	4	0	0	37	34	1	20	8	13.1	2.43	109	.234	.327	3	.214	0	2	1	3	0.4
	*Chi-N	20	4	.833	24	24	24	3	0	215	187	8	40	88	9.5	2.43	125	.224	.260	23	.223	0	9	15	3	1.6
	Yr	21	7	.750	28	28	28	3	0	252	221	9	60	96	10.0	2.43	123	.226	.271	26	.222	1	11	15	5	2.0
1886	*Chi-N	31	11	.738	42	42	38	2	0	347²	341	18	100	172	11.4	2.82	129	.253	.304	41	.236	2	19	32	2	3.4
1887	Pit-N	13	23	.361	36	36	36	0	0	322¹	377	12	84	77	13.2	4.30	90	.285	.334	33	.243	-0	-8	-15	5	-0.9
Total	10	265	214	.553	492	485	466	33	1	4275²	4092	84	749	1704	10.2	2.43	117	.242	.274	491	.236	-4	202	201	22	21.2

● JERRY McCORMICK
McCormick, John   b: Philadelphia, Pa.   d: 9/19/05, Philadelphia, Pa.   Deb: 5/1/1883 ◆

YEAR	TM/L	W	L	PCT	G	GS	CG	SH	SV	IP	H	HR	BB	SO	RAT	ERA	ERA+	OAV	OOB	BH	AVG	PB	PR	/A	PD	TPI
1884	Phi-U	0	0	—	1	0	0	0	0	2	5	1	0	3	22.5	9.00	26	.446	.446	84	.285	-0	-1	-1	-0	0.0

● MIKE McCORMICK
McCormick, Michael Francis   b: 9/29/38, Pasadena, Cal.   BL/TL, 6'2", 195 lbs.   Deb: 9/3/56

YEAR	TM/L	W	L	PCT	G	GS	CG	SH	SV	IP	H	HR	BB	SO	RAT	ERA	ERA+	OAV	OOB	BH	AVG	PB	PR	/A	PD	TPI
1956	NY-N	0	1	.000	3	2	0	0	0	6²	7	1	10	4	23.0	9.45	40	.269	.472	0	.000	-0	-4	-4	-0	-0.5
1957	NY-N	3	1	.750	24	5	1	0	0	74²	79	7	32	50	13.7	4.10	96	.280	.360	6	.273	1	-2	-1	-1	0.0
1958	SF-N	11	8	.579	42	28	8	2	1	178¹	192	19	60	82	12.9	4.59	83	.276	.336	12	.222	1	-13	-15	2	-1.2
1959	SF-N	12	16	.429	47	31	7	3	4	225²	213	24	86	151	12.0	3.99	96	.248	.317	7	.106	-2	-1	-4	1	-0.6
1960	SF-N★	15	12	.556	40	34	15	4	3	253	228	15	65	154	10.5	**2.70**	129	.241	.291	16	.182	1	**30**	22	3	2.7
1961	SF-N★	13	16	.448	40	35	13	3	0	250	235	33	75	163	11.2	3.20	119	.249	.306	15	.188	1	23	17	-2	1.7
1962	SF-N	5	5	.500	28	15	1	0	0	98²	112	18	45	42	14.4	5.38	71	.286	.361	3	.107	0	-16	-17	-1	-1.6
1963	Bal-A	6	8	.429	25	21	2	0	0	136	132	18	66	75	13.1	4.30	81	.256	.340	8	.174	1	-10	-13	-0	-1.2
1964	Bal-A	0	2	.000	4	2	0	0	0	17¹	21	1	8	13	15.1	5.19	69	.288	.358	1	.167	-0	-3	-3	-0	-0.3
1965	Was-A	8	8	.500	44	21	3	1	1	158	158	17	36	88	11.1	3.36	103	.260	.301	3	.073	-1	2	2	-1	0.0
1966	Was-A	11	14	.440	41	32	8	3	0	216	193	23	51	101	10.3	3.46	100	.236	.282	14	.212	3	-1	-0	-1	0.3
1967	SF-N	**22**	10	.688	40	35	14	5	0	262¹	220	25	81	150	10.5	2.85	115	.226	.289	10	.119	5	15	13	-2	1.3
1968	SF-N	12	14	.462	38	28	9	2	1	198¹	196	17	49	121	11.2	3.58	82	.254	.300	6	.103	1	-13	-14	-2	-2.0
1969	SF-N	11	9	.550	32	28	9	0	0	196²	175	20	77	76	11.6	3.34	105	.237	.310	9	.136	1	6	3	-1	0.3
1970	SF-N	3	4	.429	23	11	1	0	2	78¹	80	15	36	37	13.7	6.20	64	.262	.346	4	.160	-0	-19	-19	1	-1.5
	NY-A	2	0	1.000	9	4	0	0	0	20²	26	2	13	12	17.0	6.10	58	.295	.386	1	.200	0	-5	-6	-1	-0.6
1971	KC-A	0	0	—	4	0	0	0	0	9²	14	0	5	2	17.7	9.31	37	.350	.422	0	.000	-0	-6	-6	1	0.1
Total	16	134	128	.511	484	333	91	23	12	2380¹	2281	255	795	1321	11.7	3.73	96	.251	.313	115	.156	9	-18	-46	-5	-3.1

● HARRY McCORMICK
McCormick, Patrick Henry   b: 10/25/1855, Syracuse, N.Y.   d: 8/8/1889, Syracuse, N.Y.   BR/TR, 5'9", 155 lbs.   Deb: 5/1/1879

YEAR	TM/L	W	L	PCT	G	GS	CG	SH	SV	IP	H	HR	BB	SO	RAT	ERA	ERA+	OAV	OOB	BH	AVG	PB	PR	/A	PD	TPI
1879	Syr-N	18	33	.353	54	54	49	5	0	457¹	517	3	31	96	10.8	2.99	79	.266	.277	51	.222	-4	-25	-32	-7	-3.4
1881	Wor-N	1	8	.111	9	9	9	1	0	78¹	89	1	15	7	11.9	3.56	85	.275	.307	6	.133	-2	-7	-5	-1	-0.7
1882	Cin-a	14	11	.560	25	25	24	3	0	219²	177	4	33	44	9.0	1.52	174	.206	.243	12	.129	-5	29	27	0	2.1
1883	Cin-a	8	6	.571	15	15	14	1	0	128²	139	1	27	21	11.6	2.87	113	.258	.294	17	.309	4	6	5	1	0.8
Total	4	41	58	.414	103	103	96	10	0	884	922	9	115	157	10.6	2.66	98	.251	.274	86	.203	-4	3	-4	-7	-1.2

● BILL McCORRY
McCorry, William Charles   b: 7/9/1887, Saranac Lake, N.Y.   d: 3/22/73, Augusta, Ga.   BL/TR, 5'9", 157 lbs.   Deb: 9/17/09

YEAR	TM/L	W	L	PCT	G	GS	CG	SH	SV	IP	H	HR	BB	SO	RAT	ERA	ERA+	OAV	OOB	BH	AVG	PB	PR	/A	PD	TPI
1909	StL-A	0	2	.000	2	2	0	0	0	15	29	1	6	10	21.0	9.00	27	.397	.443	0	.000	-0	-11	-11	-1	-1.1

● LES McCRABB
McCrabb, Lester William "Buster"   b: 11/4/14, Wakefield, Pa.   BR/TR, 5'11", 175 lbs.   Deb: 9/7/39   C

YEAR	TM/L	W	L	PCT	G	GS	CG	SH	SV	IP	H	HR	BB	SO	RAT	ERA	ERA+	OAV	OOB	BH	AVG	PB	PR	/A	PD	TPI
1939	Phi-A	1	2	.333	5	4	2	0	0	35²	42	4	10	11	13.4	4.04	117	.290	.340	0	.000	-2	2	3	-0	0.0
1940	Phi-A	0	0	—	4	0	0	0	0	11²	19	2	2	4	17.0	6.94	64	.365	.400	1	.250	0	-3	-3	-0	0.0
1941	Phi-A	9	13	.409	26	23	11	1	2	157¹	188	16	49	40	13.7	5.49	76	.293	.346	8	.143	-2	-24	-23	-2	-3.0
1942	Phi-A	0	0	—	1	0	0	0	0	4	14	2	2	0	38.3	31.50	12	.560	.607	0	.000	-0	-12	-12	0	0.0
1950	Phi-A	0	0	—	2	0	0	0	0	1¹	7	0	0	2	47.3	27.00	17	.636	.636	0	—	-0	-3	-3	0	0.0
Total	5	10	15	.400	38	27	13	1	2	210	270	24	63	57	14.5	5.96	72	.309	.359	9	.122	-4	-40	-39	-1	-3.0

● ED McCREERY
McCreery, Esley Porterfield "Big Ed"   b: 12/24/1889, Cripple Creek, Colo.   d: 10/19/60, Sacramento, Cal.   BR/TR, 6', 190 lbs.   Deb: 8/16/14

YEAR	TM/L	W	L	PCT	G	GS	CG	SH	SV	IP	H	HR	BB	SO	RAT	ERA	ERA+	OAV	OOB	BH	AVG	PB	PR	/A	PD	TPI
1914	Det-A	1	0	1.000	3	1	0	0	0	4	6	0	3	4	20.3	11.25	25	.316	.409	0	.000	-0	-4	-4	0	-0.8

● TOM McCREERY
McCreery, Thomas Livingston   b: 10/19/1874, Beaver, Pa.   d: 7/3/41, Beaver, Pa.   BB/TR, 5'11", 180 lbs.   Deb: 6/8/1895 ◆

YEAR	TM/L	W	L	PCT	G	GS	CG	SH	SV	IP	H	HR	BB	SO	RAT	ERA	ERA+	OAV	OOB	BH	AVG	PB	PR	/A	PD	TPI
1895	Lou-N	3	1	.750	8	4	3	1	1	48²	51	0	38	14	17.4	5.36	86	.265	.400	35	.324	1	-3	-4	1	0.0
1896	Lou-N	0	1	.000	1	1	0	0	0	1	4	1	5	0	81.0	36.00	12	.582	.758	155	.351	0	-4	-4	0	-1.4
1900	Pit-N	0	0	—	1	0	0	0	0	3	3	2	1	0	12.00	12.00	30	.260	.319	29	.220	-0	-3	-3	0	0.0
Total	3	3	2	.600	10	5	3	1	1	52²	58	3	44	14	18.3	6.32	72	.276	.412	855	.290	2	-9	-10	1	-1.4

● LANCE McCULLERS
McCullers, Lance Graye   b: 3/8/64, Tampa, Fla.   BB/TR, 6'1", 218 lbs.   Deb: 8/12/85

YEAR	TM/L	W	L	PCT	G	GS	CG	SH	SV	IP	H	HR	BB	SO	RAT	ERA	ERA+	OAV	OOB	BH	AVG	PB	PR	/A	PD	TPI
1985	SD-N	0	2	.000	21	0	0	0	5	35	23	3	16	27	10.3	2.31	153	.195	.296	0	.000	-0	5	5	0	0.4
1986	SD-N	10	10	.500	70	7	0	0	5	136	103	12	58	92	10.9	2.78	131	.216	.306	2	.091	-0	14	13	-1	1.9
1987	SD-N	8	10	.444	78	0	0	0	16	123¹	115	11	59	126	12.8	3.72	106	.244	.331	1	.071	-1	5	3	1	0.5
1988	SD-N	3	6	.333	60	0	0	0	10	97²	70	8	55	81	11.5	2.49	136	.205	.315	2	.250	1	10	10	1	1.2
1989	NY-A	4	3	.571	52	0	0	0	3	84²	83	9	37	82	13.1	4.57	85	.255	.337	0	—	0	-6	-7	-0	-0.6
1990	NY-A	1	0	1.000	11	0	0	0	2	15	14	2	6	11	12.0	3.60	110	.241	.313	0	—	0	1	1	0	0.0
	Det-A	1	0	1.000	9	0	0	0	0	29²	18	2	13	20	9.4	2.73	145	.170	.261	0	—	0	4	4	-1	0.1
	Yr	2	0	1.000	20	0	0	0	2	44²	32	4	19	31	10.3	3.02	131	.194	.277	0	—	0	4	5	-1	0.1
1992	Tex-A	1	0	1.000	5	0	0	0	3	5	1	0	2	3	16.2	5.40	70	.067	.391	0	—	-0	-1	0	0	0.0
Total	7	28	31	.475	306	9	0	0	39	526¹	427	47	252	442	11.8	3.25	115	.223	.317	5	.104	-0	32	28	-1	3.5

● CHARLIE McCULLOUGH
McCullough, Charles F.   b: 1867, Dublin, Ireland   Deb: 4/23/1890

YEAR	TM/L	W	L	PCT	G	GS	CG	SH	SV	IP	H	HR	BB	SO	RAT	ERA	ERA+	OAV	OOB	BH	AVG	PB	PR	/A	PD	TPI
1890	Bro-a	4	21	.160	26	25	24	0	0	215²	247	5	102	61	15.2	4.59	85	.279	.364	2	.023	-12	-17	-17	-2	-2.7
	Syr-a	1	2	.333	3	3	3	0	0	26	29	1	14	8	14.9	7.27	49	.274	.358	1	.111	0	-10	-11	-0	-0.9
	Yr	5	23	.179	29	28	27	0	0	241²	276	6	116	69	14.6	4.88	79	.274	.349	3	.032	-12	-27	-27	-3	-3.6

● PAUL McCULLOUGH
McCullough, Paul Willard   b: 7/28/1898, New Castle, Pa.   d: 11/7/70, New Castle, Pa.   BR/TR, 5'9.5", 190 lbs.   Deb: 7/2/29

YEAR	TM/L	W	L	PCT	G	GS	CG	SH	SV	IP	H	HR	BB	SO	RAT	ERA	ERA+	OAV	OOB	BH	AVG	PB	PR	/A	PD	TPI
1929	Was-A	0	0	—	3	0	0	0	0	7¹	7	1	2	3	11.0	8.59	49	.250	.300	0	.000	-0	-4	-4	-0	0.0

● PHIL McCULLOUGH
McCullough, Pinson Lamar   b: 7/22/17, Stockbridge, Ga.   BR/TR, 6'4", 204 lbs.   Deb: 4/22/42

YEAR	TM/L	W	L	PCT	G	GS	CG	SH	SV	IP	H	HR	BB	SO	RAT	ERA	ERA+	OAV	OOB	BH	AVG	PB	PR	/A	PD	TPI
1942	Was-A	0	0	—	1	0	0	0	0	3	5	0	2	2	21.0	6.00	61	.333	.412	0	.000	-0	-1	-1	0	0.0

● LINDY McDANIEL
McDaniel, Lyndall Dale   b: 12/13/35, Hollis, Okla.   BR/TR, 6'3", 195 lbs.   Deb: 9/2/55   F

YEAR	TM/L	W	L	PCT	G	GS	CG	SH	SV	IP	H	HR	BB	SO	RAT	ERA	ERA+	OAV	OOB	BH	AVG	PB	PR	/A	PD	TPI
1955	StL-N	0	0	—	4	2	0	0	0	19	22	4	7	7	13.7	4.74	86	.293	.354	1	.200	-0	-1	-0	0	0.0
1956	StL-N	7	6	.538	39	7	1	0	0	116¹	121	7	42	59	12.6	3.40	111	.273	.335	7	.219	2	5	5	1	0.8
1957	StL-N	15	9	.625	30	26	10	1	0	191	196	13	53	75	11.9	3.49	114	.266	.317	19	.257	4	8	10	-0	1.6
1958	StL-N	5	7	.417	26	17	2	1	0	108²	139	17	31	47	14.2	5.80	71	.305	.352	2	.067	-3	-22	-20	1	-2.1
1959	StL-N	14	12	.538	62	7	1	0	15	132	144	11	41	88	12.7	3.82	111	.283	.338	1	.034	-2	2	2	1	1.3
1960	StL-N★	12	4	.750	65	2	1	0	**26**	116¹	85	8	24	105	8.5	2.09	196	.207	.253	6	.231	1	**22**	**26**	**1**	**5.0**
1961	StL-N	10	6	.625	55	1	0	0	9	94¹	117	11	30	65	14.3	4.87	90	.305	.361	4	.235	-0	-9	-5	1	-0.7
1962	StL-N	3	10	.231	55	1	0	0	14	107	96	12	29	79	10.6	4.12	104	.239	.300	2	.095	-1	-2	2	0	0.4
1963	Chi-N	13	7	.650	57	0	0	0	**22**	88	82	9	27	75	11.1	2.86	123	.251	.308	2	.091	-0	4	6	0	1.8
1964	Chi-N	1	7	.125	63	0	0	0	15	95	104	4	23	71	12.1	3.88	96	.276	.319	2	.125	-1	-4	-2	0	-0.3

YEAR TM/L	W	L	PCT	G	GS	CG	SH	SV	IP	H	HR	BB	SO	RAT	ERA	ERA+	OAV	OOB	BH	AVG	PB	PR	/A	PD	TPI
1965 Chi-N	5	6	.455	71	0	0	0	2	128^2	115	12	47	92	11.3	2.59	142	.241	.309	0	.000	-1	14	16	2	1.5
1966 SF-N	10	5	.667	64	0	0	0	6	121^2	103	6	35	93	10.2	2.66	138	.228	.284	2	.091	-1	13	14	1	1.7
1967 SF-N	2	6	.250	41	3	0	0	3	72^2	69	5	24	48	11.8	3.72	88	.248	.313	1	.091	-1	-3	-3	2	-0.3
1968 SF-N	0	0	—	12	0	0	0	0	19^1	30	2	5	9	16.3	7.45	40	.357	.393	0	.000	-0	-10	-10	0	0.0
NY-A	4	1	.800	24	0	0	0	10	51^1	30	5	12	43	7.5	1.75	165	.166	.222	0	.000	-1	7	7	2	1.1
1969 NY-A	5	6	.455	51	0	0	0	5	83^2	84	4	23	60	11.5	3.55	98	.261	.310	0	.000	-1	1	-1	1	0.0
1970 NY-A	9	5	.643	62	0	0	0	29	111^2	88	7	23	81	8.9	2.01	194	.217	.259	4	.167	-0	21	19	1	3.5
1971 NY-A	5	10	.333	44	0	0	0	4	69^2	82	12	24	39	13.7	5.04	64	.296	.352	1	.111	-1	-12	-14	0	-3.0
1972 NY-A	3	1	.750	37	0	0	0	0	68	54	4	25	47	10.5	2.25	131	.217	.288	2	.286	1	6	5	1	0.6
1973 NY-A	12	6	.667	47	3	1	0	10	160^1	148	11	49	93	11.1	2.86	128	.250	.309	0	.000	-1	17	14	3	2.0
1974 KC-A	1	4	.200	38	5	2	0	1	106^2	109	6	24	47	11.2	3.46	110	.265	.306	0	—	0	2	4	1	0.2
1975 KC-A	5	1	.833	40	0	0	0	1	78	81	3	24	40	12.1	4.15	93	.273	.327	0	—	0	-3	-3	-0	-0.3
Total 21	141	119	.542	987	74	18	2	172	2139^1	2099	172	623	1361	11.5	3.45	109	.258	.312	56	.148	-3	55	74	23	14.8

● **VON McDANIEL** McDaniel, Max Von b: 4/18/39, Hollis, Okla. BR/TR, 6'2.5", 180 lbs. Deb: 6/13/57 F

YEAR TM/L	W	L	PCT	G	GS	CG	SH	SV	IP	H	HR	BB	SO	RAT	ERA	ERA+	OAV	OOB	BH	AVG	PB	PR	/A	PD	TPI
1957 StL-N	7	5	.583	17	13	4	2	0	86^2	71	7	31	45	10.7	3.22	123	.225	.296	0	.000	-3	6	7	-1	0.5
1958 StL-N	0	0	—	2	1	0	0	0	2	5	0	5	0	45.0	13.50	31	.500	.667	0	—	0	-2	-2	-0	0.0
Total 2	7	5	.583	19	14	4	2	0	88^2	76	7	36	45	11.5	3.45	115	.233	.311	0	.000	-3	4	5	-1	0.5

● **JOE McDERMOTT** McDermott, Joseph Deb: 5/4/1871 ♦

YEAR TM/L	W	L	PCT	G	GS	CG	SH	SV	IP	H	HR	BB	SO	RAT	ERA	ERA+	OAV	OOB	BH	AVG	PB	PR	/A	PD	TPI
1872 Eck-n	0	7	.000	7	7	7	0	0	63	142	3	12	1	22.0	8.29	42	.374	.393	9	.273	1	-32	-34		-2.0

● **MICKEY McDERMOTT** McDermott, Maurice Joseph "Maury" b: 8/29/28, Poughkeepsie, N.Y. BL/TL, 6'2", 170 lbs. Deb: 4/24/48 C♦

YEAR TM/L	W	L	PCT	G	GS	CG	SH	SV	IP	H	HR	BB	SO	RAT	ERA	ERA+	OAV	OOB	BH	AVG	PB	PR	/A	PD	TPI
1948 Bos-A	0	0	—	7	0	0	0	0	23^1	16	2	35	17	20.1	6.17	71	.208	.460	3	.375	1	-5	-5	1	0.2
1949 Bos-A	5	4	.556	12	12	6	2	0	80	63	5	52	50	13.3	4.05	108	.220	.345	7	.212	1	1	3	-0	0.3
1950 Bos-A	7	3	.700	38	15	4	0	5	130	119	8	124	96	17.0	5.19	94	.249	.406	16	.364	6	-9	-4	1	0.3
1951 Bos-A	8	8	.500	34	19	9	1	0	172	141	10	92	127	12.5	3.35	133	.226	.330	18	.273	4	15	21	1	2.2
1952 Bos-A	10	9	.526	30	21	7	2	0	162	139	14	92	117	13.0	3.72	106	.234	.340	14	.226	3	-1	4	-0	0.7
1953 Bos-A	18	10	.643	32	30	8	4	0	206^1	169	9	109	92	12.2	3.01	140	.224	.323	28	.301	7	23	27	1	4.4
1954 Was-A	7	15	.318	30	26	11	1	1	196^1	172	8	110	95	13.1	3.44	103	.239	.342	19	.200	3	6	3	1	0.6
1955 Was-A	10	10	.500	31	20	8	1	1	156	140	9	100	78	14.4	3.75	102	.243	.364	25	.263	7	4	1	0	1.0
1956 *NY-A	2	6	.250	23	9	1	0	0	87	85	10	47	38	13.7	4.24	91	.261	.354	11	.212	3	-1	-4	-0	-0.1
1957 KC-A	1	4	.200	29	4	0	0	0	69	68	9	50	29	15.4	5.48	72	.266	.360	12	.245	3	-13	-12	1	0.0
1958 Det-A	0	0	—	2	0	0	0	0	2	4	1	3	1	36.0	9.00	45	.500	.571	1	.333	1	-1	-1	-0	0.0
1961 StL-N	1	0	1.000	19	0	0	0	4	27	29	3	15	15	14.7	3.67	120	.271	.361	1	.071	-1	1	2	0	0.0
KC-A	0	0	—	4	0	0	0	0	5^2	14	0	10	3	38.1	14.29	29	.452	.585	1	.200	1	-6	-6	-0	0.0
Total 12	69	69	.500	291	156	54	11	14	1316^2	1161	87	838	757	13.9	3.91	105	.240	.355	156	.252	36	14	29	4	9.6

● **MIKE McDERMOTT** McDermott, Michael Joseph b: 9/7/1862, St.Louis, Mo. d: 6/30/43, St.Louis, Mo. TR, 5'8", 145 lbs. Deb: 9/2/1889

YEAR TM/L	W	L	PCT	G	GS	CG	SH	SV	IP	H	HR	BB	SO	RAT	ERA	ERA+	OAV	OOB	BH	AVG	PB	PR	/A	PD	TPI
1889 Lou-a	1	8	.111	9	9	9	0	0	84^1	108	4	34	22	15.4	4.16	92	.302	.366	6	.182	-1	-3	-3	-0	-0.3
1895 Lou-N	4	19	.174	33	26	18	0	0	207^1	258	8	103	42	16.1	5.99	77	.300	.382	13	.159	-2	-28	-31	1	-2.5
1896 Lou-N	2	7	.222	12	10	4	0	0	65	87	4	44	12	19.0	7.34	59	.318	.423	8	.296	1	-21	-22	1	-2.0
1897 Cle-N	4	5	.444	9	7	4	0	0	62	75	2	25	12	15.0	4.50	100	.296	.367	8	.320	1	-1	-0	1	-1.2
StL-N	1	2	.333	4	4	1	0	0	21^1	23	2	19	3	17.7	9.28	47	.273	.407	2	.222	-0	-12	-12	1	-1.1
Yr	5	7	.417	13	11	5	0	0	83^1	98	4	44	15	15.3	5.72	78	.288	.370	10	.294	1	-13	-12	2	-0.9
Total 4	12	41	.226	67	56	36	1	0	440	551	20	225	91	16.3	5.79	76	.301	.385	37	.210	-1	-65	-67	4	-5.7

● **DANNY McDEVITT** McDevitt, Daniel Eugene b: 11/18/32, New York, N.Y. BL/TL, 5'10", 175 lbs. Deb: 6/17/57

YEAR TM/L	W	L	PCT	G	GS	CG	SH	SV	IP	H	HR	BB	SO	RAT	ERA	ERA+	OAV	OOB	BH	AVG	PB	PR	/A	PD	TPI
1957 Bro-N	7	4	.636	22	17	5	2	0	119	105	5	72	90	13.8	3.25	128	.238	.353	6	.154	-0	8	12	2	1.2
1958 LA-N	2	6	.250	13	10	2	0	0	48^1	71	6	31	26	19.0	7.45	55	.355	.442	2	.133	-0	-19	-18	-1	-2.5
1959 LA-N	10	8	.556	39	22	6	2	4	145	149	16	51	106	13.3	3.97	106	.263	.339	5	.109	-2	-0	4	0	0.3
1960 LA-N	0	4	.000	24	7	0	0	0	53	51	7	42	30	16.8	4.25	93	.260	.406	2	.200	0	-3	-2	-0	-0.1
1961 NY-A	1	2	.333	8	2	0	0	0	13	18	2	8	8	18.7	7.62	49	.353	.450	0	.000	-0	-5	-6	0	-1.1
Min-A	1	0	1.000	16	1	0	0	0	26^2	20	1	19	15	14.5	2.36	179	.213	.368	0	.000	-0	5	6	0	0.2
Yr	2	2	.500	24	3	0	0	0	39^2	38	3	27	23	15.7	4.08	100	.259	.388	0	.000	-0	-0	-0	0	-0.9
1962 KC-A	0	3	.000	33	1	0	0	2	51	47	5	41	28	15.7	5.82	73	.250	.387	2	.222	-0	-11	-9	1	-0.5
Total 6	21	27	.438	155	60	13	4	7	456	461	42	264	303	14.9	4.40	94	.265	.372	17	.138	-3	-25	-13	2	-2.5

● **HANK McDONALD** McDonald, Henry Monroe b: 1/16/11, Santa Monica, Cal. d: 10/17/82, Hemet, Cal. BR/TR, 6'3", 200 lbs. Deb: 4/16/31

YEAR TM/L	W	L	PCT	G	GS	CG	SH	SV	IP	H	HR	BB	SO	RAT	ERA	ERA+	OAV	OOB	BH	AVG	PB	PR	/A	PD	TPI
1931 Phi-A	2	4	.333	19	10	1	1	0	70^1	62	3	41	23	13.3	3.71	121	.239	.346	2	.095	-1	5	6	-1	0.3
1933 Phi-A	1	1	.500	4	1	0	0	0	12^1	14	0	4	1	13.1	5.11	84	.264	.316	0	.000	-0	-1	-1	-0	-0.2
StL-A	0	4	.000	25	5	0	0	0	58^1	83	6	34	22	18.5	8.64	54	.332	.418	2	.143	-1	-28	-26	-0	-1.6
Yr	1	5	.167	29	6	0	0	0	70^2	97	6	38	23	17.6	8.02	57	.320	.401	2	.111	-1	-29	-27	-0	-1.8
Total 2	3	9	.250	48	16	1	1	0	141	159	9	79	46	15.4	5.87	77	.283	.375	4	.103	-2	-24	-21	-1	-1.5

● **JIM McDONALD** McDonald, Jimmie Le Roy "Hot Rod" b: 5/17/27, Grants Pass, Ore. BR/TR, 5'10.5", 185 lbs. Deb: 7/27/50

YEAR TM/L	W	L	PCT	G	GS	CG	SH	SV	IP	H	HR	BB	SO	RAT	ERA	ERA+	OAV	OOB	BH	AVG	PB	PR	/A	PD	TPI
1950 Bos-A	1	0	1.000	9	0	0	0	0	19	23	1	10	5	16.1	3.79	129	.329	.420	1	.333	1	2	2	1	0.3
1951 StL-A	4	7	.364	16	11	5	0	1	84	84	5	46	28	14.1	4.07	108	.260	.356	6	.207	-0	0	3	1	0.4
1952 NY-A	3	4	.429	26	5	1	0	0	69^1	74	10	24	14	14.7	3.50	95	.268	.368	6	.316	3	-1	-1	3	0.5
1953 *NY-A	9	7	.563	27	18	6	2	0	129^2	128	6	39	43	11.7	3.82	97	.260	.316	4	.098	-3	3	-2	2	-0.3
1954 NY-A	4	1	.800	16	10	3	1	0	71	54	3	45	20	12.7	3.17	108	.213	.334	4	.211	2	4	2	1	0.4
1955 Bal-A	3	5	.375	21	8	0	0	0	51^2	76	5	30	20	18.5	7.14	53	.345	.424	2	.182	1	-18	-19	1	-2.3
1956 Chi-A	0	2	.000	8	3	0	0	0	18^2	29	2	7	10	17.8	8.68	47	.377	.435	0	.000	-0	-9	-9	-0	-0.9
1957 Chi-A	0	1	.000	10	0	0	0	0	22^1	18	2	10	12	11.3	2.01	185	.234	.322	0	.000	-0	4	4	-0	0.2
1958 Chi-A	0	0	—	3	0	0	0	0	2^1	6	1	4	0	38.6	19.29	19	.429	.556	0	—	0	-4	-4	0	0.0
Total 9	24	27	.471	136	55	15	3	1	468	489	24	231	158	14.0	4.27	89	.273	.359	23	.180	4	-17	-25	8	-1.7

● **JOHN McDONALD** McDonald, John Joseph (b: John Joseph McDonnell) b: 1/27/1883, Throop, Pa. d: 4/9/50, Roselle, N.J. BR/TR, 6'1", 170 lbs. Deb: 9/3/07

YEAR TM/L	W	L	PCT	G	GS	CG	SH	SV	IP	H	HR	BB	SO	RAT	ERA	ERA+	OAV	OOB	BH	AVG	PB	PR	/A	PD	TPI
1907 Was-A	0	0	—	1	0	0	0	0	6	12	0	2	3	21.0	9.00	27	.415	.453	1	.333	1	-4	-4	-0	0.1

● **BEN McDONALD** McDonald, Larry Benard b: 11/14/67, Baton Rouge, La. BR/TR, 6'7", 212 lbs. Deb: 9/6/89

YEAR TM/L	W	L	PCT	G	GS	CG	SH	SV	IP	H	HR	BB	SO	RAT	ERA	ERA+	OAV	OOB	BH	AVG	PB	PR	/A	PD	TPI
1989 Bal-A	1	0	1.000	6	0	0	0	0	7^1	8	2	4	3	14.7	8.59	44	.286	.375	0	—	0	-4	-4	0	-0.4
1990 Bal-A	8	5	.615	21	15	3	2	0	118^2	88	9	35	65	9.3	2.43	156	.205	.265	0	—	0	20	18	0	1.9
1991 Bal-A	6	8	.429	21	21	1	0	0	126^1	126	16	43	85	12.1	4.84	82	.261	.323	0	—	0	-11	-13	-1	-1.3
1992 Bal-A	13	13	.500	35	35	4	2	0	227	213	32	74	158	11.7	4.24	95	.247	.313	0	—	0	-8	-6	-1	-0.5
1993 Bal-A	13	14	.481	34	34	7	1	0	220^1	185	17	86	171	11.3	3.39	132	.228	.306	0	—	0	23	26	3	3.1
1994 Bal-A	14	7	.667	24	24	5	1	0	157^1	151	14	54	94	11.8	4.06	125	.255	.319	0	—	0	13	18	0	1.9
Total 6	55	47	.539	141	129	20	6	0	857	771	90	296	576	11.4	3.86	111	.240	.308	0	—	0	33	39	4	4.7

● **McDOOLAN** McDoolan Deb: 4/14/1873

YEAR TM/L	W	L	PCT	G	GS	CG	SH	SV	IP	H	HR	BB	SO	RAT	ERA	ERA+	OAV	OOB	BH	AVG	PB	PR	/A	PD	TPI
1873 Mar-n	0	1	.000	1	1	1	0	0	9	18	0	6	0	18.0	3.00	108	.305	.305	0	.000	-1	0	0		0.0

● **SANDY McDOUGAL** McDougal, John Auchanbolt b: 5/21/1874, Buffalo, N.Y. d: 10/2/10, Buffalo, N.Y. BR/TR, 5'10", 155 lbs. Deb: 6/12/1895

YEAR TM/L	W	L	PCT	G	GS	CG	SH	SV	IP	H	HR	BB	SO	RAT	ERA	ERA+	OAV	OOB	BH	AVG	PB	PR	/A	PD	TPI
1895 Bro-N	0	0	—	1	0	0	0	1	3	3	0	5	2	24.0	12.00	37	.256	.479	0	.000	-0	-2	-3	-0	-0.2

YEAR TM/L	W	L	PCT	G	GS	CG	SH	SV	IP	H	HR	BB	SO	RAT	ERA	ERA+	OAV	OOB	BH	AVG	PB	PR	/A	PD	TPI
1905 StL-N	1	4	.200	5	5	5	0	0	44²	50	0	12	10	12.5	3.43	87	.301	.348	2	.133	-1	-2	-2	3	0.0
Total 2	1	4	.200	6	5	5	0	1	47²	53	0	17	12	13.2	3.97	78	.298	.360	2	.125	-1	-5	-5	3	-0.2

● **DEWEY McDOUGAL**   McDougal, John H. b: 9/19/1871, Aledo, Ill. d: 4/28/36, Galesburg, Ill. TR, 170 lbs. Deb: 4/24/1895

YEAR TM/L	W	L	PCT	G	GS	CG	SH	SV	IP	H	HR	BB	SO	RAT	ERA	ERA+	OAV	OOB	BH	AVG	PB	PR	/A	PD	TPI
1895 StL-N	3	10	.231	18	14	10	0	0	114²	187	11	46	23	19.1	8.32	58	.360	.422	6	.146	-2	-45	-44	-1	-3.6
1896 StL-N	0	1	.000	3	1	0	0	0	10	13	2	4	0	16.2	8.10	54	.312	.385	0	.000	-1	-4	-4	1	-0.3
Total 2	3	11	.214	21	15	10	0	0	124²	200	13	50	23	18.8	8.30	58	.356	.420	6	.136	-3	-49	-49	-1	-3.9

● **JACK McDOWELL**   McDowell, Jack Burns b: 1/16/66, Van Nuys, Cal. BR/TR, 6'5", 180 lbs. Deb: 9/15/87

YEAR TM/L	W	L	PCT	G	GS	CG	SH	SV	IP	H	HR	BB	SO	RAT	ERA	ERA+	OAV	OOB	BH	AVG	PB	PR	/A	PD	TPI
1987 Chi-A	3	0	1.000	4	4	0	0	0	28	16	1	6	15	7.7	1.93	237	.168	.233	0	—	0	8	8	0	0.9
1988 Chi-A	5	10	.333	26	26	1	0	0	158²	147	12	68	84	12.6	3.97	100	.245	.329	0	—	0	-0	-0	-1	-0.1
1990 Chi-A	14	9	.609	33	33	4	0	0	205	189	20	77	165	12.0	3.82	100	.244	.317	0	—	0	2	0	-0	0.0
1991 Chi-A★	17	10	.630	35	35	**15**	3	0	253²	212	19	82	191	10.6	3.41	117	.228	.293	0	—	0	19	16	0	1.6
1992 Chi-A★	20	10	.667	34	34	**13**	1	0	260²	247	21	75	178	11.4	3.18	122	.251	.309	0	—	0	22	20	-1	2.1
1993 *Chi-A★	**22**	10	.688	34	34	10	**4**	0	256²	261	20	69	158	11.7	3.37	124	.266	.316	0	—	0	27	23	2	3.0
1994 Chi-A	10	9	.526	25	25	6	2	0	181	186	12	42	127	11.6	3.73	126	.266	.312	0	—	0	22	19	0	1.8
Total 7	91	58	.611	191	191	49	10	0	1343²	1258	105	419	918	11.5	3.50	117	.248	.310	0	—	0	100	87	0	9.3

● **ROGER McDOWELL**   McDowell, Roger Alan b: 12/21/60, Cincinnati, Ohio BR/TR, 6'1", 175 lbs. Deb: 4/11/85

YEAR TM/L	W	L	PCT	G	GS	CG	SH	SV	IP	H	HR	BB	SO	RAT	ERA	ERA+	OAV	OOB	BH	AVG	PB	PR	/A	PD	TPI
1985 NY-N	6	5	.545	62	2	0	0	17	127¹	108	9	37	70	10.3	2.83	122	.230	.287	3	.158	0	11	9	2	1.3
1986 *NY-N	14	9	.609	75	0	0	0	22	128	107	4	42	65	10.7	3.02	117	.228	.296	5	.278	1	10	7	3	2.0
1987 NY-N	7	5	.583	56	0	0	0	25	88²	95	7	28	32	12.7	4.16	91	.276	.334	3	.231	1	-1	-4	1	-0.5
1988 *NY-N	5	5	.500	62	0	0	0	16	89	80	1	31	46	11.5	2.63	122	.238	.308	3	.333	2	8	6	2	1.3
1989 NY-N	1	5	.167	25	0	0	0	4	35¹	34	1	16	15	13.2	3.31	99	.254	.342	1	.500	0	1	-0	2	0.2
Phi-N	3	3	.500	44	0	0	0	19	56²	45	2	22	32	10.8	1.11	319	.220	.298	0	.000	-0	15	15	1	3.0
Yr	4	8	.333	69	0	0	0	23	92	79	3	38	47	11.5	1.96	176	.231	.310	1	.333	-0	16	15	3	3.2
1990 Phi-N	6	8	.429	72	0	0	0	22	86¹	92	2	35	39	13.4	3.86	99	.286	.359	0	.000	-0	-1	-0	1	0.0
1991 Phi-N	3	6	.333	38	0	0	0	3	59	61	1	32	28	14.5	3.20	114	.266	.361	0	.000	-0	3	3	2	0.6
LA-N	6	3	.667	33	0	0	0	7	42¹	39	3	16	22	11.7	2.55	141	.257	.327	0	—	0	5	5	1	1.2
Yr	9	9	.500	71	0	0	0	10	101¹	100	4	48	50	13.1	2.93	124	.260	.343	0	.000	-0	8	8	2	1.8
1992 LA-N	6	10	.375	65	0	0	0	14	83²	103	3	42	50	15.6	4.09	84	.306	.384	0	.000	1	-5	-6	-2	-1.1
1993 LA-N	5	3	.625	54	0	0	0	2	68	76	2	30	27	14.3	2.25	170	.288	.365	1	.500	-1	14	13	3	1.7
1994 LA-N	0	3	.000	32	0	0	0	0	41¹	50	3	22	29	15.9	5.23	76	.303	.388	0	.000	-0	-5	-6	0	-0.4
Total 10	62	65	.488	618	2	0	0	151	905²	890	38	353	455	12.6	3.17	113	.260	.332	16	.222	6	55	41	19	9.3

● **SAM McDOWELL**   McDowell, Samuel Edward Thomas "Sudden Sam" b: 9/21/42, Pittsburgh, Pa. BL/TL, 6'5", 218 lbs. Deb: 9/15/61

YEAR TM/L	W	L	PCT	G	GS	CG	SH	SV	IP	H	HR	BB	SO	RAT	ERA	ERA+	OAV	OOB	BH	AVG	PB	PR	/A	PD	TPI
1961 Cle-A	0	0	—	1	1	0	0	0	6¹	3	0	5	5	11.4	0.00	—	.136	.296	0	—	-0	3	3	0	0.1
1962 Cle-A	3	7	.300	25	13	0	0	1	87²	81	9	70	70	15.9	6.06	64	.243	.381	4	.154	-1	-20	-21	-0	-2.2
1963 Cle-A	3	5	.375	14	12	3	1	0	65	63	6	44	63	14.8	4.85	75	.256	.369	4	.211	0	-9	-9	-0	-1.0
1964 Cle-A	11	6	.647	31	24	6	2	1	173¹	148	8	100	177	13.0	2.70	133	.229	.336	8	.143	0	18	17	-1	1.6
1965 Cle-A★	17	11	.607	42	35	14	3	4	273	178	9	132	**325**	10.4	**2.18**	**160**	**.185**	.287	12	.126	-3	**39**	**40**	-3	4.1
1966 Cle-A†	9	8	.529	35	28	8	**5**	3	194¹	130	12	102	**225**	11.0	2.87	120	**.188**	.298	12	.200	1	12	12	1	1.4
1967 Cle-A	13	15	.464	37	37	10	1	0	236¹	201	21	123	236	12.6	3.85	85	.233	.333	15	.183	1	-16	-15	-1	-1.7
1968 Cle-A★	15	14	.517	38	37	11	3	0	269	181	13	110	**283**	10.1	1.81	164	.189	.279	13	.153	0	35	34	-1	4.0
1969 Cle-A★	18	14	.563	39	38	18	4	1	285	222	13	102	**279**	10.5	2.94	128	.213	.288	16	.174	-1	22	26	-0	2.8
1970 Cle-A★	20	12	.625	39	39	19	1	0	**305**	236	25	131	**304**	11.0	2.92	136	.213	.300	13	.124	-3	27	**35**	-2	3.0
1971 Cle-A†	13	17	.433	35	31	8	2	1	214²	160	22	153	192	13.2	3.40	113	.207	.340	13	.178	-1	2	10	-2	1.1
1972 SF-N	10	8	.556	28	25	4	0	0	164¹	155	12	86	122	13.5	4.33	81	.253	.350	7	.119	-1	-16	-15	-0	-1.7
1973 SF-N	1	2	.333	18	3	0	0	3	40	45	4	29	35	16.6	4.50	85	.285	.396	2	.167	-0	-4	-3	0	-0.3
NY-A	5	8	.385	16	15	2	1	0	95²	73	4	64	75	12.9	3.95	93	.212	.335	0	—	0	-1	-3	0	-0.3
1974 NY-A	1	6	.143	13	7	0	0	0	48	42	6	41	33	15.6	4.69	74	.236	.379	0	—	0	-6	-6	-1	-0.9
1975 Pit-N	2	1	.667	14	1	0	0	0	34²	30	0	20	29	13.0	2.86	124	.242	.347	0	.000	-1	3	3	0	0.1
Total 15	141	134	.513	425	346	103	23	14	2492¹	1948	164	1312	2453	12.0	3.17	112	.215	.318	119	.154	-8	88	107	-5	10.0

● **CHUCK McELROY**   McElroy, Charles Dwayne b: 10/1/67, Galveston, Tex. BL/TL, 6', 160 lbs. Deb: 9/4/89

YEAR TM/L	W	L	PCT	G	GS	CG	SH	SV	IP	H	HR	BB	SO	RAT	ERA	ERA+	OAV	OOB	BH	AVG	PB	PR	/A	PD	TPI
1989 Phi-N	0	0	—	11	0	0	0	0	10¹	12	1	4	8	13.9	1.74	203	.286	.348	0	—	0	2	2	-0	0.0
1990 Phi-N	0	1	.000	16	0	0	0	0	14	24	0	10	16	21.9	7.71	50	.369	.453	0	—	0	-6	-6	-0	-0.4
1991 Chi-N	6	2	.750	71	0	0	0	3	101¹	73	7	57	92	11.5	1.95	199	.210	.322	3	.300	1	19	22	1	2.2
1992 Chi-N	4	7	.364	72	0	0	0	6	83²	73	5	51	83	13.3	3.55	101	.237	.345	4	.667	3	-0	0	-1	0.3
1993 Chi-N	2	2	.500	49	0	0	0	0	47¹	51	4	25	31	14.6	4.56	87	.280	.370	0	.000	-1	-3	-3	-0	-0.3
1994 Cin-N	1	2	.333	52	0	0	0	5	57²	52	3	15	38	10.5	2.34	178	.244	.294	1	.167	-0	12	12	-1	0.7
Total 6	13	14	.481	271	0	0	0	14	314¹	285	20	162	268	12.8	3.09	125	.246	.339	8	.286	3	24	27	-2	2.2

● **JIM McELROY**   McElroy, James D. b: 1863, San Francisco, Cal. d: 7/24/1889, Needles, Cal. 5'10", 170 lbs. Deb: 5/26/1884

YEAR TM/L	W	L	PCT	G	GS	CG	SH	SV	IP	H	HR	BB	SO	RAT	ERA	ERA+	OAV	OOB	BH	AVG	PB	PR	/A	PD	TPI
1884 Phi-N	1	12	.077	13	13	13	0	0	111	115	1	54	45	13.7	4.86	61	.254	.333	7	.146	-3	-23	-23	-0	-2.3
Wil-U	0	1	.000	1	1	0	0	0	5	10	0	0	3	18.0	10.80	25	.391	.391	0	.000	-0	-5	-5	0	-0.6
Total 1	1	13	.071	14	14	13	0	0	116	125	1	54	48	13.9	5.12	58	.261	.336	7	.140	-4	-28	-28	-0	-2.9

● **WILL McENANEY**   McEnaney, William Henry b: 2/14/52, Springfield, Ohio BL/TL, 6', 180 lbs. Deb: 7/3/74

YEAR TM/L	W	L	PCT	G	GS	CG	SH	SV	IP	H	HR	BB	SO	RAT	ERA	ERA+	OAV	OOB	BH	AVG	PB	PR	/A	PD	TPI
1974 Cin-N	2	1	.667	24	0	0	0	2	27	24	4	9	13	11.0	4.33	80	.250	.314	0	—	0	-2	-3	-1	-0.4
1975 *Cin-N	5	2	.714	70	0	0	0	15	91	92	6	23	48	11.6	2.47	145	.264	.314	0	.000	-2	12	11	-1	1.0
1976 *Cin-N	2	6	.250	55	0	0	0	7	72¹	97	3	23	28	15.1	4.85	72	.323	.373	1	.167	1	-11	-11	0	-1.3
1977 Mon-N	3	5	.375	69	0	0	0	3	86²	92	6	22	38	12.0	3.95	96	.271	.319	0	.000	-0	-0	-1	0	-0.2
1978 Pit-N	0	0	—	6	0	0	0	0	8²	15	3	4	2	18.7	10.38	36	.395	.439	0	—	0	-7	-6	0	-0.4
1979 StL-N	0	3	.000	45	0	0	0	2	64	60	3	16	15	11.0	2.95	127	.251	.304	0	.000	0	6	6	2	0.4
Total 6	12	17	.414	269	0	0	0	29	349²	380	25	95	148	12.4	3.76	97	.279	.330	1	.032	-2	-3	-4	-1	-0.5

● **LOU McEVOY**   McEvoy, Louis Anthony b: 5/30/02, Williamsburg, Kan. d: 12/17/53, Webster Groves, Mo BR/TR, 6'2.5", 203 lbs. Deb: 4/28/30

YEAR TM/L	W	L	PCT	G	GS	CG	SH	SV	IP	H	HR	BB	SO	RAT	ERA	ERA+	OAV	OOB	BH	AVG	PB	PR	/A	PD	TPI
1930 NY-A	1	3	.250	28	1	0	0	3	52¹	64	4	29	14	16.3	6.71	64	.288	.375	2	.125	-1	-12	-14	-1	-1.2
1931 NY-A	0	0	—	6	0	0	1	0	12¹	19	1	12	3	23.4	12.41	32	.358	.485	0	.000	-1	-11	-12	0	-0.2
Total 2	1	3	.250	34	1	0	0	4	64²	83	5	41	17	17.7	7.79	54	.302	.398	2	.100	-2	-23	-26	-1	-1.4

● **BARNEY McFADDEN**   McFadden, Bernard Joseph b: 2/22/1874, Eckley, Pa. d: 4/28/24, Mauch Chunk, Pa. BR/TR, 6'1", 195 lbs. Deb: 4/24/01

YEAR TM/L	W	L	PCT	G	GS	CG	SH	SV	IP	H	HR	BB	SO	RAT	ERA	ERA+	OAV	OOB	BH	AVG	PB	PR	/A	PD	TPI
1901 Cin-N	3	4	.429	8	5	4	0	0	46	54	2	40	11	19.6	6.07	53	.291	.431	3	.150	-1	-14	-15	1	-1.8
1902 Phi-N	0	1	.000	1	1	1	0	0	9	14	0	7	3	21.0	8.00	35	.354	.451	0	.000	-0	-5	-5	0	-0.5
Total 2	3	5	.375	9	6	5	0	0	55	68	2	47	14	19.8	6.38	49	.302	.435	3	.130	-2	-19	-20	1	-2.3

● **DAN McFARLAN**   McFarlan, Anderson Daniel b: 11/1/1873, Gainesville, Tex. d: 9/23/24, Louisville, Ky. Deb: 9/2/1895 F

YEAR TM/L	W	L	PCT	G	GS	CG	SH	SV	IP	H	HR	BB	SO	RAT	ERA	ERA+	OAV	OOB	BH	AVG	PB	PR	/A	PD	TPI
1895 Lou-N	0	7	.000	7	7	6	0	0	46	80	4	15	10	19.6	6.65	70	.375	.429	5	.238	-1	-10	-10	1	-1.1
1899 Bro-N	0	0	—	1	0	0	0	0	6	6	1	3	0	13.5	1.50	261	.260	.345	0	.000	-0	2	2	0	0.1
Was-N	8	18	.308	32	28	22	1	0	211²	268	5	64	41	14.6	4.76	82	.308	.363	16	.186	-0	-21	-20	-1	-2.0
Yr	8	18	.308	33	28	22	1	0	217²	274	6	67	41	14.6	4.67	84	.307	.362	16	.182	-0	-20	-18	-2	-2.0
Total 2	8	25	.242	40	35	28	1	0	263²	354	10	82	51	15.4	5.02	81	.320	.375	21	.193	-1	-29	-29	-1	-3.1

YEAR TM/L	W	L	PCT	G	GS	CG	SH	SV	IP	H	HR	BB	SO	RAT	ERA	ERA+	OAV	OOB	BH	AVG	PB	PR	/A	PD	TPI

● **CHAPPIE McFARLAND**   McFarland, Charles A.   b: 3/13/1875, Whitehill, Ill.   d: 12/14/24, Houston, Tex.   TR, 6'1",   Deb: 9/15/02   F

1902 StL-N	0	1	.000	2	1	1	0	0	11	11	1	3	3	11.5	5.73	48	.260	.309	0	.000	-1	-4	-4	0	-0.3
1903 StL-N	9	19	.321	28	26	25	1	0	229	253	2	48	76	12.1	3.07	106	.284	.325	8	.108	-4	5	5	2	0.4
1904 StL-N	14	18	.438	32	31	28	1	0	269¹	266	7	56	111	10.9	3.21	84	.248	.288	13	.131	-2	-14	-15	7	-1.3
1905 StL-N	8	18	.308	31	28	22	3	1	250¹	281	3	65	85	12.7	3.81	78	.284	.332	14	.165	1	-22	-23	1	-2.0
1906 StL-N	2	1	.667	6	4	2	0	1	37¹	33	1	8	16	9.9	1.93	136	.219	.258	2	.133	-1	3	3	1	0.3
Pit-N	1	3	.250	6	5	2	1	0	35¹	39	0	7	11	12.2	2.55	105	.298	.343	5	.385	1	0	0	0	0.2
Bro-N	0	1	.000	1	1	1	0	0	9	10	1	5	5	15.0	8.00	32	.286	.375	0	.000	-0	-5	-5	-0	-0.5
Yr	3	5	.375	13	10	5	1	1	81²	82	2	20	32	11.2	2.87	92	.257	.301	7	.226	-0	-2	-2	1	0.0
Total 5	34	61	.358	106	96	81	6	2	841¹	893	15	192	307	11.8	3.35	87	.270	.313	42	.143	-6	-37	-39	11	-3.2

● **CHRIS McFARLAND**   McFarland, Christopher   b: 8/17/1861, Fall River, Mass.   d: 5/24/18, New Bedford, Mass.   5'9", 170 lbs.   Deb: 4/19/1884   ♦

| 1884 Bal-U | 0 | 1 | .000 | 1 | 1 | 0 | 0 | 0 | 3 | 9 | 1 | 4 | 3 | 30.0 | 15.00 | 18 | .491 | .517 | 3 | .214 | -0 | -4 | -4 | -0 | -0.8 |

● **MONTE McFARLAND**   McFarland, La Mont A.   b: 1873, Illinois   d: 11/15/13, Peoria, Ill.   Deb: 9/14/1895   F

1895 Chi-N	2	0	1.000	2	2	2	0	0	14	21	1	5	10	16.7	5.14	99	.341	.390	1	.143	-1	-1	-0	0	-0.1
1896 Chi-N	0	4	.000	4	3	2	0	0	25	32	0	21	3	19.8	7.20	63	.308	.434	0	.000	-2	-8	-7	0	-1.0
Total 2	2	4	.333	6	5	4	0	0	39	53	1	26	8	18.7	6.46	73	.321	.419	1	.053	-3	-8	-7	1	-1.1

● **JACK McFETRIDGE**   McFetridge, John Reed   b: 8/25/1869, Philadelphia, Pa.   d: 1/10/17, Philadelphia, Pa.   6', 175 lbs.   Deb: 6/7/1890

1890 Phi-N	1	0	1.000	1	1	1	0	0	9	5	0	2	4	7.0	1.00	366	.158	.208	3	.750	-1	3	3	-0	0.4
1903 Phi-N	1	11	.083	14	13	11	0	0	103	120	2	49	31	15.0	4.89	67	.299	.379	6	.176	0	-19	-19	-1	-1.8
Total 2	2	11	.154	15	14	12	0	0	112	125	2	51	35	14.4	4.58	72	.288	.367	9	.237	2	-16	-16	-1	-1.4

● **ANDY McGAFFIGAN**   McGaffigan, Andrew Joseph   b: 10/25/56, W.Palm Beach, Fla.   BR/TR, 6'3", 195 lbs.   Deb: 9/22/81

1981 NY-A	0	0	—	2	0	0	0	0	7	5	1	3	2	10.3	2.57	139	.200	.286	0	—	0	1	1	-0	0.0
1982 SF-N	1	0	1.000	4	0	0	0	0	8	5	0	1	4	7.9	0.00	—	.179	.233	0	.000	-0	3	3	-0	0.4
1983 SF-N	3	9	.250	43	16	0	0	2	134¹	131	17	39	93	11.5	4.29	82	.255	.309	1	.067	-1	-10	-11	-3	-1.5
1984 Mon-N	3	4	.429	21	3	0	0	1	46	37	2	15	39	10.2	2.54	135	.220	.284	0	.000	-1	5	4	-0	0.6
Cin-N	0	2	.000	9	3	0	0	0	23	23	2	8	18	12.1	5.48	69	.261	.323	0	—	-0	-5	-4	-1	-0.4
Yr	3	6	.333	30	6	0	0	1	69	60	4	23	57	10.8	3.52	101	.233	.296	0	—	-1	1	0	-1	0.2
1985 Cin-N	3	3	.500	15	15	2	0	0	94¹	88	4	30	83	11.4	3.72	102	.247	.309	1	.034	-2	-1	1	0	-0.1
1986 Mon-N	10	5	.667	48	14	1	1	2	142²	114	9	55	104	10.8	2.65	139	.223	.301	2	.061	-2	17	17	-2	1.3
1987 Mon-N	5	2	.714	69	0	0	0	12	120¹	105	5	42	100	11.2	2.39	176	.235	.305	0	.000	-0	23	24	-0	1.7
1988 Mon-N	6	0	1.000	63	0	0	0	2	91¹	81	4	37	71	11.8	2.76	130	.233	.311	0	.000	-0	7	8	-1	0.5
1989 Mon-N	3	5	.375	57	0	0	0	2	75	85	3	30	40	14.2	4.68	75	.293	.365	1	1.000	-0	-10	-10	-1	-1.1
1990 SF-N	0	0	—	4	0	0	0	0	4²	10	2	4	4	27.0	17.36	17	.455	.538	0	—	0	-7	-7	-0	-0.5
KC-A	4	3	.571	24	11	0	0	1	78²	75	7	28	49	12.0	3.09	124	.248	.315	0	—	0	6	6	-1	0.5
1991 KC-A	0	0	—	4	0	0	0	0	8	14	0	2	3	18.0	4.50	92	.389	.421	0	—	0	-0	-0	-0	-0.0
Total 11	38	33	.535	363	62	3	1	24	833¹	773	55	294	610	11.7	3.38	110	.247	.314	6	.048	-7	30	32	-10	1.9

● **JACK McGEACHY**   McGeachy, John Charles   b: 5/23/1864, Clinton, Mass.   d: 4/5/30, Cambridge, Mass.   BR/TR, 5'8", 165 lbs.   Deb: 6/17/1886   ♦

1887 Ind-N	0	1	.000	1	0	0	0	0	6¹	13	2	4	3	24.2	11.37	36	.351	.415	109	.269	0	-5	-5	0	-0.5
1888 Ind-N	0	0	—	1	0	0	0	0	5	5	1	3	0	14.4	7.20	41	.238	.333	99	.219	0	-2	-2	-0	0.0
1889 Ind-N	0	0	—	3	0	0	0	0	4²	7	2	6	3	25.1	11.57	36	.336	.485	142	.267	0	-4	-4	-0	0.0
Total 3	0	1	.000	5	0	0	0	0	16	25	5	13	6	21.4	10.13	37	.317	.414	604	.245	0	-11	-11	-0	-0.5

● **BILL McGEE**   McGee, William Henry "Fiddler Bill"   b: 11/16/09, Batchtown, Ill.   d: 2/11/87, St.Louis, Mo.   BR/TR, 6'1", 215 lbs.   Deb: 9/29/35

1935 StL-N	1	0	1.000	1	1	1	0	0	9	3	0	1	2	4.0	1.00	410	.103	.133	1	.333	0	3	3	-0	0.3
1936 StL-N	1	1	.500	7	2	0	0	0	16	23	3	4	8	15.2	7.88	50	.359	.397	1	.250	-0	-7	-7	-0	-0.7
1937 StL-N	1	0	1.000	4	1	1	0	0	14	13	1	4	9	11.6	2.57	155	.255	.321	1	.200	-0	2	2	-0	0.2
1938 StL-N	7	12	.368	47	25	10	1	5	216	216	4	78	104	12.3	3.21	123	.257	.321	14	.209	1	14	18	-0	1.6
1939 StL-N	12	5	.706	43	17	5	4	0	156	155	14	56	96	12.3	3.81	108	.261	.328	8	.145	-2	2	5	0	0.3
1940 StL-N	16	10	.615	38	31	11	3	0	218	222	13	96	78	13.2	3.80	105	.263	.340	13	.178	-1	1	5	-3	0.1
1941 StL-N	0	1	.000	4	3	0	0	0	14	17	1	13	2	19.9	5.14	73	.298	.437	0	.000	-1	-2	-2	-0	-0.2
NY-N	2	9	.182	22	14	1	0	0	106	117	9	54	41	14.5	4.92	75	.285	.368	5	.161	-1	-15	-14	-2	-1.6
Yr	2	10	.167	26	17	1	0	0	120	134	10	67	43	15.1	4.95	75	.286	.375	5	.143	-2	-18	-17	-2	-1.8
1942 NY-N	6	3	.667	31	8	2	1	1	104	95	8	46	40	12.3	2.94	114	.244	.326	3	.103	-2	4	5	-1	0.1
Total 8	46	41	.529	197	102	31	9	6	853	861	53	355	340	12.9	3.74	104	.263	.336	46	.170	-6	2	14	-5	0.1

● **CONNY McGEEHAN**   McGeehan, Cornelius Bernard   b: 8/25/1882, Drifton, Pa.   d: 7/4/07, Hazleton, Pa.   Deb: 7/15/03   F

| 1903 Phi-A | 1 | 0 | 1.000 | 3 | 0 | 0 | 0 | 0 | 10 | 9 | 0 | 1 | 4 | 9.9 | 4.50 | 68 | .240 | .278 | 0 | .000 | -1 | -2 | -2 | 0 | -0.2 |

● **KEVIN McGEHEE**   McGehee, George Kevin   b: 1/18/69, Alexandria, La.   BR/TR, 6', 190 lbs.   Deb: 8/23/93

| 1993 Bal-A | 0 | 0 | — | 5 | 0 | 0 | 0 | 0 | 16² | 18 | 5 | 7 | 7 | 14.6 | 5.94 | 75 | .281 | .370 | 0 | — | 0 | -3 | -3 | 0 | -0.2 |

● **PAT McGEHEE**   McGehee, Patrick Henry   b: 7/2/1888, Meadville, Miss.   d: 12/30/46, Paducah, Ky.   BL/TR, 6'2.5", 180 lbs.   Deb: 8/23/12

| 1912 Det-A | 0 | 0 | — | 1 | 1 | 0 | 0 | 0 | 0 | 1 | 0 | 1 | 0 | — | — | — | 1.000 | 1.000 | 0 | — | 0 | 0 | 0 | 0 | 0.0 |

● **RANDY McGILBERRY**   McGilberry, Randall Kent   b: 10/29/53, Mobile, Ala.   BB/TR, 6'1", 195 lbs.   Deb: 9/6/77

1977 KC-A	0	1	.000	3	0	0	0	0	7	7	1	1	1	10.3	5.14	78	.280	.308	0	—	0	-1	-1	0	-0.1
1978 KC-A	0	1	.000	18	0	0	0	0	25²	27	2	18	12	15.8	4.21	91	.276	.388	0	—	0	-1	-1	-0	-0.2
Total 2	0	2	.000	21	0	0	0	0	32²	34	3	19	13	14.6	4.41	88	.276	.373	0	—	0	-2	-2	-0	-0.3

● **BILL McGILL**   McGill, William John "Parson"   b: 6/29/1880, Galva, Kan.   d: 8/7/59, Alva, Okla.   BR/TR, 6'2",   Deb: 9/16/07

| 1907 StL-A | 1 | 0 | 1.000 | 2 | 2 | 1 | 0 | 0 | 18¹ | 22 | 0 | 8 | 2 | 11.8 | 3.44 | 73 | .299 | .318 | 0 | .000 | -1 | -2 | -2 | -0 | -0.2 |

● **WILLIE McGILL**   McGill, William Vaness "Kid"   b: 11/10/1873, Atlanta, Ga.   d: 8/29/44, Indianapolis, Ind.   TL, 5'6.5", 170 lbs.   Deb: 5/8/1890

1890 Cle-P	11	9	.550	24	20	19	0	0	183²	222	5	96	82	16.2	4.12	97	.286	.373	10	.147	2	2	-3	1	0.1
1891 Cin-a	2	5	.286	8	8	6	0	0	65	69	1	37	19	15.1	4.98	83	.263	.360	2	.100	-0	-9	-6	-1	-0.6
StL-a	19	10	.655	35	31	22	1	1	249	225	10	131	154	13.4	2.93	144	.233	.333	14	.161	-1	22	35	-4	3.0
Yr	21	15	.583	43	39	28	1	1	314	294	11	168	173	13.6	3.35	125	.239	.337	16	.150	-1	13	29	-5	2.4
1892 Cin-N	1	1	.500	3	3	1	0	0	17	18	0	5	7	12.2	5.29	62	.261	.311	2	.286	-1	-4	-4	0	-0.3
1893 Chi-N	17	18	.486	39	34	26	1	0	302²	311	6	181	91	15.0	4.61	101	.258	.361	29	.234	2	1	-5	-1	-0.1
1894 Chi-N	7	19	.269	27	23	22	0	0	208	272	2	117	58	17.3	5.84	96	.312	.400	12	.244	-0	-12	-15	-2	-1.1
1895 Phi-N	10	8	.556	20	20	13	0	0	146	177	6	81	70	16.2	5.55	86	.295	.382	14	.222	-0	-12	-12	-0	-1.1
1896 Phi-N	5	4	.556	12	11	7	0	0	79²	87	6	53	29	16.3	5.31	81	.276	.386	6	.207	-0	-8	-9	-0	-0.7
Total 7	72	74	.493	168	150	116	2	1	1251	1381	26	701	510	15.4	4.59	100	.273	.368	97	.202	5	-19	-1	-11	-0.3

● **JOHN McGILLEN**   McGillen, John Joseph   b: 8/6/17, Eddystone, Pa.   d: 8/11/87, Upland, Pa.   BL/TL, 6'1", 175 lbs.   Deb: 4/20/44

| 1944 Phi-A | 0 | 0 | — | 2 | 0 | 0 | 0 | 0 | 1 | 1 | 0 | 2 | 0 | 27.0 | 18.00 | 19 | .333 | .600 | 0 | — | 0 | -2 | -2 | -0 | -0.2 |

● **JIM McGINLEY**   McGinley, James William   b: 10/2/1878, Groveland, Mass.   d: 9/20/61, Haverhill, Mass.   BR/TR, 5'9.5", 165 lbs.   Deb: 9/22/04

1904 StL-N	2	1	.667	3	3	3	0	0	27	28	0	6	6	12.3	2.00	135	.287	.325	1	.091	-1	2	2	-1	0.0
1905 StL-N	0	1	.000	1	1	0	0	0	3	5	1	2	0	21.0	15.00	20	.333	.412	1	1.000	-0	-4	-4	-0	-0.8
Total 2	2	2	.500	4	4	3	0	0	30	33	1	8	6	13.2	3.30	83	.275	.336	2	.167	-0	-2	-2	-1	-0.8

YEAR	TM/L	W	L	PCT	G	GS	CG	SH	SV	IP	H	HR	BB	SO	RAT	ERA	ERA+	OAV	OOB	BH	AVG	PB	PR	/A	PD	TPI

● DAN McGINN McGinn, Daniel Michael b: 11/29/43, Omaha, Neb. BL/TL, 6', 190 lbs. Deb: 9/3/68

1968	Cin-N	0	1	.000	14	0	0	0	0	12	13	1	11	16	18.8	5.25	60	.271	.417	0	.000	-0	-3	-3	0	-0.2
1969	Mon-N	7	10	.412	74	1	0	0	6	132¹	123	8	65	112	13.1	3.94	93	.245	.337	5	.172	1	-5	-4	1	-0.3
1970	Mon-N	7	10	.412	52	19	3	2	0	130²	154	13	78	83	16.5	5.44	76	.296	.395	4	.114	-2	-20	-19	2	-2.2
1971	Mon-N	1	4	.200	28	6	1	0	0	71	74	7	42	40	14.8	5.96	59	.274	.374	4	.235	0	-20	-19	1	-1.1
1972	Chi-N	0	5	.000	42	2	0	0	4	62²	78	5	29	42	15.9	5.89	65	.301	.380	2	.250	1	-17	-14	-1	-1.3
Total	5	15	30	.333	210	28	4	2	10	408²	442	34	225	293	15.1	5.11	74	.276	.372	15	.165	-0	-65	-59	3	-5.1

● GUS McGINNIS McGinnis, August b: 1870, Painesville, Ohio TL , 5'11", 168 lbs. Deb: 4/27/1893

1893	Chi-N	2	5	.286	13	5	3	0	0	67¹	85	2	31	13	15.9	5.35	87	.299	.374	6	.240	2	-5	-5	0	-0.2
	Phi-N	1	3	.250	5	4	4	1	0	37¹	39	0	17	12	14.0	4.34	105	.261	.344	3	.200	-1	1	1	0	0.1
	Yr	3	8	.273	18	9	7	1	0	104²	124	2	48	25	15.0	4.99	92	.284	.357	9	.225	1	-4	-4	1	-0.1

● JUMBO McGINNIS McGinnis, George Washington b: 2/22/1864, Alton, Mo. d: 5/18/34, St.Louis, Mo. 5'10", 197 lbs. Deb: 5/2/1882

1882	StL-a	25	18	.581	45	45	43	3	0	388¹	391	2	53	134	10.3	2.60	108	.245	.269	44	.217	1	4	9	-5	0.5
1883	StL-a	28	16	.636	45	45	41	6	0	382²	325	3	69	128	9.3	2.33	150	.215	.249	36	.200	-6	41	49	1	4.2
1884	StL-a	24	16	.600	40	40	39	5	0	354¹	331	4	35	141	9.6	2.84	115	.233	.258	34	.233	3	16	16	-1	1.6
1885	StL-a	6	6	.500	13	13	12	3	0	112	98	1	19	41	9.9	3.38	97	.225	.267	11	.220	0	-2	-1	-1	-0.3
1886	StL-a	5	5	.500	10	10	10	1	0	87²	107	2	27	30	14.5	3.80	91	.288	.347	7	.189	-1	-3	-3	0	-0.4
	Bal-a	11	13	.458	26	25	24	0	0	209¹	235	6	48	70	12.8	3.48	98	.280	.329	16	.188	-1	-1	-1	-0	-0.2
	Yr	16	18	.471	36	35	34	1	0	297	342	8	75	100	13.1	3.58	96	.281	.330	23	.189	-2	-4	-5	-0	-0.6
1887	Cin-a	3	5	.375	8	8	8	0	0	67	76	2	27	18	17.7	5.45	80	.296	.402	6	.194	-0	-9	-9	-0	-0.7
Total	6	102	79	.564	187	186	177	18	0	1603²	1572	21	294	562	10.7	2.95	112	.243	.281	154	.210	-5	47	61	-7	4.7

● JOE McGINNITY McGinnity, Joseph Jerome "Iron Man" (b: Joseph Jerome McGinty) b: 3/19/1871, Rock Island, Ill. d: 11/14/29, Brooklyn, N.Y. BR/TR, 5'11", 206 lbs. Deb: 4/18/1899 CH

1899	Bal-N	**28**	16	.636	48	41	38	4	2	366¹	358	3	93	74	11.7	2.68	148	.256	.314	28	.193	-5	48	52	1	5.0
1900	*Bro-N	**28**	8	.778	44	37	32	1	0	343	350	5	113	93	13.2	2.94	131	.264	.340	28	.193	-5	29	34	-2	2.3
1901	Bal-A	26	20	.565	**48**	43	**39**	1	1	382	412	7	96	75	12.5	3.56	109	.272	.324	31	.209	-4	5	13	-1	0.8
1902	Bal-A	13	10	.565	25	23	19	0	0	198²	219	3	46	39	12.4	3.44	110	.280	.326	25	.287	4	3	7	-2	1.0
	NY-N	8	8	.500	19	16	16	1	0	153	122	1	32	67	9.6	2.06	136	.219	.273	8	.121	-4	12	13	1	0.9
1903	NY-N	31	20	.608	**55**	48	**44**	3	2	434	391	4	109	171	10.8	2.43	138	.236	.291	34	.206	-2	41	**44**	-4	4.0
1904	NY-N	**35**	8	.814	51	44	38	9	5	408	307	8	86	144	9.0	**1.61**	169	.206	.256	25	.176	-1	**51**	51	3	**5.6**
1905	*NY-N	21	15	.583	**46**	38	26	2	3	320¹	289	6	71	125	10.5	2.87	102	.240	.290	28	.233	6	5	2	2	1.0
1906	NY-N	**27**	12	.692	**45**	37	32	3	2	339²	316	1	71	105	10.4	2.25	116	.246	.289	15	.130	-3	14	14	1	1.3
1907	NY-N	18	18	.500	**47**	34	23	3	**4**	310¹	320	6	58	120	11.4	3.16	78	.266	.308	18	.175	-0	-24	-24	2	-2.6
1908	NY-N	11	7	.611	37	20	7	5	**5**	186	192	8	37	55	11.4	2.27	106	.267	.310	11	.180	-0	2	3	-1	0.2
Total	10	246	142	.634	465	381	314	32	24	3441¹	3276	52	812	1068	11.2	2.66	120	.249	.302	251	.194	-14	186	207	-0	19.5

● LYNN McGLOTHEN McGlothen, Lynn Everatt b: 3/27/50, Monroe, La. d: 8/14/84, Dubach, La. BL/TR, 6'2", 195 lbs. Deb: 6/25/72

1972	Bos-A	8	7	.533	22	22	4	1	0	145	135	9	59	112	12.5	3.41	94	.247	.328	10	.189	1	-6	-3	3	0.1
1973	Bos-A	1	2	.333	6	3	0	0	0	23	39	6	8	16	18.8	8.22	49	.386	.436	0	—	0	-11	-11	-0	-1.2
1974	StL-N★	16	12	.571	31	31	8	3	0	237¹	212	12	89	142	11.5	2.69	133	.241	.312	15	.181	-1	24	23	1	2.7
1975	StL-N	15	13	.536	35	34	9	2	0	239	231	21	97	146	12.5	3.92	96	.254	.329	7	.087	-5	-8	-4	-2	-1.2
1976	StL-N	13	15	.464	33	32	10	4	0	205	209	10	68	106	12.3	3.91	90	.268	.330	15	.211	2	-9	-8	-2	-1.0
1977	SF-N	2	9	.182	21	15	2	0	0	80	94	9	52	42	16.5	5.62	69	.299	.401	2	.105	-1	-15	-15	-2	-2.0
1978	SF-N	0	0	—	5	1	0	0	0	12²	15	0	4	9	13.5	4.97	69	.313	.365	0	.000	-0	-2	-2	0	0.0
	Chi-N	5	3	.625	49	1	0	0	0	80	77	7	39	60	13.0	3.04	133	.257	.342	3	.231	1	5	9	-2	0.7
	Yr	5	3	.625	54	2	0	0	0	92²	92	7	43	69	13.1	3.30	120	.264	.344	3	.188	0	3	7	-2	0.7
1979	Chi-N	13	14	.481	42	29	6	1	2	212	236	27	55	147	12.5	4.12	100	.283	.330	16	.225	1	-9	-4	-0	-0.1
1980	Chi-N	12	14	.462	39	27	2	2	0	182¹	211	24	64	119	13.6	4.79	82	.293	.352	10	.196	2	-24	-18	-2	-2.4
1981	Chi-N	1	4	.200	20	6	0	0	0	54²	71	1	28	26	16.5	4.77	77	.317	.395	1	.083	-1	-8	-7	1	-0.6
	Chi-A	0	0	—	11	0	0	0	0	21²	14	0	7	12	9.1	4.15	86	.189	.268	0	—	0	-1	-1	0	0.0
1982	NY-A	0	0	—	4	0	0	0	0	5	9	1	2	2	19.8	10.80	37	.375	.423	0	—	0	-4	-4	0	0.0
Total	11	86	93	.480	318	201	41	13	2	1497²	1553	127	572	939	12.9	3.98	94	.270	.339	79	.173	-1	-68	-42	-7	-5.0

● PAT McGLOTHIN McGlothin, Ezra Mac b: 10/20/20, Coalfield, Tenn. BL/TR, 6'3.5", 180 lbs. Deb: 4/25/49

1949	Bro-N	1	1	.500	7	0	0	0	0	15²	13	2	5	11	10.3	4.60	89	.224	.286	0	.000	-0	-1	-1	0	-0.1
1950	Bro-N	0	0	—	1	0	0	0	0	2	5	0	1	2	27.0	13.50	30	.455	.500	0	—	0	-2	-2	-0	-0.0
Total	2	1	1	.500	8	0	0	0	0	17²	18	2	6	13	12.2	5.60	73	.261	.320	0	.000	-0	-3	-3	1	-0.1

● JIM McGLOTHLIN McGlothlin, James Milton "Red" b: 10/6/43, Los Angeles, Cal. d: 12/23/75, Union, Ky. BR/TR, 6'1", 185 lbs. Deb: 9/20/65

1965	Cal-A	0	3	.000	3	3	1	0	0	18	18	1	7	9	12.5	3.50	97	.261	.329	0	.000	-0	-0	-0	-0	-0.1
1966	Cal-A	3	1	.750	19	11	0	0	0	67²	79	9	19	41	13.2	4.52	74	.292	.340	1	.059	-0	-8	-9	-0	-0.5
1967	Cal-A★	12	8	.600	32	29	9	**6**	0	197¹	163	13	56	137	10.2	2.96	106	.226	.286	8	.140	-0	6	4	1	0.5
1968	Cal-A	10	15	.400	40	32	8	0	3	208¹	187	19	60	135	11.0	3.54	82	.244	.305	7	.111	-1	-13	-15	2	-1.8
1969	Cal-A	8	16	.333	37	35	4	1	0	201	188	19	58	96	11.2	3.18	110	.249	.307	7	.121	-1	10	7	2	0.9
1970	*Cin-N	14	10	.583	34	34	5	3	0	210²	192	19	86	87	12.0	3.59	112	.245	.322	8	.121	1	11	10	5	1.7
1971	Cin-N	8	12	.400	30	26	3	0	0	170²	151	15	47	93	10.7	3.22	104	.243	.301	7	.137	1	5	3	1	0.5
1972	*Cin-N	9	8	.529	31	24	3	1	0	145	165	14	49	69	13.3	3.91	82	.287	.343	8	.174	3	-7	-11	-0	-1.0
1973	Chi-N	3	3	.500	24	9	0	0	0	63¹	91	13	23	18	16.2	6.68	51	.340	.392	2	.125	0	-21	-23	1	-1.8
	Chi-A	0	1	.000	5	1	0	0	0	18¹	13	2	13	14	12.8	3.93	101	.203	.338	0	—	0	-0	-0	0	0.0
Total	9	67	77	.465	256	201	36	11	3	1300¹	1247	125	418	709	11.7	3.61	93	.255	.317	48	.126	2	-19	-34	11	-1.6

● STONEY McGLYNN McGlynn, Ulysses Simpson Grant b: 5/26/1872, Lancaster, Pa. d: 8/26/41, Manitowoc, Wis. BR/TR, 5'11", 185 lbs. Deb: 9/20/06

1906	StL-N	2	2	.500	6	6	6	0	0	48	43	0	15	25	11.1	2.44	108	.249	.312	1	.059	-1	7	9	2	0.2
1907	StL-N	14	25	.359	45	39	**33**	3	1	352¹	329	6	112	109	11.4	2.91	86	.251	.312	25	.200	1	-17	-16	-1	-1.6
1908	StL-N	1	6	.143	16	6	4	0	1	75²	76	0	17	23	11.3	3.45	68	.256	.301	2	.077	-1	-9	-9	1	-0.9
Total	3	17	33	.340	67	51	43	3	2	476	448	6	144	157	11.3	2.95	85	.252	.310	28	.167	0	-25	-24	2	-2.3

● MICKEY McGOWAN McGowan, Tullis Earl b: 11/26/21, Dothan, Ala. BL/TL, 6'2", 200 lbs. Deb: 4/22/48

| 1948 | NY-N | 0 | 0 | — | 3 | 0 | 0 | 0 | 0 | 3² | 3 | 1 | 4 | 2 | 17.2 | 7.36 | 53 | .231 | .412 | 0 | .000 | -0 | -1 | -1 | 0 | 0.0 |

● HOWARD McGRANER McGraner, Howard "Muck" b: 9/11/1889, Hamley Run, Ohio d: 10/22/52, Zaleski, Ohio BL/TL, 5'7", 155 lbs. Deb: 9/12/12

| 1912 | Cin-N | 1 | 0 | 1.000 | 4 | 0 | 0 | 0 | 0 | 19 | 22 | 2 | 7 | 5 | 14.2 | 7.11 | 47 | .293 | .361 | 2 | .250 | 1 | -8 | -8 | 1 | -0.2 |

● TUG McGRAW McGraw, Frank Edwin b: 8/30/44, Martinez, Cal. BR/TL, 6', 185 lbs. Deb: 4/18/65

1965	NY-N	2	7	.222	37	9	2	1	0	97²	88	8	48	57	12.8	3.32	106	.249	.344	3	.130	-1	2	2	-1	0.1
1966	NY-N	2	9	.182	15	12	1	0	0	62¹	72	11	25	34	14.0	5.34	68	.294	.359	4	.235	1	-12	-12	-0	-1.8
1967	NY-N	0	3	.000	4	4	0	0	0	17¹	13	3	13	18	13.5	7.79	44	.206	.342	1	.250	0	-9	-8	-1	-1.1
1969	*NY-N	9	3	.750	42	4	1	0	12	100¹	89	6	47	92	13.2	2.24	163	.243	.329	4	.167	0	**15**	**16**	-1	2.4
1970	NY-N	4	6	.400	57	0	0	0	10	90²	77	9	49	81	12.6	3.28	123	.231	.332	4	.308	1	8	8	1	1.2
1971	NY-N	11	4	.733	51	1	0	0	8	111	73	4	41	109	9.5	1.70	200	.189	.271	4	.222	1	**22**	**21**	-1	3.4
1972	NY-N★	8	6	.571	54	0	0	0	27	106	71	3	40	92	9.7	1.70	198	.197	.282	4	.100	-0	21	20	0	3.8
1973	*NY-N	5	6	.455	60	2	0	0	25	118²	106	11	55	81	12.4	3.87	93	.243	.331	4	.167	1	-3	-3	-0	-0.3

YEAR TM/L	W	L	PCT	G	GS	CG	SH	SV	IP	H	HR	BB	SO	RAT	ERA	ERA+	OAV	OOB	BH	AVG	PB	PR	/A	PD	TPI
1974 NY-N	6	11	.353	41	4	1	1	3	88²	96	12	32	54	13.0	4.16	86	.279	.340	1	.071	-0	-5	-6	-1	-1.2
1975 Phi-N☆	9	6	.600	56	0	0	0	14	102²	84	6	36	55	10.8	2.98	125	.226	.299	2	.154	-0	7	9	-0	1.4
1976 *Phi-N	7	6	.538	58	0	0	0	11	97¹	81	4	42	76	11.4	2.50	142	.226	.307	1	.143	0	11	11	-1	1.7
1977 *Phi-N	7	3	.700	45	0	0	0	9	79	62	6	24	58	9.9	2.62	153	.221	.284	4	.400	2	11	12	0	2.0
1978 *Phi-N	8	7	.533	55	1	0	0	9	89²	82	6	23	63	10.5	3.21	111	.245	.293	0	.000	-0	4	4	0	0.6
1979 *Phi-N	4	3	.571	65	1	0	0	16	83²	83	9	29	57	12.3	5.16	74	.259	.324	1	.167	-0	-13	-12	-1	-1.6
1980 *Phi-N	5	4	.556	57	0	0	0	20	92¹	62	3	23	75	8.5	1.46	259	.194	.253	2	.250	0	**22**	24	0	3.6
1981 *Phi-N	2	4	.333	34	0	0	0	10	44	35	2	14	26	10.0	2.66	136	.219	.282	0	.000	-0	4	5	-1	0.8
1982 Phi-N	3	3	.500	34	0	0	0	5	39²	50	3	12	25	14.3	4.31	85	.305	.356	0	.000	-0	-3	-3	0	-0.5
1983 Phi-N	2	1	.667	34	1	0	0	0	55²	58	4	19	30	12.4	3.56	100	.271	.330	1	.333	1	0	0	0	0.0
1984 Phi-N	2	0	1.000	25	0	0	0	0	38	36	1	10	26	10.9	3.79	96	.245	.293	1	.333	0	-1	-1	0	0.0
Total 19	96	92	.511	824	39	5	1	180	1514²	1318	108	582	1109	11.4	3.14	116	.237	.312	39	.182	5	81	85	-1	14.5

● **JOHN McGRAW**   McGraw, John b: 1890, d: 11/14/18, Cleveland, Ohio BR/TR, 190 lbs. Deb: 7/29/14

YEAR TM/L	W	L	PCT	G	GS	CG	SH	SV	IP	H	HR	BB	SO	RAT	ERA	ERA+	OAV	OOB	BH	AVG	PB	PR	/A	PD	TPI
1914 Bro-F	0	0	—	1	0	0	0	0	2	0	0	0	2	4.5	0.00	—	.000	.143	0	—	0	1	1	-0	0.0

● **BOB McGRAW**   McGraw, Robert Emmett b: 4/10/1895, LaVeta, Colo. d: 6/2/78, Boise, Idaho BR/TR, 6'2", 160 lbs. Deb: 9/25/17

YEAR TM/L	W	L	PCT	G	GS	CG	SH	SV	IP	H	HR	BB	SO	RAT	ERA	ERA+	OAV	OOB	BH	AVG	PB	PR	/A	PD	TPI
1917 NY-A	0	1	.000	2	1	1	0	0	11	9	0	3	3	9.8	0.82	328	.257	.316	0	.000	-0	2	2	0	0.1
1918 NY-A	0	1	.000	1	1	0	0	0	0	0	0	4	0	∞	∞	—	1.000	—	0	—	0	-4	-4	0	-0.4
1919 NY-A	1	0	1.000	6	0	0	0	0	16¹	11	1	10	3	12.1	3.31	97	.216	.355	0	.000	-0	-0	-0	-0	-0.2
Bos-A	0	2	.000	10	1	0	0	0	26²	33	0	17	6	17.9	6.75	45	.347	.461	1	.100	-1	-10	-11	-1	-0.9
Yr	1	2	.333	16	1	0	0	0	43	44	1	27	9	15.5	5.44	57	.299	.418	1	.077	-1	-11	-11	-1	-0.9
1920 NY-A	0	0	—	15	0	0	0	0	27	24	1	20	10	15.0	4.67	82	.240	.372	0	.000	-1	-3	-3	-1	-0.2
1925 Bro-N	0	2	.000	2	2	2	0	0	19²	14	0	13	3	12.4	3.20	130	.222	.355	1	.167	-0	2	2	1	0.1
1926 Bro-N	9	13	.409	33	21	10	0	1	174¹	197	12	67	49	13.7	4.59	83	.292	.358	8	.145	-2	-15	-15	-1	-1.9
1927 Bro-N	0	1	.000	1	1	0	0	0	4	5	1	2	2	15.8	9.00	44	.313	.389	0	.000	-0	-2	-2	0	-0.4
StL-N	4	5	.444	18	12	4	1	0	94	121	3	30	37	14.5	5.07	78	.323	.373	6	.182	1	-12	-12	1	-0.8
Yr	4	6	.400	19	13	4	1	0	98	126	4	32	39	14.5	5.23	75	.322	.374	6	.176	1	-14	-14	1	-1.2
1928 Phi-N	7	8	.467	39	3	0	0	1	132	150	7	56	28	14.1	4.64	92	.326	.400	4	.111	-2	-9	-5	-1	-0.8
1929 Phi-N	5	5	.500	41	4	0	0	4	86¹	113	6	43	22	16.5	5.73	91	.324	.401	4	.200	-1	-10	-5	1	-0.4
Total 9	26	38	.406	168	47	17	1	6	591¹	677	31	265	164	14.5	4.89	83	.305	.382	24	.138	-6	-61	-54	-2	-5.6

● **SCOTT McGREGOR**   McGregor, Scott Houston b: 1/18/54, Inglewood, Cal. BB/TL, 6'1", 190 lbs. Deb: 9/19/76

YEAR TM/L	W	L	PCT	G	GS	CG	SH	SV	IP	H	HR	BB	SO	RAT	ERA	ERA+	OAV	OOB	BH	AVG	PB	PR	/A	PD	TPI
1976 Bal-A	0	1	.000	3	2	0	0	0	14²	17	0	5	6	13.5	3.68	89	.293	.349	0	—	0	-0	-1	0	0.0
1977 Bal-A	3	5	.375	29	5	1	0	4	114	119	8	30	55	12.3	4.42	86	.275	.333	0	—	0	-5	-8	-1	-0.7
1978 Bal-A	15	13	.536	35	32	13	4	1	233	217	19	47	94	10.2	3.32	105	.248	.287	0	—	0	11	4	0	1.0
1979 *Bal-A	13	6	.684	27	23	7	2	0	174²	165	19	23	81	**9.8**	3.35	120	.248	**.275**	0	—	0	17	13	-1	1.4
1980 Bal-A	20	8	.714	36	36	12	4	0	252	254	16	58	119	11.2	3.32	119	.265	.308	0	—	0	20	18	-3	1.5
1981 Bal-A☆	13	5	.722	24	22	8	3	0	160	167	13	40	82	11.6	3.26	111	.273	.318	0	—	0	7	6	1	0.8
1982 Bal-A	14	12	.538	37	37	7	1	0	226¹	238	31	52	84	11.6	4.61	87	.267	.308	0	—	0	-14	-15	-1	-1.6
1983 *Bal-A	18	7	.720	36	36	12	0	0	260	271	24	45	86	11.0	3.18	124	.269	.301	0	—	0	25	22	-1	1.9
1984 Bal-A	15	12	.556	30	30	10	3	0	196¹	216	18	54	67	12.6	3.94	98	.280	.331	0	—	0	1	-2	2	0.1
1985 Bal-A	14	14	.500	35	34	8	1	0	204	226	34	65	86	12.9	4.81	84	.283	.337	0	—	0	-15	-18	-1	-2.0
1986 Bal-A	11	15	.423	34	33	4	2	0	203	216	35	57	95	12.2	4.52	91	.270	.321	0	—	0	-8	-9	-1	-0.9
1987 Bal-A	2	7	.222	26	15	1	1	0	85¹	112	15	35	39	15.8	6.64	66	.326	.393	0	—	0	-21	-21	3	-1.5
1988 Bal-A	0	3	.000	4	4	0	0	0	17¹	27	3	7	10	17.7	8.83	44	.370	.425	0	—	0	-9	-9	-1	-1.1
Total 13	138	108	.561	356	309	83	23	5	2140²	2245	235	518	904	11.7	3.99	98	.271	.316	0	—	0	10	-19	-2	-1.1

● **SLIM McGREW**   McGrew, Walter Howard b: 8/5/1899, Yoakum, Tex. d: 8/21/67, Houston, Tex. BR/TR, 6'7.5", 235 lbs. Deb: 4/18/22

YEAR TM/L	W	L	PCT	G	GS	CG	SH	SV	IP	H	HR	BB	SO	RAT	ERA	ERA+	OAV	OOB	BH	AVG	PB	PR	/A	PD	TPI
1922 Was-A	0	0	—	1	0	0	0	0	1²	4	0	1	0	32.4	10.80	36	.500	.600	0	.000	-0	-1	-1	0	0.0
1923 Was-A	0	0	—	3	0	0	0	0	5	11	0	3	1	25.2	12.60	30	.440	.500	0	.000	-0	-5	-5	0	0.0
1924 Was-A	0	1	.000	6	2	0	0	0	23¹	25	1	12	8	14.3	5.01	80	.281	.366	0	.000	-1	-2	-3	-1	-0.3
Total 3	0	1	.000	10	2	0	0	0	30	40	1	17	10	17.1	6.60	60	.328	.410	0	.000	-2	-8	-9	0	-0.3

● **McGUIRE**   McGuire Deb: 6/16/1894

YEAR TM/L	W	L	PCT	G	GS	CG	SH	SV	IP	H	HR	BB	SO	RAT	ERA	ERA+	OAV	OOB	BH	AVG	PB	PR	/A	PD	TPI
1894 Cin-N	0	0	—	1	0	0	0	0	6	15	0	5	1	30.0	10.50	53	.465	.537	1	.250	-0	-3	-3	0	0.0

● **DEACON McGUIRE**   McGuire, James Thomas b: 11/18/1863, Youngstown, Ohio d: 10/31/36, Albion, Mich. BR/TR, 6'1", 185 lbs. Deb: 6/21/1884 MC♦

YEAR TM/L	W	L	PCT	G	GS	CG	SH	SV	IP	H	HR	BB	SO	RAT	ERA	ERA+	OAV	OOB	BH	AVG	PB	PR	/A	PD	TPI
1890 Roc-a	0	0	—	1	0	0	0	0	4	10	0	1	0	24.8	6.75	53	.458	.481	99	.299	-1	-1	-1	0	0.0

● **TOM McGUIRE**   McGuire, Thomas Patrick "Elmer" b: 2/1/1892, Chicago, Ill. d: 12/7/59, Phoenix, Ariz. BR/TR, 6', 175 lbs. Deb: 4/18/14

YEAR TM/L	W	L	PCT	G	GS	CG	SH	SV	IP	H	HR	BB	SO	RAT	ERA	ERA+	OAV	OOB	BH	AVG	PB	PR	/A	PD	TPI
1914 Chi-F	5	6	.455	24	12	7	0	0	131¹	143	7	57	37	14.0	3.70	72	.288	.366	19	.271	4	-12	-15	0	-0.6
1919 Chi-A	0	0	—	1	0	0	0	0	3	5	0	3	0	24.0	9.00	35	.500	.615	0	.000	-0	-2	-2	0	0.0
Total 2	5	6	.455	25	12	7	0	0	134¹	148	7	60	37	14.2	3.82	70	.292	.371	19	.268	3	-14	-17	1	-0.6

● **BILL McGUNNIGLE**   McGunnigle, William Henry "Gunner" b: 1/1/1855, Boston, Mass. d: 3/9/1899, Brockton, Mass. BR/TR, 5'9", 155 lbs. Deb: 5/2/1879 M♦

YEAR TM/L	W	L	PCT	G	GS	CG	SH	SV	IP	H	HR	BB	SO	RAT	ERA	ERA+	OAV	OOB	BH	AVG	PB	PR	/A	PD	TPI
1879 Buf-N	9	5	.643	14	13	13	2	0	120	113	0	16	62	9.7	2.63	99	**.235**	.260	30	.175	-2	-2	-0	-1	-0.1
1880 Buf-N	2	3	.400	5	5	4	1	0	37	43	0	8	3	12.4	3.41	92	.279	.315	4	.182	-1	-4	-4	-1	-0.6
Total 2	11	8	.579	19	18	17	3	0	157	156	0	24	65	10.3	2.81	92	.246	.274	35	.173	-3	-6	-4	0	-0.7

● **MARTY McHALE**   McHale, Martin Joseph b: 10/30/1888, Stoneham, Mass. d: 5/7/79, Hempstead, N.Y. BR/TR, 5'11.5", 174 lbs. Deb: 9/28/10

YEAR TM/L	W	L	PCT	G	GS	CG	SH	SV	IP	H	HR	BB	SO	RAT	ERA	ERA+	OAV	OOB	BH	AVG	PB	PR	/A	PD	TPI
1910 Bos-A	0	2	.000	2	2	1	0	0	13²	15	0	6	14	14.5	4.61	55	.259	.338	0	.000	-1	-3	-3	-0	-0.5
1911 Bos-A	0	0	—	4	1	0	0	0	9¹	9	1	3	3	22.2	9.64	34	.475	.523	0	.000	-0	-7	-7	0	0.0
1913 NY-A	2	4	.333	7	6	4	1	0	48²	49	1	10	11	11.1	2.96	101	.266	.308	0	—	-1	-0	-0	-1	-0.2
1914 NY-A	7	16	.304	31	23	12	0	1	191	195	3	33	75	10.9	2.97	93	.268	.303	12	.200	2	-5	-4	-3	-0.7
1915 NY-A	3	7	.300	13	11	6	0	0	78¹	86	1	19	25	12.1	4.25	69	.277	.318	3	.143	1	-11	-11	0	-1.3
1916 Bos-A	0	1	.000	2	1	0	0	0	6	7	0	4	2	18.0	3.00	92	.280	.400	0	—	-0	-0	-0	0	0.1
Cle-A	0	0	—	5	0	0	0	0	11¹	10	1	6	2	12.7	5.56	54	.270	.372	0	.000	-0	-3	-3	-0	-0.1
Yr	0	1	.000	7	1	0	0	0	17¹	17	1	10	4	14.0	4.67	63	.270	.370	0	.000	-0	-4	-3	0	0.0
Total 6	12	30	.286	64	44	23	1	1	358¹	381	7	81	131	11.8	3.57	80	.275	.319	15	.140	-0	-30	-29	-4	-2.7

● **VANCE McILREE**   McIlree, Vance Elmer b: 10/14/1897, Riverside, Iowa d: 5/6/59, Kansas City, Mo. BR/TR, 6', 160 lbs. Deb: 9/13/21

YEAR TM/L	W	L	PCT	G	GS	CG	SH	SV	IP	H	HR	BB	SO	RAT	ERA	ERA+	OAV	OOB	BH	AVG	PB	PR	/A	PD	TPI
1921 Was-A	0	0	—	1	0	0	0	0	1	1	0	0	0	9.0	9.00	46	.200	.200	0	—	-0	-1	-1	-0	0.0

● **IRISH McILVEEN**   McIlveen, Henry Cooke b: 7/27/1880, Belfast, Ireland d: 10/18/60, Lorain, Ohio BL/TL, 5'11.5", 180 lbs. Deb: 7/10/06 ♦

YEAR TM/L	W	L	PCT	G	GS	CG	SH	SV	IP	H	HR	BB	SO	RAT	ERA	ERA+	OAV	OOB	BH	AVG	PB	PR	/A	PD	TPI
1906 Pit-N	0	1	.000	2	1	0	0	0	7	10	1	2	3	15.4	7.71	35	.357	.400	2	.400	1	-4	-4	0	-0.4

● **STOVER McILWAIN**   McIlwain, Stover William "Smokey" b: 9/22/39, Savannah, Ga. d: 1/15/66, Buffalo, N.Y. BR/TR, 6'2", 195 lbs. Deb: 9/25/57

YEAR TM/L	W	L	PCT	G	GS	CG	SH	SV	IP	H	HR	BB	SO	RAT	ERA	ERA+	OAV	OOB	BH	AVG	PB	PR	/A	PD	TPI
1957 Chi-A	0	0	—	1	0	0	0	0	1	2	0	1	0	27.0	—	—	.500	.600	0	—	0	0	0	0	0.0
1958 Chi-A	0	0	—	1	1	0	0	0	4	4	1	0	4	9.0	2.25	162	.250	.250	0	.000	-0	1	1	0	0.0
Total 2	0	0	—	2	1	0	0	0	5	6	1	1	4	12.6	1.80	203	.300	.333	0	.000	-0	1	1	0	0.0

● **HARRY McINTIRE**   McIntire, John Reid b: 1/11/1879, Dayton, Ohio d: 1/9/49, Daytona Beach, Fla. BR/TR, 5'11", 180 lbs. Deb: 4/14/05

YEAR TM/L	W	L	PCT	G	GS	CG	SH	SV	IP	H	HR	BB	SO	RAT	ERA	ERA+	OAV	OOB	BH	AVG	PB	PR	/A	PD	TPI
1905 Bro-N	8	25	.242	40	35	29	1	1	308²	340	6	101	135	13.4	3.70	78	.285	.351	34	.246	7	-24	-28	-3	-2.3
1906 Bro-N	13	21	.382	39	31	25	4	3	276	254	2	89	121	11.6	2.97	85	.247	.316	18	.175	1	-10	-14	-1	-1.6
1907 Bro-N	7	15	.318	28	22	19	3	0	199²	178	6	79	49	11.9	2.39	98	.248	.329	15	.217	5	2	-1	-1	0.4

YEAR	TM/L	W	L	PCT	G	GS	CG	SH	SV	IP	H	HR	BB	SO	RAT	ERA	ERA+	OAV	OOB	BH	AVG	PB	PR	/A	PD	TPI
1908	Bro-N	11	20	.355	40	35	26	4	2	288	259	5	90	108	11.5	2.69	87	.252	.324	20	.200	2	-10	-11	-2	-1.2
1909	Bro-N	7	17	.292	32	26	20	2	1	228	200	5	91	84	12.3	3.63	71	.246	.337	13	.171	1	-26	-26	-0	-2.6
1910	*Chi-N	13	9	.591	28	19	10	2	0	176	152	5	50	65	10.8	3.07	94	.240	.305	1	.258	-0	-1	-4	-1	-0.1
1911	Chi-N	11	7	.611	25	17	9	1	0	149	147	5	33	56	11.1	4.11	81	.257	.302	14	.264	4	-12	-13	-0	-1.0
1912	Chi-N	1	2	.333	4	3	2	0	0	23²	22	0	6	8	10.6	3.80	88	.256	.304	3	.300	1	-1	-1	-0	0.0
1913	Cin-N	0	1	.000	1	1	0	0	0	1	3	0	3	0	27.00	27.00	12	.600	.600	0	—	0	-3	-3	-0	-1.3
Total	9	71	117	.378	237	188	140	17	8	1650	1555	34	539	626	11.9	3.22	83	.256	.326	134	.218	24	-85	-100	-7	-9.7

● **JOE McINTOSH**   McIntosh, Joseph Anthony b: 8/4/51, Billings, Mont.   BB/TR, 6'2", 185 lbs.   Deb: 4/5/74

YEAR	TM/L	W	L	PCT	G	GS	CG	SH	SV	IP	H	HR	BB	SO	RAT	ERA	ERA+	OAV	OOB	BH	AVG	PB	PR	/A	PD	TPI
1974	SD-N	0	4	.000	10	5	0	0	0	37¹	36	3	17	22	13.0	3.62	98	.250	.333	0	—	-1	0	-0	-0	-0.2
1975	SD-N	8	15	.348	37	28	4	1	0	183	195	14	60	71	12.6	3.69	94	.273	.332	9	.188	2	-1	-4	-0	-0.3
Total	2	8	19	.296	47	33	4	1	0	220¹	231	17	77	93	12.7	3.68	95	.270	.332	9	.155	1	-1	-5	-1	-0.5

● **FRANK McINTYRE**   McIntyre, Frank W. b: 7/12/1859, Walled Lake, Mich.   d: 7/8/1887, Detroit, Mich.   Deb: 5/16/1883

YEAR	TM/L	W	L	PCT	G	GS	CG	SH	SV	IP	H	HR	BB	SO	RAT	ERA	ERA+	OAV	OOB	BH	AVG	PB	PR	/A	PD	TPI
1883	Det-N	1	0	1.000	1	1	1	0	0	11	11	0	1	0	9.8	0.82	380	.234	.250	0	.000	-0	3	3	0	0.2
	Col-a	1	1	.500	2	2	2	0	0	19	20	0	7	6	12.8	5.21	59	.253	.314	0	—	-4	-4	-5	1	-0.4
Total	1	2	1	.667	3	3	3	0	0	30	31	0	8	6	11.7	3.60	86	.246	.291	0	.000	-1	-1	-2	-1	-0.2

● **DOC McJAMES**   McJames, James McCutchen (b: James Mc Cutchen James) b: 8/27/1873, Williamsburg, S.C.   d: 9/23/01, Charleston, S.C.   TR   Deb: 9/24/1895

YEAR	TM/L	W	L	PCT	G	GS	CG	SH	SV	IP	H	HR	BB	SO	RAT	ERA	ERA+	OAV	OOB	BH	AVG	PB	PR	/A	PD	TPI
1895	Was-N	1	1	.500	2	2	2	0	0	17	17	0	16	19	17.5	1.59	302	.256	.401	1	.143	-1	6	6	0	0.5
1896	Was-N	12	20	.375	37	33	29	0	1	280¹	310	2	135	103	14.5	4.27	103	.278	.359	18	.162	-9	3	4	-0	-0.4
1897	Was-N	15	23	.395	44	39	33	3	2	323²	361	7	137	156	14.4	3.61	120	.280	.358	21	.169	-7	25	26	0	1.8
1898	Bal-N	27	15	.643	45	42	40	2	0	374	327	5	113	78	10.9	2.36	152	.234	.296	27	.181	-4	52	51	-3	4.3
1899	Bro-N	19	15	.559	37	34	27	1	1	275¹	295	4	122	105	14.0	3.50	112	.274	.353	19	.170	-5	11	13	3	1.1
1901	Bro-N	5	6	.455	13	12	6	0	0	91	104	1	40	42	14.9	4.75	71	.285	.367	1	.029	-4	-14	-14	-2	-1.9
Total	6	79	80	.497	178	162	137	6	4	1361¹	1414	19	563	593	13.4	3.43	117	.266	.343	87	.162	-30	83	86	-1	5.4

● **ARCHIE McKAIN**   McKain, Archie Richard "Happy" b: 5/12/11, Delphos, Kan.   d: 5/21/85, Salina, Kan.   BB/TL, 5'10", 175 lbs.   Deb: 4/25/37

YEAR	TM/L	W	L	PCT	G	GS	CG	SH	SV	IP	H	HR	BB	SO	RAT	ERA	ERA+	OAV	OOB	BH	AVG	PB	PR	/A	PD	TPI
1937	Bos-A	8	8	.500	36	18	3	0	6	137	152	7	64	66	14.2	4.66	102	.273	.348	13	.265	3	-1	1	0	0.4
1938	Bos-A	5	4	.556	37	5	1	0	6	99²	119	6	44	27	14.9	4.52	109	.297	.369	2	.065	-2	3	5	2	0.3
1939	Det-A	5	6	.455	32	11	4	1	4	129²	120	6	54	49	12.1	3.68	133	.247	.322	9	.220	4	14	17	-2	1.6
1940	*Det-A	5	0	1.000	27	0	0	0	3	51	48	2	25	24	12.9	2.82	168	.247	.333	1	.143	0	9	11	1	1.2
1941	Det-A	2	1	.667	15	0	0	0	0	43	58	3	11	14	14.4	5.02	90	.330	.369	0	.000	-1	-4	-2	2	0.0
	StL-A	0	1	.000	10	0	0	0	1	10	16	1	4	2	18.9	8.10	53	.364	.429	0	.000	-0	-4	-4	1	-0.4
	Yr	2	2	.500	23	0	0	0	1	53	74	5	15	16	15.3	5.60	80	.336	.381	0	.000	-1	-9	-7	3	-0.4
1943	StL-A	1	1	.500	10	0	0	0	0	16	16	0	6	6	12.4	3.94	84	.242	.306	0	.000	-0	-1	-1	0	-0.1
Total	6	26	21	.553	165	34	8	1	16	486¹	529	26	208	188	13.7	4.26	112	.275	.347	25	.176	3	15	27	4	3.0

● **HAL McKAIN**   McKain, Harold Le Roy b: 7/10/06, Logan, Iowa   d: 1/24/70, Sacramento, Cal.   BL/TR, 5'11", 185 lbs.   Deb: 9/22/27

YEAR	TM/L	W	L	PCT	G	GS	CG	SH	SV	IP	H	HR	BB	SO	RAT	ERA	ERA+	OAV	OOB	BH	AVG	PB	PR	/A	PD	TPI
1927	Cle-A	0	1	.000	2	1	0	0	0	11	18	0	4	5	18.0	4.09	103	.391	.440	0	.000	-1	0	0	0	0.0
1929	Chi-A	6	9	.400	34	10	4	1	1	158	158	10	85	33	14.4	3.65	117	.275	.378	10	.227	2	11	11	4	1.5
1930	Chi-A	6	4	.600	32	5	0	0	5	89	108	0	42	52	15.5	5.56	83	.299	.377	13	.419	7	-9	-9	1	-0.2
1931	Chi-A	6	9	.400	27	8	3	0	0	112	134	10	57	39	15.6	5.71	75	.295	.377	5	.119	-1	-16	-18	2	-1.9
1932	Chi-A	0	0	—	8	0	0	0	0	11¹	17	1	5	7	17.5	11.12	39	.340	.400	0	.000	-0	-8	-9	0	0.0
Total	5	18	23	.439	103	24	7	1	6	381¹	435	21	193	136	15.2	4.93	88	.293	.380	28	.230	8	-23	-24	7	-0.6

● **REEVE McKAY**   McKay, Reeve Stewart "Rip" b: 11/16/1881, Morgan, Tex.   d: 1/18/46, Dallas, Tex.   TR, 6'1.5", 168 lbs.   Deb: 10/2/15

YEAR	TM/L	W	L	PCT	G	GS	CG	SH	SV	IP	H	HR	BB	SO	RAT	ERA	ERA+	OAV	OOB	BH	AVG	PB	PR	/A	PD	TPI
1915	StL-A	0	0	—	1	0	0	0	0	1	1	0	0	0	9.0	9.00	32	.500	.500	0	—	0	-1	-1	0	0.0

● **JIM McKEE**   McKee, James Marion b: 2/1/47, Columbus, Ohio   BR/TR, 6'7", 215 lbs.   Deb: 9/15/72

YEAR	TM/L	W	L	PCT	G	GS	CG	SH	SV	IP	H	HR	BB	SO	RAT	ERA	ERA+	OAV	OOB	BH	AVG	PB	PR	/A	PD	TPI
1972	Pit-N	1	0	1.000	2	0	0	0	0	5	2	0	1	4	5.4	0.00	—	.125	.176	0	—	0	2	2	-0	0.4
1973	Pit-N	0	1	.000	15	1	0	0	0	27	31	2	17	13	16.3	5.67	62	.287	.389	0	.000	-0	-6	-6	-0	-0.3
Total	2	1	1	.500	17	1	0	0	0	32	33	2	18	17	14.6	4.78	73	.266	.364	0	.000	-0	-4	-5	-1	0.1

● **ROGERS McKEE**   McKee, Rogers Hornsby b: 9/16/26, Shelby, N.C.   BL/TL, 6'1", 160 lbs.   Deb: 8/18/43

YEAR	TM/L	W	L	PCT	G	GS	CG	SH	SV	IP	H	HR	BB	SO	RAT	ERA	ERA+	OAV	OOB	BH	AVG	PB	PR	/A	PD	TPI
1943	Phi-N	1	0	1.000	4	1	1	0	0	13¹	12	0	5	1	11.5	6.08	56	.226	.293	1	.200	-4	-4	0	-0.2
1944	Phi-N	0	0	—	1	0	0	0	0	2	2	1	1	0	13.5	4.50	80	.250	.333	0	—	-0	-0	0	0.0
Total	2	1	0	1.000	5	1	1	0	0	15¹	14	1	6	1	11.7	5.87	58	.230	.299	1	.200	-4	-4	0	-0.1

● **TIM McKEITHAN**   McKeithan, Emmett James b: 11/2/06, Lawndale, N.C.   d: 8/20/69, Forest City, N.C.   BR/TR, 6'2", 182 lbs.   Deb: 7/21/32

YEAR	TM/L	W	L	PCT	G	GS	CG	SH	SV	IP	H	HR	BB	SO	RAT	ERA	ERA+	OAV	OOB	BH	AVG	PB	PR	/A	PD	TPI
1932	Phi-A	0	1	.000	4	2	0	0	0	12²	18	0	5	6	16.3	7.11	64	.340	.397	0	—	-4	-4	0	-0.2
1933	Phi-A	1	0	1.000	3	1	0	0	0	9	10	0	4	3	14.0	4.00	107	.278	.350	1	.333	0	0	0	0.1
1934	Phi-A	0	0	—	3	0	0	0	0	4	7	2	5	0	27.0	15.75	28	.389	.522	0	.000	-5	-5	-0	0.0
Total	3	1	1	.500	10	3	0	0	0	25²	35	2	14	3	17.2	7.36	60	.327	.405	1	.143	-8	-8	0	-0.1

● **RUSS McKELVY**   McKelvy, Russell Errett b: 9/8/1856, Meadville, Pa.   d: 10/19/15, Omaha, Neb.   BR/TR,   Deb: 5/1/1878 ♦

YEAR	TM/L	W	L	PCT	G	GS	CG	SH	SV	IP	H	HR	BB	SO	RAT	ERA	ERA+	OAV	OOB	BH	AVG	PB	PR	/A	PD	TPI
1878	Ind-N	0	2	.000	4	1	1	0	0	25	38	1	3	3	14.8	2.16	94	.322	.339	57	.225	-0	-1	1	0.1

● **KIT McKENNA**   McKenna, James William b: 2/10/1873, Lynchburg, Va.   d: 3/31/41, Lynchburg, Va.   Deb: 7/7/1898

YEAR	TM/L	W	L	PCT	G	GS	CG	SH	SV	IP	H	HR	BB	SO	RAT	ERA	ERA+	OAV	OOB	BH	AVG	PB	PR	/A	PD	TPI
1898	Bro-N	2	6	.250	14	9	7	0	0	100²	118	4	57	27	17.2	5.63	64	.290	.399	9	.225	0	-23	-23	2	-1.3
1899	Bal-N	2	3	.400	8	4	4	0	0	45	66	1	19	7	17.6	4.60	86	.340	.407	1	.059	-1	-4	-3	-0	-0.4
Total	2	4	9	.308	22	13	11	0	0	145²	184	5	76	34	17.3	5.31	70	.306	.402	10	.175	-0	-26	-26	1	-1.7

● **LIMB McKENRY**   McKenry, Frank Gordon "Big Pete" b: 8/13/1888, Piney Flats, Tenn.   d: 11/1/56, Fresno, Cal.   BR/TR, 6'4", 205 lbs.   Deb: 8/27/15

YEAR	TM/L	W	L	PCT	G	GS	CG	SH	SV	IP	H	HR	BB	SO	RAT	ERA	ERA+	OAV	OOB	BH	AVG	PB	PR	/A	PD	TPI
1915	Cin-N	5	5	.500	21	11	5	0	0	110¹	94	3	39	37	11.1	2.94	97	.238	.311	5	.152	0	-2	-1	1	0.1
1916	Cin-N	1	1	.500	6	1	0	0	0	14²	14	0	8	2	14.7	4.30	60	.259	.375	2	.400	2	-3	-3	-0	-0.2
Total	2	6	6	.500	27	12	5	0	0	125	108	3	47	39	11.5	3.10	91	.241	.319	7	.184	2	-5	-4	1	-0.1

● **JOEL McKEON**   McKeon, Joel Jacob b: 2/25/63, Covington, Ky.   BL/TL, 6', 185 lbs.   Deb: 5/6/86

YEAR	TM/L	W	L	PCT	G	GS	CG	SH	SV	IP	H	HR	BB	SO	RAT	ERA	ERA+	OAV	OOB	BH	AVG	PB	PR	/A	PD	TPI
1986	Chi-A	3	1	.750	30	0	0	0	1	33	18	2	17	18	9.5	2.45	176	.165	.278	0	—	0	6	7	-1	0.7
1987	Chi-A	1	2	.333	13	0	0	0	0	21	27	8	15	14	18.0	9.43	49	.318	.420	0	—	0	-12	-11	-0	-1.5
Total	2	4	3	.571	43	0	0	0	1	54	45	10	32	32	12.8	5.17	85	.232	.341	0	—	0	-5	-5	-1	-0.8

● **LARRY McKEON**   McKeon, Lawrence G. b: 3/25/1866, New York   d: 7/18/15, Indianapolis, Ind   5'10", 168 lbs.   Deb: 5/1/1884

YEAR	TM/L	W	L	PCT	G	GS	CG	SH	SV	IP	H	HR	BB	SO	RAT	ERA	ERA+	OAV	OOB	BH	AVG	PB	PR	/A	PD	TPI
1884	Ind-a	18	41	.305	61	60	59	2	0	512	488	20	94	308	10.5	3.50	94	.235	.275	53	.212	-3	-14	-12	0	-0.7
1885	Cin-a	20	13	.606	33	33	32	2	0	290	273	5	50	117	10.4	2.86	114	.241	.281	20	.165	-5	13	13	-0	0.7
1886	Cin-a	8	8	.500	19	19	16	0	0	156	174	6	54	46	13.3	5.08	69	.276	.336	19	.253	1	-28	-27	1	-1.9
	KC-N	0	2	.000	3	3	3	0	0	21	44	0	8	3	22.3	10.71	35	.411	.452	0	.000	-1	-17	-16	0	-1.1
Total	3	46	64	.418	116	115	110	4	0	979	979	31	206	474	11.2	3.71	90	.248	.291	92	.202	-9	-47	-42	8	-3.0

● **DENNY McLAIN**   McLain, Dennis Dale b: 3/29/44, Chicago, Ill.   BR/TR, 6'1", 185 lbs.   Deb: 9/21/63

YEAR	TM/L	W	L	PCT	G	GS	CG	SH	SV	IP	H	HR	BB	SO	RAT	ERA	ERA+	OAV	OOB	BH	AVG	PB	PR	/A	PD	TPI
1963	Det-A	2	1	.667	3	3	2	0	0	21	20	2	16	22	15.4	4.29	87	.253	.379	1	.200	1	-2	-1	1	0.0
1964	Det-A	4	5	.444	19	16	3	0	0	100	84	16	37	70	11.0	4.05	90	.225	.297	5	.135	-1	-5	-4	-2	-0.7
1965	Det-A	16	6	.727	33	29	13	4	1	220¹	174	26	62	192	9.7	2.61	133	.216	.273	4	.054	-4	21	21	-0	1.7
1966	Det-A★	20	14	.588	38	38	14	4	0	264¹	205	42	104	192	10.6	3.92	89	.214	.294	17	.183	2	-14	-13	-1	-1.5
1967	Det-A	17	16	.515	37	37	10	3	0	235	209	35	73	161	10.9	3.79	86	.237	.297	10	.118	-3	-15	-14	-2	-2.4

YEAR TM/L	W	L	PCT	G	GS	CG	SH	SV	IP	H	HR	BB	SO	RAT	ERA	ERA+	OAV	OOB	BH	AVG	PB	PR	/A	PD	TPI
1968 *Det-A★	31	6	.838	41	41	28	6	0	336	241	31	63	280	8.3	1.96	154	.200	.243	18	.162	0	38	39	1	4.9
1969 Det-A★	24	9	.727	42	41	23	9	0	325	288	25	67	181	9.9	2.80	133	.237	.279	17	.160	-1	30	34	-5	2.7
1970 Det-A	3	5	.375	14	14	1	0	0	91¹	100	19	28	52	12.9	4.63	80	.273	.330	2	.065	-2	-9	-9	-0	-0.9
1971 Was-A	10	22	.313	33	32	9	3	0	216²	233	31	72	103	12.8	4.28	77	.281	.341	6	.103	-1	-20	-23	-1	-3.3
1972 Oak-A	1	2	.333	5	5	0	0	0	22¹	32	4	8	8	16.1	6.04	47	.323	.374	0	.000	-0	-7	-8	0	-1.0
Atl-N	3	5	.375	15	8	2	0	1	54	60	12	18	21	13.2	6.50	58	.279	.338	2	.167	-0	-18	-16	-1	-2.3
Total 10	131	91	.590	280	264	105	29	2	1886	1646	242	548	1282	10.6	3.39	101	.234	.292	82	.133	-9	-1	5	-10	-2.8

● **BARNEY McLAUGHLIN** McLaughlin, Bernard b: 1857, Ireland d: 2/13/21, Lowell, Mass. BR/TR, Deb: 8/2/1884 F♦

YEAR TM/L	W	L	PCT	G	GS	CG	SH	SV	IP	H	HR	BB	SO	RAT	ERA	ERA+	OAV	OOB	BH	AVG	PB	PR	/A	PD	TPI
1884 KC-U	1	3	.250	7	4	4	0	0	48²	62	2	15	14	14.2	5.36	42	.291	.337	37	.228	-1	-16	-17	0	-1.0

● **BYRON McLAUGHLIN** McLaughlin, Byron Scott b: 9/29/55, Van Nuys, Cal. BR/TR, 6'1", 185 lbs. Deb: 9/18/77

YEAR TM/L	W	L	PCT	G	GS	CG	SH	SV	IP	H	HR	BB	SO	RAT	ERA	ERA+	OAV	OOB	BH	AVG	PB	PR	/A	PD	TPI
1977 Sea-A	0	0	—	1	0	0	0	0	1¹	5	1	0	1	33.8	27.00	15	.625	.625	0	—	0	-3	-3	0	0.0
1978 Sea-A	4	8	.333	20	17	4	0	0	107	97	15	39	87	11.9	4.37	87	.238	.314	0	—	0	-7	-7	-2	-0.8
1979 Sea-A	7	7	.500	47	7	1	0	14	123²	114	13	60	74	12.8	4.22	103	.251	.340	0	—	0	-0	2	-2	0.0
1980 Sea-A	3	6	.333	45	4	0	0	2	90²	124	15	50	41	17.5	6.85	60	.331	.412	0	—	0	-28	-27	-2	-2.7
1983 Cal-A	2	4	.333	16	7	0	0	0	55²	63	3	22	45	14.1	5.17	78	.286	.357	0	—	0	-7	-7	-0	-0.7
Total 5	16	25	.390	129	35	5	0	16	378¹	403	47	171	248	13.9	5.11	80	.275	.356	0	—	0	-46	-43	-5	-4.2

● **FRANK McLAUGHLIN** McLaughlin, Francis Edward b: 6/19/1856, Lowell, Mass. d: 4/5/17, Lowell, Mass. BR/TR, 5'9", 160 lbs. Deb: 8/9/1882 F♦

YEAR TM/L	W	L	PCT	G	GS	CG	SH	SV	IP	H	HR	BB	SO	RAT	ERA	ERA+	OAV	OOB	BH	AVG	PB	PR	/A	PD	TPI
1883 Pit-a	0	0	—	2	0	0	0	0	9	14	0	3	1	17.0	13.00	25	.334	.378	25	.219	-0	-10	-10	-0	0.0
1884 KC-U	0	0	—	2	1	0	0	0	10	15	0	2	3	15.3	5.40	41	.325	.353	28	.228	-0	-3	-4	-1	0.0
Total 2	0	0	—	4	1	0	0	0	19	29	0	5	4	16.1	9.00	30	.329	.365	97	.228	-0	-13	-13	-1	0.0

● **JIM McLAUGHLIN** McLaughlin, James Thomas b: 11/18/1860, Cleveland, Ohio d: 11/16/1895, Cleveland, Ohio BL/TL, 157 lbs. Deb: 5/30/1884

YEAR TM/L	W	L	PCT	G	GS	CG	SH	SV	IP	H	HR	BB	SO	RAT	ERA	ERA+	OAV	OOB	BH	AVG	PB	PR	/A	PD	TPI
1884 Bal-a	1	2	.333	3	2	2	0	0	22	27	2	11	8	15.5	3.68	94	.300	.376	5	.227		-1	-1	0	0.0

● **JOEY McLAUGHLIN** McLaughlin, Joey Richard b: 7/11/56, Tulsa, Okla. BR/TR, 6'2", 205 lbs. Deb: 6/11/77

YEAR TM/L	W	L	PCT	G	GS	CG	SH	SV	IP	H	HR	BB	SO	RAT	ERA	ERA+	OAV	OOB	BH	AVG	PB	PR	/A	PD	TPI
1977 Atl-N	0	0	—	3	2	0	0	0	6	10	3	3	0	19.5	15.00	30	.385	.448	0	.000	-0	-7	-7	0	0.0
1979 Atl-N	5	3	.625	37	0	0	0	5	69	54	3	34	40	11.6	2.48	163	.224	.322	2	.182	0	10	12	-1	1.5
1980 Tor-A	6	9	.400	55	10	0	0	4	135²	159	16	53	70	11.6	4.51	95	.302	.370	0	—	0	-7	-3	-0	-0.6
1981 Tor-A	1	5	.167	40	0	0	0	10	60	55	2	21	38	11.4	2.85	138	.249	.314	0	—	0	5	7	-0	0.8
1982 Tor-A	8	6	.571	44	0	0	0	8	70	54	7	30	49	10.9	3.21	139	.212	.297	0	—	0	7	10	1	1.9
1983 Tor-A	7	4	.636	50	0	0	0	9	64²	63	11	37	47	13.9	4.45	97	.259	.357	0	—	0	-3	-1	-0	-0.2
1984 Tor-A	0	0	—	6	0	0	0	0	10²	12	0	7	3	16.0	2.53	162	.286	.388	0	—	0	2	2	0	-0.2
Tex-A	2	1	.667	15	0	0	0	0	32²	33	4	13	21	12.7	4.41	94	.260	.329	0	—	0	-2	-1	-1	-0.4
Yr	2	1	.667	21	0	0	0	0	43¹	45	4	20	24	13.5	3.95	105	.265	.342	0	—	0	0	1	-0	-0.6
Total 7	29	28	.509	250	12	0	0	36	448²	440	46	198	268	12.9	3.85	110	.262	.341	2	.167	-0	5	19	-0	2.8

● **JUD McLAUGHLIN** McLaughlin, Justin Theodore b: 3/24/12, Brighton, Mass. d: 9/27/64, Cambridge, Mass. BL/TL, 5'11", 155 lbs. Deb: 6/23/31

YEAR TM/L	W	L	PCT	G	GS	CG	SH	SV	IP	H	HR	BB	SO	RAT	ERA	ERA+	OAV	OOB	BH	AVG	PB	PR	/A	PD	TPI
1931 Bos-A	0	0	—	9	0	0	0	0	12	23	1	8	3	23.3	12.00	36	.397	.470	0	—	0	-10	-10	0	0.0
1932 Bos-A	0	0	—	1	0	0	0	0	3	5	0	4	0	27.0	15.00	30	.385	.529	0	.000	-0	-4	-4	0	0.0
1933 Bos-A	0	0	—	6	0	0	0	0	8²	14	1	5	1	19.7	6.23	70	.359	.432	0	—	0	-2	-2	-0	0.0
Total 3	0	0	—	16	0	0	0	0	23²	42	2	17	4	22.4	10.27	42	.382	.465	0	.000	-0	-16	-16	0	0.0

● **BO McLAUGHLIN** McLaughlin, Michael Duane b: 10/23/53, Oakland, Cal. BR/TR, 6'5", 210 lbs. Deb: 7/20/76

YEAR TM/L	W	L	PCT	G	GS	CG	SH	SV	IP	H	HR	BB	SO	RAT	ERA	ERA+	OAV	OOB	BH	AVG	PB	PR	/A	PD	TPI
1976 Hou-N	4	5	.444	17	11	4	2	1	79	71	6	17	32	10.3	2.85	112	.244	.290	0	.000	-1	6	3	0	0.0
1977 Hou-N	4	7	.364	46	6	0	0	5	84²	81	6	34	59	12.9	4.25	84	.260	.344	0	.000	-1	-3	-6	1	-0.9
1978 Hou-N	0	1	.000	12	1	0	0	2	23¹	30	2	16	10	18.5	5.01	66	.313	.421	0	.000	-0	-4	-4	-0	-0.3
1979 Hou-N	1	2	.333	12	0	0	0	0	16¹	22	2	4	12	14.3	5.51	64	.314	.351	0	.000	-0	-3	-4	-0	-0.6
Atl-N	1	1	.500	37	1	0	0	2	49²	63	2	16	45	14.7	4.89	83	.303	.358	0	.000	-1	-6	-5	-1	-0.3
Yr	2	3	.400	49	1	0	0	2	66	85	4	20	57	14.6	5.05	78	.305	.355	0	.000	-1	-10	-8	-1	-0.9
1981 Oak-A	0	0	—	11	0	0	0	1	11²	17	1	9	3	20.8	11.57	30	.333	.443	0		0	-10	-10	-0	-0.1
1982 Oak-A	0	4	.000	21	2	1	0	0	48¹	51	3	27	27	14.7	4.84	81	.267	.361	0	.000	-0	-4	-5	0	-0.2
Total 6	10	20	.333	156	21	5	2	9	313	335	22	123	188	13.6	4.49	80	.275	.348	0	.000	-3	-25	-32	0	-2.2

● **PAT McLAUGHLIN** McLaughlin, Patrick Elmer b: 8/17/10, Taylor, Tex. BR/TR, 6'2", 175 lbs. Deb: 4/25/37

YEAR TM/L	W	L	PCT	G	GS	CG	SH	SV	IP	H	HR	BB	SO	RAT	ERA	ERA+	OAV	OOB	BH	AVG	PB	PR	/A	PD	TPI
1937 Det-A	0	2	.000	10	3	0	0	0	32²	39	3	16	15	15.2	6.34	74	.291	.367	1	.100	-1	-6	-6	-1	-0.4
1940 Phi-A	0	0	—	1	0	0	0	0	1²	4	1	1	0	27.0	16.20	27	.444	.500	0	—	0	-2	-2	0	-0.1
1945 Det-A	0	0	—	1	0	0	0	0	1	2	0	0	0	18.0	9.00	39	.400	.400	0	—	0	-1	-1	-0	0.0
Total 3	0	2	.000	12	3	0	0	0	35¹	45	4	17	15	15.8	6.88	67	.304	.376	1	.100	-1	-9	-9	-1	-0.4

● **WARREN McLAUGHLIN** McLaughlin, Warren A. b: 1/22/1876, N.Plainfield, N.J. d: 10/22/23, Plainfield, N.J. TL, Deb: 7/7/00

YEAR TM/L	W	L	PCT	G	GS	CG	SH	SV	IP	H	HR	BB	SO	RAT	ERA	ERA+	OAV	OOB	BH	AVG	PB	PR	/A	PD	TPI
1900 Phi-N	0	0	—	1	0	0	0	0	6	4	0	6	1	15.0	4.50	80	.190	.369	1	.500	1	-1	-1	0	0.1
1902 Pit-N	3	0	1.000	3	3	3	0	0	26	27	0	9	13	12.8	2.77	99	.268	.334	4	.364	1	0	-0	-1	0.0
1903 Phi-N	0	3	.000	3	2	2	0	0	23	38	0	11	3	19.6	7.04	46	.376	.442	2	.200	0	-10	-10	-1	-1.0
Total 3	3	3	.500	7	5	5	0	0	55	69	0	26	17	15.9	4.75	64	.309	.388	7	.304	2	-10	-10	-2	-0.9

● **AL McLEAN** McLean, Albert Eldon "Elrod" b: 9/20/12, Chicago, Ill. d: 9/29/90, Asheboro, N.C. BR/TR, 6', 175 lbs. Deb: 7/16/35

YEAR TM/L	W	L	PCT	G	GS	CG	SH	SV	IP	H	HR	BB	SO	RAT	ERA	ERA+	OAV	OOB	BH	AVG	PB	PR	/A	PD	TPI
1935 Was-A	0	0	—	4	0	0	0	0	8²	12	0	5	3	17.7	7.27	59	.324	.405	0	—	0	-3	-3	-0	-0.1

● **WAYNE McLELAND** McLeland, Wayne Gaffney "Nubbin" b: 8/29/24, Milton, Iowa BR/TR, 6', 180 lbs. Deb: 4/20/51

YEAR TM/L	W	L	PCT	G	GS	CG	SH	SV	IP	H	HR	BB	SO	RAT	ERA	ERA+	OAV	OOB	BH	AVG	PB	PR	/A	PD	TPI
1951 Det-A	0	1	.000	6	1	0	0	0	11	20	1	4	0	20.5	8.18	51	.400	.455	0	.000	-0	-5	-5	0	-0.4
1952 Det-A	0	0	—	4	0	0	0	0	2²	4	0	6	0	33.8	10.13	38	.444	.667	0	—	0	-2	-2	-0	0.0
Total 2	0	1	.000	10	1	0	0	0	13²	24	1	10	0	23.0	8.56	48	.407	.500	0	.000	-0	-7	-7	0	-0.4

● **CAL McLISH** McLish, Calvin Coolidge Julius Caesar Tuskahoma "Buster" b: 12/1/25, Anadarko, Okla. BB/TR, 6'1", 200 lbs. Deb: 5/13/44 C

YEAR TM/L	W	L	PCT	G	GS	CG	SH	SV	IP	H	HR	BB	SO	RAT	ERA	ERA+	OAV	OOB	BH	AVG	PB	PR	/A	PD	TPI
1944 Bro-N	3	10	.231	23	13	3	0	0	84	110	10	48	24	17.0	7.82	45	.321	.406	7	.219	0	-39	-40	-2	-5.1
1946 Bro-N	0	0	—	1	0	0	0	0	0	1	0	0	0	—	∞	—	1.000	1.000	0	—	0	-2	-2	0	-0.2
1947 Pit-N	0	0	—	1	0	0	0	0	1	2	0	0	0	27.0	18.00	23	.400	.500	0	—	0	-2	-2	0	-0.2
1948 Pit-N	0	0	—	2	1	0	0	0	5	8	0	2	1	18.0	9.00	45	.400	.455	0	.000	-0	-3	-3	0	-0.2
1949 Chi-N	1	1	.500	8	2	0	0	0	23	31	5	12	6	16.8	5.87	69	.341	.417	3	.333	2	-5	-5	1	-0.2
1951 Chi-N	4	10	.286	30	17	5	1	0	145²	159	16	52	46	13.2	4.45	92	.283	.347	5	.119	-1	-8	-6	-0	-0.6
1956 Cle-A	2	4	.333	37	2	0	0	1	61²	67	5	32	27	14.4	4.96	85	.282	.367	1	.111	1	-6	-5	1	-0.2
1957 Cle-A	9	7	.563	42	7	2	0	0	144¹	118	11	67	88	11.7	2.74	135	.220	.309	8	.186	3	17	16	1	2.1
1958 Cle-A	16	8	.667	39	30	13	0	1	225²	214	25	70	97	11.4	2.99	122	.251	.309	6	.094	-1	19	16	0	1.6
1959 Cle-A★	19	8	.704	35	32	13	0	0	235¹	253	26	72	113	12.6	3.63	101	.270	.326	14	.189	1	6	1	3	0.6
1960 Cin-N	4	14	.222	37	21	2	0	0	151¹	170	16	48	56	13.4	4.16	92	.287	.348	2	.049	-3	-7	-6	1	-0.9
1961 Chi-A	10	13	.435	31	27	4	0	0	162¹	178	21	47	80	12.5	4.38	89	.280	.330	9	.167	-1	-6	-8	-2	-1.0
1962 Phi-N	11	5	.688	32	24	5	1	1	154²	184	15	45	71	13.4	4.25	91	.293	.343	4	.078	-2	-5	-6	-1	-0.8
1963 Phi-N	13	11	.542	32	32	10	2	0	209²	184	20	56	98	10.5	3.26	99	.239	.294	14	.203	4	1	-1	2	0.5
1964 Phi-N	0	1	.000	2	1	0	0	0	5¹	6	0	1	6	11.8	3.38	103	.261	.292	0	.000	-0	0	0	0	0.0
Total 15	92	92	.500	352	209	57	5	6	1609	1685	164	552	713	12.7	4.01	93	.270	.332	73	.186	4	-39	-50	9	-4.2

● **SAM McMACKIN** McMackin, Samuel b: 1872, Cleveland, Ohio d: 2/11/03, Columbus, Ohio BR/TL, Deb: 9/4/02

YEAR TM/L	W	L	PCT	G	GS	CG	SH	SV	IP	H	HR	BB	SO	RAT	ERA	ERA+	OAV	OOB	BH	AVG	PB	PR	/A	PD	TPI
1902 Chi-A	0	0	—	1	0	0	0	0	3	1	0	0	2	3.0	0.00	—	.105	.105	0	.000	-0	1	1	0	0.0

YEAR	TM/L	W	L	PCT	G	GS	CG	SH	SV	IP	H	HR	BB	SO	RAT	ERA	ERA+	OAV	OOB	BH	AVG	PB	PR	/A	PD	TPI
	Det-A	0	1	.000	1	1	1	0	0	8¹	9	0	4	2	15.1	3.24	113	.276	.372	2	.500	1	0	0	0	0.1
	Yr	0	1	.000	2	1	1	0	0	11¹	10	0	4	4	11.9	2.38	150	.237	.318	2	.400	0	2	2	1	0.1

● **JACK McMAHAN**   McMahan, Jack Wally b: 7/22/32, Hot Springs, Ark. BR/TL, 6′, 175 lbs. Deb: 4/18/56

YEAR	TM/L	W	L	PCT	G	GS	CG	SH	SV	IP	H	HR	BB	SO	RAT	ERA	ERA+	OAV	OOB	BH	AVG	PB	PR	/A	PD	TPI
1956	Pit-N	0	0	—	11	0	0	0	0	13¹	18	1	9	9	18.2	6.08	62	.340	.435	0	.000	-0	-3	-3	0	0.0
	KC-A	0	5	.000	23	9	0	0	0	61²	69	7	31	13	14.9	4.82	90	.290	.376	0	.000	-0	-5	-3	-0	-0.5
Total	1	0	5	.000	34	9	0	0	0	75	87	8	40	22	15.5	5.04	84	.299	.387	0	.000	-2	-8	-7	0	-0.5

● **DON McMAHON**   McMahon, Donald John b: 1/4/30, Brooklyn, N.Y. d: 7/22/87, Los Angeles, Cal. BR/TR, 6′2″, 222 lbs. Deb: 6/30/57 C

YEAR	TM/L	W	L	PCT	G	GS	CG	SH	SV	IP	H	HR	BB	SO	RAT	ERA	ERA+	OAV	OOB	BH	AVG	PB	PR	/A	PD	TPI
1957	*Mil-N	2	3	.400	32	0	0	0	9	46²	33	0	29	46	12.0	1.54	227	.196	.315	2	.250	1	12	10	-0	1.6
1958	*Mil-N☆	7	2	.778	38	0	0	0	8	58²	50	4	29	37	12.4	3.68	96	.235	.332	1	.111	0	2	-1	-0	-0.2
1959	Mil-N	5	3	.625	60	0	0	0	15	80²	81	5	37	55	13.3	2.57	138	.259	.339	2	.222	1	12	9	-1	1.3
1960	Mil-N	3	6	.333	48	0	0	0	10	63²	66	9	32	50	14.1	5.94	58	.263	.351	0	.000	-1	-15	-18	-0	-3.0
1961	Mil-N	6	4	.600	53	0	0	0	8	92	84	4	51	55	13.4	2.84	132	.249	.351	3	.188	0	12	9	1	1.2
1962	Mil-N	0	1	.000	2	0	0	0	0	3	3	1	0	3	9.0	6.00	63	.250	.250	0	—	-0	-1	-1	-0	-0.2
	Hou-N	5	5	.500	51	0	0	0	8	76²	53	4	33	69	10.2	1.53	245	.201	.292	1	.083	-1	21	19	-0	2.6
	Yr	5	6	.455	53	0	0	0	8	79²	56	5	33	72	10.2	1.69	221	.203	.290	1	.083	-1	20	18	-0	2.4
1963	Hou-N	1	5	.167	49	2	0	0	5	80	83	10	26	51	12.3	4.05	78	.270	.327	1	.083	0	-7	-8	-0	-0.7
1964	Cle-A	6	4	.600	70	0	0	0	16	101	67	7	52	92	10.8	2.41	150	.189	.297	2	.143	-0	14	13	-1	1.6
1965	Cle-A	3	3	.500	58	0	0	0	11	85	79	8	37	60	12.4	3.28	106	.248	.329	2	.222	1	2	1	0	0.3
1966	Cle-A	1	1	.500	12	0	0	0	1	12¹	8	1	6	5	10.2	2.92	118	.190	.292	0	.000	-0	1	1	-0	0.1
	Bos-A	8	7	.533	49	0	0	0	9	78	65	7	38	57	12.2	2.65	143	.232	.330	1	.091	-0	7	10	-1	2.1
	Yr	9	8	.529	61	0	0	0	10	90¹	73	8	44	62	12.0	2.69	140	.226	.324	1	.077	-0	7	11	-1	2.2
1967	Bos-A	1	2	.333	11	0	0	0	2	17²	14	4	13	10	13.8	3.57	98	.215	.346	0	.000	-0	-1	-0	-0	-0.0
	Chi-A	5	0	1.000	52	0	0	0	3	91²	54	5	27	74	8.5	1.67	186	.173	.252	2	.182	0	16	15	-0	0.9
	Yr	6	2	.750	63	0	0	0	5	109¹	68	9	40	84	9.4	1.98	160	.182	.270	2	.154	-0	15	14	-0	0.9
1968	Chi-A	2	1	.667	25	0	0	0	1	46	31	2	20	32	10.6	1.96	155	.190	.290	1	.333	0	5	5	-1	0.3
	*Det-A	3	1	.750	20	0	0	0	1	35²	22	2	10	33	8.1	2.02	149	.180	.242	0	.000	-0	4	4	-0	0.4
	Yr	5	2	.714	45	0	0	0	1	81²	53	4	30	65	9.1	1.98	152	.183	.259	1	.143	-0	9	9	-1	0.7
1969	Det-A	3	5	.375	34	0	0	0	11	37	25	2	18	38	10.7	3.89	96	.192	.295	0	.000	-1	-1	-0	-0	-0.2
	SF-N	3	1	.750	13	0	0	0	2	23²	13	1	9	21	8.4	3.04	115	.157	.239	1	.333	0	1	1	0	0.3
1970	SF-N	9	5	.643	61	0	0	0	19	94¹	70	9	45	74	11.2	2.96	134	.202	.297	2	.143	-0	11	11	-1	1.9
1971	*SF-N	10	6	.625	61	0	0	0	4	82	73	9	37	71	12.8	4.06	84	.242	.338	0	.000	-0	-5	-6	-1	-1.2
1972	SF-N	3	3	.500	44	0	0	0	5	63	46	8	21	45	9.7	3.71	94	.206	.278	1	.250	0	-2	-2	-0	-0.2
1973	SF-N	4	0	1.000	22	0	0	0	6	30¹	21	1	7	20	8.3	1.48	257	.189	.237	1	1.000	0	7	8	0	1.5
1974	SF-N	0	0	—	9	0	0	0	0	11²	12	1	5	2	11.6	3.09	123	.283	.313	0	—	0	1	1	0	0.0
Total	18	90	68	.570	874	2	0	0	153	1310²	1054	105	579	1003	11.6	2.96	119	.221	.310	23	.137	-0	96	83	-1	10.2

● **DOC McMAHON**   McMahon, Henry John b: 12/19/1886, Woburn, Mass. d: 12/11/29, Woburn, Mass. Deb: 10/6/08

YEAR	TM/L	W	L	PCT	G	GS	CG	SH	SV	IP	H	HR	BB	SO	RAT	ERA	ERA+	OAV	OOB	BH	AVG	PB	PR	/A	PD	TPI
1908	Bos-A	1	0	1.000	1	1	1	0	0	9	14	0	3	4	14.0	3.00	82	.350	.350	2	.400	1	-1	-0	0	0.0

● **SADIE McMAHON**   McMahon, John Joseph b: 9/19/1867, Wilmington, Del. d: 2/20/54, Delaware City, Del BR/TR, 5′9.5″, 165 lbs. Deb: 7/5/1889

YEAR	TM/L	W	L	PCT	G	GS	CG	SH	SV	IP	H	HR	BB	SO	RAT	ERA	ERA+	OAV	OOB	BH	AVG	PB	PR	/A	PD	TPI
1889	Phi-a	14	12	.538	28	27	27	2	0	242	230	5	102	117	12.9	3.53	107	.243	.325	16	.154	-6	8	7	4	0.4
1890	Phi-a	29	18	.617	48	46	44	0	1	410	414	5	133	225	12.4	3.34	115	.254	.318	40	.229	3	24	23	9	3.2
	Bal-a	7	3	.700	12	11	11	1	0	99	84	1	33	66	11.2	3.00	135	.223	.296	4	.103	-4	10	12	2	0.8
	Yr	36	21	.632	60	57	55	1	1	509	498	6	166	291	11.8	3.27	118	.246	.305	44	.206	-1	34	34	11	4.0
1891	Bal-a	35	24	.593	61	58	53	5	1	503	493	13	149	219	11.8	2.81	123	.248	.306	43	.205	-3	51	52	5	5.0
1892	Bal-N	19	25	.432	48	46	44	2	1	397	430	9	145	118	13.2	3.24	106	.265	.329	25	.141	-9	2	8	0	0.0
1893	Bal-N	23	18	.561	43	40	35	0	1	346¹	378	6	156	79	14.1	4.37	109	.269	.348	36	.243	-3	12	15	-1	0.9
1894	Bal-N	25	8	.758	35	33	26	0	0	275²	317	7	111	60	14.3	4.21	130	.285	.355	36	.286	-8	34	38	3	3.5
1895	*Bal-N	10	4	.714	15	15	15	4	0	122¹	110	1	32	37	10.7	2.94	162	.237	.292	16	.314	1	25	25	-1	2.2
1896	Bal-N	11	9	.550	22	22	19	0	0	175²	195	4	55	33	13.0	3.48	123	.279	.334	9	.123	-7	17	16	0	0.7
1897	Bro-N	0	6	.000	9	7	5	0	0	63	71	1	29	13	15.3	5.86	70	.293	.372	5	.200	-1	-11	-12	-0	-0.9
Total	9	173	127	.577	321	305	279	14	4	2634	2726	52	945	967	12.9	3.51	118	.260	.326	230	.204	-29	172	182	21	15.8

● **JOHN McMAKIN**   McMakin, John Weaver "Spartanburg John" b: 3/6/1878, Spartanburg, S.C. d: 9/25/56, Lyman, S.C. BR/TL, 5′11″, 165 lbs. Deb: 4/19/02

YEAR	TM/L	W	L	PCT	G	GS	CG	SH	SV	IP	H	HR	BB	SO	RAT	ERA	ERA+	OAV	OOB	BH	AVG	PB	PR	/A	PD	TPI
1902	Bro-N	2	2	.500	4	4	4	0	0	32	34	0	11	6	13.2	3.09	89	.272	.341	2	.182	1	-1	-1	-0	-0.1

● **JOE McMANUS**   McManus, Joab Logan b: 9/7/1887, Palmyra, Ill. d: 12/23/55, Beckley, W.Va. BR/TR, 5′11″, 180 lbs. Deb: 4/12/13

YEAR	TM/L	W	L	PCT	G	GS	CG	SH	SV	IP	H	HR	BB	SO	RAT	ERA	ERA+	OAV	OOB	BH	AVG	PB	PR	/A	PD	TPI
1913	Cin-N	0	0	—	1	0	0	0	0	2	3	0	4	1	31.5	18.00	18	.375	.583			0	-3	-3	0	0.0

● **PAT McMANUS**   McManus, Patrick b: Ireland d: 10/6/17, Brooklyn, N.Y. Deb: 5/22/1879

YEAR	TM/L	W	L	PCT	G	GS	CG	SH	SV	IP	H	HR	BB	SO	RAT	ERA	ERA+	OAV	OOB	BH	AVG	PB	PR	/A	PD	TPI
1879	Tro-N	0	2	.000	2	2	2	0	0	21	24	1	4	6	10.7	3.00	83	.258	.266	1	.125	0	-1	-1	-0	-0.1

● **GREG McMICHAEL**   McMichael, Gregory Winston b: 12/1/66, Knoxville, Tenn. BR/TR, 6′3″, 215 lbs. Deb: 4/12/93

YEAR	TM/L	W	L	PCT	G	GS	CG	SH	SV	IP	H	HR	BB	SO	RAT	ERA	ERA+	OAV	OOB	BH	AVG	PB	PR	/A	PD	TPI
1993	*Atl-N	2	3	.400	74	0	0	0	19	91²	68	3	29	89	9.5	2.06	195	.206	.270	0	.000	-0	20	20	2	2.0
1994	Atl-N	4	6	.400	51	0	0	0	21	58²	66	1	19	47	13.0	3.84	108	.280	.333	0	.000	-0	2	2	-1	0.4
Total	2	6	9	.400	125	0	0	0	40	150¹	134	4	48	136	10.9	2.75	148	.237	.296	0	.000	-1	23	22	1	2.4

● **GEORGE McMULLEN**   McMullen, George b: California Deb: 7/2/1887

YEAR	TM/L	W	L	PCT	G	GS	CG	SH	SV	IP	H	HR	BB	SO	RAT	ERA	ERA+	OAV	OOB	BH	AVG	PB	PR	/A	PD	TPI
1887	NY-a	2	1	.667	3	3	2	0	0	21	25	2	19	2	18.9	7.71	55	.269	.393	1	.083	-2	-8	-8	0	-0.8

● **JOHN McMULLIN**   McMullin, John F. "Lefty" b: 1848, Philadelphia, Pa. d: 4/11/1881, Philadelphia, Pa. BR/TL, 5′9″, 160 lbs. Deb: 5/9/1871 ◆

YEAR	TM/L	W	L	PCT	G	GS	CG	SH	SV	IP	H	HR	BB	SO	RAT	ERA	ERA+	OAV	OOB	BH	AVG	PB	PR	/A	PD	TPI
1871	Tro-n	12	15	.444	29	29	28	0	0	249	430	4	75	12	18.3	5.53	76	.342	.379	38	.279	1	-36	-36		-2.2
1872	Mut-n	1	0	1.000	3	1	1	0	0	15	18	0	2	1	12.0	3.60	96	.247	.267	60	.253	0	-0	-0		0.0
1873	Ath-n	1	0	1.000	1	1	1	0	0	8	10	0	1	2	12.4	2.25	152	.303	.324	62	.273	0	1	1		0.1
1875	Phi-n	0	0	—	4	0	0	0	0	12²	31	0	1	0	22.7	6.39	39	.425	.432	56	.251	2	-6	-5		0.0
Total	4 n	14	15	.483	37	31	30	0	0	284²	489	4	79	15	15.7	5.37	47	.340	.374	305	.281	2	-92	-90		-2.1

● **CRAIG McMURTRY**   McMurtry, Joe Craig b: 11/5/59, Troy, Tex. BR/TR, 6′5″, 195 lbs. Deb: 4/10/83

YEAR	TM/L	W	L	PCT	G	GS	CG	SH	SV	IP	H	HR	BB	SO	RAT	ERA	ERA+	OAV	OOB	BH	AVG	PB	PR	/A	PD	TPI
1983	Atl-N	15	9	.625	36	35	3	0	0	224²	204	13	88	105	11.7	3.08	126	.243	.315	6	.086	-4	14	20	3	2.0
1984	Atl-N	9	17	.346	37	30	0	0	0	183¹	184	16	102	99	14.1	4.32	89	.268	.363	6	.115	-1	-15	-10	4	-1.0
1985	Atl-N	0	3	.000	17	6	0	0	1	45	56	6	27	28	16.8	6.60	58	.306	.398	1	.071	-0	-15	-14	1	-0.9
1986	Atl-N	1	6	.143	37	5	0	0	0	79²	82	7	43	50	14.3	4.74	84	.265	.359	2	.125	-0	-9	-7	0	-0.6
1988	Tex-A	3	3	.500	32	0	0	0	3	60	37	5	24	35	9.3	2.25	181	.180	.270		—		11	12	1	1.3
1989	Tex-A	0	0	—	19	0	0	0	0	23	29	3	13	14	17.2	7.43	53	.312	.407		—		-9	-9	0	0.0
1990	Tex-A	0	3	.000	23	3	0	0	0	42	43	4	30	14	16.0	4.32	91	.281	.402	0	—	-0	-2	-2	1	-0.1
Total	7	28	41	.406	201	79	6	3	4	657¹	635	54	327	345	13.3	4.03	97	.257	.346	15	.099	-6	-25	-9	10	0.7

● **EDGAR McNABB**   McNabb, Edgar J. "Texas" b: 10/24/1865, Coshocton, Ohio d: 2/28/1894, Pittsburgh, Pa. BR/TR, 5′11.5″, 170 lbs. Deb: 5/12/1893

YEAR	TM/L	W	L	PCT	G	GS	CG	SH	SV	IP	H	HR	BB	SO	RAT	ERA	ERA+	OAV	OOB	BH	AVG	PB	PR	/A	PD	TPI
1893	Bal-N	8	7	.533	21	14	12	0	0	142	167	5	53	18	14.5	4.12	115	.284	.352	13	.194	-0	9	10	0	0.6

● **DAVE McNALLY**   McNally, David Arthur b: 10/31/42, Billings, Mont. BR/TL, 5′11″, 190 lbs. Deb: 9/26/62

YEAR	TM/L	W	L	PCT	G	GS	CG	SH	SV	IP	H	HR	BB	SO	RAT	ERA	ERA+	OAV	OOB	BH	AVG	PB	PR	/A	PD	TPI
1962	Bal-A	1	0	1.000	1	1	1	1	0	9	2	0	3	4	5.0	0.00	—	.071	.161	0	.000	-0	4	4	0	0.4
1963	Bal-A	7	8	.467	29	20	2	0	1	125²	133	9	55	78	13.8	4.58	76	.276	.356	2	.053	-2	-13	-15	-1	-2.0
1964	Bal-A	9	11	.450	30	23	5	3	0	159¹	157	15	51	88	12.3	3.67	97	.260	.327	7	.137	0	-1	-2	-0	-0.2

YEAR TM/L	W	L	PCT	G	GS	CG	SH	SV	IP	H	HR	BB	SO	RAT	ERA	ERA+	OAV	OOB	BH	AVG	PB	PR	/A	PD	TPI
1965 Bal-A	11	6	.647	35	29	6	2	0	198²	163	15	73	116	11.0	2.85	122	.222	.298	6	.092	-3	13	14	0	0.9
1966 *Bal-A	13	6	.684	34	33	5	1	0	213	212	22	64	158	11.8	3.17	105	.256	.313	15	.195	3	6	4	0	0.6
1967 Bal-A	7	7	.500	24	22	3	1	0	119	134	13	39	70	13.2	4.54	69	.295	.354	6	.158	-0	-17	-18	-2	-2.2
1968 Bal-A	22	10	.688	35	35	18	5	0	273	175	24	55	202	**7.9**	1.95	150	.182	.234	11	.128	4	31	30	-3	3.9
1969 *Bal-A★	20	7	.741	41	40	11	4	0	268²	232	21	84	166	10.8	3.22	111	.234	.297	8	.085	-2	12	10	-4	0.4
1970 *Bal-A☆	**24**	9	.727	40	40	16	1	0	296	277	29	78	185	11.0	3.22	113	.250	.304	14	.133	4	16	14	-2	1.6
1971 *Bal-A	21	5	**.808**	30	30	11	1	0	224¹	188	24	58	91	10.1	2.89	116	.229	.284	12	.162	3	14	12	-0	1.6
1972 Bal-A★	13	17	.433	36	36	12	6	0	241	220	15	68	120	10.8	2.95	104	.247	.302	12	.152	2	3	3	1	0.7
1973 Bal-A	17	17	.500	38	38	17	4	0	266	247	16	81	87	11.3	3.21	116	.251	.312	0	—	0	18	15	1	2.0
1974 *Bal-A	16	10	.615	39	37	13	4	1	259	260	16	81	111	12.1	3.58	96	.270	.331	0	—	0	1	-4	2	-0.1
1975 Mon-N	3	6	.333	12	12	0	0	0	77¹	88	8	36	36	14.9	5.24	73	.280	.362	4	.190	0	-14	-12	-1	-1.1
Total 14	184	119	.607	424	396	120	33	2	2730	2488	230	826	1512	11.2	3.24	106	.245	.306	97	.133	10	74	54	-8	6.5

● **TIM McNAMARA**   McNamara, Timothy Augustine b: 11/20/1898, Millville, Mass.   BR/TR, 5'11", 170 lbs.   Deb: 4/27/22

YEAR TM/L	W	L	PCT	G	GS	CG	SH	SV	IP	H	HR	BB	SO	RAT	ERA	ERA+	OAV	OOB	BH	AVG	PB	PR	/A	PD	TPI
1922 Bos-N	3	4	.429	24	5	4	2	0	70²	55	2	26	16	10.4	2.42	165	.225	.303	2	.118	-1	**13**	**12**	-0	1.0
1923 Bos-N	3	13	.188	32	16	3	0	0	139¹	185	8	29	32	14.1	4.91	81	.320	.357	7	.179	1	-14	-14	-2	-1.5
1924 Bos-N	8	12	.400	35	21	6	2	0	179	242	9	31	35	13.9	5.18	74	.334	.364	6	.140	-1	-26	-27	1	-2.6
1925 Bos-N	0	0	—	1	0	0	0	0	0²	6	0	2	1	108.0	81.00	5	.857	.889	0	—	0	-6	-6	0	-0.6
1926 NY-N	0	0	—	6	0	0	0	0	6	7	0	4	4	16.5	9.00	42	.304	.407	0	—	0	-3	-3	0	0.0
Total 5	14	29	.326	98	42	13	4	0	395²	495	19	92	88	13.6	4.78	82	.314	.355	15	.152	-1	-36	-38	-2	-3.1

● **GORDON McNAUGHTON**   McNaughton, Gordon Joseph b: 7/31/10, Chicago, Ill. d: 8/6/42, Chicago, Ill.   BR/TR, 6'1", 190 lbs.   Deb: 8/13/32

YEAR TM/L	W	L	PCT	G	GS	CG	SH	SV	IP	H	HR	BB	SO	RAT	ERA	ERA+	OAV	OOB	BH	AVG	PB	PR	/A	PD	TPI
1932 Bos-A	0	1	.000	6	2	0	0	0	21	21	1	22	6	19.7	6.43	70	.259	.434	2	.250	0	-5	-5	1	-0.1

● **HARRY McNEAL**   McNeal, John Harley b: 8/11/1877, Iberia, Ohio d: 1/11/45, Cleveland, Ohio   BR/TR, 6'3", 175 lbs.   Deb: 8/5/01

YEAR TM/L	W	L	PCT	G	GS	CG	SH	SV	IP	H	HR	BB	SO	RAT	ERA	ERA+	OAV	OOB	BH	AVG	PB	PR	/A	PD	TPI
1901 Cle-A	5	5	.500	12	10	9	0	0	85¹	120	4	30	15	16.7	4.43	80	.328	.391	6	.162	-2	-7	-8	-2	-1.1

● **ED McNICHOL**   McNichol, Edwin Briggs b: 1/10/1879, Martins Ferry, O. d: 11/1/52, Salineville, O.   BR/TR, 5'5", 170 lbs.   Deb: 7/9/04

YEAR TM/L	W	L	PCT	G	GS	CG	SH	SV	IP	H	HR	BB	SO	RAT	ERA	ERA+	OAV	OOB	BH	AVG	PB	PR	/A	PD	TPI
1904 Bos-N	2	12	.143	17	15	12	1	0	122	120	3	74	39	14.7	4.28	64	.262	.371	4	.093	-4	-21	-21	-2	-2.6

● **FRANK McPARTLIN**   McPartlin, Frank b: 2/16/1872, Hoosick Falls, N.Y d: 11/13/43, New York, N.Y.   TR, 6', 180 lbs.   Deb: 8/22/1899

YEAR TM/L	W	L	PCT	G	GS	CG	SH	SV	IP	H	HR	BB	SO	RAT	ERA	ERA+	OAV	OOB	BH	AVG	PB	PR	/A	PD	TPI
1899 NY-N	0	0	—	1	0	0	0	0	4	4	0	3	2	20.3	4.50	83	.260	.442	0	.000	-0	-0	-0	0	0.0

● **JOHN McPHERSON**   McPherson, John Jacob b: 3/9/1869, Easton, Pa. d: 9/30/41, Easton, Pa.   Deb: 7/12/01

YEAR TM/L	W	L	PCT	G	GS	CG	SH	SV	IP	H	HR	BB	SO	RAT	ERA	ERA+	OAV	OOB	BH	AVG	PB	PR	/A	PD	TPI
1901 Phi-A	0	1	.000	1	1	0	0	0	4	7	0	4	0	27.0	11.25	34	.377	.510	0	.000	-0	-3	-3	0	-0.5
1904 Phi-N	1	12	.077	15	12	11	1	0	128	130	1	46	32	12.8	3.66	73	.264	.334	3	.064	-4	-13	-14	0	-1.6
Total 2	1	13	.071	16	13	11	1	0	132	137	1	50	32	13.2	3.89	70	.268	.341	3	.063	-4	-16	-17	1	-2.1

● **HERB McQUAID**   McQuaid, Herbert George b: 3/29/1899, San Francisco, Cal d: 4/4/66, Richmond, Cal.   BR/TR, 6'2", 185 lbs.   Deb: 6/22/23

YEAR TM/L	W	L	PCT	G	GS	CG	SH	SV	IP	H	HR	BB	SO	RAT	ERA	ERA+	OAV	OOB	BH	AVG	PB	PR	/A	PD	TPI
1923 Cin-N	1	0	1.000	12	1	0	0	0	34¹	31	0	9	11	11.5	2.36	164	.238	.308	0	.000	-1	6	6	1	0.1
1926 NY-A	1	0	1.000	17	1	0	0	0	38¹	48	5	13	6	14.8	6.10	81	.329	.391	0	.000	-1	-9	-10	0	-0.3
Total 2	2	0	1.000	29	2	0	0	0	72²	79	5	23	15	13.3	4.33	89	.286	.352	0	.000	-2	-3	-4	1	-0.2

● **MIKE McQUEEN**   McQueen, Michael Robert b: 8/30/50, Oklahoma City, Okla.   BL/TL, 5'11", 190 lbs.   Deb: 10/2/69

YEAR TM/L	W	L	PCT	G	GS	CG	SH	SV	IP	H	HR	BB	SO	RAT	ERA	ERA+	OAV	OOB	BH	AVG	PB	PR	/A	PD	TPI
1969 Atl-N	0	0	—	1	1	0	0	0	3	2	0	3	3	15.0	3.00	120	.182	.357	0	—	0	0	0	-0	0.0
1970 Atl-N	1	5	.167	22	8	1	0	1	66	67	10	31	54	13.5	5.59	77	.266	.349	6	.300	2	-11	-10	-1	-0.7
1971 Atl-N	4	1	.800	17	3	0	0	1	56	47	7	23	38	11.6	3.54	105	.228	.312	4	.211	0	-0	-1	-1	0.0
1972 Atl-N	0	5	.000	23	7	1	0	1	78¹	79	11	44	40	14.2	4.60	82	.260	.355	2	.087	-2	-10	-7	-1	-0.7
1974 Cin-N	0	0	—	10	0	0	0	0	15	17	4	11	5	16.8	5.40	65	.288	.400	1	1.000	0	-3	-3	-1	-0.2
Total 5	5	11	.313	73	19	2	0	3	218¹	212	32	112	140	13.5	4.66	84	.255	.346	13	.206	1	-24	-18	-4	-1.4

● **GEORGE McQUILLAN**   McQuillan, George Watt b: 5/1/1885, Brooklyn, N.Y. d: 3/30/40, Columbus, Ohio   BR/TR, 5'11.5", 175 lbs.   Deb: 5/8/07

YEAR TM/L	W	L	PCT	G	GS	CG	SH	SV	IP	H	HR	BB	SO	RAT	ERA	ERA+	OAV	OOB	BH	AVG	PB	PR	/A	PD	TPI
1907 Phi-N	4	0	1.000	6	5	3	0	0	41	21	0	11	28	7.2	0.66	368	.158	.228	4	.364	3	8	8	-2	1.1
1908 Phi-N	23	17	.575	48	42	32	7	2	359²	263	1	91	114	9.0	1.53	159	.207	.263	18	.151	-1	33	36	-3	3.9
1909 Phi-N	13	16	.448	41	28	16	4	2	247²	202	5	54	96	9.3	2.14	121	.226	.271	9	.118	-3	13	13	-2	0.8
1910 Phi-N	9	6	.600	24	17	13	3	1	152¹	109	2	50	71	9.6	1.60	196	.204	.276	7	.149	-1	24	26	-0	2.4
1911 Cin-N	2	6	.250	19	5	2	0	0	77	92	2	31	50	14.8	4.68	71	.308	.380	2	.091	-1	-11	-12	-1	-1.3
1913 Pit-N	8	6	.571	25	16	7	0	1	141²	144	1	35	59	11.4	3.43	88	.273	.319	4	.103	-1	-4	-7	-1	-0.8
1914 Pit-N	13	17	.433	45	28	15	0	4	259¹	248	8	60	96	11.0	2.98	89	.261	.310	5	.068	-4	-6	-10	-1	-1.5
1915 Pit-N	8	10	.444	30	20	9	0	1	149	160	1	39	56	12.1	2.84	96	.284	.332	4	.091	-3	-1	-2	-0	-0.5
Phi-N	4	3	.571	9	8	5	0	0	63²	60	1	11	13	10.2	2.12	129	.247	.282	1	.043	-2	4	4	-1	0.2
Yr	12	13	.480	39	28	14	0	1	212²	220	2	50	69	11.5	2.62	104	.272	.315	5	.075	-5	3	3	-1	-0.3
1916 Phi-N	1	7	.125	21	3	1	0	2	62	58	2	15	22	11.0	2.76	96	.251	.305	1	.091	-1	-1	-0	-0.2
1918 Cle-A	0	1	.000	5	1	0	0	0	23	25	0	4	7	11.3	2.35	128	.284	.315	0	.000	-0	1	2	0	0.1
Total 10	85	89	.489	273	173	105	17	14	1576¹	1382	23	401	590	10.4	2.38	114	.241	.294	55	.117	-14	62	59	-9	4.2

● **HUGH McQUILLAN**   McQuillan, Hugh A. "Handsome Hugh" b: 9/15/1897, New York, N.Y. d: 8/26/47, New York, N.Y.   BR/TR, 6', 170 lbs.   Deb: 7/26/18

YEAR TM/L	W	L	PCT	G	GS	CG	SH	SV	IP	H	HR	BB	SO	RAT	ERA	ERA+	OAV	OOB	BH	AVG	PB	PR	/A	PD	TPI
1918 Bos-N	1	0	1.000	1	1	1	0	0	9	7	0	1	1	12.0	3.00	90	.219	.324	1	.250	0	-0	-0	0	0.0
1919 Bos-N	2	3	.400	16	7	2	0	1	60	64	4	13	12	12.2	3.45	83	.288	.332	4	.222	0	-4	-4	-1	-0.4
1920 Bos-N	11	15	.423	38	26	17	1	5	225²	230	3	70	53	12.0	3.55	86	.273	.330	19	.257	6	-10	-13	2	-0.6
1921 Bos-N	13	17	.433	45	31	13	2	5	250	284	9	90	94	13.5	4.00	91	.291	.352	18	.205	1	-6	-10	0	-0.9
1922 Bos-N	5	10	.333	28	17	7	0	0	136	154	4	56	33	14.0	4.24	94	.299	.369	7	.167	-1	-2	-4	-1	-0.4
*NY-N	6	5	.545	15	13	5	0	1	94¹	111	7	34	24	13.8	3.82	105	.301	.360	7	.189	-1	3	2	-1	0.0
Yr	11	15	.423	43	30	12	0	1	230¹	265	11	90	57	13.9	4.06	98	.299	.364	14	.177	-2	1	-2	-0	-0.4
1923 *NY-N	15	14	.517	38	32	15	5	0	229²	224	12	66	75	11.6	3.41	112	.259	.315	14	.171	-2	15	11	-1	0.8
1924 *NY-N	14	8	.636	27	23	14	1	3	184	179	8	43	49	11.0	2.69	136	.259	.304	14	.209	-1	24	20	-2	2.0
1925 NY-N	2	3	.400	14	11	2	0	1	70	95	9	23	23	15.3	6.04	67	.343	.395	3	.143	-1	-14	-16	1	-0.9
1926 NY-N	11	10	.524	33	22	12	1	0	167	171	7	42	47	11.5	3.72	101	.271	.318	7	.132	-3	2	1	2	0.0
1927 NY-N	5	4	.556	11	9	5	0	0	58	73	4	22	17	14.9	4.50	86	.309	.371	4	.211	1	-4	-4	0	-0.5
Bos-N	3	5	.375	13	11	2	0	0	78	109	2	24	17	15.6	5.54	67	.332	.381	5	.227	0	-14	-16	1	-1.3
Yr	8	9	.471	24	20	7	0	0	136	182	6	46	34	15.2	5.10	74	.322	.375	9	.220	1	-18	-20	1	-1.8
Total 10	88	94	.484	279	203	95	10	16	1561²	1703	67	489	446	12.7	3.83	95	.284	.340	103	.195	0	-10	-32	1	-2.2

● **NORM McRAE**   McRae, Norman b: 9/26/47, Elizabeth, N.J.   BR/TR, 6'1", 195 lbs.   Deb: 9/13/69

YEAR TM/L	W	L	PCT	G	GS	CG	SH	SV	IP	H	HR	BB	SO	RAT	ERA	ERA+	OAV	OOB	BH	AVG	PB	PR	/A	PD	TPI
1969 Det-A	0	0	—	3	0	0	0	0	3	2	0	1	4	9.0	6.00	62	.200	.273	0	—	0	-1	-1	-0	0.0
1970 Det-A	0	0	—	19	0	0	0	0	31¹	26	1	25	16	14.9	2.87	130	.226	.369	0	.000	-0	3	3	1	0.2
Total 2	0	0	—	22	0	0	0	0	34¹	28	1	26	19	14.4	3.15	118	.224	.362	0	.000	-0	3	3	0	0.0

● **TRICK McSORLEY**   McSorley, John Bernard b: 12/6/1858, St.Louis, Mo. d: 2/9/36, St.Louis, Mo.   TR, 5'4", 142 lbs.   Deb: 5/6/1875 ♦

YEAR TM/L	W	L	PCT	G	GS	CG	SH	SV	IP	H	HR	BB	SO	RAT	ERA	ERA+	OAV	OOB	BH	AVG	PB	PR	/A	PD	TPI
1884 Tol-a	0	0	—	1	0	0	0	0	12	5	0	2	0	22.5	4.50	76	.556	.556	17	.250	—	-0	-0	-0	0.0

● **BILL McTIGUE**   McTigue, William Patrick "Rebel" b: 1/3/1891, Nashville, Tenn. d: 5/8/20, Nashville, Tenn.   BL/TL, 6'1.5", 175 lbs.   Deb: 5/2/11 ♦

YEAR TM/L	W	L	PCT	G	GS	CG	SH	SV	IP	H	HR	BB	SO	RAT	ERA	ERA+	OAV	OOB	BH	AVG	PB	PR	/A	PD	TPI
1911 Bos-N	0	5	.000	14	8	1	0	0	37	37	3	49	23	21.4	7.05	54	.280	.481	1	.083	-1	-15	-13	-1	-1.7
1912 Bos-N	2	0	1.000	10	1	0	0	0	34²	39	0	18	17	14.8	5.45	66	.289	.373	1	.077	-1	-8	-7	1	-0.4
1916 Det-A	0	0	—	3	0	0	0	0	5¹	5	0	5	1	16.9	5.06	57	.278	.435	0	.000	-0	-1	-1	0	0.0
Total 3	2	5	.286	27	9	1	0	0	77	81	3	72	41	18.1	6.19	59	.284	.432	2	.077	-2	-24	-22	0	-2.1

YEAR TM/L	W	L	PCT	G	GS	CG	SH	SV	IP	H	HR	BB	SO	RAT	ERA	ERA+	OAV	OOB	BH	AVG	PB	PR	/A	PD	TPI

● CAL McVEY McVey, Calvin Alexander b: 8/30/1850, Montrose, Iowa d: 8/20/26, San Francisco, Cal BR/TR, 5'9", 170 lbs. Deb: 5/5/1871 M◆

1875 Bos-n	1	0	1.000	3	2	0	0	1	11	15	0	1		13.1	3.27	72	.294	.308	137	.352	2	-1	-1		0.0
1876 Chi-N	5	2	.714	11	6	5	0	2	59¹	57	0	2	9	8.9	1.52	161	.235	.241	107	.347	3	5	6	0	0.8
1877 Chi-N	4	8	.333	17	10	6	0	2	92	129	2	11	20	13.7	4.50	66	.301	.319	98	.368	6	-17	-16	-1	-1.4
1879 Cin-N	0	2	.000	3	1	1	0	0	14	34	1	2	7	23.1	8.36	28	.453	.468	105	.297	1	-9	-9	0	-0.9
Total 3	9	12	.429	31	17	12	0	4	165¹	220	3	15	36	12.8	3.76	73	.295	.309	393	.328	10	-21	-19	-1	-1.5

● DOUG McWEENY McWeeny, Douglas Lawrence "Buzz" b: 8/17/1896, Chicago, Ill. d: 1/1/53, Melrose Park, Ill. BR/TR, 6'2", 190 lbs. Deb: 4/24/21

1921 Chi-A	3	6	.333	27	8	3	0	2	97²	127	7	45	46	15.8	6.08	70	.325	.394	1	.032	-4	-20	-20	-1	-2.0
1922 Chi-A	0	1	.000	4	1	0	0	0	10²	13	0	7	5	16.9	5.91	69	.325	.426	0	.000	0	-2	-2	-0	-0.2
1924 Chi-A	1	3	.250	13	5	2	0	0	43¹	47	2	17	18	13.7	4.57	90	.294	.369	0	.000	-0	-2	-3	3	0.1
1926 Bro-N	11	13	.458	42	24	10	1	1	216¹	213	6	84	96	12.7	3.04	126	.258	.333	7	.109	-4	19	19	-1	1.4
1927 Bro-N	4	8	.333	34	22	6	0	1	164¹	167	13	70	73	13.4	3.56	111	.266	.347	2	.043	-4	7	7	1	0.2
1928 Bro-N	14	14	.500	42	32	12	4	1	244	218	11	114	79	12.4	3.17	125	.235	.322	14	.173	-1	22	23	3	2.5
1929 Bro-N	4	10	.286	36	24	4	0	1	146	167	17	93	59	16.2	6.10	76	.288	.390	5	.104	-2	-22	-24	-2	-2.2
1930 Cin-N	0	2	.000	8	2	0	0	0	25²	28	0	20	10	16.8	7.36	66	.283	.403	1	.143	-0	-7	-7	0	-0.4
Total 8	37	57	.394	206	118	37	5	6	948	980	56	450	386	13.8	4.17	98	.269	.353	30	.104	-16	-5	-7	2	-0.6

● LARRY McWILLIAMS McWilliams, Larry Dean b: 2/10/54, Wichita, Kan. BL/TL, 6'5", 180 lbs. Deb: 7/17/78

1978 Atl-N	9	3	.750	15	15	3	1	0	99¹	84	11	35	42	11.0	2.81	144	.224	.294	2	.063	-2	8	14	1	1.6
1979 Atl-N	3	2	.600	13	13	1	0	0	66¹	69	4	22	32	12.9	5.56	73	.272	.339	5	.208	1	-13	-11	1	-0.5
1980 Atl-N	9	14	.391	30	30	4	1	0	163²	188	27	39	77	12.9	4.95	76	.285	.332	8	.157	-0	-25	-22	-0	-2.8
1981 Atl-N	2	1	.667	6	5	2	1	0	37²	31	2	8	23	9.3	3.11	115	.230	.273	1	.100	-2	2	2	1	0.2
1982 Atl-N	2	3	.400	27	2	0	0	0	37²	52	3	20	24	17.7	6.21	60	.327	.409	1	.167	-0	-11	-10	2	-1.1
Pit-N	6	5	.545	19	18	2	2	1	121²	106	9	24	94	9.9	3.11	119	.232	.276	6	.188	-0	7	8	2	0.9
Yr	8	8	.500	46	20	2	2	1	159¹	158	12	44	118	11.6	3.84	97	.255	.309	7	.184	-0	-4	-2	4	-0.2
1983 Pit-N	15	8	.652	35	35	8	4	0	238	205	19	87	199	11.2	3.25	114	.230	.300	9	.114	-3	10	12	1	0.9
1984 Pit-N	12	11	.522	34	32	7	2	0	227¹	226	18	78	149	12.1	2.93	123	.263	.326	9	.122	-3	17	17	0	1.3
1985 Pit-N	7	9	.438	30	19	2	0	0	126¹	139	9	62	52	14.8	4.70	76	.283	.371	5	.125	-1	-16	-16	-0	-1.9
1986 Pit-N	3	11	.214	49	15	0	0	0	122¹	129	16	49	80	13.6	5.15	74	.268	.345	4	.138	-0	-19	-18	-0	-1.9
1987 Atl-N	0	1	.000	9	2	0	0	0	20¹	25	2	7	13	15.0	5.75	76	.301	.370	1	.200	-0	-4	-3	0	-0.1
1988 StL-N	6	9	.400	42	17	2	1	1	136	130	10	45	70	11.8	3.90	89	.253	.319	6	.162	1	-7	-6	-0	-0.7
1989 Phi-N	2	11	.154	40	16	2	1	0	120²	134	9	49	54	13.1	4.10	86	.265	.340	3	.111	-1	-8	-7	1	-0.8
KC-A	2	2	.500	8	5	1	0	0	32²	31	2	8	24	11.6	4.13	93	.254	.316	0	—	0	-1	-1	-0	-0.1
1990 KC-A	0	0	—	13	0	0	0	0	8¹	10	2	9	7	21.6	9.72	39	.313	.476	0	—	0	-5	-5	0	-0.5
Total 13	78	90	.464	370	224	34	13	3	1558¹	1548	137	542	940	12.4	3.99	93	.259	.326	60	.135	-8	-66	-48	8	-4.9

● RUSTY MEACHAM Meacham, Russell Loren b: 1/27/68, Stuart, Fla. BR/TR, 6'2", 166 lbs. Deb: 6/29/91

1991 Det-A	2	1	.667	10	4	0	0	0	27²	35	4	11	14	15.0	5.20	80	.315	.377	0	—	0	-3	-3	0	-0.4
1992 KC-A	10	4	.714	64	0	0	0	2	101²	88	5	21	64	9.7	2.74	148	.233	.275	0	—	0	13	15	2	2.0
1993 KC-A	2	2	.500	15	0	0	0	0	21	31	2	5	13	16.7	5.57	82	.326	.379	0	—	0	-3	-2	0	-0.6
1994 KC-A	3	3	.500	36	0	0	0	4	50²	51	7	12	36	11.5	3.73	139	.263	.313	0	—	0	6	8	0	0.4
Total 4	17	10	.630	125	4	0	0	6	201	205	18	49	127	11.6	3.63	121	.263	.312	0	—	0	13	17	2	1.4

● JOHNNY MEADOR Meador, John Davis b: 12/4/1892, Madison, N.C. d: 4/11/70, Winston-Salem, N.C BR/TR, 5'10.5", 165 lbs. Deb: 4/24/20

| 1920 Pit-N | 0 | 2 | .000 | 12 | 2 | 0 | 0 | 0 | 36¹ | 48 | 1 | 7 | 5 | 13.6 | 4.21 | 76 | .340 | .372 | 1 | .167 | -0 | -4 | -4 | 1 | -0.2 |

● LEE MEADOWS Meadows, Henry Lee "Specs" b: 7/12/1894, Oxford, N.C. d: 1/29/63, Daytona Beach, Fla BL/TR, 6', 190 lbs. Deb: 4/19/15

1915 StL-N	13	11	.542	39	26	14	1	0	244	232	5	88	104	12.0	2.99	93	.259	.329	8	.096	-4	-6	-5	-3	-1.2
1916 StL-N	12	23	.343	51	36	11	1	2	289	261	3	119	120	12.3	2.58	102	.247	.332	15	.158	-1	1	2	1	0.2
1917 StL-N	15	9	.625	43	37	18	4	2	265²	253	5	90	100	11.8	3.08	87	.262	.328	9	.101	-6	-11	-12	-3	-2.0
1918 StL-N	8	14	.364	30	23	12	0	1	165¹	176	1	56	49	13.2	3.59	75	.280	.348	7	.127	-2	-15	-16	-2	-2.5
1919 StL-N	4	10	.286	22	12	3	1	0	92	100	3	30	28	12.9	3.03	92	.292	.352	3	.103	-2	-1	-2	-3	-0.3
Phi-N	8	10	.444	18	17	15	3	0	158¹	128	2	49	88	10.5	2.33	138	.229	.300	6	.118	-3	10	16	-1	1.4
Yr	12	20	.375	40	29	18	4	0	250¹	228	5	79	116	11.3	2.59	118	.252	.317	9	.112	-5	9	13	2	1.1
1920 Phi-N	16	14	.533	35	33	19	3	0	247	249	5	90	95	12.6	2.84	120	.270	.341	14	.171	-3	8	16	0	1.6
1921 Phi-N	11	16	.407	28	27	15	2	0	194¹	226	10	62	52	13.5	4.31	98	.288	.343	13	.210	2	-11	-2	4	0.4
1922 Phi-N	12	18	.400	33	34	19	2	0	237	264	8	71	62	13.1	4.03	116	.288	.346	27	.314	3	2	17	3	2.6
1923 Phi-N	1	3	.250	8	5	0	0	1	19²	27	0	15	10	25.2	13.27	35	.430	.509	4	.400	-2	-20	-19	0	-2.8
Pit-N	16	10	.615	31	25	17	1	0	227	250	3	44	66	11.7	3.01	133	.284	.319	22	.250	3	25	25	2	3.1
Yr	17	13	.567	39	30	17	1	1	246²	290	3	59	76	12.8	3.83	106	.298	.339	26	.265	5	5	6	2	0.3
1924 Pit-N	13	12	.520	36	30	15	3	0	229¹	240	7	51	61	11.6	3.26	118	.278	.322	16	.195	-1	16	15	-1	1.2
1925 *Pit-N	19	10	.655	35	31	20	1	1	255¹	272	11	67	87	12.2	3.67	122	.273	.323	17	.175	-1	17	23	1	2.2
1926 Pit-N	20	9	.690	36	31	15	1	0	226²	254	10	52	54	12.3	3.97	99	.287	.329	20	.227	-1	-4	-1	3	0.1
1927 *Pit-N	19	10	.655	40	38	25	2	0	299¹	315	11	66	84	11.7	3.40	121	.273	.317	18	.157	-5	17	24	-1	1.5
1928 Pit-N	1	1	.500	4	2	1	0	0	10	18	0	5	3	20.7	8.10	50	.383	.442	2	.500	-1	-5	-4	-0	-0.7
1929 Pit-N	0	0		1	0	0	0	0	0²	1	0	0	0	40.5	13.50	35	.500	.600	0	—	-0	-1	-0	0	-0.0
Total 15	188	180	.511	490	406	219	25	7	3160²	3280	84	956	1063	12.3	3.37	106	.274	.332	201	.180	-19	22	71	6	4.8

● RUFUS MEADOWS Meadows, Rufus Rivers b: 8/25/07, Chase City, Va. d: 5/10/70, Wichita, Kan. BL/TL, 5'11", 175 lbs. Deb: 4/23/26

| 1926 Cin-N | 0 | 0 | — | 1 | 0 | 0 | 0 | 0 | 0 | 0 | 0 | 0 | 0 | — | 0.00 | — | .000 | .000 | 0 | .000 | -0 | 0 | 0 | 0 | 0.0 |

● DAVE MEADS Meads, David Donald b: 1/7/64, Montclair, N.J. BL/TL, 6' ", 175 lbs. Deb: 4/13/87

1987 Hou-N	5	3	.625	45	0	0	0	0	48²	60	8	16	32	14.2	5.55	71	.321	.377	1	.333	1	-8	-9	-1	-1.3
1988 Hou-N	3	1	.750	22	2	0	0	0	39²	37	4	14	27	11.6	3.18	105	.240	.304	1	.250	1	1	1	-0	0.1
Total 2	8	4	.667	67	2	0	0	0	88¹	97	12	30	59	13.0	4.48	81	.284	.344	2	.286	1	-7	-8	-1	-1.2

● GEORGE MEAKIM Meakim, George Clinton b: 7/11/1865, Brooklyn, N.Y. d: 2/17/23, Queens, N.Y. BR/TR, 5'7.5", 154 lbs. Deb: 5/2/1890

1890 *Lou-a	12	7	.632	28	21	16	3	1	192	173	4	63	123	11.3	2.91	132	.233	.298	11	.153	-2	21	20	-1	1.4
1891 Phi-a	1	4	.200	6	6	4	0	0	35	51	1	22	13	19.9	6.94	55	.329	.415	3	.200	-2	-13	-12	2	-1.1
1892 Chi-N	0	1	.000	1	1	1	0	0	9	18	0	2	0	20.0	11.00	30	.400	.426	2	.400	-0	-8	-8	-0	-0.5
Cin-N	1	1	.500	3	3	1	0	0	13²	19	1	9	11	19.8	8.56	38	.317	.423	0	.000	-1	-8	-8	-0	-0.9
Yr	1	2	.333	4	4	2	0	0	22²	37	1	11	11	19.9	9.53	35	.352	.424	2	.200	-1	-16	-16	-0	-1.4
1895 Lou-N	1	0	1.000	1	1	1	0	0	7	7	0	4	2	14.1	2.57	180	.256	.352	1	.333	0	2	2	0	0.2
Total 4	15	13	.536	39	32	23	3	1	256²	268	6	100	142	13.2	4.03	95	.260	.331	17	.170	-2	-6	-6	1	-0.9

● DOC MEDICH Medich, George Francis b: 12/9/48, Aliquippa, Pa. BR/TR, 6'5", 227 lbs. Deb: 9/5/72

1972 NY-A	0	0	—	1	1	0	0	0	0	2	0	2	0	—	∞	—	1.000	1.000	0	—	0	-2	-2	-1	-0.2
1973 NY-A	14	9	.609	34	32	11	3	0	235	217	20	74	145	11.3	2.95	124	.244	.300	0	—	0	23	19	-2	1.7
1974 NY-A	19	15	.559	38	38	17	4	0	279²	275	24	91	154	12.0	3.60	97	.259	.323	0	—	0	-0	-4	-1	-0.3
1975 NY-A	16	16	.500	38	37	15	2	0	272¹	271	25	74	132	11.4	3.50	104	.264	.313	0	—	0	8	4	-3	0.4
1976 Pit-N	8	11	.421	29	26	3	0	0	179	193	10	46	84	12.2	3.52	99	.281	.330	5	.096	-2	-0	-1	-1	-0.3
1977 Oak-A	10	6	.625	26	25	3	0	0	147²	155	19	49	74	12.6	4.69	86	.265	.325	0	—	0	-10	-11	-1	-1.0
Sea-A	2	0	1.000	3	3	0	0	0	22¹	26	1	4	3	12.9	3.63	113	.286	.330	0	—	0	1	1	-1	0.1
Yr	12	6	.667	29	28	3	0	0	170	181	20	53	77	12.5	4.55	89	.265	.319	0	M◆	0	-9	-10	-2	-0.9

YEAR	TM/L	W	L	PCT	G	GS	CG	SH	SV	IP	H	HR	BB	SO	RAT	ERA	ERA+	OAV	OOB	BH	AVG	PB	PR	/A	PD	TPI
	NY-N	0	1	.000	1	1	0	0	0	7	6	0	1	3	9.0	3.86	97	.261	.292	0	.000	-0	0	-0	-0	-0.1
1978	Tex-A	9	8	.529	28	22	6	2	2	171	166	10	52	71	11.6	3.74	100	.255	.313	0	—	0	0	0	1	0.1
1979	Tex-A	10	7	.588	29	19	4	1	0	149	156	9	49	58	12.6	4.17	100	.269	.330	0	—	0	1	-0	1	0.2
1980	Tex-A	14	11	.560	34	32	6	0	0	204¹	230	13	56	91	12.7	3.92	99	.285	.334	0	—	0	3	-1	-1	-0.2
1981	Tex-A	10	6	.625	20	20	4	4	0	143¹	136	8	33	65	10.7	3.08	113	.252	.297	0	—	0	9	6	1	1.1
1982	Tex-A	7	11	.389	21	21	2	0	0	122²	146	8	61	37	15.4	5.06	76	.307	.390	0	—	0	-13	-16	-0	-1.7
	*Mil-A	5	4	.556	10	10	1	0	0	63	57	4	32	36	12.9	5.00	76	.242	.335	0	—	0	-6	-9	-1	-0.6
	Yr	12	15	.444	31	31	3	0	0	185²	203	12	93	73	14.4	5.04	76	.281	.364	0	—	0	-20	-25	-0	-2.3
Total 11		124	105	.541	312	287	71	16	2	1996¹	2036	151	624	955	12.1	3.78	98	.266	.324	5	.093	-2	13	-13	-5	-0.6

● IRV MEDLINGER
Medlinger, Irving John b: 6/18/27, Chicago, Ill. d: 9/3/75, Wheeling, Ill. BL/TL, 5'11", 185 lbs. Deb: 4/20/49

YEAR	TM/L	W	L	PCT	G	GS	CG	SH	SV	IP	H	HR	BB	SO	RAT	ERA	ERA+	OAV	OOB	BH	AVG	PB	PR	/A	PD	TPI
1949	StL-A	0	0	—	3	0	0	0	0	4	11	1	3	4	31.5	27.00	17	.478	.538	0	—	0	-10	-10	-0	0.0
1951	StL-A	0	0	—	6	0	0	0	0	9²	10	1	12	5	20.5	8.38	52	.270	.449	0	—	0	-5	-4	-0	0.0
Total 2		0	0	—	9	0	0	0	0	13²	21	2	15	9	23.7	13.83	32	.350	.480	0	—	0	-15	-14	-0	0.0

● SCOTT MEDVIN
Medvin, Scott Howard b: 9/16/61, North Olmsted, O. BR/TR, 6'1", 195 lbs. Deb: 5/11/88

YEAR	TM/L	W	L	PCT	G	GS	CG	SH	SV	IP	H	HR	BB	SO	RAT	ERA	ERA+	OAV	OOB	BH	AVG	PB	PR	/A	PD	TPI
1988	Pit-N	3	0	1.000	17	0	0	0	0	27²	23	1	9	16	10.7	4.88	70	.230	.300	0	.000	-0	-4	-5	0	-0.5
1989	Pit-N	0	1	.000	6	0	0	0	0	6¹	6	0	5	4	15.6	5.68	59	.240	.367			0	-2	-2	0	-0.2
1990	Sea-A	0	1	.000	5	0	0	0	0	4¹	7	0	2	1	20.8	6.23	64	.368	.455			0	-1	-0	0	-0.2
Total 3		3	2	.600	28	0	0	0	0	38¹	36	1	16	21	12.7	5.17	67	.250	.333	0	.000	-0	-7	-7	1	-0.9

● PETE MEEGAN
Meegan, Peter J. "Steady Pete" b: 11/13/1863, San Francisco, Cal d: 3/15/05, San Francisco, Cal Deb: 8/12/1884

YEAR	TM/L	W	L	PCT	G	GS	CG	SH	SV	IP	H	HR	BB	SO	RAT	ERA	ERA+	OAV	OOB	BH	AVG	PB	PR	/A	PD	TPI
1884	Ric-a	7	12	.368	22	22	22	1	0	179	177	9	29	106	11.1	4.32	77	.246	.288	12	.160	-2	-21	-20	2	-1.7
1885	Pit-a	7	8	.467	18	16	14	1	0	146	146	1	38	58	12.0	3.39	95	.247	.303	13	.194	-1	-2	-3	-1	-0.4
Total 2		14	20	.412	40	38	36	2	0	325	323	8	67	164	11.5	3.90	84	.246	.295	25	.176	-3	-24	-23	1	-2.1

● BILL MEEHAN
Meehan, William Thomas b: 9/4/1889, Osceola Mills, Pa. d: 10/8/82, Douglas, Wyo. BR/TR, 5'9", 155 lbs. Deb: 9/17/15

YEAR	TM/L	W	L	PCT	G	GS	CG	SH	SV	IP	H	HR	BB	SO	RAT	ERA	ERA+	OAV	OOB	BH	AVG	PB	PR	/A	PD	TPI
1915	Phi-A	0	1	.000	1	1	0	0	0	4	7	0	3	4	22.5	11.25	26	.389	.476	1	1.000	0	-4	-4	0	-0.6

● ROY MEEKER
Meeker, Charles Roy b: 9/15/1900, Lead Mine, Mo. d: 3/25/29, Orlando, Fla. BL/TL, 5'9", 175 lbs. Deb: 9/22/23

YEAR	TM/L	W	L	PCT	G	GS	CG	SH	SV	IP	H	HR	BB	SO	RAT	ERA	ERA+	OAV	OOB	BH	AVG	PB	PR	/A	PD	TPI
1923	Phi-A	3	0	1.000	5	2	2	0	0	25	24	0	13	12	13.3	3.60	114	.253	.343	1	.111	-1	1	1	-0	0.1
1924	Phi-A	5	12	.294	30	14	5	1	0	146	166	4	81	37	15.5	4.68	91	.288	.381	11	.229	-1	-7	-6	-1	-0.8
1926	Cin-N	0	2	.000	7	1	1	0	0	21	24	1	9	5	14.1	6.43	57	.324	.398	0	.000	-1	-6	-6	0	-0.6
Total 3		8	14	.364	42	17	8	1	0	192	214	5	103	54	15.1	4.73	89	.287	.377	12	.190	-2	-12	-11	-1	-1.3

● JOUETT MEEKIN
Meekin, George Jouett b: 2/21/1867, New Albany, Ind. d: 12/14/44, New Albany, Ind. BR/TR, 6'1", 180 lbs. Deb: 6/13/1891

YEAR	TM/L	W	L	PCT	G	GS	CG	SH	SV	IP	H	HR	BB	SO	RAT	ERA	ERA+	OAV	OOB	BH	AVG	PB	PR	/A	PD	TPI
1891	Lou-a	10	16	.385	29	26	25	2	0	228	227	2	113	144	13.7	4.30	85	.251	.338	21	.216	4	-15	-16	-2	-1.2
1892	Lou-N	7	10	.412	19	18	17	0	0	156¹	168	3	78	67	14.5	4.03	76	.264	.350	5	.078	-5	-13	-17	-0	-1.9
	Was-N	3	10	.231	14	14	13	1	0	112	112	2	48	58	13.2	3.46	94	.250	.328	6	.133	-1	-2	-3	-0	-0.3
	Yr	10	20	.333	33	32	30	1	0	268¹	280	5	126	125	13.8	3.79	83	.257	.336	11	.101	-5	-15	-19	0	-2.2
1893	Was-N	10	15	.400	31	28	24	1	0	245	289	6	140	91	16.0	4.96	93	.285	.285	29	.257	3	-8	-9	-1	-0.4
1894	*NY-N	33	9	.786	52	48	40	1	2	409	404	13	171	133	12.9	3.70	142	.255	.332	48	.282	7	74	70	-3	5.5
1895	NY-N	16	11	.593	29	29	24	1	0	225²	296	10	73	76	15.1	5.30	88	.311	.366	28	.292	4	-13	-17	-1	-1.2
1896	NY-N	26	14	.650	*42	41	34	0	0	334¹	378	8	127	110	14.0	3.82	110	.283	.351	43	.299	12	20	14	-3	2.1
1897	NY-N	20	11	.645	37	34	30	2	0	303²	328	9	99	83	12.9	3.76	110	.273	.333	41	.299	6	19	13	-3	1.3
1898	NY-N	16	18	.471	38	37	34	1	0	320	329	9	108	82	12.6	3.77	92	.264	.328	27	.209	1	-6	-10	-5	-1.3
1899	NY-N	5	11	.313	18	18	16	0	0	148¹	169	4	70	30	15.0	4.37	86	.286	.369	12	.207	1	-8	-10	-3	-1.1
	Bos-N	7	6	.538	13	13	12	0	0	108	111	0	23	23	11.3	2.83	147	.265	.307	7	.171	-1	12	16	-2	1.3
	Yr	12	17	.414	31	31	28	0	0	256¹	280	4	93	53	13.2	3.72	105	.275	.337	19	.192	-1	4	6	-5	0.2
1900	Pit-N	0	2	.000	2	2	1	0	0	13	20	1	8	3	20.1	6.92	52	.351	.439	0	.000	-1	-5	-5	-1	-0.6
Total 10		153	133	.535	324	308	270	9	2	2603¹	2831	67	1058	900	13.8	4.07	102	.273	.345	267	.243	29	55	27	-22	2.2

● PHIL MEELER
Meeler, Charles Phillip b: 7/3/48, South Boston, Va. BR/TR, 6'5", 215 lbs. Deb: 5/10/72

YEAR	TM/L	W	L	PCT	G	GS	CG	SH	SV	IP	H	HR	BB	SO	RAT	ERA	ERA+	OAV	OOB	BH	AVG	PB	PR	/A	PD	TPI
1972	Det-A	0	1	.000	7	0	0	0	0	8¹	10	0	7	5	18.4	4.32	73	.303	.425	0	.000	-0	-1	-1	0	-0.2

● RUSS MEERS
Meers, Russell Harlan "Babe" b: 11/28/18, Tilton, Ill. BL/TL, 5'10", 170 lbs. Deb: 9/28/41

YEAR	TM/L	W	L	PCT	G	GS	CG	SH	SV	IP	H	HR	BB	SO	RAT	ERA	ERA+	OAV	OOB	BH	AVG	PB	PR	/A	PD	TPI
1941	Chi-N	0	1	.000	1	1	0	0	0	8	5	0	5	6	6.8	1.13	312	.172	.200	0	—	0	2	2	-0	0.2
1946	Chi-N	1	2	.333	7	2	0	0	0	11¹	10	0	10	2	15.9	3.18	104	.238	.385	1	1.000	0	0	0	-0	0.2
1947	Chi-N	2	0	1.000	35	1	0	0	0	64¹	61	5	38	28	14.1	4.48	88	.263	.371	2	.143	-0	-3	-4	-0	-0.2
Total 3		3	3	.500	43	4	0	0	0	83²	76	5	48	35	13.7	3.98	96	.251	.359	3	.176	-0	-0	-1	-0	0.1

● HEINIE MEINE
Meine, Henry William "The Count Of Luxemburg" b: 5/1/1896, St.Louis, Mo. d: 3/18/68, St.Louis, Mo. BR/TR, 5'11", 180 lbs. Deb: 8/16/22

YEAR	TM/L	W	L	PCT	G	GS	CG	SH	SV	IP	H	HR	BB	SO	RAT	ERA	ERA+	OAV	OOB	BH	AVG	PB	PR	/A	PD	TPI
1922	StL-A	0	0	—	1	0	0	0	0	4	5	1	2	0	15.8	4.50	92	.313	.389	0	.000	-0	-0	-0	-0	0.0
1929	Pit-N	7	6	.538	22	13	7	1	1	108	120	4	34	19	13.4	4.50	106	.291	.355	4	.103	-2	3	3	-2	0.2
1930	Pit-N	6	8	.429	20	16	4	0	1	117¹	168	6	44	18	16.6	6.14	81	.346	.406	5	.122	-3	-15	-15	3	-1.4
1931	Pit-N	**19**	13	.594	36	35	22	3	0	**284**	278	6	87	58	11.8	2.98	129	.254	.313	14	.146	-2	28	27	3	2.6
1932	Pit-N	12	9	.571	28	25	13	1	1	172¹	193	6	45	32	12.6	3.86	99	.278	.324	10	.164	-2	-0	-1	-1	-0.4
1933	Pit-N	15	8	.652	32	29	12	2	0	207¹	227	10	50	50	12.1	3.65	91	.278	.321	13	.173	-1	-7	-8	-1	-1.2
1934	Pit-N	7	6	.538	26	14	2	0	0	106¹	134	12	25	22	13.5	4.32	95	.306	.345	3	.107	-1	-3	-2	-1	-0.5
Total 7		66	50	.569	165	132	60	7	3	999¹	1125	47	287	199	12.9	3.95	101	.284	.337	49	.144	-12	5	4	-4	-0.9

● FRANK MEINKE
Meinke, Frank Louis b: 10/18/1863, Chicago, Ill. d: 11/8/31, Chicago, Ill. BR, 5'10.5", 172 lbs. Deb: 5/1/1884 F♦

YEAR	TM/L	W	L	PCT	G	GS	CG	SH	SV	IP	H	HR	BB	SO	RAT	ERA	ERA+	OAV	OOB	BH	AVG	PB	PR	/A	PD	TPI
1884	Det-N	8	23	.258	35	31	31	1	0	289	341	10	63	124	12.6	3.18	91	.275	.310	56	.164	-3	-6	-9	-2	-1.1
1885	Det-N	0	1	.000	1	1	0	0	0	5	13	0	4	0	30.6	3.60	79	.433	.500	0	.000	-0	-0	-0	-0	-0.1
Total 2		8	24	.250	36	32	31	1	0	294	354	10	67	124	12.6	3.18	91	.279	.315	56	.163	-3	-7	-9	-2	-1.2

● SAM MEJIAS
Mejias, Samuel Elias b: 5/9/52, Santiago, D.R. BR/TR, 6', 170 lbs. Deb: 9/6/76 C♦

YEAR	TM/L	W	L	PCT	G	GS	CG	SH	SV	IP	H	HR	BB	SO	RAT	ERA	ERA+	OAV	OOB	BH	AVG	PB	PR	/A	PD	TPI
1978	Mon-N	0	0	—	1	0	0	0	0	1	0	0	0	0	9.0	0.00	—	.000	.250	13	.232	0	0	0	0	0.0

● JOSE MELENDEZ
Melendez, Jose Luis (Garcia) b: 9/2/65, Naguabo, P.R. BR/TR, 6'2", 175 lbs. Deb: 9/11/90

YEAR	TM/L	W	L	PCT	G	GS	CG	SH	SV	IP	H	HR	BB	SO	RAT	ERA	ERA+	OAV	OOB	BH	AVG	PB	PR	/A	PD	TPI
1990	Sea-A	0	0	—	3	0	0	0	0	5¹	8	2	3	7	20.3	11.81	33	.333	.429	0	—	0	-5	-5	-0	0.0
1991	SD-N	8	5	.615	31	9	0	0	3	93²	77	11	24	60	9.8	3.27	116	.221	.273	2	.100	-0	4	6	-1	0.6
1992	SD-N	6	7	.462	56	3	0	0	0	89¹	82	9	20	82	10.6	2.92	122	.249	.298	0	.000	-0	6	7	-1	0.8
1993	Bos-A	2	1	.667	9	0	0	0	0	16	10	2	5	14	8.4	2.25	205	.179	.246	0	—	0	4	4	0	0.3
1994	Bos-A	0	1	.000	10	0	0	0	0	16¹	20	3	8	9	16.5	6.06	85	.323	.417	0	—	0	-2	-2	-0	-0.3
Total 5		16	14	.533	109	12	0	0	3	220²	197	27	60	172	10.8	3.47	112	.241	.298	2	.080	-1	7	10	-2	1.6

● STEVE MELTER
Melter, Stephen Blazius b: 1/2/1886, Cherokee, Iowa d: 1/28/62, Mishawaka, Ind. BR/TR, 6'2", 180 lbs. Deb: 6/27/09

YEAR	TM/L	W	L	PCT	G	GS	CG	SH	SV	IP	H	HR	BB	SO	RAT	ERA	ERA+	OAV	OOB	BH	AVG	PB	PR	/A	PD	TPI
1909	StL-N	0	1	.000	23	1	0	0	3	64¹	79	1	20	24	14.1	3.50	72	.322	.378	2	.133	-0	-6	-7	1	-0.1

● CLIFF MELTON
Melton, Clifford George "Mickey Mouse" or "Mountain Music" b: 1/3/12, Brevard, N.C. d: 7/28/86, Baltimore, Md. BL/TR, 6'5.5", 203 lbs. Deb: 4/25/37

YEAR	TM/L	W	L	PCT	G	GS	CG	SH	SV	IP	H	HR	BB	SO	RAT	ERA	ERA+	OAV	OOB	BH	AVG	PB	PR	/A	PD	TPI
1937	*NY-N	20	9	.690	46	27	14	2	**7**	248	216	9	55	142	10.1	2.61	149	.233	.280	10	.122	-5	36	**35**	4	3.9
1938	NY-N	14	14	.500	36	31	10	1	0	243	266	9	101	101	12.1	3.89	97	.276	.319	14	.175	-2	-3	-3	2	-0.3
1939	NY-N	12	15	.444	41	23	9	2	5	207¹	214	7	65	95	12.3	3.56	110	.269	.327	12	.182	-1	8	8	1	1.0
1940	NY-N	10	11	.476	37	21	4	1	2	166²	185	9	68	91	13.8	4.91	79	.285	.355	12	.222	2	-20	-19	2	-1.9

YEAR	TM/L	W	L	PCT	G	GS	CG	SH	SV	IP	H	HR	BB	SO	RAT	ERA	ERA+	OAV	OOB	BH	AVG	PB	PR	/A	PD	TPI
1941	NY-N	8	11	.421	42	22	9	3	1	194¹	181	14	61	100	11.3	3.01	123	.246	.305	7	.115	-3	13	15	4	1.4
1942	NY-N†	11	5	.688	23	17	12	2	1	143²	122	9	33	61	9.8	2.63	128	.229	.276	11	.234	2	11	12	3	1.8
1943	NY-N	9	13	.409	34	28	6	2	0	186¹	184	7	69	55	12.4	3.19	108	.257	.325	8	.148	0	4	5	3	1.0
1944	NY-N	2	2	.500	13	10	1	0	0	64¹	78	5	19	15	13.7	4.06	90	.294	.344	3	.120	-2	-3	-3	1	-0.2
Total 8		86	80	.518	272	179	65	13	16	1453²	1446	79	431	660	11.8	3.42	109	.259	.314	77	.164	-9	47	50	20	6.7

● **RUBE MELTON**   Melton, Reuben Franklin b: 2/27/17, Cramerton, N.C. d: 9/11/71, Greer, S.C. BR/TR, 6'5", 205 lbs. Deb: 4/17/41

YEAR	TM/L	W	L	PCT	G	GS	CG	SH	SV	IP	H	HR	BB	SO	RAT	ERA	ERA+	OAV	OOB	BH	AVG	PB	PR	/A	PD	TPI
1941	Phi-N	1	5	.167	25	5	2	0	0	83²	81	7	47	57	13.8	4.73	78	.258	.355	2	.105	-1	-10	-10	-1	-0.9
1942	Phi-N	9	20	.310	42	29	10	1	4	209¹	180	7	114	107	12.8	3.70	89	.234	.335	8	.123	-1	-9	-9	-2	-1.5
1943	Bro-N	5	8	.385	30	17	4	2	0	119¹	106	3	79	64	14.3	3.92	86	.243	.365	4	.105	-2	-7	-7	-1	-1.2
1944	Bro-N	9	13	.409	37	23	6	1	0	187¹	178	4	96	91	13.3	3.46	103	.254	.345	7	.123	-3	3	2	0	0.0
1946	Bro-N	6	3	.667	24	12	3	2	1	99²	72	3	52	44	11.5	1.99	170	.206	.314	3	.107	-2	16	15	-0	1.2
1947	Bro-N	0	1	.000	4	1	0	0	0	4²	7	1	7	1	27.0	13.50	31	.350	.519	1	1.000	0	-5	-5	-0	-0.8
Total 6		30	50	.375	162	87	25	6	5	704	624	22	395	363	13.2	3.62	95	.241	.344	25	.120	-9	-12	-14	-5	-3.2

● **MARIO MENDOZA**   Mendoza, Mario (Aizpuru) b: 12/26/50, Chihuahua, Mex. BR/TR, 5'11", 187 lbs. Deb: 4/26/74 ♦

YEAR	TM/L	W	L	PCT	G	GS	CG	SH	SV	IP	H	HR	BB	SO	RAT	ERA	ERA+	OAV	OOB	BH	AVG	PB	PR	/A	PD	TPI
1977	Pit-N	0	0	—	1	0	0	0	0	2	3	1	2	0	22.5	13.50	30	.375	.500	16	.198	0	-2	-2	0	0.0

● **MIKE MENDOZA**   Mendoza, Michael Joseph b: 11/26/55, Inglewood, Cal. BR/TR, 6'5", 215 lbs. Deb: 9/7/79 ♦

YEAR	TM/L	W	L	PCT	G	GS	CG	SH	SV	IP	H	HR	BB	SO	RAT	ERA	ERA+	OAV	OOB	BH	AVG	PB	PR	/A	PD	TPI
1979	Hou-N	0	0	—	1	0	0	0	0	1	0	0	0	0	0.00	0.00	—	.000	.000	0	—	0	0	0	0	0.0

● **JOCK MENEFEE**   Menefee, John b: 1/15/1868, Rowlesburg, W.Va. d: 3/11/53, Belle Vernon, Pa. BR/TR, 6', 165 lbs. Deb: 8/17/1892 ♦

YEAR	TM/L	W	L	PCT	G	GS	CG	SH	SV	IP	H	HR	BB	SO	RAT	ERA	ERA+	OAV	OOB	BH	AVG	PB	PR	/A	PD	TPI
1892	Pit-N	0	0	—	1	0	0	0	0	4	10	1	2	0	27.0	11.25	29	.455	.500	1	.000	-0	-4	-4	0	0.0
1893	Lou-N	8	7	.533	15	15	14	1	0	129¹	150	3	40	30	13.4	4.24	104	.282	.335	20	.274	4	6	2	2	0.7
1894	Lou-N	8	17	.320	28	24	20	1	0	211²	258	5	50	43	13.5	4.29	119	.297	.342	13	.165	-6	24	19	2	1.3
	Pit-N	5	8	.385	13	13	13	0	0	111²	159	4	39	33	16.1	5.40	97	.331	.383	12	.255	-1	-1	-2	2	0.0
	Yr	13	25	.342	41	37	33	1	0	323¹	417	7	89	76	14.1	4.68	110	.307	.351	25	.198	-5	23	17	4	1.3
1895	Pit-N	0	1	.000	2	1	0	0	0	1²	2	0	7	0	54.0	16.20	28	.293	.674	0	—	-0	-2	-2	0	-0.8
1898	NY-N	0	1	.000	1	1	1	0	0	9¹	11	0	2	3	14.5	4.82	72	.291	.359	0	.000	-1	-1	-1	0	-0.2
1900	Chi-N	9	4	.692	16	13	11	0	0	117	140	1	35	30	14.2	3.85	94	.296	.357	5	.109	-3	-2	-3	-2	-0.7
1901	Chi-N	8	12	.400	21	20	19	0	0	182¹	201	4	34	55	11.9	3.80	85	.278	.316	39	.257	4	-10	-11	-1	-0.6
1902	Chi-N	12	10	.545	22	21	20	4	0	197¹	202	2	26	60	10.7	2.42	112	.265	.294	50	.231	3	8	6	1	0.9
1903	Chi-N	8	10	.444	20	17	13	1	0	147	157	3	38	39	12.3	3.00	105	.275	.327	13	.203	1	4	2	3	0.6
Total 9		58	70	.453	139	125	111	7	0	1111¹	1290	20	273	293	13.0	3.81	101	.288	.335	152	.222	2	23	6	6	1.2

● **TONY MENENDEZ**   Menendez, Antonio Gustavo (Remon) b: 2/20/65, Havana, Cuba BR/TR, 6'2", 190 lbs. Deb: 6/22/92

YEAR	TM/L	W	L	PCT	G	GS	CG	SH	SV	IP	H	HR	BB	SO	RAT	ERA	ERA+	OAV	OOB	BH	AVG	PB	PR	/A	PD	TPI
1992	Cin-N	1	0	1.000	3	0	0	0	0	4²	1	1	0	5	1.9	1.93	187	.067	.067	0	—	0	1	1	-0	0.2
1993	Pit-N	2	0	1.000	14	0	0	0	0	21	24	4	4	13	10.7	3.00	135	.256	.301	0	.000	-0	2	2	-0	0.2
1994	SF-N	0	1	.000	6	0	0	0	0	3¹	8	2	2	2	27.0	21.60	19	.471	.526	0	—	-0	-6	-7	-0	-1.5
Total 3		3	1	.750	23	0	0	0	0	29	29	7	6	20	11.2	4.97	80	.264	.308	0	.000	-0	-3	-3	-1	-1.1

● **MIKE MEOLA**   Meola, Emile Michael b: 10/19/05, New York, N.Y. d: 9/1/76, Fair Lawn, N.J. BR/TR, 5'11", 175 lbs. Deb: 4/24/33

YEAR	TM/L	W	L	PCT	G	GS	CG	SH	SV	IP	H	HR	BB	SO	RAT	ERA	ERA+	OAV	OOB	BH	AVG	PB	PR	/A	PD	TPI
1933	Bos-A	0	0	—	3	0	0	0	0	2¹	5	0	2	1	27.0	23.14	19	.417	.500	0	—	0	-5	-5	-0	0.0
1936	StL-A	0	1	.000	9	0	0	0	0	19¹	29	0	13	6	20.0	9.31	58	.358	.453	1	.500	1	-9	-8	0	-0.3
	Bos-A	0	2	.000	6	3	1	0	1	21¹	29	0	10	8	16.9	5.48	97	.326	.400	1	.143	-0	-1	-1	0	0.0
	Yr	0	3	.000	15	3	1	0	1	40²	58	0	23	14	18.1	7.30	73	.339	.421	2	.222	0	-10	-9	1	-0.3
Total 2		0	3	.000	18	3	1	0	1	43	63	0	25	15	18.8	8.16	65	.346	.431	2	.222	0	-15	-14	1	-0.3

● **JOSE MERCEDES**   Mercedes, Jose Miguel b: 3/5/71, ElSeibo, D.R. BR/TR, 6'1", 180 lbs. Deb: 5/31/94

YEAR	TM/L	W	L	PCT	G	GS	CG	SH	SV	IP	H	HR	BB	SO	RAT	ERA	ERA+	OAV	OOB	BH	AVG	PB	PR	/A	PD	TPI
1994	Mil-A	2	0	1.000	19	0	0	0	0	31	22	4	16	11	11.6	2.32	212	.216	.333	0	—	0	9	9	0	0.5

● **WIN MERCER**   Mercer, George Barclay b: 6/20/1874, Chester, W.Va. d: 1/12/03, San Francisco, Cal BR/TR, 5'7", 140 lbs. Deb: 4/21/1894 ♦

YEAR	TM/L	W	L	PCT	G	GS	CG	SH	SV	IP	H	HR	BB	SO	RAT	ERA	ERA+	OAV	OOB	BH	AVG	PB	PR	/A	PD	TPI
1894	Was-N	17	23	.425	50	38	29	0	3	336¹	442	9	126	72	15.6	3.85	137	.313	.375	48	.293	3	55	53	2	5.0
1895	Was-N	13	23	.361	43	38	32	0	2	311	430	17	96	84	15.7	4.46	108	.323	.376	11	.255	0	11	12	-1	1.0
1896	Was-N	25	18	.581	46	45	38	2	0	366³	456	10	117	94	14.6	4.13	107	.302	.361	38	.244	0	10	11	1	1.1
1897	Was-N	20	20	.500	**46**	42	34	**3**	**3**	333	397	5	103	88	14.3	3.24	134	.293	.356	43	.319	8	40	41	-1	4.7
1898	Was-N	12	18	.400	33	30	24	0	0	233²	309	3	71	52	15.3	4.81	76	.316	.373	80	.321	8	-31	-30	-1	-2.5
1899	Was-N	7	14	.333	23	21	21	0	0	186	234	2	53	28	14.2	4.60	85	.307	.356	112	.299	5	-15	-14	3	-0.5
1900	NY-N	13	17	.433	33	29	26	0	0	242²	303	5	58	39	14.1	3.86	94	.305	.355	73	.294	7	-4	-7	2	0.1
1901	Was-A	9	13	.409	24	22	19	1	1	179²	217	8	50	31	13.9	4.56	80	.295	.348	42	.300	6	-18	-18	1	-1.1
1902	Det-A	15	18	.455	35	33	28	4	1	281²	282	5	80	40	11.9	3.04	120	.261	.318	18	.180	-2	17	19	4	2.1
Total 9		131	164	.444	333	298	251	11	10	2470¹	3070	64	754	528	14.5	3.99	106	.302	.359	504	.286	35	64	68	8	9.9

● **JACK MERCER**   Mercer, Harry Vernon b: 3/10/1889, Zanesville, Ohio d: 6/25/45, Dayton, Ohio Deb: 8/2/10

YEAR	TM/L	W	L	PCT	G	GS	CG	SH	SV	IP	H	HR	BB	SO	RAT	ERA	ERA+	OAV	OOB	BH	AVG	PB	PR	/A	PD	TPI
1910	Pit-N	0	0	—	1	0	0	0	0	1	0	0	2	1	18.0	0.00	—	.000	.500	0	—	0	0	0	0	0.0

● **MARK MERCER**   Mercer, Mark Kenneth b: 5/22/54, Fort Bragg, N.C. BL/TL, 6'5", 220 lbs. Deb: 9/1/81

YEAR	TM/L	W	L	PCT	G	GS	CG	SH	SV	IP	H	HR	BB	SO	RAT	ERA	ERA+	OAV	OOB	BH	AVG	PB	PR	/A	PD	TPI
1981	Tex-A	0	1	.000	7	0	0	0	2	7²	7	1	7	8	16.4	4.70	74	.241	.389	0	—	0	-1	-1	0	0.0

● **KENT MERCKER**   Mercker, Kent Franklin b: 2/1/68, Indianapolis, Ind. BL/TL, 6'1", 175 lbs. Deb: 9/22/89

YEAR	TM/L	W	L	PCT	G	GS	CG	SH	SV	IP	H	HR	BB	SO	RAT	ERA	ERA+	OAV	OOB	BH	AVG	PB	PR	/A	PD	TPI
1989	Atl-N	0	0	—	2	1	0	0	0	4¹	8	0	4	4	29.1	12.46	29	.400	.538	0	.000	-0	-4	-4	-0	0.0
1990	Atl-N	4	7	.364	36	0	0	0	7	48¹	43	6	24	39	12.8	3.17	127	.236	.332	0	.000	-0	3	5	-1	1.0
1991	*Atl-N	5	3	.625	50	4	0	0	6	73¹	56	5	35	62	11.3	2.58	151	.211	.305	1	.100	-0	9	11	-1	1.2
1992	*Atl-N	3	2	.600	53	0	0	0	6	68¹	51	4	35	49	11.7	3.42	107	.207	.313	0	—	-0	1	-2	-2	-0.1
1993	*Atl-N	3	1	.750	43	6	0	0	0	66	52	9	36	59	12.3	2.86	140	.212	.318	0	.000	-1	9	8	-1	0.2
1994	Atl-N	9	4	.692	20	17	2	1	0	112¹	90	16	45	111	10.8	3.45	120	.220	.297	2	.054	-2	10	9	-0	0.7
Total 6		24	17	.585	204	28	2	1	19	372²	342	38	181	324	11.8	3.22	123	.219	.314	3	.043	-5	27	30	-5	3.0

● **SPIKE MERENA**   Merena, John Joseph b: 11/18/09, Paterson, N.J. d: 3/9/77, Bridgeport, Conn. BL/TL, 6', 185 lbs. Deb: 9/16/34

YEAR	TM/L	W	L	PCT	G	GS	CG	SH	SV	IP	H	HR	BB	SO	RAT	ERA	ERA+	OAV	OOB	BH	AVG	PB	PR	/A	PD	TPI
1934	Bos-A	1	2	.333	4	3	2	1	0	24²	20	2	16	7	13.3	2.92	165	.222	.346	1	.143	-0	4	5	1	0.5

● **RON MERIDITH**   Meridith, Ronald Knox b: 11/26/56, San Pedro, Cal. BL/TL, 6', 175 lbs. Deb: 9/16/84

YEAR	TM/L	W	L	PCT	G	GS	CG	SH	SV	IP	H	HR	BB	SO	RAT	ERA	ERA+	OAV	OOB	BH	AVG	PB	PR	/A	PD	TPI
1984	Chi-N	0	0	—	3	0	0	0	0	5¹	6	1	2	4	13.5	3.38	116	.273	.333	0	—	0	0	0	-0	0.0
1985	Chi-N	3	2	.600	32	0	0	0	1	46¹	53	3	24	23	15.2	4.47	89	.301	.388	1	.250	0	-5	-2	0	-0.2
1986	Tex-A	1	0	1.000	5	0	0	0	0	3	2	0	1	2	9.0	3.00	143	.286	.375	0	—	0	0	0	0	0.1
1987	Tex-A	1	0	1.000	11	0	0	0	0	20²	25	7	12	17	16.1	6.10	73	.298	.385	0	—	0	-4	-4	0	-0.1
Total 4		5	2	.714	51	0	0	0	1	75¹	86	11	39	46	15.1	4.78	87	.298	.383	1	.250	0	-8	-5	1	-0.2

● **BRETT MERRIMAN**   Merriman, Brett Alan b: 7/15/66, Jacksonville, Ill. BR/TR, 6'2", 180 lbs. Deb: 4/8/93

YEAR	TM/L	W	L	PCT	G	GS	CG	SH	SV	IP	H	HR	BB	SO	RAT	ERA	ERA+	OAV	OOB	BH	AVG	PB	PR	/A	PD	TPI
1993	Min-A	1	1	.500	19	0	0	0	0	27	36	3	23	14	20.7	9.67	45	.343	.473	0	—	0	-16	-16	-0	-1.0
1994	Min-A	0	1	.000	15	0	0	0	0	17	18	0	14	10	19.1	6.35	76	.269	.424	0	—	0	-3	-3	0	-0.1
Total 2		1	2	.333	34	0	0	0	0	44	54	3	37	24	20.0	8.39	54	.314	.454	0	—	0	-19	-19	0	-1.1

● **GEORGE MERRITT**   Merritt, George Washington b: 4/14/1880, Paterson, N.J. d: 2/21/38, Memphis, Tenn. TR, 6', 160 lbs. Deb: 9/6/01 ♦

YEAR	TM/L	W	L	PCT	G	GS	CG	SH	SV	IP	H	HR	BB	SO	RAT	ERA	ERA+	OAV	OOB	BH	AVG	PB	PR	/A	PD	TPI
1901	Pit-N	3	0	1.000	3	3	3	0	0	24	28	0	5	5	13.1	4.88	67	.289	.337	3	.273	1	-4	-4	-0	-0.3

YEAR TM/L	W	L	PCT	G	GS	CG	SH	SV	IP	H	HR	BB	SO	RAT	ERA	ERA+	OAV	OOB	BH	AVG	PB	PR	/A	PD	TPI
1903 Pit-N	0	0	—	1	0	0	0	0	4	4	0	1	2	11.3	2.25	144	.267	.313	4	.148	0	0	0	-0	0.0
Total 2	3	0	1.000	4	3	3	0	0	28	32	0	6	7	12.9	4.50	73	.286	.334	10	.213	1	-4	-4	-0	-0.3

● JIM MERRITT
Merritt, James Joseph b: 12/9/43, Altadena, Cal. BL/TL, 6'2", 180 lbs. Deb: 8/2/65

YEAR TM/L	W	L	PCT	G	GS	CG	SH	SV	IP	H	HR	BB	SO	RAT	ERA	ERA+	OAV	OOB	BH	AVG	PB	PR	/A	PD	TPI
1965 *Min-A	5	4	.556	16	9	1	0	2	76²	68	11	20	61	10.3	3.17	112	.239	.289	3	.136	0	2	3	-0	0.4
1966 Min-A	7	14	.333	31	18	5	1	3	144	112	17	33	124	9.1	3.38	107	.212	.258	4	.103	-1	1	4	-0	0.4
1967 Min-A	13	7	.650	37	28	11	4	0	227²	196	21	30	161	9.2	2.53	137	.230	.262	10	.135	0	18	24	-2	2.0
1968 Min-A	12	16	.429	38	34	11	1	0	238¹	207	21	52	181	10.0	3.25	95	.232	.279	4	.141	0	-7	-4	-1	-0.5
1969 Cin-N	17	9	.654	42	36	8	1	0	251	269	33	61	144	12.0	4.37	86	.273	.318	11	.143	0	-22	-17	-3	-1.9
1970 *Cin-N★	20	12	.625	35	35	12	1	0	234	248	21	53	136	11.6	4.08	99	.270	.311	14	.169	3	-1	-1	-2	-0.1
1971 Cin-N	1	11	.083	28	11	0	0	0	107	115	14	31	38	12.5	4.37	77	.279	.334	4	.138	0	-11	-12	-2	-1.4
1972 Cin-N	1	0	1.000	4	1	0	0	0	8	13	1	2	4	16.9	4.50	71	.361	.395	0	.000	-0	-1	-1	-0	-0.2
1973 Tex-A	5	13	.278	35	19	8	1	1	160	191	18	34	65	12.7	4.05	92	.296	.332	0	—	0	-4	-6	-1	-0.5
1974 Tex-A	0	0	—	26	1	0	0	0	32²	46	3	6	18	14.3	4.13	88	.329	.356	0	—	0	-2	-2	-1	0.0
1975 Tex-A	0	0	—	5	0	0	0	0	3²	3	0	0	4	9.8	0.00	—	.214	.267	0	—	0	2	2	-0	0.0
Total 11	81	86	.485	297	192	56	9	7	1483	1468	160	322	932	11.0	3.65	98	.257	.300	56	.141	3	-25	-11	-10	-1.8

● LLOYD MERRITT
Merritt, Lloyd Wesley b: 4/8/33, St.Louis, Mo. BR/TR, 6', 189 lbs. Deb: 4/22/57

YEAR TM/L	W	L	PCT	G	GS	CG	SH	SV	IP	H	HR	BB	SO	RAT	ERA	ERA+	OAV	OOB	BH	AVG	PB	PR	/A	PD	TPI
1957 StL-N	1	2	.333	44	0	0	0	7	65¹	60	7	28	35	12.7	3.31	120	.251	.339	0	.000	-0	4	5	0	0.3

● SAM MERTES
Mertes, Samuel Blair "Sandow" b: 8/6/1872, San Francisco, Cal. d: 3/11/45, San Francisco, Cal BR/TR, 5'10", 185 lbs. Deb: 6/30/1896 ♦

YEAR TM/L	W	L	PCT	G	GS	CG	SH	SV	IP	H	HR	BB	SO	RAT	ERA	ERA+	OAV	OOB	BH	AVG	PB	PR	/A	PD	TPI
1902 Chi-A	1	0	1.000	1	0	0	0	0	8	6	0	0	6	6.8	1.13	301	.209	.209	140	.282	0	2	2	-1	0.2

● JIM MERTZ
Mertz, James Verlin b: 8/10/16, Lima, Ohio BR/TR, 5'10.5", 170 lbs. Deb: 5/1/43

YEAR TM/L	W	L	PCT	G	GS	CG	SH	SV	IP	H	HR	BB	SO	RAT	ERA	ERA+	OAV	OOB	BH	AVG	PB	PR	/A	PD	TPI
1943 Was-A	5	7	.417	33	10	2	0	3	116²	109	7	58	53	12.9	4.63	69	.251	.339	7	.184	0	-17	-18	0	-1.8

● JOSE MESA
Mesa, Jose Ramon Nova (b: Jose Ramon Nova (Mesa)) b: 5/22/66, Pueblo Viejo, D.R. BR/TR, 6'3", 220 lbs. Deb: 9/10/87

YEAR TM/L	W	L	PCT	G	GS	CG	SH	SV	IP	H	HR	BB	SO	RAT	ERA	ERA+	OAV	OOB	BH	AVG	PB	PR	/A	PD	TPI
1987 Bal-A	1	3	.250	6	5	0	0	0	31¹	38	7	15	17	15.2	6.03	73	.297	.371	0	—	0	-5	-6	-1	-0.7
1990 Bal-A	3	2	.600	7	7	0	0	0	46²	37	2	27	24	12.5	3.86	98	.218	.328	0	—	0	0	-0	-0	0.1
1991 Bal-A	6	11	.353	23	23	2	1	0	123²	151	11	62	64	15.7	5.97	66	.307	.388	0	—	0	-26	-28	1	-3.1
1992 Bal-A	3	8	.273	13	12	0	0	0	67²	77	9	27	22	14.1	5.19	78	.287	.357	0	—	0	-9	-9	0	-1.2
Cle-A	4	4	.500	15	15	1	1	0	93	92	5	43	40	13.3	4.16	94	.262	.346	0	—	0	-2	-3	-1	-0.2
Yr	7	12	.368	28	27	1	1	0	160²	169	14	70	62	13.7	4.59	86	.271	.346	0	—	0	-12	-11	-0	-1.4
1993 Cle-A	10	12	.455	34	33	3	0	0	208²	232	23	62	118	13.0	4.92	88	.286	.342	0	—	0	-14	-14	-0	-1.3
1994 Cle-A	7	5	.583	51	0	0	0	2	73	71	3	26	63	12.3	3.82	129	.254	.325	0	—	0	8	9	1	1.3
Total 6	34	45	.430	149	95	6	2	2	644	698	58	262	348	13.7	4.89	86	.279	.352	0	—	0	-49	-50	-1	-5.1

● BUD MESSENGER
Messenger, Andrew Warren b: 2/1/1898, Grand Blanc, Mich. d: 11/4/71, Lansing, Mich. BR/TR, 6', 175 lbs. Deb: 7/31/24

YEAR TM/L	W	L	PCT	G	GS	CG	SH	SV	IP	H	HR	BB	SO	RAT	ERA	ERA+	OAV	OOB	BH	AVG	PB	PR	/A	PD	TPI
1924 Cle-A	2	0	1.000	5	2	1	0	0	24	26	4	14	4	15.1	4.32	99	.283	.372	1	.125	-0	-0	-0	-0	-0.1

● ANDY MESSERSMITH
Messersmith, John Alexander b: 8/6/45, Toms River, N.J. BR/TR, 6'1", 200 lbs. Deb: 7/4/68

YEAR TM/L	W	L	PCT	G	GS	CG	SH	SV	IP	H	HR	BB	SO	RAT	ERA	ERA+	OAV	OOB	BH	AVG	PB	PR	/A	PD	TPI
1968 Cal-A	4	2	.667	28	5	2	1	4	81¹	44	3	35	74	8.9	2.21	132	.157	.253	2	.100	-1	7	6	0	0.5
1969 Cal-A	16	11	.593	40	33	10	2	2	250	169	17	100	211	9.9	2.52	138	.190	.276	12	.156	2	31	27	-1	3.0
1970 Cal-A	11	10	.524	37	26	6	1	5	194²	144	21	78	162	10.5	3.01	120	.205	.290	11	.157	0	15	13	-1	1.4
1971 Cal-A☆	20	13	.606	38	38	14	4	0	276²	224	16	121	179	11.5	2.99	108	.218	.304	16	.172	4	14	8	1	1.4
1972 Cal-A	8	11	.421	25	21	10	3	0	169²	125	5	68	142	10.3	2.81	104	.207	.290	10	.189	2	5	2	0	0.5
1973 LA-N	14	10	.583	33	33	10	3	0	249²	196	24	77	177	10.1	2.70	127	.214	.279	15	.169	2	27	20	-0	2.0
1974 *LA-N★	20	6	.769	39	39	13	3	0	292¹	227	24	94	221	10.0	2.59	132	.212	.278	23	.240	9	34	26	0	3.4
1975 LA-N☆	19	14	.576	42	40	19	7	1	321²	244	22	96	213	9.7	2.29	148	.213	.276	17	.157	2	47	40	-2	4.1
1976 Atl-N†	11	11	.500	29	28	12	3	1	207¹	166	14	74	135	10.5	3.04	125	.219	.290	12	.179	0	11	17	1	2.0
1977 Atl-N	5	4	.556	16	16	1	0	0	102¹	101	12	39	69	12.5	4.40	101	.256	.326	4	.118	-0	-6	1	-0	0.0
1978 NY-A	0	3	.000	6	5	0	0	0	22¹	24	7	15	16	16.1	5.64	64	.267	.377	0	—	0	-5	-5	-0	-0.4
1979 LA-N	2	4	.333	11	11	1	0	0	62¹	55	9	34	26	12.9	4.91	74	.244	.344	2	.091	-1	-8	-9	0	-0.8
Total 12	130	99	.568	344	295	98	27	15	2230¹	1719	174	831	1625	10.5	2.86	121	.212	.289	124	.170	20	172	145	-1	17.1

● TOM METCALF
Metcalf, Thomas John b: 7/16/40, Amherst, Wis. BR/TR, 6'2.5", 174 lbs. Deb: 8/4/63

YEAR TM/L	W	L	PCT	G	GS	CG	SH	SV	IP	H	HR	BB	SO	RAT	ERA	ERA+	OAV	OOB	BH	AVG	PB	PR	/A	PD	TPI
1963 NY-A	1	0	1.000	8	0	0	0	0	13	12	1	3	3	10.4	2.77	127	.250	.294	0	—	0	1	1	-0	0.1

● DEWEY METIVIER
Metivier, George Dewey b: 5/6/1898, Cambridge, Mass. d: 3/2/47, Cambridge, Mass. BL/TR, 5'11", 175 lbs. Deb: 9/15/22

YEAR TM/L	W	L	PCT	G	GS	CG	SH	SV	IP	H	HR	BB	SO	RAT	ERA	ERA+	OAV	OOB	BH	AVG	PB	PR	/A	PD	TPI
1922 Cle-A	2	0	1.000	2	2	1	0	0	18	18	1	3	1	11.0	4.50	89	.265	.306	1	.167	-0	-1	-1	-1	-0.1
1923 Cle-A	4	2	.667	26	5	1	0	1	73¹	111	1	38	9	18.0	6.50	61	.368	.448	3	.150	-1	-21	-21	0	-1.5
1924 Cle-A	1	5	.167	26	6	1	0	3	76¹	110	3	34	14	17.0	5.31	81	.358	.422	3	.125	-2	-9	-9	-1	-0.9
Total 3	7	7	.500	54	13	4	0	4	167²	239	5	75	24	17.2	5.74	72	.353	.423	7	.140	-2	-31	-30	-1	-2.5

● BUTCH METZGER
Metzger, Clarence Edward b: 5/23/52, Lafayette, Ind. BR/TR, 6'1", 185 lbs. Deb: 9/8/74

YEAR TM/L	W	L	PCT	G	GS	CG	SH	SV	IP	H	HR	BB	SO	RAT	ERA	ERA+	OAV	OOB	BH	AVG	PB	PR	/A	PD	TPI
1974 SF-N	1	0	1.000	10	0	0	0	0	12²	11	0	12	16	16.3	3.55	107	.239	.397	0	—	0	0	0	-0	0.0
1975 SD-N	1	0	1.000	4	0	0	0	0	4²	6	1	4	6	19.3	7.71	45	.316	.435	0	—	0	-2	-2	0	-0.4
1976 SD-N	11	4	.733	77	0	0	0	16	123¹	119	5	52	89	12.7	2.92	112	.258	.337	0	.000	-0	8	5	-0	0.7
1977 SD-N	0	0	—	17	1	0	0	0	22²	27	5	12	16	15.9	5.56	64	.307	.396	0	.000	-0	-4	-5	-0	-0.1
StL-N	4	2	.667	58	0	0	0	7	92²	78	8	38	48	11.4	3.11	124	.228	.307	0	.000	0	8	8	-1	0.4
Yr	4	2	.667	75	1	0	0	7	115¹	105	13	50	54	12.2	3.59	105	.242	.322	0	.000	-1	4	3	-1	0.3
1978 NY-N	1	3	.250	25	0	0	0	0	37¹	48	4	22	21	17.1	6.51	54	.324	.415	0	—	0	-12	-13	-1	-1.3
Total 5	18	9	.667	191	1	0	0	23	293¹	289	23	140	175	13.3	3.74	94	.262	.348	0	.000	-1	-2	-7	-2	-0.7

● BRIAN MEYER
Meyer, Brian Scott b: 1/29/63, Camden, N.J. BR/TR, 6', 190 lbs. Deb: 9/3/88

YEAR TM/L	W	L	PCT	G	GS	CG	SH	SV	IP	H	HR	BB	SO	RAT	ERA	ERA+	OAV	OOB	BH	AVG	PB	PR	/A	PD	TPI
1988 Hou-N	0	0	—	8	0	0	0	0	12¹	9	2	4	10	9.5	1.46	227	.225	.295	0	—	0	3	3	1	0.1
1989 Hou-N	0	1	.000	12	0	0	0	1	18	16	0	13	13	15.0	4.50	75	.239	.370	0	—	0	-2	-2	0	-0.1
1990 Hou-N	0	4	.000	14	0	0	0	1	20¹	16	3	6	6	9.7	2.21	168	.211	.268	0	—	0	4	4	1	0.8
Total 3	0	5	.000	34	0	0	0	2	50²	41	5	23	29	11.5	2.84	123	.224	.314	0	.000	-0	4	4	1	0.8

● JACK MEYER
Meyer, John Robert b: 3/23/32, Philadelphia, Pa. d: 3/9/67, Philadelphia, Pa. BR/TR, 6'1", 175 lbs. Deb: 4/16/55

YEAR TM/L	W	L	PCT	G	GS	CG	SH	SV	IP	H	HR	BB	SO	RAT	ERA	ERA+	OAV	OOB	BH	AVG	PB	PR	/A	PD	TPI
1955 Phi-N	6	11	.353	50	5	0	0	16	110¹	75	14	66	97	11.7	3.43	116	.190	.310	2	.100	0	8	7	-1	1.1
1956 Phi-N	7	11	.389	41	7	2	0	2	96	86	8	51	66	13.2	4.41	84	.242	.343	4	.200	1	-7	-7	0	-1.1
1957 Phi-N	0	2	.000	19	2	0	0	0	37²	44	7	24	26	15.8	5.73	66	.297	.412	1	.167	-0	-8	-8	0	-0.3
1958 Phi-N	3	6	.333	37	5	1	0	2	90¹	77	8	33	87	11.1	3.59	110	.232	.303	5	.278	1	4	4	-1	0.3
1959 Phi-N	5	3	.625	47	1	0	0	1	93²	76	9	53	71	12.5	3.36	122	.222	.328	1	.071	-1	6	7	-0	0.5
1960 Phi-N	3	1	.750	7	4	0	0	0	25	25	2	11	18	13.0	4.32	90	.272	.350	1	.125	-0	-2	-1	-0	-0.2
1961 Phi-N	0	0	—	1	0	0	0	0	2	2	1	6	2	18.0	9.00	45	.286	.444	0	—	0	-1	-1	-0	-0.0
Total 7	24	34	.414	202	24	4	0	21	455	385	49	244	375	12.6	3.92	100	.230	.332	14	.163	1	0	1	-1	0.3

● BOB MEYER
Meyer, Robert Bernard b: 8/4/39, Toledo, Ohio BR/TL, 6'2", 185 lbs. Deb: 4/20/64

YEAR TM/L	W	L	PCT	G	GS	CG	SH	SV	IP	H	HR	BB	SO	RAT	ERA	ERA+	OAV	OOB	BH	AVG	PB	PR	/A	PD	TPI
1964 NY-A	0	3	.000	7	1	0	0	0	18¹	16	1	12	12	13.7	4.91	74	.235	.350	0	.000	-0	-3	-3	1	-0.4
LA-A	1	1	.500	6	5	0	0	0	18	25	1	15	13	19.5	5.00	66	.333	.438	0	.000	-0	-3	-3	-0	-0.4
KC-A	1	4	.200	9	7	2	0	0	42	37	3	33	30	15.0	3.86	99	.248	.385	0	.000	-0	-1	-0	-1	-0.2
Yr	2	8	.200	22	13	2	0	0	78¹	78	5	58	55	15.6	4.37	84	.266	.387	0	.000	-2	-6	-6	-0	-1.0
1969 Sea-A	0	3	.000	6	5	1	0	0	32²	30	4	10	17	11.6	3.31	110	.252	.321	1	.091	-1	1	1	-1	-0.1

YEAR	TM/L	W	L	PCT	G	GS	CG	SH	SV	IP	H	HR	BB	SO	RAT	ERA	ERA+	OAV	OOB	BH	AVG	PB	PR	/A	PD	TPI
1970	Mil-A	0	1	.000	10	0	0	0	0	18¹	24	3	12	20	17.7	6.38	59	.329	.424	1	.333	0	-5	-5	-0	-0.2
Total	3	2	12	.143	38	18	3	0	0	129¹	132	12	80	92	15.0	4.38	84	.273	.379	2	.057	-3	-11	-10	-1	-1.3

● **RUSS MEYER**   Meyer, Russell Charles "Rowdy" or "The Mad Monk" b: 10/25/23, Peru, Ill.   BB/TR, 6'1", 185 lbs.   Deb: 9/13/46   C

YEAR	TM/L	W	L	PCT	G	GS	CG	SH	SV	IP	H	HR	BB	SO	RAT	ERA	ERA+	OAV	OOB	BH	AVG	PB	PR	/A	PD	TPI
1946	Chi-N	0	0		4	1	0	0	1	17	21	2	10	10	16.4	3.18	104	.309	.397	1	.200	0	0	0	0	0.0
1947	Chi-N	3	2	.600	23	2	1	0	0	45	43	4	14	22	11.6	3.40	116	.257	.319	3	.250	0	3	3	-0	0.3
1948	Chi-N	10	10	.500	29	26	8	3	0	164²	157	8	77	89	12.8	3.66	107	.254	.338	6	.107	-3	5	4	-0	0.2
1949	Phi-N	17	8	.680	37	28	14	2	1	213	199	14	70	78	11.4	3.08	128	.250	.311	10	.143	-1	23	20	-2	1.9
1950	*Phi-N	9	11	.450	32	25	3	0	1	159²	193	21	67	74	14.8	5.30	76	.304	.373	7	.140	-1	-21	-22	1	-2.4
1951	Phi-N	8	9	.471	28	24	7	2	0	168	172	13	55	65	12.3	3.48	111	.263	.322	5	.104	-2	9	7	-3	0.2
1952	Phi-N	13	14	.481	37	32	14	1	1	232²	235	10	65	92	11.7	3.14	116	.260	.311	7	.089	-2	15	13	-2	1.0
1953	*Bro-N	15	5	.750	34	32	10	2	0	191¹	201	25	63	106	12.5	4.56	93	.269	.327	11	.147	-2	-6	-6	-0	-0.8
1954	Bro-N	11	6	.647	36	28	6	2	0	180¹	193	17	49	70	12.2	3.99	102	.275	.324	2	.043	-3	2	2	-2	-0.4
1955	*Bro-N	6	2	.750	18	11	2	1	0	73	86	8	31	26	14.4	5.42	75	.300	.368	1	.037	-3	-11	-11	1	-1.2
1956	Chi-N	1	6	.143	20	9	0	0	0	57	71	11	26	28	15.6	6.32	60	.313	.388	1	.083	-1	-16	-16	2	-1.6
	Cin-N	0	0	—	1	0	0	0	0	1	1	0	0	1	9.0	0.00	—	.250	.250	0	—	0	0	0	0	0.0
	Yr	1	6	.143	21	9	0	0	0	58	72	11	26	29	15.2	6.21	61	.305	.374	1	.083	-1	-16	-16	2	-1.6
1957	Bos-A	0	0	—	2	1	0	0	0	5	10	0	3	1	23.4	5.40	74	.417	.481	1	1.000	0	-1	-1	1	0.1
1959	KC-A	1	0	1.000	18	0	0	0	1	24	24	3	11	10	13.5	4.50	89	.261	.346	0	.000	-0	-2	-1	0	-0.1
Total	13	94	73	.563	319	219	65	13	5	1531¹	1606	136	541	672	12.7	3.99	99	.271	.334	55	.114	-18	2	-8	-5	-2.8

● **LEVI MEYERLE**   Meyerle, Levi Samuel "Long Levi" b: 7/1845, Philadelphia, Pa.   d: 11/4/21, Philadelphia, Pa.   BR/TR, 6'1", 177 lbs.   Deb: 5/20/1871 ◆

YEAR	TM/L	W	L	PCT	G	GS	CG	SH	SV	IP	H	HR	BB	SO	RAT	ERA	ERA+	OAV	OOB	BH	AVG	PB	PR	/A	PD	TPI
1871	Ath-n	0	0	—	1	0	0	0	0	1	1	0	2	0	27.0	9.00	45	.250	.500	64	.492	1	-1	-1		0.0
1876	Phi-N	0	2	.000	2	2	2	0	0	18	28	0	1	0	14.5	5.00	48	.337	.345	87	.340	1	-5	-5	-0	-0.4

● **DANNY MICELI**   Miceli, Daniel b: 9/9/70, Newark, N.J.   BR/TR, 6'1", 185 lbs.   Deb: 9/9/93

YEAR	TM/L	W	L	PCT	G	GS	CG	SH	SV	IP	H	HR	BB	SO	RAT	ERA	ERA+	OAV	OOB	BH	AVG	PB	PR	/A	PD	TPI
1993	Pit-N	0	0	—	9	0	0	0	0	5¹	6	0	3	4	15.2	5.06	80	.273	.360	0		0	-1	-1	-0	0.0
1994	Pit-N	2	1	.667	28	0	0	0	2	27¹	28	5	11	27	13.5	5.93	72	.267	.347	0	.000	-0	-5	-5	-0	-0.6
Total	2	2	1	.667	37	0	0	0	2	32²	34	5	14	31	13.8	5.79	73	.268	.350	0	.000	-0	-6	-6	0	-0.6

● **GENE MICHAEL**   Michael, Eugene Richard "Stick" b: 6/2/38, Kent, Ohio   BB/TR, 6'2", 183 lbs.   Deb: 7/15/66   MC◆

YEAR	TM/L	W	L	PCT	G	GS	CG	SH	SV	IP	H	HR	BB	SO	RAT	ERA	ERA+	OAV	OOB	BH	AVG	PB	PR	/A	PD	TPI
1968	NY-A	0	0	—	1	0	0	0	0	3	5	0	0	3	18.0	0.00	—	.357	.400	23	.198	0	1	1	0	0.0

● **JOHN MICHAELS**   Michaels, John Joseph b: 7/10/07, Bridgeport, Conn.   BL/TL, 5'10.5", 154 lbs.   Deb: 4/16/32

YEAR	TM/L	W	L	PCT	G	GS	CG	SH	SV	IP	H	HR	BB	SO	RAT	ERA	ERA+	OAV	OOB	BH	AVG	PB	PR	/A	PD	TPI
1932	Bos-A	1	6	.143	28	8	2	0	0	80²	101	4	27	16	14.6	5.13	88	.304	.362	3	.143	-1	-6	-6	1	-0.4

● **JOHN MICHAELSON**   Michaelson, John August "Mike" b: 8/12/1893, Tivalkoski, Finland   d: 4/16/68, Woodruff, Wis.   BR/TR, 5'9", 165 lbs.   Deb: 8/28/21

YEAR	TM/L	W	L	PCT	G	GS	CG	SH	SV	IP	H	HR	BB	SO	RAT	ERA	ERA+	OAV	OOB	BH	AVG	PB	PR	/A	PD	TPI
1921	Chi-A	0	0	—	2	0	0	0	0	2²	4	0	1	1	16.9	10.13	42	.400	.455	0	—	0	-2	-2	-0	0.0

● **GLENN MICKENS**   Mickens, Glenn Roger b: 7/26/30, Wilmar, Cal.   BR/TR, 6', 175 lbs.   Deb: 7/19/53

YEAR	TM/L	W	L	PCT	G	GS	CG	SH	SV	IP	H	HR	BB	SO	RAT	ERA	ERA+	OAV	OOB	BH	AVG	PB	PR	/A	PD	TPI
1953	Bro-N	0	1	.000	4	2	0	0	0	6¹	11	2	4	5	21.3	11.37	37	.393	.469	0	.000	-0	-5	-5	0	-0.6

● **JIM MIDDLETON**   Middleton, James Blaine "Rifle Jim" b: 5/28/1889, Argos, Ind.   d: 1/12/74, Argos, Ind.   BR/TR, 5'11.5", 165 lbs.   Deb: 4/18/17

YEAR	TM/L	W	L	PCT	G	GS	CG	SH	SV	IP	H	HR	BB	SO	RAT	ERA	ERA+	OAV	OOB	BH	AVG	PB	PR	/A	PD	TPI
1917	NY-N	1	1	.500	13	0	0	0	1	36	35	1	8	9	11.0	2.75	93	.255	.301	0	.000	-1	-0	-1	1	-0.1
1921	Det-A	6	11	.353	38	10	2	0	7	121²	149	5	44	31	14.4	5.03	85	.302	.361	5	.147	-2	-10	-10	1	-1.4
Total	2	7	12	.368	51	10	2	0	8	157²	184	6	52	40	13.6	4.51	86	.292	.348	5	.119	-3	-10	-11	2	-1.5

● **JOHN MIDDLETON**   Middleton, John Wayne "Lefty" b: 4/11/1900, Mt.Calm, Tex.   d: 11/3/86, Amarillo, Tex.   BL/TL, 6'1", 185 lbs.   Deb: 9/6/22

YEAR	TM/L	W	L	PCT	G	GS	CG	SH	SV	IP	H	HR	BB	SO	RAT	ERA	ERA+	OAV	OOB	BH	AVG	PB	PR	/A	PD	TPI
1922	Cle-A	0	1	.000	2	1	0	0	0	7¹	8	1	6	2	17.2	7.36	54	.286	.412	1	.333	0	-3	-3	0	-0.3

● **DICK MIDKIFF**   Midkiff, Richard b: 9/28/14, Gonzales, Tex.   d: 10/30/56, Temple, Tex.   BR/TR, 6'2", 185 lbs.   Deb: 4/24/38

YEAR	TM/L	W	L	PCT	G	GS	CG	SH	SV	IP	H	HR	BB	SO	RAT	ERA	ERA+	OAV	OOB	BH	AVG	PB	PR	/A	PD	TPI
1938	Bos-A	1	1	.500	13	2	0	0	0	35¹	43	5	21	10	16.3	5.09	97	.305	.395	2	.200	0	-1	-1	0	0.0

● **GARY MIELKE**   Mielke, Gary Roger b: 1/28/63, St.James, Minn.   BR/TR, 6'3", 185 lbs.   Deb: 8/19/87

YEAR	TM/L	W	L	PCT	G	GS	CG	SH	SV	IP	H	HR	BB	SO	RAT	ERA	ERA+	OAV	OOB	BH	AVG	PB	PR	/A	PD	TPI
1987	Tex-A	0	0	—	3	0	0	0	0	3	3	2	1	3	12.0	6.00	75	.250	.308	0	—	0	-1	-1	-0	0.0
1989	Tex-A	1	0	1.000	43	0	0	0	1	49²	52	4	25	26	14.3	3.26	122	.280	.371	0	—	0	3	4	-0	0.0
1990	Tex-A	0	3	.000	33	0	0	0	0	41	42	4	15	13	13.0	3.73	105	.271	.343	0	—	0	1	1	0	0.1
Total	3	1	3	.250	79	0	0	0	1	93²	97	10	41	42	13.6	3.56	111	.275	.357	0	—	0	4	4	-0	0.1

● **PETE MIKKELSEN**   Mikkelsen, Peter James b: 10/25/39, Staten Island, N.Y.   BR/TR, 6'2", 220 lbs.   Deb: 4/17/64

YEAR	TM/L	W	L	PCT	G	GS	CG	SH	SV	IP	H	HR	BB	SO	RAT	ERA	ERA+	OAV	OOB	BH	AVG	PB	PR	/A	PD	TPI
1964	*NY-A	7	4	.636	50	0	0	0	12	86	79	3	41	63	13.0	3.56	102	.247	.340	1	.063	-1	1	1	1	0.1
1965	NY-A	4	9	.308	41	3	0	0	1	82¹	78	10	36	69	12.8	3.28	104	.249	.332	1	.100	-0	2	1	1	0.3
1966	Pit-N	9	8	.529	71	0	0	0	14	126	106	8	51	76	11.6	3.07	116	.234	.318	3	.150	-0	7	7	-0	1.0
1967	Pit-N	1	2	.333	32	0	0	0	2	56¹	50	7	19	30	11.5	4.31	78	.237	.309	0	.000	-0	-6	-6	-1	-0.5
	Chi-N	0	0	—	7	0	0	0	0	7	9	1	5	0	19.3	6.43	55	.333	.455	0	—	0	-2	-2	-0	0.0
	Yr	1	2	.333	39	0	0	0	2	63¹	59	8	24	30	11.9	4.55	74	.244	.315	0	.000	-0	-8	-8	-1	-0.5
1968	Chi-N	0	0	—	3	0	0	0	0	4²	7	3	1	5	15.4	7.71	41	.350	.381	1	1.000	0	-2	-2	0	0.1
	StL-N	0	0	—	5	0	0	0	0	16	10	0	7	8	9.6	1.13	257	.179	.270	0	.000	-0	3	3	-1	-0.1
	Yr	0	0	—	8	0	0	0	0	20²	17	3	8	13	10.9	2.61	113	.224	.298	1	.250	0	1	1	-1	0.0
1969	LA-N	7	5	.583	48	0	0	0	4	81¹	71	3	35	43	11.7	2.77	120	.193	.277	1	.167	0	7	5	1	0.9
1970	LA-N	4	2	.667	33	0	0	0	6	62	48	5	20	47	10.5	2.76	139	.211	.287	2	.333	0	9	7	0	0.9
1971	LA-N	8	5	.615	41	0	0	0	5	74	67	6	17	46	10.3	3.65	89	.242	.288	2	.200	0	-2	-3	-1	-0.5
1972	LA-N	5	5	.500	33	0	0	0	4	57²	65	3	23	41	14.5	4.06	92	.283	.360	0	.000	0	-4	-5	-0	-0.5
Total	9	45	40	.529	364	3	0	0	49	653¹	576	59	256	436	11.8	3.38	102	.237	.316	11	.133	-2	13	6	2	1.2

● **HANK MIKLOS**   Miklos, John Joseph b: 11/27/10, Chicago, Ill.   BL/TL, 5'11", 175 lbs.   Deb: 4/23/44

YEAR	TM/L	W	L	PCT	G	GS	CG	SH	SV	IP	H	HR	BB	SO	RAT	ERA	ERA+	OAV	OOB	BH	AVG	PB	PR	/A	PD	TPI
1944	Chi-N	0	0	—	7	0	0	0	0	7	9	1	3	0	15.4	7.71	46	.333	.400	0	.000	-0	-3	-3	1	0.0

● **BOB MILACKI**   Milacki, Robert b: 7/28/64, Trenton, N.J.   BR/TR, 6'4", 220 lbs.   Deb: 9/18/88

YEAR	TM/L	W	L	PCT	G	GS	CG	SH	SV	IP	H	HR	BB	SO	RAT	ERA	ERA+	OAV	OOB	BH	AVG	PB	PR	/A	PD	TPI
1988	Bal-A	2	0	1.000	3	3	1	1	0	25	9	1	9	18	6.5	0.72	542	.110	.198	0	—	0	9	9	0	0.9
1989	Bal-A	14	12	.538	37	36	3	2	0	243	233	21	88	113	12.0	3.74	101	.254	.320	0	—	0	4	1	-0	0.2
1990	Bal-A	5	8	.385	27	24	1	1	0	135¹	143	18	61	60	13.6	4.46	85	.273	.349	0	—	0	-8	-10	1	-0.8
1991	Bal-A	10	9	.526	31	26	3	1	0	184	175	17	53	108	11.2	4.01	99	.253	.307	0	—	0	2	-1	1	0.1
1992	Bal-A	6	8	.429	23	20	0	0	0	115²	140	16	44	51	14.5	5.84	69	.296	.358	0	—	0	-24	-23	1	-2.5
1993	Cle-A	1	1	.500	5	2	0	0	0	16	19	3	11	7	16.9	3.38	128	.302	.405	0	—	0	2	2	0	0.2
1994	KC-A	0	5	.000	10	10	0	0	0	55²	68	6	20	17	14.4	6.14	84	.298	.357	0	—	0	-8	-6	-0	-0.7
Total	7	38	43	.469	136	121	8	5	1	774²	787	82	286	374	12.5	4.31	92	.264	.330	0	—	0	-25	-29	1	-2.6

● **CARL MILES**   Miles, Carl Thomas b: 3/22/18, Trenton, Mo.   BB/TL, 5'11", 178 lbs.   Deb: 6/8/40

YEAR	TM/L	W	L	PCT	G	GS	CG	SH	SV	IP	H	HR	BB	SO	RAT	ERA	ERA+	OAV	OOB	BH	AVG	PB	PR	/A	PD	TPI
1940	Phi-A	0	0	—	2	0	0	0	0	8	8	1	6	2	17.2	13.50	33	.281	.425	3	.750	2	-8	-8	-0	0.2

● **JIM MILES**   Miles, James Charlie b: 8/8/43, Grenada, Miss.   BR/TR, 6'2", 210 lbs.   Deb: 9/7/68

YEAR	TM/L	W	L	PCT	G	GS	CG	SH	SV	IP	H	HR	BB	SO	RAT	ERA	ERA+	OAV	OOB	BH	AVG	PB	PR	/A	PD	TPI
1968	Was-A	0	0	—	3	0	0	0	0	4¹	8	0	2	5	20.8	12.46	23	.421	.476	0	—	0	-5	-5	-0	0.0
1969	Was-A	0	1	.000	10	1	0	0	0	20¹	19	2	15	15	16.8	6.20	56	.257	.409	1	.333	0	-6	-6	1	-0.2
Total	2	0	1	.000	13	1	0	0	0	24²	27	2	17	20	17.5	7.30	46	.290	.421	1	.333	0	-10	-11	0	-0.2

YEAR TM/L	W	L	PCT	G	GS	CG	SH	SV	IP	H	HR	BB	SO	RAT	ERA	ERA+	OAV	OOB	BH	AVG	PB	PR	/A	PD	TPI

● SAM MILITELLO Militello, Sam Salvatore b: 11/26/69, Tampa, Fla.   BR/TR, 6'3", 200 lbs.   Deb: 8/9/92

YEAR TM/L	W	L	PCT	G	GS	CG	SH	SV	IP	H	HR	BB	SO	RAT	ERA	ERA+	OAV	OOB	BH	AVG	PB	PR	/A	PD	TPI
1992 NY-A	3	3	.500	9	9	0	0	0	60	43	6	32	42	11.6	3.45	113	.195	.302	0	—	0	3	3	-1	0.2
1993 NY-A	1	1	.500	3	2	0	0	0	9¹	10	1	7	5	18.3	6.75	62	.270	.413	0	—	0	-3	-3	0	-0.4
Total 2	4	4	.500	12	11	0	0	0	69¹	53	7	39	47	12.5	3.89	101	.205	.319	0	—	0	1	0	-1	-0.2

● JOHNNY MILJUS Miljus, John Kenneth "Jovo" or "Big Serb" b: 6/30/1895, Pittsburgh, Pa. d: 2/11/76, Fort Harrison, Mont.   BR/TR, 6'1", 178 lbs. Deb: 10/2/15

YEAR TM/L	W	L	PCT	G	GS	CG	SH	SV	IP	H	HR	BB	SO	RAT	ERA	ERA+	OAV	OOB	BH	AVG	PB	PR	/A	PD	TPI
1915 Pit-F	0	0		1	0	0	0	0	1	1	0	0	0	9.0	0.00	—	.250	.250	0		0	0	0	0	0.0
1917 Bro-N	0	1	.000	4	1	1	0	0	15	14	0	8	9	15.0	0.60	466	.250	.373	0	.000	-1	4	4	-0	0.1
1920 Bro-N	1	0	1.000	9	0	0	0	0	23¹	24	2	4	9	10.8	3.09	104	.267	.298	2	.333	1	0	0	1	0.2
1921 Bro-N	6	3	.667	28	9	3	0	1	93²	115	1	27	37	13.8	4.23	92	.312	.362	5	.167	-2	-5	-4	2	-0.3
1927 *Pit-N	8	3	.727	19	6	3	2	0	75²	62	0	17	24	9.4	1.90	216	.228	.273	5	.179	-1	17	19	2	2.6
1928 Pit-N	5	7	.417	21	10	3	0	1	69²	90	2	33	26	16.3	5.30	77	.313	.389	8	.308	1	-10	-10	-0	-1.3
Cle-A	1	4	.200	11	4	1	0	1	50²	61	1	20	19	11.7	2.66	156	.243	.316	3	.200	-8	8	-0	0.7
1929 Cle-A	8	8	.500	34	15	4	0	2	128¹	174	10	64	42	16.9	5.19	86	.331	.406	11	.256	1	-13	-11	-0	-1.0
Total 7	29	26	.527	127	45	15	2	5	457¹	526	16	173	166	14.0	3.92	104	.293	.359	34	.222	0	0	7	4	1.0

● DYAR MILLER Miller, Dyar K b: 5/29/46, Batesville, Ind.   BR/TR, 6'1", 195 lbs.   Deb: 6/9/75   C

YEAR TM/L	W	L	PCT	G	GS	CG	SH	SV	IP	H	HR	BB	SO	RAT	ERA	ERA+	OAV	OOB	BH	AVG	PB	PR	/A	PD	TPI
1975 Bal-A	6	3	.667	30	0	0	0	8	46¹	32	3	16	33	9.3	2.72	129	.199	.271	0	—	0	5	4	0	1.1
1976 Bal-A	2	4	.333	49	0	0	0	7	88²	76	3	36	37	11.8	2.94	117	.246	.324	0	—	0	6	3	-1	0.2
1977 Bal-A	2	2	.500	12	0	0	0	1	22¹	25	6	10	9	14.1	5.64	67	.278	.350	0	—	0	-4	-5	-0	-0.6
Cal-A	4	4	.500	41	0	0	0	4	92¹	81	10	30	49	10.8	3.02	129	.242	.304	0	—	0	11	9	-1	0.8
Yr	6	6	.500	53	0	0	0	5	114²	106	16	40	58	11.5	3.53	110	.249	.314	0	—	0	7	5	-1	0.2
1978 Cal-A	6	2	.750	41	0	0	0	1	84²	85	3	41	34	13.9	2.66	136	.264	.356	0	—	0	10	9	-2	0.7
1979 Cal-A	1	0	1.000	14	1	0	0	0	35¹	44	2	13	16	15.0	3.31	123	.319	.386	0	—	0	4	3	-1	0.2
Tor-A	0	0	—	10	0	0	0	0	15¹	27	3	5	7	18.8	10.57	41	.391	.432	0	—	0	-11	-11	-0	-0.1
Yr	1	0	1.000	24	1	0	0	0	50²	71	5	18	23	15.8	5.51	75	.333	.385	0	—	0	-7	-8	-1	0.1
1980 NY-N	1	2	.333	31	0	0	0	1	42	37	1	11	28	10.3	1.93	184	.242	.293	0	.000	-0	8	8	-1	0.5
1981 NY-N	1	0	1.000	23	0	0	0	0	38¹	49	2	15	22	15.3	3.29	106	.327	.392	1	.333	-1	1	1	-1	0.0
Total 7	23	17	.575	251	1	0	0	22	465¹	459	35	177	235	12.5	3.23	113	.264	.335	1	.250	0	30	22	-7	2.8

● ELMER MILLER Miller, Elmer Joseph "Lefty" b: 4/17/03, Detroit, Mich. d: 1/8/87, Corona, Cal.   BL/TL, 5'11", 189 lbs.   Deb: 6/21/29 ♦

YEAR TM/L	W	L	PCT	G	GS	CG	SH	SV	IP	H	HR	BB	SO	RAT	ERA	ERA+	OAV	OOB	BH	AVG	PB	PR	/A	PD	TPI
1929 Phi-N	0	1	.000	8	2	0	0	0	11¹	12	1	21	5	28.6	11.12	47	.279	.537	9	.237	0	-8	-7	-0	-0.5

● FRANK MILLER Miller, Frank Lee "Bullet" b: 5/13/1886, Allegan, Mich. d: 2/19/74, Allegan, Mich.   BR/TR, 6', 188 lbs.   Deb: 7/12/13

YEAR TM/L	W	L	PCT	G	GS	CG	SH	SV	IP	H	HR	BB	SO	RAT	ERA	ERA+	OAV	OOB	BH	AVG	PB	PR	/A	PD	TPI
1913 Chi-A	0	1	.000	1	1	0	0	0	1²	4	0	3	2	37.8	27.00	16	.571	.700	0	—	0	-4	-4	0	-1.3
1916 Pit-N	7	10	.412	30	20	10	2	1	173	135	4	49	88	9.9	2.29	117	.226	.292	7	.137	-1	6	8	-1	0.6
1917 Pit-N	10	19	.345	38	28	14	5	1	224	216	4	60	92	11.3	3.13	91	.251	.304	9	.118	-4	-11	-7	-1	-1.4
1918 Pit-N	11	8	.579	23	23	14	2	0	170¹	152	1	37	47	10.4	2.38	121	.250	.301	6	.105	-3	7	9	-0	0.7
1919 Pit-N	13	12	.520	32	26	16	3	0	201²	170	6	34	59	9.3	3.03	100	.234	.272	7	.106	-5	-3	0	-1	-0.5
1922 Bos-N	11	13	.458	31	23	14	2	1	200	213	4	60	65	12.4	3.51	114	.279	.333	8	.118	-5	13	11	1	0.8
1923 Bos-N	0	3	.000	8	6	0	0	0	39¹	54	2	11	6	15.6	4.58	87	.335	.389	1	.143	-0	-3	-3	-1	-0.3
Total 7	52	66	.441	163	127	68	14	4	1010	944	21	254	359	10.9	3.01	104	.253	.306	38	.117	-19	7	15	1	-1.4

● FRED MILLER Miller, Frederick Holman "Speedy" b: 6/28/1886, Fairfield, Ind. d: 5/2/53, Brookville, Ind.   BL/TL, 6'2", 190 lbs.   Deb: 7/8/10

YEAR TM/L	W	L	PCT	G	GS	CG	SH	SV	IP	H	HR	BB	SO	RAT	ERA	ERA+	OAV	OOB	BH	AVG	PB	PR	/A	PD	TPI
1910 Bro-N	1	1	.500	6	2	0	0	0	21	25	1	13	2	17.6	4.71	64	.309	.423	2	.250	0	-4	-4	0	-0.3

● BERT MILLER Miller, Herbert A. b: 10/28/1875, Riley, Mich.   Deb: 7/15/1897

YEAR TM/L	W	L	PCT	G	GS	CG	SH	SV	IP	H	HR	BB	SO	RAT	ERA	ERA+	OAV	OOB	BH	AVG	PB	PR	/A	PD	TPI
1897 Lou-N	0	1	.000	4	1	1	0	0	17	32	0	3	3	18.5	7.94	54	.396	.418	1	.167	-1	-7	-7	0	-0.3

● JAKE MILLER Miller, Jacob Walter b: 2/28/1898, Wagram, Ohio d: 8/20/75, Venice, Fla.   BL/TL, 6'2", 170 lbs.   Deb: 9/11/24   F

YEAR TM/L	W	L	PCT	G	GS	CG	SH	SV	IP	H	HR	BB	SO	RAT	ERA	ERA+	OAV	OOB	BH	AVG	PB	PR	/A	PD	TPI
1924 Cle-A	0	1	.000	2	2	1	0	0	12	13	0	5	4	13.5	3.00	142	.265	.333	-1	2	2	0	0.0			
1925 Cle-A	10	13	.435	32	22	13	0	2	190¹	207	4	62	51	13.1	3.31	133	.279	.340	13	.183	-3	23	23	0	2.2
1926 Cle-A	7	4	.636	18	11	5	3	1	82²	99	1	18	24	13.0	3.27	124	.307	.348	2	.083	-2	7	7	-1	0.6
1927 Cle-A	10	8	.556	34	23	11	0	0	185¹	189	4	48	53	11.8	3.21	131	.271	.324	8	.138	-4	19	21	1	1.4
1928 Cle-A	8	9	.471	25	24	8	0	0	158	203	6	43	37	14.3	4.44	93	.332	.381	7	.135	-4	-7	-5	-1	-0.8
1929 Cle-A	14	12	.538	29	29	14	2	0	206	227	7	60	58	12.8	3.58	124	.279	.334	15	.200	-3	15	20	1	2.0
1930 Cle-A	4	4	.500	24	9	1	0	0	88¹	147	6	38	31	19.3	7.13	68	.373	.433	10	.303	1	-24	-23	1	-1.4
1931 Cle-A	2	1	.667	10	5	1	0	0	41¹	45	2	19	17	13.9	4.35	106	.273	.348	1	.077	-1	0	1	0	0.0
1933 Chi-A	5	6	.455	26	14	4	2	0	105²	130	3	47	30	15.6	5.62	75	.297	.373	7	.189	-1	-16	-16	1	-1.4
Total 9	60	58	.508	200	139	58	8	3	1069²	1260	33	340	305	13.8	4.09	106	.298	.355	63	.171	-19	19	30	6	2.6

● OX MILLER Miller, John Anthony b: 5/4/15, Gause, Tex.   BR/TR, 6'1", 190 lbs.   Deb: 8/7/43

YEAR TM/L	W	L	PCT	G	GS	CG	SH	SV	IP	H	HR	BB	SO	RAT	ERA	ERA+	OAV	OOB	BH	AVG	PB	PR	/A	PD	TPI
1943 Was-A	0	0	—	3	0	0	0	0	6	10	1	5	1	22.5	10.50	31	.370	.469	0	.000	-0	-5	-5	1	0.0
StL-A	0	0		2	0	0	0	0	6	7	2	3	3	18.0	12.00	28	.304	.429	0	.000	-0	-6	-6	1	0.0
Yr	0	0	—	5	0	0	0	0	12	17	3	8	4	20.3	11.25	29	.340	.450	0	.000	-0	-11	-11	1	0.0
1945 StL-A	2	1	.667	4	3	3	0	0	28¹	23	2	5	4	8.9	1.59	222	.219	.255	2	.182	-0	6	6	-1	0.5
1946 StL-A	1	3	.250	11	3	0	0	1	35¹	52	5	15	12	17.1	6.88	54	.338	.396	2	.286	1	-13	-12	1	-1.2
1947 Chi-N	1	2	.333	4	4	1	0	0	16	31	2	5	12	20.3	10.13	39	.397	.434	3	.429	1	-11	-11	-0	-1.4
Total 4	4	6	.400	24	10	4	0	1	91²	123	12	33	27	15.5	6.38	57	.318	.374	7	.259	2	-29	-28	1	-2.1

● JOHN MILLER Miller, John Ernest b: 5/30/41, Baltimore, Md.   BR/TR, 6'2", 210 lbs.   Deb: 9/22/62

YEAR TM/L	W	L	PCT	G	GS	CG	SH	SV	IP	H	HR	BB	SO	RAT	ERA	ERA+	OAV	OOB	BH	AVG	PB	PR	/A	PD	TPI
1962 Bal-A	1	1	.500	2	1	0	0	0	10	2	0	5	4	6.3	0.90	411	.065	.194	0	.000	-0	3	3	0	0.7
1963 Bal-A	1	1	.500	3	2	0	0	0	17	12	0	14	16	13.8	3.18	109	.194	.342	0	.000	-1	1	1	-0	0.0
1965 Bal-A	6	4	.600	16	16	1	0	0	93¹	75	4	58	71	12.9	3.18	109	.223	.338	3	.100	-1	3	3	0	0.3
1966 Bal-A	4	8	.333	23	16	0	0	0	100²	92	15	58	81	13.4	4.74	70	.241	.342	4	.118	-1	-15	-16	1	-1.8
1967 Bal-A	0	0	—	2	0	0	0	0	6	7	1	3	6	18.0	7.50	42	.304	.429	0	—	0	-3	-3	0	0.0
Total 5	12	14	.462	46	35	1	0	0	227	188	20	138	178	13.0	3.89	88	.225	.337	7	.096	-3	-10	-12	1	-0.8

● CYCLONE MILLER Miller, Joseph H. b: 9/24/1859, Springfield, Mass. d: 10/13/16, New London, Conn.   TL, 5'9.5", 165 lbs.   Deb: 7/11/1884

YEAR TM/L	W	L	PCT	G	GS	CG	SH	SV	IP	H	HR	BB	SO	RAT	ERA	ERA+	OAV	OOB	BH	AVG	PB	PR	/A	PD	TPI
1884 CP-U	1	0	1.000	1	1	1	0	0	9	4	0	0	13	4.0	1.00	244	.125	.125	1	.250	-0	1	1	1	0.2
Pro-N	3	2	.600	6	5	2	0	0	34²	36	0	11	12	12.2	2.08	136	.259	.313	1	.043	-3	3	3	-1	0.1
Phi-N	0	1	.000	1	1	0	0	0	9	17	5	6	1	23.0	10.00	30	.386	.460	0	.000	-1	-7	-7	0	-0.5
Yr	3	3	.500	7	6	3	0	0	43²	53	5	17	13	14.4	3.71	77	.290	.350	1	.037	-4	-4	-4	-1	-0.4
1886 Phi-a	10	8	.556	19	19	19	1	0	169²	168	6	59	99	11.7	2.97	118	.239	.305	9	.136	-1	9	10	1	0.9
Total 2	14	11	.560	27	26	23	1	0	222¹	215	11	76	125	11.9	3.04	110	.245	.308	11	.113	-5	7	7	0	0.7

● WHITEY MILLER Miller, Kenneth Albert b: 5/2/15, St.Louis, Mo. d: 4/3/91, St.Louis, Mo.   BR/TR, 6'1", 195 lbs.   Deb: 9/15/44

YEAR TM/L	W	L	PCT	G	GS	CG	SH	SV	IP	H	HR	BB	SO	RAT	ERA	ERA+	OAV	OOB	BH	AVG	PB	PR	/A	PD	TPI
1944 NY-N	0	1	.000	4	0	0	0	0	4	2	1	4	2	9.0	9.00		.059	.238	0	.000	-0	2	2	0	0.4

● KURT MILLER Miller, Kurt Everett b: 8/24/72, Tucson, Ariz.   BR/TR, 6'5", 205 lbs.   Deb: 6/11/94

YEAR TM/L	W	L	PCT	G	GS	CG	SH	SV	IP	H	HR	BB	SO	RAT	ERA	ERA+	OAV	OOB	BH	AVG	PB	PR	/A	PD	TPI
1994 Fla-N	1	3	.250	4	4	0	0	0	20	26	3	7	11	15.7	8.10	56	.317	.385	1	.167	-0	-9	-8	1	-1.2

● LARRY MILLER Miller, Larry Don b: 6/19/37, Topeka, Kan.   BL/TL, 6', 195 lbs.   Deb: 6/21/64

YEAR TM/L	W	L	PCT	G	GS	CG	SH	SV	IP	H	HR	BB	SO	RAT	ERA	ERA+	OAV	OOB	BH	AVG	PB	PR	/A	PD	TPI
1964 LA-N	4	8	.333	16	14	1	0	0	79²	87	1	28	50	13.2	4.18	78	.275	.338	7	.269	2	-6	-8	-1	-1.0
1965 NY-N	1	4	.200	28	5	0	0	0	57¹	66	6	25	36	14.4	5.02	70	.289	.362	2	.182	0	-9	-10	-0	-0.8

YEAR TM/L	W	L	PCT	G	GS	CG	SH	SV	IP	H	HR	BB	SO	RAT	ERA	ERA+	OAV	OOB	BH	AVG	PB	PR	/A	PD	TPI
1966 NY-N	0	2	.000	4	1	0	0	0	8¹	9	3	4	7	14.0	7.56	48	.273	.351	1	.500	0	-4	-4	-0	-0.7
Total 3	5	14	.263	48	20	1	0	0	145¹	162	10	57	93	13.7	4.71	72	.281	.349	10	.256	2	-19	-21	-1	-2.5

● **RED MILLER**   Miller, Leo Alphonso   b: 2/11/1897, Philadelphia, Pa.   d: 10/20/73, Orlando, Fla.   BR/TR, 5'11", 195 lbs.   Deb: 4/13/23

YEAR TM/L	W	L	PCT	G	GS	CG	SH	SV	IP	H	HR	BB	SO	RAT	ERA	ERA+	OAV	OOB	BH	AVG	PB	PR	/A	PD	TPI
1923 Phi-N	0	0	—	1	0	0	0	0	1²	6	0	1	0	37.8	32.40	14	.545	.583	0	.000	-0	-5	-5	-0	0.0

● **PAUL MILLER**   Miller, Paul Robert   b: 4/27/65, Burlington, Wis.   BR/TR, 6'5", 215 lbs.   Deb: 7/30/91

YEAR TM/L	W	L	PCT	G	GS	CG	SH	SV	IP	H	HR	BB	SO	RAT	ERA	ERA+	OAV	OOB	BH	AVG	PB	PR	/A	PD	TPI
1991 Pit-N	0	0	—	1	1	0	0	0	5	4	0	3	2	12.6	5.40	66	.222	.333	0	.000	-0	-1	-1	-0	-0.1
1992 Pit-N	1	0	1.000	6	0	0	0	0	11¹	11	0	1	5	9.5	2.38	144	.256	.273	0	.000	-0	1	1	-0	0.1
1993 Pit-N	0	0	—	3	2	0	0	0	10	15	2	2	2	15.3	5.40	75	.349	.378	0	.000	-0	-2	-2	-0	-0.1
Total 3	1	0	1.000	10	3	0	0	0	26¹	30	2	6	9	12.3	4.10	90	.288	.327	0	.000	-1	-1	-1	-1	-0.1

● **RALPH MILLER**   Miller, Ralph Darwin   b: 3/15/1873, Cincinnati, Ohio   d: 5/8/73, Cincinnati, Ohio   BR/TR, 5'11", 170 lbs.   Deb: 5/4/1898

YEAR TM/L	W	L	PCT	G	GS	CG	SH	SV	IP	H	HR	BB	SO	RAT	ERA	ERA+	OAV	OOB	BH	AVG	PB	PR	/A	PD	TPI
1898 Bro-N	4	14	.222	23	21	16	0	0	151²	161	4	86	43	15.4	5.34	67	.270	.374	12	.194	-1	-29	-30	3	-2.6
1899 Bal-N	1	3	.250	6	4	3	0	0	36	42	0	14	3	15.0	4.50	88	.291	.369	2	.182	1	-3	-2	-1	-0.1
Total 2	5	17	.227	29	25	19	0	0	187²	203	4	100	46	15.3	5.18	71	.274	.373	14	.192	1	-32	-32	2	-2.7

● **RALPH MILLER**   Miller, Ralph Henry "Moose" or "Lefty"   b: 1/14/1899, Vinton, Iowa   d: 2/18/67, White Bear Lake, Minn.   BR/TL, 6'1.5", 190 lbs.   Deb: 9/16/21   F

YEAR TM/L	W	L	PCT	G	GS	CG	SH	SV	IP	H	HR	BB	SO	RAT	ERA	ERA+	OAV	OOB	BH	AVG	PB	PR	/A	PD	TPI
1921 Was-A	0	0	—	1	0	0	0	0	1	0	0	0	0	0.0	0.00	—	.000	.000	—	—	0	0	0	-0	0.0

● **RANDY MILLER**   Miller, Randall Scott   b: 3/18/53, Oxnard, Cal.   BR/TR, 6'1", 180 lbs.   Deb: 9/7/77

YEAR TM/L	W	L	PCT	G	GS	CG	SH	SV	IP	H	HR	BB	SO	RAT	ERA	ERA+	OAV	OOB	BH	AVG	PB	PR	/A	PD	TPI
1977 Bal-A	0	0	—	1	0	0	0	0	0²	4	0	0	0	54.0	40.50	9	.800	.800	0	—	0	-3	-3	-0	0.0
1978 Mon-N	0	1	.000	5	0	0	0	0	7	11	1	3	6	18.0	10.29	34	.393	.452	0	.000	-0	-5	-5	0	-0.7
Total 2	0	1	.000	6	0	0	0	0	7²	15	1	3	6	21.1	12.91	27	.455	.500	0	.000	-0	-8	-8	0	-0.7

● **BOB MILLER**   Miller, Robert Gerald   b: 7/15/35, Berwyn, Ill.   BR/TL, 6'1", 185 lbs.   Deb: 6/25/53

YEAR TM/L	W	L	PCT	G	GS	CG	SH	SV	IP	H	HR	BB	SO	RAT	ERA	ERA+	OAV	OOB	BH	AVG	PB	PR	/A	PD	TPI
1953 Det-A	1	2	.333	13	1	0	0	0	36¹	43	2	21	9	16.1	5.94	68	.289	.380	1	.125	-1	-8	-8	0	-0.6
1954 Det-A	1	1	.500	32	1	0	0	1	69²	62	1	26	27	11.4	2.45	150	.244	.314	2	.133	-0	10	10	-1	0.2
1955 Det-A	2	1	.667	7	3	1	0	0	25¹	26	4	12	11	13.5	2.49	154	.263	.342	2	.222	-1	4	4	-0	0.4
1956 Det-A	0	2	.000	11	3	0	0	0	31²	37	5	22	16	16.8	5.68	72	.308	.415	1	.143	-0	-5	-6	-1	-0.3
1962 Cin-N	0	0	—	6	0	0	0	0	5¹	14	1	3	4	32.1	21.94	18	.538	.613	0	.000	-0	-11	-11	0	0.0
NY-N	2	2	.500	17	0	0	0	1	20¹	24	2	8	8	14.6	7.08	59	.312	.384	0	.000	-0	-7	-7	0	-1.2
Yr	2	2	.500	23	0	0	0	1	25²	38	3	11	12	17.5	10.17	41	.355	.420	0	.000	-0	-18	-17	0	-1.2
Total 5	6	8	.429	86	8	1	0	2	188²	206	15	92	75	14.4	4.72	83	.284	.368	6	.146	-1	-17	-17	-1	-1.5

● **BOB MILLER**   Miller, Robert John   b: 6/16/26, Detroit, Mich.   BR/TR, 6'3", 190 lbs.   Deb: 9/16/49

YEAR TM/L	W	L	PCT	G	GS	CG	SH	SV	IP	H	HR	BB	SO	RAT	ERA	ERA+	OAV	OOB	BH	AVG	PB	PR	/A	PD	TPI
1949 Phi-N	0	0	—	3	0	0	0	0	2²	2	0	2	0	13.5	0.00	—	.200	.333	0	—	0	1	1	0	0.0
1950 *Phi-N	11	6	.647	35	22	7	2	1	174	190	9	57	44	13.0	3.57	113	.277	.337	11	.180	-1	11	9	2	0.9
1951 Phi-N	2	1	.667	17	3	0	0	0	34¹	47	2	18	10	17.3	6.82	56	.331	.410	3	.429	-1	-11	-11	-0	-0.9
1952 Phi-N	0	1	.000	3	1	0	0	0	9	13	2	1	2	14.0	6.00	61	.351	.368	0	.000	-0	-2	-2	0	-0.2
1953 Phi-N	8	9	.471	35	20	8	3	2	157¹	169	14	42	63	12.2	4.00	105	.271	.319	10	.182	-1	5	4	-1	0.2
1954 Phi-N	7	9	.438	30	16	5	0	0	150	176	14	39	42	13.1	4.56	89	.300	.347	8	.160	-0	-8	-9	-1	-0.7
1955 Phi-N	8	4	.667	40	0	0	0	1	89²	80	6	28	53	10.9	2.41	165	.242	.304	5	.278	1	16	16	0	2.0
1956 Phi-N	3	6	.333	49	6	3	1	5	122¹	115	14	34	53	11.2	3.24	115	.248	.303	2	.091	-1	7	7	-0	0.4
1957 Phi-N	2	5	.286	32	1	0	0	6	60¹	61	4	17	12	11.8	2.69	142	.265	.319	2	.250	2	8	8	-1	1.1
1958 Phi-N	1	1	.500	17	0	0	0	0	22¹	36	7	9	9	18.1	11.69	34	.360	.413	0	.000	-0	-19	-19	-0	-1.5
Total 10	42	42	.500	261	69	23	6	15	822	889	72	247	263	12.6	3.96	101	.277	.332	41	.184	1	8	2	1	1.3

● **BOB MILLER**   Miller, Robert Lane (b: Robert Lane Gemeinweiser)   b: 2/18/39, St.Louis, Mo.   d: 8/6/93, Rancho Bernardo, Cal.   BR/TR, 6'1", 182 lbs.   Deb: 6/26/57   C

YEAR TM/L	W	L	PCT	G	GS	CG	SH	SV	IP	H	HR	BB	SO	RAT	ERA	ERA+	OAV	OOB	BH	AVG	PB	PR	/A	PD	TPI
1957 StL-N	0	0	—	5	0	0	0	0	9	13	2	5	7	18.0	7.00	57	.325	.400	0	—	0	-3	-3	0	0.0
1959 StL-N	4	3	.571	11	10	3	0	0	70²	66	2	21	43	11.2	3.31	128	.248	.306	5	.208	0	5	7	1	0.8
1960 StL-N	4	3	.571	15	7	0	0	0	52²	53	2	17	33	12.1	3.42	120	.262	.323	2	.143	-1	2	4	0	0.5
1961 StL-N	1	3	.250	34	5	0	0	3	74¹	82	6	46	39	15.5	4.24	104	.290	.389	5	.357	2	-2	-1	1	0.3
1962 NY-N	1	12	.077	33	21	0	0	0	143²	146	20	62	91	13.4	4.89	86	.259	.339	5	.122	-1	-15	-11	2	-0.8
1963 LA-N	10	8	.556	42	23	2	0	1	187	171	7	65	125	11.5	2.89	105	.244	.311	4	.070	-3	8	3	5	0.5
1964 LA-N	7	7	.500	**74**	2	0	0	9	137²	115	9	46	90	11.8	2.62	124	.226	.314	3	.158	1	14	10	2	1.4
1965 *LA-N	6	7	.462	61	1	0	0	9	103	82	9	26	77	9.7	2.97	110	.225	.282	0	.000	-1	7	3	2	0.5
1966 *LA-N	4	2	.667	46	0	0	0	5	84¹	70	9	29	58	10.7	2.77	119	.230	.299	1	.077	-1	8	5	1	0.5
1967 LA-N	2	9	.182	52	4	0	0	0	85²	88	9	27	32	12.4	4.31	72	.273	.335	1	.125	-0	-9	-12	1	-1.4
1968 Min-A	0	3	.000	45	0	0	0	2	72¹	65	1	24	41	11.7	2.74	113	.239	.312	1	.143	-0	2	3	1	0.2
1969 *Min-A	5	5	.500	48	11	1	0	3	119¹	118	9	32	57	11.3	3.02	121	.264	.313	-3	.000	-3	8	7	1	0.5
1970 Cle-A	2	2	.500	15	2	0	0	1	28	35	1	15	15	16.1	4.18	95	.310	.391	1	.200	-1	-1	-1	-1	-0.2
Chi-A	4	6	.400	15	12	0	0	0	70	88	11	33	36	16.1	5.01	78	.315	.396	4	.174	0	-10	-9	2	-0.9
Yr	6	8	.429	30	14	0	0	1	98	123	12	48	51	16.1	4.78	82	.313	.393	5	.179	1	-12	-9	1	-1.1
Chi-N	0	0	—	7	1	0	0	2	9	6	3	6	4	12.0	5.00	90	.194	.324	0	—	0	-1	-1	0	0.0
1971 Chi-N	0	0	—	2	0	0	0	0	7	10	1	0	1	14.1	5.14	76	.357	.379	0	.000	-0	-1	-1	0	0.0
SD-N	7	3	.700	38	0	0	0	7	63²	53	0	26	36	11.3	1.41	233	.227	.308	0	.000	-1	15	13	1	2.4
*Pit-N	1	2	.333	16	0	0	0	3	28	20	1	13	13	10.6	1.29	263	.200	.292	0	.000	-0	7	7	0	0.9
Yr	8	5	.615	56	0	0	0	10	98²	83	1	40	50	11.2	1.64	205	.229	.305	0	.000	-1	20	19	2	3.3
1972 *Pit-N	5	2	.714	36	0	0	0	5	54¹	54	3	24	24	13.1	2.65	125	.263	.343	-0	.000	-0	5	4	0	0.3
1973 SD-N	0	0	—	18	0	0	0	0	30²	29	4	12	15	12.0	4.11	84	.244	.313	0	.000	-0	-2	-2	-1	-0.1
NY-N	0	0	—	1	0	0	0	0	1	0	0	0	1	0.0	0.00	—	.000	.000	0	—	0	1	1	0	0.0
Yr	0	0	—	19	0	0	0	0	31²	29	4	12	16	11.7	3.98	87	.236	.304	0	.000	-0	-1	-2	-1	-0.1
Det-A	4	2	.667	22	0	0	0	0	42	34	3	22	23	12.0	3.43	119	.230	.329	-0	—	-0	3	3	0	0.4
1974 NY-N	2	2	.500	58	0	0	0	1	78	89	2	39	35	14.9	3.58	100	.296	.378	1	.111	-0	-0	0	0	0.3
Total 17	69	81	.460	694	99	7	0	51	1551¹	1487	101	608	895	12.3	3.37	105	.255	.328	33	.110	-8	38	31	18	5.3

● **BOB MILLER**   Miller, Robert W.   b: 1862,   Deb: 8/30/1890

YEAR TM/L	W	L	PCT	G	GS	CG	SH	SV	IP	H	HR	BB	SO	RAT	ERA	ERA+	OAV	OOB	BH	AVG	PB	PR	/A	PD	TPI
1890 Roc-a	3	7	.300	13	12	11	0	0	92¹	89	2	26	20	11.5	4.29	83	.246	.301	6	.150	-1	-4	-7	0	-0.7
1891 Was-a	2	5	.286	7	7	3	0	0	42	53	3	24	13	17.8	4.29	87	.298	.399	2	.111	-2	-3	-3	1	-0.4
Total 2	5	12	.294	20	19	14	0	1	134¹	142	5	50	33	13.5	4.29	84	.263	.335	8	.138	-3	-7	-10	1	-1.1

● **ROGER MILLER**   Miller, Roger Wesley   b: 8/1/54, Connellsville, Pa.   BR/TR, 6'3", 200 lbs.   Deb: 9/8/74

YEAR TM/L	W	L	PCT	G	GS	CG	SH	SV	IP	H	HR	BB	SO	RAT	ERA	ERA+	OAV	OOB	BH	AVG	PB	PR	/A	PD	TPI
1974 Mil-A	0	0	—	2	0	0	0	0	2¹	3	1	0	2	15.4	11.57	31	.300	.364	0	—	0	-2	-2	-0	0.0

● **RONNIE MILLER**   Miller, Roland Arthur   b: 8/28/18, Mason City, Iowa   BB/TR, 5'11", 167 lbs.   Deb: 9/10/41

YEAR TM/L	W	L	PCT	G	GS	CG	SH	SV	IP	H	HR	BB	SO	RAT	ERA	ERA+	OAV	OOB	BH	AVG	PB	PR	/A	PD	TPI
1941 Was-A	0	0	—	2	0	0	0	0	2	0	1	0	2	4.5	4.50	90	.333	.429	0	—	0	-0	-0	-0	0.0

● **ROSCOE MILLER**   Miller, Roscoe Clyde "Roxy" or "Rubberlegs"   b: 12/2/1876, Greenville, Ind.   d: 4/18/13, Corydon, Ind.   BR/TR, 6'2", 190 lbs.   Deb: 4/25/01

YEAR TM/L	W	L	PCT	G	GS	CG	SH	SV	IP	H	HR	BB	SO	RAT	ERA	ERA+	OAV	OOB	BH	AVG	PB	PR	/A	PD	TPI
1901 Det-A	23	13	.639	38	36	35	3	1	332	339	1	98	79	12.2	2.95	139	.261	.320	27	.208	-0	26	33	4	3.5
1902 Det-A	6	12	.333	20	18	15	1	0	148²	158	3	57	39	13.6	3.69	99	.273	.347	11	.183	-2	-2	-1	-1	-0.2
NY-N	1	8	.111	10	9	7	0	0	72²	77	1	11	15	11.5	4.58	61	.272	.310	1	.048	-2	-15	-14	-1	-1.8
1903 NY-N	2	5	.286	15	8	6	0	3	85	101	1	24	30	13.3	4.13	81	.302	.351	5	.161	-1	-8	-7	-1	-0.7
1904 Pit-N	7	7	.500	19	17	11	2	0	134¹	133	4	39	35	11.8	3.35	82	.256	.313	2	.043	-4	-9	-9	-1	-1.4
Total 4	39	45	.464	102	88	74	6	5	772²	808	10	229	198	12.5	3.45	100	.268	.326	46	.160	-8	-7	1	2	-0.6

YEAR TM/L	W	L	PCT	G	GS	CG	SH	SV	IP	H	HR	BB	SO	RAT	ERA	ERA+	OAV	OOB	BH	AVG	PB	PR	/A	PD	TPI
● **RUSS MILLER** Miller, Russell Lewis b: 3/25/1900, Etna, Ohio d: 4/30/62, Bucyrus, Ohio BR/TR, 5'11", 165 lbs. Deb: 9/24/27 F																									
1927 Phi-N	1	1	.500	2	2	1	0	0	15¹	21	2	3	4	14.7	5.28	78	.339	.379	1	.333	0	-2	-2	-0	-0.2
1928 Phi-N	0	12	.000	33	12	1	0	1	108	137	14	34	19	14.3	5.42	79	.315	.365	4	.148	-1	-17	-14	0	-1.4
Total 2	1	13	.071	35	14	2	0	1	123¹	158	16	37	23	14.3	5.40	79	.318	.366	5	.167	-1	-19	-16	0	-1.6
● **STU MILLER** Miller, Stuart Leonard b: 12/26/27, Northampton, Mass. BR/TR, 5'11.5", 165 lbs. Deb: 8/12/52																									
1952 StL-N	6	3	.667	12	11	6	2	0	88	63	3	26	64	9.3	2.05	182	.197	.262	3	.120	-1	16	16	3	1.8
1953 StL-N	7	8	.467	40	18	8	2	4	137²	161	19	47	79	13.7	5.56	77	.293	.351	8	.186	1	-19	-20	5	-1.5
1954 StL-N	2	3	.400	19	4	0	0	2	46²	55	5	29	22	16.8	5.79	71	.307	.412	4	.308	1	-9	-9	2	-0.6
1956 StL-N	0	1	.000	3	0	0	0	1	7¹	12	3	5	5	20.9	4.91	77	.387	.472	0	.000	-0	-1	-1	0	-0.1
Phi-N	5	8	.385	24	15	2	0	0	106²	109	16	51	55	13.8	4.47	83	.263	.349	4	.160	-2	-8	-9	0	-0.7
Yr	5	9	.357	27	15	2	0	1	114	121	19	56	60	14.3	4.50	83	.271	.357	4	.154	2	-9	-10	0	-0.8
1957 NY-N	7	9	.438	38	13	0	0	1	124	110	15	45	60	11.5	3.63	108	.242	.315	2	.057	-3	3	4	2	0.3
1958 SF-N	6	9	.400	41	20	4	1	0	182	160	16	49	119	10.4	**2.47**	**154**	.233	**.286**	6	.120	-3	30	27	1	2.2
1959 SF-N	8	7	.533	59	9	2	0	8	167²	164	15	57	95	12.1	2.84	134	.260	.326	2	.044	-3	**21**	18	3	1.7
1960 SF-N	7	6	.538	47	3	2	0	2	101²	100	9	31	65	11.9	3.90	89	.256	.315	5	.200	1	-2	-5	2	-0.3
1961 SF-N★	14	5	.737	63	0	0	0	17	122	95	4	37	89	9.8	2.66	153	.215	.277	4	.200	2	**19**	16	2	3.1
1962 ★SF-N	5	8	.385	59	0	0	0	19	107	107	8	42	78	12.7	4.12	92	.268	.341	2	.125	-0	-2	-4	0	-0.6
1963 Bal-A	5	8	.385	**71**	0	0	0	**27**	112¹	93	6	53	114	11.9	2.24	155	.232	.326	5	.313	2	17	15	2	3.0
1964 Bal-A	7	7	.500	66	0	0	0	23	97	77	7	34	87	10.6	3.06	117	.222	.297	1	.111	-0	6	5	1	1.1
1965 Bal-A	14	7	.667	67	0	0	0	24	119¹	87	5	32	104	9.1	1.89	184	.207	.265	1	.063	-1	21	21	1	**4.8**
1966 Bal-A	9	4	.692	51	0	0	0	18	92	65	5	22	67	8.9	2.25	148	.201	.260	2	.105	-1	12	11	-1	1.9
1967 Bal-A	3	10	.231	42	0	0	0	9	81¹	63	5	36	60	11.1	2.55	124	.220	.309	0	.000	-1	6	5	-0	0.9
1968 Atl-N	0	0	—	2	0	0	0	0	1¹	1	0	4	1	33.8	27.00	17	.500	.833	0	—	-0	-4	-4	0	0.0
Total 16	105	103	.505	704	93	24	5	154	1694	1522	140	600	1164	11.5	3.24	115	.242	.312	49	.133	-2	107	89	22	17.0
● **WALT MILLER** Miller, Walter W. b: 10/19/1884, Spiceland, Ind. d: 3/1/56, Marion, Ind. BR/TR, 5'11.5", 180 lbs. Deb: 9/20/11																									
1911 Bro-N	0	1	.000	3	2	0	0	0	11	16	0	6	0	18.8	6.55	51	.356	.442	0	.000	-1	-4	-4	-0	-0.4
● **BILL MILLER** Miller, William Francis "Wild Bill" b: 4/12/10, Hannibal, Mo. d: 2/26/82, Hannibal, Mo. BR/TR, 6', 180 lbs. Deb: 10/2/37																									
1937 StL-A	0	1	.000	1	1	0	0	0	4	7	1	4	1	27.0	13.50	36	.389	.522	0	.000	-0	-4	-4	0	-0.6
● **BILL MILLER** Miller, William Paul "Lefty" or "Hooks" b: 7/26/27, Minersville, Pa. BL/TL, 6', 175 lbs. Deb: 4/20/52																									
1952 NY-A	4	6	.400	21	13	5	2	0	88	78	4	49	45	13.2	3.48	96	.241	.345	6	.214	1	2	-2	-0	-0.1
1953 NY-A	2	1	.667	13	3	0	0	1	34	46	3	19	17	17.5	4.76	77	.324	.407	2	.200	-0	-3	-4	1	-0.3
1954 NY-A	0	1	.000	2	1	0	0	0	5²	9	0	1	6	15.9	6.35	54	.375	.400	0	.000	-0	-2	-2	-0	-0.3
1955 Bal-A	0	1	.000	5	1	0	0	0	4	3	0	10	4	29.3	13.50	28	.200	.520	1	1.000	0	-4	-4	-0	-0.8
Total 4	6	9	.400	41	18	5	2	1	131²	136	7	79	72	14.9	4.24	81	.270	.372	9	.225	1	-7	-12	0	-1.5
● **JOHN MILLIGAN** Milligan, John Alexander b: 1/22/04, Schuylerville, N.Y. d: 5/15/72, Fort Pierce, Fla. BR/TL, 5'10", 172 lbs. Deb: 8/11/28																									
1928 Phi-N	2	5	.286	13	7	3	0	0	68	69	2	32	22	13.5	4.37	98	.274	.358	1	.050	-2	-3	-1	1	-0.2
1929 Phi-N	0	1	.000	8	3	0	0	0	9²	29	0	10	2	38.2	16.76	31	.527	.612	1	.333	0	-13	-12	0	-1.0
1930 Phi-N	1	2	.333	9	2	1	0	0	28¹	26	0	21	7	15.6	3.18	172	.255	.392	1	.111	-1	6	7	1	0.7
1931 Phi-N	0	0	—	3	0	0	0	0	8	11	0	4	6	18.0	3.38	126	.324	.410	0	.000	0	1	1	-0	-0.1
1934 Was-A	0	0	—	2	0	0	0	0	2²	6	0	0	1	20.3	10.13	43	.500	.500	0	—	0	-2	-2	0	0.0
Total 5	3	8	.273	35	12	4	0	0	116²	141	2	67	38	16.5	5.17	90	.310	.405	3	.088	-3	-11	-7	2	-0.6
● **BILLY MILLIGAN** Milligan, William Joseph b: 8/19/1878, Buffalo, N.Y. d: 10/14/28, Buffalo, N.Y. BR/TL, 5'7", Deb: 4/30/01																									
1901 Phi-A	0	3	.000	6	3	2	0	0	33	43	1	14	5	16.1	4.36	68	.311	.383	5	.333	2	-3	-2	0	0.0
1904 NY-N	0	1	.000	5	1	1	0	2	25	36	2	4	6	14.8	5.40	51	.310	.339	1	.111	0	-7	-7	-0	-0.4
Total 2	0	4	.000	11	4	3	0	2	58	79	3	18	11	15.5	4.81	69	.311	.363	6	.250	2	-10	-10	-1	-0.4
● **BOB MILLIKEN** Milliken, Robert Fogle "Bobo" b: 8/25/26, Majorsville, W.Va. BR/TR, 6', 195 lbs. Deb: 4/22/53 C																									
1953 ★Bro-N	8	4	.667	37	10	3	0	2	117²	94	13	42	65	10.4	3.37	127	.214	.283	4	.118	-1	12	12	-2	0.8
1954 Bro-N	5	2	.714	24	3	0	0	2	62²	58	12	18	25	11.2	4.02	102	.246	.305	3	.176	-0	0	0	-1	-0.1
Total 2	13	6	.684	61	13	3	0	4	180¹	152	25	60	90	10.7	3.59	117	.225	.290	7	.137	-2	12	12	-3	0.7
● **ALAN MILLS** Mills, Alan Bernard b: 10/18/66, Lakeland, Fla. BR/TR, 6'1", 190 lbs. Deb: 4/14/90																									
1990 NY-A	1	5	.167	36	0	0	0	0	41²	48	4	33	24	17.7	4.10	97	.298	.421	0	—	0	-1	-1	0	0.0
1991 NY-A	1	1	.500	6	2	0	0	0	16¹	16	1	8	11	13.2	4.41	94	.254	.338	0	—	0	-1	-0	1	0.0
1992 Bal-A	10	4	.714	35	3	0	0	2	103¹	78	5	54	60	11.6	2.61	154	.215	.319	0	—	0	15	16	1	2.1
1993 Bal-A	5	4	.556	45	0	0	0	4	100¹	80	14	51	68	12.1	3.23	138	.225	.328	0	—	0	12	14	-0	1.2
1994 Bal-A	3	3	.500	47	0	0	0	2	45¹	43	7	24	44	13.7	5.16	98	.251	.350	0	—	0	-2	-0	0	-0.1
Total 5	20	17	.541	169	5	0	0	8	307	265	31	170	207	13.0	3.49	124	.238	.343	0	—	0	24	28	2	3.2
● **ART MILLS** Mills, Arthur Grant b: 3/2/03, Utica, N.Y. d: 7/23/75, Utica, N.Y. BR/TR, 5'10", 155 lbs. Deb: 4/16/27 FC																									
1927 Bos-N	0	1	.000	15	1	0	0	0	37²	41	1	18	7	14.8	3.82	97	.287	.378	0	.000	-1	0	-0	1	0.0
1928 Bos-N	0	0	—	4	0	0	0	0	7²	17	3	8	0	31.7	12.91	30	.472	.587	0	.000	-0	-8	-8	-0	0.0
Total 2	0	1	.000	19	1	0	0	0	45¹	58	4	26	7	17.7	5.36	70	.324	.424	0	.000	-1	-7	-8	1	0.0
● **LEFTY MILLS** Mills, Howard Robinson b: 5/12/10, Dedham, Mass. d: 9/23/82, Riverside, Cal. BL/TL, 6'1", 187 lbs. Deb: 6/10/34																									
1934 StL-A	0	0	—	4	0	0	0	0	8²	10	0	11	2	21.8	4.15	120	.303	.477	1	.333	0	0	1	-0	0.0
1937 StL-A	1	1	.500	2	1	0	0	0	12²	16	1	10	10	18.5	6.39	75	.286	.394	0	.000	-1	-2	-2	0	-0.3
1938 StL-A	10	12	.455	30	27	15	1	0	210¹	216	16	116	134	14.5	5.31	94	.262	.358	6	.091	-3	-12	-8	-2	-1.1
1939 StL-A	4	11	.267	34	14	4	0	2	144¹	147	16	113	103	16.7	6.55	74	.264	.395	11	.234	1	-31	-27	-1	-2.3
1940 StL-A	0	6	.000	26	5	1	0	0	59	64	7	52	18	18.2	7.78	59	.275	.413	2	.154	-0	-22	-21	0	-1.7
Total 5	15	30	.333	96	48	21	1	2	435	453	40	302	267	16.0	6.06	81	.266	.382	20	.149	-3	-67	-57	-3	-5.4
● **DICK MILLS** Mills, Richard Alan b: 1/29/45, Boston, Mass. BR/TR, 6'3", 195 lbs. Deb: 9/7/70																									
1970 Bos-A	0	0	—	2	0	0	0	0	3²	6	0	3	3	24.5	2.45	161	.353	.476	0	—	0	1	1	0	0.0
● **WILLIE MILLS** Mills, William Grant "Wee Willie" b: 8/15/1877, Schenevus, N.Y. d: 7/5/14, Norwood, N.Y. BR/TR, 5'7", 150 lbs. Deb: 7/13/01 F																									
1901 NY-N	0	2	.000	2	2	2	0	0	16	21	2	4	3	14.6	8.44	39	.314	.362	1	.167	0	-9	-9	-0	-0.8
● **AL MILNAR** Milnar, Albert Joseph "Happy" (b: Albert Joseph Mlinar) b: 12/26/13, Cleveland, Ohio BL/TL, 6'2", 195 lbs. Deb: 4/30/36																									
1936 Cle-A	1	2	.333	4	3	1	0	0	22	26	0	18	9	18.0	7.36	68	.286	.404	3	.300	1	-6	-6	0	-0.5
1938 Cle-A	3	1	.750	23	5	2	0	1	68¹	90	5	26	29	15.3	5.00	93	.320	.378	4	.154	-0	-2	-3	-0	-0.1
1939 Cle-A	14	12	.538	37	26	12	2	3	209	212	11	99	76	13.4	3.79	116	.264	.345	20	.253	4	19	14	0	1.9
1940 Cle-A☆	18	10	.643	37	33	15	**4**	3	242¹	242	14	99	99	12.7	3.27	129	.257	.328	17	.181	-1	30	26	-5	2.1
1941 Cle-A	12	19	.387	35	30	9	1	0	229¹	236	9	116	82	13.9	4.36	90	.266	.352	14	.171	-3	-5	-13	-3	-1.3
1942 Cle-A	6	8	.429	28	19	8	2	0	157	146	3	85	35	13.5	4.13	84	.251	.350	12	.171	2	-8	-12	1	-0.7
1943 Cle-A	1	3	.250	16	6	0	0	0	39	51	3	35	10	20.1	8.08	38	.329	.455	4	.211	4	-21	-22	0	-2.0
StL-A	1	2	.333	3	3	1	0	0	14²	23	0	9	9	19.6	5.52	60	.354	.432	2	.333	1	-4	-4	-0	-0.5
Yr	2	5	.286	19	9	1	0	0	53²	74	0	44	19	19.8	7.38	43	.335	.445	6	.240	1	-24	-25	0	-2.5
1946 StL-A	1	1	.500	4	2	1	0	0	14²	15	1	6	1	12.9	2.45	152	.278	.350	3	.750	1	2	0	0	0.4

YEAR TM/L	W	L	PCT	G	GS	CG	SH	SV	IP	H	HR	BB	SO	RAT	ERA	ERA+	OAV	OOB	BH	AVG	PB	PR	/A	PD	TPI
Phi-N	0	0	—	1	1	0	0	0	0	2	0	2	0	—	∞	—	1.000	1.000	0	—	0	-4	-4	0	-0.3
Total 8	57	58	.496	188	127	49	10	7	996¹	1043	43	495	350	14.0	4.22	96	.270	.354	79	.203	9	2	-18	-6	-1.0

● **GEORGE MILSTEAD**　　Milstead, George Earl "Cowboy"　b: 6/26/03, Cleburne, Tex.　d: 8/9/77, Cleburne, Tex.　BL/TL, 5'10", 144 lbs.　Deb: 6/27/24

1924 Chi-N	1	1	.500	13	2	1	0	0	29²	41	3	13	6	16.7	6.07	64	.328	.396	1	.167	0	-7	-7	0	-0.4
1925 Chi-N	1	1	.500	5	3	1	0	0	21	26	0	8	7	14.6	3.00	144	.310	.370	0	—	-1	3	3	0	0.2
1926 Chi-N	1	5	.167	18	4	0	0	2	55¹	63	0	24	14	14.3	3.58	107	.309	.384	1	.053	-2	2	2	2	0.2
Total 3	3	7	.300	36	9	2	0	2	106	130	3	45	27	15.0	4.16	95	.315	.385	2	.063	-3	-3	-2	3	0.0

● **LARRY MILTON**　　Milton, Samuel Lawrence "Tug"　b: 5/4/1879, Owensboro, Ky.　d: 5/16/42, Hannibal, Mo.　TR　Deb: 5/7/03

1903 StL-N	0	0	—	1	0	0	0	0	4	3	0	1	0	9.0	2.25	145	.200	.250	1	.500	0	0	0	0	0.1

● **COTTON MINAHAN**　　Minahan, Edmund Joseph　b: 12/10/1882, Springfield, Ohio　d: 5/20/58, E.Orange, N.J.　BR/TR, 6', 190 lbs.　Deb: 4/21/07

1907 Cin-N	0	2	.000	2	2	1	0	0	14	12	0	13	4	16.7	1.29	202	.261	.433	0	.000	-1	2	2	-1	0.2

● **RUDY MINARCIN**　　Minarcin, Rudy Anthony "Buster"　b: 3/25/30, N.Vandergrift, Pa.　BR/TR, 6', 195 lbs.　Deb: 4/11/55

1955 Cin-N	5	9	.357	41	12	3	1	1	115²	116	17	51	45	13.2	4.90	86	.261	.341	5	.179	-1	-11	-9	2	-0.8
1956 Bos-A	1	0	1.000	3	1	0	0	0	9²	9	2	8	5	16.8	2.79	165	.250	.400	1	.500	1	1	2	0	0.3
1957 Bos-A	0	0	—	26	0	0	0	2	44²	44	5	30	20	15.1	4.43	90	.267	.383	0	.000	0	-3	-2	-0	0.0
Total 3	6	9	.400	70	13	3	1	3	170	169	24	89	70	13.9	4.66	90	.262	.356	6	.188	0	-13	-9	2	-0.5

● **NATE MINCHEY**　　Minchey, Nathan Derek　b: 8/31/69, Austin, Tex.　BR/TR, 6'8", 225 lbs.　Deb: 9/12/93

1993 Bos-A	1	2	.333	5	5	1	0	0	33	35	5	8	18	11.7	3.55	130	.265	.307	0	—	0	3	4	-1	0.2
1994 Bos-A	2	3	.400	6	5	0	0	0	23	44	1	14	15	22.7	8.61	60	.427	.496	0	—	0	-10	-9	-0	-1.4
Total 2	3	5	.375	11	10	1	0	0	56	79	6	22	33	16.2	5.63	86	.336	.393	0	—	0	-7	-5	-1	-1.2

● **RAY MINER**　　Miner, Raymond Theadore "Lefty"　b: 4/4/1897, Glens Falls, N.Y.　d: 9/15/63, Glenridge, N.Y.　BR/TL, 5'11", 160 lbs.　Deb: 9/15/21

1921 Phi-A	0	0	—	1	0	0	0	0	1	2	0	3	0	45.0	36.00	12	.400	.625	0	—	0	-4	-4	-0	0.0

● **CRAIG MINETTO**　　Minetto, Craig Stephen　b: 4/25/54, Stockton, Cal.　BL/TL, 6', 185 lbs.　Deb: 7/4/78

1978 Oak-A	0	0	—	4	1	0	0	0	12	13	1	7	3	16.5	3.75	97	.283	.400	0	—	0	0	-0	-0	0.0
1979 Oak-A	1	5	.167	36	13	0	0	0	118¹	131	16	58	64	14.6	5.55	73	.282	.365	0	—	0	-18	-20	-2	-0.7
1980 Oak-A	0	2	.000	7	1	0	0	1	8	11	2	3	5	15.8	7.88	48	.324	.378	0	—	0	-3	-4	-0	-0.5
1981 Oak-A	0	0	—	8	0	0	0	0	6²	7	0	4	4	16.2	2.70	129	.280	.400	0	—	0	1	1	-0	0.2
Total 4	1	7	.125	55	15	0	0	1	145	162	19	72	76	14.9	5.40	73	.284	.370	0	—	0	-20	-23	-2	-1.0

● **STEVE MINGORI**　　Mingori, Stephen Bernard　b: 2/29/44, Kansas City, Mo.　BL/TL, 5'10", 170 lbs.　Deb: 8/5/70

1970 Cle-A	1	0	1.000	21	0	0	0	1	20¹	17	2	12	16	13.3	2.66	149	.227	.341	0	.000	-0	2	3	0	0.2
1971 Cle-A	1	2	.333	54	0	0	0	4	56²	31	4	24	45	8.9	1.43	268	.166	.264	1	.500	0	13	15	1	1.2
1972 Cle-A	0	6	.000	41	0	0	0	10	57	67	4	36	47	16.6	3.95	81	.293	.393	1	.125	-0	-6	-5	1	-0.7
1973 Cle-A	0	0	—	5	0	0	0	0	11²	10	3	10	4	15.4	6.17	64	.233	.377	0	—	0	-3	-3	1	0.0
KC-A	3	3	.500	19	1	0	0	1	56¹	59	6	23	46	13.6	3.04	135	.267	.344	0	—	0	5	7	-0	0.2
Yr	3	3	.500	24	1	0	0	1	68	69	9	33	50	13.8	3.57	114	.261	.350	0	—	0	2	4	1	0.2
1974 KC-A	2	3	.400	36	0	0	0	4	67¹	53	4	23	43	10.4	2.81	136	.212	.284	0	—	0	6	8	2	0.6
1975 KC-A	0	3	.000	36	0	0	0	2	50¹	42	2	20	25	11.3	2.50	154	.226	.304	0	.000	0	7	8	0	0.5
1976 *KC-A	5	5	.500	55	0	0	0	10	85¹	73	5	25	38	10.7	2.32	151	.238	.301	0	—	0	11	11	3	1.9
1977 *KC-A	2	4	.333	43	0	0	0	4	64	59	6	19	19	11.1	3.09	130	.254	.313	0	—	0	7	7	1	0.7
1978 *KC-A	1	4	.200	45	0	0	0	7	69	64	5	16	28	10.8	2.74	140	.242	.292	0	—	0	8	8	0	0.8
1979 KC-A	3	3	.500	30	0	0	0	1	46²	69	10	17	18	16.8	5.79	74	.348	.403	0	—	0	-8	-8	-1	-1.1
Total 10	18	33	.353	385	2	0	0	42	584²	544	45	225	329	12.1	3.03	126	.248	.323	2	.167	0	43	51	7	4.3

● **PAUL MINNER**　　Minner, Paul Edison "Lefty"　b: 7/30/23, New Wilmington, Pa.　BL/TL, 6'5", 210 lbs.　Deb: 9/12/46

1946 Bro-N	0	1	.000	3	0	0	0	0	4	6	1	3	3	20.3	6.75	50	.333	.429	0	—	-1	-1	-1	-0	-0.4
1948 Bro-N	4	3	.571	28	2	0	0	1	62²	61	5	26	23	12.5	2.44	164	.257	.331	4	.190	1	11	11	0	1.3
1949 *Bro-N	3	1	.750	27	1	0	0	2	47¹	49	7	18	17	12.9	3.80	108	.272	.342	3	.214	-0	1	2	0	0.2
1950 Chi-N	8	13	.381	39	24	9	1	4	190¹	217	18	72	99	13.7	4.11	102	.287	.350	14	.215	2	1	2	3	0.7
1951 Chi-N	6	17	.261	33	28	14	3	1	201²	219	20	64	68	12.6	3.79	108	.277	.331	18	.254	5	4	7	3	1.6
1952 Chi-N	14	9	.609	28	27	12	2	0	180²	180	13	54	61	11.7	3.74	103	.258	.312	15	.234	6	-0	2	1	1.1
1953 Chi-N	12	15	.444	31	27	9	2	1	201	227	15	40	64	12.1	4.21	106	.283	.320	15	.221	2	2	5	2	1.2
1954 Chi-N	11	11	.500	32	29	12	0	1	218	236	19	50	79	11.8	3.96	106	.280	.321	11	.171	3	3	6	1	1.0
1955 Chi-N	9	9	.500	22	22	7	1	0	157²	173	15	47	53	12.6	3.48	117	.283	.335	13	.232	1	10	11	2	1.5
1956 Chi-N	2	5	.286	10	9	1	0	0	47	60	9	19	14	15.5	6.89	55	.324	.393	3	.250	2	-16	-16	0	-1.8
Total 10	69	84	.451	253	169	64	9	10	1310¹	1428	122	393	481	12.6	3.94	105	.279	.332	98	.219	22	12	27	15	6.4

● **DON MINNICK**　　Minnick, Donald Athey　b: 4/14/31, Lynchburg, Va.　BR/TR, 6'3", 195 lbs.　Deb: 9/23/57

1957 Was-A	0	1	.000	2	1	0	0	0	9¹	14	1	2	7	15.4	4.82	81	.341	.372	0	.000	-0	-1	-1	-0	-0.1

● **BLAS MINOR**　　Minor, Blas　b: 3/20/66, Merced, Cal.　BR/TR, 6'3", 195 lbs.　Deb: 7/28/92

1992 Pit-N	0	0	—	1	0	0	0	0	2	3	0	0	0	13.5	4.50	76	.333	.333	0	—	-0	-0	-0	-0	0.0
1993 Pit-N	8	6	.571	65	0	0	0	2	94¹	94	8	26	84	11.8	4.10	99	.263	.320	2	.200	1	-1	-1	1	0.1
1994 Pit-N	0	1	.000	17	0	0	0	0	19	27	4	9	17	17.5	8.05	53	.351	.425	0	—	0	-8	-8	-0	-0.5
Total 3	8	7	.533	83	0	0	0	3	115¹	124	12	35	101	12.8	4.76	86	.279	.339	2	.200	0	-9	-9	1	-0.4

● **JIM MINSHALL**　　Minshall, James Edward　b: 7/4/47, Covington, Ky.　BR/TR, 6'6", 215 lbs.　Deb: 9/14/74

1974 Pit-N	0	1	.000	5	0	0	0	0	4¹	1	0	2	3	6.2	0.00	—	.083	.214	0	—	0	2	2	-0	0.4
1975 Pit-N	0	0	—	1	0	0	0	0	1	0	0	2	1	18.0	0.00	—	.000	.400	0	—	0	0	0	0	0.0
Total 2	0	1	.000	6	0	0	0	0	5¹	1	0	4	4	8.4	0.00	—	.067	.263	0	—	0	2	2	-0	0.4

● **GREG MINTON**　　Minton, Gregory Brian　b: 7/29/51, Lubbock, Tex.　BB/TR, 6'2", 190 lbs.　Deb: 9/7/75

1975 SF-N	1	1	.500	4	2	0	0	0	17	19	1	11	6	16.4	6.88	55	.288	.397	0	.000	-1	-6	-6	1	-0.6
1976 SF-N	0	3	.000	10	2	0	0	0	25²	32	0	12	7	15.8	4.91	74	.317	.395	1	.200	-0	-4	-4	-0	-0.4
1977 SF-N	1	1	.500	2	2	0	0	0	14	14	0	4	5	11.6	4.50	87	.264	.316	1	.333	1	-1	-1	0	0.0
1978 SF-N	0	1	.000	11	0	0	0	0	15²	22	3	8	6	17.8	8.04	43	.338	.419	0	—	0	-8	-8	-0	-0.5
1979 SF-N	4	3	.571	46	0	0	0	4	79²	59	0	27	33	9.9	1.81	193	.215	.289	0	.000	-0	17	15	2	1.6
1980 SF-N	4	6	.400	68	0	0	0	19	91¹	81	0	34	42	11.3	2.46	144	.243	.313	1	.125	-0	12	11	2	1.9
1981 SF-N	4	5	.444	55	0	0	0	21	84¹	84	0	36	29	12.8	2.88	119	.267	.342	0	—	0	4	3	0	0.4
1982 SF-N★	10	4	.714	78	0	0	0	30	123	108	5	42	58	11.1	1.83	196	.244	.313	3	.176	-0	**24**	**24**	1	**4.2**
1983 SF-N	7	11	.389	73	0	0	0	22	106²	117	6	47	38	13.8	3.54	100	.283	.356	6	.545	4	1	-0	-0	0.4
1984 SF-N	4	9	.308	74	1	0	0	19	124¹	130	7	57	48	13.5	3.76	93	.267	.344	1	.048	-1	-2	-4	2	-0.4
1985 SF-N	4	5	.556	68	0	0	0	0	96²	98	6	54	37	14.2	3.54	97	.272	.367	0	.000	-1	-1	-2	0	0.1
1986 SF-N	4	4	.500	48	0	0	0	5	68²	63	4	34	34	12.8	3.93	90	.251	.343	2	.400	2	-3	-3	0	-0.1
1987 SF-N	1	0	1.000	15	0	0	0	0	23¹	30	2	10	9	15.8	3.47	111	.323	.394	0	.000	-0	-0	-1	0	0.0
Cal-A	5	4	.556	44	0	0	0	10	74²	67	4	29	35	11.8	3.08	140	.255	.330	0	—	0	12	10	2	1.6
1988 Cal-A	4	5	.444	44	0	0	0	7	79	67	1	34	46	11.8	2.85	135	.233	.320	0	—	0	10	9	2	1.4
1989 Cal-A	4	3	.571	62	0	0	0	8	90	76	4	37	42	11.5	2.20	173	.230	.311	0	—	PB	17	16	2	1.7

YEAR	TM/L	W	L	PCT	G	GS	CG	SH	SV	IP	H	HR	BB	SO	RAT	ERA	ERA+	OAV	OOB	BH	AVG	PB	PR	/A	PD	TPI
1990	Cal-A	1	1	.500	11	0	0	0	0	15¹	11	1	7	4	11.2	2.35	163	.212	.317	0	—	0	3	3	0	0.4
Total	16	59	65	.476	710	7	0	0	150	1130²	1082	43	483	479	12.6	3.10	117	.257	.336	15	.146	2	80	68	19	12.4

● **GINO MINUTELLI**   Minutelli, Gino Michael b: 5/23/64, Wilmington, Del. BL/TL, 6', 180 lbs. Deb: 9/18/90

YEAR	TM/L	W	L	PCT	G	GS	CG	SH	SV	IP	H	HR	BB	SO	RAT	ERA	ERA+	OAV	OOB	BH	AVG	PB	PR	/A	PD	TPI
1990	Cin-N	0	0	—	2	0	0	0	0	1	0	0	2	0	27.0	9.00	44	.000	.500	0	—	0	-1	-1	0	0.0
1991	Cin-N	0	2	.000	16	3	0	0	0	25¹	30	5	18	21	17.1	6.04	63	.288	.393	0	.000	-0	-7	-6	0	-0.5
1993	SF-N	0	1	.000	9	0	0	0	0	14¹	7	2	15	10	13.8	3.77	104	.152	.361	0	.000	-0	0	0	-0	-0.1
Total	3	0	3	.000	27	3	0	0	0	40²	37	7	35	31	16.2	5.31	72	.242	.386	0	.000	-1	-7	-7	0	-0.6

● **PAUL MIRABELLA**   Mirabella, Paul Thomas b: 3/20/54, Belleville, N.J. BL/TL, 6'2", 196 lbs. Deb: 7/28/78

YEAR	TM/L	W	L	PCT	G	GS	CG	SH	SV	IP	H	HR	BB	SO	RAT	ERA	ERA+	OAV	OOB	BH	AVG	PB	PR	/A	PD	TPI
1978	Tex-A	3	2	.600	10	4	0	0	1	28	30	2	17	23	15.1	5.79	65	.286	.385	0	—	0	-6	-6	-0	-1.1
1979	NY-A	0	4	.000	10	1	0	0	0	14¹	16	3	10	4	17.0	8.79	46	.276	.391	0	—	0	-7	-8	-0	-1.6
1980	Tor-A	5	12	.294	33	22	3	1	0	130²	151	11	66	53	15.2	4.34	89	.294	.378	0	—	0	-4	-1	0	-0.1
1981	Tor-A	0	0	—	8	1	0	0	0	14²	20	2	7	9	17.2	7.36	53	.313	.389	0	—	0	-6	-6	-0	-0.3
1982	Tex-A	1	1	.500	40	0	0	0	3	50²	46	4	22	29	12.4	4.80	81	.241	.326	0	—	0	-4	-5	0	0.0
1983	Bal-A	0	0	—	3	2	0	0	0	9²	9	1	7	4	14.9	5.59	71	.243	.364	0	—	0	-2	-2	0	0.0
1984	Sea-A	2	5	.286	52	1	0	0	3	68	74	6	32	41	14.2	4.37	91	.282	.363	0	—	0	-3	-3	1	-0.2
1985	Sea-A	0	0	—	10	0	0	0	0	13²	9	0	4	8	9.9	1.32	320	.188	.278	0	—	0	4	4	-0	0.4
1986	Sea-A	0	0	—	8	0	0	0	0	6¹	13	1	3	6	22.7	8.53	50	.419	.471	0	—	0	-3	-3	0	-0.4
1987	Mil-A	2	1	.667	29	0	0	0	2	29¹	30	0	16	14	14.1	4.91	93	.268	.359	0	—	0	-1	-1	1	-0.1
1988	Mil-A	2	2	.500	38	0	0	0	4	60	44	3	21	33	9.8	1.65	241	.204	.274	0	—	0	15	16	1	1.3
1989	Mil-A	0	0	—	13	0	0	0	0	15¹	18	1	7	6	15.3	7.63	50	.290	.371	0	—	0	-6	-6	0	-0.1
1990	Mil-A	4	2	.667	44	2	0	0	0	59	66	9	27	28	14.5	3.97	98	.281	.360	0	—	0	-0	-1	-0	0.1
Total	13	19	29	.396	298	33	3	1	13	499²	526	43	239	258	14.0	4.45	91	.272	.356	0	—	0	-24	-21	0	-2.0

● **ANGEL MIRANDA**   Miranda, Angel Luis b: 11/9/69, Arecibo, P.R. BL/TL, 6'1", 160 lbs. Deb: 6/5/93

YEAR	TM/L	W	L	PCT	G	GS	CG	SH	SV	IP	H	HR	BB	SO	RAT	ERA	ERA+	OAV	OOB	BH	AVG	PB	PR	/A	PD	TPI
1993	Mil-A	4	5	.444	22	17	2	0	0	120	100	12	52	88	11.6	3.30	129	.226	.310	0	—	0	14	13	-1	0.8
1994	Mil-A	2	5	.286	8	8	1	0	0	46	39	8	27	24	12.9	5.28	93	.234	.340	0	—	0	-2	-2	0	-0.2
Total	2	6	10	.375	30	25	3	0	0	166	139	20	79	112	11.9	3.85	115	.228	.319	0	—	0	11	11	-1	0.6

● **ROY MITCHELL**   Mitchell, Albert Roy b: 4/19/1885, Belton, Tex. d: 9/8/59, Temple, Tex. BR/TR, 5'9.5", 170 lbs. Deb: 9/10/10

YEAR	TM/L	W	L	PCT	G	GS	CG	SH	SV	IP	H	HR	BB	SO	RAT	ERA	ERA+	OAV	OOB	BH	AVG	PB	PR	/A	PD	TPI
1910	StL-A	4	2	.667	6	6	6	0	0	52	43	0	12	23	9.9	2.60	95	.244	.300	4	.211	0	-0	-1	1	0.0
1911	StL-A	4	8	.333	28	12	8	1	0	133¹	134	4	45	40	12.5	3.85	88	.273	.341	11	.224	1	-7	-7	-0	-0.4
1912	StL-A	3	4	.429	13	7	5	0	0	62	81	2	17	22	14.8	4.65	71	.323	.375	6	.316	3	-9	-9	-1	-0.7
1913	StL-A	13	16	.448	33	27	21	4	1	245¹	265	6	47	59	11.6	3.01	98	.280	.318	13	.148	-1	-2	-2	-1	-0.4
1914	StL-A	4	5	.444	28	9	4	0	4	103¹	134	1	38	38	15.5	4.35	62	.320	.384	7	.206	1	-19	-19	0	-1.6
1918	Chi-A	0	0	—	2	2	0	0	0	12	18	1	4	3	16.5	7.50	36	.346	.393	0	.000	-0	-6	-6	-0	-0.5
	Cin-N	4	0	1.000	5	3	3	2	0	36¹	27	0	5	9	7.9	0.74	359	.208	.237	3	.214	0	8	8	-0	1.0
1919	Cin-N	0	1	.000	7	1	0	0	0	31	32	0	9	10	11.9	2.32	119	.276	.328	0	.000	-2	2	2	1	0.0
Total	7	32	37	.464	122	67	47	7	5	675¹	734	14	177	204	12.4	3.42	86	.284	.336	44	.187	3	-34	-35	-1	-2.6

● **CHARLIE MITCHELL**   Mitchell, Charles Ross b: 6/24/62, Dickson, Tenn. BR/TR, 6'3", 170 lbs. Deb: 8/9/84 F

YEAR	TM/L	W	L	PCT	G	GS	CG	SH	SV	IP	H	HR	BB	SO	RAT	ERA	ERA+	OAV	OOB	BH	AVG	PB	PR	/A	PD	TPI
1984	Bos-A	0	0	—	10	0	0	0	0	16¹	14	1	6	7	12.1	2.76	151	.226	.314	0	—	0	2	3	0	-0.1
1985	Bos-A	0	0	—	2	0	0	0	0	1²	5	1	0	2	27.0	16.20	26	.500	.500	0	—	0	-2	-2	0	0.0
Total	2	0	0	—	12	0	0	0	0	18	19	2	6	9	13.5	4.00	104	.264	.338	0	—	0	0	0	0	-0.1

● **CLARENCE MITCHELL**   Mitchell, Clarence Elmer b: 2/22/1891, Franklin, Neb. d: 11/6/63, Grand Island, Neb. BL/TL, 5'11.5", 190 lbs. Deb: 6/2/11 C◆

YEAR	TM/L	W	L	PCT	G	GS	CG	SH	SV	IP	H	HR	BB	SO	RAT	ERA	ERA+	OAV	OOB	BH	AVG	PB	PR	/A	PD	TPI
1911	Det-A	1	0	1.000	5	1	0	0	0	14¹	20	1	7	4	17.0	8.16	42	.351	.422	2	.500	1	-8	-7	1	-0.4
1916	Cin-N	11	10	.524	29	24	17	1	0	194²	211	4	45	52	12.3	3.14	83	.285	.334	28	.239	2	-11	-12	-1	-0.8
1917	Cin-N	9	15	.375	32	20	10	2	1	159¹	166	4	34	37	11.4	3.22	81	.268	.308	25	.278	4	-9	-11	0	-1.2
1918	Bro-N	0	1	.000	1	1	0	0	0	0¹	4	0	0	0	108.0	108.00	3	1.000	1.000	6	.250	1	-4	-4	0	-3.0
1919	Bro-N	7	5	.583	23	11	9	0	0	108²	123	0	23	43	12.1	3.06	97	.297	.334	18	.367	6	-2	-1	1	0.7
1920	*Bro-N	5	2	.714	19	7	3	1	1	78²	85	1	23	18	12.4	3.09	104	.288	.340	25	.234	1	0	1	1	0.4
1921	Bro-N	11	9	.550	37	18	13	3	2	190	206	7	46	39	12.2	2.89	135	.280	.327	24	.264	3	19	21	3	2.8
1922	Bro-N	0	3	.000	5	3	0	0	0	12²	28	0	7	1	25.6	14.21	29	.467	.529	45	.290	2	-14	-14	1	-2.2
1923	Phi-N	9	10	.474	29	19	8	0	0	139¹	170	8	46	41	14.2	4.72	98	.299	.355	21	.269	3	-11	-2	-3	-0.2
1924	Phi-N	6	13	.316	30	26	9	1	0	165	223	6	58	36	15.7	5.62	79	.321	.379	26	.255	-1	-32	-21	3	-1.9
1925	Phi-N	10	17	.370	32	26	12	1	1	199¹	245	23	51	46	13.6	5.28	90	.302	.347	18	.196	-2	-22	-11	4	-1.0
1926	Phi-N	9	14	.391	28	25	12	0	1	178²	232	7	55	52	14.7	4.58	90	.318	.369	19	.244	1	-15	-17	4	-0.4
1927	Phi-N	6	3	.667	13	12	8	1	0	94²	99	7	28	17	12.3	4.09	101	.271	.327	16	.238	2	-2	0	1	0.3
1928	Phi-N	0	0	—	3	0	0	0	0	5²	13	0	2	0	23.8	9.53	45	.542	.577	1	.250	0	-3	-3	0	-0.3
	*StL-N	8	9	.471	19	18	9	0	0	150	149	8	38	31	11.4	3.30	121	.265	.315	7	.125	-3	12	12	2	1.1
	Yr	8	9	.471	22	18	9	0	0	155²	162	8	40	31	11.9	3.53	114	.276	.326	8	.133	-3	8	8	3	1.1
1929	StL-N	8	11	.421	25	22	16	0	0	173	221	13	60	39	14.9	4.27	109	.320	.379	18	.273	4	9	8	-1	0.9
1930	StL-N	1	0	1.000	1	1	0	0	0	3	5	0	2	1	21.0	6.00	84	.357	.438	1	.500	0	-0	-0	-0	-0.1
	NY-N	10	3	.769	24	16	5	0	0	129	151	10	36	40	13.1	3.98	119	.298	.346	12	.255	0	14	11	2	1.1
	Yr	11	3	.786	25	17	5	0	0	132	156	10	38	41	13.3	4.02	118	.300	.349	13	.265	1	14	11	2	1.0
1931	NY-N	13	11	.542	27	25	13	0	0	190¹	221	12	52	39	13.1	4.07	91	.285	.332	16	.219	2	-4	-8	-2	-0.9
1932	NY-N	1	3	.250	8	3	1	0	2	30¹	41	1	11	7	15.7	4.15	89	.325	.384	2	.200	0	-1	-1	-1	-0.3
Total	18	125	139	.473	390	278	145	12	9	2217	2613	116	624	543	13.4	4.12	95	.297	.347	324	.252	26	-86	-54	17	-5.1

● **CRAIG MITCHELL**   Mitchell, Craig Seton b: 4/14/54, Santa Rosa, Cal. BR/TR, 6'3", 180 lbs. Deb: 9/25/75

YEAR	TM/L	W	L	PCT	G	GS	CG	SH	SV	IP	H	HR	BB	SO	RAT	ERA	ERA+	OAV	OOB	BH	AVG	PB	PR	/A	PD	TPI
1975	Oak-A	0	1	.000	1	1	0	0	0	3²	6	0	2	2	19.6	12.27	30	.375	.444	0	—	0	-3	-4	0	-0.6
1976	Oak-A	0	0	—	1	0	0	0	0	3¹	3	0	0	0	8.1	2.70	124	.231	.231	0	—	0	0	0	0	0.0
1977	Oak-A	0	1	.000	3	1	0	0	0	5²	9	1	2	1	17.5	7.94	51	.346	.393	0	—	0	-2	-2	-0	-0.3
Total	3	0	2	.000	5	2	0	0	0	12²	18	1	4	3	15.6	7.82	48	.327	.373	0	—	0	-6	-6	0	-0.9

● **FRED MITCHELL**   Mitchell, Frederick Francis (b: Frederick Francis Yapp)
b: 6/5/1878, Cambridge, Mass. d: 10/13/70, Newton, Mass. BR/TR, 5'9.5", 185 lbs. Deb: 4/27/01 MC◆

YEAR	TM/L	W	L	PCT	G	GS	CG	SH	SV	IP	H	HR	BB	SO	RAT	ERA	ERA+	OAV	OOB	BH	AVG	PB	PR	/A	PD	TPI
1901	Bos-A	6	6	.500	17	13	10	0	0	108²	115	2	51	34	14.7	3.81	93	.268	.361	7	.159	-1	-2	-3	0	-0.4
1902	Bos-A	0	1	.000	1	0	0	0	0	4	8	1	5	2	29.3	11.25	32	.414	.534	0	.000	-0	-3	-3	0	-0.5
	Phi-A	5	7	.417	18	14	9	0	1	107²	120	4	59	22	15.6	3.59	102	.282	.380	9	.188	-1	-0	1	2	0.2
	Yr	5	8	.385	19	14	9	0	1	111²	128	5	64	24	16.1	3.87	95	.288	.387	9	.184	-1	-4	-3	-3	-0.3
1903	Phi-N	11	16	.407	28	28	24	1	0	227	250	4	102	69	14.7	4.48	73	.284	.370	19	.200	-1	-31	-30	-3	-3.3
1904	Phi-N	4	7	.364	13	13	11	0	0	108²	133	3	25	29	13.7	3.40	79	.306	.353	17	.207	1	-8	-9	-3	-0.4
	Bro-N	2	5	.286	8	8	8	1	0	66	73	0	23	16	13.5	3.82	72	.291	.357	7	.292	-1	-8	-8	4	-0.4
	Yr	6	12	.333	21	21	19	1	0	174²	206	3	48	45	13.2	3.56	76	.297	.345	24	.226	4	-16	-17	4	-0.8
1905	Bro-N	3	7	.300	12	10	9	0	0	96¹	107	2	38	44	14.0	4.76	61	.285	.358	15	.190	0	-19	-20	1	-1.7
Total	5	31	49	.387	97	86	71	2	1	718²	806	16	303	216	14.6	4.10	78	.286	.366	120	.210	1	-71	-73	5	-6.5

● **JOHN MITCHELL**   Mitchell, John Kyle b: 8/11/65, Dickson, Tenn. BR/TR, 6'2", 195 lbs. Deb: 9/8/86 F

YEAR	TM/L	W	L	PCT	G	GS	CG	SH	SV	IP	H	HR	BB	SO	RAT	ERA	ERA+	OAV	OOB	BH	AVG	PB	PR	/A	PD	TPI
1986	NY-N	0	1	.000	4	1	0	0	0	10	10	1	4	2	12.6	3.60	98	.278	.350	0	.000	-0	0	0	0	0.0
1987	NY-N	3	6	.333	20	19	1	0	0	111²	124	6	36	57	13.1	4.11	92	.291	.336	4	.114	-1	-0	-4	1	-0.3
1988	NY-N	0	0	—	1	0	0	0	0	1	2	0	1	1	27.0	—	.500	.600	0	.000	-0	-1	-1	-0	0.0
1989	NY-N	0	1	.000	2	0	0	0	0	3	3	0	4	4	21.0	6.00	54	.231	.412	0	—	0	-1	-1	-0	-0.3

YEAR TM/L	W	L	PCT	G	GS	CG	SH	SV	IP	H	HR	BB	SO	RAT	ERA	ERA+	OAV	OOB	BH	AVG	PB	PR	/A	PD	TPI
1990 Bal-A	6	6	.500	24	17	1	0	0	114¹	133	7	48	43	14.5	4.64	82	.300	.372	0	—	0	-9	-11	-1	-0.8
Total 5	9	14	.391	51	37	1	0	0	240	272	14	93	107	13.9	4.35	87	.289	.356	4	.105	-1	-10	-16	2	-1.4

● **MONROE MITCHELL**   Mitchell, Monroe Barr   b: 9/11/01, Starkville, Miss.   d: 9/4/76, Valdosta, Ga.   BR/TL, 6'1.5", 170 lbs.   Deb: 7/11/23

YEAR TM/L	W	L	PCT	G	GS	CG	SH	SV	IP	H	HR	BB	SO	RAT	ERA	ERA+	OAV	OOB	BH	AVG	PB	PR	/A	PD	TPI
1923 Was-A	2	4	.333	10	6	3	1	2	41²	57	0	22	8	17.3	6.48	58	.350	.430	3	.250	1	-12	-13	-1	-1.6

● **PAUL MITCHELL**   Mitchell, Paul Michael   b: 8/19/49, Worcester, Mass.   BR/TR, 6'1", 195 lbs.   Deb: 7/1/75

YEAR TM/L	W	L	PCT	G	GS	CG	SH	SV	IP	H	HR	BB	SO	RAT	ERA	ERA+	OAV	OOB	BH	AVG	PB	PR	/A	PD	TPI
1975 Bal-A	3	0	1.000	11	4	1	0	0	57	41	8	19	31	9.5	3.63	97	.204	.273	0	—	0	1	-1	-1	-0.1
1976 Oak-A	9	7	.563	26	26	4	1	0	142	169	15	30	67	12.7	4.25	79	.294	.331	0	—	0	-11	-14	-1	-1.6
1977 Oak-A	0	3	.000	5	3	0	0	0	13²	21	3	7	5	18.4	10.54	38	.339	.406	0	—	0	-10	-10	0	-1.6
Sea-A	3	3	.500	9	9	0	0	0	39²	50	7	16	20	15.2	4.99	82	.311	.376	0	—	0	-4	-4	0	-0.4
Yr	3	6	.333	14	12	0	0	0	53¹	71	10	23	25	16.0	6.41	64	.318	.385	0	—	0	-14	-14	1	-2.0
1978 Sea-A	8	14	.364	29	29	4	2	0	168	173	21	79	75	13.6	4.18	91	.270	.352	0	—	0	-8	-7	-1	-0.9
1979 Sea-A	1	4	.200	10	6	1	0	0	36²	46	4	15	18	15.0	4.42	99	.309	.372	0	—	0	-1	-0	-0	-0.1
Mil-A	3	3	.500	18	8	0	0	0	75	81	11	10	32	11.3	5.76	72	.276	.307	0	—	0	-13	-13	-1	-1.0
Yr	4	7	.364	28	14	1	0	0	111²	127	15	25	50	12.5	5.32	79	.287	.329	0	—	0	-14	-14	-1	-1.1
1980 Mil-A	5	5	.500	17	11	1	1	1	89¹	92	7	15	29	10.9	3.53	110	.267	.300	0	—	0	5	3	0	0.4
Total 6	32	39	.451	125	96	11	4	1	621¹	673	76	191	277	12.6	4.45	85	.278	.332	0	—	0	-41	-46	-3	-5.3

● **BOBBY MITCHELL**   Mitchell, Robert McKasha   b: 2/6/1856, Cincinnati, Ohio   d: 5/1/33, Springfield, Ohio   BL/TL, 5'5", 135 lbs.   Deb: 9/6/1877   ♦

YEAR TM/L	W	L	PCT	G	GS	CG	SH	SV	IP	H	HR	BB	SO	RAT	ERA	ERA+	OAV	OOB	BH	AVG	PB	PR	/A	PD	TPI
1877 Cin-N	6	5	.545	12	12	11	0	0	100	123	0	11	41	12.1	3.51	75	.281	.299	10	.204	-0	-8	-10	-0	-0.8
1878 Cin-N	7	2	.778	9	9	9	1	0	80	69	1	18	51	9.8	2.14	100	**.223**	.265	12	.245	1	2	-0	0	0.1
1879 Cin-N	7	15	.318	23	22	20	0	0	194²	236	0	42	90	12.9	3.28	76	.283	.317	16	.147	-4	-17	-17	-4	-2.2
1882 StL-a	0	1	.000	1	1	0	0	0	7	12	0	2	2	18.0	7.71	36	.355	.391	0	.000	-1	-4	-4	-0	-0.4
Total 4	20	23	.465	45	44	40	2	0	381²	440	1	73	184	12.1	3.18	77	.272	.304	38	.180	-5	-27	-30	-4	-3.3

● **WILLIE MITCHELL**   Mitchell, William   b: 12/1/1889, Pleasant Grove, Miss.   d: 11/23/73, Sardis, Miss.   BR/TL, 6', 176 lbs.   Deb: 9/22/09

YEAR TM/L	W	L	PCT	G	GS	CG	SH	SV	IP	H	HR	BB	SO	RAT	ERA	ERA+	OAV	OOB	BH	AVG	PB	PR	/A	PD	TPI
1909 Cle-A	1	2	.333	3	3	3	0	0	23	18	0	10	8	12.5	1.57	163	.225	.340	2	.286	1	2	3	0	0.5
1910 Cle-A	12	8	.600	35	18	11	1	0	183²	155	2	55	102	11.0	2.60	100	.236	.310	10	.159	-3	-2	-0	-2	-0.6
1911 Cle-A	7	14	.333	30	22	9	0	0	177¹	190	1	60	78	13.3	3.76	91	.284	.354	7	.109	-5	-8	-7	-1	-1.3
1912 Cle-A	5	8	.385	29	15	8	0	1	163²	149	0	56	94	11.7	2.80	121	.240	.309	6	.113	-4	9	11	-3	0.1
1913 Cle-A	14	8	.636	35	22	14	4	0	217	153	1	88	141	10.3	1.91	159	.199	.288	10	.143	-2	25	27	-3	2.2
1914 Cle-A	12	17	.414	39	32	16	3	1	257	228	3	124	179	12.6	3.19	91	.238	.330	7	.086	-3	-13	-9	-5	-1.9
1915 Cle-A	11	14	.440	36	30	12	1	1	236	210	1	84	109	11.3	2.82	108	.241	.309	10	.127	-5	3	6	-4	-0.3
1916 Cle-A	2	5	.286	12	6	1	0	1	43²	55	1	19	24	15.3	5.15	58	.309	.376	0	.000	-1	-11	-10	-1	-1.8
Det-A	7	5	.583	23	17	7	2	0	127²	119	1	48	60	12.1	3.31	86	.253	.329	9	.250	2	-7	-6	-3	-0.7
Yr	9	10	.474	35	23	8	2	1	171¹	174	2	67	84	12.9	3.78	77	.269	.342	9	.191	1	-18	-17	-4	-2.5
1917 Det-A	12	8	.600	30	22	12	5	0	185¹	172	2	46	80	11.2	2.19	121	.250	.309	11	.119	-3	10	9	-2	0.4
1918 Det-A	0	1	.000	1	1	0	0	0	4	3	0	5	2	18.0	9.00	30	.200	.400	0	.000	-0	-3	-3	0	-0.5
1919 Det-A	1	2	.333	3	2	0	0	0	13²	12	2	10	4	15.1	5.27	61	.255	.397	1	.200	-0	-3	-3	-0	-0.6
Total 11	84	92	.477	276	190	93	16	4	1632	1464	14	605	921	11.8	2.88	103	.243	.320	69	.130	-24	3	18	-23	-4.5

● **VINEGAR BEND MIZELL**   Mizell, Wilmer David   b: 8/13/30, Leakesville, Miss.   BR/TL, 6'3.5", 205 lbs.   Deb: 4/22/52

YEAR TM/L	W	L	PCT	G	GS	CG	SH	SV	IP	H	HR	BB	SO	RAT	ERA	ERA+	OAV	OOB	BH	AVG	PB	PR	/A	PD	TPI
1952 StL-N	10	8	.556	30	30	7	2	0	190	171	12	103	146	13.0	3.65	102	.237	.333	3	.044	-5	2	1	-2	-0.6
1953 StL-N	13	11	.542	33	33	10	1	0	224¹	193	12	114	173	12.5	3.49	122	.227	.321	7	.084	-4	20	19	-0	1.4
1956 StL-N	14	14	.500	33	33	11	3	0	208²	172	20	92	153	11.7	3.62	104	.222	.310	8	.107	-3	3	4	0	0.2
1957 StL-N	8	10	.444	33	21	7	2	0	149¹	136	18	51	87	11.3	3.74	106	.241	.305	4	.089	-2	2	4	1	0.3
1958 StL-N	10	14	.417	30	29	8	2	0	189²	178	17	91	80	12.9	3.42	121	.252	.339	7	.115	-3	11	15	-1	1.4
1959 StL-N†	13	10	.565	31	30	8	1	0	201¹	196	21	89	108	13.1	4.20	101	.252	.334	14	.187	1	-6	1	-2	-0.1
1960 StL-N	1	3	.250	9	9	0	0	0	55¹	64	7	28	42	15.0	4.55	90	.291	.371	2	.111	-1	-5	-3	-0	-0.2
*Pit-N	13	5	.722	23	23	8	3	0	155²	141	7	46	71	11.0	3.12	120	.247	.306	7	.137	-1	11	11	-3	0.8
Yr	14	8	.636	32	32	8	3	0	211	205	14	74	113	12.0	3.50	110	.259	.325	9	.130	-1	6	8	-2	0.6
1961 Pit-N	7	10	.412	25	17	2	1	0	100	120	16	31	37	13.6	5.04	79	.299	.350	3	.130	-1	-11	-12	-3	-2.0
1962 Pit-N	1	1	.500	4	3	0	0	0	16¹	15	3	10	6	14.3	4.96	79	.254	.371	0	.000	-0	-2	-2	0	-0.2
NY-N	0	2	.000	17	2	0	0	0	38	48	10	25	15	17.5	7.34	57	.324	.425	2	.250	-0	-14	-13	-1	-0.7
Yr	1	3	.250	21	5	0	0	0	54¹	63	13	35	21	16.4	6.63	62	.301	.404	2	.143	-0	-16	-15	-0	-0.9
Total 9	90	88	.506	268	230	61	15	0	1528²	1434	143	680	918	12.6	3.85	104	.247	.329	57	.111	-19	12	25	-9	0.3

● **DAVE MLICKI**   Mlicki, David John   b: 6/8/68, Cleveland, Ohio   BR/TR, 6'4", 185 lbs.   Deb: 9/12/92

YEAR TM/L	W	L	PCT	G	GS	CG	SH	SV	IP	H	HR	BB	SO	RAT	ERA	ERA+	OAV	OOB	BH	AVG	PB	PR	/A	PD	TPI
1992 Cle-A	0	2	.000	4	4	0	0	0	21²	23	3	16	16	16.6	4.98	78	.280	.404	0	—	0	-3	-3	1	-0.1
1993 Cle-A	0	0	—	3	3	0	0	0	13¹	11	2	6	7	12.8	3.38	128	.220	.328	0	—	0	1	1	0	0.0
Total 2	0	2	.000	7	7	0	0	0	35	34	5	22	23	15.2	4.37	93	.258	.376	0	—	0	-1	-1	0	-0.1

● **KEVIN MMAHAT**   Mmahat, Kevin Paul   b: 11/9/64, Memphis, Tenn.   BL/TL, 6'5", 220 lbs.   Deb: 9/9/89

YEAR TM/L	W	L	PCT	G	GS	CG	SH	SV	IP	H	HR	BB	SO	RAT	ERA	ERA+	OAV	OOB	BH	AVG	PB	PR	/A	PD	TPI
1989 NY-A	0	2	.000	4	2	0	0	0	7²	13	2	8	3	25.8	12.91	30	.406	.537	0	—	0	-8	-8	-0	-1.5

● **MIKE MODAK**   Modak, Michael   b: 5/18/22, Campbell, Ohio   BR/TR, 5'10.5", 195 lbs.   Deb: 7/4/45

YEAR TM/L	W	L	PCT	G	GS	CG	SH	SV	IP	H	HR	BB	SO	RAT	ERA	ERA+	OAV	OOB	BH	AVG	PB	PR	/A	PD	TPI
1945 Cin-N	1	2	.333	20	3	1	1	1	42¹	52	0	23	7	15.9	5.74	65	.308	.391	1	.100	-1	-9	-9	-1	-0.8

● **DENNIS MOELLER**   Moeller, Dennis Michael   b: 9/15/67, Tarzana, Cal.   BR/TL, 6'2", 195 lbs.   Deb: 7/28/92

YEAR TM/L	W	L	PCT	G	GS	CG	SH	SV	IP	H	HR	BB	SO	RAT	ERA	ERA+	OAV	OOB	BH	AVG	PB	PR	/A	PD	TPI
1992 KC-A	0	3	.000	5	4	0	0	0	18	24	5	11	6	17.5	7.00	58	.333	.422	0	—	0	-6	-6	0	-0.9
1993 Pit-N	1	0	1.000	10	0	0	0	0	16¹	26	2	7	13	18.7	9.92	41	.356	.420	0	—	0	-11	-11	0	-0.6
Total 2	1	3	.250	15	4	0	0	0	34¹	50	7	18	19	18.1	8.39	48	.345	.421	0	—	0	-17	-17	1	-1.5

● **JOE MOELLER**   Moeller, Joseph Douglas   b: 2/15/43, Blue Island, Ill.   BR/TR, 6'5", 208 lbs.   Deb: 4/12/62

YEAR TM/L	W	L	PCT	G	GS	CG	SH	SV	IP	H	HR	BB	SO	RAT	ERA	ERA+	OAV	OOB	BH	AVG	PB	PR	/A	PD	TPI
1962 LA-N	6	5	.545	19	15	1	0	1	85²	87	10	58	46	15.2	5.25	69	.266	.377	7	.212	1	-12	-15	-1	-1.6
1964 LA-N	7	13	.350	27	24	1	0	0	145¹	153	14	31	97	11.6	4.21	77	.265	.307	3	.067	-2	-11	-16	-0	-2.2
1966 *LA-N	2	4	.333	29	8	0	0	0	78²	73	4	14	31	10.3	2.52	131	.244	.285	2	.167	1	10	7	1	0.7
1967 LA-N	0	0	—	6	0	0	0	0	5	9	1	2	3	21.6	9.00	34	.409	.480	0	—	0	-3	-3	0	0.0
1968 LA-N	1	1	.500	3	3	0	0	0	16	17	1	2	11	11.3	5.06	55	.270	.303	0	.000	-1	-4	-4	0	-0.5
1969 LA-N	1	0	1.000	23	4	0	0	0	51¹	54	6	13	25	11.7	3.33	100	.278	.324	2	.200	0	1	-0	1	0.0
1970 LA-N	7	9	.438	31	19	2	1	4	135¹	131	16	43	63	11.6	3.92	98	.248	.306	6	.154	0	2	-1	-2	-0.3
1971 LA-N	2	4	.333	28	1	0	0	2	66¹	72	5	12	32	11.4	3.80	85	.279	.311	0	.000	0	-2	-4	1	-0.4
Total 8	26	36	.419	166	74	4	1	7	583²	596	55	176	307	12.0	4.01	86	.263	.318	20	.129	-2	-20	-37	2	-4.2

● **RON MOELLER**   Moeller, Ronald Ralph "The Kid"   b: 10/13/38, Cincinnati, Ohio   BL/TL, 6', 180 lbs.   Deb: 9/8/56

YEAR TM/L	W	L	PCT	G	GS	CG	SH	SV	IP	H	HR	BB	SO	RAT	ERA	ERA+	OAV	OOB	BH	AVG	PB	PR	/A	PD	TPI
1956 Bal-A	0	1	.000	4	1	0	0	0	8²	10	0	3	2	13.5	4.15	94	.286	.342	0	.000	-0	0	-0	-0	-0.1
1958 Bal-A	0	0	—	4	0	0	0	0	4¹	6	0	3	3	18.7	4.15	87	.333	.429	0	—	0	-0	-0	0	0.0
1961 LA-A	4	8	.333	33	18	1	1	0	112²	122	15	83	87	16.5	5.83	77	.275	.392	6	.207	2	-23	-17	1	-1.3
1963 LA-A	0	0	—	3	0	0	0	0	2²	5	1	1	2	20.3	6.75	51	.385	.429	0	—	0	-1	-1	0	0.0
Was-A	2	0	1.000	8	3	0	0	0	24¹	31	4	10	10	15.5	6.29	59	.316	.385	2	.222	0	-7	-7	-1	-0.6
Yr	2	0	1.000	11	3	0	0	0	27	36	5	11	12	16.0	6.33	58	.324	.390	2	.222	0	-8	-8	-1	-0.6
Total 4	6	9	.400	52	22	1	1	0	152²	174	20	100	104	16.3	5.78	74	.287	.390	8	.205	2	-31	-25	0	-2.0

● **SAM MOFFETT**   Moffett, Samuel R.   b: 3/14/1857, Wheeling, W.Va.   d: 5/5/07, Butte, Mont.   BR/TR, 6', 175 lbs.   Deb: 5/15/1884   F♦

YEAR TM/L	W	L	PCT	G	GS	CG	SH	SV	IP	H	HR	BB	SO	RAT	ERA	ERA+	OAV	OOB	BH	AVG	PB	PR	/A	PD	TPI
1884 Cle-N	3	19	.136	24	22	21	0	0	197²	236	9	58	84	13.4	3.87	81	.284	.330	47	.184	-3	-20	-16	2	-1.4

YEAR	TM/L	W	L	PCT	G	GS	CG	SH	SV	IP	H	HR	BB	SO	RAT	ERA	ERA+	OAV	OOB	BH	AVG	PB	PR	/A	PD	TPI
1887	Ind-N	1	5	.167	6	6	6	0	0	50	47	1	23	3	13.3	3.78	110	.242	.335	5	.122	-2	2	2	-0	-0.1
1888	Ind-N	2	5	.286	7	7	6	1	0	56	62	3	17	7	13.0	4.66	64	.278	.335	4	.114	-1	-11	-11	-2	-1.3
Total	3	6	29	.171	37	35	33	1	0	303²	345	13	98	94	13.3	4.00	82	.276	.332	56	.169	-6	-29	-24	-0	-2.8

● RANDY MOFFITT
Moffitt, Randall James   b: 10/13/48, Long Beach, Cal.   BR/TR, 6'3", 190 lbs.   Deb: 6/11/72

YEAR	TM/L	W	L	PCT	G	GS	CG	SH	SV	IP	H	HR	BB	SO	RAT	ERA	ERA+	OAV	OOB	BH	AVG	PB	PR	/A	PD	TPI
1972	SF-N	1	5	.167	40	0	0	0	4	70²	72	5	30	37	13.2	3.69	94	.266	.343	0	.000	-1	-2	-2	-0	-0.2
1973	SF-N	4	4	.500	60	0	0	0	14	100¹	86	9	31	65	10.6	2.42	158	.225	.285	1	.059	-1	14	16	-1	1.4
1974	SF-N	5	7	.417	61	1	0	0	15	102	99	9	29	49	11.5	4.50	84	.256	.311	5	.313	2	-10	-8	1	-0.9
1975	SF-N	4	5	.444	55	0	0	0	11	74	73	6	32	39	13.1	3.89	98	.257	.339	3	.214	1	-2	-1	-0	-0.1
1976	SF-N	6	6	.500	58	0	0	0	14	103	92	6	35	50	11.2	2.27	160	.238	.303	2	.143	-0	14	16	-0	2.2
1977	SF-N	4	9	.308	64	0	0	0	11	87²	91	4	39	68	13.7	3.59	109	.273	.355	0	.000	-0	3	3	1	0.6
1978	SF-N	8	4	.667	70	0	0	0	12	81²	79	5	33	52	12.7	3.31	104	.258	.336	1	.143	0	2	1	-1	0.1
1979	SF-N	2	5	.286	28	0	0	0	2	35	53	5	14	16	17.7	7.71	45	.356	.418	0	.000	-0	-15	-16	-0	-3.1
1980	SF-N	1	1	.500	13	0	0	0	0	16²	18	2	4	10	12.4	4.86	73	.281	.333	0	.000	-0	-2	-2	-0	-0.3
1981	SF-N	0	0	—	10	0	0	0	0	11¹	15	2	2	11	13.5	7.94	43	.313	.340	0	—	0	-6	-6	-0	0.0
1982	Hou-N	2	4	.333	30	0	0	0	3	41²	36	3	13	20	11.7	3.02	110	.228	.307	0	.000	-0	3	1	-1	0.1
1983	Tor-A	6	2	.750	45	0	0	0	10	57¹	52	5	24	38	12.1	3.77	114	.243	.322	0	—	0	2	3	0	0.4
Total	12	43	52	.453	534	1	0	0	96	781¹	766	61	286	455	12.4	3.65	102	.257	.327	12	.140	-1	0	5	-3	0.2

● HERB MOFORD
Moford, Herbert   b: 8/6/28, Brooksville, Ky.   BR/TR, 6'1", 175 lbs.   Deb: 4/12/55

YEAR	TM/L	W	L	PCT	G	GS	CG	SH	SV	IP	H	HR	BB	SO	RAT	ERA	ERA+	OAV	OOB	BH	AVG	PB	PR	/A	PD	TPI
1955	StL-N	1	1	.500	14	1	0	0	2	24	29	5	15	8	16.9	7.88	52	.299	.398	0	.000	-0	-10	-10	1	-0.9
1958	Det-A	4	9	.308	25	11	6	0	1	109²	83	10	42	58	11.0	3.61	112	.214	.305	1	.027	-4	2	5	1	0.3
1959	Bos-A	0	2	.000	4	2	0	0	0	8²	10	3	6	7	16.6	11.42	36	.286	.390	0	.000	-0	-7	-7	-0	-1.3
1962	NY-N	0	1	.000	7	0	0	0	0	15	21	3	1	5	13.2	7.20	58	.318	.328	1	.250	-0	-5	-5	-0	-0.3
Total	4	5	13	.278	50	14	6	0	3	157¹	143	21	64	78	12.4	5.03	81	.244	.329	2	.045	-4	-21	-17	2	-2.2

● GEORGE MOGRIDGE
Mogridge, George Anthony   b: 2/18/1889, Rochester, N.Y.   d: 3/4/62, Rochester, N.Y.   BL/TL, 6'2", 165 lbs.   Deb: 8/17/11

YEAR	TM/L	W	L	PCT	G	GS	CG	SH	SV	IP	H	HR	BB	SO	RAT	ERA	ERA+	OAV	OOB	BH	AVG	PB	PR	/A	PD	TPI
1911	Chi-A	0	2	.000	4	1	0	0	0	12²	12	1	1	5	9.2	4.97	65	.255	.271	2	.400	-0	-2	-2	-0	-0.3
1912	Chi-A	3	4	.429	17	8	2	0	3	64²	69	2	15	31	11.8	4.04	79	.264	.307	2	.125	-0	-5	-6	-1	-0.7
1915	NY-A	2	3	.400	6	5	3	1	0	41	33	0	11	11	10.3	1.76	167	.219	.285	1	.083	-1	5	5	-0	0.6
1916	NY-A	6	12	.333	30	21	10	2	0	194²	174	3	45	66	10.4	2.31	125	.252	.305	14	.212	1	11	13	1	1.4
1917	NY-A	9	11	.450	29	25	15	1	0	196¹	185	5	39	46	10.7	2.98	90	.255	.301	11	.159	-1	-7	-6	1	-0.7
1918	NY-A	16	13	.552	45	19	13	1	7	239¹	232	6	43	62	10.6	2.18	130	.263	.304	15	.190	-0	16	17	3	2.5
1919	NY-A	10	7	.588	35	18	13	6	0	169	159	6	46	58	11.3	2.77	115	.250	.307	6	.125	-1	9	8	1	0.8
1920	NY-A	5	9	.357	26	15	7	0	1	125¹	146	4	36	35	13.3	4.31	89	.287	.338	7	.167	-1	-7	-7	1	-0.7
1921	Was-A	18	14	.563	38	36	21	4	0	288	301	12	66	101	11.7	3.00	137	.269	.313	15	.153	-5	41	36	2	3.0
1922	Was-A	18	13	.581	34	32	18	3	0	251²	300	12	72	61	13.7	3.58	108	.304	.358	21	.244	4	13	8	-1	1.2
1923	Was-A	13	13	.500	33	30	17	3	1	211	228	10	56	61	12.2	3.11	121	.285	.334	17	.227	1	20	15	1	2.0
1924	*Was-A	16	11	.593	30	30	13	2	0	213	217	2	61	48	12.0	3.76	107	.270	.327	13	.176	-2	11	7	0	0.5
1925	Was-A	3	4	.429	10	8	3	0	0	53	58	2	18	12	13.6	4.08	104	.291	.362	2	.105	-2	2	1	-0	-0.1
	StL-A	1	1	.500	2	2	1	0	0	15¹	17	2	5	8	13.5	5.87	80	.279	.343	0	.000	-0	-3	-2	0	-0.2
	Yr	4	5	.444	12	10	4	0	0	68¹	75	4	23	20	13.0	4.48	97	.284	.344	2	.087	-2	-1	-1	0	-0.3
1926	Bos-N	6	10	.375	39	11	0	2	3	142	173	6	36	46	13.4	4.50	79	.311	.356	8	.174	-1	-11	-15	2	-1.4
1927	Bos-N	6	4	.600	20	1	0	0	0	48²	48	4	15	26	12.0	3.70	100	.257	.319	3	.200	-0	1	0	1	0.1
Total	15	132	131	.502	398	261	138	20	20	2265²	2352	77	565	678	11.9	3.23	109	.273	.323	137	.182	-8	95	75	11	8.0

● GEORGE MOHART
Mohart, George Benjamin   b: 3/6/1892, Buffalo, N.Y.   d: 10/2/70, Silver Creek, N.Y.   BR/TR, 5'9", 165 lbs.   Deb: 4/15/20

YEAR	TM/L	W	L	PCT	G	GS	CG	SH	SV	IP	H	HR	BB	SO	RAT	ERA	ERA+	OAV	OOB	BH	AVG	PB	PR	/A	PD	TPI
1920	Bro-N	0	1	.000	13	1	0	0	0	35²	33	0	7	13	10.9	1.77	181	.250	.303	1	.125	-0	5	6	1	0.2
1921	Bro-N	0	0	—	2	0	0	0	0	7	8	0	1	1	12.9	3.86	101	.296	.345	1	.500	0	-0	0	-0	0.0
Total	2	0	1	.000	15	1	0	0	0	42²	41	0	8	14	11.2	2.11	157	.258	.310	2	.200	-0	5	6	1	0.2

● MIKE MOHLER
Mohler, Michael Ross   b: 7/26/68, Dayton, Ohio   BR/TL, 6'2", 195 lbs.   Deb: 4/7/93

YEAR	TM/L	W	L	PCT	G	GS	CG	SH	SV	IP	H	HR	BB	SO	RAT	ERA	ERA+	OAV	OOB	BH	AVG	PB	PR	/A	PD	TPI
1993	Oak-A	1	6	.143	42	9	0	0	0	64¹	57	10	44	42	14.4	5.60	73	.241	.364	0	—	0	-9	-11	0	-1.0
1994	Oak-A	0	1	.000	1	1	0	0	0	2¹	2	1	2	4	15.4	7.71	58	.167	.286	0	—	0	-1	-1	0	-0.1
Total	2	1	7	.125	43	10	0	0	0	66²	59	11	46	46	14.4	5.67	72	.237	.360	0	—	0	-10	-12	0	-1.1

● DALE MOHORCIC
Mohorcic, Dale Robert   b: 1/25/56, Cleveland, Ohio   BR/TR, 6'3", 220 lbs.   Deb: 5/31/86

YEAR	TM/L	W	L	PCT	G	GS	CG	SH	SV	IP	H	HR	BB	SO	RAT	ERA	ERA+	OAV	OOB	BH	AVG	PB	PR	/A	PD	TPI
1986	Tex-A	2	4	.333	58	0	0	0	7	79	86	5	15	29	11.6	2.51	172	.279	.315	0	—	0	15	16	0	1.4
1987	Tex-A	7	6	.538	74	0	0	0	16	99¹	88	11	19	48	9.9	2.99	150	.244	.286	0	—	0	16	16	2	2.6
1988	Tex-A	2	6	.250	43	0	0	0	5	52	62	6	20	25	15.1	4.85	84	.295	.370	0	—	0	-5	-4	0	-0.7
	NY-A	2	2	.500	13	0	0	0	1	22²	21	1	9	19	13.1	2.78	142	.239	.330	0	—	0	3	3	-1	0.5
	Yr	4	8	.333	56	0	0	0	6	74²	83	7	29	44	13.9	4.22	96	.269	.338	0	—	0	-2	-2	-0	-0.2
1989	NY-A	2	1	.667	32	0	0	0	2	57²	65	8	18	24	13.9	4.99	77	.286	.355	0	—	0	-7	-7	1	-0.3
1990	Mon-N	1	2	.333	34	0	0	0	2	53	56	6	18	29	13.2	3.23	113	.286	.358	1	.125	-0	3	2	0	0.2
Total	5	16	21	.432	254	0	0	0	33	363²	378	37	99	174	12.3	3.49	118	.272	.330	1	.125	-0	25	26	3	3.7

● BILL MOISAN
Moisan, William Joseph   b: 7/30/25, Bradford, Mass.   BL/TR, 6'1", 170 lbs.   Deb: 9/17/53

YEAR	TM/L	W	L	PCT	G	GS	CG	SH	SV	IP	H	HR	BB	SO	RAT	ERA	ERA+	OAV	OOB	BH	AVG	PB	PR	/A	PD	TPI
1953	Chi-N	0	0	—	3	0	0	0	0	5	5	0	2	1	14.4	5.40	82	.278	.381	0	—	0	-1	-1	0	0.0

● CARLTON MOLESWORTH
Molesworth, Carlton   b: 2/15/1876, Frederick, Md.   d: 7/25/61, Frederick, Md.   BL/TL, 5'6", 200 lbs.   Deb: 9/14/1895

YEAR	TM/L	W	L	PCT	G	GS	CG	SH	SV	IP	H	HR	BB	SO	RAT	ERA	ERA+	OAV	OOB	BH	AVG	PB	PR	/A	PD	TPI
1895	Was-N	0	2	.000	4	3	1	0	0	16	33	1	15	7	29.3	14.63	33	.416	.529	1	.143	-1	-17	-17	-0	-1.4

● RICHIE MOLONEY
Moloney, Richard Henry   b: 6/7/50, Brookline, Mass.   BR/TR, 6'3", 185 lbs.   Deb: 9/20/70

YEAR	TM/L	W	L	PCT	G	GS	CG	SH	SV	IP	H	HR	BB	SO	RAT	ERA	ERA+	OAV	OOB	BH	AVG	PB	PR	/A	PD	TPI
1970	Chi-A	0	0	—	1	0	0	0	0	1	2	0	0	1	18.0	0.00	—	.400	.400	0	—	0	0	0	0	0.0

● VINCE MOLYNEAUX
Molyneaux, Vincent Leo   b: 8/17/1888, Lewiston, N.Y.   d: 5/4/50, Stamford, Conn.   BR/TR, 6', 180 lbs.   Deb: 7/5/17

YEAR	TM/L	W	L	PCT	G	GS	CG	SH	SV	IP	H	HR	BB	SO	RAT	ERA	ERA+	OAV	OOB	BH	AVG	PB	PR	/A	PD	TPI
1917	StL-A	0	0	—	7	0	0	0	0	22	18	0	20	4	15.5	4.91	53	.237	.396	0	.000	-1	-5	-6	0	0.0
1918	Bos-A	1	0	1.000	6	0	0	0	0	10²	3	0	8	1	9.3	3.38	80	.086	.256	0	.000	-0	-1	-0	0	-0.1
Total	2	1	0	1.000	13	0	0	0	0	32²	21	0	28	5	13.5	4.41	60	.189	.353	0	.000	-1	-6	-6	1	-0.1

● RINTY MONAHAN
Monahan, Edward Francis   b: 4/28/28, Brooklyn, N.Y.   BR/TR, 6'1.5", 195 lbs.   Deb: 8/9/53

YEAR	TM/L	W	L	PCT	G	GS	CG	SH	SV	IP	H	HR	BB	SO	RAT	ERA	ERA+	OAV	OOB	BH	AVG	PB	PR	/A	PD	TPI
1953	Phi-N	0	0	—	4	0	0	0	0	10²	11	0	7	2	15.2	4.22	102	.275	.383	0	.000	-0	-0	0	-0	-0.1

● BILL MONBOUQUETTE
Monbouquette, William Charles   b: 8/11/36, Medford, Mass.   BR/TR, 5'11", 195 lbs.   Deb: 7/18/58   C

YEAR	TM/L	W	L	PCT	G	GS	CG	SH	SV	IP	H	HR	BB	SO	RAT	ERA	ERA+	OAV	OOB	BH	AVG	PB	PR	/A	PD	TPI
1958	Bos-A	3	4	.429	10	8	3	0	0	54¹	52	4	20	30	11.9	3.31	121	.251	.317	3	.176	-1	3	4	-1	0.4
1959	Bos-A	7	7	.500	34	17	4	0	0	151²	165	15	33	87	11.9	4.15	98	.285	.327	3	.065	-4	-5	-2	-0	-0.5
1960	Bos-A★	14	11	.560	35	30	12	3	0	215	217	18	68	134	12.0	3.64	111	.263	.320	6	.092	-3	6	10	-0	0.7
1961	Bos-A	14	14	.500	32	32	12	1	0	236¹	233	24	100	161	12.7	3.39	123	.254	.327	9	.130	-1	17	20	-1	2.1
1962	Bos-A☆	15	13	.536	35	35	11	2	0	235¹	227	22	65	153	11.3	3.33	124	.251	.303	7	.096	-3	17	21	-4	1.6
1963	Bos-A☆	20	10	.667	37	36	13	1	0	266²	258	31	42	174	10.1	3.81	99	.250	.280	10	.114	-3	-5	-1	-0	-0.4
1964	Bos-A	13	14	.481	36	35	7	5	1	234	258	34	40	120	11.5	4.04	95	.277	.308	8	.083	-2	-11	-5	-0	-0.7
1965	Bos-A	10	18	.357	35	35	10	2	0	228²	239	32	40	110	11.0	3.70	101	.269	.301	4	.059	-3	-6	-1	-0	-0.2
1966	Det-A	7	8	.467	30	14	2	1	0	102²	120	16	29	57	12.7	4.73	96	.293	.333	6	.154	-0	-15	-14	-1	-2.0
1967	Det-A	0	0	—	2	0	0	0	0	2¹	1	0	2	2	11.6	4.00	—	.143	.143	0	—	0	-0	0	-0	0.0
	NY-A	6	5	.545	33	10	2	1	1	133¹	122	6	17	53	9.7	2.36	132	.246	.277	5	.156	-0	13	11	-1	0.9
	Yr	6	5	.545	35	10	2	1	1	135¹	123	6	17	55	9.6	2.33	134	.245	.275	5	.156	-0	14	12	-1	0.9

YEAR	TM/L	W	L	PCT	G	GS	CG	SH	SV	IP	H	HR	BB	SO	RAT	ERA	ERA+	OAV	OOB	BH	AVG	PB	PR	/A	PD	TPI
1968	NY-A	5	7	.417	17	11	2	0	0	89¹	92	7	13	32	10.9	4.43	65	.264	.296	3	.115	0	-14	-15	1	-1.9
	SF-N	0	1	.000	7	0	0	0	1	12¹	11	4	2	5	9.5	3.65	81	.239	.271	0	—	0	-1	-1	0	-0.1
Total	11	114	112	.504	343	263	78	18	3	1961²	1995	211	462	1122	11.4	3.68	104	.263	.307	60	.103	-20	-2	29	-6	-0.1

● SID MONGE
Monge, Isidro Pedroza b: 4/11/51, Agua Preita, Mexico BB/TL, 6'2", 195 lbs. Deb: 9/12/75

YEAR	TM/L	W	L	PCT	G	GS	CG	SH	SV	IP	H	HR	BB	SO	RAT	ERA	ERA+	OAV	OOB	BH	AVG	PB	PR	/A	PD	TPI
1975	Cal-A	0	2	.000	4	2	0	0	0	23²	22	3	10	17	12.5	4.18	85	.242	.324	0	—	0	-1	-2	-0	0.2
1976	Cal-A	6	7	.462	32	13	2	0	0	117²	108	10	49	53	12.1	3.37	99	.248	.326	0	—	0	2	-1	-1	0.2
1977	Cal-A	0	1	.000	4	0	0	0	1	12¹	14	2	6	4	14.6	2.92	134	.304	.385	0	—	0	2	1	0	0.5
	Cle-A	1	2	.333	33	0	0	0	3	39	47	6	27	25	17.1	6.23	63	.309	.413	0	—	0	-9	-10	-1	-0.7
	Yr	1	3	.250	37	0	0	0	4	51¹	61	8	33	29	16.5	5.44	72	.307	.405	0	—	0	-8	-9	-1	-0.2
1978	Cle-A	4	3	.571	48	2	0	0	6	84²	71	4	51	54	13.0	2.76	135	.225	.332	0	—	0	9	9	-0	0.9
1979	Cle-A☆	12	10	.545	76	0	0	0	19	131	96	9	64	108	11.1	2.40	177	.209	.307	0	—	0	26	27	-0	5.0
1980	Cle-A	3	5	.375	67	0	0	0	14	94¹	80	12	40	61	11.7	3.53	115	.227	.311	0	—	0	5	6	-2	0.5
1981	Cle-A	3	5	.375	31	0	0	0	4	58	58	9	21	41	12.3	4.34	83	.266	.331	0	—	0	-4	-5	-1	-0.7
1982	Phi-N	7	1	.875	47	0	0	0	2	72	70	8	22	43	11.8	3.75	98	.256	.316	1	.111	-0	-1	-1	1	0.0
1983	Phi-N	3	0	1.000	14	0	0	0	0	11²	20	4	6	7	20.1	6.94	51	.377	.441	0	.000	-0	-4	-4	-0	-1.0
	SD-N	7	3	.700	47	0	0	0	7	68²	65	4	31	32	12.7	3.15	111	.257	.340	1	.100	-0	4	3	-0	0.3
	Yr	10	3	.769	61	0	0	0	7	80¹	85	8	37	39	13.8	3.70	95	.277	.357	1	.091	-1	-1	-2	-1	-0.7
1984	SD-N	2	1	.667	13	0	0	0	0	15	17	3	17	7	20.4	4.80	74	.293	.453	0	.000	-0	-2	-2	-0	-0.4
	Det-A	1	0	1.000	19	0	0	0	0	36	40	5	12	19	13.5	4.25	92	.282	.346	0	—	0	-1	-1	-1	-0.1
Total	10	49	40	.551	435	17	4	0	56	764	708	79	356	471	12.7	3.53	107	.248	.334	2	.095	-1	25	20	-6	4.7

● ED MONROE
Monroe, Edward Oliver "Peck" b: 2/22/1895, Louisville, Ky. d: 4/29/69, Louisville, Ky. BR/TR, 6'5", 187 lbs. Deb: 5/29/17

YEAR	TM/L	W	L	PCT	G	GS	CG	SH	SV	IP	H	HR	BB	SO	RAT	ERA	ERA+	OAV	OOB	BH	AVG	PB	PR	/A	PD	TPI
1917	NY-A	1	0	1.000	9	1	1	0	1	28²	35	1	6	12	13.5	3.45	78	.310	.355	2	.167	-0	-3	-2	-0	-0.1
1918	NY-A	0	0	—	1	0	0	0	0	2	1	0	2	1	13.5	4.50	63	.143	.333	0	—	-0	-0	-0	-0	0.0
Total	2	1	0	1.000	10	1	1	0	1	30²	36	1	8	13	13.5	3.52	77	.300	.354	2	.167	-0	-3	-3	0	-0.1

● LARRY MONROE
Monroe, Lawrence James b: 6/20/56, Detroit, Mich. BR/TR, 6'4", 200 lbs. Deb: 8/23/76

YEAR	TM/L	W	L	PCT	G	GS	CG	SH	SV	IP	H	HR	BB	SO	RAT	ERA	ERA+	OAV	OOB	BH	AVG	PB	PR	/A	PD	TPI
1976	Chi-A	0	1	.000	8	2	0	0	0	21²	23	0	13	9	15.0	4.15	86	.284	.383	0	—	0	-2	-1	-0	-0.1

● ZACH MONROE
Monroe, Zachary Charles b: 7/8/31, Peoria, Ill. BR/TR, 6', 198 lbs. Deb: 6/27/58

YEAR	TM/L	W	L	PCT	G	GS	CG	SH	SV	IP	H	HR	BB	SO	RAT	ERA	ERA+	OAV	OOB	BH	AVG	PB	PR	/A	PD	TPI
1958	*NY-A	4	2	.667	21	6	1	0	1	58	57	8	27	18	13.0	3.26	108	.263	.344	2	.118	-1	3	2	0	0.1
1959	NY-A	0	0	—	3	0	0	0	0	3¹	3	2	2	1	13.5	5.40	67	.231	.333	0	—	0	-1	-1	0	0.0
Total	2	4	2	.667	24	6	1	0	1	61¹	60	10	29	19	13.1	3.38	105	.261	.344	2	.118	-1	3	1	1	0.1

● JOHN MONTAGUE
Montague, John Evans b: 9/12/47, Newport News, Va. BR/TR, 6'2", 213 lbs. Deb: 9/9/73

YEAR	TM/L	W	L	PCT	G	GS	CG	SH	SV	IP	H	HR	BB	SO	RAT	ERA	ERA+	OAV	OOB	BH	AVG	PB	PR	/A	PD	TPI
1973	Mon-N	0	0	—	4	0	0	0	0	7²	8	0	2	7	12.9	3.52	108	.286	.355	0	.000	-0	0	0	-0	0.0
1974	Mon-N	3	4	.429	46	1	0	0	3	82²	73	5	38	43	12.5	3.16	122	.241	.333	1	.100	-0	4	6	-2	0.4
1975	Mon-N	0	1	.000	12	0	0	0	2	17²	23	4	6	9	15.8	5.60	68	.324	.392	0	.000	-0	-4	-3	-0	-0.3
	Phi-N	0	0	—	3	0	0	0	0	5	8	1	4	1	21.6	9.00	41	.400	.500	0	—	0	-3	-3	-0	-0.3
	Yr	0	1	.000	15	0	0	0	2	22²	31	5	10	10	16.3	6.35	60	.326	.390	0	.000	-0	-7	-6	0	-0.3
1977	Sea-A	8	12	.400	47	15	2	0	4	182¹	193	20	75	98	13.4	4.29	96	.272	.345	0	—	0	-5	-4	-1	-0.2
1978	Sea-A	1	3	.250	19	0	0	0	1	43²	52	2	24	14	15.7	6.18	62	.308	.394	0	—	0	-12	-12	-1	-1.1
1979	Sea-A	6	4	.600	41	1	0	0	1	116¹	125	14	47	60	13.5	5.57	78	.284	.356	0	—	0	-18	-16	-1	-1.2
	*Cal-A	2	0	1.000	14	0	0	0	6	17²	16	3	9	6	12.7	5.09	80	.242	.333	0	—	0	-2	-2	-1	-0.3
	Yr	8	4	.667	55	1	0	0	7	134	141	17	56	66	13.2	5.51	78	.273	.344	0	—	0	-19	-18	-0	-1.5
1980	Cal-A	4	2	.667	37	0	0	0	3	73²	97	8	21	22	14.5	5.13	77	.324	.371	0	—	0	-9	-10	-0	-0.7
Total	7	24	26	.480	223	17	2	0	21	546²	595	57	226	260	13.7	4.76	85	.283	.356	1	.083	-0	-47	-42	-1	-3.4

● RAFAEL MONTALVO
Montalvo, Rafael Edgardo (Torres) b: 3/31/64, Rio Piedras, P.R. BR/TR, 6', 185 lbs. Deb: 4/13/86

YEAR	TM/L	W	L	PCT	G	GS	CG	SH	SV	IP	H	HR	BB	SO	RAT	ERA	ERA+	OAV	OOB	BH	AVG	PB	PR	/A	PD	TPI
1986	Hou-N	0	0	—	1	0	0	0	0	1	1	0	2	0	27.0	9.00	40	.250	.500	0	—	0	-1	-1	0	0.0

● AURELIO MONTEAGUDO
Monteagudo, Aurelio Faustino (Cintra)
b: 11/19/43, Caibarien, Cuba d: 11/10/90, Saltillo, Mexico BR/TR, 5'11", 185 lbs. Deb: 9/1/63 F

YEAR	TM/L	W	L	PCT	G	GS	CG	SH	SV	IP	H	HR	BB	SO	RAT	ERA	ERA+	OAV	OOB	BH	AVG	PB	PR	/A	PD	TPI
1963	KC-A	0	0	—	4	0	0	0	0	7	4	3	3	9	9.0	2.57	152	.182	.280	0	—	0	1	1	0	0.0
1964	KC-A	0	4	.000	11	6	0	0	0	31¹	40	11	10	14	14.6	8.90	43	.317	.372	2	.286	1	-18	-18	-0	-1.9
1965	KC-A	0	0	—	4	0	0	0	0	7	7	4	2	5	11.6	3.86	90	.185	.290	0	—	0	-0	-0	-0	0.0
1966	KC-A	0	0	—	6	0	0	0	0	12²	12	0	7	3	13.5	2.84	120	.261	.358	0	—	0	1	1	-0	0.0
	Hou-N	0	0	—	10	0	0	0	0	15¹	14	1	11	7	14.7	4.70	73	.241	.362	0	.000	0	-2	-2	-0	-0.2
1967	Chi-A	0	1	.000	1	1	0	0	0	1¹	4	1	2	0	40.5	20.25	15	.500	.600	0	—	0	-3	-3	-0	-1.0
1970	KC-A	1	1	.500	21	0	0	0	0	27¹	20	2	9	18	9.9	2.96	126	.200	.273	0	.000	0	2	2	-1	0.1
1973	Cal-A	2	1	.667	15	0	0	0	3	30	23	2	16	8	12.9	4.20	84	.215	.339	0	—	0	-2	-2	-0	0.3
Total	7	3	7	.300	72	7	0	0	4	132	122	18	62	58	13.0	5.05	72	.247	.338	2	.200	1	-20	-21	-1	-2.6

● RENE MONTEAGUDO
Monteagudo, Rene (Miranda) b: 3/12/16, Havana, Cuba d: 9/14/73, Hialeah, Fla. BL/TL, 5'7", 165 lbs. Deb: 9/6/38 F♦

YEAR	TM/L	W	L	PCT	G	GS	CG	SH	SV	IP	H	HR	BB	SO	RAT	ERA	ERA+	OAV	OOB	BH	AVG	PB	PR	/A	PD	TPI
1938	Was-A	1	1	.500	5	3	2	0	0	22	26	3	15	13	16.8	5.73	79	.286	.387	3	.500	-1	-3	-3	-1	-0.2
1940	Was-A	2	6	.250	27	8	3	0	2	100²	128	7	52	64	16.4	6.08	69	.316	.398	6	.182	0	-19	-21	-1	-1.6
1945	Phi-N	0	0	—	14	0	0	0	0	45²	67	1	28	16	19.1	7.49	51	.347	.435	2	.301	2	-19	-19	-1	0.2
Total	3	3	7	.300	46	11	5	0	2	168¹	221	11	95	93	17.2	6.42	64	.321	.407	78	.289	4	-40	-43	-3	-1.6

● JOHN MONTEFUSCO
Montefusco, John Joseph "Count" b: 5/25/50, Long Branch, N.J. BR/TR, 6'1", 180 lbs. Deb: 9/3/74

YEAR	TM/L	W	L	PCT	G	GS	CG	SH	SV	IP	H	HR	BB	SO	RAT	ERA	ERA+	OAV	OOB	BH	AVG	PB	PR	/A	PD	TPI
1974	SF-N	3	2	.600	7	5	1	1	0	39¹	41	3	19	34	13.7	4.81	79	.256	.335	4	.286	3	-5	-4	-0	-0.3
1975	SF-N	15	9	.625	35	34	10	4	0	243²	210	11	86	215	11.2	2.88	132	.233	.305	7	.087	-2	20	25	-1	2.0
1976	SF-N★	16	14	.533	37	36	11	6	0	253¹	224	11	74	172	10.7	2.84	128	.238	.296	8	.103	-2	19	22	-4	2.0
1977	SF-N	7	12	.368	26	25	4	0	0	157¹	170	10	46	110	12.5	3.49	112	.273	.326	6	.122	-1	7	7	-2	0.5
1978	SF-N	11	9	.550	36	36	3	0	0	238²	233	25	68	177	11.5	3.81	91	.255	.310	4	.057	-3	-6	-10	-2	-1.2
1979	SF-N	3	8	.273	22	22	0	0	0	137	145	15	51	76	13.0	3.94	89	.279	.346	7	.167	2	-3	-7	-0	-0.4
1980	SF-N	4	8	.333	22	17	1	0	0	113¹	120	15	39	85	12.8	4.37	81	.265	.327	1	.033	-2	-10	-10	-1	-1.4
1981	Atl-N	2	3	.400	26	9	0	0	1	77¹	75	9	27	34	11.9	3.49	103	.260	.324	1	.067	-1	0	1	-0	0.0
1982	SD-N	10	11	.476	32	32	1	0	0	184¹	177	17	41	83	10.8	4.00	86	.251	.295	5	.086	-2	-8	-12	-1	-1.5
1983	SD-N	9	4	.692	31	10	1	0	0	95¹	94	8	32	52	12.0	3.30	105	.265	.327	1	.053	-0	3	2	-1	0.1
	NY-A	5	0	1.000	6	6	0	0	0	38	39	3	10	15	11.8	3.32	117	.271	.323	0	—	0	3	2	-1	0.3
1984	NY-A	5	3	.625	11	11	0	0	0	55¹	55	5	13	23	11.2	3.58	106	.253	.299	0	—	0	2	1	-1	0.1
1985	NY-A	0	0	—	3	1	0	0	0	7	12	3	2	2	18.0	10.29	39	.387	.424	0	—	0	-5	-5	-0	0.2
1986	NY-A	0	0	—	4	0	0	0	0	7	8	0	2	3	10.2	2.19	187	.200	.280	0	—	0	2	2	-0	0.1
Total	13	90	83	.520	298	244	32	11	5	1652¹	1604	135	513	1081	11.7	3.54	102	.255	.314	44	.097	-10	20	16	-12	0.5

● MANNY MONTEJO
Montejo, Manuel (Bofill) b: 10/16/35, Caibarien, Cuba BR/TR, 5'11", 150 lbs. Deb: 7/25/61

YEAR	TM/L	W	L	PCT	G	GS	CG	SH	SV	IP	H	HR	BB	SO	RAT	ERA	ERA+	OAV	OOB	BH	AVG	PB	PR	/A	PD	TPI
1961	Det-A	0	0	—	12	0	0	0	0	16¹	13	2	6	15	11.6	3.86	106	.217	.309	0	—	0	0	0	-1	-0.1

● RICH MONTELEONE
Monteleone, Richard b: 3/22/63, Tampa, Fla. BR/TR, 6'2", 220 lbs. Deb: 4/15/87

YEAR	TM/L	W	L	PCT	G	GS	CG	SH	SV	IP	H	HR	BB	SO	RAT	ERA	ERA+	OAV	OOB	BH	AVG	PB	PR	/A	PD	TPI
1987	Sea-A	0	0	—	3	0	0	0	0	7	10	2	4	2	19.3	6.43	73	.345	.441	0	—	0	-2	-1	0	-0.3
1988	Cal-A	0	0	—	3	0	0	0	0	4¹	4	1	2	3	12.5	0.00	—	.222	.300	0	—	0	2	2	0	0.2
1989	Cal-A	2	2	.500	24	0	0	0	0	39²	39	3	13	27	12.0	3.18	120	.255	.317	0	—	0	3	3	1	0.5
1990	NY-A	0	1	.000	5	0	0	0	0	7¹	8	0	2	8	12.3	6.14	65	.276	.323	0	—	0	-2	-2	0	-0.2

YEAR TM/L	W	L	PCT	G	GS	CG	SH	SV	IP	H	HR	BB	SO	RAT	ERA	ERA+	OAV	OOB	BH	AVG	PB	PR	/A	PD	TPI
1991 NY-A	3	1	.750	26	0	0	0	0	47	42	5	19	34	11.7	3.64	114	.236	.310	0	—	0	2	3	1	0.2
1992 NY-A	7	3	.700	47	0	0	0	0	92²	82	7	27	62	10.6	3.30	119	.235	.290	0	—	0	7	6	-1	0.6
1993 NY-A	7	4	.636	42	0	0	0	0	85²	85	14	35	50	12.6	4.94	84	.262	.333	0	—	0	-6	-7	0	-0.5
1994 SF-N	4	3	.571	39	0	0	0	0	45¹	43	6	13	16	11.1	3.18	127	.253	.306	0	.000	-0	5	4	-1	0.5
Total 8	23	14	.622	189	0	0	0	0	329	313	37	114	202	11.8	3.83	105	.250	.314	0	.000	-0	10	7	0	1.0

● **JEFF MONTGOMERY** Montgomery, Jeffrey Thomas b: 1/7/62, Wellston, Ohio BR/TR, 5'11", 180 lbs. Deb: 8/1/87

YEAR TM/L	W	L	PCT	G	GS	CG	SH	SV	IP	H	HR	BB	SO	RAT	ERA	ERA+	OAV	OOB	BH	AVG	PB	PR	/A	PD	TPI
1987 Cin-N	2	2	.500	14	1	0	0	0	19¹	25	2	9	13	15.8	6.52	65	.313	.382	0	.000	-0	-5	-5	0	-0.9
1988 KC-A	7	2	.778	45	0	0	0	1	62²	54	6	30	47	12.4	3.45	116	.231	.323	0	—	0	4	4	0	0.5
1989 KC-A	7	3	.700	63	0	0	0	18	92	66	3	25	94	9.1	1.37	281	.198	.258	0	—	0	26	25	-1	3.8
1990 KC-A	6	5	.545	73	0	0	0	24	94¹	81	6	34	94	11.4	2.39	161	.227	.303	0	—	0	16	15	0	2.7
1991 KC-A	4	4	.500	67	0	0	0	33	90	83	6	28	77	11.3	2.90	142	.246	.307	0	—	0	12	12	-0	2.0
1992 KC-A★	1	6	.143	65	0	0	0	39	82²	61	5	27	69	9.9	2.18	186	.205	.278	0	—	0	16	17	2	3.2
1993 KC-A★	7	5	.583	69	0	0	0	45	87¹	65	3	23	66	9.3	2.27	202	.206	.264	0	—	0	20	22	1	5.0
1994 KC-A	2	3	.400	42	0	0	0	27	44²	48	5	15	50	12.9	4.03	128	.276	.337	0	—	0	4	6	0	0.7
Total 8	36	30	.545	438	1	0	0	187	573	483	36	191	510	10.9	2.64	157	.227	.296	0	.000	-0	92	96	2	17.0

● **MONTY MONTGOMERY** Montgomery, Monty Bryson b: 9/1/46, Albemarle, N.C. BR/TR, 6'3", 200 lbs. Deb: 9/14/71

YEAR TM/L	W	L	PCT	G	GS	CG	SH	SV	IP	H	HR	BB	SO	RAT	ERA	ERA+	OAV	OOB	BH	AVG	PB	PR	/A	PD	TPI
1971 KC-A	3	0	1.000	3	2	0	0	0	21¹	16	1	3	12	8.0	2.11	163	.205	.235	0	.000	-0	3	3	0	0.4
1972 KC-A	3	3	.500	9	8	1	1	0	56¹	55	2	17	24	11.5	3.04	100	.263	.319	3	.176	1	-0	-0	-0	0.0
Total 2	6	3	.667	12	10	1	1	0	77²	71	2	20	36	10.5	2.78	113	.247	.296	3	.125	0	3	3	0	0.4

● **RAMON MONZANT** Monzant, Ramon Segundo (Espina) b: 1/4/33, Maracaibo, Venez. BR/TR, 6', 165 lbs. Deb: 7/2/54

YEAR TM/L	W	L	PCT	G	GS	CG	SH	SV	IP	H	HR	BB	SO	RAT	ERA	ERA+	OAV	OOB	BH	AVG	PB	PR	/A	PD	TPI
1954 NY-N	0	0	—	6	1	0	0	0	7²	8	0	11	5	22.3	4.70	86	.276	.475	0	.000	-0	-1	-1	-0	-0.1
1955 NY-N	4	8	.333	28	12	3	0	0	94²	98	11	43	54	13.7	3.99	101	.278	.361	3	.125	-1	0	0	-1	-0.2
1956 NY-N	1	0	1.000	4	1	1	0	0	13	8	4	7	11	10.4	4.15	91	.170	.278	0	.000	-1	-1	-1	-0	-0.1
1957 NY-N	3	2	.600	24	2	0	0	0	49²	55	6	16	37	13.2	3.99	99	.286	.348	3	.300	1	-1	-1	-0	-0.1
1958 SF-N	8	11	.421	43	16	4	1	1	150²	160	21	57	93	13.3	4.72	81	.273	.344	8	.163	-1	-13	-15	1	-1.7
1960 SF-N	0	0	—	1	0	0	0	0	1	1	1	0	1	9.0	9.00	39	.250	.250	0	—	0	-1	-1	0	0.0
Total 6	16	21	.432	106	32	8	1	1	316²	330	43	134	201	13.5	4.38	89	.273	.350	14	.157	-2	-15	-17	-1	-2.2

● **LEO MOON** Moon, Leo "Lefty" b: 6/22/1899, Belmont, N.C. d: 8/25/70, New Orleans, La. BR/TL, 5'11", 165 lbs. Deb: 7/9/32

YEAR TM/L	W	L	PCT	G	GS	CG	SH	SV	IP	H	HR	BB	SO	RAT	ERA	ERA+	OAV	OOB	BH	AVG	PB	PR	/A	PD	TPI
1932 Cle-A	0	0	—	1	0	0	0	0	5²	11	0	7	1	28.6	11.12	43	.379	.500	1	.500	0	-4	-4	0	-0.5

● **JIM MOONEY** Mooney, Jim Irving b: 9/4/06, Mooresburg, Tenn. d: 4/27/79, Johnson City, Tenn BR/TL, 5'11", 168 lbs. Deb: 8/14/31

YEAR TM/L	W	L	PCT	G	GS	CG	SH	SV	IP	H	HR	BB	SO	RAT	ERA	ERA+	OAV	OOB	BH	AVG	PB	PR	/A	PD	TPI
1931 NY-N	7	1	.875	10	8	6	2	0	71²	71	16	38	11.1	2.01	184	.262	.306	4	.160	0	15	13	-1	1.2	
1932 NY-N	6	10	.375	29	18	4	1	0	124³	154	18	42	37	14.1	5.05	73	.299	.352	5	.122	-2	-16	-19	-2	-2.3
1933 StL-N	2	5	.286	21	8	2	0	1	77¹	87	1	26	14	13.2	3.72	93	.296	.353	1	.050	-2	-3	-2	1	-0.3
1934 ★StL-N	2	4	.333	32	7	1	0	1	82¹	114	3	49	27	18.3	5.47	77	.326	.414	1	.053	-2	-13	-11	-1	-1.1
Total 4	17	20	.459	92	41	13	3	2	356	426	23	133	116	14.3	4.25	89	.298	.360	11	.105	-7	-18	-19	-3	-2.5

● **BILL MOONEYHAM** Mooneyham, William Craig b: 8/16/60, Livermore, Cal. BR/TR, 6', 175 lbs. Deb: 4/19/86

YEAR TM/L	W	L	PCT	G	GS	CG	SH	SV	IP	H	HR	BB	SO	RAT	ERA	ERA+	OAV	OOB	BH	AVG	PB	PR	/A	PD	TPI
1986 Oak-A	4	5	.444	45	6	0	0	2	99²	103	4	67	75	15.6	4.52	86	.270	.384	0	—	0	-4	-7	1	-0.1

● **BALOR MOORE** Moore, Balor Lilbon b: 1/25/51, Smithville, Tex. BL/TL, 6'2", 184 lbs. Deb: 5/21/70

YEAR TM/L	W	L	PCT	G	GS	CG	SH	SV	IP	H	HR	BB	SO	RAT	ERA	ERA+	OAV	OOB	BH	AVG	PB	PR	/A	PD	TPI
1970 Mon-N	0	2	.000	6	2	0	0	0	9²	14	0	8	6	20.5	7.45	55	.368	.478	1	.333	0	-4	-4	0	-0.6
1972 Mon-N	9	9	.500	22	22	6	3	0	147²	122	15	59	161	11.3	3.47	102	.226	.307	8	.145	-0	-0	1	0	0.1
1973 Mon-N	7	16	.304	35	32	3	1	0	176¹	151	18	109	151	13.4	4.49	85	.233	.346	3	.057	-3	-16	-13	-1	-2.0
1974 Mon-N	0	2	.000	8	2	0	0	0	13²	13	1	15	16	18.4	3.95	97	.245	.412	0	.000	-0	-1	-0	-0	-0.1
1977 Cal-A	0	0	.000	7	3	0	0	0	22²	28	7	10	14	16.3	3.97	99	.298	.383	0	—	0	-0	-0	-1	0.0
1978 Tor-A	6	9	.400	37	18	2	0	0	144¹	165	16	54	75	14.1	4.93	80	.294	.363	0	—	0	-19	-16	1	-1.4
1979 Tor-A	5	7	.417	34	16	5	0	0	139¹	135	17	79	51	14.3	4.84	90	.262	.369	0	—	0	-10	-8	-1	-0.7
1980 Tor-A	1	1	.500	31	3	0	0	1	64²	76	6	31	22	15.4	5.29	81	.309	.395	0	—	0	-9	-7	-0	-0.3
Total 8	28	48	.368	180	98	16	4	1	718¹	704	80	365	496	13.8	4.52	87	.261	.355	12	.106	-3	-58	-47	-1	-5.0

● **BRAD MOORE** Moore, Bradley Alan b: 6/21/64, Loveland, Colo. BR/TR, 6'1", 185 lbs. Deb: 6/14/88

YEAR TM/L	W	L	PCT	G	GS	CG	SH	SV	IP	H	HR	BB	SO	RAT	ERA	ERA+	OAV	OOB	BH	AVG	PB	PR	/A	PD	TPI
1988 Phi-N	0	0	—	5	0	0	0	0	5²	4	0	4	2	12.7	0.00	—	.267	.421	0	—	0	2	2	0	0.0
1990 Phi-N	0	0	—	3	0	0	0	0	2²	4	0	4	1	20.3	3.38	113	.400	.500	0	—	0	0	0	0	0.0
Total 2	0	0	—	8	0	0	0	0	8¹	8	0	8	3	17.3	1.08	338	.320	.452	0	—	0	2	2	0	0.0

● **CARLOS MOORE** Moore, Carlos Whitman b: 8/13/06, Clinton, Tenn. d: 7/2/58, New Orleans, La. BR/TR, 6'1.5", 180 lbs. Deb: 5/4/30

YEAR TM/L	W	L	PCT	G	GS	CG	SH	SV	IP	H	HR	BB	SO	RAT	ERA	ERA+	OAV	OOB	BH	AVG	PB	PR	/A	PD	TPI
1930 Was-A	0	0	—	11²						9	0	4	2	10.0	2.31	199	.225	.295	0	.000	-1	3	3	-0	-0.1

● **DEE MOORE** Moore, D C b: 4/6/14, Hedley, Tex. BR/TR, 5'11", 190 lbs. Deb: 9/12/36 ◆

YEAR TM/L	W	L	PCT	G	GS	CG	SH	SV	IP	H	HR	BB	SO	RAT	ERA	ERA+	OAV	OOB	BH	AVG	PB	PR	/A	PD	TPI
1936 Cin-N	0	0	—	2	1	0	0	0	7	3	0	2	3	6.4	0.00	—	.120	.185	4	.400	1	3	3	0	0.1

● **DONNIE MOORE** Moore, Donnie Ray b: 2/13/54, Lubbock, Tex. d: 7/18/89, Anaheim, Cal. BL/TR, 6', 185 lbs. Deb: 9/14/75

YEAR TM/L	W	L	PCT	G	GS	CG	SH	SV	IP	H	HR	BB	SO	RAT	ERA	ERA+	OAV	OOB	BH	AVG	PB	PR	/A	PD	TPI
1975 Chi-N	0	0	—	4	1	0	0	0	8²	12	1	4	8	16.6	4.15	92	.316	.381	0	.000	-0	-1	-0	-0	0.0
1977 Chi-N	4	2	.667	27	1	0	0	0	48²	51	1	18	34	12.8	4.07	108	.285	.350	3	.300	1	-1	2	1	0.4
1978 Chi-N	9	7	.563	71	1	0	0	4	103	117	7	31	50	13.1	4.11	98	.287	.340	4	.267	1	-6	-1	0	0.0
1979 Chi-N	1	4	.200	39	1	0	0	1	73	95	8	25	43	15.0	5.18	79	.321	.378	2	.154	0	-12	-9	1	-0.5
1980 StL-N	1	1	.500	11	0	0	0	0	21²	25	1	5	10	12.9	6.23	59	.298	.344	3	.750	2	-6	-6	-1	-0.4
1981 Mil-A	0	0	—	3	0	0	0	0	4	4	0	4	2	18.0	6.75	51	.286	.444	0	—	0	-1	-1	0	0.1
1982 ★Atl-N	3	1	.750	16	0	0	0	0	27²	32	1	7	17	13.3	4.23	88	.294	.347	0	.000	-0	-2	-2	0	-0.2
1983 Atl-N	2	3	.400	43	0	0	0	6	68²	72	6	10	41	10.7	3.67	106	.279	.306	4	.500	1	-0	2	-1	0.2
1984 Atl-N	4	5	.444	47	0	0	0	16	64¹	63	3	18	47	11.5	2.94	131	.258	.312	0	.000	-0	5	7	0	1.3
1985 Cal-A★	8	8	.500	65	0	0	0	31	103	91	9	21	72	9.8	1.92	214	.237	.277	0	—	0	25	25	-1	5.3
1986 ★Cal-A	4	5	.444	49	0	0	0	21	72²	79	8	27	53	10.2	2.97	138	.228	.288	0	—	0	10	9	-1	1.6
1987 Cal-A	2	2	.500	14	0	0	0	5	26²	28	7	13	17	13.8	2.70	159	.259	.339	0	—	0	5	5	-1	0.8
1988 Cal-A	5	2	.714	27	0	0	0	4	33	48	3	8	22	15.3	4.91	79	.343	.378	0	—	0	-3	-4	0	-0.6
Total 13	43	40	.518	416	4	0	0	89	655	698	53	186	416	12.3	3.67	110	.276	.328	16	.281	5	12	27	-1	8.0

● **EARL MOORE** Moore, Earl Alonzo "Big Ebbie" or "Crossfire" b: 7/29/1879, Pickerington, O. d: 11/28/61, Columbus, Ohio BR/TR, 6', 195 lbs. Deb: 4/25/01

YEAR TM/L	W	L	PCT	G	GS	CG	SH	SV	IP	H	HR	BB	SO	RAT	ERA	ERA+	OAV	OOB	BH	AVG	PB	PR	/A	PD	TPI
1901 Cle-A	16	14	.533	31	30	28	4	0	251²	234	4	107	99	12.5	2.90	122	.244	.325	16	.162	-5	21	18	-4	0.9
1902 Cle-A	17	17	.500	36	34	29	4	1	293	304	8	101	84	12.7	2.95	117	.268	.332	24	.212	-0	20	16	-1	1.5
1903 Cle-A	19	9	.679	29	27	27	3	1	247²	196	0	62	148	9.6	**1.74**	**164**	**.217**	.271	8	.092	-5	**34**	31	-3	2.6
1904 Cle-A	12	11	.522	26	24	22	1	0	227²	186	2	61	139	10.2	2.25	113	.224	.285	12	.140	-2	9	7	-7	-0.3
1905 Cle-A	15	15	.500	31	30	28	3	0	269	232	6	92	131	11.4	2.64	100	.234	.310	10	.104	-4	1	-0	-2	-0.8
1906 Cle-A	1	1	.500	5	4	2	0	0	29²	27	1	18	14	14.3	3.94	66	.246	.362	0	.000	-1	-4	-4	1	-0.5
1907 Cle-A	1	1	.500	3	2	1	0	0	19¹	18	0	8	7	12.6	4.66	54	.249	.332	0	.000	-1	-5	-5	-0	-0.5
NY-A	2	6	.250	12	9	3	0	0	64	72	1	30	28	14.5	3.94	71	.286	.371	6	.273	1	-10	-8	-0	-0.9
Yr	3	7	.300	15	11	4	0	0	83¹	90	1	38	35	14.3	4.10	67	.276	.359	6	.207	0	-14	-13	-0	-1.4
1908 Phi-N	2	1	.667	3	3	3	1	0	26	20	0	8	16	10.4	0.00	—	.217	.294	2	.222	1	7	7	-1	1.0
1909 Phi-N	18	12	.600	38	34	24	4	0	299²	238	7	108	173	10.7	2.10	124	.210	.283	9	.094	-4	17	17	-5	0.6
1910 Phi-N	22	15	.595	46	35	18	**6**	0	283	228	5	121	**185**	11.4	2.58	121	.228	.318	20	.230	-8	14	17	-4	2.0
1911 Phi-N	15	19	.441	42	36	21	5	0	308	265	11	164	174	12.9	2.63	131	.240	.345	11	.109	-6	27	28	-3	2.0

YEAR	TM/L	W	L	PCT	G	GS	CG	SH	SV	IP	H	HR	BB	SO	RAT	ERA	ERA+	OAV	OOB	BH	AVG	PB	PR	/A	PD	TPI
1912	Phi-N	9	14	.391	31	24	10	1	0	182¹	186	3	77	79	13.3	3.31	110	.275	.355	6	.107	-4	2	7	-2	0.1
1913	Phi-N	1	3	.250	12	5	0	0	1	52	50	3	40	24	15.8	5.02	66	.254	.382	0	.000	-2	-10	-10	1	-0.9
	Chi-N	1	1	.500	7	2	0	0	0	28¹	34	3	12	12	14.6	4.45	72	.321	.390	1	.125	-0	-4	-4	1	-0.2
	Yr	2	4	.333	19	7	0	0	1	80¹	84	6	52	36	15.2	4.82	68	.276	.382	1	.042	-2	-14	-14	2	-1.1
1914	Buf-F	11	15	.423	36	27	14	2	2	194²	184	3	99	96	13.5	4.30	69	.263	.362	9	.161	-4	-31	-29	-2	-3.9
Total	14	162	154	.513	388	326	230	34	7	2776	2474	57	1108	1403	12.0	2.78	110	.241	.321	134	.141	-34	88	88	-33	2.7

● EUEL MOORE
Moore, Euel Walton "Chief"   b: 5/27/08, Reagan, Okla.   d: 2/12/89, Tishomingo, Okla.   BR/TR, 6'2", 185 lbs.   Deb: 7/8/34

YEAR	TM/L	W	L	PCT	G	GS	CG	SH	SV	IP	H	HR	BB	SO	RAT	ERA	ERA+	OAV	OOB	BH	AVG	PB	PR	/A	PD	TPI
1934	Phi-N	5	7	.417	20	16	3	0	1	122¹	145	9	41	38	13.7	4.05	117	.288	.342	5	.109	-4	0	9	-1	0.3
1935	Phi-N	1	6	.143	15	8	1	0	1	40¹	63	5	20	15	19.0	7.81	58	.354	.425	6	.400	1	-17	-15	0	-2.0
	NY-N	1	0	1.000	6	0	0	0	0	8	9	0	4	3	14.6	5.63	69	.281	.361	-0	-1	-2	0	-0.2
	Yr	2	6	.250	21	8	1	0	1	48¹	72	5	24	18	17.9	7.45	59	.340	.407	6	.353	1	-18	-16	0	-2.2
1936	Phi-N	2	3	.400	20	5	1	0	1	54¹	76	4	12	19	14.7	6.96	65	.311	.346	4	.222	-0	-18	-15	-1	-1.3
Total	3	9	16	.360	61	29	5	0	3	225	293	18	77	75	14.9	5.48	84	.306	.360	15	.185	-3	-36	-22	-3	-3.2

● GENE MOORE
Moore, Eugene Sr. "Blue Goose"   b: 11/9/1885, Lancaster, Tex.   d: 8/31/38, Dallas, Tex.   BL/TL, 6'2", 185 lbs.   Deb: 9/28/09   F

YEAR	TM/L	W	L	PCT	G	GS	CG	SH	SV	IP	H	HR	BB	SO	RAT	ERA	ERA+	OAV	OOB	BH	AVG	PB	PR	/A	PD	TPI
1909	Pit-N	0	0	—	1	0	0	0	0	2	4	0	3	2	31.5	18.00	15	.364	.500	0	.000	-0	-3	-3	-0	0.0
1910	Pit-N	2	1	.667	4	1	0	0	0	17¹	19	1	7	9	13.5	3.12	99	.268	.333	0	.000	-1	-0	-1	-0	-0.1
1912	Cin-N	0	1	.000	5	2	0	0	1	14²	17	0	11	6	18.4	4.91	68	.304	.435	0	.000	-1	-2	-3	-0	-0.3
Total	3	2	2	.500	10	3	0	0	1	34	40	1	21	17	16.7	4.76	67	.290	.391	0	.000	-2	-6	-6	-0	-0.4

● GEORGE MOORE
Moore, George Raymond   b: 11/25/1872, Cambridge, Mass.   d: 11/17/48, Barnstable, Mass.   BB/TR, 5'10", 165 lbs.   Deb: 6/14/05

YEAR	TM/L	W	L	PCT	G	GS	CG	SH	SV	IP	H	HR	BB	SO	RAT	ERA	ERA+	OAV	OOB	BH	AVG	PB	PR	/A	PD	TPI
1905	Pit-N	0	0	—	1	0	0	0	0	3	2	0	0	1	6.0	0.00	—	.200	.200	0	.000	-0	1	1	-0	0.0

● JIM MOORE
Moore, James Stanford   b: 12/14/03, Prescott, Ark.   d: 5/19/73, Seattle, Wash.   BR/TR, 6', 165 lbs.   Deb: 9/21/28

YEAR	TM/L	W	L	PCT	G	GS	CG	SH	SV	IP	H	HR	BB	SO	RAT	ERA	ERA+	OAV	OOB	BH	AVG	PB	PR	/A	PD	TPI
1928	Cle-A	0	1	.000	1	1	1	0	0	9	5	0	5	1	10.0	2.00	207	.161	.278	0	.000	-0	2	2	-0	0.1
1929	Cle-A	0	0	—	2	0	0	0	0	5²	6	1	4	0	15.9	9.53	47	.273	.385	0	.000	-0	-3	-3	-0	0.0
1930	Chi-A	2	1	.667	9	5	2	0	1	40	42	0	12	11	12.1	3.60	128	.268	.320	3	.231	-0	5	5	-0	0.3
1931	Chi-A	0	2	.000	33	4	0	0	0	83²	93	3	27	15	13.0	4.95	86	.282	.338	1	.063	-1	-5	-6	1	-0.2
1932	Chi-A	0	0	—	1	0	0	0	0	1	1	0	1	2	18.0	0.00	—	.250	.400	0	—	-0	0	0	-0	0.0
Total	5	2	4	.333	46	10	3	0	1	139¹	147	4	49	29	12.7	4.52	97	.270	.332	4	.114	-2	-1	-2	1	0.2

● WHITEY MOORE
Moore, Lloyd Albert   b: 6/10/12, Tuscarawas, Ohio   d: 12/10/87, Uhrichsville, O.   BR/TR, 6'1", 195 lbs.   Deb: 9/27/36

YEAR	TM/L	W	L	PCT	G	GS	CG	SH	SV	IP	H	HR	BB	SO	RAT	ERA	ERA+	OAV	OOB	BH	AVG	PB	PR	/A	PD	TPI
1936	Cin-N	1	0	1.000	1	0	0	0	0	5	3	0	3	4	10.8	5.40	71	.167	.286	0	—	-0	-1	-1	-0	-0.2
1937	Cin-N	0	3	.000	13	6	0	0	0	38²	32	1	39	27	17.5	4.89	76	.239	.424	0	.000	-1	-4	-5	-0	-0.5
1938	Cin-N	6	4	.600	19	11	3	1	0	90¹	66	4	42	38	11.1	3.49	105	.205	.302	2	.077	-1	3	2	-1	-0.2
1939	*Cin-N	13	12	.520	42	24	9	2	3	187²	177	10	95	81	13.3	3.45	111	.254	.348	6	.098	-4	10	8	-1	0.5
1940	*Cin-N	8	8	.500	25	15	5	1	1	116²	100	8	56	60	12.6	3.63	104	.231	.329	5	.128	-1	3	2	-3	-0.2
1941	Cin-N	2	1	.667	23	4	1	0	0	61²	62	2	45	17	16.1	4.38	82	.256	.379	3	.167	-1	-5	-5	-1	-0.4
1942	Cin-N	0	0	—	1	0	0	0	0	1	0	0	1	0	9.0	0.00	—	.000	.250	0	—	0	0	0	0	0.0
	StL-N	0	1	.000	9	0	0	0	0	12¹	10	0	1	1	16.1	4.38	78	.217	.379	0	.000	-0	-1	-1	-1	-0.2
	Yr	0	1	.000	10	0	0	0	0	13¹	10	0	2	1	15.5	4.05	84	.204	.371	0	.000	-0	-1	-1	-1	-0.2
Total	7	30	29	.508	133	60	18	4	4	513¹	450	25	292	228	13.4	3.75	100	.237	.346	16	.103	-10	4	-0	-7	-1.2

● MARCUS MOORE
Moore, Marcus Braymont   b: 11/2/70, Oakland, Cal.   BB/TR, 6'5", 195 lbs.   Deb: 7/8/93

YEAR	TM/L	W	L	PCT	G	GS	CG	SH	SV	IP	H	HR	BB	SO	RAT	ERA	ERA+	OAV	OOB	BH	AVG	PB	PR	/A	PD	TPI
1993	Col-N	3	1	.750	27	0	0	0	0	26¹	30	4	20	13	17.4	6.84	70	.291	.411	0	.000	-0	-8	-6	-1	-0.9
1994	Col-N	1	1	.500	29	0	0	0	0	33²	33	4	21	33	15.8	6.15	81	.252	.376	0	.000	-0	-7	-4	-0	-0.3
Total	2	4	2	.667	56	0	0	0	0	60	63	8	41	46	16.5	6.45	76	.269	.391	0	.000	-0	-15	-10	-1	-1.2

● MIKE MOORE
Moore, Michael Wayne   b: 11/26/59, Eakly, Okla.   BR/TR, 6'4", 205 lbs.   Deb: 4/11/82

YEAR	TM/L	W	L	PCT	G	GS	CG	SH	SV	IP	H	HR	BB	SO	RAT	ERA	ERA+	OAV	OOB	BH	AVG	PB	PR	/A	PD	TPI
1982	Sea-A	7	14	.333	28	27	1	1	0	144¹	159	21	79	73	15.0	5.36	79	.285	.376	0	—	0	-21	-18	1	-2.2
1983	Sea-A	6	8	.429	22	21	3	2	0	128	130	10	60	108	13.6	4.71	90	.267	.352	0	—	0	-9	-6	2	-0.5
1984	Sea-A	7	17	.292	34	33	6	0	0	212	236	16	85	158	13.8	4.97	80	.282	.352	0	—	0	-23	-23	3	-2.0
1985	Sea-A	17	10	.630	35	34	14	2	0	247	230	18	70	155	11.1	3.46	122	.247	.302	0	—	0	19	21	2	2.3
1986	Sea-A	11	13	.458	38	37	11	1	1	266	279	28	94	146	13.0	4.30	99	.273	.341	0	—	0	-4	-2	-1	-0.2
1987	Sea-A	9	19	.321	33	33	12	0	0	231	268	29	84	115	13.7	4.71	100	.292	.351	0	—	0	-7	-0	1	0.1
1988	Sea-A	9	15	.375	37	32	9	3	1	228²	196	24	63	182	10.3	3.78	110	.232	.287	0	—	0	5	10	1	0.7
1989	*Oak-A★	19	11	.633	35	35	6	3	0	241²	193	14	83	172	10.4	2.61	141	.219	.288	0	—	0	34	29	2	4.0
1990	*Oak-A	13	15	.464	33	33	6	0	0	199¹	204	14	84	73	13.1	4.65	80	.267	.342	0	—	0	-16	-21	3	-2.2
1991	Oak-A	17	8	.680	33	33	3	1	0	210	176	11	105	153	12.3	2.96	130	.229	.326	0	—	0	27	20	2	2.5
1992	*Oak-A	17	12	.586	36	36	2	0	0	223	229	20	103	117	13.7	4.12	91	.268	.353	0	—	0	-4	-9	-1	-0.8
1993	Det-A	13	9	.591	36	36	4	3	0	213²	227	35	89	89	13.4	5.22	82	.271	.343	0	—	0	-21	-22	4	-1.5
1994	Det-A	11	10	.524	25	25	4	0	0	154¹	152	22	89	62	14.2	5.42	88	.263	.364	0	—	0	-11	-11	0	-1.2
Total	13	156	161	.492	425	415	78	16	2	2699	2679	267	1088	1603	12.7	4.23	97	.261	.334	0	.000	0	-32	-34	18	-1.0

● RAY MOORE
Moore, Raymond Leroy "Farmer"   b: 6/1/26, Meadows, Md.   BR/TR, 6'1", 205 lbs.   Deb: 8/1/52

YEAR	TM/L	W	L	PCT	G	GS	CG	SH	SV	IP	H	HR	BB	SO	RAT	ERA	ERA+	OAV	OOB	BH	AVG	PB	PR	/A	PD	TPI
1952	Bro-N	1	2	.333	14	2	0	0	0	28¹	29	3	26	11	18.1	4.76	76	.274	.425	0	.000	-0	-3	-4	-0	-0.4
1953	Bro-N	0	1	.000	1	1	1	0	0	8	6	1	4	4	11.3	3.38	126	.214	.313	0	.000	-0	1	1	-0	0.0
1955	Bal-A	10	10	.500	46	14	3	1	6	151²	128	14	90	114	12.7	3.92	97	.229	.329	6	.136	-2	1	-2	-2	-0.5
1956	Bal-A	12	7	.632	32	27	9	1	0	185	161	22	99	105	12.7	4.18	94	.238	.336	19	.271	-6	2	-5	-2	-0.1
1957	Bal-A	11	13	.458	34	32	7	1	0	227¹	196	17	112	117	12.3	3.72	97	.236	.328	18	.214	4	-2	-3	-2	-0.2
1958	Chi-A	9	7	.563	32	20	4	2	2	136²	107	10	70	73	11.7	3.82	95	.220	.318	9	.205	-4	-1	-4	-2	-0.2
1959	*Chi-A	3	6	.333	29	8	0	0	3	89²	86	10	46	49	13.3	4.12	91	.261	.344	2	.087	-1	-3	-4	-1	-0.5
1960	Chi-A	1	1	.500	14	0	0	0	0	20²	19	5	11	3	13.1	5.66	67	.253	.349	0	.000	-0	-4	-4	-0	-0.4
	Was-A	3	2	.600	37	0	0	0	13	65²	49	5	27	29	10.6	2.88	135	.213	.298	1	.071	-1	7	7	-2	0.6
	Yr	4	3	.571	51	0	0	0	13	86¹	68	10	38	32	11.2	3.54	109	.222	.310	1	.063	-1	3	3	-2	0.2
1961	Min-A	4	4	.500	46	0	0	0	14	56¹	49	8	38	45	14.1	3.67	115	.233	.353	0	.000	-1	-5	-5	-1	-1.0
1962	Min-A	8	3	.727	49	0	0	0	9	64²	55	8	30	58	12.1	4.73	86	.231	.322	0	.000	-1	-5	-5	-1	-1.0
1963	Min-A	1	3	.250	31	1	0	0	0	38²	50	14	17	38	15.8	6.98	52	.309	.378	1	.333	0	-14	-14	0	-1.5
Total	11	63	59	.516	365	105	24	5	46	1072²	935	101	560	612	12.7	4.06	93	.238	.335	56	.187	6	-18	-32	-10	-3.6

● BARRY MOORE
Moore, Robert Barry   b: 4/3/43, Statesville, N.C.   BL/TL, 6'1", 190 lbs.   Deb: 5/29/65

YEAR	TM/L	W	L	PCT	G	GS	CG	SH	SV	IP	H	HR	BB	SO	RAT	ERA	ERA+	OAV	OOB	BH	AVG	PB	PR	/A	PD	TPI
1965	Was-A	0	0	—	1	0	0	0	0	1	1	0	1	0	18.0	0.00	—	.333	.500	0	—	0	0	-0	0.0
1966	Was-A	3	3	.500	12	11	1	0	0	62¹	55	3	39	28	13.7	3.75	92	.240	.353	2	.105	-1	-2	-2	-0	-0.3
1967	Was-A	7	11	.389	27	26	3	1	0	143²	127	15	71	74	12.6	3.76	84	.240	.333	6	.130	-0	-8	-10	1	-1.1
1968	Was-A	4	6	.400	32	18	0	0	3	117²	116	8	42	56	12.2	3.37	87	.261	.327	3	.097	-1	-5	-6	1	-0.6
1969	Was-A	9	8	.529	31	25	4	0	0	134	123	12	67	51	12.9	4.30	81	.246	.338	9	.209	-1	-10	-12	-2	-1.5
1970	Cle-A	3	5	.375	13	12	0	0	0	70¹	70	6	46	35	15.0	4.22	90	.262	.373	2	.095	-0	-4	-2	-1	-0.3
	Chi-A	0	4	.000	24	7	0	0	0	70²	85	12	34	34	16.2	6.37	61	.302	.393	5	.263	1	-21	-19	1	-0.8
	Yr	3	9	.250	37	19	0	0	0	141	155	20	80	69	15.5	5.30	74	.281	.380	7	.175	-0	-25	-21	1	-1.1
Total	6	26	37	.413	140	99	8	1	3	599²	577	58	300	278	13.4	4.16	82	.256	.348	27	.151	-1	-50	-51	2	-4.6

● BOBBY MOORE
Moore, Robert Devell   b: 11/8/58, Sweetwater, La.   BR/TR, 6'4", 200 lbs.   Deb: 9/11/85

YEAR	TM/L	W	L	PCT	G	GS	CG	SH	SV	IP	H	HR	BB	SO	RAT	ERA	ERA+	OAV	OOB	BH	AVG	PB	PR	/A	PD	TPI
1985	SF-N	0	0	—	11	0	0	0	0	16²	18	1	10	10	15.1	3.24	106	.269	.364	0	.000	-0	1	0	-1	-0.1

YEAR TM/L	W	L	PCT	G	GS	CG	SH	SV	IP	H	HR	BB	SO	RAT	ERA	ERA+	OAV	OOB	BH	AVG	PB	PR	/A	PD	TPI
● **ROY MOORE** Moore, Roy Daniel b: 10/26/1898, Austin, Tex. d: 4/5/51, Seattle, Wash. BB/TL, 6', 185 lbs. Deb: 4/15/20																									
1920 Phi-A	1	13	.071	24	14	5	0	0	132²	161	6	64	45	15.5	4.68	86	.314	.393	10	.200	-1	-13	-10	2	-0.9
1921 Phi-A	10	10	.500	29	26	12	0	0	191²	206	4	122	64	15.6	4.51	99	.280	.385	19	.257	3	-5	-1	2	0.5
1922 Phi-A	0	3	.000	15	6	0	0	0	50²	65	1	32	29	17.8	7.64	65	.319	.418	5	.263	1	-20	-19	-0	-0.9
Det-A	0	0	—	9	0	0	0	2	19²	29	0	10	9	20.1	5.95	65	.367	.468	3	.429	1	-4	-5	0	-0.9
Yr	0	3	.000	24	6	0	0	2	70¹	94	1	42	38	18.0	7.17	58	.329	.423	8	.308	2	-24	-24	-0	-0.9
1923 Det-A	0	0	—	3	0	0	0	1	12	15	0	11	7	19.5	3.00	129	.288	.413	0	.000	-0	1	1	1	0.0
Total 4	11	26	.297	80	46	17	0	3	406²	476	11	239	154	16.2	4.98	85	.300	.397	37	.239	4	-41	-33	4	-1.3
● **TERRY MOORE** Moore, Terry Bluford b: 5/27/12, Vernon, Ala. BR/TR, 5'11", 195 lbs. Deb: 4/16/35 MC◆																									
1939 StL-N★	0	0	—	1	0	0	0	0	1	0	0	1	1	0.0	0.00	—	.000	.000	123	.295	0	0	0	0	0.0
● **TOMMY MOORE** Moore, Tommy Joe b: 7/7/48, Lynwood, Cal. BR/TR, 5'11", 175 lbs. Deb: 9/15/72																									
1972 NY-N	0	0	—	3	1	0	0	0	12¹	12	1	1	5	9.5	2.92	115	.273	.289	1	.333	0	1	1	0	0.0
1973 NY-N	0	1	.000	3	1	0	0	0	3¹	6	1	3	1	24.3	10.80	33	.400	.500	0	—	0	-3	-3	-0	-0.7
1975 StL-N	0	0	—	10	0	0	0	0	18²	15	2	12	6	13.0	3.86	97	.203	.314	1	.500	0	-0	-0	0	0.1
Tex-A	0	2	.000	12	0	0	0	0	21	31	1	12	15	18.9	8.14	46	.352	.436	0	—	0	-10	-10	0	-0.8
1977 Sea-A	2	1	.667	14	1	0	0	0	33	36	1	21	13	16.4	4.91	84	.281	.395	0	—	0	-3	-3	-1	-0.3
Total 4	2	4	.333	42	3	0	0	0	88¹	100	6	49	40	15.6	5.40	71	.287	.381	2	.400	1	-16	-15	-0	-1.7
● **CY MOORE** Moore, William Austin b: 2/7/05, Elberton, Ga. d: 3/28/72, Augusta, Ga. BR/TR, 6'1", 178 lbs. Deb: 6/7/29																									
1929 Bro-N	3	3	.500	32	4	0	0	0	68	87	3	31	17	15.6	5.56	83	.320	.389	3	.188	-0	-6	-7	-1	-0.7
1930 Bro-N	0	0	—	1	0	0	0	0	2	0	0	0	0	—	—	—	1.000	1.000	0	0	0	0	0	0	0.0
1931 Bro-N	1	2	.333	23	1	0	0	0	61²	62	5	13	35	11.5	3.79	100	.262	.311	2	.154	-1	0	0	0	-0.1
1932 Bro-N	0	3	.000	20	2	0	0	0	48²	56	3	17	21	13.7	4.81	79	.293	.354	2	.214	0	-5	-5	0	-0.2
1933 Phi-N	8	9	.471	36	18	9	3	1	161¹	177	7	42	53	12.4	3.74	102	.279	.326	3	.063	-4	-7	1	0	-0.3
1934 Phi-N	4	9	.308	35	15	3	0	0	126²	163	11	65	55	16.3	6.47	73	.309	.387	6	.143	-3	-34	-25	-1	-2.5
Total 6	16	26	.381	147	40	13	3	3	466¹	547	29	168	181	14.0	4.86	86	.293	.355	17	.128	-8	-52	-34	-2	-3.8
● **BILL MOORE** Moore, William Christopher b: 9/3/02, Corning, N.Y. d: 1/24/84, Corning, N.Y. BR/TR, 6'3", 195 lbs. Deb: 4/15/25																									
1925 Det-A	0	0	—	1	0	0	0	0	0	0	0	3	0	∞	∞	—	—	1.000	0	—	0	-2	-2	0	-0.2
● **WILCY MOORE** Moore, William Wilcy "Cy" b: 5/20/1897, Bonita, Tex. d: 3/29/63, Hollis, Okla. BR/TR, 6', 195 lbs. Deb: 4/14/27																									
1927 *NY-A	19	7	.731	50	12	6	1	**13**	213	185	3	59	75	10.4	**2.28**	**169**	**.234**	**.289**	6	.080	-7	44	37	8	4.8
1928 NY-A	4	4	.500	35	2	0	0	2	60¹	71	4	31	18	15.2	4.18	90	.286	.366	2	.143	-1	-1	-3	1	-0.3
1929 NY-A	6	4	.600	41	0	0	0	6	61	64	4	19	21	12.2	4.13	93	.268	.322	1	.067	-2	1	-2	2	-0.3
1931 Bos-A	11	13	.458	53	15	8	1	**10**	185¹	195	7	55	37	12.2	3.88	111	.269	.322	9	.161	-3	10	9	6	1.3
1932 Bos-A	4	10	.286	37	2	0	0	4	84¹	98	5	42	28	15.0	5.23	86	.284	.363	1	.045	-2	-7	-7	3	-1.0
*NY-A	2	0	1.000	10	1	0	0	4	25	27	1	6	8	11.9	2.52	162	.273	.314	0	.000	-1	5	4	0	0.3
Yr	6	10	.375	47	3	0	0	8	109¹	125	6	48	36	14.2	4.61	95	.281	.351	1	.033	-4	-2	-3	3	-0.7
1933 NY-A	5	6	.455	35	0	0	0	8	62	92	1	20	17	16.3	5.52	70	.333	.378	2	.133	-1	-9	-11	0	-2.0
Total 6	51	44	.537	261	32	14	2	49	691	732	25	232	204	12.6	3.70	110	.269	.327	21	.102	-17	44	27	20	2.8
● **BOB MOORHEAD** Moorhead, Charles Robert b: 1/23/38, Chambersburg, Pa. d: 12/3/86, Lemoyne, Pa. BR/TR, 6'1", 208 lbs. Deb: 4/11/62																									
1962 NY-N	0	2	.000	38	7	0	0	0	105¹	118	13	42	63	14.0	4.53	92	.289	.361	1	.045	-1	-7	-4	2	0.1
1965 NY-N	0	1	.000	9	0	0	0	0	14¹	16	0	5	5	13.2	4.40	80	.271	.328	0	—	-0	-1	-1	0	-0.1
Total 2	0	3	.000	47	7	0	0	0	119²	134	13	47	68	13.9	4.51	91	.287	.357	1	.045	-1	-8	-5	3	0.0
● **BOB MOOSE** Moose, Robert Ralph b: 10/9/47, Export, Pa. d: 10/9/76, Martins Ferry, Ohio BR/TR, 6', 200 lbs. Deb: 9/19/67																									
1967 Pit-N	1	0	1.000	2	2	1	0	0	14²	14	1	4	7	11.7	3.68	91	.259	.322	2	.333	1	-1	-1	-0	0.1
1968 Pit-N	8	12	.400	38	22	3	3	3	171¹	136	5	41	126	9.5	2.73	107	.218	.269	5	.093	-2	5	4	2	0.5
1969 Pit-N	14	3	.824	44	19	6	1	4	170	149	9	62	165	11.4	2.91	120	.231	.303	4	.075	-1	13	11	1	1.0
1970 *Pit-N	11	10	.524	28	27	9	2	0	189²	186	14	64	119	12.0	3.99	98	.262	.326	12	.182	3	1	-2	-1	-0.1
1971 *Pit-N	11	7	.611	30	18	3	1	1	140	169	12	35	68	13.2	4.11	82	.301	.344	4	.103	-1	-10	-11	0	-1.4
1972 *Pit-N	13	10	.565	31	30	6	3	1	226	213	14	47	144	10.5	2.91	114	.248	.290	12	.169	3	14	10	1	1.4
1973 Pit-N	12	13	.480	33	29	6	3	0	201¹	219	11	70	111	13.1	3.53	100	.280	.342	9	.134	-0	3	-0	2	0.1
1974 Pit-N	1	5	.167	7	6	0	0	0	35²	59	4	7	15	17.2	7.57	45	.386	.420	2	.182	-0	-16	-16	2	-2.0
1975 Pit-N	2	2	.500	23	5	1	0	0	67²	63	4	25	34	12.0	3.72	98	.246	.318	3	.167	-0	-1	-1	-0	-0.1
1976 Pit-N	3	9	.250	53	2	0	0	10	88	100	4	32	38	13.9	3.68	95	.294	.362	3	.250	1	-2	-2	-0	-0.1
Total 10	76	71	.517	289	160	35	13	19	1304¹	1308	75	387	827	11.9	3.50	98	.262	.319	56	.141	4	7	-9	8	-0.4
● **JAKE MOOTY** Mooty, J T b: 4/13/13, Bennett, Tex. d: 4/20/70, Fort Worth, Tex. BR/TR, 5'10.5", 170 lbs. Deb: 9/9/36																									
1936 Cin-N	0	0	—	8	0	0	0	1	13²	10	0	4	11	9.2	3.95	97	.204	.264	0	.000	-0	0	-0	-0	-0.1
1937 Cin-N	0	3	.000	14	4	0	0	1	39	54	2	22	11	17.5	8.31	45	.327	.406	0	.000	-1	-19	-20	-0	-1.5
1940 Chi-N	6	6	.500	20	12	6	0	1	114	101	11	49	42	11.9	2.92	128	.243	.325	10	.263	2	12	10	-2	1.0
1941 Chi-N	8	9	.471	33	14	7	1	4	153¹	143	9	56	45	11.8	3.35	105	.251	.320	10	.200	1	5	3	1	0.5
1942 Chi-N	2	5	.286	19	10	1	0	0	84¹	89	11	44	28	14.2	4.70	68	.265	.350	6	.214	0	-13	-14	0	-1.1
1943 Chi-N	0	0	—	2	0	0	0	0	1	2	0	1	1	27.0	0.00	—	.400	.500	0	—	0	0	0	0	0.0
1944 Det-A	0	0	—	15	0	0	0	0	28¹	34	0	18	7	16.8	4.45	80	.310	.409	1	.143	-0	-3	-3	-0	-0.1
Total 7	16	23	.410	111	38	14	1	8	433²	434	33	194	145	13.1	4.03	88	.263	.341	27	.205	1	-18	-23	-1	-1.3
● **HIKER MORAN** Moran, Albert Thomas b: 1/1/12, Rochester, N.Y. BR/TR, 6'4.5", 185 lbs. Deb: 9/29/38																									
1938 Bos-N	0	0	—	1	0	0	0	0	3	1	0	1	0	6.0	0.00	—	.111	.200	0	.000	-0	1	1	-0	0.0
1939 Bos-N	1	1	.500	6	2	1	0	0	20	21	3	11	4	14.4	4.50	82	.276	.368	1	.200	1	-1	-2	-0	-0.1
Total 2	1	1	.500	7	2	1	0	0	23	22	3	12	4	13.3	3.91	94	.259	.351	1	.167	0	-0	-1	-0	-0.1
● **BILL MORAN** Moran, Carl William "Bugs" b: 9/26/50, Portsmouth, Va. BR/TR, 6'4", 210 lbs. Deb: 4/12/74																									
1974 Chi-A	1	3	.250	15	5	0	0	0	46¹	57	5	23	17	16.7	4.66	80	.302	.394	0	—	0	-5	-5	-0	-0.5
● **CHARLIE MORAN** Moran, Charles Barthell "Uncle Charlie" b: 2/22/1878, Nashville, Tenn. d: 6/14/49, Horse Cave, Ky. BR/TR, 5'8", 180 lbs. Deb: 9/9/03 U◆																									
1903 StL-N	0	1	.000	3	2	2	0	0	24	30	0	19	7	18.8	5.25	62	.297	.413	6	.429	1	-5	-5	-1	-0.1
● **HARRY MORAN** Moran, Harry Edwin b: 4/2/1889, Slater, W.Va. d: 11/28/62, Beckley, W.Va. BL/TL, 6'1", 165 lbs. Deb: 6/23/12																									
1912 Det-A	0	1	.000	5	2	1	0	0	14²	19	1	12	3	20.3	4.91	66	.339	.471	1	.200	-0	-3	-3	-0	-0.2
1914 Buf-F	10	7	.588	34	16	7	2	2	154	159	7	53	73	13.0	4.27	69	.276	.348	10	.196	-0	-24	-22	-1	-2.4
1915 New-F	13	9	.591	34	23	13	2	0	205²	193	2	66	87	12.1	2.54	101	.262	.337	11	.180	-1	4	1	1	0.2
Total 3	23	17	.575	73	41	21	4	2	374¹	371	10	131	163	12.8	3.34	82	.271	.348	22	.188	-1	-22	-25	-0	-2.4
● **SAM MORAN** Moran, Samuel b: 9/16/1870, Rochester, N.Y. d: 8/29/1897, Rochester, N.Y. TL, 160 lbs. Deb: 8/28/1895																									
1895 Pit-N	2	4	.333	10	6	6	0	0	62²	78	2	51	19	19.0	7.47	61	.300	.421	4	.154	-1	-19	-21	0	-1.4
● **FORREST MORE** More, Forrest b: 9/30/1883, Hayden, Ind. d: 8/17/68, Columbus, Ind. BR/TR, 6', 180 lbs. Deb: 4/15/09																									
1909 StL-N	1	5	.167	15	3	1	0	0	50	48	0	20	17	12.8	5.04	50	.258	.340	2	.154	-0	-14	-14	1	-1.4
Bos-N	1	5	.167	10	4	3	0	0	48²	47	0	20	10	13.1	4.44	64	.270	.359	1	.067	-1	-10	-9	0	-1.1
Yr	2	10	.167	25	7	4	0	0	98²	95	0	40	27	12.7	4.74	56	.262	.342	3	.107	-1	-23	-23	1	-2.5

YEAR	TM/L	W	L	PCT	G	GS	CG	SH	SV	IP	H	HR	BB	SO	RAT	ERA	ERA+	OAV	OOB	BH	AVG	PB	PR	/A	PD	TPI
● DAVE MOREHEAD	Morehead, David Michael "Moe" b: 9/5/42, San Diego, Cal. BR/TR, 6'1", 185 lbs. Deb: 4/13/63																								
1963	Bos-A	10	13	.435	29	29	6	1	0	174²	137	20	99	136	12.2	3.81	99	.211	.316	6	.105	-3	-4	-1	1	-0.3
1964	Bos-A	8	15	.348	32	30	3	1	0	166²	156	14	112	139	14.7	4.97	78	.248	.365	5	.093	-2	-25	-21	-1	-2.9
1965	Bos-A	10	18	.357	34	33	5	2	0	192²	157	18	113	163	12.8	4.06	92	.217	.326	8	.131	0	-13	-7	-2	-1.2
1966	Bos-A	1	2	.333	12	5	0	0	0	28	31	7	7	20	12.2	5.46	70	.274	.317	3	.500	1	-6	-5	-0	-0.5
1967	*Bos-A	5	4	.556	10	9	1	1	0	47²	48	0	22	40	13.6	4.34	80	.264	.350	1	.083	-0	-6	-5	-1	-0.9
1968	Bos-A	1	4	.200	11	9	3	1	0	55	52	3	20	28	12.1	2.45	129	.249	.320	2	.125	-0	3	4	-1	0.2
1969	KC-A	2	3	.400	21	2	0	0	0	33	28	7	28	32	15.3	5.73	64	.239	.386	0	.000	-0	-8	-7	-0	-1.1
1970	KC-A	3	5	.375	28	17	1	0	1	121²	121	9	62	69	13.6	3.62	103	.261	.349	6	.167	-0	1	2	-2	-0.1
Total	8	40	64	.385	177	134	19	6	1	819¹	730	78	463	627	13.2	4.15	90	.237	.338	31	.127	-5	-57	-39	-7	-6.8
● SETH MOREHEAD	Morehead, Seth Marvin "Moe" b: 8/15/34, Houston, Tex. BL/TL, 6'0.5", 195 lbs. Deb: 4/27/57																								
1957	Phi-N	1	1	.500	34	1	1	0	1	58²	57	1	20	36	12.1	3.68	103	.254	.321	0	.000	-1	1	1	-1	-0.1
1958	Phi-N	1	6	.143	27	11	0	0	0	92¹	121	8	26	54	14.4	5.85	68	.319	.365	4	.182	-0	-19	-19	-2	-1.4
1959	Phi-N	0	2	.000	3	3	0	0	0	10	15	3	3	8	17.1	9.90	41	.333	.388	0	.000	-0	-7	-6	0	-1.0
	Chi-N	0	1	.000	11	2	0	0	0	18²	25	1	8	9	15.9	4.82	82	.313	.375	1	.500	1	-0	-2	-0	-0.1
	Yr	0	3	.000	14	5	0	0	0	28²	40	4	11	17	16.0	6.59	61	.317	.372	1	.200	1	-8	-8	-1	-1.1
1960	Chi-N	2	9	.182	45	7	2	0	4	123¹	123	17	46	64	12.5	3.94	96	.258	.326	4	.138	-1	-2	-2	-0	-0.3
1961	Mil-N	1	0	1.000	12	0	0	0	0	15¹	16	4	7	13	14.1	6.46	58	.271	.358	0	—	0	-4	-5	-0	-0.3
Total	5	5	19	.208	132	24	3	0	5	318¹	357	34	110	184	13.4	4.81	80	.282	.343	9	.145	-1	-33	-34	-4	-3.2
● LEW MOREN	Moren, Lewis Howard "Hicks" b: 8/4/1883, Pittsburgh, Pa. d: 11/2/66, Pittsburgh, Pa. BR/TR, 5'11", 150 lbs. Deb: 9/21/03																								
1903	Pit-N	0	1	.000	1	1	1	0	0	6	9	0	2	2	18.0	9.00	36	.346	.414	0	—	-0	-4	-4	-0	-0.5
1904	Pit-N	0	0	—	1	0	0	0	0	4	7	1	4	0	27.0	9.00	30	.412	.545	0	—	-0	-3	-3	0	0.0
1907	Phi-N	11	18	.379	37	31	21	3	1	255	202	3	101	98	11.0	2.54	95	.226	.311	6	.081	-2	-0	-1	-0	-0.7
1908	Phi-N	8	9	.471	28	16	9	4	0	154	146	1	49	72	11.5	2.92	83	.258	.320	12	.245	2	-10	-8	-0	-0.8
1909	Phi-N	16	15	.516	40	31	19	2	1	257²	226	6	93	110	11.3	2.65	98	.239	.309	10	.111	-3	-2	-2	-5	-1.1
1910	Phi-N	13	14	.481	34	26	12	1	1	205¹	207	6	82	74	13.1	3.55	88	.269	.347	11	.149	-1	-12	-10	-2	-1.4
Total	6	48	57	.457	141	105	62	10	3	882	797	17	331	356	11.8	2.95	90	.248	.323	39	.134	-5	-31	-30	-5	-4.5
● ANGEL MORENO	Moreno, Angel (Veneroso) b: 6/6/55, LaMendosa Soledad, Mex. BL/TL, 5'9", 165 lbs. Deb: 8/15/81																								
1981	Cal-A	1	3	.250	8	4	1	0	0	31¹	27	2	14	12	11.8	2.87	127	.233	.315	0	—	0	3	3	-0	0.3
1982	Cal-A	3	7	.300	13	8	2	0	1	49¹	55	7	23	22	14.4	4.74	85	.288	.367	0	—	0	-4	-4	-0	-0.7
Total	2	4	10	.286	21	12	3	0	1	80²	82	9	37	34	13.4	4.02	97	.267	.348	0	—	0	-1	-1	-0	-0.4
● JULIO MORENO	Moreno, Julio (Gonzalez) b: 1/28/21, Guines, Cuba d: 1/2/87, Miami, Fla. BR/TR, 5'8", 165 lbs. Deb: 9/8/50																								
1950	Was-A	1	1	.500	4	3	1	0	0	21¹	22	1	12	7	14.8	4.64	97	.268	.368	1	.125	-0	-0	-0	-0	-0.1
1951	Was-A	5	11	.313	31	18	5	0	2	132²	132	18	80	37	14.4	4.88	84	.256	.357	7	.175	-1	-11	-12	-1	-1.4
1952	Was-A	9	9	.500	26	22	7	0	0	147¹	154	10	52	62	12.9	3.97	90	.270	.337	6	.122	-2	-5	-7	-1	-1.1
1953	Was-A	3	1	.750	12	2	1	0	0	35¹	41	2	13	13	13.8	2.80	139	.291	.351	0	.000	-1	5	4	-0	0.3
Total	4	18	22	.450	73	45	14	0	2	336²	349	31	157	119	13.7	4.25	91	.267	.349	14	.132	-5	-12	-15	-1	-2.3
● ROGER MORET	Moret, Rogelio (Torres) b: 9/16/49, Guayama, P.R. BB/TL, 6'4", 175 lbs. Deb: 9/13/70																								
1970	Bos-A	1	0	1.000	3	1	0	0	0	8¹	7	0	4	2	11.9	3.24	122	.226	.314	0	.000	-0	0	1	-0	0.0
1971	Bos-A	4	3	.571	13	7	4	1	0	71	50	5	40	47	11.7	2.92	127	.205	.322	2	.087	-1	4	6	-0	0.5
1972	Bos-A	0	0	—	3	0	0	0	0	5	5	0	6	4	19.8	3.60	89	.263	.440	0	.000	-0	-0	-0	-0	0.0
1973	Bos-A	13	2	.867	30	15	5	2	3	156¹	138	19	67	90	12.0	3.17	127	.238	.320	0	—	0	11	15	-0	1.4
1974	Bos-A	9	10	.474	31	21	10	1	2	173¹	158	15	79	111	12.4	3.74	103	.243	.327	0	—	0	2	2	-2	-0.2
1975	*Bos-A	14	3	.824	36	16	4	1	1	145	132	8	76	80	13.0	3.60	113	.248	.344	0	—	0	3	8	-1	0.7
1976	Atl-N	3	5	.375	27	12	1	0	1	77¹	84	7	27	30	13.0	5.00	76	.280	.341	3	.130	-1	-13	-10	-1	-1.2
1977	Tex-A	3	3	.500	18	8	0	0	4	72¹	59	6	38	39	12.1	3.73	109	.220	.317	0	—	0	3	3	-1	0.1
1978	Tex-A	0	1	.000	7	2	0	0	0	14²	23	1	2	5	16.0	4.91	76	.390	.419	0	—	0	-2	-2	-0	-0.2
Total	9	47	27	.635	168	82	24	5	12	723¹	656	61	339	408	12.5	3.66	107	.245	.332	5	.100	-2	4	22	-6	1.1
● DAVE MOREY	Morey, David Beale b: 2/25/1889, Malden, Mass. d: 1/4/86, Oak Bluffs, Mass. BL/TR, 6', 185 lbs. Deb: 7/4/13																								
1913	Phi-A	0	0	—	2	0	0	0	0	4	2	0	2	1	11.3	4.50	61	.182	.357	0	.000	-0	-1	-1	0	0.0
● CY MORGAN	Morgan, Cyril Arlon b: 11/11/1895, Lakeville, Mass. d: 9/11/46, Lakeville, Mass. BR/TR, 6', 170 lbs. Deb: 6/8/21																								
1921	Bos-N	1	1	.500	17	0	0	0	1	30¹	37	0	17	8	16.3	6.53	56	.314	.404	0	.000	-1	-9	-10	1	-0.6
1922	Bos-N	0	0	—	2	0	0	0	0	1¹	8	0	2	0	67.5	27.00	15	.667	.714	0	—	0	-3	-3	-0	0.0
Total	2	1	1	.500	19	0	0	0	1	31²	45	0	19	8	7.39	7.39	50	.346	.433	0	.000	-1	-13	-13	1	-0.6
● CY MORGAN	Morgan, Harry Richard b: 11/10/1878, Pomeroy, Ohio d: 6/28/62, Wheeling, W.Va. BR/TR, 6', 175 lbs. Deb: 9/18/03																								
1903	StL-A	0	2	.000	2	1	1	0	0	13	12	6	0	6	13.8	4.15	70	.245	.350	1	.250	0	-2	-2	-0	-0.3
1904	StL-A	0	2	.000	8	3	2	0	0	51	51	3	10	24	11.1	3.71	67	.261	.304	1	.056	-2	-6	-7	1	-0.4
1905	StL-A	2	5	.286	13	8	5	1	0	77¹	82	1	37	44	14.9	3.61	71	.273	.370	2	.258	2	-8	-9	-2	-0.4
1907	StL-A	2	5	.286	10	6	4	0	0	55	77	3	17	14	15.7	6.05	42	.332	.383	2	.100	-1	-21	-22	1	-2.4
	Bos-A	6	6	.500	16	13	9	2	0	114¹	77	1	34	50	9.0	1.97	131	.193	.262	2	.057	-4	7	8	-1	0.3
	Yr	8	11	.421	26	19	13	2	0	169¹	154	4	51	64	11.1	3.30	78	.243	.303	4	.073	-5	-14	-14	1	-2.1
1908	Bos-A	14	13	.519	30	26	17	2	1	205	166	7	90	99	11.7	2.46	100	.226	.324	8	.127	-3	-1	0	1	-0.3
1909	Bos-A	2	6	.250	12	10	5	0	1	64²	52	0	31	30	12.4	2.37	106	.240	.350	1	.050	-2	1	1	2	0.2
	Phi-A	16	11	.593	28	26	21	5	0	228²	152	3	71	81	9.4	1.65	146	.191	.271	8	.108	-3	21	19	-2	1.8
	Yr	18	17	.514	40	36	26	5	1	293¹	204	3	102	111	9.9	1.81	134	**.200**	.283	9	.096	-4	22	20	1	2.0
1910	Phi-A	18	12	.600	36	34	23	3	0	290²	214	0	117	134	10.8	1.55	153	.216	.310	14	.141	-4	31	27	1	2.5
1911	Phi-A	15	7	.682	38	30	15	2	1	249²	217	0	113	136	12.7	2.70	123	.243	.341	15	.160	-5	18	13	3	0.8
1912	Phi-A	8	8	.273	16	14	5	0	0	93²	95	0	51	47	12.6	3.75	80	.226	.338	1	.033	-3	-4	-7	2	-0.8
1913	Cin-N	0	1	.000	1	1	0	0	0	2¹	5	0	1	2	27.0	15.43	21	.500	.583	0	—	0	-3	-3	-0	-0.8
Total	10	78	78	.500	210	172	107	15	3	1445¹	1180	18	578	667	11.5	2.51	105	.229	.318	61	.125	-25	32	19	12	0.2
● BILL MORGAN	Morgan, Henry William b: 10/1857, Washington, D.C. Deb: 5/4/1875 ◆																								
1875	RS-n	1	3	.250	7	4	4	1	0	42	38	0	1	0	8.4	*3.43*	71	.200	.204	18	.261	1	-5	-5		-0.2
● MIKE MORGAN	Morgan, Michael Thomas b: 10/8/59, Tulare, Cal. BR/TR, 6'3", 195 lbs. Deb: 6/11/78																								
1978	Oak-A	0	3	.000	3	3	1	0	0	12¹	19	1	8	0	19.7	7.30	50	.373	.458	0	—	0	-5	-5	1	-0.8
1979	Oak-A	2	10	.167	13	13	2	0	0	77¹	102	7	50	17	18.0	5.94	68	.332	.431	0	—	0	-15	-16	1	-1.7
1982	NY-A	7	11	.389	30	23	2	0	0	150¹	167	15	67	71	14.1	4.37	91	.285	.360	—	0	-5	-6	1	-0.6
1983	Tor-A	0	3	.000	16	4	0	0	0	45¹	48	6	21	22	13.7	5.16	83	.273	.350	—	0	-6	-4	1	-0.3
1985	Sea-A	1	1	.500	2	2	0	0	0	6	11	2	5	2	24.0	12.00	35	.393	.485	—	0	-5	-5	0	-1.1
1986	Sea-A	11	17	.393	37	33	9	1	0	216¹	243	24	86	116	13.9	4.53	94	.286	.354	—	0	-9	-7	-0	-0.9
1987	Sea-A	12	17	.414	34	31	8	2	0	207	245	25	53	85	13.2	4.65	101	.296	.342	—	0	-3	-6	2	-0.4
1988	Bal-A	1	6	.143	22	10	2	0	1	71¹	70	6	23	29	11.9	5.43	72	.255	.315	—	0	-12	-12	-0	-0.8
1989	LA-N	8	11	.421	40	19	0	0	0	152²	130	6	33	72	9.7	2.53	135	.234	.280	3	.083	-2	16	15	4	2.1
1990	LA-N	11	15	.423	33	33	6	**4**	0	211	216	19	60	106	12.0	3.75	97	.266	.314	8	.113	-2	-1	3	-0	-0.1
1991	LA-N★	14	10	.583	34	33	5	1	0	236¹	197	12	61	140	9.9	2.78	129	.226	.279	7	.092	-3	24	21	2	2.1
1992	Chi-N	16	8	.667	34	34	6	1	0	240	203	14	79	123	10.7	2.55	141	.234	.300	8	.108	-2	25	28	2	2.8

YEAR	TM/L	W	L	PCT	G	GS	CG	SH	SV	IP	H	HR	BB	SO	RAT	ERA	ERA+	OAV	OOB	BH	AVG	PB	PR	/A	PD	TPI
1993	Chi-N	10	15	.400	32	32	1	1	0	207²	206	15	74	111	12.4	4.03	99	.262	.331	4	.061	-4	0	-1	0	-0.4
1994	Chi-N	2	10	.167	15	15	1	0	0	80²	111	12	35	57	16.7	6.69	61	.338	.409	3	.125	-1	-22	-23	-1	-2.9
Total	14	95	137	.409	345	285	43	10	3	1914¹	1968	164	655	951	12.5	4.01	98	.269	.332	33	.095	-14	-16	-18	14	-2.4

● TOM MORGAN
Morgan, Tom Stephen "Plowboy"   b: 5/20/30, ElMonte, Cal.   d: 1/13/87, Anaheim, Cal.   BR/TR, 6'2", 195 lbs.   Deb: 4/20/51   C

YEAR	TM/L	W	L	PCT	G	GS	CG	SH	SV	IP	H	HR	BB	SO	RAT	ERA	ERA+	OAV	OOB	BH	AVG	PB	PR	/A	PD	TPI
1951	*NY-A	9	3	.750	27	16	4	2	2	124²	119	11	36	57	11.4	3.68	104	.253	.310	12	.273	2	6	2	2	0.5
1952	NY-A	5	4	.556	16	12	2	1	2	93²	86	8	33	35	11.8	3.07	108	.252	.325	6	.182	1	6	3	0	0.6
1954	NY-A	11	5	.688	32	17	7	4	1	143	149	8	40	34	12.2	3.34	103	.274	.330	7	.143	0	6	4	2	0.4
1955	*NY-A	7	3	.700	40	1	0	0	10	72	72	3	24	17	12.6	3.25	115	.267	.338	4	.222	0	6	4	2	0.9
1956	*NY-A	6	7	.462	41	0	0	0	11	71¹	74	7	27	20	13.1	4.16	93	.284	.357	2	.154	-0	-0	-2	1	-0.4
1957	KC-A	9	7	.563	46	13	5	0	7	143²	160	19	61	32	14.0	4.64	85	.299	.373	3	.091	-2	-14	-11	4	-1.1
1958	Det-A	2	5	.286	39	1	0	0	1	62²	70	7	4	20	10.8	3.16	128	.286	.300	2	.200	-0	4	6	-0	0.6
1959	Det-A	1	4	.200	46	1	0	0	9	92²	94	11	18	39	11.5	3.98	102	.265	.311	9	.391	4	-1	1	-0	0.4
1960	Det-A	3	2	.600	22	0	0	0	1	29	33	6	10	12	13.3	4.66	85	.295	.352	0	—	-0	-3	-2	0	-0.3
	Was-A	1	3	.250	14	0	0	0	1	24	36	6	5	11	15.8	3.75	104	.343	.378	0	.000	-1	0	-0	-0	0.0
	Yr	4	5	.444	36	0	0	0	1	53	69	12	15	23	14.4	4.25	92	.315	.362	0	.000	-1	-2	-2	0	-0.3
1961	LA-A	8	2	.800	59	0	0	0	10	91²	74	7	17	39	9.4	2.36	191	.224	.272	1	.083	-1	17	22	1	2.7
1962	LA-A	5	2	.714	48	0	0	0	9	58²	53	6	19	29	11.2	2.91	132	.247	.311	0	.000	-1	7	6	-1	0.7
1963	LA-A	0	0	—	13	0	0	0	1	16¹	20	1	6	7	16.0	5.51	62	.313	.397	0	.000	-0	-3	-4	-0	-0.1
Total	12	67	47	.588	443	61	18	7	64	1023¹	1040	95	300	364	12.1	3.61	106	.270	.329	46	.186	3	32	26	13	4.9

● GENE MORIARITY
Moriarity, Eugene John   b: 1/5/1865, Holyoke, Mass.   BL/TL, 5'8", 130 lbs.   Deb: 6/18/1884   ◆

YEAR	TM/L	W	L	PCT	G	GS	CG	SH	SV	IP	H	HR	BB	SO	RAT	ERA	ERA+	OAV	OOB	BH	AVG	PB	PR	/A	PD	TPI
1884	Ind-a	0	2	.000	2	2	2	0	0	13²	16	0	7	4	15.8	5.27	62	.267	.353	8	.216	-0	-3	-3	0	-0.3
1885	Det-N	0	0	—	1	0	0	0	0	2	3	0	1	4	18.0	9.00	32	.300	.364	1	.026	-0	-1	-1	-0	0.0
Total	2	0	2	.000	3	2	2	0	0	15²	19	0	8	5	16.1	5.74	56	.271	.354	41	.152	-0	-4	-4	0	-0.3

● JOHN MORLAN
Morlan, John Glen   b: 11/22/47, Columbus, Ohio   BR/TR, 6', 178 lbs.   Deb: 7/20/73

YEAR	TM/L	W	L	PCT	G	GS	CG	SH	SV	IP	H	HR	BB	SO	RAT	ERA	ERA+	OAV	OOB	BH	AVG	PB	PR	/A	PD	TPI
1973	Pit-N	2	2	.500	10	7	1	0	0	41	42	4	23	23	14.3	3.95	89	.276	.371	2	.182	1	-1	-2	-1	-0.2
1974	Pit-N	0	3	.000	39	0	0	0	0	65	54	2	48	38	14.5	4.29	80	.227	.363	0	.000	-1	-5	-6	-1	-0.4
Total	2	2	5	.286	49	7	1	0	0	106	96	6	71	61	14.4	4.16	83	.246	.366	2	.111	0	-6	-8	-1	-0.6

● DAN MOROGIELLO
Morogiello, Daniel Joseph   b: 3/26/55, Brooklyn, N.Y.   BL/TL, 6'1", 200 lbs.   Deb: 5/20/83

YEAR	TM/L	W	L	PCT	G	GS	CG	SH	SV	IP	H	HR	BB	SO	RAT	ERA	ERA+	OAV	OOB	BH	AVG	PB	PR	/A	PD	TPI
1983	Bal-A	0	1	.000	22	0	0	0	1	37²	39	1	10	15	11.9	2.39	165	.265	.316	0	—	0	7	7	-1	0.1

● JIM MORONEY
Moroney, James Francis   b: 12/4/1885, Boston, Mass.   d: 2/26/29, Philadelphia, Pa.   BL/TL, 6'1", 175 lbs.   Deb: 4/24/06

YEAR	TM/L	W	L	PCT	G	GS	CG	SH	SV	IP	H	HR	BB	SO	RAT	ERA	ERA+	OAV	OOB	BH	AVG	PB	PR	/A	PD	TPI
1906	Bos-N	0	3	.000	3	3	3	0	0	27	28	1	12	11	15.3	5.33	50	.259	.365	1	.100	-1	-8	-8	0	-0.8
1910	Phi-N	1	2	.333	12	2	1	0	1	42	43	1	11	13	12.4	2.14	146	.295	.360	0	.000	-1	4	5	-0	0.2
1912	Chi-N	1	1	.500	10	3	1	0	1	23²	25	0	17	5	17.5	4.56	73	.316	.460	3	.500	1	-3	-3	-0	-0.2
Total	3	2	6	.250	25	8	5	0	2	92²	96	2	40	29	14.6	3.69	83	.288	.388	4	.154	-1	-7	-7	-1	-0.8

● BILL MORRELL
Morrell, Willard Blackmer   b: 4/9/1893, Hyde Park, Mass.   d: 8/5/75, Birmingham, Ala.   BR/TR, 6', 172 lbs.   Deb: 4/20/26

YEAR	TM/L	W	L	PCT	G	GS	CG	SH	SV	IP	H	HR	BB	SO	RAT	ERA	ERA+	OAV	OOB	BH	AVG	PB	PR	/A	PD	TPI
1926	Was-A	3	3	.500	26	2	1	0	1	69²	83	5	29	16	14.7	5.30	73	.311	.383	4	.235	1	-10	-11	-1	-0.9
1930	NY-N	0	0	—	2	0	0	0	0	8	6	0	1	3	7.9	1.13	421	.214	.241	0	.000	-0	3	3	0	0.0
1931	NY-N	5	3	.625	20	7	2	0	1	66	83	4	27	16	15.0	4.36	85	.306	.369	2	.111	-0	-4	-5	-0	-0.6
Total	3	8	6	.571	48	9	3	0	2	143²	172	9	57	35	14.5	4.64	83	.304	.370	6	.162	-0	-10	-13	-1	-1.5

● JOHN MORRILL
Morrill, John Francis "Honest John"   b: 2/19/1855, Boston, Mass.   d: 4/2/32, Boston, Mass.   BR/TR, 5'10.5", 155 lbs.   Deb: 4/24/1876   M ◆

YEAR	TM/L	W	L	PCT	G	GS	CG	SH	SV	IP	H	HR	BB	SO	RAT	ERA	ERA+	OAV	OOB	BH	AVG	PB	PR	/A	PD	TPI
1880	Bos-N	0	0	—	3	0	0	0	0	10²	9	0	1	0	8.4	0.84	269	.273	.294	81	.237	0	2	2	0	0.0
1881	Bos-N	0	1	.000	3	1	0	0	1	5²	9	1	1	0	15.9	6.35	42	.333	.357	90	.289	1	-2	-2	0	-0.4
1882	Bos-N	0	0	—	1	0	0	0	0	2	3	0	0	2	13.5	0.00	—	.375	.375	101	.289	0	1	1	0	0.0
1883	Bos-N	1	0	1.000	2	1	1	0	0	13	15	0	4	5	13.2	2.77	112	.268	.317	129	.319	1	-1	-0	0	0.1
1884	Bos-N	1	1	.000	7	1	1	0	2	23	34	0	6	13	15.7	7.43	39	.315	.351	114	.260	1	-11	-12	0	-0.5
1886	Bos-N	0	0	—	1	0	0	0	0	4	5	0	0	0	11.3	0.00	—	.313	.313	106	.247	0	1	1	0	0.0
1889	Was-N	0	0	—	1	0	0	0	0	0¹	1	0	0	0	—	—	—	.000	.000	27	.185	0	0	0	0	0.0
Total	7	2	1	2	.333	18	2	58²	75	0	12	22	13.3	4.30	66	.301	.333	1275	.260	4	-9	-10	0	-0.8

● DANNY MORRIS
Morris, Danny Walker   b: 6/11/46, Greenville, Ky.   BR/TR, 6'1", 200 lbs.   Deb: 9/10/68

YEAR	TM/L	W	L	PCT	G	GS	CG	SH	SV	IP	H	HR	BB	SO	RAT	ERA	ERA+	OAV	OOB	BH	AVG	PB	PR	/A	PD	TPI
1968	Min-A	0	1	.000	3	2	0	0	0	10²	11	0	4	6	12.7	1.69	183	.262	.326	0	.000	-0	2	2	0	0.1
1969	Min-A	0	1	.000	3	1	0	0	0	5¹	5	1	4	1	15.2	5.06	72	.238	.360	0	—	0	-1	-1	-0	-0.1
Total	2	0	2	.000	6	3	0	0	0	16	16	1	8	7	13.5	2.81	117	.254	.338	0	.000	-0	1	1	0	0.0

● E. MORRIS
Morris, E.   b: Trenton, N.J.   Deb: 9/11/1884   ◆

YEAR	TM/L	W	L	PCT	G	GS	CG	SH	SV	IP	H	HR	BB	SO	RAT	ERA	ERA+	OAV	OOB	BH	AVG	PB	PR	/A	PD	TPI
1884	Bal-U	0	0	—	1	0	0	0	0	1	2	0	2	0	36.0	9.00	30	.391	.562	0	.000	-1	-1	-1	-0	0.0

● ED MORRIS
Morris, Edward "Cannonball"   b: 9/29/1862, Brooklyn, N.Y.   d: 4/12/37, Pittsburgh, Pa.   BR/TL, 165 lbs.   Deb: 5/1/1884

YEAR	TM/L	W	L	PCT	G	GS	CG	SH	SV	IP	H	HR	BB	SO	RAT	ERA	ERA+	OAV	OOB	BH	AVG	PB	PR	/A	PD	TPI
1884	Col-a	34	13	.723	52	52	47	3	0	429²	335	3	51	302	8.4	2.18	139	.204	.234	37	.186	2	51	41	2	4.2
1885	Pit-a	39	24	.619	63	63	63	7	0	581	459	5	101	298	8.9	2.35	137	.208	.247	44	.186	-5	58	56	-1	4.5
1886	Pit-a	41	20	.672	64	63	63	12	1	555¹	455	5	118	326	9.4	2.45	138	.214	.258	38	.167	-7	62	58	-1	4.4
1887	Pit-N	14	22	.389	38	38	37	1	0	317²	375	13	71	91	12.9	4.31	90	.286	.326	25	.198	-4	-8	-15	-2	-1.8
1888	Pit-N	29	23	.558	55	55	54	5	0	480	470	7	74	135	10.4	2.31	116	.245	.276	19	.101	-1	29	19	1	0.7
1889	Pit-N	6	13	.316	21	21	18	0	0	170	196	4	48	40	13.2	4.13	91	.280	.332	7	.097	-5	-2	-7	-2	-1.2
1890	Pit-P	8	7	.533	18	15	15	1	0	144¹	178	5	35	25	13.5	4.86	80	.290	.332	9	.143	-4	-10	-15	-3	-1.6
Total	7	171	122	.584	311	307	297	29	1	2678	2468	42	498	1217	10.2	2.82	116	.235	.273	179	.161	-35	179	137	-5	9.2

● JACK MORRIS
Morris, John Scott   b: 5/16/55, St.Paul, Minn.   BR/TR, 6'3", 200 lbs.   Deb: 7/26/77

YEAR	TM/L	W	L	PCT	G	GS	CG	SH	SV	IP	H	HR	BB	SO	RAT	ERA	ERA+	OAV	OOB	BH	AVG	PB	PR	/A	PD	TPI
1977	Det-A	1	1	.500	7	6	1	0	0	45²	38	4	23	28	12.0	3.74	114	.235	.330	0	—	0	2	3	-0	0.0
1978	Det-A	3	5	.375	28	7	0	0	0	106	107	8	49	48	13.5	4.33	89	.268	.352	0	—	0	-7	-5	-0	-0.5
1979	Det-A	17	7	.708	27	27	9	1	0	197²	179	19	59	113	11.0	3.28	132	.244	.304	0	—	0	21	23	-1	2.5
1980	Det-A	16	15	.516	36	36	11	2	0	250	252	20	87	112	12.3	4.18	98	.262	.326	0	—	0	-4	-2	3	0.1
1981	Det-A★	14	7	.667	25	25	15	1	0	198	153	14	78	97	10.6	3.05	124	.218	.298	0	—	0	13	16	-0	1.6
1982	Det-A	17	16	.515	37	37	17	3	0	266¹	247	37	96	135	11.6	4.06	100	.247	.312	0	—	0	1	-0	0	0.0
1983	Det-A	20	13	.606	37	37	20	0	0	293²	257	30	83	232	10.5	3.34	117	.233	.289	0	—	0	24	19	-1	1.8
1984	*Det-A★	19	11	.633	35	35	9	1	0	240¹	221	20	87	148	11.6	3.60	100	.241	.308	0	—	0	11	9	2	1.2
1985	Det-A★	16	11	.593	35	35	13	4	0	257	212	21	110	191	11.5	3.33	122	.225	.309	0	—	0	23	21	-1	2.0
1986	Det-A	21	8	.724	35	35	15	6	0	267	229	40	82	223	10.5	3.27	126	.229	.287	0	—	0	27	25	0	2.6
1987	*Det-A★	18	11	.621	34	34	13	0	0	266	227	39	93	208	10.9	3.38	125	.228	.294	0	.000	0	32	25	-2	2.2
1988	Det-A	15	13	.536	34	34	10	2	0	235	225	20	83	168	11.9	3.94	97	.251	.318	0	—	0	-1	-3	0	-0.3
1989	Det-A	6	14	.300	24	24	10	0	0	170¹	189	23	59	115	13.2	4.86	79	.283	.342	0	—	0	-19	-20	1	-2.0
1990	Det-A	15	18	.455	36	36	11	3	0	249²	231	26	97	162	12.0	4.51	88	.242	.316	0	—	0	-17	-15	-1	-1.9
1991	*Min-A★	18	12	.600	35	35	10	2	0	246²	226	18	92	163	11.8	3.43	124	.245	.317	0	—	0	18	23	-1	2.5
1992	*Tor-A	21	6	.778	34	34	6	1	0	240²	222	18	80	132	11.7	4.04	101	.246	.314	0	—	0	-3	1	1	0.0
1993	Tor-A	7	12	.368	27	27	4	1	0	152²	189	18	65	103	15.2	6.19	70	.302	.371	0	—	0	-32	-32	-2	-3.5
1994	Cle-A	10	6	.625	23	23	4	0	0	141¹	163	18	67	100	14.9	5.60	88	.292	.371	0	—	0	-13	-10	0	-1.2
Total	18	254	186	.577	549	527	175	28	0	3824	3567	389	1390	2478	11.8	3.90	105	.247	.316	0	.000	0	78	77	-5	7.1

YEAR	TM/L	W	L	PCT	G	GS	CG	SH	SV	IP	H	HR	BB	SO	RAT	ERA	ERA+	OAV	OOB	BH	AVG	PB	PR	/A	PD	TPI

● JOHN MORRIS Morris, John Wallace b: 8/23/41, Lewes, Del. BR/TL, 6'1", 198 lbs. Deb: 7/19/66

1966	Phi-N	1	1	.500	13	0	0	0	0	13²	15	2	8	8	12.5	5.27	68	.278	.328	0	—	0	-3	-3	0	-0.3
1968	Bal-A	2	0	1.000	19	0	0	0	0	31²	19	4	17	22	11.4	2.56	114	.173	.305	0	.000	-1	1	1	0	0.0
1969	Sea-A	0	0	—	6	0	0	0	0	12²	16	2	8	8	17.1	6.39	57	.308	.400	1	1.000	-4	-4	1	0.2
1970	Mil-A	4	3	.571	20	9	2	0	0	73¹	70	4	22	40	11.5	3.93	96	.253	.312	3	.176	0	-2	-1	1	0.0
1971	Mil-A	2	2	.500	43	1	0	0	1	67²	69	4	27	42	12.9	3.72	93	.270	.342	1	.200	0	-2	-2	1	0.0
1972	SF-N	0	0	—	7	0	0	0	0	6¹	9	2	2	5	15.6	4.26	82	.310	.355	0	—	0	-1	-1	0	0.0
1973	SF-N	1	0	1.000	7	0	0	0	0	6¹	12	0	3	3	21.3	8.53	45	.429	.484	0	.000	-0	-3	-3	-0	-0.5
1974	SF-N	1	1	.500	17	0	0	0	1	20²	17	1	4	9	9.1	3.05	125	.215	.253	1	1.000	0	1	2	-1	0.2
Total	8	11	7	.611	132	10	2	0	2	232¹	227	19	86	137	12.4	3.95	90	.256	.328	6	.194	1	-11	-10	3	-0.4

● BUGS MORRIS Morris, Joseph Harley (a.k.a. Joseph Harley Bennett In 1918) b: 4/19/1892, Kansas City, Mo. d: 11/21/57, Noel, Mo. BR/TR, 5'9.5", 163 lbs. Deb: 7/20/18

1918	StL-A	0	2	.000	4	2	0	0	0	10¹	12	1	7	0	16.5	3.48	79	.308	.413	1	.250	0	-1	-1	0	-0.1
1921	Chi-A	0	3	.000	3	2	1	0	0	17²	19	1	16	2	17.8	6.11	69	.297	.438	2	.333	0	-4	-4	1	-0.4
	StL-A	0	0	—	3	1	0	0	0	5²	11	1	6	3	30.2	14.29	31	.407	.543	1	1.000	0	-6	-6	-0	0.0
	Yr	0	3	.000	6	3	1	0	0	23¹	30	2	22	5	20.8	8.10	53	.330	.470	3	.429	1	-10	-10	0	-0.4
Total	2	0	5	.000	10	5	1	0	0	33²	42	3	29	5	19.5	6.68	57	.323	.453	4	.364	1	-11	-11	1	-0.5

● ED MORRIS Morris, Walter Edward "Big Ed" b: 12/7/1899, Foshee, Ala. d: 3/3/32, Century, Fla. BR/TR, 6'2", 185 lbs. Deb: 8/5/22

1922	Chi-N	0	0	—	5	0	0	0	0	12	22	1	6	5	21.0	8.25	51	.386	.444	1	.250	-0	-6	-5	-0	0.0
1928	Bos-A	19	15	.559	47	29	20	0	5	257²	255	7	80	104	11.9	3.53	117	.264	.323	14	.154	-4	15	17	-2	1.5
1929	Bos-A	14	14	.500	33	26	17	2	1	208¹	227	7	95	73	14.0	4.45	96	.282	.360	16	.232	2	-5	-4	-2	-0.4
1930	Bos-A	4	9	.308	18	9	3	0	0	65¹	67	1	38	28	14.5	4.13	112	.260	.355	6	.316	2	4	3	-0	0.7
1931	Bos-A	5	7	.417	37	14	3	0	0	130²	131	4	74	46	14.5	4.75	91	.260	.361	6	.158	-2	-5	-6	-0	-0.6
Total	5	42	45	.483	140	78	43	2	6	674	702	20	293	256	13.4	4.19	101	.271	.348	43	.195	-1	3	4	-4	1.2

● BILL MORRISETTE Morrisette, William Lee b: 1/17/1893, Baltimore, Md. d: 3/25/66, Virginia Beach, Va BR/TR, 6', 176 lbs. Deb: 9/19/15

1915	Phi-A	2	0	1.000	4	1	1	0	0	20	15	0	5	11	9.0	1.35	217	.195	.244	2	.286	0	4	4	0	0.4
1916	Phi-A	—	1	0	0	0	0	4	6	0	5	2	24.8	6.75	42	.429	.579	0	.000	0	-2	-2	1	0.1
1920	Det-A	1	1	.500	8	3	1	0	0	27	25	0	19	15	15.7	4.33	86	.245	.379	0	.000	-1	-2	-2	-0	-0.3
Total	3	3	1	.750	13	4	2	0	0	51	46	0	29	28	13.8	3.35	100	.238	.347	2	.125	-1	0	-0	0	0.2

● JIM MORRISON Morrison, James Forrest b: 9/23/52, Pensacola, Fla. BR/TR, 5'11", 182 lbs. Deb: 9/18/77 ♦

| 1988 | Atl-N | 0 | 0 | — | 3 | 0 | 0 | 0 | 0 | 3² | 3 | 0 | 2 | 1 | 12.3 | 0.00 | — | .214 | .313 | 14 | .152 | 0 | 1 | 1 | -0 | 0.0 |

● JOHNNY MORRISON Morrison, John Dewey "Jughandle Johnny" b: 10/22/1895, Pellville, Ky. d: 3/20/66, Louisville, Ky. BR/TR, 5'11", 188 lbs. Deb: 9/28/20 F

1920	Pit-N	1	0	1.000	2	1	1	0	0	7	4	0	1	3	6.4	0.00	—	.167	.200	0	.000	-0	2	3	0	0.3
1921	Pit-N	9	7	.563	21	11	7	**3**	0	144	131	4	33	52	10.3	2.88	133	.258	.305	5	.119	-1	15	15	-0	1.4
1922	Pit-N	17	11	.607	45	33	20	**5**	1	286¹	315	10	87	104	12.8	3.43	119	.286	.341	20	.198	-2	21	21	0	1.5
1923	Pit-N	25	13	.658	42	37	27	2	2	301²	287	6	110	114	12.0	3.49	115	.253	.321	21	.183	-3	17	17	-0	1.6
1924	Pit-N	11	16	.407	**41**	25	10	0	2	237²	213	7	73	85	11.0	3.75	102	.245	.307	13	.169	-2	3	2	-2	-0.2
1925	*Pit-N	17	14	.548	**44**	26	10	0	**4**	211	245	12	60	60	13.3	3.88	115	.291	.343	13	.178	-2	9	14	-2	1.3
1926	Pit-N	6	8	.429	26	13	6	2	2	122¹	119	2	44	39	12.1	3.38	116	.267	.335	3	.077	-4	6	7	-2	0.2
1927	Pit-N	3	2	.600	21	2	1	0	3	53²	63	2	21	21	14.1	4.19	98	.304	.368	2	.154	-0	-2	-0	-1	-0.2
1929	Bro-N	13	7	.650	39	10	4	0	**8**	136²	150	11	61	57	14.1	4.48	103	.279	.355	7	.163	-2	4	2	-3	-0.2
1930	Bro-N	1	2	.333	16	0	0	0	1	34²	47	4	16	11	16.4	5.45	90	.346	.414	0	.000	-1	-2	-2	-0	-0.2
Total	10	103	80	.563	297	164	90	13	23	1535	1574	57	506	546	12.4	3.65	113	.271	.332	84	.164	-18	74	79	-11	5.5

● MIKE MORRISON Morrison, Michael b: 2/6/1867, Erie, Pa. d: 6/16/55, Erie, Pa. BR/TR, 5'8.5", 156 lbs. Deb: 4/19/1887

1887	Cle-a	12	25	.324	40	40	35	0	0	316²	385	13	205	158	17.4	4.92	88	.294	.398	27	.191	-4	-22	-20	10	-1.2
1888	Cle-a	1	3	.250	4	4	4	0	0	35	40	3	19	14	15.4	5.40	57	.277	.365	4	.235	-0	-9	-9	-0	-0.8
1890	Syr-a	6	9	.400	17	14	13	1	0	127	131	4	81	69	15.9	5.88	60	.258	.374	29	.242	3	-28	-33	2	-2.5
	Bal-a	1	2	.333	4	4	3	0	0	26	15	0	20	13	12.8	3.81	107	.163	.325	1	.111	-1	0	1	1	0.1
	Yr	7	11	.389	21	18	16	1	0	153	146	4	101	82	14.6	5.53	66	.238	.348	30	.233	3	-28	-32	3	-2.4
Total	3	20	39	.339	65	62	55	1	0	504²	571	20	325	254	16.7	5.14	78	.278	.387	61	.213	-2	-59	-62	12	-4.4

● PHIL MORRISON Morrison, Philip Melvin b: 10/18/1894, Rockport, Ind. d: 1/18/55, Lexington, Ky. BB/TR, 6'2", 190 lbs. Deb: 9/30/21 F

| 1921 | Pit-N | 0 | 0 | — | 1 | 0 | 0 | 0 | 0 | 0² | 1 | 0 | 1 | 0 | 13.5 | 0.00 | — | .333 | .333 | 0 | — | 0 | 0 | 0 | 0 | 0.0 |

● HANK MORRISON Morrison, Stephen Henry b: 5/22/1866, Olneyville, R.I. d: 9/30/27, Attleboro, Mass. BR/TR, 5'10", 180 lbs. Deb: 5/28/1887

| 1887 | Ind-N | 3 | 4 | .429 | 7 | 7 | 5 | 0 | 0 | 57 | 79 | 2 | 27 | 13 | 16.9 | 7.58 | 55 | .307 | .375 | 3 | .115 | -2 | -22 | -22 | -1 | -2.0 |

● GUY MORRISON Morrison, Walter Guy b: 8/29/1895, Hinton, W.Va. d: 8/14/34, Grand Rapids, Mich BR/TR, 5'11", 185 lbs. Deb: 8/31/27

1927	Bos-N	1	2	.333	11	3	0	0	0	34¹	40	1	15	6	14.4	4.46	83	.296	.367	1	.125	1	-2	-3	1	0.0
1928	Bos-N	0	0	—	1	0	0	0	0	3	4	1	3	0	21.0	12.00	33	.308	.438	0	—	0	-3	-3	0	0.0
Total	2	1	2	.333	12	3	0	0	0	37¹	44	2	18	6	14.9	5.06	74	.297	.373	1	.125	1	-5	-6	1	0.0

● FRANK MORRISSEY Morrissey, Michael Joseph "Deacon" b: 5/5/1876, Baltimore, Md. d: 2/22/39, Baltimore, Md. TR, 5'4", 140 lbs. Deb: 7/13/01

1901	Bos-A	0	0	—	1	0	0	0	0	4¹	5	0	2	3	18.7	2.08	170	.286	.418	0	.000	-1	1	1	0	0.0
1902	Chi-N	1	3	.250	5	5	5	0	0	40	40	0	8	13	11.2	2.25	120	.260	.305	2	.091	-1	2	2	0	0.1
Total	2	1	3	.250	6	5	5	0	0	44¹	45	0	10	14	12.0	2.23	125	.263	.319	2	.080	-1	3	3	1	0.1

● CARL MORTON Morton, Carl Wendle b: 1/18/44, Kansas City, Mo. d: 4/12/83, Tulsa, Okla. BR/TR, 6', 200 lbs. Deb: 4/11/69

1969	Mon-N	0	3	.000	8	5	0	0	0	29¹	29	2	18	16	15.0	4.60	80	.264	.377	0	.000	-0	-3	-3	1	-0.3
1970	Mon-N	18	11	.621	43	37	10	4	0	284²	281	27	125	154	13.0	3.60	114	.262	.341	15	.161	2	14	16	1	1.8
1971	Mon-N	10	18	.357	36	35	9	0	1	213²	252	22	83	84	14.3	4.80	73	.289	.360	14	.182	2	-32	-30	2	-3.2
1972	Mon-N	7	13	.350	27	27	3	1	0	172	170	16	53	51	11.8	3.92	90	.258	.316	7	.135	1	-9	-7	1	-0.6
1973	Atl-N	15	10	.600	38	37	10	4	0	256²	254	16	70	112	11.5	3.41	115	.259	.311	17	.181	4	7	15	0	1.8
1974	Atl-N	16	12	.571	38	38	7	1	0	274²	293	10	89	113	12.6	3.15	120	.277	.334	10	.112	-4	14	19	-1	1.4
1975	Atl-N	17	16	.515	39	39	11	2	0	277²	302	19	82	78	12.5	3.50	108	.278	.330	15	.160	-1	4	8	0	0.9
1976	Atl-N	4	9	.308	26	24	1	0	0	140¹	172	6	45	42	14.2	4.17	91	.306	.362	8	.178	-0	-10	-6	2	-0.3
Total	8	87	92	.486	255	242	51	13	1	1648²	1753	120	565	650	12.8	3.73	102	.275	.336	86	.156	3	-15	13	6	1.5

● CHARLIE MORTON Morton, Charles Hazen b: 10/12/1854, Kingsville, Ohio d: 12/9/21, Massillon, Ohio BR/TR, 150 lbs. Deb: 5/2/1882 MU♦

| 1884 | Tol-a | 0 | 1 | .000 | 3 | 1 | 1 | 0 | 0 | 23¹ | 18 | 0 | 5 | 7 | 9.3 | 3.09 | 111 | .209 | .261 | 18 | .162 | -0 | 0 | 1 | -1 | -0.1 |

● GUY MORTON Morton, Guy Sr. "The Alabama Blossom" b: 6/1/1893, Vernon, Ala. d: 10/18/34, Sheffield, Ala. BR/TR, 6'1", 175 lbs. Deb: 6/20/14 F

1914	Cle-A	1	13	.071	25	13	6	0	1	128	116	1	55	80	12.2	3.02	95	.257	.341	1	.029	-4	-4	-2	-1	-0.8
1915	Cle-A	16	15	.516	34	27	15	6	1	240	189	5	60	134	9.4	2.14	143	.216	.268	12	.146	-4	21	24	-0	2.6
1916	Cle-A	12	8	.600	27	18	9	0	0	149²	139	1	42	88	11.1	2.89	104	.246	.302	12	.211	-1	-1	2	1	0.1
1917	Cle-A	10	10	.500	35	18	6	1	2	161	158	3	59	62	12.2	2.74	103	.266	.335	4	.085	-4	-1	2	-1	-0.5
1918	Cle-A	14	8	.636	30	23	18	3	0	214²	189	1	77	123	11.3	2.64	114	.240	.310	12	.156	-1	3	9	-1	0.6
1919	Cle-A	9	9	.500	26	20	9	3	0	147¹	128	3	47	64	10.7	2.81	119	.233	.293	9	.161	-2	7	9	-1	0.7
1920	Cle-A	8	6	.571	29	17	8	0	1	137	140	3	57	72	13.0	4.47	85	.270	.344	10	.217	-1	-10	-10	-2	-1.3
1921	Cle-A	8	3	.727	30	7	3	2	0	107²	98	1	32	45	11.0	2.76	155	.244	.303	6	.171	-2	18	18	-2	1.2

YEAR	TM/L	W	L	PCT	G	GS	CG	SH	SV	IP	H	HR	BB	SO	RAT	ERA	ERA+	OAV	OOB	BH	AVG	PB	PR	/A	PD	TPI
1922	Cle-A	14	9	.609	38	23	13	3	0	202²	218	7	85	102	13.6	4.00	100	.277	.351	13	.191	-2	1	0	3	0.2
1923	Cle-A	6	6	.500	33	14	3	2	1	129¹	133	3	56	54	13.3	4.24	93	.276	.354	7	.159	-4	-4	-4	-1	-0.6
1924	Cle-A	0	1	.000	10	0	0	0	0	12¹	12	0	13	6	18.2	6.57	65	.250	.410	0	.000	-0	-3	-3	-0	-0.3
Total	11	98	88	.527	317	185	82	19	6	1629²	1520	27	583	830	11.7	3.13	108	.251	.319	86	.157	-24	27	48	-7	1.9

● KEVIN MORTON
Morton, Kevin Joseph   b: 8/3/68, Norwalk, Conn.   BR/TL, 6'2", 185 lbs.   Deb: 7/5/91

YEAR	TM/L	W	L	PCT	G	GS	CG	SH	SV	IP	H	HR	BB	SO	RAT	ERA	ERA+	OAV	OOB	BH	AVG	PB	PR	/A	PD	TPI
1991	Bos-A	6	5	.545	16	15	1	0	0	86¹	93	9	40	45	14.0	4.59	94	.284	.363	0	—	0	-5	-3	1	-0.2

● SPARROW MORTON
Morton, William P.   TL ,   Deb: 7/15/1884

YEAR	TM/L	W	L	PCT	G	GS	CG	SH	SV	IP	H	HR	BB	SO	RAT	ERA	ERA+	OAV	OOB	BH	AVG	PB	PR	/A	PD	TPI
1884	Phi-N	0	2	.000	2	2	2	0	0	17	16	0	11	5	14.3	5.29	56	.222	.325	3	.375	1	-4	-4	-0	-0.3

● EARL MOSELEY
Moseley, Earl Victor "Vic"   b: 9/7/1884, Middleburg, Ohio   d: 7/1/63, Alliance, Ohio   BR/TR, 5'9.5", 168 lbs.   Deb: 6/17/13

YEAR	TM/L	W	L	PCT	G	GS	CG	SH	SV	IP	H	HR	BB	SO	RAT	ERA	ERA+	OAV	OOB	BH	AVG	PB	PR	/A	PD	TPI
1913	Bos-A	8	5	.615	24	15	7	3	0	120²	105	1	49	62	11.5	3.13	94	.245	.322	3	.081	-2	-3	-3	1	-0.4
1914	Ind-F	19	18	.514	43	38	29	4	1	316²	303	5	123	205	12.2	3.47	90	.258	.330	12	.110	-8	-20	-12	-0	-2.2
1915	New-F	15	15	.500	38	32	22	5	1	268	222	2	99	142	10.8	1.91	134	.229	.302	13	.148	-4	24	19	-4	1.3
1916	Cin-N	7	10	.412	31	15	7	0	1	150¹	145	5	69	60	12.8	3.89	67	.257	.338	4	.087	-3	-21	-22	-2	-2.8
Total	4	49	48	.505	136	100	65	12	3	855²	775	13	340	469	11.8	3.01	94	.247	.322	32	.114	-17	-20	-18	-5	-4.1

● WALTER MOSER
Moser, Walter Fredrick   b: 2/27/1881, Concord, N.C.   d: 12/10/46, Philadelphia, Pa.   BR/TR, 5'9", 170 lbs.   Deb: 9/3/06

YEAR	TM/L	W	L	PCT	G	GS	CG	SH	SV	IP	H	HR	BB	SO	RAT	ERA	ERA+	OAV	OOB	BH	AVG	PB	PR	/A	PD	TPI
1906	Phi-N	0	4	.000	6	4	4	0	0	42²	49	0	15	17	13.7	3.59	73	.295	.357	0	.000	-2	-5	-5	-1	-0.7
1911	Bos-A	0	1	.000	6	3	1	0	0	24²	37	0	11	11	17.9	4.01	82	.366	.434	0	.000	-1	-2	-2	0	-0.2
	StL-A				2	2	0	0	0	3¹	11	0	4	2	40.5	21.60	16	.478	.556	1	1.000	0	-7	-7	0	-2.1
	Yr	0	3	.000	8	5	1	0	0	28	48	0	15	13	20.3	6.11	54	.384	.450	1	.125	-1	-9	-9	-0	-2.3
Total	2	0	7	.000	14	9	5	0	0	70²	97	0	30	30	16.4	4.58	63	.334	.401	1	.045	-2	-13	-13	-1	-3.0

● JOHN MOSES
Moses, John William   b: 8/9/57, Los Angeles, Cal.   BB/TL, 5'10", 170 lbs.   Deb: 8/23/82   ◆

YEAR	TM/L	W	L	PCT	G	GS	CG	SH	SV	IP	H	HR	BB	SO	RAT	ERA	ERA+	OAV	OOB	BH	AVG	PB	PR	/A	PD	TPI
1989	Min-A	0	0	—	1	0	0	0	0	1	0	0	1	0	9.0	0.00	—	.000	.333	68	.281	0	0	0	-0	0.0
1990	Min-A	0	0	—	2	0	0	0	0	2	5	0	2	0	31.5	13.50	31	.455	.538	38	.221	1	-2	-2	-0	0.0
Total	2	0	0	—	3	0	0	0	0	3	5	0	3	0	24.0	9.00	46	.385	.500	438	.254	1	-2	-2	-0	0.0

● PAUL MOSKAU
Moskau, Paul Richard   b: 12/20/53, St.Joseph, Mo.   BR/TR, 6'2", 210 lbs.   Deb: 6/21/77

YEAR	TM/L	W	L	PCT	G	GS	CG	SH	SV	IP	H	HR	BB	SO	RAT	ERA	ERA+	OAV	OOB	BH	AVG	PB	PR	/A	PD	TPI
1977	Cin-N	6	6	.500	20	19	2	2	0	108	116	10	40	71	13.1	4.00	98	.278	.342	7	.184	2	-1	-1	1	0.1
1978	Cin-N	6	4	.600	26	25	2	1	1	145	139	17	57	88	12.4	3.97	89	.255	.329	10	.204	4	-6	-7	-2	-0.3
1979	Cin-N	5	4	.556	21	15	1	0	0	106¹	107	9	51	58	13.4	3.89	96	.263	.345	3	.081	-2	-2	-2	-1	-0.3
1980	Cin-N	9	7	.563	33	19	2	2	0	152²	147	13	41	94	11.1	4.01	89	.257	.308	7	.159	-0	-7	-7	0	-0.8
1981	Cin-N	2	1	.667	27	1	0	0	0	54²	54	4	32	32	14.3	4.94	72	.258	.360	0	.000	-0	-9	-9	1	-0.5
1982	Pit-N	1	3	.250	13	5	0	0	0	35	43	7	8	15	13.1	4.37	85	.303	.340	1	.091	-1	-3	-3	-0	-0.4
1983	Chi-N	3	2	.600	8	8	0	0	0	32	44	7	14	16	16.3	6.75	56	.331	.395	2	.182	-0	-11	-11	-0	-1.4
Total	7	32	27	.542	148	92	7	4	5	633²	650	67	243	374	12.8	4.22	87	.268	.336	30	.153	2	-39	-39	-0	-3.6

● JIM MOSOLF
Mosolf, James Frederick   b: 8/21/05, Puyallup, Wash.   d: 12/28/79, Dallas, Ore.   BL/TR, 5'10", 186 lbs.   Deb: 9/9/29   ◆

YEAR	TM/L	W	L	PCT	G	GS	CG	SH	SV	IP	H	HR	BB	SO	RAT	ERA	ERA+	OAV	OOB	BH	AVG	PB	PR	/A	PD	TPI
1930	Pit-N	0	0	—	1	0	0	0	0	0¹	1	0	0	1	27.0	27.00	18	.500	.500	17	.333	0	-1	-1	0	0.0

● MAL MOSS
Moss, Charles Malcolm   b: 4/18/05, Sullivan, Ind.   d: 2/5/83, Savannah, Ga.   BR/TL, 6', 175 lbs.   Deb: 4/29/30

YEAR	TM/L	W	L	PCT	G	GS	CG	SH	SV	IP	H	HR	BB	SO	RAT	ERA	ERA+	OAV	OOB	BH	AVG	PB	PR	/A	PD	TPI
1930	Chi-N	0	0	—	12	1	0	0	1	18²	18	0	14	4	15.4	6.27	78	.254	.376	3	.273	0	-3	-3	0	0.0

● RAY MOSS
Moss, Raymond Earl   b: 12/5/01, Chattanooga, Tenn.   BR/TR, 6'1", 185 lbs.   Deb: 4/17/26

YEAR	TM/L	W	L	PCT	G	GS	CG	SH	SV	IP	H	HR	BB	SO	RAT	ERA	ERA+	OAV	OOB	BH	AVG	PB	PR	/A	PD	TPI
1926	Bro-N	0	0	—	1	0	0	0	0	3	3	0	0	0	27.0	9.00	42	.600	.600	0	.000	-0	-1	-1	-0	0.0
1927	Bro-N	1	0	1.000	1	1	0	0	0	8¹	11	0	1	1	13.0	3.24	122	.333	.353	1	.333	1	1	1	-0	0.1
1928	Bro-N	0	3	.000	22	5	1	1	0	60¹	62	5	35	6	14.5	4.92	81	.279	.377	8	.320	2	-6	-6	-0	-0.1
1929	Bro-N	11	6	.647	39	20	7	2	0	182	214	9	81	59	14.9	5.04	92	.296	.373	5	.076	-5	-7	-9	-2	-1.3
1930	Bro-N	9	6	.600	36	11	5	0	1	118¹	127	13	55	30	14.1	5.10	96	.270	.352	6	.154	-2	-2	-2	-0	-0.6
1931	Bro-N	0	0	—	1	0	0	0	0	1	1	0	1	0	18.0	0.00	—	.333	.500	0	—	0	0	0	-0	0.0
	Bos-N	1	3	.250	12	5	0	0	0	45	56	2	16	14	14.4	4.60	82	.306	.362	2	.133	-1	-4	-4	-0	-0.4
	Yr	1	3	.250	13	5	0	0	0	46	57	2	17	14	14.5	4.50	84	.306	.365	2	.133	-1	-3	-4	-0	-0.4
Total	6	22	18	.550	112	42	13	3	2	416	474	29	189	109	14.6	4.95	91	.289	.367	22	.148	-5	-18	-21	-4	-2.3

● DON MOSSI
Mossi, Donald Louis "The Sphinx"   b: 1/11/29, St.Helena, Cal.   BL/TL, 6'1", 195 lbs.   Deb: 4/17/54

YEAR	TM/L	W	L	PCT	G	GS	CG	SH	SV	IP	H	HR	BB	SO	RAT	ERA	ERA+	OAV	OOB	BH	AVG	PB	PR	/A	PD	TPI
1954	*Cle-A	6	1	.857	40	5	2	0	7	93	86	5	39	55	9.3	1.94	190	.176	.268	3	.158	0	18	18	-1	1.5
1955	Cle-A	4	3	.571	57	1	0	0	9	81²	81	4	18	69	11.0	2.42	164	.253	.295	1	.111	0	14	14	2	1.7
1956	Cle-A	6	5	.545	48	3	0	0	11	87²	79	6	33	59	11.6	3.59	117	.240	.311	3	.150	0	6	6	0	0.8
1957	Cle-A★	11	10	.524	36	22	6	1	2	159	165	16	57	97	12.7	4.13	90	.265	.329	12	.218	2	-6	-7	-1	-0.8
1958	Cle-A	7	8	.467	43	5	0	0	3	101²	106	6	30	55	12.4	3.90	94	.269	.327	1	.115	-2	-1	-3	0	-0.5
1959	Det-A	17	9	.654	34	30	15	3	0	228	210	20	49	125	10.3	3.36	121	.243	.286	13	.169	-0	13	18	0	0.8
1960	Det-A	9	8	.529	23	22	9	2	0	158²	158	17	32	69	10.9	3.47	114	.258	.296	5	.116	-0	7	9	-1	0.8
1961	Det-A	15	7	.682	35	34	12	1	1	240²	237	29	47	137	10.6	2.96	139	.258	.294	13	.165	1	28	30	-2	2.7
1962	Det-A	11	13	.458	35	27	8	1	1	180¹	195	24	36	121	11.6	4.19	97	.270	.305	9	.164	1	-4	-2	-3	-0.3
1963	Det-A	7	7	.500	24	16	3	0	2	122²	110	20	17	68	9.6	3.74	100	.236	.269	8	.205	2	-0	-0	0	0.0
1964	Chi-A	3	1	.750	34	0	0	0	7	40	37	7	4	36	10.1	2.93	118	.240	.278	1	.167	-0	3	3	0	0.3
1965	KC-A	8	4	.385	51	0	0	0	7	55¹	59	0	20	41	12.8	3.74	93	.278	.341	0	.000	-1	-4	-0	0	-0.5
Total	12	101	80	.558	460	165	55	8	50	1548	1493	156	385	932	11.0	3.43	114	.252	.299	71	.163	4	74	83	-2	7.9

● EARL MOSSOR
Mossor, Earl Dalton   b: 7/21/25, Forbes, Tenn.   d: 12/29/88, Batavia, Ohio   BL/TR, 6'1", 175 lbs.   Deb: 4/30/51

YEAR	TM/L	W	L	PCT	G	GS	CG	SH	SV	IP	H	HR	BB	SO	RAT	ERA	ERA+	OAV	OOB	BH	AVG	PB	PR	/A	PD	TPI
1951	Bro-N	0	0	—	3	0	0	0	0	1²	2	1	7	1	48.6	32.40	12	.333	.692	1	1.000	0	-5	-5	-0	0.0

● GLEN MOULDER
Moulder, Glen Hubert   b: 9/28/17, Cleveland, Okla.   BR/TR, 6', 180 lbs.   Deb: 4/28/46

YEAR	TM/L	W	L	PCT	G	GS	CG	SH	SV	IP	H	HR	BB	SO	RAT	ERA	ERA+	OAV	OOB	BH	AVG	PB	PR	/A	PD	TPI
1946	Bro-N	0	0	—	1	0	0	0	0	2	2	1	1	1	13.5	4.50	75	.286	.375	0	—	0	-0	-0	-0	0.0
1947	StL-A	4	2	.667	32	2	0	0	2	73	78	4	43	23	14.9	3.82	101	.283	.379	4	.235	-0	-1	-1	0	0.1
1948	Chi-A	3	6	.333	33	9	0	0	2	85²	108	8	54	26	17.1	6.41	66	.316	.411	6	.300	2	-20	-20	1	-1.8
Total	3	7	8	.467	66	11	0	0	4	160²	188	13	98	50	16.1	5.21	78	.301	.396	10	.270	1	-21	-20	1	-1.7

● FRANK MOUNTAIN
Mountain, Frank Henry   b: 5/17/1860, Ft.Edward, N.Y.   d: 11/19/39, Schenectady, N.Y.   BR/TR, 5'11", 185 lbs.   Deb: 7/19/1880   ◆

YEAR	TM/L	W	L	PCT	G	GS	CG	SH	SV	IP	H	HR	BB	SO	RAT	ERA	ERA+	OAV	OOB	BH	AVG	PB	PR	/A	PD	TPI
1880	Tro-N	1	1	.500	2	2	2	0	0	17	23	0	6	2	15.4	5.29	48	.307	.358	2	.222	-0	-6	-5	0	-0.5
1881	Det-N	3	4	.429	7	7	7	0	0	60	80	2	18	13	14.7	5.25	56	.292	.336	4	.160	-0	-17	-16	-1	-1.5
1882	Wor-N	0	5	.000	5	5	5	0	0	42	47	0	11	5	12.4	3.00	104	.255	.297	1	.063	-0	-1	-1	-1	-0.2
	Phi-a		6	.250	8	8	8	0	0	69	72	1	11	15	10.8	3.91	76	.251	.279	12	.333	2	-9	-7	1	-0.3
	Wor-N	2	11	.154	13	13	11	0	0	102	138	4	24	24	14.3	3.97	78	.299	.334	19	.271	4	-12	-10	-1	-0.9
1883	Col-a	26	33	.441	59	59	57	4	0	503	546	8	123	159	12.0	3.60	86	.259	.300	60	.217	7	-16	-29	1	-1.9
1884	Col-a	23	17	.575	42	41	40	5	1	360²	289	7	78	156	9.4	2.45	124	.209	.257	50	.238	9	32	23	4	3.5
1885	Pit-a	1	4	.200	5	5	5	0	0	46	56	1	24	7	16.0	4.30	75	.320	.408	2	.100	-1	-5	-6	0	-0.5
1886	Pit-a	0	2	.000	2	2	2	0	0	16	22	0	14	2	23.1	7.88	43	.319	.466	8	.145	0	-8	-8	-0	-0.7
Total	7	58	83	.411	143	142	137	9	1	1215²	1273	23	309	383	11.8	3.47	88	.254	.299	158	.220	16	-41	-54	4	-3.0

● BILL MOUNTJOY
Mountjoy, William R. "Medicine Bill"   b: 1857, London, Ontaroio, Canada   d: 5/19/1894, London, Ont., Can.   BL/TR, 5'6", 150 lbs.   Deb: 9/29/1883

YEAR	TM/L	W	L	PCT	G	GS	CG	SH	SV	IP	H	HR	BB	SO	RAT	ERA	ERA+	OAV	OOB	BH	AVG	PB	PR	/A	PD	TPI
1883	Cin-a	0	1	.000	1	1	1	0	0	8	9	0	2	3	12.4	2.25	144	.266	.307	0	.000	-1	1	1	-0	0.0

YEAR	TM/L	W	L	PCT	G	GS	CG	SH	SV	IP	H	HR	BB	SO	RAT	ERA	ERA+	OAV	OOB	BH	AVG	PB	PR	/A	PD	TPI
1884	Cin-a	19	12	.613	33	33	32	3	0	289	274	5	43	96	10.4	2.93	114	.238	.275	18	.151	-3	10	13	-0	0.8
1885	Cin-a	10	7	.588	17	17	17	1	0	153²	149	5	52	50	12.2	3.16	103	.247	.314	10	.167	0	1	2	-1	0.1
	Bal-a	2	4	.333	6	6	6	1	0	53	72	1	13	15	15.1	5.43	60	.316	.363	1	.056	-0	-13	-13	1	-1.0
	Yr	12	11	.522	23	23	23	2	0	206²	221	6	65	65	12.6	3.75	87	.264	.320	11	.141	0	-11	-11	-0	-0.9
Total	3	31	24	.564	57	57	56	5	0	503²	504	11	110	164	11.5	3.25	102	.250	.297	29	.145	-4	-0	3	-1	-0.1

● **ED MOYER**   Moyer, Charles Edward b: 8/15/1885, Andover, Ohio d: 11/18/62, Jacksonville, Fla. Deb: 7/20/10

YEAR	TM/L	W	L	PCT	G	GS	CG	SH	SV	IP	H	HR	BB	SO	RAT	ERA	ERA+	OAV	OOB	BH	AVG	PB	PR	/A	PD	TPI
1910	Was-A	0	3	.000	6	3	2	0	0	25	22	1	13	3	13.7	3.24	77	.253	.369	1	.125	-1	-2	-2	1	-0.2

● **JAMIE MOYER**   Moyer, Jamie b: 11/18/62, Sellersville, Pa. BL/TL, 6', 170 lbs. Deb: 6/16/86

YEAR	TM/L	W	L	PCT	G	GS	CG	SH	SV	IP	H	HR	BB	SO	RAT	ERA	ERA+	OAV	OOB	BH	AVG	PB	PR	/A	PD	TPI
1986	Chi-N	7	4	.636	16	16	1	1	0	87¹	107	10	42	45	15.7	5.05	80	.311	.391	2	.091	-0	-13	-10	1	-1.0
1987	Chi-N	12	15	.444	35	33	1	0	0	201	210	28	97	147	14.0	5.10	84	.271	.355	14	.230	3	-23	-19	2	-1.7
1988	Chi-N	9	15	.375	34	30	3	1	0	202	212	20	55	121	12.1	3.48	104	.272	.324	5	.083	-2	-1	3	3	0.4
1989	Tex-A	4	9	.308	15	15	1	0	0	76	84	10	33	44	14.1	4.86	82	.283	.358	0	—	0	-8	-8	-1	-1.1
1990	Tex-A	2	6	.250	33	10	1	0	0	102¹	115	6	39	58	13.9	4.66	84	.290	.360	0	—	0	-9	-8	0	-0.6
1991	StL-N	0	5	.000	8	7	0	0	0	31¹	38	5	16	20	15.8	5.74	65	.319	.404	0	.000	-1	-7	-7	-0	-1.0
1993	Bal-A	12	9	.571	25	25	3	1	0	152	154	11	38	90	11.7	3.43	130	.265	.316	0	—	0	15	18	1	2.0
1994	Bal-A	5	7	.417	23	23	0	0	0	149	158	23	38	87	12.0	4.77	106	.271	.317	0	—	0	0	5	0	-0.1
Total	8	51	70	.421	189	159	10	3	0	1001	1078	113	358	612	13.2	4.42	95	.278	.343	21	.139	1	-45	-26	8	-3.1

● **RON MROZINSKI**   Mrozinski, Ronald Frank b: 9/16/30, White Haven, Pa. BR/TL, 5'11", 160 lbs. Deb: 6/20/54

YEAR	TM/L	W	L	PCT	G	GS	CG	SH	SV	IP	H	HR	BB	SO	RAT	ERA	ERA+	OAV	OOB	BH	AVG	PB	PR	/A	PD	TPI
1954	Phi-N	1	1	.500	15	4	1	0	0	48	49	10	25	26	13.9	4.50	90	.261	.347	1	.083	-1	-2	-2	-1	-0.3
1955	Phi-N	0	2	.000	22	1	0	0	1	34¹	38	2	19	18	16.0	6.55	61	.299	.407	0	.000	-1	-10	-10	-0	-0.6
Total	2	1	3	.250	37	5	1	0	1	82¹	87	12	44	44	14.8	5.36	75	.276	.372	1	.063	-2	-12	-12	-1	-0.9

● **PHIL MUDROCK**   Mudrock, Philip Ray b: 6/12/37, Louisville, Colo. BR/TR, 6'1", 190 lbs. Deb: 4/19/63

YEAR	TM/L	W	L	PCT	G	GS	CG	SH	SV	IP	H	HR	BB	SO	RAT	ERA	ERA+	OAV	OOB	BH	AVG	PB	PR	/A	PD	TPI
1963	Chi-N	0	0	—	1	0	0	0	0	1	2	0	0	0	18.0	9.00	39	.400	.400	0	—	0	-1	-1	0	0.0

● **GORDIE MUELLER**   Mueller, Joseph Gordon b: 12/10/22, Baltimore, Md. BR/TR, 6'4", 200 lbs. Deb: 4/19/50

YEAR	TM/L	W	L	PCT	G	GS	CG	SH	SV	IP	H	HR	BB	SO	RAT	ERA	ERA+	OAV	OOB	BH	AVG	PB	PR	/A	PD	TPI
1950	Bos-A	0	0	—	8	0	0	0	0	7	11	1	13	1	30.9	10.29	48	.344	.533	0	.000	-0	-4	-4	0	0.0

● **LES MUELLER**   Mueller, Leslie Clyde b: 3/4/19, Belleville, Ill. BR/TR, 6'3", 190 lbs. Deb: 8/15/41

YEAR	TM/L	W	L	PCT	G	GS	CG	SH	SV	IP	H	HR	BB	SO	RAT	ERA	ERA+	OAV	OOB	BH	AVG	PB	PR	/A	PD	TPI
1941	Det-A	0	0	—	4	0	0	0	0	13	9	1	10	8	13.2	4.85	94	.205	.352	0	.000	-0	-1	-0	0	0.0
1945	*Det-A	6	8	.429	26	18	6	2	1	134²	117	8	58	42	11.8	3.68	96	.234	.316	8	.182	0	-5	-2	-2	-0.4
Total	2	6	8	.429	30	18	6	2	1	147²	126	9	68	50	11.9	3.78	95	.231	.319	8	.170	0	-6	-3	-2	-0.4

● **WILLIE MUELLER**   Mueller, Willard Lawrence b: 8/30/56, West Bend, Wis. BR/TR, 6'4", 220 lbs. Deb: 8/12/78

YEAR	TM/L	W	L	PCT	G	GS	CG	SH	SV	IP	H	HR	BB	SO	RAT	ERA	ERA+	OAV	OOB	BH	AVG	PB	PR	/A	PD	TPI
1978	Mil-A	1	0	1.000	5	0	0	0	0	12²	16	1	6	6	15.6	6.39	59	.291	.361	0	—	0	-4	-4	0	-0.3
1981	Mil-A	0	0	—	1	0	0	0	0	2	4	0	0	1	18.0	4.50	76	.400	.400	0	—	0	-0	-0	0	0.1
Total	2	1	0	1.000	6	0	0	0	0	14²	20	1	6	7	16.0	6.14	60	.308	.366	0	—	0	-4	-4	0	-0.2

● **BILLY MUFFETT**   Muffett, Billy Arnold "Muff" b: 9/21/30, Hammond, Ind. BR/TR, 6'1", 198 lbs. Deb: 8/3/57 C

YEAR	TM/L	W	L	PCT	G	GS	CG	SH	SV	IP	H	HR	BB	SO	RAT	ERA	ERA+	OAV	OOB	BH	AVG	PB	PR	/A	PD	TPI
1957	StL-N	3	2	.600	23	0	0	0	8	44	35	1	13	21	9.8	2.25	176	.222	.281	0	.000	-1	8	8	-1	1.1
1958	StL-N	4	6	.400	35	6	1	0	5	84	107	11	42	41	16.5	4.93	84	.316	.399	4	.200	-0	-9	-7	-1	-0.9
1959	SF-N	0	0	—	5	0	0	0	0	6²	11	2	3	3	18.9	5.40	71	.407	.467	0	—	0	-1	-1	0	0.0
1960	Bos-A	6	4	.600	23	14	4	1	0	125	116	6	36	75	11.3	3.24	125	.242	.301	11	.268	2	9	11	1	1.1
1961	Bos-A	3	11	.214	38	11	2	0	2	112²	130	18	36	47	13.4	5.67	73	.291	.346	5	.217	2	-21	-19	-0	-2.0
1962	Bos-A	0	0	—	1	1	0	0	0	4	8	0	2	1	22.5	9.00	46	.471	.526	0	.000	-0	-2	-2	-0	0.0
Total	6	16	23	.410	125	32	7	1	15	376¹	407	38	132	188	13.2	4.33	94	.277	.342	20	.217	3	-16	-10	-2	-0.7

● **JOE MUICH**   Muich, Ignatius Andrew b: 11/23/03, St.Louis, Mo. d: 7/2/93, St.Louis, Mo. BR/TR, 6'2", 175 lbs. Deb: 9/4/24

YEAR	TM/L	W	L	PCT	G	GS	CG	SH	SV	IP	H	HR	BB	SO	RAT	ERA	ERA+	OAV	OOB	BH	AVG	PB	PR	/A	PD	TPI
1924	Bos-N	0	0	—	3	0	0	0	0	9	19	1	5	1	24.0	11.00	35	.432	.490	0	.000	-1	-7	-7	-0	-0.1

● **JOE MUIR**   Muir, Joseph Allen b: 11/26/22, Oriole, Md. d: 6/25/80, Baltimore, Md. BL/TL, 6'1", 172 lbs. Deb: 4/21/51

YEAR	TM/L	W	L	PCT	G	GS	CG	SH	SV	IP	H	HR	BB	SO	RAT	ERA	ERA+	OAV	OOB	BH	AVG	PB	PR	/A	PD	TPI
1951	Pit-N	0	2	.000	9	1	0	0	0	16¹	11	2	7	5	9.9	2.76	153	.180	.265	0	.000	-0	2	3	1	0.4
1952	Pit-N	2	3	.400	12	5	1	0	0	35²	42	3	18	17	15.1	6.31	63	.288	.366	1	.111	-0	-10	-9	-0	-1.2
Total	2	2	5	.286	21	6	1	0	0	52	53	5	25	22	13.5	5.19	78	.256	.336	1	.100	-0	-8	-7	1	-0.8

● **HUGH MULCAHY**   Mulcahy, Hugh Noyes "Losing Pitcher" b: 9/9/13, Brighton, Mass. BR/TR, 6'2", 190 lbs. Deb: 7/24/35 C

YEAR	TM/L	W	L	PCT	G	GS	CG	SH	SV	IP	H	HR	BB	SO	RAT	ERA	ERA+	OAV	OOB	BH	AVG	PB	PR	/A	PD	TPI
1935	Phi-N	1	5	.167	18	5	0	0	1	52²	62	2	25	11	15.7	4.78	95	.295	.383	0	.000	-2	-4	-1	1	-0.3
1936	Phi-N	1	1	.500	3	2	2	0	0	22²	20	0	12	3	13.5	3.18	143	.238	.347	2	.250	2	3	3	-0	0.3
1937	Phi-N	8	18	.308	**56**	25	9	1	3	215²	256	17	97	54	15.0	5.13	84	.296	.372	11	.151	-3	-29	-19	3	-2.0
1938	Phi-N	10	20	.333	46	34	15	0	1	267¹	294	14	120	90	14.1	4.61	84	.278	.354	16	.170	-4	-24	-22	1	-2.3
1939	Phi-N	9	16	.360	38	31	14	1	4	225²	246	19	93	59	14.0	4.99	80	.282	.359	12	.158	-3	-27	-25	0	-2.7
1940	Phi-N☆	13	22	.371	36	36	21	3	0	280	283	12	91	82	12.1	3.60	108	.261	.320	19	.202	1	8	9	3	1.5
1945	Phi-N	1	3	.250	9	6	1	0	0	28¹	33	1	9	2	13.3	3.81	101	.295	.347	0	.000	-1	-0	0	1	0.0
1946	Phi-N	2	4	.333	16	5	1	0	0	62²	69	3	33	12	15.4	4.45	77	.291	.393	3	.188	-1	-7	-7	1	-0.4
1947	Pit-N	0	0	—	2	1	0	0	0	6²	8	1	7	2	20.3	4.05	104	.333	.484	1	.333	0	0	0	1	0.1
Total	9	45	89	.336	220	143	63	5	9	1161²	1271	69	487	314	13.9	4.49	89	.280	.355	64	.165	-9	-82	-61	11	-5.8

● **TERRY MULHOLLAND**   Mulholland, Terence John b: 3/9/63, Uniontown, Pa. BR/TL, 6'3", 200 lbs. Deb: 6/8/86

YEAR	TM/L	W	L	PCT	G	GS	CG	SH	SV	IP	H	HR	BB	SO	RAT	ERA	ERA+	OAV	OOB	BH	AVG	PB	PR	/A	PD	TPI
1986	SF-N	1	7	.125	15	10	0	0	0	54²	51	3	35	27	14.3	4.94	71	.251	.364	1	.053	-1	-7	-9	-1	-1.3
1988	SF-N	2	1	.667	9	6	2	1	0	46	50	3	7	18	11.3	3.72	88	.281	.312	0	.000	-1	-1	-2	0	-0.2
1989	SF-N	0	0	—	5	1	0	0	0	11	15	0	4	6	15.5	4.09	82	.319	.373	0	.000	-1	-1	-1	0	0.0
	Phi-N	4	7	.364	20	17	2	1	0	104¹	122	8	32	60	13.6	5.00	71	.292	.348	2	.059	-2	-17	-17	1	-1.8
	Yr	4	7	.364	25	18	2	1	0	115¹	137	8	36	66	13.8	4.92	72	.295	.350	2	.056	-2	-18	-18	1	-1.8
1990	Phi-N	9	10	.474	33	26	6	1	0	180²	172	15	42	75	10.8	3.34	115	.253	.297	6	.097	-2	9	10	-3	0.4
1991	Phi-N	16	13	.552	34	34	8	3	0	232	231	15	49	142	11.0	3.61	102	.260	.301	7	.087	-4	2	1	-0	-0.4
1992	Phi-N	13	11	.542	32	32	**12**	2	0	229	227	14	46	125	10.8	3.81	92	.261	.300	8	.096	-2	-8	-8	1	-1.0
1993	*Phi-N★	12	9	.571	29	28	7	2	0	191	177	20	40	116	10.4	3.25	122	.241	.283	4	.065	-4	17	15	-1	1.0
1994	NY-A	6	7	.462	24	19	2	0	0	120²	150	24	37	72	14.2	6.49	68	.303	.355	0	—	0	-23	-28	0	-2.0
Total	8	63	65	.492	201	173	39	10	0	1169¹	1195	102	292	641	11.6	4.04	93	.265	.312	28	.079	-17	-30	-37	-4	-5.3

● **TONY MULLANE**   Mullane, Anthony John "Count" or "The Apollo Of The Box"
b: 1/20/1859, Cork, Ireland d: 4/25/44, Chicago, Ill. BB/TB, 5'10.5", 165 lbs. Deb: 8/27/1881 ◆

YEAR	TM/L	W	L	PCT	G	GS	CG	SH	SV	IP	H	HR	BB	SO	RAT	ERA	ERA+	OAV	OOB	BH	AVG	PB	PR	/A	PD	TPI
1881	Det-N	1	4	.200	5	5	5	0	0	44	55	2	17	7	14.7	4.91	59	.302	.362	5	.263	-0	-10	-10	0	-0.9
1882	Lou-a	30	24	.556	**55**	55	51	5	0	460	418	4	78	**170**	9.7	1.88	132	.226	.257	78	.257	11	41	31	11	5.1
1883	StL-a	35	15	**.700**	53	49	49	3	1	460²	372	3	74	191	8.7	2.19	**159**	.207	.238	69	.225	1	57	66	1	6.2
1884	Tol-a	36	26	.581	67	65	64	**7**	0	567	481	5	89	325	9.6	2.52	135	.214	.255	97	.276	15	46	56	10	7.7
1886	Cin-a	33	27	.550	63	56	55	1	0	529²	501	11	166	250	11.6	3.70	95	.242	.303	73	.225	2	-15	-11	-2	-0.6
1887	Cin-a	31	17	.646	48	48	47	**6**	0	416¹	414	11	121	97	12.3	3.24	134	.257	.322	44	.221	2	49	51	-1	4.5
1888	Cin-a	26	16	.619	44	42	41	4	1	380¹	341	9	75	186	10.5	2.84	112	.231	.282	44	.251	5	9	14	-0	1.8
1889	Cin-a	11	9	.550	33	25	21	1	0	220	218	4	76	113	13.1	2.99	131	.251	.329	58	.296	9	21	22	-1	2.2
1890	Cin-N	12	10	.545	25	21	21	0	1	209	175	7	94	55	12.0	2.24	159	.220	.311	79	.276	7	31	31	0	3.4
1891	Cin-N	23	26	.469	51	45	42	1	0	426¹	390	15	187	124	12.6	3.23	104	.234	.318	31	.148	-5	6	7	1	0.3
1892	Cin-N	21	13	.618	37	34	30	3	1	295	222	12	127	109	11.0	2.59	126	**.201**	.290	20	.169	-1	23	22	6	2.7

YEAR TM/L	W	L	PCT	G	GS	CG	SH	SV	IP	H	HR	BB	SO	RAT	ERA	ERA+	OAV	OOB	BH	AVG	PB	PR	/A	PD	TPI
1893 Cin-N	6	6	.500	15	13	11	0	1	122⅓	130	4	65	24	15.0	4.41	108	.264	.360	15	.288	3	3	5	0	0.6
Bal-N	12	16	.429	34	26	23	0	1	244⅔	277	4	124	71	15.0	4.45	107	.277	.360	26	.228	-3	6	8	3	0.7
Yr	18	22	.450	49	39	34	0	2	367	407	8	189	95	14.8	4.44	107	.271	.355	41	.247	-0	9	13	3	1.3
1894 Bal-N	6	9	.400	21	15	9	0	4	122⅔	155	4	90	43	18.5	6.31	87	.305	.416	21	.396	5	-13	-12	-1	-0.7
Cle-N	1	2	.333	4	4	3	0	0	33	46	3	10	3	15.3	7.64	72	.326	.371	1	.077	-1	-8	-8	2	-0.4
Yr	7	11	.389	25	19	12	0	4	155⅔	201	7	100	46	17.4	6.59	83	.306	.398	22	.333	4	-22	-20	1	-1.1
Total 13	284	220	.563	555	504	468	30	15	4531⅓	4195	98	1408	1803	11.5	3.05	118	.235	.298	661	.243	50	245	270	33	32.6

● **JOE MULLIGAN**   Mulligan, Joseph Ignatius "Big Joe" b: 7/31/13, Weymouth, Mass. d: 6/5/86, W.Roxbury, Mass. BR/TR, 6'4", 210 lbs. Deb: 6/28/34

YEAR TM/L	W	L	PCT	G	GS	CG	SH	SV	IP	H	HR	BB	SO	RAT	ERA	ERA+	OAV	OOB	BH	AVG	PB	PR	/A	PD	TPI
1934 Bos-A	1	0	1.000	14	2	1	0	0	44⅔	46	1	27	13	15.1	3.63	132	.279	.387	0	.000	-1	4	6	0	0.0

● **DICK MULLIGAN**   Mulligan, Richard Charles b: 3/18/18, Swoyersville, Pa. d: 12/15/92, Victoria, Tex. BL/TL, 6', 167 lbs. Deb: 9/24/41

YEAR TM/L	W	L	PCT	G	GS	CG	SH	SV	IP	H	HR	BB	SO	RAT	ERA	ERA+	OAV	OOB	BH	AVG	PB	PR	/A	PD	TPI
1941 Was-A	0	1	.000	1	1	0	0	0	9	11	0	2	2	13.0	5.00	81	.306	.342	0	.000	-0	-1	-1	0	-0.1
1946 Phi-N	2	2	.500	19	5	1	0	1	54⅔	61	0	27	16	15.1	4.77	72	.289	.380	0	.000	-1	-8	-8	0	-0.7
Bos-N	1	0	1.000	4	0	0	0	0	15⅓	6	1	9	4	8.8	2.35	146	.122	.259	0	.000	-0	2	2	0	0.1
Yr	3	2	.600	23	5	1	0	1	70	67	1	36	20	13.2	4.24	81	.254	.343	0	.000	-1	-6	-6	-0	-0.6
1947 Bos-N	0	0	—	1	0	0	0	0	2	4	0	1	1	22.5	9.00	43	.400	.455	0	—	-1	-1	-1	0	0.0
Total 3	3	3	.500	25	6	2	0	1	81	82	1	39	23	13.9	4.44	79	.268	.358	0	.000	-1	-8	-8	-0	-0.7

● **GEORGE MULLIN**   Mullin, George Joseph "Wabash George" b: 7/4/1880, Toledo, Ohio d: 1/7/44, Wabash, Ind. BR/TR, 5'11", 188 lbs. Deb: 5/4/02 ♦

YEAR TM/L	W	L	PCT	G	GS	CG	SH	SV	IP	H	HR	BB	SO	RAT	ERA	ERA+	OAV	OOB	BH	AVG	PB	PR	/A	PD	TPI
1902 Det-A	13	16	.448	35	30	25	0	0	260	282	4	95	78	13.3	3.67	99	.277	.343	39	.325	9	-1	2		1.1
1903 Det-A	19	15	.559	41	36	31	6	2	320⅔	284	4	106	170	11.2	2.25	130	.237	.303	45	.278	8	26	24	5	4.1
1904 Det-A	17	23	.425	45	44	42	7	0	382⅓	345	1	131	161	11.4	2.40	106	.242	.310	45	.290	11	8	6	8	3.2
1905 Det-A	21	21	.500	44	41	35	1	0	347⅔	303	4	138	168	11.6	2.51	109	.236	.314	35	.259	6	6	9	7	2.6
1906 Det-A	21	18	.538	40	40	35	2	0	330	315	4	108	123	11.9	2.78	99	.254	.322	32	.225	3	-3	-1	3	0.7
1907*Det-A	20	20	.500	46	42	35	5	3	357⅓	346	1	106	146	14.8	2.59	101	.256	.317	34	.217	3	-2	1	4	1.0
1908*Det-A	17	13	.567	39	30	26	1	0	290⅔	301	1	71	121	11.7	3.10	78	.271	.319	32	.256	8	-23	-22	1	-1.1
1909*Det-A	**29**	8	**.784**	40	35	29	3	1	303⅔	258	4	78	124	10.2	2.22	113	.234	.289	27	.214	5	9	10	1	2.0
1910 Det-A	21	12	.636	38	32	27	5	0	289	260	7	102	98	11.7	2.87	92	.254	.330	33	.256	6	-11	-8	1	-0.1
1911 Det-A	18	10	.643	30	29	25	2	0	234⅓	245	7	61	87	12.2	3.07	113	.276	.331	28	.286	8	7	10	-2	1.6
1912 Det-A	12	17	.414	30	29	22	2	0	226	214	9	92	88	12.5	3.54	92	.255	.335	25	.278	9	-6	-7	0	0.2
1913 Det-A	1	6	.143	7	7	4	0	0	52⅓	53	1	18	16	12.6	2.75	106	.268	.335	7	.350	3	1	1	1	0.5
Was-A	3	5	.375	11	9	3	0	0	57⅓	69	1	25	14	15.5	5.02	59	.283	.361	4	.190	-0	-13	-13	1	-1.5
Yr	4	11	.267	18	16	7	0	0	109⅔	122	2	43	30	14.0	3.94	75	.275	.346	11	.268	3	-12	-12	1	-1.0
1914 Ind-F	14	10	.583	36	20	11	1	2	203	202	4	91	74	13.4	2.70	115	.261	.346	24	.312	8	4	9	-4	1.5
1915 New-F	2	2	.500	5	4	3	0	0	32⅓	41	0	16	14	15.9	5.85	44	.318	.393	1	.100	-0	-11	-12	-1	-1.3
Total 14	228	196	.538	487	428	353	35	8	3686⅔	3518	42	1238	1482	11.9	2.82	101	.254	.322	401	.262	87	-11	7	28	14.5

● **DOMINIC MULRENAN**   Mulrenan, Dominic Joseph b: 12/18/1893, Woburn, Mass. d: 7/27/64, Melrose, Mass. BR/TR, 5'11", 170 lbs. Deb: 4/24/21

YEAR TM/L	W	L	PCT	G	GS	CG	SH	SV	IP	H	HR	BB	SO	RAT	ERA	ERA+	OAV	OOB	BH	AVG	PB	PR	/A	PD	TPI
1921 Chi-A	2	8	.200	12	10	3	0	0	56	84	2	36	10	19.6	7.23	59	.359	.449	3	.150	-1	-18	-19	0	-2.6

● **FRANK MULRONEY**   Mulroney, Francis Joseph b: 4/8/03, Mallard, Iowa d: 11/11/85, Aberdeen, Wash. BR/TR, 6', 170 lbs. Deb: 4/15/30

YEAR TM/L	W	L	PCT	G	GS	CG	SH	SV	IP	H	HR	BB	SO	RAT	ERA	ERA+	OAV	OOB	BH	AVG	PB	PR	/A	PD	TPI
1930 Bos-A	0	0	1.000	2	0	0	0	0	3	3	0	0	2	9.0	3.00	154	.273	.273	0	—	0	1	1	0	0.2

● **BOB MUNCRIEF**   Muncrief, Robert Cleveland b: 1/28/16, Madill, Okla. BR/TR, 6'2", 190 lbs. Deb: 9/30/37

YEAR TM/L	W	L	PCT	G	GS	CG	SH	SV	IP	H	HR	BB	SO	RAT	ERA	ERA+	OAV	OOB	BH	AVG	PB	PR	/A	PD	TPI
1937 StL-A	0	0	—	1	1	0	0	0	2	1	1	2		22.5	4.50	107	.300	.417	0	—	0	0	0	-0	0.0
1939 StL-A	0	0	—	2	0	0	0	0	3	7	1	3	1	30.0	15.00	32	.500	.588	0	—	0	-3	-3	-0	0.0
1941 StL-A	13	9	.591	36	24	12	2	1	214⅓	221	18	53	67	11.7	3.65	118	.266	.314	18	.237	2	12	15	-1	1.5
1942 StL-A	6	8	.429	24	18	7	1	0	134⅓	149	11	31	39	12.1	3.89	95	.280	.319	5	.111	-1	-3	-3	-0	-0.4
1943 StL-A	13	12	.520	35	27	12	3	1	205	211	13	48	60	11.5	2.81	118	.264	.307	10	.152	-2	11	12	-3	0.9
1944*StL-A★	13	8	.619	33	27	12	3	1	219⅓	216	11	50	88	11.0	3.08	117	.258	.302	18	.231	1	9	13	-1	1.3
1945 StL-A	13	4	.765	27	15	10	0	1	145⅔	132	8	44	54	11.0	2.72	130	.239	.297	3	.067	-4	10	13	-1	0.9
1946 StL-A	3	12	.200	29	14	4	1	0	115⅓	149	6	31	49	14.0	4.99	75	.314	.356	1	.031	-3	-19	-16	-1	-2.4
1947 StL-A	8	14	.364	31	23	7	0	0	176⅓	210	14	51	74	13.4	4.90	79	.299	.348	6	.105	-3	-23	-20	0	-2.5
1948*Cle-A	5	4	.556	21	9	1	1	0	72⅓	76	8	31	24	13.3	3.98	102	.279	.353	2	.111	-1	-8	-7	-0	-0.1
1949 Pit-N	1	5	.167	13	4	1	0	2	35⅔	44	8	13	11	14.4	6.31	67	.310	.368	4	.143	-0	-9	-8	-1	-1.3
Chi-N	5	6	.455	34	3	1	0	2	75	80	9	31	36	13.4	4.56	88	.276	.348	4	.286	1	-4	-4	0	-0.5
Yr	6	11	.353	47	7	2	0	5	110⅔	124	17	44	47	13.7	5.12	80	.287	.354	5	.238	1	-13	-13	-0	-1.8
1951 NY-A	0	0	—	2	0	0	0	0	4	5	0	3	2	27.0	9.00	43	.417	.563	0	—	-0	-2	-2	-0	0.0
Total 12	80	82	.494	288	165	67	11	9	1401⅓	1503	108	392	525	12.3	3.80	100	.275	.325	68	.155	-10	-20	-3	-7	-2.6

● **RED MUNGER**   Munger, George David b: 10/4/18, Houston, Tex. BR/TR, 6'2", 200 lbs. Deb: 5/1/43

YEAR TM/L	W	L	PCT	G	GS	CG	SH	SV	IP	H	HR	BB	SO	RAT	ERA	ERA+	OAV	OOB	BH	AVG	PB	PR	/A	PD	TPI
1943 StL-N	9	5	.643	32	9	5	0	2	93⅓	101	2	42	45	13.8	3.95	85	.281	.357	6	.214	1	-6	-6	1	-0.7
1944 StL-N†	11	3	.786	21	12	7	2	2	121	92	2	41	55	10.0	1.34	263	.212	.284	5	.114	-3	31	29	3	3.6
1946*StL-N☆	2	2	.500	10	7	2	0	1	48⅔	47	0	12	28	10.9	3.33	104	.255	.301	4	.250	1	0	1	2	0.3
1947 StL-N☆	16	5	.762	40	31	13	6	3	224⅓	218	12	76	123	11.9	3.37	123	.255	.318	15	.185	1	17	19	3	2.0
1948 StL-N	10	11	.476	39	25	7	0	0	166	179	13	74	72	13.8	4.50	91	.272	.347	8	.160	0	-10	-8	2	-0.7
1949 StL-N★	15	8	.652	35	28	12	2	1	188⅓	179	13	87	82	12.8	3.87	108	.255	.339	17	.258	4	4	6	1	1.1
1950 StL-N	7	8	.467	32	20	5	1	0	154⅔	158	15	70	61	13.4	3.90	110	.262	.342	7	.137	-2	4	7	0	0.4
1951 StL-N	4	6	.400	23	11	3	0	0	94⅔	106	13	46	44	14.5	5.32	74	.286	.365	5	.172	-0	-14	-14	2	-1.2
1952 StL-N	0	1	.000	1	1	0	0	0	4⅓	7	2	1	2	18.7	12.46	30	.389	.450	0	.000	-0	-4	-4	0	-0.6
Pit-N	0	3	.000	5	4	0	0	0	26⅓	30	6	10	8	13.7	7.18	56	.283	.345	0	.000	-1	-10	-9	1	-0.9
Yr	0	4	.000	6	5	0	0	0	30⅔	37	8	11	9	14.1	7.92	50	.296	.353	0	.000	-1	-14	-14	1	-1.5
1956 Pit-N	3	4	.429	35	13	0	0	2	107	126	8	41	45	14.0	4.04	93	.299	.361	3	.107	-0	-3	-3	-1	-0.3
Total 10	77	56	.579	273	161	54	13	12	1228⅔	1243	86	500	564	12.8	3.83	103	.264	.336	70	.174	-0	8	17	13	3.0

● **VAN MUNGO**   Mungo, Van Lingle b: 6/8/11, Pageland, S.C. d: 2/12/85, Pageland, S.C. BR/TR, 6'2", 185 lbs. Deb: 9/7/31

YEAR TM/L	W	L	PCT	G	GS	CG	SH	SV	IP	H	HR	BB	SO	RAT	ERA	ERA+	OAV	OOB	BH	AVG	PB	PR	/A	PD	TPI
1931 Bro-N	3	1	.750	5	4	2	1	0	31	27	0	13	12	11.9	2.32	164	.241	.325	3	.250	1	5	5	-1	0.7
1932 Bro-N	13	11	.542	39	33	11	1	2	223⅓	224	9	115	107	13.9	4.43	86	.260	.351	16	.203	0	-14	-15	2	-1.3
1933 Bro-N	16	15	.516	41	28	18	3	0	248	223	9	84	110	11.1	2.72	118	.236	.298	15	.179	-1	17	14	1	1.8
1934 Bro-N★	18	16	.529	45	38	22	3	3	315⅓	300	15	104	184	11.6	3.37	116	.249	.310	30	.248	4	24	19	2	2.5
1935 Bro-N	16	10	.615	37	26	18	4	2	214⅓	215	13	90	143	12.5	3.65	109	.252	.328	26	.289	5	9	8	1	1.4
1936 Bro-N☆	18	19	.486	45	37	22	3	3	311⅔	275	8	118	**238**	11.4	3.35	123	**.234**	.305	22	.179	-4	23	27	2	2.8
1937 Bro-N★	9	11	.450	25	21	14	0	3	161	136	3	56	122	10.9	2.91	139	**.229**	.298	16	.250	2	18	20	3	2.0
1938 Bro-N	4	11	.267	24	18	6	2	0	133⅓	133	11	72	72	14.0	3.92	100	.259	.353	6	.191	1	-2	-0	1	0.2
1939 Bro-N	4	5	.444	14	10	1	0	0	77⅓	70	7	33	34	12.3	3.26	124	.239	.322	10	.345	2	6	7	1	1.0
1940 Bro-N	1	0	1.000	7	0	0	0	0	22	24	1	10	19	13.9	2.45	163	.282	.358	0	.000	-1	3	4	-0	0.0
1941 Bro-N	0	0	—	2	0	0	0	0	2	1	0	2	0	13.5	4.50	81	.143	.333	0	—	-0	-0	-1	0	0.0
1942 NY-N	4	7	.333	9	5	2	0	0	36⅓	38	4	21	27	14.0	5.94	57	.273	.369	3	.214	-0	-11	-10	0	-0.8
1943 NY-N	3	7	.300	45	13	2	2	2	154⅓	140	7	79	83	13.1	3.91	88	.243	.341	7	.159	-1	-9	-8	1	-0.5
1945 NY-N†	14	7	.667	26	26	7	0	0	183	161	9	71	101	11.6	3.20	122	.238	.314	17	.233	4	12	15	0	1.9
Total 14	120	115	.511	364	259	123	20	16	2113	1957	89	868	1242	12.2	3.47	110	.245	.321	174	.221	13	83	83	11	12.8

● **MANNY MUNIZ**   Muniz, Manuel (Rodriguez) b: 12/31/47, Caguas, P.R. BR/TR, 5'11", 190 lbs. Deb: 9/3/71

YEAR TM/L	W	L	PCT	G	GS	CG	SH	SV	IP	H	HR	BB	SO	RAT	ERA	ERA+	OAV	OOB	BH	AVG	PB	PR	/A	PD	TPI
1971 Phi-N	0	1	.000	5	0	0	0	0	10⅓	9	2	8	6	14.8	6.97	51	.225	.354	0	.000	-0	-4	-4	-0	-0.4

YEAR TM/L	W	L	PCT	G	GS	CG	SH	SV	IP	H	HR	BB	SO	RAT	ERA	ERA+	OAV	OOB	BH	AVG	PB	PR	/A	PD	TPI

● **SCOTT MUNNINGHOFF** Munninghoff, Scott Andrew b: 12/5/58, Cincinnati, Ohio BR/TR, 6', 175 lbs. Deb: 4/13/80

| 1980 Phi-N | 0 | 0 | — | 4 | 0 | 0 | 0 | 0 | 6 | 8 | 0 | 5 | 2 | 19.5 | 4.50 | 84 | .320 | .433 | 1 | 1.000 | 1 | -1 | -0 | 0 | 0.1 |

● **LES MUNNS** Munns, Leslie Ernest "Big Ed" or "Nemo" b: 12/1/08, Fort Bragg, Cal. BR/TR, 6'5", 212 lbs. Deb: 4/22/34

1934 Bro-N	3	7	.300	33	9	4	0	0	99¹	106	7	60	41	15.0	4.71	83	.280	.378	7	.241	2	-7	-9	2	-0.4
1935 Bro-N	1	3	.250	21	5	0	0	1	58¹	74	5	33	13	17.1	5.55	72	.319	.413	3	.188	-0	-10	-10	-2	-0.8
1936 StL-N	0	3	.000	7	1	0	0	1	24	23	2	12	4	13.1	3.00	131	.240	.324	1	.111	-1	3	3	1	0.3
Total 3	4	13	.235	61	15	4	0	2	181²	203	14	105	58	15.5	4.76	83	.287	.382	11	.204	1	-14	-17	1	-0.9

● **MIKE MUNOZ** Munoz, Michael Anthony b: 7/12/65, Baldwin Park, Cal. BL/TL, 6'2", 190 lbs. Deb: 9/6/89

1989 LA-N	0	0	—	3	0	0	0	0	2²	5	1	2	3	23.6	16.88	20	.417	.500	0	—	0	-4	-4	0	0.0
1990 LA-N	0	1	.000	8	0	0	0	0	5²	6	0	3	2	14.3	3.18	115	.300	.391	0	.000	-0	0	0	-0	0.0
1991 Det-A	0	0	—	6	0	0	0	0	9¹	14	0	5	3	18.3	9.64	43	.350	.422	0	—	0	-6	-6	0	0.0
1992 Det-A	1	2	.333	65	0	0	0	2	48	44	3	25	23	12.9	3.00	132	.246	.338	0	—	0	5	5	2	0.5
1993 Det-A	0	1	.000	8	0	0	0	0	3	4	1	6	1	30.0	6.00	71	.308	.526	0	—	0	-1	-1	-0	-0.1
Col-N	2	1	.667	21	0	0	0	0	18	21	1	9	16	15.0	4.50	106	.309	.390	0	—	0	-1	1	0	0.1
1994 Col-N	4	2	.667	57	0	0	0	1	45²	37	3	31	32	13.4	3.74	133	.223	.345	0	—	0	2	6	0	0.9
Total 6	7	7	.500	168	0	0	0	3	132¹	131	9	81	80	14.4	4.28	103	.263	.366	0	.000	-0	-3	2	4	1.4

● **BOBBY MUNOZ** Munoz, Roberto (Sbert) b: 3/3/68, Rio Piedras, P.R. BR/TR, 6'7", 237 lbs. Deb: 5/29/93

1993 NY-A	3	3	.500	38	0	0	0	1	45²	48	1	26	33	14.6	5.32	78	.270	.363	0	—	0	-5	-6	-0	-0.5
1994 Phi-N	7	5	.583	21	14	1	0	1	104¹	101	8	35	59	11.8	2.67	154	.252	.314	7	.206	2	18	17	1	2.1
Total 2	10	8	.556	59	14	1	0	1	150	149	9	61	92	12.7	3.48	119	.257	.329	7	.206	2	13	11	1	1.6

● **STEVE MURA** Mura, Stephen Andrew b: 2/12/55, New Orleans, La. BR/TR, 6'2", 190 lbs. Deb: 9/5/78

1978 SD-N	0	2	.000	5	2	0	0	0	7²	15	1	5	5	23.5	11.74	28	.441	.513	0	.000	-0	-7	-7	-0	-1.5
1979 SD-N	4	4	.500	38	5	0	0	2	73	57	6	37	59	11.7	3.08	114	.217	.316	0	.000	-1	5	4	-0	0.2
1980 SD-N	8	7	.533	37	23	3	1	2	168²	149	9	86	109	12.7	3.68	93	.246	.343	7	.137	-0	-2	-5	0	-0.4
1981 SD-N	5	14	.263	23	22	2	0	0	138²	156	10	50	70	13.4	4.28	76	.285	.344	6	.136	-0	-12	-16	1	-1.9
1982 StL-N	12	11	.522	35	30	7	1	0	184¹	196	16	80	84	13.5	4.05	89	.278	.352	3	.057	-4	-9	-9	-1	-1.5
1983 Chi-A	0	0	—	6	0	0	0	0	12¹	13	1	6	4	13.9	4.38	96	.260	.339	0	—	0	-0	-0	-0	-0.2
1985 Oak-A	1	1	.500	23	1	0	0	1	48	41	3	25	29	12.4	4.13	93	.225	.319	0	—	0	-0	-1	-0	0.3
Total 7	30	39	.435	167	83	12	2	5	632²	627	46	289	360	13.1	4.00	88	.263	.343	16	.101	-5	-25	-35	-1	-5.0

● **MASANORI MURAKAMI** Murakami, Masanori b: 5/6/44, Otsuki, Japan BL/TL, 6', 180 lbs. Deb: 9/1/64

1964 SF-N	1	0	1.000	9	0	0	0	1	15	8	1	1	15	5.4	1.80	198	.163	.180	0	.000	-0	3	3	-1	0.1
1965 SF-N	4	1	.800	45	1	0	0	8	74¹	57	9	22	85	9.9	3.75	96	.205	.271	2	.154	-0	-2	-1	-2	-0.3
Total 2	5	1	.833	54	1	0	0	9	89¹	65	10	23	100	9.2	3.43	105	.199	.258	2	.125	-1	1	2	-2	-0.2

● **TIM MURCHISON** Murchison, Thomas Malcolm b: 10/8/1896, Liberty, N.C. d: 10/20/62, Liberty, N.C. BR/TL, 6', 185 lbs. Deb: 6/21/17

1917 StL-N	0	0	—	1	0	0	0	0	1	0	0	2	2	18.0	0.00	—	.000	.400	0	—	0	0	0	0	0.0
1920 Cle-A	0	0	—	2	0	0	0	0	5	3	0	4	0	12.6	0.00	—	.200	.368	0	.000	-0	2	2	1	0.0
Total 2	0	0	—	3	0	0	0	0	6	3	0	6	2	13.5	0.00	—	.167	.375	0	.000	-0	2	2	1	0.0

● **RED MURFF** Murff, John Robert b: 4/1/21, Burlington, Tex. BR/TR, 6'3", 195 lbs. Deb: 4/21/56

1956 Mil-N	0	0	—	14	1	0	0	1	24¹	25	3	7	18	11.8	4.44	78	.272	.323	1	.200	0	-2	-3	0	-0.0
1957 Mil-N	2	2	.500	12	1	0	0	2	26	31	3	11	13	14.5	4.85	72	.301	.368	0	.000	-1	-3	-4	1	-0.6
Total 2	2	2	.500	26	2	0	0	3	50¹	56	6	18	31	13.2	4.65	75	.287	.347	1	.091	-1	-5	-7	1	-0.6

● **CON MURPHY** Murphy, Cornelius B. "Monk" or "Razzle Dazzle" b: 10/15/1863, Worcester, Mass. d: 8/1/14, Worcester, Mass. TR, 5'9", 130 lbs. Deb: 9/11/1884

1884 Phi-N	0	3	.000	3	3	3	0	0	26	37	1	6	10	14.9	6.58	45	.319	.352	0	.000	-1	-10	-10	-0	-0.9
1890 Bro-P	4	10	.286	20	14	11	0	2	139	168	2	82	29	16.6	4.79	93	.286	.379	15	.217	-1	-9	-5	-1	-0.5
Total 2	4	13	.235	23	17	14	0	2	165	205	3	88	39	16.3	5.07	83	.292	.375	15	.190	-3	-19	-16	-1	-1.4

● **DANNY MURPHY** Murphy, Daniel Francis b: 8/23/42, Beverly, Mass. BL/TR, 5'11", 185 lbs. Deb: 6/18/60 ♦

1969 Chi-A	2	1	.667	17	0	0	0	4	31¹	28	2	10	16	11.5	2.01	192	.252	.325	0	.000	0	6	6	0	0.8
1970 Chi-A	2	3	.400	51	0	0	0	5	80²	82	11	49	42	15.1	5.69	68	.273	.382	2	.333	2	-18	-16	-1	-1.0
Total 2	4	4	.500	68	0	0	0	9	112	110	13	59	58	14.1	4.66	83	.268	.368	23	.177	2	-12	-10	-1	-0.2

● **DAN MURPHY** Murphy, Daniel Lee b: 9/18/64, Artesia, Cal. BR/TR, 6'2", 195 lbs. Deb: 8/10/89

| 1989 SD-N | 0 | 0 | — | 7 | 0 | 0 | 0 | 0 | 6¹ | 6 | 1 | 4 | 1 | 14.2 | 5.68 | 61 | .231 | .333 | 0 | — | 0 | -2 | -2 | -0 | 0.0 |

● **ED MURPHY** Murphy, Edward J. b: 1/22/1877, Auburn, N.Y. d: 1/29/35, Weedsport, N.Y. TR, 6'1", 186 lbs. Deb: 4/23/1898

1898 Phi-N	1	2	.333	7	3	2	0	0	30	41	3	10	8	15.6	5.10	67	.323	.377	5	.357	1	-5	-6	1	-0.3
1901 StL-N	10	9	.526	23	21	16	0	0	165	201	3	32	42	12.8	4.20	76	.298	.331	16	.250	3	-16	-19	2	-1.4
1902 StL-N	10	6	.625	23	17	12	1	1	164	187	7	31	37	12.1	3.02	91	.286	.321	16	.262	1	-4	-5	2	-0.2
1903 StL-N	4	8	.333	15	12	9	0	0	106	108	2	38	16	12.9	3.31	99	.262	.333	13	.203	-1	-0	-1	0	-0.1
Total 4	25	25	.500	68	53	39	1	1	465	537	17	111	103	12.7	3.64	84	.288	.331	50	.246	5	-26	-30	5	-2.0

● **JOHN MURPHY** Murphy, John H. b: 3/8/1867, Philadelphia, Pa. Deb: 4/17/1884

1884 Wil-U	0	6	.000	7	6	5	0	0	48	52	3	2	27	10.1	3.00	89	.258	.266	2	.065	-4	-3	-2	-1	-0.5
Alt-U	5	6	.455	14	10	10	0	0	111²	141	3	9	46	12.1	3.87	69	.289	.302	14	.149	-7	-18	-15	1	-1.5
Yr	5	12	.294	21	16	15	0	0	159²	193	6	11	73	11.5	3.61	74	.280	.291	16	.128	-11	-21	-17	0	-2.0

● **JOHNNY MURPHY** Murphy, John Joseph "Grandma" "Fireman" Or "Fordham Johnny" b: 7/14/08, New York, N.Y. d: 1/14/70, New York, N.Y. BR/TR, 6'2", 190 lbs. Deb: 5/19/32

1932 NY-A	0	0	—	2	0	0	0	0	3¹	7	0	3	2	27.0	16.20	25	.438	.526	1	1.000	1	-4	-4	0	0.1
1934 NY-A	14	10	.583	40	20	10	0	4	207²	193	11	76	70	11.7	3.12	130	.250	.317	7	.099	-3	32	22	1	2.1
1935 NY-A	10	5	.667	40	8	4	0	5	117	110	7	55	28	12.7	4.08	99	.243	.325	5	.156	2	5	-0	-1	0.1
1936 *NY-A	9	3	.750	27	5	2	0	5	88	90	5	36	34	13.0	3.38	138	.262	.334	13	.361	4	16	13	1	2.0
1937 *NY-A	13	4	.765	39	4	0	0	10	110	121	7	50	36	14.1	4.17	107	.277	.352	8	.229	2	5	3	4	1.0
1938 *NY-A☆	8	2	.800	32	2	1	0	11	91¹	90	5	41	43	13.0	4.24	107	.256	.336	2	.063	-3	**6**	3	1	0.2
1939 *NY-A☆	3	6	.333	38	0	0	0	19	61¹	57	2	28	30	12.5	4.40	99	.252	.335	2	.182	1	1	-0	1	0.0
1940 NY-A	8	4	.667	35	1	0	0	9	63¹	58	5	15	21	10.4	3.69	109	.247	.292	1	.077	0	5	2	1	0.3
1941 *NY-A	8	3	.727	35	0	0	0	15	77¹	68	1	40	29	12.6	1.98	199	.237	.330	1	.056	-0	**19**	**17**	-1	2.7
1942 NY-A	4	10	.286	31	0	0	0	11	58	47	2	23	24	14.1	3.41	101	.293	.364	2	.154	2	1	0	0	0.1
1943 NY-A	12	4	.750	37	0	0	0	8	68	44	2	30	31	9.8	2.51	128	.183	.273	1	.053	-2	6	5	-0	1.1
1946 NY-A	4	2	.667	27	0	0	0	7	45	40	4	19	19	11.8	3.40	102	.240	.317	0	—	0	1	0	1	0.2
1947 Bos-A	0	0	—	32	0	0	0	3	54²	41	1	28	9	11.4	2.80	139	.206	.304	3	.273	4	6	7	0	0.2
Total 13	93	53	.637	415	40	17	0	107	1045	985	52	444	378	12.4	3.50	117	.249	.326	46	.154	-0	98	68	8	10.2

● **JOE MURPHY** Murphy, Joseph Akin b: 9/7/1866, St.Louis, Mo. d: 3/28/51, Coral Gables, Fla. 5'11", 160 lbs. Deb: 4/28/1886

1886 Cin-a	2	3	.400	5	5	5	0	0	46	50	2	21	11	14.1	4.89	72	.256	.332	0	.000	-3	-7	-7	-1	-0.9
StL-N	0	4	.000	4	4	3	0	0	33	45	3	16	11	16.6	8.18	39	.349	.389	3	.214	0	-18	-18	-0	-1.5
StL-a	1	0	1.000	1	1	1	0	0	7	5	0	3	1	10.3	3.86	89	.179	.258	0	—	-1	-0	-0	-0	-0.1

YEAR TM/L	W	L	PCT	G	GS	CG	SH	SV	IP	H	HR	BB	SO	RAT	ERA	ERA+	OAV	OOB	BH	AVG	PB	PR	/A	PD	TPI
1887 StL-a	1	0	1.000	1	1	1	0	0	9	13	0	4	5	17.0	5.00	91	.317	.378	1	.167	-1	-1	-0	-0	-0.1
Total 2	4	7	.364	11	11	10	0	0	95	113	3	44	30	15.0	5.97	59	.279	.351	4	.098	-4	-26	-26	-2	-2.6

● ROB MURPHY
Murphy, Robert Albert b: 5/26/60, Miami, Fla. BL/TL, 6'2", 205 lbs. Deb: 9/13/85

YEAR TM/L	W	L	PCT	G	GS	CG	SH	SV	IP	H	HR	BB	SO	RAT	ERA	ERA+	OAV	OOB	BH	AVG	PB	PR	/A	PD	TPI
1985 Cin-N	0	0	—	2	0	0	0	0	3	2	1	2	1	12.0	6.00	63	.200	.333	0	—	0	-1	-1	-0	0.0
1986 Cin-N	6	0	1.000	34	0	0	0	1	50¹	26	0	21	36	8.4	0.72	541	.155	.249	0	.000	-0	17	18	0	2.1
1987 Cin-N	8	5	.615	87	0	0	0	3	100²	91	7	32	99	11.0	3.04	140	.239	.299	1	.200	-0	12	13	0	1.7
1988 Cin-N	0	6	.000	76	0	0	0	0	84²	69	3	38	74	11.5	3.08	116	.229	.318	0	—	0	3	5	1	0.4
1989 Bos-A	5	7	.417	74	0	0	0	9	105	97	7	41	107	11.9	2.74	149	.251	.325	0	—	0	13	16	1	1.8
1990 *Bos-A	0	6	.000	68	0	0	0	7	57	85	10	32	54	18.6	6.32	65	.348	.426	0	—	0	-15	-14	0	-1.8
1991 Sea-A	0	1	.000	57	0	0	0	4	48	47	4	19	34	12.6	3.00	137	.250	.322	0	—	0	6	6	0	0.2
1992 Hou-N	3	1	.750	59	0	0	0	0	55²	56	2	21	42	12.4	4.04	83	.260	.326	0	.000	-0	-3	-4	1	-0.2
1993 StL-N	5	7	.417	73	0	0	0	1	64²	73	8	20	41	13.1	4.87	81	.290	.344	1	.500	0	-6	-7	-0	-1.1
1994 StL-N	4	3	.571	50	0	0	0	2	40¹	35	7	13	25	10.7	3.79	107	.230	.291	0	—	0	2	1	-0	0.2
NY-A	0	0	—	3	0	0	0	0	1²	3	0	1	0	16.2	16.20	27	.375	.375	0	—	0	-2	-2	0	0.2
Total 10	31	36	.463	583	0	0	0	30	611	584	51	239	513	12.2	3.49	113	.253	.325	2	.182	-0	25	31	2	3.5

● BOB MURPHY
Murphy, Robert J. b: 12/26/1866, Dutchess Co., N.Y. Deb: 5/27/1890

YEAR TM/L	W	L	PCT	G	GS	CG	SH	SV	IP	H	HR	BB	SO	RAT	ERA	ERA+	OAV	OOB	BH	AVG	PB	PR	/A	PD	TPI
1890 NY-N	1	0	1.000	3	2	1	0	0	18	23	1	10	8	16.5	5.50	64	.301	.382	1	.111	-1	-4	-4	-0	-0.3
Bro-a	3	9	.250	12	12	10	0	0	96	121	6	46	26	16.1	5.72	68	.299	.377	9	.180	0	-20	-19	2	-1.6
Total 1	4	9	.308	15	14	11	0	0	114	144	6	56	34	16.2	5.68	67	.299	.378	10	.169	-1	-24	-23	2	-1.9

● TOM MURPHY
Murphy, Thomas Andrew b: 12/30/45, Cleveland, Ohio BR/TR, 6'3", 185 lbs. Deb: 6/13/68

YEAR TM/L	W	L	PCT	G	GS	CG	SH	SV	IP	H	HR	BB	SO	RAT	ERA	ERA+	OAV	OOB	BH	AVG	PB	PR	/A	PD	TPI
1968 Cal-A	5	6	.455	15	15	3	0	0	99¹	67	5	28	56	9.1	2.17	134	.191	.261	0	.000	-3	9	8	-1	0.5
1969 Cal-A	10	16	.385	36	35	4	0	0	215²	213	12	69	100	12.6	4.21	83	.260	.333	10	.141	-0	-14	-18	1	-1.9
1970 Cal-A	16	13	.552	39	38	5	2	0	227	223	32	81	99	12.3	4.24	85	.261	.330	14	.184	3	-13	-16	-1	-1.7
1971 Cal-A	6	17	.261	37	36	7	0	0	243¹	228	24	82	89	11.8	3.77	86	.256	.325	13	.173	1	-8	-14	1	-1.0
1972 Cal-A	0	0	—	6	0	0	0	0	10	13	0	8	2	18.9	5.40	54	.342	.457	0	—	-0	-3	-3	1	0.1
KC-A	4	4	.500	18	9	1	1	1	70¹	77	3	16	34	12.7	3.07	99	.287	.341	0	.000	-1	-0	-0	1	-0.1
Yr	4	4	.500	24	9	1	1	1	80¹	90	3	24	36	13.4	3.36	90	.293	.356	0	.000	-1	-3	-3	1	0.0
1973 StL-N	3	7	.300	19	13	2	0	0	88²	89	5	22	42	11.6	3.76	97	.269	.320	4	.174	-0	-1	-1	0	0.0
1974 Mil-A	10	10	.500	70	0	0	0	20	123	97	6	51	47	11.0	1.90	190	.224	.309	1	.500	1	23	23	2	4.9
1975 Mil-A	1	9	.100	52	0	0	0	20	72¹	85	5	27	32	14.6	4.60	83	.295	.366	0	—	0	-7	-6	0	-1.2
1976 Mil-A	1	0	1.000	15	0	0	0	0	18¹	25	2	9	7	17.7	7.36	47	.313	.396	0	—	0	-8	-8	0	-0.3
Bos-A	4	5	.444	37	0	0	0	8	81	91	5	25	32	13.1	3.44	114	.290	.346	0	—	0	1	4	-0	-0.4
Yr	4	6	.400	52	0	0	0	9	99¹	116	7	34	39	13.8	4.17	92	.293	.352	0	—	0	-7	-4	0	-0.7
1977 Bos-A	0	1	.000	16	0	0	0	2	30²	44	6	12	13	16.4	6.75	67	.338	.394	0	—	0	-9	-8	0	-1.0
Tor-A	2	1	.667	19	1	0	0	2	52	63	6	18	26	14.2	3.63	115	.304	.363	0	—	0	2	3	-0	0.1
Yr	2	2	.500	35	1	0	0	2	82²	107	12	30	39	15.0	4.79	90	.317	.374	0	—	0	-7	-4	0	-0.9
1978 Tor-A	6	9	.400	50	0	0	0	7	94	87	11	37	36	11.9	3.93	100	.256	.329	0	—	0	-2	-0	2	0.2
1979 Tor-A	1	2	.333	10	0	0	0	0	18¹	23	1	8	6	15.2	5.40	80	.311	.378	0	—	0	-2	-1	-0	-0.3
Total 12	68	101	.402	439	147	22	3	59	1444	1425	123	493	621	12.3	3.78	94	.263	.332	42	.145	0	-32	-38	7	-2.1

● WALTER MURPHY
Murphy, Walter Joseph b: 9/27/07, New York, N.Y. BR/TR, 6'1.5", 180 lbs. Deb: 4/19/31

YEAR TM/L	W	L	PCT	G	GS	CG	SH	SV	IP	H	HR	BB	SO	RAT	ERA	ERA+	OAV	OOB	BH	AVG	PB	PR	/A	PD	TPI
1931 Bos-A	0	0	—	2	0	0	0	0	2	4	0	1	0	22.5	9.00	48	.444	.500	0	—	0	-1	-1	-0	0.0

● DALE MURRAY
Murray, Dale Albert b: 2/2/50, Cuero, Tex. BR/TR, 6'4", 205 lbs. Deb: 7/7/74

YEAR TM/L	W	L	PCT	G	GS	CG	SH	SV	IP	H	HR	BB	SO	RAT	ERA	ERA+	OAV	OOB	BH	AVG	PB	PR	/A	PD	TPI
1974 Mon-N	1	1	.500	32	0	0	0	10	69²	46	1	23	31	8.9	1.03	371	.187	.257	0	.000	-1	20	22	0	1.3
1975 Mon-N	15	8	.652	63	0	0	0	9	111¹	134	0	39	43	14.2	3.96	97	.305	.365	3	.214	1	-4	-2	3	0.0
1976 Mon-N	4	9	.308	81	0	0	0	13	113¹	117	1	37	35	12.2	3.26	114	.277	.336	0	.000	-1	3	6	4	1.2
1977 Cin-N	7	2	.778	61	1	0	0	4	102	125	13	46	42	15.3	4.94	80	.314	.388	2	.167	-0	-12	-11	0	-1.0
1978 Cin-N	1	1	.500	15	0	0	0	0	32²	34	1	17	25	14.3	4.13	86	.272	.364	0	.000	-0	-2	-2	1	-0.1
NY-N	8	5	.615	53	0	0	0	5	86¹	85	4	36	37	12.8	3.65	96	.266	.345	0	.000	-0	-1	-2	2	-0.1
Yr	9	6	.600	68	0	0	0	7	119	119	5	53	62	13.2	3.78	93	.266	.346	0	.000	-1	-3	-4	2	-0.2
1979 NY-N	4	8	.333	58	0	0	0	4	97	105	6	52	37	14.6	4.82	75	.287	.376	0	.000	-0	-12	-13	1	-1.5
Mon-N	1	2	.333	9	0	0	0	1	13¹	14	1	3	4	11.5	2.70	136	.292	.333	0	.000	-0	2	1	-1	0.3
Yr	5	10	.333	67	0	0	0	5	110¹	119	7	55	41	14.2	4.57	80	.285	.369	0	.000	-0	-10	-11	0	-1.2
1980 Mon-N	0	1	.000	16	0	0	0	0	29¹	39	3	12	16	15.6	6.14	58	.315	.375	0	—	-0	-8	-8	-1	-0.7
1981 Tor-A	1	0	1.000	11	0	0	0	0	15¹	12	0	5	12	10.0	1.17	336	.211	.274	0	—	0	4	5	1	0.4
1982 Tor-A	8	7	.533	56	0	0	0	11	111	115	3	32	60	12.2	3.16	142	.268	.323	0	—	0	11	16	3	2.0
1983 NY-A	2	4	.333	40	0	0	0	1	94¹	113	5	22	45	13.0	4.48	87	.297	.337	0	—	0	-4	-6	-0	-0.1
1984 NY-A	1	2	.333	19	0	0	0	0	23²	30	2	5	13	14.1	4.94	77	.306	.352	0	—	0	-3	-3	-0	-0.1
1985 NY-A	0	0	—	3	0	0	0	0	2	4	0	4	0	18.0	13.50	30	.400	.400	0	—	0	-2	-2	-0	0.2
Tex-A	0	0	—	1	0	0	0	0	1	3	0	0	0	27.0	18.00	23	.750	.750	0	—	0	-2	-2	-0	-0.1
Yr	0	0	—	4	0	0	0	0	3	7	0	4	0	21.0	15.00	27	.500	.500	0	—	0	-4	-4	0	0.1
Total 12	53	50	.515	518	1	0	0	60	902¹	976	40	329	400	13.2	3.85	100	.282	.346	5	.077	-3	-9	-1	13	1.6

● GEORGE MURRAY
Murray, George King "Smiler" b: 9/23/1898, Charlotte, N.C. d: 10/18/55, Memphis, Tenn. BR/TR, 6'2", 200 lbs. Deb: 5/8/22

YEAR TM/L	W	L	PCT	G	GS	CG	SH	SV	IP	H	HR	BB	SO	RAT	ERA	ERA+	OAV	OOB	BH	AVG	PB	PR	/A	PD	TPI
1922 NY-A	4	2	.667	22	2	0	0	0	56²	53	0	26	14	12.7	3.97	101	.255	.340	5	.278	-2	0	0	-0	0.2
1923 Bos-A	7	11	.389	39	18	5	0	0	177²	190	9	87	40	14.4	4.91	84	.291	.380	9	.164	-1	-18	-16	-2	-1.8
1924 Bos-A	2	9	.182	28	7	0	0	0	80¹	97	6	32	27	15.2	6.72	65	.307	.383	4	.182	-1	-22	-21	0	-2.4
1926 Was-A	6	3	.667	12	12	5	0	0	81²	89	1	37	28	14.6	5.64	69	.287	.374	5	.139	-2	-15	-16	-1	-1.7
1927 Was-A	1	1	.500	7	3	0	0	0	18	18	1	15	5	17.5	7.00	58	.265	.412	1	.167	-0	-6	-6	-1	-0.6
1933 Chi-A	0	0	—	2	0	0	0	0	2¹	3	0	2	0	19.3	7.71	55	.375	.500	0	—	0	-1	-1	0	0.0
Total 6	20	26	.435	110	42	10	0	0	416¹	450	17	199	114	14.5	5.38	76	.288	.376	24	.175	-4	-61	-59	-3	-6.3

● JIM MURRAY
Murray, James Francis "Big Jim" b: 12/31/1900, Scranton, Pa. d: 7/15/73, New York, N.Y. BB/TL, 6'2", 210 lbs. Deb: 7/3/22

YEAR TM/L	W	L	PCT	G	GS	CG	SH	SV	IP	H	HR	BB	SO	RAT	ERA	ERA+	OAV	OOB	BH	AVG	PB	PR	/A	PD	TPI
1922 Bro-N	0	0	—	4	0	0	0	0	6	8	0	3	3	16.5	4.50	90	.320	.393	1	.500	0	-0	-0	-0	0.0

● AMBY MURRAY
Murray, Joseph Ambrose b: 6/4/13, Fall River, Mass. BL/TL, 5'7", 150 lbs. Deb: 7/5/36

YEAR TM/L	W	L	PCT	G	GS	CG	SH	SV	IP	H	HR	BB	SO	RAT	ERA	ERA+	OAV	OOB	BH	AVG	PB	PR	/A	PD	TPI
1936 Bos-N	0	0	—	4	1	0	0	0	11	15	1	3	2	14.7	4.09	94	.319	.360	1	.250	0	-0	-0	-0	0.0

● JOE MURRAY
Murray, Joseph Ambrose b: 11/11/20, Wilkes-Barre, Pa. BL/TL, 6', 165 lbs. Deb: 8/17/50

YEAR TM/L	W	L	PCT	G	GS	CG	SH	SV	IP	H	HR	BB	SO	RAT	ERA	ERA+	OAV	OOB	BH	AVG	PB	PR	/A	PD	TPI
1950 Phi-A	0	3	.000	8	2	0	0	0	30	34	1	21	8	16.5	5.70	80	.283	.390	0	.000	-2	-4	-4	1	-0.4

● PAT MURRAY
Murray, Patrick Joseph b: 7/18/1897, Scottsville, N.Y. d: 11/5/83, Rochester, N.Y. BR/TR, 6', 175 lbs. Deb: 7/1/19

YEAR TM/L	W	L	PCT	G	GS	CG	SH	SV	IP	H	HR	BB	SO	RAT	ERA	ERA+	OAV	OOB	BH	AVG	PB	PR	/A	PD	TPI
1919 Phi-N	0	2	.000	8	2	1	0	0	34¹	50	0	12	11	17.3	6.29	51	.347	.412	0	.000	-1	-13	-12	-0	-0.8

● DENNIS MUSGRAVES
Musgraves, Dennis Eugene b: 12/25/43, Indianapolis, Ind. BR/TR, 6'4", 188 lbs. Deb: 7/9/65

YEAR TM/L	W	L	PCT	G	GS	CG	SH	SV	IP	H	HR	BB	SO	RAT	ERA	ERA+	OAV	OOB	BH	AVG	PB	PR	/A	PD	TPI
1965 NY-N	0	0	—	5	1	0	0	0	16	11	0	7	11	11.3	0.56	627	.200	.313	0	.000	-0	5	5	-0	0.0

● STAN MUSIAL
Musial, Stanley Frank "Stan The Man" b: 11/21/20, Donora, Pa. BL/TL, 6', 175 lbs. Deb: 9/17/41 H◆

YEAR TM/L	W	L	PCT	G	GS	CG	SH	SV	IP	H	HR	BB	SO	RAT	ERA	ERA+	OAV	OOB	BH	AVG	PB	PR	/A	PD	TPI
1952 StL-N★	0	0	—	1	0	0	0	0	1	1	0	0	0	9.0	—	—	.000	.000	194	.336	1	0	0	0	0.0

● JEFF MUSSELMAN
Musselman, Jeffrey Joseph b: 6/21/63, Doylestown, Pa. BL/TL, 6', 180 lbs. Deb: 9/2/86

YEAR TM/L	W	L	PCT	G	GS	CG	SH	SV	IP	H	HR	BB	SO	RAT	ERA	ERA+	OAV	OOB	BH	AVG	PB	PR	/A	PD	TPI
1986 Tor-A	0	0	—	6	0	0	0	0	5¹	8	1	5	4	21.9	10.13	42	.333	.448	0	—	0	-4	-4	0	-0.1

YEAR	TM/L	W	L	PCT	G	GS	CG	SH	SV	IP	H	HR	BB	SO	RAT	ERA	ERA+	OAV	OOB	BH	AVG	PB	PR	/A	PD	TPI
1987	Tor-A	12	5	.706	68	1	0	0	3	89	75	7	54	54	13.3	4.15	108	.237	.354	0	—	0	3	3	1	0.5
1988	Tor-A	8	5	.615	15	15	0	0	0	85	80	4	30	39	12.0	3.18	124	.252	.322	0	—	0	7	7	-1	0.9
1989	Tor-A	0	1	.000	5	3	0	0	0	11	19	2	9	3	22.9	10.64	35	.404	.500	0	—	0	-8	-8	-0	-0.6
	NY-N	3	2	.600	20	0	0	0	0	26¹	27	1	14	11	14.0	3.08	106	.267	.357	0	—	0	1	1	2	0.3
1990	NY-N	0	2	.000	28	0	0	0	0	32	40	3	11	14	14.6	5.63	67	.310	.369	0	.000	-0	-7	-7	0	-0.4
Total 5		23	15	.605	142	19	0	0	3	248²	249	18	123	125	13.7	4.31	94	.266	.356	0	.000	-0	-7	-8	2	0.6

● RON MUSSELMAN
Musselman, Ralph Ronald b: 11/11/54, Wilmington, N.C. BR/TR, 6'2", 185 lbs. Deb: 8/18/82

YEAR	TM/L	W	L	PCT	G	GS	CG	SH	SV	IP	H	HR	BB	SO	RAT	ERA	ERA+	OAV	OOB	BH	AVG	PB	PR	/A	PD	TPI
1982	Sea-A	1	0	1.000	12	0	0	0	0	15²	18	2	6	9	14.4	3.45	123	.300	.373	0	—	0	1	1	0	-0.1
1984	Tor-A	0	2	.000	11	0	0	0	1	21¹	18	2	10	9	11.8	2.11	194	.225	.311	0	—	0	4	5	-0	0.1
1985	Tor-A	3	0	1.000	25	4	0	0	0	52¹	59	2	24	29	14.3	4.47	94	.284	.358	0	—	0	-2	-2	-1	-0.4
Total 3		4	2	.667	48	4	0	0	1	89¹	95	6	40	47	13.7	3.73	112	.273	.350	0	—	0	4	5	-1	-0.4

● PAUL MUSSER
Musser, Paul b: 6/24/1889, Millheim, Pa. d: 7/7/73, State College, Pa. BR/TR, 6', 175 lbs. Deb: 6/6/12

YEAR	TM/L	W	L	PCT	G	GS	CG	SH	SV	IP	H	HR	BB	SO	RAT	ERA	ERA+	OAV	OOB	BH	AVG	PB	PR	/A	PD	TPI
1912	Was-A	0	0	—	7	2	0	0	0	20²	16	0	16	10	14.8	2.61	128	.225	.382	0	.000	-1	2	2	0	-0.1
1919	Bos-A	0	2	.000	5	4	1	0	0	19²	26	0	8	14	15.6	4.12	73	.342	.405	0	.000	-1	-2	-2	-0	-0.4
Total 2		0	2	.000	12	6	1	0	2	40¹	42	0	24	24	15.2	3.35	95	.286	.393	0	.000	-2	-0	-1	0	-0.5

● BARNEY MUSSILL
Mussill, Bernard James b: 10/1/19, Bower Hill, Pa. BR/TL, 6'1", 200 lbs. Deb: 4/20/44

YEAR	TM/L	W	L	PCT	G	GS	CG	SH	SV	IP	H	HR	BB	SO	RAT	ERA	ERA+	OAV	OOB	BH	AVG	PB	PR	/A	PD	TPI
1944	Phi-N	0	1	.000	16	0	0	0	0	19¹	20	1	13	5	15.4	6.05	60	.267	.375	0	.000	-0	-5	-5	-0	-0.3

● MIKE MUSSINA
Mussina, Michael Cole b: 12/8/68, Williamsport, Pa. BR/TR, 6'2", 185 lbs. Deb: 8/4/91

YEAR	TM/L	W	L	PCT	G	GS	CG	SH	SV	IP	H	HR	BB	SO	RAT	ERA	ERA+	OAV	OOB	BH	AVG	PB	PR	/A	PD	TPI
1991	Bal-A	4	5	.444	12	12	2	0	0	87²	77	7	21	52	10.2	2.87	137	.239	.288	0	—	0	12	10	-0	1.1
1992	Bal-A★	18	5	**.783**	32	32	8	4	0	241	212	16	48	130	**9.8**	2.54	158	.239	**.279**	0	—	0	37	40	3	3.5
1993	Bal-A☆	14	6	.700	25	25	3	2	0	167²	163	20	44	117	11.3	4.46	100	.256	.307	0	—	0	-3	0	-0	-0.2
1994	Bal-A★	16	5	.762	24	24	3	0	0	176¹	163	19	42	99	10.5	3.06	166	.248	.294	0	—	0	34	39	0	3.8
Total 4		52	21	.712	93	93	16	6	0	672²	615	62	155	398	10.4	3.20	137	.246	.292	0	—	0	81	89	-1	8.2

● ALEX MUSTAIKIS
Mustaikis, Alexander Dominick b: 3/26/09, Chelsea, Mass. d: 1/17/70, Scranton, Pa. BR/TR, 6'3", 180 lbs. Deb: 7/7/40

YEAR	TM/L	W	L	PCT	G	GS	CG	SH	SV	IP	H	HR	BB	SO	RAT	ERA	ERA+	OAV	OOB	BH	AVG	PB	PR	/A	PD	TPI
1940	Bos-A	0	1	.000	6	1	0	0	0	15	15	1	15	6	18.0	9.00	50	.254	.405	2	.333	1	-8	-8	1	-0.3

● JEFF MUTIS
Mutis, Jeffrey Thomas b: 12/20/66, Allentown, Pa. BL/TL, 6'2", 185 lbs. Deb: 6/15/91

YEAR	TM/L	W	L	PCT	G	GS	CG	SH	SV	IP	H	HR	BB	SO	RAT	ERA	ERA+	OAV	OOB	BH	AVG	PB	PR	/A	PD	TPI
1991	Cle-A	0	3	.000	3	3	0	0	0	12¹	23	1	7	6	21.9	11.68	36	.397	.462	0	—	0	-10	-10	-0	-1.7
1992	Cle-A	0	3	.000	3	2	0	0	0	11¹	24	4	6	12	23.8	9.53	41	.429	.484	0	—	0	-7	-7	0	-0.9
1993	Cle-A	3	6	.333	17	13	1	1	0	81	94	14	33	29	14.8	5.78	75	.289	.367	0	—	0	-13	-13	1	-1.1
1994	Fla-N	1	0	1.000	35	0	0	0	0	38¹	51	6	15	30	15.7	5.40	83	.331	.394	0	.000	-0	-5	-4	0	-0.1
Total 4		4	11	.267	58	18	1	1	0	143	191	25	61	73	16.4	6.48	67	.324	.395	0	.000	-0	-36	-34	1	-3.8

● ELMER MYERS
Myers, Elmer Glenn b: 3/2/1894, York Springs, Pa. d: 7/29/76, Collingswood, N.J. BR/TR, 6'2", 185 lbs. Deb: 10/6/15

YEAR	TM/L	W	L	PCT	G	GS	CG	SH	SV	IP	H	HR	BB	SO	RAT	ERA	ERA+	OAV	OOB	BH	AVG	PB	PR	/A	PD	TPI
1915	Phi-A	1	0	1.000	1	1	1	1	0	9	2	0	5	12	7.0	0.00	—	.074	.219	0	—	0	3	3	-0	0.2
1916	Phi-A	14	23	.378	44	35	31	2	1	315	280	7	168	182	13.2	3.66	78	.248	.353	27	.214	2	-29	-28	5	-2.3
1917	Phi-A	9	16	.360	38	23	13	2	3	201²	221	2	79	88	13.6	4.42	62	.283	.353	18	.247	2	-39	-37	1	-4.1
1918	Phi-A	4	8	.333	18	15	5	1	1	95¹	101	4	42	17	13.9	4.63	63	.283	.365	5	.143	-2	-20	-18	2	-2.2
1919	Cle-A	8	7	.533	23	15	6	1	1	134²	134	3	43	38	12.5	3.74	89	.264	.334	11	.239	1	-8	-6	-1	-0.3
1920	Cle-A	2	4	.333	16	7	2	0	1	71²	93	1	23	16	15.1	4.77	80	.316	.374	6	.240	0	-8	-8	0	-0.6
	Bos-A	9	1	.900	12	10	9	1	0	97	90	1	24	34	10.8	2.13	171	.249	.299	12	.316	3	18	16	-1	1.8
	Yr	11	5	.688	28	17	11	1	1	168²	183	2	47	50	12.4	3.25	114	.277	.327	18	.286	3	10	9	-1	1.2
1921	Bos-A	8	12	.400	30	20	11	0	0	172	217	11	53	40	14.7	4.87	87	.315	.373	14	.215	-2	-11	-12	-1	-1.3
1922	Bos-A	0	1	.000	3	1	0	0	0	5²	10	1	3	1	23.8	17.47	40	.370	.469	0	—	0	-8	-8	0	-1.1
Total 8		55	72	.433	185	127	78	8	7	1102	1148	30	440	428	13.4	4.06	80	.275	.352	93	.226	4	-102	-97	8	-9.9

● HENRY MYERS
Myers, Henry C. b: 5/1858, Philadelphia, Pa. d: 4/18/1895, Philadelphia, Pa. BR/TR, 5'9", 159 lbs. Deb: 8/20/1881 M♦

YEAR	TM/L	W	L	PCT	G	GS	CG	SH	SV	IP	H	HR	BB	SO	RAT	ERA	ERA+	OAV	OOB	BH	AVG	PB	PR	/A	PD	TPI
1882	Bal-a	0	2	.000	6	2	1	0	0	26	30	2	4	7	11.8	6.58	42	.271	.296	53	.180	-1	-11	-11	-0	-0.7

● JOSEPH MYERS
Myers, Joseph William b: 3/18/1882, Wilmington, Del. d: 2/11/56, Delaware City, Del BR/TR, 5'10.5", 205 lbs. Deb: 10/7/05

YEAR	TM/L	W	L	PCT	G	GS	CG	SH	SV	IP	H	HR	BB	SO	RAT	ERA	ERA+	OAV	OOB	BH	AVG	PB	PR	/A	PD	TPI
1905	Phi-A	0	0	—	1	1	1	0	0	5	3	0	3	5	12.6	3.60	74	.175	.331	0	.000	-0	-1	-1	-0	0.0

● RANDY MYERS
Myers, Randall Kirk b: 9/19/62, Vancouver, Wash. BL/TL, 6'1", 190 lbs. Deb: 10/6/85

YEAR	TM/L	W	L	PCT	G	GS	CG	SH	SV	IP	H	HR	BB	SO	RAT	ERA	ERA+	OAV	OOB	BH	AVG	PB	PR	/A	PD	TPI
1985	NY-N	0	0	—	1	0	0	0	0	2	0	0	1	2	4.5	0.00	—	.000	.143	0	—	0	1	1	0	0.0
1986	NY-N	0	0	—	10	0	0	0	0	10²	11	1	9	13	17.7	4.22	84	.256	.396	0	—	0	-1	-1	0	0.0
1987	NY-N	3	6	.333	54	0	0	0	6	75	61	6	30	92	10.9	3.96	95	.225	.302	2	.286	1	1	-2	0	-0.1
1988	*NY-N	7	3	.700	55	0	0	0	26	68	45	5	17	69	8.5	1.72	187	.190	.250	1	.250	1	13	11	-1	2.7
1989	NY-N	7	4	.636	65	0	0	0	24	84¹	62	4	40	88	10.9	2.35	139	.206	.299	0	.000	-1	11	9	0	1.6
1990	*Cin-N★	4	6	.400	66	0	0	0	31	86²	59	6	38	98	10.4	2.08	190	.193	.288	1	.250	1	17	18	0	3.6
1991	Cin-N	6	13	.316	58	12	1	0	6	132	116	8	80	108	13.4	3.55	107	.242	.351	5	.172	0	2	4	-1	0.4
1992	SD-N	3	6	.333	66	0	0	0	38	79²	84	7	34	66	13.4	4.29	83	.279	.354	1	.143	-0	-7	-6	-0	-1.4
1993	Chi-N	2	4	.333	73	0	0	0	**53**	75¹	65	7	26	86	11.0	3.11	128	.230	.297	1	.500	1	8	7	-1	1.8
1994	Chi-N★	1	5	.167	38	0	0	0	21	40¹	40	3	16	32	12.5	3.79	108	.260	.329	0	.000	-0	2	1	0	0.3
Total 10		33	47	.412	486	12	1	0	205	654	543	47	291	654	11.6	3.11	119	.228	.314	11	.186	-0	46	43	-3	8.9

● BOB MYRICK
Myrick, Robert Howard b: 10/1/52, Hattiesburg, Miss. BR/TL, 6'1", 195 lbs. Deb: 5/28/76

YEAR	TM/L	W	L	PCT	G	GS	CG	SH	SV	IP	H	HR	BB	SO	RAT	ERA	ERA+	OAV	OOB	BH	AVG	PB	PR	/A	PD	TPI
1976	NY-N	1	1	.500	21	1	0	0	0	27²	34	2	13	11	15.3	3.25	101	.306	.379	0	.000	-0	1	1	0	0.0
1977	NY-N	2	2	.500	44	4	0	0	2	87¹	86	3	33	49	12.4	3.61	104	.265	.334	2	.182	-0	3	1	0	0.1
1978	NY-N	0	3	.000	17	0	0	0	0	24²	18	3	13	13	11.3	3.28	106	.207	.310	0	.000	-0	1	1	0	0.1
Total 3		3	6	.333	82	5	0	0	2	139²	138	10	59	73	12.8	3.48	104	.264	.340	2	.125	-1	4	2	1	0.2

● CHRIS NABHOLZ
Nabholz, Christopher William b: 1/5/67, Harrisburg, Pa. BL/TL, 6'5", 210 lbs. Deb: 6/11/90

YEAR	TM/L	W	L	PCT	G	GS	CG	SH	SV	IP	H	HR	BB	SO	RAT	ERA	ERA+	OAV	OOB	BH	AVG	PB	PR	/A	PD	TPI
1990	Mon-N	6	2	.750	11	11	1	1	0	70	43	6	32	53	9.9	2.83	129	.176	.276	0	.000	-2	7	6	-0	0.5
1991	Mon-N	8	7	.533	24	24	1	0	0	153²	134	6	57	99	11.3	3.63	100	.237	.309	6	.115	-1	1	-0	1	0.4
1992	Mon-N	11	12	.478	32	32	1	1	0	195	176	11	74	130	11.8	3.32	104	.244	.318	8	.123	-1	4	3	3	0.6
1993	Mon-N	9	8	.529	26	21	1	0	0	116²	100	9	63	74	13.2	4.09	102	.236	.346	5	.128	-1	-1	-0	1	0.0
1994	Cle-A	0	1	.000	6	4	0	0	0	11	23	1	9	5	27.0	11.45	43	.418	.508	0	—	0	-8	-8	-0	-0.6
	Bos-A	3	4	.429	8	8	0	0	0	42	44	5	29	23	16.1	6.64	77	.282	.401	0	—	0	-9	-7	0	-1.0
	Yr	3	5	.375	14	12	0	0	0	53	67	6	38	28	18.2	7.64	67	.315	.423	0	—	0	-17	-15	0	-1.6
Total 5		37	34	.521	107	100	4	2	0	588¹	520	37	264	384	12.3	3.89	98	.240	.328	19	.107	-5	-5	-5	4	-0.5

● JACK NABORS
Nabors, Herman John b: 11/19/1887, Montevallo, Ala. d: 11/20/23, Wilton, Ala. BR/TR, 6'3", 185 lbs. Deb: 8/9/15

YEAR	TM/L	W	L	PCT	G	GS	CG	SH	SV	IP	H	HR	BB	SO	RAT	ERA	ERA+	OAV	OOB	BH	AVG	PB	PR	/A	PD	TPI
1915	Phi-A	0	5	.000	10	7	2	0	0	54	54	1	35	18	16.3	5.50	53	.304	.424	2	.125	-1	-15	-15	-0	-1.4
1916	Phi-A	1	20	.048	40	30	11	0	1	212²	206	2	95	74	12.9	3.47	82	.266	.349	4	.101	-4	-15	-14	-2	-2.1
1917	Phi-A	0	0	—	2	0	0	0	0	3	2	0	1	2	9.0	3.00	92	.200	.273				-0	-0	-0	0.0
Total 3		1	25	.038	52	37	13	0	1	269²	266	3	131	94	13.5	3.87	74	.273	.364	9	.106	-6	-31	-30	-2	-3.5

● BILL NAGEL
Nagel, William Taylor b: 8/19/15, Memphis, Tenn. d: 10/8/81, Freehold, N.J. BR/TR, 6'1", 190 lbs. Deb: 4/20/39 ♦

YEAR	TM/L	W	L	PCT	G	GS	CG	SH	SV	IP	H	HR	BB	SO	RAT	ERA	ERA+	OAV	OOB	BH	AVG	PB	PR	/A	PD	TPI
1939	Phi-A	0	0	—	1	0	0	0	0	3	7	1	1	0	24.0	12.00	39	.438	.471	86	.252	0	-2	-2	-0	0.0

YEAR TM/L	W	L	PCT	G	GS	CG	SH	SV	IP	H	HR	BB	SO	RAT	ERA	ERA+	OAV	OOB	BH	AVG	PB	PR	/A	PD	TPI
● JUDGE NAGLE Nagle, Walter Harold "Lucky" b: 3/10/1880, Santa Rosa, Cal. d: 5/26/71, Santa Rosa, Cal. BR/TR, 6′, 176 lbs. Deb: 4/26/11																								
1911 Pit-N	4	2	.667	8	3	1	0	1	27¹	33	3	6	11	13.2	3.62	95	.324	.367	1	.143	-0	-1	-1	0	-0.1
Bos-A	1	1	.500	5	1	0	0	0	27	27	2	6	12	11.0	3.33	98	.262	.303	1	.100	-1	0	-0	-1	-0.2
Total 1	5	3	.625	13	4	1	0	1	54¹	60	5	12	23	12.1	3.48	96	.293	.335	2	.118	-1	-1	-1	-1	-0.3
● CHARLES NAGY Nagy, Charles Harrison b: 5/5/67, Bridgeport, Conn. BL/TR, 6′3″, 200 lbs. Deb: 6/29/90																								
1990 Cle-A	2	4	.333	9	8	0	0	0	45²	58	7	21	26	15.8	5.91	66	.315	.388	0	—	0	-10	-10	1	-1.1
1991 Cle-A	10	15	.400	33	33	6	1	0	211¹	228	15	66	109	12.8	4.13	101	.275	.333	0	—	0	-1	1	-1	-0.1
1992 Cle-A★	17	10	.630	33	33	10	3	0	252	245	11	57	169	10.9	2.96	132	.260	.303	0	—	0	27	26	3	3.1
1993 Cle-A	2	6	.250	9	9	1	0	0	48²	66	6	13	30	15.0	6.29	69	.322	.368	0	—	0	-11	-11	2	-1.2
1994 Cle-A	10	8	.556	23	23	3	0	0	169¹	175	14	48	108	12.1	3.45	143	.265	.320	0	—	0	25	28	0	2.4
Total 5	41	43	.488	107	106	20	4	0	727	772	54	205	442	12.3	3.83	111	.274	.326	0	—	0	31	34	4	3.1
● STEVE NAGY Nagy, Stephen b: 5/28/19, Franklin, N.J. BL/TL, 5′9″, 174 lbs. Deb: 4/20/47																								
1947 Pit-N	1	3	.250	6	6	1	0	0	14	18	1	9	4	17.4	5.79	73	.310	.403	1	.250	0	-3	-2	0	-0.6
1950 Was-A	2	5	.286	9	9	2	0	0	53¹	69	5	29	17	16.5	6.58	68	.307	.386	5	.227	2	-12	-12	-0	-1.1
Total 2	3	8	.273	15	15	2	0	0	67¹	87	6	38	21	16.7	6.42	69	.307	.389	6	.231	2	-15	-15	-0	-1.7
● MIKE NAGY Nagy, Michael Timothy b: 3/25/48, Bronx, N.Y. BR/TR, 6′3″, 200 lbs. Deb: 4/21/69																								
1969 Bos-A	12	2	.857	33	28	7	1	0	196²	183	10	106	84	13.7	3.11	122	.245	.347	5	.077	-2	11	15	0	0.8
1970 Bos-A	6	5	.545	23	20	4	0	0	128²	138	16	64	56	14.3	4.48	88	.275	.359	11	.250	-2	-11	-7	-1	-0.5
1971 Bos-A	1	3	.250	12	7	0	0	0	38	46	4	20	9	15.6	6.63	56	.315	.398	1	.083	-1	-13	-12	-1	-1.3
1972 Bos-A	0	0	—	1	0	0	0	0	2	3	0	0	2	18.0	9.00	36	.375	.444	0	—	-0	-1	-1	-0	0.0
1973 StL-N	0	2	.000	9	7	0	0	0	40²	44	4	15	14	13.3	4.20	87	.282	.349	1	.091	-1	-2	-3	-0	-0.2
1974 Hou-N	1	1	.500	9	0	0	0	0	12²	17	3	5	5	16.3	8.53	41	.309	.377	0	.000	-0	-7	-7	-0	-1.0
Total 6	20	13	.606	87	62	11	1	0	418²	431	37	210	170	14.1	4.15	92	.267	.357	18	.135	-2	-24	-16	-1	-2.2
● SAM NAHEM Nahem, Samuel Ralph "Subway Sam" b: 10/19/15, New York, N.Y. BR/TR, 6′1.5″, 190 lbs. Deb: 10/2/38																								
1938 Bro-N	1	0	1.000	1	1	1	0	0	9	6	0	4	2	10.0	3.00	130	.194	.286	2	.400	1	1	1	-0	0.1
1941 StL-N	5	2	.714	26	8	2	0	1	81²	76	2	38	31	12.8	2.98	126	.243	.329	4	.174	-1	6	7	1	0.6
1942 Phi-N	1	3	.250	35	2	0	0	0	74²	72	2	40	38	13.7	4.94	67	.254	.350	2	.100	-1	-13	-14	1	-0.7
1948 Phi-N	3	3	.500	28	1	0	0	0	59	68	4	45	30	17.7	7.02	56	.288	.408	2	.154	-0	-20	-20	-1	-1.9
Total 4	10	8	.556	90	12	3	0	1	224¹	222	8	127	101	14.3	4.69	78	.257	.357	10	.164	-1	-27	-26	-1	-1.9
● PETE NAKTENIS Naktenis, Peter Ernest b: 6/12/14, Aberdeen, Wash. BL/TL, 6′1″, 185 lbs. Deb: 6/13/36																								
1936 Phi-A	0	1	.000	7	1	0	0	0	18²	24	2	27	18	25.6	12.54	41	.324	.515	1	.200	-0	-16	-15	-0	-0.7
1939 Cin-N	0	0	—	3	0	0	0	0	4	2	0	0	1	9.0	2.25	170	.154	.267	0	—	0	1	1	0	0.0
Total 2	0	1	.000	10	1	0	0	0	22²	26	2	27	19	22.6	10.72	45	.299	.483	1	.200	-0	-15	-15	-0	-0.7
● BUDDY NAPIER Napier, Skelton Le Roy b: 12/18/1889, Byronville, Ga. d: 3/29/68, Hutchins, Tex. BR/TR, 5′11″, 165 lbs. Deb: 8/14/12																								
1912 StL-A	1	2	.333	7	2	0	0	0	25¹	33	0	5	10	14.6	4.97	67	.317	.366	0	.000	-1	-5	-5	-0	-0.6
1918 Chi-N	0	0	—	1	0	0	0	0	6²	10	0	4	2	18.9	5.40	52	.357	.438	1	.333	1	-2	-2	-0	0.0
1920 Cin-N	4	2	.667	9	5	5	1	0	49	47	0	7	17	10.1	1.29	236	.254	.285	3	.214	1	10	10	0	1.3
1921 Cin-N	0	2	.000	22	6	1	0	1	56²	72	2	13	14	13.5	5.56	64	.329	.366	2	.143	1	-11	-12	1	-0.2
Total 4	5	6	.455	39	13	6	1	1	137²	162	2	29	43	12.7	3.92	84	.302	.343	6	.158	1	-8	-9	1	0.5
● GONZALO NARANJO Naranjo, Lazaro Ramon Gonzalo b: 11/25/34, Havana, Cuba BL/TR, 5′11.5″, 165 lbs. Deb: 7/8/56																								
1956 Pit-N	1	2	.333	17	3	0	0	0	34¹	37	7	17	26	14.4	4.46	85	.282	.369	1	.143	0	-3	-3	1	-0.1
● RAY NARLESKI Narleski, Raymond Edmond b: 11/25/28, Camden, N.J. BR/TR, 6′1″, 175 lbs. Deb: 4/17/54 F																								
1954 ★Cle-A	3	3	.500	42	2	1	0	13	89	59	8	44	52	10.6	2.22	165	.189	.293	0	.000	-2	15	14	-1	1.1
1955 Cle-A	9	1	.900	60	1	1	0	19	111²	91	11	52	94	11.5	3.71	108	.220	.308	7	.292	1	3	3	-2	0.3
1956 Cle-A†	3	2	.600	32	0	0	0	16	59¹	36	5	19	42	8.5	1.52	277	.170	.241	2	.250	0	17	18	-1	1.6
1957 Cle-A	11	5	.688	46	15	7	1	16	154¹	136	14	70	93	12.2	3.09	120	.235	.322	4	.093	-2	12	11	-4	0.7
1958 Cle-A★	13	10	.565	44	24	7	0	1	183¹	179	21	91	102	13.4	4.07	90	.255	.343	11	.204	-1	-6	-9	-3	-1.2
1959 Det-A	4	12	.250	42	10	1	0	5	104¹	105	21	59	71	14.2	5.78	70	.254	.348	2	.095	-1	-22	-20	-2	-3.2
Total 6	43	33	.566	266	52	17	1	58	702	606	80	335	454	12.2	3.60	106	.230	.320	26	.157	-6	19	18	-12	-0.7
● BUSTER NARUM Narum, Leslie Ferdinand b: 11/16/40, Philadelphia, Pa. BR/TR, 6′1″, 200 lbs. Deb: 4/14/63																								
1963 Bal-A	0	0	—	7	0	0	0	0	9	8	0	5	5	13.0	3.00	116	.242	.342	1	1.000	1	1	0	0	0.2
1964 Was-A	9	15	.375	38	32	7	2	0	199	195	31	73	121	12.3	4.30	86	.259	.328	4	.061	-5	-15	-13	-3	-2.2
1965 Was-A	4	12	.250	46	24	2	0	0	173²	176	16	91	86	14.2	4.46	78	.267	.361	2	.043	-0	-19	-19	2	-1.6
1966 Was-A	0	0	—	3	0	0	0	0	3¹	11	2	4	0	40.5	21.60	16	.579	.652	0	—	0	-7	-7	-0	0.0
1967 Was-A	1	0	1.000	2	2	0	0	0	11²	8	1	4	8	9.3	3.09	103	.195	.267	0	.000	-1	0	0	-0	-0.1
Total 5	14	27	.341	96	58	9	2	0	396²	398	50	177	220	13.3	4.45	80	.264	.346	7	.059	-6	-40	-38	-1	-3.7
● JIM NASH Nash, James Edwin b: 2/9/45, Hawthorne, Nev. BR/TR, 6′5″, 230 lbs. Deb: 7/3/66																								
1966 KC-A	12	1	.923	18	17	5	0	1	127	95	6	47	98	10.1	2.06	165	.204	.277	5	.102	-2	19	19	-3	1.5
1967 KC-A	12	17	.414	37	34	8	2	0	222³	200	21	87	186	11.8	3.76	85	.242	.317	7	.100	-2	-13	-14	-2	-2.2
1968 Oak-A	13	13	.500	34	33	12	6	0	228²	185	19	55	169	9.6	2.28	123	.219	.270	6	.068	-3	18	14	-3	1.1
1969 Oak-A	8	8	.500	26	19	3	1	0	115¹	112	17	30	75	11.2	3.67	94	.247	.296	4	.111	-1	-3	-1	-0.5
1970 Atl-N	13	9	.591	34	33	6	2	0	212¹	211	22	90	153	13.0	4.07	105	.257	.334	7	.087	-3	1	5	0	0.2
1971 Atl-N	9	7	.563	32	19	2	0	2	133	166	17	50	65	14.6	4.94	75	.314	.374	7	.149	-1	-22	-18	-1	-2.3
1972 Atl-N	1	1	.500	11	4	0	0	1	31¹	35	2	25	10	17.2	5.46	69	.307	.432	2	.222	-1	-7	-6	-0	-0.4
Phi-N	0	8	.000	9	8	0	0	0	37¹	46	5	17	15	15.9	6.27	57	.311	.393	1	.100	-1	-12	-11	-0	-2.0
Yr	1	9	.100	20	12	0	0	1	68²	81	7	42	25	16.5	5.90	62	.305	.405	3	.158	-0	-19	-17	-0	-2.4
Total 7	68	64	.515	201	167	36	11	4	1107¹	1050	108	401	771	11.9	3.58	96	.250	.318	38	.101	-11	-18	-16	-10	-4.6
● BILLY NASH Nash, William Mitchell b: 6/24/1865, Richmond, Va. d: 11/15/29, E.Orange, N.J. BR/TR, 5′8.5″, 167 lbs. Deb: 8/5/1884 MU♦																								
1889 Bos-N	0	0	—	1	0	0	0	0	1	0	0	1	0	9.0	0.00	—	.000	.252	132	.274	0	0	-0	-0	0.0
1890 Bos-P	0	0	—	1	0	0	0	0	0¹	1	0	0	0	27.0	0.00	—	.499	.499	130	.266	0	0	0	0	0.0
Total 2	0	0	—	2	0	0	0	0	1¹	1	0	1	0	13.5	0.00	—	.201	.335	1606	.275	1	1	0	-0	0.0
● PHILIP NASTU Nastu, Philip b: 3/8/55, Bridgeport, Conn. BL/TL, 6′2″, 180 lbs. Deb: 9/15/78																								
1978 SF-N	0	1	.000	3	1	0	0	0	8	8	1	2	5	11.3	5.63	61	.258	.303	0	.000	-0	-2	-2	-0	-0.2
1979 SF-N	3	4	.429	25	14	1	0	0	100	105	14	41	47	13.3	4.32	81	.272	.345	1	.042	-1	-7	-9	0	-0.7
1980 SF-N	0	0	—	6	0	0	0	0	6	10	1	5	1	22.5	6.00	59	.357	.455	0	—	-1	-1	-2	-0	0.0
Total 3	3	5	.375	34	15	1	0	0	114	123	16	48	53	13.7	4.50	78	.276	.349	1	.040	-1	-10	-13	-0	-0.9
● JAIME NAVARRO Navarro, Jaime (Cintron) b: 3/27/67, Bayamon, P.R. BR/TR, 6′4″, 210 lbs. Deb: 6/20/89 F																								
1989 Mil-A	7	8	.467	19	19	1	1	0	109²	119	6	32	56	12.5	3.12	123	.277	.328	0	—	0	9	9	-0	1.1
1990 Mil-A	8	7	.533	32	22	3	0	0	149¹	176	16	41	75	13.3	4.46	87	.293	.343	0	—	0	-9	-10	-0	-0.9
1991 Mil-A	15	12	.556	34	34	10	2	0	234	237	15	73	114	12.2	3.92	101	.261	.320	0	—	0	4	1	-1	0.0
1992 Mil-A	17	11	.607	34	34	5	3	0	246	224	14	64	100	10.8	3.33	115	.246	.299	0	—	0	17	14	-3	1.2
1993 Mil-A	11	12	.478	35	34	5	1	0	214¹	254	21	73	114	14.2	5.33	80	.300	.363	0	—	0	-24	-26	-1	-2.5

YEAR	TM/L	W	L	PCT	G	GS	CG	SH	SV	IP	H	HR	BB	SO	RAT	ERA	ERA+	OAV	OOB	BH	AVG	PB	PR	/A	PD	TPI
1994	Mil-A	4	9	.308	29	10	0	0	0	89²	115	10	35	65	15.5	6.62	74	.314	.380	0	—	0	-18	-17	0	-2.1
Total	6	62	59	.512	183	151	24	6	1	1043	1125	80	318	524	12.7	4.30	94	.277	.334	0	—	0	-21	-29	-7	-3.2

● JULIO NAVARRO
Navarro, Julio (Ventura) "Whiplash" b: 1/9/36, Vieques, P.R. BR/TR, 5'11", 190 lbs. Deb: 9/3/62 F

YEAR	TM/L	W	L	PCT	G	GS	CG	SH	SV	IP	H	HR	BB	SO	RAT	ERA	ERA+	OAV	OOB	BH	AVG	PB	PR	/A	PD	TPI
1962	LA-A	1	1	.500	9	0	0	0	0	15¹	20	2	4	11	14.1	4.70	82	.317	.358	1	.500	0	-1	-1	-0	-0.1
1963	LA-A	4	5	.444	57	0	0	0	12	90¹	75	7	32	53	10.9	2.89	119	.228	.300	3	.200	1	7	5	1	0.9
1964	LA-A	0	0	—	5	0	0	0	1	9¹	5	0	5	8	11.6	1.93	170	.167	.324	0	.000	-0	2	1	0	0.0
	Det-A	2	1	.667	26	0	0	0	2	41	40	9	16	36	12.7	3.95	93	.250	.326	0	.000	-1	-1	-1	-0	-0.2
	Yr	2	1	.667	31	0	0	0	3	50¹	45	9	21	44	12.2	3.58	100	.234	.316	0	.000	-1	0	0	0	-0.2
1965	Det-A	0	2	.000	15	1	0	0	1	30	25	5	12	22	11.1	4.20	83	.238	.316	0	.000	-0	-2	-2	0	-0.2
1966	Det-A	0	0	—	1	0	0	0	0	0	2	2	0	0	∞	∞	—	1.000	1.000	0	—	-0	-3	-3	0	-0.3
1970	Atl-N	0	0	—	17	0	0	0	1	26¹	24	7	1	21	8.9	4.10	105	.233	.248	1	.167	-0	-0	1	0	0.0
Total	6	7	9	.438	130	1	0	0	17	212¹	191	32	70	151	11.4	3.65	99	.241	.309	5	.147	-0	1	-1	1	0.1

● EARL NAYLOR
Naylor, Earl Eugene b: 5/19/19, Kansas City, Mo. d: 1/16/90, Winter Haven, Fla. BR/TR, 6', 190 lbs. Deb: 4/15/42 ♦

YEAR	TM/L	W	L	PCT	G	GS	CG	SH	SV	IP	H	HR	BB	SO	RAT	ERA	ERA+	OAV	OOB	BH	AVG	PB	PR	/A	PD	TPI
1942	Phi-N	0	5	.000	20	4	1	0	0	60¹	68	5	29	19	14.5	6.12	54	.286	.363	33	.196	1	-19	-19	-0	-1.4

● ROLLIE NAYLOR
Naylor, Roleine Cecil b: 2/4/1892, Crum, Tex. d: 6/18/66, Fort Worth, Tex. BR/TR, 6'1.5", 180 lbs. Deb: 9/14/17

YEAR	TM/L	W	L	PCT	G	GS	CG	SH	SV	IP	H	HR	BB	SO	RAT	ERA	ERA+	OAV	OOB	BH	AVG	PB	PR	/A	PD	TPI
1917	Phi-A	2	2	.500	5	5	3	0	0	33	30	1	11	11	11.5	1.64	168	.265	.336	1	.091	-1	4	4	1	0.6
1919	Phi-A	5	18	.217	31	23	17	0	0	204²	210	3	64	68	12.2	3.34	103	.280	.339	12	.169	-2	-3	2	-0	-0.1
1920	Phi-A	10	23	.303	42	36	20	0	0	251¹	306	7	86	90	14.3	3.47	116	.312	.371	14	.163	-6	9	15	2	1.4
1921	Phi-A	3	13	.188	32	19	6	0	0	169¹	214	10	55	39	14.5	4.84	92	.315	.369	6	.115	-4	-10	-7	-2	-1.1
1922	Phi-A	10	15	.400	35	26	11	0	0	171¹	212	7	51	37	14.0	4.73	90	.309	.359	11	.200	1	-13	-9	-1	-1.0
1923	Phi-A	12	7	.632	26	20	9	2	0	143	149	5	59	27	13.1	3.46	119	.273	.344	11	.244	1	8	10	-2	1.2
1924	Phi-A	0	5	.000	10	7	1	0	0	38¹	53	2	20	10	17.1	6.34	68	.333	.408	3	.375	1	-9	-9	0	-0.8
Total	7	42	83	.336	181	136	67	2	0	1011	1174	34	346	282	13.7	3.93	102	.300	.359	58	.177	-11	-14	7	1	0.2

● MIKE NAYMICK
Naymick, Michael John b: 9/6/17, Berlin, Pa. BR/TR, 6'8", 225 lbs. Deb: 9/24/39

YEAR	TM/L	W	L	PCT	G	GS	CG	SH	SV	IP	H	HR	BB	SO	RAT	ERA	ERA+	OAV	OOB	BH	AVG	PB	PR	/A	PD	TPI
1939	Cle-A	0	1	.000	2	1	1	0	0	4²	2	0	5	3	15.4	1.93	228	.188	.381	0	.000	-0	1	1	-0	0.2
1940	Cle-A	1	2	.333	13	4	0	0	0	30	36	1	17	15	16.8	5.10	83	.290	.389	1	.167	-0	-2	-3	1	-0.2
1943	Cle-A	4	4	.500	29	4	0	0	2	62²	32	3	47	41	11.8	2.30	135	.160	.328	3	.188	-0	7	6	1	0.8
1944	Cle-A	0	0	—	7	0	0	0	0	13	16	1	10	4	18.0	9.69	34	.314	.426	0	.000	-0	-9	-9	0	0.0
	StL-N	0	0	—	1	0	0	0	0	2	2	0	1	1	13.5	4.50	78	.333	.429	0	—	-0	-0	-0	0	0.0
Total	4	5	7	.417	52	9	1	0	2	112¹	89	5	80	64	14.0	3.93	89	.224	.362	4	.154	-1	-3	-6	1	0.8

● DENNY NEAGLE
Neagle, Dennis Edward b: 9/13/68, Gambrills, Md. BL/TL, 6'4", 200 lbs. Deb: 7/27/91

YEAR	TM/L	W	L	PCT	G	GS	CG	SH	SV	IP	H	HR	BB	SO	RAT	ERA	ERA+	OAV	OOB	BH	AVG	PB	PR	/A	PD	TPI
1991	Min-A	0	1	.000	7	3	0	0	0	20	28	3	7	14	15.7	4.05	105	.329	.380	0	—	0	0	-0	-0	-0.1
1992	*Pit-N	4	6	.400	55	6	0	0	2	86¹	81	9	43	77	13.1	4.48	77	.247	.338	0	.000	-1	-9	-10	-0	-1.4
1993	Pit-N	3	5	.375	50	7	0	0	1	81¹	82	10	37	73	13.5	5.31	76	.258	.341	0	.000	-2	-11	-11	-1	-1.3
1994	Pit-N	9	10	.474	24	24	2	0	0	137	135	18	49	122	12.3	5.12	83	.259	.326	8	.190	1	-14	-13	-0	-1.5
Total	4	16	22	.421	136	40	2	0	3	324²	326	40	136	286	13.0	4.93	81	.260	.336	8	.119	-2	-35	-34	-2	-4.3

● JACK NEAGLE
Neagle, John Henry b: 1/2/1858, Syracuse, N.Y. d: 9/20/04, Syracuse, N.Y. BR/TR, 5'6", 155 lbs. Deb: 7/8/1879 ♦

YEAR	TM/L	W	L	PCT	G	GS	CG	SH	SV	IP	H	HR	BB	SO	RAT	ERA	ERA+	OAV	OOB	BH	AVG	PB	PR	/A	PD	TPI
1879	Cin-N	0	1	.000	2	2	1	0	0	13	13	0	5	4	12.5	3.46	67	.241	.305	2	.167	-0	-1	-2	-0	-0.2
1883	Phi-N	1	7	.125	8	7	6	0	0	61¹	88	0	21	13	16.0	6.90	45	.315	.363	12	.164	-2	-26	-26	-1	-2.5
	Bal-a	1	4	.200	6	5	4	0	0	46	48	1	20	9	14.3	4.89	71	.252	.323	10	.286	1	-8	-7	-0	-0.5
	Pit-a	3	12	.200	16	16	12	0	0	114	156	9	25	41	14.3	5.84	55	.306	.338	19	.188	-1	-32	-33	-1	-3.3
	Yr	4	16	.200	22	21	16	0	0	160	204	10	45	50	14.0	5.57	59	.291	.334	29	.213	-0	-40	-41	-1	-3.8
1884	Pit-a	11	26	.297	38	38	37	2	0	326	354	6	70	85	12.2	3.73	90	.285	.300	22	.149	-6	-17	-13	-3	-1.9
Total	3	16	50	.242	70	68	60	2	0	560¹	659	16	141	152	13.1	4.59	72	.272	.317	65	.176	-8	-85	-81	-5	-8.4

● JOE NEALE
Neale, Joseph Hunt b: 5/7/1866, Wadsworth, Ohio d: 12/30/13, Akron, Ohio BR/TR, 5'8", 153 lbs. Deb: 6/21/1886 ♦

YEAR	TM/L	W	L	PCT	G	GS	CG	SH	SV	IP	H	HR	BB	SO	RAT	ERA	ERA+	OAV	OOB	BH	AVG	PB	PR	/A	PD	TPI
1886	Lou-a	0	1	.000	1	1	0	0	0	7	11	0	7	0	24.4	7.71	47	.393	.528	0	.000	-0	-3	-3	1	-0.3
1887	Lou-a	1	4	.200	5	4	4	0	0	41¹	60	4	15	11	16.8	6.97	63	.326	.383	1	.053	-2	-12	-12	0	-1.1
1890	StL-a	5	3	.625	10	9	8	0	0	69	53	4	15	23	9.4	3.39	127	.206	.261	2	.067	-3	4	7	-2	0.3
1891	StL-a	6	4	.600	15	11	9	1	1	110¹	109	4	36	24	12.4	4.24	99	.249	.317	6	.118	-3	-6	-0	2	-0.2
Total	4	12	12	.500	31	25	21	1	1	227²	233	12	73	58	12.7	4.59	93	.257	.322	9	.086	-9	-18	-8	1	-1.3

● RON NECCIAI
Necciai, Ronald Andrew b: 6/18/32, Gallatin, Pa. BR/TR, 6'5", 185 lbs. Deb: 8/10/52

YEAR	TM/L	W	L	PCT	G	GS	CG	SH	SV	IP	H	HR	BB	SO	RAT	ERA	ERA+	OAV	OOB	BH	AVG	PB	PR	/A	PD	TPI
1952	Pit-N	1	6	.143	12	9	0	0	0	54²	63	5	32	31	15.8	7.08	56	.296	.390	1	.059	-1	-20	-19	-0	-2.2

● RON NEGRAY
Negray, Ronald Alvin b: 2/26/30, Akron, Ohio BR/TR, 6'1", 185 lbs. Deb: 9/14/52

YEAR	TM/L	W	L	PCT	G	GS	CG	SH	SV	IP	H	HR	BB	SO	RAT	ERA	ERA+	OAV	OOB	BH	AVG	PB	PR	/A	PD	TPI
1952	Bro-N	0	0	—	4	1	0	0	0	13	15	0	6	5	13.8	3.46	105	.294	.357	0	.000	-0	0	0	-0	0.0
1955	Phi-N	4	3	.571	19	10	2	0	0	71²	71	13	21	30	11.6	3.52	113	.257	.310	0	.000	-3	4	4	0	0.0
1956	Phi-N	2	3	.400	39	4	0	0	3	66²	72	6	24	44	13.1	4.18	89	.280	.344	3	.429	1	-3	-3	0	-0.1
1958	LA-N	0	0	—	4	0	0	0	0	11¹	12	4	7	2	15.1	7.15	57	.279	.380	0	.000	-0	-4	-4	0	0.0
Total	4	6	6	.500	66	15	2	0	3	162²	170	23	57	81	12.6	4.04	95	.271	.333	3	.086	-3	-3	-3	-1	-0.1

● JIM NEHER
Neher, James Gilmore b: 2/5/1889, Rochester, N.Y. d: 11/11/51, Buffalo, N.Y. BR/TR, 5'11", 185 lbs. Deb: 9/10/12

YEAR	TM/L	W	L	PCT	G	GS	CG	SH	SV	IP	H	HR	BB	SO	RAT	ERA	ERA+	OAV	OOB	BH	AVG	PB	PR	/A	PD	TPI
1912	Cle-A	0	0	—	1	0	0	0	0	1	0	0	0	0	0.0	0.00	—	.000	.000	0	—	0	0	0	-0	0.0

● ART NEHF
Nehf, Arthur Neukom b: 7/31/1892, Terre Haute, Ind. d: 12/18/60, Phoenix, Ariz. BL/TL, 5'9.5", 176 lbs. Deb: 8/13/15

YEAR	TM/L	W	L	PCT	G	GS	CG	SH	SV	IP	H	HR	BB	SO	RAT	ERA	ERA+	OAV	OOB	BH	AVG	PB	PR	/A	PD	TPI
1915	Bos-N	5	4	.556	12	10	6	4	0	78¹	60	0	21	39	9.7	2.53	103	.214	.276	4	.143	-1	2	1	0	0.0
1916	Bos-N	7	5	.583	22	13	6	1	0	121	110	1	20	36	9.9	2.01	124	.244	.281	5	.125	-0	8	6	-1	0.5
1917	Bos-N	17	8	.680	38	23	17	5	0	233¹	197	4	39	101	9.3	2.16	118	.231	.268	12	.171	5	14	10	1	1.7
1918	Bos-N	15	15	.500	32	31	**28**	2	0	284¹	274	2	76	96	11.3	2.69	100	.259	.312	16	.168	1	2	-0	3	0.6
1919	Bos-N	8	9	.471	22	19	13	1	0	168²	151	6	40	53	10.5	3.09	92	.242	.294	13	.206	2	-3	-4	1	-0.1
	NY-N	9	2	.818	13	12	9	2	0	102	70	2	19	24	8.0	1.50	187	.196	.240	8	.229	3	16	15	-1	2.0
	Yr	17	11	.607	35	31	22	3	0	270²	221	8	59	77	9.4	2.49	114	.224	.269	21	.214	5	13	10	1	1.9
1920	NY-N	21	12	.636	40	33	22	4	0	280²	273	8	45	79	10.2	3.08	97	.260	.291	26	.268	5	2	-3	3	0.5
1921	*NY-N	20	10	.667	41	34	18	2	1	260²	266	18	55	67	11.2	3.63	101	.271	.321	18	.202	0	5	1	3	0.4
1922	*NY-N	19	13	.594	37	35	20	2	1	268¹	286	15	64	60	11.9	3.29	122	.276	.321	25	.255	4	24	21	1	2.5
1923	*NY-N	13	10	.565	34	27	7	1	2	196	219	14	49	50	12.4	4.50	85	.281	.326	12	.190	1	-11	-15	1	-1.3
1924	*NY-N	14	4	.778	30	21	11	0	2	171²	167	14	42	72	11.1	3.62	101	.254	.301	13	.228	6	5	1	2	0.9
1925	NY-N	11	9	.550	29	20	8	1	0	155	193	7	50	63	14.2	3.77	107	.308	.360	11	.216	1	9	5	2	0.3
1926	NY-N	0	0	—	2	0	0	0	0	1²	2	0	1	0	16.2	10.80	35	.286	.375	0	.000	-0	-1	-1	0	0.0
	Cin-N	0	1	.000	7	0	0	0	0	17	25	0	4	5	16.4	3.71	100	.379	.431	1	.200	0	-0	-0	0	0.0
	Yr	0	1	.000	9	0	0	0	0	18²	27	0	6	4	16.4	4.34	85	.357	.425	1	.167	-0	-1	-1	0	0.0
1927	Cin-N	3	5	.375	21	5	1	0	0	45¹	59	2	14	21	14.5	5.56	68	.319	.367	1	.077	-1	-8	-9	1	-1.5
	Chi-N	1	1	.500	8	2	1	1	0	26¹	25	0	9	12	11.6	1.37	283	.260	.324	3	.429	1	7	7	-0	0.7
	Yr	4	6	.400	29	7	2	1	0	71²	84	2	23	33	13.4	4.02	95	.299	.352	4	.200	-0	-1	-2	1	-0.8
1928	Chi-N	13	7	.650	31	21	10	2	0	176²	190	6	52	40	12.4	2.65	145	.281	.334	11	.190	2	26	24	1	2.8
1929	*Chi-N	8	5	.615	32	15	4	0	0	120²	148	11	49	27	14.1	5.59	83	.310	.365	13	.289	4	-12	-13	1	-0.8
Total	15	184	120	.605	451	320	182	28	13	2707²	2715	107	640	844	11.3	3.20	105	.265	.310	192	.210	34	85	45	17	9.7

YEAR TM/L	W	L	PCT	G	GS	CG	SH	SV	IP	H	HR	BB	SO	RAT	ERA	ERA+	OAV	OOB	BH	AVG	PB	PR	/A	PD	TPI

● **GARY NEIBAUER**   Neibauer, Gary Wayne b: 10/29/44, Billings, Mont. BR/TR, 6'3", 200 lbs. Deb: 4/12/69

YEAR TM/L	W	L	PCT	G	GS	CG	SH	SV	IP	H	HR	BB	SO	RAT	ERA	ERA+	OAV	OOB	BH	AVG	PB	PR	/A	PD	TPI
1969 *Atl-N	1	2	.333	29	0	0	0	0	57²	42	9	31	42	11.5	3.90	92	.204	.311	0	.000	-1	-2	-2	-0	-0.2
1970 Atl-N	0	3	.000	7	0	0	0	0	12²	11	0	8	9	13.5	4.97	86	.239	.352	0	.000	-0	-1	-1	-0	-0.2
1971 Atl-N	1	0	1.000	6	1	0	0	1	21	14	3	9	6	10.3	2.14	173	.187	.282	0	.000	-1	3	4	0	0.2
1972 Atl-N	0	0	—	8	0	0	0	0	17¹	27	6	6	8	17.7	7.27	52	.360	.415	0	.000	-0	-7	-7	-0	-0.1
Phi-N	0	2	.000	9	2	0	0	0	18²	17	1	14	7	15.4	5.30	68	.239	.372	1	.250	0	-4	-4	-0	-0.4
Yr	0	2	.000	17	2	0	0	0	36	44	7	20	15	16.3	6.25	59	.297	.385	1	.125	-0	-11	-10	-1	-0.5
1973 Atl-N	2	1	.667	16	1	0	0	0	21¹	24	3	19	9	19.0	7.17	55	.282	.425	1	.250	1	-8	-8	-1	-0.9
Total 5	4	8	.333	75	4	0	0	1	148²	135	22	87	81	13.8	4.78	78	.242	.350	-1	.069	-1	-20	-17	-2	-1.6

● **JIM NEIDLINGER**   Neidlinger, James Llewellyn b: 9/24/64, Vallejo, Cal. BB/TR, 6'4", 180 lbs. Deb: 8/1/90

YEAR TM/L	W	L	PCT	G	GS	CG	SH	SV	IP	H	HR	BB	SO	RAT	ERA	ERA+	OAV	OOB	BH	AVG	PB	PR	/A	PD	TPI
1990 LA-N	5	3	.625	12	12	0	0	0	74	67	4	15	46	10.1	3.28	111	.241	.282	3	.120	-0	4	3	1	0.2

● **AL NEIGER**   Neiger, Alvin Edward b: 3/26/39, Wilmington, Del. BL/TL, 6', 195 lbs. Deb: 7/30/60

YEAR TM/L	W	L	PCT	G	GS	CG	SH	SV	IP	H	HR	BB	SO	RAT	ERA	ERA+	OAV	OOB	BH	AVG	PB	PR	/A	PD	TPI
1960 Phi-N	0	0	—	6	0	0	0	0	12²	16	2	4	3	15.6	5.68	68	.340	.415	1	.500	0	-3	-3	-0	0.0

● **ERNIE NEITZKE**   Neitzke, Ernest Fredrich b: 11/13/1894, Toledo, Ohio d: 4/27/77, Sylvania, Ohio BR/TR, 5'10", 180 lbs. Deb: 6/2/21 ♦

YEAR TM/L	W	L	PCT	G	GS	CG	SH	SV	IP	H	HR	BB	SO	RAT	ERA	ERA+	OAV	OOB	BH	AVG	PB	PR	/A	PD	TPI
1921 Bos-A	0	0	—	2	0	0	0	0	7¹	8	0	4	1	14.7	6.14	69	.333	.429	6	.240	0	-2	-2	0	0.0

● **BOTS NEKOLA**   Nekola, Francis Joseph b: 12/10/06, New York, N.Y. d: 3/11/87, Rockville, Md. BL/TL, 5'11.5", 175 lbs. Deb: 7/19/29

YEAR TM/L	W	L	PCT	G	GS	CG	SH	SV	IP	H	HR	BB	SO	RAT	ERA	ERA+	OAV	OOB	BH	AVG	PB	PR	/A	PD	TPI
1929 NY-A	0	0	—	9	1	0	0	0	18²	21	0	15	2	17.4	4.34	89	.296	.419	2	.500	1	-0	-1	1	0.2
1933 Det-A	0	0	—	2	0	0	0	0	1¹	4	1	1	0	33.8	27.00	16	.500	.556	0	—	0	-3	-3	-0	0.0
Total 2	0	0	—	11	1	0	0	0	20	25	1	16	2	18.4	5.85	66	.316	.432	2	.500	1	-4	-4	1	0.2

● **RED NELSON**   Nelson, Albert Francis (b: Albert W. Horazdovsky)
b: 5/19/1886, Cleveland, Ohio d: 10/26/56, St.Petersburg, Fla BR/TR, 5'11", 190 lbs. Deb: 9/9/10

YEAR TM/L	W	L	PCT	G	GS	CG	SH	SV	IP	H	HR	BB	SO	RAT	ERA	ERA+	OAV	OOB	BH	AVG	PB	PR	/A	PD	TPI
1910 StL-A	5	1	.833	7	6	6	1	0	60	57	0	14	30	11.3	2.55	97	.261	.318	6	.261	2	-0	-1	4	0.6
1911 StL-A	3	9	.250	16	13	6	0	0	81	103	1	44	24	17.1	5.22	65	.324	.417	3	.111	-2	-17	-17	-1	-2.3
1912 StL-A	0	2	.000	8	3	0	0	1	18	21	0	13	9	17.0	7.00	47	.318	.430	1	.333	1	-7	-7	-1	-0.8
Phi-N	2	0	1.000	4	2	1	0	0	19¹	25	2	6	2	15.4	3.72	97	.305	.367	1	.100	-1	-1	-0	-0	-0.1
1913 Phi-N	0	0	—	2	0	0	0	0	8¹	9	0	4	3	14.0	2.16	154	.290	.371	1	.333	0	1	1	0	0.1
Cin-N	0	0	—	2	0	0	0	0	1²	6	1	4	0	59.4	37.80	9	.667	.786	0	—	0	-6	-6	-0	0.0
Yr	0	0	—	4	0	0	0	0	10	15	1	8	3	21.6	8.10	41	.375	.490	1	.333	0	-5	-5	0	0.1
Total 4	10	12	.455	39	24	13	1	1	188¹	221	4	85	68	15.3	4.54	68	.305	.389	12	.182	-1	-31	-30	2	-2.5

● **ANDY NELSON**   Nelson, Andrew "Peaches" TL, Deb: 5/26/08

YEAR TM/L	W	L	PCT	G	GS	CG	SH	SV	IP	H	HR	BB	SO	RAT	ERA	ERA+	OAV	OOB	BH	AVG	PB	PR	/A	PD	TPI
1908 Chi-A	0	0	—	2	1	0	0	0	9	11	0	4	1	16.0	2.00	116	.282	.364	0	.000	0	0	0	-1	-0.1

● **EMMETT NELSON**   Nelson, George Emmett "Ramrod" b: 2/26/05, Viborg, S.Dak. d: 8/25/67, Sioux Falls, S.D. BR/TR, 6'3", 180 lbs. Deb: 6/24/35

YEAR TM/L	W	L	PCT	G	GS	CG	SH	SV	IP	H	HR	BB	SO	RAT	ERA	ERA+	OAV	OOB	BH	AVG	PB	PR	/A	PD	TPI
1935 Cin-N	4	4	.500	19	7	3	1	1	60¹	70	2	23	14	14.2	4.33	92	.295	.363	2	.133	-1	-2	-2	1	-0.3
1936 Cin-N	1	0	1.000	6	1	0	0	0	17	24	1	4	3	15.4	3.18	120	.333	.377	1	.167	-0	2	1	-0	0.0
Total 2	5	4	.556	25	8	3	1	1	77¹	94	3	27	17	14.4	4.07	97	.304	.366	3	.143	-1	-0	-1	1	-0.3

● **JIM NELSON**   Nelson, James Lorin b: 7/4/47, Birmingham, Ala. BR/TR, 6', 180 lbs. Deb: 5/30/70

YEAR TM/L	W	L	PCT	G	GS	CG	SH	SV	IP	H	HR	BB	SO	RAT	ERA	ERA+	OAV	OOB	BH	AVG	PB	PR	/A	PD	TPI
1970 Pit-N	4	2	.667	15	10	1	1	0	68¹	64	5	38	42	13.8	3.42	114	.255	.360	4	.200	0	5	4	-1	0.2
1971 Pit-N	2	2	.500	17	2	0	0	0	34²	27	0	26	11	15.1	2.34	145	.225	.384	3	.500	2	4	4	-0	0.6
Total 2	6	4	.600	32	12	1	1	0	103	91	5	64	53	14.2	3.06	122	.245	.368	7	.269	2	9	8	-1	0.8

● **JEFF NELSON**   Nelson, Jeffrey Allan b: 11/17/66, Baltimore, Md. BR/TR, 6'8", 225 lbs. Deb: 4/16/92

YEAR TM/L	W	L	PCT	G	GS	CG	SH	SV	IP	H	HR	BB	SO	RAT	ERA	ERA+	OAV	OOB	BH	AVG	PB	PR	/A	PD	TPI
1992 Sea-A	1	7	.125	66	0	0	0	6	81	71	7	44	46	13.4	3.44	115	.245	.356	0	—	0	4	5	0	0.5
1993 Sea-A	5	3	.625	71	0	0	0	1	60	57	5	34	61	14.9	4.35	101	.258	.376	0	—	0	-0	0	1	0.1
1994 Sea-A	0	0	—	28	0	0	0	0	42¹	35	3	20	44	13.4	2.76	177	.226	.344	0	—	0	10	10	0	-0.1
Total 3	6	10	.375	165	0	0	0	7	183¹	163	15	98	151	13.9	3.58	121	.245	.360	0	—	0	14	15	1	0.5

● **LUKE NELSON**   Nelson, Luther Martin b: 12/4/1893, Cable, Ill. d: 11/14/85, Moline, Ill. BR/TR, 6', 180 lbs. Deb: 5/25/19

YEAR TM/L	W	L	PCT	G	GS	CG	SH	SV	IP	H	HR	BB	SO	RAT	ERA	ERA+	OAV	OOB	BH	AVG	PB	PR	/A	PD	TPI
1919 NY-A	3	0	1.000	9	1	0	0	0	24¹	22	1	11	11	12.6	2.96	108	.244	.333	1	.143	-0	1	1	-0	0.0

● **LYNN NELSON**   Nelson, Lynn Bernard "Line Drive" b: 2/24/05, Sheldon, N.Dak. d: 2/15/55, Kansas City, Mo. BL/TR, 5'10.5", 170 lbs. Deb: 4/18/30 ♦

YEAR TM/L	W	L	PCT	G	GS	CG	SH	SV	IP	H	HR	BB	SO	RAT	ERA	ERA+	OAV	OOB	BH	AVG	PB	PR	/A	PD	TPI
1930 Chi-N	3	2	.600	37	3	0	0	0	81¹	97	10	28	29	14.5	5.09	96	.300	.367	4	.222	0	-1	-2	1	0.1
1933 Chi-N	5	5	.500	24	3	3	0	1	75²	65	2	30	20	11.3	3.21	102	.232	.306	5	.238	2	1	1	1	0.3
1934 Chi-N	0	1	.000	2	1	0	0	0	1	4	1	1	0	45.0	36.00	11	.667	.714	0	—	0	-4	-4	-0	-1.9
1937 Phi-A	4	9	.308	30	4	1	0	2	116	140	12	51	49	15.0	5.90	80	.300	.371	40	.354	6	-16	-15	-2	-0.5
1938 Phi-A	10	11	.476	32	23	13	0	2	191	215	29	79	75	14.1	5.65	85	.277	.347	31	.277	4	-18	-17	-0	-1.1
1939 Phi-A	10	13	.435	35	24	12	2	1	197²	233	27	64	75	13.7	4.78	98	.292	.347	15	.188	-2	-4	-2	-1	-0.4
1940 Det-A	1	1	.500	6	2	0	0	0	14	23	5	9	7	20.6	10.93	44	.371	.451	8	.348	2	-10	-10	-0	-0.9
Total 7	33	42	.440	166	60	29	2	6	676²	777	86	262	255	14.0	5.25	88	.287	.353	103	.281	13	-52	-49	-1	-4.4

● **MEL NELSON**   Nelson, Melvin Frederick b: 5/30/36, San Diego, Cal. BR/TL, 6', 185 lbs. Deb: 9/27/60

YEAR TM/L	W	L	PCT	G	GS	CG	SH	SV	IP	H	HR	BB	SO	RAT	ERA	ERA+	OAV	OOB	BH	AVG	PB	PR	/A	PD	TPI
1960 StL-N	0	1	.000	2	1	0	0	0	8	7	1	2	7	10.1	3.38	121	.226	.273	1	.500	0	0	1	-0	0.1
1963 LA-A	2	3	.400	36	3	0	0	1	52²	55	7	32	41	15.2	5.30	65	.263	.366	1	.091	-1	-10	-11	1	-1.0
1965 Min-A	0	4	.000	28	3	0	0	3	54²	57	7	23	31	13.5	4.12	86	.261	.337	1	.111	-0	-4	-3	1	-0.4
1967 Min-A	0	0	—	1	0	0	0	0	0¹	3	1	0	0	81.0	54.00	6	.750	.750	0	—	0	-2	-2	0	0.0
1968 *StL-N	2	1	.667	18	4	1	0	1	52²	49	3	9	16	9.9	2.91	100	.254	.287	2	.167	0	0	-0	-0	0.0
1969 StL-N	0	1	.000	8	0	0	0	0	5¹	13	0	3	3	11.81	30	.520	.571	0	—	0	-5	-5	-0	-0.8
Total 6	4	10	.286	93	11	1	0	5	173²	184	19	69	98	13.3	4.40	76	.271	.341	5	.147	-1	-20	-21	0	-2.1

● **ROGER NELSON**   Nelson, Roger Eugene "Spider" b: 6/7/44, Altadena, Cal. BR/TR, 6'3", 205 lbs. Deb: 9/9/67

YEAR TM/L	W	L	PCT	G	GS	CG	SH	SV	IP	H	HR	BB	SO	RAT	ERA	ERA+	OAV	OOB	BH	AVG	PB	PR	/A	PD	TPI
1967 Chi-A	0	1	.000	5	0	0	0	0	7	4	1	0	4	7.7	1.29	241	.182	.250	0	—	0	2	1	0	0.2
1968 Bal-A	4	3	.571	19	6	0	0	1	71	49	3	26	70	9.6	2.41	121	.192	.270	1	.063	-0	5	4	-0	0.4
1969 KC-A	7	13	.350	29	29	8	1	0	193¹	170	12	65	82	11.2	3.31	112	.243	.313	8	.138	-1	7	8	-1	0.6
1970 KC-A	0	2	.000	4	2	0	0	0	9	18	3	0	3	19.0	10.00	37	.419	.432	0	—	0	-6	-6	0	-1.1
1971 KC-A	0	1	.000	13	1	0	0	0	34	35	1	5	29	10.6	5.29	65	.269	.296	2	.333	1	-7	-7	1	-0.4
1972 KC-A	11	6	.647	34	19	10	6	3	173¹	120	13	31	120	**7.9**	2.08	146	.196	**.236**	5	.093	-2	19	18	1	1.9
1973 *Cin-N	2	2	.600	14	8	1	0	0	54²	49	4	24	17	12.5	3.46	98	.246	.336	2	.111	-1	-0	1	0	0.0
1974 Cin-N	4	4	.500	14	12	1	0	0	85¹	67	4	35	36	10.9	3.38	103	.213	.293	5	.179	0	2	1	-1	0.0
1976 KC-A	0	0	—	3	0	0	0	0	8²	4	0	4	4	10.4	2.08	169	.138	.286	0	—	0	1	1	0	0.0
Total 9	29	32	.475	135	77	20	7	5	636¹	516	44	190	371	10.2	3.06	110	.224	.288	23	.128	-3	23	21	2	2.0

● **GENE NELSON**   Nelson, Wayland Eugene b: 12/3/60, Tampa, Fla. BR/TR, 6', 174 lbs. Deb: 5/4/81

YEAR TM/L	W	L	PCT	G	GS	CG	SH	SV	IP	H	HR	BB	SO	RAT	ERA	ERA+	OAV	OOB	BH	AVG	PB	PR	/A	PD	TPI
1981 NY-A	3	1	.750	8	7	0	0	0	39¹	40	5	23	16	14.6	4.81	74	.261	.362	0	—	0	-5	-5	-0	-0.5
1982 Sea-A	6	9	.400	22	19	2	1	0	122²	133	16	60	71	14.3	4.62	92	.279	.362	0	—	0	-7	-5	1	-0.5
1983 Sea-A	0	3	.000	10	5	0	0	0	32	38	6	21	11	16.9	7.88	54	.295	.397	0	—	0	-14	-13	1	-1.1
1984 Chi-A	3	5	.375	20	9	2	0	0	74²	73	9	17	36	10.8	4.46	93	.254	.299	0	—	0	-4	-3	0	-0.2
1985 Chi-A	10	10	.500	46	18	1	0	0	145²	144	23	67	101	13.5	4.26	101	.258	.345	0	.000	0	-2	1	0	0.1
1986 Chi-A	6	6	.500	54	1	0	0	1	114²	118	6	41	70	12.7	3.85	112	.271	.338	0	—	0	4	6	1	0.7
1987 Oak-A	6	5	.545	54	6	0	0	3	123²	120	12	35	94	11.6	3.93	105	.249	.307	0	—	0	7	3	-1	0.1

YEAR TM/L	W	L	PCT	G	GS	CG	SH	SV	IP	H	HR	BB	SO	RAT	ERA	ERA+	OAV	OOB	BH	AVG	PB	PR	/A	PD	TPI
1988 *Oak-A	9	6	.600	54	1	0	0	3	111²	93	9	38	67	10.8	3.06	123	.228	.298	0	—	0	11	9	-1	1.1
1989 *Oak-A	3	5	.375	50	0	0	0	3	80	60	5	30	70	10.3	3.26	113	.203	.280	0	—	0	6	4	-1	0.2
1990 *Oak-A	3	3	.500	51	0	0	0	5	74²	55	5	17	38	9.0	1.57	237	.208	.263	0	—	0	19	18	-1	1.6
1991 Oak-A	1	5	.167	44	0	0	0	0	48²	60	12	23	23	15.9	6.84	56	.306	.387	0	—	0	-15	-16	-1	-1.8
1992 Oak-A	3	1	.750	28	2	0	0	0	51²	68	5	22	23	15.7	6.45	58	.335	.400	0	—	0	-14	-16	-1	-1.1
1993 Cal-A	0	5	.000	46	0	0	0	4	52²	50	3	23	31	12.8	3.08	146	.251	.335	0	—	0	7	8	0	0.7
Tex-A			—	6	0	0	0	1	8	10	0	1	4	12.4	3.38	123	.303	.324	0	—	0	1	1	-0	0.2
Yr	0	5	.000	52	0	0	0	5	60²	60	3	24	35	12.5	3.12	143	.252	.321	0	—	0	8	9	0	0.9
Total 13	53	64	.453	493	68	6	1	28	1080	1061	117	418	655	12.6	4.13	98	.258	.331	0	.000	0	-5	-9	-3	-0.5

● **BILL NELSON**   Nelson, William F. b: 9/28/1863, Terre Haute, Ind. d: 6/23/41, Terre Haute, Ind. TR, Deb: 9/3/1884

YEAR TM/L	W	L	PCT	G	GS	CG	SH	SV	IP	H	HR	BB	SO	RAT	ERA	ERA+	OAV	OOB	BH	AVG	PB	PR	/A	PD	TPI
1884 Pit-a	1	2	.333	3	3	3	0	0	26	26	1	8	6	13.2	4.50	75	.252	.330	2	.167	-1	-4	-3	-0	-0.4

● **ROBB NEN**   Nen, Robert Allen b: 11/28/69, San Pedro, Cal. BR/TR, 6'4", 200 lbs. Deb: 4/10/93 F

YEAR TM/L	W	L	PCT	G	GS	CG	SH	SV	IP	H	HR	BB	SO	RAT	ERA	ERA+	OAV	OOB	BH	AVG	PB	PR	/A	PD	TPI
1993 Tex-A	1	1	.500	9	3	0	0	0	22²	28	1	26	12	21.4	6.35	65	.326	.482	0	—	0	-5	-6	0	-0.2
Fla-N	1	0	1.000	15	1	0	0	0	33¹	35	5	20	27	14.9	7.02	62	.255	.350	0	.000	-0	-11	-10	-0	-0.3
1994 Fla-N	5	5	.500	44	0	0	0	15	58	46	6	17	60	9.8	2.95	153	.222	.281	0	.000	-0	8	10	-0	2.1
Total 2	7	6	.538	68	4	0	0	15	114	109	12	63	99	13.6	4.82	91	.253	.349	0	.000	-1	-8	-6	-0	1.6

● **HAL NEUBAUER**   Neubauer, Harold Charles b: 5/13/02, Hoboken, N.J. d: 9/9/49, Barrington, R.I. BR/TR, 6'0.5", 185 lbs. Deb: 6/12/25

YEAR TM/L	W	L	PCT	G	GS	CG	SH	SV	IP	H	HR	BB	SO	RAT	ERA	ERA+	OAV	OOB	BH	AVG	PB	PR	/A	PD	TPI
1925 Bos-A	1	0	1.000	7	0	0	0	0	10¹	17	2	11	4	24.4	12.19	37	.378	.500	0	—	0	-9	-9	-0	-0.7

● **TEX NEUER**   Neuer, John S. b: 6/8/1877, Fremont, Ohio d: 1/14/66, Northumberland, Pa TL, Deb: 8/28/07

YEAR TM/L	W	L	PCT	G	GS	CG	SH	SV	IP	H	HR	BB	SO	RAT	ERA	ERA+	OAV	OOB	BH	AVG	PB	PR	/A	PD	TPI
1907 NY-A	4	2	.667	7	6	6	3	0	54	40	1	19	22	9.8	2.17	129	.208	.280	2	.095	-2	2	4	-1	0.1

● **DAN NEUMEIER**   Neumeier, Daniel George b: 3/9/48, Shawano, Wis. BR/TR, 6'5", 205 lbs. Deb: 9/8/72

YEAR TM/L	W	L	PCT	G	GS	CG	SH	SV	IP	H	HR	BB	SO	RAT	ERA	ERA+	OAV	OOB	BH	AVG	PB	PR	/A	PD	TPI
1972 Chi-A	0	0	—	3	0	0	0	0	3	2	0	3	0	15.0	9.00	35	.200	.385	0	.000	-0	-2	-2	-0	0.0

● **ERNIE NEVEL**   Nevel, Ernie Wyre b: 8/17/19, Charleston, Mo. d: 7/10/88, Springfield, Mo. BR/TR, 5'11", 190 lbs. Deb: 9/26/50

YEAR TM/L	W	L	PCT	G	GS	CG	SH	SV	IP	H	HR	BB	SO	RAT	ERA	ERA+	OAV	OOB	BH	AVG	PB	PR	/A	PD	TPI
1950 NY-A	0	1	.000	3	1	0	0	0	6¹	10	0	6	3	22.7	9.95	43	.345	.457	0	.000	-0	-4	-4	0	-0.5
1951 NY-A	0	0	—	1	0	0	0	1	4	1	0	1	1	4.5	0.00	—	.083	.154	0	.000	-0	2	2	-0	0.1
1953 Cin-N	0	0	—	10	0	0	0	0	10¹	16	0	1	5	14.8	6.10	71	.390	.405	0	—	0	-2	-2	-0	0.0
Total 3	0	1	.000	14	1	0	0	1	20²	27	0	8	9	15.2	6.10	69	.329	.389	0	.000	-0	-4	-4	0	-0.4

● **ERNIE NEVERS**   Nevers, Ernest Alonzo b: 6/11/02, Willow River, Minn. d: 5/3/76, San Rafael, Cal. BR/TR, 6', 205 lbs. Deb: 4/26/26

YEAR TM/L	W	L	PCT	G	GS	CG	SH	SV	IP	H	HR	BB	SO	RAT	ERA	ERA+	OAV	OOB	BH	AVG	PB	PR	/A	PD	TPI
1926 StL-A	2	4	.333	11	7	4	0	0	74²	82	4	24	16	12.9	4.46	96	.290	.347	5	.185	-1	-4	-1	2	0.0
1927 StL-A	3	8	.273	27	5	2	0	2	94²	105	8	35	22	13.5	4.94	88	.311	.379	7	.219	-1	-8	-6	1	-0.6
1928 StL-A	1	0	1.000	6	0	0	0	0	9	9	1	2	1	11.0	3.00	140	.281	.324	0	.000	-0	1	1	0	0.1
Total 3	6	12	.333	44	12	6	0	2	178¹	196	13	61	39	13.1	4.64	93	.300	.363	12	.200	-2	-11	-6	3	-0.5

● **DON NEWCOMBE**   Newcombe, Donald "Newk" b: 6/14/26, Madison, N.J. BL/TR, 6'4", 225 lbs. Deb: 5/20/49 ♦

YEAR TM/L	W	L	PCT	G	GS	CG	SH	SV	IP	H	HR	BB	SO	RAT	ERA	ERA+	OAV	OOB	BH	AVG	PB	PR	/A	PD	TPI
1949 *Bro-N★	17	8	.680	38	31	19	5	1	244¹	223	17	73	149	11.0	3.17	129	.243	.301	22	.229	3	24	25	1	2.8
1950 Bro-N★	19	11	.633	40	35	20	4	3	267¹	258	22	75	130	11.3	3.70	111	.254	.306	24	.247	7	13	12	-0	1.8
1951 Bro-N★	20	9	.690	40	36	18	3	0	272	235	19	91	164	11.0	3.28	120	.230	.297	23	.223	5	21	20	1	2.5
1954 Bro-N	9	8	.529	29	25	6	0	0	144¹	158	24	49	82	13.2	4.55	90	.274	.337	15	.319	4	-8	-1		-0.5
1955 *Bro-N★	20	5	.800	34	31	17	1	0	233²	222	35	38	143	10.1	3.20	127	.249	.280	42	.359	20	22	22	-2	4.2
1956 *Bro-N	27	7	.794	38	36	18	5	0	268	219	33	46	139	9.0	3.06	130	.221	.257	26	.234	8	21	27	0	4.3
1957 Bro-N	11	12	.478	28	28	12	4	0	198²	199	28	33	90	10.6	3.49	119	.258	.290	17	.230	5	9	15	1	2.2
1958 LA-N	0	6	.000	11	8	1	0	0	34¹	53	11	8	16	16.0	7.86	52	.346	.379	5	.417	2	-15	-14	0	-1.9
Cin-N	7	7	.500	20	18	7	0	1	133¹	159	20	28	53	12.7	3.85	108	.298	.335	21	.350	8	2	4	-2	1.1
Yr	7	13	.350	31	26	8	0	1	167²	212	31	36	69	13.4	4.67	89	.309	.344	26	.361	10	-13	-10	-2	-0.8
1959 Cin-N	13	8	.619	30	29	17	2	1	222	216	25	27	100	10.1	3.16	128	.253	.280	32	.305	15	19	22	-1	3.5
1960 Cin-N	4	6	.400	16	15	1	0	0	82²	99	12	14	36	12.6	4.57	84	.304	.338	5	.139	-0	-7	-7	-1	-0.9
Cle-A	2	3	.400	20	2	0	0	0	54	61	6	8	27	11.5	4.33	86	.289	.315	6	.300	2	-3	-4	-1	-0.2
Total 10	149	90	.623	344	294	136	24	7	2154²	2102	252	490	1129	11.0	3.56	114	.254	.299	238	.271	79	97	116	-6	18.9

● **TOM NEWELL**   Newell, Thomas Dean b: 5/17/63, Monrovia, Cal. BR/TR, 6'1", 185 lbs. Deb: 9/9/87

YEAR TM/L	W	L	PCT	G	GS	CG	SH	SV	IP	H	HR	BB	SO	RAT	ERA	ERA+	OAV	OOB	BH	AVG	PB	PR	/A	PD	TPI
1987 Phi-N	0	0	—	2	0	0	0	0	1	4	1	3	1	63.0	36.00	12	.571	.700	0	—	0	-4	-4	0	-0.4

● **DON NEWHAUSER**   Newhauser, Donald Louis b: 11/7/47, Miami, Fla. BR/TR, 6'4", 200 lbs. Deb: 6/15/72

YEAR TM/L	W	L	PCT	G	GS	CG	SH	SV	IP	H	HR	BB	SO	RAT	ERA	ERA+	OAV	OOB	BH	AVG	PB	PR	/A	PD	TPI
1972 Bos-A	4	2	.667	31	0	0	0	4	37	30	2	25	27	13.9	2.43	132	.226	.356	0	.000	-0	3	3	-0	0.6
1973 Bos-A	0	0	—	9	0	0	0	1	12	9	0	13	8	17.3	0.00	—	.205	.397	0	—	0	5	5	-0	0.4
1974 Bos-A	0	1	.000	2	0	0	0	0	3²	5	0	4	2	22.1	9.82	39	.357	.500	0	—	0	-3	-2	-0	-0.6
Total 3	4	3	.571	42	0	0	0	5	52²	44	2	42	37	15.2	2.39	144	.230	.377	0	.000	-0	5	6	-0	0.4

● **HAL NEWHOUSER**   Newhouser, Harold b: 5/20/21, Detroit, Mich. BL/TL, 6'2", 192 lbs. Deb: 9/29/39 H

YEAR TM/L	W	L	PCT	G	GS	CG	SH	SV	IP	H	HR	BB	SO	RAT	ERA	ERA+	OAV	OOB	BH	AVG	PB	PR	/A	PD	TPI
1939 Det-A	0	1	.000	1	1	1	0	0	5	3	0	4	4	12.6	5.40	91	.188	.350	0	—	-0	-0	-0	-1	-0.1
1940 Det-A	9	9	.500	28	20	7	0	0	133¹	149	12	76	89	15.3	4.86	98	.282	.374	8	.200	-1	-7	-2	2	-0.1
1941 Det-A	9	11	.450	33	27	5	1	0	173	166	6	137	106	15.8	4.79	95	.249	.378	9	.150	-2	-12	-5	2	-0.5
1942 Det-A☆	8	14	.364	38	23	11	1	5	183²	137	4	114	103	12.4	2.45	161	.207	.325	8	.154	-1	25	31	2	4.0
1943 Det-A★	8	17	.320	37	25	10	1	1	195²	163	3	111	144	12.6	3.04	116	.224	.327	12	.185	-1	6	11	3	1.6
1944 Det-A★	29	9	.763	47	34	25	6	2	312²	264	6	102	187	10.6	2.22	161	.230	.293	29	.242	3	42	47	1	6.5
1945 *Det-A†	25	9	.735	40	36	29	8	2	313¹	239	5	110	212	10.0	1.81	194	.211	.281	28	.257	4	54	59	3	7.8
1946 Det-A★	26	9	.743	37	34	29	6	1	292²	215	10	98	275	9.7	1.94	189	.201	.269	13	.126	-1	51	56	2	7.1
1947 Det-A★	17	17	.500	40	36	24	3	0	285	268	9	110	176	12.0	2.87	131	.249	.320	19	.198	2	26	28	3	3.9
1948 Det-A★	21	12	.636	39	35	19	2	1	272¹	249	10	99	143	11.5	3.01	145	.242	.309	19	.207	1	39	41	2	4.9
1949 Det-A	18	11	.621	38	35	22	3	1	292	277	19	111	144	12.0	3.36	108	.251	.319	18	.198	2	27	26	3	2.7
1950 Det-A	15	13	.536	35	30	15	1	3	213²	232	23	81	87	13.4	4.34	108	.279	.346	13	.176	-2	6	8	0	0.8
1951 Det-A	6	6	.500	15	14	7	1	0	96¹	98	10	19	37	11.2	3.92	106	.268	.310	8	.310	2	2	3	1	0.6
1952 Det-A	9	9	.500	25	19	5	0	0	154	148	13	47	57	11.4	3.74	102	.254	.310	10	.217	3	-1	1	1	0.5
1953 Det-A	0	1	.000	7	1	0	0	0	21²	31	4	8	6	17.0	7.06	58	.348	.414	4	.500	2	-7	-7	-0	-0.2
1954 *Cle-A	7	2	.778	26	1	0	0	7	46²	34	3	18	25	10.0	2.51	147	.209	.287	2	.154	-0	6	6	0	1.3
1955 Cle-A	0	0	—	2	0	0	0	0	2¹	1	0	4	1	19.3	0.00	—	.125	.417	0	—	0	1	1	-0	0.0
Total 17	207	150	.580	488	374	212	33	26	2993	2674	137	1249	1796	11.9	3.06	130	.239	.316	201	.201	12	257	305	22	40.8

● **FLOYD NEWKIRK**   Newkirk, Floyd Elmo "Three-Finger" b: 7/16/08, Norris City, Ill. d: 4/15/76, Clayton, Mo. BR/TR, 5'11", 178 lbs. Deb: 8/21/34 F

YEAR TM/L	W	L	PCT	G	GS	CG	SH	SV	IP	H	HR	BB	SO	RAT	ERA	ERA+	OAV	OOB	BH	AVG	PB	PR	/A	PD	TPI
1934 NY-A	0	0	—	1	0	0	0	0	1	1	0	1	0	18.0	0.00	—	.333	.500	0	—	0	0	0	0	0.0

● **JOEL NEWKIRK**   Newkirk, Joel Inez "Sailor" b: 5/1/1896, Kyana, Ind. d: 1/22/66, Eldorado, Ill. BR/TR, 6', 180 lbs. Deb: 8/20/19 F

YEAR TM/L	W	L	PCT	G	GS	CG	SH	SV	IP	H	HR	BB	SO	RAT	ERA	ERA+	OAV	OOB	BH	AVG	PB	PR	/A	PD	TPI
1919 Chi-N	0	0	—	1	0	0	0	0	2	2	0	3	1	27.0	13.50	21	.286	.545	0	.000	-0	-2	-2	0	0.0
1920 Chi-N	0	1	.000	2	1	0	0	0	6²	8	1	6	2	18.9	5.40	59	.333	.467	0	.000	-0	-2	-2	-1	-0.3
Total 2	0	1	.000	3	1	0	0	0	8²	10	1	9	3	20.8	7.27	43	.323	.488	0	.000	-1	-4	-4	0	-0.3

● **MAURY NEWLIN**   Newlin, Maurice Milton b: 6/22/14, Bloomingdale, Ind d: 8/14/78, Houston, Tex. BR/TR, 6', 176 lbs. Deb: 9/20/40

YEAR TM/L	W	L	PCT	G	GS	CG	SH	SV	IP	H	HR	BB	SO	RAT	ERA	ERA+	OAV	OOB	BH	AVG	PB	PR	/A	PD	TPI
1940 StL-A	1	0	1.000	1	1	0	0	0	6	4	1	2	3	9.0	6.00	76	.190	.261	1	.500	0	-1	-1	-0	-0.1

YEAR TM/L	W	L	PCT	G	GS	CG	SH	SV	IP	H	HR	BB	SO	RAT	ERA	ERA+	OAV	OOB	BH	AVG	PB	PR	/A	PD	TPI
1941 StL-A	0	2	.000	14	0	0	0	1	27²	43	4	12	10	17.9	6.51	66	.361	.420	0	.000	-1	-7	-7	1	-0.5
Total 2	1	2	.333	15	1	0	0	1	33²	47	5	14	13	16.3	6.42	68	.336	.396	1	.125	-1	-8	-8	0	-0.6

● FRED NEWMAN
Newman, Frederick William   b: 2/21/42, Boston, Mass.   d: 6/24/87, Framingham, Mass.   BR/TR, 6'3", 190 lbs.   Deb: 9/16/62

YEAR TM/L	W	L	PCT	G	GS	CG	SH	SV	IP	H	HR	BB	SO	RAT	ERA	ERA+	OAV	OOB	BH	AVG	PB	PR	/A	PD	TPI
1962 LA-A	0	1	.000	4	1	0	0	0	6¹	11	0	3	4	19.9	9.95	39	.393	.452	0	.000	-0	-4	-4	-0	-0.6
1963 LA-A	1	5	.167	12	8	0	0	0	44	56	6	15	16	14.9	5.32	64	.316	.376	4	.250	-1	-8	-9	-0	-1.1
1964 LA-A	13	10	.565	32	28	7	2	0	190	177	9	39	83	10.6	2.75	120	.246	.291	11	.180	2	19	11	4	2.1
1965 Cal-A	14	16	.467	36	36	10	2	0	260²	225	15	64	109	10.0	2.93	116	.234	.282	7	.095	-0	15	13	8	2.4
1966 Cal-A	4	7	.364	21	19	1	0	0	102²	112	7	31	42	13.1	4.73	71	.289	.351	6	.200	1	-15	-16	1	-1.4
1967 Cal-A	1	0	1.000	3	1	0	0	0	6¹	8	1	2	0	15.6	1.42	221	.320	.393	0	.000	-0	1	1	-0	0.2
Total 6	33	39	.458	108	93	18	4	0	610	589	38	154	254	11.2	3.41	99	.256	.308	28	.153	3	8	-3	12	1.6

● JEFF NEWMAN
Newman, Jeffrey Lynn   b: 9/11/48, Fort Worth, Tex.   BR/TR, 6'2", 218 lbs.   Deb: 6/30/76   MC♦

YEAR TM/L	W	L	PCT	G	GS	CG	SH	SV	IP	H	HR	BB	SO	RAT	ERA	ERA+	OAV	OOB	BH	AVG	PB	PR	/A	PD	TPI
1977 Oak-A	0	0	—	1	0	0	0	0	1	1	0	0	0	18.0	0.00	—	.250	.400	36	.222	0	0	0	0	0.0

● RAY NEWMAN
Newman, Raymond Francis   b: 6/20/45, Evansville, Ind.   BL/TL, 6'5", 205 lbs.   Deb: 5/16/71

YEAR TM/L	W	L	PCT	G	GS	CG	SH	SV	IP	H	HR	BB	SO	RAT	ERA	ERA+	OAV	OOB	BH	AVG	PB	PR	/A	PD	TPI
1971 Chi-N	1	2	.333	30	0	0	0	2	38¹	30	4	17	35	11.0	3.52	112	.219	.305	0	.000	-1	-0	2	0	0.1
1972 Mil-A	0	0	—	4	0	0	0	1	7	4	0	2	1	7.7	0.00	—	.182	.250	1	1.000	0	2	2	0	0.2
1973 Mil-A	2	1	.667	11	0	0	0	1	18¹	19	2	5	10	11.8	2.95	128	.260	.308	0	—	0	2	2	1	0.5
Total 3	3	3	.500	45	0	0	0	4	63²	53	6	24	46	10.9	2.97	128	.228	.301	1	.143	-0	4	6	1	0.8

● BOBO NEWSOM
Newsom, Louis Norman "Buck"   b: 8/11/07, Hartsville, S.C.   d: 12/7/62, Orlando, Fla.   BR/TR, 6'3", 200 lbs.   Deb: 9/11/29

YEAR TM/L	W	L	PCT	G	GS	CG	SH	SV	IP	H	HR	BB	SO	RAT	ERA	ERA+	OAV	OOB	BH	AVG	PB	PR	/A	PD	TPI
1929 Bro-N	0	3	.000	3	2	0	0	0	9¹	15	0	5	6	19.3	10.61	44	.375	.444	0	—	0	-6	-6	0	-1.3
1930 Bro-N	0	0	—	2	0	0	0	0	3	2	0	2	1	12.0	0.00	—	.167	.286	0	—	0	2	2	-0	0.0
1932 Chi-N	0	0	—	1	0	0	0	0	1	0	0	1	0	9.0	0.00	—	.333	.333	0	—	0	0	0	0	0.0
1934 StL-A	16	20	.444	47	32	15	2	5	262¹	259	15	149	135	14.1	4.01	124	.261	.358	17	.183	-3	14	29	0	3.2
1935 StL-A	0	6	.000	7	6	1	0	1	42²	54	2	13	22	14.1	4.85	99	.303	.351	1	.091	-1	-2	-0	0	-0.1
Was-A	11	12	.478	28	23	17	2	2	198¹	222	9	84	65	14.1	4.45	97	.288	.361	22	.301	4	0	-3	-3	-0.1
Yr	11	18	.379	35	29	18	2	3	241	276	11	97	87	14.1	4.52	97	.291	.359	23	.274	3	-2	-3	-2	-0.2
1936 Was-A	17	15	.531	43	38	24	4	2	285²	294	13	146	156	14.0	4.32	111	.268	.355	23	.213	0	23	15	1	1.4
1937 Was-A	3	4	.429	11	10	3	0	0	67²	76	4	48	39	16.9	5.85	76	.287	.402	3	.120	-1	-9	-11	0	-0.9
Bos-A	13	10	.565	30	27	14	1	0	207²	193	14	119	127	13.7	4.46	106	.243	.344	19	.253	2	4	6	-2	0.6
Yr	16	14	.533	41	37	17	1	0	275²	269	18	167	166	14.3	4.81	97	.253	.356	22	.220	1	-6	-4	-1	-0.3
1938 StL-A☆	20	16	.556	44	40	31	0	1	329²	334	13	192	226	14.5	5.08	98	.265	.364	31	.250	1	-11	-4	-3	-0.4
1939 StL-A	3	1	.750	6	6	3	0	0	45²	50	5	22	28	14.4	4.73	103	.266	.346	4	.222	-0	-1	1	0	0.0
Det-A☆	17	10	.630	35	31	21	3	2	246	222	14	104	164	12.0	3.37	145	.238	.316	18	.186	-4	34	42	-1	3.6
Yr	20	11	.645	41	37	24	3	2	291²	272	19	126	192	12.3	3.58	136	.243	.320	22	.191	-4	34	42	-1	3.6
1940 *Det-A★	21	5	.808	36	34	20	3	0	264	235	19	100	164	11.5	2.83	**168**	.238	.310	23	.215	-1	46	56	-3	4.6
1941 Det-A	12	20	.375	43	36	12	2	2	250¹	265	15	118	175	13.9	4.60	99	.264	.343	10	.102	-6	-13	-22	2	-0.9
1942 Was-A	11	17	.393	30	29	15	2	0	213²	236	6	92	**113**	13.9	4.93	74	.280	.353	12	.160	-2	-30	-30	-3	-3.8
Bro-N	2	2	.500	6	5	2	1	0	32	28	1	14	21	12.1	3.38	97	.235	.321	0	.000	-1	-0	-0	-1	-0.3
1943 Bro-N	9	4	.692	22	12	6	1	1	125	113	4	57	75	12.4	3.02	111	.244	.329	11	.250	1	5	5	0	0.6
StL-A	1	6	.143	10	9	0	0	0	52¹	69	7	35	37	18.1	7.39	45	.318	.415	4	.333	1	-24	-24	-1	-2.6
Was-A	3	3	.500	6	6	2	0	0	40	38	1	21	11	13.7	3.82	84	.247	.345	2	.133	-1	-2	-3	-1	-0.6
Yr	4	9	.308	16	15	2	0	0	92¹	107	8	56	48	16.1	5.85	56	.288	.384	7	.233	-0	-26	-26	-2	-3.2
1944 Phi-A★	13	15	.464	37	33	18	2	1	265	243	11	82	142	11.2	2.82	123	.244	.304	18	.114	-6	18	19	-1	1.3
1945 Phi-A	8	20	.286	36	34	16	3	0	257¹	255	12	103	127	12.6	3.29	104	.260	.332	14	.163	-4	2	4	-4	-0.4
1946 Phi-A	3	5	.375	10	9	3	1	0	58²	61	2	30	32	14.7	3.38	105	.266	.364	2	.105	-1	1	1	-1	0.0
Was-A	11	8	.579	24	22	14	2	1	178	163	5	60	82	11.4	2.78	120	.242	.306	10	.161	-2	14	11	-3	0.6
Yr	14	13	.519	34	31	17	3	1	236²	224	7	90	114	12.0	2.93	116	.247	.316	12	.148	-3	15	12	-4	0.6
1947 Was-A	4	6	.400	14	13	1	0	0	83²	99	2	37	40	14.7	4.09	91	.296	.368	7	.241	1	-4	-3	-2	-0.5
*NY-A	7	5	.583	17	15	6	2	0	115²	109	8	30	42	11.0	2.80	126	.250	.301	4	.095	-3	12	9	-2	0.4
Yr	11	11	.500	31	28	7	2	0	199¹	208	10	67	82	12.5	3.34	108	.270	.330	11	.155	-3	8	6	-3	-0.1
1948 NY-N	0	4	.000	11	4	0	0	0	25²	35	1	13	9	16.8	4.21	94	.330	.403	1	.429	1	-1	-1	-0	-0.1
1952 Was-A	1	1	.500	10	0	0	0	2	12²	16	2	9	5	17.8	4.97	72	.302	.403	0	.000	-0	-2	-2	0	-0.4
Phi-A	3	3	.500	14	5	1	0	1	47²	38	2	23	22	11.5	3.59	110	.220	.318	2	.133	-1	0	2	0	0.2
Yr	4	4	.500	24	5	1	0	3	60¹	54	4	32	27	13.1	3.88	100	.239	.338	2	.118	-1	-1	-0	1	-0.2
1953 Phi-A	2	1	.667	17	2	1	0	0	38²	44	3	24	16	17.0	4.89	88	.282	.395	1	.167	-0	-4	-3	0	-0.2
Total 20	211	222	.487	600	483	246	31	21	3759¹	3769	206	1732	2082	13.3	3.98	107	.261	.342	253	.189	-26	67	109	-29	3.9

● DICK NEWSOME
Newsome, Heber Hampton   b: 12/13/09, Ahoskie, N.C.   d: 12/15/65, Ahoskie, N.C.   BR/TR, 6', 185 lbs.   Deb: 4/25/41

YEAR TM/L	W	L	PCT	G	GS	CG	SH	SV	IP	H	HR	BB	SO	RAT	ERA	ERA+	OAV	OOB	BH	AVG	PB	PR	/A	PD	TPI
1941 Bos-A	19	10	.655	36	29	17	2	0	213²	235	13	79	58	13.5	4.13	101	.277	.344	19	.244	3	0	1	3	0.7
1942 Bos-A	8	10	.444	24	23	11	0	0	158	174	11	67	40	13.7	5.01	74	.278	.348	13	.236	-2	-24	-23	1	-2.0
1943 Bos-A	8	13	.381	25	22	8	2	0	154¹	166	8	68	40	13.9	4.49	74	.274	.352	7	.146	-1	-20	-20	-2	-2.8
Total 3	35	33	.515	85	74	36	4	0	526	575	32	214	138	13.7	4.50	84	.276	.347	39	.215	3	-44	-42	2	-4.1

● DOC NEWTON
Newton, Eustace James   b: 10/26/1877, Indianapolis, Ind.   d: 5/14/31, Memphis, Tenn.   BL/TL, 6', 185 lbs.   Deb: 4/27/00

YEAR TM/L	W	L	PCT	G	GS	CG	SH	SV	IP	H	HR	BB	SO	RAT	ERA	ERA+	OAV	OOB	BH	AVG	PB	PR	/A	PD	TPI
1900 Cin-N	9	15	.375	35	27	22	1	0	234²	255	4	100	88	14.1	4.14	89	.276	.355	17	.198	-1	-12	-12	-2	-1.3
1901 Cin-N	4	13	.235	20	18	17	0	0	168¹	190	6	59	65	14.1	4.12	78	.282	.353	9	.130	-4	-15	-17	1	-1.8
Bro-N	6	5	.545	13	12	9	0	0	105	110	1	30	45	12.6	2.83	119	.268	.328	9	.220	1	6	6	-0	0.6
Yr	10	18	.357	33	30	26	0	0	273¹	300	7	89	110	13.0	3.62	90	.273	.332	18	.164	-4	-9	-11	1	-1.2
1902 Bro-N	15	14	.517	31	28	26	4	2	264¹	208	2	87	107	10.4	2.42	114	**.217**	.289	19	.174	-1	11	10	-2	0.8
1905 NY-A	2	2	.500	11	7	2	0	0	59²	61	1	24	15	13.1	2.11	139	.266	.340	3	.136	-1	4	5	-1	0.1
1906 NY-A	7	5	.583	21	15	6	2	0	125	118	3	33	52	11.4	3.17	94	.252	.311	9	.220	-0	-7	-3	2	-0.1
1907 NY-A	7	10	.412	19	15	10	0	0	133	132	6	31	70	11.5	3.18	88	.261	.312	4	.108	-1	-9	-6	1	-0.8
1908 NY-A	4	5	.444	23	13	6	1	1	88¹	77	0	41	49	12.8	2.95	84	.242	.341	4	.160	-0	-5	-5	0	-0.5
1909 NY-A	0	3	.000	4	4	1	0	0	22¹	27	0	11	11	16.5	2.82	90	.300	.394	1	.167	0	-1	-1	1	0.0
Total 8	54	72	.429	177	139	99	8	3	1200²	1179	17	416	502	12.5	3.22	95	.257	.329	75	.172	-9	-29	-19	-2	-3.0

● KID NICHOLS
Nichols, Charles Augustus   b: 9/14/1869, Madison, Wis.   d: 4/11/53, Kansas City, Mo.   BB/TR, 5'10.5", 175 lbs.   Deb: 4/23/1890   MH

YEAR TM/L	W	L	PCT	G	GS	CG	SH	SV	IP	H	HR	BB	SO	RAT	ERA	ERA+	OAV	OOB	BH	AVG	PB	PR	/A	PD	TPI
1890 Bos-N	27	19	.587	48	47	47	**7**	0	424	374	8	112	222	10.5	2.23	168	.229	.284	43	.247	1	63	**72**	0	6.7
1891 Bos-N	30	17	.638	52	48	45	5	3	425¹	413	15	103	240	11.3	2.39	**153**	.245	.295	36	.197	-3	**45**	**60**	6	5.8
1892 *Bos-N	35	16	.686	53	51	49	5	0	453	404	15	121	187	10.6	2.84	124	.229	.283	39	.198	1	22	34	-1	3.2
1893 Bos-N	34	14	.708	52	44	43	1	1	425	426	15	118	94	11.8	3.52	140	.253	.308	39	.220	-2	54	67	-2	5.5
1894 Bos-N	32	13	.711	50	46	40	**3**	0	407	488	23	121	113	13.7	4.75	120	.294	.345	50	.294	3	26	42	0	3.5
1895 Bos-N	26	16	.619	47	42	42	3	**3**	379²	417	15	86	140	12.0	3.41	149	.275	.316	37	.236	-4	58	71	-0	5.6
1896 Bos-N	**30**	14	.682	49	43	37	3	1	372²	387	14	101	102	12.0	2.83	161	.266	.317	28	.190	-3	**63**	71	2	6.6
1897 *Bos-N	**31**	11	.738	**46**	40	37	2	**3**	368	362	9	68	127	**10.6**	2.64	**169**	.255	**.291**	39	.265	4	68	75	-2	7.3
1898 Bos-N	**31**	12	.721	**50**	44	40	5	**4**	388	316	7	85	138	**9.6**	2.13	173	**.221**	**.272**	64	.241	3	64	67	-2	6.9
1899 Bos-N	21	19	.525	42	37	37	4	1	343¹	326	11	82	108	10.9	2.99	139	.250	.298	26	.191	-5	33	45	-1	3.9
1900 Bos-N	13	16	.448	29	27	25	**4**	0	231¹	215	14	72	53	11.6	3.07	134	.246	.311	18	.200	-2	16	27	-1	2.6
1901 Bos-N	19	16	.543	38	34	33	4	0	321	306	8	90	143	11.4	3.22	112	.250	.306	46	.282	1	4	-14	-1	2.3
1904 StL-N	21	13	.618	36	35	35	3	1	317	268	3	50	134	9.2	2.02	134	.237	.256	17	.156	-1	25	24	-1	2.4
1905 StL-N	1	5	.167	7	7	5	0	0	51²	64	1	18	16	14.3	5.40	55	.296	.350	5	.227	0	-14	-14	-1	-1.4

YEAR	TM/L	W	L	PCT	G	GS	CG	SH	SV	IP	H	HR	BB	SO	RAT	ERA	ERA+	OAV	OOB	BH	AVG	PB	PR	/A	PD	TPI
	Phi-N	10	6	.625	17	16	15	1	0	138²	129	1	28	50	10.4	2.27	129	.250	.294	10	.189	0	11	10	-4	0.7
	Yr	11	11	.500	24	23	20	1	0	190¹	193	2	46	66	11.5	3.12	94	.264	.311	15	.200	0	-2	-4	-5	-0.7
1906	Phi-N	0	1	.000	4	2	1	0	0	11	17	0	13	1	26.2	9.82	27	.386	.542	0	.000	-0	-9	-9	-1	-0.8
Total	15	361	208	.634	620	561	531	48	17	5056¹	4912	156	1268	1868	11.2	2.95	139	.250	.300	471	.226	-0	531	653	-9	60.9

● **CHET NICHOLS**   Nichols, Chester Raymond Jr. b: 2/22/31, Pawtucket, R.I. BB/TL, 6'1.5", 195 lbs. Deb: 4/19/51 F

YEAR	TM/L	W	L	PCT	G	GS	CG	SH	SV	IP	H	HR	BB	SO	RAT	ERA	ERA+	OAV	OOB	BH	AVG	PB	PR	/A	PD	TPI
1951	Bos-N	11	8	.579	33	19	12	3	2	156	142	4	69	71	12.2	**2.88**	127	.246	.327	7	.137	-2	19	14	2	1.5
1954	Mil-N	9	11	.450	35	20	5	1	1	122¹	132	5	65	55	14.8	4.41	84	.286	.379	3	.086	-3	-5	-9	1	-1.5
1955	Mil-N	9	8	.529	34	21	6	0	1	144	139	20	67	44	12.9	4.00	94	.253	.335	8	.154	-2	1	-4	2	-0.5
1956	Mil-N	0	1	.000	2	0	0	0	0	4	9	1	3	2	27.0	6.75	51	.563	.632	0	.000	-0	-1	-1	0	-0.3
1960	Bos-A	0	2	.000	6	1	0	0	0	12²	12	0	4	11	11.4	4.26	95	.240	.296	0	.000	-0	-1	-0	0	0.0
1961	Bos-A	3	2	.600	26	2	0	0	3	51²	40	3	26	20	11.5	2.09	199	.221	.319	1	.111	-0	11	12	3	1.5
1962	Bos-A	1	1	.500	29	1	0	0	3	57	61	3	22	33	13.1	3.00	138	.276	.342	0	.000	-1	6	7	1	0.4
1963	Bos-A	1	3	.250	21	7	0	0	0	52²	61	8	24	27	14.5	4.78	79	.298	.371	3	.231	-0	-7	-6	-0	-0.4
1964	Cin-N	0	0	—	3	0	0	0	0	3	4	1	0	3	12.0	6.00	60	.308	.308	0	—	0	-1	-1	-0	0.0
Total	9	34	36	.486	189	71	23	4	10	603¹	600	45	280	266	13.2	3.64	105	.264	.346	22	.127	-8	22	11	8	0.7

● **CHET NICHOLS**   Nichols, Chester Raymond Sr. "Nick" b: 7/3/1897, Woonsocket, R.I. d: 7/11/82, Pawtucket, R.I. BR/TR, 5'11", 160 lbs. Deb: 7/30/26 F

YEAR	TM/L	W	L	PCT	G	GS	CG	SH	SV	IP	H	HR	BB	SO	RAT	ERA	ERA+	OAV	OOB	BH	AVG	PB	PR	/A	PD	TPI
1926	Pit-N	0	0	—	3	0	0	0	0	7²	13	0	5	2	21.1	8.22	48	.342	.419	1	.333	0	-4	-4	0	0.0
1927	Pit-N	0	3	.000	8	0	0	0	0	27²	34	1	17	9	16.9	5.86	70	.309	.406	1	.111	-0	-6	-5	-0	-0.6
1928	NY-N	0	0	—	3	0	0	0	0	2²	11	0	3	1	50.6	23.63	17	.611	.682	0	—	0	-6	-6	0	-0.1
1930	Phi-N	1	2	.333	16	5	1	0	0	59²	76	8	16	15	14.2	6.79	80	.306	.353	6	.300	0	-12	-9	1	-0.2
1931	Phi-N	0	1	.000	3	0	0	0	0	5²	10	0	1	1	17.5	9.53	45	.435	.458	0	.000	-0	-4	-3	0	-0.5
1932	Phi-N	0	2	.000	11	0	0	0	1	19¹	23	2	14	5	17.2	6.98	63	.299	.407	0	.000	-1	-7	-6	0	-0.6
Total	6	1	8	.111	44	5	1	0	1	122²	167	11	56	33	16.7	7.19	67	.325	.395	8	.211	-1	-38	-33	1	-1.9

● **DOLAN NICHOLS**   Nichols, Dolan Levon "Nick" b: 2/28/30, Tishomingo, Miss. d: 11/20/89, Tupelo, Miss. BR/TR, 6', 195 lbs. Deb: 4/15/58

YEAR	TM/L	W	L	PCT	G	GS	CG	SH	SV	IP	H	HR	BB	SO	RAT	ERA	ERA+	OAV	OOB	BH	AVG	PB	PR	/A	PD	TPI
1958	Chi-N	0	4	.000	24	0	0	0	1	41¹	46	1	16	9	13.7	5.01	78	.295	.364	0	.000	-1	-5	-5	1	-0.4

● **TRICKY NICHOLS**   Nichols, Frederick C. b: 7/26/1850, Bridgeport, Conn. d: 8/22/1897, Bridgeport, Conn. BR/TR, 5'7.5", 150 lbs. Deb: 4/21/1875

YEAR	TM/L	W	L	PCT	G	GS	CG	SH	SV	IP	H	HR	BB	SO	RAT	ERA	ERA+	OAV	OOB	BH	AVG	PB	PR	/A	PD	TPI
1875	NH-n	4	29	.121	34	33	30	0	0	288	319	2	10		10.3	3.03	76	.243	.248	23	.192	-2	-18	-24		-2.1
1876	Bos-N	1	0	1.000	1	1	1	0	0	9	7	0	0	1	7.0	1.00	226	.200	.200	0	.000	-1	1	1	0	0.1
1877	StL-N	18	23	.439	42	39	35	1	0	350	376	2	53	80	11.0	2.60	100	.263	.289	31	.167	-6	8	-0		-0.6
1878	Pro-N	4	7	.364	11	10	10	0	0	98	157	4	8	21	15.2	4.22	52	.344	.356	9	.184	-0	-21	-22	2	-1.8
1880	Wor-N	0	2	.000	2	2	2	0	0	17²	29	0	4	4	16.8	4.08	64	.358	.388	0	.000	-1	-3	-3	-1	-0.4
1882	Bal-a	1	12	.077	16	13	12	0	0	118¹	155	2	17	21	13.1	5.02	55	.296	.319	15	.158	-2	-31	-30	-2	-2.7
Total	5	24	44	.353	72	65	60	1	0	593	724	4	82	126	12.2	3.37	76	.287	.309	55	.161	-10	-45	-53	-1	-5.4

● **ROD NICHOLS**   Nichols, Rodney Lea b: 12/29/64, Burlington, Iowa BR/TR, 6'2", 190 lbs. Deb: 7/30/88

YEAR	TM/L	W	L	PCT	G	GS	CG	SH	SV	IP	H	HR	BB	SO	RAT	ERA	ERA+	OAV	OOB	BH	AVG	PB	PR	/A	PD	TPI
1988	Cle-A	1	7	.125	11	10	3	0	0	69¹	73	5	23	31	12.7	5.06	81	.272	.334	0	—	0	-8	-7	-0	-0.8
1989	Cle-A	4	6	.400	15	11	0	0	0	71²	81	9	24	42	13.4	4.40	90	.285	.345	0	—	0	-4	-3	-0	-0.6
1990	Cle-A	0	3	.000	4	2	0	0	0	16	24	5	6	3	18.0	7.88	50	.343	.410	0	—	0	-7	-7	0	-1.0
1991	Cle-A	2	11	.154	31	16	3	1	1	137¹	145	6	30	76	11.9	3.54	117	.273	.319	0	—	0	8	9	-1	0.7
1992	Cle-A	4	3	.571	30	9	0	0	0	105¹	114	13	31	56	12.6	4.53	86	.273	.327	0	—	0	-7	-7	-0	-0.4
1993	LA-N	0	1	.000	4	0	0	0	0	6¹	9	1	2	3	15.6	5.68	67	.360	.407	0	—	0	-1	-1	0	-0.1
Total	6	11	31	.262	95	48	6	1	1	406	446	39	116	211	12.8	4.41	91	.279	.334	0	—	0	-19	-17	-1	-2.2

● **FRANK NICHOLSON**   Nicholson, Frank Collins b: 8/29/1889, Berlin, Pa. d: 11/10/72, Jersey Shore, Pa. BR/TR, 6'2", 175 lbs. Deb: 9/6/12

YEAR	TM/L	W	L	PCT	G	GS	CG	SH	SV	IP	H	HR	BB	SO	RAT	ERA	ERA+	OAV	OOB	BH	AVG	PB	PR	/A	PD	TPI
1912	Phi-N	0	0	—	2	0	0	0	0	4	8	1	2	1	22.5	6.75	54	.471	.526	0	—	0	-1	-1	0	0.0

● **GEORGE NICOL**   Nicol, George Edward b: 10/17/1870, Barry, Ill. d: 8/10/24, Milwaukee, Wis. TL, 5'7", 155 lbs. Deb: 9/23/1890 ♦

YEAR	TM/L	W	L	PCT	G	GS	CG	SH	SV	IP	H	HR	BB	SO	RAT	ERA	ERA+	OAV	OOB	BH	AVG	PB	PR	/A	PD	TPI
1890	StL-a	2	1	.667	3	3	2	0	0	17	11	1	19	16	16.9	4.76	91	.179	.389	2	.286	1	-2	-1	-0	0.0
1891	Chi-N	0	1	.000	3	2	0	0	0	11	14	0	10	12	20.5	4.91	68	.299	.432	2	.333	1	-2	-2	-1	-0.1
1894	Pit-N	3	4	.429	8	5	3	0	0	44¹	57	2	33	11	19.3	6.50	81	.309	.427	9	.450	2	-6	-6	-1	-0.6
	Lou-N	0	1	1.000	1	1	1	0	0	9	19	2	5	3	25.0	15.00	34	.423	.491	38	.352	0	-10	-10	-0	-0.6
	Yr	3	5	.375	9	6	4	0	0	53¹	76	4	38	14	19.4	7.93	66	.324	.420	47	.367	2	-15	-16	-1	-1.2
Total	3	5	7	.417	15	11	6	0	0	81¹	101	5	67	42	19.6	6.86	70	.299	.428	51	.362	5	-19	-19	-2	-1.3

● **DAVID NIED**   Nied, David Glen b: 12/22/68, Dallas, Texas BR/TR, 6'2", 175 lbs. Deb: 9/1/92

YEAR	TM/L	W	L	PCT	G	GS	CG	SH	SV	IP	H	HR	BB	SO	RAT	ERA	ERA+	OAV	OOB	BH	AVG	PB	PR	/A	PD	TPI
1992	Atl-N	3	0	1.000	6	2	0	0	0	23	10	0	5	19	5.9	1.17	312	.130	.183	2	.286	0	6	6	-0	0.9
1993	Col-N	5	9	.357	16	16	1	0	0	87	99	8	42	46	14.7	5.17	92	.296	.376	4	.174	0	-11	-4	1	-0.5
1994	Col-N	9	7	.563	22	22	2	1	0	122	137	15	47	74	13.9	4.80	104	.287	.356	4	.100	-2	-8	-2	-2	-0.1
Total	3	17	16	.515	44	40	3	1	0	232	246	23	94	139	13.4	4.58	104	.277	.349	10	.143	-2	-13	5	-1	0.3

● **TOM NIEDENFUER**   Niedenfuer, Thomas Edward b: 8/13/59, St.Louis Park, Minn. BR/TR, 6'5", 225 lbs. Deb: 8/15/81

YEAR	TM/L	W	L	PCT	G	GS	CG	SH	SV	IP	H	HR	BB	SO	RAT	ERA	ERA+	OAV	OOB	BH	AVG	PB	PR	/A	PD	TPI
1981	*LA-N	3	1	.750	17	0	0	0	2	26	25	1	6	12	11.1	3.81	87	.258	.308	0	—	0	-1	-1	-0	-0.3
1982	LA-N	3	4	.429	55	0	0	0	9	69²	71	3	25	60	12.7	2.71	128	.269	.337	0	.000	-0	7	6	-1	0.6
1983	*LA-N	8	3	.727	66	0	0	0	11	94²	55	6	29	66	8.1	1.90	189	.170	.240	0	.000	-0	18	18	-1	2.3
1984	LA-N	2	5	.286	33	0	0	0	11	47¹	39	3	23	45	12.2	2.47	143	.227	.325	0	.000	-0	6	6	-0	1.0
1985	*LA-N	7	9	.438	64	0	0	0	19	106¹	86	4	24	102	9.4	2.71	128	.223	.270	1	.111	-0	10	9	-1	1.5
1986	LA-N	6	6	.500	60	0	0	0	11	80	86	11	29	55	13.0	3.71	93	.280	.344	2	.500	1	0	-2	0	-0.3
1987	LA-N	1	0	1.000	15	0	0	0	1	16¹	13	1	9	10	12.7	2.76	144	.220	.333	0	—	0	2	2	0	0.2
	Bal-A	3	5	.375	45	0	0	0	13	52¹	55	11	22	37	13.4	4.99	88	.266	.339	0	—	0	-3	-3	-1	-0.7
1988	Bal-A	3	4	.429	52	0	0	0	18	59	59	3	19	40	12.2	3.51	111	.259	.321	0	—	0	3	3	-1	0.4
1989	Sea-A	0	3	.000	25	0	0	0	0	36¹	46	7	15	15	15.4	6.69	60	.309	.376	0	—	0	-11	-11	0	-1.0
1990	StL-N	0	6	.000	52	0	0	0	2	65	66	3	25	32	12.6	3.46	110	.269	.337	0	.000	-0	2	3	-1	0.1
Total	10	36	46	.439	484	0	0	0	97	653	601	60	226	474	11.6	3.29	112	.247	.314	3	.115	-1	34	28	-5	3.8

● **DICK NIEHAUS**   Niehaus, Richard J. b: 10/24/1892, Covington, Ky. d: 3/12/57, Atlanta, Ga. BL/TL, 5'11", 165 lbs. Deb: 9/9/13

YEAR	TM/L	W	L	PCT	G	GS	CG	SH	SV	IP	H	HR	BB	SO	RAT	ERA	ERA+	OAV	OOB	BH	AVG	PB	PR	/A	PD	TPI
1913	StL-N	0	2	.000	3	3	2	0	0	24	20	1	13	4	12.4	4.13	78	.241	.344	2	.286	1	-2	-2	0	-0.1
1914	StL-N	1	0	1.000	8	1	1	0	0	17¹	18	1	8	6	13.5	3.12	90	.269	.347	1	.250	1	-1	-1	-1	0.0
1915	StL-N	2	1	.667	15	2	0	0	0	45¹	48	3	22	21	14.1	3.97	70	.281	.366	1	.071	-1	-6	-6	-1	-0.4
1920	Cle-A	1	2	.333	19	3	0	0	2	40	42	0	16	12	13.3	3.60	106	.269	.341	4	.444	2	1	1	-1	0.1
Total	4	4	5	.444	45	9	3	0	2	126²	128	4	59	43	13.4	3.77	85	.268	.351	8	.235	2	-8	-8	-0	-0.4

● **JOE NIEKRO**   Niekro, Joseph Franklin b: 11/7/44, Martins Ferry, Ohio BR/TR, 6'1", 190 lbs. Deb: 4/16/67 F

YEAR	TM/L	W	L	PCT	G	GS	CG	SH	SV	IP	H	HR	BB	SO	RAT	ERA	ERA+	OAV	OOB	BH	AVG	PB	PR	/A	PD	TPI
1967	Chi-N	10	7	.588	36	22	7	2	0	169²	171	15	32	77	10.9	3.34	106	.257	.293	9	.196	-1	1	4	-1	0.4
1968	Chi-N	14	10	.583	34	29	2	1	2	177	204	18	59	65	13.5	4.32	73	.294	.351	6	.100	-2	-26	-23	0	-3.2
1969	Chi-N	0	1	.000	4	3	0	0	0	19¹	24	1	6	7	14.0	3.72	108	.304	.353	1	.200	-0	0	1	1	0.1
	SD-N	8	17	.320	37	31	8	3	0	202	213	15	45	55	11.5	3.70	96	.273	.312	6	.118	0	-2	-4	-1	-0.5
	Yr	8	18	.308	41	34	8	3	0	221¹	237	18	51	62	11.7	3.70	97	.275	.316	7	.125	0	-3	-3	-1	-0.4
1970	Det-A	12	13	.480	38	34	6	2	0	213	221	28	72	101	12.5	4.06	92	.266	.327	13	.197	4	-8	-8	1	-0.4
1971	Det-A	6	7	.462	31	15	0	0	0	122¹	136	14	49	43	13.8	4.49	80	.283	.352	4	.133	-0	-14	-12	1	-1.2
1972	Det-A	3	2	.600	18	7	1	0	1	47	62	3	8	24	13.6	3.83	82	.330	.360	6	.250	-1	-4	-4	-0	-0.3
1973	Atl-N	2	4	.333	20	0	0	0	3	24	23	2	11	12	12.8	4.13	95	.277	.362	1	.333	0	-1	-1	1	-0.1

YEAR	TM/L	W	L	PCT	G	GS	CG	SH	SV	IP	H	HR	BB	SO	RAT	ERA	ERA+	OAV	OOB	BH	AVG	PB	PR	/A	PD	TPI
1974	Atl-N	3	2	.600	27	2	0	0	0	43	36	5	18	31	11.7	3.56	106	.237	.326	0	.000	-1	0	1	1	0.1
1975	Hou-N	6	4	.600	40	4	1	1	4	88	79	3	39	54	12.3	3.07	110	.240	.324	3	.214	1	5	3	0	0.5
1976	Hou-N	4	8	.333	36	13	0	0	0	118	107	8	56	77	12.5	3.36	95	.238	.324	5	.185	2	2	-2	-1	0.0
1977	Hou-N	13	8	.619	44	14	9	2	5	180²	155	14	64	101	11.0	3.04	117	.237	.306	7	.140	-1	17	11	1	1.2
1978	Hou-N	14	14	.500	35	29	10	1	0	202²	190	13	73	97	12.1	3.86	86	.248	.321	9	.138	-1	-6	-13	-1	-1.8
1979	Hou-N☆	21	11	.656	38	38	11	5	0	263²	221	17	107	119	11.4	3.00	117	.228	.309	10	.120	-2	21	15	0	1.5
1980	*Hou-N	20	12	.625	37	36	11	2	0	256	268	12	79	127	12.3	3.55	93	.270	.326	22	.275	8	1	-8	-1	-0.1
1981	*Hou-N	9	9	.500	24	24	5	2	0	166	150	8	47	77	10.7	2.82	117	.243	.297	4	.176	1	12	9	-1	0.9
1982	Hou-N	17	12	.586	35	35	16	5	0	270	224	12	64	130	9.8	2.47	134	.229	.279	8	.090	-4	34	25	0	2.3
1983	Hou-N	15	14	.517	38	38	9	1	0	263²	238	15	101	152	11.7	3.48	98	.241	.313	-3	.094	-3	4	-2	-2	-0.8
1984	Hou-N	16	12	.571	38	38	6	1	0	248¹	223	16	89	127	11.5	3.04	109	.241	.310	11	.133	-2	15	8	1	0.7
1985	Hou-N	9	12	.429	32	32	4	1	0	213	197	21	99	117	12.7	3.72	93	.247	.333	17	.250	4	-3	-6	0	-0.2
	NY-A	2	1	.667	3	3	0	0	0	12¹	14	3	8	4	16.1	5.84	69	.280	.379	0	—	0	-2	-3	0	-0.5
1986	NY-A	9	10	.474	25	25	0	0	0	125²	139	15	63	59	14.5	4.87	84	.275	.356	0	—	0	-10	-11	-1	-1.5
1987	NY-A	3	4	.429	8	8	1	0	0	50²	40	4	19	30	11.2	3.55	123	.215	.301	0	—	0	5	5	-0	0.5
	*Min-A	4	9	.308	19	18	0	0	0	96¹	115	11	45	54	15.5	6.26	74	.296	.378	0	—	0	-19	-18	-1	-2.0
	Yr	7	13	.350	27	26	1	0	0	147	155	15	64	84	13.8	5.33	87	.268	.347	0	—	0	-14	-13	-1	-1.5
1988	Min-A	1	1	.500	5	2	0	0	0	11²	16	2	9	7	19.3	10.03	41	.320	.424	0	—	0	-8	-8	1	-1.0
Total	22	221	204	.520	702	500	107	29	16	3584	3466	276	1262	1747	12.0	3.59	97	.255	.321	152	.156	6	14	-38	-3	-5.4

● **PHIL NIEKRO**   Niekro, Philip Henry b: 4/1/39, Blaine, Ohio BR/TR, 6'1″, 180 lbs. Deb: 4/15/64 F

YEAR	TM/L	W	L	PCT	G	GS	CG	SH	SV	IP	H	HR	BB	SO	RAT	ERA	ERA+	OAV	OOB	BH	AVG	PB	PR	/A	PD	TPI
1964	Mil-N	0	0	—	10	0	0	0	0	15	15	1	7	8	13.8	4.80	73	.273	.365	0	—	0	-2	-2	-0	0.0
1965	Mil-N	2	3	.400	41	1	0	0	6	74²	73	5	26	49	12.3	2.89	122	.258	.327	1	.100	-0	5	5	1	0.5
1966	Atl-N	4	3	.571	28	0	0	0	2	50¹	48	4	23	17	13.1	4.11	88	.249	.335	0	.000	-1	-3	-3	2	-0.3
1967	Atl-N	11	9	.550	46	20	10	1	9	207	164	9	55	129	9.8	**1.87**	178	.218	.277	7	.123	-0	35	33	1	3.8
1968	Atl-N	14	12	.538	37	34	15	5	2	257	228	16	45	140	9.7	2.59	116	.239	.277	8	.104	-1	11	11	3	1.5
1969	*Atl-N★	23	13	.639	40	35	21	4	1	284¹	235	21	57	193	9.4	2.56	141	.221	.264	20	.211	-3	33	33	2	4.8
1970	Atl-N	12	18	.400	34	32	10	3	0	229²	222	40	68	168	11.6	4.27	100	.248	.305	12	.152	-1	-6	-0	2	0.1
1971	Atl-N	15	14	.517	42	36	18	4	2	268²	248	27	70	173	10.8	2.98	124	.245	.296	14	.152	-2	14	22	2	2.3
1972	Atl-N	16	12	.571	38	36	17	1	0	282¹	254	22	53	164	9.9	3.06	124	.236	.275	18	.194	3	12	23	1	2.5
1973	Atl-N	13	10	.565	42	30	9	1	4	245	214	21	89	131	11.3	3.31	119	.234	.306	10	.122	-1	10	17	2	1.7
1974	Atl-N	**20**	13	.606	41	39	**18**	6	1	**302**	249	19	88	195	10.2	2.38	159	.225	.286	20	.192	-0	**42**	**47**	0	**5.2**
1975	Atl-N☆	15	15	.500	39	37	13	1	0	275²	285	29	72	144	12.0	3.20	118	.269	.322	17	.172	-0	13	18	1	1.9
1976	Atl-N	17	11	.607	38	37	10	2	0	270²	249	18	101	173	11.9	3.29	115	.242	.315	18	.191	1	6	15	1	1.7
1977	Atl-N	16	20	.444	44	43	**20**	2	0	**330**	315	26	164	**262**	13.3	4.03	110	.255	.346	19	.174	-3	-5	15	2	1.4
1978	Atl-N★	19	18	.514	44	42	**22**	4	1	**334¹**	295	16	102	248	11.0	2.88	141	.235	.299	27	.225	2	26	**43**	4	**5.7**
1979	Atl-N	**21**	20	.512	44	44	**23**	1	0	**342**	311	41	113	208	11.4	3.39	119	.241	.307	24	.195	1	13	25	3	3.4
1980	Atl-N	15	18	.455	40	38	11	3	1	275	256	30	85	176	11.3	3.63	103	.249	.308	12	.133	-2	-1	3	1	0.2
1981	Atl-N	7	7	.500	22	22	3	0	0	139¹	120	6	56	62	11.4	3.10	115	.233	.310	4	.077	-4	6	7	0	0.3
1982	*Atl-N☆	17	4	**.810**	35	35	4	2	0	234¹	225	23	73	144	11.6	3.61	103	.255	.314	17	.195	2	-0	3	1	0.6
1983	Atl-N	11	10	.524	34	33	2	0	0	201²	212	18	105	128	14.2	3.97	98	.276	.364	12	.185	-0	-8	-2	0	-0.2
1984	NY-A☆	16	8	.667	32	31	5	1	0	215²	219	15	76	136	12.4	3.09	123	.267	.331	0	—	0	22	17	2	2.0
1985	NY-A	16	12	.571	33	33	7	1	0	220	203	29	120	149	13.3	4.09	98	.245	.342	0	—	0	1	-2	-2	-0.4
1986	Cle-A	11	11	.500	34	32	5	0	0	210¹	241	24	95	81	14.6	4.32	96	.287	.363	0	—	0	-3	-4	-1	-0.4
1987	Tor-A	0	2	.000	3	3	0	0	0	12	15	4	7	7	16.5	8.25	54	.306	.393	0	—	0	-5	-5	-0	-0.7
	Cle-A	7	11	.389	22	22	2	0	0	123²	142	18	53	57	14.5	5.89	77	.286	.359	0	—	0	-20	-19	0	-2.2
	Yr	7	13	.350	25	25	2	0	0	135²	157	22	60	64	14.7	6.10	74	.288	.362	0	—	0	-25	-24	-0	-2.9
	Atl-N	0	0	—	1	1	0	0	0	3	6	0	3	6	36.0	15.00	29	.429	.600	0	.000	-0	-4	-4	-0	0.0
Total	24	318	274	.537	864	716	245	45	29	5404¹	5044	482	1809	3342	11.6	3.35	115	.247	.312	260	.169	-6	192	299	28	35.4

● **JERRY NIELSEN**   Nielsen, Gerald Arthur b: 8/5/66, Sacramento, Cal. BL/TL, 6'3″, 185 lbs. Deb: 7/12/92

YEAR	TM/L	W	L	PCT	G	GS	CG	SH	SV	IP	H	HR	BB	SO	RAT	ERA	ERA+	OAV	OOB	BH	AVG	PB	PR	/A	PD	TPI
1992	NY-A	1	0	1.000	20	0	0	0	0	19²	17	1	18	12	16.0	4.58	86	.243	.398	0	—	0	-1	-1	0	0.0
1993	Cal-A	0	0	—	10	0	0	0	0	12¹	18	1	4	8	16.8	8.03	56	.340	.397	0	—	0	-5	-5	-0	0.0
Total	2	1	0	1.000	30	0	0	0	0	32	35	2	22	20	16.3	5.91	70	.285	.397	0	—	0	-6	-6	0	0.0

● **SCOTT NIELSEN**   Nielsen, Jeffrey Scott b: 12/18/58, Salt Lake City, Ut. BR/TR, 6'1″, 190 lbs. Deb: 7/7/86

YEAR	TM/L	W	L	PCT	G	GS	CG	SH	SV	IP	H	HR	BB	SO	RAT	ERA	ERA+	OAV	OOB	BH	AVG	PB	PR	/A	PD	TPI
1986	NY-A	4	4	.500	10	9	2	2	0	56	66	12	12	20	12.9	4.02	102	.299	.340	0	—	0	1	-0	-1	0.0
1987	Chi-A	3	5	.375	19	7	1	1	2	66¹	83	9	25	23	14.8	6.24	73	.307	.368	0	—	0	-13	-12	-1	-1.4
1988	NY-A	1	2	.333	7	2	0	0	0	19²	27	5	13	4	18.3	6.86	57	.333	.426	0	—	0	-6	-6	0	-0.8
1989	NY-A	1	0	1.000	2	0	0	0	0	0²	2	0	1	0	40.5	13.50	29	.500	.600	0	—	0	-1	-1	0	-0.7
Total	4	9	11	.450	38	18	3	3	2	142²	178	26	51	47	14.6	5.49	78	.309	.368	0	—	0	-19	-19	-1	-2.9

● **RANDY NIEMANN**   Niemann, Randal Harold b: 11/15/55, Scotia, Cal. BL/TL, 6'4″, 200 lbs. Deb: 5/20/79

YEAR	TM/L	W	L	PCT	G	GS	CG	SH	SV	IP	H	HR	BB	SO	RAT	ERA	ERA+	OAV	OOB	BH	AVG	PB	PR	/A	PD	TPI
1979	Hou-N	3	2	.600	26	7	3	2	1	67	64	1	22	24	12.2	3.76	93	.272	.333	2	.133	-0	-0	-2	-1	-0.2
1980	Hou-N	0	1	.000	22	1	0	0	2	33	40	2	12	18	14.2	5.45	60	.299	.356	2	.333	1	-7	-8	1	-0.1
1982	Pit-N	1	1	.500	20	0	0	0	1	35¹	34	1	17	26	13.5	5.09	73	.254	.346	2	1.000	1	-6	-5	1	-0.2
1983	Pit-N	0	1	.000	8	1	0	0	0	13²	20	2	7	8	18.4	9.22	40	.357	.438	0	.000	-0	-8	-8	0	-0.5
1984	Chi-A	0	0	—	5	0	0	0	0	5¹	5	0	5	5	16.9	1.69	246	.263	.417	0	—	0	1	1	0	0.0
1985	NY-N	0	0	—	4	0	0	0	0	4²	1	0	2	2	9.6	0.00	—	.278	.278	0	—	0	1	1	0	0.0
1986	NY-N	2	3	.400	31	1	0	0	0	35²	44	2	12	18	14.1	3.79	93	.308	.361	2	.333	1	-0	-1	1	0.0
1987	Min-A	1	0	1.000	5	0	0	0	0	5¹	3	0	7	1	20.3	8.44	55	.158	.429	0	—	0	-2	-2	0	-0.4
Total	8	7	8	.467	122	10	3	2	3	200	219	8	82	102	13.5	4.64	77	.283	.357	8	.267	2	-21	-24	2	-1.4

● **JACK NIEMES**   Niemes, Jacob Leland b: 10/19/19, Cincinnati, Ohio d: 3/4/66, Hamilton, Ohio BR/TL, 6'1″, 180 lbs. Deb: 5/30/43

YEAR	TM/L	W	L	PCT	G	GS	CG	SH	SV	IP	H	HR	BB	SO	RAT	ERA	ERA+	OAV	OOB	BH	AVG	PB	PR	/A	PD	TPI
1943	Cin-N	0	0	—	3	0	0	0	0	3	5	0	2	4	21.0	6.00	55	.385	.467	0	—	0	-1	-1	-0	0.0

● **CHUCK NIESON**   Nieson, Charles Bassett b: 9/24/42, Hanford, Cal. BR/TR, 6'2″, 185 lbs. Deb: 9/18/64

YEAR	TM/L	W	L	PCT	G	GS	CG	SH	SV	IP	H	HR	BB	SO	RAT	ERA	ERA+	OAV	OOB	BH	AVG	PB	PR	/A	PD	TPI
1964	Min-A	0	0	—	2	0	0	0	0	2	1	1	1	5	9.0	4.50	79	.143	.250	0	—	0	-0	-0	0	0.0

● **JUAN NIEVES**   Nieves, Juan Manuel (Cruz) b: 1/5/65, Las Lomas, P.R. BL/TL, 6'3″, 175 lbs. Deb: 4/10/86

YEAR	TM/L	W	L	PCT	G	GS	CG	SH	SV	IP	H	HR	BB	SO	RAT	ERA	ERA+	OAV	OOB	BH	AVG	PB	PR	/A	PD	TPI
1986	Mil-A	11	12	.478	35	33	4	3	0	184²	224	17	77	116	14.7	4.92	88	.299	.366	0	—	0	-15	-12	-2	-1.6
1987	Mil-A	14	8	.636	34	33	3	1	0	195²	199	24	100	163	13.8	4.88	94	.264	.351	0	—	0	-9	-7	-1	-0.8
1988	Mil-A	7	5	.583	25	15	1	1	1	110¹	84	13	50	73	11.0	4.08	98	.208	.297	0	—	0	-1	-0	-1	-0.2
Total	3	32	25	.561	94	81	8	5	1	490²	507	54	227	352	13.5	4.71	92	.266	.345	0	—	0	-26	-20	-4	-2.6

● **JOHNNY NIGGELING**   Niggeling, John Arnold b: 7/10/03, Remsen, Iowa d: 9/16/63, LeMars, Iowa BR/TR, 6', 170 lbs. Deb: 4/30/38

YEAR	TM/L	W	L	PCT	G	GS	CG	SH	SV	IP	H	HR	BB	SO	RAT	ERA	ERA+	OAV	OOB	BH	AVG	PB	PR	/A	PD	TPI
1938	Bos-N	1	0	1.000	2	0	0	0	0	2	4	0	1	2	22.5	9.00	38	.400	.455	0	—	0	-1	-1	-0	-0.5
1939	Cin-N	2	1	.667	10	5	2	0	0	40¹	51	3	13	20	14.7	5.80	66	.309	.367	2	.154	-0	-8	-9	-0	-0.6
1940	StL-A	7	11	.389	28	20	10	0	0	153²	148	9	69	82	13.0	4.45	103	.250	.333	9	.176	-1	-1	2	-0	0.1
1941	StL-A	7	9	.438	24	20	13	1	0	168¹	168	17	63	68	12.0	3.80	113	.255	.320	11	.167	-1	7	9	-0	0.4
1942	StL-A	15	11	.577	28	27	16	3	0	206¹	173	6	93	107	12.1	2.66	139	.226	.319	10	.139	-2	23	24	-2	2.5
1943	StL-A	6	8	.429	20	20	7	0	0	150¹	122	7	57	73	11.1	3.17	105	.220	.299	3	.061	-4	2	3	-0	-0.3
	Was-A	4	2	.667	6	6	5	3	0	51	27	0	17	24	7.8	0.88	363	.153	.227	5	.278	1	14	13	0	2.0
	Yr	10	10	.500	26	26	12	3	0	201¹	149	7	74	97	10.0	2.59	127	.202	.275	8	.119	-3	16	16	0	1.7
1944	Was-A	10	8	.556	24	24	14	2	0	206	164	5	88	121	11.2	2.32	141	.221	.307	9	.130	-2	25	21	-1	1.5

YEAR	TM/L	W	L	PCT	G	GS	CG	SH	SV	IP	H	HR	BB	SO	RAT	ERA	ERA+	OAV	OOB	BH	AVG	PB	PR	/A	PD	TPI
1945	Was-A	7	12	.368	26	25	8	2	0	176²	161	7	73	90	12.1	3.16	98	.240	.318	7	.119	-4	4	-1	-2	-0.7
1946	Was-A	3	2	.600	8	6	3	0	0	38	39	1	21	10	14.4	4.03	83	.265	.361	2	.182	0	-2	-3	-0	-0.3
	Bos-N	2	5	.286	8	8	3	0	0	58	54	2	21	24	11.8	3.26	105	.243	.311	2	.111	-1	1	1	0	0.0
Total 9		64	69	.481	184	161	81	12	0	1250²	1111	60	516	620	12.0	3.22	113	.236	.316	59	.140	-14	63	58	-7	4.2

● AL NIPPER
Nipper, Albert Samuel   b: 4/2/59, San Diego, Cal.   BR/TR, 6', 194 lbs.   Deb: 9/6/83

YEAR	TM/L	W	L	PCT	G	GS	CG	SH	SV	IP	H	HR	BB	SO	RAT	ERA	ERA+	OAV	OOB	BH	AVG	PB	PR	/A	PD	TPI
1983	Bos-A	1	1	.500	3	2	1	0	0	16	17	0	7	5	14.1	2.25	193	.293	.379	0	—	0	3	4	-0	0.2
1984	Bos-A	11	6	.647	29	24	6	0	0	182²	183	18	52	84	11.9	3.89	107	.257	.313	0	—	0	2	5	3	0.7
1985	Bos-A	9	12	.429	25	25	5	0	0	162	157	14	82	85	13.8	4.06	106	.256	.352	0	—	0	2	4	2	0.7
1986	*Bos-A	10	12	.455	26	26	3	0	0	159	186	24	47	79	13.4	5.38	77	.290	.342	0	—	0	-21	-21	3	-2.2
1987	Bos-A	11	12	.478	30	30	6	0	0	174	196	30	62	89	13.7	5.43	84	.284	.349	0	—	0	-19	-17	1	-1.8
1988	Chi-N	2	4	.333	22	12	0	0	1	80	72	9	34	27	12.3	3.04	119	.238	.322	2	.087	-1	4	5	-2	0.1
1990	Cle-A	2	3	.400	9	5	0	0	0	24	35	2	19	12	21.0	6.75	58	.354	.467	0	—	0	-8	-8	-0	-1.3
Total 7		46	50	.479	144	124	21	0	1	797²	846	97	303	381	13.3	4.52	93	.271	.342	2	.087	-1	-37	-28	7	-3.6

● MERLIN NIPPERT
Nippert, Merlin Lee   b: 9/1/38, Mangum, Okla.   BR/TR, 6'1", 175 lbs.   Deb: 9/12/62

YEAR	TM/L	W	L	PCT	G	GS	CG	SH	SV	IP	H	HR	BB	SO	RAT	ERA	ERA+	OAV	OOB	BH	AVG	PB	PR	/A	PD	TPI
1962	Bos-A	0	0	—	4	0	0	0	0	6	4	1	4	3	12.0	4.50	92	.200	.333	0	—	0	-0	-0	-0	0.0

● RON NISCHWITZ
Nischwitz, Ronald Lee   b: 7/1/37, Dayton, Ohio   BB/TL, 6'3", 205 lbs.   Deb: 9/4/61

YEAR	TM/L	W	L	PCT	G	GS	CG	SH	SV	IP	H	HR	BB	SO	RAT	ERA	ERA+	OAV	OOB	BH	AVG	PB	PR	/A	PD	TPI
1961	Det-A	0	1	.000	6	1	0	0	0	11¹	12	8	8	6	16.7	5.56	74	.295	.404	0	.000	-0	-2	-2	-0	-0.2
1962	Det-A	4	5	.444	48	0	0	0	4	64²	73	5	26	28	13.9	3.90	104	.285	.353	5	.417	2	1	1	0	0.4
1963	Cle-A	0	2	.000	14	0	0	0	1	16²	17	3	6	10	13.5	6.48	56	.262	.342	0	.000	-0	-5	-5	-0	-0.7
1965	Det-A	1	0	1.000	20	0	0	0	1	22²	21	2	6	12	10.7	2.78	125	.259	.310	0	.000	-0	2	2	-0	0.0
Total 4		5	8	.385	88	1	0	0	6	115¹	124	12	48	58	13.5	4.21	92	.278	.349	5	.278	1	-4	-4	0	-0.5

● OTHO NITCHOLAS
Nitcholas, Otho James   b: 9/13/08, McKinney, Tex.   d: 9/11/86, McKinney, Tex.   BR/TR, 6', 190 lbs.   Deb: 4/18/45

YEAR	TM/L	W	L	PCT	G	GS	CG	SH	SV	IP	H	HR	BB	SO	RAT	ERA	ERA+	OAV	OOB	BH	AVG	PB	PR	/A	PD	TPI
1945	Bro-N	1	0	1.000	7	0	0	0	0	18²	19	4	1	4	9.6	5.30	71	.257	.267	1	.250	-0	-3	-3	-0	-0.2

● WILLARD NIXON
Nixon, Willard Lee   b: 6/17/28, Taylorsville, Ga.   BL/TR, 6'2", 195 lbs.   Deb: 7/7/50

YEAR	TM/L	W	L	PCT	G	GS	CG	SH	SV	IP	H	HR	BB	SO	RAT	ERA	ERA+	OAV	OOB	BH	AVG	PB	PR	/A	PD	TPI
1950	Bos-A	8	6	.571	22	15	2	0	2	101¹	126	8	58	57	16.5	6.04	81	.310	.398	5	.139	-1	-16	-13	-0	-1.6
1951	Bos-A	7	4	.636	33	14	2	1	1	125	136	12	56	70	14.3	4.90	91	.285	.368	13	.289	3	-11	-6	-0	-0.2
1952	Bos-A	5	4	.556	23	13	5	0	0	103¹	115	12	61	50	15.6	4.86	81	.290	.390	11	.208	1	-14	-11	1	-0.7
1953	Bos-A	4	8	.333	23	15	5	1	0	116²	114	6	59	57	13.4	3.93	107	.254	.343	8	.190	0	1	4	-0	0.3
1954	Bos-A	11	12	.478	31	30	8	2	0	199²	182	16	87	102	12.5	4.06	101	.248	.335	18	.265	5	-7	1	1	0.7
1955	Bos-A	12	10	.545	31	31	7	3	0	208	207	16	85	95	12.8	4.07	105	.259	.333	18	.261	5	-2	5	2	1.2
1956	Bos-A	9	8	.529	23	22	9	1	0	145¹	142	9	57	74	12.8	4.21	110	.255	.333	11	.204	-1	-1	7	2	0.8
1957	Bos-A	12	13	.480	29	29	11	1	0	191	207	10	56	96	12.7	3.68	108	.280	.337	22	.293	5	2	7	-1	1.2
1958	Bos-A	1	7	.125	10	8	2	0	0	43¹	48	7	11	15	12.3	6.02	67	.281	.324	5	.294	1	-11	-10	0	-1.5
Total 9		69	72	.489	225	177	51	9	3	1234	1277	90	530	616	13.5	4.39	97	.270	.349	111	.242	17	-59	-16	5	0.2

● JUNIOR NOBOA
Noboa, Milciades Arturo (Diaz)   b: 11/10/64, Azua, D.R.   BR/TR, 5'10", 160 lbs.   Deb: 8/22/84 ♦

YEAR	TM/L	W	L	PCT	G	GS	CG	SH	SV	IP	H	HR	BB	SO	RAT	ERA	ERA+	OAV	OOB	BH	AVG	PB	PR	/A	PD	TPI
1990	Mon-N	0	0	—	1	0	0	0	0	0²	0	0	1	0	13.5	0.00	—	.000	.500	42	.266	0	0	0	0	0.0

● THE ONLY NOLAN
Nolan, Edward Sylvester   b: 11/7/1857, Paterson, N.J.   d: 5/18/13, Paterson, N.J.   BL/TR, 5'8", 171 lbs.   Deb: 5/1/1878

YEAR	TM/L	W	L	PCT	G	GS	CG	SH	SV	IP	H	HR	BB	SO	RAT	ERA	ERA+	OAV	OOB	BH	AVG	PB	PR	/A	PD	TPI
1878	Ind-N	13	22	.371	38	38	37	1	0	347	357	1	56	125	10.7	2.57	79	.253	.281	37	.243	6	-10	-21	2	-1.0
1881	Cle-N	8	14	.364	22	21	20	0	0	180	183	1	38	54	11.1	3.05	86	.251	.288	41	.244	1	-6	-9	-1	-0.9
1883	Pit-a	0	7	.000	7	7	6	0	0	55	81	0	10	23	14.9	4.25	75	.322	.348	8	.308	2	-6	-6	-0	-0.5
1884	Wil-U	1	4	.200	5	5	5	0	0	40	44	1	7	52	11.5	2.93	91	.261	.291	9	.273	-0	-2	-1	1	0.0
1885	Phi-N	1	5	.167	7	7	6	0	0	54	55	1	24	20	13.2	4.17	67	.256	.331	2	.077	-2	-8	-8	-1	-0.9
Total 5		23	52	.307	79	78	74	1	0	676	720	6	135	274	11.4	2.98	80	.259	.294	97	.240	7	-32	-46	1	-3.3

● GARY NOLAN
Nolan, Gary Lynn   b: 5/27/48, Herlong, Cal.   BR/TR, 6'2.5", 197 lbs.   Deb: 4/15/67

YEAR	TM/L	W	L	PCT	G	GS	CG	SH	SV	IP	H	HR	BB	SO	RAT	ERA	ERA+	OAV	OOB	BH	AVG	PB	PR	/A	PD	TPI
1967	Cin-N	14	8	.636	33	32	8	5	0	226²	193	18	62	206	10.3	2.58	145	.228	.284	7	.104	-1	20	29	-1	2.6
1968	Cin-N	9	4	.692	23	22	4	2	0	150	105	10	49	111	9.4	2.40	132	.196	.267	6	.130	2	10	13	-2	1.2
1969	Cin-N	8	8	.500	16	15	2	1	0	108²	102	11	40	83	11.8	3.56	106	.247	.313	8	.229	3	0	2	-2	0.5
1970	*Cin-N	18	7	.720	37	37	4	2	0	250²	226	26	96	181	11.6	3.27	123	.240	.311	13	.159	1	22	21	1	1.9
1971	Cin-N	12	15	.444	35	35	9	0	0	244²	208	12	59	146	9.9	3.16	106	.227	.275	11	.147	-1	8	5	1	0.5
1972	*Cin-N†	15	5	**.750**	25	25	6	2	0	176	147	13	30	90	9.1	1.99	161	.227	.262	7	.117	-1	29	24	2	2.6
1973	Cin-N	0	1	.000	2	2	0	0	0	10¹	14	6	7	3	11.3	3.48	90	.167	.302	0	.000	-0	-0	-0	0	0.0
1975	*Cin-N	15	9	.625	32	32	5	1	0	210²	202	18	29	74	9.9	3.16	114	.251	.278	12	.176	2	11	10	-2	1.1
1976	*Cin-N	15	9	.625	34	34	7	1	0	239¹	232	28	27	113	9.8	3.46	101	.254	.276	8	.101	-3	1	1	-4	-0.6
1977	Cin-N	4	1	.800	8	8	0	0	0	39¹	53	5	12	28	14.9	4.81	82	.321	.367	1	.067	-1	-4	-4	-0	-0.6
	Cal-A	0	3	.000	5	5	0	0	0	18¹	31	5	2	4	16.2	8.84	44	.365	.379	0	—	0	-10	-10	-0	-1.3
Total 10		110	70	.611	250	247	45	14	0	1674²	1505	146	413	1039	10.4	3.08	116	.239	.287	73	.138	0	87	93	-12	7.9

● DICK NOLD
Nold, Richard Louis   b: 5/4/43, San Francisco, Cal.   BR/TR, 6'2", 190 lbs.   Deb: 8/19/67

YEAR	TM/L	W	L	PCT	G	GS	CG	SH	SV	IP	H	HR	BB	SO	RAT	ERA	ERA+	OAV	OOB	BH	AVG	PB	PR	/A	PD	TPI
1967	Was-A	0	2	.000	7	3	0	0	0	20¹	19	1	13	10	14.2	4.87	65	.241	.348	0	.000	-0	-4	-4	-0	-0.4

● DICKIE NOLES
Noles, Dickie Ray   b: 11/19/56, Charlotte, N.C.   BR/TR, 6'2", 190 lbs.   Deb: 7/5/79

YEAR	TM/L	W	L	PCT	G	GS	CG	SH	SV	IP	H	HR	BB	SO	RAT	ERA	ERA+	OAV	OOB	BH	AVG	PB	PR	/A	PD	TPI
1979	Phi-N	3	4	.429	14	14	0	0	0	90	80	6	38	42	12.0	3.80	101	.246	.329	3	.100	-1	-1	0	1	0.0
1980	*Phi-N	1	4	.200	48	3	0	0	6	81	80	5	42	57	13.7	3.89	97	.254	.344	4	.308	1	-3	-1	-0	0.0
1981	*Phi-N	2	2	.500	13	8	0	0	0	58¹	57	7	23	34	12.8	4.17	95	.260	.339	2	.105	-1	-4	-4	-0	-0.5
1982	Chi-N	10	13	.435	31	30	2	2	0	171	180	11	61	85	12.9	4.42	84	.274	.340	6	.107	-2	-16	-13	-0	-1.8
1983	Chi-N	5	10	.333	24	18	1	1	0	116¹	133	9	37	59	13.2	4.72	80	.287	.341	9	.237	1	-14	-12	-1	-1.3
1984	Chi-N	2	2	.500	21	1	0	0	0	50²	60	4	16	34	13.7	5.15	76	.305	.360	0	.000	-0	-9	-7	-1	-0.7
	Tex-A	2	3	.400	18	6	0	0	0	57²	60	6	30	39	14.8	5.15	80	.262	.360	0	—	0	-7	-6	-0	-0.7
1985	Tex-A	4	8	.333	28	13	0	0	0	110¹	129	11	33	59	13.7	5.06	84	.289	.346	0	—	0	-11	-10	1	-0.9
1986	Cle-A	2	3	.600	32	0	0	0	0	54²	56	3	30	32	15.0	5.10	81	.269	.374	0	—	0	-6	-6	-0	-0.4
1987	Chi-N	4	2	.667	41	1	0	0	0	64¹	59	1	27	33	12.7	3.50	122	.239	.326	0	—	-1	4	5	1	0.5
	Det-A	0	0	—	4	0	0	0	0	2	2	0	1	0	13.5	4.50	94	.250	.333	0	—	0	-0	-0	-0	0.3
1988	Bal-A	0	2	.000	3	0	0	0	0	3¹	11	2	0	1	32.4	24.30	16	.500	.522	0	—	0	-8	-8	-0	-2.2
1990	Phi-N	0	1	.000	1	0	0	0	0	0¹	2	0	0	1	54.0	27.00	14	.667	.667	0	—	0	-1	-1	-0	-1.2
Total 11		36	53	.404	277	96	3	3	11	860	909	66	338	455	13.4	4.56	86	.272	.345	24	.136	-3	-75	-61	-2	-8.9

● ERIC NOLTE
Nolte, Eric Carl   b: 4/28/64, Canoga Park, Cal.   BL/TL, 6'3", 205 lbs.   Deb: 8/1/87

YEAR	TM/L	W	L	PCT	G	GS	CG	SH	SV	IP	H	HR	BB	SO	RAT	ERA	ERA+	OAV	OOB	BH	AVG	PB	PR	/A	PD	TPI
1987	SD-N	2	6	.250	12	12	1	0	0	67¹	57	9	36	44	12.7	3.21	123	.226	.328	2	.095	-1	7	6	-1	0.5
1988	SD-N	0	0	—	2	0	0	0	0	3	3	1	2	1	15.0	6.00	57	.273	.385	0	—	0	-1	-1	-0	0.0
1989	SD-N	0	0	—	3	1	0	0	0	9	15	1	7	8	22.0	11.00	32	.375	.468	0	—	0	-8	-8	-0	0.0
1991	SD-N	3	2	.600	6	6	0	0	0	22	37	6	10	15	19.2	11.05	34	.378	.435	1	.111	-0	-18	-18	-0	-2.9
	Tex-A	0	0	—	3	0	0	0	0	2²	3	0	3	1	20.3	3.38	119	.273	.429	0	—	0	-0	-0	-0	0.1
Total 4		5	8	.385	26	19	1	0	0	104	115	14	58	69	15.1	5.63	69	.279	.371	3	.094	-1	-20	-20	-1	-2.3

● JERRY NOPS
Nops, Jeremiah H.   b: 6/23/1875, Toledo, Ohio   d: 3/26/37, Camden, N.J.   BL/TL, 5'8.5", 168 lbs.   Deb: 9/7/1896

YEAR	TM/L	W	L	PCT	G	GS	CG	SH	SV	IP	H	HR	BB	SO	RAT	ERA	ERA+	OAV	OOB	BH	AVG	PB	PR	/A	PD	TPI
1896	Phi-N	1	0	1.000	1	1	1	0	0	7	11	0	1	1	15.4	5.14	84	.354	.374	0	.000	-1	-1	-1	-0	-0.2
	Bal-N	2	1	.667	3	3	3	0	0	22	29	0	2	8	12.7	6.14	70	.315	.329	1	.111	-1	-4	-5	-0	-0.5
	Yr	3	1	.750	4	4	4	0	0	29	40	0	3	9	13.3	5.90	73	.325	.341	1	.077	-2	-5	-5	-0	-0.7

YEAR	TM/L	W	L	PCT	G	GS	CG	SH	SV	IP	H	HR	BB	SO	RAT	ERA	ERA+	OAV	OOB	BH	AVG	PB	PR	/A	PD	TPI
1897	*Bal-N	20	6	.769	30	25	23	1	0	220²	235	5	52	69	12.1	2.81	148	.271	.318	18	.196	-3	37	33	-2	2.7
1898	Bal-N	16	9	.640	33	29	23	2	0	235	241	5	78	91	12.8	3.56	101	.263	.332	20	.220	2	1	0	-4	-0.2
1899	Bal-N	17	11	.607	33	33	26	2	0	259	296	1	71	60	13.1	4.03	98	.287	.339	29	.276	1	-5	-2	-3	-0.3
1900	Bro-N	4	4	.500	9	8	6	1	0	68	79	1	18	22	13.1	3.84	100	.290	.338	4	.160	-1	-1	0	-1	-0.2
1901	Bal-A	12	10	.545	27	23	17	1	1	176²	192	5	59	43	13.4	4.08	95	.274	.341	13	.220	-0	-8	-4	-4	-0.8
Total 6		72	41	.637	136	122	99	7	1	988¹	1083	17	281	294	12.9	3.70	106	.277	.333	85	.221	-2	19	23	-15	0.5

● **WAYNE NORDHAGEN**   Nordhagen, Wayne Oren b: 7/4/48, Thief River Falls, Minn. BR/TR, 6'2", 205 lbs. Deb: 7/16/76 ♦

YEAR	TM/L	W	L	PCT	G	GS	CG	SH	SV	IP	H	HR	BB	SO	RAT	ERA	ERA+	OAV	OOB	BH	AVG	PB	PR	/A	PD	TPI
1979	Chi-A	0	0	—	2	0	0	0	0	2	2	0	1	2	13.5	9.00	47	.286	.375	54	.280	2	-1	-1	-0	0.0

● **JOHN NORIEGA**   Noriega, John Alan b: 12/20/43, Ogden, Utah BR/TR, 6'4", 185 lbs. Deb: 5/1/69

YEAR	TM/L	W	L	PCT	G	GS	CG	SH	SV	IP	H	HR	BB	SO	RAT	ERA	ERA+	OAV	OOB	BH	AVG	PB	PR	/A	PD	TPI
1969	Cin-N	0	0	—	5	0	0	0	0	7²	12	1	3	4	17.6	5.87	64	.400	.455	0	—	0	-2	-2	-0	0.0
1970	Cin-N	0	0	—	8	0	0	0	0	18	25	0	10	6	18.5	8.00	50	.333	.425	1	.250	0	-8	-8	1	0.1
Total 2		0	0	—	13	0	0	0	0	25²	37	1	13	10	18.2	7.36	54	.352	.433	1	.250	0	-10	-10	1	0.1

● **FRED NORMAN**   Norman, Fredie Hubert b: 8/20/42, San Antonio, Tex. BB/TL, 5'8", 160 lbs. Deb: 9/21/62

YEAR	TM/L	W	L	PCT	G	GS	CG	SH	SV	IP	H	HR	BB	SO	RAT	ERA	ERA+	OAV	OOB	BH	AVG	PB	PR	/A	PD	TPI
1962	KC-A	0	0	—	2	0	0	0	0	4	4	0	1	2	11.3	2.25	188	.250	.294	0	—	0	1	1	-0	0.0
1963	KC-A	0	1	.000	2	2	0	0	0	6¹	9	1	7	6	22.7	11.37	34	.346	.485	0	.000	-0	-5	-5	0	-0.7
1964	Chi-N	0	4	.000	8	5	0	0	0	31²	34	4	21	20	15.9	6.54	57	.279	.389	1	.091	-1	-11	-10	-0	-1.2
1966	Chi-N	0	0	—	2	0	0	0	0	4	5	0	2	6	15.8	4.50	82	.313	.389	0	—	0	-0	-0	-0	0.0
1967	Chi-N	0	0	—	1	0	0	0	0	1	0	0	0	3	0.0	0.00	—	.000	.000	0	—	0	-0	-0	-0	0.0
1970	LA-N	2	0	1.000	30	0	0	0	1	62	65	8	33	47	14.5	5.23	73	.273	.366	1	.143	0	-8	-10	-1	-0.3
	StL-N	0	0	—	1	0	0	0	0	1	1	0	0	0	9.00	0.00	—	.333	.333	0	—	0	0	0	0	0.0
	Yr	2	0	1.000	31	0	0	0	1	63	66	8	33	47	14.1	5.14	75	.269	.356	1	.143	0	-8	-9	-1	-0.3
1971	StL-N	0	0	—	4	0	0	0	0	3²	7	1	7	4	34.4	12.27	29	.438	.609	0	—	0	-4	-4	-0	0.0
	SD-N	3	12	.200	20	18	5	0	0	127¹	114	7	56	77	12.2	3.32	99	.240	.323	9	.237	2	2	-0	-1	0.1
	Yr	3	12	.200	24	18	5	0	0	131	121	8	63	81	12.8	3.57	92	.246	.334	9	.237	2	-2	-4	-1	0.1
1972	SD-N	9	11	.450	42	28	10	6	2	211²	195	18	88	167	12.1	3.44	95	.244	.321	8	.125	1	0	-4	-1	-0.3
1973	SD-N	1	7	.125	12	11	1	0	0	74	72	9	29	49	12.4	4.26	82	.262	.334	3	.136	-0	-5	-6	-1	-0.7
	*Cin-N	12	6	.667	24	24	7	3	0	166¹	136	18	72	112	11.3	3.30	103	.224	.307	3	.052	-4	7	2	-1	-0.3
	Yr	13	13	.500	36	35	8	3	0	240¹	208	27	101	161	11.6	3.60	95	.235	.314	6	.075	-4	2	-5	-0	-0.9
1974	Cin-N	13	12	.520	35	26	8	2	0	186	170	15	68	141	11.6	3.14	111	.241	.309	8	.131	-2	10	7	-3	0.4
1975	*Cin-N	12	4	.750	34	26	2	0	0	188	163	23	84	119	11.8	3.73	96	.235	.318	7	.117	-2	-2	-3	-2	-0.6
1976	*Cin-N	12	7	.632	33	24	8	0	0	180¹	153	10	70	123	11.3	3.09	113	.231	.308	7	.140	-1	8	8	-3	0.4
1977	Cin-N	14	13	.519	35	34	8	1	0	221¹	200	28	98	160	12.2	3.38	116	.241	.324	8	.110	-2	13	14	-0	1.2
1978	Cin-N	11	9	.550	36	31	0	0	1	177¹	173	19	82	111	13.1	3.70	96	.255	.338	7	.140	-1	-3	-3	-1	-0.5
1979	*Cin-N	11	13	.458	34	31	5	0	0	195¹	193	14	57	95	11.5	3.64	103	.258	.311	9	.153	0	2	2	-2	0.1
1980	Mon-N	4	4	.500	48	8	2	0	4	98	96	8	40	58	12.8	4.13	86	.259	.337	1	.050	-2	-6	-6	-1	-0.9
Total 16		104	103	.502	403	268	56	15	8	1939²	1790	188	815	1303	12.2	3.64	98	.246	.324	72	.125	-11	-0	-17	-15	-3.2

● **MIKE NORRIS**   Norris, Michael Kelvin b: 3/19/55, San Francisco, Cal. BR/TR, 6'2", 175 lbs. Deb: 4/10/75

YEAR	TM/L	W	L	PCT	G	GS	CG	SH	SV	IP	H	HR	BB	SO	RAT	ERA	ERA+	OAV	OOB	BH	AVG	PB	PR	/A	PD	TPI
1975	Oak-A	1	0	1.000	4	3	1	1	0	16²	6	0	8	5	7.6	0.00	—	.107	.219	0	—	0	7	7	0	0.4
1976	Oak-A	4	5	.444	24	19	1	1	0	96	91	10	56	44	14.0	4.78	70	.250	.353	0	—	0	-13	-15	3	-1.0
1977	Oak-A	2	7	.222	16	12	1	1	0	77¹	77	14	31	35	13.0	4.77	84	.260	.338	0	.000	-0	-6	-6	1	-0.6
1978	Oak-A	0	5	.000	14	5	1	0	0	49	46	2	35	36	15.4	5.51	66	.249	.377	0	—	0	-10	-10	-0	-0.8
1979	Oak-A	5	8	.385	29	18	3	0	0	146¹	146	11	94	96	15.3	4.80	84	.265	.381	0	—	0	-9	-12	-1	-0.8
1980	Oak-A	22	9	.710	33	33	24	1	0	284¹	215	14	83	180	9.6	2.53	149	**.209**	.272	0	—	0	**47**	**39**	3	**4.7**
1981	*Oak-A★	12	9	.571	23	23	12	2	0	172²	145	17	63	78	11.4	3.75	93	.228	.308	0	—	0	-0	-6	-0	-0.6
1982	Oak-A	7	11	.389	28	28	7	1	0	166¹	154	25	84	83	13.2	4.76	82	.242	.336	0	—	0	-13	-16	1	-1.4
1983	Oak-A	5	4	.444	16	16	2	0	0	88²	68	11	36	63	10.9	3.76	103	.213	.299	0	—	0	3	1	-2	0.1
1990	Oak-A	1	0	1.000	14	0	0	0	0	27	24	0	9	16	11.7	3.00	124	.242	.318	0	—	0	3	2	0	0.2
Total 10		58	59	.496	201	157	52	7	0	1124¹	972	108	499	636	12.1	3.89	97	.233	.322	0	.000	0	7	-16	5	0.2

● **LOU NORTH**   North, Louis Alexander b: 6/15/1891, Elgin, Ill. d: 5/16/74, Shelton, Conn. BR/TR, 5'11", 175 lbs. Deb: 8/22/13

YEAR	TM/L	W	L	PCT	G	GS	CG	SH	SV	IP	H	HR	BB	SO	RAT	ERA	ERA+	OAV	OOB	BH	AVG	PB	PR	/A	PD	TPI
1913	Det-A	0	1	.000	1	1	0	0	0	6	10	1	9	3	28.5	15.00	19	.357	.514	0	.000	-0	-8	-8	-0	-0.8
1917	StL-N	0	0	—	5	0	0	0	0	11¹	14	1	4	4	13.4	3.97	68	.350	.409	0	.000	-0	-2	-2	-0	0.0
1920	StL-N	3	2	.600	24	6	3	0	1	88	90	3	32	37	12.7	3.27	91	.278	.346	7	.226	0	-1	-3	-1	-0.3
1921	StL-N	4	4	.500	40	0	0	0	7	86¹	81	5	32	28	11.9	3.54	103	.256	.327	3	.158	-1	**2**	**1**	-2	-0.2
1922	StL-N	10	3	.769	**53**	11	4	0	4	149²	164	6	64	84	14.1	4.45	87	.283	.361	11	.234	2	-6	-10	4	-0.2
1923	StL-N	3	4	.429	34	3	0	0	1	71²	90	8	31	24	15.6	5.15	76	.308	.380	4	.182	-1	-9	-10	1	-0.9
1924	StL-N	0	0	—	6	0	0	0	0	14²	15	1	9	8	14.7	6.75	56	.273	.375	1	.250	-0	-5	-5	-0	-0.6
	Bos-N	1	2	.333	9	4	1	0	0	35¹	45	1	19	11	16.3	5.35	71	.321	.403	1	.111	-1	-6	-6	-1	-0.6
	Yr	1	2	.333	15	4	1	0	0	50	60	2	28	19	15.6	5.76	66	.308	.395	2	.154	-1	-11	-11	-1	-0.6
Total 7		21	16	.568	172	25	8	0	13	463	509	24	200	199	14.0	4.43	82	.287	.363	27	.197	-1	-34	-42	0	-3.0

● **JAKE NORTHROP**   Northrop, George Howard "Jerky" b: 3/5/1888, Monroeton, Pa. d: 11/16/45, Monroeton, Pa. BL/TR, 5'11", 170 lbs. Deb: 7/29/18

YEAR	TM/L	W	L	PCT	G	GS	CG	SH	SV	IP	H	HR	BB	SO	RAT	ERA	ERA+	OAV	OOB	BH	AVG	PB	PR	/A	PD	TPI
1918	Bos-N	5	1	.833	7	4	1	0	0	40	26	0	4	6	6.5	1.35	199	.183	.200	2	.154	-1	6	6	0	0.9
1919	Bos-N	1	5	.167	11	3	2	0	0	37¹	43	2	10	9	13.0	4.58	62	.301	.351	4	.500	3	-7	-7	1	-0.7
Total 2		6	6	.500	18	7	6	1	0	77¹	69	2	13	13	9.7	2.91	95	.242	.278	6	.286	2	-1	-1	0	0.2

● **EFFIE NORTON**   Norton, Elisha Strong "Leiter" b: 8/17/1873, Conneaut, Ohio d: 3/5/50, Aspinwall, Pa. BR/TR, Deb: 8/8/1896

YEAR	TM/L	W	L	PCT	G	GS	CG	SH	SV	IP	H	HR	BB	SO	RAT	ERA	ERA+	OAV	OOB	BH	AVG	PB	PR	/A	PD	TPI
1896	Was-N	3	1	.750	8	5	2	0	0	44	49	2	14	13	14.1	3.07	144	.280	.353	4	.211	-0	6	7	-0	0.4
1897	Was-N	2	1	.667	4	2	1	0	0	17	31	0	11	3	22.2	6.88	63	.388	.463	5	.278	1	-5	-5	-0	-0.6
Total 2		5	2	.714	12	7	3	0	0	61	80	2	25	16	16.4	4.13	106	.314	.388	9	.243	0	1	2	-1	-0.2

● **TOM NORTON**   Norton, Thomas John b: 4/26/50, Elyria, Ohio BR/TR, 6'1", 200 lbs. Deb: 4/18/72

YEAR	TM/L	W	L	PCT	G	GS	CG	SH	SV	IP	H	HR	BB	SO	RAT	ERA	ERA+	OAV	OOB	BH	AVG	PB	PR	/A	PD	TPI
1972	Min-A	0	1	.000	21	0	0	0	0	32¹	31	1	14	22	12.8	2.78	115	.252	.333	0	—	0	1	2	1	0.2

● **RANDY NOSEK**   Nosek, Randall William b: 1/8/67, Omaha, Neb. BR/TR, 6'4", 215 lbs. Deb: 5/27/89

YEAR	TM/L	W	L	PCT	G	GS	CG	SH	SV	IP	H	HR	BB	SO	RAT	ERA	ERA+	OAV	OOB	BH	AVG	PB	PR	/A	PD	TPI
1989	Det-A	0	2	.000	2	2	0	0	0	5¹	7	2	10	4	28.7	13.50	28	.333	.548	0	—	0	-6	-6	-0	-1.3
1990	Det-A	1	1	.500	3	2	0	0	0	7	7	1	9	3	20.6	7.71	51	.280	.471	0	—	0	-3	-3	-0	-0.7
Total 2		1	3	.250	5	4	0	0	0	12¹	14	3	19	7	24.1	10.22	38	.304	.508	0	—	0	-9	-9	-0	-2.0

● **DON NOTTEBART**   Nottebart, Donald Edward b: 1/23/36, West Newton, Mass. BR/TR, 6'1", 190 lbs. Deb: 7/1/60

YEAR	TM/L	W	L	PCT	G	GS	CG	SH	SV	IP	H	HR	BB	SO	RAT	ERA	ERA+	OAV	OOB	BH	AVG	PB	PR	/A	PD	TPI
1960	Mil-N	1	0	1.000	5	1	0	0	1	15¹	14	0	15	8	17.0	4.11	83	.233	.387	0	.000	-1	-1	-1	1	-0.1
1961	Mil-N	6	7	.462	38	11	2	0	3	126¹	117	11	48	66	11.9	4.06	92	.251	.323	7	.184	0	-0	-4	2	-0.2
1962	Mil-N	2	2	.500	39	0	0	0	0	64	64	4	20	36	12.4	3.23	117	.258	.324	2	.333	1	5	4	2	0.5
1963	Hou-N	11	8	.579	31	27	9	2	0	193	170	10	39	118	9.8	3.17	99	.234	.275	11	.167	0	3	4	3	0.5
1964	Hou-N	6	11	.353	28	24	2	0	0	157	165	18	37	90	11.6	3.90	88	.275	.319	3	.064	-2	-6	-8	4	-0.7
1965	Hou-N	4	15	.211	29	25	3	0	0	158	166	14	55	77	12.9	4.67	72	.273	.338	5	.104	-1	-20	-23	2	-2.4
1966	Cin-N	5	4	.556	59	1	0	0	11	111¹	97	11	43	69	11.5	3.07	127	.235	.311	4	.167	-0	7	10	1	1.1
1967	Cin-N	0	3	.000	47	0	0	0	1	79¹	75	4	19	48	10.9	1.93	194	.253	.300	0	—	0	7	11	0	0.8
1969	NY-A	0	0	—	4	0	0	0	0	6	6	1	0	5	10.5	4.50	77	.261	.292	0	—	0	-1	-1	0	0.0
	Chi-N	1	1	.500	16	0	0	0	0	18	28	2	8	17	17.5	7.00	45	.350	.402	0	.000	0	-7	-6	0	-0.6
Total 9		36	51	.414	296	89	16	2	21	928¹	902	69	283	525	11.7	3.65	96	.256	.315	32	.134	-3	-8	-13	11	-1.6

YEAR TM/L	W	L	PCT	G	GS	CG	SH	SV	IP	H	HR	BB	SO	RAT	ERA	ERA+	OAV	OOB	BH	AVG	PB	PR	/A	PD	TPI
● **CHET NOURSE**			Nourse, Chester Linwood	b: 8/7/1887, Ipswich, Mass.				d: 4/20/58, Clearwater, Fla.				BR/TR, 6'3", 185 lbs.			Deb: 7/27/09										
1909 Bos-A	0	0		3	0	0	0	0	5	5	0	5	3	18.0	7.20	35	.263	.417	0	.000	-0	-3	-3	0	0.0
● **RAFAEL NOVOA**			Novoa, Rafael Angel	b: 10/26/67, New York, N.Y.				BL/TL, 6', 180 lbs.				Deb: 7/31/90													
1990 SF-N	0	1	.000	7	2	0	0	1	18²	21	3	13	14	16.4	6.75	54	.284	.391	1	.200	0	-6	-6	-1	-0.4
1993 Mil-A	0	3	.000	15	7	2	0	0	56	58	7	22	17	13.5	4.50	94	.267	.346	0	—	0	-1	-2	-1	-0.1
Total 2	0	4	.000	22	9	2	0	1	74²	79	10	35	31	14.2	5.06	81	.271	.358	1	.200	0	-7	-8	-1	-0.5
● **WIN NOYES**			Noyes, Winfield Charles	b: 6/16/1889, Pleasanton, Neb.				d: 4/8/69, Cashmere, Wash.				BR/TR, 6', 180 lbs.			Deb: 5/19/13										
1913 Bos-N	0	0		11	0	0	0	0	20²	22	1	6	5	13.9	4.79	69	.289	.372	1	.250	0	-4	-3	-0	0.0
1917 Phi-A	10	10	.500	27	22	11	1	1	171	156	5	77	64	12.5	2.95	93	.258	.345	6	.115	-2	-5	-4	-1	-0.8
1919 Phi-A	1	5	.167	10	6	3	0	0	49	66	1	15	20	15.1	5.69	60	.332	.381	2	.125	-1	-13	-12	0	-1.4
Chi-A	0	0		1	1	0	0	0	6	10	0	0	4	15.0	7.50	42	.385	.385	1	.500	0	-3	-3	-0	0.0
Yr	1	5	.167	11	7	3	0	0	55	76	1	15	24	14.9	5.89	58	.336	.378	3	.167	-1	-16	-15	0	-1.4
Total 3	11	15	.423	49	29	14	1	1	246²	254	7	98	93	13.2	3.76	78	.280	.356	10	.135	-3	-25	-22	-1	-2.2
● **EDWIN NUNEZ**			Nunez, Edwin (Martinez)	b: 5/27/63, Humacao, P.R.				BR/TR, 6'5", 237 lbs.				Deb: 4/7/82													
1982 Sea-A	1	2	.333	8	5	0	0	0	35¹	36	7	16	27	13.2	4.58	92	.269	.347	0	—	0	-2	-1	0	-0.1
1983 Sea-A	0	4	.000	14	5	0	0	0	37	40	3	22	35	15.8	4.38	97	.278	.385	0	—	0	-1	-0	0	-0.1
1984 Sea-A	2	2	.500	37	0	0	0	7	67²	55	8	21	57	10.5	3.19	125	.218	.286	0	—	0	6	6	-1	0.4
1985 Sea-A	7	3	.700	70	0	0	0	16	90¹	79	13	34	58	11.3	3.09	136	.234	.305	0	—	0	11	11	0	1.6
1986 Sea-A	1	3	.333	14	1	0	0	0	21²	25	5	5	17	12.5	5.82	73	.284	.323	0	—	0	-4	-4	0	-0.5
1987 Sea-A	3	4	.429	48	0	0	0	12	47¹	45	7	18	34	12.2	3.80	124	.262	.335	0	—	0	3	5	-0	0.5
1988 Sea-A	0	0		14	3	0	0	0	29¹	45	4	14	19	18.7	7.98	52	.366	.439	0	—	0	-13	-12	1	-1.9
NY-N	1	0	1.000	10	0	0	0	0	14	21	1	3	8	15.4	4.50	72	.339	.369	0	—	0	-2	-2	-0	-0.2
1989 Det-A	3	4	.429	27	0	0	0	1	54	49	6	36	41	14.2	4.17	92	.254	.371	0	—	0	-2	-2	1	-0.1
1990 Det-A	3	1	.750	42	0	0	0	6	80¹	65	4	37	66	11.7	2.24	177	.218	.309	0	—	0	15	15	-1	0.9
1991 Mil-A	2	1	.667	23	0	0	0	8	25¹	28	6	13	24	14.6	6.04	66	.277	.360	0	—	0	-5	-6	-0	-0.9
1992 Mil-A	1	1	.500	10	0	0	0	0	13²	12	1	6	10	11.9	2.63	146	.231	.310	0	—	0	2	2	-0	0.3
Tex-A	0	2	.000	39	0	0	0	3	45²	51	5	16	39	13.6	5.52	69	.279	.343	0	—	0	-8	-9	-1	-0.4
Yr	1	3	.250	49	0	0	0	3	59¹	63	6	22	49	13.2	4.85	78	.268	.336	0	—	0	-6	-7	-1	-0.1
1993 Oak-A	3	6	.333	56	0	0	0	1	75²	89	7	29	58	14.7	3.81	107	.298	.371	0	—	0	4	2	-0	0.4
1994 Oak-A	0	0	—	15	0	0	0	0	15	26	2	10	15	21.6	12.00	37	.382	.462	0	—	0	-12	-13	-0	0.1
Total 13	28	36	.438	427	14	0	0	54	652¹	666	74	280	508	13.3	4.19	97	.266	.344	0	—	0	-8	-8	-1	0.0
● **JOSE NUNEZ**			Nunez, Jose (Jimenez)	b: 1/13/64, Jarabacoa, D.R.				BR/TR, 6'3", 175 lbs.				Deb: 4/9/87													
1987 Tor-A	5	2	.714	37	9	0	0	0	97	91	12	58	99	13.5	5.01	90	.256	.360	0	—	0	-6	-6	-1	-0.4
1988 Tor-A	0	1	.000	13	2	0	0	0	29¹	28	3	17	18	14.1	3.07	128	.259	.365	0	—	0	3	3	-0	0.1
1989 Tor-A	0	0	—	6	1	0	0	0	10²	8	0	2	14	8.4	2.53	149	.200	.238	0	—	0	2	1	-0	0.0
1990 Chi-N	4	7	.364	21	10	0	0	0	60²	61	5	34	40	14.1	6.53	62	.270	.365	0	.000	-1	-18	-17	0	-2.6
Total 4	9	10	.474	77	22	0	0	0	197²	188	20	111	171	13.7	5.05	84	.258	.356	0	.000	-1	-20	-18	-1	-2.9
● **HOWIE NUNN**			Nunn, Howard Ralph	b: 10/18/35, Westfield, N.C.				BR/TR, 6', 173 lbs.				Deb: 4/11/59													
1959 StL-N	2	2	.500	16	0	0	0	0	21¹	23	3	15	20	16.0	7.59	56	.291	.404	0	.000	-0	-9	-8	1	-1.2
1961 Cin-N	2	1	.667	24	0	0	0	0	37²	35	0	24	26	14.3	3.58	113	.252	.366	2	.250	0	2	2	-0	0.1
1962 Cin-N	0	0	—	6	0	0	0	0	9²	15	0	3	4	16.8	5.59	72	.375	.419	0	.000	-0	-2	-2	0	0.0
Total 3	4	3	.571	46	0	0	0	0	68²	73	3	42	50	15.2	5.11	80	.283	.385	2	.200	-0	-9	-8	1	-1.1
● **JOE NUXHALL**			Nuxhall, Joseph Henry	b: 7/30/28, Hamilton, Ohio				BL/TL, 6'3", 219 lbs.				Deb: 6/10/44													
1944 Cin-N	0	0	—	1	0	0	0	0	0²	2	0	5	0	94.5	67.50	5	.500	.778	0	—	0	-5	-5	-0	0.0
1952 Cin-N	1	4	.200	37	5	2	0	1	92¹	83	4	42	52	12.5	3.22	117	.246	.334	2	.087	-1	5	6	2	0.3
1953 Cin-N	9	11	.450	30	17	5	1	2	141²	136	13	69	52	13.5	4.32	101	.252	.345	16	.327	7	-1	1	-2	0.6
1954 Cin-N	12	5	.706	35	14	5	1	0	166²	188	11	59	85	13.7	3.89	108	.292	.357	4	.173	4	3	6	0	0.9
1955 Cin-N★	17	12	.586	50	33	14	**5**	3	257	240	25	78	98	11.3	3.47	122	.249	.309	17	.198	4	16	22	-2	2.5
1956 Cin-N☆	13	11	.542	44	32	10	2	3	200²	196	14	87	120	13.0	3.72	107	.257	.338	11	.186	3	1	6	-1	0.9
1957 Cin-N	10	10	.500	39	28	6	2	1	174¹	192	24	53	99	13.0	4.75	87	.275	.332	14	.237	3	-17	-12	-2	-1.2
1958 Cin-N	12	11	.522	36	26	5	0	0	175²	169	15	63	111	11.9	3.79	109	.257	.323	13	.210	0	3	7	-0	0.7
1959 Cin-N	9	9	.500	28	21	6	1	1	131²	155	10	35	75	13.1	4.24	96	.292	.337	11	.250	3	-4	-3	-1	-0.1
1960 Cin-N	1	8	.111	38	6	0	0	0	112	130	8	27	72	12.9	4.42	86	.297	.344	2	.077	-1	-8	-7	2	-0.5
1961 KC-A	5	8	.385	37	13	1	0	1	128	135	12	65	81	14.3	5.34	78	.268	.355	19	.292	7	-19	-17	-1	-0.9
1962 LA-A	0	0	—	5	0	0	0	0	5¹	7	0	5	2	21.9	10.13	38	.304	.448	0	—	0	-4	-4	-0	0.0
Cin-N	5	0	1.000	12	9	1	0	0	66	59	4	25	57	11.6	2.45	164	.240	.313	7	.269	3	11	12	-0	1.1
1963 Cin-N	15	8	.652	35	29	14	2	2	217¹	194	14	39	169	9.9	2.61	128	.237	.277	12	.158	0	16	18	-1	1.8
1964 Cin-N	9	8	.529	32	22	7	4	2	154²	146	19	51	111	11.8	4.07	89	.250	.317	7	.130	-1	-9	-8	-2	-1.1
1965 Cin-N	11	4	.733	32	16	5	1	2	148²	142	18	31	117	10.7	3.45	109	.252	.295	8	.178	1	1	5	-3	0.3
1966 Cin-N	6	8	.429	35	16	2	1	0	130	136	14	42	71	12.9	4.50	87	.270	.338	4	.100	-2	-13	-9	-1	-1.2
Total 16	135	117	.536	526	287	83	20	19	2302²	2310	209	776	1372	12.3	3.90	102	.262	.327	152	.198	28	-21	17	-12	4.1
● **RICH NYE**			Nye, Richard Raymond	b: 8/4/44, Oakland, Cal.				BL/TL, 6'4", 185 lbs.				Deb: 9/16/66													
1966 Chi-N	0	2	.000	3	2	0	0	0	17	16	1	7	9	12.2	2.12	174	.254	.329	1	.250	0	3	3	-1	0.3
1967 Chi-N	13	10	.565	35	30	6	0	0	205	179	15	52	119	10.2	3.20	111	.234	.284	16	.213	3	4	8	-0	1.2
1968 Chi-N	7	12	.368	27	20	6	1	1	132²	145	16	34	74	12.2	3.80	83	.276	.321	8	.182	-0	-12	-9	-0	-1.4
1969 Chi-N	3	5	.375	34	5	1	0	3	68²	72	13	21	39	12.3	5.11	79	.271	.326	1	.063	-1	-12	-8	-1	-1.2
1970 StL-N	0	0	—	6	0	0	0	0	8	13	2	6	5	21.4	4.50	91	.371	.463	1	.500	1	-0	-0	0	0.1
Mon-N	3	2	.600	8	6	2	0	0	46¹	47	3	20	21	13.0	4.08	101	.260	.333	3	.176	-0	-0	0	0	0.0
Yr	3	2	.600	14	6	2	0	0	54¹	60	5	26	26	14.2	4.14	99	.276	.354	4	.211	1	-1	-0	0	0.1
Total 5	26	31	.456	113	63	16	1	4	477²	472	50	140	267	11.6	3.71	96	.257	.311	30	.190	2	-17	-7	-2	-1.0
● **JERRY NYMAN**			Nyman, Gerald Smith	b: 11/23/42, Logan, Utah				BL/TL, 5'10", 165 lbs.				Deb: 8/24/68													
1968 Chi-A	2	1	.667	8	7	1	1	0	40¹	38	1	16	27	12.0	2.01	151	.247	.318	2	.154	-0	4	5	-0	0.3
1969 Chi-A	4	4	.500	20	10	2	1	0	64²	58	7	39	40	13.5	5.29	73	.244	.350	1	.050	-1	-12	-10	-1	-1.3
1970 SD-N	0	2	.000	2	2	0	0	0	5¹	8	1	2	2	16.9	15.19	26	.364	.417	0	—	0	-7	-7	-0	-1.5
Total 3	6	7	.462	30	19	3	2	0	110¹	104	9	57	69	13.1	4.57	78	.251	.342	3	.091	-1	-14	-12	-1	-2.5
● **PRINCE OANA**			Oana, Henry Kauhane	b: 1/22/08, Waipahu, Hawaii				d: 6/19/76, Austin, Tex.				BR/TR, 6'2", 193 lbs.			Deb: 4/22/34 ◆										
1943 Det-A	3	2	.600	10	0	0	0	0	34	34	4	19	15	14.6	4.50	78	.262	.364	10	.385	4	-5	-4	-0	-0.1
1945 Det-A	0	0	—	3	1	0	0	1	11¹	3	0	7	3	7.9	1.59	221	.086	.238	6	.200	0	2	2	-0	0.0
Total 2	3	2	.600	13	1	0	0	1	45¹	37	4	26	18	12.9	3.77	93	.224	.337	16	.308	4	-2	-1	-1	-0.1
● **HENRY OBERBECK**			Oberbeck, Henry A.	b: 5/17/1858, Missouri				d: 8/26/21, St.Louis, Mo.				Deb: 5/7/1883 ◆												
1884 Bal-U	0	0		2	1	0	0	0	6¹	9	1	0	2	16.5	3.00	89	.325	.371	23	.184	-1	-0	-0	-0	-0.1
KC-U	0	5	.000	6	4	3	0	0	29¹	47	3	5	6	15.2	5.76	39	.337	.351	17	.189	-1	-11	-12	-1	-1.5
Yr	0	5	.000	8	5	3	0	0	35²	56	4	5	7	15.4	5.30	44	.335	.355	40	.186	-2	-11	-12	-1	-1.6

YEAR	TM/L	W	L	PCT	G	GS	CG	SH	SV	IP	H	HR	BB	SO	RAT	ERA	ERA+	OAV	OOB	BH	AVG	PB	PR	/A	PD	TPI

● DOC OBERLANDER   Oberlander, Hartman Louis   b: 5/12/1864, Waukegan, Ill.   d: 11/14/22, Pryor, Montana   TL ,   Deb: 5/16/1888

| 1888 | Cle-a | 1 | 2 | .333 | 3 | 3 | 3 | 0 | 0 | 25² | 27 | 2 | 18 | 23 | 16.1 | 5.26 | 59 | .261 | .375 | 3 | .214 | 0 | -6 | -6 | -0 | -0.5 |

● FRANK OBERLIN   Oberlin, Frank Rufus "Flossie"   b: 3/29/1876, Elsie, Mich.   d: 1/6/52, Ashley, Ind.   BR/TR, 6'1", 165 lbs.   Deb: 9/20/06

1906	Bos-A	1	3	.250	4	4	4	0	0	34	38	0	13	13	14.0	3.18	87	.286	.358	2	.154	-0	-2	-2	1	-0.1
1907	Bos-A	1	5	.167	12	4	2	0	0	46	48	2	24	18	14.5	4.30	60	.271	.364	2	.154	-0	-9	-9	-1	-1.1
	Was-A	2	6	.250	11	8	3	0	0	48²	57	0	12	18	13.1	4.62	52	.294	.341	1	.056	-2	-11	-12	-1	-2.0
	Yr	3	11	.214	23	12	5	0	0	94²	105	2	36	36	13.6	4.47	56	.281	.348	3	.097	-2	-20	-21	-2	-3.1
1909	Was-A	1	4	.200	9	4	1	0	0	41	41	1	16	13	13.8	3.73	65	.266	.358	2	.143	-1	-6	-6	-1	-0.9
1910	Was-A	0	6	.000	8	6	6	0	0	57¹	52	0	23	18	12.1	2.98	84	.259	.341	1	.053	-2	-3	-3	-1	-0.6
Total	4	5	24	.172	44	26	16	0	0	227	236	3	88	80	13.4	3.77	67	.275	.352	8	.104	-4	-31	-31	-3	-4.7

● DAN O'BRIEN   O'Brien, Daniel Jogues   b: 4/22/54, St.Petersburg, Fla.   BR/TR, 6'4", 215 lbs.   Deb: 9/4/78

1978	StL-N	0	2	.000	7	2	0	0	0	18	22	1	8	12	16.0	4.50	78	.301	.386	0	.000	-0	-2	-2	-0	-0.3
1979	StL-N	1	1	.500	6	0	0	0	0	11	21	0	3	5	19.6	8.18	46	.420	.453	0	.000	-0	-5	-5	-0	-0.9
Total	2	1	3	.250	13	2	0	0	0	29	43	1	11	17	17.4	5.90	61	.350	.412	0	.000	-1	-7	-7	-1	-1.2

● EDDIE O'BRIEN   O'Brien, Edward Joseph   b: 12/11/30, S.Amboy, N.J.   BR/TR, 5'9", 165 lbs.   Deb: 4/25/53   FC♦

1956	Pit-N	0	0	—	1	0	0	0	0	2	1	0	0	0	9.0	0.00	—	.167	.286	14	.264	0	1	1	-0	0.0
1957	Pit-N	1	0	1.000	3	1	1	0	0	12¹	11	2	3	10	10.2	2.19	173	.229	.275	0	.000	-1	2	2	0	0.1
1958	Pit-N	0	0	—	1	0	0	0	0	2	4	1	1	1	22.5	13.50	29	.444	.500	0	—	0	-2	-2	-0	0.0
Total	3	1	0	1.000	5	1	1	0	0	16¹	16	3	4	11	11.6	3.31	115	.254	.309	131	.236	-0	1	1	-0	0.1

● DARBY O'BRIEN   O'Brien, John F.   b: 4/15/1867, Troy, N.Y.   d: 3/11/1892, W.Troy, N.Y.   BR/TR, 5'10", 165 lbs.   Deb: 6/23/1888

1888	Cle-a	11	19	.367	30	30	30	1	0	259	245	5	99	135	12.4	3.30	94	.241	.315	20	.183	-3	-7	-6	2	-0.7
1889	Cle-N	22	17	.564	41	41	39	1	0	346²	345	9	167	122	13.9	4.15	97	.252	.343	35	.250	-4	-5	-5	2	0.1
1890	Cle-P	8	16	.333	25	25	22	0	0	206¹	229	9	93	54	14.9	3.40	117	.269	.354	15	.156	-6	19	13	-1	0.5
1891	Bos-a	18	13	.581	40	30	22	0	2	268²	300	13	127	87	15.0	3.65	96	.273	.359	30	.234	1	2	-5	-3	-0.7
Total	4	59	65	.476	136	126	113	2	2	1080²	1119	36	486	398	14.0	3.68	100	.258	.343	100	.211	-4	-9	-2	0	-0.8

● JOHNNY O'BRIEN   O'Brien, John Thomas   b: 12/11/30, S.Amboy, N.J.   BR/TR, 5'9", 170 lbs.   Deb: 4/19/53   F♦

1956	Pit-N	1	0	1.000	8	0	0	0	0	19	8	2	9	9	9.0	2.84	133	.133	.268	18	.173	-0	2	1	-0	0.0
1957	Pit-N	0	3	.000	16	1	0	0	0	40	46	7	24	19	16.0	6.07	62	.293	.390	11	.314	2	-10	-10	-1	-0.5
1958	StL-N	0	0	—	1	0	0	0	0	2	7	0	2	2	40.5	22.50	18	.538	.600	0	.000	0	-4	-4	-0	0.0
Total	3	1	3	.250	25	1	0	0	0	61	61	9	35	30	14.6	5.61	68	.265	.369	204	.250	2	-12	-12	-2	-0.5

● BOB O'BRIEN   O'Brien, Robert Allen   b: 4/23/49, Pittsburgh, Pa.   BL/TL, 5'10", 170 lbs.   Deb: 4/11/71

| 1971 | LA-N | 2 | 2 | .500 | 14 | 4 | 1 | 0 | 0 | 42 | 42 | 4 | 13 | 15 | 12.0 | 3.00 | 108 | .262 | .322 | 1 | .111 | -0 | 2 | 1 | -1 | 0.0 |

● TOM O'BRIEN   O'Brien, Thomas H.   b: 6/22/1860, Salem, Mass.   d: 4/21/21, Worcester, Mass.   BR/TR, 6'1", 185 lbs.   Deb: 6/14/1882   ♦

| 1887 | NY-a | 0 | 0 | — | 1 | 0 | 0 | 0 | 0 | 3² | 4 | 0 | 5 | 0 | 22.1 | 7.36 | 58 | .211 | .375 | 25 | .194 | -0 | -1 | -1 | -0 | 0.0 |

● BUCK O'BRIEN   O'Brien, Thomas Joseph   b: 5/9/1882, Brockton, Mass.   d: 7/25/59, Boston, Mass.   BR/TR, 5'10", 188 lbs.   Deb: 9/9/11

1911	Bos-A	5	1	.833	6	5	5	2	0	47²	30	0	21	31	9.8	0.38	868	.180	.275	2	.125	-1	16	15	1	2.0
1912	*Bos-A	20	13	.606	37	34	25	2	0	275²	237	3	90	115	11.0	2.58	132	.237	.306	13	.138	-5	23	25	1	2.4
1913	Bos-A	4	9	.308	15	12	6	0	0	90¹	103	0	35	54	13.7	3.69	80	.305	.370	5	.167	0	-8	-7	1	-0.9
	Chi-A	0	2	.000	6	3	0	0	0	18¹	21	0	13	4	16.7	3.93	74	.318	.430	0	.000	-0	-2	-2	-0	-0.3
	Yr	4	11	.267	21	15	6	0	0	108²	124	0	48	58	14.4	3.73	79	.307	.381	5	.152	-0	-10	-10	1	-1.2
Total	3	29	25	.537	64	54	36	4	0	432	391	3	159	204	11.7	2.63	125	.249	.322	20	.140	-6	29	31	1	3.2

● DARBY O'BRIEN   O'Brien, William D.   b: 9/1/1863, Peoria, Ill.   d: 6/15/1893, Peoria, Ill.   BR/TR, 6'1", 186 lbs.   Deb: 4/16/1887   ♦

| 1887 | NY-a | 0 | 0 | — | 1 | 0 | 0 | 0 | 0 | 1 | 1 | 0 | 1 | 0 | 18.0 | — | — | .333 | .500 | 157 | .301 | 0 | 0 | 0 | -0 | 0.0 |

● BILLY O'BRIEN   O'Brien, William Smith   b: 3/14/1860, Albany, N.Y.   d: 5/26/11, Kansas City, Mo.   BR , 6', 185 lbs.   Deb: 9/27/1884   ♦

| 1884 | StP-U | 1 | 0 | 1.000 | 2 | 0 | 0 | 0 | 0 | 10 | 8 | 0 | 3 | 7 | 9.9 | 1.80 | 74 | .205 | .261 | 7 | .233 | -0 | 1 | -1 | 0 | 0.0 |

● WALTER OCKEY   Ockey, Walter Andrew "Footie" (b: Walter Andrew Okpych)
b: 1/4/20, New York, N.Y.   d: 12/4/71, Staten Island, N.Y.   BR/TR, 6', 175 lbs.   Deb: 5/3/44

| 1944 | NY-N | 0 | 0 | — | 1 | 0 | 0 | 0 | 0 | 2² | 2 | 1 | 2 | 1 | 13.5 | 3.38 | 109 | .200 | .333 | 0 | — | 0 | 1 | 1 | -0 | 0.0 |

● PAT O'CONNELL   O'Connell, Patrick H.   b: 6/10/1861, Bangor, Me.   d: 1/24/43, Lewiston, Maine   BR/TR, 5'10", 175 lbs.   Deb: 7/22/1886   ♦

| 1886 | Bal-a | 0 | 0 | — | 1 | 0 | 0 | 0 | 0 | 3 | 4 | 0 | 2 | 1 | 18.0 | 6.00 | 57 | .333 | .429 | 30 | .181 | -0 | -1 | -1 | -0 | 0.0 |

● ANDY O'CONNOR   O'Connor, Andrew James   b: 9/14/1884, Roxbury, Mass.   d: 9/26/80, Norwood, Mass.   BR/TR, 6', 160 lbs.   Deb: 10/6/08

| 1908 | NY-A | 0 | 1 | .000 | 1 | 1 | 1 | 0 | 0 | 8 | 15 | 0 | 7 | 5 | 28.1 | 10.13 | 25 | .429 | .556 | 0 | .000 | -0 | -7 | -7 | -0 | -0.6 |

● FRANK O'CONNOR   O'Connor, Frank Henry   b: 9/15/1870, Keeseville, N.Y.   d: 12/26/13, Brattleboro, Vt.   BL/TL, 6', 185 lbs.   Deb: 8/3/1893

| 1893 | Phi-N | 0 | 0 | — | 3 | 1 | 0 | 0 | 1 | 4 | 2 | 0 | 9 | 0 | 24.8 | 11.25 | 41 | .145 | .482 | 2 | 1.000 | 2 | -3 | -3 | 0 | 0.0 |

● JACK O'CONNOR   O'Connor, Jack William   b: 6/2/58, Twentynine Palms, Cal.   BL/TL, 6'3", 215 lbs.   Deb: 4/9/81

1981	Min-A	3	2	.600	28	6	0	0	0	35¹	46	3	30	16	19.9	5.86	67	.336	.462		0	0	-9	-8	1	-0.9
1982	Min-A	8	9	.471	23	19	6	0	0	126	122	8	57	56	12.9	4.29	99	.255	.337		0	0	-3	-1	-3	-0.4
1983	Min-A	2	3	.400	27	8	0	0	0	83	107	13	36	56	15.5	5.86	73	.315	.380		0	0	-17	-15	-1	-1.1
1984	Min-A	0	0	—	2	0	0	0	0	4²	1	4	0	4	9.6	1.93	218	.067	.263		0	0	1	1	-0	-0.3
1985	Mon-N	0	2	.000	20	1	0	0	0	23²	21	1	13	16	12.9	4.94	69	.239	.337		0	0	-4	-4	-1	-0.4
1987	Bal-A	1	1	.500	29	0	0	0	2	46	46	5	23	33	13.5	4.30	102	.263	.348		0	0	1	0	-1	0.2
Total	6	14	17	.452	129	28	6	1	2	318²	343	36	163	177	14.4	4.89	85	.278	.364		0	0	-30	-25	-5	-2.9

● HANK O'DAY   O'Day, Henry Francis   b: 7/8/1862, Chicago, Ill.   d: 7/2/35, Chicago, Ill.   TR , 6', 180 lbs.   Deb: 5/2/1884   MU

1884	Tol-a	9	28	.243	41	40	35	2	1	326²	335	6	66	163	11.5	3.75	91	.252	.297	51	.211	-1	-18	-12	4	-0.9
1885	Pit-a	5	7	.417	12	12	10	0	0	103	110	4	16	36	11.6	3.67	88	.258	.296	12	.245	1	-5	-5	0	-0.3
1886	Was-N	2	2	.500	6	6	6	0	0	49	41	1	17	47	10.7	1.65	199	.219	.284	1	.053	-2	9	9	1	0.5
1887	Was-N	8	20	.286	30	30	29	0	0	254²	255	15	109	86	13.2	4.17	97	.254	.332	23	.198	-3	-3	-3	1	-0.5
1888	Was-N	16	29	.356	46	46	46	3	0	403	359	19	117	186	11.0	3.10	90	.232	.293	23	.139	-7	-11	-13	-3	-2.2
1889	Was-N	2	10	.167	13	13	11	0	0	108	117	7	57	23	15.0	4.33	91	.268	.360	8	.182	-1	-4	-5	0	-0.4
	*NY-N	9	1	.900	10	10	8	0	0	78	83	2	35	51	14.4	4.27	92	.264	.351	3	.097	-1	-2	-3	-1	-0.4
	Yr	11	11	.500	23	23	19	0	0	186	200	9	92	51	14.5	4.31	92	.264	.349	11	.147	-2	-6	-8	-0	-0.8
1890	NY-P	22	13	.629	43	45	33	2	3	329	350	11	163	94	14.7	4.21	108	.264	.351	34	.227	-3	1	12	-4	0.4
Total	7	73	110	.399	201	192	177	6	4	1651¹	1656	65	580	663	12.6	3.74	97	.251	.320	155	.190	-17	-33	-34	-3	-3.8

● PAUL O'DEA   O'Dea, Paul "Lefty"   b: 7/3/20, Cleveland, Ohio   d: 12/11/78, Cleveland, Ohio   BL/TL, 6', 200 lbs.   Deb: 4/19/44   ♦

1944	Cle-A	0	0	—	3	0	0	0	0	4¹	5	0	6	0	22.8	2.08	159	.333	.524	55	.318	1	1	1	-0	0.0
1945	Cle-A	0	0	—	1	0	0	0	0	2	4	0	2	0	27.0	13.50	24	.400	.500	52	.235	0	-2	-2	-0	0.0
Total	2	0	0	—	4	0	0	0	0	6¹	9	0	8	0	24.2	5.68	58	.360	.515	107	.272	1	-2	-2	-0	0.0

● BILLY O'DELL   O'Dell, William Oliver   b: 2/10/33, Whitmire, S.C.   BB/TL, 5'11", 170 lbs.   Deb: 6/20/54

| 1954 | Bal-A | 1 | 1 | .500 | 7 | 2 | 1 | 0 | 0 | 16¹ | 15 | 0 | 5 | 6 | 11.0 | 2.76 | 130 | .242 | .299 | 0 | .000 | -0 | 2 | 1 | 0 | 0.2 |

YEAR	TM/L	W	L	PCT	G	GS	CG	SH	SV	IP	H	HR	BB	SO	RAT	ERA	ERA+	OAV	OOB	BH	AVG	PB	PR	/A	PD	TPI
1956	Bal-A	0	0	—	4	1	0	0	0	8	6	0	6	6	13.5	1.13	349	.222	.364	0	.000	-0	3	2	-0	0.0
1957	Bal-A	4	10	.286	35	15	2	1	4	140¹	107	12	39	97	9.7	2.69	133	.212	.276	5	.147	-1	17	14	-2	1.1
1958	Bal-A★	14	11	.560	41	25	12	3	8	221¹	201	13	51	137	10.4	2.97	121	.241	.288	8	.111	-1	20	15	-0	1.7
1959	Bal-A★	10	12	.455	38	24	6	2	1	199¹	163	18	67	88	10.4	2.93	129	.220	.286	5	.083	-3	21	19	1	1.8
1960	SF-N	8	13	.381	43	24	6	1	2	202²	198	16	72	145	12.1	3.20	109	.252	.317	6	.107	1	13	6	-1	0.5
1961	SF-N	7	5	.583	46	14	4	1	2	130¹	132	10	33	110	11.5	3.59	106	.260	.306	4	.103	-2	6	3	-1	0.0
1962	*SF-N	19	14	.576	43	39	20	2	0	280²	282	18	66	195	11.4	3.53	108	.258	.304	12	.133	-1	13	8	-2	0.5
1963	SF-N	14	10	.583	36	33	10	3	1	222¹	218	14	70	116	11.9	3.16	101	.253	.314	16	.205	4	3	1	-4	0.0
1964	SF-N	8	7	.533	36	8	1	0	2	85	82	10	35	54	12.8	5.40	66	.252	.332	0	.000	-2	-18	-17	-1	-3.2
1965	Mil-N	10	6	.625	62	1	0	0	18	111¹	87	10	30	78	9.6	2.18	161	.215	.272	4	.174	1	17	17	-0	3.0
1966	Atl-N	2	3	.400	24	0	0	0	6	41¹	44	3	18	20	13.9	2.40	152	.272	.352	2	.250	-0	6	6	-0	0.8
	Pit-N	3	2	.600	37	2	0	0	4	71¹	74	3	23	47	12.7	2.78	129	.275	.341	1	.063	-1	7	6	-1	0.3
	Yr	5	5	.500	61	2	0	0	10	112²	118	6	41	67	13.0	2.64	136	.273	.341	3	.125	-1	12	12	-1	1.1
1967	Pit-N	5	6	.455	27	11	1	0	0	110¹	116	8	41	34	13.7	5.82	58	.265	.351	3	.115	-0	-24	-24	-1	-2.9
Total	13	105	100	.512	479	199	63	13	48	1817	1697	137	556	1133	11.4	3.29	109	.246	.306	66	.125	-7	85	59	-12	3.8

● **TED ODENWALD**   Odenwald, Theodore Joseph "Lefty"   b: 1/4/02, Hudson, Wis.   d: 10/23/65, Shakopee, Minn.   BR/TL, 5'10", 147 lbs.   Deb: 4/13/21

YEAR	TM/L	W	L	PCT	G	GS	CG	SH	SV	IP	H	HR	BB	SO	RAT	ERA	ERA+	OAV	OOB	BH	AVG	PB	PR	/A	PD	TPI
1921	Cle-A	1	0	1.000	10	0	0	0	0	17¹	16	0	6	4	11.9	1.56	274	.262	.338	0	.000	-1	5	5	0	0.2
1922	Cle-A	0	0	—	1	0	0	0	0	1¹	6	0	2	2	54.0	40.50	10	.600	.667	0	—	0	-5	-5	-0	0.0
Total	2	1	0	1.000	11	0	0	0	0	18²	22	0	8	6	14.9	4.34	98	.310	.387	0	.000	-1	-0	-0	0	0.2

● **DAVE ODOM**   Odom, David Everett "Blimp" or "Porky"   b: 6/5/18, Dinuba, Cal.   d: 11/19/87, Myrtle Beach, Fla.   BR/TR, 6'1", 220 lbs.   Deb: 5/31/43

YEAR	TM/L	W	L	PCT	G	GS	CG	SH	SV	IP	H	HR	BB	SO	RAT	ERA	ERA+	OAV	OOB	BH	AVG	PB	PR	/A	PD	TPI
1943	Bos-N	0	3	.000	22	3	1	0	2	54²	54	3	30	17	14.5	5.27	65	.269	.374	0	.000	-2	-11	-11	-1	-1.0

● **BLUE MOON ODOM**   Odom, Johnny Lee   b: 5/29/45, Macon, Ga.   BR/TR, 6', 185 lbs.   Deb: 9/5/64   ◆

YEAR	TM/L	W	L	PCT	G	GS	CG	SH	SV	IP	H	HR	BB	SO	RAT	ERA	ERA+	OAV	OOB	BH	AVG	PB	PR	/A	PD	TPI
1964	KC-A	1	2	.333	5	5	1	1	0	17	29	5	11	10	21.2	10.06	38	.363	.440	0	.000	-0	-12	-12	0	-1.7
1965	KC-A	0	0	—	1	0	0	0	0	1	2	0	2	0	36.0	9.00	39	.400	.571	0	—	0	-1	-1	0	-0.1
1966	KC-A	5	5	.500	14	14	4	2	0	90¹	70	1	53	47	12.5	2.49	136	.215	.328	3	.097	-1	9	9	2	1.1
1967	KC-A	3	8	.273	29	17	0	0	0	103²	94	9	68	67	14.3	5.04	63	.243	.360	8	.286	2	-21	-21	0	-1.9
1968	Oak-A★	16	10	.615	32	31	9	4	0	231¹	179	9	98	143	11.0	2.45	115	.216	.304	17	.218	6	14	9	1	2.0
1969	Oak-A★	15	6	.714	32	32	10	3	0	231¹	179	15	112	150	11.6	2.92	118	.215	.312	21	.266	11	18	13	1	2.5
1970	Oak-A	9	8	.529	29	29	4	1	0	156	128	14	100	88	13.6	3.80	93	.227	.351	13	.241	6	-1	-5	2	0.5
1971	Oak-A	10	12	.455	25	25	3	1	0	140²	147	13	71	69	13.9	4.29	78	.271	.355	8	.160	1	-13	-15	-1	-2.1
1972	*Oak-A	15	6	.714	31	30	4	2	0	194¹	164	10	87	86	11.8	2.50	114	.234	.321	8	.121	0	12	7	0	0.8
1973	*Oak-A	5	12	.294	30	24	3	0	0	150¹	153	14	67	83	13.3	4.49	79	.263	.341	0	.000	-0	-11	-16	-1	-1.8
1974	*Oak-A	1	5	.167	34	5	1	0	1	87¹	85	4	52	54	14.3	3.81	87	.267	.375	0	—	0	-2	-5	1	-0.3
1975	Oak-A	0	2	.000	7	2	0	0	0	11	19	1	11	4	25.4	12.27	30	.422	.544	0	—	0	-10	-11	0	-1.6
	Cle-A	1	0	1.000	3	1	1	1	0	10¹	4	1	8	10	10.5	2.61	145	.118	.286	0	—	0	1	1	-0	0.1
	Yr	1	2	.333	10	3	1	1	0	21¹	23	2	19	14	17.7	7.59	49	.284	.420	0	—	0	-9	-9	-0	-1.5
	Atl-N	1	7	.125	15	10	0	0	0	56	78	5	28	30	17.7	7.07	53	.342	.414	1	.077	-1	-21	-21	0	-2.5
1976	Chi-A	2	2	.500	8	4	0	0	0	28	31	2	20	18	16.7	5.79	62	.282	.397	0	—	0	-7	-7	-1	-0.9
Total	13	84	85	.497	295	229	40	15	1	1509	1362	103	788	857	13.0	3.70	89	.244	.341	79	.195	26	-45	-71	5	-5.8

● **GEORGE O'DONNELL**   O'Donnell, George Dana   b: 5/27/29, Winchester, Ill.   BR/TR, 6'3", 175 lbs.   Deb: 4/18/54

YEAR	TM/L	W	L	PCT	G	GS	CG	SH	SV	IP	H	HR	BB	SO	RAT	ERA	ERA+	OAV	OOB	BH	AVG	PB	PR	/A	PD	TPI
1954	Pit-N	3	9	.250	21	10	3	0	1	87¹	105	4	21	8	13.2	4.53	92	.315	.360	2	.087	-1	-4	-3	1	-0.4

● **JOHN O'DONOGHUE**   O'Donoghue, John Preston   b: 5/26/69, Wilmington, Del.   BL/TL, 6'6", 198 lbs.   Deb: 6/27/93   F

YEAR	TM/L	W	L	PCT	G	GS	CG	SH	SV	IP	H	HR	BB	SO	RAT	ERA	ERA+	OAV	OOB	BH	AVG	PB	PR	/A	PD	TPI
1993	Bal-A	0	1	.000	11	1	0	0	0	19²	22	4	10	16	15.1	4.58	98	.278	.367	0	—	0	-1	-0	-0	-0.2

● **JOHN O'DONOGHUE**   O'Donoghue, John Eugene   b: 10/7/39, Kansas City, Mo.   BR/TL, 6'3", 210 lbs.   Deb: 9/29/63   F

YEAR	TM/L	W	L	PCT	G	GS	CG	SH	SV	IP	H	HR	BB	SO	RAT	ERA	ERA+	OAV	OOB	BH	AVG	PB	PR	/A	PD	TPI
1963	KC-A	0	1	.000	1	1	0	0	0	6	6	0	2	1	12.0	1.50	260	.286	.348	0	.000	-0	1	2	-0	0.2
1964	KC-A	10	14	.417	39	32	2	1	0	173²	202	24	65	79	14.0	4.92	78	.286	.349	13	.236	2	-25	-21	-1	-2.6
1965	KC-A☆	9	18	.333	34	30	4	1	0	177²	183	15	66	82	12.7	3.95	88	.267	.332	12	.218	3	-10	-9	0	-1.0
1966	Cle-A	6	8	.429	32	13	2	0	0	108	109	13	23	49	11.2	3.83	90	.264	.306	5	.152	-1	-5	-5	1	-0.5
1967	Cle-A	8	9	.471	33	17	5	2	2	130²	120	10	33	81	10.7	3.24	101	.247	.298	4	.100	-0	0	0	3	0.4
1968	Bal-A	0	0	—	16	0	0	0	2	22	34	2	7	11	16.8	6.14	48	.374	.418	0	.000	-0	-8	-8	-0	-0.2
1969	Sea-A	2	2	.500	55	0	0	0	5	70	58	5	37	48	12.6	2.96	123	.230	.336	1	.077	-1	5	5	-0	0.3
1970	Mil-A	2	0	1.000	25	0	0	0	0	23¹	29	4	9	13	14.7	5.01	76	.299	.358	0	.000	-0	-3	-3	1	-0.6
	Mon-N	2	3	.400	9	3	0	0	0	22¹	20	2	11	6	13.3	5.24	78	.263	.371	0	.000	-0	-3	-3	-0	-0.6
1971	Mon-N	0	0	—	13	0	0	0	0	17¹	19	3	7	7	13.5	4.67	75	.271	.338	0	—	0	-2	-2	-0	0.0
Total	9	39	55	.415	257	96	13	4	10	751	780	78	260	377	12.6	4.07	87	.269	.332	35	.170	2	-49	-44	4	-4.2

● **LEFTY O'DOUL**   O'Doul, Francis Joseph   b: 3/4/1897, San Francisco, Cal.   d: 12/7/69, San Francisco, Cal.   BL/TL, 6', 180 lbs.   Deb: 4/29/19   ◆

YEAR	TM/L	W	L	PCT	G	GS	CG	SH	SV	IP	H	HR	BB	SO	RAT	ERA	ERA+	OAV	OOB	BH	AVG	PB	PR	/A	PD	TPI
1919	NY-A	0	0	—	3	0	0	0	0	5	7	0	4	2	19.8	3.60	89	.304	.407	4	.250	-1	-0	-0	-0	0.0
1920	NY-A	0	0	—	2	0	0	0	0	3²	4	0	2	2	17.2	4.91	78	.286	.412	2	.167	-0	-0	-0	-0	0.0
1922	NY-A	0	0	—	6	0	0	0	0	16	24	0	12	5	20.3	3.38	119	.353	.450	3	.333	1	1	1	0	0.1
1923	Bos-A	1	1	.500	23	1	0	0	0	53	69	2	31	10	17.7	5.43	76	.337	.433	5	.143	-1	-9	-8	1	-0.3
Total	4	1	1	.500	34	1	0	0	0	77²	104	2	49	19	18.3	4.87	83	.335	.434	1140	.349	-1	-8	-7	1	-0.2

● **BRYAN OELKERS**   Oelkers, Bryan Alois   b: 3/11/61, Zaragoza, Spain   BL/TL, 6'3", 192 lbs.   Deb: 4/9/83

YEAR	TM/L	W	L	PCT	G	GS	CG	SH	SV	IP	H	HR	BB	SO	RAT	ERA	ERA+	OAV	OOB	BH	AVG	PB	PR	/A	PD	TPI
1983	Min-A	0	5	.000	10	8	0	0	0	34¹	56	7	17	13	19.1	8.65	49	.376	.440	0	—	0	-18	-17	-1	-2.2
1986	Cle-A	3	3	.500	35	4	0	0	1	69	70	13	40	33	15.1	4.70	88	.262	.371	0	—	0	-4	-4	-1	-0.3
Total	2	3	8	.273	45	12	0	0	1	103¹	126	20	57	46	16.5	6.01	70	.303	.395	0	—	0	-21	-21	-2	-2.5

● **JOE OESCHGER**   Oeschger, Joseph Carl   b: 5/24/1892, Chicago, Ill.   d: 7/28/86, Rohnert Park, Cal   BR/TR, 6'", 190 lbs.   Deb: 4/21/14

YEAR	TM/L	W	L	PCT	G	GS	CG	SH	SV	IP	H	HR	BB	SO	RAT	ERA	ERA+	OAV	OOB	BH	AVG	PB	PR	/A	PD	TPI
1914	Phi-N	4	8	.333	32	10	5	0	1	124	129	5	54	47	14.0	3.77	78	.279	.366	3	.075	-4	-14	-11	-1	-1.6
1915	Phi-N	1	0	1.000	6	1	1	0	0	23²	21	1	9	8	11.4	3.42	80	.247	.319	0	.000	-1	-2	-2	-0	-0.2
1916	Phi-N	1	0	1.000	14	0	0	0	0	30¹	18	2	14	17	9.8	2.37	112	.184	.292	0	.000	-1	1	1	1	0.0
1917	Phi-N	15	14	.517	42	30	18	5	1	262	241	7	72	123	11.0	2.75	102	.249	.305	10	.114	-1	-1	-2	-3	-0.6
1918	Phi-N	6	18	.250	30	23	13	2	3	184	159	3	83	60	12.2	3.03	99	.238	.328	5	.083	-4	-6	-1	-2	-0.7
1919	Phi-N	0	1	1.000	5	4	2	0	0	38	52	1	16	5	16.6	5.92	54	.340	.409	0	.000	-2	-13	-11	-0	-0.5
	NY-N	0	1	1.000	5	1	0	0	0	8	12	0	2	3	15.8	4.50	62	.400	.438	0	—	0	-1	-2	-0	-0.2
	Bos-N	4	2	.667	7	7	4	1	0	56²	63	0	21	16	13.5	2.54	112	.300	.366	2	.091	-1	2	2	-1	-0.1
	Yr	4	4	.500	17	12	6	1	0	102²	127	1	39	24	14.6	3.94	76	.322	.384	2	.053	-4	-12	-11	-2	-0.8
1920	Bos-N	15	13	.536	38	30	20	5	0	299	294	10	99	80	12.1	3.46	88	.265	.329	18	.198	-3	-11	-14	-3	-1.8
1921	Bos-N	20	14	.588	46	36	19	3	0	299	303	11	97	68	12.5	3.52	104	.274	.341	28	.255	2	9	4	2	0.9
1922	Bos-N	6	21	.222	46	23	10	1	0	195²	234	8	81	51	14.9	5.06	79	.303	.375	12	.190	-0	-21	-23	1	-2.6
1923	Bos-N	5	15	.250	44	19	6	1	2	166¹	227	4	54	39	15.5	5.68	70	.330	.383	12	.231	-0	-31	-31	0	-3.2
1924	NY-N	2	0	1.000	10	2	0	0	0	29	35	1	14	10	15.5	3.10	118	.287	.360	3	.429	1	2	2	1	0.1
	Phi-N	2	7	.222	19	8	1	0	0	65¹	88	6	16	14	14.7	4.41	101	.333	.378	5	.250	-1	-4	-0	-0	0.0
	Yr	4	7	.364	29	10	1	0	0	94¹	123	7	30	18	14.9	4.01	105	.319	.372	8	.296	-1	-2	2	-1	0.1
1925	Bro-N	1	2	.333	21	3	1	0	0	65	70	7	30	18	14.9	6.08	69	.382	.452	1	.125	-0	-7	-8	-0	-0.6
Total	12	82	116	.414	365	197	99	18	8	1818	1936	61	651	535	13.1	3.81	88	.281	.349	99	.165	-18	-96	-89	-8	-11.1

YEAR TM/L	W	L	PCT	G	GS	CG	SH	SV	IP	H	HR	BB	SO	RAT	ERA	ERA+	OAV	OOB	BH	AVG	PB	PR	/A	PD	TPI

● **JACK OGDEN**   Ogden, John Mahlon b: 11/5/1897, Ogden, Pa. d: 11/9/77, Philadelphia, Pa. BR/TR, 6′, 190 lbs. Deb: 6/22/18 F

YEAR TM/L	W	L	PCT	G	GS	CG	SH	SV	IP	H	HR	BB	SO	RAT	ERA	ERA+	OAV	OOB	BH	AVG	PB	PR	/A	PD	TPI
1918 NY-N	0	0	—	5	0	0	0	0	8²	8	0	3	1	13.5	3.12	84	.296	.406	0	.000	-0	-0	-0	-0	-0.1
1928 StL-A	15	16	.484	38	31	18	1	2	242²	257	23	80	67	12.5	4.15	101	.274	.331	17	.200	-1	-3	1	-4	-0.3
1929 StL-A	4	8	.333	34	14	7	0	0	131¹	154	8	44	32	13.6	4.93	90	.301	.357	11	.244	0	-10	-7	0	-0.5
1931 Cin-N	4	8	.333	22	9	3	1	1	89	79	3	32	24	11.2	2.93	127	.242	.310	4	.148	-1	9	8	-1	0.8
1932 Cin-N	2	2	.500	24	3	1	0	0	57	72	5	22	20	14.8	5.21	74	.310	.370	2	.167	0	-8	-9	1	-0.5
Total 5	25	34	.424	123	57	29	2	3	528²	570	39	181	144	12.8	4.24	97	.280	.340	34	.200	-1	-13	-8	-4	-0.6

● **CURLY OGDEN**   Ogden, Warren Harvey b: 1/24/01, Ogden, Pa. d: 8/6/64, Chester, Pa. BR/TR, 6′1.5″, 180 lbs. Deb: 7/18/22 F

YEAR TM/L	W	L	PCT	G	GS	CG	SH	SV	IP	H	HR	BB	SO	RAT	ERA	ERA+	OAV	OOB	BH	AVG	PB	PR	/A	PD	TPI
1922 Phi-A	1	4	.200	15	6	4	0	0	72¹	59	4	33	20	12.1	3.11	137	.237	.338	7	.241	-0	8	9	-0	0.5
1923 Phi-A	1	2	.333	18	2	0	0	0	46¹	63	4	32	14	19.0	5.63	73	.330	.434	5	.294	1	-8	-8	0	-0.4
1924 Phi-A	0	3	.000	5	1	0	0	0	12²	14	1	7	4	15.6	4.97	86	.275	.373	0	.000	-1	-1	-1	-0	-0.3
*Was-A	9	5	.643	16	16	9	3	0	108	83	3	51	23	11.3	2.58	156	.221	.317	13	.277	2	20	17	-0	2.2
Yr	9	8	.529	21	17	9	3	0	120²	97	4	58	27	11.7	2.83	143	.227	.322	13	.260	1	19	16	-1	1.9
1925 Was-A	3	1	.750	17	4	2	1	0	42	45	1	18	6	13.9	4.50	94	.288	.369	3	.250	-0	-0	-1	-0	-0.1
1926 Was-A	4	4	.500	22	9	4	0	0	96¹	114	2	45	21	15.3	4.30	90	.305	.387	5	.185	-1	-3	-5	-1	-0.5
Total 5	18	19	.486	93	38	19	4	0	377²	378	13	186	88	13.9	3.79	108	.271	.364	33	.244	1	14	12	-2	1.4

● **CHAD OGEA**   Ogea, Chad Wayne b: 11/9/70, Lake Charles, La. BR/TR, 6′2″, 200 lbs. Deb: 5/3/94

YEAR TM/L	W	L	PCT	G	GS	CG	SH	SV	IP	H	HR	BB	SO	RAT	ERA	ERA+	OAV	OOB	BH	AVG	PB	PR	/A	PD	TPI
1994 Cle-A	0	1	.000	4	4	0	0	0	16¹	21	2	10	11	17.6	6.06	81	.304	.400	0	—	0	-2	-2	0	-0.1

● **JOE OGRODOWSKI**   Ogrodowski, Joseph Anthony b: 11/20/06, Hoytville, Pa. d: 6/24/59, Elmira, N.Y. BR/TR, 5′11″, 165 lbs. Deb: 4/27/25

YEAR TM/L	W	L	PCT	G	GS	CG	SH	SV	IP	H	HR	BB	SO	RAT	ERA	ERA+	OAV	OOB	BH	AVG	PB	PR	/A	PD	TPI
1925 Bos-N	0	0	—	1	0	0	0	0	1	6	0	3	0	81.0	54.00	7	.600	.692	0	—	0	-6	-6	-0	0.0

● **BILL O'HARA**   O'Hara, William Alexander b: 8/14/1883, Toronto, Ont., Can. d: 6/15/31, Jersey City, N.J. BL/TR, 5′10″, Deb: 4/15/09 ♦

YEAR TM/L	W	L	PCT	G	GS	CG	SH	SV	IP	H	HR	BB	SO	RAT	ERA	ERA+	OAV	OOB	BH	AVG	PB	PR	/A	PD	TPI
1910 StL-N	0	0	—	1	0	0	0	0	1	0	0	0	0	0.00	—	.000	.000	3	.150	-0	0	-0	0	0.0

● **JOE OHL**   Ohl, Joseph Earl (b: Joseph Earl Von Ohl) b: 1/10/1888, Jobston, N.J. d: 12/18/51, Camden, N.J. BL/TL, Deb: 7/29/09

YEAR TM/L	W	L	PCT	G	GS	CG	SH	SV	IP	H	HR	BB	SO	RAT	ERA	ERA+	OAV	OOB	BH	AVG	PB	PR	/A	PD	TPI
1909 Was-A	0	0	—	4	0	0	0	0	8²	7	0	1	2	9.3	2.08	117	.194	.237	0	.000	-0	0	0	-0	0.0

● **BOB OJEDA**   Ojeda, Robert Michael b: 12/17/57, Los Angeles, Cal. BL/TL, 6′1″, 190 lbs. Deb: 7/13/80

YEAR TM/L	W	L	PCT	G	GS	CG	SH	SV	IP	H	HR	BB	SO	RAT	ERA	ERA+	OAV	OOB	BH	AVG	PB	PR	/A	PD	TPI
1980 Bos-A	1	1	.500	7	7	0	0	0	26	39	2	14	12	18.3	6.92	61	.361	.434	0	—	0	-8	-8	-0	-0.9
1981 Bos-A	6	2	.750	10	10	2	0	0	66¹	50	6	25	28	10.4	3.12	124	.212	.293	0	—	0	4	6	-0	0.3
1982 Bos-A	4	6	.400	22	14	0	0	0	78¹	95	3	29	52	14.4	5.63	76	.296	.356	0	—	0	-14	-12	-1	-1.8
1983 Bos-A	12	7	.632	29	28	5	0	0	173²	173	15	73	94	12.9	4.04	108	.265	.342	0	—	0	4	6	0	0.2
1984 Bos-A	12	12	.500	33	32	8	5	0	216²	211	17	96	137	12.8	3.99	104	.259	.338	0	—	0	4	1	0	0.2
1985 Bos-A	9	11	.450	39	22	5	1	0	157²	166	11	48	102	12.3	4.00	107	.273	.328	0	—	0	3	5	0	0.4
1986 *NY-N	18	5	.783	32	30	7	2	0	217¹	185	15	52	148	9.9	2.57	138	.230	.279	8	.113	-2	28	23	1	2.2
1987 NY-N	3	5	.375	10	7	0	0	0	46¹	45	5	10	21	10.7	3.88	97	.253	.293	1	.071	-0	-1	-1	-0	-0.1
1988 NY-N	10	13	.435	29	29	5	5	0	190¹	158	6	33	133	9.2	2.88	112	.225	.264	10	.164	1	12	7	2	1.1
1989 NY-N	13	11	.542	31	31	5	2	0	192	179	16	78	95	12.1	3.47	94	.245	.319	7	.106	-2	1	-4	2	-0.5
1990 NY-N	7	6	.538	38	12	0	0	0	118	123	10	40	62	12.6	3.66	102	.272	.334	4	.133	-0	2	1	3	0.3
1991 LA-N	12	9	.571	31	31	2	1	0	189¹	181	15	70	120	12.1	3.18	113	.257	.326	9	.161	1	11	9	1	1.2
1992 LA-N	6	9	.400	29	29	2	1	0	166¹	169	8	81	94	13.6	3.63	95	.268	.352	5	.102	-1	-2	-3	2	-0.2
1993 Cle-A	2	1	.667	9	7	0	0	0	43	48	5	21	27	14.4	4.40	98	.289	.369	0	—	0	-0	-1	0	0.1
1994 NY-A	0	0	—	2	2	0	0	0	9	11	6	3	5	51.0	24.00	18	.611	.708	0	—	0	-6	-7	-0	0.1
Total 15	115	98	.540	351	291	41	16	1	1884¹	1833	145	676	1128	12.1	3.65	103	.257	.323	44	.127	-4	30	24	10	2.6

● **FRANK OKRIE**   Okrie, Frank Anthony "Lefty" b: 10/28/1896, Detroit, Mich. d: 10/16/59, Detroit, Mich. BL/TL, 5′11″, 175 lbs. Deb: 4/20/20 F

YEAR TM/L	W	L	PCT	G	GS	CG	SH	SV	IP	H	HR	BB	SO	RAT	ERA	ERA+	OAV	OOB	BH	AVG	PB	PR	/A	PD	TPI
1920 Det-A	1	2	.333	21	1	1	0	0	41	44	2	18	9	14.7	5.27	71	.295	.390	1	.200	-0	-7	-7	6	0.1

● **RED OLDHAM**   Oldham, John Cyrus b: 7/15/1893, Zion, Md. d: 1/28/61, Costa Mesa, Cal. BB/TL, 6′ ″, 176 lbs. Deb: 8/19/14

YEAR TM/L	W	L	PCT	G	GS	CG	SH	SV	IP	H	HR	BB	SO	RAT	ERA	ERA+	OAV	OOB	BH	AVG	PB	PR	/A	PD	TPI
1914 Det-A	2	4	.333	9	7	3	0	0	45¹	42	1	6	23	10.5	3.38	83	.243	.288	4	.267	1	-3	-3	-1	-0.4
1915 Det-A	3	0	1.000	17	2	1	0	4	57²	52	1	17	17	11.4	2.81	108	.243	.311	2	.143	-0	1	1	-1	0.0
1920 Det-A	8	13	.381	39	22	10	1	1	215¹	248	5	91	62	14.4	3.85	97	.302	.376	12	.174	-1	-1	-3	4	-0.0
1921 Det-A	11	14	.440	40	28	12	1	1	229¹	258	11	81	67	13.5	4.24	101	.288	.351	19	.224	2	1	1	1	-0.0
1922 Det-A	10	13	.435	43	27	9	0	3	212	256	14	59	72	13.8	4.67	83	.305	.358	19	.260	4	-15	-19	1	-1.3
1925 *Pit-N	3	2	.600	11	4	3	0	1	53	66	2	18	10	14.6	3.91	114	.313	.372	3	.333	2	2	3	0	0.5
1926 Pit-N	2	2	.500	17	2	0	0	2	41²	56	1	18	16	16.2	5.62	70	.359	.429	2	.222	0	-8	-8	-0	-0.7
Total 7	39	48	.448	176	92	38	2	12	854¹	978	35	292	267	13.7	4.15	93	.295	.358	64	.226	9	-23	-26	4	-1.5

● **STEVE OLIN**   Olin, Steven Robert b: 10/4/65, Portland, Ore. d: 3/22/93, Little Lake Nellie, Fla. BR/TR, 6′3″, 185 lbs. Deb: 7/29/89

YEAR TM/L	W	L	PCT	G	GS	CG	SH	SV	IP	H	HR	BB	SO	RAT	ERA	ERA+	OAV	OOB	BH	AVG	PB	PR	/A	PD	TPI
1989 Cle-A	1	4	.200	25	0	0	0	1	36	35	1	14	24	12.3	3.75	106	.255	.325	0	—	0	1	1	0	0.1
1990 Cle-A	4	4	.500	50	1	0	0	1	92¹	96	3	26	64	12.5	3.41	115	.270	.331	0	—	0	5	5	2	0.7
1991 Cle-A	3	6	.333	48	0	0	0	17	56¹	61	2	23	38	13.6	3.36	124	.274	.344	0	—	0	5	5	0	1.1
1992 Cle-A	8	5	.615	72	0	0	0	29	88¹	80	8	27	47	11.3	2.34	167	.248	.314	0	—	0	16	15	1	3.5
Total 4	16	19	.457	195	1	0	0	48	273	272	14	90	173	12.3	3.10	128	.262	.328	0	—	0	26	26	3	5.4

● **OMAR OLIVARES**   Olivares, Omar (Palqu) b: 7/6/67, Mayaguez, P.R. BR/TR, 6′1″, 185 lbs. Deb: 8/18/90 F

YEAR TM/L	W	L	PCT	G	GS	CG	SH	SV	IP	H	HR	BB	SO	RAT	ERA	ERA+	OAV	OOB	BH	AVG	PB	PR	/A	PD	TPI
1990 StL-N	1	1	.500	9	6	0	0	0	49¹	45	2	17	20	11.7	2.92	131	.249	.320	3	.176	1	5	5	1	0.4
1991 StL-N	11	7	.611	28	24	0	0	1	167¹	148	13	61	91	11.5	3.71	100	.243	.317	12	.226	3	-1	0	2	0.5
1992 StL-N	9	9	.500	32	30	1	0	0	197	189	20	63	124	11.7	3.84	88	.257	.319	16	.235	4	-7	-10	3	-0.1
1993 StL-N	5	3	.625	58	9	0	0	1	118²	134	10	54	63	14.9	4.17	95	.288	.372	7	.269	2	-2	-3	4	0.4
1994 StL-N	3	4	.429	14	12	1	0	0	73²	84	10	37	26	15.3	5.74	71	.294	.382	6	.214	2	-13	-14	1	-0.9
Total 5	29	24	.547	141	81	2	0	3	606	600	55	232	324	12.7	4.02	92	.263	.338	44	.229	12	-17	-21	9	0.3

● **DARREN OLIVER**   Oliver, Darren Christopher b: 10/6/70, Rio Linda, Cal. BR/TL, 6′, 170 lbs. Deb: 9/1/93 F

YEAR TM/L	W	L	PCT	G	GS	CG	SH	SV	IP	H	HR	BB	SO	RAT	ERA	ERA+	OAV	OOB	BH	AVG	PB	PR	/A	PD	TPI
1993 Tex-A	0	0	—	2	0	0	0	0	3¹	2	1	1	4	8.1	2.70	154	.154	.214	0	—	0	1	1	0	0.3
1994 Tex-A	4	0	1.000	43	0	0	0	2	50	40	4	35	50	14.6	3.42	132	.223	.368	0	—	0	8	6	0	0.8
Total 2	4	0	1.000	45	0	0	0	2	53¹	42	5	36	54	14.2	3.38	134	.219	.359	0	—	0	8	7	0	1.1

● **FRANCISCO OLIVERAS**   Oliveras, Francisco Javier (Noa) b: 1/31/63, Santurce, P.R. BR/TR, 5′10″, 170 lbs. Deb: 5/3/89

YEAR TM/L	W	L	PCT	G	GS	CG	SH	SV	IP	H	HR	BB	SO	RAT	ERA	ERA+	OAV	OOB	BH	AVG	PB	PR	/A	PD	TPI
1989 Min-A	3	4	.429	12	8	1	0	0	55²	64	8	15	24	12.9	4.53	91	.288	.336	0	—	0	-4	-2	-1	-0.4
1990 SF-N	2	2	.500	33	2	0	0	2	55¹	47	5	21	41	11.4	2.77	132	.230	.308	0	.000	-1	6	5	-1	0.3
1991 SF-N	6	6	.500	55	1	0	0	3	79¹	69	12	22	48	10.4	3.86	93	.242	.299	2	.200	-2	-2	-0	-0	-0.4
1992 SF-N	0	3	.000	16	7	0	0	0	44²	41	11	10	17	10.5	3.63	91	.250	.297	1	.143	0	-1	-2	-0	-0.1
Total 4	11	15	.423	116	18	1	0	5	235	221	36	68	130	11.3	3.71	99	.253	.310	3	.136	0	0	-1	-2	-0.6

● **DIOMEDES OLIVO**   Olivo, Diomedes Antonio (Maldonado) b: 1/22/19, Guayubin, D.R. d: 2/15/77, Santo Domingo, D.R. BL/TL, 6′1″, 195 lbs. Deb: 9/5/60 F

YEAR TM/L	W	L	PCT	G	GS	CG	SH	SV	IP	H	HR	BB	SO	RAT	ERA	ERA+	OAV	OOB	BH	AVG	PB	PR	/A	PD	TPI
1960 Pit-N	0	0	—	4	0	0	0	0	9²	7	1	5	10	12.1	2.79	134	.216	.310	0	.000	-0	1	1	-0	0.0
1962 Pit-N	5	1	.833	62	1	0	0	7	84¹	88	5	25	66	12.1	2.77	142	.277	.327	1	.188	1	11	11	-1	0.9
1963 StL-N	0	5	.000	19	0	0	0	0	13¹	16	1	9	9	17.6	5.40	66	.296	.406	0	—	0	-3	-3	-0	-0.9
Total 3	5	6	.455	85	1	0	0	7	107¹	112	7	39	85	12.7	3.10	125	.274	.339	1	.176	0	9	9	-0	0.0

● **CHI-CHI OLIVO**   Olivo, Federico Emilio (Maldonado) b: 3/18/28, Guayubin, D.R. d: 2/3/77, Guayubin, D.R. BR/TR, 6′2″, 215 lbs. Deb: 6/5/61 F

YEAR TM/L	W	L	PCT	G	GS	CG	SH	SV	IP	H	HR	BB	SO	RAT	ERA	ERA+	OAV	OOB	BH	AVG	PB	PR	/A	PD	TPI
1961 Mil-N	0	0	—	3	0	0	0	0	2	3	1	5	1	36.0	18.00	21	.500	.727	0	—	0	-3	-3	-0	0.0

YEAR	TM/L	W	L	PCT	G	GS	CG	SH	SV	IP	H	HR	BB	SO	RAT	ERA	ERA+	OAV	OOB	BH	AVG	PB	PR	/A	PD	TPI
1964	Mil-N	2	1	.667	38	0	0	0	5	60	55	7	21	45	11.4	3.75	94	.247	.311	1	.250	0	-1	-2	1	0.0
1965	Mil-N	0	1	.000	8	0	0	0	0	13	12	1	5	11	11.8	1.38	254	.267	.340	0	—	0	3	3	-0	0.2
1966	Atl-N	5	4	.556	47	0	0	0	7	66	59	4	19	41	10.8	4.23	86	.240	.297	1	.111	-0	-5	-4	-1	-0.8
Total	4	7	6	.538	96	0	0	0	12	141	129	13	50	98	11.5	3.96	90	.248	.315	2	.154	-0	-6	-6	-1	-0.6

● **JIM OLLOM**   Ollom, James Donald b: 7/8/45, Snohomish, Wash.   BR/TL, 6'4", 210 lbs.   Deb: 9/3/66

YEAR	TM/L	W	L	PCT	G	GS	CG	SH	SV	IP	H	HR	BB	SO	RAT	ERA	ERA+	OAV	OOB	BH	AVG	PB	PR	/A	PD	TPI
1966	Min-A	0	0	—	3	1	0	0	0	10	6	1	1	11	7.2	3.60	100	.167	.211	0	.000	-0	-0	-0	-0	0.0
1967	Min-A	0	1	.000	21	2	0	0	0	35	33	4	11	17	12.3	5.40	64	.258	.336	1	.200	0	-8	-8	-0	-0.2
Total	2	0	1	.000	24	3	0	0	0	45	39	5	12	28	11.2	5.00	70	.238	.309	1	.143	-0	-9	-8	-0	-0.2

● **FRED OLMSTEAD**   Olmstead, Frederic William b: 7/3/1881, Grand Rapids, Mich.   d: 10/22/36, Muskogee, Okla.   BR/TR, 5'11", 170 lbs.   Deb: 7/2/08

YEAR	TM/L	W	L	PCT	G	GS	CG	SH	SV	IP	H	HR	BB	SO	RAT	ERA	ERA+	OAV	OOB	BH	AVG	PB	PR	/A	PD	TPI
1908	Chi-A	0	0	—	1	0	0	0	0	2	6	0	1	1	31.5	13.50	17	.600	.636	0	.000	1	-2	-2	-0	0.0
1909	Chi-A	3	2	.600	8	6	5	0	0	54²	52	1	12	21	10.7	1.81	129	.277	.323	2	.095	-1	4	3	-0	0.2
1910	Chi-A	10	12	.455	32	20	14	4	0	184¹	174	1	50	68	11.1	1.95	123	.260	.316	10	.154	-2	12	9	1	0.9
1911	Chi-A	6	6	.500	25	11	7	1	2	117²	146	3	30	45	13.9	4.21	77	.309	.358	7	.189	-0	-11	-13	-1	-1.3
Total	4	19	20	.487	66	37	26	5	2	358²	378	5	93	135	12.1	2.74	97	.283	.334	19	.153	-3	2	-3	-0	-0.2

● **AL OLMSTED**   Olmsted, Alan Ray b: 3/18/57, St.Louis, Mo.   BR/TL, 6'2", 195 lbs.   Deb: 9/12/80

YEAR	TM/L	W	L	PCT	G	GS	CG	SH	SV	IP	H	HR	BB	SO	RAT	ERA	ERA+	OAV	OOB	BH	AVG	PB	PR	/A	PD	TPI
1980	StL-N	1	1	.500	5	5	0	0	0	34²	32	2	14	14	12.2	2.86	129	.244	.322	2	.182	-0	3	3	1	0.2

● **HANK OLMSTED**   Olmsted, Henry Theodore b: 1/12/1879, Saginaw Bay, Mich.   d: 1/6/69, Bradenton, Fla.   BR/TR, 5'8.5", 147 lbs.   Deb: 7/15/05

YEAR	TM/L	W	L	PCT	G	GS	CG	SH	SV	IP	H	HR	BB	SO	RAT	ERA	ERA+	OAV	OOB	BH	AVG	PB	PR	/A	PD	TPI
1905	Bos-A	1	2	.333	3	3	3	0	0	25	18	0	12	6	10.8	3.24	83	.203	.298	1	.125	-0	-2	-1	-0	-0.2

● **OLE OLSEN**   Olsen, Arthur b: 9/12/1894, S.Norwalk, Conn.   d: 9/12/80, Norwalk, Conn.   BR/TR, 5'10", 163 lbs.   Deb: 4/12/22

YEAR	TM/L	W	L	PCT	G	GS	CG	SH	SV	IP	H	HR	BB	SO	RAT	ERA	ERA+	OAV	OOB	BH	AVG	PB	PR	/A	PD	TPI
1922	Det-A	7	6	.538	37	15	5	0	3	137	147	8	40	52	13.2	4.53	86	.281	.348	7	.179	-1	-7	-10	1	-0.9
1923	Det-A	1	1	.500	17	2	1	0	0	41¹	42	1	17	12	13.9	6.31	61	.290	.383	1	.125	-1	-11	-11	-1	-0.6
Total	2	8	7	.533	54	17	6	0	3	178¹	189	9	57	64	13.4	4.95	78	.283	.356	8	.170	-2	-18	-21	-0	-1.5

● **VERN OLSEN**   Olsen, Vern Jarl b: 3/16/18, Hillsboro, Ore.   d: 7/13/89, Maywood, Ill.   BR/TL, 6'0.5", 175 lbs.   Deb: 9/8/39

YEAR	TM/L	W	L	PCT	G	GS	CG	SH	SV	IP	H	HR	BB	SO	RAT	ERA	ERA+	OAV	OOB	BH	AVG	PB	PR	/A	PD	TPI
1939	Chi-N	1	0	1.000	4	0	0	0	0	7²	2	0	7	3	10.6	—	.087	.300	0	.000	0	3	3	-0	0.5
1940	Chi-N	13	9	.591	34	20	9	4	0	172²	172	5	62	71	12.3	2.97	126	.260	.325	15	.263	3	17	15	4	2.6
1941	Chi-N	10	8	.556	37	23	10	2	1	185²	202	9	57	73	12.7	3.15	111	.276	.331	15	.238	3	10	7	2	1.3
1942	Chi-N	6	9	.400	32	17	4	1	1	140¹	161	6	55	46	13.9	4.49	71	.283	.347	9	.188	1	-18	-20	1	-1.8
1946	Chi-N	0	0	—	5	0	0	0	0	9²	10	0	9	8	17.7	2.79	119	.294	.442	0	—	0	1	0	0	0.0
Total	5	30	26	.536	112	60	23	7	2	516	547	18	192	201	13.0	3.40	103	.271	.335	39	.231	8	12	6	7	2.6

● **GREGG OLSON**   Olson, Greggory William b: 10/11/66, Scribner, Neb.   BR/TR, 6'4", 210 lbs.   Deb: 9/2/88

YEAR	TM/L	W	L	PCT	G	GS	CG	SH	SV	IP	H	HR	BB	SO	RAT	ERA	ERA+	OAV	OOB	BH	AVG	PB	PR	/A	PD	TPI
1988	Bal-A	1	1	.500	10	0	0	0	0	11	10	1	10	9	16.4	3.27	119	.244	.392	0	—	0	1	0	0	0.4
1989	Bal-A	5	2	.714	64	0	0	0	27	85	57	1	46	90	11.0	1.69	224	.188	.296	0	—	0	21	20	0	3.1
1990	Bal-A☆	6	5	.545	64	0	0	0	37	74¹	57	3	31	74	11.0	2.42	157	.213	.301	0	—	0	12	11	-1	3.0
1991	Bal-A	4	6	.400	72	0	0	0	31	73²	74	1	29	72	12.7	3.18	124	.261	.332	0	—	0	8	6	0	1.7
1992	Bal-A	1	5	.167	60	0	0	0	36	61¹	46	3	24	58	10.3	2.05	196	.211	.289	0	—	0	13	13	0	3.0
1993	Bal-A	0	2	.000	50	0	0	0	29	45	37	1	18	44	11.0	1.60	279	.223	.299	0	.000	0	14	14	0	2.7
1994	Atl-N	0	2	.000	16	0	0	0	1	14²	19	1	13	10	20.3	9.20	40	.317	.446	0	.000	-0	-8	-8	-1	-1.1
Total	7	17	23	.425	336	0	0	0	161	365	300	11	171	357	11.8	2.54	156	.224	.314	0	.000	0	60	58	1	12.8

● **TED OLSON**   Olson, Theodore Otto b: 8/27/12, Quincy, Mass.   d: 12/9/80, Weymouth, Mass.   BR/TR, 6'2.5", 185 lbs.   Deb: 6/21/36

YEAR	TM/L	W	L	PCT	G	GS	CG	SH	SV	IP	H	HR	BB	SO	RAT	ERA	ERA+	OAV	OOB	BH	AVG	PB	PR	/A	PD	TPI
1936	Bos-A	1	1	.500	5	3	1	0	0	18¹	24	3	8	5	15.7	7.36	72	.324	.390	1	.143	-0	-5	-4	0	-0.4
1937	Bos-A	0	0	—	11	0	0	0	0	32¹	42	4	15	11	15.9	7.24	66	.318	.388	3	.300	1	-9	-9	1	0.2
1938	Bos-A	0	0	—	2	0	0	0	0	7	9	0	2	2	14.1	6.43	77	.310	.355	0	.000	-0	-1	-1	-0	0.0
Total	3	1	1	.500	18	3	1	0	0	57²	75	7	25	18	15.6	7.18	69	.319	.385	4	.222	1	-15	-14	1	-0.2

● **ED OLWINE**   Olwine, Edward R. b: 5/28/58, Greenville, Ohio   BL/TL, 6'2", 165 lbs.   Deb: 6/2/86

YEAR	TM/L	W	L	PCT	G	GS	CG	SH	SV	IP	H	HR	BB	SO	RAT	ERA	ERA+	OAV	OOB	BH	AVG	PB	PR	/A	PD	TPI
1986	Atl-N	0	0	—	37	0	0	0	1	47²	35	5	17	37	10.0	3.40	117	.207	.283	1	.333	1	2	3	-0	0.3
1987	Atl-N	0	1	.000	27	0	0	0	0	23¹	25	4	8	12	13.1	5.01	87	.269	.333	0	—	0	-2	-2	-0	-0.1
1988	Atl-N	0	0	—	16	0	0	0	1	18²	22	4	4	5	13.0	6.75	54	.286	.329	0	—	0	-7	-6	-1	-0.1
Total	3	0	1	.000	80	0	0	0	3	89²	82	13	29	54	11.4	4.52	89	.242	.307	1	.333	1	-8	-5	-1	-0.2

● **SKINNY O'NEAL**   O'Neal, Oran Herbert b: 5/2/1899, Gatewood, Mo.   d: 6/2/81, Springfield, Mo.   BR/TR, 5'11", 160 lbs.   Deb: 4/18/25

YEAR	TM/L	W	L	PCT	G	GS	CG	SH	SV	IP	H	HR	BB	SO	RAT	ERA	ERA+	OAV	OOB	BH	AVG	PB	PR	/A	PD	TPI
1925	Phi-N	0	0	—	11	1	0	0	0	20¹	35	2	12	6	20.8	9.30	51	.407	.480	1	.167	-0	-11	-10	0	0.0
1927	Phi-N	0	0	—	2	0	0	0	0	5	9	0	2	2	19.8	9.00	46	.409	.458	0	.000	-0	-3	-3	1	0.0
Total	2	0	0	—	13	1	0	0	0	25¹	44	2	14	8	20.6	9.24	50	.407	.475	1	.143	-0	-14	-13	0	0.0

● **RANDY O'NEAL**   O'Neal, Randall Jeffrey b: 8/30/60, Ashland, Ky.   BR/TR, 6'2", 195 lbs.   Deb: 9/12/84

YEAR	TM/L	W	L	PCT	G	GS	CG	SH	SV	IP	H	HR	BB	SO	RAT	ERA	ERA+	OAV	OOB	BH	AVG	PB	PR	/A	PD	TPI
1984	Det-A	2	1	.667	4	3	0	0	0	18²	16	0	6	12	10.6	3.38	116	.222	.282	0	—	0	1	1	-0	0.1
1985	Det-A	5	5	.500	28	12	1	0	1	94¹	82	8	36	52	11.4	3.24	126	.240	.316	0	—	0	9	9	1	1.0
1986	Det-A	3	7	.300	37	11	1	0	2	122²	121	13	44	68	12.3	4.33	95	.260	.327	0	—	0	-2	-3	-1	-0.1
1987	Atl-N	4	2	.667	16	10	0	0	0	61	79	12	24	33	15.5	5.61	78	.316	.380	2	.105	-1	-10	-9	1	-0.7
	StL-N	0	0	—	1	1	0	0	0	5	2	0	2	4	7.2	1.80	231	.111	.200	1	1.000	0	1	1	0	0.1
	Yr	4	2	.667	17	11	0	0	0	66	81	12	26	37	14.5	5.32	81	.298	.359	3	.150	-0	-9	-7	1	-0.6
1988	StL-N	2	3	.400	10	8	0	0	0	53	57	7	10	20	11.7	4.58	76	.274	.314	0	.000	-2	-7	-7	1	-0.7
1989	Phi-N	0	1	.000	20	1	0	0	0	39	46	5	9	29	12.7	6.23	57	.301	.340	0	.000	-1	-12	-12	0	-0.3
1990	SF-N	1	0	1.000	26	0	0	0	0	47	58	3	18	30	14.6	3.83	95	.314	.374	1	.167	-0	-0	-1	0	0.0
Total	7	17	19	.472	142	46	2	0	3	440²	461	48	149	248	12.6	4.35	91	.272	.334	4	.080	-3	-19	-19	5	-0.6

● **ED O'NEIL**   O'Neil, Edward J. b: 3/11/1859, Fall River, Mass.   d: 9/30/1892, Fall River, Mass.   TR, 5'11", 180 lbs.   Deb: 6/20/1890

YEAR	TM/L	W	L	PCT	G	GS	CG	SH	SV	IP	H	HR	BB	SO	RAT	ERA	ERA+	OAV	OOB	BH	AVG	PB	PR	/A	PD	TPI
1890	Tol-a	0	2	.000	2	2	2	0	0	16	27	0	13	2	22.5	7.88	50	.363	.458	2	.000	-2	-7	-7	-0	-0.7
	Phi-a	0	6	.000	6	6	6	0	0	52	84	4	32	17	21.3	9.69	40	.353	.444	5	.161	-1	-34	-34	1	-2.5
	Yr	0	8	.000	8	8	8	0	0	68	111	4	45	19	21.6	9.26	42	.355	.447	5	.125	-2	-41	-41	1	-3.2

● **J. O'NEILL**   O'Neill, J. b: Bedford, Pa.   Deb: 8/20/1875

YEAR	TM/L	W	L	PCT	G	GS	CG	SH	SV	IP	H	HR	BB	SO	RAT	ERA	ERA+	OAV	OOB	BH	AVG	PB	PR	/A	PD	TPI
1875	Atl-n	0	4	.000	5	4	3	0	0	34	56	2	0	0	14.8	4.76	48	.324	.324	3	.115	-1	-9	-9		-0.9

● **TIP O'NEILL**   O'Neill, James Edward b: 5/25/1858, Woodstock, Ont., Canada   d: 12/31/15, Montreal, Que., Can   BR/TR, 6'1.5", 167 lbs.   Deb: 5/5/1883 ♦

YEAR	TM/L	W	L	PCT	G	GS	CG	SH	SV	IP	H	HR	BB	SO	RAT	ERA	ERA+	OAV	OOB	BH	AVG	PB	PR	/A	PD	TPI
1883	NY-N	5	12	.294	19	19	15	0	0	148	182	5	64	55	15.0	4.07	76	.289	.354	15	.197	-1	-15	-16	-1	-1.6
1884	StL-a	11	4	.733	17	14	14	0	0	141	125	3	51	36	11.5	2.68	124	.232	.288	82	.276	5	9	9	0	1.2
Total	2	16	16	.500	36	33	29	0	0	289	307	8	115	91	13.3	3.39	94	.256	.323	1386	.326	3	-6	-7	-1	-0.4

● **HARRY O'NEILL**   O'Neill, Joseph Henry b: 2/20/1897, Ridgetown, Ont., Canada   d: 9/5/69, Ridgetown, Ont., Can.   BR/TR, 6', 180 lbs.   Deb: 9/15/22

YEAR	TM/L	W	L	PCT	G	GS	CG	SH	SV	IP	H	HR	BB	SO	RAT	ERA	ERA+	OAV	OOB	BH	AVG	PB	PR	/A	PD	TPI
1922	Phi-A	0	0	—	1	0	0	0	0	3	2	0	1	0	12.0	3.00	142	.200	.333	0	.000	-0	0	0	0	0.0
1923	Phi-A	0	0	—	3	0	0	0	0	2	1	0	3	2	18.0	0.00	—	.167	.444	0	—	0	1	1	0	0.0
Total	2	0	0	—	4	0	0	0	0	5	3	0	4	2	14.4	1.80	233	.188	.381	0	.000	-0	1	1	0	0.0

● **MIKE O'NEILL**   O'Neill, Michael Joyce (a.k.a. Michael Joyce in 1901)
     b: 9/7/1877, Galway, Ireland   d: 8/12/59, Scranton, Pa.   BR/TR, 5'11", 185 lbs.   Deb: 9/20/01   F ♦

YEAR	TM/L	W	L	PCT	G	GS	CG	SH	SV	IP	H	HR	BB	SO	RAT	ERA	ERA+	OAV	OOB	BH	AVG	PB	PR	/A	PD	TPI
1901	StL-N	2	2	.500	5	4	4	1	0	41	29	2	10	16	9.7	1.32	242	.198	.272	6	.400	3	9	8	-1	1.0
1902	StL-N	16	15	.516	36	32	29	2	2	288¹	297	3	66	105	11.7	2.90	94	.266	.314	43	.319	9	-4	-5	0	0.8

YEAR	TM/L	W	L	PCT	G	GS	CG	SH	SV	IP	H	HR	BB	SO	RAT	ERA	ERA+	OAV	OOB	BH	AVG	PB	PR	/A	PD	TPI
1903	StL-N	4	13	.235	19	17	12	0	0	145	184	2	43	39	14.5	3.79	86	.304	.356	25	.227	2	-8	-8	-0	-0.6
1904	StL-N	10	14	.417	25	24	23	1	0	220	229	1	50	68	11.5	2.09	129	.262	.304	21	.231	5	16	15	1	2.4
Total	4	32	44	.421	85	77	68	4	2	694¹	739	8	169	228	12.1	2.73	105	.269	.318	97	.255	19	13	10	-0	3.6

● **PAUL O'NEILL** O'Neill, Paul Andrew b: 2/25/63, Columbus, Ohio BL/TL, 6'4", 205 lbs. Deb: 9/3/85 ♦

YEAR	TM/L	W	L	PCT	G	GS	CG	SH	SV	IP	H	HR	BB	SO	RAT	ERA	ERA+	OAV	OOB	BH	AVG	PB	PR	/A	PD	TPI
1987	Cin-N	0	0	—	1	0	0	0	0	2	2	1	4	2	27.0	13.50	31	.286	.545	41	.256	0	-2	-2	-0	0.0

● **EMMETT O'NEILL** O'Neill, Robert Emmett "Pinky" b: 1/13/18, San Mateo, Cal. d: 10/11/93, Sparks, Nevada BR/TR, 6'3", 185 lbs. Deb: 8/3/43

YEAR	TM/L	W	L	PCT	G	GS	CG	SH	SV	IP	H	HR	BB	SO	RAT	ERA	ERA+	OAV	OOB	BH	AVG	PB	PR	/A	PD	TPI
1943	Bos-A	1	4	.200	11	5	1	0	0	57²	56	3	46	20	16.1	4.53	73	.256	.387	3	.188	1	-8	-8	0	-0.6
1944	Bos-A	6	11	.353	28	22	8	1	0	151²	154	6	89	68	14.5	4.63	73	.265	.365	10	.182	-0	-20	-21	-2	-2.3
1945	Bos-A	8	11	.421	24	22	10	1	0	141²	134	5	117	55	16.3	5.15	66	.258	.399	9	.180	2	-28	-27	1	-3.1
1946	Chi-N	0	0	—	1	0	0	0	0	1	0	0	3	1	27.0	0.00	—	.000	.500	0	—	0	0	0	0	0.0
	Chi-A	0	0	—	2	0	0	0	0	3²	4	0	5	0	22.1	0.00	—	.333	.529	0	.000	-0	1	1	0	0.0
Total	4	15	26	.366	66	49	19	2	0	355²	348	14	260	144	15.6	4.76	71	.261	.385	22	.180	2	-54	-54	-2	-6.0

● **STEVE ONTIVEROS** Ontiveros, Steven b: 3/5/61, Tularosa, N.Mex. BR/TR, 6', 180 lbs. Deb: 6/14/85

YEAR	TM/L	W	L	PCT	G	GS	CG	SH	SV	IP	H	HR	BB	SO	RAT	ERA	ERA+	OAV	OOB	BH	AVG	PB	PR	/A	PD	TPI
1985	Oak-A	1	3	.250	39	0	0	0	8	74²	45	4	19	36	8.0	1.93	200	.174	.236	0	—	0	18	16	1	1.3
1986	Oak-A	2	2	.500	46	0	0	0	10	72²	72	10	25	54	12.1	4.71	82	.265	.329	0	—	0	-4	-7	0	-0.5
1987	Oak-A	10	8	.556	35	22	2	1	1	150²	141	19	50	97	11.6	4.00	103	.242	.306	0	—	0	8	2	2	0.5
1988	Oak-A	3	4	.429	10	10	0	0	0	54²	57	4	21	30	12.8	4.61	82	.265	.331	0	—	-0	-1	-1	-0	-0.5
1989	Phi-N	2	1	.667	6	5	0	0	0	30²	34	2	15	12	14.4	3.82	93	.288	.368	1	.083	-0	-1	-1	1	0.0
1990	Phi-N	0	0	—	5	0	0	0	0	10	9	1	3	6	10.8	2.70	142	.225	.279	0	—	0	1	1	0	0.0
1993	Sea-A	0	2	.000	14	0	0	0	0	18	18	0	6	13	12.0	1.00	440	.277	.338	0	—	0	7	7	-0	0.6
1994	Oak-A	6	4	.600	27	13	2	0	0	115¹	93	7	26	56	**9.8**	**2.65**	168	.217	**.272**	0	—	0	28	23	0	2.2
Total	8	24	24	.500	182	50	4	1	19	526²	469	47	165	304	11.1	3.43	118	.237	.300	1	.083	0	52	37	5	3.6

● **JOSE OQUENDO** Oquendo, Jose Manuel (Contreras) b: 7/4/63, Rio Piedras, P.R. BB/TR, 5'10", 160 lbs. Deb: 5/2/83 ♦

YEAR	TM/L	W	L	PCT	G	GS	CG	SH	SV	IP	H	HR	BB	SO	RAT	ERA	ERA+	OAV	OOB	BH	AVG	PB	PR	/A	PD	TPI
1987	*StL-N	0	0	—	1	0	0	0	0	1	4	0	1	0	54.0	27.00	15	.571	.667	71	.286	0	-3	-3	-0	0.0
1988	StL-N	0	1	.000	1	0	0	0	0	4	4	0	6	1	22.5	4.50	77	.267	.476	125	.277	0	-0	-0	-0	-0.1
1991	StL-N	0	0	—	1	0	0	0	0	1	2	0	2	1	36.0	27.00	14	.400	.571	88	.240	0	-3	-3	0	0.0
Total	3	0	1	.000	3	0	0	0	0	6	10	0	9	2	30.0	12.00	30	.370	.541	775	.260	1	-6	-6	-0	-0.1

● **MIKE OQUIST** Oquist, Michael Lee b: 5/30/68, LaJunta, Colo. BR/TR, 6'2", 170 lbs. Deb: 8/14/93

YEAR	TM/L	W	L	PCT	G	GS	CG	SH	SV	IP	H	HR	BB	SO	RAT	ERA	ERA+	OAV	OOB	BH	AVG	PB	PR	/A	PD	TPI
1993	Bal-A	0	0	—	5	0	0	0	0	11²	12	0	4	8	12.3	3.86	116	.261	.320	0	—	0	1	1	-0	-0.3
1994	Bal-A	3	3	.500	15	9	0	0	0	58¹	75	7	30	39	17.1	6.17	82	.319	.410	0	—	0	-9	-7	-0	-0.9
Total	2	3	3	.500	20	9	0	0	0	70	87	7	34	47	16.3	5.79	86	.310	.396	0	—	0	-8	-6	-0	-1.2

● **DON O'RILEY** O'Riley, Donald Lee b: 3/12/45, Topeka, Kan. BR/TR, 6'3", 205 lbs. Deb: 6/20/69

YEAR	TM/L	W	L	PCT	G	GS	CG	SH	SV	IP	H	HR	BB	SO	RAT	ERA	ERA+	OAV	OOB	BH	AVG	PB	PR	/A	PD	TPI
1969	KC-A	1	1	.500	18	0	0	0	1	23¹	32	0	15	10	18.1	6.94	53	.311	.398	0	.000	-0	-9	-8	-0	-0.8
1970	KC-A	0	0	—	9	2	0	0	0	23¹	26	5	9	13	13.9	5.40	69	.277	.346	0	.000	-0	-4	-4	-0	-0.1
Total	2	1	1	.500	27	2	0	0	1	46²	58	5	24	23	16.0	6.17	60	.294	.374	0	.000	-1	-13	-13	-1	-0.9

● **JESSE OROSCO** Orosco, Jesse Russell b: 4/21/57, Santa Barbara, Cal. BR/TL, 6'2", 185 lbs. Deb: 4/5/79

YEAR	TM/L	W	L	PCT	G	GS	CG	SH	SV	IP	H	HR	BB	SO	RAT	ERA	ERA+	OAV	OOB	BH	AVG	PB	PR	/A	PD	TPI
1979	NY-N	1	2	.333	18	2	0	0	0	35	33	4	22	22	14.7	4.89	74	.260	.377	0	.000	-1	-4	-5	1	-0.4
1981	NY-N	0	1	.000	8	0	0	0	1	17¹	13	2	6	18	9.9	1.56	224	.213	.284	0	.000	-0	4	4	0	0.2
1982	NY-N	4	10	.286	54	2	0	0	4	109¹	92	7	40	89	11.0	2.72	134	.230	.303	2	.143	-1	11	11	0	1.4
1983	NY-N★	13	7	.650	62	0	0	0	17	110	76	3	38	84	9.4	1.47	246	.197	.271	4	.333	1	**26**	**26**	1	**6.0**
1984	NY-N☆	10	6	.625	60	0	0	0	31	87	58	7	34	85	9.7	2.59	137	.185	.269	1	.250	1	10	9	-0	2.5
1985	NY-N	8	6	.571	54	0	0	0	17	79	66	6	34	68	11.4	2.73	126	.224	.304	3	.429	1	8	6	-1	1.4
1986	*NY-N	8	6	.571	58	0	0	0	21	81	64	6	35	62	11.3	2.33	151	.217	.306	0	.000	-0	12	11	1	2.4
1987	NY-N	3	9	.250	58	0	0	0	16	77	78	5	31	78	13.0	4.44	85	.266	.340	0	.000	-1	-3	-6	-1	-1.1
1988	*LA-N	3	2	.600	55	0	0	0	9	53	41	4	30	43	12.4	2.72	123	.215	.327	0	.000	-0	4	4	0	0.5
1989	Cle-A	3	4	.429	69	0	0	0	3	78	54	7	26	79	9.5	2.08	191	.198	.272	0	—	0	16	16	1	1.6
1990	Cle-A	5	4	.556	55	0	0	0	2	64²	58	9	38	55	13.4	3.90	101	.239	.342	0	—	0	0	1	0	0.1
1991	Cle-A	2	0	1.000	47	0	0	0	0	45²	52	4	15	36	13.4	3.74	111	.286	.343	0	—	0	2	2	-1	0.0
1992	Mil-A	3	1	.750	59	0	0	0	1	39	33	5	13	40	10.8	3.23	119	.232	.301	0	—	0	3	3	-0	0.4
1993	Mil-A	3	5	.375	57	0	0	0	8	56²	47	2	17	67	10.6	3.18	134	.224	.291	0	.000	0	7	7	3	1.3
1994	Mil-A	3	1	.750	40	0	0	0	0	39	32	4	26	36	13.8	5.08	97	.222	.349	0	—	0	-1	-1	-0	-0.2
Total	15	69	64	.519	754	4	0	0	130	971²	797	75	405	862	11.3	2.95	128	.224	.308	10	.169	2	94	88	4	16.1

● **O'ROURKE** O'Rourke Deb: 7/9/1872

YEAR	TM/L	W	L	PCT	G	GS	CG	SH	SV	IP	H	HR	BB	SO	RAT	ERA	ERA+	OAV	OOB	BH	AVG	PB	PR	/A	PD	TPI
1872	Eck-n	0	1	.000	1	1	1	0	0	9	16	0	2	0	18.0	6.00	58	.327	.353	0	.000	-1	-2	-3		-0.2

● **JIM O'ROURKE** O'Rourke, James Henry "Orator Jim" b: 9/1/1850, Bridgeport, Conn. d: 1/8/19, Bridgeport, Conn. BR/TR, 5'8", 185 lbs. Deb: 4/26/1872 FMUH♦

YEAR	TM/L	W	L	PCT	G	GS	CG	SH	SV	IP	H	HR	BB	SO	RAT	ERA	ERA+	OAV	OOB	BH	AVG	PB	PR	/A	PD	TPI
1883	Buf-N	0	0	—	2	0	0	0	1	7	10	0	1	1	14.1	6.43	49	.357	.379	1	.328	1	-3	-3	-0	-0.1
1884	Buf-N	0	1	.000	4	0	0	0	1	12²	7	0	1	3	5.7	2.84	111	.175	.195	162	.347	2	0	0	-0	0.1
Total	2	0	1	.000	6	0	0	0	2	19²	17	0	2	4	8.7	4.12	77	.250	.271	2304	.310	2	-2	-2	-1	0.1

● **MIKE O'ROURKE** O'Rourke, Michael J. Deb: 9/1/1890

YEAR	TM/L	W	L	PCT	G	GS	CG	SH	SV	IP	H	HR	BB	SO	RAT	ERA	ERA+	OAV	OOB	BH	AVG	PB	PR	/A	PD	TPI
1890	Bal-a	1	2	.333	5	5	5	0	0	41	45	0	10	8	12.7	3.95	103	.270	.323	3	.115	-1	-0	0	1	0.0

● **DAVE ORR** Orr, David L. b: 9/29/1859, New York, N.Y. d: 6/3/15, Brooklyn, N.Y. BR/TR, 5'11", 250 lbs. Deb: 5/17/1883 M♦

YEAR	TM/L	W	L	PCT	G	GS	CG	SH	SV	IP	H	HR	BB	SO	RAT	ERA	ERA+	OAV	OOB	BH	AVG	PB	PR	/A	PD	TPI
1885	NY-a	0	0	—	3	0	0	0	0	10	11	2	5	1	14.4	7.20	41	.229	.302	152	.342	2	-4	-5	-0	0.0

● **JOE ORRELL** Orrell, Forrest Gordon b: 10/6/17, National City, Cal. d: 1/12/93, Chula Vista, Cal. BR/TR, 6'4", 210 lbs. Deb: 8/12/43

YEAR	TM/L	W	L	PCT	G	GS	CG	SH	SV	IP	H	HR	BB	SO	RAT	ERA	ERA+	OAV	OOB	BH	AVG	PB	PR	/A	PD	TPI
1943	Det-A	0	0	—	10	1	0	0	0	19¹	18	0	11	6	14.4	3.72	95	.257	.373	1	.250	0	-1	-0	-0	0.0
1944	Det-A	2	1	.667	10	2	0	0	0	22¹	26	0	11	10	15.3	2.42	147	.286	.369	1	.250	0	3	3	1	0.5
1945	Det-A	2	3	.400	12	5	1	0	0	48	46	1	24	14	13.5	3.00	117	.260	.355	2	.133	-1	2	3	-0	0.1
Total	3	4	4	.500	32	7	1	0	1	89²	90	1	46	26	14.2	3.01	117	.266	.362	4	.174	-1	4	5	0	0.6

● **PHIL ORTEGA** Ortega, Filomeno Coronado "Kemo" b: 10/7/39, Gilbert, Ariz. BR/TR, 6'2", 175 lbs. Deb: 9/10/60

YEAR	TM/L	W	L	PCT	G	GS	CG	SH	SV	IP	H	HR	BB	SO	RAT	ERA	ERA+	OAV	OOB	BH	AVG	PB	PR	/A	PD	TPI
1960	LA-N	0	0	—	3	1	0	0	0	6¹	12	1	5	2	24.2	17.05	23	.400	.486	0	.000	-0	-9	-9	-0	0.0
1961	LA-N	0	2	.000	4	2	1	0	0	13	10	6	2	15	8.3	5.54	78	.208	.240	1	.250	0	-2	-2	-0	-0.2
1962	LA-N	0	2	.000	24	3	0	0	0	53²	60	8	39	30	17.1	6.88	53	.278	.394	0	.000	-0	-17	-19	-1	-0.9
1963	LA-N	0	0	—	1	0	0	0	0	1	2	1	0	1	18.0	18.00	17	.400	.400	0	—	-0	-2	-2	-0	0.0
1964	LA-N	7	9	.438	34	25	4	3	1	157¹	149	22	56	107	12.1	4.00	81	.249	.320	6	.136	-0	-8	-13	-2	-1.6
1965	Was-A	12	15	.444	35	29	4	2	0	179²	176	33	97	88	13.9	5.11	68	.262	.359	11	.208	4	-33	-33	-1	-4.1
1966	Was-A	12	12	.500	33	31	5	1	0	197¹	158	29	53	121	9.9	3.92	88	.218	.276	3	.056	-2	-11	-10	-1	-1.5
1967	Was-A	10	10	.500	34	34	5	2	0	219²	189	16	57	122	10.3	3.03	104	.231	.286	4	.061	-3	9	1	-0	-0.1
1968	Was-A	5	12	.294	31	16	1	0	0	115²	115	12	62	57	14.2	4.98	59	.263	.361	4	.167	1	-26	-27	-0	-3.6
1969	Cal-A	0	0	—	9	0	0	0	0	8	13	0	7	4	22.5	10.13	50	.333	.435	0	—	-0	-8	-7	-0	-0.6
Total	10	46	62	.426	204	141	20	9	2	951²	884	131	378	549	12.2	4.43	75	.246	.323	29	.115	-1	-109	-117	-6	-12.0

● **AL ORTH** Orth, Albert Lewis "Smiling Al" or "The Curveless Wonder" b: 9/5/1872, Tipton, Ind. d: 10/8/48, Lynchburg, Va. BL/TR, 6', 200 lbs. Deb: 8/15/1895 U♦

YEAR	TM/L	W	L	PCT	G	GS	CG	SH	SV	IP	H	HR	BB	SO	RAT	ERA	ERA+	OAV	OOB	BH	AVG	PB	PR	/A	PD	TPI
1895	Phi-N	8	1	.889	11	10	9	0	1	88	103	9	22	25	13.0	3.89	123	.288	.332	16	.356	4	9	9	-2	0.9
1896	Phi-N	15	10	.600	25	23	19	0	0	196	244	10	46	23	13.5	4.41	98	.303	.342	21	.256	3	-1	-2	1	0.1

YEAR	TM/L	W	L	PCT	G	GS	CG	SH	SV	IP	H	HR	BB	SO	RAT	ERA	ERA+	OAV	OOB	BH	AVG	PB	PR	/A	PD	TPI
1897	Phi-N	14	19	.424	36	34	29	2	0	282¹	349	12	82	64	13.9	4.62	91	.301	.350	50	.329	7	-10	-13	1	-0.4
1898	Phi-N	15	13	.536	32	28	25	1	0	250	290	4	53	52	12.6	3.02	114	.288	.329	36	.293	8	16	11	0	2.0
1899	Phi-N	14	3	.824	21	15	13	3	1	144²	149	0	19	35	10.6	2.49	148	.266	.294	13	.210	1	22	19	-4	1.6
1900	Phi-N	14	14	.500	33	30	24	2	1	262	302	4	60	68	12.9	3.78	96	.288	.335	40	.310	7	-2	-5	1	0.3
1901	Phi-N	20	12	.625	35	33	30	6	1	281²	250	3	32	92	**9.3**	2.27	150	.236	**.264**	36	.281	5	33	35	3	**4.8**
1902	Was-A	19	18	.514	38	37	36	1	0	324	367	18	40	76	11.6	3.97	93	.286	.312	38	.217	1	-14	-10	1	-0.6
1903	Was-A	10	22	.313	36	32	30	2	**2**	279²	326	8	62	88	12.7	4.34	72	.290	.331	49	.302	9	-43	-38	-0	-2.8
1904	Was-A	3	4	.429	10	7	7	0	0	73²	88	2	15	23	13.0	4.76	56	.297	.337	22	.216	0	-18	-17	0	-1.4
	NY-A	11	6	.647	20	18	11	2	0	137²	122	0	19	47	9.4	2.68	101	.238	.270	19	.297	3	-1	0	1	0.5
	Yr	14	10	.583	30	25	18	2	0	211¹	210	2	34	70	10.5	3.41	79	.259	.291	41	.247	3	-19	-17	1	-0.9
1905	NY-A	18	16	.529	40	37	26	6	0	305¹	273	8	61	121	10.1	2.86	103	.240	.283	24	.183	-1	-7	3	-0	0.1
1906	NY-A	**27**	17	.614	45	39	**36**	3	0	338²	317	2	66	133	10.2	2.34	127	.251	.288	37	.274	6	13	24	-1	**3.7**
1907	NY-A	14	21	.400	36	33	21	2	0	248²	244	2	53	78	11.0	2.61	107	.259	.302	34	.324	7	-2	5	3	1.9
1908	NY-A	2	13	.133	21	17	8	1	0	139¹	134	4	30	22	10.9	3.42	72	.255	.300	20	.290	5	-16	-15	-1	-1.1
1909	NY-A	0	0	—	1	1	0	0	0	3	4	0	0	1	21.0	12.00	16	.429	.467	9	.265	0	-3	-3	-0	0.0
Total	15	204	189	.519	440	394	324	31	6	3354²	3564	75	661	948	11.6	3.37	101	.272	.311	464	.273	63	-23	15	2	9.6

● **BABY ORTIZ**   Ortiz, Oliverio (Nunez) b: 12/5/19, Camaguey, Cuba d: 3/27/84, Central Senado, Camaguey, Cuba   BR/TR, 6', 190 lbs.   Deb: 9/23/44   F

YEAR	TM/L	W	L	PCT	G	GS	CG	SH	SV	IP	H	HR	BB	SO	RAT	ERA	ERA+	OAV	OOB	BH	AVG	PB	PR	/A	PD	TPI
1944	Was-A	0	2	.000	2	2	1	0	0	13	13	0	6	4	13.2	6.23	52	.255	.333	1	.167	-0	-4	-4	-1	-0.6

● **OSSIE ORWOLL**   Orwoll, Oswald Christian b: 11/17/1900, Portland, Ore. d: 5/8/67, Decorah, Iowa   BL/TL, 6', 174 lbs.   Deb: 4/13/28   ♦

YEAR	TM/L	W	L	PCT	G	GS	CG	SH	SV	IP	H	HR	BB	SO	RAT	ERA	ERA+	OAV	OOB	BH	AVG	PB	PR	/A	PD	TPI
1928	Phi-A	6	5	.545	27	8	3	0	2	106	110	7	50	63	13.8	4.58	87	.274	.358	52	.306	7	-6	-7	-0	-0.3
1929	Phi-A	0	2	.000	12	0	0	0	1	30	32	6	6	12	11.4	4.80	88	.278	.314	13	.255	1	-2	-2	-0	-0.1
Total	2	6	7	.462	39	8	3	0	3	136	142	13	56	65	13.2	4.63	88	.275	.348	65	.294	7	-8	-9	-1	-0.4

● **OZZIE OSBORN**   Osborn, Danny Leon b: 6/19/46, Springfield, Mo.   BR/TR, 6'2", 195 lbs.   Deb: 4/26/75

YEAR	TM/L	W	L	PCT	G	GS	CG	SH	SV	IP	H	HR	BB	SO	RAT	ERA	ERA+	OAV	OOB	BH	AVG	PB	PR	/A	PD	TPI
1975	Chi-A	3	0	1.000	24	0	0	0	0	58	57	2	37	38	14.9	4.50	86	.265	.378	0	—	0	-5	-4	-1	-0.4

● **BOB OSBORN**   Osborn, John Bode b: 4/17/03, San Diego, Tex. d: 4/19/60, Paris, Ark.   BR/TR, 6'1", 175 lbs.   Deb: 9/16/25

YEAR	TM/L	W	L	PCT	G	GS	CG	SH	SV	IP	H	HR	BB	SO	RAT	ERA	ERA+	OAV	OOB	BH	AVG	PB	PR	/A	PD	TPI
1925	Chi-N	0	0	—	1	0	0	0	0	2	6	0	0	0	27.0	0.00	—	.600	.600	0	—	0	1	1	0	0.0
1926	Chi-N	6	5	.545	31	15	6	0	1	136¹	157	3	58	43	14.2	3.63	106	.301	.371	6	.146	-3	3	3	2	0.2
1927	Chi-N	5	5	.500	24	12	2	0	0	107²	125	2	48	45	14.5	4.18	92	.294	.367	8	.205	-0	-3	-4	-1	-0.4
1929	Chi-N	0	0	—	3	1	0	0	0	9	8	0	1	2	10.0	3.00	154	.242	.286	1	.250	0	2	2	-0	0.0
1930	Chi-N	10	6	.625	35	13	3	0	1	126²	147	9	53	42	14.3	4.97	98	.300	.369	4	.095	-5	-0	-1	2	-0.4
1931	Pit-N	6	1	.857	27	2	0	0	0	64²	85	3	20	9	14.8	5.01	77	.316	.366	3	.167	-0	-8	-8	-1	-0.9
Total	6	27	17	.614	121	43	11	0	2	446¹	528	17	181	140	14.4	4.32	97	.302	.368	22	.153	-8	-6	-7	2	-1.5

● **DONOVAN OSBORNE**   Osborne, Donovan Alan b: 6/21/69, Roseville, Cal.   BB/TL, 6'2", 195 lbs.   Deb: 4/9/92

YEAR	TM/L	W	L	PCT	G	GS	CG	SH	SV	IP	H	HR	BB	SO	RAT	ERA	ERA+	OAV	OOB	BH	AVG	PB	PR	/A	PD	TPI
1992	StL-N	11	9	.550	34	29	0	0	0	179	193	14	38	104	11.7	3.77	90	.275	.314	7	.121	-1	-5	-8	-3	-1.2
1993	StL-N	10	7	.588	26	26	1	0	0	155²	153	18	47	83	12.0	3.76	105	.257	.319	10	.204	2	5	4	0	0.5
Total	2	21	16	.568	60	55	1	0	0	334²	346	32	85	187	11.8	3.76	97	.267	.316	17	.159	1	-0	-4	-3	-0.7

● **TINY OSBORNE**   Osborne, Earnest Preston b: 4/9/1893, Porterdale, Ga. d: 1/5/69, Atlanta, Ga.   BL/TR, 6'4.5", 215 lbs.   Deb: 4/15/22   F

YEAR	TM/L	W	L	PCT	G	GS	CG	SH	SV	IP	H	HR	BB	SO	RAT	ERA	ERA+	OAV	OOB	BH	AVG	PB	PR	/A	PD	TPI
1922	Chi-N	9	5	.643	41	14	7	1	3	184	183	7	95	81	14.2	4.50	93	.271	.370	9	.134	-4	-8	-6	-3	-1.0
1923	Chi-N	8	15	.348	37	25	8	1	1	179²	174	14	89	69	13.3	4.56	88	.255	.342	12	.200	-1	-11	-11	-1	-1.4
1924	Chi-N	0	0	—	2	0	0	0	1	3	3	0	2	2	15.0	3.00	130	.300	.417	0	—	0	0	0	0	0.0
	Bro-N	6	5	.545	21	13	6	0	0	104¹	123	1	54	52	15.6	5.09	74	.298	.384	9	.250	1	-14	-16	-1	-1.4
	Yr	6	5	.545	23	13	6	0	1	107¹	126	1	56	54	15.6	5.03	75	.298	.385	9	.250	1	-14	-15	-1	-1.4
1925	Bro-N	8	15	.348	41	22	10	0	1	175	210	9	75	59	14.9	4.94	85	.304	.375	14	.246	1	-13	-15	-2	-1.6
Total	4	31	40	.437	142	74	31	2	6	646	693	31	315	263	14.3	4.72	86	.280	.367	44	.200	-3	-46	-47	-6	-5.4

● **FRED OSBORNE**   Osborne, Frederick W. b: Hampton, Iowa   TL,   Deb: 7/14/1890   ♦

YEAR	TM/L	W	L	PCT	G	GS	CG	SH	SV	IP	H	HR	BB	SO	RAT	ERA	ERA+	OAV	OOB	BH	AVG	PB	PR	/A	PD	TPI
1890	Pit-N	0	5	.000	8	5	5	0	0	58	82	6	45	14	20.8	8.38	39	.323	.438	40	.238	1	-31	-33	-0	-2.0

● **WAYNE OSBORNE**   Osborne, Wayne Harold "Ossie" or "Fish Hook"   b: 10/11/12, Watsonville, Cal. d: 3/13/87, Vancouver, Wash.   BL/TR, 6'2.5", 172 lbs.   Deb: 4/18/35

YEAR	TM/L	W	L	PCT	G	GS	CG	SH	SV	IP	H	HR	BB	SO	RAT	ERA	ERA+	OAV	OOB	BH	AVG	PB	PR	/A	PD	TPI
1935	Pit-N	0	0	—	2	0	0	0	0	1¹	1	0	0	1	6.8	6.75	61	.250	.250	0	—	0	-0	-0	0	0.0
1936	Bos-N	1	1	.500	5	3	0	0	0	20	31	1	9	8	18.0	5.85	66	.352	.412	2	.250	0	-4	-4	0	-0.4
Total	2	1	1	.500	7	3	0	0	0	21¹	32	1	9	9	17.3	5.91	65	.348	.406	2	.250	0	-4	-5	0	-0.4

● **PAT OSBURN**   Osburn, Larry Patrick b: 5/4/49, Murray, Ky.   BL/TL, 6'4", 195 lbs.   Deb: 4/13/74

YEAR	TM/L	W	L	PCT	G	GS	CG	SH	SV	IP	H	HR	BB	SO	RAT	ERA	ERA+	OAV	OOB	BH	AVG	PB	PR	/A	PD	TPI
1974	Cin-N	0	0	—	6	0	0	0	0	9	11	2	4	4	15.0	8.00	44	.297	.366	0	.000	-0	-4	-5	0	-0.2
1975	Mil-A	0	1	.000	6	1	0	0	0	11²	19	2	9	1	23.1	5.40	71	.404	.517	0	—	0	-2	-2	0	-0.2
Total	2	0	1	.000	12	1	0	0	0	20²	30	4	13	5	19.6	6.53	56	.357	.455	0	.000	-0	-6	-7	1	-0.2

● **CHARLIE OSGOOD**   Osgood, Charles Benjamin b: 11/23/26, Somerville, Mass.   BR/TR, 5'10", 180 lbs.   Deb: 6/18/44

YEAR	TM/L	W	L	PCT	G	GS	CG	SH	SV	IP	H	HR	BB	SO	RAT	ERA	ERA+	OAV	OOB	BH	AVG	PB	PR	/A	PD	TPI
1944	Bro-N	0	0	—	1	0	0	0	0	3	2	0	3	0	18.0	3.00	118	.222	.462	0	—	0	0	0	-0	0.0

● **DAN OSINSKI**   Osinski, Daniel b: 11/17/33, Chicago, Ill.   BR/TR, 6'2", 195 lbs.   Deb: 4/11/62

YEAR	TM/L	W	L	PCT	G	GS	CG	SH	SV	IP	H	HR	BB	SO	RAT	ERA	ERA+	OAV	OOB	BH	AVG	PB	PR	/A	PD	TPI
1962	KC-A	0	0	—	4	0	0	0	0	4²	7	1	8	4	30.9	17.36	24	.381	.552	0	—	0	-7	-7	0	0.0
	LA-A	6	4	.600	33	0	0	0	4	54¹	45	3	30	44	12.4	2.82	137	.223	.323	0	.000	-1	7	6	0	1.1
	Yr	6	4	.600	37	0	0	0	4	59	53	4	38	48	13.9	3.97	98	.237	.347	0	.000	-1	0	-1	0	1.1
1963	LA-A	8	8	.500	47	16	4	1	0	159¹	145	15	80	100	12.8	3.28	105	.242	.333	5	.111	-2	6	3	-1	-0.1
1964	LA-A	3	3	.500	47	4	1	1	2	93	87	8	39	88	12.4	3.48	94	.244	.322	1	.056	-1	1	-2	-1	-0.1
1965	Mil-N	0	3	.000	61	0	0	0	6	83	81	4	40	54	13.2	2.82	125	.261	.348	1	.167	-0	7	6	-0	0.3
1966	Bos-A	4	3	.571	44	1	0	0	2	67¹	68	8	28	44	13.0	3.61	105	.274	.350	2	.333	0	-1	1	-1	0.1
1967	*Bos-A	3	1	.750	34	0	0	0	2	63²	61	5	14	38	10.6	2.54	137	.243	.283	3	.333	1	5	7	-0	0.5
1969	Chi-A	5	5	.500	51	0	0	0	2	60²	56	3	23	27	11.7	3.56	108	.251	.321	0	.000	-0	2	2	0	0.5
1970	Hou-N	0	1	.000	3	0	0	0	0	3²	5	0	2	1	17.2	9.82	39	.357	.438	0	—	0	-2	-2	-0	-0.5
Total	8	29	28	.509	324	21	5	2	18	589²	556	47	264	400	12.6	3.34	107	.250	.331	12	.122	-3	16	15	1	1.8

● **CLAUDE OSTEEN**   Osteen, Claude Wilson b: 8/9/39, Caney Spring, Tenn.   BL/TL, 5'11", 173 lbs.   Deb: 7/6/57   C

YEAR	TM/L	W	L	PCT	G	GS	CG	SH	SV	IP	H	HR	BB	SO	RAT	ERA	ERA+	OAV	OOB	BH	AVG	PB	PR	/A	PD	TPI
1957	Cin-N	0	0	—	3	0	0	0	0	4	4	0	3	3	15.8	2.25	183	.250	.368	0	.000	-0	1	1	-0	0.0
1959	Cin-N	0	0	—	2	0	0	0	0	7²	11	1	9	3	23.5	7.04	58	.333	.476	0	.000	-0	-3	-3	-0	0.0
1960	Cin-N	0	1	.000	20	3	0	0	0	48¹	53	5	30	15	15.6	5.03	76	.293	.396	1	.083	-1	-7	-6	0	-0.2
1961	Cin-N	0	0	—	1	0	0	0	0	0¹	0	0	0	0	0.0	0.00	—	.000	.000	0	—	0	0	0	0	0.0
	Was-A	1	1	.500	3	3	0	0	0	18¹	14	3	9	14	11.8	4.91	82	.219	.324	1	.143	-0	-2	-2	0	-0.2
1962	Was-A	8	13	.381	28	22	7	2	1	150¹	140	12	47	59	11.4	3.65	111	.246	.309	10	.208	-1	5	6	0	1.0
1963	Was-A	9	14	.391	40	29	8	2	0	212¹	222	23	60	109	12.0	3.35	111	.270	.320	12	.171	1	7	9	-1	0.8
1964	Was-A	15	13	.536	37	36	13	0	0	257	256	20	64	133	11.3	3.33	111	.259	.306	14	.156	1	8	11	2	1.5
1965	*LA-N	15	15	.500	40	40	14	7	0	287	253	19	78	162	10.5	2.79	117	.236	.290	12	.121	-1	24	15	6	2.0
1966	*LA-N	17	14	.548	39	38	8	3	0	240¹	238	6	65	137	11.4	2.85	116	.261	.312	16	.211	6	20	12	1	2.2
1967	LA-N☆	17	17	.500	39	39	14	5	0	288¹	298	14	67	137	11.0	3.22	96	.270	.304	18	.178	6	-5	-4	-0	-0.7
1968	LA-N	12	18	.400	39	36	5	3	0	253²	267	14	54	119	11.6	3.08	102	.275	.316	15	.179	2	-3	-9	-1	-0.7
1969	LA-N	20	15	.571	41	41	16	7	0	321	310	17	94	183	10.5	2.66	125	.245	.293	33	.216	9	33	24	3	3.5
1970	LA-N★	16	14	.533	37	37	11	4	0	258²	280	24	52	114	11.7	3.83	100	.276	.313	19	.204	5	6	0	-1	0.4

YEAR	TM/L	W	L	PCT	G	GS	CG	SH	SV	IP	H	HR	BB	SO	RAT	ERA	ERA+	OAV	OOB	BH	AVG	PB	PR	/A	PD	TPI
1971	LA-N	14	11	.560	38	38	11	4	0	259	262	25	63	109	11.4	3.51	92	.266	.312	16	.186	2	-1	-8	6	0.1
1972	LA-N	20	11	.645	33	33	14	4	0	252	232	16	69	100	10.9	2.64	126	.245	.299	24	.273	10	23	19	-0	3.5
1973	LA-N★	16	11	.593	33	33	12	3	0	236²	227	20	67	86	11.0	3.31	104	.258	.307	12	.154	-1	9	3	2	0.5
1974	Hou-N	9	9	.500	23	21	7	2	0	138¹	158	8	47	45	13.5	3.71	93	.292	.351	13	.283	-3	-1	-4	0	-0.1
	StL-N	0	2	.000	8	2	0	0	0	22²	26	1	11	6	14.7	4.37	82	.286	.363	0	.000	-1	-2	-2	0	-0.2
	Yr	9	11	.450	31	23	7	2	0	161	184	9	58	51	13.5	3.80	92	.288	.347	13	.245	3	-3	-6	0	-0.3
1975	Chi-A	7	16	.304	37	37	5	0	0	204¹	237	16	92	63	14.6	4.36	89	.294	.367	0	—	-0	-13	-11	1	-1.1
Total 18		196	195	.501	541	488	140	40	1	3460¹	3471	249	940	1612	11.6	3.30	104	.263	.314	207	.188	38	110	50	20	13.2

● DARRELL OSTEEN
Osteen, Milton Darrell b: 2/14/43, Oklahoma City, Okla. BR/TR, 6'1", 170 lbs. Deb: 9/2/65

YEAR	TM/L	W	L	PCT	G	GS	CG	SH	SV	IP	H	HR	BB	SO	RAT	ERA	ERA+	OAV	OOB	BH	AVG	PB	PR	/A	PD	TPI
1965	Cin-N	0	0	—	3	0	0	0	0	3	2	0	4	1	18.0	0.00	—	.200	.429	0	—	-0	1	1	0	0.0
1966	Cin-N	0	2	.000	13	0	0	0	1	15	26	3	9	17	21.0	12.00	33	.371	.443	1	.500	-0	-14	-13	-0	-1.8
1967	Cin-N	0	2	.000	10	0	0	0	2	14¹	10	1	13	13	16.3	6.28	60	.196	.388	0	.000	-0	-5	-4	0	-0.6
1970	Oak-A	1	0	1.000	3	1	0	0	0	5²	9	0	3	3	19.1	6.35	56	.346	.414	0	.000	-0	-2	-2	0	-0.3
Total 4		1	4	.200	29	1	0	0	3	38	47	4	29	34	18.7	8.05	47	.299	.418	1	.200	-0	-19	-18	-0	-2.7

● FRED OSTENDORF
Ostendorf, Frederick K. b: 8/5/1890, Baltimore, Md. d: 3/2/65, Kecoughtan, Va. BL/TL, 6'0.5", 169 lbs. Deb: 7/16/14

YEAR	TM/L	W	L	PCT	G	GS	CG	SH	SV	IP	H	HR	BB	SO	RAT	ERA	ERA+	OAV	OOB	BH	AVG	PB	PR	/A	PD	TPI
1914	Ind-F	0	0	—	1	0	0	0	0	2	5	0	2	0	36.0	22.50	14	.500	.615	0	.000	-0	-4	-4	0	0.0

● BILL OSTER
Oster, William Charles b: 1/2/33, New York, N.Y. BL/TL, 6'3", 198 lbs. Deb: 8/23/54

YEAR	TM/L	W	L	PCT	G	GS	CG	SH	SV	IP	H	HR	BB	SO	RAT	ERA	ERA+	OAV	OOB	BH	AVG	PB	PR	/A	PD	TPI
1954	Phi-A	0	1	.000	8	1	0	0	0	15²	19	2	12	5	17.8	6.32	62	.311	.425	1	.333	0	-5	-4	-0	-0.2

● FRITZ OSTERMUELLER
Ostermueller, Frederick Raymond b: 9/15/07, Quincy, Ill. d: 12/17/57, Quincy, Ill. BL/TL, 5'11", 175 lbs. Deb: 4/21/34

YEAR	TM/L	W	L	PCT	G	GS	CG	SH	SV	IP	H	HR	BB	SO	RAT	ERA	ERA+	OAV	OOB	BH	AVG	PB	PR	/A	PD	TPI
1934	Bos-A	10	13	.435	33	23	10	0	3	198²	200	7	99	75	13.6	3.49	138	.262	.348	13	.167	-2	22	29	3	3.1
1935	Bos-A	7	8	.467	22	19	10	0	1	137²	135	0	78	41	14.1	3.92	121	.257	.356	14	.286	1	8	13	-0	1.3
1936	Bos-A	10	16	.385	43	23	7	1	2	180²	210	8	84	90	14.8	4.88	109	.288	.364	15	.234	-0	3	9	3	1.3
1937	Bos-A	3	7	.300	25	7	2	0	1	86²	101	2	44	29	15.2	4.98	95	.286	.367	11	.333	3	-4	-2	0	0.0
1938	Bos-A	13	5	.722	31	18	10	1	2	176²	199	15	58	46	13.2	4.58	108	.275	.331	16	.216	2	4	7	-0	0.7
1939	Bos-A	11	7	.611	34	20	8	0	4	159¹	173	6	58	61	13.2	4.24	112	.277	.341	9	.161	-2	7	9	-1	0.7
1940	Bos-A	5	9	.357	31	16	5	0	0	143²	166	7	70	80	14.8	4.95	91	.284	.361	17	.315	4	-9	-7	-1	-0.4
1941	StL-A	0	3	.000	15	2	0	0	0	46	45	3	23	20	13.3	4.50	96	.257	.343	3	.214	0	-2	-1	0	0.0
1942	StL-A	3	1	.750	10	4	2	0	0	43²	46	4	17	21	13.0	3.71	100	.266	.332	1	.188	-0	-0	-1	-1	-0.1
1943	StL-A	0	2	.000	11	3	0	0	0	28²	36	1	13	4	15.4	5.02	66	.321	.392	2	.286	1	-5	-5	0	-0.3
	Bro-N	1	1	.500	7	1	0	0	0	27¹	21	0	12	15	10.9	3.29	102	.212	.297	0	.000	-0	0	-0	0	-0.2
1944	Bro-N	2	1	.667	10	4	3	0	1	41²	46	3	12	17	12.5	3.24	110	.267	.315	3	.154	-0	2	1	-0	0.0
	Pit-N	11	7	.611	28	24	14	1	1	204²	201	7	65	80	11.7	2.73	136	.260	.318	20	.250	-2	20	23	-1	2.0
	Yr	13	8	.619	38	28	17	1	2	246¹	247	10	77	97	11.9	2.81	131	.261	.317	22	.237	-2	22	24	-1	2.0
1945	Pit-N	5	4	.556	14	11	4	1	0	80²	74	6	37	29	12.6	4.57	86	.236	.321	9	.231	-2	-7	-6	0	-0.3
1946	Pit-N	13	10	.565	27	25	16	2	0	193¹	193	5	56	57	11.7	2.84	124	.263	.318	21	.328	6	12	15	-2	2.3
1947	Pit-N	12	10	.545	26	24	12	3	0	183	181	18	68	66	12.3	3.84	110	.254	.320	12	.188	-0	5	8	-1	0.7
1948	Pit-N	8	11	.421	23	22	10	2	0	134¹	143	16	41	43	12.4	4.42	92	.262	.315	8	.182	-0	-7	-5	-1	-0.8
Total 15		114	115	.498	390	246	113	11	15	2066²	2170	105	835	774	13.2	3.99	109	.268	.337	175	.234	16	49	85	-3	10.0

● JOE OSTROWSKI
Ostrowski, Joseph Paul "Professor" or "Specs" b: 11/15/16, W.Wyoming, Pa. BL/TL, 6', 180 lbs. Deb: 7/18/48

YEAR	TM/L	W	L	PCT	G	GS	CG	SH	SV	IP	H	HR	BB	SO	RAT	ERA	ERA+	OAV	OOB	BH	AVG	PB	PR	/A	PD	TPI
1948	StL-A	4	6	.400	26	9	3	0	3	78¹	108	6	17	20	14.4	5.97	76	.333	.367	4	.222	1	-15	-12	2	-1.2
1949	StL-A	8	8	.500	40	13	4	0	3	141	185	16	27	34	13.5	4.79	95	.307	.337	7	.189	-2	-9	-4	-1	-0.3
1950	StL-A	2	4	.333	9	7	2	0	0	57¹	57	2	7	15	10.0	2.51	197	.251	.274	4	.222	-1	13	16	-1	1.6
	NY-A	1	1	.500	21	4	1	0	3	43²	50	11	15	15	13.4	5.15	83	.294	.351	1	.111	-0	-3	-4	0	-0.2
	Yr	3	5	.375	30	11	3	0	3	101	107	13	22	30	11.5	3.65	128	.270	.308	5	.185	1	10	11	-1	1.4
1951	*NY-A	6	4	.600	34	3	2	0	5	95¹	103	4	18	30	11.5	3.49	110	.279	.314	3	.107	-2	7	4	-1	0.1
1952	NY-A	2	2	.500	20	1	0	0	2	40	56	5	14	16	16.0	5.62	59	.327	.382	0	.000	-1	-9	-10	-1	-1.2
Total 5		23	25	.479	150	37	12	0	15	455²	559	44	98	131	13.0	4.54	95	.300	.336	19	.161	1	-16	-12	-1	-1.2

● AL OSUNA
Osuna, Alfonso b: 8/10/65, Inglewood, Cal. BR/TL, 6'3", 200 lbs. Deb: 9/2/90

YEAR	TM/L	W	L	PCT	G	GS	CG	SH	SV	IP	H	HR	BB	SO	RAT	ERA	ERA+	OAV	OOB	BH	AVG	PB	PR	/A	PD	TPI
1990	Hou-N	2	0	1.000	12	0	0	0	0	11¹	10	1	6	6	15.1	4.76	78	.270	.413	0	—	0	-1	-1	-0	-0.2
1991	Hou-N	7	6	.538	71	0	0	0	12	81²	59	5	46	68	11.9	3.42	103	.201	.316	0	.000	-0	2	1	-0	0.1
1992	Hou-N	6	3	.667	66	0	0	0	0	61²	52	8	38	37	13.3	4.23	79	.236	.351	0	—	-0	-5	-6	0	-0.8
1993	Hou-N	1	1	.500	44	0	0	0	0	25¹	17	3	13	21	11.0	3.20	121	.200	.313	0	—	0	2	1	-0	0.1
1994	LA-N	2	0	1.000	15	0	0	0	0	8²	13	0	4	7	17.7	6.23	63	.333	.395	0	.000	-0	-2	-2	-0	-0.5
Total 5		18	10	.643	208	0	0	0	14	188²	151	17	107	139	12.7	3.86	92	.224	.337	0	.000	-0	-3	-7	-1	-1.3

● BILL OTEY
Otey, William Tilford "Steamboat Bill" b: 12/16/1886, Dayton, Ohio d: 4/23/31, Dayton, Ohio BL/TL, 6'2", 181 lbs. Deb: 9/27/07

YEAR	TM/L	W	L	PCT	G	GS	CG	SH	SV	IP	H	HR	BB	SO	RAT	ERA	ERA+	OAV	OOB	BH	AVG	PB	PR	/A	PD	TPI
1907	Pit-N	0	1	.000	3	2	1	0	0	16¹	23	1	4	5	15.4	4.41	55	.319	.364	1	.250	0	-4	-4	-0	-0.3
1910	Was-A	0	1	.000	9	1	1	0	0	34²	40	1	6	12	12.2	3.38	74	.301	.336	5	.385	2	-3	-3	-1	0.0
1911	Was-A	1	3	.250	12	2	0	0	0	49²	68	2	15	16	15.6	6.34	52	.333	.387	1	.059	-2	-17	-17	1	-1.2
Total 3		1	5	.167	24	5	2	0	0	100²	131	4	25	33	14.4	5.01	57	.320	.367	7	.206	0	-23	-24	-1	-1.5

● HARRY OTIS
Otis, Harry George "Cannonball" b: 10/5/1886, W.New York, N.J. d: 1/29/76, Teaneck, N.J. BR/TL, 6', 180 lbs. Deb: 9/5/09

YEAR	TM/L	W	L	PCT	G	GS	CG	SH	SV	IP	H	HR	BB	SO	RAT	ERA	ERA+	OAV	OOB	BH	AVG	PB	PR	/A	PD	TPI
1909	Cle-A	2	2	.500	5	3	0	0	0	26¹	26	0	18	6	16.1	1.37	187	.283	.416	1	.111	-0	3	3	-0	0.5

● DENNIS O'TOOLE
O'Toole, Dennis Joseph b: 3/13/49, Chicago, Ill. BR/TR, 6'3", 195 lbs. Deb: 9/8/69 F

YEAR	TM/L	W	L	PCT	G	GS	CG	SH	SV	IP	H	HR	BB	SO	RAT	ERA	ERA+	OAV	OOB	BH	AVG	PB	PR	/A	PD	TPI
1969	Chi-A	0	0	—	2	0	0	0	0	4	5	2	4	4	15.8	6.75	57	.333	.412	0	—	0	-1	-1	-0	0.0
1970	Chi-A	0	0	—	3	0	0	0	0	3¹	5	0	2	3	18.9	2.70	144	.357	.438	0	—	0	0	0	-0	0.0
1971	Chi-A	0	0	—	1	0	0	0	0	2	0	1	2	4	4.5	0	—	.000	.143	0	—	0	1	1	-0	0.0
1972	Chi-A	0	0	—	3	0	0	0	0	5	10	0	2	5	21.6	5.40	58	.417	.462	0	—	0	-1	-1	0	0.0
1973	Chi-A	0	0	—	6	0	0	0	0	16	23	3	3	8	14.6	5.63	70	.329	.356	0	—	0	-3	-3	0	-0.2
Total 5		0	0	—	15	0	0	0	0	30¹	43	3	10	22	15.7	5.04	75	.333	.381	0	—	0	-5	-4	-0	-0.2

● JIM O'TOOLE
O'Toole, James Jerome b: 1/10/37, Chicago, Ill. BB/TL, 6', 198 lbs. Deb: 9/26/58 F

YEAR	TM/L	W	L	PCT	G	GS	CG	SH	SV	IP	H	HR	BB	SO	RAT	ERA	ERA+	OAV	OOB	BH	AVG	PB	PR	/A	PD	TPI
1958	Cin-N	0	1	.000	1	1	0	0	0	7	4	0	5	4	11.6	1.29	322	.154	.290	0	.000	-0	2	2	-0	0.3
1959	Cin-N	5	8	.385	28	19	3	1	0	129¹	144	14	73	68	15.4	5.15	79	.287	.382	5	.135	-0	-17	-16	1	-1.4
1960	Cin-N	12	12	.500	34	31	7	2	1	196¹	198	14	66	124	12.3	3.80	100	.263	.325	7	.106	-3	-1	0	-3	-0.6
1961	*Cin-N	19	9	.679	39	35	11	3	2	252²	229	16	93	178	11.6	3.10	131	.240	.310	16	.172	-1	26	27	-0	2.7
1962	Cin-N	13	13	.552	36	34	11	3	0	251²	222	20	87	170	11.2	3.50	115	.238	.307	10	.110	-5	12	15	-2	0.8
1963	Cin-N★	17	14	.548	33	32	12	5	0	234¹	208	13	57	146	10.3	2.88	116	.239	.288	11	.149	-1	11	12	-3	1.2
1964	Cin-N	17	7	.708	30	30	9	3	0	220	194	8	51	145	10.0	2.66	136	.235	.279	7	.100	-1	21	23	-2	2.2
1965	Cin-N	3	10	.231	29	22	2	0	1	127²	154	14	47	71	14.4	5.92	63	.294	.355	4	.089	-2	-34	-31	-2	-3.2
1966	Cin-N	5	7	.417	25	24	2	0	0	142	139	16	49	96	12.1	3.55	110	.254	.318	6	.128	-2	1	6	-1	0.2
1967	Chi-A	4	3	.571	15	10	1	0	0	54¹	53	7	18	37	11.9	2.82	110	.251	.313	1	.077	-1	3	2	-1	0.1
Total 10		98	84	.538	270	238	58	18	4	1615¹	1545	119	546	1039	11.8	3.57	106	.251	.315	67	.125	-15	24	40	-12	2.3

● MARTY O'TOOLE
O'Toole, Martin James b: 11/27/1888, Wm.Penn, Pa. d: 2/18/49, Aberdeen, Wash. BR/TR, 5'11", 175 lbs. Deb: 9/21/08

YEAR	TM/L	W	L	PCT	G	GS	CG	SH	SV	IP	H	HR	BB	SO	RAT	ERA	ERA+	OAV	OOB	BH	AVG	PB	PR	/A	PD	TPI
1908	Cin-N	1	0	1.000	3	2	1	0	0	15	15	0	7	5	13.2	2.40	96	.273	.355	1	.200	-0	-0	-0	-0	0.0
1911	Pit-N	3	2	.600	5	5	3	0	0	38	28	1	20	34	11.4	2.37	145	.215	.320	5	.357	2	4	4	0	0.8
1912	Pit-N	15	17	.469	37	36	17	5	0	275¹	237	4	159	150	13.0	2.71	120	.241	.348	22	.222	2	21	17	1	2.0

YEAR TM/L	W	L	PCT	G	GS	CG	SH	SV	IP	H	HR	BB	SO	RAT	ERA	ERA+	OAV	OOB	BH	AVG	PB	PR	/A	PD	TPI
1913 Pit-N	6	8	.429	26	16	7	0	1	144²	148	3	55	58	12.8	3.30	91	.271	.341	7	.132	-2	-1	-5	-0	-0.7
1914 Pit-N	1	8	.111	19	9	1	0	1	92¹	92	3	47	36	13.5	4.68	57	.270	.358	5	.167	-0	-19	-21	-1	-2.0
NY-N	1	1	.500	10	5	2	0	0	34	34	0	12	13	12.2	4.24	63	.262	.324	3	.300	1	-5	-6	-0	-0.3
Yr	2	9	.182	29	14	3	0	1	126¹	126	3	59	49	13.2	4.56	58	.268	.349	8	.200	1	-25	-27	-1	-2.3
Total 5	27	36	.429	100	73	31	5	2	599¹	554	11	300	296	12.9	3.21	95	.254	.345	43	.204	2	-1	-10	-0	-0.2

● JIM OTTEN
Otten, James Edward   b: 7/1/51, Lewistown, Mont.   BR/TR, 6'2", 195 lbs.   Deb: 7/31/74

YEAR TM/L	W	L	PCT	G	GS	CG	SH	SV	IP	H	HR	BB	SO	RAT	ERA	ERA+	OAV	OOB	BH	AVG	PB	PR	/A	PD	TPI
1974 Chi-A	0	1	.000	5	1	0	0	0	16¹	22	0	12	11	19.3	5.51	68	.324	.432	0	—	0	-3	-3	-0	-0.4
1975 Chi-A	0	0	—	2	0	0	0	0	5¹	4	1	7	3	18.6	6.75	57	.235	.458	0	—	0	-2	-2	-0	-0.1
1976 Chi-A	0	0	—	2	0	0	0	0	6	9	0	2	5	16.5	4.50	79	.333	.379	0	—	0	-1	-1	-0	-0.1
1980 StL-N	0	5	.000	31	4	0	0	0	55¹	71	3	26	38	16.1	5.53	67	.323	.399	1	.200	-0	-12	-11	1	-0.9
1981 StL-N	1	0	1.000	24	0	0	0	0	35²	44	3	20	20	16.1	5.30	67	.321	.408	0	.000	-0	-7	-7	-1	-0.3
Total 5	1	6	.143	64	5	0	0	0	118²	150	7	67	75	16.7	5.46	67	.320	.408	1	.143	0	-25	-24	-1	-1.8

● DAVE OTTO
Otto, David Alan   b: 11/12/64, Chicago, Ill.   BL/TL, 6'7", 210 lbs.   Deb: 9/8/87

YEAR TM/L	W	L	PCT	G	GS	CG	SH	SV	IP	H	HR	BB	SO	RAT	ERA	ERA+	OAV	OOB	BH	AVG	PB	PR	/A	PD	TPI
1987 Oak-A	0	0	—	3	0	0	0	0	6	7	1	1	3	12.0	9.00	46	.304	.333	0	—	0	-3	-3	-0	0.0
1988 Oak-A	0	0	—	3	2	0	0	0	10	9	0	6	7	13.5	1.80	210	.243	.349	0	—	0	2	2	0	0.2
1989 Oak-A	0	0	—	1	1	0	0	0	6²	6	0	2	4	10.8	2.70	136	.261	.320	0	—	0	1	1	0	0.0
1990 Oak-A	0	0	—	2	0	0	0	0	2¹	3	0	3	2	23.1	7.71	48	.300	.462	0	—	0	-1	-1	0	0.1
1991 Cle-A	2	8	.200	18	14	1	0	0	100	108	7	47	47	12.5	4.23	98	.283	.337	0	—	0	-2	-1	-0	-0.1
1992 Cle-A	5	9	.357	18	16	0	0	0	80¹	91	12	33	32	16.1	7.06	55	.333	.396	0	—	0	-28	-28	0	-3.9
1993 Pit-N	3	4	.429	28	8	0	0	0	68	85	9	28	30	15.4	5.03	81	.317	.388	4	.222	1	-7	-7	1	-0.5
1994 Chi-N	0	1	.000	36	0	0	0	0	45	49	4	22	19	14.4	3.80	108	.283	.367	0	—	-0	2	2	-1	-0.1
Total 8	10	22	.313	109	41	1	0	0	318¹	377	33	122	144	14.4	5.06	80	.303	.369	4	.200	1	-35	-36	0	-4.3

● ORVAL OVERALL
Overall, Orval   b: 2/2/1881, Farmersville, Cal.   d: 7/14/47, Fresno, Cal.   BB/TR, 6'2", 214 lbs.   Deb: 4/16/05

YEAR TM/L	W	L	PCT	G	GS	CG	SH	SV	IP	H	HR	BB	SO	RAT	ERA	ERA+	OAV	OOB	BH	AVG	PB	PR	/A	PD	TPI
1905 Cin-N	18	23	.439	42	39	32	2	0	318	290	4	147	173	12.8	2.86	116	.252	.343	17	.145	-2	5	16	-1	1.5
1906 Cin-N	4	5	.444	13	10	6	0	0	82¹	77	1	46	33	13.9	4.26	65	.253	.359	6	.194	0	-15	-14	-1	-1.5
*Chi-N	12	3	.800	18	14	13	2	1	144	116	1	51	94	10.7	1.88	141	.217	.290	9	.170	-1	12	12	0	1.2
Yr	16	8	.667	31	24	19	2	1	226¹	193	2	97	127	11.7	2.74	98	.229	.311	15	.179	-1	-3	-2	-1	-0.3
1907 *Chi-N	23	7	.767	36	30	26	8	3	268¹	201	3	69	141	9.4	1.68	149	.208	.268	20	.213	3	24	24	2	3.5
1908 *Chi-N	15	11	.577	37	27	16	4	4	225	165	3	78	167	9.8	1.92	123	.208	.280	9	.129	-0	11	11	-1	1.1
1909 Chi-N	20	11	.645	38	32	23	9	3	285	204	0	80	**205**	9.2	1.42	179	**.198**	.262	22	.229	8	37	36	0	5.1
1910 *Chi-N	12	6	.667	23	21	11	4	1	144²	106	2	54	92	10.0	2.68	108	.212	.291	5	.122	-1	6	3	1	0.5
1913 Chi-N	4	5	.444	11	9	6	1	0	76	67	1	26	30	13.2	3.31	96	.284	.352	6	.250	-1	-1	-1	0	0.2
Total 7	108	71	.603	218	182	133	30	12	1535¹	1232	16	551	935	10.7	2.23	123	.223	.298	94	.179	9	79	87	1	11.6

● STUBBY OVERMIRE
Overmire, Frank   b: 5/16/19, Moline, Mich.   d: 3/3/77, Lakeland, Fla.   BR/TL, 5'7", 170 lbs.   Deb: 4/25/43   C

YEAR TM/L	W	L	PCT	G	GS	CG	SH	SV	IP	H	HR	BB	SO	RAT	ERA	ERA+	OAV	OOB	BH	AVG	PB	PR	/A	PD	TPI
1943 Det-A	7	6	.538	29	18	8	3	1	147	135	5	38	48	10.7	3.18	111	.243	.293	7	.167	0	2	6	-1	0.4
1944 Det-A	11	11	.500	32	28	11	3	1	199²	214	4	41	57	11.6	3.07	116	.271	.309	11	.175	1	8	11	2	1.4
1945 *Det-A	9	9	.500	31	22	9	0	4	162¹	189	6	42	36	13.0	3.88	91	.294	.341	10	.189	0	-9	-7	0	-0.7
1946 Det-A	5	7	.417	24	13	3	0	1	97¹	106	6	29	34	12.5	4.62	79	.274	.325	5	.152	-1	-12	-10	1	-1.2
1947 Det-A	11	5	.688	28	17	7	3	0	140²	142	9	44	33	12.0	3.77	100	.259	.315	7	.149	-1	-1	-0	-0	-0.1
1948 Det-A	3	4	.429	37	4	0	0	3	66¹	89	5	31	14	16.3	5.97	73	.326	.395	1	.071	-1	-12	-12	1	-1.2
1949 Det-A	1	3	.250	14	1	0	0	0	17¹	29	2	9	3	20.3	9.87	42	.377	.448	1	.333	0	-11	-11	-0	-2.0
1950 StL-A	9	12	.429	31	19	8	2	0	161	200	11	45	39	13.8	4.19	118	.298	.343	8	.167	1	7	14	-2	1.4
1951 StL-A	1	6	.143	8	7	3	0	0	53¹	61	5	21	13	13.8	3.54	124	.281	.345	1	.071	-1	3	5	-1	0.4
NY-A	1	1	.500	15	4	1	0	0	44²	50	2	18	14	14.1	4.63	83	.287	.361	1	.143	-0	-3	-4	0	-0.1
Yr	2	7	.222	23	11	4	0	0	98	111	7	39	27	14.0	4.04	102	.284	.352	2	.095	-1	1	1	-1	0.3
1952 StL-A	0	3	.000	17	4	0	0	0	41	44	3	7	10	11.2	3.73	105	.270	.300	1	.182	-0	-0	1	1	0.1
Total 10	58	67	.464	266	137	50	11	10	1130²	1259	56	325	301	12.7	3.96	98	.280	.330	54	.161	-1	-28	-8	1	-1.6

● MIKE OVERY
Overy, Harry Michael   b: 1/27/51, Clinton, Ill.   BR/TR, 6'2", 190 lbs.   Deb: 8/14/76

YEAR TM/L	W	L	PCT	G	GS	CG	SH	SV	IP	H	HR	BB	SO	RAT	ERA	ERA+	OAV	OOB	BH	AVG	PB	PR	/A	PD	TPI
1976 Cal-A	0	2	.000	5	0	0	0	0	7¹	6	1	3	8	12.3	6.14	54	.214	.313	0	—	0	-2	-2	0	-0.1

● ERNIE OVITZ
Ovitz, Ernest Gayhart   b: 10/7/1885, Mineral Point, Wis.   d: 9/11/80, Green Bay, Wis.   BR/TR, 5'8.5", 156 lbs.   Deb: 6/22/11

YEAR TM/L	W	L	PCT	G	GS	CG	SH	SV	IP	H	HR	BB	SO	RAT	ERA	ERA+	OAV	OOB	BH	AVG	PB	PR	/A	PD	TPI
1911 Chi-N	0	0	—	1	0	0	0	0	2	3	0	3	0	27.0	4.50	74	.375	.545	0	—	0	-0	-0	-0	0.0

● BOB OWCHINKO
Owchinko, Robert Dennis   b: 1/1/55, Detroit, Mich.   BL/TL, 6'2", 195 lbs.   Deb: 9/25/76

YEAR TM/L	W	L	PCT	G	GS	CG	SH	SV	IP	H	HR	BB	SO	RAT	ERA	ERA+	OAV	OOB	BH	AVG	PB	PR	/A	PD	TPI
1976 SD-N	0	2	.000	2	2	0	0	0	4¹	11	0	3	4	29.1	16.62	20	.478	.538	0	.000	-0	-6	-6	0	-1.7
1977 SD-N	9	12	.429	30	28	3	2	0	170	191	20	67	101	13.7	4.45	80	.287	.352	4	.082	-2	-10	-17	-2	-2.2
1978 SD-N	10	13	.435	36	33	4	1	0	202¹	198	14	78	94	12.3	3.56	93	.263	.333	11	.175	1	-0	-5	-1	-0.5
1979 SD-N	6	12	.333	42	20	2	0	0	149¹	144	16	55	66	12.1	3.74	94	.259	.328	4	.121	-0	0	-3	-0	-0.5
1980 Cle-A	2	9	.182	29	14	1	1	0	114¹	138	13	47	66	14.7	5.27	77	.301	.368	0	—	0	-16	-15	-1	-1.3
1981 *Oak-A	4	3	.571	29	0	0	0	0	39¹	34	2	19	26	12.4	3.20	109	.245	.340	0	—	0	2	1	-0	0.3
1982 Oak-A	2	4	.333	54	0	0	0	3	102	111	11	52	67	14.4	5.21	75	.275	.358	0	—	0	-13	-15	-1	-0.7
1983 Pit-N	0	0	—	1	0	0	0	0	0	2	1	0	0	—	∞	—	1.000	1.000	0	—	0	-1	-1	0	-0.1
1984 Cin-N	3	5	.375	49	4	0	0	0	94	91	10	39	60	12.4	4.12	92	.253	.327	2	.167	1	-6	-4	-1	-0.3
1986 Mon-N	1	0	1.000	3	3	0	0	0	15	17	1	3	6	12.0	3.60	103	.288	.323	1	.200	-0	0	-0	-0	-0.0
Total 10	37	60	.381	275	104	10	4	7	890²	937	88	363	490	13.2	4.28	85	.274	.345	22	.135	-0	-49	-66	-5	-7.0

● FRANK OWEN
Owen, Frank Malcolm "Yip"   b: 12/23/1879, Ypsilanti, Mich.   d: 11/24/42, Dearborn, Mich.   BB/TR, 5'11", 160 lbs.   Deb: 4/29/01

YEAR TM/L	W	L	PCT	G	GS	CG	SH	SV	IP	H	HR	BB	SO	RAT	ERA	ERA+	OAV	OOB	BH	AVG	PB	PR	/A	PD	TPI
1901 Det-A	1	3	.250	8	5	3	0	0	56	70	1	30	17	16.7	4.34	89	.302	.392	1	.050	-2	-4	-3	2	-0.2
1903 Chi-A	8	12	.400	26	20	15	1	1	167¹	167	1	44	66	11.7	3.50	80	.259	.314	7	.123	-1	-10	-13	4	-1.2
1904 Chi-A	21	15	.583	37	36	34	4	1	315	243	2	61	103	9.0	1.94	126	.214	.261	23	.215	-5	23	18	6	3.5
1905 Chi-A	21	13	.618	42	38	32	3	0	334	276	6	56	125	9.2	2.10	118	.226	.266	18	.145	-4	21	14	3	1.3
1906 *Chi-A	22	13	.629	42	36	27	7	0	293	289	4	54	66	10.7	2.33	109	.261	.297	14	.136	-2	12	7	4	1.0
1907 Chi-A	2	3	.400	11	4	2	0	0	47	43	1	13	15	10.7	2.49	96	.245	.297	4	.250	0	0	-0	1	0.0
1908 Chi-A	6	7	.462	25	14	5	1	0	140	142	2	37	48	11.7	3.41	68	.260	.310	9	.180	1	-16	-17	2	-1.3
1909 Chi-A	1	1	.500	3	2	1	0	0	16	19	0	3	3	12.9	4.50	52	.279	.319	1	.167	-0	-4	-4	-0	-0.5
Total 8	82	67	.550	194	155	119	16	2	1368¹	1249	17	298	443	10.4	2.55	100	.244	.290	77	.159	-3	22	1	21	2.6

● JIM OWENS
Owens, James Philip "Bear"   b: 1/16/34, Gifford, Pa.   BR/TR, 5'11", 190 lbs.   Deb: 4/19/55   C

YEAR TM/L	W	L	PCT	G	GS	CG	SH	SV	IP	H	HR	BB	SO	RAT	ERA	ERA+	OAV	OOB	BH	AVG	PB	PR	/A	PD	TPI
1955 Phi-N	0	2	.000	3	2	0	0	0	8²	16	3	2	6	20.8	8.31	48	.382	.488	0	.000	0	-4	-4	-0	-0.8
1956 Phi-N	4	0	.000	10	5	0	0	0	29²	35	3	22	22	17.9	7.28	51	.313	.434	1	.167	0	-12	-12	-0	-1.3
1958 Phi-N	1	0	1.000	1	1	0	0	0	7	4	1	5	3	11.6	2.57	154	.154	.290	0	.000	0	1	1	-0	0.1
1959 Phi-N	12	12	.500	31	30	11	1	1	221¹	203	14	73	135	11.4	3.21	128	.244	.308	9	.120	-1	18	22	3	2.1
1960 Phi-N	4	14	.222	31	22	6	0	0	150	182	21	64	83	14.8	5.04	77	.299	.367	3	.068	-3	-21	-19	-1	-2.5
1961 Phi-N	5	10	.333	20	17	3	0	0	106²	119	8	32	38	12.7	4.47	91	.287	.339	2	.074	-1	-5	-5	-2	-0.9
1962 Phi-N	2	4	.333	23	12	1	0	0	69²	90	12	33	21	15.9	6.33	61	.318	.389	2	.143	0	-18	-19	-1	-1.6
1963 Cin-N	0	0	—	4	0	0	0	0	4²	14	2	3	6	34.0	13.50	31	.350	.259	1	.125	0	-10	-9	1	-0.6
1964 Hou-N	8	7	.533	48	11	0	0	6	118	115	7	32	88	11.2	3.28	104	.262	.312	3	.103	-1	3	5	-0	0.4
1965 Hou-N	6	5	.545	50	0	0	0	8	71¹	64	4	29	53	11.7	3.28	102	.238	.312	1	.125	-0	2	1	-0	0.3
1966 Hou-N	4	7	.364	40	0	0	0	0	50	53	5	17	32	12.8	4.68	73	.273	.335	0	.000	-0	-6	-7	1	-1.5

YEAR TM/L	W	L	PCT	G	GS	CG	SH	SV	IP	H	HR	BB	SO	RAT	ERA	ERA+	OAV	OOB	BH	AVG	PB	PR	/A	PD	TPI
1967 Hou-N	0	1	.000	10	0	0	0	0	10²	12	1	2	6	11.8	4.22	78	.308	.341	0	—	0	-1	-1	-0	-0.1
Total 12	42	68	.382	286	103	21	1	21	885¹	932	84	340	516	13.0	4.31	88	.273	.340	22	.101	-7	-53	-51	-5	-7.1

● **RICK OWNBEY**   Ownbey, Richard Wayne   b: 10/20/57, Corona, Cal.   BR/TR, 6'3", 185 lbs.   Deb: 8/17/82

YEAR TM/L	W	L	PCT	G	GS	CG	SH	SV	IP	H	HR	BB	SO	RAT	ERA	ERA+	OAV	OOB	BH	AVG	PB	PR	/A	PD	TPI
1982 NY-N	1	2	.333	8	8	2	0	0	50¹	44	3	43	28	15.6	3.75	97	.242	.387	3	.200	1	-1	-1	-1	0.0
1983 NY-N	1	3	.250	10	4	0	0	0	34²	31	4	21	19	13.8	4.67	78	.240	.351	1	.111	-0	-4	-4	-0	-0.5
1984 StL-N	0	3	.000	4	4	0	0	0	19	23	1	8	11	14.7	4.74	73	.303	.369	0	.000	-0	-2	-3	-0	-0.5
1986 StL-N	1	3	.250	17	3	0	0	0	42²	47	4	19	25	14.3	3.80	96	.294	.376	0	.000	-0	-0	-1	-1	-0.2
Total 4	3	11	.214	39	19	2	0	0	146²	145	12	91	83	14.7	4.11	88	.265	.373	4	.114	-1	-8	-8	-2	-1.2

● **DOC OZMER**   Ozmer, Horace Robert   b: 5/25/01, Atlanta, Ga.   d: 12/28/70, Atlanta, Ga.   BR/TR, 5'10.5", 185 lbs.   Deb: 5/11/23

YEAR TM/L	W	L	PCT	G	GS	CG	SH	SV	IP	H	HR	BB	SO	RAT	ERA	ERA+	OAV	OOB	BH	AVG	PB	PR	/A	PD	TPI
1923 Phi-A	0	0	—	1	0	0	0	0	2	1	0	1	2	9.0	4.50	91	.167	.286	0	—	0	-0	-0	0	0.0

● **CHARLIE PABOR**   Pabor, Charles Henry   b: 9/24/1846, New York, N.Y.   d: 4/22/13, New Haven, Conn.   BL/TL, 5'8", 155 lbs.   Deb: 5/4/1871 M♦

YEAR TM/L	W	L	PCT	G	GS	CG	SH	SV	IP	H	HR	BB	SO	RAT	ERA	ERA+	OAV	OOB	BH	AVG	PB	PR	/A	PD	TPI
1871 Cle-n	0	2	.000	7	1	1	0	0	29¹	50	4	6	0	17.2	6.75	61	.325	.350	42	.296		-8	-9		-0.3
1872 Cle-n	1	1	.500	2	2	2	0	0	18	20	1	0	3	11.5	3.00	121	.253	.280	19	.211	-0	1	1		0.1
1875 Atl-n	0	1	.000	1	1	0	0	0	4	11	0	1	0	27.0	9.00	26	.440	.462	36	.235	0	-3	-3		-0.5
Total 3 n	1	4	.200	10	4	3	0	0	51¹	81	4	10	0	16.0	5.61	41	.314	.340	205	.288	-0	-18	-19		-0.7

● **JOHN PACELLA**   Pacella, John Lewis   b: 9/15/56, Brooklyn, N.Y.   BR/TR, 6'3", 195 lbs.   Deb: 9/15/77

YEAR TM/L	W	L	PCT	G	GS	CG	SH	SV	IP	H	HR	BB	SO	RAT	ERA	ERA+	OAV	OOB	BH	AVG	PB	PR	/A	PD	TPI
1977 NY-N	0	0	—	3	0	0	0	0	4	2	0	2	1	9.0	0.00	—	.133	.235	0	—	0	2	2	-0	0.0
1979 NY-N	0	2	.000	4	3	0	0	0	16¹	16	0	4	12	11.0	4.41	83	.246	.290	0	.000	-0	-1	-1	-0	-0.2
1980 NY-N	3	4	.429	32	15	0	0	0	84	89	5	59	68	16.1	5.14	69	.280	.396	2	.100	-1	-14	-15	-1	-1.3
1982 NY-A	1	0	1.000	3	1	0	0	0	10	13	0	9	2	20.7	7.20	55	.342	.479	0	—	0	-3	-4	-0	-0.2
Min-A	1	2	.333	21	4	0	0	2	51²	61	14	37	20	17.1	7.32	58	.299	.407	0	—	0	-19	-18	-1	-1.3
Yr	1	3	.250	24	5	0	0	2	61²	74	14	46	22	17.5	7.30	58	.301	.411	0	—	0	-22	-21	-2	-1.5
1984 Bal-A	0	1	.000	6	1	0	0	0	14²	15	2	9	8	14.7	6.75	57	.268	.369	0	—	0	-4	-5	-0	-0.2
1986 Det-A	0	0	—	5	0	0	0	1	11	10	0	13	5	18.8	4.09	101	.294	.489	0	—	0	0	0	1	0.1
Total 6	4	10	.286	74	21	0	0	3	191²	206	21	133	116	16.1	5.73	67	.282	.395	2	.083	-1	-40	-41	-2	-3.1

● **PAT PACILLO**   Pacillo, Patrick Michael   b: 7/23/63, Jersey City, N.J.   BR/TR, 6'2", 205 lbs.   Deb: 5/23/87

YEAR TM/L	W	L	PCT	G	GS	CG	SH	SV	IP	H	HR	BB	SO	RAT	ERA	ERA+	OAV	OOB	BH	AVG	PB	PR	/A	PD	TPI
1987 Cin-N	3	3	.500	12	7	0	0	0	39²	41	7	19	23	13.8	6.13	69	.270	.355	1	.091	-0	-9	-8	-0	-1.1
1988 Cin-N	1	0	1.000	6	0	0	0	0	10²	14	2	4	11	15.2	5.06	71	.318	.375	0	.000	-0	-2	-2	-0	-0.2
Total 2	4	3	.571	18	7	0	0	0	50¹	55	9	23	34	14.1	5.90	70	.281	.359	1	.083	-0	-11	-10	-1	-1.3

● **GENE PACKARD**   Packard, Eugene Milo   b: 7/13/1887, Colorado Springs, Colorado   d: 5/19/59, Riverside, Cal.   BL/TL, 5'10", 155 lbs.   Deb: 9/27/12

YEAR TM/L	W	L	PCT	G	GS	CG	SH	SV	IP	H	HR	BB	SO	RAT	ERA	ERA+	OAV	OOB	BH	AVG	PB	PR	/A	PD	TPI
1912 Cin-N	1	0	1.000	1	1	1	0	0	9	7	0	4	2	11.0	3.00	112	.206	.289	1	.250	1	0	0	-0	0.1
1913 Cin-N	7	11	.389	39	21	9	2	0	190²	208	7	64	73	13.2	2.97	109	.286	.350	11	.180	-0	5	6	-1	0.4
1914 KC-F	20	14	.588	42	34	24	4	5	302	282	5	88	154	11.1	2.89	96	.246	.301	28	.241	2	-0	-4	9	0.7
1915 KC-F	20	12	.625	42	31	21	5	2	281²	250	3	74	108	10.6	2.68	98	.242	.298	22	.232	2	1	-2	7	0.7
1916 Chi-N	10	6	.625	37	16	5	2	5	155¹	154	4	38	36	11.3	2.78	105	.256	.304	7	.130	-1	-3	-2	5	0.7
1917 Chi-N	0	0	—	2	0	0	0	0	1²	3	1	0	1	16.2	10.80	27	.375	.375	0	—	0	-1	-1	0	0.0
StL-N	9	6	.600	34	11	6	0	2	153¹	138	4	25	44	9.7	2.47	109	.246	.281	15	.288	3	4	4	-1	0.7
Yr	9	6	.600	36	11	6	0	2	155	141	5	25	45	9.8	2.55	105	.247	.283	15	.288	3	3	2	-0	0.7
1918 StL-N	12	12	.500	30	23	10	1	2	182¹	184	6	33	46	11.0	3.50	77	.266	.304	12	.174	-1	-15	-16	-1	-2.3
1919 Phi-N	6	8	.429	21	16	10	1	1	134¹	167	3	30	24	13.5	4.15	78	.321	.363	7	.137	-2	-19	-14	-0	-1.6
Total 8	85	69	.552	248	153	86	15	17	1410¹	1393	28	356	488	11.4	3.01	95	.262	.312	103	.205	4	-27	-25	17	-0.6

● **JOE PACTWA**   Pactwa, Joseph Martin   b: 6/2/48, Hammond, Ind.   BL/TL, 5'11", 185 lbs.   Deb: 9/15/75

YEAR TM/L	W	L	PCT	G	GS	CG	SH	SV	IP	H	HR	BB	SO	RAT	ERA	ERA+	OAV	OOB	BH	AVG	PB	PR	/A	PD	TPI
1975 Cal-A	1	0	1.000	4	3	0	0	0	16¹	23	0	10	3	18.2	3.86	92	.343	.429	0	—	0	-0	-1	-0	0.4

● **DAVE PAGAN**   Pagan, David Percy   b: 9/15/49, Nipawin, Sask., Canada   BR/TR, 6'2", 175 lbs.   Deb: 7/1/73

YEAR TM/L	W	L	PCT	G	GS	CG	SH	SV	IP	H	HR	BB	SO	RAT	ERA	ERA+	OAV	OOB	BH	AVG	PB	PR	/A	PD	TPI
1973 NY-A	0	0	—	4	1	0	0	0	12²	16	1	1	9	12.1	2.84	129	.320	.333	0	—	0	1	1	0	0.3
1974 NY-A	1	3	.250	16	6	1	0	0	49¹	49	4	28	39	14.0	5.11	68	.265	.362	0	—	0	-8	-9	-0	-0.7
1975 NY-A	0	0	—	13	0	0	0	1	31	30	2	13	18	13.1	4.06	90	.256	.341	0	—	0	-1	-1	-1	0.1
1976 NY-A	1	1	.500	7	2	1	0	0	23²	18	0	6	13	8.4	2.28	150	.222	.259	0	—	0	3	3	-1	0.3
Bal-A	1	4	.200	20	5	0	0	0	46²	54	2	23	34	15.0	5.98	55	.298	.380	0	—	0	-13	-14	-1	-1.1
Yr	2	5	.286	27	7	1	0	0	70¹	72	2	27	47	12.8	4.73	70	.273	.342	0	—	0	-9	-11	-2	-0.8
1977 Sea-A	1	1	.500	24	0	0	0	0	66	86	3	26	30	15.5	6.14	67	.323	.388	0	—	0	-15	-15	-0	-0.5
Pit-N	0	0	—	1	0	0	0	0	3	1	0	3	0	3.0	0.00	—	.100	.100	0	—	0	1	1	0	0.0
Total 5	4	9	.308	85	18	3	1	4	232¹	254	9	95	147	13.7	4.96	74	.285	.358	0	—	0	-31	-34	-2	-1.6

● **JOE PAGE**   Page, Joseph Francis "Fireman"   b: 10/28/17, Cherry Valley, Pa.   d: 4/21/80, Latrobe, Pa.   BL/TL, 6'2", 205 lbs.   Deb: 4/19/44

YEAR TM/L	W	L	PCT	G	GS	CG	SH	SV	IP	H	HR	BB	SO	RAT	ERA	ERA+	OAV	OOB	BH	AVG	PB	PR	/A	PD	TPI
1944 NY-A☆	5	7	.417	19	16	4	0	0	102²	100	3	52	63	13.6	4.56	76	.258	.351	5	.156	-0	-13	-12	-1	-1.4
1945 NY-A	6	3	.667	20	9	4	0	0	102	95	1	46	50	12.4	2.82	123	.246	.326	9	.250	1	6	7	-2	0.5
1946 NY-A	9	8	.529	31	17	6	1	3	136	126	7	72	77	13.4	3.57	97	.252	.351	4	.163	-0	-1	-2	-1	-0.3
1947 *NY-A★	14	8	.636	56	2	0	0	17	141¹	105	5	72	116	11.3	2.48	142	.208	.308	10	.217	1	19	17	-1	3.0
1948 NY-A☆	7	8	.467	55	1	0	0	16	107²	116	6	66	77	15.3	4.26	96	.275	.374	7	.292	3	0	-2	-1	-0.1
1949 *NY-A	13	8	.619	60	0	0	0	27	135¹	103	9	75	99	12.2	2.59	156	.215	.328	7	.175	-2	24	22	-2	3.8
1950 NY-A	3	7	.300	37	0	0	0	13	55¹	66	8	31	33	15.8	5.04	85	.250	.380	2	.250	-1	-3	-5	-1	-0.9
1954 Pit-N	0	0	—	7	0	0	0	0	9²	16	4	7	4	22.3	11.17	37	.364	.462	0	—	0	-8	-8	0	-0.9
Total 8	57	49	.538	285	45	14	1	76	790	727	42	421	519	13.2	3.53	106	.247	.344	47	.205	5	25	18	-7	4.6

● **PHIL PAGE**   Page, Philippe Rausac   b: 8/23/05, Springfield, Mass.   d: 7/27/58, Springfield, Mass   BR/TL, 6'2", 175 lbs.   Deb: 9/18/28 C

YEAR TM/L	W	L	PCT	G	GS	CG	SH	SV	IP	H	HR	BB	SO	RAT	ERA	ERA+	OAV	OOB	BH	AVG	PB	PR	/A	PD	TPI
1928 Det-A	2	0	1.000	3	2	2	0	0	22	21	1	10	3	12.7	2.45	167	.256	.337	2	.222	-0	4	4	1	0.4
1929 Det-A	2	0	1.000	10	4	1	0	0	25¹	29	1	19	6	17.4	8.17	53	.296	.415	1	.125	-1	-11	-11	-1	-0.8
1930 Det-A	0	1	.000	12	0	0	0	0	12	23	1	9	2	24.0	9.75	49	.434	.516	0	—	0	-7	-7	0	-0.4
1934 Bro-N	1	0	1.000	6	0	0	0	0	10	13	1	6	4	17.1	5.40	72	.342	.432	0	.000	-0	-1	-2	-1	-0.1
Total 4	3	3	.500	31	6	3	0	0	69¹	86	4	44	15	17.0	6.23	68	.317	.415	3	.167	-1	-15	-15	-1	-0.9

● **SAM PAGE**   Page, Samuel Walter   b: 2/11/16, Woodruff, S.C.   BL/TR, 6', 172 lbs.   Deb: 9/11/39

YEAR TM/L	W	L	PCT	G	GS	CG	SH	SV	IP	H	HR	BB	SO	RAT	ERA	ERA+	OAV	OOB	BH	AVG	PB	PR	/A	PD	TPI
1939 Phi-A	0	3	.000	4	3	1	0	0	22	34	1	15	11	20.0	6.95	68	.343	.430	3	.429	1	-6	-5	1	-0.4

● **VANCE PAGE**   Page, Vance Linwood   b: 9/15/05, Elm City, N.C.   d: 7/14/51, Wilson, N.C.   BR/TR, 6', 180 lbs.   Deb: 8/6/38

YEAR TM/L	W	L	PCT	G	GS	CG	SH	SV	IP	H	HR	BB	SO	RAT	ERA	ERA+	OAV	OOB	BH	AVG	PB	PR	/A	PD	TPI
1938 *Chi-N	5	4	.556	13	9	3	0	1	68	90	4	13	18	13.6	3.84	100	.323	.353	4	.154	-1	-0	-0	3	0.1
1939 Chi-N	7	7	.500	27	17	8	1	1	139¹	169	8	37	43	13.4	3.88	102	.298	.342	12	.255	3	1	1	1	0.4
1940 Chi-N	1	3	.250	30	1	0	0	0	59	65	9	26	22	13.9	4.42	85	.271	.342	4	.308	2	-4	-4	-0	-0.1
1941 Chi-N	2	2	.500	25	3	1	0	0	48¹	48	2	30	17	14.9	4.28	82	.254	.362	2	.286	1	-3	-4	-0	-0.2
Total 4	15	16	.484	95	30	12	1	2	314²	372	15	106	100	13.8	4.03	95	.292	.348	22	.237	4	-7	-8	4	0.2

● **PAT PAIGE**   Paige, George Lynn "Piggy"   b: 5/5/1883, Paw Paw, Mich.   d: 6/8/39, Berlin, Wis.   BL/TR, 5'10", 175 lbs.   Deb: 5/20/11

YEAR TM/L	W	L	PCT	G	GS	CG	SH	SV	IP	H	HR	BB	SO	RAT	ERA	ERA+	OAV	OOB	BH	AVG	PB	PR	/A	PD	TPI
1911 Cle-A	1	0	1.000	2	1	1	0	0	16	21	0	7	6	15.8	4.50	76	.339	.406	1	.143	-0	-2	-2	1	-0.1

● **SATCHEL PAIGE**   Paige, Leroy Robert   b: 7/7/06, Mobile, Ala.   d: 6/8/82, Kansas City, Mo.   BR/TR, 6'3.5", 180 lbs.   Deb: 7/9/48 CH

YEAR TM/L	W	L	PCT	G	GS	CG	SH	SV	IP	H	HR	BB	SO	RAT	ERA	ERA+	OAV	OOB	BH	AVG	PB	PR	/A	PD	TPI
1948 *Cle-A	6	1	.857	21	7	3	2	1	72²	61	2	25	45	10.8	2.48	164	.228	.297	2	.087	-2	15	13	-0	0.9
1949 Cle-A	4	7	.364	31	5	1	0	5	83	70	4	33	54	11.3	3.04	131	.230	.308	1	.063	-1	11	9	-1	1.0

YEAR	TM/L	W	L	PCT	G	GS	CG	SH	SV	IP	H	HR	BB	SO	RAT	ERA	ERA+	OAV	OOB	BH	AVG	PB	PR	/A	PD	TPI
1951	StL-A	3	4	.429	23	3	0	0	5	62	67	6	29	48	14.1	4.79	92	.276	.355	2	.125	-2	-5	-3	-1	-0.6
1952	StL-A☆	12	10	.545	46	6	3	2	10	138	116	5	57	91	11.5	3.07	128	.226	.307	5	.128	-2	9	13	0	2.0
1953	StL-A★	3	9	.250	57	4	0	0	11	117¹	114	12	39	51	11.8	3.53	119	.257	.319	2	.069	-3	6	9	-2	0.5
1965	KC-A	0	0	—	1	1	0	0	0	3	1	0	1	1	3.0	0.00	—	.100	.100	0	.000	-0	1	1	-0	0.0
Total	6	28	31	.475	179	26	4	4	32	476	429	29	183	290	11.7	3.29	124	.241	.314	12	.097	-10	37	42	-3	3.8

● PHIL PAINE   Paine, Phillips Steere "Flip"   b: 6/8/30, Chepachet, R.I.   d: 2/19/78, Lebanon, Pa.   BR/TR, 6'2", 181 lbs.   Deb: 7/14/51

YEAR	TM/L	W	L	PCT	G	GS	CG	SH	SV	IP	H	HR	BB	SO	RAT	ERA	ERA+	OAV	OOB	BH	AVG	PB	PR	/A	PD	TPI
1951	Bos-N	2	0	1.000	21	0	0	0	0	35¹	36	2	20	17	15.3	3.06	120	.271	.382	0	.000	-1	4	2	-0	0.0
1954	Mil-N	1	0	1.000	11	0	0	0	0	14	14	1	12	11	17.4	3.86	97	.292	.443	0	—	0	0	-0	-0	-0.1
1955	Mil-N	2	0	1.000	15	0	0	0	0	25¹	20	2	14	26	12.1	2.49	151	.225	.330	1	.333	0	4	4	0	0.3
1956	Mil-N	0	0	—	1	0	0	0	0	0	3	0	0	0	—	∞	—	1.000	1.000	0	—	0	-2	-2	-0	-0.2
1957	Mil-N	0	0	—	1	0	0	0	0	1	1	0	3	2	18.0	0.00	—	.143	.400	0	—	0	1	1	0	0.0
1958	StL-N	5	1	.833	46	0	0	0	1	73¹	70	7	31	45	13.0	3.56	116	.256	.343	2	.286	0	3	5	0	0.4
Total	6	10	1	.909	95	0	0	0	1	150	144	12	80	101	14.0	3.36	116	.260	.364	3	.214	-0	10	9	-0	0.4

● LANCE PAINTER   Painter, Lance Telford   b: 7/21/67, Bedford, England   BL/TL, 6'1", 195 lbs.   Deb: 5/19/93

YEAR	TM/L	W	L	PCT	G	GS	CG	SH	SV	IP	H	HR	BB	SO	RAT	ERA	ERA+	OAV	OOB	BH	AVG	PB	PR	/A	PD	TPI
1993	Col-N	2	2	.500	10	6	1	0	0	39	52	5	9	16	14.1	6.00	79	.333	.370	3	.300	1	-8	-5	0	-0.3
1994	Col-N	4	6	.400	15	14	0	0	0	73²	91	9	26	41	14.4	6.11	81	.302	.360	3	.143	-1	-16	-9	-0	-1.1
Total	2	6	8	.429	25	20	1	0	0	112²	143	14	35	57	14.3	6.07	81	.313	.363	6	.194	0	-24	-15	1	-1.4

● VICENTE PALACIOS   Palacios, Vicente (Diaz)   b: 7/19/63, Veracruz, Mex.   BR/TR, 6'3", 165 lbs.   Deb: 9/4/87

YEAR	TM/L	W	L	PCT	G	GS	CG	SH	SV	IP	H	HR	BB	SO	RAT	ERA	ERA+	OAV	OOB	BH	AVG	PB	PR	/A	PD	TPI
1987	Pit-N	2	1	.667	6	4	0	0	0	29¹	27	1	9	13	11.4	4.30	96	.250	.314	1	.111	-0	-1	-1	-1	-0.2
1988	Pit-N	1	2	.333	7	3	0	0	0	24¹	28	3	15	15	15.9	6.66	51	.295	.391	0	.000	-0	-9	-9	0	-1.0
1990	Pit-N	0	0	—	7	0	0	0	3	15	4	0	2	8	3.6	0.00	—	.083	.120	0	.000	-0	6	6	-0	0.2
1991	Pit-N	6	3	.667	36	7	1	1	3	81²	69	12	38	64	11.9	3.75	95	.228	.316	1	.071	-1	-1	-2	-1	-0.3
1992	Pit-N	3	2	.600	20	8	0	0	0	53	56	1	27	33	14.1	4.25	81	.280	.366	1	.071	-1	-4	-5	-0	-0.5
1994	StL-N	3	8	.273	31	17	1	1	1	117²	104	16	43	95	11.5	4.44	92	.245	.319	0	.000	-4	-3	-5	-0	-0.8
Total	6	15	16	.484	107	39	2	2	7	321	288	33	134	228	12.0	4.18	90	.244	.324	3	.037	-6	-11	-14	-2	-2.6

● MIKE PALAGYI   Palagyi, Michael Raymond   b: 7/4/17, Conneaut, Ohio   BR/TR, 6'2", 185 lbs.   Deb: 8/18/39

YEAR	TM/L	W	L	PCT	G	GS	CG	SH	SV	IP	H	HR	BB	SO	RAT	ERA	ERA+	OAV	OOB	BH	AVG	PB	PR	/A	PD	TPI
1939	Was-A	0	0	—	1	0	0	0	0	0	0	0	3	0	—	∞	—	—	1.000	0	—	0	-3	-3	0	-0.2

● ERV PALICA   Palica, Ervin Martin (b: Ervin Martin Pavliecivich)
        b: 2/9/28, Lomita, Cal.   d: 5/29/82, Huntington Beach, Cal.   BR/TR, 6'1.5", 180 lbs.   Deb: 4/21/45 ♦

YEAR	TM/L	W	L	PCT	G	GS	CG	SH	SV	IP	H	HR	BB	SO	RAT	ERA	ERA+	OAV	OOB	BH	AVG	PB	PR	/A	PD	TPI
1947	Bro-N	0	1	.000	3	0	0	0	0	3	2	0	2	1	15.0	3.00	138	.182	.357	0	—	0	0	0	-0	0.1
1948	Bro-N	6	6	.500	41	10	3	0	3	125¹	111	13	58	74	12.4	4.45	90	.239	.327	5	.128	0	-7	-6	-1	-0.7
1949	*Bro-N	8	9	.471	49	1	0	0	6	97	93	6	49	44	13.3	3.62	113	.261	.352	3	.158	0	5	5	-0	0.9
1950	Bro-N	13	8	.619	43	19	10	2	1	201¹	176	13	98	131	12.3	3.58	115	.237	.327	15	.221	2	13	12	-4	0.9
1951	Bro-N	2	6	.250	19	8	0	0	0	53	55	10	20	15	12.7	4.75	83	.259	.323	2	.154	0	-5	-5	1	-0.6
1953	Bro-N	0	0	—	4	0	0	0	0	6	10	1	8	3	27.0	12.00	36	.370	.514	1	1.000	0	-5	-5	0	0.1
1954	Bro-N	3	3	.500	25	3	0	0	0	67²	77	9	31	25	14.5	5.32	77	.285	.361	4	.250	1	-9	-9	-2	-0.8
1955	Bal-A	5	11	.313	33	25	5	1	0	169²	165	10	83	68	13.0	4.14	92	.260	.348	13	.236	2	-3	-6	-1	-0.3
1956	Bal-A	4	11	.267	29	14	2	0	0	116¹	117	10	50	62	13.0	4.49	87	.264	.339	5	.156	-2	-4	-7	-0	-1.0
Total	9	41	55	.427	246	80	20	3	10	839¹	806	72	399	423	13.0	4.22	94	.255	.340	48	.198	5	-16	-22	-7	-1.4

● DONN PALL   Pall, Donn Steven   b: 1/11/62, Chicago, Ill.   BR/TR, 6'2", 185 lbs.   Deb: 8/1/88

YEAR	TM/L	W	L	PCT	G	GS	CG	SH	SV	IP	H	HR	BB	SO	RAT	ERA	ERA+	OAV	OOB	BH	AVG	PB	PR	/A	PD	TPI
1988	Chi-A	0	2	.000	17	0	0	0	0	28²	39	1	8	16	14.8	3.45	115	.328	.370	0	—	0	2	1	0	0.2
1989	Chi-A	4	5	.444	53	0	0	0	6	87	90	9	19	58	12.1	3.31	115	.270	.325	0	—	0	6	5	-1	0.4
1990	Chi-A	3	5	.375	56	0	0	0	2	76	63	7	24	39	10.8	3.32	115	.232	.303	0	—	0	5	4	-0	0.4
1991	Chi-A	7	2	.778	51	0	0	0	0	71	59	7	20	40	10.4	2.41	165	.231	.295	0	—	0	13	12	-1	1.5
1992	Chi-A	5	2	.714	39	0	0	0	0	73	79	9	27	27	13.3	4.93	78	.272	.339	0	—	0	-8	-9	-1	-0.8
1993	Chi-A	2	3	.400	39	0	0	0	1	58²	62	5	11	29	11.5	3.22	130	.268	.307	0	—	0	7	6	0	0.6
	Phi-N	1	0	1.000	8	0	0	0	0	17²	15	1	3	11	9.2	2.55	156	.231	.265	0	—	0	3	3	-0	0.1
1994	NY-A	1	2	.333	26	0	0	0	0	35	43	3	9	21	13.6	3.60	123	.295	.340	0	—	0	5	3	0	0.5
	Chi-N	0	0	—	2	0	0	0	0	4	8	1	1	2	20.3	4.50	91	.444	.474	0	—	0	-0	-0	-0	-0.0
Total	7	23	21	.523	291	0	0	0	10	451	458	43	122	243	12.0	3.43	115	.265	.321	—	—	0	32	27	-2	2.9

● MIKE PALM   Palm, Richard Paul   b: 2/13/25, Boston, Mass.   BR/TR, 6'3.5", 190 lbs.   Deb: 7/11/48

YEAR	TM/L	W	L	PCT	G	GS	CG	SH	SV	IP	H	HR	BB	SO	RAT	ERA	ERA+	OAV	OOB	BH	AVG	PB	PR	/A	PD	TPI
1948	Bos-A	0	0	—	3	0	0	0	0	3	6	0	5	1	33.0	6.00	73	.400	.550	0	.000	-0	-1	-1	-0	-0.1

● PALMER   Palmer   b: St.Louis, Mo.   Deb: 5/28/1885

YEAR	TM/L	W	L	PCT	G	GS	CG	SH	SV	IP	H	HR	BB	SO	RAT	ERA	ERA+	OAV	OOB	BH	AVG	PB	PR	/A	PD	TPI
1885	StL-N	0	4	.000	4	4	4	0	0	34	46	2	20	9	17.5	3.44	80	.311	.393	1	.091	-0	-2	-3	-1	-0.4

● DAVID PALMER   Palmer, David William   b: 10/19/57, Glens Falls, N.Y.   BR/TR, 6'1", 205 lbs.   Deb: 9/9/78

YEAR	TM/L	W	L	PCT	G	GS	CG	SH	SV	IP	H	HR	BB	SO	RAT	ERA	ERA+	OAV	OOB	BH	AVG	PB	PR	/A	PD	TPI
1978	Mon-N	0	1	.000	5	1	0	0	0	9²	9	1	2	7	10.2	2.79	126	.243	.282	0	.000	-0	1	1	1	0.1
1979	Mon-N	10	2	.833	36	11	2	1	2	122²	110	10	30	72	10.4	2.64	139	.237	.286	1	.032	-3	15	14	-0	1.0
1980	Mon-N	8	6	.571	24	19	3	1	0	129²	124	11	30	73	10.8	2.98	119	.255	.301	9	.200	1	9	8	1	1.1
1982	Mon-N	6	4	.600	13	13	1	0	0	73²	60	3	36	46	12.0	3.18	115	.224	.320	1	.042	-2	3	4	0	0.3
1984	Mon-N	7	3	.700	20	19	1	0	0	105¹	101	5	44	66	12.4	3.84	89	.256	.331	4	.152	1	-3	-5	-1	-0.3
1985	Mon-N	7	10	.412	24	24	0	0	0	135²	128	5	67	106	13.1	3.71	91	.250	.341	4	.111	-0	-2	-5	2	-0.5
1986	Atl-N	11	10	.524	35	35	2	0	0	209²	181	17	102	170	12.4	3.65	109	.234	.327	12	.182	1	2	8	2	1.1
1987	Atl-N	8	11	.421	28	28	0	0	0	152¹	169	17	64	111	14.2	4.90	89	.281	.357	6	.125	0	-14	-9	1	-1.0
1988	Phi-N	7	9	.438	22	22	1	1	0	129	129	8	48	85	12.3	4.47	80	.261	.327	10	.256	5	-15	-13	-1	-1.1
1989	Det-A	0	3	.000	5	5	0	0	0	17¹	25	1	11	12	18.7	7.79	49	.342	.429	0	—	0	-8	-8	-0	-1.0
Total	10	64	59	.520	212	176	10	4	2	1085	1036	78	434	748	12.4	3.78	99	.252	.327	48	.149	2	-11	-6	5	-0.3

● JIM PALMER   Palmer, James Alvin   b: 10/15/45, New York, N.Y.   BR/TR, 6'3", 196 lbs.   Deb: 4/17/65   H

YEAR	TM/L	W	L	PCT	G	GS	CG	SH	SV	IP	H	HR	BB	SO	RAT	ERA	ERA+	OAV	OOB	BH	AVG	PB	PR	/A	PD	TPI
1965	Bal-A	5	4	.556	27	6	0	0	0	92	75	6	56	75	13.0	3.72	93	.229	.345	5	.192	1	-3	-3	-0	-0.1
1966	*Bal-A	15	10	.600	30	30	6	0	0	208¹	176	21	91	147	11.5	3.46	96	.231	.313	7	.096	-2	-0	-3	-1	-0.6
1967	*Bal-A	3	1	.750	9	9	2	1	0	49	34	6	20	23	9.9	2.94	107	.199	.283	1	.077	0	2	1	0	0.1
1969	*Bal-A	16	4	.800	26	23	11	6	0	181	131	11	64	123	9.7	2.34	152	.200	.272	13	.203	2	26	25	-4	2.6
1970	*Bal-A★	20	10	.667	39	39	17	5	0	305	263	21	100	199	10.7	2.71	134	.231	.294	17	.150	-1	34	32	-0	2.8
1971	*Bal-A★	20	9	.690	37	37	20	3	0	282	231	19	106	184	10.9	2.68	125	.225	.295	20	.196	2	24	22	1	2.4
1972	Bal-A★	21	10	.677	36	36	18	3	0	274²	219	21	70	184	9.5	2.07	149	.217	.269	22	.224	4	30	31	-1	4.2
1973	*Bal-A	22	9	.710	38	37	19	6	1	296¹	225	16	113	158	10.4	2.40	156	.211	.289	0	—	0	47	44	-1	4.5
1974	Bal-A	7	12	.368	26	26	5	2	0	178²	176	12	69	84	12.5	3.27	105	.257	.328	0	—	0	7	4	2	0.5
1975	Bal-A☆	23	11	.676	39	38	25	10	1	323	253	20	80	193	9.3	2.09	168	.216	.267	0	—	0	61	51	2	6.1
1976	Bal-A	22	13	.629	40	40	23	6	0	315	255	20	84	159	9.9	2.51	130	.224	.282	0	—	0	35	27	1	3.6
1977	Bal-A★	20	11	.645	39	39	22	3	0	319	263	24	99	193	10.3	2.91	130	.229	.292	0	—	0	41	31	0	3.3
1978	Bal-A★	21	12	.636	38	38	19	6	0	296	246	19	97	138	10.5	2.46	142	.227	.289	0	—	0	43	34	1	4.3
1979	*Bal-A	10	6	.625	23	22	7	0	0	155²	144	12	43	67	10.8	3.30	122	.246	.297	0	—	0	16	12	-0	1.4
1980	Bal-A	16	10	.615	34	33	4	0	0	224	238	26	74	109	12.7	3.98	99	.275	.334	0	—	0	-1	-1	-5	-0.1
1981	Bal-A	7	8	.467	22	22	5	0	0	127¹	117	14	46	35	11.7	3.75	97	.247	.316	0	—	0	-1	-2	-1	-0.1
1982	Bal-A	15	5	.750	36	32	8	2	1	227	195	22	63	103	10.4	3.13	129	.231	.287	0	—	0	24	23	1	2.0
1983	*Bal-A	5	4	.556	14	11	0	0	0	76²	86	11	19	34	12.3	4.23	94	.281	.323	0	—	0	-1	-2	-1	-0.3

YEAR	TM/L	W	L	PCT	G	GS	CG	SH	SV	IP	H	HR	BB	SO	RAT	ERA	ERA+	OAV	OOB	BH	AVG	PB	PR	/A	PD	TPI
1984	Bal-A	0	3	.000	5	3	0	0	0	17²	22	2	17	4	19.9	9.17	42	.319	.453	0	—	0	-10	-10	0	-1.3
Total	19	268	152	.638	558	521	211	53	4	3948	3349	303	1311	2212	10.7	2.86	125	.230	.296	85	.174	7	374	315	3	35.5

● LOWELL PALMER
Palmer, Lowell Raymond   b: 8/18/47, Sacramento, Cal.   BR/TR, 6'1", 190 lbs.   Deb: 6/21/69

YEAR	TM/L	W	L	PCT	G	GS	CG	SH	SV	IP	H	HR	BB	SO	RAT	ERA	ERA+	OAV	OOB	BH	AVG	PB	PR	/A	PD	TPI
1969	Phi-N	2	8	.200	26	9	1	1	0	90	91	12	47	68	14.4	5.20	68	.264	.362	3	.136	1	-16	-17	-0	-1.6
1970	Phi-N	1	2	.333	38	5	0	0	0	102	98	15	55	85	13.9	5.47	73	.255	.355	4	.148	1	-16	-17	-1	-0.4
1971	Phi-N	0	0	—	3	1	0	0	0	15	13	3	13	6	18.0	6.00	59	.236	.417	1	.200	-0	-4	-4	-0	-0.4
1972	StL-N	0	3	.000	16	2	0	0	0	34²	30	2	26	25	14.8	3.89	87	.244	.380	0	.000	-1	-2	-2	0	-0.2
	Cle-A	0	0	—	1	0	0	0	0	2	2	0	3	3	18.0	4.50	71	.222	.364	0	—	-0	-0	-0	-0	0.0
1974	SD-N	2	5	.286	22	8	1	0	0	73	68	9	59	52	16.5	5.67	63	.256	.404	2	.087	-1	-17	-17	-1	-1.6
Total	5	5	18	.217	106	25	2	1	0	316²	302	41	202	239	15.0	5.29	69	.255	.374	10	.122	-0	-55	-57	-1	-3.8

● EMILIO PALMERO
Palmero, Emilio Antonio "Pal"   b: 6/13/1895, Guanabacoa, Cuba   d: 7/15/70, Toledo, Ohio   BL/TL, 5'11", 157 lbs.   Deb: 9/21/15

YEAR	TM/L	W	L	PCT	G	GS	CG	SH	SV	IP	H	HR	BB	SO	RAT	ERA	ERA+	OAV	OOB	BH	AVG	PB	PR	/A	PD	TPI
1915	NY-N	0	2	.000	3	2	1	0	0	11²	10	0	9	8	17.0	3.09	83	.233	.400	1	.250	-0	-1	-1	0	-0.1
1916	NY-N	0	3	.000	4	2	0	0	0	15²	17	2	8	8	14.9	8.04	30	.288	.382	0	.000	-0	-9	-10	1	-1.5
1921	StL-A	4	7	.364	24	9	4	0	0	90	109	1	49	26	16.4	5.00	90	.319	.413	8	.216	1	-7	-5	1	-0.4
1926	Was-A	2	2	.500	7	3	0	0	0	17	22	1	15	6	20.1	4.76	81	.344	.475	1	.333	1	-2	-2	-0	-0.3
1928	Bos-N	0	1	.000	3	1	0	0	0	6²	14	0	2	0	21.6	5.40	72	.452	.485	0	.000	-0	-1	-1	-0	-0.2
Total	5	6	15	.286	41	17	5	0	0	141	172	4	83	48	17.0	5.17	77	.319	.420	10	.208	1	-19	-19	2	-2.5

● ED PALMQUIST
Palmquist, Edwin Lee   b: 6/10/33, Los Angeles, Cal.   BR/TR, 6'3", 195 lbs.   Deb: 6/10/60

YEAR	TM/L	W	L	PCT	G	GS	CG	SH	SV	IP	H	HR	BB	SO	RAT	ERA	ERA+	OAV	OOB	BH	AVG	PB	PR	/A	PD	TPI
1960	LA-N	0	1	.000	22	0	0	0	0	39	34	6	16	23	11.8	2.54	156	.243	.325	0	.000	-1	5	6	0	0.1
1961	LA-N	0	1	.000	5	0	0	0	1	8²	10	0	7	5	19.7	6.23	70	.333	.487	0	—	0	-2	-2	-0	-0.2
	Min-A	1	1	.500	9	2	0	0	0	21	33	7	13	13	21.0	9.43	45	.359	.454	0	.000	-0	-13	-12	0	-1.0
Total	2	1	3	.250	36	2	0	0	1	68²	77	13	36	41	15.6	5.11	80	.294	.391	0	.000	-0	-8	-8	0	-1.1

● JIM PANTHER
Panther, James Edward   b: 3/1/45, Burlington, Iowa   BR/TR, 6'1", 190 lbs.   Deb: 4/5/71

YEAR	TM/L	W	L	PCT	G	GS	CG	SH	SV	IP	H	HR	BB	SO	RAT	ERA	ERA+	OAV	OOB	BH	AVG	PB	PR	/A	PD	TPI
1971	Oak-A	0	1	.000	4	0	0	0	0	5²	10	1	5	4	23.8	11.12	30	.385	.484	0	—	0	-5	-5	0	-0.8
1972	Tex-A	5	9	.357	58	4	0	0	0	93²	101	8	46	44	14.6	4.13	73	.277	.365	1	.125	0	-11	-12	-1	-1.7
1973	Atl-N	2	3	.400	23	0	0	0	0	30²	45	3	9	8	15.8	7.63	52	.363	.406	0	—	0	-14	-13	-1	-1.9
Total	3	7	13	.350	85	4	0	0	0	130	156	12	60	56	15.3	5.26	61	.303	.381	1	.111	-0	-30	-29	-1	-4.4

● JOHN PAPA
Papa, John Paul   b: 12/5/40, Bridgeport, Conn.   BR/TR, 5'11", 190 lbs.   Deb: 4/11/61

YEAR	TM/L	W	L	PCT	G	GS	CG	SH	SV	IP	H	HR	BB	SO	RAT	ERA	ERA+	OAV	OOB	BH	AVG	PB	PR	/A	PD	TPI
1961	Bal-A	0	0	—	2	0	0	0	0	1	2	1	3	3	45.0	18.00	21	.400	.625	0	—	0	-2	-2	0	0.0
1962	Bal-A	0	0	—	1	0	0	0	0	1	3	0	1	0	36.0	27.00	14	.600	.667	0	—	0	-3	-3	-0	0.0
Total	2	0	0	—	3	0	0	0	0	2	5	1	4	3	40.5	22.50	17	.500	.643	0	—	0	-4	-4	0	0.0

● AL PAPAI
Papai, Alfred Thomas   b: 5/7/19, Divernon, Ill.   BR/TR, 6'3", 185 lbs.   Deb: 4/24/48

YEAR	TM/L	W	L	PCT	G	GS	CG	SH	SV	IP	H	HR	BB	SO	RAT	ERA	ERA+	OAV	OOB	BH	AVG	PB	PR	/A	PD	TPI
1948	StL-N	0	1	.000	10	0	0	0	0	16	14	3	7	8	11.8	5.06	81	.241	.323	0	.000	-0	-2	-2	0	-0.1
1949	StL-A	4	11	.267	42	15	6	0	2	142¹	175	8	81	31	16.3	5.06	90	.298	.384	3	.079	-2	-14	-8	3	-0.7
1950	Bos-A	4	2	.667	16	3	2	0	0	50²	61	5	28	19	15.8	6.75	73	.293	.377	3	.176	-0	-12	-10	-1	-1.1
	StL-A	1	0	1.000	13	0	0	0	0	19	21	0	14	7	16.6	5.21	82	.300	.417	0	.000	-0	0	0	1	-0.1
1955	Chi-A	0	0	—	7	0	0	0	0	11²	10	1	8	5	13.9	3.86	102	.244	.367	0	.000	-0	0	0	1	0.0
Total	4	9	14	.391	88	18	8	0	4	239²	281	17	138	70	15.8	5.37	84	.291	.381	6	.097	-3	-30	-22	4	-1.9

● LARRY PAPE
Pape, Laurence Albert   b: 7/21/1883, Norwood, Ohio   d: 7/21/18, Swissvale, Pa.   BR/TR, 5'11", 175 lbs.   Deb: 7/6/09

YEAR	TM/L	W	L	PCT	G	GS	CG	SH	SV	IP	H	HR	BB	SO	RAT	ERA	ERA+	OAV	OOB	BH	AVG	PB	PR	/A	PD	TPI
1909	Bos-A	2	0	1.000	11	3	2	1	2	58¹	46	0	12	18	9.7	2.01	125	.218	.276	3	.143	-1	3	3	-3	-0.2
1911	Bos-A	10	8	.556	27	19	10	1	0	176¹	167	3	63	49	11.9	2.45	134	.264	.335	13	.203	-1	18	16	5	1.8
1912	Bos-A	1	1	.500	13	2	1	0	1	48²	74	0	16	17	17.0	4.99	68	.366	.418	4	.235	1	-9	-9	-0	-0.3
Total	3	13	9	.591	51	24	13	2	3	283¹	287	3	91	84	12.4	2.80	112	.275	.339	20	.196	-1	12	11	2	1.3

● FRANK PAPISH
Papish, Frank Richard "Pap"   b: 10/21/17, Pueblo, Colo.   d: 8/30/65, Pueblo, Colo.   BR/TL, 6'2", 192 lbs.   Deb: 5/8/45

YEAR	TM/L	W	L	PCT	G	GS	CG	SH	SV	IP	H	HR	BB	SO	RAT	ERA	ERA+	OAV	OOB	BH	AVG	PB	PR	/A	PD	TPI
1945	Chi-A	4	4	.500	19	5	3	0	1	84¹	75	3	40	45	12.3	3.74	89	.241	.328	6	.231	1	-3	-4	1	-0.1
1946	Chi-A	7	5	.583	31	15	6	2	0	138	122	7	63	66	12.1	2.74	125	.243	.328	8	.186	-0	12	10	0	0.9
1947	Chi-A	12	12	.500	38	26	6	1	3	199	185	6	98	79	12.9	3.26	112	.245	.333	5	.086	-5	10	9	-1	0.4
1948	Chi-A	2	8	.200	32	14	2	0	0	95¹	97	7	75	41	16.5	5.00	85	.265	.394	5	.185	-1	-8	-8	-1	-0.9
1949	Cle-A	1	0	1.000	25	3	1	0	0	62	54	2	39	23	13.5	3.19	125	.240	.352	1	.125	0	7	5	0	0.1
1950	Pit-N	0	0	—	4	1	0	0	0	2¹	8	1	4	1	46.3	27.00	16	.533	.632	0	—	0	-6	-6	0	0.0
Total	6	26	29	.473	149	64	18	3	9	581	541	26	319	255	13.4	3.58	103	.249	.346	25	.154	-5	12	7	0	0.4

● JOHN PAPPALAU
Pappalau, John Joseph   b: 4/3/1875, Albany, N.Y.   d: 5/12/44, Albany, N.Y.   BR/TR, 6', 175 lbs.   Deb: 6/9/1897

YEAR	TM/L	W	L	PCT	G	GS	CG	SH	SV	IP	H	HR	BB	SO	RAT	ERA	ERA+	OAV	OOB	BH	AVG	PB	PR	/A	PD	TPI
1897	Cle-N	0	1	.000	2	1	1	0	0	12	22	0	6	3	22.5	10.50	43	.390	.465	0	.000	-0	-8	-8	0	-0.5

● MILT PAPPAS
Pappas, Milton Stephen "Gimpy" (b: Miltiades Stergios Papastegios)   b: 5/11/39, Detroit, Mich.   BR/TR, 6'3", 190 lbs.   Deb: 8/10/57

YEAR	TM/L	W	L	PCT	G	GS	CG	SH	SV	IP	H	HR	BB	SO	RAT	ERA	ERA+	OAV	OOB	BH	AVG	PB	PR	/A	PD	TPI
1957	Bal-A	0	0	—	4	0	0	0	0	9	6	3	4	4	11.0	1.00	359	.200	.273	0	.000	-0	3	3	0	0.0
1958	Bal-A	10	10	.500	31	21	3	0	0	135¹	135	8	48	72	12.3	4.06	89	.262	.327	6	.143	-0	-4	-7	1	-0.8
1959	Bal-A	15	9	.625	33	27	15	4	3	209¹	175	8	75	120	10.9	3.27	116	.226	.298	11	.139	-3	14	12	-1	0.9
1960	Bal-A	15	11	.577	30	27	11	0	0	205²	184	15	83	126	11.9	3.37	113	.243	.323	3	.043	-5	12	10	1	0.7
1961	Bal-A	13	9	.591	26	23	11	4	1	177²	134	16	78	89	11.1	3.04	127	.208	.301	9	.136	1	19	16	2	2.2
1962	Bal-A★	12	10	.545	35	32	9	1	0	205¹	200	31	75	130	12.1	4.03	92	.257	.324	6	.087	-0	-1	-8	3	-0.6
1963	Bal-A	16	9	.640	34	32	11	4	0	216²	186	21	69	120	10.8	3.03	115	.233	.298	9	.127	-0	14	11	3	1.4
1964	Bal-A	16	7	.696	37	36	13	7	0	251²	225	21	48	157	10.0	2.97	120	.239	.281	12	.129	-2	18	17	-1	1.7
1965	Bal-A★	13	9	.591	34	34	9	3	0	221¹	192	22	52	127	10.0	2.60	133	.233	.281	5	.071	-3	21	21	-3	1.3
1966	Cin-N	12	11	.522	33	32	6	2	0	209²	224	23	39	133	11.4	4.29	92	.275	.310	8	.107	-2	-16	-9	0	-1.1
1967	Cin-N	16	13	.552	34	32	5	3	0	217²	218	19	38	129	10.8	3.35	112	.259	.295	7	.097	-2	1	10	0	1.0
1968	Cin-N	2	5	.286	15	11	0	0	0	62²	70	9	10	43	11.8	5.60	56	.275	.307	1	.063	-1	-18	-17	-0	-1.9
	Atl-N	10	8	.556	22	19	3	1	0	121²	111	8	22	75	10.1	2.37	126	.246	.285	6	.162	2	8	8	-1	1.5
	Yr	12	13	.480	37	30	3	1	0	184	181	17	32	118	10.6	3.47	88	.255	.290	7	.132	1	-10	-9	-1	-0.4
1969	*Atl-N	6	10	.375	26	24	1	0	0	144	149	14	44	72	12.3	3.63	99	.267	.325	7	.156	3	-0	-0	-0	0.2
1970	Atl-N	2	2	.500	11	3	1	0	0	35²	44	7	6	25	13.4	6.06	71	.293	.333	0	.000	-1	-8	-7	-0	-0.8
	Chi-N	10	8	.556	21	20	6	2	0	144²	135	14	36	80	10.6	2.68	168	.248	.294	12	.240	4	22	29	-1	4.0
	Yr	12	10	.545	32	23	7	2	0	180¹	179	20	43	105	11.1	3.34	133	.256	.300	12	.200	3	14	22	-1	3.2
1971	Chi-N	17	14	.548	35	35	14	5	0	261¹	279	25	62	99	11.9	3.51	112	.274	.319	14	.154	-1	-1	12	-2	1.1
1972	Chi-N	17	7	.708	29	28	10	3	0	195	187	18	29	88	10.3	2.77	136	.251	.287	13	.191	1	15	23	0	3.1
1973	Chi-N	7	12	.368	32	30	7	1	0	162	192	20	40	48	13.1	4.28	92	.299	.344	3	.063	-3	-11	-6	-1	-1.0
Total	17	209	164	.560	520	465	129	43	4	3186	3046	298	858	1728	11.2	3.40	110	.252	.306	132	.123	-14	86	120	0	12.4

● CHAN HO PARK
Park, Chan Ho   b: 6/30/73, Kong Ju City, South Korea   BR/TR, 6'2", 185 lbs.   Deb: 4/8/94

YEAR	TM/L	W	L	PCT	G	GS	CG	SH	SV	IP	H	HR	BB	SO	RAT	ERA	ERA+	OAV	OOB	BH	AVG	PB	PR	/A	PD	TPI
1994	LA-N	0	0	—	2	0	0	0	0	4	5	1	5	6	24.8	11.25	35	.294	.478	0	—	0	-3	-3	-0	0.0

● JIM PARK
Park, James   b: 11/10/1892, Richmond, Ky.   d: 12/17/70, Lexington, Ky.   BR/TR, 6'2", 175 lbs.   Deb: 9/7/15

YEAR	TM/L	W	L	PCT	G	GS	CG	SH	SV	IP	H	HR	BB	SO	RAT	ERA	ERA+	OAV	OOB	BH	AVG	PB	PR	/A	PD	TPI
1915	StL-A	2	0	1.000	3	3	1	0	0	22²	18	1	9	5	10.7	1.19	240	.214	.290	4	.400	1	4	4	-1	0.5
1916	StL-A	1	4	.200	26	6	1	0	0	79	69	2	25	26	10.8	2.62	105	.244	.307	2	.100	-2	2	1	-2	-0.3
1917	StL-A	1	1	.500	13	0	0	0	0	20¹	27	1	12	9	17.3	6.64	39	.333	.419	0	.000	-0	-9	-9	0	-0.9
Total	3	4	5	.444	42	9	2	0	0	122	114	4	46	40	11.9	3.02	91	.254	.325	6	.188	-0	-3	-4	2	-0.7

YEAR TM/L	W	L	PCT	G	GS	CG	SH	SV	IP	H	HR	BB	SO	RAT	ERA	ERA+	OAV	OOB	BH	AVG	PB	PR	/A	PD	TPI
● **DOC PARKER**				Parker, Harley Park b: 6/14/1872, Theresa, N.Y. d: 3/3/41, Chicago, Ill. BR/TR, 6'2", 200 lbs. Deb: 7/11/1893 F																					
1893 Chi-N	0	0	—	1	0	0	0	1	2	5	0	1	0	27.0	13.50	34	.458	.503	0	.000	-0	-2	-2	-0	-0.2
1895 Chi-N	4	2	.667	7	6	5	1	0	51¹	65	1	9	9	13.5	3.68	138	.304	.341	7	.318	1	6	8	0	0.8
1896 Chi-N	1	5	.167	9	7	7	0	0	73	100	3	27	15	16.0	6.16	74	.323	.383	10	.278	0	-15	-13	1	-0.7
1901 Cin-N	0	1	.000	1	1	1	0	0	8	26	1	2	0	31.5	15.75	20	.531	.550	0	.000	-0	-11	-11	-0	-0.8
Total 4	5	8	.385	18	14	13	1	1	134¹	196	5	39	24	16.1	5.90	79	.336	.384	17	.274	0	-21	-18	1	-0.9
● **HARRY PARKER**				Parker, Harry William b: 9/14/47, Highland, Ill. BR/TR, 6'3", 190 lbs. Deb: 8/8/70																					
1970 StL-N	1	1	.500	7	4	0	0	0	22¹	24	0	15	9	15.7	3.22	128	.276	.382	2	.250	0	2	2	0	0.2
1971 StL-N	0	0	—	4	0	0	0	0	5	6	2	2	2	14.4	7.20	50	.286	.348	0	—	0	-2	-2	-0	-0.2
1973 *NY-N	8	4	.667	38	9	0	0	5	96²	79	7	36	63	11.0	3.35	108	.217	.293	4	.174	-0	3	3	-0	0.3
1974 NY-N	4	12	.250	40	16	1	0	4	131	145	10	46	58	13.3	3.92	91	.281	.343	0	.000	-4	-4	-5	-2	-1.2
1975 NY-N	2	3	.400	18	1	0	0	2	34²	37	2	19	22	14.5	4.41	78	.272	.361	0	.000	1	-3	-4	-0	-0.5
StL-N	0	1	.000	14	0	0	0	1	18²	21	3	10	13	14.9	6.27	60	.288	.373	0	.000	0	-5	-5	1	-0.2
Yr	2	4	.333	32	1	0	0	3	53¹	58	5	29	35	14.7	5.06	70	.278	.366	0	.000	1	-9	-9	0	-0.7
1976 Cle-A	0	0	—	3	0	0	0	0	7	3	0	0	5	3.9	0.00	—	.136	.136	0	—	0	3	3	0	0.2
Total 6	15	21	.417	124	30	1	0	12	315¹	315	24	128	172	12.8	3.85	94	.258	.332	6	.086	-3	-7	-8	-1	-1.4
● **CLAY PARKER**				Parker, James Clayton b: 12/19/62, Columbia, La. BR/TR, 6'1", 185 lbs. Deb: 9/14/87																					
1987 Sea-A	0	0	—	3	1	0	0	0	7²	15	2	4	3	23.5	10.57	45	.405	.476	0	—	0	-5	-5	-0	-0.3
1989 NY-A	4	5	.444	22	17	2	0	0	120	123	12	31	53	11.7	3.68	105	.264	.313	0	—	0	3	3	0	0.3
1990 NY-A	1	1	.500	5	2	0	0	0	22	19	5	7	20	10.6	4.50	88	.229	.289	0	—	0	-1	-1	-0	-0.2
Det-A	2	2	.500	24	1	0	0	0	51	45	6	25	20	12.5	3.18	125	.242	.335	0	—	0	4	4	0	0.3
Yr	3	3	.500	29	3	0	0	0	73	64	11	32	40	12.0	3.58	111	.237	.320	0	—	0	3	3	0	0.1
1992 Sea-A	0	2	.000	8	6	0	0	0	33¹	47	6	11	20	16.2	7.56	53	.338	.395	0	—	0	-13	-13	0	-0.7
Total 4	7	10	.412	62	27	2	0	0	234	249	31	78	121	12.8	4.42	89	.273	.335	0	—	0	-13	-13	0	-0.6
● **JAY PARKER**				Parker, Jay b: 7/8/1874, Theresa, N.Y. d: 6/8/35, Hartford, Mich. BR/TR, 5'11", 185 lbs. Deb: 9/27/1899 F																					
1899 Pit-N	0	0	—	1	1	1	0	0	0	0	0	2	0	—	∞	—	1.000		0	—	0	-2	-2	0	-0.2
● **ROY PARKER**				Parker, Roy William b: 2/29/1896, Union, Mo. d: 5/17/54, Tulsa, Okla. BR/TR, 6'3", 200 lbs. Deb: 9/10/19																					
1919 StL-N	0	0	—	2	0	0	0	0	2	6	0	1	0	36.0	31.50	9	.333	.400	0	—	0	-6	-6	0	0.0
● **SLICKER PARKS**				Parks, Vernon Henry b: 11/10/1895, Dallas, Mich. d: 2/21/78, Royal Oak, Mich. BR/TR, 5'10", 158 lbs. Deb: 7/11/21																					
1921 Det-A	3	2	.600	10	1	0	0	0	25¹	33	2	16	10	17.8	5.68	75	.306	.400	1	.111	-1	-4	-4	-1	-0.8
● **BILL PARKS**				Parks, William Robert b: 6/4/1849, Easton, Pa. d: 10/10/11, Easton, Pa. BR/TR, 5'8", 150 lbs. Deb: 4/26/1875 M♦																					
1875 Was-n	4	8	.333	14	11	9	0	0	106²	146	5	6		12.8	4.05	65	.281	.289	20	.179	-3	-19	-17		-1.6
Phi-n	0	0	—	2	0	0	0	0	5¹	13	0	1		23.6	6.75	37	.419	.438	1	.167	-0	-3	-3		0.0
Yr	4	8	.333	16	11	9	0	0	112	159	5	7		13.3	4.18	63	.289	.297	21	.178	-3	-21	-19		-1.6
● **ROY PARMELEE**				Parmelee, Le Roy Earl "Tarzan" b: 4/25/07, Lambertville, Mich d: 8/31/81, Monroe, Mich. BR/TR, 6'1", 190 lbs. Deb: 9/28/29																					
1929 NY-N	1	0	1.000	2	1	0	0	0	7	13	1	3	1	21.9	9.00	51	.481	.548	1	.500	0	-3	-3	0	-0.3
1930 NY-N	0	1	.000	11	1	0	0	0	21	18	3	26	19	18.9	9.43	50	.228	.419	1	.250	1	-10	-11	0	-0.4
1931 NY-N	2	2	.500	13	5	4	0	0	58²	47	1	33	30	12.7	3.68	100	.223	.336	4	.200	-0	1	0	0	0.0
1932 NY-N	0	3	.000	8	3	0	0	0	25¹	25	0	14	23	14.6	3.91	95	.250	.353	2	.400	1	-0	-1	0	0.1
1933 NY-N	13	8	.619	32	32	14	3	0	218¹	191	9	77	132	11.6	3.17	101	.232	.309	19	.235	4	4	1	0	0.5
1934 NY-N	10	6	.625	22	20	7	2	0	152²	134	6	60	83	11.8	3.42	113	**.238**	.318	11	.200	2	11	8	2	1.1
1935 NY-N	14	10	.583	34	31	13	0	0	226	214	20	97	79	12.7	4.22	91	.249	.332	18	.209	3	-5	-9	2	-0.4
1936 StL-N	11	11	.500	37	28	9	0	2	221	226	13	107	79	14.0	4.56	86	.270	.360	15	.197	0	-13	-15	-1	-1.4
1937 Chi-N	7	8	.467	33	18	8	0	0	145²	165	13	79	55	15.5	5.13	78	.286	.379	9	.173	0	-20	-19	1	-1.6
1939 Phi-A	1	6	.143	14	5	0	0	1	44²	42	2	35	13	16.1	6.45	73	.253	.369	2	.133	-1	-9	-9	0	-1.2
Total 10	59	55	.518	206	144	55	5	3	1120¹	1075	68	531	514	13.3	4.27	89	.253	.343	82	.207	9	-45	-58	5	-3.6
● **MEL PARNELL**				Parnell, Melvin Lloyd "Dusty" b: 6/13/22, New Orleans, La. BL/TL, 6', 180 lbs. Deb: 4/20/47																					
1947 Bos-A	2	3	.400	15	5	1	0	0	50²	60	1	27	23	15.6	6.39	61	.296	.381	1	.056	-2	-15	-14	-1	-1.5
1948 Bos-A	15	8	.652	35	27	16	1	0	212	205	7	90	77	12.7	3.14	140	.252	.330	13	.162	-4	27	29	2	2.7
1949 Bos-A★	**25**	7	.781	39	33	**27**	4	2	**295**	258	8	134	122	12.1	2.77	157	.237	.324	29	.254	2	**47**	**52**	-0	5.5
1950 Bos-A	18	10	.643	40	31	21	2	3	249	244	17	106	93	12.9	3.61	136	.259	.338	19	.194	-1	27	36	5	3.9
1951 Bos-A★	18	11	.621	36	29	11	3	2	221	229	11	77	77	12.5	3.26	137	.272	.333	25	.309	4	21	30	-0	**4.1**
1952 Bos-A	12	12	.500	33	29	15	3	2	214	207	13	89	107	12.7	3.62	109	.255	.332	8	.095	-3	1	8	1	0.6
1953 Bos-A	21	8	.724	38	34	12	5	0	241	217	15	116	136	12.6	3.06	137	.239	.328	21	.223	1	25	31	-2	3.4
1954 Bos-A	3	7	.300	19	15	4	1	0	92¹	104	7	35	38	13.6	3.70	111	.287	.352	3	.088	-2	0	4	0	0.2
1955 Bos-A	2	3	.400	13	9	0	0	1	46	62	12	25	18	17.2	7.83	55	.318	.398	6	.316	1	-20	-18	0	-1.6
1956 Bos-A	6	6	.538	21	20	6	1	0	131¹	129	13	59	41	12.9	3.77	123	.256	.335	7	.152	-2	6	12	-1	0.8
Total 10	123	75	.621	289	232	113	20	10	1752²	1715	104	758	732	12.8	3.50	125	.257	.336	132	.198	-7	119	170	3	18.1
● **RUBE PARNHAM**				Parnham, James Arthur b: 2/1/1894, Heidelberg, Pa. d: 11/25/63, McKeesport, Pa. BR/TR, 6'3", 185 lbs. Deb: 9/20/16																					
1916 Phi-A	2	1	.667	4	3	2	0	0	24²	27	0	13	8	14.6	4.01	71	.300	.388	3	.273	1	-3	-3	1	-0.2
1917 Phi-A	0	1	.000	2	2	0	0	0	11	12	1	9	4	17.2	4.09	67	.316	.447	0	.000	-0	-2	-2	0	-0.2
Total 2	2	2	.500	6	5	2	0	0	35²	39	1	22	12	15.4	4.04	70	.305	.407	3	.214	0	-5	-5	1	-0.4
● **JEFF PARRETT**				Parrett, Jeffrey Dale b: 8/26/61, Indianapolis, Ind. BR/TR, 6'3", 200 lbs. Deb: 4/11/86																					
1986 Mon-N	0	1	.000	12	0	0	0	0	20¹	19	3	13	21	14.2	4.87	76	.247	.356	1	.500	0	-3	-3	0	-0.1
1987 Mon-N	7	6	.538	45	0	0	0	6	62	53	8	30	56	12.0	4.21	100	.229	.318	0	.000	-1	-1	-0	-0	-0.1
1988 Mon-N	12	4	.750	61	0	0	0	6	91²	66	8	45	62	11.0	2.65	136	.214	.316	0	—	0	8	10	-1	1.7
1989 Phi-N	12	6	.667	72	0	0	0	6	105²	90	6	44	98	11.4	2.98	119	.232	.310	0	.000	-1	6	7	-1	1.0
1990 Phi-N	4	9	.308	47	5	0	0	1	81²	92	10	36	69	14.2	5.18	74	.293	.368	0	.000	-1	-13	-12	0	-1.9
Atl-N	1	1	.500	20	0	0	0	1	27	27	1	19	17	15.7	3.00	134	.281	.405	1	1.000	0	2	3	0	0.3
Yr	5	10	.333	67	5	0	0	2	108²	119	11	55	86	14.5	4.64	84	.289	.374	1	.091	-1	-10	-9	0	-1.6
1991 Atl-N	1	2	.333	18	0	0	0	0	21¹	31	2	12	14	18.1	6.33	61	.326	.402	—	—	0	-6	-6	1	-0.7
1992 *Oak-A	9	1	.900	66	0	0	0	1	98¹	81	7	42	78	11.4	3.02	124	.226	.311	0	—	0	10	8	-1	0.9
1993 Col-N	3	3	.500	40	6	0	0	1	73²	78	6	45	66	15.3	5.38	89	.274	.377	1	.091	-2	-11	-5	-0	-0.5
Total 8	49	33	.598	381	11	0	0	22	581²	537	51	286	481	12.8	3.87	100	.250	.339	3	.088	-3	-7	1	-3	0.4
● **MIKE PARROTT**				Parrott, Michael Everett Arch b: 12/6/54, Oxnard, Cal. BR/TR, 6'4", 210 lbs. Deb: 9/5/77																					
1977 Bal-A	0	0	—	3	0	0	0	0	4¹	4	0	2	2	12.5	2.08	183	.250	.333	0	—	0	1	1	-0	0.0
1978 Sea-A	1	5	.167	27	10	0	0	0	82¹	108	8	32	41	15.6	5.14	74	.316	.379	0	—	0	-13	-12	-0	-0.8
1979 Sea-A	14	12	.538	38	30	13	2	0	229²	231	17	86	127	12.7	3.77	116	.267	.338	0	—	0	11	15	3	1.7
1980 Sea-A	1	16	.059	27	16	1	0	0	94	136	16	42	53	17.1	7.28	57	.348	.412	0	—	0	-34	-33	4	-4.8
1981 Sea-A	3	6	.333	24	12	0	0	0	85	102	3	28	43	13.9	5.08	76	.299	.354	0	—	0	-13	-12	0	-1.3
Total 5	19	39	.328	119	68	14	2	0	495	581	44	190	266	14.2	4.87	85	.297	.363	0	—	0	-48	-41	6	-5.2
● **TOM PARROTT**				Parrott, Thomas William "Tacky Tom" b: 4/10/1868, Portland, Ore. d: 1/1/32, Dundee, Ore. BR/TR, 5'10.5", 170 lbs. Deb: 6/18/1893 F♦																					
1893 Chi-N	0	3	.000	4	3	2	0	0	27	35	1	17	7	17.3	6.67	69	.305	.394	7	.259	-0	-6	-6	-1	-0.5

YEAR TM/L	W	L	PCT	G	GS	CG	SH	SV	IP	H	HR	BB	SO	RAT	ERA	ERA+	OAV	OOB	BH	AVG	PB	PR	/A	PD	TPI
Cin-N	10	7	.588	22	17	11	1	0	154	174	1	70	33	14.8	4.09	117	.276	.357	13	.191	-3	10	12	2	0.9
Yr	10	10	.500	26	20	13	1	0	181	209	2	87	40	15.2	4.48	106	.281	.363	20	.211	-3	4	6	1	0.4
1894 Cin-N	17	19	.472	41	36	31	1	1	308²	402	19	126	61	15.7	5.60	99	.311	.377	74	.323	8	-9	-1	3	0.7
1895 Cin-N	11	18	.379	41	31	23	0	3	263¹	382	8	76	57	15.7	5.47	91	.333	.378	69	.343	10	-20	-14	3	-0.2
1896 StL-N	1	1	.500	7	2	2	0	0	42	62	4	18	8	17.8	6.21	70	.340	.408	138	.291	1	-9	-9	-0	-0.3
Total 4	39	48	.448	115	89	69	2	4	795	1055	33	307	166	15.7	5.33	96	.314	.376	301	.301	16	-34	-19	6	0.6

● **JIGGS PARSON**   Parson, William Edwin b: 12/28/1885, Parker, S.Dak. d: 5/19/67, Los Angeles, Cal. BR/TR, 6'2", 180 lbs. Deb: 5/16/10

YEAR TM/L	W	L	PCT	G	GS	CG	SH	SV	IP	H	HR	BB	SO	RAT	ERA	ERA+	OAV	OOB	BH	AVG	PB	PR	/A	PD	TPI
1910 Bos-N	0	2	.000	10	4	0	0	0	35¹	35	2	26	7	16.0	3.82	87	.278	.409	1	.083	-1	-3	-2	-0	-0.2
1911 Bos-N	0	1	.000	7	0	0	0	0	25	36	2	15	7	19.8	6.48	59	.375	.478	2	.200	-0	-9	-7	-1	-0.3
Total 2	0	3	.000	17	4	0	0	0	60¹	71	4	41	14	17.6	4.92	72	.320	.439	3	.136	-2	-12	-9	-1	-0.5

● **CHARLIE PARSONS**   Parsons, Charles James b: 7/18/1863, Cherry Flats, Pa. d: 3/24/36, Mansfield, Pa. BL/TL, 5'10", 160 lbs. Deb: 5/29/1886

YEAR TM/L	W	L	PCT	G	GS	CG	SH	SV	IP	H	HR	BB	SO	RAT	ERA	ERA+	OAV	OOB	BH	AVG	PB	PR	/A	PD	TPI
1886 Bos-N	0	2	.000	2	2	2	0	0	16	20	0	4	5	13.5	3.94	81	.308	.348	3	.375	-1	-1	-1	-1	-0.1
1887 NY-a	1	1	.500	4	4	4	0	0	34	51	0	6	5	15.4	4.50	94	.319	.347	3	.200	-1	-1	-1	0	-0.1
1890 Cle-N	0	1	.000	2	1	0	0	0	9	12	0	6	2	22.0	6.00	60	.310	.452	3	.750	1	-2	-2	0	-0.1
Total 3	1	4	.200	8	7	6	0	0	59	83	0	16	12	15.9	4.58	84	.315	.365	9	.333	2	-4	-5	-1	-0.3

● **TOM PARSONS**   Parsons, Thomas Anthony b: 9/13/39, Lakeville, Conn. BR/TR, 6'7", 210 lbs. Deb: 9/5/63

YEAR TM/L	W	L	PCT	G	GS	CG	SH	SV	IP	H	HR	BB	SO	RAT	ERA	ERA+	OAV	OOB	BH	AVG	PB	PR	/A	PD	TPI
1963 Pit-N	0	1	.000	1	1	0	0	0	4¹	7	1	2	2	18.7	8.31	40	.368	.429	0	.000	-0	-2	-2	0	-0.4
1964 NY-N	1	2	.333	4	2	1	0	0	19¹	20	1	6	10	12.1	4.19	85	.274	.329	0	.000	-1	-1	-1	-0	-0.3
1965 NY-N	1	10	.091	35	11	1	1	1	90²	108	17	17	58	12.4	4.67	76	.290	.321	1	.056	-0	-11	-11	1	-1.3
Total 3	2	13	.133	40	14	2	1	1	114¹	135	19	25	70	12.6	4.72	75	.291	.327	1	.037	-2	-15	-15	1	-2.0

● **BILL PARSONS**   Parsons, William Raymond b: 8/17/48, Riverside, Cal. BR/TR, 6'6", 195 lbs. Deb: 4/13/71

YEAR TM/L	W	L	PCT	G	GS	CG	SH	SV	IP	H	HR	BB	SO	RAT	ERA	ERA+	OAV	OOB	BH	AVG	PB	PR	/A	PD	TPI
1971 Mil-A	13	17	.433	36	35	12	4	0	244²	219	19	93	139	11.6	3.20	108	.241	.315	12	.167	3	7	7	0	1.3
1972 Mil-A	13	13	.500	33	30	10	2	0	214	194	27	68	111	11.1	3.91	77	.240	.301	11	.164	0	-20	-21	-3	-2.7
1973 Mil-A	3	6	.333	20	17	0	0	0	59²	59	6	67	30	19.0	6.79	55	.257	.424	0	—	0	-20	-20	-0	-2.6
1974 Oak-A	0	0	—	4	0	0	0	0	2	1	0	3	2	18.0	0.00	—	.143	.400	0	—	0	1	1	-0	0.0
Total 4	29	36	.446	93	82	22	6	0	520¹	473	52	231	282	12.3	3.89	85	.242	.325	23	.165	3	-32	-33	-3	-4.0

● **STAN PARTENHEIMER**   Partenheimer, Stanwood Wendell "Party"
b: 10/21/22, Chicopee Falls, Mass. d: 1/28/89, Wilson, N.C. BR/TL, 5'11", 175 lbs. Deb: 5/27/44 F

YEAR TM/L	W	L	PCT	G	GS	CG	SH	SV	IP	H	HR	BB	SO	RAT	ERA	ERA+	OAV	OOB	BH	AVG	PB	PR	/A	PD	TPI
1944 Bos-A	0	0	—	1	1	0	0	0	1	3	0	9	0	45.0	18.00	19	.500	.625	0	.000	-0	-2	-2	-0	0.0
1945 StL-N	0	0	—	8	2	0	0	0	13¹	12	2	16	6	18.9	6.08	62	.250	.438	0	.000	-0	-3	-3	0	0.0
Total 2	0	0	—	9	3	0	0	0	14¹	15	2	25	6	20.7	6.91	54	.278	.458	0	—	-1	-5	-5	-0	0.0

● **BILL PASCHALL**   Paschall, William Herbert b: 4/22/54, Norfolk, Va. BR/TR, 6', 175 lbs. Deb: 9/20/78

YEAR TM/L	W	L	PCT	G	GS	CG	SH	SV	IP	H	HR	BB	SO	RAT	ERA	ERA+	OAV	OOB	BH	AVG	PB	PR	/A	PD	TPI
1978 KC-A	0	1	.000	2	0	0	0	1	8	6	0	0	5	7.9	3.38	113	.207	.233	0	—	0	0	0	-0	-0.1
1979 KC-A	0	1	.000	7	0	0	0	0	13²	18	2	5	3	16.5	3.59	65	.300	.373	0	—	0	-4	-4	-0	-0.4
1981 KC-A	0	0	—	2	0	0	0	0	2	2	0	0	1	9.0	4.50	80	.286	.286	0	—	0	-0	-0	-0	0.0
Total 3	0	2	.000	11	0	0	0	1	23²	26	2	5	9	12.9	5.32	76	.271	.327	0	—	0	-3	-3	-1	-0.5

● **CAMILO PASCUAL**   Pascual, Camilo Alberto (Lus) "Little Potato" b: 1/20/34, Havana, Cuba BR/TR, 5'11", 185 lbs. Deb: 4/15/54 FC

YEAR TM/L	W	L	PCT	G	GS	CG	SH	SV	IP	H	HR	BB	SO	RAT	ERA	ERA+	OAV	OOB	BH	AVG	PB	PR	/A	PD	TPI
1954 Was-A	4	7	.364	48	4	1	0	3	119¹	126	7	61	60	14.6	4.22	108	.276	.368	4	.133	-0	-7	-9	3	-0.5
1955 Was-A	2	12	.143	43	16	1	0	3	129	158	15	70	82	16.3	6.14	62	.311	.401	7	.219	-0	-31	-33	2	-3.0
1956 Was-A	6	18	.250	39	27	6	0	2	188²	194	33	89	162	13.8	5.87	74	.261	.345	8	.138	-2	-36	-32	1	-3.6
1957 Was-A	8	17	.320	29	26	8	2	0	175²	168	17	76	113	12.7	4.10	95	.258	.338	7	.140	-2	-6	-4	2	-0.5
1958 Was-A	8	12	.400	31	27	6	2	0	177¹	166	14	60	146	11.6	3.15	121	.248	.313	9	.158	-1	12	13	1	1.4
1959 Was-A†	17	10	.630	32	30	17	6	0	238²	202	10	69	185	10.3	2.64	148	.226	.284	26	.302	6	32	34	5	**5.0**
1960 Was-A†	12	8	.600	26	22	8	3	2	151²	139	11	53	143	11.5	3.03	128	.240	.306	9	.176	3	14	15	0	2.2
1961 Min-A★	15	16	.484	35	33	15	**8**	0	252¹	205	26	100	**221**	11.0	3.46	123	.217	.294	14	.165	-0	16	22	1	2.5
1962 Min-A★	20	11	.645	34	33	**18**	**5**	0	257²	236	25	59	**206**	10.4	3.32	123	.241	.286	26	.268	8	19	22	0	3.4
1963 Min-A	21	9	.700	31	31	**18**	3	0	248¹	205	21	81	**202**	10.5	2.46	148	.224	.289	23	.250	6	32	**33**	-1	4.6
1964 Min-A★	15	12	.556	36	36	14	1	0	267¹	245	30	98	213	11.6	3.30	108	.241	.309	17	.181	4	10	8	0	1.2
1965 *Min-A	9	3	.750	27	27	5	1	0	156	126	12	63	96	11.2	3.35	106	.217	.299	12	.200	3	2	4	2	0.7
1966 Min-A	8	6	.571	21	19	2	0	0	103	113	9	30	56	12.7	4.89	73	.278	.330	9	.216	1	-17	-15	2	-1.6
1967 Was-A	12	10	.545	28	27	7	3	0	164²	147	15	43	106	10.5	3.28	105	.237	.289	9	.176	1	-1	-0	1	-0.1
1968 Was-A	13	12	.520	31	31	8	4	0	201	181	11	59	111	10.9	2.69	109	.239	.298	12	.185	1	7	5	1	0.9
1969 Was-A	2	5	.286	14	13	0	0	0	55¹	49	12	38	34	15.0	6.83	51	.239	.371	4	.235	0	-20	-21	-0	-2.2
Cin-N	0	0	—	5	1	0	0	0	7¹	14	2	4	3	22.1	8.59	44	.424	.486	0	—	0	-4	-4	0	0.0
1970 LA-N	0	0	—	10	0	0	0	0	14	12	2	5	8	11.6	2.57	149	.231	.310	0	—	0	2	2	0	0.0
1971 Cle-A	2	2	.500	9	1	0	0	0	23¹	17	0	11	20	11.2	3.09	124	.205	.305	3	.600	1	1	2	1	0.5
Total 18	174	170	.506	529	404	132	36	10	2930²	2703	256	1069	2167	11.8	3.63	103	.244	.314	198	.205	29	26	38	18	10.9

● **CARLOS PASCUAL**   Pascual, Carlos Alberto (Lus) b: 3/13/31, Havana, Cuba BR/TR, 5'6", 165 lbs. Deb: 9/24/50 F

YEAR TM/L	W	L	PCT	G	GS	CG	SH	SV	IP	H	HR	BB	SO	RAT	ERA	ERA+	OAV	OOB	BH	AVG	PB	PR	/A	PD	TPI
1950 Was-A	1	1	.500	2	2	2	0	0	17	12	0	8	3	11.1	2.12	212	.194	.296	1	.250	0	5	4	-1	0.4

● **LARRY PASHNICK**   Pashnick, Larry John b: 4/25/56, Lincoln Park, Mich. BR/TR, 6'3", 205 lbs. Deb: 4/10/82

YEAR TM/L	W	L	PCT	G	GS	CG	SH	SV	IP	H	HR	BB	SO	RAT	ERA	ERA+	OAV	OOB	BH	AVG	PB	PR	/A	PD	TPI
1982 Det-A	4	4	.500	28	13	1	0	0	94¹	110	17	25	19	13.0	4.01	101	.297	.343	0	—	0	1	1	-1	0.0
1983 Det-A	1	3	.250	12	6	0	0	0	37²	48	5	18	17	16.5	5.26	74	.308	.390	0	—	0	-5	-6	1	-0.5
1984 Min-A	2	1	.667	13	1	0	0	0	38¹	38	3	11	10	12.0	3.52	119	.260	.321	0	—	0	2	3	0	0.2
Total 3	7	8	.467	53	20	1	0	0	170¹	196	25	54	46	13.5	4.17	97	.292	.350	0	—	0	-2	-2	0	-0.3

● **CLAUDE PASSEAU**   Passeau, Claude William b: 4/9/09, Waynesboro, Miss. BR/TR, 6'3", 198 lbs. Deb: 9/29/35

YEAR TM/L	W	L	PCT	G	GS	CG	SH	SV	IP	H	HR	BB	SO	RAT	ERA	ERA+	OAV	OOB	BH	AVG	PB	PR	/A	PD	TPI
1935 Pit-N	0	1	.000	1	1	0	0	0	3	7	0	2	1	27.0	12.00	34	.500	.563	0	.000	-0	-3	-3	0	-0.6
1936 Phi-N	11	15	.423	49	21	8	2	3	217¹	247	7	55	85	12.7	3.48	130	.280	.325	22	.282	3	13	26	1	3.3
1937 Phi-N	14	18	.438	50	34	18	1	2	292¹	348	16	79	135	13.3	4.34	100	.296	.343	21	.196	-0	-14	-0	0	0.0
1938 Phi-N	11	18	.379	44	33	15	0	1	239	281	8	93	100	14.4	4.52	86	.287	.354	13	.162	-2	-19	-17	3	-1.7
1939 Phi-N	2	4	.333	8	8	4	1	0	53¹	54	1	25	29	13.5	4.22	95	.263	.346	4	.200	-2	-2	-1	0	-0.2
Chi-N	13	9	.591	34	27	13	1	3	221	215	8	48	108	10.5	3.05	129	.254	.297	12	.156	-1	21	22	1	2.0
Yr	15	13	.536	42	35	17	2	3	274¹	269	9	73	**137**	11.4	3.28	120	.255	.306	16	.165	-2	19	20	1	1.8
1940 Chi-N	20	13	.606	46	31	20	4	5	280²	259	8	59	124	10.3	2.50	150	.237	.278	20	.204	6	42	39	5	**5.3**
1941 Chi-N★	14	14	.500	34	30	20	3	0	231	262	16	52	80	12.3	3.35	105	.281	.320	19	.221	5	7	4	0	0.9
1942 Chi-N★	19	14	.576	35	34	24	3	0	278¹	284	13	74	89	11.7	2.68	119	.260	.309	19	.181	1	20	16	1	2.0
1943 Chi-N☆	15	12	.556	35	33	18	1	0	257	245	6	66	93	11.0	2.91	115	.249	.299	19	.198	1	14	12	1	1.5
1944 Chi-N	15	9	.625	34	27	18	2	0	227	234	8	50	89	11.3	2.89	122	.266	.306	13	.162	-1	18	16	1	1.6
1945 *Chi-N†	17	9	.654	34	27	19	**5**	1	227	205	4	59	98	10.5	2.46	149	.238	.289	17	.187	-2	34	**30**	3	**3.8**
1946 Chi-N★	9	8	.529	21	21	10	2	0	129¹	118	5	42	47	11.2	3.13	106	.237	.298	10	.204	3	4	3	0	0.4
1947 Chi-N	2	6	.250	19	6	1	1	2	63¹	97	7	24	26	17.3	6.25	63	.353	.407	0	.000	-2	-15	-16	-1	-2.1
Total 13	162	150	.519	444	331	188	26	21	2719²	2856	105	728	1104	12.0	3.32	113	.267	.316	189	.192	13	120	128	11	16.5

● **FRANK PASTORE**   Pastore, Frank Enrico b: 8/21/57, Alhambra, Cal. BR/TR, 6'3", 205 lbs. Deb: 4/4/79

YEAR TM/L	W	L	PCT	G	GS	CG	SH	SV	IP	H	HR	BB	SO	RAT	ERA	ERA+	OAV	OOB	BH	AVG	PB	PR	/A	PD	TPI
1979 *Cin-N	6	7	.462	30	9	2	1	4	95¹	102	8	23	63	11.9	4.25	88	.271	.315	4	.160	-0	-5	-5	0	-0.8
1980 Cin-N	13	7	.650	27	27	9	2	0	184²	161	13	42	110	9.9	3.27	109	.233	.277	10	.156	-1	7	6	-1	0.5

YEAR	TM/L	W	L	PCT	G	GS	CG	SH	SV	IP	H	HR	BB	SO	RAT	ERA	ERA+	OAV	OOB	BH	AVG	PB	PR	/A	PD	TPI
1981	Cin-N	4	9	.308	22	22	2	1	0	132	125	11	35	81	11.1	4.02	88	.247	.300	5	.114	-2	-8	-7	-2	-1.0
1982	Cin-N	8	13	.381	31	29	3	2	0	188¹	210	13	57	94	13.0	3.97	93	.286	.341	10	.172	1	-8	-6	-2	-0.7
1983	Cin-N	9	12	.429	36	29	4	1	0	184¹	207	20	64	93	13.3	4.88	78	.290	.349	11	.186	2	-26	-22	-1	-2.3
1984	Cin-N	3	8	.273	24	16	1	0	0	98¹	110	10	40	53	14.0	6.50	58	.285	.357	2	.071	-2	-32	-30	0	-3.1
1985	Cin-N	2	1	.667	17	6	1	0	0	54	60	1	16	29	12.8	3.83	99	.287	.341	2	.143	-0	-1	-0	0	0.0
1986	Min-A	3	1	.750	33	1	0	0	2	49¹	54	4	24	18	14.2	4.01	107	.283	.363	0	—	0	1	2	-1	0.0
Total	8	48	58	.453	220	139	22	7	6	986¹	1029	80	301	541	12.3	4.29	87	.270	.326	44	.151	-2	-72	-62	-5	-7.4

● **JIM PASTORIUS**   Pastorius, James W. "Sunny Jim" b: 7/12/1881, Pittsburgh, Pa. d: 5/10/41, Pittsburgh, Pa. BL/TL, 5'9", 165 lbs. Deb: 4/15/06

YEAR	TM/L	W	L	PCT	G	GS	CG	SH	SV	IP	H	HR	BB	SO	RAT	ERA	ERA+	OAV	OOB	BH	AVG	PB	PR	/A	PD	TPI
1906	Bro-N	10	14	.417	29	24	16	3	0	211²	225	4	69	58	12.6	3.61	70	.274	.333	10	.141	-0	-23	-26	-1	-2.9
1907	Bro-N	16	12	.571	28	26	20	4	0	222	218	3	77	70	12.2	2.35	100	.264	.331	15	.205	3	3	-0	-1	0.2
1908	Bro-N	4	20	.167	28	25	16	2	0	213²	171	5	74	54	10.6	2.44	96	.216	.288	8	.129	-0	-2	-2	-0	-0.3
1909	Bro-N	1	9	.100	12	9	5	1	0	79²	91	4	58	23	16.9	5.76	45	.313	.429	2	.080	-1	-28	-28	1	-3.1
Total	4	31	55	.360	97	84	57	10	0	727	705	15	278	205	12.4	3.12	78	.258	.330	35	.152	1	-50	-56	-1	-6.1

● **JOE PATE**   Pate, Joseph William b: 6/6/1892, Alice, Tex. d: 12/26/48, Fort Worth, Tex. BL/TL, 5'10", 184 lbs. Deb: 4/15/26

YEAR	TM/L	W	L	PCT	G	GS	CG	SH	SV	IP	H	HR	BB	SO	RAT	ERA	ERA+	OAV	OOB	BH	AVG	PB	PR	/A	PD	TPI
1926	Phi-A	9	0	1.000	47	2	0	0	6	113	109	3	51	24	12.9	2.71	154	.262	.345	4	.148	-0	**16**	**18**	3	1.8
1927	Phi-A	0	3	.000	32	0	0	0	6	53²	67	3	21	14	14.9	5.20	82	.318	.382	3	.300	1	-6	-6	-0	-0.3
Total	2	9	3	.750	79	2	0	0	12	166²	176	6	72	38	13.6	3.51	120	.281	.358	7	.189	1	10	13	4	1.5

● **CASE PATTEN**   Patten, Case Lyman "Casey" b: 5/7/1876, Westport, N.Y. d: 5/31/35, Rochester, N.Y. BB/TL, 6', 175 lbs. Deb: 5/4/01

YEAR	TM/L	W	L	PCT	G	GS	CG	SH	SV	IP	H	HR	BB	SO	RAT	ERA	ERA+	OAV	OOB	BH	AVG	PB	PR	/A	PD	TPI
1901	Was-A	18	10	.643	32	30	26	4	0	254¹	285	8	74	109	13.3	3.93	93	.280	.339	13	.135	-5	-7	-7	0	-1.1
1902	Was-A	17	16	.515	36	34	33	1	1	299²	331	11	89	92	12.9	4.05	91	.280	.337	12	.096	-10	-16	-12	-1	-2.1
1903	Was-A	11	22	.333	36	34	32	0	1	300	313	11	80	133	11.9	3.60	87	.268	.317	14	.132	-6	-21	-16	1	-2.1
1904	Was-A	14	23	.378	45	39	37	2	**3**	357²	367	2	79	150	11.7	3.07	87	.266	.315	16	.127	-5	-19	-16	1	-2.1
1905	Was-A	14	22	.389	42	36	29	2	0	309²	300	3	86	113	11.5	3.14	85	.255	.312	16	.155	-2	-16	-17	-2	-2.4
1906	Was-A	19	16	.543	38	32	28	7	0	282²	253	2	79	96	10.8	2.17	122	.242	.299	11	.117	-4	17	15	-1	1.3
1907	Was-A	12	16	.429	36	29	20	1	0	237¹	272	3	63	58	12.9	3.56	68	.289	.338	11	.126	-3	-27	-30	-5	-4.1
1908	Was-A	0	2	.000	4	3	1	0	0	18	25	0	6	6	15.5	3.50	65	.333	.383	1	.200	-0	-2	-2	-0	-0.3
	Bos-A	0	1	.000	1	1	0	0	0	3	8	0	1	0	27.0	15.00	16	.533	.563	0	—	-0	-4	-4	0	-0.9
	Yr	0	3	.000	5	4	1	0	0	21	33	0	7	6	17.1	5.14	45	.367	.412	1	.167	-0	-6	-7	-0	-1.2
Total	8	105	128	.451	270	238	206	17	5	2062²	2154	40	557	757	12.2	3.36	88	.269	.323	94	.127	-35	-96	-91	-7	-13.8

● **DARYL PATTERSON**   Patterson, Daryl Alan b: 11/21/43, Coalinga, Cal. BL/TR, 6'4", 195 lbs. Deb: 4/10/68

YEAR	TM/L	W	L	PCT	G	GS	CG	SH	SV	IP	H	HR	BB	SO	RAT	ERA	ERA+	OAV	OOB	BH	AVG	PB	PR	/A	PD	TPI
1968	*Det-A	2	3	.400	38	1	0	0	7	68	53	3	27	49	11.1	2.12	142	.213	.300	0	.000	-1	7	7	-0	0.5
1969	Det-A	0	2	.000	18	0	0	0	0	22¹	15	2	19	12	13.7	2.82	132	.205	.370	0	.000	-0	2	2	-1	0.1
1970	Det-A	7	1	.875	43	0	0	0	0	78	81	9	39	55	14.4	4.85	77	.269	.362	0	.000	-1	-10	-10	-1	-1.2
1971	Det-A	0	1	.000	12	0	0	0	0	9¹	14	1	6	5	20.3	4.82	74	.359	.457	0	—	-0	-1	-1	-0	-0.1
	Oak-A	0	0	—	4	0	0	0	0	5²	5	2	4	2	15.9	7.94	42	.238	.385	0	.000	-0	-3	-3	-0	0.0
	Yr	0	1	.000	16	0	0	0	0	15	19	3	10	7	18.0	6.00	58	.311	.417	0	.000	-0	-4	-4	-0	-0.1
	StL-N	0	1	.000	13	2	0	0	1	26²	20	3	15	11	11.8	4.39	82	.211	.318	0	.000	-0	-3	-2	-1	-0.2
1974	Pit-N	2	1	.667	14	0	0	0	1	21	35	3	9	8	18.9	7.29	47	.376	.431	0	.000	-0	-9	-9	0	-1.3
Total	5	11	9	.550	142	3	0	0	11	231	223	23	119	142	13.8	4.09	85	.256	.353	0	.000	-3	-17	-16	-3	-2.2

● **DAVE PATTERSON**   Patterson, David Glenn b: 7/25/56, Springfield, Mo. BR/TR, 6', 170 lbs. Deb: 6/9/79

YEAR	TM/L	W	L	PCT	G	GS	CG	SH	SV	IP	H	HR	BB	SO	RAT	ERA	ERA+	OAV	OOB	BH	AVG	PB	PR	/A	PD	TPI
1979	LA-N	4	1	.800	36	0	0	0	6	53	62	5	22	34	14.3	5.26	69	.292	.359	1	.143	-0	-9	-10	-0	-1.2

● **GIL PATTERSON**   Patterson, Gilbert Thomas b: 9/5/55, Philadelphia, Pa. BR/TR, 6'1", 185 lbs. Deb: 4/19/77

YEAR	TM/L	W	L	PCT	G	GS	CG	SH	SV	IP	H	HR	BB	SO	RAT	ERA	ERA+	OAV	OOB	BH	AVG	PB	PR	/A	PD	TPI
1977	NY-A	1	2	.333	10	6	0	0	1	33¹	38	3	20	29	16.5	5.40	73	.290	.396	0	—	0	-5	-5	1	-0.3

● **KEN PATTERSON**   Patterson, Kenneth Brian b: 7/8/64, Costa Mesa, Cal. BL/TL, 6'4", 210 lbs. Deb: 7/9/88

YEAR	TM/L	W	L	PCT	G	GS	CG	SH	SV	IP	H	HR	BB	SO	RAT	ERA	ERA+	OAV	OOB	BH	AVG	PB	PR	/A	PD	TPI
1988	Chi-A	0	2	.000	9	2	0	0	1	20²	25	2	7	8	13.9	4.79	83	.294	.348	0	—	0	-2	-2	-0	-0.2
1989	Chi-A	6	1	.857	50	1	0	0	0	65²	64	11	28	43	12.4	4.52	84	.257	.337	0	—	0	-5	-5	-1	-0.5
1990	Chi-A	2	1	.667	43	0	0	0	2	66¹	58	6	34	40	12.8	3.39	113	.242	.341	0	—	0	4	3	0	0.3
1991	Chi-A	3	0	1.000	43	0	0	0	0	63²	48	5	35	32	11.9	2.83	140	.214	.323	0	—	0	9	8	-1	0.4
1992	Chi-N	2	3	.400	32	1	0	0	0	41²	41	7	27	23	14.9	3.89	93	.268	.381	0	.000	-0	-2	-1	-0	-0.2
1993	Cal-A	1	1	.500	46	0	0	0	1	59	54	7	35	36	13.6	4.58	98	.249	.353	0	—	0	-2	-0	-1	-0.1
1994	Cal-A	0	0	—	1	0	0	0	0	0²	0	0	0	1	0.00	0.00	—	.000	.000	0	—	0	0	0	-0	0.0
Total	7	14	8	.636	224	4	0	0	5	317²	290	38	166	183	13.1	3.88	102	.248	.344	0	.000	-0	3	3	-3	-0.3

● **REGGIE PATTERSON**   Patterson, Reginald Allen b: 11/7/58, Birmingham, Ala. BR/TR, 6'4", 180 lbs. Deb: 8/13/81

YEAR	TM/L	W	L	PCT	G	GS	CG	SH	SV	IP	H	HR	BB	SO	RAT	ERA	ERA+	OAV	OOB	BH	AVG	PB	PR	/A	PD	TPI
1981	Chi-A	0	1	.000	6	1	0	0	0	7¹	14	1	6	2	24.5	13.50	26	.412	.500	0	—	0	-8	-0	0	-0.9
1983	Chi-N	1	2	.333	5	2	0	0	0	18²	17	3	6	10	11.2	4.82	79	.246	.325	0	.000	-1	-2	-2	-0	-0.4
1984	Chi-N	0	1	.000	3	1	0	0	0	6	10	1	2	5	18.0	10.50	37	.357	.400	0	.000	-0	-5	-4	0	-0.6
1985	Chi-N	3	0	1.000	8	5	1	0	0	39	36	2	10	17	10.6	3.00	133	.250	.299	1	.100	-0	3	4	0	0.3
Total	4	4	4	.500	22	9	1	0	0	71	77	7	24	34	13.1	5.20	75	.280	.342	1	.056	-1	-13	-10	0	-1.6

● **BOB PATTERSON**   Patterson, Robert Chandler b: 5/16/59, Jacksonville, Fla. BR/TL, 6'2", 195 lbs. Deb: 9/2/85

YEAR	TM/L	W	L	PCT	G	GS	CG	SH	SV	IP	H	HR	BB	SO	RAT	ERA	ERA+	OAV	OOB	BH	AVG	PB	PR	/A	PD	TPI
1985	SD-N	0	0	—	3	0	0	0	0	4	13	2	3	1	36.0	24.75	14	.565	.615	0	—	0	-9	-9	-0	0.0
1986	Pit-N	2	3	.400	11	5	0	0	0	36¹	49	0	5	20	13.4	4.95	77	.322	.344	1	.125	-0	-5	-5	1	-0.5
1987	Pit-N	1	4	.200	15	7	0	0	0	43	49	5	22	27	15.1	6.70	61	.290	.375	1	.083	-1	-13	-12	-0	-1.3
1989	Pit-N	4	3	.571	12	3	0	0	1	26²	23	3	8	20	10.5	4.05	83	.233	.290	0	.000	-0	-4	-3	-0	-0.6
1990	*Pit-N	8	5	.615	55	5	0	0	5	94²	88	9	21	70	10.6	2.95	123	.249	.296	1	.053	-0	9	7	-0	0.8
1991	*Pit-N	4	3	.571	54	1	0	0	2	65²	67	7	15	57	11.2	4.11	87	.267	.308	1	.250	-0	-3	-4	-1	-0.4
1992	*Pit-N	6	3	.667	60	0	0	0	9	64²	59	7	23	43	11.4	2.92	118	.246	.312	2	.333	-1	4	4	-1	0.7
1993	Tex-A	2	4	.333	52	0	0	0	1	52²	59	8	11	46	12.1	4.78	87	.282	.321	0	—	0	-3	-4	-0	-0.3
1994	Cal-A	2	3	.400	47	0	0	0	1	42	35	6	15	30	11.1	4.07	122	.229	.306	0	—	0	3	4	0	0.4
Total	9	29	28	.509	309	21	0	0	19	429²	442	47	123	314	12.0	4.27	90	.268	.321	6	.115	-1	-18	-21	-1	-1.2

● **ROY PATTERSON**   Patterson, Roy Lewis "Boy Wonder" b: 12/17/1876, Stoddard, Wis. d: 4/14/53, St.Croix Falls, Wis. BR/TR, 6', 185 lbs. Deb: 4/24/01

YEAR	TM/L	W	L	PCT	G	GS	CG	SH	SV	IP	H	HR	BB	SO	RAT	ERA	ERA+	OAV	OOB	BH	AVG	PB	PR	/A	PD	TPI
1901	Chi-A	20	16	.556	41	35	30	4	0	312¹	345	11	62	127	12.0	3.37	103	.277	.317	26	.222	1	10	4	0	0.4
1902	Chi-A	19	14	.576	34	30	26	2	0	268	262	5	67	61	11.1	3.06	111	.256	.304	20	.190	-2	15	10	1	1.0
1903	Chi-A	15	15	.500	34	30	26	2	1	293	275	5	69	89	10.9	2.70	104	.248	.298	11	.105	-6	8	3	0	-0.1
1904	Chi-A	9	9	.500	22	17	14	4	0	165	148	1	24	64	9.8	2.29	107	.241	.277	6	.103	-4	6	3	-1	-0.2
1905	Chi-A	4	6	.400	13	9	7	0	0	88²	73	0	16	29	9.0	1.83	135	.226	.262	8	.267	2	6	5	1	1.0
1906	Chi-A	10	7	.588	21	18	12	3	1	142	119	1	17	45	8.9	2.09	121	.231	.261	3	.061	-5	9	7	0	0.4
1907	Chi-A	4	6	.400	19	13	4	1	0	96	105	0	18	27	11.7	2.63	92	.280	.316	3	.097	-3	-1	-2	1	-0.4
Total	7	81	73	.526	184	152	119	16	2	1365	1327	23	273	442	10.8	2.75	107	.255	.297	77	.156	-16	57	31	5	2.1

● **MARTY PATTIN**   Pattin, Martin William b: 4/6/43, Charleston, Ill. BR/TR, 5'11", 180 lbs. Deb: 5/14/68 C

YEAR	TM/L	W	L	PCT	G	GS	CG	SH	SV	IP	H	HR	BB	SO	RAT	ERA	ERA+	OAV	OOB	BH	AVG	PB	PR	/A	PD	TPI
1968	Cal-A	4	4	.500	52	4	0	0	3	84	67	7	37	66	11.4	2.79	104	.221	.310	1	.083	-1	2	1	-1	-0.1
1969	Sea-A	7	12	.368	34	27	2	1	0	158²	166	20	71	126	13.6	5.62	65	.267	.335	4	.155	-1	-35	-35	-1	-3.9
1970	Mil-A	14	12	.538	37	29	11	0	0	233¹	204	20	71	161	10.8	3.39	112	.235	.298	9	.129	-2	8	10	2	1.1
1971	Mil-A☆	14	14	.500	36	36	9	5	0	264²	225	29	73	169	10.3	3.13	111	.235	.292	7	.084	-3	10	6	1	0.7
1972	Bos-A	17	13	.567	38	35	13	4	0	253	232	19	65	168	10.9	3.24	99	.243	.297	12	.140	0	-5	-1	1	0.0

YEAR	TM/L	W	L	PCT	G	GS	CG	SH	SV	IP	H	HR	BB	SO	RAT	ERA	ERA+	OAV	OOB	BH	AVG	PB	PR	/A	PD	TPI
1973	Bos-A	15	15	.500	34	30	11	2	1	219¹	238	31	69	119	12.9	4.31	93	.277	.337	0	—	0	-12	-7	1	-1.2
1974	KC-A	3	7	.300	25	11	2	0	0	117¹	121	10	28	50	11.6	3.99	96	.264	.309	0	—	0	-5	-2	-1	-0.7
1975	KC-A	10	10	.500	44	15	5	1	5	177	173	13	45	89	11.2	3.25	118	.253	.302	0	—	0	10	12	-1	1.1
1976	*KC-A	8	14	.364	44	15	4	1	5	141	114	9	38	65	9.9	2.49	141	.216	.273	0	—	0	16	16	-0	2.5
1977	*KC-A	10	3	.769	31	10	4	0	0	128¹	115	16	37	55	10.8	3.58	113	.242	.300	0	—	0	7	7	-1	0.5
1978	*KC-A	3	3	.500	32	5	2	0	4	78²	72	8	25	29	11.3	3.32	115	.248	.312	0	—	0	4	4	-2	0.1
1979	KC-A	5	2	.714	31	7	1	0	3	94¹	109	11	21	41	12.5	4.58	93	.293	.332	0	—	0	-4	-3	-1	-0.4
1980	*KC-A	4	0	1.000	37	0	0	0	4	89	97	7	23	40	12.2	3.64	111	.277	.324	0	—	0	4	4	-1	0.1
Total	13	114	109	.511	475	224	64	14	25	2038²	1933	209	603	1179	11.4	3.62	102	.250	.309	38	.123	-7	0	16	-6	-0.3

● **JIMMY PATTISON**   Pattison, James Wells b: 12/18/08, Bronx, N.Y. d: 2/22/91, Melbourne, Fla. BL/TL, 6', 185 lbs. Deb: 4/18/29

| 1929 | Bro-N | 0 | 1 | .000 | 6 | 0 | 0 | 0 | 0 | 11² | 9 | 1 | 4 | 5 | 10.0 | 4.63 | 100 | .231 | .302 | 1 | .500 | 0 | 0 | -0 | -0 | 0.0 |

● **HARRY PATTON**   Patton, Harry Claude b: 6/29/1884, Gillespie, Ill. d: 6/9/30, St.Louis, Mo. Deb: 8/22/10

| 1910 | StL-N | 0 | 0 | — | 1 | 0 | 0 | 0 | 0 | 4 | 4 | 0 | 2 | 2 | 13.5 | 2.25 | 132 | .267 | .353 | 0 | — | 0 | 0 | 0 | 0 | 0.0 |

● **MIKE PAUL**   Paul, Michael George b: 4/18/45, Detroit, Mich. BL/TL, 6', 183 lbs. Deb: 5/27/68 C

1968	Cle-A	5	8	.385	36	7	0	0	3	91²	72	11	35	87	11.0	3.93	75	.213	.296	4	.167	0	-10	-10	-1	-1.6
1969	Cle-A	5	10	.333	47	12	0	0	2	117¹	104	12	54	98	12.3	3.61	104	.241	.328	0	.000	-3	0	2	-1	-0.1
1970	Cle-A	2	8	.200	30	15	1	0	0	88	91	13	45	70	13.9	4.81	82	.271	.357	4	.154	-1	-11	-8	-2	-1.1
1971	Cle-A	2	7	.222	17	12	1	0	0	62	78	8	14	33	14.1	5.95	64	.318	.367	1	.053	-1	-17	-15	-1	-2.1
1972	Tex-A	8	9	.471	49	20	2	1	1	161²	149	4	52	108	11.3	2.17	139	.246	.308	8	.167	1	16	15	-1	1.7
1973	Tex-A	5	4	.556	36	10	1	0	2	87¹	104	9	36	49	14.9	4.95	75	.295	.368	0	—	0	-11	-12	-1	-1.1
	Chi-N	0	1	.000	11	1	0	0	0	18¹	17	2	9	6	12.8	3.44	115	.258	.347	0	.000	-0	0	1	0	0.0
1974	Chi-N	0	1	.000	2	0	0	0	0	1¹	4	1	1	1	33.8	27.00	14	.500	.556	0	—	0	-3	-3	0	-1.6
Total	7	27	48	.360	228	77	5	1	8	627²	619	60	246	452	12.7	3.91	89	.260	.334	17	.115	-4	-35	-30	-4	-5.9

● **GENE PAULETTE**   Paulette, Eugene Edward b: 5/26/1891, Centralia, Ill. d: 2/8/66, Little Rock, Ark. BR/TR, 6', 150 lbs. Deb: 6/16/11 ♦

| 1918 | StL-N | 0 | 0 | — | 1 | 0 | 0 | 0 | 0 | 0¹ | 1 | 0 | 0 | 0 | 27.0 | 0.00 | — | .500 | .500 | 126 | .273 | 0 | 0 | 0 | 0 | 0.0 |

● **GIL PAULSEN**   Paulsen, Guilford Paul Hans b: 11/14/02, Graettinger, Iowa BR/TR, 6'2.5", 190 lbs. Deb: 10/3/25

| 1925 | StL-N | 0 | 0 | — | 1 | 0 | 0 | 0 | 0 | 2 | 1 | 0 | 1 | 1 | 4.5 | 0.00 | — | .125 | .125 | 0 | — | 0 | 1 | 1 | 0 | 0.0 |

● **DAVE PAVLAS**   Pavlas, David Lee b: 8/12/62, Frankfurt, W.Germany BR/TR, 6'7", 180 lbs. Deb: 8/21/90

1990	Chi-N	2	0	1.000	13	0	0	0	0	21¹	23	2	6	12	12.2	2.11	193	.271	.319	0	.000	0	4	5	-0	0.4
1991	Chi-N	0	0	—	1	0	0	0	0	1	3	1	0	0	27.0	18.00	22	.750	.750	0	—	0	-2	-2	-0	-0.0
Total	2	2	0	1.000	14	0	0	0	0	22¹	26	3	6	12	12.9	2.82	144	.292	.337	0	.000	0	2	3	-0	0.4

● **ROGER PAVLIK**   Pavlik, Roger Allen b: 10/4/67, Houston, Tex. BB/TR, 6'3", 220 lbs. Deb: 5/2/92

1992	Tex-A	4	4	.500	13	12	1	0	0	62	66	3	34	45	15.0	4.21	90	.280	.377	0	—	0	-2	-3	-1	-0.3
1993	Tex-A	12	6	.667	26	26	2	0	0	166¹	151	18	80	131	12.8	3.41	122	.245	.336	0	—	0	17	14	1	1.6
1994	Tex-A	2	5	.286	11	11	0	0	0	50¹	61	8	30	31	17.0	7.69	59	.300	.401	0	—	0	-16	-18	-0	-1.9
Total	3	18	15	.545	50	49	3	0	0	278²	278	29	144	207	14.0	4.36	95	.263	.358	0	—	0	-1	-7	0	-0.6

● **JOHN PAWLOWSKI**   Pawlowski, John b: 9/6/63, Johnson City, N.Y. BR/TR, 6'2", 175 lbs. Deb: 9/19/87

1987	Chi-A	0	0	—	2	0	0	0	0	3²	7	0	3	2	24.5	4.91	93	.438	.526	0	—	0	-0	-0	-0	-0.1
1988	Chi-A	1	0	1.000	6	0	0	0	0	14	20	2	3	10	14.8	8.36	48	.328	.359	0	—	0	-7	-7	0	-0.4
Total	2	1	0	1.000	8	0	0	0	0	17²	27	2	6	12	16.8	7.64	54	.351	.398	0	—	0	-7	-7	-0	-0.5

● **MIKE PAXTON**   Paxton, Michael De Wayne b: 9/3/53, Memphis, Tenn. BR/TR, 5'11", 190 lbs. Deb: 5/25/77

1977	Bos-A	10	5	.667	29	12	2	1	0	108	134	7	25	58	13.5	3.83	117	.311	.353	0	—	0	3	8	-0	0.2
1978	Cle-A	12	11	.522	33	27	6	2	1	191	179	13	63	96	11.8	3.86	97	.247	.314	0	—	0	-2	-3	-1	-0.3
1979	Cle-A	8	8	.500	33	24	3	0	0	159²	210	14	52	70	14.9	5.92	72	.315	.366	0	—	0	-30	-30	0	-2.5
1980	Cle-A	0	0	—	4	0	0	0	0	7²	13	4	6	6	22.3	12.91	32	.394	.487	0	—	0	-8	-8	-0	-0.0
Total	4	30	24	.556	99	63	10	3	1	466¹	536	38	146	230	13.4	4.71	87	.289	.345	0	—	0	-37	-32	-2	-2.6

● **GEORGE PAYNE**   Payne, George Washington b: 5/23/1890, Mt.Vernon, Ky. d: 1/24/59, Bellflower, Cal. BR/TR, 5'11", 172 lbs. Deb: 5/8/20

| 1920 | Chi-A | 1 | 1 | .500 | 12 | 0 | 0 | 0 | 0 | 29² | 39 | 2 | 9 | 7 | 14.6 | 5.46 | 69 | .312 | .358 | 1 | .125 | 0 | -5 | -6 | -1 | -0.5 |

● **HARLEY PAYNE**   Payne, Harley Fenwick "Lady" b: 1/9/1868, Windsor, Ont., Can. d: 12/29/35, Orwell, Ohio BB/TL, 6', 160 lbs. Deb: 4/18/1896

1896	Bro-N	14	16	.467	34	28	24	2	0	241²	284	4	58	52	13.0	3.39	122	.290	.335	21	.214	0	26	20	3	2.2
1897	Bro-N	14	17	.452	40	38	30	1	0	280	350	6	71	86	14.1	4.63	89	.303	.353	26	.236	-0	-10	-16	1	-1.3
1898	Bro-N	1	0	1.000	1	1	1	0	0	9	11	0	3	2	14.0	4.00	90	.299	.352	3	.750	1	-0	-0	0	0.1
1899	Pit-N	1	3	.250	5	5	2	0	0	26¹	33	2	4	8	13.3	3.76	101	.306	.342	1	.100	-1	0	0	2	0.1
Total	4	30	36	.455	80	72	57	3	0	557	678	14	136	148	13.6	4.04	101	.298	.345	51	.230	0	16	3	7	1.1

● **MIKE PAYNE**   Payne, Michael Earl b: 11/15/61, Woonsocket, R.I. BR/TR, 5'11", 165 lbs. Deb: 8/22/84

| 1984 | Atl-N | 0 | 1 | .000 | 3 | 1 | 0 | 0 | 0 | 5² | 7 | 0 | 3 | 3 | 15.9 | 6.35 | 61 | .333 | .417 | 0 | .000 | -0 | -2 | -2 | 0 | -0.3 |

● **MIKE PAZIK**   Pazik, Michael Joseph b: 1/26/50, Lynn, Mass. BL/TL, 6'2", 195 lbs. Deb: 5/11/75

1975	Min-A	0	4	.000	5	3	0	0	0	19²	28	5	10	8	17.4	8.24	47	.329	.400	0	—	0	-10	-10	-1	-1.7
1976	Min-A	0	0	—	5	0	0	0	0	9	13	0	4	6	18.0	7.00	51	.342	.419	0	—	0	-3	-3	-0	-0.2
1977	Min-A	1	0	1.000	3	3	0	0	0	18	18	1	6	6	12.0	2.50	159	.265	.324	0	—	0	3	3	0	0.3
Total	3	1	4	.200	13	6	0	0	0	46²	59	6	20	20	15.4	5.79	67	.309	.377	0	—	0	-10	-10	-1	-1.6

● **FRANK PEARCE**   Pearce, Franklin Johnson b: 3/30/1860, Jefferson County, Ky. d: 11/13/26, Louisville, Ky. Deb: 10/4/1876

| 1876 | Lou-N | 0 | 0 | — | 1 | 0 | 0 | 0 | 0 | 4 | 5 | 0 | 1 | 1 | 13.5 | 4.50 | 60 | .263 | .300 | 0 | .000 | -0 | -1 | -1 | -0 | 0.0 |

● **FRANK PEARCE**   Pearce, Franklin Thomas b: 8/31/05, Middletown, Ky. d: 9/3/50, Van Buren, N.Y. BR/TR, 6', 170 lbs. Deb: 4/20/33

1933	Phi-N	5	4	.556	20	7	3	1	0	82	78	5	29	18	11.7	3.62	105	.251	.315	5	.192	-1	-3	2	0	0.1
1934	Phi-N	0	2	.000	7	1	0	0	0	20	25	4	5	4	13.5	7.20	66	.301	.341	2	.667	1	-7	-6	-1	-0.5
1935	Phi-N	0	0	—	5	0	0	0	0	13	22	0	6	7	19.4	8.31	55	.361	.418	2	.500	1	-6	-5	0	0.1
Total	3	5	6	.455	32	8	3	1	0	115	125	9	40	29	12.9	4.77	85	.275	.333	9	.273	1	-16	-9	-0	-0.3

● **GEORGE PEARCE**   Pearce, George Thomas "Filbert" b: 1/10/1888, Aurora, Ill. d: 10/11/35, Joliet, Ill. BL/TL, 5'10.5", 175 lbs. Deb: 4/16/12

1912	Chi-N	0	0	—	3	2	0	0	0	14²	15	0	12	9	16.6	5.52	60	.185	.290	1	.167	0	-3	-4	1	0.1
1913	Chi-N	13	5	.722	25	21	15	3	0	163¹	137	4	59	73	11.0	2.31	137	.234	.308	4	.073	-3	16	16	-0	1.3
1914	Chi-N	9	12	.429	30	16	4	0	0	141	122	6	65	78	12.1	3.51	79	.239	.327	4	.089	-3	-11	-11	2	-1.8
1915	Chi-N	13	9	.591	36	20	8	2	0	176	158	4	77	96	13.2	3.32	84	.244	.328	11	.196	1	-11	-11	-0	-1.2
1916	Chi-N	0	0	—	4	0	0	0	0	4¹	6	0	4	0	14.5	2.08	140	.300	.333	0	—	0	0	-0	-0	0.0
1917	StL-N	1	1	.500	5	1	0	0	1	10¹	7	0	3	4	9.6	3.48	77	.184	.262	0	.000	-1	-1	-1	0	-0.2
Total	6	36	27	.571	103	60	27	5	1	509²	445	14	217	260	11.9	3.11	94	.236	.318	20	.120	-6	-10	-10	2	-1.8

● **JIM PEARCE**   Pearce, James Madison b: 6/9/25, Zebulon, N.C. BR/TR, 6'6", 180 lbs. Deb: 9/8/49

1949	Was-A	0	1	.000	2	1	0	0	0	5	5	1	5	1	23.6	8.44	50	.375	.483	0	—	-0	-3	-2	1	-0.3
1950	Was-A	2	1	.667	20	3	1	0	0	56²	58	2	37	18	15.2	6.04	74	.270	.379	2	.154	-1	-9	-10	-0	-0.5
1953	Was-A	0	1	.000	4	1	0	0	0	9¹	15	3	6	10	20.3	7.71	51	.405	.488	0	.000	-0	-4	-4	-0	-0.4

YEAR	TM/L	W	L	PCT	G	GS	CG	SH	SV	IP	H	HR	BB	SO	RAT	ERA	ERA+	OAV	OOB	BH	AVG	PB	PR	/A	PD	TPI
1954	Cin-N	1	0	1.000	2	1	1	0	0	11	7	0	5	3	10.6	0.00	—	.194	.310	0	—	-0	5	5	0	0.4
1955	Cin-N	0	1	.000	2	1	0	0	0	3¹	8	0	0	1	21.6	10.80	39	.471	.471	0	—	-0	-3	-3	0	-0.6
Total	5	3	4	.429	30	7	2	0	0	85²	97	6	53	22	16.0	5.78	76	.295	.396	2	.105	-2	-13	-13	0	-1.4

● **DICKEY PEARCE** Pearce, Richard J. b: 2/29/1836, Brooklyn, N.Y. d: 10/12/08, Wareham, Mass. BR/TR, 5'3.5", 161 lbs. Deb: 5/18/1871 MU♦

YEAR	TM/L	W	L	PCT	G	GS	CG	SH	SV	IP	H	HR	BB	SO	RAT	ERA	ERA+	OAV	OOB	BH	AVG	PB	PR	/A	PD	TPI
1875	StL-n	0	0	—	2	0	0	0	0	5¹	10	0	0		16.9	6.75	33	.357	.357	77	.247	0	-3	-3		0.0

● **FRANK PEARS** Pears, Frank H. b: 8/30/1866, Kentucky d: 11/29/23, St.Louis, Mo. TR, 5'9", 145 lbs. Deb: 10/6/1889 U

YEAR	TM/L	W	L	PCT	G	GS	CG	SH	SV	IP	H	HR	BB	SO	RAT	ERA	ERA+	OAV	OOB	BH	AVG	PB	PR	/A	PD	TPI
1889	KC-a	0	2	.000	3	2	2	0	0	22	21	2	9	5	12.7	4.91	85	.244	.322	1	.091	-1	-3	-2	-0	-0.2
1893	StL-N	0	0	—	1	0	0	0	0	4	9	0	2	0	27.0	13.50	35	.432	.503	0	.000	-0	-4	-4	0	0.0
Total	2	0	2	.000	4	2	2	0	0	26	30	2	11	5	14.9	6.23	69	.280	.358	1	.077	-2	-7	-6	-0	-0.2

● **ALEX PEARSON** Pearson, Alexander Franklin b: 3/9/1877, Greensboro, Pa. d: 10/30/66, Rochester, Pa. BR/TR, 5'10.5", 160 lbs. Deb: 8/1/02

YEAR	TM/L	W	L	PCT	G	GS	CG	SH	SV	IP	H	HR	BB	SO	RAT	ERA	ERA+	OAV	OOB	BH	AVG	PB	PR	/A	PD	TPI
1902	StL-N	2	6	.250	11	10	8	0	0	82	90	0	22	24	12.6	3.95	69	.279	.330	9	.265	-0	-11	-11	-0	-0.9
1903	Cle-A	1	2	.333	4	3	2	0	0	30¹	34	1	3	12	11.3	3.56	80	.282	.305	1	.083	-1	-2	-2	0	-0.3
Total	2	3	8	.273	15	13	10	0	0	112¹	124	1	25	36	12.3	3.85	72	.280	.324	10	.217	-0	-13	-13	-0	-1.2

● **IKE PEARSON** Pearson, Issac Overton b: 3/1/17, Grenada, Miss. d: 3/17/85, Sarasota, Fla. BR/TR, 6'1", 180 lbs. Deb: 6/6/39

YEAR	TM/L	W	L	PCT	G	GS	CG	SH	SV	IP	H	HR	BB	SO	RAT	ERA	ERA+	OAV	OOB	BH	AVG	PB	PR	/A	PD	TPI
1939	Phi-N	2	13	.133	26	13	4	0	0	125	144	15	56	29	14.8	5.76	70	.296	.374	2	.054	-3	-26	-24	1	-2.7
1940	Phi-N	3	14	.176	29	20	5	1	1	145¹	160	13	57	43	13.6	5.45	72	.275	.343	9	.205	1	-26	-25	1	-2.4
1941	Phi-N	4	14	.222	46	10	0	0	6	136	139	8	70	38	14.4	3.57	104	.266	.361	5	.125	-2	1	2	0	0.0
1942	Phi-N	1	6	.143	35	7	0	0	0	85¹	87	4	50	21	14.9	4.54	73	.271	.376	1	.043	-2	-12	-12	-0	-1.2
1946	Phi-N	1	0	1.000	5	2	1	1	0	14¹	16	1	8	6	15.7	3.77	91	.271	.368	1	.200	1	-1	-1	0	0.1
1948	Chi-A	2	3	.400	23	2	0	0	1	53	62	8	27	12	15.5	4.92	87	.292	.378	1	.200	-0	-4	-4	1	-0.3
Total	6	13	50	.206	164	54	10	2	8	559	608	49	268	149	14.5	4.83	79	.279	.363	20	.126	-6	-66	-64	2	-6.5

● **MONTE PEARSON** Pearson, Montgomery Marcellus "Hoot" b: 9/2/09, Oakland, Cal. d: 1/27/78, Fresno, Cal. BR/TR, 6', 175 lbs. Deb: 4/22/32

YEAR	TM/L	W	L	PCT	G	GS	CG	SH	SV	IP	H	HR	BB	SO	RAT	ERA	ERA+	OAV	OOB	BH	AVG	PB	PR	/A	PD	TPI
1932	Cle-A	0	0	—	8	0	0	0	0	8	10	1	11	5	23.6	10.13	47	.323	.500	0	—	-0	-5	-5	1	0.1
1933	Cle-A	10	5	.667	19	16	10	0	0	135¹	111	5	55	54	11.0	2.33	191	.221	.297	13	.260	1	29	32	-1	3.3
1934	Cle-A	18	13	.581	39	33	19	0	2	254²	257	16	130	140	13.7	4.52	101	.260	.346	25	.272	6	-1	-1	1	0.7
1935	Cle-A	8	13	.381	30	24	10	1	0	181²	199	9	103	90	15.0	4.90	92	.279	.371	11	.177	-0	-9	-8	2	-0.6
1936	*NY-A☆	19	7	.731	33	31	15	1	1	223	191	13	135	118	13.3	3.71	125	.233	.343	23	.253	6	33	23	1	2.9
1937	*NY-A	9	3	.750	22	20	7	1	1	144²	145	6	71	63	13.9	3.17	140	.261	.339	11	.216	1	23	20	-1	1.5
1938	*NY-A	16	7	.696	28	27	13	1	0	202	198	12	113	98	13.9	3.97	114	.258	.354	13	.171	1	18	13	2	1.4
1939	*NY-A	12	5	.706	22	20	8	0	0	146¹	151	9	70	76	13.7	4.49	97	.272	.354	17	.321	1	2	-2	1	0.4
1940	NY-A☆	7	5	.583	16	16	7	1	0	109²	108	8	44	43	12.5	3.69	109	.262	.333	4	.121	-1	8	4	2	0.5
1941	Cin-N	1	3	.250	7	4	1	0	0	24¹	22	3	15	8	13.7	5.18	99	.242	.349	0	.000	-1	-4	-4	-0	-0.7
Total	10	100	61	.621	224	191	94	5	4	1429²	1392	82	740	703	13.5	4.00	112	.256	.346	117	.228	19	95	75	8	9.5

● **MARV PEASLEY** Peasley, Marvin Warren b: 7/16/1888, Jonesport, Me. d: 12/27/48, San Francisco, Cal BL/TL, 6'1", 175 lbs. Deb: 9/27/10

YEAR	TM/L	W	L	PCT	G	GS	CG	SH	SV	IP	H	HR	BB	SO	RAT	ERA	ERA+	OAV	OOB	BH	AVG	PB	PR	/A	PD	TPI
1910	Det-A	0	1	.000	2	1	0	0	0	10	13	0	11	4	22.5	8.10	32	.295	.446	0	.000	-1	-6	-6	-0	-0.5

● **GEORGE PECHINEY** Pechiney, George Adolphe "Pisch" b: 9/20/1861, Cincinnati, Ohio d: 7/14/43, Cincinnati, Ohio BR/TR, 5'9", 184 lbs. Deb: 8/4/1885

YEAR	TM/L	W	L	PCT	G	GS	CG	SH	SV	IP	H	HR	BB	SO	RAT	ERA	ERA+	OAV	OOB	BH	AVG	PB	PR	/A	PD	TPI
1885	Cin-a	7	4	.636	11	11	11	1	0	98	95	1	30	49	12.0	2.02	161	.247	.311	6	.150	-2	13	13	1	1.2
1886	Cin-a	15	21	.417	40	40	35	2	0	330¹	355	4	133	110	13.7	4.14	85	.266	.339	30	.208	-1	-25	-23	-3	-2.3
1887	Cle-a	1	9	.100	10	10	10	0	0	86	118	8	44	24	17.3	7.12	61	.303	.378	9	.250	-0	-27	-27	0	-2.1
Total	3	23	34	.404	61	61	56	3	0	514¹	568	13	207	183	14.0	4.23	85	.269	.341	45	.205	-3	-39	-36	-2	-3.2

● **BILL PECOTA** Pecota, William Joseph b: 2/16/60, Redwood City, Cal. BR/TR, 6'2", 195 lbs. Deb: 9/19/86 ♦

YEAR	TM/L	W	L	PCT	G	GS	CG	SH	SV	IP	H	HR	BB	SO	RAT	ERA	ERA+	OAV	OOB	BH	AVG	PB	PR	/A	PD	TPI
1991	KC-A	0	0	—	1	0	0	0	0	2	4	0	0	0	18.0	4.50	92	.444	.444	114	.286	0	-0	-0	-0	0.0
1992	NY-N	0	0	—	1	0	0	0	0	1	1	1	0	0	9.0	9.00	39	.250	.250	61	.227	0	-1	-1	-0	0.0
Total	2	0	0	—	2	0	0	0	0	3	5	1	0	0	15.0	6.00	65	.385	.385	380	.249	0	-1	-1	-0	0.0

● **STEVE PEEK** Peek, Stephen George b: 7/30/14, Springfield, Mass d: 9/20/91, Syracuse, N.Y. BB/TR, 6'2", 195 lbs. Deb: 4/16/41

YEAR	TM/L	W	L	PCT	G	GS	CG	SH	SV	IP	H	HR	BB	SO	RAT	ERA	ERA+	OAV	OOB	BH	AVG	PB	PR	/A	PD	TPI
1941	NY-A	4	2	.667	17	8	2	0	0	80	85	6	39	18	13.9	5.06	78	.276	.357	1	.036	-3	-8	-10	0	-0.9

● **RED PEERY** Peery, George Allan b: 8/15/06, Payson, Utah d: 5/6/85, Salt Lake City, Ut. BL/TL, 5'11", 160 lbs. Deb: 9/22/27

YEAR	TM/L	W	L	PCT	G	GS	CG	SH	SV	IP	H	HR	BB	SO	RAT	ERA	ERA+	OAV	OOB	BH	AVG	PB	PR	/A	PD	TPI
1927	Pit-N	0	0	—	1	0	0	0	0	1	0	0	1	0	9.0	0.00	—	.000	.200	0	—	0	0	0	-0	0.0
1929	Bos-N	0	1	.000	9	1	0	0	0	44	53	1	9	3	12.7	5.11	91	.305	.339	3	.214	1	-2	-2	-0	0.0
Total	2	0	1	.000	10	1	0	0	0	45	53	1	10	3	12.6	5.00	93	.298	.335	3	.214	1	-2	-2	-0	0.0

● **HEINIE PEITZ** Peitz, Henry Clement b: 11/28/1870, St.Louis, Mo. d: 10/23/43, Cincinnati, Ohio BR/TR, 5'11", 165 lbs. Deb: 10/15/1892 FC♦

YEAR	TM/L	W	L	PCT	G	GS	CG	SH	SV	IP	H	HR	BB	SO	RAT	ERA	ERA+	OAV	OOB	BH	AVG	PB	PR	/A	PD	TPI
1894	StL-N	0	0	—	1	0	0	0	0	3	7	0	2	0	30.0	9.00	60	.448	.537	89	.263	-0	-1	-1	-0	0.0
1897	Cin-N	0	1	.000	2	1	1	0	0	8	9	0	4	1	16.9	7.88	58	.282	.395	78	.293	-0	-3	-3	1	-0.2
1899	Cin-N	0	0	—	1	0	0	0	0	5	6	0	1	2	12.6	5.40	73	.297	.330	79	.272	0	-1	-1	0	0.0
Total	3	0	1	.000	4	1	1	0	0	16	22	0	7	3	18.0	7.31	62	.324	.411	1117	.271	1	-5	-5	1	-0.2

● **BARNEY PELTY** Pelty, Barney b: 9/10/1880, Farmington, Mo. d: 5/24/39, Farmington, Mo. BR/TR, 5'9", 175 lbs. Deb: 8/20/03

YEAR	TM/L	W	L	PCT	G	GS	CG	SH	SV	IP	H	HR	BB	SO	RAT	ERA	ERA+	OAV	OOB	BH	AVG	PB	PR	/A	PD	TPI
1903	StL-A	3	3	.500	7	6	5	0	1	48²	49	1	15	20	12.2	2.40	121	.261	.322	3	.150	-0	3	3	-1	0.2
1904	StL-A	15	18	.455	39	35	31	2	0	301	270	4	77	126	11.0	2.84	87	.241	.301	15	.127	-6	-8	-12	-1	-2.1
1905	StL-A	14	14	.500	31	28	27	1	0	258²	222	3	68	114	10.5	2.75	93	.233	.292	15	.153	-3	-3	-6	3	-0.7
1906	StL-A	16	11	.593	34	30	25	4	2	260²	189	1	59	92	9.2	1.59	163	.206	.267	15	.163	-3	32	29	5	3.5
1907	StL-A	12	21	.364	36	31	29	5	1	273	234	1	64	85	10.4	2.57	98	.233	.291	16	.168	-2	-1	-2	5	-0.2
1908	StL-A	7	4	.636	20	13	7	2	0	122	104	0	32	36	10.8	1.99	120	.241	.309	5	.119	-3	5	5	1	0.3
1909	StL-A	11	11	.500	27	23	17	5	0	199¹	158	0	53	88	9.8	2.30	105	.222	.281	15	.165	-0	6	3	4	0.8
1910	StL-A	5	11	.313	27	19	13	3	0	165¹	157	4	70	48	12.8	3.48	71	.263	.348	5	.089	-4	-18	-19	4	-1.7
1911	StL-A	7	15	.318	28	22	18	1	0	197	197	4	69	59	12.3	2.97	114	.265	.331	9	.138	-3	8	9	1	0.7
1912	StL-A	1	5	.167	6	6	2	0	0	38²	40	0	10	15	14.2	5.59	59	.297	.374	2	.000	-2	-10	-10	0	-1.4
	Was-A	1	4	.200	11	4	1	0	0	43²	43	0	15	15	11.1	3.30	101	.250	.310	2	.222	-0	0	-1	0	0.0
	Yr	2	9	.182	17	10	3	0	0	82¹	83	0	25	30	12.6	4.37	76	.269	.332	2	.095	-2	-10	-10	-1	-1.4
Total	10	92	117	.440	266	217	175	23	4	1908	1663	22	532	693	10.8	2.63	100	.239	.302	100	.143	-25	14	0	17	-0.6

● **ALEJANDRO PENA** Pena, Alejandro (Vasquez) b: 6/25/59, Cambiaso, D.R. BR/TR, 6'1", 205 lbs. Deb: 9/14/81

YEAR	TM/L	W	L	PCT	G	GS	CG	SH	SV	IP	H	HR	BB	SO	RAT	ERA	ERA+	OAV	OOB	BH	AVG	PB	PR	/A	PD	TPI
1981	*LA-N	1	1	.500	14	0	0	0	0	25¹	18	2	11	14	10.3	2.84	117	.194	.279	0	.000	-1	2	1	0	0.1
1982	LA-N	0	2	.000	29	0	0	0	0	35²	37	2	21	20	14.9	4.79	72	.272	.373	0	—	-0	-5	-5	1	-0.2
1983	*LA-N	12	9	.571	34	26	4	3	1	177	152	7	51	120	10.4	2.75	131	.229	.285	6	.100	-2	17	17	2	1.9
1984	LA-N	12	6	.667	28	28	8	4	0	199¹	186	7	46	135	10.6	2.48	142	.246	.292	8	.121	-1	24	23	-1	1.8
1985	LA-N	0	1	.000	2	1	0	0	0	4¹	7	1	3	2	20.8	8.31	42	.350	.435	0	.000	-0	-2	-0	-0	-0.5
1986	LA-N	1	2	.333	24	10	0	0	0	70	74	6	30	46	13.5	4.89	71	.270	.344	3	.176	-0	-9	-11	-0	-0.6
1987	LA-N	2	7	.222	37	7	0	0	11	87¹	82	9	37	76	12.5	3.50	113	.251	.331	1	.077	-1	6	4	-2	0.2
1988	LA-N	6	7	.462	60	0	0	0	12	94¹	75	4	27	83	10.0	1.91	175	.220	.281	0	—	-1	16	15	-0	2.4
1989	LA-N	4	3	.571	53	0	0	0	5	76	62	6	18	75	9.7	2.13	160	.220	.272	1	1.000	0	12	11	-1	1.1
1990	NY-N	3	3	.500	52	0	0	0	5	76	71	6	22	76	11.1	3.20	117	.245	.300	1	.167	0	5	5	-0	0.8
1991	NY-N	6	1	.857	44	0	0	0	4	63	63	5	19	49	11.7	2.71	134	.267	.322	0	.000	-0	8	7	0	0.8
	*Atl-N	2	0	1.000	15	0	0	0	11	19¹	11	1	3	13	6.5	1.40	268	.167	.203	0	.000	-0	5	5	-0	1.3
	Yr	8	1	.889	59	0	0	0	15	82¹	74	6	22	62	10.5	2.40	154	.242	.293	0	.000	-0	12	12	-0	2.1

YEAR	TM/L	W	L	PCT	G	GS	CG	SH	SV	IP	H	HR	BB	SO	RAT	ERA	ERA+	OAV	OOB	BH	AVG	PB	PR	/A	PD	TPI
1992	Atl-N	1	6	.143	41	0	0	0	15	42	40	7	13	34	11.4	4.07	90	.255	.312	0	.000	-0	-3	-2	-1	-0.6
1994	Pit-N	3	2	.600	22	0	0	0	7	28²	22	4	10	27	10.4	5.02	85	.206	.280	0	.000	-0	-3	-2	-1	-0.6
Total	13	53	50	.515	455	72	12	7	74	998¹	900	65	311	770	11.0	3.01	119	.240	.300	20	.111	-5	72	65	-7	7.4

● HIPOLITO PENA
Pena, Hipolito (Concepcion) b: 1/30/64, Fantino, D.R. BL/TL, 6'3", 165 lbs. Deb: 9/1/86

YEAR	TM/L	W	L	PCT	G	GS	CG	SH	SV	IP	H	HR	BB	SO	RAT	ERA	ERA+	OAV	OOB	BH	AVG	PB	PR	/A	PD	TPI
1986	Pit-N	0	3	.000	10	1	0	0	1	8¹	7	3	3	6	11.9	8.64	44	.206	.289	0	—	0	-5	-4	-0	-1.5
1987	Pit-N	0	3	.000	16	1	0	0	1	25²	16	2	26	16	14.7	4.56	90	.184	.372	1	.167	-0	-1	-1	-0	-0.2
1988	NY-A	1	1	.500	16	0	0	0	0	14¹	10	1	9	10	11.9	3.14	125	.192	.311	0	—	0	1	1	0	0.2
Total	3	1	7	.125	42	2	0	0	2	48¹	33	6	38	32	13.4	4.84	83	.191	.340	1	.167	-0	-5	-4	0	-1.5

● JIM PENA
Pena, James Patrick b: 9/17/64, Los Angeles, Cal. BL/TL, 6', 175 lbs. Deb: 7/7/92

YEAR	TM/L	W	L	PCT	G	GS	CG	SH	SV	IP	H	HR	BB	SO	RAT	ERA	ERA+	OAV	OOB	BH	AVG	PB	PR	/A	PD	TPI
1992	SF-N	1	1	.500	25	2	0	0	0	44	49	4	20	32	14.3	3.48	95	.282	.359	1	.200	1	0	-1	1	0.0

● JOSE PENA
Pena, Jose (Gutierrez) b: 12/3/42, Ciudad Juarez, Mex. BR/TR, 6'2", 190 lbs. Deb: 6/1/69

YEAR	TM/L	W	L	PCT	G	GS	CG	SH	SV	IP	H	HR	BB	SO	RAT	ERA	ERA+	OAV	OOB	BH	AVG	PB	PR	/A	PD	TPI
1969	Cin-N	1	1	.500	6	0	0	0	0	5	10	0	5	3	27.0	18.00	21	.400	.500	0	—	0	-8	-8	-0	-2.4
1970	LA-N	4	3	.571	29	0	0	0	4	57	51	8	29	31	13.1	4.42	87	.241	.340	1	.125	0	-2	-4	1	-0.4
1971	LA-N	2	0	1.000	21	0	0	0	0	43	32	7	18	44	10.7	3.56	91	.211	.298	2	.667	1	-0	-2	-1	0.0
1972	LA-N	0	0	—	5	0	0	0	0	7¹	13	1	6	4	23.3	8.59	39	.371	.463	0	—	0	-4	-4	-0	0.0
Total	4	7	4	.636	61	0	0	0	5	112¹	106	16	58	82	13.5	4.97	72	.250	.346	3	.273	1	-15	-18	-0	-2.8

● ORLANDO PENA
Pena, Orlando Gregorio (Quevara) b: 11/17/33, Victoria De Las Tunas, Cuba BR/TR, 5'11", 154 lbs. Deb: 8/24/58

YEAR	TM/L	W	L	PCT	G	GS	CG	SH	SV	IP	H	HR	BB	SO	RAT	ERA	ERA+	OAV	OOB	BH	AVG	PB	PR	/A	PD	TPI
1958	Cin-N	1	0	1.000	9	0	0	0	3	15	10	0	4	11	8.4	0.60	691	.185	.241	0	—	0	6	6	-0	0.6
1959	Cin-N	5	9	.357	46	8	1	0	5	136	150	26	39	76	12.5	4.76	85	.280	.329	3	.088	-0	-12	-11	-1	-1.2
1960	Cin-N	0	1	.000	4	0	0	0	0	9¹	8	0	3	9	10.6	2.89	132	.222	.282	0	.000	-0	1	1	-0	0.1
1962	KC-A	6	4	.600	13	12	6	1	0	89²	71	9	27	56	9.9	3.01	140	.213	.274	5	.161	-0	10	12	-1	1.1
1963	KC-A	12	20	.375	35	33	9	3	0	217	218	24	53	128	11.4	3.69	106	.260	.308	9	.145	-0	-1	5	-2	0.5
1964	KC-A	12	14	.462	40	32	5	0	0	219¹	231	40	73	184	12.8	4.43	86	.268	.331	12	.160	-0	-20	-15	-1	-1.8
1965	KC-A	0	6	.000	12	5	0	0	0	35¹	42	4	13	24	14.5	6.88	51	.302	.370	1	.111	-0	-13	-13	-0	-2.0
	Det-A	4	6	.400	30	0	0	0	4	57¹	54	5	20	55	11.8	2.51	138	.252	.319	2	.250	1	6	6	-1	1.1
	Yr	4	12	.250	42	5	0	0	4	92²	96	9	33	79	12.6	4.18	83	.270	.333	3	.176	1	-7	-7	-1	-0.9
1966	Det-A	4	2	.667	54	0	0	0	7	108	105	16	35	79	12.1	3.08	113	.252	.317	2	.111	-1	4	5	2	0.5
1967	Det-A	0	1	.000	2	0	0	0	0	2	2	0	0	2	27.0	13.50	24	.500	.545	0	—	0	-2	-2	-0	-0.9
	Cle-A	0	3	.000	48	1	0	0	8	88¹	67	8	22	72	9.2	3.36	97	.208	.261	0	.000	-0	-4	-3	0	-0.2
	Yr	0	4	.000	50	1	0	0	8	90¹	72	8	22	74	9.5	3.59	91	.216	.266	0	.000	-0	-4	-3	-1	-1.1
1970	Pit-N	2	1	.667	23	0	0	0	2	37²	38	6	7	25	11.0	4.78	82	.268	.307	0	.000	-0	-3	-4	1	-0.3
1971	Bal-A	0	1	.000	5	0	0	0	0	14²	16	0	5	4	12.9	3.07	109	.281	.339	0	.000	-0	1	0	0	0.0
1973	Bal-A	1	1	.500	11	2	0	0	1	44²	36	10	8	23	9.3	4.03	93	.218	.263	0	—	0	-1	-1	-0	-0.1
	StL-N	4	4	.500	42	0	0	0	6	62	60	3	14	38	10.7	2.18	167	.251	.292	1	.143	-0	10	10	0	1.5
1974	StL-N	5	2	.714	42	0	0	0	0	45	45	0	23	13.2	2.60	137	.269	.351	1	.500	0	5	5	-0	0.8
	Cal-A	0	0	—	4	0	0	0	3	8	6	0	1	5	7.9	0.00	—	.214	.241	0	—	0	2	2	-1	0.4
1975	Cal-A	0	2	.000	7	0	0	0	0	12²	13	0	8	4	14.9	2.13	166	.283	.389	0	—	0	2	2	-1	0.7
Total	14	56	77	.421	427	93	21	4	40	1202	1175	151	352	818	11.6	3.71	102	.255	.312	36	.136	-3	-7	8	-6	1.2

● RAMON PENA
Pena, Ramon Arturo (Padilla) b: 5/5/62, Santiago, D.R. BR/TR, 5'10", 155 lbs. Deb: 4/27/89 F

YEAR	TM/L	W	L	PCT	G	GS	CG	SH	SV	IP	H	HR	BB	SO	RAT	ERA	ERA+	OAV	OOB	BH	AVG	PB	PR	/A	PD	TPI
1989	Det-A	0	0	—	8	0	0	0	0	18	26	1	8	12	18.0	6.00	64	.338	.414	0	—	0	-4	-4	1	0.1

● RUSTY PENCE
Pence, Russell William b: 3/11/1900, Marine, Ill. d: 8/11/71, Hot Springs, Ark. BR/TR, 6', 185 lbs. Deb: 5/13/21

YEAR	TM/L	W	L	PCT	G	GS	CG	SH	SV	IP	H	HR	BB	SO	RAT	ERA	ERA+	OAV	OOB	BH	AVG	PB	PR	/A	PD	TPI
1921	Chi-A	0	0	—	4	0	0	0	0	5¹	6	0	7	2	23.6	8.44	50	.286	.483	0	.000	-0	-2	-2	0	0.0

● KEN PENNER
Penner, Kenneth William b: 4/24/1896, Boonville, Ind. d: 5/28/59, Sacramento, Cal. BL/TR, 5'11.5", 170 lbs. Deb: 9/11/16

YEAR	TM/L	W	L	PCT	G	GS	CG	SH	SV	IP	H	HR	BB	SO	RAT	ERA	ERA+	OAV	OOB	BH	AVG	PB	PR	/A	PD	TPI
1916	Cle-A	1	0	1.000	4	2	0	0	0	12²	14	0	4	5	12.8	4.26	71	.304	.360	0	.000	-0	-2	-2	1	-0.1
1929	Chi-N	0	1	.000	5	0	0	0	0	12²	14	1	6	3	14.2	2.84	162	.280	.357	1	.250	-0	3	2	-0	0.2
Total	2	1	1	.500	9	2	0	0	0	25¹	28	1	10	8	13.5	3.55	108	.292	.358	1	.167	-0	1	1	1	0.1

● BRAD PENNINGTON
Pennington, Brad Lee b: 4/14/69, Salem, Ind. BL/TL, 6'5", 205 lbs. Deb: 4/17/93

YEAR	TM/L	W	L	PCT	G	GS	CG	SH	SV	IP	H	HR	BB	SO	RAT	ERA	ERA+	OAV	OOB	BH	AVG	PB	PR	/A	PD	TPI
1993	Bal-A	3	2	.600	34	0	0	0	0	33	34	7	25	39	16.6	6.55	68	.266	.394	0	—	0	-8	-8	-0	-1.4
1994	Bal-A	0	1	.000	8	0	0	0	0	6	9	2	8	7	25.5	12.00	42	.346	.500	0	—	0	-5	-5	-0	-0.7
Total	2	3	3	.500	42	0	0	0	0	39	43	9	33	46	18.0	7.38	60	.279	.413	0	—	0	-13	-12	-0	-2.1

● KEWPIE PENNINGTON
Pennington, George Louis b: 9/24/1896, New York, N.Y. d: 5/3/53, Newark, N.J. BR/TR, 5'8.5", 168 lbs. Deb: 4/14/17

YEAR	TM/L	W	L	PCT	G	GS	CG	SH	SV	IP	H	HR	BB	SO	RAT	ERA	ERA+	OAV	OOB	BH	AVG	PB	PR	/A	PD	TPI
1917	StL-A	0	0	—	1	0	0	0	0	1	1	0	0	0	9.0	0.00	—	.250	.250	0	—	0	0	0	-0	0.0

● HERB PENNOCK
Pennock, Herbert Jefferis "The Knight Of Kennett Square" b: 2/10/1894, Kennett Square, Pa d: 1/30/48, New York, N.Y. BB/TL, 6', 160 lbs. Deb: 5/14/12 CH

YEAR	TM/L	W	L	PCT	G	GS	CG	SH	SV	IP	H	HR	BB	SO	RAT	ERA	ERA+	OAV	OOB	BH	AVG	PB	PR	/A	PD	TPI
1912	Phi-A	1	2	.333	17	2	1	0	2	50	48	1	30	38	14.6	4.50	68	.262	.375	2	.133	-1	-7	-8	1	-0.5
1913	Phi-A	2	1	.667	14	3	1	0	0	33¹	30	4	22	17	14.0	5.13	54	.221	.329	1	.111	-0	-8	-9	-0	-0.8
1914	*Phi-A	11	4	.733	28	14	8	3	3	151²	136	1	65	90	12.0	2.79	94	.248	.330	12	.214	-2	-3	-3	-1	-0.1
1915	Phi-A	3	6	.333	11	8	3	1	1	44	46	2	29	24	15.8	5.32	55	.266	.377	5	.278	1	-12	-12	-1	-2.0
	Bos-A	0	0	—	5	1	0	0	0	14	23	0	10	7	21.2	9.64	29	.390	.478	1	.167	0	-10	-11	-1	-0.1
	Yr	3	6	.333	16	9	3	1	1	58	69	2	39	31	16.8	6.36	45	.295	.396	6	.250	1	-22	-22	-1	-2.1
1916	Bos-A	0	2	.000	9	2	0	0	1	26²	24	0	8	12	10.8	3.04	91	.245	.311	1	.125	-0	-1	-1	-0	-0.1
1917	Bos-A	5	5	.500	24	5	4	1	1	100²	90	2	23	35	10.4	3.31	78	.243	.292	4	.167	2	-7	-8	-0	-0.7
1919	Bos-A	16	8	.667	32	26	16	5	0	219	223	2	48	70	11.3	2.71	111	.274	.316	13	.173	1	13	8	-2	0.6
1920	Bos-A	16	13	.552	37	31	19	4	2	242¹	244	9	61	68	11.5	3.68	99	.264	.312	20	.260	4	-3	-1	-3	0.1
1921	Bos-A	12	14	.462	32	32	15	1	0	222²	268	7	59	91	13.3	4.04	105	.307	.352	18	.212	2	6	5	1	0.8
1922	Bos-A	10	17	.370	32	26	15	1	0	202	230	7	74	59	13.6	4.32	95	.297	.359	9	.138	-3	-6	-5	1	-0.7
1923	*NY-A	19	6	.760	35	27	21	1	3	238¹	235	11	68	93	11.5	3.13	126	.261	.314	16	.193	-0	23	21	1	2.1
1924	NY-A	21	9	.700	40	34	25	4	3	286¹	302	13	64	101	11.5	3.23	147	.273	.314	16	.158	-2	45	42	-1	3.8
1925	NY-A	16	17	.485	47	31	21	2	2	277	267	11	71	88	11.0	2.96	144	.254	.303	20	.202	-3	44	40	-3	3.6
1926	*NY-A	23	11	.676	40	33	19	1	0	266¹	294	11	43	78	11.5	3.62	107	.282	.313	18	.212	3	12	7	1	1.1
1927	*NY-A	19	8	.704	34	26	18	1	1	209²	225	5	48	51	11.8	3.00	128	.283	.325	15	.217	-0	26	20	-2	2.1
1928	NY-A	17	6	.739	28	24	18	5	3	211	215	2	40	53	10.9	2.56	147	.267	.302	15	.203	-1	35	28	2	2.9
1929	NY-A	9	11	.450	27	23	8	1	2	157¹	205	11	28	49	13.5	4.92	78	.318	.349	9	.176	-1	-12	-19	-1	-2.1
1930	NY-A	11	7	.611	25	19	11	1	0	156¹	194	10	20	46	12.3	4.32	100	.301	.322	11	.183	-2	-6	-0	-2	-0.4
1931	NY-A	11	6	.647	25	25	12	1	0	189¹	247	7	30	65	13.2	4.28	93	.315	.342	10	.152	1	-2	-7	-1	-0.5
1932	*NY-A	9	5	.643	22	21	9	1	0	146²	191	8	38	54	14.1	4.60	89	.310	.350	8	.151	-0	-2	-9	-1	-0.7
1933	NY-A	7	4	.636	23	5	2	1	4	65	96	4	21	22	16.2	5.54	70	.342	.387	5	.238	1	-9	-12	-0	-1.8
1934	Bos-A	2	0	1.000	30	2	0	0	2	62	82	2	16	16	12.2	3.05	158	.276	.321	3	.214	-0	10	12	-1	0.8
Total	22	240	162	.597	617	420	247	35	33	3571²	3900	128	916	1227	12.2	3.60	106	.281	.328	232	.191	3	150	81	-11	6.8

● PAUL PENSON
Penson, Paul Eugene b: 7/12/31, Kansas City, Kan. BR/TR, 6'1", 185 lbs. Deb: 4/21/54

YEAR	TM/L	W	L	PCT	G	GS	CG	SH	SV	IP	H	HR	BB	SO	RAT	ERA	ERA+	OAV	OOB	BH	AVG	PB	PR	/A	PD	TPI
1954	Phi-N	1	1	.500	5	3	0	0	0	16	14	1	14	3	15.8	4.50	90	.237	.384	0	.000	-1	-1	-1	-1	-0.2

● GENE PENTZ
Pentz, Eugene David b: 6/21/53, Johnstown, Pa. BR/TR, 6'1", 200 lbs. Deb: 7/29/75

YEAR	TM/L	W	L	PCT	G	GS	CG	SH	SV	IP	H	HR	BB	SO	RAT	ERA	ERA+	OAV	OOB	BH	AVG	PB	PR	/A	PD	TPI
1975	Det-A	0	4	.000	13	0	0	0	0	25¹	27	4	20	21	16.7	3.20	126	.293	.420	0	—	0	2	2	-0	0.0
1976	Hou-N	3	3	.500	40	0	0	0	5	63²	62	5	31	36	13.3	2.97	108	.259	.347	1	.200	0	4	2	1	0.3

YEAR TM/L	W	L	PCT	G	GS	CG	SH	SV	IP	H	HR	BB	SO	RAT	ERA	ERA+	OAV	OOB	BH	AVG	PB	PR	/A	PD	TPI
1977 Hou-N	5	2	.714	41	4	0	0	2	87	76	8	44	51	12.5	3.83	93	.236	.330	0	.000	-2	1	-3	0	-0.4
1978 Hou-N	0	0	—	10	0	0	0	0	15	12	1	13	8	15.6	6.00	55	.214	.371	0	.000	-0	-4	-1	0	0.1
Total 4	8	9	.471	104	4	0	0	7	191	177	14	108	116	13.6	3.63	96	.250	.351	1	.053	-1	2	-3	1	0.1

● JIMMY PEOPLES
Peoples, James Elsworth b: 10/8/1863, Big Beaver, Mich. d: 8/29/20, Detroit, Mich. TR, 5'8", 200 lbs. Deb: 5/29/1884 U♦

YEAR TM/L	W	L	PCT	G	GS	CG	SH	SV	IP	H	HR	BB	SO	RAT	ERA	ERA+	OAV	OOB	BH	AVG	PB	PR	/A	PD	TPI
1885 Cin-a	0	2	.000	2	2	1	0	0	15	30	0	2	4	21.0	12.00	27	.390	.427	4	.182	-0	-15	-15	1	-1.2

● LAURIN PEPPER
Pepper, Hugh McLaurin b: 1/18/31, Vaughan, Miss. BR/TR, 5'11", 190 lbs. Deb: 7/4/54

YEAR TM/L	W	L	PCT	G	GS	CG	SH	SV	IP	H	HR	BB	SO	RAT	ERA	ERA+	OAV	OOB	BH	AVG	PB	PR	/A	PD	TPI
1954 Pit-N	1	5	.167	14	8	0	0	0	50^2	63	4	43	17	18.8	7.99	52	.315	.436	4	.235	0	-22	-21	1	-1.9
1955 Pit-N	0	1	.000	14	1	0	0	0	20	30	5	25	7	25.6	10.35	40	.370	.528	0	.000	-0	-14	-14	-0	-0.7
1956 Pit-N	1	1	.500	11	7	0	0	0	30	30	1	25	12	16.5	3.00	126	.256	.387	0	.000	-0	3	3	-1	0.0
1957 Pit-N	0	1	.000	5	1	0	0	0	9	11	1	5	4	16.0	8.00	47	.297	.381	0	—	-0	-4	-4	-0	-0.4
Total 4	2	8	.200	44	17	0	0	0	109^2	134	11	98	40	19.2	7.06	57	.308	.437	4	.160	-0	-38	-37	0	-3.0

● BOB PEPPER
Pepper, Robert Ernest b: 5/3/1895, Rosston, Pa. d: 4/8/68, Ford Cliff, Pa. BR/TR, 6'2", 178 lbs. Deb: 7/23/15

YEAR TM/L	W	L	PCT	G	GS	CG	SH	SV	IP	H	HR	BB	SO	RAT	ERA	ERA+	OAV	OOB	BH	AVG	PB	PR	/A	PD	TPI
1915 Phi-A	0	0	—	1	0	0	0	0	5	6	0	4	0	19.8	1.80	163	.333	.478	0	.000	-0	1	1	-0	0.0

● HARRISON PEPPERS
Peppers, Harrison (b: William Harrison Pepper) b: 9/1866, Kentucky d: 11/5/03, Webb City, Mo. BL, Deb: 6/30/1894

YEAR TM/L	W	L	PCT	G	GS	CG	SH	SV	IP	H	HR	BB	SO	RAT	ERA	ERA+	OAV	OOB	BH	AVG	PB	PR	/A	PD	TPI
1894 Lou-N	0	1	.000	2	1	0	0	0	8	10	0	4	0	15.8	6.75	75	.303	.378	0	.000	-1	-1	-1	-0	-0.2

● LUIS PERAZA
Peraza, Luis (Rios) b: 6/17/42, Rio Piedras, P.R. BR/TR, 5'11", 185 lbs. Deb: 4/9/69

YEAR TM/L	W	L	PCT	G	GS	CG	SH	SV	IP	H	HR	BB	SO	RAT	ERA	ERA+	OAV	OOB	BH	AVG	PB	PR	/A	PD	TPI
1969 Phi-N	0	0	—	8	0	0	0	0	9	12	1	2	7	14.0	6.00	59	.364	.400	0	.000	-0	-2	-2	-0	0.0

● OSWALDO PERAZA
Peraza, Oswald Jose b: 10/19/62, Puerto Cabello, Venez. BR/TR, 6'4", 172 lbs. Deb: 4/4/88

YEAR TM/L	W	L	PCT	G	GS	CG	SH	SV	IP	H	HR	BB	SO	RAT	ERA	ERA+	OAV	OOB	BH	AVG	PB	PR	/A	PD	TPI
1988 Bal-A	5	7	.417	19	15	1	0	0	86	98	10	37	61	14.3	5.55	70	.282	.355	0	—	0	-15	-16	0	-1.8

● HUB PERDUE
Perdue, Herbert Rodney "The Gallatin Squash" b: 6/7/1882, Bethpage, Tenn. d: 10/31/68, Gallatin, Tex. BR/TR, 5'10.5", 192 lbs. Deb: 4/19/11

YEAR TM/L	W	L	PCT	G	GS	CG	SH	SV	IP	H	HR	BB	SO	RAT	ERA	ERA+	OAV	OOB	BH	AVG	PB	PR	/A	PD	TPI
1911 Bos-N	6	10	.375	24	19	9	0	1	137^1	180	10	41	40	14.7	4.98	77	.321	.372	10	.208	-1	-24	-18	-0	-1.9
1912 Bos-N	13	16	.448	37	30	20	1	3	249	295	11	54	101	12.7	3.80	94	.303	.341	12	.138	-5	-11	-6	-4	-1.5
1913 Bos-N	16	13	.552	38	32	16	3	1	212^1	201	7	39	91	10.3	3.26	101	.249	.287	7	.104	-5	-1	0	-7	-1.1
1914 Bos-N	2	5	.286	9	9	2	0	0	51	60	5	11	13	13.1	5.82	47	.311	.357	1	.071	-0	-17	-17	0	-2.0
StL-N	8	8	.500	22	19	12	0	1	153^1	160	3	35	43	11.7	2.82	99	.290	.338	8	.167	-1	-0	-0	-4	-0.6
Yr	10	13	.435	31	28	14	0	1	204^1	220	8	46	56	11.9	3.57	78	.295	.340	9	.145	-1	-18	-18	-4	-2.6
1915 StL-N	6	12	.333	31	13	5	1	1	115^1	141	7	19	29	12.6	4.21	66	.311	.341	4	.111	-1	-19	-18	-0	-2.9
Total 5	51	64	.443	161	122	64	5	7	918^1	1037	43	199	317	12.3	3.85	85	.293	.334	42	.140	-13	-73	-60	-15	-10.0

● GEORGE PEREZ
Perez, George Thomas b: 12/29/37, San Fernando, Cal. BR/TR, 6'2.5", 200 lbs. Deb: 4/17/58

YEAR TM/L	W	L	PCT	G	GS	CG	SH	SV	IP	H	HR	BB	SO	RAT	ERA	ERA+	OAV	OOB	BH	AVG	PB	PR	/A	PD	TPI
1958 Pit-N	0	1	.000	4	0	0	0	1	8^1	9	1	4	2	14.0	5.40	72	.300	.382	0	.000	-0	-1	-1	-0	-0.2

● MELIDO PEREZ
Perez, Melido Turpen Gross (b: Melido Turpen Gross (Perez)) b: 2/15/66, San Cristobal, D.R. BR/TR, 6'4", 180 lbs. Deb: 9/4/87 F

YEAR TM/L	W	L	PCT	G	GS	CG	SH	SV	IP	H	HR	BB	SO	RAT	ERA	ERA+	OAV	OOB	BH	AVG	PB	PR	/A	PD	TPI
1987 KC-A	1	1	.500	3	3	0	0	0	10^1	18	2	5	5	20.0	7.84	58	.375	.434	0	—	0	-4	-4	-1	-0.6
1988 Chi-A	12	10	.545	32	32	3	1	0	197	186	26	72	138	11.9	3.79	105	.248	.316	0	—	0	4	4	2	0.2
1989 Chi-A	11	14	.440	31	31	2	0	0	183^1	187	23	90	141	13.7	5.01	76	.264	.350	0	—	0	-23	-25	-1	-3.0
1990 Chi-A	13	14	.481	35	35	3	3	0	197	177	14	86	161	12.1	4.61	83	.241	.322	0	—	0	-16	-17	-2	-2.1
1991 Chi-A	8	7	.533	49	8	0	0	1	135^2	111	15	52	128	10.9	3.12	127	.224	.299	0	—	0	15	13	1	1.5
1992 NY-A	13	16	.448	33	33	10	1	0	247^2	212	16	93	218	11.3	2.87	136	.235	.310	0	—	0	29	29	1	3.2
1993 NY-A	6	14	.300	25	25	0	0	0	163	173	22	64	148	13.1	5.19	80	.267	.334	0	—	0	-16	-19	-1	-1.9
1994 NY-A	9	4	.692	22	22	1	0	0	151^1	134	16	59	109	11.6	4.10	108	.238	.313	0	—	0	12	5	0	0.5
Total 8	73	80	.477	230	189	19	5	1	1285^1	1198	134	520	1048	12.1	4.09	98	.247	.322	0	—	0	2	-13	-6	-2.2

● MIKE PEREZ
Perez, Michael Irvin (Ortega) b: 10/19/64, Yauco, P.R. BR/TR, 6', 185 lbs. Deb: 9/5/90

YEAR TM/L	W	L	PCT	G	GS	CG	SH	SV	IP	H	HR	BB	SO	RAT	ERA	ERA+	OAV	OOB	BH	AVG	PB	PR	/A	PD	TPI
1990 StL-N	1	0	1.000	13	0	0	0	1	13^2	12	0	3	5	9.9	3.95	97	.240	.283	0	.000	-0	-0	-0	0	0.0
1991 StL-N	0	2	.000	14	0	0	0	0	17	19	1	7	7	14.3	5.82	64	.288	.365	0	—	0	-4	-4	-0	-0.5
1992 StL-N	9	3	.750	77	0	0	0	0	93	70	4	32	46	10.0	1.84	184	.210	.281	0	.000	-0	17	16	0	2.0
1993 StL-N	7	2	.778	65	0	0	0	7	72^2	65	4	20	58	10.7	2.48	160	.243	.299	0	—	0	13	12	0	1.7
1994 StL-N	2	3	.400	36	0	0	0	12	31	52	5	10	20	18.9	8.71	47	.391	.445	0	—	0	-15	-16	0	-3.5
Total 5	19	10	.655	205	0	0	0	20	227^1	218	14	72	136	11.7	3.40	109	.257	.319	0	.000	-0	10	8	1	-0.3

● PASCUAL PEREZ
Perez, Pascual Gross (b: Pascual Gross (Perez)) b: 5/17/57, San Cristobal, D.R. BR/TR, 6'2", 163 lbs. Deb: 5/7/80 F

YEAR TM/L	W	L	PCT	G	GS	CG	SH	SV	IP	H	HR	BB	SO	RAT	ERA	ERA+	OAV	OOB	BH	AVG	PB	PR	/A	PD	TPI
1980 Pit-N	0	1	.000	2	2	0	0	0	12	15	0	2	7	14.3	3.75	97	.341	.396	1	.250	0	-0	-0	-0	0.0
1981 Pit-N	2	7	.222	17	13	2	0	0	86^1	92	5	34	46	13.4	3.96	91	.273	.345	3	.136	-0	-5	-4	-0	-0.4
1982 *Atl-N	4	4	.500	16	11	0	0	0	79^1	85	4	17	29	11.6	3.06	122	.276	.314	3	.167	-1	5	6	0	0.7
1983 Atl-N★	15	8	.652	33	33	7	1	0	215^1	213	20	51	144	11.2	3.43	113	.260	.307	12	.160	-1	5	11	1	1.2
1984 Atl-N	14	8	.636	30	30	4	1	0	211^2	208	26	51	145	11.1	3.74	103	.260	.307	5	.076	-2	-4	3	3	0.4
1985 Atl-N	1	13	.071	22	22	0	0	0	95^1	115	10	57	57	16.3	6.14	63	.297	.389	3	.120	-0	-27	-24	-1	-3.2
1987 Mon-N	7	0	1.000	10	10	2	0	0	70^1	52	5	16	58	8.8	2.30	182	.206	.257	1	.042	-0	14	15	1	1.4
1988 Mon-N	12	8	.600	27	27	4	2	0	188	133	15	44	131	**8.8**	2.44	147	.196	**.253**	2	.037	-3	21	24	2	2.5
1989 Mon-N	9	13	.409	33	28	2	0	0	198^1	178	15	45	152	10.3	3.31	107	.237	.283	11	.204	-0	2	4	0	0.8
1990 NY-A	1	2	.333	3	3	0	0	0	14	8	0	3	12	7.1	1.29	309	.163	.212	0	—	0	4	4	-0	0.5
1991 NY-A	2	4	.333	14	14	0	0	0	73^2	72	7	24	41	11.2	3.18	130	.250	.311	0	—	0	8	8	0	0.5
Total 11	67	68	.496	207	193	21	4	0	1244^1	1167	107	344	822	11.1	3.44	110	.249	.303	41	.120	-5	25	47	6	4.8

● YORKIS PEREZ
Perez, Yorkis Miguel Vargas (b: Yorkis Miguel Vargas (Perez)) b: 9/30/67, Bajos De Haina, D.R. BL/TL, 6', 180 lbs. Deb: 9/30/91

YEAR TM/L	W	L	PCT	G	GS	CG	SH	SV	IP	H	HR	BB	SO	RAT	ERA	ERA+	OAV	OOB	BH	AVG	PB	PR	/A	PD	TPI
1991 Chi-N	1	0	1.000	3	0	0	0	0	4^1	2	0	2	3	8.3	2.08	187	.167	.286	0	—	0	1	1	0	0.2
1994 Fla-N	3	0	1.000	44	0	0	0	0	40^2	33	4	14	41	10.6	3.54	127	.220	.291	0	.000	-0	3	4	-1	0.2
Total 2	4	0	1.000	47	0	0	0	0	45	35	4	16	44	10.4	3.40	131	.216	.291	0	.000	-0	4	5	0	0.4

● CECIL PERKINS
Perkins, Cecil Boyce b: 12/1/40, Baltimore, Md. BR/TR, 6', 175 lbs. Deb: 7/5/67

YEAR TM/L	W	L	PCT	G	GS	CG	SH	SV	IP	H	HR	BB	SO	RAT	ERA	ERA+	OAV	OOB	BH	AVG	PB	PR	/A	PD	TPI
1967 NY-A	0	1	.000	2	1	0	0	0	5	7	1	4	1	14.4	9.00	35	.316	.381	0	.000	-0	-3	-3	0	-0.6

● CHARLIE PERKINS
Perkins, Charles Sullivan "Lefty" b: 9/9/05, Ensley, Ala. d: 5/25/88, Salem, Ore. BR/TL, 6'1", 175 lbs. Deb: 5/1/30

YEAR TM/L	W	L	PCT	G	GS	CG	SH	SV	IP	H	HR	BB	SO	RAT	ERA	ERA+	OAV	OOB	BH	AVG	PB	PR	/A	PD	TPI
1930 Phi-A	0	0	—	8	1	0	0	0	23^2	25	0	15	15	15.2	6.46	72	.313	.421	1	.125	-1	-5	-5	-0	-0.1
1934 Bro-N	0	3	.000	11	2	0	0	0	24^1	37	3	14	5	19.6	8.51	46	.336	.421	2	.286	-0	-12	-12	-1	-1.3
Total 2	0	3	.000	19	3	0	0	0	48	62	3	29	20	17.4	7.50	57	.326	.421	3	.200	-0	-17	-17	-1	-1.4

● JOHN PERKOVICH
Perkovich, John Joseph "Perky" b: 3/10/24, Chicago, Ill. BR/TR, 5'11", 170 lbs. Deb: 5/6/50

YEAR TM/L	W	L	PCT	G	GS	CG	SH	SV	IP	H	HR	BB	SO	RAT	ERA	ERA+	OAV	OOB	BH	AVG	PB	PR	/A	PD	TPI
1950 Chi-A	0	0	—	1	0	0	0	0	5	7	3	1	3	14.4	7.20	62	.318	.348	0	.000	-0	-1	-2	-0	-0.1

● HARRY PERKOWSKI
Perkowski, Harry Walter b: 9/6/22, Dante, Va. BL/TL, 6'2.5", 196 lbs. Deb: 9/13/47

YEAR TM/L	W	L	PCT	G	GS	CG	SH	SV	IP	H	HR	BB	SO	RAT	ERA	ERA+	OAV	OOB	BH	AVG	PB	PR	/A	PD	TPI
1947 Cin-N	0	0	—	3	1	0	0	0	7^1	12	1	9	3	18.4	3.68	111	.375	.429	0	.000	-0	0	0	0	0.0
1949 Cin-N	1	1	.500	5	3	2	0	0	23^2	21	2	14	3	13.3	4.56	92	.236	.340	3	.333	1	-1	-1	-1	-0.1
1950 Cin-N	0	0	—	22	0	0	0	0	34^1	36	6	23	19	15.7	5.24	81	.286	.400	7	.318	2	-4	-4	1	0.3
1951 Cin-N	4	5	.333	30	13	3	0	0	102	96	2	56	66	13.2	2.82	144	.253	.352	1	.040	-3	13	14	1	1.0
1952 Cin-N	12	10	.545	33	24	11	1	0	194	197	8	89	86	13.4	3.80	99	.265	.347	12	.160	-0	-5	-4	-0	-0.2
1953 Cin-N	12	11	.522	33	25	6	2	2	193	204	26	62	70	12.5	4.52	69	.271	.327	14	.203	1	-5	-4	-0	-0.2
1954 Cin-N	2	8	.200	28	12	3	1	0	95^2	100	16	62	32	15.3	6.11	69	.276	.384	4	.160	0	-22	-20	-1	-1.9

YEAR TM/L	W	L	PCT	G	GS	CG	SH	SV	IP	H	HR	BB	SO	RAT	ERA	ERA+	OAV	OOB	BH	AVG	PB	PR	/A	PD	TPI
1955 Chi-N	3	4	.429	25	4	0	0	2	47²	53	3	25	28	14.7	5.29	77	.283	.368	2	.154	-0	-7	-6	1	-0.8
Total 8	33	40	.452	184	76	24	4	5	697²	719	65	324	296	13.5	4.37	94	.269	.350	43	.180	1	-27	-21	2	-1.7

● **JON PERLMAN**   Perlman, Jonathan Sarnuel   b: 12/13/56, Dallas, Tex.   BL/TR, 6'3", 185 lbs.   Deb: 9/6/85

YEAR TM/L	W	L	PCT	G	GS	CG	SH	SV	IP	H	HR	BB	SO	RAT	ERA	ERA+	OAV	OOB	BH	AVG	PB	PR	/A	PD	TPI
1985 Chi-N	1	0	1.000	6	0	0	0	0	8²	10	3	8	4	18.7	11.42	35	.313	.450	0	.000	-0	-8	-7	0	-0.7
1987 SF-N	0	0	—	10	0	0	0	0	11¹	11	1	4	13	12.7	3.97	97	.256	.333	0	—	0	0	-0	-0	0.0
1988 Cle-A	0	2	.000	10	0	0	0	0	19²	25	0	11	10	16.5	5.49	75	.309	.391	0	.000	-0	-3	-3	1	-0.3
Total 3	1	2	.333	26	0	0	0	0	39²	46	4	23	17	15.9	6.35	63	.295	.389	0	.000	-0	-11	-10	1	-1.0

● **LEN PERME**   Perme, Leonard John   b: 11/25/17, Cleveland, Ohio   BL/TL, 6', 170 lbs.   Deb: 9/8/42

YEAR TM/L	W	L	PCT	G	GS	CG	SH	SV	IP	H	HR	BB	SO	RAT	ERA	ERA+	OAV	OOB	BH	AVG	PB	PR	/A	PD	TPI
1942 Chi-A	0	1	.000	4	1	1	0	0	13	5	0	4	4	6.9	1.38	260	.119	.213	1	.333	0	3	3	-0	0.2
1946 Chi-A	0	0	—	4	0	0	0	0	4¹	6	0	7	2	27.0	8.31	41	.316	.500	0	—	0	-2	-2	0	-0.1
Total 2	0	1	.000	8	1	1	0	0	17¹	11	0	11	6	11.9	3.12	114	.180	.315	1	.333	0	1	1	0	0.2

● **HUB PERNOLL**   Pernoll, Henry Hubbard   b: 3/14/1888, Grants Pass, Ore.   d: 2/18/44, Grants Pass, Ore.   BR/TL, 5'8", 175 lbs.   Deb: 4/25/10

YEAR TM/L	W	L	PCT	G	GS	CG	SH	SV	IP	H	HR	BB	SO	RAT	ERA	ERA+	OAV	OOB	BH	AVG	PB	PR	/A	PD	TPI
1910 Det-A	4	3	.571	11	5	4	0	0	54²	54	1	14	25	12.0	2.96	89	.270	.333	1	.063	-2	-3	-2	3	-0.1
1912 Det-A	0	0	—	3	0	0	0	0	9	9	0	4	3	13.0	6.00	54	.265	.342	0	.000	-0	-3	-3	0	-0.0
Total 2	4	3	.571	14	5	4	0	0	63²	63	1	18	28	12.2	3.39	80	.269	.335	1	.053	-2	-5	-5	3	-0.1

● **RON PERRANOSKI**   Perranoski, Ronald Peter (b: Ronald Peter Perzanowski)   b: 4/1/36, Paterson, N.J.   BL/TL, 6', 192 lbs.   Deb: 4/14/61   C

YEAR TM/L	W	L	PCT	G	GS	CG	SH	SV	IP	H	HR	BB	SO	RAT	ERA	ERA+	OAV	OOB	BH	AVG	PB	PR	/A	PD	TPI
1961 LA-N	7	5	.583	53	1	0	0	6	91²	82	5	41	56	12.5	2.65	164	.244	.333	1	.083	-0	14	**17**	0	2.3
1962 LA-N	6	6	.500	70	0	0	0	20	107¹	103	1	36	68	11.7	2.85	127	.255	.316	1	.071	-1	13	9	-1	1.2
1963 *LA-N	16	3	**.842**	69	0	0	0	21	129	112	7	43	75	11.1	1.67	180	.231	.299	3	.125	-0	**23**	19	0	3.7
1964 LA-N	5	7	.417	72	0	0	0	14	125¹	128	5	46	79	12.6	3.09	105	.263	.328	2	.105	-0	6	2	2	0.4
1965 *LA-N	6	6	.500	59	0	0	0	17	104²	85	2	40	53	11.0	2.24	146	.226	.305	3	.158	1	15	12	-1	1.7
1966 *LA-N	6	7	.462	55	0	0	0	7	82	82	4	31	50	12.5	3.18	104	.269	.338	2	.250	1	4	1	2	0.5
1967 LA-N	6	7	.462	70	0	0	0	16	110	97	4	45	75	11.9	2.45	126	.240	.320	1	.100	-0	11	8	1	1.3
1968 Min-A	8	7	.533	66	0	0	0	6	87	86	5	38	65	12.8	3.10	100	.252	.327	0	.000	-1	-1	-0	-0	-0.1
1969 *Min-A	9	10	.474	75	0	0	0	31	119²	85	4	52	62	10.4	2.11	173	.205	.295	2	.083	-1	20	**21**	1	**4.4**
1970 *Min-A	7	8	.467	67	0	0	0	34	111	108	7	42	55	12.2	2.43	153	.259	.328	1	.042	-2	16	16	-1	2.9
1971 Min-A	1	4	.200	36	0	0	0	5	42²	60	2	28	21	19.2	6.75	53	.337	.435	0	.000	-0	-16	-15	-0	-2.1
Det-A	0	1	.000	11	0	0	0	2	18	16	2	3	8	10.0	2.50	144	.254	.299	0	.000	-0	2	2	-0	0.1
Yr	1	5	.167	47	0	0	0	7	60²	76	4	31	29	16.5	5.49	65	.309	.388	0	.000	-1	-14	-13	-1	-2.0
1972 Det-A	0	1	.000	17	0	0	0	0	18²	23	2	8	10	15.4	7.71	41	.307	.381	0	.000	-0	-10	-9	-1	-0.6
LA-N	2	0	1.000	9	0	0	0	0	16²	19	0	8	5	14.6	2.70	123	.292	.370	0	.000	-0	1	1	-0	0.1
1973 Cal-A	2	0	2.000	8	0	0	0	0	11	11	0	7	5	15.5	4.09	87	.282	.404	0	—	-0	-0	-1	0	-0.1
Total 13	79	74	.516	737	1	0	0	179	1174²	1097	50	468	687	12.2	2.79	123	.250	.325	16	.096	-4	99	83	2	15.7

● **BILL PERRIN**   Perrin, William Joseph "Lefty"   b: 6/23/10, New Orleans, La.   d: 6/30/74, New Orleans, La.   BR/TL, 5'11", 172 lbs.   Deb: 9/30/34

YEAR TM/L	W	L	PCT	G	GS	CG	SH	SV	IP	H	HR	BB	SO	RAT	ERA	ERA+	OAV	OOB	BH	AVG	PB	PR	/A	PD	TPI
1934 Cle-A	0	1	.000	1	1	0	0	0	5	13	0	2	3	28.8	14.40	32	.520	.571	0	.000	-0	-6	-5	0	-0.7

● **GEORGE PERRING**   Perring, George Wilson   b: 8/13/1884, Sharon, Wis.   d: 8/20/60, Beloit, Wis.   BR/TR, 6', 190 lbs.   Deb: 4/25/08   ♦

YEAR TM/L	W	L	PCT	G	GS	CG	SH	SV	IP	H	HR	BB	SO	RAT	ERA	ERA+	OAV	OOB	BH	AVG	PB	PR	/A	PD	TPI
1914 KC-F	0	0	—	1	0	0	0	0	0²	2	0	1	0	40.5	13.50	21	1.000	1.000	138	.278	-0	-1	-1	-0	0.0

● **POL PERRITT**   Perritt, William Dayton   b: 8/30/1892, Arcadia, La.   d: 10/15/47, Shreveport, La.   BR/TR, 6'2", 168 lbs.   Deb: 9/7/12

YEAR TM/L	W	L	PCT	G	GS	CG	SH	SV	IP	H	HR	BB	SO	RAT	ERA	ERA+	OAV	OOB	BH	AVG	PB	PR	/A	PD	TPI
1912 StL-N	1	1	.500	6	3	1	0	0	31	25	0	10	13	10.2	3.19	107	.243	.310	2	.222	-0	1	1	0	0.0
1913 StL-N	6	14	.300	36	21	8	0	0	175	205	9	64	64	14.2	5.25	62	.300	.367	12	.203	-1	-40	-39	1	-4.0
1914 StL-N	16	13	.552	41	32	18	3	2	286	248	7	93	115	11.2	2.36	118	.245	.318	13	.141	-1	14	14	-3	0.8
1915 NY-N	12	18	.400	35	30	16	4	0	220	226	6	59	91	12.1	2.66	96	.266	.323	11	.162	-1	2	-2	-5	-1.0
1916 NY-N	18	11	.621	40	29	17	5	2	251	243	11	56	115	11.0	2.62	93	.257	.304	7	.084	-4	0	-5	-2	-1.3
1917 *NY-N	17	7	.708	35	26	14	5	1	215	186	3	45	72	10.0	1.88	135	.237	.284	11	.157	-2	20	16	1	1.7
1918 NY-N	18	13	.581	35	31	19	6	0	233	212	5	38	60	9.7	2.74	96	.246	.278	14	.175	-1	1	-3	-3	-0.8
1919 NY-N	1	1	.500	11	3	0	0	1	19	27	0	12	2	19.4	7.11	39	.386	.488	0	.000	-1	-9	-9	-0	-1.0
1920 NY-N	0	0	—	8	0	0	0	2	15	9	0	4	3	7.8	1.80	167	.167	.224	0	.000	-1	2	2	0	0.0
1921 NY-N	2	0	1.000	5	1	0	0	0	11²	17	0	5	7	18.4	3.86	95	.321	.345	0	.000	-0	-1	-1	0	-0.1
Det-A	0	0	1.000	4	2	0	0	0	13	18	0	7	3	18.0	4.85	88	.383	.473	2	.400	0	-1	-1	-0	0.0
Total 10	92	78	.541	256	178	93	23	8	1469²	1416	41	390	543	11.4	2.89	94	.259	.315	72	.151	-13	-10	-28	-11	-5.7

● **GAYLORD PERRY**   Perry, Gaylord Jackson   b: 9/15/38, Williamston, N.C.   BR/TR, 6'4", 215 lbs.   Deb: 4/14/62   FH

YEAR TM/L	W	L	PCT	G	GS	CG	SH	SV	IP	H	HR	BB	SO	RAT	ERA	ERA+	OAV	OOB	BH	AVG	PB	PR	/A	PD	TPI
1962 SF-N	3	1	.750	13	7	1	0	0	43	54	3	14	20	14.2	5.23	73	.310	.362	3	.231	0	-6	-7	-1	-0.6
1963 SF-N	1	6	.143	31	4	0	0	2	76	84	10	29	52	13.6	4.03	79	.279	.346	4	.222	1	-6	-6	-0	-0.6
1964 SF-N	12	11	.522	44	19	5	2	5	206¹	179	16	43	155	9.9	2.75	130	.232	.278	3	.054	-3	18	19	-2	1.6
1965 SF-N	8	12	.400	47	26	6	0	1	195²	194	21	70	170	12.4	4.19	86	.256	.324	10	.156	-0	-14	-13	3	-0.9
1966 SF-N★	21	8	.724	36	35	13	3	0	255²	242	15	40	201	10.1	2.99	123	.247	.280	16	.186	-0	17	19	1	2.1
1967 SF-N	15	17	.469	39	37	18	3	1	293	231	20	84	230	9.8	2.61	126	.214	.274	13	.143	-1	25	22	4	2.7
1968 SF-N	16	15	.516	39	38	19	3	1	291	240	10	59	173	9.4	2.44	120	.222	.265	11	.113	-3	18	16	4	2.0
1969 SF-N	19	14	.576	40	39	26	3	0	325¹	290	23	91	233	10.8	2.49	141	.237	.295	14	.120	-2	40	37	3	3.9
1970 SF-N★	23	13	.639	41	41	23	5	0	328²	292	27	84	214	10.5	3.20	124	.237	.290	14	.117	-4	31	28	5	3.0
1971 *SF-N	16	12	.571	37	37	14	2	0	280	255	20	67	158	10.5	2.76	123	.242	.290	10	.102	-3	22	20	0	1.6
1972 Cle-A★	24	16	.600	41	40	29	5	1	342²	253	17	82	234	9.1	1.92	168	.205	.261	17	.155	-0	**44**	49	2	**7.0**
1973 Cle-A	19	19	.500	41	41	29	7	0	344	315	34	115	238	11.4	3.38	116	.246	.311	0	—	0	17	21	1	2.3
1974 Cle-A★	21	13	.618	37	37	28	4	0	322¹	230	25	99	216	9.4	2.51	**144**	.204	.272	0	—	0	40	**39**	1	4.4
1975 Cle-A	6	9	.400	15	15	10	1	0	121²	120	16	34	85	11.5	3.55	106	.256	.308	0	—	0	3	3	1	0.5
Tex-A	12	8	.600	22	22	15	4	0	184	157	12	36	148	9.6	3.03	124	.227	.268	0	—	0	15	15	-1	1.5
Yr	18	17	.514	37	37	25	5	0	305²	277	28	70	233	10.3	3.24	116	.238	.283	0	—	0	18	18	1	2.0
1976 Tex-A	15	14	.517	32	32	21	2	0	250¹	232	14	52	143	10.2	3.24	120	.247	.287	0	—	0	18	18	0	0.6
1977 Tex-A	15	12	.556	34	34	13	4	0	238	239	21	56	177	11.3	3.37	121	.262	.308	0	—	0	18	19	-1	1.9
1978 SD-N	21	6	**.778**	37	37	5	2	0	260²	241	9	66	154	10.7	2.73	122	.248	.298	8	.092	-3	25	17	0	1.4
1979 SD-N★	12	11	.522	32	32	10	0	0	232²	225	12	67	140	11.4	3.06	115	.257	.313	6	.085	-2	17	12	1	1.1
1980 Tex-A	6	9	.400	24	24	6	2	0	155	159	12	46	107	12.3	3.43	114	.268	.328	0	—	0	10	8	1	1.1
NY-A	4	4	.500	10	8	0	0	0	50²	65	2	18	28	14.9	4.44	88	.320	.378	0	—	0	-2	-3	-0	-0.3
Yr	10	13	.435	34	32	6	2	0	205²	224	14	64	135	12.6	3.68	106	.278	.332	0	—	0	8	5	1	0.9
1981 Atl-N	8	9	.471	23	23	0	0	0	150²	182	9	24	60	12.5	3.94	91	.304	.335	12	.250	3	-8	-6	-1	-0.5
1982 Sea-A	10	12	.455	32	32	6	0	0	216²	245	24	54	116	12.6	4.40	96	.287	.332	0	—	0	-4	-0	0	-0.4
1983 Sea-A	3	10	.231	16	16	2	0	0	102	116	18	23	42	12.5	4.94	86	.286	.329	0	—	0	-10	-7	0	-0.9
KC-A	4	4	.500	14	14	1	1	0	84¹	98	6	26	40	13.3	4.27	95	.292	.344	0	—	0	-2	-2	1	-0.1
Yr	7	14	.333	30	30	3	1	0	186¹	214	24	49	82	12.8	4.64	90	.286	.331	0	—	0	-12	-10	1	-1.0
Total 22	314	265	.542	777	690	303	53	11	5350¹	4938	399	1379	3534	10.8	3.11	117	.245	.297	141	.131	-16	311	305	21	34.4

● **SCOTT PERRY**   Perry, Herbert Scott   b: 4/17/1891, Denison, Tex.   d: 10/27/59, Kansas City, Mo.   BR/TR, 6'1", 195 lbs.   Deb: 5/13/15

YEAR TM/L	W	L	PCT	G	GS	CG	SH	SV	IP	H	HR	BB	SO	RAT	ERA	ERA+	OAV	OOB	BH	AVG	PB	PR	/A	PD	TPI
1915 StL-A	0	0	—	1	1	0	0	0	2	5	0	1	0	31.5	13.50	21	.455	.538	0	—	0	-2	-2	-0	0.0
1916 Chi-N	2	1	.667	4	3	1	0	0	28¹	30	0	3	8	10.5	2.54	115	.291	.311	3	.273	1	1	0	0	0.2
1917 Cin-N	0	0	—	4	1	0	0	0	13¹	17	0	8	4	17.6	6.75	39	.321	.419	0	.000	-1	-6	-6	-0	-0.1
1918 Phi-A	20	19	.513	44	36	30	3	2	332¹	295	1	111	81	11.0	1.98	148	.247	.312	15	.134	-6	30	35	2	3.9
1919 Phi-A	4	17	.190	25	21	12	0	1	183²	193	4	72	38	13.1	3.58	96	.282	.352	8	.136	-3	-7	-3	6	0.1

YEAR	TM/L	W	L	PCT	G	GS	CG	SH	SV	IP	H	HR	BB	SO	RAT	ERA	ERA+	OAV	OOB	BH	AVG	PB	PR	/A	PD	TPI
1920	Phi-A	11	25	.306	42	34	20	1	1	263²	310	14	65	79	13.0	3.62	111	.300	.345	13	.157	-4	5	12	0	1.1
1921	Phi-A	3	6	.333	12	8	5	0	1	70	77	4	24	19	13.1	4.11	108	.288	.349	1	.038	-4	1	3	1	0.0
Total	7	40	68	.370	132	104	69	5	5	893¹	927	23	284	231	12.3	3.07	113	.277	.336	40	.135	-17	21	40	9	5.2

● **JIM PERRY**   Perry, James Evan b: 10/30/35, Williamston, N.C. BB/TR, 6'4", 200 lbs. Deb: 4/23/59 F

YEAR	TM/L	W	L	PCT	G	GS	CG	SH	SV	IP	H	HR	BB	SO	RAT	ERA	ERA+	OAV	OOB	BH	AVG	PB	PR	/A	PD	TPI
1959	Cle-A	12	10	.545	44	13	8	2	4	153	122	10	55	79	10.5	2.65	139	.225	.298	15	.300	3	21	18	-0	2.8
1960	Cle-A	**18**	10	**.643**	41	36	10	**4**	1	261¹	257	35	91	120	12.1	3.62	103	.260	.324	22	.242	3	7	4	0	0.6
1961	Cle-A☆	10	17	.370	35	35	6	1	0	223²	238	28	87	90	13.3	4.71	84	.273	.343	12	.164	-1	-17	-19	-0	-2.1
1962	Cle-A	12	12	.500	35	27	7	3	0	193²	213	21	59	74	12.7	4.14	94	.285	.339	11	.183	0	-4	-6	1	-0.5
1963	Cle-A	0	0	—	5	0	0	0	0	10¹	12	0	2	7	12.2	5.23	69	.293	.326	0	.000	-0	-2	-2	0	0.0
	Min-A	9	9	.500	35	25	5	1	1	168¹	167	17	57	65	12.1	3.74	97	.256	.318	11	.216	3	-2	-2	-1	0.0
	Yr	9	9	.500	40	25	5	1	1	178²	179	17	59	72	12.1	3.83	95	.258	.318	11	.208	3	-4	-4	-1	0.0
1964	Min-A	6	3	.667	42	1	0	0	2	65¹	61	7	23	55	11.7	3.44	104	.245	.311	2	.154	-0	1	1	-0	0.1
1965	*Min-A	12	7	.632	36	19	4	2	0	167²	142	18	47	88	10.3	2.63	135	.232	.290	9	.170	1	15	17	-1	1.9
1966	Min-A	11	7	.611	33	25	8	1	0	184¹	149	17	53	122	10.1	2.54	142	.222	.284	13	.220	4	18	22	-2	2.4
1967	Min-A	8	7	.533	37	11	3	2	0	130²	123	8	50	94	12.1	3.03	114	.255	.328	8	.190	1	3	6	-1	0.7
1968	Min-A	8	6	.571	32	18	3	2	1	139	113	8	26	69	9.3	2.27	136	.219	.263	6	.143	2	11	13	1	1.7
1969	*Min-A	20	6	.769	46	36	12	3	0	261²	244	18	66	153	11.0	2.82	129	.247	.300	16	.172	1	23	24	-2	2.2
1970	*Min-A★	**24**	12	.667	40	40	13	4	0	278²	258	20	57	168	10.5	3.04	123	.243	.287	24	.247	5	21	21	1	3.3
1971	Min-A☆	17	17	.500	40	39	8	0	1	270	263	36	102	126	12.3	4.23	84	.259	.329	17	.185	1	-23	-20	0	-2.3
1972	Min-A	13	16	.448	35	35	5	2	0	217²	191	14	60	85	10.7	3.35	96	.236	.295	11	.155	-1	-7	-3	-1	-0.7
1973	Det-A	14	13	.519	35	34	7	1	0	203	225	22	55	66	12.6	4.03	101	.282	.331	0	—	0	-5	1	-0	0.1
1974	Cle-A	17	12	.586	36	36	8	3	0	252	242	11	64	71	11.1	2.96	122	.254	.304	0	—	0	18	18	-1	2.0
1975	Cle-A	1	6	.143	8	6	0	0	0	37²	46	8	18	11	15.3	6.69	57	.309	.383	0	—	0	-12	-12	0	-1.8
	Oak-A	3	4	.429	15	11	2	1	0	67²	61	7	26	33	12.5	4.66	78	.237	.324	0	—	0	-7	-8	-1	-0.7
	Yr	4	10	.286	23	17	2	1	0	105¹	107	15	44	44	13.5	5.38	68	.264	.346	0	—	0	-19	-20	-1	-2.5
Total	17	215	174	.553	630	447	109	32	10	3285²	3127	308	998	1576	11.5	3.45	106	.252	.312	177	.199	23	61	75	-7	9.7

● **PAT PERRY**   Perry, William Patrick b: 2/4/59, Taylorsville, Ill. BL/TL, 6'1", 170 lbs. Deb: 9/12/85

YEAR	TM/L	W	L	PCT	G	GS	CG	SH	SV	IP	H	HR	BB	SO	RAT	ERA	ERA+	OAV	OOB	BH	AVG	PB	PR	/A	PD	TPI
1985	StL-N	1	0	1.000	6	0	0	0	0	12¹	3	0	3	6	4.4	0.00	—	.077	.143	1	.500	0	5	5	-0	0.4
1986	StL-N	2	3	.400	46	0	0	0	2	68²	59	5	34	29	12.2	3.80	96	.239	.331	0	.000	-1	-1	-1	1	-0.1
1987	StL-N	4	2	.667	45	0	0	0	0	65²	54	7	21	33	10.6	4.39	95	.222	.289	1	.143	-0	-2	-2	0	-0.1
	Cin-N	1	0	1.000	12	0	0	0	1	15¹	6	0	4	6	6.5	0.00	—	.122	.204	0	—	0	7	7	0	0.6
	Yr	5	2	.714	57	0	0	0	1	81	60	7	25	39	9.6	3.56	117	.203	.268	1	.143	-0	5	6	1	0.5
1988	Cin-N	2	2	.500	12	0	0	0	0	20²	21	4	9	11	13.1	5.66	63	.262	.337	0	.000	-0	-5	-0	-0	-0.9
	Chi-N	2	2	.500	35	0	0	0	0	38	40	5	7	24	11.4	3.32	109	.270	.308	1	1.000	1	1	1	-0	0.3
	Yr	4	4	.500	47	0	0	0	0	58²	61	9	16	35	12.0	4.14	87	.264	.315	1	.333	1	-5	-4	-0	-0.6
1989	Chi-N	0	1	.000	19	0	0	0	0	35²	23	2	16	20	9.8	1.77	213	.181	.281	1	.167	-0	7	8	-1	0.2
1990	LA-N	0	0	—	7	0	0	0	0	6²	9	0	5	2	20.3	8.10	45	.310	.429	0	.000	0	-3	-3	-0	0.0
Total	6	12	10	.545	182	0	0	0	6	263	215	23	99	131	10.9	3.46	110	.224	.300	4	.148	-0	8	10	-0	0.4

● **PARSON PERRYMAN**   Perryman, Emmett Key b: 10/24/1888, Everett Springs, Ga. d: 9/12/66, Starke, Fla. BR/TR, 6'4.5", 193 lbs. Deb: 4/14/15

YEAR	TM/L	W	L	PCT	G	GS	CG	SH	SV	IP	H	HR	BB	SO	RAT	ERA	ERA+	OAV	OOB	BH	AVG	PB	PR	/A	PD	TPI
1915	StL-A	2	4	.333	24	3	0	0	0	50¹	52	2	16	19	12.3	3.93	73	.281	.342	0	.000	-1	-6	-6	1	-0.7

● **BILL PERTICA**   Pertica, William Andrew b: 3/5/1897, Santa Barbara, Cal. d: 12/28/67, Los Angeles, Cal. BR/TR, 5'9", 165 lbs. Deb: 8/7/18

YEAR	TM/L	W	L	PCT	G	GS	CG	SH	SV	IP	H	HR	BB	SO	RAT	ERA	ERA+	OAV	OOB	BH	AVG	PB	PR	/A	PD	TPI
1918	Bos-A	0	0	—	1	0	0	0	0	3	3	0	0	1	9.0	3.00	89	.273	.273	0	.000	-0	-0	-0	0	0.0
1921	StL-N	14	6	.583	38	31	15	2	2	208¹	212	9	70	67	12.6	3.37	109	.267	.334	10	.143	-3	10	7	-3	0.1
1922	StL-N	8	8	.500	34	14	2	0	0	117¹	153	5	65	30	17.0	5.91	65	.333	.419	6	.182	-0	-24	-27	1	-2.9
1923	StL-N	0	0	—	1	1	0	0	0	2¹	2	0	3	0	23.1	3.86	101	.250	.500	0	—	0	-0	-0	0	0.0
Total	4	22	18	.550	74	46	17	2	2	331	370	14	138	98	14.2	4.27	87	.291	.367	16	.152	-4	-14	-20	-2	-2.8

● **STAN PERZANOWSKI**   Perzanowski, Stanley b: 8/25/50, East Chicago, Ind. BB/TR, 6'2", 170 lbs. Deb: 6/20/71

YEAR	TM/L	W	L	PCT	G	GS	CG	SH	SV	IP	H	HR	BB	SO	RAT	ERA	ERA+	OAV	OOB	BH	AVG	PB	PR	/A	PD	TPI
1971	Chi-A	0	1	.000	5	0	0	0	1	6	14	1	3	5	25.5	12.00	30	.412	.459	0	.000	-0	-6	-6	-0	-1.0
1974	Chi-A	0	0	—	2	1	0	0	0	2¹	8	1	2	2	38.6	19.29	19	.533	.588	0	—	0	-4	-4	0	-0.1
1975	Tex-A	3	3	.500	12	8	1	0	0	66	59	1	25	26	12.1	3.00	125	.246	.330	0	—	0	6	6	1	0.7
1976	Tex-A	0	0	—	5	0	0	0	0	11²	20	3	4	6	20.1	10.03	36	.385	.448	0	—	0	-8	-8	-0	-0.1
1978	Min-A	2	7	.222	13	7	1	0	0	56²	59	1	26	31	14.1	5.24	73	.276	.365	0	—	0	-9	-9	1	-1.2
Total	5	5	11	.313	37	16	2	0	2	142²	160	7	60	70	14.6	5.11	74	.288	.369	0	.000	-0	-22	-21	2	-1.7

● **JEFF PETEREK**   Peterek, Jeffrey Allen b: 9/22/63, Michigan City, Ind. BR/TR, 6'2", 195 lbs. Deb: 8/14/89

YEAR	TM/L	W	L	PCT	G	GS	CG	SH	SV	IP	H	HR	BB	SO	RAT	ERA	ERA+	OAV	OOB	BH	AVG	PB	PR	/A	PD	TPI
1989	Mil-A	0	2	.000	7	4	0	0	0	31¹	31	3	14	16	12.9	4.02	95	.252	.328	0	—	0	-0	-1	0	0.0

● **GARY PETERS**   Peters, Gary Charles b: 4/21/37, Grove City, Pa. BL/TL, 6'2", 200 lbs. Deb: 9/10/59

YEAR	TM/L	W	L	PCT	G	GS	CG	SH	SV	IP	H	HR	BB	SO	RAT	ERA	ERA+	OAV	OOB	BH	AVG	PB	PR	/A	PD	TPI
1959	Chi-A	0	0	—	2	0	0	0	0	1	2	0	2	1	36.0	0.00	—	.400	.571	0	—	0	0	0	0	0.0
1960	Chi-A	0	0	—	2	0	0	0	0	3¹	4	0	4	4	13.5	2.70	140	.286	.333	0	—	0	0	0	-0	0.0
1961	Chi-A	0	0	—	3	0	0	0	0	10¹	10	0	2	6	10.5	1.74	225	.270	.308	1	.333	-	3	2	1	0.2
1962	Chi-A	0	1	.000	5	0	0	0	0	6¹	8	0	1	4	14.2	5.68	69	.308	.357	0	—	0	-1	-1	0	-0.2
1963	Chi-A	19	8	.704	41	30	13	4	1	243	192	9	68	189	9.9	**2.33**	**150**	.216	.278	21	.259	9	**35**	32	-1	4.5
1964	Chi-A☆	**20**	8	.714	37	36	11	3	0	273²	217	20	104	205	10.8	2.50	138	.219	.297	25	.208	8	34	29	0	3.9
1965	Chi-A	10	12	.455	33	30	11	0	0	176¹	181	19	63	95	12.7	3.62	88	.265	.331	13	.181	2	-3	-8	0	-0.8
1966	Chi-A	12	10	.545	30	27	11	4	0	204²	156	11	45	129	**9.0**	**1.98**	**160**	.212	**.261**	19	.235	6	**33**	27	1	3.9
1967	Chi-A★	16	11	.593	38	36	11	3	0	260	187	15	91	215	10.0	2.28	136	**.199**	.277	21	.212	7	27	24	3	**3.7**
1968	Chi-A	4	13	.235	31	25	6	1	1	162²	146	7	60	110	11.8	3.76	80	.242	.318	15	.208	7	-14	-13	-0	-0.7
1969	Chi-A	10	15	.400	36	32	7	3	0	218²	238	21	78	140	13.2	4.53	85	.283	.347	12	.169	2	-22	-16	-2	-1.7
1970	Bos-A	16	11	.593	34	34	10	4	0	221²	221	20	83	155	12.6	4.06	98	.257	.328	20	.244	6	-9	-2	-1	-0.7
1971	Bos-A	14	11	.560	34	32	9	1	1	214	241	25	70	100	13.3	4.37	84	.288	.347	26	.271	8	-22	-16	-2	-1.2
1972	Bos-A	3	3	.500	33	4	0	0	1	85¹	74	9	35	67	13.9	4.32	74	.289	.360	6	.200	1	-12	-11	-1	-0.7
Total	14	124	103	.546	359	286	79	23	5	2081	1894	157	706	1420	11.5	3.25	106	.243	.311	179	.222	57	50	46	-1	11.1

● **JOHN PETERS**   Peters, John Paul b: 4/8/1850, Louisiana, Mo. d: 1/4/24, St.Louis, Mo. BR/TR, 5'7", 180 lbs. Deb: 5/23/1874 ♦

YEAR	TM/L	W	L	PCT	G	GS	CG	SH	SV	IP	H	HR	BB	SO	RAT	ERA	ERA+	OAV	OOB	BH	AVG	PB	PR	/A	PD	TPI
1876	Chi-N	0	0	—	1	0	0	0	0	1	1	0	1	0	18.0	0.00	—	.250	.400	111	.351	0	0	0	0	0.1

● **RUBE PETERS**   Peters, Oscar Casper b: 3/15/1885, Grantfork, Ill. d: 2/7/65, Pequannock, N.J. BR/TR, 6'1", 195 lbs. Deb: 4/13/12

YEAR	TM/L	W	L	PCT	G	GS	CG	SH	SV	IP	H	HR	BB	SO	RAT	ERA	ERA+	OAV	OOB	BH	AVG	PB	PR	/A	PD	TPI
1912	Chi-A	5	6	.455	28	11	4	0	0	108²	134	2	33	39	14.3	4.14	77	.309	.366	6	.194	-1	-10	-11	4	-0.6
1914	Bro-F	2	2	.500	11	3	1	0	0	37²	52	1	16	13	16.2	3.82	75	.335	.398	1	.091	-1	-4	-4	0	-0.5
Total	2	7	8	.467	39	14	5	0	0	146¹	186	3	49	52	14.8	4.06	77	.316	.374	7	.167	-1	-14	-15	4	-1.1

● **RAY PETERS**   Peters, Raymond James b: 8/27/46, Buffalo, N.Y. BR/TR, 6'5.5", 210 lbs. Deb: 6/4/70

YEAR	TM/L	W	L	PCT	G	GS	CG	SH	SV	IP	H	HR	BB	SO	RAT	ERA	ERA+	OAV	OOB	BH	AVG	PB	PR	/A	PD	TPI
1970	Mil-A	0	2	.000	2	2	0	0	0	2	7	0	5	1	54.0	31.50	12	.583	.706	0	—	0	-6	-6	0	-2.8

● **STEVE PETERS**   Peters, Steven Bradley b: 11/14/62, Oklahoma City, Okla BL/TL, 5'10", 170 lbs. Deb: 8/11/87

YEAR	TM/L	W	L	PCT	G	GS	CG	SH	SV	IP	H	HR	BB	SO	RAT	ERA	ERA+	OAV	OOB	BH	AVG	PB	PR	/A	PD	TPI
1987	StL-N	0	0	—	12	0	0	0	1	15	11	2	11	8	13.8	1.80	231	.298	.365	0	.000	-0	4	4	1	0.1
1988	StL-N	3	3	.500	44	0	0	0	0	45	57	7	17	30	15.8	6.40	54	.313	.387	0	.000	-0	-15	-15	-1	-1.9
Total	2	3	3	.500	56	0	0	0	1	60	74	9	28	41	15.3	5.25	69	.310	.382	0	.000	-1	-11	-11	0	-1.8

YEAR TM/L	W	L	PCT	G	GS	CG	SH	SV	IP	H	HR	BB	SO	RAT	ERA	ERA+	OAV	OOB	BH	AVG	PB	PR	/A	PD	TPI

● ADAM PETERSON
Peterson, Adam Charles b: 12/11/65, Long Beach, Cal. BR/TR, 6'3", 190 lbs. Deb: 9/19/87

YEAR TM/L	W	L	PCT	G	GS	CG	SH	SV	IP	H	HR	BB	SO	RAT	ERA	ERA+	OAV	OOB	BH	AVG	PB	PR	/A	PD	TPI
1987 Chi-A	0	0	—	1	1	0	0	0	4	8	1	3	1	24.8	13.50	34	.444	.524	0	—	0	-4	-4	-0	-0.1
1988 Chi-A	0	1	.000	2	2	0	0	0	6	6	0	6	5	18.0	13.50	29	.240	.387	0	—	0	-6	-6	-0	-0.8
1989 Chi-A	0	1	.000	3	2	0	0	0	5¹	13	1	2	3	25.3	15.19	25	.464	.500	0	—	0	-7	-7	-0	-1.0
1990 Chi-A	2	5	.286	20	11	2	0	0	85	90	12	26	29	12.5	4.55	84	.278	.335	0	—	0	-6	-7	-1	-0.5
1991 SD-N	3	4	.429	13	11	0	0	0	54²	50	10	28	37	12.8	4.45	85	.242	.332	0	.000	-1	-5	-4	-0	-0.6
Total 5	5	11	.313	39	27	2	0	0	155	167	24	65	75	13.6	5.46	70	.277	.350	0	.000	-1	-28	-28	-2	-3.0

● FRITZ PETERSON
Peterson, Fritz Fred (b: Fred Ingels Peterson) b: 2/8/42, Chicago, Ill. BB/TL, 6', 200 lbs. Deb: 4/15/66

YEAR TM/L	W	L	PCT	G	GS	CG	SH	SV	IP	H	HR	BB	SO	RAT	ERA	ERA+	OAV	OOB	BH	AVG	PB	PR	/A	PD	TPI
1966 NY-A	12	11	.522	34	32	11	2	0	215	196	15	40	96	10.0	3.31	101	.241	.279	15	.224	4	3	0	-0	0.4
1967 NY-A	8	14	.364	36	30	6	1	0	181¹	179	11	43	102	11.2	3.47	90	.256	.302	7	.146	1	-5	-7	1	-0.6
1968 NY-A	12	11	.522	36	27	6	2	0	212¹	187	13	29	115	9.3	2.63	110	.241	.272	5	.079	-2	8	6	4	1.0
1969 NY-A	17	16	.515	37	37	16	4	0	272	228	15	43	150	9.1	2.55	136	.229	.263	9	.112	-0	32	28	2	3.7
1970 NY-A★	20	11	.645	39	37	8	2	0	260¹	247	24	40	127	10.0	2.90	121	.248	.280	20	.222	5	23	18	2	2.9
1971 NY-A	15	13	.536	37	35	16	4	1	274	269	25	42	139	10.3	3.05	106	.258	.289	7	.082	-3	12	5	2	0.4
1972 NY-A	17	15	.531	35	35	12	3	0	250¹	270	17	44	100	11.5	3.24	91	.276	.310	19	.232	4	-5	-8	1	-0.5
1973 NY-A	8	15	.348	31	31	6	0	0	184¹	207	18	49	59	12.8	3.95	93	.286	.337	0	—	0	-3	-6	-0	-0.7
1974 NY-A	0	0	—	3	1	0	0	0	7²	13	1	2	5	17.6	4.70	74	.361	.395	0	—	0	-1	-1	-0	0.2
Cle-A	9	14	.391	29	29	3	0	0	152²	187	16	37	52	13.4	4.36	83	.305	.349	0	—	0	-13	-13	1	-1.6
Yr	9	14	.391	32	30	3	0	0	160¹	200	17	39	57	13.6	4.38	82	.308	.351	0	—	0	-14	-14	1	-1.4
1975 Cle-A	14	8	.636	25	25	6	2	0	146¹	154	15	40	47	12.3	3.94	96	.275	.331	0	—	0	-3	-3	-1	-0.3
1976 Cle-A	0	3	.000	9	9	0	0	0	47	59	3	10	19	13.2	5.55	63	.309	.343	0	—	0	-11	-11	-0	-0.6
Tex-A	1	0	1.000	4	2	0	0	0	15	21	0	7	4	16.8	3.60	100	.344	.412	0	—	0	-0	-0	0	-0.1
Yr	1	3	.250	13	11	0	0	0	62	80	3	17	23	14.1	5.08	69	.316	.359	0	—	0	-11	-11	0	-0.7
Total 11	133	131	.504	355	330	90	20	1	2218¹	2217	173	426	1015	10.9	3.30	101	.261	.300	82	.159	8	40	10	15	4.2

● JIM PETERSON
Peterson, James Niels b: 8/18/08, Philadelphia, Pa. d: 4/8/75, Palm Beach, Fla. BR/TR, 6'0.5", 200 lbs. Deb: 7/9/31

YEAR TM/L	W	L	PCT	G	GS	CG	SH	SV	IP	H	HR	BB	SO	RAT	ERA	ERA+	OAV	OOB	BH	AVG	PB	PR	/A	PD	TPI
1931 Phi-A	0	1	.000	6	1	1	0	0	13	18	0	4	7	15.2	6.23	72	.321	.367	1	.500	1	-3	-3	-0	-0.1
1933 Phi-A	2	5	.286	32	5	0	0	0	90²	114	6	36	18	14.9	4.96	86	.305	.366	4	.148	-1	-7	-7	2	-0.3
1937 Bro-N	0	0	—	3	0	0	0	0	5²	8	3	2	1	15.9	7.94	51	.333	.385	0	—	0	-3	-2	1	0.1
Total 3	2	6	.250	41	6	1	0	0	109¹	140	9	42	26	15.0	5.27	82	.308	.367	5	.172	0	-12	-12	3	-0.3

● KENT PETERSON
Peterson, Kent Franklin "Pete" b: 12/21/25, Goshen, Utah BR/TL, 5'10", 175 lbs. Deb: 7/15/44

YEAR TM/L	W	L	PCT	G	GS	CG	SH	SV	IP	H	HR	BB	SO	RAT	ERA	ERA+	OAV	OOB	BH	AVG	PB	PR	/A	PD	TPI
1944 Cin-N	0	0	—	1	0	0	0	0	1	0	0	0	0	0.0	0.00	—	.000	.000	0	—	0	0	0	-0	0.0
1947 Cin-N	6	13	.316	37	17	3	1	2	152¹	156	8	62	78	13.1	4.25	96	.265	.338	3	.068	-3	-3	-3	-2	-0.8
1948 Cin-N	2	15	.118	43	17	2	0	1	137	146	10	59	64	13.9	4.60	85	.271	.350	5	.139	-2	-10	-10	0	-1.3
1949 Cin-N	4	5	.444	30	7	2	0	0	66¹	66	8	46	28	15.7	6.24	67	.261	.383	1	.056	-2	-16	-15	-1	-2.0
1950 Cin-N	0	3	.000	9	2	0	0	0	20	25	4	17	6	18.9	7.20	59	.305	.424	1	.333	0	-7	-7	-1	-0.9
1951 Cin-N	1	1	.500	9	0	0	0	0	9²	13	0	8	5	20.5	6.52	63	.317	.440	0	.000	-0	-3	-3	-0	-0.5
1952 Phi-N	0	0	—	3	0	0	0	2	7	2	0	2	7	5.1	0.00	—	.091	.167	0	.000	0	3	3	-0	0.2
1953 Phi-N	0	1	.000	15	0	0	0	0	27	26	3	21	20	16.0	6.67	63	.252	.384	0	.000	-1	-7	-7	-0	-0.3
Total 8	13	38	.255	147	43	7	1	5	420¹	434	33	215	208	14.2	4.95	82	.266	.357	10	.091	-8	-43	-42	-4	-5.6

● SID PETERSON
Peterson, Sidney Herbert b: 1/31/18, Havelock, N.Dak. BR/TR, 6'3", 200 lbs. Deb: 5/4/43

YEAR TM/L	W	L	PCT	G	GS	CG	SH	SV	IP	H	HR	BB	SO	RAT	ERA	ERA+	OAV	OOB	BH	AVG	PB	PR	/A	PD	TPI
1943 StL-A	2	0	1.000	3	0	0	0	0	10	15	0	3	0	17.1	2.70	123	.341	.396	0	.000	-0	1	1	-0	0.1

● MARK PETKOVSEK
Petkovsek, Mark Joseph b: 11/18/65, Beaumont, Tex. BR/TR, 6', 185 lbs. Deb: 6/8/91

YEAR TM/L	W	L	PCT	G	GS	CG	SH	SV	IP	H	HR	BB	SO	RAT	ERA	ERA+	OAV	OOB	BH	AVG	PB	PR	/A	PD	TPI
1991 Tex-A	0	1	.000	4	1	0	0	0	9¹	21	4	4	6	24.1	14.46	28	.438	.481	0	—	0	-11	-11	-0	-0.9
1993 Pit-N	3	0	1.000	26	0	0	0	0	32¹	43	7	9	14	14.5	6.96	58	.328	.371	0	—	0	-10	-10	1	-0.8
Total 2	3	1	.750	30	1	0	0	0	41²	64	11	13	20	16.6	8.64	47	.358	.401	0	—	0	-21	-21	1	-1.7

● DAN PETRY
Petry, Daniel Joseph b: 11/13/58, Palo Alto, Cal. BR/TR, 6'4", 200 lbs. Deb: 7/8/79

YEAR TM/L	W	L	PCT	G	GS	CG	SH	SV	IP	H	HR	BB	SO	RAT	ERA	ERA+	OAV	OOB	BH	AVG	PB	PR	/A	PD	TPI
1979 Det-A	6	5	.545	15	15	2	0	0	98	90	11	33	43	11.7	3.95	110	.254	.325	0	—	0	3	4	-1	0.3
1980 Det-A	10	9	.526	27	25	4	3	0	164²	156	9	83	88	13.1	3.94	104	.253	.342	0	—	0	2	3	2	0.4
1981 Det-A	10	9	.526	23	22	7	2	0	141	115	15	57	79	11.0	3.00	126	.224	.302	0	—	0	10	12	2	1.7
1982 Det-A	15	9	.625	35	35	8	1	0	246	220	15	100	132	11.9	3.22	126	.241	.319	0	—	0	23	23	4	2.6
1983 Det-A	19	11	.633	38	38	9	2	0	266¹	256	37	99	122	12.2	3.92	100	.256	.327	0	—	0	4	-0	3	0.3
1984 *Det-L	18	8	.692	35	35	7	2	0	233¹	231	21	66	144	11.6	3.24	121	.259	.312	0	—	0	19	18	3	2.2
1985 Det-A★	15	13	.536	34	34	8	0	0	238²	190	24	81	109	10.3	3.36	121	.217	.285	0	—	0	21	19	0	2.1
1986 Det-A	5	10	.333	20	20	2	0	0	116	122	15	53	56	14.0	4.66	89	.268	.350	0	—	0	-6	-7	1	-0.7
1987 *Det-A	9	7	.563	30	21	0	0	0	134²	148	22	76	93	15.6	5.61	75	.279	.379	0	—	0	-17	-21	1	-1.8
1988 Cal-A	3	9	.250	22	22	4	1	0	139²	139	16	59	64	13.1	4.38	88	.263	.344	0	—	0	-6	-8	2	-0.3
1989 Cal-A	3	2	.600	19	4	0	0	0	51	53	8	23	21	13.6	5.47	70	.275	.355	0	—	0	-9	-9	0	-0.8
1990 Det-A	10	9	.526	32	23	0	0	0	149²	148	14	77	73	13.6	4.45	89	.263	.353	0	—	0	-9	-8	2	-0.8
1991 Det-A	2	3	.400	17	6	0	0	0	54²	66	9	19	18	14.0	4.94	84	.300	.356	0	—	0	-5	-5	2	-0.3
Atl-N	0	0	—	10	0	0	0	0	24¹	29	2	14	9	16.3	5.55	70	.296	.389	1	.200	0	-5	-4	0	0.0
Bos-A	0	0	—	13	0	0	0	1	21	21	3	12	12	13.7	4.43	97	.263	.351	0	—	0	-1	-0	0	-0.1
Total 13	125	104	.546	370	300	52	11	1	2080¹	1984	218	852	1063	12.5	3.95	102	.253	.330	1	.200	0	24	16	22	4.8

● JAY PETTIBONE
Pettibone, Harry Jonathan b: 6/21/57, Mt.Clemens, Mich. BR/TR, 6'4", 182 lbs. Deb: 9/11/83

YEAR TM/L	W	L	PCT	G	GS	CG	SH	SV	IP	H	HR	BB	SO	RAT	ERA	ERA+	OAV	OOB	BH	AVG	PB	PR	/A	PD	TPI
1983 Min-A	0	4	.000	4	4	1	0	0	27	28	8	8	10	12.7	5.33	80	.280	.345	0	—	0	-4	-3	0	-0.4

● PAUL PETTIT
Pettit, George William Paul "Lefty" b: 11/29/31, Los Angeles, Cal. BL/TL, 6'2", 195 lbs. Deb: 5/4/51

YEAR TM/L	W	L	PCT	G	GS	CG	SH	SV	IP	H	HR	BB	SO	RAT	ERA	ERA+	OAV	OOB	BH	AVG	PB	PR	/A	PD	TPI
1951 Pit-N	0	0	—	2	0	0	0	0	2²	2	1	1	0	10.1	3.38	125	.200	.273	0	.000	-0	0	0	-0	0.0
1953 Pit-N	1	2	.333	10	5	0	0	0	28	33	1	20	14	17.0	7.71	58	.297	.405	2	.250	1	-11	-10	0	-0.8
Total 2	1	2	.333	12	5	0	0	0	30²	35	2	21	14	16.4	7.34	61	.289	.394	2	.222	1	-10	-10	0	-0.8

● LEON PETTIT
Pettit, Leon Arthur "Lefty" b: 6/23/02, Waynesburg, Pa. d: 11/21/74, Columbia, Tenn. BL/TL, 5'10.5", 165 lbs. Deb: 4/18/35

YEAR TM/L	W	L	PCT	G	GS	CG	SH	SV	IP	H	HR	BB	SO	RAT	ERA	ERA+	OAV	OOB	BH	AVG	PB	PR	/A	PD	TPI
1935 Was-A	8	5	.615	41	7	1	0	3	109	129	6	58	45	15.8	4.95	87	.301	.390	2	.080	-0	-6	-6	-0	-0.8
1937 Phi-N	0	1	.000	3	1	0	0	0	4	6	1	4	0	22.5	11.25	39	.353	.476	0	—	0	-3	-3	0	-0.6
Total 2	8	6	.571	44	8	1	0	3	113	135	7	62	45	16.0	5.18	84	.303	.393	2	.080	-0	-9	-11	-0	-1.4

● BOB PETTIT
Pettit, Robert Henry b: 7/19/1861, Williamstown, Mass. d: 11/1/10, Derby, Conn. BL/TR, 5'9", 160 lbs. Deb: 9/3/1887 ♦

YEAR TM/L	W	L	PCT	G	GS	CG	SH	SV	IP	H	HR	BB	SO	RAT	ERA	ERA+	OAV	OOB	BH	AVG	PB	PR	/A	PD	TPI
1887 Chi-N	0	0	—	1	0	0	0	1	1	3	0	2	0	45.0	0.00	—	.375	.500	36	.261	0	0	0	0	0.1

● CHARLIE PETTY
Petty, Charles E. b: 6/28/1866, Nashville, Tenn. TR, Deb: 7/30/1889

YEAR TM/L	W	L	PCT	G	GS	CG	SH	SV	IP	H	HR	BB	SO	RAT	ERA	ERA+	OAV	OOB	BH	AVG	PB	PR	/A	PD	TPI
1889 Cin-a	2	3	.400	5	5	5	0	0	44	44	3	20	10	14.3	5.52	71	.252	.349	6	.300	1	-8	-8	0	-0.6
1893 NY-N	5	2	.714	9	6	4	0	0	54	66	3	28	12	15.8	3.33	140	.292	.373	7	.318	3	8	8	-0	1.0
1894 Was-N	3	8	.273	16	12	8	0	0	103	156	4	32	14	17.2	5.59	94	.345	.399	8	.195	-2	-3	-4	-1	-0.5
Cle-N	0	2	.000	4	3	2	0	0	27	42	4	14	4	19.7	8.67	63	.351	.431	1	.083	-2	-10	-10	-1	-0.7
Yr	3	10	.231	20	15	10	0	0	130	198	8	46	18	17.1	6.23	85	.341	.392	9	.170	-4	-13	-13	-1	-1.2
Total 3	10	15	.400	34	26	19	0	0	228	308	11	94	40	16.6	5.41	90	.317	.388	22	.232	-0	-13	-13	-2	-0.8

● JESSE PETTY
Petty, Jesse Lee "The Silver Fox" b: 11/23/1894, Orr, Okla. d: 10/23/71, St.Paul, Minn. BR/TL, 6', 195 lbs. Deb: 4/14/21

YEAR TM/L	W	L	PCT	G	GS	CG	SH	SV	IP	H	HR	BB	SO	RAT	ERA	ERA+	OAV	OOB	BH	AVG	PB	PR	/A	PD	TPI
1921 Cle-A	0	0	—	4	0	0	0	0	9	10	0	4	0	10.0	2.00	213	.345	.345	0	.000	-0	2	2	1	0.0

YEAR	TM/L	W	L	PCT	G	GS	CG	SH	SV	IP	H	HR	BB	SO	RAT	ERA	ERA+	OAV	OOB	BH	AVG	PB	PR	/A	PD	TPI
1925	Bro-N	9	9	.500	28	22	7	0	0	153	188	15	47	39	13.9	-4.88	86	.304	.355	7	.140	-3	-10	-12	-2	-1.5
1926	Bro-N	17	17	.500	38	33	23	1	1	275²	246	9	79	101	10.7	2.84	135	.240	.296	17	.175	-3	30	30	-4	2.7
1927	Bro-N	13	18	.419	42	33	19	2	1	271²	263	13	53	101	10.6	2.98	133	.254	.293	9	.099	-7	28	30	-3	2.1
1928	Bro-N	15	15	.500	40	31	15	2	1	234	264	18	56	74	12.5	4.04	98	.289	.334	9	.111	-5	-1	-2	-4	-1.1
1929	Pit-N	11	10	.524	36	25	12	1	0	184¹	197	12	42	58	11.7	3.71	129	.277	.317	7	.104	-5	21	22	-2	1.4
1930	Pit-N	1	6	.143	10	7	0	0	0	41¹	67	8	13	16	17.9	8.27	60	.362	.410	1	.083	-0	-15	-15	-0	-2.0
	Chi-N	1	3	.250	9	3	0	0	0	39¹	51	4	6	18	13.0	2.97	164	.317	.341	3	.231	0	9	8	-0	0.7
	Yr	2	9	.182	19	10	0	0	1	80²	118	12	19	34	15.3	5.69	87	.339	.373	4	.160	-1	-6	-7	-0	-1.3
Total	7	67	78	.462	207	154	76	6	4	1208¹	1286	77	296	407	11.9	3.68	113	.275	.320	53	.128	-25	63	63	-14	2.3

● PRETZEL PEZZULLO
Pezzullo, John b: 12/10/10, Bridgeport, Conn. d: 5/16/90, Dallas, Tex. BL/TL, 5'11.5", 180 lbs. Deb: 4/18/35

YEAR	TM/L	W	L	PCT	G	GS	CG	SH	SV	IP	H	HR	BB	SO	RAT	ERA	ERA+	OAV	OOB	BH	AVG	PB	PR	/A	PD	TPI
1935	Phi-N	3	5	.375	41	7	2	0	1	84¹	115	5	45	24	17.8	6.40	71	.321	.407	6	.250	0	-22	-18	-2	-1.6
1936	Phi-N	0	0	—	1	0	0	0	0	2	1	0	6	0	31.5	4.50	101	.167	.583	0	—	0	-0	0	-0	0.0
Total	2	3	5	.375	42	7	2	0	1	86¹	116	5	51	24	18.1	6.36	71	.319	.412	6	.250	0	-22	-18	-2	-1.6

● BILL PFANN
Pfann, William F. b: 6/1863, Hamilton, Ont., Can. d: 6/3/04, Hamilton, Ont.Can. 6', 205 lbs. Deb: 6/16/1894

YEAR	TM/L	W	L	PCT	G	GS	CG	SH	SV	IP	H	HR	BB	SO	RAT	ERA	ERA+	OAV	OOB	BH	AVG	PB	PR	/A	PD	TPI
1894	Cin-N	0	1	.000	1	1	0	0	0	3	10	1	4	0	42.0	27.00	21	.537	.618	0	.000	-0	-7	-7	0	-1.1

● JEFF PFEFFER
Pfeffer, Edward Joseph b: 3/4/1888, Seymour, Ill. d: 8/15/72, Chicago, Ill. BR/TR, 6'3", 210 lbs. Deb: 4/16/11 F

YEAR	TM/L	W	L	PCT	G	GS	CG	SH	SV	IP	H	HR	BB	SO	RAT	ERA	ERA+	OAV	OOB	BH	AVG	PB	PR	/A	PD	TPI
1911	StL-A	0	0	—	2	0	0	0	0	10	11	0	4	4	13.5	7.20	47	.297	.366	0	.000	-1	-4	-4	-0	-0.1
1913	Bro-N	0	1	.000	5	2	1	0	0	24¹	28	0	13	13	16.6	3.33	99	.311	.421	0	.000	-1	-0	-0	-0	-0.1
1914	Bro-N	23	12	.657	43	34	27	3	4	315	264	9	91	135	10.3	1.97	145	.232	.293	23	.198	-1	29	31	-4	3.1
1915	Bro-N	19	14	.576	40	34	26	6	3	291²	243	8	76	84	10.4	2.10	132	.231	.293	27	.255	5	21	22	-4	2.6
1916	*Bro-N	25	11	.694	41	36	30	6	1	328²	274	5	63	128	9.7	1.92	140	.230	.278	34	.279	7	26	28	-5	3.6
1917	Bro-N	11	15	.423	30	30	24	3	0	266	225	4	66	115	10.4	2.23	125	.234	.294	13	.130	-4	14	17	-2	0.9
1918	Bro-N	1	0	1.000	1	1	1	1	0	9	2	0	3	1	5.0	0.00	—	.071	.161	1	.250	-0	3	3	0	0.5
1919	Bro-N	17	13	.567	30	30	26	4	0	267	270	7	49	92	11.2	2.66	112	.267	.308	20	.206	1	7	9	1	1.2
1920	*Bro-N	16	9	.640	30	28	20	2	0	215	225	5	45	80	11.5	3.01	106	.273	.314	18	.243	1	3	5	-3	0.3
1921	Bro-N	1	5	.167	6	5	2	0	0	31²	36	0	9	8	13.1	4.55	86	.310	.365	0	.000	-2	-3	-2	0	-0.5
	StL-N	9	3	.750	18	13	7	1	0	98²	115	3	28	22	13.5	4.29	86	.305	.361	4	.138	-1	-6	-7	-2	-0.9
	Yr	10	8	.556	24	18	9	1	0	130¹	151	3	37	30	13.3	4.35	86	.306	.360	4	.100	-2	-8	-9	-1	-1.4
1922	StL-N	19	12	.613	44	32	19	1	2	261¹	286	12	58	83	12.2	3.58	108	.279	.324	24	.245	4	15	8	1	1.3
1923	StL-N	8	9	.471	26	18	7	1	0	152¹	171	8	40	53	13.0	4.02	97	.287	.341	7	.127	-4	-0	-2	-1	-0.7
1924	StL-N	4	5	.444	16	12	3	0	0	78	102	3	30	20	15.3	5.31	71	.318	.378	3	.115	-2	-12	-13	-1	-1.6
	Pit-N	5	3	.625	15	4	1	0	0	58²	68	3	17	19	13.0	3.07	125	.293	.341	6	.240	-0	5	5	-1	0.5
	Yr	9	8	.529	31	16	4	0	0	136²	170	6	47	39	14.3	4.35	88	.307	.361	9	.176	-3	-7	-8	-2	-1.1
Total	13	158	112	.585	347	279	194	28	10	2407¹	2320	67	592	836	11.3	2.77	114	.258	.311	180	.206	-4	97	103	-21	10.1

● BIG JEFF PFEFFER
Pfeffer, Francis Xavier b: 3/31/1882, Champaign, Ill. d: 12/19/54, Kankakee, Ill. BR/TR, 6'1", 185 lbs. Deb: 4/15/05 F

YEAR	TM/L	W	L	PCT	G	GS	CG	SH	SV	IP	H	HR	BB	SO	RAT	ERA	ERA+	OAV	OOB	BH	AVG	PB	PR	/A	PD	TPI
1905	Chi-N	4	4	.500	15	11	9	0	0	101	84	2	36	56	11.0	2.50	120	.240	.318	8	.200	1	6	5	-1	0.4
1906	Bos-N	13	22	.371	35	35	33	4	0	302¹	270	4	114	158	11.9	2.95	91	.246	.325	31	.196	3	-11	-9	2	-0.3
1907	Bos-N	6	8	.429	19	16	12	1	0	144	129	3	61	65	12.3	3.00	85	.253	.341	15	.50	3	-8	-7	-0	-0.4
1908	Bos-N	0	0	—	4	0	0	0	0	10	18	1	8	3	23.4	12.60	19	.383	.473	0	.000	-0	-11	-11	-0	-0.1
1910	Chi-N	1	0	1.000	13	1	1	0	0	41¹	43	1	16	11	13.1	3.27	88	.281	.353	3	.176	1	-1	-2	-1	0.0
1911	Bos-N	7	5	.583	26	6	4	1	2	97	116	3	57	24	16.1	4.73	81	.301	.391	9	.196	1	-14	-10	-0	-1.0
Total	6	31	39	.443	112	69	59	6	2	695²	660	14	292	317	12.7	3.30	87	.260	.342	66	.204	8	-40	-34	-0	-1.4

● FRED PFEFFER
Pfeffer, Nathaniel Frederick "Fritz" or "Dandelion" b: 3/17/1860, Louisville, Ky. d: 4/10/32, Chicago, Ill. BR/TR, 5'10.5", 184 lbs. Deb: 5/1/1882 M♦

YEAR	TM/L	W	L	PCT	G	GS	CG	SH	SV	IP	H	HR	BB	SO	RAT	ERA	ERA+	OAV	OOB	BH	AVG	PB	PR	/A	PD	TPI
1884	Chi-N	0	0	—	1	0	0	0	0	1	3	0	1	0	36.0	9.00	35	.333	.400	135	.289	0	-1	-1	0	0.0
1885	*Chi-N	2	1	.667	5	2	2	0	2	31²	26	1	8	13	9.7	2.56	119	.222	.272	113	.241	1	1	2	-1	0.2
1892	Lou-N	0	0	—	1	0	0	0	0	5	4	0	5	0	16.2	1.80	170	.211	.375	121	.257	0	1	1	0	0.0
1894	Lou-N	0	0	—	1	0	0	0	0	7	8	0	6	0	19.3	2.57	198	.284	.427	126	.308	0	2	2	-0	0.0
Total	4	2	1	.667	8	2	2	0	2	44²	41	1	20	13	12.5	2.62	130	.237	.319	1671	.255	1	3	4	-1	0.2

● JACK PFIESTER
Pfiester, John Albert "Jack The Giant Killer" (b: John Albert Hagenbush) b: 5/24/1878, Cincinnati, Ohio d: 9/3/53, Loveland, Ohio BR/TL, 5'11", 180 lbs. Deb: 9/8/03

YEAR	TM/L	W	L	PCT	G	GS	CG	SH	SV	IP	H	HR	BB	SO	RAT	ERA	ERA+	OAV	OOB	BH	AVG	PB	PR	/A	PD	TPI
1903	Pit-N	0	3	.000	3	3	1	0	0	19	26	0	10	15	18.0	6.16	53	.321	.409	0	.000	-1	-6	-6	-0	-0.8
1904	Pit-N	1	1	.500	3	2	1	0	0	20	24	0	9	6	16.6	7.20	38	.318	.381	2	.286	1	-10	-10	-0	-0.7
1906	*Chi-N	20	8	.714	31	29	20	4	0	250²	173	3	63	153	8.9	1.51	175	.194	.258	4	.048	-7	31	32	-1	2.8
1907	*Chi-N	14	9	.609	30	22	13	3	0	195	143	1	48	90	9.0	**1.15**	**216**	.207	.263	6	.094	-3	29	29	-2	3.1
1908	*Chi-N	12	10	.545	33	29	18	3	0	252	204	1	70	117	10.2	2.00	118	.223	.287	8	.101	-4	10	10	-3	0.1
1909	Chi-N	17	6	.739	29	25	13	5	0	196²	179	1	49	105	10.7	2.43	105	.240	.291	11	.169	0	4	3	3	0.4
1910	*Chi-N	6	3	.667	14	13	5	2	0	100¹	82	0	26	34	9.8	1.79	161	.225	.279	3	.091	-2	14	12	0	0.7
1911	Chi-N	1	4	.200	6	5	3	0	0	33²	34	0	18	15	14.4	4.01	83	.262	.360	2	.182	0	-2	-3	1	-0.3
Total	8	71	44	.617	149	128	75	17	0	1067¹	869	6	293	503	10.1	2.02	128	.223	.284	36	.103	-15	69	67	-3	5.5

● DAN PFISTER
Pfister, Daniel Albin b: 12/20/36, Plainfield, N.J. BR/TR, 6', 187 lbs. Deb: 9/9/61

YEAR	TM/L	W	L	PCT	G	GS	CG	SH	SV	IP	H	HR	BB	SO	RAT	ERA	ERA+	OAV	OOB	BH	AVG	PB	PR	/A	PD	TPI
1961	KC-A	0	0	—	2	0	0	0	0	2¹	3	0	4	2	34.7	15.43	27	.417	.563	0	—	0	-3	-3	-0	-0.6
1962	KC-A	4	14	.222	41	25	2	0	1	196¹	175	27	106	123	13.3	4.54	93	.238	.341	12	.185	-1	-12	-7	1	-0.6
1963	KC-A	1	0	1.000	3	1	0	0	0	9¹	8	1	3	4	11.6	1.93	202	.229	.308	0	.000	-0	2	2	0	0.2
1964	KC-A	1	5	.167	19	3	0	0	0	41¹	50	10	29	21	18.5	6.53	58	.311	.434	0	.000	-0	-13	-12	0	-1.7
Total	4	6	19	.240	65	29	2	0	1	249¹	238	40	142	156	14.3	4.87	85	.252	.359	12	.162	-2	-27	-20	1	-2.1

● LEE PFUND
Pfund, Le Roy Herbert b: 10/10/18, Oak Park, Ill. BR/TR, 6'1", 185 lbs. Deb: 4/21/45

YEAR	TM/L	W	L	PCT	G	GS	CG	SH	SV	IP	H	HR	BB	SO	RAT	ERA	ERA+	OAV	OOB	BH	AVG	PB	PR	/A	PD	TPI
1945	Bro-N	3	2	.600	15	10	2	0	0	62¹	69	4	35	27	15.7	5.20	72	.274	.373	4	.182	-0	-10	-10	1	-0.6

● BILL PHEBUS
Phebus, Raymond William b: 8/2/09, Cherryvale, Kan. d: 10/11/89, Bartow, Fla. BR/TR, 5'9", 170 lbs. Deb: 9/6/36

YEAR	TM/L	W	L	PCT	G	GS	CG	SH	SV	IP	H	HR	BB	SO	RAT	ERA	ERA+	OAV	OOB	BH	AVG	PB	PR	/A	PD	TPI
1936	Was-A	0	0	—	2	1	0	0	0	7¹	4	1	4	4	11.0	2.45	195	.114	.225	0	—	0	2	2	-0	0.0
1937	Was-A	3	2	.600	6	5	4	1	0	40²	33	2	24	12	13.1	2.21	200	.232	.351	0	.000	1	11	10	-1	1.2
1938	Was-A	0	0	—	5	0	0	0	1	6¹	9	1	7	2	22.7	11.37	40	.346	.485	0	.000	-0	-5	-5	0	-0.1
Total	3	3	2	.600	13	6	4	1	2	54¹	46	4	35	18	13.9	3.31	135	.227	.349	0	.000	1	8	7	-1	1.1

● RAY PHELPS
Phelps, Raymond Clifford b: 12/11/03, Dunlap, Tenn. d: 7/7/71, Fort Pierce, Fla. BR/TR, 6'2", 200 lbs. Deb: 4/23/30

YEAR	TM/L	W	L	PCT	G	GS	CG	SH	SV	IP	H	HR	BB	SO	RAT	ERA	ERA+	OAV	OOB	BH	AVG	PB	PR	/A	PD	TPI
1930	Bro-N	14	7	.667	36	24	11	2	0	179²	198	21	52	64	12.7	4.11	120	.280	.332	10	.147	-2	17	16	2	1.5
1931	Bro-N	7	9	.438	28	26	13	1	0	149¹	184	8	44	50	14.0	5.00	76	.306	.357	8	.157	-1	-19	-20	0	-1.9
1932	Bro-N	4	5	.444	20	8	4	0	0	79¹	101	5	27	21	14.9	5.90	65	.323	.382	2	.087	-1	-18	-18	0	-1.8
1935	Chi-A	4	8	.333	27	17	4	0	1	125	126	10	55	38	13.2	4.82	96	.262	.351	5	.122	4	-5	-3	2	-0.4
1936	Chi-A	4	6	.400	15	4	1	0	0	68²	91	4	42	17	17.7	6.03	86	.331	.423	6	.231	-1	-8	-6	1	-0.6
Total	5	33	35	.485	126	79	24	4	1	602	700	48	220	190	14.0	4.93	90	.294	.358	31	.148	-8	-32	-31	5	-3.2

● DEACON PHILLIPPE
Phillippe, Charles Louis b: 5/23/1872, Rural Retreat, Va. d: 3/30/52, Avalon, Pa. BR/TR, 6'0.5", 180 lbs. Deb: 4/21/1899

YEAR	TM/L	W	L	PCT	G	GS	CG	SH	SV	IP	H	HR	BB	SO	RAT	ERA	ERA+	OAV	OOB	BH	AVG	PB	PR	/A	PD	TPI
1899	Lou-N	21	17	.553	42	38	33	2	1	321	331	10	64	68	11.3	3.17	122	.266	.306	26	.203	-1	24	25	-0	2.3
1900	*Pit-N	20	13	.606	38	33	29	1	0	279	274	7	42	75	**10.4**	2.84	128	.256	**.289**	19	.181	-2	27	25	-2	2.0
1901	Pit-N	22	12	.647	37	32	30	1	2	296	274	1	38	103	9.8	2.22	147	.244	.275	26	.230	5	**36**	34	3	4.4
1902	Pit-N	20	9	.690	31	30	29	5	0	272	265	1	26	122	9.8	2.05	133	.255	.276	25	.221	3	22	21	-2	2.1

YEAR TM/L	W	L	PCT	G	GS	CG	SH	SV	IP	H	HR	BB	SO	RAT	ERA	ERA+	OAV	OOB	BH	AVG	PB	PR	/A	PD	TPI
1903 *Pit-N	25	9	.735	36	33	31	4	2	289¹	269	4	29	123	**9.4**	2.43	133	.241	**.263**	26	.210	2	27	26	-2	2.7
1904 Pit-N	10	10	.500	21	19	17	3	1	166²	183	1	26	82	11.4	3.24	85	.272	.302	8	.123	-4	-9	-9	-0	-1.4
1905 Pit-N	20	13	.606	38	33	25	5	0	279	235	0	48	133	9.5	2.19	137	.233	.274	9	.093	-4	25	25	-1	2.2
1906 Pit-N	15	10	.600	33	24	19	3	0	218²	216	3	26	90	10.0	2.47	108	.252	.276	20	.244	3	4	5	-1	0.8
1907 Pit-N	14	11	.560	35	26	17	1	2	214	214	2	36	61	10.7	2.61	93	.264	.300	12	.185	1	-3	-4	-2	-0.6
1908 Pit-N	0	0	—	5	0	0	0	0	12	20	0	3	1	17.3	11.25	20	.357	.390	1	.250		-0	-12	-12	-1	0.0
1909 *Pit-N	8	3	.727	22	12	7	1	0	131²	121	2	14	38	9.5	2.32	117	.253	.280	3	.071	-3	4	6	-2	-0.1
1910 Pit-N	14	2	.875	31	8	5	1	4	121²	111	4	9	30	9.1	2.29	135	.239	.258	9	.220	1	10	11	-3	1.2
1911 Pit-N	0	0	—	3	0	0	0	0	6	5	0	2	3	10.5	7.50	46	.238	.304	1	1.000	1	-3	-3	-0	0.1
Total 13	189	109	.634	372	288	242	27	12	2607	2518	41	363	929	10.1	2.59	120	.253	.283	185	.189	2	153	150	-14	15.7

● **BUZ PHILLIPS**   Phillips, Albert Abernathy   b: 5/25/04, Newton, N.C.   d: 11/6/64, Baltimore, Md.   BR/TR, 5'11.5", 185 lbs.   Deb: 8/5/30

YEAR TM/L	W	L	PCT	G	GS	CG	SH	SV	IP	H	HR	BB	SO	RAT	ERA	ERA+	OAV	OOB	BH	AVG	PB	PR	/A	PD	TPI
1930 Phi-N	0	0	—	14	1	0	0	0	43²	68	6	18	9	17.9	8.04	68	.354	.412	6	.462	2	-15	-12	-1	0.1

● **RED PHILLIPS**   Phillips, Clarence Lemuel   b: 11/3/08, Pauls Valley, Okla.   d: 2/1/88, Wichita, Kan.   BR/TR, 6'3.5", 195 lbs.   Deb: 7/24/34

YEAR TM/L	W	L	PCT	G	GS	CG	SH	SV	IP	H	HR	BB	SO	RAT	ERA	ERA+	OAV	OOB	BH	AVG	PB	PR	/A	PD	TPI
1934 Det-A	2	0	1.000	7	1	1	0	1	23¹	31	1	16	3	18.1	6.17	71	.316	.412	3	.250	1	-4	-5	-1	-0.3
1936 Det-A	2	4	.333	22	6	3	0	0	87¹	124	12	22	15	15.0	6.49	76	.332	.370	10	.303	2	-14	-15	-0	-0.7
Total 2	4	4	.500	29	7	4	0	1	110²	155	13	38	18	15.7	6.42	75	.329	.379	13	.289	3	-18	-20	-1	-1.0

● **JACK PHILLIPS**   Phillips, Jack Dorn "Stretch"   b: 9/6/21, Clarence, N.Y.   BR/TR, 6'4", 193 lbs.   Deb: 8/22/47 ♦

YEAR TM/L	W	L	PCT	G	GS	CG	SH	SV	IP	H	HR	BB	SO	RAT	ERA	ERA+	OAV	OOB	BH	AVG	PB	PR	/A	PD	TPI
1950 Pit-N	0	0	—	1	0	0	0	0	5	7	0	1	2	14.4	7.20	61	.333	.364	61	.293	0	-2	-2	-0	0.0

● **JACK PHILLIPS**   Phillips, John Stephen   b: 5/24/19, St.Louis, Mo.   d: 6/16/58, St.Louis, Mo.   BR/TR, 6'1", 185 lbs.   Deb: 7/13/45 ♦

YEAR TM/L	W	L	PCT	G	GS	CG	SH	SV	IP	H	HR	BB	SO	RAT	ERA	ERA+	OAV	OOB	BH	AVG	PB	PR	/A	PD	TPI
1945 NY-N	0	0	—	1	0	0	0	0	4¹	5	1	5	0	22.8	10.38	38	.313	.500	1	.500		-3	-3	-0	0.0

● **ED PHILLIPS**   Phillips, Norman Edwin   b: 9/20/44, Ardmore, Okla.   BR/TR, 6'1", 190 lbs.   Deb: 4/9/70

YEAR TM/L	W	L	PCT	G	GS	CG	SH	SV	IP	H	HR	BB	SO	RAT	ERA	ERA+	OAV	OOB	BH	AVG	PB	PR	/A	PD	TPI
1970 Bos-A	0	2	.000	18	0	0	0	0	23²	29	4	10	23	15.6	5.32	74	.312	.390	0	.000	-0	-4	-4	-1	-0.4

● **TOM PHILLIPS**   Phillips, Thomas Gerald   b: 4/5/1889, Philipsburg, Pa.   d: 4/12/29, Philipsburg, Pa.   BR/TR, 6'2", 190 lbs.   Deb: 9/13/15

YEAR TM/L	W	L	PCT	G	GS	CG	SH	SV	IP	H	HR	BB	SO	RAT	ERA	ERA+	OAV	OOB	BH	AVG	PB	PR	/A	PD	TPI
1915 StL-A	1	3	.250	5	4	1	0	0	27¹	27	2	12	5	13.8	2.96	97	.283	.372	1	.111	-1	-0	-0	-1	-0.2
1919 Cle-A	3	2	.600	22	3	2	0	0	55	55	2	34	18	15.1	2.95	114	.272	.385	4	.364	1	**2**	**2**	-1	0.2
1921 Was-A	1	0	1.000	1	1	1	0	0	9	9	0	3	2	12.0	2.00	206	.290	.353	0	.000	-1	2	2	-0	0.1
1922 Was-A	3	7	.300	17	7	2	1	0	70	72	2	22	19	12.6	4.89	79	.273	.338	3	.150	-1	-7	-8	-1	-1.1
Total 4	8	12	.400	45	15	6	1	0	161¹	164	6	71	44	13.6	3.74	95	.275	.361	8	.186	-1	-3	-3	-3	-1.0

● **BILL PHILLIPS**   Phillips, William Corcoran "Whoa Bill" or "Silver Bill"
b: 11/9/1868, Allenport, Pa.   d: 10/25/41, Charleroi, Pa.   BR/TR, 5'11", 180 lbs.   Deb: 8/11/1890 M

YEAR TM/L	W	L	PCT	G	GS	CG	SH	SV	IP	H	HR	BB	SO	RAT	ERA	ERA+	OAV	OOB	BH	AVG	PB	PR	/A	PD	TPI
1890 Pit-N	1	9	.100	10	10	9	0	0	82	123	8	29	25	16.8	7.57	44	.336	.386	11	.239	1	-36	-39	0	-3.2
1895 Cin-N	6	7	.462	18	9	6	2	0	109	126	6	44	15	14.6	6.03	83	.285	.359	4	.313	2	-15	-13	1	-1.0
1899 Cin-N	17	9	.654	33	27	18	1	1	227²	234	3	71	43	12.6	3.32	118	.265	.330	12	.130	-5	14	15	-0	0.9
1900 Cin-N	9	11	.450	29	24	17	3	0	208¹	229	4	67	51	13.3	4.28	86	.279	.342	13	.165	-4	-13	-14	6	-0.9
1901 Cin-N	14	18	.438	37	36	29	1	0	281¹	364	7	67	109	14.2	4.64	69	.311	.355	22	.185	-2	-41	-45	5	-3.6
1902 Cin-N	16	16	.500	33	33	30	0	0	269	267	3	55	85	11.1	2.51	119	.259	.302	39	.342	10	8	15	3	3.1
1903 Cin-N	7	6	.538	16	13	11	0	0	118¹	134	1	30	46	13.0	3.35	106	.259	.330	10	.175	-1	-1	3	2	0.3
Total 7	70	76	.479	176	152	120	6	3	1295²	1477	32	363	374	13.2	4.09	87	.284	.339	122	.224	4	-85	-77	16	-4.4

● **TAYLOR PHILLIPS**   Phillips, William Taylor "Tay"   b: 6/18/33, Atlanta, Ga.   BL/TL, 5'11", 185 lbs.   Deb: 6/8/56

YEAR TM/L	W	L	PCT	G	GS	CG	SH	SV	IP	H	HR	BB	SO	RAT	ERA	ERA+	OAV	OOB	BH	AVG	PB	PR	/A	PD	TPI
1956 Mil-N	5	3	.625	23	6	3	0	2	87²	69	6	33	36	11.2	2.26	153	.223	.311	0	.000	-2	15	12	2	1.1
1957 Mil-N	3	2	.600	27	6	0	0	2	73	82	3	40	36	15.2	5.55	63	.300	.392	2	.100	-1	-14	-17	0	-1.2
1958 Chi-N	7	10	.412	39	27	5	1	1	170¹	178	22	79	102	13.9	4.76	82	.266	.349	4	.056	-4	-15	-16	1	-1.7
1959 Chi-N	0	2	.000	7	2	0	0	0	16²	22	3	11	5	18.9	7.56	52	.319	.427	0	.000	-0	-7	-7	0	-0.7
Phi-N	1	4	.200	32	3	1	0	1	63	72	4	31	35	15.3	5.00	82	.303	.392	1	.091	-1	-7	-6	0	-0.5
Yr	1	6	.143	39	5	1	0	1	79²	94	7	42	40	15.8	5.54	74	.303	.393	1	.067	-1	-14	-13	1	-1.2
1960 Phi-N	0	1	.000	10	1	0	0	0	14	21	2	4	6	16.7	8.36	46	.356	.406	0	.000	-0	-7	-7	-0	-0.5
1963 Chi-A	0	0	—	9	0	0	0	0	14	16	1	13	13	19.3	10.29	34	.302	.448	0	.000	-0	-10	-11	0	0.0
Total 6	16	22	.421	147	45	9	1	6	438²	460	42	211	233	14.2	4.82	78	.275	.364	6	.053	-8	-46	-51	4	-3.5

● **TOM PHOEBUS**   Phoebus, Thomas Harold   b: 4/7/42, Baltimore, Md.   BR/TR, 5'8", 185 lbs.   Deb: 9/15/66

YEAR TM/L	W	L	PCT	G	GS	CG	SH	SV	IP	H	HR	BB	SO	RAT	ERA	ERA+	OAV	OOB	BH	AVG	PB	PR	/A	PD	TPI
1966 Bal-A	2	1	.667	3	3	2	2	0	22	16	0	6	17	9.0	1.23	271	.213	.272	1	.167	0	5	5	-0	0.8
1967 Bal-A	14	9	.609	33	33	7	4	0	208	177	16	114	179	12.6	3.33	95	.227	.326	11	.145	1	-2	-4	-2	-0.6
1968 Bal-A	15	15	.500	36	36	9	3	0	240²	186	10	105	193	11.0	2.62	112	.212	.299	15	.183	3	10	8	-0	1.4
1969 Bal-A	14	7	.667	35	33	6	2	0	202	180	23	87	117	12.1	3.52	101	.241	.324	15	.200	2	1	1	-1	0.1
1970 *Bal-A	5	5	.500	27	21	3	0	0	135	106	14	62	70	11.6	3.07	119	.219	.315	7	.163	-0	10	9	0	0.6
1971 SD-N	3	11	.214	29	21	2	0	0	133¹	144	14	64	80	14.2	4.45	74	.280	.363	6	.167	1	-15	-17	-1	-1.6
1972 SD-N	0	1	.000	1	1	0	0	0	5²	6	2	6	8	14.3	7.94	41	.150	.346	0	.000	-0	-3	-3	0	-0.4
Chi-A	3	3	.500	37	1	0	0	6	83¹	76	9	45	59	13.3	3.78	101	.247	.346	2	.133	-1	-3	0	1	0.0
Yr	3	4	.429	38	2	0	0	6	89	79	11	51	67	13.3	4.04	93	.241	.346	2	.118	-1	-6	-3	1	-0.4
Total 7	56	52	.519	201	149	29	11	6	1030	888	85	489	725	12.2	3.33	100	.233	.324	57	.170	6	4	-1	-3	0.3

● **STEVE PHOENIX**   Phoenix, Steven Robert   b: 1/31/68, Phoenix, Ariz.   BR/TR, 6'2", 175 lbs.   Deb: 7/30/94

YEAR TM/L	W	L	PCT	G	GS	CG	SH	SV	IP	H	HR	BB	SO	RAT	ERA	ERA+	OAV	OOB	BH	AVG	PB	PR	/A	PD	TPI
1994 Oak-A	0	0	—	2	0	0	0	0	4¹	4	0	2	3	12.5	6.23	71	.235	.316	0	—	0	-1	-1	0	0.6

● **BILL PHYLE**   Phyle, William Joseph   b: 6/25/1875, Duluth, Minn.   d: 8/6/53, Los Angeles, Cal.   TR ,   Deb: 9/17/1898 ♦

YEAR TM/L	W	L	PCT	G	GS	CG	SH	SV	IP	H	HR	BB	SO	RAT	ERA	ERA+	OAV	OOB	BH	AVG	PB	PR	/A	PD	TPI
1898 Chi-N	2	1	.667	3	3	3	2	0	23	24	0	6	4	12.5	0.78	458	.267	.327	1	.111	-0	7	7	-1	0.8
1899 Chi-N	1	8	.111	10	9	9	0	1	83²	92	2	29	10	13.4	4.20	89	.279	.344	6	.176	-2	-3	-4	1	-0.5
1901 NY-N	7	10	.412	24	19	16	0	1	168²	208	2	54	62	14.3	4.27	77	.301	.357	12	.182	-1	-18	-18	1	-1.5
Total 3	10	19	.345	37	31	28	2	2	275¹	324	4	89	76	13.9	3.96	88	.292	.351	32	.176	-4	-14	-15	2	-1.2

● **DOUG PIATT**   Piatt, Douglas William   b: 9/26/65, Beaver, Pa.   BL/TR, 6'1", 185 lbs.   Deb: 6/11/91

YEAR TM/L	W	L	PCT	G	GS	CG	SH	SV	IP	H	HR	BB	SO	RAT	ERA	ERA+	OAV	OOB	BH	AVG	PB	PR	/A	PD	TPI
1991 Mon-N	0	0	—	21	0	0	0	0	34²	29	3	17	29	11.9	2.60	139	.230	.322	0	.000	-0	4	4	0	0.0

● **WILEY PIATT**   Piatt, Wiley Harold "Iron Man"   b: 7/13/1874, Blue Creek, Ohio   d: 9/20/46, Cincinnati, Ohio   BL/TL, 5'10", 175 lbs.   Deb: 4/22/1898

YEAR TM/L	W	L	PCT	G	GS	CG	SH	SV	IP	H	HR	BB	SO	RAT	ERA	ERA+	OAV	OOB	BH	AVG	PB	PR	/A	PD	TPI
1898 Phi-N	24	14	.632	39	37	33	**6**	0	306	285	2	97	121	11.8	3.18	108	.245	.314	32	.262	4	15	9	-2	1.1
1899 Phi-N	23	15	.605	39	38	31	2	0	305	323	6	86	89	12.7	3.45	107	.271	.332	33	.270	4	14	8	-5	0.8
1900 Phi-N	9	10	.474	22	20	16	1	0	160²	194	5	71	47	15.7	4.71	77	.298	.380	17	.250	2	-18	-19	-1	-1.9
1901 Phi-A	5	12	.294	18	16	15	0	1	140	176	4	60	45	15.4	4.63	82	.303	.372	13	.224	-0	-15	-13	-4	-1.6
Chi-A	4	2	.667	7	6	4	1	0	51²	42	2	14	19	10.5	2.79	125	.220	.287	2	.118	-1	5	5	0	0.2
Yr	9	14	.391	25	22	19	1	1	191²	218	6	74	64	13.9	4.13	89	.282	.347	15	.200	-1	-10	-9	-5	-1.4
1902 Chi-A	12	12	.500	32	30	22	2	0	246	263	3	66	96	12.4	3.51	96	.274	.326	17	.200	-2	-3	-3	-3	-0.4
1903 Bos-N	9	14	.391	25	23	18	0	0	181	198	6	61	100	13.1	3.18	101	.280	.340	16	.225	2	1	1	-0	0.0
Total 6	86	79	.521	182	170	139	12	1	1390¹	1481	27	455	517	13.0	3.61	97	.272	.337	130	.239	13	-15	-20	-1	-1.8

● **HIPOLITO PICHARDO**   Pichardo, Hipolito Antonio (Balbina)   b: 8/22/69, Jicome Esperanza, D.R.   BR/TR, 6'1", 160 lbs.   Deb: 4/21/92

YEAR TM/L	W	L	PCT	G	GS	CG	SH	SV	IP	H	HR	BB	SO	RAT	ERA	ERA+	OAV	OOB	BH	AVG	PB	PR	/A	PD	TPI
1992 KC-A	9	6	.600	31	24	1	1	0	143²	148	9	49	59	12.5	3.95	103	.267	.330	0	—	0	-0	2	0	0.0
1993 KC-A	7	8	.467	30	25	2	0	0	165	183	10	53	70	13.2	4.04	113	.282	.341	0	—	0	5	10	2	0.5

YEAR TM/L	W	L	PCT	G	GS	CG	SH	SV	IP	H	HR	BB	SO	RAT	ERA	ERA+	OAV	OOB	BH	AVG	PB	PR	/A	PD	TPI
1994 KC-A	5	3	.625	45	0	0	0	3	67²	82	4	24	36	15.0	4.92	105	.308	.380	0	—	0	-1	2	0	-0.3
Total 3	21	17	.553	106	49	3	1	3	376¹	413	23	126	165	13.3	4.16	108	.281	.344	0	—	0	4	13	2	0.2

● **RON PICHE**   Piche, Ronald Jacques   b: 5/22/35, Verdun, Que., Canada   BR/TR, 5'11", 165 lbs.   Deb: 5/30/60   C

YEAR TM/L	W	L	PCT	G	GS	CG	SH	SV	IP	H	HR	BB	SO	RAT	ERA	ERA+	OAV	OOB	BH	AVG	PB	PR	/A	PD	TPI
1960 Mil-N	3	5	.375	37	0	0	0	9	48	48	3	23	38	13.9	3.56	96	.258	.349	0	.000	-0	1	-1	-1	-0.2
1961 Mil-N	2	2	.500	12	1	1	0	1	23¹	20	1	16	16	13.9	3.47	108	.238	.360	0	.000	-1	1	1	0	0.1
1962 Mil-N	3	2	.600	14	8	2	0	0	52	54	6	29	28	14.9	4.85	78	.273	.374	1	.056	-1	-5	-6	-1	-0.6
1963 Mil-N	1	1	.500	37	1	0	0	0	53	53	4	25	40	13.2	3.40	95	.256	.336	0	.000	-1	-1	-1	1	0.0
1965 Cal-A	0	3	.000	14	1	0	0	0	19²	20	5	12	14	14.6	6.86	50	.267	.368	0	.000	-0	-7	-8	-0	-1.1
1966 StL-N	1	3	.250	20	0	0	0	2	25¹	21	4	18	21	14.2	4.26	84	.214	.342	0	.000	-0	-2	-2	-0	-0.4
Total 6	10	16	.385	134	11	3	0	12	221¹	216	23	123	157	14.1	4.19	84	.255	.354	1	.024	-3	-13	-16	1	-2.2

● **CHARLIE PICKETT**   Pickett, Charles Albert   b: 3/1/1883, Delaware, Ohio   d: 5/20/69, Springfield, Ohio   BR/TR, 6'1", 175 lbs.   Deb: 6/21/10

YEAR TM/L	W	L	PCT	G	GS	CG	SH	SV	IP	H	HR	BB	SO	RAT	ERA	ERA+	OAV	OOB	BH	AVG	PB	PR	/A	PD	TPI
1910 StL-N	0	0	—	2	0	0	0	0	6	7	0	2	2	13.5	1.50	199	.280	.333	0	—	0	1	1	-0	0.0

● **CLARENCE PICKREL**   Pickrel, Clarence Douglas   b: 3/28/11, Gretna, Va.   d: 11/4/83, Rocky Mount, Va.   BR/TR, 6'1", 180 lbs.   Deb: 4/22/33

YEAR TM/L	W	L	PCT	G	GS	CG	SH	SV	IP	H	HR	BB	SO	RAT	ERA	ERA+	OAV	OOB	BH	AVG	PB	PR	/A	PD	TPI
1933 Phi-N	1	0	1.000	9	0	0	0	0	13²	20	0	3	6	15.8	3.95	97	.357	.400	0	.000	-0	-1	-0	-1	-0.1
1934 Bos-N	0	0	—	10	1	0	0	0	16	24	0	7	9	17.4	5.06	76	.333	.392	0	.000	-0	-2	-2	-1	-0.1
Total 2	1	0	1.000	19	1	0	0	0	29²	44	0	10	15	16.7	4.55	85	.344	.396	0	.000	-0	-3	-2	-1	-0.2

● **JEFF PICO**   Pico, Jeffrey Mark   b: 2/12/66, Antioch, Cal.   BR/TR, 6'1", 190 lbs.   Deb: 5/31/88

YEAR TM/L	W	L	PCT	G	GS	CG	SH	SV	IP	H	HR	BB	SO	RAT	ERA	ERA+	OAV	OOB	BH	AVG	PB	PR	/A	PD	TPI
1988 Chi-N	6	7	.462	29	13	3	2	1	112²	108	6	37	57	11.6	4.15	87	.252	.312	5	.147	-0	-9	-7	-0	-0.8
1989 Chi-N	3	1	.750	53	5	0	0	2	90²	99	8	31	38	12.9	3.77	100	.278	.336	1	.100	-1	-3	-0	1	0.1
1990 Chi-N	4	4	.500	31	8	0	0	2	92	120	7	37	37	15.5	4.79	85	.321	.383	6	.273	2	-10	-7	1	-0.3
Total 3	13	12	.520	113	26	3	2	5	295¹	327	21	105	132	13.2	4.24	90	.282	.343	12	.182	1	-22	-14	2	-1.0

● **MARIO PICONE**   Picone, Mario Peter "Babe"   b: 7/5/26, Brooklyn, N.Y.   BR/TR, 5'11", 180 lbs.   Deb: 9/27/47

YEAR TM/L	W	L	PCT	G	GS	CG	SH	SV	IP	H	HR	BB	SO	RAT	ERA	ERA+	OAV	OOB	BH	AVG	PB	PR	/A	PD	TPI
1947 NY-N	0	0	—	2	1	0	0	0	7	10	1	2	1	15.4	7.71	53	.345	.387	1	.500	-0	-3	-3	0	0.1
1952 NY-N	0	1	.000	2	1	0	0	0	9	11	2	5	3	16.0	7.00	53	.306	.390	0	.000	-0	-3	-3	0	-0.3
1954 NY-N	0	0	—	5	0	0	0	0	13²	13	1	11	6	15.8	5.27	77	.283	.421	0	.000	-0	-2	-2	0	0.0
Cin-N	0	1	.000	4	1	0	0	0	10¹	9	3	7	1	13.9	6.10	69	.243	.364	0	.000	-0	-2	-2	0	-0.1
Yr	0	1	.000	9	1	0	0	0	24	22	4	18	7	15.0	5.63	73	.265	.396	0	.000	-0	-4	-4	0	-0.1
Total 3	0	2	.000	13	3	0	0	0	40	43	7	25	11	15.3	6.30	64	.291	.393	1	.167	1	-10	-10	1	-0.3

● **AL PIECHOTA**   Piechota, Aloysius Edward "Pie"   b: 1/19/14, Chicago, Ill.   BR/TR, 6', 195 lbs.   Deb: 5/7/40

YEAR TM/L	W	L	PCT	G	GS	CG	SH	SV	IP	H	HR	BB	SO	RAT	ERA	ERA+	OAV	OOB	BH	AVG	PB	PR	/A	PD	TPI
1940 Bos-N	2	5	.286	21	8	2	0	0	61	68	6	41	18	16.1	5.75	65	.278	.381	4	.200	1	-13	-14	-0	-1.3
1941 Bos-N	0	0	—	1	0	0	0	0	1	0	0	1	0	9.00	—	.000	.250	0	—	0	0	0	0	0.0
Total 2	2	5	.286	22	8	2	0	0	62	68	6	42	18	16.0	5.66	66	.274	.379	4	.200	1	-13	-13	-0	-1.3

● **CY PIEH**   Pieh, Edwin John   b: 9/29/1886, Waunakee, Wis.   d: 9/12/45, Jacksonville, Fla   BR/TR, 6'2", 190 lbs.   Deb: 9/6/13

YEAR TM/L	W	L	PCT	G	GS	CG	SH	SV	IP	H	HR	BB	SO	RAT	ERA	ERA+	OAV	OOB	BH	AVG	PB	PR	/A	PD	TPI
1913 NY-A	1	0	1.000	4	0	0	0	0	10¹	10	0	7	6	14.8	4.35	69	.250	.362	1	.250	-0	-2	-2	1	0.0
1914 NY-A	4	4	.500	18	4	1	0	0	62¹	68	6	29	24	14.0	5.05	55	.289	.367	2	.118	-0	-16	-16	-1	-2.0
1915 NY-A	4	5	.444	21	8	3	2	0	94	78	2	39	46	11.7	2.87	102	.234	.324	2	.067	-3	1	1	0	-0.3
Total 3	9	9	.500	43	12	4	2	0	166²	156	8	75	76	12.7	3.78	76	.257	.343	5	.098	-3	-17	-17	0	-2.3

● **ED PIERCE**   Pierce, Edward John   b: 10/6/68, Arcadia, Cal.   BL/TL, 6'1", 185 lbs.   Deb: 9/6/92

YEAR TM/L	W	L	PCT	G	GS	CG	SH	SV	IP	H	HR	BB	SO	RAT	ERA	ERA+	OAV	OOB	BH	AVG	PB	PR	/A	PD	TPI
1992 KC-A	0	0	—	2	1	0	0	0	5¹	9	1	4	2	21.9	3.38	120	.429	.520	0	—	0	0	0	0	-0.2

● **RAY PIERCE**   Pierce, Raymond Lester "Lefty"   b: 6/6/1897, Emporia, Kan.   d: 5/4/63, Denver, Colo.   BL/TL, 5'7", 156 lbs.   Deb: 5/12/24

YEAR TM/L	W	L	PCT	G	GS	CG	SH	SV	IP	H	HR	BB	SO	RAT	ERA	ERA+	OAV	OOB	BH	AVG	PB	PR	/A	PD	TPI
1924 Chi-N	0	0	—	6	0	0	0	0	7¹	7	2	4	2	13.5	7.36	53	.269	.367	0	—	0	-3	-3	-0	-0.1
1925 Phi-N	5	4	.556	23	8	4	0	0	90¹	134	7	24	18	15.9	5.50	87	.356	.397	5	.179	-0	-12	-7	0	-0.6
1926 Phi-N	2	7	.222	37	7	1	0	0	84²	128	3	35	18	17.4	5.63	74	.348	.406	3	.125	-2	-17	-14	-1	-1.5
Total 3	7	11	.389	66	15	5	0	0	182	269	12	63	38	16.5	5.64	79	.349	.400	8	.154	-2	-32	-24	-1	-2.1

● **TONY PIERCE**   Pierce, Tony Michael   b: 1/29/46, Brunswick, Ga.   BR/TL, 6'1", 190 lbs.   Deb: 4/14/67

YEAR TM/L	W	L	PCT	G	GS	CG	SH	SV	IP	H	HR	BB	SO	RAT	ERA	ERA+	OAV	OOB	BH	AVG	PB	PR	/A	PD	TPI
1967 KC-A	3	4	.429	49	6	0	0	7	97²	79	6	30	61	10.5	3.04	105	.221	.290	0	.000	-2	2	2	-1	-0.2
1968 Oak-A	1	2	.333	17	3	0	0	1	32²	39	3	10	16	13.8	3.86	73	.295	.350	0	.000	-1	-3	-4	1	-0.4
Total 2	4	6	.400	66	9	0	0	8	130¹	118	9	40	77	11.3	3.25	95	.241	.306	0	.000	-3	-1	-2	-1	-0.6

● **BILLY PIERCE**   Pierce, Walter William   b: 4/2/27, Detroit, Mich.   BL/TL, 5'10", 160 lbs.   Deb: 6/1/45

YEAR TM/L	W	L	PCT	G	GS	CG	SH	SV	IP	H	HR	BB	SO	RAT	ERA	ERA+	OAV	OOB	BH	AVG	PB	PR	/A	PD	TPI
1945 Det-A	0	0	—	5	0	0	0	0	10	6	1	10	10	15.3	1.80	195	.182	.386	0	.000	-0	2	2	0	0.0
1948 Det-A	3	0	1.000	22	5	0	0	0	55¹	47	5	51	36	16.1	6.34	69	.234	.391	5	.294	-2	-13	-12	-0	-0.4
1949 Chi-A	7	15	.318	32	26	8	0	0	171²	145	11	112	95	13.5	3.88	108	.228	.344	9	.176	-1	6	6	1	0.7
1950 Chi-A	12	16	.429	33	29	15	1	1	219¹	189	11	137	118	13.5	3.98	113	.228	.339	20	.260	4	15	12	-2	1.6
1951 Chi-A	15	14	.517	37	28	18	1	2	240¹	237	14	73	113	11.6	3.03	133	.258	.313	16	.203	-0	29	27	-1	2.9
1952 Chi-A	15	12	.556	33	32	14	4	1	255¹	214	12	79	144	10.4	2.57	142	.227	.301	17	.187	-0	31	31	0	3.2
1953 Chi-A★	18	12	.600	40	33	19	7	3	271¹	216	20	102	**186**	10.6	2.72	148	**.218**	.292	11	.126	-4	**38**	**39**	-2	3.5
1954 Chi-A	9	10	.474	36	26	12	4	3	188²	179	15	86	148	12.8	3.48	107	.249	.332	11	.193	-0	5	5	-2	0.3
1955 Chi-A★	15	10	.600	33	26	16	6	1	205²	162	16	64	157	**10.0**	**1.97**	**200**	.213	**.277**	12	.171	-1	**45**	**45**	-1	**5.3**
1956 Chi-A★	20	9	.690	35	33	**21**	1	1	276¹	261	24	100	192	11.9	3.32	123	.249	.316	16	.157	-4	26	24	-3	1.5
1957 Chi-A★	**20**	12	.625	37	34	**16**	4	2	257	228	19	71	171	10.9	3.26	115	.234	.287	17	.172	-2	15	14	0	1.4
1958 Chi-A☆	17	11	.607	35	32	**19**	3	2	245	204	33	66	144	10.0	2.68	136	.227	.280	17	.205	2	30	26	-3	2.8
1959 *Chi-A☆	14	15	.483	34	33	12	2	0	224	217	26	62	114	11.3	3.62	104	.253	.306	13	.191	3	6	4	0	0.7
1960 Chi-A	14	7	.667	32	30	8	1	0	196¹	201	24	46	108	11.3	3.62	104	.266	.308	12	.179	-3	5	3	-1	0.3
1961 Chi-A☆	10	9	.526	39	28	5	1	0	180	190	17	54	106	12.3	3.80	103	.275	.328	8	.143	-2	4	2	-0	0.0
1962 *SF-N	16	6	.727	30	23	7	2	1	162¹	147	19	35	76	10.3	3.49	109	.240	.284	12	.214	2	8	5	-1	0.7
1963 SF-N	3	11	.214	38	13	1	0	8	99	106	12	20	52	11.5	4.27	75	.272	.309	4	.129	-0	-11	-12	0	-1.8
1964 SF-N	3	0	1.000	34	1	0	0	4	49	40	6	10	29	9.2	2.20	162	.222	.263	3	.333	1	7	7	-1	0.6
Total 18	211	169	.555	585	432	193	38	32	3306²	2989	284	1178	1999	11.4	3.27	119	.240	.307	203	.184	0	250	229	-15	23.3

● **BILL PIERCY**   Piercy, William Benton "Wild Bill"   b: 5/2/1896, ElMonte, Cal.   d: 8/28/51, Long Beach, Cal.   BR/TR, 6'1.5", 170 lbs.   Deb: 10/3/17

YEAR TM/L	W	L	PCT	G	GS	CG	SH	SV	IP	H	HR	BB	SO	RAT	ERA	ERA+	OAV	OOB	BH	AVG	PB	PR	/A	PD	TPI
1917 NY-A	0	1	.000	1	1	1	0	0	9	9	0	2	4	11.0	3.00	90	.257	.297	0	.000	0	-0	-0	-0	0.0
1921 *NY-A	5	4	.556	14	10	5	1	0	81²	82	4	28	35	12.9	2.98	142	.261	.337	6	.214	0	12	11	-0	1.1
1922 Bos-A	3	9	.250	29	12	7	1	0	121¹	140	2	62	24	15.4	4.67	88	.304	.394	5	.147	-3	-8	-8	2	-0.6
1923 Bos-A	8	17	.320	30	24	11	0	0	187¹	193	5	73	51	13.5	3.41	121	.277	.357	7	.132	-3	12	15	3	1.8
1924 Bos-A	5	7	.417	23	18	3	0	0	121	156	4	66	20	17.3	5.95	73	.335	.429	6	.154	-2	-23	-21	1	-1.9
1926 Chi-N	6	5	.545	19	5	1	0	0	90¹	96	1	37	31	13.8	4.48	86	.280	.360	9	.257	1	-7	-6	0	-0.6
Total 6	27	43	.386	116	70	28	2	0	610²	676	16	268	165	14.5	4.26	97	.292	.376	33	.173	-5	-15	-10	7	-0.1

● **MARINO PIERETTI**   Pieretti, Marino Paul "Chick"   b: 9/23/20, Lucca, Italy   d: 1/30/81, San Francisco, Cal.   BR/TR, 5'7", 158 lbs.   Deb: 4/19/45

YEAR TM/L	W	L	PCT	G	GS	CG	SH	SV	IP	H	HR	BB	SO	RAT	ERA	ERA+	OAV	OOB	BH	AVG	PB	PR	/A	PD	TPI
1945 Was-A	14	13	.519	44	27	14	3	2	233¹	235	3	91	66	12.6	3.32	94	.257	.325	18	.222	2	1	-6	1	-0.3
1946 Was-A	2	2	.500	20	7	2	0	0	62	70	9	40	20	16.3	5.95	56	.292	.397	3	.214	-0	-17	-18	1	-1.0
1947 Was-A	2	4	.333	23	10	2	1	0	83¹	97	3	47	32	15.8	4.21	88	.287	.377	6	.231	-0	-5	-6	1	-0.6
1948 Was-A	0	2	.000	8	1	0	0	0	11²	17	1	7	6	19.3	10.80	40	.375	.455	0	.000	-0	-8	-8	-0	-1.2
Chi-A	8	10	.444	21	18	4	0	1	120	117	6	52	28	12.7	4.95	86	.262	.339	7	.179	-1	-9	-9	1	-1.2
Yr	8	12	.400	29	19	4	0	1	131²	135	7	59	34	13.3	5.47	78	.273	.351	7	.171	-1	-17	-18	1	-2.4

YEAR	TM/L	W	L	PCT	G	GS	CG	SH	SV	IP	H	HR	BB	SO	RAT	ERA	ERA+	OAV	OOB	BH	AVG	PB	PR	/A	PD	TPI
1949	Chi-A	4	6	.400	39	9	0	0	4	116	131	10	54	25	14.4	5.51	76	.289	.364	9	.237	1	-17	-17	2	-1.2
1950	Cle-A	0	1	.000	29	1	0	0	1	47¹	45	2	30	11	14.3	4.18	104	.253	.361	2	.286	0	2	1	1	0.1
Total	6	30	38	.441	194	68	21	4	8	673²	713	34	321	188	13.9	4.53	81	.272	.353	45	.217	2	-52	-63	5	-5.1

● AL PIEROTTI
Pierotti, Albert Felix b: 10/24/1895, Boston, Mass. d: 2/12/64, Everett, Mass. BR/TR, 5'10.5", 195 lbs. Deb: 8/9/20

YEAR	TM/L	W	L	PCT	G	GS	CG	SH	SV	IP	H	HR	BB	SO	RAT	ERA	ERA+	OAV	OOB	BH	AVG	PB	PR	/A	PD	TPI
1920	Bos-N	1	1	.500	6	2	2	0	0	25	23	2	9	12	11.5	2.88	106	.250	.317	2	.250	0	1	0	-0	0.0
1921	Bos-N	0	1	.000	2	0	0	0	0	1²	3	0	3	1	32.4	21.60	17	.375	.545	0	.000	-0	-3	-3	0	-1.3
Total	2	1	2	.333	8	2	2	0	0	26²	26	2	12	13	12.8	4.05	76	.260	.339	2	.222	-0	-3	-3	-0	-1.3

● BILL PIERRO
Pierro, William Leonard "Wild Bill" b: 4/15/26, Brooklyn, N.Y. BR/TR, 6'1", 155 lbs. Deb: 7/17/50

YEAR	TM/L	W	L	PCT	G	GS	CG	SH	SV	IP	H	HR	BB	SO	RAT	ERA	ERA+	OAV	OOB	BH	AVG	PB	PR	/A	PD	TPI
1950	Pit-N	0	2	.000	12	3	0	0	0	29	33	3	28	13	19.6	10.55	42	.289	.438	2	.222	-0	-21	-20	-1	-1.2

● DAVE PIERSON
Pierson, David P. b: 8/20/1855, Wilkes-Barre, Pa. d: 11/11/22, Trenton, N.J. BR/TR, 5'7", 142 lbs. Deb: 4/25/1876 F♦

YEAR	TM/L	W	L	PCT	G	GS	CG	SH	SV	IP	H	HR	BB	SO	RAT	ERA	ERA+	OAV	OOB	BH	AVG	PB	PR	/A	PD	TPI
1876	Cin-N	0	1	.000	1	1	0	0	0	2	1	0	0	0	—	∞	—	1.000	1.000	55	.236	-0	-2	-2	0	-0.2

● WILLIAM PIERSON
Pierson, William Morris b: 6/14/1899, Atlantic City, N.J. d: 2/20/59, Atlantic City, N.J BL/TL, 6'2", 180 lbs. Deb: 7/4/18

YEAR	TM/L	W	L	PCT	G	GS	CG	SH	SV	IP	H	HR	BB	SO	RAT	ERA	ERA+	OAV	OOB	BH	AVG	PB	PR	/A	PD	TPI
1918	Phi-A	0	1	.000	8	1	0	0	0	21²	20	0	20	6	17.4	3.32	88	.286	.457	1	.250	-0	-1	-1	-1	-0.2
1919	Phi-A	0	0	—	2	1	0	0	0	7²	9	0	8	4	20.0	3.52	97	.333	.486	1	.333	0	-0	-0	0	0.1
1924	Phi-A	0	0	—	1	0	0	0	0	2²	3	0	3	0	20.3	3.38	127	.300	.462	0	—	0	0	0	0	0.0
Total	3	0	1	.000	11	2	0	0	0	32	32	0	31	10	18.3	3.38	94	.299	.464	2	.286	-0	-1	-1	-1	-0.1

● GEORGE PIKTUZIS
Piktuzis, George Richard b: 1/3/32, Chicago, Ill. BR/TL, 6'2", 200 lbs. Deb: 4/25/56

YEAR	TM/L	W	L	PCT	G	GS	CG	SH	SV	IP	H	HR	BB	SO	RAT	ERA	ERA+	OAV	OOB	BH	AVG	PB	PR	/A	PD	TPI
1956	Chi-A	0	0	—	2	0	0	0	0	5	6	1	2	3	14.4	7.20	52	.333	.400	0	—	-0	-2	-2	-0	0.0

● DUANE PILLETTE
Pillette, Duane Xavier "Dee" b: 7/24/22, Detroit, Mich. BR/TR, 6'3", 205 lbs. Deb: 7/19/49 F

YEAR	TM/L	W	L	PCT	G	GS	CG	SH	SV	IP	H	HR	BB	SO	RAT	ERA	ERA+	OAV	OOB	BH	AVG	PB	PR	/A	PD	TPI
1949	NY-A	2	4	.333	12	3	2	0	0	37¹	43	6	19	9	14.9	4.34	93	.299	.380	0	.000	-1	-1	-1	1	-0.2
1950	NY-A	0	0	—	4	0	0	0	0	7	9	0	3	4	15.4	1.29	334	.321	.387	0	—	0	3	2	-0	0.3
	StL-A	3	5	.375	24	7	1	0	2	73²	104	6	44	18	18.3	7.09	70	.337	.423	3	.136	-1	-21	-17	-0	-1.7
	Yr	3	5	.375	28	7	1	0	2	80²	113	6	47	22	18.1	6.58	74	.335	.420	3	.136	-1	-18	-15	-1	-1.7
1951	StL-A	6	14	.300	35	24	6	1	0	191	205	14	115	65	15.3	4.99	88	.276	.376	8	.136	-3	-19	-13	-1	-1.6
1952	StL-A	10	13	.435	30	30	9	1	0	205¹	222	14	55	62	12.4	3.59	109	.274	.325	12	.182	-1	2	7	-2	0.6
1953	StL-A	7	13	.350	31	25	5	1	0	166²	181	16	62	58	13.2	4.48	94	.277	.341	7	.132	-1	-9	-5	-1	-0.7
1954	Bal-A	10	14	.417	25	25	11	1	0	179	158	9	67	66	11.4	3.12	115	.234	.305	7	.132	-1	12	9	3	1.4
1955	Bal-A	0	3	.000	7	5	0	0	0	20²	31	0	14	13	19.6	6.53	58	.344	.433	1	.167	0	-6	-6	-0	-0.7
1956	Phi-N	0	0	—	20	0	0	0	0	23¹	32	7	12	10	17.0	6.56	57	.330	.404	0	.000	-0	-7	-7	0	-0.7
Total	8	38	66	.365	188	119	34	4	2	904	985	67	391	305	13.9	4.40	93	.277	.352	38	.140	-7	-45	-32	-1	-2.9

● HERMAN PILLETTE
Pillette, Herman Polycarp "Old Folks" b: 12/26/1895, St.Paul, Ore. d: 4/30/60, Sacramento, Cal. BR/TR, 6'2", 190 lbs. Deb: 7/30/17 F

YEAR	TM/L	W	L	PCT	G	GS	CG	SH	SV	IP	H	HR	BB	SO	RAT	ERA	ERA+	OAV	OOB	BH	AVG	PB	PR	/A	PD	TPI
1917	Cin-N	0	0	—	1	0	0	0	0	1	4	0	0	0	36.0	18.00	15	.571	.571	0	—	0	-2	-2	-0	0.0
1922	Det-A	19	12	.613	40	37	18	4	1	274²	270	6	95	71	12.5	2.85	136	.258	.328	17	.172	-3	36	31	3	3.2
1923	Det-A	14	19	.424	47	36	14	0	1	250¹	280	7	83	64	13.3	3.85	100	.288	.347	21	.247	4	4	4	0	0.8
1924	Det-A	1	1	.500	19	3	1	0	1	37²	46	1	14	13	15.1	4.78	86	.297	.366	4	.364	1	-2	-3	0	0.0
Total	4	34	32	.515	107	76	33	4	3	563²	600	14	192	148	13.0	3.45	113	.275	.340	42	.215	2	36	27	7	4.0

● SQUIZ PILLION
Pillion, Cecil Randolph b: 4/13/1894, Hartford, Conn. d: 9/30/62, Pittsburgh, Pa. BL/TL, 6', 178 lbs. Deb: 8/20/15

YEAR	TM/L	W	L	PCT	G	GS	CG	SH	SV	IP	H	HR	BB	SO	RAT	ERA	ERA+	OAV	OOB	BH	AVG	PB	PR	/A	PD	TPI
1915	Phi-A	0	0	—	2	0	0	0	0	5¹	10	0	2	0	21.9	6.75	43	.400	.464	0	.000	-0	-2	-2	0	0.0

● HORACIO PINA
Pina, Horacio (Garcia) b: 3/12/45, Coahuila, Mexico BR/TR, 6'2", 177 lbs. Deb: 8/14/68

YEAR	TM/L	W	L	PCT	G	GS	CG	SH	SV	IP	H	HR	BB	SO	RAT	ERA	ERA+	OAV	OOB	BH	AVG	PB	PR	/A	PD	TPI
1968	Cle-A	1	1	.500	12	3	0	0	2	31¹	24	0	15	24	11.5	1.72	172	.218	.317	0	.000	-1	4	4	0	0.3
1969	Cle-A	4	2	.667	31	4	0	0	1	46²	44	6	27	32	14.7	5.21	72	.256	.373	3	.500	1	-8	-7	0	-0.8
1970	Was-A	5	3	.625	61	0	0	0	6	71	66	4	35	41	13.2	2.79	127	.250	.344	0	.000	-0	7	6	1	0.8
1971	Was-A	1	1	.500	56	0	0	0	2	57²	47	2	31	38	12.8	3.59	92	.227	.339	0	.000	-0	-1	-2	1	0.0
1972	Tex-A	2	7	.222	60	0	0	0	15	76	61	3	43	60	13.3	3.20	94	.228	.352	1	.200	-1	-1	-3	1	0.1
1973	*Oak-A	6	3	.667	47	0	0	0	8	88	58	8	34	41	10.2	2.76	128	.193	.292	0	—	0	10	8	3	1.4
1974	Chi-N	3	4	.429	34	0	0	0	4	47¹	49	4	28	32	15.0	3.99	96	.268	.371	1	.200	-0	-2	-1	1	-0.1
	Cal-A	1	2	.333	11	0	0	0	0	11²	9	1	5	6	9.3	2.31	149	.209	.261	0	—	-0	1	1	0	0.8
1978	Phi-N	0	0	—	2	0	0	0	0	2¹	0	0	4	0	10.0	0.00	—	.000	.000	0	—	-0	1	1	0	0.0
Total	8	23	23	.500	314	7	0	0	38	432	358	28	216	278	12.6	3.25	106	.231	.336	5	.185	0	12	9	9	2.5

● ED PINKHAM
Pinkham, Edward b: 1849, Brooklyn, N.Y. TL, 5'7", 142 lbs. Deb: 5/8/1871 ♦

YEAR	TM/L	W	L	PCT	G	GS	CG	SH	SV	IP	H	HR	BB	SO	RAT	ERA	ERA+	OAV	OOB	BH	AVG	PB	PR	/A	PD	TPI
1871	Chi-n	1	0	1.000	3	0	0	0	0	10¹	10	0	3	0	11.3	3.48	132	.208	.255	25	.263	1	1	1		0.1

● GEORGE PINKNEY
Pinkney, George Burton b: 1/11/1862, Orange Prairie, Ill. d: 11/10/26, Peoria, Ill. BR/TR, 5'7", 160 lbs. Deb: 8/16/1884 ♦

YEAR	TM/L	W	L	PCT	G	GS	CG	SH	SV	IP	H	HR	BB	SO	RAT	ERA	ERA+	OAV	OOB	BH	AVG	PB	PR	/A	PD	TPI
1886	Bro-a	0	0	—	1	0	0	0	0	2	2	0	0	0	9.0	4.50	78	.400	.400	156	.261	-0	-0	-0	-0	0.0

● ED PINNANCE
Pinnance, Edward D. "Peanuts"
b: 10/22/1879, Walpole Island, Ont., Canada d: 12/12/44, Walpole Island, Ontario, Canada BL/TR, 6'1", 180 lbs. Deb: 9/14/03

YEAR	TM/L	W	L	PCT	G	GS	CG	SH	SV	IP	H	HR	BB	SO	RAT	ERA	ERA+	OAV	OOB	BH	AVG	PB	PR	/A	PD	TPI
1903	Phi-A	0	0	—	2	1	0	0	1	7	5	0	2	2	9.0	2.57	119	.200	.260	0	.000	-0	0	0	-0	0.0

● LERTON PINTO
Pinto, William Lerton b: 4/8/1899, Chillicothe, Ohio d: 5/13/83, Oxnard, Cal. BL/TL, 6', 190 lbs. Deb: 5/23/22

YEAR	TM/L	W	L	PCT	G	GS	CG	SH	SV	IP	H	HR	BB	SO	RAT	ERA	ERA+	OAV	OOB	BH	AVG	PB	PR	/A	PD	TPI
1922	Phi-N	0	1	.000	9	0	0	0	0	24²	31	1	14	14	16.4	5.11	91	.320	.405	1	.111	-1	-3	-1	-1	-0.1
1924	Phi-N	0	0	—	3	0	0	0	0	4	7	1	0	2	15.8	9.00	50	.467	.467	0	.000	-0	-2	-2	0	-0.0
Total	2	0	1	.000	12	0	0	0	0	28²	38	2	14	16	16.3	5.65	82	.339	.413	1	.100	-1	-5	-3	-1	-0.1

● ED PIPGRAS
Pipgras, Edward John b: 6/15/04, Schleswig, Iowa d: 4/13/64, Currie, Minn. BR/TR, 6'2.5", 175 lbs. Deb: 8/25/32 F

YEAR	TM/L	W	L	PCT	G	GS	CG	SH	SV	IP	H	HR	BB	SO	RAT	ERA	ERA+	OAV	OOB	BH	AVG	PB	PR	/A	PD	TPI
1932	Bro-N	0	1	.000	5	1	0	0	0	10	16	2	6	5	19.8	5.40	71	.348	.423	0	.000	-0	-2	-2	0	-0.2

● GEORGE PIPGRAS
Pipgras, George William b: 12/20/1899, Ida Grove, Iowa d: 10/19/86, Gainesville, Fla. BR/TR, 6'1.5", 185 lbs. Deb: 6/9/23 FU

YEAR	TM/L	W	L	PCT	G	GS	CG	SH	SV	IP	H	HR	BB	SO	RAT	ERA	ERA+	OAV	OOB	BH	AVG	PB	PR	/A	PD	TPI
1923	NY-A	1	3	.250	8	2	0	0	0	33¹	34	2	25	12	16.2	5.94	66	.276	.403	0	.000	-1	-7	-7	-0	-0.9
1924	NY-A	0	1	.000	9	1	0	0	1	15¹	20	0	18	4	24.7	9.98	42	.351	.532	1	.333	-2	-10	-10	1	-0.6
1927	*NY-A	10	3	.769	29	21	9	1	0	166¹	148	2	77	81	12.2	4.11	94	.247	.334	16	.239	2	1	-5	-1	-0.3
1928	*NY-A	24	13	.649	46	38	22	4	3	300²	314	4	103	139	12.6	3.38	111	.272	.333	18	.157	-4	22	13	-4	0.6
1929	NY-A	18	12	.600	39	33	13	3	0	225¹	229	16	95	125	13.1	4.23	91	.264	.340	12	.143	-4	0	-9	-3	-1.7
1930	NY-A	15	15	.500	44	30	15	**3**	4	221	230	9	70	111	12.5	4.11	105	.263	.324	12	.150	-2	13	5	-2	0.0
1931	NY-A	7	6	.538	36	14	8	1	0	137²	134	8	58	59	12.7	3.79	105	.251	.327	1	.024	-6	9	3	-2	-0.5
1932	*NY-A	16	9	.640	32	27	14	2	0	219	235	15	87	111	13.5	4.19	97	.269	.340	18	.220	-1	7	-3	-2	-0.4
1933	NY-A	2	2	.500	4	4	3	0	0	33	32	1	12	14	12.0	3.27	119	.252	.317	1	.091	4	2	1	0	0.3
	Bos-A	9	8	.529	22	17	9	1	0	128¹	140	5	45	56	13.1	4.07	108	.276	.337	9	.196	-1	3	4	-2	0.3
	Yr	11	10	.524	26	21	12	1	0	161¹	172	6	57	70	12.9	3.90	110	.271	.333	10	.175	-1	7	7	-1	0.6
1934	Bos-A	0	0	—	2	1	0	0	0	3¹	4	1	3	0	18.9	8.10	59	.308	.438	0	—	-0	-1	-0	0	-0.8
1935	Bos-A	0	1	.000	5	1	0	0	0	5	9	3	2	1	27.0	14.40	33	.391	.517	0	—	0	-6	-5	0	-0.8
Total	11	102	73	.583	276	189	93	16	12	1488¹	1529	66	598	714	13.1	4.09	98	.266	.339	88	.163	-15	35	-14	-15	-4.0

● COTTON PIPPEN
Pippen, Henry Harold b: 4/2/11, Cisco, Tex. d: 2/15/81, Williams, Cal. BR/TR, 6'2", 180 lbs. Deb: 8/28/36

YEAR	TM/L	W	L	PCT	G	GS	CG	SH	SV	IP	H	HR	BB	SO	RAT	ERA	ERA+	OAV	OOB	BH	AVG	PB	PR	/A	PD	TPI
1936	StL-N	0	2	.000	6	3	0	0	0	21	37	5	8	8	20.1	7.71	51	.402	.461	1	.167	0	-9	-9	1	-0.6
1939	Phi-A	4	11	.267	25	17	5	0	1	118²	169	13	40	33	15.9	5.99	79	.329	.378	3	.086	-2	-18	-17	2	-1.8
	Det-A	0	1	.000	3	2	0	0	0	14	18	1	6	5	15.4	7.07	69	.310	.375	2	.400	0	-4	-3	-0	-0.2

YEAR	TM/L	W	L	PCT	G	GS	CG	SH	SV	IP	H	HR	BB	SO	RAT	ERA	ERA+	OAV	OOB	BH	AVG	PB	PR	/A	PD	TPI
	Yr	4	12	.250	28	19	5	0	1	132²	187	14	46	38	15.8	6.11	77	.326	.376	5	.125	-2	-22	-20	1	-2.0
1940	Det-A	1	2	.333	4	3	0	0	0	21¹	29	3	10	9	16.9	6.75	70	.326	.400	0	.000	-1	-6	-5	0	-0.6
Total	3	5	16	.238	38	25	5	0	1	175	253	22	64	55	16.5	6.38	73	.336	.391	6	.111	-3	-36	-34	2	-3.2

● GERRY PIRTLE
Pirtle, Gerald Eugene b: 12/3/47, Tulsa, Okla. BR/TR, 6'1", 185 lbs. Deb: 7/2/78

YEAR	TM/L	W	L	PCT	G	GS	CG	SH	SV	IP	H	HR	BB	SO	RAT	ERA	ERA+	OAV	OOB	BH	AVG	PB	PR	/A	PD	TPI
1978	Mon-N	0	2	.000	19	0	0	0	0	25²	33	5	23	14	20.3	5.96	59	.314	.446	0	—	0	-7	-7	-0	-0.5

● SKIP PITLOCK
Pitlock, Lee Patrick Thomas b: 11/6/47, Hillside, Ill. BL/TL, 6'2", 180 lbs. Deb: 6/12/70

YEAR	TM/L	W	L	PCT	G	GS	CG	SH	SV	IP	H	HR	BB	SO	RAT	ERA	ERA+	OAV	OOB	BH	AVG	PB	PR	/A	PD	TPI
1970	SF-N	5	5	.500	18	15	1	0	0	87	92	13	48	56	14.9	4.66	85	.274	.371	2	.080	-0	-6	-7	0	-0.7
1974	Chi-A	3	3	.500	40	5	0	0	1	105²	103	7	55	68	14.1	4.43	84	.257	.356	0	—	0	-10	-8	-1	-0.7
1975	Chi-A	0	0	—	1	0	0	0	0	0	1	0	0	0	—	—	—	1.000	1.000	0	—	0	0	0	0	-0.1
Total	3	8	8	.500	59	20	1	0	1	192²	196	20	103	124	14.5	4.53	85	.266	.364	2	.080	-0	-15	-15	-1	-1.5

● TOGIE PITTINGER
Pittinger, Charles Reno b: 1/12/1872, Greencastle, Pa. d: 1/14/09, Greencastle, Pa. BL/TR, 6'2", 175 lbs. Deb: 4/26/00

YEAR	TM/L	W	L	PCT	G	GS	CG	SH	SV	IP	H	HR	BB	SO	RAT	ERA	ERA+	OAV	OOB	BH	AVG	PB	PR	/A	PD	TPI
1900	Bos-N	2	9	.182	18	13	8	0	0	114	135	7	54	27	15.6	5.13	80	.294	.378	6	.130	-4	-18	-13	-1	-1.4
1901	Bos-N	13	16	.448	34	33	27	1	0	281¹	288	7	76	129	11.9	3.01	120	.263	.316	11	.110	-8	10	19	3	1.2
1902	Bos-N	27	16	.628	46	40	36	7	0	389¹	360	4	128	174	11.7	2.52	112	.245	.313	20	.136	-8	11	13	-2	0.2
1903	Bos-N	18	22	.450	44	39	35	3	1	351²	352	12	143	140	14.2	3.48	92	.294	.369	14	.109	-9	-8	-11	-3	-2.1
1904	Bos-N	15	21	.417	38	38	35	5	0	335²	298	1	144	146	12.2	2.66	104	.242	.329	13	.107	-9	3	4	5	0.0
1905	Phi-N	23	14	.622	46	37	29	4	2	337¹	311	3	104	136	11.5	3.09	94	.247	.313	19	.156	-3	-3	-6	-3	-1.3
1906	Phi-N	8	10	.444	20	16	9	2	0	129²	128	2	50	43	13.2	3.40	77	.252	.334	4	.091	-1	-11	-11	-1	-1.8
1907	Phi-N	9	5	.643	16	12	8	1	0	102	101	3	35	37	12.4	3.08	81	.261	.330	5	.139	-1	-6	-7	-1	-1.0
Total	8	115	113	.504	262	228	187	23	3	2040²	2017	39	734	832	12.6	3.10	98	.260	.332	92	.124	-43	-23	-13	-2	-6.2

● STAN PITULA
Pitula, Stanley b: 3/23/31, Hackensack, N.J. d: 8/15/65, Hackensack, N.J. BR/TR, 5'10", 170 lbs. Deb: 4/24/57

YEAR	TM/L	W	L	PCT	G	GS	CG	SH	SV	IP	H	HR	BB	SO	RAT	ERA	ERA+	OAV	OOB	BH	AVG	PB	PR	/A	PD	TPI
1957	Cle-A	2	2	.500	23	5	1	0	0	59²	67	8	32	17	15.2	4.98	75	.296	.388	3	.200	0	-8	-8	-1	-0.6

● JUAN PIZARRO
Pizarro, Juan Ramon (Cordova) b: 2/7/37, Santurce, P.R. BL/TL, 5'11", 190 lbs. Deb: 5/4/57

YEAR	TM/L	W	L	PCT	G	GS	CG	SH	SV	IP	H	HR	BB	SO	RAT	ERA	ERA+	OAV	OOB	BH	AVG	PB	PR	/A	PD	TPI
1957	*Mil-N	5	6	.455	24	10	3	0	0	99¹	99	16	51	68	13.7	4.62	76	.261	.350	9	.250	3	-8	-12	-1	-1.0
1958	*Mil-N	6	4	.600	16	10	7	1	1	96²	75	12	47	84	11.7	2.70	130	.212	.312	8	.250	3	13	9	1	1.2
1959	Mil-N	6	2	.750	29	14	6	2	0	133²	117	13	70	126	13.1	3.77	94	.237	.342	5	.122	-0	3	-3	-0	-0.2
1960	Mil-N	6	7	.462	21	17	3	0	0	114²	105	13	72	88	14.2	4.55	75	.244	.357	11	.275	3	-10	-14	-1	-1.2
1961	Chi-A	14	7	.667	39	25	12	1	2	194²	164	17	89	188	11.9	3.05	128	.226	.314	17	.246	5	21	19	-1	2.3
1962	Chi-A	12	14	.462	36	32	9	1	1	203¹	182	17	97	173	12.4	3.81	103	.236	.322	11	.159	-0	4	2	-2	0.0
1963	Chi-A★	16	8	.667	32	28	10	3	1	214²	177	14	63	163	10.2	2.39	147	.224	.284	13	.178	3	30	27	-3	3.0
1964	Chi-A☆	19	9	.679	33	33	11	4	0	239	193	23	55	162	9.5	2.56	135	.219	.267	19	.211	5	28	24	-1	3.1
1965	Chi-A	6	3	.667	18	18	2	1	0	97	96	8	37	65	12.4	3.43	93	.254	.322	8	.235	3	0	-3	-0	0.1
1966	Chi-A	8	6	.571	34	9	1	0	3	88²	91	9	39	42	13.3	3.76	84	.269	.347	4	.154	-0	-3	-6	-1	-0.8
1967	Pit-N	8	10	.444	50	9	1	1	9	107	99	10	52	96	12.9	3.95	85	.245	.334	7	.259	2	-7	-7	-1	-1.2
1968	Pit-N	1	1	.500	12	0	0	0	0	11	14	2	10	6	20.5	3.27	89	.311	.446	0	.000	-0	-0	-0	-0	-0.2
	Bos-A	6	8	.429	19	12	6	0	2	107²	97	15	44	84	11.8	3.59	88	.242	.317	5	.161	1	-7	-5	2	-0.4
1969	Bos-A	0	1	.000	6	0	0	0	0	9	14	2	6	4	20.0	6.00	63	.359	.444	1	.333	0	-2	-2	-0	-0.3
	Cle-A	3	3	.500	48	4	1	0	4	82²	67	9	49	44	12.8	3.16	119	.229	.343	3	.200	0	4	6	0	0.5
	Oak-A	1	1	.500	3	0	0	0	1	7²	3	1	3	4	7.0	2.35	146	.125	.222	1	.500	0	1	1	0	0.3
	Yr	4	5	.444	57	4	1	0	7	99¹	84	9	58	52	12.9	3.35	112	.230	.335	5	.250	1	3	4	0	0.5
1970	Chi-N	0	0	—	12	0	0	0	0	15²	16	2	9	14	14.9	4.60	98	.262	.366	0	.000	-0	-1	-0	0	0.0
1971	Chi-N	7	6	.538	16	14	6	0	0	101¹	78	14	40	67	10.7	3.46	114	.209	.289	6	.176	1	5	5	0	0.8
1972	Chi-N	4	5	.444	16	7	1	0	1	59¹	66	7	32	24	15.0	3.94	97	.293	.384	3	.143	0	-3	-1	1	-0.1
1973	Chi-N	0	1	.000	2	0	0	0	0	4	6	1	3	3	18.0	11.25	35	.353	.421	0	.000	-0	-3	-0	0	-0.6
	Hou-N	2	2	.500	15	1	0	0	0	23¹	28	1	11	10	15.4	6.56	55	.301	.381	0	.000	-0	-8	-8	1	-1.1
	Yr	2	3	.400	17	1	0	0	0	27¹	34	2	12	13	15.5	7.24	51	.304	.376	0	.000	-0	-11	-11	1	-1.7
1974	*Pit-N	1	1	.500	7	0	0	0	0	24	20	2	11	7	11.6	1.88	184	.220	.304	2	.333	1	5	4	-0	0.4
Total	18	131	105	.555	488	245	79	17	28	2034¹	1807	201	888	1522	12.1	3.43	104	.237	.320	133	.202	29	55	33	-5	4.6

● GORDIE PLADSON
Pladson, Gordon Cecil b: 7/31/56, New Westminster, B.C., Canada BR/TR, 6'4", 210 lbs. Deb: 9/7/79

YEAR	TM/L	W	L	PCT	G	GS	CG	SH	SV	IP	H	HR	BB	SO	RAT	ERA	ERA+	OAV	OOB	BH	AVG	PB	PR	/A	PD	TPI
1979	Hou-N	0	0	—	4	0	0	0	0	4	9	1	2	2	24.8	4.50	78	.450	.500	0	—	0	-0	-0	-0	0.0
1980	Hou-N	0	4	.000	12	6	0	0	0	41¹	38	3	16	13	11.8	4.35	75	.244	.314	0	.000	-1	-3	-5	-0	-0.5
1981	Hou-N	0	0	—	2	0	0	0	0	4	9	0	3	2	27.0	9.00	37	.429	.500	0	—	0	-2	-3	-0	0.0
1982	Hou-N	0	0	—	2	0	0	0	0	1¹	10	0	2	1	81.0	54.00	6	.769	.800	0	—	0	-7	-8	-0	0.0
Total	4	0	4	.000	20	6	0	0	0	50²	66	4	23	18	15.8	6.04	55	.314	.382	0	.000	-1	-14	-15	-0	-0.5

● EMIL PLANETA
Planeta, Emil Joseph b: 1/31/09, Higganum, Conn. d: 2/2/63, Rocky Hill, Conn. BR/TR, 6', 190 lbs. Deb: 9/20/31

YEAR	TM/L	W	L	PCT	G	GS	CG	SH	SV	IP	H	HR	BB	SO	RAT	ERA	ERA+	OAV	OOB	BH	AVG	PB	PR	/A	PD	TPI
1931	NY-N	0	0	—	2	0	0	0	0	5¹	7	0	4	0	18.6	10.13	36	.292	.393	0	.000	-0	-4	-4	0	0.0

● ED PLANK
Plank, Edward Arthur b: 4/9/52, Chicago, Ill. BR/TR, 6'1", 205 lbs. Deb: 9/6/78

YEAR	TM/L	W	L	PCT	G	GS	CG	SH	SV	IP	H	HR	BB	SO	RAT	ERA	ERA+	OAV	OOB	BH	AVG	PB	PR	/A	PD	TPI
1978	SF-N	0	0	—	5	0	0	0	0	6²	6	1	2	1	10.8	4.05	85	.273	.333	0	—	0	-0	-0	-0	0.0
1979	SF-N	0	0	—	4	0	0	0	0	3²	9	0	2	3	27.0	7.36	47	.450	.500	0	—	0	-1	-2	-0	0.0
Total	2	0	0	—	9	0	0	0	0	10¹	15	1	4	2	16.5	5.23	64	.357	.413	0	—	0	-2	-2	-0	0.0

● EDDIE PLANK
Plank, Edward Stewart "Gettysburg Eddie" b: 8/31/1875, Gettysburg, Pa. d: 2/24/26, Gettysburg, Pa. BL/TL, 5'11.5", 175 lbs. Deb: 5/13/01 H

YEAR	TM/L	W	L	PCT	G	GS	CG	SH	SV	IP	H	HR	BB	SO	RAT	ERA	ERA+	OAV	OOB	BH	AVG	PB	PR	/A	PD	TPI
1901	Phi-A	17	13	.567	33	32	28	1	0	260²	254	2	68	90	11.4	3.31	114	.252	.304	18	.182	-3	10	13	-2	0.8
1902	Phi-A	20	15	.571	36	32	31	1	0	300	319	5	61	107	11.9	3.30	111	.273	.319	35	.292	-6	9	12	-2	1.6
1903	Phi-A	23	16	.590	43	40	33	3	0	336	317	5	65	176	10.8	2.38	128	.249	.297	25	.187	-1	22	25	-1	2.5
1904	Phi-A	26	17	.605	44	43	37	7	0	357¹	311	2	86	201	10.5	2.17	124	.235	.291	31	.240	3	17	20	-0	2.8
1905	*Phi-A	24	12	.667	41	41	35	4	0	346²	287	3	75	210	10.0	2.26	118	.227	.283	29	.230	3	15	16	-3	1.5
1906	Phi-A	19	6	.760	26	25	21	5	0	211²	173	1	51	108	10.2	2.25	121	.226	.288	17	.233	2	10	11	-2	1.3
1907	Phi-A	24	16	.600	43	40	33	8	0	343²	282	5	85	183	10.1	2.20	119	.226	.284	26	.211	2	13	16	-1	1.9
1908	Phi-A	14	16	.467	34	28	21	4	1	244²	202	1	46	135	9.5	2.17	118	.224	.269	16	.180	-1	6	11	-4	0.7
1909	Phi-A	19	10	.655	34	33	24	3	0	265¹	215	6	62	132	9.7	1.76	136	.224	.277	21	.219	-4	21	19	1	2.7
1910	Phi-A	16	10	.615	38	32	22	1	2	250¹	218	3	55	123	10.1	2.01	118	.237	.286	11	.128	-3	14	10	-3	0.4
1911	*Phi-A	23	8	.742	40	30	24	6	4	256²	237	2	77	149	11.5	2.10	110	.255	.322	18	.191	-1	35	30	1	3.4
1912	Phi-A	26	6	.813	37	30	23	5	2	259²	234	1	83	110	11.2	2.22	139	.245	.309	24	.267	4	32	25	-2	3.2
1913	*Phi-A	18	10	.643	41	30	18	7	0	242²	211	3	57	151	10.1	2.60	106	.234	.283	8	.105	-0	9	5	-1	0.3
1914	*Phi-A	15	7	.682	34	22	12	4	3	185¹	178	2	42	110	11.0	2.87	91	.266	.315	5	.105	-0	-3	-5	-3	-0.9
1915	StL-F	21	11	.656	42	31	23	6	3	268¹	212	1	54	147	9.0	2.08	138	.218	.262	24	.258	3	19	24	-3	2.9
1916	StL-A	16	15	.516	37	26	17	3	3	235²	203	6	67	88	10.5	2.33	118	.237	.297	15	.185	-0	13	11	-4	1.1
1917	StL-A	5	6	.455	20	14	8	1	1	131	105	2	38	26	10.0	1.79	145	.225	.287	4	.105	-1	13	12	-2	0.7
Total	17	326	194	.627	623	529	410	69	23	4495²	3958	41	1072	2246	10.5	2.35	122	.239	.293	331	.206	17	258	255	-32	26.9

◉ ERIK PLANTENBERG
Plantenberg, Erik John b: 10/30/68, Renton, Wash. BB/TL, 6'1", 180 lbs. Deb: 7/31/93

YEAR	TM/L	W	L	PCT	G	GS	CG	SH	SV	IP	H	HR	BB	SO	RAT	ERA	ERA+	OAV	OOB	BH	AVG	PB	PR	/A	PD	TPI
1993	Sea-A	0	0	—	20	0	0	0	1	9²	11	0	12	3	22.3	6.52	68	.282	.462	0	—	0	-2	-2	0	0.0
1994	Sea-A	0	0	—	6	0	0	0	0	7	4	0	7	1	15.4	0.00	∞	.174	.387	0	—	0	4	4	0	0.0
Total	2	0	0	—	26	0	0	0	1	16²	15	0	19	4	19.4	3.78	122	.242	.434	0	—	0	1	2	0	0.0

YEAR TM/L	W	L	PCT	G	GS	CG	SH	SV	IP	H	HR	BB	SO	RAT	ERA	ERA+	OAV	OOB	BH	AVG	PB	PR	/A	PD	TPI
● **BILL PLEIS**			Pleis, William		b: 8/5/37, St.Louis, Mo.				BL/TL, 5'10", 175 lbs.			Deb: 4/16/61													
1961 Min-A	4	2	.667	37	0	0	0	2	56¹	59	4	34	32	15.5	4.95	86	.266	.373	1	.111	-1	-6	-4	-1	-0.6
1962 Min-A	2	5	.286	21	4	0	0	3	45	46	7	14	31	12.2	4.40	93	.264	.323	4	.286	1	-2	-2	-1	-0.2
1963 Min-A	6	2	.750	36	4	1	0	0	68	67	10	16	37	11.0	4.37	83	.258	.301	2	.125	0	-6	-5	-0	-0.6
1964 Min-A	4	1	.800	47	0	0	0	4	50²	43	6	31	42	13.3	3.91	92	.232	.346	1	.250	0	-2	-2	-0	-0.1
1965 *Min-A	4	4	.500	41	2	0	0	4	51¹	49	3	27	33	13.3	2.98	119	.250	.341	0	.000	-1	3	3	-0	0.4
1966 Min-A	1	2	.333	8	0	0	0	0	9¹	5	1	4	9	8.7	1.93	186	.152	.243	0	—	0	2	2	-0	0.5
Total 6	21	16	.568	190	10	1	0	13	280²	269	31	126	184	12.9	4.07	93	.251	.334	8	.160	0	-11	-8	-3	-0.6
● **DAN PLESAC**			Plesac, Daniel Thomas		b: 2/4/62, Gary, Ind.				BL/TL, 6'5", 210 lbs.			Deb: 4/11/86													
1986 Mil-A	10	7	.588	51	0	0	0	14	91	81	5	29	75	10.9	2.97	146	.240	.301	0	—	0	12	14	-1	2.8
1987 Mil-A★	5	6	.455	57	0	0	0	23	79¹	63	8	23	89	10.1	2.61	175	.213	.276	0	—	0	16	17	0	3.2
1988 Mil-A★	1	2	.333	50	0	0	0	30	52¹	46	2	12	52	10.0	2.41	165	.234	.278	0	—	0	9	9	-0	1.7
1989 Mil-A★	3	4	.429	52	0	0	0	33	61¹	47	6	17	52	9.4	2.35	163	.213	.269	0	—	0	10	10	-0	2.4
1990 Mil-A	3	7	.300	66	0	0	0	24	69	67	5	31	65	13.2	4.43	87	.257	.342	0	—	0	-4	-4	-0	-0.9
1991 Mil-A	2	7	.222	45	10	0	0	8	92¹	92	12	39	61	13.1	4.29	93	.263	.342	0	—	0	-2	-3	-2	-0.5
1992 Mil-A	5	4	.556	44	4	0	0	1	79	64	5	35	54	11.6	2.96	130	.229	.321	0	—	0	9	8	-1	0.9
1993 Chi-N	2	1	.667	57	0	0	0	0	62²	74	10	21	47	13.6	4.74	84	.298	.353	0	.000	-0	-5	-5	-0	-0.3
1994 Chi-N	2	3	.400	54	0	0	0	1	54²	61	9	13	53	12.3	4.61	89	.279	.322	0	.000	-0	-2	-3	-1	-0.4
Total 9	33	41	.446	476	14	0	0	134	641²	595	62	220	548	11.6	3.48	117	.247	.313	0	.000	-1	43	42	-5	8.9
● **NORMAN PLITT**			Plitt, Norman William		b: 2/21/1893, York, Pa.		d: 2/1/54, New York, N.Y.		BR/TR, 5'11", 180 lbs.			Deb: 4/26/18													
1918 Bro-N	0	0	—	1	0	0	0	0	2	3	0	1	0	18.0	4.50	62	.429	.500	1	1.000	0	-0	-0	-0	0.0
1927 Bro-N	2	6	.250	19	8	1	0	0	62¹	73	3	36	9	15.9	4.91	81	.303	.396	4	.222	-0	-7	-7	0	-0.7
NY-N	1	0	1.000	3	0	0	0	0	7¹	9	0	1	0	13.5	3.68	105	.310	.355	0	.000	-0	0	0	0	0.0
Yr	3	6	.333	22	8	1	0	0	69²	82	3	37	9	15.5	4.78	83	.303	.388	4	.211	-0	-7	-6	1	-0.7
Total 2	3	6	.333	23	8	1	0	0	71²	85	3	38	9	15.7	4.77	82	.307	.394	5	.250	-0	-7	-7	1	-0.7
● **TIM PLODINEC**			Plodinec, Timothy Alfred		b: 1/27/47, Aliquippa, Pa.				BR/TR, 6'4", 190 lbs.			Deb: 6/2/72													
1972 StL-N	0	0	—	1	0	0	0	0	0¹	3	0	0	0	81.0	27.00	13	.750	.750	0	—	0	-1	-1	0	0.0
● **ERIC PLUNK**			Plunk, Eric Vaughn		b: 9/3/63, Wilmington, Cal.				BR/TR, 6'5", 210 lbs.			Deb: 5/12/86													
1986 Oak-A	4	7	.364	26	15	0	0	0	120¹	91	14	102	98	14.8	5.31	73	.214	.372	—		0	-15	-19	-2	-1.7
1987 Oak-A	4	6	.400	32	11	0	0	0	95	91	8	62	90	14.7	4.74	87	.253	.366	—		0	-3	-6	-1	-0.7
1988 *Oak-A	7	2	.778	49	0	0	0	5	78	62	6	39	79	11.8	3.00	126	.217	.313	—		0	8	7	-1	0.8
1989 Oak-A	1	1	.500	23	0	0	0	0	28²	17	1	12	24	9.4	2.20	167	.172	.268	—		0	5	5	-0	0.5
NY-A	7	5	.583	27	7	0	0	0	75²	65	9	52	61	13.9	3.69	105	.237	.359	—		0	2	2	0	0.1
Yr	8	6	.571	50	7	0	0	0	104¹	82	10	64	85	12.6	3.28	116	.219	.333	—		0	7	6	-0	0.6
1990 NY-A	6	3	.667	47	0	0	0	0	72²	58	6	43	67	12.8	2.72	146	.225	.340	—		0	10	10	2	1.3
1991 NY-A	2	5	.286	43	8	0	0	0	111²	128	18	62	103	15.4	4.76	87	.286	.374	—		0	-8	-8	-2	-0.6
1992 Cle-A	9	6	.600	58	0	0	0	0	71²	61	5	38	50	12.4	3.64	107	.229	.326	—		0	2	2	0	0.5
1993 Cle-A	4	5	.444	70	0	0	0	15	71	61	6	30	77	11.5	2.79	155	.226	.303	—		0	12	12	-1	1.8
1994 Cle-A	7	2	.778	41	0	0	0	3	71	61	3	37	73	12.7	2.54	195	.231	.330	—		0	18	19	0	2.2
Total 9	51	42	.548	416	41	0	0	30	795²	695	75	477	722	13.4	3.81	107	.236	.345	—		0	31	23	-6	4.2
● **JEFF PLYMPTON**			Plympton, Jeffrey Hunter		b: 11/24/65, Framingham, Mass.				BR/TR, 6'2", 205 lbs.			Deb: 6/15/91													
1991 Bos-A	0	0	—	4	0	0	0	0	5¹	5	0	4	2	15.2	0.00	—	.263	.391	—		0	2	3	-0	-0.1
● **RAY POAT**			Poat, Raymond Willis		b: 12/19/17, Chicago, Ill.		d: 4/29/90, Oak Lawn, Ill.		BR/TR, 6'2", 200 lbs.			Deb: 4/15/42													
1942 Cle-A	1	3	.250	4	4	1	1	0	18¹	24	1	9	8	16.7	5.40	64	.296	.374	0	.000	-0	-4	-4	0	-0.7
1943 Cle-A	2	5	.286	17	4	1	0	0	45	44	3	20	31	12.8	4.40	71	.259	.337	2	.154	-1	-6	-6	-0	-1.0
1944 Cle-A	4	8	.333	36	6	1	0	1	80²	82	9	37	40	13.3	5.13	64	.265	.343	0	.000	-2	-15	-16	-0	-2.5
1947 NY-N	7	5	.583	7	7	5	0	0	60	53	8	13	25	9.9	2.55	160	.238	.280	4	.190	2	10	10	-0	1.3
1948 NY-N	11	10	.524	39	24	7	3	0	157²	162	21	67	57	13.2	4.34	91	.262	.337	7	.125	-1	-7	-7	-2	-1.2
1949 NY-N	0	0	—	2	0	0	0	0	2¹	8	0	1	0	34.7	19.29	21	.615	.643	0	—	0	-4	-4	-0	-0.7
Pit-N	0	1	.000	11	2	0	0	0	36	52	6	15	17	16.6	6.25	67	.335	.394	1	.100	-1	-9	-8	-0	-0.3
Yr	0	1	.000	13	2	0	0	0	38¹	60	6	16	17	17.8	7.04	59	.357	.413	1	.100	-1	-13	-12	-0	-0.3
Total 6	22	30	.423	116	47	15	4	1	400	425	48	162	178	13.3	4.55	82	.271	.340	14	.115	-3	-34	-36	-3	-4.4
● **BUD PODBIELAN**			Podbielan, Clarence Anthony		b: 3/6/24, Curlew, Wash.		d: 10/26/82, Syracuse, N.Y.		BR/TR, 6'1.5", 170 lbs.			Deb: 4/25/49													
1949 Bro-N	0	1	.000	7	1	0	0	0	12¹	9	1	9	9	13.9	3.65	112	.205	.352	0	.000	-0	1	1	1	0.1
1950 Bro-N	5	4	.556	20	10	2	0	0	72²	93	10	29	28	15.4	5.33	77	.307	.371	3	.107	-1	-10	-10	1	-1.1
1951 Bro-N	2	2	.500	27	5	1	0	0	79²	67	9	36	26	11.9	3.50	112	.233	.322	7	.304	1	4	4	-0	0.3
1952 Bro-N	0	0	—	3	0	0	0	0	2	4	1	3	1	31.5	18.00	20	.444	.583	0	—	0	-3	-3	-0	0.0
Cin-N	4	5	.444	24	7	4	0	1	86²	78	8	26	22	10.9	2.80	135	.245	.304	4	.160	0	9	9	-1	0.9
Yr	4	5	.444	27	7	4	1	1	88²	82	9	29	23	11.4	3.15	120	.251	.314	4	.160	-0	6	6	-1	0.9
1953 Cin-N	6	16	.273	36	24	8	1	1	186¹	214	21	67	74	14.0	4.73	92	.290	.356	7	.125	-3	-9	-8	-0	-1.1
1954 Cin-N	7	10	.412	27	24	4	0	0	131	157	20	58	42	14.9	5.36	78	.300	.372	6	.143	-1	-19	-17	-2	-2.1
1955 Cin-N	1	2	.333	17	2	0	0	0	42	36	4	11	26	10.3	3.21	132	.234	.289	2	.400	1	4	5	0	0.4
1957 Cin-N	0	1	.000	16	1	0	0	0	16	14	4	13	12	16.6	6.19	66	.290	.333	0	.000	-0	-4	-4	0	-0.3
1959 Cle-A	0	1	.000	6	0	0	0	0	12¹	17	1	2	5	13.9	5.84	63	.354	.380	0	—	-0	-3	-3	0	-0.2
Total 9	25	42	.373	172	76	20	2	3	641	693	79	245	242	13.4	4.49	92	.279	.348	29	.154	-4	-30	-26	-2	-3.1
● **JOHNNY PODGAJNY**			Podgajny, John Sigmund "Specs"		b: 6/10/20, Chester, Pa.		d: 3/2/71, Chester, Pa.		BR/TR, 6'2", 173 lbs.			Deb: 9/15/40													
1940 Phi-N	1	3	.250	4	4	3	0	0	35	33	1	12	12	9.0	2.83	138	.250	.261	2	.167	-0	4	4	0	0.5
1941 Phi-N	9	12	.429	34	24	8	0	0	181¹	191	8	70	53	13.2	4.62	80	.270	.339	5	.129	-3	-20	-18	-1	-2.1
1942 Phi-N	6	14	.300	43	23	8	0	0	186²	191	9	63	40	12.8	3.91	85	.268	.337	11	.183	-1	-12	-12	-1	-1.4
1943 Phi-N	4	4	.500	13	5	3	0	0	64	77	4	16	13	13.1	4.22	80	.310	.352	5	.250	1	-6	-6	1	-0.5
Pit-N	0	4	.000	15	5	0	0	0	34¹	37	1	13	7	13.1	4.72	74	.266	.329	1	.143	-0	-5	-5	2	-0.4
Yr	4	8	.333	28	10	3	0	0	98¹	114	5	29	20	13.1	4.39	78	.295	.344	6	.222	0	-11	-11	3	-0.9
1946 Cle-A	0	0	—	6	0	0	0	0	9	13	0	2	4	15.0	5.00	66	.302	.333	—		0	-1	-2	0	-0.0
Total 5	20	37	.351	115	61	20	0	0	510¹	542	22	165	129	12.8	4.20	84	.273	.334	27	.168	-3	-41	-39	3	-3.9
● **JOHNNY PODRES**			Podres, John Joseph		b: 9/30/32, Witherbee, N.Y.				BL/TL, 5'11", 192 lbs.			Deb: 4/17/53	C												
1953 *Bro-N	9	4	.692	33	18	3	1	0	115	126	12	64	82	14.9	4.23	101	.282	.373	11	.306	2	1	0	-0	0.2
1954 Bro-N	11	7	.611	29	21	6	2	0	151²	147	13	53	79	11.9	4.27	96	.255	.319	17	.283	5	-3	-3	-2	0.0
1955 *Bro-N	9	10	.474	27	24	5	2	0	159¹	160	15	57	114	12.5	3.95	103	.259	.326	11	.183	-0	1	2	-1	0.0
1957 Bro-N	12	9	.571	31	27	10	**6**	3	196	168	15	44	109	**9.8**	**2.66**	**156**	**.230**	**.274**	15	.208	1	26	33	-0	3.5
1958 LA-N☆	13	15	.464	39	31	10	2	1	210¹	208	27	78	143	12.3	3.72	110	.261	.328	9	.127	-3	5	9	-2	0.6
1959 *LA-N	14	9	.609	34	29	6	2	0	195	192	23	74	145	12.4	4.11	103	.261	.331	16	.246	3	-3	3	1	0.7
1960 LA-N★	14	12	.538	34	33	8	1	0	227²	217	25	71	159	11.4	3.08	129	.250	.308	9	.136	-1	17	22	-2	2.1
1961 LA-N	18	5	**.783**	32	29	6	1	0	182²	192	27	51	124	12.2	3.74	116	.271	.324	16	.232	1	6	12	-2	1.3
1962 LA-N☆	15	13	.536	40	40	8	0	0	255	270	20	71	178	12.1	3.81	95	.272	.323	14	.159	1	-4	-5	-4	-0.8
1963 *LA-N	14	12	.538	37	34	10	5	1	198¹	196	16	64	134	11.9	3.54	85	.257	.316	9	.141	1	-6	-11	-1	-1.4
1964 LA-N	0	2	.000	2	2	0	0	0	2²	5	1	3	0	27.0	16.88	19	.417	.533	0	—	0	-4	-4	-0	-1.7

YEAR	TM/L	W	L	PCT	G	GS	CG	SH	SV	IP	H	HR	BB	SO	RAT	ERA	ERA+	OAV	OOB	BH	AVG	PB	PR	/A	PD	TPI
1965	LA-N	7	6	.538	27	22	2	1	1	134	126	17	39	63	11.2	3.43	95	.247	.303	8	.178	1	2	-2	-3	-0.4
1966	LA-N	0	0	—	1	0	0	0	0	1²	2	0	1	1	16.2	0.00	—	.400	.500	0	—	0	1	1	0	0.0
	Det-A	4	5	.444	36	13	2	1	4	107²	106	12	34	53	11.8	3.43	102	.259	.317	7	.233	2	0	1	-1	0.2
1967	Det-A	3	1	.750	21	8	0	0	1	63¹	58	12	11	34	9.9	3.84	85	.244	.280	2	.100	-1	-4	-4	-1	-0.4
1969	SD-N	5	6	.455	17	9	1	0	0	64²	66	7	28	17	13.2	4.31	82	.264	.341	1	.063	-1	-5	-6	-1	-1.1
Total	15	148	116	.561	440	340	77	24	11	2265	2239	242	743	1435	12.0	3.68	105	.259	.319	145	.190	12	37	45	-17	2.8

● **JOE POETZ**   Poetz, Joseph Frank "Bull Montana"   b: 6/22/1900, St.Louis, Mo.   d: 2/7/42, St.Louis, Mo.   BR/TR, 5'10.5", 175 lbs.   Deb: 9/14/26

1926	NY-N	0	1	.000	2	1	0	0	0	8	5	2	8	0	15.8	3.38	111	.192	.400	0	.000	0	0	0	0	0.1

● **BOOTS POFFENBERGER**   Poffenberger, Cletus Elwood   b: 7/1/15, Williamsport, Md.   BR/TR, 5'10", 178 lbs.   Deb: 6/11/37

1937	Det-A	10	5	.667	29	16	5	0	3	137¹	147	8	79	35	15.1	4.65	100	.277	.375	11	.216	-0	-1	0	1	0.1
1938	Det-A	6	7	.462	25	15	8	1	1	125	147	8	66	28	15.5	4.82	104	.297	.382	8	.182	-1	-1	2	-2	0.0
1939	Bro-N	0	0	—	3	1	0	0	0	5	7	1	4	2	19.8	5.40	75	.318	.423	0	.000	-0	-1	-0	0	0.0
Total	3	16	12	.571	57	32	13	1	4	267¹	301	17	149	65	15.4	4.75	101	.287	.379	19	.198	-2	-2	2	-0	0.1

● **TOM POHOLSKY**   Poholsky, Thomas George   b: 8/26/29, Detroit, Mich.   BR/TR, 6'3", 205 lbs.   Deb: 4/20/50

1950	StL-N	0	0	—	5	1	0	0	0	14²	16	2	3	2	11.7	3.68	117	.281	.317	0	.000	-0	1	1	-0	-0.1
1951	StL-N	7	13	.350	38	26	10	1	1	195	204	15	68	70	12.6	4.43	89	.271	.331	14	.209	0	-10	-10	1	-0.8
1954	StL-N	5	7	.417	25	13	4	0	0	106	101	11	30	55	10.6	3.06	135	.254	.296	4	.148	-1	12	12	0	1.2
1955	StL-N	9	11	.450	30	24	8	2	0	151	143	26	35	66	10.7	3.81	106	.244	.289	8	.182	-0	4	4	-1	0.4
1956	StL-N	9	14	.391	33	29	7	2	0	203	210	27	44	95	11.5	3.59	105	.268	.311	11	.159	-1	4	4	0	0.4
1957	Chi-N	1	7	.125	28	11	1	0	0	84	117	9	22	28	15.1	4.93	79	.330	.372	2	.105	-1	-10	-10	0	-0.9
Total	6	31	52	.373	159	104	30	5	1	753²	791	90	192	316	11.9	3.93	101	.270	.317	39	.171	-3	1	1	1	0.2

● **JENNINGS POINDEXTER**   Poindexter, Chester Jennings "Jinx"
b: 9/30/10, Pauls Valley, Okla.   d: 3/3/83, Norman, Okla.   BL/TL, 5'10", 165 lbs.   Deb: 9/15/36

1936	Bos-A	0	2	.000	3	3	0	0	0	10²	13	0	16	2	24.5	6.75	79	.302	.492	0	.000	-1	-2	-2	-0	-0.3
1939	Phi-N	0	0	—	11	1	0	0	0	30¹	29	0	15	12	13.1	4.15	96	.250	.336	2	.200	-0	-1	-0	0	0.0
Total	2	0	2	.000	14	4	0	0	0	41	42	0	31	14	16.0	4.83	90	.264	.384	2	.143	-1	-3	-2	-0	-0.3

● **LOU POLCHOW**   Polchow, Louis William   b: 3/14/1881, Mankato, Minn.   d: 8/15/12, Good Thunder, Minn   5'9"   Deb: 9/14/02

1902	Cle-A	0	1	.000	1	1	0	0	0	8	9	0	4	2	15.9	5.63	61	.284	.364	0	.000	-1	-2	-2	-0	-0.2

● **DICK POLE**   Pole, Richard Henry   b: 10/13/50, Trout Creek, Mich.   BR/TR, 6'3", 210 lbs.   Deb: 8/3/73   C

1973	Bos-A	3	2	.600	12	7	0	0	0	54²	70	4	18	24	14.5	5.60	72	.318	.370	0	—	0	-11	-10	-0	-1.1
1974	Bos-A	1	1	.500	15	2	0	0	1	45	55	6	13	32	13.8	4.20	91	.304	.354	0	—	0	-3	-2	1	-0.1
1975	*Bos-A	4	6	.400	18	11	2	1	0	89²	102	11	32	42	13.7	4.42	92	.290	.352	0	—	0	-6	-3	0	-0.4
1976	Bos-A	6	5	.545	31	15	1	0	0	120²	131	8	48	49	13.5	4.33	90	.279	.348	0	.000	0	-6	-1	-0	-0.6
1977	Sea-A	7	12	.368	25	24	3	0	0	122¹	127	16	57	51	14.0	5.15	80	.270	.356	0	—	0	-15	-14	-3	-2.1
1978	Sea-A	4	11	.267	21	18	2	0	0	98²	122	16	41	41	15.1	6.48	59	.306	.375	0	—	0	-30	-29	-1	-3.8
Total	6	25	37	.403	122	77	8	1	1	531	607	61	209	239	14.1	5.05	79	.290	.359	0	.000	0	-76	-63	-5	-8.1

● **KEN POLIVKA**   Polivka, Kenneth Lyle "Soup"   b: 1/21/21, Chicago, Ill.   d: 7/23/88, Aurora, Ill.   BL/TL, 5'10.5", 175 lbs.   Deb: 4/18/47

1947	Cin-N	0	0	—	2	0	0	0	0	3	3	0	3	1	18.0	3.00	137	.250	.400	0	—	0	0	0	-0	0.0

● **HOWIE POLLET**   Pollet, Howard Joseph   b: 6/26/21, New Orleans, La.   d: 8/8/74, Houston, Tex.   BL/TL, 6'1.5", 175 lbs.   Deb: 8/20/41   C

1941	StL-N	5	2	.714	9	8	6	2	0	70	55	1	27	37	10.7	1.93	195	.212	.289	5	.179	-0	13	14	1	1.5
1942	*StL-N	7	5	.583	27	13	5	2	0	109¹	102	7	39	42	11.8	2.88	119	.242	.309	7	.226	3	5	7	-2	0.8
1943	StL-N†	8	4	.667	16	14	12	5	0	118¹	83	2	32	61	8.9	1.75	192	.200	.261	7	.163	-1	21	21	-2	1.9
1946	*StL-N☆	21	10	.677	40	32	22	4	5	266	228	12	86	107	10.8	2.10	165	.234	.300	14	.161	-0	39	40	1	5.1
1947	StL-N	9	11	.450	37	24	9	0	2	176¹	195	11	87	73	14.5	4.34	95	.286	.369	15	.231	2	-5	-4	0	-0.2
1948	StL-N	13	8	.619	36	26	11	0	0	186¹	216	10	67	80	13.8	4.54	90	.289	.349	8	.118	-3	-12	-9	2	-1.1
1949	StL-N★	20	9	.690	39	28	17	5	1	230²	228	9	59	108	11.3	2.77	150	.256	.304	16	.195	1	33	36	-2	4.2
1950	StL-N	14	13	.519	37	30	14	2	2	232¹	228	19	68	117	11.5	3.29	130	.256	.310	12	.143	-2	22	26	0	2.6
1951	StL-N	0	3	.000	6	2	0	0	0	12¹	10	1	8	10	13.1	4.38	91	.208	.321	0	.000	1	-1	-1	0	0.0
	Pit-N	6	10	.375	21	21	4	1	0	128²	149	24	51	47	14.1	5.04	84	.294	.360	5	.139	1	-15	-12	-0	-1.3
	Yr	6	13	.316	27	23	4	1	1	141	159	25	59	57	14.0	4.98	84	.287	.357	5	.135	2	-16	-12	-0	-1.3
1952	Pit-N	7	16	.304	31	30	9	1	0	214	217	22	71	90	12.2	4.12	97	.266	.327	13	.191	2	-9	-3	1	0.0
1953	Pit-N	1	1	.500	5	2	0	0	0	12²	27	2	6	8	23.4	10.66	42	.482	.532	1	.333	-0	-9	-9	-0	-1.1
	Chi-N	5	6	.455	25	17	2	0	1	111¹	120	6	44	45	13.3	4.12	108	.271	.338	4	.129	-1	2	4	-1	0.2
	Yr	6	7	.462	30	19	2	0	1	124	147	8	50	53	14.4	4.79	93	.295	.360	5	.147	-1	-7	-5	-1	-0.9
1954	Chi-N	8	10	.444	20	20	4	2	0	128¹	131	14	54	58	13.0	3.58	117	.263	.335	13	.277	2	7	9	-0	1.4
1955	Chi-N	4	3	.571	24	7	1	1	5	61	62	11	27	27	13.1	5.61	73	.265	.341	6	.400	3	-11	-10	1	-0.8
1956	Chi-A	3	1	.750	11	4	0	0	0	26¹	27	2	11	14	13.0	4.10	100	.252	.322	6	.375	1	0	0	0	0.1
	Pit-N	0	4	.000	19	0	0	0	3	23¹	27	3	8	18	10.0	3.09	122	.212	.280	0	.000	1	0	0	-0	0.0
Total	14	131	116	.530	403	278	116	25	20	2107¹	2096	146	745	934	12.2	3.51	113	.260	.324	129	.185	7	82	111	0	13.7

● **LOU POLLI**   Polli, Louis Americo "Crip"   b: 7/9/01, Barre, Vt.   BR/TR, 5'10.5", 165 lbs.   Deb: 4/18/32

1932	StL-A	0	0	—	5	0	0	0	0	6²	13	0	3	5	21.6	5.40	90	.406	.457	1	.500	-0	-1	-0	-0	0.0
1944	NY-N	0	2	.000	19	0	0	0	3	35²	42	3	20	6	15.6	4.54	81	.294	.380	0	.000	-1	-4	-3	-0	-0.4
Total	2	0	2	.000	24	0	0	0	3	42¹	55	3	23	11	16.6	4.68	82	.314	.394	1	.125	-1	-4	-4	-1	-0.4

● **JOHN POLONI**   Poloni, John Paul   b: 2/28/54, Dearborn, Mich.   BL/TL, 6'5", 210 lbs.   Deb: 9/16/77

1977	Tex-A	1	0	1.000	2	1	0	0	0	7	8	1	1	5	11.6	6.43	63	.286	.310	0	—	0	-2	-2	-0	-0.3

● **JOHN POMORSKI**   Pomorski, John Leon   b: 12/30/05, Brooklyn, N.Y.   d: 12/6/77, Brampton, Ont., Can.   BR/TR, 6', 178 lbs.   Deb: 4/17/34

1934	Chi-A	0	0	—	3	0	0	0	0	1²	1	0	2	0	16.2	5.40	88	.143	.333	0	—	0	-0	-0	0	0.0

● **ARLIE POND**   Pond, Erasmus Arlington   b: 1/19/1872, Rutland, Vt.   d: 9/19/30, Cebu, Philippines   BR/TR, 5'10", 160 lbs.   Deb: 7/4/1895

1895	Bal-N	0	1	.000	6	1	1	0	2	13²	10	0	12	13	15.1	5.93	80	.202	.367	1	.333	1	-2	-2	-0	-0.1
1896	Bal-N	16	8	.667	28	26	21	0	2	214¹	232	4	57	80	12.4	3.49	123	.274	.324	19	.235	0	21	19	-2	1.5
1897	Bal-N	18	9	.667	32	28	23	0	0	248	267	4	72	59	12.8	3.52	119	.273	.332	22	.244	2	22	18	-1	1.6
1898	Bal-N	1	1	.500	3	2	1	0	0	20	8	0	7	4	8.5	0.45	796	.122	.249	2	.286	1	7	7	-1	0.7
Total	4	35	19	.648	69	57	46	0	3	496	517	8	150	156	12.5	3.45	122	.266	.327	44	.245	4	48	42	-3	3.7

● **ELMER PONDER**   Ponder, Charles Elmer   b: 6/26/1893, Reed, Okla.   d: 4/20/74, Albuquerque, N.Mex   BR/TR, 6', 178 lbs.   Deb: 9/18/17

1917	Pit-N	1	1	.500	3	2	1	0	0	21¹	12	0	6	11	8.0	1.69	168	.167	.241	0	—	-1	2	3	-1	0.0
1919	Pit-N	0	5	.000	9	5	0	0	0	47¹	55	0	6	6	12.2	3.99	76	.297	.330	2	.133	-1	-6	-5	-1	-0.7
1920	Pit-N	11	15	.423	33	23	13	2	0	196	182	3	40	62	10.3	2.62	123	.246	.286	7	.119	-4	11	13	1	1.3
1921	Pit-N	2	0	1.000	8	1	0	0	0	24²	29	1	3	2	11.7	2.19	175	.305	.327	0	.000	-2	4	5	0	0.2
	Chi-N	3	6	.333	16	11	5	0	0	89¹	117	7	17	31	13.8	4.74	81	.321	.356	4	.121	-2	-9	-9	2	-0.9
	Yr	5	6	.455	24	12	6	0	0	114	146	8	20	33	13.3	4.18	91	.317	.350	4	.093	-4	-5	-5	2	-0.7
Total	4	17	27	.386	69	42	20	3	0	378²	395	11	72	113	11.3	3.21	105	.271	.309	13	.105	-10	3	6	0	-0.1

YEAR TM/L	W	L	PCT	G	GS	CG	SH	SV	IP	H	HR	BB	SO	RAT	ERA	ERA+	OAV	OOB	BH	AVG	PB	PR	/A	PD	TPI

● ED POOLE Poole, Edward I. b: 9/7/1874, Canton, Ohio d: 3/11/19, Malvern, Ohio BR/TR, 5'10", 175 lbs. Deb: 10/6/00 ♦

1900 Pit-N	1	0	1.000	1	0	0	0	0	7	4	0	0	3	5.1	1.29	283	.167	.167	2	.500	1	2	2	0	0.4
1901 Pit-N	5	4	.556	12	10	8	1	0	80	78	3	30	26	12.8	3.60	91	.254	.332	16	.205	1	-2	-3	0	-0.2
1902 Pit-N	0	0	—	1	0	0	0	0	8	7	0	3	2	11.3	1.13	243	.235	.305	1	.250	0	1	1	-0	0.0
Cin-N	12	4	.750	16	16	16	2	0	138	129	2	54	55	12.5	2.15	139	.247	.327	7	.115	-4	10	13	0	1.0
Yr	12	4	.750	17	16	16	2	0	146	136	2	57	57	12.4	2.10	142	.247	.326	8	.123	-4	11	14	0	1.0
1903 Cin-N	7	13	.350	25	21	18	1	0	184	188	4	77	73	13.5	3.28	100	.270	.352	17	.243	0	-0	6	2	0.7
1904 Bro-N	8	14	.364	25	23	19	1	1	178	178	4	74	67	13.1	3.39	81	.268	.349	8	.129	-3	-13	-13	1	-1.5
Total 5	33	35	.485	80	70	61	5	1	595	584	13	238	226	12.9	3.04	103	.260	.340	51	.183	-6	-2	6	6	0.4

● JIM POOLE Poole, James Richard b: 4/28/66, Rochester, N.Y. BL/TL, 6'2", 190 lbs. Deb: 6/15/90

1990 LA-N	0	0	—	16	0	0	0	0	10²	7	1	8	6	12.7	4.22	87	.184	.326	0	—	0	-1	-1	-0	0.0
1991 Tex-A	0	0	—	5	0	0	0	1	6	10	3	4	4	19.5	4.50	90	.370	.433	0	—	0	-0	-0	-0	0.1
Bal-A	3	2	.600	24	0	0	0	0	36	19	3	9	34	7.0	2.00	198	.157	.215	0	—	0	8	8	0	1.4
Yr	3	2	.600	29	0	0	0	1	42	29	3	12	38	8.8	2.36	168	.195	.255	0	—	0	8	7	0	1.5
1992 Bal-A	0	0	—	6	0	0	0	0	3¹	3	0	1	3	10.8	0.00	—	.231	.286	0	—	0	1	1	0	-0.1
1993 Bal-A	2	1	.667	55	0	0	0	2	50¹	30	2	21	29	9.1	2.15	208	.175	.266	0	—	0	12	13	0	0.5
1994 Bal-A	1	0	1.000	38	0	0	0	0	20¹	32	4	11	18	19.0	6.64	76	.372	.443	0	—	0	-4	-4	0	-0.5
Total 5	6	3	.667	144	0	0	0	3	126²	101	10	53	94	10.9	3.06	141	.221	.303	0	—	0	17	18	0	1.4

● TOM POORMAN Poorman, Thomas Iverson b: 10/14/1857, Lock Haven, Pa. d: 2/18/05, Lock Haven, Pa. BL/TR, 5'7", 135 lbs. Deb: 5/5/1880 ♦

1880 Buf-N	1	8	.111	11	9	9	0	1	85	117	3	19	13	14.4	4.13	59	.307	.340	11	.157	-3	-17	-16	1	-1.6
Chi-N	2	0	1.000	2	1	0	0	0	15	12	0	8	0	12.0	2.40	101	.203	.299	5	.200	-0	-0	-1	-0.1
Yr	3	8	.273	13	10	9	0	1	100	129	3	27	13	14.0	3.87	63	.293	.334	16	.168	-3	-17	-16	1	-1.7
1884 Tol-a	0	1	.000	1	1	1	0	0	9	13	1	2	0	15.0	3.00	114	.310	.341	89	.233	0	0	0	0	0.0
1887 Phi-a	0	0	—	1	0	0	0	0	0²	5	1	1	1	81.0	40.50	11	1.250	1.200	155	.265	-0	-3	-3	0	0.0
Total 3	3	9	.250	15	11	10	0	1	109²	147	5	30	14	14.5	4.02	63	.302	.343	498	.244	-2	-19	-18	1	-1.7

● BILL POPP Popp, William Peter b: 6/7/1877, St.Louis, Mo. d: 9/5/09, St.Louis, Mo. TR, 5'10.5", 170 lbs. Deb: 4/19/02

| 1902 StL-N | 2 | 6 | .250 | 9 | 7 | 5 | 0 | 0 | 60¹ | 87 | 2 | 26 | 20 | 17.6 | 4.92 | 56 | .337 | .408 | 1 | .048 | -3 | -14 | -15 | 1 | -1.8 |

● ED PORRAY Porray, Edmund Joseph b: 12/5/1888, AtSea On Atlantic Ocean d: 7/13/54, Lackawaxen, Pa. BR/TR, 5'11", 170 lbs. Deb: 4/17/14

| 1914 Buf-F | 0 | 1 | .000 | 3 | 3 | 0 | 0 | 0 | 10¹ | 18 | 2 | 7 | 0 | 21.8 | 4.35 | 68 | .391 | .472 | 0 | .000 | -1 | -2 | -2 | 1 | -0.2 |

● CHUCK PORTER Porter, Charles William b: 1/12/56, Baltimore, Md. BR/TR, 6'3", 188 lbs. Deb: 9/14/81

1981 Mil-A	0	0	—	3	0	0	0	0	4¹	6	0	1	1	14.5	4.15	82	.316	.350	0	—	0	-0	-0	-0	0.0
1982 Mil-A	0	0	—	3	0	0	0	0	3²	3	0	1	3	9.8	4.91	77	.250	.308	0	—	0	-0	-0	-0	0.0
1983 Mil-A	7	9	.438	25	21	6	1	0	134	162	9	38	76	13.6	4.50	83	.298	.346	0	—	0	-7	-11	-0	-1.0
1984 Mil-A	6	4	.600	17	12	1	0	0	81¹	99	9	12	48	11.5	3.87	99	.284	.310	0	—	0	1	-0	-0	0.0
1985 Mil-A	0	0	—	6	1	0	0	0	13²	15	1	2	8	11.2	1.98	211	.273	.298	0	—	0	3	3	-0	0.3
Total 5	13	13	.500	54	34	7	1	0	237	278	18	54	136	12.7	4.14	92	.291	.331	0	—	0	-3	-9	-0	-1.0

● HENRY PORTER Porter, Henry b: 6/1858, Vergennes, Vt. d: 12/30/06, Brockton, Mass. BR/TR, Deb: 9/27/1884

1884 Mil-U	3	3	.500	6	6	6	1	0	51	32	1	9	71	7.2	3.00	44	.168	.205	11	.275	1	-3	-9	1	-0.7
1885 Bro-a	33	21	.611	54	54	53	2	0	481²	427	11	107	197	10.3	2.78	118	.223	.270	40	.205	-2	25	27	3	2.6
1886 Bro-a	27	19	.587	48	48	48	1	0	424	439	8	120	163	12.0	3.42	102	.252	.303	33	.179	-9	2	-3	-2	-0.7
1887 Bro-a	15	24	.385	40	40	38	1	0	339²	416	7	96	74	13.8	4.21	102	.297	.345	29	.199	-3	3	3	-2	-0.1
1888 KC-a	18	37	.327	55	54	53	4	0	474	527	16	120	145	12.7	4.16	83	.271	.321	28	.144	-13	-58	-38	4	-4.3
1889 KC-a	0	3	.000	4	4	3	0	0	23	52	0	14	9	26.2	12.52	33	.433	.496	1	.100	-1	-22	-21	0	-1.8
Total 6	96	107	.473	207	206	201	9	0	1793¹	1893	43	466	659	12.1	3.70	95	.259	.308	142	.184	-27	-53	-35	3	-5.0

● NED PORTER Porter, Ned Swindell b: 5/6/05, Apalachicola, Fla. d: 6/30/68, Gainesville, Fla. BR/TR, 6', 173 lbs. Deb: 8/7/26

1926 NY-N	0	0	—	2	0	0	0	0	2	2	1	0	1	9.0	4.50	83	.250	.250	0	—	0	-0	-0	-0	0.0
1927 NY-N	0	0	—	1	0	0	0	0	2	3	0	1	0	18.0	0.00	—	.333	.400	0	—	0	1	1	-0	0.0
Total 2	0	0	—	3	0	0	0	0	4	5	1	1	1	13.5	2.25	169	.294	.333	0	—	0	1	1	-0	0.0

● ODIE PORTER Porter, Odie Oscar b: 5/24/1877, Borden, Ind. d: 5/2/03, Borden, Ind. TL, Deb: 6/16/02

| 1902 Phi-A | 0 | 1 | .000 | 1 | 1 | 1 | 0 | 0 | 8 | 12 | 0 | 5 | 2 | 19.1 | 3.38 | 109 | .346 | .428 | 0 | — | 0 | -0 | -0 | -0 | 0.0 |

● BOB PORTERFIELD Porterfield, Erwin Coolidge b: 8/10/23, Newport, Va. d: 4/28/80, Sealy, Tex. BR/TR, 6', 190 lbs. Deb: 8/8/48

1948 NY-A	5	3	.625	16	12	2	1	0	78	85	5	34	30	13.7	4.50	91	.273	.345	6	.250	0	-2	-4	-1	-0.4
1949 NY-A	2	5	.286	12	8	3	0	0	57²	73	3	29	25	13.0	4.06	100	.251	.344	1	.053	-2	1	-0	-1	-0.2
1950 NY-A	1	1	.500	10	2	0	0	1	19²	28	1	8	9	16.5	8.69	49	.341	.400	1	.333	1	-9	-10	-0	-0.9
1951 NY-A	0	0	—	2	0	0	0	0	3	5	0	3	0	24.0	15.00	26	.385	.500	0	—	0	-4	-4	0	0.0
Was-A	9	8	.529	19	19	10	3	0	133¹	109	8	54	53	11.0	3.24	126	.224	.302	6	.130	-3	13	13	-0	1.1
Yr	9	8	.529	21	19	10	3	0	136¹	114	8	57	55	11.3	3.50	117	.228	.308	6	.130	-3	9	9	-0	1.1
1952 Was-A	13	14	.481	31	29	15	3	0	231¹	222	7	85	80	12.1	2.72	131	.254	.323	15	.190	0	24	21	-3	2.2
1953 Was-A	22	10	.688	34	32	24	9	0	255	243	19	73	77	11.2	3.35	110	.257	.310	25	.255	8	18	15	2	2.9
1954 Was-A★	13	15	.464	32	31	21	2	0	244	249	14	77	82	12.1	3.32	107	.266	.324	9	.102	-3	11	6	3	0.7
1955 Was-A	10	17	.370	30	27	8	2	0	178	197	14	54	77	12.8	4.45	86	.282	.335	12	.190	1	-10	-12	-1	-1.6
1956 Bos-A	3	12	.200	25	18	4	1	0	126	127	21	64	53	13.7	5.14	90	.260	.347	14	.326	3	-14	-7	-2	-0.6
1957 Bos-A	4	4	.500	28	9	3	1	1	102¹	107	8	30	28	12.1	4.05	99	.272	.325	5	.172	-0	-3	-1	1	0.0
1958 Bos-A	0	0	—	2	0	0	0	0	4	3	1	0	1	6.8	4.50	89	.214	.214	0	—	0	1	1	-0	0.0
Pit-N	4	6	.400	37	6	2	1	5	87²	78	7	19	39	10.1	3.29	118	.241	.285	1	.050	-1	6	6	-0	0.6
1959 Pit-N	0	0	—	6	0	0	0	0	5¹	11	1	2	1	13.5	1.69	229	.286	.348	0	—	0	1	1	-0	0.0
Chi-N	0	0	—	4	0	0	0	0	6¹	14	1	3	0	24.2	11.37	35	.424	.472	0	.000	-0	-5	-5	0	0.0
Pit-N	1	2	.333	30	0	0	0	0	36	45	3	17	18	15.5	4.75	81	.321	.395	0	.000	-0	-3	-4	1	-0.2
Yr	1	2	.333	40	0	0	0	0	47²	65	4	22	19	16.4	5.29	73	.335	.403	0	.000	-0	-7	-7	1	-0.2
Total 12	87	97	.473	318	193	92	23	8	1567²	1571	114	552	572	12.3	3.79	102	.263	.327	95	.184	4	26	16	0	3.6

● AL PORTO Porto, Alfred "Lefty" b: 6/27/26, Heilwood, Pa. BL/TL, 5'11", 176 lbs. Deb: 4/22/48

| 1948 Phi-N | 0 | 0 | — | 2 | 0 | 0 | 0 | 0 | 4 | 2 | 0 | 1 | 1 | 6.8 | 0.00 | — | .143 | .200 | 0 | — | 0 | 2 | 2 | -0 | 0.0 |

● ARNIE PORTOCARRERO Portocarrero, Arnold Mario b: 7/5/31, New York, N.Y. d: 6/21/86, Kansas City, Kan. BR/TR, 6'3", 196 lbs. Deb: 4/18/54

1954 Phi-A	9	18	.333	34	33	16	1	0	248	233	25	114	132	12.8	4.06	96	.249	.334	8	.107	-2	-9	-4	-4	-1.0
1955 KC-A	9	18	.357	24	20	4	1	0	111¹	109	12	67	34	14.6	4.77	88	.259	.366	4	.108	-1	-10	-7	-1	-1.0
1956 KC-A	0	1	.000	3	1	0	0	0	8	9	2	7	3	18.0	10.13	43	.300	.432	0	.000	-0	-5	-5	-0	-0.5
1957 KC-A	3	9	.308	33	17	1	0	0	114²	103	10	34	49	10.8	3.92	101	.240	.300	3	.107	-1	2	-0	-0	-0.2
1958 Bal-A	15	11	.577	32	27	10	3	0	204²	173	17	57	90	10.2	3.25	110	.229	.286	11	.164	0	12	8	-3	0.7
1959 Bal-A	2	7	.222	27	14	0	0	0	90	107	16	32	23	14.1	6.80	56	.294	.354	0	.000	-3	-29	-30	1	-2.8
1960 Bal-A	2	2	.600	13	5	0	0	0	40²	44	9	16	17	11.7	4.43	86	.275	.334	0	—	0	-2	-1	-0	-0.5
Total 7	38	57	.400	166	117	33	5	2	817¹	778	82	320	338	12.3	4.32	89	.252	.325	26	.108	-9	-47	-42	-9	-5.3

● MARK PORTUGAL Portugal, Mark Steven b: 10/30/62, Los Angeles, Cal. BR/TR, 6', 190 lbs. Deb: 8/14/85

| 1985 Min-A | 1 | 3 | .250 | 6 | 4 | 0 | 0 | 0 | 24¹ | 24 | 3 | 14 | 12 | 14.1 | 5.55 | 79 | .270 | .369 | 0 | — | 0 | -4 | -3 | 1 | -0.4 |

YEAR	TM/L	W	L	PCT	G	GS	CG	SH	SV	IP	H	HR	BB	SO	RAT	ERA	ERA+	OAV	OOB	BH	AVG	PB	PR	/A	PD	TPI
1986	Min-A	6	10	.375	27	15	3	0	1	112²	112	10	50	67	13.0	4.31	100	.265	.345	0	—	0	-2	-0	-0	-0.1
1987	Min-A	1	3	.250	13	7	0	0	0	44	58	13	24	28	17.0	7.77	59	.326	.409	0	—	0	-16	-15	0	-1.2
1988	Min-A	3	3	.500	26	0	0	0	3	57²	60	11	17	31	12.2	4.53	90	.274	.329	0	—	0	-4	-3	-2	-0.6
1989	Hou-N	7	1	.875	20	15	2	1	0	108	91	7	37	86	10.8	2.75	123	.232	.302	7	.206	3	9	8	0	0.9
1990	Hou-N	11	10	.524	32	32	1	0	0	196²	187	21	67	136	11.8	3.62	103	.250	.315	9	.136	-1	4	2	0	0.1
1991	Hou-N	10	12	.455	32	27	1	0	1	168¹	163	19	59	120	12.0	4.49	78	.256	.321	9	.196	3	-15	-18	-1	-2.0
1992	Hou-N	6	3	.667	18	16	1	1	0	101¹	76	7	41	62	10.5	2.66	126	.213	.296	3	.107	-1	9	8	0	0.6
1993	Hou-N	18	4	.818	33	33	1	1	0	208	194	10	77	131	11.9	2.77	140	.248	.319	15	.231	4	29	25	1	3.0
1994	SF-N	10	8	.556	21	21	1	0	0	137¹	135	17	45	87	12.2	3.93	102	.260	.326	17	.354	8	4	1	-2	0.8
Total	10	73	57	.562	228	170	10	3	5	1158¹	1100	118	431	760	12.1	3.78	101	.253	.324	60	.209	15	16	4	-3	1.1

● **BILL POSEDEL**   Posedel, William John "Sailor Bill" or "Barnacle Bill"   b: 8/2/06, San Francisco, Cal.   d: 11/28/89, Livermore, Cal.   BR/TR, 5'11", 175 lbs.   Deb: 4/23/38   C

YEAR	TM/L	W	L	PCT	G	GS	CG	SH	SV	IP	H	HR	BB	SO	RAT	ERA	ERA+	OAV	OOB	BH	AVG	PB	PR	/A	PD	TPI
1938	Bro-N	8	9	.471	33	17	6	1	1	140	178	14	46	49	14.5	5.66	69	.311	.365	10	.227	1	-29	-27	-1	-2.9
1939	Bos-N	15	13	.536	33	29	18	5	0	220²	221	8	78	73	12.2	3.92	94	.268	.331	8	.110	-4	0	-5	-1	-1.1
1940	Bos-N	12	17	.414	35	32	18	0	1	233	263	16	81	86	13.3	4.13	90	.288	.346	14	.171	1	-7	-11	-0	-0.8
1941	Bos-N	4	4	.500	18	9	3	0	0	57¹	61	6	30	10	14.4	4.87	73	.279	.368	8	.320	2	-8	-8	-0	-0.8
1946	Bos-N	2	0	1.000	19	0	0	0	4	28¹	34	4	13	9	14.9	6.99	49	.304	.376	0	.000	-0	-11	-11	-0	-1.2
Total	5	41	43	.488	138	87	45	6	6	679¹	757	48	248	227	13.4	4.56	82	.286	.349	40	.176	-0	-55	-63	-4	-7.1

● **BOB POSER**   Poser, John Falk   b: 3/16/10, Columbus, Wis.   BL/TR, 6', 173 lbs.   Deb: 4/17/32

YEAR	TM/L	W	L	PCT	G	GS	CG	SH	SV	IP	H	HR	BB	SO	RAT	ERA	ERA+	OAV	OOB	BH	AVG	PB	PR	/A	PD	TPI
1932	Chi-A	0	0	—	1	0	0	0	0	0²	3	0	2	1	67.5	27.00	16	.600	.714	0	.000	-0	-2	-2	0	0.0
1935	StL-A	1	1	.500	4	1	0	0	0	13¹	26	0	4	1	19.8	9.22	52	.400	.435	1	.250	-0	-7	-7	-1	-0.8
Total	2	1	1	.500	5	1	0	0	0	14¹	29	0	6	2	22.0	10.05	47	.414	.461	1	.143	-0	-9	-8	-1	-0.8

● **LOU POSSEHL**   Possehl, Louis Thomas   b: 4/12/26, Chicago, Ill.   BR/TR, 6'2", 180 lbs.   Deb: 8/25/46   F

YEAR	TM/L	W	L	PCT	G	GS	CG	SH	SV	IP	H	HR	BB	SO	RAT	ERA	ERA+	OAV	OOB	BH	AVG	PB	PR	/A	PD	TPI
1946	Phi-N	1	2	.333	4	4	0	0	0	13²	19	0	10	4	19.8	5.93	58	.339	.448	0	.000	-0	-4	-4	0	-0.7
1947	Phi-N	0	0	—	2	0	0	0	0	4¹	5	0	0	1	12.5	4.15	96	.385	.429	0	—	-0	-0	-0	0	0.1
1948	Phi-N	1	1	.500	3	2	1	0	0	14²	17	3	4	7	12.9	4.91	80	.304	.350	1	.250	-0	-2	-2	-0	-0.2
1951	Phi-N	0	1	.000	2	1	0	0	0	6	9	0	3	6	18.0	6.00	64	.333	.400	0	.000	-0	-1	-1	0	-0.2
1952	Phi-N	0	1	.000	4	1	0	0	0	12²	12	3	7	4	13.5	4.97	73	.235	.328	0	.000	-0	-2	-2	-0	-0.2
Total	5	2	5	.286	15	8	1	0	0	51¹	62	6	24	22	15.4	5.26	71	.305	.384	1	.100	-0	-9	-9	0	-1.2

● **NELLIE POTT**   Pott, Nelson Adolph "Lefty"   b: 7/16/1899, Cincinnati, Ohio   d: 12/3/63, Cincinnati, Ohio   BL/TL, 6', 185 lbs.   Deb: 4/19/22

YEAR	TM/L	W	L	PCT	G	GS	CG	SH	SV	IP	H	HR	BB	SO	RAT	ERA	ERA+	OAV	OOB	BH	AVG	PB	PR	/A	PD	TPI
1922	Cle-A	0	0	—	2	0	0	0	0	2	7	1	2	0	40.5	31.50	13	.583	.643	0	—	0	-6	-6	-0	0.0

● **DYKES POTTER**   Potter, Maryland Dykes   b: 9/7/10, Ashland, Ky.   BR/TR, 6', 185 lbs.   Deb: 4/26/38   F

YEAR	TM/L	W	L	PCT	G	GS	CG	SH	SV	IP	H	HR	BB	SO	RAT	ERA	ERA+	OAV	OOB	BH	AVG	PB	PR	/A	PD	TPI
1938	Bro-N	0	0	—	2	0	0	0	0	2	4	1	0	1	18.0	4.50	87	.400	.400	0	—	0	-0	-0	-0	0.0

● **NELS POTTER**   Potter, Nelson Thomas "Nellie"   b: 8/23/11, Mt.Morris, Ill.   d: 9/30/90, Mt.Morris, Ill.   BL/TR, 5'11", 180 lbs.   Deb: 4/25/36

YEAR	TM/L	W	L	PCT	G	GS	CG	SH	SV	IP	H	HR	BB	SO	RAT	ERA	ERA+	OAV	OOB	BH	AVG	PB	PR	/A	PD	TPI
1936	StL-N	0	0	—	1	0	0	0	0	1	0	0	0	0	0.0	0.00	—	.000	.000	0	—	0	0	0	0	0.0
1938	Phi-A	2	12	.143	35	9	4	0	5	111¹	139	15	49	43	15.4	6.47	66	.306	.376	10	.256	1	-21	-20	-1	-2.1
1939	Phi-A	8	12	.400	41	25	9	0	2	196¹	258	26	88	60	16.1	6.60	71	.321	.391	12	.179	-1	-43	-41	-0	-3.5
1940	Phi-A	9	14	.391	31	25	13	0	0	200²	213	18	71	73	12.8	4.44	100	.269	.330	18	.254	2	-1	0	-0	0.2
1941	Phi-A	1	1	.500	10	3	1	0	2	23¹	35	3	16	7	19.7	9.26	45	.337	.425	1	.167	-0	-13	-13	-0	-1.1
	Bos-A	2	0	1.000	10	0	0	0	0	20	21	0	16	6	16.6	4.50	93	.284	.411	0	.000	-0	-1	-1	-0	-0.1
	Yr	3	1	.750	20	3	1	0	2	43¹	56	3	32	13	18.3	7.06	59	.315	.419	1	.111	-0	-14	-14	-0	-1.2
1943	StL-A	10	5	.667	33	13	8	0	1	168¹	146	11	54	80	10.9	2.78	120	.235	.299	8	.145	-1	10	10	1	0.9
1944	*StL-A	19	7	.731	32	29	16	3	0	232	211	6	70	91	10.9	2.83	127	.244	.301	13	.159	-2	15	20	2	2.1
1945	StL-A	15	11	.577	32	32	21	3	0	255¹	212	10	68	129	9.9	2.47	143	.226	.279	28	.304	4	25	30	-1	3.5
1946	StL-A	8	9	.471	23	19	10	0	0	145	152	6	59	72	13.3	3.72	100	.268	.340	12	.231	2	-4	0	-1	0.2
1947	StL-A	4	10	.286	32	10	3	0	2	122²	130	13	44	65	12.9	4.04	96	.277	.342	9	.257	3	-5	-2	-1	0.2
1948	StL-A	1	1	.500	2	2	0	0	0	10¹	11	1	4	4	14.8	5.23	87	.262	.354	2	.500	-1	-1	-1	1	0.0
	Phi-A	2	2	.500	8	0	0	0	1	18	17	1	5	13	11.0	4.00	107	.250	.301	1	.250	0	1	1	-0	0.1
	Yr	3	3	.500	10	2	0	0	1	28¹	28	2	9	17	11.8	4.45	99	.250	.306	3	.375	1	-0	-0	0	0.1
	*Bos-N	5	2	.714	18	7	3	0	2	85	77	4	8	47	9.0	2.33	165	.245	.264	11	.379	3	15	14	1	1.6
1949	Bos-N	6	11	.353	41	3	1	0	7	96²	99	6	30	57	12.1	4.19	90	.265	.321	3	.130	-0	-2	-4	1	-0.7
Total	12	92	97	.487	349	177	89	6	22	1686	1721	123	582	747	12.4	3.99	99	.265	.328	128	.228	11	-23	-6	3	1.3

● **SQUIRE POTTER**   Potter, Robert   b: 3/18/02, Flatwoods, Ky.   d: 1/27/83, Ashland, Ky.   BR/TR, 6'1", 185 lbs.   Deb: 8/7/23   F

YEAR	TM/L	W	L	PCT	G	GS	CG	SH	SV	IP	H	HR	BB	SO	RAT	ERA	ERA+	OAV	OOB	BH	AVG	PB	PR	/A	PD	TPI
1923	Was-A	0	0	—	1	0	0	0	0	3	11	0	4	1	45.0	21.00	18	.688	.750	0	—	0	-6	-6	-0	0.0

● **BILL POUNDS**   Pounds, Jeared Wells   b: 3/11/1878, Paterson, N.J.   d: 7/7/36, Paterson, N.J.   BR/TR, 5'10.5", 178 lbs.   Deb: 5/2/03

YEAR	TM/L	W	L	PCT	G	GS	CG	SH	SV	IP	H	HR	BB	SO	RAT	ERA	ERA+	OAV	OOB	BH	AVG	PB	PR	/A	PD	TPI
1903	Cle-A	0	0	—	1	0	0	0	0	5	8	0	0	2	14.4	10.80	26	.359	.359	1	.500	1	-4	-4	-0	0.1
	Bro-N	0	0	—	1	0	0	0	0	6	8	1	2	2	15.0	6.00	53	.267	.400	2	.667	1	-2	-2	0	0.1
Total	1	0	0	—	2	0	0	0	0	11	16	1	2	4	14.7	8.18	37	.354	.381	3	.600	1	-6	-6	0	0.2

● **ABNER POWELL**   Powell, Charles Abner "Ab"   b: 12/15/1860, Shenandoah, Pa.   d: 8/7/53, New Orleans, La.   BL/TR, 5'7", 160 lbs.   Deb: 8/4/1884   ♦

YEAR	TM/L	W	L	PCT	G	GS	CG	SH	SV	IP	H	HR	BB	SO	RAT	ERA	ERA+	OAV	OOB	BH	AVG	PB	PR	/A	PD	TPI
1884	Was-U	6	12	.333	18	17	14	1	0	134	135	3	19	78	10.3	3.43	70	.245	.270	54	.283	0	-15	-15	2	-1.4
1886	Bal-a	2	5	.286	7	7	7	0	0	60	66	2	26	15	14.0	5.10	67	.264	.336	7	.179	-1	-11	-11	2	-0.9
	Cin-a	0	1	.000	4	1	1	0	0	15¹	16	0	9	4	14.7	4.70	75	.271	.368	17	.230	-0	-2	-2	-0	-0.1
	Yr	2	6	.250	11	8	8	0	0	75¹	82	2	35	19	14.0	5.02	69	.265	.339	24	.212	-1	-13	-13	1	-1.0
Total	2	8	18	.308	29	25	22	1	0	209¹	217	5	54	97	11.7	4.00	69	.252	.297	78	.257	-1	-28	-29	3	-2.4

● **DENNIS POWELL**   Powell, Dennis Clay   b: 8/13/63, Moultrie, Ga.   BR/TL, 6'3", 200 lbs.   Deb: 7/7/85

YEAR	TM/L	W	L	PCT	G	GS	CG	SH	SV	IP	H	HR	BB	SO	RAT	ERA	ERA+	OAV	OOB	BH	AVG	PB	PR	/A	PD	TPI
1985	LA-N	1	1	.500	16	2	0	0	1	29¹	30	7	13	19	13.5	5.22	67	.263	.344	0	.000	-0	-5	-6	0	-0.4
1986	LA-N	2	7	.222	27	6	0	0	0	65¹	65	5	25	31	12.5	4.27	81	.272	.343	3	.214	4	-4	-6	-1	-0.7
1987	Sea-A	1	3	.250	16	3	0	0	0	34¹	32	3	15	17	12.3	3.15	150	.250	.329	0	—	0	5	6	0	0.5
1988	Sea-A	1	3	.250	12	2	0	0	0	18²	29	2	11	15	20.3	8.68	48	.363	.452	0	—	0	-10	-9	1	-1.8
1989	Sea-A	2	2	.500	43	0	0	0	2	45	49	6	21	27	14.4	5.00	81	.285	.369	0	—	0	-6	-5	1	-0.5
1990	Sea-A	0	0	—	2	0	0	0	0	3	5	0	2	0	24.0	9.00	44	.357	.471	0	—	0	-2	-2	-0	-0.1
	Mil-A	0	4	.000	9	7	0	0	0	39¹	59	0	19	23	18.1	6.86	56	.341	.409	0	—	0	-13	-13	1	-1.0
	Yr	0	4	.000	11	7	0	0	0	42¹	64	0	21	23	18.3	7.02	55	.340	.410	0	—	0	-15	-15	1	-1.1
1992	Sea-A	4	2	.667	49	0	0	0	0	57	49	5	29	35	12.8	4.58	87	.238	.340	0	—	0	-4	-6	0	-0.4
1993	Sea-A	0	0	—	33	2	0	0	0	47²	42	7	24	32	12.7	4.15	106	.255	.353	0	—	0	0	-1	-1	-0.1
Total	8	11	22	.333	207	23	0	0	3	339²	360	35	159	199	14.1	4.95	80	.279	.363	3	.176	1	-37	-37	1	-4.5

● **GROVER POWELL**   Powell, Grover David   b: 10/10/40, Sayre, Pa.   d: 5/21/85, Raleigh, N.C.   BL/TL, 5'10", 175 lbs.   Deb: 7/13/63

YEAR	TM/L	W	L	PCT	G	GS	CG	SH	SV	IP	H	HR	BB	SO	RAT	ERA	ERA+	OAV	OOB	BH	AVG	PB	PR	/A	PD	TPI
1963	NY-N	1	1	.500	20	4	1	1	0	49²	37	2	32	39	12.7	2.72	128	.202	.324	2	.200	1	3	4	0	0.3

● **JACK POWELL**   Powell, John Joseph "Red"   b: 7/9/1874, Bloomington, Ill.   d: 10/17/44, Chicago, Ill.   BR/TR, 5'11", 195 lbs.   Deb: 6/23/1897

YEAR	TM/L	W	L	PCT	G	GS	CG	SH	SV	IP	H	HR	BB	SO	RAT	ERA	ERA+	OAV	OOB	BH	AVG	PB	PR	/A	PD	TPI
1897	Cle-N	15	10	.600	27	26	24	2	0	225	245	2	62	61	12.6	3.16	142	.275	.329	20	.206	-4	29	33	-1	2.5
1898	Cle-N	23	15	.605	42	41	36	6	0	342	328	6	112	93	12.0	3.00	121	.251	.317	18	.132	-7	23	24	-2	1.4
1899	StL-N	23	19	.548	48	43	40	4	0	373	433	15	85	75	12.7	3.52	113	.284	.330	27	.201	-1	14	19	-3	1.4
1900	StL-N	17	16	.515	38	37	28	3	0	287²	325	9	50	77	12.7	4.44	82	.284	.331	31	.284	10	-24	-26	0	-1.5
1901	StL-N	19	19	.500	45	37	33	2	3	338¹	351	14	50	133	11.0	3.54	90	.266	.299	21	.176	1	-8	-13	-5	-1.6

YEAR TM/L	W	L	PCT	G	GS	CG	SH	SV	IP	H	HR	BB	SO	RAT	ERA	ERA+	OAV	OOB	BH	AVG	PB	PR	/A	PD	TPI
1902 StL-A	22	17	.564	42	39	36	3	**2**	328^1	320	12	93	137	11.6	3.21	110	.256	.312	26	.205	4	13	12	-5	1.0
1903 StL-A	15	19	.441	38	34	33	4	**2**	306^1	294	11	58	169	10.5	2.91	100	.252	.290	25	.208	2	2	0	-1	0.2
1904 NY-A	23	19	.548	47	45	38	3	0	390^1	340	15	92	202	10.2	2.44	111	.235	.286	26	.178	-3	7	12	-6	0.3
1905 NY-A	8	13	.381	37	23	13	1	1	203	214	4	57	84	12.3	3.50	84	.272	.326	12	.185	-0	-19	-13	-6	-2.0
StL-A	2	1	.667	3	3	3	0	0	28	22	0	5	12	9.0	1.61	159	.218	.261	1	.100	-0	3	3	-1	0.1
Yr	10	14	.417	40	26	16	1	1	231	236	4	62	96	11.6	3.27	88	.264	.312	13	.173	-1	-16	-10	-7	-1.9
1906 StL-A	13	14	.481	28	26	25	3	1	244	196	2	55	132	9.6	1.77	146	.223	.275	21	.233	3	25	22	-3	2.6
1907 StL-A	13	16	.448	32	31	27	4	1	255^2	229	4	62	96	10.4	2.68	94	.241	.291	12	.132	-3	-4	-4	-3	-1.2
1908 StL-A	16	13	.552	33	32	23	5	1	256	208	1	47	85	9.2	2.11	114	.231	.274	21	.236	3	8	8	-6	0.5
1909 StL-A	12	16	.429	34	27	18	4	3	239	221	1	42	82	10.1	2.11	115	.250	.287	14	.179	0	10	8	-4	0.6
1910 StL-A	7	11	.389	21	18	8	3	0	129^1	121	0	28	52	10.4	2.30	108	.250	.292	7	.163	-1	3	3	-3	-0.2
1911 StL-A	8	19	.296	31	27	18	1	0	207^2	224	7	44	52	11.9	3.29	102	.262	.304	12	.164	-3	1	2	-5	-0.5
1912 StL-A	9	17	.346	32	27	19	0	0	235^1	248	5	52	47	11.6	3.10	107	.276	.318	15	.183	-0	6	6	-4	-0.3
Total 16	245	254	.491	578	516	422	46	15	4389	4319	110	1021	1621	11.2	2.97	106	.258	.305	309	.192	-1	90	94	-58	3.9

● **JACK POWELL**   Powell, Reginald Bertrand   b: 8/17/1891, Holcomb, Mo.   d: 3/12/30, Memphis, Tenn.   TR, 6'2", Deb: 6/14/13

YEAR TM/L	W	L	PCT	G	GS	CG	SH	SV	IP	H	HR	BB	SO	RAT	ERA	ERA+	OAV	OOB	BH	AVG	PB	PR	/A	PD	TPI
1913 StL-A	0	0	—	2	0	0	0	0	2	1	0	2	0	13.5	0.00	—	.143	.333	0	—	0	1	1	1	0.0

● **ROSS POWELL**   Powell, Ross John   b: 1/24/68, Grand Rapids, Mich.   BL/TL, 6', 180 lbs.   Deb: 9/5/93

YEAR TM/L	W	L	PCT	G	GS	CG	SH	SV	IP	H	HR	BB	SO	RAT	ERA	ERA+	OAV	OOB	BH	AVG	PB	PR	/A	PD	TPI
1993 Cin-N	0	3	.000	9	1	0	0	0	16^1	13	1	6	17	10.5	4.41	91	.224	.297	0	.000	-0	-1	-1	-0	-0.1
1994 Hou-N	0	0	—	12	0	0	0	0	7^1	6	0	5	5	14.7	1.23	332	.240	.387	0	—	0	2	2	0	0.0
Total 2	0	3	.000	21	1	0	0	0	23^2	19	1	11	22	11.8	3.42	118	.229	.326	0	.000	-0	2	2	0	-0.1

● **BILL POWELL**   Powell, William Burris "Big Bill"   b: 5/8/1885, Richmond, Va.   d: 9/28/67, E.Liverpool, Ohio   BR/TR, 6'2.5", 182 lbs.   Deb: 4/16/09

YEAR TM/L	W	L	PCT	G	GS	CG	SH	SV	IP	H	HR	BB	SO	RAT	ERA	ERA+	OAV	OOB	BH	AVG	PB	PR	/A	PD	TPI
1909 Pit-N	0	1	.000	3	1	0	0	0	7^1	7	0	6	2	17.2	3.68	74	.292	.452	1	.333	-1	-1	-1	-0	-0.1
1910 Pit-N	4	6	.400	12	9	4	2	0	75	65	0	34	23	12.5	2.40	129	.242	.338	6	.261	1	5	6	2	1.0
1912 Chi-N	0	0	—	1	0	0	0	0	2	2	0	1	0	13.5	9.00	37	.250	.333	0	—	0	-1	-1	0	0.0
1913 Cin-N	0	1	.000	1	1	0	0	0	0^1	2	0	2	0	108.0	54.00	6	1.000	1.000	0	—	0	-2	-2	0	-2.0
Total 4	4	8	.333	17	11	4	2	0	84^2	76	0	43	25	13.3	2.87	107	.251	.355	7	.269	1	1	2	2	-1.1

● **TED POWER**   Power, Ted Henry   b: 1/31/55, Guthrie, Okla.   BR/TR, 6'4", 225 lbs.   Deb: 9/9/81

YEAR TM/L	W	L	PCT	G	GS	CG	SH	SV	IP	H	HR	BB	SO	RAT	ERA	ERA+	OAV	OOB	BH	AVG	PB	PR	/A	PD	TPI
1981 LA-N	1	3	.250	5	2	0	0	0	14^1	16	0	7	15	15.1	3.14	106	.286	.375	0	.000	-0	0	0	1	0.0
1982 LA-N	1	1	.500	12	4	0	0	0	33^2	38	4	23	15	16.3	6.68	52	.288	.394	0	.000	-1	-12	-12	-0	-0.7
1983 Cin-N	5	6	.455	49	6	1	0	2	111	120	10	49	57	13.8	4.54	84	.286	.362	0	.000	-1	-11	-9	-2	-1.2
1984 Cin-N	9	7	.563	**78**	0	0	0	11	108^2	93	4	46	81	11.5	2.82	134	.237	.317	0	.000	-0	9	12	0	1.9
1985 Cin-N	8	6	.571	64	0	0	0	27	80	65	2	45	42	12.5	2.70	140	.227	.334	0	—	0	8	10	-2	2.2
1986 Cin-N	10	6	.625	56	10	0	0	1	129	115	13	52	95	11.7	3.70	105	.245	.322	3	.125	0	0	2	-0	0.3
1987 Cin-N	10	13	.435	34	34	2	1	0	204	213	28	71	133	12.7	4.50	94	.267	.329	7	.119	0	-10	-6	-3	-0.9
1988 KC-A	5	6	.455	22	12	2	2	0	80^1	98	7	30	44	14.7	5.94	67	.305	.370	0	—	0	-18	-17	-0	-2.1
Det-A	1	1	.500	4	2	0	0	0	18^2	23	1	8	13	14.9	5.79	66	.307	.373	0	—	0	-4	-4	-0	-0.3
Yr	6	7	.462	26	14	2	2	0	99	121	8	38	57	14.5	5.91	67	.300	.361	0	—	0	-21	-22	0	-2.4
1989 StL-N	7	7	.500	23	15	0	0	0	97	96	7	21	43	10.9	3.71	98	.255	.296	3	.091	-2	-2	-1	-2	-0.5
1990 *Pit-N	1	3	.250	40	0	0	0	0	51^2	50	5	17	42	11.7	3.66	99	.255	.315	1	.125	0	1	-0	-1	-0.1
1991 Cin-N	5	3	.625	68	0	0	0	3	87	87	6	31	51	12.4	3.62	105	.265	.332	0	.000	-0	1	2	-0	0.1
1992 Cle-A	3	3	.500	64	0	0	0	6	99^1	88	7	35	51	11.5	2.54	154	.248	.322	0	—	0	15	15	0	1.2
1993 Cle-A	0	2	.000	20	0	0	0	0	20	30	2	8	11	17.1	7.20	60	.333	.388	0	—	0	-6	-6	0	-0.6
Sea-A	2	2	.500	25	0	0	0	13	25^1	27	1	9	16	12.8	3.91	113	.287	.350	0	—	0	1	1	0	0.2
Yr	2	4	.333	45	0	0	0	13	45^1	57	3	17	27	14.7	5.36	81	.308	.366	0	—	0	-5	-5	0	-0.4
Total 13	68	69	.496	564	85	5	5	70	1160	1159	97	452	701	12.6	4.00	97	.264	.335	14	.089	-4	-26	-14	-10	-0.5

● **JIM POWERS**   Powers, James T.   b: 1868, New York, N.Y.   5'10", 150 lbs.   Deb: 4/18/1890

YEAR TM/L	W	L	PCT	G	GS	CG	SH	SV	IP	H	HR	BB	SO	RAT	ERA	ERA+	OAV	OOB	BH	AVG	PB	PR	/A	PD	TPI
1890 Bro-a	1	2	.333	4	2	0	0	0	30	38	1	16	3	16.5	5.70	68	.300	.382	2	.154	-0	-6	-6	-0	-0.5

● **IKE POWERS**   Powers, John Lloyd   b: 3/13/06, Hancock, Md.   d: 12/22/68, Hancock, Md.   BR/TR, 6'0.5", 188 lbs.   Deb: 7/26/27

YEAR TM/L	W	L	PCT	G	GS	CG	SH	SV	IP	H	HR	BB	SO	RAT	ERA	ERA+	OAV	OOB	BH	AVG	PB	PR	/A	PD	TPI
1927 Phi-A	1	1	.500	11	1	0	0	0	26	26	1	7	3	11.4	4.50	95	.271	.320	2	.400	1	-1	-1	-0	0.0
1928 Phi-A	1	0	1.000	9	0	0	0	2	12	8	1	10	4	14.3	4.50	89	.222	.404	0	—	0	-1	-1	1	0.0
Total 2	2	1	.667	20	1	0	0	2	38	34	2	17	7	12.3	4.50	93	.258	.347	2	.400	1	-2	-1	1	0.0

● **WILLIE PRALL**   Prall, Wilfred Anthony   b: 4/20/50, Hackensack, N.J.   BL/TL, 6'3", 200 lbs.   Deb: 9/3/75

YEAR TM/L	W	L	PCT	G	GS	CG	SH	SV	IP	H	HR	BB	SO	RAT	ERA	ERA+	OAV	OOB	BH	AVG	PB	PR	/A	PD	TPI
1975 Chi-N	0	2	.000	3	3	0	0	0	14^2	21	1	8	7	17.8	8.59	45	.339	.414	0	.000	-0	-8	-8	0	-0.9

● **AL PRATT**   Pratt, Albert George "Uncle Al"   b: 11/19/1848, Allegheny, Pa.   d: 11/21/37, Pittsburgh, Pa.   TR, 5'7", 140 lbs.   Deb: 5/4/1871   MU

YEAR TM/L	W	L	PCT	G	GS	CG	SH	SV	IP	H	HR	BB	SO	RAT	ERA	ERA+	OAV	OOB	BH	AVG	PB	PR	/A	PD	TPI
1871 Cle-n	10	17	.370	28	28	22	0	0	224^2	296	9	47	**34**	13.7	3.77	110	.277	.307	34	.262	2	11	9		0.8
1872 Cle-n	2	9	.182	15	12	8	0	0	104^2	150	3	14	7	14.1	4.39	83	.288	.307	18	.281	1	-8	-9		-0.5
Total 2 n	12	26	.316	43	40	30	0	0	329^1	446	12	61	41	13.9	3.96	92	.280	.307	52	.268	3	-9	-12		0.3

● **JOHN PREGENZER**   Pregenzer, John Arthur   b: 8/2/35, Burlington, Wis.   BR/TR, 6'5", 220 lbs.   Deb: 4/20/63

YEAR TM/L	W	L	PCT	G	GS	CG	SH	SV	IP	H	HR	BB	SO	RAT	ERA	ERA+	OAV	OOB	BH	AVG	PB	PR	/A	PD	TPI
1963 SF-N	0	0	—	6	0	0	0	1	9^1	8	0	8	5	16.4	4.82	66	.242	.405	0	—	0	-2	-2	0	0.0
1964 SF-N	2	0	1.000	13	0	0	0	0	18^1	21	1	11	8	16.2	4.91	73	.296	.398	0	—	0	-3	-3	-0	-0.3
Total 2	2	0	1.000	19	0	0	0	1	27^2	29	1	19	13	16.3	4.88	70	.279	.400	0	—	0	-4	-4	-0	-0.3

● **JIM PRENDERGAST**   Prendergast, James Bartholomew   b: 8/23/17, Brooklyn, N.Y.   d: 8/23/94, Amherst, N.Y.   BL/TL, 6'1", 208 lbs.   Deb: 4/25/48

YEAR TM/L	W	L	PCT	G	GS	CG	SH	SV	IP	H	HR	BB	SO	RAT	ERA	ERA+	OAV	OOB	BH	AVG	PB	PR	/A	PD	TPI
1948 Bos-N	1	1	.500	10	2	0	0	1	16^2	30	1	5	3	18.9	10.26	37	.380	.417	0	.000	-1	-12	-12	0	-1.4

● **MIKE PRENDERGAST**   Prendergast, Michael Thomas   b: 12/15/1888, Arlington, Ill.   d: 11/18/67, Omaha, Neb.   BR/TR, 5'9.5", 165 lbs.   Deb: 4/26/14

YEAR TM/L	W	L	PCT	G	GS	CG	SH	SV	IP	H	HR	BB	SO	RAT	ERA	ERA+	OAV	OOB	BH	AVG	PB	PR	/A	PD	TPI
1914 Chi-F	5	9	.357	30	19	7	1	0	136	131	6	40	71	11.5	2.38	114	.255	.313	4	.108	-3	8	4	-2	0.0
1915 Chi-F	14	12	.538	42	30	16	3	0	253^2	220	6	67	95	10.3	2.48	101	.240	.295	6	.075	-9	7	1	-3	-1.1
1916 Chi-N	6	11	.353	35	10	4	2	2	152	127	5	23	56	8.9	2.31	126	.228	.260	7	.152	-2	5	10	-1	0.9
1917 Chi-N	3	6	.333	35	8	1	0	1	99^1	112	6	21	43	12.1	3.35	86	.302	.339	7	.250	1	-7	-5	-1	-0.4
1918 Phi-N	13	14	.481	33	30	20	0	1	252^1	257	6	46	41	10.8	2.89	104	.273	.308	7	.082	-8	-4	-3	-2	-0.7
1919 Phi-N	0	1	1.000	5	1	0	0	0	15	20	0	10	5	18.6	8.40	38	.351	.456	1	.333	-0	-9	-9	-0	-0.5
Total 6	41	53	.436	180	98	48	6	4	908^1	867	29	207	311	10.7	2.74	102	.258	.304	32	.115	-19	0	5	-8	-1.8

● **GEORGE PRENTISS**   Prentiss, George Pepper (a.k.a. George Pepper Wilson In 1901)   b: 6/10/1876, Wilmington, Del.   d: 9/8/02, Wilmington, Del.   BB/TR, 5'11", 175 lbs.   Deb: 9/23/01

YEAR TM/L	W	L	PCT	G	GS	CG	SH	SV	IP	H	HR	BB	SO	RAT	ERA	ERA+	OAV	OOB	BH	AVG	PB	PR	/A	PD	TPI
1901 Bos-A	1	0	1.000	2	1	1	0	0	10	7	0	6	0	11.7	1.80	196	.195	.311	1	.333	1	2	2	-0	0.2
1902 Bos-A	2	2	.500	7	4	3	0	0	41	55	0	10	9	14.3	5.27	68	.321	.359	5	.313	1	-8	-8	-0	-0.6
Bal-A	0	1	.000	2	2	0	0	0	6^2	14	1	5	1	25.7	10.80	35	.426	.501	0	.000	-1	-5	-5	-0	-0.6
Yr	2	3	.400	9	6	3	0	0	47^2	69	1	15	10	15.9	6.04	60	.338	.383	5	.250	0	-13	-13	-0	-1.2
Total 2	3	3	.500	11	7	4	0	0	57^2	76	1	21	10	15.1	5.31	68	.317	.372	6	.261	1	-11	-11	-0	-1.0

● **JOE PRESKO**   Presko, Joseph Edward "Little Joe"   b: 10/7/28, Kansas City, Mo.   BR/TR, 6', 170 lbs.   Deb: 5/3/51

YEAR TM/L	W	L	PCT	G	GS	CG	SH	SV	IP	H	HR	BB	SO	RAT	ERA	ERA+	OAV	OOB	BH	AVG	PB	PR	/A	PD	TPI
1951 StL-N	7	4	.636	15	12	6	2	0	88^2	86	9	20	38	11.0	3.45	115	.251	.296	6	.162	-1	5	5	-1	0.4
1952 StL-N	7	10	.412	28	18	5	1	0	146^2	140	6	57	63	12.1	4.05	92	.247	.317	4	.093	-2	-5	-5	-1	-0.9
1953 StL-N	6	13	.316	34	25	4	0	1	161^2	165	19	65	56	13.1	5.01	85	.261	.335	13	.220	1	-13	-14	-1	-1.4
1954 StL-N	4	9	.308	37	6	1	0	1	71^2	97	14	41	36	18.0	6.91	60	.327	.417	4	.250	0	-23	-22	-0	-3.4

YEAR TM/L	W	L	PCT	G	GS	CG	SH	SV	IP	H	HR	BB	SO	RAT	ERA	ERA+	OAV	OOB	BH	AVG	PB	PR	/A	PD	TPI
1957 Det-A	1	1	.500	7	0	0	0	0	11	10	0	4	3	12.3	1.64	236	.278	.366	0	.000	-0	3	3	-0	0.4
1958 Det-A	0	0	—	7	0	0	0	2	10²	13	0	1	6	11.8	3.38	120	.317	.333	0	—	0	0	1	-0	0.1
Total 6	25	37	.403	128	61	15	2	5	490¹	511	57	188	202	13.1	4.61	87	.267	.337	27	.173	-1	-33	-33	-4	-4.8

● TOT PRESSNELL
Pressnell, Forest Charles b: 8/8/06, Findlay, Ohio BR/TR, 5'10", 175 lbs. Deb: 4/21/38

YEAR TM/L	W	L	PCT	G	GS	CG	SH	SV	IP	H	HR	BB	SO	RAT	ERA	ERA+	OAV	OOB	BH	AVG	PB	PR	/A	PD	TPI
1938 Bro-N	11	14	.440	43	19	6	1	3	192	209	11	56	57	12.8	3.56	110	.276	.332	9	.143	-1	5	7	-1	0.7
1939 Bro-N	9	7	.563	31	18	10	2	3	156²	171	8	33	43	11.8	4.02	102	.273	.311	10	.196	-1	-2	0	0	-0.1
1940 Bro-N	6	5	.545	24	4	1	1	2	68¹	58	4	17	21	10.1	3.69	108	.221	.274	0	.000	-2	1	2	-1	0.0
1941 Chi-N	5	3	.625	29	1	0	0	1	70	69	2	23	27	12.3	3.09	144	.253	.320	3	.200	-0	4	3	-1	0.3
1942 Chi-N	1	1	.500	27	0	0	0	3	39¹	40	5	5	9	11.4	5.49	58	.260	.305	2	.667	1	-10	-10	-0	-0.6
Total 5	32	30	.516	154	42	17	4	12	526¹	547	30	134	157	12.0	3.80	101	.264	.315	24	.161	-3	-1	3	-3	0.3

● JOE PRICE
Price, Joseph Walter b: 11/29/56, Inglewood, Cal. BR/TL, 6'4", 220 lbs. Deb: 6/14/80

YEAR TM/L	W	L	PCT	G	GS	CG	SH	SV	IP	H	HR	BB	SO	RAT	ERA	ERA+	OAV	OOB	BH	AVG	PB	PR	/A	PD	TPI
1980 Cin-N	7	3	.700	24	13	2	0	0	111¹	95	10	37	44	10.8	3.56	101	.236	.302	5	.128	-2	1	0	-1	-0.3
1981 Cin-N	6	1	.857	41	0	0	0	4	53²	42	3	18	41	10.1	2.52	141	.222	.290	0	.000	-0	6	6	1	0.9
1982 Cin-N	3	4	.429	59	1	0	0	3	72²	73	7	32	71	13.5	2.85	130	.263	.347	1	.333	0	6	7	-1	0.6
1983 Cin-N	10	6	.625	21	21	5	0	0	144	118	12	46	83	10.3	2.88	132	.225	.287	4	.098	-1	12	15	-0	1.4
1984 Cin-N	7	13	.350	30	30	3	1	0	171²	176	19	61	129	12.5	4.19	90	.261	.324	7	.146	-1	-12	-8	-3	-1.2
1985 Cin-N	2	2	.500	26	8	0	0	1	64²	59	10	23	52	11.4	3.90	97	.242	.307	0	.000	-1	-2	-1	-1	-0.3
1986 Cin-N	1	2	.333	25	2	0	0	0	41²	49	5	22	30	15.3	5.40	72	.293	.376	1	.143	0	-8	-7	-1	-0.6
1987 *SF-N	2	2	.500	20	0	0	0	1	35	19	5	13	42	8.5	2.57	149	.154	.241	1	.167	-0	6	5	-1	0.5
1988 SF-N	1	6	.143	38	3	0	0	4	61²	59	5	27	49	12.7	3.94	83	.249	.328	0	.000	-0	-3	-5	-0	-0.7
1989 SF-N	1	1	.500	7	1	0	0	0	14	16	3	4	10	12.9	5.79	58	.314	.364	0	.000	-0	-4	-4	-0	-0.5
Bos-A	2	5	.286	31	5	0	0	0	70¹	71	8	30	52	12.9	4.35	94	.262	.336	0	—	0	-4	-2	-1	-0.6
1990 Bal-A	3	4	.429	50	0	0	0	0	65¹	62	8	24	54	11.8	3.58	106	.253	.320	0	—	0	2	2	-0	0.3
Total 11	45	49	.479	372	84	10	1	13	906	839	95	337	657	11.8	3.65	102	.246	.316	19	.111	-5	0	8	-8	-0.5

● BILL PRICE
Price, William b: Philadelphia, Pa. Deb: 4/27/1890

YEAR TM/L	W	L	PCT	G	GS	CG	SH	SV	IP	H	HR	BB	SO	RAT	ERA	ERA+	OAV	OOB	BH	AVG	PB	PR	/A	PD	TPI
1890 Phi-a	1	0	1.000	1	1	1	0	0	9	6	0	7	1	14.0	2.00	192	.184	.344	1	.250	-0	2	2	0	0.2

● BOB PRIDDY
Priddy, Robert Simpson b: 12/10/39, Pittsburgh, Pa. BR/TR, 6'1", 200 lbs. Deb: 9/20/62

YEAR TM/L	W	L	PCT	G	GS	CG	SH	SV	IP	H	HR	BB	SO	RAT	ERA	ERA+	OAV	OOB	BH	AVG	PB	PR	/A	PD	TPI
1962 Pit-N	1	0	1.000	2	0	0	0	0	3	4	0	1	1	15.0	3.00	131	.308	.357	0	—	0	0	0	-0	0.1
1964 Pit-N	1	2	.333	19	0	0	0	1	34¹	35	2	15	23	13.4	3.93	89	.282	.364	0	.000	-0	-2	-2	-1	-0.2
1965 SF-N	1	0	1.000	8	0	0	0	0	10¹	6	1	2	7	7.0	1.74	207	.176	.222	0	.000	-0	2	2	0	0.2
1966 SF-N	6	3	.667	38	3	0	0	1	91	88	8	28	51	11.8	3.96	93	.259	.321	3	.176	-0	-4	-3	-1	-0.4
1967 Was-A	3	7	.300	46	8	1	0	4	110	98	12	33	57	10.7	3.44	92	.240	.297	4	.182	-1	-3	-3	1	0.0
1968 Chi-A	3	11	.214	35	18	2	0	0	114	106	14	41	66	11.9	3.63	83	.244	.315	1	.042	-1	-8	-8	-2	-1.2
1969 Chi-A	0	0	—	4	0	0	0	0	8	10	2	1	9	13.5	4.50	86	.303	.343	0	—	0	-1	-1	0	0.0
Cal-A	0	1	.000	15	0	0	0	0	26¹	24	4	7	15	10.6	4.78	73	.242	.292	0	.000	-0	-3	-4	0	-0.1
Yr	0	1	.000	19	0	0	0	0	34¹	34	6	9	20	11.3	4.72	76	.258	.305	0	.000	-0	-4	-4	0	-0.1
Atl-N	0	0	—	1	0	0	0	0	2	1	0	1	1	9.0	0.00	—	.143	.250	0	—	0	1	1	-0	0.0
1970 Atl-N	5	5	.500	41	0	0	0	8	73	75	9	24	32	12.6	5.42	79	.269	.333	2	.200	-0	-11	-9	1	-1.3
1971 Atl-N	4	9	.308	40	0	0	0	4	64	71	8	44	36	16.3	4.22	88	.289	.399	2	.182	-1	-5	-4	1	-0.7
Total 9	24	38	.387	249	29	3	0	18	536	518	60	198	294	12.2	4.00	87	.257	.327	13	.137	1	-33	-30	-2	-3.6

● RAY PRIM
Prim, Raymond Lee "Pop" b: 12/30/06, Salitpa, Ala. BR/TL, 6', 178 lbs. Deb: 9/24/33

YEAR TM/L	W	L	PCT	G	GS	CG	SH	SV	IP	H	HR	BB	SO	RAT	ERA	ERA+	OAV	OOB	BH	AVG	PB	PR	/A	PD	TPI
1933 Was-A	0	1	.000	2	1	0	0	0	14¹	13	0	4	9	9.4	3.14	133	.232	.259	0	.000	-1	2	2	1	0.1
1934 Was-A	0	2	.000	8	1	0	0	0	14²	19	1	8	3	16.6	6.75	64	.339	.422	0	.000	-0	-4	-4	0	-0.4
1935 Phi-N	3	4	.429	29	6	1	0	0	73¹	110	4	15	27	15.3	5.77	79	.340	.369	2	.083	-2	-14	-10	-0	-1.1
1943 Chi-N	4	3	.571	29	5	0	0	1	60	67	2	14	27	12.2	2.55	131	.282	.321	2	.167	-0	6	5	2	0.8
1945 *Chi-N	13	8	.619	34	19	9	2	2	165¹	142	9	23	88	**9.0**	**2.40**	**153**	**.228**	**.256**	13	.255	3	26	23	-1	3.0
1946 Chi-N	2	3	.400	14	2	0	0	1	23¹	28	5	10	10	14.7	5.79	57	.289	.355	1	.200	0	-6	-6	1	-1.2
Total 6	22	21	.512	116	34	10	2	4	351	379	21	72	161	11.6	3.56	107	.272	.308	18	.180	-0	9	9	3	1.2

● DON PRINCE
Prince, Donald Mark b: 4/5/38, Clarkton, N.C. BR/TR, 6'4", 200 lbs. Deb: 9/21/62

YEAR TM/L	W	L	PCT	G	GS	CG	SH	SV	IP	H	HR	BB	SO	RAT	ERA	ERA+	OAV	OOB	BH	AVG	PB	PR	/A	PD	TPI
1962 Chi-N	0	0	—	1	0	0	0	0	1	0	0	1	0	18.0	0.00	—	.000	.500	0	—	0	0	0	0	0.0

● JIM PROCTOR
Proctor, James Arthur b: 9/9/35, Brandywine, Md. BR/TR, 6', 165 lbs. Deb: 9/14/59

YEAR TM/L	W	L	PCT	G	GS	CG	SH	SV	IP	H	HR	BB	SO	RAT	ERA	ERA+	OAV	OOB	BH	AVG	PB	PR	/A	PD	TPI
1959 Det-A	0	1	.000	2	1	0	0	0	2²	8	0	3	0	37.1	16.88	24	.533	.611	0	—	0	-4	-4	0	-1.0

● RED PROCTOR
Proctor, Noah Richard b: 10/27/1900, Williamsburg, Va. d: 12/17/54, Richmond, Va. BR/TR, 6'1", 165 lbs. Deb: 8/6/23

YEAR TM/L	W	L	PCT	G	GS	CG	SH	SV	IP	H	HR	BB	SO	RAT	ERA	ERA+	OAV	OOB	BH	AVG	PB	PR	/A	PD	TPI
1923 Chi-A	0	0	—	2	0	0	0	0	4	11	0	2	0	29.3	13.50	29	.550	.591	0	—	0	-4	-4	-0	0.0

● GEORGE PROESER
Proeser, George "Yatz" b: 5/30/1864, Cincinnati, Ohio d: 10/13/41, New Burlington, O. BL/TL, 5'10", 190 lbs. Deb: 9/15/1888 ♦

YEAR TM/L	W	L	PCT	G	GS	CG	SH	SV	IP	H	HR	BB	SO	RAT	ERA	ERA+	OAV	OOB	BH	AVG	PB	PR	/A	PD	TPI
1888 Cle-a	3	4	.429	7	7	1	0	0	59	53	4	30	20	13.7	3.81	81	.231	.338	7	.304	2	-5	-5	-1	-0.4

● MIKE PROLY
Proly, Michael James b: 12/15/50, Jamaica, N.Y. BR/TR, 6', 185 lbs. Deb: 4/10/76

YEAR TM/L	W	L	PCT	G	GS	CG	SH	SV	IP	H	HR	BB	SO	RAT	ERA	ERA+	OAV	OOB	BH	AVG	PB	PR	/A	PD	TPI
1976 StL-N	1	0	1.000	14	0	0	0	2	17	21	0	6	4	14.3	3.71	95	.328	.386	0	—	0	-0	-0	0	0.0
1978 Chi-A	5	2	.714	14	6	2	0	1	65²	63	4	12	19	10.3	2.74	139	.250	.284	0	—	0	7	8	-1	0.7
1979 Chi-A	3	8	.273	38	6	0	0	9	88¹	91	6	40	32	13.2	3.87	110	.260	.339	0	—	0	3	4	1	0.6
1980 Chi-A	5	10	.333	62	3	0	0	8	146²	136	6	58	56	12.1	3.07	131	.253	.329	0	—	0	16	16	2	1.8
1981 Phi-N	2	1	.667	35	2	0	0	1	63	66	6	19	19	12.3	3.86	94	.282	.339	0	.000	-1	-3	-2	1	-0.1
1982 Chi-N	5	3	.625	44	1	0	0	1	82	77	5	22	24	11.1	2.30	162	.257	.312	4	.286	1	12	13	0	1.4
1983 Chi-N	1	5	.167	60	0	0	0	0	83	79	5	38	31	12.8	3.58	106	.259	.343	1	.091	-0	2	0	0	0.1
Total 7	22	29	.431	267	18	2	0	22	545²	531	33	195	185	12.1	3.23	121	.261	.328	5	.156	-0	36	40	4	4.5

● BILL PROUGH
Prough, Herschel Clinton "Clint" b: 11/28/1887, Markle, Ind. d: 12/29/36, Richmond, Ind. BR/TR, 6'3", 185 lbs. Deb: 4/27/12

YEAR TM/L	W	L	PCT	G	GS	CG	SH	SV	IP	H	HR	BB	SO	RAT	ERA	ERA+	OAV	OOB	BH	AVG	PB	PR	/A	PD	TPI
1912 Cin-N	0	0	—	1	0	0	0	0	3	7	0	1	0	24.0	6.00	56	.538	.571	0	.000	-0	-1	-1	-0	0.0

● AUGIE PRUDHOMME
Prudhomme, John Olgus b: 11/20/02, Frierson, La. d: 10/4/92, Shreveport, La. BR/TR, 6'2", 186 lbs. Deb: 4/19/29

YEAR TM/L	W	L	PCT	G	GS	CG	SH	SV	IP	H	HR	BB	SO	RAT	ERA	ERA+	OAV	OOB	BH	AVG	PB	PR	/A	PD	TPI
1929 Det-A	1	6	.143	34	6	2	0	1	94	119	7	53	26	16.7	6.22	69	.322	.410	5	.238	1	-21	-20	1	-1.1

● HUB PRUETT
Pruett, Hubert Shelby "Shucks" b: 9/1/1900, Malden, Mo. d: 1/28/82, Ladue, Mo. BL/TL, 5'10.5", 165 lbs. Deb: 4/26/22

YEAR TM/L	W	L	PCT	G	GS	CG	SH	SV	IP	H	HR	BB	SO	RAT	ERA	ERA+	OAV	OOB	BH	AVG	PB	PR	/A	PD	TPI
1922 StL-A	7	7	.500	39	8	4	0	7	119²	99	2	59	70	12.3	2.33	178	.235	.336	5	.147	-1	23	24	2	2.9
1923 StL-A	4	7	.364	32	8	3	0	2	104¹	109	3	64	59	15.2	4.31	97	.279	.385	3	.130	-1	-4	-2	1	-0.1
1924 StL-A	3	4	.429	33	1	0	0	0	65	64	1	42	27	15.2	4.57	99	.270	.389	3	.200	-1	-2	-0	1	0.0
1927 Phi-N	7	17	.292	31	28	12	1	0	186	238	4	89	90	16.4	6.05	68	.314	.395	13	.217	1	-44	-40	3	-3.9
1928 Phi-N	2	4	.333	13	9	4	0	0	71¹	78	2	49	35	16.4	4.54	94	.291	.406	5	.208	-0	-4	-2	0	-0.2
1930 NY-N	5	4	.556	45	8	1	0	3	135²	151	15	63	49	14.5	4.78	99	.287	.367	5	.135	-1	3	-1	1	-0.1
1932 Bos-N	1	5	.167	18	7	4	0	1	63	76	3	30	27	16.0	5.14	73	.308	.396	2	.105	-1	-9	-10	2	-0.7
Total 7	29	48	.377	211	69	28	1	13	745	816	28	396	357	15.1	4.63	92	.286	.380	36	.170	-3	-38	-29	9	-2.1

● TEX PRUIETT
Pruiett, Charles Le Roy b: 4/10/1883, Osgood, Ind. d: 3/6/53, Ventura, Cal. BL/TR, Deb: 4/26/07

YEAR TM/L	W	L	PCT	G	GS	CG	SH	SV	IP	H	HR	BB	SO	RAT	ERA	ERA+	OAV	OOB	BH	AVG	PB	PR	/A	PD	TPI
1907 Bos-A	3	11	.214	35	17	6	2	3	173²	166	1	59	54	12.1	3.11	83	.254	.323	8	.157	-1	-11	-10	1	-0.8
1908 Bos-A	1	7	.125	13	6	1	0	1	58²	55	1	21	28	12.0	1.99	124	.257	.329	1	.063	-2	3	3	0	0.3
Total 2	4	18	.182	48	23	7	2	3	232¹	221	2	80	82	12.0	2.83	90	.254	.324	9	.134	-2	-8	-7	1	-0.5

YEAR TM/L	W	L	PCT	G	GS	CG	SH	SV	IP	H	HR	BB	SO	RAT	ERA	ERA+	OAV	OOB	BH	AVG	PB	PR	/A	PD	TPI

● TROY PUCKETT
Puckett, Troy Levi b: 12/10/1889, Winchester, Ind. d: 4/13/71, Winchester, Ind. BL/TR, 6'2", 186 lbs. Deb: 10/4/11

| 1911 Phi-N | 0 | 0 | — | 1 | 0 | 0 | 0 | 0 | 2 | 4 | 0 | 2 | 1 | 31.5 | 13.50 | 26 | .444 | .583 | 0 | — | 0 | -2 | -2 | 0 | 0.0 |

● MIGUEL PUENTE
Puente, Miguel Antonio (Aguilar) b: 5/8/48, San Luis Potosi, Mex BR/TR, 6', 160 lbs. Deb: 5/3/70

| 1970 SF-N | 1 | 3 | .250 | 6 | 4 | 0 | 0 | 0 | 18² | 21 | 5 | 11 | 14 | 17.4 | 8.20 | 48 | .325 | .409 | 0 | .000 | -1 | -9 | -9 | 0 | -1.5 |

● TIM PUGH
Pugh, Timothy Dean b: 1/26/67, S.Lake Tahoe, Cal. BR/TR, 6'6", 225 lbs. Deb: 9/1/92

1992 Cin-N	4	2	.667	7	7	0	0	0	45¹	47	2	13	18	12.1	2.58	139	.276	.332	1	.077	-0	5	5	-0	0.6
1993 Cin-N	10	15	.400	31	27	3	1	0	164¹	200	19	59	94	14.6	5.26	77	.303	.366	12	.222	2	-22	-23	-0	-2.8
1994 Cin-N	3	3	.500	10	9	1	0	0	47²	60	5	26	24	16.8	6.04	69	.314	.405	5	.357	2	-10	-10	0	-0.8
Total 3	17	20	.459	48	43	4	1	0	257¹	307	26	98	136	14.5	4.93	81	.300	.368	18	.222	4	-27	-27	-1	-3.0

● CHARLIE PULEO
Puleo, Charles Michael b: 2/7/55, Glen Ridge, N.J. BR/TR, 6'3", 200 lbs.

1981 NY-N	0	0	—	4	1	0	0	0	13¹	8	0	8	8	10.8	0.00	—	.182	.308	0	.000	-0	5	5	0	0.0
1982 NY-N	9	9	.500	36	24	1	1	1	171	179	13	90	98	14.3	4.47	81	.275	.364	6	.125	-1	-17	-16	3	-1.4
1983 Cin-N	6	12	.333	27	24	0	0	0	143²	145	18	91	71	15.1	4.89	78	.269	.379	5	.100	-2	-20	-17	-2	-2.2
1984 Cin-N	1	2	.333	5	4	0	0	0	22	27	2	15	6	17.2	5.73	66	.297	.396	1	.200	0	-5	-5	-1	-0.6
1986 Atl-N	1	2	.333	5	3	1	0	0	24¹	13	4	12	18	9.6	2.96	134	.160	.277	2	.333	0	2	3	-0	0.4
1987 Atl-N	6	8	.429	35	16	1	0	0	123¹	122	11	40	99	12.0	4.23	103	.262	.325	5	.179	1	-2	2	-2	0.1
1988 Atl-N	5	5	.500	53	3	0	0	1	106¹	101	9	47	90	12.8	3.47	106	.251	.333	3	.231	-0	2	2	-0	0.2
1989 Atl-N	1	1	.500	15	1	0	0	0	29	26	2	16	17	13.0	4.66	78	.245	.344	0	.000	-0	-4	-3	-1	-0.3
Total 8	29	39	.426	180	76	3	1	2	633	621	59	319	387	13.6	4.25	90	.261	.351	22	.144	-1	-41	-30	-2	-3.8

● ALFONSO PULIDO
Pulido, Alfonso (Manzo) b: 1/23/57, Veracruz, Mexico BL/TL, 5'11", 170 lbs. Deb: 9/5/83

1983 Pit-N	0	0	—	1	1	0	0	0	2	4	2	1	1	22.5	9.00	41	.400	.455	0	—	0	-1	-1	-0	0.0
1984 Pit-N	0	0	—	1	0	0	0	0	2	3	0	1	2	18.0	9.00	40	.333	.400	0	—	0	-1	-1	-0	0.0
1986 NY-A	1	1	.500	10	3	0	0	1	30²	38	8	9	13	13.8	4.70	87	.306	.353	0	—	0	-2	-2	-0	0.0
Total 3	1	1	.500	12	4	0	0	1	34²	45	10	11	16	14.5	5.19	78	.315	.364	0	—	0	-4	-4	-0	0.0

● CARLOS PULIDO
Pulido, Juan Carlos b: 8/5/71, Caracas, Venez. BL/TL, 6', 195 lbs. Deb: 4/9/94

| 1994 Min-A | 3 | 7 | .300 | 19 | 14 | 0 | 0 | 0 | 84¹ | 87 | 17 | 40 | 32 | 13.7 | 5.98 | 81 | .273 | .356 | 0 | — | 0 | -11 | -10 | -0 | -1.0 |

● SPENCER PUMPELLY
Pumpelly, Spencer Armstrong b: 4/11/1893, Owego, N.Y. d: 12/5/73, Sayre, Pa. 5'11", 175 lbs. Deb: 7/11/25

| 1925 Was-A | 0 | 0 | — | 1 | 0 | 0 | 0 | 0 | 1 | 1 | 1 | 1 | 1 | 18.0 | 9.00 | 47 | .333 | .500 | 0 | — | 0 | -1 | -1 | -0 | 0.0 |

● BLONDIE PURCELL
Purcell, William Aloysius b: Paterson, N.J. BR/TR, 5'9.5", 159 lbs. Deb: 5/1/1879 M♦

1879 Syr-N	4	15	.211	22	17	15	0	0	179²	245	1	19	28	13.2	3.76	63	.303	.319	72	.260	3	-25	-28	-3	-2.3
Cin-N	0	2	.000	2	2	2	0	0	18	27	0	2	3	14.5	4.00	58	.355	.372	11	.220	-0	-3	-3	0	-0.3
Yr	4	17	.190	24	19	17	0	0	197²	272	1	21	31	13.3	3.78	63	.308	.324	83	.254	3	-28	-31	-2	-2.6
1880 Cin-N	3	17	.150	25	21	21	0	0	196	235	1	32	47	12.3	3.21	77	.271	.297	95	.292	4	-18	-16	-0	-1.0
1881 Buf-N	4	1	.800	9	5	5	0	0	61²	62	2	9	15	10.4	2.77	100	.248	.274	33	.292	2	0	0	1	0.2
1882 Buf-N	2	1	.667	6	3	2	0	0	31	44	2	4	9	13.9	4.94	59	.338	.358	105	.276	1	-7	-7	1	-0.4
1883 Phi-N	2	6	.250	11	9	7	0	0	80	110	0	12	30	13.7	4.39	70	.306	.329	114	.268	2	-11	-12	1	-0.6
1884 Phi-N	0	0	—	1	0	0	0	0	4	3	1	0	1	6.8	2.25	133	.188	.188	108	.252	0	0	0	-0	0.0
1885 Phi-a	0	1	.000	1	0	0	0	0	6	11	0	2	3	19.5	6.00	57	.423	.464	90	.296	0	-2	-2	0	-0.2
1886 Bal-a	0	0	—	1	0	0	0	0	1	1	0	0	0	9.0	9.00	38	.200	.200	19	.224	0	-1	-1	0	0.0
1887 Bal-a	0	0	—	1	0	0	0	0	4	8	0	4	2	29.3	15.75	26	.381	.500	142	.250	0	-5	-5	-0	0.0
Total 9	15	43	.259	79	57	52	0	0	581¹	746	7	84	138	12.9	3.73	70	.292	.314	1217	.267	12	-72	-73	-1	-4.6

● JOHN PURDIN
Purdin, John Nolan b: 7/16/42, Lynx, Ohio BR/TR, 6'2", 185 lbs. Deb: 9/16/64

1964 LA-N	2	0	1.000	3	2	1	1	0	16	6	1	6	8	6.8	0.56	576	.115	.207	1	.200	-0	5	5	-0	0.6
1965 LA-N	2	1	.667	11	2	0	0	0	22²	26	3	13	16	15.5	6.75	48	.283	.371	0	.000	-0	-8	-9	-1	-1.2
1968 LA-N	2	3	.400	35	1	0	0	2	55²	42	2	21	38	10.2	3.07	90	.206	.280	3	.500	1	-1	-2	-0	-0.1
1969 LA-N	0	0	—	9	0	0	0	0	16¹	19	7	12	6	17.1	6.06	55	.292	.403	0	.000	-0	-4	-5	-0	-0.0
Total 4	6	4	.600	58	5	1	1	2	110²	93	18	52	68	11.8	3.90	77	.225	.312	4	.250	1	-8	-11	-1	-0.7

● BOB PURKEY
Purkey, Robert Thomas b: 7/14/29, Pittsburgh, Pa. BR/TR, 6'2", 195 lbs. Deb: 4/14/54

1954 Pit-N	3	8	.273	36	11	0	0	0	131¹	145	3	62	38	14.7	5.07	83	.293	.379	2	.077	-1	-15	-13	5	-0.6
1955 Pit-N	2	7	.222	14	10	2	0	1	67²	77	5	25	24	13.8	5.32	77	.287	.353	6	.316	2	-10	-9	1	-0.8
1956 Pit-N	0	0	—	2	0	0	0	0	4	2	1	0	1	4.5	2.25	168	.143	.143	0	—	0	1	1	0	0.0
1957 Pit-N	11	14	.440	48	21	6	1	2	179²	194	10	38	51	12.0	3.86	98	.278	.322	5	.111	-0	0	-1	-1	-0.2
1958 Cin-N☆	17	11	.607	37	34	17	3	0	250	259	25	49	70	11.2	3.60	115	.268	.306	9	.111	-2	10	15	2	1.5
1959 Cin-N	13	18	.419	38	33	9	1	1	218	241	25	43	78	12.0	4.25	95	.279	.318	11	.167	-3	-7	-5	-0	-0.4
1960 Cin-N	17	11	.607	41	33	11	0	0	252²	259	23	59	97	11.6	3.60	106	.265	.312	11	.133	-2	5	6	2	0.7
1961 *Cin-N★	16	12	.571	36	34	13	1	1	246¹	245	27	51	116	11.0	3.73	109	.255	.297	8	.100	-3	8	9	6	1.2
1962 Cin-N★	23	5	**.821**	37	37	18	2	0	288¹	260	28	64	141	10.6	2.81	143	.240	.291	11	.103	-2	36	**39**	3	3.6
1963 Cin-N	6	10	.375	21	21	4	1	0	137	143	12	33	55	11.7	3.55	94	.272	.318	4	.098	-1	-4	-3	-0	-0.3
1964 Cin-N	11	9	.550	34	25	9	2	1	195²	181	16	49	78	10.9	3.04	119	.246	.299	3	.052	-4	11	13	2	1.0
1965 StL-N	10	9	.526	32	17	3	1	2	124¹	148	20	33	39	13.6	5.79	66	.294	.346	1	.029	-3	-31	-27	1	-4.0
1966 Pit-N	0	1	.000	10	0	0	0	0	19²	16	0	4	5	9.2	1.37	260	.235	.278	0	—	0	5	5	1	0.4
Total 13	129	115	.529	386	276	92	13	9	2114²	2170	195	510	793	11.7	3.79	103	.266	.315	71	.110	-13	9	30	21	2.1

● OSCAR PURNER
Purner, Oscar E. b: 1873, Washington, D.C. Deb: 9/2/1895

| 1895 Was-N | 0 | 0 | — | 1 | 0 | 0 | 0 | 0 | 2 | 4 | 1 | 3 | 0 | 31.5 | 9.00 | 53 | .408 | .547 | 0 | .000 | -0 | -1 | -1 | -0 | 0.0 |

● AMBROSE PUTTMANN
Puttmann, Ambrose Nicholas "Putty" or "Brose" b: 9/9/1880, Cincinnati, Ohio d: 6/21/36, Jamaica, N.Y. TL, 6'4", 185 lbs. Deb: 9/4/03

1903 NY-A	2	0	1.000	3	2	1	0	0	19	16	0	4	9	9.9	0.95	330	.228	.279	1	.143	-0	4	5	1	0.6
1904 NY-A	2	0	1.000	9	3	2	1	0	49¹	40	0	17	26	10.4	2.74	99	.223	.290	5	.278	2	-1	-0	0	0.2
1905 NY-A	2	7	.222	17	9	5	1	1	86¹	79	2	37	39	12.6	4.27	69	.245	.332	10	.313	3	-15	-13	-0	-1.1
1906 StL-N	2	2	.500	4	4	0	0	0	18²	23	2	9	12	16.4	5.30	50	.303	.391	2	.333	0	-6	-6	0	-1.0
Total 4	8	9	.471	33	18	8	2	1	173¹	158	4	67	85	12.1	3.58	80	.244	.322	18	.286	4	-18	-14	1	-1.3

● JOHN PYECHA
Pyecha, John Nicholas b: 11/25/31, Aliquippa, Pa. BR/TR, 6'5", 200 lbs. Deb: 4/24/54

| 1954 Chi-N | 0 | 1 | .000 | 1 | 0 | 0 | 0 | 0 | 2² | 4 | 1 | 2 | 2 | 20.3 | 10.13 | 41 | .333 | .429 | 0 | .000 | -0 | -2 | -2 | -0 | -0.5 |

● HARLAN PYLE
Pyle, Harlan Albert "Firpo" b: 11/29/05, Burchard, Neb. d: 1/13/93, Beatrice, Neb. BR/TR, 6'2", 180 lbs. Deb: 9/21/28

| 1928 Cin-N | 0 | 0 | — | 2 | 1 | 0 | 0 | 0 | 1¹ | 1 | 0 | 4 | 1 | 33.8 | 20.25 | 20 | .143 | .455 | 0 | .000 | -0 | -2 | -2 | 0 | 0.0 |

● SHADOW PYLE
Pyle, Harry Thomas b: 11/29/1861, Reading, Pa. d: 12/26/08, Reading, Pa. TL, 5'8", 136 lbs. Deb: 10/15/1884

1884 Phi-N	1	1	.500	1	1	1	0	0	9	9	0	6	4	15.0	4.00	75	.257	.366	0	.000	-1	-1	-1	-0	-0.2
1887 Chi-N	1	3	.250	4	4	3	0	0	26²	32	1	21	5	18.6	4.73	95	.291	.414	3	.188	-0	-2	-1	1	0.0
Total 2	1	4	.200	5	5	4	0	0	35²	41	1	27	9	17.7	4.54	90	.283	.402	3	.150	-1	-3	-2	1	-0.2

● EWALD PYLE
Pyle, Herbert Ewald "Lefty" b: 8/27/10, St.Louis, Mo. BL/TL, 6'0.5", 175 lbs. Deb: 4/23/39

| 1939 StL-A | 0 | 2 | .000 | 6 | 1 | 0 | 0 | 0 | 8¹ | 17 | 3 | 11 | 5 | 30.2 | 12.96 | 38 | .405 | .528 | 0 | .000 | -0 | -8 | -7 | 1 | -1.3 |

YEAR	TM/L	W	L	PCT	G	GS	CG	SH	SV	IP	H	HR	BB	SO	RAT	ERA	ERA+	OAV	OOB	BH	AVG	PB	PR	/A	PD	TPI
1942	StL-A	0	0	—	2	0	0	0	0	5^1	6	0	4	1	16.9	6.75	55	.286	.400	0	.000	-0	-2	-2	-0	-0.1
1943	Was-A	4	8	.333	18	11	2	1	1	72^2	70	0	45	25	14.4	4.09	78	.254	.360	2	.100	-1	-6	-7	-1	-1.3
1944	NY-N	7	10	.412	31	21	3	0	0	164	152	12	68	79	12.4	4.34	85	.241	.321	8	.157	-0	-13	-12	0	-1.2
1945	NY-N	0	0	—	6	1	0	0	0	6^1	16	0	4	2	28.4	17.05	23	.457	.513	0	.000	-0	-9	-9	1	0.0
	Bos-N	0	1	.000	4	2	0	0	0	13^2	16	1	18	10	22.4	7.24	53	.302	.479	2	.333	1	-5	-5	-0	-0.3
	Yr	0	1	.000	10	3	0	0	0	20	32	1	22	12	24.3	10.35	37	.364	.491	2	.250	-0	-15	-14	0	-0.3
Total	5	11	21	.344	67	36	5	1	1	270^1	277	16	150	122	14.4	5.03	71	.262	.357	12	.143	-2	-44	-43	-0	-4.2

● **TOM QUALTERS**   Qualters, Thomas Francis "Money Bags" b: 4/1/35, McKeesport, Pa. BR/TR, 6'0.5", 190 lbs. Deb: 9/13/53

YEAR	TM/L	W	L	PCT	G	GS	CG	SH	SV	IP	H	HR	BB	SO	RAT	ERA	ERA+	OAV	OOB	BH	AVG	PB	PR	/A	PD	TPI
1953	Phi-N	0	0	—	1	0	0	0	0	0^1	4	1	1	0	162.0	162.00	3	.800	.857	0	—	0	-6	-6	0	0.0
1957	Phi-N	0	0	—	6	0	0	0	0	7^1	12	0	4	6	19.6	7.36	52	.400	.471	0	—	0	-3	-3	0	0.0
1958	Phi-N	0	0	—	1	0	0	0	0	2	2	0	1	0	13.5	4.50	88	.222	.300	0	—	0	-0	-0	-0	0.0
	Chi-A	0	0	—	26	0	0	0	0	43	45	1	20	14	13.6	4.19	87	.281	.361	0	.000	0	-2	-3	1	0.1
Total	3	0	0	—	34	0	0	0	0	52^2	63	2	26	20	15.4	5.64	65	.309	.390	0	.000	0	-11	-11	1	0.1

● **PAUL QUANTRILL**   Quantrill, Paul John b: 11/3/68, London, Ont., Canada BL/TR, 6'1", 175 lbs. Deb: 7/20/92

YEAR	TM/L	W	L	PCT	G	GS	CG	SH	SV	IP	H	HR	BB	SO	RAT	ERA	ERA+	OAV	OOB	BH	AVG	PB	PR	/A	PD	TPI
1992	Bos-A	2	3	.400	27	0	0	0	1	49^1	55	1	15	24	13.0	2.19	192	.288	.343	0	—	0	10	11	-0	1.1
1993	Bos-A	6	12	.333	49	14	1	1	1	138	151	13	44	66	12.8	3.91	118	.279	.335	0	—	0	6	11	-1	1.1
1994	Bos-A	1	1	.500	17	0	0	0	0	23	25	4	5	15	12.5	3.52	146	.278	.330	0	—	0	3	4	0	-0.1
	Phi-N	2	2	.500	18	1	0	0	1	30	39	3	10	13	15.6	6.00	69	.331	.397	0	.000	-0	-6	-6	0	-0.8
Total	3	11	18	.379	111	15	1	1	3	240^1	270	21	74	118	13.2	3.78	119	.287	.344	0	.000	-0	13	20	-1	1.3

● **BILL QUARLES**   Quarles, William H. b: 1869, Petersburg, Va. d: 3/25/1897, Petersburg, Va. 6'3" Deb: 5/21/1891

YEAR	TM/L	W	L	PCT	G	GS	CG	SH	SV	IP	H	HR	BB	SO	RAT	ERA	ERA+	OAV	OOB	BH	AVG	PB	PR	/A	PD	TPI
1891	Was-a	1	1	.500	3	2	2	0	0	22	32	1	12	10	18.8	8.18	46	.328	.413	0	.000	-2	-11	-11	-0	-0.8
1893	Bos-N	2	1	.667	3	3	3	0	0	27	31	2	5	6	12.7	4.67	106	.280	.322	2	.222	0	-0	1	-0	-0.0
Total	2	3	2	.600	6	5	5	0	0	49	63	3	17	16	15.4	6.24	70	.302	.366	2	.100	-2	-11	-10	-1	-0.8

● **MEL QUEEN**   Queen, Melvin Douglas b: 3/26/42, Johnson City, N.Y. BL/TR, 6'1", 197 lbs. Deb: 4/13/64 FC♦

YEAR	TM/L	W	L	PCT	G	GS	CG	SH	SV	IP	H	HR	BB	SO	RAT	ERA	ERA+	OAV	OOB	BH	AVG	PB	PR	/A	PD	TPI
1966	Cin-N	0	0	—	7	0	0	0	1	7	11	0	6	9	21.9	6.43	61	.367	.472	7	.127	0	-2	-2	0	-0.1
1967	Cin-N	14	8	.636	31	24	6	2	0	195^2	155	17	52	154	9.8	2.76	136	.215	.273	17	.210	3	13	22	-2	2.6
1968	Cin-N	0	1	.000	5	4	0	0	0	18^1	25	7	4	20	15.2	5.89	54	.333	.383	1	.125	0	-6	-6	-0	-0.3
1969	Cin-N	1	0	1.000	2	2	0	0	0	12	7	2	3	7	8.3	2.25	167	.163	.234	1	.167	-0	2	2	-0	0.1
1970	Cal-A	3	6	.333	34	3	0	0	9	60	58	5	28	44	13.7	4.20	86	.261	.357	4	.250	-1	-3	-4	-1	-0.7
1971	Cal-A	2	2	.500	44	0	0	0	4	65^2	49	3	29	53	11.8	1.78	182	.212	.321	0	.000	-1	12	11	-1	0.6
1972	Cal-A	0	0	—	17	0	0	0	0	31	31	2	19	19	15.4	4.35	67	.265	.381	0	.000	0	-4	-5	-0	-0.2
Total	7	20	17	.541	140	33	6	2	14	389^2	336	36	143	306	11.6	3.14	113	.233	.313	49	.179	3	12	18	-4	2.2

● **MEL QUEEN**   Queen, Melvin Joseph b: 3/4/18, Maxwell, Pa. d: 4/4/82, Fort Smith, Ark. BR/TR, 6'0.5", 204 lbs. Deb: 4/18/42 F

YEAR	TM/L	W	L	PCT	G	GS	CG	SH	SV	IP	H	HR	BB	SO	RAT	ERA	ERA+	OAV	OOB	BH	AVG	PB	PR	/A	PD	TPI
1942	NY-A	1	0	1.000	4	0	0	0	0	5^2	6	0	3	0	17.5	0.00	—	.300	.440	0	—	0	2	2	0	0.4
1944	NY-A	6	3	.667	10	14	4	1	0	81^2	68	7	34	30	11.4	3.31	105	.227	.308	6	.194	0	1	2	-2	0.0
1946	NY-A	1	1	.500	14	3	1	0	0	30^1	40	2	21	26	18.1	6.53	53	.315	.412	1	.143	-0	-10	-10	-0	-0.7
1947	NY-A	0	0	—	5	0	0	0	0	6^2	9	2	4	2	18.9	9.45	37	.321	.424	0	.000	-0	-4	-4	-0	-0.2
	Pit-N	3	7	.300	14	12	2	0	0	74	70	8	51	34	14.8	4.01	105	.244	.360	2	.077	-2	0	2	-1	-0.1
1948	Pit-N	4	4	.500	25	8	0	0	0	66^1	82	8	40	34	17.0	6.65	61	.308	.405	1	.059	-2	-20	-19	-1	-2.2
1950	Pit-N	5	14	.263	33	21	4	1	0	120^1	135	18	73	76	15.7	5.98	73	.284	.381	2	.057	-3	-25	-21	-1	-3.2
1951	Pit-N	7	9	.438	39	21	4	1	0	168^1	149	21	99	123	13.3	4.44	95	.233	.337	5	.106	-3	-9	-4	-3	-0.9
1952	Pit-N	0	2	.000	2	2	0	0	0	3^1	8	2	4	3	32.4	29.70	13	.381	.480	1	—	0	-10	-10	-0	-2.6
Total	8	27	40	.403	146	77	15	3	1	556^2	567	68	329	328	14.7	5.09	80	.262	.362	17	.104	-10	-74	-63	-9	-9.3

● **EDDIE QUICK**   Quick, Edward b: 12/1881, Baltimore, Md. d: 6/19/13, Rocky Ford, Colo. TR, 5'11" Deb: 9/28/03

YEAR	TM/L	W	L	PCT	G	GS	CG	SH	SV	IP	H	HR	BB	SO	RAT	ERA	ERA+	OAV	OOB	BH	AVG	PB	PR	/A	PD	TPI
1903	NY-A	0	0	—	1	1	0	0	0	2	5	0	1	0	27.0	9.00	35	.467	.513	0	.000	-0	-1	-1	-0	0.0

● **TAD QUINN**   Quinn, Clarence Carr b: 9/21/1882, Torrington, Conn. d: 8/6/46, Waterbury, Conn. TR, 6'1", 210 lbs. Deb: 9/27/02

YEAR	TM/L	W	L	PCT	G	GS	CG	SH	SV	IP	H	HR	BB	SO	RAT	ERA	ERA+	OAV	OOB	BH	AVG	PB	PR	/A	PD	TPI
1902	Phi-A	0	1	.000	1	1	0	0	0	8	12	1	1	3	14.6	4.50	82	.346	.364	0	.000	-2	-1	-1	-0	-0.1
1903	Phi-A	0	0	—	2	0	0	0	0	9	11	0	5	1	17.0	5.00	61	.300	.398	2	.667	1	-2	-2	1	0.2
Total	2	0	1	.000	3	1	0	0	0	17	23	1	6	4	15.9	4.76	70	.322	.383	2	.333	-1	-3	-3	0	0.1

● **FRANK QUINN**   Quinn, Frank William b: 11/27/27, Springfield, Mass. d: 1/11/93, Boynton Beach, Fla. BR/TR, 6'2", 180 lbs. Deb: 5/29/49

YEAR	TM/L	W	L	PCT	G	GS	CG	SH	SV	IP	H	HR	BB	SO	RAT	ERA	ERA+	OAV	OOB	BH	AVG	PB	PR	/A	PD	TPI
1949	Bos-A	0	0	—	8	0	0	0	0	22	18	2	9	4	11.5	2.86	152	.222	.308	1	.167	-0	3	4	-0	0.0
1950	Bos-A	0	0	—	1	0	0	0	0	2	2	0	1	0	13.5	9.00	54	.250	.333	0	—	0	-1	-1	-0	0.0
Total	2	0	0	—	9	0	0	0	0	24	20	2	10	4	11.6	3.38	131	.225	.310	1	.167	-0	2	3	0	0.0

● **JACK QUINN**   Quinn, John Picus (b: John Quinn Picus) b: 7/5/1883, Janesville, Pa. d: 4/17/46, Pottsville, Pa. BR/TR, 6', 196 lbs. Deb: 4/15/09

YEAR	TM/L	W	L	PCT	G	GS	CG	SH	SV	IP	H	HR	BB	SO	RAT	ERA	ERA+	OAV	OOB	BH	AVG	PB	PR	/A	PD	TPI
1909	NY-A	9	5	.643	23	11	8	0	1	118^2	110	1	24	36	10.5	1.97	128	.252	.297	7	.156	0	7	7	3	1.3
1910	NY-A	18	12	.600	35	31	20	0	0	235^2	214	2	58	82	10.6	2.37	112	.247	.299	19	.232	4	4	8	7	2.2
1911	NY-A	8	10	.444	40	16	7	0	2	174^2	203	2	41	71	12.8	3.76	96	.297	.341	10	.164	-1	-8	-3	3	-0.1
1912	NY-A	5	7	.417	18	11	7	0	0	102^2	139	4	23	47	14.6	5.79	62	.325	.365	8	.205	-1	-28	-25	2	-2.3
1913	Bos-N	4	3	.571	8	7	6	1	0	56^1	55	1	7	33	10.1	2.40	137	.261	.288	4	.200	1	5	6	2	1.1
1914	Bal-F	26	14	.650	46	42	27	4	1	342^2	335	3	65	164	10.7	2.60	117	.266	.307	33	.273	6	11	16	1	2.7
1915	Bal-F	9	22	.290	44	31	21	0	1	273^2	289	6	63	118	11.8	3.45	83	.278	.325	29	.264	3	-22	-18	3	-1.2
1918	Chi-A	5	1	.833	6	5	5	0	0	51	38	0	7	22	7.9	2.29	119	.216	.246	4	.222	1	3	3	0	0.5
1919	NY-A	15	14	.517	38	31	18	4	0	266	263	8	65	97	10.6	2.61	123	.244	.295	19	.209	1	18	17	1	2.0
1920	NY-A	18	10	.643	41	32	17	2	0	253^1	271	8	48	101	11.4	3.20	119	.273	.308	8	.091	-5	17	18	3	1.5
1921	*NY-A	8	7	.533	33	13	6	0	0	119	158	2	32	44	14.7	3.78	112	.327	.375	9	.220	1	7	6	1	0.8
1922	Bos-A	13	16	.448	40	32	16	4	0	256	263	9	59	67	11.4	3.48	118	.267	.311	9	.099	-5	16	18	5	1.8
1923	Bos-A	13	17	.433	42	28	16	1	7	243	302	6	53	71	13.0	3.89	106	.316	.356	8	.225	-0	3	6	-1	0.6
1924	Bos-A	12	13	.480	44	25	13	2	7	228^2	241	10	52	64	12.0	3.27	134	.273	.322	14	.179	-4	24	28	4	2.9
1925	Bos-A	7	8	.467	19	15	8	0	0	105	140	3	26	24	14.5	4.37	104	.315	.357	3	.094	-2	0	2	2	0.2
	Phi-A	6	3	.667	18	14	4	0	0	99^2	119	3	16	19	12.5	3.88	120	.296	.328	3	.097	-3	6	9	1	0.5
	Yr	13	11	.542	37	29	12	0	0	204^2	259	6	42	43	13.4	4.13	111	.305	.340	6	.095	-5	6	11	3	0.7
1926	Phi-A	10	11	.476	31	21	8	1	0	163^2	191	4	36	58	12.5	3.41	122	.296	.334	8	.174	-0	11	14	1	1.7
1927	Phi-A	15	10	.600	34	25	11	3	1	201^1	211	8	37	43	11.3	3.26	131	.278	.315	6	.091	-7	20	22	-1	1.7
1928	Phi-A	18	7	.720	31	28	18	4	1	211^1	239	3	34	43	11.9	2.90	139	.286	.320	13	.165	-3	27	26	1	2.6
1929	*Phi-A	11	9	.550	35	18	7	0	2	161	182	8	39	41	12.4	3.97	107	.290	.332	8	.133	-4	5	5	0	0.1
1930	*Phi-A	9	7	.563	35	7	0	0	6	89^2	109	6	22	28	13.2	4.42	106	.302	.344	9	.265	1	**2**	**3**	2	0.7
1931	Bro-N	5	4	.556	39	1	0	0	15	64^1	65	1	24	25	12.6	2.66	143	.266	.335	3	.200	0	**9**	**8**	1	1.6
1932	Bro-N	3	7	.300	42	0	0	0	8	87^1	102	1	24	28	13.1	3.30	116	.296	.343	4	.200	0	**6**	**5**	0	0.7
1933	Cin-N	0	1	.000	14	0	0	0	0	15^2	20	0	5	3	14.4	4.02	84	.323	.373	0	.000	-0	-1	-1	0	0.0
Total	23	247	218	.531	756	444	243	28	57	3920^1	4238	102	860	1329	11.9	3.29	113	.280	.323	248	.184	-16	140	182	40	23.6

● **WIMPY QUINN**   Quinn, Wellington Hunt b: 5/12/18, Birmingham, Ala. d: 9/1/54, Santa Monica, Cal. BR/TR, 6'2", 187 lbs. Deb: 6/8/41

YEAR	TM/L	W	L	PCT	G	GS	CG	SH	SV	IP	H	HR	BB	SO	RAT	ERA	ERA+	OAV	OOB	BH	AVG	PB	PR	/A	PD	TPI
1941	Chi-N	0	0	—	3	0	0	0	0	5	3	0	3	2	10.8	7.20	49	.158	.273	1	.500	0	-2	-2	-0	0.0

● **LUIS QUINTANA**   Quintana, Luis Joaquin (Santos) b: 12/25/51, Vega Baja, P.R. BL/TL, 6'2", 175 lbs. Deb: 7/9/74

YEAR	TM/L	W	L	PCT	G	GS	CG	SH	SV	IP	H	HR	BB	SO	RAT	ERA	ERA+	OAV	OOB	BH	AVG	PB	PR	/A	PD	TPI
1974	Cal-A	2	1	.667	18	0	0	0	0	12^2	17	0	14	11	22.0	4.26	81	.327	.470	0	—	0	-1	-1	-0	0.0

YEAR	TM/L	W	L	PCT	G	GS	CG	SH	SV	IP	H	HR	BB	SO	RAT	ERA	ERA+	OAV	OOB	BH	AVG	PB	PR	/A	PD	TPI
1975	Cal-A	0	2	.000	4	0	0	0	0	7	13	2	6	5	24.4	6.43	55	.394	.487	0	—	0	-2	-2	-0	-0.6
Total	2	2	3	.400	22	0	0	0	0	19²	30	2	20	16	22.9	5.03	69	.353	.476	0	—	0	-3	-3	-0	-0.6

● ART QUIRK
Quirk, Arthur Lincoln b: 4/11/38, Providence, R.I. BR/TL, 5'11", 170 lbs. Deb: 4/17/62

YEAR	TM/L	W	L	PCT	G	GS	CG	SH	SV	IP	H	HR	BB	SO	RAT	ERA	ERA+	OAV	OOB	BH	AVG	PB	PR	/A	PD	TPI
1962	Bal-A	2	2	.500	7	5	0	0	0	27¹	36	3	18	18	17.8	5.93	62	.308	.400	1	.143	0	-6	-7	1	-0.8
1963	Was-A	1	0	1.000	7	3	0	0	0	21	23	3	8	12	13.3	4.29	87	.280	.344	1	.250	0	-2	-1	-0	-0.1
Total	2	3	2	.600	14	8	0	0	0	48¹	59	6	26	30	15.8	5.21	71	.296	.378	2	.182	0	-7	-8	0	-0.9

● DAN QUISENBERRY
Quisenberry, Daniel Raymond b: 2/7/53, Santa Monica, Cal. BR/TR, 6'2", 180 lbs. Deb: 7/8/79

YEAR	TM/L	W	L	PCT	G	GS	CG	SH	SV	IP	H	HR	BB	SO	RAT	ERA	ERA+	OAV	OOB	BH	AVG	PB	PR	/A	PD	TPI
1979	KC-A	3	2	.600	32	0	0	0	5	40	42	5	7	13	11.0	3.15	135	.278	.310	0	—	0	5	5	1	0.7
1980	*KC-A	12	7	.632	75	0	0	0	33	128¹	129	5	27	37	11.0	3.09	131	.265	.305	0	—	0	14	14	3	2.9
1981	*KC-A	1	4	.200	40	0	0	0	18	62¹	59	1	15	20	10.8	1.73	208	.258	.306	0	—	0	13	13	3	2.3
1982	KC-A★	9	7	.563	72	0	0	0	35	136²	126	12	12	46	9.1	2.57	159	.252	.270	0	—	0	23	23	6	4.5
1983	KC-A★	5	3	.625	69	0	0	0	45	139	118	6	11	48	8.4	1.94	210	.229	.245	0	◆	0	33	33	2	4.4
1984	*KC-A☆	6	3	.667	72	0	0	0	44	129¹	121	10	12	41	9.3	2.64	152	.247	.265	0	—	0	19	20	3	3.1
1985	*KC-A	8	9	.471	84	0	0	0	37	129	142	8	16	54	11.1	2.37	175	.280	.303	0	—	0	25	26	1	4.9
1986	KC-A	3	7	.300	62	0	0	0	12	81²	92	2	24	36	13.2	2.77	154	.291	.347	0	—	0	13	13	2	2.1
1987	KC-A	4	1	.800	47	0	0	0	8	49	58	3	10	17	12.7	2.76	165	.287	.324	0	—	0	9	10	2	1.3
1988	KC-A	0	1	.000	20	0	0	0	1	25¹	32	5	5	9	13.1	3.55	112	.305	.336	0	—	0	1	1	1	0.1
	StL-N	2	0	1.000	33	0	0	0	0	38	54	4	6	19	14.2	6.16	56	.344	.368	0	.000	0	-11	-11	0	-0.5
1989	StL-N	3	1	.750	63	0	0	0	6	78¹	78	2	14	37	10.6	2.64	137	.261	.294	1	.250	0	7	9	2	0.8
1990	SF-N	0	1	.000	5	0	0	0	0	6²	13	1	3	2	21.6	13.50	27	.419	.471	0	.000	-0	-7	-7	-0	-0.9
Total	12	56	46	.549	674	0	0	0	244	1043¹	1064	59	162	379	10.6	2.76	146	.267	.297	1	.167	0	144	147	25	25.7

● CHARLIE RABE
Rabe, Charles Henry b: 5/6/32, Boyce, Tex. BL/TL, 6'1", 180 lbs. Deb: 9/21/57

YEAR	TM/L	W	L	PCT	G	GS	CG	SH	SV	IP	H	HR	BB	SO	RAT	ERA	ERA+	OAV	OOB	BH	AVG	PB	PR	/A	PD	TPI
1957	Cin-N	0	1	.000	2	1	0	0	0	8¹	5	2	0	6	5.4	2.16	190	.167	.167	0	.000	-0	2	2	-0	0.1
1958	Cin-N	0	3	.000	9	1	0	0	0	18²	25	3	9	10	16.4	4.34	96	.321	.391	0	.000	-1	-1	-0	0	-0.1
Total	2	0	4	.000	11	2	0	0	0	27	30	5	9	16	13.0	3.67	113	.278	.333	0	.000	-1	1	1	0	-0.1

● STEVE RACHUNOK
Rachunok, Stephen Stepanovich "The Mad Russian" b: 12/5/16, Rittman, Ohio BR/TR, 6'4.5", 205 lbs. Deb: 9/17/40

YEAR	TM/L	W	L	PCT	G	GS	CG	SH	SV	IP	H	HR	BB	SO	RAT	ERA	ERA+	OAV	OOB	BH	AVG	PB	PR	/A	PD	TPI
1940	Bro-N	0	1	.000	2	1	0	0	0	10	9	0	5	10	12.6	4.50	89	.243	.333	0	.000	-0	-1	-1	0	-0.1

● MIKE RACZKA
Raczka, Michael b: 11/16/62, New Britain, Conn. BL/TL, 6', 200 lbs. Deb: 8/15/92

YEAR	TM/L	W	L	PCT	G	GS	CG	SH	SV	IP	H	HR	BB	SO	RAT	ERA	ERA+	OAV	OOB	BH	AVG	PB	PR	/A	PD	TPI
1992	Oak-A	0	0	—	8	0	0	0	0	6¹	8	0	5	2	18.5	8.53	44	.308	.419	0	—	0	-3	-3	-0	0.1

● DICK RADATZ
Radatz, Richard Raymond "The Monster" b: 4/2/37, Detroit, Mich. BR/TR, 6'5", 235 lbs. Deb: 4/10/62

YEAR	TM/L	W	L	PCT	G	GS	CG	SH	SV	IP	H	HR	BB	SO	RAT	ERA	ERA+	OAV	OOB	BH	AVG	PB	PR	/A	PD	TPI
1962	Bos-A	9	6	.600	62	0	0	0	24	124²	95	9	40	144	10.0	2.24	184	.211	.281	3	.097	-2	24	26	-2	3.8
1963	Bos-A★	15	6	.714	66	0	0	0	25	132¹	94	9	51	162	10.2	1.97	192	.201	.286	2	.069	-2	24	27	-2	5.0
1964	Bos-A★	16	9	.640	79	0	0	0	29	157	103	13	58	181	9.6	2.29	168	.186	.271	6	.162	-0	23	27	-2	5.3
1965	Bos-A	9	11	.450	63	0	0	0	22	124¹	104	11	53	121	11.7	3.91	95	.227	.314	5	.185	1	-6	-3	-1	-0.5
1966	Bos-A	0	2	.000	16	0	0	0	4	19	24	3	11	19	16.6	4.74	80	.304	.389	0	.000	-0	-3	-2	-1	-0.4
	Cle-A	0	3	.000	39	0	0	0	10	56²	49	6	34	49	13.7	4.61	75	.230	.348	1	.111	-0	-7	-7	-1	-0.8
	Yr	0	5	.000	55	0	0	0	14	75²	73	9	45	68	14.4	4.64	76	.253	.359	1	.091	-1	-10	-9	-2	-1.2
1967	Cle-A	0	0	—	3	0	0	0	0	3	5	1	2	1	21.0	6.00	54	.357	.438	0	—	0	-1	-1	0	0.0
	Chi-N	1	0	1.000	20	0	0	0	5	23¹	12	4	24	18	15.8	6.56	54	.154	.383	1	.250	0	-8	-8	-0	-0.7
1969	Det-A	2	2	.500	11	0	0	0	0	18²	14	3	5	18	9.2	3.38	111	.212	.268	0	.000	-0	1	1	0	0.1
	Mon-N	0	4	.000	22	0	0	0	3	34²	32	6	18	32	13.2	5.71	64	.244	.340	1	.250	0	-8	-8	-0	-1.0
Total	7	52	43	.547	381	0	0	0	122	693²	532	65	296	745	11.1	3.13	122	.212	.303	19	.131	-3	38	53	-9	10.8

● CHARLEY RADBOURN
Radbourn, Charles Gardner "Old Hoss"
b: 12/11/1854, Rochester, N.Y. d: 2/5/1897, Bloomington, Ill. BR/TR, 5'9", 168 lbs. Deb: 5/5/1880 H◆

YEAR	TM/L	W	L	PCT	G	GS	CG	SH	SV	IP	H	HR	BB	SO	RAT	ERA	ERA+	OAV	OOB	BH	AVG	PB	PR	/A	PD	TPI
1881	Pro-N	25	11	.694	41	36	34	3	0	325¹	309	1	64	117	10.3	2.43	109	.235	.270	59	.219	-1	12	8	3	0.9
1882	Pro-N	33	20	.623	55	52	51	6	0	474	429	6	51	201	9.1	2.09	135	.226	.246	78	.239	-1	43	38	1	3.4
1883	Pro-N	48	25	.658	76	68	66	4	1	632¹	563	7	56	315	8.8	2.05	151	.227	.244	108	.283	14	76	73	5	8.4
1884	*Pro-N	59	12	.831	75	73	73	11	1	678²	528	16	98	441	8.3	1.38	205	.234	.234	83	.230	6	121	109	-4	9.8
1885	Pro-N	28	21	.571	49	49	49	2	0	445²	423	4	83	154	10.2	2.20	120	.241	.275	58	.233	12	31	22	4	3.5
1886	Bos-N	27	31	.466	58	58	57	3	0	509¹	521	18	111	218	11.2	3.00	106	.254	.292	60	.237	8	17	11	2	1.9
1887	Bos-N	24	23	.511	50	50	48	1	0	425	505	20	133	87	13.8	4.55	89	.286	.340	40	.229	2	-23	-23	-3	-2.1
1888	Bos-N	7	16	.304	24	24	24	1	0	207	187	8	45	64	10.4	2.87	99	.234	.282	17	.215	1	-0	-0	-1	-0.1
1889	Bos-N	20	11	.645	33	31	28	1	0	277	282	14	72	99	11.8	3.67	113	.256	.306	23	.189	-1	11	15	2	1.4
1890	Bos-P	27	12	.692	41	38	36	1	0	343	352	8	100	80	12.1	3.31	133	.254	.309	39	.253	0	35	42	2	3.7
1891	Cin-N	11	13	.458	26	24	23	2	0	218	243	12	64	54	12.8	4.25	79	.266	.323	17	.177	-1	-22	-21	-3	-2.1
Total	11	309	195	.613	528	503	489	35	2	4535¹	4335	117	875	1830	10.4	2.67	120	.241	.278	585	.235	40	302	267	7	28.7

● GEORGE RADBOURN
Radbourn, George B. "Dordy" b: 4/8/1856, Bloomington, Ill. d: 1/1/04, Bloomington, Ill. 160 lbs. Deb: 5/30/1883

YEAR	TM/L	W	L	PCT	G	GS	CG	SH	SV	IP	H	HR	BB	SO	RAT	ERA	ERA+	OAV	OOB	BH	AVG	PB	PR	/A	PD	TPI
1883	Det-N	1	2	.333	3	3	2	0	0	22	38	1	7	2	18.4	6.55	47	.345	.385	2	.167	-1	-8	-8	0	-0.8

● ROY RADEBAUGH
Radebaugh, Roy b: 2/22/1884, Champaign, Ill. d: 1/17/45, Cedar Rapids, Iowa BR/TR, 5'7", 160 lbs. Deb: 9/22/11

YEAR	TM/L	W	L	PCT	G	GS	CG	SH	SV	IP	H	HR	BB	SO	RAT	ERA	ERA+	OAV	OOB	BH	AVG	PB	PR	/A	PD	TPI
1911	StL-N	0	0	—	2	1	0	0	0	10	6	0	4	1	9.0	2.70	125	.176	.263	0	—	0	1	1	0	0.0

● DREW RADER
Rader, Drew Leon "Lefty" b: 5/14/01, Elmira, N.Y. d: 6/5/75, Catskill, N.Y. BR/TL, 6'2", 187 lbs. Deb: 7/18/21

YEAR	TM/L	W	L	PCT	G	GS	CG	SH	SV	IP	H	HR	BB	SO	RAT	ERA	ERA+	OAV	OOB	BH	AVG	PB	PR	/A	PD	TPI
1921	Pit-N	0	0	—	1	0	0	0	0	2	2	0	0	0	9.0	0.00	—	.286	.286	0	.000	-0	1	1	-0	0.0

● PAUL RADFORD
Radford, Paul Revere "Shorty" b: 10/14/1861, Roxbury, Mass. d: 2/21/45, Boston, Mass. BR/TR, 5'6", 148 lbs. Deb: 5/1/1883 ◆

YEAR	TM/L	W	L	PCT	G	GS	CG	SH	SV	IP	H	HR	BB	SO	RAT	ERA	ERA+	OAV	OOB	BH	AVG	PB	PR	/A	PD	TPI
1884	*Pro-N	0	2	.000	2	2	1	0	0	13	27	1	0	3	20.8	7.62	37	.403	.429	70	.197	-7	-7	-0	-0.7
1885	Pro-N	0	2	.000	3	2	2	0	0	18¹	34	1	8	3	20.6	7.85	34	.378	.429	90	.243	1	-10	-11	0	-0.8
1887	NY-a	0	0	—	2	0	0	0	0	5	15	1	3	4	32.4	18.00	24	.789	.818	129	.265	1	-8	-8	-0	0.1
1890	Cle-P	0	0	—	1	0	0	0	0	5	7	1	1	0	14.4	3.60	110	.317	.347	136	.292	0	0	0	1	0.1
1891	Bos-a	0	0	—	1	0	0	0	0	1	0	0	0	0	0.0	0.00	—	.000	.000	118	.259	0	0	0	0	0.0
1893	Was-N	0	0	—	1	0	0	0	0	1	2	2	1	0	36.0	18.00	26	.403	.575	106	.228	0	-1	-1	-0	0.0
Total	6	0	4	.000	10	4	4	0	0	43¹	85	5	17	13	21.2	8.52	36	.413	.457	1206	.242	2	-25	-26	0	-1.4

● SCOTT RADINSKY
Radinsky, Scott David b: 3/3/68, Glendale, Cal. BL/TL, 6'3", 190 lbs. Deb: 4/9/90

YEAR	TM/L	W	L	PCT	G	GS	CG	SH	SV	IP	H	HR	BB	SO	RAT	ERA	ERA+	OAV	OOB	BH	AVG	PB	PR	/A	PD	TPI
1990	Chi-A	6	1	.857	62	0	0	0	4	52¹	47	1	36	46	14.6	4.82	79	.241	.365	0	—	0	-5	-6	0	-0.8
1991	Chi-A	5	5	.500	67	0	0	0	8	71¹	53	4	23	49	9.7	2.02	197	.206	.274	0	—	0	16	15	1	2.5
1992	Chi-A	3	7	.300	68	0	0	0	15	59¹	54	1	34	48	13.7	2.73	141	.243	.349	0	—	0	8	7	0	1.7
1993	*Chi-A	8	2	.800	73	0	0	0	4	54²	61	3	19	44	13.3	4.28	98	.283	.327	0	—	0	-0	-0	0	-0.0
Total	4	22	15	.595	270	0	0	0	31	237²	215	11	112	187	12.6	3.33	119	.238	.326	0	—	0	19	17	1	3.4

● HAL RAETHER
Raether, Harold Herman "Bud" b: 10/10/32, Lake Mills, Wis. BR/TR, 6'1", 185 lbs. Deb: 7/4/54

YEAR	TM/L	W	L	PCT	G	GS	CG	SH	SV	IP	H	HR	BB	SO	RAT	ERA	ERA+	OAV	OOB	BH	AVG	PB	PR	/A	PD	TPI
1954	Phi-A	0	0	—	1	0	0	0	0	2	1	0	4	0	22.5	4.50	87	.200	.556	0	—	0	-0	-0	-0	0.0
1957	KC-A	0	0	—	1	0	0	0	0	2	2	1	0	1	9.0	9.00	44	.250	.250	0	—	0	-1	-1	0	0.0
Total	2	0	0	—	2	0	0	0	0	4	3	1	4	1	15.8	6.75	58	.231	.412	0	—	0	-1	-1	-0	0.0

● KEN RAFFENSBERGER
Raffensberger, Kenneth David b: 8/8/17, York, Pa. BR/TL, 6'2", 185 lbs. Deb: 4/25/39

YEAR	TM/L	W	L	PCT	G	GS	CG	SH	SV	IP	H	HR	BB	SO	RAT	ERA	ERA+	OAV	OOB	BH	AVG	PB	PR	/A	PD	TPI
1939	StL-N	0	0	—	1	0	0	0	0	1	2	0	0	1	18.0	0.00	—	.400	.400	0	—	0	0	0	0	0.0

YEAR TM/L	W	L	PCT	G	GS	CG	SH	SV	IP	H	HR	BB	SO	RAT	ERA	ERA+	OAV	OOB	BH	AVG	PB	PR	/A	PD	TPI
1940 Chi-N	7	9	.438	43	10	3	0	3	114²	120	10	29	55	11.9	3.38	111	.271	.319	5	.167	-1	6	5	-1	0.5
1941 Chi-N	0	1	.000	10	1	0	0	0	18	17	0	7	5	12.0	4.50	78	.262	.333	0	.000	-1	-2	-2	1	-0.1
1943 Phi-N	0	1	.000	1	1	0	0	0	8	7	0	2	3	10.1	1.13	300	.241	.290	0	.000	-0	2	2	-0	0.2
1944 Phi-N★	13	20	.394	37	31	18	3	0	258²	257	9	45	136	10.6	3.06	118	.252	.285	11	.138	-3	16	16	-3	1.3
1945 Phi-N	0	3	.000	5	4	1	0	0	24¹	28	3	14	6	15.5	4.44	86	.283	.372	0	.000	-1	-2	-2	0	-0.3
1946 Phi-N	8	15	.348	39	23	14	2	6	196	203	10	39	73	11.2	3.63	95	.265	.302	10	.167	-1	-5	-4	-3	-0.8
1947 Phi-N	2	6	.250	10	7	3	1	0	41	50	4	8	16	13.0	5.49	78	.307	.343	4	.267	-1	-7	-7	1	-1.0
Cin-N	6	5	.545	19	15	7	0	1	106²	132	11	29	38	13.6	4.13	99	.305	.348	6	.162	-1	-1	-0	-1	-0.2
Yr	8	11	.421	29	22	10	1	1	147²	182	15	37	54	13.3	4.51	90	.305	.345	10	.192	-0	-7	-7	0	-1.2
1948 Cin-N	11	12	.478	40	24	7	4	0	180¹	187	15	37	57	11.2	3.84	102	.259	.296	7	.113	-3	2	1	-2	-0.3
1949 Cin-N	18	17	.514	41	38	20	5	0	284	289	23	80	103	11.8	3.39	123	.264	.315	16	.178	-1	21	25	-3	2.6
1950 Cin-N	14	19	.424	38	35	18	4	0	239	271	34	40	87	11.8	4.26	100	.279	.308	11	.134	-2	-3	-1	-2	-0.4
1951 Cin-N	16	17	.485	42	33	14	5	5	248²	232	30	38	81	**10.0**	3.44	119	.246	.279	10	.122	-3	14	18	-4	1.5
1952 Cin-N	17	13	.567	38	33	18	6	1	247	247	18	45	93	10.7	2.81	134	.261	.295	8	.107	-2	25	27	-2	2.7
1953 Cin-N	7	14	.333	26	26	9	1	0	174	200	23	33	47	12.1	3.93	111	.289	.322	8	.140	-1	7	8	2	0.9
1954 Cin-N	0	2	.000	6	1	0	0	0	10¹	15	2	3	5	15.7	7.84	53	.333	.375	1	.500	0	-4	-4	-0	-0.7
Total 15	119	154	.436	396	282	133	31	16	2151²	2257	192	449	806	11.4	3.60	110	.267	.306	97	.141	-17	71	82	-18	5.9

● **AL RAFFO**　　Raffo, Albert Martin　b: 11/27/41, San Francisco, Cal.　BR/TR, 6'5", 210 lbs.　Deb: 4/29/69

YEAR TM/L	W	L	PCT	G	GS	CG	SH	SV	IP	H	HR	BB	SO	RAT	ERA	ERA+	OAV	OOB	BH	AVG	PB	PR	/A	PD	TPI
1969 Phi-N	1	3	.250	45	0	0	0	1	72¹	81	6	25	38	13.7	4.11	86	.286	.353	1	.167	0	-4	-5	1	-0.2

● **PAT RAGAN**　　Ragan, Don Carlos Patrick　b: 11/15/1888, Blanchard, Iowa　d: 9/4/56, Los Angeles, Cal.　BR/TR, 5'10.5", 185 lbs.　Deb: 4/21/09　C

YEAR TM/L	W	L	PCT	G	GS	CG	SH	SV	IP	H	HR	BB	SO	RAT	ERA	ERA+	OAV	OOB	BH	AVG	PB	PR	/A	PD	TPI
1909 Cin-N	0	1	.000	2	0	0	0	0	8	7	0	4	2	12.4	3.38	77	.259	.355	1	.500	0	-1	-1	-0	-0.1
Chi-N	0	0	—	2	0	0	0	0	3²	4	0	1	2	12.3	2.45	104	.286	.333	0	.000	-0	0	0	-0	0.0
Yr	0	1	.000	4	0	0	0	0	11²	11	0	5	4	12.3	3.09	84	.268	.348	1	.250	0	-1	-1	-0	-0.1
1911 Bro-N	4	3	.571	22	7	5	1	1	93²	81	9	31	39	11.0	2.11	158	.252	.321	4	.138	-1	13	13	-1	0.7
1912 Bro-N	7	18	.280	36	26	12	1	1	208	211	7	65	101	12.1	3.63	92	.270	.329	4	.060	-1	-5	-7	-1	-1.5
1913 Bro-N	15	18	.455	44	32	14	0	0	264²	284	10	64	109	12.1	3.77	87	.281	.327	15	.165	-2	-17	-14	2	-1.7
1914 Bro-N	10	15	.400	38	26	14	1	3	208¹	214	5	85	106	13.0	2.98	96	.270	.343	10	.133	-3	-4	-3	0	-0.7
1915 Bro-N	1	0	1.000	5	0	0	0	0	19²	11	0	8	7	8.7	0.92	304	.164	.253	1	.167	-0	4	4	0	0.1
Bos-N	16	12	.571	33	26	13	3	0	227	208	2	59	81	10.9	2.46	105	.255	.311	12	.150	-1	7	3	-2	0.0
Yr	17	12	.586	38	26	13	3	0	246²	219	2	67	88	10.7	2.34	112	.248	.306	13	.151	-1	11	7	-2	0.1
1916 Bos-N	9	9	.500	28	23	14	5	0	182	143	3	47	63	9.4	2.08	120	.218	.270	13	.217	3	11	8	1	1.3
1917 Bos-N	9	13	.400	30	13	5	1	1	147²	138	6	35	61	10.6	2.93	87	.250	.295	6	.125	-1	-4	-6	0	-0.8
1918 Bos-N	8	17	.320	30	25	15	2	0	206¹	212	4	54	68	11.8	3.23	83	.270	.320	13	.183	-2	-11	-12	-0	-1.6
1919 Bos-N	0	2	.000	4	3	0	0	0	12²	16	0	3	3	13.5	7.11	40	.281	.317	1	.250	0	-6	-6	0	-0.8
NY-N	1	0	1.000	7	1	1	0	0	22²	19	0	14	7	13.1	1.59	177	.247	.363	3	.429	1	3	3	0	0.3
Yr	1	2	.333	11	4	1	0	0	35¹	35	0	17	10	13.2	3.57	79	.261	.344	4	.364	1	-3	-3	0	-0.5
Chi-A	0	0	—	1	0	0	0	0	1	1	0	0	0	9.0	0.00	—	.250	.250	0	—	0	0	0	0	0.0
1923 Phi-N	0	0	—	1	0	0	0	0	2	6	1	0	0	18.0	6.00	77	.400	.400	1	.500	0	-1	-0	-0	0.0
Total 11	77	104	.425	283	182	93	12	6	1608¹	1555	38	470	680	11.5	2.99	97	.260	.317	84	.154	-13	-8	-18	-2	-4.8

● **FRANK RAGLAND**　　Ragland, Frank Roland　b: 5/26/04, Water Valley, Miss.　d: 7/28/59, Paris, Miss.　BR/TR, 6'1", 186 lbs.　Deb: 4/17/32

YEAR TM/L	W	L	PCT	G	GS	CG	SH	SV	IP	H	HR	BB	SO	RAT	ERA	ERA+	OAV	OOB	BH	AVG	PB	PR	/A	PD	TPI
1932 Was-A	1	0	1.000	12	1	0	0	0	37²	54	5	21	11	18.6	7.41	58	.346	.433	3	.273	1	-12	-13	0	-0.2
1933 Phi-N	0	4	.000	11	5	0	0	0	38¹	51	1	10	4	14.6	6.81	56	.317	.360	2	.200	-0	-15	-13	1	-1.1
Total 2	1	4	.200	23	6	0	0	0	76	105	6	31	15	16.6	7.11	58	.331	.398	5	.238	1	-27	-25	1	-1.3

● **ERIC RAICH**　　Raich, Eric James　b: 11/1/51, Detroit, Mich.　BR/TR, 6'4", 225 lbs.　Deb: 5/24/75

YEAR TM/L	W	L	PCT	G	GS	CG	SH	SV	IP	H	HR	BB	SO	RAT	ERA	ERA+	OAV	OOB	BH	AVG	PB	PR	/A	PD	TPI
1975 Cle-A	7	8	.467	18	17	2	0	0	92²	118	12	31	34	14.6	5.54	68	.320	.374	0	—	0	-18	-18	-1	-2.6
1976 Cle-A	0	0	—	1	0	0	0	0	2²	7	1	0	1	23.6	16.88	21	.467	.467	0	—	0	-4	-4	-0	0.0
Total 2	7	8	.467	19	17	2	0	0	95¹	125	13	31	35	14.8	5.85	64	.326	.377	0	—	0	-22	-22	-1	-2.6

● **CHUCK RAINEY**　　Rainey, Charles David　b: 7/14/54, San Diego, Cal.　BR/TR, 5'11", 190 lbs.　Deb: 4/8/79

YEAR TM/L	W	L	PCT	G	GS	CG	SH	SV	IP	H	HR	BB	SO	RAT	ERA	ERA+	OAV	OOB	BH	AVG	PB	PR	/A	PD	TPI
1979 Bos-A	8	5	.615	20	16	4	1	1	103²	97	7	41	41	12.2	3.82	116	.250	.326	0	—	0	5	7	1	0.8
1980 Bos-A	8	3	.727	16	13	2	1	0	87	92	7	41	43	14.0	4.86	87	.273	.355	0	—	0	-8	-6	-1	-0.8
1981 Bos-A	0	1	.000	11	2	0	0	0	40	39	2	13	25	11.7	2.70	143	.252	.310	0	—	0	4	5	1	0.1
1982 Bos-A	7	5	.583	27	25	3	0	0	129	146	6	63	57	14.7	5.02	86	.294	.376	0	—	0	-14	-10	1	-0.8
1983 Chi-N	14	13	.519	34	34	1	1	0	191	219	17	74	84	13.9	4.48	85	.295	.361	9	.161	1	-18	-15	3	-1.6
1984 Chi-N	5	7	.417	17	16	0	0	0	88¹	102	4	38	45	14.5	4.28	91	.290	.362	3	.097	-1	-7	-4	1	-0.5
Oak-A	1	1	.500	16	0	0	0	1	30²	42	3	17	10	17.6	6.75	55	.333	.411	0	—	0	-9	-10	-0	-0.7
Total 6	43	35	.551	141	106	10	6	2	669²	738	53	287	300	13.9	4.50	90	.284	.358	12	.138	-1	-47	-33	5	-3.5

● **DAVE RAJSICH**　　Rajsich, David Christopher　b: 9/28/51, Youngstown, Ohio　BL/TL, 6'5", 175 lbs.　Deb: 7/2/78　F

YEAR TM/L	W	L	PCT	G	GS	CG	SH	SV	IP	H	HR	BB	SO	RAT	ERA	ERA+	OAV	OOB	BH	AVG	PB	PR	/A	PD	TPI
1978 NY-A	0	0	—	4	2	0	0	0	13¹	16	0	6	9	14.9	4.05	89	.320	.393	0	—	0	-0	-1	-0	0.0
1979 Tex-A	1	3	.250	27	3	0	0	0	53²	56	7	18	32	12.4	3.52	118	.267	.325	0	—	0	4	4	1	0.3
1980 Tex-A	2	1	.667	24	1	0	0	2	48¹	56	7	22	35	15.1	5.96	65	.295	.377	0	—	0	-10	-11	0	-0.7
Total 3	3	4	.429	55	6	0	0	2	115¹	128	14	46	76	13.8	4.60	86	.284	.355	0	—	0	-7	-8	1	-0.4

● **ED RAKOW**　　Rakow, Edward Charles "Rock"　b: 5/30/36, Pittsburgh, Pa.　BB/TR, 5'11", 178 lbs.　Deb: 4/22/60

YEAR TM/L	W	L	PCT	G	GS	CG	SH	SV	IP	H	HR	BB	SO	RAT	ERA	ERA+	OAV	OOB	BH	AVG	PB	PR	/A	PD	TPI
1960 LA-N	0	1	.000	9	2	0	0	0	22	30	5	11	9	16.8	7.36	54	.323	.394	2	.333	0	-9	-8	-0	-0.3
1961 KC-A	2	8	.200	45	11	1	0	1	124²	131	14	49	81	13.6	4.76	88	.269	.346	3	.103	-2	-10	-8	1	-0.7
1962 KC-A	14	17	.452	42	35	11	2	1	235¹	232	31	98	159	12.8	4.25	99	.260	.336	8	.098	-5	-7	-1	2	-0.4
1963 KC-A	9	10	.474	34	26	7	1	0	174¹	173	18	61	104	12.3	3.92	99	.261	.328	6	.105	-2	-6	-0	1	-0.1
1964 Det-A	8	9	.471	42	13	1	0	3	152¹	155	14	59	96	13.0	3.72	98	.266	.340	0	.000	-4	-2	-1	2	-0.3
1965 Det-A	0	0	—	6	0	0	0	0	13¹	14	2	11	10	16.9	6.08	57	.280	.410	0	.000	-0	-4	-4	-1	-0.1
1967 Atl-N	3	2	.600	17	3	0	0	0	39¹	36	4	15	25	11.9	5.26	63	.240	.313	0	.000	-0	-8	-8	-1	-1.2
Total 7	36	47	.434	195	90	20	3	5	761¹	771	88	304	484	13.0	4.33	92	.264	.339	19	.084	-13	-46	-31	4	-3.1

● **JOHN RALEIGH**　　Raleigh, John Austin　b: 4/21/1890, Elkhorn, Wis.　d: 8/24/55, Escondido, Cal.　BR/TL,　Deb: 8/4/09

YEAR TM/L	W	L	PCT	G	GS	CG	SH	SV	IP	H	HR	BB	SO	RAT	ERA	ERA+	OAV	OOB	BH	AVG	PB	PR	/A	PD	TPI
1909 StL-N	1	10	.091	15	10	3	0	0	80²	85	0	21	26	12.2	3.79	67	.285	.339	2	.087	-2	-11	-11	0	-1.6
1910 StL-N	0	0	—	3	1	0	0	0	5	8	0	0	2	14.4	9.00	33	.364	.364	0	.000	-0	-3	-3	0	0.0
Total 2	1	10	.091	18	11	3	0	0	85²	93	0	21	28	12.3	4.10	62	.291	.340	2	.083	-2	-14	-15	0	-1.6

● **PEP RAMBERT**　　Rambert, Elmer Donald　b: 8/1/16, Cleveland, Ohio　d: 11/16/74, W.Palm Beach, Fla.　BR/TR, 6', 175 lbs.　Deb: 9/23/39

YEAR TM/L	W	L	PCT	G	GS	CG	SH	SV	IP	H	HR	BB	SO	RAT	ERA	ERA+	OAV	OOB	BH	AVG	PB	PR	/A	PD	TPI
1939 Pit-N	0	0	—	2	0	0	0	0	3²	7	0	1	4	19.6	9.82	39	.389	.421	0	—	0	-2	-2	0	0.0
1940 Pit-N	0	1	.000	3	1	0	0	0	8¹	12	0	4	1	20.5	7.56	50	.333	.442	0	.000	0	-3	-3	0	-0.4
Total 2	0	1	.000	5	1	0	0	0	12	19	0	5	4	20.3	8.25	46	.352	.435	0	.000	0	-6	-6	0	-0.4

● **PETE RAMBO**　　Rambo, Warren Dawson　b: 11/1/06, Thorofare, N.J.　d: 6/19/91, Camden, N.J.　BR/TR, 5'9", 150 lbs.　Deb: 9/16/26

YEAR TM/L	W	L	PCT	G	GS	CG	SH	SV	IP	H	HR	BB	SO	RAT	ERA	ERA+	OAV	OOB	BH	AVG	PB	PR	/A	PD	TPI
1926 Phi-N	0	0	—	1	0	0	0	0	3²	6	0	4	4	24.5	14.73	28	.353	.476	1	1.000	0	-4	-4	0	0.0

● **ALLAN RAMIREZ**　　Ramirez, Daniel Allan　b: 5/1/57, Victoria, Tex.　BR/TR, 5'10", 180 lbs.　Deb: 6/8/83

YEAR TM/L	W	L	PCT	G	GS	CG	SH	SV	IP	H	HR	BB	SO	RAT	ERA	ERA+	OAV	OOB	BH	AVG	PB	PR	/A	PD	TPI
1983 Bal-A	4	4	.500	11	10	1	0	0	57	46	6	30	20	12.0	3.47	114	.229	.329	0	—	0	4	3	0	0.4

● **PEDRO RAMOS**　　Ramos, Pedro (Guerra) "Pete"　b: 4/28/35, Pinar Del Rio, Cuba　BB/TR, 6', 185 lbs.　Deb: 4/11/55　◆

YEAR TM/L	W	L	PCT	G	GS	CG	SH	SV	IP	H	HR	BB	SO	RAT	ERA	ERA+	OAV	OOB	BH	AVG	PB	PR	/A	PD	TPI
1955 Was-A	5	11	.313	45	9	3	1	5	130	121	13	39	34	11.8	3.88	99	.253	.323	3	.079	-3	1	-1	-1	-0.5

YEAR	TM/L	W	L	PCT	G	GS	CG	SH	SV	IP	H	HR	BB	SO	RAT	ERA	ERA+	OAV	OOB	BH	AVG	PB	PR	/A	PD	TPI
1956	Was-A	12	10	.545	37	18	4	0	0	152	178	23	76	54	15.2	5.27	82	.299	.381	9	.205	0	-19	-16	-0	-2.0
1957	Was-A	12	16	.429	43	30	7	1	0	231	251	43	69	91	12.7	4.79	81	.271	.327	13	.171	-1	-26	-23	-0	-2.6
1958	Was-A	14	18	.438	43	37	10	4	3	259²	277	38	77	132	12.5	4.23	90	.273	.327	21	.239	-1	-13	-12	-1	-1.3
1959	Was-A☆	13	19	.406	37	35	11	0	0	233²	233	29	52	95	11.3	4.16	94	.257	.304	11	.147	-0	-8	-6	-1	-0.8
1960	Was-A	11	18	.379	43	36	14	1	2	274	254	24	99	160	11.8	3.45	113	.245	.315	10	.116	-2	13	13	0	1.2
1961	Min-A	11	20	.355	42	34	9	3	2	264¹	265	39	79	174	11.8	3.95	107	.258	.313	16	.172	1	2	9	-3	0.8
1962	Cle-A	10	12	.455	37	27	7	2	1	201¹	189	28	85	96	12.5	3.71	104	.246	.326	10	.147	2	6	4	-0	0.6
1963	Cle-A	9	8	.529	36	22	5	0	0	184²	156	29	41	169	9.8	3.12	116	.226	.273	6	.109	1	10	10	-2	0.8
1964	Cle-A	7	10	.412	36	19	3	1	0	133	144	18	26	98	11.8	5.14	70	.273	.312	7	.179	2	-22	-23	-1	-2.5
	NY-A	1	0	1.000	13	0	0	0	8	21²	13	1	0	21	5.4	1.25	291	.183	.183	0	.000	-1	6	6	-1	0.6
	Yr	8	10	.444	49	19	3	1	8	154²	157	19	26	119	11.3	4.60	78	.259	.290	7	.159	1	-17	-17	-2	-1.9
1965	NY-A	5	5	.500	65	0	0	0	19	92¹	80	7	27	68	10.5	2.92	116	.237	.296	1	.083	-1	5	5	-1	0.6
1966	NY-A	3	9	.250	52	1	0	0	13	89²	98	10	18	58	11.7	3.61	92	.283	.321	2	.154	-0	-2	-3	-0	-0.5
1967	Phi-N	0	0	—	6	0	0	0	0	8	14	1	8	1	27.0	9.00	38	.412	.545	0	.000	-0	-5	-5	1	0.1
1969	Pit-N	0	1	.000	5	0	0	0	0	6	8	2	0	4	12.0	6.00	58	.320	.320	0	.000	-0	-2	-2	0	-0.3
	Cin-N	4	3	.571	38	0	0	0	2	66¹	73	8	24	40	13.8	5.16	73	.284	.357	0	.000	-1	-12	-10	-0	-1.1
	Yr	4	4	.500	43	0	0	0	2	72¹	81	10	24	44	13.7	5.23	72	.287	.354	0	.000	-1	-13	-12	-0	-1.4
1970	Was-A	0	0	—	4	0	0	0	0	8¹	10	2	4	10	15.1	7.56	47	.294	.368	0	.000	-0	-4	-4	0	0.0
Total	15	117	160	.422	582	268	73	13	55	2355²	2364	315	724	1305	12.1	4.08	95	.261	.320	109	.155	-0	-68	-58	-9	-6.9

● WILLIE RAMSDELL
Ramsdell, James Willard "The Knuck"   b: 4/4/16, Williamsburg, Kan.   d: 10/8/69, Wichita, Kan.   BR/TR, 5'10", 180 lbs.   Deb: 9/24/47

YEAR	TM/L	W	L	PCT	G	GS	CG	SH	SV	IP	H	HR	BB	SO	RAT	ERA	ERA+	OAV	OOB	BH	AVG	PB	PR	/A	PD	TPI
1947	Bro-N	1	1	.500	2	0	0	0	0	2²	4	0	3	3	27.0	6.75	61	.333	.500	1	1.000	0	-1	-1	0	-0.4
1948	Bro-N	4	4	.500	27	1	0	0	4	50¹	48	6	41	34	16.5	5.19	77	.251	.391	1	.091	-1	-7	-7	1	-1.0
1950	Bro-N	1	2	.333	5	0	0	0	0	6¹	7	0	2	2	14.2	2.84	144	.292	.370	0	.000	-0	1	1	0	0.4
	Cin-N	7	12	.368	27	22	8	1	0	157¹	151	17	75	83	13.0	3.72	114	.255	.341	10	.200	1	7	9	-1	0.9
	Yr	8	14	.364	32	22	8	1	1	163²	158	17	77	85	13.0	3.68	115	.256	.341	10	.189	1	8	10	-1	1.3
1951	Cin-N	9	17	.346	31	31	10	1	0	196	204	18	70	88	12.9	4.04	101	.266	.333	9	.155	-1	-2	1	-2	-0.2
1952	Chi-N	2	3	.400	19	4	0	0	0	67	41	5	24	30	9.4	2.42	159	.173	.263	1	.056	-1	10	11	-1	0.6
Total	5	24	39	.381	111	58	18	2	5	479²	455	46	215	240	12.9	3.83	107	.250	.335	22	.156	-2	9	14	-2	0.3

● TOAD RAMSEY
Ramsey, Thomas A.   b: 8/8/1864, Indianapolis, Ind.   d: 3/27/06, Indianapolis, Ind.   BR/TL,   Deb: 9/5/1885

YEAR	TM/L	W	L	PCT	G	GS	CG	SH	SV	IP	H	HR	BB	SO	RAT	ERA	ERA+	OAV	OOB	BH	AVG	PB	PR	/A	PD	TPI
1885	Lou-a	3	6	.333	9	9	9	0	0	79	44	1	28	83	8.3	1.94	167	.150	.227	4	.129	-2	12	11	-0	0.8
1886	Lou-a	38	27	.585	67	67	**66**	3	0	588²	447	3	207	499	10.2	2.45	149	**.198**	.269	58	.241	-3	66	**78**	-3	6.5
1887	Lou-a	37	27	.578	65	64	61	0	0	561	544	9	167	**355**	11.7	3.43	128	.242	.299	43	.191	-10	54	60	-3	3.5
1888	Lou-a	8	30	.211	40	40	37	0	0	342¹	362	10	86	228	12.1	3.42	90	.262	.310	17	.120	-7	-13	-13	-4	-2.1
1889	Lou-a	1	16	.059	18	18	15	0	0	140	175	7	71	60	15.9	5.59	69	.297	.374	15	.263	0	-27	-27	-2	-2.5
	StL-a	3	1	.750	5	3	3	0	0	41	44	0	10	33	12.1	3.95	107	.266	.312	5	.294	0	-0	1	-1	0.1
	Yr	4	17	.190	23	21	18	0	0	181	219	7	81	93	15.0	5.22	75	.289	.359	20	.270	1	-28	-26	-2	-2.4
1890	StL-a	24	17	.585	44	40	34	1	0	348²	325	10	102	257	11.2	3.69	117	.239	.296	33	.228	-1	7	24	-7	1.5
Total	6	114	124	.479	248	241	225	5	0	2100²	1941	40	671	1515	11.4	3.29	117	.234	.295	175	.204	-22	97	134	-25	7.8

● RIBS RANEY
Raney, Frank Robert Donald (b: Frank Robert Donald Raniszewski)   b: 2/16/23, Detroit, Mich.   BR/TR, 6'4", 190 lbs.   Deb: 9/18/49

YEAR	TM/L	W	L	PCT	G	GS	CG	SH	SV	IP	H	HR	BB	SO	RAT	ERA	ERA+	OAV	OOB	BH	AVG	PB	PR	/A	PD	TPI
1949	StL-A	1	2	.333	3	3	1	0	0	16¹	23	2	12	5	19.3	7.71	59	.333	.432	0	.000	-1	-6	-6	-0	-0.9
1950	StL-A	0	1	.000	1	0	0	0	0	2	2	0	2	2	18.0	4.50	110	.250	.400	0	.000	0	0	0	0	0.0
Total	2	1	3	.250	4	3	1	0	0	18¹	25	2	14	7	19.1	7.36	62	.325	.429	0	.000	-1	-6	-6	-0	-0.9

● PAT RAPP
Rapp, Patrick Leland   b: 7/13/67, Jennings, La.   BR/TR, 6'3", 195 lbs.   Deb: 7/10/92

YEAR	TM/L	W	L	PCT	G	GS	CG	SH	SV	IP	H	HR	BB	SO	RAT	ERA	ERA+	OAV	OOB	BH	AVG	PB	PR	/A	PD	TPI
1992	SF-N	0	2	.000	3	2	0	0	0	10	8	0	6	3	13.5	7.20	46	.235	.366	0	.000	-0	-4	-4	0	-0.7
1993	Fla-N	4	6	.400	16	16	1	0	0	94	101	7	39	57	13.6	4.02	107	.281	.355	6	.194	0	0	3	0	0.4
1994	Fla-N	7	8	.467	24	23	2	1	0	133¹	132	13	69	75	14.0	3.85	117	.266	.364	5	.122	-1	5	10	-1	0.7
Total	3	11	16	.407	43	41	3	1	0	237¹	241	20	114	135	13.8	4.06	108	.271	.360	11	.149	-1	1	8	-1	0.4

● VIC RASCHI
Raschi, Victor John Angelo   b: 3/28/19, W.Springfield, Mass.   d: 10/14/88, Groveland, N.Y.   BR/TR, 6'1", 205 lbs.   Deb: 9/23/46

YEAR	TM/L	W	L	PCT	G	GS	CG	SH	SV	IP	H	HR	BB	SO	RAT	ERA	ERA+	OAV	OOB	BH	AVG	PB	PR	/A	PD	TPI
1946	NY-A	2	0	1.000	2	2	2	0	0	16	14	0	5	11	10.7	3.94	88	.230	.288	1	.250	-1	-1	-1	0	-0.1
1947	*NY-A	7	2	.778	15	14	6	1	0	104²	89	11	38	51	11.0	3.87	91	.226	.296	10	.250	2	-2	-4	-0	-0.2
1948	NY-A★	19	8	.704	36	31	18	6	1	222²	208	15	74	124	11.5	3.84	106	.247	.310	19	.235	2	11	6	-1	0.7
1949	*NY-A★	21	10	.677	38	37	21	3	0	274²	247	16	138	124	12.8	3.34	121	.241	.334	13	.157	1	26	21	1	2.3
1950	*NY-A★	21	8	**.724**	33	32	17	2	1	256²	232	19	116	155	12.3	4.00	107	.243	.327	17	.198	1	17	8	-3	1.2
1951	*NY-A	21	10	.677	35	34	15	4	0	258¹	233	20	103	**164**	11.9	3.27	117	.242	.319	15	.176	-2	24	16	-3	1.2
1952	*NY-A★	16	6	.727	31	31	13	4	0	223	174	13	91	127	10.9	2.78	119	.216	.300	13	.188	-3	22	13	-4	1.1
1953	*NY-A	13	6	.684	28	26	7	4	1	181	150	11	55	76	**10.2**	3.33	111	.224	**.283**	9	.143	-2	13	7	-2	0.3
1954	StL-N	8	9	.471	30	29	6	2	0	179	182	24	71	73	12.7	4.73	87	.268	.337	9	.141	-2	-13	-12	1	-1.1
1955	StL-N	1	0	1.000	1	1	0	0	0	1²	5	0	1	2	32.4	21.60	19	.556	.600	0	—	-0	-3	-3	-0	-1.0
	KC-A	4	6	.400	20	18	1	0	0	101¹	132	16	35	49	14.9	5.42	77	.312	.366	6	.182	-0	-16	-14	1	-1.1
Total	10	132	66	.667	269	255	106	26	3	1819	1666	139	727	944	12.0	3.72	105	.244	.319	112	.184	3	78	38	-9	2.8

● DENNIS RASMUSSEN
Rasmussen, Dennis Lee   b: 4/18/59, Los Angeles, Cal.   BL/TL, 6'7", 230 lbs.   Deb: 9/16/83   F

YEAR	TM/L	W	L	PCT	G	GS	CG	SH	SV	IP	H	HR	BB	SO	RAT	ERA	ERA+	OAV	OOB	BH	AVG	PB	PR	/A	PD	TPI
1983	SD-N	0	0	—	4	1	0	0	0	13²	10	1	8	13	11.9	1.98	176	.200	.310	0	.000	-0	3	2	1	0.0
1984	NY-A	9	6	.600	24	24	1	0	0	147²	127	16	60	110	11.6	4.57	83	.234	.315	—	0	-10	-13	-1	-1.0	
1985	NY-A	3	5	.375	22	16	2	0	0	101²	97	10	42	63	12.4	3.98	100	.255	.331	—	0	2	0	0	0.2	
1986	NY-A	18	6	.750	31	31	3	1	0	202	160	28	74	131	10.5	3.88	105	.217	.290	0	7	5	-1	0.5		
1987	NY-A	9	7	.563	26	25	2	0	0	146	145	31	55	89	12.6	4.75	92	.260	.331	0	-5	-6	-0	-0.5		
	Cin-N	4	1	.800	7	7	0	0	0	45¹	39	5	12	39	10.3	3.97	107	.229	.284	1	.067	-1	1	1	0	0.1
1988	Cin-N	2	6	.250	11	11	1	0	0	56¹	68	8	22	27	14.7	5.75	62	.300	.367	5	.227	-1	-14	-14	0	-1.6
	SD-N	14	4	.778	20	20	6	0	0	148¹	131	9	36	85	10.3	2.55	133	.238	.287	9	.188	2	15	14	2	2.2
	Yr	16	10	.615	31	31	7	1	0	204²	199	17	58	112	11.4	3.43	100	.254	.308	14	.200	3	0	0	2	0.6
1989	SD-N	10	10	.500	33	33	1	0	0	183²	190	18	72	87	13.0	4.26	82	.270	.340	11	.169	1	-16	-16	-1	-1.4
1990	SD-N	11	15	.423	32	32	3	1	0	187²	217	28	62	86	13.5	4.51	85	.292	.349	18	.290	5	-15	-14	-0	-1.3
1991	SD-N	6	13	.316	24	24	1	1	0	146²	155	12	49	75	12.6	3.74	101	.271	.331	6	.136	1	-1	1	0	0.4
1992	Chi-N	0	0	—	3	1	0	0	0	5	7	2	2	0	18.0	10.80	33	.350	.435	0	—	0	-4	-4	0	0.0
	KC-A	4	1	.800	5	5	1	1	0	37²	25	0	6	12	7.4	1.43	283	.197	.233	0	—	0	10	11	1	1.5
1993	KC-A	1	2	.333	9	4	0	0	0	29	40	4	14	12	17.1	7.45	61	.328	.401	0	—	0	-10	-9	-0	-0.8
Total	11	91	76	.545	251	234	21	5	0	1450²	1411	172	514	829	12.1	4.11	94	.256	.323	50	.193	8	-37	-41	2	-1.9

● ERIC RASMUSSEN
Rasmussen, Eric Ralph (Born Harold Ralph Rasmussen)   b: 3/22/52, Racine, Wis.   BR/TR, 6'3", 205 lbs.   Deb: 7/21/75

YEAR	TM/L	W	L	PCT	G	GS	CG	SH	SV	IP	H	HR	BB	SO	RAT	ERA	ERA+	OAV	OOB	BH	AVG	PB	PR	/A	PD	TPI
1975	StL-N	5	5	.500	14	13	2	1	0	81	86	8	20	59	11.8	3.78	99	.264	.306	4	.154	-0	-1	-1	0	-0.1
1976	StL-N	6	12	.333	43	17	2	1	0	150¹	139	10	54	76	11.7	3.53	100	.247	.315	4	.105	-1	1	0	3	0.2
1977	StL-N	11	17	.393	34	34	11	3	0	233	223	24	63	120	11.2	3.48	111	.254	.308	10	.139	-1	11	10	-1	1.0
1978	StL-N	2	5	.286	10	10	2	1	0	60¹	61	4	20	32	12.1	4.18	84	.270	.329	2	.111	-1	-4	-4	0	-0.6
	SD-N	12	10	.545	27	24	3	0	0	146¹	154	16	43	59	12.2	4.06	82	.277	.333	7	.152	-1	-8	-12	1	-1.6
	Yr	14	15	.483	37	34	5	0	0	206²	215	20	63	91	12.1	4.09	83	.274	.329	9	.141	-2	-12	-16	1	-2.2
1979	SD-N	6	9	.400	45	20	5	3	3	156²	142	9	42	69	10.6	3.27	108	.244	.295	2	.056	-2	8	4	-1	0.2
1980	SD-N	4	11	.267	40	14	0	0	0	111¹	130	6	33	50	13.4	4.37	79	.295	.349	2	.095	-1	-9	-12	-0	-1.6
1982	StL-N	1	2	.333	8	3	0	0	0	18¹	21	2	8	15	14.2	4.42	82	.288	.358	0	.000	-1	-2	-2	0	-0.2

YEAR TM/L	W	L	PCT	G	GS	CG	SH	SV	IP	H	HR	BB	SO	RAT	ERA	ERA+	OAV	OOB	BH	AVG	PB	PR	/A	PD	TPI
1983 StL-N	0	0	—	6	0	0	0	1	7²	16	1	4	6	23.5	11.74	31	.444	.500	0	—	0	-7	-7	0	-0.2
KC-A	3	6	.333	11	9	2	1	0	52²	61	4	22	18	14.2	4.78	85	.289	.356	0	—	0	-4	-4	-0	-0.6
Total 8	50	77	.394	238	144	27	12	5	1017²	1033	87	309	489	12.0	3.85	94	.266	.321	31	.119	-5	-17	-27	2	-3.5

● HANS RASMUSSEN
Rasmussen, Henry Florian b: 4/18/1895, Chicago, Ill. d: 1/1/49, Chicago, Ill. BR/TR, 6'6", 220 lbs. Deb: 8/11/15

YEAR TM/L	W	L	PCT	G	GS	CG	SH	SV	IP	H	HR	BB	SO	RAT	ERA	ERA+	OAV	OOB	BH	AVG	PB	PR	/A	PD	TPI
1915 Chi-F	0	0	—	2	0	0	0	0	2	3	0	2	2	22.5	13.50	19	.600	.714	0	.000	-0	-2	-2	0	0.0

● FRED RATH
Rath, Frederick Helsher b: 9/1/43, Little Rock, Ark. BR/TR, 6'3", 200 lbs. Deb: 9/10/68

YEAR TM/L	W	L	PCT	G	GS	CG	SH	SV	IP	H	HR	BB	SO	RAT	ERA	ERA+	OAV	OOB	BH	AVG	PB	PR	/A	PD	TPI
1968 Chi-A	0	0	—	5	0	0	0	0	11¹	8	0	3	3	9.5	1.59	191	.182	.250	0	—	0	2	2	0	0.0
1969 Chi-A	0	2	.000	3	2	0	0	0	11²	11	4	8	4	14.7	7.71	50	.256	.373	0	.000	-0	-5	-5	0	-0.7
Total 2	0	2	.000	8	2	0	0	0	23	19	4	11	7	12.1	4.70	73	.218	.313	0	.000	-0	-4	-3	0	-0.7

● STEVE RATZER
Ratzer, Steven Wayne b: 9/9/53, Paterson, N.J. BR/TR, 6'1", 192 lbs. Deb: 10/5/80

YEAR TM/L	W	L	PCT	G	GS	CG	SH	SV	IP	H	HR	BB	SO	RAT	ERA	ERA+	OAV	OOB	BH	AVG	PB	PR	/A	PD	TPI
1980 Mon-N	0	0	—	1	1	0	0	0	4	9	0	2	0	24.8	11.25	32	.450	.500	0	.000	-0	-3	-3	0	0.0
1981 Mon-N	1	1	.500	12	0	0	0	0	17¹	23	2	7	4	15.6	6.23	56	.311	.370	0	.000	-0	-5	-5	1	-0.5
Total 2	1	1	.500	13	1	0	0	0	21¹	32	2	9	4	17.3	7.17	49	.340	.398	0	.000	-0	-9	-9	1	-0.5

● DOUG RAU
Rau, Douglas James b: 12/15/48, Columbus, Tex. BL/TL, 6'2", 175 lbs. Deb: 9/2/72

YEAR TM/L	W	L	PCT	G	GS	CG	SH	SV	IP	H	HR	BB	SO	RAT	ERA	ERA+	OAV	OOB	BH	AVG	PB	PR	/A	PD	TPI
1972 LA-N	2	2	.500	7	3	2	0	0	32²	18	1	11	19	8.3	2.20	151	.159	.240	1	.143	1	5	4	0	0.6
1973 LA-N	4	2	.667	31	3	0	0	3	63²	64	5	28	51	13.1	3.96	87	.259	.337	1	.091	-1	-2	-4	-0	-0.5
1974 *LA-N	13	11	.542	36	35	3	1	0	198¹	191	20	70	126	12.0	3.72	91	.251	.318	9	.141	-1	-2	-7	-0	-0.9
1975 LA-N	15	9	.625	38	38	8	2	0	257²	227	18	61	151	10.2	3.11	109	.236	.283	17	.195	2	15	8	-1	0.9
1976 LA-N	16	12	.571	34	32	8	3	0	231	221	18	69	98	11.6	2.57	132	.258	.318	9	.150	1	24	21	-0	2.6
1977 *LA-N	14	8	.636	32	32	4	2	0	212¹	232	15	49	126	12.2	3.43	111	.282	.327	10	.141	-0	11	9	-1	0.7
1978 LA-N	15	9	.625	30	30	7	2	0	199	219	17	68	95	13.1	3.26	108	.284	.344	9	.143	-1	7	6	-2	0.3
1979 LA-N	1	5	.167	11	11	1	1	0	56	73	6	22	28	15.9	5.30	69	.320	.390	2	.143	1	-10	-10	-0	-0.9
1981 Cal-A	1	2	.333	3	3	0	0	0	10¹	14	2	4	3	15.7	8.71	42	.341	.400	0	—	0	-6	-6	-0	-1.3
Total 9	81	60	.574	222	187	33	11	3	1261	1259	99	382	697	11.9	3.35	104	.262	.320	58	.154	2	41	21	-6	1.5

● BOB RAUCH
Rauch, Robert John b: 6/16/49, Brookings, S.D. BR/TR, 6'4", 200 lbs. Deb: 6/29/72

YEAR TM/L	W	L	PCT	G	GS	CG	SH	SV	IP	H	HR	BB	SO	RAT	ERA	ERA+	OAV	OOB	BH	AVG	PB	PR	/A	PD	TPI
1972 NY-N	0	1	.000	19	0	0	0	1	27	27	3	21	23	16.0	5.00	67	.273	.400	0	.000	-0	-5	-5	0	-0.2

● LANCE RAUTZHAN
Rautzhan, Clarence George b: 8/20/52, Pottsville, Pa. BR/TL, 6'1", 195 lbs. Deb: 7/23/77

YEAR TM/L	W	L	PCT	G	GS	CG	SH	SV	IP	H	HR	BB	SO	RAT	ERA	ERA+	OAV	OOB	BH	AVG	PB	PR	/A	PD	TPI
1977 *LA-N	4	1	.800	25	0	0	0	2	20²	19	7	13	13.9	4.35	88	.313	.368	0	—	-0	-1	-1	0	-0.3	
1978 *LA-N	2	1	.667	43	0	0	0	4	61¹	61	1	19	26	11.5	2.93	120	.263	.321	0	.000	-1	4	4	2	0.4
1979 LA-N	0	2	.000	12	0	0	0	1	9²	9	1	11	5	19.6	7.45	49	.273	.467	0	—	0	-4	-4	0	-0.8
Mil-A	0	0	—	3	0	0	0	0	3	3	0	10	2	39.0	9.00	46	.300	.650	0	—	0	-2	-2	0	0.0
Total 3	6	4	.600	83	0	0	0	7	94²	98	1	47	45	14.0	3.90	93	.276	.364	0	.000	-1	-2	-3	2	-0.7

● SHANE RAWLEY
Rawley, Shane William b: 7/27/55, Racine, Wis. BR/TL, 6', 180 lbs. Deb: 4/6/78

YEAR TM/L	W	L	PCT	G	GS	CG	SH	SV	IP	H	HR	BB	SO	RAT	ERA	ERA+	OAV	OOB	BH	AVG	PB	PR	/A	PD	TPI
1978 Sea-A	4	9	.308	52	2	0	0	4	111¹	114	7	51	66	13.7	4.12	92	.275	.362	0	—	0	-4	-4	1	-0.3
1979 Sea-A	5	9	.357	48	3	0	0	11	84¹	88	2	40	48	13.8	3.84	113	.278	.361	0	—	0	3	5	1	0.8
1980 Sea-A	7	7	.500	59	0	0	0	13	113²	103	3	63	68	13.4	3.33	124	.257	.363	0	—	0	9	10	2	1.6
1981 Sea-A	4	6	.400	46	0	0	0	8	68¹	64	1	38	35	13.6	3.95	97	.257	.358	0	—	0	-2	-1	0	-0.3
1982 NY-A	11	10	.524	47	17	3	0	3	164	165	10	54	111	12.1	4.06	98	.267	.328	0	—	0	-1	1	1	0.1
1983 NY-A	14	14	.500	34	33	13	2	1	238¹	246	19	79	124	12.4	3.78	103	.269	.329	0	—	0	8	3	0	0.5
1984 NY-A	2	3	.400	11	10	0	0	0	42	46	0	27	24	15.6	6.21	61	.272	.372	0	—	0	-10	-11	-0	-0.9
Phi-N	10	6	.625	18	18	3	0	0	120¹	117	13	27	58	10.8	3.81	95	.257	.300	5	.116	-2	-3	-2	-1	-0.6
1985 Phi-N	13	8	.619	36	31	6	2	0	198²	188	16	81	106	12.3	3.31	111	.249	.323	8	.138	0	8	1	1	1.0
1986 Phi-N☆	11	7	.611	23	23	7	1	0	157²	166	13	50	73	12.4	3.54	109	.270	.326	9	.173	0	3	5	-0	0.6
1987 Phi-N	17	11	.607	36	36	4	1	0	229²	250	23	86	123	13.4	4.39	97	.279	.344	12	.152	-0	-8	-4	-1	-0.6
1988 Phi-N	8	16	.333	32	32	4	1	0	198	220	27	78	87	13.7	4.18	85	.286	.355	6	.105	-1	-16	-14	-0	-1.7
1989 Min-A	5	12	.294	27	25	1	0	0	145	167	19	60	68	14.1	5.21	79	.293	.361	0	—	0	-21	-17	-1	-1.9
Total 12	111	118	.485	469	230	41	7	40	1871¹	1934	153	734	991	13.0	4.02	97	.271	.341	40	.138	-3	-36	-22	2	-1.7

● CARL RAY
Ray, Carl Grady b: 1/31/1889, Danbury, N.C. d: 4/3/70, Walnut Cove, N.C. BL/TL, 5'11", 170 lbs. Deb: 9/25/15

YEAR TM/L	W	L	PCT	G	GS	CG	SH	SV	IP	H	HR	BB	SO	RAT	ERA	ERA+	OAV	OOB	BH	AVG	PB	PR	/A	PD	TPI
1915 Phi-A	0	1	.000	2	1	0	0	0	7¹	11	0	6	6	25.8	4.91	60	.333	.488	0	.000	-0	-2	-1	0	-0.2
1916 Phi-A	0	1	.000	3	1	0	0	0	9¹	9	0	14	5	23.1	4.82	59	.257	.480	0	.000	-0	-2	-4	-1	-0.3
Total 2	0	2	.000	5	2	0	0	0	16²	20	0	20	11	24.3	4.86	59	.294	.484	0	.000	-0	-4	-4	-1	-0.5

● JIM RAY
Ray, James Francis "Sting" b: 12/1/44, Rock Hill, S.C. BR/TR, 6'1", 195 lbs. Deb: 9/16/65

YEAR TM/L	W	L	PCT	G	GS	CG	SH	SV	IP	H	HR	BB	SO	RAT	ERA	ERA+	OAV	OOB	BH	AVG	PB	PR	/A	PD	TPI
1965 Hou-N	0	2	.000	3	2	0	0	0	7²	11	1	6	7	20.0	10.57	32	.355	.459	0	.000	-0	-6	-6	0	-1.2
1966 Hou-N	0	0	—	1	0	0	0	0	0	0	0	1	0	—	∞	—	—	1.000	0	—	0	-1	-1	0	-0.1
1968 Hou-N	2	3	.400	41	2	1	0	1	80²	65	5	25	71	10.2	2.68	110	.220	.283	1	.067	-1	3	2	-1	0.0
1969 Hou-N	8	2	.800	40	13	0	0	0	115	105	11	48	115	12.1	3.91	90	.245	.324	4	.115	-1	-4	-5	-1	-0.6
1970 Hou-N	6	3	.667	52	0	0	0	5	105	97	13	49	67	12.5	3.26	119	.251	.336	5	.185	-0	9	7	0	0.6
1971 Hou-N	10	4	.714	47	1	0	0	3	97²	72	3	31	46	9.7	2.12	159	.211	.281	3	.167	-1	15	14	-2	1.8
1972 Hou-N	10	9	.526	54	0	0	0	6	90¹	77	10	44	50	12.4	4.28	79	.227	.321	1	.063	-1	-8	-9	-1	-2.3
1973 Hou-N	6	4	.600	42	0	0	0	6	69	65	5	38	25	13.8	4.43	82	.253	.356	3	.231	-0	-6	-6	-1	-1.0
1974 Det-A	1	3	.250	28	0	0	0	2	52¹	49	4	29	26	13.6	4.47	85	.254	.354	0	—	0	-5	-4	0	-0.5
Total 9	43	30	.589	308	20	1	0	25	617²	541	52	271	407	12.0	3.61	97	.238	.323	16	.137	-3	-4	-8	-6	-3.3

● FARMER RAY
Ray, Robert Henry b: 9/17/1886, Ft.Lyon, Colo. d: 3/11/63, Electra, Tex. BL/TR, 5'11", 160 lbs. Deb: 6/13/10

YEAR TM/L	W	L	PCT	G	GS	CG	SH	SV	IP	H	HR	BB	SO	RAT	ERA	ERA+	OAV	OOB	BH	AVG	PB	PR	/A	PD	TPI
1910 StL-A	4	10	.286	21	16	11	0	0	140²	146	3	49	35	12.9	3.58	69	.285	.356	7	.175	0	-17	-17	-3	-1.9

● CURT RAYDON
Raydon, Curtis Lowell b: 11/18/33, Bloomington, Ill. BR/TR, 6'4", 190 lbs. Deb: 4/15/58

YEAR TM/L	W	L	PCT	G	GS	CG	SH	SV	IP	H	HR	BB	SO	RAT	ERA	ERA+	OAV	OOB	BH	AVG	PB	PR	/A	PD	TPI
1958 Pit-N	8	4	.667	31	20	2	1	1	134¹	118	18	61	85	12.3	3.62	107	.236	.326	1	.026	-2	5	4	-3	-0.2

● BUGS RAYMOND
Raymond, Arthur Lawrence b: 2/24/1882, Chicago, Ill. d: 9/7/12, Chicago, Ill. BR/TR, 5'10", 180 lbs. Deb: 9/23/04

YEAR TM/L	W	L	PCT	G	GS	CG	SH	SV	IP	H	HR	BB	SO	RAT	ERA	ERA+	OAV	OOB	BH	AVG	PB	PR	/A	PD	TPI
1904 Det-A	0	1	.000	5	2	1	0	0	14²	14	0	6	7	13.5	3.07	83	.252	.346	0	—	-1	-1	-1	1	0.0
1907 StL-N	2	4	.333	8	6	6	1	0	64²	56	3	21	34	10.9	1.67	150	.230	.294	2	.091	-0	6	6	0	0.6
1908 StL-N	15	25	.375	48	37	23	5	2	324¹	236	2	95	145	9.6	2.03	116	.207	.277	17	.189	1	12	12	3	2.1
1909 NY-N	18	12	.600	39	31	18	2	0	270	239	7	87	121	11.1	2.47	104	.245	.311	13	.146	0	4	3	2	0.5
1910 NY-N	4	11	.267	19	11	6	0	0	99¹	106	2	40	55	14.0	3.81	78	.280	.362	5	.156	-1	-9	-9	-2	-1.1
1911 NY-N	6	4	.600	17	9	4	1	0	81²	73	1	33	39	11.9	3.31	102	.248	.328	5	.200	1	1	1	0	0.1
Total 6	45	57	.441	136	96	58	9	2	854²	724	15	282	401	10.9	2.49	105	.235	.306	42	.160	0	14	11	9	2.2

● HARRY RAYMOND
Raymond, Harry H. "Jack" b: 2/20/1862, Utica, N.Y. d: 3/21/25, San Diego, Cal. 5'9", 179 lbs. Deb: 9/9/1888 ◆

YEAR TM/L	W	L	PCT	G	GS	CG	SH	SV	IP	H	HR	BB	SO	RAT	ERA	ERA+	OAV	OOB	BH	AVG	PB	PR	/A	PD	TPI
1889 Lou-a	1	0	1.000	1	1	1	0	0	9	8	0	11	1	19.0	1.00	385	.231	.416	123	.239	0	3	3	-0	0.2

● CLAUDE RAYMOND
Raymond, Joseph Claude Marc "Frenchy" b: 5/7/37, St.Jean, Que., Canada BR/TR, 5'10", 175 lbs. Deb: 4/15/59

YEAR TM/L	W	L	PCT	G	GS	CG	SH	SV	IP	H	HR	BB	SO	RAT	ERA	ERA+	OAV	OOB	BH	AVG	PB	PR	/A	PD	TPI
1959 Chi-A	0	0	—	3	0	0	0	0	4	5	2	4	2	15.8	9.00	42	.333	.412	0	—	-0	-2	-2	0	0.0
1961 Mil-N	0	0	—	13	0	0	0	0	20¹	22	2	4	14	14.2	3.98	94	.275	.356	0	.000	-0	-0	-1	0	0.0
1962 Mil-N	5	5	.500	26	0	0	0	10	42²	37	5	10	40	11.4	2.74	138	.236	.310	0	.000	-1	6	5	-1	1.2
1963 Mil-N	4	6	.400	45	0	0	0	0	53¹	57	12	27	44	14.9	5.40	60	.268	.361	2	.500	2	-13	-13	1	-2.3
1964 Hou-N	5	5	.500	38	0	0	0	0	79²	64	3	22	56	10.1	2.82	121	.229	.292	1	.071	-0	6	5	1	0.7

YEAR	TM/L	W	L	PCT	G	GS	CG	SH	SV	IP	H	HR	BB	SO	RAT	ERA	ERA+	OAV	OOB	BH	AVG	PB	PR	/A	PD	TPI
1965	Hou-N	7	4	.636	33	7	2	0	5	96¹	87	6	16	79	10.1	2.90	116	.244	.286	3	.115	-1	7	5	-0	0.5
1966	Hou-N☆	7	5	.583	62	0	0	0	16	92	85	10	25	73	11.2	3.13	109	.242	.300	1	.111	-0	5	3	-2	0.3
1967	Hou-N	0	4	.000	21	0	0	0	5	31	31	5	7	17	11.6	3.19	104	.256	.308	1	.200	0	1	0	-0	0.1
	Atl-N	4	1	.800	28	0	0	0	5	34¹	33	2	11	14	11.5	2.62	127	.260	.319	0	.000	-0	3	3	-0	0.5
	Yr	4	5	.444	49	0	0	0	10	65¹	64	7	18	31	11.3	2.89	115	.255	.305	1	.143	-0	4	3	-0	0.6
1968	Atl-N	3	5	.375	36	0	0	0	10	60¹	56	4	18	37	11.2	2.83	106	.256	.315	1	.143	-0	1	1	-0	0.2
1969	Atl-N	2	2	.500	33	0	0	0	1	48	56	4	13	15	13.3	5.25	69	.298	.350	2	.286	0	-9	-9	-1	-0.8
	Mon-N	1	2	.333	15	0	0	0	1	22	21	2	8	11	12.7	4.09	90	.256	.337	0	.000	-0	-1	-1	1	-0.1
	Yr	3	4	.429	48	0	0	0	2	70	77	6	21	26	12.9	4.89	74	.281	.337	2	.182	-0	-10	-10	-0	-0.9
1970	Mon-N	6	7	.462	59	0	0	0	23	83¹	76	13	27	68	11.3	4.43	93	.240	.303	0	.000	-1	-4	-3	-1	-0.8
1971	Mon-N	1	7	.125	37	0	0	0	0	53²	81	5	25	29	17.8	4.70	75	.373	.438	0	.000	-1	-7	-7	1	-0.9
Total	12	46	53	.465	449	7	2	0	83	721	711	75	225	497	12.0	3.66	96	.261	.324	11	.109	-2	-7	-13	-0	-1.4

● BARRY RAZIANO
Raziano, Barry John   b: 2/5/47, New Orleans, La.   BB/TR, 5'10", 175 lbs.   Deb: 8/18/73

YEAR	TM/L	W	L	PCT	G	GS	CG	SH	SV	IP	H	HR	BB	SO	RAT	ERA	ERA+	OAV	OOB	BH	AVG	PB	PR	/A	PD	TPI
1973	KC-A	0	0	—	2	0	0	0	0	5	6	1	1	0	14.4	5.40	76	.316	.381	0	—	0	-1	-1	0	0.0
1974	Cal-A	1	2	.333	13	0	0	0	1	16²	15	1	8	9	12.4	6.48	53	.246	.333	0	—	0	-5	-6	-0	-0.7
Total	2	1	2	.333	15	0	0	0	1	21²	21	2	9	9	12.9	6.23	58	.262	.344	0	—	0	-6	-6	-0	-0.7

● RIP REAGAN
Reagan, Arthur (b: Arthur Edgar Ragan)   b: 6/5/1878, Lincoln, Ill.   d: 6/8/53, Kansas City, Mo.   BR/TR, 5'11", 170 lbs.   Deb: 9/19/03

YEAR	TM/L	W	L	PCT	G	GS	CG	SH	SV	IP	H	HR	BB	SO	RAT	ERA	ERA+	OAV	OOB	BH	AVG	PB	PR	/A	PD	TPI
1903	Cin-N	0	2	.000	3	2	2	0	0	18	40	0	7	7	24.0	6.00	59	.455	.500	2	.250	—	-5	-5	-0	-0.4

● JIM REARDON
Reardon, James Matthew   b: 1866, Hoosick Falls, N.Y.   d: 2/25/1891, Hoosick Falls, N.Y   Deb: 7/17/1886

YEAR	TM/L	W	L	PCT	G	GS	CG	SH	SV	IP	H	HR	BB	SO	RAT	ERA	ERA+	OAV	OOB	BH	AVG	PB	PR	/A	PD	TPI
1886	StL-N	0	1	.000	1	1	1	0	0	8	10	1	5	0	16.9	6.75	48	.323	.417	1	.250	—	-3	-3	-0	-0.3
	Cin-a	0	1	.000	1	1	0	0	0	2	5	0	4	0	40.5	18.00	30	.500	.643	0	.000	-1	-3	-3	-0	-0.9
Total	1	0	2	.000	2	2	1	0	0	10	15	1	9	0	21.6	9.00	36	.366	.480	1	.143	-1	-6	-6	-0	-1.2

● JEFF REARDON
Reardon, Jeffrey James   b: 10/1/55, Dalton, Mass.   BR/TR, 6'1", 195 lbs.   Deb: 8/25/79

YEAR	TM/L	W	L	PCT	G	GS	CG	SH	SV	IP	H	HR	BB	SO	RAT	ERA	ERA+	OAV	OOB	BH	AVG	PB	PR	/A	PD	TPI
1979	NY-N	1	2	.333	18	0	0	0	2	20²	12	2	9	10	9.1	1.74	209	.174	.269	0	—	0	5	4	-0	0.7
1980	NY-N	8	7	.533	61	0	0	0	6	110¹	96	10	47	101	11.7	2.61	136	.231	.310	0	.000	-1	12	12	-2	1.3
1981	NY-N	1	0	1.000	18	0	0	0	2	28²	27	2	12	28	12.6	3.45	107	.245	.325	0	.000	-0	0	0	-1	-0.1
	*Mon-N	2	0	1.000	25	0	0	0	6	41²	21	3	9	21	6.7	1.30	269	.148	.204	0	.000	-0	10	10	-1	0.7
	Yr	3	0	1.000	43	0	0	0	8	70¹	48	5	21	49	9.0	2.18	160	.189	.254	0	.000	-1	10	10	-2	0.6
1982	Mon-N	7	4	.636	75	0	0	0	26	109	87	6	36	86	10.2	2.06	176	.221	.289	1	.100	-0	19	19	-1	2.8
1983	Mon-N	7	9	.438	66	0	0	0	21	92	87	7	44	78	12.9	3.03	118	.250	.336	1	.125	-0	6	6	-2	1.0
1984	Mon-N	7	7	.500	68	0	0	0	23	87	70	5	37	79	11.4	2.90	118	.220	.307	0	.000	-0	7	5	-0	0.8
1985	Mon-N★	2	8	.200	63	0	0	0	41	87²	68	7	26	67	9.8	3.18	107	.209	.270	2	.286	-1	4	2	-1	0.4
1986	Mon-N☆	7	9	.438	62	0	0	0	35	89	83	12	26	67	11.1	3.94	94	.251	.307	1	.125	-0	-2	-3	-0	-0.7
1987	*Min-A	8	8	.500	63	0	0	0	31	80¹	70	14	28	83	11.3	4.48	103	.232	.303	0	—	-0	0	1	-1	0.2
1988	Min-A☆	2	4	.333	63	0	0	0	42	73	68	6	15	56	10.5	2.47	165	.245	.289	0	—	0	12	13	-2	2.3
1989	Min-A	5	4	.556	65	0	0	0	31	73	68	8	12	46	10.2	4.07	102	.246	.285	0	—	-0	4	5	-1	-0.5
1990	*Bos-A	5	3	.625	47	0	0	0	21	51¹	39	5	19	33	10.3	3.16	129	.206	.282	0	—	-0	4	5	-1	0.9
1991	Bos-A★	1	4	.200	57	0	0	0	40	59¹	54	9	16	44	10.8	3.03	142	.236	.289	0	—	-1	7	8	-2	1.5
1992	Bos-A	2	2	.500	46	0	0	0	27	42¹	53	4	7	32	13.0	4.25	99	.308	.339	0	—	-0	-1	-0	-0	-0.2
	*Atl-N	3	0	1.000	14	0	0	0	3	15²	14	0	2	7	9.8	1.15	318	.241	.279	0	—	0	4	4	-0	1.0
1993	Cin-N	4	6	.400	58	0	0	0	8	61²	66	4	10	35	11.8	4.09	98	.270	.313	0	.000	-0	-0	-1	-2	-0.2
1994	NY-A	1	0	1.000	11	0	0	0	2	9²	17	3	3	4	18.6	8.38	53	.386	.426	0	—	0	-4	-4	0	-0.3
Total	16	73	77	.487	880	0	0	0	367	1132¹	1000	109	358	877	11.0	3.16	121	.236	.299	5	.088	-3	80	83	-18	11.6

● FRANK REBERGER
Reberger, Frank Beall "Crane"   b: 6/7/44, Caldwell, Idaho   BL/TR, 6'5", 200 lbs.   Deb: 6/6/68   C

YEAR	TM/L	W	L	PCT	G	GS	CG	SH	SV	IP	H	HR	BB	SO	RAT	ERA	ERA+	OAV	OOB	BH	AVG	PB	PR	/A	PD	TPI
1968	Chi-N	0	1	.000	3	1	0	0	0	6	9	1	2	3	16.5	4.50	70	.346	.393	0	—	0	-1	-1	-0	-0.1
1969	SD-N	1	2	.333	67	0	0	0	6	87²	83	6	41	65	12.9	3.59	98	.258	.345	1	.200	—	0	-1	2	0.2
1970	SF-N	7	8	.467	45	18	3	0	2	152	178	13	98	117	16.8	5.57	71	.293	.397	11	.234	1	-26	-27	-0	-2.3
1971	SF-N	3	0	1.000	13	7	0	0	0	43²	37	5	19	21	12.0	3.92	87	.228	.317	3	.231	0	-2	-3	0	-0.1
1972	SF-N	3	4	.429	20	11	2	0	0	99¹	97	10	37	52	12.6	3.99	87	.257	.332	8	.229	2	-6	-6	1	0.0
Total	5	14	15	.483	148	37	5	0	8	388²	404	35	197	258	14.3	4.52	81	.270	.361	23	.230	4	-35	-36	4	-2.3

● JOHN RECCIUS
Reccius, John   b: 10/29/1859, Louisville, Ky.   d: 9/1/30, Louisville, Ky.   5'6.5",   Deb: 5/2/1882   F♦

YEAR	TM/L	W	L	PCT	G	GS	CG	SH	SV	IP	H	HR	BB	SO	RAT	ERA	ERA+	OAV	OOB	BH	AVG	PB	PR	/A	PD	TPI
1882	Lou-a	4	6	.400	13	10	9	1	0	95	106	3	22	31	12.1	3.03	82	.264	.302	63	.237	3	-4	-6	-1	-0.4
1883	Lou-a	0	0	—	1	0	0	0	0	4	10	0	0	0	22.5	2.25	133	.446	.446	9	.143	-0	0	0	-0	0.0
Total	2	4	6	.400	14	10	9	1	0	99	116	3	22	31	12.5	3.00	83	.274	.310	72	.219	3	-4	-6	-1	-0.4

● PHIL RECCIUS
Reccius, Phillip   b: 6/7/1862, Louisville, Ky.   d: 2/15/03, Louisville, Ky.   5'9", 163 lbs.   Deb: 9/25/1882   F♦

YEAR	TM/L	W	L	PCT	G	GS	CG	SH	SV	IP	H	HR	BB	SO	RAT	ERA	ERA+	OAV	OOB	BH	AVG	PB	PR	/A	PD	TPI
1884	Lou-a	6	7	.462	18	11	11	0	0	129¹	118	2	19	46	9.8	2.71	114	.228	.261	63	.240	2	8	5	0	0.6
1885	Lou-a	0	4	.000	7	5	4	0	1	40	46	0	11	10	13.0	3.82	84	.253	.299	97	.241	1	-3	-3	1	-0.1
1886	Lou-a	0	1	.000	1	1	0	0	1	3	7	0	3	0	30.0	9.00	40	.467	.556	4	.308	0	-2	-2	-0	-0.4
1887	Cle-a	0	0	—	1	0	0	0	0	7	8	0	5	0	16.7	7.71	56	.320	.433	47	.205	-0	-3	-3	0	0.0
Total	4	6	12	.333	27	17	15	0	1	179¹	179	2	38	56	11.1	3.26	97	.242	.284	225	.231	4	1	-2	1	0.1

● PHIL REDDING
Redding, Philip Hayden   b: 1/25/1890, Crystal Springs, Miss.   d: 3/30/29, Greenwood, Miss.   BL/TR, 5'11.5", 190 lbs.   Deb: 9/14/12

YEAR	TM/L	W	L	PCT	G	GS	CG	SH	SV	IP	H	HR	BB	SO	RAT	ERA	ERA+	OAV	OOB	BH	AVG	PB	PR	/A	PD	TPI
1912	StL-N	2	1	.667	3	3	2	0	0	25¹	31	2	11	9	14.9	4.97	69	.313	.382	0	.000	-1	-4	-4	-0	-0.5
1913	StL-N	0	0	—	1	0	0	0	0	2²	2	0	1	1	10.1	6.75	48	.286	.375	0	.000	-0	-1	-1	-0	0.0
Total	2	2	1	.667	4	3	2	0	0	28	33	2	12	10	14.5	5.14	66	.311	.381	0	.000	-1	-5	-5	-0	-0.5

● PETE REDFERN
Redfern, Peter Irvine   b: 8/25/54, Glendale, Cal.   BR/TR, 6'2", 195 lbs.   Deb: 5/15/76

YEAR	TM/L	W	L	PCT	G	GS	CG	SH	SV	IP	H	HR	BB	SO	RAT	ERA	ERA+	OAV	OOB	BH	AVG	PB	PR	/A	PD	TPI
1976	Min-A	8	8	.500	23	23	1	1	0	118	105	6	63	74	13.0	3.51	103	.241	.341	0	—	0	1	1	-1	-0.1
1977	Min-A	6	9	.400	30	28	1	0	0	137¹	164	13	66	73	15.3	5.18	77	.304	.384	0	—	0	-17	-18	1	-1.6
1978	Min-A	0	2	.000	3	2	0	0	0	9²	10	2	6	4	14.9	6.52	59	.294	.400	0	—	0	-3	-3	-0	-0.6
1979	Min-A	7	3	.700	40	6	0	0	1	108¹	106	8	35	85	11.8	3.49	126	.258	.318	0	—	0	9	11	-5	0.5
1980	Min-A	7	8	.500	23	16	2	0	2	104²	116	11	33	73	12.9	4.56	96	.283	.336	0	—	0	-6	-6	-1	-0.4
1981	Min-A	9	8	.529	24	23	3	0	0	141²	140	12	52	77	12.3	4.07	97	.261	.328	0	—	0	-6	-2	-1	-0.6
1982	Min-A	5	11	.313	27	13	2	0	0	94¹	122	16	51	40	16.6	6.58	64	.322	.404	0	—	0	-26	-25	1	-3.5
Total	7	42	48	.467	170	111	9	1	3	714	764	68	306	426	13.6	4.54	89	.278	.353	0	—	0	-50	-38	-2	-6.3

● HOWIE REED
Reed, Howard Dean "Diz"   b: 12/21/36, Dallas, Tex.   d: 12/7/84, Corpus Christi, Tex.   BR/TR, 6'1", 210 lbs.   Deb: 9/13/58

YEAR	TM/L	W	L	PCT	G	GS	CG	SH	SV	IP	H	HR	BB	SO	RAT	ERA	ERA+	OAV	OOB	BH	AVG	PB	PR	/A	PD	TPI
1958	KC-A	1	0	1.000	3	1	0	0	0	10¹	5	0	4	5	7.8	0.87	449	.132	.214	0	.000	—	3	3	-0	0.3
1959	KC-A	0	3	.000	6	3	0	0	0	20²	26	3	10	11	15.7	7.40	54	.313	.387	0	.000	—	-8	-8	-1	-1.0
1960	KC-A	0	0	—	1	0	0	0	0	1²	0	1	0	0	10.8	0.00	—	.286	.286	0	—	—	0	0	-0	0.0
1964	LA-N	3	4	.429	26	7	0	0	1	90	79	4	36	52	11.5	3.20	101	.236	.310	2	.100	-1	0	0	-0	0.1
1965	*LA-N	4	5	.583	38	5	0	0	0	78	73	6	27	47	11.9	3.12	105	.243	.312	0	.000	0	3	3	-0	0.3
1966	LA-N	0	0	—	1	0	0	0	0	1²	0	0	1	0	5.4	0.00	—	.167	.167	0	—	-0	0	0	-0	0.0
	Cal-A	0	1	.000	19	1	0	0	5	43	39	5	15	17	11.3	2.93	115	.247	.312	0	.000	-1	2	2	-0	-0.1
1967	Hou-N	1	1	.500	4	2	0	0	0	18¹	19	0	7	9	10.3	3.44	96	.268	.328	0	.000	-0	0	0	-0	0.0
1969	Mon-N	6	7	.462	31	15	3	0	0	106	119	7	50	59	14.5	4.84	76	.290	.369	4	.125	1	-15	-14	2	-1.2
1970	Mon-N	6	5	.545	57	1	0	0	5	89	81	7	40	42	12.4	3.13	131	.252	.339	0	.000	-PB	9	10	0	1.2

YEAR TM/L	W	L	PCT	G	GS	CG	SH	SV	IP	H	HR	BB	SO	RAT	ERA	ERA+	OAV	OOB	BH	AVG	PB	PR	/A	PD	TPI
1971 Mon-N	2	3	.400	43	0	0	0	0	56²	66	8	24	25	14.3	4.29	82	.296	.364	0	.000	-0	-5	-5	0	-0.4
Total 10	26	29	.473	229	35	3	1	9	515¹	510	41	208	268	12.7	3.72	96	.261	.334	6	.066	-1	-5	-9	3	-0.9

● **JERRY REED**   Reed, Jerry Maxwell b: 10/8/55, Bryson City, N.C. BR/TR, 6'1", 190 lbs. Deb: 9/11/81

YEAR TM/L	W	L	PCT	G	GS	CG	SH	SV	IP	H	HR	BB	SO	RAT	ERA	ERA+	OAV	OOB	BH	AVG	PB	PR	/A	PD	TPI
1981 Phi-N	0	1	.000	4	0	0	0	0	4²	7	0	6	5	25.1	7.71	47	.333	.481	0	—	0	-2	-2	0	-0.4
1982 Phi-N	1	0	1.000	7	0	0	0	0	8²	11	0	3	1	15.6	5.19	71	.324	.395	0	—	0	-2	-1	-0	-0.2
Cle-A	1	1	.500	6	1	0	0	0	15²	15	1	3	10	10.3	3.45	118	.250	.286	0	—	0	1	1	0	0.1
1983 Cle-A	0	0	—	7	0	0	0	0	21¹	26	4	9	11	14.8	7.17	59	.310	.376	0	—	0	-7	-7	1	0.1
1985 Cle-A	3	5	.375	33	5	0	0	8	72¹	67	12	19	37	11.1	4.11	101	.245	.302	0	—	0	0	0	1	0.1
1986 Sea-A	4	0	1.000	11	4	0	0	0	34²	38	3	13	16	13.2	3.12	136	.273	.336	0	—	0	4	4	-0	0.4
1987 Sea-A	1	2	.333	39	1	0	0	7	81²	79	7	24	51	11.7	3.42	138	.255	.315	0	—	0	9	12	-0	0.2
1988 Sea-A	1	1	.500	46	0	0	0	1	86¹	82	8	33	48	12.2	3.96	105	.256	.330	0	—	0	2	1	0	0.1
1989 Sea-A	7	7	.500	52	1	0	0	0	101²	89	10	43	50	11.8	3.19	126	.235	.314	0	—	0	8	9	-0	1.0
1990 Sea-A	0	1	.000	4	0	0	0	0	7¹	8	1	3	2	13.5	4.91	81	.286	.355	0	—	0	-1	-1	0	-0.1
Bos-A	2	1	.667	29	0	0	0	2	45	55	1	16	17	14.2	4.80	85	.302	.359	0	—	0	-4	-4	-0	-0.5
Yr	2	2	.500	33	0	0	0	2	52¹	63	2	19	19	14.1	4.82	84	.300	.358	0	—	0	-5	-4	0	-0.6
Total 9	20	19	.513	238	12	0	0	18	479¹	477	47	172	248	12.4	3.94	107	.261	.328	0	—	0	6	14	2	0.7

● **RICK REED**   Reed, Richard Allen b: 8/16/64, Huntington, W.Va. BR/TR, 6', 195 lbs. Deb: 8/8/88

YEAR TM/L	W	L	PCT	G	GS	CG	SH	SV	IP	H	HR	BB	SO	RAT	ERA	ERA+	OAV	OOB	BH	AVG	PB	PR	/A	PD	TPI
1988 Pit-N	1	0	1.000	2	2	0	0	0	12	10	1	2	6	9.0	3.00	113	.233	.267	0	.000	-0	1	1	0	0.0
1989 Pit-N	1	4	.200	15	7	0	0	0	54²	62	5	11	34	12.3	5.60	60	.290	.330	1	.077	-0	-13	-14	-0	-1.2
1990 Pit-N	2	3	.400	13	8	1	1	0	53²	62	6	12	27	12.6	4.36	83	.279	.319	4	.250	1	-3	-4	-1	-0.3
1991 Pit-N	0	0	—	1	1	0	0	0	4¹	8	1	1	2	18.7	10.38	34	.400	.429	1	.500	1	-3	-3	-0	0.1
1992 KC-A	3	7	.300	19	18	1	1	0	100¹	105	10	20	49	11.7	3.68	110	.271	.316	0	—	0	3	4	1	0.3
1993 KC-A	0	0	—	1	0	0	0	0	3²	6	0	1	3	19.6	9.82	47	.375	.444	0	—	0	-2	-2	-0	-0.2
Tex-A	1	0	1.000	2	0	0	0	0	4	6	1	1	2	18.0	2.25	184	.375	.444	0	—	0	1	1	0	0.3
Yr	1	0	1.000	3	0	0	0	0	7²	12	1	2	5	17.6	5.87	74	.364	.417	0	—	0	-1	-1	0	0.1
1994 Tex-A	1	1	.500	4	3	0	0	0	16²	17	3	7	12	13.5	5.94	76	.254	.333	0	—	0	-2	-3	-0	0.1
Total 7	9	15	.375	57	39	2	2	1	249¹	276	27	55	135	12.3	4.55	84	.280	.325	6	.171	1	-19	-21	0	-0.9

● **BOB REED**   Reed, Robert Edward b: 1/12/45, Boston, Mass. BR/TR, 5'10", 175 lbs. Deb: 9/5/69

YEAR TM/L	W	L	PCT	G	GS	CG	SH	SV	IP	H	HR	BB	SO	RAT	ERA	ERA+	OAV	OOB	BH	AVG	PB	PR	/A	PD	TPI
1969 Det-A	0	0	—	8	0	0	0	0	14²	9	0	9	9	10.4	1.84	203	.184	.298	1	.500	-0	3	3	0	0.1
1970 Det-A	2	4	.333	16	4	0	0	2	46¹	54	5	14	26	13.2	4.86	77	.292	.342	1	.083	-0	-6	-6	-1	-0.9
Total 2	2	4	.333	24	5	0	0	2	61	63	5	22	35	12.5	4.13	90	.269	.332	2	.143	-0	-3	-3	-0	-0.8

● **RON REED**   Reed, Ronald Lee b: 11/2/42, LaPorte, Ind. BR/TR, 6'6", 215 lbs. Deb: 9/26/66

YEAR TM/L	W	L	PCT	G	GS	CG	SH	SV	IP	H	HR	BB	SO	RAT	ERA	ERA+	OAV	OOB	BH	AVG	PB	PR	/A	PD	TPI
1966 Atl-N	1	1	.500	2	2	0	0	0	8¹	7	1	4	6	11.9	2.16	168	.226	.314	0	.000	-0	1	1	-0	0.3
1967 Atl-N	1	1	.500	3	3	0	0	0	21¹	21	1	3	11	11.0	2.95	112	.262	.306	0	.000	-1	1	1	1	0.1
1968 Atl-N★	11	10	.524	35	28	6	1	0	201²	189	10	49	111	10.9	3.35	89	.246	.297	10	.161	1	-8	-8	0	-0.7
1969 *Atl-N	18	10	.643	36	33	7	1	0	241¹	227	24	56	160	10.8	3.47	104	.246	.294	10	.125	-2	3	4	-1	0.1
1970 Atl-N	7	10	.412	21	18	6	0	0	134²	140	16	39	68	12.1	4.41	97	.266	.319	4	.091	-2	-5	-2	-1	-0.4
1971 Atl-N	13	14	.481	32	32	8	1	0	222¹	221	26	54	129	11.2	3.72	100	.261	.306	11	.149	-3	-6	-6	-1	-0.4
1972 Atl-N	11	15	.423	31	30	11	1	0	213	222	18	60	111	12.2	3.93	96	.270	.325	13	.178	-1	-11	-3	1	-0.4
1973 Atl-N	4	11	.267	20	19	2	0	1	116¹	133	7	31	64	12.9	4.41	89	.287	.335	9	.200	-0	-10	-6	1	-0.6
1974 Atl-N	10	11	.476	28	28	6	2	0	186	171	16	41	78	10.4	3.39	112	.243	.286	6	.105	-3	5	8	-2	0.3
1975 Atl-N	4	5	.444	10	10	1	0	0	74²	93	1	16	40	13.1	4.22	89	.304	.339	6	.231	1	-5	-4	-0	-0.3
StL-N	9	8	.529	24	24	7	2	0	175²	181	4	37	99	11.4	3.23	116	.263	.305	9	.161	-0	8	10	-1	0.8
Yr	13	13	.500	34	34	8	2	0	250¹	274	5	53	139	11.9	3.52	107	.275	.314	15	.183	-1	3	7	-1	0.5
1976 *Phi-N	8	7	.533	59	4	1	0	14	128	88	8	32	96	8.6	2.46	144	.193	.249	4	.167	-0	15	15	-1	2.1
1977 *Phi-N	7	5	.583	60	3	0	0	15	124¹	101	9	37	84	10.1	2.75	145	.223	.283	2	.111	-0	16	17	-1	1.9
1978 *Phi-N	3	4	.429	66	0	0	0	17	108²	87	6	23	85	9.5	2.24	160	.223	.275	0	.000	-0	16	16	-2	1.4
1979 *Phi-N	13	8	.619	61	0	0	0	5	102	110	9	32	58	12.7	4.15	92	.278	.335	3	.300	1	-5	-4	-0	-0.6
1980 *Phi-N	7	5	.583	55	0	0	0	9	91¹	88	4	30	54	11.7	4.04	94	.253	.314	3	.300	1	-4	-3	1	-0.2
1981 *Phi-N	5	3	.625	39	0	0	0	8	61¹	54	6	17	40	10.6	3.08	118	.237	.293	3	.500	1	3	4	-1	0.7
1982 Phi-N	5	5	.500	57	2	0	0	14	98	85	4	24	57	10.3	2.66	138	.235	.289	4	.333	2	10	11	2	1.8
1983 *Phi-N	9	1	.900	61	0	0	0	8	95²	89	5	34	73	11.7	3.48	102	.248	.315	1	.167	-0	2	1	-2	-0.1
1984 Chi-A	0	6	.000	51	0	0	0	12	73	67	6	14	57	10.1	3.08	135	.248	.288	0	.000	-0	7	9	0	1.0
Total 19	146	140	.510	751	236	55	8	103	2477²	2374	182	633	1481	11.1	3.46	107	.252	.303	98	.158	-6	32	68	-3	6.8

● **STEVE REED**   Reed, Steven Vincent b: 3/11/66, Los Angeles, Cal. BR/TR, 6'2", 200 lbs. Deb: 8/30/92

YEAR TM/L	W	L	PCT	G	GS	CG	SH	SV	IP	H	HR	BB	SO	RAT	ERA	ERA+	OAV	OOB	BH	AVG	PB	PR	/A	PD	TPI
1992 SF-N	1	0	1.000	18	0	0	0	0	15²	13	2	3	11	9.8	2.30	144	.220	.270	0	—	0	2	2	1	0.2
1993 Col-N	9	5	.643	64	0	0	0	3	84¹	80	13	30	51	12.1	4.48	106	.259	.330	0	—	-1	-4	3	0	0.3
1994 Col-N	3	2	.600	**61**	0	0	0	3	64	79	9	26	51	15.6	3.94	126	.306	.383	0	.000	-0	2	7	-1	0.5
Total 3	13	7	.650	143	0	0	0	6	164	172	24	59	113	13.2	4.06	116	.275	.347	0	.000	-1	-0	12	-0	1.0

● **BILL REEDER**   Reeder, William Edgar b: 2/20/22, Dike, Texas BR/TR, 6'5", 205 lbs. Deb: 4/23/49

YEAR TM/L	W	L	PCT	G	GS	CG	SH	SV	IP	H	HR	BB	SO	RAT	ERA	ERA+	OAV	OOB	BH	AVG	PB	PR	/A	PD	TPI
1949 StL-N	1	1	.500	21	1	0	0	0	33²	33	2	30	21	17.1	5.08	82	.270	.418	0	.000	-0	-4	-3	-0	-0.2

● **STAN REES**   Rees, Stanley Milton "Nellie" b: 2/25/1899, Cynthiana, Ky. d: 8/30/37, Lexington, Ky. BL/TL, 6'3", 190 lbs. Deb: 6/12/18

YEAR TM/L	W	L	PCT	G	GS	CG	SH	SV	IP	H	HR	BB	SO	RAT	ERA	ERA+	OAV	OOB	BH	AVG	PB	PR	/A	PD	TPI
1918 Was-A	1	0	1.000	2	0	0	0	0	2	3	0	4	1	31.5	0.00	—	.500	.700	0	—	0	1	1	0	0.3

● **BOBBY REEVES**   Reeves, Robert Edwin "Gunner" b: 6/24/04, Hill City, Tenn. d: 6/4/93, Chattanooga, Tenn. BR/TR, 5'11", 170 lbs. Deb: 6/9/26 ♦

YEAR TM/L	W	L	PCT	G	GS	CG	SH	SV	IP	H	HR	BB	SO	RAT	ERA	ERA+	OAV	OOB	BH	AVG	PB	PR	/A	PD	TPI
1931 Bos-A	0	0	—	1	0	0	0	0	7¹	6	0	1	0	8.6	3.68	117	.214	.241	14	.167	0	1	1	0	0.0

● **MIKE REGAN**   Regan, Michael Joseph b: 11/19/1887, Phoenix, N.Y. d: 5/22/61, Albany, N.Y. BR/TR, 5'11", 165 lbs. Deb: 5/13/17

YEAR TM/L	W	L	PCT	G	GS	CG	SH	SV	IP	H	HR	BB	SO	RAT	ERA	ERA+	OAV	OOB	BH	AVG	PB	PR	/A	PD	TPI
1917 Cin-N	11	10	.524	32	26	16	1	0	216	228	4	41	50	11.4	2.71	97	.273	.310	15	.200	1	0	-2	3	0.2
1918 Cin-N	5	5	.500	22	6	4	3	2	80	77	0	29	15	11.9	3.26	82	.262	.328	8	.296	2	-4	-5	-1	-0.5
1919 Cin-N	0	0	—	1	0	0	0	0	2¹	1	0	0	1	3.9	0.00	—	.143	.143	0	.000	-0	1	1	-0	0.0
Total 3	16	15	.516	55	32	20	4	2	298¹	306	4	70	66	11.5	2.84	93	.269	.314	23	.223	3	-4	-7	2	-0.3

● **PHIL REGAN**   Regan, Philip Raymond "The Vulture" b: 4/6/37, Otsego, Mich. BR/TR, 6'3", 200 lbs. Deb: 7/19/60 C

YEAR TM/L	W	L	PCT	G	GS	CG	SH	SV	IP	H	HR	BB	SO	RAT	ERA	ERA+	OAV	OOB	BH	AVG	PB	PR	/A	PD	TPI
1960 Det-A	0	4	.000	17	7	0	0	1	68	70	11	25	38	12.8	4.50	88	.267	.336	1	.059	-1	-5	-4	-1	-0.4
1961 Det-A	10	7	.588	32	16	6	0	2	120	134	19	41	46	13.2	5.25	78	.281	.339	3	.075	-2	-16	-15	-3	-2.4
1962 Det-A	11	9	.550	35	23	6	0	0	171¹	169	23	64	87	12.3	4.04	101	.254	.320	13	.206	-1	-1	0	-2	-0.1
1963 Det-A	15	9	.625	38	27	5	1	1	189	179	14	59	115	11.7	3.86	97	.245	.308	9	.143	-1	-5	-2	-3	-0.6
1964 Det-A	5	10	.333	32	21	2	0	1	146²	162	21	49	91	13.3	5.03	73	.282	.344	13	.317	5	-23	-22	-0	-1.6
1965 Det-A	1	5	.167	16	7	1	0	0	51²	57	6	20	37	13.4	5.05	69	.282	.347	1	.083	-0	-9	-9	-0	-1.1
1966 *LA-N☆	14	1	.933	65	0	0	0	21	116²	85	6	24	88	8.4	1.62	203	.207	.251	3	.143	0	**26**	22	1	3.8
1967 LA-N	6	9	.400	55	0	0	0	6	96¹	108	9	32	53	13.3	2.99	104	.284	.343	1	.100	-0	4	1	1	0.2
1968 LA-N	1	0	1.000	5	0	0	0	0	7²	7	1	1	7	12.9	3.52	78	.313	.333	0	.000	-0	-0	-1	-0	-0.2
Chi-N	10	5	.667	68	0	0	0	25	127	109	9	24	60	9.6	2.20	144	.232	.272	3	.150	-0	11	14	0	2.4
Yr	12	5	.706	73	0	0	0	25	134²	119	10	25	67	9.8	2.27	138	.237	.276	3	.143	-0	11	13	-0	2.2
1969 Chi-N	12	6	.667	71	0	0	0	17	112	109	6	35	56	12.6	3.70	109	.263	.339	1	.067	-0	1	0	1	0.8
1970 Chi-N	5	9	.357	54	0	0	0	12	75²	81	8	32	31	13.6	4.76	95	.287	.362	0	.000	-0	-6	-2	0	-0.3
1971 Chi-N	5	5	.500	48	1	0	0	6	73¹	84	4	33	28	14.6	3.93	100	.301	.379	0	.000	-1	-4	0	1	0.0

YEAR	TM/L	W	L	PCT	G	GS	CG	SH	SV	IP	H	HR	BB	SO	RAT	ERA	ERA+	OAV	OOB	BH	AVG	PB	PR	/A	PD	TPI
1972	Chi-N	0	1	.000	5	0	0	0	0	4	6	0	2	2	18.0	2.25	169	.400	.471	0	—	0	1	1	-0	0.2
	Chi-A	0	1	.000	10	0	0	0	0	13¹	18	1	6	4	16.9	4.05	77	.346	.424	1	1.000	0	-1	-1	0	0.0
Total	13	96	81	.542	551	105	20	1	92	1372²	1392	150	447	743	12.2	3.84	97	.265	.325	49	.153	1	-31	-16	-4	0.7

● EARL REID   Reid, Earl Percy b: 6/8/13, Bangor, Ala.   d: 5/11/84, Cullman, Ala.   BL/TR, 6'3", 190 lbs.   Deb: 5/8/46

YEAR	TM/L	W	L	PCT	G	GS	CG	SH	SV	IP	H	HR	BB	SO	RAT	ERA	ERA+	OAV	OOB	BH	AVG	PB	PR	/A	PD	TPI
1946	Bos-N	1	0	1.000	2	0	0	0	0	3	4	0	3	2	21.0	3.00	114	.308	.438	0	—	0	0	0	-0	0.0

● BILL REIDY   Reidy, William Joseph b: 10/9/1873, Cleveland, Ohio d: 10/14/15, Cleveland, Ohio   BR/TR, 5'10", 175 lbs.   Deb: 7/21/1896

YEAR	TM/L	W	L	PCT	G	GS	CG	SH	SV	IP	H	HR	BB	SO	RAT	ERA	ERA+	OAV	OOB	BH	AVG	PB	PR	/A	PD	TPI
1896	NY-N	0	1	.000	2	1	1	0	0	13	24	0	2	1	20.1	7.62	55	.391	.437	0	.000	-1	-5	-5	0	-0.3
1899	Bro-N	1	0	1.000	2	1	1	0	1	7	9	0	2	2	14.1	2.57	152	.311	.356	0	.000	-1	1	1	0	0.1
1901	Mil-A	16	20	.444	37	33	28	2	0	301¹	364	14	62	50	13.0	4.21	85	.295	.333	16	.143	-6	-18	-21	-3	-2.7
1902	StL-A	3	5	.375	12	9	7	0	0	95	111	0	13	16	12.4	4.45	79	.292	.327	8	.195	-0	-9	-10	1	-0.6
1903	StL-A	1	4	.200	7	5	5	0	0	43	53	1	7	8	13.2	3.98	73	.302	.339	1	.067	-2	-5	-5	-1	-0.8
	Bro-N	6	7	.462	15	13	11	0	0	104	130	6	14	21	13.0	3.46	92	.315	.346	9	.243	1	-2	-3	-1	-0.4
1904	Bro-N	0	4	.000	6	4	2	0	1	38¹	49	0	6	11	13.4	4.46	62	.293	.326	5	.156	-0	-7	-7	-1	-0.8
Total	6	27	41	.397	79	66	55	3	2	601²	740	15	106	109	13.1	4.17	82	.301	.337	39	.159	-9	-46	-50	-5	-5.5

● ART REINHART   Reinhart, Arthur Conrad b: 5/29/1899, Ackley, Iowa d: 11/11/46, Houston, Tex.   BL/TL, 6'1", 170 lbs.   Deb: 4/26/19

YEAR	TM/L	W	L	PCT	G	GS	CG	SH	SV	IP	H	HR	BB	SO	RAT	ERA	ERA+	OAV	OOB	BH	AVG	PB	PR	/A	PD	TPI
1919	StL-N	0	0	—	1	0	0	0	0	0	0	0	0	0	—	—	—	1.000	0	—	0	0	0	0	0.0
1925	StL-N	11	5	.688	20	16	15	1	0	144²	149	7	47	26	12.4	3.05	142	.278	.341	22	.328	5	20	20	-0	2.5
1926	*StL-N	10	5	.667	27	11	9	0	0	143	159	5	47	26	13.2	4.22	93	.295	.355	20	.317	4	-6	-5	1	0.0
1927	StL-N	5	2	.714	21	9	4	2	1	81²	82	5	36	15	13.0	4.19	94	.267	.344	10	.313	2	-2	-2	-1	-0.1
1928	StL-N	4	6	.400	23	9	3	1	2	75¹	80	3	27	12	12.8	2.87	139	.272	.333	4	.167	-0	9	9	-1	1.1
Total	5	30	18	.625	92	45	31	4	3	444²	470	20	157	79	12.9	3.60	113	.280	.345	56	.301	10	20	23	-1	3.5

● JACK REIS   Reis, Harrie Crane b: 6/14/1890, Cincinnati, Ohio d: 7/20/39, Cincinnati, Ohio   BR/TR, 5'10.5", 160 lbs.   Deb: 9/9/11

YEAR	TM/L	W	L	PCT	G	GS	CG	SH	SV	IP	H	HR	BB	SO	RAT	ERA	ERA+	OAV	OOB	BH	AVG	PB	PR	/A	PD	TPI
1911	StL-N	0	0	—	3	0	0	0	0	9¹	5	0	4	4	12.5	0.96	350	.156	.325	0	.000	-0	3	3	0	0.0

● LAURIE REIS   Reis, Lawrence P. b: 11/20/1858, Illinois d: 1/24/21, Chicago, Ill.   BR/TR, 160 lbs.   Deb: 10/1/1877

YEAR	TM/L	W	L	PCT	G	GS	CG	SH	SV	IP	H	HR	BB	SO	RAT	ERA	ERA+	OAV	OOB	BH	AVG	PB	PR	/A	PD	TPI
1877	Chi-N	3	1	.750	4	4	4	1	0	36	29	1	6	11	8.8	0.75	396	.213	.246	2	.125	-2	8	9	-0	0.7
1878	Chi-N	1	3	.250	4	4	4	0	0	36	55	0	4	8	14.8	3.25	75	.335	.351	3	.150	-1	-4	-3	-1	-0.5
Total	2	4	4	.500	8	8	8	1	0	72	84	1	10	19	11.8	2.00	135	.280	.303	5	.139	-2	4	6	-2	0.2

● BOBBY REIS   Reis, Robert Joseph Thomas b: 1/2/09, Woodside, N.Y. d: 5/1/73, St.Paul, Minn.   BR/TR, 6'1", 175 lbs.   Deb: 9/19/31 ♦

YEAR	TM/L	W	L	PCT	G	GS	CG	SH	SV	IP	H	HR	BB	SO	RAT	ERA	ERA+	OAV	OOB	BH	AVG	PB	PR	/A	PD	TPI
1935	Bro-N	3	2	.600	14	2	1	0	2	41¹	46	0	24	7	15.5	2.83	140	.277	.372	21	.247	1	5	5	1	0.8
1936	Bos-N	6	5	.545	35	5	3	0	0	138²	152	7	74	25	15.0	4.48	86	.283	.375	13	.217	1	-7	-10	4	-0.2
1937	Bos-N	0	0	—	4	0	0	0	0	5	3	0	5	0	14.4	1.80	199	.158	.333	2	.244	1	1	1	-0	0.0
1938	Bos-N	1	6	.143	16	2	1	0	0	57²	61	5	41	20	16.9	4.99	69	.271	.397	9	.184	-0	-8	-10	0	-1.0
Total	4	10	13	.435	69	9	5	0	2	242²	262	12	144	52	15.5	4.27	88	.277	.379	70	.233	3	-8	-14	5	-0.4

● TOMMY REIS   Reis, Thomas Edward b: 8/6/14, Newport, Ky.   BR/TR, 6'2", 180 lbs.   Deb: 4/27/38

YEAR	TM/L	W	L	PCT	G	GS	CG	SH	SV	IP	H	HR	BB	SO	RAT	ERA	ERA+	OAV	OOB	BH	AVG	PB	PR	/A	PD	TPI
1938	Phi-N	0	1	.000	4	0	0	0	0	4²	8	0	2	2	30.9	19.29	20	.364	.533	0	.000	-0	-8	-8	0	-1.3
	Bos-N	0	0	—	4	0	0	0	0	6¹	8	1	4	2	12.8	7.11	48	.296	.321	0	—	-2	-3	-0	0.0
Yr	0	1	.000	8	0	0	0	0	11	16	1	6	4	20.5	12.27	30	.327	.431	0	—	-0	-10	-11	-0	-1.3

● BUGS REISIGL   Reisigl, Jacob b: 12/12/1887, Brooklyn, N.Y. d: 2/24/57, Amsterdam, N.Y.   BR/TR, 5'10.5", 175 lbs.   Deb: 9/20/11

YEAR	TM/L	W	L	PCT	G	GS	CG	SH	SV	IP	H	HR	BB	SO	RAT	ERA	ERA+	OAV	OOB	BH	AVG	PB	PR	/A	PD	TPI
1911	Cle-A	0	1	.000	2	1	0	0	0	13	16	1	3	6	13.1	6.23	55	.271	.314	0	—	-1	-4	-4	0	-0.3

● DOC REISLING   Reisling, Frank Carl b: 7/25/1874, Martins Ferry, O. d: 3/4/55, Tulsa, Okla.   BR/TR, 5'10", 180 lbs.   Deb: 9/10/04

YEAR	TM/L	W	L	PCT	G	GS	CG	SH	SV	IP	H	HR	BB	SO	RAT	ERA	ERA+	OAV	OOB	BH	AVG	PB	PR	/A	PD	TPI
1904	Bro-N	3	4	.429	7	7	6	1	0	51	45	0	10	19	11.3	2.12	130	.238	.308	2	.154	0	4	4	0	0.5
1905	Bro-N	0	1	.000	2	0	0	0	0	3	3	0	4	2	21.0	3.00	96	.273	.467	0	.000	0	-0	-0	0	0.0
1909	Was-A	2	4	.333	10	6	6	1	0	66²	70	0	17	22	11.7	2.43	100	.270	.315	4	.167	0	0	0	-1	-0.1
1910	Was-A	10	10	.500	30	20	13	2	1	191	185	3	44	57	11.0	2.54	98	.264	.312	12	.200	2	-1	-1	0	0.1
Total	4	15	19	.441	49	33	25	4	1	311²	303	3	75	100	11.3	2.45	103	.261	.314	18	.184	2	3	2	-1	0.5

● MIKE REMLINGER   Remlinger, Michael John b: 3/23/66, Middletown, N.Y.   BL/TL, 6', 195 lbs.   Deb: 6/15/91

YEAR	TM/L	W	L	PCT	G	GS	CG	SH	SV	IP	H	HR	BB	SO	RAT	ERA	ERA+	OAV	OOB	BH	AVG	PB	PR	/A	PD	TPI
1991	SF-N	2	1	.667	8	6	1	0	0	35	36	5	20	19	14.4	4.37	82	.271	.366	0	—	-3	-3	-0	-0.3
1994	NY-N	1	5	.167	10	9	0	0	0	54²	55	9	35	33	15.0	4.61	92	.261	.368	0	.000	-2	-2	-1	-0.5
Total	2	3	6	.333	18	15	1	0	0	89²	91	14	55	52	14.8	4.52	88	.265	.368	0	.000	-5	-5	-1	-0.8

● WIN REMMERSWAAL   Remmerswaal, Wilhelmus Abraham b: 3/8/54, The Hague, Holland   BR/TR, 6'2", 160 lbs.   Deb: 8/3/79

YEAR	TM/L	W	L	PCT	G	GS	CG	SH	SV	IP	H	HR	BB	SO	RAT	ERA	ERA+	OAV	OOB	BH	AVG	PB	PR	/A	PD	TPI
1979	Bos-A	1	0	1.000	8	0	0	0	0	20¹	26	1	12	16	17.3	7.08	62	.317	.411	0	—	0	-6	-6	0	-0.7
1980	Bos-A	2	1	.667	14	0	0	0	0	35¹	39	4	9	20	12.2	4.58	92	.295	.340	0	—	0	-2	-1	-1	-0.2
Total	2	3	1	.750	22	0	0	0	0	55²	65	5	21	36	14.1	5.50	78	.304	.369	0	—	0	-9	-7	-1	-0.9

● ALEX REMNEAS   Remneas, Alexander Norman b: 2/21/1886, Minneapolis, Minn. d: 8/27/75, Phoenix, Ariz.   BR/TR, 6'1", 180 lbs.   Deb: 4/15/12

YEAR	TM/L	W	L	PCT	G	GS	CG	SH	SV	IP	H	HR	BB	SO	RAT	ERA	ERA+	OAV	OOB	BH	AVG	PB	PR	/A	PD	TPI
1912	Det-A	0	0	—	1	0	0	0	0	1²	5	0	0	0	27.0	27.00	12	.455	.455	0	—	-0	-4	-4	0	0.0
1915	StL-A	0	0	—	2	0	0	0	0	6	3	0	3	5	10.5	1.50	191	.136	.269	0	.000	-0	1	1	0	0.0
Total	2	0	0	—	3	0	0	0	0	7²	8	0	3	5	14.1	7.04	42	.242	.324	0	.000	-0	-3	-3	0	0.0

● ERWIN RENFER   Renfer, Erwin Arthur b: 12/11/1891, Elgin, Ill. d: 10/26/57, Sycamore, Ill.   BR/TR, 6', 180 lbs.   Deb: 9/18/13

YEAR	TM/L	W	L	PCT	G	GS	CG	SH	SV	IP	H	HR	BB	SO	RAT	ERA	ERA+	OAV	OOB	BH	AVG	PB	PR	/A	PD	TPI
1913	Det-A	0	1	.000	1	1	0	0	0	6	5	3	0	1	13.5	6.00	49	.227	.346	0	—	-0	-2	-2	0	-0.3

● LADDIE RENFROE   Renfroe, Cohen Williams b: 5/9/62, Natchez, Miss.   BB/TR, 5'11", 200 lbs.   Deb: 7/3/91

YEAR	TM/L	W	L	PCT	G	GS	CG	SH	SV	IP	H	HR	BB	SO	RAT	ERA	ERA+	OAV	OOB	BH	AVG	PB	PR	/A	PD	TPI
1991	Chi-N	0	1	.000	4	0	0	0	0	4²	11	1	2	4	25.1	13.50	29	.440	.481	0	.000	-0	-5	-5	0	-0.9

● MARSHALL RENFROE   Renfroe, Marshall Daniel b: 5/25/36, Century, Fla. d: 12/10/70, Pensacola, Fla.   BL/TL, 6', 180 lbs.   Deb: 9/27/59

YEAR	TM/L	W	L	PCT	G	GS	CG	SH	SV	IP	H	HR	BB	SO	RAT	ERA	ERA+	OAV	OOB	BH	AVG	PB	PR	/A	PD	TPI
1959	SF-N	0	0	—	1	1	0	0	0	2	3	1	3	3	27.0	27.00	14	.333	.500	0	—	-5	-5	-0	0.0

● HAL RENIFF   Reniff, Harold Eugene "Porky" b: 7/2/38, Warren, Ohio   BR/TR, 6', 215 lbs.   Deb: 6/8/61

YEAR	TM/L	W	L	PCT	G	GS	CG	SH	SV	IP	H	HR	BB	SO	RAT	ERA	ERA+	OAV	OOB	BH	AVG	PB	PR	/A	PD	TPI
1961	NY-A	2	0	1.000	25	0	0	0	2	45¹	31	1	31	21	12.3	2.58	144	.197	.330	0	.000	-1	7	6	-1	0.2
1962	NY-A	0	0	—	2	0	0	0	0	3²	6	0	5	1	29.5	7.36	51	.400	.571	0	—	0	-1	-1	-0	0.0
1963	*NY-A	4	3	.571	48	0	0	0	18	89¹	63	3	42	56	10.8	2.62	134	.202	.301	0	.000	-1	10	9	3	1.2
1964	*NY-A	6	4	.600	41	0	0	0	9	69¹	47	3	30	38	10.0	3.12	116	.199	.289	1	.100	-1	4	4	0	0.6
1965	NY-A	3	4	.429	51	0	0	0	3	85¹	74	4	48	74	13.4	3.80	90	.232	.341	0	.000	-0	-3	-4	-0	-0.1
1966	NY-A	3	7	.300	56	0	0	0	9	95¹	80	7	49	79	12.7	3.21	104	.229	.333	4	.286	1	2	1	-1	0.2
1967	NY-A	0	2	.000	24	0	0	0	0	40	40	0	14	24	12.8	4.27	73	.256	.329	0	.000	-0	-5	-5	-1	-0.3
	NY-N	3	3	.500	29	0	0	0	4	43	42	1	23	21	13.8	3.35	101	.266	.363	0	.000	-0	1	1	-1	0.2
Total	7	21	23	.477	276	0	0	0	45	471¹	383	14	242	314	12.3	3.27	106	.225	.327	5	.096	-2	14	10	-0	1.4

● JIM RENINGER   Reninger, James David b: 3/7/13, Aurora, Ill.   BR/TR, 6'3", 210 lbs.   Deb: 9/17/38

YEAR	TM/L	W	L	PCT	G	GS	CG	SH	SV	IP	H	HR	BB	SO	RAT	ERA	ERA+	OAV	OOB	BH	AVG	PB	PR	/A	PD	TPI
1938	Phi-A	0	2	.000	4	4	1	0	0	22²	28	3	14	9	16.7	7.15	68	.295	.385	0	.000	-0	-6	-6	0	-0.4
1939	Phi-A	0	2	.000	4	2	0	0	0	16¹	24	3	12	8	19.8	7.71	61	.369	.468	1	.167	-0	-6	-5	-1	-0.5
Total	2	0	4	.000	8	6	1	0	0	39	52	6	26	12	18.0	7.38	65	.321	.419	1	.077	-1	-12	-11	-1	-0.9

● STEVE RENKO   Renko, Steven b: 12/10/44, Kansas City, Kan.   BR/TR, 6'5", 230 lbs.   Deb: 6/27/69

YEAR	TM/L	W	L	PCT	G	GS	CG	SH	SV	IP	H	HR	BB	SO	RAT	ERA	ERA+	OAV	OOB	BH	AVG	PB	PR	/A	PD	TPI
1969	Mon-N	6	7	.462	18	15	4	0	0	103¹	94	14	50	68	12.7	4.01	92	.243	.333	6	.167	1	-5	-4	-1	-0.4

YEAR	TM/L	W	L	PCT	G	GS	CG	SH	SV	IP	H	HR	BB	SO	RAT	ERA	ERA+	OAV	OOB	BH	AVG	PB	PR	/A	PD	TPI
1970	Mon-N	13	11	.542	41	33	7	1	1	222²	203	27	104	142	12.7	4.32	95	.241	.329	16	.200	2	-7	-5	-0	-0.3
1971	Mon-N	15	14	.517	40	37	9	3	0	275²	256	24	135	129	12.9	3.75	94	.247	.336	21	.210	4	-9	-7	-2	-0.4
1972	Mon-N	1	10	.091	30	12	0	0	0	97	96	11	67	66	15.1	5.20	68	.262	.376	1	.292	1	-19	-18	1	-1.7
1973	Mon-N	15	11	.577	36	34	9	0	1	249²	201	26	108	164	11.2	2.81	136	.218	.300	24	.273	7	24	28	-2	3.6
1974	Mon-N	12	16	.429	37	35	8	1	0	227²	222	17	81	138	12.0	4.03	95	.257	.321	17	.210	3	-10	-5	3	0.1
1975	Mon-N	6	12	.333	31	25	3	1	1	170¹	175	20	76	99	13.3	4.07	94	.265	.341	8	.278	5	-8	-5	-0	0.0
1976	Mon-N	0	1	.000	5	1	0	0	0	13	15	2	3	4	12.5	5.54	67	.288	.327	1	.333	1	-3	-3	-1	-0.2
	Chi-N	8	11	.421	28	27	4	1	0	163¹	164	12	43	112	11.4	3.86	100	.258	.305	5	.094	-3	-6	0	-1	-0.5
	Yr	8	12	.400	33	28	4	1	0	176¹	179	14	46	116	11.5	3.98	97	.260	.307	6	.107	-3	-9	-3	-2	-0.7
1977	Chi-N	2	2	.500	13	8	0	0	1	51¹	51	10	21	34	12.8	4.56	96	.258	.332	2	.167	0	-4	-1	-1	-0.2
	Chi-A	5	0	1.000	8	8	0	0	0	53¹	55	3	17	36	12.3	3.54	115	.274	.333	0	—	0	3	3	0	0.3
1978	Oak-A	6	12	.333	27	25	3	1	0	151	152	10	67	89	13.2	4.29	85	.265	.344	0	—	0	-9	-11	-0	-0.8
1979	Bos-A	11	9	.550	27	27	4	1	0	171	174	22	53	99	12.1	4.11	107	.260	.317	0	—	0	2	6	-1	0.3
1980	Bos-A	9	9	.500	32	23	1	0	0	165¹	180	17	56	90	12.9	4.19	101	.281	.340	0	—	0	-3	0	-1	-0.2
1981	Cal-A	8	4	.667	22	15	0	0	1	102	93	7	42	50	12.0	3.44	106	.250	.328	0	—	0	2	2	-2	0.1
1982	Cal-A	11	6	.647	31	23	4	0	0	156	163	17	51	81	12.4	4.44	91	.269	.327	0	—	0	-6	-7	-2	-0.8
1983	KC-A	6	11	.353	25	17	1	0	1	121¹	144	9	36	54	13.4	4.30	95	.293	.343	0	—	0	-4	-1	-1	-0.5
Total	15	134	146	.479	451	365	57	9	6	2494	2438	248	1010	1455	12.5	3.99	98	.256	.329	114	.215	21	-62	-27	-9	-1.6

● **ANDY REPLOGLE**　　Replogle, Andrew David　b: 10/7/53, South Bend, Ind.　BR/TR, 6'5", 205 lbs.　Deb: 4/11/78

YEAR	TM/L	W	L	PCT	G	GS	CG	SH	SV	IP	H	HR	BB	SO	RAT	ERA	ERA+	OAV	OOB	BH	AVG	PB	PR	/A	PD	TPI
1978	Mil-A	9	5	.643	32	18	3	2	0	149¹	177	14	47	41	13.6	3.92	96	.301	.353	0	—	0	-3	-3	-2	-0.5
1979	Mil-A	0	0	—	3	0	0	0	0	8	13	0	2	2	16.9	5.63	74	.382	.417	0	—	0	-1	-1	0	0.0
Total	2	9	5	.643	35	18	3	2	0	157¹	190	14	49	43	13.7	4.00	94	.305	.357	0	—	0	-4	-4	-2	-0.5

● **XAVIER RESCIGNO**　　Rescigno, Xavier Frederick "Mr. X"　b: 10/13/13, New York, N.Y.　BR/TR, 5'10.5", 175 lbs.　Deb: 4/22/43

YEAR	TM/L	W	L	PCT	G	GS	CG	SH	SV	IP	H	HR	BB	SO	RAT	ERA	ERA+	OAV	OOB	BH	AVG	PB	PR	/A	PD	TPI
1943	Pit-N	6	9	.400	37	14	5	1	2	132²	125	6	45	41	11.7	2.98	117	.252	.317	5	.143	9	6	7	-2	0.6
1944	Pit-N	10	8	.556	48	6	2	0	5	124	146	9	34	45	13.1	4.35	85	.291	.337	2	.091	-1	-10	-9	-0	-1.3
1945	Pit-N	3	5	.375	44	1	0	0	9	78²	95	6	34	29	14.9	5.72	69	.303	.372	2	.133	-0	-17	-16	-0	-1.8
Total	3	19	22	.463	129	21	7	1	16	335¹	366	21	113	115	13.0	4.13	89	.279	.338	9	.125	-1	-21	-17	-3	-2.5

● **GEORGE RETTGER**　　Rettger, George Edward　b: 7/29/1868, Cleveland, Ohio　d: 6/5/21, Lakewood, Ohio　BR/TR, 5'11", 175 lbs.　Deb: 8/13/1891

YEAR	TM/L	W	L	PCT	G	GS	CG	SH	SV	IP	H	HR	BB	SO	RAT	ERA	ERA+	OAV	OOB	BH	AVG	PB	PR	/A	PD	TPI
1891	StL-a	7	3	.700	14	12	10	1	1	92²	85	4	51	49	14.0	3.40	124	.236	.343	3	.071	-3	3	8	-1	0.4
1892	Cle-N	1	3	.250	6	5	3	0	0	38	32	2	31	12	15.2	4.26	80	.219	.360	2	.133	-0	-4	-4	-0	-0.4
	Cin-N	1	0	1.000	1	1	1	0	0	9	8	0	1	1	19.0	4.00	82	.229	.413	1	.125	-0	-1	-1	-0	-0.1
	Yr	2	3	.400	7	6	4	0	0	47	40	2	41	13	15.7	4.21	80	.220	.366	3	.130	-0	-5	-4	-1	-0.5
Total	2	9	6	.600	21	18	14	1	1	139²	125	6	92	62	14.6	3.67	107	.231	.353	6	.092	-3	-1	4	-1	-0.1

● **OTTO RETTIG**　　Rettig, Adolph John　b: 1/29/1894, New York, N.Y.　d: 6/16/77, Stuart, Fla.　BR/TR, 5'11", 165 lbs.　Deb: 7/19/22

YEAR	TM/L	W	L	PCT	G	GS	CG	SH	SV	IP	H	HR	BB	SO	RAT	ERA	ERA+	OAV	OOB	BH	AVG	PB	PR	/A	PD	TPI
1922	Phi-A	1	2	.333	4	4	1	0	0	18¹	18	0	12	3	15.2	4.91	87	.265	.383	1	.000	-1	-1	-0	0	-0.3

● **ED REULBACH**　　Reulbach, Edward Marvin "Big Ed"　b: 12/1/1882, Detroit, Mich.　d: 7/17/61, Glens Falls, N.Y.　BR/TR, 6'1", 190 lbs.　Deb: 5/16/05

YEAR	TM/L	W	L	PCT	G	GS	CG	SH	SV	IP	H	HR	BB	SO	RAT	ERA	ERA+	OAV	OOB	BH	AVG	PB	PR	/A	PD	TPI
1905	Chi-N	18	14	.563	34	29	28	5	1	291²	208	1	73	152	9.2	1.42	210	.201	.266	14	.127	-6	51	51	-1	4.8
1906	*Chi-N	19	4	**.826**	33	24	20	6	3	218	129	2	92	94	9.7	1.65	160	**.175**	.278	13	.157	-2	24	24	3	2.8
1907	*Chi-N	17	4	**.810**	27	22	16	4	0	192	147	1	64	96	10.3	1.69	148	.217	.294	11	.175	0	17	17	1	2.1
1908	*Chi-N	24	7	**.774**	46	35	25	7	1	297²	227	2	106	133	10.4	2.03	116	.214	.292	23	.232	7	11	11	-1	1.7
1909	Chi-N	19	10	.655	35	32	23	6	0	262²	194	1	82	105	9.8	1.78	143	.212	.285	12	.140	-1	24	22	4	2.9
1910	Chi-N	12	8	.600	24	23	14	1	0	173¹	162	1	49	56	11.4	3.12	92	.251	.313	6	.107	-3	-2	-5	-1	-0.8
1911	Chi-N	16	9	.640	33	29	15	2	0	221¹	191	3	103	79	12.1	2.96	112	.236	.325	6	.090	-1	11	9	3	1.0
1912	Chi-N	10	6	.625	39	19	8	0	4	169	161	7	60	75	12.2	3.78	88	.259	.332	6	.109	-3	-7	-8	4	-0.6
1913	Chi-N	1	3	.250	10	3	1	0	0	38²	41	1	21	10	14.7	4.42	72	.281	.375	3	.250	-1	-5	-5	-0	-0.5
	Bro-N	7	6	.538	15	12	8	2	0	110	77	3	34	46	9.4	2.05	161	.202	.274	3	.103	0	14	15	-1	1.7
	Yr	8	9	.471	25	15	9	2	0	148²	118	4	55	56	10.7	2.66	123	.223	.301	6	.146	0	9	10	-1	1.2
1914	Bro-N	11	18	.379	44	29	14	3	3	256	228	5	83	119	11.3	2.64	108	.242	.310	9	.125	-0	4	6	1	0.8
1915	New-F	21	10	.677	33	30	23	4	1	270	233	3	69	117	10.2	2.23	115	.236	.287	18	.196	-2	15	10	1	1.1
1916	Bos-N	7	6	.538	21	11	6	0	0	109¹	99	1	41	47	11.9	2.47	101	.251	.328	3	.091	-1	2	0	5	0.5
1917	Bos-N	0	1	.000	5	2	0	0	0	22¹	21	0	15	9	14.9	2.82	90	.256	.378	0	.000	-1	-0	-1	-1	0.2
Total	13	182	106	.632	399	300	201	40	13	2632¹	2118	33	892	1138	10.7	2.28	122	.224	.299	127	.147	-11	159	146	22	17.7

● **PAUL REUSCHEL**　　Reuschel, Paul Richard　b: 1/12/47, Quincy, Ill.　BR/TR, 6'4", 225 lbs.　Deb: 7/25/75　F

YEAR	TM/L	W	L	PCT	G	GS	CG	SH	SV	IP	H	HR	BB	SO	RAT	ERA	ERA+	OAV	OOB	BH	AVG	PB	PR	/A	PD	TPI
1975	Chi-N	1	3	.250	28	0	0	0	5	36	44	1	13	12	14.5	3.50	110	.312	.374	0	.000	-0	0	1	0	0.2
1976	Chi-N	4	2	.667	50	2	0	0	3	87	94	12	33	55	13.2	4.55	85	.278	.344	2	.154	-0	-10	-7	1	-0.4
1977	Chi-N	5	6	.455	69	0	0	0	4	107	105	9	40	62	12.2	4.37	100	.262	.329	0	.000	-1	-6	0	2	0.1
1978	Chi-N	2	0	1.000	16	0	0	0	0	28	29	4	13	13	13.8	5.14	78	.269	.352	0	—	0	-5	-3	-0	-0.3
	Cle-A	2	4	.333	18	6	1	0	0	89²	95	5	22	24	11.9	3.11	120	.271	.318	0	—	0	6	6	1	0.5
1979	Cle-A	2	1	.667	17	1	0	0	1	45¹	73	7	11	22	16.7	7.94	54	.365	.398	0	—	0	-19	-19	1	-1.1
Total	5	16	16	.500	198	9	1	0	13	393	440	38	132	188	13.2	4.51	89	.286	.344	2	.063	-2	-32	-21	5	-1.0

● **RICK REUSCHEL**　　Reuschel, Rickey Eugene　b: 5/16/49, Quincy, Ill.　BR/TR, 6'3", 235 lbs.　Deb: 6/19/72　F

YEAR	TM/L	W	L	PCT	G	GS	CG	SH	SV	IP	H	HR	BB	SO	RAT	ERA	ERA+	OAV	OOB	BH	AVG	PB	PR	/A	PD	TPI
1972	Chi-N	10	8	.556	21	18	5	4	0	129	127	3	29	87	11.0	2.93	130	.259	.303	6	.136	-1	7	13	-0	1.6
1973	Chi-N	14	15	.483	36	36	7	3	0	237	244	15	62	168	11.8	3.00	131	.263	.312	9	.123	-3	17	25	4	3.0
1974	Chi-N	13	12	.520	41	38	8	2	0	240²	262	18	83	160	13.1	4.30	89	.276	.338	19	.221	2	-18	-13	5	-0.6
1975	Chi-N	11	17	.393	38	37	6	0	1	234	244	17	67	155	12.2	3.73	103	.268	.323	16	.208	2	-3	3	3	0.8
1976	Chi-N	14	12	.538	38	37	9	2	0	260	260	17	64	146	11.5	3.46	111	.265	.315	19	.229	4	1	11	3	1.9
1977	Chi-N★	20	10	.667	39	37	8	4	1	252	233	13	74	166	11.1	2.79	157	.247	.305	18	.207	1	31	**45**	3	5.8
1978	Chi-N	14	15	.483	35	35	9	1	0	242²	235	16	54	115	10.9	3.41	118	.254	.299	10	.137	-1	4	17	2	2.0
1979	Chi-N	18	12	.600	36	36	5	1	0	239	251	16	75	125	12.7	3.62	114	.274	.335	13	.165	1	3	13	5	2.1
1980	Chi-N	11	13	.458	38	38	6	0	0	257	281	13	76	140	12.6	3.40	115	.286	.340	13	.159	-1	6	15	5	1.8
1981	Chi-N	4	7	.364	13	13	1	0	0	85²	87	4	23	53	12.0	3.47	107	.267	.323	2	.080	-1	0	2	2	0.3
	*NY-A	4	4	.500	12	11	3	0	0	70²	75	4	10	22	11.0	2.67	134	.280	.308	0	—	0	8	7	1	0.9
1983	Chi-N	1	1	.500	4	4	0	0	0	20²	18	1	10	9	12.2	3.92	97	.234	.322	1	.143	-0	-1	-1	1	0.1
1984	Chi-N	5	5	.500	19	14	0	0	0	92¹	123	7	23	43	14.5	5.17	76	.339	.383	7	.241	2	-16	-13	1	-1.0
1985	Pit-N	14	8	.636	31	26	9	1	0	194	153	7	52	138	9.6	2.27	157	.215	.272	10	.169	-1	28	28	4	4.0
1986	Pit-N	9	16	.360	35	34	4	2	0	215²	232	20	57	125	12.4	3.96	97	.274	.326	11	.157	-0	-6	-3	3	0.0
1987	Pit-N★	8	6	.571	25	25	9	3	0	177	163	12	30	80	10.4	2.75	150	.246	.290	9	.150	-2	26	27	1	2.3
	*SF-N	5	3	.625	9	8	3	1	0	50	44	1	7	27	9.5	4.32	89	.230	.265	2	.105	-0	-1	-3	0	-0.4
	Yr	13	9	.591	34	33	**12**	**4**	0	227	207	13	42	107	**10.0**	3.09	131	.242	.285	11	.139	-2	25	24	1	1.9
1988	SF-N	19	11	.633	36	36	**7**	3	0	245	242	11	42	92	10.7	3.12	104	.260	.297	8	.110	-1	9	4	-2	0.0
1989	*SF-N★	17	8	.680	32	32	2	0	0	208¹	195	18	54	111	10.8	2.94	115	.247	.297	10	.164	1	13	10	-1	1.3
1990	SF-N	3	6	.333	15	13	0	0	0	87	102	8	31	49	13.9	3.93	93	.297	.357	4	.154	0	-1	-3	-0	-0.2
1991	SF-N	0	2	.000	4	1	0	0	0	10²	17	0	7	4	20.3	4.22	85	.370	.453	0	—	0	-1	-1	0	-0.2
Total	19	214	191	.528	557	529	102	26	5	3548¹	3588	221	935	2015	11.7	3.37	114	.264	.316	187	.168	8	108	183	39	25.5

● **JERRY REUSS**　　Reuss, Jerry　b: 6/19/49, St.Louis, Mo.　BL/TL, 6'5", 217 lbs.　Deb: 9/27/69

YEAR	TM/L	W	L	PCT	G	GS	CG	SH	SV	IP	H	HR	BB	SO	RAT	ERA	ERA+	OAV	OOB	BH	AVG	PB	PR	/A	PD	TPI
1969	StL-N	1	0	1.000	1	1	0	0	0	7	2	0	3	3	9.0	0.00	—	.091	.259	1	.333	0	3	3	0	0.6
1970	StL-N	7	8	.467	20	20	5	2	0	127¹	132	9	49	74	12.9	4.10	100	.271	.339	2	.050	-3	-1	0	-0	-0.2

YEAR	TM/L	W	L	PCT	G	GS	CG	SH	SV	IP	H	HR	BB	SO	RAT	ERA	ERA+	OAV	OOB	BH	AVG	PB	PR	/A	PD	TPI
1971	StL-N	14	14	.500	36	35	7	2	0	211	228	15	109	131	14.7	4.78	75	.279	.368	8	.123	0	-31	-28	-2	-3.5
1972	Hou-N	9	13	.409	33	30	4	1	1	192	177	14	83	174	12.7	4.17	81	.246	.332	7	.106	-1	-15	-17	-1	-2.0
1973	Hou-N	16	13	.552	41	40	12	3	0	279¹	271	17	117	177	12.6	3.74	97	.256	.332	13	.137	-1	-2	-3	-2	-0.7
1974	*Pit-N	16	11	.593	35	35	14	1	0	260	259	20	101	105	12.5	3.50	99	.261	.329	13	.151	0	4	-1	-2	-0.3
1975	*Pit-N★	18	11	.621	32	32	15	6	0	237¹	224	10	78	131	11.5	2.54	139	.253	.314	14	.197	2	28	26	2	3.7
1976	Pit-N	14	9	.609	31	29	11	3	2	209¹	209	16	51	108	11.3	3.53	99	.256	.301	16	.242	6	-1	-1	-2	0.3
1977	Pit-N	10	13	.435	33	33	8	2	0	208	225	11	71	116	13.0	4.11	97	.280	.341	12	.171	1	-5	-3	1	-0.1
1978	Pit-N	3	2	.600	23	12	3	1	0	82²	97	5	23	42	13.4	4.90	76	.297	.348	5	.185	0	-12	-11	-0	-0.6
1979	LA-N	7	14	.333	39	21	4	1	3	160	178	4	60	83	13.6	3.54	103	.282	.347	7	.167	1	3	2	1	0.5
1980	LA-N★	18	6	.750	37	29	10	**6**	3	229¹	193	12	40	111	9.1	2.51	139	.227	.261	6	.088	-1	28	25	1	2.7
1981	*LA-N	10	4	.714	22	22	8	2	0	152²	138	6	27	51	10.0	2.30	144	.243	.282	10	.196	0	20	17	3	1.9
1982	*LA-N	18	11	.621	39	37	8	4	0	254²	232	11	50	138	10.0	3.11	111	.240	.278	17	.221	3	14	10	2	1.6
1983	*LA-N	12	11	.522	32	31	7	0	0	223¹	233	12	50	143	11.5	2.94	122	.271	.313	20	.282	5	17	16	4	2.7
1984	LA-N	5	7	.417	30	15	2	0	1	99	102	4	31	44	12.1	3.82	92	.266	.321	4	.167	1	-3	-3	-0	-0.3
1985	*LA-N	14	10	.583	34	33	5	3	0	212²	210	13	58	84	11.5	2.92	119	.260	.312	10	.135	-1	16	13	-2	1.1
1986	LA-N	2	6	.250	19	13	0	0	1	74	96	13	17	29	14.0	5.84	59	.313	.353	5	.250	2	-17	-20	1	-1.7
1987	LA-N	0	0	—	1	0	0	0	0	2	2	0	0	2	9.0	4.50	88	.333	.333	0	—	-0	-0	-0	0.0
	Cin-N	0	5	.000	7	7	0	0	0	34²	52	2	12	10	16.9	7.79	54	.351	.404	1	.125	0	-14	-14	-1	-1.6
	Yr	0	5	.000	8	7	0	0	0	36²	54	2	12	12	16.4	7.61	56	.348	.399	1	.125	0	-14	-14	-1	-1.6
	Cal-A	4	5	.444	17	16	1	1	0	82¹	112	16	17	37	14.3	5.25	82	.327	.362	0	—	0	-7	-9	2	-0.7
1988	Chi-A	13	9	.591	32	29	2	0	0	183	183	15	43	73	11.3	3.44	115	.263	.309	0	—	0	11	11	0	1.2
1989	Chi-A	8	5	.615	23	19	1	1	0	106²	135	12	21	27	13.4	5.06	75	.308	.344	0	—	0	-14	-15	-2	-1.8
	Mil-A	1	4	.200	7	7	0	0	0	33²	36	7	13	13	13.4	5.35	72	.273	.342	0	—	0	-5	-6	-0	-0.7
	Yr	9	9	.500	30	26	1	1	0	140¹	171	19	34	40	13.2	5.13	74	.295	.336	0	—	0	-19	-21	-2	-2.5
1990	Pit-N	0	0	—	4	1	0	0	0	7²	8	1	3	1	12.9	3.52	103	.267	.333	0	—	0	0	0	0	0.0
Total	22	220	191	.535	628	547	127	39	11	3669²	3734	245	1127	1907	12.1	3.64	100	.265	.322	171	.167	15	16	-7	2	2.1

● **TODD REVENIG**   Revenig, Todd Michael b: 6/28/69, Brainerd, Minn.   BR/TR, 6'1", 185 lbs.   Deb: 8/24/92

YEAR	TM/L	W	L	PCT	G	GS	CG	SH	SV	IP	H	HR	BB	SO	RAT	ERA	ERA+	OAV	OOB	BH	AVG	PB	PR	/A	PD	TPI
1992	Oak-A	0	0	—	2	0	0	0	0	2	2	0	1	0	9.0	0.00	—	.286	.286	0	—	0	1	1	-0	0.4

● **CARLOS REYES**   Reyes, Carlos Alberto b: 4/4/69, Miami, Fla.   BB/TR, 6'1", 190 lbs.   Deb: 4/7/94

YEAR	TM/L	W	L	PCT	G	GS	CG	SH	SV	IP	H	HR	BB	SO	RAT	ERA	ERA+	OAV	OOB	BH	AVG	PB	PR	/A	PD	TPI
1994	Oak-A	0	3	.000	27	9	0	0	1	78	71	10	44	57	13.5	4.15	107	.242	.345	0	—	0	6	3	0	0.6

● **ALLIE REYNOLDS**   Reynolds, Allie Pierce "Superchief" b: 2/10/15, Bethany, Okla.   BR/TR, 6', 195 lbs.   Deb: 9/17/42

YEAR	TM/L	W	L	PCT	G	GS	CG	SH	SV	IP	H	HR	BB	SO	RAT	ERA	ERA+	OAV	OOB	BH	AVG	PB	PR	/A	PD	TPI
1942	Cle-A	0	0	—	2	0	0	0	0	5	5	0	4	2	16.2	0.00	—	.250	.375	0	.000	-0	2	2	-0	0.0
1943	Cle-A	11	12	.478	34	21	11	3	3	198²	140	3	109	**151**	11.6	2.99	104	**.202**	.316	10	.149	-1	7	3	-0	0.1
1944	Cle-A	11	8	.579	28	21	5	1	1	158	141	2	91	84	13.4	3.30	100	.240	.346	7	.123	-3	2	-0	-1	-0.4
1945	Cle-A†	18	12	.600	44	30	16	2	4	247¹	227	7	130	112	13.2	3.20	101	.247	.343	8	.094	-7	5	1	-1	-0.7
1946	Cle-A	11	15	.423	31	28	9	3	0	183¹	180	10	108	107	14.2	3.88	85	.259	.359	14	.222	1	-8	-12	-1	-1.5
1947	*NY-A	19	8	**.704**	34	30	17	4	2	241²	207	23	123	129	12.4	3.20	110	.227	.322	13	.146	-2	13	9	-2	0.6
1948	NY-A	16	7	.696	39	31	11	1	3	236¹	240	17	111	101	13.5	3.77	108	.268	.351	16	.193	0	14	8	-3	0.4
1949	*NY-A☆	17	6	.739	35	31	4	2	1	213²	200	15	123	105	13.8	4.00	101	.250	.353	17	.218	6	5	1	-0	0.6
1950	*NY-A★	16	12	.571	35	29	14	2	2	240²	215	12	138	160	13.5	3.74	115	.242	.349	15	.185	1	22	15	-1	1.5
1951	*NY-A	17	8	.680	40	26	16	**7**	**7**	221	171	12	100	126	11.2	3.05	125	**.213**	.304	14	.184	0	26	19	-3	1.8
1952	*NY-A☆	20	8	.714	35	29	24	**6**	6	244¹	194	10	97	**160**	11.0	**2.06**	**161**	.218	.300	13	.153	-1	**44**	34	-1	3.9
1953	*NY-A★	13	7	.650	41	15	5	1	13	145	140	9	61	86	12.8	3.41	108	.253	.333	5	.122	1	9	4	-2	0.5
1954	NY-A†	13	4	.765	36	18	5	4	7	157¹	133	13	66	100	11.6	3.32	104	.233	.316	8	.160	-0	7	2	-0	0.1
Total	13	182	107	.630	434	309	137	36	49	2492¹	2193	133	1261	1423	12.7	3.30	110	.238	.333	140	.163	-5	149	87	-16	6.9

● **ARCHIE REYNOLDS**   Reynolds, Archie Edward b: 1/3/46, Glendale, Cal.   BR/TR, 6'2", 205 lbs.   Deb: 8/15/68

YEAR	TM/L	W	L	PCT	G	GS	CG	SH	SV	IP	H	HR	BB	SO	RAT	ERA	ERA+	OAV	OOB	BH	AVG	PB	PR	/A	PD	TPI
1968	Chi-N	0	1	.000	7	1	0	0	0	13¹	14	1	7	6	14.9	6.75	47	.259	.355	1	.500	1	-6	-5	-0	-0.4
1969	Chi-N	0	1	.000	2	2	0	0	0	7¹	11	1	7	4	22.1	2.45	164	.379	.500	0	.000	0	1	1	-0	0.2
1970	Chi-N	0	2	.000	7	1	0	0	0	15	17	2	9	9	16.2	6.60	68	.298	.403	0	.000	0	-4	-3	-0	-0.4
1971	Cal-A	0	3	.000	15	1	0	0	0	27¹	32	2	18	15	16.5	4.61	70	.305	.407	0	.000	0	-3	-4	0	-0.4
1972	Mil-A	0	1	.000	5	2	0	0	0	18²	26	2	8	13	16.4	7.23	42	.338	.400	2	.500	1	-9	-9	-1	-0.4
Total	5	0	8	.000	36	7	0	0	0	81²	100	8	49	47	16.6	5.73	61	.311	.405	3	.273	2	-21	-21	-1	-1.4

● **CHARLIE REYNOLDS**   Reynolds, Charles E. b: 7/31/1857, Allegany, N.Y.   d: 5/1/13, Buffalo, N.Y.   Deb: 5/18/1882

YEAR	TM/L	W	L	PCT	G	GS	CG	SH	SV	IP	H	HR	BB	SO	RAT	ERA	ERA+	OAV	OOB	BH	AVG	PB	PR	/A	PD	TPI
1882	Phi-a	1	1	.500	2	2	1	0	0	12	18	0	3	4	15.8	5.25	57	.325	.360	1	.125	-1	-3	-3	-1	-0.5

● **CRAIG REYNOLDS**   Reynolds, Gordon Craig b: 12/27/52, Houston, Tex.   BL/TR, 6'1", 175 lbs.   Deb: 8/1/75   ♦

YEAR	TM/L	W	L	PCT	G	GS	CG	SH	SV	IP	H	HR	BB	SO	RAT	ERA	ERA+	OAV	OOB	BH	AVG	PB	PR	/A	PD	TPI
1986	*Hou-N	0	0	—	1	0	0	0	0	1	3	0	2	1	45.0	27.00	13	.500	.625	78	.249	0	-3	-3	0	0.0
1989	Hou-N	0	0	—	1	0	0	0	0	1	3	0	1	0	45.0	27.00	13	.500	.625	38	.201	0	-3	-3	0	0.0
Total	2	0	0	—	2	0	0	0	0	2	6	0	3	1	45.0	27.00	13	.500	.625	1142	.256	0	-5	-5	0	0.0

● **KEN REYNOLDS**   Reynolds, Kenneth Lee b: 1/4/47, Trevose, Pa.   BL/TL, 6', 180 lbs.   Deb: 9/5/70

YEAR	TM/L	W	L	PCT	G	GS	CG	SH	SV	IP	H	HR	BB	SO	RAT	ERA	ERA+	OAV	OOB	BH	AVG	PB	PR	/A	PD	TPI
1970	Phi-N	0	0	—	4	0	0	0	0	2¹	3	0	4	1	27.0	0.00	—	.333	.538	0	—	0	1	1	0	0.0
1971	Phi-N	5	9	.357	35	25	2	1	0	162¹	163	11	82	81	13.9	4.49	78	.269	.361	10	.200	2	-19	-17	-1	-1.3
1972	Phi-N	2	15	.118	33	23	2	0	0	154¹	149	17	60	87	12.2	4.26	84	.258	.329	8	.200	1	-14	-11	-0	-1.1
1973	Mil-A	0	1	.000	2	1	0	0	0	7¹	5	1	9	3	17.2	7.36	51	.200	.444	0	—	0	-3	-3	1	-0.2
1975	StL-N	0	1	.000	10	0	0	0	0	17	12	0	11	7	12.2	1.59	236	.214	.343	0	—	-0	4	4	1	0.3
1976	SD-N	0	3	.000	19	2	0	0	1	32¹	38	0	29	18	18.6	6.40	51	.309	.441	0	.000	-1	-10	-11	-0	-1.1
Total	6	7	29	.194	103	51	4	1	1	375²	370	29	196	197	13.8	4.46	80	.265	.358	18	.186	2	-41	-38	0	-3.4

● **SHANE REYNOLDS**   Reynolds, Richard Shane b: 3/26/68, Bastrop, La.   BR/TR, 6'3", 210 lbs.   Deb: 7/20/92

YEAR	TM/L	W	L	PCT	G	GS	CG	SH	SV	IP	H	HR	BB	SO	RAT	ERA	ERA+	OAV	OOB	BH	AVG	PB	PR	/A	PD	TPI
1992	Hou-N	1	3	.250	8	5	0	0	0	25¹	42	2	6	10	17.1	7.11	47	.385	.417	2	.500	1	-10	-11	0	-1.3
1993	Hou-N	0	0	—	5	1	0	0	0	11	11	0	6	10	13.9	0.82	473	.256	.347	1	.500	0	4	4	-0	0.4
1994	Hou-N	8	5	.615	33	14	1	1	0	124	128	10	21	110	11.3	3.05	133	.263	.302	3	.091	-2	16	14	0	1.2
Total	3	9	8	.529	46	20	1	1	0	160¹	181	12	33	130	12.3	3.54	111	.284	.325	6	.154	-0	10	7	1	-0.1

● **BOB REYNOLDS**   Reynolds, Robert Allen b: 1/21/47, Seattle, Wash.   BR/TR, 6', 205 lbs.   Deb: 9/19/69

YEAR	TM/L	W	L	PCT	G	GS	CG	SH	SV	IP	H	HR	BB	SO	RAT	ERA	ERA+	OAV	OOB	BH	AVG	PB	PR	/A	PD	TPI
1969	Mon-N	0	0	—	1	1	0	0	0	1¹	3	0	3	2	40.5	20.25	18	.429	.600	0	—	0	-2	-2	0	0.0
1971	StL-N	0	0	—	4	0	0	0	0	7	15	2	6	4	28.3	10.29	35	.441	.537	0	.000	-0	-5	-5	-0	0.0
	Mil-A	0	1	.000	3	0	0	0	0	6	4	0	3	1	10.5	3.00	116	.222	.333	0	.000	0	0	0	0	0.0
1972	Bal-A	0	0	—	3	0	0	0	0	9²	8	0	7	5	14.0	1.86	165	.258	.395	0	.000	-0	1	1	-0	0.0
1973	*Bal-A	7	5	.583	42	1	0	0	9	111	88	3	31	77	9.6	1.95	192	.219	.275	0	—	0	23	22	-2	2.5
1974	*Bal-A	7	5	.583	54	0	0	0	7	69¹	75	4	14	43	11.7	2.73	127	.278	.316	0	—	0	7	6	-0	1.0
1975	Bal-A	0	1	.000	7	0	0	0	0	6	11	1	1	1	18.0	9.00	39	.423	.444	0	—	0	-3	-4	0	-0.1
	Det-A	0	2	.000	21	0	0	0	3	34²	40	8	14	26	14.3	4.67	86	.288	.357	0	—	0	-3	-3	-0	-0.5
	Cle-A	0	2	.000	5	0	0	0	0	9²	11	0	3	5	13.0	4.66	81	.289	.341	0	—	0	-1	-1	-0	-0.2
	Yr	0	5	.000	33	0	0	0	5	50¹	62	9	18	32	14.3	5.19	75	.301	.357	0	—	0	-8	-7	-0	-0.8
Total	6	14	16	.467	140	2	0	0	21	254²	255	18	82	167	12.0	3.15	116	.264	.324	0	.000	-0	16	14	-3	2.7

● **ROSS REYNOLDS**   Reynolds, Ross Ernest "Doc" b: 8/20/1887, Barksdale, Tex.   d: 6/23/70, Ada, Okla.   BR/TR, 6'2", 185 lbs.   Deb: 5/2/14

YEAR	TM/L	W	L	PCT	G	GS	CG	SH	SV	IP	H	HR	BB	SO	RAT	ERA	ERA+	OAV	OOB	BH	AVG	PB	PR	/A	PD	TPI
1914	Det-A	5	3	.625	26	7	3	1	0	78	62	0	39	31	12.3	2.08	135	.230	.340	1	.048	-2	6	6	-1	0.3

YEAR	TM/L	W	L	PCT	G	GS	CG	SH	SV	IP	H	HR	BB	SO	RAT	ERA	ERA+	OAV	OOB	BH	AVG	PB	PR	/A	PD	TPI
1915	Det-A	0	1	.000	4	2	0	0	0	11¹	17	0	5	2	18.3	6.35	48	.378	.451	0	.000	-0	-4	-4	0	-0.3
Total	2	5	4	.556	30	9	3	1	0	89¹	79	0	44	33	13.1	2.62	108	.251	.355	1	.042	-2	1	2	-1	0.0

● ARMANDO REYNOSO
Reynoso, Armando Martin (Gutierrez) b: 5/1/66, San Luis Potosi, Mex. BR/TR, 6', 186 lbs. Deb: 8/11/91

YEAR	TM/L	W	L	PCT	G	GS	CG	SH	SV	IP	H	HR	BB	SO	RAT	ERA	ERA+	OAV	OOB	BH	AVG	PB	PR	/A	PD	TPI
1991	Atl-N	2	1	.667	6	5	0	0	0	23¹	26	4	10	10	15.0	6.17	63	.299	.390	0	.000	-0	-6	-6	2	-0.5
1992	Atl-N	1	0	1.000	3	1	0	0	1	7²	11	2	2	2	16.4	4.70	78	.393	.452	0	.000	-0	-1	-1	0	-0.1
1993	Col-N	12	11	.522	30	30	4	0	0	189	206	22	63	117	13.2	4.00	119	.277	.340	8	.127	-1	1	16	2	1.9
1994	Col-N	3	4	.429	9	9	1	0	0	52¹	54	5	22	25	14.1	4.82	103	.278	.369	3	.176	-0	-4	1	2	0.3
Total	4	18	16	.529	48	45	5	0	1	272¹	297	33	97	154	13.6	4.36	108	.282	.353	11	.124	-2	-10	10	6	1.6

● FLINT RHEM
Rhem, Charles Flint "Shad" b: 1/24/01, Rhems, S.C. d: 7/30/69, Columbia, S.C. BR/TR, 6'2", 180 lbs. Deb: 9/6/24

YEAR	TM/L	W	L	PCT	G	GS	CG	SH	SV	IP	H	HR	BB	SO	RAT	ERA	ERA+	OAV	OOB	BH	AVG	PB	PR	/A	PD	TPI
1924	StL-N	2	2	.500	6	3	3	0	1	32¹	31	1	17	20	13.4	4.45	85	.254	.345	2	.167	-0	-2	-2	0	-0.3
1925	StL-N	8	13	.381	30	23	8	1	1	170	204	16	58	66	14.1	4.92	88	.299	.357	14	.237	1	-12	-11	0	-1.1
1926	*StL-N	**20**	7	.741	34	34	20	1	0	258	241	12	75	72	11.1	3.21	122	.250	.305	18	.188	-2	18	20	1	1.8
1927	StL-N	10	12	.455	27	26	9	2	0	169¹	189	6	54	51	13.1	4.41	90	.285	.342	4	.068	-5	-9	-9	-3	-1.8
1928	*StL-N	11	8	.579	28	22	9	0	3	169²	199	13	71	47	14.5	4.14	97	.296	.365	11	.164	-1	-3	-3	2	-0.3
1930	*StL-N	12	8	.600	26	19	9	0	0	139²	173	11	37	47	13.7	4.45	113	.306	.352	12	.231	-1	8	9	-3	0.7
1931	*StL-N	11	10	.524	33	26	10	2	1	207¹	214	17	60	72	12.0	3.56	111	.268	.321	9	.130	-4	7	9	-2	0.2
1932	StL-N	4	2	.667	6	6	5	1	0	50	48	3	10	18	10.4	3.06	129	.257	.294	3	.188	0	5	5	0	0.6
	Phi-N	11	7	.611	26	20	10	0	1	168²	177	13	49	35	12.1	3.74	118	.269	.319	7	.113	-5	3	13	-0	0.7
	Yr	15	9	.625	32	26	15	1	1	218²	225	16	59	53	11.7	3.58	120	.266	.314	10	.128	-5	7	18	-0	1.3
1933	Phi-N	5	14	.263	28	19	3	0	2	125	182	10	33	27	15.6	6.62	58	.340	.381	4	.087	-4	-46	-39	-0	-5.5
1934	StL-N	1	0	1.000	5	1	0	0	1	15²	26	0	7	6	19.0	4.60	92	.394	.452	0	.000	-0	-1	-1	-0	-0.1
	Bos-N	8	8	.500	25	20	5	1	0	152²	164	5	38	56	11.9	3.60	106	.273	.317	3	.058	-5	8	4	1	0.0
	Yr	9	8	.529	30	21	5	1	1	168¹	190	5	45	62	12.6	3.69	105	.285	.331	3	.056	-5	7	3	1	-0.1
1935	Bos-N	0	5	.000	10	6	0	0	0	40¹	61	4	11	10	16.1	5.36	71	.341	.379	0	.000	-1	-6	-7	0	-0.8
1936	StL-N	2	1	.667	10	4	0	0	0	26²	49	2	9	7	19.6	6.75	58	.405	.446	1	.125	-0	-8	-8	-1	-0.9
Total	12	105	97	.520	294	229	91	8	10	1725¹	1958	113	529	534	13.1	4.20	98	.287	.340	88	.144	-28	-39	-20	-3	-6.8

● BILLY RHINES
Rhines, William Pearl "Bunker" b: 3/14/1869, Ridgway, Pa. d: 1/30/22, Ridgway, Pa. BR/TR, 5'11", 168 lbs. Deb: 4/22/1890

YEAR	TM/L	W	L	PCT	G	GS	CG	SH	SV	IP	H	HR	BB	SO	RAT	ERA	ERA+	OAV	OOB	BH	AVG	PB	PR	/A	PD	TPI
1890	Cin-N	28	17	.622	46	45	45	6	0	401¹	337	6	113	182	**10.4**	**1.95**	**182**	.221	**.281**	29	.188	-5	**72**	72	1	6.5
1891	Cin-N	17	24	.415	48	43	40	1	1	372²	364	4	124	138	12.3	2.87	117	.246	.314	18	.122	-9	20	21	3	1.3
1892	Cin-N	4	7	.364	12	10	7	0	0	83²	113	0	36	12	16.5	5.06	65	.310	.379	5	.167	1	-16	-17	-1	-1.7
1893	Lou-N	1	4	.200	5	5	3	0	0	31	49	3	19	0	20.6	8.71	51	.348	.436	1	.091	-2	-14	-15	0	-1.6
1895	Cin-N	19	10	.655	38	33	25	0	0	267²	322	4	76	72	14.1	4.81	103	.293	.351	25	.221	-4	-1	5	-0	0.1
1896	Cin-N	8	6	.571	19	17	11	3	0	143	128	1	48	32	**11.6**	**2.45**	**188**	.238	**.311**	10	.192	-3	30	34	0	2.5
1897	Cin-N	21	15	.583	41	32	26	1	0	288²	311	4	86	65	12.9	4.08	112	.273	.333	17	.159	-6	7	15	-2	0.7
1898	Pit-N	12	16	.429	31	29	27	2	0	258	289	0	61	48	12.7	3.52	101	.281	.329	15	.150	-4	2	1	5	0.2
1899	Pit-N	4	4	.500	9	9	4	0	0	54	59	3	13	6	12.7	6.00	64	.278	.331	10	.435	4	-13	-13	-1	-1.2
Total	9	114	103	.525	249	223	188	13	1	1900	1972	25	576	555	12.6	3.47	114	.262	.323	130	.176	-27	88	101	4	6.8

● BOB RHOADS
Rhoads, Robert Barton "Dusty" b: 10/4/1879, Wooster, Ohio d: 2/12/67, San Bernardino, Cal. BR/TR, 6'1", 215 lbs. Deb: 4/19/02

YEAR	TM/L	W	L	PCT	G	GS	CG	SH	SV	IP	H	HR	BB	SO	RAT	ERA	ERA+	OAV	OOB	BH	AVG	PB	PR	/A	PD	TPI
1902	Chi-N	4	8	.333	16	12	12	1	1	118	131	1	42	43	13.7	3.20	84	.281	.348	10	.222	0	-6	-7	-1	-0.7
1903	StL-N	5	8	.385	17	13	12	1	0	129	154	3	47	52	14.2	4.60	71	.303	.366	7	.140	-2	-19	-19	-1	-1.9
	Cle-A	2	3	.400	5	5	5	0	0	41	55	2	3	21	13.2	5.27	54	.320	.339	2	.118	-1	-10	-11	-0	-1.2
1904	Cle-A	10	9	.526	22	19	18	0	0	175¹	175	1	48	72	11.7	2.87	88	.261	.315	18	.196	0	-5	-7	-1	-0.8
1905	Cle-A	16	9	.640	28	26	24	4	0	235	219	4	55	61	10.9	2.83	93	.248	.300	21	.221	4	-5	-5	-0	-0.1
1906	Cle-A	22	10	.688	38	34	31	7	0	315	259	6	92	89	10.2	1.80	145	.227	.288	19	.161	-3	31	29	-2	2.4
1907	Cle-A	15	14	.517	35	31	23	5	1	275	258	0	84	76	11.7	2.29	110	.250	.315	17	.185	-1	8	7	-1	0.4
1908	Cle-A	18	12	.600	37	30	20	1	0	270	229	2	73	62	10.3	1.77	135	.239	.298	20	.222	4	19	19	2	2.9
1909	Cle-A	5	9	.357	20	15	9	2	0	131²	124	1	50	46	12.2	2.90	88	.281	.361	7	.163	-0	-6	-5	1	-0.5
Total	8	97	82	.542	218	185	154	21	2	1691²	1604	19	494	522	11.5	2.61	100	.256	.316	121	.188	-0	7	1	-3	0.5

● RICK RHODEN
Rhoden, Richard Alan b: 5/16/53, Boynton Beach, Fla. BR/TR, 6'3", 195 lbs. Deb: 7/5/74

YEAR	TM/L	W	L	PCT	G	GS	CG	SH	SV	IP	H	HR	BB	SO	RAT	ERA	ERA+	OAV	OOB	BH	AVG	PB	PR	/A	PD	TPI
1974	LA-N	1	0	1.000	4	0	0	0	0	9	5	1	4	7	9.0	2.00	170	.161	.257	1	.500	0	2	1	-0	0.2
1975	LA-N	3	3	.500	26	11	1	0	0	99¹	94	8	32	40	11.5	3.08	110	.253	.314	2	.071	-2	6	4	0	0.0
1976	LA-N★	12	3	.800	27	26	10	3	0	181	165	17	53	77	10.9	2.98	113	.242	.298	20	.308	7	10	8	-2	1.2
1977	*LA-N	16	10	.615	31	31	4	1	0	216¹	223	20	63	122	12.0	3.74	102	.270	.323	18	.231	5	4	2	-3	0.4
1978	*LA-N	10	8	.556	30	23	6	3	0	164²	160	13	51	79	11.7	3.66	96	.255	.314	7	.135	-0	-2	-3	-1	-0.5
1979	Pit-N	0	1	.000	1	1	0	0	0	5	5	0	2	2	12.6	7.20	54	.263	.333	1	1.000	0	-2	-2	0	-0.2
1980	Pit-N	7	5	.583	20	19	2	0	0	126²	133	9	40	70	12.5	3.84	95	.273	.332	15	.375	6	-3	-3	0	-0.3
1981	Pit-N	9	4	.692	21	21	4	2	0	136¹	147	6	53	76	13.3	3.89	92	.283	.352	9	.188	1	-6	-5	1	-0.3
1982	Pit-N	11	14	.440	35	35	6	1	0	230¹	239	14	70	128	12.2	4.14	89	.267	.321	22	.265	8	-14	-11	2	0.0
1983	Pit-N	13	13	.500	36	35	7	2	1	244¹	256	16	68	153	12.0	3.09	120	.276	.327	13	.151	-2	14	17	1	1.4
1984	Pit-N	14	9	.609	33	33	6	3	0	238¹	216	13	62	136	10.5	2.72	132	.243	.293	28	.333	10	23	**23**	2	3.5
1985	Pit-N	10	15	.400	35	35	4	0	0	213¹	254	18	69	128	13.9	4.47	80	.296	.352	14	.189	2	-21	-21	-0	-2.1
1986	Pit-N☆	15	12	.556	34	34	12	1	0	253²	211	17	76	159	10.3	2.84	135	.228	.288	25	.278	9	25	28	1	4.0
1987	NY-A	16	10	.615	30	29	4	0	0	181²	184	22	61	107	12.3	3.86	113	.268	.330	0	.000	0	12	10	-0	1.4
1988	NY-A	12	12	.500	30	30	4	0	0	197	206	20	56	94	12.3	4.29	92	.269	.325	0	.000	0	-7	-8	-1	-0.9
1989	Hou-N	2	6	.250	20	17	0	0	0	96²	108	7	41	41	14.2	4.28	79	.289	.364	6	.207	1	-8	-10	1	-0.6
Total	16	151	125	.547	413	380	69	17	1	2593²	2606	198	801	1419	12.0	3.59	103	.264	.321	181	.238	45	33	32	1	8.1

● ARTHUR LEE RHODES
Rhodes, Arthur Lee b: 10/24/69, Waco, Tex. BL/TL, 6'2", 190 lbs. Deb: 8/21/91

YEAR	TM/L	W	L	PCT	G	GS	CG	SH	SV	IP	H	HR	BB	SO	RAT	ERA	ERA+	OAV	OOB	BH	AVG	PB	PR	/A	PD	TPI
1991	Bal-A	0	3	.000	8	8	0	0	0	36	47	4	23	23	17.5	8.00	49	.320	.412	0	—	0	-16	-16	-1	-0.9
1992	Bal-A	7	5	.583	15	15	2	1	0	94¹	87	6	38	77	12.0	3.63	111	.249	.325	0	—	0	3	4	0	0.4
1993	Bal-A	5	6	.455	17	17	0	0	0	85²	91	16	49	49	14.8	6.51	69	.274	.369	0	—	0	-21	-19	-1	-2.4
1994	Bal-A	3	5	.375	10	10	3	2	0	52²	51	8	30	47	14.2	5.81	78	.254	.356	0	—	0	-6	-4	0	-0.7
Total	4	15	19	.441	50	50	5	3	0	268²	276	34	140	196	14.1	5.56	78	.268	.358	0	—	0	-39	-36	-2	-3.6

● CHARLIE RHODES
Rhodes, Charles Anderson "Dusty" b: 4/7/1885, Caney, Kan. d: 10/26/18, Caney, Kan. BR/TR, 5'7", 180 lbs. Deb: 7/26/06

YEAR	TM/L	W	L	PCT	G	GS	CG	SH	SV	IP	H	HR	BB	SO	RAT	ERA	ERA+	OAV	OOB	BH	AVG	PB	PR	/A	PD	TPI
1906	StL-N	3	4	.429	9	6	3	0	0	45	37	0	20	32	12.6	3.40	77	.223	.328	3	.188	-0	-4	-4	0	-0.6
1908	Cin-N	0	0	—	1	0	0	0	0	4	1	0	2	4	9.0	0.00	—	.077	.250	0	.000	-0	1	1	0	0.1
	StL-N	1	2	.333	4	4	3	0	0	33	23	2	12	15	9.8	3.00	79	.200	.281	3	.250	1	-2	-2	1	-0.1
	Yr	1	2	.333	5	4	3	0	0	37	24	2	14	19	9.5	2.68	88	.186	.271	3	.231	1	-1	-1	1	-0.1
1909	StL-N	3	5	.375	12	10	4	0	0	61	55	0	33	25	13.3	3.98	64	.256	.360	4	.211	1	-9	-10	2	-0.9
Total	3	7	11	.389	26	20	10	0	0	143	116	2	67	76	12.1	3.46	73	.228	.329	10	.208	2	-14	-15	4	-1.6

● GORDON RHODES
Rhodes, John Gordon "Dusty" b: 8/11/07, Winnemucca, Nev. d: 3/24/60, Long Beach, Cal. BR/TR, 6', 187 lbs. Deb: 4/29/29

YEAR	TM/L	W	L	PCT	G	GS	CG	SH	SV	IP	H	HR	BB	SO	RAT	ERA	ERA+	OAV	OOB	BH	AVG	PB	PR	/A	PD	TPI
1929	NY-A	0	4	.000	10	4	0	0	0	42²	57	3	16	13	15.8	4.85	80	.333	.397	3	.300	1	-3	-5	-1	-0.4
1930	NY-A	3	0	1.000	3	0	0	0	0	2	3	0	4	1	31.5	9.00	48	.500	.700	0	—	0	-1	-1	0	-0.0
1931	NY-A	6	3	.667	18	11	4	0	0	87	82	3	52	36	13.9	3.41	116	.235	.334	6	.214	1	9	5	0	0.6
1932	NY-A	1	2	.333	6	2	0	0	1	24	25	0	21	15	17.3	7.88	52	.275	.411	2	.286	-0	-9	-10	1	-0.8
	Bos-A	1	8	.111	16	11	5	0	0	79¹	79	5	31	22	12.5	5.11	88	.261	.329	2	.074	-2	-6	-5	-0	-0.7
	Yr	2	10	.167	22	13	5	0	1	103¹	104	5	52	37	13.6	5.75	76	.264	.350	4	.118	-2	-15	-16	1	-1.5
1933	Bos-A	12	15	.444	34	29	14	0	0	232	242	13	93	85	13.0	4.03	109	.265	.334	23	.267	4	6	9	-1	1.3

YEAR TM/L	W	L	PCT	G	GS	CG	SH	SV	IP	H	HR	BB	SO	RAT	ERA	ERA+	OAV	OOB	BH	AVG	PB	PR	/A	PD	TPI
1934 Bos-A	12	12	.500	44	31	10	0	2	219	247	10	98	79	14.3	4.56	105	.285	.360	10	.133	-3	-2	6	1	0.3
1935 Bos-A	2	10	.167	34	19	1	0	2	146¹	195	14	60	44	15.7	5.41	88	.324	.387	7	.146	-4	-16	-11	-1	-1.1
1936 Phi-A	9	20	.310	35	28	13	1	1	216¹	266	26	102	61	15.4	5.74	89	.304	.378	16	.213	-2	-17	-15	-3	-2.0
Total 8	43	74	.368	200	135	47	1	5	1048²	1196	74	477	356	14.4	4.85	95	.286	.361	69	.194	-5	-37	-28	-3	-2.8

● **BILL RHODES**   Rhodes, William Clarence b: Pottstown, Pa. Deb: 6/14/1893

YEAR TM/L	W	L	PCT	G	GS	CG	SH	SV	IP	H	HR	BB	SO	RAT	ERA	ERA+	OAV	OOB	BH	AVG	PB	PR	/A	PD	TPI
1893 Lou-N	5	12	.294	20	19	17	0	0	151²	244	10	66	22	19.0	7.60	58	.352	.416	9	.129	-4	-49	-54	-2	-4.4

● **DENNIS RIBANT**   Ribant, Dennis Joseph b: 9/20/41, Detroit, Mich. BR/TR, 5'11", 175 lbs. Deb: 8/9/64

YEAR TM/L	W	L	PCT	G	GS	CG	SH	SV	IP	H	HR	BB	SO	RAT	ERA	ERA+	OAV	OOB	BH	AVG	PB	PR	/A	PD	TPI
1964 NY-N	1	5	.167	14	7	1	1	1	57²	65	8	9	35	11.5	5.15	69	.281	.308	2	.100	-0	-10	-10	-1	-1.1
1965 NY-N	1	3	.250	19	1	0	0	3	35¹	29	5	6	13	8.9	3.82	92	.228	.263	0	.000	-1	-1	-1	-0	-0.3
1966 NY-N	11	9	.550	39	26	10	1	3	188¹	184	20	40	84	10.8	3.20	114	.254	.294	12	.197	0	8	9	0	1.1
1967 Pit-N	9	8	.529	38	22	2	0	0	172	186	16	40	75	12.0	4.08	82	.280	.324	16	.267	5	-14	-14	2	-0.6
1968 Det-A	2	2	.500	14	0	0	0	1	24¹	20	1	10	7	11.5	2.22	136	.217	.301	1	.200	-0	2	2	-1	0.4
Chi-A	0	2	.000	17	0	0	0	1	31¹	42	3	17	20	17.5	6.03	50	.318	.404	0	.000	-1	-11	-10	-0	-0.8
Yr	2	4	.333	31	0	0	0	2	55²	62	4	27	27	14.7	4.37	69	.276	.358	1	.083	-0	-9	-8	-0	-0.4
1969 StL-N	0	0	—	1	0	0	0	0	1¹	1	1	1	0	33.8	13.50	26	.571	.625	0	—	0	-1	-1	-0	0.0
Cin-N	0	0	—	7	0	0	0	0	8¹	6	1	3	7	9.7	1.08	348	.188	.257	0	—	0	2	2	-0	0.0
Yr	0	0	—	8	0	0	0	0	9²	10	2	4	7	13.0	2.79	134	.250	.318	0	—	0	1	1	-0	0.0
Total 6	24	29	.453	149	56	13	2	9	518²	536	55	126	241	11.6	3.87	90	.267	.312	31	.195	4	-24	-23	0	-1.3

● **FRANK RICCELLI**   Riccelli, Frank Joseph b: 2/24/53, Syracuse, N.Y. BL/TL, 6'3", 205 lbs. Deb: 9/11/76

YEAR TM/L	W	L	PCT	G	GS	CG	SH	SV	IP	H	HR	BB	SO	RAT	ERA	ERA+	OAV	OOB	BH	AVG	PB	PR	/A	PD	TPI
1976 SF-N	1	1	.500	4	3	0	0	0	16	16	1	5	11	11.8	5.63	64	.258	.313	1	.167	-0	-4	-4	-0	-0.4
1978 Hou-N	0	0	—	2	0	0	0	0	3	1	0	1	3	3.0	0.00	—	.100	.100	0	—	0	1	1	-0	0.0
1979 Hou-N	2	2	.500	11	2	0	0	0	22	22	0	18	20	16.4	4.09	86	.262	.392	2	.333	1	-1	-1	1	-0.1
Total 3	3	3	.500	17	5	0	0	0	41	39	1	23	32	13.6	4.39	81	.250	.346	3	.250	1	-3	-4	0	-0.5

● **SAM RICE**   Rice, Edgar Charles b: 2/20/1890, Morocco, Ind. d: 10/13/74, Rossmoor, Md. BL/TR, 5'9", 150 lbs. Deb: 8/7/15 H♦

YEAR TM/L	W	L	PCT	G	GS	CG	SH	SV	IP	H	HR	BB	SO	RAT	ERA	ERA+	OAV	OOB	BH	AVG	PB	PR	/A	PD	TPI
1915 Was-A	1	0	1.000	4	2	1	0	0	18	13	0	9	11	11.0	2.00	148	.213	.314	1	.375	2	2	2	-0	0.2
1916 Was-A	0	1	.000	5	1	0	0	0	21¹	18	0	10	3	11.8	2.95	95	.237	.326	59	.299	2	-0	-0	-0	0.1
Total 2	1	1	.500	9	3	1	0	0	39¹	31	0	19	12	11.4	2.52	114	.226	.321	2987	.322	2	2	2	-0	0.3

● **PAT RICE**   Rice, Patrick Edward b: 11/2/63, Rapid City, S.Dak. BR/TR, 6'2", 200 lbs. Deb: 5/18/91

YEAR TM/L	W	L	PCT	G	GS	CG	SH	SV	IP	H	HR	BB	SO	RAT	ERA	ERA+	OAV	OOB	BH	AVG	PB	PR	/A	PD	TPI
1991 Sea-A	1	1	.500	7	2	0	0	0	21	18	3	10	12	12.4	3.00	137	.234	.330	0	—	0	3	3	-0	0.2

● **WOODY RICH**   Rich, Woodrow Earl b: 3/9/16, Morganton, N.C. d: 4/18/83, Morganton, N.C. BL/TR, 6'2", 185 lbs. Deb: 4/22/39

YEAR TM/L	W	L	PCT	G	GS	CG	SH	SV	IP	H	HR	BB	SO	RAT	ERA	ERA+	OAV	OOB	BH	AVG	PB	PR	/A	PD	TPI
1939 Bos-A	4	3	.571	21	12	3	0	1	77	78	2	35	24	13.8	4.91	96	.264	.352	7	.259	0	-2	-2	1	0.0
1940 Bos-A	1	0	1.000	3	1	1	0	0	11²	9	1	8	7	7.7	0.77	583	.214	.233	0	.000	-1	5	5	-0	0.3
1941 Bos-A	0	0	—	2	1	0	0	0	3²	8	1	2	4	24.5	17.18	24	.421	.476	0	—	-1	-5	-5	-0	0.0
1944 Bos-N	1	1	.500	7	2	1	0	0	25	32	3	12	6	16.9	5.76	66	.327	.416	1	.125	-1	-6	-5	0	-0.4
Total 4	6	4	.600	33	16	5	0	1	117¹	127	8	50	42	14.2	5.06	89	.280	.361	8	.205	-1	-9	-7	2	-0.1

● **J.R. RICHARD**   Richard, James Rodney b: 3/7/50, Vienna, La. BR/TR, 6'8", 222 lbs. Deb: 9/5/71

YEAR TM/L	W	L	PCT	G	GS	CG	SH	SV	IP	H	HR	BB	SO	RAT	ERA	ERA+	OAV	OOB	BH	AVG	PB	PR	/A	PD	TPI
1971 Hou-N	2	1	.667	4	4	1	0	0	21	17	1	16	29	14.1	3.43	98	.215	.347	0	.000	-0	0	-0	-0	-0.1
1972 Hou-N	1	0	1.000	4	1	0	0	0	6	10	0	8	8	30.0	13.50	25	.385	.556	0	—	0	-7	-7	-0	-0.9
1973 Hou-N	6	2	.750	16	10	2	1	0	72	54	2	38	75	11.6	4.00	91	.210	.314	5	.179	0	-3	-3	-1	-0.4
1974 Hou-N	2	3	.400	15	9	0	0	0	64²	58	3	36	42	13.2	4.18	83	.243	.344	3	.143	0	-4	-5	-1	-0.4
1975 Hou-N	12	10	.545	33	31	7	1	0	203	178	8	138	176	14.2	4.39	77	.203	.359	4	.203	15	-23	-22	-2	-2.0
1976 Hou-N	20	15	.571	39	39	14	3	0	291	221	14	151	214	11.6	2.75	116	**.212**	.314	14	.140	0	24	14	-1	1.6
1977 Hou-N	18	12	.600	36	36	13	3	0	267	212	18	104	214	10.7	2.97	120	.218	.293	20	.230	6	28	18	3	2.9
1978 Hou-N	18	11	.621	36	36	16	3	0	275¹	192	12	141	303	11.0	3.11	107	**.196**	.299	18	.178	1	14	6	2	1.0
1979 Hou-N	18	13	.581	38	38	19	4	0	292¹	220	13	98	313	9.9	2.71	130	**.209**	.278	12	.126	-0	**33**	**26**	-1	2.5
1980 Hou-N★	10	4	.714	17	17	4	4	0	113²	65	2	40	119	8.3	1.90	173	.166	.244	6	.154	1	21	18	-1	2.2
Total 10	107	71	.601	238	221	76	19	0	1606	1227	73	770	1493	11.3	3.15	108	.212	.306	93	.168	12	91	44	0	6.4

● **DUANE RICHARDS**   Richards, Duane Lee b: 12/16/36, Spartanburg, Ind. BR/TR, 6'3", 200 lbs. Deb: 9/25/60

YEAR TM/L	W	L	PCT	G	GS	CG	SH	SV	IP	H	HR	BB	SO	RAT	ERA	ERA+	OAV	OOB	BH	AVG	PB	PR	/A	PD	TPI
1960 Cin-N	0	0	—	2	0	0	0	0	3	5	0	2	2	21.0	9.00	42	.385	.467	0	—	0	-2	-2	0	0.0

● **RUSTY RICHARDS**   Richards, Russell Earl b: 1/27/65, Houston, Tex. BL/TL, 6'4", 200 lbs. Deb: 9/20/89

YEAR TM/L	W	L	PCT	G	GS	CG	SH	SV	IP	H	HR	BB	SO	RAT	ERA	ERA+	OAV	OOB	BH	AVG	PB	PR	/A	PD	TPI
1989 Atl-N	0	0	—	2	2	0	0	0	9¹	10	2	6	4	16.4	4.82	76	.278	.395	0	.000	-0	-1	-1	0	0.0
1990 Atl-N	0	0	—	1	0	0	0	0	1	2	1	1	0	27.0	27.00	15	.400	.500	0	—	0	-3	-3	0	0.0
Total 2	0	0	—	3	2	0	0	0	10¹	12	3	7	4	17.4	6.97	53	.293	.408	0	.000	-0	-4	-4	0	0.0

● **HARDY RICHARDSON**   Richardson, Abram Harding "Old True Blue"
b: 4/21/1855, Clarksboro, N.J. d: 1/14/31, Utica, N.Y. BR/TR, 5'9.5", 170 lbs. Deb: 5/1/1879 ♦

YEAR TM/L	W	L	PCT	G	GS	CG	SH	SV	IP	H	HR	BB	SO	RAT	ERA	ERA+	OAV	OOB	BH	AVG	PB	PR	/A	PD	TPI
1885 Buf-N	0	0	—	1	0	0	0	0	4	5	0	3	1	18.0	2.25	132	.294	.400	136	.319	0	0	0	0	0.0
1886 Det-N	3	0	1.000	4	0	0	0	0	12	11	1	10	5	15.8	4.50	74	.208	.343	189	.351	2	-2	-0	-3	-0.3
Total 2	3	0	1.000	5	0	0	0	0	16	16	1	13	6	16.3	3.94	82	.229	.349	1688	.299	3	-1	-1	0	-0.3

● **DANNY RICHARDSON**   Richardson, Daniel b: 1/25/1863, Elmira, N.Y. d: 9/12/26, New York, N.Y. BR/TR, 5'8", 165 lbs. Deb: 5/22/1884 M♦

YEAR TM/L	W	L	PCT	G	GS	CG	SH	SV	IP	H	HR	BB	SO	RAT	ERA	ERA+	OAV	OOB	BH	AVG	PB	PR	/A	PD	TPI
1885 NY-N	7	1	.875	9	8	7	1	0	75	58	0	18	21	9.1	2.40	111	.205	.252	52	.263	2	4	2	-1	0.3
1886 NY-N	0	2	.000	5	1	1	0	0	25	33	1	17	17	15.8	5.76	56	.320	.386	55	.232	1	-7	-7	1	-0.3
1887 NY-N	0	0	—	1	0	0	0	0	0	0	0	0	1	—	—	—	1.000	125	.278	0	0	0	0	0.0
Total 3	7	3	.700	15	9	8	1	0	100	91	1	30	38	10.9	3.24	86	.236	.291	1129	.254	3	-3	-5	-2	-0.6

● **GORDIE RICHARDSON**   Richardson, Gordon Clark b: 7/19/38, Colquitt, Ga. BR/TL, 6', 185 lbs. Deb: 7/26/64

YEAR TM/L	W	L	PCT	G	GS	CG	SH	SV	IP	H	HR	BB	SO	RAT	ERA	ERA+	OAV	OOB	BH	AVG	PB	PR	/A	PD	TPI
1964 *StL-N	4	2	.667	19	6	1	0	1	47	42	2	15	28	10.7	2.30	166	.231	.296	1	.077	-0	6	8	-1	0.9
1965 NY-N	2	2	.500	35	0	0	0	2	52¹	41	5	16	43	10.1	3.78	93	.224	.294	0	.000	-1	-1	-1	-0	-0.2
1966 NY-N	0	2	.000	15	1	0	0	1	18²	24	7	6	15	14.5	9.16	40	.312	.361	0	.000	-0	-12	-11	-0	-1.3
Total 3	6	6	.500	69	7	1	0	4	118	105	14	37	86	11.1	4.04	90	.242	.307	1	.048	-1	-6	-5	-2	-0.6

● **JEFF RICHARDSON**   Richardson, Jeffrey Scott b: 8/29/63, Wichita, Kan. BR/TR, 6'3", 185 lbs. Deb: 9/19/90

YEAR TM/L	W	L	PCT	G	GS	CG	SH	SV	IP	H	HR	BB	SO	RAT	ERA	ERA+	OAV	OOB	BH	AVG	PB	PR	/A	PD	TPI
1990 Cal-A	0	0	—	1	0	0	0	0	0¹	1	0	0	0	27.0	—	—	.500	.500	0	—	0	0	0	0	0.0

● **JACK RICHARDSON**   Richardson, John William b: 10/3/1891, Central City, Ill. d: 1/18/70, Marion, Ill. BB/TR, 6'3", 197 lbs. Deb: 9/17/15

YEAR TM/L	W	L	PCT	G	GS	CG	SH	SV	IP	H	HR	BB	SO	RAT	ERA	ERA+	OAV	OOB	BH	AVG	PB	PR	/A	PD	TPI
1915 Phi-A	0	1	.000	3	3	2	0	0	24	21	0	14	11	13.5	2.63	111	.253	.367	0	.000	-1	1	1	-0	-0.1
1916 Phi-A	0	0	—	1	0	0	0	0	0²	2	0	1	1	40.5	40.50	7	.667	.750	0	—	0	-3	-3	-0	0.0
Total 2	0	1	.000	4	3	2	0	0	24²	23	0	15	12	14.2	3.65	80	.267	.382	0	.000	-1	-2	-2	-0	-0.1

● **PETE RICHERT**   Richert, Peter Gerard b: 10/29/39, Floral Park, N.Y. BL/TL, 6', 184 lbs. Deb: 4/12/62

YEAR TM/L	W	L	PCT	G	GS	CG	SH	SV	IP	H	HR	BB	SO	RAT	ERA	ERA+	OAV	OOB	BH	AVG	PB	PR	/A	PD	TPI
1962 LA-N	5	4	.556	19	12	1	0	0	81¹	77	6	45	75	13.6	3.87	94	.249	.346	2	.080	-1	-2	-2	1	-0.3
1963 LA-N	5	3	.625	20	12	1	0	0	78	80	7	28	54	12.6	4.50	67	.262	.326	4	.182	1	-11	-13	-1	-1.4
1964 LA-N	2	3	.400	8	6	1	0	0	34²	38	2	18	25	15.1	4.15	78	.271	.363	1	.091	-0	-2	-4	1	-0.4
1965 Was-A★	15	12	.556	34	29	6	0	0	194	146	8	84	161	10.8	2.60	134	.210	.297	10	.156	-0	19	19	-0	2.5
1966 Was-A★	14	14	.500	36	34	7	0	0	245²	196	36	69	195	9.7	3.37	103	.215	.271	14	.163	2	2	2	-2	0.2
1967 Was-A	2	6	.250	11	10	1	1	0	54¹	49	5	15	41	10.8	4.64	68	.237	.291	1	.059	-1	-8	-9	-1	-1.5

YEAR	TM/L	W	L	PCT	G	GS	CG	SH	SV	IP	H	HR	BB	SO	RAT	ERA	ERA+	OAV	OOB	BH	AVG	PB	PR	/A	PD	TPI
	Bal-A	7	10	.412	26	19	5	1	2	132¹	107	11	41	90	10.1	2.99	105	.220	.282	4	.108	-1	4	2	1	0.3
	Yr	9	16	.360	37	29	6	2	2	186²	156	16	56	131	10.3	3.47	91	.223	.282	5	.093	-2	-5	-7	-1	-1.2
1968	Bal-A	6	3	.667	36	0	0	0	6	62¹	51	7	12	47	9.5	3.47	84	.225	.273	2	.200	0	-3	-4	1	-0.5
1969	*Bal-A	7	4	.636	44	0	0	0	12	57¹	42	7	14	54	8.8	2.20	162	.202	.252	1	.125	-0	9	9	-1	2.0
1970	*Bal-A	7	2	.778	50	0	0	0	13	54²	36	5	24	66	10.0	1.98	185	.194	.289	0	.000	-0	11	10	0	2.2
1971	*Bal-A	3	5	.375	35	0	0	0	4	36¹	26	3	22	35	12.1	3.47	97	.205	.327	0	.000	-0	-0	-0	0	-0.1
1972	LA-N	2	3	.400	37	0	0	0	6	52	42	3	18	38	10.6	2.25	148	.219	.289	3	.500	1	7	6	-0	0.8
1973	LA-N	3	3	.500	39	0	0	0	7	51	44	5	19	31	11.3	3.18	108	.234	.308	1	.200	0	3	1	1	0.3
1974	StL-N	0	0	—	13	0	0	0	1	11¹	10	1	11	4	16.7	2.38	150	.244	.404	0	—	0	2	2	-0	0.5
	Phi-N	2	1	.667	21	0	0	0	0	20¹	15	0	4	9	8.4	2.21	171	.205	.247	0	—	0	3	4	-0	0.5
	Yr	2	1	.667	34	0	0	0	1	31²	25	1	15	13	11.4	2.27	163	.216	.305	0	—	0	5	5	-1	0.5
Total 13		80	73	.523	429	122	22	3	51	1165²	959	116	424	925	10.8	3.19	106	.223	.295	43	.145	-1	34	24	-3	4.7

● LEW RICHIE
Richie, Lewis A. b: 8/23/1883, Ambler, Pa. d: 8/15/36, South Montain, Pa. BR/TR, 5'8", 165 lbs. Deb: 5/8/06

YEAR	TM/L	W	L	PCT	G	GS	CG	SH	SV	IP	H	HR	BB	SO	RAT	ERA	ERA+	OAV	OOB	BH	AVG	PB	PR	/A	PD	TPI
1906	Phi-N	9	11	.450	33	22	14	3	0	205²	170	3	79	65	11.2	2.41	109	.230	.309	3	.050	-3	5	5	-3	-0.2
1907	Phi-N	6	6	.500	25	12	9	2	0	117	88	0	38	40	10.1	1.77	137	.215	.290	7	.163	0	9	8	-1	0.8
1908	Phi-N	7	10	.412	25	15	13	2	1	157²	125	1	49	58	10.3	1.83	133	.233	.304	11	.212	2	9	10	-1	1.2
1909	Phi-N	1	1	.500	11	1	0	0	1	45	40	0	18	11	12.0	2.00	130	.263	.349	4	.250	1	3	3	-1	0.2
	Bos-N	7	7	.500	22	13	9	2	2	131²	118	2	44	42	11.1	2.32	121	.247	.312	5	.114	-2	4	7	-3	0.2
	Yr	8	8	.500	33	14	9	2	3	176²	158	2	62	53	11.3	2.24	123	.250	.318	9	.150	-1	7	10	-4	0.4
1910	Bos-N	0	3	.000	4	2	0	0	0	16¹	20	0	9	7	16.0	2.76	121	.317	.403	0	.000	-1	1	1	1	0.2
	*Chi-N	11	4	.733	30	11	8	3	4	130	117	1	51	52	11.8	2.70	107	.257	.336	9	.225	3	5	3	1	0.6
	Yr	11	7	.611	34	13	8	3	4	146¹	137	1	60	59	12.3	2.71	108	.264	.344	9	.205	2	5	4	1	0.8
1911	Chi-N	15	11	.577	36	28	18	4	1	253	213	6	103	98	11.3	2.31	143	.235	.315	14	.154	-3	31	28	0	2.4
1912	Chi-N	16	8	.667	39	27	15	4	0	238	222	5	74	69	11.4	2.95	113	.261	.324	10	.132	-3	12	10	-2	0.3
1913	Chi-N	2	4	.333	16	5	0	0	0	65	77	3	30	15	15.0	5.82	55	.304	.380	2	.118	-0	-19	-19	-1	-1.7
Total 8		74	65	.532	241	136	86	20	9	1359¹	1190	21	495	437	11.4	2.54	115	.246	.320	65	.147	-7	60	58	-11	4.0

● BERYL RICHMOND
Richmond, Beryl Justice b: 8/24/07, Glen Easton, W.Va. d: 4/24/80, Cameron, W.Va. BB/TL, 6'1", 185 lbs. Deb: 4/21/33

YEAR	TM/L	W	L	PCT	G	GS	CG	SH	SV	IP	H	HR	BB	SO	RAT	ERA	ERA+	OAV	OOB	BH	AVG	PB	PR	/A	PD	TPI
1933	Chi-N	0	0	—	4	0	0	0	0	4²	10	0	2	2	23.1	1.93	170	.455	.500	0	.000	-0	1	1	-0	0.0
1934	Cin-N	1	2	.333	6	2	1	0	0	19¹	23	0	10	9	15.4	3.72	110	.303	.384	0	.000	-1	1	1	-0	0.0
Total 2		1	2	.333	10	2	1	0	0	24	33	0	12	11	16.9	3.38	116	.337	.409	0	.000	-1	1	1	-0	0.0

● LEE RICHMOND
Richmond, J. Lee b: 5/5/1857, Sheffield, Ohio d: 10/1/29, Toledo, Ohio TL, 5'10", 142 lbs. Deb: 9/27/1879 ♦

YEAR	TM/L	W	L	PCT	G	GS	CG	SH	SV	IP	H	HR	BB	SO	RAT	ERA	ERA+	OAV	OOB	BH	AVG	PB	PR	/A	PD	TPI
1879	Bos-N	1	0	1.000	1	1	1	0	0	9	4	0	1	11	5.0	2.00	124	.114	.139	2	.333	0	0	0	-0	0.1
1880	Wor-N	32	32	.500	74	66	57	5	3	590²	541	7	74	243	9.4	2.15	121	.232	.255	70	.227	-4	15	29	-6	1.9
1881	Wor-N	25	26	.490	53	52	50	3	0	462¹	547	7	68	156	12.0	3.39	89	.284	.309	63	.250	-1	-31	-19	2	-1.5
1882	Wor-N	14	33	.298	48	46	44	0	0	411	525	11	88	123	13.4	3.74	83	.294	.327	64	.281	-7	-39	-29	3	-1.7
1883	Pro-N	3	7	.300	12	12	8	0	0	92	122	2	27	13	14.6	3.33	93	.314	.358	55	.284	3	-2	-2	-0	-0.7
1886	Cin-a	0	2	.000	3	2	1	0	0	18	24	0	11	6	18.5	8.00	44	.308	.407	8	.276	0	-9	-9	-0	-0.7
Total 6		75	100	.429	191	179	161	8	3	1583	1763	27	269	552	11.6	3.06	95	.269	.298	262	.257	7	-66	-28	-1	-1.9

● RAY RICHMOND
Richmond, Raymond Sinclair b: 6/15/1896, Fillmore, Ill. d: 10/21/69, DeSoto, Mo. BR/TR, 6', 175 lbs. Deb: 9/25/20

YEAR	TM/L	W	L	PCT	G	GS	CG	SH	SV	IP	H	HR	BB	SO	RAT	ERA	ERA+	OAV	OOB	BH	AVG	PB	PR	/A	PD	TPI
1920	StL-A	2	0	1.000	2	2	1	0	0	17	18	0	9	4	14.3	6.35	62	.273	.360	1	.167	-0	-5	-5	0	-0.4
1921	StL-A	0	1	.000	6	2	0	0	0	14¹	21	1	13	6	23.2	11.30	40	.362	.500	0	.000	-1	-11	-11	-0	-0.7
Total 2		2	1	.667	8	4	1	0	0	31¹	39	1	22	10	18.4	8.62	48	.315	.430	1	.100	-1	-16	-15	0	-1.1

● REGGIE RICHTER
Richter, Emil Henry b: 9/14/1888, Dusseldorf, Germany d: 8/2/34, Winfield, Ill. BR/TR, 6'2", 180 lbs. Deb: 5/30/11

YEAR	TM/L	W	L	PCT	G	GS	CG	SH	SV	IP	H	HR	BB	SO	RAT	ERA	ERA+	OAV	OOB	BH	AVG	PB	PR	/A	PD	TPI
1911	Chi-N	1	3	.250	22	5	0	0	2	54²	62	1	20	34	14.0	3.13	106	.307	.378	1	.100	-1	2	1	-0	0.0

● DICK RICKETTS
Ricketts, Richard James b: 12/4/33, Pottstown, Pa. d: 3/6/88, Rochester, N.Y. BL/TR, 6'7", 215 lbs. Deb: 6/14/59 F

YEAR	TM/L	W	L	PCT	G	GS	CG	SH	SV	IP	H	HR	BB	SO	RAT	ERA	ERA+	OAV	OOB	BH	AVG	PB	PR	/A	PD	TPI
1959	StL-N	1	6	.143	12	9	0	0	0	55²	68	7	30	25	15.8	5.82	73	.301	.383	1	.056	-2	-12	-10	-2	-1.4

● ELMER RIDDLE
Riddle, Elmer Ray b: 7/31/14, Columbus, Ga. d: 5/14/84, Columbus, Ga. BR/TR, 5'11.5", 170 lbs. Deb: 10/1/39 F

YEAR	TM/L	W	L	PCT	G	GS	CG	SH	SV	IP	H	HR	BB	SO	RAT	ERA	ERA+	OAV	OOB	BH	AVG	PB	PR	/A	PD	TPI
1939	Cin-N	0	0	—	1	0	0	0	0	2	1	0	0	0	4.5	0.00	—	.143	.143	0	—	0	1	1	-0	0.0
1940	*Cin-N	1	2	.333	15	1	1	0	2	33²	30	0	17	14	12.6	1.87	202	.236	.343	1	.143	0	7	7	-0	0.7
1941	Cin-N	19	4	.826	33	22	15	4	1	216²	180	8	59	80	10.1	2.24	160	.224	.282	16	.225	3	33	33	-1	3.6
1942	Cin-N	7	11	.389	29	19	7	1	0	158¹	157	7	79	78	13.6	3.69	89	.260	.349	15	.259	3	-7	-7	-1	-0.6
1943	Cin-N	21	11	.656	36	33	19	5	3	260¹	235	6	107	69	11.9	2.63	126	.245	.322	18	.194	1	22	20	-1	2.5
1944	Cin-N	2	2	.500	4	4	2	0	0	26²	25	0	12	6	12.5	4.05	86	.250	.330	1	.125	-0	-2	-1	-0	-0.2
1945	Cin-N	1	4	.200	12	3	0	0	0	29²	39	4	20	5	20.0	8.19	46	.333	.458	3	.273	1	-14	-15	-2	-1.9
1947	Cin-N	1	0	1.000	16	3	0	0	0	30¹	42	5	31	8	22.0	8.31	49	.333	.468	0	.000	-0	-14	-14	-1	-0.5
1948	Pit-N☆	12	10	.545	28	27	12	3	1	191	184	20	81	63	12.6	3.49	117	.250	.327	12	.188	1	10	12	0	1.5
1949	Pit-N	1	8	.111	16	12	1	0	1	74¹	81	9	45	24	15.7	5.33	79	.281	.386	3	.136	-1	-11	-9	-2	-1.2
Total 10		65	52	.556	190	124	57	13	8	1023	974	59	458	342	12.8	3.40	107	.252	.335	69	.204	7	26	25	-4	3.9

● DENNY RIDDLEBERGER
Riddleberger, Dennis Michael b: 11/22/45, Clifton Forge, Va. BR/TL, 6'3", 195 lbs. Deb: 9/15/70

YEAR	TM/L	W	L	PCT	G	GS	CG	SH	SV	IP	H	HR	BB	SO	RAT	ERA	ERA+	OAV	OOB	BH	AVG	PB	PR	/A	PD	TPI
1970	Was-A	0	0	—	8	0	0	0	0	9¹	7	1	2	5	8.7	0.96	369	.219	.265	0	—	0	3	3	-0	0.0
1971	Was-A	3	1	.750	57	0	0	0	0	69²	67	9	32	56	12.9	3.23	102	.260	.344	0	.000	0	2	1	-0	0.0
1972	Cle-A	1	3	.250	38	0	0	0	1	54	45	5	22	34	11.5	2.50	129	.237	.322	0	.000	0	3	4	-1	0.3
Total 3		4	4	.500	103	0	0	0	1	133	119	15	56	95	12.0	2.77	119	.248	.330	0	.000	0	8	8	-1	0.3

● DORSEY RIDDLEMOSER
Riddlemoser, Dorsey Lee b: 3/25/1875, Frederick, Md. d: 5/11/54, Frederick, Md. BR/TR, Deb: 8/22/1899

YEAR	TM/L	W	L	PCT	G	GS	CG	SH	SV	IP	H	HR	BB	SO	RAT	ERA	ERA+	OAV	OOB	BH	AVG	PB	PR	/A	PD	TPI
1899	Was-N	0	0	—	1	0	0	0	0	2	7	0	2	0	40.5	18.00	22	.552	.613	0	.000	-0	-3	-3	0	0.0

● JACK RIDGWAY
Ridgway, Jacob A. b: 7/23/1889, Philadelphia, Pa. d: 2/23/28, Philadelphia, Pa. BL/TR, 5'11", 174 lbs. Deb: 5/20/14

YEAR	TM/L	W	L	PCT	G	GS	CG	SH	SV	IP	H	HR	BB	SO	RAT	ERA	ERA+	OAV	OOB	BH	AVG	PB	PR	/A	PD	TPI
1914	Bal-F	0	1	.000	4	1	0	0	0	9	20	1	3	2	24.0	11.00	28	.444	.490	0	.000	-0	-8	-8	0	-0.7

● STEVE RIDZIK
Ridzik, Stephen George b: 4/29/29, Yonkers, N.Y. BR/TR, 5'11", 170 lbs. Deb: 9/4/50

YEAR	TM/L	W	L	PCT	G	GS	CG	SH	SV	IP	H	HR	BB	SO	RAT	ERA	ERA+	OAV	OOB	BH	AVG	PB	PR	/A	PD	TPI
1950	Phi-N	0	0	—	1	0	0	0	0	3	3	1	1	2	12.0	6.00	67	.300	.364	0	—	0	-1	-1	-0	0.0
1952	Phi-N	4	2	.667	24	9	2	0	0	92²	74	10	37	43	10.9	3.01	121	.218	.297	3	.136	0	7	7	-2	0.2
1953	Phi-N	9	6	.600	42	12	1	0	0	124	119	15	48	53	12.5	3.77	112	.256	.332	7	.194	2	7	6	-1	0.8
1954	Phi-N	4	5	.444	35	6	0	0	0	80²	72	7	44	45	12.9	4.13	98	.233	.329	5	.227	1	-1	-1	-0	0.0
1955	Phi-N	0	1	.000	9	0	0	0	0	11	7	1	8	3	14.7	2.45	162	.179	.360	0	.000	-1	2	2	-0	0.1
	Cin-N	0	3	.000	13	2	0	0	0	30	35	4	14	6	15.0	4.50	94	.299	.379	1	.167	-0	-1	-1	-0	-0.2
	Yr	0	4	.000	16	3	0	0	0	41	42	5	22	12	14.3	3.95	105	.264	.357	1	.100	-0	1	1	-1	-0.1
1956	NY-N	6	2	.750	41	5	1	1	0	92¹	80	7	65	53	14.6	3.80	99	.240	.371	7	.250	1	-0	-0	-0	-0.1
1957	NY-N	0	2	.000	15	0	0	0	0	26²	19	3	19	13	13.5	4.73	83	.213	.364	1	.200	-0	-3	-2	-0	-0.1
1958	Cle-A	0	2	.000	6	0	0	0	0	8²	9	1	5	4	14.5	2.08	176	.257	.350	0	.000	-0	2	2	-0	0.0
1963	Was-A	5	6	.455	20	13	1	0	0	89²	82	16	35	47	12.2	4.82	77	.240	.319	5	.172	-1	-12	-11	-0	-1.3
1964	Was-A	5	5	.500	49	3	0	0	1	112	96	10	31	60	10.8	2.89	128	.236	.301	6	.222	1	9	10	-1	0.9
1965	Was-A	6	4	.600	63	0	0	0	8	109²	108	7	32	72	13.0	4.02	86	.257	.335	3	.167	-1	-7	-7	-0	-0.6
1966	Phi-N	0	0	—	2	0	0	0	0	2¹	5	0	1	0	23.1	7.71	47	.455	.500	0	—	0	-1	-1	-0	0.0
Total 12		39	38	.506	314	48	4	1	11	782²	709	93	351	406	12.6	3.79	101	.243	.332	38	.192	4	2	3	-4	0.2

YEAR TM/L	W	L	PCT	G	GS	CG	SH	SV	IP	H	HR	BB	SO	RAT	ERA	ERA+	OAV	OOB	BH	AVG	PB	PR	/A	PD	TPI
● ELMER RIEGER				Rieger, Elmer Jay b: 2/25/1889, Perris, Cal. d: 10/21/59, Los Angeles, Cal. BB/TR, 6', 175 lbs. Deb: 4/20/10																				
1910 StL-N	0	2	.000	13	2	0	0	0	21¹	26	1	7	9	14.3	5.48	54	.325	.386	0	.000	0	-6	-6	0	-0.5
● DAVE RIGHETTI				Righetti, David Allan b: 11/28/58, San Jose, Cal. BL/TL, 6'3", 198 lbs. Deb: 9/16/79																				
1979 NY-A	0	1	.000	3	3	0	0	0	17¹	10	2	10	13	10.4	3.63	112	.182	.308	0	—	0	1	1	0	0.3
1981 *NY-A	8	4	.667	15	15	2	0	0	105¹	75	1	38	89	9.7	2.05	174	.196	.269	0	—	0	19	18	-1	2.0
1982 NY-A	11	10	.524	33	27	4	0	1	183	155	11	108	163	13.2	3.79	105	.229	.340	0	—	0	6	4	-2	0.4
1983 NY-A	14	8	.636	31	31	7	2	0	217	194	12	67	169	10.9	3.44	113	.237	.297	0	—	0	15	11	-1	0.9
1984 NY-A	5	6	.455	64	0	0	0	31	96¹	79	5	37	90	10.8	2.34	162	.223	.296	0	—	0	18	16	-0	2.8
1985 NY-A	12	7	.632	74	0	0	0	29	107	96	5	45	92	11.9	2.78	144	.241	.318	0	—	0	16	15	-1	3.4
1986 NY-A★	8	8	.500	74	0	0	0	46	106²	88	4	35	83	10.5	2.45	167	.226	.293	0	—	0	20	19	-1	4.6
1987 NY-A★	8	6	.571	60	0	0	0	31	95	95	9	44	77	13.4	3.51	125	.262	.346	0	—	0	10	9	-0	1.9
1988 NY-A	5	4	.556	60	0	0	0	25	87	86	5	37	70	12.8	3.52	112	.257	.332	0	—	0	4	4	-1	0.6
1989 NY-A	2	6	.250	55	0	0	0	25	69	73	3	26	51	13.0	3.00	129	.277	.344	0	—	0	7	7	-0	1.2
1990 NY-A	1	1	.500	53	0	0	0	36	53	48	8	26	43	12.9	3.57	111	.234	.326	0	—	0	2	2	-1	0.3
1991 SF-N	2	7	.222	61	0	0	0	24	71²	64	4	28	51	11.9	3.39	106	.240	.319	0	.000	-0	2	2	1	0.3
1992 SF-N	2	7	.222	54	4	0	0	1	78¹	79	4	36	47	13.2	5.06	65	.269	.348	1	.143	-0	-14	-15	-2	-2.0
1993 SF-N	1	1	.500	51	0	0	0	1	47¹	58	11	17	31	14.5	5.70	69	.305	.365	1	1.000	0	-9	-9	-0	-0.4
1994 Oak-A	0	0	—	7	0	0	0	0	7	13	3	4	4	29.6	16.71	27	.419	.561	0	—	0	-9	-10	0	0.2
Tor-A	0	1	.000	13	0	0	0	0	13¹	9	2	10	10	12.8	6.75	71	.188	.328	0	—	0	-3	-3	0	-0.2
Yr	0	1	.000	20	0	0	0	0	20¹	22	5	14	14	18.1	10.18	46	.272	.410	0	—	0	-12	-12	0	-0.0
Total 15	79	77	.506	708	80	13	2	252	1354¹	1222	89	573	1083	12.1	3.44	113	.241	.321	2	.182	0	86	70	-10	16.3
● JOHNNY RIGNEY				Rigney, John Dungan b: 10/28/14, Oak Park, Ill. d: 10/21/84, Lombard, Ill. BR/TR, 6'2", 190 lbs. Deb: 4/21/37																				
1937 Chi-A	2	5	.286	22	4	0	0	1	90²	107	10	46	38	15.5	4.96	93	.290	.373	5	.167	-0	-3	-4	-1	-0.3
1938 Chi-A	9	9	.500	38	12	7	1	1	167	164	16	72	84	12.8	3.56	138	.256	.333	3	.145	-3	23	25	0	2.0
1939 Chi-A	15	8	.652	35	29	11	2	0	218²	208	10	84	119	12.1	3.70	128	.247	.316	16	.200	-1	22	25	-2	2.0
1940 Chi-A	14	18	.438	39	33	19	2	3	280²	240	22	90	141	10.6	3.11	142	.230	.292	20	.215	1	40	41	-1	4.2
1941 Chi-A	13	13	.500	30	29	18	3	0	237	224	21	92	119	12.1	3.84	107	.249	.320	17	.202	2	8	7	-0	0.8
1942 Chi-A	3	3	.500	7	7	6	0	0	59	40	2	16	34	8.7	3.20	112	.185	.245	1	.053	-1	3	3	0	0.1
1946 Chi-A	5	5	.500	15	11	3	2	0	82²	76	6	35	51	12.3	4.03	85	.240	.319	4	.154	-1	-5	-6	-1	-0.8
1947 Chi-A	2	3	.400	11	7	2	0	0	50²	42	3	15	19	10.1	1.95	187	.228	.286	0	.000	-2	10	10	1	0.8
Total 8	63	64	.496	197	132	66	10	5	1186¹	1101	90	450	605	11.9	3.59	121	.244	.314	71	.177	-6	98	100	-3	8.8
● JOSE RIJO				Rijo, Jose Antonio (Abreu) b: 5/13/65, San Cristobal, D.R. BR/TR, 6'1", 200 lbs. Deb: 4/5/84																				
1984 NY-A	2	8	.200	24	5	0	0	2	62¹	74	5	33	47	15.6	4.76	80	.298	.383	0	—	0	-5	-7	-1	-0.9
1985 Oak-A	6	4	.600	12	9	0	0	0	63²	57	6	28	65	12.2	3.53	109	.239	.322	0	—	0	4	2	-1	0.8
1986 Oak-A	9	11	.450	39	26	4	0	1	193²	172	24	108	176	13.2	4.65	83	.237	.339	0	—	0	-10	-17	-1	-1.0
1987 Oak-A	2	7	.222	21	14	1	0	0	82¹	106	10	41	67	16.3	5.90	70	.305	.381	0	—	0	-13	-16	0	-1.1
1988 Cin-N	13	8	.619	49	19	0	0	0	162	120	9	63	160	10.3	2.39	150	.209	.291	2	.054	-2	19	21	0	2.6
1989 Cin-N	7	6	.538	19	19	1	1	0	111	101	6	48	86	12.2	2.84	127	.249	.332	8	.211	1	8	9	-0	1.2
1990 *Cin-N	14	8	.636	29	29	7	1	0	197	151	10	78	152	10.6	2.70	146	.212	.292	10	.161	0	24	27	1	3.1
1991 Cin-N	15	6	.714	30	30	3	1	0	204¹	165	8	55	172	9.8	2.51	151	.219	.274	14	.209	1	27	29	-0	3.0
1992 Cin-N	15	10	.600	33	33	2	0	0	211	185	15	44	171	9.9	2.56	141	.238	.292	14	.194	1	22	24	1	3.2
1993 Cin-N	14	9	.609	36	36	2	1	0	257¹	218	19	62	227	9.9	2.48	162	.230	.278	22	.268	7	45	44	3	4.8
1994 Cin-N†	9	6	.600	26	26	2	0	0	172¹	177	16	52	171	12.2	3.08	135	.265	.322	10	.204	2	22	21	2	0.0
Total 11	106	83	.561	318	246	22	4	3	1717	1526	126	612	1494	11.3	3.12	124	.239	.308	80	.197	10	142	141	5	17.7
● GEORGE RILEY				Riley, George Michael b: 10/6/56, Philadelphia, Pa. BL/TL, 6'2", 210 lbs. Deb: 9/15/79																				
1979 Chi-N	0	1	.000	4	1	0	0	0	13	16	1	6	16.6		5.54	74	.320	.414	0	.000	-0	-3	-2	0	-0.1
1980 Chi-N	0	4	.000	22	6	0	0	0	36	41	2	20	18	15.8	5.75	68	.293	.389	0	.000	-0	-9	-7	1	-0.7
1984 SF-N	1	0	1.000	5	4	0	0	0	29¹	39	1	7	12	14.7	3.99	88	.315	.361	1	.100	-0	-1	-2	-0	-0.1
1986 Mon-N	0	0	—	10	0	0	0	0	8²	7	0	8	5	16.6	4.15	89	.212	.381	0	—	0	-0	-0	0	-0.0
Total 4	1	5	.167	41	5	0	0	0	87	103	4	41	40	15.6	4.97	76	.297	.382	1	.077	-1	-13	-11	1	-0.9
● ANDY RINCON				Rincon, Andrew John b: 3/5/59, Monterey Park, Cal. BR/TR, 6'3", 195 lbs. Deb: 9/15/80																				
1980 StL-N	3	1	.750	4	4	1	0	0	31	23	1	7	22	8.7	2.61	141	.215	.263	3	.250	0	3	4	0	0.6
1981 StL-N	3	1	.750	5	5	1	1	0	35²	27	0	5	13	8.6	1.77	201	.214	.256	3	.231	1	7	7	-0	0.9
1982 StL-N	2	3	.400	11	6	1	0	0	40	35	1	25	11	13.5	4.72	77	.241	.353	1	.100	-0	-5	-5	-1	-0.6
Total 3	8	5	.615	20	15	3	1	0	106²	85	2	37	46	10.5	3.12	116	.225	.297	7	.200	1	5	6	-1	0.9
● JEFF RINEER				Rineer, Jeffrey Alan b: 7/3/55, Lancaster, Pa. BL/TL, 6'4", 205 lbs. Deb: 9/30/79																				
1979 Bal-A	0	0	—	1	1	0	0	0	1	1	0	0	0	0.00	—	.000	.000	0	—	0	0	0	0	0.4
● JIMMY RING				Ring, James Joseph b: 2/15/1895, Brooklyn, N.Y. d: 7/6/65, New York, N.Y. BR/TR, 6'1", 170 lbs. Deb: 4/13/17																				
1917 Cin-N	3	7	.300	24	7	3	0	2	88	90	7	35	33	12.9	4.40	60	.272	.343	2	.077	-2	-16	-17	0	-2.2
1918 Cin-N	9	5	.643	21	18	13	4	0	142¹	130	5	48	26	11.4	2.85	94	.247	.314	6	.120	-3	-1	-3	-3	-0.9
1919 *Cin-N	10	9	.526	32	18	12	2	3	183	150	1	51	61	10.0	2.26	123	.232	.291	6	.097	-5	13	10	-3	0.9
1920 Cin-N	17	16	.515	42	33	18	1	1	266²	268	5	92	73	12.3	3.54	86	.264	.329	19	.198	-0	-12	-15	1	-1.8
1921 Phi-N	10	19	.345	34	30	21	0	1	246	258	6	88	88	12.8	4.24	100	.274	.340	12	.145	-4	-13	-13	0	-0.2
1922 Phi-N	12	18	.400	40	33	17	0	1	249¹	292	19	103	116	14.4	4.58	102	.297	.365	13	.148	-5	-13	2	4	0.2
1923 Phi-N	18	16	.529	39	36	23	0	0	304¹	336	13	115	112	13.4	3.87	119	.283	.347	12	.106	-9	4	25	3	1.8
1924 Phi-N	10	12	.455	32	31	16	1	0	215¹	236	6	108	72	14.5	3.97	112	.286	.371	17	.230	-1	-2	12	2	1.3
1925 Phi-N	14	16	.467	38	37	21	1	0	270	325	14	119	93	14.8	4.37	109	.297	.367	11	.109	-7	-3	12	2	0.7
1926 NY-N	11	10	.524	39	23	5	0	2	183¹	207	12	74	76	13.8	4.57	82	.290	.357	3	.375	1	-15	-17	-1	-2.1
1927 StL-N	0	4	.000	13	1	0	0	0	33	39	3	17	13	15.5	6.55	60	.300	.385	3	.375	1	-10	-10	1	-0.8
1928 Phi-N	4	17	.190	35	25	4	0	1	173	214	14	103	72	16.6	6.40	67	.316	.407	11	.183	-2	-46	-41	6	-4.2
Total 12	118	149	.442	389	294	154	9	11	2354¹	2545	104	953	835	13.5	4.12	95	.281	.351	120	.147	-40	-115	-50	16	-7.3
● ALLEN RIPLEY				Ripley, Allen Stevens b: 10/18/52, Norwood, Mass. BR/TR, 6'3", 190 lbs. Deb: 4/10/78 F																				
1978 Bos-A	2	5	.286	15	11	1	0	0	73	92	10	22	26	14.4	5.55	74	.311	.364	0	—	0	-14	-12	-1	-1.9
1979 Bos-A	3	1	.750	16	3	0	0	1	64²	77	9	25	34	14.6	5.15	86	.295	.363	0	—	0	-7	-5	-1	-0.9
1980 SF-N	9	10	.474	23	20	2	0	0	112²	119	10	36	65	12.7	4.15	85	.274	.335	6	.150	-0	-7	-8	0	-1.2
1981 SF-N	4	4	.500	19	14	1	0	0	90²	103	5	27	47	13.2	4.07	84	.289	.345	4	.133	-1	-6	-6	1	-0.6
1982 Chi-N	5	7	.417	28	19	0	0	0	122²	130	12	38	57	12.5	4.26	88	.285	.343	5	.132	-1	-9	-7	-0	-0.7
Total 5	23	27	.460	101	67	4	0	1	463²	521	46	148	229	13.3	4.52	83	.289	.348	15	.139	-3	-43	-38	-0	-5.3
● WALT RIPLEY				Ripley, Walter Franklin b: 11/26/16, Worcester, Mass. d: 10/7/90, Attleboro, Mass. BR/TR, 6', 168 lbs. Deb: 8/17/35 F																				
1935 Bos-A	0	0	—	2	0	0	0	0	4	7	0	3	0	22.5	9.00	53	.412	.500	0	—	0	-2	-2	0	-0.0
● RAY RIPPELMEYER				Rippelmeyer, Raymond Roy b: 7/9/33, Valmeyer, Ill. BR/TR, 6'3", 200 lbs. Deb: 4/14/62 C																				
1962 Was-A	1	2	.333	18	1	0	0	0	39¹	47	7	17	17	14.6	5.49	74	.294	.362	3	.500	2	-7	-6	2	0.0
● CHARLIE RIPPLE				Ripple, Charles Dawson b: 12/1/21, Bolton, N.C. d: 5/6/79, Wilmington, N.C. BL/TL, 6'2", 210 lbs. Deb: 9/25/44																				
1944 Phi-N	0	0	—	1	1	0	0	0	2¹	6	0	4	2	38.6	15.43	23	.500	.625	1	1.000	0	-3	-3	-0	0.0

YEAR	TM/L	W	L	PCT	G	GS	CG	SH	SV	IP	H	HR	BB	SO	RAT	ERA	ERA+	OAV	OOB	BH	AVG	PB	PR	/A	PD	TPI
1945	Phi-N	0	1	.000	4	0	0	0	0	7²	7	0	10	5	20.0	7.04	54	.241	.436	0	.000	-0	-3	-3	-0	-0.3
1946	Phi-N	1	0	1.000	6	0	0	0	0	3¹	5	0	6	3	29.7	10.80	32	.385	.579	0	—	0	-3	-3	-0	-0.7
Total	3	1	1	.500	11	1	0	0	0	13¹	18	0	20	10	25.7	9.45	39	.333	.514	1	.500	0	-9	-9	-0	-1.0

● BILL RISLEY
Risley, William Charles b: 5/29/67, Chicago, Ill. BR/TR, 6'2", 215 lbs. Deb: 7/8/92

YEAR	TM/L	W	L	PCT	G	GS	CG	SH	SV	IP	H	HR	BB	SO	RAT	ERA	ERA+	OAV	OOB	BH	AVG	PB	PR	/A	PD	TPI
1992	Mon-N	1	0	1.000	1	1	0	0	0	5	4	0	1	2	9.0	1.80	193	.235	.278	0	.000	-0	1	1	0	0.2
1993	Mon-N	0	0	—	2	0	0	0	0	3	2	1	2	2	15.0	6.00	70	.200	.385	0	—	0	-1	-1	0	0.0
1994	Sea-A	9	6	.600	37	0	0	0	0	52¹	31	7	19	61	8.6	3.44	143	.170	.249	0	—	0	8	9	0	2.1
Total	3	10	6	.625	40	1	0	0	0	60¹	37	8	22	65	9.0	3.43	138	.177	.259	0	.000	-0	8	9	0	2.3

● JAY RITCHIE
Ritchie, Jay Seay b: 11/20/36, Salisbury, N.C. BR/TR, 6'4", 190 lbs. Deb: 8/4/64

YEAR	TM/L	W	L	PCT	G	GS	CG	SH	SV	IP	H	HR	BB	SO	RAT	ERA	ERA+	OAV	OOB	BH	AVG	PB	PR	/A	PD	TPI
1964	Bos-A	1	1	.500	21	0	0	0	0	46	43	4	14	35	11.2	2.74	141	.249	.305	1	.111	-1	5	6	-0	0.2
1965	Bos-A	1	2	.333	44	0	0	0	2	71	83	3	26	55	13.9	3.17	118	.302	.364	1	.200	0	2	4	0	0.2
1966	Atl-N	0	1	.000	22	0	0	0	4	35¹	32	3	12	33	11.2	4.08	89	.241	.303	2	.500	1	-2	-2	0	0.0
1967	Atl-N	4	6	.400	52	0	0	0	2	82¹	75	6	29	57	11.8	3.17	105	.245	.319	3	.300	1	2	1	1	0.4
1968	Cin-N	2	3	.400	28	2	0	0	0	56²	68	7	13	32	13.0	4.61	69	.293	.333	0	.000	-1	-10	-9	-1	-1.0
Total	5	8	13	.381	167	2	0	0	8	291¹	301	23	94	212	12.4	3.49	101	.269	.329	7	.200	1	-3	-1	-0	-0.2

● WALLY RITCHIE
Ritchie, Wallace Reid b: 7/12/65, Glendale, Cal. BL/TL, 6'2", 180 lbs. Deb: 5/1/87

YEAR	TM/L	W	L	PCT	G	GS	CG	SH	SV	IP	H	HR	BB	SO	RAT	ERA	ERA+	OAV	OOB	BH	AVG	PB	PR	/A	PD	TPI
1987	Phi-N	3	2	.600	49	0	0	0	3	62¹	60	8	29	45	13.0	3.75	113	.254	.338	1	.250	0	2	3	-0	0.3
1988	Phi-N	0	0	—	19	0	0	0	0	26	19	1	17	8	12.8	3.12	114	.207	.336	0	—	0	1	1	-0	0.0
1991	Phi-N	1	2	.333	39	0	0	0	0	50¹	44	4	17	26	11.3	2.50	146	.234	.304	0	.000	-0	7	7	-0	0.3
1992	Phi-N	2	1	.667	40	0	0	0	1	39	44	4	17	19	14.1	3.00	116	.288	.359	0	.000	0	2	2	-0	0.2
Total	4	6	5	.545	147	0	0	0	4	177²	167	16	80	98	12.7	3.14	121	.250	.333	1	.125	0	12	13	-1	0.8

● REGGIE RITTER
Ritter, Reggie Blake b: 1/23/60, Malvern, Ark. BL/TR, 6'2", 195 lbs. Deb: 5/17/86

YEAR	TM/L	W	L	PCT	G	GS	CG	SH	SV	IP	H	HR	BB	SO	RAT	ERA	ERA+	OAV	OOB	BH	AVG	PB	PR	/A	PD	TPI
1986	Cle-A	0	0	—	5	0	0	0	0	10	14	1	4	6	17.1	6.30	66	.341	.413	0	—	0	-2	-2	0	0.2
1987	Cle-A	1	1	.500	14	0	0	0	0	26²	33	5	16	11	16.5	6.08	74	.300	.389	0	—	0	-5	-5	0	-0.3
Total	2	1	1	.500	19	0	0	0	0	36²	47	6	20	17	16.7	6.14	72	.311	.395	0	—	0	-7	-7	1	-0.1

● HANK RITTER
Ritter, William Herbert b: 10/12/1893, McCoysville, Pa. d: 9/3/64, Akron, Ohio BR/TR, 6', 180 lbs. Deb: 8/3/12

YEAR	TM/L	W	L	PCT	G	GS	CG	SH	SV	IP	H	HR	BB	SO	RAT	ERA	ERA+	OAV	OOB	BH	AVG	PB	PR	/A	PD	TPI
1912	Phi-N	0	0	—	3	0	0	0	0	6	5	0	5	1	15.0	4.50	81	.192	.323	0	.000	-0	-1	-1	-0	-0.1
1914	NY-N	1	0	1.000	1	0	0	0	0	8	4	0	4	4	9.0	1.13	236	.160	.276	0	.000	-0	1	1	-0	0.1
1915	NY-N	2	1	.667	22	2	0	0	0	58¹	66	4	15	33	13.3	4.63	55	.291	.348	2	.125	-1	-12	-13	-0	-0.9
1916	NY-N	1	0	1.000	3	0	0	0	0	5	3	0	0	3	7.2	0.00	—	.200	.250	0	—	1	1	1	-0	0.2
Total	4	4	1	.800	29	2	0	0	2	77¹	78	4	24	43	12.6	3.96	67	.266	.334	2	.100	-0	-10	-11	-1	-0.5

● JIM RITTWAGE
Rittwage, James Michael b: 10/23/44, Cleveland, Ohio BR/TR, 6'3", 190 lbs. Deb: 9/7/70

YEAR	TM/L	W	L	PCT	G	GS	CG	SH	SV	IP	H	HR	BB	SO	RAT	ERA	ERA+	OAV	OOB	BH	AVG	PB	PR	/A	PD	TPI
1970	Cle-A	1	1	.500	8	3	1	0	0	26	18	0	21	16	13.5	4.15	95	.194	.342	3	.375	1	-1	-1	0	0.1

● KEVIN RITZ
Ritz, Kevin D b: 6/8/65, Eatontown, N.J. BR/TR, 6'4", 195 lbs. Deb: 7/15/89

YEAR	TM/L	W	L	PCT	G	GS	CG	SH	SV	IP	H	HR	BB	SO	RAT	ERA	ERA+	OAV	OOB	BH	AVG	PB	PR	/A	PD	TPI
1989	Det-A	4	6	.400	12	12	0	0	0	74	75	2	44	56	14.6	4.38	87	.265	.366	0	—	0	-4	-5	0	-0.5
1990	Det-A	0	4	.000	4	4	0	0	0	7¹	14	1	14	3	34.4	11.05	36	.400	.571	0	—	0	-6	-6	1	-2.1
1991	Det-A	0	3	.000	11	5	0	0	0	15¹	17	1	22	9	24.1	11.74	35	.288	.494	0	—	0	-13	-13	0	-2.1
1992	Det-A	2	5	.286	23	11	0	0	0	80¹	88	4	44	57	15.1	5.60	71	.278	.372	0	—	0	-15	-15	0	-1.2
1994	Col-N	5	6	.455	15	15	0	0	0	73²	88	5	35	53	15.5	5.62	88	.303	.386	0	.000	-2	-12	-5	1	-0.8
Total	5	11	24	.314	65	47	1	0	0	250²	282	12	159	178	16.2	5.78	73	.287	.391	0	.000	-2	-49	-44	2	-6.7

● BEN RIVERA
Rivera, Bienvenido Santana b: 1/11/68, San Pedro De Macoris, D.R. BR/TR, 6'6", 210 lbs. Deb: 4/9/92

YEAR	TM/L	W	L	PCT	G	GS	CG	SH	SV	IP	H	HR	BB	SO	RAT	ERA	ERA+	OAV	OOB	BH	AVG	PB	PR	/A	PD	TPI
1992	Atl-N	0	1	.000	8	0	0	0	0	15¹	21	1	13	11	21.1	4.70	78	.339	.468	0	.000	-0	-2	-2	-0	-0.1
	Phi-N	7	3	.700	20	14	4	1	0	102	78	8	32	66	9.9	2.82	124	.211	.278	3	.094	-1	8	8	-0	0.6
	Yr	7	4	.636	28	14	4	1	0	117¹	99	9	45	77	11.2	3.07	114	.228	.304	3	.091	-1	6	6	-0	0.5
1993	*Phi-N	13	9	.591	30	28	1	1	0	163	175	16	85	123	14.7	5.02	79	.273	.363	5	.098	-2	-18	-19	-2	-2.6
1994	Phi-N	3	4	.429	9	7	0	0	0	38	40	7	22	19	14.9	6.87	60	.274	.373	0	.000	-1	-11	-12	0	-1.8
Total	3	23	17	.575	67	49	5	2	0	318¹	314	32	152	219	13.5	4.52	84	.258	.345	8	.086	-3	-23	-25	-2	-3.9

● TINK RIVIERE
Riviere, Arthur Bernard b: 8/2/1899, Liberty, Tex. d: 9/27/65, Liberty, Tex. BR/TR, 5'10", 167 lbs. Deb: 4/15/21

YEAR	TM/L	W	L	PCT	G	GS	CG	SH	SV	IP	H	HR	BB	SO	RAT	ERA	ERA+	OAV	OOB	BH	AVG	PB	PR	/A	PD	TPI
1921	StL-N	1	0	1.000	18	2	0	0	0	38¹	45	2	20	15	15.7	6.10	60	.280	.366	3	.375	2	-10	-10	-2	-0.2
1925	Chi-A	0	0	—	3	0	0	0	0	4²	6	0	7	1	27.0	13.50	31	.429	.636	0	.000	-0	-5	-5	1	0.0
Total	2	1	0	1.000	21	2	0	0	0	43	51	2	27	16	17.0	6.91	54	.291	.395	3	.333	2	-15	-15	-1	-0.2

● EPPA RIXEY
Rixey, Eppa "Jeptha" b: 5/3/1891, Culpeper, Va. d: 2/28/63, Cincinnati, Ohio BR/TL, 6'5", 210 lbs. Deb: 6/21/12 H

YEAR	TM/L	W	L	PCT	G	GS	CG	SH	SV	IP	H	HR	BB	SO	RAT	ERA	ERA+	OAV	OOB	BH	AVG	PB	PR	/A	PD	TPI
1912	Phi-N	10	10	.500	23	20	10	3	0	162	147	2	54	59	11.3	2.50	145	.256	.322	9	.170	-2	16	16	-1	2.0
1913	Phi-N	9	5	.643	35	19	9	1	2	155²	148	4	56	75	12.1	3.12	107	.258	.331	9	.191	-0	1	4	-0	0.3
1914	Phi-N	2	11	.154	24	15	2	0	0	103	124	0	45	41	15.0	4.37	67	.313	.387	1	.038	-1	-18	-16	-2	-2.0
1915	*Phi-N	11	12	.478	29	22	10	2	1	176²	163	2	64	88	11.7	2.39	150	.250	.319	9	.164	-0	7	7	-0	0.9
1916	Phi-N	22	10	.688	38	33	20	3	0	287	239	4	74	134	10.0	1.85	143	.229	.284	15	.155	-2	25	26	3	3.2
1917	Phi-N	16	21	.432	39	36	23	4	1	281¹	249	1	67	121	10.3	2.27	124	.241	.290	18	.191	-1	14	17	4	2.6
1919	Phi-N	6	12	.333	23	18	11	1	0	154	160	4	50	63	12.4	3.97	81	.278	.339	7	.149	-2	-18	-13	-2	-1.4
1920	Phi-N	11	22	.333	41	34	25	0	2	284¹	288	5	69	109	11.4	3.48	98	.274	.321	25	.248	1	-11	-2	3	0.3
1921	Cin-N	19	18	.514	40	36	21	2	1	301	324	1	66	76	11.8	2.78	129	.282	.324	13	.129	-5	34	27	3	2.8
1922	Cin-N	**25**	13	.658	40	38	26	2	0	313¹	337	13	45	80	11.1	3.53	113	.275	.303	21	.193	-5	20	16	-0	1.5
1923	Cin-N	20	15	.571	42	37	23	3	1	309	334	3	65	97	11.7	2.80	138	.280	.320	17	.159	-5	41	37	2	3.4
1924	Cin-N	15	14	.517	35	29	15	4	1	238¹	219	3	47	57	10.1	2.76	137	.246	.285	18	.214	-1	29	27	-1	3.1
1925	Cin-N	21	11	.656	39	36	22	2	1	287¹	302	8	47	69	11.2	2.88	143	.273	.307	22	.214	-1	44	39	-2	3.6
1926	Cin-N	14	8	.636	37	29	14	3	0	233	231	12	58	61	11.2	3.40	109	.265	.313	19	.226	0	11	8	-2	0.5
1927	Cin-N	12	10	.545	34	29	11	1	1	219²	240	3	43	42	11.7	3.48	109	.287	.325	20	.247	4	11	7	-1	1.0
1928	Cin-N	19	18	.514	43	37	17	3	2	291¹	317	4	67	58	12.0	3.43	115	.288	.330	18	.173	-1	18	17	-0	1.8
1929	Cin-N	10	13	.435	35	24	11	0	0	201	235	6	60	37	13.3	4.16	110	.296	.348	15	.231	0	12	9	-1	0.8
1930	Cin-N	9	13	.409	32	21	5	0	0	164	207	11	47	37	14.3	5.10	93	.317	.370	11	.200	-1	-2	-5	-0	-0.6
1931	Cin-N	4	7	.364	22	17	4	0	0	126²	143	4	30	22	12.3	3.91	96	.291	.332	6	.150	-1	-1	-2	4	0.1
1932	Cin-N	5	5	.500	25	11	6	2	0	111²	108	3	16	14	10.3	2.66	145	.254	.288	9	.265	1	15	15	1	1.4
1933	Cin-N	6	3	.667	16	12	5	1	0	94¹	94	2	12	10	12.4	3.15	108	.298	.319	2	.257	2	2	3	1	0.6
Total	21	266	251	.515	692	553	290	37	14	4494²	4633	92	1082	1350	11.6	3.15	116	.272	.318	291	.191	-15	251	248	16	25.9

● JOHN ROACH
Roach, John F. b: Farrandsville, Pa. BR/TL, 5'9", 175 lbs. Deb: 5/14/1887

YEAR	TM/L	W	L	PCT	G	GS	CG	SH	SV	IP	H	HR	BB	SO	RAT	ERA	ERA+	OAV	OOB	BH	AVG	PB	PR	/A	PD	TPI
1887	NY-N	0	1	.000	1	1	1	0	0	8	18	0	4	3	25.9	11.25	33	.419	.479	1	.250	-0	-6	-7	-0	-0.5

● SKEL ROACH
Roach, Rudolph Charles (b: Rudolph Charles Weichbrodt) b: 10/20/1871, Germany d: 3/9/58, Oak Park, Ill. BR/TR, 6'2", Deb: 8/9/1899

YEAR	TM/L	W	L	PCT	G	GS	CG	SH	SV	IP	H	HR	BB	SO	RAT	ERA	ERA+	OAV	OOB	BH	AVG	PB	PR	/A	PD	TPI
1899	Chi-N	1	0	1.000	1	1	1	0	0	9	13	0	1	4	14.0	3.00	125	.337	.354	0	.000	-1	1	1	0	0.1

● BRUCE ROBBINS
Robbins, Bruce Duane b: 9/10/59, Portland, Ind. BL/TL, 6'1", 190 lbs. Deb: 7/28/79

YEAR	TM/L	W	L	PCT	G	GS	CG	SH	SV	IP	H	HR	BB	SO	RAT	ERA	ERA+	OAV	OOB	BH	AVG	PB	PR	/A	PD	TPI
1979	Det-A	3	3	.500	10	8	0	0	0	46	45	3	21	22	12.9	3.91	111	.265	.346	0	—	0	2	2	-0	0.1
1980	Det-A	4	2	.667	15	6	0	0	0	51²	60	12	28	23	15.3	6.62	62	.287	.371	0	—	0	-15	-14	-0	-1.6
Total	2	7	5	.583	25	14	0	0	0	97²	105	15	49	45	14.2	5.34	79	.277	.360	0	—	0	-13	-12	-0	-1.5

YEAR	TM/L	W	L	PCT	G	GS	CG	SH	SV	IP	H	HR	BB	SO	RAT	ERA	ERA+	OAV	OOB	BH	AVG	PB	PR	/A	PD	TPI

● BERT ROBERGE
Roberge, Bertrand Roland   b: 10/3/54, Lewiston, Maine   BR/TR, 6'4", 190 lbs.   Deb: 5/28/79

YEAR	TM/L	W	L	PCT	G	GS	CG	SH	SV	IP	H	HR	BB	SO	RAT	ERA	ERA+	OAV	OOB	BH	AVG	PB	PR	/A	PD	TPI
1979	Hou-N	3	0	1.000	26	0	0	0	4	32	20	0	17	13	10.4	1.69	208	.196	.311	0	.000	-0	7	6	-0	0.7
1980	Hou-N	2	0	1.000	14	0	0	0	0	24¹	24	2	10	9	13.3	5.92	56	.261	.346	0	.000	-0	-6	-7	0	-0.6
1982	Hou-N	1	2	.333	22	0	0	0	3	25²	29	0	6	18	12.3	4.21	79	.284	.324	0	.000	-0	-2	-3	-0	-0.4
1984	Chi-A	3	3	.500	21	0	0	0	0	40²	36	2	15	25	12.0	3.76	111	.240	.321	0	—	0	1	2	1	0.2
1985	Mon-N	3	3	.500	42	0	0	0	2	68	58	5	22	34	10.9	3.44	99	.232	.299	0	.000	-0	1	-0	0	0.0
1986	Mon-N	0	4	.000	21	0	0	0	1	28²	33	2	10	20	13.8	6.28	59	.295	.358	0	.000	-0	-8	-8	-0	-1.1
Total	6	12	12	.500	146	0	0	0	10	219¹	200	11	80	119	11.8	3.98	90	.248	.321	0	.000	-1	-7	-10	1	-1.2

● DALE ROBERTS
Roberts, Dale "Mountain Man"   b: 4/12/42, Owenton, Ky.   BR/TL, 6'4", 180 lbs.   Deb: 9/9/67

YEAR	TM/L	W	L	PCT	G	GS	CG	SH	SV	IP	H	HR	BB	SO	RAT	ERA	ERA+	OAV	OOB	BH	AVG	PB	PR	/A	PD	TPI
1967	NY-A	0	0	—	2	0	0	0	0	2	3	0	2	0	31.5	9.00	35	.429	.636	0	—	0	-1	-1	0	0.0

● DAVE ROBERTS
Roberts, David Arthur   b: 9/11/44, Gallipolis, Ohio   BL/TL, 6'2", 197 lbs.   Deb: 7/6/69

YEAR	TM/L	W	L	PCT	G	GS	CG	SH	SV	IP	H	HR	BB	SO	RAT	ERA	ERA+	OAV	OOB	BH	AVG	PB	PR	/A	PD	TPI
1969	SD-N	0	3	.000	22	5	0	0	1	48²	65	5	19	19	16.1	4.81	74	.322	.388	4	.267	1	-7	-7	0	-0.3
1970	SD-N	8	14	.364	43	21	3	2	1	181²	182	16	43	102	11.2	3.81	104	.261	.305	9	.153	1	5	3	-0	0.5
1971	SD-N	14	17	.452	37	34	14	2	0	269²	238	9	61	135	10.1	2.10	157	.240	.288	19	.221	2	41	36	1	4.6
1972	Hou-N	12	7	.632	35	28	7	3	2	192	227	18	57	111	13.4	4.50	75	.296	.346	16	.239	6	-22	-24	-1	-1.9
1973	Hou-N	17	11	.607	39	36	12	6	0	249¹	264	15	62	119	11.8	2.85	127	.271	.316	11	.129	-3	22	22	-1	2.0
1974	Hou-N	10	12	.455	34	30	8	2	1	204	216	6	65	72	12.5	3.40	102	.276	.333	16	.219	5	5	1	2	0.9
1975	Hou-N	8	14	.364	32	27	7	0	1	198¹	182	13	73	101	11.7	4.27	79	.244	.313	9	.143	-1	-14	-20	1	-1.9
1976	Det-A	16	17	.485	36	36	18	4	0	252	254	16	63	79	11.5	4.00	93	.264	.312	0	—	0	-13	-8	-2	-1.1
1977	Det-A	4	10	.286	22	22	5	0	0	129¹	143	20	41	46	12.9	5.15	83	.274	.330	0	—	0	-16	-12	-0	-1.5
	Chi-N	1	1	.500	17	6	1	0	1	53	55	1	12	23	11.5	3.23	136	.275	.319	1	.059	-2	4	7	2	0.3
1978	Chi-N	6	8	.429	35	20	2	1	1	142¹	159	17	56	54	13.8	5.25	77	.288	.357	17	.327	6	-26	-19	1	-1.1
1979	SF-N	0	2	.000	26	1	0	0	3	42	42	3	18	23	13.1	2.57	136	.262	.341	0	.000	-1	5	4	1	0.3
	*Pit-N	5	2	.714	21	3	0	0	1	38²	47	1	12	15	14.0	3.26	119	.318	.373	0	.000	-1	2	3	0	0.5
	Yr	5	4	.556	47	4	0	0	4	80²	89	4	30	38	13.4	2.90	127	.287	.352	0	.000	-1	7	7	1	0.8
1980	Pit-N	0	1	.000	2	0	0	0	0	2¹	2	0	1	1	11.6	3.86	94	.250	.333	0	—	0	-0	-0	-0	0.0
	Sea-A	2	3	.400	37	4	0	0	3	80¹	87	7	27	47	12.8	4.37	95	.270	.329	0	.000	0	-3	-2	-1	-0.3
1981	NY-N	0	3	.000	7	4	0	0	0	15¹	26	5	5	10	18.2	9.39	37	.366	.408	1	.250	0	-10	-10	0	-1.6
Total	13	103	125	.452	445	277	77	20	15	2099	2188	155	615	957	12.2	3.78	97	.270	.324	103	.194	15	-27	-28	7	-0.6

● JIM ROBERTS
Roberts, James Newson "Big Jim"   b: 10/13/1895, Artesia, Miss.   d: 6/24/84, Columbus, Miss.   BR/TR, 6'3", 205 lbs.   Deb: 7/27/24

YEAR	TM/L	W	L	PCT	G	GS	CG	SH	SV	IP	H	HR	BB	SO	RAT	ERA	ERA+	OAV	OOB	BH	AVG	PB	PR	/A	PD	TPI
1924	Bro-N	0	3	.000	11	5	0	0	0	25¹	41	1	8	10	18.1	7.46	50	.360	.411	1	.143	-0	-10	-10	-0	-1.1
1925	Bro-N	0	0	—	1	0	0	0	0	1	1	0	0	0	9.0	0.00	—	.500	.500	0	—	0	0	0	0	0.0
Total	2	0	3	.000	12	5	0	0	0	26¹	42	1	8	10	17.8	7.18	52	.362	.413	1	.143	-0	-10	-10	-0	-1.1

● LEON ROBERTS
Roberts, Leon Kauffman   b: 1/22/51, Vicksburg, Mich.   BR/TR, 6'3", 200 lbs.   Deb: 9/3/74 ♦

YEAR	TM/L	W	L	PCT	G	GS	CG	SH	SV	IP	H	HR	BB	SO	RAT	ERA	ERA+	OAV	OOB	BH	AVG	PB	PR	/A	PD	TPI
1984	KC-A	0	0	—	1	0	0	0	0	1	4	1	1	1	45.0	27.00	15	.571	.625	10	.222	0	-3	-3	0	0.0

● RAY ROBERTS
Roberts, Raymond   b: 8/25/1895, Cruger, Miss.   d: 1/30/62, Cruger, Miss.   BL/TR, 5'11", 180 lbs.   Deb: 9/12/19

YEAR	TM/L	W	L	PCT	G	GS	CG	SH	SV	IP	H	HR	BB	SO	RAT	ERA	ERA+	OAV	OOB	BH	AVG	PB	PR	/A	PD	TPI
1919	Phi-A	0	2	.000	3	2	0	0	0	14	21	0	3	2	15.4	7.71	44	.368	.400	1	.250	-0	-7	-7	-0	-0.8

● ROBIN ROBERTS
Roberts, Robin Evan   b: 9/30/26, Springfield, Ill.   BB/TR, 6', 190 lbs.   Deb: 6/18/48   H

YEAR	TM/L	W	L	PCT	G	GS	CG	SH	SV	IP	H	HR	BB	SO	RAT	ERA	ERA+	OAV	OOB	BH	AVG	PB	PR	/A	PD	TPI
1948	Phi-N	7	9	.438	20	20	9	0	0	146²	148	10	61	84	13.1	3.19	124	.278	.356	11	.250	4	12	12	-2	1.5
1949	Phi-N	15	15	.500	43	31	11	3	4	226²	229	15	75	95	12.3	3.69	107	.273	.337	5	.075	-3	9	6	-3	0.1
1950	*Phi-N★	20	11	.645	40	39	21	**5**	1	304¹	282	29	77	146	10.7	3.02	134	.248	.297	12	.118	-4	**38**	35	0	2.9
1951	Phi-N★	21	15	.583	44	39	22	6	2	315	284	20	64	127	10.0	3.03	127	.237	**.278**	15	.172	5	33	29	-3	**3.4**
1952	Phi-N☆	**28**	7	.800	39	37	**30**	3	2	330	292	22	45	148	9.3	2.59	141	.234	.263	14	.125	3	**42**	39	-3	4.0
1953	Phi-N★	**23**	16	.590	44	41	**33**	5	2	346²	324	30	61	**198**	10.0	2.75	153	.242	.276	22	.179	5	59	**56**	-1	6.1
1954	Phi-N★	**23**	15	.605	45	38	**29**	4	4	336²	289	35	56	**185**	**9.4**	2.97	136	.231	**.267**	15	.123	-3	41	40	-4	3.6
1955	Phi-N★	**23**	14	.622	41	38	**26**	1	3	305	292	41	53	160	10.2	3.28	121	.246	**.280**	27	.252	14	26	24	-5	3.7
1956	Phi-N☆	19	18	.514	43	37	**22**	1	3	297¹	328	46	40	157	11.2	4.45	84	.282	.307	20	.200	4	-22	-24	-0	-2.4
1957	Phi-N	10	22	.313	39	32	14	2	2	249²	246	40	43	128	10.5	4.07	93	.252	.284	13	.162	0	-5	-7	0	-0.8
1958	Phi-N	17	14	.548	35	34	21	1	0	269²	270	30	51	130	10.8	3.24	122	.259	.294	20	.202	4	21	22	-2	2.5
1959	Phi-N	15	17	.469	35	35	19	2	0	257¹	267	34	35	137	10.7	4.27	96	.263	.291	17	.191	3	-9	-5	-0	-0.8
1960	Phi-N	12	16	.429	35	33	13	2	1	237¹	256	31	34	122	11.1	4.02	97	.275	.302	12	.152	-1	-7	-4	-3	-0.5
1961	Phi-N	1	10	.091	26	18	2	0	0	117	154	19	23	54	13.8	5.85	70	.326	.360	-2	.091	-2	-24	-23	-2	-2.2
1962	Bal-A	10	9	.526	27	25	6	0	0	191¹	176	17	41	102	10.4	2.78	133	.244	.289	10	.192	2	25	20	-1	2.0
1963	Bal-A	14	13	.519	35	35	9	2	0	251¹	230	35	40	124	9.8	3.33	104	.240	**.272**	16	.203	2	8	4	-2	0.5
1964	Bal-A	13	7	.650	31	31	8	4	0	204	203	18	52	109	11.4	2.91	123	.261	.310	9	.132	-1	16	16	-2	1.1
1965	Bal-A	5	7	.417	20	15	5	1	0	114²	110	17	20	63	10.3	3.38	103	.252	.286	6	.171	1	1	1	-1	0.1
	Hou-N	5	2	.714	10	10	3	2	0	76	61	6	10	34	8.4	1.89	177	.216	.243	3	.238	3	14	12	1	1.4
1966	Hou-N	3	5	.375	13	12	1	1	1	63²	79	7	10	26	12.7	3.82	90	.307	.336	1	.063	-1	-1	-3	-1	-0.5
	Chi-N	2	3	.400	11	9	1	0	0	48¹	62	8	11	28	13.6	6.14	60	.313	.349	2	.200	-1	-14	-13	-0	-1.1
	Yr	5	8	.385	24	21	2	1	1	112	141	15	21	54	13.0	4.82	73	.307	.337	3	.115	-0	-15	-16	-0	-1.6
Total	19	286	245	.539	676	609	305	45	25	4688²	4582	505	902	2357	10.6	3.41	113	.255	.293	255	.167	34	264	236	-35	24.9

● CHARLIE ROBERTSON
Robertson, Charles Culbertson   b: 1/31/1896, Dexter, Tex.   d: 8/23/84, Fort Worth, Tex.   BL/TR, 6', 175 lbs.   Deb: 5/13/19

YEAR	TM/L	W	L	PCT	G	GS	CG	SH	SV	IP	H	HR	BB	SO	RAT	ERA	ERA+	OAV	OOB	BH	AVG	PB	PR	/A	PD	TPI
1919	Chi-A	0	1	.000	1	1	0	0	0	2	5	0	0	1	22.5	9.00	35	.556	.556	0	—	-0	-1	-1	-0	-0.5
1922	Chi-A	14	15	.483	37	34	21	3	0	272	294	9	89	83	12.8	3.64	112	.286	.345	16	.184	-2	12	13	-5	0.6
1923	Chi-A	13	18	.419	38	34	18	1	0	255	262	8	104	91	13.1	3.81	104	.277	.346	21	.247	0	5	4	-2	0.3
1924	Chi-A	4	10	.286	17	14	5	0	0	97¹	108	2	54	29	15.0	4.99	83	.293	.383	6	.182	-1	-8	-9	-2	-1.4
1925	Chi-A	8	12	.400	24	23	6	2	0	137	181	5	47	27	15.1	5.26	79	.327	.381	10	.222	0	-13	-17	-2	-2.1
1926	StL-A	1	2	.333	8	7	1	0	0	28	38	4	21	13	19.6	8.36	51	.333	.445	3	.300	1	-13	-13	-0	-1.0
1927	Bos-N	7	17	.292	28	22	6	0	0	154¹	188	2	46	49	13.9	4.72	79	.308	.360	12	.240	1	-14	-17	-1	-2.4
1928	Bos-N	2	5	.286	13	7	3	0	1	59¹	73	5	16	17	13.5	5.31	74	.308	.352	0	.000	-1	-9	-9	-1	-1.1
Total	8	49	80	.380	166	142	60	6	1	1005	1149	38	377	310	13.8	4.44	90	.296	.361	68	.208	-2	-42	-49	-13	-7.6

● JERRY ROBERTSON
Robertson, Jerry Lee   b: 10/13/43, Winchester, Kan.   BB/TR, 6'2", 205 lbs.   Deb: 4/8/69

YEAR	TM/L	W	L	PCT	G	GS	CG	SH	SV	IP	H	HR	BB	SO	RAT	ERA	ERA+	OAV	OOB	BH	AVG	PB	PR	/A	PD	TPI
1969	Mon-N	5	16	.238	38	27	3	0	1	179²	186	17	81	133	13.6	3.96	93	.272	.352	5	.089	-3	-7	-6	-3	-1.1
1970	Det-A	0	0	—	11	0	0	0	0	14²	19	1	5	11	14.7	3.68	101	.306	.358	0	—	0	0	0	0	0.0
Total	2	5	16	.238	49	27	3	0	1	194¹	205	18	86	144	13.7	3.94	93	.274	.352	5	.089	-3	-7	-6	-3	-1.1

● DICK ROBERTSON
Robertson, Preston   b: 1891, Washington, D.C.   d: 10/2/44, New Orleans, La.   BR/TR, 5'9", 160 lbs.   Deb: 9/16/13

YEAR	TM/L	W	L	PCT	G	GS	CG	SH	SV	IP	H	HR	BB	SO	RAT	ERA	ERA+	OAV	OOB	BH	AVG	PB	PR	/A	PD	TPI
1913	Cin-N	0	1	.000	2	1	1	0	0	10	13	0	9	1	19.8	7.20	45	.342	.468	-0	—	0	-4	-4	-0	-0.4
1918	Bro-N	3	6	.333	13	9	7	1	0	87	87	6	28	18	11.9	2.59	108	.272	.330	9	.300	2	2	2	-0	0.4
1919	Was-A	0	1	.000	7	4	0	0	0	27²	25	1	9	7	11.1	2.28	141	.253	.315	0	.000	-1	3	3	0	0.0
Total	3	3	8	.273	22	14	8	1	0	124²	125	7	46	26	12.3	2.89	101	.274	.340	9	.225	0	2	2	-0	0.0

● RICH ROBERTSON
Robertson, Richard Paul   b: 10/14/44, Albany, Cal.   BR/TR, 6'2", 210 lbs.   Deb: 9/10/66

YEAR	TM/L	W	L	PCT	G	GS	CG	SH	SV	IP	H	HR	BB	SO	RAT	ERA	ERA+	OAV	OOB	BH	AVG	PB	PR	/A	PD	TPI
1966	SF-N	0	0	—	1	0	0	0	0	2¹	3	0	2	2	19.3	7.71	48	.300	.417	0	—	0	-1	-1	-0	0.0
1967	SF-N	0	0	—	2	0	0	0	0	2	3	0	0	1	13.5	4.50	73	.333	.333	0	—	0	-0	-0	0	0.0
1968	SF-N	2	0	1.000	3	1	1	0	0	9	9	0	3	8	12.0	6.00	49	.265	.324	1	.500	-0	-3	-3	-0	-0.6
1969	SF-N	1	3	.250	17	1	1	0	0	44¹	54	4	21	20	15.2	5.48	64	.298	.375	0	.000	-1	-9	-10	-0	-0.9

YEAR	TM/L	W	L	PCT	G	GS	CG	SH	SV	IP	H	HR	BB	SO	RAT	ERA	ERA+	OAV	OOB	BH	AVG	PB	PR	/A	PD	TPI
1970	SF-N	8	9	.471	41	26	6	0	1	183²	199	22	96	121	14.5	4.85	82	.277	.363	6	.102	-1	-16	-18	-0	-1.6
1971	SF-N	2	2	.500	23	6	1	0	1	61	66	5	31	32	14.6	4.57	74	.267	.354	1	.067	-1	-8	-8	-1	-0.7
Total	6	13	14	.481	86	40	8	1	2	302¹	333	31	153	184	14.6	4.94	76	.278	.362	8	.093	-2	-38	-40	-1	-3.8

● RICH ROBERTSON

Robertson, Richard Wayne b: 9/15/68, Nacogdoches, Tex.   BL/TL, 6'4", 175 lbs.   Deb: 4/30/93

YEAR	TM/L	W	L	PCT	G	GS	CG	SH	SV	IP	H	HR	BB	SO	RAT	ERA	ERA+	OAV	OOB	BH	AVG	PB	PR	/A	PD	TPI
1993	Pit-N	0	1	.000	9	0	0	0	0	9	15	0	4	5	19.0	6.00	67	.385	.442	0	—	0	-2	-2	-0	-0.2
1994	Pit-N	0	0	—	8	0	0	0	0	15²	20	2	10	8	17.2	6.89	62	.313	.405	1	.250	0	-5	-5	-1	0.0
Total	2	0	1	.000	17	0	0	0	0	24²	35	2	14	13	17.9	6.57	64	.340	.419	1	.250	0	-7	-7	-1	-0.2

● DEWEY ROBINSON

Robinson, Dewey Everett b: 4/28/55, Evanston, Ill.   BR/TR, 6', 180 lbs.   Deb: 4/6/79

YEAR	TM/L	W	L	PCT	G	GS	CG	SH	SV	IP	H	HR	BB	SO	RAT	ERA	ERA+	OAV	OOB	BH	AVG	PB	PR	/A	PD	TPI
1979	Chi-A	0	1	.000	11	0	0	0	0	14¹	11	1	9	5	12.6	6.28	68	.212	.328	0	—	0	-3	-3	-0	-0.2
1980	Chi-A	1	1	.500	15	0	0	0	0	35	26	2	16	28	10.8	3.09	131	.215	.307	0	—	0	4	4	0	0.2
1981	Chi-A	1	0	1.000	4	0	0	0	0	4	5	1	3	2	18.0	4.50	79	.357	.471	0	—	0	-0	-0	-0	-0.1
Total	3	2	2	.500	30	0	0	0	0	53¹	42	4	28	35	11.8	4.05	100	.225	.326	0	—	0	0	0	-0	-0.1

● DON ROBINSON

Robinson, Don Allen b: 6/8/57, Ashland, Ky.   BR/TR, 6'4", 231 lbs.   Deb: 4/10/78

YEAR	TM/L	W	L	PCT	G	GS	CG	SH	SV	IP	H	HR	BB	SO	RAT	ERA	ERA+	OAV	OOB	BH	AVG	PB	PR	/A	PD	TPI
1978	Pit-N	14	6	.700	35	32	9	1	1	228¹	203	20	57	135	10.4	3.47	107	.236	.286	20	.235	2	3	6	-1	0.6
1979	*Pit-N	8	8	.500	29	25	4	0	0	160²	171	12	52	96	12.7	3.87	100	.277	.337	10	.204	1	-2	0	-3	-0.2
1980	Pit-N	7	10	.412	29	24	3	2	1	160¹	157	14	45	103	11.6	3.99	91	.257	.314	19	.333	6	-7	-6	0	0.0
1981	Pit-N	0	3	.000	16	2	0	0	2	38¹	47	4	23	17	16.4	5.87	61	.313	.405	3	.250	1	-10	-10	1	-0.7
1982	Pit-N	15	13	.536	38	30	6	0	0	227	213	26	103	165	12.6	4.28	87	.250	.333	24	.282	8	-17	-15	-2	-1.0
1983	Pit-N	2	2	.500	9	6	0	0	0	36¹	43	5	21	28	15.9	4.46	83	.297	.386	2	.154	1	-3	-3	-0	-0.2
1984	Pit-N	5	6	.455	51	1	0	0	10	122	99	6	49	110	10.9	3.02	119	.226	.304	9	.290	4	8	8	1	1.3
1985	Pit-N	5	11	.313	44	6	0	0	3	95¹	95	6	42	65	13.1	3.87	92	.255	.334	5	.238	3	-3	-3	-0	-0.3
1986	Pit-N	3	4	.429	50	0	0	0	14	69¹	54	5	27	53	11.7	3.38	114	.237	.315	4	.667	2	3	4	0	0.7
1987	Pit-N	6	6	.500	42	0	0	0	12	65¹	66	6	22	53	12.1	3.86	107	.267	.327	1	.143	0	2	2	0	0.4
	*SF-N	5	1	.833	25	0	0	0	7	42²	39	1	18	26	12.0	2.74	140	.239	.315	3	.273	0	6	5	-1	1.0
	Yr	11	7	.611	67	0	0	0	19	108	105	7	40	79	12.1	3.42	117	.255	.322	4	.222	0	8	7	-1	1.4
1988	SF-N	10	5	.667	51	19	3	2	6	176²	152	11	49	122	10.4	2.45	133	.231	.287	13	.173	4	20	16	-2	1.6
1989	*SF-N	12	11	.522	34	32	5	1	0	197	184	22	37	96	10.2	3.43	98	.248	.285	15	.185	4	-1	-4	-4	-0.2
1990	SF-N	10	7	.588	26	25	4	0	0	157²	173	18	41	78	12.3	4.57	80	.280	.326	9	.143	1	-14	-16	-2	-1.6
1991	SF-N	5	9	.357	34	16	0	0	1	121¹	123	12	50	78	12.9	4.38	82	.265	.337	6	.150	0	-9	-11	-1	-1.2
1992	Cal-A	1	0	1.000	3	3	0	0	0	16¹	19	1	3	9	12.1	2.20	181	.292	.324	0	—	0	3	3	-1	0.1
	Phi-N	1	4	.200	8	8	0	0	0	43²	49	4	12	11	11.1	6.18	56	.290	.310	7	.389	3	-13	-13	-1	-1.1
Total	15	109	106	.507	524	229	34	6	57	1958¹	1894	175	643	1251	11.8	3.79	96	.255	.317	146	.231	41	-34	-34	-14	-0.8

● HUMBERTO ROBINSON

Robinson, Humberto Valentino b: 6/25/30, Colon, Panama   BR/TR, 6'1", 155 lbs.   Deb: 4/20/55

YEAR	TM/L	W	L	PCT	G	GS	CG	SH	SV	IP	H	HR	BB	SO	RAT	ERA	ERA+	OAV	OOB	BH	AVG	PB	PR	/A	PD	TPI
1955	Mil-N	3	1	.750	13	2	1	0	2	38	31	1	25	19	14.2	3.08	122	.235	.373	1	.077	-1	4	3	0	0.2
1956	Mil-N	0	0	—	1	0	0	0	0	2	1	0	2	0	13.5	0.00	—	.167	.375	0	—	0	1	1	0	0.0
1958	Mil-N	2	4	.333	19	0	0	0	1	41²	30	4	13	26	9.7	3.02	116	.203	.276	1	.167	1	4	2	1	0.5
1959	Cle-A	1	0	1.000	5	0	0	0	0	8²	9	0	4	6	13.5	4.15	89	.281	.361	0	—	0	-0	-0	0	0.0
	Phi-N	2	4	.333	31	4	1	0	1	73	70	6	24	32	11.6	3.33	123	.251	.310	3	.231	1	5	6	0	0.7
1960	Phi-N	0	4	.000	33	1	0	0	0	49²	48	6	22	31	12.7	3.44	113	.255	.333	1	.167	-0	2	2	0	0.2
Total	5	8	13	.381	102	7	2	0	4	213	189	17	90	114	12.0	3.25	119	.241	.323	6	.158	0	16	14	2	1.6

● JEFF ROBINSON

Robinson, Jeffrey Daniel b: 12/13/60, Santa Ana, Cal.   BR/TR, 6'4", 200 lbs.   Deb: 4/7/84

YEAR	TM/L	W	L	PCT	G	GS	CG	SH	SV	IP	H	HR	BB	SO	RAT	ERA	ERA+	OAV	OOB	BH	AVG	PB	PR	/A	PD	TPI
1984	SF-N	7	15	.318	34	33	1	1	0	171²	195	12	52	102	13.3	4.56	77	.288	.345	7	.115	-2	-19	-20	0	-2.5
1985	SF-N	0	0	—	8	0	0	0	0	12¹	12	2	10	8	19.0	5.11	67	.333	.448	0	—	0	-2	-2	-0	0.0
1986	SF-N	6	3	.667	64	1	0	0	8	104¹	92	6	32	90	10.8	3.36	105	.234	.293	1	.067	-1	4	2	-1	0.0
1987	SF-N	6	8	.429	63	0	0	0	10	96²	69	10	48	82	11.0	2.79	138	.207	.309	2	.111	-1	14	11	1	1.8
	Pit-N	2	1	.667	18	0	0	0	4	26²	20	1	6	19	8.8	3.04	135	.215	.263	1	.250	1	3	3	0	0.6
	Yr	8	9	.471	81	0	0	0	14	123¹	89	11	54	101	10.4	2.85	137	.206	.295	3	.136	0	17	14	1	2.4
1988	Pit-N	11	5	.688	75	0	0	0	9	124²	113	6	39	87	11.2	3.03	112	.244	.307	6	.188	0	6	5	0	0.8
1989	Pit-N	7	13	.350	50	19	0	0	4	141¹	161	14	59	95	14.1	4.58	73	.283	.351	8	.229	2	-17	-19	1	-2.3
1990	NY-A	3	6	.333	54	4	1	0	0	88²	82	8	34	43	11.9	3.45	115	.248	.320	0	—	0	4	5	2	0.7
1991	Cal-A	0	3	.000	39	0	0	0	0	57	56	9	29	57	13.7	5.37	76	.259	.352	0	—	0	-8	-8	0	-0.5
1992	Chi-N	4	3	.571	49	5	0	0	1	78	76	5	46	46	13.6	3.00	120	.263	.356	0	.000	-1	5	5	1	0.4
Total	9	46	57	.447	454	62	2	1	39	901¹	880	75	349	629	12.5	3.79	95	.258	.330	22	.137	-1	-10	-18	4	-1.0

● JEFF ROBINSON

Robinson, Jeffrey Mark b: 12/14/61, Ventura, Cal.   BR/TR, 6'6", 240 lbs.   Deb: 4/12/87

YEAR	TM/L	W	L	PCT	G	GS	CG	SH	SV	IP	H	HR	BB	SO	RAT	ERA	ERA+	OAV	OOB	BH	AVG	PB	PR	/A	PD	TPI
1987	*Det-A	9	6	.600	29	21	2	1	0	127¹	132	16	54	98	13.6	5.37	79	.262	.342	0	—	0	-13	-16	-1	-1.6
1988	Det-A	13	6	.684	24	23	6	2	0	172	121	19	72	114	10.3	2.98	128	**.197**	.284	0	—	0	19	16	-0	1.7
1989	Det-A	4	5	.444	16	16	1	1	0	78	76	10	46	40	14.2	4.73	81	.259	.361	0	—	0	-7	-8	-1	-0.9
1990	Det-A	10	9	.526	27	27	1	1	0	145	141	23	88	76	14.6	5.96	66	.255	.364	0	—	0	-33	-32	-1	-3.7
1991	Bal-A	4	9	.308	21	19	0	0	0	104¹	119	12	51	65	15.2	5.18	76	.289	.375	0	—	0	-13	-14	-1	-1.4
1992	Tex-A	4	4	.500	16	4	0	0	0	45²	50	6	21	18	14.0	5.72	66	.281	.357	0	—	0	-9	-10	-1	-1.4
	Pit-N	3	1	.750	8	7	0	0	0	36¹	33	2	15	14	12.1	4.46	77	.244	.325	1	.091	-1	-4	-4	0	-0.5
Total	6	47	40	.540	141	117	10	5	0	708²	672	88	347	425	13.2	4.79	82	.250	.341	1	.091	-1	-60	-68	-4	-7.8

● JACK ROBINSON

Robinson, John Edward b: 2/20/21, Orange, N.J.   BR/TR, 6', 175 lbs.   Deb: 5/4/49

YEAR	TM/L	W	L	PCT	G	GS	CG	SH	SV	IP	H	HR	BB	SO	RAT	ERA	ERA+	OAV	OOB	BH	AVG	PB	PR	/A	PD	TPI
1949	Bos-A	0	0	—	3	0	0	0	0	4	4	0	1	1	13.5	2.25	194	.267	.353	0	—	0	1	1	0	0.0

● HANK ROBINSON

Robinson, John Henry "Rube" (b: John Henry Roberson)
b: 8/16/1889, Floyd, Ark.   d: 7/3/65, N.Little Rock, Ark   BR/TL, 5'11.5", 160 lbs.   Deb: 9/2/11

YEAR	TM/L	W	L	PCT	G	GS	CG	SH	SV	IP	H	HR	BB	SO	RAT	ERA	ERA+	OAV	OOB	BH	AVG	PB	PR	/A	PD	TPI
1911	Pit-N	0	1	.000	8	1	0	0	0	13	13	0	5	8	13.2	2.77	124	.283	.365	0	.000	-0	1	1	1	0.1
1912	*Pit-N	12	7	.632	33	16	11	0	2	175	146	3	30	79	9.6	2.26	144	.237	.284	15	.254	3	22	19	-1	2.1
1913	Pit-N	14	9	.609	43	23	8	1	0	196¹	184	4	41	50	10.6	2.38	126	.255	.301	11	.180	-1	18	14	-2	1.3
1914	StL-N	7	8	.467	26	16	6	1	0	126	128	1	32	30	11.7	3.00	93	.274	.325	6	.171	-0	-3	-3	2	-0.2
1915	StL-N	7	8	.467	32	15	6	1	0	143	128	1	35	57	10.7	2.45	114	.245	.301	5	.106	-2	5	5	1	0.4
1918	NY-A	2	4	.333	11	3	1	0	0	48	47	0	16	14	12.4	3.00	94	.269	.340	0	.000	-2	-1	-1	-0	-0.4
Total	6	42	37	.532	150	73	32	3	2	701¹	646	6	159	238	10.7	2.53	118	.253	.305	37	.170	-3	42	36	1	3.3

● RON ROBINSON

Robinson, Ronald Dean b: 3/24/62, Exeter, Cal.   BR/TR, 6'4", 235 lbs.   Deb: 8/14/84

YEAR	TM/L	W	L	PCT	G	GS	CG	SH	SV	IP	H	HR	BB	SO	RAT	ERA	ERA+	OAV	OOB	BH	AVG	PB	PR	/A	PD	TPI
1984	Cin-N	1	2	.333	12	5	1	0	0	39²	35	3	24	24	10.9	2.72	139	.232	.293	0	.000	-1	4	5	0	0.2
1985	Cin-N	7	7	.500	33	12	0	0	1	108¹	107	11	32	76	11.6	3.99	95	.259	.314	2	.091	-1	-5	-2	1	-0.4
1986	Cin-N	10	3	.769	70	0	0	0	14	116²	110	10	43	117	12.0	3.24	119	.253	.323	1	.071	-1	6	8	1	1.1
1987	Cin-N	7	5	.583	48	18	0	0	1	154	148	14	43	99	11.2	3.68	115	.256	.308	7	.194	0	7	10	-2	0.5
1988	Cin-N	3	7	.300	17	16	0	0	0	78²	88	5	26	38	13.3	4.12	87	.285	.344	5	.200	1	-6	-5	-0	-0.5
1989	Cin-N	5	3	.625	15	15	0	0	0	83¹	80	8	21	36	11.9	3.35	108	.252	.317	6	.214	1	4	2	-0	0.4
1990	Cin-N	2	2	.500	6	5	0	0	0	31¹	36	2	14	14	14.4	4.88	81	.295	.368	1	.091	-1	-4	-3	0	-0.4
	Mil-A	12	5	.706	22	22	7	2	0	148¹	158	5	22	57	10.9	2.91	133	.274	.326	0	—	0	16	16	0	1.7
1991	Mil-A	0	1	.000	1	1	0	0	0	4¹	6	0	4	1	20.8	6.23	64	.353	.476	0	—	0	-1	-0	-0	-0.1
1992	Mil-A	1	4	.200	8	8	0	0	0	35¹	51	3	14	12	17.1	5.86	65	.331	.394	0	—	0	-8	-9	-1	-0.9
Total	9	48	39	.552	232	102	C8	2	19	800	819	61	253	473	12.3	3.63	107	.267	.326	22	.153	-2	12	21	-1	1.5

YEAR TM/L	W	L	PCT	G	GS	CG	SH	SV	IP	H	HR	BB	SO	RAT	ERA	ERA+	OAV	OOB	BH	AVG	PB	PR	/A	PD	TPI
● **BILL ROBINSON** Robinson, William (b: William Anderson) b: Taylorsville, Ky. Deb: 8/12/1889																									
1889 Lou-a	0	1	.000	1	1	1	0	0	8	10	2	6	2	18.0	10.13	38	.297	.403	1	.333	0	-6	-6	0	-0.4
● **YANK ROBINSON** Robinson, William H. b: 9/19/1859, Philadelphia, Pa. d: 8/25/1894, St.Louis, Mo. BR/TR, 5'6.5", 170 lbs. Deb: 8/24/1882 ♦																									
1882 Det-N	0	0	—	1	0	0	0	0	2	0	0	1	0	4.5	0.00	—	.000	.125	7	.179	-0	1	1	0	0.0
1884 Bal-U	3	3	.500	11	3	3	0	0	75	96	1	18	61	13.7	3.48	77	.291	.328	111	.267	-0	-9	-7	-3	-0.7
1886 *StL-a	0	1	.000	1	1	1	0	0	9	10	0	7	1	17.0	3.00	115	.286	.405	132	.274	0	0	0	-0	0.1
1887 *StL-a	0	0	—	1	0	0	0	1	3	3	0	3	0	21.0	3.00	151	.333	.538	131	.305	0	0	1	-0	0.0
Total 4	3	4	.429	14	4	4	0	1	89	109	1	29	62	14.1	3.34	85	.287	.339	825	.241	-0	-7	-5	-3	-0.6
● **CHICK ROBITAILLE** Robitaille, Joseph Anthony b: 3/2/1879, Whitehall, N.Y. d: 7/30/47, Waterford, N.Y. BR/TR, 5'8", 150 lbs. Deb: 9/2/04																									
1904 Pit-N	4	3	.571	9	8	8	0	0	66	52	1	13	34	9.0	1.91	144	.208	.250	2	.095	-2	6	6	-1	0.3
1905 Pit-N	8	5	.615	17	12	10	0	0	120¹	126	1	28	32	11.7	2.92	103	.276	.322	6	.133	-2	1	1	-0	-0.1
Total 2	12	8	.600	26	20	18	0	0	186¹	178	2	41	66	10.8	2.56	114	.252	.297	8	.121	-4	7	7	-1	0.2
● **ARMANDO ROCHE** Roche, Armando (Baez) b: 12/7/26, Havana, Cuba BR/TR, 6', 190 lbs. Deb: 5/10/45																									
1945 Was-A	0	0	—	2	0	0	0	0	6	10	2	2	0	18.0	6.00	52	.400	.444	0	.000	-0	-2	-2	0	0.0
● **MIKE ROCHFORD** Rochford, Michael Joseph b: 3/14/63, Methuen, Mass. BL/TL, 6'4", 205 lbs. Deb: 9/3/88																									
1988 Bos-A	0	0	—	2	0	0	0	0	2¹	4	1	1	1	19.3	19.30		.364	.417	0	—	0	1	1	0	0.0
1989 Bos-A	0	0	—	4	0	0	0	0	4	4	1	4	1	18.0	6.75	61	.267	.421	0	—	0	-1	-1	-0	0.0
1990 Bos-A	0	1	.000	2	1	0	0	0	4	10	1	4	0	31.5	18.00	23	.526	.609	0	—	0	-6	-6	-0	-1.1
Total 3	0	1	.000	8	1	0	0	0	10¹	18	2	9	2	23.5	9.58	43	.400	.500	0	—	0	-7	-6	-0	-1.1
● **RICH RODAS** Rodas, Richard Martin b: 11/7/59, Roseville, Cal. BL/TL, 6'1", 180 lbs. Deb: 9/6/83																									
1983 LA-N	0	0	—	7	0	0	0	0	4²	4	0	3	5	13.5	1.93	186	.222	.333	0	—	0	1	1	-0	0.0
1984 LA-N	0	0	—	3	0	0	0	0	5	5	2	1	1	10.8	5.40	65	.250	.286	0	.000	-0	-1	-1	0	0.0
Total 2	0	0	—	10	0	0	0	0	9²	9	2	4	6	12.1	3.72	96	.237	.310	0	.000	-0	-0	-0	0	0.0
● **EDUARDO RODRIGUEZ** Rodriguez, Eduardo (Reyes) b: 3/6/52, Barceloneta, P.R. BR/TR, 6', 185 lbs. Deb: 6/20/73																									
1973 Mil-A	9	7	.563	30	6	2	0	5	76¹	71	6	47	49	14.1	3.30	114	.247	.357	1	1.000	1	4	4	-0	0.9
1974 Mil-A	7	4	.636	43	6	0	0	4	111²	97	7	51	58	12.3	3.63	100	.241	.333	0	—	0	-0	-0	-0	0.0
1975 Mil-A	7	0	1.000	43	1	0	0	7	87²	77	9	44	65	12.9	3.49	110	.235	.334	0	—	0	3	3	-2	0.1
1976 Mil-A	5	13	.278	45	12	3	0	8	136	124	10	65	77	12.7	3.64	96	.249	.339	0	—	0	-2	-2	-1	-0.3
1977 Mil-A	5	6	.455	42	5	1	1	4	142²	126	15	56	104	11.7	4.35	93	.236	.311	0	—	0	-5	-5	-1	-0.4
1978 Mil-A	5	5	.500	32	8	0	0	2	105¹	107	9	26	51	11.5	3.93	96	.262	.310	0	—	0	-0	-0	-2	-0.2
1979 KC-A	4	1	.800	29	1	1	0	2	74¹	79	9	34	26	14.0	4.84	88	.276	.359	0	—	0	-5	-5	-1	-0.5
Total 7	42	36	.538	264	39	7	1	32	734	681	65	323	430	12.6	3.89	98	.248	.332	1	1.000	1	-7	-7	-5	-0.4
● **FREDDY RODRIGUEZ** Rodriguez, Fernando Pedro (Borrego) b: 4/29/24, Havana, Cuba BR/TR, 6', 180 lbs. Deb: 4/18/58																									
1958 Chi-N	0	0	—	7	0	0	0	2	7¹	8	2	5	5	17.2	7.36	53	.267	.389	0	.000	-0	-3	-3	-0	-0.2
1959 Phi-N	0	0	—	1	0	0	0	0	2	4	1	0	1	22.5	13.50	30	.400	.455	0	—	0	-2	-2	-0	0.0
Total 2	0	0	—	8	0	0	0	2	9¹	12	3	5	6	18.3	8.68	46	.300	.404	0	.000	-0	-5	-5	-0	-0.2
● **RICK RODRIGUEZ** Rodriguez, Ricardo b: 9/21/60, Oakland, Cal. BR/TR, 6'3", 190 lbs. Deb: 9/17/86																									
1986 Oak-A	1	2	.333	3	3	0	0	0	16¹	17	4	7	2	13.2	6.61	58	.262	.333	0	—	0	-4	-5	2	-0.5
1987 Oak-A	1	0	1.000	15	0	0	0	0	24¹	32	1	15	9	17.8	2.96	139	.337	.432	0	—	0	4	3	1	0.2
1988 Cle-A	1	2	.333	10	5	0	0	0	33	43	4	17	9	16.6	7.09	58	.323	.404	0	—	0	-11	-11	1	-0.8
1990 SF-N	0	0	—	3	0	0	0	0	3¹	5	0	2	2	18.9	8.10	45	.357	.438	0	—	0	-2	-2	0	0.0
Total 4	3	4	.429	31	8	0	0	0	77	97	9	41	22	16.4	5.73	71	.316	.400	0	—	0	-13	-14	2	-1.1
● **RICH RODRIGUEZ** Rodriguez, Richard Anthony b: 3/1/63, Downey, Cal. BL/TL, 5'10", 194 lbs. Deb: 6/30/90																									
1990 SD-N	1	1	.500	32	0	0	0	1	47²	52	2	16	22	13.0	2.83	135	.287	.348	0	.000	-0	5	5	1	0.3
1991 SD-N	3	1	.750	64	1	0	0	0	80	66	8	44	40	12.4	3.26	116	.234	.337	0	.000	-1	4	5	-0	0.2
1992 SD-N	6	3	.667	61	1	0	0	0	91	77	4	29	64	10.5	2.37	151	.229	.290	0	.000	-0	11	12	1	1.2
1993 SD-N	2	3	.400	34	1	0	0	0	30	34	2	9	22	13.2	3.30	125	.281	.336	0	.000	-0	2	3	-1	0.4
Fla-N	0	1	.000	36	0	0	0	0	46	39	8	24	21	12.5	4.11	105	.229	.328	0	.000	-0	1	1	1	0.1
Yr	2	4	.333	70	1	0	0	0	76	73	10	33	43	12.7	3.79	112	.250	.328	0	.000	-0	2	4	0	0.5
1994 StL-N	3	5	.375	56	0	0	0	0	60¹	62	6	26	43	13.3	4.03	101	.270	.346	0	.000	-1	0	0	-0	0.0
Total 5	15	14	.517	283	2	0	0	4	355	330	30	148	212	12.2	3.22	121	.250	.327	0	.000	-1	24	26	-0	2.1
● **ROSARIO RODRIGUEZ** Rodriguez, Rosario Isabel (Echavarria) b: 7/8/69, Los Mochis, Mexico BR/TL, 6', 185 lbs. Deb: 9/1/89																									
1989 Cin-N	1	1	.500	7	0	0	0	0	4¹	3	0	2	0	12.5	4.15	87	.188	.316	0	—	0	-0	-0	0	-0.1
1990 Cin-N	0	0	—	9	0	0	0	0	10¹	15	3	2	8	15.7	6.10	65	.357	.400	0	—	0	-3	-2	0	0.0
1991 *Pit-N	1	1	.500	18	0	0	0	6	15¹	14	1	8	10	13.5	4.11	87	.246	.348	0	.000	-0	-1	-1	0	-0.2
Total 3	2	2	.500	34	0	0	0	6	30	32	4	13	18	14.1	4.80	77	.278	.362	0	.000	-0	-4	-4	1	-0.3
● **ROBERTO RODRIQUEZ** Rodriguez, Roberto (Munoz) b: 11/29/41, Caracas, Venez. BR/TR, 6'3", 185 lbs. Deb: 5/13/67																									
1967 KC-A	1	1	.500	15	5	0	0	0	40¹	42	4	14	29	12.7	3.57	89	.268	.331	0	.000	-1	-2	-2	-0	-0.3
1970 Oak-A	0	0	—	6	0	0	0	0	12¹	10	2	3	8	9.5	2.92	121	.227	.277	0	.000	-0	1	1	0	0.0
SD-N	0	0	—	10	0	0	0	0	16¹	26	5	6	17	17.1	6.61	60	.366	.408	0	.000	-0	-5	-5	-0	-0.2
Chi-N	3	2	.600	26	0	0	0	5	43¹	50	6	15	46	13.5	5.82	77	.289	.346	1	.125	1	-9	-6	-0	-0.6
Yr	3	2	.600	36	0	0	0	5	59²	76	7	20	54	14.5	6.03	72	.311	.364	1	.091	0	-13	-11	-0	-0.8
Total 2	4	3	.571	57	5	0	0	7	112¹	128	13	37	91	13.3	4.81	80	.288	.344	1	.048	-1	-14	-12	-0	-1.1
● **PREACHER ROE** Roe, Elwin Charles b: 2/26/15, Ash Flat, Ark. BR/TL, 6'2", 170 lbs. Deb: 8/22/38																									
1938 StL-N	0	0	—	1	0	0	0	0	2²	6	0	2	1	27.0	13.50	29	.429	.500	0	.000	-0	0	0	-0	0.0
1944 Pit-N	13	11	.542	39	25	7	1	1	185¹	182	7	59	88	11.8	3.11	120	.253	.311	7	.132	-2	10	13	-1	1.2
1945 Pit-N†	14	13	.519	33	31	15	3	1	235	228	11	46	**148**	10.5	2.87	137	.259	.296	8	.107	-3	24	28	1	2.8
1946 Pit-N	3	8	.273	21	10	1	0	2	70	83	5	25	28	14.1	5.14	69	.294	.356	1	.067	-1	-13	-13	-0	-1.9
1947 Pit-N	4	15	.211	38	22	4	1	0	144	163	19	63	59	13.7	5.25	80	.276	.348	5	.125	-2	-19	-16	-1	-2.2
1948 Bro-N	12	8	.600	34	22	8	2	2	177²	156	14	33	86	9.7	2.63	152	.233	.271	5	.098	-2	26	27	-1	2.6
1949 *Bro-N★	15	6	.714	30	27	13	3	1	212²	201	25	44	109	10.5	2.79	147	.252	.293	8	.114	-2	29	31	-2	2.4
1950 Bro-N☆	19	11	.633	36	32	16	2	1	250²	245	34	66	125	11.3	3.30	124	.257	.308	14	.154	-3	23	22	-1	1.9
1951 Bro-N☆	22	3	**.880**	34	33	19	2	0	257²	247	30	64	113	10.9	3.04	129	.258	.304	10	.112	-5	26	25	-1	1.7
1952 *Bro-N†	11	2	.846	27	25	8	2	0	158²	163	16	39	83	11.6	3.12	117	.270	.317	4	.070	-3	11	9	-1	0.9
1953 *Bro-N	11	3	.786	25	24	9	1	0	157	171	27	40	85	12.2	4.36	98	.278	.323	3	.053	-4	-1	-2	-1	-0.5
1954 Bro-N	3	4	.429	15	7	0	0	1	69	71	11	23	31	13.1	5.00	82	.279	.341	3	.088	-1	-3	-3	-0	-0.3
Total 12	127	84	.602	333	261	101	17	10	1914¹	1907	199	504	956	11.4	3.43	116	.261	.310	68	.110	-27	108	115	-9	7.5
● **CLAY ROE** Roe, James Clay "Shad" b: 1/7/04, Greenbriar, Tenn. d: 4/4/56, Cleveland, Miss. BL/TL, 6'1", 180 lbs. Deb: 10/3/23																									
1923 Was-A	0	1	.000	1	1	0	0	0	1²	0	0	6	2	32.4	0.00	—	.000	.500	0	—	0	1	1	-0	0.5
● **ED ROEBUCK** Roebuck, Edward Jack b: 7/3/31, East Millsboro, Pa. BR/TR, 6'2", 185 lbs. Deb: 4/18/55																									
1955 *Bro-N	5	6	.455	47	0	0	0	12	84	96	14	24	33	13.2	4.71	86	.288	.342	2	.111	-1	-6	-6	1	-0.9
1956 *Bro-N	5	4	.556	43	0	0	0	1	89¹	83	15	29	60	11.5	3.93	101	.251	.315	6	.333	2	-2	0	1	0.3

YEAR	TM/L	W	L	PCT	G	GS	CG	SH	SV	IP	H	HR	BB	SO	RAT	ERA	ERA+	OAV	OOB	BH	AVG	PB	PR	/A	PD	TPI
1957	Bro-N	8	2	.800	44	1	0	0	8	96¹	70	9	46	73	11.0	2.71	154	.205	.303	5	.238	2	13	16	2	2.3
1958	LA-N	0	1	.000	32	0	0	0	5	44	45	9	15	26	12.7	3.48	118	.271	.339	2	.500	1	2	3	-0	0.2
1960	LA-N	8	3	.727	58	0	0	0	8	116²	109	13	38	77	11.3	2.78	143	.256	.317	4	.167	-0	13	15	2	1.8
1961	LA-N	2	0	1.000	5	0	0	0	0	9	12	1	2	9	14.0	5.00	87	.324	.359	0	.000	-0	-1	-1	-0	-0.2
1962	LA-N	10	2	.833	64	0	0	0	9	119¹	102	11	54	72	12.2	3.09	117	.232	.325	6	.214	1	11	7	0	0.9
1963	LA-N	2	4	.333	29	0	0	0	0	40¹	54	4	21	26	17.2	4.24	71	.321	.403	1	.250	0	-4	-5	1	-0.7
	Was-A	2	1	.667	26	0	0	0	4	57¹	63	5	29	25	14.8	3.30	113	.284	.372	2	.182	0	2	3	1	0.2
1964	Was-A	0	0	—	2	0	0	0	0	1	0	0	2	0	18.0	9.00	41	.000	.333	0	—	-0	-1	-1	0	0.0
	Phi-N	5	3	.625	60	0	0	0	12	77¹	55	7	25	42	9.8	2.21	157	.196	.272	0	.000	-1	11	11	1	1.5
1965	Phi-N	5	3	.625	44	0	0	0	3	50¹	55	2	15	29	13.4	3.40	102	.288	.355	0	.000	0	1	0	-1	-0.1
1966	Phi-N	0	2	.000	6	0	0	0	0	6	9	0	2	5	16.5	6.00	60	.333	.379	0	—	-0	-2	-2	-0	-0.5
Total	11	52	31	.627	460	1	0	0	62	791	753	90	302	477	12.3	3.35	114	.254	.329	28	.204	3	38	41	7	4.8

● **MIKE ROESLER**   Roesler, Michael Joseph   b: 9/12/63, Fort Wayne, Ind.   BR/TR, 6'5", 195 lbs.   Deb: 8/9/89

YEAR	TM/L	W	L	PCT	G	GS	CG	SH	SV	IP	H	HR	BB	SO	RAT	ERA	ERA+	OAV	OOB	BH	AVG	PB	PR	/A	PD	TPI
1989	Cin-N	0	1	.000	17	0	0	0	0	25	22	4	9	14	11.2	3.96	91	.239	.307	0	—	0	-1	-1	-1	-0.1
1990	Pit-N	1	0	1.000	5	0	0	0	0	6	5	1	2	4	10.5	3.00	121	.217	.280	0	.000	-0	1	0	-0	0.0
Total	2	1	1	.500	22	0	0	0	0	31	27	5	11	18	11.0	3.77	96	.235	.302	0	—	-0	-1	-1	-1	-0.1

● **OSCAR ROETTGER**   Roettger, Oscar Frederick Louis "Okkie"   b: 2/19/1900, St.Louis, Mo.   d: 7/4/86, St.Louis, Mo.   BR/TR, 6', 170 lbs.   Deb: 7/7/23   F♦

YEAR	TM/L	W	L	PCT	G	GS	CG	SH	SV	IP	H	HR	BB	SO	RAT	ERA	ERA+	OAV	OOB	BH	AVG	PB	PR	/A	PD	TPI
1923	NY-A	0	0	—	5	0	0	0	1	11²	16	3	12	7	22.4	8.49	46	.340	.483	0	.000	-0	-6	-6	0	-0.1
1924	NY-A	0	0	—	1	0	0	0	0	0	1	0	2	0	—	—	—	1.000	1.000	0	—	-0				
Total	2	0	0	—	6	0	0	0	1	11²	17	3	14	7	24.7	8.49	46	.354	.508	14	.212	-0	-6	-6	0	-0.1

● **JOE ROGALSKI**   Rogalski, Joseph Anthony   b: 7/15/12, Ashland, Wis.   d: 11/20/51, Ashland, Wis.   BR/TR, 6'2", 187 lbs.   Deb: 9/14/38

YEAR	TM/L	W	L	PCT	G	GS	CG	SH	SV	IP	H	HR	BB	SO	RAT	ERA	ERA+	OAV	OOB	BH	AVG	PB	PR	/A	PD	TPI
1938	Det-A	0	0	—	2	0	0	0	0	7	12	0	0	2	15.4	2.57	194	.400	.400	0	.000	-0	2	2	-0	0.0

● **KEVIN ROGERS**   Rogers, Charles Kevin   b: 8/20/68, Cleveland, Miss.   BB/TL, 6'2", 190 lbs.   Deb: 9/4/92

YEAR	TM/L	W	L	PCT	G	GS	CG	SH	SV	IP	H	HR	BB	SO	RAT	ERA	ERA+	OAV	OOB	BH	AVG	PB	PR	/A	PD	TPI
1992	SF-N	0	2	.000	6	6	0	0	0	34	37	4	13	26	13.5	4.24	78	.280	.349	2	.222	0	-3	-4	-1	-0.2
1993	SF-N	2	2	.500	64	0	0	0	0	80²	71	3	28	62	11.5	2.68	146	.236	.309	0	—	-0	12	11	-1	0.4
1994	SF-N	0	0	—	9	0	0	0	0	10¹	10	1	6	7	13.9	3.48	115	.250	.348	0	—	-0	1	1	-0	0.0
Total	3	2	4	.333	79	6	0	0	0	125	118	8	47	95	12.2	3.17	118	.249	.324	2	.167	-0	10	8	-2	0.2

● **KENNY ROGERS**   Rogers, Kenneth Scott   b: 11/10/64, Savannah, Ga.   BL/TL, 6'1", 200 lbs.   Deb: 4/6/89

YEAR	TM/L	W	L	PCT	G	GS	CG	SH	SV	IP	H	HR	BB	SO	RAT	ERA	ERA+	OAV	OOB	BH	AVG	PB	PR	/A	PD	TPI
1989	Tex-A	3	4	.429	73	0	0	0	2	73²	60	4	42	63	13.0	2.93	135	.232	.348	0	—	0	8	8	2	1.0
1990	Tex-A	10	6	.625	69	3	0	0	15	97²	93	6	42	74	12.5	3.13	125	.249	.326	0	—	0	8	9	2	1.8
1991	Tex-A	10	10	.500	63	9	0	0	5	109²	121	14	61	73	15.4	5.42	74	.281	.378	0	—	-16	-17	-0	-2.9	
1992	Tex-A	3	6	.333	81	0	0	0	6	78²	80	7	26	70	12.1	3.09	123	.261	.319	0	—	0	7	6	1	1.1
1993	Tex-A	16	10	.615	35	33	5	0	0	208¹	210	18	71	140	12.3	4.10	101	.263	.326	0	—	0	5	1	4	0.8
1994	Tex-A	11	8	.579	24	24	6	2	0	167¹	169	24	52	120	12.0	4.46	102	.260	.318	0	—	0	6	1	0	0.5
Total	6	53	44	.546	345	69	11	2	28	735¹	733	71	294	540	12.8	4.03	103	.260	.334	0	—	0	19	9	9	2.3

● **LEE ROGERS**   Rogers, Lee Otis "Buck"   b: 10/8/13, Tuscaloosa, Ala.   BR/TL, 5'11", 170 lbs.   Deb: 4/27/38

YEAR	TM/L	W	L	PCT	G	GS	CG	SH	SV	IP	H	HR	BB	SO	RAT	ERA	ERA+	OAV	OOB	BH	AVG	PB	PR	/A	PD	TPI
1938	Bos-A	1	1	.500	14	2	0	0	0	27²	32	4	18	7	16.3¹	6.51	76	.302	.403	0	.000	-0	-5	-5	1	-0.2
	Bro-N	0	2	.000	12	2	0	0	0	23²	23	0	10	11	12.9	5.70	68	.256	.337	0	.000	-0	-5	-5	1	-0.2
Total	1	1	3	.250	26	4	0	0	0	51¹	55	4	28	18	14.7	6.14	73	.281	.373	0	.000	0	-10	-10	2	-0.4

● **BUCK ROGERS**   Rogers, Orlin Woodrow "Lefty"   b: 11/5/12, Spring Garden, Va.   BR/TL, 5'8.5", 164 lbs.   Deb: 9/15/35

YEAR	TM/L	W	L	PCT	G	GS	CG	SH	SV	IP	H	HR	BB	SO	RAT	ERA	ERA+	OAV	OOB	BH	AVG	PB	PR	/A	PD	TPI
1935	Was-A	0	1	.000	2	1	0	0	0	10	16	0	6	7	19.8	7.20	60	.340	.415	0	.000	-1	-3	-3	-0	-0.3

● **STEVE ROGERS**   Rogers, Stephen Douglas   b: 10/26/49, Jefferson City, Mo.   BR/TR, 6'1", 182 lbs.   Deb: 7/18/73

YEAR	TM/L	W	L	PCT	G	GS	CG	SH	SV	IP	H	HR	BB	SO	RAT	ERA	ERA+	OAV	OOB	BH	AVG	PB	PR	/A	PD	TPI
1973	Mon-N	10	5	.667	17	17	7	3	0	134	93	5	49	64	9.6	1.54	247	.199	.276	4	.098	-1	31	34	1	4.1
1974	Mon-N☆	15	22	.405	38	38	11	1	0	253²	255	19	80	154	12.1	4.47	86	.265	.324	11	.139	-1	-24	-18	3	-2.2
1975	Mon-N	11	12	.478	35	35	12	3	0	251²	248	13	88	137	12.2	3.29	116	.260	.325	13	.169	1	9	15	0	1.5
1976	Mon-N	7	17	.292	33	32	8	4	1	230	212	10	69	150	11.2	3.21	116	.256	.309	11	.149	-2	7	13	5	1.7
1977	Mon-N	17	16	.515	40	40	17	4	0	301²	272	16	81	206	10.7	3.10	123	.242	.296	10	.104	-5	27	24	4	2.3
1978	Mon-N★	13	10	.565	30	29	11	1	1	219	186	12	64	126	10.4	2.47	143	.235	.294	8	.113	-2	27	26	1	2.6
1979	Mon-N★	13	12	.520	37	37	13	5	0	248²	232	14	78	143	11.4	3.00	122	.251	.312	12	.156	1	20	18	2	2.1
1980	Mon-N	16	11	.593	37	37	14	4	0	281	247	16	85	147	10.7	2.98	120	.238	.298	13	.160	1	19	18	-1	1.9
1981	*Mon-N	12	8	.600	22	22	7	3	0	160²	149	7	41	87	10.8	3.42	102	.248	.298	8	.145	-1	1	1	-1	0.0
1982	Mon-N★	19	8	.704	35	35	14	4	0	277	245	12	65	179	10.3	2.40	151	.237	.286	11	.129	0	37	38	0	3.7
1983	Mon-N☆	17	12	.586	36	36	13	5	0	273	258	14	78	146	11.2	3.23	111	.250	.308	12	.146	-1	12	11	-2	0.8
1984	Mon-N	6	15	.286	31	28	1	0	0	169¹	171	12	78	64	13.3	4.31	80	.267	.348	7	.143	1	-13	-17	0	-1.3
1985	Mon-N	2	4	.333	8	7	1	0	0	38	51	1	20	18	16.8	5.68	60	.329	.406	2	.143	0	-9	-10	1	-1.2
Total	13	158	152	.510	399	393	129	37	2	2837²	2619	151	876	1621	11.2	3.17	115	.248	.308	122	.138	-8	146	154	14	15.3

● **TOM ROGERS**   Rogers, Thomas Andrew "Shotgun"   b: 2/12/1892, Sparta, Tenn.   d: 3/7/36, Nashville, Tenn.   BR/TR, 6'0.5", 180 lbs.   Deb: 4/14/17

YEAR	TM/L	W	L	PCT	G	GS	CG	SH	SV	IP	H	HR	BB	SO	RAT	ERA	ERA+	OAV	OOB	BH	AVG	PB	PR	/A	PD	TPI
1917	StL-A	3	6	.333	24	8	3	0	0	108²	112	2	44	27	13.2	3.89	67	.277	.352	5	.172	-1	-15	-16	-0	-1.4
1918	StL-A	8	10	.444	29	16	11	0	2	154	148	3	49	29	11.7	3.27	84	.267	.330	13	.245	2	-8	-9	2	-0.7
1919	StL-A	0	1	.000	2	0	0	0	0	1	7	0	0	1	63.0	27.00	12	.700	.700	0	—	-0	-3	-3	0	-1.6
	Phi-A	4	12	.250	23	18	7	1	0	140	152	9	60	37	13.8	4.31	80	.292	.369	11	.224	-0	-17	-14	4	-1.0
	Yr	4	13	.235	25	18	7	1	0	141	159	9	60	38	14.2	4.47	77	.300	.374	11	.224	-0	-19	-16	4	-2.6
1921	*NY-A	0	1	.000	5	0	0	0	1	11	12	1	9	0	18.0	7.36	58	.300	.440	1	.333	-0	-4	-4	1	-0.3
Total	4	15	30	.333	83	42	21	1	3	414²	431	15	162	94	13.1	3.95	75	.282	.354	30	.224	1	-46	-45	6	-5.0

● **CLINT ROGGE**   Rogge, Francis Clinton   b: 7/19/1889, Memphis, Mich.   d: 1/6/69, Mt.Clemens, Mich.   BL/TR, 5'10", 185 lbs.   Deb: 4/11/15

YEAR	TM/L	W	L	PCT	G	GS	CG	SH	SV	IP	H	HR	BB	SO	RAT	ERA	ERA+	OAV	OOB	BH	AVG	PB	PR	/A	PD	TPI
1915	Pit-F	17	11	.607	37	31	17	5	0	254¹	240	6	93	93	12.1	2.55	106	.257	.330	14	.173	-1	5	5	1	0.5
1921	Cin-N	1	2	.333	6	3	0	0	0	35¹	43	2	9	12	13.2	4.08	88	.307	.349	1	.100	-0	-1	-2	0	-0.1
Total	2	18	13	.581	43	34	17	5	0	289²	283	8	102	105	12.2	2.73	103	.264	.332	15	.165	-1	4	3	1	0.4

● **GARRY ROGGENBURK**   Roggenburk, Garry Earl   b: 4/16/40, Cleveland, Ohio   BR/TL, 6'6", 195 lbs.   Deb: 4/20/63

YEAR	TM/L	W	L	PCT	G	GS	CG	SH	SV	IP	H	HR	BB	SO	RAT	ERA	ERA+	OAV	OOB	BH	AVG	PB	PR	/A	PD	TPI
1963	Min-A	2	4	.333	36	2	0	0	4	50	47	3	22	24	13.3	2.16	169	.253	.347	1	.143	-0	8	8	1	1.2
1965	Min-A	1	0	1.000	12	0	0	0	0	21	21	1	9	6	14.1	3.43	104	.266	.363	0	.000	-0	0	0	-1	-0.0
1966	Min-A	1	2	.333	12	0	0	0	1	12¹	14	4	10	3	17.5	5.84	62	.292	.414	0	—	-0	-3	-3	0	-0.8
	Bos-A	0	0	—	1	0	0	0	0	0¹	1	0	1	0	54.0	0.00	—	.500	.667	0	—	-0	0	0	0	0.0
	Yr	1	2	.333	13	0	0	0	1	12²	15	4	11	3	18.5	5.68	66	.300	.426	0	—	-0	-3	-3	0	-0.8
1968	Bos-A	0	0	—	4	0	0	0	0	8¹	9	0	4	4	13.0	2.16	146	.257	.316	0	—	0	1	1	0	0.1
1969	Bos-A	0	1	.000	7	0	0	0	0	9²	13	1	5	8	17.7	8.38	45	.342	.432	0	.000	-0	-5	-5	0	-0.5
	Sea-A	2	2	.500	7	0	0	0	1	24¹	27	6	11	11	14.4	4.44	82	.276	.355	1	.125	-0	-2	-2	0	-0.4
	Yr	2	3	.400	14	0	0	0	1	34	40	7	16	19	15.1	5.56	66	.292	.370	1	.100	-1	-7	-7	0	-0.9
Total	5	6	9	.400	79	2	0	0	7	126	132	15	64	56	14.5	3.64	99	.272	.364	2	.100	-1	-1	-1	0	-0.5

● **SAUL ROGOVIN**   Rogovin, Saul Walter   b: 10/10/23, Brooklyn, N.Y.   BR/TR, 6'2", 205 lbs.   Deb: 4/28/49

YEAR	TM/L	W	L	PCT	G	GS	CG	SH	SV	IP	H	HR	BB	SO	RAT	ERA	ERA+	OAV	OOB	BH	AVG	PB	PR	/A	PD	TPI
1949	Det-A	0	1	.000	5	0	0	0	0	5²	13	1	7	2	31.8	14.29	29	.464	.571	0	—	0	-6	-6	-0	-0.9
1950	Det-A	2	1	.667	11	5	1	0	0	40	39	5	26	11	15.5	4.50	104	.258	.374	3	.188	0	0	1	-0	0.0
1951	Det-A	1	1	.500	5	4	0	0	0	24	23	4	7	11	11.3	5.25	80	.247	.300	2	.286	1	-3	-3	0	-0.1
	Chi-A	11	7	.611	22	22	17	3	0	192²	166	11	67	77	10.9	2.48	163	.234	.301	15	.203	-0	35	33	-1	2.9

YEAR	TM/L	W	L	PCT	G	GS	CG	SH	SV	IP	H	HR	BB	SO	RAT	ERA	ERA+	OAV	OOB	BH	AVG	PB	PR	/A	PD	TPI
	Yr	12	8	.600	27	26	17	3	0	216²	189	15	74	82	11.0	**2.78**	**146**	.235	.301	17	.210	1	32	**31**	-0	2.8
1952	Chi-A	14	9	.609	33	30	12	3	1	231²	224	14	79	121	11.9	3.85	95	.255	.318	17	.202	3	-4	-5	-0	-0.2
1953	Chi-A	7	12	.368	22	19	4	1	1	131	151	17	48	62	13.8	5.22	77	.289	.351	5	.135	-0	-18	-17	-0	-2.2
1955	Bal-A	1	8	.111	14	12	1	0	0	71	79	5	27	35	13.7	4.56	84	.288	.356	2	.091	-1	-5	-6	-0	-0.9
	Phi-N	5	3	.625	12	11	5	2	0	73	60	3	17	27	9.5	3.08	129	.230	.277	6	.250	2	8	7	-1	0.9
1956	Phi-N	7	6	.538	22	18	3	0	0	106²	122	22	37	48	12.6	4.98	75	.282	.325	4	.111	-2	-14	-15	-1	-1.9
1957	Phi-N	0	0	—	4	0	0	0	0	8	11	1	3	0	15.8	9.00	42	.333	.389	0	—	0	-5	-5	-0	0.0
Total	8	48	48	.500	150	121	43	9	2	883²	888	83	308	388	12.3	4.06	96	.262	.326	54	.180	2	-12	-16	-4	-2.4

● LES ROHR
Rohr, Leslie Norvin   b: 3/5/46, Lowestoft, England   BL/TL, 6'5", 205 lbs.   Deb: 9/19/67

YEAR	TM/L	W	L	PCT	G	GS	CG	SH	SV	IP	H	HR	BB	SO	RAT	ERA	ERA+	OAV	OOB	BH	AVG	PB	PR	/A	PD	TPI
1967	NY-N	2	1	.667	3	3	0	0	0	17	13	1	9	15	11.6	2.12	160	.224	.328	0	.000	-1	2	2	-1	0.3
1968	NY-N	0	2	.000	2	1	0	0	0	6	9	0	7	5	24.0	4.50	67	.333	.471	0	—	0	-1	-1	0	-0.3
1969	NY-N	0	0	—	1	0	0	0	0	1¹	5	0	1	0	40.5	20.25	18	.625	.667	0	—	0	-2	-2	-0	0.0
Total	3	2	3	.400	6	4	0	0	0	24¹	27	1	17	20	16.3	3.70	90	.290	.400	0	.000	-0	-1	-1	-1	0.0

● BILLY ROHR
Rohr, William Joseph   b: 7/1/45, San Diego, Cal.   BL/TL, 6'3", 170 lbs.   Deb: 4/14/67

YEAR	TM/L	W	L	PCT	G	GS	CG	SH	SV	IP	H	HR	BB	SO	RAT	ERA	ERA+	OAV	OOB	BH	AVG	PB	PR	/A	PD	TPI
1967	Bos-A	2	3	.400	10	8	2	1	0	42¹	43	4	22	16	14.2	5.10	68	.256	.349	0	.000	-1	-9	-8	-0	-0.9
1968	Cle-A	1	0	1.000	17	0	0	0	1	18¹	18	5	10	5	13.7	6.87	43	.265	.359	0	.000	-0	-8	-8	0	-0.6
Total	2	3	3	.500	27	8	2	1	1	60²	61	9	32	21	14.1	5.64	59	.258	.352	0	.000	-1	-17	-16	-0	-1.5

● MEL ROJAS
Rojas, Melquiades (Medrano)   b: 12/10/66, Haina, D.R.   BR/TR, 5'11", 175 lbs.   Deb: 8/1/90

YEAR	TM/L	W	L	PCT	G	GS	CG	SH	SV	IP	H	HR	BB	SO	RAT	ERA	ERA+	OAV	OOB	BH	AVG	PB	PR	/A	PD	TPI
1990	Mon-N	3	1	.750	23	0	0	0	1	40	34	5	24	26	13.5	3.60	101	.234	.351	0	.000	-0	1	0	-0	-0.1
1991	Mon-N	3	3	.500	37	0	0	0	6	48	42	4	13	37	10.5	3.75	96	.228	.283	0	—	-0	-0	-1	-0	-0.2
1992	Mon-N	7	1	.875	68	0	0	0	10	100²	71	2	34	70	9.6	1.43	242	.199	.272	1	.067	-1	23	23	-0	2.2
1993	Mon-N	5	8	.385	66	0	0	0	10	88¹	80	6	30	48	11.6	2.95	141	.242	.313	1	.083	-1	11	12	-1	1.8
1994	Mon-N	3	2	.600	58	0	0	0	16	84	71	11	21	84	10.3	3.32	128	.227	.284	2	.200	-0	8	9	0	0.9
Total	5	21	15	.583	252	0	0	0	43	361	298	28	122	265	10.8	2.79	138	.224	.296	4	.091	-2	43	43	-2	4.6

● MINNIE ROJAS
Rojas, Minervino Alejandro (Landin)   b: 11/26/38, Remidios, Las Villas, Cuba   BR/TR, 6'1", 170 lbs.   Deb: 5/30/66

YEAR	TM/L	W	L	PCT	G	GS	CG	SH	SV	IP	H	HR	BB	SO	RAT	ERA	ERA+	OAV	OOB	BH	AVG	PB	PR	/A	PD	TPI
1966	Cal-A	7	4	.636	47	2	0	0	10	84¹	83	9	15	37	10.6	2.88	117	.262	.297	1	.071	-0	5	4	-1	0.5
1967	Cal-A	12	9	.571	72	0	0	0	**27**	121²	106	7	38	83	10.9	2.52	125	.232	.296	1	.059	-1	10	8	-2	1.6
1968	Cal-A	4	3	.571	38	0	0	0	6	55	55	11	15	33	11.5	4.25	68	.252	.300	1	.100	-0	-8	-8	-1	-1.4
Total	3	23	16	.590	157	2	0	0	43	261	244	27	68	153	10.9	3.00	105	.246	.297	3	.073	-2	7	5	-4	0.7

● COOKIE ROJAS
Rojas, Octavio Victor (Rivas)   b: 3/6/39, Havana, Cuba   BR/TR, 5'10", 170 lbs.   Deb: 4/10/62   MC♦

YEAR	TM/L	W	L	PCT	G	GS	CG	SH	SV	IP	H	HR	BB	SO	RAT	ERA	ERA+	OAV	OOB	BH	AVG	PB	PR	/A	PD	TPI
1967	Phi-N	0	0	—	1	0	0	0	0	1	1	0	0	0	9.0	0.00	—	.200	.200	137	.259	0	0	0	-0	0.0

● JIM ROLAND
Roland, James Ivan   b: 12/14/42, Franklin, N.C.   BR/TL, 6'3", 190 lbs.   Deb: 9/20/62

YEAR	TM/L	W	L	PCT	G	GS	CG	SH	SV	IP	H	HR	BB	SO	RAT	ERA	ERA+	OAV	OOB	BH	AVG	PB	PR	/A	PD	TPI
1962	Min-A	0	0	—	1	0	0	0	0	2	1	0	0	1	4.5	0.00	—	.143	.143	0	—	0	1	1	-0	0.0
1963	Min-A	4	1	.800	10	7	2	1	0	49	32	4	27	34	10.8	2.57	142	.185	.295	0	.000	-2	6	6	0	0.4
1964	Min-A	2	6	.250	30	13	1	0	3	94¹	76	12	55	63	12.9	4.10	87	.218	.332	4	.148	-1	-5	-6	-1	-0.7
1966	Min-A	0	0	—	1	0	0	0	0	2	0	0	0	0	0.0	0.00	—	.000	.000	0	—	0	1	1	0	0.0
1967	Min-A	0	1	.000	25	0	0	0	2	35²	33	3	17	16	12.6	3.03	114	.244	.329	0	.000	-0	1	2	-0	0.0
1968	Min-A	4	1	.800	28	4	1	0	0	61²	55	3	24	36	11.8	3.50	88	.238	.315	0	.000	-1	-4	-3	1	-0.2
1969	Oak-A	5	1	.833	39	3	2	0	1	86¹	59	2	46	48	11.6	2.19	157	.197	.316	2	.095	-1	14	12	0	0.7
1970	Oak-A	3	3	.500	28	2	0	0	2	43¹	28	2	23	26	10.6	2.70	131	.181	.287	0	.000	-0	5	4	1	0.6
1971	Oak-A	1	3	.250	31	0	0	0	1	45¹	34	4	19	30	11.5	3.18	105	.214	.317	0	.000	-0	1	1	-1	0.0
1972	Oak-A	0	0	—	2	0	0	0	0	2¹	5	0	0	0	19.3	3.86	74	.455	.455		—	0	-0	-0	-0	0.0
	NY-A	0	1	.000	16	0	0	0	0	25	27	3	16	13	15.8	5.04	58	.287	.396	0	.000	-0	-6	-6	-0	-0.3
	Tex-A	0	0	—	5	0	0	0	0	3¹	7	1	2	4	27.0	8.10	37	.412	.500		—	0	-2	-2	-0	0.0
	Yr	0	1	.000	23	0	0	0	0	30²	39	4	18	17	17.0	5.28	56	.317	.408	0	.000	-0	-8	-8	-0	-0.3
Total	10	19	17	.528	216	29	6	1	9	450¹	357	34	229	272	12.1	3.22	106	.218	.321	6	.071	-5	12	10	-1	0.5

● JOSE ROMAN
Roman, Jose Rafael (Sarita)   b: 5/21/63, Santo Domingo, D.R.   BR/TR, 6', 175 lbs.   Deb: 9/5/84

YEAR	TM/L	W	L	PCT	G	GS	CG	SH	SV	IP	H	HR	BB	SO	RAT	ERA	ERA+	OAV	OOB	BH	AVG	PB	PR	/A	PD	TPI
1984	Cle-A	0	2	.000	3	2	0	0	0	6	9	1	11	3	30.0	18.00	23	.391	.588		—	0	-9	-9	-0	-2.0
1985	Cle-A	0	4	.000	5	3	0	0	0	16¹	13	3	14	12	14.9	6.61	63	.230	.342		—	0	-4	-4	-0	-0.9
1986	Cle-A	1	2	.333	6	5	0	0	0	22	23	3	17	9	16.8	6.55	63	.280	.410		—	0	-6	-6	-1	-0.7
Total	3	1	8	.111	14	10	0	0	0	44¹	45	7	42	24	17.9	8.12	51	.265	.413		—	0	-20	-20	-1	-3.6

● RON ROMANICK
Romanick, Ronald James   b: 11/6/60, Burley, Idaho   BR/TR, 6'4", 195 lbs.   Deb: 4/5/84

YEAR	TM/L	W	L	PCT	G	GS	CG	SH	SV	IP	H	HR	BB	SO	RAT	ERA	ERA+	OAV	OOB	BH	AVG	PB	PR	/A	PD	TPI
1984	Cal-A	12	12	.500	33	33	8	2	0	229²	240	23	61	87	12.0	3.76	105	.270	.320		—	0	6	5	-2	0.3
1985	Cal-A	14	9	.609	31	31	6	1	0	195	210	29	62	64	12.7	4.11	100	.280	.338		—	0	1	0	-3	-0.3
1986	Cal-A	5	8	.385	18	18	1	1	0	106¹	124	13	44	38	14.2	5.50	75	.297	.364		—	0	-16	-16	-1	-1.8
Total	3	31	29	.517	82	82	15	4	0	531	574	65	167	189	12.7	4.24	96	.279	.336		—	0	-9	-11	-6	-1.8

● JIM ROMANO
Romano, James King   b: 4/6/27, Brooklyn, N.Y.   d: 9/12/90, New York, N.Y.   BR/TR, 6'4", 190 lbs.   Deb: 9/21/50

YEAR	TM/L	W	L	PCT	G	GS	CG	SH	SV	IP	H	HR	BB	SO	RAT	ERA	ERA+	OAV	OOB	BH	AVG	PB	PR	/A	PD	TPI
1950	Bro-N	0	0	—	3	1	0	0	0	6¹	8	0	2	8	14.2	5.68	72	.296	.345	0	.000	-0	-1	-1	0	0.0

● DUTCH ROMBERGER
Romberger, Allen Isaiah   b: 5/26/27, Klingerstown, Pa.   d: 5/26/83, Weikert, Pa.   BR/TR, 6', 185 lbs.   Deb: 5/31/54

YEAR	TM/L	W	L	PCT	G	GS	CG	SH	SV	IP	H	HR	BB	SO	RAT	ERA	ERA+	OAV	OOB	BH	AVG	PB	PR	/A	PD	TPI
1954	Phi-A	1	1	.500	10	0	0	0	0	15²	28	3	12	6	23.0	11.49	34	.406	.494	0	.000	-0	-14	-13	-0	-1.5

● RAMON ROMERO
Romero, Ramon (De Los Santos)   b: 1/8/59, San Pedro De Macoris, D.R.   BL/TL, 6'4", 170 lbs.   Deb: 9/18/84

YEAR	TM/L	W	L	PCT	G	GS	CG	SH	SV	IP	H	HR	BB	SO	RAT	ERA	ERA+	OAV	OOB	BH	AVG	PB	PR	/A	PD	TPI
1984	Cle-A	0	0	—	1	0	0	0	0	3	3	0	0	3	3.0	0.00	—	.000	.111	—		0	1	1	-0	-0.1
1985	Cle-A	2	3	.400	19	10	0	0	0	64¹	69	13	38	38	15.7	6.58	63	.276	.382	—		0	-17	-17	-1	-1.2
Total	2	2	3	.400	20	10	0	0	0	67¹	69	13	38	41	15.1	6.28	66	.267	.374	—		0	-16	-16	-1	-1.3

● EDDIE ROMMEL
Rommel, Edwin Americus   b: 9/13/1897, Baltimore, Md.   d: 8/26/70, Baltimore, Md.   BR/TR, 6'2", 197 lbs.   Deb: 4/19/20   CU

YEAR	TM/L	W	L	PCT	G	GS	CG	SH	SV	IP	H	HR	BB	SO	RAT	ERA	ERA+	OAV	OOB	BH	AVG	PB	PR	/A	PD	TPI
1920	Phi-A	7	7	.500	33	12	8	2	1	173²	165	5	43	43	11.0	2.85	141	.259	.309	11	.216	-0	18	23	5	2.2
1921	Phi-A	16	23	.410	46	32	20	0	3	285¹	312	21	87	71	12.6	3.94	113	.284	.337	18	.191	-2	11	16	3	2.0
1922	Phi-A	**27**	13	.675	**51**	33	22	3	2	294	294	21	63	54	11.1	3.28	130	.267	.309	17	.181	-3	25	32	3	4.0
1923	Phi-A	18	19	.486	**56**	31	19	3	5	297²	306	14	108	76	12.6	3.27	126	.271	.336	24	.238	1	24	28	6	**4.0**
1924	Phi-A	18	15	.545	43	34	21	0	1	278	302	8	94	72	12.9	3.95	108	.284	.344	15	.158	-6	9	10	8	1.2
1925	Phi-A	**21**	10	.677	52	28	14	1	3	261	285	10	95	67	13.3	3.69	126	.281	.346	15	.185	-1	20	28	5	3.3
1926	Phi-A	11	11	.500	37	26	12	3	0	219	225	10	54	52	11.5	3.08	135	.268	.314	6	.098	-4	23	26	2	2.3
1927	Phi-A	11	3	.786	30	17	8	2	1	146²	166	6	48	33	13.3	4.36	98	.286	.343	8	.157	-2	-4	-2	3	-0.1
1928	Phi-A	13	5	.722	43	11	6	0	4	173²	177	11	26	37	10.6	3.06	131	.266	.295	12	.255	-0	19	18	3	2.3
1929	*Phi-A	12	2	.857	32	6	3	0	1	113²	135	10	34	25	13.5	2.85	148	.294	.344	8	.205	-0	18	17	1	2.0
1930	Phi-A	9	4	.692	35	9	5	0	3	130¹	142	11	27	35	11.7	4.28	109	.277	.315	10	.263	3	5	6	1	0.9
1931	*Phi-A	7	5	.583	25	10	8	1	0	118	136	5	27	18	12.5	2.97	151	.291	.331	14	.259	-2	18	20	-0	1.9
1932	Phi-A	1	2	.333	17	0	0	0	2	65¹	84	6	18	16	14.1	5.51	82	.315	.358	6	.300	2	-7	-7	2	0.0
Total	13	171	119	.590	500	249	147	18	29	2556¹	2729	138	724	599	12.3	3.54	122	.277	.329	164	.199	-7	179	217	42	26.0

● ENRIQUE ROMO
Romo, Enrique (Navarro)   b: 7/15/47, Santa Rosalia, Mex   BR/TR, 5'11", 185 lbs.   Deb: 4/7/77   F

YEAR	TM/L	W	L	PCT	G	GS	CG	SH	SV	IP	H	HR	BB	SO	RAT	ERA	ERA+	OAV	OOB	BH	AVG	PB	PR	/A	PD	TPI
1977	Sea-A	8	10	.444	58	3	0	0	16	114¹	93	8	39	105	10.8	2.83	145	.227	.302	0	—	0	16	16	1	3.0
1978	Sea-A	11	7	.611	56	0	0	0	10	107¹	88	12	39	62	11.1	3.69	103	.227	.306	0	—	0	1	1	-1	0.1
1979	*Pit-N	10	5	.667	84	0	0	0	5	129¹	122	11	43	106	11.7	2.99	130	.253	.318	2	.167	-0	11	13	2	1.7

YEAR	TM/L	W	L	PCT	G	GS	CG	SH	SV	IP	H	HR	BB	SO	RAT	ERA	ERA+	OAV	OOB	BH	AVG	PB	PR	/A	PD	TPI
1980	Pit-N	5	5	.500	74	0	0	0	11	123²	117	10	28	82	10.6	3.27	111	.252	.296	5	.455	3	4	5	1	0.9
1981	Pit-N	1	3	.250	33	0	0	0	9	41²	47	5	18	23	14.0	4.54	79	.288	.359	0	.000	-0	-5	-4	-0	-0.7
1982	Pit-N	9	3	.750	45	0	0	0	1	86²	81	11	36	58	12.3	4.36	85	.245	.322	3	.300	1	-7	-6	-0	-0.8
Total	6	44	33	.571	350	3	0	0	52	603	548	57	203	436	11.4	3.45	111	.245	.312	10	.270	4	19	25	2	4.2

● VICENTE ROMO
Romo, Vicente (Navarro) "Huevo" b: 4/12/43, Santa Rosalia, Mex. BR/TR, 6'1", 195 lbs. Deb: 4/11/68 F

YEAR	TM/L	W	L	PCT	G	GS	CG	SH	SV	IP	H	HR	BB	SO	RAT	ERA	ERA+	OAV	OOB	BH	AVG	PB	PR	/A	PD	TPI
1968	LA-N				1	0	0	0	0	1	1	0	0	0	9.0	0.00	—	.250	.250	0	—	0	0	0	0	0.0
	Cle-A	5	3	.625	40	1	0	0	12	83¹	43	5	32	54	8.3	1.62	183	.154	.245	2	.143	-0	13	12	-0	1.7
1969	Cle-A	1	1	.500	3	0	0	0	0	8	7	0	3	7	11.3	2.25	167	.233	.303	1	.500	0	1	1	-0	0.4
	Bos-A	7	9	.438	52	11	4	1	11	127¹	116	14	50	89	11.8	3.18	120	.247	.321	4	.129	-1	6	9	0	1.2
	Yr	8	10	.444	55	11	4	1	11	135¹	123	14	53	96	11.8	3.13	122	.246	.319	5	.152	-0	7	10	0	1.6
1970	Bos-A	7	3	.700	48	10	0	0	6	108	115	14	43	71	13.2	4.08	97	.273	.340	4	.148	-0	-4	-1	1	0.0
1971	Chi-A	1	7	.125	45	2	0	0	5	72	52	5	37	48	11.1	3.38	106	.202	.303	4	.364	1	1	2	1	0.5
1972	Chi-A	3	0	1.000	28	0	0	0	0	51²	47	5	18	46	11.5	3.31	94	.246	.314	0	.000	-1	-1	-1	1	-0.1
1973	SD-N	2	3	.400	49	1	0	0	7	87²	85	11	46	51	13.4	3.70	94	.260	.351	2	.125	-1	-0	-2	0	-0.2
1974	SD-N	5	5	.500	54	1	0	0	9	71	78	6	37	26	14.8	4.56	78	.290	.380	0	.000	-1	-7	-8	2	-1.2
1982	LA-N	1	2	.333	15	6	0	0	0	35²	25	1	14	24	10.3	3.03	114	.195	.285	1	.200	0	2	2	1	0.2
Total	8	32	33	.492	335	32	4	1	52	645²	569	61	280	416	11.9	3.36	106	.239	.322	18	.149	-1	10	13	5	2.5

● JOHN ROMONOSKY
Romonosky, John b: 7/7/29, Harrisburg, Ill. BR/TR, 6'2", 195 lbs. Deb: 9/6/53

YEAR	TM/L	W	L	PCT	G	GS	CG	SH	SV	IP	H	HR	BB	SO	RAT	ERA	ERA+	OAV	OOB	BH	AVG	PB	PR	/A	PD	TPI
1953	StL-N	0	0		2	2	0	0	0	7²	9	1	4	3	16.4	4.70	91	.281	.378	0	.000	-0	-0	-0	-0	-0.1
1958	Was-A	2	4	.333	18	5	1	0	0	55¹	52	6	28	38	13.0	6.51	59	.243	.331	4	.308	2	-17	-17	0	-1.3
1959	Was-A	1	0	1.000	12	2	0	0	0	38¹	36	4	19	22	13.6	3.29	119	.254	.354	2	.182	0	2	3	-0	0.1
Total	3	3	4	.429	32	9	1	0	0	101¹	97	11	51	63	13.5	5.15	75	.250	.343	6	.231	2	-15	-14	-0	-1.3

● GILBERTO RONDON
Rondon, Gilberto b: 11/18/53, Bronx, N.Y. BR/TR, 6'2", 200 lbs. Deb: 4/10/76 F

YEAR	TM/L	W	L	PCT	G	GS	CG	SH	SV	IP	H	HR	BB	SO	RAT	ERA	ERA+	OAV	OOB	BH	AVG	PB	PR	/A	PD	TPI
1976	Hou-N	2	2	.500	19	7	0	0	0	53²	70	6	39	21	18.3	5.70	56	.315	.418	4	.286	1	-13	-15	-1	-1.0
1979	Chi-A	0	0	—	4	0	0	0	0	9²	11	2	6	3	15.8	3.72	114	.282	.378	0	—	0	1	1	-0	0.0
Total	2	2	2	.500	23	7	0	0	0	63¹	81	8	45	24	17.9	5.40	62	.310	.412	4	.286	1	-13	-14	-1	-1.0

● JIM ROOKER
Rooker, James Phillip b: 9/23/42, Lakeview, Ore. BR/TL, 6', 201 lbs. Deb: 6/30/68

YEAR	TM/L	W	L	PCT	G	GS	CG	SH	SV	IP	H	HR	BB	SO	RAT	ERA	ERA+	OAV	OOB	BH	AVG	PB	PR	/A	PD	TPI
1968	Det-A	0	0	—	2	0	0	0	0	4²	4	0	1	4	9.6	3.86	78	.235	.278	0	.000	-0	-0	-0	0	0.0
1969	KC-A	4	16	.200	28	22	8	1	0	158¹	136	13	73	108	11.9	3.75	98	.229	.315	16	.281	8	-2	-1	-1	0.6
1970	KC-A	10	15	.400	38	29	6	3	1	203²	190	11	102	117	12.9	3.54	106	.252	.341	14	.200	3	4	5	-0	0.9
1971	KC-A	2	7	.222	20	7	1	1	0	54	59	2	24	31	14.0	5.33	64	.284	.361	0	.000	-1	-11	-11	-1	-1.9
1972	KC-A	5	6	.455	18	14	6	2	0	72	78	3	24	44	12.9	4.38	69	.280	.339	2	.100	-1	-11	-11	1	-1.6
1973	Pit-N	10	6	.625	41	18	6	3	5	170¹	143	12	52	122	10.4	2.85	123	.229	.290	12	.245	3	15	13	1	1.6
1974	*Pit-N	15	11	.577	33	33	15	1	0	262²	228	11	83	139	10.8	2.78	124	.238	.301	29	.305	11	25	20	1	3.2
1975	*Pit-N	13	11	.542	28	28	7	1	0	196²	177	16	76	102	11.7	2.97	119	.238	.311	6	.095	-3	14	12	0	1.2
1976	Pit-N	15	8	.652	30	29	10	1	1	198²	201	12	72	92	12.5	3.35	104	.263	.328	16	.216	3	3	3	-1	0.6
1977	Pit-N	14	9	.609	30	30	7	2	0	204¹	196	24	64	89	11.5	3.08	129	.253	.310	13	.186	0	19	20	-2	2.0
1978	Pit-N	9	11	.450	28	28	1	0	0	163¹	160	13	81	76	13.4	4.24	87	.259	.348	9	.161	0	-12	-10	1	-1.0
1979	*Pit-N	4	7	.364	19	11	1	0	0	103²	106	11	39	44	12.6	4.60	84	.266	.331	4	.121	-1	-10	-8	-1	-1.0
1980	Pit-N	2	2	.500	4	4	0	0	0	18	16	0	12	8	14.0	3.50	104	.262	.384	1	.143	1	0	0	0	0.2
Total	13	103	109	.486	319	255	66	15	7	1810¹	1694	128	703	976	12.0	3.46	104	.249	.321	122	.201	23	34	30	-2	4.8

● CHARLIE ROOT
Root, Charles Henry "Chinski" b: 3/17/1899, Middletown, Ohio d: 11/5/70, Hollister, Cal. BR/TR, 5'10.5", 190 lbs. Deb: 4/18/23 C

YEAR	TM/L	W	L	PCT	G	GS	CG	SH	SV	IP	H	HR	BB	SO	RAT	ERA	ERA+	OAV	OOB	BH	AVG	PB	PR	/A	PD	TPI
1923	StL-A	0	4	.000	27	2	0	0	0	60	68	4	18	27	13.8	5.70	73	.302	.369	1	.077	-1	-11	-10	-1	-0.8
1926	Chi-N	18	17	.514	42	32	21	2	2	271¹	267	10	62	127	11.1	2.82	136	.264	.310	13	.143	-4	30	31	-1	3.2
1927	Chi-N	26	15	.634	48	36	21	4	2	309	296	16	117	145	12.3	3.76	103	.254	.326	27	.221	3	6	4	-4	0.3
1928	Chi-N	14	18	.438	40	30	13	1	2	237	214	19	73	122	11.2	3.57	108	.242	.305	13	.178	-0	11	7	-3	0.6
1929	*Chi-N	19	6	.760	43	31	19	4	5	272	286	12	83	124	12.3	3.47	133	.275	.330	15	.156	0	38	35	-4	2.4
1930	Chi-N	16	14	.533	37	30	15	4	3	220¹	247	17	63	124	12.9	4.33	113	.281	.334	21	.262	5	16	14	-3	1.7
1931	Chi-N	17	14	.548	39	31	19	3	2	251	240	7	71	131	11.4	3.48	111	.252	.309	20	.222	3	11	13	-3	1.2
1932	*Chi-N	15	10	.600	39	23	11	0	3	216¹	211	10	55	96	11.3	3.58	105	.253	.303	13	.171	-1	7	5	-3	0.1
1933	Chi-N	15	10	.600	35	30	20	2	0	242¹	232	6	86	86	11.3	2.60	126	.252	.306	8	.094	-4	20	18	-3	1.0
1934	Chi-N	4	7	.364	34	9	2	0	0	117²	141	8	53	46	15.2	4.28	90	.298	.375	7	.175	2	-3	-5	-1	-0.4
1935	*Chi-N	15	8	.652	38	18	11	1	2	201¹	193	15	47	94	10.9	3.08	127	.252	.298	14	.203	2	21	19	-3	1.4
1936	Chi-N	3	6	.333	33	4	0	0	1	73²	81	3	20	32	12.6	4.15	96	.280	.331	5	.333	1	-1	-1	-1	-0.1
1937	Chi-N	13	5	.722	46	15	5	0	0	178²	173	18	74	70	10.5	3.38	118	.253	.290	12	.179	0	11	12	-1	1.1
1938	*Chi-N	8	7	.533	44	11	5	0	0	160²	163	10	30	70	10.9	2.86	134	.258	.294	8	.167	-0	17	17	-2	1.4
1939	Chi-N	8	8	.500	35	16	8	0	4	167¹	189	11	34	65	12.1	4.03	98	.286	.323	10	.175	2	-2	-2	-3	-0.3
1940	Chi-N	2	4	.333	36	8	1	0	1	112	118	9	35	50	12.2	3.86	97	.265	.317	4	.129	-1	-0	-1	-0	-0.1
1941	Chi-N	8	7	.533	19	15	6	0	0	106²	133	8	37	46	14.3	5.40	65	.306	.360	5	.152	2	-21	-22	-1	-2.6
Total	17	201	160	.557	632	341	177	21	40	3197¹	3252	187	889	1459	11.9	3.59	110	.264	.318	196	.180	8	148	129	-35	10.5

● JOHN ROPER
Roper, John Christopher b: 11/21/71, Southern Pines, N.C. BR/TR, 6', 175 lbs. Deb: 5/16/93

YEAR	TM/L	W	L	PCT	G	GS	CG	SH	SV	IP	H	HR	BB	SO	RAT	ERA	ERA+	OAV	OOB	BH	AVG	PB	PR	/A	PD	TPI
1993	Cin-N	2	5	.286	16	15	0	0	0	80	92	10	36	54	14.8	5.62	72	.295	.375	5	.179	-0	-14	-14	-0	-1.1
1994	Cin-N	6	2	.750	16	15	0	0	0	92	90	16	30	51	12.1	4.50	92	.255	.320	6	.182	0	-3	-4	-0	-0.3
Total	2	8	7	.533	32	30	0	0	0	172	182	26	66	105	13.4	5.02	82	.274	.346	11	.180	0	-17	-18	-1	-1.4

● CHUCK ROSE
Rose, Charles Alfred b: 9/1/1885, Macon, Mo. d: 8/4/61, Salina, Kan. BL/TL, 5'8.5", 158 lbs. Deb: 9/13/09

YEAR	TM/L	W	L	PCT	G	GS	CG	SH	SV	IP	H	HR	BB	SO	RAT	ERA	ERA+	OAV	OOB	BH	AVG	PB	PR	/A	PD	TPI
1909	StL-A	1	2	.333	3	3	3	0	0	25	32	1	7	6	15.1	5.40	45	.330	.393	0	.000	-1	-8	-8	-1	-1.0

● DON ROSE
Rose, Donald Gary b: 3/19/47, Covina, Cal. BR/TR, 6'3", 195 lbs. Deb: 9/15/71

YEAR	TM/L	W	L	PCT	G	GS	CG	SH	SV	IP	H	HR	BB	SO	RAT	ERA	ERA+	OAV	OOB	BH	AVG	PB	PR	/A	PD	TPI
1971	NY-N	0	0	—	1	0	0	0	0	2	2	0	0	1	9.0	0.00	—	.286	.286	0		0	1	1	-0	0.0
1972	Cal-A	1	4	.200	16	4	0	0	0	42²	49	9	19	39	14.3	4.22	69	.283	.354	2	.200	1	-5	-6	-0	-0.6
1974	SF-N	0	0	—	2	0	0	0	0	1	4	0	1	0	45.0	9.00	42	.667	.714	0	—	0	-1	-1	-0	0.0
Total	3	1	4	.200	19	4	0	0	0	45²	55	9	20	40	14.8	4.14	71	.296	.364	2	.200	1	-5	-6	-1	-0.6

● ZEKE ROSEBRAUGH
Rosebraugh, Eli Ethelbert b: 9/8/1870, Charleston, Ill. d: 7/16/30, Fresno, Cal. TL , Deb: 9/21/1898

YEAR	TM/L	W	L	PCT	G	GS	CG	SH	SV	IP	H	HR	BB	SO	RAT	ERA	ERA+	OAV	OOB	BH	AVG	PB	PR	/A	PD	TPI
1898	Pit-N	0	2	.000	4	2	2	0	0	21²	23	0	9	6	14.5	3.32	107	.270	.360	3	.375	1	1	1	-0	0.1
1899	Pit-N	0	1	.000	2	2	0	0	0	6	14	0	3	0	27.0	9.00	42	.451	.513	0	.000	-0	-3	-3	-0	-0.5
Total	2	0	3	.000	6	4	2	0	0	27²	37	0	12	6	17.2	4.55	79	.318	.401	3	.300	1	-3	-3	-0	-0.4

● CHIEF ROSEMAN
Roseman, James John b: 1856, New York, N.Y. d: 7/4/38, Brooklyn, N.Y. BR/TR, 5'7", 167 lbs. Deb: 5/1/1882 M♦

YEAR	TM/L	W	L	PCT	G	GS	CG	SH	SV	IP	H	HR	BB	SO	RAT	ERA	ERA+	OAV	OOB	BH	AVG	PB	PR	/A	PD	TPI
1885	NY-a	0	1	.000	1	1	0	0	0	1	3	0	2	0	45.0	27.00	11	.333	.455	114	.278	-4	-3	-3	0	-1.2
1886	NY-a	0	0	—	1	0	0	0	0	7	6	0	0	0	7.7	5.14	66	.240	.240	127	.227	4	-1	-1	0	0.0
1887	NY-a	0	0	—	2	0	0	0	0	8	11	0	5	1	20.3	7.88	48	.407	.529	56	.228	-0	-3	-3	-0	-0.0
Total	3	0	1	.000	4	1	0	0	0	16	20	0	7	1	16.3	7.88	48	.328	.414	726	.263	0	-7	-7	-0	-1.2

● STEVE ROSENBERG
Rosenberg, Steven Allen b: 10/31/64, Brooklyn, N.Y. BL/TL, 6', 186 lbs. Deb: 6/4/88

YEAR	TM/L	W	L	PCT	G	GS	CG	SH	SV	IP	H	HR	BB	SO	RAT	ERA	ERA+	OAV	OOB	BH	AVG	PB	PR	/A	PD	TPI
1988	Chi-A	0	1	.000	33	0	0	0	0	46	53	5	19	28	14.1	4.30	92	.298	.365	0		0	-2	-2	-0	-0.1
1989	Chi-A	4	13	.235	38	21	2	0	0	142	148	14	58	77	13.1	4.94	77	.273	.344	0	—	0	-17	-18	-0	-1.9
1990	Chi-A	1	0	1.000	6	0	0	0	0	10	10	2	5	4	13.5	5.40	71	.256	.341	0		0	-2	-2	0	-0.1

YEAR	TM/L	W	L	PCT	G	GS	CG	SH	SV	IP	H	HR	BB	SO	RAT	ERA	ERA+	OAV	OOB	BH	AVG	PB	PR	/A	PD	TPI
1991	SD-N	1	1	.500	10	0	0	0	0	11²	11	3	5	6	12.3	6.94	55	.250	.327	0	.000	-0	-4	-4	-0	-0.7
Total 4		6	15	.286	87	21	2	0	1	209²	222	24	87	115	13.3	4.94	78	.276	.348	0	.000	-0	-24	-26	-0	-2.8

● **WAYNE ROSENTHAL**   Rosenthal, Wayne Scott b: 2/19/65, Brooklyn, N.Y. BR/TR, 6'5", 220 lbs. Deb: 6/26/91

YEAR	TM/L	W	L	PCT	G	GS	CG	SH	SV	IP	H	HR	BB	SO	RAT	ERA	ERA+	OAV	OOB	BH	AVG	PB	PR	/A	PD	TPI
1991	Tex-A	1	4	.200	36	0	0	0	1	70¹	72	9	36	61	13.9	5.25	77	.257	.344	0	—	0	-9	-10	-1	-0.7
1992	Tex-A	0	0	—	6	0	0	0	0	4²	7	1	2	1	17.4	7.71	49	.333	.391	0	—	0	-2	-2	0	0.0
Total 2		1	4	.200	42	0	0	0	1	75	79	10	38	62	14.2	5.40	74	.262	.347	0	—	0	-11	-12	-1	-0.7

● **STEVE ROSER**   Roser, Emerson Corey b: 1/25/18, Rome, N.Y. BR/TR, 6'4", 220 lbs. Deb: 5/5/44

YEAR	TM/L	W	L	PCT	G	GS	CG	SH	SV	IP	H	HR	BB	SO	RAT	ERA	ERA+	OAV	OOB	BH	AVG	PB	PR	/A	PD	TPI
1944	NY-A	4	3	.571	16	6	1	0	1	84	80	3	34	34	12.2	3.86	90	.256	.329	3	.100	-2	-4	-3	-1	-0.5
1945	NY-A	0	0	—	11	0	0	0	0	27	27	1	8	11	11.7	3.67	94	.262	.315	1	.125	-0	-1	-1	0	0.0
1946	NY-A	1	1	.500	4	1	0	0	0	3¹	7	0	4	1	29.7	16.20	21	.438	.550	0	—	0	-5	-5	-0	-2.0
	Bos-N	1	1	.500	14	1	0	0	1	35	33	1	18	18	13.1	3.60	95	.250	.340	0	.000	-1	-1	-1	-0	-0.1
Total 3		6	5	.545	45	8	1	0	2	149¹	147	5	64	64	12.7	4.04	86	.261	.336	4	.093	-3	-10	-9	-1	-2.6

● **BUSTER ROSS**   Ross, Chester Franklin b: 3/11/03, Kuttawa, Ky. d: 4/24/82, Mayfield, Ky. BL/TL, 6'1", 195 lbs. Deb: 6/15/24

YEAR	TM/L	W	L	PCT	G	GS	CG	SH	SV	IP	H	HR	BB	SO	RAT	ERA	ERA+	OAV	OOB	BH	AVG	PB	PR	/A	PD	TPI
1924	Bos-A	4	3	.571	30	2	1	1	1	93¹	109	3	30	16	13.4	3.47	126	.307	.361	5	.200	-0	8	9	-1	0.5
1925	Bos-A	3	8	.273	33	8	0	0	0	94¹	119	9	40	15	15.6	6.20	73	.313	.386	3	.125	-1	-19	-17	-1	-1.8
1926	Bos-A	0	1	.000	1	0	0	0	0	2²	5	0	4	0	30.4	16.88	24	.385	.529	0	.000	-0	-4	-4	-0	-0.8
Total 3		7	12	.368	64	10	1	1	1	190¹	233	12	74	31	14.8	5.01	89	.311	.377	8	.160	-2	-15	-12	-2	-2.1

● **CLIFF ROSS**   Ross, Clifford Davis b: 8/3/28, Philadelphia, Pa. BL/TL, 6'4", 195 lbs. Deb: 9/11/54

YEAR	TM/L	W	L	PCT	G	GS	CG	SH	SV	IP	H	HR	BB	SO	RAT	ERA	ERA+	OAV	OOB	BH	AVG	PB	PR	/A	PD	TPI
1954	Cin-N	0	0	—	4	0	0	0	0	2²	0	0	0	1	0.0	0.00	—	.000	.000	0	—	0	1	1	0	0.1

● **ERNIE ROSS**   Ross, Ernest Bertram "Curly" b: 3/31/1880, Toronto, Ont., Can. d: 3/28/50, Toronto, Ont., Can. BL/TL, 5'8", 150 lbs. Deb: 9/17/02

YEAR	TM/L	W	L	PCT	G	GS	CG	SH	SV	IP	H	HR	BB	SO	RAT	ERA	ERA+	OAV	OOB	BH	AVG	PB	PR	/A	PD	TPI
1902	Bal-A	1	1	.500	2	2	2	0	0	17	20	0	12	2	17.5	7.41	51	.293	.406	0	.000	-1	-7	-7	-1	-0.7

● **BOB ROSS**   Ross, Floyd Robert b: 11/2/28, Fullerton, Cal. BR/TL, 6', 165 lbs. Deb: 6/16/50

YEAR	TM/L	W	L	PCT	G	GS	CG	SH	SV	IP	H	HR	BB	SO	RAT	ERA	ERA+	OAV	OOB	BH	AVG	PB	PR	/A	PD	TPI
1950	Was-A	0	1	.000	6	2	0	0	0	12²	15	1	15	2	21.3	8.53	53	.300	.462	0	.000	-0	-6	-6	0	-0.4
1951	Was-A	0	1	.000	11	1	0	0	0	31²	36	3	21	23	16.2	6.54	63	.295	.399	1	.111	-0	-8	-9	-1	-0.3
1956	Phi-N	0	0	—	3	0	0	0	0	3¹	4	1	2	4	16.2	8.10	46	.333	.429	0	—	0	-2	-2	0	0.0
Total 3		0	2	.000	20	3	0	0	0	47²	55	5	38	29	17.6	7.17	58	.299	.419	1	.083	-1	-16	-16	0	-0.7

● **GARY ROSS**   Ross, Gary Douglas b: 9/16/47, McKeesport, Pa. BR/TR, 6'1", 190 lbs. Deb: 6/28/68

YEAR	TM/L	W	L	PCT	G	GS	CG	SH	SV	IP	H	HR	BB	SO	RAT	ERA	ERA+	OAV	OOB	BH	AVG	PB	PR	/A	PD	TPI
1968	Chi-N	1	1	.500	13	5	1	0	0	41	44	3	25	31	15.1	4.17	76	.288	.388	1	.091	-1	-5	-5	-0	-0.3
1969	Chi-N	0	0	—	2	1	0	0	0	2	1	0	2	2	13.5	13.50	30	.143	.333	0	—	0	-2	-2	-0	0.0
	SD-N	3	12	.200	46	7	0	0	3	109²	104	5	56	58	13.5	4.19	84	.252	.348	0	.000	-2	-7	-8	2	-1.1
	Yr	3	12	.200	48	8	0	0	3	111²	105	5	58	60	13.5	4.35	81	.250	.348	0	.000	-2	-9	-10	2	-1.1
1970	SD-N	2	3	.400	33	2	0	0	1	62¹	72	8	36	39	16.0	5.20	76	.305	.404	4	.500	2	-8	-8	1	-0.4
1971	SD-N	1	3	.250	13	0	0	0	0	24¹	27	0	11	13	14.4	2.96	111	.300	.382	0	.000	-0	1	1	0	0.1
1972	SD-N	4	3	.571	60	0	0	0	3	91²	87	2	49	46	13.7	2.45	134	.261	.363	2	.154	-0	10	8	1	0.8
1973	SD-N	4	4	.500	58	0	0	0	0	76¹	93	8	33	44	15.3	5.42	64	.304	.379	0	.000	-0	-15	-17	-1	-1.6
1974	SD-N	0	0	—	9	0	0	0	0	18	23	1	6	11	14.5	4.50	79	.315	.367	0	.000	-0	-2	-2	0	0.0
1975	Cal-A	0	1	.000	1	0	0	0	0	5	6	1	1	4	12.6	5.40	66	.273	.304	0	—	0	-1	-0	-0	-0.1
1976	Cal-A	8	16	.333	34	31	7	2	0	225	224	12	58	100	11.5	3.00	111	.258	.308	0	—	0	13	8	5	1.4
1977	Cal-A	2	4	.333	14	12	0	0	0	58¹	83	10	11	30	14.8	5.55	70	.337	.371	0	—	0	-10	-11	1	-0.9
Total 10		25	47	.347	283	59	8	2	7	713²	764	48	288	378	13.6	3.92	89	.278	.352	7	.115	-2	-26	-36	9	-2.1

● **GEORGE ROSS**   Ross, George Sidney b: 6/27/1892, San Rafael, Cal. d: 4/22/35, Amityville, N.Y. BL/TL, 5'10.5", 175 lbs. Deb: 6/27/18

YEAR	TM/L	W	L	PCT	G	GS	CG	SH	SV	IP	H	HR	BB	SO	RAT	ERA	ERA+	OAV	OOB	BH	AVG	PB	PR	/A	PD	TPI
1918	NY-N	0	0	—	1	0	0	0	1	2¹	2	0	3	2	19.3	0.00	—	.222	.417	0	.000	-0	1	1	-0	0.1

● **BUCK ROSS**   Ross, Lee Ravon b: 2/2/15, Norwood, N.C. d: 11/23/78, Charlotte, N.C. BR/TR, 6'2", 170 lbs. Deb: 5/7/36

YEAR	TM/L	W	L	PCT	G	GS	CG	SH	SV	IP	H	HR	BB	SO	RAT	ERA	ERA+	OAV	OOB	BH	AVG	PB	PR	/A	PD	TPI
1936	Phi-A	9	14	.391	30	27	12	1	0	200²	253	17	83	47	15.1	5.83	88	.304	.367	12	.169	-1	-18	-16	-2	-1.7
1937	Phi-A	5	10	.333	28	22	7	1	0	147¹	183	12	63	37	15.1	4.89	96	.306	.373	5	.102	-3	-4	-3	-0	-0.5
1938	Phi-A	9	16	.360	29	28	10	0	0	184¹	218	23	80	54	14.5	5.32	91	.289	.357	12	.190	-0	-11	-10	-1	-1.1
1939	Phi-A	6	14	.300	29	28	6	1	0	174	216	17	69	43	16.1	6.00	78	.302	.384	12	.207	-1	-27	-25	-2	-2.5
1940	Phi-A	5	10	.333	24	19	10	0	1	156¹	160	15	60	43	12.7	4.38	102	.256	.322	7	.132	-2	0	1	-1	-0.2
1941	Phi-A	0	1	.000	1	1	0	0	0	4	10	2	2	0	27.0	18.00	23	.435	.480	0	.000	-0	-6	-6	0	-0.9
	Chi-A	3	8	.273	20	11	7	0	0	108¹	99	6	43	30	11.9	3.16	130	.239	.312	7	.219	1	12	11	-2	1.0
	Yr	3	9	.250	21	12	7	0	0	112¹	109	8	45	30	12.4	3.69	111	.249	.321	7	.212	1	6	5	-2	0.1
1942	Chi-A	5	7	.417	22	14	7	0	0	113¹	118	6	39	37	12.5	5.00	72	.264	.323	6	.158	-0	-17	-18	-3	-1.9
1943	Chi-A	11	7	.611	21	21	7	1	0	149¹	140	6	56	41	11.9	3.19	105	.253	.324	4	.087	-1	2	2	-1	0.0
1944	Chi-A	2	7	.222	20	9	2	0	0	90¹	97	7	35	20	13.4	5.18	66	.280	.350	2	.077	-2	-18	-18	-2	-2.0
1945	Chi-A	1	1	.500	13	2	0	0	0	37¹	51	3	17	8	16.4	5.79	57	.327	.393	2	.182	-0	-10	-10	-1	-0.6
Total 10		56	95	.371	237	182	65	6	2	1365¹	1545	114	573	360	14.0	4.94	88	.283	.351	69	.154	-11	-97	-91	-13	-10.4

● **MARK ROSS**   Ross, Mark Joseph b: 8/8/57, Galveston, Tex. BR/TR, 6', 195 lbs. Deb: 9/12/82

YEAR	TM/L	W	L	PCT	G	GS	CG	SH	SV	IP	H	HR	BB	SO	RAT	ERA	ERA+	OAV	OOB	BH	AVG	PB	PR	/A	PD	TPI
1982	Hou-N	0	0	—	4	0	0	0	0	6	3	0	0	4	4.5	1.50	221	.143	.143	0	—	0	1	1	0	0.0
1984	Hou-N	1	0	1.000	2	0	0	0	0	2¹	1	0	0	1	3.9	0.00	—	.125	.125	0	—	0	1	1	-0	0.4
1985	Hou-N	0	2	.000	8	0	0	0	0	13	12	2	3	9	9.7	4.85	71	.240	.269	0	.000	-0	-2	-2	-0	-0.3
1987	Pit-N	0	0	—	1	0	0	0	0	1	1	0	0	0	9.0	9.00	46	.250	.250	0	—	0	-0	-0	0	0.0
1988	Tor-A	0	0	—	3	0	0	0	0	7¹	5	0	4	4	11.0	4.91	80	.185	.290	0	—	0	-1	-1	-0	0.0
1990	Pit-N	1	0	1.000	9	0	0	0	0	12²	11	2	4	5	10.7	3.55	102	.244	.306	0	.000	-0	0	0	0	0.0
Total 6		2	2	.500	27	0	0	0	0	42¹	33	5	10	17	9.1	3.83	93	.213	.261	0	.000	-0	-1	-0	0	0.1

● **FRANK ROSSO**   Rosso, Francis James b: 3/1/21, Agawam, Mass. d: 1/26/80, Springfield, Mass. BR/TR, 5'11", 180 lbs. Deb: 9/15/44

YEAR	TM/L	W	L	PCT	G	GS	CG	SH	SV	IP	H	HR	BB	SO	RAT	ERA	ERA+	OAV	OOB	BH	AVG	PB	PR	/A	PD	TPI
1944	NY-N	0	0	—	2	0	0	0	0	4	11	0	3	1	31.5	9.00	41	.550	.609	0	—	0	-2	-2	0	-0.2

● **MARV ROTBLATT**   Rotblatt, Marvin "Rotty" b: 10/18/27, Chicago, Ill. BB/TL, 5'7", 160 lbs. Deb: 7/4/48

YEAR	TM/L	W	L	PCT	G	GS	CG	SH	SV	IP	H	HR	BB	SO	RAT	ERA	ERA+	OAV	OOB	BH	AVG	PB	PR	/A	PD	TPI
1948	Chi-A	0	1	.000	7	2	0	0	0	18¹	19	0	23	4	21.1	7.85	54	.271	.457	0	.000	-0	-7	-7	-1	-0.4
1950	Chi-A	0	0	—	2	0	0	0	0	8²	11	2	5	6	16.6	6.23	72	.344	.432	0	.000	-0	-2	-2	0	-0.0
1951	Chi-A	4	2	.667	26	2	0	0	2	47²	44	4	23	20	12.8	3.40	119	.244	.333	0	.000	-2	4	3	1	0.3
Total 3		4	3	.571	35	4	0	0	2	74²	74	6	51	30	15.3	4.82	86	.262	.379	0	.000	-2	-5	-6	1	-0.1

● **JACK ROTHROCK**   Rothrock, John Houston b: 3/14/05, Long Beach, Cal. d: 2/2/80, San Bernardino, Cal BB/TR, 5'11.5", 165 lbs. Deb: 7/28/25 ◆

YEAR	TM/L	W	L	PCT	G	GS	CG	SH	SV	IP	H	HR	BB	SO	RAT	ERA	ERA+	OAV	OOB	BH	AVG	PB	PR	/A	PD	TPI
1928	Bos-A	0	0	—	1	0	0	0	0	1	0	0	0	0	0.0	0.00	—	.000	.000	92	.267	0	0	0	0	0.0

● **LARRY ROTHSCHILD**   Rothschild, Lawrence Lee b: 3/12/54, Chicago, Ill. BL/TR, 6'2", 180 lbs. Deb: 9/11/81 C

YEAR	TM/L	W	L	PCT	G	GS	CG	SH	SV	IP	H	HR	BB	SO	RAT	ERA	ERA+	OAV	OOB	BH	AVG	PB	PR	/A	PD	TPI
1981	Det-A	0	0	—	5	0	0	0	1	5²	4	1	2	1	15.9	1.59	237	.190	.385	0	—	0	1	1	0	0.1
1982	Det-A	0	0	—	2	0	0	0	0	2²	4	1	2	1	20.3	13.50	30	.333	.429	0	—	0	-3	-3	-0	-0.1
Total 2		0	0	—	7	0	0	0	1	8¹	8	1	4	1	17.3	5.40	72	.250	.400	0	—	0	-1	-1	0	0.1

● **GENE ROUNSAVILLE**   Rounsaville, Virle Gene b: 9/27/44, Konawa, Okla. BR/TR, 6'3", 205 lbs. Deb: 4/7/70

YEAR	TM/L	W	L	PCT	G	GS	CG	SH	SV	IP	H	HR	BB	SO	RAT	ERA	ERA+	OAV	OOB	BH	AVG	PB	PR	/A	PD	TPI
1970	Chi-A	0	1	.000	8	0	0	0	0	6¹	10	1	2	3	17.1	9.95	39	.357	.400	0	—	0	-4	-4	-0	-0.6

YEAR	TM/L	W	L	PCT	G	GS	CG	SH	SV	IP	H	HR	BB	SO	RAT	ERA	ERA+	OAV	OOB	BH	AVG	PB	PR	/A	PD	TPI

● JACK ROWAN   Rowan, John Albert b: 6/16/1887, New Castle, Pa. d: 9/29/66, Dayton, Ohio BR/TR, 6'1", 210 lbs. Deb: 9/6/06

1906	Det-A	0	1	.000	1	1	1	0	0	9	15	0	6	0	21.0	11.00	25	.373	.455	1	.250	0	-8	-8	-0	-0.6
1908	Cin-N	3	3	.500	8	7	4	1	0	49¹	46	0	16	24	11.3	1.82	126	.253	.313	1	.071	-0	3	3	1	0.3
1909	Cin-N	11	12	.478	38	23	14	0	0	225²	185	0	104	81	11.6	2.79	93	.233	.324	6	.092	-1	-5	-5	-0	-1.1
1910	Cin-N	14	13	.519	42	30	18	4	1	261	242	4	105	108	12.3	2.93	99	.254	.334	19	.229	3	3	-0	-4	-0.2
1911	Phi-N	2	4	.333	12	6	2	0	0	45²	59	3	20	17	15.8	4.73	73	.316	.385	1	.077	-1	-7	-7	1	-0.8
	Chi-N	0	0	—	1	0	0	0	0	2	1	0	2	0	18.0	4.50	74	.143	.400	0	.000	-0	-0	-0	0	0.0
	Yr	2	4	.333	13	6	2	0	0	47²	60	3	22	17	15.7	4.72	73	.308	.381	1	.071	-1	-7	-7	1	-0.8
1913	Cin-N	0	4	.000	5	5	5	0	0	39	37	0	9	21	10.8	3.00	108	.264	.313	2	.182	1	1	1	-0	0.2
1914	Cin-N	1	3	.250	12	2	0	0	0	39	38	1	10	16	11.1	3.46	85	.262	.310	0	.000	-1	-3	-2	-1	-0.4
Total	7	31	40	.437	119	74	44	5	3	670²	623	8	272	267	12.2	3.07	92	.255	.333	30	.151		-16	-19	-9	-2.6

● DAVE ROWE   Rowe, David Elwood b: 10/9/1854, Harrisburg, Pa. d: 12/9/30, Glendale, Cal. BR/TR, 5'9", 180 lbs. Deb: 5/30/1877 FM♦

1877	Chi-N	0	1	.000	1	1	1	0	0	1	3	0	2	0	45.0	18.00	17	.600	.714	2	.286	0	-2	-2	0	-0.9
1882	Cle-N	0	1	.000	1	1	1	0	0	9	29	3	7	0	36.0	12.00	23	.492	.545	25	.258	0	-9	-9	-0	-0.6
1883	Bal-a	0	0	—	1	0	0	0	0	4	12	1	2	1	31.5	20.25	17	.492	.530	80	.313	0	-8	-7	-0	0.0
1884	StL-U	1	0	1.000	1	1	0	0	0	9	10	0	0	2	10.0	2.00	120	.263	.263	142	.293	0	0	0	0	0.1
Total	4	1	2	.333	4	3	2	0	0	23	54	4	11	3	25.4	9.78	28	.427	.473	383	.263	0	-18	-18	-0	-1.4

● DON ROWE   Rowe, Donald Howard b: 4/3/36, Brawley, Cal. BL/TL, 6', 180 lbs. Deb: 4/9/63 C

| 1963 | NY-N | 0 | 0 | — | 26 | 1 | 0 | 0 | 0 | 54² | 59 | 6 | 21 | 27 | 13.3 | 4.28 | 81 | .280 | .348 | 3 | .231 | 0 | -6 | -5 | -1 | -0.1 |

● KEN ROWE   Rowe, Kenneth Darrell b: 12/31/33, Ferndale, Mich. BR/TR, 6'2", 185 lbs. Deb: 4/14/63 C

1963	LA-N	1	1	.500	14	0	0	0	0	27²	28	2	11	12	13.0	2.93	103	.264	.339	0	.000	-1	1	0	-0	-0.1
1964	Bal-A	1	0	1.000	6	0	0	0	0	4¹	10	1	4	4	22.8	8.31	43	.455	.478	0	—	0	-2	-2	0	-0.4
1965	Bal-A	0	0	—	6	0	0	0	0	13¹	17	0	2	3	12.8	3.38	103	.321	.345	1	1.000	0	0	-1	0	0.0
Total	3	2	1	.667	26	0	0	0	1	45¹	55	3	14	19	13.9	3.57	90	.304	.357	1	.167	-0	-1	-2	-1	-0.5

● SCHOOLBOY ROWE   Rowe, Lynwood Thomas b: 1/11/10, Waco, Tex. d: 1/8/61, ElDorado, Ark. BR/TR, 6'4.5", 210 lbs. Deb: 4/15/33 C♦

1933	Det-A	7	4	.636	19	15	8	1	0	123¹	129	7	31	75	11.7	3.58	121	.269	.315	11	.220	-0	10	10	2	0.9
1934	*Det-A	24	8	.750	45	30	20	3	1	266	259	12	81	149	11.5	3.45	127	.256	.312	33	.303	12	31	28	-0	4.0
1935	*Det-A☆	19	13	.594	42	34	21	**6**	3	275²	272	11	68	140	11.2	3.69	113	.255	**.301**	34	.312	14	23	15	-2	2.6
1936	Det-A★	19	10	.655	41	35	19	4	3	245¹	266	16	64	115	12.2	4.51	110	.275	.321	23	.256	7	14	12	2	2.0
1937	Det-A	1	4	.200	10	2	1	0	0	31¹	49	7	9	6	16.9	8.62	54	.350	.393	2	.200	-0	-14	-14	-0	-1.6
1938	Det-A	0	2	.000	4	3	0	0	0	21	20	1	11	4	13.3	3.00	167	.256	.348	1	.167	-0	4	5	1	0.4
1939	Det-A	10	12	.455	28	24	8	1	0	164	192	17	61	51	14.0	4.99	98	.291	.353	15	.246	2	-7	-2	-0	-0.6
1940	*Det-A	16	3	**.842**	27	23	11	1	0	169	170	15	43	61	11.4	3.46	137	.259	.305	18	.269	5	17	24	-0	2.9
1941	Det-A	8	6	.571	27	14	4	0	1	139	155	6	33	54	12.2	4.14	110	.278	.318	15	.273	6	6	6	1	1.1
1942	Det-A	1	0	1.000	2	1	0	0	0	10¹	9	0	2	7	9.6	0.00	—	.220	.256	0	.000	-1	4	5	0	0.4
	Bro-N	1	0	1.000	9	2	0	0	0	30¹	36	2	12	6	14.5	5.34	61	.288	.355	4	.211	0	-7	-7	0	-0.2
1943	Phi-N	14	8	.636	27	25	11	3	1	199	196	7	29	52	10.3	2.94	115	.249	.279	36	.300	16	10	10	3	3.1
1946	Phi-N	11	4	.733	17	16	9	2	0	136	112	3	21	51	9.2	2.12	162	.224	.263	11	.180	2	20	20	-2	2.3
1947	Phi-N★	14	10	.583	31	28	15	1	1	195²	232	22	45	74	12.9	4.32	93	.292	.333	22	.278	10	-6	-7	-1	0.1
1948	Phi-N	10	10	.500	30	20	8	0	0	148	167	14	31	46	12.4	4.07	97	.281	.319	10	.192	-2	-2	-1	1	-0.0
1949	Phi-N	3	7	.300	23	6	2	0	0	65¹	68	2	17	22	12.0	4.82	82	.300	.354	4	.235	2	-6	-6	1	-0.6
Total	15	158	101	.610	382	278	137	22	12	2219¹	2332	132	558	913	11.8	3.87	110	.269	.315	239	.263	76	93	96	2	17.4

● MIKE ROWLAND   Rowland, Michael Evan b: 1/31/53, Chicago, Ill. BR/TR, 6'3", 205 lbs. Deb: 7/25/80

1980	SF-N	1	1	.500	19	0	0	0	0	27	20	2	8	9	9.7	2.33	152	.206	.274	0	—	0	4	4	-0	0.2
1981	SF-N	0	1	.000	9	1	0	0	0	15²	13	1	6	8	11.5	3.45	100	.232	.317	1	1.000	0	0	-0	-0	0.0
Total	2	1	2	.333	28	1	0	0	0	42²	33	3	14	16	10.3	2.74	128	.216	.290	1	1.000	0	4	4	-0	0.2

● CHARLIE ROY   Roy, Charles Robert b: 6/22/1884, Beaulieu, Minn. d: 2/10/50, Blackfoot, Idaho BR/TR, 5'10", 190 lbs. Deb: 6/27/06 F

| 1906 | Phi-N | 0 | 1 | .000 | 7 | 1 | 0 | 0 | 0 | 18¹ | 24 | 0 | 5 | 6 | 14.7 | 4.91 | 53 | .316 | .366 | 0 | .000 | -1 | -5 | -5 | -0 | -0.3 |

● EMILE ROY   Roy, Emile Arthur b: 5/26/07, Brighton, Mass. BR/TR, 5'11", 180 lbs. Deb: 9/30/33

| 1933 | Phi-A | 0 | 1 | .000 | 1 | 1 | 0 | 0 | 0 | 2¹ | 4 | 0 | 4 | 3 | 30.9 | 27.00 | 16 | .364 | .533 | 0 | — | 0 | -6 | -6 | -0 | -1.2 |

● JEAN-PIERRE ROY   Roy, Jean-Pierre b: 6/26/20, Montreal, Que., Can. BB/TR, 5'10", 160 lbs. Deb: 5/5/46

| 1946 | Bro-N | 0 | 0 | — | 3 | 1 | 0 | 0 | 0 | 6¹ | 5 | 2 | 5 | 6 | 14.2 | 9.95 | 34 | .200 | .333 | 0 | .000 | -0 | -5 | -5 | -0 | -0.1 |

● LUTHER ROY   Roy, Luther Franklin b: 7/29/02, Ooltewah, Tenn. d: 7/24/63, Grand Rapids, Mich. BR/TR, 5'10.5", 161 lbs. Deb: 6/12/24 F

1924	Cle-A	0	5	.000	16	5	2	0	0	48²	62	3	31	14	17.2	7.77	55	.318	.412	4	.267	-0	-19	-19	1	-1.5
1925	Cle-A	0	0	—	6	1	0	0	0	10	14	1	11	1	22.5	3.60	123	.368	.510	0	.000	-0	1	1	-0	-0.1
1927	Chi-N	3	1	.750	11	0	0	0	0	19²	14	0	11	5	11.9	2.29	169	.209	.329	1	.333	0	4	3	0	0.7
1929	Phi-N	3	6	.333	21	12	1	0	0	88²	137	11	37	16	18.0	8.42	62	.350	.411	9	.281	2	-37	-32	1	-2.2
	Bro-N	0	0	—	3	0	0	0	0	3²	4	0	2	0	14.7	4.91	94	.286	.375	0	.000	-0	-0	-0	0	0.0
	Yr	3	6	.333	23	12	1	0	0	92¹	141	11	39	16	17.5	8.29	62	.346	.403	9	.273	2	-37	-32	1	-2.2
Total	4	6	12	.333	56	18	3	0	0	170²	231	15	92	36	17.2	7.17	66	.328	.408	14	.264	2	-51	-47	1	-3.1

● NORMIE ROY   Roy, Norman Brooks "Jumbo" b: 11/15/28, Newton, Mass. BR/TR, 6', 200 lbs. Deb: 4/23/50

| 1950 | Bos-N | 4 | 3 | .571 | 19 | 6 | 2 | 0 | 1 | 59² | 72 | 7 | 39 | 25 | 17.0 | 5.13 | 75 | .305 | .408 | 3 | .167 | 0 | -7 | -8 | 0 | -0.9 |

● DICK ROZEK   Rozek, Richard Louis b: 3/27/27, Cedar Rapids, Iowa BL/TL, 6'0.5", 190 lbs. Deb: 4/29/50

1950	Cle-A	0	0	—	12	2	0	0	0	25¹	28	3	19	14	16.7	4.97	87	.283	.398	0	.000	-1	-1	-2	-1	-0.1
1951	Cle-A	0	0	—	7	1	0	0	0	15¹	18	1	11	5	17.6	2.93	129	.286	.400	1	.333	0	2	1	-1	0.0
1952	Cle-A	1	0	1.000	10	1	0	0	0	12²	11	0	13	5	17.1	4.97	82	.224	.387	0	.000	-0	-2	-2	-0	-0.2
1953	Phi-A	0	0	—	2	0	0	0	0	10²	8	3	9	2	14.3	5.06	85	.222	.378	0	.000	-1	-1	-1	0	-0.1
1954	Phi-A	0	0	—	2	0	0	0	0	1¹	0	0	3	0	27.0	6.75	58	.000	.571	0	—	0	-0	-0	0	0.0
Total	5	1	0	1.000	33	4	0	0	0	65¹	65	7	55	26	16.8	4.55	88	.260	.397	1	.083	-1	-3	-4	-2	-0.3

● DAVE ROZEMA   Rozema, David Scott b: 8/5/56, Grand Rapids, Mich. BR/TR, 6'4", 200 lbs. Deb: 4/11/77

1977	Det-A	15	7	.682	28	28	16	1	0	218	222	25	34	92	10.8	3.09	139	.265	.299	0	—	0	23	29	0	2.8
1978	Det-A	9	12	.429	28	28	11	2	0	209¹	205	17	41	57	10.7	3.14	123	.260	.298	0	—	0	15	17	-1	1.5
1979	Det-A	4	4	.500	16	16	4	1	0	97¹	101	9	30	33	12.7	3.51	123	.270	.334	0	—	0	8	9	0	0.6
1980	Det-A	6	9	.400	42	13	2	1	4	144²	152	11	49	49	12.8	3.92	105	.277	.342	0	—	0	2	3	1	0.3
1981	Det-A	5	5	.500	28	9	2	2	3	104	99	12	25	46	11.0	3.63	104	.256	.306	0	—	0	1	1	1	0.1
1982	Det-A	3	0	1.000	8	2	0	0	1	27²	17	2	7	15	8.1	1.63	250	.179	.243	0	—	0	8	7	1	0.7
1983	Det-A	8	3	.727	29	16	1	0	2	105	100	16	29	63	11.1	3.43	114	.248	.300	0	—	0	7	6	1	0.7
1984	Det-A	7	6	.538	29	16	0	0	0	101	110	13	18	48	11.6	3.74	105	.271	.309	0	—	0	3	2	1	0.1
1985	Tex-A	3	7	.300	34	4	0	0	7	88	100	10	22	42	12.7	4.19	101	.287	.333	0	—	0	-0	-1	1	0.1
1986	Tex-A	0	0	—	6	0	0	0	0	10²	19	1	3	3	18.6	5.91	73	.404	.440	0	—	0	-2	-2	0	0.0
Total	10	60	53	.531	248	132	36	7	17	1106	1125	113	258	448	11.5	3.47	117	.266	.313	0	—	0	63	73	3	7.3

YEAR TM/L	W	L	PCT	G	GS	CG	SH	SV	IP	H	HR	BB	SO	RAT	ERA	ERA+	OAV	OOB	BH	AVG	PB	PR	/A	PD	TPI
● JORGE RUBIO				Rubio, Jorge Jesus (Chavez) b: 4/23/45, Mexicali, Mexico BR/TR, 6'3", 200 lbs. Deb: 4/21/66																					
1966 Cal-A	2	1	.667	7	4	1	1	0	27¹	22	2	16	27	12.8	2.96	113	.220	.333	0	.000	-1	1	1	-0	0.0
1967 Cal-A	0	2	.000	3	3	0	0	0	15	18	2	9	4	18.6	3.60	87	.316	.443	1	.333	1	-1	-1	0	0.0
Total 2	2	3	.400	10	7	1	1	0	42¹	40	4	25	31	14.9	3.19	103	.255	.374	1	.091	-0	1	0	-0	0.0
● DAVE RUCKER				Rucker, David Michael b: 9/1/57, San Bernardino, Cal BL/TL, 6'1", 190 lbs. Deb: 4/12/81																					
1981 Det-A	0	0	—	2	0	0	0	0	4	3	0	1	2	11.3	6.75	56	.188	.278	0	—	0	-1	-1	-0	0.0
1982 Det-A	5	6	.455	27	4	1	0	0	64	62	4	23	31	12.2	3.38	120	.251	.320	0	—	0	5	5	0	0.8
1983 Det-A	1	2	.333	4	3	0	0	0	9	18	2	8	6	27.0	17.00	23	.419	.519	0	—	0	-13	-13	-0	-2.7
StL-N	5	3	.625	34	0	0	0	0	37	36	1	18	22	13.4	2.43	149	.263	.353	0	.000	-0	5	5	0	1.0
1984 StL-N	2	3	.400	50	0	0	0	0	73	62	3	34	38	12.0	2.10	166	.237	.327	1	.143	0	12	11	-1	0.6
1985 Phi-N	3	2	.600	39	3	0	0	1	79¹	82	6	40	41	14.2	4.31	85	.279	.368	4	.333	2	-6	-6	0	-0.1
1986 Phi-N	0	2	.000	19	0	0	0	0	25	34	4	14	14	17.3	5.76	67	.340	.421	0	.000	-0	-6	-5	0	-0.4
1988 Pit-N	0	2	.000	31	0	0	0	0	28¹	39	2	9	16	15.2	4.76	71	.328	.375	0	.000	-0	-4	-4	-0	-0.3
Total 7	16	20	.444	206	10	1	0	1	319²	337	19	147	170	13.9	3.94	94	.276	.357	5	.192	1	-8	-9	0	-1.1
● NAP RUCKER				Rucker, George b: 9/30/1884, Crabapple, Ga. d: 12/19/70, Alpharetta, Ga. BR/TL, 5'11", 190 lbs. Deb: 4/15/07																					
1907 Bro-N	15	13	.536	37	30	26	4	0	275¹	242	3	80	131	10.8	2.06	114	.242	.303	15	.155	-1	13	9	-1	0.7
1908 Bro-N	17	19	.472	42	35	30	6	1	333¹	265	1	125	199	11.0	2.08	113	.231	.317	21	.179	-1	11	10	4	1.5
1909 Bro-N	13	19	.406	38	33	28	6	1	309¹	245	6	101	201	10.5	2.24	116	.228	.303	12	.119	-5	12	12	-2	0.5
1910 Bro-N	17	18	.486	41	39	**27**	**6**	0	320¹	293	5	84	147	10.8	2.58	117	.251	.306	23	.209	-1	16	16	-2	1.3
1911 Bro-N	22	18	.550	48	33	23	5	4	315²	255	12	110	190	10.5	2.71	123	.226	.300	21	.202	2	24	22	2	3.0
1912 Bro-N	18	21	.462	45	34	23	**6**	4	297²	272	6	72	151	10.5	2.21	152	.250	.298	25	.245	2	40	38	2	**5.2**
1913 Bro-N	14	15	.483	41	33	16	4	3	260	236	3	67	111	10.7	2.87	115	.249	.304	21	.241	2	10	12	-4	1.1
1914 Bro-N	7	6	.538	16	16	5	0	0	103²	113	2	27	35	12.3	3.39	84	.275	.323	9	.265	2	-7	-6	-0	-0.5
1915 Bro-N	9	4	.692	19	15	7	1	1	122²	134	3	28	38	12.0	2.42	115	.279	.322	9	.214	-1	4	5	1	0.8
1916 *Bro-N	2	1	.667	9	3	1	0	0	37¹	34	0	7	14	10.1	1.69	159	.241	.282	1	.091	-1	4	4	0	0.2
Total 10	134	134	.500	336	271	186	38	14	2375¹	2089	41	701	1217	10.8	2.42	119	.243	.306	157	.195	1	127	121	1	13.8
● ERNIE RUDOLPH				Rudolph, Ernest William b: 2/13/10, Black River Falls, Wis. BL/TR, 5'8", 165 lbs. Deb: 6/16/45																					
1945 Bro-N	1	0	1.000	7	0	0	0	0	8²	12	1	7	3	19.7	5.19	72	.333	.442	0	—	1	-1	-1	0	-0.1
● DON RUDOLPH				Rudolph, Frederick Donald b: 8/16/31, Baltimore, Md. d: 9/12/68, Granada Hills, Cal BL/TL, 5'11", 195 lbs. Deb: 9/21/57																					
1957 Chi-A	1	0	1.000	5	0	0	0	0	12	6	2	2	6	6.0	2.25	166	.146	.186	1	.500	1	2	2	-0	0.2
1958 Chi-A	1	0	1.000	7	0	0	0	0	7	4	0	5	2	11.6	2.57	141	.190	.346	0	—	0	1	1	0	0.2
1959 Chi-A	0	0	—	4	0	0	0	1	3	4	0	2	0	18.0	0.00	—	.333	.429	0	—	0	1	1	0	0.1
Cin-N	0	0	—	5	0	0	0	0	7¹	13	1	3	8	19.6	4.91	83	.394	.444	0	.000	-0	-1	-1	0	0.0
1962 Cle-A	0	0	—	1	0	0	0	0	0¹	1	0	0	0	27.0	—	—	1.000	1.000	0	—	0	0	0	0	0.0
Was-A	8	10	.444	37	23	6	2	0	176¹	187	13	42	68	11.8	3.62	111	.274	.319	10	.175	1	7	8	-1	0.8
Yr	8	10	.444	38	23	6	2	0	176²	188	13	42	68	11.9	3.62	112	.275	.320	10	.175	1	7	8	-1	0.8
1963 Was-A	7	19	.269	37	26	4	0	1	174	189	28	36	70	11.9	4.55	82	.275	.317	8	.178	2	-18	-16	-1	-2.1
1964 Was-A	1	3	.250	28	8	0	0	1	70¹	81	10	12	32	11.9	4.09	90	.290	.320	1	.067	-1	-4	-3	-0	-0.3
Total 6	18	32	.360	124	57	10	2	3	450¹	485	54	102	182	11.9	4.00	96	.276	.319	20	.167	3	-11	-8	-1	-1.1
● DICK RUDOLPH				Rudolph, Richard "Baldy" b: 8/25/1887, New York, N.Y. d: 10/20/49, Bronx, N.Y. BR/TR, 5'9.5", 160 lbs. Deb: 9/30/10 C																					
1910 NY-N	0	1	.000	3	1	1	0	0	12	21	0	2	10	17.3	7.50	40	.350	.371	1	.250	0	-6	-6	-0	-0.7
1911 NY-N	0	0	—	1	0	0	0	0	2	2	0	0	0	9.00	37	.250	.250	1	1.000	0	-1	-1	-0	0.0
1913 Bos-N	14	13	.519	33	22	17	2	0	249¹	258	4	59	109	11.5	2.92	112	.276	.320	21	.239	4	8	10	5	1.9
1914 *Bos-N	26	10	.722	42	36	31	6	0	336¹	288	9	61	138	**9.4**	2.35	117	.238	.276	15	.125	-1	16	15	2	1.7
1915 Bos-N	22	19	.537	44	43	30	3	1	341¹	304	4	64	147	9.9	2.37	109	.242	.282	23	.198	6	14	8	1	1.7
1916 Bos-N	19	12	.613	41	38	27	5	3	312	266	7	38	133	**8.9**	2.16	115	.235	**.261**	16	.158	1	16	11	6	1.9
1917 Bos-N	13	13	.500	31	30	22	5	0	242²	252	1	54	96	11.5	3.41	75	.272	.314	20	.230	3	-19	-23	-7	-2.1
1918 Bos-N	9	10	.474	21	20	15	3	0	154	144	2	30	48	10.2	2.57	104	.255	.292	10	.185	-1	3	2	1	0.3
1919 Bos-N	13	18	.419	37	32	24	2	2	273²	282	2	54	76	11.1	2.17	132	.276	.314	17	.193	3	23	21	0	2.9
1920 Bos-N	4	8	.333	18	11	3	0	0	89	104	4	24	24	13.3	4.04	75	.294	.346	5	.185	-0	-9	-10	-0	-1.2
1922 Bos-N	0	2	.000	3	3	1	0	0	16	22	2	5	3	15.2	5.06	79	.328	.375	2	.400	1	-2	-2	0	-0.1
1923 Bos-N	1	2	.333	4	4	1	1	0	19¹	27	1	6	3	17.7	3.72	107	.333	.413	0	.000	-1	1	1	0	0.0
1927 Bos-N	0	0	—	1	0	0	0	0	1¹	1	0	1	0	13.5	0.00	—	.200	.333	0	—	0	1	1	-0	0.0
Total 13	121	108	.528	279	240	172	27	8	2049	1971	35	402	786	10.8	2.66	104	.258	.298	131	.188	14	44	25	15	6.3
● KIRK RUETER				Rueter, Kirk Wesley b: 12/1/70, Hoyleton, Ill. BL/TL, 6'3", 190 lbs. Deb: 7/7/93																					
1993 Mon-N	8	0	1.000	14	14	1	0	0	85²	85	5	18	31	10.8	2.73	153	.264	.303	2	.077	-1	12	14	2	1.3
1994 Mon-N	7	3	.700	20	20	0	0	0	92¹	106	11	23	50	12.8	5.17	82	.294	.340	4	.118	-1	-10	-9	0	-1.0
Total 2	15	3	.833	34	34	1	0	0	178	191	16	41	81	11.8	3.99	105	.280	.323	6	.100	-2	3	4	2	0.3
● DUTCH RUETHER				Ruether, Walter Henry b: 9/13/1893, Alameda, Cal. d: 5/16/70, Phoenix, Ariz. BL/TL, 6'1.5", 180 lbs. Deb: 4/13/17 ♦																					
1917 Chi-N	2	0	1.000	10	4	1	0	0	36¹	37	0	12	23	12.9	2.48	117	.285	.359	12	.273	2	1	2	1	0.4
Cin-N	1	2	.333	7	4	1	1	0	35²	43	0	14	12	14.9	3.53	74	.323	.396	5	.208	1	-3	-4	-2	-0.2
Yr	3	2	.600	17	8	2	1	0	72	80	0	26	35	13.5	3.00	92	.301	.367	17	.250	3	-2	-2	0	0.2
1918 Cin-N	0	1	.000	2	2	1	0	0	10	10	0	3	10	12.6	2.70	99	.244	.311	0	.000	-0	0	-0	-0	-0.1
1919 *Cin-N	19	6	**.760**	33	29	20	3	0	242²	195	1	83	78	10.6	1.82	153	.223	.295	24	.261	6	30	26	-3	3.1
1920 Cin-N	16	12	.571	37	33	23	5	3	265²	235	2	96	99	11.5	2.47	123	.247	.321	20	.192	-1	20	17	0	1.7
1921 Bro-N	10	13	.435	36	27	12	1	2	211¹	247	7	67	78	13.7	4.26	91	.299	.356	34	.351	11	-11	-9	-1	0.2
1922 Bro-N	21	12	.636	35	35	26	2	0	267¹	290	11	92	89	13.1	3.53	115	.282	.345	26	.208	4	17	16	-0	2.2
1923 Bro-N	15	14	.517	34	34	20	0	0	275	308	11	86	87	13.1	4.22	92	.287	.343	32	.274	4	-7	-10	-2	-0.6
1924 Bro-N	8	13	.381	30	21	13	2	0	168	190	4	45	63	12.9	3.91	96	.282	.332	15	.242	2	-1	-3	1	-0.2
1925 *Was-A	18	7	.720	30	29	16	1	0	223¹	241	6	105	68	14.3	3.87	109	.281	.365	36	.333	6	13	9	-3	1.6
1926 Was-A	12	6	.667	23	23	9	0	0	169¹	214	5	64	46	16.1	4.84	80	.311	.375	23	.250	4	-15	-18	-1	-1.4
*NY-A	2	3	.400	5	5	1	0	0	36	32	0	18	12	12.8	3.50	110	.248	.345	2	.095	-2	2	1	-1	-0.1
Yr	14	9	.609	28	28	10	0	0	205¹	246	5	84	56	14.5	4.60	84	.300	.366	25	.221	3	-13	-17	-3	-1.5
1927 NY-A	13	6	.684	27	26	12	3	0	184	202	8	52	45	12.8	3.38	114	.287	.343	21	.262	5	16	10	0	1.4
Total 11	137	95	.591	309	272	155	18	8	2124²	2244	54	739	708	12.9	3.50	104	.277	.342	250	.258	45	60	36	-9	8.2
● SCOTT RUFFCORN				Ruffcorn, Scott Patrick b: 12/12/69, Austin, Tex. BR/TR, 6'4", 215 lbs. Deb: 6/19/93																					
1993 Chi-A	0	2	.000	3	2	0	0	0	10	9	2	10	2	17.1	8.10	52	.265	.432	0	—	0	-4	-4	-1	-0.7
1994 Chi-A	0	2	.000	2	2	0	0	0	6¹	15	1	5	3	28.4	12.79	37	.455	.526	0	—	0	-6	-6	-0	-1.1
Total 2	0	4	.000	5	4	0	0	0	16¹	24	3	15	5	21.5	9.92	44	.358	.476	0	—	0	-10	-10	-1	-1.8
● BRUCE RUFFIN				Ruffin, Bruce Wayne b: 10/4/63, Lubbock, Tex BB/TL, 6'2", 205 lbs. Deb: 6/28/86																					
1986 Phi-N	9	4	.692	21	21	6	0	0	146¹	138	6	44	70	11.3	2.46	157	.251	.308	4	.073	-3	20	23	-1	1.5
1987 Phi-N	11	14	.440	35	35	3	1	0	204²	236	17	73	93	13.7	4.35	97	.298	.359	4	.055	-5	-6	-3	-1	-0.8
1988 Phi-N	6	10	.375	55	15	3	0	0	144¹	151	6	80	82	14.6	4.43	80	.275	.370	4	.121	-0	-16	-14	1	-1.5
1989 Phi-N	6	10	.375	24	23	3	0	0	125²	152	10	62	70	15.3	4.44	80	.301	.377	6	.176	2	-13	-13	2	-1.1
1990 Phi-N	6	13	.316	32	25	2	1	0	149	178	14	62	79	14.6	5.38	71	.297	.364	3	.068	-2	-26	-26	0	-3.1
1991 Phi-N	4	7	.364	31	15	1	1	0	119	125	6	38	85	12.4	3.78	97	.272	.329	0	.000	-1	-1	-2	-0	-0.3

YEAR	TM/L	W	L	PCT	G	GS	CG	SH	SV	IP	H	HR	BB	SO	RAT	ERA	ERA+	OAV	OOB	BH	AVG	PB	PR	/A	PD	TPI
1992	Mil-A	1	6	.143	25	6	1	0	0	58	66	7	41	45	16.6	6.67	57	.293	.402				-18	-18	-0	-2.0
1993	Col-N	6	5	.545	59	12	0	0	2	139²	145	11	69	126	13.9	3.87	123	.269	.352	2	.080	-1	3	14	-0	0.9
1994	Col-N	4	5	.444	56	0	0	0	16	55²	55	6	30	65	13.9	4.04	123	.253	.347	1	.250	0	1	6	1	1.3
Total 9		53	74	.417	338	152	17	3	21	1142¹	1246	83	499	715	13.8	4.25	94	.281	.355	24	.082	-10	-56	-33	1	-5.1

● **JOHNNY RUFFIN**   Ruffin, Johnny Renando b: 7/29/71, Butler, Ala.   BR/TR, 6'3", 172 lbs.   Deb: 8/8/93

YEAR	TM/L	W	L	PCT	G	GS	CG	SH	SV	IP	H	HR	BB	SO	RAT	ERA	ERA+	OAV	OOB	BH	AVG	PB	PR	/A	PD	TPI
1993	Cin-N	2	1	.667	21	0	0	0	2	37²	36	4	11	30	11.5	3.58	112	.247	.304	1	.333	0	2	2	0	0.2
1994	Cin-N	7	2	.778	51	0	0	0	1	70	57	7	27	44	10.8	3.09	135	.223	.297	0	.000	-1	9	8	-1	0.8
Total 2		9	3	.750	72	0	0	0	3	107²	93	11	38	74	11.0	3.26	126	.231	.299	1	.091	-1	11	10	-1	1.0

● **RED RUFFING**   Ruffing, Charles Herbert b: 5/3/04, Granville, Ill. d: 2/17/86, Mayfield Hts., O.   BR/TR, 6'1.5", 205 lbs.   Deb: 5/31/24 CH♦

YEAR	TM/L	W	L	PCT	G	GS	CG	SH	SV	IP	H	HR	BB	SO	RAT	ERA	ERA+	OAV	OOB	BH	AVG	PB	PR	/A	PD	TPI
1924	Bos-A	0	0	—	8	2	0	0	0	23	29	4	9	10	16.0	6.65	66	.333	.414	1	.143	-0	-6	-6	-1	0.0
1925	Bos-A	9	18	.333	37	27	13	3	1	217¹	253	10	75	64	13.7	5.01	91	.299	.357	17	.215	-0	-15	-11	-1	-1.2
1926	Bos-A	6	15	.286	37	22	6	0	2	166	169	4	68	58	13.1	4.39	93	.274	.351	10	.196	0	-7	-6	-1	-0.8
1927	Bos-A	5	13	.278	26	18	10	0	2	158¹	160	7	87	77	14.3	4.66	91	.277	.375	14	.255	1	-9	-8	0	-0.6
1928	Bos-A	10	25	.286	42	34	**25**	1	2	289¹	303	8	96	118	12.7	3.89	106	.275	.339	38	.314	11	5	7	-3	1.7
1929	Bos-A	9	22	.290	35	30	18	1	1	244¹	280	17	118	109	14.7	4.86	88	.297	.376	35	.307	5	-17	-16	-1	-1.0
1930	Bos-A	0	3	.000	4	3	1	0	0	24	32	1	6	14	14.6	6.38	72	.323	.368	3	.273	1	-5	-5	-1	-0.5
	NY-A	15	5	.750	34	25	12	2	1	197²	200	10	62	117	13.0	4.14	104	.260	.317	37	.374	17	11	3	-2	1.6
	Yr	15	8	.652	38	28	13	2	1	221²	232	11	68	131	12.3	4.38	99	.267	.322	40	.364	18	7	-1	-3	1.1
1931	NY-A	16	14	.533	37	30	19	1	2	237	240	11	87	132	12.6	4.41	90	.256	.323	36	.330	11	-1	-12	-3	-0.3
1932	*NY-A	18	7	.720	35	29	22	3	2	259	219	16	115	**190**	11.7	3.09	132	**.226**	.311	38	.306	14	40	28	-2	3.5
1933	NY-A	9	14	.391	35	28	18	0	3	235	230	7	93	122	12.5	3.91	99	.258	.330	29	.252	8	10	-1	-0	0.7
1934	NY-A★	19	11	.633	36	31	19	5	0	256¹	232	18	104	149	11.8	3.93	103	.236	.310	28	.248	7	16	4	-3	0.7
1935	NY-A	16	11	.593	30	29	19	2	0	222	201	17	76	81	11.3	3.12	130	.239	.303	37	.339	14	33	23	-2	3.5
1936	*NY-A	20	12	.625	33	33	25	3	0	271	274	22	90	102	12.2	3.85	121	.263	.323	37	.291	16	36	24	2	3.9
1937	*NY-A	20	7	.741	31	31	22	4	0	256¹	242	17	68	131	10.9	2.98	149	.247	.296	26	.202	3	47	42	-4	3.7
1938	*NY-A☆	**21**	7	**.750**	31	31	22	3	0	247¹	246	16	82	127	11.9	3.31	137	.258	.317	24	.224	10	**41**	34	-2	**4.0**
1939	*NY-A★	21	7	.750	28	28	22	**5**	0	233¹	211	15	75	95	11.1	2.93	149	.240	.301	35	.307	9	44	37	-2	4.7
1940	NY-A★	15	12	.556	30	30	20	3	0	226	218	24	76	97	11.8	3.38	119	.252	.314	11	.124	-3	25	16	-3	1.1
1941	*NY-A	15	6	.714	23	23	13	0	0	185²	177	17	54	60	11.2	3.54	111	.252	.306	27	.303	12	13	8	-3	1.6
1942	*NY-A☆	14	7	.667	24	24	16	4	0	193²	183	10	41	60	10.5	3.21	107	.250	.292	20	.250	7	10	5	-2	1.0
1945	NY-A	7	3	.700	11	11	8	1	0	87¹	85	7	20	24	10.9	2.89	120	.251	.294	10	.217	1	5	6	-2	0.5
1946	NY-A	5	1	.833	8	8	4	2	0	61	37	2	19	19	8.9	1.77	195	.171	.251	3	.120	-1	12	11	-1	0.9
1947	Chi-A	3	5	.375	9	9	1	0	0	53	63	7	16	13	13.4	6.11	60	.290	.339	5	.208	-0	-14	-14	-0	-1.8
Total 22		273	225	.548	624	536	335	45	16	4344	4284	254	1541	1987	12.2	3.80	109	.258	.323	521	.269	143	272	174	-34	26.9

● **VERN RUHLE**   Ruhle, Vernon Gerald b: 1/25/51, Coleman, Mich.   BR/TR, 6'1", 187 lbs.   Deb: 9/9/74

YEAR	TM/L	W	L	PCT	G	GS	CG	SH	SV	IP	H	HR	BB	SO	RAT	ERA	ERA+	OAV	OOB	BH	AVG	PB	PR	/A	PD	TPI
1974	Det-A	2	0	1.000	5	3	1	0	0	33	35	1	6	10	11.5	2.73	139	.273	.311	0	—	0	3	4	-1	-0.1
1975	Det-A	11	12	.478	32	31	8	3	0	190	199	17	65	67	12.8	4.03	100	.266	.330	0	—	0	-5	-0	-2	-0.5
1976	Det-A	9	12	.429	32	32	5	1	0	199²	227	19	59	88	13.1	3.92	95	.288	.340	0	—	0	-9	-5	-0	-0.7
1977	Det-A	3	5	.375	14	10	0	0	0	66¹	83	9	15	27	13.7	5.70	75	.305	.348	0	—	0	-12	-10	-1	-1.1
1978	Hou-N	3	3	.500	13	10	2	2	0	68	57	9	20	27	10.3	2.12	156	.224	.283	1	.056	-1	11	9	-1	0.6
1979	Hou-N	2	6	.250	13	10	2	2	0	66¹	64	9	8	33	10.0	4.07	86	.249	.277	1	.053	-0	-2	-4	-1	-0.6
1980	*Hou-N	12	4	.750	28	22	6	2	0	159¹	148	7	29	55	10.2	2.37	139	.251	.289	12	.245	4	22	16	-2	1.9
1981	*Hou-N	4	6	.400	20	15	1	0	1	102	97	6	20	39	10.4	2.91	113	.250	.289	6	.250	1	3	4	-2	0.6
1982	Hou-N	9	13	.409	31	21	3	2	1	149	169	12	24	56	11.9	3.93	84	.289	.321	4	.098	-0	-5	-10	-1	-1.5
1983	Hou-N	8	5	.615	41	9	0	0	3	114²	107	13	36	43	11.5	3.69	92	.249	.312	2	.105	-1	-1	-4	0	-0.3
1984	Hou-N	1	9	.100	40	6	0	0	1	90¹	112	5	29	60	14.3	4.58	72	.309	.365	1	.083	-1	-10	-13	-1	-1.3
1985	Cle-A	2	10	.167	42	16	1	0	3	125	139	16	30	54	12.3	4.32	96	.283	.326	0	—	0	-2	-3	-0	-0.3
1986	*Cal-A	1	3	.250	19	1	0	0	1	47²	46	5	7	23	10.2	4.15	99	.247	.278	0	—	0	0	0	1	0.0
Total 13		67	88	.432	327	188	29	12	11	1411¹	1483	119	348	582	11.9	3.73	97	.270	.318	27	.148	6	-5	-16	-8	-3.3

● **ANDY RUSH**   Rush, Jesse Howard b: 12/26/1889, Longton, Kan. d: 3/16/69, Fresno, Cal. BR/TR, 6'3", 180 lbs. Deb: 4/16/25

YEAR	TM/L	W	L	PCT	G	GS	CG	SH	SV	IP	H	HR	BB	SO	RAT	ERA	ERA+	OAV	OOB	BH	AVG	PB	PR	/A	PD	TPI
1925	Bro-N	0	1	.000	4	2	0	0	0	9²	16	3	5	4	19.6	9.31	45	.364	.429	0	.000	-0	-5	-6	0	-0.5

● **BOB RUSH**   Rush, Robert Ransom b: 12/21/25, Battle Creek, Mich   BR/TR, 6'4", 205 lbs. Deb: 4/22/48

YEAR	TM/L	W	L	PCT	G	GS	CG	SH	SV	IP	H	HR	BB	SO	RAT	ERA	ERA+	OAV	OOB	BH	AVG	PB	PR	/A	PD	TPI
1948	Chi-N	5	11	.313	36	16	4	0	0	133¹	153	8	37	72	12.9	3.92	100	.287	.335	5	.128	-2	1	-0	1	-0.1
1949	Chi-N	10	18	.357	35	27	9	1	4	201	197	10	79	80	12.4	4.07	99	.255	.324	2	.032	-7	-1	-1	1	-0.7
1950	Chi-N☆	13	20	.394	39	34	19	1	1	254²	261	11	93	93	12.7	3.71	113	.265	.332	15	.167	-1	12	14	2	1.8
1951	Chi-N	11	12	.478	37	29	12	2	2	211¹	212	16	68	129	12.1	3.83	107	.254	.312	13	.191	-0	3	6	1	0.7
1952	Chi-N★	17	13	.567	34	32	17	4	0	250¹	205	14	81	157	10.5	2.70	143	.216	.282	28	.292	7	29	32	2	**5.0**
1953	Chi-N	9	14	.391	29	28	8	1	0	166²	177	17	66	84	13.4	4.54	98	.270	.341	6	.111	-2	-5	-2	-1	-0.3
1954	Chi-N	13	15	.464	33	32	11	0	0	236¹	213	12	103	124	12.2	3.77	111	.243	.326	23	.277	7	8	11	3	2.3
1955	Chi-N	13	11	.542	33	33	14	3	0	234	204	19	73	130	10.7	3.50	117	.234	.295	9	.110	-4	14	15	1	1.2
1956	Chi-N	13	10	.565	32	32	13	1	0	239²	210	30	59	104	10.3	3.19	118	.233	.282	8	.098	-3	15	15	-2	0.9
1957	Chi-N	6	16	.273	31	29	5	0	0	205¹	211	16	66	103	12.2	4.38	88	.265	.323	14	.203	2	-12	-12	-2	-1.1
1958	*Mil-N	10	6	.625	28	20	5	2	0	147¹	142	13	31	84	10.6	3.42	103	.253	.293	9	.200	2	9	7	-2	0.2
1959	Mil-N	5	6	.455	31	9	1	1	0	101¹	102	5	23	64	11.2	2.40	148	.257	.299	6	.188	0	17	13	-1	1.3
1960	Mil-N	2	0	1.000	10	0	0	0	0	15	24	4	5	8	17.4	4.20	82	.369	.414	1	.333	1	-1	-1	-0	-0.1
	Chi-A	0	0	—	9	0	0	0	0	14¹	14	5	6	12	13.2	5.65	67	.302	.362	1	1.000	1	-3	-3	0	0.1
Total 13		127	152	.455	417	321	118	16	8	2410²	2327	177	789	1244	11.6	3.65	109	.255	.313	140	.173	0	88	99	7	11.2

● **AMOS RUSIE**   Rusie, Amos Wilson "The Hoosier Thunderbolt" b: 5/30/1871, Mooresville, Ind. d: 12/6/42, Seattle, Wash. BR/TR, 6'1", 200 lbs. Deb: 5/9/1889 H

YEAR	TM/L	W	L	PCT	G	GS	CG	SH	SV	IP	H	HR	BB	SO	RAT	ERA	ERA+	OAV	OOB	BH	AVG	PB	PR	/A	PD	TPI
1889	Ind-N	12	10	.545	33	22	19	1	0	225	246	12	116	109	14.8	5.32	78	.273	.358	18	.175	-3	-33	-29	-2	-2.5
1890	NY-N	29	34	.460	67	63	56	4	1	548²	436	3	289	**341**	12.3	2.56	137	**.212**	.316	79	.278	10	62	58	6	**6.9**
1891	NY-N	33	20	.623	61	57	52	**6**	1	500¹	391	6	262	337	12.1	2.55	125	**.207**	.310	54	.245	4	44	36	2	3.7
1892	NY-N	31	31	.500	64	61	58	2	0	532	405	7	267	288	11.6	2.88	112	.202	.300	53	.210	-0	24	20	5	2.5
1893	NY-N	33	21	.611	**56**	52	**50**	4	1	**482**	451	15	218	**208**	12.8	3.23	144	**.240**	.324	57	.269	3	**77**	76	3	**7.2**
1894	*NY-N	**36**	13	.735	54	50	45	**3**	1	444	426	10	200	**195**	**12.8**	**2.78**	**189**	**.250**	**.330**	52	.280	2	126	122	8	**11.0**
1895	NY-N	23	23	.500	49	47	42	**4**	0	393¹	384	11	159	201	12.6	3.73	124	.252	.325	44	.246	-5	46	40	3	3.3
1897	NY-N	28	10	.737	38	37	35	2	0	322¹	314	6	87	135	11.5	2.54	164	.253	.308	40	.278	3	64	58	2	6.1
1898	NY-N	20	11	.645	37	36	33	4	1	300	288	6	103	114	12.0	3.03	115	.251	.317	29	.210	-1	19	15	-0	1.2
1901	Cin-N	0	1	.000	3	2	2	0	0	22	43	1	3	6	18.8	8.59	37	.405	.422	1	.125	-0	-13	-13	0	-0.5
Total 10		245	174	.585	462	427	392	30	5	3769²	3384	75	1704	1934	12.4	3.07	130	.234	.319	427	.247	12	416	381	27	38.9

◉ **SCOTT RUSKIN**   Ruskin, Scott Drew b: 6/8/63, Jacksonville, Fla.   BR/TL, 6'2", 185 lbs. Deb: 4/9/90

YEAR	TM/L	W	L	PCT	G	GS	CG	SH	SV	IP	H	HR	BB	SO	RAT	ERA	ERA+	OAV	OOB	BH	AVG	PB	PR	/A	PD	TPI
1990	Pit-N	2	2	.500	44	0	0	0	2	47²	41	2	28	34	15.1	3.02	120	.246	.370	2	.333	4	3	0	0	0.4
	Mon-N	1	0	1.000	23	0	0	0	0	27²	25	2	10	23	11.4	2.28	160	.243	.310	0	.000	-0	5	4	0	0.2
	Yr	3	2	.600	67	0	0	0	2	75¹	75	4	38	57	13.5	2.75	132	.256	.341	2	.250	1	9	7	0	0.6
1991	Mon-N	4	4	.500	64	0	0	0	6	63²	57	4	30	46	12.7	4.24	85	.241	.333	0	.000	-0	-4	-4	-0	-0.6
1992	Cin-N	4	3	.571	57	0	0	0	0	53²	56	6	20	43	13.3	5.03	72	.275	.342	0	.000	-0	-9	-9	-1	-1.1
1993	Cin-N	0	0	—	4	0	0	0	0	1	3	1	2	0	45.0	18.00	22	.500	.625	0	.000	-0	-2	-2	0	-0.1
Total 4		11	9	.550	192	0	0	0	8	193²	191	15	90	146	13.3	3.95	92	.260	.345	2	.154	1	-6	-7	1	-1.1

YEAR TM/L	W	L	PCT	G	GS	CG	SH	SV	IP	H	HR	BB	SO	RAT	ERA	ERA+	OAV	OOB	BH	AVG	PB	PR	/A	PD	TPI
● JOHN RUSS — Russ, John b: 4/1/1858, Cannelton, Ind. d: 1/18/12, Louisville, Ky. Deb: 7/4/1882 ♦																									
1882 Bal-a	0	1	.000	1	1	0	0	0	5	10	0	1	0	19.8	7.20	38	.391	.414	1	.333	0	-3	-2	-0	-0.3
● ALLAN RUSSELL — Russell, Allan E. "Rubberarm" b: 7/31/1893, Baltimore, Md. d: 10/20/72, Baltimore, Md. BB/TR, 5'11", 165 lbs. Deb: 9/13/15 F																									
1915 NY-A	1	2	.333	5	3	1	0	0	27	21	1	21	21	14.3	2.67	110	.228	.377	2	.250	-1	1	1	-0	0.1
1916 NY-A	6	10	.375	34	19	8	1	6	171¹	138	8	75	104	11.6	3.20	90	.232	.324	2	.044	-3	-7	-6	0	-0.9
1917 NY-A	7	8	.467	25	10	6	0	2	104¹	89	3	39	55	11.6	2.24	120	.236	.319	10	.323	3	5	5	-1	1.1
1918 NY-A	7	11	.389	27	18	7	2	4	141	139	6	73	54	13.9	3.26	87	.267	.363	7	.167	-1	-7	-7	-1	-1.1
1919 NY-A	5	5	.500	23	9	4	1	1	90²	89	6	32	50	12.2	3.47	92	.251	.317	7	.233	0	-2	-3	0	-0.2
Bos-A	10	4	.714	21	11	9	1	4	121¹	105	0	39	63	10.8	2.52	120	.246	.310	5	.122	-1	10	7	-1	0.6
Yr	15	9	.625	44	20	13	2	5	212	194	6	71	113	11.3	2.93	106	.248	.311	12	.169	-1	7	4	-0	0.4
1920 Bos-A	5	6	.455	16	10	7	0	1	107²	100	3	38	53	11.8	3.01	121	.251	.321	5	.122	-2	9	8	1	0.6
1921 Bos-A	7	11	.389	39	13	7	0	3	173	204	10	77	60	15.1	4.11	103	.303	.382	7	.123	-5	3	2	0	-0.3
1922 Bos-A	6	7	.462	34	11	1	0	2	125²	152	6	57	34	15.3	5.01	82	.314	.392	3	.079	-3	-14	-13	2	-1.2
1923 Was-A	10	7	.588	52	5	4	0	9	181¹	177	9	77	67	12.7	3.03	124	.270	.348	10	.200	-2	19	15	-3	1.2
1924 *Was-A	5	1	.833	37	0	0	0	8	82¹	83	1	45	17	14.1	4.37	92	.282	.379	5	.278	2	-1	-3	-0	-0.1
1925 Was-A	2	4	.333	32	2	0	0	2	68²	85	6	37	25	16.1	5.77	72	.315	.399	2	.143	-1	-10	-12	2	-0.8
Total 11	71	76	.483	345	111	54	5	42	1394¹	1382	59	610	603	13.1	3.52	99	.269	.351	65	.157	-10	5	-4	-0	-1.0
● LEFTY RUSSELL — Russell, Clarence Dickson b: 7/8/1890, Baltimore, Md. d: 1/22/62, Baltimore, Md. BL/TL, 6'1", 165 lbs. Deb: 10/1/10 F																									
1910 Phi-A	1	0	1.000	1	1	1	1	0	9	8	0	2	5	10.0	0.00	—	.258	.303	0	.000	-0	3	2	0	0.3
1911 Phi-A	0	3	.000	7	2	0	0	0	31²	45	1	18	7	19.3	7.67	41	.357	.456	5	.385	1	-15	-16	1	-1.0
1912 Phi-A	0	2	.000	5	2	1	0	0	17¹	18	1	14	9	18.2	7.27	42	.265	.412	0	.000	-0	-8	-8	0	-0.8
Total 3	1	5	.167	13	5	2	1	0	58	71	2	34	21	17.5	6.36	47	.316	.423	5	.250	1	-20	-22	1	-1.5
● REB RUSSELL — Russell, Ewell Albert b: 4/12/1889, Jackson, Miss. d: 9/30/73, Indianapolis, Ind BL/TL, 5'11", 185 lbs. Deb: 4/18/13 ♦																									
1913 Chi-A	22	16	.579	52	36	26	8	4	316²	250	2	79	122	9.5	1.90	154	.219	.273	20	.189	3	36	36	-5	4.2
1914 Chi-A	8	12	.400	38	23	8	1	1	167¹	168	3	33	79	11.0	2.90	92	.268	.308	17	.266	4	-3	-4	0	-0.1
1915 Chi-A	11	10	.524	41	25	10	3	2	229¹	215	0	47	90	10.5	2.59	115	.249	.292	21	.244	4	9	10	-2	1.1
1916 Chi-A	18	11	.621	56	25	16	5	3	264¹	207	1	42	112	**8.5**	2.42	114	.220	**.254**	13	.143	-4	12	10	-2	0.5
1917 *Chi-A	15	5	**.750**	35	24	11	5	3	189¹	170	1	32	54	9.6	1.95	136	.245	.279	19	.279	5	15	15	-1	2.2
1918 Chi-A	7	5	.583	19	15	10	2	0	124²	117	0	33	38	10.8	2.60	105	.252	.302	7	.140	-1	2	2	-1	-0.2
1919 Chi-A	0	0	—	1	0	0	0	0	1	0	0	0	0			—	1.000	1.000	0	.000	-0	0	0	0	0.0
Total 7	81	59	.579	242	148	81	24	13	1291²	1128	7	267	495	9.8	2.33	120	.238	.281	262	.268	10	72	69	-11	7.7
● JACK RUSSELL — Russell, Jack Erwin b: 10/24/05, Paris, Tex. d: 11/3/90, Clearwater, Fla. BR/TR, 6'1.5", 178 lbs. Deb: 5/5/26																									
1926 Bos-A	0	5	.000	36	5	1	0	0	98	94	2	24	17	10.9	3.58	114	.268	.316	4	.190	-0	5	5	4	0.6
1927 Bos-A	4	9	.308	34	15	4	1	0	147	172	5	40	25	13.3	4.10	103	.298	.348	4	.125	-3	1	2	1	0.0
1928 Bos-A	11	14	.440	32	26	10	2	0	201¹	233	6	41	27	12.4	3.84	107	.294	.332	13	.210	-0	4	6	1	0.8
1929 Bos-A	6	18	.250	35	32	13	0	0	227¹	263	12	40	37	12.1	3.92	109	.290	.322	9	.129	-4	8	9	4	0.8
1930 Bos-A	9	20	.310	35	30	15	0	0	229²	302	11	53	53	14.0	5.45	85	.321	.359	14	.177	-3	-20	-21	2	-2.2
1931 Bos-A	10	18	.357	36	31	13	0	0	232	298	7	65	45	14.2	5.16	83	.310	.355	16	.195	-0	-20	-22	3	-1.8
1932 Bos-A	1	7	.125	11	6	1	0	0	39²	61	2	15	7	17.2	6.81	66	.343	.394	1	.091	-1	-10	-10	2	-1.7
Cle-A	5	7	.417	18	11	6	0	1	113	146	5	27	27	13.9	4.70	101	.310	.349	12	.300	2	-3	-1	1	0.4
Yr	6	14	.300	29	17	7	0	1	152²	207	7	42	34	14.7	5.25	89	.319	.361	13	.255	1	-13	-10	2	-1.3
1933 *Was-A	12	6	.667	50	3	2	0	13	124	119	3	32	28	11.0	2.69	156	.255	.305	5	.147	-1	22	21	4	3.4
1934 Was-A☆	5	10	.333	54	9	3	0	7	157²	179	6	56	38	13.5	4.17	104	.287	.348	7	.159	3	6	3	3	-1.4
1935 Was-A	4	9	.308	43	7	2	0	3	126	170	10	37	30	14.9	5.71	76	.324	.371	4	.200	1	-18	-20	3	-1.4
1936 Was-A	3	2	.600	18	5	1	0	3	49²	66	3	25	6	16.5	6.34	75	.317	.391	0	.000	-2	-7	-9	1	-0.9
Bos-A	0	3	.000	23	2	0	0	0	40	57	2	16	9	16.4	5.62	94	.345	.403	2	.286	-0	-3	-1	2	0.1
Yr	3	5	.375	41	7	1	0	3	89²	123	5	41	15	16.5	6.02	83	.330	.396	2	.091	-2	-10	-10	3	-0.8
1937 Det-A	2	5	.286	25	0	0	0	4	40¹	63	4	20	10	18.7	7.59	62	.362	.431	0	.000	-0	-13	-13	1	-2.0
1938 *Chi-N	6	1	.857	42	0	0	0	3	102¹	100	1	30	29	11.5	3.34	115	.258	.313	7	.219	1	5	6	3	0.8
1939 Chi-N	3	5	.571	39	0	0	0	0	68²	78	3	24	32	13.4	3.67	107	.282	.339	0	.000	-2	2	2	1	0.0
1940 StL-N	3	4	.429	26	0	0	0	1	54	53	1	26	16	13.2	2.50	160	.252	.335	0	.000	-2	8	9	1	1.1
Total 15	85	141	.376	557	182	71	3	38	2050²	2454	83	571	418	13.4	4.46	97	.299	.346	103	.167	-11	-33	-33	36	-1.2
● JEFF RUSSELL — Russell, Jeffrey Lee b: 9/2/61, Cincinnati, Ohio BR/TR, 6'3", 210 lbs. Deb: 8/13/83																									
1983 Cin-N	4	5	.444	10	10	0	0	0	68¹	58	7	22	40	10.5	3.03	126	.233	.295	3	.143	1	5	6	-0	0.8
1984 Cin-N	6	18	.250	33	30	4	2	0	181²	186	15	65	101	12.6	4.26	89	.263	.329	8	.140	-0	-14	-10	1	-1.1
1985 Tex-A	3	6	.333	13	13	0	0	0	62	85	10	27	44	16.5	7.55	56	.324	.392	0	—	0	-23	-23	1	-2.6
1986 Tex-A	5	2	.714	37	0	0	0	0	82	74	11	31	54	11.6	3.40	126	.244	.316	0	—	0	7	8	2	0.8
1987 Tex-A	5	4	.556	52	2	0	0	3	97¹	109	9	52	56	15.1	4.44	101	.285	.373	0	—	0	0	0	1	0.2
1988 Tex-A★	10	9	.526	34	24	5	0	0	188²	183	15	66	88	12.2	3.82	107	.257	.326	0	.000	-0	-3	-3	3	0.0
1989 Tex-A★	6	4	.600	71	0	0	0	38	72²	45	4	24	77	8.9	1.98	200	.182	.263	0	—	0	15	16	2	4.2
1990 Tex-A	1	5	.167	27	0	0	0	10	25¹	23	1	16	16	13.9	4.26	92	.253	.364	0	—	0	-1	-1	0	-0.3
1991 Tex-A	6	4	.600	68	0	0	0	30	79¹	71	11	26	52	11.1	3.29	122	.235	.298	0	—	0	7	7	1	1.5
1992 Tex-A	2	3	.400	51	0	0	0	28	56²	51	3	22	43	11.9	1.91	199	.238	.315	0	—	0	13	12	1	2.5
*Oak-A	2	0	1.000	8	0	0	0	2	9²	4	0	3	5	6.5	0.00	—	.125	.200	0	—	0	4	4	0	1.0
Yr	4	3	.571	59	0	0	0	30	66¹	55	3	25	48	10.9	1.63	233	.220	.291	0	—	0	17	16	0	3.5
1993 Bos-A	1	4	.200	51	0	0	0	33	46²	43	3	14	45	10.4	2.70	171	.231	.293	0	—	0	8	10	1	2.6
1994 Bos-A	0	5	.000	29	0	0	0	12	28	30	3	13	18	14.1	5.14	100	.270	.352	0	—	0	-1	-0	0	0.0
Cle-A	1	1	.500	13	0	0	0	5	12²	13	2	3	10	11.4	4.97	99	.265	.308	0	—	0	-0	-0	0	0.0
Yr	1	6	.143	42	0	0	0	17	40²	43	5	16	28	13.1	5.09	100	.264	.330	0	—	0	-2	-0	0	0.0
Total 12	52	70	.426	497	79	11	2	163	1011	971	92	384	649	12.3	3.79	108	.253	.325	11	.139	1	23	35	11	10.3
● JOHN RUSSELL — Russell, John Albert b: 10/20/1894, San Mateo, Cal. d: 11/19/30, Ely, Nev. BL/TL, 6'2", 195 lbs. Deb: 7/4/17																									
1917 Bro-N	0	1	.000	5	1	1	0	0	16	12	1	6	1	10.1	4.50	62	.222	.300	1	.250	0	-3	-3	-0	-0.2
1918 Bro-N	0	0	—	1	0	0	0	0	1	2	0	1	0	27.0	18.00	15	.500	.600	0	—	0	-2	-2	0	-0.3
1921 Chi-A	2	5	.286	11	9	4	0	1	66¹	82	3	35	15	16.0	5.29	80	.314	.397	10	.400	3	-7	-8	-1	-0.4
1922 Chi-A	0	1	.000	6²	7	0	4	3	14.9	6.75	60	.280	.379	0	—	0	-2	-1	0	-0.3					
Total 4	2	7	.222	21	11	5	0	1	90	103	4	46	19	15.0	5.40	73	.299	.384	11	.367	3	-14	-14	-1	-0.9
● JOHN RUSSELL — Russell, John William b: 1/5/61, Oklahoma City, Okla. BR/TR, 6', 200 lbs. Deb: 6/22/84 ♦																									
1989 Atl-N	0	0	—	1	0	0	0	0	0¹	0	0	0	0	0.0	0.00	—	.000	.000	29	.182	0	0	0	0	0.0
● MARIUS RUSSO — Russo, Marius Ugo "Lefty" b: 7/19/14, Brooklyn, N.Y. BR/TL, 6'1", 190 lbs. Deb: 6/6/39																									
1939 NY-A	8	3	.727	21	11	8	2	0	116	86	6	41	55	9.9	2.41	181	.210	.283	10	.244	1	29	25	2	2.5
1940 NY-A	14	8	.636	30	24	15	0	1	189¹	181	17	55	87	11.3	3.28	123	.249	.303	12	.188	2	23	16	3	2.2
1941 *NY-A☆	14	10	.583	28	27	17	3	1	209¹	195	8	87	105	12.1	3.09	127	.247	.322	18	.231	3	25	20	2	2.5
1942 NY-A	4	1	.800	9	5	2	0	0	45¹	41	2	14	15	11.1	2.78	124	.244	.306	4	.235	0	4	3	0	0.5
1943 *NY-A	5	10	.333	24	14	5	1	0	101²	89	4	27	43	12.0	3.72	87	.235	.319	6	.194	0	-5	-6	0	-0.7
1946 NY-A	0	2	.000	8	3	0	0	0	18²	26	1	11	7	17.8	4.34	80	.333	.416	0	.000	-1	-2	-2	0	-0.2
Total 6	45	34	.570	120	84	47	6	2	680²	618	41	253	311	11.6	3.13	124	.242	.312	50	.213	8	74	57	8	6.8

YEAR	TM/L	W	L	PCT	G	GS	CG	SH	SV	IP	H	HR	BB	SO	RAT	ERA	ERA+	OAV	OOB	BH	AVG	PB	PR	/A	PD	TPI

● **DICK RUSTECK**   Rusteck, Richard Frank b: 7/12/41, Chicago, Ill.   BR/TL, 6'1", 175 lbs.   Deb: 6/10/66

| 1966 | NY-N | 1 | 2 | .333 | 8 | 3 | 1 | 1 | 0 | 24 | 24 | 1 | 8 | 9 | 12.0 | 3.00 | 121 | .276 | .337 | 0 | .000 | -1 | 2 | 2 | -0 | 0.1 |

● **BABE RUTH**   Ruth, George Herman "The Bambino" or "The Sultan Of Swat"
b: 2/6/1895, Baltimore, Md.   d: 8/16/48, New York, N.Y.   BL/TL, 6'2", 215 lbs.   Deb: 7/11/14 CH♦

1914	Bos-A	2	1	.667	4	3	1	0	0	23	21	1	7	3	11.0	3.91	94	.236	.292	2	.200	0	-3	-3	-0	-0.4
1915	*Bos-A	18	8	.692	32	28	16	1	0	217²	166	3	85	112	10.6	2.44	114	.212	.294	29	.315	16	12	8	1	2.8
1916	*Bos-A	23	12	.657	44	41	23	9	1	323²	230	0	118	170	9.9	**1.75**	158	**.201**	.280	37	.272	14	**39**	37	0	**5.9**
1917	Bos-A	24	13	.649	41	38	**35**	6	2	326¹	244	2	108	128	10.0	2.01	128	.211	.284	40	.325	17	24	21	2	4.8
1918	*Bos-A	13	7	.650	20	19	18	1	0	166¹	125	1	49	40	9.5	2.22	121	.214	.277	95	.300	12	10	9	4	2.9
1919	Bos-A	9	5	.643	17	15	12	0	1	133¹	148	2	58	30	14.0	2.97	102	.290	.365	139	.322	14	4	1	0	1.5
1920	NY-A	1	0	1.000	1	1	0	0	0	4	3	0	2	0	11.3	4.50	85	.200	.294	172	.376	1	-0	-0	-0	0.0
1921	*NY-A	2	0	1.000	2	1	0	0	0	9	14	1	9	2	23.0	9.00	47	.350	.469	204	.378	2	-5	-5	-0	-0.7
1930	NY-A	1	0	1.000	1	1	1	0	0	9	11	0	2	3	13.0	3.00	143	.306	.342	186	.359	1	2	1	1	0.3
1933	NY-A★	1	0	1.000	1	1	1	0	0	9	12	0	3	0	15.0	5.00	78	.308	.357	138	.301	1	-1	-1	-0	0.0
Total	10	94	46	.671	163	148	107	17	4	1221¹	974	10	441	488	10.6	2.28	122	.221	.297	2873	.342	78	81	67	8	17.1

● **JOHNNY RUTHERFORD**   Rutherford, John William "Doc" b: 5/5/25, Belleville, Ont., Canada BL/TR, 5'10.5", 170 lbs.   Deb: 4/30/52

| 1952 | *Bro-N | 7 | 7 | .500 | 22 | 11 | 4 | 0 | 2 | 97¹ | 97 | 9 | 29 | 29 | 11.8 | 4.25 | 86 | .262 | .319 | 9 | .290 | 2 | -6 | -7 | 1 | -0.6 |

● **DICK RUTHVEN**   Ruthven, Richard David b: 3/27/51, Sacramento, Cal.   BR/TR, 6'3", 190 lbs.   Deb: 4/17/73

1973	Phi-N	6	9	.400	25	23	3	1	1	128¹	125	10	75	98	14.2	4.21	90	.257	.360	5	.132	-1	-8	-6	1	-0.7
1974	Phi-N	9	13	.409	35	35	6	0	0	212²	182	11	116	153	12.7	4.02	94	.231	.332	13	.191	-1	-10	-6	-1	-0.8
1975	Phi-N	2	2	.500	11	7	0	0	0	40²	37	4	22	26	13.3	4.20	89	.243	.343	2	.154	-0	-3	-2	-0	-0.3
1976	Atl-N☆	14	17	.452	36	36	8	4	0	240¹	255	14	90	142	13.2	4.19	90	.275	.345	13	.171	-0	-19	-11	2	-1.1
1977	Atl-N	7	13	.350	25	23	6	2	0	151	158	14	62	84	13.2	4.23	105	.267	.338	12	.267	1	-5	-4	-2	0.6
1978	Atl-N	2	6	.250	13	13	2	1	0	81	78	8	28	45	11.8	4.11	98	.257	.319	2	.083	-2	-5	-1	-0	-0.2
	*Phi-N	13	5	.722	20	20	9	2	0	150²	136	13	28	75	9.9	2.99	119	.248	.285	15	.283	4	10	10	-0	1.6
	Yr	15	11	.577	33	33	11	3	0	231²	214	21	56	120	10.5	3.38	111	.250	.297	17	.221	3	5	9	-1	1.4
1979	Phi-N	7	5	.583	20	20	3	2	0	122¹	121	10	37	58	11.8	4.27	90	.256	.313	6	.146	-0	-7	-6	-2	-0.7
1980	*Phi-N	17	10	.630	33	33	6	1	0	223¹	241	9	74	86	12.8	3.55	107	.283	.342	16	.235	4	1	6	-0	1.0
1981	*Phi-N★	12	7	.632	23	22	5	0	0	146²	162	10	54	69	13.4	5.15	70	.281	.346	7	.140	-0	-27	-25	-1	-3.0
1982	Phi-N	11	11	.500	33	31	8	2	0	204¹	189	16	59	115	11.2	3.79	97	.246	.305	7	.109	-2	-4	-3	-2	-0.8
1983	Phi-N	1	3	.250	7	7	0	0	0	33²	46	5	10	26	15.0	5.61	64	.333	.378	1	.111	-1	-7	-8	-0	-0.8
	Chi-N	12	9	.571	25	25	5	2	0	149¹	156	17	28	73	11.3	4.10	92	.269	.306	12	.226	2	-8	-5	2	-0.3
	Yr	13	12	.520	32	32	5	2	0	183	202	22	38	99	12.2	4.38	86	.279	.318	13	.210	2	-15	-13	2	-1.1
1984	Chi-N	6	10	.375	23	22	0	0	0	126²	154	14	41	55	14.1	5.04	77	.302	.359	7	.159	-0	-21	-16	-0	-1.8
1985	Chi-N	4	7	.364	20	15	0	0	0	87¹	103	6	37	26	14.4	4.53	88	.299	.367	5	.208	0	-9	-5	-1	-0.8
1986	Chi-N	0	0	—	6	0	0	0	0	10²	12	4	6	3	15.2	5.06	80	.293	.383	0	.000	-0	-2	-1	-0	0.0
Total	14	123	127	.492	355	332	61	17	1	2109	2155	165	767	1145	12.6	4.14	92	.267	.333	123	.183	6	-123	-75	-4	-8.1

● **CYCLONE RYAN**   Ryan, Daniel R. b: 1866, Cappagh White, Ireland d: 1/30/17, Medfield, Mass.   TR, 6',   Deb: 8/8/1887 ♦

1887	NY-a	0	1	.000	2	1	0	0	0	2¹	5	1	6	0	42.4	23.14	18	.455	.647	7	.219	-0	-5	-5	-0	-1.2
1891	Bos-N	0	0	—	1	0	0	0	0	3	2	0	1	0	9.0	0.00	—	.182	.251	0	.000	-0	1	1	0	0.0
Total	2	0	1	.000	3	1	0	0	0	5¹	7	1	7	0	23.6	10.13	39	.319	.483	7	.212	-0	-4	-4	0	-1.2

● **JACK RYAN**   Ryan, Jack "Gulfport" b: 9/19/1884, Lawrenceville, Ill.   d: 10/16/49, Hondsboro, Miss.   BR/TR, 5'10", 165 lbs.   Deb: 7/2/08

1908	Cle-A	1	1	.500	8	1	1	0	1	35²	27	3	2	7	7.6	2.27	105	.220	.238	1	.091	0	0	0	-0	0.1
1909	Bos-A	4	3	.571	13	8	2	0	0	61¹	65	0	20	24	13.1	3.23	77	.281	.349	4	.211	-0	-5	-5	-1	-0.6
1911	Bro-N	0	1	.000	3	1	0	0	0	6	9	1	4	1	21.0	3.00	111	.375	.483	0	.000	0	0	0	-0	0.0
Total	3	5	5	.500	24	10	3	0	1	103	101	4	26	32	11.6	2.88	87	.267	.324	5	.161	1	-4	-4	-0	-0.5

● **JIMMY RYAN**   Ryan, James Edward "Pony" b: 2/11/1863, Clinton, Mass.   d: 10/26/23, Chicago, Ill.   BR/TL, 5'9", 162 lbs.   Deb: 10/8/1885 ♦

1886	*Chi-N	0	0	—	5	0	0	0	1	23¹	19	2	13	15	12.3	4.63	79	.257	.368	100	.306	1	-3	-3	0	0.1
1887	Chi-N	2	1	.667	8	3	2	0	0	45	53	3	17	14	15.2	4.20	107	.305	.386	145	.285	2	-1	-1	0	0.3
1888	Chi-N	4	0	1.000	8	2	1	0	0	38¹	40	2	10	13	13.9	3.05	99	.297	.347	182	.332	4	-1	-0	0	0.2
1891	Chi-N	0	0	—	2	0	0	0	1	5²	11	0	2	2	20.6	1.59	210	.394	.434	140	.277	1	1	1	-0	0.1
1893	Chi-N	0	0	—	1	0	0	0	0	4²	3	0	0	1	5.8	0.00	—	.178	.178	102	.299	1	2	2	0	0.0
Total	5	6	1	.857	24	5	3	0	2	117	133	7	44	43	14.1	3.62	105	.295	.365	2502	.306	9	-1	2	2	0.6

● **JOHN RYAN**   Ryan, John A. (Played 1 Game Under Real Name Of Daniel Sheehan) b: Birmingham, Mich.   TR,   Deb: 4/19/1884

| 1884 | Bal-U | 3 | 2 | .600 | 6 | 6 | 5 | 0 | 0 | 51 | 61 | 1 | 16 | 33 | 13.6 | 3.35 | 80 | .278 | .327 | 2 | .080 | -3 | -5 | -4 | -0 | -0.6 |

● **JOHNNY RYAN**   Ryan, John Joseph b: 10/1853, Philadelphia, Pa.   d: 3/22/02, Philadelphia, Pa.   5'7.5", 150 lbs.   Deb: 8/19/1873 ♦

1874	Bal-n	0	0	—	1	0	0	0	0	1¹	9	0	0	0	60.8	13.50	23	.643	.643	33	.179	-0	-2	-2		0.0
1875	NH-n	1	5	.167	10	6	4	0	0	59¹	69	1	0	9	11.8	3.34	69	.256	.280	23	.158	-1	-6	-7		-0.6
1876	Lou-N	0	0	—	1	0	0	0	1	8	22	0	0	1	24.8	5.63	48	.449	.449	61	.253	-0	-3	-3	-0	0.0
Total	2 n	1	5	.167	11	6	4	0	0	60²	78	1	0	9	12.9	3.56	65	.275	.297	58	.172	-2	-7	-8		-0.6

● **KEN RYAN**   Ryan, Kenneth Frederick b: 10/24/68, Pawtucket, R.I.   BR/TR, 6'3", 200 lbs.   Deb: 8/31/92

1992	Bos-A	0	0	—	7	0	0	0	1	7	4	2	5	11	16.4	6.43	66	.174	.321	0		0	-2	-2	0	0.0
1993	Bos-A	7	2	.778	47	0	0	0	1	50	43	2	29	49	13.5	3.60	128	.235	.349	0		0	4	6	0	0.9
1994	Bos-A	2	3	.400	42	0	0	0	13	48	46	1	17	32	12.0	2.44	211	.256	.323	0		0	13	14	0	2.1
Total	3	9	5	.643	96	0	0	0	15	105	93	5	51	86	12.7	3.26	148	.241	.336	0		0	15	18	1	3.0

● **NOLAN RYAN**   Ryan, Lynn Nolan b: 1/31/47, Refugio, Tex.   BR/TR, 6'2", 195 lbs.   Deb: 9/11/66

1966	NY-N	0	1	.000	2	1	0	0	0	3	5	1	3	6	24.0	15.00	24	.357	.471	0		0	-4	-4	0	-0.9
1968	NY-N	6	9	.400	21	18	3	0	0	134	93	12	75	133	11.6	3.09	98	.200	.317	5	.114	-1	-2	-2	-0	-0.5
1969	*NY-N	6	3	.667	25	10	2	0	1	89¹	60	3	53	92	11.5	3.53	104	.189	.307	3	.103	-1	-1	-1	-2	-0.3
1970	NY-N	7	11	.389	27	19	5	2	0	131²	86	10	97	125	12.8	3.42	118	.188	.335	8	.178	-1	9	9	-1	1.0
1971	NY-N	10	14	.417	30	26	3	0	0	152	125	8	116	137	15.2	3.97	86	.219	.365	6	.128	-0	-8	-9	-1	-1.6
1972	Cal-A☆	19	16	.543	39	39	20	**9**	0	284	166	14	157	**329**	10.6	2.28	128	**.171**	.292	13	.135	-0	25	20	-2	2.4
1973	Cal-A★	21	16	.568	41	39	26	4	1	326	238	18	162	**383**	11.2	2.87	123	.203	.304	0		0	34	24	-2	2.9
1974	Cal-A	22	16	.579	42	41	26	3	0	332²	221	14	202	**367**	11.7	2.89	119	**.190**	.314	0		0	27	20	2	2.8
1975	Cal-A☆	14	12	.538	28	28	10	5	0	198	152	13	132	186	13.2	3.45	103	.213	.342	0		0	7	2	-2	0.5
1976	Cal-A	17	18	.486	39	39	21	**7**	0	284¹	193	13	183	**327**	12.1	3.36	99	**.195**	.323	0		0	5	-1	0	0.3
1977	Cal-A†	19	16	.543	37	37	**22**	4	0	299	198	12	204	**341**	12.4	2.77	141	**.193**	.331	0		0	43	38	0	4.2
1978	Cal-A	10	13	.435	31	31	14	3	0	234²	183	12	148	**260**	12.8	3.72	97	.220	.340	0		0	1	-3	1	0.1
1979	*Cal-A★	16	14	.533	34	34	17	**5**	0	222²	169	15	114	**223**	11.7	3.60	113	**.212**	.314	0		0	15	12	-0	1.6
1980	*Hou-N	11	10	.524	35	35	4	2	0	233²	205	10	98	200	11.8	3.35	98	.236	.316	6	.086	-1	6	-2	-1	-0.5
1981	*Hou-N★	11	5	.688	21	21	5	3	0	149	99	2	68	140	10.1	**1.69**	195	**.188**	.281	11	.216	3	**30**	27	-1	**3.3**
1982	Hou-N	16	12	.571	35	35	10	3	0	250¹	196	10	109	245	11.3	3.16	105	**.213**	.302	10	.120	-1	12	4	-0	0.3
1983	Hou-N	14	9	.609	29	29	5	2	0	196¹	134	9	101	183	11.0	2.98	114	**.195**	.302	5	.072	-4	14	9	-0	0.6
1984	Hou-N	12	11	.522	30	30	5	2	0	183²	143	12	69	197	10.6	3.04	109	.211	.288	6	.098	-2	11	6	-3	0.3
1985	Hou-N★	10	12	.455	35	35	4	0	0	232	205	12	95	209	12.0	3.80	91	.239	.322	7	.111	-1	-5	-9	-3	-1.2

YEAR	TM/L	W	L	PCT	G	GS	CG	SH	SV	IP	H	HR	BB	SO	RAT	ERA	ERA+	OAV	OOB	BH	AVG	PB	PR	/A	PD	TPI
1986	*Hou-N	12	8	.600	30	30	1	0	0	178	119	14	82	194	10.4	3.34	108	.188	.285	6	.102	-2	8	5	-1	0.1
1987	Hou-N	8	16	.333	34	34	0	0	0	211²	154	14	87	**270**	10.4	**2.76**	**142**	**.199**	.284	4	.062	-3	**31**	**27**	-1	2.5
1988	Hou-N	12	11	.522	33	33	4	1	0	220	186	18	87	**228**	11.5	3.52	94	.227	.307	4	.057	-3	-2	-5	-3	-1.1
1989	Tex-A★	16	10	.615	32	32	6	2	0	239¹	162	17	98	**301**	10.1	3.20	124	**.187**	.276	0	—	0	18	20	-1	1.9
1990	Tex-A	13	9	.591	30	30	5	2	0	204	137	18	74	**232**	**9.6**	3.44	114	**.188**	**.269**	0	—	0	11	11	-2	0.9
1991	Tex-A	12	6	.667	27	27	2	2	0	173	102	12	72	203	**9.3**	2.91	138	**.172**	**.267**	0	—	0	23	21	-1	2.0
1992	Tex-A	5	9	.357	27	27	2	0	0	157¹	138	9	69	157	12.5	3.72	102	.238	.331	0	—	0	4	1	-1	0.0
1993	Tex-A	5	5	.500	13	13	0	0	0	66¹	54	5	40	46	12.9	4.88	85	.220	.331	0	—	0	-4	-5	-2	-0.8
Total	27	324	292	.526	807	773	222	61	3	5386	3923	321	2795	5714	11.5	3.19	111	.204	.309	94	.110	-17	309	218	-29	20.8

● **ROSY RYAN**   Ryan, Wilfred Patrick Dolan   b: 3/15/1898, Worcester, Mass.   d: 12/10/80, Scottsdale, Ariz.   BL/TR, 6', 185 lbs.   Deb: 9/7/19

YEAR	TM/L	W	L	PCT	G	GS	CG	SH	SV	IP	H	HR	BB	SO	RAT	ERA	ERA+	OAV	OOB	BH	AVG	PB	PR	/A	PD	TPI
1919	NY-N	1	2	.333	4	3	1	0	0	20¹	20	0	9	7	13.3	3.10	91	.260	.345	0	.000	-1	-0	-1	-1	-0.2
1920	NY-N	0	1	.000	3	1	1	0	0	15¹	14	1	4	5	10.6	1.76	170	.259	.310	0	.000	-1	2	2	0	0.1
1921	NY-N	7	10	.412	36	16	5	0	3	147¹	140	6	32	58	12.7	3.73	98	.255	.297	9	.200	1	1	-1	-1	-0.2
1922	*NY-N	17	12	.586	46	20	12	1	3	191²	194	5	74	75	12.7	3.01	133	.269	.338	12	.194	1	23	21	-1	2.8
1923	*NY-N	16	5	.762	**45**	15	7	0	4	172²	169	8	46	58	11.3	3.49	109	.257	.308	11	.208	0	10	6	0	0.7
1924	*NY-N	8	6	.571	37	9	2	0	5	124²	137	1	37	36	12.7	4.26	86	.285	.339	1	.139	-1	-5	-8	-2	-1.2
1925	Bos-N	2	8	.200	37	7	1	0	2	122¹	152	7	52	48	15.0	6.31	64	.303	.368	11	.282	3	-28	-31	-1	-2.0
1926	Bos-N	0	2	.000	7	2	0	0	0	19	29	1	7	1	17.1	7.58	47	.392	.444	1	.200	-0	-8	-9	-0	-0.8
1928	NY-N	0	0	—	3	0	0	0	0	6	17	1	1	5	27.0	16.50	23	.486	.500	0	.000	-1	-8	-8	-0	-0.1
1933	Bro-N	1	1	.500	30	0	0	0	0	61¹	69	3	16	22	12.9	4.55	71	.276	.327	2	.154	0	-8	-9	-0	-0.4
Total	10	52	47	.525	248	73	29	1	19	881	941	33	278	315	12.6	4.14	91	.277	.333	51	.190	1	-22	-38	-5	-1.3

● **MIKE RYBA**   Ryba, Dominic Joseph   b: 6/9/03, DeLancey, Pa.   d: 12/13/71, Brookline Station, Mo.   BR/TR, 5'11", 180 lbs.   Deb: 9/22/35   C

YEAR	TM/L	W	L	PCT	G	GS	CG	SH	SV	IP	H	HR	BB	SO	RAT	ERA	ERA+	OAV	OOB	BH	AVG	PB	PR	/A	PD	TPI
1935	StL-N	1	1	.500	2	1	1	0	0	16	15	0	1	6	9.0	3.38	121	.242	.254	2	.400	1	1	1	0	0.2
1936	StL-N	5	1	.833	14	0	0	0	0	45	55	3	16	25	14.6	5.40	73	.294	.356	3	.167	-0	-7	-7	-1	-1.0
1937	StL-N	9	6	.600	38	8	5	0	0	135	152	8	40	57	12.9	4.13	96	.284	.336	15	.313	4	-3	-2	0	0.2
1938	StL-N	1	1	.500	3	0	0	0	0	5	8	0	1	0	16.2	5.40	73	.348	.375	0	—	0	-1	-1	0	-0.3
1941	Bos-A	7	3	.700	40	3	0	0	6	121	143	14	42	54	13.8	4.46	93	.297	.353	8	.216	1	-4	-4	2	0.0
1942	Bos-A	3	3	.500	18	0	0	0	3	44¹	49	5	13	16	12.8	3.86	97	.278	.332	5	.294	1	-1	-1	1	0.0
1943	Bos-A	7	5	.583	40	8	4	1	2	143²	142	4	57	50	13.5	3.26	102	.262	.333	8	.186	1	1	1	-1	0.0
1944	Bos-A	12	7	.632	42	7	2	0	2	138	119	7	39	50	10.3	3.33	102	.233	.287	6	.146	-0	2	1	3	0.4
1945	Bos-A	7	6	.538	34	9	4	1	2	123	122	5	33	44	11.5	2.49	137	.259	.310	9	.250	1	12	13	-1	1.5
1946	*Bos-A	0	1	.000	9	0	0	0	1	12²	12	1	5	5	12.3	3.55	103	.261	.333	2	1.000	1	-0	-0	-0	0.1
Total	10	52	34	.605	240	36	16	2	16	783²	817	47	247	307	12.3	3.66	100	.269	.326	58	.235	9	-1	1	3	1.1

● **GARY RYERSON**   Ryerson, Gary Lawrence   b: 6/7/48, Los Angeles, Cal.   BR/TL, 6'1", 175 lbs.   Deb: 6/28/72

YEAR	TM/L	W	L	PCT	G	GS	CG	SH	SV	IP	H	HR	BB	SO	RAT	ERA	ERA+	OAV	OOB	BH	AVG	PB	PR	/A	PD	TPI
1972	Mil-A	3	8	.273	20	14	4	1	0	102	119	9	21	45	12.4	3.62	84	.290	.324	1	.042	-1	-6	-7	-1	-1.0
1973	Mil-A	0	1	.000	9	4	0	0	0	23	32	6	7	10	15.3	7.83	48	.327	.371	0	—	0	-10	-10	0	-0.3
Total	2	3	9	.250	29	18	4	1	0	125	151	9	28	55	12.9	4.39	72	.297	.333	1	.042	-1	-17	-17	-1	-1.3

● **BRET SABERHAGEN**   Saberhagen, Bret William   b: 4/11/64, Chicago Heights, Ill.   BR/TR, 6'1", 195 lbs.   Deb: 4/4/84

YEAR	TM/L	W	L	PCT	G	GS	CG	SH	SV	IP	H	HR	BB	SO	RAT	ERA	ERA+	OAV	OOB	BH	AVG	PB	PR	/A	PD	TPI
1984	*KC-A	10	11	.476	38	18	2	1	1	157²	138	13	36	73	10.0	3.48	116	.237	.283	0	—	0	9	10	1	1.2
1985	*KC-A	20	6	.769	32	32	10	1	0	235¹	211	19	38	158	**9.6**	2.87	145	.241	**.273**	0	—	0	33	34	2	3.8
1986	KC-A	7	12	.368	30	25	4	2	0	156	165	15	29	112	11.3	4.15	102	.268	.303	0	—	0	0	2	1	0.3
1987	KC-A★	18	10	.643	33	33	15	4	0	257	246	27	53	163	10.7	3.36	135	.252	.295	0	—	0	31	34	1	3.4
1988	KC-A	14	16	.467	35	35	9	0	0	260²	271	18	59	171	11.5	3.80	105	.269	.312	0	—	0	5	5	0	0.6
1989	KC-A	23	6	**.793**	36	35	**12**	4	0	**262¹**	209	13	43	193	**8.7**	**2.16**	**178**	.217	**.252**	0	—	0	**50**	**49**	0	**5.5**
1990	KC-A★	5	9	.357	20	20	5	0	0	135	146	9	28	87	11.7	3.27	117	.279	.316	0	—	0	10	8	3	1.2
1991	KC-A	13	8	.619	28	28	7	2	0	196¹	165	12	45	136	10.0	3.07	134	.228	.281	0	—	0	22	23	1	2.4
1992	NY-N	3	5	.375	17	15	1	1	0	97²	84	6	27	81	10.6	3.50	99	.233	.294	3	.107	-1	0	-0	3	0.2
1993	NY-N	7	7	.500	19	19	4	1	0	139¹	131	11	17	93	9.8	3.29	122	.250	.278	5	.111	-0	12	11	3	1.3
1994	NY-N☆	14	4	**.778**	24	24	4	0	0	177¹	169	13	13	143	9.4	2.74	156	.254	.273	10	.172	1	29	30	2	3.2
Total	11	134	94	.588	312	284	73	16	1	2074²	1935	156	388	1410	10.2	3.19	128	.248	.286	18	.137	0	201	205	17	23.1

● **RAY SADECKI**   Sadecki, Raymond Michael   b: 12/26/40, Kansas City, Kan.   BL/TL, 5'11", 180 lbs.   Deb: 5/19/60

YEAR	TM/L	W	L	PCT	G	GS	CG	SH	SV	IP	H	HR	BB	SO	RAT	ERA	ERA+	OAV	OOB	BH	AVG	PB	PR	/A	PD	TPI
1960	StL-N	9	9	.500	26	26	7	1	0	157	148	15	86	95	13.4	3.78	109	.249	.345	12	.211	-0	-0	6	-2	0.4
1961	StL-N	14	10	.583	31	31	13	0	1	222²	196	28	102	114	12.2	3.72	118	.238	.324	22	.253	2	8	17	-5	1.3
1962	StL-N	6	8	.429	22	17	4	1	1	102¹	121	13	43	50	14.7	5.54	77	.296	.367	3	.081	-2	-18	-14	-2	-2.1
1963	StL-N	10	10	.500	36	28	4	1	1	193¹	198	25	78	136	13.0	4.10	87	.266	.339	4	.141	-1	-17	-12	-3	-1.6
1964	*StL-N	20	11	.645	37	32	9	2	1	220	232	16	60	119	12.0	3.68	103	.273	.322	12	.160	-1	-4	3	-3	0.3
1965	StL-N	6	15	.286	36	28	4	0	1	172²	192	26	64	122	13.3	5.21	74	.284	.346	11	.200	2	-32	-26	-2	-3.0
1966	StL-N	2	1	.667	5	3	1	0	0	24¹	16	2	9	21	9.2	2.22	162	.188	.266	3	.429	1	4	4	0	0.7
	SF-N	3	7	.300	26	19	3	1	0	105	125	20	39	62	14.4	5.40	68	.293	.358	11	.324	5	-21	-20	-2	-1.4
	Yr	5	8	.385	31	22	4	1	0	129¹	141	22	48	83	13.4	4.80	76	.276	.343	14	.341	7	-17	-17	-2	-0.7
1967	SF-N	12	6	.667	35	24	10	2	0	188	165	8	58	145	10.9	2.78	118	.238	.301	18	.247	4	13	11	-1	1.4
1968	SF-N	12	18	.400	38	36	13	6	0	254	225	14	70	206	10.6	2.91	101	.237	.292	8	.094	-1	2	1	-2	-0.3
1969	SF-N	5	8	.385	29	17	4	3	0	138¹	137	18	53	104	12.5	4.23	83	.259	.329	5	.125	-2	-10	-11	-2	-0.6
1970	NY-N	8	4	.667	28	19	4	0	0	138²	134	16	52	89	12.1	3.89	103	.255	.322	8	.205	1	2	-2	0	0.0
1971	NY-N	7	7	.500	34	20	5	1	0	163¹	139	10	44	120	10.3	2.92	117	.234	.285	10	.200	1	10	9	-2	0.6
1972	NY-N	2	1	.667	34	2	0	0	1	75²	73	3	31	38	12.6	3.09	109	.257	.334	2	.154	-0	3	2	-1	-0.1
1973	*NY-N	5	4	.556	31	11	0	0	1	116²	109	11	41	87	11.6	3.39	107	.248	.314	7	.226	1	3	3	-3	0.1
1974	NY-N	8	8	.500	34	10	3	1	0	103	107	7	35	64	12.6	3.41	105	.274	.337	7	.259	1	2	2	-0	0.0
1975	StL-N	1	0	1.000	8	0	0	0	0	11	13	0	7	8	16.4	3.27	115	.289	.385	0	—	0	1	1	-0	0.0
	Atl-N	2	3	.400	25	5	0	0	1	66¹	73	3	21	24	13.3	4.21	90	.286	.350	3	.200	0	-4	-3	-1	-0.3
	Yr	3	3	.500	33	5	0	0	1	77¹	86	3	28	32	13.7	4.07	93	.285	.353	3	.200	0	-4	-3	-1	-0.3
	KC-A	1	0	1.000	3	0	0	0	0	3	5	0	3	6	20.0	3.00	128	.333	.444	0	—	0	0	2	-0	-0.1
1976	KC-A	0	0	—	3	0	0	0	0	4²	7	0	3	1	19.3	0.00	—	.368	.455	0	—	0	2	2	0	0.2
	Mil-A	2	0	1.000	36	0	0	0	0	37¹	38	2	20	27	14.7	4.34	81	.262	.363	0	—	0	-4	-4	-1	-0.3
	Yr	2	0	1.000	39	0	0	0	0	42	45	2	23	28	15.2	3.86	91	.274	.374	0	—	0	-2	-2	-1	-0.3
1977	NY-N	1	0	1.000	3	1	0	0	0	3	3	0	0	4	9.0	6.00	62	.300	.462	0	—	0	-1	-1	-0	-0.2
Total	18	135	131	.508	563	328	85	20	7	2500²	2456	240	922	1614	12.3	3.78	97	.258	.326	151	.191	19	-61	-32	-30	-4.9

● **JIM SADOWSKI**   Sadowski, James Michael   b: 8/7/51, Pittsburgh, Pa.   BR/TR, 6'3", 195 lbs.   Deb: 4/27/74

YEAR	TM/L	W	L	PCT	G	GS	CG	SH	SV	IP	H	HR	BB	SO	RAT	ERA	ERA+	OAV	OOB	BH	AVG	PB	PR	/A	PD	TPI
1974	Pit-N	0	1	.000	4	0	0	0	0	9	7	1	9	4	16.0	6.00	57	.233	.410	0	.000	0	-2	-3	1	-0.2

● **BOB SADOWSKI**   Sadowski, Robert   b: 2/19/38, Pittsburgh, Pa.   BR/TR, 6'2", 195 lbs.   Deb: 6/19/63   F

YEAR	TM/L	W	L	PCT	G	GS	CG	SH	SV	IP	H	HR	BB	SO	RAT	ERA	ERA+	OAV	OOB	BH	AVG	PB	PR	/A	PD	TPI
1963	Mil-N	5	7	.417	19	18	5	1	0	116²	99	8	30	72	10.3	2.62	123	.231	.289	2	.057	-2	9	8	1	0.6
1964	Mil-N	9	10	.474	51	18	5	0	5	166²	159	18	56	96	12.0	4.10	86	.251	.319	8	.154	0	-11	-11	3	-1.0
1965	Mil-N	5	9	.357	34	13	3	0	1	123	117	13	35	78	11.3	4.32	82	.250	.306	3	.086	-1	-11	-11	-1	-1.5
1966	Bos-A	1	1	.500	11	5	0	0	2	33¹	41	4	9	11	13.8	5.40	70	.311	.359	0	.000	-1	-7	-6	-0	-0.4
Total	4	20	27	.426	115	54	13	1	8	439²	416	41	130	257	11.5	3.87	90	.250	.311	13	.101	-4	-20	-20	2	-2.3

● **TED SADOWSKI**   Sadowski, Theodore   b: 4/1/36, Pittsburgh, Pa.   d: 7/18/93, Shaler Twsp., Pa.   BR/TR, 6'1.5", 190 lbs.   Deb: 9/2/60   F

YEAR	TM/L	W	L	PCT	G	GS	CG	SH	SV	IP	H	HR	BB	SO	RAT	ERA	ERA+	OAV	OOB	BH	AVG	PB	PR	/A	PD	TPI
1960	Was-A	1	0	1.000	9	1	0	0	1	17¹	17	4	9	12	14.0	5.19	75	.258	.355	0	.000	-0	-3	-3	-0	-0.2

YEAR	TM/L	W	L	PCT	G	GS	CG	SH	SV	IP	H	HR	BB	SO	RAT	ERA	ERA+	OAV	OOB	BH	AVG	PB	PR	/A	PD	TPI
1961	Min-A	0	2	.000	15	1	0	0	0	33	49	6	11	12	16.6	6.82	62	.348	.399	0	.000	-1	-10	-9	1	-0.5
1962	Min-A	1	1	.500	19	0	0	0	0	34	37	6	11	15	13.0	5.03	81	.301	.363	2	.500	1	-4	-4	0	-0.1
Total 3		2	3	.400	43	2	0	0	1	84¹	103	16	31	39	14.6	5.76	71	.312	.376	2	.154	-0	-17	-16	1	-0.8

● A. J. SAGER
Sager, Anthony Joseph b: 3/3/65, Columbus, Ohio BR/TR, 6'4", 220 lbs. Deb: 4/4/94

YEAR	TM/L	W	L	PCT	G	GS	CG	SH	SV	IP	H	HR	BB	SO	RAT	ERA	ERA+	OAV	OOB	BH	AVG	PB	PR	/A	PD	TPI
1994	SD-N	1	4	.200	22	3	0	0	0	46²	62	4	16	26	15.4	5.98	70	.325	.383	1	.100	0	-9	-9	2	-0.7

● JOHNNY SAIN
Sain, John Franklin b: 9/25/17, Havana, Ark. BR/TR, 6'2", 200 lbs. Deb: 4/24/42 C

YEAR	TM/L	W	L	PCT	G	GS	CG	SH	SV	IP	H	HR	BB	SO	RAT	ERA	ERA+	OAV	OOB	BH	AVG	PB	PR	/A	PD	TPI
1942	Bos-N	4	7	.364	40	3	0	0	6	97	79	8	63	68	13.6	3.90	86	.228	.354	2	.074	-2	-6	-6	1	-0.8
1946	Bos-N	20	14	.588	37	34	24	3	2	265	225	8	87	129	10.7	2.21	155	.230	.294	28	.298	5	35	36	3	5.9
1947	Bos-N★	21	12	.636	38	35	22	3	1	266	265	19	79	132	11.8	3.52	111	.255	.310	37	.346	12	16	11	1	2.6
1948	*Bos-N★	24	15	.615	42	39	28	4	1	314²	297	19	83	137	11.0	2.60	147	.245	.296	25	.217	3	47	43	-2	5.3
1949	Bos-N	10	17	.370	37	36	16	1	0	243	285	15	75	73	13.5	4.81	78	.291	.344	20	.206	1	-21	-28	-2	-2.7
1950	Bos-N	20	13	.606	37	37	25	3	0	278²	294	34	70	96	11.8	3.94	98	.269	.314	21	.206	4	-6	-3	-2	-0.2
1951	Bos-N	5	13	.278	26	22	6	1	1	160¹	195	16	45	63	13.6	4.21	87	.299	.347	11	.212	3	-4	-10	0	-0.7
	*NY-A	2	1	.667	7	4	1	0	1	37	41	5	8	21	11.9	4.14	93	.281	.318	4	.286	1	-0	-1	1	0.0
1952	*NY-A	11	6	.647	35	16	8	0	7	148¹	149	15	38	57	11.5	3.46	96	.261	.310	19	.268	7	4	-2	-1	0.3
1953	*NY-A☆	14	7	.667	40	19	10	1	9	189	189	16	45	84	11.3	3.00	123	.262	.308	17	.250	5	21	15	-0	2.1
1954	NY-A	6	6	.500	45	0	0	0	22	77	66	11	14	33	9.5	3.16	109	.229	.267	6	.353	3	5	2	-0	0.7
1955	NY-A	0	0	—	3	0	0	0	0	5¹	6	1	3	4	11.8	6.75	55	.300	.333	0	.000	-0	-2	-2	0	0.0
	KC-A	2	5	.286	25	0	0	0	1	44²	54	10	10	12	12.9	5.44	77	.297	.333	0	.000	-1	-7	-6	-1	-1.1
	Yr	2	5	.286	28	0	0	0	1	50	60	14	11	17	12.8	5.58	74	.297	.333	0	.000	-1	-9	-8	-1	-1.1
Total 11		139	116	.545	412	245	140	16	51	2125²	2145	180	619	910	11.8	3.49	106	.261	.315	190	.245	40	94	50	-2	11.4

● RANDY ST.CLAIRE
St.Claire, Randy Anthony b: 8/23/60, Glens Falls, N.Y. BR/TR, 6'2", 190 lbs. Deb: 9/11/84 F

YEAR	TM/L	W	L	PCT	G	GS	CG	SH	SV	IP	H	HR	BB	SO	RAT	ERA	ERA+	OAV	OOB	BH	AVG	PB	PR	/A	PD	TPI
1984	Mon-N	0	0	—	4	0	0	0	0	8	11	0	2	4	15.8	4.50	76	.344	.400	0	—	0	-1	-1	-0	0.0
1985	Mon-N	5	3	.625	42	0	0	0	0	68²	69	3	26	25	12.6	3.93	86	.265	.334	1	.200	1	-3	-4	0	-0.3
1986	Mon-N	2	0	1.000	11	0	0	0	1	19	13	2	6	21	9.0	2.37	156	.186	.250	0	.000	-0	3	3	1	0.4
1987	Mon-N	3	3	.500	44	0	0	0	7	67	64	9	20	43	11.4	4.03	104	.249	.306	2	.333	1	0	1	-0	0.1
1988	Mon-N	0	0	—	6	0	0	0	0	7¹	11	2	5	6	19.6	6.14	59	.344	.432	0	—	0	-2	-2	0	0.0
	Cin-N	1	0	1.000	10	0	0	0	0	13²	13	3	9	8	11.9	2.63	136	.241	.305	0	.000	-0	1	1	-0	0.1
	Yr	1	0	1.000	16	0	0	0	0	21	24	5	14	14	14.6	3.86	93	.276	.351	0	.000	-0	-1	-1	0	0.1
1989	Min-A	1	0	1.000	14	0	0	0	0	22¹	24	5	10	14	12.5	5.24	79	.226	.323	0	—	0	-3	-3	0	-0.1
1991	*Atl-N	0	0	—	10	0	0	0	0	28²	31	4	9	30	12.6	4.08	95	.282	.336	1	.500	1	-1	-1	0	0.1
1992	Atl-N	0	0	—	10	0	0	0	0	15¹	17	1	8	14	14.7	5.87	62	.283	.368	0	—	0	-4	-4	0	0.0
1994	Tor-A	0	0	—	2	0	0	0	0	2	4	0	2	2	27.0	9.00	54	.444	.545	0	—	0	-1	-1	0	0.0
Total 9		12	6	.667	162	0	0	0	9	252	252	28	93	160	12.5	4.14	92	.260	.328	4	.267	1	-11	-10	1	0.3

● JIM ST.VRAIN
St.Vrain, James Marcellin b: 6/6/1883, Ralls County, Mo. d: 6/12/37, Butte, Montana BR/TL, 5'9", 175 lbs. Deb: 4/20/02

YEAR	TM/L	W	L	PCT	G	GS	CG	SH	SV	IP	H	HR	BB	SO	RAT	ERA	ERA+	OAV	OOB	BH	AVG	PB	PR	/A	PD	TPI
1902	Chi-N	4	6	.400	12	11	10	1	0	95	88	0	25	51	11.2	2.08	130	.246	.304	3	.097	-2	7	7	0	0.5

● LUIS SALAZAR
Salazar, Luis Ernesto (Garcia) b: 5/19/56, Barcelona, Venez. BR/TR, 5'9", 180 lbs. Deb: 8/15/80 ♦

YEAR	TM/L	W	L	PCT	G	GS	CG	SH	SV	IP	H	HR	BB	SO	RAT	ERA	ERA+	OAV	OOB	BH	AVG	PB	PR	/A	PD	TPI
1987	SD-N	0	0	—	2	0	0	0	0	2	2	0	1	0	13.5	4.50	88	.250	.333	48	.254	0	-0	-0	0	0.0

● FREDDY SALE
Sale, Frederick Link b: 5/2/02, Chester, S.C. d: 5/27/56, Hermosa Beach, Cal. BR/TR, 5'9", 160 lbs. Deb: 6/30/24

YEAR	TM/L	W	L	PCT	G	GS	CG	SH	SV	IP	H	HR	BB	SO	RAT	ERA	ERA+	OAV	OOB	BH	AVG	PB	PR	/A	PD	TPI
1924	Pit-N	0	0	—	1	0	0	0	0	1	2	0	2	0	18.0	0.00	—	.500	.500	0	—	0	0	0	-0	0.0

● HARRY SALISBURY
Salisbury, Henry H. b: 5/15/1855, Providence, R.I. d: 3/29/33, Chicago, Ill. BL Deb: 8/28/1879

YEAR	TM/L	W	L	PCT	G	GS	CG	SH	SV	IP	H	HR	BB	SO	RAT	ERA	ERA+	OAV	OOB	BH	AVG	PB	PR	/A	PD	TPI
1879	Tro-N	4	6	.400	10	10	9	0	0	89	103	0	11	31	11.5	2.22	112	.265	.285	2	.056	-4	3	3	2	0.0
1882	Pit-a	20	18	.526	38	38	38	1	0	335	315	1	37	135	9.5	2.63	99	.232	.253	22	.152	-6	2	-1	-2	-0.8
Total 2		24	24	.500	48	48	47	1	0	424	418	1	48	166	9.9	2.55	102	.239	.260	24	.133	-10	5	2	-1	-0.8

● BILL SALISBURY
Salisbury, William Ansel "Solly" b: 11/12/1876, Algona, Iowa d: 1/17/52, Rowena, Ore. BR/TR, 6', 180 lbs. Deb: 4/19/02

YEAR	TM/L	W	L	PCT	G	GS	CG	SH	SV	IP	H	HR	BB	SO	RAT	ERA	ERA+	OAV	OOB	BH	AVG	PB	PR	/A	PD	TPI
1902	Phi-N	0	0	—	2	1	0	0	0	6	15	1	2	0	27.0	13.50	21	.468	.513	0	.000	-0	-7	-7	-1	-0.1

● ROGER SALKELD
Salkeld, Roger William b: 3/6/71, Burbank, Cal. BR/TR, 6'5", 215 lbs. Deb: 9/8/93 F

YEAR	TM/L	W	L	PCT	G	GS	CG	SH	SV	IP	H	HR	BB	SO	RAT	ERA	ERA+	OAV	OOB	BH	AVG	PB	PR	/A	PD	TPI
1993	Sea-A	0	0	—	3	2	0	0	0	14¹	13	0	4	13	11.3	2.51	175	.232	.295	0	—	0	3	3	0	0.0
1994	Sea-A	2	5	.286	13	13	0	0	0	59	76	7	45	46	18.6	7.17	68	.314	.424	0	—	0	-16	-15	-0	-1.4
Total 2		2	5	.286	16	15	0	0	0	73¹	89	7	49	59	17.2	6.26	77	.299	.401	0	—	0	-13	-12	0	-1.4

● SLIM SALLEE
Sallee, Harry Franklin "Scatter" b: 2/3/1885, Higginsport, Ohio d: 3/23/50, Higginsport, Ohio BL/TL, 6'3", 180 lbs. Deb: 4/16/08

YEAR	TM/L	W	L	PCT	G	GS	CG	SH	SV	IP	H	HR	BB	SO	RAT	ERA	ERA+	OAV	OOB	BH	AVG	PB	PR	/A	PD	TPI
1908	StL-N	3	8	.273	25	12	7	1	0	128²	144	1	36	39	12.8	3.15	75	.274	.324	2	.049	-3	-11	-11	-0	-1.3
1909	StL-N	10	11	.476	32	27	12	1	0	219	223	3	59	55	11.8	2.42	104	.264	.315	8	.113	-2	4	3	0	0.0
1910	StL-N	7	8	.467	18	13	9	1	2	115	112	4	24	46	10.7	2.97	100	.251	.290	4	.108	-2	1	0	-0	-0.2
1911	StL-N	15	9	.625	36	30	18	1	3	245	234	6	64	74	11.1	2.76	123	.257	.309	15	.169	-2	18	17	-3	1.1
1912	StL-N	16	17	.485	48	32	20	3	6	294	289	6	72	108	11.2	2.60	132	.266	.315	14	.136	-4	26	27	-2	2.3
1913	StL-N	19	15	.559	50	31	18	3	5	276	257	11	60	106	10.5	2.71	119	.255	.301	20	.211	2	15	16	1	2.2
1914	StL-N	18	17	.514	46	30	18	3	6	282¹	252	5	72	105	10.6	2.10	133	.242	.302	21	.231	2	22	22	-2	2.9
1915	StL-N	13	17	.433	46	33	17	2	3	275¹	245	6	57	91	10.0	2.84	98	.238	.280	11	.120	-3	-3	-2	-1	-0.7
1916	StL-N	5	5	.500	16	7	4	2	1	70	75	2	9	28	12.9	3.47	76	.290	.352	3	.167	-0	-7	-6	-1	-1.1
	NY-N	9	4	.692	15	11	7	2	0	111²	96	2	10	35	8.5	1.37	178	.234	.252	9	.257	2	15	13	-3	1.6
	Yr	14	9	.609	31	18	11	4	1	181²	171	4	33	63	10.1	2.18	115	.255	.290	12	.226	2	9	7	-4	0.5
1917	*NY-N	18	7	.720	34	24	18	1	4	215²	199	4	34	54	9.8	2.17	118	.249	.280	17	.221	1	13	9	-4	2.0
1918	NY-N	8	8	.500	18	16	12	1	2	132	122	3	12	33	9.1	2.25	117	.241	.259	5	.122	-2	8	6	-2	0.3
1919	*Cin-N	21	7	.750	29	28	22	4	0	227²	221	4	20	24	9.6	2.06	135	.258	.276	14	.189	2	22	18	-5	2.0
1920	Cin-N	5	6	.455	21	12	6	0	2	116	129	4	16	13	11.4	3.34	91	.293	.320	6	.171	-1	-3	-4	-3	-0.8
	NY-N	1	0	1.000	5	2	1	0	0	17	16	0	0	2	8.5	1.59	189	.239	.239	1	.333	1	3	3	-0	0.2
	Yr	6	6	.500	26	14	7	0	2	133	145	4	16	15	10.9	3.11	97	.284	.306	7	.184	-0	-1	-4	-3	-0.6
1921	NY-N	6	4	.600	37	8	1	0	4	96¹	115	7	14	23	12.1	3.64	101	.307	.332	8	.364	2	1	-0	-2	0.0
Total 14		174	143	.549	476	308	189	25	36	2821²	2729	68	573	836	10.7	2.56	114	.258	.299	158	.171	-8	125	110	-26	9.4

● ROGER SALMON
Salmon, Roger Elliott b: 5/11/1891, Newark, N.J. d: 6/17/74, Belfast, Me. BL/TL, 6'2", 170 lbs. Deb: 5/3/12

YEAR	TM/L	W	L	PCT	G	GS	CG	SH	SV	IP	H	HR	BB	SO	RAT	ERA	ERA+	OAV	OOB	BH	AVG	PB	PR	/A	PD	TPI
1912	Phi-A	1	0	1.000	2	1	0	0	0	5	7	0	4	5	19.8	9.00	34	.318	.423	0	.000	-0	-3	-3	-0	-0.5

● GUS SALVE
Salve, Augustus William b: 12/29/1885, Boston, Mass. d: 3/29/71, Providence, R.I. BL/TL, 6', 190 lbs. Deb: 9/14/08

YEAR	TM/L	W	L	PCT	G	GS	CG	SH	SV	IP	H	HR	BB	SO	RAT	ERA	ERA+	OAV	OOB	BH	AVG	PB	PR	/A	PD	TPI
1908	Phi-A	0	1	.000	2	1	1	0	0	15¹	17	1	9	6	15.8	4.11	62	.266	.365	0	.000	-1	-3	-3	-1	-0.3

● JACK SALVESON
Salveson, John Theodore b: 1/5/14, Fullerton, Cal. d: 12/28/74, Norwalk, Cal. BR/TR, 6'0.5", 180 lbs. Deb: 6/3/33

YEAR	TM/L	W	L	PCT	G	GS	CG	SH	SV	IP	H	HR	BB	SO	RAT	ERA	ERA+	OAV	OOB	BH	AVG	PB	PR	/A	PD	TPI
1933	NY-N	0	2	.000	8	2	0	0	0	30²	30	4	14	8	12.9	3.82	84	.252	.331	1	.111	-1	-2	-2	0	-0.2
1934	NY-N	3	1	.750	12	4	0	0	0	38¹	42	3	13	18	13.1	3.52	110	.281	.337	3	.300	1	2	1	1	0.2
1935	Pit-N	0	1	.000	5	0	0	0	0	7	11	1	5	2	21.9	9.00	46	.306	.405	0	—	-0	-4	-4	-1	-0.4
	Chi-A	1	2	.333	20	2	2	0	0	66²	79	6	23	22	13.8	4.86	95	.298	.354	6	.300	2	-3	-2	0	-0.1
1943	Cle-A	5	2	.625	23	11	4	3	3	86	81	6	11	29	11.9	3.35	93	.266	.322	6	.231	2	-0	-2	0	0.1
1945	Cle-A	0	1	.000	19	0	0	0	1	44	52	1	8	6	14.1	3.68	88	.294	.321	4	.400	1	2	1	0	0.4
Total 5		9	9	.500	87	19	6	3	4	272²	302	21	87	85	12.9	3.99	91	.280	.336	20	.260	7	-8	-11	2	0.1

YEAR TM/L	W	L	PCT	G	GS	CG	SH	SV	IP	H	HR	BB	SO	RAT	ERA	ERA+	OAV	OOB	BH	AVG	PB	PR	/A	PD	TPI

● **MANNY SALVO**   Salvo, Manuel "Gyp"   b: 6/30/13, Sacramento, Cal.   BR/TR, 6'4", 210 lbs.   Deb: 4/22/39

YEAR TM/L	W	L	PCT	G	GS	CG	SH	SV	IP	H	HR	BB	SO	RAT	ERA	ERA+	OAV	OOB	BH	AVG	PB	PR	/A	PD	TPI
1939 NY-N	4	10	.286	32	18	4	0	1	136	150	11	75	69	15.2	4.63	85	.285	.380	4	.098	-2	-11	-11	-1	-1.0
1940 Bos-N	10	9	.526	21	20	14	5	0	160²	151	9	43	60	11.0	3.08	121	.248	.300	6	.103	-3	14	11	-1	0.8
1941 Bos-N	7	16	.304	35	27	11	2	0	195	192	9	93	67	13.3	4.06	88	.255	.340	7	.113	-0	-9	-11	-0	-1.2
1942 Bos-N	7	8	.467	25	14	6	1	0	130²	129	7	41	25	12.0	3.03	110	.260	.322	4	.122	-1	4	4	-1	0.2
1943 Bos-N	0	1	.000	1	1	0	0	0	5	5	0	6	1	19.8	7.20	47	.250	.423	2	1.000	2	-2	-2	-0	-0.2
Phi-N	0	0	—	1	0	0	0	0	0¹	2	0	1	0	81.0	27.00	12	.667	.750	0	—	0	-1	-1	0	0.0
Bos-N	5	6	.455	20	13	5	1	0	93²	94	6	25	25	11.5	3.27	105	.261	.311	6	.214	1	1	2	-1	0.2
Yr	5	7	.417	22	14	5	1	0	99	101	6	32	26	12.2	3.55	96	.264	.322	8	.267	2	-2	-1	-1	0.0
Total 5	33	50	.398	135	93	40	9	1	721¹	723	42	284	247	12.8	3.69	98	.261	.334	30	.129	-4	-4	-7	-3	-1.2

● **JOE SAMBITO**   Sambito, Joseph Charles   b: 6/28/52, Brooklyn, N.Y.   BL/TL, 6'1", 190 lbs.   Deb: 7/20/76

YEAR TM/L	W	L	PCT	G	GS	CG	SH	SV	IP	H	HR	BB	SO	RAT	ERA	ERA+	OAV	OOB	BH	AVG	PB	PR	/A	PD	TPI
1976 Hou-N	3	2	.600	20	4	1	1	1	53¹	45	4	14	26	10.0	3.54	90	.237	.289	2	.222	1	-0	-2	1	0.0
1977 Hou-N	5	5	.500	54	1	0	0	7	89	77	6	24	67	10.2	2.33	153	.235	.287	2	.154	-0	16	12	1	1.5
1978 Hou-N	4	9	.308	62	0	0	0	11	88	85	5	32	96	12.0	3.07	108	.260	.326	1	.167	0	5	2	1	0.6
1979 Hou-N★	8	7	.533	63	0	0	0	22	91¹	80	8	23	83	10.5	1.77	198	.235	.292	2	.286	2	**20**	18	1	4.1
1980 *Hou-N	8	4	.667	64	0	0	0	17	90¹	65	3	22	75	8.9	2.19	150	.200	.255	0	.000	—	14	11	0	1.9
1981 *Hou-N	5	5	.500	49	0	0	0	10	63²	43	4	22	41	9.5	1.84	179	.192	.270	0	.000	—	12	10	1	2.0
1982 Hou-N	0	0	—	9	0	0	0	4	12²	7	0	2	7	6.4	0.71	467	.159	.196	0	.000	—	4	4	0	0.3
1984 Hou-N	0	0	—	32	0	0	0	0	47²	39	5	16	26	10.4	3.02	110	.228	.294	0	.000	—	3	2	-1	-0.1
1985 NY-N	0	0	—	8	0	0	0	0	10²	21	1	8	3	24.5	12.66	27	.420	.500	0	—	0	-11	-11	-0	0.0
1986 *Bos-A	2	0	1.000	53	0	0	0	12	44²	54	4	16	30	14.5	4.84	86	.298	.362	0	—	0	-3	-3	0	-0.3
1987 Bos-A	2	6	.250	47	0	0	0	0	37²	46	8	16	35	14.8	6.93	65	.301	.367	0	—	0	-10	-10	-0	-1.9
Total 11	37	38	.493	461	5	1	1	84	629	562	48	195	489	11.0	3.03	115	.241	.302	7	.135	2	49	32	4	8.1

● **BILL SAMPEN**   Sampen, William Albert   b: 1/18/63, Lincoln, Ill.   BR/TR, 6'1", 185 lbs.   Deb: 4/10/90

YEAR TM/L	W	L	PCT	G	GS	CG	SH	SV	IP	H	HR	BB	SO	RAT	ERA	ERA+	OAV	OOB	BH	AVG	PB	PR	/A	PD	TPI
1990 Mon-N	12	7	.632	59	4	0	0	2	90¹	94	7	33	69	12.9	2.99	122	.268	.334	0	.000	-1	8	7	-1	1.2
1991 Mon-N	9	5	.643	43	8	0	0	0	92¹	96	13	46	52	14.1	4.00	91	.273	.362	3	.231	0	-3	-4	-1	-0.6
1992 Mon-N	1	4	.200	44	1	0	0	0	63¹	62	4	29	23	13.1	3.13	111	.268	.352	0	.000	-1	3	2	1	0.2
KC-A	0	2	.000	8	0	0	0	0	19²	21	0	3	14	12.4	3.66	111	.292	.346	0	—	0	1	1	0	0.1
1993 KC-A	2	2	.500	18	0	0	0	0	18¹	25	1	9	9	18.7	5.89	78	.338	.437	0	—	0	-3	-3	0	-0.9
1994 Cal-A	1	1	.500	10	0	0	0	0	15¹	14	1	13	9	17.6	6.46	77	.241	.405	0	—	0	-3	-3	0	-0.4
Total 5	25	21	.543	182	14	0	0	2	299¹	312	26	133	176	13.9	3.73	100	.274	.358	3	.111	-1	2	1	-1	-0.4

● **JOE SAMUELS**   Samuels, Joseph Jonas "Skabotch"   b: 3/21/05, Scranton, Pa.   BR/TR, 6'1.5", 196 lbs.   Deb: 4/23/30

YEAR TM/L	W	L	PCT	G	GS	CG	SH	SV	IP	H	HR	BB	SO	RAT	ERA	ERA+	OAV	OOB	BH	AVG	PB	PR	/A	PD	TPI
1930 Det-A	0	0	—	2	0	0	0	0	6	10	1	6	1	24.0	16.50	29	.417	.533	0	.000	-0	-8	-8	-0	0.0

● **ROGER SAMUELS**   Samuels, Roger Howard   b: 1/5/61, San Jose, Cal.   BL/TL, 6'5", 210 lbs.   Deb: 7/20/88

YEAR TM/L	W	L	PCT	G	GS	CG	SH	SV	IP	H	HR	BB	SO	RAT	ERA	ERA+	OAV	OOB	BH	AVG	PB	PR	/A	PD	TPI
1988 SF-N	1	2	.333	15	0	0	0	0	23¹	17	4	7	22	9.6	3.47	94	.202	.272	0	.000	-0	-0	-1	0	-0.1
1989 Pit-N	0	0	—	5	0	0	0	0	3²	9	1	4	2	31.9	9.82	34	.474	.565	0	—	0	-3	-3	-0	0.0
Total 2	1	2	.333	20	0	0	0	0	27	26	5	11	24	12.7	4.33	76	.252	.330	0	.000	-0	-3	-3	-0	-0.1

● **ALEX SANCHEZ**   Sanchez, Alex Anthony   b: 4/8/66, Concord, Cal.   BR/TR, 6'2", 185 lbs.   Deb: 5/23/89

YEAR TM/L	W	L	PCT	G	GS	CG	SH	SV	IP	H	HR	BB	SO	RAT	ERA	ERA+	OAV	OOB	BH	AVG	PB	PR	/A	PD	TPI
1989 Tor-A	0	1	.000	4	3	0	0	0	11²	16	1	14	4	23.1	10.03	38	.356	.508	0	—	0	-8	-8	1	-0.5

● **ISRAEL SANCHEZ**   Sanchez, Israel (Matos)   b: 8/20/63, Falcon Lasvias, Cuba   BL/TL, 5'9", 170 lbs.   Deb: 7/7/88

YEAR TM/L	W	L	PCT	G	GS	CG	SH	SV	IP	H	HR	BB	SO	RAT	ERA	ERA+	OAV	OOB	BH	AVG	PB	PR	/A	PD	TPI
1988 KC-A	3	2	.600	19	1	0	0	1	35²	36	0	18	14	13.6	4.54	88	.265	.351	0	—	0	-2	-3	0	-0.3
1990 KC-A	0	0	—	11	0	0	0	0	9²	16	1	3	5	18.6	8.38	46	.381	.435	0	—	0	-5	-5	-0	0.0
Total 2	3	2	.600	30	1	0	0	1	45¹	52	1	21	19	14.7	5.36	74	.292	.370	0	—	0	-7	-7	0	-0.3

● **LUIS SANCHEZ**   Sanchez, Luis Mercedes (b: Luis Mercedes Escoba (Sanchez))   b: 8/24/53, Cariaco, Ven.   BR/TR, 6'2", 210 lbs.   Deb: 4/10/81

YEAR TM/L	W	L	PCT	G	GS	CG	SH	SV	IP	H	HR	BB	SO	RAT	ERA	ERA+	OAV	OOB	BH	AVG	PB	PR	/A	PD	TPI
1981 Cal-A	0	2	.000	17	0	0	0	0	33²	39	4	11	13	13.6	2.94	124	.287	.345	0	—	0	3	3	-0	0.2
1982 *Cal-A	7	4	.636	46	0	0	0	5	92²	89	3	34	58	12.6	3.21	126	.259	.339	0	—	0	9	9	1	1.1
1983 Cal-A	10	8	.556	56	1	0	0	7	98¹	92	6	40	49	12.4	3.66	110	.254	.333	0	—	0	4	4	2	0.9
1984 Cal-A	9	7	.563	49	0	0	0	11	83²	84	10	33	62	12.9	3.33	119	.268	.343	0	—	0	6	6	-0	1.2
1985 Cal-A	2	0	1.000	26	0	0	0	2	61¹	67	9	27	34	13.9	5.72	72	.283	.358	0	—	0	-11	-11	-0	-0.3
Total 5	28	21	.571	194	1	0	0	27	369²	371	32	145	216	12.9	3.75	107	.267	.342	0	—	0	11	10	2	3.1

● **RAUL SANCHEZ**   Sanchez, Raul Guadalupe (Rodriguez)   b: 12/12/30, Marianao, Cuba   BR/TR, 6', 150 lbs.   Deb: 4/17/52

YEAR TM/L	W	L	PCT	G	GS	CG	SH	SV	IP	H	HR	BB	SO	RAT	ERA	ERA+	OAV	OOB	BH	AVG	PB	PR	/A	PD	TPI
1952 Was-A	1	1	.500	3	2	1	1	0	12²	13	0	7	6	14.2	3.55	100	.260	.351	0	.000	-1	0	0	-0	-0.1
1957 Cin-N	3	2	.600	38	0	0	0	5	62¹	61	7	25	37	13.0	4.76	86	.262	.344	2	.286	1	-6	-5	1	-0.3
1960 Cin-N	1	0	1.000	8	0	0	0	0	14²	12	1	11	5	16.0	4.91	78	.226	.388	1	.500	0	-2	-2	0	-0.1
Total 3	5	3	.625	49	2	1	1	5	89²	86	8	43	48	13.7	4.62	86	.256	.352	3	.214	0	-8	-6	1	-0.5

● **BEN SANDERS**   Sanders, Alexander Bennett   b: 2/16/1865, Catharpin, Va.   d: 8/29/30, Memphis, Tenn.   BR/TR, 6', 210 lbs.   Deb: 6/6/1888   ♦

YEAR TM/L	W	L	PCT	G	GS	CG	SH	SV	IP	H	HR	BB	SO	RAT	ERA	ERA+	OAV	OOB	BH	AVG	PB	PR	/A	PD	TPI
1888 Phi-N	19	10	.655	31	29	28	**8**	0	275¹	240	3	33	121	9.0	1.90	157	.228	.253	58	.246	5	29	33	4	4.2
1889 Phi-N	19	18	.514	44	39	34	1	0	349¹	406	9	96	123	13.0	3.55	122	.282	.328	47	.278	6	18	31	-2	3.0
1890 Phi-P	19	18	.514	43	40	37	2	1	346²	412	13	69	107	12.7	3.76	114	.283	.320	59	.312	9	18	20	1	2.4
1891 Phi-a	11	5	.688	19	18	15	0	1	145	157	3	37	40	12.5	3.79	101	.267	.319	39	.250	-1	1	1	-1	0.2
1892 Lou-N	12	19	.387	31	31	30	3	0	268¹	281	6	62	77	11.6	3.22	95	.259	.300	54	.273	10	2	-5	-1	0.5
Total 5	80	70	.533	168	157	144	14	2	1385	1496	34	297	468	11.8	3.24	116	.266	.306	257	.271	33	66	79	1	10.3

● **DEE SANDERS**   Sanders, Dee Wilma   b: 4/8/21, Quitman, Tex.   BR/TR, 6'3", 195 lbs.   Deb: 8/12/45

YEAR TM/L	W	L	PCT	G	GS	CG	SH	SV	IP	H	HR	BB	SO	RAT	ERA	ERA+	OAV	OOB	BH	AVG	PB	PR	/A	PD	TPI
1945 StL-A	0	0	—	2	0	0	0	0	1¹	7	0	1	1	54.0	40.50	9	.700	.727	0	—	0	-6	-5	0	0.0

● **KEN SANDERS**   Sanders, Kenneth George "Daffy"   b: 7/8/41, St.Louis, Mo.   BR/TR, 5'11", 185 lbs.   Deb: 8/6/64

YEAR TM/L	W	L	PCT	G	GS	CG	SH	SV	IP	H	HR	BB	SO	RAT	ERA	ERA+	OAV	OOB	BH	AVG	PB	PR	/A	PD	TPI
1964 KC-A	0	2	.000	21	0	0	0	2	27	23	2	17	18	13.7	3.67	104	.232	.350	0	—	0	-0	0	1	0.1
1966 Bos-A	3	6	.333	24	0	0	0	2	47¹	36	2	28	33	12.5	3.80	100	.214	.333	0	.000	-0	-2	-1	-0	0.0
KC-A	3	4	.429	38	1	0	0	1	65¹	59	7	48	41	14.9	3.72	91	.250	.379	2	.250	-2	-2	-1	-1	-0.1
Yr	6	10	.375	62	1	0	0	3	112²	95	9	76	74	13.7	3.75	95	.233	.355	2	.143	-2	-4	-2	-1	-0.1
1968 Oak-A	0	1	.000	7	0	0	0	0	10²	8	1	8	6	13.5	3.38	84	.229	.372	0	—	0	-0	-1	0	-0.1
1970 Mil-A	5	2	.714	50	0	0	0	13	92¹	64	1	25	64	9.1	1.75	216	.201	.268	3	.231	0	20	21	1	2.5
1971 Mil-A	7	12	.368	**83**	0	0	0	**31**	136¹	111	9	34	80	9.8	1.91	181	.227	.282	0	.000	-1	**23**	24	2	4.7
1972 Mil-A	2	9	.182	62	0	0	0	17	92¹	88	9	31	51	11.8	3.12	97	.245	.309	1	.143	0	-1	-1	0	0.0
1973 Min-A	2	4	.333	27	0	0	0	8	44¹	53	4	21	19	15.4	6.09	65	.299	.380	0	—	0	-11	-11	-0	-1.7
Cle-A	5	1	.833	15	0	0	0	5	27¹	18	1	9	14	8.9	1.65	238	.188	.257	0	—	0	7	7	0	1.8
Yr	7	5	.583	42	0	0	0	13	71²	71	6	30	33	12.7	4.40	90	.255	.328	0	—	0	-5	-4	0	0.1
1974 Cle-A	0	1	.000	9	0	0	0	0	11	21	5	5	4	21.3	9.82	37	.404	.456	0	—	0	-8	-8	-0	-0.7
Cal-A	0	0	—	9	0	0	0	0	9²	10	0	3	4	12.1	2.79	123	.278	.333	0	—	0	1	1	0	0.5
Yr	0	1	.000	18	0	0	0	0	20²	31	5	8	8	17.0	6.53	54	.352	.406	0	—	0	-7	-7	-1	-0.2
1975 NY-N	1	1	.500	29	0	0	0	5	43	31	2	14	19	9.4	2.30	150	.205	.273	0	.000	0	6	5	0	0.4
1976 NY-N	1	2	.333	31	0	0	0	0	47	39	6	11	17	10.0	2.87	115	.231	.286	0	.000	0	3	2	1	0.5
KC-A	0	0	—	2	0	0	0	0	2	3	0	0	0	18.0	0.00	—	.273	.429	0	—	0	1	1	0	0.1
Total 10	29	45	.392	408	1	0	0	86	656²	564	49	258	360	11.5	2.97	118	.235	.314	6	.115	-0	38	39	7	7.5

YEAR TM/L	W	L	PCT	G	GS	CG	SH	SV	IP	H	HR	BB	SO	RAT	ERA	ERA+	OAV	OOB	BH	AVG	PB	PR	/A	PD	TPI
● ROY SANDERS Sanders, Roy Garvin "Butch" or "Pepe" b: 8/1/1892, Stafford, Kan. d: 1/17/50, Kansas City, Mo. BR/TR, 6'0.5", 195 lbs. Deb: 4/16/17																									
1917 Cin-N	0	1	.000	2	2	1	0	0	14	12	0	16	3	18.6	4.50	58	.273	.475	0	.000	-1	-3	-3	1	-0.2
1918 Pit-N	7	9	.438	28	14	6	1	1	156	135	1	52	55	10.9	2.60	111	.239	.305	8	.151	-1	3	5	2	0.6
Total 2	7	10	.412	30	16	7	1	1	170	147	1	68	58	11.5	2.75	104	.241	.321	8	.136	-2	0	2	2	0.4
● ROY SANDERS Sanders, Roy Lee "Simon" b: 6/10/1894, Missouri d: 7/8/63, Louisville, Ky. BR/TR, 6', 185 lbs. Deb: 8/6/18																									
1918 NY-A	0	2	.000	6	2	0	0	0	25²	28	0	16	8	16.1	4.21	67	.301	.414	0	.000	-1	-4	-4	-1	-0.5
1920 StL-A	1	1	.500	8	1	0	0	0	17¹	20	1	17	2	19.7	5.19	75	.313	.463	0	.000	-1	-3	-2	-1	-0.4
Total 2	1	3	.250	14	3	0	0	0	43	48	1	33	10	17.6	4.60	71	.306	.435	0	.000	-2	-7	-6	-1	-0.9
● SCOTT SANDERS Sanders, Scott Gerald b: 3/25/69, Hannibal, Mo. BR/TR, 6'4", 220 lbs. Deb: 8/6/93																									
1993 SD-N	3	3	.500	9	9	0	0	0	52¹	54	4	23	37	13.4	4.13	100	.265	.342	1	.063	-1	-1	0	-1	-0.2
1994 SD-N	4	8	.333	23	20	0	0	1	111	103	10	48	109	12.6	4.78	88	.245	.329	4	.125	-0	-7	-7	1	-0.7
Total 2	7	11	.389	32	29	0	0	1	163¹	157	14	71	146	12.9	4.57	91	.251	.333	5	.104	-2	-8	-7	-1	-0.9
● WAR SANDERS Sanders, Warren Williams b: 8/2/1877, Maynardville, Tenn. d: 8/3/62, Chattanooga, Tenn. BR/TL, 5'10", 160 lbs. Deb: 4/18/03																									
1903 StL-N	1	6	.143	8	6	3	0	0	40	48	0	21	9	16.0	6.07	54	.286	.372	1	.067	-2	-12	-12	-1	-1.9
1904 StL-N	1	2	.333	4	3	1	0	0	19	25	1	1	11	12.8	4.74	57	.298	.314	0	.000	-1	-4	-4	0	-0.6
Total 2	2	8	.200	12	9	4	0	0	59	73	1	22	20	14.9	5.64	55	.290	.354	1	.048	-2	-17	-17	-0	-2.5
● SCOTT SANDERSON Sanderson, Scott Douglas b: 7/22/56, Dearborn, Mich. BR/TR, 6'5", 200 lbs. Deb: 8/6/78																									
1978 Mon-N	4	2	.667	10	9	1	1	0	61	52	3	21	50	10.9	2.51	140	.232	.301	2	.105	-1	7	7	-1	0.5
1979 Mon-N	9	8	.529	34	24	5	3	1	168	148	16	54	138	11.0	3.43	107	.236	.300	8	.160	-0	6	4	-2	0.2
1980 Mon-N	16	11	.593	33	33	7	3	0	211¹	206	18	56	125	11.3	3.11	115	.257	.308	5	.078	-3	12	11	-2	0.8
1981 *Mon-N	9	7	.563	22	22	4	1	0	137¹	122	10	31	77	10.1	2.95	118	.236	.281	4	.114	2	8	8	-2	1.0
1982 Mon-N	12	12	.500	32	32	7	0	0	224	212	24	58	158	11.0	3.46	105	.251	.301	8	.140	1	4	5	-3	0.2
1983 Mon-N	6	7	.462	18	16	0	0	1	81¹	98	12	20	55	13.1	4.65	77	.303	.344	4	.143	-0	-9	-10	-1	-1.5
1984 *Chi-N	8	5	.615	24	24	3	0	0	140²	140	6	24	76	10.6	3.14	125	.264	.298	5	.119	-1	7	12	1	1.1
1985 Chi-N	5	6	.455	19	19	2	0	0	121	100	13	27	80	9.4	3.12	128	.228	.273	2	.065	-2	6	12	1	1.0
1986 Chi-N	9	11	.450	37	28	1	1	1	169²	165	21	37	124	10.8	4.19	96	.255	.297	3	.059	-1	-9	-3	-1	-0.8
1987 Chi-N	8	9	.471	32	22	0	0	2	144²	156	23	50	106	13.0	4.29	100	.274	.336	1	.075	-1	-3	-3	-1	-0.2
1988 Chi-N	1	2	.333	11	0	0	0	0	15¹	13	1	3	6	9.4	5.28	68	.232	.271	0	—	0	-3	-3	-0	-0.6
1989 *Chi-N	11	9	.550	37	23	2	0	0	146¹	155	16	31	86	11.6	3.94	95	.273	.313	2	.047	-1	-7	-3	-2	-0.8
1990 *Oak-A	17	11	.607	34	34	2	1	0	206¹	205	27	66	128	12.0	3.88	96	.255	.315	0	—	0	4	8	-3	-0.6
1991 NY-A☆	16	10	.615	34	34	2	2	0	208	200	22	29	130	10.0	3.81	109	.252	.281	0	—	0	7	8	-3	0.6
1992 NY-A	12	11	.522	33	33	2	1	0	193¹	220	28	64	104	13.4	4.93	79	.286	.344	0	—	0	-21	-22	-2	-2.5
1993 Cal-A	7	11	.389	21	21	4	1	0	135¹	153	15	27	66	12.3	4.46	101	.289	.329	0	—	0	-2	-1	-1	-0.2
SF-N	4	2	.667	11	8	0	0	0	48²	48	12	7	36	10.4	3.51	111	.255	.286	0	.000	-1	3	2	0	0.1
1994 Chi-A	8	4	.667	18	14	1	0	0	92	110	20	12	36	12.1	5.09	92	.296	.322	0	—	0	-3	-4	0	-0.4
Total 17	162	138	.540	460	396	43	14	5	2504¹	2503	286	617	1581	11.4	3.81	102	.261	.308	46	.097	-12	1	22	-21	-2.1
● FRED SANFORD Sanford, John Frederick b: 8/9/19, Garfield, Utah BB/TR, 6'1", 200 lbs. Deb: 5/5/43																									
1943 StL-A	0	0	—	3	0	0	0	0	9¹	7	0	4	2	10.6	1.93	172	.219	.306	0	—	0	1	0	0	0.0
1946 StL-A	2	1	.667	22	3	2	2	0	22	19	0	9	8	11.5	2.05	182	.235	.311	2	.286	1	4	4	-0	0.7
1947 StL-A	7	16	.304	34	23	9	0	4	186²	186	17	76	62	12.6	3.71	104	.261	.332	11	.204	-0	-0	3	-1	0.2
1948 StL-A	12	21	.364	42	33	9	1	2	227	250	19	91	79	13.6	4.64	98	.279	.347	11	.151	-2	-9	-2	1	-0.4
1949 NY-A	7	3	.700	29	11	3	0	0	95¹	100	9	57	51	14.8	3.87	105	.270	.367	4	.118	-2	3	2	-0	-0.1
1950 NY-A	5	4	.556	26	12	0	0	0	112²	103	9	79	54	14.6	4.55	94	.252	.374	8	.229	1	0	-3	3	0.1
1951 NY-A	0	3	.000	11	2	0	0	0	26²	15	2	25	10	13.5	3.71	103	.169	.351	0	.000	-1	1	0	1	0.0
Was-A	2	3	.400	7	7	0	0	0	37	51	5	27	12	19.0	6.57	62	.329	.429	1	.071	-1	-10	-10	-1	-1.3
StL-A	2	4	.333	9	7	1	0	0	27¹	37	6	23	7	19.8	10.21	43	.308	.420	2	.286	1	-18	-18	-0	-2.9
Yr	4	10	.286	27	16	1	0	0	91	103	13	75	29	17.6	6.82	60	.283	.405	3	.115	-1	-27	-27	-0	-4.2
Total 7	37	55	.402	164	98	26	3	6	744	768	67	391	285	14.1	4.45	94	.268	.357	39	.170	-4	-28	-21	2	-3.7
● JACK SANFORD Sanford, John Stanley b: 5/18/29, Wellesley Hills, Mass. BR/TR, 6', 190 lbs. Deb: 9/16/56 C																									
1956 Phi-N	1	0	1.000	3	1	0	0	0	13	7	0	13	6	14.5	1.38	269	.184	.404	1	.333	0	3	3	0	0.3
1957 Phi-N★	19	8	.704	33	33	15	3	0	236²	194	22	94	**188**	11.1	3.08	124	**.221**	.298	15	.169	-1	21	19	-1	1.9
1958 Phi-N	10	13	.435	38	27	7	2	0	186¹	197	15	81	106	13.6	4.44	89	.274	.350	10	.169	1	-10	-10	-2	-1.1
1959 SF-N	15	12	.556	36	31	10	0	1	222¹	198	22	70	132	11.1	3.16	121	.235	.300	8	.111	-1	20	16	-1	1.6
1960 SF-N	12	14	.462	37	34	11	**6**	0	219	199	11	99	125	12.3	3.82	90	.243	.326	13	.176	1	-1	-8	-1	-0.9
1961 SF-N	13	9	.591	38	33	6	0	0	217¹	203	22	87	112	12.2	4.22	90	.249	.325	16	.216	6	-5	-10	-1	-0.4
1962 *SF-N	24	7	.774	39	38	13	2	0	265¹	233	23	92	147	11.1	3.43	111	.234	.301	15	.153	0	15	11	2	1.3
1963 SF-N	16	13	.552	42	42	11	0	0	284¹	273	21	76	158	11.2	3.51	91	.251	.303	13	.138	3	-7	-10	3	-0.4
1964 SF-N	5	7	.417	18	17	3	1	1	106¹	91	7	37	64	11.2	3.30	108	.228	.300	4	.133	1	3	3	1	0.4
1965 SF-N	4	5	.444	23	16	0	0	2	91	92	11	30	43	12.8	3.96	91	.256	.325	3	.120	-0	-4	-4	-1	-0.4
Cal-A	1	2	.333	9	5	0	0	1	29¹	35	2	10	13	13.8	4.60	74	.324	.381	1	.143	-0	-4	-4	1	-0.4
1966 Cal-A	13	7	.650	50	6	0	0	5	108	108	11	27	54	11.6	3.83	88	.271	.323	3	.136	1	-5	-6	1	-0.9
1967 Cal-A	3	2	.600	12	9	0	0	0	48¹	53	6	7	21	11.2	4.47	70	.288	.314	3	.200	1	-7	-7	1	-0.5
KC-A	1	2	.333	10	1	0	0	0	22	24	1	14	13	16.4	6.55	49	.296	.412	0	.000	-0	-8	-8	1	-1.0
Yr	4	4	.500	22	10	0	0	0	70¹	77	7	21	34	12.8	5.12	62	.288	.345	3	.167	1	-15	-15	2	-1.5
Total 12	137	101	.576	388	293	76	14	11	2049¹	1907	174	737	1182	11.8	3.69	98	.247	.316	105	.158	12	11	-14	3	-0.5
● MO SANFORD Sanford, Meredith Leroy b: 12/24/66, Americus, Ga. BR/TR, 6'6", 220 lbs. Deb: 8/9/91																									
1991 Cin-N	1	2	.333	5	5	0	0	0	28	19	3	15	31	11.3	3.86	99	.186	.297	0	.000	-1	-0	-0	-0	-0.1
1993 Col-N	1	2	.333	11	6	0	0	0	35²	37	4	27	36	16.1	5.30	90	.278	.400	0	.000	-1	-5	-2	-1	-0.3
Total 2	2	4	.333	16	11	0	0	0	63²	56	7	42	67	14.0	4.66	93	.238	.356	0	.000	-2	-6	-2	-1	-0.4
● JOSE SANTIAGO Santiago, Jose Guillermo (Guzman) "Pants" b: 9/4/28, Coamo, P.R. BR/TR, 5'10", 175 lbs. Deb: 4/17/54																									
1954 Cle-A	0	0	—	1	0	0	0	0	1²	2	1	2	1	10.8	0.00	—	.000	.286	0	—	0	1	1	-0	0.0
1955 Cle-A	2	0	1.000	17	0	0	0	0	32²	31	1	14	19	13.8	2.48	161	.256	.357	2	.500	1	5	5	0	0.4
1956 KC-A	1	2	.333	9	5	0	0	0	21²	36	6	17	9	24.1	8.31	52	.387	.504	2	.400	0	-10	-10	-1	-1.0
Total 3	3	2	.600	27	5	0	0	0	56	67	3	33	29	17.7	4.66	88	.306	.420	4	.444	2	-4	-3	0	-0.6
● JOSE SANTIAGO Santiago, Jose Rafael (Alfonso) b: 8/15/40, Juana Diaz, P.R. BR/TR, 6'2", 185 lbs. Deb: 9/9/63																									
1963 KC-A	1	0	1.000	4	0	0	0	0	7	5	2	4	5	12.9	9.00	43	.276	.323	0	—	0	-4	-4	0	-0.5
1964 KC-A	0	6	.000	34	8	0	0	0	83²	84	9	35	64	13.2	4.73	81	.258	.337	0	.000	-2	-10	-9	-1	-0.8
1965 KC-A	0	0	—	4	0	0	0	0	5	8	1	4	4	21.6	9.00	39	.364	.462	0	—	0	-3	-3	0	0.0
1966 Bos-A	12	13	.480	35	28	7	1	2	172	155	17	58	119	11.3	3.66	104	.238	.302	11	.196	0	-4	3	-1	0.3
1967 *Bos-A	12	4	.750	50	11	2	0	5	145¹	138	14	47	109	11.6	3.59	97	.251	.313	8	.190	2	-6	-2	0	0.1
1968 Bos-A†	9	4	.692	18	18	7	2	0	124	96	13	42	86	10.2	2.25	140	.215	.287	7	.163	1	10	13	-0	1.4
1969 Bos-A	0	0	—	10	0	0	0	0	7²	11	2	4	2	17.6	3.52	108	.324	.395	0	—	0	0	0	-0	0.0
1970 Bos-A	0	2	.000	8	0	0	0	1	11¹	18	0	6	8	20.6	10.32	38	.353	.441	2	.667	1	-8	-8	-0	-1.3
Total 8	34	29	.540	163	65	16	3	8	556	518	56	200	404	11.8	3.74	96	.246	.314	28	.173	2	-26	-10	-2	-0.8

YEAR TM/L	W	L	PCT	G	GS	CG	SH	SV	IP	H	HR	BB	SO	RAT	ERA	ERA+	OAV	OOB	BH	AVG	PB	PR	/A	PD	TPI
● **AL SANTORINI**			Santorini, Alan Joel b: 5/19/48, Irvington, N.J. BR/TR, 6', 190 lbs. Deb: 9/10/68																					
1968 Atl-N	0	1	.000	1	1	0	0	0	3	4	1	0	0	12.0	0.00	—	.286	.286	0	—	0	1	1	-0	0.4
1969 SD-N	8	14	.364	32	30	2	1	0	184²	194	11	73	111	13.4	3.95	90	.270	.343	7	.111	-1	-7	-8	1	-1.0
1970 SD-N	1	8	.111	21	12	0	0	1	75²	91	11	43	41	16.3	6.07	66	.294	.385	0	.000	-2	-17	-18	-1	-2.1
1971 SD-N	0	2	.000	18	3	0	0	0	38¹	43	4	11	21	12.7	3.76	88	.285	.333	2	.400	1	-1	-2	-1	-0.1
StL-N	0	2	.000	19	5	0	0	2	49²	51	2	19	21	12.9	3.81	95	.270	.340	3	.300	1	-2	-1	-0	0.0
Yr	0	4	.000	37	8	0	0	2	88	94	6	30	42	12.8	3.78	92	.275	.335	5	.333	1	-3	-3	-1	-0.1
1972 StL-N	8	11	.421	30	19	3	3	0	133²	136	6	46	72	12.3	4.11	83	.263	.324	3	.075	-2	-10	-10	-1	-1.7
1973 StL-N	0	0	—	6	0	0	0	0	8¹	14	1	2	2	18.4	5.40	67	.400	.447	0	.000	-0	-2	-2	-0	0.0
Total 6	17	38	.309	127	70	5	4	3	493¹	533	36	194	268	13.5	4.29	83	.276	.346	15	.109	-4	-38	-40	-3	-4.5
● **MANNY SARMIENTO**			Sarmiento, Manuel Eduardo (Apónte) b: 2/2/56, Cagua, Venez. BR/TR, 6', 170 lbs. Deb: 7/30/76																					
1976 *Cin-N	5	1	.833	22	0	0	0	0	43²	36	1	12	20	10.1	2.06	170	.222	.280	0	.000	0	7	7	-1	0.7
1977 Cin-N	0	0	—	24	0	0	0	0	40¹	28	6	11	23	8.7	2.45	160	.196	.253	0	.000	-0	7	7	-1	-0.1
1978 Cin-N	9	7	.563	63	4	0	0	5	127¹	109	16	54	72	11.6	4.38	81	.234	.315	0	.000	-1	-11	-12	-1	-1.7
1979 Cin-N	0	4	.000	23	1	0	0	0	38²	47	2	7	23	12.8	4.66	80	.311	.346	0	.000	-1	-4	-4	-0	-0.5
1980 Sea-A	0	1	.000	9	0	0	0	1	14²	14	2	6	15	12.3	3.68	112	.255	.328	0	—	0	1	1	-0	0.0
1982 Pit-N	9	4	.692	35	17	4	0	1	164²	153	7	46	81	10.9	3.39	109	.246	.298	9	.191	1	4	6	-2	0.3
1983 Pit-N	3	5	.375	52	0	0	0	4	84¹	74	8	36	49	11.7	2.99	124	.243	.324	0	.000	-1	6	7	-1	0.5
Total 7	26	22	.542	228	22	4	0	12	513²	461	42	172	283	11.1	3.49	106	.242	.306	9	.103	-3	9	11	-6	-0.8
● **KEVIN SAUCIER**			Saucier, Kevin Andrew b: 8/9/56, Pensacola, Fla. BR/TL, 6'1", 196 lbs. Deb: 10/1/78																					
1978 Phi-N	1	0	1.000	1	0	0	0	0	2	4	0	1	2	27.0	18.00	20	.400	.500	0	—	0	-3	-3	-0	-0.9
1979 Phi-N	1	4	.200	29	2	0	0	1	62¹	68	4	33	21	15.0	4.19	91	.291	.385	1	.100	-1	-3	-3	-0	-0.2
1980 *Phi-N	7	3	.700	40	0	0	0	0	50	50	2	20	25	13.3	3.42	111	.281	.366	0	.000	-1	1	2	-0	0.3
1981 Det-A	4	2	.667	38	0	0	0	13	49	26	1	21	23	9.6	1.65	228	.160	.277	0	—	0	11	12	-0	2.0
1982 Det-A	3	1	.750	31	1	0	0	5	40¹	35	0	29	23	14.7	3.12	130	.254	.391	0	—	0	4	4	-0	0.5
Total 5	15	11	.577	139	3	0	0	19	203²	183	7	104	94	13.3	3.31	116	.253	.359	1	.056	-2	10	12	-1	1.7
● **DENNIS SAUNDERS**			Saunders, Dennis James b: 1/4/49, Alhambra, Cal. BB/TR, 6'3", 195 lbs. Deb: 5/21/70																					
1970 Det-A	1	1	.500	8	0	0	0	1	14	16	1	5	8	14.1	3.21	116	.286	.355	0	.000	-1	1	1	-0	0.1
● **RICH SAUVEUR**			Sauveur, Richard Daniel b: 11/23/63, Arlington, Va. BL/TL, 6'4", 163 lbs. Deb: 7/1/86																					
1986 Pit-N	0	0	—	3	3	0	0	0	12	17	3	6	6	18.8	6.00	64	.354	.446	1	.333	0	-3	-3	1	0.1
1988 Mon-N	0	0	—	4	0	0	0	0	3	3	1	2	3	15.0	6.00	60	.250	.357	0	—	0	-1	-1	-0	0.0
1991 NY-N	0	0	—	4	0	0	0	0	3¹	7	1	2	4	24.3	10.80	34	.467	.529	0	—	0	-3	-3	-0	0.0
1992 KC-A	0	1	.000	8	0	0	0	0	14¹	15	1	8	7	15.7	4.40	92	.273	.385	0	—	0	-1	-1	-0	-0.1
Total 4	0	1	.000	21	3	0	0	0	32²	42	6	18	20	17.6	5.79	67	.323	.421	1	.333	0	-7	-7	1	0.0
● **JACK SAVAGE**			Savage, John Joseph b: 4/22/64, Louisville, Ky. BR/TR, 6'3", 190 lbs. Deb: 9/14/87																					
1987 LA-N	0	0	—	3	0	0	0	0	3¹	4	0	4	0	10.8	2.70	147	.286	.286	0	—	0	1	0	-0	0.0
1990 Min-A	0	2	.000	17	0	0	0	0	26	37	3	11	12	16.6	8.31	50	.339	.400	0	—	0	-13	-12	-0	-0.9
Total 2	0	2	.000	20	0	0	0	0	29¹	41	3	11	12	16.6	7.67	54	.333	.388	0	—	0	-12	-12	-0	-0.9
● **BOB SAVAGE**			Savage, John Robert b: 12/1/21, Manchester, N.H. BR/TR, 6'2", 180 lbs. Deb: 6/24/42																					
1942 Phi-A	0	1	.000	8	3	0	0	0	30²	24	0	31	10	16.1	3.23	117	.220	.393	1	.111	0	1	2	-0	0.0
1946 Phi-A	3	15	.167	40	19	7	1	2	164	164	5	93	78	14.2	4.06	87	.259	.355	5	.122	1	-10	-9	-3	-1.2
1947 Phi-A	8	10	.444	44	8	2	1	6	146	135	8	55	56	11.7	3.76	101	.245	.314	2	.050	-4	-1	1	-2	-0.5
1948 Phi-A	5	1	.833	33	1	1	0	5	75¹	98	9	33	26	15.7	6.21	69	.318	.384	1	.077	-1	-16	-16	-1	-1.4
1949 StL-A	0	0	—	4	0	0	0	0	7	12	1	3	1	19.3	6.43	70	.400	.455	0	.000	-0	-2	-1	-0	0.0
Total 5	16	27	.372	129	31	10	2	9	423	433	23	215	171	13.8	4.32	88	.265	.352	9	.087	-3	-27	-24	-6	-3.1
● **DON SAVIDGE**			Savidge, Donald Snyder b: 8/28/08, Berwick, Pa. d: 3/22/83, Santa Barbara, Cal BR/TR, 6'1", 180 lbs. Deb: 8/6/29 F																					
1929 Was-A	0	0	—	3	0	0	0	0	6	12	1	2	2	21.0	9.00	47	.414	.452			0	-3	-3	0	0.0
● **RALPH SAVIDGE**			Savidge, Ralph Austin "The Human Whipcord" b: 2/3/1879, Jerseytown, Pa. d: 7/22/59, Berwick, Pa. BR/TR, 6'2", 210 lbs. Deb: 9/22/08 F																					
1908 Cin-N	0	1	.000	4	1	1	0	0	21	18	0	8	7	11.1	2.57	90	.247	.321	0	.000	-1	-0	-1	-1	-0.2
1909 Cin-N	0	0	—	1	0	0	0	0	4	10	1	3	2	31.5	22.50	12	.588	.667	0	.000	-0	-9	-9	-0	0.0
Total 2	0	1	.000	5	1	1	0	0	25	28	1	11	9	14.4	5.76	41	.311	.392	0	.000	-1	-9	-9	-1	-0.2
● **MOE SAVRANSKY**			Savransky, Morris b: 1/13/29, Cleveland, Ohio BL/TL, 5'11", 175 lbs. Deb: 4/23/54																					
1954 Cin-N	0	2	.000	16	0	0	0	0	24	23	6	8	7	12.4	4.88	86	.247	.320	1	.500	1	-2	-2	1	0.0
● **RICK SAWYER**			Sawyer, Richard Clyde b: 4/7/48, Bakersfield, Cal. BR/TR, 6'2", 205 lbs. Deb: 4/28/74																					
1974 NY-A	0	0	—	1	0	0	0	0	1²	2	0	1	1	16.2	16.20	22	.500	.600	0	—	0	-2	-2	-0	0.2
1975 NY-A	0	0	—	4	0	0	0	0	6	7	0	2	3	13.5	3.00	121	.304	.360	0	—	0	1	0	-0	0.0
1976 SD-N	5	3	.625	13	11	4	2	0	81²	84	2	38	33	13.6	2.53	129	.272	.353	5	.208	1	9	7	-0	0.7
1977 SD-N	7	6	.538	56	9	0	0	0	111	136	15	55	45	16.1	5.84	61	.316	.402	3	.150	1	-24	-28	1	-2.7
Total 4	12	9	.571	74	20	4	2	0	200¹	229	17	96	82	15.0	4.49	76	.299	.382	8	.182	2	-17	-24	1	-1.8
● **WILL SAWYER**			Sawyer, Willard Newton b: 7/29/1864, Brimfield, Ohio d: 1/5/36, Kent, Ohio BL/TL, Deb: 7/21/1883																					
1883 Cle-N	4	10	.286	17	15	15	0	0	141	119	1	47	76	10.6	2.36	133	**.217**	.279	1	.021	-7	12	12	-3	0.1
● **BILL SAYLES**			Sayles, William Nisbeth b: 7/27/17, Portland, Ore. BR/TR, 6'2", 175 lbs. Deb: 7/17/39																					
1939 Bos-A	0	0	—	5	0	0	0	0	14	14	1	13	9	17.4	7.07	67	.264	.409	1	.143	-0	-4	-4	0	0.0
1943 NY-N	1	3	.250	18	3	1	0	0	53	60	4	23	38	14.1	4.75	72	.284	.355	4	.308	1	-8	-8	-0	-0.5
Bro-N	0	0	—	5	0	0	0	0	11²	13	0	10	5	17.7	7.71	44	.271	.397	1	.500	1	-6	-6	-0	0.0
Yr	1	3	.250	23	3	1	0	0	64²	73	4	33	43	14.8	5.29	65	.282	.363	5	.333	1	-14	-13	-1	-0.5
Total 2	1	3	.250	28	3	1	0	0	78²	87	4	46	52	15.2	5.61	65	.279	.372	6	.273	1	-17	-17	-0	-0.5
● **PHIL SAYLOR**			Saylor, Philip Andrew "Lefty" b: 1/2/1871, Van Wert Co., Ohio d: 7/23/37, W.Alexandria, O. TL, Deb: 7/11/1891																					
1891 Phi-N	0	0	—	1	0	0	0	0	3	2	1	0	0	6.0	6.00	57	.182	.182	0	.000	-0	-1	-1	-0	0.0
● **FRANK SCANLAN**			Scanlan, Frank Aloysius b: 4/28/1890, Syracuse, N.Y. d: 4/9/69, Brooklyn, N.Y. BL/TL, 6'1.5", 175 lbs. Deb: 8/6/09 F																					
1909 Phi-N	0	0	—	6	0	0	0	1	11	8	0	5	5	10.6	1.64	159	.211	.302	0	.000	-1	1	1	-0	-0.1
● **BOB SCANLAN**			Scanlan, Robert Guy b: 8/9/66, Los Angeles, Cal. BR/TR, 6'7", 215 lbs. Deb: 5/7/91																					
1991 Chi-N	7	8	.467	40	13	0	0	1	111	114	5	40	44	12.7	3.89	100	.268	.335	1	.042	-2	-3	-0	-0	-0.2
1992 Chi-N	3	6	.333	69	0	0	0	14	87¹	76	4	30	42	11.0	2.89	125	.235	.302	0	—	0	6	7	1	1.1
1993 Chi-N	4	5	.444	70	0	0	0	0	75¹	79	6	28	44	13.1	4.54	88	.278	.349	1	.500	0	-4	-5	-1	-0.6
1994 Mil-A	2	6	.250	30	12	0	0	0	103	117	11	28	65	13.0	4.11	120	.288	.340	0	—	0	8	9	-0	0.6
Total 4	16	25	.390	209	25	0	0	17	376²	386	26	126	195	12.5	3.85	107	.268	.332	2	.067	-2	7	12	-0	0.9
● **DOC SCANLAN**			Scanlan, William Dennis b: 3/7/1881, Syracuse, N.Y. d: 5/29/49, Brooklyn, N.Y. BL/TR, 5'8", 165 lbs. Deb: 9/24/03 F																					
1903 Pit-N	0	1	.000	1	1	0	0	0	9	5	0	6	0	11.0	4.00	81	.167	.306	0	.000	-1	-1	-1	-0	-0.1
1904 Pit-N	1	3	.250	4	3	1	0	0	22	21	0	20	10	17.6	4.91	56	.236	.387	0	.000	-1	-5	-5	-0	-0.9

YEAR	TM/L	W	L	PCT	G	GS	CG	SH	SV	IP	H	HR	BB	SO	RAT	ERA	ERA+	OAV	OOB	BH	AVG	PB	PR	/A	PD	TPI
	Bro-N	6	6	.500	13	12	11	3	0	104	94	0	40	40	11.8	2.16	127	.242	.316	5	.143	-2	7	7	-2	0.4
	Yr	7	9	.438	17	15	12	3	0	126	115	0	60	50	12.6	2.64	104	.240	.327	5	.122	-2	1	1	-2	-0.5
1905	Bro-N	14	12	.538	33	28	22	2	0	249²	220	4	104	135	12.0	2.92	99	.237	.319	16	.167	-2	2	-1	-2	-0.4
1906	Bro-N	18	13	.581	38	33	28	6	2	288	230	5	127	120	11.3	3.19	79	.214	.301	18	.186	3	-18	-21	-7	-2.7
1907	Bro-N	6	8	.429	17	15	10	2	0	107	90	1	61	59	13.0	3.20	73	.239	.349	9	.265	5	-9	-10	-2	-0.9
1909	Bro-N	8	7	.533	19	17	12	2	0	141¹	125	2	65	72	12.4	2.93	89	.252	.343	12	.273	5	-5	-5	-1	-0.1
1910	Bro-N	9	11	.450	34	25	14	0	2	217¹	175	1	116	103	12.3	2.61	116	.234	.341	14	.203	1	10	10	-2	0.8
1911	Bro-N	3	10	.231	22	15	3	0	1	113²	101	2	69	45	13.9	3.64	92	.256	.374	4	.121	-2	-3	-4	-1	-0.7
Total 8		65	71	.478	181	149	102	15	5	1252	1061	15	608	584	12.3	3.00	93	.234	.330	78	.188	8	-21	-31	-17	-4.6

● **PAT SCANTLEBURY**   Scantlebury, Patricio Athelstan b: 11/11/17, Gatun, Canal Zone d: 5/24/91, Glen Ridge, N.J. BL/TL, 6'1", 180 lbs. Deb: 4/19/56

YEAR	TM/L	W	L	PCT	G	GS	CG	SH	SV	IP	H	HR	BB	SO	RAT	ERA	ERA+	OAV	OOB	BH	AVG	PB	PR	/A	PD	TPI
1956	Cin-N	0	1	.000	6	2	0	0	0	19	24	5	5	10	13.7	6.63	60	.293	.333	0	.000	-0	-6	-6	-0	-0.3

● **RANDY SCARBERY**   Scarbery, Randy James b: 6/22/52, Fresno, Cal. BB/TR, 6'1", 185 lbs. Deb: 4/16/79

YEAR	TM/L	W	L	PCT	G	GS	CG	SH	SV	IP	H	HR	BB	SO	RAT	ERA	ERA+	OAV	OOB	BH	AVG	PB	PR	/A	PD	TPI
1979	Chi-A	2	8	.200	45	5	0	0	4	101¹	102	9	34	45	12.3	4.62	92	.262	.326	0	—	0	-5	-4	0	-0.4
1980	Chi-A	1	2	.333	15	0	0	0	2	28²	24	1	7	18	10.4	4.08	99	.238	.300	0	—	-0	-0	-0	-0	0.0
Total 2		3	10	.231	60	5	0	0	6	130	126	10	41	63	11.9	4.50	93	.257	.320	0	—	0	-5	-4	0	-0.4

● **RAY SCARBOROUGH**   Scarborough, Ray Wilson (b: Rae Wilson Scarborough)
b: 7/23/17, Mt.Gilead, N.C. d: 7/1/82, Mount Olive, N.C. BR/TR, 6', 185 lbs. Deb: 6/26/42 C

YEAR	TM/L	W	L	PCT	G	GS	CG	SH	SV	IP	H	HR	BB	SO	RAT	ERA	ERA+	OAV	OOB	BH	AVG	PB	PR	/A	PD	TPI
1942	Was-A	2	1	.667	17	5	1	1	0	63¹	68	2	32	16	14.2	4.12	89	.272	.355	4	.190	0	-3	-3	1	-0.1
1943	Was-A	4	4	.500	24	6	2	0	3	86	93	2	46	43	14.5	2.83	113	.273	.359	8	.333	2	5	4	-0	0.6
1946	Was-A	7	11	.389	32	20	6	1	1	155²	176	8	74	46	14.5	4.05	83	.286	.364	7	.140	-2	-9	-12	2	-1.3
1947	Was-A	6	13	.316	33	18	8	2	0	161	165	5	67	63	13.0	3.41	109	.267	.339	6	.120	-3	5	6	-0	0.3
1948	Was-A	15	8	.652	31	26	9	0	1	185¹	166	10	72	76	11.7	2.82	154	.233	.307	14	.219	-0	30	31	1	3.8
1949	Was-A	13	11	.542	34	27	11	1	0	199²	204	10	88	81	13.5	4.60	93	.265	.346	13	.194	-0	-9	-8	1	-0.7
1950	Was-A	3	5	.375	8	8	4	2	0	58¹	62	1	22	24	13.3	4.01	112	.276	.345	2	.100	-1	4	3	1	0.3
	Chi-A☆	10	13	.435	27	23	8	1	1	149¹	160	10	62	70	13.6	5.30	85	.274	.347	8	.174	-1	-12	-14	-1	-1.9
	Yr	13	18	.419	35	31	12	3	1	207²	222	11	84	94	13.4	4.94	91	.273	.344	10	.152	-3	-8	-10	-0	-1.6
1951	Bos-A	12	9	.571	37	22	8	0	0	184	201	21	61	71	13.5	5.09	88	.275	.342	13	.191	-2	-20	-13	1	-1.5
1952	Bos-A	1	5	.167	28	8	1	1	4	76²	79	8	35	29	13.9	4.81	82	.266	.351	4	.222	0	-10	-7	0	-0.6
	*NY-A	5	1	.833	9	4	1	0	0	34	27	4	15	13	11.4	2.91	114	.223	.314	5	.357	2	3	2	-0	0.4
	Yr	6	6	.500	37	12	2	1	4	110²	106	12	50	42	12.8	4.23	89	.251	.332	9	.281	2	-7	-6	0	-0.2
1953	NY-A	2	2	.500	25	1	0	0	0	54²	52	6	26	20	13.5	3.29	112	.250	.345	1	.083	-0	4	2	0	0.2
	Det-A	0	2	.000	13	0	0	0	0	20²	34	3	11	12	20.9	8.27	49	.354	.436	0	.000	-0	-10	-10	-0	-1.1
	Yr	2	4	.333	38	1	0	0	0	75¹	86	7	37	32	15.1	4.66	81	.279	.362	1	.071	-0	-6	-7	-0	-0.9
Total 10		80	85	.485	318	168	59	9	12	1428²	1487	88	611	564	13.5	4.13	97	.267	.344	85	.186	-6	-22	-19	4	-1.6

● **MAC SCARCE**   Scarce, Guerrant McCurdy b: 4/8/49, Danville, Va. BL/TL, 6'3", 200 lbs. Deb: 7/10/72

YEAR	TM/L	W	L	PCT	G	GS	CG	SH	SV	IP	H	HR	BB	SO	RAT	ERA	ERA+	OAV	OOB	BH	AVG	PB	PR	/A	PD	TPI
1972	Phi-N	1	2	.333	31	0	0	0	4	36²	30	6	20	40	12.8	3.44	105	.222	.331	0	.000	-1	0	1	1	0.1
1973	Phi-N	1	8	.111	52	0	0	0	12	70²	54	3	47	57	13.0	2.42	157	.220	.347	0	.000	-1	10	11	-1	1.6
1974	Phi-N	3	8	.273	58	0	0	0	5	70¹	72	6	35	50	13.9	4.99	76	.275	.365	0	.000	-1	-11	-9	-1	-1.7
1975	NY-N	0	0	—	1	0	0	0	0	0	1	0	0	0	—	—	—	1.000	1.000	0	—	0	-0	-0	0	0.0
1978	Min-A	1	1	.500	17	0	0	0	0	32	35	5	15	17	14.9	3.94	97	.292	.384	0	—	0	-1	-0	-1	-0.1
Total 5		6	19	.240	159	0	0	0	21	209²	192	20	117	164	13.6	3.69	102	.251	.357	0	.000	-2	-2	2	-2	-0.1

● **AL SCHACHT**   Schacht, Alexander b: 11/11/1892, New York, N.Y. d: 7/14/84, Waterbury, Conn. BR/TR, 5'11", 142 lbs. Deb: 9/18/19 C

YEAR	TM/L	W	L	PCT	G	GS	CG	SH	SV	IP	H	HR	BB	SO	RAT	ERA	ERA+	OAV	OOB	BH	AVG	PB	PR	/A	PD	TPI
1919	Was-A	2	0	1.000	2	2	1	0	0	15	14	0	4	4	10.8	2.40	134	.233	.281	0	.000	0	1	1	-0	0.2
1920	Was-A	6	4	.600	22	11	5	1	1	99¹	130	2	30	19	14.6	4.44	84	.319	.367	5	.192	1	-7	-8	-2	-0.4
1921	Was-A	6	6	.500	29	5	2	0	1	82²	110	2	27	15	15.1	4.90	84	.332	.386	5	.227	1	-6	-7	-3	-1.1
Total 3		14	10	.583	53	18	8	1	2	197	254	4	61	38	14.5	4.48	86	.318	.368	10	.196	2	-11	-14	-2	-1.3

● **SID SCHACHT**   Schacht, Sidney b: 2/3/18, Bogota, N.J. BR/TR, 5'11", 170 lbs. Deb: 4/23/50

YEAR	TM/L	W	L	PCT	G	GS	CG	SH	SV	IP	H	HR	BB	SO	RAT	ERA	ERA+	OAV	OOB	BH	AVG	PB	PR	/A	PD	TPI
1950	StL-A	0	0	—	8	1	0	0	0	10²	24	5	14	7	32.1	16.03	31	.429	.543	0	.000	-0	-14	-13	-0	0.0
1951	StL-A	0	0	—	6	0	0	0	1	6	14	1	5	4	28.5	21.00	21	.452	.528	0	—	0	-11	-11	-0	-0.4
	Bos-N	0	2	.000	5	0	0	0	0	4²	6	0	2	1	15.4	1.93	191	.300	.364	0	—	0	1	1	-0	0.3
Total 2		0	2	.000	19	1	0	0	1	21¹	44	6	21	12	27.4	14.34	31	.411	.508	0	.000	-0	-24	-23	-1	-0.1

● **HAL SCHACKER**   Schacker, Harold b: 4/6/25, Brooklyn, N.Y. BR/TR, 6', 190 lbs. Deb: 5/9/45

YEAR	TM/L	W	L	PCT	G	GS	CG	SH	SV	IP	H	HR	BB	SO	RAT	ERA	ERA+	OAV	OOB	BH	AVG	PB	PR	/A	PD	TPI
1945	Bos-N	0	1	.000	6	0	0	0	0	15¹	14	2	9	6	13.5	5.28	73	.241	.343	0	.000	0	-3	-2	-0	-0.2

● **GERMANY SCHAEFER**   Schaefer, Herman A. b: 2/4/1877, Chicago, Ill. d: 5/16/19, Saranac Lake, N.Y. BR/TR, 5'9", 175 lbs. Deb: 10/5/01 ♦

YEAR	TM/L	W	L	PCT	G	GS	CG	SH	SV	IP	H	HR	BB	SO	RAT	ERA	ERA+	OAV	OOB	BH	AVG	PB	PR	/A	PD	TPI
1912	Was-A	0	0	—	1	0	0	0	0	0²	1	0	0	0	13.5	0.00	—	.333	.333	41	.247	0	0	0	-0	0.0
1913	Was-A	0	0	—	1	0	0	0	0	0¹	2	0	1	0	54.0	54.00	9	.667	.667	32	.320	0	-2	-2	0	0.0
Total 2		0	0	—	2	0	0	0	0	1	3	0	1	0	27.0	18.00	18	.500	.500	972	.257	0	-2	-2	0	0.0

● **HARRY SCHAEFFER**   Schaeffer, Harry Edward "Lefty" b: 6/23/24, Reading, Pa. BL/TL, 6'2.5", 175 lbs. Deb: 7/28/52

YEAR	TM/L	W	L	PCT	G	GS	CG	SH	SV	IP	H	HR	BB	SO	RAT	ERA	ERA+	OAV	OOB	BH	AVG	PB	PR	/A	PD	TPI
1952	NY-A	0	1	.000	5	2	0	0	0	17	18	2	18	15	19.1	5.29	63	.265	.419			-0	-3	-4	-0	-0.2

● **MARK SCHAEFFER**   Schaeffer, Mark Philip b: 6/5/48, Santa Monica, Cal. BL/TL, 6'5", 215 lbs. Deb: 4/18/72

YEAR	TM/L	W	L	PCT	G	GS	CG	SH	SV	IP	H	HR	BB	SO	RAT	ERA	ERA+	OAV	OOB	BH	AVG	PB	PR	/A	PD	TPI
1972	SD-N	2	0	1.000	41	0	0	0	0	41	52	3	28	25	18.0	4.61	71	.319	.425			-0	-5	-6	1	-0.3

● **JOE SCHAFFERNOTH**   Schaffernoth, Joseph Arthur b: 8/6/37, Trenton, N.J. BR/TR, 6'4.5", 195 lbs. Deb: 4/15/59

YEAR	TM/L	W	L	PCT	G	GS	CG	SH	SV	IP	H	HR	BB	SO	RAT	ERA	ERA+	OAV	OOB	BH	AVG	PB	PR	/A	PD	TPI
1959	Chi-N	1	0	1.000	5	1	0	0	0	7²	11	1	4	3	17.6	8.22	48	.355	.429	0	.000	-0	-4	-4	-0	-0.5
1960	Chi-N	2	3	.400	33	0	0	0	3	55	46	2	17	33	10.5	2.78	136	.235	.299	2	.286	0	6	6	0	0.7
1961	Chi-N	0	4	.000	21	0	0	0	0	38¹	43	7	18	23	14.6	6.34	66	.293	.373	0	.000	-1	-10	-9	-0	-0.9
	Cle-A	0	1	.000	15	0	0	0	0	17	16	2	14	9	16.4	4.76	83	.242	.383	0	.000	-0	-1	-2	1	0.0
Total 3		3	8	.273	74	1	0	0	3	118	116	12	53	68	13.1	4.58	86	.264	.347	2	.125	-1	-9	-8	1	-0.7

● **ART SCHALLOCK**   Schallock, Arthur Lawrence b: 4/25/24, Mill Valley, Cal. BL/TL, 5'9", 160 lbs. Deb: 7/16/51

YEAR	TM/L	W	L	PCT	G	GS	CG	SH	SV	IP	H	HR	BB	SO	RAT	ERA	ERA+	OAV	OOB	BH	AVG	PB	PR	/A	PD	TPI
1951	NY-A	3	1	.750	11	6	3	0	0	46¹	50	3	20	19	13.8	3.88	99	.272	.346	5	.294	1	1	-0	0	0.1
1952	NY-A	0	0	—	2	0	0	0	0	2	3	0	2	1	22.5	9.00	37	.375	.500	0	—	0	-1	-1	-0	0.0
1953	*NY-A	0	0	—	7	1	0	0	0	21¹	30	2	15	13	19.4	2.95	125	.345	.447	2	.333	1	2	2	-0	0.0
1954	NY-A	1	0	1.000	8	1	0	0	0	17¹	20	3	11	9	16.6	4.15	83	.282	.386	0	—	-0	-1	-1	-0	-0.2
1955	NY-A	0	0	—	2	0	0	0	0	3	4	1	4	2	15.0	6.00	62	.333	.385	0	—	0	-1	-1	0	0.0
	Bal-A	3	5	.375	30	6	1	0	0	80¹	92	2	42	33	15.2	4.15	92	.294	.381	2	.105	-1	-2	-3	-1	-0.4
	Yr	3	5	.375	32	6	1	0	0	83¹	96	3	43	35	15.2	4.21	90	.295	.381	2	.105	-1	-3	-4	-1	-0.4
Total 5		6	7	.462	58	14	3	0	1	170¹	199	11	91	77	15.6	4.02	94	.295	.383	9	.200	1	-1	-5	-1	-0.5

● **CHARLEY SCHANZ**   Schanz, Charles Murrell b: 6/8/19, Anacortes, Wash. d: 5/28/92, Sacramento, Cal. BR/TR, 6'3.5", 215 lbs. Deb: 4/20/44

YEAR	TM/L	W	L	PCT	G	GS	CG	SH	SV	IP	H	HR	BB	SO	RAT	ERA	ERA+	OAV	OOB	BH	AVG	PB	PR	/A	PD	TPI
1944	Phi-N	13	16	.448	40	30	13	1	3	241¹	231	6	103	84	12.7	3.32	109	.254	.334	12	.148	-1	8	8	-0	0.8
1945	Phi-N	4	15	.211	35	21	5	1	5	144²	165	5	87	56	16.2	4.35	88	.285	.387	6	.154	-0	-9	-8	1	-1.0
1946	Phi-N	6	6	.500	32	15	4	0	2	116¹	130	8	71	47	15.9	5.80	59	.285	.389	3	.083	-0	-31	-31	1	-3.2
1947	Phi-N	2	4	.333	34	6	1	0	2	101²	107	7	47	42	13.9	4.16	96	.295	.380	4	.148	-1	-1	-2	-0	-0.2
1950	Bos-A	3	2	.600	14	0	0	0	2	22²	25	3	24	14	19.9	8.34	59	.281	.439	1	.091	-1	-9	-9	0	-1.6
Total 5		28	43	.394	155	72	23	2	14	626²	658	29	332	243	14.6	4.34	86	.275	.369	26	.134	-5	-43	-42	1	-5.2

YEAR TM/L	W	L	PCT	G	GS	CG	SH	SV	IP	H	HR	BB	SO	RAT	ERA	ERA+	OAV	OOB	BH	AVG	PB	PR	/A	PD	TPI
● **JOHN SCHAPPERT** Schappert, John b: Brooklyn, N.Y. d: 7/29/16, Rockaway Beach, N.Y. BR/TR, 5'10", 170 lbs. Deb: 5/3/1882
1882 StL-a	8	7	.533	15	14	13	0	0	128	131	2	32	38	11.5	3.52	80	.248	.291	9	.180	0	-12	-10	-2	-1.1
● **BILL SCHARDT** Schardt, Wilburt "Big Bill" b: 1/20/1886, Cleveland, Ohio d: 7/20/64, Vermilion, Ohio BR/TR, 6'4", 210 lbs. Deb: 4/14/11
1911 Bro-N	5	15	.250	39	22	10	1	4	195¹	190	4	91	77	13.3	3.59	93	.266	.355	10	.169	0	-4	-6	0	-0.5
1912 Bro-N	0	1	.000	7	0	0	0	1	20²	25	1	6	7	14.4	4.35	77	.321	.384	0	.000	-1	-2	-2	2	0.0
Total 2	5	16	.238	46	22	10	1	5	216	215	5	97	84	13.4	3.67	91	.271	.358	10	.154	-1	-6	-8	2	-0.5
● **JEFF SCHATTINGER** Schattinger, Jeffrey Charles b: 10/25/55, Fresno, Cal. BL/TR, 6'5", 200 lbs. Deb: 9/21/81
1981 KC-A	0	0	—	1	0	0	0	0	3	2	0	1	1	15.0	0.00	—	.182	.357	0	—	0	1	1	-0	0.0
● **DAN SCHATZEDER** Schatzeder, Daniel Ernest b: 12/1/54, Elmhurst, Ill. BL/TL, 6', 195 lbs. Deb: 9/4/77
1977 Mon-N	2	1	.667	6	3	1	1	0	21²	16	0	13	14	12.0	2.49	153	.203	.315	2	.333	0	3	3	-0	0.5
1978 Mon-N	7	7	.500	29	18	2	0	0	143²	108	10	68	69	11.2	3.07	115	.213	.308	10	.222	3	8	7	-2	0.8
1979 Mon-N	10	5	.667	32	21	3	0	1	162	136	17	59	106	10.9	2.83	129	.225	.295	11	.216	4	16	15	-3	1.5
1980 Det-A	11	13	.458	32	26	9	2	0	192²	178	23	58	94	11.2	4.02	102	.246	.304	0	—	0	2	2	-0	0.0
1981 Det-A	6	8	.429	17	14	1	0	0	71¹	74	13	29	20	13.2	6.06	62	.265	.339	0	—	0	-19	-18	-0	-3.1
1982 SF-N	1	4	.200	13	3	0	0	0	33¹	47	3	12	18	15.9	7.29	49	.333	.386	1	.125	-0	-14	-14	0	-1.8
Mon-N	0	2	.000	26	1	0	0	0	36	37	1	12	15	12.8	3.50	104	.276	.345	2	.400	1	0	1	-0	0.1
Yr	1	6	.143	39	4	0	0	0	69¹	84	4	24	33	14.3	5.32	68	.304	.364	3	.231	1	-13	-13	-0	-1.7
1983 Mon-N	5	2	.714	58	2	0	0	2	87	88	3	25	48	12.2	3.21	112	.265	.326	2	.200	0	4	4	-1	0.2
1984 Mon-N	7	7	.500	36	14	1	1	1	136	132	13	36	89	9.9	2.71	126	.224	.278	11	.314	5	13	11	-3	1.3
1985 Mon-N	3	5	.375	24	15	1	0	0	104¹	101	13	31	64	11.4	3.80	89	.259	.314	6	.194	3	-2	-5	-0	0.0
1986 Mon-N	3	2	.600	30	1	0	0	0	59	53	6	19	33	11.0	3.20	115	.240	.300	9	.429	6	3	3	-1	0.8
Phi-N	3	3	.500	25	0	0	0	0	29¹	28	3	16	14	13.5	3.38	114	.252	.346	1	.200	0	1	2	-0	0.3
Yr	6	5	.545	55	1	0	0	0	88¹	81	9	35	47	11.8	3.26	115	.243	.314	10	.385	7	4	5	-1	1.1
1987 Phi-N	3	1	.750	26	0	0	0	0	37²	40	4	14	28	12.9	4.06	104	.278	.342	2	.167	0	0	1	-0	0.0
*Min-A	3	1	.750	30	1	0	0	0	43²	64	8	18	30	17.1	6.39	72	.342	.403	0	—	0	-9	-9	-0	-0.7
1988 Cle-A	0	2	.000	15	0	0	0	3	16	26	6	2	10	16.3	9.56	45	.351	.377	0	—	0	-10	-10	-1	-1.6
Min-A	0	1	.000	10	0	0	0	0	10¹	8	1	5	7	12.2	1.74	234	.216	.326	0	—	0	3	3	0	0.1
Yr	0	3	.000	25	0	0	0	3	26¹	34	7	7	17	14.4	6.49	63	.304	.350	0	—	0	-7	-7	-0	-1.5
1989 Hou-N	4	1	.800	36	0	0	0	1	56²	64	4	28	46	15.1	4.45	76	.287	.374	0	.000	-1	-6	-7	-0	-0.7
1990 Hou-N	1	3	.250	45	2	0	0	0	64	61	2	23	37	11.8	2.39	155	.261	.327	1	.250	0	10	9	-0	0.5
NY-N	0	0	—	6	0	0	0	0	5²	5	0	0	2	7.9	0.00	—	.263	.263	0	—	0	2	2	-0	0.0
Yr	1	3	.250	51	2	0	0	0	69²	66	2	23	39	11.5	2.20	169	.256	.317	1	.250	0	12	12	-0	0.5
1991 KC-A	0	0	—	8	0	0	0	0	6²	11	0	7	4	24.3	9.45	44	.367	.486	0	—	0	-4	-4	-0	0.0
Total 15	69	68	.504	504	121	18	4	10	1317	1257	128	475	748	12.0	3.74	99	.253	.321	58	.240	22	1	-4	-13	-1.8
● **RUBE SCHAUER** Schauer, Alexander John (b: Dimitri Ivanovich Dimitrihoff) b: 3/19/1891, Odessa, Russia d: 4/15/57, Minneapolis, Minn. BR/TR, 6'2", 192 lbs. Deb: 8/27/13
1913 NY-N	0	1	.000	3	1	1	0	0	12	14	0	9	7	17.3	7.50	42	.292	.404	0	.000	-0	-6	-6	0	-0.4
1914 NY-N	0	0	—	6	0	0	0	0	22¹	16	2	8	6	9.7	3.22	82	.205	.279	1	.143	-0	-1	-1	-1	-0.1
1915 NY-N	2	8	.200	32	7	4	0	0	105¹	101	4	35	65	11.8	3.50	73	.258	.322	2	.077	-2	-9	-11	-0	-1.3
1916 NY-N	1	4	.200	19	3	1	0	0	45²	44	0	16	24	12.2	2.96	82	.257	.328	2	.222	-0	-2	-3	-0	-0.3
1917 Phi-A	7	16	.304	33	21	10	0	1	215	209	6	69	62	11.8	3.14	88	.263	.324	11	.145	-2	-11	-9	0	-1.2
Total 5	10	29	.256	93	32	16	0	1	400¹	384	12	137	164	11.9	3.35	80	.259	.324	16	.132	-4	-29	-30	-1	-3.3
● **OWEN SCHEETZ** Scheetz, Owen Franklin b: 12/24/13, New Bedford, Ohio BR/TR, 6', 190 lbs. Deb: 4/22/43
1943 Was-A	0	0	—	6	0	0	0	1	9	16	0	4	5	20.0	7.00	46	.381	.435	0	.000	0	-4	-4	0	-0.1
● **LEFTY SCHEGG** Schegg, Gilbert Eugene (b: Gilbert Eugene Price) b: 8/28/1889, Leesville, Ohio d: 2/27/63, Niles, Ohio BL/TL, 5'11", 180 lbs. Deb: 8/20/12
1912 Was-A	0	0	—	2	1	0	0	0	5¹	7	0	4	3	18.6	3.38	99	.333	.440	0	.000	-0	-0	-0	-1	-0.1
● **CARL SCHEIB** Scheib, Carl Alvin b: 1/1/27, Gratz, Pa. BR/TR, 6'1", 192 lbs. Deb: 9/6/43
1943 Phi-A	0	1	.000	6	0	0	0	0	18²	24	4	3	3	13.5	4.34	78	.308	.341	0	.000	-1	-2	-2	-1	-0.2
1944 Phi-A	0	0	—	15	0	0	0	0	36¹	36	1	11	13	12.6	4.21	83	.257	.329	3	.300	1	-3	-3	1	0.2
1945 Phi-A	0	0	—	4	0	0	0	0	8²	6	0	4	2	10.4	3.12	110	.207	.303	0	.000	0	0	0	0	0.0
1947 Phi-A	4	6	.400	21	12	6	2	0	116	121	11	55	26	13.8	5.04	76	.274	.357	6	.133	-2	-17	-16	-2	-1.6
1948 Phi-A	14	8	.636	32	24	15	1	0	198²	219	14	76	44	13.4	3.94	109	.286	.351	31	.298	7	8	8	1	1.9
1949 Phi-A	9	12	.429	38	23	11	2	0	182²	191	16	118	43	15.3	5.12	80	.275	.382	17	.236	3	-19	-21	-3	-2.0
1950 Phi-A	3	10	.231	43	8	1	0	3	106	138	13	70	37	17.7	7.22	63	.317	.411	13	.250	-1	-31	-31	-1	-3.2
1951 Phi-A	1	12	.077	46	11	3	0	0	143	132	7	71	49	13.3	4.47	96	.250	.347	21	.396	8	-6	-3	4	1.0
1952 Phi-A	11	7	.611	30	19	8	1	2	158	153	21	50	42	11.8	4.39	90	.253	.314	18	.220	-1	-12	-8	-0	-0.8
1953 Phi-A	3	7	.300	28	8	3	0	2	96	99	7	29	25	12.7	4.88	88	.261	.325	8	.195	-1	-9	-6	-0	-0.7
1954 Phi-A	0	1	.000	1	1	0	0	0	2	5	1	4	1	31.5	22.50	17	.500	.583	0	—	-0	-4	-4	-1	-1.1
StL-N	0	1	.000	3	1	0	0	0	4²	3	1	5	5	21.2	11.57	36	.300	.440	0	.000	-0	-4	-4	-0	-0.7
Total 11	45	65	.409	267	107	47	6	17	1070²	1130	99	493	290	13.9	4.88	85	.274	.355	117	.250	16	-100	-89	0	-7.2
● **FRANK SCHEIBECK** Scheibeck, Frank S. b: 6/28/1865, Detroit, Mich. d: 10/22/56, Detroit, Mich. BR/TR, 5'7", 145 lbs. Deb: 5/9/1887 ♦
1887 Cle-a	0	1	.000	1	1	1	0	0	9	17	1	4	3	22.0	12.00	36	.362	.423	2	.222	0	-8	-8	-0	-0.5
● **JACK SCHEIBLE** Scheible, John G. b: 2/16/1866, Youngstown, Ohio d: 8/9/1897, Youngstown, Ohio TL , Deb: 9/8/1893
1893 Cle-N	1	1	.500	2	2	2	1	0	18	15	0	11	1	13.0	2.00	244	.220	.328	1	.143	-0	5	6	-0	0.5
1894 Phi-N	0	1	.000	1	1	0	0	0	0¹	6	0	2	0	243.0	189.00	3	.862	.904	0	—	-0	-7	-7	-0	-3.9
Total 2	1	2	.333	3	3	2	1	0	18¹	21	0	13	1	17.2	5.40	91	.259	.392	1	.143	-0	-1	-1	-0	-3.4
● **RICH SCHEID** Scheid, Richard Paul b: 2/3/65, Staten Island, N.Y. BL/TL, 6'3", 185 lbs. Deb: 9/11/92
1992 Hou-N	0	1	.000	7	1	0	0	0	12	14	2	6	8	15.0	6.00	56	.280	.357	0	.000	-0	-3	-4	-0	-0.3
1994 Fla-N	1	3	.250	8	5	0	0	0	32¹	35	4	8	17	12.5	3.34	135	.269	.321	0	.000	-1	3	4	-1	0.3
Total 2	1	4	.200	15	6	0	0	0	44¹	49	6	14	25	13.2	4.06	103	.272	.332	0	.000	-1	-0	1	-0	0.0
● **JIM SCHELLE** Schelle, Gerard Anthony b: 4/13/17, Baltimore, Md. d: 5/4/90, Weymouth, Mass. BR/TR, 6'3", 204 lbs. Deb: 7/23/39
1939 Phi-A	0	0	—	1	0	0	0	0	0	1	0	3	0	—	∞	—	1.000	1.000	0	—	0	-3	-3	0	-0.2
● **FRED SCHEMANSKE** Schemanske, Frederick George "Buck" b: 4/28/03, Detroit, Mich. d: 2/18/60, Detroit, Mich. BR/TR, 6'2", 190 lbs. Deb: 9/15/23 ♦
1923 Was-A	0	0	—	1	0	0	0	0	1	3	0	0	0	27.0	27.00	14	.600	.600	2	1.000	1	-3	-3	-0	0.1
● **BILL SCHENCK** Schenck, William G. b: Brooklyn, N.Y. 5'7", 171 lbs. Deb: 5/29/1882 ♦
1882 Lou-a	1	0	1.000	2	1	1	0	0	10	6	0	1	4	6.3	0.90	275	.162	.184	60	.260	0	2	2	-0	0.1
● **JOHN SCHENEBERG** Scheneberg, John Bluford b: 11/20/1887, Guyandotte, W.Va. d: 9/26/50, Huntington, W.Va. BB/TR, 6'1", 180 lbs. Deb: 9/23/13
1913 Pit-N	0	1	.000	1	1	0	0	0	6	10	0	3	1	18.0	6.00	50	.400	.444	1	.500	0	-2	-2	-0	-0.2
1920 StL-A	0	0	—	1	0	0	0	0	2	7	0	0	0	36.0	27.00	15	.583	.615	0	—	0	-5	-5	-0	0.0
Total 2	0	1	.000	2	1	0	0	0	8	17	0	3	1	22.5	11.25	29	.459	.500	1	.500	0	-7	-7	-0	-0.2

YEAR	TM/L	W	L	PCT	G	GS	CG	SH	SV	IP	H	HR	BB	SO	RAT	ERA	ERA+	OAV	OOB	BH	AVG	PB	PR	/A	PD	TPI

● **FRED SCHERMAN** Scherman, Frederick John b: 7/25/44, Dayton, Ohio BL/TL, 6'1", 195 lbs. Deb: 4/26/69

YEAR	TM/L	W	L	PCT	G	GS	CG	SH	SV	IP	H	HR	BB	SO	RAT	ERA	ERA+	OAV	OOB	BH	AVG	PB	PR	/A	PD	TPI
1969	Det-A	1	0	1.000	4	0	0	0	0	4	6	2	0	3	13.5	6.75	55	.333	.333	0	—	0	-1	-1	0	-0.3
1970	Det-A	4	4	.500	48	0	0	0	1	69²	61	5	28	58	11.6	3.23	115	.237	.315	2	.167	-0	4	4	0	0.4
1971	Det-A	11	6	.647	69	1	1	0	20	113	91	11	49	46	11.5	2.71	133	.226	.318	5	.208	1	9	11	1	2.3
1972	*Det-A	7	3	.700	57	3	0	0	12	94	91	5	53	53	14.3	3.64	86	.269	.376	2	.091	-1	-6	-5	-1	-0.9
1973	Det-A	2	2	.500	34	0	0	0	1	61²	59	6	30	28	13.4	4.23	97	.258	.351	0	—	0	-3	-1	-1	-0.2
1974	Hou-N	2	5	.286	53	0	0	0	4	61¹	67	5	26	35	14.7	4.11	84	.284	.372	0	.000	-0	-3	-4	-0	-0.6
1975	Hou-N	0	1	.000	16	0	0	0	0	16¹	21	4	4	13	14.3	4.96	68	.318	.366	0	.000	-0	-2	-3	0	-0.2
	Mon-N	4	3	.571	34	7	0	0	0	76¹	84	3	41	43	15.3	3.54	108	.283	.379	1	.063	-1	1	2	1	0.2
	Yr	4	4	.500	50	7	0	0	0	92²	105	7	45	56	15.1	3.79	99	.288	.373	1	.059	-1	-2	-0	1	0.0
1976	Mon-N	2	2	.500	31	0	0	0	1	40	42	5	14	18	13.3	4.95	75	.261	.331	1	.250	-0	-6	-5	-1	-0.6
Total	8	33	26	.559	346	11	1	0	39	536¹	522	46	245	297	13.4	3.66	99	.260	.350	11	.134	-1	-9	-3	-1	0.1

● **BILL SCHERRER** Scherrer, William Joseph b: 1/20/58, Tonawanda, N.Y. BL/TL, 6'4", 180 lbs. Deb: 9/7/82

YEAR	TM/L	W	L	PCT	G	GS	CG	SH	SV	IP	H	HR	BB	SO	RAT	ERA	ERA+	OAV	OOB	BH	AVG	PB	PR	/A	PD	TPI
1982	Cin-N	0	1	.000	5	2	0	0	0	17¹	17	0	0	7	8.8	2.60	142	.250	.250	1	.500	1	2	2	-0	0.2
1983	Cin-N	2	3	.400	73	0	0	0	10	92	73	6	33	57	10.4	2.74	139	.225	.296	1	.091	-0	9	11	1	0.9
1984	Cin-N	1	1	.500	36	0	0	0	1	52¹	64	6	15	35	13.6	4.99	76	.300	.346	0	.000	-0	-8	-7	-0	-0.3
	*Det-A	1	0	1.000	18	0	0	0	1	19	14	1	8	16	10.4	1.89	207	.206	.289	0	—	0	4	4	0	0.2
1985	Det-A	3	2	.600	48	0	0	0	0	66	62	10	41	46	14.2	4.36	93	.248	.356	0	—	0	-2	-1	1	-0.1
1986	Det-A	0	1	.000	13	0	0	0	0	21	19	3	22	16	18.0	7.29	57	.244	.416	0	—	0	-7	-7	-0	-0.3
1987	Cin-N	1	1	.500	23	0	0	0	0	33	43	3	16	24	16.1	4.36	97	.328	.401	0	.000	-0	-1	-0	-0	-0.1
1988	Bal-A	0	1	.000	4	0	0	0	0	4	8	2	3	3	24.8	13.50	29	.400	.478	0	—	0	-4	-4	-0	-0.7
	Phi-N	0	0	—	8	0	0	0	0	6²	7	0	2	3	12.2	5.40	66	.269	.321	0	—	0	-1	-1	0	0.0
Total	7	8	10	.444	228	2	0	0	11	311¹	307	31	140	207	13.0	4.08	96	.260	.340	2	.118	-0	-8	-5	1	-0.2

● **DUTCH SCHESLER** Schesler, Charles b: 6/1/1900, Frankfurt, Germany d: 11/19/53, Harrisburg, Pa. BR/TR, 6'2", 185 lbs. Deb: 4/16/31

YEAR	TM/L	W	L	PCT	G	GS	CG	SH	SV	IP	H	HR	BB	SO	RAT	ERA	ERA+	OAV	OOB	BH	AVG	PB	PR	/A	PD	TPI
1931	Phi-N	0	0	—	17	0	0	0	0	38¹	65	4	18	14	20.4	7.28	58	.385	.455	1	.111	-0	-15	-13	0	0.0

● **LOU SCHETTLER** Schettler, Louis Martin b: 6/12/1886, Pittsburgh, Pa. d: 5/1/60, Youngstown, Ohio BR/TR, 5'11", 160 lbs. Deb: 4/25/10

YEAR	TM/L	W	L	PCT	G	GS	CG	SH	SV	IP	H	HR	BB	SO	RAT	ERA	ERA+	OAV	OOB	BH	AVG	PB	PR	/A	PD	TPI
1910	Phi-N	2	6	.250	27	7	3	0	1	107	96	2	51	62	12.5	3.20	98	.247	.337	7	.171	-1	-2	-1	-1	-0.3

● **CURT SCHILLING** Schilling, Curtis Montague b: 11/14/66, Anchorage, Alaska BR/TR, 6'5", 205 lbs. Deb: 9/7/88

YEAR	TM/L	W	L	PCT	G	GS	CG	SH	SV	IP	H	HR	BB	SO	RAT	ERA	ERA+	OAV	OOB	BH	AVG	PB	PR	/A	PD	TPI
1988	Bal-A	0	3	.000	4	4	0	0	0	14²	22	3	10	4	20.3	9.82	40	.355	.452	0	—	0	-10	-10	-1	-1.4
1989	Bal-A	0	1	.000	5	1	0	0	0	8²	10	3	3	6	13.5	6.23	61	.286	.342	0	—	0	-2	-2	-0	-0.3
1990	Bal-A	1	2	.333	35	0	0	0	3	46	38	1	19	32	11.2	2.54	149	.229	.308	0	—	0	7	6	-1	0.5
1991	Hou-N	3	5	.375	56	0	0	0	8	75²	79	2	39	71	14.0	3.81	92	.271	.358	1	.333	-0	-1	-3	-1	-0.4
1992	Phi-N	14	11	.560	42	26	10	4	2	226¹	165	11	59	147	**8.9**	2.35	149	**.201**	**.256**	10	.156	-0	29	29	-3	3.0
1993	*Phi-N	16	7	.696	34	34	7	2	0	235¹	234	23	57	186	11.5	4.02	99	.259	.305	11	.147	-1	1	-1	-0	-0.2
1994	Phi-N	2	8	.200	13	13	1	0	0	82¹	87	10	28	58	12.9	4.48	92	.270	.334	3	.107	-1	-2	-3	-1	-0.5
Total	7	36	37	.493	189	78	18	6	13	689	635	52	215	504	11.2	3.55	106	.244	.304	25	.147	-2	21	16	-5	0.7

● **RED SCHILLINGS** Schillings, Elbert Isaiah b: 3/29/1900, Deport, Tex. d: 1/7/54, Oklahoma City, Okla BR/TR, 5'10", 180 lbs. Deb: 9/11/22

YEAR	TM/L	W	L	PCT	G	GS	CG	SH	SV	IP	H	HR	BB	SO	RAT	ERA	ERA+	OAV	OOB	BH	AVG	PB	PR	/A	PD	TPI
1922	Phi-A	0	0	—	4	0	0	0	0	8	10	1	11	4	23.6	6.75	63	.313	.488	0	.000	-0	-2	-1	-0	0.0

● **CALVIN SCHIRALDI** Schiraldi, Calvin Drew b: 6/16/62, Houston, Tex. BR/TR, 6'4", 200 lbs. Deb: 9/1/84

YEAR	TM/L	W	L	PCT	G	GS	CG	SH	SV	IP	H	HR	BB	SO	RAT	ERA	ERA+	OAV	OOB	BH	AVG	PB	PR	/A	PD	TPI
1984	NY-N	0	2	.000	5	3	0	0	0	17¹	20	3	10	16	15.6	5.71	62	.286	.375	0	.000	-0	-4	-4	-0	-0.4
1985	NY-N	2	1	.667	10	4	0	0	0	26¹	43	4	11	21	19.5	8.89	39	.368	.435	1	.125	-0	-15	-16	0	-1.6
1986	*Bos-A	4	2	.667	25	0	0	0	9	51	36	5	14	55	9.2	1.41	295	.201	.267	0	—	0	16	16	-1	2.3
1987	Bos-A	8	5	.615	62	1	0	0	6	83²	75	15	40	93	12.5	4.41	103	.240	.328	0	—	0	1	-0	0	0.2
1988	Chi-N	9	13	.409	29	27	1	1	1	166¹	166	13	63	140	12.5	4.38	82	.257	.325	6	.100	-2	-17	-14	-2	-2.2
1989	Chi-N	3	6	.333	54	0	0	0	4	78²	60	7	50	54	12.7	3.78	100	.209	.328	0	.000	-1	-2	-0	-1	-0.2
	SD-N	3	1	.750	21¹	12	1	13	17	10.5	2.53	138	.162	.287	1	.143	1	2	2	-0	0.5
	Yr	6	7	.462	59	4	0	0	4	100	72	8	63	71	12.2	3.51	105	.198	.316	1	.063	-0	0	2	-2	0.3
1990	SD-N	3	8	.273	42	8	0	0	1	104	105	11	60	74	14.4	4.41	87	.264	.362	4	.190	2	-7	-7	-1	-0.6
1991	Tex-A	0	1	.000	3	0	0	0	0	4²	5	3	5	1	19.3	11.57	35	.263	.417	0	—	0	-4	-4	0	-0.6
Total	8	32	39	.451	235	47	2	1	21	553¹	522	62	267	471	13.0	4.28	90	.248	.336	12	.111	-1	-32	-26	-5	-2.6

● **BIFF SCHLITZER** Schlitzer, Victor Joseph b: 12/4/1884, Rochester, N.Y. d: 1/4/48, Wellesley Hills, Mass. BR/TR, 5'11", 175 lbs. Deb: 4/17/08

YEAR	TM/L	W	L	PCT	G	GS	CG	SH	SV	IP	H	HR	BB	SO	RAT	ERA	ERA+	OAV	OOB	BH	AVG	PB	PR	/A	PD	TPI
1908	Phi-A	6	8	.429	24	18	11	2	0	131	110	1	45	57	10.8	3.16	81	.234	.303	9	.196	-1	-11	-9	-2	-1.3
1909	Phi-A	0	3	.000	4	3	0	0	0	13¹	13	0	7	6	15.5	5.40	45	.245	.365	1	.250	-0	-4	-4	1	-0.8
	Bos-A	4	4	.500	13	8	5	0	1	69²	68	0	17	23	11.1	3.49	72	.234	.279	4	.154	-0	-8	-8	1	-0.8
	Yr	4	7	.364	17	11	5	0	1	83	81	0	24	29	11.5	3.80	65	.234	.286	5	.167	-0	-12	-12	2	-1.6
1914	Buf-F	0	0	—	3	0	0	0	0	3¹	7	3	2	1	24.3	16.20	18	.438	.500	1	1.000	-0	-5	-5	-0	0.0
Total	3	10	15	.400	44	29	16	2	1	217¹	198	4	71	87	11.4	3.60	71	.239	.303	15	.195	-0	-28	-26	-0	-2.9

● **GEORGE SCHMEES** Schmees, George Edward "Rocky" b: 9/6/24, Cincinnati, Ohio BL/TL, 6', 190 lbs. Deb: 4/15/52 ♦

YEAR	TM/L	W	L	PCT	G	GS	CG	SH	SV	IP	H	HR	BB	SO	RAT	ERA	ERA+	OAV	OOB	BH	AVG	PB	PR	/A	PD	TPI
1952	Bos-A	0	0	—	2	1	0	0	0	6	9	0	2	2	16.5	3.00	131	.346	.393	13	.203	0	0	1	1	0.1

● **AL SCHMELZ** Schmelz, Alan George b: 11/12/43, Whittier, Cal. BR/TR, 6'4", 210 lbs. Deb: 9/7/67

YEAR	TM/L	W	L	PCT	G	GS	CG	SH	SV	IP	H	HR	BB	SO	RAT	ERA	ERA+	OAV	OOB	BH	AVG	PB	PR	/A	PD	TPI
1967	NY-N	0	0	—	2	0	0	0	0	3	4	1	1	2	15.0	3.00	113	.364	.417	0	—	0	0	0	0	0.0

● **BUTCH SCHMIDT** Schmidt, Charles John "Butcher Boy" b: 7/19/1886, Baltimore, Md. d: 9/4/52, Baltimore, Md. BL/TL, 6'1.5", 200 lbs. Deb: 5/11/09 ♦

YEAR	TM/L	W	L	PCT	G	GS	CG	SH	SV	IP	H	HR	BB	SO	RAT	ERA	ERA+	OAV	OOB	BH	AVG	PB	PR	/A	PD	TPI
1909	NY-A	0	0	—	1	0	0	0	0	5	10	0	1	2	19.8	7.20	35	.435	.458	0	.000	-0	-3	-3	-0	-0.1

● **DAVE SCHMIDT** Schmidt, David Joseph b: 4/22/57, Niles, Mich. BR/TR, 6'1", 185 lbs. Deb: 5/1/81

YEAR	TM/L	W	L	PCT	G	GS	CG	SH	SV	IP	H	HR	BB	SO	RAT	ERA	ERA+	OAV	OOB	BH	AVG	PB	PR	/A	PD	TPI
1981	Tex-A	0	1	.000	14	1	0	0	1	31²	31	1	11	13	12.2	3.13	111	.258	.326	0	—	0	2	1	0	0.1
1982	Tex-A	4	6	.400	33	8	0	0	6	109²	118	5	25	69	12.1	3.20	121	.279	.327	0	—	0	11	8	-0	1.0
1983	Tex-A	3	3	.500	31	0	0	0	0	46¹	42	3	14	29	11.1	3.88	103	.241	.302	0	—	0	1	1	0	0.2
1984	Tex-A	6	6	.500	43	0	0	0	12	70¹	69	6	20	46	11.4	2.56	162	.262	.314	0	—	0	11	12	-1	2.6
1985	Tex-A	7	6	.538	51	4	1	1	6	85²	81	6	22	46	10.8	3.15	134	.246	.293	0	—	0	9	10	1	1.7
1986	Chi-A	3	6	.333	49	1	0	0	0	92¹	94	10	27	67	12.3	3.31	130	.264	.325	0	—	0	9	10	-1	1.0
1987	Bal-A	10	5	.667	35	14	2	1	0	124	128	13	26	70	11.3	3.77	117	.263	.302	0	—	0	9	9	-1	0.8
1988	Bal-A	8	5	.615	41	9	0	0	2	129²	129	14	38	67	11.8	3.40	115	.262	.319	0	—	0	8	7	2	1.0
1989	Bal-A	10	13	.435	38	26	2	0	0	156²	196	24	36	46	13.4	5.69	67	.310	.349	0	—	0	-31	-33	1	-4.1
1990	Mon-N	3	3	.500	34	0	0	0	13	48	58	3	13	22	13.3	4.31	85	.297	.341	0	.000	-0	-3	-4	-0	-0.6
1991	Mon-N	0	1	.000	4	0	0	0	0	4¹	9	2	2	3	22.8	10.38	35	.429	.478	0	—	0	-3	-3	0	-0.6
1992	Sea-A	0	0	—	3	0	0	0	0	3¹	7	1	3	1	27.0	18.90	21	.438	.526	0	—	0	-6	-6	0	0.0
Total	12	54	55	.495	376	63	5	3	50	902	962	85	237	479	12.1	3.88	103	.274	.323	0	.000	-0	17	13	3	3.1

● **FREDDY SCHMIDT** Schmidt, Frederick Albert b: 2/9/16, Hartford, Conn. BR/TR, 6'1", 185 lbs. Deb: 4/25/44

YEAR	TM/L	W	L	PCT	G	GS	CG	SH	SV	IP	H	HR	BB	SO	RAT	ERA	ERA+	OAV	OOB	BH	AVG	PB	PR	/A	PD	TPI
1944	*StL-N	7	3	.700	37	9	3	2	5	114¹	94	5	58	58	12.0	3.15	112	.222	.317	7	.206	-0	6	5	-1	0.3
1946	StL-N	1	0	1.000	16	0	0	0	0	27¹	27	0	15	14	14.8	3.29	105	.276	.388	0	.000	-0	1	1	-1	0.0
1947	StL-N	0	0	—	2	0	0	0	0	4	5	1	1	2	13.5	2.25	184	.333	.375	0	—	0	1	1	-0	0.0
	Phi-N	5	8	.385	29	5	0	0	0	76²	76	4	43	24	14.4	4.70	85	.285	.392	1	.050	-2	-5	-6	-1	-1.1
	Chi-N	0	0	—	1	1	0	0	0	3	4	0	5	0	27.0	9.00	44	.333	.529	0	—	0	-2	-2	-0	0.0

YEAR TM/L	W	L	PCT	G	GS	CG	SH	SV	IP	H	HR	BB	SO	RAT	ERA	ERA+	OAV	OOB	BH	AVG	PB	PR	/A	PD	TPI
Yr	5	8	.385	32	6	0	0	0	83²	85	5	49	26	14.4	4.73	85	.285	.386	1	.045	-2	-6	-7	-1	-1.1
Total 3	13	11	.542	85	15	3	2	5	225¹	206	10	122	98	13.4	3.75	98	.252	.355	8	.140	-2	-0	-1	-1	-0.8

● **PETE SCHMIDT**   Schmidt, Friedrich Christoph Herman b: 7/23/1890, Lowden, Iowa d: 3/11/73, Pembroke, Ont., Can BR/TR, 5'11", 175 lbs. Deb: 7/14/13

YEAR TM/L	W	L	PCT	G	GS	CG	SH	SV	IP	H	HR	BB	SO	RAT	ERA	ERA+	OAV	OOB	BH	AVG	PB	PR	/A	PD	TPI
1913 StL-A	0	0	—	1	0	0	0	1	2	3	0	2	0	22.5	4.50	65	.333	.455	0	—	0	-0	-0	-0	-0.1

● **HENRY SCHMIDT**   Schmidt, Henry Martin b: 6/26/1873, Brownsville, Tex. d: 4/23/26, Nashville, Tenn. BR/TR, 5'11", 170 lbs. Deb: 4/17/03

YEAR TM/L	W	L	PCT	G	GS	CG	SH	SV	IP	H	HR	BB	SO	RAT	ERA	ERA+	OAV	OOB	BH	AVG	PB	PR	/A	PD	TPI
1903 Bro-N	22	13	.629	40	36	29	5	2	301	321	5	120	96	13.8	3.83	83	.280	.359	21	.196	3	-19	-21	6	-1.3

● **WILLARD SCHMIDT**   Schmidt, Willard Raymond b: 5/29/28, Hays, Kan. BR/TR, 6'1", 187 lbs. Deb: 4/19/52

YEAR TM/L	W	L	PCT	G	GS	CG	SH	SV	IP	H	HR	BB	SO	RAT	ERA	ERA+	OAV	OOB	BH	AVG	PB	PR	/A	PD	TPI
1952 StL-N	2	3	.400	18	3	0	0	1	34²	36	6	18	30	14.5	5.19	72	.267	.361	1	.125	-0	-6	-6	1	-0.7
1953 StL-N	0	2	.000	6	2	0	0	0	17²	21	1	13	11	17.8	9.17	46	.288	.402	0	.000	-1	-10	-10	-0	-0.9
1955 StL-N	7	6	.538	20	15	8	1	0	129²	89	7	57	86	10.3	2.78	146	.197	.291	5	.119	-3	18	19	1	1.5
1956 StL-N	6	8	.429	33	21	2	0	1	147²	131	18	78	52	12.8	3.84	99	.246	.344	10	.233	1	-1	-1	2	0.2
1957 StL-N	10	3	.769	40	8	1	0	0	116²	146	13	49	63	15.2	4.78	83	.312	.380	7	.212	0	-12	-11	1	-1.0
1958 Cin-N	3	5	.375	41	2	0	0	0	69¹	60	8	31	41	12.2	2.86	145	.235	.325	1	.091	-1	8	10	1	1.1
1959 Cin-N	3	2	.600	36	4	0	0	0	70²	80	4	30	40	14.1	3.95	103	.296	.369	1	.083	-0	-0	1	1	0.2
Total 7	31	29	.517	194	55	11	1	2	586¹	563	57	278	323	13.1	3.93	101	.258	.344	25	.163	-2	-1	2	6	0.4

● **CRAZY SCHMIT**   Schmit, Frederick M. "Germany" b: 2/13/1866, Chicago, Ill. d: 10/5/40, Chicago, Ill. BL/TL, 5'10.5", 165 lbs. Deb: 4/21/1890

YEAR TM/L	W	L	PCT	G	GS	CG	SH	SV	IP	H	HR	BB	SO	RAT	ERA	ERA+	OAV	OOB	BH	AVG	PB	PR	/A	PD	TPI
1890 Pit-N	1	9	.100	11	10	9	1	0	83¹	108	3	42	35	17.1	5.83	57	.304	.390	2	.061	-3	-21	-23	-0	-2.3
1892 Bal-N	1	4	.200	6	6	6	0	0	47¹	37	0	26	17	12.0	3.23	106	.207	.307	2	.105	-1	0	1	1	0.1
1893 Bal-N	3	2	.600	9	6	4	0	0	49	67	1	22	10	16.7	6.61	72	.316	.386	5	.238	-0	-11	-10	-1	-0.8
NY-N	0	2	.000	4	4	1	0	0	20²	30	0	17	5	21.3	7.40	63	.329	.445	4	.444	2	-6	-6	0	-0.3
Yr	3	4	.429	13	10	5	0	0	69²	97	1	39	15	17.8	6.85	69	.318	.399	9	.300	1	-17	-16	-1	-1.1
1899 Cle-N	2	17	.105	20	19	16	0	0	138¹	197	3	62	24	17.8	5.86	63	.334	.410	11	.157	-2	-31	-33	2	-3.4
1901 Bal-A	0	2	.000	4	3	1	0	0	22²	25	0	16	2	16.3	1.99	195	.276	.385	2	.222	0	4	5	1	0.5
Total 5	7	36	.163	54	48	37	1	0	361¹	464	7	185	93	16.8	5.45	69	.306	.390	26	.161	-4	-64	-68	2	-6.2

● **JOHNNY SCHMITZ**   Schmitz, John Albert "Bear Tracks" b: 11/27/20, Wausau, Wis. BR/TL, 6', 170 lbs. Deb: 9/6/41

YEAR TM/L	W	L	PCT	G	GS	CG	SH	SV	IP	H	HR	BB	SO	RAT	ERA	ERA+	OAV	OOB	BH	AVG	PB	PR	/A	PD	TPI
1941 Chi-N	2	0	1.000	5	3	1	0	0	20²	12	0	9	11	9.6	1.31	269	.182	.289	4	.571	2	5	5	1	0.8
1942 Chi-N	3	7	.300	23	10	1	0	2	86²	70	3	45	51	12.3	3.43	93	.230	.335	4	.154	-1	-1	-2	4	0.1
1946 Chi-N☆	11	11	.500	41	31	14	2	2	224¹	184	6	94	**135**	11.2	2.61	127	**.221**	.302	9	.130	-2	20	18	2	1.8
1947 Chi-N	13	18	.419	38	28	10	3	4	207	209	8	80	97	12.7	3.22	123	.262	.330	9	.132	-2	19	17	2	2.4
1948 Chi-N★	18	13	.581	34	30	18	2	1	242	186	11	97	100	10.6	2.64	148	**.215**	.295	11	.131	-2	35	34	5	4.6
1949 Chi-N	11	13	.458	36	31	9	3	3	207	227	11	92	75	14.0	4.35	93	.287	.363	10	.143	-1	-7	-7	5	-0.3
1950 Chi-N	10	16	.385	39	27	8	3	0	193	217	23	91	75	14.5	4.99	84	.284	.363	8	.119	-3	-18	-17	5	-1.7
1951 Chi-N	1	2	.333	8	3	0	0	0	18	22	1	15	6	18.5	8.00	51	.301	.420	1	.167	-0	-8	-8	1	-1.0
Bro-N	1	4	.200	16	7	0	0	0	55²	55	4	28	20	13.7	5.34	74	.259	.351	4	.222	2	-9	-9	1	-0.4
Yr	2	6	.250	24	10	0	0	0	73²	77	5	43	26	14.9	5.99	66	.270	.370	5	.208	1	-17	-17	2	-1.4
1952 Bro-N	1	1	.500	10	3	1	0	0	33¹	29	3	18	11	13.0	4.32	84	.238	.340	1	.125	-0	-2	-3	1	-0.0
NY-A	1	1	.500	5	2	1	0	1	15	15	0	9	3	15.0	3.60	92	.263	.373	3	.600	2	0	-0	0	0.2
Cin-N	1	0	1.000	3	0	0	0	0	5	3	0	2	3	10.8	0.00	—	.188	.316	0	—	0	2	2	0	0.4
1953 NY-A	0	0	—	3	0	0	0	2	4¹	2	1	3	0	10.4	2.08	178	.143	.294	0	—	0	1	1	0	0.1
Was-A	2	7	.222	24	13	5	0	4	107²	118	9	37	39	13.3	3.68	106	.286	.351	2	.059	-4	4	3	1	-0.1
Yr	2	7	.222	27	13	5	0	6	112	120	10	40	39	13.2	3.62	108	.284	.349	2	.059	-4	5	4	1	0.0
1954 Was-A	11	8	.579	29	23	12	2	1	185¹	176	6	64	56	11.8	2.91	122	.255	.321	7	.117	-3	17	13	2	1.2
1955 Was-A	7	10	.412	32	21	6	1	1	165	187	8	54	49	13.5	3.71	103	.291	.352	10	.185	-0	5	2	2	0.5
1956 Bos-N	0	0	—	2	0	0	0	0	4¹	5	0	4	0	18.7	0.00	—	.278	.409	0	.000	-0	2	2	0	0.0
Bal-A	0	3	.000	18	3	0	0	0	38¹	49	3	14	15	15.0	3.99	98	.318	.379	0	.000	-1	1	-0	1	-0.1
Yr	0	3	.000	20	3	0	0	0	42²	54	3	18	15	15.4	3.59	111	.314	.382	0	.000	-2	3	2	1	-0.1
Total 13	93	114	.449	366	235	86	16	21	1812²	1766	97	757	746	12.7	3.55	107	.258	.335	83	.141	-14	66	50	35	8.5

● **CHARLIE SCHMUTZ**   Schmutz, Charles Otto "King" b: 1/1/1890, San Diego, Cal. d: 6/27/62, Seattle, Wash. BR/TR, 6'1.5", 195 lbs. Deb: 5/13/14

YEAR TM/L	W	L	PCT	G	GS	CG	SH	SV	IP	H	HR	BB	SO	RAT	ERA	ERA+	OAV	OOB	BH	AVG	PB	PR	/A	PD	TPI
1914 Bro-N	1	3	.250	18	5	1	0	0	57¹	57	1	13	21	11.1	3.30	87	.265	.310	3	.188	1	-3	-3	0	-0.1
1915 Bro-N	0	0	—	1	0	0	0	0	4	7	0	1	1	18.0	6.75	41	.438	.471	0	.000	-0	-2	-2	0	-0.0
Total 2	1	3	.250	19	5	1	0	0	61¹	64	1	14	22	11.6	3.52	81	.277	.321	3	.176	1	-5	-5	1	-0.1

● **FRANK SCHNEIBERG**   Schneiberg, Frank Frederick b: 3/12/1882, Milwaukee, Wis. d: 5/18/48, Milwaukee, Wis. TR, Deb: 6/8/10

YEAR TM/L	W	L	PCT	G	GS	CG	SH	SV	IP	H	HR	BB	SO	RAT	ERA	ERA+	OAV	OOB	BH	AVG	PB	PR	/A	PD	TPI
1910 Bro-N	0	0	—	1	0	0	0	0	1	5	0	4	0	81.0	63.00	5	.625	.750	0	—	0	-7	-7	-0	0.0

● **DAN SCHNEIDER**   Schneider, Daniel Louis b: 8/29/42, Evansville, Ind. BL/TL, 6'3", 170 lbs. Deb: 5/12/63

YEAR TM/L	W	L	PCT	G	GS	CG	SH	SV	IP	H	HR	BB	SO	RAT	ERA	ERA+	OAV	OOB	BH	AVG	PB	PR	/A	PD	TPI
1963 Mil-N	1	0	1.000	30	3	0	0	0	43²	36	2	20	19	11.5	3.09	104	.225	.311	0	.000	-1	1	1	-1	-0.2
1964 Mil-N	1	2	.333	13	5	0	0	0	36¹	38	6	13	14	12.6	5.45	65	.270	.331	0	.000	-1	-8	-8	1	-0.6
1966 Atl-N	0	0	—	14	0	0	0	0	26¹	35	1	5	11	14.0	3.42	106	.324	.360	4	.500	1	1	1	-0	0.1
1967 Hou-N	0	2	.000	54	0	0	0	0	52²	60	5	27	39	15.2	4.96	67	.296	.384	1	.200	-0	-9	-10	1	-0.3
1969 Hou-N	0	1	.000	6	0	0	0	0	7¹	16	2	5	3	25.8	13.50	26	.485	.553	0	.000	-0	-8	-8	0	-0.9
Total 5	2	5	.286	117	8	0	0	0	166¹	185	16	70	86	14.0	4.71	72	.287	.359	5	.172	-1	-24	-24	1	-1.9

● **JEFF SCHNEIDER**   Schneider, Jeffrey Theodore b: 12/6/52, Bremerton, Wash. BB/TL, 6'3", 195 lbs. Deb: 8/12/81

YEAR TM/L	W	L	PCT	G	GS	CG	SH	SV	IP	H	HR	BB	SO	RAT	ERA	ERA+	OAV	OOB	BH	AVG	PB	PR	/A	PD	TPI
1981 Bal-A	0	0	—	11	0	0	0	1	24	27	4	12	17	15.0	4.88	74	.290	.377	0	—	0	-3	-3	-0	-0.1

● **PETE SCHNEIDER**   Schneider, Peter Joseph b: 8/20/1895, Los Angeles, Cal. d: 6/1/57, Los Angeles, Cal. BR/TR, 6'1", 194 lbs. Deb: 6/20/14

YEAR TM/L	W	L	PCT	G	GS	CG	SH	SV	IP	H	HR	BB	SO	RAT	ERA	ERA+	OAV	OOB	BH	AVG	PB	PR	/A	PD	TPI
1914 Cin-N	5	13	.278	29	20	11	1	1	144¹	143	1	56	62	12.8	2.81	104	.269	.347	8	.178	1	-0	-2	-1	0.2
1915 Cin-N	14	19	.424	48	35	16	5	2	275²	254	4	104	108	11.9	2.48	115	.251	.325	23	.245	5	8	12	-1	2.0
1916 Cin-N	10	19	.345	44	31	16	2	1	274¹	259	4	82	117	11.6	2.69	96	.255	.319	21	.236	2	-2	-3	-3	-0.3
1917 Cin-N	20	19	.513	46	42	24	0	1	333²	311	4	117	138	11.8	2.10	124	.255	.326	19	.167	-0	23	19	-5	1.8
1918 Cin-N	10	15	.400	33	30	17	2	0	217	213	2	117	51	14.1	3.53	76	.272	.374	24	.289	1	-18	-21	-3	-2.0
1919 NY-A	0	1	.000	7	4	0	0	0	29	19	1	22	11	13.7	3.41	94	.192	.355	1	.111	-1	-1	-1	-0	-0.2
Total 6	59	86	.407	207	162	84	10	4	1274	1199	16	498	487	12.4	2.66	102	.257	.336	96	.221	14	9	8	-13	1.5

● **KARL SCHNELL**   Schnell, Karl Otto b: 9/20/1899, Los Angeles, Cal. d: 5/31/92, Palo Alto, Cal. BR/TR, 6'1", 176 lbs. Deb: 4/24/22

YEAR TM/L	W	L	PCT	G	GS	CG	SH	SV	IP	H	HR	BB	SO	RAT	ERA	ERA+	OAV	OOB	BH	AVG	PB	PR	/A	PD	TPI
1922 Cin-N	0	0	—	10	0	0	0	0	20	21	0	18	5	17.5	2.70	148	.300	.443	1	.250	0	3	3	0	0.0
1923 Cin-N	0	0	—	1	0	0	0	0	1	2	0	2	0	36.0	36.00	11	.667	.800	0	—	0	-4	-4	-0	0.0
Total 2	0	0	—	11	0	0	0	0	21	23	0	20	5	18.4	4.29	92	.315	.462	1	.250	0	-0	-0	0	0.0

● **GERRY SCHOEN**   Schoen, Gerald Thomas b: 1/15/47, New Orleans, La. BR/TR, 6'3", 215 lbs. Deb: 9/14/68

YEAR TM/L	W	L	PCT	G	GS	CG	SH	SV	IP	H	HR	BB	SO	RAT	ERA	ERA+	OAV	OOB	BH	AVG	PB	PR	/A	PD	TPI
1968 Was-A	0	1	.000	1	1	0	0	0	3²	6	1	4	2	17.2	7.36	40	.400	.438	0	.000	-0	-2	-2	-0	-0.4

● **JUMBO SCHOENECK**   Schoeneck, Louis N. b: 3/3/1862, Chicago, Ill. d: 1/20/30, Chicago, Ill. BR/TR, 6'3", 223 lbs. Deb: 4/20/1884 ♦

YEAR TM/L	W	L	PCT	G	GS	CG	SH	SV	IP	H	HR	BB	SO	RAT	ERA	ERA+	OAV	OOB	BH	AVG	PB	PR	/A	PD	TPI
1888 Ind-N	0	0	—	2	0	0	0	0	4¹	5	0	1	2	12.5	0.00	—	.227	.261	40	.237			1	1	-0	0.0

● **MIKE SCHOOLER**   Schooler, Michael Ralph b: 8/10/62, Anaheim, Cal. BR/TR, 6'3", 220 lbs. Deb: 6/10/88

YEAR TM/L	W	L	PCT	G	GS	CG	SH	SV	IP	H	HR	BB	SO	RAT	ERA	ERA+	OAV	OOB	BH	AVG	PB	PR	/A	PD	TPI
1988 Sea-A	5	8	.385	40	0	0	0	15	48¹	45	4	24	54	13.0	3.54	118	.245	.335	0	—	0	2	3	-0	0.7
1989 Sea-A	1	7	.125	67	0	0	0	33	77	81	2	19	69	11.9	2.81	144	.266	.314	0	—	0	9	10	1	2.0
1990 Sea-A	1	4	.200	49	0	0	0	30	56	47	5	16	45	10.3	2.25	176	.227	.286	0	.000	0	10	11	0	2.3

YEAR	TM/L	W	L	PCT	G	GS	CG	SH	SV	IP	H	HR	BB	SO	RAT	ERA	ERA+	OAV	OOB	BH	AVG	PB	PR	/A	PD	TPI
1991	Sea-A	3	3	.500	34	0	0	0	7	34¹	25	2	10	31	9.2	3.67	112	.198	.257	0	—	0	2	2	-0	0.3
1992	Sea-A	2	7	.222	53	0	0	0	13	51²	55	7	24	33	13.9	4.70	84	.275	.356	0	—	0	-4	-4	1	-0.8
1993	Tex-A	3	0	1.000	17	0	0	0	0	24¹	30	3	10	16	14.8	5.55	75	.303	.367	0	—	0	-3	-4	-0	-0.4
Total	6	15	29	.341	260	0	0	0	98	291²	283	23	103	248	12.1	3.49	116	.253	.318	0	.000	0	16	18	1	4.1

● **ED SCHORR**   Schorr, Edward Walter   b: 2/14/1891, Bremen, Ohio   d: 9/12/69, Atlantic City, N.J.   BR/TR, 6'2.5", 180 lbs.   Deb: 4/26/15

YEAR	TM/L	W	L	PCT	G	GS	CG	SH	SV	IP	H	HR	BB	SO	RAT	ERA	ERA+	OAV	OOB	BH	AVG	PB	PR	/A	PD	TPI
1915	Chi-N	0	0	—	2	0	0	0	0	6	9	0	5	3	21.0	7.50	37	.409	.519	1	.500	0	-3	-3	0	0.0

● **GENE SCHOTT**   Schott, Arthur Eugene   b: 7/14/13, Batavia, Ohio   d: 11/16/92, Sun City Center, Fla.   BR/TR, 6'2", 185 lbs.   Deb: 4/16/35   ♦

YEAR	TM/L	W	L	PCT	G	GS	CG	SH	SV	IP	H	HR	BB	SO	RAT	ERA	ERA+	OAV	OOB	BH	AVG	PB	PR	/A	PD	TPI
1935	Cin-N	8	11	.421	33	19	9	1	0	159	153	5	64	49	12.3	3.91	102	.253	.326	12	.200	—	2	1	3	0.5
1936	Cin-N	11	11	.500	31	22	8	0	1	180	184	7	73	65	13.1	3.80	101	.262	.335	18	.300	7	4	0	1	0.9
1937	Cin-N	4	13	.235	37	17	7	2	1	154¹	150	2	48	56	11.6	2.97	125	.253	.310	7	.143	-1	16	13	1	1.3
1938	Cin-N	5	5	.500	31	4	0	0	2	83	89	8	32	21	13.2	4.45	82	.279	.347	3	.125	-1	-6	-7	1	-0.9
1939	Phi-N	0	1	.000	4	0	0	0	0	11	14	0	5	1	17.2	4.91	82	.326	.420	2	.333	1	-1	-1	-1	0.0
Total	5	28	41	.406	136	62	24	3	4	587¹	590	22	222	192	12.6	3.72	103	.261	.329	42	.211	6	15	6	6	1.8

● **PETE SCHOUREK**   Schourek, Peter Alan   b: 5/10/69, Austin, Tex.   BL/TL, 6'5", 195 lbs.   Deb: 4/9/91

YEAR	TM/L	W	L	PCT	G	GS	CG	SH	SV	IP	H	HR	BB	SO	RAT	ERA	ERA+	OAV	OOB	BH	AVG	PB	PR	/A	PD	TPI
1991	NY-N	5	4	.556	35	8	1	1	2	86¹	82	7	43	67	13.2	4.27	85	.248	.338	3	.136	0	-6	-6	1	-0.5
1992	NY-N	6	8	.429	22	21	0	0	0	136	137	9	44	60	12.1	3.64	95	.261	.321	2	.048	-3	-2	-3	-2	-0.8
1993	NY-N	5	12	.294	41	18	0	0	0	128¹	168	13	45	72	15.1	5.96	67	.319	.376	7	.219	2	-27	-28	0	-3.1
1994	Cin-N	7	2	.778	22	10	0	0	0	81¹	90	11	29	69	13.5	4.09	102	.287	.353	4	.174	1	1	1	0	0.2
Total	4	23	26	.469	120	57	1	1	2	432	477	40	161	268	13.5	4.54	84	.281	.347	16	.134	-0	-34	-36	-1	-4.2

● **BARNEY SCHREIBER**   Schreiber, David Henry   b: 5/8/1882, Waverly, Ohio   d: 10/6/64, Chillicothe, Ohio   BL/TL, 6', 185 lbs.   Deb: 5/15/11

YEAR	TM/L	W	L	PCT	G	GS	CG	SH	SV	IP	H	HR	BB	SO	RAT	ERA	ERA+	OAV	OOB	BH	AVG	PB	PR	/A	PD	TPI
1911	Cin-N	0	0	—	3	0	0	0	1	10	19	2	2	5	18.9	5.40	61	.413	.438	0	.000	-0	-2	-2	-0	-0.1

● **PAUL SCHREIBER**   Schreiber, Paul Frederick "Von"   b: 10/8/02, Jacksonville, Fla.   d: 1/28/82, Sarasota, Fla.   BR/TR, 6'2", 180 lbs.   Deb: 9/2/22   C

YEAR	TM/L	W	L	PCT	G	GS	CG	SH	SV	IP	H	HR	BB	SO	RAT	ERA	ERA+	OAV	OOB	BH	AVG	PB	PR	/A	PD	TPI
1922	Bro-N	0	0	—	1	0	0	0	0	1	2	0	0	0	18.0	0.00	—	.500	.500	0	—	0	0	0	0	0.0
1923	Bro-N	0	0	—	9	0	0	0	1	15	16	1	8	1	15.6	4.20	92	.276	.382	0	.000	-0	-0	-1	-0	-0.1
1945	NY-A	0	0	—	2	0	0	0	0	4¹	4	0	2	1	12.5	4.15	83	.267	.353	0	—	0	-0	-0	1	0.1
Total	3	0	0	—	12	0	0	0	1	20¹	22	1	10	5	15.0	3.98	96	.286	.382	0	.000	-0	-0	-1	1	0.0

● **AL SCHROLL**   Schroll, Albert Bringhurst "Bull"   b: 3/22/32, New Orleans, La.   BR/TR, 6'2", 210 lbs.   Deb: 4/20/58

YEAR	TM/L	W	L	PCT	G	GS	CG	SH	SV	IP	H	HR	BB	SO	RAT	ERA	ERA+	OAV	OOB	BH	AVG	PB	PR	/A	PD	TPI
1958	Bos-A	0	0	—	5	0	0	0	0	10	6	1	4	7	9.0	4.50	89	.176	.263	1	1.000	0	-1	-1	0	0.1
1959	Phi-N	1	1	.500	3	0	0	0	0	9¹	12	1	6	4	17.4	8.68	47	.353	.450	1	.250	0	-5	-5	-0	-0.8
	Bos-A	1	4	.200	14	5	1	0	0	46	47	3	22	26	13.7	4.70	86	.269	.354	1	.111	0	-4	-3	-1	-0.3
1960	Chi-N	0	0	—	2	0	0	0	0	2²	3	1	5	2	27.0	10.13	37	.273	.500	1	1.000	0	-2	-2	-0	0.0
1961	Min-A	4	4	.500	11	8	2	0	0	50	53	5	27	24	14.8	5.22	81	.266	.360	5	.278	0	-7	-5	-0	-0.6
Total	4	6	9	.400	35	13	4	0	0	118	121	11	64	63	14.3	5.34	77	.267	.362	9	.273	4	-19	-16	-1	-1.6

● **KEN SCHROM**   Schrom, Kenneth Marvin   b: 11/23/54, Grangeville, Idaho   BR/TR, 6'2", 195 lbs.   Deb: 8/8/80

YEAR	TM/L	W	L	PCT	G	GS	CG	SH	SV	IP	H	HR	BB	SO	RAT	ERA	ERA+	OAV	OOB	BH	AVG	PB	PR	/A	PD	TPI
1980	Tor-A	1	0	1.000	17	0	0	0	1	31	32	3	19	13	14.8	5.23	82	.274	.375	0	—	0	-4	-3	0	-0.1
1982	Tor-A	1	0	1.000	6	0	0	0	0	15¹	13	3	15	8	16.4	5.87	76	.232	.394	0	—	0	-3	-2	-1	-0.6
1983	Min-A	15	8	.652	33	28	6	1	0	196¹	196	14	80	80	13.1	3.71	114	.266	.345	0	—	0	8	12	-3	0.9
1984	Min-A	5	11	.313	25	21	3	0	0	137	156	15	41	49	13.0	4.47	94	.285	.336	0	—	0	-7	-4	-2	-0.8
1985	Min-A	9	12	.429	29	26	6	0	0	160²	164	28	59	74	12.5	4.99	88	.272	.337	0	—	0	-15	-10	1	-1.2
1986	Cle-A☆	14	7	.667	34	33	3	1	0	206	217	34	49	87	12.1	4.54	91	.271	.322	0	—	0	-8	-9	-3	-1.1
1987	Cle-A	6	13	.316	32	29	4	1	0	153²	185	24	57	61	14.3	6.50	70	.298	.360	0	—	0	-35	-34	-2	-3.6
Total	7	51	51	.500	176	137	22	3	1	900	963	125	320	372	13.1	4.81	89	.276	.342	0	—	0	-65	-51	-10	-6.5

● **RON SCHUELER**   Schueler, Ronald Richard   b: 4/18/48, Catharine, Kan.   BR/TR, 6'4", 205 lbs.   Deb: 4/16/72   C

YEAR	TM/L	W	L	PCT	G	GS	CG	SH	SV	IP	H	HR	BB	SO	RAT	ERA	ERA+	OAV	OOB	BH	AVG	PB	PR	/A	PD	TPI
1972	Atl-N	5	8	.385	37	18	3	0	2	144²	122	16	60	96	11.4	3.67	103	.227	.307	8	.190	0	-3	2	-1	0.1
1973	Atl-N	8	7	.533	39	20	4	2	2	186	179	24	66	124	11.9	3.87	102	.255	.319	11	.177	-1	-4	1	-1	-0.1
1974	Phi-N	11	16	.407	44	27	5	0	1	203¹	202	17	98	109	13.5	3.72	102	.264	.351	6	.118	-2	-2	1	-2	-0.4
1975	Phi-N	4	4	.500	46	6	1	0	0	92²	88	6	40	69	12.5	5.24	71	.258	.338	2	.154	-0	-17	-16	1	-1.2
1976	Phi-N	1	0	1.000	35	0	0	0	3	49²	44	4	16	43	11.2	2.90	122	.243	.312	0	.000	0	3	4	-1	0.2
1977	Min-A	8	7	.533	52	7	0	0	3	134²	131	16	61	93	13.2	4.41	90	.260	.347	0	—	0	-5	-6	2	-0.4
1978	Chi-A	3	5	.375	30	7	0	0	0	81²	76	10	39	39	13.4	4.30	88	.251	.350	0	—	0	-5	-5	-0	-0.4
1979	Chi-A	0	1	.000	8	1	0	0	0	19²	19	3	13	6	15.6	7.32	58	.264	.391	0	—	0	-7	-7	-0	-0.3
Total	8	40	48	.455	291	86	13	2	11	912¹	861	96	393	563	12.6	4.08	94	.253	.334	27	.159	-3	-40	-25	-2	-2.7

● **DAVE SCHULER**   Schuler, David Paul   b: 10/4/53, Framingham, Mass.   BR/TL, 6'4", 210 lbs.   Deb: 9/17/79

YEAR	TM/L	W	L	PCT	G	GS	CG	SH	SV	IP	H	HR	BB	SO	RAT	ERA	ERA+	OAV	OOB	BH	AVG	PB	PR	/A	PD	TPI
1979	Cal-A	0	0	—	1	0	0	0	0	1²	2	1	0	0	10.8	10.80	38	.333	.333	0	—	0	-1	-1	-0	0.2
1980	Cal-A	0	1	.000	8	0	0	0	0	12²	13	3	2	7	10.7	3.55	111	.271	.300	0	—	0	1	1	-0	0.00
1985	Atl-N	0	0	—	9	0	0	0	0	10²	19	4	3	10	18.6	6.75	57	.404	.440	0	—	0	-4	-3	-0	0.0
Total	3	0	1	.000	18	0	0	0	0	25	34	8	5	17	14.0	5.40	72	.337	.368	0	—	0	-4	-4	-1	0.2

● **ERIK SCHULLSTROM**   Schullstrom, Erik Paul   b: 3/25/69, San Diego, Cal.   BR/TR, 6'5", 220 lbs.   Deb: 7/18/94

YEAR	TM/L	W	L	PCT	G	GS	CG	SH	SV	IP	H	HR	BB	SO	RAT	ERA	ERA+	OAV	OOB	BH	AVG	PB	PR	/A	PD	TPI
1994	Min-A	0	0	—	9	0	0	0	1	13	13	0	5	13	13.2	2.77	175	.260	.339	0	—	0	3	3	0	0.0

● **BUDDY SCHULTZ**   Schultz, Charles Budd   b: 9/19/50, Cleveland, Ohio   BR/TL, 6', 175 lbs.   Deb: 9/3/75

YEAR	TM/L	W	L	PCT	G	GS	CG	SH	SV	IP	H	HR	BB	SO	RAT	ERA	ERA+	OAV	OOB	BH	AVG	PB	PR	/A	PD	TPI
1975	Chi-N	2	0	1.000	6	0	0	0	0	5²	11	0	5	4	25.4	6.35	60	.367	.457	0	—	0	-2	-2	-0	-0.5
1976	Chi-N	1	1	.500	29	0	0	0	2	23²	37	3	9	15	17.5	6.08	63	.356	.407	0	.000	-0	-7	-6	1	-0.6
1977	StL-N	6	1	.857	40	3	0	0	1	85¹	76	5	24	66	10.5	2.32	166	.245	.299	2	.167	0	15	14	-1	1.1
1978	StL-N	2	4	.333	62	0	0	0	6	83	68	4	36	70	11.3	3.80	93	.226	.309	1	.200	1	-2	-3	-1	-0.2
1979	StL-N	4	3	.571	31	0	0	0	3	42¹	40	7	14	38	11.5	4.46	84	.256	.318	0	.000	-0	-3	-3	-0	-0.6
Total	5	15	9	.625	168	3	0	0	12	240	232	21	88	193	12.0	3.68	101	.257	.324	3	.120	0	1	1	-1	-0.8

● **BARNEY SCHULTZ**   Schultz, George Warren   b: 8/15/26, Beverly, N.J.   BR/TR, 6'2", 200 lbs.   Deb: 4/12/55   C

YEAR	TM/L	W	L	PCT	G	GS	CG	SH	SV	IP	H	HR	BB	SO	RAT	ERA	ERA+	OAV	OOB	BH	AVG	PB	PR	/A	PD	TPI
1955	StL-N	1	2	.333	19	0	0	0	4	29²	25	5	19	14.3	7.89	52	.259	.370	0	.000	-1	-13	-13	1	-1.4	
1959	Det-A	1	2	.333	13	0	0	0	0	18¹	17	1	14	17	15.7	4.42	92	.254	.390	2	1.000	1	-1	-1	-0	0.0
1961	Chi-N	7	6	.538	41	0	0	0	7	66²	57	6	25	59	11.6	2.70	155	.228	.308	1	.100	-1	10	11	-0	2.1
1962	Chi-N	5	5	.500	51	0	0	0	5	77²	66	7	23	58	10.8	3.82	108	.231	.297	0	.000	-0	1	3	0	0.3
1963	Chi-N	1	0	1.000	15	0	0	0	0	27¹	25	5	9	18	11.2	3.62	97	.263	.327	0	—	0	-1	-0	-0	0.0
	StL-N	2	0	1.000	24	0	0	0	0	35¹	36	5	8	26	11.7	3.57	99	.263	.313	0	—	0	-0	-0	-0	0.0
	Yr	3	0	1.000	39	0	0	0	0	62²	61	10	17	44	11.5	3.59	98	.263	.319	0	.000	-0	-1	-0	-0	0.0
1964	*StL-N	1	3	.250	30	0	0	0	14	49¹	35	1	11	29	8.4	1.64	232	.201	.249	1	.167	0	10	12	-1	1.7
1965	StL-N	2	2	.500	34	0	0	0	0	42¹	39	8	11	38	10.6	3.83	100	.242	.291	0	.000	-0	-1	-0	0	0.0
Total	7	20	20	.500	227	0	0	0	35	346²	303	38	116	264	11.3	3.63	109	.237	.308	4	.121	-1	4	12	-0	2.7

● **BOB SCHULTZ**   Schultz, Robert Duffy   b: 11/27/23, Louisville, Ky.   d: 3/31/79, Nashville, Tenn.   BR/TL, 6'3", 200 lbs.   Deb: 4/20/51

YEAR	TM/L	W	L	PCT	G	GS	CG	SH	SV	IP	H	HR	BB	SO	RAT	ERA	ERA+	OAV	OOB	BH	AVG	PB	PR	/A	PD	TPI
1951	Chi-N	3	6	.333	17	10	2	0	0	77¹	75	9	51	27	14.9	5.24	78	.251	.364	4	.138	-1	-11	-10	-1	-1.2
1952	Chi-N	6	3	.667	29	5	1	0	0	74	63	9	31	41	14.1	4.01	96	.232	.357	4	.222	-0	-2	-1	-2	-0.3
1953	Chi-N	0	2	.000	7	2	0	0	0	11²	13	2	11	4	19.3	5.40	82	.289	.439	0	.000	-0	-1	-1	-0	-0.3
	Pit-N	0	2	.000	11	2	0	0	0	18²	26	3	10	5	18.3	8.20	55	.321	.409	0	—	0	-8	-8	-0	-0.7
	Yr	0	4	.000	18	4	0	0	0	30¹	39	5	21	9	18.4	7.12	63	.307	.413	0	.000	-0	-10	-9	-1	-1.0

YEAR TM/L	W	L	PCT	G	GS	CG	SH	SV	IP	H	HR	BB	SO	RAT	ERA	ERA+	OAV	OOB	BH	AVG	PB	PR	/A	PD	TPI
1955 Det-A	0	0	—	1	0	0	0	0	1¹	2	0	2	0	27.0	20.25	19	.333	.500	0	—	0	-2	-2	-0	0.0
Total 4	9	13	.409	65	19	3	0	0	183	179	17	125	67	15.3	5.16	79	.255	.372	8	.154	-1	-25	-23	-4	-2.5

● WEBB SCHULTZ   Schultz, Webb Carl b: 1/31/1898, Wautoma, Wis. d: 7/26/86, Delavan, Wis. BR/TR, 5'11", 172 lbs. Deb: 8/3/24

YEAR TM/L	W	L	PCT	G	GS	CG	SH	SV	IP	H	HR	BB	SO	RAT	ERA	ERA+	OAV	OOB	BH	AVG	PB	PR	/A	PD	TPI
1924 Chi-A	0	0	—	1	0	0	0	0	1	1	0	0	0	9.0	9.00	46	.250	.250	0	—	0	-1	-1	-0	0.0

● MIKE SCHULTZ   Schultz, William Michael b: 12/17/20, Syracuse, N.Y. BL/TL, 6'1", 175 lbs. Deb: 4/20/47

| 1947 Cin-N | 0 | 0 | — | 1 | 0 | 0 | 0 | 0 | 2 | 4 | 0 | 2 | 0 | 27.0 | 4.50 | 91 | .444 | .545 | 0 | — | 0 | -0 | -0 | -0 | 0.0 |

● JOHN SCHULTZE   Schultze, John F. b: Burlington, N.J. 6'0.5", 165 lbs. Deb: 5/6/1891

| 1891 Phi-N | 0 | 1 | .000 | 6 | 1 | 0 | 0 | 0 | 15 | 18 | 1 | 11 | 4 | 17.4 | 6.60 | 52 | .286 | .393 | 1 | .167 | — | -5 | -5 | -1 | -0.3 |

● AL SCHULZ   Schulz, Albert Christopher b: 5/12/1889, Toledo, Ohio d: 12/13/31, Gallipolis, Ohio BR/TL, 6', 182 lbs. Deb: 9/25/12

1912 NY-A	1	1	.500	3	1	1	0	0	16¹	11	0	11	8	12.1	2.20	163	.183	.310	0	.000	-0	2	3	1	0.3
1913 NY-A	7	13	.350	38	22	9	0	0	193	197	4	69	77	12.6	3.73	80	.266	.333	11	.175	-4	-17	-16	-1	-1.6
1914 NY-A	1	3	.250	6	4	1	0	0	28¹	27	0	10	18	12.4	4.76	58	.237	.310	0	.000	—	-6	-6	1	-0.8
Buf-F	9	12	.429	27	23	10	0	2	171	160	3	77	87	12.6	3.37	88	.259	.343	10	.179	-1	-9	-8	2	-0.8
1915 Buf-F	21	14	.600	42	38	25	5	0	309²	264	8	149	160	12.2	3.08	91	.238	.332	18	.165	-4	-12	-10	1	-1.3
1916 Cin-N	8	19	.296	44	22	10	0	2	215	208	4	93	95	12.8	3.14	85	.268	.350	8	.125	-3	-12	-13	0	-2.0
Total 5	47	62	.431	160	110	56	5	4	933¹	867	19	409	445	12.5	3.32	85	.254	.337	47	.155	-9	-55	-50	3	-6.2

● WALT SCHULZ   Schulz, Walter Frederick b: 4/16/1900, St.Louis, Mo. d: 2/27/28, Prescott, Ark. BR/TR, 6', 170 lbs. Deb: 9/24/20

| 1920 StL-N | 0 | 0 | — | 2 | 0 | 0 | 0 | 0 | 6 | 10 | 1 | 2 | 0 | 18.0 | 6.00 | 50 | .370 | .414 | 0 | .000 | -0 | -2 | -2 | 0 | 0.0 |

● DON SCHULZE   Schulze, Donald Arthur b: 9/27/62, Roselle, Ill. BR/TR, 6'3", 225 lbs. Deb: 9/13/83

1983 Chi-N	0	1	.000	4	3	0	0	0	14	19	1	7	8	17.4	7.07	54	.322	.403	0	.000	0	-5	-5	0	-0.3
1984 Chi-N	0	0	—	1	1	0	0	0	3	8	0	1	2	27.0	12.00	33	.571	.600	0	—	0	-3	-3	0	0.0
Cle-A	3	6	.333	19	14	2	0	0	85²	105	9	27	39	13.9	4.83	85	.302	.352	0	—	0	-8	-7	-0	-0.7
1985 Cle-A	4	10	.286	19	18	1	0	0	94¹	128	10	19	37	14.4	6.01	69	.322	.360	0	—	0	-20	-20	1	-2.4
1986 Cle-A	4	4	.500	19	13	1	0	0	84²	88	9	34	33	13.5	5.00	83	.266	.343	0	—	0	-8	-8	-1	-0.7
1987 NY-N	1	2	.333	5	4	0	0	0	21²	24	4	6	5	12.9	6.23	61	.296	.352	0	.000	—	-5	-6	1	-0.6
1989 NY-A	1	1	.500	2	2	0	0	0	11	12	1	5	5	14.7	4.09	95	.300	.391	0	—	-0	-0	-0	-0	-0.1
SD-N	2	1	.667	7	4	0	0	0	24¹	38	6	6	15	16.3	5.55	63	.352	.386	0	.000	-0	-6	-6	1	-0.6
Total 6	15	25	.375	76	59	4	0	0	338²	422	40	105	144	14.3	5.47	74	.306	.361	0	—	-0	-54	-54	1	-5.4

● HAL SCHUMACHER   Schumacher, Harold Henry "Prince Hal" b: 11/23/10, Hinckley, N.Y. d: 4/21/93, Cooperstown, N.Y. BR/TR, 6', 190 lbs. Deb: 4/15/31

1931 NY-N	1	1	.500	8	2	1	0	1	18¹	31	3	14	11	22.1	10.80	34	.387	.479	1	.143	-0	-14	-14	1	-1.4
1932 NY-N	5	6	.455	27	13	2	1	0	101¹	119	3	39	38	14.2	3.55	104	.288	.352	7	.226	1	4	2	2	0.5
1933 *NY-N☆	19	12	.613	35	33	21	7	1	258²	199	9	84	96	9.9	2.16	149	**.214**	.280	21	.214	1	34	30	3	4.2
1934 NY-N	23	10	.697	41	36	18	2	0	297	299	16	89	112	11.8	3.18	122	.259	.313	28	.239	10	29	23	3	3.5
1935 NY-N★	19	9	.679	33	33	19	3	0	261²	235	11	70	79	10.7	2.89	133	.238	.292	21	.196	2	33	28	7	3.7
1936 *NY-N	11	13	.458	35	30	9	3	1	215¹	234	15	69	75	12.7	3.47	112	.280	.336	16	.216	2	13	10	4	1.6
1937 *NY-N	13	12	.520	38	29	10	1	1	217²	222	11	89	100	12.9	3.60	108	.264	.335	18	.222	3	8	7	1	1.1
1938 NY-N	13	8	.619	28	28	12	3	0	185	178	12	50	54	11.2	3.50	108	.248	.299	16	.239	4	6	5	2	1.2
1939 NY-N	13	10	.565	29	27	8	0	0	181²	199	14	89	58	14.4	4.81	82	.276	.358	14	.203	1	-18	-18	0	-1.9
1940 NY-N	13	13	.500	34	30	12	1	1	227	218	14	96	123	12.4	3.25	119	.251	.325	15	.192	2	15	16	4	2.4
1941 NY-N	12	10	.545	30	26	12	1	0	206	187	11	79	63	11.8	3.36	110	.243	.317	10	.152	-1	6	8	-1	0.6
1942 NY-N	12	13	.480	29	29	12	3	0	216	208	12	82	49	12.2	3.04	111	.251	.321	13	.173	1	7	8	2	1.2
1946 NY-N	4	4	.500	24	13	2	0	1	96²	95	8	52	48	13.7	3.91	88	.255	.347	1	.038	-2	-5	-5	3	-0.4
Total 13	158	121	.566	391	329	138	27	7	2482¹	2424	139	902	906	12.1	3.36	111	.255	.321	181	.202	24	117	100	30	16.3

● HACK SCHUMANN   Schumann, Carl J. b: 8/13/1884, Buffalo, N.Y. d: 3/25/46, Mill Grove, N.Y. TR, 6'2", 230 lbs. Deb: 9/19/06

| 1906 Phi-A | 0 | 2 | .000 | 4 | 2 | 1 | 0 | 0 | 18 | 21 | 0 | 8 | 9 | 15.5 | 4.00 | 68 | .294 | .381 | 0 | .000 | -1 | -3 | -3 | -0 | -0.4 |

● FERDIE SCHUPP   Schupp, Ferdinand Maurice b: 1/16/1891, Louisville, Ky. d: 12/16/71, Los Angeles, Cal. BR/TR, 5'10", 150 lbs. Deb: 4/19/13

1913 NY-N	0	0	—	5	1	0	0	0	12	10	0	3	2	9.8	0.75	416	.244	.295	1	.333	1	3	3	-0	0.1
1914 NY-N	0	0	—	8	0	0	0	1	17	19	0	9	9	15.9	5.82	46	.306	.411	0	.000	-0	-6	-6	-0	-0.1
1915 NY-N	1	0	1.000	23	1	0	0	0	54²	57	1	29	28	14.7	5.10	50	.281	.379	2	.200	1	-14	-15	0	-0.2
1916 NY-N	9	3	.750	30	11	8	4	1	140¹	79	1	37	86	7.8	0.90	271	.167	.235	4	.098	-2	27	24	-3	1.6
1917 *NY-N	21	7	**.750**	36	32	25	6	0	272	202	7	70	147	9.1	1.95	131	**.209**	.265	15	.161	1	23	18	-3	1.7
1918 NY-N	1	0	1.000	10	2	1	0	0	33¹	42	1	27	22	19.4	7.56	30	.328	.456	1	.111	—	-18	-18	0	-0.6
1919 NY-N	1	3	.250	9	4	0	0	1	32	32	1	18	17	14.1	5.63	50	.269	.365	2	.333	-1	-10	-10	-1	-1.3
StL-N	4	4	.500	10	10	6	0	0	69²	55	2	30	31	11.1	3.75	75	.221	.307	1	.050	-0	-6	-7	-1	-0.9
Yr	5	7	.417	19	14	6	0	1	101²	87	4	48	54	12.0	4.34	64	.236	.326	3	.115	-1	-16	-17	-2	-2.2
1920 StL-N	16	13	.552	38	37	17	0	0	250²	246	5	127	119	13.7	3.52	85	.265	.358	22	.256	6	-11	-15	-2	-1.3
1921 StL-N	2	0	1.000	9	4	1	0	1	37¹	42	5	21	22	15.7	4.10	89	.276	.371	4	.286	1	-1	-2	-0	-0.1
Bro-N	3	4	.429	20	7	1	0	2	61	75	2	27	26	15.3	4.57	85	.310	.384	1	.083	-1	-5	-5	-0	-0.6
Yr	5	4	.556	29	11	2	0	3	98¹	117	7	48	48	15.3	4.39	87	.295	.374	5	.192	-0	-7	-6	-0	-0.7
1922 Chi-A	4	4	.500	18	12	3	1	0	74	79	4	66	38	17.9	6.08	67	.284	.425	5	.217	1	-17	-17	-0	-1.5
Total 10	61	39	.610	216	121	62	11	6	1054	938	30	464	553	12.3	3.32	87	.244	.331	58	.182	-5	-35	-51	-10	-3.2

● WAYNE SCHURR   Schurr, Wayne Allen b: 8/6/37, Garrett, Ind. BR/TR, 6'4", 185 lbs. Deb: 4/15/64

| 1964 Chi-N | 0 | 0 | — | 26 | 0 | 0 | 0 | 0 | 48¹ | 57 | 3 | 11 | 29 | 12.7 | 3.72 | 100 | .298 | .337 | 0 | .000 | -0 | -1 | -0 | -0 | -0.1 |

● MIKE SCHWABE   Schwabe, Michael Scott b: 7/12/64, Ft.Dodge, Iowa BR/TR, 6'4", 200 lbs. Deb: 5/27/89

1989 Det-A	2	4	.333	13	14	0	0	0	44²	58	6	16	13	15.1	6.04	63	.307	.364	0	—	0	-11	-11	1	-1.2
1990 Det-A	0	0	—	1	0	0	0	0	3²	5	0	1	1	12.3	2.45	161	.357	.357	0	—	0	1	1	0	0.0
Total 2	2	4	.333	14	4	0	0	0	48¹	63	6	16	14	14.9	5.77	66	.310	.364	0	—	0	-10	-10	1	-1.2

● DON SCHWALL   Schwall, Donald Bernard b: 3/2/36, Wilkes-Barre, Pa. BR/TR, 6'6", 200 lbs. Deb: 5/21/61

1961 Bos-A★	15	7	.682	25	25	10	2	0	178²	167	8	110	91	14.3	3.22	129	.255	.368	11	.180	-0	16	19	1	2.2
1962 Bos-A	9	15	.375	33	32	5	1	0	182¹	180	18	121	89	15.4	4.94	84	.260	.378	9	.136	-2	-20	-16	0	-2.1
1963 Pit-N	6	12	.333	33	24	3	2	0	167²	158	13	74	86	12.8	3.33	99	.255	.340	8	.160	-0	-1	-1	2	0.1
1964 Pit-N	4	3	.571	15	9	0	0	0	49²	53	1	15	36	12.3	4.35	81	.269	.321	5	.263	-2	-4	-5	0	-0.4
1965 Pit-N	9	6	.600	43	1	0	0	4	77	77	5	30	55	12.7	2.92	120	.269	.343	0	.000	-2	5	5	2	1.0
1966 Pit-N	3	2	.600	11	4	0	0	0	41²	31	3	21	24	11.4	2.16	165	.209	.250	1	.100	-0	7	7	0	0.8
Atl-N	3	3	.500	11	8	0	0	0	45¹	44	2	19	27	12.9	4.37	83	.256	.337	0	.000	-2	-4	-4	0	-0.6
Yr	6	5	.545	22	12	0	0	0	87¹	75	5	40	51	12.1	3.31	109	.234	.322	1	.043	-2	3	3	-0	0.2
1967 Atl-N	0	0	—	1	0	0	0	0	0²	1	0	1	0	13.5	0.00	—	.000	.500	0	—	0	0	0	0	0.0
Total 7	49	48	.505	172	103	18	5	4	743	710	50	391	408	13.7	3.72	102	.257	.354	34	.145	-5	-1	5	4	1.0

● BLACKIE SCHWAMB   Schwamb, Ralph Richard b: 8/6/26, Lancaster, Cal. d: 12/21/89, Los Angeles, Cal. BR/TR, 6'5.5", 198 lbs. Deb: 7/25/48

| 1948 StL-A | 1 | 1 | .500 | 12 | 5 | 0 | 0 | 0 | 31² | 44 | 3 | 21 | 7 | 18.5 | 8.53 | 53 | .331 | .422 | 3 | .300 | -1 | -15 | -14 | 0 | -0.6 |

● JEFF SCHWARZ   Schwarz, Jeffrey William b: 5/20/64, Fort Pierce, Fla. BR/TR, 6'5", 190 lbs. Deb: 4/24/93

| 1993 Chi-A | 2 | 2 | .500 | 41 | 0 | 0 | 0 | 0 | 51 | 35 | 1 | 38 | 41 | 13.4 | 3.71 | 113 | .201 | .353 | 0 | — | 0 | 3 | 3 | -1 | 0.1 |

YEAR TM/L	W	L	PCT	G	GS	CG	SH	SV	IP	H	HR	BB	SO	RAT	ERA	ERA+	OAV	OOB	BH	AVG	PB	PR	/A	PD	TPI
1994 Chi-A	0	0	—	9	0	0	0	0	11¹	9	0	16	14	19.9	6.35	74	.205	.417	0	—	0	-2	-2	0	0.0
Cal-A	0	0	—	4	0	0	0	0	6²	5	0	6	4	14.9	4.05	123	.250	.423	0	—	0	1	1	0	-0.1
Yr	0	0	—	13	0	0	0	0	18	14	0	22	18	18.0	5.50	87	.219	.419	0	—	0	-1	-1	0	-0.1
Total 2	2	2	.500	54	0	0	0	0	69	49	1	60	59	14.6	4.17	104	.206	.372	0	—	0	2	1	-1	0.0

● **RUDY SCHWENCK** Schwenck, Rudolph Christian b: 4/6/1884, Louisville, Ky. d: 11/27/41, Anchorage, Ky. BL/TL, 6', 174 lbs. Deb: 9/23/09

YEAR TM/L	W	L	PCT	G	GS	CG	SH	SV	IP	H	HR	BB	SO	RAT	ERA	ERA+	OAV	OOB	BH	AVG	PB	PR	/A	PD	TPI
1909 Chi-N	1	1	.500	3	2	0	0	0	4	16	0	3	3	45.0	13.50	19	.308	.357	1	.250	0	-5	-5	1	-1.6

● **HAL SCHWENK** Schwenk, Harold Edward b: 8/23/1890, Schuylkill Haven, Pa. d: 9/3/55, Kansas City, Mo. BL/TL, 6', 185 lbs. Deb: 9/4/13

YEAR TM/L	W	L	PCT	G	GS	CG	SH	SV	IP	H	HR	BB	SO	RAT	ERA	ERA+	OAV	OOB	BH	AVG	PB	PR	/A	PD	TPI
1913 StL-A	1	0	1.000	11	1	1	0	0	11	12	0	4	3	13.1	3.27	90	.333	.400	1	.333	1	-0	-0	-0	0.0

● **JIM SCOGGINS** Scoggins, Lynn J. "Lefty" b: 7/19/1891, Killeen, Tex. d: 8/16/23, Columbia, S.C. BL/TL, 5'11", 165 lbs. Deb: 8/26/13

YEAR TM/L	W	L	PCT	G	GS	CG	SH	SV	IP	H	HR	BB	SO	RAT	ERA	ERA+	OAV	OOB	BH	AVG	PB	PR	/A	PD	TPI
1913 Chi-A	0	1	.000	1	1	0	0	0	1	0	0	1	0	9.0	.000		.000	.500	0	—	0	0	0	0	0.0

● **HERB SCORE** Score, Herbert Jude b: 6/7/33, Rosedale, N.Y. BL/TL, 6'2", 185 lbs. Deb: 4/15/55

YEAR TM/L	W	L	PCT	G	GS	CG	SH	SV	IP	H	HR	BB	SO	RAT	ERA	ERA+	OAV	OOB	BH	AVG	PB	PR	/A	PD	TPI
1955 Cle-A☆	16	10	.615	33	32	11	2	0	227¹	158	18	154	**245**	12.4	2.85	140	.194	.323	10	.119	-4	28	29	-4	2.2
1956 Cle-A★	20	9	.690	35	33	16	**5**	0	249¹	162	18	129	**263**	10.6	2.53	166	**.186**	.292	16	.184	1	45	46	-4	4.8
1957 Cle-A	2	1	.667	5	5	3	1	0	36	18	0	26	39	11.3	2.00	186	.149	.304	1	.091	-0	7	7	0	0.5
1958 Cle-A	2	3	.400	12	5	2	1	3	41	29	1	34	48	13.8	3.95	92	.197	.348	1	.091	-0	-1	-1	-3	-0.3
1959 Cle-A	9	11	.450	30	25	9	1	0	160²	123	28	115	147	13.4	4.71	78	**.210**	.341	5	.096	-3	-15	-18	-3	-2.6
1960 Chi-A	5	10	.333	23	22	5	1	0	113²	91	10	87	78	14.3	3.72	102	.226	.366	3	.100	-0	2	1	-1	0.0
1961 Chi-A	1	2	.333	8	5	1	0	0	24¹	22	3	24	14	17.0	6.66	59	.259	.422	0	.000	-1	-7	-7	-0	-0.8
1962 Chi-A	0	0	—	4	0	0	0	0	6	6	1	4	3	15.0	4.50	87	.261	.370	0	—	-0	-0	-0	-0	0.0
Total 8	55	46	.545	150	127	47	11	3	858¹	609	79	573	837	12.5	3.36	117	.200	.328	36	.128	-8	59	55	-12	3.8

● **DICK SCOTT** Scott, Amos Richard b: 2/5/1883, Bethel, Ohio d: 1/18/11, Chicago, Ill. BR/TR, 6', 180 lbs. Deb: 6/26/01

YEAR TM/L	W	L	PCT	G	GS	CG	SH	SV	IP	H	HR	BB	SO	RAT	ERA	ERA+	OAV	OOB	BH	AVG	PB	PR	/A	PD	TPI
1901 Cin-N	0	2	.000	3	3	2	0	0	21	26	2	9	7	16.3	5.14	62	.302	.387	0	.000	-1	-4	-5	-1	-0.5

● **DARRYL SCOTT** Scott, Darryl Nelson b: 8/6/68, Fresno, Cal. BR/TR, 6'1", 185 lbs. Deb: 5/31/93

YEAR TM/L	W	L	PCT	G	GS	CG	SH	SV	IP	H	HR	BB	SO	RAT	ERA	ERA+	OAV	OOB	BH	AVG	PB	PR	/A	PD	TPI
1993 Cal-A	1	2	.333	16	0	0	0	0	20	19	1	11	13	13.9	5.85	77	.250	.352	0	—	0	-3	-3	-1	-0.5

● **ED SCOTT** Scott, Edward b: 8/12/1870, Walbridge, Ohio d: 11/1/33, Toledo, Ohio BR/TR, 6'3", Deb: 4/19/00

YEAR TM/L	W	L	PCT	G	GS	CG	SH	SV	IP	H	HR	BB	SO	RAT	ERA	ERA+	OAV	OOB	BH	AVG	PB	PR	/A	PD	TPI
1900 Cin-N	17	20	.459	42	35	31	0	1	315	370	10	65	87	12.8	3.86	95	.292	.334	19	.154	-5	-6	-6	9	-0.2
1901 Cle-A	6	6	.500	17	16	11	0	1	124²	149	2	38	23	14.0	4.40	81	.293	.350	10	.208	1	-10	-12	2	-0.7
Total 2	23	26	.469	59	51	42	0	2	439²	519	12	103	110	13.2	4.01	91	.292	.338	29	.170	-4	-16	-18	11	-0.9

● **GEORGE SCOTT** Scott, George William b: 11/17/1896, Trenton, Mo. BR/TR, 6'1", 175 lbs. Deb: 9/13/20

YEAR TM/L	W	L	PCT	G	GS	CG	SH	SV	IP	H	HR	BB	SO	RAT	ERA	ERA+	OAV	OOB	BH	AVG	PB	PR	/A	PD	TPI
1920 StL-N	0	0	—	2	0	0	0	0	6	4	0	3	1	10.5	4.50	66	.200	.304	0	.000	-0	-1	-1	-0	-0.1

● **JIM SCOTT** Scott, James "Death Valley Jim" b: 4/23/1888, Deadwood, S.Dak. d: 4/7/57, Jacumba, Cal. BR/TR, 6'1", 235 lbs. Deb: 4/25/09

YEAR TM/L	W	L	PCT	G	GS	CG	SH	SV	IP	H	HR	BB	SO	RAT	ERA	ERA+	OAV	OOB	BH	AVG	PB	PR	/A	PD	TPI
1909 Chi-A	12	12	.500	36	29	20	4	0	250¹	194	0	93	135	10.9	2.30	102	.223	.310	9	.106	-1	5	1	-1	-0.2
1910 Chi-A	8	18	.308	41	23	14	2	1	229²	182	5	86	135	10.7	2.43	99	.226	.303	15	.203	2	2	-1	3	0.4
1911 Chi-A	14	11	.560	39	26	13	3	0	222	195	3	81	128	11.4	2.39	135	.240	.311	11	.155	-2	24	21	-4	1.5
1912 Chi-A	2	2	.500	6	4	2	1	0	37²	36	0	15	23	12.4	2.15	149	.265	.342	0	.000	-2	5	4	-0	0.2
1913 Chi-A	20	20	.500	48	38	25	4	1	312¹	252	2	86	158	10.0	1.90	154	.221	.281	7	.072	-7	36	36	3	3.8
1914 Chi-A	14	18	.438	43	33	12	2	1	253¹	228	5	75	138	10.9	2.84	94	.246	.306	14	.163	-0	-3	-4	3	-0.4
1915 Chi-A	24	11	.686	48	35	23	**7**	2	296¹	256	3	78	120	10.3	2.03	146	.238	.292	12	.126	-5	30	31	2	3.4
1916 Chi-A	7	14	.333	32	21	8	1	3	165¹	155	3	53	71	11.5	2.72	101	.258	.321	6	.115	-3	2	1	-1	-0.4
1917 Chi-A	6	7	.462	24	17	6	1	1	125	126	0	42	37	12.5	1.87	142	.272	.341	5	.119	-2	11	11	0	1.0
Total 9	107	113	.486	317	226	123	26	9	1892	1624	21	609	945	10.9	2.30	120	.238	.305	79	.129	-21	111	99	3	9.3

● **JACK SCOTT** Scott, John William b: 4/18/1892, Ridgeway, N.C. d: 11/30/59, Durham, N.C. BL/TR, 6'2.5", 199 lbs. Deb: 9/6/16

YEAR TM/L	W	L	PCT	G	GS	CG	SH	SV	IP	H	HR	BB	SO	RAT	ERA	ERA+	OAV	OOB	BH	AVG	PB	PR	/A	PD	TPI
1916 Pit-N	0	0	—	1	0	0	0	0	5	5	3	4	4	14.4	10.80	25	.278	.381	0	.000	-0	-5	-5	0	0.0
1917 Bos-N	1	2	.333	7	3	3	0	0	39²	36	0	5	21	10.0	1.82	141	.255	.295	2	.125	-1	4	3	-1	0.1
1919 Bos-N	6	6	.500	19	12	7	0	1	103²	109	3	39	44	12.9	3.13	91	.275	.341	7	.175	-1	-2	-3	-3	-0.7
1920 Bos-N	10	21	.323	44	33	22	3	1	291	308	6	85	94	12.6	3.53	87	.277	.336	21	.212	0	-13	-15	-4	-2.0
1921 Bos-N	15	13	.536	**47**	29	16	2	3	233²	258	9	57	83	12.4	3.70	99	.283	.330	30	.341	10	2	-1	-1	0.7
1922 Cin-N	0	0	—	1	0	0	0	0	1	2	0	1	0	27.0	9.00	44	.500	.600	0	.000	-0	-1	-1	-0	0.0
*NY-N	8	2	.800	17	10	5	0	2	79²	83	7	23	37	12.2	4.41	91	.265	.320	1	.267	1	-3	-4	-0	-0.4
Yr	8	2	.800	18	10	5	0	2	80²	85	7	24	37	12.4	4.46	90	.268	.324	1	.258	1	-3	-4	-1	-0.4
1923 *NY-N	16	7	.696	40	25	9	3	1	220	223	15	65	79	11.9	3.89	98	.267	.323	25	.316	7	-3	-2	-2	0.3
1925 NY-N	14	15	.483	36	28	18	2	3	239²	251	10	55	87	11.6	3.15	128	.269	.313	21	.241	6	30	24	2	3.3
1926 NY-N	13	15	.464	**50**	22	13	0	5	226	242	13	53	82	11.9	4.34	86	.276	.319	28	.337	9	-13	-15	-1	-0.9
1927 Phi-N	9	21	.300	**48**	25	17	1	1	233¹	304	15	69	69	14.5	5.09	81	.330	.379	33	.289	8	-30	-25	-0	-2.0
1928 NY-N	4	1	.800	16	3	3	0	1	50¹	59	3	11	17	12.9	3.58	109	.295	.338	4	.267	1	2	2	0	0.3
1929 NY-N	7	6	.538	30	6	2	0	1	91²	89	12	42	40	11.4	3.53	130	.260	.314	8	.308	3	12	11	1	1.6
Total 12	103	109	.486	356	196	115	11	19	1814²	1969	94	493	657	12.4	3.85	96	.281	.332	187	.275	44	-13	-30	-9	0.3

● **LEFTY SCOTT** Scott, Marshall b: 7/15/15, Roswell, N.Mex. d: 3/3/64, Houston, Tex. BR/TL, 6'0.5", 165 lbs. Deb: 6/15/45

YEAR TM/L	W	L	PCT	G	GS	CG	SH	SV	IP	H	HR	BB	SO	RAT	ERA	ERA+	OAV	OOB	BH	AVG	PB	PR	/A	PD	TPI
1945 Phi-N	0	2	.000	8	2	0	0	0	22¹	29	1	12	5	16.5	4.43	86	.312	.390	0	.000	-0	-2	-1	-1	-0.2

● **MIKE SCOTT** Scott, Michael Warren b: 4/26/55, Santa Monica, Cal. BR/TR, 6'3", 215 lbs. Deb: 4/18/79

YEAR TM/L	W	L	PCT	G	GS	CG	SH	SV	IP	H	HR	BB	SO	RAT	ERA	ERA+	OAV	OOB	BH	AVG	PB	PR	/A	PD	TPI
1979 NY-N	1	3	.250	18	9	0	0	0	52¹	59	4	20	21	13.6	5.33	68	.289	.353	0	.000	-1	-9	-10	-0	-0.8
1980 NY-N	1	1	.500	6	6	1	0	0	29¹	40	1	8	13	14.7	4.30	83	.331	.372	1	.111	0	-2	-2	-0	-0.1
1981 NY-N	5	10	.333	23	23	1	0	0	136	130	11	34	54	10.9	3.90	89	.261	.309	3	.073	-2	-6	-6	3	-0.5
1982 NY-N	7	13	.350	37	22	1	0	3	147	185	13	60	63	15.1	5.14	71	.321	.387	7	.146	0	-25	-25	4	-2.8
1983 Hou-N	10	6	.625	24	24	2	2	0	145	143	8	46	73	12.0	3.72	91	.258	.320	6	.167	1	-2	-5	-0	-0.4
1984 Hou-N	5	11	.313	31	29	0	0	0	154	179	7	43	83	13.1	4.68	71	.293	.343	6	.128	-0	-19	-23	-2	-2.2
1985 Hou-N	18	8	.692	36	35	4	2	0	221²	194	20	80	137	11.2	3.29	105	.235	.304	11	.153	2	7	4	-2	0.6
1986 *Hou-N★	18	10	.643	37	37	7	**5**	0	275¹	182	17	72	**306**	8.4	2.22	162	**.186**	**.244**	12	.126	-2	46	42	2	4.3
1987 Hou-N★	16	13	.552	36	36	8	3	0	247²	199	21	79	233	10.2	3.23	121	.217	**.282**	10	.125	-1	23	19	0	1.9
1988 Hou-N	14	8	.636	32	32	8	5	0	218²	162	19	53	190	9.2	2.92	114	.204	.261	6	.085	-3	13	10	-1	0.6
1989 Hou-N†	**20**	10	.667	33	32	9	2	0	229	180	23	62	172	9.6	3.10	109	.212	.268	10	.133	-0	10	7	-2	0.6
1990 Hou-N	9	13	.409	32	32	4	0	0	205²	194	27	66	121	11.4	3.81	98	.260	.305	7	.130	-0	-7	-8	-2	-1.3
1991 Hou-N	0	2	.000	2	2	0	0	0	7	11	2	4	3	20.6	12.86	27	.367	.457	0	.000	-0	-7	-7	-0	-1.3
Total 13	124	108	.534	347	319	45	22	3	2068²	1858	173	627	1469	11.0	3.54	100	.240	.300	81	.124	-6	28	1	3	-0.5

● **MILT SCOTT** Scott, Milton Parker "Mikado Milt" b: 1/17/1866, Chicago, Ill. d: 11/3/38, Baltimore, Md. BR, 5'9", 160 lbs. Deb: 9/30/1882 ♦

YEAR TM/L	W	L	PCT	G	GS	CG	SH	SV	IP	H	HR	BB	SO	RAT	ERA	ERA+	OAV	OOB	BH	AVG	PB	PR	/A	PD	TPI
1886 Bal-a	0	0	—	1	0	0	0	0	3	2	0	2	0	15.0	3.00	114	.125	.263	92	.190	-0	0	-0	-0	0.0

● **MICKEY SCOTT** Scott, Ralph Robert b: 7/25/47, Weimar, Germany BL/TL, 6'1", 165 lbs. Deb: 5/6/72

YEAR TM/L	W	L	PCT	G	GS	CG	SH	SV	IP	H	HR	BB	SO	RAT	ERA	ERA+	OAV	OOB	BH	AVG	PB	PR	/A	PD	TPI
1972 Bal-A	0	1	.000	15	0	0	0	0	23	23	2	5	11	11.3	2.74	112	.277	.326	0	.000	1	1	1	-0	0.1
1973 Bal-A	0	0	—	1	0	0	0	0	1²	3	0	1	2	21.6	5.40	69	.286	.444	0	—	0	-0	-0	-0	0.0
Mon-N	1	2	.333	22	0	0	0	0	24	27	3	9	11	14.3	5.25	73	.287	.362	0	.000	-0	-4	-4	-0	-0.5
1975 Cal-A	4	2	.667	50	0	0	0	3	68¹	59	8	18	31	10.3	3.29	108	.233	.287	0	—	0	4	2	-1	0.7
1976 Cal-A	3	0	1.000	33	0	0	0	3	39	47	3	12	10	13.6	3.23	103	.307	.358	0	—	0	1	0	-0	0.0

YEAR TM/L	W	L	PCT	G	GS	CG	SH	SV	IP	H	HR	BB	SO	RAT	ERA	ERA+	OAV	OOB	BH	AVG	PB	PR	/A	PD	TPI
1977 Cal-A	0	2	.000	12	0	0	0	0	16	19	1	4	5	12.9	5.63	70	.302	.343	0	—	0	-3	-3	-0	-0.2
Total 5	8	7	.533	133	0	0	0	4	172	177	18	50	70	12.1	3.72	94	.271	.327	0	.000	0	-2	-4	-1	0.2

● **DICK SCOTT**   Scott, Richard Lewis b: 3/15/33, Portsmouth, N.H.   BR/TL, 6'2", 185 lbs.   Deb: 5/8/63

YEAR TM/L	W	L	PCT	G	GS	CG	SH	SV	IP	H	HR	BB	SO	RAT	ERA	ERA+	OAV	OOB	BH	AVG	PB	PR	/A	PD	TPI
1963 LA-N	0	0	—	9	0	0	0	2	12	17	6	3	6	15.0	6.75	45	.340	.377	0	—	0	-5	-5	0	-0.2
1964 Chi-N	0	0	—	3	0	0	0	0	4¹	10	2	1	1	22.8	12.46	30	.417	.440	0	—	0	-4	-4	0	0.0
Total 2	0	0	—	12	0	0	0	2	16¹	27	8	4	7	17.1	8.27	39	.365	.397	0	—	0	-9	-9	0	-0.2

● **TIM SCOTT**   Scott, Timothy Dale b: 11/16/66, Hanford, Cal.   BR/TR, 6'2", 185 lbs.   Deb: 6/25/91

YEAR TM/L	W	L	PCT	G	GS	CG	SH	SV	IP	H	HR	BB	SO	RAT	ERA	ERA+	OAV	OOB	BH	AVG	PB	PR	/A	PD	TPI
1991 SD-N	0	0	—	2	0	0	0	0	1	2	0	0	1	18.0	9.00	42	.400	.400	0	—	0	-1	-1	-0	-0.1
1992 SD-N	4	1	.800	34	0	0	0	0	37²	39	4	21	30	14.6	5.26	68	.267	.363	0	—	0	-7	-7	-1	-0.9
1993 SD-N	2	0	1.000	24	0	0	0	0	37²	38	1	15	30	13.6	2.39	173	.260	.345	0	.000	-0	7	7	0	0.3
Mon-N	5	2	.714	32	0	0	0	0	34	31	3	19	35	13.2	3.71	113	.242	.340	0	.000	-0	1	2	-0	0.3
Yr	7	2	.778	56	0	0	0	0	71²	69	4	34	65	13.2	3.01	138	.246	.328	0	.000	-0	8	9	0	0.6
1994 Mon-N	5	2	.714	40	0	0	0	1	53¹	51	0	18	37	12.0	2.70	157	.251	.318	0	.000	-0	9	9	-2	0.9
Total 4	16	5	.762	132	0	0	0	2	163²	161	8	73	133	13.3	3.46	117	.256	.340	0	.000	-1	9	11	-3	0.6

● **SCOTT SCUDDER**   Scudder, William Scott b: 2/14/68, Paris, Tex.   BR/TR, 6'2", 180 lbs.   Deb: 6/6/89

YEAR TM/L	W	L	PCT	G	GS	CG	SH	SV	IP	H	HR	BB	SO	RAT	ERA	ERA+	OAV	OOB	BH	AVG	PB	PR	/A	PD	TPI
1989 Cin-N	4	9	.308	23	17	0	0	0	100¹	91	14	61	66	13.7	4.49	80	.239	.346	4	.167	1	-11	-10	-1	-1.2
1990 *Cin-N	5	5	.500	21	10	0	0	0	71²	74	12	30	42	13.4	4.90	81	.265	.343	1	.056	-1	-9	-8	-1	-1.1
1991 Cin-N	6	9	.400	27	14	0	0	0	101¹	91	6	56	51	13.6	4.35	87	.246	.354	3	.103	-0	-8	-6	-1	-1.0
1992 Cle-A	6	10	.375	23	22	0	0	0	109	134	10	55	66	15.8	5.28	74	.303	.383	0	—	0	-16	-17	-2	-2.1
1993 Cle-A	0	1	.000	2	1	0	0	0	4	5	0	4	1	22.5	9.00	44	.333	.500	0	—	0	-2	-2	-0	-0.4
Total 5	21	34	.382	96	64	0	0	0	386¹	395	42	206	226	14.3	4.80	79	.266	.360	8	.113	-0	-46	-42	-3	-5.8

● **ROD SCURRY**   Scurry, Rodney Grant b: 3/17/56, Sacramento, Cal. d: 11/5/92, Reno, Nev.   BL/TL, 6'2", 180 lbs.   Deb: 4/17/80

YEAR TM/L	W	L	PCT	G	GS	CG	SH	SV	IP	H	HR	BB	SO	RAT	ERA	ERA+	OAV	OOB	BH	AVG	PB	PR	/A	PD	TPI
1980 Pit-N	0	2	.000	20	0	0	0	0	37²	23	2	17	28	10.0	2.15	169	.176	.280	1	.250	0	6	6	-0	0.3
1981 Pit-N	4	5	.444	27	7	0	0	7	74	74	6	40	65	14.2	3.77	95	.261	.358	3	.158	0	-2	-1	-1	-0.3
1982 Pit-N	4	5	.444	76	0	0	0	14	103²	79	3	64	94	12.8	1.74	213	.212	.334	5	.238	1	21	23	-1	2.7
1983 Pit-N	4	9	.308	61	0	0	0	7	68	63	6	53	67	15.9	5.56	67	.249	.387	0	.000	-1	-15	-14	-0	-2.9
1984 Pit-N	5	6	.455	43	0	0	0	2	46¹	28	1	22	48	9.7	2.53	143	.175	.275	0	.000	-0	5	6	0	1.4
1985 Pit-N	0	1	.000	30	0	0	0	2	47²	42	4	28	43	13.2	3.21	111	.236	.340	0	.000	-0	2	2	0	0.1
NY-A	1	0	1.000	5	0	0	0	1	12²	12	0	7	17	12.1	2.84	141	.125	.300	0	—	0	2	2	-0	0.1
1986 NY-A	2	1	.333	31	0	0	0	0	39¹	38	1	22	36	14.2	3.66	112	.252	.354	0	—	0	2	2	-0	0.2
1988 Sea-A	0	2	.000	39	0	0	0	2	31¹	32	6	18	33	15.5	4.02	103	.258	.370	0	—	0	-0	0	-0	-0.1
Total 8	19	32	.373	332	7	0	0	39	460²	384	31	274	431	13.2	3.24	115	.227	.341	9	.164	0	22	25	-0	1.5

● **JOHNNIE SEALE**   Seale, Johnny Ray "Durango Kid" b: 11/14/38, Edgewater, Colo.   BL/TL, 5'10", 155 lbs.   Deb: 9/20/64

YEAR TM/L	W	L	PCT	G	GS	CG	SH	SV	IP	H	HR	BB	SO	RAT	ERA	ERA+	OAV	OOB	BH	AVG	PB	PR	/A	PD	TPI
1964 Det-A	1	0	1.000	4	0	0	0	0	10	6	1	4	5	9.0	3.60	102	.171	.256	0	.000	-0	0	0	1	0.0
1965 Det-A	0	0	—	4	0	0	0	0	3	7	1	2	3	27.0	12.00	29	.500	.563	0	—	-0	-3	-3	-0	0.0
Total 2	1	0	1.000	8	0	0	0	0	13	13	2	6	8	13.2	5.54	65	.265	.345	0	.000	-0	-3	-3	-0	0.0

● **KIM SEAMAN**   Seaman, Kim Michael b: 5/6/57, Pascagoula, Miss.   BL/TL, 6'4", 205 lbs.   Deb: 9/28/79

YEAR TM/L	W	L	PCT	G	GS	CG	SH	SV	IP	H	HR	BB	SO	RAT	ERA	ERA+	OAV	OOB	BH	AVG	PB	PR	/A	PD	TPI
1979 StL-N	0	0	—	1	0	0	0	0	2	0	0	2	1	9.0	0.00	—	.000	.250	0	—	0	1	1	0	0.0
1980 StL-N	3	2	.600	26	0	0	0	4	23²	16	2	13	10	11.0	3.42	108	.188	.296	0	.000	-0	0	1	-0	0.1
Total 2	3	2	.600	27	0	0	0	4	25²	16	2	15	10	10.9	3.16	117	.176	.292	0	.000	-0	1	2	-0	0.1

● **RUDY SEANEZ**   Seanez, Rudy Caballero b: 10/20/68, Brawley, Cal.   BR/TR, 5'10", 185 lbs.   Deb: 9/7/89

YEAR TM/L	W	L	PCT	G	GS	CG	SH	SV	IP	H	HR	BB	SO	RAT	ERA	ERA+	OAV	OOB	BH	AVG	PB	PR	/A	PD	TPI
1989 Cle-A	0	0	—	5	0	0	0	0	5	1	0	4	7	9.0	3.60	110	.071	.278	0	—	0	-0	-0	-0	0.0
1990 Cle-A	2	1	.667	24	0	0	0	0	27¹	22	2	25	24	15.8	5.60	70	.220	.381	0	—	0	-5	-5	-1	-0.5
1991 Cle-A	0	0	—	5	0	0	0	0	5	10	2	7	7	30.6	16.20	26	.385	.515	0	—	0	-7	-7	-0	-0.6
1993 SD-N	0	0	—	3	0	0	0	0	3¹	8	1	2	1	27.0	13.50	31	.471	.526	0	—	0	-4	-3	0	0.0
1994 LA-N	1	1	.500	17	0	0	0	0	23²	24	2	9	18	12.9	2.66	148	.273	.347	0	.000	-0	4	3	0	0.2
Total 5	3	2	.600	54	0	0	0	0	64¹	65	7	47	57	15.9	5.60	71	.265	.388	0	.000	-0	-11	-12	-1	-0.3

● **RAY SEARAGE**   Searage, Raymond Mark b: 5/1/55, Freeport, N.Y.   BL/TL, 6'1", 180 lbs.   Deb: 6/11/81

YEAR TM/L	W	L	PCT	G	GS	CG	SH	SV	IP	H	HR	BB	SO	RAT	ERA	ERA+	OAV	OOB	BH	AVG	PB	PR	/A	PD	TPI
1981 NY-N	1	0	1.000	26	0	0	0	1	36²	34	2	17	16	12.5	3.68	95	.252	.336	1	1.000	0	-1	-1	-0	0.0
1984 Mil-A	2	1	.667	21	0	0	0	6	38¹	20	0	16	29	8.7	0.70	546	.155	.253	0	—	0	14	13	0	1.5
1985 Mil-A	1	4	.200	33	0	0	0	1	38	54	2	24	36	18.5	5.92	70	.338	.424	0	—	0	-7	-7	-1	-1.0
1986 Mil-A	0	1	.000	17	0	0	0	0	22	29	6	9	10	16.0	6.95	62	.315	.382	0	—	0	-7	-6	-0	-0.4
Chi-A	1	0	1.000	29	0	0	0	1	29	15	1	19	26	10.6	0.62	694	.156	.296	0	—	0	11	12	0	0.3
Yr	1	1	.500	46	0	0	0	1	51	44	7	28	36	12.7	3.35	129	.233	.332	0	—	0	5	5	-0	-0.1
1987 Chi-A	2	3	.400	58	0	0	0	2	55²	56	9	24	33	13.1	4.20	109	.264	.342	0	—	0	2	2	-0	0.1
1989 LA-N	3	4	.429	41	0	0	0	0	35²	29	1	18	24	11.9	3.53	97	.225	.320	0	—	0	-0	-0	1	0.0
1990 LA-N	1	0	1.000	29	0	0	0	0	32¹	30	1	10	19	11.1	2.78	131	.250	.308	0	.000	-0	4	3	1	0.1
Total 7	11	13	.458	254	0	0	0	11	287²	267	22	137	193	12.7	3.50	114	.249	.336	1	.333	0	15	15	0	0.6

● **STEVE SEARCY**   Searcy, William Steven b: 6/4/64, Knoxville, Tenn.   BL/TL, 6'1", 190 lbs.   Deb: 8/29/88

YEAR TM/L	W	L	PCT	G	GS	CG	SH	SV	IP	H	HR	BB	SO	RAT	ERA	ERA+	OAV	OOB	BH	AVG	PB	PR	/A	PD	TPI
1988 Det-A	0	2	.000	2	2	0	0	0	8	8	3	4	5	13.5	5.63	68	.242	.324	—	—	0	-1	-2	-0	-0.2
1989 Det-A	1	1	.500	8	2	0	0	0	22¹	27	3	12	11	15.7	6.04	63	.307	.390	—	—	0	-5	-6	-0	-0.5
1990 Det-A	2	7	.222	16	12	1	0	0	75¹	76	9	51	66	15.2	4.66	85	.270	.381	—	—	0	-6	-6	-0	-0.7
1991 Det-A	1	2	.333	16	5	0	0	0	40²	52	8	30	32	18.1	8.41	49	.313	.418	—	—	0	-19	-19	-0	-1.2
Phi-N	2	1	.667	18	0	0	0	0	30¹	29	2	14	21	12.8	4.15	88	.252	.333	0	.000	0	-2	-2	-0	-0.2
1992 Phi-N	0	0	—	10	0	0	0	0	10¹	13	0	8	5	18.3	6.10	57	.325	.438	—	—	0	-3	-3	0	0.0
Total 5	6	13	.316	70	21	1	0	0	187	205	25	119	140	15.6	5.68	69	.283	.384	0	.000	0	-37	-37	-1	-2.8

● **TOM SEATON**   Seaton, Thomas Gordon b: 8/30/1887, Blair, Neb. d: 4/10/40, ElPaso, Tex.   BB/TR, 6', 175 lbs.   Deb: 4/13/12

YEAR TM/L	W	L	PCT	G	GS	CG	SH	SV	IP	H	HR	BB	SO	RAT	ERA	ERA+	OAV	OOB	BH	AVG	PB	PR	/A	PD	TPI
1912 Phi-N	16	12	.571	44	27	16	2	2	255	246	8	106	118	12.7	3.28	111	.261	.342	18	.217	-0	4	10	-2	0.8
1913 Phi-N	**27**	12	.692	52	35	21	5	1	**322¹**	262	6	136	**168**	11.4	2.60	128	.226	.313	12	.109	-5	22	26	2	2.7
1914 Bro-F	25	14	.641	44	38	26	7	2	302²	299	6	102	172	12.3	3.03	95	.259	.326	22	.206	2	-5	-5	-0	-0.4
1915 Bro-F	12	11	.522	32	23	13	0	3	189¹	199	4	99	86	14.3	4.56	60	.273	.362	16	.242	3	-39	-39	1	-4.0
New-F	2	6	.250	12	10	7	0	1	75	61	1	21	28	10.1	2.28	112	.224	.285	4	.154	0	4	3	1	0.3
Yr	14	17	.452	44	33	20	0	4	264¹	260	7	120	114	13.0	3.92	68	.259	.339	20	.217	3	-35	-36	2	-3.7
1916 Chi-N	6	6	.500	31	12	4	0	1	121	108	3	43	45	11.5	3.27	89	.246	.319	7	.184	-0	-9	-5	1	-0.4
1917 Chi-N	5	4	.556	16	9	3	1	0	74²	60	0	23	27	10.1	2.53	114	.227	.292	5	.238	1	1	3	1	0.6
Total 5	93	65	.589	231	154	90	15	11	1340	1235	30	530	644	12.1	3.14	98	.249	.327	84	.186	-0	-22	-12	4	-0.4

● **TOM SEATS**   Seats, Thomas Edward b: 9/24/10, Farmington, N.C. d: 5/10/92, San Ramon, Cal.   BR/TL, 5'11", 190 lbs.   Deb: 5/4/40

YEAR TM/L	W	L	PCT	G	GS	CG	SH	SV	IP	H	HR	BB	SO	RAT	ERA	ERA+	OAV	OOB	BH	AVG	PB	PR	/A	PD	TPI
1940 Det-A	2	2	.500	26	2	0	0	0	55²	67	4	21	25	14.2	4.69	101	.290	.349	1	.083	-1	-2	0	0	-0.1
1945 Bro-N	10	7	.588	31	18	6	2	0	121²	127	8	37	44	12.5	4.36	86	.261	.320	9	.209	0	-8	-8	-0	-1.0
Total 2	12	9	.571	57	20	6	2	1	177¹	194	12	58	69	13.0	4.47	91	.271	.329	10	.182	-1	-10	-8	0	-1.1

● **TOM SEAVER**   Seaver, George Thomas "Tom Terrific" b: 11/17/44, Fresno, Cal.   BR/TR, 6'1", 206 lbs.   Deb: 4/13/67   H

YEAR TM/L	W	L	PCT	G	GS	CG	SH	SV	IP	H	HR	BB	SO	RAT	ERA	ERA+	OAV	OOB	BH	AVG	PB	PR	/A	PD	TPI
1967 NY-N★	16	13	.552	35	34	18	2	0	251	224	19	78	170	11.0	2.76	123	.241	.303	2	.143	-0	17	18	0	2.3
1968 NY-N★	16	12	.571	36	35	14	5	1	277²	224	15	48	205	9.1	2.20	137	.222	.262	15	.158	-0	24	25	2	3.1
1969 *NY-N☆	25	7	**.781**	36	35	18	5	0	273¹	202	24	82	208	9.6	2.21	166	**.207**	.273	11	.121	-0	42	44	2	5.6

YEAR	TM/L	W	L	PCT	G	GS	CG	SH	SV	IP	H	HR	BB	SO	RAT	ERA	ERA+	OAV	OOB	BH	AVG	PB	PR	/A	PD	TPI
1970	NY-N★	18	12	.600	37	36	19	2	0	290²	230	21	83	**283**	9.8	**2.82**	**143**	.214	.273	17	.179	4	**40**	**39**	2	**4.5**
1971	NY-N☆	20	10	.667	36	35	21	4	0	286¹	210	18	61	**289**	8.6	**1.76**	**194**	.206	**.253**	18	.196	4	**54**	**52**	1	**6.5**
1972	NY-N☆	21	12	.636	35	35	13	3	0	262	215	19	77	249	10.2	2.92	115	.224	.285	13	.146	4	16	13	2	2.3
1973	*NY-N	19	10	.655	36	36	**18**	3	0	290	219	23	64	**251**	8.9	**2.08**	**174**	**.206**	.254	15	.161	3	51	50	-0	**5.4**
1974	NY-N	11	11	.500	32	32	12	5	0	236	199	19	75	201	10.6	3.20	111	.230	.283	7	.099	-2	11	9	2	0.9
1975	NY-N★	**22**	9	.710	36	36	15	5	0	280¹	217	11	88	**243**	9.9	2.38	145	.214	.280	17	.179	3	39	33	2	4.3
1976	NY-N★	14	11	.560	35	34	13	5	0	271	211	14	77	**235**	9.7	2.59	127	.213	.273	7	.085	-2	**27**	21	1	1.9
1977	NY-N	7	3	.700	13	13	5	3	0	96	79	7	28	72	10.0	3.00	125	.221	.277	5	.161	-0	10	8	1	0.8
	Cin-N★	14	3	.824	20	20	14	4	0	165¹	120	12	38	124	8.6	2.34	168	.201	.249	12	.218	4	29	29	-1	3.3
	Yr	21	6	.778	33	33	19	**7**	0	261¹	199	19	66	196	**9.1**	2.58	149	**.208**	**.259**	17	.198	4	39	37	-0	4.1
1978	Cin-N☆	16	14	.533	36	36	8	1	0	259²	218	26	89	226	10.6	2.88	123	.227	.292	9	.122	-0	20	19	-2	2.0
1979	*Cin-N	16	6	**.727**	32	32	9	**5**	0	215	187	16	61	131	10.4	3.14	119	.236	.291	12	.158	2	14	14	0	1.6
1980	Cin-N	10	8	.556	26	26	5	1	0	168	140	24	59	101	10.7	3.64	98	.225	.293	6	.130	1	-1	-1	1	0.1
1981	Cin-N★	**14**	**2**	**.875**	23	23	6	1	0	166¹	120	10	66	87	10.2	2.54	140	.205	.289	11	.200	1	17	19	-1	2.1
1982	Cin-N	5	13	.278	21	21	0	0	0	111¹	136	14	44	62	14.8	5.50	67	.302	.368	6	.176	1	-23	-22	-1	-3.2
1983	NY-N	9	14	.391	34	34	5	2	0	231	201	18	86	135	11.3	3.55	102	.235	.308	10	.156	2	2	2	-1	0.3
1984	Chi-A	15	11	.577	34	33	10	4	0	236²	216	27	61	131	10.6	3.95	105	.240	.290	0	—	0	1	5	1	0.7
1985	Chi-A	16	11	.593	35	33	6	1	0	238²	223	22	69	134	11.3	3.17	136	.248	.307	0	—	0	26	30	2	3.5
1986	Chi-A	2	6	.250	12	12	1	0	0	72	66	9	27	31	12.3	4.38	99	.242	.321	0	—	0	-2	-1	-1	-0.2
	Bos-A	5	7	.417	16	16	1	0	0	104¹	114	8	29	72	12.5	3.80	110	.271	.329	0	—	0	4	4	-0	0.4
	Yr	7	13	.350	28	28	2	0	0	176¹	180	17	56	103	12.1	4.03	105	.261	.318	0	—	0	3	4	-1	0.2
Total	20	311	205	.603	656	647	231	61	1	4782²	3971	380	1390	3640	10.2	2.86	127	.226	.285	202	.154	28	419	411	13	48.2

● **BOB SEBRA**   Sebra, Robert Bush b: 12/11/61, Ridgewood, N.J.   BR/TR, 6'2", 200 lbs.   Deb: 6/26/85

YEAR	TM/L	W	L	PCT	G	GS	CG	SH	SV	IP	H	HR	BB	SO	RAT	ERA	ERA+	OAV	OOB	BH	AVG	PB	PR	/A	PD	TPI
1985	Tex-A	0	2	.000	7	4	0	0	0	20¹	26	4	14	13	18.1	7.52	56	.306	.410	0	—	0	-8	-7	-0	-0.6
1986	Mon-N	5	5	.500	17	13	3	1	0	91¹	82	9	25	66	10.8	3.55	104	.239	.296	6	.207	1	2	1	-1	0.2
1987	Mon-N	6	15	.286	36	27	4	1	0	177¹	184	15	67	156	12.9	4.42	95	.272	.340	8	.157	0	-7	-4	-1	-0.5
1988	Phi-N	1	2	.333	3	3	0	0	0	11¹	15	0	10	7	19.9	7.94	45	.333	.455	0	.000	-0	-6	-6	-0	-1.2
1989	Phi-N	2	3	.400	6	5	0	0	0	34¹	41	6	10	21	14.4	4.46	80	.295	.359	0	.000	-0	-3	-0	-0	-0.5
	Cin-N	0	0	—	15	0	0	0	1	21	24	2	18	14	19.3	6.43	56	.296	.441	0	.000	-0	-7	-7	-0	-0.1
	Yr	2	3	.400	21	5	0	0	1	55¹	65	8	28	35	15.6	5.20	68	.289	.375	0	.000	-1	-11	-10	-0	-0.6
1990	Mil-A	1	2	.333	10	0	0	0	0	11	20	1	5	4	21.3	8.18	47	.408	.473	0	—	0	-5	-5	1	-1.2
Total	6	15	29	.341	94	52	7	2	1	366²	392	37	149	281	13.6	4.71	84	.276	.351	14	.146	-0	-34	-31	-2	-3.9

● **DOC SECHRIST**   Sechrist, Theodore O'Hara b: 2/10/1876, Williamstown, Ky. d: 4/2/50, Louisville, Ky.   BR/TR, 5'9", 160 lbs.   Deb: 4/28/1899

YEAR	TM/L	W	L	PCT	G	GS	CG	SH	SV	IP	H	HR	BB	SO	RAT	ERA	ERA+	OAV	OOB	BH	AVG	PB	PR	/A	PD	TPI
1899	NY-N	0	0	—	1	0	0	0	0	2	0	0	2	1	9.0	—	—	—	1.000	0	—	—	0	0	0	0.0

● **DON SECRIST**   Secrist, Donald Laverne b: 2/26/44, Seattle, Wash.   BL/TL, 6'2", 195 lbs.   Deb: 4/11/69

YEAR	TM/L	W	L	PCT	G	GS	CG	SH	SV	IP	H	HR	BB	SO	RAT	ERA	ERA+	OAV	OOB	BH	AVG	PB	PR	/A	PD	TPI
1969	Chi-A	0	1	.000	19	0	0	0	0	40	35	7	14	23	11.2	6.07	63	.227	.296	1	.143	0	-11	-10	0	-0.2
1970	Chi-A	0	0	—	9	0	0	0	0	14²	19	2	12	9	19.0	5.52	71	.333	.449	0	—	0	-3	-3	0	-0.0
Total	2	0	1	.000	28	0	0	0	0	54²	54	9	26	32	13.3	5.93	65	.256	.340	1	.143	0	-14	-13	0	-0.2

● **DUKE SEDGWICK**   Sedgwick, Henry Kenneth b: 6/1/1898, Martins Ferry, O. d: 12/4/82, Clearwater, Fla.   BR/TR, 6', 175 lbs.   Deb: 7/12/21

YEAR	TM/L	W	L	PCT	G	GS	CG	SH	SV	IP	H	HR	BB	SO	RAT	ERA	ERA+	OAV	OOB	BH	AVG	PB	PR	/A	PD	TPI
1921	Phi-N	1	3	.250	16	5	1	0	0	71¹	81	3	32	21	14.8	4.92	86	.283	.363	5	.208	-1	-9	-5	-1	-0.5
1923	Was-A	0	1	.000	5	2	1	0	0	16	27	1	6	4	18.6	7.88	48	.415	.465	0	.000	-1	-7	-7	1	-0.4
Total	2	1	4	.200	21	7	2	0	0	87¹	108	4	38	25	15.5	5.46	76	.308	.382	5	.172	-2	-16	-13	-0	-0.9

● **CHARLIE SEE**   See, Charles Henry "Chad" b: 10/13/1896, Pleasantville, N.Y d: 7/19/48, Bridgeport, Conn.   BL/TR, 5'10.5", 175 lbs.   Deb: 8/6/19 ♦

YEAR	TM/L	W	L	PCT	G	GS	CG	SH	SV	IP	H	HR	BB	SO	RAT	ERA	ERA+	OAV	OOB	BH	AVG	PB	PR	/A	PD	TPI
1920	Cin-N	0	0	—	1	0	0	0	0	6	6	0	4	3	15.0	6.00	51	.286	.400	25	.305	0	-2	-2	-0	0.0

● **CHUCK SEELBACH**   Seelbach, Charles Frederick b: 3/20/48, Lakewood, Ohio   BR/TR, 6', 180 lbs.   Deb: 6/29/71

YEAR	TM/L	W	L	PCT	G	GS	CG	SH	SV	IP	H	HR	BB	SO	RAT	ERA	ERA+	OAV	OOB	BH	AVG	PB	PR	/A	PD	TPI
1971	Det-A	0	0	—	5	0	0	0	0	4	6	2	7	1	31.5	13.50	27	.375	.583	0	—	0	-4	-4	0	0.0
1972	*Det-A	9	8	.529	61	3	0	0	14	112	96	6	39	76	11.1	2.89	109	.238	.310	3	.143	1	2	3	-1	0.7
1973	Det-A	1	0	1.000	5	0	0	0	0	7	7	2	2	2	11.6	3.86	106	.241	.300	0	—	0	0	0	1	-0.4
1974	Det-A	0	0	—	4	0	0	0	0	7²	9	2	3	0	15.3	4.70	81	.300	.382	0	—	0	-1	-1	0	-0.3
Total	4	10	8	.556	75	3	0	0	14	130²	118	11	51	79	12.0	3.38	96	.247	.326	3	.143	1	-3	-2	-0	-0.0

● **EMMETT SEERY**   Seery, John Emmett b: 2/13/1861, Princeville, Ill. d: 8/8/30, Saranac Lake, N.Y.   BL/TR,   Deb: 4/17/1884 ♦

YEAR	TM/L	W	L	PCT	G	GS	CG	SH	SV	IP	H	HR	BB	SO	RAT	ERA	ERA+	OAV	OOB	BH	AVG	PB	PR	/A	PD	TPI
1886	StL-N	0	0	—	2	0	0	0	0	7	8	1	3	2	14.1	7.71	42	.320	.393	108	.238	0	-3	-3	-0	0.0

● **HERMAN SEGELKE**   Segelke, Herman Neils b: 4/24/58, San Mateo, Cal.   BR/TR, 6'4", 200 lbs.   Deb: 4/7/82

YEAR	TM/L	W	L	PCT	G	GS	CG	SH	SV	IP	H	HR	BB	SO	RAT	ERA	ERA+	OAV	OOB	BH	AVG	PB	PR	/A	PD	TPI
1982	Chi-N	0	0	—	3	0	0	0	0	4¹	6	1	6	4	24.9	8.31	45	.316	.480	0	—	0	-2	-2	0	0.0

● **DIEGO SEGUI**   Segui, Diego Pablo (Gonzalez) b: 8/17/37, Holguin, Cuba   BR/TR, 6', 190 lbs.   Deb: 4/12/62 F

YEAR	TM/L	W	L	PCT	G	GS	CG	SH	SV	IP	H	HR	BB	SO	RAT	ERA	ERA+	OAV	OOB	BH	AVG	PB	PR	/A	PD	TPI
1962	KC-A	8	5	.615	37	13	2	0	6	116²	89	16	46	71	10.5	3.86	109	.211	.291	8	.235	2	1	5	0	0.7
1963	KC-A	9	6	.600	38	23	4	1	0	167	173	17	73	116	13.4	3.77	103	.267	.343	12	.218	1	-3	2	1	0.4
1964	KC-A	8	17	.320	40	35	5	2	0	217	219	30	94	155	13.0	4.56	84	.260	.335	11	.155	-0	-23	-18	2	-1.7
1965	KC-A	5	15	.250	40	25	5	1	0	163	166	18	67	119	13.0	4.64	75	.261	.334	9	.191	2	-21	-21	-1	-2.2
1966	Was-A	3	7	.300	21	13	1	1	0	72	82	8	24	54	13.3	5.00	69	.291	.346	2	.111	-1	-13	-12	-1	-1.7
1967	KC-A	3	4	.429	36	3	0	0	1	70	62	4	31	52	12.2	3.09	103	.238	.324	0	.000	-1	1	1	-0	-0.1
1968	Oak-A	6	5	.545	52	0	0	0	6	83	51	7	32	72	9.0	2.39	118	.173	.255	1	.111	0	5	4	-0	0.5
1969	Sea-A	12	6	.667	66	8	2	0	12	142¹	127	14	61	113	12.0	3.35	108	.238	.319	4	.148	-0	4	4	-1	0.7
1970	Oak-A	10	10	.500	47	19	3	2	2	162	130	9	66	95	11.1	**2.56**	**138**	.222	.305	5	.116	-2	21	18	-1	1.8
1971	*Oak-A	10	8	.556	26	25	5	0	0	146¹	122	13	63	81	11.6	3.14	106	.229	.316	4	.085	-1	5	3	-1	0.2
1972	Oak-A	0	1	.000	7	3	0	0	0	22²	25	2	7	11	12.7	3.57	80	.287	.340	1	.143	-0	-1	-2	-0	-0.1
	StL-N	3	1	.750	55²	47	2	32	54	12.8	3.07	111	.229	.333	1	.143	0	2	2	1	0.3					
1973	StL-N	7	6	.538	65	0	0	0	17	100¹	78	6	53	93	11.8	2.78	131	.222	.310	0	.000	-1	10	10	1	1.4
1974	Bos-A	6	8	.429	58	0	0	0	10	108	106	9	49	76	13.0	4.00	96	.257	.337	0	—	0	-5	-2	-1	-0.8
1975	*Bos-A	2	5	.286	33	1	0	0	6	71	71	10	43	45	14.5	4.82	85	.270	.373	0	—	0	-8	-6	-0	-0.7
1977	Sea-A	0	7	.000	40	7	0	0	2	110²	128	17	70	91	12.4	5.69	72	.291	.321	0	—	0	-20	-19	-0	-1.1
Total	15	92	111	.453	639	171	28	7	71	1807²	1656	185	786	1298	12.2	3.81	96	.243	.323	58	.151	-1	-43	-32	-3	-2.4

● **JOSE SEGURA**   Segura, Jose Altagracia (Mota) b: 1/26/63, Fundacion, D.R.   BR/TR, 5'11", 180 lbs.   Deb: 4/10/88

YEAR	TM/L	W	L	PCT	G	GS	CG	SH	SV	IP	H	HR	BB	SO	RAT	ERA	ERA+	OAV	OOB	BH	AVG	PB	PR	/A	PD	TPI
1988	Chi-A	0	0	—	4	0	0	0	0	8²	19	1	2	8	28.0	13.50	29	.432	.519	0	—	0	-9	-9	0	-1.0
1989	Chi-A	0	1	.000	7	0	0	0	0	6	13	2	4	4	24.0	15.00	25	.464	.516	0	—	0	-7	-7	0	-1.0
1991	SF-N	0	1	.000	11	0	0	0	0	16¹	20	1	10	8	13.8	4.41	81	.303	.352	0	—	0	-1	-2	-0	-0.1
Total	3	0	2	.000	22	0	0	0	0	31	52	4	16	16	19.7	9.00	41	.377	.442	0	—	0	-18	-18	0	-1.1

● **SOCKS SEIBOLD**   Seibold, Harry b: 4/3/1896, Philadelphia, Pa. d: 9/21/65, Philadelphia, Pa.   BR/TR, 5'8.5", 162 lbs.   Deb: 9/18/15 ♦

YEAR	TM/L	W	L	PCT	G	GS	CG	SH	SV	IP	H	HR	BB	SO	RAT	ERA	ERA+	OAV	OOB	BH	AVG	PB	PR	/A	PD	TPI
1916	Phi-A	1	2	.333	3	2	1	0	0	21²	22	0	6	5	12.9	4.15	69	.272	.344	2	.167	-0	-3	-3	1	-0.3
1917	Phi-A	4	16	.200	33	15	9	1	1	160	141	1	85	55	12.9	3.94	70	.243	.343	13	.220	2	-23	-21	-1	-2.5
1919	Phi-A	2	3	.400	14	4	1	0	0	45²	58	2	26	19	17.3	5.32	64	.322	.419	2	.154	-1	-11	-10	-0	-1.0
1929	Bos-N	12	17	.414	38	27	16	1	1	205²	208	17	80	54	13.6	4.73	99	.285	.352	20	.288	-0	-1	-1	0	0.2
1930	Bos-N	15	16	.484	36	33	20	1	2	251	288	16	65	70	13.4	4.12	120	.290	.348	19	.211	0	24	23	-3	2.1
1931	Bos-N	10	18	.357	33	29	10	3	0	206¹	226	12	65	50	12.8	4.67	81	.279	.335	9	.129	-4	-18	-20	0	-2.7

YEAR TM/L	W	L	PCT	G	GS	CG	SH	SV	IP	H	HR	BB	SO	RAT	ERA	ERA+	OAV	OOB	BH	AVG	PB	PR	/A	PD	TPI
1932 Bos-N	3	10	.231	28	20	6	1	0	136²	173	12	41	33	14.2	4.68	80	.309	.358	7	.152	-2	-12	-14	2	-1.1
1933 Bos-N	1	4	.200	11	5	1	0	1	36²	43	0	14	10	14.0	3.68	83	.295	.356	1	.111	0	-1	-3	0	-0.3
Total 8	48	86	.358	191	135	64	8	5	1063²	1179	60	405	296	13.5	4.43	91	.284	.350	76	.192	-0	-45	-48	-1	-5.6

● KEVIN SEITZER   Seitzer, Kevin Lee b: 3/26/62, Springfield, Ill.   BR/TR, 5′11″, 180 lbs.   Deb: 9/3/86 ◆

YEAR TM/L	W	L	PCT	G	GS	CG	SH	SV	IP	H	HR	BB	SO	RAT	ERA	ERA+	OAV	OOB	BH	AVG	PB	PR	/A	PD	TPI
1993 Oak-A	0	0	—	1	0	0	0	0	0¹	0	0	0	1	0.0	0.00	—	.000	.000	65	.255	1	0	0	0	0.0

● AARON SELE   Sele, Aaron Helmer b: 6/25/70, Golden Valley, Minn.   BR/TR, 6′5″, 205 lbs.   Deb: 6/23/93

YEAR TM/L	W	L	PCT	G	GS	CG	SH	SV	IP	H	HR	BB	SO	RAT	ERA	ERA+	OAV	OOB	BH	AVG	PB	PR	/A	PD	TPI
1993 Bos-A	7	2	.778	18	18	0	0	0	111²	100	5	48	93	12.5	2.74	168	.237	.325	0	—	0	20	23	-2	1.4
1994 Bos-A	8	7	.533	22	22	2	0	0	143¹	140	13	60	105	13.1	3.83	134	.261	.345	0	—	0	15	21	0	1.6
Total 2	15	9	.625	40	40	2	0	0	255	240	18	108	198	12.8	3.35	146	.250	.336	0	—	0	35	44	-2	3.0

● EPP SELL   Sell, Lester Elwood b: 4/26/1897, Llewellyn, Pa. d: 2/19/61, Reading, Pa.   BR/TR, 6′, 175 lbs.   Deb: 9/1/22

YEAR TM/L	W	L	PCT	G	GS	CG	SH	SV	IP	H	HR	BB	SO	RAT	ERA	ERA+	OAV	OOB	BH	AVG	PB	PR	/A	PD	TPI
1922 StL-N	4	2	.667	7	5	0	0	0	33	47	2	6	5	15.0	6.82	57	.338	.374	4	.333	1	-10	-11	1	-1.3
1923 StL-N	0	1	.000	5	1	0	0	0	15	16	1	8	2	14.4	6.00	65	.291	.381	0	.000	-1	-3	-3	-0	-0.3
Total 2	4	3	.571	12	6	0	0	0	48	63	3	14	7	14.8	6.56	59	.325	.376	4	.211	0	-13	-14	0	-1.6

● JEFF SELLERS   Sellers, Jeffrey Doyle b: 5/11/64, Compton, Cal.   BR/TR, 6′1″, 175 lbs.   Deb: 9/15/85

YEAR TM/L	W	L	PCT	G	GS	CG	SH	SV	IP	H	HR	BB	SO	RAT	ERA	ERA+	OAV	OOB	BH	AVG	PB	PR	/A	PD	TPI
1985 Bos-A	2	0	1.000	4	4	1	0	0	22¹	24	1	7	6	12.5	3.63	118	.273	.326	0	—	0	1	1	-0	0.1
1986 Bos-A	3	7	.300	14	13	1	0	0	82	90	13	40	51	14.6	4.94	84	.282	.367	0	—	0	-7	-7	0	-0.7
1987 Bos-A	7	8	.467	25	22	4	2	0	139²	161	10	61	99	14.5	5.28	86	.298	.373	0	—	0	-13	-12	1	-1.2
1988 Bos-A	1	7	.125	18	12	1	0	0	85²	89	9	56	70	15.5	4.83	85	.268	.379	0	—	0	-8	-7	-0	-0.9
Total 4	13	22	.371	61	51	7	2	0	329²	364	33	164	226	14.7	4.97	87	.285	.370	0	—	0	-27	-24	0	-2.7

● DAVE SELLS   Sells, David Wayne b: 9/18/46, Vacaville, Cal.   BR/TR, 5′11″, 175 lbs.   Deb: 8/2/72

YEAR TM/L	W	L	PCT	G	GS	CG	SH	SV	IP	H	HR	BB	SO	RAT	ERA	ERA+	OAV	OOB	BH	AVG	PB	PR	/A	PD	TPI
1972 Cal-A	2	0	1.000	10	0	0	0	0	16	11	0	5	2	9.0	2.81	103	.196	.262	0	—	0	0	0	0	0.1
1973 Cal-A	7	2	.778	51	0	0	0	10	68	72	3	35	25	14.8	3.71	96	.277	.373	0	—	0	1	-1	0	0.4
1974 Cal-A	2	3	.400	20	0	0	0	2	39	48	3	16	14	15.5	3.69	93	.312	.387	0	—	0	-0	-1	0	0.3
1975 Cal-A	0	0	—	4	0	0	0	0	8¹	9	3	8	7	18.4	8.64	41	.250	.386	0	—	0	-5	-5	0	0.0
LA-N	0	2	.000	5	0	0	0	0	7	6	2	3	1	11.6	3.86	88	.222	.300	1	1.000	1	-0	-0	0	0.0
Total 4	11	7	.611	90	0	0	0	12	138¹	146	10	67	49	14.4	3.90	88	.274	.363	1	1.000	1	-4	-7	1	0.8

● DICK SELMA   Selma, Richard Jay b: 11/4/43, Santa Ana, Cal.   BR/TR, 5′11″, 175 lbs.   Deb: 9/2/65

YEAR TM/L	W	L	PCT	G	GS	CG	SH	SV	IP	H	HR	BB	SO	RAT	ERA	ERA+	OAV	OOB	BH	AVG	PB	PR	/A	PD	TPI
1965 NY-N	2	1	.667	4	4	1	1	0	26²	22	2	9	26	10.8	3.71	95	.229	.302	2	.222	0	-1	-1	1	0.0
1966 NY-N	4	6	.400	30	7	0	0	1	80²	84	11	39	58	14.1	4.24	86	.274	.361	1	.071	-0	-6	-5	2	-0.4
1967 NY-N	2	4	.333	38	8	0	0	2	81¹	71	3	36	52	12.1	2.77	122	.241	.328	2	.091	-1	6	6	1	0.4
1968 NY-N	9	10	.474	33	23	4	3	0	169²	148	11	54	117	11.0	2.76	110	.233	.298	12	.207	2	4	5	2	1.0
1969 SD-N	2	2	.500	4	3	1	0	0	22	19	3	9	20	11.5	4.09	86	.229	.304	2	.286	0	-1	-1	0	-0.2
Chi-N	10	8	.556	36	25	4	2	1	168²	137	13	72	161	11.3	3.63	111	.222	.307	8	.154	-0	-1	7	-1	0.6
Yr	12	10	.545	40	28	5	2	1	190²	156	16	81	181	11.3	3.68	108	.223	.307	10	.169	-0	-2	6	-1	0.4
1970 Phi-N	8	9	.471	73	0	0	0	22	134¹	108	8	59	153	11.5	2.75	145	.226	.317	3	.150	0	**19**	**19**	2	3.1
1971 Phi-N	0	2	.000	17	0	0	0	1	24²	21	2	8	15	11.3	3.28	107	.231	.307	1	1.000	0	1	0	0	0.1
1972 Phi-N	2	9	.182	46	10	0	0	3	98²	91	13	73	58	15.4	5.56	65	.249	.381	4	.200	1	-23	-22	1	-2.3
1973 Phi-N	1	1	.500	6	0	0	0	0	8	6	1	5	4	12.4	5.63	67	.240	.367	0	—	0	-2	-2	1	-0.3
1974 Cal-A	2	2	.500	18	0	0	0	0	23	22	2	17	15	15.7	5.09	68	.272	.404	0	—	0	-4	-4	1	-0.2
Mil-A	0	0	—	2	0	0	0	0	2¹	5	0	2	2	23.1	19.29	18	.455	.500	0	—	0	-4	-4	-0	-0.0
Yr	2	2	.500	20	0	0	0	1	25¹	27	2	17	17	16.0	6.39	54	.290	.405	0	—	0	-8	-8	1	-0.2
Total 10	42	54	.438	307	76	11	6	31	840	734	69	381	681	12.2	3.62	100	.238	.327	35	.172	2	-11	-2	8	1.8

● FRANK SELMAN   Selman, Frank C. (a.k.a. Frank C. Williams 1871-75) b: Baltimore, Md.   Deb: 5/4/1871 ◆

YEAR TM/L	W	L	PCT	G	GS	CG	SH	SV	IP	H	HR	BB	SO	RAT	ERA	ERA+	OAV	OOB	BH	AVG	PB	PR	/A	PD	TPI
1873 Mar-n	0	1	.000	1	1	1	0	0	9	21	0	0	0	21.0	8.00	40	.350	.350	1	.333	0	-5	-5		-0.3

● CARROLL SEMBERA   Sembera, Carroll William b: 7/26/41, Shiner, Tex.   BR/TR, 6′, 155 lbs.   Deb: 9/28/65

YEAR TM/L	W	L	PCT	G	GS	CG	SH	SV	IP	H	HR	BB	SO	RAT	ERA	ERA+	OAV	OOB	BH	AVG	PB	PR	/A	PD	TPI
1965 Hou-N	0	1	.000	2	1	0	0	0	7¹	5	0	3	4	9.8	3.68	91	.185	.267	0	.000	-0	-0	-0	0	0.0
1966 Hou-N	1	2	.333	24	0	0	0	1	33	36	3	16	21	14.2	3.00	114	.288	.369	0	—	0	2	2	0	0.1
1967 Hou-N	2	6	.250	45	0	0	0	3	59²	66	7	19	48	13.0	4.83	69	.269	.325	1	.143	-0	-10	-10	1	-1.3
1969 Mon-N	0	2	.000	23	0	0	0	2	33	28	1	24	15	14.7	3.55	104	.246	.386	1	.250	0	0	0	-0	0.0
1970 Mon-N	0	0	—	5	0	0	0	0	6²	14	2	11	6	35.1	18.90	22	.424	.578	0	—	0	-11	-11	0	0.0
Total 5	3	11	.214	99	1	0	0	7	139²	149	13	73	94	14.6	4.70	74	.274	.364	2	.133	-0	-18	-19	1	-1.2

● FRANK SEMINARA   Seminara, Frank Peter b: 5/16/67, Brooklyn, N.Y.   BR/TR, 6′2″, 205 lbs.   Deb: 6/2/92

YEAR TM/L	W	L	PCT	G	GS	CG	SH	SV	IP	H	HR	BB	SO	RAT	ERA	ERA+	OAV	OOB	BH	AVG	PB	PR	/A	PD	TPI
1992 SD-N	9	4	.692	19	18	0	0	0	100¹	98	5	46	61	13.2	3.68	97	.257	.342	4	.118	-1	-2	-1	2	-0.1
1993 SD-N	3	3	.500	18	7	0	0	0	46¹	53	5	21	22	15.0	4.47	93	.294	.377	2	.200	0	-2	-2	0	-0.2
1994 NY-N	0	2	.000	10	1	0	0	0	17	20	2	8	7	14.8	5.82	73	.303	.378	0	.000	0	-3	-3	-1	-0.4
Total 3	12	9	.571	47	26	0	0	0	163²	171	12	75	90	13.9	4.12	92	.273	.356	6	.128	-1	-7	-6	1	-0.7

● RAY SEMPROCH   Semproch, Roman Anthony "Baby" b: 1/7/31, Cleveland, Ohio   BR/TR, 5′11″, 180 lbs.   Deb: 4/15/58

YEAR TM/L	W	L	PCT	G	GS	CG	SH	SV	IP	H	HR	BB	SO	RAT	ERA	ERA+	OAV	OOB	BH	AVG	PB	PR	/A	PD	TPI
1958 Phi-N	13	11	.542	36	30	12	2	0	204¹	211	25	58	92	12.1	3.92	101	.264	.319	7	.095	-5	1	1	-1	-0.4
1959 Phi-N	3	10	.231	30	18	2	0	3	111²	119	12	59	54	14.6	5.40	76	.277	.368	6	.176	-0	-18	-16	1	-1.7
1960 Det-A	3	0	1.000	17	0	0	0	0	27	29	2	16	9	15.0	4.00	99	.269	.363	0	.000	-0	-0	-0	1	0.1
1961 LA-A	0	0	—	2	0	0	0	0	1	1	0	3	1	36.0	9.00	50	.333	.667	0	—	0	-1	-0	0	0.0
Total 4	19	21	.475	85	48	14	2	3	344	360	39	136	156	13.2	4.42	91	.269	.340	13	.116	-5	-18	-16	1	-2.0

● STEVE SENTENEY   Senteney, Stephen Leonard b: 8/7/55, Indianapolis, Ind. d: 6/19/89, Colusa, Cal.   BR/TR, 6′2″, 205 lbs.   Deb: 6/6/82

YEAR TM/L	W	L	PCT	G	GS	CG	SH	SV	IP	H	HR	BB	SO	RAT	ERA	ERA+	OAV	OOB	BH	AVG	PB	PR	/A	PD	TPI
1982 Tor-A	0	0	—	11	0	0	0	0	22	32	5	6	20	11.9	4.91	91	.247	.293	0	—	0	-2	-1	-0	-0.1

● MANNY SEOANE   Seoane, Manuel Modesto b: 6/26/55, Tampa, Fla.   BR/TR, 6′3″, 187 lbs.   Deb: 9/18/77

YEAR TM/L	W	L	PCT	G	GS	CG	SH	SV	IP	H	HR	BB	SO	RAT	ERA	ERA+	OAV	OOB	BH	AVG	PB	PR	/A	PD	TPI
1977 Phi-N	0	0	—	2	1	0	0	0	6	11	3	4	2	21.0	6.00	67	.407	.467	1	.500	0	-1	-1	-0	0.0
1978 Chi-N	1	0	1.000	7	1	0	0	0	8¹	11	0	5	3	18.4	5.40	75	.297	.395	0	—	0	-2	-1	-0	-0.2
Total 2	1	0	1.000	9	2	0	0	0	14¹	22	0	9	9	19.5	5.65	71	.344	.425	1	.500	0	-3	-3	-1	-0.2

● BILLY SERAD   Serad, William I. b: 1863, Philadelphia, Pa. d: 11/1/25, Chester, Pa.   BR/TR, 5′7″, 156 lbs.   Deb: 5/5/1884

YEAR TM/L	W	L	PCT	G	GS	CG	SH	SV	IP	H	HR	BB	SO	RAT	ERA	ERA+	OAV	OOB	BH	AVG	PB	PR	/A	PD	TPI
1884 Buf-N	16	20	.444	37	37	34	2	0	308	373	21	111	150	14.1	4.27	74	.281	.336	24	.175	-7	-44	-38	-3	-4.2
1885 Buf-N	7	21	.250	30	29	27	0	0	241¹	299	5	80	90	14.1	4.10	73	.293	.344	16	.154	-6	-34	-30	-3	-3.5
1887 Cin-a	10	11	.476	22	21	20	2	1	187¹	201	7	80	34	13.9	4.08	106	.266	.343	14	.177	-4	4	5	-1	0.1
1888 Cin-a	2	3	.400	6	5	5	0	0	50²	62	1	19	4	15.5	3.55	89	.291	.365	3	.130	-1	-3	-2	-1	-0.4
Total 4	35	55	.389	95	92	86	4	1	787¹	935	34	290	278	14.2	4.13	82	.282	.342	57	.166	-17	-77	-64	-7	-8.0

● GARY SERUM   Serum, Gary Wayne b: 10/24/56, Fargo, N.D.   BR/TR, 6′1″, 180 lbs.   Deb: 7/22/77

YEAR TM/L	W	L	PCT	G	GS	CG	SH	SV	IP	H	HR	BB	SO	RAT	ERA	ERA+	OAV	OOB	BH	AVG	PB	PR	/A	PD	TPI
1977 Min-A	0	0	—	8	0	0	0	0	22²	22	4	10	14	13.5	4.37	91	.268	.362	0	—	0	-1	-1	-0	0.0
1978 Min-A	9	9	.500	34	23	6	1	1	184¹	188	14	44	80	11.5	4.10	93	.266	.311	0	—	0	-7	-6	0	-0.6
1979 Min-A	1	3	.250	20	5	0	0	0	64	93	10	20	31	15.9	6.61	66	.354	.399	0	—	0	-17	-16	0	-0.9
Total 3	10	12	.455	62	28	6	1	1	271	303	28	74	125	12.7	4.72	84	.288	.337	0	—	0	-25	-23	-0	-1.5

● SCOTT SERVICE   Service, Scott David b: 2/26/67, Cincinnati, Ohio   BR/TR, 6′6″, 230 lbs.   Deb: 9/5/88

YEAR TM/L	W	L	PCT	G	GS	CG	SH	SV	IP	H	HR	BB	SO	RAT	ERA	ERA+	OAV	OOB	BH	AVG	PB	PR	/A	PD	TPI
1988 Phi-N	0	0	—	5	0	0	0	0	5¹	7	0	1	6	15.2	1.69	211	.333	.391	0	—	0	1	1	-0	0.0

YEAR	TM/L	W	L	PCT	G	GS	CG	SH	SV	IP	H	HR	BB	SO	RAT	ERA	ERA+	OAV	OOB	BH	AVG	PB	PR	/A	PD	TPI
1992	Mon-N	0	0	—	5	0	0	0	0	7	15	1	5	11	25.7	14.14	25	.417	.488	0	.000	-0	-8	-8	-0	0.0
1993	Col-N	0	0	—	3	0	0	0	0	4²	8	1	1	3	19.3	9.64	49	.400	.455	0	—	0	-3	-3	-0	0.0
	Cin-N	2	2	.500	26	0	0	0	2	41¹	36	5	15	40	11.3	3.70	109	.235	.308	1	.143	-0	2	1	-0	0.1
	Yr	2	2	.500	29	0	0	0	2	46	44	6	16	43	11.9	4.30	95	.250	.316	1	.143	-0	-1	-1	-0	0.1
1994	Cin-N	1	2	.333	6	0	0	0	0	7¹	8	2	3	5	13.5	7.36	56	.267	.333	0	—	-0	-3	-3	0	-0.8
Total	4	3	4	.429	45	0	0	0	2	65²	74	9	25	65	14.0	5.48	73	.285	.354	1	.111	-0	-11	-11	0	-0.7

● **MERLE SETTLEMIRE**   Settlemire, Edgar Merle "Lefty"   b: 1/19/03, Santa Fe, Ohio   d: 6/12/88, Russells Point, Ohio   BL/TL, 5'9", 156 lbs.   Deb: 4/13/28

1928	Bos-A	0	6	.000	30	9	0	0	0	82¹	116	2	34	12	17.1	5.47	75	.345	.415	3	.176	-1	-13	-12	2	-0.6

● **AL SEVERINSEN**   Severinsen, Albert Henry   b: 11/9/44, Brooklyn, N.Y.   BR/TR, 6'3", 220 lbs.   Deb: 7/1/69

1969	Bal-A	1	1	.500	12	0	0	0	0	19²	14	2	10	13	11.0	2.29	156	.206	.308	1	.333	0	3	3	0	0.3
1971	SD-N	2	5	.286	59	0	0	0	8	70	77	4	30	31	14.0	3.47	95	.292	.368	0	.000	-0	-0	-1	1	0.0
1972	SD-N	0	1	.000	17	0	0	0	1	21¹	13	1	7	9	9.3	2.53	130	.173	.262	0	.000	-0	2	2	0	0.1
Total	3	3	7	.300	88	0	0	0	9	111	104	7	47	53	12.6	3.08	108	.256	.338	1	.200	0	5	3	2	0.4

● **ED SEWARD**   Seward, Edward William (b: Edward William Sourhardt)   b: 6/29/1867, Cleveland, Ohio   d: 7/30/47, Cleveland, Ohio   TR, 5'7", 175 lbs.   Deb: 9/30/1885   U♦

1885	Pro-N	0	0	—	1	0	0	0	0	6	2	0	1	1	3.0	0.00	—	.100	.100	0	.000	-0	2	2	1	0.0
1887	Phi-a	25	25	.500	55	52	52	3	0	470²	445	7	140	155	11.6	4.13	104	.244	.306	50	.188	-4	9	8	-2	0.0
1888	Phi-a	35	19	.648	57	57	57	6	0	518²	388	4	127	272	9.3	2.01	149	.200	.258	32	.142	-4	61	56	3	4.9
1889	Phi-a	21	15	.583	39	38	35	3	0	320	353	8	101	102	13.1	3.97	95	.271	.330	31	.217	6	-4	-6	-2	-0.2
1890	Phi-a	6	12	.333	21	19	15	1	0	154	165	4	72	55	14.3	4.73	81	.266	.349	10	.139	-1	-15	-15	-0	-1.5
1891	Cle-N	2	1	.667	3	3	0	0	0	16¹	16	0	4	4	9.4	3.86	90	.247	.258	4	.211	0	-1	-1	-1	-0.1
Total	6	89	72	.553	176	169	159	13	0	1485²	1369	23	441	589	11.4	3.40	108	.237	.299	127	.174	-3	51	43	-2	3.1

● **FRANK SEWARD**   Seward, Frank Martin   b: 4/7/21, Pennsauken, N.J.   BR/TR, 6'3", 200 lbs.   Deb: 9/28/43

1943	NY-N	0	1	.000	1	1	0	0	0	9	12	0	5	2	17.0	3.00	115	.324	.405	0	.000	-1	0	0	-0	-0.1
1944	NY-N	3	2	.600	25	7	2	0	0	78¹	98	8	32	16	15.2	5.40	68	.306	.373	2	.083	-2	-16	-15	-1	-1.2
Total	2	3	3	.500	26	8	3	0	0	87¹	110	8	37	18	15.4	5.15	71	.308	.376	2	.071	-2	-15	-15	-2	-1.3

● **RIP SEWELL**   Sewell, Truett Banks   b: 5/11/07, Decatur, Ala.   d: 9/3/89, Plant City, Fla.   BL/TR, 6'1", 180 lbs.   Deb: 6/14/32   C

1932	Det-A	0	0	—	5	0	0	0	0	10²	19	2	4	4	22.8	12.66	37	.388	.474	1	.500	0	-10	-9	0	0.0
1938	Pit-N	0	1	.000	17	0	0	0	1	38¹	41	3	21	17	15.0	4.23	90	.275	.372	1	.083	-1	-2	-2	1	0.0
1939	Pit-N	10	9	.526	52	12	5	1	2	176¹	177	10	73	69	12.8	4.08	94	.265	.339	11	.200	1	-3	-5	3	-0.1
1940	Pit-N	16	5	.762	33	23	14	2	1	189²	169	6	67	60	11.3	2.80	136	.238	.307	14	.192	2	22	21	2	2.7
1941	Pit-N	14	17	.452	39	32	18	2	2	249	225	18	84	76	11.3	3.72	97	.235	.299	16	.174	-0	-2	-3	2	-0.1
1942	Pit-N	17	15	.531	40	33	18	5	2	248	259	13	72	69	12.1	3.41	99	.265	.317	13	.149	-2	-3	-1	-0	-0.3
1943	Pit-N★	**21**	9	.700	35	31	**25**	2	3	265¹	267	6	75	65	11.7	2.54	137	.260	.312	30	.286	6	25	28	1	**4.0**
1944	Pit-N★	21	12	.636	38	33	24	3	2	286	263	15	99	87	11.5	3.18	117	.240	.304	25	.223	3	14	17	-1	2.1
1945	Pit-N†	11	9	.550	33	24	9	1	1	188	212	9	91	60	14.6	4.07	97	.279	.357	20	.313	6	-6	-3	0	0.3
1946	Pit-N★	8	12	.400	25	20	11	2	0	149¹	140	6	53	33	11.7	3.68	96	.245	.310	9	.180	-0	-4	-3	-1	-0.4
1947	Pit-N	6	4	.600	24	12	4	1	0	121	121	11	36	36	11.9	3.57	118	.263	.321	5	.125	-1	7	9	1	0.7
1948	Pit-N	13	3	.813	21	17	7	0	0	121²	126	9	37	36	12.1	3.48	117	.262	.317	6	.143	1	6	8	-0	1.1
1949	Pit-N	6	1	.857	28	6	2	1	0	76	82	6	32	26	13.5	3.91	108	.280	.351	1	.063	-0	1	2	-1	0.1
Total	13	143	97	.596	390	243	137	20	15	2119¹	2101	116	748	636	12.2	3.48	107	.256	.320	152	.203	16	45	60	7	10.1

● **ELMER SEXAUER**   Sexauer, Elmer George   b: 5/21/26, St.Louis Co., Mo.   BR/TR, 6'4", 220 lbs.   Deb: 9/6/48

1948	Bro-N	0	0	—	2	0	0	0	0	0²	0	0	2	0	27.0	13.50	30	.000	.500	0	—	0	-1	-1	-0	0.0

● **FRANK SEXTON**   Sexton, Frank Joseph   b: 7/8/1872, Brockton, Mass.   d: 1/4/38, Brighton, Mass.   160 lbs.   Deb: 6/21/1895

1895	Bos-N	1	5	.167	7	5	4	0	0	49	59	2	22	14	15.2	5.69	90	.293	.369	5	.227	-1	-5	-3	-1	-0.4

● **GORDON SEYFRIED**   Seyfried, Gordon Clay   b: 7/4/37, Long Beach, Cal.   BR/TR, 6', 185 lbs.   Deb: 9/13/63

1963	Cle-A	0	1	.000	3	1	0	0	0	7¹	9	0	3	1	14.7	1.23	295	.300	.364	0	.000	-0	2	2	0	0.3
1964	Cle-A	0	0	—	2	0	0	0	0	2¹	4	0	0	0	15.4	0.00	—	.444	.444	0	—	0	1	1	-0	0.0
Total	2	0	1	.000	5	1	0	0	0	9²	13	0	3	1	14.9	0.93	388	.333	.381	0	.000	-0	3	3	0	0.3

● **JAKE SEYMOUR**   Seymour, Jacob (b: Jacob Semer)   b: 1854, Pittsburgh, Pa.   d: 8/1/1897, Allegheny, Pa.   Deb: 9/23/1882

1882	Pit-a	0	1	.000	1	1	1	0	0	8	16	0	2	2	20.3	7.88	33	.391	.420	0	.000	-1	-5	-5	-0	-0.4

● **CY SEYMOUR**   Seymour, James Bentley   b: 12/9/1872, Albany, N.Y.   d: 9/20/19, New York, N.Y.   BL/TL, 6', 200 lbs.   Deb: 4/22/1896   ♦

1896	NY-N	2	4	.333	11	8	4	0	0	70¹	75	8	51	33	16.5	6.40	66	.271	.390	7	.219	-1	-16	-17	1	-1.1
1897	NY-N	18	14	.563	38	33	28	2	1	277²	254	4	164	149	14.2	3.37	123	**.242**	.355	33	.241	1	29	24	8	3.0
1898	NY-N	25	19	.568	45	43	39	4	0	356²	313	4	213	**239**	14.1	3.18	109	.234	.353	82	.276	7	17	12	8	2.7
1899	NY-N	14	18	.438	32	32	31	0	0	268¹	247	5	170	142	14.7	3.56	106	.245	.364	52	.327	8	9	6	5	1.9
1900	NY-N	2	1	.667	13	7	2	0	0	53	58	4	54	19	20.7	6.96	52	.278	.447	12	.300	1	-19	-20	1	-0.7
1902	Cin-N	0	0	—	1	0	0	0	0	3	4	0	3	2	21.0	9.00	33	.319	.451	33	.340	16	-2	-2	-0	0.0
Total	6	61	56	.521	140	123	104	6	1	1029	951	25	655	584	14.8	3.76	101	.244	.365	1723	.303	16	18	3	23	5.8

● **JOHN SHAFFER**   Shaffer, John W. "Cannon Ball"   b: 2/18/1864, Lock Haven, Pa.   d: 11/21/26, Endicott, N.Y.   Deb: 9/13/1886

1886	NY-a	5	3	.625	8	8	1	0	0	69	40	0	29	36	9.1	1.96	174	.164	.255	6	.240	1	11	11	-1	1.1
1887	NY-a	2	11	.154	13	13	10	0	0	112	148	3	53	22	17.0	6.19	69	.310	.391	8	.167	-3	-24	-24	2	-2.0
Total	2	7	14	.333	21	21	21	1	0	181	188	3	82	58	14.0	4.57	86	.260	.346	14	.192	-2	-12	-13	1	-0.9

● **GUS SHALLIX**   Shallix, August (b: August Schallick)   b: 3/29/1858, Paderborn, Westphalia, Germany   d: 10/28/37, Cincinnati, Ohio   BR/TR, 5'11", 165 lbs.   Deb: 6/22/1884

1884	Cin-a	11	10	.524	23	23	23	0	0	199²	163	6	53	78	10.9	3.70	90	.212	.286	3	.036	-10	-10	-8	1	-1.5
1885	Cin-a	6	4	.600	13	12	7	0	0	91¹	95	1	33	15	13.9	3.25	100	.265	.349	5	.128	-2	-0	1	1	-0.1
Total	2	17	14	.548	36	35	30	0	0	291	258	7	86	93	11.8	3.56	93	.229	.306	8	.065	-12	-10	-8	2	-1.6

● **GREG SHANAHAN**   Shanahan, Paul Gregory   b: 12/11/47, Eureka, Cal.   BR/TR, 6'2", 190 lbs.   Deb: 9/4/73

1973	LA-N	0	0	—	7	0	0	0	1	15²	14	2	4	11	10.3	3.45	100	.230	.277	0	—	-0	-0	-0	0	0.0
1974	LA-N	0	0	—	4	0	0	0	0	7	7	1	5	2	15.4	3.86	88	.259	.375	0	—	-0	-0	-0	-0	0.0
Total	2	0	0	—	11	0	0	0	1	22²	21	3	9	13	11.9	3.57	96	.239	.309	0	.000	-0	-0	-0	0	0.0

● **HARVEY SHANK**   Shank, Harvey Tillman   b: 7/29/46, Toronto, Ont., Can.   BR/TR, 6'4", 220 lbs.   Deb: 5/16/70

1970	Cal-A	0	0	—	1	0	0	0	0	3	2	0	2	1	12.0	0.00	—	.182	.308	0	—	0	1	1	-0	0.0

● **BILL SHANNER**   Shanner, Wilfred William   b: 11/4/1894, Oakland City, Ind.   d: 12/18/86, Evansville, Ind.   BL/TR,   Deb: 10/1/20

1920	Phi-A	0	0	—	1	0	0	0	0	4	6	2	1	0	15.8	6.75	60	.353	.389	0	.000	-0	-1	-1	0	0.0

● **BOBBY SHANTZ**   Shantz, Robert Clayton   b: 9/26/25, Pottstown, Pa.   BR/TL, 5'6", 142 lbs.   Deb: 5/1/49   F

1949	Phi-A	6	8	.429	33	7	4	1	2	127	100	9	74	58	12.5	3.40	121	.221	.334	7	.189	1	11	10	4	1.5
1950	Phi-A	8	14	.364	36	23	16	0	0	214²	251	18	85	93	14.4	4.61	90	.299	.362	11	.167	-0	-1	-4	0	-0.2
1951	Phi-A☆	18	10	.643	32	25	13	3	0	205¹	213	15	70	77	12.6	3.94	108	.270	.333	18	.250	2	4	-8	3	1.5
1952	Phi-A★	**24**	7	**.774**	33	33	27	5	0	279²	230	21	63	152	**9.6**	2.48	160	.225	**.272**	19	.198	2	37	**46**	2	5.5

YEAR TM/L	W	L	PCT	G	GS	CG	SH	SV	IP	H	HR	BB	SO	RAT	ERA	ERA+	OAV	OOB	BH	AVG	PB	PR	/A	PD	TPI
1953 Phi-A	5	9	.357	16	16	6	0	0	105²	107	10	26	58	11.3	4.09	105	.263	.307	9	.237	1	-1	2	2	0.6
1954 Phi-A	1	0	1.000	2	1	0	0	0	8	12	2	3	3	18.0	7.88	50	.364	.432	1	.333	0	-4	-4	0	-0.3
1955 KC-A	5	10	.333	23	17	4	1	0	125	124	8	66	58	13.8	4.54	92	.264	.356	6	.146	-2	-8	-5	1	-0.6
1956 KC-A	2	7	.222	45	2	1	0	9	101¹	95	12	37	67	12.0	4.35	99	.248	.319	2	.091	-1	-2	-0	1	0.0
1957 *NY-A☆	11	5	.688	30	21	9	1	5	173	157	15	40	72	10.6	**2.45**	147	.248	.299	10	.179	2	26	22	6	3.1
1958 NY-A	7	6	.538	33	13	3	0	0	126	127	8	35	80	11.7	3.36	105	.262	.315	8	.229	2	6	2	3	0.8
1959 NY-A	7	3	.700	33	4	2	2	3	94²	64	4	33	66	9.2	2.38	153	.189	.261	5	.217	1	16	13	1	1.7
1960 *NY-A	5	4	.556	42	0	0	0	11	67²	57	5	24	54	11.0	2.79	128	.235	.309	1	.100	-0	8	6	1	1.0
1961 Pit-N	6	3	.667	43	6	2	1	2	89¹	91	5	26	61	12.2	3.32	120	.271	.331	7	.438	3	7	7	2	1.1
1962 Hou-N	1	1	.500	3	3	1	0	0	20²	15	1	5	14	8.7	1.31	286	.208	.260	0	.000	-1	6	6	2	0.7
StL-N	5	3	.625	28	0	0	0	4	57²	45	7	20	47	10.3	2.18	195	.211	.282	2	.154	-0	11	13	1	2.0
Yr	6	4	.600	31	3	1	0	4	78¹	60	8	25	61	9.9	1.95	211	.210	.276	2	.095	-1	17	19	3	2.7
1963 StL-N	6	4	.600	55	0	0	0	11	79¹	55	6	17	70	8.4	2.61	136	.192	.243	1	.143	-0	6	8	3	1.6
1964 StL-N	1	3	.250	16	0	0	0	0	17¹	14	2	7	12	10.9	3.12	122	.226	.304	0	—	-0	1	1	1	0.4
Chi-N	0	1	.000	20	0	0	0	1	11¹	15	2	6	12	16.7	5.56	67	.319	.396	0	—	-0	-3	-2	0	-0.2
Phi-N	1	1	.500	14	0	0	0	0	32	23	1	6	18	8.2	2.25	154	.204	.244	0	.000	-0	5	4	2	0.5
Yr	2	5	.286	50	0	0	0	1	60²	52	5	19	42	10.5	3.12	116	.233	.293	0	.000	-0	3	3	4	0.7
Total 16	119	99	.546	537	171	78	15	48	1935²	1795	151	643	1072	11.5	3.38	119	.248	.313	107	.195	11	125	137	39	21.1

● **GEORGE SHARROTT**   Sharrott, George Oscar b: 11/2/1869, W.New Brighton, S.I., N.Y. d: 1/6/32, Jamaica, N.Y. BL/TL, 5′8″, 164 lbs. Deb: 7/27/1893

YEAR TM/L	W	L	PCT	G	GS	CG	SH	SV	IP	H	HR	BB	SO	RAT	ERA	ERA+	OAV	OOB	BH	AVG	PB	PR	/A	PD	TPI
1893 Bro-N	4	6	.400	13	10	10	0	1	95	114	3	58	24	17.1	5.87	75	.289	.390	9	.231	0	-13	-15	-1	-1.2
1894 Bro-N	0	1	.000	2	2	1	0	0	9	7	0	5	2	15.0	7.00	71	.213	.367	1	.333	0	-2	-2	-0	-0.2
Total 2	4	7	.364	15	12	11	0	1	104	121	3	63	26	16.9	5.97	75	.283	.388	10	.238	0	-14	-17	-1	-1.4

● **JACK SHARROTT**   Sharrott, John Henry b: 8/13/1869, Bangor, Me. d: 12/31/27, Los Angeles, Cal. BR/TR, 5′9″, 165 lbs. Deb: 4/22/1890 ♦

YEAR TM/L	W	L	PCT	G	GS	CG	SH	SV	IP	H	HR	BB	SO	RAT	ERA	ERA+	OAV	OOB	BH	AVG	PB	PR	/A	PD	TPI
1890 NY-N	11	10	.524	25	20	18	0	0	184	162	3	88	84	12.7	2.89	121	.229	.322	22	.202	-2	14	13	3	1.2
1891 NY-N	5	5	.500	10	9	6	0	1	69¹	47	2	35	41	11.2	2.60	123	.185	.293	10	.333	4	6	5	1	1.0
1892 NY-N	0	0	—	1	0	0	0	0	2	2	0	1	1	13.5	4.50	72	.250	.333	1	.125	-0	0	0	-0	0.0
1893 Phi-N	4	2	.667	12	4	2	0	0	56	53	1	33	11	14.5	4.50	102	.242	.352	38	.250	0	1	0	0	0.1
Total 4	20	17	.541	48	33	26	0	1	311¹	264	6	157	137	12.7	3.12	116	.222	.322	71	.237	2	21	17	3	2.3

● **JOE SHAUTE**   Shaute, Joseph Benjamin "Lefty" b: 8/1/1899, Peckville, Pa. d: 2/21/70, Scranton, Pa. BL/TL, 6′, 190 lbs. Deb: 7/6/22

YEAR TM/L	W	L	PCT	G	GS	CG	SH	SV	IP	H	HR	BB	SO	RAT	ERA	ERA+	OAV	OOB	BH	AVG	PB	PR	/A	PD	TPI
1922 Cle-A	0	0	—	2	0	0	0	0	3²	7	2	3	3	24.5	19.64	20	.389	.476	0	.000	-0	-6	-6	-0	-0.1
1923 Cle-A	10	8	.556	33	16	7	0	0	172	176	4	53	61	12.0	3.51	113	.275	.332	11	.162	-4	9	9	-2	0.3
1924 Cle-A	20	17	.541	46	34	21	2	2	283	317	8	83	68	12.9	3.75	114	.287	.340	34	.318	9	15	16	-2	2.6
1925 Cle-A	4	12	.250	26	17	10	1	4	131	160	6	44	34	14.1	5.43	81	.304	.358	16	.302	3	-15	-15	-2	-1.4
1926 Cle-A	14	10	.583	34	25	15	1	1	206²	215	6	65	47	12.3	3.53	115	.278	.337	20	.274	4	11	12	-5	1.2
1927 Cle-A	9	16	.360	45	28	14	0	2	230¹	255	9	75	63	13.0	4.22	100	.286	.343	27	.325	6	-2	-0	-2	0.3
1928 Cle-A	13	17	.433	36	31	21	0	2	253²	295	9	68	81	13.1	4.04	102	.299	.348	21	.228	3	-0	3	1	0.7
1929 Cle-A	8	8	.500	26	24	8	0	0	162	211	6	52	43	14.7	4.28	104	.320	.370	17	.293	3	-1	3	-3	0.3
1930 Cle-A	0	0	—	4	0	0	0	0	4²	11	1	3	2	23.1	15.43	31	.333	.429	0	—	-0	-6	-5	-0	0.0
1931 Bro-N	11	8	.579	25	19	6	0	0	128²	162	9	32	50	13.6	4.83	79	.305	.346	8	.178	-0	-14	-14	-0	-1.9
1932 Bro-N	7	7	.500	34	9	1	0	4	117	147	8	21	32	13.1	4.54	84	.301	.333	9	.200	1	-9	-9	-2	-1.1
1933 Bro-N	3	4	.429	41	4	0	0	2	108¹	125	4	31	26	13.0	3.49	92	.287	.336	6	.222	1	-2	-3	1	0.0
1934 Cin-N	0	2	.000	8	1	0	0	1	17¹	19	1	3	2	11.4	4.15	98	.268	.297	1	.250	-0	-0	-0	-1	-0.1
Total 13	99	109	.476	360	208	103	5	18	1818¹	2097	75	534	512	13.1	4.15	99	.293	.345	170	.258	25	-18	-12	-14	0.8

● **JEFF SHAVER**   Shaver, Jeffrey Thomas b: 7/30/63, Beaver, Pa. BR/TR, 6′3″, 195 lbs. Deb: 7/6/88

YEAR TM/L	W	L	PCT	G	GS	CG	SH	SV	IP	H	HR	BB	SO	RAT	ERA	ERA+	OAV	OOB	BH	AVG	PB	PR	/A	PD	TPI
1988 Oak-A	0	0	—	1	0	0	0	0	1	0	0	0	0	9.0	0.00	—	.000	.333	0	—	0	0	0	0	0.3

● **DON SHAW**   Shaw, Donald Wellington b: 2/23/44, Pittsburgh, Pa. BL/TL, 6′, 185 lbs. Deb: 4/11/67

YEAR TM/L	W	L	PCT	G	GS	CG	SH	SV	IP	H	HR	BB	SO	RAT	ERA	ERA+	OAV	OOB	BH	AVG	PB	PR	/A	PD	TPI
1967 NY-N	4	5	.444	40	0	0	0	3	51¹	40	5	23	44	11.0	2.98	114	.219	.306	0	.000	0	2	2	-1	0.4
1968 NY-N	0	0	—	7	0	0	0	0	12¹	3	1	5	11	5.8	0.73	414	.086	.200	0	—	0	3	3	0	0.0
1969 Mon-N	2	5	.286	35	1	0	0	1	65²	61	9	37	45	13.7	5.21	71	.254	.358	0	—	-0	-12	-11	1	-1.1
1971 StL-N	7	2	.778	45	0	0	0	2	51	45	1	31	19	13.6	2.65	136	.237	.347	0	—	0	5	5	0	0.9
1972 StL-N	0	1	.000	8	0	0	0	0	3	5	1	3	2	24.0	9.00	38	.417	.533	0	—	-0	-2	-2	-0	-0.6
Oak-A	0	1	.000	3	0	0	0	0	5	12	2	2	4	23.6	16.88	17	.500	.538	0	—	-0	-8	-8	-1	-1.2
Total 5	13	14	.481	138	1	0	0	6	188²	166	19	101	123	12.9	4.01	87	.243	.343	0	—	0	-12	-11	-1	-1.6

● **DUPEE SHAW**   Shaw, Frederick Lander b: 5/31/1859, Charlestown, Mass. d: 6/11/38, Wakefield, Mass. BL/TL, 5′8″, 165 lbs. Deb: 6/18/1883

YEAR TM/L	W	L	PCT	G	GS	CG	SH	SV	IP	H	HR	BB	SO	RAT	ERA	ERA+	OAV	OOB	BH	AVG	PB	PR	/A	PD	TPI
1883 Det-N	10	15	.400	26	25	23	1	0	227	238	3	44	73	11.2	2.50	124	.256	.290	29	.206	-3	16	15	0	1.2
1884 Det-N	9	18	.333	28	28	25	1	0	227²	219	8	72	142	11.5	3.04	95	.237	.292	26	.191	-1	-2	-4	2	-0.3
Bos-U	21	15	.583	39	38	35	5	0	315²	227	1	37	309	7.5	1.77	135	.188	.212	37	.242	-5	**24**	22	-0	1.5
1885 Pro-N	23	26	.469	49	49	47	6	0	399²	343	7	99	194	10.0	2.57	103	.209	.254	22	.133	-10	11	4	-2	-0.7
1886 Was-N	13	31	.295	45	44	43	1	0	385²	384	6	91	177	11.1	3.34	98	.250	.291	13	.088	-10	-1	-2	-1	-1.3
1887 Was-N	7	13	.350	21	20	20	0	0	181¹	263	8	46	47	15.5	6.45	63	.328	.366	13	.186	-2	-48	-48	-2	-4.0
1888 Was-N	0	3	.000	3	3	3	0	0	25	36	2	7	8	15.5	6.48	43	.333	.374	0	.000	-1	-10	-10	-1	-1.1
Total 6	83	121	.407	211	207	196	13	0	1762	1710	41	396	950	10.8	3.10	96	.239	.279	140	.170	-32	-10	-25	-5	-4.7

● **JIM SHAW**   Shaw, James Aloysius "Grunting Jim" b: 8/19/1893, Pittsburgh, Pa. d: 1/27/62, Washington, D.C. BR/TR, 6′, 180 lbs. Deb: 9/15/13

YEAR TM/L	W	L	PCT	G	GS	CG	SH	SV	IP	H	HR	BB	SO	RAT	ERA	ERA+	OAV	OOB	BH	AVG	PB	PR	/A	PD	TPI
1913 Was-A	0	1	.000	2	1	0	0	0	13	8	0	7	14	11.1	2.08	142	.205	.340	0	.000	-0	1	1	1	0.2
1914 Was-A	15	17	.469	48	31	15	5	**4**	257	198	3	137	164	12.0	2.70	104	.216	.324	10	.118	-3	1	3	1	0.2
1915 Was-A	6	11	.353	25	18	7	1	0	133	102	4	76	78	12.2	2.50	119	.220	.333	10	.233	1	6	7	-1	0.9
1916 Was-A	3	8	.273	26	9	5	2	1	106¹	86	1	50	44	11.7	2.62	106	.227	.320	5	.156	-0	2	2	-3	-0.1
1917 Was-A	15	14	.517	47	31	15	2	1	266¹	233	1	123	118	12.1	3.21	82	.242	.328	14	.154	-2	-16	-17	-3	-2.4
1918 Was-A	16	12	.571	41	30	14	4	1	241¹	201	2	90	129	10.9	2.42	113	.228	.300	11	.133	-5	9	8	-5	-0.1
1919 Was-A	17	17	.500	**45**	37	23	3	**5**	**306**	274	5	101	128	11.2	2.73	118	.244	.309	17	.160	-1	17	16	-6	1.1
1920 Was-A	11	18	.379	38	32	19	0	0	236¹	285	12	87	88	14.3	4.27	87	.314	.376	14	.189	0	-12	-14	-4	-1.8
1921 Was-A	1	0	1.000	15	4	0	0	3	40¹	59	2	17	4	17.0	7.36	56	.345	.404	5	.417	2	-14	-15	0	-0.3
Total 9	84	98	.462	287	193	96	17	17	1600¹	1446	28	688	767	12.1	3.07	99	.247	.329	86	.163	-8	-4	-7	-19	-2.3

● **JEFF SHAW**   Shaw, Jeffrey Lee b: 7/7/66, Washington Court House, Ohio BR/TR, 6′2″, 185 lbs. Deb: 4/30/90

YEAR TM/L	W	L	PCT	G	GS	CG	SH	SV	IP	H	HR	BB	SO	RAT	ERA	ERA+	OAV	OOB	BH	AVG	PB	PR	/A	PD	TPI
1990 Cle-A	3	4	.429	12	9	0	0	0	48²	73	11	20	25	17.2	6.66	59	.356	.413	0	—	-0	-15	-15	0	-1.7
1991 Cle-A	0	5	.000	29	1	0	0	1	72¹	72	6	27	31	12.8	3.36	124	.262	.337	0	—	0	6	6	0	0.4
1992 Cle-A	0	1	.000	2	1	0	0	0	7²	7	2	4	3	12.9	8.22	48	.259	.355	0	—	-0	-4	-4	0	-0.3
1993 Mon-N	2	7	.222	55	8	0	0	0	95²	91	12	32	50	12.2	4.14	101	.254	.327	1	.067	-1	-1	0	1	0.0
1994 Mon-N	5	2	.714	46	0	0	0	1	67¹	67	8	15	47	11.2	3.88	109	.254	.299	2	.286	1	3	3	1	0.4
Total 5	10	19	.345	144	19	0	0	2	291²	310	39	98	156	13.0	4.41	99	.275	.340	3	.136	-0	-11	-9	2	-1.2

● **BOB SHAW**   Shaw, Robert John b: 6/29/33, Bronx, N.Y. BR/TR, 6′2″, 195 lbs. Deb: 8/11/57 C

YEAR TM/L	W	L	PCT	G	GS	CG	SH	SV	IP	H	HR	BB	SO	RAT	ERA	ERA+	OAV	OOB	BH	AVG	PB	PR	/A	PD	TPI
1957 Det-A	0	1	.000	7	0	0	0	0	9²	11	2	7	4	16.8	7.45	52	.289	.400	0	.000	-0	-4	-4	-0	-0.4
1958 Det-A	1	2	.333	11	2	0	0	0	26²	32	2	13	14	15.2	5.06	80	.302	.378	3	.375	1	-4	-3	1	-0.2
Chi-A	4	2	.667	29	3	0	0	0	64	67	8	28	18	13.6	4.64	78	.271	.350	0	—	-0	-6	-7	-2	-0.6
Yr	5	4	.556	40	5	0	0	0	90²	99	10	41	35	14.1	4.76	79	.280	.358	3	.136	-0	-10	-10	-2	-0.8
1959 *Chi-A	18	6	**.750**	47	26	8	3	3	230²	217	15	54	89	10.8	2.69	140	.249	.297	9	.123	-2	30	27	1	2.6

YEAR	TM/L	W	L	PCT	G	GS	CG	SH	SV	IP	H	HR	BB	SO	RAT	ERA	ERA+	OAV	OOB	BH	AVG	PB	PR	/A	PD	TPI
1960	Chi-A	13	13	.500	36	32	7	1	0	192²	221	16	62	46	13.4	4.06	93	.292	.348	8	.138	-0	-4	-6	-1	-0.9
1961	Chi-A	3	4	.429	14	10	3	0	0	71¹	85	11	20	31	13.4	3.79	103	.302	.351	4	.000	-1	2	1	-0	-0.1
	KC-A	9	10	.474	26	24	6	0	0	150¹	165	13	58	60	13.8	4.31	97	.281	.352	11	.200	-1	-5	-2	-0	-0.3
	Yr	12	14	.462	40	34	9	0	0	221²	250	24	78	91	13.6	4.14	99	.286	.349	11	.151	-2	-3	-1	-0	-0.4
1962	Mil-N★	15	9	.625	38	29	12	3	2	225	223	20	44	124	11.2	2.80	136	.260	.305	10	.137	1	29	25	-0	2.6
1963	Mil-N	7	11	.389	48	16	3	3	13	159	144	10	55	105	11.5	2.66	121	.243	.312	5	.122	0	11	10	-2	1.2
1964	SF-N	7	6	.538	61	1	0	0	11	93¹	105	5	31	57	13.6	3.76	95	.286	.350	0	.000	-1	-2	-2	-2	-0.6
1965	SF-N	16	9	.640	42	33	6	1	2	235	231	17	53	148	10.3	2.64	136	.236	.280	8	.101	-3	23	25	1	2.4
1966	SF-N	1	4	.200	13	6	0	0	0	31²	45	9	7	21	14.8	6.25	59	.324	.356	0	.000	-1	-9	-9	-1	-1.4
	NY-N	11	10	.524	26	25	7	2	0	167²	171	12	42	104	11.8	3.92	93	.261	.313	13	.260	3	-6	-5	-1	-0.2
	Yr	12	14	.462	39	31	7	2	0	199¹	216	21	49	125	12.3	4.29	85	.272	.320	13	.232	2	-15	-14	0	-1.6
1967	NY-N	3	9	.250	23	13	3	1	0	98²	105	9	28	49	12.3	4.29	79	.273	.326	1	.040	-1	-10	-10	-1	-1.4
	Chi-N	0	2	.000	9	3	0	0	0	22¹	33	0	9	7	18.5	6.04	59	.351	.430	1	.250	0	-7	-6	-0	-0.6
	Yr	3	11	.214	32	16	3	1	0	121	138	9	37	56	13.3	4.61	74	.286	.342	2	.069	-1	-17	-16	-2	-2.0
Total	11	108	98	.524	430	223	55	14	32	1778	1837	149	511	880	12.2	3.52	105	.267	.323	69	.133	-7	38	34	-2	2.1

● SAM SHAW
Shaw, Samuel E. b: 5/1864, Baltimore, Md. BR/TR, 5'5", 140 lbs. Deb: 5/3/1888

YEAR	TM/L	W	L	PCT	G	GS	CG	SH	SV	IP	H	HR	BB	SO	RAT	ERA	ERA+	OAV	OOB	BH	AVG	PB	PR	/A	PD	TPI
1888	Bal-a	2	4	.333	6	6	6	0	0	53	65	2	15	22	14.3	3.40	88	.291	.347	3	.150	-1	-2	-2	-1	-0.4
1893	Chi-N	1	0	1.000	2	2	1	0	0	16	12	2	13	1	19.1	5.63	82	.202	.418	2	.286	-0	-2	-2	-0	-0.1
Total	2	3	4	.429	8	8	7	0	0	69	77	4	28	23	15.4	3.91	86	.273	.365	5	.185	-1	-4	-4	-1	-0.5

● BOB SHAWKEY
Shawkey, James Robert b: 12/4/1890, Sigel, Pa. d: 12/31/80, Syracuse, N.Y. BR/TR, 5'11", 168 lbs. Deb: 7/16/13 MC

YEAR	TM/L	W	L	PCT	G	GS	CG	SH	SV	IP	H	HR	BB	SO	RAT	ERA	ERA+	OAV	OOB	BH	AVG	PB	PR	/A	PD	TPI
1913	Phi-A	6	5	.545	18	15	8	1	0	111¹	92	2	50	52	11.7	2.34	118	.207	.291	6	.136	-2	7	5	1	0.4
1914	*Phi-A	16	8	.667	38	31	18	5	2	237	223	4	75	89	11.4	2.73	96	.262	.323	17	.205	2	0	-3	-2	-0.3
1915	Phi-A	6	6	.500	17	13	7	1	0	100	103	3	38	56	12.8	4.05	72	.278	.346	4	.129	-1	-12	-12	0	-1.4
	NY-A	4	7	.364	16	9	5	1	0	85²	78	2	35	31	12.1	3.26	90	.265	.347	7	.241	1	-3	-3	-1	-0.3
	Yr	10	13	.435	33	22	12	2	0	185²	181	5	73	87	12.4	3.68	80	.272	.345	11	.183	1	-15	-16	-1	-1.7
1916	NY-A	24	14	.632	53	27	21	4	8	276²	204	4	81	122	9.5	2.21	131	.209	.273	17	.183	-1	19	21	0	2.9
1917	NY-A	13	15	.464	32	26	16	2	0	236¹	207	2	72	97	10.9	2.44	110	.243	.306	16	.190	-0	6	7	3	1.1
1918	NY-A	1	1	.500	3	2	1	1	0	16	7	0	10	9	9.6	1.13	251	.143	.288	3	.750	2	3	3	0	0.7
1919	NY-A	20	11	.645	41	27	22	3	5	261¹	218	7	92	122	11.0	2.72	117	.231	.303	22	.234	-0	15	14	-1	1.5
1920	NY-A	20	13	.606	38	31	20	5	2	267²	246	10	85	126	11.2	**2.45**	**156**	.248	.308	23	.230	-0	40	41	-3	4.3
1921	*NY-A	18	12	.600	38	31	18	3	2	245	245	16	86	126	12.4	4.08	104	.263	.329	27	.300	4	6	4	-0	0.4
1922	*NY-A	20	12	.625	39	34	22	3	1	299²	286	16	98	130	11.5	2.91	138	.256	.316	21	.183	-3	38	36	-0	3.2
1923	*NY-A	16	11	.593	36	31	17	1	1	258²	232	17	102	125	11.8	3.51	112	**.246**	.322	14	.202	-3	14	12	-1	0.8
1924	NY-A	16	11	.593	38	25	10	1	0	207²	226	11	74	114	13.1	4.12	101	.286	.350	22	.319	8	3	1	-1	0.7
1925	NY-A	6	14	.300	33	20	9	1	0	186	209	12	67	81	13.6	4.11	104	.294	.359	10	.147	-4	6	3	-1	-0.2
1926	*NY-A	8	7	.533	29	10	3	1	3	104¹	102	8	37	63	12.2	3.62	106	.263	.330	9	.257	2	5	3	-0	0.5
1927	NY-A	2	3	.400	19	2	0	0	0	43²	44	1	16	23	12.6	2.89	134	.262	.330	1	.091	-1	4	5	-0	0.5
Total	15	196	150	.566	488	334	197	33	28	2937	2722	114	1018	1360	11.6	3.09	114	.251	.319	225	.214	4	151	136	-10	14.8

● SPEC SHEA
Shea, Francis Joseph "The Naugatuck Nugget" (b: Francis Joseph O'shea) b: 10/2/20, Naugatuck, Conn. BR/TR, 6', 195 lbs. Deb: 4/19/47

YEAR	TM/L	W	L	PCT	G	GS	CG	SH	SV	IP	H	HR	BB	SO	RAT	ERA	ERA+	OAV	OOB	BH	AVG	PB	PR	/A	PD	TPI
1947	*NY-A★	14	5	.737	27	23	13	1	0	178²	127	10	89	89	11.1	3.07	115	**.200**	.303	11	.196	2	13	9	-3	0.8
1948	NY-A	9	10	.474	28	22	8	3	1	155²	117	10	87	71	11.9	3.41	120	**.208**	.316	7	.149	1	15	12	-2	1.1
1949	NY-A	1	1	.500	20	3	0	0	1	52¹	48	5	43	22	15.6	5.33	76	.250	.387	3	.250	1	-7	-7	-0	-0.2
1951	NY-A	5	5	.500	25	11	2	2	0	95²	112	11	50	38	15.6	4.33	88	.300	.389	6	.214	1	-2	-5	-0	-0.4
1952	Was-A	11	7	.611	22	21	12	2	0	169	144	6	92	65	12.7	2.93	121	.231	.331	15	.238	2	14	12	-1	1.3
1953	Was-A	12	7	.632	23	23	11	1	0	164²	151	11	75	38	12.6	3.94	99	.244	.329	11	.177	-1	1	-1	-1	-0.3
1954	Was-A	2	9	.182	23	11	1	0	0	71¹	97	9	34	22	16.8	6.18	58	.340	.414	1	.050	-2	-19	-21	1	-2.9
1955	Was-A	2	2	.500	27	4	1	1	2	56¹	53	4	27	16	12.9	3.99	96	.251	.339	4	.400	1	-0	-1	-1	0.0
Total	8	56	46	.549	195	118	48	12	5	943²	849	66	497	361	13.0	3.80	99	.243	.340	58	.195	6	14	-3	-8	-0.6

● JOHN SHEA
Shea, John Michael Joseph "Lefty" b: 12/27/04, Everett, Mass. d: 11/30/56, Malden, Mass. BL/TL, 5'10.5", 171 lbs. Deb: 6/30/28

YEAR	TM/L	W	L	PCT	G	GS	CG	SH	SV	IP	H	HR	BB	SO	RAT	ERA	ERA+	OAV	OOB	BH	AVG	PB	PR	/A	PD	TPI
1928	Bos-A	0	0	—	1	0	0	0	0	1	1	0	1	0	18.0	18.00	23	.250	.400	0	—	0	-2	-2	0	0.0

● MIKE SHEA
Shea, Michael J. b: 3/10/1867, New Orleans, La. TR, 5'10", 170 lbs. Deb: 4/20/1887

YEAR	TM/L	W	L	PCT	G	GS	CG	SH	SV	IP	H	HR	BB	SO	RAT	ERA	ERA+	OAV	OOB	BH	AVG	PB	PR	/A	PD	TPI
1887	Cin-a	1	1	.500	2	2	2	0	0	16²	26	0	10	2	19.4	7.02	62	.333	.409	2	.250	0	-5	-5	1	-0.3

● RED SHEA
Shea, Patrick Henry b: 11/29/1898, Ware, Mass. d: 11/17/81, Stafford Springs, Conn. BR/TR, 6', 165 lbs. Deb: 5/6/18

YEAR	TM/L	W	L	PCT	G	GS	CG	SH	SV	IP	H	HR	BB	SO	RAT	ERA	ERA+	OAV	OOB	BH	AVG	PB	PR	/A	PD	TPI
1918	Phi-A	0	0	—	3	0	0	0	0	9	14	0	2	2	16.0	4.00	73	.378	.410	0	.000	-0	-1	-1	-0	-0.1
1921	NY-N	5	2	.714	9	2	1	0	0	32	28	2	2	10	9.3	3.09	119	.239	.270	1	.111	-1	2	2	-1	0.3
1922	NY-N	0	3	.000	11	2	0	0	0	23	22	2	11	5	12.9	4.70	85	.256	.340	0	.000	-1	-2	-2	-1	-0.2
Total	3	5	5	.500	23	4	1	0	0	64	64	4	15	17	11.5	3.80	97	.267	.318	1	.053	-2	-0	-1	-0	0.0

● STEVE SHEA
Shea, Steven Francis b: 12/5/42, Worcester, Mass. BR/TR, 6'3", 215 lbs. Deb: 7/14/68

YEAR	TM/L	W	L	PCT	G	GS	CG	SH	SV	IP	H	HR	BB	SO	RAT	ERA	ERA+	OAV	OOB	BH	AVG	PB	PR	/A	PD	TPI
1968	Hou-N	4	4	.500	30	0	0	0	6	34²	27	0	11	15	10.6	3.38	88	.229	.311	0	.000	-1	-2	-2	1	-0.4
1969	Mon-N	0	0	—	10	0	0	0	0	15²	18	2	8	11	14.9	2.87	128	.300	.382	0	—	0	1	1	0	0.9
Total	2	4	4	.500	40	0	0	0	6	50¹	45	2	19	26	12.0	3.22	99	.253	.335	0	.000	-1	-0	-1	1	0.4

● AL SHEALY
Shealy, Albert Berley b: 3/20/1900, Chapin, S.C. d: 3/7/67, Hagerstown, Md. BR/TR, 5'11", 175 lbs. Deb: 4/13/28

YEAR	TM/L	W	L	PCT	G	GS	CG	SH	SV	IP	H	HR	BB	SO	RAT	ERA	ERA+	OAV	OOB	BH	AVG	PB	PR	/A	PD	TPI
1928	NY-A	8	6	.571	23	12	3	0	2	96	124	6	42	39	15.7	5.06	74	.308	.375	9	.237	2	-11	-14	0	-1.6
1930	Chi-N	0	0	—	24	0	0	0	0	27	37	2	14	14	17.0	8.00	61	.327	.402	3	.600	1	-9	-9	-0	0.1
Total	2	8	6	.571	47	12	3	0	2	123	161	8	56	53	16.0	5.71	70	.313	.381	12	.279	4	-20	-23	-0	-1.5

● JOHN SHEARON
Shearon, John M. b: 1870, Pittsburgh, Pa. d: 2/1/23, Bradford, Pa. Deb: 7/28/1891 ◆

YEAR	TM/L	W	L	PCT	G	GS	CG	SH	SV	IP	H	HR	BB	SO	RAT	ERA	ERA+	OAV	OOB	BH	AVG	PB	PR	/A	PD	TPI
1891	Cle-N	1	3	.250	6	5	4	0	0	46	57	2	24	19	16.0	3.52	98	.293	.373	30	.242	-0	-1	-0	-0	0.0

● GEORGE SHEARS
Shears, George Penfield b: 4/13/1890, Marshall, Mo. d: 11/12/78, Loveland, Colo. BR/TL, 6'3", 180 lbs. Deb: 4/24/12

YEAR	TM/L	W	L	PCT	G	GS	CG	SH	SV	IP	H	HR	BB	SO	RAT	ERA	ERA+	OAV	OOB	BH	AVG	PB	PR	/A	PD	TPI
1912	NY-A	0	0	—	4	0	0	0	0	15	24	1	11	9	21.0	5.40	67	.364	.455	1	.167	0	-3	-3	0	0.0

● TOM SHEEHAN
Sheehan, Thomas Clancy b: 3/31/1894, Grand Ridge, Ill. d: 10/29/82, Chillicothe, Ohio. BR/TR, 6'2.5", 190 lbs. Deb: 7/14/15 MC

YEAR	TM/L	W	L	PCT	G	GS	CG	SH	SV	IP	H	HR	BB	SO	RAT	ERA	ERA+	OAV	OOB	BH	AVG	PB	PR	/A	PD	TPI
1915	Phi-A	4	9	.308	15	13	8	1	0	102	131	1	38	22	15.0	4.15	71	.335	.395	4	.118	-3	-14	-14	-1	-1.9
1916	Phi-A	1	16	.059	38	17	8	0	0	188	197	2	94	54	14.0	3.69	84	.287	.374	7	.125	-2	-18	-17	3	-1.4
1921	NY-A	1	0	1.000	12	1	0	0	1	33	43	4	19	7	17.2	5.45	78	.326	.414	5	.625	-2	-4	-2	2	0.2
1924	Cin-N	9	11	.450	39	16	8	2	1	166²	170	5	54	52	12.1	3.24	116	.269	.328	18	.310	4	12	10	-2	1.2
1925	Cin-N	1	0	1.000	10	3	1	0	2	29	37	3	12	5	15.2	8.07	50	.298	.360	1	.200	-1	-12	-13	-1	-0.4
	Pit-N	1	1	.500	23	0	0	0	2	57¹	63	2	13	13	11.9	2.67	167	.286	.326	3	.150	-1	10	11	0	0.3
	Yr	2	1	.667	33	3	1	0	4	86¹	100	5	25	18	13.0	4.48	97	.291	.339	4	.160	-0	-2	-1	-1	-0.1
1926	Pit-N	2	2	.000	9	4	1	0	0	31	36	0	12	16	14.5	6.68	58	.289	.370	1	.111	-1	-10	-9	-0	-0.6
Total	6	17	39	.304	146	54	26	3	5	607	677	14	242	169	13.7	4.00	86	.294	.362	39	.205	-4	-36	-36	1	-2.6

● ROLLIE SHELDON
Sheldon, Roland Frank b: 12/17/36, Putnam, Conn. BR/TR, 6'4", 190 lbs. Deb: 4/23/61

YEAR	TM/L	W	L	PCT	G	GS	CG	SH	SV	IP	H	HR	BB	SO	RAT	ERA	ERA+	OAV	OOB	BH	AVG	PB	PR	/A	PD	TPI
1961	NY-A	11	5	.688	35	21	2	0	0	162²	149	17	55	84	11.4	3.60	103	.246	.311	7	.125	-2	8	2	1	0.1
1962	NY-A	7	8	.467	34	16	2	0	1	118	136	12	28	54	12.6	5.49	68	.289	.331	2	.077	0	-20	-23	-2	-2.7
1964	*NY-A	5	2	.714	19	12	3	0	1	102¹	92	18	18	57	9.8	3.61	100	.243	.279	3	.088	-2	0	0	-1	-0.1
1965	NY-A	0	0	—	3	0	0	0	0	6¹	5	0	1	7	8.5	1.42	240	.238	.273	0	.000	-0	1	1	0	0.0

YEAR	TM/L	W	L	PCT	G	GS	CG	SH	SV	IP	H	HR	BB	SO	RAT	ERA	ERA+	OAV	OOB	BH	AVG	PB	PR	/A	PD	TPI
	KC-A	10	8	.556	32	29	4	1	0	186²	180	22	56	105	11.7	3.95	88	.251	.312	4	.078	-3	-10	-10	-0	-1.2
	Yr	10	8	.556	35	29	4	1	0	193	185	22	57	112	11.6	3.87	90	.251	.310	4	.077	-3	-9	-8	0	-1.2
1966	KC-A	4	7	.364	14	13	1	1	0	69	73	3	26	26	13.0	3.13	109	.275	.342	2	.087	-1	2	2	0	0.2
	Bos-A	1	6	.143	23	10	1	0	0	79²	106	15	23	38	14.8	4.97	77	.320	.368	2	.111	-1	-14	-10	-0	-0.9
	Yr	5	13	.278	37	23	2	1	0	148²	179	18	49	64	13.9	4.12	88	.297	.352	4	.098	-2	-11	-8	1	-0.7
Total	5	38	36	.514	160	101	17	4	2	724²	741	87	207	371	11.9	4.09	89	.266	.320	20	.096	-9	-32	-36	0	-4.6

● FRANK SHELLENBACK
Shellenback, Frank Victor b: 12/16/1898, Joplin, Mo. d: 8/17/69, Newton, Mass. BR/TR, 6'2", 192 lbs. Deb: 5/8/18 C

YEAR	TM/L	W	L	PCT	G	GS	CG	SH	SV	IP	H	HR	BB	SO	RAT	ERA	ERA+	OAV	OOB	BH	AVG	PB	PR	/A	PD	TPI
1918	Chi-A	9	12	.429	28	21	10	2	2	182²	180	1	74	47	12.7	2.66	103	.262	.338	7	.130	-1	2	2	-5	-0.5
1919	Chi-A	1	3	.250	8	4	2	0	0	35	40	1	16	10	14.4	5.14	62	.303	.378	1	.091	-0	-7	-8	-0	-0.8
Total	2	10	15	.400	36	25	12	2	2	217²	220	2	90	57	13.0	3.06	92	.269	.344	8	.123	-1	-5	-6	-5	-1.3

● JIM SHELLENBACK
Shellenback, James Philip b: 11/18/43, Riverside, Cal. BL/TL, 6'2", 200 lbs. Deb: 9/15/66 C

YEAR	TM/L	W	L	PCT	G	GS	CG	SH	SV	IP	H	HR	BB	SO	RAT	ERA	ERA+	OAV	OOB	BH	AVG	PB	PR	/A	PD	TPI
1966	Pit-N	0	0	—	2	0	0	0	0	3	3	2	3	3	18.0	9.00	40	.300	.462	0	—	0	-2	-2	0	0.0
1967	Pit-N	1	1	.500	6	2	1	0	0	23¹	23	1	12	11	13.9	2.70	125	.250	.343	1	.167	-0	2	2	-0	0.1
1969	Pit-N	0	0	—	8	0	0	0	0	16²	14	1	4	7	9.7	3.24	108	.233	.281	0	.000	-0	1	0	1	0.1
	Was-A	4	7	.364	30	11	2	0	1	84²	87	8	48	50	14.5	4.04	86	.268	.364	5	.185	-0	-4	-5	2	-0.5
1970	Was-A	6	7	.462	39	14	2	1	0	117¹	107	6	51	57	12.1	3.68	97	.246	.325	2	.067	-2	0	-2	-1	-0.4
1971	Was-A	3	11	.214	40	15	3	1	0	120	123	10	49	47	13.1	3.53	94	.267	.342	5	.167	-0	-1	-3	1	-0.2
1972	Tex-A	2	4	.333	22	6	0	0	1	57	46	6	16	30	10.1	3.47	87	.221	.283	1	.100	-0	3	-3	-1	-0.4
1973	Tex-A	0	0	—	2	0	0	0	0	1²	0	0	0	3	0.0	0.00	—	.000	.000	0	—	0	1	1	0	0.1
1974	Tex-A	0	0	—	11	0	0	0	0	24²	30	5	12	14	15.7	5.84	61	.306	.387	0	—	-0	-6	-6	0	-0.5
1977	Min-A	0	0	—	5	0	0	0	0	5²	10	1	5	3	23.8	7.94	50	.385	.484	0	—	-0	-2	-2	0	0.0
Total	9	16	30	.348	165	48	8	2	2	454	443	40	200	222	12.9	3.81	89	.258	.338	14	.135	-2	-14	-21	3	-1.2

● BERT SHEPARD
Shepard, Bert Robert b: 6/28/20, Dana, Ind. BL/TL, 5'11", 185 lbs. Deb: 8/4/45

YEAR	TM/L	W	L	PCT	G	GS	CG	SH	SV	IP	H	HR	BB	SO	RAT	ERA	ERA+	OAV	OOB	BH	AVG	PB	PR	/A	PD	TPI
1945	Was-A	0	0	—	1	0	0	0	0	5¹	3	0	1	2	8.4	1.69	184	.167	.250	0	.000	-0	1	1	0	0.0

● KEITH SHEPHERD
Shepherd, Keith Wayne b: 1/21/68, Wabash, Ind. BR/TR, 6'2", 205 lbs. Deb: 9/6/92

YEAR	TM/L	W	L	PCT	G	GS	CG	SH	SV	IP	H	HR	BB	SO	RAT	ERA	ERA+	OAV	OOB	BH	AVG	PB	PR	/A	PD	TPI
1992	Phi-N	1	1	.500	12	0	0	0	2	22	19	0	6	10	10.2	3.27	107	.244	.298	0	—	0	1	1	0	0.1
1993	Col-N	1	3	.250	14	1	0	0	1	19¹	26	4	4	7	14.4	6.98	68	.333	.373	0	.000	-0	-6	-5	-0	-0.9
Total	2	2	4	.333	26	1	0	0	3	41¹	45	4	10	17	12.2	5.01	81	.288	.335	0	.000	-0	-6	-4	0	-0.8

● BILL SHERDEL
Sherdel, William Henry "Wee Willie" b: 8/15/1896, McSherrystown, Pa d: 11/14/68, McSherrystown, Pa BL/TL, 5'10", 160 lbs. Deb: 4/22/18

YEAR	TM/L	W	L	PCT	G	GS	CG	SH	SV	IP	H	HR	BB	SO	RAT	ERA	ERA+	OAV	OOB	BH	AVG	PB	PR	/A	PD	TPI
1918	StL-N	6	12	.333	35	16	9	1	0	182¹	174	3	49	40	11.2	2.71	100	.259	.313	15	.242	3	1	-0	-2	0.2
1919	StL-N	5	9	.357	36	11	7	0	1	137¹	137	3	42	52	11.9	3.47	80	.270	.328	13	.271	2	-9	-10	1	-0.7
1920	StL-N	11	10	.524	43	7	4	0	6	170	183	1	40	74	12.4	3.28	91	.297	.350	14	.222	2	-3	-6	1	-0.4
1921	StL-N	9	8	.529	38	8	5	1	1	144¹	137	7	38	57	11.1	3.18	115	.247	.299	5	.114	-2	10	8	1	0.6
1922	StL-N	17	13	.567	47	31	15	3	2	242	298	12	62	79	13.6	3.87	100	.303	.348	17	.193	1	6	-0	-3	-0.3
1923	StL-N	15	13	.536	39	26	14	0	1	225	270	15	59	78	13.4	4.32	90	.296	.343	28	.337	9	-8	-10	-3	-0.6
1924	StL-N	8	9	.471	35	10	6	0	1	168²	188	9	38	57	12.3	3.42	111	.291	.335	15	.200	2	8	7	-2	0.7
1925	StL-N	15	6	.714	32	21	17	2	1	200	216	8	42	53	11.7	3.11	139	.277	.316	15	.205	2	26	27	-1	2.6
1926	*StL-N	16	12	.571	34	29	17	3	0	234²	255	15	49	59	11.9	3.49	112	.278	.318	22	.244	2	9	11	-3	1.1
1927	StL-N	17	12	.586	39	28	18	0	6	232¹	241	17	48	59	11.3	3.53	112	.269	.308	14	.194	1	10	11	-4	1.1
1928	*StL-N	21	10	.677	38	27	20	0	5	248²	251	17	56	72	11.2	2.86	140	.261	.303	19	.226	4	31	31	-5	3.7
1929	StL-N	10	15	.400	33	22	11	1	0	195²	278	14	58	69	15.5	5.93	79	.337	.382	16	.229	2	-26	-28	-2	-2.8
1930	StL-N	3	2	.600	13	7	1	0	0	64	86	5	13	29	14.1	4.64	108	.325	.358	2	.105	-1	2	3	-1	0.0
	Bos-N	6	5	.545	21	14	7	0	1	119¹	131	6	30	26	12.3	4.75	104	.283	.329	4	.095	-4	3	2	-1	-0.2
	Yr	9	7	.563	34	21	8	0	1	183¹	217	11	43	55	12.9	4.71	105	.298	.339	6	.098	-5	5	5	-1	-0.2
1931	Bos-N	6	10	.375	27	16	8	0	0	137²	163	13	35	34	13.0	4.25	89	.294	.337	14	.304	-0	-6	-7	-2	-0.6
1932	Bos-N	0	0	—	1	0	0	0	0	1²	3	0	1	0	21.6	0.00	—	.375	.444	0	—	0	1	1	-0	0.0
	StL-N	0	0	—	3	0	0	0	0	5²	7	0	1	1	12.7	4.76	83	.304	.333	1	1.000	1	-1	-1	0	0.1
	Yr	0	0	—	4	0	0	0	0	7¹	10	0	2	1	13.5	3.68	106	.323	.364	1	1.000	1	0	0	0	0.1
Total	15	165	146	.531	514	273	159	11	26	2709¹	3018	149	661	839	12.4	3.72	103	.285	.330	214	.223	27	55	38	-25	4.4

● ROY SHERID
Sherid, Royden Richard b: 1/25/07, Norristown, Pa. d: 2/28/82, Parker Ford, Pa. BR/TR, 6'2", 185 lbs. Deb: 5/11/29

YEAR	TM/L	W	L	PCT	G	GS	CG	SH	SV	IP	H	HR	BB	SO	RAT	ERA	ERA+	OAV	OOB	BH	AVG	PB	PR	/A	PD	TPI
1929	NY-A	6	6	.500	33	15	9	1	1	154²	165	6	55	51	13.1	3.61	107	.277	.343	9	.180	-1	11	4	-1	0.2
1930	NY-A	12	13	.480	37	21	8	0	4	184	214	13	87	59	15.0	5.23	82	.289	.368	7	.101	-6	-12	-19	-2	-2.7
1931	NY-A	5	5	.500	17	8	3	0	2	74¹	94	4	24	39	14.7	5.69	70	.306	.362	10	.333	1	-11	-14	0	-1.4
Total	3	23	24	.489	87	44	20	0	7	413	473	23	166	149	14.2	4.71	87	.288	.358	26	.174	-4	-12	-29	-2	-3.9

● JOE SHERMAN
Sherman, Joel Powers b: 11/4/1890, Yarmouth, Mass. d: 12/21/87, Cape Coral, Fla. BR/TR, 6', 165 lbs. Deb: 9/24/15

YEAR	TM/L	W	L	PCT	G	GS	CG	SH	SV	IP	H	HR	BB	SO	RAT	ERA	ERA+	OAV	OOB	BH	AVG	PB	PR	/A	PD	TPI
1915	Phi-A	1	0	1.000	2	1	1	0	0	15	15	0	5	1	10.8	2.40	122	.259	.295	2	.333	1	1	1	-0	0.0

● DAN SHERMAN
Sherman, Lester Daniel "Babe" b: 5/9/1890, Hubbardsville, N.Y. d: 9/16/55, Highland Park, Mich. BR/TR, 5'6", 145 lbs. Deb: 6/4/14

YEAR	TM/L	W	L	PCT	G	GS	CG	SH	SV	IP	H	HR	BB	SO	RAT	ERA	ERA+	OAV	OOB	BH	AVG	PB	PR	/A	PD	TPI
1914	Chi-F	0	1	.000	1	1	0	0	0	0	2	0	2	0	54.0	—	—	.000	.667	0	—	0	0	0	1	0.3

● TIM SHERRILL
Sherrill, Timothy Shawn b: 9/10/65, Harrison, Ark. BL/TL, 5'11", 170 lbs. Deb: 8/14/90

YEAR	TM/L	W	L	PCT	G	GS	CG	SH	SV	IP	H	HR	BB	SO	RAT	ERA	ERA+	OAV	OOB	BH	AVG	PB	PR	/A	PD	TPI
1990	StL-N	0	0	—	8	0	0	0	0	4¹	10	1	3	3	27.0	6.23	61	.476	.542	0	—	0	-1	-1	0	0.0
1991	StL-N	0	0	—	10	0	0	0	0	14¹	20	1	3	14	15.7	8.16	46	.339	.391	0	—	0	-7	-7	0	-0.7
Total	2	0	0	—	18	0	0	0	0	18²	30	2	6	17	18.3	7.71	48	.375	.432	0	—	0	-8	-8	0	-0.8

● FRED SHERRY
Sherry, Fred Peter (b: Fred Peter Schuerholz) b: 1/13/1889, Honesdale, Pa. d: 7/27/75, Honesdale, Pa. BR/TR, 6', 170 lbs. Deb: 4/25/11

YEAR	TM/L	W	L	PCT	G	GS	CG	SH	SV	IP	H	HR	BB	SO	RAT	ERA	ERA+	OAV	OOB	BH	AVG	PB	PR	/A	PD	TPI
1911	Was-A	0	4	.000	10	3	2	0	0	52¹	63	1	19	20	14.1	4.30	76	.310	.369	3	.158	-0	-6	-6	0	-0.4

● LARRY SHERRY
Sherry, Lawrence b: 7/25/35, Los Angeles, Cal. BR/TR, 6'2", 204 lbs. Deb: 4/17/58 FC

YEAR	TM/L	W	L	PCT	G	GS	CG	SH	SV	IP	H	HR	BB	SO	RAT	ERA	ERA+	OAV	OOB	BH	AVG	PB	PR	/A	PD	TPI
1958	LA-N	0	0	—	5	0	0	0	0	4¹	10	0	7	2	37.4	12.46	33	.476	.621	0	—	0	-4	-4	0	0.0
1959	*LA-N	7	2	.778	23	9	1	0	3	94¹	75	9	43	72	11.4	2.19	193	.218	.308	7	.219	2	18	21	-1	2.2
1960	LA-N	14	10	.583	57	3	1	0	7	142¹	125	14	82	114	13.5	3.79	105	.238	.347	6	.162	1	-1	3	1	0.6
1961	LA-N	4	4	.500	53	1	0	0	15	94²	90	10	39	79	12.6	3.90	111	.252	.333	2	.154	-1	1	5	-2	0.3
1962	LA-N	3	4	.700	58	0	0	0	11	90	81	8	44	71	13.1	3.20	113	.241	.339	2	.118	-0	7	4	-0	0.5
1963	LA-N	2	6	.250	36	3	0	0	0	79²	82	9	24	47	12.4	3.73	81	.265	.325	1	.111	1	-4	-6	-0	-0.6
1964	Det-A	7	5	.583	38	0	0	0	11	66¹	52	7	37	58	12.5	3.66	100	.216	.327	0	.000	-2	-0	-0	-0	-0.2
1965	Det-A	3	6	.333	39	0	0	0	5	78¹	71	5	40	46	12.9	3.10	112	.254	.349	3	.300	3	5	5	-0	0.4
1966	Det-A	8	5	.615	55	0	0	0	20	77²	66	8	36	63	12.2	3.82	91	.232	.325	4	.400	-3	-3	-1	-0	-0.5
1967	Det-A	0	1	.000	20	0	0	0	2	28	35	3	7	20	13.8	6.43	51	.289	.333	-0	—	-0	-10	-10	0	-0.4
	Hou-N	1	2	.333	29	0	0	0	0	40²	53	4	13	32	14.8	4.87	68	.327	.381	0	.000	-1	-7	-7	1	-0.7
1968	Cal-A	0	0	—	3	0	0	0	0	3	2	1	2	2	27.0	6.00	49	.467	.529	0	—	-0	-1	-1	-0	0.0
Total	11	53	44	.546	416	16	2	1	82	799¹	747	78	374	606	13.0	3.67	101	.249	.339	25	.169	4	0	5	-2	1.8

● BEN SHIELDS
Shields, Benjamin Cowan "Big Ben" or "Lefty" b: 6/17/03, Huntersville, N.C d: 1/24/82, Woodruff, S.C. BR/TL, 6'1.5", 195 lbs. Deb: 4/17/24

YEAR	TM/L	W	L	PCT	G	GS	CG	SH	SV	IP	H	HR	BB	SO	RAT	ERA	ERA+	OAV	OOB	BH	AVG	PB	PR	/A	PD	TPI
1924	NY-A	0	0	—	2	0	0	0	0	2	6	0	2	0	36.0	27.00	15	.545	.615	0	—	0	-5	-5	-0	0.0
1925	NY-A	3	0	1.000	4	2	2	0	0	24	24	2	12	5	14.3	4.88	87	.267	.365	1	.125	-1	-1	-2	-1	-0.3
1930	Bos-N	0	0	—	3	0	0	0	0	10	16	0	6	1	19.8	9.00	51	.400	.478	0	.000	-0	-5	-5	0	0.0
1931	Phi-N	1	0	1.000	4	0	0	0	0	5¹	9	1	7	3	27.0	15.19	28	.391	.533	0	.000	-0	-7	-6	-0	-1.0
Total	4	4	0	1.000	13	2	2	0	0	41¹	55	3	27	9	18.3	8.27	53	.335	.435	1	.077	-2	-18	-18	-1	-1.3

YEAR	TM/L	W	L	PCT	G	GS	CG	SH	SV	IP	H	HR	BB	SO	RAT	ERA	ERA+	OAV	OOB	BH	AVG	PB	PR	/A	PD	TPI

● CHARLIE SHIELDS Shields, Charles S. b: 12/10/1879, Jackson, Tenn. d: 8/27/53, Memphis, Tenn. BL/TL, Deb: 4/23/02

1902	Bal-A	4	11	.267	23	15	10	1	1	142¹	201	7	32	28	14.9	4.24	89	.333	.368	8	.167	-1	-10	-7	-4	-1.1
	StL-A	3	0	1.000	4	4	3	0	0	30	37	1	7	6	13.2	3.30	107	.303	.341	6	.462	2	1	1	-1	0.3
	Yr	7	11	.389	27	19	13	1	1	172¹	238	8	39	34	14.5	4.07	92	.327	.361	14	.230	1	-10	-7	-5	-0.8
1907	StL-N	0	2	.000	3	2	0	0	0	6²	12	0	7	1	28.4	9.45	46	.444	.583	0	.000	-0	-5	-5	0	-1.2
Total	2	7	13	.350	30	21	13	1	1	179	250	8	46	35	15.1	4.27	86	.332	.373	14	.222	1	-15	-12	-4	-2.0

● STEVE SHIELDS Shields, Stephen Mack b: 11/30/58, Gadsden, Ala. BR/TR, 6'5", 230 lbs. Deb: 6/1/85

1985	Atl-N	1	2	.333	23	6	0	0	0	68	86	9	32	29	15.8	5.16	75	.320	.394	2	.111	-1	-12	-10	-1	-0.6
1986	Atl-N	0	0	—	6	0	0	0	0	12²	13	4	7	6	14.2	7.11	56	.271	.364	0	.000	-0	-5	-4	-0	0.0
	KC-A	0	0	—	3	0	0	0	0	8²	3	1	4	2	7.3	2.08	205	.111	.226	0	—	0	2	2	-0	-0.1
1987	Sea-A	2	0	1.000	20	0	0	0	0	30	43	7	12	22	16.5	6.60	71	.333	.390	0	—	0	-7	-6	-0	-0.8
1988	NY-A	5	5	.500	39	0	0	0	0	82¹	96	8	30	55	14.0	4.37	90	.298	.362	0	—	0	-4	-4	0	-0.4
1989	Min-A	0	1	.000	11	0	0	0	0	17¹	28	3	6	12	17.7	7.79	53	.354	.400	0	—	0	-8	-7	-0	-0.5
Total	5	8	8	.500	102	6	0	0	3	219	269	32	91	126	14.9	5.26	77	.308	.375	2	.105	-1	-33	-29	-1	-2.4

● VINCE SHIELDS Shields, Vincent William b: 11/18/1900, Fredericton, N.B., Canada d: 10/17/52, Plaster Rock, N.B., Canada BL/TL, 5'11", 185 lbs. Deb: 9/20/24

| 1924 | StL-N | 1 | 1 | .500 | 2 | 1 | 0 | 0 | 0 | 12 | 10 | 1 | 3 | 4 | 12.0 | 3.00 | 126 | .227 | .320 | 2 | .400 | 0 | 1 | 1 | -1 | 0.2 |

● GARLAND SHIFFLETT Shifflett, Garland Jessie "Duck" b: 3/28/35, Elkton, Va. BR/TR, 5'10.5", 165 lbs. Deb: 4/22/57

1957	Was-A	0	0	—	6	1	0	0	0	8	6	0	10	2	18.0	10.13	38	.222	.432	0	—	0	-6	-6	-0	0.0
1964	Min-A	0	2	.000	10	0	0	0	1	17²	22	1	7	8	15.3	4.58	78	.297	.366	0	.000	-0	-2	-2	0	-0.2
Total	2	0	2	.000	16	1	0	0	1	25²	28	1	17	10	16.1	6.31	58	.277	.387	0	.000	-0	-8	-8	-0	-0.2

● STEVE SHIFFLETT Shifflett, Stephen Earl b: 1/5/66, Kansas City, Mo. BR/TR, 6'1", 205 lbs. Deb: 7/3/92

| 1992 | KC-A | 1 | 4 | .200 | 34 | 0 | 0 | 0 | 0 | 52 | 55 | 6 | 17 | 25 | 12.8 | 2.60 | 156 | .279 | .343 | 0 | — | 0 | 8 | 8 | 0 | 0.8 |

● ZAK SHINALL Shinall, Zakary Sebastien b: 10/14/68, St.Louis, Mo. BR/TR, 6'3", 215 lbs. Deb: 5/12/93

| 1993 | Sea-A | 0 | 0 | — | 1 | 0 | 0 | 0 | 0 | 2² | 4 | 1 | 2 | 0 | 20.3 | 3.38 | 130 | .333 | .429 | 0 | — | 0 | 0 | 0 | 0 | 0.0 |

● RAZOR SHINES Shines, Anthony Raymond "Ray" b: 7/18/56, Durham, N.C. BB/TR, 6'1", 210 lbs. Deb: 9/9/83 ◆

| 1985 | Mon-N | 0 | 0 | — | 1 | 0 | 0 | 0 | 0 | 1 | 1 | 0 | 0 | 0 | 9.0 | 0.00 | — | .250 | .250 | 6 | .120 | -0 | 0 | 0 | 0 | 0.0 |

● DAVE SHIPANOFF Shipanoff, David Noel b: 11/13/59, Edmonton, Alb., Can. BR/TR, 6'2", 185 lbs. Deb: 8/9/85

| 1985 | Phi-N | 1 | 2 | .333 | 26 | 0 | 0 | 0 | 3 | 36¹ | 33 | 3 | 16 | 26 | 12.4 | 3.22 | 114 | .231 | .313 | 0 | .000 | -0 | 1 | 2 | 0 | 0.1 |

● JOE SHIPLEY Shipley, Joseph Clark "Moses" b: 5/9/35, Morristown, Tenn. BR/TR, 6'4", 210 lbs. Deb: 7/14/58

1958	SF-N	0	0	—	1	0	0	0	0	1¹	3	0	3	0	54.0	33.75	11	.429	.667	0	—	0	-4	-4	-0	-0.1
1959	SF-N	0	0	—	10	1	0	0	0	18	16	2	17	11	17.0	4.50	85	.239	.400	0	.000	-0	-1	-1	-0	-0.1
1960	SF-N	0	0	—	15	0	0	0	0	20	20	2	9	9	14.4	5.40	64	.274	.376	0	—	0	-4	-4	1	0.1
1963	Chi-A	0	1	.000	3	0	0	0	0	4²	9	0	6	3	28.9	5.79	61	.409	.536	0	.000	-0	-1	-1	0	-0.3
Total	4	0	1	.000	29	1	0	0	0	44	48	4	35	23	18.2	5.93	61	.284	.424	0	.000	-1	-10	-11	0	-0.3

● DUKE SHIREY Shirey, Clair Lee b: 6/20/1898, Jersey Shore, Pa. d: 9/1/62, Hagerstown, Md. BR/TR, 6'1", 175 lbs. Deb: 9/28/20

| 1920 | Was-A | 0 | 1 | .000 | 2 | 1 | 0 | 0 | 0 | 4 | 5 | 0 | 2 | 0 | 18.0 | 6.75 | 55 | .313 | .421 | 0 | .000 | -0 | -1 | -1 | -0 | -0.3 |

● TEX SHIRLEY Shirley, Alvis Newman b: 4/25/18, Birthright, Tex. d: 11/7/93, DeSoto, Tex. BB/TR, 6'1", 175 lbs. Deb: 9/6/41

1941	Phi-A	0	1	.000	5	0	0	0	1	7¹	8	1	6	1	17.2	2.45	171	.286	.412	0	.000	-0	1	1	0	0.2
1942	Phi-A	0	1	.000	15	1	0	0	1	35²	37	0	22	10	15.4	5.30	71	.272	.381	0	.000	-1	-7	-6	-1	-0.4
1944	*StL-A	5	4	.556	23	11	2	1	0	80¹	59	4	64	35	13.9	4.15	87	.203	.348	4	.143	-2	-6	-5	-1	-0.8
1945	StL-A	8	12	.400	32	24	10	2	0	183²	191	8	93	77	14.0	3.63	97	.274	.360	20	.286	-2	-5	-2	-1	-0.1
1946	StL-A	6	12	.333	27	18	7	0	0	139²	148	7	105	45	16.4	4.96	75	.273	.391	10	.196	-0	-23	-19	-1	-2.3
Total	5	19	30	.388	102	54	19	3	2	446²	443	20	290	168	14.9	4.25	85	.261	.371	34	.214	-1	-39	-31	-3	-3.4

● BOB SHIRLEY Shirley, Robert Charles b: 6/25/54, Cushing, Okla. BR/TL, 5'11", 185 lbs. Deb: 4/10/77

1977	SD-N	12	18	.400	39	35	1	0	0	214	215	22	100	146	13.4	3.70	96	.259	.341	9	.122	-2	5	4	1	-0.6
1978	SD-N	8	11	.421	50	20	2	0	1	166	164	10	61	102	12.4	3.69	90	.262	.330	5	.125	-0	-2	-7	2	-0.6
1979	SD-N	8	16	.333	49	25	4	1	0	205	196	15	59	117	11.5	3.38	104	.257	.316	5	.091	-2	8	3	0	0.2
1980	SD-N	11	12	.478	59	12	3	0	7	137	143	12	54	67	12.9	3.55	97	.276	.344	1	.033	-2	1	-2	2	-0.3
1981	StL-N	6	4	.600	28	11	1	0	0	79¹	78	6	34	36	12.8	4.08	87	.260	.337	3	.136	-1	0	-3	0	-0.8
1982	Cin-N	8	13	.381	41	20	1	0	0	152²	138	17	73	89	12.6	3.60	103	.248	.338	6	.143	-1	0	2	1	0.2
1983	NY-A	5	8	.385	25	17	1	1	0	108	122	10	36	53	13.2	5.08	77	.293	.350	0	—	0	-12	-14	1	-1.3
1984	NY-A	3	3	.500	41	7	1	0	0	114¹	119	8	38	48	12.4	3.38	112	.274	.333	0	—	0	8	5	0	0.5
1985	NY-A	5	5	.500	48	8	2	0	0	109	103	5	26	55	10.7	2.64	151	.251	.295	0	—	0	18	16	-1	1.4
1986	NY-A	0	4	.000	39	6	0	0	3	105¹	108	11	40	64	12.9	5.04	81	.271	.342	0	—	0	-10	-11	1	-0.3
1987	NY-A	1	0	1.000	12	1	0	0	0	34	36	4	16	12	13.8	4.50	97	.277	.356	0	—	0	-0	-1	0	-0.2
	KC-A	0	0	—	3	0	0	0	0	7¹	10	5	6	1	19.6	14.73	31	.323	.432	0	—	0	-8	-8	-0	-0.2
	Yr	1	0	1.000	15	1	0	0	0	41¹	46	9	22	13	14.8	6.31	70	.275	.360	0	—	0	-9	-9	-1	-0.2
Total	11	67	94	.416	434	162	16	2	18	1432	1432	127	543	790	12.5	3.82	96	.264	.334	29	.110	-8	2	-24	5	-1.8

● STEVE SHIRLEY Shirley, Steven Brian b: 10/12/56, San Francisco, Cal. BL/TL, 6', 185 lbs. Deb: 6/21/82

| 1982 | LA-N | 1 | 1 | .500 | 11 | 0 | 0 | 0 | 0 | 12² | 15 | 0 | 7 | 8 | 15.6 | 4.26 | 81 | .300 | .386 | 1 | 1.000 | 0 | -1 | -1 | 0 | -0.1 |

● GEORGE SHOCH Shoch, George Quintus b: 1/6/1859, Philadelphia, Pa. d: 9/30/37, Philadelphia, Pa. BR/TR, 5'6", 158 lbs. Deb: 9/10/1886 ◆

| 1888 | Was-N | 0 | 0 | — | 1 | 0 | 0 | 0 | 0 | 3 | 2 | 0 | 1 | 0 | 9.0 | 0.00 | — | .167 | .231 | 58 | .183 | 0 | 1 | 1 | -0 | 0.0 |

● URBAN SHOCKER Shocker, Urban James (b: Urbain Jacques Shockcor) b: 8/22/1890, Cleveland, Ohio d: 9/9/28, Denver, Colo. BR/TR, 5'10", 170 lbs. Deb: 4/24/16

1916	NY-A	4	3	.571	12	9	4	1	0	82¹	67	2	32	43	11.5	2.62	110	.230	.319	4	.190	1	2	2	-0	0.3
1917	NY-A	8	5	.615	26	13	7	0	1	145	124	4	46	68	10.6	2.61	103	.241	.303	8	.178	-1	1	1	2	0.2
1918	StL-A	6	5	.545	14	9	7	0	2	94²	69	0	40	33	10.5	1.81	152	.209	.296	11	.324	4	10	10	1	1.8
1919	StL-A	13	11	.542	30	25	14	5	0	211	193	6	55	86	10.7	2.69	123	.244	.296	13	.138	-0	13	15	-1	1.4
1920	StL-A	20	10	.667	38	28	22	0	**5**	245²	224	10	70	107	10.9	2.71	145	.248	.305	18	.225	2	30	33	0	4.0
1921	StL-A	**27**	12	.692	47	38	30	4	4	326²	345	21	86	132	12.0	3.55	126	.270	.319	27	.260	5	26	34	3	4.3
1922	StL-A	24	17	.585	48	38	29	2	3	348	365	22	57	**149**	11.0	2.97	139	.272	.304	22	.191	2	41	45	-3	4.8
1923	StL-A	20	12	.625	43	35	24	3	1	277¹	292	12	49	109	**11.2**	3.41	122	.272	**.306**	16	.200	2	18	24	-3	2.3
1924	StL-A	16	13	.552	40	33	17	4	1	246¹	270	11	52	88	11.9	4.20	107	.277	.315	16	.239	5	1	9	-2	1.2
1925	NY-A	12	12	.500	30	30	15	2	2	244¹	278	17	58	74	12.5	3.65	117	.294	.336	11	.172	5	20	17	-2	1.7
1926	*NY-A	19	11	.633	41	32	18	0	2	258¹	272	13	71	59	12.0	3.38	114	.269	.318	13	.171	1	18	14	-2	1.3
1927	NY-A	18	6	.750	31	27	13	2	0	200	207	8	41	35	11.2	2.84	136	.268	.306	13	.241	3	29	23	-2	2.5
1928	NY-A	0	0	—	1	0	0	0	0	2	1	0	0	0	13.5	0.00	—	.429	.429	0	—	0	1	1	-0	0.0
Total	13	187	117	.615	412	317	200	28	25	2681²	2709	126	657	983	11.4	3.17	124	.265	.311	167	.209	28	210	226	-9	25.8

● MILT SHOFFNER Shoffner, Milburn James b: 11/13/05, Sherman, Tex. d: 1/19/78, Madison, Ohio BL/TL, 6'1.5", 184 lbs. Deb: 7/20/29

| 1929 | Cle-A | 2 | 3 | .400 | 11 | 3 | 1 | 0 | 0 | 44² | 46 | 4 | 22 | 15 | 14.3 | 5.04 | 88 | .284 | .380 | 0 | .000 | -2 | -4 | -3 | 0 | -0.5 |

YEAR TM/L	W	L	PCT	G	GS	CG	SH	SV	IP	H	HR	BB	SO	RAT	ERA	ERA+	OAV	OOB	BH	AVG	PB	PR	/A	PD	TPI
1930 Cle-A	3	4	.429	24	10	1	0	0	84²	129	8	50	17	19.1	7.97	61	.362	.442	7	.212	1	-31	-30	-0	-1.8
1931 Cle-A	2	3	.400	12	4	1	0	0	41	55	4	26	12	18.2	7.24	64	.320	.415	1	.077	-1	-13	-12	-0	-1.3
1937 Bos-N	3	1	.750	6	5	3	1	1	42²	38	1	9	13	10.1	2.53	142	.239	.284	2	.125	1	7	5	1	0.6
1938 Bos-N	8	7	.533	26	15	9	1	1	139²	147	7	36	49	11.9	3.54	97	.270	.317	12	.211	3	4	-2	-2	-0.1
1939 Bos-N	4	6	.400	25	11	7	0	1	132¹	133	4	42	51	12.0	3.13	118	.265	.324	7	.159	-1	12	8	0	0.6
Cin-N	2	2	.500	10	3	0	0	0	37²	43	3	11	6	13.4	3.35	115	.289	.346	1	.091	-1	2	2	-0	0.1
Yr	6	8	.429	35	14	7	0	1	170	176	7	53	57	12.2	3.18	117	.270	.327	8	.145	-1	14	10	0	0.7
1940 Cin-N	1	0	1.000	20	0	0	0	0	54¹	56	3	18	17	12.3	5.63	67	.268	.326	2	.125	-1	-11	-11	-1	-0.3
Total 7	25	26	.490	134	51	22	2	3	577	647	34	214	180	13.6	4.59	85	.287	.352	32	.156	-0	-35	-43	-2	-2.7

● ERNIE SHORE
Shore, Ernest Grady　b: 3/24/1891, East Bend, N.C.　d: 9/24/80, Winston-Salem, N.C.　BR/TR, 6'4", 220 lbs.　Deb: 6/20/12

YEAR TM/L	W	L	PCT	G	GS	CG	SH	SV	IP	H	HR	BB	SO	RAT	ERA	ERA+	OAV	OOB	BH	AVG	PB	PR	/A	PD	TPI
1912 NY-N	0	0	—	1	0	0	1	1	1	8	1	1	1	81.0	27.00	13	.667	.692	0	—	0	-3	-3	-0	-0.5
1914 Bos-A	10	5	.667	20	16	10	1	1	139²	103	1	34	51	9.2	2.00	135	.204	.261	5	.102	-3	12	11	2	1.1
1915 *Bos-A	19	8	.704	38	32	17	4	0	247	207	3	66	102	10.1	1.64	169	.228	.283	8	.101	-3	36	31	4	3.5
1916 *Bos-A	16	10	.615	38	28	10	3	1	225²	221	1	49	62	10.9	2.63	105	.259	.302	7	.091	-5	5	3	5	0.4
1917 Bos-A	13	10	.565	29	27	14	1	1	226²	201	1	55	57	10.6	2.22	116	.240	.297	13	.167	-1	11	9	3	1.1
1919 NY-A	5	8	.385	20	13	3	0	0	95	105	4	44	24	14.2	4.17	77	.288	.366	4	.143	-2	-10	-10	0	-1.4
1920 NY-A	2	2	.500	14	5	2	0	1	44¹	61	1	21	12	16.8	4.87	78	.333	.405	2	.182	-0	-5	-5	1	-0.4
Total 7	65	43	.602	160	121	56	9	5	979¹	906	12	270	309	11.1	2.47	113	.247	.304	39	.121	-14	45	36	14	3.8

● RAY SHORE
Shore, Raymond Everett　b: 6/9/21, Cincinnati, Ohio　BR/TR, 6'3", 210 lbs.　Deb: 9/21/46　C

YEAR TM/L	W	L	PCT	G	GS	CG	SH	SV	IP	H	HR	BB	SO	RAT	ERA	ERA+	OAV	OOB	BH	AVG	PB	PR	/A	PD	TPI
1946 StL-A	0	0	—	1	0	0	0	0	1	3	0	1	0	36.0	18.00	21	.500	.571	0	—	0	-2	-2	0	0.0
1948 StL-A	1	2	.333	17	4	0	0	0	38	40	2	35	12	18.7	6.39	71	.270	.422	0	.000	-1	-9	-8	0	-0.6
1949 StL-A	0	1	.000	13	0	0	0	0	23¹	27	3	31	13	23.1	10.80	42	.297	.484	0	.000	-1	-17	-16	1	-0.6
Total 3	1	3	.250	31	4	0	0	0	62¹	70	5	67	26	20.6	8.23	55	.286	.450	0	.000	-2	-28	-26	1	-1.2

● BILL SHORES
Shores, William David　b: 5/26/04, Abilene, Tex.　d: 2/19/84, Purcell, Okla.　BR/TR, 6', 185 lbs.　Deb: 4/11/28

YEAR TM/L	W	L	PCT	G	GS	CG	SH	SV	IP	H	HR	BB	SO	RAT	ERA	ERA+	OAV	OOB	BH	AVG	PB	PR	/A	PD	TPI
1928 Phi-A	1	1	.500	3	2	1	0	0	14	13	0	7	5	12.9	3.21	125	.250	.339	0	.000	-1	1	1	-0	0.0
1929 Phi-A	11	6	.647	39	13	5	1	7	152²	150	9	59	49	12.5	3.60	118	.262	.334	5	.125	-2	11	11	-1	0.9
1930 *Phi-A	12	4	.750	31	19	7	1	0	159	169	11	70	48	13.7	4.19	112	.276	.353	11	.193	-2	8	9	0	0.5
1931 Phi-A	0	3	.000	6	2	0	0	0	16	26	3	10	2	20.3	5.06	89	.361	.439	1	.333	0	-1	-1	-0	-0.1
1933 NY-N	2	1	.667	8	3	1	0	0	36²	41	4	14	20	13.5	3.93	82	.291	.355	3	.273	1	-2	-3	1	0.0
1936 Chi-A	0	0	—	9	0	0	0	0	17	26	1	8	5	18.0	9.53	55	.356	.420	1	.200	-0	-8	-7	-1	-0.1
Total 6	26	15	.634	96	39	14	2	7	395¹	425	28	168	129	13.6	4.17	105	.279	.353	21	.174	-4	8	8	1	1.3

● CHRIS SHORT
Short, Christopher Joseph　b: 9/19/37, Milford, Del.　d: 8/1/91, Wilmington, Del.　BR/TL, 6'4", 205 lbs.　Deb: 4/19/59

YEAR TM/L	W	L	PCT	G	GS	CG	SH	SV	IP	H	HR	BB	SO	RAT	ERA	ERA+	OAV	OOB	BH	AVG	PB	PR	/A	PD	TPI
1959 Phi-N	0	0	—	3	2	0	0	0	14¹	19	3	10	8	18.8	8.16	50	.317	.423	0	—	-1	-7	-6	-0	-0.1
1960 Phi-N	6	9	.400	42	10	2	0	3	107¹	101	8	52	54	13.1	3.94	99	.249	.339	0	.000	-3	-2	-1	0	-0.4
1961 Phi-N	6	12	.333	39	16	1	0	1	127¹	157	12	71	80	16.3	5.94	69	.304	.391	6	.162	-1	-27	-26	-1	-3.3
1962 Phi-N	11	9	.550	47	12	4	0	3	142	149	13	56	91	13.5	3.42	113	.272	.348	8	.222	1	8	7	0	1.1
1963 Phi-N	9	12	.429	38	27	6	3	0	198	185	12	69	160	11.7	2.95	109	.248	.315	7	.106	-2	7	6	4	0.8
1964 Phi-N★	17	9	.654	42	31	12	4	2	220²	174	10	51	181	9.3	2.20	158	.217	.268	7	.108	-1	33	31	-1	3.5
1965 Phi-N	18	11	.621	47	40	15	5	2	297¹	260	18	89	237	10.7	2.82	123	.235	.295	13	.131	-4	24	21	-3	1.5
1966 Phi-N	20	10	.667	47	39	19	4	0	272	257	28	68	177	11.1	3.54	102	.250	.302	22	.208	1	2	2	0	0.3
1967 Phi-N★	9	11	.450	29	26	8	2	1	199¹	163	9	74	142	10.9	2.39	142	.225	.300	6	.091	-2	22	22	0	2.1
1968 Phi-N	19	13	.594	42	36	9	2	1	269²	236	25	81	202	10.9	2.94	110	.236	.299	12	.152	0	1	2	-1	0.2
1969 Phi-N	0	0	—	2	2	0	0	0	10	11	2	4	5	14.4	7.20	49	.282	.364	0	.000	-0	-4	-4	0	-0.4
1970 Phi-N	9	16	.360	36	34	7	2	1	199	211	13	66	133	12.8	4.30	93	.272	.334	3	.049	-5	-6	-7	-2	-1.5
1971 Phi-N	7	14	.333	31	26	5	2	1	173	182	22	63	95	12.9	3.85	92	.274	.339	4	.083	-1	-7	-6	-1	-0.9
1972 Phi-N	1	1	.500	19	0	0	0	1	23	24	3	8	20	12.5	3.91	92	.267	.327	0	—	0	-1	-1	-0	-0.1
1973 Mil-A	3	5	.375	42	7	0	0	0	72	86	5	44	44	16.5	5.13	73	.299	.395	0	—	0	-10	-11	-0	-1.2
Total 15	135	132	.506	501	308	88	24	18	2325	2215	183	806	1629	11.9	3.43	103	.252	.319	88	.126	-17	33	30	-4	2.0

● BILL SHORT
Short, William Ross　b: 11/27/37, Kingston, N.Y.　BL/TL, 5'9", 170 lbs.　Deb: 4/23/60

YEAR TM/L	W	L	PCT	G	GS	CG	SH	SV	IP	H	HR	BB	SO	RAT	ERA	ERA+	OAV	OOB	BH	AVG	PB	PR	/A	PD	TPI
1960 NY-A	3	5	.375	10	10	2	0	0	47	49	5	30	14	15.3	4.79	75	.282	.390	3	.200	1	-5	-6	-1	-0.9
1962 Bal-A	0	0	—	5	0	0	0	0	4	8	1	0	3	33.8	15.75	23	.381	.536	0	.000	-1	-5	-5	0	-0.9
1966 Bal-A	2	3	.400	6	6	1	1	0	37²	34	2	10	27	10.5	2.87	116	.239	.289	1	.091	-1	2	1	1	0.2
Bos-A	0	0	—	8	0	0	0	0	8¹	10	1	2	2	13.0	4.32	88	.294	.333	-0	—	0	-1	-0	0	-0.1
Yr	2	3	.400	14	6	1	1	0	46	44	3	12	29	11.0	3.13	109	.247	.295	1	.083	-1	2	1	1	0.2
1967 Pit-N	0	0	—	6	0	0	0	0	2¹	1	0	1	1	7.7	3.86	87	.143	.250	-0	—	0	-0	-0	0	0.0
1968 NY-N	0	3	.000	34	0	0	0	0	30¹	24	0	14	24	11.6	4.75	64	.220	.315	0	.000	-0	-6	-6	1	-0.6
1969 Cin-N	0	0	—	4	0	0	0	0	2¹	4	0	1	0	19.3	15.43	24	.400	.455	0	.000	-0	-3	-3	-0	-0.6
Total 6	5	11	.313	73	16	3	1	0	132	130	8	64	71	13.4	4.70	73	.262	.349	4	.125	-1	-18	-19	2	-1.3

● CLYDE SHOUN
Shoun, Clyde Mitchell "Hardrock"　b: 3/20/12, Mountain City, Tenn.　d: 3/20/68, Mountain Home, Tenn.　BL/TL, 6'1", 188 lbs.　Deb: 8/7/35

YEAR TM/L	W	L	PCT	G	GS	CG	SH	SV	IP	H	HR	BB	SO	RAT	ERA	ERA+	OAV	OOB	BH	AVG	PB	PR	/A	PD	TPI
1935 Chi-N	1	0	1.000	5	1	0	0	0	12²	14	2	5	5	13.5	2.84	138	.298	.365	0	.000	-0	2	2	-0	0.0
1936 Chi-N	0	0	—	4	0	0	0	0	4¹	3	0	6	1	18.7	12.46	32	.200	.429	0	—	-0	-4	-4	0	0.0
1937 Chi-N	7	7	.500	37	9	2	0	0	93	118	9	45	43	15.8	5.61	71	.309	.382	4	.138	-1	-18	-17	-1	-2.4
1938 StL-N	6	6	.500	40	12	3	0	1	117¹	130	8	43	37	13.3	4.14	96	.283	.345	8	.258	0	-5	-2	-1	-0.3
1939 StL-N	3	1	.750	53	2	0	0	9	103	98	4	42	50	12.4	3.76	109	.248	.328	3	.115	-1	2	4	-1	0.1
1940 StL-N	13	11	.542	54	19	13	1	5	197¹	193	13	46	82	11.0	3.92	102	.255	.299	12	.190	-1	-2	-1	-0	0.0
1941 StL-N	3	5	.375	26	6	0	0	0	70	98	9	20	34	15.2	5.66	67	.337	.379	4	.182	0	-16	-15	1	-1.4
1942 StL-N	0	0	—	2	0	0	0	0	1²	1	0	0	0	5.4	0.00	—	.167	.167	0	—	0	1	1	0	0.0
Cin-N	1	3	.250	34	0	0	0	0	72²	55	2	24	32	9.8	2.23	147	.216	.283	4	.308	1	9	9	1	0.6
Yr	1	3	.250	36	0	0	0	0	74¹	56	2	24	32	9.7	2.18	151	.215	.281	4	.308	1	9	9	1	0.6
1943 Cin-N	14	5	.737	45	5	2	0	7	147	131	5	46	61	10.8	3.06	108	.241	.300	13	.310	4	5	4	1	1.0
1944 Cin-N	13	10	.565	38	21	12	1	2	202²	193	10	24	59	10.6	3.02	116	.248	.284	13	.224	1	13	11	-3	0.9
1946 Cin-N	1	6	.143	27	5	0	0	0	79	87	3	26	20	13.0	4.10	82	.292	.351	2	.095	-1	-6	-7	-2	-0.9
1947 Cin-N	0	0	—	10	0	0	0	0	14¹	16	2	5	7	13.8	5.02	82	.320	.393	0	—	-2	-2	-1	-0	-0.0
Bos-N	5	3	.625	26	3	1	1	1	73²	73	6	21	23	11.5	4.40	89	.254	.305	3	.158	-1	-3	-4	-1	-0.6
Yr	5	3	.625	36	3	1	1	1	88	89	8	26	30	11.8	4.50	87	.263	.316	3	.158	-1	-4	-6	-1	-0.6
1948 Bos-N	5	1	.833	36	3	0	0	4	74	77	7	20	25	11.8	4.01	96	.267	.315	4	.190	0	-0	-1	-2	-0.3
1949 Bos-N	0	0	—	1	0	0	0	0	1	1	0	0	0	9.0	0.00	—	.250	.250	0	—	0	0	0	0	0.0
Chi-A	1	0	1.000	16	0	0	0	0	23¹	14	3	13	8	19.3	5.79	72	.370	.442	1	.200	-0	-4	-4	-1	-0.5
Total 14	73	59	.553	454	85	34	3	29	1287	1325	81	404	483	12.2	3.91	96	.270	.324	73	.202	1	-27	-25	-9	-3.6

● BRIAN SHOUSE
Shouse, Brian Douglas　b: 9/26/68, Effingham, Ill.　BL/TL, 5'11", 180 lbs.　Deb: 7/31/93　♦

YEAR TM/L	W	L	PCT	G	GS	CG	SH	SV	IP	H	HR	BB	SO	RAT	ERA	ERA+	OAV	OOB	BH	AVG	PB	PR	/A	PD	TPI
1993 Pit-N	0	0	—	6	0	0	0	0	4	7	1	2	3	20.3	9.00	45	.368	.429	0	—	0	-2	-2	0	0.0

● ERIC SHOW
Show, Eric Vaughn　b: 5/19/56, Riverside, Cal.　d: 3/16/94, Dulzura, Cal.　BR/TR, 6'1", 185 lbs.　Deb: 9/2/81

YEAR TM/L	W	L	PCT	G	GS	CG	SH	SV	IP	H	HR	BB	SO	RAT	ERA	ERA+	OAV	OOB	BH	AVG	PB	PR	/A	PD	TPI
1981 SD-N	1	3	.250	15	0	0	0	0	23	17	2	9	22	10.6	3.13	104	.213	.300	0	—	0	1	0	0	0.1
1982 SD-N	10	6	.625	47	14	2	2	3	150	117	10	48	88	10.2	2.64	130	.217	.287	6	.146	-1	16	13	2	1.5
1983 SD-N	15	12	.556	35	33	4	2	0	200²	201	25	74	120	12.6	4.17	84	.263	.330	11	.172	-1	-12	-15	-2	-2.0
1984 *SD-N	15	9	.625	32	32	3	1	0	206²	175	18	88	104	11.6	3.40	105	.234	.317	17	.246	PB	4	4	-1	0.7
1985 SD-N	12	11	.522	35	35	5	2	0	233	212	27	87	141	11.7	3.09	114	.243	.316	10	.127	-1	13	11	-3	0.7

YEAR	TM/L	W	L	PCT	G	GS	CG	SH	SV	IP	H	HR	BB	SO	RAT	ERA	ERA+	OAV	OOB	BH	AVG	PB	PR	/A	PD	TPI
1986	SD-N	9	5	.643	24	22	2	0	0	136¹	109	11	69	94	12.0	2.97	123	.225	.326	7	.163	1	11	10	-2	0.9
1987	SD-N	8	16	.333	34	34	5	3	0	206¹	188	26	85	117	12.3	3.84	103	.241	.323	5	.071	-4	6	3	-1	-0.2
1988	SD-N	16	11	.593	32	32	13	1	0	234²	201	22	53	144	10.0	3.26	104	.231	.280	12	.148	-0	5	4	-4	-0.1
1989	SD-N	8	6	.571	16	16	1	0	0	106¹	113	9	66	66	13.0	4.23	83	.274	.340	8	.235	2	-9	-9	-1	-1.0
1990	SD-N	6	8	.429	39	12	0	0	1	106¹	131	16	41	55	14.9	5.76	66	.306	.372	5	.200	1	-23	-23	-1	-2.7
1991	Oak-A	1	2	.333	23	5	0	0	0	51²	62	5	17	20	13.8	5.92	65	.298	.351	0	—	0	-10	-12	-1	-0.6
Total	11	101	89	.532	332	235	35	11	7	1655	1526	171	610	971	11.9	3.66	98	.247	.319	81	.160	3	1	-13	-13	-2.4

● **LEV SHREVE**   Shreve, Leven Lawrence b: 1/14/1869, Louisville, Ky. d: 10/18/42, Detroit, Mich.   BR/TR, 5'11", 150 lbs.   Deb: 5/2/1887

YEAR	TM/L	W	L	PCT	G	GS	CG	SH	SV	IP	H	HR	BB	SO	RAT	ERA	ERA+	OAV	OOB	BH	AVG	PB	PR	/A	PD	TPI
1887	Bal-a	3	1	.750	5	5	4	1	0	38	33	0	19	13	12.6	3.79	108	.228	.321	4	.167	-1	2	1	0	0.0
	Ind-N	5	9	.357	14	14	14	1	0	122	141	5	65	22	15.5	4.72	88	.278	.365	13	.265	0	-9	-8	-2	-0.8
1888	Ind-N	11	24	.314	35	35	34	1	0	297²	352	23	93	101	13.7	4.63	64	.288	.342	21	.183	-1	-59	-55	0	-5.4
1889	Ind-N	0	3	.000	3	3	1	0	0	15²	25	3	12	5	21.8	13.79	30	.350	.450	0	.000	-1	-17	-17	0	-1.9
Total	3	19	37	.339	57	57	53	3	0	473¹	551	31	189	141	14.3	4.89	70	.283	.351	38	.195	-3	-82	-78	-2	-8.1

● **HARRY SHRIVER**   Shriver, Harry Graydon "Pop" b: 9/2/1896, Wadestown, W.Va. d: 1/21/70, Morgantown, W.Va. BR/TR, 6'2", 180 lbs.   Deb: 4/14/22

YEAR	TM/L	W	L	PCT	G	GS	CG	SH	SV	IP	H	HR	BB	SO	RAT	ERA	ERA+	OAV	OOB	BH	AVG	PB	PR	/A	PD	TPI
1922	Bro-N	4	6	.400	25	14	4	2	0	108¹	114	5	48	38	13.6	2.99	136	.287	.367	1	.037	-3	13	13	-2	0.5
1923	Bro-N	0	0	—	1	1	0	0	0	4	8	0	0	1	18.0	6.75	58	.444	.444	0	.000	-0	-1	-1	-0	0.0
Total	2	4	6	.400	26	15	4	2	0	112¹	122	5	48	39	13.8	3.12	130	.294	.370	1	.036	-3	12	12	-3	0.5

● **PAUL SHUEY**   Shuey, Paul Kenneth b: 9/16/70, Lima, Ohio   BR/TR, 6'3", 215 lbs.   Deb: 5/8/94

YEAR	TM/L	W	L	PCT	G	GS	CG	SH	SV	IP	H	HR	BB	SO	RAT	ERA	ERA+	OAV	OOB	BH	AVG	PB	PR	/A	PD	TPI
1994	Cle-A	0	1	.000	14	0	0	0	5	11²	14	1	12	16	20.1	8.49	58	.280	.419	0	—	0	-5	-5	0	-0.9

● **TOOTS SHULTZ**   Shultz, Wallace Luther b: 10/10/1888, Homestead, Pa. d: 1/30/59, McKeesport, Pa.   BR/TR, 5'10", 175 lbs.   Deb: 5/5/11

YEAR	TM/L	W	L	PCT	G	GS	CG	SH	SV	IP	H	HR	BB	SO	RAT	ERA	ERA+	OAV	OOB	BH	AVG	PB	PR	/A	PD	TPI
1911	Phi-N	0	3	.000	5	3	2	0	0	25	30	5	15	9	17.6	9.36	37	.300	.412	2	.250	0	-17	-16	0	-1.5
1912	Phi-N	1	4	.200	22	4	1	0	1	59	75	2	35	20	17.2	4.58	79	.333	.430	5	.238	0	-8	-6	0	-0.4
Total	2	1	7	.125	27	7	3	0	1	84	105	7	50	29	17.4	6.00	60	.323	.424	7	.241	0	-24	-23	1	-1.9

● **HARRY SHUMAN**   Shuman, Harry b: 3/5/16, Philadelphia, Pa. BR/TR, 6'2", 195 lbs.   Deb: 9/14/42

YEAR	TM/L	W	L	PCT	G	GS	CG	SH	SV	IP	H	HR	BB	SO	RAT	ERA	ERA+	OAV	OOB	BH	AVG	PB	PR	/A	PD	TPI
1942	Pit-N	0	0	—	1	0	0	0	0	2	0	0	1	1	4.5	0.00	—	.000	.167	0	—	0	1	1	-0	0.0
1943	Pit-N	0	0	—	11	0	0	0	0	22	30	0	8	5	16.4	5.32	65	.337	.404	0	.000	-0	-5	-4	0	0.0
1944	Phi-N	0	0	—	18	0	0	0	0	26²	26	1	11	4	12.5	4.05	89	.245	.316	0	.000	-0	-1	-1	0	0.0
Total	3	0	0	—	30	0	0	0	0	50²	56	1	20	10	13.9	4.44	80	.280	.351	0	.000	-0	-5	-5	0	0.0

● **PAUL SIEBERT**   Siebert, Paul Edward b: 6/5/53, Minneapolis, Minn.   BL/TL, 6'2", 205 lbs.   Deb: 9/7/74   F

YEAR	TM/L	W	L	PCT	G	GS	CG	SH	SV	IP	H	HR	BB	SO	RAT	ERA	ERA+	OAV	OOB	BH	AVG	PB	PR	/A	PD	TPI
1974	Hou-N	1	1	.500	5	5	1	1	0	25¹	21	3	11	10	11.4	3.55	97	.236	.320	0	.000	-1	0	-0	1	0.0
1975	Hou-N	0	2	.000	7	2	0	0	2	18¹	20	0	6	6	13.3	2.95	114	.294	.360	0	.000	-0	1	1	0	0.1
1976	Hou-N	0	2	.000	19	0	0	0	0	25²	29	0	18	10	16.8	3.16	101	.296	.410	0	.000	-0	1	0	-1	-0.1
1977	SD-N	0	0	—	4	0	0	0	0	3²	3	1	4	1	17.2	2.45	144	.214	.389	0	—	-0	1	0	-0	0.0
	NY-N	2	1	.667	25	0	0	0	0	28	27	0	13	20	13.2	3.86	97	.257	.345	0	.000	-0	0	-0	-0	-0.1
	Yr	2	1	.667	29	0	0	0	0	31²	30	1	17	21	13.6	3.69	101	.250	.348	0	.000	-0	1	0	-0	-0.1
1978	NY-N	0	2	.000	27	0	0	1	1	28	30	2	21	12	16.7	5.14	68	.283	.406	0	—	-0	-5	-5	0	-0.4
Total	5	3	8	.273	87	7	1	1	3	129	130	6	73	59	14.4	3.77	92	.271	.372	0	.000	-2	-2	-4	0	-0.5

● **SONNY SIEBERT**   Siebert, Wilfred Charles b: 1/14/37, St.Marys, Mo.   BR/TR, 6'3", 198 lbs.   Deb: 4/26/64   C

YEAR	TM/L	W	L	PCT	G	GS	CG	SH	SV	IP	H	HR	BB	SO	RAT	ERA	ERA+	OAV	OOB	BH	AVG	PB	PR	/A	PD	TPI
1964	Cle-A	7	9	.438	41	14	3	1	3	156	142	15	57	144	11.6	3.23	111	.243	.313	13	.265	5	7	6	-2	1.1
1965	Cle-A	16	8	.667	39	27	4	1	1	188²	139	14	46	191	9.1	2.43	143	.206	**.262**	7	.106	-2	22	22	1	2.8
1966	Cle-A★	16	8	**.667**	34	32	11	1	1	241	193	25	62	163	9.7	2.80	123	.221	.278	11	.129	-2	17	17	2	1.7
1967	Cle-A	10	12	.455	34	26	7	1	4	185¹	136	17	54	136	9.5	2.38	137	.202	.268	7	.135	1	18	18	-2	2.3
1968	Cle-A	12	10	.545	31	30	8	4	0	206	145	12	88	146	10.5	2.97	100	.198	.290	11	.157	1	0	-0	-1	0.2
1969	Cle-A	0	1	.000	2	2	0	0	0	14	10	1	8	6	11.6	3.21	117	.196	.305	1	.250	0	1	1	-0	0.1
	Bos-A	14	10	.583	43	22	2	0	5	163¹	151	21	68	127	12.3	3.80	100	.245	.324	8	.151	1	-3	0	2	0.3
	Yr	14	11	.560	45	24	2	0	5	177¹	161	22	76	133	12.2	3.76	101	.241	.322	9	.158	1	-3	1	2	0.4
1970	Bos-A	15	8	.652	33	33	7	2	0	222²	207	29	60	142	11.0	3.44	115	.248	.303	10	.130	-2	7	13	0	1.1
1971	Bos-A☆	16	10	.615	32	32	12	4	0	235¹	220	20	61	131	10.8	2.91	127	.266	.300	21	.266	10	15	21	1	3.5
1972	Bos-A	12	12	.500	32	30	7	3	0	196¹	204	17	59	123	12.4	3.80	84	.264	.322	17	.236	6	-16	-13	1	-0.8
1973	Bos-A	0	1	.000	2	2	0	0	0	2¹	5	1	1	5	23.1	7.71	52	.417	.462	0	—	0	-1	-1	0	-0.3
	Tex-A	7	11	.389	25	20	1	2	0	119²	120	11	37	76	12.0	3.99	93	.258	.317	0	—	0	-2	-1	2	-0.3
	Yr	7	12	.368	27	20	1	1	2	122	125	12	38	81	12.2	4.06	92	.262	.320	0	—	0	-3	-4	2	-0.6
1974	StL-N	8	8	.500	28	20	5	3	0	133²	150	8	51	68	13.7	3.84	93	.288	.355	5	.114	-2	-3	-4	-1	-0.7
1975	SD-N	3	2	.600	6	6	0	0	0	26²	37	2	10	10	16.2	4.39	79	.330	.390	3	.375	2	-2	-3	0	-0.3
	Oak-A	4	4	.500	11	9	1	0	0	61	64	3	14	43	13.4	3.69	98	.252	.338	0	.000	-0	1	-0	-1	-0.2
Total	12	140	114	.551	399	307	67	21	16	2152	1919	197	692	1512	11.1	3.21	110	.238	.303	114	.173	18	57	73	5	10.5

● **DWIGHT SIEBLER**   Siebler, Dwight Leroy b: 8/5/37, Columbus, Neb.   BR/TR, 6'2", 184 lbs.   Deb: 8/26/63

YEAR	TM/L	W	L	PCT	G	GS	CG	SH	SV	IP	H	HR	BB	SO	RAT	ERA	ERA+	OAV	OOB	BH	AVG	PB	PR	/A	PD	TPI
1963	Min-A	2	1	.667	7	5	2	0	0	38²	25	6	12	22	8.8	2.79	130	.182	.253	2	.133	0	4	4	-1	0.1
1964	Min-A	0	0	—	9	0	0	0	0	11	10	1	6	10	13.1	4.91	73	.256	.356	0	—	-0	-2	-2	-0	-0.1
1965	Min-A	0	0	—	7	1	0	0	0	15	11	2	11	15	13.2	4.20	85	.193	.324	0	.000	-0	-1	-1	0	0.0
1966	Min-A	2	2	.500	23	2	0	0	1	49²	47	6	14	24	11.2	3.44	104	.253	.308	0	.000	-0	1	1	-1	-0.1
1967	Min-A	0	0	—	2	0	0	0	0	3	4	0	1	0	15.0	3.00	115	.364	.417	0	—	-0	0	0	-0	0.0
Total	5	4	3	.571	48	8	2	0	1	117¹	97	15	44	71	11.0	3.45	104	.226	.300	2	.074	-1	2	2	-2	0.0

● **CANDY SIERRA**   Sierra, Ulises (Pizarro) b: 3/27/67, Rio Piedras, P.R.   BR/TR, 6'2", 190 lbs.   Deb: 4/6/88

YEAR	TM/L	W	L	PCT	G	GS	CG	SH	SV	IP	H	HR	BB	SO	RAT	ERA	ERA+	OAV	OOB	BH	AVG	PB	PR	/A	PD	TPI
1988	SD-N	0	1	.000	15	0	0	0	0	23²	36	2	11	20	17.9	5.70	60	.379	.443	0	.000	-0	-6	-6	-0	-0.3
	Cin-N	0	0	—	1	0	0	0	0	4	5	0	1	4	13.5	4.50	80	.294	.333	0	.000	-0	-0	-0	0	0.0
	Yr	0	1	.000	16	0	0	0	0	27²	41	2	12	24	17.2	5.53	62	.363	.424	0	.000	-0	-6	-6	-0	-0.3

● **ED SIEVER**   Siever, Edward Tilden b: 4/2/1877, Goddard, Kan. d: 2/4/20, Detroit, Mich.   BL/TL, 5'11.5", 190 lbs.   Deb: 4/26/01

YEAR	TM/L	W	L	PCT	G	GS	CG	SH	SV	IP	H	HR	BB	SO	RAT	ERA	ERA+	OAV	OOB	BH	AVG	PB	PR	/A	PD	TPI
1901	Det-A	18	15	.545	38	33	30	2	0	288²	334	9	65	85	12.7	3.24	119	.286	.328	18	.168	-5	14	19	-1	1.3
1902	Det-A	8	11	.421	25	23	17	4	1	188¹	166	0	32	36	9.6	**1.91**	**191**	.237	.273	10	.152	-4	35	36	-4	2.6
1903	StL-A	13	14	.481	31	27	24	1	0	254	245	6	39	90	10.2	2.48	117	.253	.285	13	.140	-4	14	12	2	1.0
1904	StL-A	10	15	.400	29	24	19	2	0	217	235	3	65	77	12.6	2.65	93	.277	.330	11	.155	-1	-1	-4	1	-0.6
1906	Det-A	14	11	.560	30	25	20	1	0	222²	240	4	45	71	11.9	2.71	102	.278	.321	12	.156	-3	-0	1	-2	-0.5
1907	*Det-A	18	11	.621	39	33	22	3	1	274²	256	1	52	88	10.5	2.16	121	.249	.292	15	.160	-3	12	14	-4	0.6
1908	Det-A	2	6	.250	11	9	4	1	0	61²	74	0	13	23	12.7	3.50	69	.302	.337	3	.167	-1	-8	-7	-1	-1.1
Total	7	83	83	.500	203	174	136	14	2	1507	1550	24	311	470	11.3	2.60	116	.266	.308	82	.156	-21	65	70	-9	3.3

● **WALTER SIGNER**   Signer, Walter Donald Aloysius b: 10/12/10, New York, N.Y. d: 7/23/74, Greenwich, Conn.   BR/TR, 6', 185 lbs.   Deb: 9/18/43

YEAR	TM/L	W	L	PCT	G	GS	CG	SH	SV	IP	H	HR	BB	SO	RAT	ERA	ERA+	OAV	OOB	BH	AVG	PB	PR	/A	PD	TPI
1943	Chi-N	2	1	.667	4	2	1	0	0	25	24	3	4	6	10.1	2.88	116	.245	.275	2	.250	1	3	4	0	0.2
1945	Chi-N	0	0	—	6	0	0	0	0	8	11	1	6	5	18.0	3.38	108	.256	.333	0	.000	-0	-0	-1	-0	0.0
Total	2	2	1	.667	10	2	1	0	1	33	35	4	9	5	12.0	3.00	114	.248	.293	2	.222	1	2	2	-0	0.2

● **SETH SIGSBY**   Sigsby, Seth De Witt (b: Seth De Witt) b: 4/30/1874, Cobleskill, N.Y. d: 9/15/53, Schenectady, N.Y   6', 175 lbs.   Deb: 6/27/1893

YEAR	TM/L	W	L	PCT	G	GS	CG	SH	SV	IP	H	HR	BB	SO	RAT	ERA	ERA+	OAV	OOB	BH	AVG	PB	PR	/A	PD	TPI
1893	NY-N	0	0	—	1	0	0	0	0	3	1	0	4	2	18.0	9.00	52	.101	.403	0	.000	-0	-1	-1	-0	0.0

AL SIMA
Sima, Albert b: 10/7/21, Mahwah, N.J. d: 8/17/93, Suffern, N.Y. BR/TL, 6', 187 lbs. Deb: 6/28/50

YEAR	TM/L	W	L	PCT	G	GS	CG	SH	SV	IP	H	HR	BB	SO	RAT	ERA	ERA+	OAV	OOB	BH	AVG	PB	PR	/A	PD	TPI
1950	Was-A	4	5	.444	17	9	1	0	0	77	89	9	26	23	13.6	4.79	94	.291	.348	3	.115	-2	-2	-3	-1	-0.6
1951	Was-A	3	7	.300	18	8	1	0	0	77	79	5	41	14	14.0	4.79	85	.261	.349	3	.176	1	-6	-6	-1	-0.6
1953	Was-A	2	3	.400	31	5	1	0	1	68¹	63	7	31	25	12.8	3.42	114	.249	.338	2	.118	-1	4	4	1	0.2
1954	Chi-A	0	1	.000	5	1	0	0	1	7	11	1	2	1	16.7	5.14	73	.393	.433	0	.000	-0	-1	-1	0	-0.2
	Phi-A	2	5	.286	29	7	1	0	2	79¹	101	9	32	36	15.1	5.22	75	.309	.370	1	.050	-2	-13	-12	-1	-1.3
	Yr	2	6	.250	34	8	1	0	3	86¹	112	10	34	37	15.2	5.21	75	.314	.373	1	.045	-2	-14	-13	-1	-1.5
Total 4		11	21	.344	100	30	4	0	4	308²	343	31	132	111	14.0	4.61	89	.282	.354	9	.110	-5	-18	-17	-2	-2.5

CURT SIMMONS
Simmons, Curtis Thomas b: 5/19/29, Egypt, Pa. BL/TL, 6', 187 lbs. Deb: 9/28/47

YEAR	TM/L	W	L	PCT	G	GS	CG	SH	SV	IP	H	HR	BB	SO	RAT	ERA	ERA+	OAV	OOB	BH	AVG	PB	PR	/A	PD	TPI
1947	Phi-N	1	0	1.000	1	1	1	0	0	9	5	0	6	9	11.0	1.00	401	.161	.297	1	.500	0	3	3	-0	0.4
1948	Phi-N	7	13	.350	31	22	7	0	0	170	169	8	108	86	14.8	4.87	81	.266	.374	7	.137	-1	-17	-17	1	-1.8
1949	Phi-N	4	10	.286	38	14	2	0	1	131¹	133	7	55	83	13.0	4.59	86	.275	.350	7	.171	-1	-8	-9	-0	-1.0
1950	Phi-N	17	8	.680	31	27	11	2	1	214²	178	19	88	146	11.2	3.40	119	.223	.302	12	.156	-1	18	16	-0	1.5
1952	Phi-N★	14	8	.636	28	28	15	6	0	201¹	170	11	70	141	10.8	2.82	130	.227	.294	11	.164	2	20	19	-3	1.9
1953	Phi-N★	16	13	.552	32	30	19	4	0	238	211	17	82	138	11.2	3.21	131	.236	.302	13	.140	-3	28	26	-3	2.4
1954	Phi-N	14	15	.483	34	33	21	3	1	253	226	14	98	125	11.7	2.81	144	.239	.314	16	.176	-1	35	35	-3	3.3
1955	Phi-N	8	8	.500	25	22	3	0	0	130	148	15	50	58	13.9	4.92	81	.290	.356	8	.174	-1	-13	-14	-1	-1.6
1956	Phi-N	15	10	.600	33	27	14	0	0	198	186	17	65	88	11.5	3.36	111	.248	.311	17	.236	3	9	8	-1	1.3
1957	Phi-N★	12	11	.522	32	29	9	2	0	212	214	11	50	92	11.3	3.44	111	.264	.309	17	.239	4	10	9	-3	1.0
1958	Phi-N	7	14	.333	29	27	7	1	1	168¹	196	11	40	78	12.8	4.38	90	.293	.336	12	.203	0	-8	-8	-1	-1.0
1959	Phi-N	0	0	—	7	0	0	0	0	10	16	2	0	4	15.3	4.50	91	.400	.415	0	—	0	-1	-0	0	0.0
1960	Phi-N	0	0	—	4	2	0	0	0	4	13	3	6	4	42.8	18.00	22	.542	.633	0	—	0	-6	-6	1	0.0
	StL-N	7	4	.636	23	17	3	1	0	152	149	11	31	63	10.7	2.66	154	.257	.295	10	.213	1	19	24	0	1.8
	Yr	7	4	.636	27	19	3	1	0	156	162	14	37	67	11.5	3.06	134	.269	.311	10	.213	1	12	18	1	1.8
1961	StL-N	9	10	.474	30	29	6	2	0	195²	203	14	64	99	12.5	3.13	141	.269	.329	20	.303	5	20	28	-0	3.0
1962	StL-N	10	10	.500	31	22	9	4	0	154	167	18	32	74	11.8	3.51	122	.280	.320	8	.160	0	7	13	-1	1.5
1963	StL-N	15	9	.625	32	32	11	6	0	232²	209	13	48	127	10.2	2.48	143	.239	.283	13	.160	0	21	28	-4	2.5
1964	*StL-N	18	9	.667	34	34	12	3	0	244	233	24	49	104	10.6	3.43	111	.249	.290	3	.106	-3	3	10	-1	0.6
1965	StL-N	9	15	.375	34	32	5	0	0	203	229	19	54	96	12.7	4.08	94	.283	.331	3	.047	-5	-12	-5	-2	-1.3
1966	StL-N	1	1	.500	10	5	1	0	0	33¹	35	3	14	14	13.2	4.59	78	.269	.340	1	.125	-0	-4	-4	-1	-0.2
	Chi-N	4	7	.364	19	10	3	1	0	77¹	79	7	21	24	11.8	4.07	90	.268	.319	2	.111	-0	-2	-3	-0	-0.4
	Yr	5	8	.385	29	15	4	1	0	110²	114	10	35	38	12.2	4.23	86	.268	.325	3	.115	-0	-8	-7	-1	-0.6
1967	Chi-N	3	7	.300	17	14	3	0	0	82	100	10	23	31	13.7	4.94	72	.300	.349	4	.143	-1	-14	-13	-0	-1.5
	Cal-A	2	1	.667	14	4	1	1	1	34²	44	1	9	13	14.3	2.60	121	.321	.372	2	.222	1	2	2	-1	0.2
Total 20		193	183	.513	569	461	163	36	5	3348²	3313	255	1063	1697	11.9	3.54	111	.259	.319	194	.171	1	109	142	-21	12.6

PAT SIMMONS
Simmons, Patrick Clement (b: Patrick Clement Simoni) b: 11/29/08, Watervliet, N.Y. d: 7/3/68, Albany, N.Y. BR/TR, 5'11", 172 lbs. Deb: 4/18/28

YEAR	TM/L	W	L	PCT	G	GS	CG	SH	SV	IP	H	HR	BB	SO	RAT	ERA	ERA+	OAV	OOB	BH	AVG	PB	PR	/A	PD	TPI
1928	Bos-A	0	2	.000	31	3	0	0	1	69	69	4	38	16	14.1	4.04	102	.271	.367	2	.133	-1	0	1	-0	-0.1
1929	Bos-A	0	0	—	2	0	0	0	1	7	6	0	3	2	11.6	0.00	—	.231	.310	0	.000	-0	3	3	0	0.1
Total 2		0	2	.000	33	3	0	0	2	76	75	4	41	18	13.9	3.67	112	.267	.362	2	.125	-1	3	4	-0	0.0

DOUG SIMONS
Simons, Douglas Eugene b: 9/15/66, Bakersfield, Cal. BL/TL, 6', 170 lbs. Deb: 4/9/91

YEAR	TM/L	W	L	PCT	G	GS	CG	SH	SV	IP	H	HR	BB	SO	RAT	ERA	ERA+	OAV	OOB	BH	AVG	PB	PR	/A	PD	TPI
1991	NY-N	2	3	.400	42	1	0	0	1	60²	55	5	19	38	11.3	5.19	70	.246	.310	0	.000	-0	-10	-10	2	-0.7
1992	Mon-N	0	0	—	7	0	0	0	0	5¹	15	3	2	6	30.4	23.63	15	.500	.545	0	—	0	-12	-12	-0	0.0
Total 2		2	3	.400	49	1	0	0	1	66	70	8	21	44	12.8	6.68	54	.276	.338	0	.000	-0	-22	-22	2	-0.7

JOE SIMPSON
Simpson, Joe Allen b: 12/31/51, Purcell, Okla. BL/TL, 6'3", 175 lbs. Deb: 9/2/75 ♦

YEAR	TM/L	W	L	PCT	G	GS	CG	SH	SV	IP	H	HR	BB	SO	RAT	ERA	ERA+	OAV	OOB	BH	AVG	PB	PR	/A	PD	TPI
1983	KC-A	0	0	—	2	0	0	0	0	1	4	2	1	0	18.0	0.00	136	.308	.400	20	.168	1	0	0	-0	0.0

STEVE SIMPSON
Simpson, Steven Edward b: 8/30/48, St.Joseph, Mo. d: 11/2/89, Omaha, Neb. BR/TR, 6'3", 200 lbs. Deb: 9/10/72

YEAR	TM/L	W	L	PCT	G	GS	CG	SH	SV	IP	H	HR	BB	SO	RAT	ERA	ERA+	OAV	OOB	BH	AVG	PB	PR	/A	PD	TPI
1972	SD-N	0	2	.000	9	0	0	0	2	11¹	10	0	8	9	14.3	4.76	69	.238	.360	0	—	0	-2	-2	-0	-0.4

DUKE SIMPSON
Simpson, Thomas Leo b: 9/15/27, Columbus, Ohio BR/TR, 6'1.5", 190 lbs. Deb: 5/6/53

YEAR	TM/L	W	L	PCT	G	GS	CG	SH	SV	IP	H	HR	BB	SO	RAT	ERA	ERA+	OAV	OOB	BH	AVG	PB	PR	/A	PD	TPI
1953	Chi-N	1	2	.333	30	1	0	0	0	45	60	8	25	21	17.2	8.00	56	.314	.396	2	.250	0	-19	-18	-0	-1.0

WAYNE SIMPSON
Simpson, Wayne Kirby b: 12/2/48, Los Angeles, Cal. BR/TR, 6'3", 220 lbs. Deb: 4/9/70

YEAR	TM/L	W	L	PCT	G	GS	CG	SH	SV	IP	H	HR	BB	SO	RAT	ERA	ERA+	OAV	OOB	BH	AVG	PB	PR	/A	PD	TPI
1970	Cin-N☆	14	3	.824	26	26	10	2	0	176	125	15	81	119	11.0	3.02	134	.198	.298	6	.094	-4	20	20	2	1.6
1971	Cin-N	4	7	.364	22	21	1	0	0	117¹	106	9	77	61	14.3	4.76	71	.244	.361	1	.031	-2	-17	-18	2	-1.6
1972	Cin-N	8	5	.615	24	22	1	0	0	130¹	124	17	49	70	12.1	4.14	78	.247	.316	3	.063	-3	-10	-13	-3	-1.8
1973	KC-A	3	4	.429	16	10	1	0	0	59²	66	1	35	29	15.4	5.73	72	.284	.381	0	—	0	-13	-11	-0	-1.1
1975	Phi-N	1	0	1.000	7	5	0	0	0	30²	31	1	11	19	12.6	3.23	116	.263	.331	2	.222	0	1	2	0	0.1
1977	Cal-A	6	12	.333	27	23	0	0	0	122	154	14	62	55	16.5	5.83	67	.308	.392	0	—	0	-24	-26	-1	-3.3
Total 6		36	31	.537	122	107	13	2	0	636	606	57	315	353	13.4	4.37	85	.251	.343	12	.078	-8	-42	-47	0	-6.1

PETE SIMS
Sims, Clarence b: 5/24/1891, Crown City, Ohio d: 12/2/68, Dallas, Tex. BR/TR, 5'11.5", 165 lbs. Deb: 9/16/15

YEAR	TM/L	W	L	PCT	G	GS	CG	SH	SV	IP	H	HR	BB	SO	RAT	ERA	ERA+	OAV	OOB	BH	AVG	PB	PR	/A	PD	TPI
1915	StL-A	1	0	1.000	3	2	0	0	0	8¹	6	0	6	4	13.0	4.32	66	.214	.353	1	1.000	1	-1	-1	-0	-0.1

BERT SINCOCK
Sincock, Herbert Sylvester b: 9/8/1887, Barkerville, B.C., Canada d: 8/1/46, Houghton, Mich. BL/TL, 5'10.5", 165 lbs. Deb: 6/25/08

YEAR	TM/L	W	L	PCT	G	GS	CG	SH	SV	IP	H	HR	BB	SO	RAT	ERA	ERA+	OAV	OOB	BH	AVG	PB	PR	/A	PD	TPI
1908	Cin-N	0	0	—	1	0	0	0	0	4²	3	0	0	1	5.8	3.86	60	.176	.176	0	.000	-0	-1	-1	-0	0.0

BILL SINGER
Singer, William Robert "The Singer Throwing Machine" b: 4/24/44, Los Angeles, Cal. BR/TR, 6'4", 200 lbs. Deb: 9/24/64

YEAR	TM/L	W	L	PCT	G	GS	CG	SH	SV	IP	H	HR	BB	SO	RAT	ERA	ERA+	OAV	OOB	BH	AVG	PB	PR	/A	PD	TPI
1964	LA-N	0	1	.000	2	2	0	0	0	14	11	0	12	3	14.8	3.21	101	.216	.365	1	.167	-0	1	0	-0	0.0
1965	LA-N	0	0	—	2	0	0	0	0	1	2	0	2	1	36.0	0.00	—	.400	.571	0	—	0	0	0	0	0.0
1966	LA-N	0	0	—	3	0	0	0	0	4	4	0	0	4	13.5	0.00	—	.286	.375	0	—	0	2	1	0	0.0
1967	LA-N	12	8	.600	32	29	7	3	0	204¹	185	5	61	169	11.2	2.64	117	.239	.301	6	.090	-3	17	10	1	0.7
1968	LA-N	13	17	.433	37	36	12	6	0	256¹	227	14	78	227	10.9	2.88	96	.237	.298	12	.148	3	3	-3	0	-0.2
1969	LA-N★	20	12	.625	41	40	16	2	1	315²	244	22	74	247	9.4	2.34	142	.210	.263	11	.102	-4	44	35	-2	2.8
1970	LA-N	8	5	.615	16	16	5	3	0	106¹	79	2	52	93	9.6	3.13	122	.203	.267	5	.132	-0	11	8	-1	0.8
1971	LA-N	10	17	.370	31	31	8	1	0	203¹	195	19	71	144	12.0	4.16	78	.252	.318	6	.103	-0	-16	-21	-1	-2.7
1972	LA-N	6	16	.273	26	25	4	3	0	169¹	148	8	60	101	11.3	3.67	91	.237	.309	4	.073	-3	-4	-6	-1	-1.0
1973	Cal-A★	20	14	.588	40	40	19	2	0	315²	280	15	130	241	11.9	3.22	110	.235	.314	0	—	0	21	11	-2	1.0
1974	Cal-A	7	4	.636	14	14	8	0	0	108²	102	3	47	77	12.1	2.98	115	.250	.321	0	—	0	8	5	0	0.6
1975	Cal-A	7	15	.318	29	27	8	0	0	179	171	18	81	78	13.0	4.98	71	.257	.343	0	—	0	-24	-28	-1	-3.1
1976	Tex-A	4	1	.800	10	10	2	1	0	64²	56	4	27	34	12.2	3.48	103	.239	.331	0	—	0	0	1	-0	0.0
	Min-A	9	9	.500	26	26	4	3	0	172	177	12	69	63	13.2	3.77	96	.274	.349	0	—	0	-5	-3	-2	-0.5
	Yr	13	10	.565	36	36	7	4	0	236²	233	13	96	97	12.7	3.69	97	.262	.338	0	—	0	-4	-2	-2	-0.5
1977	Tor-A	2	8	.200	13	12	0	0	0	59²	71	5	39	33	16.9	6.79	62	.296	.399	0	—	0	-18	-17	-0	-2.3
Total 14		118	127	.482	322	308	94	24	2	2174	1952	132	781	1515	11.6	3.39	99	.240	.311	45	.109	-7	39	-7	-7	-3.7

ELMER SINGLETON
Singleton, Bert Elmer "Smoky" b: 6/26/18, Ogden, Utah BR/TR, 6'2", 174 lbs. Deb: 8/20/45

YEAR	TM/L	W	L	PCT	G	GS	CG	SH	SV	IP	H	HR	BB	SO	RAT	ERA	ERA+	OAV	OOB	BH	AVG	PB	PR	/A	PD	TPI
1945	Bos-N	1	4	.200	7	5	1	0	0	37¹	35	1	14	14	12.1	4.82	79	.248	.321	0	.000	-1	-4	-4	-0	-0.6
1946	Bos-N	0	1	.000	15	2	0	0	0	33²	27	3	21	17	13.1	3.74	92	.247	.340	0	.000	-1	-1	-1	-0	-0.1
1947	Pit-N	2	2	.500	36	3	0	0	1	67	70	9	39	24	14.9	6.31	67	.267	.366	4	.308	1	-17	-16	0	-0.7
1948	Pit-N	4	6	.400	38	5	1	0	2	92¹	90	11	40	53	12.8	4.97	82	.253	.330	2	.087	-2	-10	-9	1	-1.0

YEAR TM/L	W	L	PCT	G	GS	CG	SH	SV	IP	H	HR	BB	SO	RAT	ERA	ERA+	OAV	OOB	BH	AVG	PB	PR	/A	PD	TPI
1950 Was-A	1	2	.333	21	1	0	0	0	36¹	39	4	17	19	13.9	5.20	86	.291	.371	3	.429	1	-3	-3	1	0.0
1957 Chi-N	0	1	.000	5	2	0	0	0	13¹	20	3	2	6	14.9	6.75	57	.333	.355	0	.000	-0	-4	-4	0	-0.3
1958 Chi-N	1	0	1.000	2	0	0	0	0	4²	1	0	1	2	3.9	0.00	—	.071	.133	0	.000	-0	2	2	-0	0.4
1959 Chi-N	2	1	.667	21	1	0	0	0	43	40	2	12	25	10.9	2.72	145	.252	.304	0	.000	-1	6	6	1	0.4
Total 8	11	17	.393	145	19	2	0	4	327²	322	33	146	160	13.0	4.83	83	.258	.338	9	.132	-3	-32	-29	3	-1.9

● **JOHN SINGLETON**   Singleton, John Edward "Sheriff"   b: 11/27/1896, Gallipolis, Ohio   d: 10/23/37, Dayton, Ohio   BR/TR, 5'11", 171 lbs.   Deb: 6/8/22

1922 Phi-N	1	10	.091	22	9	3	1	0	93	127	6	38	27	16.5	5.90	79	.346	.415	5	.139	-2	-19	-13	-1	-1.5

● **DOUG SISK**   Sisk, Douglas Randall   b: 9/26/57, Renton, Wash.   BR/TR, 6'2", 210 lbs.   Deb: 9/6/82

1982 NY-N	0	1	.000	8	0	0	0	1	8²	5	1	4	4	10.4	1.04	349	.172	.294	0	—	0	2	2	0	0.4
1983 NY-N	5	4	.556	67	0	0	0	11	104¹	88	1	59	33	13.0	2.24	162	.235	.346	3	.500	1	16	16	-1	1.8
1984 NY-N	1	3	.250	50	0	0	0	15	77²	57	1	54	32	13.2	2.09	169	.215	.354	1	.091	-0	13	12	0	1.2
1985 NY-N	4	5	.444	42	0	0	0	2	73	86	3	40	26	15.8	5.30	65	.291	.379	0	.000	-1	-14	-15	1	-1.9
1986 *NY-N	4	2	.667	41	0	0	0	1	70²	77	0	31	31	14.4	3.06	116	.282	.366	0	.000	-0	5	4	-1	0.2
1987 NY-N	3	1	.750	55	0	0	0	3	78	83	5	22	37	12.5	3.46	109	.270	.325	0	.000	-1	5	3	1	0.2
1988 Bal-A	3	3	.500	52	0	0	0	0	94¹	109	3	45	26	14.9	3.72	105	.306	.387	0	—	0	3	2	1	0.2
1990 Atl-N	0	0	—	3	0	0	0	0	2¹	1	0	4	1	19.3	3.86	105	.143	.455	0	—	0	-0	-0	0	0.0
1991 Atl-N	2	1	.667	14	0	0	0	0	14¹	21	1	8	5	18.2	5.02	77	.333	.408	0	—	0	-2	-2	0	-0.3
Total 9	22	20	.524	332	0	0	0	33	523¹	527	15	267	195	14.0	3.27	112	.268	.361	4	.105	-1	29	23	2	1.8

● **TOMMIE SISK**   Sisk, Tommie Wayne   b: 4/12/42, Ardmore, Okla.   BR/TR, 6'3", 195 lbs.   Deb: 7/19/62

1962 Pit-N	0	2	.000	5	3	1	0	0	17²	18	1	8	6	13.8	4.08	97	.257	.342	1	.200	0	-0	-0	-0	-0.1
1963 Pit-N	1	3	.250	57	4	1	0	1	108	85	6	45	73	10.9	2.92	113	.222	.305	1	.063	-0	4	5	1	0.2
1964 Pit-N	1	4	.200	42	1	0	0	0	61¹	91	4	29	35	18.0	6.16	57	.364	.436	0	.000	-1	-18	-18	2	-1.3
1965 Pit-N	7	3	.700	38	12	1	1	0	111¹	103	6	50	66	12.4	3.40	103	.248	.330	2	.061	-2	2	1	-1	0.2
1966 Pit-N	10	5	.667	34	23	4	1	1	150	146	14	52	60	12.1	4.14	86	.256	.323	5	.098	-1	-9	-9	0	-1.0
1967 Pit-N	13	13	.500	37	31	11	2	1	207²	196	6	78	85	12.0	3.34	101	.253	.324	7	.101	-2	1	1	-1	-0.1
1968 Pit-N	5	5	.500	33	11	0	0	1	96	101	3	35	41	13.0	3.28	89	.282	.351	2	.083	-1	4	-3	-0	-0.5
1969 SD-N	2	13	.133	53	13	1	0	6	143	160	11	48	59	13.2	4.78	74	.285	.342	3	.120	-1	-19	-20	1	-2.0
1970 Chi-A	1	1	.500	17	1	0	0	0	33¹	37	6	13	16	13.5	5.40	72	.276	.340	1	.250	0	-6	-6	1	-0.2
Total 9	40	49	.449	316	99	19	4	10	928¹	937	57	358	441	12.7	3.92	88	.266	.337	22	.094	-7	-48	-50	3	-5.2

● **DAVE SISLER**   Sisler, David Michael   b: 10/16/31, St.Louis, Mo.   BR/TR, 6'4", 200 lbs.   Deb: 4/21/56   F

1956 Bos-A	9	8	.529	39	14	3	0	3	142¹	120	13	72	93	12.6	4.62	100	.227	.328	5	.119	-2	-7	0	0	-0.2
1957 Bos-A	7	8	.467	22	19	5	0	1	122¹	135	15	61	55	14.6	4.71	85	.280	.363	7	.167	-0	-12	-10	1	-1.1
1958 Bos-A	8	9	.471	30	25	4	1	0	149¹	157	22	79	71	14.3	4.94	81	.276	.366	9	.196	0	-19	-16	-1	-1.6
1959 Bos-A	0	0	—	3	0	0	0	0	6²	9	3	1	3	13.5	6.75	60	.310	.333	1	.500	0	-2	-2	-0	0.0
Det-A	1	3	.250	32	0	0	0	7	51²	46	4	36	29	14.5	4.01	101	.242	.366	1	.200	-0	-1	0	-1	0.0
Yr	1	3	.250	35	0	0	0	7	58¹	55	7	37	32	14.3	4.32	94	.251	.362	2	.286	-0	-3	-2	-1	0.0
1960 Det-A	7	5	.583	41	0	0	0	6	80	56	3	45	47	11.6	2.47	160	.199	.314	0	.000	-1	12	13	1	2.2
1961 Was-A	2	8	.200	45	1	0	0	11	60¹	55	6	48	30	15.8	4.18	96	.241	.393	0	.000	-0	-1	-0	-2	-0.2
1962 Cin-N	4	3	.571	35	0	0	0	1	43²	44	4	26	27	14.4	3.92	103	.270	.370	0	—	0	0	1	-1	0.0
Total 7	38	44	.463	247	59	12	1	29	656¹	622	70	368	355	13.8	4.33	95	.253	.354	25	.157	-2	-31	-15	1	-0.9

● **GEORGE SISLER**   Sisler, George Harold "Georgeous George"   b: 3/24/1893, Manchester, Ohio   d: 3/26/73, Richmond Heights, Mo.   BL/TL, 5'11", 170 lbs.   Deb: 6/28/15   FMCH♦

1915 StL-A	4	4	.500	15	8	6	0	0	70	62	0	38	41	13.4	2.83	101	.247	.355	78	.285	3	1	0	0	0.2
1916 StL-A	1	2	.333	3	3	3	1	0	27	18	0	6	12	8.3	1.00	275	.198	.255	177	.305	1	5	5	1	0.9
1918 StL-A	0	0	—	2	1	0	0	1	8	10	0	4	4	16.9	4.50	61	.286	.375	154	.341	1	-2	-2	0	0.0
1920 StL-A	0	0	—	1	0	0	0	1	1	0	0	2	0	0.00	—	.000	.000	257	.407	1	0	0	0	0.1
1925 StL-A	0	0	—	1	0	0	0	0	2	1	0	1	1	9.0	0.00	—	.167	.286	224	.345	0	1	1	0	0.0
1926 StL-A	0	0	—	1	0	0	0	1	2	0	0	3	0	9.0	0.00	—	.000	.286	178	.290	0	1	0	0	0.1
1928 Bos-N	0	0	—	1	0	0	0	0	1	0	0	1	1	9.0	0.00	—	.000	.333	167	.340	0	0	0	-0	0.0
Total 7	5	6	.455	24	12	9	1	3	111	91	0	52	63	12.1	2.35	123	.231	.330	2812	.340	7	8	7	1	1.3

● **CARL SITTON**   Sitton, Carl Vetter   b: 9/22/1882, Pendleton, S.C.   d: 9/11/31, Valdosta, Ga.   BR/TR, 5'10.5", 170 lbs.   Deb: 4/24/09

1909 Cle-A	3	2	.600	14	5	3	0	0	50	50	1	16	16	12.2	2.88	89	.263	.327	2	.154	0	-2	-2	-1	-0.2

● **PETE SIVESS**   Sivess, Peter   b: 9/23/13, South River, N.J.   BR/TR, 6'3.5", 195 lbs.   Deb: 6/13/36

1936 Phi-N	3	4	.429	17	6	2	0	0	65	84	6	36	22	16.8	4.57	99	.310	.393	3	.120	-2	-4	-0	-2	-0.4
1937 Phi-N	1	1	.500	6	2	1	0	0	23	30	5	11	4	16.0	7.04	62	.330	.402	0	.000	-1	-8	-7	-1	-0.6
1938 Phi-N	3	6	.333	39	8	2	0	3	116	143	12	69	32	16.5	5.51	71	.306	.397	6	.188	-1	-22	-21	-1	-1.7
Total 3	7	11	.389	62	16	5	0	3	204	257	23	116	58	16.5	5.38	77	.310	.396	9	.143	-4	-34	-28	-3	-2.7

● **JIM SIWY**   Siwy, James Gerard   b: 9/20/58, Central Falls, R.I   BR/TR, 6'4", 200 lbs.   Deb: 8/20/82

1982 Chi-A	0	0	—	2	1	0	0	0	7	10	1	5	3	19.3	10.29	39	.385	.484	0	—	0	-5	-5	-0	-0.2
1984 Chi-A	0	0	—	1	0	0	0	0	4¹	3	0	2	1	10.4	2.08	200	.231	.333	0	—	0	1	1	-0	-0.2
Total 2	0	0	—	3	1	0	0	0	11¹	13	1	7	4	15.9	7.15	57	.333	.435	0	—	0	-4	-4	-0	-0.2

● **JOE SKALSKI**   Skalski, Joseph Douglas   b: 9/26/64, Burnham, Ill.   BR/TR, 6'3", 190 lbs.   Deb: 4/10/89

1989 Cle-A	0	2	.000	2	1	0	0	0	6²	7	0	4	3	17.6	6.75	59	.259	.394	0	—	0	-2	-2	-0	-0.5

● **DAVE SKAUGSTAD**   Skaugstad, David Wendell   b: 1/10/40, Algona, Iowa   BL/TL, 6'1", 179 lbs.   Deb: 9/25/57

1957 Cin-N	0	0	—	2	0	0	0	0	5²	4	0	6	4	15.9	1.59	259	.190	.370	0	.000	0	1	2	0	0.0

● **DAVE SKEELS**   Skeels, David   b: 12/29/1892, Addy, Wash.   d: 12/2/26, Spokane, Wash.   BL/TR, 6'1", 187 lbs.   Deb: 9/14/10

1910 Det-A	0	0	—	1	1	0	0	0	6	9	0	4	2	21.0	12.00	22	.333	.438	0	.000	-0	-6	-6	0	0.0

● **CRAIG SKOK**   Skok, Craig Richard   b: 9/1/47, Dobbs Ferry, N.Y.   BR/TL, 6', 190 lbs.   Deb: 5/4/73

1973 Bos-A	0	1	.000	11	0	0	0	1	28²	35	2	11	22	14.4	6.28	64	.304	.365	0	—	0	-8	-7	-0	-0.3
1976 Tex-A	0	1	.000	9	0	0	0	0	5	13	2	3	5	28.8	12.60	28	.481	.533	0	—	0	-5	-5	-0	-1.0
1978 Atl-N	3	2	.600	43	0	0	0	0	62	64	8	27	28	13.2	4.35	93	.266	.340	2	.250	-0	-5	-2	-0	-0.2
1979 Atl-N	1	3	.250	44	0	0	0	2	54¹	58	7	17	30	12.9	3.98	102	.282	.345	0	.000	-1	-1	0	-0	0.1
Total 4	4	7	.364	107	0	0	0	5	150	170	19	58	85	13.9	4.86	83	.289	.355	2	.182	-1	-20	-14	-0	-1.4

● **JOHN SKOPEC**   Skopec, John S. "Buckshot"   b: 5/8/1880, Chicago, Ill.   d: 10/20/12, Chicago, Ill.   BR/TL, 5'10", 190 lbs.   Deb: 4/25/01

1901 Chi-A	6	3	.667	9	9	6	0	0	68¹	72	1	45	24	15.1	3.16	110	.239	.388	10	.333	3	4	2	3	0.8
1903 Det-A	2	2	.500	6	5	3	0	0	39¹	46	0	13	14	14.0	3.43	85	.291	.352	2	.154	-0	-2	-0	-0	-0.1
Total 2	8	5	.615	15	14	9	0	0	107²	108	1	58	38	14.7	3.26	101	.259	.363	12	.279	3	2	1	3	0.6

● **JOHN SLAGLE**   Slagle, John A.   b: Lawrence, Ind.   BL/TR,   Deb: 4/30/1891

1891 Cin-a	0	0	—	1	0	0	0	1	1¹	3	0	1	1	27.0	0.00	—	.431	.502	0	.000	-0	1	1	0	0.1

● **ROGER SLAGLE**   Slagle, Roger Lee   b: 11/4/53, Wichita, Kan.   BR/TR, 6'3", 190 lbs.   Deb: 9/7/79

1979 NY-A	0	0	—	1	0	0	0	0	2	0	0	2	0	0.0	0.00	—	.000	.000	0	—	0	1	1	0	0.0

YEAR TM/L	W	L	PCT	G	GS	CG	SH	SV	IP	H	HR	BB	SO	RAT	ERA	ERA+	OAV	OOB	BH	AVG	PB	PR	/A	PD	TPI
● WALT SLAGLE Slagle, Walter Jennings b: 12/15/1878, Kenton, Ohio d: 6/17/74, San Gabriel, Cal. BB/TR, 6′, 165 lbs. Deb: 5/4/10																									
1910 Cin-N	0	0		1	0	0	0	0	1	0	0	3	0	36.0	9.00	32	.000	.571	0	—	0	-1	-1	-0	0.0
● CY SLAPNICKA Slapnicka, Cyril Charles b: 3/23/1886, Cedar Rapids, Iowa d: 10/20/79, Cedar Rapids, Iowa BB/TR, 5′10″, 165 lbs. Deb: 9/26/11																									
1911 Chi-N	0	2	.000	3	2	1	0	0	24	21	0	7	10	11.6	3.38	98	.236	.313	2	.222	-0	0	-0	1	0.1
1918 Pit-N	1	4	.200	7	6	4	0	1	49¹	50	2	22	3	14.0	4.74	61	.269	.362	1	.071	-1	-11	-10	-0	-1.1
Total 2	1	6	.143	10	8	5	0	1	73¹	71	2	29	13	13.3	4.30	70	.258	.346	3	.130	-1	-11	-10	0	-1.0
● JOHN SLAPPEY Slappey, John Henry b: 8/8/1898, Albany, Ga. d: 6/10/57, Marietta, Ga. BL/TL, 6′4″, 170 lbs. Deb: 8/23/20																									
1920 Phi-A	0	1	.000	3	1	0	0	0	6¹	15	0	4	1	27.0	7.11	57	.441	.500	1	.500	1	-2	-2	-0	-0.2
● JIM SLATON Slaton, James Michael b: 6/19/50, Long Beach, Cal. BR/TR, 6′, 185 lbs. Deb: 4/14/71																									
1971 Mil-A	10	8	.556	26	23	5	4	0	147²	140	16	71	63	12.9	3.78	92	.253	.339	5	.109	-1	-5	-5	-2	-0.9
1972 Mil-A	1	6	.143	9	8	0	0	0	44	50	3	21	17	14.7	5.52	55	.287	.367	1	.091	-1	-12	-12	1	-1.8
1973 Mil-A	13	15	.464	38	38	13	3	0	276¹	266	30	99	134	11.9	3.71	101	.251	.316	0	—	0	3	1	-3	-0.2
1974 Mil-A	13	16	.448	40	35	10	3	0	250	255	22	102	126	13.0	3.92	92	.268	.341	0	—	0	-9	-9	0	-0.9
1975 Mil-A	11	18	.379	37	33	10	3	0	217	238	28	90	119	13.7	4.52	85	.276	.346	0	—	0	-18	-17	1	-2.0
1976 Mil-A	14	15	.483	38	38	12	2	0	292²	287	14	94	138	11.9	3.44	101	.259	.320	0	—	0	2	2	-0	0.3
1977 Mil-A☆	10	14	.417	32	31	7	1	0	221	223	25	77	104	12.7	3.58	113	.266	.336	0	—	0	12	12	0	1.2
1978 Det-A	17	11	.607	35	34	11	2	0	233²	235	27	85	92	12.6	4.12	94	.263	.332	0	—	0	-9	-7	-1	-0.9
1979 Mil-A	15	9	.625	32	31	12	3	0	213	229	16	54	80	12.0	3.63	115	.278	.323	0	—	0	14	13	1	1.3
1980 Mil-A	1	1	.500	3	3	0	0	0	16¹	17	3	5	4	12.1	4.41	88	.270	.324	0	—	0	-1	-1	-0	-0.1
1981 *Mil-A	5	7	.417	24	21	0	0	0	117¹	120	10	50	47	13.2	4.37	78	.273	.350	0	—	0	-9	-12	-0	-0.9
1982 *Mil-A	10	6	.625	39	7	0	0	6	117²	117	14	41	59	12.2	3.29	115	.264	.327	0	—	0	10	6	-0	0.8
1983 Mil-A	14	6	.700	46	0	0	0	5	112¹	112	12	56	38	13.7	4.33	86	.272	.363	0	—	0	-3	-7	-0	-1.2
1984 Cal-A	7	10	.412	32	22	5	1	0	163	192	22	56	67	13.8	4.97	80	.295	.353	0	—	0	-18	-18	0	-1.6
1985 Cal-A	6	10	.375	29	24	1	0	1	148¹	162	22	63	60	13.8	4.52	84	.284	.357	0	—	0	-4	-4	-0	-0.4
1986 Cal-A	4	6	.400	14	12	0	0	0	73¹	84	9	29	31	14.1	5.65	73	.295	.364	0	—	0	-12	-13	1	-1.4
Det-A	0	0	—	22	0	0	0	2	40	46	5	11	12	13.0	4.05	102	.287	.337	0	—	0	1	0	-0	0.0
Yr	4	6	.400	36	12	0	0	2	113¹	130	14	40	43	13.6	5.08	81	.287	.346	0	—	0	-11	-12	1	-1.4
Total 16	151	158	.489	496	360	86	22	14	2683²	2773	277	1004	1191	12.8	4.03	94	.270	.337	6	.105	-2	-58	-70	-4	-8.7
● PHIL SLATTERY Slattery, Philip Ryan b: 2/25/1893, Harper, Iowa d: 3/2/68, Long Beach, Cal. BR/TL, 5′11″, 160 lbs. Deb: 9/16/15																									
1915 Pit-N	0	0	—	3	0	0	0	0	8	5	0	1	1	9.0	0.00	—	.185	.267	0	.000	-0	2	2	-1	-0.1
● BARNEY SLAUGHTER Slaughter, Byron Atkins b: 10/6/1884, Smyrna, Del. d: 5/17/61, Philadelphia, Pa. BR/TR, 5′11.5″, 165 lbs. Deb: 8/9/10																									
1910 Phi-N	0	1	.000	8	1	0	0	1	18	21	0	11	7	16.0	5.50	57	.318	.416	1	.200	0	-5	-5	-0	-0.3
● STERLING SLAUGHTER Slaughter, Sterling Feore b: 11/18/41, Danville, Ill. BR/TR, 5′11″, 165 lbs. Deb: 4/19/64																									
1964 Chi-N	2	4	.333	20	6	1	0	0	51²	56	4	32	32	16.7	5.75	65	.305	.397	1	.083	-0	-13	-12	-1	-1.4
● BILL SLAYBACK Slayback, William Grover b: 2/21/48, Hollywood, Cal. BR/TR, 6′4″, 200 lbs. Deb: 6/26/72																									
1972 Det-A	5	6	.455	23	13	3	1	0	81²	74	4	25	65	11.0	3.20	98	.239	.298	4	.174	-1	-1	-0	1	0.0
1973 Det-A	0	0	—	3	0	0	0	0	2	5	0	0	1	27.0	4.50	91	.417	.462	0	—	0	-0	-0	-0	0.0
1974 Det-A	1	3	.250	16	4	0	0	0	54²	57	1	26	23	14.2	4.77	80	.273	.361	0	—	0	-7	-6	-0	-0.5
Total 3	6	9	.400	42	17	3	1	0	138¹	136	5	51	89	12.5	3.84	89	.256	.327	4	.174	-1	-8	-7	0	-0.5
● STEVE SLAYTON Slayton, Foster Herbert b: 4/26/02, Barre, Vt. d: 12/20/84, Manchester, N.H. BR/TR, 6′, 163 lbs. Deb: 7/21/28																									
1928 Bos-A	0	0	—	3	0	0	0	0	7	6	0	3	2	11.6	3.86	107	.240	.321	0	.000	-0	0	-0	-0	0.0
● LOU SLEATER Sleater, Louis Mortimer b: 9/8/26, St.Louis, Mo. BL/TL, 5′10″, 185 lbs. Deb: 4/25/50																									
1950 StL-A	0	0	—	1	0	0	0	0	1	0	0	1	0	1.0	0.00	—	.000	.000	0	—	0	1	1	0	0.0
1951 StL-A	1	9	.100	20	8	4	0	1	81	88	7	53	33	16.2	5.11	86	.271	.381	7	.226	0	-9	-6	-1	-0.8
1952 StL-A	0	1	.000	4	2	0	0	0	8²	9	1	5	1	14.5	7.27	54	.265	.359	0	.000	-0	-3	-3	0	-0.4
Was-A	4	2	.667	14	9	3	1	0	57	56	4	30	22	13.9	3.63	98	.260	.356	1	.050	-2	-0	-1	-0	-0.4
Yr	4	3	.571	18	11	3	1	0	65²	65	5	35	23	14.0	4.11	88	.261	.357	1	.045	-2	-3	-4	-0	-0.8
1955 KC-A	1	1	.500	16	1	0	0	0	25²	33	3	21	11	18.9	7.71	54	.324	.439	1	.154	-1	-11	-10	-0	-0.8
1956 Mil-N	2	2	.500	25	1	0	0	0	45²	42	6	27	32	13.6	3.15	110	.240	.342	1	.500	3	2	3	1	0.5
1957 Det-A	3	3	.500	41	0	0	0	2	69¹	67	9	28	43	11.7	3.76	102	.250	.315	5	.250	0	1	0	0	0.4
1958 Det-A	0	0	—	4	0	0	0	0	5¹	3	2	6	4	15.2	6.75	60	.158	.360	1	1.000	1	-2	-2	0	0.2
Bal-A	1	0	1.000	6	0	0	0	0	7	14	0	2	5	20.6	12.86	28	.438	.471	0	.000	-0	-7	-7	0	-0.9
Yr	1	0	1.000	10	0	0	0	0	12¹	17	2	8	9	18.2	10.22	37	.333	.424	1	.143	0	-9	-9	0	-0.7
Total 7	12	18	.400	131	21	7	1	5	300²	306	32	172	152	14.5	4.70	83	.263	.362	21	.204	3	-28	-26	-2	-2.2
● LEFTY SLOAT Sloat, Dwain Clifford b: 12/1/18, Nokomis, Ill. BR/TL, 6′, 168 lbs. Deb: 4/24/48																									
1948 Bro-N	0	1	.000	4	1	0	0	0	7¹	7	0	8	1	18.4	6.14	65	.280	.455	0	.000	-0	-2	-1	1	-0.2
1949 Chi-N	0	0	—	5	1	0	0	0	9	14	0	3	3	17.0	7.00	58	.400	.447	0	—	0	-3	-3	0	0.0
Total 2	0	1	.000	9	2	0	0	0	16¹	21	0	11	4	17.6	6.61	61	.350	.451	0	.000	-0	-5	-5	1	-0.2
● HEATHCLIFF SLOCUMB Slocumb, Heathcliff b: 6/7/66, Jamaica, N.Y. BR/TR, 6′3″, 210 lbs. Deb: 4/11/91																									
1991 Chi-N	2	1	.667	52	0	0	0	1	62²	52	3	30	34	12.4	3.45	113	.231	.328	0	.000	-0	2	3	0	0.1
1992 Chi-N	0	3	.000	30	0	0	0	1	36	52	3	21	27	18.5	6.50	55	.351	.435	0	.000	-0	-12	-12	-0	-1.1
1993 Chi-N	1	0	1.000	10	0	0	0	0	10²	7	0	4	9	9.3	3.38	118	.189	.268	0	.000	-0	1	1	0	0.1
Cle-A	3	1	.750	20	0	0	0	0	27¹	28	3	16	18	14.5	4.28	101	.272	.370	0	—	0	-0	0	0	0.0
1994 Phi-N	5	1	.833	52	0	0	0	0	72¹	75	0	28	58	13.1	2.86	144	.262	.332	1	.250	0	11	10	0	0.8
Total 4	11	6	.647	164	0	0	0	2	209	215	9	99	141	13.8	3.88	103	.268	.352	1	.100	-0	1	3	-0	-0.1
● JOE SLUSARSKI Slusarski, Joseph Andrew b: 12/19/66, Indianapolis, Ind. BR/TR, 6′4″, 195 lbs. Deb: 4/11/91																									
1991 Oak-A	5	7	.417	20	19	1	0	0	109¹	121	14	52	60	14.6	5.27	73	.283	.366	0	—	0	-14	-17	-1	-1.6
1992 Oak-A	5	5	.500	15	14	0	0	0	76	85	15	27	38	14.0	5.45	69	.284	.355	0	—	0	-13	-14	-1	-1.7
1993 Oak-A	0	0	—	2	1	0	0	0	8²	9	1	11	1	20.8	5.19	78	.300	.488	0	—	0	-1	-1	0	0.0
Total 3	10	12	.455	37	34	1	0	0	194	215	30	90	99	14.6	5.34	71	.284	.368	0	—	0	-28	-33	-2	-3.3
● AARON SMALL Small, Aaron James b: 11/23/71, Oxnard, Cal. BR/TR, 6′5″, 200 lbs. Deb: 6/11/94																									
1994 Tor-A	0	0	—	1	0	0	0	0	2	5	1	2	0	31.5	9.00	54	.500	.583	0	—	0	-1	-1	0	0.0
● WALT SMALLWOOD Smallwood, Walter Clayton b: 4/24/1893, Dayton, Md. d: 4/29/67, Baltimore, Md. BR/TR, 6′2″, 190 lbs. Deb: 9/19/17																									
1917 NY-A	0	0	—	2	0	0	0	0	2	1	0	4	1	—	—	—	.167	.286	0	—	0	1	1	0	0.0
1919 NY-A	0	0	—	6	0	0	0	0	21²	20	1	6	6	12.9	4.98	64	.263	.356	0	.000	-1	-4	-4	-0	-0.1
Total 2	0	0	—	8	0	0	0	0	23²	21	1	10	7	12.5	4.56	69	.256	.351	0	.000	-1	-4	-4	-0	-0.1
● JOHN SMILEY Smiley, John Patrick b: 3/17/65, Phoenixville, Pa. BL/TL, 6′4″, 195 lbs. Deb: 9/1/86																									
1986 Pit-N	1	0	1.000	12	0	0	0	0	11²	4	2	4	9	6.2	3.86	99	.105	.190	0	—	0	3	3	0	0.2
1987 Pit-N	5	5	.500	63	0	0	0	4	75	69	7	50	58	14.3	5.76	71	.244	.357	1	.143	0	-14	-14	0	-1.8
1988 Pit-N	13	11	.542	34	32	5	1	0	205	185	15	46	129	10.3	3.25	105	.241	.287	5	.079	-2	5	3	-1	0.1
1989 Pit-N	12	8	.600	28	28	8	1	0	205¹	174	22	49	123	9.9	2.81	120	.226	.276	9	.138	1	16	13	-2	1.0

YEAR	TM/L	W	L	PCT	G	GS	CG	SH	SV	IP	H	HR	BB	SO	RAT	ERA	ERA+	OAV	OOB	BH	AVG	PB	PR	/A	PD	TPI
1990	*Pit-N	9	10	.474	26	25	2	0	0	149¹	161	15	36	86	12.0	4.64	78	.275	.319	6	.122	-0	-14	-17	0	-1.9
1991	*Pit-N★	**20**	8	**.714**	33	32	2	1	0	207²	194	17	44	129	10.4	3.08	116	.251	.294	7	.100	-2	14	11	0	1.2
1992	Min-A	16	9	.640	34	34	5	2	0	241	205	17	65	163	10.3	3.21	126	.231	.288	0	—	0	19	23	0	2.2
1993	Cin-N	3	9	.250	18	18	2	0	0	105²	117	15	31	60	12.8	5.62	72	.286	.339	8	.250	2	-19	-19	0	-1.6
1994	Cin-N	11	10	.524	24	24	1	1	0	158²	169	18	37	112	11.9	3.86	108	.275	.320	11	.200	5	6	5	-1	0.8
Total	9	90	70	.563	272	193	25	6	4	1359¹	1278	128	362	869	11.0	3.70	101	.249	.302	47	.138	0	13	5	-3	0.0

● **SMITH**   Smith   Deb: 6/5/1884

YEAR	TM/L	W	L	PCT	G	GS	CG	SH	SV	IP	H	HR	BB	SO	RAT	ERA	ERA+	OAV	OOB	BH	AVG	PB	PR	/A	PD	TPI
1884	Bal-U	0	0	—	1	1	0	0	0	6	12	0	2	2	21.0	9.00	30	.391	.429	1	.200	-1	-4	-4	-0	-0.1

● **SMITH**   Smith   Deb: 5/31/1886

1886	Cin-a	0	1	.000	1	1	1	0	0	9	8	0	10	1	18.0	4.00	88	.229	.400	1	.250	-0	-1	-0	0	0.0

● **AL SMITH**   Smith, Alfred John   b: 10/12/07, Belleville, Ill.   d: 4/28/77, Brownsville, Tex.   BL/TL, 5'11", 180 lbs.   Deb: 5/5/34   C

YEAR	TM/L	W	L	PCT	G	GS	CG	SH	SV	IP	H	HR	BB	SO	RAT	ERA	ERA+	OAV	OOB	BH	AVG	PB	PR	/A	PD	TPI
1934	NY-N	3	5	.375	30	5	0	0	5	66²	70	2	21	27	12.3	4.32	90	.266	.320	4	.286	1	-2	-3	-0	-0.4
1935	NY-N	10	8	.556	40	10	4	1	5	124	125	6	32	44	11.9	3.41	113	.263	.319	4	.118	-0	8	6	-1	0.7
1936	*NY-N	14	13	.519	43	30	9	**4**	2	209¹	217	16	69	89	12.5	3.78	103	.274	.335	10	.137	-1	6	3	-1	0.1
1937	*NY-N	5	4	.556	33	9	2	0	0	85²	91	8	30	41	12.9	4.20	93	.275	.339	3	.120	-2	-3	-3	-1	-0.5
1938	Phi-N	1	4	.200	37	1	0	0	1	86	115	7	40	46	16.2	6.28	62	.320	.388	0	.000	-2	-24	-23	0	-1.4
1939	Phi-N	0	0	—	5	0	0	0	0	9	11	1	5	2	18.0	4.00	100	.314	.429	0	.000	-0	-0	0	0	0.0
1940	Cle-A	15	7	.682	31	24	11	6	2	183	187	2	55	46	12.3	3.44	122	.270	.329	19	.306	7	19	16	2	2.6
1941	Cle-A	12	13	.480	29	27	13	2	0	206²	204	12	75	76	12.2	3.83	103	.256	.321	11	.155	2	7	2	2	0.6
1942	Cle-A	10	15	.400	30	24	7	1	0	168¹	163	9	71	66	12.8	3.96	87	.251	.329	15	.250	3	-6	-9	-1	-1.0
1943	Cle-A☆	17	7	.708	29	27	14	3	1	208¹	186	7	72	72	11.1	2.55	122	.239	.303	14	.206	3	17	13	-0	1.9
1944	Cle-A	7	13	.350	28	26	7	1	0	181²	197	6	69	44	13.3	3.42	96	.280	.347	10	.156	1	0	-2	1	-0.2
1945	Cle-A	5	12	.294	21	19	8	3	1	133²	141	8	48	34	12.9	3.84	85	.275	.340	12	.293	4	-7	-9	2	-0.4
Total	12	99	101	.495	356	202	75	16	17	1662¹	1707	94	587	587	12.6	3.72	99	.267	.332	102	.191	14	17	-10	4	2.0

● **AL SMITH**   Smith, Alfred Kendricks   b: 12/13/03, Norristown, Pa.   BR/TR, 6', 170 lbs.   Deb: 6/18/26

1926	NY-N	0	0	—	1	0	0	0	0	2	4	0	2	0	27.0	9.00	42	.444	.545	0	—	0	-1	-1	-0	0.0

● **ART SMITH**   Smith, Arthur Laird   b: 6/21/06, Boston, Mass.   BR/TR, 6', 175 lbs.   Deb: 6/9/32

1932	Chi-A	0	1	.000	3	2	0	0	0	7	17	1	4	1	27.0	11.57	37	.500	.553	0	—	-0	-6	-6	1	-0.6

● **BILLY SMITH**   Smith, Billy Lavern   b: 9/13/54, LaMarque, Tex.   BR/TR, 6'7", 200 lbs.   Deb: 6/9/81

1981	*Hou-N	1	1	.500	10	1	0	0	1	20²	20	3	3	3	10.0	3.05	108	.263	.291	0	—	0	1	1	0	0.0

● **BRYN SMITH**   Smith, Bryn Nelson   b: 8/11/55, Marietta, Ga.   BR/TR, 6'2", 205 lbs.   Deb: 9/8/81

YEAR	TM/L	W	L	PCT	G	GS	CG	SH	SV	IP	H	HR	BB	SO	RAT	ERA	ERA+	OAV	OOB	BH	AVG	PB	PR	/A	PD	TPI
1981	Mon-N	1	0	1.000	7	0	0	0	0	13	14	1	3	9	11.8	2.77	126	.280	.321	0	.000	-0	1	1	-0	0.1
1982	Mon-N	2	4	.333	47	1	0	0	3	79¹	81	5	23	50	11.8	4.20	87	.264	.315	0	.000	-0	-5	-5	0	-0.4
1983	Mon-N	6	11	.353	49	12	5	3	3	155¹	142	13	43	101	11.0	2.49	144	.248	.306	5	.167	0	20	19	0	2.1
1984	Mon-N	12	13	.480	28	28	4	2	0	179	178	15	51	101	11.7	3.32	103	.259	.313	7	.132	1	5	2	2	0.6
1985	Mon-N	18	5	.783	32	32	4	2	0	222¹	193	12	41	127	9.5	2.91	116	.232	.269	14	.194	3	17	12	-1	1.4
1986	Mon-N	10	8	.556	30	30	1	0	0	187¹	182	15	63	105	12.1	3.94	94	.251	.316	8	.138	1	-5	-5	3	-0.3
1987	Mon-N	10	9	.526	26	26	2	1	0	150¹	164	16	31	94	11.8	4.37	96	.274	.312	6	.136	1	-5	-3	-0	-0.3
1988	Mon-N	12	10	.545	32	32	1	0	0	198	179	15	32	122	10.0	3.00	120	.243	.284	6	.109	-1	10	13	-2	1.1
1989	Mon-N	10	11	.476	33	32	3	1	0	215²	177	16	54	129	9.8	2.84	124	.223	.276	4	.065	-2	16	17	2	1.6
1990	StL-N	9	8	.529	26	25	0	0	0	141¹	160	11	30	78	12.4	4.27	89	.286	.327	10	.256	3	-7	-7	-1	-0.5
1991	StL-N	12	9	.571	31	31	3	0	0	198²	188	16	45	94	10.9	3.85	97	.251	.300	16	.246	3	-4	-3	-1	-0.1
1992	StL-N	4	2	.667	13	1	0	0	0	21¹	20	3	5	9	11.8	4.64	73	.247	.315	0	.000	-0	-3	-3	0	-0.8
1993	Col-N	2	4	.333	11	5	0	0	0	29²	47	2	11	9	18.5	8.49	56	.362	.424	0	.000	-0	-15	-12	1	-2.0
Total	13	108	94	.535	365	255	23	8	6	1791¹	1725	140	432	1028	11.1	3.53	104	.253	.302	76	.153	7	25	24	4	2.7

● **CHARLIE SMITH**   Smith, Charles Edwin   b: 4/20/1880, Cleveland, Ohio   d: 1/3/29, Wickliffe, Ohio   BR/TR, 6'1", 185 lbs.   Deb: 8/6/02   F

YEAR	TM/L	W	L	PCT	G	GS	CG	SH	SV	IP	H	HR	BB	SO	RAT	ERA	ERA+	OAV	OOB	BH	AVG	PB	PR	/A	PD	TPI
1902	Cle-A	2	1	.667	3	3	2	1	0	20	23	0	5	5	12.6	4.05	85	.289	.331	1	.125	-0	-1	-1	0	-0.2
1906	Was-A	9	16	.360	33	22	17	2	0	235¹	250	2	75	105	12.7	2.91	91	.275	.336	16	.184	-1	-6	-7	-2	-1.0
1907	Was-A	10	20	.333	36	31	21	3	0	258²	254	0	51	119	10.6	2.61	93	.259	.296	12	.143	-3	-2	-5	3	-0.6
1908	Was-A	9	13	.409	26	23	14	1	1	184	166	2	60	83	11.2	2.40	96	.247	.311	8	.123	-2	0	-2	-1	-0.6
1909	Was-A	3	12	.200	23	15	7	1	0	145²	140	4	37	72	11.2	3.27	74	.250	.303	7	.156	-1	-13	-14	0	-1.4
	Bos-A	3	0	1.000	3	3	2	0	0	25	23	2	2	11	9.4	2.16	116	.237	.260	3	.300	1	1	1	0	0.2
	Yr	6	12	.333	26	18	9	1	0	170²	163	6	39	83	10.7	3.11	78	.247	.290	10	.182	-0	-12	-13	1	-1.2
1910	Bos-A	11	6	.647	24	18	11	0	1	156¹	141	4	35	53	10.2	2.30	111	.248	.294	5	.114	-2	4	4	-2	-0.1
1911	Bos-A	0	0	—	1	1	0	0	0	2	2	1	1	0	13.5	9.00	36	.250	.333	0	—	0	-1	-1	0	0.0
	Chi-N	3	2	.600	7	5	3	1	0	38	31	0	7	11	9.2	1.42	233	.228	.271	1	.077	-1	8	8	-1	0.8
1912	Chi-N	7	4	.636	20	5	1	0	1	94	92	2	31	47	12.1	4.21	79	.269	.335	9	.257	1	-8	-9	-1	-0.7
1913	Chi-N	7	9	.438	20	17	8	1	0	137²	138	2	34	47	11.5	2.55	125	.274	.325	4	.089	-3	10	10	0	0.7
1914	Chi-N	2	4	.333	16	5	1	0	0	53²	49	3	15	17	10.9	3.86	72	.251	.308	1	.091	-1	-6	-6	-1	-0.9
Total	10	66	87	.431	212	148	87	10	3	1350¹	1309	22	353	570	11.3	2.81	94	.259	.311	67	.150	-13	-14	-24	-2	-3.8

● **POP SMITH**   Smith, Charles Marvin   b: 10/12/1856, Digby, N.S., Canada   d: 4/18/27, Boston, Mass.   BR/TR, 5'11", 170 lbs.   Deb: 5/1/1880   U♦

1883	Col-a	0	0	—	3	0	0	0	0	5²	10	0	0	0	15.9	6.35	48	.363	.363	106	.262	1	-2	-2	-0	0.0

● **POP-BOY SMITH**   Smith, Clarence Ossie   b: 5/23/1892, Newport, Tenn.   d: 2/16/24, Sweetwater, Tex.   BR/TR, 6'1", 176 lbs.   Deb: 4/19/13

YEAR	TM/L	W	L	PCT	G	GS	CG	SH	SV	IP	H	HR	BB	SO	RAT	ERA	ERA+	OAV	OOB	BH	AVG	PB	PR	/A	PD	TPI
1913	Chi-A	0	1	.000	15	2	0	0	0	32	31	0	11	13	12.7	3.38	87	.261	.338	0	.000	-1	-2	-2	1	0.0
1916	Cle-A	1	2	.333	5	3	0	0	1	25²	25	1	11	4	13.0	3.86	78	.253	.333	2	.286	0	-3	-2	-0	-0.3
1917	Cle-A	0	1	.000	6	0	0	0	0	8²	14	0	4	3	19.7	8.31	34	.368	.442	0	.000	-0	-5	-5	1	-0.5
Total	3	1	4	.200	26	5	0	0	1	66¹	70	1	26	20	13.7	4.21	70	.273	.352	2	.154	-1	-10	-9	2	-0.8

● **CLAY SMITH**   Smith, Clay Jamieson   b: 9/11/14, Cambridge, Kan.   BR/TR, 6'2", 190 lbs.   Deb: 9/13/38

1938	Cle-A	0	0	—	4	0	0	0	0	11	18	1	2	3	16.4	6.55	71	.367	.392	0	.000	-0	-2	-2	0	0.0
1940	*Det-A	1	1	.500	14	1	0	0	0	28¹	32	3	13	14	14.6	5.08	94	.283	.362	0	.000	-0	-2	-1	1	-0.1
Total	2	1	1	.500	18	1	0	0	0	39¹	50	4	15	17	15.1	5.49	86	.309	.371	0	.000	-1	-4	-3	1	-0.1

● **DAN SMITH**   Smith, Daniel Scott   b: 4/20/69, St.Paul, Minn.   BL/TL, 6'5", 190 lbs.   Deb: 9/12/92

1992	Tex-A	0	3	.000	4	2	0	0	0	14¹	18	1	8	5	16.3	5.02	76	.321	.406	0	—	0	-2	-2	-0	-0.4
1994	Tex-A	1	2	.333	13	0	0	0	0	14²	18	2	12	9	18.4	4.30	105	.281	.395	0	—	0	1	0	0	0.1
Total	2	1	5	.167	17	2	0	0	0	29	36	3	20	14	17.4	4.66	90	.300	.400	0	—	0	-1	-2	-0	-0.3

● **DARYL SMITH**   Smith, Daryl Clinton   b: 7/29/60, Baltimore, Md.   BR/TR, 6'4", 185 lbs.   Deb: 9/18/90

1990	KC-A	0	1	.000	2	1	0	0	0	6²	5	0	4	6	12.2	4.05	95	.238	.360	0	—	0	-0	-0	-0	0.0

● **DAVE SMITH**   Smith, David Merwin   b: 12/17/14, Sellers, S.C.   BR/TR, 5'10", 170 lbs.   Deb: 6/16/38

1938	Phi-A	2	1	.667	21	0	0	0	0	44¹	50	0	28	13	16.0	5.08	95	.284	.385	0	.000	-1	-1	-1	-0	-0.2
1939	Phi-A	0	0	—	1	0	0	0	0	0	1	0	2	0	—	—	—	1.000	1.000	0	—	-0	-0	-0	0	0.0
Total	2	2	1	.667	22	0	0	0	0	44¹	51	0	30	13	16.6	5.08	95	.288	.394	0	.000	-1	-1	-1	-0	-0.2

YEAR TM/L	W	L	PCT	G	GS	CG	SH	SV	IP	H	HR	BB	SO	RAT	ERA	ERA+	OAV	OOB	BH	AVG	PB	PR	/A	PD	TPI

● DAVE SMITH Smith, David Stanley b: 1/21/55, Richmond, Cal. BR/TR, 6'1", 195 lbs. Deb: 4/11/80

1980 *Hou-N	7	5	.583	57	0	0	0	10	102²	90	1	32	85	11.0	1.93	170	.237	.304	0	.000	-1	19	15	-1	1.9
1981 *Hou-N	5	3	.625	42	0	0	0	8	75	54	2	23	52	9.5	2.76	119	.198	.265	2	.250	0	6	4	-0	0.6
1982 Hou-N	5	4	.556	49	1	0	0	11	63¹	69	4	31	28	14.2	3.84	86	.285	.366	0	.000	-0	-2	-4	-1	-0.7
1983 Hou-N	3	1	.750	42	0	0	0	6	72²	72	2	36	41	13.4	3.10	110	.258	.343	0	.000	-1	4	2	-2	-0.1
1984 Hou-N	5	4	.556	53	0	0	0	5	77¹	60	5	20	45	9.4	2.21	150	.214	.269	0	.000	-0	12	10	-1	1.1
1985 Hou-N	9	5	.643	64	0	0	0	27	79¹	69	3	17	40	9.9	2.27	153	.235	.280	0	.000	0	12	11	-1	2.5
1986 *Hou-N☆	4	7	.364	54	0	0	0	33	56	39	5	22	46	10.0	2.73	132	.200	.284	0	.000	-0	6	5	0	1.7
1987 Hou-N	2	3	.400	50	0	0	0	24	60	39	0	21	73	9.2	1.65	237	.182	.258	1	.500	1	16	15	-0	2.6
1988 Hou-N	4	5	.444	51	0	0	0	27	57¹	60	1	19	38	12.6	2.67	124	.268	.328	0	.000	-0	5	4	-0	1.1
1989 Hou-N	3	4	.429	52	0	0	0	25	58	49	1	19	31	10.7	2.64	128	.233	.300	0	.000	-0	6	5	1	1.1
1990 Hou-N★	6	6	.500	49	0	0	0	23	60¹	45	4	20	50	9.7	2.39	156	.210	.278	0	.000	0	9	9	-1	2.4
1991 Chi-N	0	6	.000	35	0	0	0	17	33	39	6	19	16	16.1	6.00	65	.302	.396	0	.000	-0	-8	-8	-0	-2.2
1992 Chi-N	0	0	—	11	0	0	0	0	14¹	15	0	4	3	11.9	2.51	143	.273	.322	0	—	0	2	2	-0	0.0
Total 13	53	53	.500	609	1	0	0	216	809¹	700	34	283	548	11.1	2.67	130	.234	.303	3	.068	-2	87	71	-7	12.0

● DAVE SMITH Smith, David Wayne b: 8/30/57, Tomball, Tex. BR/TR, 6'1", 190 lbs. Deb: 9/18/84

1984 Cal-A	0	0	—	1	0	0	0	0	1	4	1	0	0	36.0	18.00	22	.571	.571	0	—	0	-2	-2	0	0.0
1985 Cal-A	0	0	—	4	0	0	0	0	5	5	1	1	3	10.8	7.20	57	.278	.316	0	—	0	-2	-2	0	0.0
Total 2	0	0	—	5	0	0	0	0	6	9	2	1	3	15.0	9.00	45	.360	.385	0	—	0	-3	-3	0	0.0

● DOUG SMITH Smith, Douglass Weldon b: 5/25/1892, Millers Falls, Mass. d: 9/18/73, Greenfield, Mass. BL/TL, 5'10", 168 lbs. Deb: 7/10/12

| 1912 Bos-A | 0 | 0 | — | 1 | 0 | 0 | 0 | 0 | 3 | 4 | 0 | 0 | 1 | 12.0 | 3.00 | 113 | .364 | .364 | 0 | — | 0 | 0 | 0 | -0 | 0.0 |

● EDDIE SMITH Smith, Edgar b: 12/14/13, Mansfield, N.J. d: 1/2/94, Willingboro, N.J. BB/TL, 5'10", 174 lbs. Deb: 9/20/36

1936 Phi-A	1	1	.500	2	2	2	0	0	19	22	3	8	7	14.2	1.89	269	.275	.341	1	.125	-1	7	7	0	0.6
1937 Phi-A	4	17	.190	38	23	14	1	5	196²	178	18	90	79	12.4	3.94	120	.242	.327	17	.233	1	15	17	-2	1.7
1938 Phi-A	3	10	.231	43	7	0	0	4	130²	151	13	76	78	15.9	5.92	82	.287	.381	12	.286	3	-16	-16	0	-1.1
1939 Phi-A	1	0	1.000	3	0	0	0	0	3²	7	0	2	3	22.1	9.82	48	.412	.474	0	—	0	-2	-2	-0	-0.4
Chi-A	9	11	.450	29	22	7	1	0	176²	161	11	90	67	13.0	3.67	129	.247	.342	6	.115	-1	19	21	-2	1.7
Yr	10	11	.476	32	22	7	1	0	180¹	168	11	92	70	13.2	3.79	125	.251	.346	6	.115	-1	17	19	-2	1.3
1940 Chi-A	14	9	.609	32	28	12	0	0	207¹	179	16	95	119	12.0	3.21	138	.228	.313	15	.217	2	27	28	-1	2.9
1941 Chi-A★	13	17	.433	34	33	21	1	1	263¹	243	13	114	111	12.4	3.18	129	.246	.328	19	.216	4	28	27	0	3.2
1942 Chi-A☆	7	20	.259	29	28	18	2	1	215	223	17	86	78	13.1	3.98	90	.269	.341	9	.123	-2	-8	-9	2	-1.0
1943 Chi-A	11	11	.500	25	25	14	2	0	187²	197	2	76	66	13.3	3.69	90	.277	.351	11	.159	-1	-8	-7	1	-0.9
1946 Chi-A	8	11	.421	24	21	3	1	1	145¹	135	9	60	59	12.3	2.85	120	.246	.325	8	.178	0	11	9	-0	1.2
1947 Chi-A	1	3	.250	15	5	0	0	0	33¹	40	1	24	12	17.3	7.29	50	.299	.405	1	.167	-0	-13	-13	-1	-1.5
Bos-A	1	3	.250	8	3	0	0	0	17	18	3	18	15	19.1	7.41	52	.290	.424	1	.167	-0	-7	-7	-0	-1.3
Yr	2	6	.250	23	8	0	0	0	50¹	58	4	42	27	17.9	7.33	51	.289	.412	2	.167	-0	-20	-20	-1	-2.8
Total 10	73	113	.392	282	197	91	8	12	1595²	1554	106	739	694	13.1	3.82	108	.256	.340	100	.188	5	51	53	-3	5.1

● EDGAR SMITH Smith, Edgar Eugene b: 6/12/1862, Providence, R.I. d: 11/3/1892, Providence, R.I. BR/TR, 5'10", 160 lbs. Deb: 5/25/1883 ♦

1883 Phi-N	0	1	.000	1	1	1	0	0	7	18	0	3	2	27.0	15.43	20	.409	.447	3	.750	1	-10	-10	-0	-0.7
1884 Was-a	0	2	.000	3	2	2	0	0	22	27	0	5	4	13.5	4.91	62	.276	.317	5	.088	-1	-4	-5	-0	-0.4
1885 Pro-N	1	0	1.000	1	1	1	0	0	9	9	0	1	1	9.0	1.00	265	.273	.273	1	.250	0	2	2	0	0.2
1890 Cle-N	1	4	.200	6	6	5	0	0	44	42	1	10	11	10.8	4.30	83	.244	.289	7	.292	2	-4	-3	2	0.0
Total 4	2	7	.222	11	10	8	0	0	82	96	1	18	18	12.7	5.05	65	.276	.316	18	.184	2	-15	-16	1	-0.9

● ELMER SMITH Smith, Elmer Ellsworth b: 3/23/1868, Pittsburgh, Pa. d: 11/3/45, Pittsburgh, Pa. BL/TL, 5'11", 178 lbs. Deb: 9/10/1886 ♦

1886 Cin-a	4	4	.500	9	9	8	0	0	72²	57	1	44	40	12.9	3.72	95	.211	.328	8	.286	4	-2	-2	0	0.2
1887 Cin-a	34	17	.667	52	52	49	3	0	447¹	400	5	126	176	10.8	2.94	148	.230	.286	47	.253	5	68	70	-5	6.0
1888 Cin-a	22	17	.564	40	40	37	5	0	348¹	309	11	89	154	10.8	2.74	116	.229	.286	29	.225	4	13	17	-5	1.4
1889 Cin-a	9	12	.429	29	22	16	0	0	203	253	11	101	104	16.0	4.88	80	.296	.375	23	.277	6	-23	-22	-4	-1.6
1892 Pit-N	6	7	.462	17	13	12	1	0	134	140	2	58	51	13.4	3.63	91	.258	.331	140	.274	6	-5	-5	-1	-0.1
1894 Pit-N	0	0	—	1	0	0	0	0	4	6	0	1	0	18.0	4.50	116	.342	.410	174	.356	0	-0	-0	-0	0.0
1898 Cin-N	0	0	—	1	0	0	0	0	1	2	0	3	0	45.0	18.00	21	.411	.635	166	.342	0	-2	-2	-0	0.0
Total 7	75	57	.568	149	136	122	9	0	1210¹	1167	20	422	525	12.1	3.35	113	.244	.311	1454	.310	25	48	58	-16	5.9

● BILL SMITH Smith, F. William b: 1863, New Orleans, La. TR, 5'8", 152 lbs. Deb: 7/6/1886

| 1886 Det-N | 5 | 4 | .556 | 9 | 9 | 9 | 0 | 0 | 77 | 81 | 0 | 30 | 36 | 13.0 | 4.09 | 81 | .259 | .324 | 7 | .184 | -1 | -7 | -7 | -1 | -0.8 |

● FRANK SMITH Smith, Frank Elmer "Nig" or "Piano Mover" (b: Frank Elmer Schmidt)
b: 10/28/1879, Pittsburgh, Pa. d: 11/3/52, Pittsburgh, Pa. BR/TR, 5'10.5", 194 lbs. Deb: 4/22/04

1904 Chi-A	16	9	.640	26	23	22	4	0	202¹	157	0	58	107	10.1	2.09	117	.215	.284	18	.250	4	11	8	-2	1.3
1905 Chi-A	19	13	.594	39	31	27	4	0	291²	215	0	107	171	10.1	2.13	116	.207	.286	24	.226	7	17	11	-0	1.9
1906 Chi-A	5	5	.500	20	13	8	1	1	122	124	1	37	53	12.2	3.39	75	.267	.327	12	.293	5	-10	-12	1	-0.3
1907 Chi-A	23	10	.697	41	37	29	3	0	310	280	3	111	139	11.4	2.47	97	.243	.311	18	.196	5	3	-2	4	0.7
1908 Chi-A	16	17	.485	41	35	24	3	1	297²	213	2	73	129	8.7	2.03	114	.203	.256	20	.189	4	12	10	3	1.7
1909 Chi-A	25	17	.595	51	40	37	7	1	365	278	1	70	177	8.7	1.80	130	.214	.257	22	.173	6	27	22	10	4.6
1910 Chi-A	4	9	.308	19	15	9	3	0	128²	91	1	40	50	9.3	2.03	118	.204	.272	8	.186	2	7	5	4	1.2
Bos-A	1	2	.333	4	3	2	0	0	28	22	0	11	8	10.9	4.82	53	.234	.321	1	.111	-0	-7	-7	-0	-0.7
Yr	5	11	.313	23	18	11	3	0	156²	113	1	51	58	9.5	2.53	96	.208	.277	9	.173	2	-0	-2	4	0.5
1911 Bos-A	0	0	—	1	1	0	0	0	2¹	6	0	3	1	34.7	15.43	21	.500	.600	0	—	0	-3	-3	0	0.1
Cin-N	10	14	.417	34	18	10	0	1	176¹	198	1	55	67	13.1	3.98	83	.289	.345	12	.214	3	-11	-13	4	-0.9
1912 Cin-N	1	1	.500	7	3	1	0	0	22²	34	1	15	5	19.5	6.35	53	.370	.458	0	.000	-0	-7	-8	-0	-0.6
1914 Bal-F	10	8	.556	39	22	9	1	2	174²	180	8	47	83	11.7	2.99	101	.259	.306	12	.203	0	-2	1	2	0.3
1915 Bal-F	4	4	.500	17	9	2	0	0	88²	108	5	31	37	14.1	4.67	61	.312	.369	5	.172	0	-19	-18	-0	-1.4
Bro-F	5	2	.714	15	5	4	1	0	63	69	2	18	24	12.4	3.14	87	.290	.340	4	.200	1	-3	-3	1	-0.2
Yr	9	6	.600	32	14	6	1	0	151²	177	7	49	61	13.4	4.04	70	.303	.357	9	.184	1	-22	-21	1	-1.6
Total 11	139	111	.556	354	255	184	27	6	2273	1975	27	676	1051	10.7	2.59	99	.237	.297	156	.204	35	16	-9	27	7.7

● FRANK SMITH Smith, Frank Thomas b: 4/4/28, Pierrepont Manor, N.Y. BR/TR, 6'3", 200 lbs. Deb: 4/18/50

1950 Cin-N	2	7	.222	38	4	0	0	3	90²	73	12	39	55	11.9	3.87	109	.216	.312	2	.095	-2	3	4	-1	0.1
1951 Cin-N	5	5	.500	50	0	0	0	11	76	65	7	22	34	10.8	3.20	128	.230	.295	0	.000	-1	6	7	0	1.1
1952 Cin-N	12	11	.522	53	2	1	0	7	122¹	109	13	41	77	11.6	3.75	101	.242	.315	5	.172	0	-0	0	-2	-0.1
1953 Cin-N	8	1	.889	50	1	0	0	2	83²	89	15	25	42	12.6	5.49	79	.272	.330	2	.154	-1	-11	-11	1	-1.0
1954 Cin-N	5	8	.385	50	0	0	0	20	81	60	15	29	51	10.2	2.67	157	.211	.291	1	.100	1	13	14	0	2.9
1955 StL-N	3	1	.750	28	0	0	0	1	39	27	3	23	17	12.7	3.23	126	.205	.344	0	.000	-0	3	4	-0	0.3
1956 Cin-N	0	0	—	2	0	0	0	0	3	3	2	2	1	15.0	12.00	33	.300	.417	0	—	0	-3	-3	-0	0.0
Total 7	35	33	.515	271	7	1	0	44	495²	426	67	181	277	11.6	3.81	107	.234	.313	10	.115	-3	11	16	-2	3.3

● FRED SMITH Smith, Frederick b: 11/24/1878, New Diggings, Wis. d: 2/4/64, Los Angeles, Cal. BL/TR, 6', 186 lbs. Deb: 6/14/07

| 1907 Cin-N | 2 | 7 | .222 | 18 | 9 | 5 | 0 | 1 | 85¹ | 90 | 3 | 24 | 19 | 12.4 | 2.85 | 91 | .274 | .331 | 3 | .107 | -2 | -4 | -2 | 0 | -0.4 |

● FRED SMITH — Smith, Frederick C. b: 3/25/1863, Greene, N.Y. d: 1/9/41, Syracuse, N.Y. BL/TR, 5'11", 156 lbs. Deb: 4/18/1890

YEAR TM/L	W	L	PCT	G	GS	CG	SH	SV	IP	H	HR	BB	SO	RAT	ERA	ERA+	OAV	OOB	BH	AVG	PB	PR	/A	PD	TPI
1890 Tol-a	19	13	.594	35	34	31	2	0	286	273	13	90	116	11.8	3.27	121	.244	.307	21	.167	-2	19	22	3	2.0

● GEORGE SMITH — Smith, George Allen "Columbia George" b: 5/31/1892, Byram, Conn. d: 1/7/65, Greenwich, Conn. BR/TR, 6'2", 163 lbs. Deb: 8/9/16

YEAR TM/L	W	L	PCT	G	GS	CG	SH	SV	IP	H	HR	BB	SO	RAT	ERA	ERA+	OAV	OOB	BH	AVG	PB	PR	/A	PD	TPI
1916 NY-N	3	0	1.000	9	1	0	0	0	20^2	14	0	6	9	9.1	2.61	93	.197	.269	0	.000	-0	-0	-0	0	0.0
1917 NY-N	0	3	.000	14	1	1	0	0	38	38	1	11	16	11.8	2.84	90	.270	.327	0	.000	-1	-1	-1	-0	-0.2
1918 Cin-N	2	3	.400	10	6	4	1	0	55^1	71	3	11	19	13.3	4.07	66	.329	.361	0	.000	-2	-8	-9	1	-0.9
NY-N	2	3	.400	5	2	1	0	0	26^2	26	0	6	4	11.1	4.05	65	.255	.303	2	.250	0	-4	-4	-1	-0.8
Bro-N	4	1	.800	8	5	4	0	0	50	43	0	5	18	9.0	2.34	119	.249	.278	3	.200	2	1	2	1	0.4
Yr	8	7	.533	23	13	9	1	0	132	140	3	22	41	11.2	3.41	79	.285	.318	5	.125	-2	-9	-10	-1	-1.3
1919 NY-N	0	2	.000	3	2	0	0	0	11	18	1	4	0	18.0	5.73	49	.383	.431	0	.000	-0	-3	-4	-0	-0.7
Phi-N	5	11	.313	31	19	11	1	0	184^2	194	7	46	42	11.8	3.22	100	.278	.326	8	.133	-3	-6	0	-1	-0.4
Yr	5	13	.278	34	21	11	1	0	195^2	212	8	50	42	12.2	3.36	95	.285	.332	8	.127	-4	-10	-3	-1	-1.1
1920 Phi-N	13	18	.419	43	28	10	1	2	250^2	265	10	51	51	11.6	3.45	99	.283	.324	7	.097	-6	-9	-1	-2	-0.9
1921 Phi-N	4	20	.167	39	28	12	1	1	221^1	303	12	52	45	14.6	4.76	89	.335	.373	4	.056	-8	-24	-13	-2	-2.1
1922 Phi-N	5	14	.263	42	18	6	1	0	194	250	16	35	44	13.5	4.78	98	.350	.350	5	.076	-7	-15	-2	-1	-1.0
1923 Bro-N	3	6	.333	25	7	3	0	1	91	99	4	28	15	12.9	3.66	106	.278	.336	5	.192	-1	3	2	-2	-0.1
Total 8	41	81	.336	229	117	52	5	4	1143^1	1321	54	255	263	12.6	3.89	94	.298	.340	34	.097	-29	-63	-31	-8	-6.7

● HEINIE SMITH — Smith, George Henry b: 10/24/1871, Pittsburgh, Pa. d: 6/25/39, Buffalo, N.Y. BR/TR, 5'9.5", 160 lbs. Deb: 9/8/1897 M♦

YEAR TM/L	W	L	PCT	G	GS	CG	SH	SV	IP	H	HR	BB	SO	RAT	ERA	ERA+	OAV	OOB	BH	AVG	PB	PR	/A	PD	TPI
1901 NY-N	0	1	.000	2	1	1	0	0	13^1	24	0	5	5	21.6	8.10	41	.386	.456	6	.207	0	-7	-7	-0	-0.4

● GERMANY SMITH — Smith, George J. b: 4/21/1863, Pittsburgh, Pa. d: 12/1/27, Altoona, Pa. BR/TR, 6', 175 lbs. Deb: 4/17/1884 ♦

YEAR TM/L	W	L	PCT	G	GS	CG	SH	SV	IP	H	HR	BB	SO	RAT	ERA	ERA+	OAV	OOB	BH	AVG	PB	PR	/A	PD	TPI
1884 Alt-U	0	0	—	1	1	0	0	0	1	3	0	0	1	27.0	9.00	30	.491	.491	34	.315	0	-1	-1	0	0.0

● GEORGE SMITH — Smith, George Shelby b: 10/27/01, Louisville, Ky. d: 5/26/81, Richmond, Va. BR/TR, 6'1", 175 lbs. Deb: 4/21/26

YEAR TM/L	W	L	PCT	G	GS	CG	SH	SV	IP	H	HR	BB	SO	RAT	ERA	ERA+	OAV	OOB	BH	AVG	PB	PR	/A	PD	TPI
1926 Det-A	1	2	.333	23	1	0	0	0	44	55	3	33	15	18.4	6.95	58	.318	.433	0	.000	-0	-14	-14	-1	-0.9
1927 Det-A	4	1	.800	29	0	0	0	0	71^1	62	3	50	32	14.4	3.91	108	.240	.368	7	.368	3	2	2	-1	0.4
1928 Det-A	1	1	.500	39	2	0	0	3	106	103	3	50	54	13.0	4.42	93	.263	.346	3	.111	-2	-4	-4	-2	-0.5
1929 Det-A	3	2	.600	14	2	1	0	0	35^2	42	1	36	13	19.7	5.80	74	.307	.451	5	.417	2	-6	-6	1	-0.3
1930 Bos-A	1	2	.333	27	2	0	0	0	73^2	92	7	49	21	17.3	6.60	70	.317	.418	8	.333	2	-16	-16	0	-0.3
Total 5	10	8	.556	132	7	1	0	3	330^2	354	17	218	135	15.7	5.28	81	.283	.392	23	.264	4	-39	-38	-2	-1.7

● HAL SMITH — Smith, Harold Laverne b: 6/30/02, Creston, Iowa d: 9/27/92, Ft.Lauderdale, Fla. BR/TR, 6'3", 195 lbs. Deb: 9/14/32

YEAR TM/L	W	L	PCT	G	GS	CG	SH	SV	IP	H	HR	BB	SO	RAT	ERA	ERA+	OAV	OOB	BH	AVG	PB	PR	/A	PD	TPI
1932 Pit-N	1	0	1.000	2	1	1	0	0	12	9	0	4	2	8.3	0.75	508	.209	.244	0	.000	-0	4	4	0	0.3
1933 Pit-N	8	7	.533	28	19	8	2	1	145	149	5	31	40	11.5	2.86	116	.261	.305	6	.128	-2	8	7	-2	0.4
1934 Pit-N	3	4	.429	20	5	1	0	0	50	72	3	18	15	16.9	7.20	57	.343	.405	1	.059	-2	-17	-17	-0	-2.2
1935 Pit-N	0	0	—	1	0	0	0	0	3	2	0	1	2	9.0	3.00	137	.200	.273	0	—	0	0	0	-0	-0.0
Total 4	12	11	.522	51	25	10	3	1	210	232	8	52	59	12.6	3.77	94	.279	.328	7	.104	-4	-5	-5	-2	-1.5

● HARRY SMITH — Smith, Harrison Morton b: 8/15/1889, Union, Neb. d: 7/26/64, Dunbar, Neb. BR/TR, 5'9", 160 lbs. Deb: 10/6/12

YEAR TM/L	W	L	PCT	G	GS	CG	SH	SV	IP	H	HR	BB	SO	RAT	ERA	ERA+	OAV	OOB	BH	AVG	PB	PR	/A	PD	TPI
1912 Chi-A	1	0	1.000	1	1	0	0	0	5	6	0	0	1	10.8	1.80	178	.333	.333	0	.000	-0	1	1	-0	0.1

● JACK SMITH — Smith, Jack Hatfield b: 11/15/35, Pikeville, Ky. BR/TR, 6', 185 lbs. Deb: 9/10/62

YEAR TM/L	W	L	PCT	G	GS	CG	SH	SV	IP	H	HR	BB	SO	RAT	ERA	ERA+	OAV	OOB	BH	AVG	PB	PR	/A	PD	TPI
1962 LA-N	0	0	—	8	0	0	0	1	10	10	0	4	7	12.6	4.50	81	.263	.333	0	.000	-0	-1	-1	-0	-0.1
1963 LA-N	0	0	—	4	0	0	0	0	8^1	10	2	2	5	15.1	7.56	40	.303	.378	0	.000	-0	-4	-4	0	0.0
1964 Mil-N	2	2	.500	22	0	0	0	1	31	28	3	11	19	11.3	3.77	93	.254	.302	1	.333	-1	-1	-1	1	0.0
Total 3	2	2	.500	34	0	0	0	1	49^1	48	5	17	31	12.2	4.56	76	.254	.322	1	.167	-1	-5	-6	1	-0.1

● JAKE SMITH — Smith, Jacob (b: Jacob Schmidt) b: 6/10/1887, Dravosburg, Pa d: 11/7/48, E.McKeesport, Pa. BB/TL, 6'5", 200 lbs. Deb: 10/3/11

YEAR TM/L	W	L	PCT	G	GS	CG	SH	SV	IP	H	HR	BB	SO	RAT	ERA	ERA+	OAV	OOB	BH	AVG	PB	PR	/A	PD	TPI
1911 Phi-N	0	0	—	2	0	0	0	0	5	3	0	2	1	9.0	0.00	—	.176	.263	0	.000	-0	2	2	0	0.0

● PHENOMENAL SMITH — Smith, John Francis (b: John Francis Gammon) b: 12/12/1864, Philadelphia, Pa. d: 4/3/52, Manchester, N.H. BL/TL, 5'6.5", 161 lbs. Deb: 4/18/1884

YEAR TM/L	W	L	PCT	G	GS	CG	SH	SV	IP	H	HR	BB	SO	RAT	ERA	ERA+	OAV	OOB	BH	AVG	PB	PR	/A	PD	TPI
1884 Bal-U	3	4	.429	9	8	5	0	0	62	86	2	17	13	15.0	3.48	77	.308	.348	5	.147	-4	-7	-6	-1	-0.9
Phi-a	0	1	.000	1	1	1	0	0	9	14	0	1	3	15.0	4.00	85	.368	.385	1	.250	-0	-1	-1	0	-0.5
Pit-a	0	1	.000	1	1	1	0	0	8	11	0	2	4	15.8	9.00	37	.306	.359	0	.000	-1	-5	-5	0	-0.5
Yr	0	2	.000	2	2	2	0	0	17	25	0	3	7	15.4	6.35	53	.338	.372	1	.125	-1	-6	-6	0	-0.5
1885 Bro-a	0	1	.000	1	1	1	0	0	8	12	0	6	2	21.4	12.38	27	.300	.404	1	.333	0	-8	-8	0	-0.6
Phi-a	0	1	.000	1	1	1	0	0	4	7	0	4	7	27.0	9.00	38	.368	.500	0	.000	-0	-3	-2	-0	-0.4
Yr	0	2	.000	2	2	1	0	0	12	19	0	10	9	22.5	11.25	30	.317	.423	1	.200	-0	-11	-11	0	-1.0
1886 Det-N	1	1	.500	3	3	3	0	0	25	16	0		15	8.6	2.16	153	.174	.240	1	.111	-1	3	3	-1	0.1
1887 Bal-a	25	30	.455	58	55	54	1	0	491^1	526	7	176	206	13.1	3.79	108	.261	.325	48	.234	8	28	17	-1	2.0
1888 Bal-a	14	19	.424	35	32	31	0	0	292	249	5	137	152	12.6	3.61	83	.222	.320	27	.248	8	-18	-20	-4	-1.5
Phi-a	2	1	.667	3	3	3	0	0	22	21	0	10	19	12.7	2.86	104	.242	.321	3	.333	1	0	0	-0	0.1
Yr	16	20	.444	38	35	34	0	0	314	270	5	147	171	12.0	3.55	84	.219	.303	30	.254	9	-17	-20	-4	-1.4
1889 Phi-a	2	3	.400	5	5	5	0	0	43	53	2	25	12	17.0	4.40	86	.294	.389	3	.188	0	-3	-3	-1	-0.3
1890 Phi-N	8	12	.400	24	20	19	1	0	204	209	5	89	81	13.5	4.28	85	.257	.336	24	.279	4	-16	-14	-2	-0.9
Pit-N	1	3	.250	5	5	5	0	0	44	39	0	13	15	10.8	3.07	107	.230	.289	7	.412	2	2	1	-0	0.3
Yr	9	15	.375	29	25	24	1	0	248	248	5	102	96	12.7	4.06	88	.255	.321	31	.301	6	-14	-13	-3	-0.6
1891 Phi-N	1	1	.500	3	2	0	0	0	19	20	1	8	3	13.3	4.26	80	.260	.330	3	.375	-1	-2	-2	-1	-0.1
Total 8	57	78	.422	149	137	128	2	0	1231^1	1263	22	496	532	13.2	3.87	93	.254	.329	123	.243	19	-28	-38	-10	-2.7

● CHICK SMITH — Smith, John William (b: Jan Smadt) b: 12/2/1892, Dayton, Ky. d: 10/11/35, Dayton, Ohio BL/TL, 5'8", 165 lbs. Deb: 4/12/13

YEAR TM/L	W	L	PCT	G	GS	CG	SH	SV	IP	H	HR	BB	SO	RAT	ERA	ERA+	OAV	OOB	BH	AVG	PB	PR	/A	PD	TPI
1913 Cin-N	0	1	.000	5	1	0	0	0	17^2	15	1	11	11	13.2	3.57	91	.238	.351	0	.000	-1	-1	-1	0	-0.1

● LEE SMITH — Smith, Lee Arthur b: 12/4/57, Shreveport, La. BR/TR, 6'6", 225 lbs. Deb: 9/1/80

YEAR TM/L	W	L	PCT	G	GS	CG	SH	SV	IP	H	HR	BB	SO	RAT	ERA	ERA+	OAV	OOB	BH	AVG	PB	PR	/A	PD	TPI
1980 Chi-N	2	0	1.000	18	0	0	0	0	21^2	21	0	14	17	14.5	2.91	135	.259	.368	0	—	0	2	2	-0	0.2
1981 Chi-N	3	6	.333	40	1	0	0	1	66^2	57	2	31	50	12.0	3.51	105	.239	.330	0	.000	-1	-0	1	-0	0.1
1982 Chi-N	2	5	.286	72	5	0	0	17	117	105	5	37	99	11.2	2.69	139	.245	.309	1	.063	-0	12	14	-1	1.2
1983 Chi-N★	4	10	.286	66	0	0	0	**29**	103^1	70	5	41	91	9.8	1.65	229	.194	.279	1	.111	-0	23	25	-1	4.9
1984 *Chi-N	9	7	.563	69	0	0	0	33	101	98	6	35	86	11.9	3.65	107	.255	.317	1	.077	-1	3	3	0	0.6
1985 Chi-N	7	4	.636	65	0	0	0	33	97^2	87	9	32	112	11.1	3.04	131	.242	.305	0	.000	-0	6	10	-1	1.9
1986 Chi-N	9	9	.500	66	0	0	0	31	90^1	69	7	42	93	11.1	3.09	131	.215	.306	0	.000	-0	6	10	-0	2.5
1987 Chi-N★	4	10	.286	62	0	0	0	36	83^2	84	4	32	96	12.5	3.12	137	.259	.326	0	.000	-0	9	11	-2	2.6
1988 *Bos-A	4	5	.444	64	0	0	0	29	83^2	72	7	37	96	11.8	2.80	147	.225	.307	0	—	0	11	12	-1	2.1
1989 Bos-A	6	1	.857	64	0	0	0	25	70^2	53	6	33	96	11.0	3.57	115	.209	.301	0	—	0	2	4	-0	0.9
1990 Bos-A	2	1	.667	11	0	0	0	4	14^1	13	0	9	17	13.8	1.88	216	.236	.344	0	—	0	3	3	-0	0.9
StL-N	3	4	.429	53	0	0	0	27	68^2	58	3	20	70	10.2	2.10	182	.227	.284	0	.000	-0	13	13	-2	2.3
1991 StL-N☆	6	3	.667	67	0	0	0	**47**	73	70	5	13	67	10.2	2.34	159	.249	.282	0	—	0	11	11	-1	3.0
1992 StL-N☆	4	9	.308	70	0	0	0	**43**	75	62	4	26	60	10.6	3.12	109	.221	.287	0	—	0	3	2	-1	0.6
1993 StL-N☆	2	4	.333	55	0	0	0	43	50	49	11	9	49	10.4	4.50	88	.251	.284	0	.000	-0	-3	-3	-1	-1.0
NY-A	0	0	—	8	0	0	0	0	8	0	0	1	11	10.1	0.00	—	.148	.222	0	—	0	3	3	-0	0.9
1994 Bal-A★	1	4	.200	41	0	0	0	**33**	38^1	34	6	11	42	10.6	3.29	154	.239	.294	0	—	0	6	8	-0	2.2
Total 15	68	82	.453	891	6	0	0	434	1163	1006	80	427	1152	11.1	2.93	134	.234	.304	3	.047	-4	108	130	-9	24.7

YEAR TM/L	W	L	PCT	G	GS	CG	SH	SV	IP	H	HR	BB	SO	RAT	ERA	ERA+	OAV	OOB	BH	AVG	PB	PR	/A	PD	TPI

● ROY SMITH Smith, Le Roy Purdy b: 9/6/61, Mt.Vernon, N.Y. BR/TR, 6'3", 200 lbs. Deb: 6/23/84

1984 Cle-A	5	5	.500	22	14	1	0	0	86¹	91	14	40	55	13.8	4.59	89	.270	.349	0	—	0	-6	-5	-2	-0.7
1985 Cle-A	1	4	.200	12	11	1	0	0	62¹	84	8	17	28	14.7	5.34	77	.321	.364	0	—	0	-8	-8	-1	-0.6
1986 Min-A	0	2	.000	5	0	0	0	0	10¹	13	1	5	8	16.5	6.97	62	.295	.380	0	—	0	-3	-3	-0	-0.6
1987 Min-A	1	0	1.000	7	1	0	0	0	16¹	20	3	6	6	15.4	4.96	93	.290	.364	0	—	0	-1	-1	-0	-0.1
1988 Min-A	3	0	1.000	9	4	0	0	0	37	29	3	12	17	10.2	2.68	152	.210	.278	0	—	0	5	6	-1	0.4
1989 Min-A	10	6	.625	32	26	2	0	1	172¹	180	22	51	92	12.3	3.92	106	.269	.326	0	—	0	-1	4	-3	-0.2
1990 Min-A	5	10	.333	32	23	1	1	0	153¹	191	20	47	87	14.0	4.81	86	.313	.362	0	—	0	-15	-11	-2	-1.3
1991 Bal-A	5	4	.556	17	14	0	0	0	80¹	99	9	24	25	13.9	5.60	71	.311	.362	0	—	0	-13	-15	-1	-1.3
Total 8	30	31	.492	136	93	4	1	1	618¹	707	80	202	320	13.4	4.60	90	.289	.346	0	—	0	-42	-33	-9	-4.4

● MARK SMITH Smith, Mark Christopher b: 11/23/55, Arlington, Va. BR/TR, 6'2", 215 lbs. Deb: 8/12/83

| 1983 Oak-A | 1 | 0 | 1.000 | 8 | 1 | 0 | 0 | 0 | 14² | 24 | 0 | 6 | 10 | 19.0 | 6.75 | 57 | .387 | .449 | 0 | — | 0 | -4 | -5 | -0 | 0.0 |

● MIKE SMITH Smith, Michael Anthony b: 2/23/61, Jackson, Miss. BR/TR, 6'1", 195 lbs. Deb: 4/6/84

1984 Cin-N	1	0	1.000	8	0	0	0	0	10¹	12	1	5	7	14.8	5.23	72	.286	.362	0	—	0	-2	-2	-0	-0.2
1985 Cin-N	0	0	—	2	0	0	0	0	3¹	2	2	1	2	8.1	5.40	70	.167	.231	0	—	0	-1	-1	0	0.0
1986 Cin-N	0	0	—	2	1	0	0	0	3¹	7	0	1	1	21.6	13.50	29	.412	.444	0	—	0	-4	-4	0	0.0
1988 Mon-N	0	0	—	5	0	0	0	1	8²	6	0	5	4	11.4	3.12	115	.207	.324	0	.000	0	0	0	0	0.0
1989 Pit-N	0	1	.000	16	0	0	0	0	24	28	1	10	12	14.3	3.75	89	.301	.369	0	.000	-0	-1	-1	1	0.0
Total 5	1	1	.500	33	1	0	0	1	49²	55	4	22	26	14.0	4.71	75	.285	.358	0	.000	-1	-7	-6	0	-0.2

● MIKE SMITH Smith, Michael Anthony b: 10/31/63, San Antonio, Tex. BR/TR, 6'3", 180 lbs. Deb: 6/30/89

1989 Bal-A	2	0	1.000	13	1	0	0	0	20	25	3	14	12	17.5	7.65	50	.313	.415	0	—	0	-8	-9	-0	-0.6
1990 Bal-A	0	0	—	2	0	0	0	0	3	4	2	1	2	15.0	12.00	32	.308	.357	0	—	0	-3	-3	-0	0.0
Total 2	2	0	1.000	15	1	0	0	0	23	29	5	15	14	17.2	8.22	46	.312	.407	0	—	0	-11	-11	0	-0.6

● PETE SMITH Smith, Peter John b: 2/27/66, Abington, Mass. BR/TR, 6'3", 200 lbs. Deb: 9/8/87

1987 Atl-N	1	2	.333	6	6	0	0	0	31²	39	3	14	11	15.1	4.83	90	.307	.376	1	.091	-1	-3	-2	-1	-0.3
1988 Atl-N	7	15	.318	32	32	5	3	0	195¹	183	15	88	124	12.5	3.69	100	.250	.331	6	.113	-1	-5	-0	-3	-0.4
1989 Atl-N	5	14	.263	28	27	1	0	0	142	144	13	57	115	12.7	4.75	77	.263	.333	4	.098	-0	-20	-17	-1	-2.3
1990 Atl-N	5	6	.455	13	13	3	0	0	77	77	11	24	56	11.8	4.79	84	.260	.316	2	.087	-1	-9	-6	-1	-1.0
1991 Atl-N	1	3	.250	14	10	0	0	0	48	48	5	22	29	13.1	5.06	77	.262	.341	2	.167	-0	-7	-6	-1	-0.4
1992 *Atl-N	7	0	1.000	12	11	2	1	0	79	63	8	28	43	10.4	2.05	178	.217	.286	1	.038	-1	13	14	-0	1.1
1993 Atl-N	4	8	.333	20	14	0	0	0	90²	92	15	36	53	12.9	4.37	92	.270	.343	6	.222	1	-3	-4	0	-0.3
1994 NY-N	4	10	.286	21	21	1	0	0	131¹	145	25	42	62	13.0	5.55	77	.285	.342	5	.135	0	-20	-19	1	-1.6
Total 8	34	58	.370	146	134	12	4	0	795	791	90	311	493	12.5	4.34	90	.261	.331	27	.117	-0	-54	-40	-4	-5.2

● PETE SMITH Smith, Peter Luke b: 3/19/40, Natick, Mass. BR/TR, 6'2", 190 lbs. Deb: 9/13/62

1962 Bos-A	0	1	.000	1	1	0	0	0	3²	7	3	2	1	22.1	19.64	21	.438	.500	0	.000	—	-6	-6	0	-0.9
1963 Bos-A	0	0	—	6	1	0	0	0	15	11	2	6	6	10.2	3.60	105	.212	.293	0	.000	-0	0	0	0	0.0
Total 2	0	1	.000	7	2	0	0	0	18²	18	5	8	7	12.5	6.75	57	.265	.342	0	.000	-0	-6	-6	0	-0.9

● REGGIE SMITH Smith, Reginald b: Louisville, Ky. Deb: 7/11/1886

| 1886 Phi-a | 0 | 1 | .000 | 1 | 1 | 1 | 0 | 0 | 9 | 15 | 0 | 5 | 4 | 20.0 | 7.00 | 50 | .385 | .455 | 0 | .000 | -1 | -4 | -3 | -0 | -0.3 |

● ED SMITH Smith, Rhesa Edward b: 2/21/1879, Mentone, Ind. d: 3/20/55, Tarpon Springs, Fla. BR/TR, 5'11", 170 lbs. Deb: 4/27/06

| 1906 StL-A | 8 | 11 | .421 | 19 | 18 | 13 | 0 | 0 | 154² | 153 | 3 | 53 | 45 | 12.5 | 3.72 | 69 | .261 | .331 | 11 | .204 | 2 | -18 | -20 | 1 | -1.9 |

● BOB SMITH Smith, Robert Ashley (a.k.a. Robert M. Brown in 1914)
b: 7/20/1890, Woodbury, Vt. d: 12/27/65, West Los Angeles, Cal. BR/TR, 5'11", 160 lbs. Deb: 4/19/13

1913 Chi-A	0	0	—	1	0	0	0	0	2	3	0	3	1	27.0	13.50	22	.273	.429	0	—	0	-2	-2	-0	0.0
1914 Buf-F	0	0	—	15	1	0	0	3	36²	39	3	16	13	14.0	3.44	86	.281	.363	2	.222	0	-2	-1	1	0.1
1915 Buf-F	0	0	—	1	0	0	0	0	1	1	0	2	0	36.0	18.00	16	.333	.667	0	—	0	-2	-2	0	0.0
Total 3	0	0	—	17	1	0	0	3	39²	43	3	21	14	15.2	4.31	69	.281	.379	2	.222	0	-6	-6	1	0.1

● BOB SMITH Smith, Robert Eldridge b: 4/22/1895, Rogersville, Tenn. d: 7/19/87, Waycross, Ga. BR/TR, 5'10", 175 lbs. Deb: 4/19/23 ♦

1925 Bos-N	5	3	.625	13	10	6	0	0	92²	110	6	36	19	14.2	4.47	90	.304	.367	49	.282	3	-2	-5	-0	-0.1
1926 Bos-N	10	13	.435	33	23	14	4	1	201¹	199	10	75	44	12.2	3.75	94	.269	.336	25	.298	7	2	-5	2	0.5
1927 Bos-N	10	18	.357	41	32	16	1	3	260²	297	9	75	81	12.9	3.76	99	.301	.351	27	.248	4	4	-1	2	0.6
1928 Bos-N	13	17	.433	38	25	14	0	2	244¹	274	11	74	59	12.9	3.87	101	.289	.342	23	.250	3	3	1	3	0.7
1929 Bos-N	11	17	.393	34	29	19	1	3	231	256	20	71	65	12.8	4.68	100	.285	.338	17	.172	-1	1	0	1	0.1
1930 Bos-N	10	14	.417	38	24	14	2	5	219²	247	25	85	84	13.7	4.26	116	.290	.357	19	.235	-1	17	16	2	1.6
1931 Chi-N	15	12	.556	36	29	18	2	2	240¹	239	10	62	63	11.3	3.22	120	.256	.303	19	.218	2	17	17	1	2.0
1932 *Chi-N	4	3	.571	34	11	4	1	2	119	148	4	36	35	14.1	4.61	82	.303	.355	10	.238	2	-10	-11	-1	-0.4
1933 Cin-N	4	4	.500	16	6	4	0	0	73²	75	3	11	18	10.5	2.20	154	.260	.287	5	.200	0	9	10	0	1.0
Bos-N	4	3	.571	14	4	3	1	1	58²	68	3	7	16	11.5	3.22	95	.296	.316	4	.200	1	1	-1	0	0.0
Yr	8	7	.533	30	10	7	1	1	132¹	143	6	18	34	10.9	2.65	123	.276	.300	9	.200	1	10	9	1	1.0
1934 Bos-N	6	9	.400	39	5	3	0	5	121²	133	9	36	26	12.5	4.66	82	.277	.328	9	.250	1	-8	-11	1	-1.1
1935 Bos-N	8	18	.308	46	20	8	2	5	203¹	232	13	61	58	13.1	3.94	96	.285	.337	17	.270	2	2	-3	2	-0.2
1936 Bos-N	6	7	.462	35	11	5	2	8	136	142	3	35	36	11.8	3.77	102	.264	.311	10	.222	0	4	1	1	0.2
1937 Bos-N	0	1	.000	18	0	0	0	3	44	52	6	14	12	12.3	4.09	88	.295	.326	2	.200	1	-1	-2	-1	-0.1
Total 13	106	139	.433	435	229	128	16	40	2246¹	2472	132	670	618	12.7	3.94	100	.283	.335	409	.242	23	40	4	12	4.8

● BOB SMITH Smith, Robert Gilchrist b: 2/1/31, Woodsville, N.H. BR/TL, 6'1.5", 190 lbs. Deb: 4/29/55

1955 Bos-A	0	0	—	1	0	0	0	0	1²	1	0	1	1	10.8	0.00	—	.200	.333	0	—	0	1	1	-0	0.0
1957 StL-N	0	0	—	6	0	0	0	1	9²	12	0	6	11	17.7	4.66	85	.267	.365	0	.000	-0	-1	-1	0	0.0
Pit-N	2	4	.333	20	4	2	0	0	55	48	2	25	35	12.1	3.11	122	.229	.314	1	.077	-1	5	4	-1	0.2
Yr	2	4	.333	26	4	2	0	1	64²	60	2	31	46	12.8	3.34	114	.234	.319	1	.067	-1	4	3	-1	0.2
1958 Pit-N	2	2	.500	35	4	0	0	1	61	61	6	31	24	13.9	4.43	87	.262	.353	1	.091	-1	-3	-4	-1	-0.2
1959 Pit-N	0	0	—	20	0	0	0	0	28¹	32	1	17	12	15.6	3.49	111	.291	.386	0	.000	-1	1	1	-0	-0.1
Det-A	0	3	.000	9	0	0	0	0	11	20	5	3	10	18.8	8.18	50	.417	.451	0	.000	-0	-5	-5	0	-1.2
Total 4	4	9	.308	91	8	2	0	2	166²	174	14	83	93	14.1	4.05	95	.267	.354	2	.069	-2	-2	-3	-0	-1.3

● BOB SMITH Smith, Robert Walkay "Riverboat" b: 5/13/28, Clarence, Mo. BL/TL, 6', 185 lbs. Deb: 4/22/58

1958 Bos-A	4	3	.571	17	5	0	0	0	66²	61	4	46	43	14.3	3.78	106	.248	.364	2	.105	-1	-0	2	1	0.1
1959 Chi-N	0	0	—	1	0	0	0	0	0²	5	0	2	0	94.5	81.00	5	.833	.875	0	—	0	-6	-6	0	0.0
Cle-A	0	1	.000	12	5	0	0	0	29¹	31	2	12	17	13.2	5.22	71	.282	.352	0	.000	-1	-4	-5	-0	-0.2
Total 2	4	4	.500	30	10	0	0	0	96²	97	6	59	60	14.5	4.75	82	.268	.371	2	.080	-2	-10	-9	1	-0.1

● RUFUS SMITH Smith, Rufus Frazier "Shirt" b: 1/24/05, Guilford College, N.C. d: 8/21/84, Aiken, S.C. BR/TL, 5'8", 165 lbs. Deb: 10/2/27

| 1927 Det-A | 0 | 0 | — | 1 | 1 | 0 | 0 | 0 | 8 | 8 | 0 | 3 | 2 | 13.5 | 3.38 | 125 | .242 | .324 | 0 | .000 | -1 | 1 | 1 | -0 | -0.1 |

● SHERRY SMITH Smith, Sherrod Malone b: 2/18/1891, Monticello, Ga. d: 9/12/49, Reidsville, Ga. BR/TL, 6'1", 170 lbs. Deb: 5/11/11

| 1911 Pit-N | 0 | 0 | — | 1 | 0 | 0 | 0 | 0 | 0² | 4 | 0 | 1 | 0 | 67.5 | 54.00 | 6 | .667 | .714 | 0 | — | 0 | -4 | -4 | -0 | 0.0 |
| 1912 Pit-N | 0 | 0 | — | 3 | 0 | 0 | 0 | 1 | 4 | 6 | 0 | 1 | 3 | 15.8 | 6.75 | 48 | .600 | .636 | 0 | — | 0 | -1 | -2 | -0 | -0.1 |

YEAR TM/L	W	L	PCT	G	GS	CG	SH	SV	IP	H	HR	BB	SO	RAT	ERA	ERA+	OAV	OOB	BH	AVG	PB	PR	/A	PD	TPI
1915 Bro-N	14	8	.636	29	20	11	2	2	173²	169	3	42	52	11.2	2.59	107	.264	.315	14	.246	3	3	4	-0	0.7
1916 *Bro-N	14	10	.583	36	25	15	4	1	219	193	5	45	67	9.9	2.34	114	.239	.282	21	.273	5	7	8	0	1.6
1917 Bro-N	12	12	.500	38	23	15	0	3	211²	210	5	51	58	11.2	3.32	84	.265	.311	15	.195	2	-14	-12	3	-0.8
1919 Bro-N	7	12	.368	30	19	13	2	1	173	181	3	29	40	11.1	2.24	133	.278	.313	8	.148	-2	13	14	3	1.7
1920 *Bro-N	11	9	.550	33	13	6	2	3	136¹	134	1	27	33	10.8	1.85	173	.264	.304	10	.233	2	19	21	5	4.0
1921 Bro-N	7	11	.389	35	17	9	0	4	175¹	232	4	34	36	13.7	3.90	100	.319	.350	13	.228	1	-2	-0	5	0.5
1922 Bro-N	4	8	.333	28	9	3	1	2	108²	128	6	35	15	14.1	4.56	89	.309	.373	9	.257	2	-5	-6	1	-0.3
Cle-A	1	0	1.000	2	2	1	0	0	15²	18	0	3	4	12.1	3.45	116	.295	.328	2	.333	1	1	1	0	0.1
1923 Cle-A	9	6	.600	30	16	10	1	1	124	129	4	37	23	12.2	3.27	121	.269	.324	11	.244	1	10	10	2	1.3
1924 Cle-A	12	14	.462	39	27	20	2	1	247²	267	5	42	34	11.5	3.02	142	.277	.312	18	.202	-1	33	35	3	3.4
1925 Cle-A	11	14	.440	31	30	22	1	1	237	296	11	48	30	13.3	4.86	91	.306	.342	28	.304	7	-12	-12	-0	-0.4
1926 Cle-A	11	10	.524	27	24	16	1	0	188¹	214	4	31	25	11.9	3.73	109	.292	.324	14	.215	2	6	7	3	1.2
1927 Cle-A	1	4	.200	11	2	1	0	1	38	53	2	14	8	15.6	5.45	77	.342	.396	2	.167	-0	-6	-5	-0	-0.6
Total 14	114	118	.491	373	227	142	16	21	2052²	2234	57	440	428	11.9	3.32	108	.282	.324	165	.233	22	48	59	26	12.3

● **TOM SMITH**   Smith, Thomas Edward   b: 12/5/1871, Boston, Mass.   d: 3/2/29, Dorchester, Mass.   BR/TR, 5'7.5", 165 lbs.   Deb: 6/6/1894

YEAR TM/L	W	L	PCT	G	GS	CG	SH	SV	IP	H	HR	BB	SO	RAT	ERA	ERA+	OAV	OOB	BH	AVG	PB	PR	/A	PD	TPI
1894 Bos-N	0	0	—	2	0	0	0	1	6	8	2	6	2	27.0	15.00	38	.316	.510	0	.000	-0	-6	-6	-0	-0.2
1895 Phi-N	2	3	.400	11	7	4	0	0	68	76	1	53	21	18.0	6.88	70	.278	.408	8	.242	-0	-16	-16	-1	-0.9
1896 Lou-N	2	3	.400	11	5	4	0	0	55	73	2	25	14	16.7	5.40	80	.316	.393	8	.205	-0	-6	-7	1	-0.4
1898 StL-N	0	1	.000	1	1	1	0	0	9	9	0	5	1	16.0	2.00	189	.258	.383	1	.500	1	2	2	0	0.3
Total 4	4	7	.364	25	13	9	0	1	138	166	5	89	38	17.7	6.33	72	.294	.406	17	.224	-0	-27	-27	-0	-1.2

● **BILL SMITH**   Smith, William Garland   b: 6/8/34, Washington, D.C.   BL/TL, 6', 190 lbs.   Deb: 9/13/58

YEAR TM/L	W	L	PCT	G	GS	CG	SH	SV	IP	H	HR	BB	SO	RAT	ERA	ERA+	OAV	OOB	BH	AVG	PB	PR	/A	PD	TPI
1958 StL-N	0	1	.000	2	1	0	0	0	9²	12	0	4	4	14.9	6.52	63	.324	.390	0	.000	-0	-3	-3	-0	-0.2
1959 StL-N	0	0	—	6	0	0	0	1	8¹	11	0	3	4	15.1	1.08	393	.333	.389	0	.000	-0	3	3	-0	0.1
1962 Phi-N	1	5	.167	24	5	0	0	0	50¹	59	8	10	26	12.5	4.29	90	.295	.332	2	.182	1	-2	-2	-0	-0.2
Total 3	1	6	.143	32	6	0	0	1	68¹	82	8	17	34	13.2	4.21	94	.304	.347	2	.143	0	-2	-2	-0	-0.3

● **WILLIE SMITH**   Smith, Willie   b: 2/11/39, Anniston, Ala.   BL/TL, 6', 190 lbs.   Deb: 6/18/63   ◆

YEAR TM/L	W	L	PCT	G	GS	CG	SH	SV	IP	H	HR	BB	SO	RAT	ERA	ERA+	OAV	OOB	BH	AVG	PB	PR	/A	PD	TPI
1963 Det-A	1	0	1.000	11	2	0	0	2	21²	24	2	13	16	15.4	4.57	82	.300	.398	1	.125	-0	-2	-2	-0	-0.2
1964 LA-A	1	4	.200	15	1	0	0	0	31²	34	5	10	20	12.8	2.84	116	.293	.354	108	.301	6	3	2	0	0.5
1968 Cle-A	0	0	—	2	0	0	0	0	5	2	0	1	1	5.4	0.00	—	.125	.176	6	.143	-0	2	2	0	0.0
Chi-N	0	0	—	1	0	0	0	0	2²	0	0	0	2	0.0	0.00	—	.000	.000	39	.275	-0	1	1	0	0.1
Total 3	2	4	.333	29	3	0	0	2	61	60	7	24	39	12.5	3.10	110	.273	.347	410	.248	6	3	2	1	0.4

● **WILLIE SMITH**   Smith, Willie Everett   b: 8/27/67, Savannah, Ga.   BR/TR, 6'6", 250 lbs.   Deb: 4/25/94

YEAR TM/L	W	L	PCT	G	GS	CG	SH	SV	IP	H	HR	BB	SO	RAT	ERA	ERA+	OAV	OOB	BH	AVG	PB	PR	/A	PD	TPI
1994 StL-N	1	1	.500	8	0	0	0	0	7	9	4	3	7	15.4	9.00	45	.300	.364	0	—	0	-4	-4	-0	-0.9

● **ZANE SMITH**   Smith, Zane William   b: 12/28/60, Madison, Wis.   BL/TL, 6'2", 195 lbs.   Deb: 9/10/84

YEAR TM/L	W	L	PCT	G	GS	CG	SH	SV	IP	H	HR	BB	SO	RAT	ERA	ERA+	OAV	OOB	BH	AVG	PB	PR	/A	PD	TPI
1984 Atl-N	1	0	1.000	3	3	0	0	0	20	16	1	13	16	13.0	2.25	171	.219	.337	5	.556	2	3	4	0	0.4
1985 Atl-N	9	10	.474	42	18	2	2	0	147	135	4	80	85	13.3	3.80	101	.254	.355	6	.162	-0	-3	1	2	0.3
1986 Atl-N	8	16	.333	38	32	3	1	1	204²	209	8	105	139	14.0	4.05	98	.275	.367	5	.085	-3	-7	-2	3	-0.2
1987 Atl-N	15	10	.600	36	36	9	0	0	242	245	19	91	130	12.7	4.09	106	.266	.335	10	.132	-1	-0	7	1	0.8
1988 Atl-N	5	10	.333	23	22	3	0	0	140¹	159	8	44	59	13.2	4.30	86	.292	.348	7	.167	0	-13	-10	3	-0.6
1989 Atl-N	1	12	.077	17	17	0	0	0	99	102	5	33	58	12.5	4.45	82	.267	.329	5	.179	-0	-11	-9	2	-0.9
Mon-N	0	1	.000	31	0	0	0	2	48	39	2	19	35	11.1	1.50	235	.220	.299	1	.250	0	11	11	1	0.5
Yr	1	13	.071	48	17	0	0	2	147	141	7	52	93	11.9	3.49	103	.249	.313	6	.188	0	0	2	3	-0.4
1990 Mon-N	6	7	.462	22	21	1	0	0	139¹	141	11	41	80	11.9	3.23	113	.266	.322	7	.175	1	9	6	1	0.8
*Pit-N	6	2	.750	11	10	3	2	0	76	55	4	9	50	7.6	1.30	278	.203	.229	4	.143	1	21	20	-0	2.2
Yr	12	9	.571	33	31	4	2	0	215¹	196	15	50	130	10.3	2.55	143	.243	.287	11	.162	2	30	26	1	3.0
1991 *Pit-N	16	10	.615	35	35	6	3	0	228	234	15	29	120	10.5	3.20	112	.268	.293	13	.183	3	12	9	1	1.4
1992 Pit-N	8	8	.500	23	22	4	3	0	141	138	8	19	56	10.1	3.06	112	.261	.289	6	.122	-0	7	6	1	0.7
1993 Pit-N	3	7	.300	14	14	1	0	0	83	97	5	22	32	12.9	4.55	89	.298	.343	2	.080	-2	-5	-5	-1	-0.7
1994 Pit-N	10	8	.556	25	24	2	1	0	157	162	18	34	57	11.2	3.27	130	.270	.309	12	.211	1	16	17	3	2.2
Total 11	88	101	.466	320	254	34	15	3	1725¹	1732	108	539	917	12.0	3.56	108	.266	.324	83	.158	1	39	56	17	6.9

● **ROGER SMITHBERG**   Smithberg, Roger Craig   b: 3/21/66, Elgin, Ill.   BR/TR, 6'3", 205 lbs.   Deb: 9/1/93

YEAR TM/L	W	L	PCT	G	GS	CG	SH	SV	IP	H	HR	BB	SO	RAT	ERA	ERA+	OAV	OOB	BH	AVG	PB	PR	/A	PD	TPI
1993 Oak-A	1	2	.333	13	0	0	0	3	19²	13	2	7	4	9.6	2.75	148	.197	.284	0	—	0	3	3	1	0.6
1994 Oak-A	0	0	—	2	0	0	0	0	2¹	6	1	1	3	27.0	15.43	29	.500	.538	0	—	0	-3	-3	0	0.0
Total 2	1	2	.333	15	0	0	0	3	22	19	3	8	7	11.5	4.09	101	.244	.322	0	—	0	1	0	1	0.6

● **MIKE SMITHSON**   Smithson, Billy Mike   b: 1/21/55, Centerville, Tenn.   BL/TR, 6'8", 215 lbs.   Deb: 8/27/82

YEAR TM/L	W	L	PCT	G	GS	CG	SH	SV	IP	H	HR	BB	SO	RAT	ERA	ERA+	OAV	OOB	BH	AVG	PB	PR	/A	PD	TPI
1982 Tex-A	3	4	.429	8	8	3	0	0	46²	51	5	13	24	12.9	5.01	77	.282	.340	0	—	0	-5	-6	-1	-0.8
1983 Tex-A	10	14	.417	33	33	10	0	0	223¹	233	14	71	135	12.6	3.91	102	.269	.330	0	—	0	4	2	1	0.4
1984 Min-A	15	13	.536	36	36	10	1	0	252	246	35	54	144	11.0	3.68	114	.252	.296	0	—	0	9	15	-1	1.4
1985 Min-A	15	14	.517	37	37	8	3	0	257	264	25	78	127	12.5	4.34	101	.270	.333	0	—	0	-6	-2	-2	-0.0
1986 Min-A	13	14	.481	34	33	8	1	0	198	234	26	57	114	13.9	4.77	90	.294	.352	0	—	0	-13	-10	1	-1.3
1987 Min-A	4	7	.364	21	20	0	0	0	109	126	17	38	53	14.3	5.94	78	.286	.355	0	—	0	-18	-16	-1	-1.5
1988 *Bos-A	9	6	.600	31	18	1	0	0	126²	149	25	37	73	13.6	5.97	69	.292	.347	0	—	0	-28	-26	-1	-2.8
1989 Bos-A	7	14	.333	40	19	1	1	2	143²	170	21	35	61	13.5	4.95	83	.297	.348	0	—	0	-17	-14	-1	-2.1
Total 8	76	86	.469	240	204	41	6	2	1356¹	1473	168	383	731	12.8	4.58	92	.277	.334	0	—	0	-74	-53	-4	-6.7

● **LEFTY SMOLL**   Smoll, Clyde Hetrick   b: 4/17/14, Quakertown, Pa.   d: 8/31/85, Quakertown, Pa.   BB/TL, 5'10", 175 lbs.   Deb: 4/26/40

YEAR TM/L	W	L	PCT	G	GS	CG	SH	SV	IP	H	HR	BB	SO	RAT	ERA	ERA+	OAV	OOB	BH	AVG	PB	PR	/A	PD	TPI
1940 Phi-N	2	8	.200	33	9	0	0	0	109	145	6	36	31	15.3	5.37	73	.322	.378	5	.161	-1	-18	-18	-2	-1.7

● **JOHN SMOLTZ**   Smoltz, John Andrew   b: 5/15/67, Detroit, Mich.   BR/TR, 6'3", 210 lbs.   Deb: 7/23/88

YEAR TM/L	W	L	PCT	G	GS	CG	SH	SV	IP	H	HR	BB	SO	RAT	ERA	ERA+	OAV	OOB	BH	AVG	PB	PR	/A	PD	TPI
1988 Atl-N	2	7	.222	12	12	0	0	0	64	74	10	33	37	15.3	5.48	67	.285	.369	2	.118	-0	-14	-13	-1	-1.7
1989 Atl-N★	12	11	.522	29	29	5	0	0	208	160	15	72	168	10.1	2.94	124	.212	.282	7	.113	1	13	16	2	2.1
1990 Atl-N	14	11	.560	34	34	6	2	0	231¹	206	20	90	170	11.6	3.85	105	.240	.313	12	.162	1	-2	5	1	0.7
1991 *Atl-N	14	13	.519	36	36	5	0	0	229²	206	16	77	148	11.2	3.80	102	.243	.308	7	.108	-1	-3	2	0	0.2
1992 *Atl-N★	15	12	.556	35	35	9	3	0	246²	206	17	80	**215**	10.6	2.85	129	.224	.289	12	.160	2	18	22	-1	2.6
1993 *Atl-N★	15	11	.577	35	35	3	1	0	243²	208	23	100	208	11.6	3.62	111	.230	.311	13	.183	3	11	11	-0	1.3
1994 Atl-N	6	10	.375	21	21	1	0	0	134²	120	15	48	113	11.5	4.14	100	.239	.310	6	.162	1	1	0	0	0.2
Total 7	78	75	.510	202	202	29	6	0	1358	1180	116	500	1059	11.3	3.59	108	.234	.305	59	.147	8	24	44	2	5.4

● **HARRY SMYTHE**   Smythe, William Henry   b: 10/24/04, Augusta, Ga.   d: 8/28/80, Augusta, Ga.   BL/TL, 5'10.5", 179 lbs.   Deb: 7/21/29

YEAR TM/L	W	L	PCT	G	GS	CG	SH	SV	IP	H	HR	BB	SO	RAT	ERA	ERA+	OAV	OOB	BH	AVG	PB	PR	/A	PD	TPI
1929 Phi-N	4	6	.400	19	7	2	0	1	68²	94	3	15	12	14.4	5.24	99	.330	.365	5	.192	-1	-4	-0	2	0.0
1930 Phi-N	0	3	.000	25	3	0	0	2	49²	84	3	31	9	21.4	7.79	70	.368	.450	4	.286	-0	-16	-13	-1	-0.8
1934 NY-A	0	2	.000	8	0	0	0	0	15	24	1	4	7	19.2	7.80	52	.381	.451	1	.200	-0	-6	-6	1	-0.7
Bro-N	1	1	.500	8	0	0	0	1	21¹	30	3	8	5	16.5	5.91	66	.337	.398	3	.333	1	-4	-5	1	-0.2
Total 3	5	12	.294	60	10	2	0	4	154²	232	10	62	33	17.4	6.40	78	.349	.408	13	.241	0	-29	-24	2	-1.7

● **NATE SNELL**   Snell, Nathaniel   b: 9/2/52, Orangeburg, S.C.   BR/TR, 6'4", 190 lbs.   Deb: 9/20/84

YEAR TM/L	W	L	PCT	G	GS	CG	SH	SV	IP	H	HR	BB	SO	RAT	ERA	ERA+	OAV	OOB	BH	AVG	PB	PR	/A	PD	TPI
1984 Bal-A	1	1	.500	5	0	0	0	0	7²	8	1	1	7	10.6	2.35	165	.258	.281	0	—	0	1	1	-0	0.3
1985 Bal-A	3	2	.600	43	0	0	0	5	100¹	100	4	30	41	11.8	2.69	150	.260	.315	0	—	0	16	15	1	1.0

YEAR	TM/L	W	L	PCT	G	GS	CG	SH	SV	IP	H	HR	BB	SO	RAT	ERA	ERA+	OAV	OOB	BH	AVG	PB	PR	/A	PD	TPI
1986	Bal-A	2	1	.667	34	0	0	0	0	72¹	69	9	22	29	11.4	3.86	107	.257	.316	0	—	0	3	2	1	0.3
1987	Det-A	1	2	.333	22	2	0	0	0	38²	39	5	19	19	13.5	3.96	107	.267	.352	0	—	0	2	1	-1	0.1
Total	4	7	6	.538	104	2	0	0	5	219	216	19	72	96	11.9	3.29	125	.260	.321	0	—	0	22	20	1	1.7

● **FRANK SNOOK**　　Snook, Frank Walter　b: 3/28/49, Somerville, N.J.　BR/TR, 6'2", 180 lbs.　Deb: 7/13/73

YEAR	TM/L	W	L	PCT	G	GS	CG	SH	SV	IP	H	HR	BB	SO	RAT	ERA	ERA+	OAV	OOB	BH	AVG	PB	PR	/A	PD	TPI
1973	SD-N	0	2	.000	18	0	0	0	1	27¹	19	4	18	13	12.2	3.62	96	.200	.327	0	.000	-0	0	-0	1	0.0

● **COLONEL SNOVER**　　Snover, Colonel Lester "Bosco"　b: 5/16/1895, Hallstead, Pa.　d: 4/30/69, Rochester, N.Y.　BL/TL, 6'0.5", 200 lbs.　Deb: 9/18/19

YEAR	TM/L	W	L	PCT	G	GS	CG	SH	SV	IP	H	HR	BB	SO	RAT	ERA	ERA+	OAV	OOB	BH	AVG	PB	PR	/A	PD	TPI
1919	NY-N	0	1	.000	2	1	0	0	0	9	7	0	3	4	11.0	1.00	281	.212	.297	0	.000	0	2	2	-0	0.2

● **BRIAN SNYDER**　　Snyder, Brian Robert　b: 2/20/58, Flemington, N.J.　BL/TL, 6'3", 185 lbs.　Deb: 5/25/85

YEAR	TM/L	W	L	PCT	G	GS	CG	SH	SV	IP	H	HR	BB	SO	RAT	ERA	ERA+	OAV	OOB	BH	AVG	PB	PR	/A	PD	TPI
1985	Sea-A	1	2	.333	15	6	0	0	1	35¹	44	2	19	23	16.3	6.37	66	.306	.390	0	—	0	-9	-8	1	-0.6
1989	Oak-A	0	0	—	2	0	0	0	0	0²	2	1	2	1	54.0	27.00	14	.500	.667	0	—	0	-2	-2	0	0.2
Total	2	1	2	.333	17	6	0	0	1	36	46	3	21	24	17.0	6.75	62	.311	.400	0	—	0	-10	-10	1	-0.4

● **GENE SNYDER**　　Snyder, Gene Walter　b: 3/31/31, York, Pa.　BR/TL, 5'11", 175 lbs.　Deb: 4/26/59

YEAR	TM/L	W	L	PCT	G	GS	CG	SH	SV	IP	H	HR	BB	SO	RAT	ERA	ERA+	OAV	OOB	BH	AVG	PB	PR	/A	PD	TPI
1959	LA-N	1	1	.500	11	2	0	0	0	26¹	32	1	20	20	17.8	5.47	77	.299	.409	0	.000	-0	-4	-4	-0	-0.3

● **GEORGE SNYDER**　　Snyder, George T.　b: 8/1848, Philadelphia, Pa.　d: 8/2/05, Philadelphia, Pa.　Deb: 9/30/1882

YEAR	TM/L	W	L	PCT	G	GS	CG	SH	SV	IP	H	HR	BB	SO	RAT	ERA	ERA+	OAV	OOB	BH	AVG	PB	PR	/A	PD	TPI
1882	Phi-a	1	0	1.000	1	1	1	0	0	9	4	0	2	0	6.0	0.00	—	.125	.177	1	.333	0	3	3	0	0.3

● **BILL SNYDER**　　Snyder, William Nicholas　b: 1/28/1898, Mansfield, Ohio　d: 10/8/34, Vicksburg, Mich.　BR/TR,　Deb: 9/4/19

YEAR	TM/L	W	L	PCT	G	GS	CG	SH	SV	IP	H	HR	BB	SO	RAT	ERA	ERA+	OAV	OOB	BH	AVG	PB	PR	/A	PD	TPI
1919	Was-A	0	1	.000	2	1	0	0	0	8	6	0	3	5	10.1	1.13	285	.200	.273	0	.000	-0	2	2	-0	0.2
1920	Was-A	2	1	.667	16	4	1	0	1	54	59	1	28	17	15.5	4.17	90	.280	.380	6	.316	1	-2	-3	-1	-0.1
Total	2	2	2	.500	18	5	1	0	1	62	65	1	31	22	14.8	3.77	97	.270	.367	6	.286	1	-0	-1	-1	0.1

● **RAY SOFF**　　Soff, Raymond John　b: 10/31/58, Adrian, Mich.　BR/TR, 6', 185 lbs.　Deb: 7/17/86

YEAR	TM/L	W	L	PCT	G	GS	CG	SH	SV	IP	H	HR	BB	SO	RAT	ERA	ERA+	OAV	OOB	BH	AVG	PB	PR	/A	PD	TPI
1986	StL-N	4	2	.667	30	0	0	0	0	38¹	37	4	13	22	11.7	3.29	111	.255	.316	0	.000	-0	2	1	0	0.2
1987	StL-N	1	0	1.000	12	0	0	0	0	15¹	18	3	5	9	14.1	6.46	64	.295	.358	0	.000	-0	-4	-4	-0	-0.2
Total	2	5	2	.714	42	0	0	0	0	53²	55	7	18	31	12.4	4.19	90	.267	.329	0	.000	-0	-2	-2	0	0.0

● **JULIO SOLANO**　　Solano, Julio Cesar　b: 1/8/60, Aqua Blanca, D.R.　BR/TR, 6'1", 160 lbs.　Deb: 4/5/83

YEAR	TM/L	W	L	PCT	G	GS	CG	SH	SV	IP	H	HR	BB	SO	RAT	ERA	ERA+	OAV	OOB	BH	AVG	PB	PR	/A	PD	TPI
1983	Hou-N	0	2	.000	4	0	0	0	0	6	5	1	4	3	13.5	6.00	57	.217	.333	0	—	0	-2	-2	-0	-0.5
1984	Hou-N	1	3	.250	31	0	0	0	0	50²	31	3	18	33	8.7	1.95	170	.179	.257	1	.333	0	9	8	-1	0.5
1985	Hou-N	2	2	.500	20	0	0	0	0	33²	34	5	13	17	12.6	3.48	100	.262	.329	0	.000	-0	0	-0	-1	-0.1
1986	Hou-N	3	1	.750	16	1	0	0	0	32	39	5	22	21	18.0	7.59	47	.310	.424	0	.000	-1	-14	-14	-0	-1.7
1987	Hou-N	0	0	—	11	0	0	0	0	20	25	5	9	12	15.3	7.65	51	.298	.366	0	—	0	-8	-8	0	0.0
1988	Sea-A	0	0	—	17	0	0	0	0	22	22	3	12	10	13.9	4.09	102	.268	.362	0	—	0	-0	-0	-1	-0.2
1989	Sea-A	0	0	—	7	0	0	0	0	9²	6	1	4	6	10.2	5.59	72	.176	.282	0	—	0	-2	-2	-0	-0.2
Total	7	6	8	.429	106	1	0	0	3	174	162	23	82	102	12.8	4.55	79	.248	.336	1	.077	-1	-16	-18	-2	-2.2

● **MARCELINO SOLIS**　　Solis, Marcelino　b: 7/19/30, San Luis Potosi, Mexico　BL/TL, 6'1", 185 lbs.　Deb: 7/16/58

YEAR	TM/L	W	L	PCT	G	GS	CG	SH	SV	IP	H	HR	BB	SO	RAT	ERA	ERA+	OAV	OOB	BH	AVG	PB	PR	/A	PD	TPI
1958	Chi-N	3	3	.500	15	4	0	0	0	52	74	4	20	15	17.0	6.06	65	.339	.405	5	.250	1	-12	-12	-0	-1.1

● **EDDIE SOLOMON**　　Solomon, Eddie "Buddy"　b: 2/9/51, Perry, Ga.　d: 1/12/86, Macon, Ga.　BR/TR, 6'3", 190 lbs.　Deb: 9/2/73

YEAR	TM/L	W	L	PCT	G	GS	CG	SH	SV	IP	H	HR	BB	SO	RAT	ERA	ERA+	OAV	OOB	BH	AVG	PB	PR	/A	PD	TPI
1973	LA-N	0	0	—	4	0	0	0	0	6¹	10	3	4	6	21.3	7.11	48	.357	.455	0	.000	-0	-2	-3	-0	0.0
1974	*LA-N	0	0	—	4	0	0	0	1	6	5	1	2	4	10.5	1.50	227	.217	.280	0	—	0	1	1	0	0.1
1975	Chi-N	0	0	—	6	0	0	0	0	6²	7	1	6	3	17.6	1.35	285	.269	.406	0	—	0	2	2	0	0.0
1976	StL-N	1	1	.500	26	2	0	0	0	37	45	2	16	19	15.1	4.86	73	.306	.378	2	.400	1	-6	-5	1	-0.1
1977	Atl-N	6	6	.500	18	16	0	0	0	88²	110	10	34	54	14.8	4.57	97	.305	.368	4	.129	-1	-6	-1	-0	-0.3
1978	Atl-N	4	6	.400	37	8	0	0	2	106	98	12	50	64	12.7	4.08	99	.247	.335	4	.138	-1	-6	-0	-0	-0.1
1979	Atl-N	7	14	.333	31	30	4	0	0	186	184	19	51	96	11.7	4.21	96	.254	.308	13	.203	1	-10	-3	-1	-0.4
1980	Pit-N	7	3	.700	26	12	2	0	0	100¹	96	8	37	35	12.3	2.69	135	.253	.325	7	.219	1	10	11	-0	1.1
1981	Pit-N	8	6	.571	22	17	2	0	0	127	133	6	27	38	11.6	3.12	115	.278	.321	7	.163	-1	5	7	-1	0.5
1982	Pit-N	2	6	.250	11	10	0	0	0	46²	69	9	18	18	17.0	6.75	55	.347	.404	2	.133	-1	-16	-16	-2	-2.4
	Chi-A	1	0	1.000	6	0	0	0	0	7¹	7	1	2	2	11.0	3.68	110	.241	.290	0	—	0	0	0	-0	0.0
Total	10	36	42	.462	191	95	8	0	4	718	764	76	247	337	12.9	4.00	97	.274	.337	39	.177	-1	-28	-8	-3	-1.6

● **JOE SOMMER**　　Sommer, Joseph John　b: 11/20/1858, Covington, Ky.　d: 1/16/38, Cincinnati, Ohio　BR/TR,　Deb: 7/8/1880　♦

YEAR	TM/L	W	L	PCT	G	GS	CG	SH	SV	IP	H	HR	BB	SO	RAT	ERA	ERA+	OAV	OOB	BH	AVG	PB	PR	/A	PD	TPI
1883	Cin-a	0	0	—	1	0	0	0	0	5	9	0	1	2	18.0	5.40	60	.367	.392	115	.278	0	-1	-1	-0	0.0
1885	Bal-a	0	0	—	2	0	0	0	1	3	6	0	0	1	18.0	9.00	36	.429	.429	118	.251	0	-2	-2	-0	-0.1
1886	Bal-a	0	0	—	1	0	0	0	0	4	14	0	3	1	38.3	18.00	19	.519	.567	117	.209	-0	-6	-6	-0	0.0
1887	Bal-a	0	0	—	1	0	0	0	0	1	2	1	2	0	27.0	9.00	46	.333	.429	123	.266	0	-1	-1	-0	0.0
1890	Cle-N	0	0	—	1	0	0	0	0	1	2	1	1	0	36.0	0.00	—	.403	.575	8	.229	-0	-0	-0	-0	0.0
Total	5	0	0	—	6	0	0	0	1	14	33	1	7	3	25.7	9.64	35	.432	.479	911	.248	1	-10	-10	-1	-0.1

● **RUDY SOMMERS**　　Sommers, Rudolph　b: 10/30/1888, Cincinnati, Ohio　d: 3/18/49, Louisville, Ky.　BB/TL, 5'11", 165 lbs.　Deb: 9/8/12

YEAR	TM/L	W	L	PCT	G	GS	CG	SH	SV	IP	H	HR	BB	SO	RAT	ERA	ERA+	OAV	OOB	BH	AVG	PB	PR	/A	PD	TPI
1912	Chi-N	0	1	.000	1	0	0	0	0	3	4	0	2	2	18.0	3.00	111	.333	.429	0	.000	0	0	0	-0	0.0
1914	Bro-F	2	7	.222	23	8	2	0	2	82	88	3	34	40	13.7	4.06	71	.282	.358	6	.250	2	-11	-11	-1	-1.0
1926	Bos-A	0	0	—	2	0	0	0	0	2	3	0	3	0	27.0	13.50	30	.333	.500	0	—	0	-2	-2	-0	0.0
1927	Bos-A	0	0	—	7	0	0	0	0	14	18	1	14	2	20.6	8.36	51	.353	.492	1	.500	0	-7	-6	1	0.1
Total	4	2	8	.200	33	8	2	0	2	101	113	4	53	44	15.1	4.81	64	.294	.384	7	.259	2	-19	-19	-0	-0.9

● **ANDY SOMMERVILLE**　　Sommerville, Andrew Henry (b: Henry Travers Summersgill)　b: 2/6/1876, Brooklyn, N.Y.　d: 6/16/31, Richmond Hill, N.Y.　Deb: 8/8/1894

YEAR	TM/L	W	L	PCT	G	GS	CG	SH	SV	IP	H	HR	BB	SO	RAT	ERA	ERA+	OAV	OOB	BH	AVG	PB	PR	/A	PD	TPI
1894	Bro-N	0	1	.000	1	1	0	0	0	0¹	1	0	5	0	162.0	162.00	3	.510	.862	0	—	0	-6	-6	0	-3.6

● **DON SONGER**　　Songer, Donald C.　b: 1/31/1900, Walnut, Kan.　d: 10/3/62, Kansas City, Mo.　BL/TL, 6', 165 lbs.　Deb: 9/21/24

YEAR	TM/L	W	L	PCT	G	GS	CG	SH	SV	IP	H	HR	BB	SO	RAT	ERA	ERA+	OAV	OOB	BH	AVG	PB	PR	/A	PD	TPI
1924	Pit-N	0	0	—	4	1	0	0	1	9¹	14	1	3	3	16.4	6.75	57	.333	.378	0	.000	-0	-3	-3	-0	-0.1
1925	Pit-N	0	1	.000	8	0	0	0	0	11²	14	0	4	4	17.0	2.31	193	.298	.400	0	.000	-0	3	3	-0	0.2
1926	Pit-N	7	8	.467	35	14	5	1	2	126¹	118	4	52	27	12.9	3.13	126	.252	.340	4	.105	-2	10	11	1	1.1
1927	Pit-N	0	0	—	2	0	0	0	0	4²	10	4	0	4	28.9	11.57	36	.526	.625	0	.000	-0	-4	-4	-0	0.0
	NY-N	3	5	.375	22	1	0	0	1	50¹	48	4	31	9	14.3	2.86	135	.261	.370	3	.300	1	6	6	1	1.0
	Yr	3	5	.375	24	1	0	0	1	55	58	8	31	13	15.4	3.60	108	.284	.392	3	.273	1	2	2	1	1.0
Total	4	10	14	.417	71	16	5	1	4	202¹	204	9	98	44	14.0	3.38	117	.268	.361	7	.132	-2	11	13	2	2.2

● **LARY SORENSEN**　　Sorensen, Lary Alan　b: 10/4/55, Detroit, Mich.　BR/TR, 6'2", 210 lbs.　Deb: 6/7/77

YEAR	TM/L	W	L	PCT	G	GS	CG	SH	SV	IP	H	HR	BB	SO	RAT	ERA	ERA+	OAV	OOB	BH	AVG	PB	PR	/A	PD	TPI
1977	Mil-A	7	10	.412	23	20	9	0	0	142¹	147	10	36	57	11.6	4.36	93	.270	.316	0	—	0	-5	-5	1	-0.4
1978	Mil-A★	18	12	.600	37	36	17	3	1	280²	277	14	50	78	10.6	3.21	117	.259	.295	0	—	0	17	17	1	1.8
1979	Mil-A	15	14	.517	34	34	16	2	0	235¹	250	30	42	63	11.3	3.98	105	.275	.310	0	—	0	6	5	1	0.6
1980	Mil-A	12	10	.545	35	29	8	1	0	195²	242	13	45	54	13.3	3.68	105	.311	.351	0	—	0	8	4	1	0.7
1981	StL-N	7	7	.500	23	23	3	1	0	140¹	149	8	26	52	11.3	3.27	109	.271	.305	3	.065	-3	3	4	0	0.1
1982	Cle-A	10	15	.400	32	30	6	1	0	189¹	251	19	52	62	14.7	5.61	73	.322	.369	0	—	0	-32	-32	-1	-3.7
1983	Cle-A	12	11	.522	36	34	8	1	0	222²	238	21	65	76	12.3	4.24	100	.276	.328	0	—	0	-5	-0	2	0.1
1984	Oak-A	6	13	.316	46	21	2	0	1	183¹	240	24	44	63	14.2	4.91	76	.317	.359	0	—	0	-19	-24	-1	-2.3
1985	Chi-N	3	7	.300	45	3	0	0	0	82¹	86	8	24	34	12.5	4.26	94	.274	.333	0	—	-0	-6	-3	-0	-0.3
1987	Mon-N	3	4	.429	23	5	0	0	1	47²	56	7	12	21	13.4	4.72	89	.286	.336	0	.000	-1	-3	-3	-1	-0.5

YEAR TM/L	W	L	PCT	G	GS	CG	SH	SV	IP	H	HR	BB	SO	RAT	ERA	ERA+	OAV	OOB	BH	AVG	PB	PR	/A	PD	TPI
1988 SF-N	0	0	—	12	0	0	0	2	16²	24	1	3	9	14.6	4.86	67	.329	.355	0	.000	-0	-3	-3	-0	-0.1
Total 11	93	103	.474	346	235	69	10	6	1736¹	1960	147	402	569	12.4	4.15	95	.287	.329	3	.049	-4	-38	-38	1	-4.0

● VIC SORRELL
Sorrell, Victor Garland b: 4/9/01, Morrisville, N.C. d: 5/4/72, Raleigh, N.C. BR/TR, 5'10", 180 lbs. Deb: 4/22/28

YEAR TM/L	W	L	PCT	G	GS	CG	SH	SV	IP	H	HR	BB	SO	RAT	ERA	ERA+	OAV	OOB	BH	AVG	PB	PR	/A	PD	TPI
1928 Det-A	8	11	.421	29	23	8	0	0	171	182	9	83	67	14.2	4.79	86	.277	.363	6	.109	-5	-14	-13	-3	-1.9
1929 Det-A	14	15	.483	36	31	13	1	1	226	270	15	106	81	15.1	5.18	83	.302	.377	12	.145	-6	-23	-22	-1	-3.0
1930 Det-A	16	11	.593	35	30	14	2	1	233¹	245	13	106	97	13.5	3.86	124	.274	.351	15	.188	-3	21	24	-3	1.8
1931 Det-A	13	14	.481	35	32	19	1	1	245	267	8	114	99	14.0	4.15	110	.278	.355	14	.159	-4	6	12	1	0.8
1932 Det-A	14	14	.500	32	31	13	1	0	234¹	234	11	77	84	12.1	4.03	117	.259	.319	9	.118	-4	12	17	-2	1.3
1933 Det-A	11	15	.423	36	28	13	1	1	232²	233	18	78	75	12.1	3.79	114	.260	.321	11	.149	-2	13	13	-0	1.0
1934 Det-A	6	9	.400	28	19	6	1	2	129²	146	13	45	46	13.5	4.79	92	.283	.345	4	.108	-1	-4	-6	2	-0.5
1935 Det-A	4	3	.571	12	6	4	0	0	51¹	65	2	25	22	16.1	4.03	103	.319	.398	0	.000	-3	2	1	-0	-0.2
1936 Det-A	6	7	.462	30	14	5	1	3	131¹	153	9	64	37	15.0	5.28	94	.294	.373	6	.154	1	-3	-5	2	-0.2
1937 Det-A	0	2	.000	7	2	0	0	1	17	25	3	8	11	17.5	9.00	52	.338	.402	0	.000	-0	-8	-8	0	-0.9
Total 10	92	101	.477	280	216	95	8	10	1671²	1820	101	706	619	13.7	4.43	102	.279	.351	77	.139	-27	-0	14	-4	-1.8

● ELIAS SOSA
Sosa, Elias (Martinez) b: 6/10/50, LaVega, D.R. BR/TR, 6'2", 190 lbs. Deb: 9/8/72

YEAR TM/L	W	L	PCT	G	GS	CG	SH	SV	IP	H	HR	BB	SO	RAT	ERA	ERA+	OAV	OOB	BH	AVG	PB	PR	/A	PD	TPI
1972 SF-N	0	1	.000	8	0	0	0	3	15²	10	0	12	10	12.6	2.30	152	.189	.338	0	.000	-0	2	2	-0	0.2
1973 SF-N	10	4	.714	71	1	0	0	18	107	95	7	41	70	11.8	3.28	116	.241	.318	1	.071	-0	5	6	-1	0.9
1974 SF-N	9	7	.563	68	0	0	0	6	101	94	8	45	48	12.5	3.48	109	.252	.334	1	.067	-1	2	4	-1	0.4
1975 StL-N	0	3	.000	14	1	0	0	0	27¹	22	3	14	15	12.2	3.95	95	.227	.330	1	.125	-0	-1	-1	-0	-0.1
Atl-N	2	2	.500	43	0	0	0	2	62¹	70	3	29	31	14.7	4.48	84	.294	.378	1	.143	-0	-6	-5	-0	-0.4
Yr	2	5	.286	57	1	0	0	2	89²	92	6	43	46	13.9	4.32	87	.271	.358	2	.133	-1	-7	-5	-0	-0.5
1976 Atl-N	4	4	.500	21	0	0	0	3	35¹	41	3	13	32	14.0	5.35	71	.287	.350	1	.143	-0	-7	-6	-0	-1.5
LA-N	2	4	.333	24	0	0	0	1	33²	30	0	12	20	11.2	3.48	97	.242	.309	0	—	0	-0	-0	-0	-0.1
Yr	6	8	.429	45	0	0	0	4	69	71	3	25	52	12.5	4.43	81	.263	.325	1	.143	-0	-7	-6	-0	-1.6
1977 *LA-N	2	2	.500	44	0	0	0	1	63²	42	7	12	47	7.8	1.98	193	.189	.234	1	.250	1	14	13	-0	0.8
1978 Oak-A	8	2	.800	68	0	0	0	14	109	106	5	44	61	12.5	2.64	138	.264	.338	0	—	0	14	12	0	1.5
1979 Mon-N	8	7	.533	62	0	0	0	18	96²	77	2	37	59	10.8	1.96	187	.219	.297	2	.154	0	19	18	-1	3.3
1980 Mon-N	9	6	.600	67	0	0	0	9	93²	104	5	19	58	11.9	3.07	116	.286	.323	1	.091	-0	5	5	-0	0.8
1981 *Mon-N	1	2	.333	32	0	0	0	3	39¹	46	3	8	18	12.6	3.66	95	.297	.335	2	1.000	1	-1	0	-0	0.1
1982 Det-A	3	3	.500	38	0	0	0	4	61	64	11	18	24	12.4	4.43	92	.270	.327	0	—	0	-2	-2	1	-0.2
1983 SD-N	1	4	.200	41	1	0	0	1	72¹	72	7	30	45	13.1	4.35	80	.268	.348	1	.143	-0	-6	-7	-1	-0.6
Total 12	59	51	.536	601	4	0	0	83	918	873	64	334	538	12.0	3.32	111	.255	.325	12	.130	-3	37	39	-3	5.1

● JOSE SOSA
Sosa, Jose Ynocencio (b: Jose Ynocencio (Sosa)) b: 12/28/52, Santo Domingo, D.R. BR/TR, 5'11", 158 lbs. Deb: 7/22/75

YEAR TM/L	W	L	PCT	G	GS	CG	SH	SV	IP	H	HR	BB	SO	RAT	ERA	ERA+	OAV	OOB	BH	AVG	PB	PR	/A	PD	TPI
1975 Hou-N	1	3	.250	25	2	0	0	1	47	51	5	23	31	14.4	4.02	84	.291	.377	3	.333	2	-2	-3	-1	-0.2
1976 Hou-N	0	0	—	9	0	0	0	0	11²	16	0	6	5	19.3	6.94	46	.340	.446	0	—	0	-4	-5	1	0.1
Total 2	1	3	.250	34	2	0	0	1	58²	67	5	29	36	15.3	4.60	72	.302	.392	3	.333	2	-7	-8	-0	-0.1

● ALLEN SOTHORON
Sothoron, Allen Sutton b: 4/27/1893, Bradford, Ohio d: 6/17/39, St.Louis, Mo. BB/TR, 5'11", 182 lbs. Deb: 9/17/14 MC

YEAR TM/L	W	L	PCT	G	GS	CG	SH	SV	IP	H	HR	BB	SO	RAT	ERA	ERA+	OAV	OOB	BH	AVG	PB	PR	/A	PD	TPI
1914 StL-A	0	0	—	1	0	0	0	0	6	6	0	4	3	15.0	6.00	45	.261	.370	0	.000	-0	-2	-2	-0	0.0
1915 StL-A	0	1	.000	3	1	0	0	0	3²	8	0	5	2	31.9	7.36	39	.400	.520	0	.000	-0	-2	-2	-0	-0.4
1917 StL-A	14	19	.424	48	32	17	3	4	276²	259	2	96	85	11.8	2.83	92	.251	.320	20	.217	3	-5	-7	-1	-0.6
1918 StL-A	12	12	.500	29	24	14	2	0	209	152	3	67	71	9.6	1.94	141	**.205**	.274	10	.159	-2	20	19	-3	1.6
1919 StL-A	20	13	.606	40	30	21	3	3	270	256	4	87	106	11.8	2.20	151	.246	.311	17	.175	-2	31	34	-7	3.1
1920 StL-A	8	15	.348	36	26	12	1	2	218¹	263	6	89	81	14.8	4.70	83	.307	.376	16	.222	-1	-22	-19	-2	-2.1
1921 StL-A	1	2	.333	5	4	1	0	0	27²	33	2	13	9	13.7	5.20	86	.314	.368	1	.111	-1	-6	-6	0	-0.3
Bos-A	0	2	.000	2	2	0	0	0	6	15	0	5	2	30.0	13.50	31	.455	.526	1	.500	1	-6	-6	0	-1.2
Cle-A	12	4	.750	22	16	10	2	0	144²	146	6	58	61	13.1	3.24	132	.279	.358	16	.276	2	17	17	-2	1.5
Yr	13	8	.619	29	22	11	2	0	178¹	194	8	76	72	13.7	3.89	111	.293	.367	18	.261	2	8	8	-2	0.0
1922 Cle-A	1	3	.250	6	4	2	0	0	25¹	26	1	14	8	14.9	6.39	63	.274	.378	4	.444	1	-7	-7	-0	-0.8
1924 StL-N	10	16	.385	29	28	16	**4**	0	196²	209	9	84	62	13.9	3.57	106	.275	.354	14	.194	-2	7	5	-3	0.0
1925 StL-N	10	10	.500	28	23	8	2	0	155²	173	7	63	67	14.0	4.05	107	.280	.353	11	.196	-1	4	5	-4	0.0
1926 StL-N	3	3	.500	15	4	1	0	0	42²	37	2	16	19	11.2	4.22	93	.247	.319	3	.231	-0	-2	-1	-1	-0.3
Total 11	91	100	.476	264	194	102	17	9	1582¹	1583	34	596	576	12.7	3.31	105	.264	.336	113	.207	-2	29	30	-24	0.5

● MARIO SOTO
Soto, Mario Melvin b: 7/12/56, Bani, D.R. BR/TR, 6', 185 lbs. Deb: 7/21/77

YEAR TM/L	W	L	PCT	G	GS	CG	SH	SV	IP	H	HR	BB	SO	RAT	ERA	ERA+	OAV	OOB	BH	AVG	PB	PR	/A	PD	TPI
1977 Cin-N	2	6	.250	12	10	2	1	0	60²	60	12	26	44	13.2	5.34	74	.258	.340	1	.077	-0	-10	-10	0	-1.1
1978 Cin-N	1	0	1.000	5	1	0	0	0	18	13	1	13	13	13.0	2.50	142	.197	.329	0	.000	-0	2	2	-0	0.0
1979 *Cin-N	3	2	.600	25	0	0	0	0	37¹	33	2	30	32	15.4	5.30	70	.243	.383	4	.571	-2	-7	-7	-1	-0.7
1980 Cin-N	10	8	.556	53	12	3	1	4	190¹	126	11	84	182	10.4	3.07	116	**.187**	.279	2	.043	-4	11	11	0	0.6
1981 Cin-N	9	7	.563	25	25	10	3	0	175	142	13	61	151	10.6	3.29	108	.220	.290	4	.068	-4	4	5	-1	0.0
1982 Cin-N★	14	13	.519	35	34	13	2	0	257²	202	19	71	274	**9.7**	2.79	132	.215	**.273**	14	.167	1	23	26	-1	2.7
1983 Cin-N★	17	13	.567	34	34	**18**	3	0	273²	207	28	95	242	10.1	2.70	141	.208	.280	11	.125	-1	28	**34**	-1	3.3
1984 Cin-N★	18	7	.720	33	33	**13**	0	0	237¹	181	26	87	185	10.4	3.53	107	.209	.286	18	.207	3	2	7	-3	0.7
1985 Cin-N	12	15	.444	36	36	9	1	0	256²	196	30	104	214	10.6	3.58	106	.211	.292	11	.133	-2	0	6	-1	0.3
1986 Cin-N	5	10	.333	19	19	1	0	0	105	113	15	46	67	13.7	4.71	82	.280	.355	3	.111	-1	-12	-10	-1	-1.4
1987 Cin-N	3	2	.600	6	6	0	0	0	31²	34	7	12	11	13.1	5.12	83	.279	.343	1	.083	-1	-4	-3	0	-0.5
1988 Cin-N	3	7	.300	13	14	1	0	0	87	88	8	28	34	12.2	4.66	77	.267	.328	1	.045	-1	-12	-10	-1	-1.3
Total 12	100	92	.521	297	224	72	13	4	1730¹	1395	172	657	1449	10.8	3.47	108	.220	.296	70	.132	-10	27	51	-8	2.6

● MARK SOUZA
Souza, Kenneth Mark b: 2/1/55, Redwood City, Cal. BL/TL, 6', 180 lbs. Deb: 4/22/80

YEAR TM/L	W	L	PCT	G	GS	CG	SH	SV	IP	H	HR	BB	SO	RAT	ERA	ERA+	OAV	OOB	BH	AVG	PB	PR	/A	PD	TPI
1980 Oak-A	—	5	0	0	0	0	7	9	1	5	2	18.0	7.71	49	.310	.412	0		0	-3	-3	-0	0.4			

● JOHN SOWDERS
Sowders, John b: 12/10/1866, Louisville, Ky. d: 7/29/39, Indianapolis, Ind BR/TL, 6', Deb: 6/28/1887 F◆

YEAR TM/L	W	L	PCT	G	GS	CG	SH	SV	IP	H	HR	BB	SO	RAT	ERA	ERA+	OAV	OOB	BH	AVG	PB	PR	/A	PD	TPI
1887 Ind-N	0	0	—	1	0	0	0	0	3	11	0	5	0	48.0	21.00	20	.500	.593	0	.000	-0	-6	-6	-0	0.0
1889 KC-a	6	16	.273	25	23	20	0	1	185	204	9	105	104	15.4	4.82	87	.271	.366	19	.218	-2	-20	-13	-2	-1.4
1890 Bro-P	19	16	.543	39	37	28	1	0	309	358	3	161	91	15.4	3.82	117	.278	.363	25	.189	-5	14	22	-2	1.3
Total 3	25	32	.439	65	60	48	1	1	497	573	12	271	195	15.6	4.29	97	.278	.366	44	.199	-7	-11	4	-4	-0.1

● BILL SOWDERS
Sowders, William Jefferson "Little Bill" b: 11/29/1864, Louisville, Ky. d: 2/2/51, Indianapolis, Ind. BR/TR, 6', 155 lbs. Deb: 4/24/1888 F

YEAR TM/L	W	L	PCT	G	GS	CG	SH	SV	IP	H	HR	BB	SO	RAT	ERA	ERA+	OAV	OOB	BH	AVG	PB	PR	/A	PD	TPI
1888 Bos-N	19	15	.559	36	35	34	2	0	317	278	3	73	132	10.2	2.07	138	.226	.275	18	.148	-4	27	27	1	2.3
1889 Bos-N	1	2	.333	7	4	3	0	2	42	53	1	23	10	16.7	5.14	81	.299	.385	4	.235	-0	-5	-5	1	-0.2
Pit-N	6	5	.545	13	11	9	0	0	52²	94	1	29	33	21.7	7.35	51	.376	.449	13	.271	2	-19	-21	2	-2.7
Yr	7	7	.500	20	15	12	0	**2**	94²	147	2	52	43	19.3	6.37	62	.342	.418	17	.262	2	-25	-26	3	-2.9
1890 Pit-N	3	8	.273	15	11	9	0	0	106	117	1	24	30	12.1	4.42	75	.271	.313	9	.180	-2	-10	-13	2	-1.4
Total 3	29	30	.492	71	61	55	2	2	517²	542	8	149	205	12.3	3.34	94	.260	.314	44	.186	-4	-7	-11	2	-2.0

● BOB SPADE
Spade, Robert b: 1/4/1877, Akron, Ohio d: 9/7/24, Cincinnati, Ohio BR/TR, 5'10", 190 lbs. Deb: 9/22/07

YEAR TM/L	W	L	PCT	G	GS	CG	SH	SV	IP	H	HR	BB	SO	RAT	ERA	ERA+	OAV	OOB	BH	AVG	PB	PR	/A	PD	TPI
1907 Cin-N	1	2	.333	3	3	3	0	0	27	21	0	9	7	10.3	1.00	260	.219	.292	2	.286	1	4	5	-1	0.7
1908 Cin-N	17	12	.586	35	28	22	2	1	249¹	230	2	85	74	11.6	2.74	84	.250	.317	17	.195	1	-11	-12	-4	-1.8
1909 Cin-N	5	5	.500	14	13	8	0	0	98	91	0	39	31	12.3	2.85	91	.236	.313	10	.294	-4	-3	-3	-4	-0.3
1910 Cin-N	1	2	.333	3	3	1	0	0	17¹	35	1	9	1	23.4	6.75	43	.479	.542	0	.000	-0	-7	-7	1	-1.1

YEAR TM/L	W	L	PCT	G	GS	CG	SH	SV	IP	H	HR	BB	SO	RAT	ERA	ERA+	OAV	OOB	BH	AVG	PB	PR	/A	PD	TPI
StL-A	1	3	.250	7	5	2	1	0	34²	34	1	17	8	13.5	4.41	56	.270	.361	3	.273	2	-7	-7	-1	-0.7
Total 4	25	24	.510	62	52	36	4	1	426¹	411	4	159	121	12.3	2.96	82	.257	.329	32	.222	7	-23	-25	-9	-3.2

● WARREN SPAHN   Spahn, Warren Edward b: 4/23/21, Buffalo, N.Y. BL/TL, 6', 175 lbs. Deb: 4/19/42 CH

YEAR TM/L	W	L	PCT	G	GS	CG	SH	SV	IP	H	HR	BB	SO	RAT	ERA	ERA+	OAV	OOB	BH	AVG	PB	PR	/A	PD	TPI
1942 Bos-N	0	0	—	4	2	1	0	0	15²	25	0	11	7	20.7	5.74	58	.368	.456	1	.167	-0	-4	-4	-0	0.0
1946 Bos-N	8	5	.615	24	16	8	0	1	125²	107	6	36	67	10.3	2.94	117	.228	.285	7	.163	-1	7	7	-2	0.4
1947 Bos-N★	21	10	.677	40	35	22	7	3	289²	245	15	84	123	10.3	2.33	167	.226	.283	16	.163	1	56	50	-2	5.1
1948 *Bos-N	15	12	.556	36	35	16	3	1	257	237	19	77	114	11.0	3.71	103	.242	.298	15	.167	2	7	3	0	0.5
1949 Bos-N★	21	14	.600	38	38	25	4	0	302¹	283	27	86	151	11.1	3.07	123	.245	.299	18	.162	-0	33	24	-2	2.3
1950 Bos-N☆	21	17	.553	41	39	25	1	1	293	248	22	111	191	11.1	3.16	122	.227	.299	23	.217	4	32	22	0	3.1
1951 Bos-N☆	22	14	.611	39	36	26	7	0	310²	278	20	109	164	11.2	2.98	123	.238	.304	22	.190	5	34	24	-2	2.9
1952 Bos-N☆	14	19	.424	40	35	19	5	3	290	263	19	73	183	10.6	2.98	121	.240	.291	18	.161	2	24	20	1	2.7
1953 Mil-N★	23	7	.767	35	32	24	5	3	265²	211	14	70	148	9.6	2.10	187	.217	.270	23	.219	5	65	54	2	6.6
1954 Mil-N★	21	12	.636	39	34	23	1	3	283¹	262	24	86	136	11.1	3.14	118	.245	.302	21	.208	6	29	18	1	2.7
1955 Mil-N	17	14	.548	39	32	16	1	1	245²	249	25	65	110	11.6	3.26	115	.265	.314	17	.210	5	21	14	0	2.1
1956 Mil-N	20	11	.645	39	35	20	3	3	281¹	249	25	52	128	9.7	2.78	124	.238	.276	22	.210	8	31	21	-1	2.9
1957 *Mil-N☆	21	11	.656	39	35	18	4	3	271	241	23	78	111	10.7	2.69	130	.237	.293	13	.138	1	36	24	0	3.0
1958 *Mil-N☆	22	11	.667	38	36	23	2	1	290	257	29	76	150	10.4	3.07	115	.237	.288	36	.333	18	28	14	4	3.9
1959 Mil-N☆	21	15	.583	40	36	21	4	0	292	282	21	70	143	10.9	2.96	120	.253	.298	24	.231	7	32	19	-1	2.8
1960 Mil-N	21	10	.677	40	33	18	4	2	267²	254	20	74	154	11.2	3.50	98	.250	.303	14	.147	3	-2	-3	3	0.3
1961 Mil-N★	21	13	.618	38	34	21	4	0	262²	236	24	64	115	10.4	3.02	124	.243	.293	21	.223	10	30	21	3	3.9
1962 Mil-N☆	18	14	.563	34	34	22	0	0	269¹	248	25	55	118	10.2	3.04	125	.246	.287	18	.184	4	27	23	1	3.1
1963 Mil-N☆	23	7	.767	33	33	22	7	0	259²	241	23	49	102	10.1	2.60	124	.248	.284	16	.178	5	20	18	4	3.2
1964 Mil-N	6	13	.316	38	25	4	1	4	173²	204	23	52	78	13.4	5.29	67	.297	.348	11	.186	2	-34	-34	-1	-3.5
1965 NY-N	4	12	.250	20	19	5	0	0	126	140	18	35	56	12.6	4.36	81	.281	.331	4	.114	1	-11	-12	0	-1.2
SF-N	3	4	.429	16	11	3	0	0	71²	70	8	21	34	11.6	3.39	106	.256	.312	3	.143	0	1	2	1	0.2
Yr	7	16	.304	36	30	8	0	0	197²	210	26	56	90	12.2	4.01	89	.271	.321	7	.125	1	-10	-10	1	-1.0
Total 21	363	245	.597	750	665	382	63	29	5243²	4830	434	1434	2583	10.8	3.09	118	.244	.297	363	.194	88	470	330	9	47.0

● AL SPALDING   Spalding, Albert Goodwill b: 9/2/1850, Byron, Ill. d: 9/9/15, San Diego, Cal. BR/TR, 6'1", 170 lbs. Deb: 5/5/1871 MH♦

YEAR TM/L	W	L	PCT	G	GS	CG	SH	SV	IP	H	HR	BB	SO	RAT	ERA	ERA+	OAV	OOB	BH	AVG	PB	PR	/A	PD	TPI
1871 Bos-n	19	10	.655	31	31	22	1	0	257¹	333	2	38	23	13.0	3.36	124	.268	.290	39	.271	2	25	23		1.6
1872 Bos-n	38	8	.826	48	48	41	3	0	404²	412	0	27	27	9.8	1.98	188	.240	.252	87	.357	19	78	79		7.1
1873 Bos-n	41	14	.745	60	55	48	1	2	497²	643	5	28	31	12.1	2.46	135	.283	.292	106	.329	19	44	47		4.3
1874 Bos-n	52	16	.765	71	69	65	4	0	616¹	753	1	23		11.3	2.35	126	.273	.279	119	.331	22	44	42		4.6
1875 Bos-n	55	5	.917	72	63	52	7	8	575	571	1	14		9.2	1.52	156	.244	.249	22	.312	22	60	54		6.0
1876 Chi-N	47	12	.797	61	60	53	8	0	528²	542	6	26	39	9.7	1.75	139	.247	.256	91	.312	9	33	41	4	4.6
1877 Chi-N	1	0	1.000	4	1	0	0	1	11	17	0	0	2	13.9	3.27	91	.321	.321	65	.256		-1	-0	1	0.0
Total 5 n	205	53	.795	282	266	228	16	10	2351	2712	9	130	81	10.9	2.22	142	.263	.272	458	.324	84	251	244		23.6
Total 2	48	12	.800	65	61	53	8	1	539²	559	6	26	41	9.8	1.78	138	.249	.257	158	.287	84	32	40	5	4.6

● BILL SPANSWICK   Spanswick, William Henry b: 7/8/38, Springfield, Mass. BL/TL, 6'3", 195 lbs. Deb: 4/18/64

YEAR TM/L	W	L	PCT	G	GS	CG	SH	SV	IP	H	HR	BB	SO	RAT	ERA	ERA+	OAV	OOB	BH	AVG	PB	PR	/A	PD	TPI
1964 Bos-A	2	3	.400	29	7	0	0	0	65¹	75	9	44	55	16.8	6.89	56	.306	.418	4	.286	1	-24	-22	1	-1.3

● TULLY SPARKS   Sparks, Thomas Frank b: 12/12/1874, Etna, Ga. d: 7/15/37, Anniston, Ala. BR/TR, Deb: 9/15/1897

YEAR TM/L	W	L	PCT	G	GS	CG	SH	SV	IP	H	HR	BB	SO	RAT	ERA	ERA+	OAV	OOB	BH	AVG	PB	PR	/A	PD	TPI
1897 Phi-N	0	1	.000	1	1	1	0	0	8	12	0	4	0	18.0	10.13	41	.343	.411	0	.000	-1	-5	-5	0	-0.4
1899 Pit-N	8	6	.571	28	17	8	0	0	170	180	1	82	53	14.4	3.86	99	.271	.360	8	.129	-2	-0	-1	-1	-0.3
1901 Mil-A	7	16	.304	29	26	18	0	0	210	228	6	93	62	14.4	3.51	102	.273	.356	12	.169	-1	4	2	-0	0.1
1902 NY-N	4	10	.286	15	13	11	0	1	115	123	2	40	41	13.1	3.76	75	.273	.338	5	.135	-1	-12	-12	3	-1.2
Bos-N	7	9	.438	17	15	15	1	0	142²	151	4	40	37	12.5	3.47	103	.272	.329	8	.154	-1	2	2	0	0.0
1903 Phi-N	11	15	.423	28	28	27	0	0	248	248	3	56	88	11.3	2.72	120	.263	.310	10	.109	-5	15	15	-2	0.7
1904 Phi-N	7	16	.304	26	25	19	3	0	200²	208	1	43	67	11.5	2.65	101	.260	.302	8	.105	-5	2	1	-4	-0.8
1905 Phi-N	14	11	.560	34	26	20	3	1	259²	217	2	73	98	10.4	2.18	134	.236	.298	12	.128	-2	24	21	-6	1.1
1906 Phi-N	19	16	.543	42	37	29	6	3	316²	244	4	62	114	9.0	2.16	121	.211	.257	16	.154	-0	17	16	-4	1.4
1907 Phi-N	22	8	.733	33	31	24	3	1	265	221	2	51	90	9.5	2.00	121	.228	.271	3	.034	-8	14	14	-5	-0.1
1908 Phi-N	16	15	.516	33	31	24	2	2	263¹	225	3	51	85	10.6	2.60	93	.257	.300	4	.052	-6	-5	-5	-1	-1.5
1909 Phi-N	6	11	.353	24	16	6	1	0	121²	126	4	32	40	11.9	2.96	88	.280	.320	5	.139	-5	-5	-5	-0	-0.9
1910 Phi-N	0	2	.000	3	3	0	0	0	15	22	2	4	2	15.6	6.00	52	.324	.361	0	.000	-0	-5	-5	0	-0.6
Total 12	121	136	.471	313	269	202	19	8	2335²	2231	33	629	778	11.4	2.79	105	.253	.309	91	.114	-33	42	37	-21	-2.5

● JOE SPARMA   Sparma, Joseph Blase b: 2/4/42, Massillon, Ohio d: 5/14/86, Columbus, Ohio BR/TR, 6', 195 lbs. Deb: 5/20/64

YEAR TM/L	W	L	PCT	G	GS	CG	SH	SV	IP	H	HR	BB	SO	RAT	ERA	ERA+	OAV	OOB	BH	AVG	PB	PR	/A	PD	TPI
1964 Det-A	5	6	.455	21	11	3	2	0	84	62	4	45	71	11.8	3.00	122	.207	.316	4	.160	-1	6	6	1	1.0
1965 Det-A	13	8	.619	30	28	6	0	0	167	142	13	75	127	11.9	3.18	109	.228	.314	7	.135	-0	5	6	-0	0.6
1966 Det-A	2	7	.222	29	13	0	0	0	91²	103	14	52	61	15.5	5.30	66	.288	.383	5	.217	1	-19	-19	-2	-1.8
1967 Det-A	16	9	.640	37	37	11	5	0	217²	186	20	85	153	11.5	3.76	87	.227	.306	4	.054	-5	-13	-12	-2	-2.1
1968 *Det-A	10	10	.500	34	31	7	1	0	182¹	169	14	77	110	12.5	3.70	81	.246	.328	8	.133	-1	-15	-14	-2	-1.9
1969 Det-A	6	8	.429	23	16	3	2	0	92²	78	9	77	41	15.2	4.76	78	.231	.375	4	.138	-1	-12	-11	-1	-1.6
1970 Mon-N	0	4	.000	9	6	1	0	0	29¹	34	7	25	23	18.7	7.06	58	.296	.430	0	.000	-0	-10	-10	-0	-1.2
Total 7	52	52	.500	183	142	31	10	0	864²	774	77	436	586	12.9	3.94	86	.239	.334	32	.119	-6	-57	-53	-7	-7.0

● TRIS SPEAKER   Speaker, Tristram E "The Grey Eagle" b: 4/4/1888, Hubbard, Tex. d: 12/8/58, Lake Whitney, Tex. BL/TL, 5'11.5", 193 lbs. Deb: 9/14/07 MH♦

YEAR TM/L	W	L	PCT	G	GS	CG	SH	SV	IP	H	HR	BB	SO	RAT	ERA	ERA+	OAV	OOB	BH	AVG	PB	PR	/A	PD	TPI
1914 Bos-A	0	0	—	1	0	0	0	0	1	2	0	0	0	18.0	9.00	30	.500	.500	193	.338	1	-1	-1	0	0.0

● CLIFF SPECK   Speck, Robert Clifford b: 8/8/56, Portland, Ore. BR/TR, 6'4", 195 lbs. Deb: 7/30/86

YEAR TM/L	W	L	PCT	G	GS	CG	SH	SV	IP	H	HR	BB	SO	RAT	ERA	ERA+	OAV	OOB	BH	AVG	PB	PR	/A	PD	TPI
1986 Atl-N	2	1	.667	13	1	0	0	0	28¹	25	2	15	21	13.0	4.13	96	.238	.339	0	.000	-0	-1	-0	0	0.0

● BY SPEECE   Speece, Byron Franklin b: 1/6/1897, West Baden, Ind. d: 9/29/74, Elgin, Ore. BR/TR, 5'11", 170 lbs. Deb: 4/21/24

YEAR TM/L	W	L	PCT	G	GS	CG	SH	SV	IP	H	HR	BB	SO	RAT	ERA	ERA+	OAV	OOB	BH	AVG	PB	PR	/A	PD	TPI
1924 *Was-A	2	1	.667	21	1	0	0	0	54¹	60	0	27	15	14.7	2.65	152	.303	.392	3	.150	-1	10	8	1	0.4
1925 Cle-A	3	5	.375	28	3	3	0	1	90¹	106	0	28	26	13.6	4.28	103	.297	.353	5	.161	-2	1	1	0	0.0
1926 Cle-A	0	0	—	2	0	0	0	0	3	1	0	2	1	9.0	0.00	—	.125	.300	0	—	0	1	1	0	0.0
1930 Phi-N	0	0	—	11	0	0	0	0	19²	41	1	4	9	20.6	13.27	41	.432	.455	1	.333	-0	-18	-17	0	0.0
Total 4	5	6	.455	62	4	3	0	1	167¹	208	1	61	51	14.7	4.73	93	.316	.378	9	.167	-2	-6	-6	2	0.4

● FLOYD SPEER   Speer, Floyd Vernie b: 1/27/13, Booneville, Ark. d: 3/22/69, Little Rock, Ark. BR/TR, 6', 180 lbs. Deb: 4/25/43

YEAR TM/L	W	L	PCT	G	GS	CG	SH	SV	IP	H	HR	BB	SO	RAT	ERA	ERA+	OAV	OOB	BH	AVG	PB	PR	/A	PD	TPI
1943 Chi-A	0	0	—	1	0	0	0	0	1	1	0	1	0	27.0	9.00	37	.250	.500	0	—	-0	-1	-1	0	0.0
1944 Chi-A	0	0	—	2	0	0	0	0	2	4	0	1	0	18.0	9.00	38	.500	.500	0	—	-0	-1	-1	0	0.0
Total 2	0	0	—	3	0	0	0	0	3	5	0	2	0	21.0	9.00	38	.417	.500	0	—	-0	-2	-2	0	0.0

● KID SPEER   Speer, George Nathan b: 6/16/1886, Corning, Mo. d: 1/13/46, Edmonton, Alberta, Canada BL/TL, 5'9", 152 lbs. Deb: 4/24/09

YEAR TM/L	W	L	PCT	G	GS	CG	SH	SV	IP	H	HR	BB	SO	RAT	ERA	ERA+	OAV	OOB	BH	AVG	PB	PR	/A	PD	TPI
1909 Det-A	4	4	.500	12	8	4	0	1	76¹	88	2	13	12	12.4	2.83	89	.293	.331	3	.120	-0	-3	-3	1	-0.3

● HACK SPENCER   Spencer, Fred Calvin b: 4/25/1885, St.Cloud, Minn. d: 2/5/69, St.Anthony, Minn. BR/TR, 5'10.5", 172 lbs. Deb: 4/18/12

YEAR TM/L	W	L	PCT	G	GS	CG	SH	SV	IP	H	HR	BB	SO	RAT	ERA	ERA+	OAV	OOB	BH	AVG	PB	PR	/A	PD	TPI
1912 StL-A	0	0	—	1	0	0	0	0	1²	2	0	0	0	10.8	0.00	—	.286	.286	0	—	0	1	1	0	0.0

● GEORGE SPENCER   Spencer, George Elwell b: 7/7/26, Columbus, Ohio BR/TR, 6'1", 215 lbs. Deb: 8/17/50

YEAR TM/L	W	L	PCT	G	GS	CG	SH	SV	IP	H	HR	BB	SO	RAT	ERA	ERA+	OAV	OOB	BH	AVG	PB	PR	/A	PD	TPI
1950 NY-N	1	0	1.000	10	1	1	0	0	25¹	12	3	7	5	6.8	2.49	165	.141	.207	0	.000	-1	5	5	0	0.1
1951 *NY-N	10	4	.714	57	4	2	0	6	132	125	21	56	36	12.4	3.75	104	.254	.332	4	.125	-1	3	2	1	0.3

YEAR	TM/L	W	L	PCT	G	GS	CG	SH	SV	IP	H	HR	BB	SO	RAT	ERA	ERA+	OAV	OOB	BH	AVG	PB	PR	/A	PD	TPI
1952	NY-N	3	5	.375	35	4	0	0	3	60	57	13	21	27	12.2	5.55	67	.251	.323	2	.200	0	-12	-12	-0	-1.6
1953	NY-N	0	0	—	1	0	0	0	0	2¹	3	0	2	1	19.3	7.71	56	.300	.417	0	—	0	-1	-1	-0	0.0
1954	NY-N	1	0	1.000	6	0	0	0	0	12¹	9	1	8	4	12.4	3.65	111	.209	.333	0	.000	-0	1	1	1	0.1
1955	NY-N	0	0	—	1	0	0	0	0	1²	1	1	3	1	21.6	5.40	75	.167	.444	0	—	0	-0	0	-0	0.0
1958	Det-A	1	0	1.000	7	0	0	0	0	10	11	0	4	5	13.5	2.70	149	.289	.357	0	—	0	1	1	0	0.2
1960	Det-A	0	1	.000	5	0	0	0	0	7²	10	1	5	4	17.6	3.52	112	.323	.417	0	.000	-0	0	0	-0	0.0
Total	8	16	10	.615	122	9	3	0	9	251¹	228	40	106	82	12.1	4.05	96	.245	.324	6	.120	-2	-3	-4	2	-0.9

● GLENN SPENCER   Spencer, Glenn Edward b: 9/11/05, Corning, N.Y. d: 12/30/58, Binghamton, N.Y. BR/TR, 5'11", 155 lbs. Deb: 4/11/28

YEAR	TM/L	W	L	PCT	G	GS	CG	SH	SV	IP	H	HR	BB	SO	RAT	ERA	ERA+	OAV	OOB	BH	AVG	PB	PR	/A	PD	TPI
1928	Pit-N	0	0	—	4	0	0	0	0	5²	4	0	3	2	11.1	1.59	255	.200	.304	0	—	0	2	2	-0	-0.1
1930	Pit-N	8	9	.471	41	10	5	0	4	156²	185	16	63	60	14.4	5.40	92	.305	.372	6	.113	-4	-7	-7	-2	-1.2
1931	Pit-N	11	12	.478	38	18	11	1	3	186²	180	8	65	51	12.1	3.42	112	.260	.328	5	.096	-3	9	9	-0	0.7
1932	Pit-N	4	8	.333	39	13	5	1	1	137²	167	10	44	35	14.0	4.97	77	.288	.341	6	.162	-1	-17	-18	-1	-1.6
1933	NY-N	0	2	.000	17	3	1	0	0	47¹	52	3	26	14	15.0	5.13	63	.284	.376	2	.167	-0	-9	-10	0	-0.4
Total	5	23	31	.426	139	44	22	2	8	534	588	37	201	162	13.5	4.53	91	.282	.349	19	.123	-9	-23	-25	-3	-2.6

● BOB SPICER   Spicer, Robert Oberton b: 4/11/25, Richmond, Va. BL/TR, 5'10", 173 lbs. Deb: 4/17/55

YEAR	TM/L	W	L	PCT	G	GS	CG	SH	SV	IP	H	HR	BB	SO	RAT	ERA	ERA+	OAV	OOB	BH	AVG	PB	PR	/A	PD	TPI
1955	KC-A	0	0	—	2	0	0	0	0	2²	9	2	4	2	47.3	33.75	12	.529	.636	0	.000	-0	-9	-9	-0	0.0
1956	KC-A	0	0	—	2	0	0	0	0	2¹	6	1	1	0	30.9	19.29	22	.545	.615	0	—	0	-4	-4	0	0.0
Total	2	0	0	—	4	0	0	0	0	5	15	3	5	2	39.6	27.00	16	.536	.629	0	.000	-0	-13	-13	0	0.0

● DAN SPILLNER   Spillner, Daniel Ray b: 11/27/51, Casper, Wyo. BR/TR, 6'1", 190 lbs. Deb: 5/21/74

YEAR	TM/L	W	L	PCT	G	GS	CG	SH	SV	IP	H	HR	BB	SO	RAT	ERA	ERA+	OAV	OOB	BH	AVG	PB	PR	/A	PD	TPI
1974	SD-N	9	11	.450	30	25	5	2	0	148	153	15	70	95	13.6	4.01	89	.267	.346	1	.023	-4	-7	-8	-1	-1.5
1975	SD-N	5	13	.278	37	25	3	0	1	166²	194	14	63	104	14.0	4.27	81	.293	.356	6	.133	1	-12	-15	-0	-1.4
1976	SD-N	2	11	.154	32	14	0	0	0	106²	120	11	55	57	14.8	5.06	65	.291	.374	1	.040	-1	-19	-21	1	-2.4
1977	SD-N	7	6	.538	76	0	0	0	6	123	130	12	60	74	14.0	3.73	95	.280	.363	2	.118	1	2	-3	-2	-0.4
1978	SD-N	1	0	1.000	17	0	0	0	0	25²	32	2	7	16	13.7	4.56	73	.317	.361	0	—	0	-3	-4	-0	-0.1
	Cle-A	3	1	.750	36	0	0	0	3	56¹	54	2	21	48	12.1	3.67	102	.254	.323	0	—	0	1	0	-1	-0.1
1979	Cle-A	9	5	.643	49	13	3	0	1	157²	153	16	64	97	12.6	4.62	92	.256	.331	0	—	0	-7	-6	-1	-0.6
1980	Cle-A	16	11	.593	34	30	7	1	0	194¹	225	23	74	100	14.0	5.28	77	.288	.352	0	—	0	-27	-26	-2	-3.3
1981	Cle-A	4	4	.500	32	5	1	0	7	97¹	86	3	39	59	11.6	3.14	115	.240	.314	0	—	0	6	5	0	0.6
1982	Cle-A	12	10	.545	65	0	0	0	21	133²	117	9	45	90	10.9	2.49	164	.235	.299	0	—	0	**24**	**24**	-3	4.2
1983	Cle-A	2	9	.182	60	0	0	0	8	92¹	117	7	38	48	15.3	5.07	84	.315	.382	0	—	0	-10	-9	-1	-1.3
1984	Cle-A	0	5	.000	14	8	0	0	0	51	70	3	22	26	16.2	5.65	72	.332	.395	0	—	0	-9	-9	-1	-0.7
	Chi-A	1	0	1.000	22	0	0	0	1	48¹	51	7	14	26	12.3	4.10	101	.276	.330	0	—	0	-1	-0	-0	0.0
	Yr	1	5	.167	36	8	0	0	2	99¹	121	10	36	49	14.3	4.89	84	.301	.360	0	—	0	-10	-9	-1	-0.7
1985	Chi-A	4	3	.571	52	3	0	0	1	91²	83	10	33	41	11.4	3.44	126	.245	.312	0	—	0	7	9	-3	0.4
Total	12	75	89	.457	556	123	19	3	50	1492²	1585	134	605	878	13.3	4.21	91	.275	.345	10	.077	-3	-55	-62	-12	-6.6

● SCIPIO SPINKS   Spinks, Scipio Ronald b: 7/12/47, Chicago, Ill. BR/TR, 6'1", 185 lbs. Deb: 9/16/69

YEAR	TM/L	W	L	PCT	G	GS	CG	SH	SV	IP	H	HR	BB	SO	RAT	ERA	ERA+	OAV	OOB	BH	AVG	PB	PR	/A	PD	TPI
1969	Hou-N	0	0	—	1	0	0	0	0	2	1	0	1	4	9.0	0.00	—	.143	.250	0	—	0	1	1	0	0.0
1970	Hou-N	0	1	.000	5	2	0	0	0	13²	17	5	9	9	17.1	9.88	39	.293	.388	0	.000	-0	-9	-9	-1	-0.6
1971	Hou-N	1	0	1.000	5	3	1	0	0	29¹	22	2	13	26	11.0	3.68	91	.210	.303	2	.222	1	-1	-1	0	0.0
1972	StL-N	5	5	.500	16	16	6	0	0	118	96	5	59	93	12.0	2.67	127	.221	.317	7	.167	-1	10	10	1	0.8
1973	StL-N	1	5	.167	8	8	0	0	0	38²	39	4	25	25	14.9	4.89	75	.269	.376	2	.182	1	-5	-5	1	-0.6
Total	5	7	11	.389	35	29	7	0	0	201²	175	16	107	154	12.7	3.70	94	.234	.332	11	.169	0	-4	-5	1	-0.4

● PAUL SPLITTORFF   Splittorff, Paul William b: 10/8/46, Evansville, Ind. BL/TL, 6'3", 210 lbs. Deb: 9/23/70

YEAR	TM/L	W	L	PCT	G	GS	CG	SH	SV	IP	H	HR	BB	SO	RAT	ERA	ERA+	OAV	OOB	BH	AVG	PB	PR	/A	PD	TPI
1970	KC-A	0	1	.000	2	1	0	0	0	8²	16	1	5	10	21.8	7.27	51	.390	.457	1	.500	0	-3	-3	-0	-0.3
1971	KC-A	8	9	.471	22	22	6	3	0	144¹	129	4	35	80	10.5	2.68	128	.243	.295	5	.104	-1	13	12	2	1.5
1972	KC-A	12	12	.500	35	33	12	2	0	216	189	11	67	140	10.8	3.13	97	.241	.304	16	.225	4	-2	-2	4	0.6
1973	KC-A	20	11	.645	38	38	12	3	0	262	279	19	78	110	12.4	3.98	103	.272	.327	0	—	0	-5	4	1	0.0
1974	KC-A	13	19	.406	36	36	8	1	0	226	252	23	75	90	13.1	4.10	93	.285	.342	0	—	0	-12	-7	0	-1.3
1975	KC-A	9	10	.474	35	23	6	1	3	159	156	10	56	76	12.1	3.17	121	.255	.319	0	—	0	11	12	2	1.5
1976	*KC-A	11	8	.579	26	23	5	1	0	158²	169	11	59	59	13.1	3.97	88	.277	.343	0	—	0	-8	-8	1	-0.8
1977	*KC-A	16	6	**.727**	37	37	6	2	0	229	243	11	83	99	12.9	3.69	109	.278	.342	0	—	0	9	9	-0	0.7
1978	*KC-A	19	13	.594	39	38	13	2	0	262	244	21	60	76	10.5	3.40	112	.247	.293	0	—	0	11	12	1	1.5
1979	KC-A	15	17	.469	36	35	11	0	0	240	248	25	77	77	12.4	4.24	101	.268	.328	0	—	0	-1	1	-2	-0.2
1980	*KC-A	14	11	.560	34	33	4	0	0	204	236	17	43	53	12.4	4.15	98	.296	.333	0	—	0	-3	-2	-0	-0.3
1981	KC-A	5	5	.500	21	15	1	0	0	99	111	12	23	48	12.3	4.36	83	.294	.337	0	—	0	-8	-8	1	-0.7
1982	KC-A	10	10	.500	29	28	6	0	0	162	166	20	57	74	12.6	4.28	95	.266	.330	0	—	0	-4	-4	0	-0.4
1983	KC-A	13	8	.619	27	27	4	0	0	156	159	9	52	61	12.2	3.63	112	.262	.322	0	—	0	7	8	0	0.9
1984	KC-A	1	3	.250	12	3	0	0	0	28	47	3	10	4	18.3	7.71	52	.376	.422	0	—	0	-12	-11	1	-1.3
Total	15	166	143	.537	429	392	88	17	1	2554²	2644	192	780	1057	12.2	3.81	101	.270	.326	22	.182	3	-6	10	10	1.4

● PAUL SPOLJARIC   Spoljaric, Paul Nikola b: 9/24/70, Kelowna, B.C., Canada BR/TL, 6'3", 205 lbs. Deb: 4/6/94

YEAR	TM/L	W	L	PCT	G	GS	CG	SH	SV	IP	H	HR	BB	SO	RAT	ERA	ERA+	OAV	OOB	BH	AVG	PB	PR	/A	PD	TPI
1994	Tor-A	0	1	.000	2	1	0	0	0	2¹	5	3	9	2	54.0	38.57	13	.417	.667	0	—	0	-9	-9	0	-1.9

● CARL SPONGBERG   Spongberg, Carl Gustav b: 5/21/1884, Idaho Falls, Idaho d: 7/21/38, Los Angeles, Cal. BR/TR, 6'2", 208 lbs. Deb: 8/1/08

YEAR	TM/L	W	L	PCT	G	GS	CG	SH	SV	IP	H	HR	BB	SO	RAT	ERA	ERA+	OAV	OOB	BH	AVG	PB	PR	/A	PD	TPI
1908	Chi-N	0	0	—	1	0	0	0	0	7	9	1	6	4	21.9	9.00	26	.321	.472	2	.667	1	-5	-5	0	0.1

● KARL SPOONER   Spooner, Karl Benjamin b: 6/23/31, Oriskany Falls, N.Y. d: 4/10/84, Vero Beach, Fla. BR/TL, 6', 185 lbs. Deb: 9/22/54

YEAR	TM/L	W	L	PCT	G	GS	CG	SH	SV	IP	H	HR	BB	SO	RAT	ERA	ERA+	OAV	OOB	BH	AVG	PB	PR	/A	PD	TPI
1954	Bro-N	2	0	1.000	2	2	2	2	0	18	7	0	6	27	6.5	0.00	—	.113	.191	1	.167	0	8	8	-0	1.1
1955	*Bro-N	8	6	.571	29	14	2	1	2	98²	79	8	41	78	11.4	3.65	111	.215	.302	8	.286	3	4	5	-0	0.8
Total	2	10	6	.625	31	16	4	3	2	116²	86	8	47	105	10.6	3.09	132	.200	.286	9	.265	3	12	13	-1	1.9

● JERRY SPRADLIN   Spradlin, Jerry Carl b: 6/14/67, Fullerton, Cal. BB/TR, 6'7", 230 lbs. Deb: 7/2/93

YEAR	TM/L	W	L	PCT	G	GS	CG	SH	SV	IP	H	HR	BB	SO	RAT	ERA	ERA+	OAV	OOB	BH	AVG	PB	PR	/A	PD	TPI
1993	Cin-N	2	1	.667	37	0	0	0	2	49	44	4	9	24	9.7	3.49	115	.249	.285	0	—	-0	3	3	-1	0.0
1994	Cin-N	0	0	—	6	0	0	0	0	8	12	2	2	4	15.8	10.13	41	.353	.389	0	—	-0	-5	-5	0	0.0
Total	2	2	1	.667	43	0	0	0	2	57	56	6	11	28	10.6	4.42	91	.265	.302	0	.000	-0	-2	-2	-1	0.0

● HOMER SPRAGINS   Spragins, Homer Franklin b: 11/9/20, Grenada, Miss. BR/TR, 6'1", 190 lbs. Deb: 9/13/47

YEAR	TM/L	W	L	PCT	G	GS	CG	SH	SV	IP	H	HR	BB	SO	RAT	ERA	ERA+	OAV	OOB	BH	AVG	PB	PR	/A	PD	TPI
1947	Phi-N	0	0	—	4	0	0	0	0	5¹	3	0	3	3	10.1	6.75	59	.158	.273	0	—	0	-2	-2	0	0.0

● CHARLIE SPRAGUE   Sprague, Charles Wellington b: 10/10/1864, Cleveland, Ohio d: 12/31/12, Des Moines, Iowa BL/TL, 5'11", 150 lbs. Deb: 9/17/1887 ◆

YEAR	TM/L	W	L	PCT	G	GS	CG	SH	SV	IP	H	HR	BB	SO	RAT	ERA	ERA+	OAV	OOB	BH	AVG	PB	PR	/A	PD	TPI
1887	Chi-N	1	0	1.000	3	3	2	0	0	22	24	1	13	9	16.8	4.91	91	.276	.394	2	.154	-1	-2	-1	-1	-0.2
1889	Cle-N	0	2	.000	2	2	2	0	0	17	27	0	10	8	20.6	8.47	48	.349	.437	1	.143	-0	-8	-8	1	-0.6
1890	Tol-a	9	5	.643	19	12	9	0	0	122²	111	0	78	59	15.2	3.89	102	.234	.363	47	.236	3	-0	-1	-2	0.1
Total	3	10	7	.588	24	17	13	0	0	161²	162	1	101	76	16.0	4.51	89	.254	.376	50	.228	1	-11	-9	-2	-0.7

● ED SPRAGUE   Sprague, Edward Nelson Sr. b: 9/16/45, Boston, Mass. BR/TR, 6'4", 195 lbs. Deb: 4/10/68 F

YEAR	TM/L	W	L	PCT	G	GS	CG	SH	SV	IP	H	HR	BB	SO	RAT	ERA	ERA+	OAV	OOB	BH	AVG	PB	PR	/A	PD	TPI
1968	Oak-A	3	4	.429	47	1	0	0	4	68²	51	5	34	34	11.4	3.28	86	.209	.311	0	.000	-1	-2	-3	1	-0.4
1969	Oak-A	1	1	.500	27	0	0	0	2	46¹	47	4	31	20	15.5	4.47	77	.267	.383	1	.200	0	-4	-5	2	0.0
1971	Cin-N	1	0	1.000	7	0	0	0	0	11	8	0	1	7	7.4	0.00	—	.195	.214	0	—	0	4	4	0	0.3
1972	Cin-N	3	3	.500	33	0	0	0	2	56²	55	6	26	26	13.3	4.13	78	.261	.350	0	.000	-1	-4	-6	-1	-0.7
1973	Cin-N	1	3	.250	28	0	0	0	1	38²	35	3	22	19	13.7	5.12	66	.246	.355	0	.000	-0	-6	-7	0	-0.7

YEAR	TM/L	W	L	PCT	G	GS	CG	SH	SV	IP	H	HR	BB	SO	RAT	ERA	ERA+	OAV	OOB	BH	AVG	PB	PR	/A	PD	TPI
	StL-N	0	0	—	8	0	0	0	0	8	8	1	4	2	13.5	2.25	162	.276	.364	0	—	0	1	1	0	0.0
	Yr	1	3	.250	36	0	0	0	1	46²	43	4	26	21	13.3	4.63	74	.247	.345	0	.000	-0	-5	-6	1	-0.7
	Mil-A	0	1	.000	9²	0	0	0	1	9²	13	0	14	3	27.0	9.31	40	.317	.509	0	—	-0	-6	-6	-0	-0.6
1974	Mil-A	7	2	.778	20	10	3	0	0	94	94	3	31	57	12.4	2.39	151	.266	.332	0	—	0	13	13	-1	1.2
1975	Mil-A	1	7	.125	18	11	0	0	1	67¹	81	5	40	21	16.4	4.68	82	.297	.390	0	—	-0	-7	-6	-1	-0.8
1976	Mil-A	0	2	.000	3	0	0	0	0	7²	14	0	3	0	20.0	7.04	50	.438	.486	0	—	-0	-3	-3	1	-0.6
Total	8	17	23	.425	198	23	3	0	9	408	406	27	206	188	13.9	3.84	89	.263	.356	1	.045	-1	-15	-19	2	-2.3

● **JACK SPRING**   Spring, Jack Russell   b: 3/11/33, Spokane, Wash.   BR/TL, 6'1", 180 lbs.   Deb: 4/16/55

YEAR	TM/L	W	L	PCT	G	GS	CG	SH	SV	IP	H	HR	BB	SO	RAT	ERA	ERA+	OAV	OOB	BH	AVG	PB	PR	/A	PD	TPI
1955	Phi-N	0	1	.000	2	0	0	0	0	2²	2	2	1	2	10.1	6.75	59	.200	.273	0	.000	-0	-1	-1	-0	-0.3
1957	Bos-A	0	0	—	1	0	0	0	0	1	0	0	1	2	9.0	0.00	—	.000	.000	0	—	0	0	0	0	0.0
1958	Was-A	0	0	—	3	1	0	0	0	7	16	1	7	1	29.6	14.14	27	.457	.548	0	.000	-0	-8	-8	-0	-1.1
1961	LA-A	3	0	1.000	18	4	0	0	0	38	35	4	15	27	12.6	4.26	106	.243	.327	0	.000	-1	-1	-1	-0	0.0
1962	LA-A	4	2	.667	57	0	0	0	6	65	66	7	30	31	13.6	4.02	96	.270	.355	1	.091	-1	-0	-1	1	-0.1
1963	LA-A	3	0	1.000	45	0	0	0	2	38¹	40	3	9	13	11.5	3.05	112	.268	.310	1	.333	0	2	2	1	0.2
1964	LA-A	1	0	1.000	6	0	0	0	0	3¹	3	1	3	0	16.2	2.70	122	.273	.429	0	—	0	0	0	-0	0.0
	Chi-N	0	0	—	7	0	0	0	0	6	4	0	2	1	9.0	6.00	62	.200	.273	0	—	0	-2	-2	0	0.0
	StL-N	0	0	—	2	0	0	0	0	3	8	1	1	1	27.0	3.00	127	.471	.500	0	—	0	0	0	0	0.0
	Yr	0	0	—	9	0	0	0	0	9	12	1	3	1	15.0	5.00	75	.316	.366	0	—	0	-1	-1	0	0.0
1965	Cle-A	1	2	.333	14	0	0	0	0	21²	21	2	10	9	12.9	3.74	93	.259	.341	1	.333	-1	-1	-1	-1	-0.1
Total	8	12	5	.706	155	5	0	0	8	186	195	21	78	86	13.5	4.26	90	.273	.349	3	.107	-1	-9	-9	1	-0.3

● **BRAD SPRINGER**   Springer, Bradford Louis   b: 5/9/04, Detroit, Mich.   d: 1/4/70, Birmingham, Mich.   BL/TL, 6', 155 lbs.   Deb: 5/1/25

YEAR	TM/L	W	L	PCT	G	GS	CG	SH	SV	IP	H	HR	BB	SO	RAT	ERA	ERA+	OAV	OOB	BH	AVG	PB	PR	/A	PD	TPI
1925	StL-A	0	0	—	2	0	0	0	0	3	1	0	7	0	24.0	3.00	156	.200	.667	0	—	0	1	1	0	0.0
1926	Cin-N	0	0	—	1	0	0	0	0	1¹	2	0	2	1	33.8	6.75	55	.286	.500	0	.000	-0	-0	-0	0	0.0
Total	2	0	0	—	3	0	0	0	0	4¹	3	0	9	1	27.0	4.15	105	.250	.591	0	.000	-0	-0	-0	0	0.0

● **ED SPRINGER**   Springer, Edward H.   b: 2/9/1861, California   d: 4/24/26, Los Angeles Co., Cal.   6'2", 187 lbs.   Deb: 7/12/1889

YEAR	TM/L	W	L	PCT	G	GS	CG	SH	SV	IP	H	HR	BB	SO	RAT	ERA	ERA+	OAV	OOB	BH	AVG	PB	PR	/A	PD	TPI
1889	Lou-a	0	1	.000	1	1	1	0	0	5	8	0	2	1	21.6	9.00	43	.351	.447	0	.000	-0	-3	-3	-0	-0.4

● **RUSS SPRINGER**   Springer, Russell Paul   b: 11/7/68, Alexandria, La.   BR/TR, 6'4", 195 lbs.   Deb: 4/17/92

YEAR	TM/L	W	L	PCT	G	GS	CG	SH	SV	IP	H	HR	BB	SO	RAT	ERA	ERA+	OAV	OOB	BH	AVG	PB	PR	/A	PD	TPI
1992	NY-A	0	0	—	14	0	0	0	0	16	18	0	10	12	16.3	6.19	63	.281	.387		0	0	-4	-4	-0	-0.5
1993	Cal-A	1	6	.143	14	9	1	0	0	60	73	11	32	31	16.2	7.20	63	.303	.391		0	6	-19	-18	-1	-2.0
1994	Cal-A	2	2	.500	18	5	0	0	2	45²	53	9	14	28	13.2	5.52	90	.291	.342		0	0	-4	-3	-0	-0.4
Total	3	3	8	.273	46	14	1	0	2	121²	144	20	56	71	15.1	6.44	72	.296	.373		0	0	-27	-25	-2	-2.4

● **CHARLIE SPROULL**   Sproull, Charles William   b: 1/9/19, Taylorsville, Ga.   d: 1/13/80, Rockford, Ill.   BR/TR, 6'3", 185 lbs.   Deb: 4/19/45

YEAR	TM/L	W	L	PCT	G	GS	CG	SH	SV	IP	H	HR	BB	SO	RAT	ERA	ERA+	OAV	OOB	BH	AVG	PB	PR	/A	PD	TPI
1945	Phi-N	4	10	.286	34	19	2	0	1	130¹	158	10	80	47	16.4	5.94	65	.298	.390	5	.143	-1	-31	-31	-1	-3.1

● **BOB SPROUT**   Sprout, Robert Samuel   b: 12/5/41, Florin, Pa.   BL/TL, 6', 165 lbs.   Deb: 9/27/61

YEAR	TM/L	W	L	PCT	G	GS	CG	SH	SV	IP	H	HR	BB	SO	RAT	ERA	ERA+	OAV	OOB	BH	AVG	PB	PR	/A	PD	TPI
1961	LA-A	0	0	—	1	1	0	0	0	4	4	0	3	2	15.8	4.50	100	.267	.389	0	—	0	-0	-0	-0	0.0

● **BOBBY SPROWL**   Sprowl, Robert John   b: 4/14/56, Sandusky, Ohio   BL/TL, 6'2", 190 lbs.   Deb: 9/5/78

YEAR	TM/L	W	L	PCT	G	GS	CG	SH	SV	IP	H	HR	BB	SO	RAT	ERA	ERA+	OAV	OOB	BH	AVG	PB	PR	/A	PD	TPI
1978	Bos-A	0	2	.000	3	3	0	0	0	12²	12	3	10	10	15.6	6.39	64	.245	.373	0	—	0	-4	-3	-0	-0.5
1979	Hou-N	0	0	—	3	0	0	0	0	4	1	0	2	3	6.8	0.00	—	.083	.214	0	—	0	2	2	-0	0.0
1980	Hou-N	0	0	—	1	0	0	0	0	1	1	0	1	3	18.0	0.00	—	.250	.400	0	—	0	0	0	0	0.0
1981	Hou-N	0	1	.000	15	1	0	0	0	28²	40	1	14	18	17.0	5.97	55	.333	.403	1	.167	-0	-8	-9	-0	-0.3
Total	4	0	3	.000	22	4	0	0	0	46¹	54	4	27	34	15.7	5.44	65	.292	.382	1	.167	-0	-10	-10	-1	-0.8

● **MIKE SQUIRES**   Squires, Michael Lynn   b: 3/5/52, Kalamazoo, Mich.   BL/TL, 5'11", 185 lbs.   Deb: 9/1/75   C◆

YEAR	TM/L	W	L	PCT	G	GS	CG	SH	SV	IP	H	HR	BB	SO	RAT	ERA	ERA+	OAV	OOB	BH	AVG	PB	PR	/A	PD	TPI
1984	Chi-A	0	0	—	1	0	0	0	0	0¹	0	0	0	0				.000	.000	15	.183	0	0	0	0	0.0

● **GEORGE STABLEIN**   Stablein, George Charles   b: 10/29/57, Inglewood, Cal.   BR/TR, 6'4", 185 lbs.   Deb: 9/20/80

YEAR	TM/L	W	L	PCT	G	GS	CG	SH	SV	IP	H	HR	BB	SO	RAT	ERA	ERA+	OAV	OOB	BH	AVG	PB	PR	/A	PD	TPI
1980	SD-N	0	1	.000	4	2	0	0	0	11²	16	0	3	4	14.7	3.09	111	.340	.380	0	—	-0	1	0	-0	0.0

● **EDDIE STACK**   Stack, William Edward   b: 10/24/1887, Chicago, Ill.   d: 8/28/58, Chicago, Ill.   BR/TR, 6', 175 lbs.   Deb: 6/7/10

YEAR	TM/L	W	L	PCT	G	GS	CG	SH	SV	IP	H	HR	BB	SO	RAT	ERA	ERA+	OAV	OOB	BH	AVG	PB	PR	/A	PD	TPI
1910	Phi-N	6	7	.462	20	16	8	1	0	117	115	7	34	48	11.8	4.00	78	.266	.326	3	.083	-3	-13	-11	-1	-1.6
1911	Phi-N	5	5	.500	13	10	5	0	0	77²	67	3	41	36	13.2	3.59	96	.234	.342	2	.083	-2	-2	-1	0	-0.3
1912	Bro-N	7	5	.583	28	17	4	0	1	142	139	6	55	45	12.9	3.36	100	.264	.343	7	.135	-3	1	-0	-1	-0.4
1913	Bro-N	4	4	.500	23	9	4	1	0	87	79	0	32	34	11.6	2.38	138	.250	.321	4	.160	-1	8	9	-2	0.4
	Chi-N	4	2	.667	11	7	3	1	1	51	56	1	15	28	12.9	4.24	75	.280	.336	1	.063	-1	-6	-6	-1	-0.9
	Yr	8	6	.571	34	16	7	2	1	138	135	1	47	62	12.0	3.07	106	.261	.325	5	.122	-2	2	3	-3	-0.5
1914	Chi-N	0	1	.000	7	1	0	0	0	16¹	13	0	11	9	13.2	4.96	56	.220	.343	0	—	-0	-4	-4	-0	-0.2
Total	5	26	24	.520	102	60	24	3	2	491	469	14	188	200	12.4	3.52	93	.258	.334	17	.108	-10	-15	-14	-4	-3.0

● **GENERAL STAFFORD**   Stafford, James Joseph "Jamsey"   b: 7/9/1868, Webster, Mass.   d: 9/18/23, Worcester, Mass.   BR/TR, 5'8", 165 lbs.   Deb: 8/27/1890   F◆

YEAR	TM/L	W	L	PCT	G	GS	CG	SH	SV	IP	H	HR	BB	SO	RAT	ERA	ERA+	OAV	OOB	BH	AVG	PB	PR	/A	PD	TPI
1890	Buf-P	3	9	.250	12	12	11	0	0	98	123	8	43	21	15.6	5.14	80	.294	.365	7	.143	-2	-10	-11	-1	-1.1

● **JOHN STAFFORD**   Stafford, John Henry "Doc"   b: 4/8/1870, Dudley, Mass.   d: 7/3/40, Worcester, Mass.   BR/TR, 5'10", 170 lbs.   Deb: 6/15/1893   F

YEAR	TM/L	W	L	PCT	G	GS	CG	SH	SV	IP	H	HR	BB	SO	RAT	ERA	ERA+	OAV	OOB	BH	AVG	PB	PR	/A	PD	TPI
1893	Cle-N	0	1	.000	2	0	0	0	0	7	12	1	7	4	24.4	14.14	35	.367	.478	0	.000	-0	-7	-7	-0	-0.7

● **BILL STAFFORD**   Stafford, William Charles   b: 8/13/39, Catskill, N.Y.   BR/TR, 6'2", 193 lbs.   Deb: 4/17/60

YEAR	TM/L	W	L	PCT	G	GS	CG	SH	SV	IP	H	HR	BB	SO	RAT	ERA	ERA+	OAV	OOB	BH	AVG	PB	PR	/A	PD	TPI
1960	*NY-A	3	1	.750	11	8	2	1	0	60	50	3	18	36	10.4	2.25	159	.226	.287	1	.045	-2	11	9	1	0.4
1961	*NY-A	14	9	.609	36	25	8	3	2	195	168	13	59	101	10.7	2.68	139	.232	.294	12	.179	2	29	23	-1	2.6
1962	*NY-A	14	9	.609	35	33	7	2	0	213¹	188	23	77	109	11.3	3.67	102	.233	.303	17	.218	3	7	2	-1	0.3
1963	NY-A	4	8	.333	28	14	0	0	3	89²	104	16	42	52	15.0	6.02	58	.287	.366	7	.292	3	-24	-25	-0	-3.0
1964	NY-A	5	0	1.000	31	1	0	0	4	60²	50	4	22	39	11.0	2.67	136	.231	.308	1	.077	-1	6	6	0	0.6
1965	NY-A	3	8	.273	22	15	1	0	0	111¹	93	16	31	71	10.2	3.56	96	.229	.286	0	.000	-3	-1	-2	-1	-0.5
1966	KC-A	0	4	.000	39	2	0	0	0	39²	42	2	12	38	12.7	4.99	68	.273	.333	0	—	-0	-7	-7	-1	-0.8
1967	KC-A	0	1	.000	14	0	0	0	0	16	12	0	9	10	11.8	1.69	189	.214	.323	0	.000	-0	3	3	0	0.2
Total	8	43	40	.518	186	104	18	6	9	785²	707	77	270	449	11.4	3.52	103	.240	.308	38	.155	-0	24	9	-2	-0.2

● **CHICK STAHL**   Stahl, Charles Sylvester   b: 1/10/1873, Avila, Ind.   d: 3/28/07, W.Baden, Ind.   BL/TL, 5'10", 160 lbs.   Deb: 4/19/1897   M◆

YEAR	TM/L	W	L	PCT	G	GS	CG	SH	SV	IP	H	HR	BB	SO	RAT	ERA	ERA+	OAV	OOB	BH	AVG	PB	PR	/A	PD	TPI
1899	Bos-N	0	0	—	1	0	0	0	0	2	2	0	3	0	22.5	9.00	46	.260	.468	202	.351	0	-1	-1	0	0.0

● **GERRY STALEY**   Staley, Gerald Lee   b: 8/21/20, Brush Prairie, Wash.   BR/TR, 6', 195 lbs.   Deb: 4/20/47

YEAR	TM/L	W	L	PCT	G	GS	CG	SH	SV	IP	H	HR	BB	SO	RAT	ERA	ERA+	OAV	OOB	BH	AVG	PB	PR	/A	PD	TPI
1947	StL-N	1	0	1.000	18	1	1	0	0	29¹	33	2	8	14	12.9	2.76	150	.287	.339	0	.000	-1	4	4	1	0.1
1948	StL-N	4	4	.500	31	3	0	0	0	52	61	5	21	23	14.2	6.92	59	.288	.352	2	.222	1	-17	-16	1	-2.0
1949	StL-N	10	10	.500	45	17	5	2	6	171¹	154	7	41	55	10.4	2.73	152	**.238**	.286	5	.122	-0	25	27	3	3.5
1950	StL-N	13	13	.500	42	22	7	1	3	169²	201	14	61	62	14.3	4.99	86	.300	.365	8	.145	-1	-16	-13	3	-1.6
1951	StL-N	19	13	.594	42	30	10	4	3	227	244	14	71	67	12.9	3.81	104	.275	.337	13	.160	-1	4	3	3	0.6
1952	StL-N☆	17	14	.548	35	33	15	0	1	239²	238	21	52	93	11.2	3.27	114	.256	.301	13	.153	-2	12	12	4	1.6
1953	StL-N☆	18	9	.667	40	32	15	1	4	230	243	31	54	81	12.3	3.99	107	.269	.322	8	.103	-5	8	7	2	0.5
1954	StL-N	7	13	.350	48	20	3	1	2	155²	198	16	51	51	14.5	5.26	78	.308	.361	5	.139	-1	-21	-20	2	-2.1
1955	Cin-N	5	8	.385	30	18	2	0	0	119²	146	22	28	40	13.3	4.66	91	.309	.351	2	.056	-4	-8	-6	1	-0.8
	NY-A	0	0	—	2	0	0	0	0	2	5	1	1	0	27.0	13.50	28	.417	.462	0	—	0	-2	-2	0	0.0

YEAR TM/L	W	L	PCT	G	GS	CG	SH	SV	IP	H	HR	BB	SO	RAT	ERA	ERA+	OAV	OOB	BH	AVG	PB	PR	/A	PD	TPI
1956 NY-A	0	0	—	1	0	0	0	0	0¹	4	0	0	1	108.0	108.00	4	.800	.800	0	.000	-0	-4	-4	0	0.0
Chi-A	8	3	.727	26	10	5	0	0	101²	98	11	20	25	11.0	2.92	140	.251	.298	3	.094	-2	14	13	1	1.1
Yr	8	3	.727	27	10	5	0	0	102	102	11	20	26	11.3	3.26	126	.258	.304	3	.091	-3	10	9	1	1.1
1957 Chi-A	5	1	.833	47	0	0	0	7	105	95	7	27	44	10.5	2.06	182	.244	.293	1	.045	-1	**20**	**20**	2	1.4
1958 Chi-A	4	5	.444	50	0	0	0	8	85¹	81	10	24	27	11.1	3.16	115	.259	.312	0	.000	-1	6	4	3	0.7
1959 *Chi-A	8	5	.615	67	0	0	0	14	116¹	111	11	25	54	10.5	2.24	167	.259	.300	2	.154	0	**21**	**20**	-0	2.6
1960 Chi-A★	13	8	.619	64	0	0	0	10	115¹	94	8	25	52	9.5	2.42	156	.227	.276	4	.235	1	**19**	**17**	3	**3.7**
1961 Chi-A	0	3	.000	16	0	0	0	0	18	17	3	5	8	11.0	5.00	78	.246	.297	0	—	-0	-2	-2	0	-0.3
KC-A	1	1	.500	23	0	0	0	2	30	32	4	10	16	13.2	3.60	116	.278	.346	0	.000	0	1	2	1	0.2
Det-A	1	1	.500	13	0	0	0	2	13¹	15	1	6	8	13.3	3.38	121	.288	.362	0	.000	-0	1	1	0	0.2
Yr	2	5	.286	52	0	0	0	4	61¹	64	8	21	32	12.5	3.96	103	.267	.326	0	.000	-0	0	1	1	0.1
Total 15	134	111	.547	640	186	58	9	61	1981²	2070	187	529	727	12.1	3.70	108	.270	.322	66	.126	-16	65	68	29	9.4

● **HARRY STALEY**   Staley, Henry E. b: 11/3/1866, Jacksonville, Ill. d: 1/12/10, Battle Creek, Mich BR/TR, 5'10", 175 lbs. Deb: 6/23/1888

YEAR TM/L	W	L	PCT	G	GS	CG	SH	SV	IP	H	HR	BB	SO	RAT	ERA	ERA+	OAV	OOB	BH	AVG	PB	PR	/A	PD	TPI
1888 Pit-N	12	12	.500	25	24	24	2	0	207¹	185	6	53	89	10.6	2.69	99	.235	.289	11	.129	-4	4	-1	-1	-0.5
1889 Pit-N	21	26	.447	49	47	46	1	1	420	433	11	116	159	11.9	3.51	107	.258	.309	30	.161	-7	23	11	2	0.6
1890 Pit-P	21	25	.457	46	46	44	3	0	387²	392	5	74	145	**11.1**	3.23	121	.251	**.290**	34	.207	1	43	29	-2	2.5
1891 Pit-N	4	5	.444	9	7	6	0	0	71²	77	4	11	25	11.3	2.89	114	.264	.296	7	.226	1	4	3	0	0.4
Bos-N	20	8	.714	31	30	26	1	0	252¹	236	11	69	114	11.0	2.50	146	.238	.291	17	.167	-2	24	33	-1	2.7
Yr	24	13	.649	40	37	32	1	0	324	313	15	80	139	11.0	2.58	138	.244	**.290**	24	.180	-1	28	36	-1	3.1
1892 *Bos-N	22	10	.688	37	35	31	3	0	299²	273	10	97	93	11.2	3.03	116	.233	.293	16	.131	-6	8	16	-2	0.7
1893 Bos-N	18	10	.643	36	31	23	0	0	263	344	22	81	61	14.7	5.13	96	.307	.356	30	.265	3	-14	-6	-1	-0.4
1894 Bos-N	12	10	.545	27	21	18	0	0	208²	305	15	61	32	16.0	6.81	83	.337	.382	20	.235	0	-35	-26	-3	-2.1
1895 StL-N	6	13	.316	23	16	13	0	0	158²	223	8	39	28	15.0	5.22	93	.326	.365	9	.134	-6	-8	-7	-2	-1.2
Total 8	136	119	.533	283	257	231	10	1	2269	2468	92	601	746	12.4	3.80	105	.269	.317	174	.182	-19	51	51	-9	2.7

● **TRACY STALLARD**   Stallard, Evan Tracy b: 8/31/37, Coeburn, Va. BR/TR, 6'5", 205 lbs. Deb: 9/24/60

YEAR TM/L	W	L	PCT	G	GS	CG	SH	SV	IP	H	HR	BB	SO	RAT	ERA	ERA+	OAV	OOB	BH	AVG	PB	PR	/A	PD	TPI
1960 Bos-A	0	0	—	4	0	0	0	0	0²	2	0	0	2	4.5	0.00	—	.000	.133	0	—	0	2	2	0	0.0
1961 Bos-A	2	7	.222	43	14	1	0	2	132²	110	15	96	109	14.0	4.88	85	.229	.359	3	.083	-2	-13	-11	-2	-1.1
1962 Bos-A	0	0	—	1	0	0	0	0	1	0	0	0	0	0.0	0.00	—	.000	.000	0	—	0	0	0	0	0.0
1963 NY-N	6	17	.261	39	23	5	0	1	154²	156	23	77	110	13.6	4.71	74	.262	.347	3	.063	-3	-24	-21	-1	-3.3
1964 NY-N	10	20	.333	36	34	11	2	0	225²	213	16	73	118	11.6	3.79	94	.252	.316	15	.190	2	-6	-5	-2	-0.7
1965 StL-N	11	8	.579	40	26	4	1	0	194¹	172	25	70	99	11.5	3.38	114	.235	.307	6	.088	-4	3	10	-2	0.3
1966 StL-N	1	5	.167	20	7	0	0	1	52¹	65	9	25	35	15.8	5.68	63	.305	.383	0	.000	0	-12	-12	0	-1.5
Total 7	30	57	.345	183	104	21	3	4	764²	716	92	343	477	12.7	4.17	90	.248	.332	27	.110	-9	-50	-37	-7	-6.3

● **CHARLEY STANCEU**   Stanceu, Charles b: 1/9/16, Canton, Ohio d: 4/3/69, Canton, Ohio BR/TR, 6'2", 190 lbs. Deb: 4/16/41

YEAR TM/L	W	L	PCT	G	GS	CG	SH	SV	IP	H	HR	BB	SO	RAT	ERA	ERA+	OAV	OOB	BH	AVG	PB	PR	/A	PD	TPI
1941 NY-A	3	3	.500	22	2	0	0	0	48	58	3	35	21	17.6	5.63	70	.296	.405	0	.000	-2	-8	-9	-1	-1.2
1946 NY-A	0	0	—	3	0	0	0	0	4	6	0	5	3	24.8	9.00	38	.316	.458	0	—	0	-2	-2	0	0.0
Phi-N	2	4	.333	14	11	1	0	0	70¹	71	4	39	23	14.1	4.22	81	.270	.364	0	.000	-2	-6	-6	-1	-0.8
Total 2	5	7	.417	39	13	1	0	0	122¹	135	7	79	47	15.8	4.93	74	.282	.385	0	.000	-4	-17	-18	-2	-2.0

● **PETE STANDRIDGE**   Standridge, Alfred Peter b: 4/25/1891, Black Diamond, Wash. d: 8/2/63, San Francisco, Cal. BR/TR, 5'10.5", 165 lbs. Deb: 9/19/11

YEAR TM/L	W	L	PCT	G	GS	CG	SH	SV	IP	H	HR	BB	SO	RAT	ERA	ERA+	OAV	OOB	BH	AVG	PB	PR	/A	PD	TPI
1911 StL-N	0	0	—	2	0	0	0	0	4²	10	0	4	3	28.9	9.64	35	.435	.536	0	.000	-0	-3	-3	0	0.0
1915 Chi-N	4	1	.800	29	3	2	0	0	112¹	120	2	36	42	12.7	3.61	77	.274	.332	9	.225	3	-11	-10	0	-0.2
Total 2	4	1	.800	31	3	2	0	0	117	130	2	40	45	13.3	3.85	73	.282	.343	9	.220	3	-14	-14	0	-0.2

● **AL STANEK**   Stanek, Albert Wilfred "Lefty" b: 12/24/43, Springfield, Mass. BL/TL, 5'11.5", 190 lbs. Deb: 4/26/63

YEAR TM/L	W	L	PCT	G	GS	CG	SH	SV	IP	H	HR	BB	SO	RAT	ERA	ERA+	OAV	OOB	BH	AVG	PB	PR	/A	PD	TPI
1963 SF-N	0	0	—	11	0	0	0	0	13¹	10	1	12	5	14.9	4.73	68	.217	.379	0	.000	-0	-2	-2	1	0.1

● **KEVIN STANFIELD**   Stanfield, Kevin Bruce b: 12/19/55, Huron, S.Dak. BL/TL, 6', 190 lbs. Deb: 9/14/79

YEAR TM/L	W	L	PCT	G	GS	CG	SH	SV	IP	H	HR	BB	SO	RAT	ERA	ERA+	OAV	OOB	BH	AVG	PB	PR	/A	PD	TPI
1979 Min-A	0	0	—	3	0	0	0	0	3	6	0	0	0	6.0	6.00	73	.200	.200	0	—	0	-1	-1	0	0.0

● **LEE STANGE**   Stange, Albert Lee b: 10/27/36, Chicago, Ill. BR/TR, 5'10", 170 lbs. Deb: 4/15/61 C

YEAR TM/L	W	L	PCT	G	GS	CG	SH	SV	IP	H	HR	BB	SO	RAT	ERA	ERA+	OAV	OOB	BH	AVG	PB	PR	/A	PD	TPI
1961 Min-A	1	0	1.000	7	0	0	0	0	12¹	15	1	10	10	18.2	2.92	145	.294	.410	0	.000	-0	2	2	0	0.1
1962 Min-A	4	3	.571	44	6	1	0	3	95	98	14	39	70	13.1	4.45	92	.271	.343	1	.059	-1	-5	-4	-0	-0.4
1963 Min-A	12	5	.706	32	20	7	2	0	164²	145	21	43	100	10.3	2.62	139	.233	.283	5	.096	-1	18	19	-0	1.7
1964 Min-A	3	6	.333	14	11	2	0	0	79²	78	13	19	54	11.0	4.74	75	.255	.298	1	.040	-1	-10	-10	1	-1.1
Cle-A	4	8	.333	23	14	0	0	0	91²	98	14	31	78	12.8	4.12	87	.270	.329	2	.080	-1	-5	-5	-0	-0.8
Yr	7	14	.333	37	25	2	0	0	171¹	176	27	50	132	11.9	4.41	81	.262	.314	3	.060	-2	-15	-16	0	-1.9
1965 Cle-A	8	4	.667	41	12	4	2	0	132	122	13	26	80	10.2	3.34	104	.247	.286	3	.107	1	2	2	-2	0.1
1966 Cle-A	1	0	1.000	8	2	1	0	0	16	17	1	3	8	11.8	2.81	122	.279	.323	1	.250	1	1	1	-0	0.1
Bos-A	7	9	.438	28	19	8	2	0	153¹	140	17	43	77	10.8	3.35	114	.246	.300	3	.063	-3	2	8	-1	0.3
Yr	8	9	.471	36	21	9	2	0	169¹	157	18	46	85	10.8	3.30	114	.248	.300	4	.077	-3	3	9	-2	0.4
1967 *Bos-A	8	10	.444	35	24	6	2	1	181²	171	14	32	101	10.2	2.77	126	.246	.282	3	.061	-3	9	14	-3	0.9
1968 Bos-A	5	5	.500	50	2	1	0	12	103	89	10	25	53	10.0	3.93	80	.237	.286	2	.133	0	-11	-9	-1	-1.3
1969 Bos-A	6	9	.400	41	15	2	0	3	137	137	14	56	59	13.1	3.68	103	.256	.333	3	.086	-2	-1	2	-2	-0.1
1970 Bos-A	2	2	.500	20	0	0	0	2	27¹	34	5	12	14	15.8	5.60	71	.301	.378	0	.000	-0	-6	-5	0	-0.8
Chi-A	1	0	1.000	16	0	0	0	0	22¹	28	5	5	14	13.3	5.24	74	.295	.330	0	.000	-0	-4	-3	-0	-0.2
Yr	3	2	.600	36	0	0	0	2	49²	62	10	17	28	14.3	5.44	72	.291	.343	0	.000	-0	-10	-8	-0	-1.0
Total 10	62	61	.504	359	125	32	8	21	1216	1172	142	344	718	11.3	3.56	102	.252	.306	24	.079	-11	-8	12	-9	-1.5

● **DON STANHOUSE**   Stanhouse, Donald Joseph b: 2/12/51, DuQuoin, Ill. BR/TR, 6'2", 195 lbs. Deb: 4/19/72

YEAR TM/L	W	L	PCT	G	GS	CG	SH	SV	IP	H	HR	BB	SO	RAT	ERA	ERA+	OAV	OOB	BH	AVG	PB	PR	/A	PD	TPI
1972 Tex-A	2	9	.182	24	16	1	0	0	104²	83	8	73	78	13.5	3.78	80	.223	.351	4	.129	-0	-8	-9	2	-0.8
1973 Tex-A	1	7	.125	21	5	1	0	1	70	70	5	44	42	14.9	4.76	78	.262	.371	0	—	0	-7	-8	2	-0.6
1974 Tex-A	1	1	.500	18	0	0	0	0	31¹	38	4	17	26	16.4	4.88	73	.302	.393	0	—	0	-4	-5	1	0.0
1975 Mon-N	0	0	—	4	3	0	0	0	13	19	1	11	5	20.8	8.31	46	.345	.455	1	.333	0	-7	-6	-0	0.0
1976 Mon-N	9	12	.429	34	26	8	1	1	184	182	7	92	79	13.6	3.77	99	.263	.352	11	.212	2	-5	-1	3	0.4
1977 Mon-N	10	10	.500	47	16	1	0	10	158¹	147	12	84	89	13.4	3.41	112	.251	.349	9	.191	1	9	7	-1	0.9
1978 Bal-A	6	9	.400	56	0	0	0	24	74²	60	4	52	42	13.5	2.89	121	.230	.358	0	—	0	7	5	0	1.4
1979 *Bal-A☆	7	3	.700	52	0	0	0	21	72²	49	4	51	34	12.5	2.85	141	.202	.342	0	—	0	11	9	1	1.9
1980 LA-N	2	2	.500	21	0	0	0	7	25	30	4	19	15	16.6	5.04	69	.306	.404	0	.000	-0	-4	-4	1	-0.8
1982 Bal-A	0	1	.000	17	0	0	0	0	26²	29	3	15	20	15.5	5.40	75	.276	.377	0	.000	-0	-4	-4	0	-0.1
Total 10	38	54	.413	294	66	11	2	64	760¹	707	48	455	408	13.9	3.84	95	.252	.359	25	.185	4	-13	-16	8	2.3

● **JOE STANKA**   Stanka, Joe Donald b: 7/23/31, Hammon, Okla. BR/TR, 6'5", 201 lbs. Deb: 9/2/59

YEAR TM/L	W	L	PCT	G	GS	CG	SH	SV	IP	H	HR	BB	SO	RAT	ERA	ERA+	OAV	OOB	BH	AVG	PB	PR	/A	PD	TPI
1959 Chi-A	1	0	1.000	2	0	0	0	0	5¹	2	1	4	3	10.1	3.38	111	.111	.273	1	.333	0	0	0	-0	0.0

● **BUCK STANLEY**   Stanley, John Leonard b: 11/13/1889, Washington, D.C. d: 8/13/40, Norfolk, Va. BL/TL, 5'10", 160 lbs. Deb: 9/12/11 F

YEAR TM/L	W	L	PCT	G	GS	CG	SH	SV	IP	H	HR	BB	SO	RAT	ERA	ERA+	OAV	OOB	BH	AVG	PB	PR	/A	PD	TPI
1911 Phi-N	0	0	—	4	0	0	0	0	11¹	14	0	9	5	18.3	6.35	54	.326	.442	0	.000	-1	-4	-4	-1	-0.1

● **JOE STANLEY**   Stanley, Joseph Bernard b: 4/2/1881, Washington, D.C. d: 9/13/67, Detroit, Mich. BB/TR, 5'9.5", 150 lbs. Deb: 9/11/1897 F♦

YEAR TM/L	W	L	PCT	G	GS	CG	SH	SV	IP	H	HR	BB	SO	RAT	ERA	ERA+	OAV	OOB	BH	AVG	PB	PR	/A	PD	TPI
1897 Was-N	0	0	—	1	0	0	0	0	0²	0	0	0	0	0.0	0.00	—	.000	.000	0	.000	-0	0	0	-0	0.0
1903 Bos-N	0	0	—	1	0	0	0	0	4	4	0	4	0	20.3	9.00	36	.286	.474	77	.250	0	-3	-3	-0	0.0

YEAR TM/L	W	L	PCT	G	GS	CG	SH	SV	IP	H	HR	BB	SO	RAT	ERA	ERA+	OAV	OOB	BH	AVG	PB	PR	/A	PD	TPI
1906 Was-A	0	0	—	1	0	0	0	0	3	3	1	1	0	15.0	12.00	22	.263	.373	36	.163		-3	-3	-0	0.0
Total 3	0	0	—	3	0	0	0	0	7²	7	1	5	4	16.4	9.39	33	.256	.408	148	.213	0	-5	-5	-1	0.0

● **BOB STANLEY**   Stanley, Robert William b: 11/10/54, Portland, Maine BR/TR, 6'4", 215 lbs. Deb: 4/16/77

YEAR TM/L	W	L	PCT	G	GS	CG	SH	SV	IP	H	HR	BB	SO	RAT	ERA	ERA+	OAV	OOB	BH	AVG	PB	PR	/A	PD	TPI
1977 Bos-A	8	7	.533	41	13	3	1	3	151	176	10	43	44	13.2	3.99	112	.294	.344	0	—	0	1	8	4	0.8
1978 Bos-A	15	2	.882	52	3	0	0	10	141²	142	5	34	38	11.2	2.60	158	.266	.312	0	—	0	18	24	2	3.2
1979 Bos-A★	16	12	.571	40	30	9	4	1	216²	250	14	44	56	12.4	3.99	111	.294	.332	0	—	0	5	10	2	1.3
1980 Bos-A	10	8	.556	52	17	5	1	14	175	186	11	52	71	12.6	3.39	124	.278	.337	0	—	0	12	16	3	2.1
1981 Bos-A	10	8	.556	35	1	0	0	0	98²	110	3	38	28	14.0	3.83	101	.294	.368	0	—	0	-2	0	3	0.3
1982 Bos-A	12	7	.632	48	0	0	0	14	168¹	161	11	50	83	11.5	3.10	**139**	.255	.313	0	—	0	18	23	4	3.1
1983 Bos-A★	8	10	.444	64	0	0	0	33	145¹	145	7	38	65	11.5	2.85	153	.266	.317	0	—	0	20	24	-1	3.9
1984 Bos-A	9	10	.474	57	0	0	0	22	106²	113	9	23	52	11.6	3.54	117	.267	.308	0	—	0	5	7	3	1.8
1985 Bos-A	6	6	.500	48	0	0	0	10	87²	76	7	30	46	11.1	2.87	149	.237	.306	0	—	0	12	14	0	2.1
1986 *Bos-A	6	6	.500	66	1	0	0	16	82¹	109	9	22	54	14.3	4.37	95	.322	.364	0	—	0	-2	-2	1	-0.3
1987 Bos-A	4	15	.211	34	20	4	1	0	152²	198	17	42	67	14.2	5.01	91	.321	.366	0	—	0	-9	-8	1	-0.9
1988 *Bos-A	6	4	.600	57	0	0	0	5	101²	90	6	29	57	11.2	3.19	129	.242	.309	0	—	0	9	10	-0	0.9
1989 Bos-A	5	2	.714	43	0	0	0	4	79¹	102	4	26	32	14.6	4.88	84	.321	.374	0	—	0	-9	-7	1	-0.7
Total 13	115	97	.542	637	85	21	7	132	1707	1858	113	471	693	12.5	3.64	117	.282	.334	0	—	0	80	121	22	17.6

● **MIKE STANTON**   Stanton, Michael Thomas b: 9/25/52, Phenix City, Ala. BB/TR, 6'2", 205 lbs. Deb: 7/9/75

YEAR TM/L	W	L	PCT	G	GS	CG	SH	SV	IP	H	HR	BB	SO	RAT	ERA	ERA+	OAV	OOB	BH	AVG	PB	PR	/A	PD	TPI
1975 Hou-N	0	2	.000	7	2	0	0	1	17¹	20	1	20	16	20.8	7.27	46	.290	.449	1	.250	0	-7	-8	0	-0.8
1980 Cle-A	1	3	.250	51	0	0	0	5	85²	98	5	44	74	15.2	5.46	75	.297	.385	0	—	0	-14	-13	1	-0.6
1981 Cle-A	3	3	.500	24	0	0	0	2	43¹	43	4	18	34	12.7	4.36	83	.262	.335	0	—	0	-3	-4	-1	-0.5
1982 Sea-A	2	4	.333	56	1	0	0	7	71¹	70	5	21	49	11.5	4.16	102	.260	.314	0	—	0	-1	1	1	0.1
1983 Sea-A	2	3	.400	50	0	0	0	8	65	65	3	28	47	13.0	3.32	128	.273	.352	0	—	0	5	7	-0	0.5
1984 Sea-A	4	4	.500	54	0	0	0	8	61	55	3	22	55	11.7	3.54	113	.241	.313	0	—	0	3	3	-1	0.4
1985 Sea-A	1	2	.333	24	0	0	0	1	29	32	4	21	17	17.4	5.28	80	.278	.403	0	—	0	-4	-3	1	-0.3
Chi-A	0	1	.000	11	0	0	0	0	11²	15	2	8	12	17.7	9.26	47	.294	.390	0	—	0	-7	-6	0	-0.5
Yr	1	3	.250	35	0	0	0	1	40²	47	6	29	29	16.8	6.42	66	.278	.384	0	—	0	-10	-10	1	-0.8
Total 7	13	22	.371	277	3	0	0	31	384¹	398	27	182	304	13.8	4.61	88	.272	.356	1	.250	0	-27	-24	1	-1.7

● **MIKE STANTON**   Stanton, William Michael b: 6/2/67, Houston, Tex. BL/TL, 6'1", 190 lbs. Deb: 8/24/89

YEAR TM/L	W	L	PCT	G	GS	CG	SH	SV	IP	H	HR	BB	SO	RAT	ERA	ERA+	OAV	OOB	BH	AVG	PB	PR	/A	PD	TPI
1989 Atl-N	0	1	.000	20	0	0	0	7	24	17	0	8	27	9.4	1.50	243	.207	.278	0	—	0	5	6	-0	0.6
1990 Atl-N	0	3	.000	7	0	0	0	2	7	16	1	4	7	27.0	18.00	22	.444	.512	0	—	0	-11	-11	0	-3.7
1991 *Atl-N	5	5	.500	74	0	0	0	7	78	62	6	21	54	9.7	2.88	135	.217	.273	3	.500	2	7	9	1	1.5
1992 *Atl-N	5	4	.556	65	0	0	0	8	63²	59	6	20	44	11.5	4.10	89	.247	.310	1	.500	0	-4	-3	0	-0.5
1993 Atl-N	4	6	.400	63	0	0	0	27	52	51	4	29	43	13.8	4.67	86	.255	.349	0	—	0	-4	-4	-1	-1.1
1994 Atl-N	3	1	.750	49	0	0	0	3	45²	41	2	26	35	13.8	3.55	117	.248	.361	2	.667	1	3	3	1	0.4
Total 6	17	20	.459	278	0	0	0	54	270¹	246	19	108	210	12.0	3.90	100	.244	.321	6	.545	3	-3	-0	2	-2.8

● **DAVE STAPLETON**   Stapleton, David Earl b: 10/16/61, Miami, Ariz. BL/TL, 6'1", 185 lbs. Deb: 9/14/87

YEAR TM/L	W	L	PCT	G	GS	CG	SH	SV	IP	H	HR	BB	SO	RAT	ERA	ERA+	OAV	OOB	BH	AVG	PB	PR	/A	PD	TPI
1987 Mil-A	2	0	1.000	4	0	0	0	0	14²	13	0	3	14	9.8	1.84	248	.241	.281	0	—	0	4	4	-0	0.5
1988 Mil-A	0	0	—	6	0	0	0	0	13²	20	1	9	6	19.8	5.93	67	.339	.435	0	—	0	-3	-3	-0	0.0
Total 2	2	0	1.000	10	0	0	0	0	28¹	33	1	12	20	14.6	3.81	112	.292	.365	0	—	0	1	1	-0	0.5

● **CON STARKEL**   Starkel, Conrad b: 11/16/1880, Germany d: 1/19/33, Tacoma, Wash. BR/TR, 6', 200 lbs. Deb: 4/19/06

YEAR TM/L	W	L	PCT	G	GS	CG	SH	SV	IP	H	HR	BB	SO	RAT	ERA	ERA+	OAV	OOB	BH	AVG	PB	PR	/A	PD	TPI
1906 Was-A	0	0	—	1	0	0	0	0	3	7	1	2	1	27.0	18.00	15	.455	.518	0	—	0	-5	-5	0	-0.1

● **RAY STARR**   Starr, Raymond Francis "Iron Man" b: 4/23/06, Nowata, Okla. d: 2/9/63, Baylis, Ill. BR/TR, 6'1", 178 lbs. Deb: 9/11/32

YEAR TM/L	W	L	PCT	G	GS	CG	SH	SV	IP	H	HR	BB	SO	RAT	ERA	ERA+	OAV	OOB	BH	AVG	PB	PR	/A	PD	TPI
1932 StL-N	1	1	.500	3	2	1	1	0	20	19	2	10	6	13.5	2.70	146	.284	.385	1	.250	0	3	3	1	0.3
1933 NY-N	0	1	.000	6	2	0	0	0	13¹	19	0	10	2	20.3	5.40	59	.339	.448	0	.000	-0	-3	-3	-0	-0.3
Bos-N	0	1	.000	9	1	0	0	0	28	32	4	9	15	13.5	3.86	79	.296	.356	1	.143	0	-2	-2	0	0.0
Yr	0	2	.000	15	3	0	0	0	41¹	51	4	19	17	15.5	4.35	71	.309	.384	1	.100	0	-5	-6	0	-0.3
1941 Cin-N	3	2	.600	7	4	3	2	0	34	28	1	6	11	9.3	2.65	136	.219	.259	2	.182	-0	4	4	0	0.5
1942 Cin-N☆	15	13	.536	37	33	17	4	1	276²	228	10	106	83	11.0	2.67	123	.226	.301	8	.091	-5	20	19	-2	1.2
1943 Cin-N	11	10	.524	36	33	9	2	1	217¹	201	9	91	42	12.3	3.64	91	.248	.328	9	.122	-4	-6	-8	-0	-1.2
1944 Pit-N	6	5	.545	27	12	5	0	3	89²	116	6	36	25	15.4	5.02	74	.314	.377	3	.136	.1	-14	-13	-1	-1.5
1945 Pit-N	0	2	.000	4	0	0	0	3	6²	10	1	4	0	18.9	9.45	42	.370	.452	1	1.000	1	-4	-4	0	-0.9
Chi-N	1	0	1.000	9	1	0	0	0	13¹	17	1	7	5	16.2	7.43	49	.298	.375	1	.500	1	-5	-6	0	-0.3
Yr	1	2	.333	13	1	0	0	0	20	27	1	11	5	17.1	8.10	46	.321	.400	2	.667	1	-10	-10	0	-1.2
Total 7	37	35	.514	138	88	35	9	4	699	670	33	279	189	12.4	3.53	96	.255	.329	26	.123	-7	-8	-11	-1	-2.2

● **DICK STARR**   Starr, Richard Eugene b: 3/2/21, Kittanning, Pa. BR/TR, 6'3", 190 lbs. Deb: 9/5/47

YEAR TM/L	W	L	PCT	G	GS	CG	SH	SV	IP	H	HR	BB	SO	RAT	ERA	ERA+	OAV	OOB	BH	AVG	PB	PR	/A	PD	TPI
1947 NY-A	1	0	1.000	4	1	0	0	0	12¹	12	1	8	1	14.6	1.46	242	.250	.357	1	.333	1	3	3	0	0.3
1948 NY-A	0	0	—	2	0	0	0	0	2	0	0	2	2	9.0	4.50	91	.000	.250	0	—	0	-0	-0	-0	0.0
1949 StL-A	1	7	.125	30	8	1	1	0	83¹	96	6	48	44	15.7	4.32	105	.292	.384	2	.087	-1	-1	-2	-1	0.0
1950 StL-A	7	5	.583	32	16	4	1	2	123²	140	11	74	30	16.1	5.02	99	.287	.389	5	.139	-3	-6	-1	-1	-0.4
1951 StL-A	2	5	.286	15	9	0	0	0	62	66	10	42	26	16.0	7.40	59	.273	.385	4	.222	0	-23	-21	-1	-2.0
Was-A	1	7	.125	11	11	1	0	0	61¹	76	12	24	17	14.7	5.58	73	.304	.365	3	.176	1	-10	-10	-2	-1.2
Yr	3	12	.200	26	20	1	0	0	123¹	142	22	66	43	15.5	6.49	65	.287	.371	7	.200	1	-33	-31	-2	-3.2
Total 5	12	24	.333	93	45	7	2	2	344²	390	40	198	120	15.6	5.25	86	.286	.381	15	.155	-2	-37	-27	-4	-3.3

● **HERMAN STARRETTE**   Starrette, Herman Paul b: 11/20/38, Statesville, N.C. BR/TR, 6', 175 lbs. Deb: 7/1/63 C

YEAR TM/L	W	L	PCT	G	GS	CG	SH	SV	IP	H	HR	BB	SO	RAT	ERA	ERA+	OAV	OOB	BH	AVG	PB	PR	/A	PD	TPI
1963 Bal-A	0	1	.000	18	0	0	0	0	26	26	1	7	13	12.1	3.46	100	.271	.333	0	.000	0	0	0	1	0.1
1964 Bal-A	1	0	1.000	5	0	0	0	0	11	9	0	6	5	12.3	1.64	218	.250	.357	0	.000	-0	2	2	-0	0.1
1965 Bal-A	0	0	—	4	0	0	0	0	9	8	0	3	3	11.0	1.00	347	.258	.324	0	.000	0	2	2	0	0.0
Total 3	1	1	.500	27	0	0	0	0	46	43	1	16	21	11.9	2.54	137	.264	.337	0	.000	-0	5	5	1	0.2

● **ED STAUFFER**   Stauffer, Charles Edward b: 1/10/1898, Emsworth, Pa. d: 7/2/79, St.Petersburg, Fla BR/TR, 5'11", 185 lbs. Deb: 4/26/23

YEAR TM/L	W	L	PCT	G	GS	CG	SH	SV	IP	H	HR	BB	SO	RAT	ERA	ERA+	OAV	OOB	BH	AVG	PB	PR	/A	PD	TPI
1923 Chi-N	0	0	—	1	0	0	0	0	2	7	0	0	0	27.0	13.50	30	.556	.600	0	—	0	-2	-2	-0	-0.2
1925 StL-A	0	1	.000	20	1	0	0	0	30¹	34	1	21	13	16.3	5.34	87	.283	.390	1	.250	-0	-3	-2	-1	-0.2
Total 2	0	1	.000	21	1	0	0	0	32¹	39	1	22	13	17.0	5.85	79	.302	.404	1	.250	-0	-5	-4	-1	-0.2

● **BILL STEARNS**   Stearns, William E. b: 3/20/1853, Washington, D.C. d: 12/30/1898, Washington, D.C. TR Deb: 6/26/1871

YEAR TM/L	W	L	PCT	G	GS	CG	SH	SV	IP	H	HR	BB	SO	RAT	ERA	ERA+	OAV	OOB	BH	AVG	PB	PR	/A	PD	TPI
1871 Oly-n	2	0	1.000	2	2	2	0	0	18	10	0	8	0	9.0	2.50	167	.149	.240	0	.000		3	3		0.1
1872 Nat-n	0	11	.000	11	11	11	0	0	99	194	3	2	0	17.9	6.91	68	.339	.343	11	.234	-4	-35	-24		-1.8
1873 Was-n	7	25	.219	32	32	32	0	0	283	481	8	15	4	15.8	4.55	74	.330	.337	24	.180	-6	-41	-38		-2.9
1874 Har-n	2	14	.125	22	18	14	0	1	164	255	1	13		14.7	4.50	70	.311	.322	21	.159	-5	-27	-24		-1.9
1875 Was-n	1	14	.067	17	16	14	0	0	141	243	0	5	2	15.8	5.36	49	.332	.335	20	.260	-1	-45	-43		-3.1
Total 5 n	12	64	.158	84	79	73	0	1	705	1183	12	43	6	15.7	4.98	53	.324	.332	76	.191	-16	-197	-185		-9.6

● **CHARLIE STECHER**   Stecher, Charles b: Bordentown, N.J. Deb: 9/6/1890

YEAR TM/L	W	L	PCT	G	GS	CG	SH	SV	IP	H	HR	BB	SO	RAT	ERA	ERA+	OAV	OOB	BH	AVG	PB	PR	/A	PD	TPI
1890 Phi-a	0	10	.000	10	10	9	0	0	68	111	4	60	18	24.5	10.32	37	.355	.479	7	.241	1	-49	-49	2	-4.4

● **ELMER STEELE**   Steele, Elmer Rae b: 5/17/1886, Poughkeepsie, N.Y. d: 3/9/66, Rhinebeck, N.Y. BB/TR, 5'11", 200 lbs. Deb: 9/12/07

YEAR TM/L	W	L	PCT	G	GS	CG	SH	SV	IP	H	HR	BB	SO	RAT	ERA	ERA+	OAV	OOB	BH	AVG	PB	PR	/A	PD	TPI
1907 Bos-A	0	1	.000	4	1	0	0	0	11¹	11	0	1	10	9.5	1.59	162	.256	.273	0	.000	-1	1	1	0	0.1

YEAR TM/L	W	L	PCT	G	GS	CG	SH	SV	IP	H	HR	BB	SO	RAT	ERA	ERA+	OAV	OOB	BH	AVG	PB	PR	/A	PD	TPI
1908 Bos-A	5	7	.417	16	13	9	1	0	118	85	1	13	37	7.7	1.83	135	.209	.239	2	.051	-4	7	8	-1	0.3
1909 Bos-A	4	4	.500	16	8	2	0	1	75²	75	1	15	32	10.8	2.85	88	.255	.294	6	.250	1	-3	-3	0	-0.2
1910 Pit-N	0	3	.000	3	3	2	0	0	24	19	0	3	7	8.3	2.25	138	.221	.247	0	.000	-1	2	2	1	0.3
1911 Pit-N	9	9	.500	31	16	7	2	2	166	153	5	31	52	10.2	2.60	132	.256	.297	11	.180	-0	15	15	2	1.7
Bro-N	0	0	—	5	2	0	0	0	23	24	0	5	9	11.3	3.13	107	.258	.296	0	.000	-1	1	1	0	-0.1
Yr	9	9	.500	36	18	7	2	2	189	177	5	36	61	10.1	2.67	128	.255	.292	11	.157	-1	15	16	2	1.6
Total 5	18	24	.429	75	43	20	3	3	418	367	7	68	147	9.5	2.41	122	.241	.278	19	.132	-5	23	25	3	2.1

● **BOB STEELE**   Steele, Robert Wesley b: 1/5/1894, Cassburn, Ont., Can. d: 1/27/62, Ocala, Fla. BB/TL, 5'10.5", 175 lbs. Deb: 4/17/16

YEAR TM/L	W	L	PCT	G	GS	CG	SH	SV	IP	H	HR	BB	SO	RAT	ERA	ERA+	OAV	OOB	BH	AVG	PB	PR	/A	PD	TPI
1916 StL-N	5	15	.250	29	21	7	1	0	148	156	6	42	67	12.2	3.41	78	.285	.340	10	.196	-1	-13	-13	-3	-2.0
1917 StL-N	1	3	.250	12	6	1	0	0	42	33	1	19	23	11.1	3.21	84	.223	.311	5	.385	2	-2	-2	-1	-0.1
Pit-N	5	11	.313	27	19	13	1	1	179²	158	0	53	82	10.8	2.76	103	.237	.298	17	.224	1	-1	-2	-1	0.0
Yr	6	14	.300	39	25	14	1	1	221²	191	1	72	105	10.9	2.84	99	.235	.301	22	.247	2	-3	-1	-2	-0.1
1918 Pit-N	2	3	.400	10	4	2	1	1	49	44	2	17	21	11.6	3.31	87	.240	.312	2	.125	-0	-3	-2	-0	-0.3
NY-N	3	5	.375	12	7	5	1	1	66	56	1	11	24	9.5	2.59	101	.226	.267	6	.286	2	1	0	-2	0.0
Yr	5	8	.385	22	11	7	2	2	115	100	3	28	45	10.3	2.90	94	.231	.282	8	.216	2	-2	-2	-3	-0.3
1919 NY-N	0	1	.000	1	0	0	0	0	3	3	0	2	0	15.0	6.00	47	.250	.357	0	.000	-0	-1	-1	-0	-0.3
Total 4	16	38	.296	91	57	28	4	3	487²	450	10	144	217	11.2	3.05	90	.249	.310	40	.225	3	-19	-16	-8	-2.7

● **BILL STEELE**   Steele, William Mitchell "Big Bill" b: 10/5/1885, Milford, Pa. d: 10/19/49, Overland, Mo. BR/TR, 5'11", 200 lbs. Deb: 9/10/10

YEAR TM/L	W	L	PCT	G	GS	CG	SH	SV	IP	H	HR	BB	SO	RAT	ERA	ERA+	OAV	OOB	BH	AVG	PB	PR	/A	PD	TPI
1910 StL-N	4	4	.500	9	8	8	0	1	71²	71	1	24	25	12.7	3.27	91	.264	.338	8	.258	-1	-2	-2	-1	0.0
1911 StL-N	18	19	.486	43	34	23	1	3	287¹	287	8	113	115	12.8	3.73	91	.269	.345	21	.208	4	-10	-11	3	-0.6
1912 StL-N	9	13	.409	40	25	7	0	2	194	245	5	66	67	14.8	4.69	73	.322	.381	11	.180	1	-27	-27	4	-2.2
1913 StL-N	4	4	.500	12	9	2	0	0	54	58	3	18	10	13.2	5.00	65	.286	.353	1	.056	-1	-11	-11	-1	-1.6
1914 StL-N	1	2	.333	17	2	0	0	0	53¹	55	3	7	16	11.0	2.70	104	.274	.308	5	.294	2	1	1	1	0.3
Bro-N	1	1	.500	8	1	0	0	1	16¹	17	1	7	3	13.2	5.51	52	.258	.329	1	.333	1	-5	-5	-0	-0.6
Yr	2	3	.400	25	3	0	0	1	69²	72	4	14	19	11.1	3.36	84	.267	.303	6	.300	2	-4	-4	1	-0.3
Total 5	37	43	.463	129	79	40	1	7	676²	733	21	235	236	13.3	4.02	82	.286	.352	47	.203	8	-55	-55	8	-4.7

● **BILL STEEN**   Steen, William John b: 11/11/1887, Pittsburgh, Pa. d: 3/13/79, Signal Hill, Cal. BR/TR, 6'0.5", 180 lbs. Deb: 4/15/12

YEAR TM/L	W	L	PCT	G	GS	CG	SH	SV	IP	H	HR	BB	SO	RAT	ERA	ERA+	OAV	OOB	BH	AVG	PB	PR	/A	PD	TPI
1912 Cle-A	9	8	.529	26	16	6	1	0	143¹	163	3	45	61	13.1	3.77	90	.298	.352	13	.271	2	-7	-6	-1	-0.5
1913 Cle-A	4	5	.444	22	13	7	2	2	128¹	113	3	49	57	11.6	2.45	124	.237	.313	7	.171	-0	7	8	-0	0.5
1914 Cle-A	9	14	.391	30	22	13	1	0	200²	201	4	68	97	12.2	2.60	111	.272	.337	14	.200	1	3	6	0	0.8
1915 Cle-A	1	4	.200	10	7	2	0	0	45¹	51	1	15	22	13.5	4.96	61	.290	.352	3	.188	-1	-10	-10	2	-0.8
Det-A	5	1	.833	20	7	3	0	4	79¹	83	0	22	28	12.0	2.72	111	.269	.319	5	.179	-1	2	3	2	0.3
Yr	6	5	.545	30	14	5	0	4	124²	134	1	37	50	12.4	3.54	86	.275	.328	8	.182	-1	-8	-7	4	-0.5
Total 4	28	32	.467	108	65	31	4	6	597	611	7	199	265	12.4	3.05	101	.272	.334	42	.207	1	-6	2	2	0.3

● **MILT STEENGRAFE**   Steengrafe, Milton Henry b: 5/26/1900, San Francisco, Cal d: 6/2/77, BR/TR, 6', 170 lbs. Deb: 5/5/24

YEAR TM/L	W	L	PCT	G	GS	CG	SH	SV	IP	H	HR	BB	SO	RAT	ERA	ERA+	OAV	OOB	BH	AVG	PB	PR	/A	PD	TPI
1924 Chi-A	0	0	—	3	0	0	0	0	5²	15	0	4	3	30.2	12.71	32	.484	.543	0	.000	-0	-5	-5	0	0.0
1926 Chi-A	1	1	.500	13	1	0	0	0	38¹	43	1	19	10	15.0	3.99	97	.295	.383	0	.000	-2	0	-1	-1	-0.3
Total 2	1	1	.500	16	1	0	0	0	44	58	1	23	13	17.0	5.11	76	.328	.411	0	.000	-2	-5	-6	-1	-0.3

● **MORRIE STEEVENS**   Steevens, Morris Dale b: 10/7/40, Salem, Ill. BL/TL, 6'2", 175 lbs. Deb: 4/13/62

YEAR TM/L	W	L	PCT	G	GS	CG	SH	SV	IP	H	HR	BB	SO	RAT	ERA	ERA+	OAV	OOB	BH	AVG	PB	PR	/A	PD	TPI
1962 Chi-N	0	1	.000	12	0	0	0	0	15	10	0	11	5	13.2	2.40	173	.196	.349	0	.000	-0	3	3	0	0.2
1964 Phi-N	0	0	—	4	0	0	0	0	2²	5	0	1	3	20.3	3.38	103	.385	.429	0	—	0	0	0	0	0.0
1965 Phi-N	0	1	.000	6	0	0	0	0	2²	5	1	4	3	30.4	16.88	20	.417	.563	0	—	-0	-4	-4	-0	-1.3
Total 3	0	2	.000	22	1	0	0	0	20¹	20	1	16	11	16.4	4.43	90	.263	.398	0	.000	-0	-1	-1	-0	-1.1

● **ED STEIN**   Stein, Edward F. b: 9/5/1869, Detroit, Mich. d: 5/10/28, Detroit, Mich. BR/TR, 5'11", 170 lbs. Deb: 7/24/1890

YEAR TM/L	W	L	PCT	G	GS	CG	SH	SV	IP	H	HR	BB	SO	RAT	ERA	ERA+	OAV	OOB	BH	AVG	PB	PR	/A	PD	TPI
1890 Chi-N	12	6	.667	20	18	14	1	0	160²	147	9	83	65	13.5	3.81	96	.236	.336	9	.153	-2	-4	-3	-1	-0.5
1891 Chi-N	7	6	.538	14	10	9	1	0	101	99	7	57	38	14.1	3.74	89	.247	.343	7	.163	-1	-4	-5	2	-0.4
1892 Bro-N	27	16	.628	48	42	38	6	1	377¹	310	6	150	190	11.3	2.84	111	.215	.296	31	.215	4	19	14	2	1.8
1893 Bro-N	19	15	.559	37	34	28	1	0	298¹	294	4	119	81	12.7	3.77	117	.250	.323	25	.212	-3	30	22	2	1.7
1894 Bro-N	26	14	.650	44	40	37	2	1	350	388	10	170	84	14.7	4.63	107	.278	.362	38	.259	5	27	12	-0	1.3
1895 Bro-N	15	13	.536	32	27	24	1	0	255¹	282	9	89	55	13.4	4.72	93	.276	.340	26	.250	2	2	-9	1	-0.5
1896 Bro-N	3	6	.333	17	10	6	0	0	90¹	130	6	51	16	18.2	4.88	84	.334	.414	10	.256	-0	-5	-8	0	-0.5
1898 Bro-N	0	2	.000	3	2	2	0	0	23	39	0	9	6	18.8	5.48	65	.372	.421	4	.400	1	-5	-5	-0	-0.3
Total 8	109	78	.583	215	183	158	12	3	1656	1689	51	732	535	13.5	3.97	103	.258	.338	150	.226	5	59	22	5	2.6

● **IRV STEIN**   Stein, Irvin Michael b: 5/21/11, Madisonville, La. d: 1/7/81, Covington, La. BR/TR, 6'2", 170 lbs. Deb: 7/7/32

YEAR TM/L	W	L	PCT	G	GS	CG	SH	SV	IP	H	HR	BB	SO	RAT	ERA	ERA+	OAV	OOB	BH	AVG	PB	PR	/A	PD	TPI
1932 Phi-A	0	0	—	1	0	0	0	0	3	7	2	1	0	24.0	12.00	38	.500	.533	0	.000	-0	-3	-2	0	0.0

● **RANDY STEIN**   Stein, William Randolph b: 3/7/53, Pomona, Cal. BR/TR, 6'4", 210 lbs. Deb: 4/17/78

YEAR TM/L	W	L	PCT	G	GS	CG	SH	SV	IP	H	HR	BB	SO	RAT	ERA	ERA+	OAV	OOB	BH	AVG	PB	PR	/A	PD	TPI
1978 Mil-A	3	2	.600	31	1	0	0	1	72²	78	5	39	42	15.0	5.33	71	.280	.376	0	—	0	-13	-13	0	-0.8
1979 Sea-A	2	3	.400	23	1	0	0	0	41¹	48	7	27	39	16.5	5.88	74	.291	.394	0	—	0	-8	-7	-1	-0.8
1981 Sea-A	0	1	1.000	5	0	0	0	0	9¹	18	1	8	6	25.1	10.61	36	.429	.520	0	—	0	-7	-7	0	-0.7
1982 Chi-N	0	0	—	6	0	0	0	0	10¹	7	2	7	6	12.2	3.48	107	.200	.333	0	—	0	0	-0	0	0.0
Total 4	5	6	.455	65	2	0	0	1	133²	151	15	81	93	16.0	5.72	69	.290	.390	0	—	0	-27	-26	-1	-2.3

● **RAY STEINEDER**   Steineder, Raymond J. b: 11/13/1895, Salem, N.J. d: 8/25/82, Vineland, N.J. BR/TR, 6'0.5", 160 lbs. Deb: 7/16/23

YEAR TM/L	W	L	PCT	G	GS	CG	SH	SV	IP	H	HR	BB	SO	RAT	ERA	ERA+	OAV	OOB	BH	AVG	PB	PR	/A	PD	TPI
1923 Pit-N	2	0	1.000	15	2	1	0	0	55	58	3	18	23	12.8	4.75	85	.278	.341	7	.467	3	-5	-4	-1	0.0
1924 Pit-N	0	1	.000	5	0	0	0	0	2²	6	0	5	0	37.1	13.50	28	.400	.550	0	—	0	-3	-3	0	-0.9
Phi-N	1	1	.500	9	0	0	0	0	28²	29	1	16	11	14.1	4.40	101	.266	.360	3	.300	0	-2	-0	0	0.1
Yr	1	2	.333	14	0	0	0	0	31¹	35	1	21	11	16.1	5.17	85	.282	.386	3	.300	0	-5	-3	0	-0.8
Total 2	3	2	.600	29	2	1	0	0	86¹	93	4	39	34	14.0	4.90	85	.279	.358	10	.400	3	-9	-7	-1	-0.8

● **RICK STEIRER**   Steirer, Ricky Francis b: 8/27/56, Baltimore, Md. BR/TR, 6'4", 200 lbs. Deb: 8/5/82

YEAR TM/L	W	L	PCT	G	GS	CG	SH	SV	IP	H	HR	BB	SO	RAT	ERA	ERA+	OAV	OOB	BH	AVG	PB	PR	/A	PD	TPI
1982 Cal-A	1	0	1.000	10	1	0	0	0	26¹	25	2	11	14	12.6	3.76	108	.243	.322	0	—	0	1	1	0	0.1
1983 Cal-A	3	2	.600	19	5	0	0	0	61²	77	3	18	25	14.3	4.82	83	.302	.355	0	—	0	-5	-6	1	-0.3
1984 Cal-A	0	1	.000	1	1	0	0	0	2²	6	0	2	2	27.0	16.88	24	.500	.571	0	—	0	-4	-4	0	-0.8
Total 3	4	3	.571	30	7	0	0	0	90²	108	5	31	41	14.2	4.86	83	.292	.353	0	—	0	-8	-8	1	-1.0

● **BILL STELLBERGER**   Stellberger, William F. b: 4/22/1865, Detroit, Mich. d: 11/9/36, Detroit, Mich. BL/TL, Deb: 10/1/1885

YEAR TM/L	W	L	PCT	G	GS	CG	SH	SV	IP	H	HR	BB	SO	RAT	ERA	ERA+	OAV	OOB	BH	AVG	PB	PR	/A	PD	TPI
1885 Pro-N	0	1	.000	1	1	1	0	0	8	14	0	4	0	20.3	7.88	34	.389	.450	0	.000	-1	-4	-5	0	-0.4

● **JEFF STEMBER**   Stember, Jeffrey Alan b: 3/2/58, Elizabeth, N.J. BR/TR, 6'5", 220 lbs. Deb: 8/5/80

YEAR TM/L	W	L	PCT	G	GS	CG	SH	SV	IP	H	HR	BB	SO	RAT	ERA	ERA+	OAV	OOB	BH	AVG	PB	PR	/A	PD	TPI
1980 SF-N	0	0	—	1	1	0	0	0	3	2	1	2	0	12.0	3.00	118	.167	.286	0	.000	-0	0	-0	0	0.0

● **BILL STEMMEYER**   Stemmeyer, William "Cannon Ball" b: 5/6/1865, Cleveland, Ohio d: 5/3/45, Cleveland, Ohio BR/TR, 6'2", 190 lbs. Deb: 10/3/1885

YEAR TM/L	W	L	PCT	G	GS	CG	SH	SV	IP	H	HR	BB	SO	RAT	ERA	ERA+	OAV	OOB	BH	AVG	PB	PR	/A	PD	TPI
1885 Bos-N	1	1	.500	2	2	2	1	0	11	7	1	8	14	14.7	0.00	—	.194	.383	3	.429	1	3	3	0	0.8
1886 Bos-N	22	18	.550	41	41	41	0	0	348²	300	11	144	239	11.5	3.02	106	.218	.292	41	.277	9	11	7	-3	1.2
1887 Bos-N	6	8	.429	15	14	14	0	1	119¹	138	4	41	41	13.7	5.20	78	.274	.331	12	.255	2	-15	-15	-2	-1.3
1888 Cle-a	0	2	.000	2	2	2	0	0	16	37	0	9	7	26.4	9.00	34	.437	.496	4	.400	1	-11	-11	-0	-0.8
Total 4	29	29	.500	60	59	59	1	1	495	482	15	205	295	12.5	3.67	92	.241	.312	60	.283	14	-11	-16	-4	-0.1

YEAR TM/L	W	L	PCT	G	GS	CG	SH	SV	IP	H	HR	BB	SO	RAT	ERA	ERA+	OAV	OOB	BH	AVG	PB	PR	/A	PD	TPI

● DAVE STENHOUSE Stenhouse, David Rotchford b: 9/12/33, Westerly, R.I. BR/TR, 6', 195 lbs. Deb: 4/18/62 F

1962 Was-A★	11	12	.478	34	26	9	2	0	197	169	24	90	123	11.9	3.65	110	.234	.320	3	.052	-5	7	8	2	0.6
1963 Was-A	3	9	.250	16	16	2	1	0	87	90	12	45	47	14.1	4.55	82	.260	.347	2	.080	-1	-9	-8	0	-1.1
1964 Was-A	2	7	.222	26	14	1	0	1	88	80	12	39	44	12.3	4.81	77	.239	.320	6	.300	2	-12	-11	-0	-0.9
Total 3	16	28	.364	76	56	12	3	1	372	339	48	174	214	12.5	4.14	94	.241	.327	11	.107	-4	-14	-11	1	-1.4

● BUZZ STEPHEN Stephen, Louis Roberts b: 7/13/44, Porterville, Cal. BR/TR, 6'4", 205 lbs. Deb: 9/20/68

| 1968 Min-A | 1 | 1 | .500 | 2 | 2 | 0 | 0 | 0 | 11¹ | 11 | 0 | 7 | 4 | 15.1 | 4.76 | 65 | .275 | .396 | 0 | .000 | -0 | -2 | -2 | 0 | -0.4 |

● BRYAN STEPHENS Stephens, Bryan Maris b: 7/14/20, Fayetteville, Ark d: 11/21/91, Santa Ana, Cal. BR/TR, 6'4", 175 lbs. Deb: 5/15/47

1947 Cle-A	5	10	.333	31	5	1	0	1	92	79	6	39	34	11.7	4.01	87	.230	.312	3	.111	-2	-3	-5	-1	-1.1
1948 StL-A	3	6	.333	43	12	2	0	3	122²	141	14	67	35	15.6	6.02	76	.289	.379	4	.125	-1	-24	-20	-1	-1.5
Total 2	8	16	.333	74	17	3	0	4	214²	220	20	106	69	13.9	5.16	79	.264	.352	7	.119	-3	-27	-26	-2	-2.6

● CLARENCE STEPHENS Stephens, Clarence Wright b: 8/19/1863, Cincinnati, Ohio d: 2/28/45, Cincinnati, Ohio TR , Deb: 10/8/1886

1886 Cin-a	1	0	1.000	1	1	1	0	0	8	9	0	5	6	16.9	5.63	63	.273	.385	3	.600	1	-2	-2	0	-0.1
1891 Cin-N	0	1	.000	1	1	1	0	0	8	9	1	3	3	13.5	7.88	43	.273	.334	0	.000	-0	-4	-4	-0	-0.4
1892 Cin-N	0	1	.000	1	1	0	0	0	7	12	0	4	1	20.6	1.29	254	.364	.432	0	.000	-0	2	2	0	0.2
Total 3	1	2	.333	3	3	2	0	0	23	30	1	12	10	16.8	5.09	67	.303	.384	3	.300	0	-4	-4	0	-0.3

● BEN STEPHENS Stephens, George Benjamin b: 9/28/1867, Romeo, Mich. d: 8/5/1896, Armada, Mich. 5'10.5", 170 lbs. Deb: 8/5/1892

1892 Bal-N	1	1	.500	5	2	1	0	1	29	37	2	9	7	14.6	2.79	123	.298	.351	0	.000	-2	2	2	-0	0.0
1893 Was-N	0	6	.000	9	6	6	0	0	63²	83	1	31	14	16.7	5.80	80	.306	.385	3	.103	-4	-8	-8	1	-0.8
1894 Was-N	0	0	—	3	2	1	0	0	11	19	1	8	1	22.9	4.91	107	.375	.469	1	.250	-0	1	0	0	0.0
Total 3	1	7	.125	17	10	9	0	1	103²	139	4	48	22	16.8	4.86	90	.312	.386	4	.087	-5	-6	-6	1	-0.8

● EARL STEPHENSON Stephenson, Chester Earl b: 7/31/47, Benson, N.C. BL/TL, 6'3", 175 lbs. Deb: 4/7/71

1971 Chi-N	1	0	1.000	16	0	0	0	0	20¹	24	1	11	11	15.5	4.43	89	.316	.402	0	.000	-0	-2	-1	0	-0.1
1972 Mil-A	3	5	.375	35	8	1	0	0	80¹	79	5	33	33	12.9	3.25	93	.262	.340	0	.000	-2	-2	-2	-0	-0.4
1977 Bal-A	0	0	—	1	0	0	0	0	3	5	1	0	2	15.0	9.00	42	.357	.357	0	—	0	-2	-2	-0	0.6
1978 Bal-A	0	0	—	2	0	0	0	0	9²	10	0	5	4	14.0	2.79	125	.294	.385	0	—	0	1	1	-0	0.3
Total 4	4	5	.444	54	8	1	0	1	113¹	118	7	49	50	13.5	3.57	91	.277	.356	0	.000	-2	-4	-4	-0	0.4

● JERRY STEPHENSON Stephenson, Jerry Joseph b: 10/6/43, Detroit, Mich. BL/TR, 6'2", 185 lbs. Deb: 4/14/63 F

1963 Bos-A	0	0	—	1	1	0	0	0	2¹	5	0	2	3	27.0	7.71	49	.556	.636	0	.000	-0	-1	-1	-0	0.0
1965 Bos-A	1	5	.167	15	8	0	0	0	52	62	7	33	49	16.6	6.23	60	.287	.384	3	.231	-1	-16	-14	0	-1.4
1966 Bos-A	2	5	.286	15	11	1	0	0	66¹	68	6	44	50	15.3	5.83	65	.264	.373	2	.118	-1	-18	-15	0	-1.5
1967 *Bos-A	3	1	.750	8	6	0	0	0	39²	32	4	16	24	11.1	3.86	90	.227	.310	4	.250	0	-3	-2	0	-0.1
1968 Bos-A	2	8	.200	23	7	2	0	0	68²	81	4	42	51	16.4	5.64	56	.295	.392	6	.353	2	-20	-19	1	-2.4
1969 Sea-A	0	0	—	2	0	0	0	0	2²	6	0	3	1	33.8	10.13	36	.429	.556	0	—	-0	-2	-2	0	0.0
1970 LA-N	0	0	—	3	0	0	0	0	6²	11	0	5	6	21.6	9.45	41	.379	.471	0	.000	-0	-4	-4	-0	0.0
Total 7	8	19	.296	67	33	3	0	1	238¹	265	21	145	184	15.7	5.70	62	.281	.381	15	.231	2	-64	-57	1	-5.4

● JOHN STERLING Sterling, John A. b: Philadelphia, Pa. Deb: 10/12/1890

| 1890 Phi-a | 0 | 1 | .000 | 1 | 1 | 1 | 0 | 0 | 5 | 16 | 1 | 4 | 1 | 37.8 | 21.60 | 18 | .519 | .586 | 0 | .000 | -0 | -10 | -10 | -0 | -1.0 |

● RANDY STERLING Sterling, Randall Wayne b: 4/21/51, Key West, Fla. BB/TR, 6'2", 195 lbs. Deb: 9/16/74

| 1974 NY-N | 1 | 1 | .500 | 3 | 2 | 0 | 0 | 0 | 9¹ | 13 | 0 | 3 | 2 | 16.4 | 4.82 | 74 | .351 | .415 | 0 | .000 | -0 | -1 | -1 | 0 | -0.2 |

● DAVE STEVENS Stevens, David James b: 3/4/70, Fullerton, Cal. BR/TR, 6'3", 210 lbs. Deb: 5/20/94

| 1994 Min-A | 5 | 2 | .714 | 24 | 0 | 0 | 0 | 0 | 45 | 55 | 6 | 23 | 24 | 15.8 | 6.80 | 71 | .302 | .383 | 0 | — | 0 | -10 | -10 | -1 | -1.2 |

● JIM STEVENS Stevens, James Arthur "Steve" b: 8/25/1889, Williamsburg, Md. d: 9/25/66, Baltimore, Md. BR/TR, 5'11", 180 lbs. Deb: 8/24/14

| 1914 Was-A | 0 | 0 | — | 2 | 0 | 0 | 0 | 0 | 3 | 4 | 0 | 2 | 0 | 21.0 | 9.00 | 31 | .364 | .500 | 0 | .000 | -0 | -2 | -2 | -0 | 0.0 |

● DAVE STEWART Stewart, David Keith b: 2/19/57, Oakland, Cal. BR/TR, 6'2", 200 lbs. Deb: 9/22/78

1978 LA-N	0	0	—	1	0	0	0	0	2	1	0	1	1	4.5	0.00	—	.167	.167	0	—	0	1	1	-0	0.0
1981 *LA-N	4	3	.571	32	0	0	0	6	43¹	40	3	14	29	11.2	2.49	133	.250	.310	2	.400	2	5	4	0	1.0
1982 LA-N	9	8	.529	45	14	0	0	1	146¹	137	14	49	80	11.6	3.81	91	.249	.313	7	.179	1	-3	-6	-1	-0.6
1983 LA-N	5	2	.714	46	1	0	0	8	76	67	4	33	54	12.1	2.96	121	.237	.321	1	.143	-0	6	5	-1	0.5
Tex-A	5	2	.714	8	8	2	0	0	59	50	2	17	24	10.5	2.14	188	.233	.295	0	—	0	13	12	0	1.5
1984 Tex-A	7	14	.333	32	27	3	0	0	192¹	193	26	87	119	13.3	4.73	88	.258	.339	0	—	0	-16	-12	-1	-1.4
1985 Tex-A	0	6	.000	42	5	0	0	4	81¹	86	13	37	64	13.8	5.42	78	.273	.353	0	—	0	-12	-11	-0	-0.8
Phi-N	0	0	—	4	0	0	0	0	4¹	5	0	4	2	18.7	6.23	59	.278	.409	0	—	0	-1	-1	-0	0.0
1986 Phi-N	0	0	—	8	0	0	0	0	12¹	15	1	4	9	13.9	6.57	59	.306	.358	0	—	0	-4	-4	-0	0.0
Oak-A	9	5	.643	29	17	4	1	0	149¹	137	15	65	102	12.4	3.74	103	.241	.322	0	—	0	7	2	-0	0.2
1987 Oak-A	**20**	13	.606	37	37	8	1	0	261¹	224	24	105	205	11.5	3.68	112	.229	.307	0	—	0	22	13	-3	1.5
1988 *Oak-A	21	12	.636	37	37	**14**	2	0	**275²**	240	14	110	192	11.5	3.23	117	.234	.310	0	—	0	22	17	-3	1.7
1989 *Oak-A★	21	9	.700	36	36	8	0	0	257²	260	23	69	155	11.7	3.32	111	.263	.315	0	—	0	16	10	-1	1.2
1990 *Oak-A	22	11	.667	36	36	**11**	**4**	0	**267**	226	16	83	166	10.6	2.56	145	.231	.294	0	—	0	40	34	-2	4.1
1991 Oak-A	11	11	.500	35	35	2	1	0	226	245	24	105	144	14.3	5.18	74	.278	.361	0	—	0	-27	-34	-2	-3.0
1992 *Oak-A	12	10	.545	31	31	6	0	0	199¹	175	25	79	130	11.8	3.66	102	.237	.318	0	—	0	6	2	-3	0.1
1993 *Tor-A	12	8	.600	26	26	0	0	0	162	146	23	72	96	12.3	4.44	97	.242	.326	0	—	0	-2	-2	-0	-0.5
1994 Tor-A	7	8	.467	22	22	1	0	0	133¹	151	26	62	111	14.6	5.87	82	.285	.364	0	—	0	-16	-16	0	-1.5
Total 15	165	122	.575	507	332	55	9	19	2548²	2398	253	995	1683	12.2	3.86	101	.249	.323	10	.196	2	57	15	-20	4.0

● FRANK STEWART Stewart, Frank "Stewy" b: 9/8/06, Minneapolis, Minn. BR/TR, 6'1.5", 180 lbs. Deb: 10/2/27

| 1927 Chi-A | 0 | 1 | .000 | 1 | 1 | 0 | 0 | 0 | 4 | 5 | 0 | 4 | 0 | 20.3 | 9.00 | 45 | .357 | .500 | 0 | .000 | -0 | -2 | -2 | 1 | -0.4 |

● JOE STEWART Stewart, Joseph Lawrence "Ace" b: 3/11/1879, Monroe, N.C. d: 2/9/13, Youngstown, Ohio TR , 5'11", 175 lbs. Deb: 9/13/04

| 1904 Bos-N | 0 | 0 | — | 2 | 0 | 0 | 0 | 0 | 9¹ | 12 | 0 | 4 | 1 | 16.4 | 9.64 | 29 | .286 | .362 | 1 | .200 | -0 | -7 | -7 | -0 | 0.0 |

● SAMMY STEWART Stewart, Samuel Lee b: 10/28/54, Asheville, N.C. BR/TR, 6'3", 208 lbs. Deb: 9/1/78

1978 Bal-A	1	1	.500	2	2	0	0	0	11¹	11	0	6	11	10.3	3.18	110	.238	.289	0	—	0	1	0	0	0.4
1979 *Bal-A	8	5	.615	31	3	1	0	1	117²	96	11	71	71	13.2	3.52	114	.232	.351	0	—	0	9	6	3	1.0
1980 Bal-A	7	7	.500	33	3	2	0	3	118²	103	9	60	78	12.5	3.56	111	.235	.330	0	—	0	6	5	-0	0.6
1981 Bal-A	4	8	.333	29	3	0	0	0	112¹	89	8	57	57	11.9	2.32	156	.225	.327	0	—	0	17	16	-0	1.8
1982 Bal-A	10	9	.526	38	12	1	1	5	139	140	9	62	69	13.2	4.14	97	.263	.342	0	—	0	-1	-2	-1	-0.2
1983 *Bal-A	9	4	.692	58	0	0	0	7	144¹	138	7	67	95	12.8	3.62	109	.253	.336	0	—	0	7	5	-1	0.4
1984 Bal-A	7	4	.636	60	0	0	0	13	93	81	7	47	56	12.5	3.29	118	.241	.336	0	—	0	7	6	0	0.9
1985 Bal-A	5	7	.417	56	1	0	0	0	129²	117	15	66	77	12.8	3.61	112	.246	.339	0	—	0	8	6	-1	0.6
1986 Bos-A	4	1	.800	27	0	0	0	0	63²	64	7	48	47	15.8	4.38	95	.266	.388	0	—	0	-1	-2	-0	-0.2
1987 Cle-A	4	2	.667	25	0	0	0	3	27	25	4	21	25	15.7	5.67	80	.234	.364	0	—	0	-4	-3	-0	-0.7
Total 10	59	48	.551	359	25	4	1	45	956²	863	77	502	586	13.0	3.59	110	.245	.341	0	—	0	49	39	1	4.6

YEAR TM/L	W	L	PCT	G	GS	CG	SH	SV	IP	H	HR	BB	SO	RAT	ERA	ERA+	OAV	OOB	BH	AVG	PB	PR	/A	PD	TPI

● BUNKY STEWART   Stewart, Veston Goff b: 1/7/31, Jasper, N.C.   BL/TL, 6', 155 lbs.   Deb: 5/4/52

1952 Was-A	0	0	—	1	0	0	0	0	1	2	0	1	1	27.0	18.00	20	.500	.600	0	—	-0	-2	-2	0	-0.2
1953 Was-A	0	2	.000	2	2	1	0	0	15¹	17	1	11	3	17.0	4.70	83	.283	.403	1	.200	-0	-1	-1	-0	-0.2
1954 Was-A	0	2	.000	29	2	0	0	1	50²	67	3	27	27	17.4	7.64	47	.324	.412	0	.000	0	-22	-23	1	-0.8
1955 Was-A	0	0	—	7	1	0	0	0	15¹	18	0	6	10	14.1	4.11	93	.295	.358	0	-0	-0	-0	-0	0	-0.0
1956 Was-A	5	7	.417	33	9	1	0	2	105	111	15	82	36	17.0	5.57	78	.276	.405	7	.250	-0	-16	-15	1	-1.4
Total 5	5	11	.313	72	14	2	0	3	187¹	215	19	127	77	16.9	6.01	67	.293	.404	8	.211	-0	-42	-41	2	-2.4

● LEFTY STEWART   Stewart, Walter Cleveland b: 9/23/1900, Sparta, Tenn.   d: 9/26/74, Knoxville, Tenn.   BR/TL, 5'10", 160 lbs.   Deb: 4/20/21

1921 Det-A	0	0	—	5	0	0	0	1	9	20	0	5	4	25.0	12.00	36	.455	.510	0	.000	-0	-8	-8	0	-0.2
1927 StL-A	8	11	.421	27	19	11	0	1	155²	187	7	43	43	13.4	4.28	102	.310	.357	15	.306	3	-2	1	2	0.5
1928 StL-A	7	9	.438	29	17	7	1	3	142²	173	5	32	25	13.1	4.67	90	.310	.350	14	.275	4	-10	-7	-0	-0.5
1929 StL-A	9	6	.600	23	18	8	1	0	149²	137	11	49	47	11.4	3.25	136	.246	.312	6	.118	-4	17	20	-0	1.3
1930 StL-A	20	12	.625	35	33	23	1	0	271	281	21	70	79	11.7	3.45	141	.268	.315	22	.244	2	36	43	0	4.7
1931 StL-A	14	17	.452	36	33	20	1	0	258	287	17	85	89	13.1	4.40	105	.277	.334	22	.250	6	-0	7	1	1.4
1932 StL-A	15	19	.441	41	32	18	2	1	259²	269	22	99	86	12.9	4.61	105	.270	.338	12	.146	-2	-4	-1	-0	0.6
1933 *Was-A	15	6	.714	34	31	11	1	0	230²	227	19	60	69	11.2	3.82	109	.256	.304	11	.143	1	12	9	1	0.8
1934 Was-A	7	11	.389	24	22	7	1	0	152	184	8	36	46	13.1	4.03	107	.303	.343	7	.156	-1	8	5	-0	0.3
1935 Was-A	0	1	.000	1	1	0	0	0	2²	8	1	2	1	33.8	13.50	32	.533	.588	0	.000	-0	-3	-3	-0	-0.6
Cle-A	6	6	.500	24	10	2	0	2	91	122	6	17	18	13.8	5.44	83	.312	.342	6	.200	-1	-10	-9	-1	-1.3
Yr	6	7	.462	25	11	2	0	2	93²	130	7	19	25	14.4	5.67	79	.320	.352	6	.194	-1	-13	-12	-1	-1.9
Total 10	101	98	.508	279	216	107	8	8	1722	1895	117	498	503	12.6	4.19	108	.281	.332	115	.204	6	35	64	0	7.0

● MACK STEWART   Stewart, William Macklin b: 9/23/14, Stevenson, Ala.   d: 3/21/60, Macon, Ga.   BR/TR, 6', 167 lbs.   Deb: 7/7/44

1944 Chi-N	0	0	—	8	0	0	0	0	12¹	11	1	4	3	10.9	1.46	242	.239	.300	0	.000	-0	3	3	-0	0.0
1945 Chi-N	0	1	.000	16	1	0	0	0	28¹	37	0	14	9	14.6	4.76	77	.322	.395	1	.333	0	-3	-4	0	-0.1
Total 2	0	1	.000	24	1	0	0	0	40²	48	1	18	12	14.6	3.76	96	.298	.369	1	.250	-0	-0	-1	0	-0.1

● PHIL STIDHAM   Stidham, Phillip Wayne b: 11/18/68, Tulsa, Okla.   BR/TR, 6', 180 lbs.   Deb: 6/4/94

| 1994 Det-A | 0 | 0 | — | 5 | 0 | 0 | 0 | 0 | 4¹ | 12 | 3 | 4 | 4 | 33.2 | 24.92 | 19 | .571 | .640 | 0 | — | 0 | -10 | -10 | 0 | 0.0 |

● DAVE STIEB   Stieb, David Andrew b: 7/22/57, Santa Ana, Cal.   BR/TR, 6'1", 195 lbs.   Deb: 6/29/79

1979 Tor-A	8	8	.500	18	18	7	1	0	129¹	139	11	48	52	13.3	4.31	101	.276	.344	18	—	0	-1	-3	3	0.3
1980 Tor-A★	12	15	.444	34	32	14	4	0	242²	232	12	83	108	11.9	3.71	116	.260	.327	0	.000	0	9	16	5	2.2
1981 Tor-A★	11	10	.524	25	25	11	2	0	183²	148	10	61	89	10.8	3.19	124	.223	.299	0	—	0	10	15	2	1.9
1982 Tor-A	17	14	.548	38	38	19	5	0	288¹	271	27	75	141	11.0	3.25	138	.248	.299	0	—	0	27	39	4	4.2
1983 Tor-A	17	12	.586	36	36	14	4	0	278	223	21	93	187	10.7	3.04	141	.219	.293	0	—	0	31	39	1	3.9
1984 Tor-A★	16	8	.667	35	35	11	2	0	267	215	19	88	198	10.6	2.83	145	.221	.293	0	—	0	34	37	1	3.3
1985 *Tor-A★	14	13	.519	36	36	8	2	0	265	206	22	96	167	10.6	2.48	170	.213	.290	0	—	0	49	51	5	5.5
1986 Tor-A	7	12	.368	37	34	1	1	1	205	239	29	87	127	15.0	4.74	89	.297	.376	0	—	0	-13	-12	1	-0.8
1987 Tor-A	13	9	.591	33	31	3	1	0	185	164	16	87	115	12.6	4.09	110	.239	.331	0	—	0	8	8	1	1.0
1988 Tor-A★	16	8	.667	32	31	8	4	0	207¹	157	15	79	147	10.8	3.04	129	.210	.296	0	—	0	21	21	1	2.3
1989 *Tor-A	17	8	.680	33	33	3	2	0	206²	164	12	76	101	11.0	3.35	112	.219	.302	0	—	0	12	10	0	1.2
1990 Tor-A	18	6	.750	33	33	2	2	0	208²	179	11	64	125	10.9	2.93	134	.230	.297	0	—	0	23	23	3	2.9
1991 Tor-A	4	3	.571	9	9	1	0	0	59²	52	4	23	29	11.6	3.17	133	.243	.322	0	—	0	6	7	1	0.8
1992 Tor-A	4	6	.400	21	14	1	0	0	96¹	98	9	43	45	13.5	5.04	81	.275	.359	0	—	0	-12	-10	2	-0.9
1993 Chi-A	1	3	.250	22	11	0	0	0	22¹	27	1	14	11	16.5	6.04	69	.300	.394	0	—	0	-4	-5	-0	-0.6
Total 15	175	135	.565	424	409	103	30	1	2845	2514	219	1017	1642	11.6	3.41	122	.239	.313	0	.000	0	199	240	29	27.2

● FRED STIELY   Stiely, Fred Warren "Lefty" b: 6/1/01, Pillow, Pa.   d: 1/6/81, Valley View, Pa.   BL/TL, 5'8", 170 lbs.   Deb: 10/6/29

1929 StL-A	1	0	1.000	1	1	1	0	0	9	11	0	3	2	15.0	0.00	—	.297	.366	2	.667	1	4	4	0	0.7
1930 StL-A	0	1	.000	4	2	1	0	0	19	27	4	8	5	17.1	8.53	57	.346	.414	3	.429	1	-8	-8	-0	-0.2
1931 StL-A	0	0	—	4	0	0	0	0	6²	7	0	3	2	14.9	6.75	69	.269	.367	0	—	0	-2	-2	-0	0.0
Total 3	1	1	.500	9	3	2	0	0	34²	45	4	14	9	16.1	5.97	79	.319	.392	5	.500	2	-6	-5	-1	0.5

● DICK STIGMAN   Stigman, Richard Lewis b: 1/24/36, Nimrod, Minn.   BR/TL, 6'3", 200 lbs.   Deb: 4/22/60

1960 Cle-A☆	5	11	.313	41	18	3	0	9	133²	118	13	87	104	13.8	4.51	83	.238	.352	8	.222	2	-9	-11	-2	-1.4
1961 Cle-A	2	5	.286	22	6	0	0	0	64¹	65	9	25	48	12.6	4.62	85	.264	.332	2	.125	-1	-4	-5	0	-0.5
1962 Min-A	12	5	.706	40	15	6	0	3	142²	122	19	64	116	11.9	3.66	112	.233	.319	2	.044	-4	5	7	-2	0.2
1963 Min-A	15	15	.500	33	33	15	3	0	241	210	32	81	193	10.9	3.25	112	.231	.294	9	.107	-2	10	11	-4	0.6
1964 Min-A	6	15	.286	32	29	5	1	0	190	160	31	70	159	11.1	4.03	89	.225	.299	7	.101	-3	-8	-9	-3	-1.5
1965 Min-A	4	2	.667	33	8	0	0	4	70	59	14	33	70	11.8	4.37	81	.227	.314	2	.133	-0	-7	-6	-1	-0.7
1966 Bos-A	2	1	.667	34	10	1	1	0	81	85	15	46	65	14.7	5.44	70	.268	.363	2	.118	-1	-18	-15	-1	-0.7
Total 7	46	54	.460	235	119	30	5	16	922²	819	133	406	755	12.0	4.03	93	.237	.318	32	.113	-8	-32	-29	-13	-4.0

● ROLLIE STILES   Stiles, Rolland Mays "Lena" b: 11/17/06, Ratcliff, Ark.   BR/TR, 6'1.5", 180 lbs.   Deb: 6/19/30

1930 StL-A	3	6	.333	20	7	3	0	0	102	136	10	41	25	15.7	5.91	82	.337	.399	10	.270	-0	-14	-12	-1	-0.9
1931 StL-A	3	1	.750	34	2	0	0	0	81	112	6	60	32	19.3	7.22	64	.352	.458	1	.045	-2	-26	-23	-0	-1.2
1933 StL-A	3	7	.300	31	9	6	1	1	115	154	0	47	29	15.9	5.01	93	.327	.390	2	.061	-3	-9	-5	-1	-0.7
Total 3	9	14	.391	85	18	9	1	1	298	402	16	148	86	16.8	5.92	80	.337	.412	13	.141	-5	-49	-40	-2	-2.8

● ARCHIE STIMMEL   Stimmel, Archibald May "Lumbago" b: 5/30/1873, Woodsboro, Md.   d: 8/18/58, Frederick, Md.   BR/TR, 6', 175 lbs.   Deb: 7/3/00

1900 Cin-N	1	1	.500	2	1	1	0	0	13	18	1	4	2	15.2	6.92	53	.327	.373	1	.200	-0	-5	-5	-0	-0.6
1901 Cin-N	4	14	.222	20	18	14	1	0	153¹	170	10	44	55	13.3	4.11	78	.279	.340	5	.081	-5	-13	-15	-3	-2.2
1902 Cin-N	0	4	.000	4	3	3	0	0	26	37	1	12	7	17.7	3.46	87	.334	.408	2	.200	-0	-2	-1	-0	-0.2
Total 3	5	19	.208	26	22	18	1	0	192¹	225	12	60	64	14.0	4.21	76	.290	.352	8	.104	-5	-20	-21	-3	-3.0

● CARL STIMSON   Stimson, Carl Remus b: 7/18/1894, Hamburg, Iowa   d: 11/9/36, Omaha, Neb.   BB/TR, 6'5", 190 lbs.   Deb: 6/6/23

| 1923 Bos-A | 0 | 0 | — | 2 | 0 | 0 | 0 | 0 | 4 | 12 | 0 | 5 | 1 | 40.5 | 22.50 | 18 | .750 | .818 | 0 | .000 | -0 | -8 | -8 | 0 | 0.0 |

● HARRY STINE   Stine, Harry C. b: 2/20/1864, Shenandoah, Pa.   d: 6/5/24, Niagara Falls, N.Y.   TL, 5'6", 150 lbs.   Deb: 7/22/1890

| 1890 Phi-a | 0 | 1 | .000 | 1 | 1 | 1 | 0 | 0 | 8 | 17 | 0 | 4 | 1 | 23.6 | 9.00 | 43 | .418 | .470 | 0 | .000 | -0 | -5 | -5 | -0 | -0.4 |

● LEE STINE   Stine, Lee Elbert b: 11/17/13, Stillwater, Okla.   BR/TR, 5'11", 185 lbs.   Deb: 4/17/34

1934 Chi-A	0	0	—	4	0	0	0	0	11	11	2	10	8	18.0	8.18	58	.268	.423	0	.000	-0	-5	-4	-0	0.0
1935 Chi-A	0	0	—	1	0	0	0	0	2	2	1	3	1	22.5	9.00	51	.286	.500	0	—	-1	-1	-1	0	0.1
1936 Cin-N	3	8	.273	40	13	5	1	2	121²	157	6	41	26	15.2	5.03	76	.318	.379	8	.296	3	-14	-16	2	-0.9
1938 NY-A	0	0	—	4	0	0	0	0	8²	9	0	1	4	10.4	1.04	437	.333	.357	1	.500	0	4	3	0	0.0
Total 4	3	8	.273	49	13	5	1	2	143¹	179	9	55	39	15.3	5.09	78	.315	.384	9	.300	2	-16	-18	2	-0.8

● JACK STIVETTS   Stivetts, John Elmer "Happy Jack" b: 3/31/1868, Ashland, Pa.   d: 4/18/30, Ashland, Pa.   BR/TR, 6'2", 185 lbs.   Deb: 6/26/1889 ♦

1889 StL-a	12	7	.632	26	20	18	2	1	191²	174	4	68	143	10.6	2.25	188	.212	.285	18	.228	17	34	42	0	3.3
1890 StL-a	27	21	.563	54	46	41	3	0	419¹	399	14	179	289	12.5	3.52	123	.243	.324	65	.288	14	16	37	3	4.9
1891 StL-a	33	22	.600	64	56	40	3	0	440	357	15	232	259	12.4	2.86	147	.214	.317	92	.305	9	42	66	3	7.7
1892 *Bos-N	35	16	.686	54	48	45	3	1	415²	346	12	171	180	11.4	3.03	116	.217	.297	71	.296	15	12	22	1	3.7

YEAR	TM/L	W	L	PCT	G	GS	CG	SH	SV	IP	H	HR	BB	SO	RAT	ERA	ERA+	OAV	OOB	BH	AVG	PB	PR	/A	PD	TPI
1893	Bos-N	20	12	.625	38	34	29	1	1	283²	315	17	115	61	14.0	4.41	112	.273	.344	51	.297	7	8	17	-2	1.7
1894	Bos-N	26	14	.650	45	39	30	0	0	338	429	27	127	76	15.2	4.90	116	.306	.369	80	.328	10	16	29	-3	3.0
1895	Bos-N	17	17	.500	38	34	30	0	0	291	341	15	89	111	13.7	4.64	110	.288	.344	30	.190	-7	5	15	-1	0.5
1896	Bos-N	22	14	.611	42	36	31	2	0	329	353	20	99	71	12.6	4.10	111	.272	.327	76	.344	11	9	16	-3	2.1
1897	*Bos-N	11	4	.733	18	15	10	0	0	129¹	147	5	43	27	13.6	3.41	131	.284	.344	73	.367	7	13	15	1	2.1
1898	Bos-N	0	1	.000	2	1	1	0	0	12	17	2	7	1	18.0	8.25	45	.331	.411	28	.252	0	-6	-6	0	-0.3
1899	Cle-N	7	4	.800	7	4	3	0	0	48	56	0	25	5	17.8	5.68	65	.308	.410	8	.205	1	-8	-2	2	-0.3
Total	11	203	132	.606	388	333	278	14	4	2887²	2905	131	1155	1223	13.0	3.74	121	.255	.329	592	.297	65	141	247	0	28.2

● CHUCK STOBBS

Stobbs, Charles Klein b: 7/2/29, Wheeling, W.Va.   BL/TL, 6'1", 185 lbs.   Deb: 9/15/47

YEAR	TM/L	W	L	PCT	G	GS	CG	SH	SV	IP	H	HR	BB	SO	RAT	ERA	ERA+	OAV	OOB	BH	AVG	PB	PR	/A	PD	TPI
1947	Bos-A	0	1	.000	4	1	0	0	0	9	10	0	10	5	20.0	6.00	65	.294	.455	0	.000	-0	-2	-2	0	-0.2
1948	Bos-A	0	0	—	6	0	0	0	0	7	9	0	7	4	20.6	6.43	68	.321	.457	0	.000	-0	-2	-2	0	0.0
1949	Bos-A	11	6	.647	26	19	10	0	0	152	145	10	75	70	13.1	4.03	108	.254	.343	11	.208	-0	3	6	-1	0.5
1950	Bos-A	12	7	.632	32	21	6	0	1	169¹	158	17	88	78	13.3	5.10	96	.250	.346	14	.246	3	-10	-4	1	0.0
1951	Bos-A	10	9	.526	34	25	6	0	0	170	180	15	74	75	13.7	4.76	94	.271	.349	11	.180	-2	-12	-6	-2	-1.0
1952	Chi-A	7	12	.368	38	17	2	0	0	135	118	9	72	73	13.0	3.13	116	.237	.339	3	.079	-1	8	8	1	1.0
1953	Was-A	11	8	.579	27	20	8	0	0	153	146	11	44	67	11.2	3.29	118	.246	.299	10	.227	1	12	10	-0	1.3
1954	Was-A	11	11	.500	31	24	10	3	0	182	189	6	67	67	12.7	4.10	87	.270	.335	7	.137	0	-8	-11	-1	-1.1
1955	Was-A	4	14	.222	41	16	2	0	3	140¹	169	13	57	60	14.6	5.00	77	.302	.368	6	.171	2	-16	-18	1	-1.8
1956	Was-A	15	15	.500	37	33	15	1	1	240	264	29	54	97	12.0	3.60	120	.279	.328	15	.179	-2	15	19	1	2.1
1957	Was-A	8	20	.286	42	31	5	2	1	211²	235	28	80	114	13.6	5.36	73	.279	.345	16	.211	1	-37	-34	-3	-4.2
1958	Was-A	2	6	.250	19	8	0	0	0	56²	87	7	16	23	16.7	6.04	63	.369	.413	0	.000	-2	-14	-14	0	-1.9
	StL-N	1	3	.250	17	0	0	0	0	39²	40	4	14	25	12.3	3.63	114	.261	.323	1	.250	0	1	2	1	0.3
1959	Was-A	1	8	.111	41	7	0	0	7	90²	82	13	24	50	10.7	2.98	131	.238	.291	2	.105	-1	9	9	-0	0.8
1960	Was-A	12	7	.632	40	13	1	1	2	119¹	115	13	38	72	11.8	3.32	117	.252	.313	3	.088	-2	7	8	-2	0.8
1961	Min-A	2	3	.400	24	3	0	0	2	44²	56	8	15	17	14.7	7.46	57	.311	.371	3	.375	1	-17	-16	-1	-1.7
Total	15	107	130	.451	459	238	65	7	19	1920¹	2003	183	735	897	13.0	4.29	95	.269	.338	102	.176	-1	-63	-46	-3	-5.0

● WES STOCK

Stock, Wesley Gay b: 4/10/34, Longview, Wash.   BR/TR, 6'2", 188 lbs.   Deb: 4/19/59   C

YEAR	TM/L	W	L	PCT	G	GS	CG	SH	SV	IP	H	HR	BB	SO	RAT	ERA	ERA+	OAV	OOB	BH	AVG	PB	PR	/A	PD	TPI
1959	Bal-A	0	0	—	7	0	0	0	0	12²	16	1	2	8	12.8	3.55	107	.302	.327	0	.000	-0	0	0	-0	0.0
1960	Bal-A	2	2	.500	17	0	0	0	2	34¹	26	2	14	23	10.7	2.88	132	.218	.306	0	.000	-0	4	4	1	0.4
1961	Bal-A	5	0	1.000	35	1	0	0	3	71²	58	3	27	47	10.9	3.01	128	.225	.303	0	.000	-1	8	7	2	0.6
1962	Bal-A	3	2	.600	53	0	0	0	3	65	50	7	36	34	12.0	4.43	83	.217	.326	0	.000	-0	-3	-5	3	-0.1
1963	Bal-A	7	0	1.000	47	0	0	0	1	75¹	69	11	31	55	11.9	3.94	88	.246	.321	0	.000	-1	-3	-4	1	-0.4
1964	Bal-A	2	0	1.000	14	0	0	0	0	20²	17	5	8	14	10.9	3.92	91	.233	.309	0	.000	-1	-1	-0	1	-0.1
	KC-A	6	3	.667	50	0	0	0	5	93	69	10	34	101	10.4	1.94	197	.213	.296	3	.200	0	17	19	-1	2.0
	Yr	8	3	.727	64	0	0	0	5	113²	86	15	42	115	10.5	2.30	164	.216	.297	3	.158	-0	17	19	-0	1.9
1965	KC-A	0	4	.000	62	0	0	0	4	99²	96	18	40	52	12.6	5.24	67	.251	.328	0	.000	-1	-20	-19	2	-0.8
1966	KC-A	2	2	.500	35	0	0	0	3	44	30	3	21	31	11.0	2.66	128	.199	.309	0	.000	-0	4	4	-0	0.3
1967	KC-A	0	0	—	1	0	0	0	0	1	3	0	2	0	45.0	18.00	18	.500	.625	0	—	0	-2	-2	-0	0.0
Total	9	27	13	.675	321	3	0	0	22	517¹	434	60	215	365	11.6	3.60	101	.231	.315	3	.051	-4	6	3	7	1.9

● OTIS STOCKSDALE

Stocksdale, Otis Hinkley "Old Gray Fox"
b: 8/7/1871, Near Arcadia, Md.   d: 3/15/33, Pennsville, N.J.   BL/TR, 5'10.5", 180 lbs.   Deb: 7/24/1893

YEAR	TM/L	W	L	PCT	G	GS	CG	SH	SV	IP	H	HR	BB	SO	RAT	ERA	ERA+	OAV	OOB	BH	AVG	PB	PR	/A	PD	TPI
1893	Was-N	2	8	.200	11	11	7	0	0	69	111	4	32	12	19.3	8.22	56	.352	.420	12	.300	2	-27	-28	1	-2.5
1894	Was-N	5	9	.357	18	14	11	0	0	117¹	176	10	42	10	17.8	5.06	104	.342	.407	23	.324	1	3	3	1	0.3
1895	Was-N	6	11	.353	20	17	11	0	1	136	199	7	52	23	17.1	6.09	79	.335	.396	23	.311	2	-20	-19	-0	-1.5
	Bos-N	2	2	.500	4	4	1	0	0	23	31	2	8	2	15.3	5.87	87	.317	.369	4	.267	0	-3	-2	-0	-0.3
	Yr	8	13	.381	24	21	12	0	1	159	230	9	60	25	16.4	6.06	80	.329	.382	27	.303	2	-23	-21	-1	-1.8
1896	Bal-N	1	0	1.000	1	0	0	0	0	2	4	0	2	1	37.8	16.20	26	.455	.594	1	.333	1	-2	-2	-0	-0.7
Total	4	15	31	.326	54	46	30	0	1	347	521	23	136	48	17.6	6.20	80	.341	.405	63	.310	5	-49	-48	1	-4.7

● BOB STODDARD

Stoddard, Robert Lyle b: 3/8/57, San Jose, Cal.   BR/TR, 6'1", 200 lbs.   Deb: 9/4/81

YEAR	TM/L	W	L	PCT	G	GS	CG	SH	SV	IP	H	HR	BB	SO	RAT	ERA	ERA+	OAV	OOB	BH	AVG	PB	PR	/A	PD	TPI
1981	Sea-A	2	1	.667	5	5	1	0	0	34²	35	3	9	22	11.7	2.60	148	.269	.321	0		0	4	5	-0	0.4
1982	Sea-A	3	3	.500	9	9	2	1	0	67¹	48	7	18	24	9.2	2.41	176	.205	.271	0	—	0	12	14	0	1.2
1983	Sea-A	9	17	.346	35	23	2	1	0	175²	182	29	58	87	12.5	4.41	97	.274	.336	0	—	0	-3	-3	3	-0.1
1984	Sea-A	2	3	.400	27	6	0	0	0	79	86	10	37	39	14.2	5.13	78	.274	.359	0	—	0	-10	-10	1	-0.5
1985	Det-A	0	0	—	8	0	0	0	0	13¹	15	3	5	11	13.5	6.75	60	.268	.328	0	—	0	-4	-4	1	0.0
1986	SD-N	1	0	1.000	18	0	0	0	0	23¹	20	1	11	17	12.3	2.31	158	.227	.320	0	.000	-0	4	3	-0	0.1
1987	KC-A	1	3	.250	17	2	0	0	1	40	51	3	22	23	17.1	4.27	107	.313	.404	0	—	-0	0	1	1	0.2
Total	7	18	27	.400	119	45	5	2	3	433¹	437	56	160	223	12.7	4.03	103	.266	.336	0	.000	-0	0	6	5	1.3

● TIM STODDARD

Stoddard, Timothy Paul b: 1/24/53, E.Chicago, Ind.   BR/TR, 6'7", 250 lbs.   Deb: 9/7/75

YEAR	TM/L	W	L	PCT	G	GS	CG	SH	SV	IP	H	HR	BB	SO	RAT	ERA	ERA+	OAV	OOB	BH	AVG	PB	PR	/A	PD	TPI
1975	Chi-A	0	0	—	1	0	0	0	0	1	2	1	0	0	9.00	9.00	40	.400	.400	0		0	-1	-1	0	0.0
1978	Bal-A	0	1	.000	8	0	0	0	0	18	22	3	8	14	16.0	6.00	58	.301	.386	0		0	-4	-5	0	0.0
1979	*Bal-A	3	1	.750	29	0	0	0	3	58	44	3	19	47	9.8	1.71	235	.212	.278	0		0	16	15	-0	1.2
1980	Bal-A	5	3	.625	64	0	0	0	26	86	72	2	38	64	11.6	2.51	157	.233	.319	0		0	15	14	-1	2.1
1981	Bal-A	4	2	.667	31	0	0	0	7	37¹	38	6	18	32	14.0	3.86	94	.268	.358	0		0	-1	-1	-0	-0.2
1982	Bal-A	3	4	.429	50	0	0	0	12	56	53	4	29	43	13.3	4.02	100	.249	.342	0		0	-0	-0	0	0.0
1983	Bal-A	4	3	.571	47	0	0	0	9	57²	65	10	29	50	14.8	6.09	65	.293	.377	0		0	-13	-14	0	-1.9
1984	*Chi-N	10	6	.625	58	0	0	0	7	92	77	9	57	87	13.2	3.82	102	.236	.352	1	.091	-1	-2	-1	-1	-1.0
1985	SD-N	1	6	.143	44	0	0	0	0	60	63	9	37	42	15.0	4.65	76	.269	.369	0	.000	-1	-7	-7	-1	-1.0
1986	SD-N	1	3	.250	30	0	0	0	0	45¹	33	6	34	47	13.3	3.77	97	.200	.337	1	.250	1	-0	-1	0	0.1
	NY-A	4	1	.800	24	0	0	0	4	49¹	41	6	23	34	11.7	3.83	107	.232	.320	0		0	0	0	1	0.1
1987	NY-A	4	3	.571	57	0	0	0	8	92²	83	13	30	78	11.0	3.50	125	.235	.295	0		0	10	9	-1	0.7
1988	NY-A	2	2	.500	28	0	0	0	3	55	62	6	27	33	14.9	6.38	62	.286	.370	0		0	-15	-15	0	-1.1
1989	Cle-A	0	0	—	14	0	0	0	0	21¹	26	1	7	12	13.5	2.95	134	.313	.368	0		0	2	2	-0	-0.1
Total	13	41	35	.539	485	0	0	0	76	729²	680	72	356	582	12.9	3.95	100	.250	.339	2	.100	-1	-2	-0	-3	-0.1

● ART STOKES

Stokes, Arthur Milton b: 9/13/1896, Emmitsburg, Md.   d: 6/3/62, Titusville, Pa.   BR/TR, 5'10.5", 155 lbs.   Deb: 5/5/25

YEAR	TM/L	W	L	PCT	G	GS	CG	SH	SV	IP	H	HR	BB	SO	RAT	ERA	ERA+	OAV	OOB	BH	AVG	PB	PR	/A	PD	TPI
1925	Phi-A	1	1	.500	12	0	0	0	0	24¹	24	0	10	7	13.3	4.07	114	.270	.356	0	.000	-0	1	-0	-0	0.0

● DICK STONE

Stone, Charles Richard b: 12/5/11, Oklahoma City, Okla   d: 2/18/80, Oklahoma City, Okla.   BL/TL, 5'9", 153 lbs.   Deb: 8/26/45

YEAR	TM/L	W	L	PCT	G	GS	CG	SH	SV	IP	H	HR	BB	SO	RAT	ERA	ERA+	OAV	OOB	BH	AVG	PB	PR	/A	PD	TPI
1945	Was-A	0	0	—	3	0	0	0	0	5	6	0	2	0	14.4	0.00	—	.316	.381	0	—	0	2	2	0	0.0

● DEAN STONE

Stone, Darrah Dean b: 9/1/30, Moline, Ill.   BL/TL, 6'4", 205 lbs.   Deb: 9/13/53

YEAR	TM/L	W	L	PCT	G	GS	CG	SH	SV	IP	H	HR	BB	SO	RAT	ERA	ERA+	OAV	OOB	BH	AVG	PB	PR	/A	PD	TPI
1953	Was-A	0	1	.000	3	1	0	0	0	8²	13	1	6	5	18.7	8.31	47	.361	.439	0	.000	-0	-4	-4	0	-0.4
1954	Was-A★	12	10	.545	31	23	10	2	0	178²	161	7	69	87	11.6	3.22	110	.240	.312	5	.096	-0	10	7	-3	0.5
1955	Was-A	6	13	.316	43	24	5	1	0	180	180	14	114	84	14.9	4.15	92	.267	.375	2	.043	-4	-6	-2	1	-1.1
1956	Was-A	5	7	.417	41	21	2	0	3	132	148	10	93	86	16.9	6.27	69	.282	.397	3	.088	-2	-31	-29	-1	-2.5
1957	Was-A	0	0	—	3	0	0	0	0	3¹	5	0	2	3	18.9	8.10	48	.357	.438	0	—	0	-2	-2	-0	0.0
	Bos-A	1	3	.250	17	8	0	1	0	51¹	56	5	35	35	16.0	5.08	78	.284	.392	0	—	0	-7	-6	1	-0.5
	Yr	1	3	.250	20	8	0	1	0	54²	61	5	37	35	16.1	5.27	73	.290	.397	0	—	0	-8	-8	1	-0.4
1959	StL-N	0	1	.000	18	1	0	0	0	30	30	4	16	17	13.8	4.20	101	.273	.365	0	—	0	-1	0	-0	-0.1
1962	Hou-N	3	2	.600	15	7	2	2	0	52¹	61	4	20	31	14.1	4.47	84	.295	.360	4	.250	1	-3	-4	0	-0.2

YEAR TM/L	W	L	PCT	G	GS	CG	SH	SV	IP	H	HR	BB	SO	RAT	ERA	ERA+	OAV	OOB	BH	AVG	PB	PR	/A	PD	TPI
Chi-A	1	0	1.000	27	0	0	0	5	30¹	28	3	9	23	11.3	3.26	120	.255	.317	1	.500	1	2	2	-0	0.2
1963 Bal-A	1	2	.333	17	0	0	0	0	19¹	23	0	10	12	15.4	5.12	68	.307	.388	0		0	-3	-4	0	-0.5
Total 8	29	39	.426	215	85	19	5	12	686	705	47	373	380	14.3	4.47	86	.269	.363	15	.088	-6	-43	-46	-5	-4.6

● DWIGHT STONE
Stone, Dwight Ely b: 8/2/1886, Holt Co., Neb. d: 6/3/76, Glendale, Cal. BR/TR, 6'1.5", 170 lbs. Deb: 4/13/13

YEAR TM/L	W	L	PCT	G	GS	CG	SH	SV	IP	H	HR	BB	SO	RAT	ERA	ERA+	OAV	OOB	BH	AVG	PB	PR	/A	PD	TPI
1913 StL-A	2	6	.250	18	7	4	1	0	91	94	0	46	37	14.5	3.56	82	.267	.363	9	.273	2	-6	-6	1	-0.2
1914 KC-F	8	14	.364	39	22	6	0	0	186²	205	8	77	88	14.0	4.34	64	.281	.356	7	.121	-4	-30	-32	1	-3.7
Total 2	10	20	.333	57	29	10	1	0	277²	299	8	123	125	14.2	4.08	69	.276	.358	16	.176	-2	-36	-39	2	-3.9

● ARNIE STONE
Stone, Edwin Arnold b: 10/9/1892, North Creek, N.Y. d: 7/29/48, Hudson Falls, N.Y BR/TL, 6', 180 lbs. Deb: 8/7/23

YEAR TM/L	W	L	PCT	G	GS	CG	SH	SV	IP	H	HR	BB	SO	RAT	ERA	ERA+	OAV	OOB	BH	AVG	PB	PR	/A	PD	TPI
1923 Pit-N	0	1	.000	9	0	0	0	0	12¹	19	0	4	2	16.8	8.03	50	.352	.397	0	.000	-0	-6	-6	-1	-0.4
1924 Pit-N	4	2	.667	26	2	1	0	0	64	57	0	15	7	10.1	2.95	130	.259	.306	2	.133	-1	6	6	0	0.4
Total 2	4	3	.571	35	2	1	0	0	76¹	76	0	19	9	11.2	3.77	102	.277	.324	2	.125	-1	1	1	-0	0.0

● GEORGE STONE
Stone, George Heard b: 7/9/46, Ruston, La. BL/TL, 6'3", 205 lbs. Deb: 9/15/67

YEAR TM/L	W	L	PCT	G	GS	CG	SH	SV	IP	H	HR	BB	SO	RAT	ERA	ERA+	OAV	OOB	BH	AVG	PB	PR	/A	PD	TPI
1967 Atl-N	0	0	—	2	1	0	0	0	7¹	8	0	1	5	11.0	4.91	68	.267	.290	0	.000	-0	-1	-1	0	0.0
1968 Atl-N	7	4	.636	17	10	2	0	0	75	52	9	19	52	9.8	2.76	108	.222	.271	9	.333	3	2	2	-1	0.5
1969 *Atl-N	13	10	.565	36	20	3	0	3	165¹	166	20	48	102	11.9	3.65	99	.260	.317	11	.186	1	-1	-1	-1	0.7
1970 Atl-N	11	11	.500	35	30	9	2	0	207¹	218	27	50	131	11.9	3.86	111	.267	.314	17	.236	4	4	10	3	1.6
1971 Atl-N	6	8	.429	27	24	4	2	0	172²	186	19	35	110	11.8	3.60	103	.274	.315	11	.177	-0	-3	2	-0	0.1
1972 Atl-N	6	11	.353	31	16	2	1	1	111	143	18	44	63	15.5	5.51	69	.315	.380	5	.200	1	-25	-21	1	-2.8
1973 *NY-N	12	3	.800	27	20	2	0	1	148	157	16	31	77	11.4	2.80	129	.274	.311	13	.271	2	14	13	1	1.7
1974 NY-N	2	7	.222	15	13	1	0	0	77	103	10	21	29	14.5	5.03	71	.322	.364	3	.115	-1	-12	-13	0	-1.4
1975 NY-N	3	3	.500	13	11	1	0	0	57	75	3	21	21	15.2	5.05	68	.323	.379	3	.167	-0	-9	-10	1	-0.9
Total 9	60	57	.513	203	145	24	5	5	1020²	1119	122	270	590	12.4	3.89	96	.278	.326	72	.212	10	-31	-19	4	-1.2

● ROCKY STONE
Stone, John Vernon b: 8/23/18, Redding, Cal. d: 11/12/86, Fountain Valley, Cal. BR/TR, 6', 200 lbs. Deb: 5/2/43

YEAR TM/L	W	L	PCT	G	GS	CG	SH	SV	IP	H	HR	BB	SO	RAT	ERA	ERA+	OAV	OOB	BH	AVG	PB	PR	/A	PD	TPI
1943 Cin-N	0	1	.000	13	0	0	0	0	24²	23	0	8	11	11.3	4.38	76	.237	.295	1	.250	0	-3	-3	-1	-0.2

● STEVE STONE
Stone, Steven Michael b: 7/14/47, Euclid, Ohio BR/TR, 5'10", 175 lbs. Deb: 4/8/71

YEAR TM/L	W	L	PCT	G	GS	CG	SH	SV	IP	H	HR	BB	SO	RAT	ERA	ERA+	OAV	OOB	BH	AVG	PB	PR	/A	PD	TPI
1971 SF-N	5	9	.357	24	19	2	2	0	110²	110	9	55	63	13.7	4.15	82	.259	.349	0	.000	-2	-8	-9	2	-1.2
1972 SF-N	6	8	.429	27	16	4	1	0	123²	97	11	49	85	10.8	2.98	117	.218	.298	4	.118	-1	6	7	0	0.7
1973 Chi-N	6	11	.353	36	22	3	0	1	176¹	163	11	62	138	12.9	4.24	93	.245	.335	0	—	-0	-8	-5	0	-0.5
1974 Chi-N	8	6	.571	38	23	1	0	0	169²	185	19	64	90	13.4	4.14	92	.278	.345	7	.121	-3	-10	-6	1	-0.7
1975 Chi-N	12	8	.600	33	32	6	1	0	214¹	198	24	80	139	11.9	3.95	97	.245	.317	8	.111	-2	-8	-3	0	-0.4
1976 Chi-N	3	6	.333	17	15	1	1	0	75	70	6	21	33	11.3	4.08	95	.250	.309	3	.143	-1	-5	-2	-1	-0.4
1977 Chi-A	15	12	.556	31	31	8	0	0	207¹	228	25	80	124	13.6	4.51	90	.281	.350	0	—	0	-10	-10	-0	-1.1
1978 Chi-A	12	12	.500	30	30	6	1	0	212	196	19	84	118	12.0	4.37	87	.247	.321	0	—	0	-14	-13	1	-1.5
1979 *Bal-A	11	7	.611	32	32	3	0	0	186	173	31	73	96	12.0	3.77	106	.248	.320	0	—	0	9	5	1	0.6
1980 Bal-A★	25	7	.781	37	37	9	1	0	250²	224	22	101	149	11.9	3.23	122	.240	.319	0	—	0	22	20	-2	2.2
1981 Bal-A	4	7	.364	15	12	0	0	0	62²	63	7	27	30	13.1	4.60	79	.266	.343	0	—	0	-7	-7	-0	-1.1
Total 11	107	93	.535	320	269	43	7	1	1788¹	1707	184	716	1065	12.4	3.97	97	.253	.328	22	.100	-9	-32	-22	-0	-3.4

● TIGE STONE
Stone, William Arthur b: 9/18/01, Macon, Ga. d: 1/1/60, Jacksonville, Fla. BR/TR, 5'8", 145 lbs. Deb: 8/23/23 ♦

YEAR TM/L	W	L	PCT	G	GS	CG	SH	SV	IP	H	HR	BB	SO	RAT	ERA	ERA+	OAV	OOB	BH	AVG	PB	PR	/A	PD	TPI
1923 StL-N	0	0	—	1	0	0	0	0	3	5	1	3	1	24.0	12.00	33	.455	.571	1	1.000	0	-3	-3	0	0.1

● BILL STONEMAN
Stoneman, William Hambly b: 4/7/44, Oak Park, Ill. BR/TR, 5'10", 170 lbs. Deb: 7/16/67

YEAR TM/L	W	L	PCT	G	GS	CG	SH	SV	IP	H	HR	BB	SO	RAT	ERA	ERA+	OAV	OOB	BH	AVG	PB	PR	/A	PD	TPI
1967 Chi-N	2	4	.333	28	2	0	0	4	63	51	7	22	52	10.4	3.29	108	.223	.291	0	.000	-1	1	2	-1	0.0
1968 Chi-N	0	1	.000	18	0	0	0	0	29¹	24	6	14	18	15.3	5.52	57	.310	.391	0	.000	-0	-8	-8	-0	-0.3
1969 Mon-N	11	19	.367	42	36	8	5	0	235²	233	26	123	185	14.1	4.39	84	.261	.358	4	.055	-3	-21	-19	-1	-2.6
1970 Mon-N	7	15	.318	40	30	5	3	0	207²	209	26	109	176	14.4	4.59	90	.263	.361	6	.100	-2	-13	-11	-1	-1.4
1971 Mon-N	17	16	.515	39	39	20	3	0	294²	243	20	146	251	12.0	3.15	112	.225	.321	12	.129	-1	10	12	0	1.4
1972 Mon-N★	12	14	.462	36	35	13	4	0	250²	213	15	102	171	11.4	2.98	119	.229	.308	6	.080	-4	13	16	0	1.1
1973 Mon-N	4	8	.333	29	17	0	0	1	96²	120	12	55	48	16.9	6.80	56	.310	.404	1	.050	-1	-34	-32	0	-3.6
1974 Cal-A	1	8	.111	13	11	0	0	0	58²	78	8	31	33	17.0	6.14	56	.322	.404	0	—	0	-16	-18	0	-2.3
Total 8	54	85	.388	245	170	46	15	5	1236¹	1182	94	602	934	13.3	4.08	90	.253	.344	29	.086	-13	-68	-57	-3	-7.7

● LIL STONER
Stoner, Ulysses Simpson Grant b: 2/28/1899, Bowie, Tex. d: 6/26/66, Enid, Okla. BR/TR, 5'9.5", 180 lbs. Deb: 4/15/22

YEAR TM/L	W	L	PCT	G	GS	CG	SH	SV	IP	H	HR	BB	SO	RAT	ERA	ERA+	OAV	OOB	BH	AVG	PB	PR	/A	PD	TPI
1922 Det-A	4	4	.500	17	7	2	0	0	62²	76	3	35	18	16.4	7.04	55	.315	.409	2	.100	-1	-21	-22	1	-2.3
1924 Det-A	11	11	.500	36	25	10	1	0	215²	271	13	65	66	14.2	4.72	87	.316	.367	15	.195	1	-12	-14	-1	-1.2
1925 Det-A	10	9	.526	34	18	8	0	1	152	166	6	53	51	13.5	4.26	101	.283	.352	16	.291	4	2	1	-3	0.1
1926 Det-A	7	10	.412	32	22	7	0	0	159²	179	11	63	57	13.8	5.47	74	.291	.359	9	.170	-2	-26	-25	-0	-2.4
1927 Det-A	10	13	.435	38	24	13	0	5	215	251	9	77	63	13.9	3.98	106	.301	.362	8	.108	-6	4	6	-2	-0.2
1928 Det-A	5	8	.385	36	11	4	0	4	126¹	151	16	42	29	14.0	4.35	95	.296	.353	7	.179	-1	-4	-3	-2	-0.6
1929 Det-A	3	3	.500	24	5	1	0	4	53	57	2	31	12	15.3	5.26	82	.288	.390	1	.067	-2	-6	-6	2	-0.7
1930 Pit-N	0	0	—	5	0	0	0	0	5²	7	2	3	1	15.9	4.76	105	.318	.400	0	—	0	0	0	0	0.0
1931 Phi-N	0	0	—	7	0	0	0	0	13²	22	0	5	2	17.8	6.59	64	.373	.422	0	.000	-1	-4	-4	-0	-0.1
Total 9	50	58	.463	229	111	45	1	14	1003²	1180	62	374	299	14.2	4.76	87	.301	.366	58	.172	-7	-66	-67	-5	-7.4

● MEL STOTTLEMYRE
Stottlemyre, Melvin Leon Jr. b: 12/28/63, Prosser, Wash. BR/TR, 6', 190 lbs. Deb: 7/17/90 F

YEAR TM/L	W	L	PCT	G	GS	CG	SH	SV	IP	H	HR	BB	SO	RAT	ERA	ERA+	OAV	OOB	BH	AVG	PB	PR	/A	PD	TPI
1990 KC-A	0	1	.000	13	2	0	0	0	31¹	35	3	12	14	13.5	4.88	78	.280	.343	0	—	0	-3	-4	0	-0.1

● MEL STOTTLEMYRE
Stottlemyre, Melvin Leon Sr. b: 11/13/41, Hazelton, Mo. BR/TR, 6'2", 190 lbs. Deb: 8/12/64 FC

YEAR TM/L	W	L	PCT	G	GS	CG	SH	SV	IP	H	HR	BB	SO	RAT	ERA	ERA+	OAV	OOB	BH	AVG	PB	PR	/A	PD	TPI
1964 *NY-A	9	3	.750	13	12	5	2	0	96	77	3	35	49	10.7	2.06	176	.219	.294	9	.243	2	17	17	1	2.5
1965 NY-A☆	20	9	.690	37	37	18	4	0	291	250	18	88	155	10.7	2.63	129	.233	.295	13	.131	1	27	25	6	3.2
1966 NY-A★	12	20	.375	37	35	9	3	1	251	239	18	82	146	11.5	3.80	87	.253	.313	11	.138	1	-10	-13	4	-1.1
1967 NY-A	15	15	.500	36	36	10	4	0	255	235	20	88	151	11.5	2.96	105	.248	.313	8	.098	-3	8	5	0	0.8
1968 NY-A★	21	12	.636	36	36	19	6	0	278²	243	21	65	140	10.0	2.45	118	.234	.281	13	.143	2	16	14	2	2.2
1969 NY-A★	20	14	.588	39	39	24	3	0	303	267	19	97	113	11.0	2.82	123	.239	.303	18	.178	5	27	22	8	3.8
1970 NY-A★	15	13	.536	37	37	14	0	0	271	262	23	84	126	11.7	3.09	114	.255	.315	16	.188	9	19	13	2	2.5
1971 NY-A	16	12	.571	35	35	19	7	0	269²	234	16	69	132	10.2	2.87	113	.233	.285	16	.170	9	18	11	3	1.7
1972 NY-A	14	18	.438	36	36	9	2	0	260	250	13	85	110	11.7	3.22	92	.254	.316	16	.200	3	-5	-8	3	-0.3
1973 NY-A	16	16	.500	38	38	19	4	0	273	259	13	79	95	11.3	3.07	119	.253	.310	0	—	0	23	18	2	2.2
1974 NY-A	6	7	.462	16	16	7	1	0	113	99	7	37	40	12.7	3.58	97	.272	.335	0	—	0	0	-1	-1	-0.2
Total 11	164	139	.541	360	356	152	40	1	2661¹	2435	171	809	1257	11.1	2.97	112	.245	.304	120	.160	21	139	102	36	17.3

● TODD STOTTLEMYRE
Stottlemyre, Todd Vernon b: 5/20/65, Sunnyside, Wash. BL/TR, 6'3", 195 lbs. Deb: 4/6/88 F

YEAR TM/L	W	L	PCT	G	GS	CG	SH	SV	IP	H	HR	BB	SO	RAT	ERA	ERA+	OAV	OOB	BH	AVG	PB	PR	/A	PD	TPI
1988 Tor-A	4	8	.333	28	16	0	0	0	98	109	15	46	67	14.6	5.69	69	.283	.366	0	—	0	-19	-19	-0	-2.1
1989 *Tor-A	7	7	.500	27	18	0	0	0	127²	137	11	44	63	13.1	3.88	97	.282	.348	0	—	0	-2	-1	-0	-0.8
1990 Tor-A	13	17	.433	33	33	4	0	0	203	214	18	69	115	12.9	4.34	91	.274	.339	0	—	0	-10	-9	-0	-1.1
1991 *Tor-A	15	8	.652	34	34	1	0	0	219	194	21	75	116	11.5	3.78	111	.235	.308	0	—	0	8	10	0	0.8
1992 *Tor-A	12	11	.522	28	27	6	2	0	174	175	20	63	98	12.8	4.50	91	.262	.320	0	—	0	-8	-6	-1	-1.2
1993 *Tor-A	11	12	.478	30	28	1	1	0	176²	204	11	69	98	14.1	4.84	89	.292	.358	0	—	0	-10	-10	-1	-1.2
1994 Tor-A	7	7	.500	26	19	3	1	0	140²	149	19	48	105	13.1	4.22	114	.275	.342	0	—	0	9	9	0	0.8
Total 7	69	70	.496	206	175	15	4	1	1139	1182	115	414	662	13.0	4.39	95	.269	.339	0	—	0	-33	-28	-3	-4.3

YEAR	TM/L	W	L	PCT	G	GS	CG	SH	SV	IP	H	HR	BB	SO	RAT	ERA	ERA+	OAV	OOB	BH	AVG	PB	PR	/A	PD	TPI

● **ALLYN STOUT** Stout, Allyn McClelland "Fish Hook" b: 10/31/04, Peoria, Ill. d: 12/22/74, Sikeston, Mo. BR/TR, 5'10", 167 lbs. Deb: 5/16/31

YEAR	TM/L	W	L	PCT	G	GS	CG	SH	SV	IP	H	HR	BB	SO	RAT	ERA	ERA+	OAV	OOB	BH	AVG	PB	PR	/A	PD	TPI
1931	StL-N	6	0	1.000	30	3	1	0	3	72²	87	2	34	40	15.1	4.21	93	.305	.381	2	.105	-1	-3	-2	1	-0.2
1932	StL-N	4	5	.444	36	3	1	0	1	73²	87	5	28	32	14.5	4.40	89	.305	.375	2	.100	-1	-4	-4	1	-0.5
1933	StL-N	0	0	—	1	0	0	0	0	2	1	0	1	1	9.0	0.00	—	.167	.286	—	—	0	1	1	0	0.0
	Cin-N	2	3	.400	23	5	2	0	0	71¹	85	3	26	29	14.0	3.79	90	.295	.354	4	.182	-0	-4	-3	-1	-0.3
	Yr	2	3	.400	24	5	2	0	0	73¹	86	3	27	30	13.9	3.68	92	.293	.352	4	.182	-0	-3	-2	-1	-0.3
1934	Cin-N	6	8	.429	41	16	4	0	1	140²	170	10	47	51	14.1	4.86	84	.297	.354	8	.186	0	-13	-12	-0	-1.1
1935	NY-N	1	4	.200	40	2	0	0	5	88	99	7	37	29	14.3	4.91	79	.289	.365	2	.133	0	-9	-10	-1	-0.7
1943	Bos-N	1	0	1.000	9	0	0	0	0	9¹	17	1	4	3	20.3	6.75	51	.378	.429	0	.000	0	-3	-3	-0	-0.3
Total	6	20	20	.500	180	29	8	0	11	457²	546	28	177	185	14.5	4.54	85	.299	.365	18	.149	-3	-35	-34	-1	-3.3

● **JESSE STOVALL** Stovall, Jesse Cramer "Scout" b: 7/24/1875, Independence, Mo. d: 7/12/55, San Diego, Cal. BL/TR, 6', 175 lbs. Deb: 8/31/03 F

YEAR	TM/L	W	L	PCT	G	GS	CG	SH	SV	IP	H	HR	BB	SO	RAT	ERA	ERA+	OAV	OOB	BH	AVG	PB	PR	/A	PD	TPI
1903	Cle-A	5	1	.833	6	6	6	2	0	57	44	0	21	12	10.7	2.05	139	.213	.295	1	.045	-2	6	5	-1	0.2
1904	Det-A	3	13	.188	22	17	13	1	0	146²	170	3	45	41	14.2	4.42	58	.291	.358	11	.196	0	-30	-30	-0	-3.0
Total	2	8	14	.364	28	23	19	3	0	203²	214	3	66	53	13.2	3.76	70	.270	.341	12	.154	-2	-24	-25	-0	-2.8

● **HARRY STOVEY** Stovey, Harry Duffield (b: Harry Duffield Stowe) b: 12/20/1856, Philadelphia, Pa. d: 9/20/37, New Bedford, Mass BR/TR, 5'11.5", 175 lbs. Deb: 5/1/1880 M♦

YEAR	TM/L	W	L	PCT	G	GS	CG	SH	SV	IP	H	HR	BB	SO	RAT	ERA	ERA+	OAV	OOB	BH	AVG	PB	PR	/A	PD	TPI
1880	Wor-N	0	0	—	2	0	0	0	0	6	8	0	3	3	16.5	4.50	58	.308	.379	94	.265	0	-1	-1	-0	0.0
1883	Phi-a	0	0	—	1	0	0	0	0	3	5	0	0	4	15.0	9.00	39	.349	.349	128	.304	0	-2	-2	-0	0.0
1886	Phi-a	0	0	—	1	0	0	0	0	0¹	2	0	0	0	54.0	27.00	13	.667	.667	144	.294	0	-1	-1	-0	0.0
Total	3	0	0	—	4	0	0	0	0	9¹	15	0	3	7	17.4	6.75	43	.346	.389	1770	.288	1	-4	-4	-0	0.0

● **HAL STOWE** Stowe, Harold Rudolph b: 8/29/37, Gastonia, N.C. BL/TL, 6', 170 lbs. Deb: 9/30/60

YEAR	TM/L	W	L	PCT	G	GS	CG	SH	SV	IP	H	HR	BB	SO	RAT	ERA	ERA+	OAV	OOB	BH	AVG	PB	PR	/A	PD	TPI
1960	NY-A	0	0	—	1	0	0	0	0	1	0	0	1	0	9.0	9.00	40	.000	.500	0	—	0	-1	-1	-0	0.0

● **MIKE STRAHLER** Strahler, Michael Wayne b: 3/14/47, Chicago, Ill. BR/TR, 6'4", 180 lbs. Deb: 9/12/70

YEAR	TM/L	W	L	PCT	G	GS	CG	SH	SV	IP	H	HR	BB	SO	RAT	ERA	ERA+	OAV	OOB	BH	AVG	PB	PR	/A	PD	TPI
1970	LA-N	1	1	.500	6	0	0	0	0	18²	13	1	10	11	11.1	1.45	265	.194	.299	2	.250	0	5	5	0	0.6
1971	LA-N	0	0	—	6	0	0	0	0	12²	10	1	8	7	12.8	2.84	114	.217	.333	0	.000	-0	1	1	-0	0.0
1972	LA-N	1	2	.333	19	2	1	0	0	47	42	5	22	25	12.4	3.26	102	.237	.325	2	.182	1	1	0	-0	0.1
1973	Det-A	4	5	.444	22	11	1	0	0	80¹	84	7	39	37	13.9	4.37	94	.273	.356	0	—	-0	-5	-3	-1	-0.3
Total	4	6	8	.429	53	13	2	0	1	158²	149	14	79	80	13.0	3.57	105	.249	.339	4	.200	1	2	3	-1	0.4

● **DICK STRAHS** Strahs, Richard Bernard b: 12/4/23, Evanston, Ill. d: 5/26/88, Las Vegas, Nev. BL/TR, 6', 192 lbs. Deb: 7/24/54

YEAR	TM/L	W	L	PCT	G	GS	CG	SH	SV	IP	H	HR	BB	SO	RAT	ERA	ERA+	OAV	OOB	BH	AVG	PB	PR	/A	PD	TPI
1954	Chi-A	0	0	—	9	0	0	0	1	14¹	16	0	8	8	15.1	5.65	66	.271	.358	0	.000	-0	-3	-3	-0	0.0

● **LES STRAKER** Straker, Lester Paul (Bolnalda) b: 10/10/59, Ciudad Bolivar, Ven BR/TR, 6'1", 193 lbs. Deb: 4/11/87

YEAR	TM/L	W	L	PCT	G	GS	CG	SH	SV	IP	H	HR	BB	SO	RAT	ERA	ERA+	OAV	OOB	BH	AVG	PB	PR	/A	PD	TPI
1987	*Min-A	8	10	.444	31	26	1	0	0	154¹	150	24	59	76	12.3	4.37	106	.257	.328	0	—	0	1	4	-2	0.3
1988	Min-A	2	5	.286	16	14	1	1	1	82²	86	8	25	23	12.1	3.92	104	.276	.329	0	—	0	1	1	0	0.1
Total	2	10	15	.400	47	40	2	1	1	237	236	32	84	99	12.2	4.22	105	.264	.328	0	—	0	2	5	-1	0.4

● **BOB STRAMPE** Strampe, Robert Edwin b: 6/13/50, Janesville, Wis. BB/TR, 6'1", 185 lbs. Deb: 5/10/72

YEAR	TM/L	W	L	PCT	G	GS	CG	SH	SV	IP	H	HR	BB	SO	RAT	ERA	ERA+	OAV	OOB	BH	AVG	PB	PR	/A	PD	TPI
1972	Det-A	0	0	—	7	0	0	0	0	4²	6	0	7	4	25.1	11.57	27	.300	.481	0	—	0	-4	-4	-0	0.0

● **PAUL STRAND** Strand, Paul Edward b: 12/19/1893, Carbonado, Wash. d: 7/2/74, Salt Lake City, Utah BR/TL, 6'0.5", 190 lbs. Deb: 5/15/13 ♦

YEAR	TM/L	W	L	PCT	G	GS	CG	SH	SV	IP	H	HR	BB	SO	RAT	ERA	ERA+	OAV	OOB	BH	AVG	PB	PR	/A	PD	TPI
1913	Bos-N	0	0	—	7	0	0	0	0	17	22	1	12	6	18.0	2.12	155	.393	.500	1	.167	-2	2	2	0	0.0
1914	Bos-N	6	2	.750	16	3	1	0	1	55¹	47	1	23	33	11.5	2.44	113	.235	.317	8	.333	2	2	2	-0	0.5
1915	Bos-N	1	1	.500	6	2	2	0	1	22²	26	0	3	13	11.5	2.38	109	.295	.319	2	.091	-2	1	1	-1	-0.1
Total	3	7	3	.700	29	5	3	0	2	95	95	2	38	52	12.7	2.37	119	.276	.350	49	.224	-2	5	5	-1	0.4

● **SCOTT STRATTON** Stratton, C. Scott b: 10/2/1869, Campbellsburg, Ky. d: 3/8/39, Louisville, Ky. BL/TR, 6', 180 lbs. Deb: 4/21/1888 ♦

YEAR	TM/L	W	L	PCT	G	GS	CG	SH	SV	IP	H	HR	BB	SO	RAT	ERA	ERA+	OAV	OOB	BH	AVG	PB	PR	/A	PD	TPI
1888	Lou-a	10	17	.370	33	28	28	2	0	269²	287	7	53	97	11.8	3.64	85	.263	.306	64	.257	5	-17	-17	-1	-1.0
1889	Lou-a	3	13	.188	19	17	13	0	1	133²	157	6	42	42	13.9	3.23	119	.284	.342	66	.288	4	9	9	2	1.4
1890	*Lou-a	34	14	**.708**	50	49	44	4	0	431	398	3	61	207	**9.9**	**2.36**	**163**	.238	**.270**	61	.323	16	**72**	**71**	6	**8.9**
1891	Pit-N	2	2	.000	2	2	2	0	0	18¹	16	0	5	5	10.3	2.45	134	.226	.277	1	.125	-1	2	2	1	0.2
	Lou-a	6	13	.316	20	20	20	1	0	172	204	10	34	52	12.4	4.08	90	.285	.324	27	.235	-1	-7	-8	3	-0.4
1892	Lou-N	21	19	.525	42	40	39	2	0	351²	342	1	70	119	10.8	2.92	105	.245	.285	12	.256	10	14	6	2	1.8
1893	Lou-N	12	23	.343	37	35	34	1	0	314²	445	8	100	43	15.8	5.43	81	.323	.373	49	.226	3	-27	-36	6	-2.1
1894	Lou-N	1	5	.167	7	5	4	0	0	43	72	3	13	3	18.4	8.37	61	.368	.415	12	.324	2	-15	-16	0	-1.2
	Chi-N	8	5	.615	15	12	11	0	0	119¹	198	5	40	23	18.2	6.03	93	.366	.412	36	.375	7	-9	-6	0	0.1
	Yr	9	10	.474	22	17	15	0	0	162¹	270	8	53	26	18.1	6.65	82	.365	.409	48	.361	8	-24	-21	1	-1.1
1895	Chi-N	2	3	.400	5	5	3	0	0	30	51	1	14	4	20.7	9.60	53	.370	.442	7	.292	1	-16	-15	1	-1.5
Total	8	97	114	.460	230	213	198	10	1	1883¹	2170	44	432	569	12.8	3.87	99	.280	.324	379	.274	48	7	-10	20	6.2

● **MONTY STRATTON** Stratton, Monty Franklin Pierce "Gander" b: 5/21/12, Celeste, Tex. d: 9/29/82, Greenville, Tex. BR/TR, 6'5", 180 lbs. Deb: 6/2/34 C

YEAR	TM/L	W	L	PCT	G	GS	CG	SH	SV	IP	H	HR	BB	SO	RAT	ERA	ERA+	OAV	OOB	BH	AVG	PB	PR	/A	PD	TPI
1934	Chi-A	0	0	—	1	0	0	0	0	3¹	4	0	1	0	13.5	5.40	88	.333	.385	0	.000	-0	-2	-1	0	0.0
1935	Chi-A	1	2	.333	5	5	2	0	0	38	40	0	9	8	12.1	4.03	115	.274	.325	2	.143	-1	2	3	0	0.1
1936	Chi-A	5	7	.417	16	14	3	0	0	95	117	8	46	37	15.5	5.21	100	.305	.381	8	.216	1	-2	-0	2	0.2
1937	Chi-A†	15	5	.750	22	21	14	5	0	164²	142	6	37	69	**9.9**	2.40	**191**	.234	**.280**	12	.200	-0	41	40	1	4.5
1938	Chi-A	15	9	.625	26	22	17	0	2	186¹	186	18	56	82	12.0	4.01	122	.255	.315	21	.266	5	16	18	0	2.6
Total	5	36	23	.610	70	62	36	5	2	487¹	489	32	149	196	12.0	3.71	130	.261	.319	43	.224	5	56	61	3	7.4

● **ED STRATTON** Stratton, William Edward b: Baltimore, Md. Deb: 5/14/1873

YEAR	TM/L	W	L	PCT	G	GS	CG	SH	SV	IP	H	HR	BB	SO	RAT	ERA	ERA+	OAV	OOB	BH	AVG	PB	PR	/A	PD	TPI
1873	Mar-n	0	3	.000	3	3	3	0	0	27	75	3	0	0	25.0	8.33	39	.410	.410	2	.125	-1	-15	-15		-1.0

● **JOE STRAUSS** Strauss, Joseph "Dutch" or "The Socker" (b: Joseph Strasser) b: 11/16/1858, Cincinnati, Ohio d: 6/24/06, Cincinnati, Ohio BR/TR, Deb: 7/27/1884 ♦

YEAR	TM/L	W	L	PCT	G	GS	CG	SH	SV	IP	H	HR	BB	SO	RAT	ERA	ERA+	OAV	OOB	BH	AVG	PB	PR	/A	PD	TPI
1886	Lou-a	0	0	—	2	0	0	0	0	4	6	0	3	0	20.3	4.50	81	.231	.310	64	.215	-0	-0	-0	-0	0.0

● **OSCAR STREIT** Streit, Oscar William b: 7/7/1873, Florence, Ala. d: 10/10/35, Birmingham, Ala. BL/TL, 6'5", 190 lbs. Deb: 4/21/1899

YEAR	TM/L	W	L	PCT	G	GS	CG	SH	SV	IP	H	HR	BB	SO	RAT	ERA	ERA+	OAV	OOB	BH	AVG	PB	PR	/A	PD	TPI
1899	Bos-N	1	0	1.000	2	1	0	0	0	14²	15	1	15	0	19.6	6.75	62	.264	.434	0	.000	-1	-5	-4	0	-0.3
1902	Cle-A	0	7	.000	8	7	4	0	0	51²	72	3	25	10	17.4	5.23	66	.330	.406	4	.211	1	-9	-10	-1	-1.1
Total	2	1	7	.125	10	8	5	0	0	66¹	87	4	40	10	17.9	5.56	65	.316	.412	4	.154	-0	-14	-14	-1	-1.4

● **ED STRELECKI** Strelecki, Edward Harold b: 4/10/05, Newark, N.J. d: 1/9/68, Newark, N.J. BR/TR, 5'11.5", 180 lbs. Deb: 4/16/28

YEAR	TM/L	W	L	PCT	G	GS	CG	SH	SV	IP	H	HR	BB	SO	RAT	ERA	ERA+	OAV	OOB	BH	AVG	PB	PR	/A	PD	TPI
1928	StL-A	0	2	.000	22	2	1	0	1	50¹	49	4	17	8	12.0	4.29	98	.269	.335	2	.200	-1	-1	-1	-0	0.0
1929	StL-A	1	1	.500	7	0	0	0	0	11	12	1	6	2	15.5	4.91	90	.279	.380	0	.000	-0	-1	-1	-0	-0.1
1931	Cin-N	0	0	—	13	0	0	0	0	24¹	37	2	9	3	18.1	9.25	40	.394	.462	1	.200	0	-15	-15	0	0.1
Total	3	1	3	.250	42	2	1	0	1	85²	98	7	32	13	14.2	5.78	71	.307	.379	3	.176	0	-17	-16	1	0.0

● **PHIL STREMMEL** Stremmel, Philip b: 4/16/1880, Zanesville, Ohio d: 12/26/47, Chicago, Ill. BR/TR, 6', 175 lbs. Deb: 9/16/09

YEAR	TM/L	W	L	PCT	G	GS	CG	SH	SV	IP	H	HR	BB	SO	RAT	ERA	ERA+	OAV	OOB	BH	AVG	PB	PR	/A	PD	TPI
1909	StL-A	0	2	.000	2	2	2	0	0	18	20	1	4	6	12.5	4.50	54	.308	.357	0	.000	-1	-4	-4	0	-0.4
1910	StL-A	0	2	.000	5	2	2	0	0	29	31	0	16	7	14.6	3.72	86	.287	.395	1	.125	0	-4	-4	2	-0.1
Total	2	0	4	.000	7	4	4	0	0	47	51	1	20	13	13.8	4.02	61	.295	.371	1	.071	-1	-8	-8	2	-0.5

YEAR TM/L	W	L	PCT	G	GS	CG	SH	SV	IP	H	HR	BB	SO	RAT	ERA	ERA+	OAV	OOB	BH	AVG	PB	PR	/A	PD	TPI
● CUB STRICKER Stricker, John A. (b: John A. Streaker) b: 2/15/1860, Philadelphia, Pa. d: 11/19/37, Philadelphia, Pa. BR/TR, 5'3", 138 lbs. Deb: 5/2/1882 M♦																									
1882 Phi-a	1	0	1.000	2	0	0	0	0	7	3	0	1	2	5.1	1.29	232	.121	.155	59	.217	-0	1	1	-0	0.1
1884 Phi-a	0	0	—	1	0	0	0	0	3	6	0	1	1	21.0	6.00	56	.333	.368	92	.231	0	-1	-1	-0	0.0
1887 Cle-a	0	0	—	3	0	0	0	1	5²	5	0	7	2	19.1	3.18	137	.238	.429	141	.264	0	1	1	-0	0.1
1888 Cle-a	1	0	1.000	2	0	0	0	0	12	16	0	2	5	14.3	4.50	69	.309	.347	115	.233	0	-2	-2	-0	-0.1
Total 4	2	0	1.000	8	0	0	0	1	27²	30	0	11	10	13.7	3.58	94	.260	.329	1107	.239	1	-1	-1	-0	0.1
● JIM STRICKLAND Strickland, James Michael b: 6/12/46, Los Angeles, Cal. BL/TL, 6', 175 lbs. Deb: 5/19/71																									
1971 Min-A	1	0	1.000	24	0	0	0	0	31¹	20	2	18	21	11.5	1.44	247	.183	.310	0	.000	0	7	7	0	0.3
1972 Min-A	3	1	.750	25	0	0	0	3	36	28	7	19	30	11.8	2.50	128	.214	.313	1	.333	1	2	3	0	0.5
1973 Min-A	0	1	.000	7	0	0	0	0	5¹	11	0	5	6	27.0	11.81	34	.440	.533	0	—	0	-5	-5	-0	-0.7
1975 Cle-A	0	0	—	4	0	0	0	1	4²	4	0	2	3	13.5	1.93	196	.222	.333	0	—	0	1	1	-0	0.0
Total 4	4	2	.667	60	0	0	0	5	77¹	63	9	44	60	12.8	2.68	128	.223	.333	1	.250	1	6	7	0	0.1
● BILL STRICKLAND Strickland, William Goss b: 3/29/08, Nashville, Ga. BR/TR, 6'2", 170 lbs. Deb: 9/16/37																									
1937 StL-A	0	0	—	9	0	0	0	0	21¹	28	2	15	6	19.0	5.91	82	.341	.455	1	.167	-0	-3	-3	-0	0.0
● ELMER STRICKLETT Stricklett, Elmer Griffin "Spitball" b: 8/29/1876, Glasco, Kan. d: 6/7/64, Santa Cruz, Cal. BR/TR, 5'6", 140 lbs. Deb: 4/22/04																									
1904 Chi-A	0	1	.000	1	1	0	0	0	7	12	0	2	3	18.0	10.29	24	.377	.414	0	.000	-0	-6	-6	0	-0.6
1905 Bro-N	9	18	.333	33	28	25	1	1	237¹	259	0	71	77	13.0	3.34	87	.282	.343	13	.148	-1	-9	-12	9	-0.4
1906 Bro-N	14	18	.438	41	35	28	5	5	291²	273	2	77	88	11.0	2.72	93	.253	.306	20	.206	5	-3	-6	9	0.9
1907 Bro-N	12	14	.462	29	26	25	4	0	229²	211	1	65	69	11.1	2.27	103	.255	.315	12	.148	1	5	2	7	1.1
Total 4	35	51	.407	104	90	78	10	6	765²	755	3	215	237	11.7	2.84	91	.264	.322	45	.167	4	-12	-22	25	1.0
● JOHN STRIKE Strike, John b: 1865, Pennsylvania Deb: 9/24/1886																									
1886 Phi-N	1	1	.500	2	2	1	0	0	15	19	1	7	11	15.6	4.80	69	.311	.382	0	.000	-1	-2	-2	-1	-0.4
● JAKE STRIKER Striker, Wilbur Scott b: 10/23/33, New Washington, O. BL/TL, 6'2", 200 lbs. Deb: 9/25/59																									
1959 Cle-A	1	0	1.000	1	1	0	0	0	6²	8	0	4	5	16.2	2.70	136	.296	.387	0	.000	1	1	1	0	0.2
1960 Chi-A	0	0	—	2	0	0	0	0	3²	5	1	1	1	17.2	4.91	77	.357	.438	0	—	0	-0	-0	-0	0.0
Total 2	1	0	1.000	3	1	0	0	0	10¹	13	1	5	6	16.5	3.48	107	.317	.404	0	.000	1	0	0	-0	0.2
● NICK STRINCEVICH Strincevich, Nicholas "Jumbo" b: 3/1/15, Gary, Ind. BR/TR, 6'1", 180 lbs. Deb: 4/23/40																									
1940 Bos-N	4	8	.333	32	14	5	0	1	128²	142	17	63	54	14.9	5.53	67	.278	.367	5	.116	-2	-24	-26	-2	-2.5
1941 Bos-N	0	0	—	3	0	0	0	0	3¹	7	0	6	1	37.8	10.80	33	.412	.583	0	—	0	-3	-3	0	0.0
Pit-N	1	2	.333	12	3	0	0	0	31	35	4	13	12	14.2	5.23	69	.280	.353	3	.429	1	-5	-6	0	-0.4
Yr	1	2	.333	15	3	0	0	0	34¹	42	4	19	13	16.3	5.77	63	.294	.380	3	.429	1	-8	-8	0	-0.4
1942 Pit-N	0	0	—	7	1	0	0	0	22¹	19	2	9	10	11.7	2.82	120	.229	.312	0	.000	-1	1	1	-0	-0.1
1944 Pit-N	14	7	.667	40	26	11	0	2	190	190	5	37	47	10.9	3.08	121	.257	.296	9	.158	-1	11	13	5	1.9
1945 Pit-N	16	10	.615	36	29	18	1	2	228¹	235	7	49	74	11.3	3.31	119	.260	.301	17	.202	0	12	16	-2	1.6
1946 Pit-N	10	15	.400	32	22	11	3	1	176	185	7	44	49	11.9	3.58	98	.268	.316	8	.154	1	-3	-1	-2	-0.3
1947 Pit-N	1	6	.143	32	7	1	0	0	89	111	7	37	22	15.2	5.26	80	.316	.385	1	.048	-2	-12	-10	-0	-0.9
1948 Pit-N	0	0	—	3	0	0	0	0	4¹	8	0	2	1	20.8	8.31	49	.444	.500	0	—	0	-2	-2	0	0.0
Phi-N	0	1	.000	6	1	0	0	0	16²	26	1	10	19	19.4	9.18	43	.347	.424	0	.000	-1	-10	-10	-1	-0.6
Yr	0	1	.000	9	1	0	0	0	21	34	1	12	5	19.7	9.00	44	.366	.438	0	.000	-1	-12	-12	-0	-0.6
Total 8	46	49	.484	203	103	46	4	6	889²	958	52	270	274	12.7	4.05	93	.273	.329	43	.158	-4	-34	-26	-0	-1.3
● JOHN STROHMAYER Strohmayer, John Emery b: 10/13/46, Belle Fourche, S.D. BR/TR, 6'1", 181 lbs. Deb: 4/29/70																									
1970 Mon-N	3	1	.750	42	0	0	0	0	76	85	7	39	74	14.9	4.86	85	.279	.364	1	.167	-0	-7	-6	-0	-0.3
1971 Mon-N	7	5	.583	27	14	2	0	1	114	124	16	31	56	12.6	4.34	81	.281	.333	8	.229	1	-11	-10	-1	-1.1
1972 Mon-N	1	2	.333	48	0	0	0	3	76²	73	6	31	50	12.3	3.52	101	.256	.331	0	.000	-0	-1	0	1	0.1
1973 Mon-N	0	1	.000	17	3	0	0	0	34²	34	4	22	15	14.8	5.19	73	.260	.370	1	.200	-0	-6	-5	0	-0.1
NY-N	0	0	—	7	0	0	0	0	10	13	2	4	5	15.3	8.10	45	.310	.370	0	—	0	-5	-5	0	0.0
Yr	0	1	.000	24	3	0	0	0	44²	47	6	26	20	14.7	5.84	65	.270	.365	1	.200	-0	-11	-10	-0	-0.1
1974 NY-N	0	0	—	1	0	0	0	0	1	0	0	1	0	9.0	0.00	—	.000	.250	0	—	0	0	0	0	0.0
Total 5	11	9	.550	142	17	2	0	4	312¹	329	35	128	200	13.4	4.47	83	.272	.346	10	.200	1	-29	-26	-0	-1.4
● BRENT STROM Strom, Brent Terry b: 10/14/48, San Diego, Cal. BR/TL, 6'3", 190 lbs. Deb: 7/31/72																									
1972 NY-N	0	3	.000	11	5	0	0	0	30¹	34	7	15	20	14.5	6.82	49	.296	.377	0	.000	-1	-12	-11	-1	-1.2
1973 Cle-A	2	10	.167	27	18	2	0	0	123	134	18	47	91	13.5	4.61	85	.278	.346	0	—	0	-11	-9	1	-0.8
1975 SD-N	8	8	.500	18	16	6	2	0	120¹	103	6	33	56	10.3	2.54	137	.233	.289	3	.100	-1	14	12	0	1.6
1976 SD-N	12	16	.429	36	33	8	1	0	210²	188	15	73	103	11.2	3.29	99	.239	.305	4	.063	-2	5	-0	0	-0.3
1977 SD-N	0	2	.000	8	3	0	0	0	16²	23	5	12	8	18.9	12.42	28	.329	.427	1	.333	0	-16	-16	-0	-1.6
Total 5	22	39	.361	100	75	16	3	0	501	482	51	180	278	12.0	3.95	88	.254	.321	8	.078	-3	-19	-26	0	-2.3
● FLOYD STROMME Stromme, Floyd Marvin "Rock" b: 8/1/16, Cooperstown, N.Dak. BR/TR, 5'11", 170 lbs. Deb: 7/5/39																									
1939 Cle-A	0	1	.000	5	0	0	0	0	13	13	1	13	4	18.0	4.85	91	.265	.419	1	.333	0	-0	-1	-0	0.0
● SAILOR STROUD Stroud, Ralph Vivian b: 5/15/1885, Ironia, N.J. d: 4/11/70, Stockton, Cal. BR/TR, 6', 160 lbs. Deb: 4/29/10																									
1910 Det-A	5	9	.357	28	15	7	3	1	130¹	123	9	41	63	11.8	3.25	81	.257	.325	1	.026	-4	-11	-9	-4	-1.8
1915 NY-N	12	9	.571	32	22	8	0	1	184	194	3	35	62	11.5	2.79	92	.281	.321	9	.161	-1	-1	-5	-0	-0.6
1916 NY-N	3	2	.600	10	4	0	0	1	46²	47	1	9	16	11.0	2.70	90	.266	.305	1	.071	-1	-0	-0	-0	-0.3
Total 3	20	20	.500	70	41	15	3	3	361	364	13	85	141	11.5	2.94	88	.271	.321	11	.101	-6	-12	-15	-4	-2.7
● STEAMBOAT STRUSS Struss, Clarence Herbert b: 2/24/09, Riverdale, Ill. d: 9/12/85, Grand Rapids, Mich. BR/TR, 5'11", 163 lbs. Deb: 9/30/34																									
1934 Pit-N	0	1	.000	1	1	0	0	0	7	6	0	3	6	16.7	6.43	64	.250	.382	1	.333	-0	-2	-2	0	-0.2
● DUTCH STRYKER Stryker, Sterling Alpa b: 7/29/1895, Atlantic Highlands, N.J. d: 11/5/64, Red Bank, N.J. BR/TR, 5'11.5", 180 lbs. Deb: 4/16/24																									
1924 Bos-N	3	8	.273	20	10	2	0	0	73¹	90	4	22	22	13.9	6.01	64	.314	.365	5	.217	-0	-17	-18	2	-2.1
1926 Bro-N	0	0	—	2	0	0	0	0	2	8	0	1	0	40.5	27.00	14	.571	.600	0	—	0	-5	-5	-0	0.0
Total 2	3	8	.273	22	10	2	0	0	75¹	98	4	23	22	14.6	6.57	58	.326	.375	5	.217	-0	-23	-23	2	-2.1
● JOHNNY STUART Stuart, John Davis "Stud" b: 4/27/01, Clinton, Tenn. d: 5/13/70, Charleston, W.Va. BR/TR, 5'11", 170 lbs. Deb: 7/27/22																									
1922 StL-N	0	0	—	2	1	0	0	0	2	2	2	7	2	22.5	9.00	43	.222	.417	0	—	0	-1	-1	-0	0.0
1923 StL-N	9	5	.643	37	10	7	1	0	149²	139	11	70	55	13.1	4.27	91	.252	.345	14	.246	1	-4	-6	-1	-0.6
1924 StL-N	9	11	.450	28	22	13	0	0	159	167	12	60	54	13.1	4.75	80	.273	.343	11	.204	-1	-16	-17	-3	-2.2
1925 StL-N	2	2	.500	15	1	1	0	0	47	52	6	24	14	14.9	6.13	71	.278	.366	4	.250	-1	-10	-9	-0	-0.6
Total 4	20	18	.526	82	34	21	1	3	357²	360	29	156	124	13.4	4.76	82	.265	.348	29	.228	-1	-31	-34	-5	-3.4
● MARLIN STUART Stuart, Marlin Henry b: 8/8/18, Paragould, Ark. d: 6/16/94, Paragould, Ark. BL/TR, 6'2", 185 lbs. Deb: 4/26/49																									
1949 Det-A	0	2	.000	14	2	0	0	0	29²	39	3	35	14	22.4	9.10	46	.348	.503	2	.333	1	-16	-16	0	-0.9
1950 Det-A	3	1	.750	19	1	0	0	2	43²	59	6	22	19	16.9	5.56	84	.330	.406	1	.083	-1	-5	-4	0	-0.5
1951 Det-A	4	6	.400	29	15	5	0	1	124	119	9	71	46	14.3	3.77	111	.258	.365	10	.233	1	5	6	0	0.6
1952 Det-A	3	2	.600	30	9	2	0	1	91¹	91	8	48	32	14.0	4.93	77	.265	.360	2	.087	-1	-13	-10	-1	-0.7
StL-A	1	2	.333	12	2	0	0	1	26	26	3	9	13	12.1	4.15	94	.260	.321	0	.000	-1	-1	-1	-1	0.0
Yr	4	4	.500	42	11	2	0	2	117¹	117	11	57	45	13.3	4.76	81	.262	.346	2	.069	-2	-14	-12	-1	-0.9

YEAR TM/L	W	L	PCT	G	GS	CG	SH	SV	IP	H	HR	BB	SO	RAT	ERA	ERA+	OAV	OOB	BH	AVG	PB	PR	/A	PD	TPI
1953 StL-A	8	2	.800	60	2	0	0	7	114^1	136	6	44	46	14.2	3.94	107	.300	.363	5	.192	-1	1	3	-0	0.2
1954 Bal-A	1	2	.333	22	0	0	0	2	38^1	46	2	15	13	14.8	4.46	80	.303	.373	0	.000	-0	-3	-4	-0	-0.3
NY-A	3	0	1.000	10	0	0	0	1	18^1	28	0	12	2	19.6	5.40	64	.350	.435	2	.333	0	-3	-4	0	-0.6
Yr	4	2	.667	32	0	0	0	3	56^2	74	2	27	15	16.0	4.76	74	.315	.385	2	.222	-0	-7	-8	1	-0.9
Total 6	23	17	.575	196	31	7	0	15	485^2	544	37	256	185	15.1	4.65	87	.289	.378	22	.176	-1	-36	-31	-0	-2.4

● **GEORGE STUELAND**   Stueland, George Anton b: 3/2/1899, Algona, Iowa d: 9/9/64, Onawa, Iowa BB/TR, 6'1.5", 174 lbs. Deb: 9/15/21

YEAR TM/L	W	L	PCT	G	GS	CG	SH	SV	IP	H	HR	BB	SO	RAT	ERA	ERA+	OAV	OOB	BH	AVG	PB	PR	/A	PD	TPI
1921 Chi-N	0	1	.000	2	1	0	0	0	11	11	0	7	4	14.7	5.73	67	.282	.391	1	.333	0	-2	-2	-0	-0.2
1922 Chi-N	9	4	.692	35	12	4	0	0	113	129	9	49	44	14.6	5.81	72	.297	.374	4	.129	-2	-22	-20	-1	-2.2
1923 Chi-N	0	1	.000	6	0	0	0	0	8	11	0	5	2	18.0	5.63	71	.478	.571	0	—	0	-1	-1	0	-0.1
1925 Chi-N	0	0	—	2	0	0	0	0	3	2	0	3	2	15.0	3.00	144	.182	.357	1	1.000	0	0	0	0	0.1
Total 4	9	6	.600	45	13	4	0	0	135	153	9	64	52	14.8	5.73	73	.301	.385	6	.171	-1	-25	-24	-1	-2.4

● **PAUL STUFFEL**   Stuffel, Paul Harrington "Stu" b: 3/22/27, Canton, Ohio BR/TR, 6'2", 185 lbs. Deb: 9/16/50

YEAR TM/L	W	L	PCT	G	GS	CG	SH	SV	IP	H	HR	BB	SO	RAT	ERA	ERA+	OAV	OOB	BH	AVG	PB	PR	/A	PD	TPI
1950 Phi-N	0	0	—	3	0	0	0	0	5	4	0	1	3	10.8	1.80	225	.211	.286	0	—	0	1	1	0	0.0
1952 Phi-N	1	0	1.000	2	1	0	0	0	6	5	0	7	3	18.0	3.00	122	.217	.400	0	.000	-0	0	0	0	0.1
1953 Phi-N	0	0	—	2	0	0	0	0	0	0	0	4	0		∞	—	—	1.000	0	—	0	-4	-4	0	-0.4
Total 3	1	0	1.000	7	1	0	0	0	11	9	0	12	6	18.0	5.73	67	.214	.400	0	.000	-0	-2	-2	0	-0.3

● **GEORGE STULTZ**   Stultz, George Irvin b: 6/30/1873, Louisville, Ky. d: 3/19/55, Louisville, Ky. 5'10", 150 lbs. Deb: 9/22/1894

YEAR TM/L	W	L	PCT	G	GS	CG	SH	SV	IP	H	HR	BB	SO	RAT	ERA	ERA+	OAV	OOB	BH	AVG	PB	PR	/A	PD	TPI
1894 Bos-N	1	0	1.000	1	1	1	0	0	9	4	0	5	1	9.0	0.00		.134	.258	1	.333	-0	5	6	1	0.6

● **JIM STUMP**   Stump, James Gilbert b: 2/10/32, Lansing, Mich. BR/TR, 6', 188 lbs. Deb: 8/29/57

YEAR TM/L	W	L	PCT	G	GS	CG	SH	SV	IP	H	HR	BB	SO	RAT	ERA	ERA+	OAV	OOB	BH	AVG	PB	PR	/A	PD	TPI
1957 Det-A	1	0	1.000	6	0	0	0	0	13^1	11	1	8	2	12.8	2.03	190	.220	.328	1	.500	0	3	3	0	0.2
1959 Det-A	0	0	—	5	0	0	0	0	11^1	12	1	4	6	12.7	2.38	170	.279	.340	1	1.000	1	2	2	0	0.1
Total 2	1	0	1.000	11	0	0	0	0	24^2	23	2	12	8	12.8	2.19	180	.247	.333	2	.667	1	4	5	0	0.3

● **JOHN STUPER**   Stuper, John Anton b: 5/9/57, Butler, Pa. BR/TR, 6'2", 200 lbs. Deb: 6/1/82

YEAR TM/L	W	L	PCT	G	GS	CG	SH	SV	IP	H	HR	BB	SO	RAT	ERA	ERA+	OAV	OOB	BH	AVG	PB	PR	/A	PD	TPI
1982 *StL-N	9	7	.563	23	21	2	0	0	136^2	137	8	55	53	12.6	3.36	108	.266	.337	5	.119	-1	4	4	-3	0.0
1983 StL-N	12	11	.522	40	30	6	1	1	198	202	15	71	81	12.5	3.68	98	.265	.329	8	.136	-1	-1	-1	-1	-0.4
1984 StL-N	3	5	.375	15	12	0	0	0	61^1	73	4	20	19	13.9	5.28	66	.297	.354	1	.063	-1	-12	-12	0	-1.5
1985 Cin-N	8	5	.615	33	13	1	0	0	99	116	8	37	38	13.9	4.55	83	.303	.364	1	.059	-0	-10	-8	0	-1.1
Total 4	32	28	.533	111	76	9	1	1	495	528	35	183	191	13.0	3.96	92	.277	.341	15	.112	-3	-20	-18	-4	-3.0

● **TOM STURDIVANT**   Sturdivant, Thomas Virgil "Snake" b: 4/28/30, Gordon, Kan. BL/TR, 6'1", 186 lbs. Deb: 4/14/55

YEAR TM/L	W	L	PCT	G	GS	CG	SH	SV	IP	H	HR	BB	SO	RAT	ERA	ERA+	OAV	OOB	BH	AVG	PB	PR	/A	PD	TPI
1955 *NY-A	1	3	.250	33	1	0	0	0	68^1	48	6	42	48	12.1	3.16	118	.203	.329	1	.083	-1	6	4	-0	0.1
1956 *NY-A	16	8	.667	32	17	6	2	5	158^1	134	15	52	110	10.8	3.30	117	.224	**.291**	20	.313	4	15	10	-2	1.7
1957 *NY-A	16	6	**.727**	28	28	7	2	0	201^2	170	14	80	118	11.3	2.54	141	.232	.311	13	.183	1	28	23	-2	2.3
1958 NY-A	3	6	.333	15	10	0	0	0	70^2	77	6	38	41	15.0	4.20	84	.274	.366	4	.190	0	-3	-5	-2	-0.7
1959 NY-A	0	2	.000	7	3	0	0	0	25^1	20	4	9	16	10.3	4.97	73	.222	.293	0	.000	-1	-3	-4	0	-0.3
KC-A	2	6	.250	36	3	0	0	0	71^2	70	9	34	57	13.8	4.65	86	.258	.354	1	.059	-2	-6	-5	1	-0.6
Yr	2	8	.200	43	6	0	0	0	97	90	13	43	73	12.9	4.73	83	.249	.338	1	.043	-3	-9	-9	2	-0.9
1960 Bos-A	3	3	.500	40	3	0	0	0	101^1	106	16	45	67	13.0	4.97	81	.279	.358	4	.182	-1	-12	-10	0	-0.7
1961 Was-A	2	6	.250	15	10	1	1	0	80	67	6	40	39	12.4	4.61	87	.233	.332	2	.077	-1	-5	-5	1	-0.5
Pit-N	5	2	.714	13	11	6	1	1	85^2	81	6	17	45	10.4	2.84	141	.249	.289	8	.250	1	11	11	-1	0.8
1962 Pit-N	9	5	.643	49	12	2	1	2	125^1	120	12	39	76	11.6	3.73	105	.260	.321	6	.182	0	3	3	0	0.3
1963 Pit-N	0	0	—	3	0	0	0	0	8^1	8	1	4	6	13.0	6.48	51	.267	.353	0	.000	-0	-3	-3	0	0.0
Det-A	1	2	.333	28	0	0	0	0	55	43	7	24	36	11.1	3.76	99	.221	.309	0	.000	-1	-1	-0	1	-0.1
KC-A	1	2	.333	17	3	0	0	0	53	47	3	17	26	11.0	3.74	104	.237	.301	0	.000	-1	-1	-1	0	-0.1
Yr	2	4	.333	45	3	0	0	0	108	90	10	41	62	11.0	3.75	102	.226	.300	0	.000	-2	-1	1	1	-0.2
1964 KC-A	0	0	—	3	0	0	0	0	3^2	4	1	2	1	17.2	9.82	39	.308	.438	1	1.000	0	-3	-2	-0	-0.1
NY-N	0	0	—	16	0	0	0	1	28^2	34	2	7	18	13.5	5.97	60	.306	.358	0	.000	-0	-8	-8	-0	-0.1
Total 10	59	51	.536	335	101	22	7	17	1137	1029	107	449	704	12.0	3.74	102	.244	.322	60	.183	-1	18	10	-4	2.1

● **DICK SUCH**   Such, Richard Stanley b: 10/15/44, Sanford, N.C. BL/TR, 6'4", 190 lbs. Deb: 4/6/70 C

YEAR TM/L	W	L	PCT	G	GS	CG	SH	SV	IP	H	HR	BB	SO	RAT	ERA	ERA+	OAV	OOB	BH	AVG	PB	PR	/A	PD	TPI
1970 Was-A	1	5	.167	21	5	0	0	0	54	58	8	45	41	17.3	7.56	47	.258	.410	3	.231	1	-21	-22	0	-2.2

● **CHARLEY SUCHE**   Suche, Charles Morris b: 8/5/15, Cranes Mill, Tex. d: 2/11/84, San Antonio, Tex. BR/TL, 6'2", 190 lbs. Deb: 9/18/38

YEAR TM/L	W	L	PCT	G	GS	CG	SH	SV	IP	H	HR	BB	SO	RAT	ERA	ERA+	OAV	OOB	BH	AVG	PB	PR	/A	PD	TPI
1938 Cle-A	0	0	—	1	0	0	0	0	1^1	3	0	0	0	47.3	27.00	17	.571	.700	1	1.000	1	-3	-3	0	0.1

● **JIM SUCHECKI**   Suchecki, James Joseph b: 8/25/27, Chicago, Ill. BR/TR, 6', 185 lbs. Deb: 5/20/50

YEAR TM/L	W	L	PCT	G	GS	CG	SH	SV	IP	H	HR	BB	SO	RAT	ERA	ERA+	OAV	OOB	BH	AVG	PB	PR	/A	PD	TPI
1950 Bos-A	0	0	—	4	0	0	0	0	4	3	0	4	3	15.8	4.50	109	.231	.412	0	—		0	0	0	0.0
1951 StL-A	0	6	.000	29	6	0	0	0	89^2	113	8	42	47	15.7	5.42	81	.299	.371	2	.100	-2	-13	-10	-1	-0.8
1952 Pit-N	0	0	—	5	0	0	0	0	10	14	1	4	6	17.1	5.40	74	.326	.396	0	.000	-0	-2	-2	-0	0.0
Total 3	0	6	.000	38	6	0	0	0	103^2	130	9	50	56	15.8	5.38	81	.300	.374	2	.091	-2	-15	-12	-1	-0.8

● **WILLIE SUDHOFF**   Sudhoff, John William "Wee Willie" b: 9/17/1874, St.Louis, Mo. d: 5/25/17, St.Louis, Mo. BR/TR, 5'7", 165 lbs. Deb: 8/20/1897

YEAR TM/L	W	L	PCT	G	GS	CG	SH	SV	IP	H	HR	BB	SO	RAT	ERA	ERA+	OAV	OOB	BH	AVG	PB	PR	/A	PD	TPI
1897 StL-N	2	7	.222	11	9	9	0	0	92^2	126	8	21	19	14.3	4.47	99	.321	.356	10	.238	-1	-2	-1	2	0.0
1898 StL-N	11	27	.289	41	38	35	0	0	315	355	11	102	65	13.8	4.34	87	.282	.349	19	.158	-6	-26	-19	8	-1.8
1899 Cle-N	3	8	.273	11	10	8	0	0	86^1	131	3	25	10	17.0	6.98	53	.348	.399	2	.065	-2	-30	-32	2	-2.9
StL-N	13	10	.565	26	24	18	0	0	189^1	203	6	67	33	13.5	3.61	110	.274	.346	14	.206	-0	5	8	4	1.2
Yr	16	18	.471	37	34	26	0	0	275^2	334	9	92	43	14.4	4.67	83	.297	.358	16	.162	-2	-25	-24	6	-1.7
1900 StL-N	6	8	.429	16	14	13	0	0	127	128	3	37	29	12.3	2.76	132	.261	.324	20	.189	-0	13	12	1	1.2
1901 StL-N	17	11	.607	38	26	25	1	2	276^1	281	6	92	78	12.7	3.52	90	.262	.330	19	.176	3	-6	-10	2	-0.4
1902 StL-A	12	12	.500	30	25	20	0	0	220	213	6	67	42	11.9	2.86	123	.255	.319	13	.169	-2	17	16	3	1.7
1903 StL-A	21	15	.583	38	35	30	5	0	293^2	262	4	56	104	12.0	2.27	128	.238	.281	20	.182	-1	23	21	3	2.7
1904 StL-A	8	15	.348	27	24	20	1	0	222^1	232	6	54	63	12.0	3.76	66	.269	.320	14	.165	-0	-29	-32	5	-2.5
1905 StL-A	10	20	.333	32	30	23	1	0	244	222	7	78	70	11.5	2.99	85	.244	.312	16	.186	2	-9	-12	4	-0.8
1906 Was-A	0	2	.000	9	5	0	0	0	19^2	30	1	9	7	18.8	9.15	29	.353	.427	3	.429	1	-14	-14	1	-1.1
Total 10	103	135	.433	279	240	201	10	3	2086^1	2183	62	608	520	12.6	3.56	92	.269	.329	150	.179	-6	-57	-65	34	-2.7

● **JOE SUGDEN**   Sugden, Joseph b: 7/31/1870, Philadelphia, Pa. d: 6/28/59, Philadelphia, Pa. BB/TR, 5'10", 180 lbs. Deb: 7/20/1893 C♦

YEAR TM/L	W	L	PCT	G	GS	CG	SH	SV	IP	H	HR	BB	SO	RAT	ERA	ERA+	OAV	OOB	BH	AVG	PB	PR	/A	PD	TPI
1902 StL-A	0	0	—	1	0	0	0	0	1	1	0	0	0	9.0	0.00		.261	.261	50	.250	0	0	0	0	0.0

● **GEORGE SUGGS**   Suggs, George Franklin b: 7/7/1882, Kinston, N.C. d: 4/4/49, Kinston, N.C. BR/TR, 5'7.5", 168 lbs. Deb: 4/21/08

YEAR TM/L	W	L	PCT	G	GS	CG	SH	SV	IP	H	HR	BB	SO	RAT	ERA	ERA+	OAV	OOB	BH	AVG	PB	PR	/A	PD	TPI
1908 Det-A	1	1	.500	6	1	0	1	1	27	32	0	2	8	11.3	1.67	145	.299	.312	2	.200	0	2	2	-1	0.1
1909 Det-A	1	3	.250	9	4	2	0	1	44^1	34	1	10	18	9.5	2.03	124	.228	.290	1	.067	-1	2	2	-0	0.1
1910 Cin-N	20	12	.625	35	30	23	2	0	266	248	6	48	91	10.5	2.40	121	.253	.297	14	.165	2	19	15	1	2.1
1911 Cin-N	15	13	.536	36	29	17	1	0	260^2	258	3	79	91	12.0	3.00	110	.268	.330	23	.256	6	12	9	3	1.9
1912 Cin-N	19	16	.543	42	36	25	5	3	303	320	8	56	104	11.5	2.94	114	.278	.318	17	.160	-1	16	14	1	1.5
1913 Cin-N	4	15	.348	36	25	17	2	2	199	220	6	35	73	11.6	4.03	81	.292	.329	17	.254	2	-18	-17	3	-1.3
1914 Bal-F	24	14	.632	46	38	26	6	4	319^1	322	6	57	132	11.0	2.90	104	.266	.304	21	.212	2	-1	5	6	1.3
1915 Bal-F	11	17	.393	35	25	12	0	3	232^2	288	2	68	71	14.0	4.14	69	.318	.370	17	.221	5	-36	-33	2	-3.5
Total 8	99	91	.521	245	185	115	16	17	1652	1722	40	355	588	11.7	3.11	100	.277	.322	112	.204	11	-5	-1	14	2.2

YEAR TM/L	W	L	PCT	G	GS	CG	SH	SV	IP	H	HR	BB	SO	RAT	ERA	ERA+	OAV	OOB	BH	AVG	PB	PR	/A	PD	TPI

● ED SUKLA
Sukla, Edward Anthony (b: Edward Anthony Suckla) b: 3/3/43, Long Beach, Cal. BR/TR, 5'11", 170 lbs. Deb: 9/17/64

YEAR TM/L	W	L	PCT	G	GS	CG	SH	SV	IP	H	HR	BB	SO	RAT	ERA	ERA+	OAV	OOB	BH	AVG	PB	PR	/A	PD	TPI
1964 LA-A	0	1	1.000	2	0	0	0	0	2^2	2	1	1	3	10.1	6.75	49	.200	.273	0	—	0	-1	-1	0	-0.3
1965 Cal-A	2	3	.400	25	0	0	0	3	32	32	3	10	12	12.1	4.50	76	.264	.326	0	—	0	-4	-4	1	-0.6
1966 Cal-A	1	1	.500	12	0	0	0	1	16^2	18	4	6	8	13.0	6.48	52	.281	.343	0	.000	-0	-6	-6	-1	-0.8
Total 3	3	5	.375	39	0	0	0	4	51^1	52	8	17	26	12.3	5.26	64	.267	.329	0	.000	-0	-10	-11	0	-1.7

● CHARLIE SULLIVAN
Sullivan, Charles Edward b: 5/23/03, Yadkin Valley, N.C. d: 5/28/35, Maiden, N.C. BL/TR, 6'1", 185 lbs. Deb: 4/21/28

YEAR TM/L	W	L	PCT	G	GS	CG	SH	SV	IP	H	HR	BB	SO	RAT	ERA	ERA+	OAV	OOB	BH	AVG	PB	PR	/A	PD	TPI
1928 Det-A	0	2	.000	3	2	0	0	0	12^1	18	1	6	2	17.5	6.57	63	.360	.429	0	.000	-1	-3	-3	0	-0.5
1930 Det-A	1	5	.167	40	3	2	0	5	93^2	112	9	53	18	16.0	6.53	73	.311	.401	7	.292	2	-20	-18	1	-0.9
1931 Det-A	3	2	.600	31	4	2	0	0	95	109	6	46	28	14.8	4.93	93	.288	.366	4	.167	-1	-6	-4	-0	-0.3
Total 3	4	9	.308	74	9	4	0	5	201	239	16	105	68	15.5	5.78	81	.303	.386	11	.212	-0	-29	-25	1	-1.7

● FLEURY SULLIVAN
Sullivan, Florence P. b: 1862, E.St.Louis, Ill. d: 2/15/1897, E.St.Louis, Ill. Deb: 5/3/1884

YEAR TM/L	W	L	PCT	G	GS	CG	SH	SV	IP	H	HR	BB	SO	RAT	ERA	ERA+	OAV	OOB	BH	AVG	PB	PR	/A	PD	TPI
1884 Pit-a	16	35	.314	51	51	51	2	0	441	496	15	96	189	12.5	4.20	80	.268	.311	29	.153	-9	-47	-41	1	-4.5

● FRANK SULLIVAN
Sullivan, Franklin Leal b: 1/23/30, Hollywood, Cal. BR/TR, 6'6.5", 215 lbs. Deb: 7/31/53

YEAR TM/L	W	L	PCT	G	GS	CG	SH	SV	IP	H	HR	BB	SO	RAT	ERA	ERA+	OAV	OOB	BH	AVG	PB	PR	/A	PD	TPI
1953 Bos-A	1	1	.500	14	0	0	0	0	25^2	24	3	11	17	12.6	5.61	75	.264	.350	1	.250	-1	-5	-4	-0	-0.3
1954 Bos-A	15	12	.556	36	26	11	3	1	206^1	185	18	66	124	11.2	3.14	131	.240	.305	7	.103	-3	13	22	-1	2.7
1955 Bos-A★	**18**	13	.581	35	35	16	3	0	**260**	235	23	100	129	11.8	2.91	147	.241	.316	10	.112	-4	30	40	1	4.2
1956 Bos-A☆	14	7	.667	34	33	12	1	0	242	253	22	82	116	12.8	3.42	135	.268	.332	12	.141	-5	20	32	0	2.0
1957 Bos-A	14	11	.560	31	30	14	3	0	240^2	206	16	48	127	**9.8**	2.73	146	.230	**.275**	13	.165	-2	28	34	2	**3.5**
1958 Bos-A	13	9	.591	32	29	10	2	3	199^1	216	18	49	103	12.1	3.57	112	.278	.324	11	.164	-1	4	10	-1	0.9
1959 Bos-A	9	11	.450	30	26	5	2	1	177^2	172	17	67	107	12.5	3.95	103	.258	.332	12	.200	-1	-2	2	-1	0.0
1960 Bos-A	6	16	.273	40	22	4	0	1	153^2	164	12	52	98	13.0	5.10	79	.269	.332	5	.125	-1	-21	-18	-1	-2.5
1961 Phi-N	3	16	.158	49	18	1	1	6	159^1	161	19	55	114	12.5	4.29	95	.262	.327	5	.152	0	-5	-4	-1	-0.3
1962 Phi-N	0	2	.000	19	0	0	0	0	23	38	2	12	12	20.3	6.26	62	.396	.473	0	—	0	-6	-6	0	-0.4
Min-A	4	1	.800	21	0	0	0	5	33^1	33	3	13	10	12.4	3.24	126	.258	.326	0	.000	-0	3	3	0	0.5
1963 Min-A	1	0	1.000	11	0	0	0	1	11	15	1	4	2	15.5	5.73	64	.349	.404	0	—	0	-3	-3	0	-0.2
Total 11	97	100	.492	351	219	73	15	18	1732	1702	148	559	959	12.0	3.60	116	.257	.320	76	.144	-17	59	108	3	10.1

● HARRY SULLIVAN
Sullivan, Harry Andrew b: 4/12/1888, Rockford, Ill. d: 9/22/19, Rockford, Ill. BL/TL, Deb: 8/11/09

YEAR TM/L	W	L	PCT	G	GS	CG	SH	SV	IP	H	HR	BB	SO	RAT	ERA	ERA+	OAV	OOB	BH	AVG	PB	PR	/A	PD	TPI
1909 StL-N	0	0	—	2	1	0	0	0	1	4	1	2	1	54.0	36.00	7	.500	.600	0	.000	-0	-4	-4	-0	0.0

● JIM SULLIVAN
Sullivan, James E. b: 4/25/1869, Charlestown, Mass. d: 11/30/01, Roxbury, Mass. BR/TR, 5'10", 155 lbs. Deb: 4/22/1891

YEAR TM/L	W	L	PCT	G	GS	CG	SH	SV	IP	H	HR	BB	SO	RAT	ERA	ERA+	OAV	OOB	BH	AVG	PB	PR	/A	PD	TPI
1891 Bos-N	0	0	—	1	0	0	0	0	0^1	2	0	5	0	189.0	81.00	5	.667	.875	0	—	-0	-3	-3	-0	0.0
Col-a	0	1	.000	1	1	1	0	0	9	10	1	5	1	16.0	4.00	87	.272	.374	0	.000	-1	-0	-1	1	-0.1
1895 Bos-N	11	9	.550	21	19	16	0	0	179^1	236	10	58	46	15.6	4.82	109	.312	.374	5	.176	-6	-1	6	-2	-0.2
1896 Bos-N	11	12	.478	31	26	21	1	1	225^1	268	12	68	33	13.7	4.03	113	.293	.346	19	.216	-3	8	13	-3	0.5
1897 *Bos-N	4	5	.444	13	9	8	1	2	89	91	1	26	17	12.0	3.94	113	.263	.318	6	.182	-3	4	5	-1	0.1
Total 4	26	27	.491	67	55	46	2	3	503	607	24	162	97	14.2	4.35	108	.295	.354	40	.190	-11	8	20	-6	0.3

● JIM SULLIVAN
Sullivan, James Richard b: 4/5/1894, Mine Run, Va. d: 2/12/72, Burtonsville, Md. BR/TR, 5'11", 165 lbs. Deb: 9/27/21

YEAR TM/L	W	L	PCT	G	GS	CG	SH	SV	IP	H	HR	BB	SO	RAT	ERA	ERA+	OAV	OOB	BH	AVG	PB	PR	/A	PD	TPI
1921 Phi-A	0	2	.000	2	2	2	0	0	17	20	0	7	8	14.3	3.18	140	.294	.360	0	.000	-1	2	2	-0	0.1
1922 Phi-A	0	2	.000	20	2	1	0	0	51^1	76	3	25	15	17.9	5.44	78	.373	.443	1	.091	-0	-8	-7	-0	-0.3
1923 Cle-A	0	1	.000	3	0	0	0	0	5	10	0	5	4	28.8	14.40	28	.476	.593	0	.000	-0	-6	-6	-0	-0.9
Total 3	0	5	.000	25	4	3	0	0	73^1	106	3	37	27	17.8	5.52	78	.362	.437	1	.056	-2	-12	-10	-1	-1.1

● JOHN SULLIVAN
Sullivan, John Jeremiah "Lefty" b: 5/31/1894, Chicago, Ill. d: 7/7/58, Chicago, Ill. BL/TL, 5'11", 165 lbs. Deb: 7/18/19

YEAR TM/L	W	L	PCT	G	GS	CG	SH	SV	IP	H	HR	BB	SO	RAT	ERA	ERA+	OAV	OOB	BH	AVG	PB	PR	/A	PD	TPI
1919 Chi-A	0	1	.000	4	2	1	0	0	15	24	1	8	9	19.8	4.20	76	.364	.440	0	.000	-0	-2	-2	-1	-0.2

● JOE SULLIVAN
Sullivan, Joe b: 9/26/10, Mason City, Ill. d: 4/8/85, Sequim, Wash. BL/TL, 5'11", 175 lbs. Deb: 4/20/35

YEAR TM/L	W	L	PCT	G	GS	CG	SH	SV	IP	H	HR	BB	SO	RAT	ERA	ERA+	OAV	OOB	BH	AVG	PB	PR	/A	PD	TPI
1935 Det-A	6	6	.500	25	12	5	0	0	125^2	119	4	71	53	13.8	3.51	119	.244	.344	7	.163	-1	13	9	-1	0.6
1936 Det-A	2	5	.286	26	4	1	0	1	79^2	111	4	40	32	17.3	6.78	73	.331	.406	5	.179	-1	-15	-16	-1	-1.3
1939 Bos-N	6	9	.400	31	11	7	0	2	113^2	114	9	50	46	13.1	3.64	101	.266	.346	12	.300	3	3	1	0	0.4
1940 Bos-N	10	14	.417	36	22	7	0	1	177^1	157	9	89	64	12.9	3.55	105	.240	.339	14	.197	-0	6	3	0	0.4
1941 Bos-N	2	2	.500	16	2	0	0	0	52^1	60	2	26	11	15.1	4.13	86	.290	.374	1	.067	-1	-3	-3	1	-0.3
Pit-N	4	1	.800	16	4	0	0	1	39^1	40	2	22	10	14.2	2.97	121	.258	.350	4	.364	1	3	3	0	0.5
Yr	6	3	.667	32	6	0	0	1	91^2	100	4	48	21	14.5	3.63	99	.275	.359	5	.192	-0	-0	-1	1	0.2
Total 5	30	37	.448	150	55	20	0	5	588	601	25	298	216	14.0	4.01	99	.265	.355	43	.207	1	7	-3	0	0.3

● MARTY SULLIVAN
Sullivan, Martin C. b: 10/20/1862, Lowell, Mass. d: 1/6/1894, Lowell, Mass. BR/TR, Deb: 4/30/1887 ♦

YEAR TM/L	W	L	PCT	G	GS	CG	SH	SV	IP	H	HR	BB	SO	RAT	ERA	ERA+	OAV	OOB	BH	AVG	PB	PR	/A	PD	TPI
1887 Chi-N	0	0	—	1	0	0	0	0	2^1	6	0	1	1	27.0	7.71	58	.500	.538	134	.284	0	-1	-1	-0	0.0

● MIKE SULLIVAN
Sullivan, Michael Joseph "Big Mike" b: 10/23/1866, Boston, Mass. d: 6/14/06, Boston, Mass. BL, 6'1", 210 lbs. Deb: 6/17/1889

YEAR TM/L	W	L	PCT	G	GS	CG	SH	SV	IP	H	HR	BB	SO	RAT	ERA	ERA+	OAV	OOB	BH	AVG	PB	PR	/A	PD	TPI
1889 Was-N	0	3	.000	9	3	3	0	0	41	47	2	32	15	18.0	7.24	54	.279	.403	1	.053	-2	-15	-15	-0	-1.0
1890 Chi-N	5	6	.455	12	12	10	0	0	96	108	3	58	33	15.9	4.59	80	.275	.374	5	.125	-3	-11	-10	-0	-1.2
1891 Phi-a	0	2	.000	2	2	2	0	0	18	17	2	10	7	15.0	3.50	109	.241	.359	0	.000	-1	0	1	-0	-0.1
NY-N	1	2	.333	3	3	3	0	0	24	24	0	8	11	12.4	3.38	95	.251	.315	2	.200	-0	-0	-0	-0	-0.1
1892 Cin-N	12	4	.750	21	16	15	0	0	166^1	174	4	56	44	12.2	3.08	106	.264	.344	13	.176	-2	4	3	-2	-0.1
1893 Cin-N	8	11	.421	27	18	14	0	1	183^2	200	5	103	40	15.7	5.05	95	.269	.371	16	.203	-3	-8	-5	-0	-0.7
1894 Was-N	2	10	.167	20	12	11	0	1	117^2	166	10	74	21	19.0	6.58	80	.329	.423	9	.158	-4	-16	-17	-0	-1.5
Cle-N	6	5	.545	13	11	9	0	0	90^2	128	4	47	19	17.7	6.35	86	.329	.405	13	.295	-0	-10	-9	-1	-0.8
Yr	8	15	.348	33	23	20	0	1	208^1	294	14	121	40	18.1	6.48	83	.326	.407	22	.218	-4	-27	-26	-1	-2.3
1895 Cle-N	1	2	.333	4	3	2	0	0	31	42	1	16	5	17.1	8.42	59	.318	.396	2	.133	-2	-13	-12	-0	-0.9
1896 NY-N	10	13	.435	25	22	18	0	0	185^1	188	3	71	42	13.2	4.66	90	.261	.338	16	.208	-3	-6	-9	0	-1.2
1897 NY-N	8	7	.533	23	16	11	1	2	148^2	183	6	71	35	16.2	5.09	82	.300	.386	18	.273	0	-13	-15	-1	-1.1
1898 Bos-N	0	1	.000	3	2	0	0	0	12	19	1	9	1	21.8	12.00	31	.356	.457	1	.333	0	-11	-11	-0	-0.7
1899 Bos-N	1	0	1.000	1	1	1	0	0	9	10	1	4	1	15.0	5.00	83	.281	.369	1	.333	0	-1	-1	-0	-0.1
Total 11	54	66	.450	163	121	99	1	4	1123^1	1311	46	577	286	15.8	5.11	84	.285	.375	97	.196	-21	-100	-102	-5	-9.5

● PAT SULLIVAN
Sullivan, Patrick J. b: 12/22/1862, Milwaukee, Wis. TR, 5'11", 165 lbs. Deb: 8/30/1884 ♦

YEAR TM/L	W	L	PCT	G	GS	CG	SH	SV	IP	H	HR	BB	SO	RAT	ERA	ERA+	OAV	OOB	BH	AVG	PB	PR	/A	PD	TPI
1884 KC-U	0	1	.000	1	1	0	0	0	7	15	1	5	1	25.7	11.57	19	.408	.479	22	.193	-0	-7	-7	-0	-0.6

● LEFTY SULLIVAN
Sullivan, Paul Thomas b: 9/7/16, Nashville, Tenn. d: 11/1/88, Scottsdale, Ariz. BL/TL, 6'3", 204 lbs. Deb: 5/6/39

YEAR TM/L	W	L	PCT	G	GS	CG	SH	SV	IP	H	HR	BB	SO	RAT	ERA	ERA+	OAV	OOB	BH	AVG	PB	PR	/A	PD	TPI
1939 Cle-A	0	1	.000	7	1	0	0	0	12^2	9	0	9	4	13.5	4.26	103	.214	.365	0	.000	-0	1	0	-1	-0.1

● SUTER SULLIVAN
Sullivan, Suter G. b: 10/14/1872, Baltimore, Md. d: 4/19/25, Baltimore, Md. 6', 170 lbs. Deb: 7/24/1898 ♦

YEAR TM/L	W	L	PCT	G	GS	CG	SH	SV	IP	H	HR	BB	SO	RAT	ERA	ERA+	OAV	OOB	BH	AVG	PB	PR	/A	PD	TPI
1898 StL-N	0	0	—	1	0	0	0	0	6	10	0	4	3	21.0	1.50	253	.367	.449	32	.222	0	1	2	-0	0.0

● TOM SULLIVAN
Sullivan, Thomas b: 3/1/1860, New York, N.Y. d: 4/12/47, Cincinnati, Ohio Deb: 9/27/1884

YEAR TM/L	W	L	PCT	G	GS	CG	SH	SV	IP	H	HR	BB	SO	RAT	ERA	ERA+	OAV	OOB	BH	AVG	PB	PR	/A	PD	TPI
1884 Col-a	2	2	.500	4	4	4	0	0	31	42	3	12	3	13.1	4.06	75	.318	.333	1	.091	-1	-3	-4	-1	-0.5
1886 Lou-a	2	7	.222	9	9	8	0	0	75	94	6	33	27	15.5	3.96	92	.305	.376	3	.111	-2	-4	-3	0	-0.4
1888 KC-a	8	16	.333	24	24	24	0	0	214^2	227	2	68	84	13.4	3.40	101	.262	.332	10	.109	-6	-8	1	5	0.0
1889 KC-a	2	8	.200	10	10	10	0	0	87^1	111	2	48	24	17.1	5.67	74	.300	.391	5	.152	-1	-18	-14	-1	-1.3
Total 4	14	33	.298	47	47	46	0	0	408	474	12	152	147	14.5	4.04	89	.283	.354	19	.117	-9	-33	-20	4	-2.2

● TOM SULLIVAN — Sullivan, Thomas Augustin b: 10/18/1895, Boston, Mass. d: 9/23/62, Boston, Mass. BL/TL, 5'11", 178 lbs. Deb: 5/15/22

YEAR TM/L	W	L	PCT	G	GS	CG	SH	SV	IP	H	HR	BB	SO	RAT	ERA	ERA+	OAV	OOB	BH	AVG	PB	PR	/A	PD	TPI
1922 Phi-N	0	0	—	3	0	0	0	0	8	16	0	5	2	24.8	11.25	41	.410	.489	1	.250	1	-6	-6	0	0.1

● SLEEPER SULLIVAN — Sullivan, Thomas Jefferson "Old Iron Hands" b: St.Louis, Mo. d: 9/25/1899, Camden, N.J. BR/TR, 175 lbs. Deb: 5/3/1881 ♦

YEAR TM/L	W	L	PCT	G	GS	CG	SH	SV	IP	H	HR	BB	SO	RAT	ERA	ERA+	OAV	OOB	BH	AVG	PB	PR	/A	PD	TPI
1884 StL-U	1	0	1.000	1	1	0	0	0	6	10	0	1	4	15.0	4.50	53	.349	.349	1	.111	-1	-1	-1	-0	-0.2

● BILL SULLIVAN — Sullivan, William T. Deb: 4/19/1890

YEAR TM/L	W	L	PCT	G	GS	CG	SH	SV	IP	H	HR	BB	SO	RAT	ERA	ERA+	OAV	OOB	BH	AVG	PB	PR	/A	PD	TPI
1890 Syr-a	1	4	.200	6	6	4	0	0	42	51	2	27	13	18.0	7.93	45	.291	.403	2	.091	-2	-19	-21	-0	-1.8

● ED SUMMERS — Summers, Oron Edgar "Kickapoo Ed" or "Chief" b: 12/5/1884, Ladoga, Ind. d: 5/12/53, Indianapolis, Ind. BB/TR, 6'2", 180 lbs. Deb: 4/16/08

YEAR TM/L	W	L	PCT	G	GS	CG	SH	SV	IP	H	HR	BB	SO	RAT	ERA	ERA+	OAV	OOB	BH	AVG	PB	PR	/A	PD	TPI
1908 *Det-A	24	12	.667	40	32	23	5	1	301	271	3	55	103	10.3	1.64	147	.242	.290	14	.124	-6	25	26	-1	2.4
1909 *Det-A	19	9	.679	35	32	24	3	1	281²	243	4	52	107	9.7	2.24	113	.227	.269	10	.106	-4	8	9	1	0.5
1910 Det-A	13	12	.520	30	25	18	1	0	220¹	211	8	60	82	11.3	2.53	104	.254	.308	14	.184	-0	-2	1	0	0.3
1911 Det-A	11	11	.500	30	20	13	0	1	179¹	189	3	51	65	12.6	3.66	95	.274	.334	16	.254	1	-6	-4	-1	-0.5
1912 Det-A	1	1	.500	3	3	1	0	0	16²	16	1	3	5	10.3	4.86	67	.250	.284	3	.500	1	-3	-3	0	-0.2
Total 5	68	45	.602	138	112	79	9	3	999	930	19	221	362	10.8	2.42	111	.246	.296	57	.162	-9	23	30	-0	2.5

● BILLY SUNDAY — Sunday, William Ashley "Parson" or "The Evangelist" b: 11/19/1862, Ames, Iowa d: 11/6/35, Chicago, Ill. BL/TR, 5'10", 160 lbs. Deb: 5/22/1883 ♦

YEAR TM/L	W	L	PCT	G	GS	CG	SH	SV	IP	H	HR	BB	SO	RAT	ERA	ERA+	OAV	OOB	BH	AVG	PB	PR	/A	PD	TPI
1890 Pit-N	0	0	—	1	0	0	0	0	1	0	0	0	0		∞	—	1.000	1.000	92	.257	-2	-2	-2	0	-0.2

● GORDIE SUNDIN — Sundin, Gordon Vincent b: 10/10/37, Minneapolis, Minn. BR/TR, 6'4", 215 lbs. Deb: 9/19/56

YEAR TM/L	W	L	PCT	G	GS	CG	SH	SV	IP	H	HR	BB	SO	RAT	ERA	ERA+	OAV	OOB	BH	AVG	PB	PR	/A	PD	TPI
1956 Bal-A	0	0	—	1	0	0	0	0	0	0	0	2	0	—	∞	—	—	1.000	0	—		-1	-1	-0	-0.1

● STEVE SUNDRA — Sundra, Stephen Richard "Smokey" b: 3/27/10, Luxor, Pa. d: 3/23/52, Cleveland, Ohio BR/TR, 6'2", 190 lbs. Deb: 4/17/36

YEAR TM/L	W	L	PCT	G	GS	CG	SH	SV	IP	H	HR	BB	SO	RAT	ERA	ERA+	OAV	OOB	BH	AVG	PB	PR	/A	PD	TPI
1936 NY-A	0	0	—	1	0	0	0	0	2	2	0	2	0	18.0	0.00	—	.286	.444	0	.000	-0	1	1	-0	0.0
1938 NY-A	6	4	.600	25	8	3	0	0	93²	107	7	43	33	14.4	4.80	94	.291	.365	6	.182	1	-0	-3	1	-0.1
1939 *NY-A	11	1	.917	24	11	8	1	0	120²	110	7	56	27	12.4	2.76	158	.240	.323	13	.265	4	25	21	1	2.2
1940 NY-A	4	6	.400	27	8	2	0	2	99¹	121	11	42	26	14.9	5.53	73	.299	.366	4	.138	-1	-13	-16	0	-1.5
1941 Was-A	9	13	.409	28	23	11	0	0	168¹	203	11	61	50	14.2	5.29	76	.294	.352	13	.217	2	-21	-23	-1	-2.4
1942 Was-A	1	3	.250	6	4	2	0	0	33²	43	1	15	5	15.8	5.61	65	.305	.376	2	.167	-0	-7	-7	-0	-0.8
StL-A	8	3	.727	20	13	6	0	0	110²	122	2	29	26	12.3	3.82	97	.275	.319	9	.225	3	-2	-1	-0	0.1
Yr	9	6	.600	26	17	8	0	0	144¹	165	3	44	31	13.0	4.24	87	.282	.332	11	.212	2	-9	-9	-0	-0.7
1943 StL-A	15	11	.577	32	29	13	3	0	208	212	11	66	44	12.0	3.25	103	.266	.322	16	.219	1	1	2	0	0.4
1944 StL-A	2	0	1.000	3	3	2	0	0	19	15	1	4	1	9.0	1.42	253	.211	.253	0	.000	-0	4	5	0	0.5
1946 StL-A	0	0	—	2	0	0	0	0	4	9	0	3	1	27.0	11.25	37	.409	.480	0	—	-0	-1	-0	0	-0.1
Total 9	56	41	.577	168	99	47	4	2	859¹	944	50	321	214	13.3	4.17	94	.277	.340	63	.209	10	-16	-24	1	-1.6

● TOM SUNKEL — Sunkel, Thomas Jacob "Lefty" b: 8/9/12, Paris, Ill. BL/TL, 6'1", 190 lbs. Deb: 8/26/37

YEAR TM/L	W	L	PCT	G	GS	CG	SH	SV	IP	H	HR	BB	SO	RAT	ERA	ERA+	OAV	OOB	BH	AVG	PB	PR	/A	PD	TPI
1937 StL-N	0	0	—	9	1	0	0	1	29¹	24	0	11	9	10.7	2.76	144	.214	.285	1	.111	-1	4	4	-0	-0.1
1939 StL-N	4	4	.500	20	11	2	1	0	85¹	79	4	56	54	14.3	4.22	98	.242	.354	9	.321	2	-3	-1	-1	0.0
1941 NY-N	1	1	.500	2	2	1	1	0	15¹	7	0	12	14	11.7	2.93	126	.140	.317	2	.333	0	1	1	-0	0.2
1942 NY-N	3	6	.333	19	11	3	0	0	63²	65	5	41	29	15.0	4.81	70	.269	.375	2	.105	-1	-11	-10	-2	-1.6
1943 NY-N	0	1	.000	1	1	0	0	0	2²	4	1	3	0	23.6	10.13	34	.308	.438	0	—	0	-2	-2	0	-0.5
1944 Bro-N	1	3	.250	12	3	0	0	2	24	39	1	10	6	18.4	7.50	47	.368	.422	0	.000	-1	-10	-11	-1	-1.7
Total 6	9	15	.375	63	29	6	2	2	220¹	218	11	133	112	14.4	4.53	83	.256	.358	14	.212	-1	-21	-19	-4	-3.7

● RICK SURHOFF — Surhoff, Richard Clifford b: 10/3/62, Bronx, N.Y. BR/TR, 6'3", 210 lbs. Deb: 9/8/85 F

YEAR TM/L	W	L	PCT	G	GS	CG	SH	SV	IP	H	HR	BB	SO	RAT	ERA	ERA+	OAV	OOB	BH	AVG	PB	PR	/A	PD	TPI
1985 Phi-N	0	1	.000	2	0	0	0	0	1	2	0	1	1	18.0		—	.500	.500	0		0	0	0	0	0.4
Tex-A	0	0	—	7	0	0	0	0	8¹	12	3	2	8	16.2	7.56	56	.343	.395	0		0	-3	-3	-0	-0.6
Total 1	1	1	.500	9	0	0	0	2	9¹	14	2	3	9	16.4	6.75	62	.359	.405	0		0	-3	-3	-0	-0.2

● MAX SURKONT — Surkont, Matthew Constantine b: 6/16/22, Central Falls, R.I. d: 10/8/86, Largo, Fla. BR/TR, 6', 205 lbs. Deb: 4/19/49

YEAR TM/L	W	L	PCT	G	GS	CG	SH	SV	IP	H	HR	BB	SO	RAT	ERA	ERA+	OAV	OOB	BH	AVG	PB	PR	/A	PD	TPI
1949 Chi-A	3	5	.375	44	2	0	0	4	96	92	9	60	38	14.5	4.78	87	.255	.366	1	.045	-1	-6	-7	-1	-0.8
1950 Bos-N	9	6	.714	9	6	2	0	0	55²	63	5	20	21	13.7	3.23	119	.285	.350	5	.435	5	6	4	-1	0.9
1951 Bos-N	12	16	.429	37	33	11	2	1	237	230	21	89	110	12.4	3.99	92	.252	.323	11	.151	-1	-1	-8	-3	-1.1
1952 Bos-N	12	13	.480	31	29	12	3	0	215	201	14	76	125	11.7	3.77	96	.245	.311	7	.111	-1	-1	-4	-1	-0.6
1953 Mil-N	11	5	.688	28	24	11	2	0	170	168	22	64	83	12.3	4.18	94	.255	.321	16	.286	7	2	-5	1	0.3
1954 Pit-N	9	18	.333	33	29	11	0	0	208¹	216	25	78	78	12.9	4.41	95	.268	.335	10	.167	-8	-8	-5	0	-0.5
1955 Pit-N	7	14	.333	35	22	5	0	2	166¹	194	23	78	84	14.9	5.57	74	.298	.376	7	.140	-1	-28	-27	-2	-3.2
1956 Pit-N	0	0	—	1	0	0	0	0	2	0	0	3	1	22.5	4.50	84	.333	.556	0	—	-0	-0	-0	0	0.0
StL-N	0	0	—	5	0	0	0	0	5²	10	3	2	5	19.1	9.53	40	.417	.462	0	—	-0	-4	-4	-0	0.0
NY-N	2	2	.500	8	4	1	0	1	32	24	5	9	18	9.3	4.78	79	.202	.258	1	.111	-0	-4	-4	-0	-0.5
Yr	2	2	.500	14	4	1	0	1	39²	36	8	14	24	11.3	5.45	69	.240	.305	1	.100	-0	-7	-7	-1	-0.5
1957 NY-N	0	1	.000	5	0	0	0	0	14²	24	4	9	2	21.5	9.95	40	.321	.367	0	—	-0	-4	-4	-0	-0.6
Total 9	61	76	.445	236	149	53	7	8	1194¹	1209	134	481	571	12.9	4.38	89	.262	.335	63	.176	8	-48	-63	-5	-6.1

● GEORGE SUSCE — Susce, George Daniel b: 9/13/31, Pittsburgh, Pa. BR/TR, 6'1", 180 lbs. Deb: 4/15/55 F

YEAR TM/L	W	L	PCT	G	GS	CG	SH	SV	IP	H	HR	BB	SO	RAT	ERA	ERA+	OAV	OOB	BH	AVG	PB	PR	/A	PD	TPI
1955 Bos-A	9	7	.563	29	15	6	1	1	144¹	123	12	49	60	11.2	3.06	140	.232	.306	7	.143	-2	15	20	-0	1.8
1956 Bos-A	2	4	.333	21	6	0	0	0	69²	71	4	44	26	15.4	6.20	74	.262	.373	4	.222	1	-16	-12	-0	-0.8
1957 Bos-A	7	3	.700	29	5	0	0	1	88¹	93	6	41	40	14.0	4.28	93	.274	.358	3	.120	-1	-5	-3	-1	-0.5
1958 Bos-A	0	0	—	2	0	0	0	0	2	6	1	1	0	31.5	18.00	22	.600	.636	0	—	-0	-3	-3	-0	0.0
Det-A	4	3	.571	27	10	2	0	0	90²	90	7	26	42	11.8	3.67	110	.259	.316	3	.125	-1	1	4	-2	0.0
Yr	4	3	.571	29	10	2	0	0	92²	96	8	27	42	12.2	3.98	101	.268	.325	3	.125	-1	-2	1	-2	0.0
1959 Det-A	0	0	—	9	0	0	0	0	14²	24	4	9	9	21.5	12.89	32	.358	.449	0	.000	-0	-15	-14	0	-0.5
Total 5	22	17	.564	117	36	8	1	2	409²	407	44	170	177	13.1	4.42	95	.260	.340	17	.145	-2	-23	-9	-4	0.5

● RICK SUTCLIFFE — Sutcliffe, Richard Lee b: 6/21/56, Independence, Mo. BL/TR, 6'7", 215 lbs. Deb: 9/29/76

YEAR TM/L	W	L	PCT	G	GS	CG	SH	SV	IP	H	HR	BB	SO	RAT	ERA	ERA+	OAV	OOB	BH	AVG	PB	PR	/A	PD	TPI
1976 LA-N	0	0	—	1	1	0	0	0	5	2	0	1	3	5.4	0.00	—	.125	.176	0	.000	-0	2	2	-0	0.0
1978 LA-N	0	0	—	2	0	0	0	0	1²	2	1	2	1	21.6	0.00	—	.286	.444	0		0	1	1	0	0.0
1979 LA-N	17	10	.630	39	30	5	1	0	242	217	16	97	117	11.8	3.46	105	.243	.319	21	.247	5	7	5	-2	0.8
1980 LA-N	3	9	.250	42	10	1	1	5	110	122	10	55	59	14.6	5.56	63	.285	.368	4	.148	-0	-24	-25	-1	-2.9
1981 LA-N	2	2	.500	14	6	0	0	0	47	41	5	20	16	12.1	4.02	83	.238	.325	2	.182	1	-3	-4	0	-0.2
1982 Cle-A	14	8	.636	34	27	6	1	1	216	174	16	98	142	11.5	**2.96**	138	**.226**	.317	0		0	**27**	27	1	2.7
1983 Cle-A☆	17	11	.607	36	35	10	2	0	243¹	251	23	102	160	13.3	4.29	99	.268	.344	0		0	-6	-1	-2	-0.2
1984 Cle-A	5	5	.444	15	15	2	0	0	94¹	111	7	46	58	15.2	5.15	79	.298	.378	0		0	-12	-11	-0	-1.0
*Chi-N	16	1	**.941**	20	20	7	3	0	150¹	123	9	39	155	9.8	2.69	145	.220	.272	14	.250	3	15	20	2	2.8
1985 Chi-N	8	8	.500	20	20	6	0	0	130	119	13	44	102	11.5	3.18	126	.240	.306	2	.105	0	6	12	1	1.8
1986 Chi-N	5	14	.263	28	27	4	1	0	176²	166	18	96	122	13.4	4.64	87	.252	.348	11	.208	1	-18	-12	1	-0.8
1987 Chi-N★	**18**	10	.643	34	34	6	1	0	237¹	223	24	106	174	12.6	3.68	116	.252	.335	12	.148	2	11	16	4	2.4
1988 Chi-N	13	14	.481	32	32	12	2	0	226	232	18	70	144	12.1	3.86	93	.269	.325	12	.160	-1	-10	-6	-1	-0.3
1989 *Chi-N★	16	11	.593	35	34	5	1	0	229	202	18	69	153	10.7	3.66	101	.243	.310	10	.143	1	9	12	-0	0.6
1990 Chi-N	0	2	.000	5	5	0	0	0	21¹	25	2	12	7	15.6	5.91	69	.305	.394	0	—	-0	-5	-4	0	-0.3
1991 Chi-N	6	5	.545	19	18	0	0	0	96²	96	8	45	52	13.1	4.10	95	.264	.345	3	.094	-1	-4	-2	0	-0.4
1992 Bal-A	16	15	.516	36	36	5	2	0	237¹	251	20	74	109	12.6	4.47	90	.273	.332	0		0	-14	-12	-2	-1.8

YEAR	TM/L	W	L	PCT	G	GS	CG	SH	SV	IP	H	HR	BB	SO	RAT	ERA	ERA+	OAV	OOB	BH	AVG	PB	PR	/A	PD	TPI
1993	Bal-A	10	10	.500	29	28	3	0	0	166	212	23	74	80	15.8	5.75	78	.314	.386	0	—	0	-26	-24	1	-2.5
1994	StL-N	6	4	.600	16	14	0	0	0	67²	93	11	32	26	16.9	6.52	62	.331	.403	3	.130	-0	-17	-18	1	-2.2
Total	18	171	139	.552	457	392	72	18	6	2697²	2662	236	1081	1679	12.6	4.08	97	.260	.334	102	.181	17	-77	-35	10	-1.5

● HARRY SUTER
Suter, Harry Richard "Handsome Harry" or "Rube" b: 9/15/1887, Independence, Mo. d: 7/24/71, Topeka, Kan. BL/TL, 5'10", 190 lbs. Deb: 4/16/09

YEAR	TM/L	W	L	PCT	G	GS	CG	SH	SV	IP	H	HR	BB	SO	RAT	ERA	ERA+	OAV	OOB	BH	AVG	PB	PR	/A	PD	TPI
1909	Chi-A	2	3	.400	18	7	3	1	1	87¹	72	2	28	53	10.7	2.47	95	.199	.264	3	.094	-1	0	-1	-1	-0.3

● DARRELL SUTHERLAND
Sutherland, Darrell Wayne b: 11/14/41, Glendale, Cal. BR/TR, 6'4", 169 lbs. Deb: 6/28/64 F

YEAR	TM/L	W	L	PCT	G	GS	CG	SH	SV	IP	H	HR	BB	SO	RAT	ERA	ERA+	OAV	OOB	BH	AVG	PB	PR	/A	PD	TPI
1964	NY-N	0	3	.000	10	4	0	0	0	26²	32	1	12	9	15.5	7.76	46	.302	.383	1	.200	0	-13	-12	1	-1.1
1965	NY-N	3	1	.750	18	2	0	0	0	48	33	4	17	16	10.1	2.81	125	.199	.289	2	.154	0	4	4	2	0.5
1966	NY-N	2	0	1.000	31	0	0	0	1	44¹	60	6	25	23	17.7	4.87	75	.339	.426	2	.667	-1	-6	-6	1	-0.1
1968	Cle-A	0	0	—	3	0	0	0	0	3¹	6	0	4	2	27.0	8.10	37	.375	.500	0	—	0	-2	-2	-0	0.0
Total	4	5	4	.556	62	6	0	0	1	122¹	131	11	58	50	14.5	4.78	75	.282	.371	5	.238	1	-17	-17	3	-0.7

● SUDS SUTHERLAND
Sutherland, Harvey Scott b: 2/20/1894, Beaverton, Ore. d: 5/11/72, Portland, Ore. BR/TR, 6', 180 lbs. Deb: 4/14/21

YEAR	TM/L	W	L	PCT	G	GS	CG	SH	SV	IP	H	HR	BB	SO	RAT	ERA	ERA+	OAV	OOB	BH	AVG	PB	PR	/A	PD	TPI
1921	Det-A	6	2	.750	13	8	3	0	0	58	80	1	18	18	15.2	4.97	86	.328	.374	11	.407	2	-4	-4	2	-0.1

● DIZZY SUTHERLAND
Sutherland, Howard Alvin b: 4/9/22, Washington, D.C. d: 8/26/79, Washington, D.C. BL/TL, 6', 200 lbs. Deb: 9/20/49

YEAR	TM/L	W	L	PCT	G	GS	CG	SH	SV	IP	H	HR	BB	SO	RAT	ERA	ERA+	OAV	OOB	BH	AVG	PB	PR	/A	PD	TPI
1949	Was-A	0	1	.000	1	1	0	0	0	1	2	0	6	0	72.0	45.00	9	.400	.727	0	—	0	-5	-5	0	-1.7

● BRUCE SUTTER
Sutter, Howard Bruce b: 1/8/53, Lancaster, Pa. BR/TR, 6'2", 190 lbs. Deb: 5/9/76

YEAR	TM/L	W	L	PCT	G	GS	CG	SH	SV	IP	H	HR	BB	SO	RAT	ERA	ERA+	OAV	OOB	BH	AVG	PB	PR	/A	PD	TPI
1976	Chi-N	6	3	.667	52	0	0	0	10	83¹	63	4	26	73	9.6	2.70	143	.209	.272	0	.000	-1	7	11	-0	1.3
1977	Chi-N†	7	3	.700	62	0	0	0	31	107¹	69	5	23	129	7.8	1.34	327	.183	.232	3	.150	-0	31	36	1	5.8
1978	Chi-N★	8	10	.444	64	0	0	0	27	99	82	10	34	106	10.6	3.18	127	.220	.287	1	.077	-0	4	9	0	2.2
1979	Chi-N★	6	6	.500	62	0	0	0	37	101¹	67	3	32	110	8.8	2.22	185	.186	.252	3	.250	-1	17	21	1	4.5
1980	Chi-N★	5	8	.385	60	0	0	0	28	102¹	90	5	34	76	11.0	2.64	148	.242	.307	1	.111	-1	11	14	-0	2.7
1981	StL-N★	3	5	.375	48	0	0	0	25	82¹	64	5	24	57	9.7	2.62	136	.218	.279	0	.000	-1	8	9	1	1.3
1982	*StL-N	9	8	.529	70	0	0	0	36	102¹	88	8	34	61	11.0	2.90	125	.235	.303	1	.125	-0	8	8	0	2.0
1983	StL-N	9	10	.474	60	0	0	0	21	89¹	90	8	30	64	12.2	4.23	86	.262	.324	0	.000	-1	-6	-6	2	-1.4
1984	StL-N☆	5	7	.417	71	0	0	0	45	122²	109	6	23	77	9.8	1.54	225	.245	.284	0	.000	-0	28	26	1	4.9
1985	Atl-N	7	7	.500	58	0	0	0	23	88¹	91	13	29	52	12.5	4.48	86	.267	.330	0	.000	-0	-9	-6	-0	-1.4
1986	Atl-N	2	0	1.000	16	0	0	0	3	18²	17	3	9	16	12.5	4.34	92	.243	.329	0	.000	-0	-1	-1	0	-0.1
1988	Atl-N	1	4	.200	38	0	0	0	14	45¹	49	4	11	40	12.1	4.76	77	.275	.321	0	.000	-0	-7	-5	0	-0.1
Total	12	68	71	.489	661	0	0	0	300	1042¹	879	77	309	861	10.4	2.83	135	.230	.289	9	.088	-5	91	116	4	20.8

● JACK SUTTHOFF
Sutthoff, John Gerhard "Sunny Jack" b: 6/29/1873, Cincinnati, Ohio d: 8/3/42, Cincinnati, Ohio BL/TR, 5'9", 175 lbs. Deb: 9/15/1898

YEAR	TM/L	W	L	PCT	G	GS	CG	SH	SV	IP	H	HR	BB	SO	RAT	ERA	ERA+	OAV	OOB	BH	AVG	PB	PR	/A	PD	TPI
1898	Was-N	0	0	—	2	1	0	0	0	8¹	16	1	8	3	25.9	12.96	28	.401	.501	1	.333	-9	-9	0	0.0
1899	StL-N	0	2	.000	2	2	1	0	0	13	19	0	10	4	20.1	10.38	38	.339	.440	0	.000	-1	-9	-9	1	-1.0
1901	Cin-N	1	6	.143	10	4	4	0	0	70¹	82	2	39	12	15.7	5.50	58	.289	.379	3	.107	-2	-17	-18	-1	-1.7
1903	Cin-N	16	9	.640	30	27	21	3	0	224²	207	6	79	76	12.1	2.80	127	.246	.323	12	.143	-3	12	19	-1	1.4
1904	Cin-N	5	6	.455	12	10	8	1	0	90	83	1	43	27	12.9	2.30	127	.255	.348	6	.182	-0	4	6	-2	0.5
	Phi-N	6	13	.316	19	18	17	0	0	163²	172	2	71	46	13.9	3.68	73	.272	.354	10	.164	-0	-17	-18	-1	-2.1
	Yr	11	19	.367	31	28	25	0	0	253²	255	2	114	73	13.4	3.19	87	.266	.349	16	.170	-1	-13	-12	-3	-1.6
1905	Phi-N	3	4	.429	13	6	4	1	0	77²	82	2	36	26	14.1	3.82	76	.290	.378	2	.080	-1	-7	-8	0	-0.7
Total	6	31	40	.437	88	68	55	4	0	647²	661	10	286	194	13.6	3.65	86	.269	.353	34	.142	-7	-43	-37	-5	-3.6

● DON SUTTON
Sutton, Donald Howard b: 4/2/45, Clio, Ala. BR/TR, 6'1", 185 lbs. Deb: 4/14/66

YEAR	TM/L	W	L	PCT	G	GS	CG	SH	SV	IP	H	HR	BB	SO	RAT	ERA	ERA+	OAV	OOB	BH	AVG	PB	PR	/A	PD	TPI
1966	LA-N	12	12	.500	37	35	6	2	0	225²	192	19	52	209	9.9	2.99	110	.228	.276	15	.183	1	15	8	-0	0.9
1967	LA-N	11	15	.423	37	34	11	3	1	232²	223	18	57	169	11.1	3.95	79	.250	.300	10	.133	-0	-15	-22	-2	-2.5
1968	LA-N	11	15	.423	35	27	7	2	1	207²	179	6	59	162	10.4	2.60	106	.232	.288	11	.177	1	9	4	-1	0.5
1969	LA-N	17	18	.486	41	41	11	4	0	293¹	269	25	91	217	11.1	3.47	96	.242	.301	15	.153	-1	4	-5	0	-0.6
1970	LA-N	15	13	.536	38	38	10	4	0	260¹	251	38	78	201	11.7	4.08	94	.249	.310	13	.155	3	-1	-7	-1	-0.5
1971	LA-N	17	12	.586	38	37	12	4	1	265¹	231	10	55	194	9.9	2.54	127	.238	.282	19	.216	3	27	20	-1	2.5
1972	LA-N★	19	9	.679	33	33	18	9	0	272²	186	13	63	207	8.4	2.08	160	.189	.240	13	.143	-1	42	38	-0	3.9
1973	LA-N★	18	10	.643	33	33	14	3	0	256¹	196	18	56	200	9.0	2.42	142	.209	.258	10	.119	-2	35	29	-1	2.9
1974	*LA-N	19	9	.679	40	40	14	5	0	276	241	23	80	179	10.7	3.23	105	.229	.288	18	.184	1	12	5	-1	0.4
1975	LA-N★	16	13	.552	35	35	11	6	0	254¹	202	11	62	175	9.4	2.87	119	.213	.264	11	.138	-1	21	15	-1	1.4
1976	LA-N	21	10	.677	35	34	15	6	0	267²	231	8	82	161	10.6	3.06	111	.234	.295	7	.083	-3	13	10	-3	0.5
1977	*LA-N★	14	8	.636	33	33	9	3	0	240¹	207	23	69	150	10.4	3.18	120	.233	.291	11	.151	1	19	17	-1	1.4
1978	*LA-N	15	11	.577	34	34	12	2	0	238¹	228	29	54	154	10.8	3.55	99	.250	.295	6	.083	-1	1	-1	-2	-0.7
1979	LA-N	12	15	.444	33	32	6	1	1	226	201	21	61	146	10.5	3.82	95	.239	.291	11	.143	-2	-2	-5	-1	-0.8
1980	LA-N	13	5	.722	32	31	4	2	0	212¹	163	20	47	128	9.0	2.20	159	.211	.258	5	.078	-4	33	30	-0	2.1
1981	Hou-N	11	9	.550	23	23	6	3	0	158²	132	6	29	104	9.2	2.61	126	.230	.268	7	.137	0	16	12	0	1.6
1982	Hou-N	13	8	.619	27	27	4	0	0	195	169	10	46	139	10.0	3.00	111	.232	.279	11	.162	-0	13	7	-1	0.6
	*Mil-A	4	1	.800	7	7	2	1	0	54²	55	8	18	36	12.0	3.29	115	.263	.322	0	—	0	5	3	1	0.7
1983	Mil-A	8	13	.381	31	31	4	0	0	220¹	209	21	54	134	10.9	4.08	91	.246	.295	0	—	0	-5	-9	-1	-0.5
1984	Mil-A	14	12	.538	33	33	1	0	0	212²	224	24	51	143	11.8	3.77	102	.266	.310	0	—	0	5	-2	-2	0.3
1985	Oak-A	13	8	.619	29	29	1	0	0	194¹	194	19	51	91	11.3	3.89	99	.256	.302	0	—	0	6	-1	0	0.3
	Cal-A	2	2	.500	5	5	0	0	0	31²	27	6	8	16	9.9	3.69	111	.233	.282	0	—	0	2	1	1	0.1
	Yr	15	10	.600	34	34	1	0	0	226	221	25	59	107	11.2	3.86	101	.251	.299	0	—	0	7	1	-1	0.4
1986	*Cal-A	15	11	.577	34	34	3	0	0	207	192	31	49	116	10.6	3.74	110	.242	.288	0	—	0	10	9	-3	0.8
1987	Cal-A	11	11	.500	35	34	1	0	0	191²	199	38	41	99	11.6	4.70	92	.269	.313	0	—	0	-5	-8	-3	-0.9
1988	LA-N	3	6	.333	16	16	0	0	0	87¹	91	7	30	44	12.6	3.92	85	.270	.332	2	.087	-1	-6	-6	-1	-0.7
Total	23	324	256	.559	774	756	178	58	5	5282¹	4692	472	1343	3574	10.4	3.26	108	.236	.287	195	.144	-7	259	146	-26	13.6

● EZRA SUTTON
Sutton, Ezra Ballou b: 9/17/1850, Palmyra, N.Y. d: 6/20/07, Braintree, Mass. BR/TR, 5'8.5", 153 lbs. Deb: 5/4/1871 ♦

YEAR	TM/L	W	L	PCT	G	GS	CG	SH	SV	IP	H	HR	BB	SO	RAT	ERA	ERA+	OAV	OOB	BH	AVG	PB	PR	/A	PD	TPI
1875	Ath-n	0	0	—	2	0	0	0	0	6	14	0	0	0	21.0	7.50	35	.412	.412	116	.324	1	-3	-3	0.0

● JOHN SUTTON
Sutton, Johnny Ike b: 11/13/52, Dallas, Tex. BR/TR, 5'11", 185 lbs. Deb: 4/7/77

YEAR	TM/L	W	L	PCT	G	GS	CG	SH	SV	IP	H	HR	BB	SO	RAT	ERA	ERA+	OAV	OOB	BH	AVG	PB	PR	/A	PD	TPI
1977	StL-N	2	1	.667	14	0	0	0	0	24¹	28	1	9	9	13.7	2.59	149	.315	.378	0	.000	0	4	3	0	0.4
1978	Min-A	0	0	—	17	0	0	0	0	44¹	46	3	15	18	12.6	3.45	111	.264	.326	0	—	0	2	2	-0	-0.2
Total	2	2	1	.667	31	0	0	0	0	68²	74	4	24	27	13.0	3.15	122	.281	.344	0	.000	-0	5	5	0	0.2

● BILL SWABACH
Swabach, William Deb: 7/9/1887

YEAR	TM/L	W	L	PCT	G	GS	CG	SH	SV	IP	H	HR	BB	SO	RAT	ERA	ERA+	OAV	OOB	BH	AVG	PB	PR	/A	PD	TPI
1887	NY-N	0	2	.000	2	2	2	0	0	16	27	1	6	6	19.1	5.06	74	.346	.400	0	.000	-1	-2	-2	0	-0.3

● BILL SWAGGERTY
Swaggerty, William David b: 12/5/56, Sanford, Fla. BR/TR, 6'2", 186 lbs. Deb: 8/13/83

YEAR	TM/L	W	L	PCT	G	GS	CG	SH	SV	IP	H	HR	BB	SO	RAT	ERA	ERA+	OAV	OOB	BH	AVG	PB	PR	/A	PD	TPI
1983	Bal-A	1	1	.500	7	2	0	0	0	21²	21	1	6	7	12.0	2.91	136	.267	.315	0	—	0	3	3	1	0.4
1984	Bal-A	3	2	.600	23	6	0	0	0	57	68	7	21	18	14.1	5.21	74	.302	.362	0	—	0	-8	-8	-1	-0.7
1985	Bal-A	0	0	—	1	0	0	0	0	1²	3	0	2	2	27.0	5.40	75	.375	.500	0	—	0	-0	-1	0	0.1
1986	Bal-A	0	0	—	1	0	0	0	0	1	8	0	1	1	63.0	18.00	23	.750	.778	0	—	0	-2	-2	0	0.1
Total	4	4	3	.571	32	8	0	0	0	81¹	100	8	30	28	14.4	4.76	82	.306	.364	0	—	0	-7	-8	0	-0.1

● CY SWAIM
Swaim, John Hillary b: 3/11/1874, Cadwallader, Ohio 6'6", 180 lbs. Deb: 5/3/1897

YEAR	TM/L	W	L	PCT	G	GS	CG	SH	SV	IP	H	HR	BB	SO	RAT	ERA	ERA+	OAV	OOB	BH	AVG	PB	PR	/A	PD	TPI
1897	Was-N	10	11	.476	27	20	15	0	0	193	225	5	60	55	13.8	4.43	98	.289	.347	17	.227	-3	-2	-2	-3	-0.7

YEAR TM/L	W	L	PCT	G	GS	CG	SH	SV	IP	H	HR	BB	SO	RAT	ERA	ERA+	OAV	OOB	BH	AVG	PB	PR	/A	PD	TPI
1898 Was-N	3	11	.214	16	13	9	0	1	101¹	119	4	28	30	13.4	4.26	86	.290	.342	5	.143	-3	-7	-7	-1	-1.1
Total 2	13	22	.371	43	33	24	0	1	294¹	344	9	88	85	13.6	4.37	94	.289	.346	22	.200	-6	-10	-9	-5	-1.8

● **CRAIG SWAN**   Swan, Craig Steven b: 11/30/50, Van Nuys, Cal.   BR/TR, 6'3", 215 lbs.   Deb: 9/3/73

YEAR TM/L	W	L	PCT	G	GS	CG	SH	SV	IP	H	HR	BB	SO	RAT	ERA	ERA+	OAV	OOB	BH	AVG	PB	PR	/A	PD	TPI
1973 NY-N	0	1	.000	3	1	0	0	0	8¹	16	2	2	4	19.4	8.64	42	.432	.462	0	.000	-0	-5	-5	-0	-0.5
1974 NY-N	1	3	.250	7	5	0	0	0	30¹	28	1	21	10	14.5	4.45	80	.255	.374	4	.364	-1	-3	-3	0	-0.2
1975 NY-N	1	3	.250	6	6	0	0	0	31	38	4	13	19	15.1	6.39	54	.302	.371	0	.000	-1	-10	-10	-1	-1.2
1976 NY-N	6	9	.400	23	22	2	1	0	132¹	129	11	44	89	12.1	3.54	93	.254	.320	4	.103	-1	-1	-4	-1	-0.5
1977 NY-N	9	10	.474	26	24	2	1	0	146²	153	10	56	71	12.9	4.23	88	.268	.334	8	.188	-0	-5	-8	-2	-1.2
1978 NY-N	9	6	.600	29	28	5	1	0	207¹	164	12	58	125	**9.7**	**2.43**	**143**	.219	.277	10	.154	-0	26	24	1	1.8
1979 NY-N	14	13	.519	35	35	10	3	0	251¹	241	20	57	145	10.7	3.29	110	.255	.299	10	.123	-1	12	10	-1	0.8
1980 NY-N	5	9	.357	21	21	4	1	0	128¹	117	20	30	79	10.3	3.58	99	.247	.292	7	.219	-2	-0	-2	-0	-0.1
1981 NY-N	0	2	.000	5	3	0	0	0	13²	10	0	1	9	7.2	3.29	106	.204	.220	0	—	0	0	0	-0	0.0
1982 NY-N	11	7	.611	37	21	2	0	1	166¹	165	13	37	67	10.9	3.35	108	.256	.297	8	.182	3	5	5	-1	0.7
1983 NY-N	2	8	.200	27	18	0	0	1	96¹	112	14	42	43	14.4	5.51	66	.299	.369	2	.077	-2	-20	-20	-1	-2.2
1984 NY-N	1	0	1.000	10	0	0	0	0	18²	18	5	7	10	12.1	8.20	43	.247	.313	0	—	0	-10	-10	-0	-0.5
Cal-A	0	1	.000	2	1	0	0	0	5	8	3	0	2	14.4	10.80	37	.348	.348	0	—	0	-4	-4	-0	-0.6
Total 12	59	72	.450	231	185	25	7	2	1235²	1199	115	368	673	11.5	3.74	95	.256	.312	54	.151	1	-13	-24	-10	-3.7

● **DUCKY SWAN**   Swan, Harry Gordon b: 8/11/1887, Lancaster, Pa. d: 5/8/46, Pittsburgh, Pa.   BR/TR, 5'10", 165 lbs.   Deb: 4/28/14

YEAR TM/L	W	L	PCT	G	GS	CG	SH	SV	IP	H	HR	BB	SO	RAT	ERA	ERA+	OAV	OOB	BH	AVG	PB	PR	/A	PD	TPI
1914 KC-F	0	0	—	1	0	0	0	0	1	0	0	1	1	9.0	0.00	—	.000	.250	0	—	0	0	0	-0	0.0

● **RUSS SWAN**   Swan, Russell Howard b: 1/3/64, Fremont, Cal.   BL/TL, 6'4", 210 lbs.   Deb: 8/3/89

YEAR TM/L	W	L	PCT	G	GS	CG	SH	SV	IP	H	HR	BB	SO	RAT	ERA	ERA+	OAV	OOB	BH	AVG	PB	PR	/A	PD	TPI
1989 SF-N	0	2	.000	2	2	0	0	0	6²	11	4	4	2	20.3	10.80	31	.393	.469	0	.000	-0	-5	-6	0	-1.2
1990 SF-N	0	1	.000	2	1	0	0	0	2¹	6	0	4	1	38.6	3.86	94	.429	.556	0	.000	-0	-0	-0	0	0.0
Sea-A	2	3	.400	11	8	0	0	0	47	42	3	18	15	11.5	3.64	109	.244	.316	0	—	0	1	2	0	0.1
1991 Sea-A	6	2	.750	63	0	0	0	2	78²	81	8	28	33	12.5	3.43	120	.269	.331	0	—	0	6	6	1	0.6
1992 Sea-A	3	10	.231	55	9	1	0	9	104¹	104	8	45	45	13.1	4.74	84	.262	.342	0	—	0	-9	-9	2	-1.0
1993 Sea-A	3	3	.500	23	0	0	0	0	19²	25	2	18	10	20.6	9.15	48	.316	.455	0	—	0	-11	-10	1	-2.6
1994 Cle-A	0	1	.000	12	0	0	0	0	8	13	1	7	2	22.5	11.25	44	.382	.488	0	—	0	-6	-6	0	-0.6
Total 6	14	22	.389	168	20	1	0	11	266²	282	26	124	108	13.9	4.83	84	.275	.356	0	.000	-0	-24	-23	3	-4.7

● **RED SWANSON**   Swanson, Arthur Leonard b: 10/15/36, Baton Rouge, La.   BR/TR, 6'1.5", 175 lbs.   Deb: 9/10/55

YEAR TM/L	W	L	PCT	G	GS	CG	SH	SV	IP	H	HR	BB	SO	RAT	ERA	ERA+	OAV	OOB	BH	AVG	PB	PR	/A	PD	TPI
1955 Pit-N	0	0	—	1	0	0	0	0	2	1	1	3	2	22.5	18.00	23	.286	.500	0	—	0	-3	-3	-0	0.0
1956 Pit-N	0	0	—	9	0	0	0	0	11²	21	1	8	5	22.4	10.03	38	.438	.518	0	—	0	-8	-8	1	0.1
1957 Pit-N	3	3	.500	32	8	1	0	0	72²	69	9	31	29	12.4	3.72	102	.248	.327	0	.000	-1	1	-1	-0	-0.2
Total 3	3	3	.500	42	8	1	0	0	86¹	91	11	42	34	14.0	4.90	77	.277	.360	0	.000	-1	-10	-11	-0	-0.1

● **ED SWARTWOOD**   Swartwood, Cyrus Edward b: 1/12/1859, Rockford, Ill. d: 5/15/24, Pittsburgh, Pa.   BL/TR, 198 lbs.   Deb: 8/11/1881   U♦

YEAR TM/L	W	L	PCT	G	GS	CG	SH	SV	IP	H	HR	BB	SO	RAT	ERA	ERA+	OAV	OOB	BH	AVG	PB	PR	/A	PD	TPI
1884 Pit-a	0	0	—	1	0	0	0	0	2¹	6	0	1	0	27.0	11.57	29	.400	.438	115	.288	-2	-2	-2	-0	0.0
1890 Tol-a	0	0	—	1	0	0	0	0	3	2	0	1	1	6.0	3.00	132	.184	.184	151	.327	0	0	0	-0	0.0
Total 2	0	0	—	2	0	0	0	0	5¹	8	0	1	1	15.2	6.75	55	.309	.335	861	.299	-2	-2	-2	-0	0.0

● **BUD SWARTZ**   Swartz, Sherwin Merle b: 6/13/29, Tulsa, Okla.   BL/TL, 6'2.5", 180 lbs.   Deb: 7/12/47

YEAR TM/L	W	L	PCT	G	GS	CG	SH	SV	IP	H	HR	BB	SO	RAT	ERA	ERA+	OAV	OOB	BH	AVG	PB	PR	/A	PD	TPI
1947 StL-A	0	0	—	5	0	0	0	0	5¹	9	1	7	1	27.0	6.75	57	.360	.500	1	1.000	0	-2	-2	-0	0.0

● **MONTY SWARTZ**   Swartz, Vernon Monroe "Dazzy" b: 1/1/1897, Farmersville, Ohio d: 1/13/80, Germantown, Ohio   BR/TR, 5'11", 182 lbs.   Deb: 10/3/20

YEAR TM/L	W	L	PCT	G	GS	CG	SH	SV	IP	H	HR	BB	SO	RAT	ERA	ERA+	OAV	OOB	BH	AVG	PB	PR	/A	PD	TPI
1920 Cin-N	0	1	.000	1	1	1	0	0	12	17	0	2	2	14.3	4.50	68	.333	.358	2	.500	-1	-1	-1	-0	-0.1

● **PARK SWARTZEL**   Swartzel, Park B. b: 11/21/1865, Knightstown, Ind. d: 1/3/40, Los Angeles, Cal.   BR/TR,   Deb: 4/17/1889

YEAR TM/L	W	L	PCT	G	GS	CG	SH	SV	IP	H	HR	BB	SO	RAT	ERA	ERA+	OAV	OOB	BH	AVG	PB	PR	/A	PD	TPI
1889 KC-a	19	27	.413	48	47	45	0	1	410¹	481	21	117	147	13.6	4.32	97	.283	.338	25	.144	-9	-22	-6	9	-0.5

● **CHARLIE SWEENEY**   Sweeney, Charles J. b: 4/13/1863, San Francisco, Cal d: 4/4/02, San Francisco, Cal.   BR/TR, 5'10.5", 181 lbs.   Deb: 5/11/1882   ♦

YEAR TM/L	W	L	PCT	G	GS	CG	SH	SV	IP	H	HR	BB	SO	RAT	ERA	ERA+	OAV	OOB	BH	AVG	PB	PR	/A	PD	TPI
1883 Pro-N	7	7	.500	20	18	14	0	0	146²	142	3	28	48	10.4	3.13	99	.237	.272	19	.218	-1	0	-1	1	-0.1
1884 Pro-N	17	8	.680	27	24	22	4	1	221	153	4	29	145	**7.4**	1.55	182	**.187**	**.215**	50	.298	6	35	31	1	3.9
StL-U	24	7	.774	33	32	31	2	0	271	207	4	13	192	7.3	1.83	131	.197	.207	54	.316	6	19	17	5	2.4
1885 StL-N	11	21	.344	35	35	32	2	0	275	276	6	50	84	10.9	3.93	70	.250	.282	55	.206	-0	-34	-36	0	-3.3
1886 StL-N	5	6	.455	11	11	11	0	0	93	108	4	39	28	14.2	4.16	78	.285	.352	16	.250	1	-9	-10	0	-0.8
1887 Cle-a	0	3	.000	3	3	3	0	0	24	42	1	13	8	20.6	8.25	53	.372	.437	30	.226	-2	-11	-10	0	-0.8
Total 5	64	52	.552	129	123	113	8	1	1030²	928	24	172	505	9.6	2.87	97	.228	.260	224	.251	14	1	-8	8	1.3

● **BILL SWEENEY**   Sweeney, William J. b: Philadelphia, Pa. d: 8/2/03, Philadelphia, Pa.   TR ,   Deb: 6/27/1882

YEAR TM/L	W	L	PCT	G	GS	CG	SH	SV	IP	H	HR	BB	SO	RAT	ERA	ERA+	OAV	OOB	BH	AVG	PB	PR	/A	PD	TPI
1882 Phi-a	9	10	.474	20	20	18	0	0	170	178	4	42	48	11.6	2.91	102	.252	.294	14	.159	-3	-4	-1	-1	-0.2
1884 Bal-U	**40**	21	.656	**62**	60	**58**	4	0	**538**	522	13	74	374	10.0	2.59	103	.238	.263	71	.240	-16	-9	5	1	-0.7
Total 2	49	31	.613	82	80	76	4	0	708	700	17	116	422	10.4	2.67	103	.241	.270	85	.221	-19	-13	7	1	-0.9

● **LES SWEETLAND**   Sweetland, Lester Leo (Born Leo Sweetland) b: 8/15/01, St.Ignace, Mich. d: 3/4/74, Melbourne, Fla.   BR/TL, 5'11.5", 155 lbs.   Deb: 7/4/27

YEAR TM/L	W	L	PCT	G	GS	CG	SH	SV	IP	H	HR	BB	SO	RAT	ERA	ERA+	OAV	OOB	BH	AVG	PB	PR	/A	PD	TPI
1927 Phi-N	2	10	.167	21	13	6	0	0	103²	147	3	53	21	17.6	6.16	67	.348	.425	12	.316	3	-26	-23	5	-1.5
1928 Phi-N	3	15	.167	37	18	5	0	2	135¹	163	15	97	23	18.3	6.58	65	.306	.426	9	.191	1	-39	-35	2	-3.7
1929 Phi-N	13	11	.542	43	25	10	2	2	204¹	255	23	87	47	15.5	5.11	102	.316	.389	26	.292	3	-9	-2	4	0.8
1930 Phi-N	7	15	.318	34	25	9	1	0	167	271	24	60	36	18.1	7.71	71	.373	.425	16	.281	4	-51	-42	-3	-3.7
1931 Chi-N	8	7	.533	26	14	9	0	0	130¹	156	3	61	32	15.3	5.04	77	.297	.375	15	.268	5	-17	-17	-1	-1.3
Total 5	33	58	.363	161	95	39	3	4	740²	992	68	358	159	16.9	6.10	77	.329	.407	78	.272	16	-142	-116	12	-9.4

● **STEVE SWETONIC**   Swetonic, Stephen Albert b: 8/13/03, Mt.Pleasant, Pa. d: 4/22/74, Canonsburg, Pa.   BR/TR, 5'11", 185 lbs.   Deb: 4/17/29   ♦

YEAR TM/L	W	L	PCT	G	GS	CG	SH	SV	IP	H	HR	BB	SO	RAT	ERA	ERA+	OAV	OOB	BH	AVG	PB	PR	/A	PD	TPI
1929 Pit-N	8	10	.444	41	12	3	0	5	143²	172	6	50	35	14.2	4.82	99	.299	.360	13	.271	-3	-2	-1	2	0.3
1930 Pit-N	6	6	.500	23	6	3	1	5	96²	107	7	27	35	12.5	4.47	111	.276	.323	4	.111	-3	5	5	-1	0.3
1931 Pit-N	0	2	.000	14	0	0	0	1	27²	28	0	16	8	14.3	3.90	99	.264	.361	1	.143	-0	-0	-0	-0	0.0
1932 Pit-N	11	6	.647	24	19	11	**4**	0	162²	134	11	55	39	10.5	2.82	135	**.221**	.286	5	.093	-4	19	18	-1	1.2
1933 Pit-N	12	12	.500	31	21	8	3	0	164²	166	10	64	37	12.5	3.50	95	.260	.330	11	.200	1	-3	-3	-1	-0.5
Total 5	37	36	.507	133	58	25	8	11	595²	607	34	212	154	12.5	3.81	107	.262	.326	34	.170	-3	20	19	-2	1.3

● **BILL SWIFT**   Swift, William Charles b: 10/27/61, Portland, Maine   BR/TR, 6', 180 lbs.   Deb: 6/7/85

YEAR TM/L	W	L	PCT	G	GS	CG	SH	SV	IP	H	HR	BB	SO	RAT	ERA	ERA+	OAV	OOB	BH	AVG	PB	PR	/A	PD	TPI
1985 Sea-A	6	10	.375	23	21	0	0	0	120²	131	9	48	55	13.7	4.77	88	.279	.352	0	—	0	-8	-8	0	-0.9
1986 Sea-A	2	9	.182	29	17	1	0	0	115¹	148	6	55	55	16.4	5.46	78	.319	.399	0	—	0	-16	-16	1	-1.2
1988 Sea-A	8	12	.400	38	24	6	1	0	174²	199	10	65	47	14.0	4.59	91	.294	.363	0	—	0	-12	-8	-2	-0.9
1989 Sea-A	7	3	.700	37	16	0	0	1	130	140	7	38	45	12.5	4.43	91	.278	.331	0	—	0	-8	-6	5	-0.1
1990 Sea-A	6	4	.600	55	8	0	0	6	128	135	4	21	42	11.5	2.39	166	.272	.311	0	—	0	22	22	0	1.9
1991 Sea-A	1	2	.333	71	0	0	0	17	90¹	74	3	26	48	10.1	1.99	207	.224	.283	0	—	0	21	21	3	1.8
1992 SF-N	10	4	.714	30	22	3	1	1	164²	144	6	43	77	10.4	**2.08**	159	.239	.293	8	.157	1	26	22	2	2.3
1993 SF-N	21	8	.724	34	34	1	0	1	232²	195	18	55	157	9.9	2.82	138	.226	.278	21	.262	6	31	28	4	4.2
1994 SF-N	8	7	.533	17	17	0	0	0	109¹	109	10	31	62	11.6	3.38	119	.262	.315	6	.188	2	10	8	-1	1.1
Total 9	69	59	.539	334	159	11	4	25	1265²	1275	74	382	588	12.1	3.51	113	.265	.324	47	.215	14	66	64	15	8.2

● **BILL SWIFT**   Swift, William Vincent b: 1/10/08, Elmira, N.Y. d: 2/23/69, Bartow, Fla.   BR/TR, 6'1.5", 192 lbs.   Deb: 4/12/32

YEAR TM/L	W	L	PCT	G	GS	CG	SH	SV	IP	H	HR	BB	SO	RAT	ERA	ERA+	OAV	OOB	BH	AVG	PB	PR	/A	PD	TPI
1932 Pit-N	14	10	.583	39	23	11	0	4	214¹	205	15	26	64	9.8	3.61	106	.248	.272	15	.192	-1	6	5	-4	0.0

YEAR TM/L	W	L	PCT	G	GS	CG	SH	SV	IP	H	HR	BB	SO	RAT	ERA	ERA+	OAV	OOB	BH	AVG	PB	PR	/A	PD	TPI
1933 Pit-N	14	10	.583	37	29	13	2	0	218^1	214	11	36	64	10.5	3.13	106	.251	.285	20	.244	3	5	5	-2	0.6
1934 Pit-N	11	13	.458	37	24	13	1	0	212^2	244	15	46	81	12.6	3.98	103	.284	.326	18	.214	2	2	3	-1	0.3
1935 Pit-N	15	8	.652	39	21	11	3	1	203^2	193	6	37	74	10.2	2.70	152	.247	.282	19	.244	3	30	32	-4	3.2
1936 Pit-N	16	16	.500	45	31	17	0	2	262^1	275	18	63	92	11.8	4.01	101	.265	.310	31	.295	9	0	1	-5	0.5
1937 Pit-N	9	10	.474	36	17	9	0	3	164	160	14	34	84	10.8	3.95	98	.256	.297	9	.167	-1	-1	2	-3	-0.5
1938 Pit-N	7	5	.583	36	9	2	0	4	150	155	9	40	77	11.9	3.24	117	.271	.323	10	.200	2	9	9	-1	0.8
1939 Pit-N	5	7	.417	36	8	2	1	4	129^2	150	6	28	56	12.6	3.89	99	.293	.333	10	.238	2	0	-1	-3	0.2
1940 Bos-N	1	1	.500	4	0	0	0	1	9^1	12	0	7	7	18.3	2.89	129	.308	.413		.000	-0	1	1	0	0.2
1941 Bro-N	3	0	1.000	9	0	0	0	1	22	26	4	7	9	13.5	3.27	112	.289	.340	1	.200	-0	1	1	-0	0.1
1943 Chi-A	0	2	.000	18	1	0	0	0	51^1	48	5	27	28	14.2	4.21	79	.246	.355	1	.100	0	-5	-5	-2	-0.4
Total 11	95	82	.537	336	163	78	7	20	1637^2	1682	103	351	636	11.4	3.58	108	.263	.305	134	.227	18	49	49	-25	4.6

● **OAD SWIGART**   Swigart, Oadis Vaughn   b: 2/13/15, Archie, Mo.   BL/TR, 6', 175 lbs.   Deb: 9/14/39

YEAR TM/L	W	L	PCT	G	GS	CG	SH	SV	IP	H	HR	BB	SO	RAT	ERA	ERA+	OAV	OOB	BH	AVG	PB	PR	/A	PD	TPI
1939 Pit-N	1	1	.500	3	3	1	1	0	24^1	27	1	6	8	12.2	4.44	87	.293	.337	2	.250	-0	-1	-2	-0	-0.1
1940 Pit-N	0	2	.000	7	2	0	0	0	22^1	27	1	10	9	14.9	4.43	86	.297	.366	1	.200	-0	-1	-2	0	-0.1
Total 2	1	3	.250	10	5	1	1	0	46^2	54	2	16	17	13.5	4.44	86	.295	.352	3	.231	0	-3	-3	0	-0.2

● **AD SWIGLER**   Swigler, Adam William "Doc"   b: 9/21/1895, Philadelphia, Pa.   d: 2/5/75, Philadelphia, Pa.   BR/TR, 5'10", 180 lbs.   Deb: 9/25/17

YEAR TM/L	W	L	PCT	G	GS	CG	SH	SV	IP	H	HR	BB	SO	RAT	ERA	ERA+	OAV	OOB	BH	AVG	PB	PR	/A	PD	TPI
1917 NY-N	0	1	.000	1	1	0	0	0	6	7	0	8	4	22.5	6.00	43	.333	.517	0	.000	-0	-2	-2	0	-0.3

● **GREG SWINDELL**   Swindell, Forest Gregory   b: 1/2/65, Fort Worth, Tex.   BR/TL, 6'2", 225 lbs.   Deb: 8/21/86

YEAR TM/L	W	L	PCT	G	GS	CG	SH	SV	IP	H	HR	BB	SO	RAT	ERA	ERA+	OAV	OOB	BH	AVG	PB	PR	/A	PD	TPI
1986 Cle-A	5	2	.714	9	9	1	0	0	61^2	57	9	15	46	10.7	4.23	98	.243	.291	0	—	0	-0	-1	1	0.1
1987 Cle-A	3	8	.273	16	15	4	1	0	102^1	112	18	37	97	13.2	5.10	89	.283	.346	0	—	0	-7	-7	-0	-0.7
1988 Cle-A	18	14	.563	33	33	12	4	0	242	234	18	45	180	10.4	3.20	129	.252	.287	0	—	0	21	25	-1	2.9
1989 Cle-A★	13	6	.684	28	28	5	2	0	184^1	170	16	51	129	10.8	3.37	118	.246	.298	0	—	0	11	12	-0	1.0
1990 Cle-A	12	9	.571	34	34	3	0	0	214^2	245	27	47	135	12.3	4.40	89	.288	.326	0	—	0	-12	-12	-2	-1.2
1991 Cle-A	9	16	.360	33	33	7	0	0	238	241	21	31	169	10.4	3.48	119	.263	.289	0	—	0	16	18	-1	1.6
1992 Cin-N	12	8	.600	31	30	5	3	0	213^2	210	14	41	138	10.7	2.70	133	.260	.297	10	.125	-2	19	21	-1	1.8
1993 Hou-N	12	13	.480	31	30	1	1	0	190^1	215	24	40	124	12.1	4.16	93	.283	.319	11	.183	0	-3	-6	0	-0.7
1994 Hou-N	8	9	.471	24	24	1	0	0	148^1	175	20	26	74	12.3	4.37	93	.302	.333	11	.250	3	-3	-5	-2	-0.5
Total 9	92	85	.520	239	236	39	11	0	1595^1	1659	167	333	1092	11.3	3.74	107	.269	.308	32	.174	2	42	47	-7	4.3

● **JOSH SWINDELL**   Swindell, Joshua Ernest   b: 7/5/1883, Rose Hill, Kan.   d: 3/19/69, Fruita, Colo.   BR/TR, 6', 180 lbs.   Deb: 9/16/11 ♦

YEAR TM/L	W	L	PCT	G	GS	CG	SH	SV	IP	H	HR	BB	SO	RAT	ERA	ERA+	OAV	OOB	BH	AVG	PB	PR	/A	PD	TPI
1911 Cle-A	0	1	.000	4	1	1	0	0	17^1	19	0	4	6	12.5	2.08	164	.257	.304	1	.250	-0	2	3	0	0.1

● **PAUL SWINGLE**   Swingle, Paul Christopher   b: 12/21/66, Inglewood, Cal.   BR/TR, 6', 185 lbs.   Deb: 9/7/93

YEAR TM/L	W	L	PCT	G	GS	CG	SH	SV	IP	H	HR	BB	SO	RAT	ERA	ERA+	OAV	OOB	BH	AVG	PB	PR	/A	PD	TPI
1993 Cal-A	0	1	.000	9	0	0	0	0	9^2	15	2	6	6	19.6	8.38	54	.357	.438	0	—	0	-4	-4	-0	-0.4

● **LEN SWORMSTEDT**   Swormstedt, Leonard Jordan   b: 10/6/1878, Cincinnati, Ohio   d: 7/19/64, Salem, Mass.   BR/TR, 5'11.5", 165 lbs.   Deb: 9/29/01

YEAR TM/L	W	L	PCT	G	GS	CG	SH	SV	IP	H	HR	BB	SO	RAT	ERA	ERA+	OAV	OOB	BH	AVG	PB	PR	/A	PD	TPI
1901 Cin-N	2	1	.667	3	3	3	0	0	26	19	2	5	13	9.0	1.73	185	.203	.259	0	.000	-1	5	4	0	0.3
1902 Cin-N	0	2	.000	2	2	2	0	0	18	22	1	5	3	13.5	4.00	75	.301	.345	0	.000	-1	-2	-2	-0	-0.3
1906 Bos-A	1	1	.500	3	2	2	0	0	21	17	0	0	6	7.7	1.29	214	.224	.235	1	.125	-1	3	3	-1	0.2
Total 3	3	4	.429	8	7	7	0	0	65	58	3	10	22	9.8	2.22	136	.239	.278	1	.043	-3	5	6	-1	0.2

● **BOB SYKES**   Sykes, Robert Joseph   b: 12/11/54, Neptune, N.J.   BB/TL, 6'2", 200 lbs.   Deb: 4/9/77

YEAR TM/L	W	L	PCT	G	GS	CG	SH	SV	IP	H	HR	BB	SO	RAT	ERA	ERA+	OAV	OOB	BH	AVG	PB	PR	/A	PD	TPI
1977 Det-A	5	7	.417	32	20	3	0	0	132^2	141	15	50	58	13.1	4.41	97	.271	.337	0	—	0	-5	-2	-0	-0.5
1978 Det-A	6	6	.500	22	10	3	2	2	93^2	99	14	34	58	12.9	3.94	98	.275	.339	0	—	0	-2	-1	-2	-0.5
1979 StL-N	4	3	.571	13	11	0	0	0	67	86	11	34	35	16.3	6.18	61	.315	.393	2	.095	-0	-18	-18	-1	-1.7
1980 StL-N	6	10	.375	27	19	4	3	0	126	134	12	54	50	13.4	4.64	79	.277	.350	4	.103	-1	-15	-13	-2	-1.9
1981 StL-N	2	0	1.000	22	1	0	0	0	37^1	37	2	18	14	13.5	4.58	78	.266	.354	0	.000	-0	-5	-4	1	-0.1
Total 5	23	26	.469	116	61	10	5	2	456^2	497	54	190	215	13.6	4.65	84	.280	.351	6	.097	-2	-44	-38	-4	-4.7

● **LOU SYLVESTER**   Sylvester, Louis J.   b: 2/14/1855, Springfield, Ill.   BR/TR, 5'3", 165 lbs.   Deb: 4/18/1884 ♦

YEAR TM/L	W	L	PCT	G	GS	CG	SH	SV	IP	H	HR	BB	SO	RAT	ERA	ERA+	OAV	OOB	BH	AVG	PB	PR	/A	PD	TPI
1884 Cin-U	0	1	.000	6	1	1	0	1	32^2	32	0	6	7	10.5	3.58	72	.239	.272	89	.267	-0	-4	-4	-1	-0.2

● **JEFF TABAKA**   Tabaka, Jeffrey Jon   b: 1/17/64, Barberton, Ohio   BR/TL, 6'2", 195 lbs.   Deb: 4/19/94

YEAR TM/L	W	L	PCT	G	GS	CG	SH	SV	IP	H	HR	BB	SO	RAT	ERA	ERA+	OAV	OOB	BH	AVG	PB	PR	/A	PD	TPI
1994 Pit-N	0	0	—	5	0	0	0	0	4	4	1	8	2	27.0	18.00	24	.250	.500	0	—	0	-6	-6	-0	0.0
SD-N	3	1	.750	34	0	0	0	1	37	30	0	19	30	11.4	3.89	108	.209	.307	1	1.000	1	1	1	-0	0.2
Yr	3	1	.750	39	0	0	0	1	41	32	1	27	32	13.0	5.27	80	.213	.333	1	1.000	1	-5	-5	-0	0.2

● **LEFTY TABER**   Taber, Edward Timothy   b: 1/11/1900, Rock Island, Ill.   d: 11/5/83, Lincoln, Neb.   BL/TL, 6', 180 lbs.   Deb: 9/4/26

YEAR TM/L	W	L	PCT	G	GS	CG	SH	SV	IP	H	HR	BB	SO	RAT	ERA	ERA+	OAV	OOB	BH	AVG	PB	PR	/A	PD	TPI
1926 Phi-N	0	0	—	6	0	0	0	0	8^1	8	0	6	0	16.2	7.56	55	.242	.375	0	.000	-0	-3	-3	-0	0.0
1927 Phi-N	0	1	.000	3	1	0	0	0	3^1	8	0	5	0	37.8	18.90	22	.533	.667	0	.000	-0	-6	-5	0	-1.2
Total 2	0	1	.000	9	1	0	0	0	11^2	16	0	10	0	22.4	10.80	38	.333	.475	0	.000	-0	-9	-9	0	-1.2

● **JOHN TABER**   Taber, John Pardon   b: 6/28/1868, Acushnet, Mass.   d: 2/21/40, Boston, Mass.   BR/TR, 5'8",   Deb: 4/30/1890

YEAR TM/L	W	L	PCT	G	GS	CG	SH	SV	IP	H	HR	BB	SO	RAT	ERA	ERA+	OAV	OOB	BH	AVG	PB	PR	/A	PD	TPI
1890 Bos-N	0	1	.000	2	1	1	0	0	13	11	0	8	3	13.2	4.15	90	.222	.330	1	.000	-1	-1	-1	0	-0.1

● **JEFF TACKETT**   Tackett, Jeffrey Wilson   b: 12/1/65, Fresno, Cal.   BR/TR, 6'2", 200 lbs.   Deb: 9/11/91 ♦

YEAR TM/L	W	L	PCT	G	GS	CG	SH	SV	IP	H	HR	BB	SO	RAT	ERA	ERA+	OAV	OOB	BH	AVG	PB	PR	/A	PD	TPI
1993 Bal-A	0	0	—	1	0	0	0	0	1	1	0	1	0	18.0			.250	.400	15	.172	1	0	0	0	0.0

● **JOHN TAFF**   Taff, John Gallatin   b: 6/3/1890, Austin, Tex.   d: 5/15/61, Houston, Tex.   BR/TR, 6', 170 lbs.   Deb: 5/11/13

YEAR TM/L	W	L	PCT	G	GS	CG	SH	SV	IP	H	HR	BB	SO	RAT	ERA	ERA+	OAV	OOB	BH	AVG	PB	PR	/A	PD	TPI
1913 Phi-A	0	1	.000	7	1	0	0	1	17^2	22	0	5	9	13.8	6.62	42	.293	.338	1	.200	-0	-7	-8	0	-0.5

● **DOUG TAITT**   Taitt, Douglas John "Poco"   b: 8/3/02, Bay City, Mich.   d: 12/12/70, Portland, Ore.   BL/TR, 6', 176 lbs.   Deb: 4/10/28 ♦

YEAR TM/L	W	L	PCT	G	GS	CG	SH	SV	IP	H	HR	BB	SO	RAT	ERA	ERA+	OAV	OOB	BH	AVG	PB	PR	/A	PD	TPI
1928 Bos-A	0	0	—	1	0	0	0	0	1	2	0	2	1	36.0	27.00	15	.400	.571	144	.299	0	-3	-3	0	0.0

● **FRED TALBOT**   Talbot, Frederick Lealand "Bubby"   b: 6/28/41, Washington, D.C.   BR/TR, 6'2", 195 lbs.   Deb: 9/28/63

YEAR TM/L	W	L	PCT	G	GS	CG	SH	SV	IP	H	HR	BB	SO	RAT	ERA	ERA+	OAV	OOB	BH	AVG	PB	PR	/A	PD	TPI
1963 Chi-A	0	0	—	1	1	0	0	0	3	2	0	4	2	18.0	3.00	117	.222	.462	0	.000	-0	0	0	0	0.0
1964 Chi-A	4	5	.444	17	12	3	2	0	75^1	83	7	20	34	12.8	3.70	93	.288	.343	5	.263	3	-1	-2	-1	0.0
1965 KC-A	10	12	.455	39	33	7	1	0	198	188	25	86	117	12.7	4.14	84	.251	.333	14	.200	3	-15	-14	-1	-1.2
1966 KC-A	4	4	.500	11	11	0	0	0	67^2	65	6	28	37	12.6	4.79	77	.248	.325	3	.150	0	-10	-10	-0	-1.1
NY-A	7	7	.500	23	19	3	0	0	124^1	123	16	45	48	12.4	4.13	81	.262	.331	5	.143	1	-10	-11	-0	-1.1
Yr	11	11	.500	34	30	3	0	0	192	188	22	73	85	12.4	4.36	77	.256	.326	8	.145	1	-20	-22	-0	-2.2
1967 NY-A	6	8	.429	29	22	2	0	0	138^2	132	20	54	61	12.5	4.22	74	.252	.329	6	.158	3	-15	-17	2	-0.4
1968 NY-A	1	9	.100	29	11	1	0	0	99	89	6	42	67	12.1	3.36	86	.241	.322	2	.118	1	-4	-5	1	-0.4
1969 NY-A	0	0	—	8	0	0	0	0	12^1	13	1	6	7	13.9	5.11	68	.283	.365	0	.000	-0	-2	-2	0	-0.2
Sea-A	5	8	.385	25	16	1	1	0	114^2	125	12	41	67	13.3	4.16	87	.278	.343	6	.162	2	-7	-7	0	-0.5
Oak-A	1	2	.333	12	2	0	0	0	19	22	2	7	9	13.7	5.21	66	.297	.358	1	.333	0	-3	-4	0	-0.6
Yr	6	10	.375	45	18	1	1	0	146	160	15	54	83	13.2	4.38	82	.277	.339	7	.171	2	-12	-13	0	-1.1
1970 Oak-A	0	1	.000	3	0	0	0	0	1^2	2	1	1	0	16.2	10.80	33	.286	.375	0	.000	-0	-1	-1	0	-0.5
Total 8	38	56	.404	195	126	12	4	1	853^2	844	96	334	449	12.7	4.12	81	.260	.334	42	.174	13	-68	-74	2	-6.4

● **ROY TALCOTT**   Talcott, Le Roy Everett   b: 1/16/20, Brookline, Mass.   BR/TR, 6'1.5", 180 lbs.   Deb: 6/24/43

YEAR TM/L	W	L	PCT	G	GS	CG	SH	SV	IP	H	HR	BB	SO	RAT	ERA	ERA+	OAV	OOB	BH	AVG	PB	PR	/A	PD	TPI
1943 Bos-N	0	0	—	1	0	0	0	0	1	2	0	1	0	40.5	27.00		.333	.600				-2	-2	0	0.0

YEAR	TM/L	W	L	PCT	G	GS	CG	SH	SV	IP	H	HR	BB	SO	RAT	ERA	ERA+	OAV	OOB	BH	AVG	PB	PR	/A	PD	TPI

● **VITO TAMULIS**   Tamulis, Vitautis Casimirus   b: 7/11/11, Cambridge, Mass.   d: 5/5/74, Nashville, Tenn.   BL/TL, 5'9", 170 lbs.   Deb: 9/25/34

1934	NY-A	1	0	1.000	1	1	1	1	0	9	7	0	1	5	8.0	0.00	—	.219	.242	1	.250	0	4	4	0	0.5
1935	NY-A	10	5	.667	30	19	9	3	1	160²	178	7	55	57	13.2	4.09	99	.280	.339	14	.246	4	7	-1	-1	0.2
1938	StL-A	0	3	.000	3	2	0	0	0	15¹	26	2	10	11	21.1	7.63	65	.366	.444	2	.400	1	-5	-5	0	-0.6
	Bro-N	12	6	.667	38	18	9	0	2	159²	181	11	40	70	12.6	3.83	102	.288	.333	7	.127	-3	-1	1	-2	-0.3
1939	Bro-N	9	8	.529	39	17	8	1	4	158²	177	10	45	83	13.0	4.37	92	.287	.343	10	.182	-1	-8	-6	0	-0.7
1940	Bro-N	8	5	.615	41	12	4	1	2	154¹	147	5	34	55	10.7	3.09	129	.244	.288	6	.130	-1	13	16	-1	1.0
1941	Phi-N	0	1	.000	6	1	0	0	0	12	21	1	7	7	21.8	9.00	41	.382	.460	0	.000	-0	-7	-7	0	-0.5
	Bro-N	0	0	—	12	0	0	0	1	22	21	1	10	8	12.7	3.68	100	.244	.323	0	.000	-1	-0	-0	0	-0.1
	Yr	0	1	.000	18	1	0	0	1	34	42	2	17	15	15.6	5.56	66	.296	.371	0	.000	-1	-7	-7	0	-0.6
Total	6	40	28	.588	170	70	31	6	10	691²	758	37	202	294	12.7	3.97	101	.278	.331	40	.175	-1	3	4	-2	-0.5

● **FRANK TANANA**   Tanana, Frank Daryl   b: 7/3/53, Detroit, Mich.   BL/TL, 6'3", 195 lbs.   Deb: 9/9/73

1973	Cal-A	2	2	.500	4	4	2	1	0	26¹	20	2	8	22	9.6	3.08	115	.200	.259	0	—	0	2	1	0	0.3
1974	Cal-A	14	19	.424	39	35	12	4	0	268²	262	27	77	180	11.6	3.12	110	.255	.312	0	—	0	15	10	0	1.6
1975	Cal-A	16	9	.640	34	33	16	5	0	257¹	211	21	73	**269**	10.2	2.62	135	.226	.288	0	—	0	33	26	3	3.3
1976	Cal-A★	19	10	.655	34	34	23	2	0	288¹	212	24	73	261	**9.2**	2.43	137	.203	**.261**	0	—	0	35	29	1	3.2
1977	Cal-A†	15	9	.625	31	31	20	**7**	0	241¹	201	19	61	205	10.2	**2.54**	154	.227	.286	0	—	0	41	37	1	3.7
1978	Cal-A☆	18	12	.600	33	33	10	4	0	239	239	26	60	137	11.6	3.65	99	.258	.309	0	—	0	3	-1	-2	-0.4
1979	*Cal-A	7	5	.583	18	17	2	1	0	90¹	93	9	25	46	12.0	3.89	105	.264	.317	0	—	0	3	2	-1	0.4
1980	Cal-A	11	12	.478	32	31	7	0	0	204	223	18	45	113	12.2	4.15	95	.277	.322	0	—	0	-3	-5	-1	-0.6
1981	Bos-A	4	10	.286	24	23	5	2	0	141¹	142	17	43	78	12.0	4.01	96	.265	.324	0	—	0	-6	-7	1	-0.2
1982	Tex-A	7	18	.280	30	30	7	0	0	194¹	199	16	55	87	12.1	4.21	92	.264	.320	0	—	0	-3	-7	-0	-0.7
1983	Tex-A	7	9	.438	29	22	3	0	0	159¹	144	14	49	108	11.3	3.16	127	.240	.304	0	—	0	16	15	3	1.8
1984	Tex-A	15	15	.500	35	35	9	1	0	246¹	234	30	81	141	11.7	3.25	127	.245	.308	0	—	0	20	24	1	2.7
1985	Tex-A	2	7	.222	13	13	0	0	0	77²	89	15	23	52	13.1	5.91	72	.287	.338	0	—	0	-15	-15	0	-1.5
	Det-A	10	7	.588	20	20	4	0	0	137¹	131	13	34	107	10.9	3.34	122	.250	.298	0	—	0	12	11	1	1.4
	Yr	12	14	.462	33	33	4	0	0	215	220	28	57	159	11.7	4.27	97	.262	.311	0	—	0	-3	-3	1	-0.1
1986	Det-A	12	9	.571	32	31	3	1	0	188¹	196	23	65	119	12.6	4.16	99	.268	.330	0	—	0	0	-1	1	0.1
1987	*Det-A	15	10	.600	34	34	5	3	0	218²	216	27	56	146	11.4	3.91	108	.256	.306	0	—	0	13	8	1	0.9
1988	Det-A	14	11	.560	32	32	2	0	0	203	213	25	64	127	12.5	4.21	91	.267	.324	0	—	0	-6	-9	1	-0.7
1989	Det-A	10	14	.417	33	33	6	1	0	223²	227	21	74	147	12.4	3.58	107	.265	.329	0	—	0	7	6	2	1.0
1990	Det-A	9	8	.529	34	29	1	0	1	176¹	190	25	66	114	13.5	5.31	75	.280	.352	0	—	0	-27	-26	0	-2.2
1991	Det-A	13	12	.520	33	33	2	0	0	217¹	217	26	78	107	12.3	3.77	110	.265	.330	0	.000	0	8	9	1	1.1
1992	Det-A	13	11	.542	32	31	3	0	0	186²	188	22	90	91	13.7	4.39	90	.267	.356	0	—	0	-9	-9	-1	-1.0
1993	NY-N	7	15	.318	29	29	0	0	0	183	198	26	48	104	12.5	4.48	90	.278	.332	9	.155	—	-9	-9	-1	-1.1
	NY-A	0	2	.000	3	3	0	0	0	19²	18	2	7	12	11.4	3.20	130	.222	.284	0	—	0	2	-1	0	0.2
Total	21	240	236	.504	638	616	143	34	1	4188¹	4063	448	1255	2773	11.7	3.66	106	.254	.314	9	.153	1	134	95	14	13.3

● **JESSE TANNEHILL**   Tannehill, Jesse Niles "Powder"   b: 7/14/1874, Dayton, Ky.   d: 9/22/56, Dayton, Ky.   BB/TL, 5'8", 150 lbs.   Deb: 6/17/1894   FC◆

1894	Cin-N	1	0	1.000	5	1	1	0	1	29	37	1	16	7	16.8	7.14	78	.307	.393	0	.000	-2	-6	-5	-1	-0.4
1897	Pit-N	9	9	.500	21	16	11	1	0	142	172	1	24	40	12.9	4.25	98	.297	.334	49	.266	3	1	-1	3	0.3
1898	Pit-N	25	13	.658	43	38	34	5	2	326²	338	2	63	93	11.4	2.95	121	.265	.306	44	.289	7	24	22	3	3.5
1899	Pit-N	24	14	.632	40	35	32	3	1	313	354	4	51	61	12.0	2.73	140	.285	.320	34	.258	5	39	38	4	4.8
1900	Pit-N	20	6	.769	29	27	23	2	0	234	247	3	43	50	11.8	2.88	126	.270	.315	37	.336	8	21	19	1	2.7
1901	Pit-N	18	10	.643	32	30	25	4	1	252¹	240	1	36	118	10.2	**2.18**	150	.249	.283	33	.244	5	32	31	-3	3.2
1902	Pit-N	20	6	.769	26	24	23	2	0	231	203	0	25	100	9.3	1.95	140	.236	.266	43	.291	7	21	20	-0	3.1
1903	NY-A	15	15	.500	32	31	22	2	0	239²	258	3	34	106	11.3	3.27	96	.274	.306	26	.234	5	-8	-4	2	0.3
1904	Bos-A	21	11	.656	33	31	30	4	0	281²	256	5	33	116	9.6	2.04	131	.243	.275	24	.197	3	17	20	3	3.0
1905	Bos-A	22	9	.710	37	32	27	6	0	271²	238	7	59	113	10.3	2.48	109	.237	.288	21	.226	6	5	7	2	1.7
1906	Bos-A	13	11	.542	27	26	18	2	0	196¹	207	9	39	82	11.7	3.16	87	.274	.318	22	.278	6	-10	-9	-0	-0.4
1907	Bos-A	6	7	.462	18	16	10	2	0	131	131	3	20	29	10.7	2.47	104	.262	.297	10	.196	1	1	2	0	0.3
1908	Bos-A	0	0	—	1	1	0	0	0	5	4	0	3	2	12.6	3.60	68	.200	.304	1	.500	0	-1	-1	0	0.1
	Was-A	2	4	.333	10	9	5	0	0	71²	77	0	21	26	13.3	3.77	61	.276	.346	11	.256	2	-11	-12	1	-0.6
	Yr	2	4	.333	11	10	5	0	0	76²	81	0	26	16	13.3	3.76	61	.273	.343	12	.267	2	-12	-12	2	-0.4
1909	Was-A	1	1	.500	3	2	1	0	0	21	19	1	5	8	10.7	3.43	71	.268	.325	6	.167	-0	-2	-2	1	-0.1
1911	Cin-N	0	0	—	1	0	0	0	0	4¹	6	0	3	1	18.7	6.23	53	.316	.409	0	.000	-0	-1	-1	0	0.0
Total	15	197	116	.629	358	319	263	34	7	2750¹	2787	40	477	940	11.1	2.79	115	.263	.303	361	.256	55	123	125	16	21.5

● **BRUCE TANNER**   Tanner, Bruce Matthew   b: 12/9/61, New Castle, Pa.   BL/TR, 6'3", 220 lbs.   Deb: 6/12/85   F

| 1985 | Chi-A | 1 | 2 | .333 | 10 | 4 | 0 | 0 | 0 | 27 | 34 | 1 | 13 | 9 | 16.3 | 5.33 | 81 | .309 | .392 | 0 | — | 0 | -4 | -3 | 1 | -0.4 |

● **KEVIN TAPANI**   Tapani, Kevin Ray   b: 2/18/64, Des Moines, Iowa   BR/TR, 6', 180 lbs.   Deb: 7/4/89

1989	NY-N	0	0	—	3	0	0	0	0	7¹	5	1	4	2	11.0	3.68	89	.192	.300	0	.000	—	-0	-0	0	0.0
	Min-A	2	2	.500	5	5	0	0	0	32²	34	2	8	21	11.6	3.86	107	.266	.309	0	—	0	0	1	-0	-0.2
1990	Min-A	12	8	.600	28	28	1	1	0	159¹	164	12	29	101	11.0	4.07	102	.264	.299	0	—	0	-3	2	0	0.0
1991	*Min-A	16	9	.640	34	34	4	1	0	244	225	23	40	135	9.8	2.99	143	.245	.278	0	—	0	30	35	-0	3.3
1992	Min-A	16	11	.593	34	34	4	1	0	220	226	17	48	138	11.4	3.97	102	.269	.313	0	—	0	-0	2	1	-0.1
1993	Min-A	12	15	.444	36	35	3	1	0	225²	243	21	57	150	12.2	4.43	98	.272	.320	0	—	0	-3	-2	1	-0.1
1994	Min-A	11	7	.611	24	24	4	0	0	156	181	13	39	91	12.9	4.62	105	.291	.337	0	—	0	3	4	0	0.4
Total	6	69	52	.570	164	160	16	5	0	1045	1078	89	225	638	11.4	3.94	109	.266	.308	0	—	0	27	42	1	3.5

● **RANDY TATE**   Tate, Randall Lee   b: 10/23/52, Florence, Ala.   BR/TR, 6'3", 190 lbs.   Deb: 4/14/75

| 1975 | NY-N | 5 | 13 | .278 | 26 | 23 | 2 | 0 | 0 | 137² | 121 | 8 | 86 | 99 | 13.9 | 4.45 | 78 | .240 | .356 | 0 | .000 | -4 | -13 | -15 | 0 | -2.3 |

● **STU TATE**   Tate, Stuart Douglas   b: 6/17/62, Huntsville, Ala.   BR/TR, 6'3", 205 lbs.   Deb: 9/20/89

| 1989 | SF-N | 0 | 0 | — | 2 | 0 | 0 | 0 | 0 | 2² | 3 | 0 | 4 | 4 | 10.1 | 3.38 | 100 | .250 | .250 | 0 | — | 0 | 0 | -0 | -0 | 0.0 |

● **AL TATE**   Tate, Walter Alvin   b: 7/1/18, Coleman, Okla.   d: 5/8/93, Bountiful, Utah   BR/TR, 6', 180 lbs.   Deb: 9/27/46

| 1946 | Pit-N | 0 | 1 | .000 | 2 | 1 | 1 | 0 | 0 | 9 | 8 | 0 | 7 | 2 | 15.0 | 5.00 | 70 | .267 | .405 | 1 | .333 | 0 | -2 | -1 | 0 | -0.1 |

● **KEN TATUM**   Tatum, Kenneth Ray   b: 4/25/44, Alexandria, La.   BR/TR, 6'2", 205 lbs.   Deb: 5/28/69

1969	Cal-A	7	2	.778	45	0	0	0	22	86¹	51	1	39	65	9.8	1.36	257	.172	.277	6	.286	4	**22**	20	-0	3.8
1970	Cal-A	7	4	.636	62	0	0	0	17	88²	68	12	26	50	10.0	2.94	123	.208	.277	2	.182	1	8	7	0	1.2
1971	Bos-A	2	4	.333	36	1	0	0	9	53²	50	3	25	21	13.9	4.19	88	.255	.362	3	.300	2	-4	-3	0	-0.2
1972	Bos-A	0	2	.000	22	0	0	0	4	29¹	32	3	15	15	15.0	3.07	105	.283	.377	0	.000	-0	-0	-0	-0	0.0
1973	Bos-A	0	0	—	1	0	0	0	0	4	6	2	3	0	20.3	9.00	45	.462	.563	0	—	0	-2	-2	-0	0.0
1974	Chi-A	0	0	—	10	1	0	0	0	20²	23	3	9	5	13.9	4.79	78	.274	.344	0	.000	-0	-3	-2	1	0.0
Total	6	16	12	.571	176	2	0	0	52	282²	230	24	117	156	11.7	2.93	122	.224	.314	11	.244	7	20	20	0	4.8

● **WALT TAUSCHER**   Tauscher, Walter Edward   b: 11/22/01, LaSalle, Ill.   d: 11/27/92, Winter Park, Fla.   BR/TR, 6'1", 186 lbs.   Deb: 4/19/28

1928	Pit-N	0	0	—	17	0	0	0	1	29¹	28	0	12	7	13.2	4.91	83	.280	.374	1	.167	-0	-3	-3	-0	-0.1
1931	Was-A	1	0	1.000	6	0	0	0	0	12	24	2	4	5	21.0	7.50	57	.429	.467	0	—	0	-4	-4	2	-0.2
Total	2	1	0	1.000	23	0	0	0	1	41¹	52	2	16	12	15.5	5.66	73	.333	.406	1	.167	-0	-7	-7	1	-0.3

YEAR	TM/L	W	L	PCT	G	GS	CG	SH	SV	IP	H	HR	BB	SO	RAT	ERA	ERA+	OAV	OOB	BH	AVG	PB	PR	/A	PD	TPI
● **JULIAN TAVAREZ**					Tavarez, Julian (Carmen) b: 5/22/73, Santiago, D.R. BR/TR, 6'2", 165 lbs. Deb: 8/7/93																				
1993	Cle-A	2	2	.500	8	7	0	0	0	37	53	7	13	19	16.5	6.57	66	.340	.398	0	—	0	-9	-9	-0	-0.8
1994	Cle-A	0	1	.000	1	1	0	0	0	1²	6	1	1	0	37.8	21.60	23	.500	.538	0	—	0	-3	-3	0	-1.1
Total	2	2	3	.400	9	8	0	0	0	38²	59	8	14	19	17.5	7.22	60	.351	.408	0	—	0	-12	-12	-0	-1.9
● **ARLAS TAYLOR**					Taylor, Arlas Walter "Lefty" or "Foxy" b: 3/16/1896, Warrick County, Ind. d: 9/10/58, Dade City, Fla. BR/TL, 5'11" Deb: 9/15/21																				
1921	Phi-A	0	1	.000	1	1	0	0	0	2	7	1	2	1	40.5	22.50	20	.636	.692	0	—	0	-4	-4	-0	-1.0
● **BEN TAYLOR**					Taylor, Benjamin Harrison b: 4/2/1889, Paoli, Ind. d: 11/3/46, Martin County, Ind. BR/TR, 5'11", 163 lbs. Deb: 6/28/12																				
1912	Cin-N	0	0	—	2	0	0	0	0	5²	9	0	3	2	20.6	3.18	106	.360	.448	0	.000	0	0	0	-0	0.0
● **BRUCE TAYLOR**					Taylor, Bruce Bell b: 4/16/53, Holden, Mass. BR/TR, 6', 178 lbs. Deb: 8/5/77																				
1977	Det-A	1	0	1.000	19	0	0	0	2	29¹	23	2	10	19	10.4	3.38	127	.219	.293	0	—	0	2	3	0	0.0
1978	Det-A	0	0	—	1	0	0	0	0	1	0	0	0	0	0.0	0.00	—	.000	.000	0	—	0	0	0	0	0.0
1979	Det-A	1	2	.333	10	0	0	0	0	18²	16	1	7	8	12.1	4.82	90	.242	.333	0	—	0	-1	-1	0	-0.3
Total	3	2	2	.500	30	0	0	0	2	49	39	3	17	27	10.8	3.86	111	.224	.304	0	—	0	1	2	0	-0.3
● **CHUCK TAYLOR**					Taylor, Charles Gilbert b: 4/18/42, Murfreesboro, Tenn. BR/TR, 6'2", 195 lbs. Deb: 5/27/69																				
1969	StL-N	7	5	.583	27	13	5	1	0	126²	108	8	30	62	10.0	2.56	140	.235	.287	7	.179	1	15	14	-2	1.2
1970	StL-N	6	7	.462	56	7	1	0	8	124¹	116	5	31	64	10.8	3.11	132	.256	.306	3	.115	-1	13	14	1	1.5
1971	StL-N	3	1	.750	43	1	0	0	3	71¹	72	7	25	46	12.4	3.53	102	.267	.331	2	.167	0	-1	1	0	0.1
1972	NY-N	0	0	—	20	0	0	0	2	31	44	2	9	9	15.7	5.52	61	.341	.388	0	.000	0	-7	-7	1	0.0
	Mil-A	0	0	—	5	0	0	0	1	11²	8	0	3	6	9.3	1.54	196	.200	.273	1	.500	0	2	2	0	0.1
1973	Mon-N	2	0	1.000	8	0	0	0	0	20¹	17	3	2	10	8.4	1.77	215	.230	.250	0	.000	0	4	5	1	0.5
1974	Mon-N	6	2	.750	61	0	0	0	11	107²	101	8	25	43	10.8	2.17	177	.256	.305	3	.300	1	17	20	1	2.0
1975	Mon-N	2	2	.500	54	0	0	0	6	74	72	6	24	29	11.8	3.53	108	.264	.326	0	.000	0	1	2	0	0.1
1976	Mon-N	2	3	.400	31	0	0	0	0	40	38	4	13	14	11.5	4.50	83	.273	.336	0	.000	0	-4	-3	-0	-0.5
Total	8	28	20	.583	305	21	6	2	31	607	576	43	162	282	11.1	3.07	123	.258	.312	16	.158	0	40	47	1	5.0
● **DORN TAYLOR**					Taylor, Donald Clyde b: 8/11/58, Abington, Pa. BR/TR, 6'2", 180 lbs. Deb: 4/30/87																				
1987	Pit-N	2	3	.400	14	8	0	0	0	53¹	48	10	28	37	13.0	5.74	72	.247	.345	3	.167	-0	-10	-10	-1	-0.8
1989	Pit-N	1	1	.500	9	0	0	0	0	10²	14	0	5	3	16.0	5.06	66	.333	.404	0	.000	-0	-2	-2	-0	-0.4
1990	Bal-A	0	1	.000	4	0	0	0	0	3²	4	0	2	4	14.7	2.45	155	.250	.333	0	—	0	1	1	0	0.3
Total	3	3	5	.375	27	8	0	0	0	67²	66	10	35	44	13.6	5.45	73	.262	.354	3	.158	-1	-11	-11	-1	-0.9
● **ED TAYLOR**					Taylor, Edgar Ruben "Rube" b: 3/23/1877, Palestine, Tex. d: 1/31/12, Dallas, Tex. TL, Deb: 8/8/03																				
1903	StL-N	0	0	—	1	0	0	0	0	3	0	0	1	0	0.0	0.00	—	.000	.000	0	.000	0	1	1	0	0.1
● **GARY TAYLOR**					Taylor, Gary William b: 10/19/45, Detroit, Mich. BR/TR, 6'2", 190 lbs. Deb: 9/2/69																				
1969	Det-A	0	1	.000	7	0	0	0	0	10¹	10	2	6	3	13.9	5.23	71	.244	.340	0	.000	-0	-2	-2	0	-0.2
● **HARRY TAYLOR**					Taylor, Harry Evans b: 12/2/35, San Angelo, Tex. BR/TR, 6', 185 lbs. Deb: 9/17/57																				
1957	KC-A	0	0	—	2	0	0	0	0	8²	11	0	4	4	16.6	3.12	127	.314	.400	1	.250	0	1	1	-0	0.0
● **HARRY TAYLOR**					Taylor, James Harry b: 5/20/19, E.Glenn, Ind. BR/TR, 6'1", 175 lbs. Deb: 9/22/46																				
1946	Bro-N	0	0	—	4	0	0	0	1	4²	5	0	1	6	11.6	3.86	88	.313	.353	0	—	0	-0	-0	0	0.0
1947	*Bro-N	10	5	.667	33	20	10	2	1	162	130	10	83	58	12.1	3.11	133	**.225**	.327	8	.129	-2	17	18	1	1.5
1948	Bro-N	2	7	.222	17	13	2	0	0	80²	90	8	61	32	17.2	5.36	75	.288	.408	6	.273	1	-13	-12	2	-0.9
1950	Bos-A	2	0	1.000	3	2	2	1	0	19	13	0	8	8	9.9	1.42	345	.197	.284	2	.286	0	7	7	0	0.8
1951	Bos-A	4	9	.308	31	8	1	0	2	81¹	100	6	42	22	15.8	5.75	78	.307	.388	3	.103	-3	-15	-12	1	-1.8
1952	Bos-A	1	0	1.000	2	1	1	0	0	11	6	1	6	1	11.7	1.80	219	.176	.317	1	.250	0	2	2	0	0.2
Total	6	19	21	.475	90	44	16	3	4	357²	344	25	201	127	14.0	4.10	102	.258	.359	20	.161	-3	-2	4	4	-0.2
● **JACK TAYLOR**					Taylor, John Budd "Brewery Jack" b: 5/23/1873, W.New Brighton, N.Y. d: 2/7/1900, Staten Island, N.Y. BR/TR, 6'1", 190 lbs. Deb: 9/16/1891																				
1891	NY-N	0	1	.000	1	1	1	0	0	8	4	1	3	3	7.9	1.13	285	.143	.226	0	.000	0	2	2	-0	0.2
1892	Phi-N	1	0	1.000	3	3	2	0	0	26	28	2	10	7	13.2	1.38	234	.264	.328	2	.167	-0	5	5	-1	0.0
1893	Phi-N	10	9	.526	25	16	14	0	1	170	189	8	77	41	14.6	4.24	108	.273	.354	20	.215	-2	8	6	2	0.5
1894	Phi-N	23	13	.639	41	34	31	1	1	298	347	13	96	76	13.9	4.08	125	.288	.349	48	.333	8	41	34	2	3.7
1895	Phi-N	26	14	.650	41	37	33	1	1	335	403	7	83	93	13.5	4.49	107	.293	.340	45	.290	7	11	11	4	1.9
1896	Phi-N	20	21	.488	45	41	35	1	1	359	459	17	112	97	14.8	4.79	90	.308	.364	29	.185	-6	-17	-19	4	-1.9
1897	Phi-N	16	20	.444	40	37	35	2	2	317¹	376	5	76	88	13.6	4.23	99	.292	.345	35	.252	2	3	-1	3	0.3
1898	StL-N	15	29	.341	50	47	42	0	1	397¹	465	14	83	89	13.0	3.90	97	.290	.335	38	.242	3	-13	-5	8	0.7
1899	Cin-N	9	10	.474	24	18	15	2	2	168¹	197	7	41	34	13.3	4.12	95	.292	.341	17	.250	-0	-5	-4	-1	-0.5
Total	9	120	117	.506	270	234	208	7	9	2079	2468	74	581	528	13.7	4.23	103	.292	.346	234	.252	11	36	34	21	4.9
● **JACK TAYLOR**					Taylor, John W. b: 1/14/1874, New Straitsville, Ohio d: 3/4/38, Columbus, Ohio BR/TR, 5'10", 170 lbs. Deb: 9/25/1898																				
1898	Chi-N	5	0	1.000	5	5	5	0	0	41	32	0	10	11	9.4	2.20	163	.214	.268	3	.200	1	6	6	-0	0.8
1899	Chi-N	18	21	.462	41	39	39	1	0	354²	380	6	84	67	12.3	3.76	100	.274	.325	37	.266	10	4	0	1	1.0
1900	Chi-N	10	17	.370	28	26	25	2	1	222¹	226	4	58	57	11.8	2.55	141	.263	.316	19	.235	2	28	26	-3	2.7
1901	Chi-N	13	19	.406	33	31	30	0	0	275²	341	5	44	68	12.8	3.36	96	.301	.332	23	.217	2	-1	-4	2	0.0
1902	Chi-N	23	11	.676	36	33	33	7	1	324²	271	2	43	83	**9.0**	**1.33**	203	.227	**.260**	44	.237	3	**52**	49	1	**6.3**
1903	Chi-N	21	14	.600	37	33	33	1	1	312¹	277	2	57	83	9.8	2.45	128	.235	.273	28	.222	4	28	24	1	2.6
1904	StL-N	20	19	.513	41	39	39	3	1	352	297	5	82	103	10.0	2.22	121	.220	.271	28	.211	4	20	19	1	2.6
1905	StL-N	15	21	.417	37	34	34	3	1	309	302	10	85	102	11.6	3.44	87	.259	.315	23	.190	4	-15	-16	-2	-1.5
1906	StL-N	8	9	.471	17	17	17	1	0	155	133	3	47	27	10.9	2.15	122	.227	.292	11	.208	3	8	8	1	1.4
	Chi-N	12	3	.800	17	16	15	2	0	147¹	116	1	39	34	9.8	1.83	144	.223	.285	11	.208	2	13	13	-0	1.5
	Yr	20	12	.625	34	33	32	3	0	302¹	249	4	86	61	10.2	1.99	132	.224	.283	22	.208	5	21	21	0	2.9
1907	Chi-N	7	5	.583	17	13	8	0	0	123	127	3	33	22	11.8	3.29	76	.268	.318	9	.191	0	-11	-11	1	-1.0
Total	10	152	139	.522	310	286	278	19	5	2617	2502	41	582	657	10.9	2.66	115	.250	.298	236	.223	35	134	116	5	16.7
● **KERRY TAYLOR**					Taylor, Kerry Thomas b: 1/25/71, Bemidji, Minn. BR/TR, 6'3", 200 lbs. Deb: 4/13/93																				
1993	SD-N	0	5	.000	36	7	0	0	0	68¹	72	5	49	45	16.5	6.45	64	.277	.399	0	.000	-1	-18	-18	-1	-1.3
1994	SD-N	0	0	—	1	1	0	0	0	4¹	9	1	1	3	22.8	8.31	51	.409	.458	0	.000	-0	-2	-2	-0	0.0
Total	2	0	5	.000	37	8	0	0	0	72²	81	6	50	48	16.8	6.56	63	.287	.404	0	.000	-2	-20	-20	-1	-1.3
● **DUMMY TAYLOR**					Taylor, Luther Haden b: 2/21/1875, Oskaloosa, Kan. d: 8/22/58, Jacksonville, Ill. BR/TR, 6'1", 160 lbs. Deb: 8/27/00																				
1900	NY-N	4	3	.571	11	7	6	0	0	62¹	74	0	24	16	14.9	2.45	147	.294	.367	3	.136	-1	9	8	-2	0.5
1901	NY-N	18	27	.400	45	43	37	4	0	353¹	377	8	112	136	12.9	3.18	104	.271	.333	18	.132	-8	5	5	1	-0.2
1902	Cle-A	1	3	.250	4	4	4	0	0	34	37	0	8	8	12.4	1.59	217	.277	.328	1	.100	-0	8	7	1	0.9
	NY-N	7	15	.318	26	25	18	0	0	200²	194	4	55	87	11.8	2.29	123	.254	.316	6	.092	-5	11	12	-1	0.6
1903	NY-N	13	13	.500	33	31	18	1	0	244²	306	6	89	94	14.7	4.23	79	.314	.374	12	.146	-2	-26	-24	-1	-2.4
1904	NY-N	21	15	.583	37	36	29	5	0	296¹	231	6	75	138	9.6	2.34	117	.214	.270	16	.157	-1	13	13	3	1.6
1905	NY-N	16	9	.640	32	28	18	4	0	213¹	200	6	51	91	10.9	2.66	110	.247	.298	9	.130	-1	8	6	1	0.6
1906	NY-N	17	9	.654	31	27	13	2	0	213	186	4	57	91	10.5	2.20	119	.233	.289	14	.184	-1	10	10	-1	1.1
1907	NY-N	11	7	.611	28	21	11	3	1	171	145	1	46	56	10.2	2.42	102	.232	.288	6	.125	-1	1	1	-1	-0.1

YEAR TM/L	W	L	PCT	G	GS	CG	SH	SV	IP	H	HR	BB	SO	RAT	ERA	ERA+	OAV	OOB	BH	AVG	PB	PR	/A	PD	TPI
1908 NY-N	8	5	.615	27	15	6	1	2	127²	127	5	34	50	11.6	2.33	104	.253	.306	8	.229	2	1	1	-0	0.3
Total 9	116	106	.523	274	237	160	21	3	1916¹	1877	39	551	767	11.7	2.75	107	.256	.314	93	.144	-17	40	39	0	2.9

● **WILEY TAYLOR**   Taylor, Philip Wiley   b: 3/18/1888, Wamego, Kan.   d: 7/8/54, Westmoreland, Kan.   BR/TR, 6'1", 175 lbs.   Deb: 9/6/11

YEAR TM/L	W	L	PCT	G	GS	CG	SH	SV	IP	H	HR	BB	SO	RAT	ERA	ERA+	OAV	OOB	BH	AVG	PB	PR	/A	PD	TPI
1911 Det-A	0	2	.000	3	2	1	0	0	19	18	0	10	9	13.7	3.79	91	.247	.345	0	.000	-1	-1	-1	-1	-0.2
1912 Chi-A	0	1	.000	3	3	0	0	0	20	21	0	14	4	15.7	4.95	65	.309	.427	0	.000	-1	-4	-4	-0	-0.2
1913 StL-A	0	2	.000	5	4	1	0	0	31²	33	0	16	12	13.9	4.83	61	.280	.366	0	.000	-1	-7	-7	-0	-0.5
1914 StL-A	2	5	.286	16	8	2	1	0	50	41	0	25	20	12.2	3.42	79	.209	.305	2	.167	-0	-4	-4	-0	-0.6
Total 4	2	10	.167	27	17	4	1	0	120²	113	0	65	45	13.5	4.10	72	.248	.346	2	.061	-3	-15	-15	-0	-1.5

● **SCOTT TAYLOR**   Taylor, Rodney Scott   b: 8/2/67, Defiance, Ohio   BL/TL, 6'1", 185 lbs.   Deb: 9/17/92

YEAR TM/L	W	L	PCT	G	GS	CG	SH	SV	IP	H	HR	BB	SO	RAT	ERA	ERA+	OAV	OOB	BH	AVG	PB	PR	/A	PD	TPI
1992 Bos-A	1	1	.500	4	1	0	0	0	14²	13	4	4	7	10.4	4.91	86	.245	.298	0	—	0	-2	-1	-0	-0.1
1993 Bos-A	0	1	1.000	16	0	0	0	0	11	14	1	12	8	22.1	8.18	56	.311	.466	0	—	0	-5	-4	-0	-0.8
Total 2	1	2	.333	20	1	0	0	0	25²	27	5	16	15	15.4	6.31	69	.276	.383	0	—	0	-6	-5	-0	-0.9

● **RON TAYLOR**   Taylor, Ronald Wesley   b: 12/13/37, Toronto, Ont., Can.   BR/TR, 6'1", 195 lbs.   Deb: 4/11/62

YEAR TM/L	W	L	PCT	G	GS	CG	SH	SV	IP	H	HR	BB	SO	RAT	ERA	ERA+	OAV	OOB	BH	AVG	PB	PR	/A	PD	TPI
1962 Cle-A	2	2	.500	8	4	1	0	0	33¹	36	6	13	15	13.5	5.94	65	.281	.352	3	.273	0	-7	-8	-0	-0.8
1963 StL-N	9	7	.563	54	9	2	0	11	133¹	119	10	30	91	10.3	2.84	125	.243	.293	1	.031	-3	7	11	-3	0.9
1964 *StL-N	8	4	.667	63	2	0	0	7	101¹	109	15	33	69	12.7	4.62	82	.274	.331	2	.133	-0	-12	-9	-2	-1.0
1965 StL-N	2	1	.667	25	0	0	0	1	43²	43	6	15	26	12.2	4.53	85	.261	.326	2	.400	1	-5	-3	-0	-0.2
Hou-N	1	5	.167	32	1	0	0	4	57²	68	5	16	37	13.9	6.40	52	.305	.365	0	.000	-1	-18	-19	-1	-2.4
Yr	3	6	.333	57	1	0	0	5	101¹	111	11	31	63	13.1	5.60	64	.283	.343	2	.111	-1	-23	-23	-1	-2.6
1966 Hou-N	2	3	.400	36	1	0	0	4	64²	89	5	10	29	14.5	5.71	60	.333	.369	2	.167	-0	-15	-16	-1	-1.3
1967 NY-N	4	6	.400	50	0	0	0	8	73	60	1	23	46	10.4	2.34	145	.230	.295	0	.000	-1	8	8	0	1.3
1968 NY-N	1	5	.167	58	0	0	0	13	76²	64	4	18	49	9.7	2.70	112	.228	.277	0	.000	-1	2	3	1	0.3
1969 *NY-N	9	4	.692	59	0	0	0	13	76	61	7	24	42	10.2	2.72	134	.222	.289	1	.250	0	7	8	0	1.7
1970 NY-N	5	4	.556	57	0	0	0	13	66¹	65	5	16	28	11.0	3.93	102	.265	.310	0	.000	-1	1	1	0	0.1
1971 NY-N	2	2	.500	45	0	0	0	2	69	71	7	11	32	10.8	3.65	93	.269	.301	1	.250	1	-1	-2	-0	-0.1
1972 SD-N	0	0	—	4	0	0	0	0	5	9	5	1	4	16.2	12.60	26	.375	.375	0	—	0	-5	-5	-0	-0.3
Total 11	45	43	.511	491	17	3	0	72	800	794	76	209	464	11.5	3.93	91	.264	.316	12	.103	-5	-39	-32	-2	-1.5

● **TERRY TAYLOR**   Taylor, Terry Derrell   b: 7/28/64, Crestview, Fla.   BR/TR, 6'1", 180 lbs.   Deb: 8/19/88

YEAR TM/L	W	L	PCT	G	GS	CG	SH	SV	IP	H	HR	BB	SO	RAT	ERA	ERA+	OAV	OOB	BH	AVG	PB	PR	/A	PD	TPI
1988 Sea-A	0	1	.000	8	2	0	0	0	23	26	2	11	9	14.5	6.26	66	.295	.374	0	—	0	-6	-5	-1	-0.6

● **PETE TAYLOR**   Taylor, Vernon Charles   b: 11/26/27, Severn, Md.   BR/TR, 6'1", 170 lbs.   Deb: 5/2/52

YEAR TM/L	W	L	PCT	G	GS	CG	SH	SV	IP	H	HR	BB	SO	RAT	ERA	ERA+	OAV	OOB	BH	AVG	PB	PR	/A	PD	TPI
1952 StL-A	0	0	—	1	0	0	0	0	2	4	0	3	2	31.5	13.50	29	.500	.636	0	—	0	-2	-2	0	0.0

● **WADE TAYLOR**   Taylor, Wade Eric   b: 10/19/65, Mobile, Ala.   BR/TR, 6'1", 185 lbs.   Deb: 6/2/91

YEAR TM/L	W	L	PCT	G	GS	CG	SH	SV	IP	H	HR	BB	SO	RAT	ERA	ERA+	OAV	OOB	BH	AVG	PB	PR	/A	PD	TPI
1991 NY-A	7	12	.368	23	22	0	0	0	116¹	144	13	53	72	15.8	6.27	66	.314	.393	0	—	0	-28	-27	1	-3.6

● **BILLY TAYLOR**   Taylor, William Henry "Bollicky Bill"   b: 1855, Washington, D.C.   d: 5/14/1900, Jacksonville, Fla.   BR/TR, 5'11.5", 204 lbs.   Deb: 5/21/1881   ♦

YEAR TM/L	W	L	PCT	G	GS	CG	SH	SV	IP	H	HR	BB	SO	RAT	ERA	ERA+	OAV	OOB	BH	AVG	PB	PR	/A	PD	TPI
1881 Wor-N	0	1	.000	1	1	1	0	0	8	15	0	6	0	23.6	7.88	38	.366	.447	3	.107	-0	-5	-4	-0	-0.4
Cle-N	0	0	—	1	0	0	0	0	3	0	0	1	2	3.0	0.00	—	.000	.100	25	.243	-0	1	1	-0	0.0
Yr	0	1	.000	2	1	1	0	0	11	15	0	7	2	18.0	5.73	51	.300	.300	28	.214	-0	-4	-3	-0	-0.4
1882 Pit-a	0	1	.000	1	0	0	0	0	5	11	0	4	1	27.0	16.20	16	.414	.491	84	.281	0	-8	-8	-0	-0.8
1883 Pit-a	4	7	.364	19	9	8	0	0	127	166	4	34	41	14.2	5.39	60	.296	.337	96	.260	3	-29	-31	-2	-1.9
1884 StL-U	25	4	.862	33	29	29	2	4	263	222	2	40	154	9.0	1.68	143	.213	.243	68	.366	13	22	21	-1	**2.8**
Phi-a	18	12	.600	30	30	30	1	0	260	232	3	44	100	10.0	2.53	134	.219	.252	28	.252	3	21	25	2	2.9
1885 Phi-a	1	5	.167	6	6	6	0	0	52¹	68	0	9	11	13.4	3.27	105	.343	.375	4	.190	-1	-0	1	-1	-0.1
1886 Bal-a	1	6	.143	8	8	8	0	0	72¹	87	1	20	37	13.6	5.72	60	.284	.332	12	.308	1	-18	-18	-0	-1.2
1887 Phi-a	1	0	1.000	1	1	1	0	0	9	10	1	7	1	17.0	3.00	143	.286	.405	1	.250	-0	1	1	-0	0.1
Total 7	50	36	.581	100	84	83	3	4	799²	811	11	165	376	11.2	3.17	96	.248	.287	323	.277	20	-14	-13	-4	1.4

● **BILLY TAYLOR**   Taylor, William Howell   b: 10/16/61, Monticello, Fla.   BR/TR, 6'8", 200 lbs.   Deb: 4/5/94

YEAR TM/L	W	L	PCT	G	GS	CG	SH	SV	IP	H	HR	BB	SO	RAT	ERA	ERA+	OAV	OOB	BH	AVG	PB	PR	/A	PD	TPI
1994 Oak-A	1	3	.250	41	0	0	0	1	46¹	38	4	18	48	11.3	3.50	127	.220	.301	0	—	0	7	5	0	0.9

● **BUD TEACHOUT**   Teachout, Arthur John   b: 2/27/04, Los Angeles, Cal.   d: 5/11/85, Laguna Beach, Cal   BR/TL, 6'2", 183 lbs.   Deb: 5/12/30

YEAR TM/L	W	L	PCT	G	GS	CG	SH	SV	IP	H	HR	BB	SO	RAT	ERA	ERA+	OAV	OOB	BH	AVG	PB	PR	/A	PD	TPI
1930 Chi-N	11	4	.733	40	16	6	0	0	153	178	16	48	59	13.3	4.06	120	.296	.348	17	.270	3	16	14	-1	1.3
1931 Chi-N	1	2	.333	27	3	1	0	0	61¹	79	6	28	14	15.8	5.72	67	.305	.375	5	.238	0	-13	-13	1	-0.4
1932 StL-N	0	0	—	1	0	0	0	0	1	2	0	0	0	18.0	0.00	—	.400	.400	0	—	0	0	0	-0	0.0
Total 3	12	6	.667	68	19	7	0	0	215¹	259	22	76	73	14.0	4.51	102	.299	.356	22	.262	3	3	2	0	0.9

● **GEORGE TEBEAU**   Tebeau, George E. "White Wings"   b: 12/26/1861, St.Louis, Mo.   d: 2/4/23, Denver, Colo.   BR/TR, 5'9", 175 lbs.   Deb: 4/16/1887   F♦

YEAR TM/L	W	L	PCT	G	GS	CG	SH	SV	IP	H	HR	BB	SO	RAT	ERA	ERA+	OAV	OOB	BH	AVG	PB	PR	/A	PD	TPI
1887 Cin-a	0	1	.000	1	1	1	0	0	8	21	0	3	1	28.1	13.50	32	.488	.532	94	.296	0	-8	-8	0	-0.5
1890 Tol-a	0	0	—	1	0	0	0	0	5	9	0	5	0	25.2	9.00	44	.378	.486	102	.268	0	-3	-3	-0	0.0
Total 2	0	1	.000	2	1	1	0	0	13	30	0	8	1	27.0	11.77	36	.449	.514	622	.269	1	-11	-11	0	-0.5

● **PATSY TEBEAU**   Tebeau, Oliver Wendell   b: 12/5/1864, St.Louis, Mo.   d: 5/15/18, St.Louis, Mo.   BR/TR, 5'8", 163 lbs.   Deb: 9/20/1887   FM♦

YEAR TM/L	W	L	PCT	G	GS	CG	SH	SV	IP	H	HR	BB	SO	RAT	ERA	ERA+	OAV	OOB	BH	AVG	PB	PR	/A	PD	TPI
1896 *Cle-N	0	0	—	1	0	0	0	0	0	1	0	0	0	—	—	—	1.000	1.000	146	.269	0	0	0	0	0.0

● **AL TEDROW**   Tedrow, Allen Seymour   b: 12/14/1891, Westerville, Ohio   d: 1/23/58, Westerville, Ohio   BR/TL, 6', 180 lbs.   Deb: 9/15/14

YEAR TM/L	W	L	PCT	G	GS	CG	SH	SV	IP	H	HR	BB	SO	RAT	ERA	ERA+	OAV	OOB	BH	AVG	PB	PR	/A	PD	TPI
1914 Cle-A	1	2	.333	4	3	1	0	0	22¹	19	0	14	4	14.5	1.21	239	.235	.367	1	.167	0	4	4	-0	0.6

● **KENT TEKULVE**   Tekulve, Kenton Charles   b: 3/5/47, Cincinnati, Ohio   BR/TR, 6'4", 180 lbs.   Deb: 5/20/74

YEAR TM/L	W	L	PCT	G	GS	CG	SH	SV	IP	H	HR	BB	SO	RAT	ERA	ERA+	OAV	OOB	BH	AVG	PB	PR	/A	PD	TPI
1974 Pit-N	1	1	.500	8	0	0	0	0	9	12	1	5	6	18.0	6.00	57	.343	.439	0	—	0	-2	-3	1	-0.5
1975 *Pit-N	1	2	.333	34	0	0	0	5	56	43	2	23	28	10.8	2.25	157	.215	.299	1	.091	-0	9	8	2	0.7
1976 Pit-N	5	3	.625	64	0	0	0	9	102²	91	3	25	68	10.2	2.45	142	.241	.288	0	.000	-1	12	12	2	1.2
1977 Pit-N	10	1	.909	72	0	0	0	7	103	89	5	33	59	10.7	3.06	130	.236	.299	3	.250	-1	10	11	3	1.6
1978 Pit-N	8	7	.533	91	0	0	0	31	135	115	5	55	77	11.5	2.33	159	.228	.306	2	.095	-1	**19**	21	3	3.6
1979 *Pit-N	10	8	.556	94	0	0	0	31	134¹	109	9	49	75	10.7	2.75	141	.222	.296	2	.133	-0	15	17	2	3.2
1980 Pit-N☆	8	12	.400	78	0	0	0	21	93	96	6	40	47	13.3	3.39	107	.267	.342	0	.000	-1	2	3	1	0.7
1981 Pit-N	5	5	.500	45	0	0	0	3	65	61	1	17	34	10.9	2.49	144	.250	.302	0	.000	-1	7	8	1	1.4
1982 Pit-N	12	8	.600	85	0	0	0	20	128²	113	7	46	66	11.3	2.87	129	.237	.309	1	.071	-0	10	12	2	2.3
1983 Pit-N	7	5	.583	76	0	0	0	18	99	78	1	36	52	10.4	1.64	226	.223	.296	0	.000	-1	22	23	1	3.7
1984 Pit-N	3	9	.250	72	0	0	0	13	88	86	4	33	36	12.3	2.66	135	.262	.331	0	.000	-1	9	9	3	1.7
1985 Pit-N	0	0	—	2	0	0	0	0	3¹	7	1	5	4	32.4	16.20	22	.467	.600	0	—	0	-5	-5	0	-0.3
Phi-N	4	10	.286	58	0	0	0	14	72¹	67	4	25	36	11.7	2.99	123	.246	.314	0	.000	-0	5	6	1	1.3
Yr	4	10	.286	61	0	0	0	14	75²	74	5	30	40	12.6	3.57	103	.258	.332	0	.000	-0	1	1	1	1.3
1986 Phi-N	11	5	.688	73	0	0	0	4	110	99	5	25	57	10.1	2.54	152	.240	.283	0	.000	-1	14	16	0	2.4
1987 Phi-N	6	4	.600	90	0	0	0	8	105	96	8	29	66	10.7	3.09	137	.243	.295	0	.000	-1	12	13	1	1.4
1988 Phi-N	3	7	.300	70	0	0	0	0	80	87	3	22	43	12.5	3.60	99	.276	.327	1	.500	0	-1	-0	1	-0.1
1989 Cin-N	0	3	.000	37	0	0	0	1	52	56	5	23	31	13.7	5.02	72	.272	.345	1	.500	0	-9	-8	-0	-0.4
Total 16	94	90	.511	1050	0	0	0	184	1436¹	1305	63	491	779	11.4	2.85	131	.244	.309	10	.083	-6	128	141	22	24.3

● **ANTHONY TELFORD**   Telford, Anthony Charles   b: 3/6/66, San Jose, Cal.   BR/TR, 6', 175 lbs.   Deb: 8/19/90

YEAR TM/L	W	L	PCT	G	GS	CG	SH	SV	IP	H	HR	BB	SO	RAT	ERA	ERA+	OAV	OOB	BH	AVG	PB	PR	/A	PD	TPI
1990 Bal-A	3	3	.500	8	8	0	0	0	36¹	43	4	19	20	15.6	4.95	77	.295	.380	0	—	0	-4	-5	0	-0.5

YEAR	TM/L	W	L	PCT	G	GS	CG	SH	SV	IP	H	HR	BB	SO	RAT	ERA	ERA+	OAV	OOB	BH	AVG	PB	PR	/A	PD	TPI
1991	Bal-A	0	0	—	9	1	0	0	0	26²	27	3	6	24	11.1	4.05	98	.265	.306	0	—	0	0	-0	-0	0.0
1993	Bal-A	0	0	—	3	0	0	0	0	7¹	11	3	1	6	16.0	9.82	46	.344	.382	0	—	0	-4	-4	0	-0.3
Total	3	3	3	.500	20	9	0	0	0	70¹	81	10	26	50	13.9	5.12	77	.289	.354	0	—	0	-9	-9	0	-0.8

● **DAVE TELGHEDER**   Telgheder, David William b: 11/11/66, Middletown, N.Y.   BR/TR, 6'3", 212 lbs.   Deb: 6/12/93

YEAR	TM/L	W	L	PCT	G	GS	CG	SH	SV	IP	H	HR	BB	SO	RAT	ERA	ERA+	OAV	OOB	BH	AVG	PB	PR	/A	PD	TPI
1993	NY-N	6	2	.750	24	7	0	0	0	75²	82	10	21	35	12.7	4.76	84	.276	.332	1	.067	-0	-6	-6	-1	-0.7
1994	NY-N	0	1	.000	6	0	0	0	0	10	11	2	8	4	17.1	7.20	59	.282	.404	0	—	0	-3	-3	-0	-0.3
Total	2	6	3	.667	30	7	0	0	0	85²	93	12	29	39	13.2	5.04	80	.277	.341	1	.067	-0	-9	-10	-1	-1.0

● **TOM TELLMANN**   Tellmann, Thomas John b: 3/29/54, Warren, Pa.   BR/TR, 6'3", 195 lbs.   Deb: 6/9/79

YEAR	TM/L	W	L	PCT	G	GS	CG	SH	SV	IP	H	HR	BB	SO	RAT	ERA	ERA+	OAV	OOB	BH	AVG	PB	PR	/A	PD	TPI
1979	SD-N	0	0	—	1	0	0	0	0	2²	7	1	0	1	23.6	16.88	21	.467	.467	0	.000	-0	-4	-4	0	0.0
1980	SD-N	3	0	1.000	6	2	2	0	1	22¹	23	0	8	9	12.5	1.61	213	.264	.326	1	.125	-0	5	5	0	0.6
1983	Mil-A	9	4	.692	44	0	0	0	8	99²	95	7	35	48	11.9	2.80	133	.259	.327	0	—	0	14	10	3	2.2
1984	Mil-A	6	3	.667	50	0	0	0	4	81	82	6	31	28	12.7	2.78	138	.272	.342	0	—	0	11	10	1	1.2
1985	Oak-A	0	0	—	11	0	0	0	0	21¹	33	3	9	8	18.1	5.06	76	.347	.410	0	—	0	-2	-3	0	0.1
Total	5	18	7	.720	112	2	2	0	13	227	240	17	83	94	13.0	3.05	123	.277	.343	1	.111	-0	24	18	4	4.1

● **CHUCK TEMPLETON**   Templeton, Charles Sherman b: 6/1/32, Detroit, Mich.   BR/TL, 6'3", 210 lbs.   Deb: 9/9/55

YEAR	TM/L	W	L	PCT	G	GS	CG	SH	SV	IP	H	HR	BB	SO	RAT	ERA	ERA+	OAV	OOB	BH	AVG	PB	PR	/A	PD	TPI
1955	Bro-N	0	1	.000	4	0	0	0	0	4²	4	1	5	3	21.2	11.57	35	.294	.478	0	—	0	-4	-4	-0	-0.7
1956	Bro-N	0	1	.000	6	4	0	0	0	16¹	20	2	10	8	16.5	6.61	60	.294	.385	0	.000	-0	-5	-5	-0	-0.3
Total	2	0	2	.000	10	4	0	0	0	21	25	4	15	11	17.6	7.71	52	.294	.406	0	.000	-0	-9	-9	-0	-1.0

● **JOHN TENER**   Tener, John Kinley b: 7/25/1863, County Tyrone, Ireland d: 5/19/46, Pittsburgh, Pa.   BR/TR, 6'4", 180 lbs.   Deb: 6/8/1885 ♦

YEAR	TM/L	W	L	PCT	G	GS	CG	SH	SV	IP	H	HR	BB	SO	RAT	ERA	ERA+	OAV	OOB	BH	AVG	PB	PR	/A	PD	TPI
1888	Chi-N	7	5	.583	12	12	11	1	0	102	90	6	25	39	10.9	2.74	111	.228	.288	9	.196	-0	1	3	1	0.4
1889	Chi-N	15	15	.500	35	30	28	1	0	287	302	16	105	105	13.0	3.64	114	.262	.328	41	.273	5	12	17	3	2.1
1890	Pit-P	3	11	.214	14	14	13	0	0	117	160	6	70	30	18.1	7.31	53	.312	.400	12	.190	4	-40	-44	4	-3.1
Total	3	25	31	.446	61	56	52	2	0	506	552	28	200	174	13.7	4.30	90	.268	.339	62	.236	6	-27	-23	8	-0.6

● **JIM TENNANT**   Tennant, James McDonnell b: 3/3/07, Shepherdstown, W.Va d: 4/16/67, Trumbull, Conn.   BR/TR, 6'1", 190 lbs.   Deb: 9/28/29

YEAR	TM/L	W	L	PCT	G	GS	CG	SH	SV	IP	H	HR	BB	SO	RAT	ERA	ERA+	OAV	OOB	BH	AVG	PB	PR	/A	PD	TPI
1929	NY-N	0	0	—	1	0	0	0	0	1	1	0	1	0	1	9.0	0.00	—	.333	.333	0	—	0	1	1	0	0.0

● **FRED TENNEY**   Tenney, Fred Clay b: 7/9/1859, Marlborough, N.H. d: 6/15/19, Fall River, Mass.   Deb: 4/28/1884 ♦

YEAR	TM/L	W	L	PCT	G	GS	CG	SH	SV	IP	H	HR	BB	SO	RAT	ERA	ERA+	OAV	OOB	BH	AVG	PB	PR	/A	PD	TPI
1884	Bos-U	3	1	.750	4	4	4	0	0	35	31	6	5	18	9.3	2.31	103	.222	.248	2	.118	-3	0	0	-1	-0.3
	Wil-U	0	1	.000	1	1	1	0	0	8	6	0	4	10	11.3	1.13	137	.194	.287	0	.000	-1	1	1	0	0.1
	Yr	3	2	.600	5	5	5	0	0	43	37	6	9	28	9.6	2.09	116	.217	.256	2	.100	-3	2	2	-1	-0.3

● **FRED TENNEY**   Tenney, Frederick b: 11/26/1871, Georgetown, Mass. d: 7/3/52, Boston, Mass.   BL/TL, 5'9", 155 lbs.   Deb: 6/16/1894 M♦

YEAR	TM/L	W	L	PCT	G	GS	CG	SH	SV	IP	H	HR	BB	SO	RAT	ERA	ERA+	OAV	OOB	BH	AVG	PB	PR	/A	PD	TPI
1905	Bos-N	0	0	—	1	0	0	0	0	2	5	0	1	0	27.0	4.50	69	.417	.462	158	.288	0	-0	-0	-0	0.0

● **BOB TERLECKI**   Terlecki, Robert Joseph b: 2/14/45, Trenton, N.J.   BR/TR, 5'8", 185 lbs.   Deb: 8/16/72

YEAR	TM/L	W	L	PCT	G	GS	CG	SH	SV	IP	H	HR	BB	SO	RAT	ERA	ERA+	OAV	OOB	BH	AVG	PB	PR	/A	PD	TPI
1972	Phi-N	0	0	—	9	0	0	0	0	13¹	16	2	10	5	17.6	4.73	76	.308	.419	0	—	0	-2	-2	0	0.0

● **GREG TERLECKY**   Terlecky, Gregory John b: 3/20/52, Culver City, Cal.   BR/TR, 6'3", 200 lbs.   Deb: 6/12/75

YEAR	TM/L	W	L	PCT	G	GS	CG	SH	SV	IP	H	HR	BB	SO	RAT	ERA	ERA+	OAV	OOB	BH	AVG	PB	PR	/A	PD	TPI
1975	StL-N	0	1	.000	20	0	0	0	0	30¹	38	4	12	13	14.8	4.45	84	.306	.368	1	.333	0	-3	-2	0	0.0

● **JEFF TERPKO**   Terpko, Jeffrey Michael b: 10/16/50, Sayre, Pa.   BR/TR, 6', 180 lbs.   Deb: 9/21/74

YEAR	TM/L	W	L	PCT	G	GS	CG	SH	SV	IP	H	HR	BB	SO	RAT	ERA	ERA+	OAV	OOB	BH	AVG	PB	PR	/A	PD	TPI
1974	Tex-A	0	0	—	3	0	0	0	0	7	6	0	4	3	12.9	1.29	277	.231	.333	0	—	0	2	2	-0	0.2
1976	Tex-A	3	3	.500	32	0	0	0	0	52²	42	3	29	24	12.1	2.39	150	.223	.327	0	—	0	7	7	-0	0.6
1977	Mon-N	0	1	.000	13	0	0	0	0	20²	28	2	15	14	18.7	5.66	67	.346	.448	0	.000	-0	-4	-4	-0	-0.2
Total	3	3	4	.429	48	0	0	0	0	80¹	76	5	48	41	13.9	3.14	116	.258	.362	0	.000	-0	4	5	-1	0.6

● **WALT TERRELL**   Terrell, Charles Walter b: 5/11/58, Jeffersonville, Ind   BL/TR, 6'2", 205 lbs.   Deb: 9/8/82

YEAR	TM/L	W	L	PCT	G	GS	CG	SH	SV	IP	H	HR	BB	SO	RAT	ERA	ERA+	OAV	OOB	BH	AVG	PB	PR	/A	PD	TPI
1982	NY-N	0	3	.000	3	3	0	0	0	21	22	2	14	8	15.4	3.43	106	.268	.375	2	.400	1	0	0	-0	0.1
1983	NY-N	8	8	.500	21	20	4	2	0	133²	123	7	55	59	12.1	3.57	102	.251	.329	8	.182	3	1	1	-0	0.4
1984	NY-N	11	12	.478	33	33	3	1	0	215	232	16	80	114	13.2	3.52	101	.282	.348	6	.080	-4	2	0	-0	-0.3
1985	Det-A	15	10	.600	34	34	5	3	0	229	221	9	95	130	12.6	3.85	106	.255	.332	0	—	0	7	6	3	0.9
1986	Det-A	15	12	.556	34	33	9	2	0	217¹	199	30	98	93	12.4	4.56	90	.245	.329	0	—	0	-9	-10	2	-1.0
1987	*Det-A	17	10	.630	35	35	10	1	0	244²	254	30	94	143	12.9	4.05	104	.268	.336	0	—	0	11	5	-1	0.7
1988	Det-A	7	16	.304	29	29	11	1	0	206¹	199	20	78	84	12.2	3.97	96	.251	.328	0	—	0	-0	-4	1	0.0
1989	SD-N	5	13	.278	19	19	4	1	0	123¹	134	14	26	63	11.7	4.01	87	.277	.314	4	.100	-0	-7	-7	3	-0.7
	NY-A	6	5	.545	13	13	1	1	0	83	102	9	24	30	13.9	5.20	74	.307	.358	0	—	0	-12	-12	-0	-1.4
1990	Pit-N	2	7	.222	16	16	0	0	0	82²	98	13	33	34	14.7	5.88	62	.295	.366	3	.107	-1	-19	-21	1	-2.0
	Det-A	6	4	.600	13	12	0	0	0	75¹	86	7	24	30	14.1	4.54	87	.290	.359	0	—	0	-5	-5	-1	-0.7
1991	Det-A	12	14	.462	35	33	8	2	0	218²	257	16	79	80	13.9	4.24	98	.301	.361	0	—	0	-4	-2	-1	-0.3
1992	Det-A	7	10	.412	36	14	1	0	0	136²	163	16	48	61	14.1	5.20	76	.298	.358	0	—	0	-19	-19	1	-2.0
Total	11	111	124	.472	321	294	56	14	0	1986²	2090	187	748	929	13.0	4.22	93	.274	.341	23	.120	-1	-54	-68	8	-6.3

● **JERRY TERRELL**   Terrell, Jerry Wayne b: 7/13/46, Waseca, Minn.   BR/TR, 6', 170 lbs.   Deb: 4/14/73 ♦

YEAR	TM/L	W	L	PCT	G	GS	CG	SH	SV	IP	H	HR	BB	SO	RAT	ERA	ERA+	OAV	OOB	BH	AVG	PB	PR	/A	PD	TPI
1979	KC-A	0	0	—	1	0	0	0	0	1	0	0	0	0	0.0	0.00	—	.000	.000	12	.300	0	0	0	0	0.0
1980	KC-A	0	0	—	1	0	0	0	0	1	1	0	1	0	18.0	0.00	—	.250	.400	1	.063	0	0	0	0	0.0
Total	2	0	0	—	2	0	0	0	0	2	1	0	1	0	9.0	0.00	—	.143	.250	412	.253	0	1	1	0	0.0

● **JOHN TERRY**   Terry, John Burchard b: 11/1/1879, Waterbury, Conn. d: 4/27/33, Kansas City, Mo.   Deb: 9/17/02

YEAR	TM/L	W	L	PCT	G	GS	CG	SH	SV	IP	H	HR	BB	SO	RAT	ERA	ERA+	OAV	OOB	BH	AVG	PB	PR	/A	PD	TPI
1902	Det-A	0	1	.000	1	1	1	0	0	5	8	0	1	0	16.2	3.60	101	.361	.388	0	.000	-0	-0	0	-0	-0.1
1903	StL-A	1	1	.500	3	1	1	0	0	17²	21	0	4	2	14.3	2.55	114	.294	.357	0	.000	-1	1	1	-0	-0.1
Total	2	1	2	.333	4	2	2	0	0	22²	29	0	5	2	14.7	2.78	111	.310	.364	0	.000	-2	1	1	-0	-0.2

● **YANK TERRY**   Terry, Lancelot Yank b: 2/11/11, Bedford, Ind. d: 11/4/79, Bloomington, Ind.   BR/TR, 6'1", 180 lbs.   Deb: 8/3/40

YEAR	TM/L	W	L	PCT	G	GS	CG	SH	SV	IP	H	HR	BB	SO	RAT	ERA	ERA+	OAV	OOB	BH	AVG	PB	PR	/A	PD	TPI
1940	Bos-A	1	0	1.000	5	2	1	0	0	19¹	24	2	11	9	16.3	8.84	51	.304	.389	2	.250	0	-10	-9	0	-0.4
1942	Bos-A	6	5	.545	20	11	3	0	1	85	82	5	43	37	13.4	3.92	95	.248	.339	3	.111	-1	-2	-2	-0	-0.4
1943	Bos-A	7	9	.438	30	22	7	0	1	163²	147	8	63	63	11.6	3.52	94	.242	.314	3	.067	-3	-4	-4	0	-0.6
1944	Bos-A	6	10	.375	27	17	3	0	0	132²	142	10	65	30	14.2	4.21	81	.276	.361	11	.234	1	-11	-12	0	-1.2
1945	Bos-A	0	4	.000	12	4	1	0	0	56²	68	8	14	28	13.0	4.13	82	.296	.336	2	.111	-2	-5	-5	-1	-0.5
Total	5	20	28	.417	93	55	14	0	2	457¹	463	33	196	167	13.1	4.09	85	.263	.339	21	.145	-4	-32	-31	-1	-3.1

● **RALPH TERRY**   Terry, Ralph Willard b: 1/9/36, Big Cabin, Okla.   BR/TR, 6'3", 195 lbs.   Deb: 8/6/56

YEAR	TM/L	W	L	PCT	G	GS	CG	SH	SV	IP	H	HR	BB	SO	RAT	ERA	ERA+	OAV	OOB	BH	AVG	PB	PR	/A	PD	TPI
1956	NY-A	1	2	.333	3	3	0	0	0	13¹	17	2	11	8	18.9	9.45	41	.347	.467	1	.167	-0	-8	-8	-0	-1.3
1957	NY-A	1	1	.500	7	2	1	1	0	20²	18	1	8	7	11.3	3.05	118	.240	.313	1	.250	-0	2	1	0	0.2
	KC-A	4	11	.267	21	19	3	1	0	130²	119	15	47	80	11.7	3.38	117	.239	.310	6	.143	-2	6	8	0	0.7
	Yr	5	12	.294	28	21	4	2	0	151¹	137	16	55	87	11.7	3.33	117	.239	.310	7	.152	-3	8	10	0	0.9
1958	KC-A	11	13	.458	40	33	8	3	2	216²	217	29	61	134	11.6	4.24	92	.262	.314	14	.197	-0	-11	-8	-2	-1.1
1959	KC-A	2	4	.333	9	7	2	0	0	46¹	56	9	19	36	14.8	5.24	76	.308	.376	3	.176	-1	-6	-6	-1	-0.7
	NY-A	3	7	.300	24	16	5	1	0	127¹	130	7	30	55	11.5	3.39	107	.270	.316	4	.098	-3	7	4	-0	-0.1
	Yr	5	11	.313	33	23	7	1	0	173²	186	16	49	90	12.3	3.89	96	.280	.331	7	.121	-3	-0	-3	-0	-0.8
1960	*NY-A	10	8	.556	35	23	7	3	1	166²	149	15	52	92	11.1	3.40	105	.237	.300	6	.122	-2	9	3	0	0.1
1961	*NY-A	16	3	.842	31	27	9	2	0	188¹	162	19	42	86	9.8	3.15	118	.232	.277	15	.227	2	18	12	1	1.4

YEAR TM/L	W	L	PCT	G	GS	CG	SH	SV	IP	H	HR	BB	SO	RAT	ERA	ERA+	OAV	OOB	BH	AVG	PB	PR	/A	PD	TPI
1962 *NY-A☆	23	12	.657	43	39	14	3	2	298²	257	40	57	176	9.6	3.19	117	.231	.270	20	.189	1	26	18	-4	1.7
1963 *NY-A	17	15	.531	40	37	18	3	1	268	246	29	39	114	9.7	3.22	109	.242	.273	7	.080	-6	12	9	-1	0.2
1964 *NY-A	7	11	.389	27	14	2	1	4	115	130	20	31	77	12.7	4.54	80	.283	.329	7	.200	1	-12	-12	-0	-1.7
1965 Cle-A	11	6	.647	30	26	6	2	0	165²	154	22	23	84	9.7	3.69	94	.242	.269	4	.143	2	-4	-4	-4	-0.6
1966 KC-A	1	5	.167	15	10	0	0	0	64	65	7	15	33	11.4	3.80	89	.263	.308	3	.214	1	-3	-3	-1	-0.2
NY-N	0	1	.000	11	1	0	0	1	24²	27	1	11	14	13.9	4.74	77	.293	.369	1	.167	-0	-3	-3	-0	-0.2
1967 NY-N	0	0	—	2	0	0	0	0	3¹	1	0	1	5	2.7	0.00	—	.091	.091	0	—	0	1	1	0	0.0
Total 12	107	99	.519	338	257	75	20	11	1849¹	1748	216	446	1000	10.8	3.62	102	.249	.296	95	.160	-6	32	13	-11	-1.6

● SCOTT TERRY
Terry, Scott Ray b: 11/21/59, Hobbs, N.Mex. BR/TR, 5'11", 195 lbs. Deb: 4/9/86

YEAR TM/L	W	L	PCT	G	GS	CG	SH	SV	IP	H	HR	BB	SO	RAT	ERA	ERA+	OAV	OOB	BH	AVG	PB	PR	/A	PD	TPI
1986 Cin-N	1	2	.333	28	3	0	0	0	55²	66	8	32	32	15.8	6.14	63	.300	.389	1	.250	0	-15	-14	0	-0.7
1987 StL-N	0	0	—	11	0	0	0	0	13¹	13	0	8	9	14.2	3.38	123	.260	.362	0	.000	-0	1	1	0	0.0
1988 StL-N	9	6	.600	51	11	1	0	3	129¹	119	5	34	65	10.6	2.92	119	.247	.297	7	.250	2	8	8	0	1.2
1989 StL-N	8	10	.444	31	24	1	0	2	148²	142	14	43	69	11.4	3.57	102	.253	.310	7	.156	2	-1	1	2	0.5
1990 StL-N	2	6	.250	50	2	0	0	2	72	75	7	27	35	13.3	4.75	80	.264	.337	5	.455	2	-8	-7	0	-0.6
1991 StL-N	4	4	.500	65	0	0	0	1	80¹	76	1	32	52	12.1	2.80	133	.249	.320	1	.143	-0	8	8	1	0.9
Total 6	24	28	.462	236	40	2	0	8	499¹	491	35	176	262	12.1	3.73	98	.258	.323	21	.216	6	-7	-3	4	1.3

● ADONIS TERRY
Terry, William H b: 8/7/1864, Westfield, Mass. d: 2/24/15, Milwaukee, Wis. BR/TR, 5'11.5", 168 lbs. Deb: 5/1/1884 U◆

YEAR TM/L	W	L	PCT	G	GS	CG	SH	SV	IP	H	HR	BB	SO	RAT	ERA	ERA+	OAV	OOB	BH	AVG	PB	PR	/A	PD	TPI
1884 Bro-a	19	35	.352	56	55	54	2	0	476	486	10	72	230	10.7	3.55	93	.248	.277	55	.233	3	-16	-12	-3	-1.2
1885 Bro-a	6	17	.261	25	23	23	0	1	209	213	9	42	96	11.2	4.26	77	.262	.301	45	.170	-3	-24	-22	1	-2.1
1886 Bro-a	18	16	.529	34	34	32	5	0	288¹	263	1	115	162	12.3	3.09	113	.231	.310	71	.237	2	12	13	4	1.8
1887 Bro-a	16	16	.500	40	35	35	1	3	318	331	10	99	138	12.4	4.02	107	.262	.320	103	.293	7	10	10	5	1.6
1888 Bro-a	13	8	.619	23	23	20	2	0	195	145	2	67	138	10.2	2.03	147	**.199**	.275	29	.252	3	22	21	7	2.2
1889 *Bro-a	22	15	.595	41	39	35	2	0	326	285	6	126	186	11.8	3.29	113	.228	.306	48	.300	12	20	16	6	2.9
1890 *Bro-N	26	16	.619	46	44	38	1	0	370	362	3	133	185	12.4	2.94	117	.248	.318	101	.278	15	26	20	1	3.1
1891 Bro-N	6	16	.273	25	22	18	1	1	194	207	5	80	65	13.6	4.22	78	.263	.336	19	.209	3	-19	-20	-1	-1.5
1892 Bal-N	0	1	.000	1	1	1	0	0	9	7	0	7	3	14.0	4.00	86	.206	.342	0	.000	-1	-1	-1	0	-0.1
Pit-N	18	7	.720	30	26	24	2	1	240	185	4	106	95	11.2	2.51	131	.204	.293	16	.160	1	21	21	1	2.1
Yr	18	8	.692	31	27	25	2	1	249	192	4	113	98	11.3	2.57	129	.205	.295	16	.154	1	20	20	1	2.0
1893 Pit-N	12	8	.600	26	19	14	0	0	170	177	5	99	52	15.2	4.45	102	.260	.363	18	.254	2	4	2	0	0.4
1894 Pit-N	0	1	.000	1	1	0	0	0	0²	2	0	4	0	81.0	67.50	8	.510	.758	0	—	0	-5	-5	-2	-2.1
Chi-N	5	11	.313	23	21	16	0	0	163¹	232	12	123	39	20.4	5.84	96	.330	.441	33	.347	4	-9	-4	-1	-0.0
Yr	5	12	.294	24	22	16	0	0	164	234	12	127	39	20.7	6.09	92	.331	.444	33	.347	4	-14	-9	-1	-2.1
1895 Chi-N	21	14	.600	38	34	31	0	0	311¹	346	4	131	88	14.3	4.80	106	.277	.354	30	.219	-6	-1	10	2	0.5
1896 Chi-N	15	14	.517	30	28	25	1	0	235¹	268	6	88	74	14.0	4.28	106	.284	.351	26	.263	2	2	7	-2	0.7
1897 Chi-N	0	0	—	1	1	0	0	0	7	6	1	3	0	21.4	10.13	44	.324	.453	0	.000	-1	-5	-5	0	-0.4
Total 14	197	196	.501	440	406	367	17	6	3514	3520	76	1298	1552	12.7	3.73	103	.252	.322	594	.249	45	38	47	15	7.9

● DICK TERWILLIGER
Terwilliger, Richard Martin b: 6/27/06, Sand Lake, Mich. d: 1/21/69, Greenville, Mich. BR/TR, 5'11", 178 lbs. Deb: 8/18/32

YEAR TM/L	W	L	PCT	G	GS	CG	SH	SV	IP	H	HR	BB	SO	RAT	ERA	ERA+	OAV	OOB	BH	AVG	PB	PR	/A	PD	TPI
1932 StL-N	0	0	—	1	0	0	0	0	3	1	0	2	2	11.0	0.00	—	.143	.400	0	.000	-0	1	1	0	0.0

● JEFF TESREAU
Tesreau, Charles Monroe b: 3/5/1889, Silver Mine, Mo. d: 9/24/46, Hanover, N.H. BR/TR, 6'2", 218 lbs. Deb: 4/12/12

YEAR TM/L	W	L	PCT	G	GS	CG	SH	SV	IP	H	HR	BB	SO	RAT	ERA	ERA+	OAV	OOB	BH	AVG	PB	PR	/A	PD	TPI
1912 *NY-N	17	7	.708	36	28	19	3	1	243	177	2	106	119	10.9	**1.96**	172	**.204**	.298	12	.146	-2	39	38	1	3.3
1913 *NY-N	22	13	.629	41	38	17	1	0	282	222	7	119	167	11.1	2.17	144	**.220**	.306	21	.221	2	32	30	1	3.9
1914 NY-N	26	10	.722	42	40	26	8	1	322¹	238	8	128	189	10.4	2.37	112	**.209**	.293	28	.239	6	15	10	-2	1.5
1915 NY-N	19	16	.543	43	38	24	8	3	306	235	4	75	176	9.3	2.29	112	.215	.269	24	.233	6	16	9	1	1.8
1916 NY-N	14	14	.500	40	32	23	5	2	268¹	249	9	65	113	10.7	2.92	83	.250	.300	18	.191	2	-9	-14	-0	-1.4
1917 *NY-N	13	8	.619	33	20	11	1	2	183²	168	6	58	85	11.2	3.09	83	.249	.312	14	.230	2	-8	-11	2	-1.0
1918 NY-N	4	4	.500	12	9	3	1	0	73²	61	1	21	31	10.0	2.32	113	.227	.283	7	.318	2	4	3	1	0.6
Total 7	115	72	.615	247	205	123	27	9	1679	1350	37	572	880	10.5	2.43	114	.223	.295	124	.216	17	89	63	3	8.7

● BOB TEWKSBURY
Tewksbury, Robert Alan b: 11/30/60, Concord, N.H. BR/TR, 6'4", 200 lbs. Deb: 4/11/86

YEAR TM/L	W	L	PCT	G	GS	CG	SH	SV	IP	H	HR	BB	SO	RAT	ERA	ERA+	OAV	OOB	BH	AVG	PB	PR	/A	PD	TPI
1986 NY-A	9	5	.643	23	20	2	0	0	130¹	144	8	31	49	12.4	3.31	123	.282	.329	0	—	0	12	11	2	1.3
1987 NY-A	1	4	.200	8	6	0	0	0	33¹	47	5	7	12	14.9	6.75	65	.338	.374	0	—	0	-9	-9	0	-1.0
Chi-N	0	4	.000	7	3	0	0	0	18	32	1	13	10	22.5	6.50	66	.421	.506	0	.000	-1	-5	-4	-1	-0.9
1988 Chi-N	0	0	—	1	1	0	0	0	3¹	6	1	2	1	21.6	8.10	45	.400	.471	0	.000	-0	-2	-2	0	-0.0
1989 StL-N	1	0	1.000	7	4	1	1	0	30	25	2	10	17	11.1	3.30	110	.225	.301	1	.111	-0	1	1	0	0.0
1990 StL-N	10	9	.526	28	20	3	2	1	145¹	151	7	15	50	10.5	3.47	110	.267	.290	7	.171	1	5	6	-1	0.8
1991 StL-N	11	12	.478	30	30	3	0	0	191	206	13	38	75	11.7	3.25	114	.281	.321	9	.155	1	9	10	1	1.3
1992 StL-N★	16	5	**.762**	33	32	5	0	0	233	217	15	20	91	9.3	2.16	157	.248	.267	6	.086	-2	35	32	0	2.7
1993 StL-N	17	10	.630	32	32	2	0	0	213²	258	15	20	97	12.0	3.83	103	.301	.322	14	.203	2	5	3	3	0.9
1994 StL-N	12	10	.545	24	24	4	1	0	155²	190	19	22	79	12.4	5.32	76	.304	.337	10	.185	1	-19	-22	2	-2.3
Total 9	77	59	.566	193	172	20	4	1	1153²	1276	86	178	481	11.6	3.62	106	.283	.314	47	.153	2	33	26	6	2.8

● GRANT THATCHER
Thatcher, Ulysses Grant b: 2/23/1877, Maytown, Pa. d: 3/17/36, Lancaster, Pa. TR, 5'10.5", 180 lbs. Deb: 9/9/03

YEAR TM/L	W	L	PCT	G	GS	CG	SH	SV	IP	H	HR	BB	SO	RAT	ERA	ERA+	OAV	OOB	BH	AVG	PB	PR	/A	PD	TPI
1903 Bro-N	3	1	.750	4	4	4	0	0	28	33	1	7	9	12.9	2.89	110	.292	.333	2	.182	0	1	1	-0	0.1
1904 Bro-N	1	0	1.000	1	0	0	0	0	9	9	0	2	4	11.0	4.00	69	.281	.324	1	.250	0	-1	-1	-0	-0.1
Total 2	4	1	.800	5	4	4	0	0	37	42	1	9	13	12.4	3.16	98	.290	.331	3	.200	0	-0	-0	-0	0.0

● GREG THAYER
Thayer, Gregory Allen b: 10/23/49, Cedar Rapids, Iowa BR/TR, 5'11", 182 lbs. Deb: 4/7/78

YEAR TM/L	W	L	PCT	G	GS	CG	SH	SV	IP	H	HR	BB	SO	RAT	ERA	ERA+	OAV	OOB	BH	AVG	PB	PR	/A	PD	TPI
1978 Min-A	1	1	.500	20	0	0	0	0	45	40	5	30	30	14.6	3.80	100	.258	.388	0	—	0	-0	-0	-1	-0.0

● JACK THEIS
Theis, John Louis b: 7/23/1891, Georgetown, Ohio d: 7/6/41, Georgetown, Ohio BR/TR, 6', 190 lbs. Deb: 7/5/20

YEAR TM/L	W	L	PCT	G	GS	CG	SH	SV	IP	H	HR	BB	SO	RAT	ERA	ERA+	OAV	OOB	BH	AVG	PB	PR	/A	PD	TPI
1920 Cin-N	0	0	—	1	0	0	0	0	2	1	0	3	0	18.0	0.00	—	.143	.400	0	—	0	1	1	-0	0.0

● DUANE THEISS
Theiss, Duane Charles b: 11/20/53, Zanesville, Ohio BR/TR, 6'3", 185 lbs. Deb: 8/5/77

YEAR TM/L	W	L	PCT	G	GS	CG	SH	SV	IP	H	HR	BB	SO	RAT	ERA	ERA+	OAV	OOB	BH	AVG	PB	PR	/A	PD	TPI
1977 Atl-N	1	1	.500	17	0	0	0	0	20²	24	1	16	7	18.7	6.53	68	.338	.457	0	.000	-0	-6	-5	0	-0.4
1978 Atl-N	0	0	—	3	0	0	0	0	6¹	3	0	3	3	9.9	1.42	285	.158	.304	0	.000	0	2	2	0	0.0
Total 2	1	1	.500	20	0	0	0	0	27	29	1	19	10	16.7	5.33	82	.302	.427	0	.000	-0	-5	-3	0	-0.4

● JUG THESENGA
Thesenga, Arnold Joseph b: 4/27/14, Jefferson, S.Dak. BR/TR, 6', 200 lbs. Deb: 9/1/44

YEAR TM/L	W	L	PCT	G	GS	CG	SH	SV	IP	H	HR	BB	SO	RAT	ERA	ERA+	OAV	OOB	BH	AVG	PB	PR	/A	PD	TPI
1944 Was-A	0	0	—	5	1	0	0	0	12¹	18	0	12	2	21.9	5.11	64	.340	.462	0	.000	-0	-2	-3	0	0.0

● BERT THIEL
Thiel, Maynard Bert b: 5/4/26, Marion, Wis. BR/TR, 5'10", 185 lbs. Deb: 4/17/52

YEAR TM/L	W	L	PCT	G	GS	CG	SH	SV	IP	H	HR	BB	SO	RAT	ERA	ERA+	OAV	OOB	BH	AVG	PB	PR	/A	PD	TPI
1952 Bos-N	1	1	.500	4	0	0	0	0	7	11	1	4	6	21.9	7.71	47	.344	.447	0	—	0	-3	-3	-0	-0.8

● HENRY THIELMAN
Thielman, Henry Joseph b: 10/3/1880, St.Cloud, Minn. d: 9/2/42, New York, N.Y. BR/TR, 5'11", 175 lbs. Deb: 4/17/02 F◆

YEAR TM/L	W	L	PCT	G	GS	CG	SH	SV	IP	H	HR	BB	SO	RAT	ERA	ERA+	OAV	OOB	BH	AVG	PB	PR	/A	PD	TPI
1902 NY-N	0	1	.000	2	2	0	0	0	6	8	0	6	5	21.0	1.50	187	.319	.451	1	.111	-0	1	1	0	0.2
Cin-N	9	15	.375	25	23	22	0	1	211	201	2	78	49	12.7	3.24	92	.251	.332	12	.132	-4	-11	-6	-1	-1.1
Yr	9	16	.360	27	25	22	0	1	217	209	2	84	54	12.9	3.19	94	.253	.336	13	.130	-4	-10	-5	-1	-0.9
1903 Bro-N	0	3	.000	4	3	3	0	0	29	31	3	10	10	14.6	4.66	69	.330	.427	5	.217	1	-4	-5	1	-0.2
Total 2	9	19	.321	31	28	25	0	1	246	240	5	94	64	13.1	3.37	90	.261	.346	18	.146	-3	-14	-9	-0	-1.1

● JAKE THIELMAN
Thielman, John Peter b: 5/20/1879, St.Cloud, Minn. d: 1/28/28, Minneapolis, Minn. BR/TR, 5'11", 175 lbs. Deb: 4/23/05 F

YEAR TM/L	W	L	PCT	G	GS	CG	SH	SV	IP	H	HR	BB	SO	RAT	ERA	ERA+	OAV	OOB	BH	AVG	PB	PR	/A	PD	TPI
1905 StL-N	15	16	.484	32	29	26	0	0	242	265	4	62	87	12.6	3.50	85	.281	.333	21	.231	8	-13	-14	3	-0.5

YEAR TM/L	W	L	PCT	G	GS	CG	SH	SV	IP	H	HR	BB	SO	RAT	ERA	ERA+	OAV	OOB	BH	AVG	PB	PR	/A	PD	TPI
1906 StL-N	0	1	.000	1	1	0	0	0	5	5	0	2	0	12.6	3.60	73	.263	.333	1	.500	0	-1	-1	-0	-0.1
1907 Cle-A	11	8	.579	20	18	18	3	0	166	151	2	34	56	10.4	2.33	108	.244	.291	12	.203	1	4	3	-3	0.2
1908 Cle-A	4	3	.571	11	8	5	0	0	61^2	59	2	9	15	10.5	3.65	66	.260	.300	8	.348	4	-9	-9	2	-0.4
Bos-A	0	0	—	1	0	0	0	0	0^2	3	1	0	0	40.5	40.50	6	.600	.600	0	—	0	-3	-3	-0	0.0
Yr	4	3	.571	12	8	5	0	0	62^1	62	3	9	15	10.3	4.04	59	.263	.290	8	.348	4	-11	-11	1	-0.4
Total 4	30	28	.517	65	56	49	3	0	475^1	483	9	107	158	11.6	3.16	86	.266	.315	42	.240	13	-21	-23	2	-0.8

● DAVE THIES
Thies, David Robert b: 3/21/37, Minneapolis, Minn. BR/TR, 6'4", 205 lbs. Deb: 4/20/63

YEAR TM/L	W	L	PCT	G	GS	CG	SH	SV	IP	H	HR	BB	SO	RAT	ERA	ERA+	OAV	OOB	BH	AVG	PB	PR	/A	PD	TPI
1963 KC-A	0	1	.000	9	2	0	0	0	25^1	26	2	12	9	14.2	4.62	84	.274	.367	2	.333	1	-3	-2	0	0.0

● JAKE THIES
Thies, Vernon Arthur b: 4/1/26, St.Louis, Mo. BR/TR, 5'11", 170 lbs. Deb: 4/24/54

YEAR TM/L	W	L	PCT	G	GS	CG	SH	SV	IP	H	HR	BB	SO	RAT	ERA	ERA+	OAV	OOB	BH	AVG	PB	PR	/A	PD	TPI
1954 Pit-N	3	9	.250	33	18	3	1	0	130^1	120	13	49	57	11.9	3.87	108	.244	.317	1	.030	-2	3	5	0	0.2
1955 Pit-N	0	1	.000	1	1	0	0	0	3^2	5	0	3	0	22.1	4.91	84	.357	.500	-	0	-0	-0	-0	-0	-0.1
Total 2	3	10	.231	34	19	3	1	0	134	125	13	52	57	12.2	3.90	107	.248	.323	1	.030	-2	3	4	0	0.1

● BOBBY THIGPEN
Thigpen, Robert Thomas b: 7/17/63, Tallahassee, Fla. BR/TR, 6'3", 195 lbs. Deb: 8/6/86

YEAR TM/L	W	L	PCT	G	GS	CG	SH	SV	IP	H	HR	BB	SO	RAT	ERA	ERA+	OAV	OOB	BH	AVG	PB	PR	/A	PD	TPI
1986 Chi-A	2	0	1.000	20	0	0	0	7	35^2	26	1	12	20	9.8	1.77	244	.205	.279	0	—	0	10	10	-0	0.8
1987 Chi-A	7	5	.583	51	0	0	0	16	89	86	10	24	52	11.4	2.73	168	.256	.311	0	—	0	17	18	0	2.9
1988 Chi-A	5	8	.385	68	0	0	0	34	90	96	6	33	62	13.3	3.30	120	.273	.342	0	—	0	7	7	0	1.5
1989 Chi-A	2	6	.250	61	0	0	0	34	79	62	10	40	47	11.7	3.76	101	.218	.316	0	—	0	1	0	-1	0.1
1990 Chi-A★	4	6	.400	77	0	0	0	57	88^2	60	5	32	70	9.4	1.83	209	.195	.274	0	—	0	20	20	0	5.3
1991 Chi-A	7	5	.583	67	0	0	0	30	69^2	63	10	38	47	13.6	3.49	114	.245	.351	0	—	0	5	4	1	1.2
1992 Chi-A	1	3	.250	55	0	0	0	22	55	58	4	33	45	15.4	4.75	81	.275	.381	0	—	0	-5	-5	1	-0.7
1993 Chi-A	0	0	—	25	0	0	0	1	34^2	51	5	12	19	17.7	5.71	73	.349	.417	0	—	0	-5	-6	-1	-0.9
*Phi-N	3	1	.750	17	0	0	0	0	19^1	23	2	9	10	15.4	6.05	66	.307	.388	0	.000	-0	-4	-4	0	-0.8
1994 Sea-A	0	2	.000	7	0	0	0	0	7^2	12	3	5	4	20.0	9.39	52	.353	.436	0	—	0	-4	-4	0	-0.9
Total 9	31	36	.463	448	0	0	0	201	568^2	537	56	238	376	12.6	3.43	118	.252	.334	0	.000	-0	41	39	1	9.5

● DICK THOENEN
Thoenen, Richard Crispin b: 1/9/44, Mexico, Mo. BR/TR, 6'6", 215 lbs. Deb: 9/16/67

YEAR TM/L	W	L	PCT	G	GS	CG	SH	SV	IP	H	HR	BB	SO	RAT	ERA	ERA+	OAV	OOB	BH	AVG	PB	PR	/A	PD	TPI
1967 Phi-N	0	0	—	1	0	0	0	0	1	2	0	0	0	18.0	9.00	38	.500	.500	0	—	0	-1	-1	0	0.0

● TOMMY THOMAS
Thomas, Alphonse b: 12/23/1899, Baltimore, Md. d: 4/27/88, Dallastown, Pa. BR/TR, 5'10", 175 lbs. Deb: 4/17/26

YEAR TM/L	W	L	PCT	G	GS	CG	SH	SV	IP	H	HR	BB	SO	RAT	ERA	ERA+	OAV	OOB	BH	AVG	PB	PR	/A	PD	TPI
1926 Chi-A	15	12	.556	44	32	13	2	2	249	225	7	110	127	12.1	3.80	102	.244	.325	16	.186	-1	6	2	-3	-0.2
1927 Chi-A	19	16	.543	40	36	24	3	1	307^2	271	16	94	107	10.7	2.98	136	.244	.303	14	.147	-3	40	36	-4	2.9
1928 Chi-A	17	16	.515	36	32	24	3	2	283	277	16	76	129	11.4	3.08	131	.259	.310	21	.219	3	30	30	-3	3.3
1929 Chi-A	14	18	.438	36	31	24	2	1	259^2	270	17	60	62	11.4	3.19	134	.269	.310	25	.255	2	30	32	-3	3.4
1930 Chi-A	5	13	.278	34	27	7	0	0	169	229	13	44	58	14.6	5.22	89	.323	.364	7	.125	-4	-11	-11	0	-1.3
1931 Chi-A	10	14	.417	43	36	11	2	2	245^1	298	17	69	72	13.6	4.73	90	.292	.340	21	.241	1	-10	-13	-1	-1.0
1932 Chi-A	3	3	.500	12	3	1	0	0	43^2	55	6	15	11	14.6	6.18	70	.307	.364	1	.077	-1	-8	-9	-0	-1.1
Was-A	8	7	.533	18	14	7	1	0	117	114	5	46	36	12.3	3.54	122	.255	.325	10	.238	1	12	10	-2	1.0
Yr	11	10	.524	30	17	8	1	0	160^2	169	11	61	47	12.9	4.26	101	.270	.334	11	.200	0	4	1	-2	-0.1
1933 *Was-A	7	7	.500	35	14	2	0	3	135	149	9	49	35	13.3	4.80	87	.273	.336	10	.238	1	-8	-9	-2	-0.9
1934 Was-A	8	9	.471	33	18	7	1	1	133^1	154	9	58	42	14.5	5.47	79	.294	.368	7	.184	-0	-14	-17	-2	-2.0
1935 Was-A	0	0	—	1	0	0	0	0	0^1	3	0	0	0	81.0	54.00	8	.750	.750	0	—	0	-2	-2	0	0.0
Phi-N	0	1	.000	4	1	0	0	0	12	15	2	5	3	15.0	5.25	86	.313	.377	0	.000	-0	-2	-1	-0	-0.1
1936 StL-N	11	9	.550	36	21	8	1	0	179^2	219	25	72	40	14.8	5.26	102	.297	.362	8	.138	-3	-4	2	-2	-0.3
1937 StL-N	0	1	.000	17	2	0	0	0	30^2	46	2	10	10	16.7	7.04	69	.348	.399	0	.000	-1	-8	-8	0	-0.3
Bos-A	0	2	.000	9	0	0	0	0	11	16	2	4	4	17.2	4.09	116	.340	.404	1	.250	-0	1	1	0	0.1
Yr	0	3	.000	26	2	0	0	0	41^2	62	4	14	14	16.6	6.26	77	.344	.395	1	.125	-1	-7	-7	0	-0.2
Total 12	117	128	.478	398	267	128	15	12	2176^1	2341	144	712	736	12.7	4.11	104	.275	.333	141	.195	-5	52	43	-22	3.5

● BLAINE THOMAS
Thomas, Blaine M. "Baldy" b: 8/1888, Glendora, Cal. d: 8/21/15, Glendora, Cal. BR/TR, 5'10", 165 lbs. Deb: 8/25/11

YEAR TM/L	W	L	PCT	G	GS	CG	SH	SV	IP	H	HR	BB	SO	RAT	ERA	ERA+	OAV	OOB	BH	AVG	PB	PR	/A	PD	TPI
1911 Bos-A	0	0	—	2	2	0	0	0	4^2	3	0	7	0	21.2	0.00	—	.273	.579	1	.500	0	2	2	0	0.0

● CARL THOMAS
Thomas, Carl Leslie b: 5/28/32, Minneapolis, Minn. BR/TR, 6'5", 245 lbs. Deb: 4/19/60

YEAR TM/L	W	L	PCT	G	GS	CG	SH	SV	IP	H	HR	BB	SO	RAT	ERA	ERA+	OAV	OOB	BH	AVG	PB	PR	/A	PD	TPI
1960 Cle-A	1	0	1.000	4	0	0	0	0	9^2	8	1	10	5	17.7	7.45	50	.229	.413	1	.333	1	-4	-4	0	-0.3

● LEFTY THOMAS
Thomas, Clarence Fletcher b: 10/4/03, Glade Spring, Va. d: 3/21/52, Charlottesville, Va. BL/TL, 6', 183 lbs. Deb: 9/26/25

YEAR TM/L	W	L	PCT	G	GS	CG	SH	SV	IP	H	HR	BB	SO	RAT	ERA	ERA+	OAV	OOB	BH	AVG	PB	PR	/A	PD	TPI
1925 Was-A	0	2	.000	2	2	1	0	0	13	14	0	7	10	14.5	2.08	204	.264	.350	0	.000	-1	3	3	0	0.3
1926 Was-A	0	0	—	6	0	0	0	0	8^2	8	0	10	3	18.7	5.19	74	.267	.450	0	.000	0	-1	-1	-1	0.0
Total 2	0	2	.000	8	2	1	0	0	21^2	22	0	17	13	16.2	3.32	123	.265	.390	0	.000	-1	2	2	-1	0.3

● CLAUDE THOMAS
Thomas, Claude Alfred "Lefty" b: 5/15/1890, Stanberry, Mo. d: 3/6/46, Sulphur, Okla. BL/TL, 6'1", 180 lbs. Deb: 9/14/16

YEAR TM/L	W	L	PCT	G	GS	CG	SH	SV	IP	H	HR	BB	SO	RAT	ERA	ERA+	OAV	OOB	BH	AVG	PB	PR	/A	PD	TPI
1916 Was-A	1	2	.333	7	4	1	1	0	28^1	27	1	12	7	13.0	4.13	68	.265	.353	1	.100	-1	-4	-4	-0	-0.5

● FAY THOMAS
Thomas, Fay Wesley "Scow" b: 10/10/04, Holyrood, Kan. d: 8/16/90, Chatsworth, Cal. BR/TR, 6'2", 195 lbs. Deb: 6/27/27

YEAR TM/L	W	L	PCT	G	GS	CG	SH	SV	IP	H	HR	BB	SO	RAT	ERA	ERA+	OAV	OOB	BH	AVG	PB	PR	/A	PD	TPI
1927 NY-N	0	0	—	9	0	0	0	0	16^1	19	3	4	11	13.2	3.31	117	.302	.353	0	.000	-0	1	1	-0	-0.1
1931 Cle-A	2	4	.333	16	2	1	0	0	48^2	63	2	32	25	17.8	5.18	89	.323	.421	2	.154	-1	-4	-3	-1	-0.4
1932 Bro-N	0	1	.000	7	2	0	0	0	17	22	0	8	9	15.9	7.41	51	.306	.375	0	.000	-0	-7	-7	0	-0.4
1935 StL-A	7	15	.318	49	19	4	0	1	147	165	11	89	67	15.7	4.78	100	.289	.388	4	.105	-3	-5	-2	1	0.0
Total 4	9	20	.310	81	23	5	0	1	229	269	16	133	112	16.0	4.95	93	.299	.392	6	.107	-4	-15	-9	1	-0.9

● FROSTY THOMAS
Thomas, Forrest b: 5/23/1881, Faucett, Mo. d: 3/18/70, St.Joseph, Mo. BR/TR, 6', 185 lbs. Deb: 5/1/05

YEAR TM/L	W	L	PCT	G	GS	CG	SH	SV	IP	H	HR	BB	SO	RAT	ERA	ERA+	OAV	OOB	BH	AVG	PB	PR	/A	PD	TPI
1905 Det-A	0	1	.000	2	1	0	0	0	6	10	0	3	5	21.0	7.50	37	.371	.452	0	.000	-0	-3	-3	0	-0.4

● BUD THOMAS
Thomas, Luther Baxter b: 9/9/10, Faber, Va. BR/TR, 6', 180 lbs. Deb: 9/13/32

YEAR TM/L	W	L	PCT	G	GS	CG	SH	SV	IP	H	HR	BB	SO	RAT	ERA	ERA+	OAV	OOB	BH	AVG	PB	PR	/A	PD	TPI
1932 Was-A	0	0	—	2	0	0	0	0	3	1	0	2	1	9.0	—		.100	.250	0	—	0	1	1	0	0.0
1933 Was-A	0	0	—	2	0	0	0	0	4	11	1	2	1	31.5	15.75	27	.550	.609	0	.000	-0	-5	-5	0	0.0
1937 Phi-A	8	15	.348	35	26	6	1	0	169^2	208	15	52	54	13.8	4.99	95	.295	.344	6	.128	-1	-7	-5	-3	-0.9
1938 Phi-A	9	14	.391	42	29	7	1	0	212^1	259	23	62	48	13.7	4.92	98	.295	.347	9	.130	-3	-3	-2	-1	-0.5
1939 Phi-A	0	1	.000	6	2	0	0	0	4	8	2	1	0	20.3	15.75	30	.421	.450	0	.000	-0	-5	-5	-0	-0.9
Was-A	0	0	—	4	0	0	0	0	9	11	0	2	0	13.0	6.00	72	.306	.342	0	.000	-0	-1	-2	0	0.0
Det-A	7	0	1.000	27	0	0	0	0	47^1	45	7	20	14	12.4	4.18	117	.254	.330	1	.111	-0	2	4	0	0.4
Yr	7	1	.875	33	2	0	0	0	60^1	64	9	23	14	12.5	5.22	92	.276	.341	1	.071	-0	-3	-3	-0	-0.1
1940 Det-A	0	1	.000	3	0	0	0	0	4	8	1	3	0	24.8	9.00	53	.421	.500	0	—	0	-2	-2	1	-0.3
1941 Det-A	1	3	.250	26	1	0	0	2	72^2	74	4	22	17	11.9	4.21	108	.260	.313	2	.105	-1	-1	3	2	0.2
Total 7	25	34	.424	143	58	13	2	3	526	625	53	166	135	13.6	4.96	93	.292	.345	18	.120	-7	-20	-13	-1	-2.0

● MYLES THOMAS
Thomas, Myles Lewis b: 10/22/1897, State College, Pa. d: 12/12/63, Toledo, Ohio BR/TR, 5'9.5", 170 lbs. Deb: 4/18/26

YEAR TM/L	W	L	PCT	G	GS	CG	SH	SV	IP	H	HR	BB	SO	RAT	ERA	ERA+	OAV	OOB	BH	AVG	PB	PR	/A	PD	TPI
1926 *NY-A	6	6	.500	33	13	3	0	0	140^1	140	6	65	38	13.3	4.23	91	.271	.356	5	.116	-3	-6	-1	-0	-0.7
1927 NY-A	7	4	.636	21	9	1	0	0	88^2	111	4	43	25	15.7	4.87	79	.322	.398	9	.333	2	-7	-10	-0	-0.9
1928 NY-A	1	0	1.000	12	1	0	0	0	31^2	33	3	9	10	11.9	3.41	110	.277	.328	4	.400	1	2	1	-0	0.1
1929 NY-A	0	2	.000	5	1	0	0	0	15	27	1	4	5	21.6	10.80	36	.409	.480	1	.143	-1	-11	-12	1	-1.2
Was-A	7	8	.467	22	14	7	0	2	125^1	139	3	48	33	13.4	3.52	121	.288	.352	14	.292	2	10	10	1	1.3
Yr	7	10	.412	27	15	7	0	2	140^1	166	4	57	36	14.3	4.30	98	.302	.368	15	.273	1	-1	-2	1	0.1

YEAR TM/L	W	L	PCT	G	GS	CG	SH	SV	IP	H	HR	BB	SO	RAT	ERA	ERA+	OAV	OOB	BH	AVG	PB	PR	/A	PD	TPI
1930 Was-A	2	2	.500	12	2	0	0	0	33²	49	3	15	12	17.1	8.29	55	.358	.421	2	.182	-1	-14	-14	-1	-1.4
Total 5	23	22	.511	105	40	11	0	2	434²	499	20	189	121	14.3	4.64	87	.299	.372	35	.240	0	-23	-30	1	-2.8

● ROY THOMAS
Thomas, Roy Allen b: 3/24/1874, Norristown, Pa. d: 11/20/59, Norristown, Pa. BL/TL, 5'11", 150 lbs. Deb: 4/14/1899 FC♦

YEAR TM/L	W	L	PCT	G	GS	CG	SH	SV	IP	H	HR	BB	SO	RAT	ERA	ERA+	OAV	OOB	BH	AVG	PB	PR	/A	PD	TPI
1900 Phi-N	0	0	—	1	0	0	0	0	2²	4	0	0	0	13.5	3.38	107	.345	.345	168	.316	—	0	0	-0	0.0

● ROY THOMAS
Thomas, Roy Justin b: 6/22/53, Quantico, Va. BR/TR, 6'6", 200 lbs. Deb: 9/21/77

YEAR TM/L	W	L	PCT	G	GS	CG	SH	SV	IP	H	HR	BB	SO	RAT	ERA	ERA+	OAV	OOB	BH	AVG	PB	PR	/A	PD	TPI
1977 Hou-N	0	0	—	4	0	0	0	0	6¹	5	0	3	4	11.4	2.84	125	.208	.296	0	—	0	1	1	0	0.0
1978 StL-N	1	1	.500	16	1	0	0	3	28¹	21	0	16	16	11.8	3.81	92	.216	.327	1	.250	0	-1	-1	1	0.0
1979 StL-N	3	4	.429	26	6	0	0	1	77	66	9	24	44	10.5	2.92	129	.237	.298	1	.059	-1	7	7	1	0.6
1980 StL-N	2	3	.400	24	5	0	0	1	55	59	3	25	22	14.2	4.75	78	.274	.358	2	.154	-0	-7	-6	1	-0.5
1983 Sea-A	3	1	.750	43	0	0	0	1	88²	95	3	32	77	13.1	3.45	123	.275	.340	0	—	0	6	8	-0	0.1
1984 Sea-A	3	2	.600	21	1	0	0	1	49²	52	8	37	42	16.9	5.26	76	.280	.410	0	—	0	-7	-7	0	-0.6
1985 Sea-A	7	0	1.000	40	0	0	0	1	93²	66	8	48	70	11.1	3.36	125	.202	.309	0	—	0	8	9	-1	0.5
1987 Sea-A	1	0	1.000	8	0	0	0	0	20²	23	2	11	14	15.2	5.23	90	.299	.393	0	—	0	-2	-1	-1	-0.2
Total 8	20	11	.645	182	13	0	0	7	419¹	387	33	196	289	12.8	3.82	105	.250	.339	4	.118	-1	5	9	1	-0.1

● STAN THOMAS
Thomas, Stanley Brown b: 7/11/49, Rumford, Me. BR/TR, 6'2", 185 lbs. Deb: 7/5/74

YEAR TM/L	W	L	PCT	G	GS	CG	SH	SV	IP	H	HR	BB	SO	RAT	ERA	ERA+	OAV	OOB	BH	AVG	PB	PR	/A	PD	TPI
1974 Tex-A	0	0	—	12	0	0	0	0	13²	22	1	6	8	18.4	6.59	54	.379	.438	0	—	0	-5	-5	0	0.0
1975 Tex-A	4	4	.500	46	1	0	0	3	81¹	72	2	34	46	12.1	3.10	121	.239	.322	0	—	0	6	6	0	0.7
1976 Cle-A	4	4	.500	37	7	2	0	6	105²	88	5	41	54	11.3	2.30	152	.229	.310	0	—	0	14	14	3	1.6
1977 Sea-A	2	6	.250	13	9	1	0	0	58¹	74	8	25	14	15.7	6.02	68	.310	.382	0	—	0	-13	-12	-0	-1.4
NY-A	1	0	1.000	3	0	0	0	0	6¹	7	0	4	1	15.6	7.11	55	.280	.379	0	—	0	-2	-2	-0	-0.3
Yr	3	6	.333	16	9	1	0	0	64²	81	8	29	15	15.3	6.12	67	.300	.368	0	—	0	-15	-15	-1	-1.7
Total 4	11	14	.440	111	17	3	0	9	265¹	263	16	110	123	13.0	3.70	101	.261	.340	0	—	0	1	1	3	0.6

● TOM THOMAS
Thomas, Thomas R. "Savage Tom" b: 12/27/1873, Shawnee, Ohio d: 9/23/42, Shawnee, Ohio BR/TR, 6'4", 195 lbs. Deb: 9/20/1894

YEAR TM/L	W	L	PCT	G	GS	CG	SH	SV	IP	H	HR	BB	SO	RAT	ERA	ERA+	OAV	OOB	BH	AVG	PB	PR	/A	PD	TPI
1894 Cle-N	0	0	—	1	0	0	0	0	0¹	2	0	0	2	54.0	27.00	20	.000	.676	0	—	0	-1	-1	0	0.0
1899 StL-N	1	1	.500	4	2	2	0	0	25	22	1	4	8	9.4	2.52	158	.236	.268	3	.250	0	4	4	0	0.3
1900 StL-N	2	2	.500	5	1	1	0	0	26¹	38	2	4	7	14.7	3.76	97	.336	.364	1	.091	-1	-0	-0	-1	-0.2
Total 3	3	3	.500	10	3	3	0	0	51²	60	3	10	15	12.4	3.31	115	.290	.326	4	.174	-1	3	3	-1	0.1

● ERSKINE THOMASON
Thomason, Melvin Erskine b: 8/13/48, Laurens, S.C. BR/TR, 6'1", 190 lbs. Deb: 9/18/74

YEAR TM/L	W	L	PCT	G	GS	CG	SH	SV	IP	H	HR	BB	SO	RAT	ERA	ERA+	OAV	OOB	BH	AVG	PB	PR	/A	PD	TPI
1974 Phi-N	0	0	—	1	0	0	0	0	1	0	0	1	0	0.0	0.00	—	.000	.000	0	—	0	0	0	0	0.0

● ART THOMPSON
Thompson, Arthur J. Deb: 6/17/1884

YEAR TM/L	W	L	PCT	G	GS	CG	SH	SV	IP	H	HR	BB	SO	RAT	ERA	ERA+	OAV	OOB	BH	AVG	PB	PR	/A	PD	TPI
1884 Was-U	0	1	.000	1	1	1	0	0	8	10	0	3	8	14.6	6.75	36	.287	.343	0	.000	-1	-4	-4	0	-0.4

● FORREST THOMPSON
Thompson, David Forrest b: 3/3/18, Mooresville, N.C. d: 2/26/79, Charlotte, N.C. BL/TL, 5'11", 195 lbs. Deb: 4/26/48

YEAR TM/L	W	L	PCT	G	GS	CG	SH	SV	IP	H	HR	BB	SO	RAT	ERA	ERA+	OAV	OOB	BH	AVG	PB	PR	/A	PD	TPI
1948 Was-A	6	10	.375	46	7	0	4	4	131¹	134	9	54	40	13.0	3.84	113	.262	.334	10	.286	2	7	7	-0	1.1
1949 Was-A	1	3	.250	9	1	0	0	0	16¹	22	1	9	8	17.6	4.41	97	.328	.416	3	.600	2	-0	-0	0	0.1
Total 2	7	13	.350	55	8	1	0	4	147²	156	10	63	48	13.5	3.90	111	.270	.344	13	.325	4	6	7	-0	1.2

● JUNIOR THOMPSON
Thompson, Eugene Earl b: 6/7/17, Latham, Ill. BR/TR, 6'1", 185 lbs. Deb: 4/26/39

YEAR TM/L	W	L	PCT	G	GS	CG	SH	SV	IP	H	HR	BB	SO	RAT	ERA	ERA+	OAV	OOB	BH	AVG	PB	PR	/A	PD	TPI
1939 *Cin-N	13	5	.722	42	11	5	3	2	152¹	130	6	55	87	11.1	2.54	151	.236	.309	11	.229	0	23	22	-1	2.3
1940 *Cin-N	16	9	.640	33	31	17	3	0	225¹	197	10	96	103	11.8	3.32	114	.233	.313	18	.228	3	13	12	-1	1.4
1941 Cin-N	6	6	.500	27	15	4	0	1	109	117	6	57	46	14.6	4.87	74	.272	.361	7	.233	1	-15	-15	2	-1.3
1942 Cin-N	4	7	.364	29	10	1	0	0	101²	86	5	53	35	12.5	3.36	98	.226	.324	8	.267	2	-1	-1	4	0.5
1946 NY-N	4	6	.400	39	1	0	0	4	62²	36	5	40	31	10.9	1.29	266	.190	.332	1	.143	0	15	15	2	2.8
1947 NY-N	4	2	.667	15	0	0	0	0	35²	36	3	27	13	16.1	4.29	95	.279	.408	0	.000	-1	-1	-1	-1	-0.1
Total 6	47	35	.573	185	68	27	6	7	686²	602	35	328	315	12.3	3.26	113	.239	.329	45	.225	6	35	32	6	5.6

● FULLER THOMPSON
Thompson, Fuller Weidner b: 5/1/1889, Los Angeles, Cal. d: 2/19/72, Los Angeles, Cal. BR/TR, 5'11.5", 164 lbs. Deb: 8/19/11

YEAR TM/L	W	L	PCT	G	GS	CG	SH	SV	IP	H	HR	BB	SO	RAT	ERA	ERA+	OAV	OOB	BH	AVG	PB	PR	/A	PD	TPI
1911 Bos-N	0	0	—	3	0	0	0	0	4²	5	0	2	0	13.5	3.86	99	.294	.368	0	—	0	-0	-0	0	0.0

● HARRY THOMPSON
Thompson, Harold b: 9/9/1889, Nanticoke, Pa. d: 2/14/51, Reno, Nev. BL/TL, 5'8", 150 lbs. Deb: 4/24/19

YEAR TM/L	W	L	PCT	G	GS	CG	SH	SV	IP	H	HR	BB	SO	RAT	ERA	ERA+	OAV	OOB	BH	AVG	PB	PR	/A	PD	TPI
1919 Was-A	0	3	.000	12	2	0	0	1	43¹	48	0	8	10	12.0	3.53	91	.293	.333	8	.250	1	-1	-2	0	0.0
Phi-A	0	1	.000	3	0	0	0	0	12	16	4	3	1	14.3	6.75	51	.327	.365	0	.000	-1	-5	-4	0	-0.4
Yr	0	4	.000	15	2	0	0	1	55¹	64	4	11	11	12.2	4.23	77	.298	.332	8	.211	0	-6	-6	1	-0.4

● LEE THOMPSON
Thompson, John Dudley "Lefty" b: 2/26/1898, Smithfield, Utah d: 2/17/63, Santa Barbara, Cal BL/TL, 6'1", 185 lbs. Deb: 9/4/21

YEAR TM/L	W	L	PCT	G	GS	CG	SH	SV	IP	H	HR	BB	SO	RAT	ERA	ERA+	OAV	OOB	BH	AVG	PB	PR	/A	PD	TPI
1921 Chi-A	0	3	.000	4	4	0	0	0	20²	32	0	6	4	16.5	8.27	51	.333	.373	2	.286	0	-9	-9	-1	-1.0

● GUS THOMPSON
Thompson, John Gustav b: 6/22/1877, Humboldt, Iowa d: 3/28/58, Kalispell, Mont. 6'2", 185 lbs. Deb: 8/31/03

YEAR TM/L	W	L	PCT	G	GS	CG	SH	SV	IP	H	HR	BB	SO	RAT	ERA	ERA+	OAV	OOB	BH	AVG	PB	PR	/A	PD	TPI
1903 *Pit-N	2	2	.500	5	4	3	0	0	43	52	1	16	22	14.4	3.56	91	.295	.358	4	.250	0	-1	-2	-1	-0.2
1906 StL-N	2	11	.154	17	12	8	0	0	103	111	2	25	36	12.3	4.28	61	.285	.336	6	.176	-1	-19	-19	1	-2.2
Total 2	4	13	.235	22	16	11	0	0	146	163	3	41	58	12.9	4.07	69	.288	.343	10	.200	0	-20	-20	0	-2.4

● JOCKO THOMPSON
Thompson, John Samuel b: 1/17/17, Beverly, Mass. d: 2/3/88, Olney, Md. BL/TL, 6', 185 lbs. Deb: 9/21/48

YEAR TM/L	W	L	PCT	G	GS	CG	SH	SV	IP	H	HR	BB	SO	RAT	ERA	ERA+	OAV	OOB	BH	AVG	PB	PR	/A	PD	TPI
1948 Phi-N	1	0	1.000	2	2	1	0	0	13	10	0	9	7	13.2	2.77	142	.233	.365	0	.000	-0	2	2	-0	0.1
1949 Phi-N	1	3	.250	8	5	1	0	0	31¹	38	6	11	12	14.1	6.89	57	.314	.371	2	.182	-0	-10	-10	-1	-1.1
1950 Phi-N	0	0	—	2	0	0	0	0	4	1	0	4	2	11.3	0.00	—	.077	.294	0	—	0	2	2	0	0.0
1951 Phi-N	4	8	.333	29	14	3	2	1	119¹	102	12	59	60	12.3	3.85	100	.231	.325	4	.103	-1	2	0	-1	-0.2
Total 4	6	11	.353	41	21	5	2	1	167²	151	18	83	81	12.7	4.24	91	.244	.336	6	.113	-1	-5	-7	-1	-1.2

● MARK THOMPSON
Thompson, Mark Radford b: 4/7/71, Russellville, Ky. BR/TR, 6'2", 205 lbs. Deb: 7/26/94

YEAR TM/L	W	L	PCT	G	GS	CG	SH	SV	IP	H	HR	BB	SO	RAT	ERA	ERA+	OAV	OOB	BH	AVG	PB	PR	/A	PD	TPI
1994 Col-N	1	1	.500	2	2	0	0	0	9	16	2	8	5	25.0	9.00	55	.400	.510	0	.000	-0	-5	-4	-0	-0.7

● MIKE THOMPSON
Thompson, Michael Wayne b: 9/6/49, Denver, Colo. BR/TR, 6'3", 190 lbs. Deb: 5/19/71

YEAR TM/L	W	L	PCT	G	GS	CG	SH	SV	IP	H	HR	BB	SO	RAT	ERA	ERA+	OAV	OOB	BH	AVG	PB	PR	/A	PD	TPI
1971 Was-A	1	6	.143	16	12	0	0	0	66²	53	3	54	41	14.9	4.86	68	.222	.372	2	.118	0	-10	-12	-1	-1.1
1973 StL-N	0	0	—	2	2	0	0	0	4	1	0	5	3	13.5	0.00	—	.077	.333	0	.000	-0	2	2	-0	0.0
1974 StL-N	0	3	.000	19	4	0	0	0	38¹	37	1	35	25	17.4	5.63	63	.274	.430	0	.000	-1	-9	-9	0	-0.7
Atl-N	0	0	—	1	1	0	0	0	4	7	0	2	2	20.3	4.50	84	.412	.474	1	1.000	-0	-0	-0	0	0.1
Yr	0	3	.000	20	5	0	0	0	42¹	44	1	37	27	17.2	5.53	65	.286	.424	1	.111	-1	-9	-9	0	-0.6
1975 Atl-N	0	6	.000	16	10	0	0	0	51²	60	2	32	42	16.0	4.70	80	.305	.402	1	.071	-1	-6	-5	1	-0.6
Total 4	1	15	.063	54	29	0	0	0	164²	158	6	128	113	15.9	4.86	73	.263	.396	4	.098	-1	-24	-24	1	-2.3

● RICH THOMPSON
Thompson, Richard Neil b: 11/1/58, New York, N.Y. BR/TR, 6'3", 225 lbs. Deb: 4/28/85

YEAR TM/L	W	L	PCT	G	GS	CG	SH	SV	IP	H	HR	BB	SO	RAT	ERA	ERA+	OAV	OOB	BH	AVG	PB	PR	/A	PD	TPI
1985 Cle-A	3	8	.273	57	0	0	0	3	80	95	8	48	30	16.8	6.30	66	.303	.405	0	—	0	-19	-19	-2	-2.6
1989 Mon-N	0	2	.000	19	1	0	0	2	33	27	2	11	15	10.9	2.18	162	.241	.320	0	.000	0	5	5	0	0.3
1990 Mon-N	0	0	—	1	0	0	0	0	1	1	0	0	0	9.0	0.00	—	.250	.250	0	—	0	0	0	0	0.0
Total 3	3	10	.231	77	1	0	0	5	114	123	10	59	45	15.0	5.05	78	.286	.382	0	.000	0	-14	-14	-2	-2.3

● TOMMY THOMPSON
Thompson, Thomas Carl b: 11/7/1889, Spring City, Tenn. d: 1/16/63, LaJolla, Cal. BR/TR, 5'9.5", 170 lbs. Deb: 6/5/12 F

YEAR TM/L	W	L	PCT	G	GS	CG	SH	SV	IP	H	HR	BB	SO	RAT	ERA	ERA+	OAV	OOB	BH	AVG	PB	PR	/A	PD	TPI
1912 NY-A	0	2	.000	7	2	1	0	0	32²	43	0	13	15	16.3	6.06	59	.341	.415	3	.300	1	-10	-9	-1	-0.5

YEAR	TM/L	W	L	PCT	G	GS	CG	SH	SV	IP	H	HR	BB	SO	RAT	ERA	ERA+	OAV	OOB	BH	AVG	PB	PR	/A	PD	TPI

● **WILL THOMPSON**   Thompson, Will McLain   b: 8/30/1870, Pittsburgh, Pa.   d: 6/9/62, Pittsburgh, Pa.   BR/TR, 5'11.5", 190 lbs.   Deb: 7/9/1892

| 1892 | Pit-N | 0 | 1 | .000 | 1 | 1 | 0 | 0 | 0 | 3 | 0 | 5 | 0 | 27.0 | 3.00 | 110 | .250 | .500 | 0 | — | 0 | 0 | 0 | 0 | 0.1 |

● **HANK THORMAHLEN**   Thormahlen, Herbert Ehler "Lefty"   b: 7/5/1896, Jersey City, N.J.   d: 2/6/55, Los Angeles, Cal.   BL/TL, 6', 180 lbs.   Deb: 9/29/17

1917	NY-A	0	1	.000	1	1	0	0	0	8	9	0	4	5	15.8	2.25	119	.281	.378	0	.000	-0	0	0	0	0.0
1918	NY-A	7	3	.700	16	12	5	2	0	112²	85	1	52	22	11.4	2.48	114	.217	.318	3	.077	-3	4	4	0	0.0
1919	NY-A	12	10	.545	30	25	13	2	1	188²	155	10	61	62	10.5	2.62	122	.228	.295	11	.186	-0	13	12	-1	1.2
1920	NY-A	9	6	.600	29	15	6	0	1	143¹	178	5	43	35	14.0	4.14	92	.312	.362	10	.222	1	-6	-5	1	-0.3
1921	Bos-A	1	7	.125	23	9	3	0	0	96¹	101	3	34	17	13.2	4.48	94	.277	.349	4	.174	-1	-2	-3	-0	-0.2
1925	Bro-N	0	3	.000	5	2	0	0	0	16	22	0	9	7	18.6	3.94	106	.333	.429	1	.200	0	1	0	0	0.2
Total	6	29	30	.492	104	64	27	4	2	565	550	19	203	148	12.3	3.33	105	.261	.332	29	.168	-3	10	9	0	0.9

● **PAUL THORMODSGARD**   Thormodsgard, Paul Gayton   b: 11/10/53, San Francisco, Cal.   BR/TR, 6'2", 190 lbs.   Deb: 4/10/77

1977	Min-A	11	15	.423	37	37	8	1	0	218	236	25	65	94	12.6	4.62	86	.280	.333	0	—	0	-14	-16	-1	-1.6
1978	Min-A	1	6	.143	12	12	1	0	0	66	81	7	17	23	13.5	5.05	76	.308	.352	0	—	0	-9	-9	-1	-1.0
1979	Min-A	0	0	—	1	0	0	0	0	1	3	1	0	1	27.0	9.00	49	.500	.500	0	—	0	-1	-1	0	0.0
Total	3	12	21	.364	50	49	9	1	0	285	320	33	82	118	12.8	4.74	83	.288	.339	0	—	0	-24	-25	-2	-2.6

● **JOHN THORNTON**   Thornton, John   b: 1870, Washington, D.C.   5'10.5", 175 lbs.   Deb: 8/14/1889   ♦

1889	Was-N	0	1	.000	1	1	1	0	0	9	8	0	3	2	15.0	5.00	79	.231	.360	0	.000	-1	-1	-1	-0	-0.2
1891	Phi-N	15	16	.484	37	32	23	1	2	269	268	3	115	52	13.1	3.68	93	.250	.328	17	.138	-7	-10	-8	2	-1.3
1892	Phi-N	0	2	.000	3	2	1	0	0	12	16	1	17	2	24.8	12.75	25	.308	.478	5	.385	1	-13	-13	0	-1.3
Total	3	15	19	.441	41	35	25	1	2	290	292	4	139	57	13.7	4.10	83	.252	.337	22	.154	-7	-24	-22	2	-2.8

● **WALTER THORNTON**   Thornton, Walter Miller   b: 2/18/1875, Lewiston, Maine   d: 7/14/60, Los Angeles, Cal.   BL/TL, 6'1", 180 lbs.   Deb: 7/1/1895   ♦

1895	Chi-N	2	0	1.000	7	2	2	0	1	40	58	3	31	13	21.1	6.07	84	.333	.448	7	.318	2	-6	-4	-1	-0.1
1896	Chi-N	2	1	.667	5	5	2	0	0	23²	30	1	13	10	16.4	5.70	80	.306	.388	2	.364	2	-4	-3	-1	-0.2
1897	Chi-N	6	7	.462	16	16	15	0	0	130¹	164	4	51	56	15.3	4.70	95	.305	.371	85	.321	4	-6	-6	-1	0.1
1898	Chi-N	13	10	.565	28	25	21	2	0	215¹	226	4	56	56	12.5	3.34	107	.268	.327	62	.295	6	6	6	-1	0.9
Total	4	23	18	.561	56	48	40	2	1	409¹	478	12	151	134	14.5	4.18	97	.289	.359	162	.312	13	-8	-6	-2	0.7

● **BOB THORPE**   Thorpe, Robert Joseph   b: 1/12/35, San Diego, Cal.   d: 3/17/60, San Diego, Cal.   BR/TR, 6'1", 170 lbs.   Deb: 4/17/55

| 1955 | Chi-N | 0 | 0 | — | 2 | 0 | 0 | 0 | 0 | 3 | 4 | 0 | 4 | 0 | 12.0 | 3.00 | 136 | .333 | .333 | 0 | — | 0 | 0 | 0 | 0 | 0.0 |

● **GEORGE THROOP**   Throop, George Lynford   b: 11/24/50, Pasadena, Cal.   BR/TR, 6'7", 205 lbs.   Deb: 9/7/75

1975	KC-A	0	0	—	7	0	0	0	2	9	8	1	2	8	10.0	4.00	96	.250	.294	0	—	0	-0	-0	0	-0.1
1977	KC-A	0	0	—	4	0	0	0	1	5¹	1	1	4	1	8.4	3.38	120	.059	.238	0	—	0	0	0	0	0.0
1978	KC-A	1	0	1.000	1	0	0	0	0	3	2	0	3	2	15.0	0.00	—	.222	.417	0	—	0	1	1	0	0.3
1979	KC-A	0	0	—	4	0	0	0	0	2²	7	0	5	1	40.5	13.50	32	.467	.600	0	—	0	-3	-3	-0	-0.1
	Hou-N	1	0	1.000	14	0	0	0	0	22¹	23	4	11	15	14.1	3.22	109	.271	.361	0	.000	-0	1	1	-0	0.0
Total	4	2	0	1.000	30	0	0	0	3	42¹	41	6	25	27	14.2	3.83	97	.259	.364	0	.000	-0	-1	-0	0	0.1

● **LOU THUMAN**   Thuman, Louis Charles Frank   b: 12/13/16, Baltimore, Md.   BR/TR, 6'2", 185 lbs.   Deb: 9/8/39

1939	Was-A	0	0	—	3	0	0	0	0	4	5	0	2	1	15.8	9.00	48	.278	.350	0	—	0	-2	-2	0	-0.2
1940	Was-A	0	1	.000	2	0	0	0	0	5	10	0	7	0	30.6	14.40	29	.400	.531	0	.000	-0	-6	-6	0	-0.8
Total	2	0	1	.000	5	0	0	0	0	9	15	0	9	1	24.0	12.00	35	.349	.462	0	.000	-0	-8	-8	0	-0.8

● **MARK THURMOND**   Thurmond, Mark Anthony   b: 9/12/56, Houston, Tex.   BL/TL, 6', 193 lbs.   Deb: 5/14/83

1983	SD-N	7	3	.700	21	18	2	0	0	115¹	104	7	33	49	10.8	2.65	131	.248	.306	2	.054	-2	12	11	1	0.8
1984	*SD-N	14	8	.636	32	29	1	1	0	178²	174	12	55	57	11.5	2.97	120	.256	.311	11	.190	1	12	12	1	1.8
1985	SD-N	7	11	.389	36	23	1	1	2	138¹	154	9	44	57	13.1	3.97	89	.291	.349	3	.088	-2	-6	-7	1	-0.9
1986	SD-N	3	7	.300	17	15	2	1	0	70²	96	7	27	32	15.7	6.50	56	.325	.382	6	.250	1	-22	-22	0	-2.6
	Det-A	4	1	.800	25	4	0	0	5	51²	44	7	17	17	10.6	1.92	215	.234	.298	0	—	0	13	13	-1	1.2
1987	*Det-A	0	1	.000	48	0	0	0	5	61²	83	5	24	21	15.6	4.23	100	.331	.389	0	—	0	2	-0	-0	0.0
1988	Bal-A	1	8	.111	43	6	0	0	3	74²	80	10	27	29	13.1	4.58	85	.277	.343	0	—	0	-5	-6	-1	-0.7
1989	Bal-A	2	4	.333	49	2	0	0	4	90	102	6	17	34	12.0	3.90	97	.288	.323	0	—	0	-0	-1	-1	-0.1
1990	SF-N	2	3	.400	43	0	0	0	0	56²	53	6	18	24	11.3	3.34	109	.257	.317	0	.000	-1	3	2	1	0.3
Total	8	40	46	.465	314	97	6	3	21	837²	890	69	262	320	12.5	3.69	100	.277	.333	22	.139	-1	9	1	2	-0.2

● **SLOPPY THURSTON**   Thurston, Hollis John   b: 6/2/1899, Fremont, Neb.   d: 9/14/73, Los Angeles, Cal.   BR/TR, 5'11", 165 lbs.   Deb: 4/19/23

1923	StL-A	0	0	—	2	1	0	0	0	4	8	0	2	0	22.5	6.75	62	.421	.476	0	—	0	-1	-1	-0	0.0
	Chi-A	7	8	.467	44	12	8	0	4	191²	223	11	36	55	12.2	3.05	130	.308	.341	25	.316	6	20	19	-0	2.0
	Yr	7	8	.467	46	13	8	0	4	195²	231	11	38	55	12.4	3.13	127	.310	.345	25	.316	6	19	18	-1	2.0
1924	Chi-A	20	14	.588	38	36	**28**	1	1	291	330	17	60	37	12.2	3.80	108	.290	.329	31	.254	4	14	10	1	1.6
1925	Chi-A	10	14	.417	36	25	9	0	1	183	250	14	47	35	14.9	5.95	70	.335	.378	24	.286	7	-32	-37	2	-3.1
1926	Chi-A	6	8	.429	31	13	6	1	3	134¹	164	10	36	35	13.5	5.02	77	.311	.356	19	.311	6	-15	-17	-1	-1.3
1927	Was-A	13	13	.500	29	28	13	2	0	205¹	254	16	60	38	13.9	4.47	91	.308	.356	29	.315	9	-8	-9	-1	-0.2
1930	Bro-N	6	4	.600	24	11	5	2	0	106	110	4	17	26	10.8	3.40	145	.266	.295	10	.200	-0	19	18	2	1.5
1931	Bro-N	9	9	.500	24	11	11	0	0	143	175	3	39	35	13.7	3.97	96	.301	.346	13	.217	2	-2	-2	-1	-0.1
1932	Bro-N	12	8	.600	28	20	10	2	0	153	174	14	38	35	12.5	4.06	94	.287	.330	17	.304	5	-3	-4	1	0.1
1933	Bro-N	6	8	.429	32	15	5	0	3	131¹	171	6	34	12	14.5	4.52	71	.319	.366	7	.159	-1	-17	-19	2	-1.9
Total	9	89	86	.509	288	178	95	8	13	1542²	1859	93	369	306	13.1	4.24	94	.304	.346	175	.270	38	-25	-42	3	-1.4

● **LUIS TIANT**   Tiant, Luis Clemente (Vega)   b: 11/23/40, Marianao, Cuba   BR/TR, 5'11", 190 lbs.   Deb: 7/19/64

1964	Cle-A	10	4	.714	19	16	9	3	1	127	94	13	47	105	10.1	2.83	127	.207	.284	5	.111	-1	11	11	0	1.1
1965	Cle-A	11	11	.500	41	30	10	2	1	196¹	166	20	66	152	10.8	3.53	99	.228	.295	6	.088	-2	-2	-1	-0	-0.3
1966	Cle-A	12	11	.522	46	16	7	**5**	8	155	121	16	50	145	10.6	2.79	123	.213	.279	4	.111	-1	11	11	-1	1.6
1967	Cle-A	12	9	.571	33	29	9	1	2	213²	177	24	67	219	10.3	2.74	119	.221	.282	18	.254	5	12	13	-2	1.6
1968	Cle-A★	21	9	.700	34	32	19	**9**	0	258¹	152	16	73	264	8.0	**1.60**	**185**	**.168**	**.233**	7	.080	-5	**40**	39	-3	4.2
1969	Cle-A	9	20	.310	38	37	9	1	0	249²	229	37	129	156	13.2	3.71	101	.246	.343	11	.235	-6	-3	-1	-1	0.7
1970	*Min-A	7	3	.700	18	17	2	1	0	92²	84	12	41	50	12.3	3.40	109	.246	.330	13	.406	5	3	3	-0	0.9
1971	Bos-A	1	7	.125	21	10	1	0	0	72¹	73	8	32	59	13.2	4.85	76	.259	.337	3	.158	-0	-11	-9	-0	-1.0
1972	Bos-A	15	6	.714	43	19	12	6	3	179	128	7	65	123	9.7	**1.91**	**168**	.202	.277	6	.107	-2	23	26	-1	3.0
1973	Bos-A	20	13	.606	35	35	23	0	0	272	217	36	78	206	**10.0**	3.34	120	.219	**.281**	0	—	0	14	20	-1	2.0
1974	Bos-A★	22	13	.629	38	38	25	**7**	0	311¹	281	21	82	176	10.6	2.92	132	.241	.293	0	.000	0	24	32	-3	3.0
1975	*Bos-A	18	14	.563	35	35	18	2	0	260	262	25	72	142	11.7	4.02	101	.264	.316	0	.000	-0	-7	2	-3	-0.2
1976	Bos-A★	21	12	.636	38	38	19	3	0	279	274	25	64	131	11.0	3.06	128	.260	.304	0	.000	-0	14	26	-2	2.8
1977	Bos-A	12	8	.600	32	32	3	0	0	188²	210	26	51	124	12.5	4.53	99	.279	.327	0	—	0	-10	-1	-2	-1.0
1978	Bos-A	13	8	.619	32	31	12	5	0	212¹	185	26	57	114	10.5	3.31	124	.234	.290	0	—	0	11	19	-2	0.8
1979	NY-A	13	8	.619	30	30	5	1	0	195²	190	22	53	104	11.2	3.91	104	.251	.300	0	—	0	7	4	-0	0.5
1980	NY-A	8	9	.471	25	25	3	0	0	136¹	139	10	50	84	12.5	4.89	80	.265	.330	0	—	0	-13	-15	1	-1.4
1981	Pit-N	2	5	.286	9	9	1	0	0	57¹	54	7	20	28	11.5	3.92	92	.243	.303	3	.188	1	-3	-2	-1	-0.3
1982	Cal-A	2	2	.500	6	6	0	0	0	29²	39	3	8	30	14.3	5.76	70	.310	.351	0	—	0	-6	-6	-1	-0.7
Total	19	229	172	.571	573	484	187	49	15	3486¹	3075	346	1104	2416	10.9	3.30	113	.236	.298	84	.164	6	116	173	-21	17.3

YEAR TM/L	W	L	PCT	G	GS	CG	SH	SV	IP	H	HR	BB	SO	RAT	ERA	ERA+	OAV	OOB	BH	AVG	PB	PR	/A	PD	TPI

● **JAY TIBBS** Tibbs, Jay Lindsey b: 1/4/62, Birmingham, Ala. BR/TR, 6'3", 185 lbs. Deb: 7/15/84

1984 Cin-N	6	2	.750	14	14	3	1	0	100²	87	4	33	40	10.7	2.86	132	.238	.302	5	.139	-1	8	10	-1	0.6
1985 Cin-N	10	16	.385	35	34	5	2	0	218	216	14	83	98	12.3	3.92	97	.262	.329	6	.092	-3	-8	-3	1	-0.6
1986 Mon-N	7	9	.438	35	31	3	2	0	190¹	181	12	70	117	12.0	3.97	93	.256	.326	7	.130	-0	-5	-6	-1	-0.5
1987 Mon-N	4	5	.444	19	12	0	0	0	83	95	10	34	54	14.0	4.99	84	.289	.355	3	.120	0	-8	-7	-1	-0.7
1988 Bal-A	4	15	.211	30	24	1	0	0	158²	184	18	63	82	14.2	5.39	72	.293	.360	0	—	0	-25	-26	0	-2.7
1989 Bal-A	5	0	1.000	10	8	1	0	0	54¹	62	2	20	30	13.6	2.82	135	.287	.347	0	—	0	6	6	-0	0.5
1990 Bal-A	2	7	.222	10	10	0	0	0	50²	55	8	14	23	12.3	5.68	67	.279	.327	0	—	0	-10	-11	0	-1.5
Pit-N	1	0	1.000	5	0	0	0	0	7	7	0	2	4	11.6	2.57	141	.259	.310	0	—	0	1	1	0	0.1
Total 7	39	54	.419	158	133	13	5	0	862²	887	68	319	448	12.6	4.20	91	.269	.335	21	.117	-4	-41	-36	-1	-4.8

● **DICK TIDROW** Tidrow, Richard William b: 5/14/47, San Francisco, Cal. BR/TR, 6'4", 213 lbs. Deb: 4/18/72

1972 Cle-A	14	15	.483	39	34	10	3	0	237¹	200	21	70	123	10.5	2.77	116	.230	.291	7	.100	-3	8	12	-4	0.7
1973 Cle-A	14	16	.467	42	40	13	2	0	274²	289	31	95	138	12.8	4.42	89	.270	.334	0	—	0	-19	-15	-2	-1.7
1974 Cle-A	1	3	.250	4	4	0	0	0	19	21	4	13	8	17.1	7.11	51	.276	.396	0	—	0	-7	-7	-0	-1.2
NY-A	11	9	.550	33	25	5	0	1	190²	205	14	53	100	12.4	3.87	90	.279	.331	0	—	0	-5	-8	-2	-0.9
Yr	12	12	.500	37	29	5	0	1	209²	226	18	66	108	12.7	4.16	84	.278	.335	0	—	0	-13	-15	-1	-2.1
1975 NY-A	6	3	.667	37	0	0	0	5	69¹	65	5	31	38	12.9	3.12	117	.256	.344	0	—	0	5	4	-1	0.5
1976 *NY-A	4	5	.444	47	2	0	0	10	92¹	80	5	24	65	10.2	2.63	130	.233	.285	0	—	0	9	8	-1	0.8
1977 *NY-A	11	4	.733	49	7	0	0	5	151	143	20	41	83	11.1	3.16	125	.250	.303	0	—	0	15	13	-1	1.3
1978 *NY-A	7	11	.389	31	25	4	0	0	185¹	191	13	53	73	12.1	3.84	94	.267	.322	0	—	0	-2	-4	-2	-0.4
1979 NY-A	2	1	.667	14	0	0	0	2	22²	38	5	4	7	16.7	7.94	51	.409	.433	0	—	0	-9	-10	-1	-1.0
Chi-N	11	5	.688	63	0	0	0	4	102²	86	5	42	68	11.4	2.72	151	.231	.313	2	.200	0	12	16	1	2.7
1980 Chi-N	6	5	.545	**84**	0	0	0	6	116	97	10	53	97	12.0	2.79	140	.229	.322	0	.000	0	10	14	1	1.4
1981 Chi-N	3	10	.231	51	0	0	0	6	74²	73	6	30	39	12.5	5.06	73	.256	.329	0	.000	-1	-13	-11	-1	-2.3
1982 Chi-N	8	3	.727	65	0	0	0	6	103²	106	6	29	62	12.0	3.39	110	.265	.319	0	.000	-1	2	4	-2	0.2
1983 *Chi-A	2	4	.333	50	1	0	0	7	91²	86	13	34	66	11.9	4.22	99	.242	.310	0	—	0	-2	-0	1	-0.2
1984 NY-N	0	0	—	11	0	0	0	0	15²	25	5	7	8	18.4	9.19	38	.357	.416	0	—	0	-10	-10	0	0.0
Total 13	100	94	.515	620	138	32	5	55	1746²	1705	163	579	975	12.0	3.68	101	.257	.321	9	.095	-5	-5	-6	-11	-0.1

● **BOBBY TIEFENAUER** Tiefenauer, Bobby Gene b: 10/10/29, Desloge, Mo. BR/TR, 6'2", 185 lbs. Deb: 7/14/52 C

1952 StL-N	0	0	—	6	0	0	0	0	8	12	1	7	3	21.4	7.88	47	.343	.452	0	.000	-0	-4	-4	0	0.0
1955 StL-N	1	4	.200	18	0	0	0	0	32²	31	6	10	16	12.4	4.41	92	.261	.338	0	.000	-0	-1	-1	0	-0.2
1960 Cle-A	0	1	.000	6	0	0	0	0	9	6	0	3	2	11.0	2.00	187	.242	.306	0	.000	0	2	2	-0	0.2
1961 StL-N	0	0	—	3	0	0	0	0	4¹	9	0	4	3	27.0	6.23	71	.450	.542	0	—	0	-1	-1	-0	0.0
1962 Hou-N	2	4	.333	43	0	0	0	1	85	91	6	21	60	12.1	4.34	86	.277	.324	1	.111	0	-4	-6	-2	-0.5
1963 Mil-N	1	1	.500	12	0	0	0	2	29²	20	1	4	22	7.3	1.21	265	.194	.224	0	.000	0	7	7	1	0.6
1964 Mil-N	4	6	.400	46	0	0	0	13	73	61	6	15	48	9.7	3.21	110	.225	.273	0	.000	-1	3	3	-1	0.2
1965 Mil-N	0	1	.000	6	0	0	0	0	7	8	1	3	7	15.4	7.71	46	.286	.375	0	—	0	-3	-3	-0	-0.4
NY-A	1	1	.500	10	0	0	0	2	20¹	19	3	5	15	11.1	3.54	96	.253	.309	0	.000	0	-0	-0	-0	-0.0
Cle-A	0	5	.000	15	0	0	0	4	22¹	24	3	10	13	14.1	4.84	72	.277	.354	0	.000	-1	-0	-0	-0	-0.9
Yr	1	6	.143	25	0	0	0	6	42²	43	6	15	28	12.4	4.22	82	.259	.324	0	.000	-0	-4	-4	-0	-0.9
1967 Cle-A	0	0	—	5	0	0	0	0	11¹	9	0	3	6	9.5	0.79	411	.225	.279	0	—	0	3	3	-1	0.2
1968 Chi-N	0	1	.000	9	0	0	0	1	13¹	20	2	9	14.9	6.08	52	.351	.373	0	.000	-0	-5	-4	-0	-0.4
Total 10	9	25	.265	179	0	0	0	23	316	312	29	87	204	11.7	3.84	94	.260	.317	1	.026	-1	-7	-9	-2	-1.2

● **VERLE TIEFENTHALER** Tiefenthaler, Verle Matthew b: 7/11/37, Breda, Iowa BL/TR, 6'1", 190 lbs. Deb: 4/19/62

1962 Chi-A	0	0	—	3	0	0	0	0	3²	6	1	7	1	31.9	9.82	40	.353	.542	0	—	0	-2	-2	0	0.0

● **EDDIE TIEMEYER** Tiemeyer, Edward Carl b: 5/9/1885, Cincinnati, Ohio d: 9/27/46, Cincinnati, Ohio BR/TR, 5'11.5", 185 lbs. Deb: 8/19/06 ♦

1906 Cin-N	0	0	—	1	0	0	0	0	1	1	0	1	1	18.0	0.00	—	.500	.667	2	.182	0	0	-0	-0	0.0

● **MIKE TIERNAN** Tiernan, Michael Joseph "Silent Mike" b: 1/21/1867, Trenton, N.J. d: 11/9/18, New York, N.Y. BL/TL, 5'11", 165 lbs. Deb: 4/30/1887 ♦

1887 NY-N	1	2	.333	5	0	0	0	1	**1**	19²	33	2	7	3	18.8	8.69	43	.398	.451	117	.287	2	-10	-11	-0	-1.2

● **LES TIETJE** Tietje, Leslie William "Toots" b: 9/11/11, Sumner, Iowa BR/TR, 6'0.5", 178 lbs. Deb: 9/18/33

1933 Chi-A	2	0	1.000	3	3	1	0	0	22¹	16	1	15	9	12.5	2.42	175	.203	.330	1	.125	0	5	5	0	0.4
1934 Chi-A	5	14	.263	34	22	6	1	0	176	174	20	96	81	13.9	4.81	98	.257	.351	1	.017	-7	-6	-1	2	-0.7
1935 Chi-A	9	15	.375	30	21	9	1	0	169²	184	14	81	64	14.2	4.30	108	.277	.357	12	.197	-1	3	6	-2	0.5
1936 Chi-A	0	0	—	2	0	0	0	0	2¹	6	0	5	3	42.4	27.00	19	.462	.611	0	—	0	-6	-6	-0	-0.0
StL-A	3	5	.375	14	7	2	0	0	50¹	65	2	30	16	17.3	6.62	81	.310	.401	1	.067	-1	-9	-7	1	-0.9
Yr	3	5	.375	16	7	2	0	0	52²	71	2	35	19	18.5	7.52	71	.318	.415	1	.067	-1	-15	-13	1	-0.9
1937 StL-A	1	2	.333	5	4	2	0	0	30	32	0	17	5	14.7	4.20	115	.283	.377	0	.000	-2	1	2	-1	0.0
1938 StL-A	2	5	.286	17	8	2	1	0	62	83	8	38	15	17.6	7.55	66	.327	.414	2	.111	-1	-19	-18	-1	-1.7
Total 6	22	41	.349	105	65	22	3	0	512²	560	45	282	193	14.9	5.11	93	.279	.369	17	.099	-12	-31	-19	0	-2.4

● **RAY TIFT** Tift, Raymond Frank b: 6/21/1884, Fitchburg, Mass. d: 3/29/45, Verona, N.J. TL, Deb: 8/7/07

1907 NY-A	0	0	—	4	1	0	0	0	19	33	0	4	6	17.5	4.74	59	.382	.409	0	.000	-0	-5	-4	-1	-0.1

● **JOHNNY TILLMAN** Tillman, John Lawrence "Ducky" b: 10/6/1893, Bridgeport, Conn. d: 4/7/64, Harrisburg, Pa. BB/TR, 5'11", 170 lbs. Deb: 9/20/15

1915 StL-A	1	0	1.000	2	1	0	0	0	10	6	0	4	6	9.0	0.90	318	.176	.263	0	.000	-0	2	2	0	0.2

● **THAD TILLOTSON** Tillotson, Thaddeus Asa b: 12/20/40, Merced, Cal. BR/TR, 6'2.5", 195 lbs. Deb: 4/14/67

1967 NY-A	3	9	.250	43	5	1	0	2	98¹	99	9	39	62	12.8	4.03	78	.261	.333	1	.063	-0	-9	-10	0	-1.2
1968 NY-A	1	0	1.000	7	0	0	0	0	10¹	11	0	7	1	15.7	4.35	67	.282	.391	0	.000	-0	-2	-2	0	-0.1
Total 2	4	9	.308	50	5	1	0	2	108²	110	9	46	63	13.1	4.06	77	.263	.339	1	.059	-1	-10	-11	1	-1.3

● **GARY TIMBERLAKE** Timberlake, Gary Dale b: 8/8/48, Laconia, Ind. BR/TL, 6'2", 205 lbs. Deb: 6/18/69

1969 Sea-A	0	0	—	2	2	0	0	0	6	7	0	9	4	24.0	7.50	48	.269	.457	0	.000	-0	-3	-3	-0	-0.1

● **MIKE TIMLIN** Timlin, Michael August b: 3/10/66, Midland, Tex. BR/TR, 6'4", 205 lbs. Deb: 4/8/91

1991 *Tor-A	11	6	.647	63	3	0	0	3	108¹	94	6	50	85	12.0	3.16	133	.233	.319	0	—	0	11	13	1	1.9
1992 Tor-A	0	2	.000	26	0	0	0	1	43²	45	0	20	35	13.6	4.12	99	.271	.353	0	—	0	-1	-0	-0	-0.1
1993 *Tor-A	4	2	.667	54	0	0	0	1	55²	63	7	27	49	14.7	4.69	92	.284	.364	0	—	0	-2	-2	-1	-0.1
1994 Tor-A	0	1	.000	34	0	0	0	2	40	41	5	20	38	14.2	5.17	93	.261	.352	0	—	0	-2	-2	-0	-0.1
Total 4	15	11	.577	177	3	0	0	7	247²	243	18	117	207	13.3	4.00	108	.256	.341	0	—	0	6	9	2	1.6

● **TOM TIMMERMANN** Timmermann, Thomas Henry b: 5/12/40, Breese, Ill. BR/TR, 6'4", 215 lbs. Deb: 6/18/69

1969 Det-A	4	3	.571	31	1	1	0	3	55²	50	1	26	42	12.6	2.75	136	.238	.328	1	.111	-0	5	6	-1	0.6
1970 Det-A	6	7	.462	61	0	0	0	27	85¹	90	3	34	49	13.3	4.11	91	.273	.344	0	.000	-2	-4	-4	-0	-1.0
1971 Det-A	7	6	.538	52	2	0	0	4	84	82	6	37	51	13.1	3.86	93	.262	.346	1	.053	-1	3	4	-2	0.3
1972 Det-A	8	10	.444	34	25	3	0	1	149²	121	12	41	88	10.0	2.89	109	.216	.276	6	.136	-1	3	4	-2	0.3
1973 Det-A	1	1	.500	17	1	0	0	1	39	39	4	11	21	11.5	3.69	111	.258	.309	0	—	0	1	2	-1	-0.2
Cle-A	8	7	.533	29	15	4	0	2	124¹	117	15	54	62	12.6	4.92	80	.251	.332	0	—	0	-15	-14	-1	-1.6
Yr	9	8	.529	46	16	4	0	3	163¹	156	19	65	83	12.3	4.63	86	.252	.327	0	—	0	-15	-12	-1	-1.8

YEAR TM/L	W	L	PCT	G	GS	CG	SH	SV	IP	H	HR	BB	SO	RAT	ERA	ERA+	OAV	OOB	BH	AVG	PB	PR	/A	PD	TPI
1974 Cle-A	1	1	.500	4	0	0	0	0	10	9	1	5	2	12.6	5.40	67	.250	.341	0	—	0	-2	-2	1	-0.3
Total 6	35	35	.500	228	44	8	2	35	548	508	42	208	315	12.0	3.78	96	.246	.319	8	.091	-4	-16	-10	-3	-2.7

● BEN TINCUP
Tincup, Austin Ben b: 12/14/1890, Adair, Okla. d: 7/5/80, Claremore, Okla. BL/TR, 6'1", 180 lbs. Deb: 5/22/14 C♦

YEAR TM/L	W	L	PCT	G	GS	CG	SH	SV	IP	H	HR	BB	SO	RAT	ERA	ERA+	OAV	OOB	BH	AVG	PB	PR	/A	PD	TPI
1914 Phi-N	8	10	.444	28	17	9	3	2	155	165	0	62	108	13.4	2.61	113	.286	.359	9	.170	-1	3	6	1	0.7
1915 Phi-N	0	0	—	10	0	0	0	0	31	31	1	9	10	10.2	2.03	135	.263	.324	0	.000	-1	2	2	0	-0.1
1918 Phi-N	0	1	.000	8	1	0	0	0	16²	24	0	6	6	16.2	7.56	40	.329	.380	1	.125	-0	-9	-8	1	-0.4
1928 Chi-N	0	0	—	2	0	0	0	0	9	14	0	1	3	15.0	7.00	55	.378	.395	0	.000	-0	-3	-3	0	-0.1
Total 4	8	11	.421	48	18	9	3	2	211²	229	1	78	127	13.2	3.10	95	.291	.358	10	.135	-3	-6	-3	3	0.2

● BUD TINNING
Tinning, Lyle Forrest b: 3/12/06, Pilger, Neb. d: 1/17/61, Evansville, Ind. BB/TR, 5'11", 198 lbs. Deb: 4/20/32

YEAR TM/L	W	L	PCT	G	GS	CG	SH	SV	IP	H	HR	BB	SO	RAT	ERA	ERA+	OAV	OOB	BH	AVG	PB	PR	/A	PD	TPI
1932 *Chi-N	5	3	.625	24	7	2	0	0	93¹	93	3	24	30	11.5	2.80	135	.263	.313	2	.087	-1	11	10	0	0.7
1933 Chi-N	13	6	.684	32	21	10	3	1	175¹	169	3	60	59	12.0	3.18	103	.255	.320	14	.209	1	3	2	-2	0.0
1934 Chi-N	4	6	.400	39	7	1	1	3	129¹	134	9	46	44	12.6	3.34	116	.269	.332	7	.179	-1	10	8	-1	0.4
1935 StL-N	0	0	—	4	0	0	0	0	7²	9	1	5	2	17.6	5.87	70	.300	.417	0	.000	-0	-2	-2	0	0.0
Total 4	22	15	.595	99	35	13	4	4	405²	405	16	135	135	12.2	3.19	113	.262	.325	23	.177	-1	23	18	-4	1.1

● DAN TIPPLE
Tipple, Daniel E. "Big Dan" or "Rusty" b: 2/13/1890, Rockford, Ill. d: 3/26/60, Omaha, Neb. BR/TR, 6', 176 lbs. Deb: 9/18/15

YEAR TM/L	W	L	PCT	G	GS	CG	SH	SV	IP	H	HR	BB	SO	RAT	ERA	ERA+	OAV	OOB	BH	AVG	PB	PR	/A	PD	TPI
1915 NY-A	1	1	.500	3	2	2	0	0	19	14	1	11	14	11.8	0.95	310	.203	.313	0	.000	-1	4	4	-1	0.2

● JACK TISING
Tising, Johnnie Joseph b: 10/9/03, High Point, Mo. d: 9/5/67, Leadville, Colo. BL/TR, 6'2", 180 lbs. Deb: 4/24/36

YEAR TM/L	W	L	PCT	G	GS	CG	SH	SV	IP	H	HR	BB	SO	RAT	ERA	ERA+	OAV	OOB	BH	AVG	PB	PR	/A	PD	TPI
1936 Pit-N	1	3	.250	10	6	1	0	0	47	52	5	24	27	14.6	4.21	96	.272	.353	3	.273	0	-1	-1	-0	-0.1

● CANNONBALL TITCOMB
Titcomb, Ledell b: 8/21/1866, W.Baldwin, Me. d: 6/8/50, Kingston, N.H. BL/TL, 5'6", 157 lbs. Deb: 5/5/1886

YEAR TM/L	W	L	PCT	G	GS	CG	SH	SV	IP	H	HR	BB	SO	RAT	ERA	ERA+	OAV	OOB	BH	AVG	PB	PR	/A	PD	TPI
1886 Phi-N	0	5	.000	5	5	5	0	0	41	43	1	24	24	14.7	3.73	88	.244	.335	1	.063	-2	-2	-2	1	-0.3
1887 Phi-a	1	2	.333	3	3	3	0	0	24	31	1	19	16	18.8	6.75	64	.298	.407	0	.000	-1	-7	-7	-1	-0.7
NY-N	4	3	.571	9	9	9	0	0	72	68	3	37	34	13.3	3.88	97	.233	.321	2	.069	-4	-2	-1	-1	-0.5
1888 *NY-N	14	8	.636	23	23	22	4	0	197	149	4	46	129	9.1	2.24	122	.201	.253	10	.122	-4	13	11	-4	0.2
1889 NY-N	1	2	.333	3	3	3	0	0	26	27	1	16	7	15.6	6.58	60	.260	.369	1	.083	-1	-7	-8	-0	-0.7
1890 Roc-a	10	9	.526	20	19	19	1	0	168²	168	6	97	73	14.9	3.74	95	.252	.358	8	.107	-5	-3	-3	-3	-1.0
Total 5	30	29	.508	63	62	61	5	0	528²	486	16	239	283	12.7	3.47	96	.233	.318	22	.098	-18	2	-9	-8	-3.0

● DAVE TOBIK
Tobik, David Vance b: 3/2/53, Euclid, Ohio BR/TR, 6'1", 195 lbs. Deb: 8/26/78

YEAR TM/L	W	L	PCT	G	GS	CG	SH	SV	IP	H	HR	BB	SO	RAT	ERA	ERA+	OAV	OOB	BH	AVG	PB	PR	/A	PD	TPI
1978 Det-A	0	0	—	5	0	0	0	0	12	12	1	3	11	11.3	3.75	103	.261	.306	0	—	0	0	0	-0	-0.2
1979 Det-A	3	5	.375	37	0	0	0	3	68²	59	12	25	48	11.0	4.33	100	.231	.300	0	—	0	-1	-0	-1	-0.3
1980 Det-A	1	0	1.000	17	1	0	0	0	61	61	7	21	34	12.1	3.98	103	.266	.328	0	—	0	1	0	-0	-0.1
1981 Det-A	2	2	.500	27	0	0	0	1	60¹	47	7	33	32	11.9	2.69	140	.215	.317	0	—	0	7	7	-1	0.7
1982 Det-A	4	9	.308	51	0	0	0	9	98²	86	8	38	63	11.4	3.56	114	.241	.316	0	—	0	6	6	-1	0.7
1983 Tex-A	2	1	.667	27	0	0	0	0	44	36	2	13	30	10.0	3.68	109	.222	.280	0	—	0	2	2	0	0.3
1984 Tex-A	1	6	.143	24	0	0	0	5	42¹	44	5	17	30	13.2	3.61	115	.265	.337	0	—	0	2	1	0	0.2
1985 Sea-A	1	0	1.000	8	0	0	0	1	9	10	2	3	8	13.0	6.00	70	.286	.342	0	—	0	-2	-2	-0	-0.2
Total 8	14	23	.378	196	2	0	0	28	396	355	44	153	256	11.6	3.70	110	.242	.314	0	—	0	13	16	-3	0.6

● JIM TOBIN
Tobin, James Anthony "Abba Dabba" b: 12/27/12, Oakland, Cal. d: 5/19/69, Oakland, Cal. BR/TR, 6', 185 lbs. Deb: 4/30/37 F♦

YEAR TM/L	W	L	PCT	G	GS	CG	SH	SV	IP	H	HR	BB	SO	RAT	ERA	ERA+	OAV	OOB	BH	AVG	PB	PR	/A	PD	TPI
1937 Pit-N	6	3	.667	20	8	7	0	1	87	74	1	28	37	10.7	3.00	129	.226	.289	15	.441	7	9	8	-2	1.4
1938 Pit-N	14	12	.538	40	33	14	2	0	241¹	254	17	66	70	12.2	3.47	109	.270	.321	25	.243	7	9	9	-2	1.3
1939 Pit-N	9	9	.500	25	19	8	0	0	145¹	194	7	33	43	14.2	4.52	85	.319	.356	18	.243	5	-10	-11	-1	-0.8
1940 Bos-N	7	3	.700	15	11	9	0	0	96¹	102	8	24	29	11.8	3.83	97	.264	.307	12	.279	3	0	-1	-1	0.2
1941 Bos-N	12	12	.500	33	26	20	3	0	238	229	12	60	61	10.9	3.10	115	.253	.300	19	.184	3	14	14	2	2.0
1942 Bos-N	12	21	.364	37	33	**28**	1	0	287²	283	20	96	71	12.0	3.97	84	.257	.320	28	.246	14	-21	-20	6	-0.1
1943 Bos-N	14	14	.500	33	30	24	1	0	250	241	12	69	52	11.2	2.66	128	.251	.303	30	.280	6	20	21	2	3.5
1944 Bos-N★	18	19	.486	43	36	**28**	5	3	299¹	271	18	97	83	11.3	3.01	127	.240	.302	22	.190	5	20	27	7	4.7
1945 Bos-N	9	14	.391	27	25	16	0	0	196²	220	10	56	38	12.9	3.84	100	.282	.334	11	.143	-5	-1	-0	2	0.7
*Det-A	4	5	.444	14	6	2	0	1	58¹	61	2	28	14	14.3	3.55	99	.274	.365	3	.120	-1	-1	-0	1	0.1
Total 9	105	112	.484	287	227	156	12	5	1900	1929	107	557	498	11.9	3.44	106	.262	.316	183	.230	54	39	45	16	13.0

● PAT TOBIN
Tobin, Marion Brooks b: 1/28/16, Hermitage, Ark. d: 1/21/75, Shreveport, La. BR/TR, 6'1", 198 lbs. Deb: 8/21/41

YEAR TM/L	W	L	PCT	G	GS	CG	SH	SV	IP	H	HR	BB	SO	RAT	ERA	ERA+	OAV	OOB	BH	AVG	PB	PR	/A	PD	TPI
1941 Phi-A	0	0	—	1	0	0	0	0	1	4	0	2	0	54.0	36.00	12	.571	.667	0	—	0	-4	-4	0	0.0

● FRANK TODD
Todd, George Franklin b: 10/18/1869, Aberdeen, Md. d: 8/11/19, Havre De Grace, Md. TL, Deb: 7/14/1898

YEAR TM/L	W	L	PCT	G	GS	CG	SH	SV	IP	H	HR	BB	SO	RAT	ERA	ERA+	OAV	OOB	BH	AVG	PB	PR	/A	PD	TPI
1898 Lou-N	0	2	.000	4	2	0	0	0	11	23	0	8	5	27.0	13.91	26	.422	.511	1	.200	0	-13	-13	-1	-1.6

● JACKSON TODD
Todd, Jackson A b: 11/20/51, Tulsa, Okla. BR/TR, 6'2", 180 lbs. Deb: 5/5/77

YEAR TM/L	W	L	PCT	G	GS	CG	SH	SV	IP	H	HR	BB	SO	RAT	ERA	ERA+	OAV	OOB	BH	AVG	PB	PR	/A	PD	TPI
1977 NY-N	3	6	.333	19	10	0	0	0	71²	78	8	20	39	12.6	4.77	78	.273	.325	1	.059	-1	-7	-8	0	-1.0
1979 Tor-A	0	1	.000	12	1	0	0	0	32¹	40	7	7	14	13.4	5.85	74	.299	.338	0	—	0	-6	-5	0	-0.2
1980 Tor-A	5	2	.714	12	12	4	0	0	85	90	14	30	44	12.9	4.02	107	.276	.341	0	—	0	0	3	1	0.1
1981 Tor-A	2	7	.222	21	13	3	0	0	97²	94	10	31	41	11.9	3.96	99	.251	.315	0	—	0	-3	-0	1	-0.1
Total 4	10	16	.385	64	36	7	0	0	286²	302	39	88	138	12.5	4.40	90	.270	.328	1	.059	-1	-16	-11	2	-1.2

● JIM TODD
Todd, James Richard b: 9/21/47, Lancaster, Pa. BL/TR, 6'2", 190 lbs. Deb: 4/29/74

YEAR TM/L	W	L	PCT	G	GS	CG	SH	SV	IP	H	HR	BB	SO	RAT	ERA	ERA+	OAV	OOB	BH	AVG	PB	PR	/A	PD	TPI
1974 Chi-N	4	2	.667	43	6	0	0	3	88	82	7	41	42	12.9	3.89	98	.252	.341	1	.063	-1	-3	-1	1	-0.1
1975 *Oak-A	8	3	.727	58	0	0	0	12	122	104	6	33	50	10.3	2.29	159	.234	.292	0	—	0	20	18	4	2.3
1976 Oak-A	7	8	.467	49	0	0	0	4	82²	87	6	34	22	13.8	3.81	88	.276	.358	0	—	0	-3	-4	2	-0.6
1977 Chi-N	1	1	.500	20	0	0	0	0	30²	47	1	19	17	20.0	9.10	48	.336	.422	0	.000	-0	-18	-16	0	-0.9
1978 Sea-A	3	4	.429	49	2	0	0	3	106²	113	4	61	37	14.7	3.88	98	.280	.375	0	—	0	-1	-1	0	0.0
1979 Oak-A	2	5	.286	51	0	0	0	2	81	108	12	51	26	17.9	6.56	62	.329	.423	0	—	0	-21	-23	0	-1.4
Total 6	25	23	.521	270	8	0	0	24	511	541	34	239	194	14.0	4.23	89	.277	.360	1	.059	-2	-25	-26	7	-0.7

● HAL TOENES
Toenes, William Harrel b: 10/8/17, Mobile, Ala. BR/TR, 5'11.5", 175 lbs. Deb: 9/17/47

YEAR TM/L	W	L	PCT	G	GS	CG	SH	SV	IP	H	HR	BB	SO	RAT	ERA	ERA+	OAV	OOB	BH	AVG	PB	PR	/A	PD	TPI
1947 Was-A	0	1	.000	3	1	0	0	0	6²	11	0	2	5	17.6	6.75	55	.379	.419	0	.000	-0	-2	-2	-0	-0.3

● FREDDIE TOLIVER
Toliver, Freddie Lee b: 2/3/61, Natchez, Miss. BR/TR, 6'1", 170 lbs. Deb: 9/15/84

YEAR TM/L	W	L	PCT	G	GS	CG	SH	SV	IP	H	HR	BB	SO	RAT	ERA	ERA+	OAV	OOB	BH	AVG	PB	PR	/A	PD	TPI
1984 Cin-N	0	0	—	3	1	0	0	0	10	7	0	7	4	12.6	0.90	420	.206	.341	0	.000	-0	3	3	-0	0.0
1985 Phi-N	0	4	.000	11	3	0	0	0	25	27	1	17	23	15.8	4.68	79	.273	.379	2	.500	-1	-3	-3	-0	-0.4
1986 Phi-N	0	2	.000	5	5	0	0	0	25²	28	0	11	20	13.7	3.51	110	.286	.358	0	.000	-1	-0	-0	0	0.0
1987 Phi-N	1	1	.500	10	4	0	0	0	30¹	34	2	17	25	15.4	5.64	75	.291	.385	0	.000	-1	-5	-5	-0	-0.3
1988 Min-A	7	6	.538	21	19	4	0	0	114²	116	8	52	69	13.3	4.24	96	.270	.350	0	—	0	-3	-2	-0	0.0
1989 Min-A	1	3	.250	7	5	0	0	0	29	39	2	15	11	17.1	7.76	53	.317	.396	0	—	0	-12	-12	1	-1.2
SD-N	0	0	—	9	0	0	0	0	14	17	5	9	14	17.4	7.07	49	.321	.429	0	—	0	-6	-6	-0	-0.1
1993 Pit-N	1	0	1.000	12	0	0	0	0	21²	20	2	8	14	12.5	3.74	108	.267	.353	0	.000	-0	1	1	0	0.0
Total 7	10	16	.385	78	37	0	0	0	270¹	288	21	136	180	14.3	4.73	85	.280	.367	2	.111	-4	-25	-22	1	-2.0

● DICK TOMANEK
Tomanek, Richard Carl "Bones" b: 1/6/31, Avon Lake, Ohio BL/TL, 6'1", 175 lbs. Deb: 9/25/53

YEAR TM/L	W	L	PCT	G	GS	CG	SH	SV	IP	H	HR	BB	SO	RAT	ERA	ERA+	OAV	OOB	BH	AVG	PB	PR	/A	PD	TPI
1953 Cle-A	1	0	1.000	1	1	1	0	0	9	6	1	6	6	13.0	2.00	188	.176	.317	0	.000	-1	2	2	-0	0.1
1954 Cle-A	0	0	—	1	0	0	0	0	1²	1	1	1	0	10.8	5.40	68	.167	.286	0	—	0	-0	-0	-0	0.0
1957 Cle-A	2	1	.667	34	0	0	0	0	69²	67	13	37	55	13.6	5.68	65	.248	.341	3	.231	0	-15	-15	-0	-0.5

YEAR	TM/L	W	L	PCT	G	GS	CG	SH	SV	IP	H	HR	BB	SO	RAT	ERA	ERA+	OAV	OOB	BH	AVG	PB	PR	/A	PD	TPI
1958	Cle-A	2	3	.400	18	6	2	0	0	57²	61	8	28	42	14.2	5.62	65	.276	.363	2	.118	0	-12	-13	0	-0.9
	KC-A	5	5	.500	36	2	1	0	5	72¹	69	5	28	50	12.1	3.61	108	.252	.321	3	.231	1	1	2	-0	0.4
	Yr	7	8	.467	54	8	3	0	5	130	130	13	56	92	12.9	4.50	84	.261	.336	5	.167	1	-11	-10	0	-0.5
1959	KC-A	0	1	.000	16	0	0	0	2	20²	27	6	12	13	17.9	6.53	61	.310	.406	1	.500	0	-6	-6	0	-0.3
Total	5	10	10	.500	106	11	4	0	7	231	231	34	112	166	13.6	4.95	77	.259	.346	9	.180	1	-30	-30	1	-1.2

● **ANDY TOMASIC** Tomasic, Andrew John b: 12/10/19, Hokendauqua, Pa. BR/TR, 6', 175 lbs. Deb: 4/28/49

YEAR	TM/L	W	L	PCT	G	GS	CG	SH	SV	IP	H	HR	BB	SO	RAT	ERA	ERA+	OAV	OOB	BH	AVG	PB	PR	/A	PD	TPI
1949	NY-N	0	1	.000	2	0	0	0	0	5	9	2	5	2	25.2	18.00	22	.375	.483	0	.000	-0	-8	-8	-0	-1.1

● **ANDY TOMBERLIN** Tomberlin, Andy Lee b: 11/7/66, Monroe, N.C. BL/TL, 5'11", 160 lbs. Deb: 8/12/93 ♦

YEAR	TM/L	W	L	PCT	G	GS	CG	SH	SV	IP	H	HR	BB	SO	RAT	ERA	ERA+	OAV	OOB	BH	AVG	PB	PR	/A	PD	TPI
1994	Bos-A	0	0	—	1	0	0	0	0	2	1	0	1	1	9.0	0.00	—	.143	.250	7	.194	1	1	1	0	0.0

● **DAVE TOMLIN** Tomlin, David Allen b: 6/22/49, Maysville, Ky. BL/TL, 6'3", 185 lbs. Deb: 9/2/72

YEAR	TM/L	W	L	PCT	G	GS	CG	SH	SV	IP	H	HR	BB	SO	RAT	ERA	ERA+	OAV	OOB	BH	AVG	PB	PR	/A	PD	TPI
1972	Cin-N	0	0	—	3	0	0	0	0	4	7	2	1	2	18.0	9.00	36	.412	.444	0	—	0	-2	-3	0	0.0
1973	*Cin-N	1	2	.333	16	0	0	0	1	27²	24	5	15	20	12.7	4.88	70	.238	.336	0	.000	-0	-4	-5	0	-0.5
1974	SD-N	2	0	1.000	47	0	0	0	2	58	59	4	30	29	14.1	4.34	82	.271	.364	0	.000	-0	-5	-5	1	-0.2
1975	SD-N	4	2	.667	67	0	0	0	1	83	87	5	31	48	13.0	3.25	107	.275	.344	1	.200	1	3	2	3	0.6
1976	SD-N	0	1	.000	49	1	0	0	0	73	62	4	20	43	10.2	2.84	115	.235	.291	0	.000	-1	5	4	2	0.2
1977	SD-N	4	4	.500	76	0	0	0	3	101²	98	3	32	55	11.7	3.01	118	.259	.320	2	.286	0	10	6	1	0.7
1978	Cin-N	9	1	.900	57	0	0	0	4	62¹	88	3	30	32	17.5	5.78	61	.326	.399	1	.200	0	-15	-15	1	-2.5
1979	*Cin-N	2	2	.500	53	0	0	0	0	58¹	59	3	18	30	12.0	2.62	142	.269	.328	1	.500	0	7	7	0	0.5
1980	Cin-N	3	0	1.000	27	0	0	0	0	26	38	2	11	6	17.0	5.54	65	.355	.415	0	—	0	-6	-6	0	-0.5
1982	Mon-N	0	0	—	1	0	0	0	0	2	1	0	1	2	9.0	4.50	81	.167	.286	0	—	0	-0	-0	0	0.0
1983	Pit-N	0	0	—	5	0	0	0	0	4	6	0	1	5	15.8	6.75	55	.316	.350	0	—	0	-1	-1	-0	0.0
1985	Pit-N	0	0	—	1	0	0	0	0	1	1	0	1	0	18.0	0.00	—	.333	.500	0	—	0	0	0	0	0.0
1986	Mon-N	0	0	—	7	0	0	0	0	10¹	13	1	7	6	18.3	5.23	71	.317	.429	0	—	0	-2	-2	0	0.0
Total	13	25	12	.676	409	1	0	0	12	511¹	543	32	198	278	13.3	3.82	92	.277	.347	5	.147	0	-9	-17	9	-1.7

● **RANDY TOMLIN** Tomlin, Randy Leon b: 6/14/66, Bainbridge, Md. BL/TL, 5'11", 179 lbs. Deb: 8/6/90

YEAR	TM/L	W	L	PCT	G	GS	CG	SH	SV	IP	H	HR	BB	SO	RAT	ERA	ERA+	OAV	OOB	BH	AVG	PB	PR	/A	PD	TPI
1990	Pit-N	4	4	.500	12	12	2	1	0	77²	62	5	12	42	8.7	2.55	142	.221	.256	1	.040	-1	11	9	1	0.9
1991	*Pit-N	8	7	.533	31	27	4	2	0	175	170	9	54	104	11.8	2.98	120	.254	.316	10	.192	1	14	11	2	1.3
1992	*Pit-N	14	9	.609	35	33	1	1	0	208²	226	11	42	90	11.8	3.41	101	.282	.322	9	.138	-0	2	1	3	0.4
1993	Pit-N	4	8	.333	18	18	1	0	0	98¹	109	11	15	44	11.8	4.85	83	.291	.327	6	.182	0	-9	-9	1	-0.8
1994	Pit-N	0	3	.000	10	4	0	0	0	20²	23	1	10	17	14.4	3.92	108	.291	.371	3	.500	1	1	1	0	0.2
Total	5	30	31	.492	106	94	8	3	0	580¹	590	37	133	297	11.5	3.43	106	.268	.314	29	.160	1	18	13	7	2.0

● **CHUCK TOMPKINS** Tompkins, Charles Herbert b: 9/1/1889, Prescott, Ark. d: 9/20/75, Prescott, Ark. BR/TR, 6', 185 lbs. Deb: 6/25/12

YEAR	TM/L	W	L	PCT	G	GS	CG	SH	SV	IP	H	HR	BB	SO	RAT	ERA	ERA+	OAV	OOB	BH	AVG	PB	PR	/A	PD	TPI
1912	Cin-N	0	0	—	1	0	0	0	0	3	5	0	0	1	15.0	0.00	—	.357	.357	1	1.000	0	1	1	-0	0.0

● **RON TOMPKINS** Tompkins, Ronald Everett "Stretch" b: 11/27/44, San Diego, Cal. BR/TR, 6'4", 198 lbs. Deb: 9/9/65

YEAR	TM/L	W	L	PCT	G	GS	CG	SH	SV	IP	H	HR	BB	SO	RAT	ERA	ERA+	OAV	OOB	BH	AVG	PB	PR	/A	PD	TPI
1965	KC-A	0	0	—	5	1	0	0	0	10¹	9	0	3	4	11.3	3.48	100	.237	.310	0	.000	-0	-0	0	0	0.0
1971	Chi-N	0	2	.000	35	0	0	0	3	39²	31	3	21	20	12.5	4.08	96	.214	.325	0	—	0	-3	-1	1	0.1
Total	2	0	2	.000	40	1	0	0	3	50	40	3	24	24	12.2	3.96	97	.219	.322	0	.000	-0	-3	-1	1	0.1

● **TOMMY TOMS** Toms, Thomas Howard b: 10/15/51, Charlottesville, Va BR/TR, 6'4", 195 lbs. Deb: 5/4/75

YEAR	TM/L	W	L	PCT	G	GS	CG	SH	SV	IP	H	HR	BB	SO	RAT	ERA	ERA+	OAV	OOB	BH	AVG	PB	PR	/A	PD	TPI
1975	SF-N	0	1	.000	7	0	0	0	0	10¹	13	1	6	6	16.5	6.10	62	.317	.404	0	—	0	-3	-3	-0	-0.2
1976	SF-N	0	1	.000	7	0	0	0	1	8²	13	1	4	4	14.5	6.23	58	.351	.368	0	—	0	-3	-3	-0	-0.3
1977	SF-N	0	1	.000	4	0	0	0	0	4¹	7	0	2	2	18.7	2.08	188	.333	.391	0	—	0	1	1	-0	0.2
Total	3	0	3	.000	18	0	0	0	1	23¹	33	2	9	12	16.2	5.40	70	.333	.389	0	—	0	-5	-4	-0	-0.3

● **FRED TONEY** Toney, Fred Alexandra b: 12/11/1888, Nashville, Tenn. d: 3/11/53, Nashville, Tenn. BR/TR, 6'1", 195 lbs. Deb: 4/15/11

YEAR	TM/L	W	L	PCT	G	GS	CG	SH	SV	IP	H	HR	BB	SO	RAT	ERA	ERA+	OAV	OOB	BH	AVG	PB	PR	/A	PD	TPI
1911	Chi-N	1	1	.500	18	4	1	0	0	67	55	2	35	27	12.8	2.42	137	.229	.339	2	.111	-1	7	7	1	0.1
1912	Chi-N	1	2	.333	9	2	0	0	0	24	21	0	11	9	12.4	5.25	63	.247	.340	0	.000	-0	-5	-5	-1	-0.6
1913	Chi-N	2	2	.500	7	5	2	0	0	39	52	1	22	12	17.3	6.00	53	.327	.412	3	.250	1	-12	-12	0	-1.0
1915	Cin-N	17	6	.739	36	23	18	6	2	222²	160	3	73	108	9.5	1.58	181	.207	.278	7	.095	-5	29	32	3	3.1
1916	Cin-N	14	17	.452	41	38	21	3	1	300	247	6	78	146	10.0	2.28	114	.231	.288	12	.121	-4	11	11	-4	0.2
1917	Cin-N	24	16	.600	43	42	31	7	1	339²	300	4	77	123	10.1	2.20	119	.238	.286	13	.112	-6	19	16	-5	0.7
1918	Cin-N	6	10	.375	21	19	9	1	1	136²	148	2	31	32	11.8	2.90	92	.282	.322	9	.214	-0	-2	-3	-1	-0.3
	NY-N	6	2	.750	11	9	7	1	1	85¹	55	1	7	19	6.8	1.69	156	.192	.216	6	.188	-1	10	9	-1	0.7
	Yr	12	12	.500	32	28	16	2	**3**	222	203	3	38	51	9.9	2.43	109	.250	.285	15	.203	-0	8	5	0	0.4
1919	NY-N	13	6	.684	24	20	14	4	1	181	157	6	35	40	9.6	1.84	152	.235	.276	15	.227	1	22	19	-3	1.9
1920	NY-N	21	11	.656	42	37	17	4	1	278¹	266	8	57	81	10.6	2.65	113	.259	.302	23	.240	3	15	11	-2	1.2
1921	*NY-N	18	11	.621	42	32	16	1	3	249¹	274	14	65	63	12.4	3.61	102	.289	.338	18	.209	2	5	2	-1	0.3
1922	NY-N	5	6	.455	13	12	6	0	0	86¹	91	5	31	10	12.9	4.17	96	.277	.343	2	.067	-3	-1	-2	-2	-0.6
1923	StL-N	11	12	.478	29	28	16	1	0	196²	211	6	61	48	12.7	3.84	102	.282	.341	8	.116	-5	3	1	3	0.0
Total	12	139	102	.577	336	271	158	28	12	2206	2037	59	583	718	10.9	2.69	113	.251	.305	118	.159	-18	102	85	-12	5.7

● **DOC TONKIN** Tonkin, Harry Glenville b: 8/11/1881, Concord, N.H. d: 5/30/59, Miami, Fla. BL/TL, 5'9", 165 lbs. Deb: 8/19/07

YEAR	TM/L	W	L	PCT	G	GS	CG	SH	SV	IP	H	HR	BB	SO	RAT	ERA	ERA+	OAV	OOB	BH	AVG	PB	PR	/A	PD	TPI
1907	Was-A	0	0	—	1	0	0	0	0	2²	6	0	5	0	37.1	6.75	36	.444	.594	2	1.000	1	-1	-1	0	0.1

● **STEVE TOOLE** Toole, Stephen John b: 4/9/1859, New Orleans, La. d: 3/28/19, Pittsburgh, Pa. BR/TL, 6', 170 lbs. Deb: 4/20/1886 U

YEAR	TM/L	W	L	PCT	G	GS	CG	SH	SV	IP	H	HR	BB	SO	RAT	ERA	ERA+	OAV	OOB	BH	AVG	PB	PR	/A	PD	TPI
1886	Bro-a	6	6	.500	13	12	11	0	0	104	100	1	64	48	14.9	4.41	79	.246	.359	20	.351	4	-11	-11	2	-0.5
1887	Bro-a	14	10	.583	24	24	22	1	0	194	186	1	106	48	14.1	4.31	100	.254	.358	24	.233	-1	-0	-0	-1	-0.2
1888	KC-a	5	6	.455	12	10	10	0	0	91²	124	4	50	35	17.6	6.68	51	.312	.396	10	.208	-0	-37	-33	0	-2.9
1890	Bro-a	2	4	.333	6	6	6	0	0	53¹	47	0	39	10	15.2	4.05	96	.229	.363	6	.300	2	-1	-1	0	0.1
Total	4	27	26	.509	55	52	49	1	0	443	457	5	259	141	15.1	4.79	81	.262	.367	60	.263	5	-49	-44	2	-3.5

● **RUPE TOPPIN** Toppin, Ruperto b: 12/7/41, Panama City, Panama BR/TR, 6', 185 lbs. Deb: 7/28/62

YEAR	TM/L	W	L	PCT	G	GS	CG	SH	SV	IP	H	HR	BB	SO	RAT	ERA	ERA+	OAV	OOB	BH	AVG	PB	PR	/A	PD	TPI
1962	KC-A	0	0	—	2	0	0	0	0	2	1	0	5	1	27.0	13.50	31	.167	.545	1	1.000	0	-2	-2	-0	0.0

● **RED TORKELSON** Torkelson, Chester Leroy b: 3/19/1894, Chicago, Ill. d: 9/22/64, Chicago, Ill. BR/TR, 6', 175 lbs. Deb: 8/29/17

YEAR	TM/L	W	L	PCT	G	GS	CG	SH	SV	IP	H	HR	BB	SO	RAT	ERA	ERA+	OAV	OOB	BH	AVG	PB	PR	/A	PD	TPI
1917	Cle-A	2	1	.667	4	3	0	0	0	22¹	33	1	13	10	19.3	7.66	37	.333	.421	2	.222	-0	-12	-12	0	-1.3

● **PABLO TORREALBA** Torrealba, Pablo Arnoldo (Torrealba) b: 4/28/48, Barquisimeto, Ven. BL/TL, 5'9", 175 lbs. Deb: 4/9/75

YEAR	TM/L	W	L	PCT	G	GS	CG	SH	SV	IP	H	HR	BB	SO	RAT	ERA	ERA+	OAV	OOB	BH	AVG	PB	PR	/A	PD	TPI
1975	Atl-N	0	1	.000	6	0	0	0	0	6²	7	0	3	5	13.5	1.35	279	.250	.323	1	1.000	0	2	2	1	0.4
1976	Atl-N	0	0	—	36	0	0	0	0	53	67	0	22	33	15.6	3.57	106	.315	.387	0	-0	1	1	1	0.0
1977	Oak-A	4	6	.400	41	10	3	0	2	116²	127	5	38	51	12.9	2.62	153	.279	.337	0	—	-0	19	18	2	1.7
1978	Chi-A	2	4	.333	25	3	1	1	1	57¹	69	6	39	23	17.4	4.71	81	.301	.410	0	—	0	-6	-6	-1	-0.8
1979	Chi-A	0	0	—	3	0	0	0	0	5²	5	1	2	1	11.1	1.59	268	.250	.318	0	—	0	2	2	0	0.0
Total	5	6	13	.316	111	13	4	1	5	239¹	275	12	104	113	14.6	3.27	120	.291	.366	1	.200	0	16	17	2	1.4

● **ANGEL TORRES** Torres, Angel Rafael (Ruiz) b: 10/24/52, Las Ciengas, Azua, D.R. BL/TL, 5'11", 168 lbs. Deb: 9/12/77

YEAR	TM/L	W	L	PCT	G	GS	CG	SH	SV	IP	H	HR	BB	SO	RAT	ERA	ERA+	OAV	OOB	BH	AVG	PB	PR	/A	PD	TPI
1977	Cin-N	0	0	—	5	0	0	0	0	8	7	2	8	4	16.2	2.16	187	.233	.395	0	—	—	2	2	0	0.0

● **GIL TORRES** Torres, Don Gilberto (Nunez) b: 8/23/15, Regla, Cuba d: 1/10/83, Regla, Cuba BR/TR, 6', 155 lbs. Deb: 4/25/40 F♦

YEAR	TM/L	W	L	PCT	G	GS	CG	SH	SV	IP	H	HR	BB	SO	RAT	ERA	ERA+	OAV	OOB	BH	AVG	PB	PR	/A	PD	TPI
1940	Was-A	0	0	—	2	0	0	0	0	2²	3	0	0	1	10.1	0.00	—	.273	.273	0	—	0	1	1	0	0.0

YEAR	TM/L	W	L	PCT	G	GS	CG	SH	SV	IP	H	HR	BB	SO	RAT	ERA	ERA+	OAV	OOB	BH	AVG	PB	PR	/A	PD	TPI
1946	Was-A	0	0	—	3	0	0	0	1	7	9	0	3	2	15.4	7.71	43	.310	.375	47	.254	1	-3	-3	-0	-0.1
Total	2	0	0	—	5	0	0	0	1	9²	12	0	3	3	14.0	5.59	64	.300	.349	320	.252	1	-2	-2	-0	-0.1

● **HECTOR TORRES**   Torres, Hector Epitacio (Marroquin) b: 9/16/45, Monterrey, Mexico   BR/TR, 6', 175 lbs.   Deb: 4/10/68   C ♦

YEAR	TM/L	W	L	PCT	G	GS	CG	SH	SV	IP	H	HR	BB	SO	RAT	ERA	ERA+	OAV	OOB	BH	AVG	PB	PR	/A	PD	TPI
1972	Mon-N	0	0	—	1	0	0	0	0	0²	5	0	0	0	67.5	27.00	13	.714	.714	28	.155	0	-2	-2	0	0.0

● **SALOMON TORRES**   Torres, Salomon (Ramirez) b: 3/11/72, San Pedro De Macoris, D.R.   BR/TR, 5'11", 150 lbs.   Deb: 8/29/93

YEAR	TM/L	W	L	PCT	G	GS	CG	SH	SV	IP	H	HR	BB	SO	RAT	ERA	ERA+	OAV	OOB	BH	AVG	PB	PR	/A	PD	TPI
1993	SF-N	3	5	.375	8	8	0	0	0	44²	37	5	27	23	13.1	4.03	97	.231	.346	3	.231	0	0	-1	1	0.0
1994	SF-N	2	8	.200	16	14	1	0	0	84¹	95	10	34	42	14.5	5.44	74	.292	.372	4	.154	-0	-12	-13	-2	-1.5
Total	2	5	13	.278	24	22	1	0	0	129	132	15	61	65	14.0	4.95	80	.272	.363	7	.179	-0	-11	-14	-1	-1.5

● **MIKE TORREZ**   Torrez, Michael Augustine b: 8/28/46, Topeka, Kan.   BR/TR, 6'5", 220 lbs.   Deb: 9/10/67

YEAR	TM/L	W	L	PCT	G	GS	CG	SH	SV	IP	H	HR	BB	SO	RAT	ERA	ERA+	OAV	OOB	BH	AVG	PB	PR	/A	PD	TPI
1967	StL-N	0	1	.000	3	1	0	0	0	5²	5	0	1	5	11.1	3.18	103	.238	.304	0	.000	0	0	0	-0	0.0
1968	StL-N	2	1	.667	5	2	0	0	0	19¹	20	1	12	6	15.4	2.79	104	.286	.398	2	.286	0	0	0	0	0.1
1969	StL-N	10	4	.714	24	15	3	0	0	107²	96	7	62	61	13.5	3.59	99	.240	.346	3	.073	-2	-0	-0	0	-0.2
1970	StL-N	8	10	.444	30	28	5	1	0	179¹	168	12	103	100	13.8	4.22	98	.248	.350	17	.270	4	-3	-2	-0	0.2
1971	StL-N	1	2	.333	9	6	0	0	0	36	41	2	30	8	18.0	6.00	60	.304	.434	1	.143	1	-10	-10	0	-0.6
	Mon-N	0	0	—	1	0	0	0	0	3	4	0	1	2	15.0	0.00	—	.308	.357	0	—	0	1	1	0	0.0
	Yr	1	2	.333	10	6	0	0	0	39	45	2	31	10	17.5	5.54	65	.300	.420	1	.143	1	-9	-8	1	-0.6
1972	Mon-N	16	12	.571	34	33	13	0	0	243¹	215	15	103	112	12.0	3.33	107	.242	.325	15	.176	0	3	6	2	1.0
1973	Mon-N	9	12	.429	35	34	8	3	1	208	207	17	115	90	14.1	4.46	86	.262	.359	12	.174	-1	-18	-15	2	-1.3
1974	Mon-N	15	8	.652	32	30	6	1	0	186¹	184	10	84	92	13.1	3.57	107	.257	.337	8	.125	-3	1	5	5	0.8
1975	Bal-A	20	9	**.690**	36	36	16	2	0	270²	238	15	133	119	12.5	3.06	115	.239	.332	0	—	0	22	14	1	1.4
1976	Oak-A	16	12	.571	39	39	13	4	0	266²	231	15	87	115	10.9	2.50	134	.235	.301	0	—	0	30	25	-1	2.7
1977	Oak-A	3	1	.750	4	4	2	0	0	26¹	23	3	11	12	12.0	4.44	91	.242	.327	0	—	0	-1	-1	-0	-0.2
	*NY-A	14	12	.538	31	31	15	2	0	217	212	20	75	90	12.2	3.82	103	.259	.326	0	—	0	6	3	-2	0.1
	Yr	17	13	.567	35	35	17	2	0	243¹	235	23	86	102	12.1	3.88	102	.256	.324	0	—	0	5	2	-2	-0.1
1978	Bos-A	16	13	.552	36	36	15	2	0	250	272	19	99	120	13.5	3.96	104	.281	.349	0	—	0	-6	4	-2	0.2
1979	Bos-A	16	13	.552	36	36	12	1	0	252¹	254	20	121	125	13.6	4.49	98	.264	.349	0	—	0	-8	-2	-0	-0.4
1980	Bos-A	9	16	.360	36	32	6	1	0	207¹	256	18	75	97	14.4	5.08	83	.313	.371	0	—	0	-24	-20	2	-2.0
1981	Bos-A	10	3	.769	22	22	2	0	0	127¹	130	10	51	54	12.8	3.68	105	.267	.337	0	—	0	-0	3	-1	0.1
1982	Bos-A	9	9	.500	31	31	1	0	0	175²	196	20	74	84	14.1	5.23	82	.282	.356	0	—	0	-22	-18	-2	-1.9
1983	NY-N	10	17	.370	39	34	5	0	0	222¹	227	16	113	104	13.8	4.37	83	.271	.358	3	.046	-5	-18	-18	-0	-2.5
1984	NY-N	1	5	.167	9	8	0	0	0	37²	55	3	18	16	17.9	5.02	70	.369	.444	3	.300	1	-6	-6	0	-0.8
	Oak-A	0	0	—	2	0	0	0	0	2¹	9	0	3	2	46.3	27.00	14	.563	.632	0	—	0	-6	-6	-0	0.3
Total	18	185	160	.536	494	458	117	15	0	3044	3043	223	1371	1404	13.2	3.96	97	.264	.345	64	.155	-4	-60	-38	3	-3.0

● **LOU TOST**   Tost, Louis Eugene b: 6/1/11, Cumberland, Wash.   d: 2/22/67, Santa Clara, Cal.   BL/TL, 6', 175 lbs.   Deb: 4/20/42

YEAR	TM/L	W	L	PCT	G	GS	CG	SH	SV	IP	H	HR	BB	SO	RAT	ERA	ERA+	OAV	OOB	BH	AVG	PB	PR	/A	PD	TPI
1942	Bos-N	10	10	.500	35	22	5	1	0	147²	146	12	52	43	12.3	3.53	94	.256	.322	9	.176	0	-4	-3	-1	-0.5
1943	Bos-N	0	1	.000	3	1	0	0	0	6²	10	2	4	3	18.9	5.40	63	.357	.438	0	.000	-0	-1	-1	0	-0.2
1947	Pit-N	0	0	—	1	0	0	0	0	1	3	0	0	0	27.0	9.00	47	.600	.600	0	—	-0	-1	-1	0	0.0
Total	3	10	11	.476	39	23	5	1	0	155¹	159	14	56	46	12.7	3.65	92	.263	.330	9	.173	-0	-6	-5	-1	-0.7

● **PAUL TOTH**   Toth, Paul Louis b: 6/30/35, McRoberts, Ky.   BR/TR, 6'1", 175 lbs.   Deb: 4/22/62

YEAR	TM/L	W	L	PCT	G	GS	CG	SH	SV	IP	H	HR	BB	SO	RAT	ERA	ERA+	OAV	OOB	BH	AVG	PB	PR	/A	PD	TPI
1962	StL-N	1	0	1.000	6	1	0	0	0	16²	18	1	4	5	11.9	5.40	79	.295	.338	2	.400	0	-3	-2	-0	-0.1
	Chi-N	3	1	.750	6	4	1	0	0	34	29	2	10	11	10.9	4.24	98	.240	.308	2	.182	0	-1	-0	-0	-0.1
	Yr	4	1	.800	12	5	2	0	0	50²	47	3	14	16	11.2	4.62	91	.257	.317	4	.250	1	-4	-2	-1	-0.2
1963	Chi-N	5	9	.357	27	14	3	2	0	130²	115	9	35	66	10.5	3.10	113	.240	.294	1	.026	-3	3	6	-1	0.2
1964	Chi-N	0	2	.000	4	2	0	0	0	10²	15	2	5	0	16.9	8.44	44	.341	.408	1	.333	0	-6	-6	1	-0.8
Total	3	9	12	.429	43	21	5	2	0	192	177	14	54	82	11.0	3.80	97	.251	.326	6	.103	-2	-7	-2	-1	-0.8

● **CLAY TOUCHSTONE**   Touchstone, Clayland Maffitt b: 1/24/03, Moore, Pa.   d: 4/28/49, Beaumont, Tex.   BR/TR, 5'9", 175 lbs.   Deb: 9/4/28

YEAR	TM/L	W	L	PCT	G	GS	CG	SH	SV	IP	H	HR	BB	SO	RAT	ERA	ERA+	OAV	OOB	BH	AVG	PB	PR	/A	PD	TPI
1928	Bos-N	0	0	—	5	0	0	0	0	8	15	0	2	1	20.3	4.50	87	.417	.462	0	.000	-0	-1	-1	0	0.0
1929	Bos-N	0	0	—	1	0	0	0	0	2²	6	1	0	1	20.3	16.88	28	.429	.429	1	1.000	0	-4	-4	0	0.0
1945	Chi-A	0	0	—	6	0	0	0	0	10	14	1	6	4	18.9	5.40	61	.311	.404	0	.000	-0	-2	-2	0	0.0
Total	3	0	0	—	12	0	0	0	0	20²	35	2	8	6	19.6	6.53	57	.368	.429	1	.250	-0	-6	-6	0	0.0

● **CESAR TOVAR**   Tovar, Cesar Leonardo "Pepito" (b: Cesar Leonard Perez (Tovar))
b: 7/3/40, Caracas, Venez.   d: 7/14/94, Caracas, Venez.   BR/TR, 5'9", 155 lbs.   Deb: 4/12/65   ♦

YEAR	TM/L	W	L	PCT	G	GS	CG	SH	SV	IP	H	HR	BB	SO	RAT	ERA	ERA+	OAV	OOB	BH	AVG	PB	PR	/A	PD	TPI
1968	Min-A	0	0	—	1	1	0	0	0	1	0	0	1	1	9.0	0.00	—	.000	.250	167	.272	0	0	0	0	0.0

● **IRA TOWNSEND**   Townsend, Ira Dance "Pat" b: 1/9/1894, Weimar, Tex.   d: 7/21/65, Schulenberg, Tex.   BR/TR, 6'1", 180 lbs.   Deb: 8/25/20

YEAR	TM/L	W	L	PCT	G	GS	CG	SH	SV	IP	H	HR	BB	SO	RAT	ERA	ERA+	OAV	OOB	BH	AVG	PB	PR	/A	PD	TPI
1920	Bos-N	0	0	—	4	1	0	0	0	6²	10	0	2	1	17.6	1.35	226	.370	.433	0	.000	-0	1	1	-0	0.0
1921	Bos-N	0	0	—	4	0	0	0	0	7¹	11	1	4	0	20.9	6.14	59	.344	.447	0	.000	-0	-2	-2	0	0.0
Total	2	0	0	—	8	1	0	0	0	14	21	1	6	1	19.3	3.86	87	.356	.441	0	.000	-1	-1	-1	-0	0.0

● **HAPPY TOWNSEND**   Townsend, John b: 4/9/1879, Townsend, Del.   d: 12/21/63, Wilmington, Del.   BR/TR, 6', 190 lbs.   Deb: 4/19/01

YEAR	TM/L	W	L	PCT	G	GS	CG	SH	SV	IP	H	HR	BB	SO	RAT	ERA	ERA+	OAV	OOB	BH	AVG	PB	PR	/A	PD	TPI
1901	Phi-N	9	6	.600	19	16	14	2	0	143²	118	3	64	72	11.7	3.45	99	**.223**	.312	7	.109	-4	-2	-1	-2	-0.7
1902	Was-A	9	16	.360	27	26	22	0	0	220	233	12	89	71	13.7	4.45	80	.272	.349	23	.264	3	-21	-18	-1	-1.5
1903	Was-A	2	11	.154	20	13	10	0	0	126²	145	3	48	54	14.4	4.76	66	.286	.359	2	.045	-4	-25	-23	-0	-2.4
1904	Was-A	5	26	.161	36	34	31	2	0	291¹	319	3	100	143	13.2	3.58	74	.279	.342	20	.168	-2	-32	-30	-1	-3.3
1905	Was-A	7	16	.304	34	24	22	0	0	263	247	2	84	102	11.8	2.63	101	.250	.318	15	.181	1	1	1	-3	-0.1
1906	Cle-A	3	7	.300	17	12	8	1	0	92²	92	1	31	31	12.5	2.91	90	.262	.332	4	.133	-1	-2	-3	-0	-0.5
Total	6	35	82	.299	153	125	107	5	0	1137²	1154	24	416	473	12.9	3.59	84	.264	.335	71	.166	-8	-82	-75	-7	-8.5

● **LEO TOWNSEND**   Townsend, Leo Alphonse "Lefty" b: 1/15/1891, Mobile, Ala.   d: 12/3/76, Mobile, Ala.   BL/TL, 5'10", 160 lbs.   Deb: 9/8/20

YEAR	TM/L	W	L	PCT	G	GS	CG	SH	SV	IP	H	HR	BB	SO	RAT	ERA	ERA+	OAV	OOB	BH	AVG	PB	PR	/A	PD	TPI
1920	Bos-N	2	2	.500	7	1	1	0	0	24¹	18	1	2	0	7.4	1.48	206	.220	.238	1	.167	0	4	4	0	0.7
1921	Bos-N	0	1	.000	1	1	0	0	0	1¹	2	0	3	0	33.8	27.00	14	.400	.625	0	—	0	-3	-3	0	-1.2
Total	2	2	3	.400	8	2	1	0	0	25²	20	1	5	0	8.8	2.81	110	.230	.272	1	.167	0	1	1	0	-0.5

● **BILL TOZER**   Tozer, William Louis b: 7/3/1882, St.Louis, Mo.   d: 2/23/55, Belmont, Cal.   BR/TR, 6', 200 lbs.   Deb: 4/16/08

YEAR	TM/L	W	L	PCT	G	GS	CG	SH	SV	IP	H	HR	BB	SO	RAT	ERA	ERA+	OAV	OOB	BH	AVG	PB	PR	/A	PD	TPI
1908	Cin-N	0	0	—	4	0	0	0	0	10²	11	0	4	5	13.5	1.69	137	.268	.348	0	.000	-0	1	1	-0	0.0

● **STEVE TRACHSEL**   Trachsel, Stephen Christopher b: 10/31/70, Oxnard, Cal.   BR/TR, 6'3", 185 lbs.   Deb: 9/19/93

YEAR	TM/L	W	L	PCT	G	GS	CG	SH	SV	IP	H	HR	BB	SO	RAT	ERA	ERA+	OAV	OOB	BH	AVG	PB	PR	/A	PD	TPI
1993	Chi-N	0	2	.000	3	3	0	0	0	19²	16	4	3	14	8.7	4.58	87	.219	.250	1	.167	0	-1	-1	0	0.0
1994	Chi-N	9	7	.563	22	22	1	0	0	146	133	19	54	108	11.7	3.21	128	.242	.314	8	.186	1	16	15	2	1.7
Total	2	9	9	.500	25	25	1	0	0	165²	149	23	57	122	11.4	3.37	122	.240	.306	9	.184	1	15	13	3	1.7

● **FRED TRAUTMAN**   Trautman, Frederick Orlando b: 3/24/1892, Bucyrus, Ohio   d: 2/15/64, Bucyrus, Ohio   BR/TR, 6'1", 175 lbs.   Deb: 4/27/15

YEAR	TM/L	W	L	PCT	G	GS	CG	SH	SV	IP	H	HR	BB	SO	RAT	ERA	ERA+	OAV	OOB	BH	AVG	PB	PR	/A	PD	TPI
1915	New-F	0	0	—	1	0	0	0	0	3	4	0	1	2	18.0	6.00	43	.364	.462	0	.000	-0	-1	-1	-0	0.0

● **JOHN TRAUTWEIN**   Trautwein, John Howard b: 8/7/62, Lafayette Hill, Pa.   BR/TR, 6'3", 205 lbs.   Deb: 4/7/88

YEAR	TM/L	W	L	PCT	G	GS	CG	SH	SV	IP	H	HR	BB	SO	RAT	ERA	ERA+	OAV	OOB	BH	AVG	PB	PR	/A	PD	TPI
1988	Bos-A	0	1	.000	9	0	0	0	0	16	26	2	9	8	20.3	9.00	46	.382	.462	0	—	0	-9	-9	0	-0.7

● **ALLAN TRAVERS**   Travers, Aloysius Joseph "Joe" b: 5/7/1892, Philadelphia, Pa.   d: 4/19/68, Philadelphia, Pa.   BR/TR, 6'1", 180 lbs.   Deb: 5/18/12

YEAR	TM/L	W	L	PCT	G	GS	CG	SH	SV	IP	H	HR	BB	SO	RAT	ERA	ERA+	OAV	OOB	BH	AVG	PB	PR	/A	PD	TPI
1912	Det-A	0	1	.000	1	1	1	0	0	8	26	0	7	1	37.1	15.75	21	.605	.660	0	.000	-0	-11	-11	1	-0.8

YEAR TM/L	W	L	PCT	G	GS	CG	SH	SV	IP	H	HR	BB	SO	RAT	ERA	ERA+	OAV	OOB	BH	AVG	PB	PR	/A	PD	TPI
● **BILL TRAVERS**			Travers, William Edward	b: 10/27/52, Norwood, Mass.					BL/TL, 6'6", 200 lbs.		Deb: 5/19/74														
1974 Mil-A	2	3	.400	23	1	0	0	0	53	59	4	30	31	15.3	4.92	73	.296	.391	0	—	0	-8	-8	0	-0.6
1975 Mil-A	6	11	.353	28	23	5	0	1	136¹	130	15	60	57	13.3	4.29	89	.251	.342	0	—	0	-8	-7	-1	-0.9
1976 Mil-A☆	15	16	.484	34	34	15	3	0	240	211	21	95	120	11.8	2.81	124	.237	.316	0	—	0	19	18	-1	2.3
1977 Mil-A	4	12	.250	19	19	2	1	0	121²	140	13	57	49	15.1	5.25	77	.291	.374	0	—	0	-16	-16	0	-1.8
1978 Mil-A	12	11	.522	28	28	8	3	0	175²	184	20	58	66	12.7	4.41	85	.268	.331	0	—	0	-13	-13	1	-1.4
1979 Mil-A	14	8	.636	30	27	9	2	0	187¹	196	33	45	74	11.7	3.89	107	.270	.315	0	—	0	7	6	-2	0.4
1980 Mil-A	12	6	.667	29	25	7	1	0	154²	147	20	47	62	11.7	3.91	99	.249	.311	0	—	0	2	-1	-1	0.1
1981 Cal-A	0	1	.000	4	4	0	0	0	9²	14	2	4	5	16.8	8.38	44	.333	.391	0	—	0	-5	-5	-0	-0.5
1983 Cal-A	0	3	.000	10	7	0	0	0	42²	58	4	19	24	16.7	5.91	68	.331	.403	0	—	0	-9	-9	0	-0.5
Total 9	65	71	.478	205	168	46	10	1	1120²	1139	134	415	488	12.6	4.10	93	.264	.335	0	—	0	-30	-34	-3	-2.9
● **HARRY TREKELL**			Trekell, Harry Roy	b: 11/18/1892, Breda, Ill.		d: 11/4/65, Spokane, Wash.			BR/TR, 6'1.5", 170 lbs.		Deb: 8/16/13														
1913 StL-N	0	1	.000	7	1	1	0	0	30	25	2	8	15	10.5	4.50	72	.221	.285	1	.111	-0	-4	-4	-0	-0.2
● **BILL TREMEL**			Tremel, William Leonard "Mumbles"	b: 7/4/29, Lilly, Pa.		5'11", 180 lbs.		Deb: 6/12/54																	
1954 Chi-N	1	2	.333	17	0	0	0	4	51¹	45	3	28	21	12.8	4.21	100	.243	.343	2	.250	0	-1	-0	-1	-0.1
1955 Chi-N	3	0	1.000	23	0	0	0	0	38²	33	2	18	13	11.9	3.72	110	.239	.327	2	.286	0	1	2	-1	0.1
1956 Chi-N	0	0	—	1	0	0	0	0	1	3	0	0	0	27.0	9.00	42	.600	.600	0	—	0	-1	-1	-0	0.0
Total 3	4	2	.667	57	0	0	0	6	91	81	5	46	34	12.6	4.05	102	.247	.340	4	.267	0	-0	1	-2	0.0
● **BOB TRICE**			Trice, Robert Lee	b: 8/28/26, Newton, Ga.		d: 9/16/88, Weirton, W.Va.			BR/TR, 6'3", 190 lbs.		Deb: 9/13/53														
1953 Phi-A	2	1	.667	3	3	1	0	0	23	25	4	6	4	12.1	5.48	78	.275	.320	1	.143	0	-4	-3	1	-0.2
1954 Phi-A	7	8	.467	19	18	8	1	0	119	146	14	48	22	14.7	5.60	70	.305	.369	12	.286	4	-25	-22	0	-2.0
1955 KC-A	0	0	—	4	0	0	0	0	10	14	4	6	2	18.0	9.00	46	.326	.408	2	.667	1	-6	-5	1	0.1
Total 3	9	9	.500	26	21	9	1	0	152	185	22	60	28	14.5	5.80	69	.302	.365	15	.288	5	-34	-31	2	-2.1
● **JOE TRIMBLE**			Trimble, Joseph Gerard	b: 10/12/30, Providence, R.I.		BR/TR, 6'1", 190 lbs.		Deb: 4/29/55																	
1955 Bos-A	0	0	—	2	0	0	0	0	2	0	3	1	13.5	0.00	—	.000	.375	0	—	0	1	1	0	0.0
1957 Pit-N	0	2	.000	5	4	0	0	0	19²	23	7	13	9	16.9	8.24	46	.291	.398	1	.143	-0	-10	-10	0	-0.8
Total 2	0	2	.000	7	4	0	0	0	21²	23	7	16	10	16.6	7.48	51	.274	.396	1	.143	-0	-9	-9	0	-0.8
● **KEN TRINKLE**			Trinkle, Kenneth Wayne	b: 12/15/19, Paoli, Ind.		d: 5/10/76, Paoli, Ind.			BR/TR, 6'1.5", 175 lbs.		Deb: 4/25/43														
1943 NY-N	1	5	.167	11	6	1	0	0	45²	51	3	15	10	13.2	3.74	92	.276	.333	3	.250	1	-2	-2	1	0.0
1946 NY-N	7	14	.333	**48**	13	2	0	2	151	146	8	74	49	13.2	3.87	89	.253	.340	3	.079	-2	-8	-7	-0	-1.2
1947 NY-N	8	4	.667	**62**	0	0	0	10	93²	100	3	48	37	14.3	3.75	109	.278	.364	3	.188	0	3	3	2	0.6
1948 NY-N	4	5	.444	53	0	0	0	7	70²	66	6	41	20	14.0	3.18	124	.244	.350	2	.250	-0	6	6	1	1.0
1949 Phi-N	1	1	.500	42	0	0	0	2	74¹	79	3	30	14	13.6	4.00	99	.299	.377	0	.000	-0	0	-0	1	0.1
Total 5	21	29	.420	216	19	3	0	21	435¹	442	23	208	130	13.6	3.74	100	.267	.352	11	.138	-2	0	0	6	0.5
● **RICKY TRLICEK**			Trlicek, Richard Alan	b: 4/26/69, Houston, Tex.		BR/TR, 6'3", 200 lbs.		Deb: 4/8/92																	
1992 Tor-A	0	0	—	2	0	0	0	0	1²	2	0	2	1	21.6	10.80	38	.286	.444	0	—	0	-1	-1	-0	-0.1
1993 LA-N	1	2	.333	41	0	0	0	1	64	59	3	21	41	11.6	4.08	94	.244	.309	1	.250	0	-0	-2	1	-0.0
1994 Bos-A	1	1	.500	12	1	0	0	0	22¹	32	5	16	7	19.3	8.06	64	.330	.425	0	—	0	-8	-7	0	-0.8
Total 3	2	3	.400	55	1	0	0	1	88	93	8	39	49	13.7	5.22	79	.269	.346	1	.250	0	-10	-11	1	-0.9
● **RICH TROEDSON**			Troedson, Richard La Monte	b: 5/1/50, Palo Alto, Cal.		BL/TL, 6'1", 170 lbs.		Deb: 4/9/73																	
1973 SD-N	7	9	.438	50	18	2	0	1	152¹	167	12	59	81	13.4	4.25	82	.284	.351	7	.175	0	-10	-13	2	-1.1
1974 SD-N	1	1	.500	15	1	0	0	1	18²	24	6	8	11	15.9	8.68	41	.300	.371	0	.000	-0	-10	-11	-0	-1.1
Total 2	8	10	.444	65	19	2	0	2	171	191	18	67	92	13.7	4.74	73	.286	.353	7	.171	0	-21	-24	2	-2.2
● **MIKE TROMBLEY**			Trombley, Michael Scott	b: 4/14/67, Springfield, Mass.		BR/TR, 6'2", 200 lbs.		Deb: 8/19/92																	
1992 Min-A	3	2	.600	10	7	0	0	0	46¹	43	5	17	38	11.8	3.30	123	.247	.318	0	—	0	3	4	0	0.3
1993 Min-A	6	6	.500	44	10	0	0	2	114¹	131	15	41	85	13.8	4.88	89	.290	.353	0	—	0	-7	-7	1	-0.5
1994 Min-A	2	0	1.000	24	0	0	0	0	48¹	56	10	18	32	14.3	6.33	77	.287	.356	0	—	0	-8	-8	0	-0.3
Total 3	11	8	.579	78	17	0	0	2	209	230	30	76	155	13.5	4.87	91	.280	.346	0	—	0	-12	-11	1	-0.5
● **HAL TROSKY**			Trosky, Harold Arthur Jr. "Hoot" (b: Harold Arthur Troyavesky Jr.)	b: 9/29/36, Cleveland, Ohio		BR/TR, 6'3", 205 lbs.		Deb: 9/25/58 F																
1958 Chi-A	1	0	1.000	2	0	0	0	0	3	5	0	2	1	21.0	6.00	61	.385	.467	0	—	0	-1	-1	0	-0.2
● **BILL TROTTER**			Trotter, William Felix	b: 8/10/08, Cisne, Ill.		d: 8/26/84, Arlington, Mass.			BR/TR, 6'2", 195 lbs.		Deb: 4/23/37														
1937 StL-A	2	9	.182	34	12	4	0	0	122¹	150	14	50	37	15.2	5.81	83	.304	.376	1	.030	-3	-16	-13	-2	-1.4
1938 StL-A	0	1	.000	1	1	1	0	0	8	8	0	0	1	9.0	5.63	88	.242	.242	0	.000	-0	-1	-1	1	0.0
1939 StL-A	6	13	.316	41	13	4	0	0	156²	205	16	54	61	15.2	5.34	91	.316	.378	4	.108	-1	-13	-8	1	-0.8
1940 StL-A	7	6	.538	36	4	1	0	2	98	117	5	31	29	13.7	3.77	122	.300	.353	1	.045	-2	7	**9**	1	0.2
1941 StL-A	4	2	.667	29	0	0	0	0	49²	68	2	19	17	16.1	5.98	72	.332	.394	0	.000	-1	-10	-9	1	-1.0
1942 StL-A	0	1	.000	3	0	0	0	0	2	5	0	2	0	31.5	18.00	21	.385	.467	0	—	0	-3	-3	0	-1.2
Was-A	3	1	.750	17	0	0	0	0	40²	52	4	14	13	14.6	5.75	63	.304	.357	0	.000	-0	-9	-9	-0	-0.8
Yr	3	2	.600	20	0	0	0	0	42²	57	4	16	13	15.4	6.33	58	.310	.365	0	.000	-0	-13	-13	1	-2.0
1944 StL-N	0	1	.000	2	1	0	0	0	6	14	5	4	0	27.0	13.50	26	.467	.529	0	.000	-0	-7	-7	0	-0.8
Total 7	22	34	.393	163	31	9	0	3	483¹	619	46	174	158	15.0	5.40	85	.313	.373	6	.055	-7	-52	-42	2	-5.1
● **DIZZY TROUT**			Trout, Paul Howard	b: 6/29/15, Sandcut, Ind.		d: 2/28/72, Harvey, Ill.			BR/TR, 6'2.5", 195 lbs.		Deb: 4/25/39 F														
1939 Det-A	9	10	.474	33	22	6	0	2	162	168	5	74	72	13.7	3.61	135	.270	.351	12	.211	-0	18	23	-1	2.2
1940 *Det-A	3	7	.300	33	10	1	0	0	100²	125	4	54	64	16.3	4.47	106	.307	.392	4	.129	-2	-1	3	2	0.3
1941 Det-A	9	9	.500	37	18	6	1	2	151²	144	7	84	88	13.6	3.74	122	.252	.350	9	.180	0	7	14	1	1.6
1942 Det-A	12	18	.400	35	29	13	1	0	223	214	15	89	91	12.4	3.43	115	.249	.322	16	.213	2	6	13	4	2.3
1943 Det-A	**20**	12	.625	44	30	18	**5**	6	246²	204	6	101	111	11.1	2.48	142	.227	.305	20	.220	2	22	29	4	4.7
1944 Det-A☆	27	14	.659	49	40	**33**	**7**	0	**352¹**	314	9	83	144	10.2	**2.12**	**168**	.237	.284	36	.271	12	**51**	**57**	**7**	**9.1**
1945 *Det-A	18	15	.545	41	31	18	4	2	246¹	252	8	79	97	12.1	3.14	112	.267	.324	25	.245	4	6	10	3	2.1
1946 Det-A	17	13	.567	38	32	23	5	3	276¹	244	11	97	151	11.2	2.34	156	.238	.306	20	.194	3	36	40	4	5.3
1947 Det-A☆	10	11	.476	32	26	9	2	2	186¹	186	6	65	74	12.3	3.48	108	.261	.325	11	.162	3	5	6	3	1.4
1948 Det-A	10	14	.417	32	23	11	2	2	183²	193	6	73	91	13.1	3.43	127	.269	.338	15	.217	2	18	19	2	2.6
1949 Det-A	3	6	.333	19	4	0	0	0	59¹	72	4	21	19	13.5	4.40	95	.292	.350	2	.143	-0	-1	-2	0	-0.1
1950 Det-A	13	5	.722	34	20	11	1	4	184²	190	13	64	88	13.2	3.75	125	.267	.332	12	.190	1	17	19	3	2.1
1951 Det-A	9	14	.391	42	22	7	0	5	191²	172	13	75	89	11.6	4.04	103	.240	.312	14	.269	5	2	3	4	1.2
1952 Det-A	1	5	.167	10	2	0	0	0	27	30	4	19	20	16.3	5.33	71	.286	.395	3	.333	1	-5	-5	1	-0.8
Bos-A	9	8	.529	26	17	2	0	1	133²	133	3	68	57	13.7	3.64	108	.263	.354	6	.136	-1	1	5	1	0.5
Yr	10	13	.435	36	19	2	0	1	160²	163	7	87	77	14.2	3.92	100	.267	.361	9	.170	-1	-4	-0	2	-0.3
1957 Bal-A	0	0	—	2	0	0	0	0	0¹	4	0	0	0	108.0	81.00	4	.800	.800	0	—	0	-3	-3	0	0.0
Total 15	170	161	.514	521	322	158	28	35	2725²	2641	112	1046	1256	12.3	3.23	124	.255	.325	205	.213	31	177	232	38	34.5
● **STEVE TROUT**			Trout, Steven Russell	b: 7/30/57, Detroit, Mich.		BL/TL, 6'4", 195 lbs.		Deb: 7/1/78 F																
1978 Chi-A	3	0	1.000	4	3	1	0	0	22¹	19	10	11	11	12.1	4.03	94	.229	.319	0	—	0	-1	-1	-0	-0.1
1979 Chi-A	11	8	.579	34	18	6	2	4	155	165	10	59	76	13.3	3.89	109	.273	.343	0	—	0	6	6	2	0.9

YEAR	TM/L	W	L	PCT	G	GS	CG	SH	SV	IP	H	HR	BB	SO	RAT	ERA	ERA+	OAV	OOB	BH	AVG	PB	PR	/A	PD	TPI
1980	Chi-A	9	16	.360	32	30	7	2	0	199²	229	14	49	89	12.9	3.70	109	.290	.338	0	—	0	8	7	3	1.1
1981	Chi-A	8	7	.533	20	18	3	0	0	124²	122	7	38	54	11.8	3.47	103	.261	.322	0	—	0	3	2	0	0.3
1982	Chi-A	6	9	.400	25	19	2	0	0	120¹	130	9	50	62	13.6	4.26	95	.273	.344	0	—	0	-3	-3	0	-0.3
1983	Chi-N	10	14	.417	34	32	1	0	0	180	217	13	59	80	13.9	4.65	82	.305	.360	12	.194	1	-20	-17	2	-1.8
1984	*Chi-N	13	7	.650	32	31	6	2	0	190	205	7	59	81	12.6	3.41	115	.285	.341	8	.131	-1	4	10	4	1.3
1985	Chi-N	9	7	.563	24	24	3	1	0	140²	142	8	63	44	13.2	3.39	118	.270	.350	5	.109	-2	3	9	2	1.1
1986	Chi-N	5	7	.417	37	25	0	0	0	161	184	6	78	69	14.7	4.75	85	.298	.378	9	.209	1	-19	-13	1	-0.7
1987	Chi-N	6	3	.667	11	11	3	2	0	75	72	9	27	32	12.0	3.00	143	.260	.328	4	.154	1	9	11	0	1.2
	NY-A	0	4	.000	14	9	0	0	0	46¹	51	4	37	27	17.3	6.60	66	.274	.397	0	—	0	-11	-11	0	-0.7
1988	Sea-A	4	7	.364	15	13	0	0	0	56¹	86	6	31	14	19.5	7.83	53	.361	.445	0	—	0	-24	-23	0	-3.8
1989	Sea-A	4	3	.571	19	3	0	0	0	30	43	3	17	17	18.0	6.60	61	.333	.411	0	—	0	-9	-9	0	-1.9
Total	12	88	92	.489	301	236	32	9	4	1501¹	1665	90	578	656	13.6	4.18	96	.286	.354	38	.160	-2	-55	-30	14	-3.4

● **BOB TROWBRIDGE**   Trowbridge, Robert   b: 6/27/30, Hudson, N.Y.   d: 4/3/80, Hudson, N.Y.   BR/TR, 6'1", 190 lbs.   Deb: 4/22/56

YEAR	TM/L	W	L	PCT	G	GS	CG	SH	SV	IP	H	HR	BB	SO	RAT	ERA	ERA+	OAV	OOB	BH	AVG	PB	PR	/A	PD	TPI
1956	Mil-N	3	2	.600	19	4	1	0	0	50²	38	4	34	40	13.1	2.66	130	.210	.341	0	.000	-1	6	4	0	0.4
1957	*Mil-N	7	5	.583	32	16	3	1	1	126	118	9	52	75	12.2	3.64	96	.248	.323	4	.103	-2	3	-2	-1	-0.4
1958	Mil-N	1	3	.250	27	4	0	0	1	55	53	4	26	31	13.1	3.93	90	.252	.338	1	.111	-1	0	-2	-1	-0.3
1959	Mil-N	1	0	1.000	16	0	0	0	1	30¹	45	2	10	22	16.3	5.93	60	.344	.390	0	.000	-0	-7	-8	-0	-0.4
1960	KC-A	1	3	.250	22	1	0	0	2	68¹	70	6	34	33	13.8	4.61	86	.281	.370	1	.056	-1	-6	-5	0	-0.4
Total	5	13	13	.500	116	25	4	1	5	330¹	324	25	156	201	13.2	3.95	91	.260	.344	6	.078	-5	-3	-13	-1	-1.1

● **BUN TROY**   Troy, Robert   b: 8/22/1888, Germany   d: 10/7/18, Meuse, France   BR/TR, 6'4", 195 lbs.   Deb: 9/15/12

YEAR	TM/L	W	L	PCT	G	GS	CG	SH	SV	IP	H	HR	BB	SO	RAT	ERA	ERA+	OAV	OOB	BH	AVG	PB	PR	/A	PD	TPI
1912	Det-A	0	1	.000	1	1	0	0	0	6²	9	0	3	1	17.6	5.40	60	.346	.433	0	.000	-0	-2	-2	-0	-0.2

● **VIRGIL TRUCKS**   Trucks, Virgil Oliver "Fire"   b: 4/26/17, Birmingham, Ala.   BR/TR, 5'11", 198 lbs.   Deb: 9/27/41   C

YEAR	TM/L	W	L	PCT	G	GS	CG	SH	SV	IP	H	HR	BB	SO	RAT	ERA	ERA+	OAV	OOB	BH	AVG	PB	PR	/A	PD	TPI
1941	Det-A	0	0	—	1	0	0	0	0	2	4	0	0	3	18.0	9.00	50	.500	.500	0	—	0	-1	-1	0	0.0
1942	Det-A	14	8	.636	28	20	8	2	0	167²	147	3	74	91	12.0	2.74	144	.231	.314	8	.123	-4	17	23	-2	2.3
1943	Det-A	16	10	.615	33	25	10	2	2	202²	170	11	52	118	9.9	2.84	124	.225	.276	13	.181	-2	10	15	-2	1.6
1945	*Det-A	0	0	—	1	1	0	0	0	5¹	3	0	2	3	8.4	1.69	208	.176	.263	0	.000	-0	1	1	0	0.0
1946	Det-A	14	9	.609	32	29	15	2	0	236²	217	23	75	161	11.2	3.23	113	.241	.302	17	.179	-1	7	11	-1	0.8
1947	Det-A	10	12	.455	36	26	8	2	2	180²	186	14	79	108	13.3	4.53	83	.263	.339	19	.271	-2	-17	-15	-1	-1.6
1948	Det-A	14	13	.519	43	26	7	0	2	211²	190	14	85	123	11.8	3.78	115	.240	.315	13	.165	-3	12	14	-1	1.1
1949	Det-A★	19	11	.633	41	32	17	**6**	4	275	209	16	124	**153**	11.0	2.81	148	.211	.301	12	.120	-6	42	41	-3	3.3
1950	Det-A	3	1	.750	7	7	3	1	0	48¹	48	6	21	25	12.5	3.54	133	.243	.324	3	.150	-1	6	6	1	0.4
1951	Det-A	13	8	.619	37	18	6	1	1	153²	153	9	75	89	13.6	4.33	96	.262	.350	13	.236	-0	-4	-3	-2	-0.2
1952	Det-A	5	19	.208	35	29	8	3	1	197	190	12	82	129	12.7	3.97	96	.251	.330	12	.188	-0	-7	-4	2	-0.2
1953	StL-A	5	4	.556	16	12	4	2	2	88	83	4	32	47	12.2	3.07	137	.249	.322	4	.160	-1	9	11	-1	0.9
	Chi-A	15	6	.714	24	21	13	3	1	176¹	151	14	67	102	11.3	2.86	141	.232	.306	15	.238	2	22	23	1	2.9
	Yr	20	10	.667	40	33	17	5	3	264¹	234	18	99	149	11.4	2.93	139	.237	.308	19	.216	1	31	34	0	3.8
1954	Chi-A★	19	12	.613	40	33	16	**5**	3	264²	224	13	95	152	10.9	2.79	134	.228	.297	17	.183	-1	27	28	1	3.2
1955	Chi-A	13	8	.619	32	26	7	3	0	175	176	16	61	91	12.3	3.96	100	.260	.323	8	.125	-3	0	0	0	-0.3
1956	Det-A	6	5	.545	22	16	3	1	1	120	104	16	63	43	13.0	3.83	108	.239	.343	11	.244	1	4	4	-1	0.2
1957	KC-A	9	7	.563	48	7	0	0	0	116	106	12	62	55	13.2	3.03	131	.248	.346	4	.143	-1	10	12	0	1.6
1958	KC-A	0	1	.000	16	0	0	0	3	22	18	2	15	15	13.5	2.05	191	.222	.344	0	.000	-0	4	5	0	0.3
	NY-A	2	1	.667	25	0	0	0	1	39²	40	1	24	26	15.0	4.54	78	.265	.373	2	.250	-0	-3	-4	-0	-0.4
	Yr	2	2	.500	41	0	0	0	4	61²	58	3	39	41	14.4	3.65	100	.249	.361	2	.222	-0	1	0	-0	-0.1
Total	17	177	135	.567	517	328	124	33	30	2682²	2416	188	1088	1534	11.9	3.39	117	.240	.317	171	.180	-19	141	167	-5	15.9

● **MIKE TRUJILLO**   Trujillo, Michael Andrew   b: 1/12/60, Denver, Colo.   BR/TR, 6'1", 180 lbs.   Deb: 4/14/85

YEAR	TM/L	W	L	PCT	G	GS	CG	SH	SV	IP	H	HR	BB	SO	RAT	ERA	ERA+	OAV	OOB	BH	AVG	PB	PR	/A	PD	TPI
1985	Bos-A	4	4	.500	27	7	1	0	1	84	112	7	23	19	14.8	4.82	89	.320	.367	0	—	0	-6	-5	2	-0.6
1986	Bos-A	0	0	—	3	0	0	0	0	5²	7	0	6	4	20.6	9.53	44	.304	.448	0	—	0	-3	-3	1	0.0
	Sea-A	3	2	.600	11	4	1	1	1	41¹	32	5	15	19	10.2	2.40	177	.215	.287	0	—	0	8	8	-0	0.9
	Yr	3	2	.600	14	4	1	1	1	47	39	5	21	23	11.5	3.26	130	.227	.311	0	—	0	5	5	0	0.9
1987	Sea-A	4	4	.500	28	7	0	0	1	65²	70	12	26	36	13.4	6.17	76	.277	.349	0	—	0	-12	-11	-1	-1.6
1988	Det-A	0	0	—	6	0	0	0	0	12¹	11	2	5	5	11.7	5.11	75	.234	.308	0	—	0	-2	-2	0	0.3
1989	Det-A	1	2	.333	8	4	1	0	0	25²	35	3	13	13	16.8	5.96	64	.333	.407	0	—	0	-6	-6	0	-0.5
Total	5	12	12	.500	83	22	3	1	3	234²	267	29	88	96	13.8	5.02	86	.288	.353	0	—	0	-21	-19	2	-1.5

● **ED TRUMBULL**   Trumbull, Edward J. (b: Edward J. Trembly)   b: 11/3/1860, Chicopee, Mass.   d: 1/14/37, Kingston, Pa.   Deb: 5/10/1884   ♦

YEAR	TM/L	W	L	PCT	G	GS	CG	SH	SV	IP	H	HR	BB	SO	RAT	ERA	ERA+	OAV	OOB	BH	AVG	PB	PR	/A	PD	TPI
1884	Was-a	1	9	.100	10	10	10	0	0	84	108	4	31	43	15.0	4.71	64	.295	.352	10	.116	-2	-14	-16	-1	-1.7

● **GEORGE TSAMIS**   Tsamis, George Alex   b: 6/14/67, Campbell, Cal.   BR/TL, 6'2", 190 lbs.   Deb: 4/26/93

YEAR	TM/L	W	L	PCT	G	GS	CG	SH	SV	IP	H	HR	BB	SO	RAT	ERA	ERA+	OAV	OOB	BH	AVG	PB	PR	/A	PD	TPI
1993	Min-A	1	2	.333	41	0	0	0	1	68¹	86	9	27	30	15.3	6.19	70	.317	.385	0	—	0	-14	-14	1	-0.5

● **JOHN TSITOURIS**   Tsitouris, John Philip   b: 5/4/36, Monroe, N.C.   BR/TR, 6', 175 lbs.   Deb: 6/13/57

YEAR	TM/L	W	L	PCT	G	GS	CG	SH	SV	IP	H	HR	BB	SO	RAT	ERA	ERA+	OAV	OOB	BH	AVG	PB	PR	/A	PD	TPI
1957	Det-A	1	0	1.000	2	0	0	0	0	3¹	8	0	2	2	27.0	8.10	48	.500	.556	0	.000	-0	-2	-2	0	-0.4
1958	KC-A	0	0	—	1	1	0	0	0	3	2	0	2	1	12.0	3.00	130	.182	.308	0	.000	-0	0	0	0	0.0
1959	KC-A	4	3	.571	24	10	0	0	0	83¹	90	3	35	50	13.8	4.97	81	.271	.346	3	.150	-1	-10	-9	-1	-0.8
1960	KC-A	0	2	.000	14	2	0	0	0	33	38	3	21	12	18.3	6.55	61	.297	.427	0	.000	-1	-10	-9	-0	-0.6
1962	Cin-N	1	0	1.000	4	2	1	1	0	21¹	13	0	7	7	9.7	0.84	477	.181	.280	0	.000	-0	7	8	0	0.2
1963	Cin-N	12	8	.600	30	21	8	3	0	191	167	20	38	113	10.2	3.16	106	.232	.281	5	.081	-3	3	4	-3	-0.3
1964	Cin-N	9	13	.409	37	24	6	1	2	175¹	178	20	75	146	13.2	3.80	95	.263	.340	11	.190	2	-5	-4	-1	-0.3
1965	Cin-N	6	9	.400	31	20	3	0	1	131	134	18	65	91	14.3	4.95	76	.265	.359	3	.070	-2	-20	-17	-1	-2.2
1966	Cin-N	0	0	—	1	0	0	0	0	1	3	0	0	1	36.0	18.00	22	.750	.800	0	—	0	-2	-2	0	0.0
1967	Cin-N	1	0	1.000	2	1	0	0	0	8	4	1	6	4	11.3	3.38	111	.154	.313	0	—	0	0	0	0	0.1
1968	Cin-N	0	3	.000	3	3	0	0	0	12²	16	6	8	6	17.8	7.11	44	.302	.403	0	.000	-0	-6	-6	0	-1.1
Total	11	34	38	.472	149	84	18	5	3	663	653	71	260	432	12.9	4.13	88	.257	.335	22	.111	-6	-44	-36	-5	-5.4

● **TOMMY TUCKER**   Tucker, Thomas Joseph "Foghorn"   b: 10/28/1863, Holyoke, Mass.   d: 10/22/35, Montague, Mass.   BB/TR, 5'11", 165 lbs.   Deb: 4/16/1887   ♦

YEAR	TM/L	W	L	PCT	G	GS	CG	SH	SV	IP	H	HR	BB	SO	RAT	ERA	ERA+	OAV	OOB	BH	AVG	PB	PR	/A	PD	TPI
1888	Bal-a	0	0	—	1	0	0	0	0	2¹	4	0	0	2	15.4	3.86	77	.365	.365	149	.287	0	-0	-0	-0	0.0
1891	Bos-N	0	0	—	1	0	0	0	0	1	3	0	0	0	27.0	9.00	41	.501	.501	148	.270	0	-1	-1	-0	0.0
Total	2	0	0	—	2	0	0	0	0	3¹	7	0	0	2	18.9	5.40	59	.413	.413	1882	.290	0	-1	-1	-0	0.0

● **TOM TUCKEY**   Tuckey, Thomas H. "Tabasco Tom"   b: 10/7/1883, Connecticut   d: 10/17/50, New York, N.Y.   TL, 6'3",   Deb: 8/11/08

YEAR	TM/L	W	L	PCT	G	GS	CG	SH	SV	IP	H	HR	BB	SO	RAT	ERA	ERA+	OAV	OOB	BH	AVG	PB	PR	/A	PD	TPI
1908	Bos-N	3	3	.500	8	8	3	1	0	72	60	2	20	26	10.5	2.50	96	.265	.336	1	.050	-2	-1	-1	0	-0.2
1909	Bos-N	0	9	.000	17	10	4	0	0	90²	104	1	22	16	12.6	4.27	66	.295	.342	4	.138	-1	-17	-15	1	-1.4
Total	2	3	12	.200	25	18	7	1	0	162²	164	3	42	42	11.8	3.49	76	.284	.340	5	.102	-3	-18	-15	1	-1.6

● **JOHN TUDOR**   Tudor, John Thomas   b: 2/2/54, Schenectady, N.Y.   BL/TL, 6', 185 lbs.   Deb: 8/16/79

YEAR	TM/L	W	L	PCT	G	GS	CG	SH	SV	IP	H	HR	BB	SO	RAT	ERA	ERA+	OAV	OOB	BH	AVG	PB	PR	/A	PD	TPI
1979	Bos-A	1	2	.333	6	6	1	0	0	28	39	2	9	11	15.4	6.43	69	.345	.393	0	—	0	-7	-6	1	-0.5
1980	Bos-A	8	5	.615	16	13	5	0	0	92¹	81	4	31	45	11.2	3.02	140	.238	.307	0	—	0	10	12	2	1.4
1981	Bos-A	4	3	.571	18	11	2	0	1	78²	74	11	28	43	12.3	4.58	85	.252	.323	0	—	0	-8	-6	1	-0.8
1982	Bos-A	13	10	.565	32	30	6	1	0	195²	215	20	59	146	13.0	3.63	119	.280	.338	0	—	0	10	15	2	1.4
1983	Bos-A	13	12	.520	34	34	6	1	0	242	236	32	81	136	11.9	4.09	106	.255	.317	0	—	0	-1	7	-1	0.2
1984	Pit-N	12	11	.522	32	32	6	1	0	212	200	19	56	117	10.9	3.27	110	.248	.297	16	.211	2	8	8	-1	1.0

YEAR TM/L	W	L	PCT	G	GS	CG	SH	SV	IP	H	HR	BB	SO	RAT	ERA	ERA+	OAV	OOB	BH	AVG	PB	PR	/A	PD	TPI
1985 *StL-N	21	8	.724	36	36	14	**10**	0	275	209	14	49	169	**8.6**	1.93	183	.209	**.249**	13	.138	1	51	49	1	5.5
1986 StL-N	13	7	.650	30	30	3	0	0	219	197	22	53	107	10.3	2.92	125	.244	.291	11	.153	-0	19	18	1	1.6
1987 *StL-N	10	2	.833	16	16	0	0	0	96	100	11	32	54	12.5	3.84	108	.272	.333	7	.200	1	3	3	1	0.6
1988 StL-N	6	5	.545	21	21	4	1	0	145¹	131	5	31	55	10.1	2.29	152	.247	.290	5	.109	-1	19	19	1	1.5
*LA-N	4	3	.571	9	9	1	0	0	52¹	58	5	10	32	11.7	2.41	138	.284	.318	0	.000	-1	6	5	0	0.6
Yr	10	8	.556	30	30	5	1	0	197²	189	10	41	87	10.5	2.32	148	.254	.294	5	.085	-2	25	24	1	2.1
1989 LA-N	0	0	—	6	3	0	0	0	14¹	17	1	6	9	14.4	3.14	109	.309	.377	0	.000	-0	1	0	0	0.0
1990 StL-N	12	4	.750	25	22	1	1	0	146¹	120	11	30	63	9.3	2.40	159	.225	.269	7	.152	0	23	23	2	2.7
Total 12	117	72	.619	281	263	50	16	1	1797	1677	156	475	988	10.9	3.12	123	.248	.301	59	.154	3	132	146	9	15.2

● **OSCAR TUERO**   Tuero, Oscar (Monzon) (b: Oscar Tuero Monzon) b: 12/17/1898, Canada d: 10/21/60, Houston, Tex. BR/TR, 5'8.5", 158 lbs. Deb: 5/30/18

YEAR TM/L	W	L	PCT	G	GS	CG	SH	SV	IP	H	HR	BB	SO	RAT	ERA	ERA+	OAV	OOB	BH	AVG	PB	PR	/A	PD	TPI
1918 StL-N	1	2	.333	11	3	2	0	0	44¹	32	0	10	13	9.1	1.02	267	.208	.269	3	.250	0	9	8	-1	0.5
1919 StL-N	5	7	.417	**45**	16	4	0	**4**	154²	137	4	42	45	11.0	3.20	87	.242	.306	8	.205	1	-5	-7	-0	-0.5
1920 StL-N	0	0	—	2	0	0	0	0	0²	5	0	1	0	81.0	54.00	6	.833	.857	0	—	0	-4	-4	-0	0.0
Total 3	6	9	.400	58	19	6	0	4	199²	174	4	53	58	10.8	2.88	96	.240	.303	11	.216	1	0	-2	-1	0.0

● **BOB TUFTS**   Tufts, Robert Malcolm b: 11/2/55, Medford, Mass. BL/TL, 6'5", 215 lbs. Deb: 8/10/81

YEAR TM/L	W	L	PCT	G	GS	CG	SH	SV	IP	H	HR	BB	SO	RAT	ERA	ERA+	OAV	OOB	BH	AVG	PB	PR	/A	PD	TPI
1981 SF-N	0	0	—	11	0	0	0	0	15¹	20	1	6	12	15.8	3.52	97	.308	.375	0	.000	-0	-0	-0	1	0.1
1982 KC-A	2	0	1.000	10	0	0	0	2	20	24	3	3	13	12.1	4.50	91	.293	.318	0	—	-0	-1	-1	-1	-0.2
1983 KC-A	0	0	—	6	0	0	0	0	6²	16	1	5	3	29.7	8.10	50	.444	.524	0	—	-0	-3	-3	0	0.0
Total 3	2	0	1.000	27	0	0	0	2	42	60	5	14	28	16.3	4.71	81	.328	.382	0	.000	-0	-4	-4	-0	-0.1

● **LEE TUNNELL**   Tunnell, Byron Lee b: 10/30/60, Tyler, Tex. BR/TR, 6'1", 180 lbs. Deb: 9/4/82

YEAR TM/L	W	L	PCT	G	GS	CG	SH	SV	IP	H	HR	BB	SO	RAT	ERA	ERA+	OAV	OOB	BH	AVG	PB	PR	/A	PD	TPI
1982 Pit-N	1	1	.500	5	3	0	0	0	18¹	17	1	5	4	11.8	3.93	94	.254	.324	0	.000	-0	-1	-0	1	-0.1
1983 Pit-N	11	6	.647	35	25	5	3	0	177²	167	15	58	95	11.5	3.65	102	.252	.314	7	.121	-1	-0	1	2	0.2
1984 Pit-N	1	7	.125	26	6	0	0	0	68¹	81	6	40	51	15.9	5.27	68	.298	.388	1	.083	-1	-13	-13	1	-1.3
1985 Pit-N	4	10	.286	24	23	0	0	0	132¹	126	11	57	74	12.5	4.01	89	.251	.329	4	.085	-2	-6	-6	1	-0.8
1987 *StL-N	4	4	.500	32	9	0	0	0	74¹	90	5	34	49	15.1	4.84	86	.307	.381	4	.235	-0	-6	-6	0	-0.5
1989 Min-A	1	0	1.000	10	0	0	0	0	12	18	1	6	7	18.0	6.00	69	.340	.407	0	—	-0	-3	-2	-0	-0.6
Total 6	22	28	.440	132	66	5	3	1	483	499	39	200	280	13.1	4.23	88	.270	.343	16	.116	-4	-29	-27	4	-3.1

● **GEORGE TURBEVILLE**   Turbeville, George Elkins b: 8/24/14, Turbeville, S.C. d: 10/5/83, Salisbury, N.C. BR/TL, 6'1", 175 lbs. Deb: 7/20/35

YEAR TM/L	W	L	PCT	G	GS	CG	SH	SV	IP	H	HR	BB	SO	RAT	ERA	ERA+	OAV	OOB	BH	AVG	PB	PR	/A	PD	TPI
1935 Phi-A	0	3	.000	19	6	2	0	0	63²	74	2	69	20	20.2	7.63	60	.312	.467	2	.105	-2	-22	-22	-1	-1.1
1936 Phi-A	2	5	.286	12	6	2	0	0	43²	42	6	32	10	16.5	6.39	80	.258	.398	2	.143	-1	-7	-6	-0	-0.8
1937 Phi-A	0	4	.000	31	3	0	0	0	77¹	80	2	56	17	15.8	4.77	99	.266	.381	6	.231	-1	-1	-1	-1	-0.1
Total 3	2	12	.143	62	15	4	0	0	184²	196	10	157	47	17.5	6.14	77	.280	.416	10	.169	-2	-30	-29	-2	-2.0

● **LUCAS TURK**   Turk, Lucas Newton "Harlem" or "Chief" b: 5/2/1898, Homer, Ga. d: 1/11/94, Homer, Ga. BR/TR, 6', 165 lbs. Deb: 6/7/22

YEAR TM/L	W	L	PCT	G	GS	CG	SH	SV	IP	H	HR	BB	SO	RAT	ERA	ERA+	OAV	OOB	BH	AVG	PB	PR	/A	PD	TPI
1922 Was-A	0	0	—	5	0	0	0	0	11²	16	0	5	1	16.2	6.94	56	.340	.404	1	.250	0	-4	-4	-1	-0.1

● **BOB TURLEY**   Turley, Robert Lee "Bullet Bob" b: 9/19/30, Troy, Ill. BR/TR, 6'2", 215 lbs. Deb: 9/29/51   C

YEAR TM/L	W	L	PCT	G	GS	CG	SH	SV	IP	H	HR	BB	SO	RAT	ERA	ERA+	OAV	OOB	BH	AVG	PB	PR	/A	PD	TPI
1951 StL-A	0	1	.000	1	1	0	0	0	7¹	5	1	10	3	17.2	7.36	60	.355	.412	0	.000	-0	-3	-2	0	-0.3
1953 StL-A	2	6	.250	10	7	3	1	0	60¹	39	4	44	61	12.7	3.28	128	.184	.329	5	.278	1	5	6	-1	0.9
1954 Bal-A☆	14	15	.483	35	35	14	0	0	247¹	178	7	181	**185**	13.3	3.46	104	**.203**	.343	11	.136	-3	7	3	-1	0.1
1955 *NY-A☆	17	13	.567	36	34	13	6	1	246²	168	16	177	210	12.8	3.06	122	**.193**	.333	11	.134	-0	25	19	-2	1.9
1956 *NY-A	8	4	.667	27	21	5	1	0	132	138	13	103	91	16.7	5.05	77	.273	.400	8	.174	-0	-13	-17	-1	-1.5
1957 *NY-A	13	6	.684	32	23	9	4	3	176¹	120	17	85	152	10.9	2.71	133	**.194**	.300	5	.088	-2	21	17	-0	1.6
1958 *NY-A★	**21**	7	**.750**	33	31	**19**	6	1	245¹	178	24	128	168	11.5	2.97	119	**.206**	.313	12	.136	-1	22	15	-2	1.4
1959 *NY-A	8	11	.421	33	22	7	3	0	154¹	141	15	83	111	13.2	4.32	84	.245	.343	4	.087	-2	-8	-11	-1	-1.5
1960 *NY-A	9	3	.750	34	24	4	1	5	173¹	138	14	87	87	11.9	3.27	110	.222	.322	4	.073	-4	12	6	-1	-0.1
1961 NY-A	3	5	.375	15	12	1	0	0	72	74	11	51	48	16.1	5.75	65	.269	.391	2	.095	-1	-14	-16	-1	-1.7
1962 NY-A	3	3	.500	24	8	0	0	1	69	68	8	47	42	15.5	4.57	82	.263	.384	0	.000	-1	-5	-6	1	-0.6
1963 LA-A	2	7	.222	19	12	3	2	0	87¹	71	5	51	70	12.8	3.30	104	.222	.332	4	.160	1	3	1	-0	0.2
Bos-A	1	4	.200	11	7	0	0	0	41¹	42	6	28	35	15.5	6.10	62	.256	.368	3	.214	0	-11	-11	-0	-1.2
Yr	3	11	.214	30	19	3	2	0	128²	113	11	79	105	13.5	4.20	84	.232	.340	7	.179	1	-8	-9	-1	-1.0
Total 12	101	85	.543	310	237	78	24	12	1712²	1366	140	1068	1265	13.1	3.64	101	.220	.340	69	.126	-12	41	4	-9	-0.8

● **TUCK TURNER**   Turner, George A. b: 2/13/1873, W.New Brighton, N.Y. d: 7/16/45, Staten Island, N.Y. BB/TL, 5'6.5", 155 lbs. Deb: 8/18/1893 ♦

YEAR TM/L	W	L	PCT	G	GS	CG	SH	SV	IP	H	HR	BB	SO	RAT	ERA	ERA+	OAV	OOB	BH	AVG	PB	PR	/A	PD	TPI
1894 Phi-N	0	0	—	1	0	0	0	0	6	9	1	2	3	18.0	7.50	68	.342	.410	141	.416	1	-1	-2	-0	0.0

● **JIM TURNER**   Turner, James Riley "Milkman Jim" b: 8/6/03, Antioch, Tenn. BL/TR, 6', 185 lbs. Deb: 4/30/37   C

YEAR TM/L	W	L	PCT	G	GS	CG	SH	SV	IP	H	HR	BB	SO	RAT	ERA	ERA+	OAV	OOB	BH	AVG	PB	PR	/A	PD	TPI
1937 Bos-N	20	11	.645	33	34	24	**5**	1	256²	228	13	52	69	**9.8**	2.38	150	.235	**.274**	24	.250	4	**44**	34	0	**4.5**
1938 Bos-N☆	14	18	.438	35	34	22	3	0	268	267	21	54	71	10.9	3.46	99	.259	.299	22	.229	4	10	-1	4	0.7
1939 Bos-N	4	11	.267	25	22	9	0	0	157²	181	10	51	50	13.5	4.28	86	.293	.351	13	.236	2	-6	-10	1	-0.5
1940 *Cin-N	14	7	.667	24	23	11	0	0	187	187	9	32	53	10.5	2.89	131	.264	.296	18	.240	3	20	19	-1	2.2
1941 Cin-N	6	4	.600	23	10	3	0	0	113	120	5	24	34	11.5	3.11	116	.277	.317	6	.146	-1	7	6	2	0.6
1942 Cin-N	0	0	—	3	0	0	0	0	3¹	5	1	3	0	21.6	10.80	30	.333	.444	0	.000	-0	-3	-3	0	-0.4
*NY-A	1	1	.500	5	0	0	0	0	7	4	0	1	2	6.4	1.29	268	.167	.200	0	.000	-0	2	2	0	0.6
1943 NY-A	3	1	1.000	18	0	0	0	0	43¹	44	1	13	15	11.8	3.53	91	.260	.313	1	.077	-1	-1	-2	-0	-0.3
1944 NY-A	4	4	.500	35	0	0	0	7	41²	42	3	22	13	13.8	3.46	101	.264	.354	2	.200	-0	-0	-1	-0	-0.1
1945 NY-A	3	4	.429	30	0	0	0	**10**	54¹	45	4	31	22	12.6	3.64	95	.225	.329	1	.091	-1	-2	-1	1	-0.2
Total 9	69	60	.535	231	119	69	8	20	1132	1123	67	283	329	11.3	3.22	111	.260	.307	87	.218	12	70	45	6	7.6

● **KEN TURNER**   Turner, Kenneth Charles b: 8/17/43, Framingham, Mass. BR/TL, 6'2", 190 lbs. Deb: 6/11/67

YEAR TM/L	W	L	PCT	G	GS	CG	SH	SV	IP	H	HR	BB	SO	RAT	ERA	ERA+	OAV	OOB	BH	AVG	PB	PR	/A	PD	TPI
1967 Cal-A	1	2	.333	13	1	0	0	0	17¹	16	4	4	6	10.9	4.15	76	.239	.292	0	.000	-0	-2	-2	0	-0.3

● **TED TURNER**   Turner, Theodore Holhot b: 5/4/1892, Lawrenceburg, Ky. d: 2/4/58, Lexington, Ky. BR/TR, 6', 180 lbs. Deb: 4/20/20

YEAR TM/L	W	L	PCT	G	GS	CG	SH	SV	IP	H	HR	BB	SO	RAT	ERA	ERA+	OAV	OOB	BH	AVG	PB	PR	/A	PD	TPI
1920 Chi-N	0	0	—	1	0	0	0	0	1¹	2	0	1	0	20.3	13.50	24	.400	.500	0	.000	-0	-2	-2	0	0.0

● **TINK TURNER**   Turner, Thomas Lovatt b: 2/20/1890, Swarthmore, Pa. d: 2/25/62, Philadelphia, Pa. BR/TR, 6'1", 190 lbs. Deb: 9/24/15

YEAR TM/L	W	L	PCT	G	GS	CG	SH	SV	IP	H	HR	BB	SO	RAT	ERA	ERA+	OAV	OOB	BH	AVG	PB	PR	/A	PD	TPI
1915 Phi-A	0	1	.000	1	1	0	0	0	2	5	1	3	0	36.0	22.50	13	.500	.615	0	—	0	-4	-4	-0	-1.1

● **MATT TURNER**   Turner, William Matthew b: 2/18/67, Lexington, Ky. BR/TR, 6'5", 215 lbs. Deb: 4/23/93

YEAR TM/L	W	L	PCT	G	GS	CG	SH	SV	IP	H	HR	BB	SO	RAT	ERA	ERA+	OAV	OOB	BH	AVG	PB	PR	/A	PD	TPI
1993 Fla-N	4	5	.444	55	0	0	0	0	68	57	7	26	59	10.9	2.91	148	.227	.305	0	.000	-0	9	11	0	1.3
1994 Cle-A	1	0	1.000	9	0	0	0	0	12²	13	0	7	5	16.3	2.13	232	.241	.359	0	—	-0	4	4	0	0.2
Total 2	5	5	.500	64	0	0	0	0	80²	68	7	33	64	11.7	2.79	159	.230	.315	0	.000	-0	12	15	0	1.5

● **ELMER TUTWILER**   Tutwiler, Elmer Strange b: 11/19/05, Carbon Hill, Ala. d: 5/3/76, Pensacola, Fla. BR/TR, 5'11", 158 lbs. Deb: 8/20/28

YEAR TM/L	W	L	PCT	G	GS	CG	SH	SV	IP	H	HR	BB	SO	RAT	ERA	ERA+	OAV	OOB	BH	AVG	PB	PR	/A	PD	TPI
1928 Pit-N	0	0	—	2	0	0	0	0	3²	4	0	0	4	9.8	4.91	83	.267	.267	0	—	-0	-0	-0	-0	0.0

● **TWINK TWINING**   Twining, Howard Earle "Doc" b: 5/30/1894, Horsham, Pa. d: 6/14/73, Lansdale, Pa. BR/TR, 6', 168 lbs. Deb: 7/9/16

YEAR TM/L	W	L	PCT	G	GS	CG	SH	SV	IP	H	HR	BB	SO	RAT	ERA	ERA+	OAV	OOB	BH	AVG	PB	PR	/A	PD	TPI
1916 Cin-N	0	0	—	1	0	0	0	0	2	4	1	1	0	27.0	13.50	19	.444	.545	0	—	0	-2	-2	0	0.0

● **LARRY TWITCHELL**   Twitchell, Lawrence Grant b: 2/18/1864, Cleveland, Ohio d: 8/23/30, Cleveland, Ohio BR/TR, 6', 185 lbs. Deb: 4/30/1886 ♦

YEAR TM/L	W	L	PCT	G	GS	CG	SH	SV	IP	H	HR	BB	SO	RAT	ERA	ERA+	OAV	OOB	BH	AVG	PB	PR	/A	PD	TPI
1886 Det-N	0	2	.000	4	4	2	0	0	25	35	1	12	6	16.9	6.48	51	.347	.416	1	.063	-2	-9	-9	1	-0.6
1887 *Det-N	11	1	.917	15	12	11	0	**1**	112¹	120	3	36	24	13.3	4.33	94	.268	.336	88	.333	4	-3	-3	-1	-0.2

YEAR TM/L	W	L	PCT	G	GS	CG	SH	SV	IP	H	HR	BB	SO	RAT	ERA	ERA+	OAV	OOB	BH	AVG	PB	PR	/A	PD	TPI
1888 Det-N	0	0	—	2	0	0	0	1	4	6	1	0	3	13.5	6.75	41	.375	.375	128	.244	0	-2	-2	0	-0.1
1889 Cle-N	0	0	—	1	0	0	0	0	1	0	0	1	0	9.0	0.00	—	.000	.252	151	.275	0	0	0	-0	0.0
1890 Buf-P	5	7	.417	13	12	12	0	0	104¹	112	3	72	29	17.2	4.57	90	.263	.388	38	.221	1	-4	-5	2	-0.2
1891 Col-a	1	1	.500	6	1	1	0	0	31	29	1	13	8	13.1	4.06	85	.239	.328	62	.277	2	-1	-2	-0	0.0
1894 Lou-N	0	0	—	1	0	0	0	0	3	5	1	1	0	18.0	6.00	85	.367	.410	56	.267	0	-0	-0	0	0.0
Total 7	17	11	.607	42	29	26	0	2	280²	307	10	135	70	15.1	4.62	85	.272	.364	676	.263	7	-19	-21	1	-1.1

● WAYNE TWITCHELL
Twitchell, Wayne Lee b: 3/10/48, Portland, Ore. BR/TR, 6'6", 220 lbs. Deb: 9/7/70

YEAR TM/L	W	L	PCT	G	GS	CG	SH	SV	IP	H	HR	BB	SO	RAT	ERA	ERA+	OAV	OOB	BH	AVG	PB	PR	/A	PD	TPI
1970 Mil-A	0	0	—	2	0	0	0	0	1²	3	0	1	5	21.6	10.80	35	.333	.400	0	—	0	-1	-1	0	0.0
1971 Phi-N	1	0	1.000	6	1	0	0	0	16	8	1	10	15	10.7	0.00	—	.145	.288	0	.000	-0	6	6	0	0.3
1972 Phi-N	5	9	.357	49	15	1	1	1	139²	138	6	56	112	12.6	4.06	88	.259	.332	2	.071	-2	-9	-7	-1	-1.0
1973 Phi-N★	13	9	.591	34	28	10	5	0	223¹	172	16	99	169	11.3	2.50	152	.219	.314	7	.097	-4	29	32	-3	2.3
1974 Phi-N	6	9	.400	25	18	2	0	0	112¹	122	11	65	72	15.5	5.21	73	.276	.377	6	.171	-1	-20	-18	-2	-2.3
1975 Phi-N	5	10	.333	36	20	0	0	0	134¹	132	10	78	101	14.1	4.42	84	.261	.361	4	.088	-2	-12	-10	-3	-1.5
1976 Phi-N	3	1	.750	26	2	0	0	1	61²	55	3	18	67	11.1	1.75	203	.241	.305	1	.167	-0	12	12	0	0.9
1977 Phi-N	0	5	.000	12	8	0	0	0	45²	50	3	25	37	14.8	4.53	88	.287	.377	1	.091	-0	-3	-3	1	-0.3
Mon-N	6	5	.545	22	22	2	0	0	139	116	18	49	93	11.0	4.21	90	.230	.304	2	.205	2	-5	-6	-1	-0.3
Yr	6	10	.375	34	30	2	0	0	184²	166	21	74	130	11.9	4.29	90	.244	.323	9	.180	2	-8	-9	-0	-0.6
1978 Mon-N	4	12	.250	33	15	0	0	0	112	121	16	71	69	15.8	5.38	65	.286	.395	2	.083	-1	-22	-23	-1	-3.2
1979 NY-N	5	3	.625	33	2	0	0	0	63²	55	5	44	55	16.1	5.23	70	.243	.400	3	.375	1	-11	-11	-0	-1.2
Sea-A	0	2	.000						13²	11	2	10	5	15.1	5.27	83	.220	.371	0	—	0	-2	-1	-0	-0.2
Total 10	48	65	.425	282	133	15	6	2	1063	983	92	537	789	13.2	3.98	94	.250	.346	33	.127	-6	-38	-31	-10	-6.5

● JEFF TWITTY
Twitty, Jeffrey Dean b: 11/10/57, Lancaster, S.C. BL/TL, 6'2", 185 lbs. Deb: 7/5/80

YEAR TM/L	W	L	PCT	G	GS	CG	SH	SV	IP	H	HR	BB	SO	RAT	ERA	ERA+	OAV	OOB	BH	AVG	PB	PR	/A	PD	TPI
1980 KC-A	2	1	.667	13	0	0	0	0	22¹	33	4	7	9	16.1	6.04	67	.351	.396	0	—	0	-5	-5	0	-0.6

● CY TWOMBLY
Twombly, Edwin Parker b: 6/15/1897, Groveland, Mass. d: 12/3/74, Savannah, Ga. BL/TL, 5'10.5", 170 lbs. Deb: 6/25/21

YEAR TM/L	W	L	PCT	G	GS	CG	SH	SV	IP	H	HR	BB	SO	RAT	ERA	ERA+	OAV	OOB	BH	AVG	PB	PR	/A	PD	TPI
1921 Chi-A	1	2	.333	7	4	0	0	0	27²	26	1	25	7	17.2	5.86	72	.283	.445	0	.000	-2	-5	-5	1	-0.5

● LEFTY TYLER
Tyler, George Albert b: 12/14/1889, Derry, N.H. d: 9/29/53, Lowell, Mass. BL/TL, 6', 175 lbs. Deb: 9/20/10 F

YEAR TM/L	W	L	PCT	G	GS	CG	SH	SV	IP	H	HR	BB	SO	RAT	ERA	ERA+	OAV	OOB	BH	AVG	PB	PR	/A	PD	TPI
1910 Bos-N	0	0	—	2	0	0	0	0	11¹	11	1	6	6	13.5	2.38	140	.275	.370	2	.500	1	1	1	-0	0.1
1911 Bos-N	7	10	.412	28	20	10	1	0	165¹	150	11	109	90	14.6	5.06	76	.243	.365	10	.164	-1	-31	-23	3	-1.8
1912 Bos-N	12	22	.353	42	29	15	1	0	256¹	262	8	126	144	14.0	4.18	86	.276	.367	19	.198	-1	-22	-17	4	-1.8
1913 Bos-N	16	17	.485	39	34	28	4	2	290¹	245	2	108	143	11.3	2.79	118	.235	.313	21	.206	4	13	16	7	2.9
1914 *Bos-N	16	13	.552	38	34	21	5	2	271¹	247	7	101	140	12.0	2.69	103	.249	.327	19	.202	1	3	2	-2	0.1
1915 Bos-N	10	9	.526	32	24	15	1	0	204²	182	6	84	89	11.9	2.86	91	.243	.324	23	.261	8	-2	-6	-1	0.2
1916 Bos-N	17	9	.654	34	28	21	6	1	249¹	200	6	58	117	9.4	2.02	123	.226	.276	19	.204	7	17	13	2	2.5
1917 Bos-N	14	12	.538	32	28	22	4	1	239	203	1	86	98	11.1	2.52	101	.240	.314	31	.231	4	5	1	3	1.1
1918 *Chi-N	19	8	.704	33	30	22	6	1	269¹	218	1	67	102	9.7	2.00	139	.226	.279	21	.210	1	23	23	3	3.0
1919 Chi-N	2	2	.500	6	5	3	0	0	30	20	0	13	9	9.9	2.10	137	.196	.287	1	.143	1	3	3	0	0.6
1920 Chi-N	11	12	.478	27	27	18	2	0	193	193	6	57	57	11.8	3.31	97	.268	.324	17	.262	4	-4	-2	3	0.5
1921 Chi-N	3	2	.600	10	6	4	0	0	50	59	2	15	8	13.1	3.24	118	.294	.340	6	.231	1	3	3	-1	0.3
Total 12	127	116	.523	323	265	179	30	7	2230	1990	51	829	1003	11.6	2.95	101	.245	.320	189	.217	30	9	11	21	7.7

● JIM TYNG
Tyng, James Alexander b: 3/27/1856, Philadelphia, Pa. d: 10/30/31, New York, N.Y. 5'9", 155 lbs. Deb: 9/23/1879

YEAR TM/L	W	L	PCT	G	GS	CG	SH	SV	IP	H	HR	BB	SO	RAT	ERA	ERA+	OAV	OOB	BH	AVG	PB	PR	/A	PD	TPI
1879 Bos-N	1	2	.333	3	3	3	0	0	27	35	0	6	7	13.7	5.00	50	.292	.325	5	.357	1	-8	-8	0	-0.5
1888 Phi-N	0	0	—	1	0	0	0	1	4	8	0	2	2	24.8	4.50	66	.381	.458	0	.000	-0	-1	-1	0	0.0
Total 2	1	2	.333	4	3	3	0	1	31	43	0	8	9	15.1	4.94	51	.305	.347	5	.333	1	-8	-8	0	-0.5

● DAVE TYRIVER
Tyriver, David Burton b: 10/31/37, Oshkosh, Wis. d: 10/28/88, Oshkosh, Wis. BR/TR, 6' ", 175 lbs. Deb: 8/21/62

YEAR TM/L	W	L	PCT	G	GS	CG	SH	SV	IP	H	HR	BB	SO	RAT	ERA	ERA+	OAV	OOB	BH	AVG	PB	PR	/A	PD	TPI
1962 Cle-A	0	0	—	4	0	0	0	0	10²	10	2	7	7	15.2	4.22	92	.250	.375	0	.000	-0	-0	-0	0	0.0

● JIMMY UCHRINSCKO
Uchrinscko, James Emerson b: 10/20/1900, W.Newton, Pa. BL/TL, 6', 180 lbs. Deb: 7/20/26

YEAR TM/L	W	L	PCT	G	GS	CG	SH	SV	IP	H	HR	BB	SO	RAT	ERA	ERA+	OAV	OOB	BH	AVG	PB	PR	/A	PD	TPI
1926 Was-A	0	0	—	3	0	0	0	0	8	13	0	8	0	23.6	10.13	38	.433	.553	0	.000	-0	-5	-6	0	0.0

● BOB UHL
Uhl, Robert Ellwood "Lefty" b: 9/17/13, San Francisco, Cal. d: 8/21/90, Santa Rosa, Cal. BB/TL, 5'11", 175 lbs. Deb: 5/8/38

YEAR TM/L	W	L	PCT	G	GS	CG	SH	SV	IP	H	HR	BB	SO	RAT	ERA	ERA+	OAV	OOB	BH	AVG	PB	PR	/A	PD	TPI
1938 Chi-A	0	0	—	1	0	0	0	0	2	1	0	0	0	4.5	0.00	—	.167	.167	0	—	0	1	1	-0	0.0
1940 Det-A	0	0	—	1	0	0	0	0	0	4	0	2	0	—	∞	—	1.000	1.000	0	—	0	-4	-4	0	-0.3
Total 2	0	0	—	2	0	0	0	0	2	5	0	2	0	31.5	18.00	27	.500	.583	0	—	0	-3	-3	-0	-0.3

● GEORGE UHLE
Uhle, George Ernest "The Bull" b: 9/18/1898, Cleveland, Ohio d: 2/26/85, Lakewood, Ohio BR/TR, 6', 190 lbs. Deb: 4/30/19 C♦

YEAR TM/L	W	L	PCT	G	GS	CG	SH	SV	IP	H	HR	BB	SO	RAT	ERA	ERA+	OAV	OOB	BH	AVG	PB	PR	/A	PD	TPI
1919 Cle-A	10	5	.667	26	12	7	1	0	127	129	1	43	50	12.7	2.91	115	.261	.329	13	.302	3	5	6	0	1.0
1920 *Cle-A	4	5	.444	27	6	2	0	1	84²	98	3	29	27	14.4	5.21	73	.296	.367	11	.344	2	-13	-13	0	-1.0
1921 Cle-A	16	13	.552	41	28	13	2	2	238	288	9	63	63	13.4	4.01	106	.306	.352	23	.245	3	7	7	-3	0.7
1922 Cle-A	22	16	.579	50	40	23	5	3	287¹	328	6	89	82	13.5	4.07	98	.290	.348	29	.266	9	-1	-2	-3	0.1
1923 Cle-A	26	16	.619	54	44	29	1	3	357²	378	8	102	109	12.4	3.77	105	.271	.326	52	.361	16	8	8	0	2.4
1924 Cle-A	9	15	.375	28	25	15	0	1	196¹	238	6	75	57	14.9	4.77	90	.306	.376	33	.308	7	-12	-11	1	-0.4
1925 Cle-A	13	11	.542	29	26	17	1	0	210²	218	5	78	68	13.0	4.10	108	.268	.339	29	.287	6	7	7	-3	1.0
1926 Cle-A	27	11	.711	39	36	32	3	1	318¹	300	7	118	159	12.2	2.83	143	.253	.328	30	.227	4	42	43	-0	5.2
1927 Cle-A	8	9	.471	25	22	10	1	0	153¹	187	3	59	69	15.0	4.34	97	.310	.379	21	.266	4	-3	-2	-1	1.1
1928 Cle-A	12	17	.414	31	28	18	2	1	214¹	252	9	84	74	12.9	4.07	102	.300	.344	28	.286	7	-1	2	3	1.1
1929 Det-A	15	11	.577	32	30	21	1	0	249	283	9	58	100	12.4	4.08	105	.287	.328	37	.343	8	26	30	-3	3.2
1930 Det-A	12	12	.500	33	29	18	1	3	239	239	18	75	117	12.0	3.65	131	.264	.323	36	.308	8	26	30	-3	3.2
1931 Det-A	11	12	.478	29	18	15	2	2	193	190	10	49	63	11.3	3.50	131	.255	.304	22	.244	5	19	23	-1	2.9
1932 Det-A	6	6	.500	33	15	6	1	5	146²	152	15	42	51	12.1	4.48	105	.266	.320	10	.182	1	-0	4	1	0.3
1933 Det-A	0	0	—	1	0	0	0	0	0²	2	1	0	1	27.0	27.00	16	.500	.500	0	—	0	-2	-2	-0	-0.0
NY-N	1	1	.500	6	1	0	0	0	13²	16	1	6	4	14.5	7.90	41	.302	.373	0	.000	-0	-7	-7	0	-0.9
NY-A	6	1	.857	12	6	4	0	0	61	63	4	9	26	12.7	5.16	75	.257	.321	8	.400	4	-6	-9	-1	-0.5
1934 NY-A	2	4	.333	10	2	0	0	0	16¹	30	3	7	10	20.4	9.92	41	.400	.451	3	.600	2	-10	-11	-0	-2.7
1936 Cle-A	0	1	.000	7	0	0	0	0	12²	26	2	5	5	22.0	8.53	59	.419	.463	3	.381	4	-5	-5	1	-0.8
Total 17	200	166	.546	513	368	232	21	25	3119²	3417	119	966	1135	13.0	3.99	105	.281	.340	393	.289	92	60	74	-15	13.5

● JERRY UJDUR
Ujdur, Gerald Raymond b: 3/5/57, Duluth, Minn. BR/TR, 6'1", 195 lbs. Deb: 8/17/80

YEAR TM/L	W	L	PCT	G	GS	CG	SH	SV	IP	H	HR	BB	SO	RAT	ERA	ERA+	OAV	OOB	BH	AVG	PB	PR	/A	PD	TPI
1980 Det-A	1	0	1.000	9	2	0	0	0	21¹	36	5	10	9	19.8	7.59	54	.383	.448	0	—	0	-8	-8	-1	-0.6
1981 Det-A	0	0	—	4	4	0	0	0	14	19	2	5	5	15.4	6.43	64	.339	.322	0	—	0	-4	-4	0	0.0
1982 Det-A	10	10	.500	25	25	7	0	0	178	150	29	69	86	11.2	3.69	110	.230	.306	0	—	0	8	7	-1	0.6
1983 Det-A	0	4	.000	11	6	0	0	0	34	41	6	20	13	16.4	7.15	55	.293	.385	0	—	0	-12	-12	-1	-1.2
1984 Cle-A	1	2	.333	4	3	0	0	0	14¹	22	1	6	5	18.8	6.91	59	.355	.429	0	—	0	-5	-4	-1	-0.9
Total 5	12	16	.429	53	40	7	0	0	261²	268	43	110	118	13.2	4.78	84	.266	.342	0	—	0	-21	-22	-3	-2.1

● SANDY ULLRICH
Ullrich, Carlos Santiago (Castello) b: 7/25/21, Havana, Cuba BR/TR, 6'1", 180 lbs. Deb: 5/3/44

YEAR TM/L	W	L	PCT	G	GS	CG	SH	SV	IP	H	HR	BB	SO	RAT	ERA	ERA+	OAV	OOB	BH	AVG	PB	PR	/A	PD	TPI
1944 Was-A	0	0	—						9²	9	2	4	2	20.5	9.31	35	.386	.449	1	.333	-0	-6	-7	0	-0.1
1945 Was-A	3	3	.500	28	6	0	0	1	81¹	91	3	34	26	13.8	4.54	68	.276	.343	6	.273	1	-11	-13	1	-0.7
Total 2	3	3	.500	31	6	0	0	1	91	108	5	38	28	14.5	5.04	62	.289	.356	7	.280	1	-17	-19	2	-0.7

YEAR TM/L	W	L	PCT	G	GS	CG	SH	SV	IP	H	HR	BB	SO	RAT	ERA	ERA+	OAV	OOB	BH	AVG	PB	PR	/A	PD	TPI

● **DUTCH ULRICH** — Ulrich, Frank W. b: 11/18/1899, Baltimore, Md. d: 2/11/29, Baltimore, Md. BR/TR, 6'2", 195 lbs. Deb: 4/18/25

YEAR TM/L	W	L	PCT	G	GS	CG	SH	SV	IP	H	HR	BB	SO	RAT	ERA	ERA+	OAV	OOB	BH	AVG	PB	PR	/A	PD	TPI
1925 Phi-N	3	3	.500	21	4	2	1	0	65	73	6	12	29	11.9	3.05	157	.285	.320	2	.125	-1	9	12	1	1.0
1926 Phi-N	8	13	.381	45	17	8	1	1	147²	178	9	37	52	13.2	4.08	101	.304	.347	12	.245	1	-4	1	-0	0.3
1927 Phi-N	8	11	.421	32	18	14	1	1	193¹	201	6	40	42	11.2	3.17	131	.271	.308	9	.123	-6	16	21	-2	1.1
Total 3	19	27	.413	98	39	24	3	2	406	452	21	89	123	12.0	3.48	122	.286	.324	23	.167	-5	21	34	-2	2.4

● **ARNOLD UMBACH** — Umbach, Arnold William b: 12/6/42, Williamsburg, Va. BR/TR, 6'1", 180 lbs. Deb: 10/3/64

YEAR TM/L	W	L	PCT	G	GS	CG	SH	SV	IP	H	HR	BB	SO	RAT	ERA	ERA+	OAV	OOB	BH	AVG	PB	PR	/A	PD	TPI
1964 Mil-N	1	0	1.000	1	1	0	0	0	8¹	11	0	4	7	16.2	3.24	109	.333	.405	0	.000	0	0	0	-0	0.0
1966 Atl-N	0	2	.000	22	3	0	0	0	40²	40	1	18	23	13.3	3.10	117	.256	.341	1	.200	0	2	2	-0	0.1
Total 2	1	2	.333	23	4	0	0	0	49	51	1	22	30	13.8	3.12	116	.270	.352	1	.125	0	3	3	-0	0.1

● **JIM UMBARGER** — Umbarger, James Harold b: 2/17/53, Burbank, Cal. BL/TL, 6'6", 200 lbs. Deb: 4/8/75

YEAR TM/L	W	L	PCT	G	GS	CG	SH	SV	IP	H	HR	BB	SO	RAT	ERA	ERA+	OAV	OOB	BH	AVG	PB	PR	/A	PD	TPI
1975 Tex-A	8	7	.533	56	12	3	2	2	131	134	11	59	50	13.4	4.12	91	.276	.357	0	—	0	-5	-5	1	-0.5
1976 Tex-A	10	12	.455	30	30	10	3	0	197¹	208	12	54	105	12.0	3.15	114	.274	.324	0	—	0	8	10	-0	1.0
1977 Oak-A	1	5	.167	12	8	1	0	0	44	62	3	28	24	19.2	6.55	61	.354	.454	0	—	0	-12	-12	0	-1.3
Tex-A	1	1	.500	3	2	0	0	0	13	14	2	4	5	12.5	5.54	74	.275	.327	0	—	0	-2	-2	-0	-0.3
Yr	2	6	.250	15	10	1	0	0	57	76	5	32	29	17.1	6.32	64	.326	.408	0	—	0	-14	-14	0	-1.6
1978 Tex-A	5	8	.385	32	9	1	0	0	97²	116	9	36	60	14.2	4.88	77	.299	.362	0	—	0	-12	-12	1	-1.5
Total 4	25	33	.431	133	61	15	5	3	483	534	37	181	244	13.5	4.14	90	.287	.354	0	—	0	-23	-22	2	-2.6

● **JIM UMBRICHT** — Umbricht, James b: 9/17/30, Chicago, Ill. d: 4/8/64, Houston, Tex. BR/TR, 6'4", 215 lbs. Deb: 9/26/59

YEAR TM/L	W	L	PCT	G	GS	CG	SH	SV	IP	H	HR	BB	SO	RAT	ERA	ERA+	OAV	OOB	BH	AVG	PB	PR	/A	PD	TPI
1959 Pit-N	0	0	—	1	1	0	0	0	7	7	3	4	3	14.1	6.43	60	.259	.355	0	.000	-0	-2	-2	0	0.0
1960 Pit-N	1	2	.333	17	3	0	0	1	40²	40	5	27	26	14.8	5.09	74	.270	.383	2	.333	0	-6	-6	-1	-0.5
1961 Pit-N	0	0	—	1	0	0	0	0	3¹	5	0	2	1	18.9	2.70	148	.333	.412	1	1.000	0	0	0	-0	0.0
1962 Hou-N	4	0	1.000	34	0	0	0	2	67	51	3	17	55	9.4	2.01	185	.213	.270	1	.111	-0	14	13	1	0.8
1963 Hou-N	4	3	.571	35	3	0	0	0	76	52	6	21	48	8.8	2.61	121	.195	.256	1	.111	-0	6	5	1	0.5
Total 5	9	5	.643	88	7	0	0	3	194	155	17	71	133	10.6	3.06	115	.222	.297	5	.179	-0	13	10	0	0.8

● **WILLIE UNDERHILL** — Underhill, Willie Vern b: 9/6/04, Yowell, Tex. d: 10/26/70, Bay City, Tex. BR/TR, 6'2", 185 lbs. Deb: 9/8/27

YEAR TM/L	W	L	PCT	G	GS	CG	SH	SV	IP	H	HR	BB	SO	RAT	ERA	ERA+	OAV	OOB	BH	AVG	PB	PR	/A	PD	TPI
1927 Cle-A	0	2	.000	4	1	0	0	0	8¹	12	0	11	4	24.8	9.72	43	.375	.535	0	.000	-0	-5	-5	0	-0.9
1928 Cle-A	1	2	.333	11	3	1	0	0	28	33	0	20	16	17.4	4.50	92	.306	.419	4	.364	2	-1	-1	0	0.1
Total 2	1	4	.200	15	4	1	0	0	36¹	45	0	31	20	19.1	5.70	73	.321	.448	4	.333	1	-7	-6	0	-0.8

● **FRED UNDERWOOD** — Underwood, Frederick Theodore b: 10/14/1868, St.Louis Co., Mo. d: 1/26/06, Kansas City, Mo. 170 lbs. Deb: 7/18/1894

YEAR TM/L	W	L	PCT	G	GS	CG	SH	SV	IP	H	HR	BB	SO	RAT	ERA	ERA+	OAV	OOB	BH	AVG	PB	PR	/A	PD	TPI
1894 Bro-N	2	4	.333	7	6	5	0	0	47	80	1	30	10	21.4	7.85	63	.371	.453	7	.389	2	-13	-15	-0	-1.1

● **PAT UNDERWOOD** — Underwood, Patrick John b: 2/9/57, Kokomo, Ind. BL/TL, 6', 175 lbs. Deb: 5/31/79 F

YEAR TM/L	W	L	PCT	G	GS	CG	SH	SV	IP	H	HR	BB	SO	RAT	ERA	ERA+	OAV	OOB	BH	AVG	PB	PR	/A	PD	TPI
1979 Det-A	6	4	.600	27	15	1	0	0	121²	126	17	29	83	11.6	4.59	94	.269	.314	0	—	0	-5	-4	-1	-0.4
1980 Det-A	3	6	.333	49	7	0	0	5	112²	121	12	35	60	12.6	3.59	114	.277	.333	0	—	0	6	6	-0	0.3
1982 Det-A	4	8	.333	33	12	0	0	3	99	108	17	22	43	11.8	4.73	86	.269	.307	0	—	0	-7	-7	1	-0.8
1983 Det-A	0	0	—	4	0	0	0	0	10¹	11	1	6	2	14.8	8.71	45	.289	.386	0	—	0	-5	-6	-0	-0.5
Total 4	13	18	.419	113	34	3	0	8	343²	366	47	92	188	12.1	4.43	94	.272	.320	0	—	0	-12	-10	-1	-0.9

● **TOM UNDERWOOD** — Underwood, Thomas Gerald b: 12/22/53, Kokomo, Ind. BR/TL, 5'11", 170 lbs. Deb: 8/19/74 F

YEAR TM/L	W	L	PCT	G	GS	CG	SH	SV	IP	H	HR	BB	SO	RAT	ERA	ERA+	OAV	OOB	BH	AVG	PB	PR	/A	PD	TPI
1974 Phi-N	1	0	1.000	7	0	0	0	0	13	15	1	5	8	13.8	4.85	78	.313	.377	0	.000	-0	-2	-2	-0	-0.2
1975 Phi-N	14	13	.519	35	35	7	2	0	219¹	221	12	84	123	12.8	4.14	90	.262	.333	9	.122	-2	-13	-10	-4	-1.7
1976 *Phi-N	10	5	.667	33	25	3	0	2	155²	154	9	63	94	12.6	3.53	101	.260	.332	5	.109	-1	-0	-0	-2	-0.3
1977 Phi-N	3	2	.600	14	0	0	0	1	33¹	44	2	18	20	16.7	5.13	78	.328	.408	0	.000	-0	-5	-4	-0	-0.6
StL-N	6	9	.400	19	17	1	0	0	100	104	7	57	66	14.6	4.95	78	.278	.375	4	.133	-0	-12	-12	-1	-1.7
Yr	9	11	.450	33	17	1	0	1	133¹	148	9	75	86	15.1	4.99	78	.290	.382	4	.121	-0	-16	-16	-2	-2.3
1978 Tor-A	6	14	.300	31	30	7	1	0	197²	201	23	87	139	13.2	4.10	96	.263	.340	0	—	0	-7	-4	-3	-0.7
1979 Tor-A	9	16	.360	33	32	12	1	0	227	213	23	95	127	12.6	3.69	118	.253	.335	0	—	0	13	17	-0	1.6
1980 *NY-A	13	9	.591	38	27	2	2	2	187	163	15	66	116	11.2	3.66	107	.237	.307	0	—	0	8	5	-0	0.7
1981 NY-A	1	4	.200	9	6	0	0	0	32²	32	2	13	29	12.4	4.41	81	.262	.333	0	—	0	-3	-3	-0	-0.4
*Oak-A	3	2	.600	16	5	1	0	1	51	37	4	25	46	11.3	3.18	109	.202	.305	0	—	0	3	2	0	0.2
Yr	4	6	.400	25	11	1	0	1	83²	69	6	38	75	11.7	3.66	96	.226	.316	0	—	0	-0	-1	-0	-0.2
1982 Oak-A	10	6	.625	56	10	2	0	7	153	136	14	68	79	12.1	3.29	119	.241	.324	0	—	0	13	10	-2	0.8
1983 Oak-A	9	7	.563	51	15	0	0	4	144²	156	13	50	62	12.9	4.04	95	.277	.338	0	—	0	0	-3	-3	-0.2
1984 Bal-A	1	0	1.000	37	1	0	0	0	71²	71	8	31	39	13.7	3.52	110	.282	.354	0	—	0	4	3	1	0.3
Total 11	86	87	.497	379	203	35	6	18	1586	1554	130	662	948	12.7	3.89	100	.259	.336	18	.117	-4	-0	-0	-15	-2.3

● **WOODY UPCHURCH** — Upchurch, Jefferson Woodrow b: 4/13/11, Buies Creek, N.C. d: 10/23/71, Buies Creek, N.C. BR/TL, 6', 180 lbs. Deb: 9/14/35

YEAR TM/L	W	L	PCT	G	GS	CG	SH	SV	IP	H	HR	BB	SO	RAT	ERA	ERA+	OAV	OOB	BH	AVG	PB	PR	/A	PD	TPI
1935 Phi-A	0	2	.000	3	3	1	0	0	21¹	23	3	12	2	14.8	5.06	90	.271	.361	2	.286	-1	-1	-1	-0	-0.1
1936 Phi-A	0	2	.000	7	2	1	0	0	22¹	36	7	14	6	20.1	9.67	53	.353	.431	1	.143	-0	-12	-11	-1	-0.9
Total 2	0	4	.000	10	5	2	0	0	43²	59	10	26	8	17.5	7.42	65	.316	.399	3	.214	-0	-13	-13	-1	-1.0

● **JOHN UPHAM** — Upham, John Leslie b: 12/29/41, Windsor, Ont., Can. BL/TL, 6', 180 lbs. Deb: 4/16/67 ♦

YEAR TM/L	W	L	PCT	G	GS	CG	SH	SV	IP	H	HR	BB	SO	RAT	ERA	ERA+	OAV	OOB	BH	AVG	PB	PR	/A	PD	TPI
1967 Chi-N	0	1	.000	5	0	0	0	0	1¹	4	1	2	2	40.5	33.75	11	.571	.667	2	.667	1	-5	-4	0	-2.4
1968 Chi-N	0	0	—	2	0	0	0	0	7	2	0	3	2	7.0	0.00	—	.087	.222	2	.200	0	2	2	0	0.0
Total 2	0	1	.000	7	0	0	0	0	8¹	6	1	5	4	13.0	5.40	60	.200	.333	4	.308	1	-2	-2	0	-2.4

● **BILL UPHAM** — Upham, William Lawrence b: 4/4/1888, Akron, Ohio d: 9/14/59, Newark, N.J. BB/TR, 6', 178 lbs. Deb: 4/10/15

YEAR TM/L	W	L	PCT	G	GS	CG	SH	SV	IP	H	HR	BB	SO	RAT	ERA	ERA+	OAV	OOB	BH	AVG	PB	PR	/A	PD	TPI
1915 Bro-F	6	8	.429	33	11	4	2	5	121	129	6	40	46	12.6	3.05	89	.274	.331	4	.111	-2	-4	-4	2	-0.6
1918 Bos-N	1	1	.500	3	2	2	0	0	20²	28	2	1	8	12.6	5.23	51	.326	.333	2	.222	0	-6	-6	-0	-0.5
Total 2	7	9	.438	36	13	6	2	5	141²	157	8	41	54	12.6	3.37	81	.282	.332	6	.133	-2	-10	-10	2	-1.1

● **JERRY UPP** — Upp, George Henry b: 12/10/1883, Sandusky, Ohio d: 6/30/37, Sandusky, Ohio TL, Deb: 9/2/09

YEAR TM/L	W	L	PCT	G	GS	CG	SH	SV	IP	H	HR	BB	SO	RAT	ERA	ERA+	OAV	OOB	BH	AVG	PB	PR	/A	PD	TPI
1909 Cle-A	2	1	.667	7	4	2	0	0	26²	26	0	12	13	12.8	1.69	152	.260	.339	2	.222	1	2	3	1	0.4

● **CECIL UPSHAW** — Upshaw, Cecil Lee b: 10/22/42, Spearsville, La. BR/TR, 6'6", 205 lbs. Deb: 10/1/66

YEAR TM/L	W	L	PCT	G	GS	CG	SH	SV	IP	H	HR	BB	SO	RAT	ERA	ERA+	OAV	OOB	BH	AVG	PB	PR	/A	PD	TPI
1966 Atl-N	0	0	—	1	0	0	0	0	3	0	0	3	2	9.0	0.00	—	.000	.273	1	1.000	0	1	1	-0	0.0
1967 Atl-N	2	3	.400	30	0	0	0	8	45¹	42	4	8	31	10.7	2.58	129	.247	.297	1	.167	1	4	4	0	0.6
1968 Atl-N	8	7	.533	52	0	0	0	13	116²	98	6	24	74	9.7	2.47	121	.229	.276	4	.174	0	7	7	-0	1.1
1969 *Atl-N	6	4	.600	62	0	0	0	27	105¹	102	7	29	57	11.3	2.91	124	.259	.311	5	.238	2	8	11	1	1.5
1971 Atl-N	11	6	.647	49	0	0	0	17	82	95	5	28	56	13.7	3.51	106	.292	.352	0	.000	-2	-0	-2	-1	0.2
1972 Atl-N	3	5	.375	42	0	0	0	13	53²	50	5	19	23	11.7	3.69	103	.249	.317	1	.143	-0	-1	1	1	0.2
1973 Atl-N	0	1	.000	5	0	0	0	0	3²	8	0	2	3	24.5	9.82	40	.444	.500	0	—	0	-3	-2	0	-0.6
Hou-N	2	3	.400	35	0	0	0	2	38¹	38	3	15	21	12.7	4.46	81	.259	.331	0	.000	-0	-3	-4	1	-0.4
Yr	2	4	.333	40	0	0	0	2	42	46	3	17	24	13.7	4.93	74	.277	.348	0	.000	-0	-6	-6	1	-1.0
1974 Cle-A	0	1	.000	7	0	0	0	0	8	10	1	4	7	15.8	3.38	107	.345	.424	0	—	0	-0	-0	-0	0.0
NY-A	1	5	.167	36	0	0	0	6	59²	53	1	24	30	12.1	3.02	116	.254	.339	0	—	0	4	3	1	0.5
Yr	1	6	.143	43	0	0	0	6	67²	63	2	28	34	12.5	3.15	112	.262	.347	0	—	0	3	3	1	0.5
1975 Chi-A	1	1	.500	29	0	0	0	1	47¹	49	5	21	24	14.1	3.23	120	.271	.359	3	—	0	3	3	-0	0.1
Total 9	34	36	.486	348	0	0	0	86	563	545	37	177	323	11.9	3.13	112	.258	.322	12	.160	1	19	23	2	3.2

YEAR TM/L	W	L	PCT	G	GS	CG	SH	SV	IP	H	HR	BB	SO	RAT	ERA	ERA+	OAV	OOB	BH	AVG	PB	PR	/A	PD	TPI

● BILL UPTON　Upton, William Ray b: 6/18/29, Esther, Mo. d: 1/2/87, San Diego, Cal. BR/TR, 6', 167 lbs. Deb: 4/13/54 F

| 1954 Phi-A | 0 | 0 | — | 2 | 0 | 0 | 0 | 0 | 5 | 6 | 1 | 1 | 2 | 12.6 | 1.80 | 217 | .300 | .333 | 0 | — | 0 | 1 | 1 | 0 | 0.1 |

● JACK URBAN　Urban, Jack Elmer b: 12/5/28, Omaha, Neb. BR/TR, 5'8", 155 lbs. Deb: 6/13/57

1957 KC-A	7	4	.636	31	13	3	0	0	129¹	111	7	45	55	10.9	3.34	118	.237	.305	11	.282	2	6	9	2	1.1
1958 KC-A	8	11	.421	30	24	5	1	1	132	150	17	51	54	13.8	5.93	66	.286	.351	7	.152	-2	-32	-30	-1	-4.0
1959 StL-N	0	0	—	8	0	0	0	0	10²	18	1	7	4	21.1	9.28	46	.409	.490	0	.000	-0	-6	-6	-0	0.0
Total 3	15	15	.500	69	37	8	1	1	272	279	25	103	113	12.7	4.83	82	.269	.337	18	.209	0	-32	-27	-0	-2.9

● TOM URBANI　Urbani, Thomas James b: 1/21/68, Santa Cruz, Cal. BL/TL, 6'1", 190 lbs. Deb: 4/21/93

1993 StL-N	1	3	.250	18	9	0	0	0	62	73	4	26	33	14.4	4.65	85	.296	.363	3	.188	1	-4	-5	0	-0.2
1994 StL-N	3	7	.300	20	10	0	0	0	80¹	98	12	21	43	13.7	5.15	79	.302	.350	6	.250	2	-8	-10	0	-0.9
Total 2	4	10	.286	38	19	0	0	0	142¹	171	16	47	76	14.0	4.93	82	.299	.355	9	.225	2	-13	-14	1	-1.1

● JOHN URREA　Urrea, John Godoy b: 2/9/55, Los Angeles, Cal. BR/TR, 6'3", 205 lbs. Deb: 4/10/77

1977 StL-N	7	6	.538	41	12	2	1	4	139²	126	13	35	81	10.4	3.16	122	.244	.292	4	.138	2	12	11	1	1.2
1978 StL-N	4	9	.308	27	12	1	0	0	98²	108	4	47	61	14.8	5.38	65	.284	.373	3	.125	-1	-20	-20	0	-2.5
1979 StL-N	0	0	—	3	2	0	0	0	11¹	13	0	9	5	17.5	3.97	95	.310	.431	1	.250	0	-0	-0	0	0.0
1980 StL-N	4	1	.800	30	1	0	0	3	64²	57	2	41	36	13.9	3.48	106	.239	.356	3	.231	0	1	2	-1	0.0
1981 SD-N	2	2	.500	38	0	0	0	2	49	43	1	28	19	13.6	2.39	136	.239	.351	1	.250	0	6	5	-1	0.3
Total 5	17	18	.486	139	27	3	1	9	363¹	347	20	160	202	12.9	3.74	97	.256	.339	12	.162	2	-2	-4	-1	-1.0

● BOB VAIL　Vail, Robert Garfield "Doc" b: 9/24/1881, Linneus, Maine d: 3/22/42, Philadelphia, Pa. BR/TR, 5'10", 165 lbs. Deb: 8/27/08

| 1908 Pit-N | 1 | 2 | .333 | 4 | 1 | 0 | 0 | 0 | 15 | 15 | 0 | 7 | 9 | 13.8 | 6.00 | 38 | .268 | .359 | 1 | .333 | 1 | -6 | -6 | -1 | -1.1 |

● ISMAEL VALDES　Valdes, Ismael b: 8/21/73, Victoria, Mex. BR/TR, 6'3", 185 lbs. Deb: 6/15/94

| 1994 LA-N | 3 | 1 | .750 | 21 | 1 | 0 | 0 | 0 | 28¹ | 21 | 2 | 10 | 28 | 9.8 | 3.18 | 124 | .206 | .277 | 0 | .000 | -0 | 3 | 2 | 1 | 0.4 |

● EFRAIN VALDEZ　Valdez, Efrain Antonio b: 7/11/66, Nizao Bani, D.R. BL/TL, 5'11", 180 lbs. Deb: 8/13/90

1990 Cle-A	1	1	.500	13	0	0	0	0	23²	20	2	14	13	12.9	3.04	129	.233	.340	0	—	0	2	2	0	0.2
1991 Cle-A	0	0	—	7	0	0	0	0	6	5	0	3	1	13.5	1.50	277	.238	.360	0	—	0	2	2	0	0.0
Total 2	1	1	.500	20	0	0	0	0	29²	25	2	17	14	13.0	2.73	145	.234	.344	0	—	0	4	4	-0	0.2

● RAFAEL VALDEZ　Valdez, Rafael Emilio (Diaz) b: 12/17/67, Nizao Bani, D.R. BR/TR, 5'11", 165 lbs. Deb: 4/18/90

| 1990 SD-N | 0 | 1 | .000 | 3 | 0 | 0 | 0 | 0 | 5² | 11 | 4 | 3 | 3 | 20.6 | 11.12 | 34 | .393 | .433 | 0 | .000 | -0 | -5 | -5 | -0 | -0.7 |

● RENE VALDEZ　Valdez, Rene Gutierrez (b: Rene Gutierrez (Valdez)) b: 6/2/29, Guanabacoa, Cuba BR/TR, 6'3", 175 lbs. Deb: 4/21/57

| 1957 Bro-N | 1 | 1 | .500 | 5 | 1 | 0 | 0 | 0 | 13 | 13 | 1 | 7 | 10 | 13.8 | 5.54 | 75 | .265 | .357 | 0 | .000 | -0 | -2 | -2 | -0 | -0.3 |

● SERGIO VALDEZ　Valdez, Sergio Sanchez (b: Sergio Sanchez (Valdez)) b: 9/7/64, Elias Pina, D.R. BR/TR, 6', 165 lbs. Deb: 9/10/86

1986 Mon-N	0	4	.000	5	5	0	0	0	25	39	2	11	20	18.4	6.84	54	.361	.425	1	.125	-0	-9	-9	-0	-1.2
1989 Atl-N	1	2	.333	19	1	0	0	0	32²	31	5	17	26	13.2	6.06	60	.246	.336	1	1.000	0	-9	-9	-1	-0.8
1990 Atl-N	0	0	—	6	0	0	0	0	5¹	6	0	3	2	15.2	6.75	60	.273	.360	0	—	0	-2	-2	0	0.0
Cle-A	6	6	.500	24	13	0	0	0	102¹	109	17	35	63	12.8	4.75	82	.276	.336	0	—	0	-10	-9	-0	-1.0
1991 Cle-A	0	1	.000	6	0	0	0	0	16¹	15	3	5	11	11.0	5.51	75	.238	.294	0	—	0	-3	-2	-1	-0.2
1992 Mon-N	0	2	.000	27	0	0	0	0	37¹	25	2	12	32	8.9	2.41	144	.185	.252	0	.000	-0	5	4	0	0.2
1993 Mon-N	0	0	—	4	0	0	0	0	3	4	1	1	2	15.0	9.00	46	.308	.357	0	—	0	-2	-2	-0	0.0
1994 Bos-A	0	1	.000	12	1	0	0	0	14¹	25	4	8	4	20.7	8.16	63	.391	.458	0	—	0	-5	-5	-0	-0.4
Total 7	8	15	.348	103	20	0	0	0	236¹	254	34	92	161	13.3	5.14	75	.274	.341	2	.167	-0	-34	-33	-1	-3.4

● CORKY VALENTINE　Valentine, Harold Lewis b: 1/4/29, Troy, Ohio BR/TR, 6'1", 203 lbs. Deb: 4/17/54

1954 Cin-N	12	11	.522	36	28	7	3	1	194¹	211	24	60	73	12.7	4.45	94	.282	.339	9	.138	-2	-8	-5	-2	-0.9
1955 Cin-N	2	1	.667	10	5	0	0	0	26²	29	5	16	14	15.5	7.43	57	.276	.377	0	.000	-1	-10	-9	1	-0.9
Total 2	14	12	.538	46	33	7	3	1	221	240	29	76	87	13.1	4.81	87	.282	.344	9	.125	-3	-18	-15	-1	-1.8

● JOHN VALENTINE　Valentine, John Gill b: 11/21/1855, Brooklyn, N.Y. d: 10/10/03, Central Islip, N.Y Deb: 5/3/1883

| 1883 Col-a | 2 | 10 | .167 | 13 | 12 | 11 | 0 | 0 | 102 | 130 | 0 | 18 | 13 | 13.0 | 3.53 | 87 | .291 | .317 | 17 | .283 | 3 | -3 | -5 | 1 | -0.1 |

● VITO VALENTINETTI　Valentinetti, Vito John b: 9/16/28, W.New York, N.J. BR/TR, 6', 195 lbs. Deb: 6/20/54

1954 Chi-A	0	0	—	1	0	0	0	0	1	4	1	2	1	54.0	54.00	7	.571	.667	0	—	0	-6	-6	-0	0.0
1956 Chi-N	6	4	.600	42	6	0	0	1	95¹	84	10	36	26	11.4	3.78	100	.243	.317	2	.100	-1	-0	-0	-1	-0.3
1957 Chi-N	0	0	—	9	0	0	0	0	12	12	1	7	8	14.3	2.25	172	.255	.352	0	.000	0	2	2	-0	0.0
Cle-A	2	2	.500	11	2	1	0	0	23²	26	3	13	9	15.2	4.94	75	.289	.385	1	.200	-0	-3	-3	-0	-0.5
1958 Det-A	1	0	1.000	15	0	0	0	2	18²	18	4	5	10	11.6	3.38	120	.257	.316	0	—	0	1	1	-0	0.1
Was-A	4	6	.400	23	10	2	0	0	95²	106	16	49	33	14.8	5.08	75	.286	.373	9	.321	2	-14	-13	2	-0.9
Yr	5	6	.455	38	10	2	0	2	114¹	124	20	54	43	14.2	4.80	80	.281	.362	9	.321	2	-13	-12	1	-0.8
1959 Was-A	0	2	.000	7	1	0	0	0	10²	16	0	10	7	22.8	10.13	39	.356	.482	0	—	0	-7	-7	0	-1.1
Total 5	13	14	.481	108	15	3	0	3	257	266	35	122	94	13.8	4.73	81	.273	.358	12	.218	1	-27	-26	0	-2.7

● FERNANDO VALENZUELA　Valenzuela, Fernando (Anguamea) b: 11/1/60, Navojoa, Mexico BL/TL, 5'11", 195 lbs. Deb: 9/15/80

1980 LA-N	2	0	1.000	10	0	0	0	1	17²	8	0	5	16	6.6	0.00	—	.136	.203	0	.000	-0	7	7	0	0.9
1981 *LA-N★	13	7	.650	25	25	**11**	**8**	0	**192¹**	140	11	61	**180**	9.5	2.48	134	.205	.271	16	.250	3	22	18	2	2.5
1982 LA-N★	19	13	.594	37	37	18	4	0	285	247	13	83	199	10.5	2.87	121	.236	.294	16	.168	1	23	19	5	2.7
1983 *LA-N☆	15	10	.600	35	35	9	4	0	257	245	16	99	189	12.2	3.75	96	.255	.327	17	.187	-2	-3	-4	4	0.2
1984 LA-N★	12	17	.414	34	34	12	2	0	261	218	14	106	240	11.2	3.03	116	.229	.308	15	.190	4	16	14	4	2.5
1985 *LA-N★	17	10	.630	35	35	14	5	0	272¹	211	14	101	208	10.3	2.45	142	.214	.288	21	.216	4	35	31	2	3.6
1986 LA-N★	**21**	11	.656	34	34	**20**	3	0	269¹	226	18	85	242	10.4	3.14	110	.226	.288	24	.220	5	17	9	4	1.9
1987 LA-N	14	14	.500	34	34	**12**	1	0	251	254	25	124	190	13.7	3.98	100	.262	.349	13	.141	-1	3	-0	3	0.2
1988 LA-N	5	8	.385	23	22	3	0	1	142¹	142	11	76	64	13.8	4.24	79	.268	.360	8	.182	1	-12	-14	3	-0.8
1989 LA-N	10	13	.435	31	31	3	0	0	196²	185	11	98	116	13.0	3.43	99	.251	.340	12	.182	1	-0	-2	0	0.2
1990 LA-N	13	13	.500	33	33	5	2	0	204	223	19	77	115	13.2	4.59	80	.276	.339	21	.304	8	-18	-21	-0	-1.6
1991 Cal-A	0	2	.000	2	2	0	0	0	6²	14	3	3	5	23.0	12.15	34	.452	.500	0	—	0	-6	-6	0	-1.2
1993 Bal-A	8	10	.444	32	31	5	2	0	178²	179	18	79	78	13.2	4.94	91	.266	.346	0	—	0	-12	-9	2	-0.7
1994 Phi-N	1	2	.333	8	7	0	0	0	45	42	2	7	19	9.8	3.00	130	.247	.277	3	.250	1	6	6	0	0.4
Total 14	150	130	.536	373	360	112	31	2	2579	2334	181	1004	1861	11.7	3.44	105	.243	.316	166	.203	30	78	47	29	10.8

● JULIO VALERA　Valera, Julio Enrique (Torres) b: 10/13/68, Aguadilla, P.R. BR/TR, 6'2", 185 lbs. Deb: 9/1/90

1990 NY-N	1	1	.500	3	3	0	0	0	13	20	1	7	4	18.7	6.92	54	.351	.422	1	.200	0	-5	-5	-1	-0.6
1991 NY-N	0	0	—	2	0	0	0	0	2	1	0	4	3	22.5	0.00	—	.143	.455	0	—	0	1	1	0	0.0
1992 Cal-A	8	11	.421	30	28	4	2	0	188	188	15	64	113	12.2	3.73	107	.262	.324	0	—	0	-4	-5	-2	-2.0
1993 Cal-A	3	6	.333	19	5	0	0	4	53	77	8	15	28	16.0	6.62	68	.344	.390	0	—	0	-14	-12	-0	-2.0
Total 4	12	18	.400	54	36	4	2	4	256	286	24	90	148	13.4	4.46	91	.284	.345	1	.200	0	-13	-11	-3	-2.4

● CLAY Van ALSTYNE　Van Alstyne, Clayton Emory "Spike" b: 5/24/1900, Stuyvesant, N.Y. d: 1/5/60, Hudson, N.Y. BR/TR, 5'11", 180 lbs. Deb: 8/20/27

| 1927 Was-A | 0 | 0 | — | 2 | 0 | 0 | 0 | 0 | 3 | 3 | 0 | 0 | 0 | 9.0 | 3.00 | 136 | .250 | .250 | 0 | — | 0 | 0 | 0 | 0 | 0.0 |

YEAR TM/L	W	L	PCT	G	GS	CG	SH	SV	IP	H	HR	BB	SO	RAT	ERA	ERA+	OAV	OOB	BH	AVG	PB	PR	/A	PD	TPI
1928 Was-A	0	0	—	4	0	0	0	0	21¹	26	0	13	5	16.9	5.48	73	.329	.430	2	.250	1	-3	-3	1	0.2
Total 2	0	0	—	6	0	0	0	0	24¹	29	0	13	5	15.9	5.18	78	.319	.410	2	.250	1	-3	-3	1	0.2

● RUSS Van ATTA
Van Atta, Russell "Sheriff" b: 6/21/06, Augusta, N.J. d: 10/10/86, Andover, N.J. BL/TL, 6', 184 lbs. Deb: 4/25/33

YEAR TM/L	W	L	PCT	G	GS	CG	SH	SV	IP	H	HR	BB	SO	RAT	ERA	ERA+	OAV	OOB	BH	AVG	PB	PR	/A	PD	TPI
1933 NY-A	12	4	.750	26	22	10	2	1	157	160	8	63	76	12.8	4.18	93	.262	.332	17	.283	4	2	-5	0	-0.1
1934 NY-A	3	5	.375	28	9	0	0	0	88	107	4	46	39	15.9	6.34	64	.307	.390	6	.207	1	-18	-22	-1	-1.6
1935 NY-A	0	0	—	5	0	0	0	0	4²	5	0	4	3	17.4	3.86	105	.263	.391	0	.000	0	0	0	0	0.0
StL-A	9	16	.360	53	17	1	0	3	170¹	201	10	87	87	15.4	5.34	90	.292	.374	9	.214	-1	-17	-10	-1	-1.5
Yr	9	16	.360	58	17	1	0	3	175	206	10	91	90	15.4	5.30	90	.291	.375	9	.209	-1	-16	-10	-2	-1.5
1936 StL-A	4	7	.364	52	9	2	0	2	122²	164	9	68	59	17.2	6.60	81	.320	.401	5	.172	-1	-21	-17	1	-1.2
1937 StL-A	1	2	.333	16	6	1	0	0	58²	74	2	32	34	16.3	5.52	87	.307	.388	6	.462	3	-6	-5	1	0.2
1938 StL-A	4	7	.364	25	12	3	1	0	104	118	7	61	35	15.6	6.06	82	.289	.382	4	.133	-1	-15	-13	0	-1.1
1939 StL-A	0	0	—	2	1	0	0	0	7	9	0	7	6	21.9	11.57	42	.310	.459	0	.000	-0	-5	-5	-0	0.2
Total 7	33	41	.446	207	76	17	3	6	712¹	838	39	368	339	15.4	5.60	82	.293	.376	47	.228	5	-80	-78	-1	-5.3

● OZZIE Van BRABANT
Van Brabant, Camille Oscar b: 9/28/26, Kingsville, Ont., Canada BR/TR, 6'1", 165 lbs. Deb: 4/13/54

YEAR TM/L	W	L	PCT	G	GS	CG	SH	SV	IP	H	HR	BB	SO	RAT	ERA	ERA+	OAV	OOB	BH	AVG	PB	PR	/A	PD	TPI
1954 Phi-A	0	2	.000	9	2	0	0	0	26²	35	3	18	10	18.2	7.09	55	.347	.450	1	.200	0	-10	-9	1	-0.5
1955 KC-A	0	0	—	2	0	0	0	0	2	4	1	2	1	27.0	18.00	23	.400	.500	0	—	0	-3	-3	-0	-0.1
Total 2	0	2	.000	11	2	0	0	0	28²	39	4	20	11	18.8	7.85	50	.351	.455	1	.200	0	-13	-13	1	-0.5

● DAZZY VANCE
Vance, Clarence Arthur b: 3/4/1891, Orient, Iowa d: 2/16/61, Homosassa Springs, Fla. BR/TR, 6'2", 200 lbs. Deb: 4/16/15 H

YEAR TM/L	W	L	PCT	G	GS	CG	SH	SV	IP	H	HR	BB	SO	RAT	ERA	ERA+	OAV	OOB	BH	AVG	PB	PR	/A	PD	TPI
1915 Pit-N	0	1	.000	1	1	0	0	0	2²	3	0	5	0	30.4	10.13	27	.375	.643	0	.000	-0	-2	-2	0	-0.6
NY-A	0	3	.000	8	3	1	0	0	28	23	1	16	18	13.2	3.54	83	.232	.350	2	.667	2	-2	-2	-0	0.0
1918 NY-A	0	0	—	2	0	0	0	0	2¹	9	0	2	0	42.4	15.43	18	.692	.733	0	—	0	-3	-3	-0	0.0
1922 Bro-N	18	12	.600	36	30	16	5	0	245²	259	9	94	134	13.2	3.70	110	.276	.347	20	.225	1	11	10	0	1.3
1923 Bro-N	18	15	.545	37	35	21	3	0	280¹	263	10	100	197	12.0	3.50	111	.250	.322	7	.084	-3	16	12	0	0.9
1924 Bro-N	28	6	.824	35	34	30	3	0	308¹	238	11	77	262	9.5	2.16	173	.213	.269	16	.151	-2	58	54	1	5.7
1925 Bro-N	22	9	.710	31	31	26	4	0	265¹	247	8	66	221	11.0	3.53	118	.250	.304	14	.143	-0	22	19	1	2.1
1926 Bro-N	9	10	.474	24	22	12	0	1	169	172	7	58	140	12.3	3.89	98	.271	.333	10	.182	-1	-1	-1	2	-0.1
1927 Bro-N	16	15	.516	34	32	25	2	1	273¹	242	12	69	184	10.4	2.70	147	.239	.291	15	.167	-2	37	38	-2	3.8
1928 Bro-N	22	10	.688	38	32	24	4	2	280¹	226	11	72	200	9.8	2.09	190	.221	.277	17	.177	2	59	59	1	7.0
1929 Bro-N	14	13	.519	31	26	17	1	0	231¹	244	15	47	126	11.7	3.89	119	.274	.316	10	.135	-2	21	19	1	1.7
1930 Bro-N	17	15	.531	35	31	20	4	0	258²	241	15	55	173	10.5	2.61	188	.246	.289	12	.135	-5	68	66	-1	6.6
1931 Bro-N	11	13	.458	30	29	12	2	0	218²	221	12	53	150	11.3	3.38	113	.261	.304	9	.134	-2	12	11	1	0.9
1932 Bro-N	12	11	.522	27	24	9	1	1	175²	171	10	57	103	11.7	4.20	91	.256	.315	5	.089	-4	-6	-7	-0	-1.2
1933 StL-N	6	2	.750	28	11	2	0	3	99	105	3	28	67	12.2	3.55	98	.267	.318	5	.179	-1	-2	-1	-1	-0.2
1934 Cin-N	0	2	.000	6	2	0	0	0	18	28	1	11	9	20.0	7.50	54	.350	.435	1	.250	0	-7	-7	-0	-0.6
*StL-N	1	1	.500	19	4	1	0	1	59	62	4	14	33	11.9	3.66	115	.271	.318	2	.133	-0	3	4	-0	0.1
Yr	1	3	.250	25	6	1	0	1	77	90	5	25	42	13.7	4.56	92	.290	.347	3	.158	-0	-4	-3	-0	-0.5
1935 Bro-N	3	2	.600	25	6	1	0	1	51	55	3	16	28	13.1	4.41	90	.268	.330	1	.059	-2	-2	-2	-0	-0.4
Total 16	197	140	.585	442	347	216	29	11	2966²	2809	132	840	2045	11.3	3.24	125	.251	.308	146	.150	-18	281	266	3	27.0

● SANDY VANCE
Vance, Gene Covington b: 1/5/47, Lamar, Colo. BR/TR, 6'2", 180 lbs. Deb: 4/26/70

YEAR TM/L	W	L	PCT	G	GS	CG	SH	SV	IP	H	HR	BB	SO	RAT	ERA	ERA+	OAV	OOB	BH	AVG	PB	PR	/A	PD	TPI
1970 LA-N	7	7	.500	20	18	2	0	0	115	109	9	37	45	11.5	3.13	122	.248	.308	7	.189	1	12	9	-3	0.8
1971 LA-N	2	1	.667	10	3	0	0	0	26	38	1	9	11	16.3	6.92	47	.355	.405	0	.000	-0	-10	-11	-0	-1.2
Total 2	9	8	.529	30	21	2	0	0	141	147	10	46	56	12.4	3.83	97	.269	.327	7	.167	0	2	-2	-3	-0.4

● JOE VANCE
Vance, Joseph Albert "Sandy" b: 9/16/05, Devine, Tex. d: 7/4/78, Devine, Tex. BR/TR, 6'1.5", 190 lbs. Deb: 4/18/35

YEAR TM/L	W	L	PCT	G	GS	CG	SH	SV	IP	H	HR	BB	SO	RAT	ERA	ERA+	OAV	OOB	BH	AVG	PB	PR	/A	PD	TPI
1935 Chi-A	2	2	.500	10	0	0	0	0	31	36	4	21	12	16.5	6.68	69	.295	.399	2	.182	-1	-8	-7	1	-0.8
1937 NY-A	1	0	1.000	2	2	0	0	0	15	11	2	9	3	12.0	3.00	148	.204	.317	0	.000	-1	3	2	1	0.1
1938 NY-A	0	0	—	3	1	0	0	0	11¹	20	2	4	2	19.1	7.15	63	.408	.453	3	.750	2	-3	-3	0	0.2
Total 3	3	2	.600	15	3	0	0	0	57¹	67	5	34	17	15.9	5.81	79	.298	.390	5	.250	1	-8	-8	1	-0.5

● CHRIS Van CUYK
Van Cuyk, Christian Gerald b: 1/3/27, Kimberly, Wis. d: 11/3/92, Hudson, Fla. BL/TL, 6'6", 215 lbs. Deb: 7/16/50 F

YEAR TM/L	W	L	PCT	G	GS	CG	SH	SV	IP	H	HR	BB	SO	RAT	ERA	ERA+	OAV	OOB	BH	AVG	PB	PR	/A	PD	TPI
1950 Bro-N	1	3	.250	12	4	1	0	0	33¹	33	3	12	21	12.4	4.86	84	.266	.336	1	.100	-1	-3	-3	-1	-0.4
1951 Bro-N	1	2	.333	9	6	0	0	0	29¹	33	4	11	16	14.7	5.52	71	.295	.378	2	.250	0	-5	-5	-0	-0.4
1952 Bro-N	5	6	.455	23	16	4	0	1	97²	104	12	40	66	13.7	5.16	71	.271	.347	8	.242	2	-16	-17	-1	-1.7
Total 3	7	11	.389	44	26	5	0	1	160¹	170	19	63	103	13.6	5.16	73	.274	.351	11	.216	1	-23	-25	-2	-2.5

● JOHNNY Van CUYK
Van Cuyk, John Henry b: 7/7/21, Little Chute, Wis. BL/TL, 6'1", 190 lbs. Deb: 9/18/47 F

YEAR TM/L	W	L	PCT	G	GS	CG	SH	SV	IP	H	HR	BB	SO	RAT	ERA	ERA+	OAV	OOB	BH	AVG	PB	PR	/A	PD	TPI
1947 Bro-N	0	0	—	2	0	0	0	0	3¹	5	0	1	2	16.2	5.40	77	.357	.400	0	—	0	-0	-0	0	0.0
1948 Bro-N	0	0	—	3	0	0	0	0	5	4	1	1	1	9.0	3.60	111	.200	.238	0	—	0	0	0	0	0.0
1949 Bro-N	0	0	—	2	0	0	0	0	2	3	0	1	0	18.0	9.00	46	.429	.500	0	—	0	-1	-1	-0	0.0
Total 3	0	0	—	7	0	0	0	0	10¹	12	1	3	3	13.1	5.23	78	.293	.341	0	—	0	-1	-1	0	0.0

● ED VANDE BERG
Vande Berg, Edward John b: 10/26/58, Redlands, Cal. BR/TL, 6'2", 180 lbs. Deb: 4/7/82

YEAR TM/L	W	L	PCT	G	GS	CG	SH	SV	IP	H	HR	BB	SO	RAT	ERA	ERA+	OAV	OOB	BH	AVG	PB	PR	/A	PD	TPI
1982 Sea-A	9	4	.692	78	0	0	0	5	76	54	5	32	60	10.4	2.37	179	.207	.298	0	—	0	14	16	2	2.9
1983 Sea-A	2	4	.333	68	0	0	0	5	64¹	59	6	22	49	11.5	3.36	127	.246	.312	0	—	0	5	6	0	0.5
1984 Sea-A	8	12	.400	50	17	2	0	7	130¹	165	18	50	71	14.8	4.76	84	.313	.373	0	—	0	-11	-11	-0	-1.7
1985 Sea-A	2	1	.667	76	0	0	0	3	67²	71	4	31	34	13.7	3.72	113	.274	.354	0	—	0	3	4	1	0.2
1986 LA-N	1	5	.167	60	0	0	0	0	71¹	83	8	33	42	14.8	3.41	101	.290	.366	0	.000	-0	2	1	1	0.1
1987 Cle-A	1	0	1.000	55	0	0	0	0	72¹	96	9	21	40	14.6	5.10	89	.325	.370	0	—	0	-5	-5	0	0.0
1988 Tex-A	2	2	.500	26	0	0	0	0	37	44	2	11	18	13.4	4.14	99	.308	.357	0	—	0	-1	-1	0	-0.2
Total 7	25	28	.472	413	17	2	0	22	519	572	52	200	314	13.5	3.92	104	.284	.351	0	.000	-0	8	10	3	1.8

● HY VANDENBERG
Vandenberg, Harold Harris b: 3/17/06, Abilene, Kan. d: 7/31/94, Bloomington, Minn. BR/TR, 6'4", 220 lbs. Deb: 6/8/35

YEAR TM/L	W	L	PCT	G	GS	CG	SH	SV	IP	H	HR	BB	SO	RAT	ERA	ERA+	OAV	OOB	BH	AVG	PB	PR	/A	PD	TPI
1935 Bos-A	0	0	—	3	0	0	0	0	5¹	15	1	4	2	32.1	20.25	23	.500	.559	1	1.000	0	-9	-9	0	0.0
1937 NY-N	0	1	.000	1	1	1	0	0	8	10	1	6	2	18.0	7.88	49	.313	.421	0	.000	-1	-4	-4	1	-0.3
1938 NY-N	0	1	.000	6	1	0	0	0	18	28	2	7	20	20.0	7.50	50	.368	.455	0	.000	-1	-7	-7	1	-0.3
1939 NY-N	0	0	—	2	0	0	0	0	6¹	10	0	6	3	22.7	5.68	69	.345	.457	0	.000	-1	-1	-1	0	0.0
1940 NY-N	1	1	.500	13	3	1	0	1	32¹	27	2	16	17	12.2	3.90	100	.227	.324	1	.125	-0	-0	-1	-0	-0.1
1944 Chi-N	7	4	.636	35	9	2	0	0	126¹	123	8	51	54	12.5	3.63	97	.255	.327	1	.237	-1	-0	-1	-0	-0.1
1945 *Chi-N	7	3	.700	30	7	3	1	2	95¹	91	3	33	35	12.1	3.49	105	.259	.330	4	.125	-1	2	1	0	0.0
Total 7	15	10	.600	90	22	7	1	5	291²	304	17	128	120	13.5	4.32	85	.259	.349	15	.169	-1	-19	-21	2	-0.7

● JOHNNY VANDER MEER
Vander Meer, John Samuel "Double No-Hit" or "The Dutch Master"
b: 11/2/14, Prospect Park, N.J. BB/TL, 6'1", 190 lbs. Deb: 4/22/37

YEAR TM/L	W	L	PCT	G	GS	CG	SH	SV	IP	H	HR	BB	SO	RAT	ERA	ERA+	OAV	OOB	BH	AVG	PB	PR	/A	PD	TPI
1937 Cin-N	3	5	.375	19	9	4	0	0	84¹	63	0	69	52	14.3	3.84	97	.209	.359	5	.217	1	1	-1	2	0.2
1938 Cin-N★	15	10	.600	32	29	16	3	0	225¹	177	12	103	125	11.3	3.12	117	.213	.302	15	.181	-2	17	13	-1	1.0
1939 Cin-N☆	5	9	.357	30	21	8	0	0	129	128	7	95	102	15.7	4.67	82	.264	.387	4	.111	-1	-11	-12	-1	-1.4
1940 *Cin-N	3	1	.750	10	7	2	0	0	48	38	3	41	41	15.0	3.75	101	.211	.360	6	.300	2	0	0	1	0.2
1941 Cin-N	16	13	.552	33	32	18	6	0	226¹	172	8	162	202	11.9	2.82	127	.214	.321	10	.132	-3	20	19	2	2.3
1942 Cin-N★	18	12	.600	33	33	21	4	0	244	188	6	102	186	10.7	2.43	135	.208	.290	11	.147	-1	24	23	1	2.9
1943 Cin-N★	15	16	.484	36	36	21	3	0	289	228	6	162	174	12.2	2.87	116	.224	.332	13	.137	-2	17	14	3	1.6
1946 Cin-N	10	12	.455	29	25	11	4	0	204¹	175	11	78	94	11.1	3.17	105	.233	.305	18	.247	2	5	4	-2	0.5

YEAR	TM/L	W	L	PCT	G	GS	CG	SH	SV	IP	H	HR	BB	SO	RAT	ERA	ERA+	OAV	OOB	BH	AVG	PB	PR	/A	PD	TPI
1947	Cin-N	9	14	.391	30	29	9	3	0	186	186	11	87	79	13.4	4.40	93	.261	.343	5	.088	-3	-7	-6	-1	-1.0
1948	Cin-N	17	14	.548	33	33	14	3	0	232	204	15	124	120	12.8	3.41	115	.239	.336	11	.141	0	14	13	-1	1.6
1949	Cin-N	5	10	.333	28	24	7	3	0	159²	172	12	85	76	14.6	4.90	85	.281	.370	4	.077	-3	-15	-13	1	-1.2
1950	Chi-N	3	4	.429	32	6	0	0	1	73²	60	10	59	41	14.8	3.79	111	.221	.363	2	.125	-0	3	3	-0	0.3
1951	Cle-A	0	1	.000	1	1	0	0	0	3	3	0	1	2	27.0	18.00	21	.500	.529	0	.000	-0	-5	-5	1	-0.9
Total	13	119	121	.496	346	285	131	29	2	2104²	1799	100	1132	1294	12.6	3.44	107	.232	.332	104	.152	-9	63	53	3	6.1

● BEN Van DYKE
Van Dyke, Benjamin Harrison b: 8/15/1888, Clintonville, Pa. d: 10/22/73, Sarasota, Fla. BR/TL, 6'1", 150 lbs. Deb: 5/11/09

YEAR	TM/L	W	L	PCT	G	GS	CG	SH	SV	IP	H	HR	BB	SO	RAT	ERA	ERA+	OAV	OOB	BH	AVG	PB	PR	/A	PD	TPI
1909	Phi-N	0	0	—	2	0	0	0	0	7¹	7	0	4	5	13.5	3.68	71	.269	.367	0	.000	-0	-1	-1	-0	-0.1
1912	Bos-A	0	0	—	3	1	0	0	0	14¹	13	0	7	8	13.2	3.14	108	.245	.344	1	.250	-0	0	0	-1	-0.1
Total	2	0	0	—	5	1	0	0	0	21²	20	0	11	13	13.3	3.32	94	.253	.352	1	.143	-0	-1	-0	-1	-0.2

● TIM VANEGMOND
Vanegmond, Timothy Layne b: 5/31/69, Shreveport, La. BR/TR, 6'2", 185 lbs. Deb: 6/26/94

YEAR	TM/L	W	L	PCT	G	GS	CG	SH	SV	IP	H	HR	BB	SO	RAT	ERA	ERA+	OAV	OOB	BH	AVG	PB	PR	/A	PD	TPI
1994	Bos-A	2	3	.400	7	7	1	0	0	38	38	7	21	22	13.9	6.34	81	.255	.347	0	—	0	-7	-5	0	-0.6

● ELAM VANGILDER
Vangilder, Elam Russell b: 4/23/1896, Cape Girardeau, Mo d: 4/30/77, Cape Girardeau, Mo BR/TR, 6'1", 192 lbs. Deb: 9/18/19

YEAR	TM/L	W	L	PCT	G	GS	CG	SH	SV	IP	H	HR	BB	SO	RAT	ERA	ERA+	OAV	OOB	BH	AVG	PB	PR	/A	PD	TPI
1919	StL-A	1	0	1.000	3	1	1	0	0	13	15	0	3	6	12.5	2.08	160	.306	.346	2	.667	1	2	2	1	0.3
1920	StL-A	3	8	.273	24	13	4	0	0	104²	131	7	40	25	15.0	5.50	71	.310	.373	4	.133	-2	-20	-18	-0	-1.8
1921	StL-A	11	12	.478	31	21	10	1	0	180¹	196	10	67	48	13.2	3.94	114	.278	.342	13	.200	-2	7	11	-3	1.0
1922	StL-A	19	13	.594	43	30	19	3	4	245	248	13	48	63	11.1	3.42	121	.270	.310	32	.344	13	17	20	-3	3.4
1923	StL-A	16	17	.485	41	35	20	4	1	282²	276	11	120	74	12.8	3.06	136	.266	.345	24	.218	-0	29	35	-4	3.3
1924	StL-A	5	10	.333	43	18	5	0	1	145¹	183	10	55	49	15.3	5.64	80	.317	.385	13	.295	3	-23	-18	2	-1.2
1925	StL-A	14	8	.636	52	16	4	1	6	193¹	225	11	92	61	15.0	4.70	99	.303	.385	13	.183	-1	-7	-1	-0	-0.3
1926	StL-A	9	11	.450	42	19	8	1	0	181	196	12	98	40	14.7	5.17	83	.285	.376	11	.190	1	-23	-18	-2	-1.8
1927	StL-A	10	12	.455	44	23	12	3	1	203	245	13	102	62	15.6	4.79	91	.310	.392	19	.279	2	-15	-10	-4	-1.0
1928	Det-A	11	10	.524	38	11	7	0	5	156¹	163	4	67	43	13.4	3.91	105	.272	.348	15	.259	2	2	3	0	0.6
1929	Det-A	0	1	.000	6	0	0	0	0	11¹	16	1	7	3	18.3	6.35	68	.348	.434	0	.000	-0	-3	-3	1	-0.1
Total	11	99	102	.493	367	187	90	13	19	1715²	1894	92	699	474	13.8	4.28	100	.288	.360	146	.243	15	-33	-3	-9	2.4

● GEORGE Van HALTREN
Van Haltren, George Edward Martin "Rip"
b: 3/30/1866, St.Louis, Mo d: 9/29/45, Oakland, Cal. BL/TL, 5'11", 170 lbs. Deb: 6/27/1887 M♦

YEAR	TM/L	W	L	PCT	G	GS	CG	SH	SV	IP	H	HR	BB	SO	RAT	ERA	ERA+	OAV	OOB	BH	AVG	PB	PR	/A	PD	TPI
1887	Chi-N	11	7	.611	20	18	18	1	1	161	177	6	66	76	14.5	3.86	116	.277	.359	35	.203	-2	4	11	-0	0.8
1888	Chi-N	13	13	.500	30	24	24	4	1	245²	263	15	60	139	12.3	3.52	86	.267	.318	90	.283	11	-18	-13	2	-0.1
1890	Bro-P	15	10	.600	28	25	23	0	2	223	272	8	89	48	15.4	4.28	104	.288	.362	126	.335	10	-1	4	3	1.3
1891	Bal-a	0	1	.000	6	1	0	0	0	23	38	1	10	7	20.3	5.09	73	.357	.432	180	.318	3	-3	-3	-0	0.0
1892	Bal-N	0	0	—	4	0	0	0	0	14²	28	1	7	5	21.5	9.20	37	.389	.443	168	.302	2	-10	-9	-0	0.1
1895	NY-N	1	0	—	1	0	0	0	0	5	13	0	2	1	30.6	12.60	37	.473	.540	177	.340	-0	-4	-4	-0	0.0
1896	NY-N	1	0	1.000	2	0	0	0	0	8	5	1	2	3	6.8	2.25	187	.179	.207	197	.351	1	2	2	-0	0.2
1900	NY-N	0	0	—	1	0	0	0	0	3	1	0	3	0	12.0	0.00	—	.105	.319	180	.315	0	1	1	-0	0.0
1901	NY-N	0	0	—	1	0	0	0	0	6	6	1	2	2	28.5	3.00	110	.411	.525	182	.335	0	0	1	-0	0.1
Total	9	40	31	.563	93	68	65	5	4	689¹	809	33	244	281	14.5	4.05	96	.285	.353	2532	.316	25	-30	-12	6	2.4

● BILL Van LANDINGHAM
Van Landingham, William Joseph b: 7/16/70, Columbia, Tenn. BR/TR, 6'2", 210 lbs. Deb: 5/21/94

YEAR	TM/L	W	L	PCT	G	GS	CG	SH	SV	IP	H	HR	BB	SO	RAT	ERA	ERA+	OAV	OOB	BH	AVG	PB	PR	/A	PD	TPI
1994	SF-N	8	2	.800	16	14	0	0	0	84	70	4	43	56	12.3	3.54	114	.223	.320	2	.065	-2	6	5	0	0.2

● TODD Van POPPEL
Van Poppel, Todd Matthew b: 12/9/71, Hinsdale, Ill. BR/TR, 6'5", 210 lbs. Deb: 9/11/91

YEAR	TM/L	W	L	PCT	G	GS	CG	SH	SV	IP	H	HR	BB	SO	RAT	ERA	ERA+	OAV	OOB	BH	AVG	PB	PR	/A	PD	TPI
1991	Oak-A	0	0	—	1	1	0	0	0	4²	7	1	2	6	17.4	9.64	40	.368	.429	0	—	0	-3	-3	0	0.3
1993	Oak-A	6	6	.500	16	16	0	0	0	84	76	10	62	47	15.0	5.04	81	.243	.371	0	—	0	-7	-9	-1	-1.2
1994	Oak-A	7	10	.412	23	23	0	0	0	116²	108	20	89	83	15.4	6.09	73	.250	.382	0	—	0	-17	-21	0	-2.4
Total	3	13	16	.448	40	40	0	0	0	205¹	191	31	153	136	15.3	5.74	75	.250	.379	0	—	0	-26	-33	-1	-3.3

● IKE Van ZANDT
Van Zandt, Charles Isaac b: 1877, Brooklyn, N.Y. d: 9/14/08, Nashua, N.H. BL, Deb: 8/5/01 ♦

YEAR	TM/L	W	L	PCT	G	GS	CG	SH	SV	IP	H	HR	BB	SO	RAT	ERA	ERA+	OAV	OOB	BH	AVG	PB	PR	/A	PD	TPI
1901	NY-N	0	0	—	2	0	0	0	0	12²	16	0	4	3	17.8	7.11	47	.306	.408	1	.167	-0	-5	-5	-1	-0.1
1905	StL-A	0	0	—	1	0	0	0	0	6²	2	0	2	3	6.8	0.00	—	.096	.210	75	.233	0	2	2	0	0.0
Total	2	0	0	—	3	0	0	0	0	19¹	18	0	10	5	14.0	4.66	65	.246	.352	76	.224	-0	-3	-3	-1	-0.1

● ANDY VARGA
Varga, Andrew William b: 12/11/30, Chicago, Ill. d: 11/4/92, Orlando, Fla. BR/TL, 6'4", 187 lbs. Deb: 9/9/50

YEAR	TM/L	W	L	PCT	G	GS	CG	SH	SV	IP	H	HR	BB	SO	RAT	ERA	ERA+	OAV	OOB	BH	AVG	PB	PR	/A	PD	TPI
1950	Chi-N	0	0	—	1	0	0	0	0	1	0	0	1	0	9.0	0.00	—	.000	.333	0	—	0	0	0	-0	0.0
1951	Chi-N	0	0	—	2	0	0	0	0	3	2	0	6	1	24.0	3.00	136	.200	.500	0	—	0	1	1	-0	0.0
Total	2	0	0	—	3	0	0	0	0	4	2	0	7	1	20.3	2.25	183	.167	.474	0	—	0	1	1	-0	0.0

● ROBERTO VARGAS
Vargas, Roberto Enrique b: 5/29/29, Santurce, P.R. BL/TL, 5'11", 170 lbs. Deb: 4/17/55

YEAR	TM/L	W	L	PCT	G	GS	CG	SH	SV	IP	H	HR	BB	SO	RAT	ERA	ERA+	OAV	OOB	BH	AVG	PB	PR	/A	PD	TPI
1955	Mil-N	0	0	—	25	0	0	0	0	24²	39	4	14	13	19.7	8.76	43	.355	.432	1	.500	0	-13	-14	1	-0.1

● BILL VARGUS
Vargus, William Fay b: 11/11/1899, N.Scituate, Mass. d: 2/12/79, Hyannis, Mass. BL/TL, 6', 165 lbs. Deb: 6/23/25

YEAR	TM/L	W	L	PCT	G	GS	CG	SH	SV	IP	H	HR	BB	SO	RAT	ERA	ERA+	OAV	OOB	BH	AVG	PB	PR	/A	PD	TPI
1925	Bos-N	1	1	.500	11	2	1	0	0	36¹	45	1	13	6	14.9	3.96	101	.302	.366	3	.250	0	1	0	0	0.0
1926	Bos-N	0	0	—	4	0	0	0	0	3	4	0	2	0	15.0	3.00	118	.333	.385	0	—	0	0	0	-0	0.0
Total	2	1	1	.500	15	2	1	0	0	39¹	49	1	14	6	14.9	3.89	102	.304	.367	3	.250	0	1	0	0	0.0

● DIKE VARNEY
Varney, Lawrence Delano (b: Lawrence Delano De Varney)
b: 8/9/1880, Dover, N.H. d: 4/23/50, Long Island City, N.Y. BL/TL, 6', 165 lbs. Deb: 7/3/02

YEAR	TM/L	W	L	PCT	G	GS	CG	SH	SV	IP	H	HR	BB	SO	RAT	ERA	ERA+	OAV	OOB	BH	AVG	PB	PR	/A	PD	TPI
1902	Cle-A	1	1	.500	3	3	0	0	0	14²	14	0	12	7	19.0	6.14	56	.252	.427	1	.167	-0	-4	-4	0	-0.5

● CAL VASBINDER
Vasbinder, Moses Calhoun b: 7/19/1880, Scio, Ohio d: 12/22/50, Cadiz, Ohio BR/TR, 6'2", Deb: 4/27/02

YEAR	TM/L	W	L	PCT	G	GS	CG	SH	SV	IP	H	HR	BB	SO	RAT	ERA	ERA+	OAV	OOB	BH	AVG	PB	PR	/A	PD	TPI
1902	Cle-A	0	0	—	2	0	0	0	0	5	5	1	8	2	23.4	9.00	38	.261	.478	1	.500	0	-3	-3	0	0.0

● RAFAEL VASQUEZ
Vasquez, Rafael b: 6/28/58, LaRomana, D.R. BR/TR, 6', 160 lbs. Deb: 4/6/79

YEAR	TM/L	W	L	PCT	G	GS	CG	SH	SV	IP	H	HR	BB	SO	RAT	ERA	ERA+	OAV	OOB	BH	AVG	PB	PR	/A	PD	TPI
1979	Sea-A	1	0	1.000	9	0	0	0	0	16	23	4	6	9	16.9	5.06	86	.354	.417	0	—	0	-2	-1	-0	-0.1

● PORTER VAUGHAN
Vaughan, Cecil Porter "Lefty" b: 5/11/19, Stevensville, Va. BR/TL, 6'1", 178 lbs. Deb: 6/16/40

YEAR	TM/L	W	L	PCT	G	GS	CG	SH	SV	IP	H	HR	BB	SO	RAT	ERA	ERA+	OAV	OOB	BH	AVG	PB	PR	/A	PD	TPI
1940	Phi-A	2	9	.182	18	15	6	0	2	99¹	104	9	61	46	15.2	5.35	83	.264	.367	8	.235	0	-11	-10	-1	-1.0
1941	Phi-A	0	2	.000	5	3	0	0	0	22²	32	3	12	6	17.5	7.94	53	.327	.400	1	.143	-0	-10	-9	-0	-0.7
1946	Phi-A	0	0	—	1	0	0	0	0	0	1	0	1	0	—	—	—	1.000	1.000	0	—	0	0	0	0	0.0
Total	3	2	11	.154	24	18	6	0	2	122	137	12	74	52	15.8	5.83	75	.278	.375	9	.220	-0	-20	-19	-1	-1.7

● CHARLIE VAUGHAN
Vaughan, Charles Wayne b: 10/6/47, Mercedes, Tex. BR/TL, 6'1.5", 185 lbs. Deb: 9/3/66

YEAR	TM/L	W	L	PCT	G	GS	CG	SH	SV	IP	H	HR	BB	SO	RAT	ERA	ERA+	OAV	OOB	BH	AVG	PB	PR	/A	PD	TPI
1966	Atl-N	1	0	1.000	1	1	0	0	0	7	9	2	6	4	14.1	2.57	141	.296	.367	1	.250	-0	1	1	0	0.1
1969	Atl-N	0	0	—	1	0	0	0	0	1	1	0	3	1	36.0	18.00	20	.250	.571	0	—	0	-2	-2	-0	0.0
Total	2	1	0	1.000	2	1	0	0	0	8	10	2	9	5	16.9	4.50	81	.290	.405	1	.250	-0	-1	-0	0	0.1

● ROY VAUGHN
Vaughn, Clarence Leroy b: 9/4/11, Sedalia, Mo. d: 3/1/37, Martinsville, Va. BB/TR, 6'0.5", 178 lbs. Deb: 7/1/34

YEAR	TM/L	W	L	PCT	G	GS	CG	SH	SV	IP	H	HR	BB	SO	RAT	ERA	ERA+	OAV	OOB	BH	AVG	PB	PR	/A	PD	TPI
1934	Phi-A	0	0	—	2	0	0	0	0	4¹	3	1	3	1	12.5	2.08	211	.176	.300	0	.000	-0	1	1	-0	0.0

● DE WAYNE VAUGHN
Vaughn, De Wayne Mathew b: 7/22/59, Oklahoma City, Okla BR/TR, 5'11", 180 lbs. Deb: 4/17/88

YEAR	TM/L	W	L	PCT	G	GS	CG	SH	SV	IP	H	HR	BB	SO	RAT	ERA	ERA+	OAV	OOB	BH	AVG	PB	PR	/A	PD	TPI
1988	Tex-A	0	0	—	8	0	0	0	0	15¹	24	4	4	8	16.4	7.63	53	.348	.384	0	—	0	-6	-6	-1	-0.1

YEAR TM/L	W	L	PCT	G	GS	CG	SH	SV	IP	H	HR	BB	SO	RAT	ERA	ERA+	OAV	OOB	BH	AVG	PB	PR	/A	PD	TPI

● **FARMER VAUGHN**   Vaughn, Harry Francis b: 3/1/1864, Ruraldale, Ohio d: 2/21/14, Cincinnati, Ohio BR/TR, 6'3", 177 lbs. Deb: 10/7/1886 ♦

| 1891 Cin-a | 0 | 0 | — | 1 | 0 | 0 | 0 | 0 | 7 | 12 | 0 | 1 | 0 | 18.0 | 3.86 | 107 | .366 | .402 | 45 | .257 | 0 | -0 | 0 | -0 | 0.0 |

● **HIPPO VAUGHN**   Vaughn, James Leslie b: 4/9/1888, Weatherford, Tex. d: 5/29/66, Chicago, Ill. BB/TL, 6'4", 215 lbs. Deb: 6/19/08

1908 NY-A	0	0	—	2	0	0	0	0	2¹	1	0	4	2	19.3	3.86	64	.167	.500	0	.000	-0	-0	-0	0	0.0
1910 NY-A	13	11	.542	30	25	18	5	1	221²	190	1	58	107	10.5	1.83	146	.237	.297	10	.133	-2	17	20	-0	2.0
1911 NY-A	8	10	.444	26	19	10	0	0	145²	158	2	54	74	13.5	4.39	82	.284	.354	7	.143	-1	-17	-13	1	-1.4
1912 NY-A	2	8	.200	15	10	5	1	0	63	66	0	37	46	14.9	5.14	70	.264	.361	2	.095	-2	-13	-11	1	-1.5
Was-A	4	3	.571	12	8	4	0	0	81	75	0	43	49	13.6	2.89	115	.253	.356	6	.200	-1	4	4	2	0.4
Yr	6	11	.353	27	18	9	1	0	144	141	0	80	95	14.1	3.88	89	.258	.357	8	.157	-2	-9	-7	3	-1.1
1913 Chi-N	5	1	.833	7	6	5	2	0	56	37	0	27	36	10.6	1.45	220	.182	.284	4	.190	-1	11	11	0	1.1
1914 Chi-N	21	13	.618	42	35	23	4	1	293²	236	1	109	165	10.8	2.05	135	.222	.299	14	.144	-0	24	24	-0	2.7
1915 Chi-N	20	12	.625	41	34	18	4	1	269²	240	0	77	148	10.9	2.87	97	.238	.299	14	.163	1	-4	-3	-1	-0.3
1916 Chi-N	17	15	.531	44	35	21	4	1	294	269	4	67	144	10.5	2.20	132	.250	.298	14	.135	-0	14	23	1	2.2
1917 Chi-N	23	13	.639	41	38	27	5	0	295²	255	3	91	195	10.8	2.01	144	.235	.300	16	.160	-1	23	29	3	4.1
1918 *Chi-N	**22**	10	.688	35	33	27	**8**	0	**290¹**	216	1	76	**148**	9.3	**1.74**	**160**	**.208**	.266	23	.240	-1	**33**	**34**	-1	**4.4**
1919 Chi-N	21	14	.600	38	37	25	4	1	**306²**	264	3	62	**141**	9.7	1.79	161	.234	.278	17	.173	-0	**38**	**37**	-3	4.2
1920 Chi-N	19	16	.543	40	38	24	4	0	301	301	8	81	131	11.7	2.54	126	.264	.318	22	.216	4	20	22	-2	2.7
1921 Chi-N	3	11	.214	17	14	7	0	0	109¹	153	4	31	30	15.6	6.01	64	.341	.390	10	.244	2	-27	-27	-1	-2.7
Total 13	178	137	.565	390	332	214	41	5	2730	2461	39	817	1416	11.1	2.49	120	.244	.306	159	.173	-1	123	152	-1	17.9

● **AL VEACH**   Veach, Alvis Lindel b: 8/6/09, Maylene, Ala. d: 9/6/90, Charlotte, N.C. BR/TR, 5'11", 178 lbs. Deb: 9/22/35

| 1935 Phi-A | 0 | 2 | .000 | 2 | 2 | 1 | 0 | 0 | 10 | 20 | 1 | 9 | 3 | 26.1 | 11.70 | 39 | .417 | .509 | 0 | .000 | -1 | -8 | -8 | 0 | -1.1 |

● **BOBBY VEACH**   Veach, Robert Hayes b: 6/29/1888, Island, Ky. d: 8/7/45, Detroit, Mich. BL/TR, 5'11", 160 lbs. Deb: 8/6/12 ♦

| 1918 Det-A | 0 | 0 | — | 1 | 0 | 0 | 0 | 1 | 2 | 2 | 0 | 2 | 0 | 18.0 | 4.50 | 59 | .286 | .444 | 139 | .279 | 0 | -0 | -0 | -0 | -0.1 |

● **PEEK-A-BOO VEACH**   Veach, William Walter b: 6/15/1862, Indianapolis, Ind d: 11/12/37, Indianapolis, Ind. Deb: 8/24/1884 ♦

1884 KC-U	3	9	.250	12	12	12	0	0	104	95	1	10	62	9.1	2.42	92	.227	.245	11	.134	-3	0	-2	1	-0.4
1887 Lou-a	0	1	.000	1	1	1	0	0	9	5	1	8	2	13.0	4.00	110	.172	.351	0	.000	-0	0	-0	-0	0.0
Total 2	3	10	.231	13	13	13	0	0	113	100	2	18	64	9.4	2.55	94	.223	.253	76	.215	-4	1	-2	1	-0.4

● **BOB VEALE**   Veale, Robert Andrew b: 10/28/35, Birmingham, Ala. BB/TL, 6'6", 212 lbs. Deb: 4/16/62

1962 Pit-N	2	2	.500	11	6	2	0	1	45²	39	2	25	42	12.6	3.74	105	.235	.335	4	.250	1	1	1	-0	0.1
1963 Pit-N	5	2	.714	34	7	3	2	3	77²	59	1	40	68	11.6	1.04	316	.215	.317	2	.087	-0	19	**19**	0	1.9
1964 Pit-N	18	12	.600	40	38	14	1	0	279²	222	8	124	**250**	11.2	2.74	128	.217	.303	15	.156	-0	25	24	-1	2.4
1965 Pit-N☆	17	12	.586	39	37	14	7	0	266	221	5	119	276	11.7	2.84	124	.225	.313	8	.086	-4	21	20	-2	1.5
1966 Pit-N☆	16	12	.571	38	37	12	3	0	268¹	228	18	102	229	11.2	3.02	118	.232	.307	13	.138	-2	18	17	-2	1.2
1967 Pit-N	16	8	.667	33	31	6	1	0	203	184	12	119	179	13.7	3.64	93	.245	.352	3	.043	-5	-6	-1	1	-1.1
1968 Pit-N	13	14	.481	36	33	13	4	0	245¹	187	13	94	171	10.4	2.05	142	.211	.288	9	.110	-2	25	24	-2	2.3
1969 Pit-N	13	14	.481	34	34	9	1	0	225²	232	8	91	213	13.0	3.23	108	.267	.338	4	.051	-5	9	6	-0	0.1
1970 Pit-N	10	15	.400	34	32	5	1	0	202	189	14	99	178	12.7	3.92	100	.246	.331	11	.164	1	-3	-0	-2	-0.1
1971 *Pit-N	6	0	1.000	37	0	0	0	2	46¹	59	5	24	40	16.1	6.99	48	.314	.392	3	.333	1	-18	-19	-2	-2.5
1972 Pit-N	0	0	—	5	0	0	0	0	9	10	0	7	6	17.0	6.00	55	.313	.436	0	.000	-0	-3	-3	-0	-0.1
Bos-A	2	0	1.000	6	0	0	0	0	8	2	0	3	10	5.6	0.00	—	.083	.185	0	.000	-0	3	3	0	1.0
1973 Bos-A	2	3	.400	32	0	0	0	11	36¹	37	2	12	25	12.1	3.47	116	.268	.327	0	—	0	1	2	1	0.5
1974 Bos-A	0	1	.000	18	0	0	0	0	13	15	2	4	16	13.2	5.54	69	.283	.333	0	—	-0	-3	-2	-0	-0.3
Total 13	120	95	.558	397	255	78	20	21	1926	1684	91	858	1703	12.0	3.07	113	.236	.320	72	.114	-17	96	86	-9	6.9

● **LOU VEDDER**   Vedder, Louis Edward b: 4/20/1897, Oakville, Mich. d: 3/9/90, Lake Placid, Fla. BR/TR, 5'10.5", 175 lbs. Deb: 9/18/20

| 1920 Det-A | 0 | 0 | — | 1 | 0 | 0 | 0 | 0 | 2 | 0 | 0 | 1 | 0 | 0.00 | — | .000 | .000 | 0 | — | 0 | 1 | 1 | 0 | 0.0 |

● **AL VEIGEL**   Veigel, Allen Francis b: 1/30/17, Dover, Ohio BR/TR, 6'1", 180 lbs. Deb: 9/21/39

| 1939 Bos-N | 0 | 1 | .000 | 2 | 2 | 0 | 0 | 0 | 2² | 3 | 0 | 5 | 1 | 27.0 | 6.75 | 55 | .250 | .471 | 0 | .000 | -0 | -1 | -1 | -0 | -0.3 |

● **BUCKY VEIL**   Veil, Frederick William b: 8/2/1881, Tyrone, Pa. d: 4/16/31, Altoona, Pa. BR/TR, 5'10", 165 lbs. Deb: 4/19/03

1903 *Pit-N	5	3	.625	12	6	4	0	0	70²	70	1	36	20	13.8	3.82	85	.269	.362	6	.207	-0	-4	-5	-0	-0.5
1904 Pit-N	0	0	—	1	1	0	0	0	4²	4	0	4	1	17.4	5.79	47	.250	.429	1	1.000	0	-2	-2	0	0.1
Total 2	5	3	.625	13	7	4	0	0	75¹	74	1	40	21	14.0	3.94	81	.268	.367	7	.233	-0	-6	-6	-0	-0.4

● **CARLOS VELAZQUEZ**   Velazquez, Carlos (Quinones) b: 3/22/48, Loiza, P.R. BR/TR, 5'11", 180 lbs. Deb: 7/20/73

| 1973 Mil-A | 2 | 2 | .500 | 18 | 0 | 0 | 0 | 1 | 38¹ | 46 | 5 | 10 | 12 | 13.1 | 2.58 | 146 | .297 | .339 | 0 | — | 0 | 5 | 5 | 0 | 0.6 |

● **JOE VERBANIC**   Verbanic, Joseph Michael b: 4/24/43, Washington, Pa. BR/TR, 6', 155 lbs. Deb: 7/22/66

1966 Phi-N	1	1	.500	17	0	0	0	0	14	12	2	10	7	14.1	5.14	70	.226	.349	0	—	0	-2	-2	-0	-0.3
1967 NY-A	4	3	.571	28	6	1	1	2	80¹	74	6	21	39	10.9	2.80	112	.249	.303	2	.111	-0	4	3	2	0.4
1968 NY-A	6	7	.462	40	11	2	1	4	97	104	6	41	40	14.0	3.15	92	.284	.366	2	.080	-1	-2	-3	1	-0.4
1970 NY-A	1	0	1.000	7	0	0	0	0	15²	20	1	12	8	19.0	4.60	76	.323	.440	1	.333	-2	-2	-1	0	-0.0
Total 4	12	11	.522	92	17	3	2	6	207	210	15	84	94	13.2	3.26	95	.270	.348	5	.109	-1	-2	-4	4	-0.3

● **AL VERDEL**   Verdel, Albert Alfred "Stumpy" b: 6/10/21, Punxsutawney, Pa. BR/TR, 5'9.5", 186 lbs. Deb: 4/20/44

| 1944 Phi-N | 0 | 0 | — | 1 | 0 | 0 | 0 | 0 | 1 | 0 | 0 | 0 | 0 | 0.00 | — | .000 | .000 | 0 | — | 0 | 0 | 0 | 0 | 0.0 |

● **DAVE VERES**   Veres, David Scott b: 10/19/66, Montgomery, Ala. BR/TR, 6'2", 195 lbs. Deb: 5/10/94

| 1994 Hou-N | 3 | 3 | .500 | 32 | 0 | 0 | 0 | 1 | 41 | 39 | 4 | 7 | 28 | 10.3 | 2.41 | 169 | .247 | .283 | 1 | .500 | 1 | 8 | 8 | -1 | 1.1 |

● **RANDY VERES**   Veres, Randolf Ruhland b: 11/25/65, Sacramento, Cal. BR/TR, 6'3", 190 lbs. Deb: 7/1/89

1989 Mil-A	0	1	.000	3	1	0	0	0	8¹	9	0	4	8	14.0	4.32	89	.290	.371	0	—	0	-0	-0	0	0.0
1990 Mil-A	0	3	.000	26	0	0	0	1	41²	38	5	16	16	11.9	3.67	105	.247	.322	0	—	0	1	1	1	0.2
1994 Chi-N	1	1	.500	10	0	0	0	0	9²	12	3	2	5	14.0	5.59	74	.308	.357	0	.000	-0	-1	-2	0	-0.3
Total 3	1	5	.167	39	1	0	0	1	59²	59	8	22	29	12.5	4.07	96	.263	.335	0	.000	-0	-1	-1	1	-0.1

● **TOMMY VEREKER**   Vereker, John James b: 12/2/1893, Baltimore, Md. d: 4/2/74, Baltimore, Md. 5'10", 185 lbs. Deb: 6/17/15

| 1915 Bal-F | 0 | 0 | — | 2 | 0 | 0 | 0 | 0 | 3 | 3 | 1 | 2 | 1 | 18.0 | 15.00 | 19 | .273 | .429 | 0 | — | 0 | -4 | -4 | 0 | 0.0 |

● **JOHN VERHOEVEN**   Verhoeven, John C b: 7/3/53, Long Beach, Cal. BR/TR, 6'5", 200 lbs. Deb: 7/6/76

1976 Cal-A	0	2	.000	21	0	0	0	4	37¹	35	2	14	23	11.8	3.38	99	.252	.320	0	—	0	1	-0	1	0.2
1977 Cal-A	0	2	.000	3	0	0	0	0	4²	4	0	4	3	17.4	3.86	101	.222	.391	0	—	0	0	0	0	0.2
Chi-A	0	0	—	6	0	0	0	0	10¹	7	0	2	6	9.6	2.61	156	.184	.268	0	—	0	2	2	1	0.1
Yr	0	2	.000	9	0	0	0	0	15	11	0	6	9	11.4	3.00	134	.224	.297	0	—	0	2	2	1	0.3
1980 Min-A	3	4	.429	44	0	0	0	1	99²	109	10	29	42	12.7	3.97	110	.289	.345	0	—	0	1	4	-0	-0.1
1981 Min-A	0	0	—	25	0	0	0	0	52	57	4	14	16	12.6	3.98	99	.288	.341	0	—	0	-2	-0	0	-0.2
Total 4	3	8	.273	99	0	0	0	5	204	214	16	63	90	12.5	3.79	106	.278	.337	0	—	0	1	5	2	0.2

● **JOE VERNON**   Vernon, Joseph Henry b: 11/25/1889, Mansfield, Mass. d: 3/13/55, Philadelphia, Pa. BR/TR, 5'11", 160 lbs. Deb: 7/20/12

| 1912 Chi-N | 0 | 0 | — | 1 | 0 | 0 | 0 | 0 | 4 | 4 | 0 | 6 | 1 | 24.8 | 11.25 | 30 | .286 | .524 | 0 | .000 | -0 | -3 | -4 | -0 | -0.1 |

YEAR	TM/L	W	L	PCT	G	GS	CG	SH	SV	IP	H	HR	BB	SO	RAT	ERA	ERA+	OAV	OOB	BH	AVG	PB	PR	/A	PD	TPI
1914	Bro-F	0	0	—	1	1	0	0	0	3¹	4	0	5	0	24.3	10.80	27	.308	.500	0	.000	-0	-3	-3	-0	0.0
Total	2	0	0	—	2	1	0	0	0	7¹	8	0	11	1	24.5	11.05	28	.296	.513	0	.000	-0	-6	-6	-0	-0.1

● **BOB VESELIC**   Veselic, Robert Michael   b: 9/27/55, Pittsburgh, Pa.   BR/TR, 6', 175 lbs.   Deb: 9/18/80

YEAR	TM/L	W	L	PCT	G	GS	CG	SH	SV	IP	H	HR	BB	SO	RAT	ERA	ERA+	OAV	OOB	BH	AVG	PB	PR	/A	PD	TPI
1980	Min-A	0	0	—	1	0	0	0	0	4	3	1	2	2	9.0	4.50	97	.214	.267	0	—	0	-0	-0	-0	-0.3
1981	Min-A	1	1	.500	5	0	0	0	0	22²	22	1	12	13	13.5	3.18	124	.250	.340	0	—	0	1	2	-1	-0.1
Total	2	1	1	.500	6	0	0	0	0	26²	25	2	13	15	13.5	3.38	119	.245	.330	0	—	0	1	2	-1	-0.4

● **LEE VIAU**   Viau, Leon A.   b: 7/5/1866, Corinth, Vt.   d: 12/17/47, Hopewell, N.J.   BR/TR, 5'4", 160 lbs.   Deb: 4/22/1888

YEAR	TM/L	W	L	PCT	G	GS	CG	SH	SV	IP	H	HR	BB	SO	RAT	ERA	ERA+	OAV	OOB	BH	AVG	PB	PR	/A	PD	TPI
1888	Cin-a	27	14	.659	42	42	42	1	0	387²	331	7	110	164	10.7	2.65	120	.222	.285	13	.087	-11	18	23	-2	0.7
1889	Cin-a	22	20	.524	47	42	38	1	1	373	379	8	136	152	12.7	3.79	103	.255	.322	21	.143	-9	3	5	-3	-0.6
1890	Cin-N	7	5	.583	13	10	7	1	0	90	97	8	39	41	13.7	4.50	79	.267	.339	5	.139	-2	-9	-9	1	-1.1
	Cle-N	4	9	.308	13	13	13	1	0	107	101	4	42	30	12.4	3.36	106	.242	.318	7	.163	-2	2	3	-1	0.0
	Yr	11	14	.440	26	23	20	2	0	197	198	12	81	71	13.0	3.88	92	.253	.327	12	.152	-4	-7	-7	0	-1.1
1891	Cle-N	18	17	.514	45	38	31	0	0	343²	367	3	138	130	13.6	3.01	115	.263	.336	23	.160	-3	13	17	1	1.2
1892	Cle-N	0	1	.000	1	1	0	0	0	1	5	0	1	0	54.0	36.00	9	.625	.667	0	—	-0	-4	-4	-0	-1.5
	Lou-N	4	11	.267	16	15	14	1	0	130²	156	7	56	36	14.6	3.99	77	.285	.351	13	.197	1	-10	-13	2	-0.9
	Bos-N	1	0	1.000	1	1	1	0	0	9	5	0	4	1	9.0	—	—	.156	.250	0	.000	-0	3	4	-0	0.3
	Yr	5	12	.294	18	17	15	1	0	140²	166	7	61	37	14.5	3.97	78	.282	.350	13	.188	1	-11	-14	2	-2.1
Total	5	83	77	.519	178	162	146	5	1	1442	1441	37	526	554	12.6	3.33	105	.251	.320	82	.139	-27	16	25	-1	-1.9

● **RUBE VICKERS**   Vickers, Harry Porter   b: 5/17/1878, St.Marys, Ont., Can   d: 12/9/58, Belleville, Mich.   BL/TR, 6'2", 225 lbs.   Deb: 9/21/02

YEAR	TM/L	W	L	PCT	G	GS	CG	SH	SV	IP	H	HR	BB	SO	RAT	ERA	ERA+	OAV	OOB	BH	AVG	PB	PR	/A	PD	TPI
1902	Cin-N	0	3	.000	3	3	3	0	0	21	31	0	8	6	17.1	6.00	50	.342	.401	4	.364	1	-8	-7	-1	-0.8
1903	Bro-N	0	1	.000	4	1	1	0	0	14	27	0	9	5	23.8	10.93	29	.415	.493	1	.100	-1	-12	-12	1	-0.6
1907	Phi-A	2	2	.500	10	4	3	1	0	50¹	44	1	12	21	10.2	3.40	77	.237	.287	3	.150	-1	-5	-4	0	-0.4
1908	Phi-A	18	19	.486	53	34	21	6	1	317	264	0	71	156	9.8	2.21	116	.231	.282	17	.160	-1	6	12	-3	1.0
1909	Phi-A	2	2	.500	18	3	1	0	1	55²	60	0	19	25	13.1	3.40	71	.274	.338	1	.063	-1	-6	-6	-1	-0.8
Total	5	22	27	.449	88	45	29	7	2	458	426	1	119	213	11.0	2.93	89	.250	.305	26	.160	-3	-23	-17	-4	-1.6

● **TOM VICKERY**   Vickery, Thomas Gill "Vinegar Tom"   b: 5/5/1867, Milford, N.J.   d: 3/21/21, Burlington, N.J.   TR, 6', 170 lbs.   Deb: 4/21/1890

YEAR	TM/L	W	L	PCT	G	GS	CG	SH	SV	IP	H	HR	BB	SO	RAT	ERA	ERA+	OAV	OOB	BH	AVG	PB	PR	/A	PD	TPI
1890	Phi-N	24	22	.522	46	46	41	2	0	382	405	8	184	162	14.6	3.44	106	.264	.353	33	.208	-4	6	9	-2	0.3
1891	Chi-N	6	5	.545	14	12	7	0	0	79²	72	4	44	39	13.7	4.07	82	.232	.337	7	.179	-2	-6	-7	1	-0.8
1892	Bal-N	8	10	.444	24	21	17	0	0	176	189	3	87	49	14.6	3.53	97	.264	.351	18	.243	-2	-5	-2	-2	-0.1
1893	Phi-N	4	5	.444	13	11	7	0	0	80	100	1	37	15	16.1	5.40	85	.297	.377	11	.314	1	-7	-7	2	-0.3
Total	4	42	42	.500	97	90	72	2	0	717²	766	16	352	265	14.6	3.75	98	.264	.354	69	.225	-3	-12	-6	-1	-0.9

● **BOB VINES**   Vines, Robert Earl   b: 2/25/1897, Waxahachie, Tex.   d: 10/18/82, Orlando, Fla.   BR/TR, 6'4", 184 lbs.   Deb: 9/3/24

YEAR	TM/L	W	L	PCT	G	GS	CG	SH	SV	IP	H	HR	BB	SO	RAT	ERA	ERA+	OAV	OOB	BH	AVG	PB	PR	/A	PD	TPI
1924	StL-N	0	0	—	2	0	0	0	0	10²	23	1	0	0	19.4	9.28	41	.426	.426	0	.000	-1	-6	-7	-0	-0.1
1925	Phi-N	0	0	—	3	0	0	0	0	4	9	0	3	0	27.0	11.25	42	.450	.522	0	—	0	-3	-3	0	0.0
Total	2	0	0	—	5	0	0	0	0	14²	32	1	3	0	21.5	9.82	41	.432	.455	0	.000	-1	-10	-9	-0	-0.1

● **DAVE VINEYARD**   Vineyard, David Kent   b: 2/25/41, Clay, W.Va.   BR/TR, 6'3", 195 lbs.   Deb: 7/18/64

YEAR	TM/L	W	L	PCT	G	GS	CG	SH	SV	IP	H	HR	BB	SO	RAT	ERA	ERA+	OAV	OOB	BH	AVG	PB	PR	/A	PD	TPI
1964	Bal-A	2	5	.286	19	6	1	0	0	54	57	5	27	50	14.0	4.17	86	.274	.357	2	.167	0	-3	-4	-1	-0.5

● **BILL VINTON**   Vinton, William Miller   b: 4/27/1865, Winthrop, Mass.   d: 9/3/1893, Pawtucket, R.I.   BR/TR, 6'1", 160 lbs.   Deb: 7/3/1884

YEAR	TM/L	W	L	PCT	G	GS	CG	SH	SV	IP	H	HR	BB	SO	RAT	ERA	ERA+	OAV	OOB	BH	AVG	PB	PR	/A	PD	TPI
1884	Phi-N	10	10	.500	21	21	20	0	0	182	166	6	35	105	9.9	2.23	134	.220	.255	9	.115	-6	15	15	3	1.1
1885	Phi-N	3	6	.333	9	9	8	0	0	77	90	0	23	21	13.2	3.04	92	.269	.317	2	.067	-3	-2	-2	0	-0.5
	Phi-a	4	3	.571	7	7	6	2	0	55	46	1	15	34	10.6	2.45	140	.200	.261	4	.154	-0	5	6	-0	0.6
Total	2	17	19	.472	37	37	34	2	0	314	302	7	73	160	10.9	2.64	122	.229	.272	15	.112	-10	18	19	3	1.2

● **FRANK VIOLA**   Viola, Frank John   b: 4/19/60, Hempstead, N.Y.   BL/TL, 6'4", 209 lbs.   Deb: 6/6/82

YEAR	TM/L	W	L	PCT	G	GS	CG	SH	SV	IP	H	HR	BB	SO	RAT	ERA	ERA+	OAV	OOB	BH	AVG	PB	PR	/A	PD	TPI
1982	Min-A	4	10	.286	22	22	3	1	0	126	152	22	38	84	13.6	5.21	81	.302	.351	0	—	0	-16	-14	-1	-1.4
1983	Min-A	7	15	.318	35	34	4	0	0	210	242	34	92	127	14.7	5.49	77	.287	.363	0	—	0	-33	-29	-1	-2.7
1984	Min-A	18	12	.600	35	35	10	4	0	257²	225	28	73	149	10.5	3.21	131	.233	.290	0	—	0	22	28	-3	2.8
1985	Min-A	18	14	.563	36	36	9	0	0	250²	262	26	68	135	11.9	4.09	108	.268	.316	0	—	0	1	9	-2	0.8
1986	Min-A	16	13	.552	37	37	7	1	0	245²	257	37	83	191	12.6	4.51	96	.268	.329	0	—	0	-9	-5	-3	-0.9
1987	*Min-A	17	10	.630	36	36	7	1	0	251²	230	29	66	197	10.8	2.90	159	.241	.294	0	—	0	44	48	-1	**4.6**
1988	Min-A★	**24**	7	**.774**	35	35	7	2	0	255¹	236	20	54	193	10.3	2.64	154	.245	.288	0	—	0	38	**40**	-1	**4.6**
1989	Min-A	8	12	.400	24	24	7	1	0	175²	171	16	47	138	11.3	3.79	109	.256	.308	0	—	0	2	7	0	0.7
	NY-N	5	5	.500	12	12	2	1	0	85¹	75	5	27	73	10.9	3.38	97	.236	.298	3	.130	-0	1	-1	-1	-0.2
1990	NY-N★	20	12	.625	35	35	7	3	0	**249²**	227	15	60	182	10.4	2.67	140	.242	.289	13	.153	-1	**31**	30	-0	**3.6**
1991	NY-N★	13	15	.464	35	35	3	0	0	231¹	259	25	54	132	12.2	3.97	92	.286	.327	9	.127	-1	-7	-8	-1	-1.2
1992	Bos-A	13	12	.520	35	35	6	1	0	238	214	13	89	121	11.7	3.44	122	.242	.316	0	—	0	13	20	3	1.8
1993	Bos-A	11	8	.579	29	29	2	1	0	183²	180	12	72	91	12.6	3.14	147	.259	.334	0	—	0	24	30	0	2.9
1994	Bos-A	1	1	.500	6	6	0	0	0	31	34	2	17	9	14.8	4.65	111	.296	.386	0	—	0	1	2	-0	-0.3
Total	13	175	146	.545	412	411	74	16	0	2791²	2764	285	840	1822	11.8	3.67	114	.259	.315	25	.140	-2	111	155	-11	15.1

● **JAKE VIRTUE**   Virtue, Jacob Kitchline "Guesses"   b: 3/2/1865, Philadelphia, Pa.   d: 2/3/43, Camden, N.J.   BB/TL, 5'9.5", 165 lbs.   Deb: 7/21/1890   ♦

YEAR	TM/L	W	L	PCT	G	GS	CG	SH	SV	IP	H	HR	BB	SO	RAT	ERA	ERA+	OAV	OOB	BH	AVG	PB	PR	/A	PD	TPI
1893	Cle-N	0	0	—	1	0	0	0	0	5	3	0	3	2	10.8	1.80	271	.169	.289	100	.265	0	2	2	-0	0.0
1894	Cle-N	0	0	—	1	0	0	0	0	0	0	0	1	0	—	—	—	—	1.000	23	.258	0	0	0	0	0.0
Total	2	0	0	—	2	0	0	0	0	5	3	0	4	2	12.6	1.80	271	.169	.321	483	.274	0	2	2	-0	0.0

● **JOE VITELLI**   Vitelli, Antonio Joseph   b: 4/12/08, McKees Rocks, Pa.   d: 2/7/67, Pittsburgh, Pa.   BR/TR, 6'1", 195 lbs.   Deb: 5/30/44   ♦

YEAR	TM/L	W	L	PCT	G	GS	CG	SH	SV	IP	H	HR	BB	SO	RAT	ERA	ERA+	OAV	OOB	BH	AVG	PB	PR	/A	PD	TPI
1944	Pit-N	0	0	—	4	0	0	0	0	7	5	1	7	2	16.7	2.57	145	.185	.371	0	.000	-0	1	1	0	0.0

● **JOE VITKO**   Vitko, Joseph John   b: 2/1/70, Somerville, N.J.   BR/TR, 6'8", 210 lbs.   Deb: 9/18/92

YEAR	TM/L	W	L	PCT	G	GS	CG	SH	SV	IP	H	HR	BB	SO	RAT	ERA	ERA+	OAV	OOB	BH	AVG	PB	PR	/A	PD	TPI
1992	NY-N	0	1	.000	3	1	0	0	0	4²	12	1	1	6	25.1	13.50	26	.444	.464	0	—	0	-5	-5	-0	-0.9

● **OLLIE VOIGT**   Voigt, Olen Edward "Ode"   b: 1/29/1900, Wheaton, Ill.   d: 4/7/70, Scottsdale, Ariz.   BL/TR, 6'1", 170 lbs.   Deb: 4/19/24

YEAR	TM/L	W	L	PCT	G	GS	CG	SH	SV	IP	H	HR	BB	SO	RAT	ERA	ERA+	OAV	OOB	BH	AVG	PB	PR	/A	PD	TPI
1924	StL-A	1	0	1.000	8	1	0	0	0	16¹	21	1	13	4	18.7	5.51	82	.356	.472	1	.250	1	-2	-2	1	0.1

● **BILL VOISELLE**   Voiselle, William Symmes "Big Bill" or "Ninety-Six"   b: 1/29/19, Greenwood, S.C.   BR/TR, 6'4", 200 lbs.   Deb: 9/1/42

YEAR	TM/L	W	L	PCT	G	GS	CG	SH	SV	IP	H	HR	BB	SO	RAT	ERA	ERA+	OAV	OOB	BH	AVG	PB	PR	/A	PD	TPI
1942	NY-N	0	1	.000	2	1	0	0	0	9	6	1	4	5	10.0	2.00	168	.176	.263	0	.000	0	1	1	-0	0.2
1943	NY-N	1	2	.333	4	4	3	0	0	31	18	1	14	19	9.3	2.03	170	.154	.244	1	.111	-1	5	5	-1	0.3
1944	NY-N☆	21	16	.568	43	41	25	1	0	312²	276	31	118	**161**	11.5	3.02	121	.232	.303	22	.210	3	20	22	-3	2.5
1945	NY-N	14	14	.500	41	35	14	4	0	232¹	249	15	97	115	13.6	4.49	87	.273	.345	10	.127	-3	-18	-15	-0	-1.9
1946	NY-N	9	15	.375	36	25	10	2	0	178	171	14	85	89	12.9	3.74	92	.248	.330	9	.164	-1	-7	-6	-0	-0.9
1947	NY-N	1	4	.200	11	5	1	0	0	42²	44	4	22	20	14.1	4.64	88	.284	.376	2	.133	-1	-3	-3	-0	-0.4
	Bos-N	8	7	.533	22	20	7	0	0	131¹	146	6	51	59	13.6	4.32	90	.280	.345	9	.170	-1	-4	-6	1	-0.6
	Yr	9	11	.450	33	25	8	0	0	174	190	4	73	79	13.7	4.40	90	.280	.351	11	.162	-1	-7	-9	1	-1.0
1948	*Bos-N	13	13	.500	37	30	9	2	2	215²	226	18	90	89	13.3	3.63	106	.272	.345	7	.097	-4	8	5	-3	-0.1
1949	Bos-N	7	8	.467	30	22	5	4	0	169¹	170	14	78	63	13.2	4.04	94	.263	.343	7	.115	-2	0	-5	1	-0.5
1950	Chi-N	0	4	.000	19	7	0	0	0	51¹	64	7	29	25	16.5	5.79	73	.303	.390	1	.077	-1	-9	-9	-0	-0.8
Total	9	74	84	.468	245	190	74	13	2	1373¹	1370	115	588	645	12.9	3.83	100	.258	.334	68	.147	-10	-6	-10	-6	-2.2

YEAR TM/L	W	L	PCT	G	GS	CG	SH	SV	IP	H	HR	BB	SO	RAT	ERA	ERA+	OAV	OOB	BH	AVG	PB	PR	/A	PD	TPI
● **JAKE VOLZ**			Volz, Jacob Phillip "Silent Jake"	b: 4/4/1878, San Antonio, Tex.									d: 8/11/62, San Antonio, Tex.		BR/TR, 5'10", 175 lbs.			Deb: 9/28/01						
1901 Bos-A	1	0	1.000	1	1	1	0	0	7	6	2	9	5	19.3	9.00	39	.229	.426	0	.000	-1	-4	-4	-1	-0.5
1905 Bos-N	0	2	.000	3	2	0	0	0	8²	12	0	8	1	21.8	10.38	30	.364	.500	0	.000	-0	-7	-7	-1	-1.3
1908 Cin-N	1	2	.333	7	4	1	0	0	22²	16	1	12	6	11.9	3.57	65	.195	.313	1	.250	-0	-3	-3	-1	-0.5
Total 3	2	4	.333	11	7	2	0	0	38¹	34	3	29	12	15.5	6.10	44	.241	.381	1	.100	-1	-14	-14	-2	-2.3
● **TONY Von FRICKEN**			Von Fricken, Anthony	b: 5/30/1870, Brooklyn, N.Y.									d: 3/22/47, Troy, N.Y.		BB/TR, 5'11.5", 160 lbs.			Deb: 5/9/1890						
1890 Bos-N	0	1	.000	1	1	1	0	0	8	23	0	8	2	34.9	10.13	37	.493	.567	0	.000	-1	-6	-6	-0	-0.5
● **BRUCE Von HOFF**			Von Hoff, Bruce Frederick	b: 11/17/43, Oakland, Cal.							BR/TR, 6', 187 lbs.			Deb: 9/28/65											
1965 Hou-N	0	0	—	3	0	0	0	0	3	3	0	2	1	15.0	9.00	37	.250	.357	0	—	0	-2	-2	-0	0.0
1967 Hou-N	0	3	.000	10	10	0	0	0	50¹	52	3	28	22	14.3	4.83	69	.268	.360	1	.067	-1	-8	-8	-1	-0.6
Total 2	0	3	.000	13	10	0	0	0	53¹	55	3	30	23	14.3	5.06	65	.267	.360	1	.067	-1	-10	-10	-1	-0.6
● **DAVE Von OHLEN**			Von Ohlen, David	b: 10/25/58, Flushing, N.Y.							BL/TL, 6'2", 200 lbs.			Deb: 5/13/83											
1983 StL-N	3	2	.600	46	0	0	0	2	68¹	71	3	25	21	13.0	3.29	110	.280	.351	1	.143	0	3	2	-0	0.2
1984 StL-N	1	0	1.000	27	0	0	0	1	34²	39	0	8	19	12.2	3.12	111	.300	.341	1	1.000	0	2	1	1	0.2
1985 Cle-A	3	2	.600	26	0	0	0	1	43¹	47	3	20	12	13.9	2.91	142	.288	.366	0	—	0	6	6	1	0.7
1986 Oak-A	0	3	.000	24	0	0	0	0	15¹	18	0	7	4	14.7	3.52	110	.300	.373	0	—	0	1	1	0	0.2
1987 Oak-A	0	0	—	4	0	0	0	0	6	10	1	1	3	16.5	7.50	55	.400	.423	0	—	0	-2	-2	-0	0.0
Total 5	7	7	.500	127	0	0	0	4	167²	185	7	61	59	13.4	3.33	113	.293	.358	2	.250	1	9	8	1	1.3
● **CY VORHEES**			Vorhees, Henry Bert	b: 9/30/1874, Lodi, Ohio							d: 2/8/10, Perry, Ohio		6'3", 200 lbs.		Deb: 4/17/02											
1902 Phi-N	3	3	.500	10	4	3	1	0	53²	63	1	20	24	14.1	3.86	73	.292	.355	7	.350	2	-6	-6	-1	-0.5
Was-A	0	1	.000	1	1	1	0	0	8	10	0	2	1	13.5	4.50	82	.306	.346	2	.667	1	-1	-1	-0	0.0
Total 1	3	4	.429	11	5	4	1	0	61²	73	1	22	25	14.0	3.94	74	.294	.354	9	.391	3	-7	-7	-1	-0.5
● **ED VOSBERG**			Vosberg, Edward John	b: 9/28/61, Tucson, Ariz.							BL/TL, 6'1", 190 lbs.			Deb: 9/17/86											
1986 SD-N	0	1	.000	5	3	0	0	0	13²	17	1	9	8	17.1	6.59	55	.304	.400	0	.000	-0	-4	-4	-0	-0.4
1990 SF-N	1	1	.500	18	0	0	0	0	24¹	21	3	12	12	12.2	5.55	66	.233	.324	0	—	0	-5	-5	-0	-0.4
1994 Oak-A	0	2	.000	16	0	0	0	0	13²	16	2	5	12	13.8	3.95	112	.320	.382	0	—	0	1	1	0	0.3
Total 3	1	4	.200	39	3	0	0	0	51²	54	6	32	32	13.9	5.40	72	.276	.360	0	.000	-0	-8	-9	-1	-0.5
● **ALEX VOSS**			Voss, Alexander	b: 5/16/1858, Roswell, Ga.						d: 8/31/06, Cincinnati, Ohio		BR/TR, 6'1", 180 lbs.		Deb: 4/17/1884	♦											
1884 Was-U	5	14	.263	27	20	18	0	0	186¹	206	2	32	112	11.5	3.57	67	.262	.291	47	.192	-9	-23	-24	3	-2.2
KC-U	0	6	.000	7	6	6	0	0	53	74	2	7	17	13.8	4.25	53	.310	.329	4	.089	-4	-11	-12	1	-1.3
Yr	5	20	.200	34	26	24	0	0	239¹	280	4	39	129	12.0	3.72	63	.273	.300	51	.176	-13	-34	-36	3	-3.5
● **RIP VOWINKEL**			Vowinkel, John Henry	b: 11/18/1884, Oswego, N.Y.						d: 7/13/66, Oswego, N.Y.		BR/TR, 5'10", 195 lbs.		Deb: 9/5/05											
1905 Cin-N	3	3	.500	6	6	4	0	0	45¹	52	2	10	7	12.5	4.17	79	.302	.344	1	.071	-0	-6	-4	-2	-0.7
● **PETE VUCKOVICH**			Vuckovich, Peter Dennis	b: 10/27/52, Johnstown, Pa.							BR/TR, 6'4", 220 lbs.			Deb: 8/3/75											
1975 Chi-A	0	1	.000	4	2	0	0	0	10¹	17	0	7	5	20.9	13.06	30	.386	.471	0	—	0	-11	-11	0	-0.9
1976 Chi-A	7	4	.636	33	7	1	0	0	110¹	122	3	60	62	15.2	4.65	77	.287	.380	0	—	0	-14	-13	0	-1.3
1977 Tor-A	7	7	.500	53	8	3	1	8	148	143	13	59	123	12.6	3.47	121	.257	.333	0	—	0	12	12	1	1.2
1978 StL-N	12	12	.500	45	23	6	2	1	198¹	187	9	59	149	11.3	2.54	138	.253	.310	8	.138	-1	23	21	2	2.6
1979 StL-N	15	10	.600	34	32	9	0	0	233	229	22	64	145	11.4	3.59	105	.260	.312	12	.152	-2	4	4	-1	0.1
1980 StL-N	12	9	.571	32	30	7	3	1	222¹	203	18	60	132	11.1	3.40	109	.247	.306	13	.183	-1	5	7	-1	0.8
1981 *Mil-A	14	4	.778	24	23	2	1	0	149²	137	9	57	84	11.9	3.55	96	.249	.324	0	—	0	2	-2	1	0.0
1982 *Mil-A	18	6	.750	30	30	9	1	0	223²	234	14	102	105	13.7	3.34	113	.275	.356	0	—	0	18	11	1	1.2
1983 Mil-A	0	2	.000	3	3	0	0	0	14²	15	0	10	10	16.0	4.91	76	.259	.377	0	—	0	-1	-2	-0	-0.2
1985 Mil-A	6	10	.375	22	22	1	0	0	112²	134	16	48	55	15.1	5.51	76	.298	.374	0	—	0	-17	-17	-1	-2.1
1986 Mil-A	2	4	.333	6	6	0	0	0	32¹	33	3	11	12	12.8	3.06	141	.273	.343	0	—	0	4	5	0	0.8
Total 11	93	69	.574	286	186	38	8	10	1455¹	1454	107	545	882	12.6	3.66	103	.264	.334	33	.159	-2	22	16	2	2.2
● **PAUL WACHTEL**			Wachtel, Paul Horine	b: 4/30/1888, Myersville, Md.						d: 12/15/64, San Antonio, Tex.		BR/TR, 5'11", 175 lbs.		Deb: 9/18/17											
1917 Bro-N	0	0	—	2	0	0	0	0	6	9	0	4	3	19.5	10.50	27	.375	.464	1	.333	0	-5	-5	-0	0.0
● **CHARLIE WACKER**			Wacker, Charles James	b: 12/8/1883, Jeffersonville, Ind						d: 8/7/48, Evansville, Ind.		BL/TL, 5'9",		Deb: 4/28/09											
1909 Pit-N	0	0	—	1	0	0	0	0	2	2	0	1	0	13.5	0.00	—	.400	.500	0	—	0	1	1	0	0.0
● **RUBE WADDELL**			Waddell, George Edward	b: 10/13/1876, Bradford, Pa.						d: 4/1/14, San Antonio, Tex.		BR/TL, 6'1.5", 196 lbs.		Deb: 9/8/1897	H											
1897 Lou-N	0	1	.000	2	1	1	0	0	14	17	0	6	5	15.4	3.21	133	.297	.374	0	.000	-1	2	2	0	0.0
1899 Lou-N	7	2	.778	10	9	9	1	1	79	69	4	14	44	10.4	3.08	125	.235	.288	8	.235	-0	7	7	-1	0.6
1900 *Pit-N	8	13	.381	29	22	16	2	0	208²	176	3	55	130	10.5	2.37	153	.229	.291	14	.173	-2	31	29	1	2.4
1901 Pit-N	0	2	.000	2	2	0	0	0	7²	10	0	9	4	23.5	9.39	35	.313	.476	0	.000	-0	-5	-5	-0	-0.9
Chi-N	14	14	.500	29	28	26	0	0	243²	239	5	66	168	11.6	2.81	115	.255	.310	25	.255	6	14	12	3	2.2
Yr	14	16	.467	31	30	26	0	0	251¹	249	5	75	172	11.9	3.01	108	.257	.316	25	.248	6	9	6	4	1.3
1902 Phi-A	24	7	.774	33	27	26	3	0	276¹	224	7	64	210	9.7	2.05	179	.222	.276	32	.286	7	47	50	7	5.9
1903 Phi-A	21	16	.568	39	38	34	4	0	324	274	8	85	302	10.2	2.44	125	.229	.284	14	.122	6	19	22	0	1.7
1904 Phi-A	25	19	.568	46	46	39	8	0	383	307	6	91	349	9.7	1.62	165	.225	.284	17	.132	-7	42	45	2	4.9
1905 Phi-A	27	10	.730	46	34	27	7	0	328²	231	5	90	287	9.1	1.48	180	.199	.263	20	.172	-1	43	43	-0	4.9
1906 Phi-A	15	17	.469	43	34	22	8	0	272²	221	1	92	196	10.7	2.21	123	.225	.298	14	.163	-0	15	16	-2	1.6
1907 Phi-A	19	13	.594	44	33	20	7	0	284²	234	2	73	232	10.2	2.15	121	.226	.284	12	.119	-5	13	15	-2	0.8
1908 StL-A	19	14	.576	43	36	25	5	3	285²	223	0	90	232	10.1	1.89	127	.213	.281	10	.110	-1	16	16	-1	1.4
1909 StL-A	11	14	.440	31	28	16	5	0	220¹	204	1	57	141	10.9	2.37	102	.267	.323	5	.067	-5	3	1	-1	-0.6
1910 StL-A	3	1	.750	10	2	0	0	1	33	31	1	11	16	11.7	3.55	70	.242	.307	1	.111	-0	-4	-4	-0	-0.6
Total 13	193	143	.574	407	340	261	50	5	2961¹	2460	37	803	2316	10.3	2.16	135	.228	.288	172	.161	-17	241	248	-1	24.6
● **TOM WADDELL**			Waddell, Thomas David	b: 9/17/58, Dundee, Scotland						BR/TR, 6'1", 185 lbs.		Deb: 4/15/84													
1984 Cle-A	7	4	.636	58	0	0	0	6	97	68	12	37	59	9.8	3.06	133	.202	.283	0	—	0	10	11	-1	1.2
1985 Cle-A	8	6	.571	49	9	1	0	9	112²	104	20	39	53	11.5	4.87	85	.246	.312	0	—	0	-9	-9	0	-1.1
1987 Cle-A	0	1	.000	6	0	0	0	0	5²	7	1	7	6	23.8	14.29	32	.292	.469	0	—	0	-6	-6	-0	-0.9
Total 3	15	11	.577	113	9	1	0	15	215¹	179	33	83	118	11.1	4.30	96	.229	.305	0	—	0	-5	-4	-1	-0.8
● **BEN WADE**			Wade, Benjamin Styron	b: 11/26/22, Morehead City, N.C						BR/TR, 6'3", 205 lbs.		Deb: 4/30/48	F												
1948 Chi-N	0	1	.000	2	0	0	0	0	5	4	1	4	1	14.4	7.20	54	.211	.348	0	.000	-0	-2	-2	-0	-0.3
1952 Bro-N	11	9	.550	37	24	5	1	3	180	166	19	94	118	13.1	3.60	101	.246	.340	7	.117	-1	3	1	-2	0.0
1953 *Bro-N	7	5	.583	32	9	1	0	3	90¹	79	15	33	65	11.6	3.79	113	.232	.308	4	.167	0	5	5	-2	0.4
1954 Bro-N	1	1	.500	23	0	0	0	0	45	62	9	21	25	16.6	8.20	50	.339	.407	0	.000	-1	-21	-21	-1	-1.2
StL-N	0	0	—	13	0	0	0	0	23	27	3	15	19	17.2	5.48	75	.303	.415	0	—	0	-3	-3	-0	—
Yr	1	1	.500	36	0	0	0	0	68	89	12	36	44	16.8	7.28	56	.319	.401	0	—	-1	-24	-24	-1	-1.2
1955 Pit-N	0	1	.000	11	0	0	0	0	28	26	3	14	7	13.2	3.21	128	.252	.347	0	—	0	3	3	-0	0.1
Total 5	19	17	.528	118	25	6	1	10	371¹	364	49	181	235	13.4	4.34	90	.259	.347	11	.112	-0	-16	-18	-5	-1.0

YEAR	TM/L	W	L	PCT	G	GS	CG	SH	SV	IP	H	HR	BB	SO	RAT	ERA	ERA+	OAV	OOB	BH	AVG	PB	PR	/A	PD	TPI

● JAKE WADE Wade, Jacob Fields "Whistling Jake" b: 4/1/12, Morehead City, N.C. BL/TL, 6'2", 175 lbs. Deb: 4/22/36 F

1936	Det-A	4	5	.444	13	11	4	1	0	78¹	93	7	52	30	16.8	5.29	94	.296	.398	5	.172	-0	-2	-3	-1	-0.4
1937	Det-A	7	10	.412	33	25	7	1	0	165¹	160	13	107	69	14.7	5.39	87	.257	.368	11	.186	-1	-14	-13	1	-1.2
1938	Det-A	3	2	.600	27	2	0	0	0	70	73	9	48	23	15.6	6.56	76	.268	.378	1	.048	-2	-14	-12	0	-0.9
1939	Bos-A	1	4	.200	20	6	1	0	0	47²	68	1	37	21	19.8	6.23	76	.358	.463	0	.000	-2	-9	-8	-0	-0.9
	StL-A	0	2	.000	4	2	1	0	0	16¹	26	1	19	9	24.8	11.02	44	.356	.489	0	.000	-1	-12	-11	0	-1.0
	Yr	1	6	.143	24	8	2	0	0	64	94	2	56	30	21.1	7.45	64	.357	.470	0	.000	-3	-20	-19	0	-1.9
1942	Chi-A	5	5	.500	15	10	3	0	0	85²	84	2	56	32	14.7	4.10	88	.255	.363	7	.241	-1	-4	-5	1	-0.3
1943	Chi-A	3	7	.300	21	9	3	1	0	83²	66	3	54	41	13.3	3.01	111	.222	.349	4	.148	-0	3	3	-1	0.2
1944	Chi-A	2	4	.333	19	5	1	0	2	74²	75	3	41	35	14.0	4.82	71	.261	.354	7	.292	1	-12	-12	-2	-1.0
1946	NY-A	2	1	.667	13	1	0	0	1	35¹	33	2	14	22	12.2	2.29	151	.250	.327	1	.111	-0	5	5	0	0.4
	Was-A	0	0	—	6	0	0	0	0	11¹	12	1	12	9	19.1	4.76	70	.279	.436	0	.000	-0	-2	-2	0	-0.0
	Yr	2	1	.667	19	1	0	0	1	46²	45	3	26	31	13.7	2.89	118	.256	.351	1	.100	-0	3	3	1	0.4
Total	8	27	40	.403	171	71	20	3	3	668¹	690	42	440	291	15.3	5.00	84	.269	.378	36	.167	-5	-60	-58	-1	-5.1

● JACK WADSWORTH Wadsworth, John L. b: 12/17/1867, Wellington, Ohio d: 7/8/41, Elyria, Ohio BL/TR, 180 lbs. Deb: 5/1/1890

1890	Cle-N	2	16	.111	20	19	19	0	0	169²	202	6	81	26	15.3	5.20	69	.287	.365	12	.176	-3	-31	-30	-1	-2.7
1893	Bal-N	0	3	.000	3	3	0	0	0	16	37	0	8	2	25.3	11.25	42	.439	.487	3	.429	1	-12	-12	-1	-1.3
1894	Lou-N	4	18	.182	22	22	20	0	0	173	261	10	103	57	19.1	7.60	67	.344	.425	19	.257	-0	-44	-48	-0	-3.9
1895	Lou-N	0	1	.000	2	0	0	0	0	9	24	0	7	2	31.0	16.00	29	.479	.543	1	.250	-0	-11	-11	0	-0.8
Total	4	6	38	.136	47	44	39	0	0	367²	524	16	199	87	17.9	6.85	64	.328	.406	35	.229	-2	-97	-101	-1	-8.7

● CHARLIE WAGNER Wagner, Charles Thomas "Broadway" b: 12/3/12, Reading, Pa. BR/TR, 5'11", 170 lbs. Deb: 4/19/38 C

1938	Bos-A	1	3	.250	13	6	1	0	0	36²	47	5	24	14	17.7	8.35	59	.309	.407	2	.167	-1	-14	-14	-1	-1.3
1939	Bos-A	3	1	.750	9	5	0	0	0	38¹	49	3	14	13	14.8	4.23	112	.320	.377	1	.071	-2	2	2	-0	0.1
1940	Bos-A	1	0	1.000	12	1	0	0	0	29¹	45	5	8	13	16.3	5.52	81	.344	.381	1	.200	-0	-4	-3	-0	-0.1
1941	Bos-A	12	8	.600	29	25	12	3	0	187¹	175	14	85	51	12.5	3.07	136	.245	.326	10	.159	-1	22	23	-0	2.1
1942	Bos-A	14	11	.560	29	26	17	2	0	205¹	184	5	95	52	12.4	3.29	113	.247	.336	5	.077	-5	8	10	1	0.7
1946	Bos-A	1	0	1.000	8	4	0	0	0	30²	32	6	19	14	15.0	5.87	62	.276	.378	1	.091	-0	-8	-8	-0	-0.3
Total	6	32	23	.582	100	67	30	5	0	527²	532	38	245	157	13.4	3.91	104	.264	.346	20	.118	-9	6	10	-1	1.1

● GARY WAGNER Wagner, Gary Edward b: 6/28/40, Bridgeport, Ill. BR/TR, 6'4", 191 lbs. Deb: 4/18/65

1965	Phi-N	7	7	.500	59	0	0	0	7	105	87	6	49	91	11.8	3.00	115	.233	.325	1	.077	-0	6	5	1	0.8
1966	Phi-N	0	1	.000	5	1	0	0	0	6¹	8	1	5	2	18.5	8.53	42	.333	.448	0	—	0	-3	-3	-0	-0.5
1967	Phi-N	0	0	—	1	0	0	0	0	2	1	0	1	4	4.5	0.00	—	.167	.167	0	—	0	1	1	0	0.0
1968	Phi-N	4	4	.500	44	0	0	0	8	78	69	0	31	43	12.1	3.00	100	.243	.328	1	.083	-1	-0	0	1	0.0
1969	Phi-N	0	3	.000	9	2	0	0	0	19¹	31	3	7	8	17.7	7.91	45	.365	.413	0	.000	-0	-9	-9	-1	-1.4
	Bos-A	1	3	.250	6	1	0	0	0	16¹	18	1	15	9	18.2	6.06	63	.300	.440	0	.000	-0	-4	-4	-0	-0.9
1970	Bos-A	3	1	.750	38	0	0	0	7	40¹	36	3	19	20	12.7	3.35	118	.232	.324	1	.167	-0	2	3	-1	0.3
Total	6	15	19	.441	162	4	0	0	22	267¹	250	14	126	174	13.0	3.70	93	.253	.343	3	.081	-2	-9	-8	1	-1.7

● HECTOR WAGNER Wagner, Hector Raul Guerrero (b: Hector Raul Guerrero (Wagner)) b: 11/26/68, San Juan, D.R. BR/TR, 6'3", 185 lbs. Deb: 9/10/90

1990	KC-A	0	2	.000	5	5	0	0	0	23¹	32	4	11	14	16.6	8.10	47	.323	.391	0	—	0	-11	-11	0	-0.7
1991	KC-A	1	1	.500	2	2	0	0	0	10	16	2	3	5	17.1	7.20	57	.348	.388	0	—	0	-3	-3	-0	-0.6
Total	2	1	3	.250	7	7	0	0	0	33¹	48	6	14	19	16.7	7.83	50	.331	.390	0	—	0	-14	-14	0	-1.3

● HONUS WAGNER Wagner, John Peter "The Flying Dutchman" b: 2/24/1874, Mansfield, Pa. d: 12/6/55, Carnegie, Pa. BR/TR, 5'11", 200 lbs. Deb: 7/19/1897 FMCH ♦

1900	*Pit-N	0	0	—	1	0	0	0	0	3	3	0	4	1	21.0	0.00	—	.260	.450	201	.381	1	1	1	-0	0.0
1902	Pit-N	0	0	—	1	0	0	0	0	5¹	4	0	2	5	10.1	0.00	—	.209	.284	176	.330	1	2	2	-0	0.0
Total	2	0	0	—	2	0	0	0	0	8¹	7	0	6	6	14.0	0.00	—	.228	.354	3415	.327	1	3	3	-0	0.0

● MARK WAGNER Wagner, Mark Duane b: 3/4/54, Conneaut, Ohio BR/TR, 6'1", 175 lbs. Deb: 8/20/76 ♦

1984	Oak-A	0	0	—	1	0	0	0	0	1²	2	0	1	1	16.2	0.00	—	.400	.500	20	.230	0	1	1	-0	0.0

● PAUL WAGNER Wagner, Paul Alan b: 11/14/67, Milwaukee, Wis. BR/TR, 6'3", 205 lbs. Deb: 7/26/92

1992	Pit-N	2	0	1.000	6	1	0	0	0	13	9	0	5	5	9.7	0.69	451	.191	.269	1	.333	0	4	4	0	0.7
1993	Pit-N	8	8	.500	44	17	1	1	2	141¹	143	15	42	114	11.8	4.27	95	.263	.317	8	.190	0	-4	-3	-1	-0.4
1994	Pit-N	7	8	.467	29	17	1	0	0	119²	136	7	50	86	14.6	4.59	93	.293	.372	6	.162	-0	-5	-5	2	-0.3
Total	3	17	16	.515	79	35	2	1	2	274	288	22	97	205	12.9	4.24	97	.273	.340	15	.183	-0	-4	-4	2	-0.0

● BULL WAGNER Wagner, William George b: 1/1/1888, Lilley, Mich. d: 10/2/67, Muskegon, Mich. BR/TR, 6'0.5", 225 lbs. Deb: 6/2/13

1913	Bro-N	4	2	.667	18	1	0	0	0	70²	77	5	30	11	14.0	5.48	60	.285	.363	6	.231	0	-18	-17	-2	-1.4
1914	Bro-N	0	1	.000	6	0	0	0	0	12¹	14	0	12	4	19.7	6.57	44	.311	.466	0	.000	-0	-5	-5	-0	-0.4
Total	2	4	3	.571	24	1	0	0	0	83	91	5	42	15	14.9	5.64	57	.289	.380	6	.222	-0	-23	-22	-2	-1.8

● DAVE WAINHOUSE Wainhouse, David Paul b: 11/7/67, Toronto, Ont., Can. BL/TR, 6'2", 190 lbs. Deb: 8/3/91

1991	Mon-N	0	1	.000	2	0	0	0	0	2²	2	0	4	1	20.3	6.75	54	.222	.462	0	—	0	-1	-1	-0	-0.3
1993	Sea-A	0	0	—	3	0	0	0	0	2¹	7	1	5	2	50.1	27.00	16	.500	.650	0	—	0	-6	-6	-0	0.0
Total	2	0	1	.000	5	0	0	0	0	5	9	1	9	3	34.2	16.20	25	.391	.576	0	—	0	-7	-7	-0	-0.3

● RICK WAITS Waits, Michael Richard b: 5/15/52, Atlanta, Ga. BL/TL, 6'3", 195 lbs. Deb: 9/17/73

1973	Tex-A	0	0	—	1	0	0	0	1	1	1	0	1	0	18.0	9.00	41	.333	.500	0	—	0	-1	-1	-0	-0.1
1975	Cle-A	6	2	.750	16	7	3	0	1	70¹	57	3	25	34	10.6	2.94	128	.221	.292	0	—	0	7	7	0	0.8
1976	Cle-A	7	9	.438	26	22	4	2	0	123²	143	7	54	65	14.3	4.00	87	.297	.368	0	—	0	-7	-7	1	-0.9
1977	Cle-A	9	7	.563	37	16	1	0	2	135¹	132	8	64	62	13.1	3.99	99	.262	.347	0	—	0	-1	-1	-0	-0.1
1978	Cle-A	13	15	.464	34	33	15	2	0	230¹	206	16	86	97	11.5	3.20	117	.240	.310	0	—	0	14	14	3	2.0
1979	Cle-A	16	13	.552	34	34	8	3	0	231	230	26	91	91	12.7	4.44	96	.264	.336	0	—	0	-6	-5	2	-0.4
1980	Cle-A	13	14	.481	33	33	9	2	0	224¹	231	18	82	109	12.6	4.45	91	.270	.335	0	—	0	-10	-10	-1	-1.1
1981	Cle-A	8	10	.444	22	21	5	1	0	126¹	173	7	44	51	15.5	4.92	74	.330	.383	0	—	0	-18	-18	2	-2.1
1982	Cle-A	2	13	.133	25	21	2	0	0	115	128	13	57	44	14.6	5.40	76	.290	.372	0	—	0	-17	-17	1	-1.8
1983	Cle-A	0	1	.000	8	0	0	0	0	19²	23	1	9	13	14.6	4.58	93	.307	.381	0	—	0	-1	-1	0	0.0
	Mil-A	0	2	.000	10	2	0	0	0	30	39	1	11	20	15.0	5.10	73	.320	.376	0	—	0	-3	-5	-0	-0.3
	Yr	0	3	.000	18	2	0	0	0	49²	62	2	20	33	14.9	4.89	80	.308	.371	0	—	0	-5	-5	-0	-0.3
1984	Mil-A	2	4	.333	47	1	0	0	3	73	84	4	24	49	13.3	3.58	108	.297	.352	0	—	0	3	2	0	0.3
1985	Mil-A	3	2	.600	24	0	0	0	0	47	67	3	20	24	16.7	6.51	64	.340	.401	0	.000	0	-12	-12	0	-1.2
Total	12	79	92	.462	317	190	47	10	8	1427	1514	110	568	659	13.2	4.25	92	.277	.346	0	.000	0	-50	-53	8	-4.9

● TIM WAKEFIELD Wakefield, Timothy Stephen b: 8/2/66, Melbourne, Fla. BR/TR, 6'2", 195 lbs. Deb: 7/31/92

1992	*Pit-N	8	1	.889	13	13	4	1	0	92	76	3	35	51	11.0	2.15	160	.232	.309	2	.071	-1	14	13	1	1.3
1993	Pit-N	6	11	.353	24	20	3	2	0	128¹	145	14	75	59	16.1	5.61	72	.291	.393	7	.163	1	-22	-22	-1	-2.5
Total	2	14	12	.538	37	33	7	3	0	220¹	221	17	110	110	13.9	4.17	91	.268	.360	9	.127	-0	-9	-9	-0	-1.2

● BILL WAKEFIELD Wakefield, William Sumner b: 5/24/41, Kansas City, Mo. BR/TR, 6', 175 lbs. Deb: 4/18/64

1964	NY-N	3	5	.375	62	4	0	0	2	119²	103	10	61	61	13.0	3.61	99	.235	.341	4	.167	-0	-1	-0	0	0.0

RUBE WALBERG
Walberg, George Elvin b: 7/27/1896, Pine City, Minn. d: 10/27/78, Tempe, Ariz. BL/TL, 6'1.5", 190 lbs. Deb: 4/29/23

YEAR TM/L	W	L	PCT	G	GS	CG	SH	SV	IP	H	HR	BB	SO	RAT	ERA	ERA+	OAV	OOB	BH	AVG	PB	PR	/A	PD	TPI
1923 NY-N	0	0	—	2	0	0	0	0	5	4	0	1	1	9.0	1.80	212	.211	.250	0	.000	-0	1	1	-0	0.0
Phi-A	4	8	.333	26	10	4	0	0	115	122	10	60	38	14.4	5.32	77	.280	.369	13	.317	3	-17	-16	1	-1.1
1924 Phi-A	0	0	—	6	2	0	0	0	7	10	0	10	3	25.7	12.86	33	.345	.513	1	.500	0	-7	-7	0	0.0
1925 Phi-A	8	14	.364	53	20	7	0	7	191²	197	11	77	82	13.0	3.99	117	.269	.340	10	.156	-4	9	14	1	1.2
1926 Phi-A	12	10	.545	40	19	5	2	2	151	168	4	60	72	13.9	2.80	149	.292	.365	7	.152	-2	20	23	-1	2.8
1927 Phi-A	16	12	.571	46	34	15	0	4	249¹	257	18	91	136	12.7	3.93	108	.271	.337	18	.207	3	6	9	-0	1.2
1928 Phi-A	17	12	.586	38	30	16	3	1	235²	236	19	64	112	11.6	3.55	113	.265	.317	18	.209	1	13	12	1	1.5
1929 *Phi-A	18	11	.621	40	33	20	3	4	267²	256	22	99	94	11.9	3.60	118	.254	.320	23	.223	-0	19	19	-2	1.6
1930 *Phi-A	13	12	.520	38	30	12	2	1	205¹	207	6	85	100	12.9	4.69	100	.262	.335	12	.164	-3	-1	-0	-1	-0.4
1931 *Phi-A	20	12	.625	44	35	19	1	3	291	298	16	109	106	12.6	3.74	120	.266	.331	13	.124	-6	21	24	-1	1.6
1932 Phi-A	17	10	.630	41	34	19	3	0	272	305	16	103	96	13.5	4.73	96	.282	.344	16	.170	-3	-8	-6	-0	-0.8
1933 Phi-A	9	13	.409	40	20	10	1	4	201	224	12	95	68	14.3	4.88	88	.278	.354	9	.132	-1	-13	-13	-1	-1.4
1934 Bos-A	6	7	.462	30	10	2	0	0	104²	118	5	41	38	13.8	4.04	119	.284	.350	6	.188	-1	5	9	1	1.0
1935 Bos-A	5	9	.357	44	10	4	0	3	142²	152	10	54	44	13.1	3.91	121	.273	.340	6	.162	-2	9	13	-1	0.9
1936 Bos-A	5	4	.556	24	9	5	0	0	100¹	98	7	36	49	12.1	4.40	121	.257	.323	5	.156	-1	7	10	1	0.7
1937 Bos-A	5	7	.417	32	11	3	0	1	104²	143	7	46	46	16.5	5.59	85	.332	.400	5	.122	-1	-11	-10	-0	-1.1
Total 15	155	141	.524	544	307	140	15	32	2644	2795	163	1031	1085	13.1	4.16	107	.273	.341	162	.179	-18	53	82	-2	7.7

DOC WALDBAUER
Waldbauer, Albert Charles b: 2/22/1892, Richmond, Va. d: 7/16/69, Yakima, Wash. BR/TR, 6', 172 lbs. Deb: 9/24/17

YEAR TM/L	W	L	PCT	G	GS	CG	SH	SV	IP	H	HR	BB	SO	RAT	ERA	ERA+	OAV	OOB	BH	AVG	PB	PR	/A	PD	TPI
1917 Was-A	0	0	—	2	0	0	0	1	5	10	0	2	2	21.6	7.20	36	.476	.522	0	.000	-0	-3	-3	0	-0.1

BOB WALK
Walk, Robert Vernon b: 11/26/56, Van Nuys, Cal. BR/TR, 6'4", 208 lbs. Deb: 5/26/80

YEAR TM/L	W	L	PCT	G	GS	CG	SH	SV	IP	H	HR	BB	SO	RAT	ERA	ERA+	OAV	OOB	BH	AVG	PB	PR	/A	PD	TPI
1980 *Phi-N	11	7	.611	27	27	0	0	0	151²	163	8	71	94	14.0	4.57	83	.276	.356	7	.140	-0	-16	-13	-1	-1.5
1981 Atl-N	1	4	.200	12	8	0	0	0	43¹	41	6	23	16	13.3	4.57	78	.250	.342	1	.143	-0	-5	-5	-1	-0.6
1982 *Atl-N	11	9	.550	32	27	3	1	0	164¹	179	19	59	84	13.4	4.87	77	.280	.347	10	.196	2	-23	-21	-2	-2.4
1983 Atl-N	0	0	—	1	1	0	0	0	3²	7	0	2	4	22.1	7.36	53	.412	.474	0	.000	-0	-2	-1	-0	0.0
1984 Pit-N	1	1	.500	2	2	0	0	0	10¹	8	1	4	10	10.5	2.61	138	.200	.273	0	.000	-0	1	1	-0	0.1
1985 Pit-N	2	3	.400	9	9	1	1	0	58²	60	3	18	40	12.0	3.68	97	.265	.320	0	.000	-1	-1	-1	-1	-0.3
1986 Pit-N	7	8	.467	44	15	1	1	2	141²	129	14	64	78	12.5	3.75	102	.251	.337	6	.154	-0	-0	1	2	0.3
1987 Pit-N	8	2	.800	39	12	1	1	0	117	107	11	51	78	12.4	3.31	124	.245	.329	6	.231	1	10	10	1	1.0
1988 Pit-N★	12	10	.545	32	32	1	1	0	212²	183	6	65	81	10.6	2.71	126	.230	.290	6	.087	-2	17	16	0	1.5
1989 Pit-N	13	10	.565	33	31	1	0	0	196	208	6	65	83	12.7	4.41	76	.271	.331	13	.186	-3	-20	-23	1	-2.2
1990 *Pit-N	7	5	.583	26	24	1	1	1	129²	136	17	36	73	12.2	3.75	97	.270	.324	6	.162	1	1	-2	-0	-0.2
1991 *Pit-N	9	2	.818	25	20	0	0	0	115	104	10	35	67	11.3	3.60	99	.240	.304	8	.205	2	1	-0	-0	0.2
1992 *Pit-N	10	6	.625	36	19	1	0	0	135	132	10	43	60	12.1	3.20	108	.258	.323	4	.093	-2	5	4	1	0.4
1993 Pit-N	13	14	.481	32	32	3	0	0	187	214	23	70	80	13.9	5.68	71	.294	.360	7	.121	-2	-34	-34	-1	-4.3
Total 14	105	81	.565	350	259	16	6	5	1666	1671	143	606	848	12.5	4.03	91	.263	.330	74	.145	1	-66	-67	-1	-8.0

ED WALKER
Walker, Edward Harrison b: 8/11/1874, Cambois, England d: 9/29/47, Akron, Ohio BL/TL, 6'5", 242 lbs. Deb: 9/26/02

YEAR TM/L	W	L	PCT	G	GS	CG	SH	SV	IP	H	HR	BB	SO	RAT	ERA	ERA+	OAV	OOB	BH	AVG	PB	PR	/A	PD	TPI
1902 Cle-A	0	1	.000	1	1	1	0	0	8	11	0	3	1	15.8	3.38	102	.327	.382	1	.333	0	0	0	0	0.0
1903 Cle-A	0	0	—	3	3	0	0	0	12	13	0	10	4	17.3	5.25	54	.275	.402	0	.000	-0	-3	-3	-1	-0.1
Total 2	0	1	.000	4	4	1	0	0	20	24	0	13	5	16.6	4.50	69	.297	.394	1	.167	0	-3	-3	-1	-0.1

DIXIE WALKER
Walker, Ewart Gladstone b: 6/1/1887, Brownsville, Pa. d: 11/14/65, Leeds, Ala. BL/TR, 6', 192 lbs. Deb: 9/17/09 F

YEAR TM/L	W	L	PCT	G	GS	CG	SH	SV	IP	H	HR	BB	SO	RAT	ERA	ERA+	OAV	OOB	BH	AVG	PB	PR	/A	PD	TPI
1909 Was-A	3	1	.750	4	4	4	0	0	36	31	0	6	25	9.3	2.50	97	.217	.248	2	.154	-0	-0	-0	-0	-0.1
1910 Was-A	11	11	.500	29	26	16	3	0	199¹	177	2	68	84	11.4	3.30	76	.245	.317	9	.130	-3	-17	-18	-1	-2.3
1911 Was-A	8	13	.381	32	24	15	2	0	185²	205	2	50	65	12.7	3.39	97	.286	.339	20	.303	4	-1	-2	-1	-1.0
1912 Was-A	3	6	.333	9	8	5	0	0	60	72	2	18	29	14.1	5.25	64	.300	.359	2	.125	1	-13	-13	-0	-1.5
Total 4	25	31	.446	74	62	40	5	0	481	485	6	142	203	12.1	3.52	82	.266	.326	33	.201	2	-31	-33	-3	-3.9

MYSTERIOUS WALKER
Walker, Frederick Mitchell b: 3/21/1884, Utica, Neb. d: 2/1/58, Oak Park, Ill. BR/TR, 5'10.5", 185 lbs. Deb: 6/28/10

YEAR TM/L	W	L	PCT	G	GS	CG	SH	SV	IP	H	HR	BB	SO	RAT	ERA	ERA+	OAV	OOB	BH	AVG	PB	PR	/A	PD	TPI
1910 Cin-N	0	0	—	1	0	0	0	0	3	4	0	4	1	24.0	3.00	97	.333	.500	0	.000	-0	-0	-0	-0	0.0
1912 Cle-A	0	0	—	1	0	0	0	0	1	0	0	1	0	9.0	0.00	—	.000	.200	0	—	-0	0	0	-0	0.0
1913 Bro-N	1	3	.250	11	8	3	0	0	58¹	44	2	35	35	13.0	3.55	93	.233	.367	3	.167	-0	-2	-2	2	0.0
1914 Pit-F	4	16	.200	35	21	12	0	0	169¹	197	3	74	79	14.6	4.31	67	.294	.367	6	.113	-3	-27	-27	3	-2.8
1915 Bro-F	2	4	.333	13	7	2	0	1	65²	61	3	22	28	11.4	3.70	73	.242	.303	6	.222	-0	-7	-7	1	-0.5
Total 5	7	23	.233	61	36	17	0	1	297¹	306	9	136	143	13.6	4.00	73	.272	.354	15	.152	-3	-36	-36	6	-3.3

GEORGE WALKER
Walker, George A. b: 1863, Hamilton, Ontario, Canada TR, 5'9", 184 lbs. Deb: 8/1/1888

YEAR TM/L	W	L	PCT	G	GS	CG	SH	SV	IP	H	HR	BB	SO	RAT	ERA	ERA+	OAV	OOB	BH	AVG	PB	PR	/A	PD	TPI
1888 Bal-a	1	3	.250	4	4	4	0	0	35	36	2	14	18	12.9	5.91	50	.256	.324	1	.077	-1	-11	-11	-0	-1.1

LUKE WALKER
Walker, James Luke b: 9/2/43, DeKalb, Tex. BL/TL, 6'1.5", 192 lbs. Deb: 9/7/65

YEAR TM/L	W	L	PCT	G	GS	CG	SH	SV	IP	H	HR	BB	SO	RAT	ERA	ERA+	OAV	OOB	BH	AVG	PB	PR	/A	PD	TPI
1965 Pit-N	0	0	—	2	0	0	0	0	5	2	0	1	5	5.4	0.00	—	.118	.167	0	—	0	2	2	0	0.0
1966 Pit-N	0	1	.000	10	1	0	0	0	10	8	0	15	7	21.6	4.50	79	.205	.436	0	.000	-0	-1	-1	-0	-0.1
1968 Pit-N	0	3	.000	39	2	0	0	3	61²	42	1	39	66	12.0	2.04	143	.190	.314	0	.000	-1	6	6	1	0.4
1969 Pit-N	4	6	.400	31	15	3	0	1	118²	98	5	57	96	11.9	3.64	96	.226	.319	0	.000	-3	-1	-2	1	-0.4
1970 *Pit-N	15	6	.714	42	19	5	3	3	163	129	6	89	124	12.1	3.04	128	.219	.323	6	.130	-1	18	16	-0	1.8
1971 *Pit-N	10	8	.556	28	24	4	2	0	159²	157	9	53	88	13.5	3.55	95	.262	.324	1	.022	-3	-3	-3	-2	-0.8
1972 *Pit-N	4	6	.400	26	12	2	0	2	92²	84	9	34	48	12.8	3.40	98	.278	.342	2	.083	-1	-1	-0	-0	-0.3
1973 Pit-N	7	12	.368	37	18	2	1	1	122	129	9	66	74	14.5	4.65	76	.270	.360	2	.067	-2	-13	-15	-1	-2.5
1974 Det-A	5	5	.500	28	9	0	0	0	92	100	4	54	52	15.3	4.99	76	.278	.375	0	—	-0	-14	-12	-0	-1.3
Total 9	45	47	.489	243	100	16	7	9	824²	763	43	408	558	12.9	3.65	97	.247	.337	11	.059	-11	-3	-11	-2	-3.2

ROY WALKER
Walker, James Roy "Dixie" b: 4/13/1893, Lawrenceburg, Tenn d: 2/10/62, New Orleans, La. BR/TR, 6'1.5", 180 lbs. Deb: 9/16/12

YEAR TM/L	W	L	PCT	G	GS	CG	SH	SV	IP	H	HR	BB	SO	RAT	ERA	ERA+	OAV	OOB	BH	AVG	PB	PR	/A	PD	TPI
1912 Cle-A	0	0	—	1	0	0	0	0	2	0	0	2	1	9.0	0.00	—	.000	.250	0	—	-0	1	1	-0	0.0
1915 Cle-A	4	9	.308	25	15	4	0	1	131	122	1	65	57	13.3	3.98	77	.261	.360	5	.132	-2	-15	-14	-2	-1.8
1917 Chi-N	0	1	.000	2	1	0	0	0	7	8	0	5	4	16.7	3.86	75	.286	.394	0	.000	-0	-1	-1	-0	-0.1
1918 Chi-N	1	3	.250	13	7	2	0	1	43¹	50	1	15	20	13.7	2.70	103	.298	.359	0	.000	-1	0	0	-0	-0.1
1921 StL-N	11	12	.478	38	24	11	0	3	170²	194	10	53	52	13.1	4.22	87	.293	.347	11	.204	-0	-8	-10	-1	-1.4
1922 StL-N	1	2	.333	12	2	0	0	0	32	34	1	15	14	13.8	4.78	81	.293	.374	1	.143	-0	-2	-3	-1	-0.4
Total 6	17	27	.386	91	49	17	0	5	386	408	13	155	148	13.3	3.99	85	.282	.355	17	.153	-4	-26	-26	-5	-3.8

JERRY WALKER
Walker, Jerry Allen b: 2/12/39, Ada, Okla. BB/TR, 6'1", 195 lbs. Deb: 7/6/57 C

YEAR TM/L	W	L	PCT	G	GS	CG	SH	SV	IP	H	HR	BB	SO	RAT	ERA	ERA+	OAV	OOB	BH	AVG	PB	PR	/A	PD	TPI
1957 Bal-A	1	0	1.000	13	3	1	1	1	27²	24	1	14	13	12.4	2.93	124	.245	.339	0	.000	-1	3	2	-0	0.0
1958 Bal-A	0	0	—	6	0	0	0	0	10¹	16	2	5	6	18.3	6.97	52	.340	.404	0	.000	-0	-4	-4	-0	-0.1
1959 Bal-A★	11	10	.524	30	22	7	2	4	182	160	15	52	100	10.6	2.92	130	.240	.297	11	.169	-1	19	18	-0	1.9
1960 Bal-A	3	4	.429	29	18	1	0	9	118	107	15	56	48	12.7	3.74	102	.247	.337	14	.368	5	2	1	1	0.6
1961 KC-A	8	14	.364	36	24	4	0	2	168	160	21	66	56	14.3	4.82	87	.253	.359	16	.250	3	-15	-12	-1	-1.1
1962 KC-A	8	9	.471	31	21	3	1	0	143¹	165	27	78	57	15.7	5.90	72	.288	.381	15	.263	5	-31	-27	-2	-2.2
1963 Cle-A	6	6	.500	39	2	0	0	1	88	92	6	36	41	13.3	4.91	74	.265	.338	2	.105	-0	-13	-13	-0	-1.7
1964 Cle-A	0	1	.000	6	0	0	0	0	9²	9	1	4	5	12.1	4.66	77	.257	.333	0	.000	-0	-1	-1	-0	-0.2
Total 8	37	44	.457	190	90	16	4	13	747	734	97	341	326	13.3	4.36	90	.259	.343	58	.230	10	-39	-36	1	-2.7

YEAR	TM/L	W	L	PCT	G	GS	CG	SH	SV	IP	H	HR	BB	SO	RAT	ERA	ERA+	OAV	OOB	BH	AVG	PB	PR	/A	PD	TPI

● **MARTY WALKER**　Walker, Martin Van Buren "Buddy"　b: 3/27/1899, Philadelphia, Pa.　d: 4/24/78, Philadelphia, Pa.　BL/TL, 6', 170 lbs.　Deb: 9/30/28

| 1928 | Phi-N | 0 | 1 | .000 | 1 | 1 | 0 | 0 | 0 | 0 | 2 | 0 | 3 | 0 | — | ∞ | — | 1.000 | 1.000 | 0 | — | 0 | -2 | -2 | 0 | -0.2 |

● **MIKE WALKER**　Walker, Michael Aaron　b: 6/23/65, Houston, Tex.　BR/TR, 6'3", 205 lbs.　Deb: 6/16/92

| 1992 | Sea-A | 0 | 3 | .000 | 5 | 3 | 0 | 0 | 0 | 14² | 21 | 4 | 9 | 5 | 18.4 | 7.36 | 54 | .333 | .417 | 0 | — | 0 | -6 | -6 | 0 | -0.9 |

● **MIKE WALKER**　Walker, Michael Charles　b: 10/4/66, Chicago, Ill.　BR/TR, 6'2", 195 lbs.　Deb: 9/9/88

1988	Cle-A	0	1	.000	3	1	0	0	0	8²	8	0	10	7	18.7	7.27	57	.258	.439	0	—	0	-3	-3	0	-0.4
1990	Cle-A	2	6	.250	18	11	0	0	0	75²	82	6	42	34	15.5	4.88	80	.277	.378	0	—	0	-8	-8	-0	-0.8
1991	Cle-A	0	1	.000	5	0	0	0	0	4¹	6	0	2	2	18.7	2.08	200	.316	.409	0	—	0	1	1	0	0.2
Total	3	2	8	.200	26	12	0	0	0	88²	96	6	54	43	15.9	4.97	79	.277	.386	0	—	0	-10	-10	0	-1.0

● **TOM WALKER**　Walker, Robert Thomas　b: 11/7/48, Tampa, Fla.　BR/TR, 6'1", 188 lbs.　Deb: 4/23/72

1972	Mon-N	2	2	.500	46	0	0	0	2	74²	71	4	22	42	11.3	2.89	123	.248	.304	0	.000	-0	5	5	-0	0.3
1973	Mon-N	7	5	.583	54	0	0	0	4	91²	95	7	42	68	13.7	3.63	105	.274	.357	0	.000	-1	0	2	-0	0.2
1974	Mon-N	4	5	.444	33	8	1	0	2	91²	96	7	28	70	12.4	3.83	100	.266	.322	3	.188	0	-2	0	-1	0.0
1975	Det-A	3	8	.273	36	9	1	0	0	115¹	116	16	40	60	12.6	4.45	90	.261	.329	0	—	0	-9	-6	-2	-0.9
1976	StL-N	1	2	.333	10	0	0	0	3	19²	22	2	3	11	11.4	4.12	86	.265	.291	2	.400	1	-1	-1	-1	-0.2
1977	Mon-N	1	1	.500	11	0	0	0	0	19	15	2	7	10	10.4	4.74	80	.221	.293	0	.000	-0	-2	-2	-0	-0.2
	Cal-A	0	0	—	1	0	0	0	0	2	3	2	0	1	13.5	9.00	43	.375	.375	0	—	-0	-1	-1	-0	0.0
Total	6	18	23	.439	191	17	2	0	11	414	418	40	142	262	12.4	3.87	99	.262	.326	5	.152	-0	-10	-3	-3	-0.8

● **TOM WALKER**　Walker, Thomas William　b: 8/1/1881, Philadelphia, Pa.　d: 7/10/44, Woodbury Heights, N.J.　BR/TR, 5'11", 170 lbs.　Deb: 9/27/02

1902	Phi-A	0	1	.000	1	1	1	0	0	8	10	0	0	4	5.63	65	.306	.327	1	.250	-0	-2	-2	1	-0.1
1904	Cin-N	15	8	.652	24	24	22	2	0	217	196	2	53	64	11.1	2.24	131	.238	.299	9	.117	-4	12	17	-2	1.0
1905	Cin-N	9	7	.563	23	19	12	1	0	144²	171	3	44	28	13.7	3.24	102	.305	.362	7	.137	-1	-4	1	-0	-0.1
Total	3	24	16	.600	48	44	35	3	0	369²	377	5	97	94	12.1	2.70	114	.266	.325	17	.129	-6	6	16	-1	0.8

● **BILL WALKER**　Walker, William Henry　b: 10/7/03, E.St.Louis, Ill.　d: 6/14/66, E.St.Louis, Ill.　BR/TL, 6', 175 lbs.　Deb: 9/13/27

1927	NY-N	0	0	—	3	0	0	0	0	4	6	0	5	4	24.8	9.00	43	.429	.579	0	—	-2	-2	-2	-0	0.0
1928	NY-N	3	6	.333	22	8	1	0	0	76¹	79	9	31	39	13.1	4.72	83	.275	.348	2	.091	-2	-6	-7	-0	-0.9
1929	NY-N	14	7	.667	29	23	13	1	0	177²	188	11	57	65	12.6	**3.09**	148	.274	.334	7	.115	-3	32	29	-3	2.3
1930	NY-N	17	15	.531	39	34	13	2	1	245¹	258	19	88	105	12.9	3.93	121	.266	.334	16	.186	-1	29	22	-1	2.1
1931	NY-N	16	9	.640	37	28	19	**6**	3	239¹	212	6	49	121	10.5	**2.26**	**164**	.231	.283	5	.065	-6	**43**	**38**	-4	2.8
1932	NY-N	8	12	.400	31	22	9	0	2	163	177	23	55	74	13.0	4.14	90	.274	.334	7	.135	-2	-5	-8	2	-0.9
1933	StL-N	9	10	.474	29	20	6	2	0	158	168	8	67	41	13.4	3.42	102	.273	.346	7	.132	-2	-1	1	1	0.0
1934	*StL-N	12	4	.750	24	19	10	1	0	153	160	11	66	76	13.4	3.12	136	.270	.345	5	.093	-4	16	19	-1	1.2
1935	StL-N★	13	8	.619	37	25	8	2	1	193¹	222	7	78	79	14.2	3.82	107	.288	.357	6	.102	-4	4	6	-1	0.2
1936	StL-N	5	6	.455	21	13	4	1	1	79²	106	5	27	22	15.3	5.87	67	.318	.373	7	.280	2	-16	-17	1	-1.8
Total	10	97	77	.557	272	192	83	15	8	1489²	1576	99	538	626	12.9	3.59	114	.271	.335	62	.127	-23	93	83	-7	5.0

● **JIM WALKUP**　Walkup, James Elton　b: 12/14/09, Havana, Ark.　BR/TR, 6'1", 170 lbs.　Deb: 9/22/34

1934	StL-A	0	0	—	3	0	0	0	0	8¹	6	1	6	1	11.9	2.16	231	.200	.314	1	.333	0	2	3	-0	0.4
1935	StL-A	6	9	.400	55	20	4	1	0	181¹	226	17	104	44	16.5	6.25	77	.305	.392	6	.128	-3	-36	-29	-1	-2.4
1936	StL-A	0	3	.000	5	2	0	0	0	15²	20	0	6	5	14.9	8.04	67	.308	.366	0	.000	-1	-5	-5	1	-0.7
1937	StL-A	9	12	.429	27	18	6	0	0	150¹	218	16	83	46	18.0	7.36	66	.347	.423	14	.241	-1	-46	-42	2	-4.4
1938	StL-A	1	12	.077	18	13	1	0	0	94	127	13	53	28	17.5	6.80	73	.329	.414	4	.138	-2	-21	-19	-0	-2.1
1939	StL-A	0	1	.000	1	0	0	0	0	0²	2	0	1	0	40.5	0.00	—	.500	.600	0	—	0	0	0	0	0.6
	Det-A	0	1	.000	7	0	0	0	0	12	15	3	4	5	17.3	7.50	65	.319	.418	1	.500	-0	-4	-3	0	-0.2
	Yr	0	2	.000	8	0	0	0	0	12²	17	3	5	5	18.5	7.11	69	.333	.433	1	.500	-0	-3	-3	0	0.4
Total	6	16	38	.296	116	53	11	1	0	462¹	614	49	260	134	17.1	6.74	72	.323	.406	26	.182	-6	-110	-96	1	-9.2

● **JIM WALKUP**　Walkup, James Huey　b: 11/3/1895, Havana, Ark.　d: 6/12/90, Duncan, Okla.　BR/TL, 5'8", 150 lbs.　Deb: 4/30/27

| 1927 | Det-A | 0 | 0 | — | 2 | 0 | 0 | 0 | 0 | 1² | 3 | 0 | 0 | 0 | 16.2 | 5.40 | 78 | .429 | .429 | 0 | .000 | -0 | -0 | -0 | 0 | 0.0 |

● **MURRAY WALL**　Wall, Murray Wesley　b: 9/19/26, Dallas, Tex.　d: 10/8/71, Lone Oak, Tex.　BR/TR, 6'3", 185 lbs.　Deb: 7/4/50

1950	Bos-N	0	0	—	1	0	0	0	0	4	6	0	2	2	18.0	9.00	43	.333	.400	0	.000	-0	-2	-2	-0	0.0
1957	Bos-A	3	0	1.000	11	0	0	0	0	24¹	21	3	2	13	8.5	3.33	120	.233	.250	2	.333	0	1	2	1	0.4
1958	Bos-A	8	9	.471	52	1	0	0	10	114¹	109	14	33	53	11.6	3.62	111	.255	.316	3	.107	-0	2	5	3	0.9
1959	Bos-A	1	4	.200	15	0	0	0	3	31²	31	5	15	8	13.1	5.40	75	.267	.351	0	.000	-1	-5	-5	-1	-0.8
	Was-A	0	0	—	1	0	0	0	0	1¹	3	1	0	1	20.3	6.75	58	.600	.600	0	.000	-0	-0	-0	-0	0.0
	Bos-A	1	1	.500	11	0	0	0	0	17¹	26	2	11	6	19.7	5.71	71	.371	.463	0	.000	-0	-4	-3	-0	-0.4
	Yr	2	5	.286	27	0	0	0	3	50¹	60	8	26	14	15.6	5.54	73	.313	.397	0	.000	-1	-9	-8	1	-1.2
Total	4	13	14	.481	91	1	0	0	14	193	196	25	63	82	12.4	4.20	96	.270	.333	5	.109	-3	-8	-4	5	0.1

● **STAN WALL**　Wall, Stanley Arthur　b: 6/16/51, Butler, Mo.　BL/TL, 6'1", 175 lbs.　Deb: 7/19/75

1975	LA-N	0	1	.000	10	0	0	0	0	16	12	0	7	6	11.3	1.69	201	.222	.323	0	—	0	3	3	0	0.2
1976	LA-N	2	2	.500	31	0	0	0	1	50	50	5	15	27	12.1	3.60	94	.269	.330	0	.000	-1	-1	-1	-1	-0.2
1977	LA-N	2	3	.400	25	0	0	0	0	32	36	3	13	22	14.1	5.34	72	.279	.350	0	.000	-1	-5	-5	-1	-0.8
Total	3	4	6	.400	66	0	0	0	1	98	98	8	35	55	12.6	3.86	91	.266	.336	0	.000	-1	-2	-2	-2	-0.8

● **DAVE WALLACE**　Wallace, David William　b: 9/7/47, Waterbury, Conn.　BR/TR, 5'10", 185 lbs.　Deb: 7/18/73

1973	Phi-N	0	0	—	4	0	0	0	0	3²	13	1	2	2	36.8	22.09	17	.591	.625	0	—	0	-8	-7	0	0.0
1974	Phi-N	0	1	.000	3	0	0	0	0	3	4	2	3	3	21.0	9.00	42	.308	.438	0	—	0	-2	-2	0	-0.5
1978	Tor-A	0	0	—	6	0	0	0	0	14	12	1	11	7	14.8	3.86	102	.245	.383	0	—	0	-0	-0	-0	0.0
Total	3	0	1	.000	13	0	0	0	0	20²	29	4	16	12	19.6	7.84	49	.345	.450	0	—	0	-9	-9	0	-0.5

● **HUCK WALLACE**　Wallace, Harry Clinton "Lefty"　b: 7/27/1882, Richmond, Ind.　d: 7/6/51, Cleveland, Ohio　BL/TL, 5'6", 160 lbs.　Deb: 6/5/12

| 1912 | Phi-N | 0 | 0 | — | 4 | 0 | 0 | 0 | 0 | 4² | 7 | 0 | 4 | 4 | 21.2 | 0.00 | — | .350 | .458 | 0 | — | 0 | 2 | 2 | 0 | 0.0 |

● **LEFTY WALLACE**　Wallace, James Harold　b: 8/12/21, Evansville, Ind.　d: 7/28/82, Evansville, Ind.　BL/TL, 5'11", 160 lbs.　Deb: 5/5/42

1942	Bos-N	1	3	.250	19	3	1	0	0	49¹	39	3	24	20	11.9	3.83	87	.217	.316	2	.143	-0	-3	-3	-1	-0.3
1945	Bos-N	1	0	1.000	5	3	1	0	0	20	18	1	9	4	12.6	4.50	85	.240	.329	0	.000	-1	-2	-1	0	-0.1
1946	Bos-N	3	3	.500	27	8	2	0	0	75¹	76	5	31	27	12.9	4.18	82	.253	.325	1	.056	-1	-6	-6	2	-0.4
Total	3	5	6	.455	51	14	4	0	0	144²	133	9	64	51	12.5	4.11	84	.240	.323	3	.079	-2	-11	-10	1	-0.8

● **MIKE WALLACE**　Wallace, Michael Sherman　b: 2/3/51, Gastonia, N.C.　BL/TL, 6'2", 204 lbs.　Deb: 6/27/73

1973	Phi-N	1	1	.500	20	3	1	0	1	33¹	38	1	15	20	14.3	3.78	100	.304	.379	0	.000	-0	-0	0	-0	-0.1
1974	Phi-N	1	0	1.000	8	0	0	0	0	8¹	12	0	2	1	15.1	5.40	70	.324	.359	0	—	0	-2	-2	-0	-0.2
	NY-A	6	0	1.000	23	1	0	0	0	52¹	42	3	35	34	13.2	2.41	145	.222	.344	0	—	0	7	6	-1	0.6
1975	NY-A	0	0	—	3	0	0	0	0	4¹	11	1	1	2	24.9	14.54	25	.458	.480	0	—	0	-5	-5	0	-0.2
	StL-N	0	0	—	9	0	0	0	0	8²	9	0	5	6	14.5	2.08	181	.281	.378	0	—	0	2	2	0	0.1
1976	StL-N	3	2	.600	49	0	0	0	2	66¹	66	3	39	40	14.2	4.07	87	.264	.363	1	.333	0	-4	-4	0	-0.3
1977	Tex-A	0	0	—	5	0	0	0	0	8¹	10	1	10	2	21.6	7.56	54	.323	.488	0	—	0	-3	-3	0	-0.2
Total	5	11	3	.786	117	4	1	0	3	181²	188	9	107	105	14.6	3.91	92	.273	.371	1	.143	-0	-6	-6	-1	-0.2

YEAR TM/L	W	L	PCT	G	GS	CG	SH	SV	IP	H	HR	BB	SO	RAT	ERA	ERA+	OAV	OOB	BH	AVG	PB	PR	/A	PD	TPI

● **BOBBY WALLACE**   Wallace, Rhoderick John   b: 11/4/1873, Pittsburgh, Pa.   d: 11/3/60, Torrance, Cal.   BR/TR, 5'8", 170 lbs.   Deb: 9/15/1894   MUCH♦

1894 Cle-N	2	1	.667	4	3	2	0	0	26	28	1	20	10	17.0	5.19	105	.272	.396	2	.154	-1	0	1	1	0.0
1895 Cle-N	12	14	.462	30	28	22	1	1	228²	271	3	87	63	14.4	4.09	122	.290	.356	21	.214	-3	17	23	3	2.0
1896 *Cle-N	10	7	.588	22	16	13	2	0	145¹	167	2	49	46	13.6	3.34	136	.286	.345	35	.235	0	16	19	-0	1.8
1902 StL-A	0	0	—	1	1	0	0	0	2	3	0	0	1	13.5			.346	.346	141	.285	0	1	1	0	0.0
Total 4	24	22	.522	57	48	37	3	1	402	469	6	156	120	14.3	3.87	125	.288	.355	2309	.268	-3	35	44	4	3.8

● **TIM WALLACH**   Wallach, Timothy Charles   b: 9/14/57, Huntington Park, Cal.   BR/TR, 6'3", 200 lbs.   Deb: 9/6/80 ♦

1987 Mon-N★	0	0	—	1	0	0	0	0	1	1	0	0	0	9.0	0.00		.333	.333	177	.298	1	0	0	-0	0.0
1989 Mon-N★	0	0	—	1	0	0	0	0	1	2	0	0	0	18.0	9.00	39	.500	.500	159	.277	0	-1	-1	0	0.0
Total 2	0	0	—	2	0	0	0	0	2	3	0	0	0	13.5	4.50	86	.429	.429	1916	.258	-0	-0	-0	-0	0.0

● **RED WALLER**   Waller, John Francis   b: 6/16/1883, Washington, D.C.   d: 2/9/15, Secaucus, N.J.   Deb: 4/27/09

| 1909 NY-N | 0 | 0 | — | 1 | 0 | 0 | 0 | 0 | 1 | 3 | 0 | 1 | 0 | 36.0 | 0.00 | — | .429 | .500 | 0 | — | 0 | 0 | 0 | 0 | 0.0 |

● **AUGIE WALSH**   Walsh, August Sothley   b: 8/17/04, Wilmington, Del.   d: 11/12/85, San Rafael, Cal.   BR/TR, 6', 175 lbs.   Deb: 10/2/27

1927 Phi-N	0	1	.000	1	1	1	0	0	10	12	3	5	0	15.3	4.50	92	.333	.415	1	.250	-0	-1	-0	-0	-0.1
1928 Phi-N	4	9	.308	38	11	2	0	2	122¹	160	13	40	38	15.1	6.18	69	.321	.378	10	.256	2	-30	-26	-2	-2.4
Total 2	4	10	.286	39	12	3	0	2	132¹	172	16	45	38	15.1	6.05	70	.322	.380	11	.256	2	-30	-26	-2	-2.5

● **CONNIE WALSH**   Walsh, Cornelius R.   b: 4/23/1882, St.Louis, Mo.   d: 4/5/53, St.Louis, Mo.   Deb: 9/16/07

| 1907 Pit-N | 0 | 0 | — | 1 | 0 | 0 | 0 | 0 | 1 | 1 | 0 | 1 | 0 | 18.0 | 9.00 | 27 | .250 | .400 | 0 | — | 0 | -1 | -1 | -0 | 0.0 |

● **DAVE WALSH**   Walsh, David Peter   b: 9/25/60, Arlington, Mass.   BL/TL, 6'1", 185 lbs.   Deb: 8/13/90

| 1990 LA-N | 1 | 0 | 1.000 | 20 | 0 | 0 | 0 | 0 | 16¹ | 15 | 1 | 6 | 15 | 11.6 | 3.86 | 95 | .242 | .309 | 0 | — | 0 | -0 | -0 | 0 | 0.0 |

● **ED WALSH**   Walsh, Edward Arthur   b: 2/11/05, Meriden, Conn.   d: 10/31/37, Meriden, Conn.   BR/TR, 6'1", 180 lbs.   Deb: 7/4/28   F

1928 Chi-A	4	7	.364	14	10	3	0	0	78	86	4	42	32	15.3	4.96	82	.290	.387	3	.111	-2	-8	-8	-1	-1.2
1929 Chi-A	6	11	.353	24	20	7	0	0	129	156	9	64	31	15.6	5.65	76	.312	.394	10	.233	2	-20	-20	1	-1.9
1930 Chi-A	1	4	.200	37	4	0	0	0	103²	131	6	30	37	14.3	5.38	86	.316	.367	9	.265	1	-8	-9	-1	-0.2
1932 Chi-A	0	2	.000	4	4	1	0	0	20¹	26	3	13	7	17.3	8.41	51	.299	.390	2	.286	0	-9	-9	-0	-0.7
Total 4	11	24	.314	79	38	11	0	0	331	399	22	149	107	15.3	5.57	78	.307	.384	24	.216	1	-45	-45	1	-4.0

● **ED WALSH**   Walsh, Edward Augustine "Big Ed"   b: 5/14/1881, Plains, Pa.   d: 5/26/59, Pompano Beach, Fla   BR/TR, 6'1", 193 lbs.   Deb: 5/7/04   FMUCH

1904 Chi-A	6	3	.667	18	8	6	1	1	110²	90	1	32	57	10.2	2.60	94	.223	.285	9	.220	3	-0	-2	1	0.2
1905 Chi-A	8	3	.727	22	13	9	1	0	136²	121	0	29	71	10.1	2.17	114	.239	.284	9	.155	-0	7	5	0	0.4
1906 *Chi-A	17	13	.567	41	31	24	**10**	1	278¹	215	1	58	171	9.1	1.88	135	.216	.265	14	.141	-2	25	21	8	3.0
1907 Chi-A	24	18	.571	**56**	46	**37**	5	4	**422¹**	341	3	87	206	9.3	**1.60**	150	.223	.268	25	.162	-1	**45**	**38**	22	**6.4**
1908 Chi-A	**40**	15	**.727**	**66**	49	**42**	11	6	**464**	343	2	56	**269**	9.1	1.42	146	.203	.232	27	.172	2	**51**	**47**	14	**8.1**
1909 Chi-A	15	11	.577	31	28	20	8	2	230¹	166	0	50	127	**8.6**	1.41	166	.203	**.253**	18	.214	4	**27**	24	7	4.4
1910 Chi-A	18	20	.474	**45**	36	33	7	**5**	369²	242	5	61	258	**7.5**	**1.27**	**189**	**.187**	**.226**	30	.217	4	**52**	46	10	**7.1**
1911 Chi-A	27	18	.600	**56**	37	33	5	4	**368²**	327	4	72	255	9.9	2.22	145	.239	**.280**	34	.215	-2	46	41	15	6.2
1912 Chi-A	27	17	.614	**62**	41	32	6	**10**	**393**	332	6	94	254	9.8	2.15	149	.231	.279	33	.243	6	51	46	7	6.6
1913 Chi-A	8	3	.727	16	14	7	1	1	97²	91	1	39	34	12.3	2.58	113	.243	.321	5	.156	-1	4	4	1	0.4
1914 Chi-A	2	3	.400	8	5	3	1	0	44²	33	0	20	15	10.9	2.82	95	.212	.305	1	.063	-1	-0	-1	1	-0.1
1915 Chi-A	3	0	1.000	3	3	1	0	0	27	19	0	7	12	8.7	1.33	223	.202	.257	4	.364	1	5	5	-1	0.6
1916 Chi-A	0	1	.000	2	1	0	0	0	3¹	4	0	3	3	18.9	2.70	102	.286	.412	0	—	0	0	0	0	0.0
1917 Bos-N	0	1	.000	4	3	1	0	0	18	22	0	9	4	16.0	3.50	73	.314	.400	1	.250	1	-2	-2	0	0.0
Total 14	195	126	.607	430	315	250	57	34	2964¹	2346	23	617	1736	9.2	1.82	145	.218	.264	210	.193	14	310	270	83	43.3

● **JUNIOR WALSH**   Walsh, James Gerald   b: 3/7/19, Newark, N.J.   d: 11/12/90, Olyphant, Pa.   BR/TR, 5'11", 185 lbs.   Deb: 9/14/46

1946 Pit-N	0	1	.000	4	2	0	0	0	10¹	9	0	10	2	17.4	5.23	67	.237	.408	0	.000	-1	-2	-2	-0	-0.2
1948 Pit-N	1	0	1.000	2	0	0	0	0	4¹	4	1	5	0	18.7	10.38	39	.235	.409	0	—	-0	-3	-3	-0	-0.5
1949 Pit-N	1	4	.200	9	7	1	1	0	42²	40	5	16	24	11.8	5.06	83	.244	.311	0	.000	-1	-5	-4	-1	-0.6
1950 Pit-N	1	1	.500	38	2	0	0	0	62¹	56	6	34	33	13.1	5.05	87	.246	.346	1	.167	1	-6	-5	-0	-0.1
1951 Pit-N	1	4	.200	36	1	0	0	2	73¹	92	9	46	32	17.1	6.87	61	.304	.397	1	.143	-1	-24	-22	1	-1.3
Total 5	4	10	.286	89	12	1	1	2	193	201	21	111	91	14.7	5.88	72	.268	.365	2	.065	-1	-40	-35	-0	-2.7

● **JIM WALSH**   Walsh, James Thomas   b: 7/10/1894, Roxbury, Mass.   d: 5/13/67, Boston, Mass.   BL/TL, 5'11", 175 lbs.   Deb: 8/25/21

| 1921 Det-A | 0 | 0 | — | 3 | 0 | 0 | 0 | 0 | 4 | 2 | 0 | 1 | 3 | 6.8 | 2.25 | 190 | .125 | .176 | 0 | — | 0 | 1 | 1 | 0 | 0.0 |

● **DEE WALSH**   Walsh, Leo Thomas   b: 3/28/1890, St.Louis, Mo.   d: 7/14/71, St.Louis, Mo.   BB/TR, 5'9.5", 165 lbs.   Deb: 4/10/13 ♦

| 1915 StL-A | 0 | 0 | — | 1 | 0 | 0 | 0 | 0 | 2 | 2 | 0 | 2 | 0 | 18.0 | 13.50 | 21 | .222 | .364 | 33 | .220 | 0 | -2 | -2 | -0 | 0.0 |

● **JIMMY WALSH**   Walsh, Michael Timothy "Runt"   b: 3/25/1886, Lima, Ohio   d: 1/21/47, Baltimore, Md.   BR/TR, 5'9", 174 lbs.   Deb: 4/25/10 ♦

| 1911 Phi-N | 0 | 1 | .000 | 1 | 0 | 0 | 0 | 0 | 2² | 7 | 1 | 1 | 1 | 27.0 | 13.50 | 26 | .500 | .533 | 78 | .270 | -0 | -3 | -3 | -0 | -0.7 |

● **GENE WALTER**   Walter, Gene Winston   b: 11/22/60, Chicago, Ill.   BL/TL, 6'4", 200 lbs.   Deb: 8/9/85

1985 SD-N	0	2	.000	15	0	0	0	3	22	12	0	18	18	8.2	2.05	173	.158	.238	0	.000	0	4	4	0	0.5
1986 SD-N	2	2	.500	57	0	0	0	0	98	89	7	49	84	13.0	3.86	95	.247	.343	2	.200	1	-2	-2	1	0.1
1987 NY-N	1	2	.333	21	0	0	0	0	19²	18	1	13	11	14.6	3.20	118	.243	.364	0	.000	0	2	1	-0	0.2
1988 NY-N	0	1	.000	19	0	0	0	0	16²	21	0	11	14	17.3	3.78	85	.309	.405	0	—	0	-1	-1	-0	-0.1
Sea-A	1	0	1.000	16	0	0	0	1	26¹	21	0	15	13	13.0	5.13	81	.216	.333	0	—	0	-3	-3	-0	-0.3
Total 4	4	7	.364	128	0	0	0	4	182²	161	8	96	140	13.0	3.74	98	.238	.339	2	.167	1	0	-1	0	0.4

● **BERNIE WALTER**   Walter, James Bernard   b: 8/15/08, Dover, Tenn.   d: 10/30/88, Nashville, Tenn.   BR/TR, 6'1", 175 lbs.   Deb: 8/16/30

| 1930 Pit-N | 0 | 0 | — | 1 | 0 | 0 | 0 | 0 | 1 | 0 | 0 | 0 | 1 | 0.0 | 0.00 | — | .000 | .000 | 0 | — | 0 | 1 | 1 | 0 | 0.0 |

● **CHARLIE WALTERS**   Walters, Charles Leonard   b: 2/21/47, Minneapolis, Minn.   BR/TR, 6'4", 190 lbs.   Deb: 4/11/69

| 1969 Min-A | 0 | 0 | — | 6 | 0 | 0 | 0 | 0 | 6² | 6 | 1 | 3 | 2 | 13.5 | 5.40 | 68 | .240 | .345 | 0 | — | 0 | -1 | -1 | -0 | 0.0 |

● **MIKE WALTERS**   Walters, Michael Charles   b: 10/18/57, St.Louis, Mo.   BR/TR, 6'5", 203 lbs.   Deb: 7/8/83

1983 Min-A	1	1	.500	23	0	0	0	2	59	52	4	20	21	11.3	4.12	103	.243	.314	0	—	0	-0	-0	-0	-0.1
1984 Min-A	0	3	.000	23	0	0	0	2	29	31	1	14	10	14.3	3.72	113	.287	.374	0	—	0	1	2	0	-0.1
Total 2	1	4	.200	46	0	0	0	4	88	83	5	34	31	12.3	3.99	106	.258	.334	0	—	0	0	2	0	-0.2

● **BUCKY WALTERS**   Walters, William Henry   b: 4/19/09, Philadelphia, Pa.   d: 4/20/91, Abington, Pa.   BR/TR, 6'1", 180 lbs.   Deb: 9/18/31   MC♦

1934 Phi-N	0	0	—	2	1	0	0	0	7	8	1	2	2	14.1	1.29	367	.296	.367	78	.260	-0	2	3	1	0.1
1935 Phi-N	9	9	.500	24	22	8	2	0	151	168	9	68	40	14.5	4.17	109	.289	.370	24	.250	1	-3	6	2	1.1
1936 Phi-N	11	21	.344	40	33	15	**4**	0	258	284	11	115	66	14.1	4.26	107	.277	.353	29	.240	2	-7	8	9	2.2
1937 Phi-N★	14	15	.483	37	34	15	3	0	246¹	292	14	86	87	13.9	4.75	91	.295	.353	38	.277	4	-23	-11	5	-0.2
1938 Phi-N	4	8	.333	12	12	9	1	0	82²	91	4	42	28	14.8	5.23	74	.276	.363	10	.286	3	-13	-12	0	-1.2
Cin-N	11	6	.647	27	22	11	1	0	168¹	168	12	66	62	12.6	3.69	99	.255	.321	9	.141	-2	-2	-2	0	0.1
Yr	15	14	.517	39	34	20	3	1	251	259	16	108	90	13.2	4.20	89	.264	.335	19	.192	1	-11	-13	3	-1.1
1939 *Cin-N☆	27	11	.711	39	36	**31**	2	0	**319**	250	15	109	**137**	10.3	**2.29**	168	**.220**	.291	39	.325	13	**58**	55	4	8.5
1940 *Cin-N★	22	10	.688	36	36	**29**	3	0	**305**	241	19	92	115	10.0	**2.48**	153	.220	.283	24	.205	2	46	44	-1	4.7

YEAR TM/L	W	L	PCT	G	GS	CG	SH	SV	IP	H	HR	BB	SO	RAT	ERA	ERA+	OAV	OOB	BH	AVG	PB	PR	/A	PD	TPI
1941 Cin-N★	19	15	.559	37	35	27	5	2	302	292	10	88	129	11.4	2.83	127	.255	.309	20	.189	2	27	26	2	3.3
1942 Cin-N★	15	14	.517	34	32	21	2	0	253²	223	8	73	109	10.7	2.66	123	.231	.289	24	.242	6	18	18	1	3.0
1943 Cin-N	15	15	.500	34	34	21	5	0	246¹	244	8	109	80	12.9	3.54	94	.264	.342	24	.267	8	-4	-6	1	0.2
1944 Cin-N★	23	8	.742	34	32	27	6	1	285	233	10	87	77	10.2	2.40	145	.219	.281	30	.280	8	38	34	1	4.7
1945 Cin-N	10	10	.500	22	22	12	3	0	168	166	6	51	45	11.7	2.68	140	.259	.316	14	.230	5	21	20	-0	2.9
1946 Cin-N	10	7	.588	22	22	10	2	0	151¹	146	9	64	60	12.6	2.56	131	.258	.336	7	.127	-1	14	13	2	1.6
1947 Cin-N	8	8	.500	20	20	5	2	0	122	137	15	49	43	13.9	5.75	71	.278	.347	12	.267	3	-23	-22	-1	-2.3
1948 Cin-N	0	3	.000	7	5	1	0	0	35	42	6	18	19	15.4	4.63	84	.316	.397	4	.267	-0	-3	-3	1	-0.1
1950 Bos-N	0	0	—	1	0	0	0	0	4	5	0	2	0	15.8	4.50	86	.313	.389	0	.000	-0	-0	-0	-0	0.0
Total 16	198	160	.553	428	398	242	42	4	3104²	2990	154	1121	1107	12.1	3.30	115	.253	.321	477	.243	57	152	168	27	28.6

● **BRUCE WALTON**   Walton, Bruce Kenneth b: 12/25/62, Bakersfield, Cal. BR/TR, 6'2", 195 lbs. Deb: 5/11/91

YEAR TM/L	W	L	PCT	G	GS	CG	SH	SV	IP	H	HR	BB	SO	RAT	ERA	ERA+	OAV	OOB	BH	AVG	PB	PR	/A	PD	TPI
1991 Oak-A	1	0	1.000	12	0	0	0	0	13	11	3	6	10	12.5	6.23	62	.229	.327	0	—	0	-3	-3	-0	-0.2
1992 Oak-A	0	0	—	7	0	0	0	0	10	17	1	3	7	18.0	9.90	38	.378	.417	0	—	0	-7	-7	-0	0.0
1993 Mon-N	0	0	—	4	0	0	0	0	5²	11	1	3	0	22.2	9.53	44	.407	.467	0	.000	-0	-3	-3	0	0.0
1994 Col-N	1	0	1.000	4	0	0	0	0	5¹	6	1	3	1	15.2	8.44	59	.273	.360	0	—	0	-3	-2	0	-0.3
Total 4	2	0	1.000	27	0	0	0	0	34	45	6	15	18	16.1	8.21	49	.317	.386	0	.000	-0	-16	-16	-1	-0.5

● **DICK WANTZ**   Wantz, Richard Carter b: 4/11/40, South Gate, Cal. d: 5/13/65, Inglewood, Cal. BR/TR, 6'5", 175 lbs. Deb: 4/13/65

YEAR TM/L	W	L	PCT	G	GS	CG	SH	SV	IP	H	HR	BB	SO	RAT	ERA	ERA+	OAV	OOB	BH	AVG	PB	PR	/A	PD	TPI
1965 Cal-A	0	0	—	1	0	0	0	0	1	3	0	0	2	27.0	18.00	19	.500	.500	0	—	0	-2	-2	0	0.0

● **STEVE WAPNICK**   Wapnick, Steven Lee b: 9/25/65, Panorama City, Cal. BR/TR, 6'2", 200 lbs. Deb: 4/14/90

YEAR TM/L	W	L	PCT	G	GS	CG	SH	SV	IP	H	HR	BB	SO	RAT	ERA	ERA+	OAV	OOB	BH	AVG	PB	PR	/A	PD	TPI
1990 Det-A	0	0	—	4	0	0	0	0	7	6	0	10	6	23.1	6.43	62	.296	.486	0	—	0	-2	-2	-0	0.0
1991 Chi-A	0	1	.000	6	0	0	0	0	5	2	0	4	1	10.8	1.80	221	.111	.273	0	—	0	1	1	-0	0.2
Total 2	0	1	.000	10	0	0	0	0	12	10	0	14	7	18.0	4.50	88	.222	.407	0	—	0	-1	-1	-0	0.2

● **COLIN WARD**   Ward, Colin Norval b: 11/22/60, Los Angeles, Cal. BL/TL, 6'3", 190 lbs. Deb: 9/21/85

YEAR TM/L	W	L	PCT	G	GS	CG	SH	SV	IP	H	HR	BB	SO	RAT	ERA	ERA+	OAV	OOB	BH	AVG	PB	PR	/A	PD	TPI
1985 SF-N	0	0	—	6	2	0	0	0	12¹	10	0	7	8	12.4	4.38	78	.233	.340	0	.000	-0	-1	-1	0	0.0

● **JOHNNY WARD**   Ward, John b: East St.Louis, Ill. Deb: 9/19/1885

YEAR TM/L	W	L	PCT	G	GS	CG	SH	SV	IP	H	HR	BB	SO	RAT	ERA	ERA+	OAV	OOB	BH	AVG	PB	PR	/A	PD	TPI
1885 Pro-N	0	1	.000	1	1	1	0	0	8	10	0	1	3	12.4	4.50	59	.286	.306	0	.000	-0	-1	-1	-0	-0.2

● **JOHN WARD**   Ward, John Montgomery b: 3/3/1860, Bellefonte, Pa. d: 3/4/25, Augusta, Ga. BL/TR, 5'9", 165 lbs. Deb: 7/15/1878 MH♦

YEAR TM/L	W	L	PCT	G	GS	CG	SH	SV	IP	H	HR	BB	SO	RAT	ERA	ERA+	OAV	OOB	BH	AVG	PB	PR	/A	PD	TPI
1878 Pro-N	22	13	.629	37	37	37	6	0	334	308	3	34	116	9.2	1.51	146	.231	.251	27	.196	8	30	26	2	2.6
1879 Pro-N	47	19	.712	70	60	58	2	1	587	571	5	36	239	9.3	2.15	110	.239	.250	104	.286	17	23	13	4	2.9
1880 Pro-N	39	24	.619	70	67	59	8	1	595	501	5	45	230	8.3	1.74	127	.217	.232	81	.228	1	42	31	5	3.4
1881 Pro-N	18	18	.500	39	35	32	3	0	330	326	2	53	119	10.3	2.13	125	.242	.271	87	.244	3	24	19	5	2.5
1882 Pro-N	19	12	.613	33	32	29	4	1	278	261	6	36	72	9.6	2.59	109	.232	.256	87	.245	4	10	7	4	1.0
1883 NY-N	16	13	.552	34	25	24	1	0	277	278	4	31	121	10.0	2.70	115	.246	.267	97	.255	6	14	12	4	1.8
1884 NY-N	3	3	.500	9	5	5	0	0	60²	72	2	18	23	13.4	3.41	87	.280	.327	12	.253	-1	-3	-3	1	-0.1
Total 7	164	102	.617	292	261	244	24	3	2461²	2317	26	253	920	9.4	2.10	118	.235	.254	495	.275	31	138	105	24	14.1

● **DICK WARD**   Ward, Richard Ole b: 5/21/09, Herrick, S.Dak. d: 5/30/66, Freeland, Wash. BR/TR, 6'1", 198 lbs. Deb: 5/3/34

YEAR TM/L	W	L	PCT	G	GS	CG	SH	SV	IP	H	HR	BB	SO	RAT	ERA	ERA+	OAV	OOB	BH	AVG	PB	PR	/A	PD	TPI
1934 Chi-N	0	0	—	3	0	0	0	0	6	9	0	2	1	16.5	3.00	129	.375	.423	0	.000	-0	1	1	-0	0.0
1935 StL-N	0	0	—	1	0	0	0	0	0	0	0	1	0	—	—	—	—	1.000	0	—	0	0	0	0	0.0
Total 2	0	0	—	4	0	0	0	0	6	9	0	3	1	18.0	3.00	129	.375	.444	0	.000	-0	1	1	-0	0.0

● **COLBY WARD**   Ward, Robert Colby b: 1/2/64, Lansing, Mich. BR/TR, 6'2", 185 lbs. Deb: 7/27/90

YEAR TM/L	W	L	PCT	G	GS	CG	SH	SV	IP	H	HR	BB	SO	RAT	ERA	ERA+	OAV	OOB	BH	AVG	PB	PR	/A	PD	TPI
1990 Cle-A	1	3	.250	22	0	0	0	1	36	31	3	21	23	13.3	4.25	92	.238	.349	0	—	0	-1	-1	-0	-0.1

● **DUANE WARD**   Ward, Roy Duane b: 5/28/64, Park View, N.Mex. BR/TR, 6'4", 215 lbs. Deb: 4/12/86

YEAR TM/L	W	L	PCT	G	GS	CG	SH	SV	IP	H	HR	BB	SO	RAT	ERA	ERA+	OAV	OOB	BH	AVG	PB	PR	/A	PD	TPI
1986 Atl-N	0	1	.000	10	0	0	0	0	16	22	2	8	16	16.9	7.31	54	.349	.423	0	—	-0	-6	-6	1	-0.3
Tor-A	0	1	.000	2	1	0	0	0	2	3	0	4	1	36.0	13.50	31	.300	.533	0	—	0	-2	-2	0	-0.3
1987 Tor-A	1	0	1.000	12	1	0	0	0	11²	14	0	12	10	20.1	6.94	65	.326	.473	0	—	0	-3	-3	0	-0.3
1988 Tor-A	9	3	.750	64	0	0	0	15	111²	101	5	60	91	13.4	3.30	119	.245	.347	0	—	0	8	8	-0	0.9
1989 *Tor-A	4	10	.286	66	0	0	0	15	114²	94	4	58	122	12.3	3.77	100	.230	.333	0	—	0	1	2	1	0.6
1990 Tor-A	2	8	.200	73	0	0	0	11	127²	101	9	42	112	10.2	3.45	114	.221	.288	0	—	0	6	7	1	0.6
1991 *Tor-A	7	6	.538	81	0	0	0	23	107¹	80	5	33	132	9.6	2.77	152	.207	.273	0	—	0	16	17	0	2.8
1992 *Tor-A	7	4	.636	79	0	0	0	12	101¹	76	5	39	103	10.3	1.95	209	.207	.285	0	—	0	22	24	-0	3.1
1993 *Tor-A★	2	3	.400	71	0	0	0	45	71²	49	4	25	97	9.4	2.13	202	.193	.268	0	—	0	17	17	-1	3.5
Total 8	32	36	.471	458	2	0	0	121	664	540	32	281	676	11.3	3.19	126	.225	.310	0	.000	-0	60	62	1	9.7

● **JON WARDEN**   Warden, Jonathan Edgar "Warbler" b: 10/1/46, Columbus, Ohio BB/TL, 6', 205 lbs. Deb: 4/11/68

YEAR TM/L	W	L	PCT	G	GS	CG	SH	SV	IP	H	HR	BB	SO	RAT	ERA	ERA+	OAV	OOB	BH	AVG	PB	PR	/A	PD	TPI
1968 Det-A	4	1	.800	28	0	0	0	3	37¹	30	5	15	25	10.8	3.62	83	.217	.294	0	.000	-0	-3	-3	-1	-0.5

● **CURT WARDLE**   Wardle, Curtis Ray b: 11/16/60, Downey, Cal. BL/TL, 6'5", 220 lbs. Deb: 8/30/84

YEAR TM/L	W	L	PCT	G	GS	CG	SH	SV	IP	H	HR	BB	SO	RAT	ERA	ERA+	OAV	OOB	BH	AVG	PB	PR	/A	PD	TPI
1984 Min-A	0	0	—	2	0	0	0	0	4	3	2	0	5	6.8	4.50	93	.200	.200	0	—	0	-0	-0	0	-0.3
1985 Min-A	1	3	.250	35	0	0	0	1	49	49	9	28	47	14.3	5.51	80	.266	.366	0	—	0	-7	-6	1	-0.8
Cle-A	7	6	.538	15	12	0	0	0	66	78	11	34	37	15.4	6.68	62	.297	.379	0	—	0	-19	-19	-1	-3.0
Yr	8	9	.471	50	12	0	0	1	115	127	20	62	84	14.9	6.18	69	.283	.371	0	—	0	-26	-25	0	-3.8
Total 2	8	9	.471	52	12	0	0	1	119	130	22	62	89	14.7	6.13	69	.281	.369	0	—	0	-26	-25	0	-4.1

● **JACK WARHOP**   Warhop, John Milton "Chief" or "Crab" (b: John Milton Wauhop) b: 7/4/1884, Hinton, W.Va. d: 10/4/60, Freeport, Ill. BR/TR, 5'9.5", 168 lbs. Deb: 9/19/08

YEAR TM/L	W	L	PCT	G	GS	CG	SH	SV	IP	H	HR	BB	SO	RAT	ERA	ERA+	OAV	OOB	BH	AVG	PB	PR	/A	PD	TPI
1908 NY-A	1	2	.333	5	4	3	0	0	36¹	40	0	8	11	12.9	4.46	56	.292	.349	1	.063	-1	-8	-8	0	-0.7
1909 NY-A	13	15	.464	36	23	21	3	2	243¹	197	2	81	95	11.2	2.40	105	.233	.319	11	.128	-2	2	3	1	0.3
1910 NY-A	14	14	.500	37	27	20	0	2	243	219	1	79	75	11.7	3.00	89	.246	.320	14	.177	-1	-13	-9	-4	-1.6
1911 NY-A	12	13	.480	31	25	17	1	0	209²	239	6	44	71	12.8	4.16	86	.286	.333	12	.153	-4	-19	-13	-2	-1.9
1912 NY-A	10	19	.345	39	22	16	0	3	258	256	7	59	110	11.5	2.86	126	.266	.319	19	.207	-1	13	21	-3	1.9
1913 NY-A	4	6	.400	15	7	1	0	0	62¹	69	1	33	11	16.5	3.75	80	.292	.406	3	.130	-0	-6	-5	-2	-1.0
1914 NY-A	8	15	.348	37	23	15	0	0	216²	182	8	44	56	9.8	2.37	117	.235	.286	10	.141	-1	9	9	-2	0.9
1915 NY-A	7	9	.438	21	19	12	0	0	143¹	164	3	52	34	14.3	3.96	74	.309	.384	7	.137	-2	-16	-16	-3	-2.0
Total 8	69	93	.426	221	150	105	4	7	1412²	1366	28	400	463	12.0	3.12	96	.262	.328	77	.156	-12	-38	-19	-13	-4.3

● **CY WARMOTH**   Warmoth, Wallace Walter b: 2/2/1893, Bone Gap, Ill. d: 6/20/57, Mt.Carmel, Ill. BL/TL, 5'11", 158 lbs. Deb: 8/31/16

YEAR TM/L	W	L	PCT	G	GS	CG	SH	SV	IP	H	HR	BB	SO	RAT	ERA	ERA+	OAV	OOB	BH	AVG	PB	PR	/A	PD	TPI
1916 StL-N	0	0	—	3	0	0	0	0	5	12	0	4	1	30.6	14.40	19	.500	.586	0	.000	-0	-7	-7	-0	0.0
1922 Was-A	1	0	1.000	7	1	0	0	0	19	15	0	9	8	11.4	1.42	272	.205	.293	1	.143	-0	6	5	-0	0.2
1923 Was-A	7	5	.583	21	13	4	0	0	105	103	4	76	45	15.4	4.29	88	.261	.381	8	.222	2	-4	-6	0	-0.4
Total 3	8	5	.615	29	14	5	0	0	129	130	4	89	54	15.4	4.26	88	.264	.379	9	.200	2	-5	-7	-0	-0.2

● **LON WARNEKE**   Warneke, Lonnie "The Arkansas Hummingbird" b: 3/28/09, Mt.Ida, Ark. d: 6/23/76, Hot Springs, Ark. BR/TR, 6'2", 185 lbs. Deb: 4/18/30 U

YEAR TM/L	W	L	PCT	G	GS	CG	SH	SV	IP	H	HR	BB	SO	RAT	ERA	ERA+	OAV	OOB	BH	AVG	PB	PR	/A	PD	TPI
1930 Chi-N	0	0	—	1	0	0	0	0	1¹	2	0	5	0	47.3	33.75	14	.400	.700	0	—	0	-4	-4	0	0.0
1931 Chi-N	2	4	.333	20	7	3	0	0	64¹	67	1	37	27	15.0	3.22	120	.269	.370	5	.263	1	5	5	-1	0.4
1932 *Chi-N	22	6	.786	35	32	25	4	0	277	247	12	64	106	10.2	2.37	159	.243	.283	19	.192	-0	46	43	-0	4.1
1933 Chi-N★	18	13	.581	36	34	26	4	1	287¹	262	8	75	133	10.6	2.00	163	.244	.295	30	.300	10	43	40	3	6.2
1934 Chi-N★	22	10	.688	43	35	23	3	3	291¹	273	16	66	143	10.5	3.21	121	.244	.287	22	.195	-1	27	21	0	2.1

YEAR TM/L	W	L	PCT	G	GS	CG	SH	SV	IP	H	HR	BB	SO	RAT	ERA	ERA+	OAV	OOB	BH	AVG	PB	PR	/A	PD	TPI
1935 *Chi-N	20	13	.606	42	30	20	1	4	261²	257	19	50	120	10.7	3.06	128	.257	.294	20	.220	1	28	25	-1	3.0
1936 Chi-N★	16	13	.552	40	29	13	4	1	240¹	246	10	76	113	12.2	3.45	116	.264	.322	17	.202	0	15	14	-1	1.5
1937 StL-N	18	11	.621	36	33	18	2	0	238²	280	32	69	87	13.2	4.53	88	.287	.335	21	.262	4	-16	-14	-3	-1.4
1938 StL-N	13	8	.619	31	26	12	4	0	197	199	14	64	89	12.1	3.97	100	.256	.314	23	.324	5	-4	-0	-2	0.3
1939 StL-N☆	13	7	.650	34	21	6	2	2	162	160	14	49	59	11.7	3.78	109	.259	.316	10	.192	1	3	6	-0	0.7
1940 StL-N	16	10	.615	33	31	17	1	0	232	235	17	47	85	11.1	3.14	127	.257	.296	18	.209	2	18	22	1	2.6
1941 StL-N☆	17	9	.654	37	30	12	4	0	246	227	19	82	83	11.4	3.15	120	.249	.313	9	.117	-2	13	17	-2	1.3
1942 StL-N	6	4	.600	12	12	5	0	0	82	76	8	15	31	10.0	3.29	104	.238	.272	10	.333	3	0	1	-1	0.3
Chi-N	5	7	.417	15	12	8	1	2	99	97	2	21	28	10.7	2.27	141	.259	.298	6	.188	-0	11	10	-0	1.2
Yr	11	11	.500	27	24	13	1	2	181	173	10	36	59	10.4	2.73	121	.249	.286	16	.258	2	12	11	-1	1.5
1943 Chi-N	4	5	.444	21	10	4	0	0	88¹	82	3	18	30	10.2	3.16	106	.246	.285	5	.192	1	2	2	1	0.4
1945 Chi-N	0	1	.000	9	1	0	0	0	14	16	0	1	6	10.9	3.86	95	.267	.279	0	.000	0	-0	-0	0	0.0
Total 15	192	121	.613	445	343	192	30	13	2782¹	2726	175	739	1140	11.3	3.18	119	.255	.304	215	.223	27	188	188	-5	22.7

● **ED WARNER**   Warner, Edward Emory b: 6/20/1889, Fitchburg, Mass. d: 2/5/54, New York, N.Y. BR/TL, 5'10.5", 165 lbs. Deb: 7/2/12

YEAR TM/L	W	L	PCT	G	GS	CG	SH	SV	IP	H	HR	BB	SO	RAT	ERA	ERA+	OAV	OOB	BH	AVG	PB	PR	/A	PD	TPI
1912 Pit-N	1	1	.500	11	3	1	1	0	45	40	0	18	13	12.2	3.60	91	.242	.328	2	.133	-1	-1	-2	1	-0.1

● **JACK WARNER**   Warner, Jack Dyer b: 7/12/40, Brandywine, W.Va. BR/TR, 5'11", 190 lbs. Deb: 4/10/62

YEAR TM/L	W	L	PCT	G	GS	CG	SH	SV	IP	H	HR	BB	SO	RAT	ERA	ERA+	OAV	OOB	BH	AVG	PB	PR	/A	PD	TPI
1962 Chi-N	0	0	—	7	0	0	0	0	7	9	3	0	3	11.6	7.71	54	.321	.321	0	—	0	-3	-3	0	0.0
1963 Chi-N	0	0	.000	8	0	0	0	0	22²	21	1	8	7	11.5	2.78	126	.256	.322	1	.250	0	1	2	-0	0.1
1964 Chi-N	0	0	—	7	0	0	0	0	9¹	12	0	4	6	15.4	2.89	128	.333	.400	0	—	0	1	1	0	0.0
1965 Chi-N	0	1	.000	11	0	0	0	0	15²	22	1	9	7	17.8	8.62	43	.355	.437	0	.000	-0	-9	-9	0	-0.5
Total 4	0	2	.000	33	0	0	0	0	54²	64	5	21	23	14.0	5.10	72	.308	.371	1	.200	0	-10	-9	0	-0.4

● **MIKE WARREN**   Warren, Michael Bruce b: 3/26/61, Inglewood, Cal. BR/TR, 6'1", 175 lbs. Deb: 6/12/83

YEAR TM/L	W	L	PCT	G	GS	CG	SH	SV	IP	H	HR	BB	SO	RAT	ERA	ERA+	OAV	OOB	BH	AVG	PB	PR	/A	PD	TPI
1983 Oak-A	5	3	.625	12	9	3	1	0	65²	54	18	30	9.6	—	4.11	94	.215	.273	0	—	0	-0	-2	-1	0.2
1984 Oak-A	3	6	.333	24	12	0	0	0	90	104	11	44	61	15.1	4.90	76	.291	.373	0	—	0	-9	-12	-2	-0.7
1985 Oak-A	1	4	.200	16	6	0	0	0	49	52	13	38	48	17.3	6.61	58	.261	.390	0	—	0	-13	-15	-1	-0.9
Total 3	9	13	.409	52	27	3	1	0	204²	207	28	100	139	13.9	5.06	75	.261	.349	0	—	0	-23	-28	-4	-1.4

● **TOMMY WARREN**   Warren, Thomas Gentry b: 7/5/17, Tulsa, Okla. d: 1/2/68, Tulsa, Okla. BB/TL, 6'1", 190 lbs. Deb: 4/18/44

YEAR TM/L	W	L	PCT	G	GS	CG	SH	SV	IP	H	HR	BB	SO	RAT	ERA	ERA+	OAV	OOB	BH	AVG	PB	PR	/A	PD	TPI
1944 Bro-N	1	4	.200	22	4	2	0	0	68²	74	4	40	18	14.9	4.98	71	.270	.363	11	.256	2	-10	-11	0	-0.6

● **DAN WARTHEN**   Warthen, Daniel Dean b: 12/1/52, Omaha, Neb. BB/TL, 6', 200 lbs. Deb: 5/18/75 C

YEAR TM/L	W	L	PCT	G	GS	CG	SH	SV	IP	H	HR	BB	SO	RAT	ERA	ERA+	OAV	OOB	BH	AVG	PB	PR	/A	PD	TPI
1975 Mon-N	8	6	.571	40	18	2	0	3	167²	130	8	87	128	11.7	3.11	123	.217	.317	6	.118	-2	9	13	1	0.9
1976 Mon-N	2	10	.167	23	16	2	1	0	90	76	8	66	67	14.4	5.30	70	.232	.364	0	.000	-3	-18	-16	0	-2.2
1977 Mon-N	2	3	.400	12	6	1	0	0	35	33	7	38	26	18.3	7.97	48	.262	.433	1	.111	-0	-16	-16	1	-1.9
Phi-N	0	1	.000	3	0	0	0	0	3²	4	0	5	1	22.1	0.00	—	.267	.450	0	—	0	2	2	-0	0.4
Yr	2	4	.333	15	6	1	0	0	38²	37	7	43	27	18.6	7.22	53	.261	.432	1	.111	-0	-14	-15	0	-1.5
1978 Hou-N	0	1	.000	5	1	0	0	0	10²	10	3	2	2	10.1	4.22	78	.250	.286	0	.000	-0	-1	-1	-0	-0.1
Total 4	12	21	.364	83	41	5	1	3	307	253	26	198	224	13.3	4.31	88	.228	.347	7	.079	-6	-23	-18	1	-2.9

◉ **GEORGE WASHBURN**   Washburn, George Edward b: 10/6/14, Solon, Me. d: 1/5/79, Baton Rouge, La. BL/TR, 6'1", 175 lbs. Deb: 5/4/41

YEAR TM/L	W	L	PCT	G	GS	CG	SH	SV	IP	H	HR	BB	SO	RAT	ERA	ERA+	OAV	OOB	BH	AVG	PB	PR	/A	PD	TPI
1941 NY-A	0	1	.000	1	1	0	0	0	2	2	0	5	1	31.5	13.50	29	.286	.583	0	.000	-0	-2	-2	0	-0.7

● **GREG WASHBURN**   Washburn, Gregory James b: 12/3/46, Coal City, Ill. BR/TR, 6', 190 lbs. Deb: 6/7/69

YEAR TM/L	W	L	PCT	G	GS	CG	SH	SV	IP	H	HR	BB	SO	RAT	ERA	ERA+	OAV	OOB	BH	AVG	PB	PR	/A	PD	TPI
1969 Cal-A	0	2	.000	8	2	0	0	0	11¹	21	0	5	4	21.4	7.94	44	.404	.466	0	—	0	-5	-6	0	-0.9

● **LIBE WASHBURN**   Washburn, Libeus b: 6/16/1874, Lyme, N.H. d: 3/22/40, Malone, N.Y. BB/TL, 5'10", 180 lbs. Deb: 5/30/02 ♦

YEAR TM/L	W	L	PCT	G	GS	CG	SH	SV	IP	H	HR	BB	SO	RAT	ERA	ERA+	OAV	OOB	BH	AVG	PB	PR	/A	PD	TPI
1903 Phi-N	0	4	.000	4	4	4	0	0	35	44	0	11	9	14.1	4.37	75	.326	.377	3	.167	-0	-4	-4	-1	-0.5

● **RAY WASHBURN**   Washburn, Ray Clark b: 5/31/38, Pasco, Wash. BR/TR, 6'1", 205 lbs. Deb: 9/20/61

YEAR TM/L	W	L	PCT	G	GS	CG	SH	SV	IP	H	HR	BB	SO	RAT	ERA	ERA+	OAV	OOB	BH	AVG	PB	PR	/A	PD	TPI
1961 StL-N	1	1	.500	3	2	1	0	0	20¹	10	1	7	12	8.0	1.77	248	.152	.243	1	.125	-1	5	6	0	0.5
1962 StL-N	12	9	.571	34	25	2	1	0	175²	187	25	58	109	12.7	4.10	104	.273	.332	10	.179	-1	-3	-3	1	0.5
1963 StL-N	5	3	.625	11	11	4	2	0	64¹	50	5	14	47	9.1	3.08	115	.212	.259	1	.053	-1	2	3	1	0.4
1964 StL-N	3	4	.429	15	10	0	0	2	60	60	4	17	28	12.3	4.05	94	.264	.329	2	.133	-0	-3	-2	1	-0.1
1965 StL-N	9	11	.450	28	16	1	1	0	119¹	114	15	44	69	10.8	3.62	106	.254	.300	5	.152	0	-1	-3	-1	0.4
1966 StL-N	11	9	.550	27	26	4	1	0	170	183	15	44	90	12.1	3.76	95	.280	.326	5	.093	-1	-3	-3	-1	0.4
1967 *StL-N	10	7	.588	27	27	3	1	0	186¹	190	14	42	98	11.4	3.53	93	.265	.309	6	.091	-2	-3	-5	-2	-0.1
1968 *StL-N	14	8	.636	31	30	8	4	0	215	191	9	47	124	10.0	2.26	128	.239	.283	5	.083	-0	17	15	-2	1.4
1969 StL-N	3	8	.273	28	16	2	0	1	132¹	133	9	49	80	12.4	3.06	117	.261	.327	3	.081	-2	8	8	1	0.5
1970 *Cin-N	4	4	.500	35	3	0	0	0	66¹	90	7	48	37	18.7	6.92	58	.324	.423	0	.000	-1	-21	-21	1	-2.2
Total 10	72	64	.529	239	166	25	10	5	1209²	1208	107	354	700	11.8	3.53	101	.261	.316	38	.105	-7	-3	6	4	0.6

● **BUCK WASHER**   Washer, William b: 10/11/1882, Akron, Ohio d: 12/8/55, Akron, Ohio BR/TR, 5'10", 175 lbs. Deb: 4/25/05

YEAR TM/L	W	L	PCT	G	GS	CG	SH	SV	IP	H	HR	BB	SO	RAT	ERA	ERA+	OAV	OOB	BH	AVG	PB	PR	/A	PD	TPI
1905 Phi-N	0	0	—	1	0	0	0	0	3	4	0	5	0	27.0	6.00	49	—	1.800	0	.000	-0	-1	-1	0	0.0

● **GARY WASLEWSKI**   Waslewski, Gary Lee b: 7/21/41, Meriden, Conn. BR/TR, 6'4", 195 lbs. Deb: 6/11/67

YEAR TM/L	W	L	PCT	G	GS	CG	SH	SV	IP	H	HR	BB	SO	RAT	ERA	ERA+	OAV	OOB	BH	AVG	PB	PR	/A	PD	TPI
1967 *Bos-A	2	2	.500	12	8	0	0	0	42	34	3	20	20	11.8	3.21	108	.225	.320	1	.091	-1	0	1	0	0.1
1968 Bos-A	4	7	.364	34	11	2	0	2	105¹	108	9	40	59	13.2	3.67	86	.269	.344	1	.038	-2	-8	-6	2	-0.7
1969 StL-N	0	2	.000	12	0	0	0	0	20²	19	3	8	16	12.2	3.92	91	.244	.322	0	.000	-0	-1	-1	0	0.0
Mon-N	3	7	.300	30	14	3	1	1	109¹	102	5	63	63	14.2	3.29	112	.252	.364	1	.033	-2	4	5	1	0.2
Yr	3	9	.250	42	14	3	1	1	130	121	8	71	79	13.8	3.39	108	.250	.355	1	.032	-2	3	4	1	0.2
1970 Mon-N	0	2	.000	6	4	0	0	0	24²	24	3	15	19	13.9	5.11	80	.247	.352	0	.000	-0	-3	-3	1	-0.2
NY-A	2	2	.500	26	5	0	0	4	55	42	4	27	27	11.9	3.11	113	.219	.327	1	.100	-1	4	2	1	0.0
1971 NY-A	0	1	.000	24	0	0	0	0	35²	28	2	16	17	11.4	3.28	98	.214	.304	0	.000	-0	1	-0	0	0.0
1972 Oak-A	0	3	.000	8	0	0	0	0	17²	12	3	8	8	10.2	2.04	140	.190	.282	0	.000	-0	2	1	0	0.3
Total 6	11	26	.297	152	42	5	1	5	410¹	368	32	197	229	12.9	3.44	100	.243	.338	4	.045	-6	-2	1	4	-0.1

● **STEVE WATERBURY**   Waterbury, Steven Craig b: 4/6/52, Carbondale, Ill. BR/TR, 6'5", 190 lbs. Deb: 9/14/76

YEAR TM/L	W	L	PCT	G	GS	CG	SH	SV	IP	H	HR	BB	SO	RAT	ERA	ERA+	OAV	OOB	BH	AVG	PB	PR	/A	PD	TPI
1976 StL-N	0	0	—	6	0	0	0	0	7	10	3	4	4	15.0	6.00	59	.304	.385	0	—	0	-2	-2	-0	-0.1

● **FRED WATERS**   Waters, Fred Warren b: 2/2/27, Benton, Miss. d: 8/28/89, Pensacola, Fla. BL/TL, 5'11", 185 lbs. Deb: 9/20/55

YEAR TM/L	W	L	PCT	G	GS	CG	SH	SV	IP	H	HR	BB	SO	RAT	ERA	ERA+	OAV	OOB	BH	AVG	PB	PR	/A	PD	TPI
1955 Pit-N	0	0	—	2	0	0	0	0	5	7	1	2	0	16.2	3.60	114	.318	.375	0	.000	-0	0	0	0	0.0
1956 Pit-N	2	2	.500	23	5	1	0	0	51	48	3	30	14	13.9	2.82	134	.258	.364	1	.050	-1	5	5	-1	0.1
Total 2	2	2	.500	25	5	1	0	0	56	55	4	32	14	14.1	2.89	131	.264	.365	1	.048	-1	6	6	-1	0.1

● **BOB WATKINS**   Watkins, Robert Cecil b: 3/12/48, San Francisco, Cal. BR/TR, 6'1", 170 lbs. Deb: 9/6/69

YEAR TM/L	W	L	PCT	G	GS	CG	SH	SV	IP	H	HR	BB	SO	RAT	ERA	ERA+	OAV	OOB	BH	AVG	PB	PR	/A	PD	TPI
1969 Hou-N	0	0	—	5	0	0	0	0	15²	13	1	13	11	14.9	5.17	68	.241	.388	0	.000	-0	-3	-3	-0	-0.1

● **ALLEN WATSON**   Watson, Allen Kenneth b: 11/18/70, Jamaica, N.Y. BL/TL, 6'3", 195 lbs. Deb: 7/8/93

YEAR TM/L	W	L	PCT	G	GS	CG	SH	SV	IP	H	HR	BB	SO	RAT	ERA	ERA+	OAV	OOB	BH	AVG	PB	PR	/A	PD	TPI
1993 StL-N	6	7	.462	16	15	0	0	0	86	90	11	28	49	12.7	4.60	86	.271	.333	6	.231	2	-5	-6	-1	-0.7
1994 StL-N	6	5	.545	22	22	0	0	0	115²	130	15	53	74	13.9	5.52	74	.286	.370	6	.158	1	-17	-19	-1	-1.5
Total 2	12	12	.500	38	37	0	0	0	201²	220	26	81	123	13.9	5.13	78	.280	.355	12	.188	3	-22	-25	-2	-2.2

DOC WATSON
Watson, Charles John b: 1/30/1886, Kensington, Ohio d: 12/30/49, San Diego, Cal. BR/TL, 6', 170 lbs. Deb: 9/3/13

YEAR	TM/L	W	L	PCT	G	GS	CG	SH	SV	IP	H	HR	BB	SO	RAT	ERA	ERA+	OAV	OOB	BH	AVG	PB	PR	/A	PD	TPI
1913	Chi-N	1	0	1.000	1	1	1	0	0	9	8	0	6	1	15.0	1.00	318	.242	.375	0	.000	0	2	2	-1	0.2
1914	Chi-F	9	8	.529	26	18	10	3	1	172	145	4	49	69	10.3	2.04	130	.236	.295	5	.093	-5	16	12	-1	0.5
	StL-F	3	4	.429	9	7	4	2	0	56	41	1	24	18	11.1	1.93	158	.211	.311	2	.125	-1	6	7	-1	0.6
	Yr	12	12	.500	35	25	14	5	1	228	186	3	73	87	10.4	2.01	137	.229	.296	7	.100	-6	22	19	-2	1.1
1915	StL-F	9	9	.500	33	20	6	0	0	135²	132	1	58	45	12.9	3.98	72	.273	.355	5	.125	-3	-19	-17	-4	-2.8
Total 3		22	21	.512	69	46	21	5	1	372²	326	4	137	133	11.5	2.70	104	.246	.322	12	.107	-9	5	4	-7	-1.5

MULE WATSON
Watson, John Reeves b: 10/15/1896, Homer, La. d: 8/25/49, Shreveport, La. BR/TR, 6'1.5", 185 lbs. Deb: 7/4/18

YEAR	TM/L	W	L	PCT	G	GS	CG	SH	SV	IP	H	HR	BB	SO	RAT	ERA	ERA+	OAV	OOB	BH	AVG	PB	PR	/A	PD	TPI
1918	Phi-A	7	10	.412	21	19	11	3	0	141²	139	0	44	30	11.8	3.37	87	.288	.350	6	.128	-3	-9	-7	-2	-1.3
1919	Phi-A	0	1	.000	4	2	0	0	0	14¹	17	2	7	6	15.1	6.91	50	.309	.387	0	.000	-1	-6	-6	1	-0.3
1920	Bos-N	0	0	—	1	0	0	0	0	3	0	0	0	0	0.00	0.00	—	.000	.000	0	.000	-0	1	1	0	0.0
	Pit-N	0	0	—	5	0	0	0	0	11¹	15	2	7	1	17.5	8.74	37	.326	.415	0	.000	-0	-7	-7	0	-0.1
	Bos-N	5	4	.556	12	10	4	2	0	71²	79	0	17	16	12.2	3.77	81	.298	.343	3	.130	-1	-5	-6	-0	-0.8
	Yr	5	4	.556	18	10	4	2	0	86	94	2	24	17	12.5	4.29	72	.294	.345	3	.111	-2	-11	-12	-0	-0.9
1921	Bos-N	14	13	.519	44	31	15	1	2	259¹	269	11	57	48	11.6	3.85	95	.270	.314	12	.138	-4	-2	-6	-1	-1.0
1922	Bos-N	8	14	.364	41	29	8	1	1	201	262	9	59	53	14.6	4.70	85	.317	.366	13	.197	-0	-13	-16	-0	-1.5
1923	Bos-N	1	2	.333	11	4	1	0	1	31¹	42	2	20	10	17.8	5.17	77	.339	.431	2	.250	-0	-4	-4	0	-0.4
	*NY-N	8	5	.615	17	15	8	0	0	108¹	117	11	21	26	11.5	3.41	112	.280	.316	8	.174	-1	7	5	-1	0.3
	Yr	9	7	.563	28	19	9	0	1	139²	159	13	41	36	13.0	3.80	101	.293	.344	10	.185	-1	3	1	-1	-0.1
1924	*NY-N	7	4	.636	22	16	6	1	0	99²	122	7	24	18	13.3	3.79	97	.303	.343	9	.257	4	1	-1	-1	0.2
Total 7		50	53	.485	178	126	53	8	4	941²	1062	44	256	208	12.8	4.03	89	.293	.342	53	.165	-8	-38	-45	-3	-4.9

MILT WATSON
Watson, Milton Wilson "Mule" b: 1/10/1890, Flovilla, Ga. d: 4/10/62, Pine Bluff, Ark. BR/TR, 6'1", 180 lbs. Deb: 7/26/16

YEAR	TM/L	W	L	PCT	G	GS	CG	SH	SV	IP	H	HR	BB	SO	RAT	ERA	ERA+	OAV	OOB	BH	AVG	PB	PR	/A	PD	TPI
1916	StL-N	4	6	.400	18	13	5	2	0	103	109	3	33	27	12.8	3.06	86	.283	.346	7	.219	-0	-5	-5	-1	-0.5
1917	StL-N	10	13	.435	41	20	5	3	0	161¹	149	5	51	45	11.7	3.51	77	.252	.321	5	.098	-4	-14	-15	1	-2.3
1918	Phi-N	5	7	.417	23	11	6	0	0	112²	126	1	36	29	13.1	3.43	87	.293	.350	3	.075	-4	-8	-5	-1	-1.1
1919	Phi-N	2	4	.333	8	4	3	0	0	47	51	3	19	12	13.8	5.17	62	.282	.356	1	.063	-0	-12	-10	0	-1.3
Total 4		21	30	.412	90	48	19	5	0	424	435	10	139	113	12.5	3.57	79	.274	.339	16	.115	-9	-40	-35	-0	-5.2

MOTHER WATSON
Watson, Walter L. b: 1/27/1865, Middleport, Ohio d: 11/23/1898, Middleport, Ohio 5'9", 145 lbs. Deb: 5/19/1887

YEAR	TM/L	W	L	PCT	G	GS	CG	SH	SV	IP	H	HR	BB	SO	RAT	ERA	ERA+	OAV	OOB	BH	AVG	PB	PR	/A	PD	TPI
1887	Cin-a	0	1	.000	2	2	1	0	0	14	22	0	6	1	18.0	5.79	75	.328	.384	1	.125	-0	-2	-2	-1	-0.2

EDDIE WATT
Watt, Edward Dean b: 4/4/41, Lamoni, Iowa BR/TR, 5'10", 197 lbs. Deb: 4/12/66

YEAR	TM/L	W	L	PCT	G	GS	CG	SH	SV	IP	H	HR	BB	SO	RAT	ERA	ERA+	OAV	OOB	BH	AVG	PB	PR	/A	PD	TPI
1966	Bal-A	9	7	.563	43	13	1	0	4	145²	123	11	44	102	10.6	3.83	87	.230	.295	14	.304	6	-6	-8	-2	-0.5
1967	Bal-A	3	5	.375	49	0	0	0	8	103²	67	5	37	93	9.3	2.26	140	.183	.263	4	.182	2	11	10	0	1.2
1968	Bal-A	5	5	.500	59	0	0	0	11	83¹	63	1	35	72	10.8	2.27	129	.209	.295	0	.000	-0	7	6	0	0.9
1969	*Bal-A	5	2	.714	56	0	0	0	16	71	49	3	26	46	9.8	1.65	216	.194	.274	0	.000	-0	16	15	-0	2.2
1970	*Bal-A	7	7	.500	53	0	0	0	12	55¹	44	3	29	33	12.7	3.25	112	.239	.358	1	.125	-0	3	2	0	0.7
1971	*Bal-A	3	1	.750	35	0	0	0	11	39²	39	1	8	26	10.7	1.82	185	.260	.297	0	.000	-0	7	7	-1	1.1
1972	Bal-A	2	3	.400	45	0	0	0	7	45²	30	2	20	34	10.2	2.17	142	.191	.291	0	.000	-0	5	5	-0	0.7
1973	*Bal-A	3	4	.429	30	0	0	0	5	71	62	8	21	38	10.8	3.30	113	.235	.296	0	—	-1	4	3	-1	0.7
1974	Phi-N	1	1	.500	42	0	0	0	6	38¹	39	3	26	23	15.7	3.99	95	.275	.394	0	.000	-0	-2	-1	0	-0.1
1975	Chi-N	0	1	.000	6	0	0	0	0	6	14	0	6	4	34.5	13.50	28	.452	.575	0	—	-0	-7	-6	0	-0.9
Total 10		38	36	.514	411	13	1	0	80	659²	530	37	254	462	11.0	2.91	116	.222	.304	19	.190	6	38	33	-3	5.6

FRANK WATT
Watt, Frank Marion "Kilo" b: 12/15/02, Washington, D.C. d: 8/31/56, Washington, D.C. BR/TR, 6'1", 205 lbs. Deb: 4/14/31 F

YEAR	TM/L	W	L	PCT	G	GS	CG	SH	SV	IP	H	HR	BB	SO	RAT	ERA	ERA+	OAV	OOB	BH	AVG	PB	PR	/A	PD	TPI
1931	Phi-N	5	5	.500	38	12	5	0	2	122²	147	5	49	25	14.6	4.84	88	.296	.362	8	.205	0	-13	-8	-2	-0.8

JIM WAUGH
Waugh, James Elden b: 11/25/33, Lancaster, Ohio BR/TR, 6'3", 185 lbs. Deb: 4/19/52

YEAR	TM/L	W	L	PCT	G	GS	CG	SH	SV	IP	H	HR	BB	SO	RAT	ERA	ERA+	OAV	OOB	BH	AVG	PB	PR	/A	PD	TPI
1952	Pit-N	1	6	.143	17	7	1	0	0	52¹	61	4	32	18	16.3	6.36	63	.285	.383	1	.100	-0	-15	-14	-0	-1.6
1953	Pit-N	4	5	.444	29	11	1	0	0	90¹	108	21	56	23	16.3	6.48	69	.295	.389	5	.227	0	-22	-20	-1	-1.7
Total 2		5	11	.313	46	18	2	0	0	142²	169	25	88	41	16.3	6.43	67	.291	.387	6	.188	0	-37	-34	-1	-3.3

FRANK WAYENBERG
Wayenberg, Frank b: 8/27/1898, Franklin, Kan. d: 4/16/75, Zanesville, Ohio BR/TR, 6'0.5", 172 lbs. Deb: 8/25/24

YEAR	TM/L	W	L	PCT	G	GS	CG	SH	SV	IP	H	HR	BB	SO	RAT	ERA	ERA+	OAV	OOB	BH	AVG	PB	PR	/A	PD	TPI
1924	Cle-A	0	0	—	2	1	0	0	0	6²	7	0	5	3	17.6	5.40	79	.259	.394	1	.500	0	-1	-1	-0	0.0

GARY WAYNE
Wayne, Gary Anthony b: 11/30/62, Dearborn, Mich. BL/TL, 6'3", 185 lbs. Deb: 4/7/89

YEAR	TM/L	W	L	PCT	G	GS	CG	SH	SV	IP	H	HR	BB	SO	RAT	ERA	ERA+	OAV	OOB	BH	AVG	PB	PR	/A	PD	TPI
1989	Min-A	3	4	.429	60	0	0	0	1	71	55	4	36	41	11.7	3.30	126	.212	.311	0	—	0	5	7	-0	0.3
1990	Min-A	1	1	.500	38	0	0	0	1	38²	38	5	13	28	12.1	4.19	99	.255	.319	0	—	0	-1	-0	-0	-0.1
1991	Min-A	1	0	1.000	8	0	0	0	1	12¹	11	1	4	7	11.7	5.11	84	.244	.320	0	—	0	-1	-1	-0	-0.1
1992	Min-A	3	3	.500	41	0	0	0	1	48	46	2	19	29	12.8	2.63	154	.260	.342	0	—	0	7	8	1	1.0
1993	Col-N	5	3	.625	65	0	0	0	1	62¹	68	8	26	49	13.7	5.05	94	.276	.348	1	1.000	0	-7	-2	-0	-0.2
1994	LA-N	1	3	.250	19	0	0	0	0	17¹	19	2	6	10	14.5	4.67	85	.279	.364	0	.000	-0	-1	-1	0	-0.3
Total 6		14	14	.500	231	0	0	0	4	249²	237	22	104	164	12.7	3.93	109	.251	.332	1	.500	0	1	10	1	0.6

KEN WEAFER
Weafer, Kenneth Albert "Al" b: 2/6/14, Woburn, Mass. BR/TR, 6'0.5", 183 lbs. Deb: 5/29/36

YEAR	TM/L	W	L	PCT	G	GS	CG	SH	SV	IP	H	HR	BB	SO	RAT	ERA	ERA+	OAV	OOB	BH	AVG	PB	PR	/A	PD	TPI
1936	Bos-N	0	0	—	1	0	0	0	0	3	6	1	3	0	27.0	12.00	32	.375	.474	0	.000	-0	-3	-3	-0	0.0

DAVE WEATHERS
Weathers, John David b: 9/25/69, Lawrenceburg, Tenn. BR/TR, 6'3", 205 lbs. Deb: 8/2/91

YEAR	TM/L	W	L	PCT	G	GS	CG	SH	SV	IP	H	HR	BB	SO	RAT	ERA	ERA+	OAV	OOB	BH	AVG	PB	PR	/A	PD	TPI
1991	Tor-A	1	0	1.000	15	0	0	0	0	14²	15	1	17	13	20.9	4.91	86	.263	.447	0	—	0	-1	-1	-0	-0.1
1992	Tor-A	0	0	—	2	0	0	0	0	3¹	5	1	2	3	18.9	8.10	50	.385	.467	0	—	0	-2	-1	-0	-0.5
1993	Fla-N	2	3	.400	14	6	0	0	0	45²	57	3	13	34	14.0	5.12	84	.306	.355	1	.100	-1	-5	-4	-0	-0.5
1994	Fla-N	8	12	.400	24	24	0	0	0	135	166	13	59	72	15.3	5.27	85	.306	.379	3	.068	-3	-16	-11	-1	-1.7
Total 4		11	15	.423	55	30	0	0	0	198²	243	18	91	122	15.4	5.26	84	.305	.381	4	.074	-3	-24	-18	-1	-2.3

FLOYD WEAVER
Weaver, David Floyd b: 5/12/41, Ben Franklin, Tex. BR/TR, 6'4", 195 lbs. Deb: 9/30/62

YEAR	TM/L	W	L	PCT	G	GS	CG	SH	SV	IP	H	HR	BB	SO	RAT	ERA	ERA+	OAV	OOB	BH	AVG	PB	PR	/A	PD	TPI
1962	Cle-A	1	0	1.000	1	1	0	0	0	5	3	1	4	8	5.4	1.80	215	.167	.167	1	.500	0	1	1	-0	0.3
1965	Cle-A	2	2	.500	32	1	0	0	0	61¹	61	10	24	37	13.2	5.43	64	.265	.347	1	.091	-0	-13	-13	-0	-0.9
1970	Chi-A	1	2	.333	31	3	0	0	0	61²	52	7	31	51	12.4	4.38	89	.233	.332	0	—	0	-5	-3	-0	-0.3
1971	Mil-A	0	1	.000	21	0	0	0	0	27¹	33	3	18	12	17.1	7.24	48	.320	.426	0	—	0	-11	-11	-0	-0.4
Total 4		4	5	.444	85	5	0	0	0	155¹	149	21	73	108	13.3	5.21	70	.260	.351	2	.100	0	-28	-27	-1	-1.3

HARRY WEAVER
Weaver, Harry Abraham b: 2/26/1892, Clarendon, Pa. d: 5/30/83, Rochester, N.Y. BR/TR, 5'11", 160 lbs. Deb: 9/18/15

YEAR	TM/L	W	L	PCT	G	GS	CG	SH	SV	IP	H	HR	BB	SO	RAT	ERA	ERA+	OAV	OOB	BH	AVG	PB	PR	/A	PD	TPI
1915	Phi-A	0	2	.000	2	2	2	0	0	18	18	1	10	1	14.5	3.00	98	.290	.397	1	.167	-0	-0	-1	1	0.1
1916	Phi-A	0	0	—	3	0	0	0	0	8	14	0	5	2	21.4	10.13	28	.424	.500	1	.500	0	-6	-6	0	-0.2
1917	Chi-N	1	1	.500	4	2	1	0	0	19²	17	0	7	8	11.0	2.75	105	.230	.296	1	.200	-0	-0	0	1	0.1
1918	Chi-N	2	2	.500	8	3	1	1	1	32²	27	1	7	9	9.4	2.20	126	.227	.270	2	.250	-0	2	1	0	0.4
1919	Chi-N	0	1	.000	2	0	0	0	0	3¹	6	0	2	1	24.3	10.80	27	.375	.474	0	.000	-0	-3	-3	-0	-0.1
Total 5		3	6	.333	19	8	4	2	1	81²	82	2	31	21	12.7	3.64	78	.270	.341	5	.227	-0	-8	-7	2	-0.1

JIM WEAVER
Weaver, James Brian "Fluff" b: 2/19/39, Lancaster, Pa. BL/TL, 6', 178 lbs. Deb: 8/13/67

YEAR	TM/L	W	L	PCT	G	GS	CG	SH	SV	IP	H	HR	BB	SO	RAT	ERA	ERA+	OAV	OOB	BH	AVG	PB	PR	/A	PD	TPI
1967	Cal-A	3	0	1.000	13	2	0	0	1	30¹	26	2	9	20	10.7	2.67	118	.232	.295	0	.000	-1	2	2	2	0.3
1968	Cal-A	0	1	.000	14	0	0	0	0	22²	22	4	10	8	12.7	2.38	122	.259	.337	0	.000	-0	2	1	-1	0.0
Total 2		3	1	.750	27	2	0	0	1	53	48	6	19	28	11.5	2.55	119	.244	.313	0	.000	-1	3	3	1	0.3

YEAR	TM/L	W	L	PCT	G	GS	CG	SH	SV	IP	H	HR	BB	SO	RAT	ERA	ERA+	OAV	OOB	BH	AVG	PB	PR	/A	PD	TPI
● **JIM WEAVER**				Weaver, James Dement "Big Jim"			b: 11/25/03, Obion County, Tenn.			d: 12/12/83, Lakeland, Fla.			BR/TR, 6'6", 230 lbs.			Deb: 8/27/28									
1928	Was-A	0	0	—	3	0	0	0	0	6	2	0	6	2	13.5	1.50	267	.143	.429	0	.000	-0	2	2	0	0.0
1931	NY-A	2	1	.667	17	5	2	0	0	57²	66	1	29	28	15.0	5.31	75	.280	.361	1	.050	-3	-6	-9	0	-0.6
1934	StL-A	2	0	1.000	5	5	2	0	0	19²	17	3	20	11	16.9	6.41	78	.236	.402	1	.143	-0	-4	-3	1	-0.2
	Chi-N	11	9	.550	27	20	8	1	0	159	163	5	54	98	12.5	3.91	99	.263	.326	3	.058	-5	3	-1	1	-0.6
1935	Pit-N	14	8	.636	33	22	11	4	0	176¹	177	9	58	87	12.1	3.42	120	.254	.313	4	.071	-4	12	13	1	1.2
1936	Pit-N	14	8	.636	38	31	11	1	0	225²	239	12	74	108	12.5	4.31	94	.272	.329	8	.101	-5	-7	-6	-2	-1.2
1937	Pit-N	8	5	.615	32	9	2	1	0	109²	106	2	31	44	11.2	3.20	121	.255	.307	4	.148	-0	9	8	-2	0.7
1938	StL-A	0	1	.000	1	1	0	0	0	7	9	0	9	4	23.1	9.00	55	.321	.486	0	.000	-0	-3	-3	-0	-0.3
	Cin-N	6	4	.600	30	15	2	0	3	129¹	109	6	54	64	11.4	3.13	117	.227	.306	9	.205	0	9	7	-1	0.5
1939	Cin-N	0	0	—	3	0	0	0	0	3	3	0	1	3	12.0	3.00	128	.250	.308	0	.000	-0	0	0	0	0.0
Total	8	57	36	.613	189	108	38	7	3	893¹	891	38	336	449	12.5	3.88	102	.258	.326	30	.104	-17	14	9	-4	-0.5
● **MONTE WEAVER**				Weaver, Montie Morton "Prof"			b: 6/15/06, Helton, N.C.			d: 6/14/94, Orlando, Fla.			BL/TR, 6', 170 lbs.			Deb: 9/20/31									
1931	Was-A	1	0	1.000	3	1	1	0	0	10	11	0	6	6	15.3	4.50	95	.268	.362	-0	-0	-0	-0	0	0.0	
1932	Was-A	22	10	.688	43	30	13	1	2	234	236	9	112	83	13.4	4.08	106	.261	.342	27	.287	6	10	6	-2	1.0
1933	*Was-A	10	5	.667	23	21	12	1	0	152¹	147	3	53	45	11.9	3.25	129	.257	.322	7	.125	-3	17	16	-1	1.0
1934	Was-A	11	15	.423	31	31	11	0	0	204²	255	16	63	51	14.0	4.79	90	.306	.355	13	.162	-2	-7	-11	-2	-1.5
1935	Was-A	1	1	.500	5	2	0	0	0	12	16	1	6	4	16.5	5.25	82	.320	.393	1	.333	-1	-1	-1	-0	-0.2
1936	Was-A	6	4	.600	26	5	3	0	1	91	92	3	38	15	12.9	4.35	110	.262	.334	5	.200	1	7	4	-0	0.4
1937	Was-A	12	9	.571	30	26	9	0	0	188²	197	21	70	44	12.7	4.20	105	.266	.330	14	.206	1	9	5	1	0.6
1938	Was-A	7	6	.538	31	18	7	0	0	139	157	9	74	43	15.2	5.24	86	.282	.370	12	.267	4	-7	-11	-1	-0.6
1939	Bos-A	1	0	1.000	9	1	1	0	1	20¹	26	0	13	6	17.7	6.64	71	.321	.421	0	.000	-1	-5	-4	-1	-0.3
Total	9	71	50	.587	201	135	57	2	4	1052	1137	62	435	297	13.5	4.36	101	.276	.345	79	.209	5	24	3	-6	0.4
● **ORLIE WEAVER**				Weaver, Orville Forest		b: 6/4/1886, Newport, Ky.			d: 11/28/70, New Orleans, La.			BR/TR, 6', 180 lbs.			Deb: 9/14/10										
1910	Chi-N	1	1	.500	7	2	2	0	0	32	34	2	15	22	14.1	3.66	79	.270	.352	2	.154	-1	-2	-3	-1	-0.3
1911	Chi-N	2	2	.500	6	4	1	1	0	43²	29	0	17	20	10.3	2.06	161	.196	.296	1	.059	-1	7	6	-0	0.3
	Bos-N	3	12	.200	27	17	4	0	0	121	140	9	84	50	17.2	6.47	59	.303	.418	5	.122	-2	-41	-36	-2	-4.1
	Yr	5	14	.263	33	21	5	1	0	164²	169	9	101	70	15.1	5.30	70	.275	.384	6	.103	-4	-35	-29	-3	-3.8
Total	2	6	15	.286	40	23	7	1	0	196²	203	11	116	92	15.1	5.03	71	.276	.383	8	.113	-4	-37	-32	-4	-4.1
● **ROGER WEAVER**				Weaver, Roger Edward		b: 10/6/54, Amsterdam, N.Y.			BR/TR, 6'3", 190 lbs.			Deb: 6/6/80												
1980	Det-A	3	4	.429	19	6	0	0	0	63²	56	5	34	42	12.9	4.10	100	.247	.347	0	—	0	-0	0	1	-0.1
● **SAM WEAVER**				Weaver, Samuel H.		b: 7/10/1855, Philadelphia, Pa.			d: 2/1/14, Philadelphia, Pa.			BR/TR, 5'10", 175 lbs.			Deb: 10/25/1875									
1875	Phi-n	1	0	1.000	1	1	1	0	0	6	6	0	2		12.0	1.50	168	.240	.296	1	.250	0	1	1	0	0.1
1878	Mil-N	12	31	.279	45	43	39	1	0	383	371	2	21	95	9.2	1.95	135	.237	.247	34	.200	-3	15	29	0	2.7
1882	Phi-a	26	15	.634	42	41	41	2	0	371	374	6	35	104	9.9	2.74	109	.245	.262	36	.232	1	-2	10	1	1.1
1883	Lou-a	26	22	.542	48	48	47	4	0	418²	468	3	38	116	10.9	3.70	81	.265	.280	39	.192	-0	-18	-33	0	-2.9
1884	Phi-U	5	10	.333	17	17	14	0	0	136	206	3	11	40	14.4	5.76	40	.327	.339	18	.214	-5	-50	-52	-1	-4.4
1886	Phi-a	0	2	.000	2	2	1	0	0	11	30	0	2	2	27.0	14.73	24	.423	.446	1	.143	-1	-14	-14	-0	-1.4
Total	5	69	80	.463	154	151	142	7	0	1319²	1449	14	107	357	10.6	3.23	88	.260	.275	128	.207	-8	-69	-55	0	-4.9
● **LEFTY WEBB**				Webb, Cleon Earl		b: 3/1/1885, Mt.Gilead, Ohio			d: 1/12/58, Circleville, Ohio			BB/TL, 5'11", 165 lbs.			Deb: 5/23/10								
1910	Pit-N	2	1	.667	7	3	2	0	0	27	29	0	9	6	13.3	5.67	55	.266	.333	2	.200	-0	-8	-8	-0	-0.8
● **HANK WEBB**				Webb, Henry Gaylon Matthew		b: 5/21/50, Copiague, N.Y.			BR/TR, 6'3", 175 lbs.			Deb: 9/5/72										
1972	NY-N	0	0	—	6	2	0	0	0	18¹	18	1	9	15	13.3	4.42	76	.261	.346	0	.000	-1	-2	-2	1	0.0
1973	NY-N	0	0	—	2	0	0	0	0	1²	2	1	2	1	21.6	10.80	33	.286	.444	0	—	0	-1	-1	-0	0.0
1974	NY-N	0	2	.000	3	2	0	0	0	10	15	1	10	8	23.4	7.20	49	.341	.473	0	.000	-0	-4	-4	-0	-0.7
1975	NY-N	7	6	.538	29	15	3	1	0	115	102	12	62	38	12.9	4.07	85	.236	.333	8	.258	2	-6	-8	-1	-0.7
1976	NY-N	0	1	.000	8	0	0	0	0	16	17	2	7	7	14.6	4.50	73	.274	.366	0	.000	-0	-2	-2	-0	-0.1
1977	LA-N	0	0	—	5	0	0	0	0	8	5	1	1	2	7.9	2.25	170	.192	.250	-0	1	1	-0	0.0	
Total	6	7	9	.438	53	19	3	1	0	169	159	18	91	71	13.6	4.31	80	.248	.346	8	.200	1	-13	-16	-1	-1.5
● **RED WEBB**				Webb, Samuel Henry		b: 9/25/24, Washington, D.C.			BL/TR, 6', 175 lbs.			Deb: 9/15/48											
1948	NY-N	2	1	.667	5	3	2	0	0	28	27	2	10	9	12.2	3.21	122	.248	.317	2	.222	2	2	2	0	0.2
1949	NY-N	1	1	.500	20	0	0	0	0	44²	41	3	21	9	12.5	4.03	99	.248	.333	4	.400	2	0	-0	2	0.4
Total	2	3	2	.600	25	3	2	0	0	72²	68	5	31	18	12.4	3.72	107	.248	.327	6	.316	2	2	2	2	0.6
● **BILL WEBB**				Webb, William Frederick		b: 12/12/13, Atlanta, Ga.			d: 6/1/94, Austell, Ga.			BR/TR, 6'2", 180 lbs.			Deb: 5/15/43									
1943	Phi-N	0	0	—	1	0	0	0	0	1	1	1	0	1	18.0	9.00	37	.333	.500	0	—	0	-1	-1	-0	-0.1
● **LES WEBBER**				Webber, Lester Elmer		b: 5/6/15, Kelseyville, Cal.			d: 11/13/86, Santa Maria, Cal.			BR/TR, 6'0.5", 185 lbs.			Deb: 5/17/42									
1942	Bro-N	3	2	.600	19	3	1	0	1	51²	46	2	22	23	11.8	2.96	110	.230	.306	1	.071	-1	2	2	1	0.1
1943	Bro-N	2	2	.500	54	0	0	0	10	115²	112	6	69	24	14.5	3.81	88	.264	.373	3	.120	-1	-6	-6	2	-0.2
1944	Bro-N	7	8	.467	48	9	1	0	3	140¹	157	9	64	42	14.2	4.94	72	.282	.357	8	.205	1	-21	-22	4	-1.7
1945	Bro-N	7	3	.700	17	7	5	0	0	75¹	69	3	25	30	11.3	3.58	105	.237	.300	2	.091	-1	2	1	-1	0.0
1946	Bro-N	3	3	.500	11	4	0	0	0	43	34	5	15	16	10.3	2.30	147	.225	.295	1	.100	-1	5	5	-1	0.6
	Cle-A	1	1	.500	4	2	0	0	0	5¹	13	4	0	5	30.4	23.63	14	.464	.545	0	.000	-0	-12	-12	0	-2.8
1948	Cle-A	0	0	—	1	0	0	0	0	0²	3	0	1	1	54.0	40.50	10	.750	.800	0	—	-0	-3	-3	0	0.0
Total	6	23	19	.548	154	25	7	0	14	432	434	25	201	141	13.4	4.19	83	.262	.345	15	.135	-2	-32	-34	5	-4.0
● **CHARLIE WEBER**				Weber, Charles P. "Count"		b: 10/22/1868, Cincinnati, Ohio			d: 6/13/14, Beaumont, Tex.			Deb: 7/30/1898										
1898	Was-N	0	1	.000	1	1	0	0	0	4	9	1	0	2	27.0	15.75	23	.440	.511	0	.000	-0	-5	-5	-0	-0.8
● **MIKE WEGENER**				Wegener, Michael Denis		b: 10/8/46, Denver, Colo.			BR/TR, 6'4", 215 lbs.			Deb: 4/9/69										
1969	Mon-N	5	14	.263	32	26	4	1	0	165²	150	10	96	124	13.6	4.40	84	.243	.349	13	.241	2	-15	-13	1	-1.0
1970	Mon-N	3	6	.333	25	16	1	0	0	104¹	100	16	56	35	13.8	5.26	78	.252	.350	4	.118	-2	-14	-13	-1	-1.2
Total	2	8	20	.286	57	42	5	1	0	270	250	26	152	159	13.7	4.73	81	.247	.349	17	.193	0	-29	-27	1	-2.2
● **BILL WEGMAN**				Wegman, William Edward		b: 12/19/62, Cincinnati, Ohio			BR/TR, 6'5", 200 lbs.			Deb: 9/14/85										
1985	Mil-A	2	0	1.000	3	3	0	0	0	17²	17	3	3	6	10.2	3.57	117	.246	.278	0		0	1	1	-0	0.1
1986	Mil-A	5	12	.294	35	32	2	0	0	198¹	217	32	43	82	12.1	5.13	84	.279	.323	0		0	-21	-18	-1	-1.4
1987	Mil-A	12	11	.522	34	33	7	0	0	225	229	31	53	102	11.5	4.24	108	.265	.312	0		0	5	8	-0	0.7
1988	Mil-A	13	13	.500	32	31	4	1	0	199	207	24	50	84	11.8	4.12	97	.265	.313	0		0	-3	-3	-1	-0.5
1989	Mil-A	2	6	.250	11	8	0	0	0	51	69	6	21	27	15.9	6.71	57	.321	.381	0		0	-16	-16	1	-2.0
1990	Mil-A	2	2	.500	8	5	1	1	0	29²	37	6	6	20	13.0	4.85	80	.298	.331	0		0	-3	-3	-1	-0.4
1991	Mil-A	15	7	.682	28	28	7	2	0	193¹	176	16	40	89	10.4	2.84	140	.242	.288	0		0	27	24	2	2.9
1992	Mil-A	13	14	.481	35	35	7	0	0	261²	251	28	55	127	10.8	3.20	120	.250	.295	0		0	22	19	4	2.2
1993	Mil-A	4	14	.222	20	18	5	0	0	120²	135	14	34	50	12.8	4.48	95	.291	.342	0		0	-5	-8	-1	-0.3
1994	Mil-A	8	4	.667	19	19	0	0	0	115²	140	14	26	59	13.1	4.51	109	.305	.343	0		0	4	5	0	0.5
Total	10	76	83	.478	225	212	33	4	0	1412	1478	173	331	646	11.8	4.10	102	.269	.315	0		0	13	14	5	1.8

YEAR TM/L	W	L	PCT	G	GS	CG	SH	SV	IP	H	HR	BB	SO	RAT	ERA	ERA+	OAV	OOB	BH	AVG	PB	PR	/A	PD	TPI

● BIGGS WEHDE
Wehde, Wilbur b: 11/23/06, Holstein, Iowa d: 9/21/70, Sioux Falls, S.Dak. BR/TR, 5'10.5", 180 lbs. Deb: 9/15/30

YEAR TM/L	W	L	PCT	G	GS	CG	SH	SV	IP	H	HR	BB	SO	RAT	ERA	ERA+	OAV	OOB	BH	AVG	PB	PR	/A	PD	TPI
1930 Chi-A	0	0	—	4	0	0	0	0	6¹	7	1	7	3	21.3	9.95	46	.304	.484	0	.000	-0	-4	-4	1	0.1
1931 Chi-A	1	0	1.000	8	0	0	0	0	16	19	0	10	3	17.4	6.75	63	.333	.449	0	.000	-0	-4	-4	1	-0.2
Total 2	1	0	1.000	12	0	0	0	0	22¹	26	1	17	6	18.5	7.66	57	.325	.460	0	.000	-1	-8	-8	1	-0.1

● HERM WEHMEIER
Wehmeier, Herman Ralph b: 2/18/27, Cincinnati, Ohio d: 5/21/73, Dallas, Tex. BR/TR, 6'2", 200 lbs. Deb: 9/7/45

YEAR TM/L	W	L	PCT	G	GS	CG	SH	SV	IP	H	HR	BB	SO	RAT	ERA	ERA+	OAV	OOB	BH	AVG	PB	PR	/A	PD	TPI
1945 Cin-N	0	1	.000	2	2	0	0	0	5	10	0	4	0	25.2	12.60	30	.435	.519	0	.000	-0	-5	-5	0	-0.7
1947 Cin-N	0	0	—	1	0	0	0	0	1	0	0	0	0	0.00	—	.000	.000	0	—	0	0	0	0	0.0
1948 Cin-N	11	8	.579	33	24	6	0	0	147¹	179	21	75	56	15.6	5.86	67	.299	.379	5	.091	-3	-31	-32	-0	-3.8
1949 Cin-N	11	12	.478	33	29	11	1	0	213¹	202	20	117	80	13.8	4.68	89	.253	.353	20	.256	2	-15	-12	-2	-1.1
1950 Cin-N	10	18	.357	41	32	12	0	4	230	255	27	135	121	15.4	5.67	75	.281	.376	14	.152	-3	-39	-37	-3	-4.4
1951 Cin-N	7	10	.412	39	22	10	2	2	184²	167	15	89	93	12.7	3.70	110	.241	.330	17	.288	3	5	8	-2	0.8
1952 Cin-N	9	11	.450	33	26	6	1	0	190¹	197	23	103	83	14.5	5.15	73	.269	.365	12	.188	2	-30	-29	-4	-2.9
1953 Cin-N	1	6	.143	28	10	2	0	0	81²	100	20	47	32	16.2	7.16	61	.299	.385	4	.200	-0	-26	-25	-1	-1.9
1954 Cin-N	0	3	.000	12	3	0	0	2	33²	36	6	21	13	15.5	6.68	63	.271	.374	0	.000	-1	-10	-9	1	-0.8
Phi-N	10	8	.556	25	17	10	2	0	138	117	10	51	49	11.4	3.85	105	.231	.302	6	.120	-2	3	3	-0	0.1
Yr	10	11	.476	37	20	10	2	2	171²	153	16	72	62	11.8	4.40	92	.238	.316	6	.102	-3	-6	-6	1	-0.7
1955 Phi-N	10	12	.455	31	29	10	1	0	193²	176	21	67	85	11.4	4.41	90	.241	.307	20	.278	-4	-8	-10	-1	-0.7
1956 Phi-N	0	2	.000	3	3	0	0	0	20	18	2	11	8	13.0	4.05	92	.240	.337	0	.000	-1	-1	-1	-1	-0.2
StL-N	12	9	.571	34	19	7	2	1	170²	150	16	71	68	11.7	3.69	102	.240	.319	13	.224	4	2	2	-1	0.5
Yr	12	11	.522	37	22	7	2	1	190²	168	18	82	76	11.8	3.73	101	.240	.320	13	.197	3	1	1	-2	0.3
1957 StL-N	10	7	.588	36	18	5	0	0	165	165	25	54	91	12.1	4.31	92	.253	.312	12	.203	0	-6	-6	-0	-0.8
1958 StL-N	0	1	.000	3	3	0	0	0	6	13	2	4	2	22.5	13.50	31	.448	.484	1	.500	1	-6	-6	0	-0.8
Det-A	1	0	1.000	7	3	0	0	0	22²	21	2	5	11	10.3	2.38	169	.241	.283	0	.000	-1	3	4	-0	0.1
Total 13	92	108	.460	361	240	79	9	9	1803	1806	210	852	794	13.4	4.80	84	.260	.344	124	.196	5	-165	-156	-14	-16.4

● DAVE WEHRMEISTER
Wehrmeister, David Thomas b: 11/9/52, Berwyn, Ill. BR/TR, 6'4", 195 lbs. Deb: 4/16/76

YEAR TM/L	W	L	PCT	G	GS	CG	SH	SV	IP	H	HR	BB	SO	RAT	ERA	ERA+	OAV	OOB	BH	AVG	PB	PR	/A	PD	TPI
1976 SD-N	0	4	.000	7	4	0	0	0	19¹	27	0	11	10	17.7	7.45	44	.333	.413	0	.000	-1	-8	-9	0	-1.6
1977 SD-N	1	3	.250	30	6	0	0	0	69²	81	8	44	32	16.5	6.07	58	.293	.396	2	.167	0	-17	-20	-1	-1.0
1978 SD-N	1	0	1.000	4	0	0	0	0	7¹	8	1	5	2	16.0	6.14	54	.276	.382	0	—	0	-2	-2	-0	-0.3
1981 NY-A	0	0	—	5	0	0	0	0	7	6	0	7	7	16.7	5.14	69	.240	.406	0	—	0	-1	-1	0	0.1
1984 Phi-N	0	0	—	7	0	0	0	0	15	18	1	7	13	15.6	7.20	50	.300	.382	0	.000	-0	-6	-6	0	0.0
1985 Chi-A	2	2	.500	23	0	0	0	2	39¹	35	4	10	32	11.0	3.43	126	.241	.304	0	—	0	3	4	0	0.4
Total 6	4	9	.308	76	10	0	0	2	157²	175	14	84	96	15.2	5.65	65	.284	.376	2	.100	-1	-31	-34	0	-2.4

● STUMP WEIDMAN
Weidman, George E. b: 2/17/1861, Rochester, N.Y. d: 3/2/05, New York, N.Y. BR/TR, 5'7.5", 165 lbs. Deb: 8/26/1880 U ◆

YEAR TM/L	W	L	PCT	G	GS	CG	SH	SV	IP	H	HR	BB	SO	RAT	ERA	ERA+	OAV	OOB	BH	AVG	PB	PR	/A	PD	TPI
1880 Buf-N	0	9	.000	17	13	9	0	0	113²	141	1	9	25	11.9	3.40	72	.291	.304	8	.103	-5	-13	-12	-1	-1.3
1881 Det-N	8	5	.615	13	13	13	1	0	115	108	1	12	26	9.4	1.80	162	.238	.258	12	.255	0	12	14	-2	1.3
1882 Det-N	25	20	.556	46	45	43	4	0	411	391	10	39	161	9.4	2.63	112	.236	.253	42	.218	-5	12	14	-0	0.7
1883 Det-N	20	24	.455	52	47	41	3	2	402¹	435	8	72	183	11.3	3.53	88	.257	.288	58	.185	-8	-18	-19	2	-2.2
1884 Det-N	4	21	.160	26	26	24	0	0	212²	257	9	57	96	13.3	3.72	78	.273	.314	49	.163	-4	-18	-20	-1	-2.1
1885 Det-N	14	24	.368	38	38	37	3	0	330	343	7	63	149	11.1	3.14	91	.252	.286	24	.157	-4	-12	-11	-3	-1.7
1886 KC-N	12	36	.250	51	51	48	1	0	427²	549	11	112	168	13.9	4.50	84	.303	.344	30	.168	-10	-57	-35	-4	-3.5
1887 Det-N	13	7	.650	21	21	20	0	0	183	221	9	60	56	14.3	5.36	76	.296	.356	17	.207	-3	-26	-27	-0	-2.4
NY-a	4	8	.333	12	12	11	1	0	97	122	3	25	37	13.7	4.64	92	.292	.333	7	.152	-2	-4	-4	1	-0.4
NY-N	0	1	.000	1	1	1	0	0	8	10	0	2	4	13.5	1.13	335	.286	.324	1	.333	0	3	3	-0	0.2
1888 NY-N	1	1	.500	2	2	2	0	0	18	17	2	8	5	13.5	3.50	78	.230	.321	0	.000	-0	-1	-2	-0	-0.2
Total 9	101	156	.393	279	269	249	13	2	2318¹	2594	61	459	910	11.9	3.60	89	.268	.302	248	.177	-42	-120	-98	-2	-11.6

● DICK WEIK
Weik, Richard Henry "Legs" b: 11/17/27, Waterloo, Iowa d: 4/21/91, Harvey, Ill. BR/TR, 6'3.5", 184 lbs. Deb: 9/8/48 ◆

YEAR TM/L	W	L	PCT	G	GS	CG	SH	SV	IP	H	HR	BB	SO	RAT	ERA	ERA+	OAV	OOB	BH	AVG	PB	PR	/A	PD	TPI
1948 Was-A	1	2	.333	3	3	0	0	0	12²	14	1	22	8	25.6	5.68	76	.311	.537	3	.750	-2	-2	-2	-0	-0.2
1949 Was-A	3	12	.200	27	14	2	2	1	95¹	78	5	103	58	17.1	5.38	79	.230	.410	5	.179	-1	-13	-12	1	-1.6
1950 Was-A	1	3	.250	14	5	1	0	0	44	38	2	47	26	17.4	4.30	105	.236	.409	2	.154	-1	1	1	-1	-0.1
Cle-A	1	3	.250	11	2	0	0	0	26	18	1	26	16	15.6	3.81	114	.205	.391	1	.200	0	2	2	0	0.2
Yr	2	6	.250	25	7	1	0	0	70	56	3	73	42	16.7	4.11	108	.225	.402	3	.167	-1	4	2	-1	0.1
1953 Det-A	0	1	.000	12	1	0	0	0	19¹	32	3	23	6	25.6	13.97	29	.386	.519	1	.500	1	-21	-21	-0	-0.9
1954 Det-A	0	1	.000	9	1	0	0	0	16¹	23	3	16	9	22.0	7.16	52	.354	.488	0	.000	-1	-6	-6	-1	-0.4
Total 5	6	22	.214	76	26	3	2	1	213²	203	15	237	123	18.6	5.90	72	.260	.433	12	.226	-1	-39	-39	0	-3.0

● ED WEILAND
Weiland, Edwin Nicholas b: 11/26/14, Evanston, Ill. d: 7/12/71, Chicago, Ill. BL/TR, 5'11", 180 lbs. Deb: 5/1/40 F

YEAR TM/L	W	L	PCT	G	GS	CG	SH	SV	IP	H	HR	BB	SO	RAT	ERA	ERA+	OAV	OOB	BH	AVG	PB	PR	/A	PD	TPI
1940 Chi-A	0	0	—	5	0	0	0	0	14¹	15	5	7	3	13.8	8.79	50	.263	.344	1	.200	-0	-7	-7	-0	-0.1
1942 Chi-A	0	0	—	5	0	0	0	0	9²	18	0	3	4	19.6	7.45	48	.383	.420	0	.000	-0	-4	-4	-0	-0.1
Total 2	0	0	—	10	0	0	0	0	24	33	5	10	7	16.1	8.25	50	.317	.377	1	.143	-0	-11	-11	-1	-0.2

● BOB WEILAND
Weiland, Robert George "Lefty" b: 12/14/05, Chicago, Ill. d: 11/9/88, Chicago, Ill. BL/TL, 6'4", 215 lbs. Deb: 9/30/28 F

YEAR TM/L	W	L	PCT	G	GS	CG	SH	SV	IP	H	HR	BB	SO	RAT	ERA	ERA+	OAV	OOB	BH	AVG	PB	PR	/A	PD	TPI
1928 Chi-A	1	0	1.000	1	1	1	1	0	7	0	5	9	13.0	0.00	—	.212	.333	1	.333	0	4	4	0	0.5
1929 Chi-A	2	4	.333	15	9	1	0	1	62	62	3	43	25	15.7	5.81	74	.268	.390	2	.111	-1	-11	-10	-1	-1.1
1930 Chi-A	0	4	.000	14	3	0	0	0	32²	38	1	21	15	16.8	6.61	70	.297	.404	0	.000	-1	-7	-0	-0	-0.8
1931 Chi-A	2	7	.222	15	8	3	0	0	75	75	3	46	38	15.0	5.16	83	.259	.368	4	.182	1	-7	-8	1	-0.6
1932 Bos-A	6	16	.273	43	27	7	0	1	195²	231	11	97	63	15.4	4.51	100	.295	.377	9	.148	-1	-1	-0	3	0.2
1933 Bos-A	8	14	.364	39	27	12	0	3	216¹	197	19	100	97	12.6	3.87	113	.244	.331	7	.108	-4	10	12	-2	0.6
1934 Bos-A	1	5	.167	11	7	2	0	0	55²	63	4	27	29	14.6	5.50	87	.293	.372	2	.105	-1	-6	-4	0	-0.4
Cle-A	1	5	.167	16	7	2	0	0	70	71	5	30	42	13.0	4.11	111	.262	.336	3	.125	-0	3	3	-1	0.2
Yr	2	10	.167	27	14	4	0	0	125²	134	9	57	71	13.7	4.73	99	.276	.352	5	.116	-1	-3	-1	-0	-0.2
1935 StL-A	0	2	.000	14	4	0	0	0	32	39	6	31	11	20.0	9.56	50	.298	.436	0	.000	-0	-18	-17	-1	-1.0
1937 StL-N	15	14	.517	41	34	21	2	0	264¹	283	14	94	105	13.6	3.54	112	.276	.339	15	.169	-1	11	13	-2	1.1
1938 StL-N	16	11	.593	35	29	11	1	1	228¹	248	14	67	117	12.6	3.59	110	.272	.324	11	.138	-3	5	9	-4	0.6
1939 StL-N	10	12	.455	32	23	6	3	1	146¹	146	4	50	63	12.4	3.57	115	.264	.331	3	.065	-4	6	9	-1	0.7
1940 StL-N	0	0	—	1	0	0	0	0	1	3	1	0	0	27.0	27.00	15	.600	.600	—	0	-3	-3	-0	0.0
Total 12	62	94	.397	277	179	66	7	7	1388¹	1463	85	611	614	13.7	4.24	100	.272	.350	57	.129	-16	-13	2	-4	0.0

● CARL WEILMAN
Weilman, Carl Woolworth "Zeke" (b: Carl Woolworth Weilenmann) b: 11/29/1889, Hamilton, Ohio d: 5/25/24, Hamilton, Ohio BL/TL, 6'5.5", 187 lbs. Deb: 8/24/12

YEAR TM/L	W	L	PCT	G	GS	CG	SH	SV	IP	H	HR	BB	SO	RAT	ERA	ERA+	OAV	OOB	BH	AVG	PB	PR	/A	PD	TPI
1912 StL-A	2	4	.333	8	6	5	2	1	48¹	42	0	3	24	8.4	2.79	119	.227	.239	2	.118	-1	3	3	0	0.3
1913 StL-A	10	20	.333	39	28	17	2	0	251²	262	2	60	79	11.7	3.40	86	.281	.328	12	.146	-3	-13	-13	1	-1.6
1914 StL-A	18	13	.581	44	36	20	3	1	299	260	1	84	119	10.7	2.08	130	.237	.298	15	.149	-1	22	21	1	2.2
1915 StL-A	18	19	.486	47	31	19	3	4	295²	240	6	83	125	9.9	2.34	122	.229	.287	23	.230	2	19	17	-1	2.3
1916 StL-A	17	18	.486	46	31	19	1	2	276	237	3	76	91	10.5	2.15	128	.242	.301	14	.154	-1	21	18	-3	1.9
1917 StL-A	1	2	.333	5	3	0	0	0	19	19	1	6	9	11.8	1.89	137	.268	.325	0	.000	-1	2	1	-0	0.1
1919 StL-A	10	6	.625	20	20	12	3	0	148	133	3	45	44	11.0	2.07	160	.244	.305	9	.191	0	19	21	-0	2.2
1920 StL-A	9	13	.409	30	24	13	1	2	183¹	201	6	61	45	13.0	4.47	88	.291	.351	11	.175	-2	-14	-11	1	-1.3
Total 8	85	95	.472	239	179	105	15	10	1521	1394	22	418	536	10.9	2.67	114	.251	.306	86	.170	-7	59	56	1	6.3

YEAR TM/L	W	L	PCT	G	GS	CG	SH	SV	IP	H	HR	BB	SO	RAT	ERA	ERA+	OAV	OOB	BH	AVG	PB	PR	/A	PD	TPI
● **JAKE WEIMER** Weimer, Jacob "Tornado Jake" b: 11/29/1873, Ottumwa, Iowa d: 6/19/28, Chicago, Ill. BR/TL, 5'11", 175 lbs. Deb: 4/17/03																								
1903 Chi-N	20	8	.714	35	33	27	3	0	282	241	4	104	128	11.4	2.30	136	**.225**	.301	21	.196	2	30	26	-1	2.4
1904 Chi-N	20	14	.588	37	37	31	5	0	307	229	1	97	177	9.8	1.91	140	.204	.272	21	.183	-1	28	26	3	2.9
1905 Chi-N	18	12	.600	33	30	26	2	1	250¹	212	1	80	107	10.9	2.26	132	.229	.299	19	.207	2	21	20	-1	2.4
1906 Cin-N	20	14	.588	41	39	31	6	1	304²	263	0	99	141	11.1	2.22	124	.236	.306	29	.269	6	14	18	1	2.9
1907 Cin-N	11	14	.440	29	26	19	3	0	209	165	6	63	67	10.8	2.41	108	.226	.308	14	.194	2	1	4	2	1.0
1908 Cin-N	8	7	.533	15	15	9	2	0	116²	110	2	50	36	12.8	2.39	96	.255	.341	11	.244	2	-0	-1	1	0.2
1909 NY-N	0	0	—	1	0	0	0	0	3	7	0	0	1	24.0	9.00	28	.467	.500	0	.000	-0	-2	-2	-0	0.0
Total 7	97	69	.584	191	180	143	21	2	1472²	1227	14	493	657	11.0	2.23	125	.227	.300	115	.213	11	93	93	5	11.8
● **LEFTY WEINERT** Weinert, Phillip Walter b: 4/21/02, Philadelphia, Pa. d: 4/17/73, Rockledge, Fla. BL/TL, 6'1", 195 lbs. Deb: 9/24/19																								
1919 Phi-N	0	0	—	1	0	0	0	0	4	11	0	2	0	29.3	18.00	18	.478	.520	2	1.000	1	-7	-7	0	0.2
1920 Phi-N	1	1	.500	10	2	0	0	0	22	27	1	19	10	19.2	6.14	56	.333	.465	0	.000	-1	-7	-7	-0	-0.7
1921 Phi-N	1	0	1.000	8	0	0	0	0	12¹	8	1	5	2	10.2	1.46	290	.216	.326	1	1.000	0	3	4	-1	0.3
1922 Phi-N	8	11	.421	34	22	10	0	1	166²	189	10	70	58	14.3	3.40	137	.289	.362	14	.241	-0	13	23	-2	2.3
1923 Phi-N	4	17	.190	38	20	8	0	1	156	207	10	81	46	17.1	5.42	85	.327	.410	19	.322	2	-25	-14	-3	-1.7
1924 Phi-N	1	0	1.000	8	1	0	0	0	14²	10	0	11	7	12.9	2.45	182	.204	.350	0	.000	-1	2	3	0	0.2
1927 Chi-N	1	1	.500	5	3	1	0	0	19²	21	2	6	5	12.4	4.58	84	.259	.310	1	.200	0	-1	-2	-0	-0.2
1928 Chi-N	1	0	1.000	10	1	0	0	0	17	24	0	9	8	18.0	5.29	73	.393	.479	0	.000	0	-2	-3	-1	-0.2
1931 NY-A	2	2	.500	17	0	0	0	2	24²	31	2	19	24	20.1	6.20	64	.316	.451	0	.000	-0	-5	-6	0	-0.8
Total 9	18	33	.353	131	49	19	0	2	437	528	26	222	160	15.9	4.59	97	.308	.393	37	.261	2	-29	-7	-6	-0.6
● **ROY WEIR** Weir, William Franklin "Bill" b: 2/25/11, Portland, Maine d: 9/30/89, Anaheim, Cal. BL/TL, 5'8.5", 170 lbs. Deb: 6/25/36																								
1936 Bos-N	4	3	.571	12	7	3	2	0	57¹	53	0	24	29	12.1	2.83	136	.241	.316	5	.278	2	8	6	1	1.0
1937 Bos-N	1	1	.500	10	4	1	0	0	33	27	0	19	8	12.5	3.82	94	.227	.333	0	.000	-1	0	-1	1	-0.1
1938 Bos-N	1	0	1.000	5	0	0	0	0	13¹	14	4	6	3	13.5	6.75	51	.269	.345	1	.333	0	-4	-5	0	-0.3
1939 Bos-N	0	0	—	2	0	0	0	0	2²	1	0	1	2	6.8	0.00	—	.125	.222	0	.000	-0	1	1	0	0.0
Total 4	6	4	.600	29	11	4	2	0	106¹	95	4	50	42	12.3	3.55	104	.238	.323	6	.188	1	5	2	2	0.6
● **CURT WELCH** Welch, Curtis Benton b: 2/11/1862, E.Liverpool, Ohio d: 8/29/1896, E.Liverpool, Ohio BR/TR, 5'10", 175 lbs. Deb: 5/1/1884 ◆																								
1890 Phi-a	0	0	—	1	0	0	0	0	1	6	0	6	0	54.0	54.00	7	.670	.670	106	.268	0	-6	-6	0	0.0
● **TED WELCH** Welch, Floyd John b: 10/17/1892, Coyville, Kan. d: 1/6/43, Great Bend, Kan. BL/TR, 5'9.5", 160 lbs. Deb: 5/15/14																								
1914 StL-F	0	0	—	3	0	0	0	0	6	6	0	3	2	18.0	6.00	51	.273	.429	0	.000	-0	-2	-2	-0	0.0
● **JOHNNY WELCH** Welch, John Vernon b: 12/2/06, Washington, D.C. d: 9/2/40, St.Louis, Mo. BL/TR, 6'3", 184 lbs. Deb: 5/22/26																								
1926 Chi-N	0	0	—	3	0	0	0	0	4¹	5	0	1	0	12.5	2.08	185	.357	.400	1	1.000	0	1	1	-0	0.0
1927 Chi-N	0	0	—	1	0	0	0	0	1	0	0	3	1	27.0	9.00	43	.000	.500	0	—	0	-1	-1	0	0.0
1928 Chi-N	0	0	—	3	0	0	0	0	4	13	0	0	2	29.3	15.75	24	.591	.591	0	—	0	-5	-5	0	0.0
1931 Chi-N	2	1	.667	8	3	1	0	0	33²	39	2	10	7	13.4	3.74	103	.291	.345	5	.417	2	0	0	0	0.2
1932 Bos-A	4	6	.400	20	8	3	1	0	72¹	93	3	38	26	16.7	5.23	86	.312	.395	9	.250	2	-6	-6	0	-0.5
1933 Bos-A	4	9	.308	47	7	1	0	3	129	142	6	67	68	14.7	4.60	95	.283	.370	6	.162	-1	-5	-3	1	-0.3
1934 Bos-A	13	15	.464	41	22	8	1	0	206¹	223	14	76	91	13.4	4.49	107	.274	.342	15	.203	-1	0	7	1	0.7
1935 Bos-A	10	9	.526	31	19	10	1	2	143	155	4	53	48	13.3	4.47	106	.273	.339	9	.180	-0	0	4	0	0.5
1936 Bos-A	2	1	.667	9	3	1	0	0	32²	43	4	8	9	14.1	5.51	96	.305	.342	3	.273	1	-2	-1	0	0.0
Pit-N	0	0	—	9	1	0	0	1	22	22	3	6	5	11.5	4.50	90	.265	.315	2	.286	1	-1	-1	-1	0.0
Total 9	35	41	.461	172	63	24	3	6	648¹	735	36	262	257	14.1	4.66	99	.285	.355	50	.219	4	-18	-4	1	0.6
● **MICKEY WELCH** Welch, Michael Francis "Smiling Mickey" b: 7/4/1859, Brooklyn, N.Y. d: 7/30/41, Concord, N.H. BR/TR, 5'8", 160 lbs. Deb: 5/1/1880 H																								
1880 Tro-N	34	30	.531	65	64	64	4	0	574	575	7	80	123	10.3	2.54	99	.249	.274	72	.287	10	-11	-1	-7	0.3
1881 Tro-N	21	18	.538	40	40	40	4	0	368	371	7	78	104	11.0	2.67	111	.255	.293	30	.203	-4	4	12	-6	0.1
1882 Tro-N	14	16	.467	33	33	30	5	0	281	334	7	62	53	12.7	3.46	82	.280	.315	37	.245	1	-17	-20	-3	-1.9
1883 NY-N	25	23	.521	54	52	46	4	0	426	431	11	66	144	10.5	2.73	114	.244	.272	75	.234	3	20	18	-6	1.3
1884 NY-N	39	21	.650	65	65	62	4	0	557¹	528	12	146	345	10.9	2.50	119	.237	.284	60	.241	9	30	29	-5	2.9
1885 NY-N	44	11	**.800**	56	55	55	7	1	492	372	4	131	258	9.2	1.66	160	.203	.256	41	.206	5	63	55	-8	5.0
1886 NY-N	33	22	.600	59	59	56	1	0	500	514	13	163	272	12.2	2.99	108	.259	.315	46	.216	1	18	12	-2	0.8
1887 NY-N	22	15	.595	40	40	39	2	0	346	339	7	91	115	11.3	3.36	112	.253	.303	36	.243	4	28	16	-2	1.3
1888 *NY-N	26	19	.578	47	47	47	5	0	425¹	328	12	108	167	9.5	1.93	154	.207	.263	32	.189	1	44	38	-4	3.3
1889 *NY-N	27	12	.692	45	41	39	3	**2**	375	340	14	149	125	12.0	3.02	130	.234	.310	30	.192	-4	41	38	-3	2.8
1890 NY-N	17	14	.548	37	37	33	2	0	292¹	268	5	122	97	12.4	2.99	117	.236	.317	22	.179	-3	19	17	-3	0.8
1891 NY-N	5	9	.357	22	15	14	0	1	160	176	7	97	46	16.0	4.27	75	.269	.372	10	.141	-4	-16	-19	-3	-1.9
1892 NY-N	0	0	—	1	1	0	0	0	5	11	0	4	1	27.0	14.40	22	.423	.500	1	.333	0	-6	-6	-0	0.0
Total 13	307	210	.594	564	549	525	41	4	4802	4587	106	1297	1850	11.1	2.71	114	.242	.292	492	.224	21	216	196	-52	14.8
● **BOB WELCH** Welch, Robert Lynn b: 11/3/56, Detroit, Mich. BR/TR, 6'3", 190 lbs. Deb: 6/20/78																								
1978 *LA-N	7	4	.636	23	13	4	3	3	111¹	92	6	26	66	9.6	2.02	174	.229	.277	5	.172	0	19	18	-1	1.8
1979 LA-N	5	6	.455	25	12	1	0	5	81¹	82	7	32	64	12.9	3.98	91	.265	.340	3	.158	-0	-2	-3	-1	-0.5
1980 LA-N★	14	9	.609	32	32	3	2	0	213²	190	15	79	141	11.5	3.29	106	.242	.314	17	.243	3	7	5	-1	0.8
1981 *LA-N	9	5	.643	23	23	2	1	0	141¹	141	11	41	88	11.8	3.44	96	.259	.315	10	.222	2	-1	-2	-1	-0.1
1982 LA-N	16	11	.593	36	36	9	3	0	235²	199	19	81	176	10.9	3.36	103	.229	.299	12	.141	-1	9	8	-1	0.8
1983 *LA-N	15	12	.556	31	31	4	3	0	204	164	13	72	156	10.5	2.65	136	.222	.294	7	.096	-2	22	21	-0	2.5
1984 LA-N	13	13	.500	31	31	4	1	0	178²	191	11	58	126	12.6	3.78	93	.273	.331	4	.078	-3	-4	-5	2	-0.8
1985 LA-N	14	4	.778	23	23	8	3	0	167¹	141	16	35	96	9.8	2.31	150	.225	.273	9	.180	1	24	22	1	2.6
1986 LA-N	7	13	.350	33	33	7	3	0	235²	227	14	55	183	11.0	3.28	105	.251	.299	8	.105	-0	11	4	-1	0.2
1987 LA-N	15	9	.625	35	35	6	**4**	0	251²	204	21	86	196	10.5	3.22	123	.221	.291	13	.157	1	24	21	2	2.2
1988 *Oak-A	17	9	.654	36	36	4	2	0	244²	237	22	81	158	12.1	3.64	104	.257	.323	0	—	0	9	4	0	0.6
1989 *Oak-A	17	8	.680	33	33	1	0	0	209²	191	13	78	137	11.8	3.00	122	.241	.314	0	—	0	20	16	0	1.8
1990 *Oak-A★	**27**	6	**.818**	35	35	2	2	0	238	214	26	77	127	11.2	2.95	126	.242	.306	0	—	0	25	20	0	3.0
1991 Oak-A	12	13	.480	35	35	7	1	0	220	220	25	91	101	13.2	4.58	84	.263	.343	0	—	0	-12	-18	-1	-1.9
1992 Oak-A	11	7	.611	20	20	0	0	0	123²	114	13	43	47	11.6	3.27	114	.247	.314	0	—	0	9	6	-1	0.0
1993 Oak-A	9	11	.450	30	28	0	0	0	166²	208	25	56	63	14.6	5.29	77	.310	.370	0	—	0	-18	-23	1	-2.1
1994 Oak-A	3	6	.333	25	8	0	0	0	68²	79	10	43	44	16.1	7.08	63	.290	.389	0	.000	0	-17	-20	0	-2.1
Total 17	211	146	.591	506	462	61	28	8	3092	2894	267	1034	1969	11.7	3.47	106	.249	.314	88	.151	2	126	70	-2	9.0
● **DON WELCHEL** Welchel, Donald Ray b: 2/3/57, Atlanta, Tex. BR/TR, 6'4", 205 lbs. Deb: 9/15/82																								
1982 Bal-A	1	0	1.000	2	0	0	0	0	4¹	6	0	2	3	16.6	8.31	49	.300	.364	0	—	0	-2	-3	-0	-0.4
1983 Bal-A	0	2	.000	11	0	0	0	0	26²	33	1	10	16	14.5	5.40	73	.297	.355	0	—	0	-4	-4	-0	-0.3
Total 2	1	2	.333	13	0	0	0	0	31	39	1	12	19	14.8	5.81	68	.298	.357	0	—	0	-6	-6	-0	-0.7
● **DAVID WELLS** Wells, David Lee b: 5/20/63, Torrance, Cal. BL/TL, 6'3", 225 lbs. Deb: 6/30/87																								
1987 Tor-A	4	3	.571	18	2	0	0	1	29¹	37	0	12	32	15.0	3.99	113	.311	.374	0	—	0	2	2	0	0.4
1988 Tor-A	3	5	.375	41	0	0	0	4	64¹	65	12	31	56	13.7	4.62	85	.269	.356	0	—	0	-5	-5	-0	-0.7
1989 *Tor-A	7	4	.636	54	0	0	0	2	86¹	66	5	28	78	9.8	2.40	157	.207	.271	0	—	0	16	15	0	1.5
1990 Tor-A	11	6	.647	43	25	0	0	3	189	165	14	45	115	10.1	3.14	125	.235	.283	0	—	0	16	17	1	1.5
1991 *Tor-A	15	10	.600	40	28	2	0	1	198¹	188	24	49	106	10.8	3.72	113	.251	.299	0	—	0	8	11	1	1.3

YEAR TM/L	W	L	PCT	G	GS	CG	SH	SV	IP	H	HR	BB	SO	RAT	ERA	ERA+	OAV	OOB	BH	AVG	PB	PR	/A	PD	TPI
1992 *Tor-A	7	9	.438	41	14	0	0	2	120	138	16	36	62	13.7	5.40	76	.289	.349	0	—	0	-19	-18	-0	-2.3
1993 Det-A	11	9	.550	32	30	0	0	0	187	183	26	42	139	11.2	4.19	102	.254	.301	0	—	0	3	2	-1	0.1
1994 Det-A	5	7	.417	16	16	5	1	0	111¹	113	13	24	71	11.2	3.96	120	.260	.302	0	—	0	10	10	0	0.9
Total 8	63	53	.543	285	115	7	1	13	985²	955	110	267	659	11.4	3.88	107	.254	.307	0	—	0	29	32	1	2.9

● ED WELLS
Wells, Edwin Lee "Satchelfoot" b: 6/7/1900, Ashland, Ohio d: 5/1/86, Montgomery, Ala. BL/TL, 6'1.5", 183 lbs. Deb: 6/16/23

YEAR TM/L	W	L	PCT	G	GS	CG	SH	SV	IP	H	HR	BB	SO	RAT	ERA	ERA+	OAV	OOB	BH	AVG	PB	PR	/A	PD	TPI
1923 Det-A	0	0	—	7	0	0	0	0	10	11	0	6	6	15.3	5.40	72	.306	.405	0	.000	-0	-2	-2	-0	0.0
1924 Det-A	6	8	.429	29	15	5	0	4	102	117	2	42	33	14.1	4.06	101	.291	.360	7	.212	-1	2	1	1	0.1
1925 Det-A	6	9	.400	35	14	5	0	2	134¹	190	8	62	45	17.0	6.23	69	.345	.413	12	.279	3	-27	-29	1	-2.5
1926 Det-A	12	10	.545	36	26	9	4	0	178	201	7	76	58	14.1	4.15	98	.297	.370	15	.205	0	-2	-2	-3	-0.4
1927 Det-A	0	1	.000	8	1	0	0	1	20	28	3	5	5	14.8	6.75	62	.333	.371	2	.286	0	-6	-6	1	-0.2
1929 NY-A	13	9	.591	31	23	10	3	0	193¹	179	19	81	78	12.1	4.33	89	.248	.324	17	.230	2	-2	-10	-4	-1.2
1930 NY-A	12	3	.800	27	21	7	0	0	150²	185	11	49	46	14.2	5.20	83	.302	.358	15	.259	0	-9	-15	-2	-1.4
1931 NY-A	9	5	.643	27	10	6	0	2	116²	130	7	37	34	13.0	4.32	92	.286	.341	10	.222	1	1	-5	-2	-0.5
1932 NY-A	3	3	.500	22	0	0	0	2	31²	38	1	12	13	14.2	4.26	96	.302	.362	0	.000	-1	1	-1	-0	-0.2
1933 StL-A	6	14	.300	36	22	10	0	1	203²	230	13	63	58	13.0	4.20	111	.278	.330	14	.197	-1	2	10	-3	0.5
1934 StL-A	1	7	.125	33	8	2	0	1	92	108	7	35	27	14.0	4.79	104	.292	.353	1	.045	-2	3	2	1	0.1
Total 11	68	69	.496	291	140	54	7	13	1232¹	1417	78	468	403	13.9	4.65	91	.291	.355	93	.215	1	-46	-55	-10	-5.7

● JOHN WELLS
Wells, John Frederick b: 11/25/22, Junction City, Kan. d: 10/23/93, Olean, N.Y. BR/TR, 5'11.5", 180 lbs. Deb: 9/14/44

YEAR TM/L	W	L	PCT	G	GS	CG	SH	SV	IP	H	HR	BB	SO	RAT	ERA	ERA+	OAV	OOB	BH	AVG	PB	PR	/A	PD	TPI
1944 Bro-N	0	2	.000	4	2	0	0	0	15	18	1	11	7	17.4	5.40	66	.316	.426	1	.250	0	-3	-3	-0	-0.4

● BOB WELLS
Wells, Robert Lee b: 11/1/66, Yakima, Wash. BR/TR, 6', 180 lbs. Deb: 5/16/94

YEAR TM/L	W	L	PCT	G	GS	CG	SH	SV	IP	H	HR	BB	SO	RAT	ERA	ERA+	OAV	OOB	BH	AVG	PB	PR	/A	PD	TPI
1994 Phi-N	1	0	1.000	6	0	0	0	0	5	4	0	3	3	14.4	1.80	229	.235	.381	0	—	0	1	1	-0	0.2
Sea-A	1	0	1.000	1	0	0	0	0	4	4	0	1	3	11.3	2.25	218	.250	.294	0	—	0	1	1	-0	0.3
Total 1	2	0	1.000	7	0	0	0	0	9	8	0	4	6	13.0	2.00	223	.242	.342	0	—	0	2	2	-0	0.5

● TERRY WELLS
Wells, Terry b: 9/10/63, Kankakee, Ill. BL/TL, 6'3", 205 lbs. Deb: 7/3/90

YEAR TM/L	W	L	PCT	G	GS	CG	SH	SV	IP	H	HR	BB	SO	RAT	ERA	ERA+	OAV	OOB	BH	AVG	PB	PR	/A	PD	TPI
1990 LA-N	1	2	.333	5	5	0	0	0	20²	25	4	14	18	17.0	7.84	47	.287	.386	0	.000	-1	-9	-10	-1	-1.3

● CHRIS WELSH
Welsh, Christopher Charles b: 4/14/55, Wilmington, Del. BL/TL, 6'2", 185 lbs. Deb: 4/12/81

YEAR TM/L	W	L	PCT	G	GS	CG	SH	SV	IP	H	HR	BB	SO	RAT	ERA	ERA+	OAV	OOB	BH	AVG	PB	PR	/A	PD	TPI
1981 SD-N	6	7	.462	22	19	4	2	0	123²	122	9	41	51	11.9	3.78	86	.264	.325	6	.146	0	-4	-7	1	-0.6
1982 SD-N	8	8	.500	28	20	3	1	0	139¹	146	16	63	48	13.7	4.91	70	.268	.347	11	.262	4	-20	-23	1	-2.0
1983 SD-N	0	1	.000	7	1	0	0	0	14¹	13	2	2	5	9.4	2.51	139	.236	.263	0	.000	-0	2	2	-0	0.1
Mon-N	0	1	.000	16	5	0	0	0	44²	46	5	18	17	13.7	5.04	71	.267	.351	4	.286	1	-7	-7	1	0.1
Yr	0	2	.000	23	6	0	0	0	59	59	7	20	22	12.7	4.42	81	.260	.331	4	.222	1	-5	-6	1	0.1
1985 Tex-A	2	5	.286	25	6	0	0	0	76¹	101	11	25	31	15.3	4.13	102	.316	.372	0	0	1	0	1	-1	0.0
1986 Cin-N	6	9	.400	24	24	1	0	0	139¹	163	16	40	40	13.3	4.78	81	.301	.353	5	.119	0	-16	-14	-1	-1.4
Total 5	22	31	.415	122	76	8	3	0	537²	591	52	189	192	13.3	4.45	81	.282	.346	26	.182	5	-46	-49	2	-3.9

● DICK WELTEROTH
Welteroth, Richard John b: 8/3/27, Williamsport, Pa. BR/TR, 5'11", 165 lbs. Deb: 5/16/48

YEAR TM/L	W	L	PCT	G	GS	CG	SH	SV	IP	H	HR	BB	SO	RAT	ERA	ERA+	OAV	OOB	BH	AVG	PB	PR	/A	PD	TPI
1948 Was-A	2	1	.667	33	2	0	0	1	65¹	73	6	50	16	17.1	5.51	79	.286	.405	1	.100	-1	-9	-8	-0	-0.5
1949 Was-A	2	5	.286	52	0	0	0	2	95¹	107	6	89	37	18.6	7.36	58	.296	.437	1	.059	-1	-34	-33	-0	-2.3
1950 Was-A	0	0	—	5	0	0	0	0	6	5	0	6	2	16.5	3.00	150	.217	.379	0	—	0	1	1	0	0.0
Total 3	4	6	.400	90	4	0	0	3	166²	185	12	145	55	17.9	6.48	66	.290	.422	2	.074	-2	-41	-40	-0	-2.8

● TONY WELZER
Welzer, Anton Frank b: 4/5/1899, Germany d: 3/18/71, Milwaukee, Wis. BR/TR, 5'11", 160 lbs. Deb: 4/13/26

YEAR TM/L	W	L	PCT	G	GS	CG	SH	SV	IP	H	HR	BB	SO	RAT	ERA	ERA+	OAV	OOB	BH	AVG	PB	PR	/A	PD	TPI
1926 Bos-A	4	3	.571	39	6	1	0	1	139	167	5	53	29	14.4	4.86	84	.308	.373	8	.211	2	-13	-12	4	0.0
1927 Bos-A	6	11	.353	37	19	8	1	0	171²	214	10	71	56	15.2	4.72	89	.318	.386	4	.095	-2	-11	-9	1	-0.9
Total 2	10	14	.417	76	25	9	1	1	310²	381	15	124	85	14.8	4.78	87	.313	.380	12	.150	-0	-24	-22	4	-0.9

● TURK WENDELL
Wendell, Steven John b: 5/19/67, Pittsfield, Mass. BB/TR, 6'2", 180 lbs. Deb: 6/17/93

YEAR TM/L	W	L	PCT	G	GS	CG	SH	SV	IP	H	HR	BB	SO	RAT	ERA	ERA+	OAV	OOB	BH	AVG	PB	PR	/A	PD	TPI
1993 Chi-N	1	2	.333	7	4	0	0	0	22²	24	0	8	15	12.7	4.37	91	.273	.333	1	.143	-0	-1	-1	0	-0.1
1994 Chi-N	0	1	.000	6	2	0	0	0	14¹	22	3	10	9	20.1	11.93	34	.349	.438	0	.000	0	-12	-12	-0	-0.7
Total 2	1	3	.250	13	6	0	0	0	37	46	3	18	24	15.6	7.30	55	.305	.379	1	.111	-0	-13	-13	0	-0.8

● BUTCH WENSLOFF
Wensloff, Charles William b: 12/3/15, Sausalito, Cal. BR/TR, 5'11", 185 lbs. Deb: 5/2/43

YEAR TM/L	W	L	PCT	G	GS	CG	SH	SV	IP	H	HR	BB	SO	RAT	ERA	ERA+	OAV	OOB	BH	AVG	PB	PR	/A	PD	TPI
1943 NY-A	13	11	.542	29	27	18	1	0	223¹	179	7	70	105	10.1	2.54	127	.219	.282	14	.177	-0	19	17	-1	1.7
1947 *NY-A	3	1	.750	11	5	1	0	0	51²	41	3	22	18	11.0	2.61	135	.217	.299	5	.263	1	6	5	-1	0.4
1948 Cle-A	0	1	.000	1	0	0	0	0	1²	2	1	3	2	27.0	10.80	38	.286	.500	0	—	0	-1	-1	-0	-0.5
Total 3	16	13	.552	41	32	19	1	0	276²	222	11	95	125	10.3	2.60	126	.219	.287	19	.194	0	24	21	-2	1.6

● FRED WENZ
Wenz, Frederick Charles "Fireball" b: 8/26/41, Bound Brook, N.J. BR/TR, 6'3", 214 lbs. Deb: 6/4/68

YEAR TM/L	W	L	PCT	G	GS	CG	SH	SV	IP	H	HR	BB	SO	RAT	ERA	ERA+	OAV	OOB	BH	AVG	PB	PR	/A	PD	TPI
1968 Bos-A	0	0	—	1	0	0	0	0	1	0	0	2	3	18.0	0.00	—	.000	.400	0	—	0	0	0	-0	0.0
1969 Bos-A	1	0	1.000	8	0	0	0	0	11	9	7	10	11	15.5	5.73	66	.225	.380	0	—	0	-3	-2	0	-0.2
1970 Phi-N	2	0	1.000	22	0	0	0	1	30¹	27	2	13	24	12.2	4.45	90	.237	.320	0	.000	-1	-1	-2	-1	-0.2
Total 3	3	0	1.000	31	0	0	0	1	42¹	36	9	25	38	13.2	4.68	84	.229	.339	0	.000	-0	-4	-4	-1	-0.4

● PERRY WERDEN
Werden, Percival Wheritt b: 7/21/1865, St.Louis, Mo. d: 1/9/34, Minneapolis, Minn. BR/TR, 6'2", 220 lbs. Deb: 4/24/1884 ◆

YEAR TM/L	W	L	PCT	G	GS	CG	SH	SV	IP	H	HR	BB	SO	RAT	ERA	ERA+	OAV	OOB	BH	AVG	PB	PR	/A	PD	TPI
1884 StL-U	12	1	.923	16	16	12	1	0	141¹	113	1	22	64	8.6	1.97	121	.204	.235	18	.237	-4	7	7	1	0.2

● BILL WERLE
Werle, William George "Bugs" b: 12/21/20, Oakland, Cal. BL/TL, 6'2.5", 182 lbs. Deb: 4/22/49 C

YEAR TM/L	W	L	PCT	G	GS	CG	SH	SV	IP	H	HR	BB	SO	RAT	ERA	ERA+	OAV	OOB	BH	AVG	PB	PR	/A	PD	TPI
1949 Pit-N	12	13	.480	35	29	10	2	0	221	243	22	51	106	12.3	4.24	99	.278	.324	9	.117	-3	-5	-7	1	-0.3
1950 Pit-N	8	16	.333	48	22	6	0	2	215¹	249	20	65	78	13.4	4.60	95	.290	.344	13	.194	1	-11	-5	4	-0.1
1951 Pit-N	8	6	.571	59	9	2	0	6	149²	181	20	51	57	14.3	5.65	75	.304	.364	12	.300	3	-28	-24	3	-1.5
1952 Pit-N	0	0	—	5	0	0	0	0	4	9	1	1	1	22.5	9.00	44	.429	.455	0	—	0	-2	-2	0	0.0
StL-N	1	2	.333	19	0	0	0	1	39	40	6	15	23	12.9	4.85	77	.268	.339	1	.111	-0	-5	-5	1	-0.3
Yr	1	2	.333	24	0	0	0	1	43	49	7	16	24	13.8	5.23	71	.288	.353	1	.111	-0	-7	-7	2	-0.3
1953 Bos-A	0	1	.000	5	0	0	0	0	11²	7	1	1	4	6.2	1.54	273	.179	.200	0	.000	0	3	3	1	0.4
1954 Bos-A	0	1	.000	14	0	0	0	0	24	41	5	10	14	19.3	4.38	94	.376	.438	0	.000	-0	-2	-1	-0	-0.1
Total 6	29	39	.426	185	60	18	2	15	665¹	770	80	194	283	13.4	4.69	90	.291	.345	35	.176	1	-50	-34	10	-1.9

● GEORGE WERLEY
Werley, George William b: 9/8/38, St.Louis, Mo. BR/TR, 6'2", 196 lbs. Deb: 9/29/56

YEAR TM/L	W	L	PCT	G	GS	CG	SH	SV	IP	H	HR	BB	SO	RAT	ERA	ERA+	OAV	OOB	BH	AVG	PB	PR	/A	PD	TPI
1956 Bal-A	0	0	—	1	0	0	0	0	1	1	0	2	0	27.0	9.00	44	.250	.500	0	—	0	-1	-1	0	0.0

● JOHNNY WERTS
Werts, Henry Levi b: 4/20/1898, Pomaria, S.C. d: 9/24/90, Newberry, S.C. BR/TR, 5'10", 180 lbs. Deb: 4/14/26

YEAR TM/L	W	L	PCT	G	GS	CG	SH	SV	IP	H	HR	BB	SO	RAT	ERA	ERA+	OAV	OOB	BH	AVG	PB	PR	/A	PD	TPI
1926 Bos-N	11	9	.550	32	23	7	1	0	189¹	212	6	47	65	12.8	3.28	108	.287	.338	17	.266	4	11	6	2	1.2
1927 Bos-N	4	10	.286	42	15	4	0	1	164¹	204	5	52	39	14.2	4.55	82	.315	.369	7	.163	-0	-11	-15	-1	-1.3
1928 Bos-N	0	2	.000	10	2	0	0	0	18¹	31	2	8	5	19.1	10.31	38	.369	.424	1	.333	0	-13	-13	0	-1.1
1929 Bos-N	0	0	—	4	0	0	0	1	6	13	1	4	2	25.5	10.50	45	.433	.500	1	1.000	0	-4	-4	-0	-0.1
Total 4	15	21	.417	88	40	11	1	2	378	460	14	111	111	13.9	4.29	85	.307	.360	26	.234	4	-17	-27	1	-1.3

● BILL WERTZ
Wertz, William Charles b: 1/15/67, Cleveland, Ohio BR/TR, 6'6", 220 lbs. Deb: 5/22/93

YEAR TM/L	W	L	PCT	G	GS	CG	SH	SV	IP	H	HR	BB	SO	RAT	ERA	ERA+	OAV	OOB	BH	AVG	PB	PR	/A	PD	TPI
1993 Cle-A	2	3	.400	34	0	0	0	0	59²	54	5	32	53	13.1	3.62	119	.238	.335	0	—	0	5	5	-2	0.2
1994 Cle-A	0	0	—	1	0	0	0	0	4¹	9	0	1	1	20.8	10.38	48	.409	.435	0	—	0	-3	-3	-0	0.0
Total 2	2	3	.400	35	0	0	0	0	64	63	5	33	54	13.6	4.08	107	.253	.343	0	—	0	2	2	-2	0.2

YEAR	TM/L	W	L	PCT	G	GS	CG	SH	SV	IP	H	HR	BB	SO	RAT	ERA	ERA+	OAV	OOB	BH	AVG	PB	PR	/A	PD	TPI

● DAVID WEST
West, David Lee b: 9/1/64, Memphis, Tenn. BL/TL, 6'6", 230 lbs. Deb: 9/24/88

YEAR	TM/L	W	L	PCT	G	GS	CG	SH	SV	IP	H	HR	BB	SO	RAT	ERA	ERA+	OAV	OOB	BH	AVG	PB	PR	/A	PD	TPI
1988	NY-N	1	0	1.000	2	1	0	0	0	6	6	0	3	3	13.5	3.00	107	.273	.360	2	1.000	1	0	0	-0	0.2
1989	NY-N	0	2	.000	11	2	0	0	0	24¹	25	4	14	19	14.8	7.40	44	.260	.360	1	.200	0	-11	-11	-1	-0.9
	Min-A	3	2	.600	10	5	0	0	0	39¹	48	5	19	31	15.8	6.41	65	.306	.388	0	—	0	-11	-10	-1	-1.3
1990	Min-A	7	9	.438	29	27	2	0	0	146¹	142	21	78	92	13.8	5.10	81	.256	.352	0	—	0	-19	-15	-1	-2.0
1991	*Min-A	4	4	.500	15	12	0	0	0	71¹	66	13	28	52	12.0	4.54	94	.244	.317	0	—	0	-4	-2	0	-0.2
1992	Min-A	1	3	.250	9	3	0	0	0	28¹	32	3	20	19	16.8	6.99	58	.276	.387	0	—	0	-10	-9	-0	-1.2
1993	*Phi-N	6	4	.600	76	0	0	0	3	86¹	60	6	51	87	12.1	2.92	136	.194	.318	2	.400	1	11	10	-2	1.1
1994	Phi-N	4	10	.286	31	14	0	0	0	99	74	7	61	83	12.4	3.55	116	.205	.322	2	.071	-2	7	6	-2	0.4
Total	7	26	34	.433	183	64	2	0	3	501	453	59	274	386	13.3	4.63	88	.240	.341	7	.175	0	-36	-31	-6	-3.9

● FRANK WEST
West, Frank b: 1873, Wilmerding, Pa. 180 lbs. Deb: 7/11/1894

YEAR	TM/L	W	L	PCT	G	GS	CG	SH	SV	IP	H	HR	BB	SO	RAT	ERA	ERA+	OAV	OOB	BH	AVG	PB	PR	/A	PD	TPI
1894	Bos-N	0	0	—	1	0	0	0	0	3	5	0	2	1	21.0	9.00	63	.367	.448	0	.000	-0	-1	-1	-0	0.0

● HI WEST
West, James Hiram b: 8/8/1884, Roseville, Ill. d: 5/25/63, Los Angeles, Cal. BR/TR, 6', 185 lbs. Deb: 9/8/05

YEAR	TM/L	W	L	PCT	G	GS	CG	SH	SV	IP	H	HR	BB	SO	RAT	ERA	ERA+	OAV	OOB	BH	AVG	PB	PR	/A	PD	TPI
1905	Cle-A	2	2	.500	6	4	4	1	0	33	43	0	10	15	15.3	4.09	64	.316	.375	1	.077	-1	-5	-5	-2	-0.9
1911	Cle-A	3	4	.429	13	8	3	0	1	64²	84	1	18	17	14.6	3.76	91	.343	.395	3	.130	-2	-3	-2	-1	-0.5
Total	2	5	6	.455	19	12	7	1	1	97²	127	1	28	32	14.8	3.87	81	.333	.388	4	.111	-3	-8	-8	-3	-1.4

● LEFTY WEST
West, Weldon Edison b: 9/3/15, Gibsonville, N.C. d: 7/23/79, Hendersonville, N.C. BR/TL, 6', 165 lbs. Deb: 4/30/44

YEAR	TM/L	W	L	PCT	G	GS	CG	SH	SV	IP	H	HR	BB	SO	RAT	ERA	ERA+	OAV	OOB	BH	AVG	PB	PR	/A	PD	TPI
1944	StL-A	0	0	—	11	0	0	0	0	24¹	34	1	19	11	20.0	6.29	57	.366	.478	1	.143	-0	-8	-7	-0	-0.1
1945	StL-A	3	4	.429	24	8	1	0	0	74¹	71	2	31	38	12.3	3.63	97	.245	.318	2	.074	-3	-2	-1	-2	-0.5
Total	2	3	4	.429	35	8	1	0	0	98²	105	3	50	49	14.2	4.29	83	.274	.359	3	.088	-3	-10	-8	-2	-0.6

● HUYLER WESTERVELT
Westervelt, Huyler b: 10/1/1870, Piermont, N.Y. 5'9", 170 lbs. Deb: 4/21/1894

YEAR	TM/L	W	L	PCT	G	GS	CG	SH	SV	IP	H	HR	BB	SO	RAT	ERA	ERA+	OAV	OOB	BH	AVG	PB	PR	/A	PD	TPI
1894	NY-N	7	10	.412	23	18	11	1	0	141	170	4	76	35	16.0	5.04	104	.295	.382	8	.143	-5	4	3	0	-0.1

● MICKEY WESTON
Weston, Michael Lee b: 3/26/61, Flint, Mich. BR/TR, 6'1", 180 lbs. Deb: 6/18/89

YEAR	TM/L	W	L	PCT	G	GS	CG	SH	SV	IP	H	HR	BB	SO	RAT	ERA	ERA+	OAV	OOB	BH	AVG	PB	PR	/A	PD	TPI
1989	Bal-A	1	0	1.000	7	0	0	0	1	13	18	1	2	7	14.5	5.54	68	.346	.382	0	—	0	-2	-3	-0	-0.2
1990	Bal-A	0	1	.000	9	2	0	0	0	21	28	6	6	9	14.6	7.71	49	.322	.366	0	—	0	-9	-9	-0	-0.3
1991	Tor-A	0	0	—	2	0	0	0	0	2	1	0	1	1	9.0	0.00	—	.143	.250	0	—	0	1	1	-0	0.0
1992	Phi-N	0	1	.000	1	1	0	0	0	3²	7	1	1	0	22.1	12.27	28	.412	.474	0	.000	-0	-4	-4	-0	-0.7
1993	NY-N	0	0	—	4	0	0	0	0	5²	11	0	1	2	20.6	7.94	51	.393	.433	0	—	0	-2	-2	-0	0.0
Total	5	1	2	.333	23	3	0	0	1	45¹	65	8	11	19	15.7	7.15	53	.340	.385	0	.000	0	-16	-17	-1	-1.2

● JOHN WETTELAND
Wetteland, John Karl b: 8/21/66, San Mateo, Cal. BR/TR, 6'2", 195 lbs. Deb: 5/31/89

YEAR	TM/L	W	L	PCT	G	GS	CG	SH	SV	IP	H	HR	BB	SO	RAT	ERA	ERA+	OAV	OOB	BH	AVG	PB	PR	/A	PD	TPI
1989	LA-N	5	8	.385	31	12	0	0	1	102²	81	8	34	96	10.1	3.77	91	.218	.284	3	.143	-0	-3	-4	-1	-0.7
1990	LA-N	2	4	.333	22	5	0	0	0	43	44	6	17	36	13.6	4.81	76	.263	.346	1	.143	1	-5	-6	-1	-0.7
1991	LA-N	1	0	1.000	6	0	0	0	0	9	5	0	3	9	9.0	0.00	—	.161	.257	0	—	0	4	4	0	0.4
1992	Mon-N	4	4	.500	67	0	0	0	37	83¹	64	6	36	99	11.2	2.92	119	.213	.305	1	.200	0	5	5	-1	1.0
1993	Mon-N	9	3	.750	70	0	0	0	43	85¹	58	3	28	113	9.3	1.37	304	.188	.260	0	.000	-0	25	27	-1	**6.5**
1994	Mon-N	4	6	.400	52	0	0	0	25	63²	46	5	21	68	9.9	2.83	150	.202	.278	1	.250	-0	10	10	-1	2.2
Total	6	25	25	.500	248	17	0	0	106	387	298	28	139	421	10.5	2.93	128	.212	.289	6	.146	0	36	35	-5	8.7

● BUZZ WETZEL
Wetzel, Charles Edward b: 8/25/1894, Jay, Okla. d: 3/7/41, Globe, Ariz. BR/TR, 6'1", 162 lbs. Deb: 7/25/27

YEAR	TM/L	W	L	PCT	G	GS	CG	SH	SV	IP	H	HR	BB	SO	RAT	ERA	ERA+	OAV	OOB	BH	AVG	PB	PR	/A	PD	TPI
1927	Phi-A	0	0	—	2	1	0	0	0	4²	8	0	5	0	25.1	7.71	54	.400	.520	1	1.000	0	-2	-2	0	0.1

● SHORTY WETZEL
Wetzel, George William b: 1868, Philadelphia, Pa. d: 2/25/1899, Dayton, Ohio Deb: 8/26/1885

YEAR	TM/L	W	L	PCT	G	GS	CG	SH	SV	IP	H	HR	BB	SO	RAT	ERA	ERA+	OAV	OOB	BH	AVG	PB	PR	/A	PD	TPI
1885	Bal-a	0	2	.000	2	2	1	0	0	17	27	0	9	6	20.6	8.47	38	.333	.419	0	.000	-1	-10	-10	1	-0.8

● STEFAN WEVER
Wever, Stefan Matthew b: 4/22/58, Marburg, W.Germ BR/TR, 6'8", 245 lbs. Deb: 9/17/82

YEAR	TM/L	W	L	PCT	G	GS	CG	SH	SV	IP	H	HR	BB	SO	RAT	ERA	ERA+	OAV	OOB	BH	AVG	PB	PR	/A	PD	TPI
1982	NY-A	0	1	.000	1	1	0	0	0	2²	6	1	3	2	30.4	27.00	15	.429	.529	0	—	0	-7	-7	-0	-1.2

● GUS WEYHING
Weyhing, August "Cannonball" b: 9/29/1866, Louisville, Ky. d: 9/4/55, Louisville, Ky. BR/TR, 5'10", 145 lbs. Deb: 5/2/1887 F

YEAR	TM/L	W	L	PCT	G	GS	CG	SH	SV	IP	H	HR	BB	SO	RAT	ERA	ERA+	OAV	OOB	BH	AVG	PB	PR	/A	PD	TPI
1887	Phi-a	26	28	.481	55	55	53	2	0	466¹	465	12	167	193	12.9	4.27	101	.253	.328	42	.201	-9	2	1	-2	-0.8
1888	Phi-a	28	18	.609	47	47	45	3	0	404	314	4	111	204	10.4	2.25	133	.207	.279	40	.217	4	36	33	1	3.7
1889	Phi-a	30	21	.588	54	53	50	4	0	449	382	15	212	213	12.6	2.95	128	.223	.321	25	.131	-15	45	42	-3	2.1
1890	Bro-P	30	16	.652	49	46	38	3	0	390	419	10	179	177	14.2	3.60	124	.263	.343	27	.164	-6	27	37	-9	1.9
1891	Phi-a	31	20	.608	52	51	51	3	0	450	428	12	161	219	12.4	3.18	120	.242	.317	22	.111	-16	27	32	-5	1.0
1892	Phi-N	32	21	.604	59	49	46	6	**3**	469²	411	9	168	202	11.4	2.66	122	.226	.298	29	.136	-10	33	30	-9	1.1
1893	Phi-N	23	16	.590	42	40	33	2	0	345¹	399	11	145	101	14.7	4.74	96	.281	.350	22	.150	-3	-6	-2	-5	-1.5
1894	Phi-N	16	14	.533	38	34	25	2	1	266¹	365	12	116	81	16.8	5.81	88	.322	.393	20	.174	-9	-14	-21	-3	-2.5
1895	Phi-N	0	2	.000	2	2	0	0	0	9	23	0	13	3	36.0	20.00	24	.469	.580	0	.000	-1	-15	-15	0	-1.7
	Pit-N	1	0	1.000	1	1	1	0	0	9	10	0	5	3	15.0	1.00	452	.277	.365	1	.250	1	4	4	1	0.4
	Lou-N	7	19	.269	28	25	22	1	0	213	285	9	66	55	15.2	5.41	86	.316	.368	20	.225	-0	-15	-18	0	-1.6
	Yr	8	21	.276	31	28	23	1	0	231	318	9	84	61	16.0	5.81	80	.322	.380	21	.216	-1	-26	-30	1	-2.9
1896	Lou-N	2	3	.400	5	5	4	0	0	42	62	6	15	9	16.9	6.64	65	.340	.396	2	.133	-1	-11	-11	1	-0.9
1898	Was-N	15	26	.366	45	42	39	0	0	361	428	10	84	92	13.2	4.51	81	.292	.338	25	.177	-5	-36	-34	-2	-3.8
1899	Was-N	17	21	.447	43	38	34	2	0	334²	414	8	76	96	13.9	4.54	86	.303	.352	26	.206	-6	-26	-24	-6	-2.8
1900	StL-N	3	2	.600	7	5	3	0	0	46²	60	2	21	6	15.8	4.63	79	.311	.382	2	.095	-1	-5	-5	-1	-0.7
	Bro-N	3	4	.429	8	8	3	0	0	48	66	1	20	8	16.5	4.31	89	.326	.392	4	.222	-0	-3	-3	-1	-0.4
	Yr	6	6	.500	15	13	6	0	0	94²	126	3	41	14	16.1	4.47	84	.318	.384	6	.154	-3	-8	-8	-1	-1.1
1901	Cle-A	0	0	—	2	1	0	0	0	11¹	20	0	5	0	23.0	7.94	45	.379	.470	0	.000	-1	-5	-6	-0	-0.1
	Cin-N	0	1	.000	1	1	1	0	0	9	11	0	2	3	15.0	3.00	107	.299	.368	0	.000	-0	0	0	-0	-0.1
Total	14	264	232	.532	538	503	448	28	4	4324¹	4562	120	1566	1665	13.3	3.89	102	.264	.335	307	.166	-83	41	38	-39	-6.7

● JOHN WEYHING
Weyhing, John b: 6/24/1869, Louisville, Ky. d: 6/20/1890, Louisville, Ky. BL/TL, 6'2", 185 lbs. Deb: 7/13/1888 F

YEAR	TM/L	W	L	PCT	G	GS	CG	SH	SV	IP	H	HR	BB	SO	RAT	ERA	ERA+	OAV	OOB	BH	AVG	PB	PR	/A	PD	TPI
1888	Cin-a	3	4	.429	8	8	7	0	0	65²	52	0	17	30	9.6	1.23	257	.210	.263	3	.130	-2	13	14	-1	1.1
1889	Col-a	0	0	—	1	0	0	0	0	1	1	0	4	0	45.0	27.00	13	.252	.628	0	—	0	-3	-3	-0	0.0
Total	2	3	4	.429	9	8	7	0	0	66²	53	0	21	30	10.1	1.62	196	.210	.274	3	.130	-2	11	12	-1	1.1

● LEE WHEAT
Wheat, Leroy William b: 9/15/29, Edwardsville, Ill BR/TR, 6'4", 200 lbs. Deb: 4/21/54

YEAR	TM/L	W	L	PCT	G	GS	CG	SH	SV	IP	H	HR	BB	SO	RAT	ERA	ERA+	OAV	OOB	BH	AVG	PB	PR	/A	PD	TPI
1954	Phi-A	0	2	.000	8	1	0	0	0	28¹	38	1	9	7	15.2	5.72	68	.304	.356	1	.125	-0	-6	-6	-0	-0.4
1955	KC-A	0	0	—	3	0	0	0	0	2	8	1	3	1	49.5	22.50	19	.533	.611	0	—	0	-4	-4	0	0.0
Total	2	0	2	.000	11	1	0	0	0	30¹	46	2	12	8	17.5	6.82	57	.329	.386	1	.125	-0	-10	-10	-0	-0.4

● CHARLIE WHEATLEY
Wheatley, Charles b: 6/27/1893, Rosedale, Kan. d: 12/10/82, Tulsa, Okla. BR/TR, 5'11", 174 lbs. Deb: 9/6/12

YEAR	TM/L	W	L	PCT	G	GS	CG	SH	SV	IP	H	HR	BB	SO	RAT	ERA	ERA+	OAV	OOB	BH	AVG	PB	PR	/A	PD	TPI
1912	Det-A	1	4	.200	5	5	2	0	0	35	45	1	17	14	16.5	6.17	53	.331	.413	0	.000	-2	-11	-11	0	-1.4

● WOODY WHEATON
Wheaton, Elwood Pierce b: 10/3/14, Philadelphia, Pa. BL/TL, 5'8.5", 160 lbs. Deb: 9/28/43 ♦

YEAR	TM/L	W	L	PCT	G	GS	CG	SH	SV	IP	H	HR	BB	SO	RAT	ERA	ERA+	OAV	OOB	BH	AVG	PB	PR	/A	PD	TPI
1944	Phi-A	0	1	.000	11	1	0	0	0	38	36	1	20	15	13.5	3.55	98	.255	.352	11	.186	0	-1	-0	-1	-0.1

● RIP WHEELER
Wheeler, Floyd Clark b: 3/2/1898, Marion, Ky. d: 9/18/68, Marion, Ky. BR/TR, 6', 180 lbs. Deb: 9/30/21

YEAR	TM/L	W	L	PCT	G	GS	CG	SH	SV	IP	H	HR	BB	SO	RAT	ERA	ERA+	OAV	OOB	BH	AVG	PB	PR	/A	PD	TPI
1921	Pit-N	0	0	—	1	0	0	0	0	3	6	0	1	0	24.0	9.00	43	.500	.571	0	.000	-2	-2	-0	0	0.0
1922	Pit-N	0	0	—	1	0	0	0	0	1	1	0	2	0	27.0	0.00	—	.333	.600	0	0	0	0	0	0	0.0
1923	Chi-N	1	2	.333	3	3	1	0	0	24	28	2	5	5	13.5	4.88	82	.298	.353	1	.111	-1	-2	-2	1	-0.2

YEAR TM/L	W	L	PCT	G	GS	CG	SH	SV	IP	H	HR	BB	SO	RAT	ERA	ERA+	OAV	OOB	BH	AVG	PB	PR	/A	PD	TPI
1924 Chi-N	3	6	.333	29	4	0	0	0	101¹	103	8	21	16	11.0	3.91	100	.265	.303	7	.219	-1	-0	-0	0	-0.1
Total 4	4	8	.333	34	7	1	0	0	129¹	138	10	29	21	11.9	4.18	94	.278	.323	8	.190	-2	-4	-4	2	-0.3

● **GEORGE WHEELER** Wheeler, George L. (b: George L. Heroux) b: 8/3/1869, Methuen, Mass. d: 3/23/46, Santa Ana, Cal. BB/TB Deb: 9/18/1896

YEAR TM/L	W	L	PCT	G	GS	CG	SH	SV	IP	H	HR	BB	SO	RAT	ERA	ERA+	OAV	OOB	BH	AVG	PB	PR	/A	PD	TPI
1896 Phi-N	1	1	.500	3	2	2	0	0	16¹	18	0	5	2	13.8	3.86	112	.277	.348	1	.111	-1	1	1	0	0.0
1897 Phi-N	11	10	.524	26	19	17	0	0	191	229	3	62	35	13.9	3.96	106	.295	.349	16	.203	-1	8	5	1	0.4
1898 Phi-N	6	8	.429	15	13	10	0	0	112¹	155	1	36	20	15.8	4.17	82	.325	.379	8	.186	-1	-7	-9	3	-0.8
1899 Phi-N	3	1	.750	6	5	3	0	0	39	44	1	13	3	13.8	6.00	61	.284	.351	4	.235	1	-9	-10	0	-0.7
Total 4	21	20	.512	50	39	32	0	0	358²	446	5	116	60	14.5	4.24	92	.303	.359	29	.196	-2	-8	-13	4	-1.1

● **HARRY WHEELER** Wheeler, Harry Eugene b: 3/3/1858, Versailles, Ind. d: 10/9/1900, Cincinnati, Ohio BR/TR, 5'11", 165 lbs. Deb: 6/19/1878 M♦

YEAR TM/L	W	L	PCT	G	GS	CG	SH	SV	IP	H	HR	BB	SO	RAT	ERA	ERA+	OAV	OOB	BH	AVG	PB	PR	/A	PD	TPI
1878 Pro-N	6	1	.857	7	6	6	0	0	62	70	1	25	25	13.8	3.48	63	.275	.339	4	.148	-1	-8	-9	-2	-1.0
1879 Cin-N	0	1	.000	1	1	0	0	0	1	6	0	4	0	90.0	81.00	3	.667	.769	0	.000	-0	-9	-9	-0	-2.5
1882 Cin-a	1	2	.333	4	1	1	0	0	21²	21	0	12	10	13.7	5.40	49	.238	.329	86	.250	1	-7	-7	-0	-0.7
1883 Col-a	0	1	.000	1	1	0	0	0	5	13	0	2	0	27.0	7.20	43	.456	.492	84	.226	0	-2	-2	-0	-0.3
1884 KC-U	0	1	.000	1	1	1	0	0	8	7	0	6	6	7.9	1.13	199	.220	.220	16	.258	-0	1	1	0	0.1
Total 5	7	6	.538	14	10	8	0	0	97²	117	1	43	41	14.7	4.70	50	.283	.351	256	.228	-1	-24	-26	-2	-4.4

● **GARY WHEELOCK** Wheelock, Gary Richard b: 11/29/51, Bakersfield, Cal. BR/TR, 6'3", 205 lbs. Deb: 9/17/76

YEAR TM/L	W	L	PCT	G	GS	CG	SH	SV	IP	H	HR	BB	SO	RAT	ERA	ERA+	OAV	OOB	BH	AVG	PB	PR	/A	PD	TPI
1976 Cal-A	0	0	—	2	0	0	0	0	2	6	0	1	2	36.0	27.00	12	.500	.571	0	—	0	-5	-5	-0	-0.1
1977 Sea-A	6	9	.400	17	17	2	0	0	88¹	94	16	26	47	12.4	4.89	84	.268	.322	0	—	0	-8	-8	-1	-1.2
1980 Sea-A	0	0	—	1	1	0	0	0	3	4	0	1	1	15.0	6.00	69	.333	.385	0	—	0	-1	-1	0	0.0
Total 3	6	9	.400	20	18	2	0	0	93¹	104	16	28	50	13.0	5.40	76	.277	.333	0	—	0	-14	-14	-0	-1.2

● **JACK WHILLOCK** Whillock, Jack Franklin b: 11/4/42, Clinton, Ark. BR/TR, 6'3", 195 lbs. Deb: 8/29/71

YEAR TM/L	W	L	PCT	G	GS	CG	SH	SV	IP	H	HR	BB	SO	RAT	ERA	ERA+	OAV	OOB	BH	AVG	PB	PR	/A	PD	TPI
1971 Det-A	0	2	.000	7	0	0	0	1	8	10	0	2	6	13.5	5.63	64	.323	.364	0	.000	-0	-2	-2	0	-0.5

● **PAT WHITAKER** Whitaker, William H. b: 11/1864, St.Louis, Mo. d: 7/15/02, St.Louis, Mo. TR Deb: 10/11/1888

YEAR TM/L	W	L	PCT	G	GS	CG	SH	SV	IP	H	HR	BB	SO	RAT	ERA	ERA+	OAV	OOB	BH	AVG	PB	PR	/A	PD	TPI
1888 Bal-a	1	1	.500	2	2	2	0	0	14	13	0	6	6	13.5	5.14	58	.237	.335	0	.000	-1	-3	-3	2	-0.3
1889 Bal-a	1	0	1.000	1	1	1	0	0	9	10	0	4	1	14.0	2.00	197	.273	.344	1	.250	-0	2	2	0	0.2
Total 2	2	1	.667	3	3	3	0	0	23	23	0	10	6	13.7	3.91	86	.251	.338	1	.100	-1	-1	-1	2	-0.1

● **BILL WHITBY** Whitby, William Edward b: 7/29/43, Crewe, Va. BR/TR, 6'1", 190 lbs. Deb: 6/17/64

YEAR TM/L	W	L	PCT	G	GS	CG	SH	SV	IP	H	HR	BB	SO	RAT	ERA	ERA+	OAV	OOB	BH	AVG	PB	PR	/A	PD	TPI
1964 Min-A	0	0	—	4	0	0	0	0	6¹	8	3	1	2	12.8	8.53	42	.308	.333	0	.000	-1	-3	-3	-0	0.0

● **BOB WHITCHER** Whitcher, Robert Arthur b: 4/29/17, Berlin, N.H. BL/TL, 5'8", 165 lbs. Deb: 8/20/45

YEAR TM/L	W	L	PCT	G	GS	CG	SH	SV	IP	H	HR	BB	SO	RAT	ERA	ERA+	OAV	OOB	BH	AVG	PB	PR	/A	PD	TPI
1945 Bos-N	0	2	.000	6	3	0	0	0	15²	12	1	12	6	13.8	2.87	133	.235	.381	1	.333	0	2	2	-0	0.2

● **ABE WHITE** White, Adel b: 5/16/04, Winder, Ga. d: 10/1/78, Atlanta, Ga. BR/TL, 6', 185 lbs. Deb: 7/10/37

YEAR TM/L	W	L	PCT	G	GS	CG	SH	SV	IP	H	HR	BB	SO	RAT	ERA	ERA+	OAV	OOB	BH	AVG	PB	PR	/A	PD	TPI
1937 StL-N	0	1	.000	5	0	0	0	0	9¹	14	1	3	2	16.4	6.75	59	.341	.386	1	1.000	0	-3	-3	-0	-0.2

● **ERNIE WHITE** White, Ernest Daniel b: 9/5/16, Pacolet Mills, S.C. d: 5/22/74, Augusta, Ga. BR/TL, 5'11.5", 175 lbs. Deb: 5/9/40 C

YEAR TM/L	W	L	PCT	G	GS	CG	SH	SV	IP	H	HR	BB	SO	RAT	ERA	ERA+	OAV	OOB	BH	AVG	PB	PR	/A	PD	TPI
1940 StL-N	1	1	.500	8	1	0	0	0	21²	29	0	14	15	18.3	4.15	96	.315	.411	3	.429	1	-1	-0	1	0.1
1941 StL-N	17	7	.708	32	25	12	3	2	210	169	12	70	117	10.5	2.40	157	.217	.287	15	.190	0	29	32	-4	3.3
1942 *StL-N	7	5	.583	26	19	7	1	2	128¹	113	11	41	67	10.9	2.52	136	.232	.294	8	.195	0	11	13	-2	1.0
1943 *StL-N	5	5	.500	14	10	5	1	0	78²	78	4	33	28	12.8	3.78	89	.257	.332	6	.214	0	-3	-4	-1	-0.5
1946 Bos-N	0	1	.000	12	1	0	0	0	23²	22	1	8	8	12.9	4.18	82	.256	.347	1	.250	0	-2	-2	-1	-0.1
1947 Bos-N	0	0	—	1	1	0	0	0	4	1	0	1	1	4.5	0.00	—	.083	.154	1	1.000	0	2	2	0	0.0
1948 Bos-N	0	2	.000	15	0	0	0	2	23	13	0	17	8	11.7	1.96	196	.167	.316	0	.000	-0	5	5	-1	0.4
Total 7	30	21	.588	108	57	24	5	6	489¹	425	28	188	244	11.5	2.78	130	.231	.306	34	.209	2	41	45	-8	4.2

● **GABE WHITE** White, Gabriel Allen b: 11/20/71, Sebring, Fla. BL/TL, 6'2", 200 lbs. Deb: 5/27/94

YEAR TM/L	W	L	PCT	G	GS	CG	SH	SV	IP	H	HR	BB	SO	RAT	ERA	ERA+	OAV	OOB	BH	AVG	PB	PR	/A	PD	TPI
1994 Mon-N	1	1	.500	7	5	0	0	1	23²	24	4	11	17	13.7	6.08	70	.261	.346	0	.000	-0	-5	-5	-0	-0.5

● **DEKE WHITE** White, George Frederick b: 9/8/1872, Albany, N.Y. d: 11/5/57, Ilion, N.Y. BB/TL, Deb: 9/14/1895

YEAR TM/L	W	L	PCT	G	GS	CG	SH	SV	IP	H	HR	BB	SO	RAT	ERA	ERA+	OAV	OOB	BH	AVG	PB	PR	/A	PD	TPI
1895 Phi-N	1	0	1.000	3	1	1	0	1	17¹	17	1	13	6	16.6	9.87	49	.253	.389	1	.125	-1	-10	-10	-0	-0.6

● **DOC WHITE** White, Guy Harris b: 4/9/1879, Washington, D.C. d: 2/19/69, Silver Spring, Md. BL/TL, 6'1", 150 lbs. Deb: 4/22/01 ♦

YEAR TM/L	W	L	PCT	G	GS	CG	SH	SV	IP	H	HR	BB	SO	RAT	ERA	ERA+	OAV	OOB	BH	AVG	PB	PR	/A	PD	TPI
1901 Phi-N	14	13	.519	31	27	22	0	0	236²	241	2	56	132	11.8	3.19	106	.262	.314	27	.276	5	3	5	3	1.3
1902 Phi-N	16	20	.444	36	35	34	3	0	306	277	3	72	185	10.6	2.53	111	.242	.294	47	.263	4	9	10	2	2.0
1903 Chi-A	17	16	.515	37	36	29	3	0	300	258	4	69	114	10.2	2.13	132	.232	.285	20	.202	6	28	23	3	3.3
1904 Chi-A	16	12	.571	30	30	23	7	0	228	201	6	68	115	11.0	1.78	138	.238	.301	12	.158	0	21	17	1	2.4
1905 Chi-A	17	13	.567	36	33	25	4	0	260¹	204	2	58	120	9.4	1.76	140	.217	.269	15	.167	0	26	21	-0	2.4
1906 *Chi-A	18	6	.750	28	24	20	7	0	219¹	160	2	38	95	**8.3**	**1.52**	**167**	**.207**	**.249**	12	.185	4	29	25	2	3.6
1907 Chi-A	**27**	13	.675	46	35	24	6	1	291	270	3	38	141	9.7	2.26	106	.248	.277	20	.222	4	9	5	1	1.6
1908 Chi-A	18	13	.581	37	34	25	0	0	296	267	3	69	126	10.5	2.55	91	.244	.295	25	.229	4	-5	-8	7	0.4
1909 Chi-A	11	9	.550	24	21	14	3	0	177²	149	1	31	77	9.5	1.72	136	.226	.269	45	.234	6	15	12	-1	2.1
1910 Chi-A	15	13	.536	33	29	20	2	1	236²	219	2	50	111	10.7	2.66	90	.243	.291	25	.198	2	-4	-7	2	-0.3
1911 Chi-A	10	14	.417	34	29	16	4	2	214¹	219	2	35	72	11.0	2.98	108	.271	.309	20	.256	3	9	6	-1	0.8
1912 Chi-A	8	10	.444	32	19	9	1	0	172	172	1	47	57	13.0	3.24	99	.262	.325	7	.125	-1	-1	-1	-0	-0.3
1913 Chi-A	2	4	.333	19	8	2	0	0	103	106	2	39	39	13.1	3.50	84	.278	.353	3	.120	-1	-6	-7	2	-0.2
Total 13	189	156	.548	427	363	262	45	5	3041	2743	33	670	1384	10.5	2.39	112	.242	.292	278	.217	37	134	100	24	19.1

● **HAL WHITE** White, Harold George b: 3/18/19, Utica, N.Y. BR/TR, 5'10", 170 lbs. Deb: 4/22/41

YEAR TM/L	W	L	PCT	G	GS	CG	SH	SV	IP	H	HR	BB	SO	RAT	ERA	ERA+	OAV	OOB	BH	AVG	PB	PR	/A	PD	TPI
1941 Det-A	0	0	—	4	0	0	0	0	9	11	0	6	2	17.0	6.00	76	.306	.405	0	.000	-0	-2	-1	0	0.0
1942 Det-A	12	12	.500	34	25	12	4	1	216²	212	6	82	93	12.4	2.91	136	.252	.323	13	.169	-1	18	25	0	2.6
1943 Det-A	7	12	.368	32	24	7	2	2	177²	150	6	71	58	11.2	3.39	104	.228	.304	8	.140	-1	-2	3	0	-0.2
1946 Det-A	1	1	.500	11	1	1	0	0	27¹	34	5	15	12	16.1	5.60	65	.312	.395	0	.000	-1	-6	-6	1	-0.4
1947 Det-A	4	5	.444	35	5	0	0	2	84²	91	4	47	33	14.9	3.61	104	.279	.373	3	.167	0	1	1	1	0.3
1948 Det-A	2	1	.667	27	0	0	0	1	42²	46	2	26	17	15.4	6.12	71	.272	.372	2	.154	0	-9	-8	-1	-0.6
1949 Det-A	1	0	1.000	9	0	0	0	2	12	5	0	4	4	6.8	0.00	—	.125	.205	1	.333	0	6	6	1	0.7
1950 Det-A	9	6	.600	42	8	3	1	1	111	96	7	65	53	13.1	4.54	103	.239	.347	4	.121	-2	0	2	0	0.0
1951 Det-A	3	4	.429	38	6	1	0	0	76	74	7	49	23	14.8	4.74	88	.264	.378	4	.250	0	-5	-5	2	-0.3
1952 Det-A	1	8	.111	41	6	1	0	5	63¹	53	1	39	18	13.1	3.69	103	.237	.350	2	.182	0	1	1	2	0.2
1953 StL-A	0	0	—	10	0	0	0	0	10¹	8	1	3	2	10.5	2.61	161	.205	.279	0	.000	0	2	2	0	0.1
StL-N	6	5	.545	49	0	0	0	7	84²	84	5	39	32	13.1	2.98	143	.272	.353	0	.000	-2	12	11	1	1.5
1954 StL-N	0	0	—	5	0	0	0	0	4	4	1	2	2	28.8	19.80	21	.400	.533	0	—	0	-9	-9	-0	-0.6
Total 12	46	54	.460	336	67	23	7	25	920¹	875	47	450	349	13.1	3.78	106	.253	.342	37	.145	-7	8	23	6	4.3

● **DEACON WHITE** White, James Laurie b: 12/7/1847, Caton, N.Y. d: 7/7/39, Aurora, Ill. BL/TR, 5'11", 175 lbs. Deb: 5/4/1871 FM♦

YEAR TM/L	W	L	PCT	G	GS	CG	SH	SV	IP	H	HR	BB	SO	RAT	ERA	ERA+	OAV	OOB	BH	AVG	PB	PR	/A	PD	TPI
1876 Chi-N	0	0	—	1	0	0	0	0	2	1	0	3	0	4.5	0.00	—	.143	.143	104	.343	1	1	0	0	0.1
1890 Buf-P	0	0	—	1	0	0	0	0	8	18	0	2	0	22.5	9.00	46	.427	.453	114	.260	0	-4	-4	-0	0.0
Total 2	0	0	—	2	0	0	0	0	10	19	0	5	0	18.9	7.20	53	.387	.411	1619	.303	1	-4	-4	-0	0.1

● **LARRY WHITE** White, Larry David b: 9/25/58, San Fernando, Cal. BR/TR, 6'5", 190 lbs. Deb: 9/20/83

YEAR TM/L	W	L	PCT	G	GS	CG	SH	SV	IP	H	HR	BB	SO	RAT	ERA	ERA+	OAV	OOB	BH	AVG	PB	PR	/A	PD	TPI
1983 LA-N	0	0	—	4	0	0	0	0	7	4	0	3	5	9.0	1.29	279	.174	.269	0	—	0	2	2	0	0.0

YEAR TM/L	W	L	PCT	G	GS	CG	SH	SV	IP	H	HR	BB	SO	RAT	ERA	ERA+	OAV	OOB	BH	AVG	PB	PR	/A	PD	TPI
1984 LA-N	0	1	.000	7	1	0	0	0	12	9	2	6	10	11.3	3.00	118	.209	.306	0	.000	-0	1	1	-0	0.0
Total 2	0	1	.000	11	1	0	0	0	19	13	2	9	15	10.4	2.37	150	.197	.293	0	.000	-0	3	3	-0	0.0

● **KIRBY WHITE**   White, Oliver Kirby "Red" or "Buck" b: 1/3/1884, Hillsboro, Ohio d: 4/22/43, Hillsboro, Ohio BL/TR, 6', 190 lbs. Deb: 5/4/09

YEAR TM/L	W	L	PCT	G	GS	CG	SH	SV	IP	H	HR	BB	SO	RAT	ERA	ERA+	OAV	OOB	BH	AVG	PB	PR	/A	PD	TPI
1909 Bos-N	6	13	.316	23	19	11	1	0	148¹	134	5	80	53	13.0	3.22	88	.245	.343	8	.160	-1	-10	-6	-1	-1.0
1910 Bos-N	1	2	.333	3	3	3	0	0	26	15	2	12	6	10.4	1.38	240	.188	.316	2	.333	1	5	6	0	0.8
Pit-N	10	9	.526	30	21	7	3	2	153¹	142	2	75	42	13.0	3.46	90	.258	.352	12	.261	-3	-7	-6	-3	-0.7
Yr	11	11	.500	33	24	10	3	2	179¹	157	4	87	48	12.5	3.16	99	.248	.343	14	.269	4	-3	-1	-3	0.1
1911 Pit-N	0	1	.000	2	1	0	0	0	3	3	1	1	1	12.0	9.00	38	.250	.308	0	.000	-0	-2	-2	0	-0.5
Total 3	17	25	.405	58	44	21	4	2	330²	294	10	168	102	12.8	3.24	93	.247	.345	22	.214	3	-15	-9	-4	-1.4

● **RICK WHITE**   White, Richard Allen b: 12/23/68, Springfield, Ohio BR/TR, 6'4", 215 lbs. Deb: 4/6/94

YEAR TM/L	W	L	PCT	G	GS	CG	SH	SV	IP	H	HR	BB	SO	RAT	ERA	ERA+	OAV	OOB	BH	AVG	PB	PR	/A	PD	TPI
1994 Pit-N	4	5	.444	43	5	0	0	6	75¹	79	9	17	38	12.2	3.82	111	.280	.334	1	.077	-1	3	4	-1	0.3

● **STEVE WHITE**   White, Stephen Vincent b: 12/21/1884, Dorchester, Mass. d: 1/29/75, Braintree, Mass. BR/TR, 5'10", 160 lbs. Deb: 5/29/12

YEAR TM/L	W	L	PCT	G	GS	CG	SH	SV	IP	H	HR	BB	SO	RAT	ERA	ERA+	OAV	OOB	BH	AVG	PB	PR	/A	PD	TPI
1912 Was-A	0	0	—	1	0	0	0	0	0²	2	1	1	0	27.0	9.00	—	.667	.667	0	—	-0	0	0	-0	0.0
Bos-N	0	0	—	3	0	0	0	0	6	9	0	5	2	22.5	6.00	60	.429	.556	0	.000	-0	-2	-2	0	0.0
Total 1	0	0	—	4	0	0	0	0	6²	11	1	5	3	23.0	5.40	66	.458	.567	0	.000	-0	-1	-1	-0	0.0

● **BILL WHITE**   White, William Dighton b: 5/1/1860, Bridgeport, Ohio d: 12/29/24, Bellaire, Ohio TR, Deb: 5/3/1884 ♦

YEAR TM/L	W	L	PCT	G	GS	CG	SH	SV	IP	H	HR	BB	SO	RAT	ERA	ERA+	OAV	OOB	BH	AVG	PB	PR	/A	PD	TPI
1886 Lou-a	0	0	—	1	0	0	0	0	1	2	0	2	1	36.0	9.00	40	.400	.571	143	.257	0	-1	-1	0	0.0

● **WILL WHITE**   White, William Henry "Whoop-La" b: 10/11/1854, Caton, N.Y. d: 8/31/11, Port Carling, Ont., Canada BB/TR, 5'9.5", 175 lbs. Deb: 7/20/1877 FM

YEAR TM/L	W	L	PCT	G	GS	CG	SH	SV	IP	H	HR	BB	SO	RAT	ERA	ERA+	OAV	OOB	BH	AVG	PB	PR	/A	PD	TPI
1877 Bos-N	2	1	.667	3	3	3	1	0	27	27	0	2	7	9.7	3.00	94	.243	.257	3	.200	-1	-1	-1	-1	-0.2
1878 Cin-N	30	21	.588	52	52	52	5	0	468	477	1	45	169	10.0	1.79	119	.252	.269	28	.142	-8	27	18	-2	0.7
1879 Cin-N	43	31	.581	76	75	75	4	0	680	676	10	68	232	9.8	1.99	117	.238	.256	40	.136	-17	38	26	-7	0.2
1880 Cin-N	18	42	.300	62	62	58	3	0	517¹	550	9	56	161	10.5	2.14	116	.255	.273	35	.169	-9	13	20	-7	0.5
1881 Det-N	0	2	.000	2	2	2	0	0	18	24	1	2	5	13.0	5.00	58	.296	.313	0	.000	-1	-4	-4	-1	-0.5
1882 Cin-a	40	12	.769	54	54	52	8	0	480	411	3	71	122	9.0	1.54	172	.216	.244	55	.266	6	61	59	13	7.3
1883 Cin-a	43	22	.662	65	64	64	6	0	577	473	16	104	141	9.0	2.09	155	.209	.244	54	.225	3	78	74	-3	6.6
1884 Cin-a	34	18	.654	52	52	52	7	0	456	479	16	74	118	11.6	3.32	101	.255	.296	35	.190	-2	-3	1	-6	-0.8
1885 Cin-a	18	15	.545	34	34	33	2	0	293¹	295	9	64	80	11.8	3.53	92	.255	.309	20	.169	-3	-9	-9	-3	-1.4
1886 Cin-a	1	2	.333	3	3	3	0	0	26	28	1	10	6	15.2	4.15	85	.280	.379	1	.111	-1	-2	-2	-0	-0.2
Total 10	229	166	.580	403	401	394	36	0	3542²	3440	65	496	1041	10.2	2.28	120	.239	.268	271	.183	-33	198	179	-17	12.2

● **JOHN WHITEHEAD**   Whitehead, John Henderson "Silent John" b: 4/27/09, Coleman, Tex. d: 10/20/64, Bonham, Tex. BR/TR, 6'2", 195 lbs. Deb: 4/19/35

YEAR TM/L	W	L	PCT	G	GS	CG	SH	SV	IP	H	HR	BB	SO	RAT	ERA	ERA+	OAV	OOB	BH	AVG	PB	PR	/A	PD	TPI
1935 Chi-A	13	13	.500	28	27	18	1	0	222¹	209	17	101	72	12.6	3.72	124	.250	.332	12	.146	-5	18	22	3	2.0
1936 Chi-A	13	13	.500	34	32	15	1	1	230²	254	9	98	70	13.9	4.64	112	.276	.349	21	.241	1	10	14	3	1.7
1937 Chi-A	11	8	.579	26	24	8	4	0	165¹	191	14	56	45	13.7	4.07	113	.294	.354	13	.224	1	10	10	-1	0.9
1938 Chi-A	10	11	.476	32	24	10	2	0	183¹	218	12	80	38	14.8	4.76	103	.299	.370	6	.100	-4	1	3	-1	-0.1
1939 Chi-A	0	3	.000	7	4	0	0	0	32	60	4	5	9	18.3	8.16	58	.408	.428	0	.000	-1	-13	-12	0	-1.0
StL-A	1	3	.250	26	4	0	0	1	66	88	10	17	9	14.6	5.86	83	.321	.365	1	.059	-1	-9	-7	1	-0.4
Yr	1	6	.143	33	8	0	0	1	98	148	14	22	18	15.8	6.61	73	.352	.387	1	.038	-3	-22	-20	1	-1.4
1940 StL-A	1	3	.250	15	4	1	1	0	40	46	3	14	11	13.5	5.40	85	.286	.343	2	.167	-1	-5	-4	-1	-0.4
1942 StL-A	0	0	—	4	0	0	0	0	4	8	0	1	0	22.5	6.75	55	.421	.476	0	—	0	-1	-1	0	0.0
Total 7	49	54	.476	172	119	52	9	4	944	1074	69	372	254	14.0	4.60	105	.287	.355	55	.169	-11	11	24	5	2.7

● **MILT WHITEHEAD**   Whitehead, Milton P. b: 1862, Canada d: 8/15/01, Highland, Cal. BB, Deb: 4/20/1884 ♦

YEAR TM/L	W	L	PCT	G	GS	CG	SH	SV	IP	H	HR	BB	SO	RAT	ERA	ERA+	OAV	OOB	BH	AVG	PB	PR	/A	PD	TPI
1884 StL-U	0	1	.000	1	1	0	0	0	8	12	0	2	2	18.0	9.00	27	.360	.391	83	.211	-0	-6	-6	0	-0.5

● **EARL WHITEHILL**   Whitehill, Earl Oliver b: 2/7/1900, Cedar Rapids, Iowa d: 10/22/54, Omaha, Neb. BL/TL, 5'9.5", 174 lbs. Deb: 9/15/23 C

YEAR TM/L	W	L	PCT	G	GS	CG	SH	SV	IP	H	HR	BB	SO	RAT	ERA	ERA+	OAV	OOB	BH	AVG	PB	PR	/A	PD	TPI
1923 Det-A	2	0	1.000	8	3	1	0	0	33	22	2	15	19	10.9	2.73	142	.188	.296	4	.364	1	5	4	-0	0.3
1924 Det-A	17	9	.654	35	32	16	2	0	233	260	8	79	65	13.6	3.86	106	.288	.353	19	.213	1	10	6	-0	0.7
1925 Det-A	11	11	.500	35	33	15	1	2	239¹	267	13	88	83	13.7	4.66	92	.293	.361	19	.218	0	-7	-9	-1	-0.8
1926 Det-A	16	13	.552	36	34	13	0	0	252¹	271	7	79	109	12.8	3.99	102	.277	.336	23	.253	4	1	2	-1	0.5
1927 Det-A	16	14	.533	41	31	17	3	3	236	238	4	105	95	13.4	3.36	125	.267	.350	16	.205	-0	21	22	-3	2.3
1928 Det-A	11	16	.407	31	30	12	1	0	196¹	214	8	78	93	13.4	4.31	95	.277	.344	13	.194	-1	-6	-4	1	-0.6
1929 Det-A	14	15	.483	38	28	18	1	1	245¹	267	16	96	103	13.4	4.62	93	.280	.348	23	.256	5	-10	-9	-0	-0.5
1930 Det-A	17	13	.567	34	31	16	0	1	220²	248	8	80	109	13.7	4.24	113	.285	.351	16	.193	-4	10	14	-2	1.0
1931 Det-A	13	16	.448	34	34	22	0	0	271¹	287	22	118	81	13.6	4.08	112	.274	.351	15	.155	-5	9	15	2	1.1
1932 Det-A	16	12	.571	33	31	17	3	0	244	255	17	93	81	13.0	4.54	104	.269	.337	22	.244	1	-2	-5	-2	0.4
1933 *Was-A	22	8	.733	39	37	19	2	1	270	271	9	100	96	12.5	3.33	125	.262	.329	24	.222	2	28	25	-2	2.5
1934 Was-A	14	11	.560	32	31	15	0	0	235	269	10	94	96	14.0	4.52	96	.290	.357	17	.200	4	-1	-5	-0	-0.2
1935 Was-A	14	11	.519	34	34	19	1	0	279¹	318	16	104	102	13.8	4.29	101	.289	.354	19	.183	-1	5	1	1	0.1
1936 Was-A	14	11	.560	28	28	14	0	0	212¹	252	17	89	63	14.6	4.87	98	.294	.362	13	.169	-0	4	-2	-1	-0.3
1937 Cle-A	8	8	.500	33	22	6	1	2	147	189	14	80	53	16.8	6.49	71	.322	.409	11	.224	1	-31	-31	1	-2.5
1938 Cle-A	9	8	.529	26	23	6	0	0	160¹	187	18	83	60	15.7	5.56	83	.289	.378	7	.125	-2	-14	-16	-2	-1.6
1939 Chi-N	4	7	.364	24	11	2	1	1	89¹	102	8	50	42	15.8	5.14	77	.292	.389	3	.103	-2	-12	-12	-1	-1.6
Total 17	218	185	.541	541	473	226	16	11	3564²	3917	192	1431	1350	13.8	4.36	100	.282	.353	264	.204	4	10	6	-9	0.8

● **CHARLIE WHITEHOUSE**   Whitehouse, Charles Evis "Lefty" b: 1/25/1894, Charleston, Ill. d: 7/19/60, Indianapolis, Ind BB/TL, 6', 152 lbs. Deb: 8/29/14

YEAR TM/L	W	L	PCT	G	GS	CG	SH	SV	IP	H	HR	BB	SO	RAT	ERA	ERA+	OAV	OOB	BH	AVG	PB	PR	/A	PD	TPI
1914 Ind-F	2	0	1.000	8	2	2	0	0	26	34	0	5	10	13.8	4.85	64	.324	.360	0	.000	-1	-6	-5	-0	-0.5
1915 New-F	2	2	.500	11	3	1	0	0	39²	46	0	17	18	15.4	4.31	59	.299	.386	0	.000	-1	-7	-8	-1	-0.9
1919 Was-A	0	1	.000	6	1	0	0	0	12	13	1	6	5	14.3	4.50	71	.283	.365	0	.000	-0	-2	-2	-0	-0.2
Total 3	4	3	.571	25	6	3	0	0	77²	93	1	28	33	14.7	4.52	63	.305	.375	0	.000	-1	-14	-14	-1	-1.6

● **GIL WHITEHOUSE**   Whitehouse, Gilbert Arthur b: 10/15/1893, Somerville, Mass. d: 2/14/26, Brewer, Me. BB/TR, 5'10", 170 lbs. Deb: 6/20/12 ♦

YEAR TM/L	W	L	PCT	G	GS	CG	SH	SV	IP	H	HR	BB	SO	RAT	ERA	ERA+	OAV	OOB	BH	AVG	PB	PR	/A	PD	TPI
1915 New-F	0	0	—	1	0	0	0	0	1	0	0	1	0	9.0	0.00	—	.000	.250	27	.225	0	0	-0	-0	0.0

● **LEN WHITEHOUSE**   Whitehouse, Leonard Joseph b: 9/10/57, Burlington, Vt. BL/TL, 5'11", 175 lbs. Deb: 9/1/81

YEAR TM/L	W	L	PCT	G	GS	CG	SH	SV	IP	H	HR	BB	SO	RAT	ERA	ERA+	OAV	OOB	BH	AVG	PB	PR	/A	PD	TPI
1981 Tex-A	0	1	.000	2	1	0	0	0	3¹	8	1	2	2	27.0	16.20	21	.500	.556	0	—	0	-5	-5	-0	-0.9
1983 Min-A	7	1	.875	60	0	0	0	0	73²	70	6	44	44	14.2	4.15	102	.261	.369	0	—	0	-1	1	-1	-0.3
1984 Min-A	2	2	.500	30	0	0	0	1	31¹	29	3	17	18	13.8	3.16	133	.254	.361	0	—	0	3	4	-0	0.2
1985 Min-A	0	0	—	5	0	0	0	0	7¹	12	4	2	4	17.2	11.05	40	.353	.389	0	—	0	-6	-5	-0	-0.5
Total 4	9	4	.692	97	1	0	0	1	115²	119	14	65	68	14.6	4.67	90	.275	.375	0	—	0	-6	-6	-1	-1.5

● **WALLY WHITEHURST**   Whitehurst, Walter Richard b: 4/11/64, Shreveport, La. BR/TR, 6'3", 180 lbs. Deb: 7/17/89

YEAR TM/L	W	L	PCT	G	GS	CG	SH	SV	IP	H	HR	BB	SO	RAT	ERA	ERA+	OAV	OOB	BH	AVG	PB	PR	/A	PD	TPI
1989 NY-N	0	1	.000	9	1	0	0	0	14	17	2	5	9	14.1	4.50	73	.293	.349	0	.000	0	-2	-2	-0	-0.1
1990 NY-N	1	0	1.000	38	0	0	0	0	65²	63	5	9	46	9.9	3.29	114	.251	.277	2	.250	0	4	3	0	0.1
1991 NY-N	7	12	.368	36	20	0	0	1	133¹	142	12	25	87	11.5	4.18	87	.274	.313	6	.182	1	-7	-8	1	-0.8
1992 NY-N	3	9	.250	44	11	0	0	0	97	99	4	33	70	12.6	3.62	96	.264	.330	4	.182	1	-1	-2	-1	-0.1
1993 SD-N	4	7	.364	21	19	0	0	0	105²	109	11	30	57	12.1	3.83	108	.276	.332	2	.083	-2	2	4	0	0.2
1994 SD-N	4	7	.364	13	13	0	0	0	64	84	8	26	43	15.6	4.92	85	.319	.383	2	.105	-0	-5	-5	0	-0.8
Total 6	19	36	.345	161	64	0	0	3	479²	514	42	128	312	12.3	3.98	95	.276	.327	16	.150	1	-9	-10	2	-1.5

YEAR TM/L	W	L	PCT	G	GS	CG	SH	SV	IP	H	HR	BB	SO	RAT	ERA	ERA+	OAV	OOB	BH	AVG	PB	PR	/A	PD	TPI
● **MATT WHITESIDE** Whiteside, Matthew Christopher b: 8/8/67, Charleston, Mo. BR/TR, 6', 185 lbs. Deb: 8/5/92
1992 Tex-A	1	1	.500	20	0	0	0	4	28	26	1	11	13	11.9	1.93	197	.245	.316	0	—	0	6	6	-0	0.8
1993 Tex-A	2	1	.667	60	0	0	0	1	73	78	7	23	39	12.6	4.32	96	.281	.338	0	—	0	0	-1	-1	0.2
1994 Tex-A	2	2	.500	47	0	0	0	1	61	68	6	28	37	14.3	5.02	90	.286	.363	0	—	0	-1	-3	0	0.2
Total 3	5	4	.556	127	0	0	0	6	162	172	14	62	89	13.1	4.17	102	.277	.344	0	—	0	5	1	-1	1.2
● **JESSE WHITING** Whiting, Jesse W. b: 5/30/1879, Philadelphia, Pa. d: 10/28/37, Philadelphia, Pa. Deb: 9/27/02
1902 Phi-N	0	1	.000	1	1	1	0	0	9	13	0	6	0	19.0	5.00	56	.337	.426	1	.333	0	-2	-2	0	-0.2
1906 Bro-N	1	1	.500	3	2	2	1	0	24²	26	0	6	7	12.0	2.92	86	.286	.337	3	.300	1	-1	-1	1	0.1
1907 Bro-N	0	0	—	1	0	0	0	0	3	3	0	3	2	18.0	12.00	20	.273	.429	0	.000	-0	-3	-3	0	0.0
Total 3	1	2	.333	5	3	3	1	0	36²	42	0	15	9	14.2	4.17	62	.299	.370	4	.267	0	-6	-6	1	-0.1
● **ART WHITNEY** Whitney, Arthur Wilson b: 1/16/1858, Brockton, Mass. d: 8/15/43, Lowell, Mass. BR/TR, 5'8", 155 lbs. Deb: 5/1/1880 F♦
1882 Det-N	0	1	.000	3	2	1	0	0	18	31	1	8	11	19.5	6.00	49	.373	.429	21	.183	-1	-6	-6	-1	-0.3
1886 Pit-a	0	0	—	1	0	0	0	0	6	7	0	3	2	15.0	3.00	113	.304	.385	122	.239	0	0	0	-0	0.0
1889 *NY-N	0	1	.000	1	0	0	0	0	6	7	0	3	3	15.0	3.00	131	.283	.360	103	.218	0	1	1	-0	0.1
Total 3	0	2	.000	5	2	1	0	0	30	45	1	14	16	17.7	4.80	67	.344	.408	820	.223	-1	-5	-5	-1	-0.2
● **JIM WHITNEY** Whitney, James Evans "Grasshopper Jim" b: 11/10/1857, Conklin, N.Y. d: 5/21/1891, Binghamton, N.Y. BL/TR, 6'2", 172 lbs. Deb: 5/2/1881 ♦
1881 Bos-N	31	33	.484	66	63	57	6	0	552¹	548	6	90	162	10.4	2.48	107	.248	.277	72	.255	11	18	11	-4	1.9
1882 Bos-N	24	21	.533	49	48	46	3	0	420	404	3	41	180	9.5	2.64	109	.237	.255	81	.323	23	12	11	1	3.1
1883 Bos-N	37	21	.638	62	56	54	1	2	514	492	7	35	345	9.2	2.24	138	.238	.251	115	.281	20	51	49	0	6.0
1884 Bos-N	23	14	.622	38	37	35	6	0	336	272	12	27	270	8.0	2.09	138	.207	.223	70	.259	10	33	30	4	4.0
1885 Bos-N	18	32	.360	51	50	50	2	0	441¹	503	14	37	200	11.0	2.98	90	.272	.286	68	.234	7	-8	-14	6	-0.2
1886 KC-N	12	32	.273	46	44	42	3	0	393	465	9	55	167	11.9	4.49	84	.284	.308	59	.239	5	-51	-31	6	-1.7
1887 Was-N	24	21	.533	47	47	46	2	0	404²	430	16	42	146	10.9	3.22	126	.259	.284	53	.264	9	38	38	4	4.7
1888 Was-N	18	21	.462	39	39	37	2	0	325	317	7	54	79	10.5	3.05	92	.245	.280	24	.170	-1	-7	-9	-1	-1.1
1889 Ind-N	2	7	.222	9	8	7	0	0	70	106	4	19	16	16.3	6.81	61	.338	.380	12	.375	5	-22	-21	-1	-1.5
1890 Phi-a	2	2	.500	6	4	3	0	0	40	61	1	11	6	16.4	5.17	74	.340	.381	5	.238	-0	-6	-6	-0	-0.5
Total 10	191	204	.484	413	396	377	25	2	3496³	3598	79	411	1571	10.4	2.97	105	.253	.275	559	.261	89	60	55	15	14.7
● **BILL WHITROCK** Whitrock, William Franklin b: 3/4/1870, Cincinnati, Ohio d: 7/26/35, Derby, Conn. TR, 5'7.5", 170 lbs. Deb: 5/3/1890
1890 StL-a	5	6	.455	16	11	10	0	1	105	104	2	40	39	12.9	3.51	123	.251	.327	7	.146	-3	4	9	0	0.6
1893 Lou-N	2	5	.286	8	8	5	0	0	46²	64	3	18	8	16.6	8.10	54	.317	.384	7	.280	1	-18	-19	0	-1.8
1894 Lou-N	0	1	.000	1	1	0	0	0	4	8	0	2	0	22.5	9.00	57	.410	.465	0	.000	-0	-2	-2	-0	-0.3
Cin-N	2	6	.250	10	8	8	0	0	70¹	110	7	39	9	20.2	6.65	84	.352	.438	13	.217	-2	-10	-9	0	-0.8
Yr	2	7	.222	11	9	8	0	0	74¹	118	7	41	9	20.3	6.78	82	.355	.440	13	.210	-3	-12	-10	0	-1.1
1896 Phi-N	0	1	.000	2	1	1	0	0	9	10	0	3	1	13.0	3.00	144	.303	.335	0	.000	-0	1	1	0	0.1
Total 4	9	19	.321	37	29	24	0	1	235	296	12	102	57	16.0	5.44	87	.301	.378	27	.196	-5	-24	-18	0	-2.2
● **ED WHITSON** Whitson, Eddie Lee b: 5/19/55, Johnson City, Tenn. BR/TR, 6'3", 195 lbs. Deb: 9/4/77
1977 Pit-N	1	0	1.000	5	0	0	0	0	15²	11	0	9	10	11.5	3.45	116	.204	.317	0	.000	-0	1	1	-0	0.0
1978 Pit-N	5	6	.455	43	0	0	0	4	74¹	66	5	37	64	12.7	3.27	113	.243	.338	2	.182	-0	3	4	-1	0.5
1979 Pit-N	2	3	.400	19	7	0	0	1	57²	53	6	36	31	14.0	4.37	89	.238	.346	0	.000	-1	-4	-3	-1	-0.4
SF-N	5	8	.385	18	17	2	0	0	100¹	98	5	39	62	12.6	3.95	89	.254	.329	5	.156	-1	-2	-5	-0	-0.7
Yr	7	11	.389	37	24	2	0	1	158	151	11	75	93	13.1	4.10	89	.248	.334	5	.111	-2	-6	-8	-1	-1.1
1980 SF-N☆	11	13	.458	34	34	6	2	0	211²	222	7	56	90	12.0	3.10	114	.271	.321	6	.091	-4	12	10	-2	0.5
1981 SF-N	6	9	.400	22	22	2	1	0	123	130	10	47	65	13.1	4.02	85	.273	.340	3	.091	-1	-7	-8	-2	-1.2
1982 Cle-A	4	2	.667	40	9	1	1	2	107²	91	6	58	61	12.5	3.26	125	.231	.330	0	—	0	10	10	-2	0.4
1983 SD-N	5	7	.417	31	21	2	0	1	144¹	143	6	50	81	12.1	4.30	81	.256	.318	8	.182	1	-11	-13	-4	-1.3
1984 *SD-N	14	8	.636	31	31	1	0	0	189	181	16	42	103	10.8	3.24	110	.255	.299	3	.049	-5	7	7	1	0.4
1985 NY-A	10	8	.556	30	30	2	2	0	158²	201	19	43	89	14.0	4.88	83	.309	.354	0	—	0	-13	-15	-2	-1.5
1986 NY-A	5	2	.714	14	4	0	0	0	37	54	5	23	27	18.7	7.54	54	.335	.418	0	—	0	-14	-14	-0	-2.1
SD-N	1	7	.125	17	12	0	0	0	75²	85	8	37	46	14.5	5.59	65	.287	.366	3	.167	1	-16	-16	-0	-1.5
1987 SD-N	10	13	.435	36	36	3	1	0	205²	197	36	64	135	11.6	4.73	84	.251	.310	8	.123	-1	-15	-18	-2	-2.1
1988 SD-N	13	11	.542	34	33	0	0	0	205¹	202	17	45	118	10.9	3.77	90	.259	.301	11	.167	1	-7	-9	-1	-0.9
1989 SD-N	16	11	.593	33	33	5	1	0	227	198	22	48	117	10.0	2.66	132	.235	.281	10	.139	1	21	21	-2	2.4
1990 SD-N	14	9	.609	32	32	6	3	0	228²	215	13	47	127	10.4	2.60	147	.251	.291	10	.149	1	30	31	3	3.4
1991 SD-N	4	6	.400	13	12	2	0	0	78²	93	13	17	40	12.6	5.03	75	.299	.335	3	.125	-1	-12	-11	-1	-1.3
Total 15	126	123	.506	452	333	35	12	8	2240¹	2240	211	698	1266	11.9	3.79	97	.261	.319	72	.125	-11	-17	-28	-14	-5.4
● **WALT WHITTAKER** Whittaker, Walter Elton "Doc" b: 6/11/1894, Chelsea, Mass. d: 8/9/65, Pembroke, Mass. BL/TR, 5'9.5", 165 lbs. Deb: 7/6/16
1916 Phi-A	0	0	—	1	0	0	0	0	2	3	0	2	0	22.5	4.50	63	.375	.500	0	—	0	-0	-0	0	0.0
● **KEVIN WICKANDER** Wickander, Kevin Dean b: 1/4/65, Fort Dodge, Iowa BL/TL, 6'2", 202 lbs. Deb: 8/10/89
1989 Cle-A	0	0	—	2	0	0	0	0	2²	6	0	2	0	27.0	3.38	117	.462	.533	0	—	0	0	0	-0	-0.1
1990 Cle-A	0	1	.000	10	0	0	0	0	12¹	14	0	4	10	13.9	3.65	107	.304	.373	0	—	0	0	0	0	0.0
1992 Cle-A	2	0	1.000	44	0	0	0	1	41	39	1	28	38	15.6	3.07	127	.258	.388	0	—	0	4	4	0	0.3
1993 Cle-A	0	0	—	11	0	0	0	0	8²	15	3	3	3	18.7	4.15	104	.366	.409	0	—	0	0	0	-0	-0.1
Cin-N	1	0	1.000	33	0	0	0	0	25¹	32	5	19	20	18.8	6.75	60	.308	.424	0	.000	-0	-8	-8	-0	-0.3
Total 5	3	1	.750	100	0	0	0	1	90	106	9	56	71	16.9	4.30	88	.299	.404	0	.000	-0	-3	-3	-1	-0.1
● **KEMP WICKER** Wicker, Kemp Caswell (b: Kemp Caswell Whicker) b: 8/13/06, Kernersville, N.C. d: 6/11/73, Kernersville, N.C BR/TL, 5'11", 182 lbs. Deb: 8/14/36
1936 NY-A	1	2	.333	7	0	0	0	0	20	31	2	11	5	18.9	7.65	61	.356	.429	1	.143	-0	-6	-7	0	-0.8
1937 *NY-A	7	3	.700	16	10	6	1	0	88	107	8	26	14	13.6	4.40	101	.296	.343	4	.114	-3	2	0	-2	-0.4
1938 NY-A	1	0	1.000	1	0	0	0	0	1	0	0	1	0	9.00	.000	.250	0	—	0	1	1	-0	0.5
1941 Bro-N	1	2	.333	16	2	0	0	1	32	30	3	14	8	12.4	3.66	100	.252	.331	1	.250	1	-0	-0	-0	0.0
Total 4	10	7	.588	40	12	6	1	1	141	168	13	52	27	14.0	4.66	92	.294	.353	6	.130	-2	-3	-5	-2	-0.7
● **BOB WICKER** Wicker, Robert Kitridge b: 5/24/1878, Bedford, Ind. d: 1/22/55, Evanston, Ill. BR/TR, 6'2", 180 lbs. Deb: 8/11/01
1901 StL-N	0	0	—	1	0	0	0	0	3	4	0	1	2	15.0	0.00	—	.317	.368	1	.333	0	1	1	-0	0.0
1902 StL-N	5	12	.294	22	16	14	1	0	152¹	159	1	45	78	12.2	3.19	86	.269	.322	18	.234	1	-7	-8	3	-0.4
1903 StL-N	0	0	—	2	0	0	0	0	5	6	0	3	2	12.6	0.00	—	.174	.269	0	.000	-0	2	2	1	0.0
Chi-N	20	9	.690	32	27	24	1	1	247	236	3	74	110	11.4	3.02	104	.253	.311	24	.245	6	7	3	-5	0.4
Yr	20	9	.690	33	27	24	1	1	252	240	3	77	113	11.4	2.96	106	.252	.309	24	.240	6	9	5	-4	0.4
1904 Chi-N	17	9	.654	30	27	23	4	0	229	201	6	58	99	10.3	2.67	100	.232	.282	34	.219	1	22	20	-5	1.4
1905 Chi-N	13	6	.684	22	22	17	4	0	178	139	4	47	86	9.5	2.02	147	.221	.276	10	.139	-2	19	19	-3	1.4
1906 Chi-N	3	5	.375	10	8	5	0	0	72¹	70	1	19	25	11.1	2.99	88	.257	.306	2	.100	-1	-3	-3	-1	-0.5
Cin-N	6	11	.353	20	17	14	0	0	150	150	3	46	69	11.8	2.70	102	.263	.319	9	.180	2	-1	-1	-4	-0.1
Yr	9	16	.360	30	25	19	0	0	222¹	220	3	65	94	11.6	2.79	97	.261	.315	11	.157	1	-4	-4	-5	-0.1
Total 6	64	52	.552	138	117	97	10	1	1036²	963	16	293	472	11.0	2.73	105	.247	.301	98	.205	6	20	16	-15	0.3
● **DAVE WICKERSHAM** Wickersham, David Clifford b: 9/27/35, Erie, Pa. BR/TR, 6'3", 190 lbs. Deb: 9/18/60
1960 KC-A	0	0	—	5	0	0	0	2	8¹	4	0	1	3	5.4	1.08	369	.148	.179	0	.000	-0	3	3	0	0.1

YEAR TM/L	W	L	PCT	G	GS	CG	SH	SV	IP	H	HR	BB	SO	RAT	ERA	ERA+	OAV	OOB	BH	AVG	PB	PR	/A	PD	TPI
1961 KC-A	2	1	.667	17	0	0	0	2	21	25	0	5	10	13.7	5.14	81	.309	.364	2	.667	1	-3	-2	0	-0.2
1962 KC-A	11	4	.733	30	9	3	0	1	110	105	13	43	61	12.8	4.17	101	.257	.340	2	.057	-3	-2	1	1	-0.1
1963 KC-A	12	15	.444	38	34	4	1	1	237^2	244	21	79	118	12.6	4.09	95	.268	.333	11	.138	-3	-12	-5	1	-0.8
1964 Det-A	19	12	.613	40	36	11	1	1	254	224	28	81	164	11.2	3.44	106	.232	.299	5	.073	-5	5	6	-0	0.1
1965 Det-A	9	14	.391	34	27	8	3	0	195^1	179	12	61	109	11.6	3.78	92	.241	.308	4	.069	-4	-7	-7	1	-1.0
1966 Det-A	8	3	.727	38	14	3	0	1	140^2	139	14	54	93	12.9	3.20	109	.261	.338	2	.044	-3	4	4	1	0.1
1967 Det-A	4	5	.444	36	4	0	0	4	85^1	72	6	33	44	11.5	2.74	119	.235	.318	0	.000	-2	5	5	1	0.5
1968 Pit-N	1	0	1.000	11	0	0	0	1	20^2	21	0	13	9	14.8	3.48	84	.276	.382	1	.333		-1	-1	-0	-0.1
1969 KC-A	2	3	.400	34	0	0	0	5	50	58	6	14	27	13.3	3.96	93	.294	.347	0	.000	0	-2	-2	0	-0.1
Total 10	68	57	.544	283	124	29	5	18	1123	1071	100	384	638	12.1	3.66	100	.252	.323	28	.086	-18	-11	2	4	-1.5

● BOB WICKMAN
Wickman, Robert Joe b: 2/6/69, Green Bay, Wis. BR/TR, 6'1", 207 lbs. Deb: 8/24/92

YEAR TM/L	W	L	PCT	G	GS	CG	SH	SV	IP	H	HR	BB	SO	RAT	ERA	ERA+	OAV	OOB	BH	AVG	PB	PR	/A	PD	TPI
1992 NY-A	6	1	.857	8	8	0	0	0	50^1	51	2	20	21	13.1	4.11	95	.273	.349	0	—	0	-1	-1	0	-0.1
1993 NY-A	14	4	.778	41	19	1	1	4	140	156	13	69	70	14.8	4.63	90	.284	.369	0	—	0	-5	-7	-1	-0.7
1994 NY-A	5	4	.556	**53**	0	0	0	6	70	54	3	27	56	10.5	3.09	144	.213	.292	0	—	0	13	10	0	1.7
Total 3	25	9	.735	102	27	1	1	10	260^1	261	18	116	147	13.3	4.11	102	.264	.346	0	—	0	8	2	-0	0.9

● AL WIDMAR
Widmar, Albert Joseph b: 3/20/25, Cleveland, Ohio BR/TR, 6'3", 185 lbs. Deb: 4/25/47 C

YEAR TM/L	W	L	PCT	G	GS	CG	SH	SV	IP	H	HR	BB	SO	RAT	ERA	ERA+	OAV	OOB	BH	AVG	PB	PR	/A	PD	TPI
1947 Bos-A	0	0	—	2	0	0	0	0	1^1	1	1	2	1	20.3	13.50	29	.200	.429	0	—	0	-1	-1	0	0.0
1948 StL-A	2	6	.250	49	0	0	0	1	82^2	88	4	48	34	14.8	4.46	102	.275	.370	3	.300	1	-2	1	2	0.3
1950 StL-A	7	15	.318	36	26	8	1	4	194^2	211	16	74	78	13.3	4.76	104	.271	.337	10	.149	-3	-4	4	1	0.2
1951 StL-A	4	9	.308	26	16	4	0	0	107^2	157	19	52	28	17.6	6.52	67	.344	.414	5	.167	-1	-29	-25	1	-2.6
1952 Chi-A	0	0	—	1	0	0	0	0	2	4	1	0	2	18.0	4.50	81	.444	.444	0	—	-0	-0	-0	-0	0.0
Total 5	13	30	.302	114	42	12	1	5	388^1	461	41	176	143	14.9	5.21	90	.294	.367	18	.168	-4	-36	-22	3	-2.1

● WILD BILL WIDNER
Widner, William Waterfield b: 6/3/1867, Cincinnati, Ohio d: 12/10/08, Cincinnati, Ohio BR/TR, 6', 180 lbs. Deb: 6/8/1887

YEAR TM/L	W	L	PCT	G	GS	CG	SH	SV	IP	H	HR	BB	SO	RAT	ERA	ERA+	OAV	OOB	BH	AVG	PB	PR	/A	PD	TPI
1887 Cin-a	1	0	1.000	1	1	1	0	0	9	11	2	2	0	14.0	5.00	87	.275	.326	1	.250	-1	-1	-1	0	-0.1
1888 Was-N	5	7	.417	13	13	13	0	0	115	111	7	22	33	10.9	2.82	100	.247	.291	12	.200	-1	0	-0	-0	-0.1
1889 Col-a	12	20	.375	41	34	25	2	1	294	368	11	85	63	14.4	5.20	70	.297	.351	28	.211	-2	-44	-52	0	-4.2
1890 Col-a	4	8	.333	13	10	8	1	0	96	103	3	24	14	12.2	3.28	109	.266	.314	8	.195	-1	6	3	2	0.4
1891 Cin-a	0	1	.000	1	1	1	0	0	8	13	0	4	0	21.4	7.88	52	.353	.444	1	.250	-0	-4	-3	0	-0.3
Total 5	22	36	.379	69	59	48	3	1	522	606	23	137	110	13.3	4.36	79	.281	.333	50	.207	-3	-42	-52	2	-4.2

● TED WIEAND
Wieand, Franklin Delano Roosevelt b: 4/4/33, Walnutport, Pa. BR/TR, 6'2", 195 lbs. Deb: 9/27/58

YEAR TM/L	W	L	PCT	G	GS	CG	SH	SV	IP	H	HR	BB	SO	RAT	ERA	ERA+	OAV	OOB	BH	AVG	PB	PR	/A	PD	TPI
1958 Cin-N	0	0	—	1	0	0	0	0	2	4	1	0	2	18.0	9.00	46	.400	.400	0	—	0	-1	-1	-0	0.0
1960 Cin-N	0	1	.000	5	0	0	0	0	4^1	4	2	5	3	18.7	10.38	37	.250	.429	0	—	0	-3	-3	0	-0.6
Total 2	0	1	.000	6	0	0	0	0	6^1	8	3	5	5	18.5	9.95	39	.308	.419	0	—	0	-4	-4	0	-0.6

● CHARLIE WIEDEMEYER
Wiedemeyer, Charles John "Chick" b: 1/31/14, Chicago, Ill. d: 10/27/79, Lake Geneva, Fla. BL/TL, 6'3", 180 lbs. Deb: 9/9/34

YEAR TM/L	W	L	PCT	G	GS	CG	SH	SV	IP	H	HR	BB	SO	RAT	ERA	ERA+	OAV	OOB	BH	AVG	PB	PR	/A	PD	TPI
1934 Chi-N	0	0	—	4	1	0	0	0	8^1	11	2	4	2	22.7	9.72	40	.432	.500	0	—	-0	-5	-5	0	0.0

● JACK WIENEKE
Wieneke, John b: 3/10/1894, Saltsburg, Pa. d: 3/16/33, Pleasant Ridge, Mich. BR/TL, 6', 182 lbs. Deb: 7/4/21

YEAR TM/L	W	L	PCT	G	GS	CG	SH	SV	IP	H	HR	BB	SO	RAT	ERA	ERA+	OAV	OOB	BH	AVG	PB	PR	/A	PD	TPI
1921 Chi-A	0	1	.000	10	3	0	0	0	25^1	39	4	17	10	20.3	8.17	52	.351	.442	1	.111	-1	-11	-11	0	-0.4

● BOB WIESLER
Wiesler, Robert George b: 8/13/30, St.Louis, Mo. BB/TL, 6'2", 195 lbs. Deb: 8/3/51

YEAR TM/L	W	L	PCT	G	GS	CG	SH	SV	IP	H	HR	BB	SO	RAT	ERA	ERA+	OAV	OOB	BH	AVG	PB	PR	/A	PD	TPI
1951 NY-A	0	2	.000	4	3	0	0	0	9^1	13	0	11	3	23.1	13.50	28	.361	.511	0	.000	-1	-10	-10	0	-1.6
1954 NY-A	3	2	.600	6	5	0	0	0	30^1	28	0	30	25	17.2	4.15	83	.259	.420	3	.273	1	-1	-2	-1	-0.3
1955 NY-A	0	2	.000	16	7	0	0	0	53	39	1	49	25	15.1	3.91	96	.212	.380	2	.143	1	0	-1	1	0.0
1956 Was-A	3	12	.200	37	21	3	0	0	123	141	11	112	49	18.7	6.44	67	.300	.438	3	.091	-3	-31	-29	1	-3.1
1957 Was-A	1	1	.500	3	2	1	0	0	16^1	15	2	11	9	14.9	4.41	88	.250	.375	1	.167		-1	-1	0	-0.1
1958 Was-A	0	0	—	4	0	0	0	0	9^1	14	2	5	5	19.3	6.75	56	.359	.444	0	.000	-0	-3	-3	1	0.0
Total 6	7	19	.269	70	38	4	0	0	241^1	250	16	218	113	17.7	5.74	70	.279	.423	9	.130	-3	-46	-46	3	-5.1

● WHITEY WIETELMANN
Wietelmann, William Frederick b: 3/15/19, Zanesville, Ohio BB/TR, 6', 170 lbs. Deb: 9/6/39 C♦

YEAR TM/L	W	L	PCT	G	GS	CG	SH	SV	IP	H	HR	BB	SO	RAT	ERA	ERA+	OAV	OOB	BH	AVG	PB	PR	/A	PD	TPI
1945 Bos-N	0	0	—	1	0	0	0	0	1	6	0	2	0	72.0	54.00	7	.667	.727	116	.271	0	-6	-6	-0	0.0
1946 Bos-N	0	0	—	3	0	0	0	0	6^2	9	1	4	2	18.9	8.10	42	.310	.412	16	.205	0	-3	-3	-0	0.0
Total 2	0	0	—	4	0	0	0	0	7^2	15	1	6	2	25.8	14.09	25	.395	.489	409	.232		-9	-9	0	0.0

● JIMMY WIGGS
Wiggs, James Alvin "Big Jim" b: 9/1/1876, Trondheim, Norway d: 1/20/63, Xenia, Ohio BB/TR, 6'4", 200 lbs. Deb: 4/23/03

YEAR TM/L	W	L	PCT	G	GS	CG	SH	SV	IP	H	HR	BB	SO	RAT	ERA	ERA+	OAV	OOB	BH	AVG	PB	PR	/A	PD	TPI
1903 Cin-N	0	1	.000	2	1	0	0	0	5	12	0	2	2	27.0	5.40	66	.500	.556	0	.000	-0	-1	-1	-0	-0.2
1905 Det-A	3	3	.500	7	7	4	0	0	41^1	30	0	29	37	13.1	3.27	84	.204	.339	2	.133	-0	-3	-2	-0	-0.4
1906 Det-A	0	0	—	4	1	0	0	0	10^1	11	1	7	7	17.4	5.23	53	.276	.409	1	.333	-0	-3	-3	0	0.0
Total 3	3	4	.429	13	9	4	0	0	56^2	53	1	38	46	15.1	3.81	74	.252	.376	3	.158	-0	-7	-6	0	-0.5

● BILL WIGHT
Wight, William Robert "Lefty" b: 4/12/22, Rio Vista, Cal. BL/TL, 6'1", 180 lbs. Deb: 4/17/46

YEAR TM/L	W	L	PCT	G	GS	CG	SH	SV	IP	H	HR	BB	SO	RAT	ERA	ERA+	OAV	OOB	BH	AVG	PB	PR	/A	PD	TPI
1946 NY-A	2	2	.500	14	4	1	0	0	40^1	44	1	30	11	16.7	4.46	77	.289	.410	0	.000	-1	-4	-5	0	-0.5
1947 NY-A	1	0	1.000	1	1	1	0	0	9	8	0	2	3	10.0	1.00	353	.242	.286	0	.000	0	3	3	0	0.4
1948 Chi-A	9	20	.310	34	32	7	1	1	223^1	238	9	135	68	15.1	4.80	89	.278	.377	6	.082	-7	-13	-13	1	-2.0
1949 Chi-A	15	13	.536	35	33	14	3	1	245	254	6	96	78	12.9	3.31	126	.275	.343	14	.165	-1	24	24	0	2.3
1950 Chi-A	10	16	.385	30	28	13	3	0	206	213	10	79	62	12.8	3.58	125	.270	.336	0	.000	-9	23	21	2	1.6
1951 Bos-A	7	7	.500	34	17	4	2	0	118^1	128	5	63	38	14.5	5.10	88	.282	.369	4	.073	-4	-13	-8	1	-1.2
1952 Bos-A	2	1	.667	10	2	0	0	0	24^1	14	3	14	5	10.7	2.96	133	.169	.296	1	.143		2	3	0	0.3
Det-A	5	9	.357	23	19	8	3	0	143^2	167	7	55	65	13.9	3.88	98	.291	.354	11	.220	1	-3	-1	2	0.5
Yr	7	10	.412	33	21	8	3	0	168	181	10	69	70	13.4	3.75	102	.275	.344	12	.211	1	-1	1	2	0.5
1953 Det-A	0	3	.000	13	4	0	0	0	25^1	35	4	14	10	17.4	8.88	46	.333	.412	3	.429	1	-14	-14	-1	-1.3
Cle-A	2	1	.667	20	0	0	0	1	26^2	29	1	16	14	15.2	3.71	101	.282	.378	0	.000	-1	1	0	0	0.0
Yr	2	4	.333	33	4	0	0	1	52	64	5	30	24	16.3	6.23	63	.308	.395	3	.250		-13	-13	-0	-1.3
1955 Cle-A	0	0	—	17	0	0	0	1	24	24	0	9	12	14.2	2.63	152	.261	.327	0	—	0	2	2	0	0.2
Bal-A	6	8	.429	19	14	8	2	2	117^1	111	6	39	54	11.6	2.45	155	.252	.315	3	.083	-2	20	18	2	2.1
Yr	6	8	.429	36	14	8	2	3	141^1	135	6	48	63	11.7	2.48	155	.254	.317	3	.083	-2	23	21	4	2.3
1956 Bal-A	9	12	.429	35	26	7	1	0	174^2	198	7	72	84	14.2	4.02	89	.289	.362	12	.200	-1	3	-2	-1	-0.3
1957 Bal-A	6	6	.500	27	17	2	0	0	121	122	4	54	50	13.4	3.64	99	.271	.354	1	.029	-3	2	-1	-1	-0.5
1958 Cin-N	0	1	.000	7	0	0	0	0	6^2	7	1	4	5	14.9	4.05	102	.292	.393	0	—	-0	-0	-0	0	0.0
StL-N	3	0	1.000	28	1	1	0	2	57^1	64	7	32	16	15.1	5.02	82	.290	.379	1	.100	-0	-7	-6	1	-0.3
Yr	3	1	.750	35	1	1	0	2	64	71	8	36	21	15.0	4.92	84	.290	.381	1	.077	-0	-7	-6	1	-0.3
Total 12	77	99	.438	347	198	66	15	8	1563	1656	74	714	574	13.7	3.95	103	.277	.355	55	.115	-28	27	22	9	2.7

● FRED WIGINGTON
Wigington, Fred Thomas b: 12/16/1897, Rogers, Neb. d: 5/8/80, Mesa, Ariz. BR/TR, 5'10", 168 lbs. Deb: 4/20/23

YEAR TM/L	W	L	PCT	G	GS	CG	SH	SV	IP	H	HR	BB	SO	RAT	ERA	ERA+	OAV	OOB	BH	AVG	PB	PR	/A	PD	TPI
1923 StL-N	0	0	—	4	0	0	0	0	8^1	11	0	5	2	17.3	3.24	121	.367	.457	0	.000	0	1	1	0	0.0

● SANDY WIHTOL
Wihtol, Alexander Ames b: 6/1/55, Palo Alto, Cal. BR/TR, 6'1", 195 lbs. Deb: 9/7/79

YEAR TM/L	W	L	PCT	G	GS	CG	SH	SV	IP	H	HR	BB	SO	RAT	ERA	ERA+	OAV	OOB	BH	AVG	PB	PR	/A	PD	TPI
1979 Cle-A	0	0	—	5	0	0	0	0	10^2	10	0	3	6	11.0	3.38	126	.238	.289	0	—	0	1	1	0	0.0
1980 Cle-A	1	0	1.000	17	0	0	0	1	35^1	35	2	14	20	13.0	3.57	114	.257	.336	0	—	0	2	2	-1	0.0
1982 Cle-A	0	0	—	6	0	0	0	0	11^2	9	1	7	8	13.1	4.63	88	.220	.347	0	—	0	-1	-1	-0	0.0
Total 3	1	0	1.000	28	0	0	0	1	57^2	54	3	24	34	12.6	3.75	110	.247	.329	0	—	0	2	2	0	0.0

YEAR TM/L	W	L	PCT	G	GS	CG	SH	SV	IP	H	HR	BB	SO	RAT	ERA	ERA+	OAV	OOB	BH	AVG	PB	PR	/A	PD	TPI
● MILT WILCOX Wilcox, Milton Edward b: 4/20/50, Honolulu, Hawaii BR/TR, 6'2", 185 lbs. Deb: 9/5/70
1970 *Cin-N	3	1	.750	5	2	1	1	1	22¹	19	2	7	13	10.9	2.42	167	.229	.297	1	.200	0	4	4	0	0.8
1971 Cin-N	2	2	.500	18	3	0	0	1	43¹	43	2	17	21	12.9	3.32	101	.269	.346	0	.000	-1	1	0	0	-0.1
1972 Cle-A	7	14	.333	32	27	4	2	0	156	145	18	72	90	12.8	3.40	94	.251	.339	9	.200	1	-6	-3	-3	-0.6
1973 Cle-A	8	10	.444	26	19	4	0	0	134¹	143	14	68	82	14.7	5.83	67	.275	.367	0	—	0	-30	-29	1	-3.2
1974 Cle-A	2	2	.500	41	2	1	0	4	71¹	74	10	24	33	13.0	4.67	77	.271	.341	0	—	0	-8	-8	1	-0.5
1975 Chi-N	0	1	.000	25	0	0	0	0	38¹	50	4	17	21	16.0	5.63	68	.323	.393	1	.333	0	-9	-8	0	-0.1
1977 Det-A	6	2	.750	20	13	1	0	0	106¹	96	13	37	82	11.3	3.64	118	.241	.307	0	—	0	5	8	-0	0.5
1978 Det-A	13	12	.520	29	27	16	2	0	215¹	208	22	68	132	11.9	3.76	103	.255	.318	0	—	0	2	1	0	0.4
1979 Det-A	12	10	.545	33	29	7	0	0	196¹	201	18	73	109	13.1	4.35	99	.267	.341	0	—	0	-3	-1	3	0.2
1980 Det-A	13	11	.542	32	31	13	1	0	198²	201	24	68	97	12.5	4.48	92	.262	.327	0	—	0	-10	-8	1	-0.8
1981 Det-A	12	9	.571	24	24	8	1	0	166¹	152	10	52	79	11.4	3.03	124	.247	.312	0	—	0	12	14	1	1.7
1982 Det-A	12	10	.545	29	29	9	1	0	193²	187	18	85	112	13.0	3.62	112	.257	.340	0	—	0	10	9	3	1.2
1983 Det-A	11	10	.524	26	26	9	2	0	186	164	19	74	101	11.7	3.97	98	.237	.314	0	—	0	2	-1	3	0.3
1984 *Det-A	17	8	.680	33	33	0	0	0	193²	183	13	66	119	11.9	4.00	98	.252	.321	0	—	0	-0	-2	1	0.0
1985 Det-A	1	3	.250	8	8	0	0	0	39	51	6	14	20	15.0	4.85	84	.315	.369	0	—	0	-3	-3	1	-0.1
1986 Sea-A	0	8	.000	13	10	0	0	0	55²	74	11	28	26	16.7	5.50	77	.327	.404	0	—	0	-8	-8	0	-0.9
Total 16	119	113	.513	394	283	73	10	6	2016²	1991	204	770	1137	12.7	4.07	96	.260	.334	11	.177	0	-44	-33	14	-1.2
● RANDY WILES Wiles, Randall E b: 9/10/51, Fort Belvoir, Va. BL/TL, 6'1", 185 lbs. Deb: 8/7/77
1977 Chi-A	1	1	.500	5	0	0	0	0	2²	5	1	3	0	27.0	10.13	40	.417	.533	0	—	0	-2	-2	0	-1.1
● MARK WILEY Wiley, Mark Eugene b: 2/28/48, National City, Cal. BR/TR, 6'1", 200 lbs. Deb: 6/17/75 C
1975 Min-A	1	3	.250	15	3	1	0	2	38²	50	4	13	15	14.9	6.05	64	.325	.381	0	—	0	-10	-9	-1	-1.0
1978 SD-N	1	0	1.000	4	1	0	0	0	7²	11	1	1	1	14.1	5.87	57	.324	.343	0	.000	-0	-2	-2	-0	-0.3
Tor-A	0	0	—	2	0	0	0	0	2²	3	0	1	2	13.5	6.75	58	.273	.333	0	—	0	-1	-1	-0	-0.1
Total 2	2	3	.400	21	4	1	0	2	49	64	5	15	18	14.7	6.06	62	.322	.372	0	.000	-0	-13	-12	-1	-1.3
● HARRY WILHELM Wilhelm, Harry Lester b: 4/7/1874, Uniontown, Pa. d: 2/20/44, Republic, Pa. BR/TR, 5'7", 155 lbs. Deb: 8/12/1899
1899 Lou-N	1	1	.500	5	3	2	0	0	25	36	1	3	6	14.4	6.12	63	.336	.360	3	.250	2	-6	-6	0	-0.2
● KAISER WILHELM Wilhelm, Irvin Key b: 1/26/1874, Wooster, Ohio d: 5/21/36, Rochester, N.Y. BR/TR, 6', 162 lbs. Deb: 4/18/03 MUC
1903 Pit-N	5	3	.625	12	9	7	1	0	86	88	0	25	20	12.1	3.24	100	.264	.321	3	.088	-2	0	-0	2	-0.1
1904 Bos-N	14	20	.412	39	36	30	3	0	288	316	8	74	73	12.4	3.69	75	.285	.333	7	.070	-8	-30	-30	1	-3.9
1905 Bos-N	3	23	.115	34	27	23	0	0	242¹	287	7	75	76	13.6	4.53	68	.295	.349	16	.160	-2	-41	-39	2	-3.7
1908 Bro-N	16	22	.421	42	36	33	6	0	332	266	3	83	99	9.6	1.87	125	.217	.271	12	.108	-4	18	18	3	1.9
1909 Bro-N	3	13	.188	22	17	14	1	0	163	176	3	59	45	13.1	3.26	80	.289	.353	13	.228	2	-12	-12	1	-0.8
1910 Bro-N	3	7	.300	15	5	0	0	0	68¹	88	3	18	17	14.1	4.74	64	.314	.358	6	.316	2	-13	-13	1	-1.4
1914 Bal-F	12	17	.414	47	27	11	1	5	243²	263	10	81	113	12.7	4.03	75	.291	.349	21	.250	1	-31	-27	3	-2.6
1915 Bal-F	0	0	—	1	0	0	0	0	1	0	0	0	0	0.0	0.00	—	.000	.000	0	—	0	0	0	0	0.0
1921 Phi-N	0	0	—	4	0	0	0	0	8	11	0	3	1	15.8	3.38	125	.393	.452	0	.000	-0	1	0	0	0.0
Total 9	56	105	.348	216	157	118	12	5	1432¹	1495	34	418	444	12.2	3.44	81	.274	.328	78	.154	-12	-108	-102	11	-10.6
● HOYT WILHELM Wilhelm, James Hoyt b: 7/26/23, Huntersville, N.C. BR/TR, 6', 195 lbs. Deb: 4/19/52 H
1952 NY-N	15	3	**.833**	**71**	0	0	0	11	159¹	127	12	57	108	10.7	**2.43**	152	.220	.296	6	.158	0	23	23	1	2.9
1953 NY-N☆	7	8	.467	**68**	0	0	0	15	145	127	13	77	71	12.9	3.04	141	.238	.339	5	.152	1	**20**	**20**	-1	2.3
1954 *NY-N	12	4	.750	57	0	0	0	7	111¹	77	5	52	64	10.8	2.10	192	.198	.300	1	.048	-2	**24**	**24**	1	3.4
1955 NY-N	4	1	.800	59	0	0	0	0	103	104	10	40	71	12.8	3.93	102	.266	.337	3	.158	-1	1	1	3	0.2
1956 NY-N	4	9	.308	64	0	0	0	8	89¹	97	7	43	71	14.3	3.83	99	.280	.362	2	.222	0	-1	-0	2	0.1
1957 StL-N	1	4	.200	40	0	0	0	11	55	52	7	21	29	12.4	4.25	93	.254	.332	0	.000	-1	-2	-2	-0	-0.3
Cle-A	1	0	1.000	2	0	0	0	1	3²	2	1	1	0	9.8	2.45	151	.154	.267	0	—	0	1	1	-0	0.1
1958 Cle-A	2	7	.222	30	6	1	0	5	90¹	70	4	35	57	10.6	2.49	146	.215	.294	2	.095	-1	13	12	1	1.2
Bal-A	1	3	.250	9	4	3	1	0	40²	25	2	10	35	8.0	1.99	180	.179	.238	1	.091	-1	8	7	-0	0.6
Yr	3	10	.231	39	10	4	1	5	131	95	6	45	92	9.7	2.34	155	.203	.274	3	.094	-2	21	19	1	1.8
1959 Bal-A★	15	11	.577	32	27	13	3	0	226	178	13	77	139	10.6	**2.19**	173	.224	.301	4	.053	-6	**42**	**40**	-1	3.7
1960 Bal-A	11	8	.579	41	11	3	1	7	147	125	13	39	107	10.1	3.31	115	.228	.280	3	.071	-3	9	8	1	0.9
1961 Bal-A★	9	7	.563	51	1	0	0	18	109²	89	5	41	87	11.0	2.30	167	.219	.296	1	.050	-1	21	19	1	3.2
1962 Bal-A†	7	10	.412	52	0	0	0	15	93	64	5	34	90	9.8	1.94	191	.197	.279	2	.125	-0	21	18	0	3.8
1963 Chi-A	5	8	.385	55	3	0	0	21	136¹	106	8	30	111	9.2	2.64	133	.215	.265	2	.069	-1	15	13	1	1.6
1964 Chi-A	12	9	.571	73	0	0	0	27	131¹	94	7	30	95	8.6	1.99	174	.202	.254	3	.143	-1	24	21	-1	4.3
1965 Chi-A	7	7	.500	66	0	0	0	20	144	88	11	32	106	7.6	1.81	176	.177	.229	0	.000	-2	**26**	**22**	-1	2.6
1966 Chi-A	5	2	.714	46	0	0	0	6	81¹	50	6	17	61	7.5	1.66	191	.178	.227	1	.125	0	16	14	-1	1.3
1967 Chi-A	8	3	.727	49	0	0	0	12	89	58	2	34	76	9.7	1.31	236	.183	.270	1	.077	-1	**19**	**18**	-1	2.7
1968 Chi-A	4	4	.500	72	0	0	0	12	93²	69	4	24	72	9.1	1.73	175	.205	.262	0	.000	-0	13	13	-1	1.5
1969 Cal-A	5	7	.417	44	0	0	0	10	65²	44	5	18	53	9.0	2.47	141	.194	.261	0	.000	-1	8	7	-0	1.4
Atl-N	2	0	1.000	8	0	0	0	4	12¹	5	0	4	14	7.3	0.73	494	.119	.213	0	.000	-0	4	4	0	0.7
1970 Atl-N☆	6	4	.600	50	0	0	0	13	78¹	69	7	39	67	12.5	3.10	138	.234	.325	1	.091	-0	8	10	0	1.6
Chi-N	0	1	.000	3	0	0	0	0	3²	4	1	3	2	17.2	9.82	46	.286	.412	0	—	-0	-2	-2	-0	-0.4
Yr	6	5	.545	53	0	0	0	13	82	73	8	42	68	12.6	3.40	126	.234	.325	1	.091	-0	6	8	1	1.2
1971 Atl-N	0	0	—	3	0	0	0	0	2¹	6	2	1	1	27.0	15.43	24	.500	.538	0	—	0	-3	-3	0	0.0
LA-N	0	1	.000	9	0	0	0	3	17²	6	1	4	15	5.1	1.02	317	.111	.172	0	.000	0	5	4	0	0.4
Yr	0	1	.000	12	0	0	0	3	20	12	3	5	16	7.6	2.70	122	.182	.239	0	.000	-0	2	1	0	0.4
1972 LA-N	0	1	.000	16	0	0	0	1	25¹	20	0	15	9	12.4	4.62	72	.217	.327	0	—	0	-3	-4	0	-0.1
Total 21	143	122	.540	1070	52	20	5	227	2254¹	1757	150	778	1610	10.4	2.52	146	.216	.290	38	.088	-21	310	288	5	40.0
● LEFTY WILKIE Wilkie, Aldon Jay b: 10/30/14, Zealandia, Sask., Canada d: 8/5/92, Tualatin, Ore. BL/TL, 5'11.5", 175 lbs. Deb: 4/22/41
1941 Pit-N	2	4	.333	26	6	2	1	2	79	90	1	40	16	14.9	4.56	79	.289	.372	7	.292	1	-8	-8	1	-0.4
1942 Pit-N	6	7	.462	35	6	3	0	1	107¹	112	4	37	18	12.6	4.19	81	.269	.330	10	.263	2	-10	-10	2	-0.7
1946 Pit-N	0	0	—	7	0	0	0	0	7²	13	0	3	3	18.8	10.57	33	.382	.432	0	—	0	-6	-6	-0	-0.0
Total 3	8	11	.421	68	12	5	1	3	194	215	5	80	37	13.8	4.59	76	.283	.352	17	.274	3	-25	-24	3	-1.1
● DEAN WILKINS Wilkins, Dean Allan b: 8/24/66, Blue Island, Ill. BR/TR, 6'1", 170 lbs. Deb: 8/21/89
1989 Chi-N	1	0	1.000	11	0	0	0	0	15²	13	2	9	14	12.6	4.60	82	.228	.333	0	.000	-0	-2	-1	0	-0.1
1990 Chi-N	0	0	—	7	0	0	0	0	7¹	11	1	7	3	23.3	9.82	42	.333	.463	0	.000	-0	-5	-5	-0	-0.2
1991 Hou-N	2	1	.667	7	0	0	0	2	8	16	0	10	4	29.3	11.25	31	.410	.531	0	.000	-0	-7	-7	-0	-2.2
Total 3	3	1	.750	25	0	0	0	2	31	40	3	26	21	19.5	7.55	50	.310	.429	0	.000	-0	-14	-13	0	-2.5
● ERIC WILKINS Wilkins, Eric Lamoine b: 12/9/56, St.Louis, Mo. BR/TR, 6'1", 190 lbs. Deb: 4/11/79
1979 Cle-A	2	4	.333	16	14	0	0	0	69²	77	4	38	52	15.4	4.39	97	.289	.386	0	—	0	-1	-1	0	-0.1
● ROY WILKINSON Wilkinson, Roy Hamilton b: 5/8/1893, Canandaigua, N.Y. d: 7/2/56, Louisville, Ky. BR/TR, 6'1", 170 lbs. Deb: 4/29/18
1918 Cle-A	0	0	—	1	0	0	0	0	1	0	0	0	0	0.0	0.00	—	.000	.000	0	—	0	0	0	-0	0.0
1919 *Chi-A	1	1	.500	4	1	1	1	0	22	21	0	10	5	12.7	2.05	156	.266	.348	3	.375	2	3	3	1	0.5
1920 Chi-A	7	9	.438	34	12	8	0	2	145	162	6	48	30	13.2	4.03	93	.297	.356	7	.146	-3	-4	-4	-3	-0.9
1921 Chi-A	4	20	.167	36	23	11	0	3	198¹	259	4	78	50	15.5	5.13	83	.334	.397	8	.123	-4	-19	-20	5	-1.8

YEAR TM/L	W	L	PCT	G	GS	CG	SH	SV	IP	H	HR	BB	SO	RAT	ERA	ERA+	OAV	OOB	BH	AVG	PB	PR	/A	PD	TPI
1922 Chi-A	0	1	.000	4	1	0	0	1	14¹	24	1	6	3	19.5	8.79	46	.393	.456	0	.000	-0	-8	-8	-0	-0.6
Total 5	12	31	.279	79	37	20	1	6	380²	466	11	142	88	14.5	4.66	86	.318	.381	18	.145	-5	-27	-28	4	-2.8

● BILL WILKINSON
Wilkinson, William Carl b: 8/10/64, Greybull, Wyoming BR/TL, 5'10", 160 lbs. Deb: 6/13/85 F

YEAR TM/L	W	L	PCT	G	GS	CG	SH	SV	IP	H	HR	BB	SO	RAT	ERA	ERA+	OAV	OOB	BH	AVG	PB	PR	/A	PD	TPI
1985 Sea-A	0	2	.000	2	2	0	0	0	6	8	2	6	5	21.0	13.50	31	.333	.467	0	—	0	-6	-6	0	-1.3
1987 Sea-A	3	4	.429	56	0	0	0	10	76¹	61	8	21	73	9.7	3.66	129	.223	.278	0	—	0	7	9	-1	0.8
1988 Sea-A	2	2	.500	30	0	0	0	2	31	28	3	15	25	12.5	3.48	119	.233	.319	0	—	0	2	2	-1	0.1
Total 3	5	8	.385	88	2	0	0	12	113¹	97	13	42	103	11.0	4.13	110	.232	.302	0	—	0	2	5	-1	-0.4

● TED WILKS
Wilks, Theodore "Cork" b: 11/13/15, Fulton, N.Y. d: 8/21/89, Houston, Tex. BR/TR, 5'9.5", 178 lbs. Deb: 4/25/44 C

YEAR TM/L	W	L	PCT	G	GS	CG	SH	SV	IP	H	HR	BB	SO	RAT	ERA	ERA+	OAV	OOB	BH	AVG	PB	PR	/A	PD	TPI
1944 *StL-N	17	4	.810	36	21	16	4	0	207²	173	12	49	70	9.7	2.64	133	.227	.275	9	.141	-1	22	20	-4	1.4
1945 StL-N	4	7	.364	18	16	4	1	0	98¹	103	9	29	28	12.1	2.93	128	.270	.324	4	.133	-0	10	9	-2	0.7
1946 *StL-N	8	0	1.000	40	4	0	0	1	95	88	13	38	40	12.1	3.41	101	.248	.324	5	.208	0	0	0	-1	0.0
1947 StL-N	4	0	1.000	37	0	0	0	5	50¹	57	10	11	28	12.5	5.01	83	.279	.323	1	.167	-0	-5	-5	-0	-0.4
1948 StL-N	6	6	.500	57	2	1	0	13	130²	113	6	39	71	10.5	2.62	156	.235	.293	5	.167	-1	19	21	-1	2.2
1949 StL-N	10	3	.769	59	0	0	0	9	118¹	105	7	38	71	10.9	3.73	112	.240	.301	1	.037	-3	4	6	-2	0.1
1950 StL-N	2	0	1.000	18	0	0	0	0	24¹	27	4	9	15	13.7	6.66	65	.287	.356	0	.000	-0	-7	-6	-0	-0.5
1951 StL-N	0	0	—	17	0	0	0	0	18	19	1	5	5	12.0	3.00	132	.279	.329	0	.000	-0	2	2	-1	0.0
Pit-N	3	5	.375	48	1	1	0	12	82²	69	6	24	43	10.3	2.83	149	.231	.292	1	.083	-1	10	13	1	1.6
Yr	3	5	.375	65	1	1	0	13	100²	88	7	29	48	10.6	2.86	146	.240	.299	1	.077	-1	12	15	0	1.6
1952 Pit-N	5	5	.500	44	0	0	0	4	72¹	65	9	31	24	12.2	3.61	111	.245	.329	1	.125	-0	1	3	-1	0.3
Cle-A	0	0	—	7	0	0	0	0	11²	8	0	7	6	11.6	3.86	87	.186	.300	0	—	0	-0	-1	-0	0.0
1953 Cle-A	0	0	—	4	0	0	0	0	3²	5	0	3	2	19.6	7.36	51	.278	.381	0	.000	0	-1	-1	-0	0.0
Total 10	59	30	.663	385	44	22	5	46	913	832	76	283	403	11.1	3.26	118	.244	.304	27	.131	-5	55	61	-11	5.4

● ED WILLETT
Willett, Robert Edgar b: 3/7/1884, Norfolk, Va. d: 5/10/34, Wellington, Kan. BR/TR, 6', 183 lbs. Deb: 9/5/06

YEAR TM/L	W	L	PCT	G	GS	CG	SH	SV	IP	H	HR	BB	SO	RAT	ERA	ERA+	OAV	OOB	BH	AVG	PB	PR	/A	PD	TPI
1906 Det-A	0	3	.000	3	3	3	0	0	25	24	0	8	16	12.2	3.96	70	.256	.327	1	.000	-1	-4	-3	1	-0.4
1907 Det-A	1	5	.167	10	6	1	0	0	48²	47	0	20	27	12.8	3.70	71	.256	.335	1	.077	-1	-6	-6	1	-0.7
1908 Det-A	15	8	.652	30	23	18	2	1	197¹	186	2	60	77	11.9	2.28	106	.261	.331	11	.164	-2	3	3	5	0.6
1909 *Det-A	21	10	.677	41	34	25	3	1	292²	239	5	76	89	10.1	2.34	108	.221	.281	22	.196	3	5	6	-1	0.8
1910 Det-A	16	11	.593	37	25	18	4	0	224¹	175	2	74	66	10.7	2.37	111	.217	.296	11	.133	-2	4	7	7	1.3
1911 Det-A	13	14	.481	38	27	15	2	1	231¹	261	5	80	86	13.8	3.66	95	.295	.363	22	.268	7	-8	-5	3	0.4
1912 Det-A	17	15	.531	37	31	28	1	0	284¹	281	3	84	89	12.1	3.29	99	.262	.326	19	.165	-1	1	-1	5	0.3
1913 Det-A	13	14	.481	34	30	19	0	0	242	237	0	89	59	12.5	3.09	95	.260	.333	26	.283	7	-4	-5	3	0.2
1914 StL-F	4	16	.200	27	21	14	0	0	175	208	4	56	73	14.1	4.22	72	.295	.355	15	.234	1	-26	-23	5	-1.7
1915 StL-F	2	3	.400	17	2	1	0	2	52²	61	2	18	19	14.0	4.61	62	.295	.360	3	.200	0	-11	-10	0	-1.0
Total 10	102	99	.507	274	202	142	12	5	1773¹	1719	24	565	600	12.1	3.08	94	.258	.326	130	.199	11	-47	-37	28	0.3

● CARL WILLEY
Willey, Carlton Francis b: 6/6/31, Cherryfield, Me. BR/TR, 6', 175 lbs. Deb: 4/30/58

YEAR TM/L	W	L	PCT	G	GS	CG	SH	SV	IP	H	HR	BB	SO	RAT	ERA	ERA+	OAV	OOB	BH	AVG	PB	PR	/A	PD	TPI
1958 *Mil-N	9	7	.563	23	19	9	4	0	140	110	14	53	74	10.6	2.70	130	.215	.291	5	.104	-2	19	13	-2	0.9
1959 Mil-N	5	9	.357	26	15	5	2	0	117	126	12	31	51	12.2	4.15	85	.273	.322	4	.103	-1	-3	-8	-1	-1.1
1960 Mil-N	6	7	.462	28	21	2	1	0	144²	136	19	65	109	12.9	4.35	79	.248	.335	7	.146	1	-10	-15	-1	-1.2
1961 Mil-N	6	12	.333	35	22	4	0	0	159²	147	20	65	91	12.1	3.83	98	.247	.323	1	.019	-6	4	-2	3	-0.5
1962 Mil-N	2	5	.286	30	6	0	0	1	73¹	95	9	20	40	14.2	5.40	70	.319	.364	3	.273	-1	-12	-13	-0	-1.1
1963 NY-N	9	14	.391	30	28	7	4	0	183	149	24	69	101	10.9	3.10	113	.220	.296	6	.111	-1	4	8	0	0.9
1964 NY-N	0	2	.000	14	3	0	0	0	30	37	5	8	14	13.8	3.60	99	.301	.348	0	.000	-0	-0	-1	-1	-0.2
1965 NY-N	1	2	.333	13	3	1	0	0	28	30	2	15	13	15.1	4.18	84	.270	.367	0	.000	-1	-2	-1	-0	-0.3
Total 8	38	58	.396	199	117	28	11	1	875²	830	105	326	493	12.1	3.76	95	.250	.320	26	.099	-9	1	-17	-3	-2.6

● NICK WILLHITE
Willhite, Jon Nicholas b: 1/27/41, Tulsa, Okla. BL/TL, 6'2", 195 lbs. Deb: 6/16/63

YEAR TM/L	W	L	PCT	G	GS	CG	SH	SV	IP	H	HR	BB	SO	RAT	ERA	ERA+	OAV	OOB	BH	AVG	PB	PR	/A	PD	TPI
1963 LA-N	2	3	.400	8	8	1	1	0	38	44	5	10	28	12.8	3.79	80	.286	.329	3	.300	1	-2	-3	-1	-0.4
1964 LA-N	2	4	.333	10	7	2	0	0	43²	43	4	13	24	11.5	3.71	87	.264	.318	0	.000	-0	-1	-2	1	-0.2
1965 Was-A	0	0	—	5	0	0	0	0	6¹	10	2	4	3	19.9	7.11	49	.345	.424	0	—	0	-3	-3	-0	0.0
LA-N	2	2	.500	15	6	0	0	1	42	47	7	22	28	15.2	5.36	61	.288	.380	4	.400	3	-8	-10	-0	-0.6
1966 LA-N	0	0	—	6	0	0	0	0	4¹	3	0	5	4	16.6	2.08	159	.214	.421	0	—	0	1	1	0	0.0
1967 Cal-A	0	2	.000	10	7	0	0	0	39¹	39	6	16	22	12.6	4.35	72	.258	.329	0	.000	-0	-5	-5	-0	-0.4
NY-N	0	1	.000	4	1	0	0	0	8¹	9	1	5	9	15.1	8.64	39	.257	.350	0	.000	-0	-5	-5	-0	-0.5
Total 6	6	12	.333	58	29	3	1	1	182	195	27	75	118	13.5	4.55	70	.275	.346	7	.163	4	-23	-27	0	-2.1

● ALBERT WILLIAMS
Williams, Albert Hamilton (De Souza) b: 5/6/54, Lagunas De Perlas, Nic. BR/TR, 6'4", 190 lbs. Deb: 5/7/80

YEAR TM/L	W	L	PCT	G	GS	CG	SH	SV	IP	H	HR	BB	SO	RAT	ERA	ERA+	OAV	OOB	BH	AVG	PB	PR	/A	PD	TPI
1980 Min-A	6	2	.750	18	9	3	0	1	77	73	9	30	35	12.0	3.51	124	.253	.323	0	—	0	5	7	-1	0.2
1981 Min-A	6	10	.375	23	22	4	0	0	150	160	11	52	76	12.8	4.08	97	.276	.337	0	—	0	-7	-2	-2	-0.7
1982 Min-A	9	7	.563	26	26	3	0	0	153²	166	18	55	61	12.9	4.22	101	.276	.337	0	—	0	-2	0	0	0.0
1983 Min-A	11	14	.440	36	29	4	1	1	193¹	196	21	68	68	12.5	4.14	103	.262	.327	0	—	0	-2	2	-2	-0.1
1984 Min-A	3	5	.375	17	11	1	0	0	68²	75	9	22	22	13.6	5.77	73	.284	.355	0	—	0	-14	-12	-0	-1.3
Total 5	35	38	.479	120	97	15	1	2	642²	670	68	227	262	12.7	4.24	99	.270	.334	0	—	0	-20	-4	-4	-1.7

● AL WILLIAMS
Williams, Almon Edward b: 5/11/14, Valhermoso Springs, Ala. d: 7/19/69, Groves, Tex. BR/TR, 6'3", 200 lbs. Deb: 4/19/37

YEAR TM/L	W	L	PCT	G	GS	CG	SH	SV	IP	H	HR	BB	SO	RAT	ERA	ERA+	OAV	OOB	BH	AVG	PB	PR	/A	PD	TPI
1937 Phi-A	4	1	.800	16	8	2	0	1	75¹	88	0	49	27	16.5	5.38	88	.300	.402	2	.083	-2	-6	-6	0	-0.5
1938 Phi-A	0	7	.000	30	8	1	0	0	93¹	128	6	54	25	17.6	6.94	70	.324	.407	3	.040	-3	-22	-22	-0	-1.5
Total 2	4	8	.333	46	16	3	0	1	168²	216	6	103	52	17.1	6.24	77	.314	.405	5	.061	-5	-29	-27	0	-2.0

● GUS WILLIAMS
Williams, Augustine H. b: 1870, New York, N.Y. d: 10/14/1890, New York, N.Y. 5'11", 170 lbs. Deb: 4/18/1890

YEAR TM/L	W	L	PCT	G	GS	CG	SH	SV	IP	H	HR	BB	SO	RAT	ERA	ERA+	OAV	OOB	BH	AVG	PB	PR	/A	PD	TPI
1890 Bro-a	0	1	.000	2	2	1	0	0	12	13	0	12	2	18.8	7.50	52	.268	.413	2	.500	1	-5	-5	-1	-0.3

● BRIAN WILLIAMS
Williams, Brian O'Neal b: 2/15/69, Lancaster, S.C. BR/TR, 6'3", 205 lbs. Deb: 9/16/91

YEAR TM/L	W	L	PCT	G	GS	CG	SH	SV	IP	H	HR	BB	SO	RAT	ERA	ERA+	OAV	OOB	BH	AVG	PB	PR	/A	PD	TPI
1991 Hou-N	0	1	.000	2	2	0	0	0	12	11	2	4	12	12.0	3.75	94	.250	.327	0	.000	-0	-0	-0	0	-0.1
1992 Hou-N	7	6	.538	16	16	0	0	0	96¹	92	10	42	54	12.5	3.92	86	.255	.333	4	.133	-0	-4	-6	0	-0.8
1993 Hou-N	4	4	.500	42	5	0	0	3	82	76	7	38	56	13.0	4.83	80	.248	.338	2	.200	-0	-7	-9	2	-0.6
1994 Hou-N	6	5	.545	20	13	0	0	0	78¹	112	9	41	49	18.0	5.74	71	.343	.422	6	.261	1	-13	-15	-1	-1.7
Total 4	17	16	.515	80	36	0	0	3	268²	291	28	125	163	14.2	4.72	79	.280	.362	12	.182	1	-25	-30	1	-3.2

● CHARLIE WILLIAMS
Williams, Charles Prosek b: 10/11/47, Flushing, N.Y. BR/TR, 6'2", 200 lbs. Deb: 4/23/71

YEAR TM/L	W	L	PCT	G	GS	CG	SH	SV	IP	H	HR	BB	SO	RAT	ERA	ERA+	OAV	OOB	BH	AVG	PB	PR	/A	PD	TPI
1971 NY-N	5	6	.455	31	9	1	0	0	90¹	92	7	41	53	13.5	4.78	71	.267	.348	2	.087	-1	-13	-14	-1	-1.8
1972 SF-N	0	2	.000	3	2	0	0	0	9¹	14	3	3	9	16.4	8.68	40	.333	.378	0	.000	-0	-5	-5	-0	-1.0
1973 SF-N	3	0	1.000	12	2	0	0	0	23	32	2	7	11	15.3	6.65	57	.330	.375	1	.333	0	-8	-8	-0	-0.8
1974 SF-N	1	3	.250	39	7	0	0	0	100¹	93	6	31	48	11.3	2.78	137	.250	.311	3	.136	-1	9	11	3	0.6
1975 SF-N	5	3	.625	55	1	0	0	0	98	94	6	66	45	15.1	3.49	109	.261	.381	2	.125	0	1	3	2	0.5
1976 SF-N	2	0	1.000	53	0	0	0	4	85	80	4	39	34	12.8	2.96	122	.256	.343	1	.125	-0	5	6	1	0.2
1977 SF-N	6	5	.545	55	8	1	0	0	119¹	116	9	60	41	13.5	4.00	98	.222	.354	4	.222	0	-1	-1	-0	-0.1
1978 SF-N	1	3	.250	25	4	0	0	0	48	60	6	28	22	16.7	5.44	63	.314	.405	0	.000	-1	-10	-11	0	-0.9
Total 8	23	22	.511	268	33	2	0	4	573¹	581	38	275	257	13.7	3.97	93	.269	.355	13	.134	-2	-22	-17	3	-3.3

● LEFTY WILLIAMS
Williams, Claude Preston b: 3/9/1893, Aurora, Mo. d: 11/4/59, Laguna Beach, Cal. BR/TL, 5'9", 160 lbs. Deb: 9/17/13

YEAR TM/L	W	L	PCT	G	GS	CG	SH	SV	IP	H	HR	BB	SO	RAT	ERA	ERA+	OAV	OOB	BH	AVG	PB	PR	/A	PD	TPI
1913 Det-A	1	3	.250	5	4	3	0	1	29	34	0	4	9	12.1	4.97	59	.286	.315	1	.100	-0	-7	-7	-1	-1.0

YEAR TM/L	W	L	PCT	G	GS	CG	SH	SV	IP	H	HR	BB	SO	RAT	ERA	ERA+	OAV	OOB	BH	AVG	PB	PR	/A	PD	TPI
1914 Det-A	0	1	.000	1	1	0	0	0	1	3	0	2	0	45.0	0.00	—	.429	.556	0	—	0	0	0	-0	0.4
1916 Chi-A	13	7	.650	43	26	10	2	1	224^1	220	5	65	138	11.8	2.89	96	.267	.327	10	.135	-0	-1	-3	-4	-0.8
1917 *Chi-A	17	8	.680	45	29	8	1	1	230	221	8	81	85	12.2	2.97	89	.252	.321	6	.090	-3	-8	-8	-5	-1.7
1918 Chi-A	6	4	.600	15	14	7	2	1	105^2	76	0	47	30	10.9	2.73	100	.209	.308	5	.132	-2	1	0	-2	-0.5
1919 *Chi-A	23	11	.676	41	40	27	5	1	297	265	7	58	125	10.1	2.64	121	.244	.289	17	.181	1	20	18	-5	1.5
1920 Chi-A	22	14	.611	39	38	25	0	0	299	302	15	90	128	12.2	3.91	96	.271	.332	22	.218	-0	-4	-5	-3	-0.8
Total 7	82	48	.631	189	152	80	10	5	1186	1121	30	347	515	11.5	3.13	99	.255	.316	61	.159	-4	1	-4	-21	-2.9

● **MUTT WILLIAMS** Williams, David Carter b: 7/31/1891, Ozark, Ark. d: 3/30/62, Fayetteville, Ark. BR/TR, 6'3.5", 195 lbs. Deb: 10/4/13

YEAR TM/L	W	L	PCT	G	GS	CG	SH	SV	IP	H	HR	BB	SO	RAT	ERA	ERA+	OAV	OOB	BH	AVG	PB	PR	/A	PD	TPI
1913 Was-A	1	0	1.000	1	1	0	0	0	4	4	1	2	1	13.5	4.50	66	.286	.375	1	.500	0	-1	-1	0	-0.1
1914 Was-A	0	0	—	5	0	0	0	1	7	5	0	4	3	11.6	5.14	55	.227	.346	0	—	0	-2	-2	-0	-0.1
Total 2	1	0	1.000	6	1	0	0	1	11	9	1	6	4	12.3	4.91	58	.250	.357	1	.500	0	-3	-2	-0	-0.2

● **DAVE WILLIAMS** Williams, David Owen b: 2/7/1881, Scranton, Pa. d: 4/25/18, Hot Springs, Ark. BR/TL, 5'11.5", 167 lbs. Deb: 7/2/02

YEAR TM/L	W	L	PCT	G	GS	CG	SH	SV	IP	H	HR	BB	SO	RAT	ERA	ERA+	OAV	OOB	BH	AVG	PB	PR	/A	PD	TPI
1902 Bos-A	0	0	—	3	0	0	0	0	18^2	22	0	11	7	16.4	5.30	67	.294	.391	3	.333	1	-4	-4	-1	0.0

● **DON WILLIAMS** Williams, Donald Fred b: 9/14/31, Floyd, Va. BR/TR, 6'2", 180 lbs. Deb: 9/12/58

YEAR TM/L	W	L	PCT	G	GS	CG	SH	SV	IP	H	HR	BB	SO	RAT	ERA	ERA+	OAV	OOB	BH	AVG	PB	PR	/A	PD	TPI
1958 Pit-N	0	0	—	2	0	0	0	0	4	6	1	1	3	15.8	6.75	57	.375	.412	0	—	0	-1	-1	0	0.0
1959 Pit-N	0	0	—	6	0	0	0	0	12	17	1	3	3	15.0	6.75	57	.362	.400	1	.333	1	-4	-4	-1	0.0
1962 KC-A	0	0	—	3	0	0	0	0	4	6	0	1	1	15.8	9.00	47	.353	.389	0	.000	-0	-2	-2	-0	0.0
Total 3	0	0	—	11	0	0	0	0	20	29	2	4	7	15.3	7.20	55	.363	.400	1	.250	1	-7	-7	-1	0.0

● **DON WILLIAMS** Williams, Donald Reid "Dino" b: 9/2/35, Los Angeles, Cal. d: 12/20/91, LaJolla, Cal. BR/TR, 6'5", 218 lbs. Deb: 8/4/63

YEAR TM/L	W	L	PCT	G	GS	CG	SH	SV	IP	H	HR	BB	SO	RAT	ERA	ERA+	OAV	OOB	BH	AVG	PB	PR	/A	PD	TPI
1963 Min-A	0	0	—	3	0	0	0	0	4^1	8	1	6	2	29.1	10.38	35	.381	.519	0	—	0	-3	-3	0	0.0

● **DALE WILLIAMS** Williams, Elisha Alphonso b: 10/6/1855, Ludlow, Ky. d: 10/22/39, Covington, Ky. BR/TR, 5'9", 175 lbs. Deb: 8/12/1876

YEAR TM/L	W	L	PCT	G	GS	CG	SH	SV	IP	H	HR	BB	SO	RAT	ERA	ERA+	OAV	OOB	BH	AVG	PB	PR	/A	PD	TPI
1876 Cin-N	1	8	.111	9	9	9	0	0	83	123	1	4	6		4.23	52	.339	.346	7	.200	-2	-18	-19	-0	-1.6

● **FRANK WILLIAMS** Williams, Frank Lee b: 2/13/58, Seattle, Wash. BR/TR, 6'1", 190 lbs. Deb: 4/5/84

YEAR TM/L	W	L	PCT	G	GS	CG	SH	SV	IP	H	HR	BB	SO	RAT	ERA	ERA+	OAV	OOB	BH	AVG	PB	PR	/A	PD	TPI
1984 SF-N	9	4	.692	61	1	1	1	3	106^1	88	2	51	91	12.0	3.55	99	.226	.321	4	.222	1	0	-1	4	0.5
1985 SF-N	2	4	.333	49	0	0	0	1	73	65	5	35	54	13.1	4.19	82	.242	.342	0	.000	-0	-5	-6	0	-0.5
1986 SF-N	3	1	.750	36	0	0	0	1	52^1	35	0	21	33	10.3	1.20	292	.212	.316	1	.500	0	15	13	1	1.1
1987 Cin-N	4	0	1.000	85	0	0	0	2	105^2	101	5	39	60	12.1	2.30	185	.254	.324	0	.000	-1	21	23	1	0.9
1988 Cin-N	3	2	.600	60	0	0	0	1	62^2	59	6	35	43	13.8	2.59	139	.252	.354	0	.000	-0	6	7	0	0.6
1989 Det-A	3	3	.500	42	0	0	0	1	71^2	70	5	46	33	14.9	3.64	105	.254	.366	0	—	0	2	1	-0	0.1
Total 6	24	14	.632	333	1	1	1	8	471^2	418	23	227	314	12.7	3.00	124	.242	.336	5	.172	1	39	38	5	2.7

● **WOODY WILLIAMS** Williams, Gregory Scott b: 8/19/66, Houston, Tex. BR/TR, 6', 180 lbs. Deb: 5/14/93

YEAR TM/L	W	L	PCT	G	GS	CG	SH	SV	IP	H	HR	BB	SO	RAT	ERA	ERA+	OAV	OOB	BH	AVG	PB	PR	/A	PD	TPI
1993 Tor-A	3	1	.750	30	0	0	0	0	37	40	2	22	24	15.3	4.38	99	.274	.373	0	—	0	-0	-1	1	0.0
1994 Tor-A	1	3	.250	38	0	0	0	0	59^1	44	5	33	56	12.0	3.64	133	.205	.316	0	—	0	8	8	0	0.4
Total 2	4	4	.500	68	0	0	0	0	96^1	84	7	55	80	13.3	3.92	118	.233	.339	0	—	0	7	8	1	0.4

● **JOHNNIE WILLIAMS** Williams, John Brodie "Honolulu Johnnie" b: 7/16/1889, Honolulu, Hawaii d: 9/8/63, Long Beach, Cal. BR/TR, 6', 180 lbs. Deb: 4/21/14

YEAR TM/L	W	L	PCT	G	GS	CG	SH	SV	IP	H	HR	BB	SO	RAT	ERA	ERA+	OAV	OOB	BH	AVG	PB	PR	/A	PD	TPI
1914 Det-A	0	2	.000	4	3	1	0	0	11^1	17	0	5	4	17.5	6.35	44	.378	.440	0	.000	-0	-5	-4	-0	-0.8

● **LEON WILLIAMS** Williams, Leon Theo "Lefty" b: 12/2/05, Macon, Ga. d: 11/20/84, Atlanta, Ga. BL/TL, 5'10.5", 154 lbs. Deb: 6/2/26

YEAR TM/L	W	L	PCT	G	GS	CG	SH	SV	IP	H	HR	BB	SO	RAT	ERA	ERA+	OAV	OOB	BH	AVG	PB	PR	/A	PD	TPI
1926 Bro-N	0	0	—	8	0	0	0	0	8^1	16	0	2	3	19.4	5.40	71	.421	.450	1	.200	0	-1	-1	1	0.1

● **MARSH WILLIAMS** Williams, Marshall McDiarmid "Cap" b: 2/21/1893, Faison, N.C. d: 2/22/35, Tucson, Ariz. BR/TR, 6', 180 lbs. Deb: 7/7/16

YEAR TM/L	W	L	PCT	G	GS	CG	SH	SV	IP	H	HR	BB	SO	RAT	ERA	ERA+	OAV	OOB	BH	AVG	PB	PR	/A	PD	TPI
1916 Phi-A	0	6	.000	10	4	3	0	0	51^1	71	4	31	17	17.9	7.89	36	.350	.436	2	.105	-1	-29	-29	-1	-3.0

● **MATT WILLIAMS** Williams, Matthew Evan b: 7/25/59, Houston, Tex. BR/TR, 6'1", 200 lbs. Deb: 8/2/83

YEAR TM/L	W	L	PCT	G	GS	CG	SH	SV	IP	H	HR	BB	SO	RAT	ERA	ERA+	OAV	OOB	BH	AVG	PB	PR	/A	PD	TPI
1983 Tor-A	1	1	.500	4	3	0	0	0	8	13	5	7	5	23.6	14.63	29	.361	.477	0	—	0	-9	-9	-0	-1.6
1985 Tex-A	2	1	.667	6	3	0	0	0	26	20	3	10	22	10.4	2.42	175	.211	.286	0	—	0	5	5	-1	0.4
Total 2	3	2	.600	10	6	0	0	0	34	33	8	17	27	13.5	5.29	80	.252	.342	0	—	0	-4	-4	-1	-1.2

● **MIKE WILLIAMS** Williams, Michael Darren b: 7/29/69, Radford, Va. BR/TR, 6'2", 190 lbs. Deb: 6/30/92

YEAR TM/L	W	L	PCT	G	GS	CG	SH	SV	IP	H	HR	BB	SO	RAT	ERA	ERA+	OAV	OOB	BH	AVG	PB	PR	/A	PD	TPI
1992 Phi-N	1	1	.500	5	5	0	0	0	28^2	29	3	7	5	11.3	5.34	65	.259	.303	4	.400	1	-6	-6	-0	-0.3
1993 Phi-N	1	3	.250	17	4	0	0	0	51	50	5	22	33	12.7	5.29	75	.253	.327	1	.083	-1	-7	-8	-0	-0.6
1994 Phi-N	2	4	.333	12	8	0	0	0	50^1	61	7	20	29	14.5	5.01	82	.310	.373	2	.167	0	-4	-5	-0	-0.5
Total 3	4	8	.333	34	17	1	0	0	130	140	15	49	67	13.1	5.19	76	.276	.340	7	.206	1	-17	-18	-1	-1.4

● **MITCH WILLIAMS** Williams, Mitchell Steven "Wild Thing" b: 11/17/64, Santa Ana, Cal. BL/TL, 6'4", 205 lbs. Deb: 4/9/86

YEAR TM/L	W	L	PCT	G	GS	CG	SH	SV	IP	H	HR	BB	SO	RAT	ERA	ERA+	OAV	OOB	BH	AVG	PB	PR	/A	PD	TPI
1986 Tex-A	8	6	.571	**80**	0	0	0	8	98	69	8	79	90	14.6	3.58	120	.202	.369	0	—	0	6	8	-1	1.0
1987 Tex-A	8	6	.571	85	1	0	0	6	108^2	63	9	94	129	13.6	3.23	138	.175	.355	0	—	0	15	15	1	1.9
1988 Tex-A	2	7	.222	67	0	0	0	18	68	48	4	47	61	13.4	4.63	88	.203	.349	0	—	0	-5	-4	0	-0.8
1989 *Chi-N★	4	4	.500	76	0	0	0	36	81^2	71	6	52	67	14.4	2.76	136	.238	.366	1	.200	1	7	9	-1	1.0
1990 Chi-N	1	8	.111	59	2	0	0	16	66^1	60	4	50	55	15.1	3.93	104	.239	.368	0	—	-1	-1	1	-1	0.0
1991 Phi-N	12	5	.706	69	0	0	0	30	88^1	56	4	62	84	12.8	2.34	156	.182	.333	0	.000	0	13	13	-1	3.4
1992 Phi-N	5	8	.385	66	0	0	0	29	81	69	4	64	74	15.4	3.78	92	.240	.389	1	.250	0	-2	-3	-1	-0.7
1993 *Phi-N	3	7	.300	65	0	0	0	43	62	56	4	60	74	14.8	3.34	119	.245	.371	1	1.000	0	5	4	-1	1.2
1994 Hou-N	1	4	.200	25	0	0	0	6	20	21	4	24	21	20.7	7.65	53	.269	.447	0	—	0	-8	-8	-0	-2.2
Total 9	44	55	.444	592	3	0	0	192	674	513	46	516	641	14.4	3.53	114	.215	.365	3	.188	1	30	36	-5	5.7

● **STEAMBOAT WILLIAMS** Williams, Rees Gephardt b: 1/31/1892, Cascade, Mont. d: 6/29/79, Deer River, Minn. BL/TR, 5'11", 170 lbs. Deb: 7/12/14

YEAR TM/L	W	L	PCT	G	GS	CG	SH	SV	IP	H	HR	BB	SO	RAT	ERA	ERA+	OAV	OOB	BH	AVG	PB	PR	/A	PD	TPI
1914 StL-N	0	1	.000	5	1	0	0	0	11	13	1	6	2	15.5	6.55	43	.295	.380	0	.000	-0	-5	-5	-0	-0.4
1916 StL-N	6	7	.462	36	8	5	0	1	105	121	6	27	25	12.8	4.20	63	.291	.336	5	.208	1	-18	-18	-0	-2.2
Total 2	6	8	.429	41	9	5	0	1	116	134	7	33	27	13.0	4.42	60	.291	.340	5	.200	1	-23	-23	-0	-2.6

● **RICK WILLIAMS** Williams, Richard Allen b: 11/9/52, Merced, Cal. BR/TR, 6'1", 180 lbs. Deb: 6/12/78

YEAR TM/L	W	L	PCT	G	GS	CG	SH	SV	IP	H	HR	BB	SO	RAT	ERA	ERA+	OAV	OOB	BH	AVG	PB	PR	/A	PD	TPI
1978 Hou-N	1	2	.333	17	0	0	0	0	34^2	43	2	10	17	13.8	4.67	71	.301	.346	0	.000	-1	-4	-5	-0	-0.5
1979 Hou-N	4	7	.364	31	16	2	2	0	121^1	122	6	30	37	11.4	3.26	108	.261	.308	8	.258	3	6	3	0	0.6
Total 2	5	9	.357	48	17	2	2	0	156	165	8	40	54	11.9	3.58	97	.270	.317	8	.222	2	2	-2	1	0.1

● **ACE WILLIAMS** Williams, Robert Fulton b: 3/18/17, Montclair, N.J. BR/TL, 6'2", 174 lbs. Deb: 7/15/40

YEAR TM/L	W	L	PCT	G	GS	CG	SH	SV	IP	H	HR	BB	SO	RAT	ERA	ERA+	OAV	OOB	BH	AVG	PB	PR	/A	PD	TPI
1940 Bos-N	0	0	—	5	0	0	0	0	9	21	0	12	5	34.0	16.00	23	.375	.493	0	.000	-0	-12	-12	0	0.0
1946 Bos-N	0	0	—	1	0	0	0	0	0	1	0	1	0	—	—	—	1.000	1.000	0	—	0	-0	-0	-0	0.0
Total 2	0	0	—	6	0	0	0	0	9	22	0	13	5	36.0	16.00	23	.386	.507	0	.000	0	-12	-12	0	0.0

● **STAN WILLIAMS** Williams, Stanley Wilson b: 9/14/36, Enfield, N.H. BR/TR, 6'5", 230 lbs. Deb: 5/17/58 C

YEAR TM/L	W	L	PCT	G	GS	CG	SH	SV	IP	H	HR	BB	SO	RAT	ERA	ERA+	OAV	OOB	BH	AVG	PB	PR	/A	PD	TPI
1958 LA-N	9	7	.563	27	21	3	2	0	119	99	10	65	80	12.9	4.01	102	.228	.338	2	.050	-3	-1	1	0	-0.1
1959 *LA-N	5	5	.500	35	15	2	0	0	124^2	102	12	86	89	14.2	3.97	106	.238	.363	7	.194	1	0	0	0	0.3
1960 LA-N★	14	10	.583	38	30	9	2	1	207^1	162	26	72	175	10.4	3.00	133	.210	.282	0	.141	0	18	22	1	2.4
1961 LA-N	15	12	.556	41	35	6	2	0	235^1	213	21	108	205	12.5	3.90	111	.242	.329	13	.167	-1	3	12	-1	1.1
1962 LA-N	14	12	.538	40	28	4	1	1	185^2	184	16	98	108	13.7	4.46	81	.253	.341	5	.076	-2	-11	-17	-1	-2.4
1963 *NY-A	9	8	.529	29	21	6	1	0	146	137	7	57	98	12.3	3.21	110	.249	.326	5	.102	-1	7	5	1	0.5
1964 NY-A	1	5	.167	21	10	1	0	0	82	76	7	38	54	12.5	3.84	94	.248	.330	3	.143	-0	-2	-2	1	-0.1

YEAR TM/L	W	L	PCT	G	GS	CG	SH	SV	IP	H	HR	BB	SO	RAT	ERA	ERA+	OAV	OOB	BH	AVG	PB	PR	/A	PD	TPI
1965 Cle-A	0	0	—	3	0	0	0	0	4¹	6	1	3	1	18.7	6.23	56	.353	.450	0	—	0	-1	-1	0	0.0
1967 Cle-A	6	4	.600	16	8	2	1	1	79	64	6	24	75	10.1	2.62	125	.218	.279	2	.091	-1	5	6	-2	0.4
1968 Cle-A	13	11	.542	44	24	6	2	9	194¹	163	14	51	147	10.4	2.50	118	.225	.285	9	.161	1	10	10	-1	1.5
1969 Cle-A	6	14	.300	61	15	3	0	12	178¹	155	25	67	139	11.8	3.94	96	.235	.317	4	.100	-1	-6	-3	-1	-0.5
1970 *Min-A	10	1	.909	68	0	0	0	15	113¹	85	8	32	76	9.7	1.99	187	.208	.274	0	.000	-2	22	22	-2	2.3
1971 Min-A	4	5	.444	46	1	0	0	4	78	63	7	44	47	13.3	4.15	86	.220	.340	0	.000	-1	-6	-5	-1	-0.8
StL-N	3	0	1.000	10	0	0	0	0	12²	13	0	2	8	12.1	1.42	253	.265	.321	0	.000	-0	3	3	0	0.8
1972 Bos-A	0	0	—	3	0	0	0	0	4¹	5	0	1	3	12.5	6.23	52	.294	.333	0	—	0	-2	-1	0	0.0
Total 14	109	94	.537	482	208	42	11	43	1764¹	1527	160	748	1305	12.0	3.48	108	.232	.317	59	.118	-10	39	53	-4	5.6

● **TED WILLIAMS**   Williams, Theodore Samuel "The Kid", "The Thumper" or "The Splendid Splinter"
b: 8/30/18, San Diego, Cal. BL/TR, 6'3", 205 lbs. Deb: 4/20/39 MH♦

| 1940 Bos-A★ | 0 | 0 | — | 1 | 0 | 0 | 0 | 0 | 2 | 3 | 0 | 1 | 1 | 13.5 | 4.50 | 100 | .333 | .333 | 193 | .344 | 1 | -0 | -1 | 0 | 0.0 |

● **TOM WILLIAMS**   Williams, Thomas C. b: 8/19/1870, Minersville, Ohio d: 7/27/40, Columbus, Ohio Deb: 5/1/1892

1892 Cle-N	1	0	1.000	2	1	1	0	0	9	9	1	1	3	10.0	3.00	113	.250	.270	1	.100	-1	0	0	-0	0.0
1893 Cle-N	1	1	.500	5	2	2	0	0	24	33	1	10	6	16.5	4.88	100	.317	.383	5	.278	0	-1	0	0	0.0
Total 2	2	1	.667	7	3	3	0	0	33	42	2	11	9	14.7	4.36	102	.300	.355	6	.214	-0	-0	0	-0	0.0

● **POP WILLIAMS**   Williams, Walter Merrill b: 5/19/1874, Bowdoinham, Me. d: 8/4/59, Topsham, Maine BL/5'11", 190 lbs. Deb: 9/14/1898

1898 Was-N	0	2	.000	2	2	2	0	0	17	32	0	7	3	20.6	8.47	43	.396	.444	3	.375	1	-9	-9	-1	-0.7
1902 Chi-N	11	16	.407	31	31	26	1	0	254¹	259	2	63	94	11.7	2.51	107	.264	.313	23	.198	2	8	5	3	1.1
1903 Chi-N	0	1	.000	1	1	1	0	0	5	9	0	0	2	16.2	5.40	58	.409	.409	0	.000	0	-1	-1	-0	-0.2
Phi-N	1	1	.500	2	2	2	0	0	18	21	0	6	8	14.0	3.00	109	.304	.368	2	.286	0	1	1	1	0.2
Bos-N	4	5	.444	10	10	9	1	0	83	97	3	37	20	15.5	4.12	78	.295	.381	10	.238	-0	-8	-8	-1	-0.8
Yr	5	7	.417	13	13	12	1	0	106	127	3	43	30	15.2	3.99	81	.302	.378	12	.235	0	-8	-9	-0	-0.8
Total 3	16	25	.390	46	46	40	2	0	377¹	418	5	113	127	13.1	3.20	90	.282	.340	38	.217	4	-10	-13	2	-0.4

● **WASH WILLIAMS**   Williams, Washington J. b: Philadelphia, Pa. d: 1/1890, Philadelphia, Pa. 5'11", 180 lbs. Deb: 8/5/1884 ♦

| 1885 Chi-N | 0 | 0 | — | 1 | 1 | 0 | 0 | 0 | 2 | 2 | 0 | 5 | 0 | 31.5 | 13.50 | 22 | .400 | .700 | 1 | .250 | -0 | -2 | -2 | 0 | 0.0 |

● **NED WILLIAMSON**   Williamson, Edward Nagle b: 10/24/1857, Philadelphia, Pa. d: 3/3/1894, Willow Springs, Ark BR/TR, 5'11", 210 lbs. Deb: 5/1/1878 ♦

1881 Chi-N	1	1	.500	3	1	1	0	0	18	14	0	0	2	7.0	2.00	137	.209	.209	92	.268	1	2	1	-0	0.1
1882 Chi-N	0	0	—	1	0	0	0	0	3	9	1	1	0	30.0	6.00	48	.500	.526	98	.282	0	-1	-1	0	0.0
1883 Chi-N	0	0	—	1	0	0	0	0	1	1	0	1	0	18.0	9.00	35	.167	.286	111	.276	0	-1	-1	0	0.0
1884 Chi-N	0	0	—	2	0	0	0	0	2	8	0	2	0	45.0	18.00	17	.500	.556	116	.278	1	-3	-3	0	0.0
1885 *Chi-N	0	0	—	2	0	0	0	2	6	2	0	3	0	3.0	0.00	—	.080	.080	97	.238	0	2	2	0	0.2
1886 *Chi-N	0	0	—	2	0	0	0	1	3	2	0	1	0	6.0	0.00	—	.143	.143	93	.216	0	1	1	-0	0.1
1887 Chi-N	0	0	—	1	0	0	0	0	2	2	0	1	0	13.5	9.00	50	.222	.300	117	.267	0	-1	-1	0	0.0
Total 7	1	1	.500	12	1	1	0	3	35	38	1	5	7	11.1	3.34	90	.245	.269	1159	.255	3	-2	-1	0	0.4

● **MARK WILLIAMSON**   Williamson, Mark Alan b: 7/21/59, Corpus Christi, Tex. BR/TR, 6', 171 lbs. Deb: 4/8/87

1987 Bal-A	8	9	.471	61	2	0	0	3	125	122	12	41	73	12.0	4.03	109	.261	.324	0	—	0	6	5	1	0.9
1988 Bal-A	5	8	.385	37	10	2	0	2	117²	125	14	40	69	12.8	4.90	80	.272	.333	0	—	0	-12	-13	-0	-1.3
1989 Bal-A	10	5	.667	65	0	0	0	9	107¹	105	4	30	55	11.5	2.93	129	.261	.315	0	—	0	11	10	-1	1.5
1990 Bal-A	8	2	.800	49	0	0	0	1	85¹	65	8	28	60	9.8	2.21	171	.215	.282	0	—	0	16	15	1	1.8
1991 Bal-A	5	5	.500	65	0	0	0	4	80¹	87	9	35	53	13.7	4.48	88	.275	.348	0	—	0	-3	-5	-0	-0.6
1992 Bal-A	0	0	—	12	0	0	0	1	18²	16	1	14	12	15.5	0.96	417	.239	.338	0	—	0	6	6	-1	0.0
1993 Bal-A	7	5	.583	48	1	0	0	0	88	106	5	25	45	13.4	4.91	91	.304	.350	0	—	0	-6	-4	-0	-0.6
1994 Bal-A	3	1	.750	28	2	0	0	1	67¹	75	9	17	28	12.6	4.01	127	.278	.325	0	—	0	6	8	0	0.3
Total 8	46	35	.568	365	15	2	0	21	689²	701	62	226	397	12.2	3.86	107	.266	.326	0	—	0	24	22	-0	2.0

● **AL WILLIAMSON**   Williamson, Silas Albert b: 2/20/1900, Buckville, Ark. d: 11/29/78, Hot Springs, Ark. BR/TR, 5'11", 160 lbs. Deb: 4/27/28

| 1928 Chi-A | 0 | 0 | — | 1 | 0 | 0 | 0 | 0 | 2 | 1 | 0 | 0 | 0 | 4.5 | 0.00 | — | .167 | .167 | 0 | — | 0 | 1 | 1 | 0 | 0.0 |

● **CARL WILLIS**   Willis, Carl Blake b: 12/28/60, Danville, Va. BL/TR, 6'4", 210 lbs. Deb: 6/9/84

1984 Det-A	0	2	.000	10	2	0	0	0	16	25	1	5	4	16.9	7.31	54	.362	.405	0	—	0	-6	-6	0	-0.6
Cin-N				7	0	0	0	0	9²	8	1	2	8	9.3	3.72	101	.222	.263	0	—	0	-0	-0	0	0.0
1985 Cin-N	1	0	1.000	11	0	0	0	1	13²	21	3	5	6	17.1	9.22	41	.344	.394	0	.000	0	-9	-8	-0	-0.7
1986 Cin-N	1	3	.250	29	0	0	0	0	52¹	54	4	32	24	15.0	4.47	87	.278	.383	1	.333	0	-4	-4	1	-0.2
1988 Chi-A	0	0	—	6	0	0	0	0	12	17	3	7	6	18.0	8.25	48	.362	.444	0	—	0	-6	-6	-0	0.0
1991 *Min-A	8	3	.727	40	0	0	0	2	89	76	4	19	53	9.7	2.63	162	.232	.276	0	—	0	14	16	-1	1.8
1992 Min-A	7	3	.700	59	0	0	0	1	79¹	73	4	11	45	9.5	2.72	149	.246	.273	0	—	0	11	12	-1	1.3
1993 Min-A	3	0	1.000	53	0	0	0	5	58	56	2	17	44	11.3	3.10	140	.259	.313	0	—	0	8	8	-0	0.5
1994 Min-A	2	4	.333	49	0	0	0	1	59¹	89	6	12	37	15.3	5.92	82	.335	.363	0	—	0	-7	-7	0	-0.7
Total 8	22	16	.579	264	2	0	0	13	389¹	419	28	110	222	12.3	4.09	103	.277	.327	1	.250	0	1	6	-2	1.4

● **LEFTY WILLIS**   Willis, Charles William b: 11/4/05, Leetown, W.Va. d: 5/10/62, Bethesda, Md. BL/TL, 6'1", 175 lbs. Deb: 10/3/25

1925 Phi-A	0	0	—	1	1	0	0	0	5	9	2	3	0	19.8	10.80	43	.409	.458	0	.000	-1	-4	-3	0	0.0
1926 Phi-A	0	0	—	13	1	0	0	1	32¹	31	0	12	13	12.2	1.39	300	.270	.344	2	.222	-0	9	10	-0	0.0
1927 Phi-A	3	1	.750	15	2	1	0	0	27	32	2	11	7	14.3	5.67	75	.308	.374	0	.000	-1	-5	-4	1	-0.5
Total 3	3	1	.750	29	4	1	0	1	64¹	72	4	25	23	13.7	3.92	108	.299	.367	2	.111	-1	1	2	1	-0.5

● **DALE WILLIS**   Willis, Dale Jerome b: 5/29/38, Calhoun, Ga. BR/TR, 5'11", 165 lbs. Deb: 4/14/63

| 1963 KC-A | 0 | 2 | .000 | 25 | 0 | 0 | 0 | 1 | 44² | 46 | 3 | 25 | 47 | 15.1 | 5.04 | 77 | .266 | .371 | 1 | .167 | -0 | -7 | -6 | 1 | -0.2 |

● **JIM WILLIS**   Willis, James Gladden b: 3/20/27, Doyline, La. BL/TR, 6'3", 175 lbs. Deb: 4/22/53

1953 Chi-N	2	1	.667	13	3	2	0	0	43¹	37	3	17	15	11.8	3.12	143	.228	.313	0	.000	-1	6	6	1	0.4
1954 Chi-N	0	1	.000	14	1	0	0	0	23	22	1	18	5	16.8	3.91	107	.256	.402	0	.000	-1	0	1	1	0.0
Total 2	2	2	.500	27	4	2	0	0	66¹	59	4	35	20	13.6	3.39	129	.238	.346	0	.000	-2	6	7	2	0.4

● **JOE WILLIS**   Willis, Joseph Denk b: 4/9/1890, Coal Grove, Ohio d: 12/4/66, Ironton, Ohio BR/TL, 6'1", 185 lbs. Deb: 5/3/11

1911 StL-A	0	1	.000	1	1	0	0	0	7	8	0	4	3	14.1	5.14	66	.308	.379	0	—	0	-1	-1	-1	-0.2
StL-N	0	1	.000	2	2	1	0	0	15	13	0	4	5	10.2	4.20	80	.232	.283	0	.000	-1	-1	-1	0	-0.1
1912 StL-N	4	9	.308	31	17	4	0	2	129²	143	4	62	55	14.6	4.44	77	.288	.372	6	.158	-2	-15	-15	-1	-1.5
1913 StL-N	0	0	—	7	0	0	0	0	9²	9	0	11	6	18.6	7.45	43	.257	.435	0	.000	-0	-5	-5	-0	-0.2
Total 3	4	11	.267	41	20	5	0	2	161¹	173	4	80	66	14.4	4.63	74	.282	.369	6	.125	-2	-22	-22	-2	-2.0

● **LES WILLIS**   Willis, Lester Evans "Wimpy" or "Lefty" b: 1/17/08, Nacogdoches, Tex. d: 1/22/82, Jasper, Tex. BL/TL, 5'9.5", 195 lbs. Deb: 4/28/47

| 1947 Cle-A | 0 | 2 | .000 | 4 | 4 | 1 | 0 | 0 | 23 | 24 | 1 | 10 | 16.8 | 3.48 | 100 | .324 | .404 | 1 | .091 | -1 | 1 | 0 | -1 | -0.2 |

● **MIKE WILLIS**   Willis, Michael Henry b: 12/26/50, Oklahoma City, Okla BL/TL, 6'2", 210 lbs. Deb: 4/13/77

1977 Tor-A	2	6	.250	43	3	0	0	5	107¹	105	15	38	59	12.0	3.94	106	.260	.324	0	—	0	1	3	1	0.3
1978 Tor-A	3	7	.300	44	2	1	0	7	100²	104	11	39	52	12.8	4.56	86	.271	.338	0	—	0	-9	-7	0	-0.8
1979 Tor-A	0	3	.000	17	0	0	0	0	26²	35	1	16	8	17.6	8.44	51	.333	.426	0	—	0	-13	-12	0	-1.2
1980 Tor-A	2	1	.667	20	0	0	0	3	26¹	25	3	11	14	12.6	1.71	252	.248	.327	0	—	0	7	8	0	0.7

YEAR TM/L	W	L	PCT	G	GS	CG	SH	SV	IP	H	HR	BB	SO	RAT	ERA	ERA+	OAV	OOB	BH	AVG	PB	PR	/A	PD	TPI
1981 Tor-A	0	4	.000	20	0	0	0	0	35	43	6	20	16	16.5	5.91	67	.301	.390	0	—	0	-9	-8	0	-0.8
Total 5	7	21	.250	144	6	1	0	15	296	312	36	124	149	13.3	4.59	89	.274	.347	0	—	0	-22	-16	1	-1.8

● **RON WILLIS**　　Willis, Ronald Earl　b: 7/12/43, Willisville, Tenn.　d: 11/21/77, Memphis, Tenn.　BR/TR, 6'2", 195 lbs.　Deb: 9/20/66

YEAR TM/L	W	L	PCT	G	GS	CG	SH	SV	IP	H	HR	BB	SO	RAT	ERA	ERA+	OAV	OOB	BH	AVG	PB	PR	/A	PD	TPI
1966 StL-N	0	0	—	4	0	0	0	1	3	1	0	1	2	6.0	0.00	—	.100	.182	0	—	0	1	1	-0	0.1
1967 *StL-N	6	5	.545	65	0	0	0	10	81	76	3	43	42	13.6	2.67	123	.257	.357	3	.375	1	6	6	2	1.3
1968 *StL-N	2	3	.400	48	0	0	0	4	63²	50	4	28	39	11.2	3.39	85	.213	.299	0	—	-1	-3	-4	1	-0.4
1969 StL-N	1	2	.333	26	0	0	0	0	32¹	26	4	19	23	12.8	4.18	86	.224	.338	1	1.000	0	-2	-2	1	0.0
Hou-N	0	0	—	3	0	0	0	0	2¹	3	0	0	2	11.6	0.00	—	.300	.300	0	—	0	1	1	-0	0.0
Yr	1	2	.333	29	0	0	0	0	34²	29	4	19	25	12.5	3.89	92	.223	.322	1	1.000	0	-1	-1	1	0.0
1970 SD-N	2	2	.500	42	0	0	0	4	56	53	4	28	20	13.7	4.02	99	.247	.344	0	.000	-1	0	-0	1	0.1
Total 5	11	12	.478	188	0	0	0	19	238¹	209	15	119	128	12.7	3.32	102	.237	.334	4	.160	0	4	2	5	1.1

● **VIC WILLIS**　　Willis, Victor Gazaway　b: 4/12/1876, Cecil Co., Md.　d: 8/3/47, Elkton, Md.　BR/TR, 6'2", 185 lbs.　Deb: 4/20/1898

YEAR TM/L	W	L	PCT	G	GS	CG	SH	SV	IP	H	HR	BB	SO	RAT	ERA	ERA+	OAV	OOB	BH	AVG	PB	PR	/A	PD	TPI
1898 Bos-N	25	13	.658	41	38	29	1	0	311	264	5	148	160	12.8	2.84	130	.228	.331	17	.145	-6	27	30	-0	2.5
1899 Bos-N	27	8	.771	41	38	35	5	2	342²	277	6	117	120	11.1	2.50	167	.221	.303	29	.216	-4	52	63	0	5.3
1900 Bos-N	10	17	.370	32	29	22	2	0	236	258	11	106	53	14.3	4.19	98	.277	.359	12	.136	-6	-13	-2	-2	-0.9
1901 Bos-N	20	17	.541	38	35	33	6	0	305¹	262	6	78	133	10.3	2.36	153	.230	.286	20	.187	-1	33	43	-1	4.6
1902 Bos-N	27	20	.574	51	46	45	4	3	410	372	6	101	225	10.7	2.20	129	.242	.295	23	.153	-6	27	29	4	3.1
1903 Bos-N	12	18	.400	33	32	29	2	0	278	256	3	88	125	11.5	2.98	108	.251	.317	24	.188	-1	9	7	3	0.8
1904 Bos-N	18	25	.419	43	43	39	2	0	350	357	7	109	196	12.3	2.85	97	.266	.327	27	.182	1	-4	-4	7	0.4
1905 Bos-N	12	29	.293	41	41	36	4	0	342	340	7	107	149	12.1	3.21	97	.265	.328	20	.153	-3	-8	-4	6	-0.1
1906 Pit-N	23	13	.639	41	36	32	6	1	322	295	0	76	124	10.5	1.73	154	.250	.298	20	.174	-1	32	34	5	4.5
1907 Pit-N	21	11	.656	39	37	27	6	1	292²	234	4	69	107	9.5	2.34	104	.219	.271	14	.136	-2	4	3	2	0.3
1908 Pit-N	23	11	.676	41	38	25	7	0	304²	239	2	69	97	9.3	2.07	111	.213	.262	17	.165	-1	10	8	-1	0.7
1909 *Pit-N	22	11	.667	39	35	24	4	1	289²	243	3	83	95	10.3	2.24	122	.231	.289	14	.136	-2	12	16	1	1.6
1910 StL-N	9	12	.429	33	23	12	1	3	212	224	6	61	67	12.1	3.35	89	.275	.326	11	.167	-2	-8	-9	2	-0.8
Total 13	249	205	.548	513	471	388	50	11	3996	3621	66	1212	1651	11.2	2.63	118	.243	.307	248	.166	-33	172	208	27	22.0

● **CLAUDE WILLOUGHBY**　　Willoughby, Claude William "Flunky" or "Weeping Willie"　b: 11/14/1898, Fredonia, Kan.　d: 8/14/73, McPherson, Kan.　BR/TR, 5'9.5", 165 lbs.　Deb: 9/18/25

YEAR TM/L	W	L	PCT	G	GS	CG	SH	SV	IP	H	HR	BB	SO	RAT	ERA	ERA+	OAV	OOB	BH	AVG	PB	PR	/A	PD	TPI
1925 Phi-N	2	1	.667	3	3	1	0	0	23	26	0	11	6	14.9	1.96	244	.295	.380	1	.000	-1	6	7	-1	0.7
1926 Phi-N	8	12	.400	47	18	6	0	1	168	218	11	71	37	15.8	5.95	70	.327	.396	11	.212	-1	-40	-34	3	-3.3
1927 Phi-N	3	7	.300	35	6	1	1	2	97²	126	7	53	14	16.7	6.54	63	.321	.404	2	.077	-2	-28	-26	-1	-2.6
1928 Phi-N	6	5	.545	35	13	5	1	1	130²	180	6	83	26	18.3	5.30	80	.340	.432	6	.150	-1	-19	-15	-1	-1.2
1929 Phi-N	15	14	.517	49	34	14	1	4	243¹	288	15	108	50	14.8	4.99	104	.296	.370	13	.143	-5	-7	-5	4	0.5
1930 Phi-N	4	17	.190	41	24	5	1	1	153	241	17	68	38	18.3	7.59	72	.369	.430	5	.104	-4	-44	-36	2	-3.9
1931 Pit-N	0	2	.000	9	2	1	0	0	25²	32	4	12	4	15.4	6.31	61	.305	.376	2	.286	0	-7	-7	0	-0.4
Total 7	38	58	.396	219	100	33	4	9	841¹	1111	56	406	175	16.4	5.84	81	.326	.401	39	.143	-14	-140	-106	8	-10.2

● **JIM WILLOUGHBY**　　Willoughby, James Arthur　b: 1/31/49, Salinas, Cal.　BR/TR, 6'2", 185 lbs.　Deb: 9/5/71

YEAR TM/L	W	L	PCT	G	GS	CG	SH	SV	IP	H	HR	BB	SO	RAT	ERA	ERA+	OAV	OOB	BH	AVG	PB	PR	/A	PD	TPI
1971 SF-N	0	1	.000	2	1	0	0	0	4	8	0	1	3	20.3	9.00	38	.400	.429	0	.000	-0	-2	-2	0	-0.5
1972 SF-N	6	4	.600	11	11	7	0	0	87²	72	8	14	40	9.0	2.36	148	.222	.259	5	.185	0	11	11	0	1.4
1973 SF-N	4	5	.444	39	12	1	1	1	123	138	21	37	60	13.0	4.68	82	.295	.350	4	.143	1	-14	-12	-1	-0.8
1974 SF-N	1	4	.200	18	4	0	0	0	40²	51	7	9	12	13.3	4.65	82	.304	.339	1	.100	-0	-5	-4	1	-0.4
1975 *Bos-A	5	2	.714	24	0	0	0	8	48¹	46	6	16	29	11.9	3.54	115	.247	.314	0	—	0	1	3	0	0.3
1976 Bos-A	3	12	.200	54	0	0	0	10	99	94	4	31	37	12.1	2.82	139	.256	.328	0	.000	0	8	12	1	2.2
1977 Bos-A	6	2	.750	31	0	0	0	2	54²	54	5	18	33	12.2	4.94	91	.258	.323	0	—	0	-5	-3	1	-0.3
1978 Chi-A	1	6	.143	59	0	0	0	13	93¹	95	6	19	36	11.4	3.86	99	.275	.320	0	—	0	-1	-1	2	0.1
Total 8	26	36	.419	238	28	8	1	34	550²	558	57	145	250	11.8	3.79	102	.267	.321	10	.149	1	-8	4	5	2.0

● **FRANK WILLS**　　Wills, Frank Lee　b: 10/26/58, New Orleans, La.　BR/TR, 6'2", 202 lbs.　Deb: 7/31/83

YEAR TM/L	W	L	PCT	G	GS	CG	SH	SV	IP	H	HR	BB	SO	RAT	ERA	ERA+	OAV	OOB	BH	AVG	PB	PR	/A	PD	TPI
1983 KC-A	2	1	.667	6	4	0	0	0	34²	35	2	15	23	13.0	4.15	98	.259	.333	0	—	0	-0	-0	-0	-0.1
1984 KC-A	2	3	.400	10	5	0	0	0	37	39	3	13	21	12.6	5.11	79	.271	.331	0	—	0	-5	-4	-1	-0.6
1985 Sea-A	5	11	.313	24	18	1	0	1	123	122	16	68	67	14.1	6.00	70	.266	.365	0	—	0	-25	-24	0	-2.7
1986 Cle-A	4	4	.500	26	0	0	0	4	40¹	43	6	16	32	13.2	4.91	84	.272	.339	0	—	0	-3	-3	0	-0.6
1987 Cle-A	0	1	.000	6	0	0	0	0	5¹	3	0	7	4	16.9	5.06	89	.176	.417	0	—	0	-0	-0	-0	-0.1
1988 Tor-A	0	0	—	10	0	0	0	0	20²	22	2	6	19	12.2	5.23	75	.272	.322	0	—	0	-3	-3	1	-0.2
1989 Tor-A	3	1	.750	24	4	0	0	0	71¹	65	4	30	41	12.1	3.66	103	.242	.320	0	—	0	2	1	-0	0.1
1990 Tor-A	6	4	.600	44	4	0	0	1	99	101	13	38	72	12.7	4.73	83	.266	.334	0	—	0	-9	-9	0	-0.8
1991 Tor-A	0	1	.000	4	0	0	0	0	4¹	8	2	5	2	29.1	16.62	25	.421	.560	0	—	0	-6	-6	0	-1.1
Total 9	22	26	.458	154	35	1	0	6	435²	438	50	198	281	13.3	5.06	80	.264	.344	0	—	0	-50	-50	0	-5.9

● **TED WILLS**　　Wills, Theodore Carl　b: 2/9/34, Fresno, Cal.　BL/TL, 6'2", 200 lbs.　Deb: 5/24/59

YEAR TM/L	W	L	PCT	G	GS	CG	SH	SV	IP	H	HR	BB	SO	RAT	ERA	ERA+	OAV	OOB	BH	AVG	PB	PR	/A	PD	TPI
1959 Bos-A	2	6	.250	9	8	2	0	0	56¹	68	9	24	24	14.9	5.27	77	.302	.372	4	.250	1	-9	-8	-0	-0.9
1960 Bos-A	1	1	.500	15	0	0	0	1	30¹	38	4	16	28	16.9	7.42	55	.317	.410	2	.250	1	-12	-11	1	-0.6
1961 Bos-A	3	2	.600	17	0	0	0	1	19²	24	2	19	11	19.7	5.95	70	.304	.439	0	.000	-0	-4	-4	0	-0.9
1962 Bos-A	0	0	—	1	0	0	0	0	0	2	0	1	0	—	∞	—	1.000	1.000	0	—	0	-1	-1	0	-0.1
Cin-N	0	2	.000	26	0	0	0	3	61	61	12	23	58	13.1	5.31	76	.266	.346	5	.313	1	-9	-9	-0	-0.3
1965 Chi-A	2	0	1.000	15	0	0	0	0	19	17	2	14	12	15.2	2.84	112	.258	.395	0	.000	0	1	1	0	0.1
Total 5	8	11	.421	83	13	2	0	5	186¹	210	29	97	133	15.3	5.51	72	.291	.383	11	.250	3	-34	-32	1	-2.7

● **PAUL WILMET**　　Wilmet, Paul Richard　b: 11/8/58, Green Bay, Wis.　BR/TR, 5'11", 170 lbs.　Deb: 7/25/89

YEAR TM/L	W	L	PCT	G	GS	CG	SH	SV	IP	H	HR	BB	SO	RAT	ERA	ERA+	OAV	OOB	BH	AVG	PB	PR	/A	PD	TPI
1989 Tex-A	0	0	—	3	0	0	0	0	2¹	5	0	2	1	27.0	15.43	26	.417	.500	0	—	0	-3	-3	0	0.0

● **WHITEY WILSHERE**　　Wilshere, Vernon Sprague　b: 8/3/12, Poplar Ridge, N.Y.　d: 5/23/85, Cooperstown, N.Y.　BL/TL, 6', 180 lbs.　Deb: 6/24/34

YEAR TM/L	W	L	PCT	G	GS	CG	SH	SV	IP	H	HR	BB	SO	RAT	ERA	ERA+	OAV	OOB	BH	AVG	PB	PR	/A	PD	TPI
1934 Phi-A	0	1	.000	9	2	0	0	0	21²	39	0	15	19	22.8	12.05	36	.394	.478	0	.000	-0	-18	-18	-1	-0.8
1935 Phi-A	9	9	.500	27	18	7	3	1	142¹	136	8	78	80	14.2	4.05	112	.253	.358	4	.093	-4	6	8	-0	0.5
1936 Phi-A	1	2	.333	5	3	0	0	0	18¹	21	1	19	4	19.6	6.87	74	.288	.435	0	.000	-0	-4	-4	-0	-0.5
Total 3	10	12	.455	41	23	7	3	1	182¹	196	9	112	103	15.7	5.28	87	.276	.383	4	.080	-4	-15	-14	-1	-0.8

● **TERRY WILSHUSEN**　　Wilshusen, Terry Wayne　b: 3/22/49, Atascadero, Cal.　BR/TR, 6'2", 210 lbs.　Deb: 4/7/73

YEAR TM/L	W	L	PCT	G	GS	CG	SH	SV	IP	H	HR	BB	SO	RAT	ERA	ERA+	OAV	OOB	BH	AVG	PB	PR	/A	PD	TPI
1973 Cal-A	0	0	—	1	0	0	0	0	0¹	0	0	2	0	81.0	81.00	4	.000	.750	0	—	0	-3	-3	0	0.4

● **DON WILSON**　　Wilson, Donald Edward　b: 2/12/45, Monroe, La.　d: 1/5/75, Houston, Tex.　BR/TR, 6'3", 205 lbs.　Deb: 9/29/66

YEAR TM/L	W	L	PCT	G	GS	CG	SH	SV	IP	H	HR	BB	SO	RAT	ERA	ERA+	OAV	OOB	BH	AVG	PB	PR	/A	PD	TPI
1966 Hou-N	1	0	1.000	1	0	0	0	0	6	5	1	4	7	9.0	3.00	114	.238	.273	1	.500	1	0	0	0	0.1
1967 Hou-N	10	9	.526	31	28	7	3	0	184	141	10	69	159	10.6	2.79	119	.209	.289	6	.091	-2	12	11	-2	0.7
1968 Hou-N	13	16	.448	33	30	9	1	0	208²	197	9	70	175	11.3	3.28	90	.236	.302	15	.214	-4	-7	-7	-2	-0.8
1969 Hou-N	16	12	.571	34	34	13	1	0	225	210	16	97	235	12.6	4.00	89	.245	.328	8	.099	-1	-10	-11	-0	-1.5
1970 Hou-N	11	6	.647	29	27	3	0	0	184¹	188	15	66	94	12.7	3.91	99	.259	.327	8	.116	-2	3	-1	-3	-0.6
1971 Hou-N★	16	10	.615	35	34	18	3	0	268	195	15	79	180	9.4	2.45	137	.202	.268	14	.154	-1	30	27	-3	2.2
1972 Hou-N	15	10	.600	33	33	13	3	0	228¹	196	16	66	172	10.4	2.68	125	.233	.290	8	.105	-2	20	17	1	1.7
1973 Hou-N	11	16	.407	37	32	10	3	0	239¹	187	21	92	149	10.8	3.20	114	.213	.293	14	.177	1	12	12	-2	1.1
1974 Hou-N	11	13	.458	33	27	5	4	0	204²	170	16	100	112	12.0	3.08	112	.227	.321	13	.206	2	12	9	-3	1.0
Total 9	104	92	.531	266	245	78	20	2	1748¹	1479	119	640	1283	11.2	3.15	109	.228	.301	87	.146	-1	73	57	-14	3.9

YEAR TM/L	W	L	PCT	G	GS	CG	SH	SV	IP	H	HR	BB	SO	RAT	ERA	ERA+	OAV	OOB	BH	AVG	PB	PR	/A	PD	TPI

● DUANE WILSON Wilson, Duane Lewis b: 6/29/34, Wichita, Kan. BL/TL, 6'1", 185 lbs. Deb: 7/3/58

| 1958 Bos-A | 0 | 0 | — | 2 | 2 | 0 | 0 | 0 | 6¹ | 10 | 0 | 7 | 3 | 24.2 | 5.68 | 70 | .400 | .531 | 0 | .000 | -0 | -1 | -1 | 0 | 0.0 |

● FIN WILSON Wilson, Finis Elbert b: 12/9/1889, East Fork, Ky. d: 3/9/59, Coral Gables, Fla. BL/TL, 6'1", 194 lbs. Deb: 9/26/14

1914 Bro-F	0	1	.000	2	1	1	0	0	7	7	0	11	4	23.1	7.71	37	.269	.486	1	.500	1	-4	-4	-0	-0.4
1915 Bro-F	1	8	.111	18	11	5	0	0	102¹	85	2	53	47	12.5	3.78	72	.249	.356	11	.314	2	-12	-12	0	-0.7
Total 2	1	9	.100	20	12	6	0	0	109¹	92	2	64	51	13.2	4.03	68	.250	.367	12	.324	3	-16	-16	-0	-1.1

● ZEKE WILSON Wilson, Frank Ealton b: 12/24/1869, Benton, Ala. d: 4/26/28, Montgomery, Ala. BR/TR, 5'10", 165 lbs. Deb: 4/23/1895

1895 Bos-N	2	4	.333	6	6	4	0	0	45	54	1	27	5	16.2	5.20	98	.293	.383	6	.316	1	-2	-0	1	0.1
Cle-N	3	1	.750	8	7	3	0	0	44²	63	3	20	16	17.1	4.23	118	.327	.396	2	.111	-2	3	4	-0	0.0
Yr	5	5	.500	14	13	7	0	0	89²	117	4	47	21	16.7	4.72	107	.310	.390	8	.216	-2	1	3	1	0.1
1896 Cle-N	17	9	.654	33	29	20	1	1	240	265	9	81	56	13.3	4.01	113	.278	.339	27	.270	2	9	14	6	1.8
1897 Cle-N	16	11	.593	34	30	26	1	0	263²	323	6	83	69	14.2	4.16	108	.299	.354	26	.224	-3	4	10	1	0.6
1898 Cle-N	13	18	.419	33	31	28	0	0	254²	307	4	51	45	12.9	3.60	100	.296	.333	21	.178	-3	0	0	4	0.1
1899 StL-N	1	1	.500	5	2	2	0	0	26	30	0	4	3	12.5	4.50	88	.289	.327	0	.000	-1	-2	-1	1	-0.1
Total 5	52	44	.542	119	105	83	3	1	874	1042	26	266	194	13.8	4.03	106	.293	.347	82	.215	-8	13	25	14	2.5

● GARY WILSON Wilson, Gary Steven b: 11/21/54, Camden, Ark. BR/TR, 6'2", 185 lbs. Deb: 4/13/79

| 1979 Hou-N | 0 | 0 | — | 6 | 0 | 0 | 0 | 0 | 7¹ | 15 | 2 | 6 | 6 | 25.8 | 12.27 | 29 | .441 | .525 | 0 | — | -0 | -7 | -7 | -0 | -0.7 |

● GLENN WILSON Wilson, Glenn Dwight b: 12/22/58, Baytown, Tex. BR/TR, 6'1", 190 lbs. Deb: 4/15/82 ♦

| 1987 Phi-N | 0 | 0 | — | 1 | 0 | 0 | 0 | 0 | 1 | 0 | 0 | 0 | 1 | 0.00 | .000 | .000 | 150 | .264 | 0 | 0 | 0 | 0 | 0.0 |

● TEX WILSON Wilson, Gomer Russell b: 7/8/01, Trenton, Tex. d: 9/15/46, Sulphur Springs, Tex. BR/TL, 5'10", 170 lbs. Deb: 9/2/24

| 1924 Bro-N | 0 | 0 | — | 2 | 0 | 0 | 0 | 0 | 3² | 7 | 0 | 1 | 1 | 19.6 | 14.73 | 25 | .412 | .444 | 0 | .000 | -0 | -4 | -4 | 0 | -0.4 |

● HIGHBALL WILSON Wilson, Howard Paul b: 8/9/1878, Philadelphia, Pa. d: 10/16/34, Havre De Grace, Md TR , Deb: 9/13/1899

1899 Cle-N	0	1	.000	1	1	1	0	0	8	12	0	5	1	19.1	9.00	41	.345	.428	1	.333	0	-5	-5	-0	-0.4
1902 Phi-A	7	5	.583	13	10	8	0	0	96¹	103	1	19	18	12.2	2.43	151	.274	.324	6	.171	-1	12	13	-1	1.2
1903 Was-A	7	18	.280	30	28	25	1	0	242¹	269	7	43	56	12.0	3.31	95	.280	.318	17	.200	2	-9	-5	-4	-0.6
1904 Was-A	0	3	.000	3	3	3	0	0	25	33	0	4	11	14.0	4.68	57	.318	.355	2	.222	1	-6	-6	-0	-0.5
Total 4	14	27	.341	47	42	37	1	0	371²	417	8	71	86	12.3	3.29	99	.283	.325	26	.197	2	-7	-2	-5	-0.3

● JIM WILSON Wilson, James Alger b: 2/20/22, San Diego, Cal. d: 9/2/86, Newport Beach, Cal BR/TR, 6'1.5", 200 lbs. Deb: 4/18/45

1945 Bos-A	6	8	.429	23	21	8	2	0	144¹	121	7	88	50	13.1	3.30	103	.228	.339	13	.245	2	1	2	-2	0.1
1946 Bos-A	0	0	—	1	0	0	0	0	0²	2	1	0	0	27.0	27.00	14	.500	.500	0	—	0	-2	-2	-0	0.0
1948 StL-A	0	0	—	4	0	0	0	0	2²	5	0	5	1	33.8	13.50	34	.417	.588	0	—	0	-3	-3	0	0.0
1949 Phi-A	0	0	—	2	0	0	0	0	5	7	2	5	2	21.6	14.40	29	.350	.480	0	.000	-0	-6	-6	-0	-0.1
1951 Bos-N	7	7	.500	20	15	5	0	1	110	131	14	40	33	14.3	5.40	68	.294	.357	7	.179	0	-18	-21	-1	-2.4
1952 Bos-N	12	14	.462	33	33	14	0	0	234	234	19	90	104	12.6	4.23	85	.262	.333	14	.163	-0	-13	-16	-1	-1.8
1953 Mil-N	4	9	.308	20	18	5	0	0	114	107	16	43	71	12.1	4.34	90	.243	.315	6	.167	1	-1	-5	1	-0.3
1954 Mil-N☆	8	2	.800	27	19	6	4	0	127²	129	12	36	52	12.0	3.52	106	.266	.323	7	.159	0	8	3	1	0.3
1955 Bal-A☆	12	18	.400	34	31	14	4	0	235¹	200	17	87	96	11.1	3.44	111	.228	.300	15	.169	-2	14	10	-0	1.0
1956 Bal-A	4	2	.667	7	7	1	0	0	48¹	49	5	16	31	12.5	5.03	78	.268	.333	4	.267	2	-5	-6	-0	-0.4
Chi-A★	9	12	.429	28	21	6	3	0	159²	149	15	70	82	12.5	4.06	101	.248	.329	19	.306	4	2	1	-0	0.5
Yr	13	14	.481	35	28	7	3	0	208	198	20	86	113	12.4	4.28	95	.252	.327	23	.299	6	-3	-5	0	0.1
1957 Chi-A	15	8	.652	30	29	12	5	0	201²	189	22	65	100	11.5	3.48	107	.249	.310	10	.147	-0	7	6	-2	0.4
1958 Chi-A	9	9	.500	28	23	4	1	1	155²	146	21	63	70	12.7	4.10	89	.268	.341	4	.078	-3	-6	-8	-1	-1.3
Total 12	86	89	.491	257	217	75	19	2	1539	1479	151	608	692	12.4	4.01	93	.254	.327	99	.181	4	-21	-45	-5	-4.0

● JACK WILSON Wilson, John Francis "Black Jack" b: 4/12/12, Portland, Ore. BR/TR, 5'11", 210 lbs. Deb: 9/9/34

1934 Phi-A	0	1	.000	2	2	1	0	0	9	15	1	9	2	24.0	12.00	37	.405	.522	0	.000	-0	-8	-8	-0	-0.6
1935 Bos-A	3	4	.429	23	6	2	0	1	64	72	0	36	19	15.5	4.22	112	.290	.385	5	.313	2	2	4	1	0.7
1936 Bos-A	6	8	.429	43	9	2	0	3	136¹	152	4	86	74	15.8	4.42	120	.284	.384	11	.220	-0	9	13	0	1.1
1937 Bos-A	16	10	.615	51	21	14	1	7	221¹	209	11	119	137	13.5	3.70	128	.248	.343	14	.165	-3	23	26	1	2.5
1938 Bos-A	15	15	.500	37	27	11	3	1	194²	200	16	91	96	13.5	4.30	115	.262	.342	15	.221	0	11	14	-1	1.7
1939 Bos-A	11	11	.500	36	22	6	0	0	177¹	198	10	75	80	13.9	4.67	101	.281	.351	10	.159	-4	-1	-1	-0	-0.2
1940 Bos-A	12	6	.667	41	16	9	0	5	157²	170	17	87	102	14.8	5.08	89	.270	.362	18	.273	4	-12	-10	-2	-0.8
1941 Bos-A	4	13	.235	27	12	4	1	0	116¹	140	7	70	55	16.6	5.03	83	.300	.397	7	.159	-1	-11	-11	-1	-1.3
1942 Was-A	1	4	.200	12	6	1	0	0	42	57	2	23	18	17.4	6.64	55	.322	.403	2	.118	-1	-14	-14	-1	-1.6
Det-A	0	0	—	9	0	0	0	0	13	20	3	5	7	17.3	4.85	81	.351	.403	0	.000	-0	-2	-1	0	0.0
Yr	1	4	.200	21	6	1	0	0	55	77	5	28	25	17.2	6.22	60	.328	.399	2	.111	-1	-16	-15	-0	-1.6
Total 9	68	72	.486	281	121	50	5	20	1131²	1233	73	601	590	14.7	4.59	102	.276	.364	82	.199	-3	-4	13	1	1.5

● JOHN WILSON Wilson, John Nicodemus b: 6/15/1890, Boonsboro, Md. d: 9/23/54, Annapolis, Md. BR/TL, 6'1", 185 lbs. Deb: 6/11/13

| 1913 Was-A | 0 | 0 | — | 3 | 0 | 0 | 0 | 0 | 4 | 4 | 0 | 3 | 1 | 15.8 | 4.50 | 66 | .267 | .389 | 0 | — | 0 | -1 | -1 | 0 | 0.0 |

● JOHN WILSON Wilson, John Samuel b: 4/25/03, Coal City, Ala. d: 8/27/80, Chattanooga, Tenn. BR/TR, 6'2", 164 lbs. Deb: 5/9/27

1927 Bos-A	0	2	.000	5	2	2	0	0	25¹	31	1	13	8	15.6	3.55	119	.326	.407	1	.111	-1	2	2	-0	0.0
1928 Bos-A	0	0	—	2	0	0	0	0	5	6	0	6	1	21.6	9.00	46	.333	.500	0	.000	-0	-3	-3	0	0.0
Total 2	0	2	.000	7	2	2	0	0	30¹	37	1	19	9	16.6	4.45	94	.327	.424	1	.100	-1	-1	-1	-0	0.0

● MAX WILSON Wilson, Max b: 6/3/16, Haw River, N.C. d: 1/2/77, Greensboro, N.C. BL/TL, 5'7", 160 lbs. Deb: 9/10/40

1940 Phi-N	0	0	—	3	0	0	0	0	7	16	1	2	3	23.1	12.86	30	.444	.474	0	.000	-0	-7	-7	0	0.0
1946 Was-A	0	1	.000	9	0	0	0	0	12²	16	1	9	8	17.8	7.11	47	.320	.424	0	.000	0	-5	-5	-0	-0.4
Total 2	0	1	.000	12	0	0	0	0	19²	32	2	11	11	19.7	9.15	39	.372	.443	0	.000	-0	-12	-12	-0	-0.4

● PETE WILSON Wilson, Peter Alex b: 10/9/1885, Springfield, Mass. d: 6/5/57, St.Petersburg, Fla TL , Deb: 9/15/08

1908 NY-A	3	3	.500	6	6	4	1	0	39	27	0	33	28	14.1	3.46	72	.191	.349	1	.071	-1	-5	-4	-0	-0.7
1909 NY-A	6	5	.545	14	13	7	1	0	93²	82	2	43	44	12.4	3.17	80	.230	.320	4	.118	-1	-7	-7	-1	-1.0
Total 2	9	8	.529	20	19	11	2	0	132²	109	2	76	72	12.9	3.26	77	.219	.329	5	.104	-2	-12	-11	-1	-1.7

● EARL WILSON Wilson, Robert Earl (Name Changed From Wilson, Earl Lawrence) b: 10/2/34, Ponchatoula, La. BR/TR, 6'3", 216 lbs. Deb: 7/28/59

1959 Bos-A	1	1	.500	9	4	0	0	0	23²	21	2	31	17	19.8	6.08	67	.241	.441	4	.500	2	-6	-5	0	-0.2
1960 Bos-A	3	2	.600	13	9	2	0	0	65	61	4	48	40	15.1	4.71	86	.247	.369	4	.174	-0	-6	-5	-0	-0.3
1962 Bos-A	12	8	.600	31	28	4	1	0	191¹	163	21	111	137	13.2	3.90	106	.231	.340	12	.174	-3	1	5	-1	0.7
1963 Bos-A	11	16	.407	37	34	6	3	0	210²	184	18	105	123	12.4	3.76	101	.234	.325	15	.208	5	-3	1	1	0.7
1964 Bos-A	11	12	.478	33	31	5	0	0	202¹	213	37	73	166	12.8	4.49	86	.269	.332	15	.205	8	-20	-14	0	-0.7
1965 Bos-A	13	14	.481	36	36	8	1	0	230²	221	25	77	164	11.8	3.98	94	.250	.313	14	.177	8	-13	-7	-1	0.0
1966 Bos-A	5	5	.500	15	14	5	1	0	100²	88	9	36	67	11.3	3.84	99	.235	.306	8	.250	3	-5	-0	-0	0.3
Det-A	13	6	.684	23	23	8	2	0	163¹	126	16	38	133	9.3	2.59	134	.213	.265	15	.234	9	15	16	2	3.2
Yr	18	11	.621	38	37	13	3	0	264	214	25	74	200	10.0	3.07	117	.220	.278	23	.240	12	11	16	2	3.5
1967 Det-A	22	11	.667	39	38	12	0	0	264	216	34	92	184	10.6	3.27	100	.224	.294	20	.185	7	-1	-0	2	0.9
1968 *Det-A	13	12	.520	34	33	10	3	0	224¹	192	25	65	168	10.3	2.85	106	.231	.287	20	.227	10	3	4	1	1.7

YEAR	TM/L	W	L	PCT	G	GS	CG	SH	SV	IP	H	HR	BB	SO	RAT	ERA	ERA+	OAV	OOB	BH	AVG	PB	PR	/A	PD	TPI
1969	Det-A	12	10	.545	35	35	5	1	0	214²	209	23	69	150	11.8	3.31	113	.256	.317	10	.132	-0	7	10	1	1.1
1970	Det-A	4	6	.400	18	16	4	1	0	96	87	15	32	74	11.3	4.41	85	.238	.303	6	.194	2	-7	-7	-0	-0.5
	SD-N	1	6	.143	15	9	0	0	0	65	82	5	19	29	14.3	4.85	82	.309	.360	1	.059	0	-6	-6	-1	-0.7
Total	11	121	109	.526	338	310	69	13	0	2051²	1863	236	796	1452	11.8	3.69	99	.242	.315	144	.195	57	-39	-10	2	6.2

● **ROY WILSON**   Wilson, Roy Edward "Lefty" b: 9/13/1896, Foster, Iowa d: 12/3/69, Clarion, Iowa BL/TL, 6′, 175 lbs. Deb: 4/18/28

YEAR	TM/L	W	L	PCT	G	GS	CG	SH	SV	IP	H	HR	BB	SO	RAT	ERA	ERA+	OAV	OOB	BH	AVG	PB	PR	/A	PD	TPI
1928	Chi-A	0	0	—	1	0	0	0	0	3¹	2	0	3	2	13.5	0.00	—	.167	.333	0	.000	-0	1	2	0	0.0

● **STEVE WILSON**   Wilson, Stephen Douglas b: 12/13/64, Victoria, B.C., Can. BL/TL, 6′4″, 205 lbs. Deb: 9/16/88

YEAR	TM/L	W	L	PCT	G	GS	CG	SH	SV	IP	H	HR	BB	SO	RAT	ERA	ERA+	OAV	OOB	BH	AVG	PB	PR	/A	PD	TPI
1988	Tex-A	0	0	—	3	0	0	0	0	7²	7	1	4	1	12.9	5.87	70	.259	.355	0	—	0	-2	-2	-0	-0.1
1989	*Chi-N	6	4	.600	53	8	0	0	2	85²	83	6	31	65	12.1	4.20	89	.257	.324	1	.063	-1	-7	-4	0	-0.6
1990	Chi-N	4	9	.308	45	15	1	0	1	139	140	17	43	95	12.0	4.79	85	.259	.316	6	.162	0	-15	-11	-1	-1.0
1991	Chi-N	0	0	—	8	0	0	0	0	12¹	13	1	5	9	13.1	4.38	89	.277	.346	0	.000	-0	-1	-1	-0	-0.1
	LA-N	0	0	—	11	0	0	0	2	8¹	1	0	4	5	5.4	0.00	—	.042	.179	0	.000	-0	3	3	-0	0.1
	Yr	0	0	—	19	0	0	0	2	20²	14	1	9	14	10.0	2.61	144	.194	.284	0	.000	-0	2	3	-1	0.0
1992	LA-N	2	5	.286	60	0	0	0	0	66²	74	6	29	54	14.0	4.18	82	.282	.356	1	.333	-0	-5	-5	-0	-0.6
1993	LA-N	1	0	1.000	25	0	0	0	1	25²	30	2	14	23	15.8	4.56	84	.288	.378	0	.000	-0	-1	-2	0	-0.1
Total	6	13	18	.419	205	23	1	0	6	345¹	348	33	130	252	12.6	4.40	87	.262	.330	8	.133	-1	-28	-22	-2	-2.4

● **TREVOR WILSON**   Wilson, Trevor Kirk b: 6/7/66, Torrance, Cal. BL/TL, 6′, 190 lbs. Deb: 9/5/88

YEAR	TM/L	W	L	PCT	G	GS	CG	SH	SV	IP	H	HR	BB	SO	RAT	ERA	ERA+	OAV	OOB	BH	AVG	PB	PR	/A	PD	TPI
1988	SF-N	0	2	.000	4	4	0	0	0	22	25	1	8	15	13.5	4.09	80	.298	.359	2	.286	1	-2	-2	-1	-0.2
1989	SF-N	2	3	.400	14	4	0	0	0	39¹	28	2	24	22	12.8	4.35	78	.207	.344	2	.250	1	-4	-4	-0	-0.4
1990	SF-N	8	7	.533	27	17	3	2	0	110¹	87	11	49	66	11.2	4.00	91	.218	.305	4	.138	0	-3	-4	-2	-0.4
1991	SF-N	13	11	.542	44	29	2	1	0	202	173	13	77	139	11.4	3.56	100	.234	.310	12	.235	5	3	0	3	0.8
1992	SF-N	8	14	.364	26	26	1	1	0	154	152	18	64	88	13.0	4.21	79	.265	.345	3	.077	-1	-12	-15	1	-2.0
1993	SF-N	7	5	.583	22	18	1	0	0	110	110	8	40	57	12.8	3.60	109	.275	.350	4	.138	1	5	4	-1	0.4
Total	6	38	42	.475	137	98	7	4	0	637²	575	53	262	387	12.1	3.87	92	.247	.328	27	.166	6	-12	-22	4	-1.8

● **WALTER WILSON**   Wilson, Walter Wood b: 11/24/13, Glenn, Ga. d: 4/17/94, Bremen, Ga. BL/TR, 6′4″, 190 lbs. Deb: 4/17/45

YEAR	TM/L	W	L	PCT	G	GS	CG	SH	SV	IP	H	HR	BB	SO	RAT	ERA	ERA+	OAV	OOB	BH	AVG	PB	PR	/A	PD	TPI
1945	Det-A	1	3	.250	25	4	1	0	0	70¹	76	4	35	28	14.6	4.61	76	.284	.373	1	.053	-2	-10	-9	1	-0.6

● **WILLY WILSON**   Wilson, William b: 1/7/1884, Columbus, Ohio d: 10/28/25, Seattle, Wash. BR/TR, Deb: 10/3/06

YEAR	TM/L	W	L	PCT	G	GS	CG	SH	SV	IP	H	HR	BB	SO	RAT	ERA	ERA+	OAV	OOB	BH	AVG	PB	PR	/A	PD	TPI
1906	Was-A	0	1	.000	1	1	1	0	0	7	3	0	2	1	7.7	2.57	102	.133	.235	0	.000	-0	0	0	0	0.0

● **MUTT WILSON**   Wilson, William Clarence "Lank" b: 7/20/1896, Kiser, N.C. d: 8/31/62, Wildwood, Fla. BR/TR, 6′3″, 167 lbs. Deb: 9/11/20

YEAR	TM/L	W	L	PCT	G	GS	CG	SH	SV	IP	H	HR	BB	SO	RAT	ERA	ERA+	OAV	OOB	BH	AVG	PB	PR	/A	PD	TPI
1920	Det-A	1	1	.500	3	2	1	0	0	13	12	0	5	4	11.8	3.46	108	.240	.309	1	.250	-0	0	0	-1	0.0

● **BILL WILSON**   Wilson, William Donald b: 11/6/28, Central City, Neb. BR/TR, 6′2″, 200 lbs. Deb: 9/24/50 ♦

YEAR	TM/L	W	L	PCT	G	GS	CG	SH	SV	IP	H	HR	BB	SO	RAT	ERA	ERA+	OAV	OOB	BH	AVG	PB	PR	/A	PD	TPI
1955	KC-A	0	0	—	1	0	0	0	0	1	1	0	1	1	18.0	0.00	—	.250	.400	61	.223	0	0	0	0	0.0

● **BILL WILSON**   Wilson, William Harlan b: 9/21/42, Pomeroy, Ohio BR/TR, 6′2″, 200 lbs. Deb: 4/8/69

YEAR	TM/L	W	L	PCT	G	GS	CG	SH	SV	IP	H	HR	BB	SO	RAT	ERA	ERA+	OAV	OOB	BH	AVG	PB	PR	/A	PD	TPI
1969	Phi-N	2	5	.286	37	0	0	0	0	62¹	53	6	36	48	13.0	3.32	107	.231	.338	0	.000	-0	2	2	-1	0.0
1970	Phi-N	1	0	1.000	37	0	0	0	0	58¹	57	5	33	41	13.9	4.78	83	.263	.360	1	.250	0	-5	-5	-0	-0.1
1971	Phi-N	4	6	.400	38	0	0	0	7	58²	39	4	22	40	9.5	3.07	115	.188	.268	1	.100	-1	3	3	2	0.7
1972	Phi-N	1	1	.500	23	0	0	0	0	30	26	1	11	18	11.1	3.30	109	.234	.303	0	—	0	1	1	0	0.1
1973	Phi-N	1	3	.250	44	0	0	0	4	48²	54	7	29	24	15.3	6.66	57	.293	.390	0	.000	-0	-16	-15	-0	-1.5
Total	5	9	15	.375	179	0	0	0	17	258	229	23	131	171	12.6	4.22	88	.241	.335	2	.083	-1	-16	-15	0	-0.8

● **HOOKS WILTSE**   Wiltse, George Leroy b: 9/7/1880, Hamilton, N.Y. d: 1/21/59, Long Beach, N.Y. BR/TL, 6′, 185 lbs. Deb: 4/21/04 FC

YEAR	TM/L	W	L	PCT	G	GS	CG	SH	SV	IP	H	HR	BB	SO	RAT	ERA	ERA+	OAV	OOB	BH	AVG	PB	PR	/A	PD	TPI
1904	NY-N	13	3	.813	24	16	14	2	3	164²	150	8	61	105	11.8	2.84	96	.240	.313	15	.224	3	-2	-2	3	0.4
1905	NY-N	15	6	.714	32	19	18	1	3	197	158	5	61	120	10.4	2.47	119	.219	.284	20	.278	7	12	10	5	2.4
1906	NY-N	16	11	.593	38	26	21	4	6	249¹	227	3	58	125	10.4	2.27	115	.241	.288	18	.191	2	10	9	-1	1.2
1907	NY-N	13	12	.520	33	21	14	3	2	190¹	171	4	48	79	10.6	2.18	114	.241	.294	9	.134	0	6	6	2	1.1
1908	NY-N	23	14	.622	44	38	30	7	2	330	266	4	73	118	9.5	2.24	108	.224	.274	26	.236	6	5	7	-0	1.4
1909	NY-N	20	11	.645	37	30	22	4	3	269¹	228	9	51	119	9.5	2.00	138	.233	.275	19	.200	2	18	17	-2	1.9
1910	NY-N	14	12	.538	36	30	18	2	2	235¹	232	4	52	88	10.9	2.72	109	.261	.303	13	.176	0	8	7	-3	0.4
1911	*NY-N	12	9	.571	30	24	11	4	0	187¹	177	7	39	92	10.5	3.27	103	.251	.292	13	.188	-1	3	2	0	0.1
1912	NY-N	9	6	.600	28	17	5	0	3	134	140	7	28	58	11.4	3.16	107	.273	.312	15	.326	4	3	2	2	0.8
1913	*NY-N	0	0	—	17	2	0	0	3	57²	53	1	8	25	9.7	1.56	200	.237	.266	5	.208	0	11	10	0	0.8
1914	NY-N	1	1	.500	20	0	0	0	1	38	41	2	12	19	12.6	2.84	93	.289	.344	2	.667	2	-0	-1	0	0.1
1915	Bro-F	3	5	.375	18	3	1	0	5	59¹	49	1	7	17	8.8	2.28	120	.226	.277	1	.045	-3	3	3	-1	0.1
Total	12	139	90	.607	357	226	154	27	34	2112¹	1892	54	498	965	10.4	2.47	112	.241	.290	156	.210	22	77	72	5	10.1

● **HAL WILTSE**   Wiltse, Harold James "Whitey" b: 8/6/03, Clay City, Ill. d: 11/2/83, Bunkie, La. BL/TL, 5′9″, 168 lbs. Deb: 4/13/26

YEAR	TM/L	W	L	PCT	G	GS	CG	SH	SV	IP	H	HR	BB	SO	RAT	ERA	ERA+	OAV	OOB	BH	AVG	PB	PR	/A	PD	TPI
1926	Bos-A	8	15	.348	37	29	9	1	0	196¹	201	6	99	59	14.0	4.22	97	.273	.363	5	.085	-5	-4	-3	0	-0.7
1927	Bos-A	10	18	.357	36	29	13	1	1	219	276	5	76	47	14.6	5.10	83	.321	.379	16	.208	-2	-23	-21	1	-2.3
1928	Bos-A	0	2	.000	2	2	1	0	0	12	16	1	1	5	15.0	9.00	46	.314	.364	0	.000	-1	-7	-7	-0	-0.8
	StL-A	2	5	.286	26	5	0	0	0	72	93	4	35	23	16.4	5.25	80	.316	.395	5	.227	-0	-10	-8	0	-0.7
	Yr	2	7	.222	28	7	1	0	0	84	109	5	36	28	15.9	5.79	72	.313	.382	5	.192	-1	-16	-15	0	-1.5
1931	Phi-N	0	0	—	1	0	0	0	0	1	3	0	0	0	27.0	9.00	47	.600	.600	0	—	0	-1	-1	0	0.0
Total	4	20	40	.333	102	65	23	2	1	500¹	589	16	211	134	14.7	4.87	85	.303	.375	26	.160	-7	-44	-40	2	-4.5

● **SNAKE WILTSE**   Wiltse, Lewis De Witt b: 12/5/1871, Bouckville, N.Y. d: 8/25/28, Harrisburg, Pa. BR/TL, Deb: 5/5/01 F

YEAR	TM/L	W	L	PCT	G	GS	CG	SH	SV	IP	H	HR	BB	SO	RAT	ERA	ERA+	OAV	OOB	BH	AVG	PB	PR	/A	PD	TPI
1901	Pit-N	1	4	.200	7	5	3	0	0	44¹	57	2	13	10	15.2	4.26	77	.310	.371	3	.158	-1	-5	-5	1	-0.5
	Phi-A	13	5	.722	19	19	18	2	0	166	185	1	35	40	12.3	3.58	105	.279	.321	25	.373	8	2	4	1	1.2
1902	Phi-A	8	8	.500	19	17	13	0	1	138	182	7	41	28	14.9	5.15	71	.318	.368	10	.175	-0	-24	-23	-1	-2.3
	Bal-A	7	11	.389	19	18	18	0	0	164	215	4	51	37	15.0	5.10	74	.316	.371	39	.295	6	-28	-24	-0	-1.7
	Yr	15	19	.441	38	35	31	0	1	302	397	11	92	65	14.8	5.13	73	.316	.366	49	.259	5	-52	-47	-1	-4.0
1903	NY-A	0	3	.000	4	3	2	0	1	25	35	1	6	6	15.1	5.40	58	.329	.371	2	.222	0	-7	-6	0	-0.7
Total	3	29	31	.483	68	62	54	2	2	537¹	674	15	146	121	14.2	4.59	80	.305	.356	79	.278	13	-62	-55	0	-4.0

● **FRED WINCHELL**   Winchell, Frederick Russell (b: Frederick Cook) b: 1/23/1882, Arlington, Mass. d: 8/8/58, Toronto, Ont., Can. TR, 5′8″, Deb: 9/16/09

YEAR	TM/L	W	L	PCT	G	GS	CG	SH	SV	IP	H	HR	BB	SO	RAT	ERA	ERA+	OAV	OOB	BH	AVG	PB	PR	/A	PD	TPI
1909	Cle-A	0	3	.000	4	3	0	0	1	14¹	16	0	2	7	11.3	6.28	41	.296	.321	1	.200	0	-6	-6	-0	-1.2

● **ED WINEAPPLE**   Wineapple, Edward "Lefty" b: 8/10/05, Boston, Mass. BL/TL, 6′, 210 lbs. Deb: 9/15/29

YEAR	TM/L	W	L	PCT	G	GS	CG	SH	SV	IP	H	HR	BB	SO	RAT	ERA	ERA+	OAV	OOB	BH	AVG	PB	PR	/A	PD	TPI
1929	Was-A	0	0	—	1	0	0	0	0	4	7	0	3	1	22.5	4.50	94	.467	.556	0	.000	-0	-0	-0	-0	0.0

● **RALPH WINEGARNER**   Winegarner, Ralph Lee b: 10/29/09, Benton, Kan. d: 4/14/88, Wichita, Kan. BR/TR, 6′, 182 lbs. Deb: 9/20/30 C♦

YEAR	TM/L	W	L	PCT	G	GS	CG	SH	SV	IP	H	HR	BB	SO	RAT	ERA	ERA+	OAV	OOB	BH	AVG	PB	PR	/A	PD	TPI
1932	Cle-A	1	0	1.000	5	1	1	0	0	17¹	7	0	13	13	10.4	1.04	457	.123	.286	1	.143	-0	7	7	-0	0.3
1934	Cle-A	5	4	.556	22	6	4	0	0	78¹	91	7	39	32	15.2	5.51	82	.289	.371	10	.196	1	-9	-9	-0	-0.7
1935	Cle-A	2	2	.500	25	4	2	0	0	67¹	89	10	29	41	15.9	5.75	78	.313	.379	26	.310	4	-10	-9	0	-0.1
1936	Cle-A	0	0	—	9	0	0	0	0	14²	18	0	6	3	14.7	4.91	103	.295	.358	2	.125	-1	0	0	0	-0.1
1949	StL-A	0	0	—	9	0	0	0	0	16²	24	0	2	0	14.0	7.56	60	.329	.347	2	.400	2	-6	-6	-0	0.0
Total	5	8	6	.571	70	11	7	0	0	194¹	229	13	89	89	14.9	5.33	86	.290	.364	51	.278	5	-18	-16	-1	-0.4

YEAR TM/L	W	L	PCT	G	GS	CG	SH	SV	IP	H	HR	BB	SO	RAT	ERA	ERA+	OAV	OOB	BH	AVG	PB	PR	/A	PD	TPI
● **JIM WINFORD** Winford, James Head "Cowboy" b: 10/9/09, Shelbyville, Tenn. d: 12/16/70, Miami, Okla. BR/TR, 6'1", 180 lbs. Deb: 9/10/32																									
1932 StL-N	1	1	.500	4	1	0	0	0	8¹	9	0	5	4	15.1	6.48	61	.273	.368	2	.667	1	-2	-2	0	-0.4
1934 StL-N	0	2	.000	5	1	0	0	0	12²	17	0	6	3	17.8	7.82	54	.327	.417	0	.000	-0	-5	-5	-0	-0.6
1935 StL-N	0	0	—	2	1	0	0	0	11¹	13	1	5	7	14.3	3.97	103	.283	.353	0	.000	-0	0	0	-1	-0.1
1936 StL-N	11	10	.524	39	23	10	1	3	192	203	10	68	72	12.9	3.80	104	.269	.333	5	.085	-4	5	3	-4	-0.5
1937 StL-N	2	4	.333	16	4	0	0	0	46¹	56	2	27	17	16.1	5.83	68	.311	.401	1	.125	-1	-10	-10	-0	-1.1
1938 Bro-N	0	1	.000	2	1	0	0	0	5²	9	1	4	4	20.6	11.12	35	.346	.433	0	.000	-0	-5	-5	-0	-0.6
Total 6	14	18	.438	68	31	10	1	3	276¹	307	14	115	107	14.0	4.56	87	.281	.353	8	.108	-3	-17	-18	-5	-3.3
● **ERNIE WINGARD** Wingard, Ernest James "Jim" b: 10/17/1900, Prattville, Ala. d: 1/17/77, Prattville, Ala. BL/TL, 6'2", 176 lbs. Deb: 5/1/24																									
1924 StL-A	13	12	.520	36	26	14	0	1	218	215	6	85	23	12.5	3.51	129	.262	.334	18	.234	2	17	24	-3	2.4
1925 StL-A	9	10	.474	32	18	8	0	0	145	183	10	77	20	16.3	5.52	85	.319	.403	15	.288	3	-18	-14	2	-1.0
1926 StL-A	5	8	.385	39	16	7	0	3	169	188	9	76	30	14.3	3.57	120	.290	.369	14	.230	1	8	14	3	1.4
1927 StL-A	2	13	.133	38	17	7	0	0	156¹	213	7	79	28	16.9	6.56	66	.340	.415	10	.179	2	-42	-38	2	-2.7
Total 4	29	43	.403	145	77	36	0	4	688¹	799	32	317	101	14.8	4.64	96	.299	.377	57	.232	7	-34	-14	4	0.1
● **TED WINGFIELD** Wingfield, Frederick Davis b: 8/7/1899, Bedford, Va. d: 7/18/75, Johnson City, Tenn. BR/TR, 5'11", 168 lbs. Deb: 9/23/23																									
1923 Was-A	0	0	—	1	0	0	0	0	1	0	0	1	0	9.0	0.00	—	.000	.000	0	—	0	0	0	0	0.0
1924 Was-A	0	0	—	4	0	0	0	0	7	9	0	4	2	16.7	2.57	157	.300	.382	0	.000	-0	1	1	-0	0.0
Bos-A	0	2	.000	4	3	2	0	0	25²	23	0	8	4	11.2	2.45	178	.240	.298	3	.333	1	5	5	0	0.5
Yr	0	2	.000	8	3	2	0	0	32²	32	0	12	6	12.1	2.48	173	.254	.319	3	.273	0	6	7	-0	0.5
1925 Bos-A	12	19	.387	41	26	18	2	2	254¹	267	11	92	30	13.0	3.96	115	.278	.346	23	.245	1	12	16	7	2.5
1926 Bos-A	11	16	.407	43	20	9	1	3	190²	220	11	50	30	12.8	4.44	92	.298	.344	15	.217	-0	-9	-8	2	-0.8
1927 Bos-A	1	7	.125	20	8	2	0	0	74²	105	2	27	1	16.3	5.06	83	.357	.417	4	.222	1	-8	-7	2	-0.4
Total 5	24	44	.353	113	57	31	3	5	553¹	624	24	181	68	13.3	4.18	103	.294	.353	45	.234	1	3	9	11	1.8
● **LAVE WINHAM** Winham, Lafayette Sharkey "Lefty" b: 10/23/1881, Brooklyn, N.Y. d: 9/12/51, Brooklyn, N.Y. BL/TL, 5'11", 200 lbs. Deb: 4/21/02																									
1902 Bro-N	0	0	—	1	0	0	0	0	3	4	0	2	1	18.0	0.00	—	.319	.413	0	.000	-0	1	1	0	0.0
1903 Pit-N	3	1	.750	5	4	3	1	0	36	33	0	21	22	13.5	2.25	144	.231	.329	1	.071	-1	4	4	-1	0.1
Total 2	3	1	.750	6	4	3	1	0	39	37	0	23	23	13.8	2.08	154	.238	.336	1	.063	-2	5	5	-1	0.1
● **GEORGE WINKELMAN** Winkelman, George Edward b: 2/18/1865, Washington, D.C. d: 5/19/60, Washington, D.C. BL/TL, Deb: 8/4/1883 ◆																									
1886 Was-N	0	1	.000	1	1	0	0	0	6	12	0	5	4	25.5	10.50	31	.400	.486	1	.200	-0	-5	-5	-0	-0.5
● **GEORGE WINN** Winn, George Benjamin "Breezy" or "Lefty" b: 10/26/1897, Perry, Ga. d: 11/1/69, Roberta, Ga. BL/TL, 5'11", 170 lbs. Deb: 4/29/19																									
1919 Bos-A	0	0	—	3	0	0	0	0	4²	6	0	1	0	13.5	7.71	39	.353	.389	0	.000	-0	-2	-2	0	0.0
1922 Cle-A	1	2	.333	8	3	1	0	0	33²	44	2	5	7	13.1	4.54	88	.317	.340	3	.333	1	-2	-2	0	-0.1
1923 Cle-A	0	0	—	1	0	0	0	0	2	0	0	1	0	4.5	0.00	—	.000	.143	0	—	0	1	1	-0	0.0
Total 3	1	2	.333	12	3	1	0	0	40¹	50	2	7	7	12.7	4.69	83	.309	.337	3	.300	1	-3	-4	-0	-0.1
● **JIM WINN** Winn, James Francis b: 9/23/59, Stockton, Cal. BR/TR, 6'3", 210 lbs. Deb: 4/10/83																									
1983 Pit-N	0	0	—	7	0	0	0	0	11	12	2	6	4	14.7	7.36	50	.267	.353	0	—	0	-5	-4	0	0.0
1984 Pit-N	1	0	1.000	9	0	0	0	0	18²	19	2	9	11	13.5	3.86	93	.264	.346	0	.000	-0	-1	-1	0	0.0
1985 Pit-N	3	6	.333	30	7	0	0	0	75²	77	4	31	22	13.1	5.23	68	.266	.341	2	.111	-0	-14	-14	2	-1.4
1986 Pit-N	3	5	.375	50	3	0	0	3	88	85	9	38	70	12.8	3.58	107	.258	.338	1	.063	-1	1	2	1	0.3
1987 Chi-A	4	6	.400	56	0	0	0	7	94	95	10	62	44	15.6	4.79	96	.271	.390	0	—	-0	-3	-2	3	-0.1
1988 Min-A	1	0	1.000	9	0	0	0	0	21	33	4	10	9	18.4	6.00	68	.355	.417	0	—	0	-5	-5	0	-0.4
Total 6	12	17	.414	161	10	0	0	10	308¹	321	31	156	159	14.2	4.67	85	.272	.362	3	.086	-1	-26	-23	6	-1.6
● **TOM WINSETT** Winsett, John Thomas "Long Tom" b: 11/24/09, McKenzie, Tenn. BL/TR, 6'2", 190 lbs. Deb: 4/20/30 ◆																									
1937 Bro-N	0	0	—	1	0	0	0	0	1	3	0	2	0	45.0	18.00	22	.600	.714	83	.237	0	-2	-2	-0	0.0
● **HANK WINSTON** Winston, Henry Rudolph b: 6/15/04, Youngville, N.C. d: 2/4/74, Jacksonville, Fla. BL/TR, 6'3.5", 226 lbs. Deb: 9/30/33																									
1933 Phi-A	0	0	—	1	0	0	0	0	6²	7	0	6	2	17.6	6.75	67	.280	.419	0	.000	-0	-2	-2	-0	0.0
1936 Bro-N	1	3	.250	14	0	0	0	0	32¹	40	2	16	8	15.9	6.12	67	.301	.380	1	.091	-1	-8	-7	-0	-0.8
Total 2	1	3	.250	15	0	0	0	0	39	47	2	22	10	16.2	6.23	67	.297	.387	1	.071	-1	-9	-9	0	-0.8
● **GEORGE WINTER** Winter, George Lovington "Sassafras" b: 4/27/1878, New Providence, Pa d: 5/26/51, Franklin Lakes, N.J. TR, 5'8", 155 lbs. Deb: 6/15/01																									
1901 Bos-A	16	12	.571	28	28	26	1	0	241	234	4	66	63	11.4	2.80	126	.252	.304	19	.190	-4	23	20	-1	1.5
1902 Bos-A	11	9	.550	20	20	18	0	0	168¹	149	2	53	51	11.2	2.99	119	.238	.305	10	.164	-2	11	11	-0	0.8
1903 Bos-A	9	8	.529	24	19	14	0	0	178¹	182	4	37	64	11.4	3.08	99	.264	.308	7	.106	-4	-2	-1	-0	-0.6
1904 Bos-A	8	4	.667	20	16	12	1	0	135²	126	4	27	31	10.5	2.32	115	.247	.293	5	.116	-2	4	5	-2	0.1
1905 Bos-A	16	17	.485	35	27	24	0	0	264¹	249	5	54	119	10.5	2.96	91	.250	.292	24	.261	3	-9	-8	0	-0.6
1906 Bos-A	6	18	.250	29	22	18	1	2	207²	215	8	38	72	11.2	4.12	67	.270	.308	17	.246	-2	-33	-32	-0	-3.3
1907 Bos-A	12	15	.444	35	27	21	4	1	256²	198	2	61	88	9.2	2.07	125	.215	.266	21	.223	1	14	15	-2	1.5
1908 Bos-A	4	14	.222	22	17	8	0	1	147²	150	3	34	55	11.5	3.05	81	.274	.321	9	.184	-1	-11	-10	-0	-1.3
*Det-A	1	5	.167	7	6	5	0	1	56¹	49	0	7	25	9.4	1.60	152	.240	.276	2	.111	-1	5	5	1	0.6
Yr	5	19	.208	29	23	13	0	1	204	199	3	41	80	10.7	2.65	93	.263	.304	11	.164	-2	-6	-4	1	-0.7
Total 8	83	102	.449	220	182	146	9	4	1656	1552	32	377	568	10.7	2.87	101	.250	.297	114	.193	-8	2	7	-4	-1.3
● **CLARENCE WINTERS** Winters, Clarence John b: 9/7/1898, Detroit, Mich. d: 6/29/45, Detroit, Mich. Deb: 8/28/24																									
1924 Bos-A	0	1	.000	4	2	0	0	0	7	22	0	4	3	33.4	20.57	21	.512	.553	1	.333	0	-13	-13	0	-1.3
● **JESSE WINTERS** Winters, Jesse Franklin "Buck" or "T-Bone" b: 12/22/1893, Stephenville, Tex. d: 6/5/86, Abilene, Texas BR/TR, 6'1", 165 lbs. Deb: 5/3/19																									
1919 NY-N	1	2	.333	16	2	0	0	3	28	39	1	13	6	17.7	5.46	51	.339	.420	0	.000	-0	-8	-8	-0	-1.1
1920 NY-N	0	0	—	21	0	0	0	0	46¹	37	1	28	14	13.4	3.50	86	.233	.361	0	.000	-1	-2	-3	1	0.0
1921 Phi-N	5	10	.333	18	14	10	0	0	114	142	4	28	22	13.7	3.63	116	.310	.355	5	.128	-3	2	8	2	0.8
1922 Phi-N	6	6	.500	34	9	4	0	2	138¹	176	8	56	29	15.4	5.33	87	.319	.386	11	.256	-0	-19	-10	-1	-0.7
1923 Phi-N	1	6	.143	21	6	1	0	1	78¹	116	7	39	23	18.3	7.35	63	.348	.423	4	.160	-1	-29	-24	-1	-1.9
Total 5	13	24	.351	110	31	15	0	6	405	510	21	164	94	15.4	5.04	84	.316	.385	20	.171	-5	-56	-39	2	-2.9
● **ALAN WIRTH** Wirth, Alan Lee b: 12/8/56, Mesa, Ariz. BR/TR, 6'4", 190 lbs. Deb: 4/9/78																									
1978 Oak-A	5	6	.455	16	14	2	1	0	81¹	72	6	34	31	12.1	3.43	106	.252	.337	0	—	0	3	4	0	0.3
1979 Oak-A	1	0	1.000	5	1	0	0	0	12	14	2	8	7	17.3	6.00	67	.298	.411	0	—	0	-2	-3	0	0.2
1980 Oak-A	0	0	—	2	0	0	0	0	2	3	0	0	1	13.5	4.50	84	.333	.333	0	—	-0	-0	-0	-0	0.7
Total 3	6	6	.500	23	15	2	1	0	95¹	89	8	42	39	12.7	3.78	98	.260	.348	0	—	0	1	-1	-1	1.2
● **ARCHIE WISE** Wise, Archibald Edwin b: 7/31/12, Waxahachie, Tex. d: 2/2/78, Dallas, Tex. BR/TR, 6', 165 lbs. Deb: 7/24/32																									
1932 Chi-A	0	0	—	2	0	0	0	0	7¹	8	1	5	2	17.2	4.91	88	.258	.378	0	.000	-1	-0	-0	0	-0.1
● **RICK WISE** Wise, Richard Charles b: 9/13/45, Jackson, Mich. BR/TR, 6'2", 195 lbs. Deb: 4/18/64																									
1964 Phi-N	5	3	.625	25	8	0	0	0	69	78	7	25	39	13.8	4.04	86	.277	.342	5	.294	2	-4	-4	-2	-0.4
1966 Phi-N	5	6	.455	22	13	2	1	0	99¹	100	5	24	58	11.5	3.71	97	.262	.311	0	—	-4	-1	-1	-1	-0.6
1967 Phi-N	11	11	.500	36	25	6	3	0	181¹	177	16	45	111	11.2	3.28	104	.259	.308	11	.208	3	2	3	1	0.7
1968 Phi-N	9	15	.375	30	30	7	1	0	182	210	12	37	97	12.5	4.55	66	.292	.332	14	.241	7	-32	-31	1	-3.2
1969 Phi-N	15	13	.536	33	31	14	3	0	220	215	19	61	144	11.4	3.23	110	.257	.309	20	.270	1	9	8	1	1.9

YEAR	TM/L	W	L	PCT	G	GS	CG	SH	SV	IP	H	HR	BB	SO	RAT	ERA	ERA+	OAV	OOB	BH	AVG	PB	PR	/A	PD	TPI
1970	Phi-N	13	14	.481	35	34	5	1	0	220¹	253	15	65	113	13.1	4.17	96	.287	.338	15	.200	5	-3	-4	1	0.1
1971	Phi-N☆	17	14	.548	38	37	17	4	0	272¹	261	20	70	155	11.1	2.88	123	.254	.304	23	.237	10	18	20	0	3.4
1972	StL-N	16	16	.500	35	35	20	2	0	269	250	16	71	142	10.8	3.11	109	.251	.301	16	.172	1	10	9	2	1.4
1973	StL-N★	16	12	.571	35	34	14	5	0	259	259	18	59	144	11.2	3.37	108	.257	.300	17	.193	6	8	8	-1	1.4
1974	Bos-A	3	4	.429	9	9	1	0	0	49	47	2	16	25	11.8	3.86	100	.251	.314	0	—	0	-1	-0	-0	-0.1
1975	*Bos-A	19	12	.613	35	35	17	1	0	255¹	262	34	72	141	11.9	3.95	103	.266	.315	0	—	0	-5	4	-1	0.1
1976	Bos-A	14	11	.560	34	34	11	4	0	224¹	218	18	48	93	10.8	3.53	111	.255	.296	0	—	0	-0	9	2	1.2
1977	Bos-A	11	5	.688	26	20	4	2	0	128¹	151	19	28	85	12.8	4.77	94	.291	.332	0	—	0	-10	-4	1	-0.4
1978	Cle-A	9	19	.321	33	31	9	1	0	211²	226	22	59	106	12.2	4.34	86	.275	.325	0	—	0	-14	-14	-0	-1.7
1979	Cle-A	15	10	.600	34	34	9	2	0	231²	229	24	68	108	11.6	3.73	114	.256	.309	0	—	0	12	13	4	1.7
1980	SD-N	6	8	.429	27	27	1	0	0	154¹	172	14	37	59	12.2	3.67	93	.285	.326	8	.138	-1	-1	-4	-1	-0.5
1981	SD-N	4	8	.333	18	18	0	0	0	98	116	10	19	27	12.4	3.77	86	.296	.328	1	.040	-2	-3	-6	0	-0.8
1982	SD-N	0	0	—	1	0	0	0	0	2	3	0	0	0	13.5	9.00	38	.333	.333	0	—	0	-1	-1	0	0.0
Total	18	188	181	.509	506	455	138	30	0	3127	3227	261	804	1647	11.7	3.69	100	.267	.315	130	.195	34	-15	2	9	4.2

● **ROY WISE**　　Wise, Roy Ogden b: 11/18/24, Springfield, Ill. BB/TR, 6'2", 170 lbs. Deb: 5/13/44

YEAR	TM/L	W	L	PCT	G	GS	CG	SH	SV	IP	H	HR	BB	SO	RAT	ERA	ERA+	OAV	OOB	BH	AVG	PB	PR	/A	PD	TPI
1944	Pit-N	0	0	—	2	0	0	0	0	3	4	0	3	1	21.0	9.00	41	.333	.467	0	—	0	-2	-2	-0	0.0

● **BILL WISE**　　Wise, William E. b: 3/15/1861, Washington, D.C. d: 5/5/40, Washington, D.C. Deb: 5/2/1882

YEAR	TM/L	W	L	PCT	G	GS	CG	SH	SV	IP	H	HR	BB	SO	RAT	ERA	ERA+	OAV	OOB	BH	AVG	PB	PR	/A	PD	TPI
1882	Bal-a	1	2	.333	3	3	3	0	0	26	30	1	4	9	11.8	2.77	99	.271	.296	2	.100	-1	-0	-0	-0	-0.1
1884	Was-U	23	18	.561	50	41	34	4	0	364¹	383	5	60	268	10.9	3.04	79	.253	.281	79	.233	-8	-24	-26	5	-2.4
1886	Was-N	0	1	.000	1	1	0	0	0	3	6	0	2	0	24.0	9.00	37	.400	.471	0	.000	-0	-2	-2	-0	-0.4
Total	3	24	21	.533	54	45	37	4	0	393¹	419	6	66	277	11.1	3.07	79	.255	.284	81	.224	-9	-26	-28	4	-2.9

● **JACK WISNER**　　Wisner, John Henry b: 11/5/1899, Grand Rapids, Mich. d: 12/15/81, Jackson, Mich. BR/TR, 6'3", 195 lbs. Deb: 9/12/19

YEAR	TM/L	W	L	PCT	G	GS	CG	SH	SV	IP	H	HR	BB	SO	RAT	ERA	ERA+	OAV	OOB	BH	AVG	PB	PR	/A	PD	TPI
1919	Pit-N	1	0	1.000	4	1	1	0	0	18²	12	0	7	4	9.6	0.96	313	.185	.274	0	.000	-1	4	4	-0	0.1
1920	Pit-N	1	3	.250	17	2	1	0	0	44²	46	1	10	13	11.5	3.43	94	.274	.318	0	.000	-1	-1	-1	1	-0.1
1925	NY-N	0	0	—	25	0	0	0	0	40¹	33	4	14	13	10.9	3.79	106	.228	.304	0	.000	-1	2	1	-0	-0.1
1926	NY-N	2	2	.500	5	3	2	0	0	28	21	4	10	5	10.0	3.54	106	.208	.279	2	.200	-0	1	1	-0	-0.1
Total	4	4	5	.444	51	6	4	0	0	131²	112	9	41	35	10.7	3.21	111	.234	.300	2	.065	-3	6	5	1	-0.1

● **WHITEY WISTERT**　　Wistert, Francis Michael b: 2/20/12, Chicago, Ill. d: 4/23/85, Painesville, Ohio BR/TR, 6'4", 210 lbs. Deb: 9/11/34

YEAR	TM/L	W	L	PCT	G	GS	CG	SH	SV	IP	H	HR	BB	SO	RAT	ERA	ERA+	OAV	OOB	BH	AVG	PB	PR	/A	PD	TPI
1934	Cin-N	0	1	.000	2	1	0	0	0	8	5	1	5	2	11.3	1.13	363	.185	.313	0	—	-0	3	3	-0	0.2

● **WITHEROW**　　Witherow Deb: 7/1/1875

YEAR	TM/L	W	L	PCT	G	GS	CG	SH	SV	IP	H	HR	BB	SO	RAT	ERA	ERA+	OAV	OOB	BH	AVG	PB	PR	/A	PD	TPI
1875	Was-n	0	1	.000	1	1	0	0	0	1	5	0	0	0	45.0	18.00	15	.625	.625	0	.000	0	-2	-2		-0.9

● **ROY WITHERUP**　　Witherup, Foster Leroy b: 7/26/1886, N.Washington, Pa. d: 12/23/41, New Bethlehem, Pa. BR/TR, 6', 185 lbs. Deb: 5/14/06

YEAR	TM/L	W	L	PCT	G	GS	CG	SH	SV	IP	H	HR	BB	SO	RAT	ERA	ERA+	OAV	OOB	BH	AVG	PB	PR	/A	PD	TPI
1906	Bos-N	0	3	.000	8	3	3	0	0	46	59	2	19	14	15.5	6.26	43	.322	.389	2	.133	-1	-19	-18	-1	-1.2
1908	Was-A	2	4	.333	6	6	4	0	0	48¹	51	0	8	31	11.2	2.98	77	.264	.297	3	.167	-1	-3	-4	0	-0.5
1909	Was-A	1	5	.167	12	8	5	0	0	68	79	1	20	26	13.1	4.24	57	.306	.356	1	.053	-2	-13	-14	-2	-1.5
Total	3	3	12	.200	26	17	12	0	0	162¹	189	3	47	71	13.2	4.44	55	.298	.348	6	.115	-3	-35	-36	-2	-3.2

● **GEORGE WITT**　　Witt, George Adrian "Red" b: 11/9/33, Long Beach, Cal. BR/TR, 6'3", 200 lbs. Deb: 9/21/57

YEAR	TM/L	W	L	PCT	G	GS	CG	SH	SV	IP	H	HR	BB	SO	RAT	ERA	ERA+	OAV	OOB	BH	AVG	PB	PR	/A	PD	TPI
1957	Pit-N	0	1	.000	1	1	0	0	0	1¹	4	1	5	0	60.8	40.50	9	.500	.692	0	—	0	-5	-5	-0	-1.6
1958	Pit-N	9	2	.818	18	15	5	3	0	106	78	2	59	81	11.8	1.61	240	.209	.320	6	.154	-1	28	27	-0	2.5
1959	Pit-N	0	7	.000	15	11	0	0	0	50²	58	7	32	30	16.2	6.93	56	.293	.394	0	.000	-1	-17	-17	-0	-2.1
1960	*Pit-N	1	2	.333	10	6	0	0	0	30	33	3	12	15	13.5	4.20	89	.300	.369	0	.000	-1	-1	-1	-0	-0.3
1961	Pit-N	0	1	.000	9	1	0	0	0	15²	17	5	9	9	12.6	6.32	63	.274	.328	1	.500	-1	-4	-4	-1	-0.2
1962	LA-A	1	1	.500	5	2	0	0	0	10	15	4	5	10	18.0	8.10	48	.349	.417	1	.333	0	-5	-5	-0	-0.8
	Hou-N	0	2	.000	8	2	0	0	0	15¹	20	2	9	10	17.6	7.04	53	.339	.435	1	.250	0	-5	-6	-0	-0.6
Total	6	11	16	.407	66	38	5	3	0	229	225	24	127	156	14.0	4.32	89	.263	.361	9	.130	-2	-10	-12	-2	-3.1

● **MIKE WITT**　　Witt, Michael Atwater b: 7/20/60, Fullerton, Cal. BR/TR, 6'7", 192 lbs. Deb: 4/11/81

YEAR	TM/L	W	L	PCT	G	GS	CG	SH	SV	IP	H	HR	BB	SO	RAT	ERA	ERA+	OAV	OOB	BH	AVG	PB	PR	/A	PD	TPI
1981	Cal-A	8	9	.471	22	21	7	1	0	129	123	9	47	75	12.6	3.28	111	.251	.330	0	—	0	5	5	-1	0.5
1982	*Cal-A	8	6	.571	33	26	5	1	0	179²	177	8	47	85	11.6	3.51	116	.260	.314	0	—	0	11	11	-0	0.7
1983	Cal-A	7	14	.333	43	19	2	0	5	154	173	14	75	77	14.8	4.91	82	.293	.379	0	—	0	-14	-15	-1	-1.9
1984	Cal-A	15	11	.577	34	34	9	2	0	246²	227	17	84	196	11.5	3.47	114	.244	.310	0	—	0	14	14	-1	1.3
1985	Cal-A	15	9	.625	35	35	6	1	0	250	228	22	98	180	11.9	3.56	115	.243	.317	0	—	0	16	15	0	1.4
1986	*Cal-A☆	18	10	.643	34	34	14	3	0	269	218	22	73	208	9.8	2.84	144	.221	.277	—	—	0	40	38	2	4.0
1987	Cal-A☆	16	14	.533	36	36	10	0	0	247	252	34	84	192	12.4	4.01	107	.261	.323	0	—	0	12	8	-1	1.1
1988	Cal-A	13	16	.448	34	34	12	2	0	249²	263	14	87	133	12.8	4.15	93	.272	.335	0	—	0	-5	-8	-0	-0.7
1989	Cal-A	9	15	.375	33	33	5	0	0	220	252	26	48	123	12.4	4.54	84	.292	.330	0	—	0	-16	-18	4	-1.3
1990	Cal-A	0	3	.000	10	10	1	0	1	20¹	19	1	13	14	14.6	1.77	216	.250	.367	0	—	0	5	5	1	0.9
	NY-A	5	6	.455	16	16	2	1	0	96²	87	8	34	60	11.6	4.47	89	.240	.312	0	—	0	-6	-5	-0	-0.5
	Yr	5	9	.357	26	26	2	1	1	117	106	9	47	74	12.1	4.00	99	.240	.319	0	—	0	-1	-1	1	0.4
1991	NY-A	0	1	.000	2	2	0	0	0	5¹	8	1	1	0	15.2	10.13	41	.320	.346	0	—	0	-4	-4	0	-0.5
1993	NY-A	3	2	.600	9	9	0	0	0	41	39	7	22	30	14.0	5.27	79	.248	.352	0	—	0	-4	-5	0	-0.3
Total	12	117	116	.502	341	299	72	11	6	2108¹	2066	183	713	1373	12.1	3.83	105	.257	.322	0	—	0	55	41	4	4.7

● **BOBBY WITT**　　Witt, Robert Andrew b: 5/11/64, Arlington, Mass. BR/TR, 6'2", 205 lbs. Deb: 4/10/86

YEAR	TM/L	W	L	PCT	G	GS	CG	SH	SV	IP	H	HR	BB	SO	RAT	ERA	ERA+	OAV	OOB	BH	AVG	PB	PR	/A	PD	TPI
1986	Tex-A	11	9	.550	31	31	0	0	0	157²	130	18	143	174	15.8	5.48	78	.223	.379	0	—	0	-23	-21	0	-2.4
1987	Tex-A	8	10	.444	26	25	1	0	0	143	114	10	140	160	16.2	4.91	91	.219	.388	0	.000	0	-7	-7	0	-0.7
1988	Tex-A	8	10	.444	22	22	13	2	0	174¹	134	13	101	148	12.2	3.92	104	.216	.326	0	—	0	1	3	-1	0.0
1989	Tex-A	12	13	.480	31	31	5	1	0	194¹	182	14	114	166	13.8	5.14	77	.248	.351	0	—	0	-27	-25	0	-2.9
1990	Tex-A	17	10	.630	33	32	7	1	0	222	197	12	110	221	12.6	3.36	116	.238	.330	0	—	0	13	14	-1	1.5
1991	Tex-A	3	7	.300	17	16	1	1	0	88²	84	7	74	82	16.1	6.09	66	.254	.392	0	—	0	-20	-20	-1	-2.0
1992	Tex-A	9	13	.409	25	25	0	0	0	161¹	152	14	95	100	13.9	4.46	85	.254	.358	0	—	0	-9	-12	-0	-1.4
	*Oak-A	1	1	.500	6	6	0	0	0	31²	31	2	19	25	14.2	3.41	110	.265	.368	0	—	0	2	1	0	0.2
	Yr	10	14	.417	31	31	0	0	0	193	183	16	114	125	13.8	4.29	88	.252	.354	0	—	0	-8	-11	-0	-1.2
1993	Oak-A	14	13	.519	35	33	5	1	0	220	226	16	91	131	13.1	4.21	97	.269	.343	0	—	0	3	-3	2	0.2
1994	Oak-A	8	10	.444	24	24	5	3	0	135²	151	22	70	111	15.0	5.04	88	.283	.371	0	—	0	-6	-7	0	-0.7
Total	9	91	96	.487	250	245	37	9	0	1528²	1401	125	957	1318	14.0	4.56	90	.246	.356	0	.000	0	-71	-79	-1	-8.2

● **JOHNNIE WITTIG**　　Wittig, John Carl "Hans" b: 6/16/14, Baltimore, Md. BR/TR, 6', 180 lbs. Deb: 8/4/38

YEAR	TM/L	W	L	PCT	G	GS	CG	SH	SV	IP	H	HR	BB	SO	RAT	ERA	ERA+	OAV	OOB	BH	AVG	PB	PR	/A	PD	TPI
1938	NY-N	2	3	.400	13	6	2	0	0	39¹	41	4	26	14	15.3	4.81	78	.263	.368	0	.000	-1	-4	-5	-1	-0.8
1939	NY-N	0	2	.000	5	2	1	0	0	16²	18	0	14	4	17.8	7.56	52	.281	.418	0	.000	-1	-7	-7	0	-0.7
1941	NY-N	3	5	.375	25	9	0	0	0	85¹	111	5	45	47	16.6	5.59	66	.319	.398	5	.200	-1	-19	-18	-2	-1.7
1943	NY-N	5	15	.250	40	22	4	1	4	164	172	14	76	56	13.6	4.23	82	.273	.352	5	.098	-3	-15	-14	-3	-2.3
1949	Bos-A	0	0	—	1	0	0	0	0	2	2	0	2	0	18.0	9.00	48	.286	.444	0	—	0	-1	-1	0	-0.1
Total	5	10	25	.286	84	39	7	1	4	307¹	344	23	163	121	14.9	4.89	73	.286	.372	10	.110	-6	-46	-44	-6	-5.5

● **MARK WOHLERS**　　Wohlers, Mark Edward b: 1/23/70, Holyoke, Mass. BR/TR, 6'4", 207 lbs. Deb: 8/17/91

YEAR	TM/L	W	L	PCT	G	GS	CG	SH	SV	IP	H	HR	BB	SO	RAT	ERA	ERA+	OAV	OOB	BH	AVG	PB	PR	/A	PD	TPI
1991	*Atl-N	3	1	.750	17	0	0	0	2	19²	17	1	13	13	14.6	3.20	121	.239	.372	0	.000	-0	1	1	0	0.3
1992	*Atl-N	1	2	.333	32	0	0	0	4	35¹	28	0	14	17	11.0	2.55	144	.235	.321	0	.000	-0	4	4	0	0.5

YEAR TM/L	W	L	PCT	G	GS	CG	SH	SV	IP	H	HR	BB	SO	RAT	ERA	ERA+	OAV	OOB	BH	AVG	PB	PR	/A	PD	TPI
1993 *Atl-N	6	2	.750	46	0	0	0	0	48	37	2	22	45	11.3	4.50	89	.218	.311	0	—	0	-2	-3	0	-0.3
1994 Atl-N	7	2	.778	51	0	0	0	1	51	51	1	33	58	14.8	4.59	90	.264	.372	1	1.000	0	-2	-2	0	-0.3
Total 4	17	7	.708	146	0	0	0	7	154	133	4	82	133	12.8	3.92	101	.241	.343	1	.250	0	0	1	1	0.2

● PETE WOJEY
Wojey, Peter Paul b: 12/1/19, Stowe, Pa. BR/TR, 5'11", 185 lbs. Deb: 7/2/54

YEAR TM/L	W	L	PCT	G	GS	CG	SH	SV	IP	H	HR	BB	SO	RAT	ERA	ERA+	OAV	OOB	BH	AVG	PB	PR	/A	PD	TPI
1954 Bro-N	1	1	.500	14	1	0	0	1	27²	24	3	14	21	13.0	3.25	126	.242	.348	0	.000	-0	3	3	1	0.2
1956 Det-A	0	0	—	2	0	0	0	0	4	2	0	1	1	6.8	2.25	183	.167	.231	0	—	0	1	1	0	0.0
1957 Det-A	0	0	—	2	0	0	0	0	1¹	1	0	0	0	6.8	0.00	—	.200	.200	0	—	0	1	1	0	0.0
Total 3	1	1	.500	18	1	0	0	1	33	27	3	15	22	12.0	3.00	136	.233	.331	0	.000	-0	4	4	1	0.2

● ED WOJNA
Wojna, Edward David b: 8/20/60, Bridgeport, Conn. BR/TR, 6'1", 185 lbs. Deb: 6/16/85

YEAR TM/L	W	L	PCT	G	GS	CG	SH	SV	IP	H	HR	BB	SO	RAT	ERA	ERA+	OAV	OOB	BH	AVG	PB	PR	/A	PD	TPI
1985 SD-N	2	4	.333	15	7	0	0	0	42	53	6	19	18	16.1	5.79	61	.312	.391	2	.167	-0	-10	-11	-0	-1.3
1986 SD-N	2	2	.500	7	7	1	0	0	39	42	2	16	19	13.6	3.23	113	.268	.339	2	.143	-0	2	2	-1	0.1
1987 SD-N	0	3	.000	5	3	0	0	0	18¹	25	2	6	13	15.7	5.89	67	.333	.390	0	.000	-1	-4	-4	1	-0.5
1989 Cle-A	0	1	.000	9	3	0	0	0	33	31	0	14	10	12.3	4.09	97	.254	.331	0	—	0	-1	-0	1	0.0
Total 4	4	10	.286	36	20	1	0	0	132¹	151	10	55	60	14.4	4.62	81	.288	.361	4	.129	-1	-13	-13	1	-1.7

● ERNIE WOLF
Wolf, Ernest Adolph b: 2/2/1889, Newark, N.J. d: 5/23/64, Atlantic Highlands, N.J. BR/TR, 5'11", 174 lbs. Deb: 9/10/12

YEAR TM/L	W	L	PCT	G	GS	CG	SH	SV	IP	H	HR	BB	SO	RAT	ERA	ERA+	OAV	OOB	BH	AVG	PB	PR	/A	PD	TPI
1912 Cle-A	0	0	—	1	0	0	0	0	5²	8	0	4	1	19.1	6.35	54	.348	.444	0	—	-0	-2	-2	-0	-0.1

● WALLY WOLF
Wolf, Walter Beck b: 1/5/42, Los Angeles, Cal. BR/TR, 6'0.5", 191 lbs. Deb: 9/27/69

YEAR TM/L	W	L	PCT	G	GS	CG	SH	SV	IP	H	HR	BB	SO	RAT	ERA	ERA+	OAV	OOB	BH	AVG	PB	PR	/A	PD	TPI
1969 Cal-A	0	0	—	2	0	0	0	0	2¹	3	1	3	2	23.1	11.57	30	.333	.500	0	—	0	-2	-2	-0	0.0
1970 Cal-A	0	0	—	4	0	0	0	0	5¹	3	1	4	5	11.8	5.06	71	.176	.333	0	—	0	-1	-1	-0	0.0
Total 2	0	0	—	6	0	0	0	0	7²	6	2	7	7	15.3	7.04	51	.231	.394	0	—	0	-3	-3	-0	0.0

● LEFTY WOLF
Wolf, Walter Francis b: 6/10/1900, Hartford, Conn. d: 9/25/71, New Orleans, La. BR/TL, 5'10", 163 lbs. Deb: 7/4/21

YEAR TM/L	W	L	PCT	G	GS	CG	SH	SV	IP	H	HR	BB	SO	RAT	ERA	ERA+	OAV	OOB	BH	AVG	PB	PR	/A	PD	TPI
1921 Phi-A	0	0	—	8	0	0	0	0	15	15	0	16	11	19.8	7.20	62	.273	.452	1	.250	-0	-5	-5	-0	0.0

● JIMMY WOLF
Wolf, William Van Winkle "Chicken" b: 5/12/1862, Louisville, Ky. d: 5/16/03, Louisville, Ky. BR/TR, 5'9", 190 lbs. Deb: 5/2/1882 M♦

YEAR TM/L	W	L	PCT	G	GS	CG	SH	SV	IP	H	HR	BB	SO	RAT	ERA	ERA+	OAV	OOB	BH	AVG	PB	PR	/A	PD	TPI
1882 Lou-a	0	0	—	1	0	0	0	0	6	11	0	3	1	21.0	9.00	28	.371	.429	95	.299	0	-4	-4	-0	0.0
1885 Lou-a	0	0	—	1	0	0	0	0	1	1	0	0	1	9.0	9.00	36	.200	.200	141	.292	0	-1	-1	0	0.0
1886 Lou-a	0	0	—	1	0	0	0	0	3	7	0	0	0	21.0	15.00	24	.350	.350	148	.272	0	-4	-4	-0	0.0
Total 3	0	0	—	3	0	0	0	0	10	19	0	3	2	19.8	10.80	27	.348	.382	1440	.290	1	-9	-9	-0	0.0

● CHUCK WOLFE
Wolfe, Charles Hunt b: 2/15/1897, Wolfsburg, Pa. d: 11/27/57, Schellsburg, Pa. BL/TR, 5'7", 175 lbs. Deb: 8/2/23

YEAR TM/L	W	L	PCT	G	GS	CG	SH	SV	IP	H	HR	BB	SO	RAT	ERA	ERA+	OAV	OOB	BH	AVG	PB	PR	/A	PD	TPI
1923 Phi-A	0	0	—	3	0	0	0	0	9²	6	1	8	1	13.0	3.72	110	.194	.359	1	.333	0	0	-0	-0	0.0

● ED WOLFE
Wolfe, Edward Anthony b: 1/2/29, Los Angeles, Cal. BR/TR, 6'3", 185 lbs. Deb: 4/19/52

YEAR TM/L	W	L	PCT	G	GS	CG	SH	SV	IP	H	HR	BB	SO	RAT	ERA	ERA+	OAV	OOB	BH	AVG	PB	PR	/A	PD	TPI
1952 Pit-N	0	0	—	3	0	0	0	0	3²	7	1	5	1	31.9	7.36	54	.467	.619	0	—	0	-1	-1	0	0.0

● BARNEY WOLFE
Wolfe, Wilbert Otto b: 1/9/1876, Independence, Pa. d: 2/27/53, N.Charleroi, Pa. BR/TR, 6'1", Deb: 4/24/03

YEAR TM/L	W	L	PCT	G	GS	CG	SH	SV	IP	H	HR	BB	SO	RAT	ERA	ERA+	OAV	OOB	BH	AVG	PB	PR	/A	PD	TPI
1903 NY-A	6	9	.400	20	16	12	1	0	148¹	143	1	26	48	10.6	2.97	105	.253	.293	4	.075	-4	-0	2	-0	-0.2
1904 NY-A	0	3	.000	7	3	2	0	0	33²	31	1	4	8	9.9	3.21	85	.246	.280	0	.000	-1	-2	-2	-0	-0.3
Was-A	6	9	.400	17	16	13	2	0	126²	131	0	22	44	11.7	3.27	81	.268	.314	5	.119	-2	-9	-9	-2	-1.3
Yr	6	12	.333	24	19	15	2	0	160¹	162	1	26	52	11.2	3.26	82	.262	.304	5	.096	-3	-12	-10	-2	-1.6
1905 Was-A	9	13	.409	28	23	17	1	1	182	162	1	37	52	10.2	2.57	103	.240	.287	8	.127	-1	2	2	-2	-0.2
1906 Was-A	0	3	.000	4	3	2	0	0	20	17	0	10	8	13.0	4.05	65	.233	.341	2	.286	0	-3	-3	0	-0.4
Total 4	21	37	.362	76	61	46	4	1	510²	484	3	99	160	10.8	2.96	94	.251	.297	19	.109	-8	-13	-10	-4	-2.4

● BILL WOLFE
Wolfe, William b: Jersey City, N.J. Deb: 9/10/02

YEAR TM/L	W	L	PCT	G	GS	CG	SH	SV	IP	H	HR	BB	SO	RAT	ERA	ERA+	OAV	OOB	BH	AVG	PB	PR	/A	PD	TPI
1902 Phi-N	0	1	.000	1	1	1	0	0	9	11	0	4	3	16.0	4.00	70	.301	.385	1	.333	0	-1	-1	0	-0.1

● ROGER WOLFF
Wolff, Roger Francis b: 4/10/11, Evansville, Ill. d: 3/23/94, Chester, Ill. BR/TR, 6'0.5", 208 lbs. Deb: 9/20/41

YEAR TM/L	W	L	PCT	G	GS	CG	SH	SV	IP	H	HR	BB	SO	RAT	ERA	ERA+	OAV	OOB	BH	AVG	PB	PR	/A	PD	TPI
1941 Phi-A	0	2	.000	2	2	2	0	0	17	15	0	4	2	10.1	3.18	132	.231	.275	1	.200	-0	2	2	-0	0.2
1942 Phi-A	12	15	.444	32	25	15	2	3	214¹	206	16	69	94	11.7	3.32	114	.249	.309	6	.088	-3	8	11	0	1.0
1943 Phi-A	10	15	.400	41	26	13	2	6	221	232	11	72	91	12.5	3.54	96	.274	.334	9	.122	-4	-6	-4	-3	-1.1
1944 Was-A	4	15	.211	33	21	5	0	0	155	186	4	60	73	14.6	4.99	65	.295	.362	12	.218	1	-27	-30	2	-3.1
1945 Was-A	20	10	.667	33	29	21	4	2	250	200	4	53	108	**9.1**	2.12	146	.215	**.258**	9	.107	-5	35	27	-1	2.7
1946 Was-A	5	8	.385	21	17	6	0	0	122	115	8	30	50	11.1	2.58	130	.249	.302	4	.103	-0	12	10	-1	0.9
1947 Cle-A	—	—	—	7	2	0	0	0	16	15	1	10	5	15.2	3.94	88	.259	.386	0	.000	-0	-0	-1	-1	0.0
Pit-N	1	4	.200	13	6	1	0	0	30	49	4	18	7	20.4	8.70	49	.368	.447	0	.000	-1	-15	-15	-1	-2.1
Total 7	52	69	.430	182	128	63	8	13	1025¹	1018	56	316	430	11.9	3.41	100	.258	.316	41	.122	-13	8	1	-3	-1.5

● MELLIE WOLFGANG
Wolfgang, Meldon John "Red" b: 3/20/1890, Albany, N.Y. d: 6/30/47, Albany, N.Y. BR/TR, 5'9", 160 lbs. Deb: 4/18/14

YEAR TM/L	W	L	PCT	G	GS	CG	SH	SV	IP	H	HR	BB	SO	RAT	ERA	ERA+	OAV	OOB	BH	AVG	PB	PR	/A	PD	TPI
1914 Chi-A	9	5	.643	24	11	9	2	0	119¹	96	0	32	50	9.7	1.89	142	.219	.272	7	.175	-0	11	11	4	1.7
1915 Chi-A	2	2	.500	17	2	0	0	0	53²	39	0	12	21	8.7	1.84	161	.211	.263	2	.118	-1	7	7	-1	0.2
1916 Chi-A	4	6	.400	27	14	6	1	0	127	103	2	42	36	10.6	1.98	139	.228	.296	9	.225	0	12	11	1	1.0
1917 Chi-A	0	0	—	5	0	0	0	0	17²	18	1	6	3	12.7	5.09	52	.305	.379	0	.000	-1	-5	-5	-0	-0.1
1918 Chi-A	0	1	.000	4	0	0	0	0	8¹	12	0	3	1	16.2	5.40	51	.333	.385	1	.500	0	-2	-2	0	-0.2
Total 5	15	14	.517	77	27	15	3	0	326	268	3	95	111	10.1	2.18	127	.229	.289	19	.184	-1	23	21	4	2.6

● HARRY WOLTER
Wolter, Harry Meigs b: 7/11/1884, Monterey, Cal. d: 7/7/70, Palo Alto, Cal. BL/TL, 5'10", 175 lbs. Deb: 5/14/07 ♦

YEAR TM/L	W	L	PCT	G	GS	CG	SH	SV	IP	H	HR	BB	SO	RAT	ERA	ERA+	OAV	OOB	BH	AVG	PB	PR	/A	PD	TPI
1907 Pit-N	0	0	—	1	0	0	0	0	2	2	0	2	0	22.5	4.50	54	.333	.455	0	.000	-0	-0	-0	-0	0.0
StL-N	0	2	.000	3	3	1	0	0	23	27	1	18	8	18.4	4.30	58	.318	.448	16	.340	1	-5	-5	-1	-0.4
Yr	0	2	.000	4	3	1	0	0	25	30	1	20	8	18.7	4.32	58	.319	.448	16	.333	1	-5	-5	-1	-0.4
1909 Bos-A	4	4	.500	11	6	0	0	0	59	66	0	30	21	15.3	3.51	71	.303	.397	30	.246	2	-7	-7	-1	-0.8
Total 2	4	6	.400	15	9	1	0	0	84	96	1	50	29	16.3	3.75	67	.308	.413	515	.270	3	-12	-12	-2	-1.2

● RYNIE WOLTERS
Wolters, Reinder Albertus b: 12/18/1842, U.S.A. d: 1/3/17, Newark, N.J. TR, 6', 165 lbs. Deb: 5/18/1871

YEAR TM/L	W	L	PCT	G	GS	CG	SH	SV	IP	H	HR	BB	SO	RAT	ERA	ERA+	OAV	OOB	BH	AVG	PB	PR	/A	PD	TPI
1871 Mut-n	16	16	.500	**32**	32	**31**	**1**	0	283	345	7	39	22	12.2	3.43	110	**.263**	.285	51	.370	20	25	11		2.0
1872 Cle-n	3	6	.333	12	8	5	0	0	76¹	119	3	7	4	14.9	5.19	70	.302	.314	16	.232	-0	-12	-13		-0.9
1873 Res-n	0	1	.000	1	1	1	0	0	9	13	0	1	1	14.0	0.00	—	.220	.233	0	.000	-0	3	3		0.2
Total 3 n	19	23	.452	45	41	37	1	0	368¹	477	10	47	27	12.8	3.71	90	.271	.290	67	.318	19	-19	-15		1.3

● DOOLEY WOMACK
Womack, Horace Guy b: 8/25/39, Columbia, S.C. BL/TR, 6', 170 lbs. Deb: 4/14/66

YEAR TM/L	W	L	PCT	G	GS	CG	SH	SV	IP	H	HR	BB	SO	RAT	ERA	ERA+	OAV	OOB	BH	AVG	PB	PR	/A	PD	TPI
1966 NY-A	7	3	.700	42	1	0	0	4	75	52	6	23	50	9.4	2.64	126	.198	.270	1	.200	0	7	6	2	1.1
1967 NY-A	5	6	.455	65	0	0	0	18	97	80	6	35	57	10.9	2.41	130	.230	.306	4	.286	1	9	8	4	1.8
1968 NY-A	3	7	.300	45	0	0	0	6	61²	53	6	29	27	12.1	3.21	90	.244	.336	1	.200	0	-2	-2	2	-0.1
1969 Hou-N	2	1	.667	30	0	0	0	2	51¹	49	1	20	32	12.6	3.51	101	.259	.340	1	.167	-0	2	2	0	0.2
Sea-A	2	1	.667	9	0	0	0	0	14¹	15	0	3	8	11.3	2.51	145	.273	.310	0	.000	-0	2	2	0	0.4
1970 Oak-A	0	0	—	2	0	0	0	0	3	4	2	1	3	15.0	15.00	24	.308	.357	0	—	0	-4	-4	0	0.0
Total 5	19	18	.514	193	1	0	0	24	302¹	253	21	111	177	11.1	2.95	110	.239	.310	7	.226	1	12	9	11	3.4

● SPADES WOOD
Wood, Charles Asher b: 1/13/09, Spartanburg, S.C. d: 5/18/86, Wichita, Kan. BL/TL, 5'10.5", 150 lbs. Deb: 8/16/30

YEAR TM/L	W	L	PCT	G	GS	CG	SH	SV	IP	H	HR	BB	SO	RAT	ERA	ERA+	OAV	OOB	BH	AVG	PB	PR	/A	PD	TPI
1930 Pit-N	4	3	.571	9	7	4	2	0	58	61	4	32	23	14.4	5.12	97	.270	.360	5	.250	1	-1	-1	-2	-0.2

YEAR TM/L	W	L	PCT	G	GS	CG	SH	SV	IP	H	HR	BB	SO	RAT	ERA	ERA+	OAV	OOB	BH	AVG	PB	PR	/A	PD	TPI
1931 Pit-N	2	6	.250	15	10	2	0	0	64	69	2	46	33	16.3	6.05	64	.273	.387	5	.227	1	-16	-16	-0	-1.6
Total 2	6	9	.400	24	17	6	2	0	122	130	6	78	56	15.4	5.61	78	.271	.375	10	.238	1	-16	-17	-2	-1.8

● GEORGE WOOD
Wood, George A. "Dandy"   b: 11/9/1858, Boston, Mass.   d: 4/4/24, Harrisburg, Pa.   BL/TR, 5'10.5", 175 lbs.   Deb: 5/1/1880   MU♦

YEAR TM/L	W	L	PCT	G	GS	CG	SH	SV	IP	H	HR	BB	SO	RAT	ERA	ERA+	OAV	OOB	BH	AVG	PB	PR	/A	PD	TPI
1883 Det-N	0	0	—	1	0	0	0	0	5	8	0	3	0	19.8	7.20	43	.348	.423	133	.302	0	-2	-2	0	0.1
1885 Det-N	0	0	—	1	0	0	0	0	4	5	0	1	1	13.5	0.00	—	.333	.375	105	.290	0	1	1	-0	0.0
1888 Phi-N	0	0	—	2	0	0	0	2	2	3	0	1	0	18.0	4.50	66	.300	.364	99	.229	1	-0	-0	0	-0.1
1889 Phi-N	0	0	—	1	0	0	0	0	1	2	0	0	2	18.0	18.00	24	.403	.403	106	.251	0	-2	-2	0	0.0
Total 4	0	0	—	5	0	0	0	2	12	18	0	5	3	17.3	5.25	59	.340	.397	1467	.273	1	-3	-3	0	0.0

● JOE WOOD
Wood, Joe "Smokey Joe" (b: Howard Ellsworth Wood)   b: 10/25/1889, Kansas City, Mo.   d: 7/27/85, West Haven, Conn.   BR/TR, 5'11", 180 lbs.   Deb: 8/24/08   F♦

YEAR TM/L	W	L	PCT	G	GS	CG	SH	SV	IP	H	HR	BB	SO	RAT	ERA	ERA+	OAV	OOB	BH	AVG	PB	PR	/A	PD	TPI
1908 Bos-A	1	1	.500	6	2	1	1	0	22²	14	0	16	11	12.3	2.38	103	.161	.298	0	.000	-1	0	0	-0	-0.1
1909 Bos-A	11	7	.611	24	19	13	4	0	160²	121	1	43	88	9.5	2.18	114	.209	.270	9	.164	-0	5	6	-4	0.2
1910 Bos-A	12	13	.480	35	17	14	3	0	198²	155	3	56	145	10.0	1.68	152	.220	.287	18	.261	5	19	19	2	3.4
1911 Bos-A	23	17	.575	44	33	25	5	3	275²	226	2	76	231	10.2	2.02	162	.223	.284	23	.261	9	40	38	7	**6.5**
1912 *Bos-A	**34**	**5**	**.872**	43	38	**35**	**10**	1	344	267	2	82	258	9.4	1.91	178	.216	.272	36	.290	11	54	57	8	8.6
1913 Bos-A	11	5	.688	23	18	12	1	2	145²	120	0	61	123	11.7	2.29	129	.229	.319	15	.268	4	10	11	4	2.1
1914 Bos-A	9	3	.750	18	14	11	1	1	113¹	94	1	34	67	10.2	2.62	103	.229	.288	6	.140	0	2	1	1	0.1
1915 Bos-A	15	5	**.750**	25	16	10	3	2	157¹	120	1	44	63	9.4	**1.49**	187	.216	.275	14	.259	4	25	23	1	3.6
1917 Cle-A	0	1	.000	5	1	0	0	1	15²	17	0	7	2	13.8	3.45	82	.309	.387	0	.000	-1	-1	-1	0	-0.2
1919 Cle-A	0	0	—	1	0	0	0	0	0²	0	0	0	0	0.0	0.00	—	.000	.000	49	.255	0	0	0	-0	0.1
1920 *Cle-A	0	0	—	1	0	0	0	0	2	4	0	2	1	27.0	22.50	17	.444	.545	37	.270	0	-4	-4	0	0.1
Total 11	116	57	.671	225	158	121	28	11	1436¹	1138	10	421	989	10.1	2.03	146	.220	.285	553	.283	31	150	150	14	24.3

● JOHN WOOD
Wood, John B.   b: 1871,   5'7", 142 lbs.   Deb: 5/9/1896

YEAR TM/L	W	L	PCT	G	GS	CG	SH	SV	IP	H	HR	BB	SO	RAT	ERA	ERA+	OAV	OOB	BH	AVG	PB	PR	/A	PD	TPI
1896 StL-N	0	0	—	1	0	0	0	0	0	1	0	2	0		∞	—	1.000	1.000	0	—	0	-1	-1	0	-0.1

● JOE WOOD
Wood, Joseph Frank   b: 5/20/16, Shohola, Pa.   BR/TR, 6', 190 lbs.   Deb: 5/1/44   F

YEAR TM/L	W	L	PCT	G	GS	CG	SH	SV	IP	H	HR	BB	SO	RAT	ERA	ERA+	OAV	OOB	BH	AVG	PB	PR	/A	PD	TPI
1944 Bos-A	0	1	.000	3	1	0	0	0	9²	13	0	3	5	14.9	6.52	52	.317	.364	0	.000	-0	-3	-3	0	-0.3

● PETE WOOD
Wood, Peter Burke   b: 2/1/1857, Hamilton, Ont., Can.   d: 3/15/23, Chicago, Ill.   TR, 5'7", 185 lbs.   Deb: 7/15/1885   F

YEAR TM/L	W	L	PCT	G	GS	CG	SH	SV	IP	H	HR	BB	SO	RAT	ERA	ERA+	OAV	OOB	BH	AVG	PB	PR	/A	PD	TPI
1885 Buf-N	8	15	.348	24	22	21	0	0	198²	235	4	66	38	13.6	4.44	67	.280	.332	23	.221	-1	-36	-32	-1	-3.1
1889 Phi-N	1	1	.500	3	2	2	0	0	19	28	0	3	8	14.7	5.21	83	.332	.355	0	.000	-1	-3	-2	-0	-0.3
Total 2	9	16	.360	27	24	23	0	0	217²	263	4	69	46	13.7	4.51	69	.285	.334	23	.205	-2	-38	-34	-1	-3.4

● WILBUR WOOD
Wood, Wilbur Forrester   b: 10/22/41, Cambridge, Mass.   BR/TL, 6', 180 lbs.   Deb: 6/30/61

YEAR TM/L	W	L	PCT	G	GS	CG	SH	SV	IP	H	HR	BB	SO	RAT	ERA	ERA+	OAV	OOB	BH	AVG	PB	PR	/A	PD	TPI
1961 Bos-A	0	0	—	6	1	0	0	0	13	14	2	7	7	14.5	5.54	75	.269	.356	0	.000	-0	-2	-2	-0	-0.1
1962 Bos-A	0	0	—	1	1	0	0	0	7²	6	0	3	3	10.6	3.52	117	.214	.290	0	.000	-0	0	1	0	0.0
1963 Bos-A	0	5	.000	25	6	0	0	0	64²	67	10	13	28	11.6	3.76	101	.257	.314	0	.000	-1	-1	0	-1	-0.2
1964 Bos-A	0	0	—	4	0	0	0	0	5²	13	1	3	5	25.4	17.47	22	.433	.485	0	.000	-9	-9	-9	0	-0.1
Pit-N	0	2	.000	3	2	1	0	0	17¹	16	0	11	7	15.1	3.63	97	.246	.372	0	.000	-0	-0	-1	-0	-0.1
1965 Pit-N	1	1	.500	34	1	0	0	0	51¹	44	3	16	29	10.7	3.16	111	.237	.300	0	.000	-1	2	2	-1	-0.1
1967 Chi-A	4	2	.667	51	8	0	0	4	95¹	95	2	28	47	11.7	2.45	126	.260	.315	1	.063	-0	8	7	-1	0.4
1968 Chi-A	13	12	.520	**88**	2	0	0	16	159	127	8	33	74	9.2	1.87	162	.222	.268	2	.091	-1	**20**	**20**	-0	3.9
1969 Chi-A	10	11	.476	**76**	0	0	0	15	119²	113	13	44	73	11.7	3.01	128	.248	.313	0	.000	-1	8	11	1	2.1
1970 Chi-A	9	13	.409	**77**	0	0	0	21	121²	118	7	36	85	11.5	2.81	139	.258	.315	2	.111	-1	12	15	2	3.3
1971 Chi-A☆	22	13	.629	44	42	22	7	1	334	272	21	62	210	9.2	1.91	**188**	.222	.264	5	.052	-5	**57**	**62**	2	**6.6**
1972 Chi-A★	**24**	17	.585	49	49	20	8	0	**376²**	325	28	74	193	9.7	2.51	125	.235	.277	17	.136	-2	23	26	4	3.1
1973 Chi-A	**24**	20	.545	49	48	21	4	0	**359¹**	381	25	91	199	12.0	3.46	114	.270	.318	0	—	0	14	20	1	2.3
1974 Chi-A☆	20	19	.513	42	42	22	1	0	320¹	305	27	80	169	11.1	3.60	104	.254	.305	0	—	0	5	3	0	0.7
1975 Chi-A	16	20	.444	43	43	14	2	0	291¹	309	26	92	140	12.5	4.11	94	.272	.329	0	—	0	-11	-8	1	-0.8
1976 Chi-A	4	3	.571	7	7	5	1	0	56¹	51	3	11	31	9.9	2.24	159	.242	.279	0	—	0	8	8	1	1.1
1977 Chi-A	7	8	.467	24	18	5	1	0	122²	139	10	50	42	14.6	4.99	82	.293	.373	0	—	0	-13	-12	2	-1.1
1978 Chi-A	10	10	.500	28	27	4	0	0	168	187	23	74	69	14.1	5.20	73	.285	.361	0	—	0	-27	-26	2	-2.5
Total 17	164	156	.512	651	297	114	24	57	2684	2582	209	724	1411	11.3	3.24	112	.254	.308	27	.084	-14	92	120	15	18.6

● BRAD WOODALL
Woodall, David Bradley   b: 6/25/69, Atlanta, Ga.   BB/TL, 6', 175 lbs.   Deb: 7/22/94

YEAR TM/L	W	L	PCT	G	GS	CG	SH	SV	IP	H	HR	BB	SO	RAT	ERA	ERA+	OAV	OOB	BH	AVG	PB	PR	/A	PD	TPI
1994 Atl-N	0	1	.000	1	1	0	0	0	6	5	2	2	2	10.5	4.50	92	.227	.292	1	.500	0	-0	-0	1	0.0

● GENE WOODBURN
Woodburn, Eugene Stewart   b: 8/20/1886, Bellaire, Ohio   d: 1/18/61, Sandusky, Ohio   BR/TR, 6', 175 lbs.   Deb: 7/27/11

YEAR TM/L	W	L	PCT	G	GS	CG	SH	SV	IP	H	HR	BB	SO	RAT	ERA	ERA+	OAV	OOB	BH	AVG	PB	PR	/A	PD	TPI
1911 StL-N	1	5	.167	11	6	1	0	0	38¹	22	0	40	23	16.0	5.40	63	.167	.382	1	.167	1	-9	-9	1	-1.0
1912 StL-N	1	4	.200	20	5	1	0	0	48¹	60	0	42	25	19.7	5.59	61	.306	.438	0	.000	-2	-12	-12	-1	-1.3
Total 2	2	9	.182	31	11	2	0	0	86²	82	0	82	48	18.1	5.50	62	.250	.414	1	.053	-0	-20	-20	0	-2.3

● FRED WOODCOCK
Woodcock, Fred Wayland   b: 5/17/1868, Winchendon, Mass.   d: 8/11/43, Ashburnham, Mass.   BL/TL, 6'2", 190 lbs.   Deb: 5/17/1892

YEAR TM/L	W	L	PCT	G	GS	CG	SH	SV	IP	H	HR	BB	SO	RAT	ERA	ERA+	OAV	OOB	BH	AVG	PB	PR	/A	PD	TPI
1892 Pit-N	1	2	.333	5	4	3	0	0	33	42	1	17	8	16.6	3.55	93	.298	.381	3	.200	-1	-1	-1	0	0.0

● GEORGE WOODEND
Woodend, George Anthony   b: 12/9/17, Hartford, Conn.   d: 2/6/80, Hartford, Conn.   BR/TR, 6', 200 lbs.   Deb: 4/22/44

YEAR TM/L	W	L	PCT	G	GS	CG	SH	SV	IP	H	HR	BB	SO	RAT	ERA	ERA+	OAV	OOB	BH	AVG	PB	PR	/A	PD	TPI
1944 Bos-N	0	0	—	3	0	0	0	0	2	5	0	5	0	45.0	13.50	28	.556	.714	0	—	0	-2	-2	0	0.0

● HAL WOODESHICK
Woodeshick, Harold Joseph   b: 8/24/32, Wilkes-Barre, Pa.   BR/TL, 6'3", 200 lbs.   Deb: 9/14/56

YEAR TM/L	W	L	PCT	G	GS	CG	SH	SV	IP	H	HR	BB	SO	RAT	ERA	ERA+	OAV	OOB	BH	AVG	PB	PR	/A	PD	TPI
1956 Det-A	0	2	.000	2	2	0	0	0	5¹	12	1	3	1	25.3	13.50	30	.444	.500	0	—	0	-6	-6	0	-1.3
1958 Cle-A	6	6	.500	14	9	3	0	0	71²	71	4	25	27	12.8	3.64	100	.265	.341	4	.167	-1	1	0	3	0.2
1959 Was-A	2	4	.333	31	3	0	0	0	61	58	2	36	30	14.0	3.69	106	.253	.357	0	.000	-1	1	2	1	0.1
1960 Was-A	4	5	.444	41	14	1	0	4	115	131	7	60	46	15.2	4.70	83	.289	.375	2	.069	-2	-11	-10	2	-0.8
1961 Was-A	3	2	.600	7	6	1	0	0	40¹	38	3	24	24	14.5	4.02	100	.257	.371	2	.125	-1	-0	-1	0	-0.7
Det-A	1	1	.500	12	2	0	0	0	18¹	25	3	17	13	20.6	7.85	52	.316	.438	0	.000	-0	-8	-8	0	-0.7
Yr	4	3	.571	19	8	1	0	0	58²	63	6	41	37	16.0	5.22	77	.273	.382	2	.100	-1	-8	-8	2	-0.7
1962 Hou-N	5	16	.238	31	26	2	1	0	139¹	161	3	54	82	14.1	4.39	85	.290	.356	3	.081	-1	-7	-10	0	-1.5
1963 Hou-N★	11	9	.550	55	0	0	0	10	114	75	3	42	94	9.7	1.97	160	.186	.273	3	.130	-0	17	15	3	3.3
1964 Hou-N	2	9	.182	61	0	0	0	**23**	78¹	73	3	32	58	12.9	2.76	124	.249	.337	0	.000	-0	7	6	2	1.3
1965 Hou-N	3	4	.429	27	0	0	0	1	32¹	27	3	18	22	12.5	3.06	110	.227	.328	1	.167	-0	2	1	1	0.3
StL-N	3	2	.600	51	0	0	0	15	59²	47	1	27	37	11.5	1.81	212	.221	.314	0	.000	-1	11	13	2	2.0
Yr	6	6	.500	78	0	0	0	18	92	74	4	45	59	11.8	2.25	163	.223	.319	1	.071	-1	13	15	2	2.3
1966 StL-N	2	1	.667	59	0	0	0	4	70¹	57	5	23	30	10.4	1.92	187	.224	.290	1	.200	-0	13	13	3	1.1
1967 *StL-N	2	1	.667	36	0	0	0	0	41²	41	2	28	20	15.6	5.18	63	.252	.371	0	.000	-0	-8	-9	1	-0.7
Total 11	44	62	.415	427	62	7	1	61	847¹	816	40	389	484	13.2	3.56	102	.254	.342	16	.092	-7	13	7	18	3.3

● DAN WOODMAN
Woodman, Daniel Courtenay "Cocoa"   b: 7/8/1893, Danvers, Mass.   d: 12/14/62, Danvers, Mass.   BR/TR, 5'8", 160 lbs.   Deb: 7/10/14

YEAR TM/L	W	L	PCT	G	GS	CG	SH	SV	IP	H	HR	BB	SO	RAT	ERA	ERA+	OAV	OOB	BH	AVG	PB	PR	/A	PD	TPI
1914 Buf-F	0	0	—	13	0	0	0	1	33²	30	0	11	13	11.2	2.41	123	.246	.313	1	.143	-1	2	2	-1	-0.1
1915 Buf-F	0	0	—	5	1	0	0	0	15¹	14	0	9	1	13.5	4.11	68	.246	.348	1	.250	-0	-2	-2	1	0.1
Total 2	0	0	—	18	1	0	0	1	49	44	0	20	14	11.9	2.94	99	.246	.325	2	.182	-1	-1	-0	0	0.0

● CLARENCE WOODS
Woods, Clarence Cofield   b: 6/11/1892, Woods Ridge, Ohio County, Ind.   d: 7/2/69, Rising Sun, Ind.   BR/TR, 6'5", 230 lbs.   Deb: 8/8/14

YEAR TM/L	W	L	PCT	G	GS	CG	SH	SV	IP	H	HR	BB	SO	RAT	ERA	ERA+	OAV	OOB	BH	AVG	PB	PR	/A	PD	TPI
1914 Ind-F	0	0	—	2	0	0	0	1	2	1	0	2	1	13.5	4.50	69	.167	.375	0	—	0	-0	-0	0	0.0

YEAR	TM/L	W	L	PCT	G	GS	CG	SH	SV	IP	H	HR	BB	SO	RAT	ERA	ERA+	OAV	OOB	BH	AVG	PB	PR	/A	PD	TPI

● **PINKY WOODS**   Woods, George Rowland b: 5/22/15, Waterbury, Conn. d: 10/30/82, Los Angeles, Cal. BR/TR, 6'5", 225 lbs. Deb: 6/20/43

1943	Bos-A	5	6	.455	23	12	2	0	1	100²	109	6	55	32	14.8	4.92	67	.284	.375	8	.222	-0	-18	-18	-0	-1.9
1944	Bos-A	4	8	.333	38	20	5	1	0	170²	171	4	88	56	14.0	3.27	104	.266	.360	7	.146	-1	3	2	2	0.2
1945	Bos-A	4	7	.364	24	12	3	0	2	107¹	108	3	63	36	14.4	4.19	81	.268	.368	9	.214	1	-10	-9	1	-0.7
Total	3	13	21	.382	85	44	10	1	3	378²	388	13	206	124	14.3	3.97	85	.272	.366	24	.190	-1	-25	-25	3	-2.4

● **JOHN WOODS**   Woods, John Fulton "Abe" b: 1/18/1898, Princeton, W.Va. d: 10/4/46, Norfolk, Va. BR/TR, 6', 175 lbs. Deb: 9/16/24

| 1924 | Bos-A | 0 | 0 | — | 1 | 0 | 0 | 0 | 0 | 1 | 0 | 0 | 3 | 0 | 27.0 | 0.00 | — | — | .500 | | | 0 | 0 | 0 | -0 | 0.0 |

● **WALT WOODS**   Woods, Walter Sydney b: 4/28/1875, Rye, N.H. d: 10/30/51, Portsmouth, N.H. BR/TR, 5'9.5", 165 lbs. Deb: 4/20/1898

1898	Chi-N	9	13	.409	27	22	18	3	0	215	224	7	59	26	12.3	3.14	114	.266	.322	27	.175	-4	11	11	1	0.6
1899	Lou-N	9	13	.409	26	21	17	0	0	186¹	216	9	37	21	12.6	3.28	117	.290	.329	19	.151	-3	12	12	5	1.3
1900	Pit-N	0	0	—	1	0	0	0	0	3	9	0	1	1	30.0	21.00	17	.513	.539	0	.000	-0	-6	-6	-0	0.0
Total	3	18	26	.409	54	43	35	3	0	404¹	449	16	97	48	12.5	3.34	111	.280	.328	46	.164	-7	17	17	5	1.9

● **DICK WOODSON**   Woodson, Richard Lee b: 3/30/45, Oelwein, Iowa BR/TR, 6'5", 207 lbs. Deb: 4/8/69

1969	*Min-A	7	5	.583	44	10	2	0	1	110¹	99	11	49	66	12.3	3.67	99	.237	.322	2	.074	-1	-1	-0	1	-0.1
1970	*Min-A	1	2	.333	21	0	0	0	1	30²	29	2	19	22	14.1	3.82	98	.244	.348	0	.000	-0	-0	-0	-0	0.0
1972	Min-A	14	14	.500	36	36	9	3	0	251²	193	19	101	150	10.6	2.72	118	.211	.291	7	.080	-5	10	14	1	1.1
1973	Min-A	10	8	.556	23	23	4	2	0	141¹	137	12	68	53	13.2	3.95	100	.254	.339	0	—	0	-2	-0	-2	-0.2
1974	Min-A	1	1	.500	5	4	0	0	0	27	30	5	4	12	11.7	4.33	87	.273	.304	0	—	0	-2	-2	1	-0.3
	NY-A	1	2	.333	8	3	0	0	0	28	34	6	12	12	15.1	5.79	60	.301	.373	0	—	0	-7	-7	-1	-0.6
	Yr	2	3	.400	13	7	0	0	0	55	64	11	16	24	13.3	5.07	71	.286	.336	0	—	0	-9	-9	-0	-0.9
Total	5	34	32	.515	137	76	15	5	2	589	522	55	253	315	12.0	3.47	102	.236	.317	9	.077	-7	-2	5	-0	-0.1

● **KERRY WOODSON**   Woodson, Walter Browne b: 5/18/69, Jacksonville, Fla. BR/TR, 6'2", 190 lbs. Deb: 7/19/92

| 1992 | Sea-A | 0 | 1 | .000 | 8 | 1 | 0 | 0 | 0 | 13² | 12 | 0 | 11 | 6 | 15.0 | 3.29 | 121 | .245 | .403 | 0 | — | 0 | 1 | 1 | 0 | 0.1 |

● **FRANK WOODWARD**   Woodward, Frank Russell b: 5/17/1894, New Haven, Conn. d: 6/11/61, New Haven, Conn. BR/TR, 5'10", 175 lbs. Deb: 4/17/18

1918	Phi-N	0	0	—	2	0	0	0	0	6	6	0	4	4	15.0	6.00	50	.250	.357	1	.333	0	-2	-2	-0	0.0
1919	Phi-N	6	9	.400	17	12	6	0	0	100²	109	5	35	27	13.3	4.74	68	.291	.359	6	.207	1	-20	-17	-2	-2.4
	StL-N	3	5	.375	17	7	2	0	1	72	65	1	28	18	11.8	2.63	106	.248	.323	1	.048	-2	2	1	-0	-0.1
	Yr	9	14	.391	34	19	8	0	1	172²	174	6	63	45	12.4	3.86	79	.271	.337	7	.140	-1	-18	-16	-2	-2.5
1921	Was-A	0	0	—	3	1	0	0	0	10²	11	0	3	4	11.8	5.91	70	.282	.333	1	.333	0	-2	-2	-0	0.0
1922	Was-A	0	0	—	1	0	0	0	0	2¹	3	0	3	2	23.1	11.57	33	.375	.545	0	.000	-0	-2	-2	-0	-0.1
1923	Chi-A	0	1	.000	2	1	0	0	0	2	5	0	1	0	27.0	13.50	29	.500	.545	0	—	0	-2	-2	-0	-0.7
Total	5	9	15	.375	42	21	8	0	1	193²	199	6	74	55	13.0	4.23	74	.277	.350	9	.158	-1	-26	-24	-2	-3.2

● **BOB WOODWARD**   Woodward, Robert John b: 9/28/62, Hanover, N.H. BR/TR, 6'3", 185 lbs. Deb: 9/5/85

1985	Bos-A	1	0	1.000	5	2	0	0	0	26²	17	0	9	16	9.5	1.69	254	.168	.250	0	—	0	7	8	-1	-0.1
1986	Bos-A	2	3	.400	9	6	0	0	0	35²	46	4	11	14	14.6	5.30	79	.313	.365	0	—	0	-4	-5	0	-0.5
1987	Bos-A	1	1	.500	9	6	0	0	0	37	53	6	15	15	16.8	7.05	64	.338	.399	0	—	0	-11	-10	-1	-0.6
1988	Bos-A	0	0	—	1	0	0	0	0	0²	2	0	1	0	40.5	13.50	30	.500	.600	0	—	0	-1	-1	0	0.0
Total	4	4	4	.500	24	14	0	0	0	100	118	10	36	45	14.2	5.04	86	.289	.352	0	—	0	-9	-8	-1	-1.2

● **FLOYD WOOLDRIDGE**   Wooldridge, Floyd Lewis b: 8/25/28, Jerico Springs, Mo BR/TR, 6'1", 185 lbs. Deb: 5/1/55

| 1955 | StL-N | 2 | 4 | .333 | 18 | 8 | 2 | 0 | 0 | 57² | 64 | 9 | 27 | 14 | 14.4 | 4.84 | 84 | .281 | .359 | 4 | .222 | 0 | -5 | -5 | -1 | -0.6 |

● **JUNIOR WOOTEN**   Wooten, Earl Hazwell b: 1/16/24, Pelzer, S.C. BR/TL, 5'11", 160 lbs. Deb: 9/16/47 ♦

| 1948 | Was-A | 0 | 0 | — | 1 | 0 | 0 | 0 | 0 | 2 | 2 | 0 | 2 | 1 | 18.0 | 9.00 | 48 | .250 | .400 | 66 | .256 | 0 | -1 | -1 | 0 | 0.0 |

● **FRED WORDEN**   Worden, Frederick Bamford b: 9/4/1894, St.Louis, Mo. d: 11/9/41, St.Louis, Mo. BR/TR, Deb: 9/28/14

| 1914 | Phi-A | 0 | 0 | — | 1 | 0 | 0 | 0 | 0 | 2 | 8 | 0 | 1 | 0 | 36.0 | 18.00 | 15 | .615 | .615 | 0 | .000 | -0 | -3 | -3 | 0 | 0.0 |

● **HOGE WORKMAN**   Workman, Harry Hall b: 9/25/1899, Huntington, W.Va. d: 5/20/72, Ft.Myers, Fla. BR/TR, 5'11", 170 lbs. Deb: 6/27/24

| 1924 | Bos-A | 0 | 0 | — | 11 | 1 | 0 | 0 | 0 | 18 | 25 | 2 | 11 | 7 | 19.0 | 8.50 | 51 | .325 | .422 | 0 | .000 | -0 | -9 | -8 | 0 | 0.0 |

● **RALPH WORKS**   Works, Ralph Talmadge "Judge" b: 3/16/1888, Payson, Ill. d: 8/8/41, Pasadena, Cal. BL/TR, 6'2.5", 185 lbs. Deb: 5/1/09

1909	*Det-A	4	1	.800	16	4	4	0	2	64	62	0	17	31	11.3	1.97	128	.261	.313	1	.059	-2	4	4	-1	0.1
1910	Det-A	3	6	.333	18	10	5	0	1	85²	73	1	39	36	12.2	3.57	74	.235	.328	8	.267	1	-10	-9	-1	-0.9
1911	Det-A	11	5	.688	30	15	9	3	0	167¹	173	6	67	68	13.2	3.87	89	.268	.342	9	.148	-3	-10	-8	-4	-1.7
1912	Det-A	5	10	.333	27	16	9	1	1	157	185	4	66	64	14.8	4.24	77	.308	.383	8	.143	-3	-16	-17	-0	-1.7
	Cin-N	1	1	.500	3	1	1	0	0	9²	4	0	5	5	9.3	2.79	120	.133	.278	1	.200	-0	1	1	-0	0.1
1913	Cin-N	0	1	.000	5	2	0	0	0	15	15	0	8	4	15.6	7.80	42	.242	.356	1	.167	-1	-8	-8	-0	-0.4
Total	5	24	24	.500	99	48	28	4	4	498²	512	5	202	208	13.3	3.79	83	.271	.348	28	.160	-8	-39	-37	-6	-4.2

● **TIM WORRELL**   Worrell, Timothy Howard b: 7/5/67, Pasadena, Cal. BR/TR, 6'4", 215 lbs. Deb: 6/25/93 F

1993	SD-N	2	7	.222	21	16	0	0	0	100²	104	11	43	52	13.1	4.92	84	.269	.342	1	.032	-3	-10	-9	-1	-1.0
1994	SD-N	0	1	.000	3	3	0	0	0	14²	9	0	5	14	8.6	3.68	114	.170	.241	1	.500	1	1	1	0	0.2
Total	2	2	8	.200	24	19	0	0	0	115¹	113	11	48	66	12.6	4.76	87	.257	.330	2	.061	-2	-9	-8	-1	-0.8

● **TODD WORRELL**   Worrell, Todd Roland b: 9/28/59, Arcadia, Cal. BR/TR, 6'5", 215 lbs. Deb: 8/28/85 F

1985	*StL-N	3	0	1.000	17	0	0	0	5	21²	17	2	7	17	10.0	2.91	122	.215	.279	0	.000	-0	2	2	-0	0.2
1986	StL-N	9	10	.474	74	0	0	0	**36**	103²	86	9	41	73	11.1	2.08	175	.229	.307	1	.143	0	**19**	**18**	-2	**4.5**
1987	*StL-N	8	6	.571	75	0	0	0	33	94²	86	8	34	92	11.4	2.66	156	.242	.308	1	.100	0	15	16	0	3.4
1988	StL-N★	5	9	.357	68	0	0	0	32	90	69	7	34	78	10.4	3.00	116	.214	.291	0	.000	0	4	5	-0	1.1
1989	StL-N	3	5	.375	47	0	0	0	20	51²	42	4	26	41	11.8	2.96	123	.222	.316	0	.000	0	3	4	1	1.0
1992	StL-N	5	3	.625	67	0	0	0	3	64	45	4	25	64	10.0	2.11	161	.198	.281	0	—	0	10	9	-1	1.1
1993	LA-N	1	1	.500	35	0	0	0	5	38²	46	6	11	31	13.3	6.05	63	.313	.361	0	—	0	-9	-10	-0	-0.8
1994	LA-N	6	5	.545	38	0	0	0	11	42	37	4	12	44	10.7	4.29	92	.236	.294	0	—	0	-2	-0	-0	-0.5
Total	8	40	39	.506	421	0	0	0	145	506¹	428	44	190	440	11.1	2.97	124	.225	.304	2	.080	-0	44	42	-4	10.0

● **RICH WORTHAM**   Wortham, Richard Cooper b: 10/22/53, Odessa, Tex. BR/TL, 6', 185 lbs. Deb: 5/3/78

1978	Chi-A	3	2	.600	8	8	2	0	0	59	59	1	23	25	12.5	3.05	125	.267	.336	0	—	0	5	5	-0	0.4
1979	Chi-A	14	14	.500	34	33	5	0	0	204	195	21	100	119	13.1	4.90	87	.255	.343	0	—	0	-15	-15	-2	-1.9
1980	Chi-A	4	7	.364	41	10	0	0	1	92	102	4	58	45	15.9	5.97	67	.285	.389	0	—	0	-20	-20	1	-2.0
1983	Oak-A	0	0	—	1	0	0	0	0	0	3	0	1	0	—	∞		1.000	1.000	0	—	0	-1	-1	-0	0.1
Total	4	21	23	.477	84	51	7	0	1	355	359	26	182	189	13.9	4.89	84	.266	.356	0	—	0	-32	-31	-1	-3.4

● **AL WORTHINGTON**   Worthington, Allan Fulton "Red" b: 2/5/29, Birmingham, Ala. BR/TR, 6'2", 205 lbs. Deb: 7/6/53 C

1953	NY-N	4	8	.333	20	17	8	6	0	102	103	6	54	52	14.0	3.44	125	.258	.349	2	.065	-2	10	10	0	0.8
1954	NY-N	0	2	.000	10	1	0	0	0	18	21	0	15	8	18.0	3.50	115	.333	.462	0	.000	-1	1	1	0	0.1
1956	NY-N	7	14	.333	28	24	4	0	0	165²	159	7	74	95	12.6	3.97	95	.254	.333	12	.235	2	-4	-3	2	0.0
1957	NY-N	8	11	.421	55	12	1	1	4	157²	140	19	56	90	11.5	4.22	93	.237	.309	4	.100	-2	-6	-5	0	-0.8
1958	SF-N	11	7	.611	54	12	1	0	6	151¹	152	17	55	76	12.5	3.63	105	.255	.322	8	.182	0	5	5	0	0.4
1959	SF-N	2	3	.400	42	3	0	0	2	73¹	68	8	37	45	13.5	3.68	103	.253	.354	1	.077	-1	2	1	1	0.1

YEAR	TM/L	W	L	PCT	G	GS	CG	SH	SV	IP	H	HR	BB	SO	RAT	ERA	ERA+	OAV	OOB	BH	AVG	PB	PR	/A	PD	TPI
1960	Bos-A	0	1	.000	6	0	0	0	0	11²	17	1	11	7	21.6	7.71	52	.340	.459	0	.000	-0	-5	-5	0	-0.4
	Chi-A	1	1	.500	4	0	0	0	0	5¹	3	0	4	1	11.8	3.38	112	.176	.333	2	1.000	1	0	0	0	0.2
	Yr	1	2	.333	10	0	0	0	0	17	20	1	15	8	18.5	6.35	62	.299	.427	2	.667	1	-5	-5	0	-0.2
1963	Cin-N	4	4	.500	50	0	0	0	10	81¹	75	6	31	55	12.1	2.99	112	.248	.324	1	.083	-0	3	3	2	0.6
1964	Cin-N	1	0	1.000	6	0	0	0	0	7	14	0	2	6	21.9	10.29	35	.400	.447	0	—	-5	-5	-5	-0	-0.7
	Min-A	5	6	.455	41	0	0	0	14	72¹	47	4	28	59	9.3	1.37	261	.183	.263	1	.063	-1	18	18	1	3.5
1965	*Min-A	10	7	.588	62	0	0	0	21	80¹	57	4	41	59	11.3	2.13	167	.207	.316	1	.100	-0	12	13	2	3.7
1966	Min-A	6	3	.667	65	0	0	0	16	91¹	66	6	27	93	9.3	2.46	146	.199	.261	3	.273	1	10	11	1	1.8
1967	Min-A	8	9	.471	59	0	0	0	16	92	77	6	38	80	11.3	2.84	122	.229	.309	0	.000	-1	4	6	0	1.4
1968	Min-A	4	5	.444	54	0	0	0	**18**	76¹	67	1	32	57	11.7	2.71	114	.238	.315	0	.000	-1	2	3	0	0.5
1969	*Min-A	4	1	.800	46	0	0	0	3	61	65	7	20	51	12.5	4.57	80	.278	.335	0	.000	-1	-6	-6	-1	-0.7
Total	14	75	82	.478	602	69	11	3	110	1246²	1130	105	527	834	12.2	3.39	110	.243	.323	35	.137	-5	41	46	7	10.5

● **GENE WRIGHT**   Wright, Clarence Eugene "Big Gene" b: 12/11/1878, Cleveland, Ohio d: 10/29/30, Barberton, Ohio BR/TR, 6'2", 185 lbs. Deb: 10/5/01

1901	Bro-N	1	0	1.000	1	1	0	0	0	9	6	0	1	6	7.0	1.00	335	.189	.213	1	.333	2	2	-0	0.3
1902	Cle-A	7	11	.389	21	18	15	1	1	148	150	6	75	52	14.2	3.95	87	.263	.357	10	.143	-2	-6	-8	-2	-1.2
1903	Cle-A	3	9	.250	15	12	8	0	0	101²	122	1	58	42	16.3	5.75	50	.296	.388	9	.209	2	-32	-33	2	-2.9
	StL-A	3	5	.375	8	8	7	1	0	61	73	2	16	37	13.7	3.69	79	.296	.348	3	.143	-1	-5	-5	1	-0.6
	Yr	6	14	.300	23	20	15	1	0	162²	195	3	74	79	15.1	4.98	58	.294	.368	12	.188	2	-36	-38	3	-3.5
1904	StL-A	0	1	.000	1	1	0	0	0	4	10	0	2	3	27.0	13.50	18	.469	.515	0	.000	-0	-5	-5	1	-0.8
Total	4	14	26	.350	46	40	31	2	1	323²	361	9	152	140	14.7	4.50	70	.282	.365	23	.167	-1	-45	-49	1	-5.2

● **CLYDE WRIGHT**   Wright, Clyde b: 2/20/41, Jefferson City, Tenn. BR/TL, 6'1", 185 lbs. Deb: 6/15/66

1966	Cal-A	4	7	.364	20	13	3	1	0	91¹	92	11	25	37	11.6	3.74	90	.265	.316	3	.103	-1	-3	-4	0	-0.6
1967	Cal-A	5	5	.500	20	11	1	0	0	77¹	76	5	24	35	11.8	3.26	96	.260	.319	6	.273	2	-0	-1	0	0.1
1968	Cal-A	10	6	.625	41	13	2	1	3	125²	123	13	44	71	12.1	3.94	74	.256	.321	8	.216	2	-13	-14	-1	-1.8
1969	Cal-A	1	8	.111	37	5	0	0	0	63²	66	4	30	31	13.7	4.10	85	.278	.362	2	.182	0	-3	-4	0	-0.5
1970	Cal-A★	22	12	.647	39	39	7	2	0	260²	226	24	88	110	11.1	2.83	128	.232	.300	18	.171	3	26	23	-2	3.0
1971	Cal-A	16	17	.485	37	37	10	2	0	276²	225	17	82	135	10.1	2.99	108	.226	.287	14	.154	2	14	8	4	1.5
1972	Cal-A	18	11	.621	35	35	15	2	0	251	229	14	80	87	11.2	2.98	98	.246	.308	18	.217	7	2	-2	3	0.9
1973	Cal-A	11	19	.367	37	36	13	1	0	257	273	26	76	65	12.3	3.68	96	.273	.326	0	—	0	4	-4	4	0.2
1974	Mil-A	9	20	.310	38	32	15	0	0	232	264	22	54	64	12.3	4.42	82	.284	.323	0	—	0	-21	-21	2	-2.2
1975	Tex-A	4	6	.400	25	14	1	0	0	93¹	105	7	47	32	14.8	4.44	85	.294	.378	0	—	0	-7	-7	2	-0.5
Total	10	100	111	.474	329	235	67	9	3	1728²	1679	143	550	667	11.7	3.50	96	.256	.316	69	.183	14	-1	-27	13	0.1

● **DAVE WRIGHT**   Wright, David William b: 8/27/1875, Dennison, Ohio d: 1/18/46, Dennison, Ohio BR/TR, 6', 185 lbs. Deb: 7/22/1895

1895	Pit-N	0	0	—	1	0	0	0	0	2	6	0	1	0	31.5	27.00	17	.509	.547	0	.000	-0	-5	-5	0	0.0
1897	Chi-N	1	0	1.000	1	1	1	0	0	7	17	1	2	4	27.0	15.43	29	.458	.511	1	.333	0	-9	-9	0	-0.7
Total	2	1	0	1.000	2	1	1	0	0	9	23	1	3	4	28.0	18.00	25	.470	.520	1	.250	0	-14	-14	0	-0.7

● **GEORGE WRIGHT**   Wright, George b: 1/28/1847, Yonkers, N.Y. d: 8/21/37, Boston, Mass. BR/TR, 5'9.5", 150 lbs. Deb: 5/5/1871 FMH♦

1875	Bos-n	0	1	.000	2	0	0	0	0	4	5	0	0	0	11.3	2.25	105	.263	.263	135	.333	1	0	0	0.0
1876	Bos-N	0	0	—	1	0	0	0	0	1	1	0	0	1	9.0	0.00	—	.250	.250	100	.299	0	0	0	0	0.0

● **ED WRIGHT**   Wright, Henderson Edward b: 5/15/19, Dyersburg, Tenn. BR/TR, 6'1", 180 lbs. Deb: 7/29/45

1945	Bos-N	8	3	.727	15	12	7	1	0	111¹	104	7	33	24	11.1	2.51	153	.254	.310	5	.128	-2	16	16	-1	1.2
1946	Bos-N	12	9	.571	36	21	8	2	0	176¹	164	8	71	44	12.1	3.52	97	.250	.325	18	.305	6	-2	-2	0	0.4
1947	Bos-N	3	3	.500	23	6	1	0	0	64²	80	9	35	14	16.3	6.40	61	.305	.391	3	.130	-0	-17	-18	-0	-1.5
1948	Bos-N	0	0	—	3	0	0	0	0	4²	9	0	2	2	21.2	1.93	199	.474	.524	0	—	0	1	1	0	0.0
1952	Phi-A	2	1	.667	24	0	0	0	1	41¹	55	6	20	9	17.0	6.53	61	.320	.400	1	.143	-0	-13	-12	0	-0.9
Total	5	25	16	.610	101	39	16	3	1	398¹	412	30	161	93	13.1	4.00	92	.271	.344	27	.211	3	-15	-14	-2	-0.8

● **JIM WRIGHT**   Wright, James "Jiggs" b: 9/19/1900, Hyde, England d: 4/10/63, Oakland, Cal. BR/TR, 6'2.5", 195 lbs. Deb: 9/14/27

1927	StL-A	1	0	1.000	2	1	1	0	0	12	8	0	4	4	9.0	4.50	97	.182	.250	0	.000	-0	-0	-0	-0	-0.1
1928	StL-A	0	0	—	2	0	0	0	0	2	3	0	2	2	22.5	13.50	31	.375	.500	0	—	-2	-2	0	0.0
Total	2	1	0	1.000	4	1	1	0	0	14	11	0	6	6	10.9	5.79	75	.212	.293	0	.000	-0	-3	-2	0	-0.1

● **JIM WRIGHT**   Wright, James Clifton b: 12/21/50, Reed City, Mich. BR/TR, 6'1", 165 lbs. Deb: 4/15/78

1978	Bos-A	8	4	.667	24	16	5	3	0	116	122	8	24	56	11.9	3.57	115	.276	.323	0	—	0	7	7	-2	0.5
1979	Bos-A	1	0	1.000	11	1	0	0	0	23	19	5	7	15	11.3	5.09	87	.226	.309	0	—	0	-2	-2	-0	-0.4
Total	2	9	4	.692	35	17	5	3	0	139	141	13	31	71	11.8	3.82	109	.268	.321	0	—	0	5	5	-2	0.1

● **JIM WRIGHT**   Wright, James Leon b: 3/3/55, St.Joseph, Mo. BR/TR, 6'5", 205 lbs. Deb: 4/22/81

1981	KC-A	2	3	.400	17	4	0	0	0	52	57	5	21	27	13.8	3.46	104	.277	.349	0	—	0	1	1	-1	0.0
1982	KC-A	0	0	—	7	0	0	0	0	23²	32	3	6	9	14.5	5.32	77	.320	.358	0	—	0	-3	-3	-1	-0.1
Total	2	2	3	.400	24	4	0	0	0	75²	89	8	27	36	14.0	4.04	93	.291	.352	0	—	0	-2	-2	-1	-0.1

● **RICKY WRIGHT**   Wright, James Richard b: 11/22/58, Paris, Tex. BL/TL, 6'3", 175 lbs. Deb: 7/28/82

1982	LA-N	2	1	.667	14	5	0	0	0	32²	28	1	20	24	13.2	3.03	114	.233	.343	1	.125	0	2	2	0	0.2
1983	LA-N	0	0	—	6	0	0	0	0	6¹	5	0	2	5	9.9	2.84	126	.227	.292	0	—	0	1	1	-0	0.0
	Tex-A	0	0	—	1	0	0	0	0	2	0	0	1	2	4.5	0.00	—	.000	.167	0	—	0	1	1	-0	0.2
1984	Tex-A	0	2	.000	8	1	0	0	0	14²	20	3	11	6	19.0	6.14	68	.357	.463	0	—	0	-3	-3	0	-0.5
1985	Tex-A	0	0	—	5	0	0	0	0	7²	5	0	5	7	11.7	4.70	90	.185	.313	0	—	0	-0	-0	0	-0.1
1986	Tex-A	1	0	1.000	21	1	0	0	0	39¹	44	1	21	23	14.9	5.03	85	.284	.369	0	—	0	-4	-3	1	0.0
Total	5	3	3	.500	55	7	0	0	0	102²	102	5	60	67	14.2	4.30	92	.265	.364	1	.125	0	-4	-4	1	-0.2

● **KEN WRIGHT**   Wright, Kenneth Warren b: 9/4/46, Pensacola, Fla. BR/TR, 6'2", 210 lbs. Deb: 4/10/70

1970	KC-A	1	2	.333	47	0	0	0	3	53¹	49	2	29	30	14.3	5.23	71	.261	.379	0	.000	-0	-9	-9	-0	-0.7
1971	KC-A	3	6	.333	21	12	1	1	1	78	66	6	47	56	13.4	3.69	93	.230	.344	2	.091	-1	-2	-1	1	-0.3
1972	KC-A	1	2	.333	17	0	0	0	4	18¹	15	0	15	18	15.2	4.91	62	.231	.383	0	.000	-0	-4	-4	0	-0.9
1973	KC-A	6	5	.545	25	12	1	0	0	80²	60	6	82	75	15.8	4.91	84	.210	.386	0	—	0	-10	-7	-1	-1.1
1974	NY-A	0	0	—	3	0	0	0	0	5²	5	0	7	2	19.1	3.18	110	.227	.414	0	—	0	0	0	0	0.2
Total	5	11	15	.423	113	24	2	1	8	236	195	14	180	181	14.7	4.54	81	.230	.372	2	.071	-2	-24	-22	-1	-2.8

● **MEL WRIGHT**   Wright, Melvin James b: 5/11/28, Manila, Ark. d: 5/16/83, Houston, Tex. BR/TR, 6'3", 210 lbs. Deb: 4/17/54 C

1954	StL-N	0	0	—	9	0	0	0	0	10¹	16	2	11	4	25.3	10.45	39	.348	.492	0	.000	-0	-7	-7	0	0.0
1955	StL-N	2	2	.500	29	0	0	0	0	36¹	44	4	19	18	13.4	6.19	66	.308	.353	0	.000	-1	-9	-9	0	-0.9
1960	Chi-N	0	1	1.000	16	0	0	0	2	16¹	17	1	3	8	11.0	4.96	76	.279	.313	0	.000	-0	-2	-2	-1	-0.3
1961	Chi-N	0	1	.000	11	0	0	0	1	21	42	3	4	6	19.7	10.71	39	.416	.438	0	.000	-0	-16	-15	1	-0.6
Total	4	2	4	.333	58	0	0	0	3	84	119	10	27	36	16.0	7.61	53	.339	.391	0	.000	-2	-34	-33	1	-1.8

● **BOB WRIGHT**   Wright, Robert Cassius b: 12/13/1891, Decatur Co., Ind. d: 7/30/93, Carmichael, Cal. BR/TR, 6'1.5", 175 lbs. Deb: 9/21/15

1915	Chi-N	0	0	—	2	0	0	0	0	4	6	0	0	3	13.5	2.25	123	.353	.353	0	—	0	0	0	0	0.0

● **ROY WRIGHT**   Wright, Roy Earl b: 9/26/33, Buchtel, Ohio BR/TR, 6'2", 170 lbs. Deb: 9/30/56

1956	NY-N	0	1	.000	1	1	0	0	0	2²	8	1	2	0	33.8	16.88	22	.533	.588	0	.000	-0	-4	-4	0	-0.9

YEAR TM/L	W	L	PCT	G	GS	CG	SH	SV	IP	H	HR	BB	SO	RAT	ERA	ERA+	OAV	OOB	BH	AVG	PB	PR	/A	PD	TPI

● RASTY WRIGHT   Wright, Wayne Bromley   b: 11/5/1895, Ceredo, W.Va.   d: 6/12/48, Columbus, Ohio   BR/TR, 5'11", 160 lbs.   Deb: 6/22/17

1917 StL-A	0	1	.000	16	1	0	0	0	39²	48	0	10	5	13.4	5.45	48	.300	.345	2	.200		-12	-13	0	-0.2
1918 StL-A	8	2	.800	18	13	6	1	0	111¹	99	1	18	25	9.9	2.51	109	.244	.285	10	.294	3	3	3	-1	0.5
1919 StL-A	0	5	.000	24	5	2	0	0	63¹	79	1	20	14	14.2	5.54	60	.315	.368	1	.083	-1	-16	-16	0	-1.2
1922 StL-A	9	7	.563	31	16	5	0	5	154	148	7	50	44	12.0	2.92	142	.262	.331	7	.140	-2	19	21	1	2.0
1923 StL-A	7	4	.636	20	8	4	0	0	82²	107	6	34	26	15.9	6.42	65	.317	.387	6	.222	0	-22	-21	0	-2.2
Total 5	24	19	.558	109	43	17	1	5	451	481	15	132	114	12.6	4.05	87	.280	.338	26	.195	1	-28	-26	0	-1.1

● HARRY WRIGHT   Wright, William Henry   b: 1/10/1835, Sheffield, England   d: 10/3/1895, Atlantic City, N.J.   BR/TR, 5'9.5", 157 lbs.   Deb: 5/5/1871   FMH♦

1871 Bos-n	1	0	1.000	9	0	0	0	**3**	18²	34	0	4	0	18.3	6.27	66	.337	.362	44	.299	1	-4	-4		-0.2
1872 Bos-n	1	0	1.000	7	0	0	0	1	25²	26	0	0	1	9.1	2.10	177	.241	.241	54	.260	0	**5**	**5**		0.1
1873 Bos-n	2	2	.500	12	5	0	0	1	38¹	65	0	7	0	16.9	4.23	78	.330	.353	67	.252	1	-4	-4		-0.3
1874 Bos-n	0	2	.000	6	2	0	0	**3**	16²	24	0	4		15.1	2.70	110	.338	.373	56	.304	2	1	0		0.1
Total 4 n	4	4	.500	34	7	0	0	8	99¹	149	0	15	1	14.9	*3.81*	78	.312	.333	222	.274	5	-9	-9		-0.3

● LUCKY WRIGHT   Wright, William Simmons "William The Red" or "Deacon"   b: 2/21/1880, Tontogany, Ohio   d: 7/6/41, Tontogany, Ohio   BR/TR, 6', 178 lbs.   Deb: 4/18/09

1909 Cle-A	0	4	.000	5	4	3	0	0	28	21	0	7	5	9.0	3.21	80	.223	.277	0	.000	-1	-2	-2	-0	-0.4

● FRANK WURM   Wurm, Frank James   b: 4/27/24, Cambridge, N.Y.   BB/TL, 6'1", 175 lbs.   Deb: 9/4/44

1944 Bro-N	0	0	—	1	1	0	0	0	0¹	1	0	5	1	162.0	108.00	3	.500	.857	0	—	0	-4	-4	0	0.0

● JOHN WYATT   Wyatt, John Thomas   b: 4/19/35, Chicago, Ill.   BR/TR, 5'11.5", 200 lbs.   Deb: 9/8/61

1961 KC-A	0	0	—	5	0	0	0	1	7¹	8	0	4	6	16.0	2.45	170	.296	.406	0	—	0	1	1	0	0.1
1962 KC-A	10	7	.588	59	9	0	0	11	125	121	12	80	106	14.8	4.46	95	.253	.366	3	.103	-2	-7	-3	-1	-0.7
1963 KC-A	6	4	.600	63	0	0	0	21	92	83	12	43	81	12.3	3.13	125	.239	.323	0	.000	-1	5	8	-1	1.1
1964 KC-A★	9	8	.529	**81**	0	0	0	20	128	111	23	52	74	11.5	3.59	106	.236	.314	0	.000	-1	1	3	-1	0.3
1965 KC-A	2	6	.250	65	0	0	0	18	88²	78	8	53	70	13.7	3.25	107	.241	.354	0	.000	-0	2	2	0	0.3
1966 KC-A	0	3	.000	19	0	0	0	0	23²	19	3	16	25	14.1	5.32	64	.213	.346	0	—	0	-5	-5	1	-0.7
Bos-A	3	4	.429	42	0	0	0	10	71²	59	3	27	63	11.3	3.14	121	.229	.311	0	.000	-1	2	5	-1	0.4
Yr	3	7	.300	61	0	0	0	10	95¹	78	6	43	88	11.8	3.68	101	.223	.316	0	.000	-1	-3	0	-1	-0.3
1967 *Bos-A	10	7	.588	60	0	0	0	20	93¹	71	6	39	68	10.8	2.60	134	.217	.304	1	.083	-0	7	9	1	2.2
1968 Bos-A	1	2	.333	8	0	0	0	0	10²	9	2	6	11	13.5	4.22	75	.231	.348	0	—	-1	-1	0	-0	-0.3
NY-A	0	2	.000	7	0	0	0	0	8¹	7	1	9	6	17.3	2.16	134	.219	.390	0	—	-0	1	1	-0	0.2
Det-A	1	0	1.000	22	0	0	0	1	30¹	26	2	11	25	11.3	2.37	127	.236	.311	0	.000	-0	2	2	0	0.1
Yr	2	4	.333	37	0	0	0	1	49¹	42	5	26	42	12.6	2.74	110	.230	.329	0	.000	-0	2	2	-0	-0.0
1969 Oak-A	0	1	.000	9	0	0	0	0	8¹	8	0	6	5	15.3	5.40	64	.250	.400	0	.000	-0	-2	-2	-0	-0.2
Total 9	42	44	.488	435	9	0	0	103	687¹	600	72	346	540	12.7	3.47	108	.237	.334	4	.048	-6	6	21	-2	2.8

● WHIT WYATT   Wyatt, John Whitlow   b: 9/27/07, Kensington, Ga.   BR/TR, 6'1", 185 lbs.   Deb: 9/16/29   C

1929 Det-A	0	1	.000	4	4	1	0	0	25¹	30	1	18	14	17.4	6.75	64	.309	.422	1	.100	-1	-7	-7	1	-0.3
1930 Det-A	4	5	.444	21	7	2	0	2	85²	76	6	35	68	12.0	3.57	134	.239	.320	12	.353	3	10	12	0	1.4
1931 Det-A	4	2	.000	4	1	1	0	0	20¹	30	2	12	8	19.0	8.85	52	.361	.448	2	.286	0	-10	-10	-1	-0.8
1932 Det-A	9	13	.409	43	22	10	0	1	205²	228	12	102	82	14.6	5.03	93	.286	.369	15	.192	0	-13	-8	-1	-0.8
1933 Det-A	0	1	.000	10	0	0	0	0	17	20	1	9	9	16.4	4.24	102	.299	.397	0	.000	-0	0	0	-0	-0.0
Chi-A	3	4	.429	26	7	2	0	1	87²	91	7	45	31	14.2	4.62	92	.266	.355	6	.214	-0	-3	-4	-0	-0.2
Yr	3	5	.375	36	7	2	0	1	104²	111	8	54	40	14.4	4.56	93	.270	.358	6	.200	-0	-3	-4	-0	-0.2
1934 Chi-A	4	11	.267	23	6	2	0	2	67²	83	10	37	36	16.1	7.18	66	.303	.388	6	.231	0	-20	-18	0	-3.2
1935 Chi-A	4	3	.571	30	1	0	0	5	52	65	6	25	22	15.9	6.75	68	.308	.387	3	.231	1	-13	-12	-1	-1.4
1936 Chi-A	0	0	—	3	0	0	0	1	3	3	0	0	0	9.0	0.00	—	.273	.273	0	—	-0	2	2	-0	0.1
1937 Cle-A	2	3	.400	29	4	2	0	0	73	67	3	40	52	13.2	4.44	104	.244	.340	7	.389	3	1	1	0	0.3
1939 Bro-N☆	8	3	.727	16	14	6	2	0	109	88	3	39	52	10.7	2.31	174	.224	.297	6	.167	-0	19	21	1	2.1
1940 Bro-N★	15	14	.517	37	34	16	**5**	0	239¹	213	19	82	124	11.3	3.46	116	.254	.304	14	.175	-0	14	14	-2	1.3
1941 *Bro-N★	**22**	10	.688	38	35	23	**7**	1	288¹	223	10	82	176	**9.6**	2.34	157	**.212**	**.270**	26	.239	7	**41**	**42**	-1	**5.3**
1942 Bro-N☆	19	7	.731	31	30	16	0	0	217¹	185	9	63	104	10.6	2.73	119	.225	.286	14	.182	1	14	13	-1	1.4
1943 Bro-N	14	5	.737	26	26	13	3	0	180²	139	5	43	80	**9.1**	2.49	135	**.207**	**.255**	17	.283	4	18	17	-2	2.1
1944 Bro-N	2	6	.250	9	9	1	0	0	37²	51	1	16	4	16.5	7.17	50	.311	.379	2	.154	-0	-15	-15	-0	-2.6
1945 Phi-N	0	7	.000	10	10	2	0	0	51¹	72	3	14	10	15.1	5.26	73	.330	.371	2	.125	0	-8	-8	1	-0.9
Total 16	106	95	.527	360	210	97	17	13	1761	1684	98	642	872	12.1	3.79	105	.251	.319	133	.219	18	27	39	-6	3.8

● WELDON WYCKOFF   Wyckoff, John Weldon   b: 2/19/1892, Williamsport, Pa.   d: 5/8/61, Sheboygan Falls, Wis.   BR/TR, 6'1", 175 lbs.   Deb: 4/19/13

1913 Phi-A	2	4	.333	17	7	4	0	0	61²	56	1	46	31	15.3	4.38	63	.233	.363	4	.190	-0	-10	-11	0	-1.0
1914 *Phi-A	11	7	.611	32	20	11	0	2	185	153	2	103	86	12.6	3.02	87	.228	.334	11	.147	-0	-6	-8	-5	-1.3
1915 Phi-A	10	22	.313	43	34	20	1	0	276	238	1	165	157	13.3	3.52	83	.246	.359	12	.125	-4	-18	-18	2	-2.2
1916 Phi-A	0	1	.000	7	2	1	0	0	21¹	20	1	20	4	17.3	5.48	52	.247	.402	3	.375	1	-6	-6	0	-0.2
Bos-A	0	0	—	8	0	0	0	1	22²	19	0	18	18	14.7	4.76	58	.232	.370	1	.167	-0	-5	-5	-1	-0.2
Yr	0	1	.000	15	2	1	0	1	44	39	1	38	22	15.8	5.11	55	.238	.381	4	.286	1	-11	-11	-1	-0.4
1917 Bos-A	0	0	—	1	0	0	0	0	5	4	0	4	1	16.2	1.80	143	.222	.391	0	.000	-0	0	0	0	0.0
1918 Bos-A	0	0	—	1	0	0	0	0	2	4	0	2	1	22.5	0.00	—	.400	.455	0	.000	-0	1	1	-0	0.0
Total 6	23	34	.404	109	63	36	1	3	573²	494	5	357	299	13.6	3.55	79	.239	.355	31	.149	-4	-44	-48	-3	-4.9

● FRANK WYMAN   Wyman, Frank H.   b: 5/10/1862, Haverhill, Mass.   d: 2/4/16, Everett, Mass.   Deb: 6/10/1884   ♦

1884 KC-U	0	1	.000	3	1	1	0	0	21	37	0	3	9	17.1	6.86	33	.362	.380	27	.218	-1	-10	-11	-1	-0.5

● EARLY WYNN   Wynn, Early "Gus"   b: 1/6/20, Hartford, Ala.   BB/TR, 6', 200 lbs.   Deb: 9/13/39   CH♦

1939 Was-A	0	2	.000	3	3	1	0	0	20¹	26	0	10	1	15.9	5.75	76	.313	.387	1	.167	-0	-3	-3	-1	-0.3
1941 Was-A	3	1	.750	5	5	4	0	0	40	35	1	10	15	10.1	1.57	257	.226	.273	2	.133	-0	11	11	0	1.1
1942 Was-A	10	16	.385	30	28	10	1	0	190	246	6	73	58	15.3	5.12	71	.314	.374	15	.217	2	-31	-31	-1	-3.6
1943 Was-A	18	12	.600	37	33	12	3	0	256²	232	15	83	89	11.1	2.91	110	.240	.301	29	.296	7	11	8	-2	1.6
1944 Was-A	8	17	.320	33	25	19	2	2	207²	221	3	67	65	12.6	3.38	96	.277	.334	19	.207	2	-3	-2	-0	-0.4
1946 Was-A	8	5	.615	17	12	9	0	0	107	112	8	33	36	12.4	3.11	108	.267	.325	15	.319	7	5	3	-0	1.1
1947 Was-A	17	15	.531	33	31	22	2	0	247	251	13	90	73	12.6	3.64	102	.262	.329	33	.275	7	2	-1	0	0.9
1948 Was-A	8	19	.296	33	31	15	1	0	198	236	18	94	49	15.0	5.82	75	.295	.370	23	.217	3	-34	-32	-1	-3.4
1949 Cle-A	11	7	.611	26	23	6	0	0	164²	186	8	57	62	13.3	4.15	96	.282	.340	10	.143	-2	-1	-3	1	-0.3
1950 Cle-A	18	8	.692	32	28	14	2	0	213²	166	20	101	143	**11.4**	**3.20**	135	**.212**	**.305**	18	.234	7	33	27	0	3.6
1951 Cle-A	20	13	.606	37	34	21	3	1	274¹	227	18	107	133	11.1	3.02	126	.225	.301	20	.185	2	**34**	23	-1	2.6
1952 Cle-A	23	12	.657	42	33	19	4	3	285²	239	23	132	153	11.7	2.90	115	.231	.318	22	.222	5	25	14	-1	2.1
1953 Cle-A	17	12	.586	36	34	16	1	0	251²	234	19	107	138	12.3	3.93	95	.245	.324	25	.275	9	-5	-5	1	0.2
1954 *Cle-A	**23**	11	.676	40	36	20	3	2	**270²**	225	21	83	155	10.2	2.73	135	.225	.284	17	.183	1	30	29	-3	3.3
1955 Cle-A	17	11	.607	32	31	16	5	0	230	207	19	80	122	11.3	2.82	142	.240	.307	15	.179	1	29	30	-3	3.3
1956 Cle-A★	20	9	.690	38	35	18	4	2	277²	233	26	91	158	10.7	2.72	154	.228	.294	23	.228	3	44	46	1	5.1
1957 Cle-A★	14	17	.452	40	37	13	1	1	263	270	32	104	**184**	13.0	4.31	86	.265	.336	10	.116	-1	-15	-17	-1	-2.1
1958 Chi-A★	14	16	.467	40	34	11	4	2	239²	214	27	104	**179**	12.2	4.13	88	.242	.325	15	.200	3	-10	-13	-2	-1.5
1959 *Chi-A★	**22**	10	.688	37	37	14	5	0	**255²**	202	20	119	179	11.6	3.17	119	.216	.310	22	.244	9	20	17	-1	2.8

YEAR	TM/L	W	L	PCT	G	GS	CG	SH	SV	IP	H	HR	BB	SO	RAT	ERA	ERA+	OAV	OOB	BH	AVG	PB	PR	/A	PD	TPI
1960	Chi-A★	13	12	.520	36	35	13	4	1	237¹	220	20	112	158	12.7	3.49	108	.247	.334	15	.200	7	10	8	-2	1.2
1961	Chi-A	8	2	.800	17	16	5	0	0	110¹	88	11	47	64	11.1	3.51	112	.220	.304	6	.162	-0	6	5	-2	0.2
1962	Chi-A	7	15	.318	27	26	11	3	0	167²	171	15	56	91	12.3	4.46	88	.264	.326	7	.130	0	-9	-10	-2	-1.4
1963	Cle-A	5	1	0	20	5	1	0	1	55¹	50	2	15	29	10.6	2.28	159	.250	.302	3	.273	1	8	8	-0	0.5
Total 23		300	244	.551	691	612	290	49	15	4564	4291	338	1775	2334	12.1	3.54	106	.248	.321	365	.214	72	170	112	-25	16.6

● BILLY WYNNE
Wynne, Billy Vernon   b: 7/31/43, Williamston, N.C.   BL/TR, 6′5″, 206 lbs.   Deb: 8/6/67

YEAR	TM/L	W	L	PCT	G	GS	CG	SH	SV	IP	H	HR	BB	SO	RAT	ERA	ERA+	OAV	OOB	BH	AVG	PB	PR	/A	PD	TPI
1967	NY-N	0	0	—	6	1	0	0	0	8²	12	0	2	4	14.5	3.12	109	.324	.359	0	.000	-0	0	0	-0	0.0
1968	Chi-A	0	0	—	1	0	0	0	0	2	2	0	2	1	18.0	4.50	67	.250	.400	0	—	0	-0	-0	-0	0.0
1969	Chi-A	7	7	.500	20	20	6	1	0	128²	143	14	50	67	13.7	4.06	95	.283	.351	5	.122	-1	-6	-3	-0	-0.3
1970	Chi-A	1	4	.200	12	9	0	0	0	44	54	8	22	19	15.8	5.32	73	.298	.377	1	.077	-0	-8	-7	1	-0.7
1971	Cal-A	0	0	—	3	0	0	0	0	3²	6	0	2	6	19.6	4.91	66	.375	.444	0	—	-0	-1	-1	-0	0.0
Total 5		8	11	.421	42	30	6	1	0	187	217	22	78	97	14.4	4.33	88	.290	.361	6	.109	-2	-15	-11	1	-1.0

● BILL WYNNE
Wynne, William Andrew   b: 3/27/1869, Neuse, N.C.   d: 8/7/51, Raleigh, N.C.   BR/TR, 5′11.5″, 161 lbs.   Deb: 8/31/1894

YEAR	TM/L	W	L	PCT	G	GS	CG	SH	SV	IP	H	HR	BB	SO	RAT	ERA	ERA+	OAV	OOB	BH	AVG	PB	PR	/A	PD	TPI
1894	Was-N	0	1	.000	1	1	1	0	0	8	10	1	8	2	22.5	6.75	78	.303	.465	0	.000	-0	-1	-1	-0	-0.1

● HANK WYSE
Wyse, Henry Washington "Hooks"   b: 3/1/18, Lunsford, Ark.   BR/TR, 5′11.5″, 185 lbs.   Deb: 9/7/42

YEAR	TM/L	W	L	PCT	G	GS	CG	SH	SV	IP	H	HR	BB	SO	RAT	ERA	ERA+	OAV	OOB	BH	AVG	PB	PR	/A	PD	TPI
1942	Chi-N	2	1	.667	4	4	1	0	2	28	33	1	6	8	12.5	1.93	166	.287	.322	1	.125	-0	4	4	-0	0.4
1943	Chi-N	9	7	.563	38	15	8	2	5	156	159	4	34	45	11.3	2.94	113	.264	.306	4	.080	-4	8	7	3	0.7
1944	Chi-N	16	15	.516	41	34	14	3	1	257¹	277	9	57	86	11.8	3.15	112	.278	.318	16	.178	-1	13	11	0	1.1
1945	*Chi-N†	22	10	.688	38	34	23	2	0	278¹	272	17	55	77	10.7	2.68	136	.256	.296	17	.168	-2	35	30	2	3.2
1946	Chi-N	14	12	.538	40	27	12	2	1	201¹	206	7	52	62	11.7	2.68	124	.265	.313	18	.243	-1	16	14	2	2.2
1947	Chi-N	6	9	.400	37	19	5	1	1	142	158	12	64	53	14.3	4.31	92	.286	.363	5	.111	-1	-4	-6	1	-0.5
1950	Phi-A	9	14	.391	41	23	4	0	0	170²	192	16	87	33	15.1	5.85	78	.287	.376	9	.153	-3	-24	-25	0	-3.0
1951	Phi-A	1	2	.333	9	1	0	0	0	14²	24	0	8	5	19.6	7.98	54	.381	.451	1	.250	-0	-6	-6	0	-1.0
	Was-A	0	0	—	3	2	0	0	0	9¹	17	0	10	0	27.0	9.64	42	.378	.500	0	.000	-1	-6	-6	0	-0.1
	Yr	1	2	.333	12	3	0	0	0	24	41	0	18	5	22.5	8.63	49	.380	.472	1	.125	-1	-12	-12	0	-1.1
Total 8		79	70	.530	251	159	67	11	8	1257²	1338	66	373	362	12.4	3.52	105	.274	.329	71	.163	-11	36	24	9	3.0

● BIFF WYSONG
Wysong, Harlan   b: 4/13/05, Clarksville, Ohio   d: 8/8/51, Xenia, Ohio   BL/TL, 6′3″, 195 lbs.   Deb: 8/10/30

YEAR	TM/L	W	L	PCT	G	GS	CG	SH	SV	IP	H	HR	BB	SO	RAT	ERA	ERA+	OAV	OOB	BH	AVG	PB	PR	/A	PD	TPI
1930	Cin-N	0	1	.000	1	1	0	0	0	2¹	6	0	3	1	34.7	19.29	25	.545	.643	0	—	0	-4	-4	-0	-0.9
1931	Cin-N	0	2	.000	12	2	0	0	0	21²	25	2	23	5	19.9	7.89	47	.298	.449	1	.250	-0	-10	-10	-1	-0.8
1932	Cin-N	1	0	1.000	7	0	0	0	0	12¹	13	0	8	5	15.3	3.65	106	.277	.382	0	.000	-0	0	0	-0	0.0
Total 3		1	3	.250	20	3	0	0	0	36¹	44	2	34	11	19.3	7.18	54	.310	.443	1	.167	-0	-13	-13	-0	-1.7

● RUSTY YARNALL
Yarnall, Waldo William   b: 10/22/02, Chicago, Ill.   d: 10/9/85, Lowell, Mass.   BR/TR, 6′, 175 lbs.   Deb: 6/30/26

YEAR	TM/L	W	L	PCT	G	GS	CG	SH	SV	IP	H	HR	BB	SO	RAT	ERA	ERA+	OAV	OOB	BH	AVG	PB	PR	/A	PD	TPI
1926	Phi-N	0	1	.000	1	0	0	0	0	1	3	0	1	0	36.0	18.00	23	.500	.571	0	.000	-0	-2	-2	0	-0.9

● RUBE YARRISON
Yarrison, Byron Wardsworth   b: 3/9/1896, Montgomery, Pa.   d: 4/22/77, Williamsport, Pa.   BR/TR, 5′11″, 165 lbs.   Deb: 4/13/22

YEAR	TM/L	W	L	PCT	G	GS	CG	SH	SV	IP	H	HR	BB	SO	RAT	ERA	ERA+	OAV	OOB	BH	AVG	PB	PR	/A	PD	TPI
1922	Phi-A	1	2	.333	18	0	0	0	0	33²	50	4	12	10	17.1	8.29	51	.362	.421	1	.167	-0	-16	-15	-0	-1.2
1924	Bro-N	0	2	.000	3	0	0	0	0	11	12	0	3	2	13.1	6.55	57	.267	.327	0	.000	-0	-3	-3	0	-0.5
Total 2		1	4	.200	21	0	0	0	0	44²	62	4	15	12	16.1	7.86	53	.339	.398	1	.125	-0	-19	-19	0	-1.7

● EMIL YDE
Yde, Emil Ogden   b: 1/28/1900, Great Lakes, Ill.   d: 12/4/68, Leesburg, Fla.   BB/TL, 5′11″, 165 lbs.   Deb: 4/21/24

YEAR	TM/L	W	L	PCT	G	GS	CG	SH	SV	IP	H	HR	BB	SO	RAT	ERA	ERA+	OAV	OOB	BH	AVG	PB	PR	/A	PD	TPI
1924	Pit-N	16	3	.842	33	22	14	4	0	194	171	3	62	53	11.1	2.83	136	.244	.311	21	.239	2	22	22	1	2.3
1925	*Pit-N	17	9	.654	33	28	13	0	0	207	254	11	75	41	14.4	4.13	108	.309	.369	17	.191	-2	3	8	-0	0.6
1926	Pit-N	8	7	.533	37	22	12	1	0	187¹	181	3	81	34	12.7	3.65	108	.260	.339	17	.230	3	4	6	0	0.7
1927	*Pit-N	1	3	.250	9	2	0	0	0	29²	45	1	15	9	18.8	9.71	42	.375	.453	3	.167	-0	-19	-18	1	-1.9
1929	Det-A	7	3	.700	29	6	4	1	0	86²	100	8	63	23	16.9	5.30	81	.296	.406	16	.333	-2	-10	-10	-1	-0.7
Total 5		49	25	.662	141	80	43	6	0	704²	751	26	296	160	13.5	4.02	102	.281	.355	74	.233	5	-0	7	1	1.0

● JOE YEAGER
Yeager, Joseph F. "Little Joe"   b: 8/28/1875, Philadelphia, Pa.   d: 7/2/37, Detroit, Mich.   BR/TR, 5′10″, 160 lbs.   Deb: 4/22/1898 ◆

YEAR	TM/L	W	L	PCT	G	GS	CG	SH	SV	IP	H	HR	BB	SO	RAT	ERA	ERA+	OAV	OOB	BH	AVG	PB	PR	/A	PD	TPI
1898	Bro-N	12	22	.353	36	33	32	0	0	291¹	333	4	80	70	12.9	3.65	98	.285	.334	23	.172	-3	-1	-2	5	0.0
1899	Bro-N	2	2	.500	10	4	2	1	1	47²	56	1	16	6	14.0	4.72	83	.292	.353	9	.191	1	-5	-4	1	-0.2
1900	Bro-N	1	1	.500	2	2	2	0	0	17	21	1	4	3	13.8	6.88	56	.303	.349	2	.333	-0	-6	-6	-0	-0.5
1901	Det-A	12	11	.522	26	25	22	2	1	199²	209	4	46	38	11.9	2.61	147	.266	.313	37	.296	5	23	27	2	3.5
1902	Det-A	6	12	.333	19	15	14	0	0	140	171	5	41	28	13.9	4.82	76	.301	.354	39	.242	3	-19	-18	3	-1.4
1903	Det-A	0	1	.000	1	1	1	0	0	9	15	0	1	0	15.0	4.00	73	.369	.369	103	.256	0	-1	-1	-0	-0.1
Total 6		33	49	.402	94	80	73	3	2	704²	805	15	188	145	13.0	3.74	99	.285	.334	467	.252	6	-9	-4	11	1.3

● AL YEARGIN
Yeargin, James Almond   b: 10/16/01, Mauldin, S.C.   d: 5/8/37, Greenville, S.C.   BR/TR, 5′11″, 170 lbs.   Deb: 10/1/22

YEAR	TM/L	W	L	PCT	G	GS	CG	SH	SV	IP	H	HR	BB	SO	RAT	ERA	ERA+	OAV	OOB	BH	AVG	PB	PR	/A	PD	TPI
1922	Bos-N	0	1	.000	1	1	1	0	0	7	5	1	2	4	9.0	1.29	311	.192	.250	0	.000	-0	2	2	0	0.2
1924	Bos-N	1	11	.083	32	12	6	0	0	141¹	162	7	42	34	13.2	5.09	75	.293	.346	6	.143	-2	-19	-20	4	-1.3
Total 2		1	12	.077	33	13	7	0	0	148¹	167	8	44	35	13.0	4.91	78	.288	.342	6	.133	-2	-17	-18	4	-1.1

● LARRY YELLEN
Yellen, Lawrence Alan   b: 1/4/43, Brooklyn, N.Y.   BR/TR, 5′11″, 190 lbs.   Deb: 9/26/63

YEAR	TM/L	W	L	PCT	G	GS	CG	SH	SV	IP	H	HR	BB	SO	RAT	ERA	ERA+	OAV	OOB	BH	AVG	PB	PR	/A	PD	TPI
1963	Hou-N	0	0	—	1	1	0	0	0	5	7	0	1	3	14.4	3.60	88	.280	.308	0	—	-0	-0	-0	0	0.0
1964	Hou-N	0	0	—	13	1	0	0	0	21	27	4	10	9	15.9	6.86	50	.297	.366	0	.000	-0	-8	-8	-0	0.0
Total 2		0	0	—	14	2	0	0	0	26	34	4	11	12	15.6	6.23	54	.293	.354	0	.000	-0	-8	-8	0	0.0

● CHIEF YELLOWHORSE
Yellowhorse, Moses J.   b: 1/28/1898, Pawnee, Okla.   d: 4/10/64, Pawnee, Okla.   BR/TR, 5′10″, 180 lbs.   Deb: 4/15/21

YEAR	TM/L	W	L	PCT	G	GS	CG	SH	SV	IP	H	HR	BB	SO	RAT	ERA	ERA+	OAV	OOB	BH	AVG	PB	PR	/A	PD	TPI
1921	Pit-N	5	3	.625	10	4	1	0	1	48¹	45	1	13	19	10.8	2.98	129	.254	.305	0	.000	-2	4	5	-2	0.3
1922	Pit-N	3	1	.750	28	5	2	0	0	77²	92	0	20	24	13.2	4.52	90	.305	.352	6	.316	-1	-4	-4	-1	-0.1
Total 2		8	4	.667	38	9	3	0	1	126	137	1	33	43	12.3	3.93	101	.286	.335	6	.167	-2	1	1	-3	0.2

● CARROLL YERKES
Yerkes, Charles Carroll "Lefty"   b: 6/13/03, McSherrystown, Pa.   d: 12/20/50, Oakland, Cal.   BR/TL, 5′11″, 180 lbs.   Deb: 5/31/27

YEAR	TM/L	W	L	PCT	G	GS	CG	SH	SV	IP	H	HR	BB	SO	RAT	ERA	ERA+	OAV	OOB	BH	AVG	PB	PR	/A	PD	TPI
1927	Phi-A	0	0	—	1	0	0	0	0	1	1	0	1	0	9.0	0.00	—	.000	.333	0	—	0	0	0	0	0.0
1928	Phi-A	0	1	.000	2	1	1	0	0	8²	7	0	2	1	9.3	2.08	193	.233	.281	0	.000	-0	2	2	1	0.2
1929	Phi-A	1	0	1.000	19	2	0	0	0	37¹	47	3	13	11	14.7	4.58	92	.329	.389	0	.000	-2	-1	-2	2	0.0
1932	Chi-N	0	0	—	2	0	0	0	0	9	5	2	3	4	8.0	3.00	126	.167	.242	1	.333	0	1	1	-0	0.0
1933	Chi-N	0	0	—	1	0	0	0	0	2	2	0	1	0	13.5	4.50	73	.286	.375	0	—	-0	-0	-0	0	0.0
Total 5		1	1	.500	25	3	1	0	1	58	61	5	20	16	12.7	3.88	106	.288	.352	1	.063	-2	2	1	3	0.2

● STAN YERKES
Yerkes, Stanley Lewis "Yank"   b: 11/28/1874, Cheltenham, Pa.   d: 7/28/40, Boston, Mass.   BR/TR, 5′10″, 165 lbs.   Deb: 5/3/01

YEAR	TM/L	W	L	PCT	G	GS	CG	SH	SV	IP	H	HR	BB	SO	RAT	ERA	ERA+	OAV	OOB	BH	AVG	PB	PR	/A	PD	TPI
1901	Bal-A	0	1	.000	1	1	1	0	0	8	12	1	2	4	15.8	6.75	57	.342	.377	1	.333	0	-3	-3	0	-0.2
	StL-N	3	1	.750	8	4	4	0	0	34	35	2	6	15	11.1	3.18	100	.264	.301	1	.083	-1	1	1	-0	-0.1
1902	StL-N	12	21	.364	39	37	27	1	0	272²	341	0	79	81	13.9	3.66	75	.306	.353	12	.132	-3	-27	-28	-2	-3.6
1903	StL-N	0	1	.000	1	1	0	0	0	5	8	0	0	3	14.4	1.80	181	.333	.333	0	.000	-0	1	1	-0	0.1
Total 3		15	24	.385	45	43	32	1	0	319²	396	3	87	103	13.7	3.66	77	.303	.348	14	.130	-4	-28	-30	-3	-3.8

● RICH YETT
Yett, Richard Martin   b: 10/6/62, Pomona, Cal.   BR/TR, 6′2″, 187 lbs.   Deb: 4/13/85

YEAR	TM/L	W	L	PCT	G	GS	CG	SH	SV	IP	H	HR	BB	SO	RAT	ERA	ERA+	OAV	OOB	BH	AVG	PB	PR	/A	PD	TPI
1985	Min-A	0	0	—	2	0	0	0	0	0¹	1	0	0	16	81.0	27.00	16	.333	.600	0	—	-1	-1	-0	-0	-0.0
1986	Cle-A	5	3	.625	39	3	1	1	1	78²	84	11	37	50	14.0	5.15	80	.275	.355	0	—	0	-8	-9	-1	-0.9
1987	Cle-A	3	9	.250	37	11	2	0	1	97²	96	21	49	59	13.6	5.25	86	.257	.347	0	—	0	-9	-8	-1	-0.9
1988	Cle-A	9	6	.600	23	22	0	0	0	134¹	146	11	55	71	13.5	4.62	89	.275	.344	0	—	0	-10	-8	-2	-1.0

YEAR	TM/L	W	L	PCT	G	GS	CG	SH	SV	IP	H	HR	BB	SO	RAT	ERA	ERA+	OAV	OOB	BH	AVG	PB	PR	/A	PD	TPI
1989	Cle-A	5	6	.455	32	12	1	0	0	99	111	10	47	47	14.5	5.00	79	.283	.363	0	—	0	-12	-11	-1	-1.4
1990	Min-A	0	0	—	4	0	0	0	0	4¹	6	1	1	2	14.5	2.08	200	.353	.389	0	—	0	1	1	0	-0.3
Total	6	22	24	.478	136	49	4	1	2	414¹	444	53	191	229	13.9	4.95	84	.274	.353	0	—	0	-39	-36	-5	-4.7

● EARL YINGLING
Yingling, Earl Hershey "Chink" b: 10/29/1888, Chillicothe, Ohio d: 10/2/62, Columbus, Ohio BL/TL, 5'11.5", 180 lbs. Deb: 4/12/11

YEAR	TM/L	W	L	PCT	G	GS	CG	SH	SV	IP	H	HR	BB	SO	RAT	ERA	ERA+	OAV	OOB	BH	AVG	PB	PR	/A	PD	TPI
1911	Cle-A	1	0	1.000	4	3	1	0	0	22¹	30	1	9	6	16.1	4.43	77	.326	.392	3	.273	0	-3	-3	0	-0.1
1912	Bro-N	6	11	.353	25	16	12	0	0	163	186	10	56	51	13.4	3.59	93	.293	.351	16	.250	3	-3	-4	-1	-0.2
1913	Bro-N	8	8	.500	26	13	8	2	0	146²	158	2	10	40	10.4	2.58	128	.280	.295	23	.383	8	10	12	-1	2.0
1914	Cin-N	9	13	.409	34	27	8	3	0	198	207	6	54	80	12.1	3.45	85	.274	.328	23	.192	1	-15	-12	-2	-1.2
1918	Was-A	1	2	.333	5	2	2	0	0	38	30	0	12	15	9.9	2.13	128	.238	.304	7	.467	3	3	3	1	0.7
Total	5	25	34	.424	94	61	31	5	0	568	611	19	141	201	12.1	3.22	98	.281	.328	72	.267	16	-8	-4	-3	1.2

● JOE YINGLING
Yingling, Joseph Granville b: 7/23/1866, Westminster, Md. d: 10/24/46, Manchester, Md. BR/TL, 5'7.5", 145 lbs. Deb: 5/28/1886 ♦

YEAR	TM/L	W	L	PCT	G	GS	CG	SH	SV	IP	H	HR	BB	SO	RAT	ERA	ERA+	OAV	OOB	BH	AVG	PB	PR	/A	PD	TPI
1886	Was-N	0	0	—	1	0	0	0	0	3	7	0	1	0	24.0	12.00	27	.412	.444	0	.000	-0	-3	-3	0	-0.3

● LEN YOCHIM
Yochim, Leonard Joseph b: 10/16/28, New Orleans, La. BL/TL, 6'2", 200 lbs. Deb: 9/18/51 F

YEAR	TM/L	W	L	PCT	G	GS	CG	SH	SV	IP	H	HR	BB	SO	RAT	ERA	ERA+	OAV	OOB	BH	AVG	PB	PR	/A	PD	TPI
1951	Pit-N	1	1	.500	2	2	0	0	0	8²	10	0	11	5	22.8	8.31	51	.278	.458	0	.000	-0	-4	-4	0	-0.7
1954	Pit-N	0	1	.000	10	1	0	0	0	19²	30	2	8	7	17.4	7.32	57	.361	.418	1	.500	0	-7	-7	1	-0.2
Total	2	1	2	.333	12	3	0	0	0	28¹	40	2	19	12	19.1	7.62	55	.336	.432	1	.200	-0	-11	-11	1	-0.9

● RAY YOCHIM
Yochim, Raymond Austin Aloysius b: 7/19/22, New Orleans, La. BR/TR, 6'1", 170 lbs. Deb: 5/2/48 F

YEAR	TM/L	W	L	PCT	G	GS	CG	SH	SV	IP	H	HR	BB	SO	RAT	ERA	ERA+	OAV	OOB	BH	AVG	PB	PR	/A	PD	TPI
1948	StL-N	0	0	—	1	0	0	0	0	1	0	0	3	1	27.0	0.00	—	.000	.500	0	—	0	0	0	0	0.0
1949	StL-N	0	0	—	3	0	0	0	0	2¹	3	1	4	3	27.0	15.43	27	.273	.467	0	—	0	-3	-3	-0	0.0
Total	2	0	0	—	4	0	0	0	0	3¹	3	1	7	4	27.0	10.80	38	.214	.476	0	—	0	-2	-2	-0	0.0

● LEFTY YORK
York, James Edward b: 11/1/1892, West Fork, Ark. d: 4/9/61, York, Pa. BL/TL, 5'10", 185 lbs. Deb: 9/12/19

YEAR	TM/L	W	L	PCT	G	GS	CG	SH	SV	IP	H	HR	BB	SO	RAT	ERA	ERA+	OAV	OOB	BH	AVG	PB	PR	/A	PD	TPI
1919	Phi-A	0	2	.000	2	2	0	0	0	4¹	13	0	5	2	37.4	24.92	14	.500	.581	0	.000	-0	-10	-10	0	-2.4
1921	Chi-N	5	9	.357	40	10	4	1	1	139	170	5	63	57	15.4	4.73	81	.308	.384	5	.128	-2	-15	-14	-3	-1.8
Total	2	5	11	.313	42	12	4	1	1	143¹	183	5	68	59	16.1	5.34	71	.317	.393	5	.125	-2	-25	-24	-3	-4.2

● JIM YORK
York, James Harlan b: 8/27/47, Maywood, Cal. BR/TR, 6'3", 200 lbs. Deb: 9/21/70

YEAR	TM/L	W	L	PCT	G	GS	CG	SH	SV	IP	H	HR	BB	SO	RAT	ERA	ERA+	OAV	OOB	BH	AVG	PB	PR	/A	PD	TPI
1970	KC-A	1	1	.500	4	0	0	0	0	8	5	2	2	6	7.9	3.38	111	.179	.233	0	.000	-0	0	0	0	0.0
1971	KC-A	5	5	.500	53	0	0	0	3	93¹	70	7	44	103	11.3	2.89	119	.203	.299	2	.118	1	6	6	-0	0.7
1972	Hou-N	0	1	.000	26	0	0	0	0	36	45	3	18	25	16.0	5.25	64	.321	.403	0	.000	-0	-7	-8	0	-0.2
1973	Hou-N	3	4	.429	41	0	0	0	6	53	65	4	20	22	14.6	4.42	82	.305	.368	0	.000	-0	-4	-5	0	-0.7
1974	Hou-N	2	2	.500	28	0	0	0	1	38¹	48	1	19	15	16.0	3.29	105	.298	.376	0	.000	-1	1	1	0	0.0
1975	Hou-N	4	4	.500	19	4	0	0	1	46²	43	1	25	17	14.1	3.86	87	.251	.363	1	.091	-0	-1	-3	-1	-0.6
1976	NY-N	1	0	1.000	3	0	0	0	0	9²	14	1	4	6	17.7	5.59	61	.333	.404	0	—	0	-2	-2	-0	-0.2
Total	7	16	17	.485	174	4	0	0	10	285	290	19	132	194	13.7	3.79	91	.264	.349	3	.075	-1	-7	-10	-1	-1.0

● MIKE YORK
York, Michael David b: 9/6/64, Oak Park, Ill. BR/TR, 6'1", 187 lbs. Deb: 8/17/90

YEAR	TM/L	W	L	PCT	G	GS	CG	SH	SV	IP	H	HR	BB	SO	RAT	ERA	ERA+	OAV	OOB	BH	AVG	PB	PR	/A	PD	TPI
1990	Pit-N	1	1	.500	4	1	0	0	0	12²	13	0	5	4	13.5	2.84	127	.277	.358	1	.333	0	1	1	0	0.2
1991	Cle-A	1	4	.200	14	4	0	0	0	34²	45	2	19	19	17.1	6.75	62	.333	.423	0	—	0	-10	-10	-0	-1.3
Total	2	2	5	.286	18	5	0	0	0	47¹	58	2	24	23	16.2	5.70	70	.319	.407	1	.333	-0	-9	-9	-0	-1.1

● GUS YOST
Yost, August 6'5", Deb: 6/12/1893

YEAR	TM/L	W	L	PCT	G	GS	CG	SH	SV	IP	H	HR	BB	SO	RAT	ERA	ERA+	OAV	OOB	BH	AVG	PB	PR	/A	PD	TPI
1893	Chi-N	0	1	.000	1	1	0	0	0	2²	3	0	8	1	37.1	13.50	34	.275	.582	0	.000	-0	-3	-3	0	-0.6

● FLOYD YOUMANS
Youmans, Floyd Everett b: 5/11/64, Tampa, Fla. BR/TR, 6'1", 190 lbs. Deb: 7/1/85

YEAR	TM/L	W	L	PCT	G	GS	CG	SH	SV	IP	H	HR	BB	SO	RAT	ERA	ERA+	OAV	OOB	BH	AVG	PB	PR	/A	PD	TPI
1985	Mon-N	4	3	.571	14	12	0	0	0	77	57	3	49	54	12.5	2.45	138	.206	.327	1	.053	-0	10	8	-2	0.5
1986	Mon-N	13	12	.520	33	32	6	2	0	219	145	14	118	202	11.0	3.53	104	.188	.299	12	.160	2	4	4	-3	0.2
1987	Mon-N	9	8	.529	23	23	3	3	0	116¹	112	13	47	94	12.4	4.64	91	.251	.324	6	.150	-1	-7	-6	-0	-0.7
1988	Mon-N	3	6	.333	14	13	1	1	0	84	64	4	41	54	11.5	3.21	112	.213	.311	4	.154	-0	2	4	-1	0.3
1989	Phi-N	1	5	.167	10	10	0	0	0	42²	50	7	25	20	16.2	5.70	62	.299	.397	1	.077	-1	-10	-10	0	-1.3
Total	5	30	34	.469	94	90	10	6	0	539	428	45	280	424	12.0	3.74	100	.218	.319	24	.139	-1	-1	-6	-6	-1.0

● ANTHONY YOUNG
Young, Anthony Wayne b: 1/19/66, Houston, Tex. BR/TR, 6'2", 200 lbs. Deb: 8/5/91

YEAR	TM/L	W	L	PCT	G	GS	CG	SH	SV	IP	H	HR	BB	SO	RAT	ERA	ERA+	OAV	OOB	BH	AVG	PB	PR	/A	PD	TPI
1991	NY-N	2	5	.286	10	8	0	0	0	49¹	48	4	12	20	11.1	3.10	117	.257	.305	2	.143	0	3	3	-1	0.3
1992	NY-N	2	14	.125	52	13	1	0	15	121	134	8	31	64	12.3	4.17	83	.285	.331	3	.111	-1	-9	-9	-0	-1.6
1993	NY-N	1	16	.059	39	10	1	0	3	100¹	103	8	42	62	13.1	3.77	107	.265	.339	2	.143	-0	3	3	0	0.4
1994	Chi-N	4	6	.400	20	19	0	0	0	114²	103	12	46	65	11.7	3.92	105	.246	.320	6	.176	-0	4	2	1	0.3
Total	4	9	41	.180	121	50	2	0	18	385¹	388	32	131	211	12.2	3.85	99	.265	.327	13	.146	-1	1	-1	-1	-0.6

● PETE YOUNG
Young, Bryan Owen b: 3/19/68, Meadville, Miss. BR/TR, 6', 225 lbs. Deb: 6/5/92

YEAR	TM/L	W	L	PCT	G	GS	CG	SH	SV	IP	H	HR	BB	SO	RAT	ERA	ERA+	OAV	OOB	BH	AVG	PB	PR	/A	PD	TPI
1992	Mon-N	0	0	—	13	0	0	0	0	20¹	18	0	9	11	12.4	3.98	87	.247	.337	0	—	0	-1	-1	-0	0.0
1993	Mon-N	1	0	1.000	4	0	0	0	0	5¹	4	0	0	3	6.8	3.38	124	.211	.211	0	.000	-0	0	0	0	0.1
Total	2	1	0	1.000	17	0	0	0	0	25²	22	0	9	14	11.2	3.86	94	.239	.314	0	.000	-0	-1	-1	-0	0.1

● CHARLIE YOUNG
Young, Charles "Cy" b: 1/12/1893, Philadelphia, Pa. d: 5/12/52, Riverside, N.J. BB/TR, 5'10.5", 155 lbs. Deb: 9/5/15

YEAR	TM/L	W	L	PCT	G	GS	CG	SH	SV	IP	H	HR	BB	SO	RAT	ERA	ERA+	OAV	OOB	BH	AVG	PB	PR	/A	PD	TPI
1915	Bal-F	2	3	.400	9	5	1	0	0	35	39	0	21	13	16.5	5.91	49	.289	.400	2	.222	0	-12	-12	2	-1.3

● CLIFF YOUNG
Young, Clifford Raphael b: 8/2/64, Willis, Tex. d: 11/4/93, Montgomery Co., Tex. BL/TL, 6'4", 200 lbs. Deb: 7/14/90

YEAR	TM/L	W	L	PCT	G	GS	CG	SH	SV	IP	H	HR	BB	SO	RAT	ERA	ERA+	OAV	OOB	BH	AVG	PB	PR	/A	PD	TPI
1990	Cal-A	1	1	.500	17	0	0	0	0	30²	40	2	7	19	14.1	3.52	108	.325	.366	0	—	0	1	1	-0	0.2
1991	Cal-A	1	0	1.000	11	0	0	0	0	12²	12	3	3	6	10.7	4.26	96	.261	.306	0	—	0	-0	-0	0	-0.0
1993	Cle-A	3	3	.500	21	7	0	0	1	60¹	74	9	18	31	14.2	4.62	94	.298	.353	0	—	0	-2	-2	-1	-0.2
Total	3	5	4	.556	49	7	0	0	1	103²	126	14	28	56	13.7	4.25	97	.302	.352	0	—	0	-1	-1	-1	0.0

● CURT YOUNG
Young, Curtis Allen b: 4/16/60, Saginaw, Mich. BR/TR, 6'1", 180 lbs. Deb: 6/24/83

YEAR	TM/L	W	L	PCT	G	GS	CG	SH	SV	IP	H	HR	BB	SO	RAT	ERA	ERA+	OAV	OOB	BH	AVG	PB	PR	/A	PD	TPI
1983	Oak-A	0	1	.000	8	2	0	0	0	9	17	1	5	5	23.0	16.00	24	.386	.460	0	—	0	-12	-12	-0	-1.0
1984	Oak-A	9	4	.692	20	17	2	1	0	108²	118	9	31	41	13.0	4.06	92	.274	.334	0	—	0	-1	-4	-1	-0.3
1985	Oak-A	0	4	.000	19	7	0	0	0	46	57	15	22	19	15.7	7.24	53	.300	.376	0	—	0	-16	-17	-1	-1.0
1986	Oak-A	13	9	.591	29	27	5	2	0	198	176	19	57	116	10.9	3.45	112	.236	.297	0	—	0	16	9	-0	1.1
1987	Oak-A	13	7	.650	31	31	6	0	0	203	194	38	44	124	10.7	4.08	101	.252	.295	0	.000	0	8	1	0	0.1
1988	*Oak-A	11	8	.579	26	26	1	0	0	156¹	162	23	50	69	12.4	4.14	91	.275	.336	0	—	0	-3	-6	-1	-0.8
1989	Oak-A	5	9	.357	25	20	1	0	0	111	117	10	47	55	13.5	3.73	99	.264	.338	0	—	0	2	-1	-1	0.1
1990	*Oak-A	9	6	.600	26	21	0	0	0	124¹	124	17	53	56	13.0	4.85	77	.266	.344	0	—	0	-13	-16	-0	-1.5
1991	Oak-A	4	2	.667	41	1	0	0	0	68¹	74	8	34	27	14.5	5.00	77	.278	.364	0	—	0	-7	-9	-1	-0.6
1992	KC-A	1	2	.333	10	2	0	0	0	24¹	29	1	7	7	13.3	5.18	78	.293	.340	0	—	0	-3	-3	-0	-0.4
	NY-A	3	0	1.000	13	5	0	0	0	43¹	51	1	10	13	13.1	3.32	118	.298	.344	0	—	0	3	3	0	0.2
	Yr	4	2	.667	23	7	0	0	0	67²	80	2	17	20	13.2	3.99	99	.295	.341	0	—	0	-0	-0	-0	-0.2
1993	Oak-A	1	1	.500	14	2	0	0	0	14²	14	5	6	4	12.3	4.30	95	.241	.313	0	—	0	-1	-1	-1	0.0
Total	11	69	53	.566	251	162	15	3	0	1107	1133	147	366	536	12.5	4.31	90	.265	.328	0	.000	0	-26	-55	-3	-4.1

● CY YOUNG
Young, Denton True b: 3/29/1867, Gilmore, Ohio d: 11/4/55, Newcomerstown, Ohio BR/TR, 6'2", 210 lbs. Deb: 8/6/1890 MH

YEAR	TM/L	W	L	PCT	G	GS	CG	SH	SV	IP	H	HR	BB	SO	RAT	ERA	ERA+	OAV	OOB	BH	AVG	PB	PR	/A	PD	TPI
1890	Cle-N	9	7	.563	17	16	16	0	0	147²	145	6	30	39	11.2	3.47	103	.249	.295	8	.123	-6	2	2	1	-0.3
1891	Cle-N	27	22	.551	55	46	43	0	2	423²	431	4	140	147	12.3	2.85	122	.254	.314	29	.167	-3	24	29	-1	2.4

YEAR TM/L	W	L	PCT	G	GS	CG	SH	SV	IP	H	HR	BB	SO	RAT	ERA	ERA+	OAV	OOB	BH	AVG	PB	PR	/A	PD	TPI
1892 *Cle-N	36	12	.750	53	49	48	9	0	453	363	8	118	168	9.8	1.93	176	.211	.266	31	.158	-8	68	74	5	6.6
1893 Cle-N	34	16	.680	53	46	42	1	1	422²	442	10	103	102	11.8	3.36	145	.261	.307	44	.235	-6	61	71	4	6.4
1894 Cle-N	26	21	.553	52	47	44	2	1	408²	488	19	106	108	13.2	3.94	139	.293	.337	40	.215	-8	63	69	7	5.6
1895 *Cle-N	35	10	.778	47	40	36	4	0	369²	363	10	75	121	10.9	3.26	153	.253	.294	30	.214	-4	62	71	8	7.0
1896 *Cle-N	28	15	.651	51	46	42	5	3	414¹	477	7	62	140	11.9	3.24	140	.286	.316	52	.289	7	52	60	8	6.4
1897 Cle-N	21	19	.525	46	38	35	2	0	335²	391	7	49	88	12.0	3.78	119	.289	.318	34	.222	-4	20	27	3	2.3
1898 Cle-N	25	13	.658	46	41	40	1	0	377²	387	6	41	101	10.4	2.53	143	.263	.287	39	.253	5	45	46	7	5.3
1899 StL-N	26	16	.619	44	42	40	4	1	369¹	368	10	44	111	10.2	2.58	154	.259	.285	32	.216	-1	52	57	6	6.2
1900 StL-N	19	19	.500	41	35	32	4	0	321¹	337	7	36	115	10.5	3.00	121	.269	.291	22	.177	-2	25	23	0	2.1
1901 Bos-A	33	10	.767	43	41	38	5	0	371¹	324	6	37	158	8.9	1.62	217	.232	.256	32	.209	0	84	79	1	8.3
1902 Bos-A	32	11	.744	45	43	41	3	0	384²	350	6	53	160	9.7	2.15	166	.243	.276	34	.230	2	61	61	-6	5.8
1903 *Bos-A	28	9	.757	40	35	34	7	2	341²	294	6	37	176	9.2	2.08	146	.232	.259	44	.321	12	34	36	-3	4.9
1904 Bos-A	26	16	.619	43	41	40	10	1	380	327	6	29	200	8.5	1.97	136	.233	.251	33	.223	2	27	30	-5	3.1
1905 Bos-A	18	19	.486	38	33	31	4	0	320²	248	3	30	210	8.0	1.82	148	.215	.240	18	.150	-2	30	31	-2	3.3
1906 Bos-A	13	21	.382	39	34	28	0	2	287²	288	3	25	140	10.0	3.19	86	.264	.285	16	.154	-4	-16	-14	-1	-2.0
1907 Bos-A	21	15	.583	43	37	33	6	2	343¹	286	9	51	147	9.0	1.99	130	.228	.263	27	.216	0	21	22	-6	1.8
1908 Bos-A	21	11	.656	36	33	30	3	2	299	230	1	37	150	8.1	1.26	195	.213	.240	26	.226	1	38	40	-6	4.1
1909 Cle-A	19	15	.559	35	34	30	3	0	295	267	4	59	109	10.2	2.26	113	.250	.294	21	.196	-0	7	10	-1	1.0
1910 Cle-A	7	10	.412	21	20	14	1	0	163¹	149	0	27	58	9.9	2.53	102	.252	.289	8	.145	-0	-0	1	1	0.2
1911 Cle-A	3	4	.429	7	7	4	0	0	46¹	54	4	13	20	13.2	3.88	88	.298	.349	1	.063	-2	-3	-2	-0	-0.5
Bos-N	4	5	.444	11	11	8	2	0	80	83	4	15	35	11.4	3.71	103	.268	.308	2	.080	-2	-3	1	0	-0.1
Total 22	511	316	.618	906	815	749	76	17	7356²	7092	138	1217	2803	10.4	2.63	138	.252	.286	623	.210	-22	754	820	19	79.9

● **HARLEY YOUNG** Young, Harlan Edward "Cy The Third" b: 9/28/1883, Portland, Ind. d: 3/26/75, Jacksonville, Fla. BR/TR, 6'2", Deb: 4/21/08

YEAR TM/L	W	L	PCT	G	GS	CG	SH	SV	IP	H	HR	BB	SO	RAT	ERA	ERA+	OAV	OOB	BH	AVG	PB	PR	/A	PD	TPI
1908 Pit-N	0	2	.000	8	3	0	0	0	48¹	40	0	10	17	10.2	2.23	104	.233	.296	1	.083	-1	1	0	1	0.0
Bos-N	0	1	.000	6	2	1	0	0	27¹	29	0	4	12	11.9	3.29	73	.269	.313	2	.200	-0	-3	-3	-0	-0.1
Yr	0	3	.000	14	5	1	0	0	75²	69	0	14	29	10.2	2.62	89	.243	.286	3	.136	-0	-2	-2	1	-0.1

● **IRV YOUNG** Young, Irving Melrose "Young Cy" or "Cy The Second" b: 7/21/1877, Columbia Falls, Maine d: 1/14/35, Brewer, Maine BL/TL, 5'10", 170 lbs. Deb: 4/14/05

YEAR TM/L	W	L	PCT	G	GS	CG	SH	SV	IP	H	HR	BB	SO	RAT	ERA	ERA+	OAV	OOB	BH	AVG	PB	PR	/A	PD	TPI
1905 Bos-N	20	21	.488	43	42	41	7	0	378	337	6	71	156	9.9	2.90	107	.241	.282	14	.103	-8	8	4	4	0.4
1906 Bos-N	16	25	.390	43	41	37	4	0	358¹	349	6	83	151	11.0	2.91	92	.263	.309	12	.096	-7	-11	-9	3	-1.5
1907 Bos-N	10	23	.303	40	32	22	3	1	245¹	287	5	58	86	13.1	3.96	64	.306	.354	13	.162	-1	-41	-38	1	-4.9
1908 Bos-N	4	9	.308	16	11	7	1	0	85	94	2	19	32	12.2	2.86	84	.289	.332	5	.156	-1	-5	-4	-1	-0.9
Pit-N	4	3	.571	16	7	3	1	0	89²	73	1	21	31	9.9	2.01	115	.225	.283	6	.200	1	4	3	-1	0.3
Yr	8	12	.400	32	18	10	2	1	174²	167	3	40	63	10.9	2.42	97	.257	.305	11	.177	0	-1	-1	-2	-0.6
1910 Chi-A	4	8	.333	27	17	7	4	0	135²	122	0	39	64	10.9	2.72	88	.247	.306	5	.114	-2	-3	-5	-0	-0.7
1911 Chi-A	5	6	.455	24	11	3	1	2	92²	99	2	25	40	12.0	4.37	74	.229	.271	5	.179	-5	-11	-12	1	-1.2
Total 6	63	95	.399	209	161	120	21	4	1384²	1361	23	316	560	11.1	3.11	88	.260	.307	60	.126	-18	-62	-57	6	-8.5

● **J. B. YOUNG** Young, J. B. b: Mt.Carmel, Pa. Deb: 6/10/1892

YEAR TM/L	W	L	PCT	G	GS	CG	SH	SV	IP	H	HR	BB	SO	RAT	ERA	ERA+	OAV	OOB	BH	AVG	PB	PR	/A	PD	TPI
1892 StL-N	0	0	—	1	0	0	0	0	2	9	0	2	1	49.5	22.50	14	.600	.647	0	.000	-0	-4	-4	-0	0.0

● **KIP YOUNG** Young, Kip Lane b: 10/29/54, Georgetown, Ohio BR/TR, 5'11", 175 lbs. Deb: 7/21/78

YEAR TM/L	W	L	PCT	G	GS	CG	SH	SV	IP	H	HR	BB	SO	RAT	ERA	ERA+	OAV	OOB	BH	AVG	PB	PR	/A	PD	TPI
1978 Det-A	6	7	.462	14	13	7	0	0	105²	94	9	30	49	10.7	2.81	137	.246	.304	0	—	0	11	12	-2	1.1
1979 Det-A	2	2	.500	13	7	0	0	0	43²	60	11	11	22	14.8	6.39	68	.323	.364	0	—	0	-11	-10	1	-0.9
Total 2	8	9	.471	27	20	7	0	0	149¹	154	20	41	71	11.9	3.86	104	.271	.324	0	—	0	1	2	-1	0.2

● **MATT YOUNG** Young, Matthew John b: 8/9/58, Pasadena, Cal. BL/TL, 6'3", 205 lbs. Deb: 4/6/83

YEAR TM/L	W	L	PCT	G	GS	CG	SH	SV	IP	H	HR	BB	SO	RAT	ERA	ERA+	OAV	OOB	BH	AVG	PB	PR	/A	PD	TPI
1983 Sea-A★	11	15	.423	33	32	5	2	0	203²	178	17	79	130	11.7	3.27	130	.236	.315	0	—	0	18	22	2	2.8
1984 Sea-A	6	8	.429	22	22	1	0	0	113¹	141	11	57	73	15.8	5.72	70	.307	.384	0	—	0	-22	-22	1	-2.2
1985 Sea-A	12	19	.387	37	35	5	2	1	218¹	242	23	76	136	13.4	4.91	86	.282	.345	0	—	0	-18	-17	-2	-2.3
1986 Sea-A	8	6	.571	65	5	1	0	13	103²	108	9	46	82	14.1	3.82	111	.272	.359	0	—	0	4	5	-1	0.6
1987 LA-N	5	8	.385	47	0	0	0	11	54¹	62	3	17	42	13.1	4.47	89	.288	.341	0	.000	-0	-2	-3	-2	-1.0
1989 *Oak-A	1	4	.200	26	4	0	0	0	37¹	42	2	31	27	17.6	6.75	55	.286	.410	0	—	0	-12	-13	-1	-1.3
1990 Sea-A	8	18	.308	34	33	7	1	0	225¹	198	15	107	176	12.4	3.51	113	.237	.328	0	—	0	10	11	-0	1.2
1991 Bos-A	3	7	.300	19	16	0	0	0	88²	92	4	53	69	14.9	5.18	83	.266	.367	0	—	0	-11	-9	-0	-1.0
1992 Bos-A	0	4	.000	28	8	1	0	0	70²	69	7	42	57	14.5	4.58	92	.257	.363	0	—	0	-5	-3	-1	-0.6
1993 Cle-A	1	6	.143	22	0	0	0	0	74¹	75	8	57	65	16.3	5.21	83	.266	.395	0	—	0	-7	-7	0	-0.6
Total 10	55	95	.367	333	163	20	5	25	1189²	1207	99	565	857	13.7	4.40	94	.265	.350	0	.000	-0	-46	-35	-3	-4.1

● **CHIEF YOUNGBLOOD** Youngblood, Albert Clyde b: 6/13/1900, Hillsboro, Tex. d: 7/6/68, Amarillo, Tex. BL/TR, 6'3", 202 lbs. Deb: 7/16/22

YEAR TM/L	W	L	PCT	G	GS	CG	SH	SV	IP	H	HR	BB	SO	RAT	ERA	ERA+	OAV	OOB	BH	AVG	PB	PR	/A	PD	TPI
1922 Was-A	0	0	—	2	0	0	0	0	4¹	9	0	7	0	37.4	14.54	27	.429	.600	0	.000	-0	-5	-5	0	0.0

● **DUCKY YOUNT** Yount, Herbert Macon "Hub" b: 12/7/1885, Iredell Co., N.C. d: 5/9/70, Winston-Salem, N.C. BR/TR, 6'2", 178 lbs. Deb: 5/20/14

YEAR TM/L	W	L	PCT	G	GS	CG	SH	SV	IP	H	HR	BB	SO	RAT	ERA	ERA+	OAV	OOB	BH	AVG	PB	PR	/A	PD	TPI
1914 Bal-F	1	1	.500	13	1	1	0	0	41¹	44	2	19	19	14.2	4.14	73	.280	.365	1	.083	-1	-6	-5	1	-0.3

● **LARRY YOUNT** Yount, Lawrence King b: 2/15/50, Houston, Tex. BR/TR, 6'2", 185 lbs. Deb: 9/15/71 F

YEAR TM/L	W	L	PCT	G	GS	CG	SH	SV	IP	H	HR	BB	SO	RAT	ERA	ERA+	OAV	OOB	BH	AVG	PB	PR	/A	PD	TPI
1971 Hou-N	0	0	—	1	0	0	0	0	0	0	0	0	0	—	—	—	—	—	0	—	0	0	0	0	0.0

● **CARL YOWELL** Yowell, Carl Columbus "Sundown" b: 12/20/02, Madison, Va. d: 7/27/85, Jacksonville, Tex. BL/TL, 6'4", 180 lbs. Deb: 9/5/24

YEAR TM/L	W	L	PCT	G	GS	CG	SH	SV	IP	H	HR	BB	SO	RAT	ERA	ERA+	OAV	OOB	BH	AVG	PB	PR	/A	PD	TPI
1924 Cle-A	1	1	.500	4	2	2	0	0	27	37	1	13	8	16.7	6.67	64	.343	.413	2	.182	-1	-7	-7	-0	-0.5
1925 Cle-A	2	3	.400	12	4	1	0	0	36¹	40	1	17	12	14.4	4.46	99	.310	.395	1	.125	-1	-0	-0	0	-0.1
Total 2	3	4	.429	16	6	3	0	0	63¹	77	2	30	20	15.3	5.40	81	.325	.403	3	.158	-1	-8	-7	0	-0.6

● **EDDIE YUHAS** Yuhas, John Edward b: 8/5/24, Youngstown, Ohio d: 7/6/86, Winston-Salem, N.C BR/TR, 6'1", 180 lbs. Deb: 4/17/52

YEAR TM/L	W	L	PCT	G	GS	CG	SH	SV	IP	H	HR	BB	SO	RAT	ERA	ERA+	OAV	OOB	BH	AVG	PB	PR	/A	PD	TPI
1952 StL-N	12	2	.857	54	2	0	0	6	99¹	90	5	35	39	11.5	2.72	137	.243	.312	4	.190	1	11	11	-1	1.6
1953 StL-N	0	0	—	2	0	0	0	0	1	3	0	0	0	27.0	18.00	24	.500	.500	0	—	0	-2	-2	-0	0.0
Total 2	12	2	.857	56	2	0	0	6	100¹	93	5	35	39	11.7	2.87	130	.247	.315	4	.190	1	10	9	-1	1.6

● **ADRIAN ZABALA** Zabala, Adrian (Rodriguez) b: 8/26/16, San Antonio De Los Banos, Cuba BL/TL, 5'11", 165 lbs. Deb: 8/11/45

YEAR TM/L	W	L	PCT	G	GS	CG	SH	SV	IP	H	HR	BB	SO	RAT	ERA	ERA+	OAV	OOB	BH	AVG	PB	PR	/A	PD	TPI
1945 NY-N	2	4	.333	11	5	2	1	0	43¹	46	2	20	14	13.7	4.78	82	.284	.363	3	.231	1	-5	-4	0	-0.4
1949 NY-N	2	3	.400	15	4	1	1	0	41	44	5	10	13	12.1	5.27	76	.278	.325	1	.077	-1	-6	-6	-1	-0.9
Total 2	4	7	.364	26	9	3	1	1	84¹	90	7	30	27	12.9	5.02	79	.281	.345	4	.154	-0	-10	-10	-1	-1.3

● **ZIP ZABEL** Zabel, George Washington b: 2/18/1891, Wetmore, Kan. d: 5/31/70, Beloit, Wis. BR/TR, 6'1.5", 185 lbs. Deb: 10/5/13

YEAR TM/L	W	L	PCT	G	GS	CG	SH	SV	IP	H	HR	BB	SO	RAT	ERA	ERA+	OAV	OOB	BH	AVG	PB	PR	/A	PD	TPI
1913 Chi-N	1	0	1.000	1	1	0	0	0	5	3	0	1	0	7.2	0.00	—	.167	.211	0	.000	0	2	2	0	0.4
1914 Chi-N	4	4	.500	29	7	2	0	3	128	104	5	45	50	10.6	2.18	128	.235	.309	7	.184	-1	9	9	-1	0.4
1915 Chi-N	7	10	.412	36	17	8	1	0	163	124	3	84	60	11.7	3.20	87	.218	.323	4	.074	-4	-8	-8	3	-0.8
Total 3	12	14	.462	66	25	10	1	3	296	231	8	130	110	11.2	2.71	103	.224	.315	11	.117	-4	2	3	2	0.0

● **CHINK ZACHARY** Zachary, Albert Myron (b: Albert Myron Zarski) b: 10/19/17, Brooklyn, N.Y. BR/TR, 5'11", 182 lbs. Deb: 4/23/44

YEAR TM/L	W	L	PCT	G	GS	CG	SH	SV	IP	H	HR	BB	SO	RAT	ERA	ERA+	OAV	OOB	BH	AVG	PB	PR	/A	PD	TPI
1944 Bro-N	0	2	.000	4	2	0	0	0	10¹	10	2	7	3	15.7	9.58	37	.238	.360	0	.000	-0	-7	-7	-0	-1.1

YEAR TM/L	W	L	PCT	G	GS	CG	SH	SV	IP	H	HR	BB	SO	RAT	ERA	ERA+	OAV	OOB	BH	AVG	PB	PR	/A	PD	TPI

● TOM ZACHARY
Zachary, Jonathan Thompson Walton (a.k.a. Zach Walton In 1918)
b: 5/7/1896, Graham, N.C. d: 1/24/69, Burlington, N.C. BL/TL, 6'1", 187 lbs. Deb: 7/11/18

YEAR TM/L	W	L	PCT	G	GS	CG	SH	SV	IP	H	HR	BB	SO	RAT	ERA	ERA+	OAV	OOB	BH	AVG	PB	PR	/A	PD	TPI
1918 Phi-A	2	0	1.000	2	2	0	0	0	8	9	0	7	1	18.0	5.63	52	.321	.457	2	.500	1	-3	-2	-0	-0.5
1919 Was-A	1	5	.167	17	7	0	0	0	61²	68	0	20	9	13.0	2.92	110	.292	.350	5	.333	2	2	2	-1	0.3
1920 Was-A	15	16	.484	44	31	19	3	2	262²	289	7	78	53	12.7	3.77	99	.285	.339	29	.261	6	1	-1	0	0.4
1921 Was-A	18	16	.529	39	31	17	2	1	250	314	10	59	53	13.6	3.96	104	.319	.361	23	.256	3	9	4	-0	0.8
1922 Was-A	15	10	.600	32	25	13	1	1	184²	190	6	43	37	11.5	3.12	124	.275	.321	21	.296	5	19	15	0	2.4
1923 Was-A	10	16	.385	35	29	10	0	0	204¹	270	9	63	40	14.8	4.49	84	.321	.372	15	.192	-0	-12	-17	-1	-1.9
1924 *Was-A	15	9	.625	33	27	13	1	2	202²	198	5	53	45	11.3	2.75	147	.264	.315	22	.306	4	33	29	2	3.7
1925 *Was-A	12	15	.444	38	33	11	1	2	217²	247	10	74	58	13.4	3.85	110	.296	.355	12	.174	-2	13	9	-0	0.8
1926 StL-A	14	15	.483	34	31	18	3	0	247¹	264	14	97	53	13.4	3.60	119	.288	.359	23	.267	4	11	19	3	2.7
1927 StL-A	4	6	.400	13	12	6	0	0	78¹	110	4	27	13	15.7	4.37	100	.345	.396	3	.107	-2	-2	-0	-1	-0.3
Was-A	4	7	.364	15	14	5	1	0	102²	116	2	30	13	13.0	3.94	103	.290	.343	5	.139	-2	2	-1	-3	-0.3
Yr	8	13	.381	28	26	11	1	0	181	226	6	57	26	14.2	4.13	102	.314	.366	8	.125	-4	0	-1	-3	-0.6
1928 Was-A	6	9	.400	20	14	5	1	0	102²	130	5	40	19	15.0	5.44	74	.322	.384	10	.303	1	-16	-16	-1	-1.7
*NY-A	3	3	.500	7	6	3	0	1	45²	54	1	15	7	13.6	3.94	95	.320	.375	2	.133	-0	1	-1	1	-0.1
Yr	9	12	.429	27	20	8	1	1	148¹	184	6	55	26	14.5	4.98	79	.321	.380	12	.250	1	-15	-17	2	-1.8
1929 NY-A	12	0	1.000	26	11	7	2	2	119²	131	5	30	35	12.3	2.48	155	.277	.323	10	.238	1	23	18	-3	1.5
1930 NY-A	1	1	.500	3	3	0	0	0	16²	18	0	9	1	14.6	6.48	66	.269	.355	2	.250	1	-3	-4	1	-0.3
Bos-N	11	5	.688	24	22	10	1	0	151¹	192	9	50	57	14.4	4.58	108	.317	.369	13	.241	2	7	6	-1	0.6
1931 Bos-N	11	15	.423	33	28	16	3	2	229	243	8	53	64	11.7	3.10	122	.272	.314	14	.167	-1	19	17	2	2.0
1932 Bos-N	12	11	.522	32	24	12	1	0	212	231	6	55	67	12.2	3.10	121	.280	.326	21	.273	5	18	16	-2	1.9
1933 Bos-N	7	9	.438	26	20	6	2	2	125	134	1	35	22	12.2	3.53	87	.276	.325	5	.119	-2	-3	-6	-1	-1.0
1934 Bos-N	1	2	.333	5	4	2	1	0	24	27	1	8	4	13.1	3.38	113	.278	.333	0	.000	-1	2	1	-0	0.0
Bro-N	5	6	.455	22	12	4	0	2	101²	122	5	21	28	12.8	4.43	88	.301	.339	7	.184	1	-4	-6	-1	-0.5
Yr	6	8	.429	27	16	6	1	2	125²	149	6	29	32	12.9	4.23	92	.297	.338	7	.152	-0	-2	-5	-1	-0.5
1935 Bro-N	7	12	.368	25	21	9	1	4	158	193	10	35	33	13.1	3.59	111	.297	.335	7	.135	-1	8	7	0	0.7
1936 Bro-N	0	0	—	1	0	0	0	0	0¹	2	0	1	0	81.0	54.00	8	1.000	1.000	0	—	-0	-2	-2	-0	0.0
Phi-N	0	3	.000	7	2	0	0	1	20¹	28	2	11	8	17.3	7.97	57	.329	.406	3	.333	1	-9	-8	-0	-0.9
Yr	0	3	.000	8	2	0	0	1	20²	30	2	12	8	18.3	8.71	52	.345	.424	3	.333	1	-11	-10	-0	-0.9
Total 19	186	191	.493	533	409	186	24	22	3126¹	3580	119	914	720	13.1	3.73	106	.294	.345	254	.226	25	116	82	-2	10.3

● CHRIS ZACHARY
Zachary, William Christopher b: 2/19/44, Knoxville, Tenn. BL/TR, 6'2", 200 lbs. Deb: 4/11/63

YEAR TM/L	W	L	PCT	G	GS	CG	SH	SV	IP	H	HR	BB	SO	RAT	ERA	ERA+	OAV	OOB	BH	AVG	PB	PR	/A	PD	TPI
1963 Hou-N	2	2	.500	22	7	0	0	0	57	62	5	22	42	13.7	4.89	64	.272	.344	0	.000	-1	-10	-11	1	-0.7
1964 Hou-N	0	1	.000	1	1	0	0	0	4	6	1	1	2	15.8	9.00	38	.333	.368	-0	-2	-2	-0	-0.4	
1965 Hou-N	0	2	.000	4	2	0	0	0	10²	12	0	6	4	15.2	4.22	80	.273	.360	0	.000	-0	-1	-1	-0	-0.2
1966 Hou-N	3	5	.375	10	8	0	0	0	55	44	1	32	37	12.6	3.44	100	.221	.332	4	.222	1	1	-0	-1	0.0
1967 Hou-N	1	6	.143	9	7	0	0	0	36¹	42	5	12	18	13.9	5.70	58	.290	.352	1	.100	-0	-9	-10	-1	-1.7
1969 KC-A	0	1	.000	8	2	0	0	0	18¹	27	4	7	6	16.7	7.85	47	.346	.400	1	.500	0	-9	-8	-0	-0.4
1971 StL-N	3	10	.231	23	12	1	1	0	89²	114	3	26	48	14.5	5.32	68	.316	.368	8	.242	1	-18	-17	0	-2.2
1972 *Det-A	1	1	.500	25	1	0	0	1	38¹	27	2	15	21	10.1	1.41	223	.201	.287	1	.500	1	7	7	-0	0.5
1973 Pit-N	0	1	.000	6	0	0	0	1	12	10	1	1	6	8.3	3.00	117	.222	.239	0	.000	-0	1	1	-0	0.0
Total 9	10	29	.256	108	40	1	1	2	321¹	344	22	122	184	13.4	4.57	74	.275	.344	15	.181	1	-41	-42	-1	-5.1

● PAT ZACHRY
Zachry, Patrick Paul b: 4/24/52, Richmond, Tex. BR/TR, 6'5", 180 lbs. Deb: 4/11/76

YEAR TM/L	W	L	PCT	G	GS	CG	SH	SV	IP	H	HR	BB	SO	RAT	ERA	ERA+	OAV	OOB	BH	AVG	PB	PR	/A	PD	TPI
1976 *Cin-N	14	7	.667	38	28	6	1	0	204	170	8	83	143	11.3	2.74	128	.228	.307	7	.113	-2	17	17	-2	1.4
1977 Cin-N	3	7	.300	12	12	3	0	0	75	78	7	29	36	13.0	5.04	78	.273	.342	3	.136	-1	-9	-9	1	-1.0
NY-N	7	6	.538	19	19	2	1	0	119²	129	14	48	63	13.5	3.76	99	.278	.350	6	.143	-1	2	-0	-2	-0.3
Yr	10	13	.435	31	31	5	1	0	194²	207	21	77	99	13.3	4.25	90	.274	.344	9	.141	-2	-7	-10	-0	-1.3
1978 NY-N☆	10	6	.625	21	21	5	2	0	138	120	9	60	78	11.8	3.33	105	.236	.318	3	.070	-2	4	2	1	0.2
1979 NY-N	5	1	.833	7	7	1	0	0	42²	44	3	21	17	14.1	3.59	101	.267	.356	2	.125	-1	1	0	0	0.0
1980 NY-N	6	10	.375	28	26	7	3	0	164²	145	16	58	88	11.4	3.01	118	.240	.312	4	.043	-4	11	10	-2	0.4
1981 NY-N	7	14	.333	24	24	3	0	0	139	151	13	56	76	13.7	4.14	84	.282	.354	6	.158	0	-10	-10	1	-1.4
1982 NY-N	6	9	.400	36	16	2	0	1	137²	149	10	57	69	13.5	4.05	90	.279	.349	3	.079	-2	-7	-6	-0	-0.9
1983 *LA-N	6	1	.857	40	1	0	0	0	61¹	63	6	21	36	12.5	2.49	144	.278	.341	2	.500	1	8	7	0	0.9
1984 LA-N	5	6	.455	58	0	0	0	2	82²	84	3	51	55	14.9	3.81	93	.267	.372	2	.333	1	-2	-3	1	-0.2
1985 Phi-N	0	0	—	3	0	0	0	0	8¹	8	1	11	8	17.8	4.26	86	.280	.410	0	—	-0	-1	-1	1	0.0
Total 10	69	67	.507	293	154	29	7	3	1177¹	1147	88	495	669	12.7	3.52	102	.259	.336	36	.113	-11	13	8	-1	-0.9

● GEORGE ZACKERT
Zackert, George Carl "Zeke" b: 12/24/1884, Buchanan Co., Mo. d: 2/18/77, Burlington, Iowa BL/TL, 6', 177 lbs. Deb: 9/22/11

YEAR TM/L	W	L	PCT	G	GS	CG	SH	SV	IP	H	HR	BB	SO	RAT	ERA	ERA+	OAV	OOB	BH	AVG	PB	PR	/A	PD	TPI
1911 StL-N	0	2	.000	4	1	0	0	0	7¹	17	0	6	6	28.2	11.05	31	.486	.561	0	.000	-0	-6	-6	1	-1.3
1912 StL-N	0	0	—	1	0	0	0	0	1	2	0	1	0	36.0	18.00	19	.667	.800	0	—	0	-2	-2	0	0.0
Total 2	0	2	.000	5	1	0	0	0	8¹	19	0	7	6	29.2	11.88	28	.500	.587	0	.000	-0	-8	-8	1	-1.3

● GEOFF ZAHN
Zahn, Geoffrey Clayton b: 12/19/45, Baltimore, Md. BL/TL, 6'1", 180 lbs. Deb: 9/2/73

YEAR TM/L	W	L	PCT	G	GS	CG	SH	SV	IP	H	HR	BB	SO	RAT	ERA	ERA+	OAV	OOB	BH	AVG	PB	PR	/A	PD	TPI
1973 LA-N	1	0	1.000	6	1	0	0	0	13¹	5	2	2	9	4.7	1.35	255	.116	.156	0	.000	-0	3	3	0	0.2
1974 LA-N	3	5	.375	21	10	1	0	0	79²	78	3	16	33	10.8	2.03	167	.254	.295	4	.174	—	0	14	12	0	1.1
1975 LA-N	0	1	.000	2	0	0	0	0	3	2	0	5	1	21.0	9.00	38	.222	.500	0	—	0	-2	-2	-0	-0.5
Chi-N	2	7	.222	16	10	1	0	1	62²	67	2	26	21	13.4	4.45	86	.282	.352	2	.133	-1	-6	-4	1	-0.5
Yr	2	8	.200	18	10	1	0	1	65²	69	2	31	22	13.7	4.66	82	.279	.360	2	.133	-1	-8	-6	1	-1.0
1976 Chi-N	0	1	.000	3	2	0	0	0	8¹	16	0	2	4	20.5	10.80	36	.410	.452	0	.000	-0	-7	-6	0	-0.7
1977 Min-A	12	14	.462	34	32	7	1	0	198	234	20	66	88	13.9	4.68	85	.299	.358	0	—	0	-14	-15	2	-1.4
1978 Min-A	14	14	.500	35	35	12	1	0	252¹	260	18	81	106	12.3	3.03	126	.274	.334	0	—	0	20	22	-0	2.3
1979 Min-A	13	7	.650	26	24	4	0	0	169	181	13	41	58	11.8	3.57	123	.279	.322	0	—	0	12	15	2	1.5
1980 Min-A	14	18	.438	38	35	13	5	0	232²	273	17	66	96	13.2	4.41	99	.302	.351	0	—	0	-10	-1	0	-0.7
1981 Cal-A	10	11	.476	25	25	9	0	0	161¹	181	18	43	52	12.5	4.41	83	.285	.330	0	—	0	-13	-14	-1	-1.6
1982 *Cal-A	18	8	.692	34	34	12	4	0	229¹	225	18	65	81	11.5	3.73	109	.259	.314	0	—	0	9	8	-1	0.7
1983 Cal-A	9	11	.450	29	28	11	3	0	203	212	22	51	81	11.7	3.33	121	.269	.314	0	—	0	17	16	-2	1.3
1984 Cal-A	13	10	.565	28	27	9	**5**	0	199¹	200	11	48	61	11.2	3.12	127	.263	.308	0	—	0	19	19	1	2.2
1985 Cal-A	2	2	.500	7	7	1	0	0	37	44	5	14	14	14.1	4.38	94	.299	.360	0	—	0	-1	-1	1	0.0
Total 13	111	109	.505	304	270	79	20	1	1849	1978	149	526	705	12.3	3.74	107	.278	.329	6	.140	-2	43	51	4	3.9

● PAUL ZAHNISER
Zahniser, Paul Vernon b: 9/6/1896, Sac City, Iowa d: 9/26/64, Klamath Falls, Ore. BR/TR, 5'10.5", 170 lbs. Deb: 5/18/23

YEAR TM/L	W	L	PCT	G	GS	CG	SH	SV	IP	H	HR	BB	SO	RAT	ERA	ERA+	OAV	OOB	BH	AVG	PB	PR	/A	PD	TPI
1923 Was-A	9	10	.474	33	21	10	1	0	177	201	7	76	52	14.2	3.86	97	.291	.364	5	.096	-1	-2	-2	-2	-0.5
1924 Was-A	5	7	.417	24	14	5	1	0	92	98	2	49	28	14.8	4.40	92	.283	.378	4	.129	-2	-2	-4	-2	-0.7
1925 Bos-A	5	12	.294	37	21	7	1	1	176²	232	6	89	30	16.4	5.15	88	.327	.403	8	.138	-4	-15	-12	-2	-1.5
1926 Bos-A	6	18	.250	30	24	7	1	0	172	213	5	69	35	14.9	4.97	82	.321	.387	8	.163	-1	-18	-17	-3	-1.8
1929 Cin-N	0	0	—	1	0	0	0	0	1	2	1	1	0	27.0	27.00	17	.400	.500	0	—	0	-2	-2	0	0.0
Total 5	25	47	.347	125	80	29	4	1	618²	746	21	284	145	15.1	4.66	88	.309	.384	25	.132	-8	-35	-37	-2	-4.5

● CARL ZAMLOCH
Zamloch, Carl Eugene b: 10/6/1889, Oakland, Cal. d: 8/19/63, Santa Barbara, Cal BR/TR, 6'1", 176 lbs. Deb: 5/7/13

YEAR TM/L	W	L	PCT	G	GS	CG	SH	SV	IP	H	HR	BB	SO	RAT	ERA	ERA+	OAV	OOB	BH	AVG	PB	PR	/A	PD	TPI
1913 Det-A	1	6	.143	17	5	3	0	1	69²	66	1	23	28	11.9	2.45	119	.257	.325	4	.182	-1	4	4	-1	0.2

YEAR TM/L	W	L	PCT	G	GS	CG	SH	SV	IP	H	HR	BB	SO	RAT	ERA	ERA+	OAV	OOB	BH	AVG	PB	PR	/A	PD	TPI
● **OSCAR ZAMORA**				Zamora, Oscar Jose (Sosa)		b: 9/23/44, Camaguey, Cuba			BR/TR, 5'10", 178 lbs.			Deb: 6/18/74													
1974 Chi-N	3	9	.250	56	0	0	0	10	83²	82	6	19	38	10.9	3.12	122	.264	.306	2	.182	-0	5	6	0	1.0
1975 Chi-N	5	2	.714	52	0	0	0	10	71	84	17	15	28	12.5	5.07	76	.298	.333	1	.167	-0	-11	-10	-0	-1.3
1976 Chi-N	5	3	.625	40	2	0	0	3	55	70	8	17	27	14.4	5.24	74	.317	.368	0	.000	-1	-11	-8	-1	-1.4
1978 Hou-N	0	0	—	10	0	0	0	0	15	20	2	7	6	16.2	7.20	46	.328	.397	0	.000	-0	-6	-6	0	0.0
Total 4	13	14	.481	158	2	0	0	23	224²	256	33	58	99	12.6	4.53	84	.293	.337	3	.107	-2	-23	-18	-1	-1.7
● **DOM ZANNI**				Zanni, Dominick Thomas		b: 3/1/32, Bronx, N.Y.			BR/TR, 5'11", 180 lbs.			Deb: 9/28/58													
1958 SF-N	1	0	1.000	1	0	0	0	0	4	7	1	1	3	18.0	2.25	169	.412	.444	0	.000	-0	1	1	-0	0.1
1959 SF-N	0	0	—	9	0	0	0	0	11	12	2	8	11	17.2	6.55	58	.273	.396	0	—	-0	-3	-3	1	0.1
1961 SF-N	1	0	1.000	8	0	0	0	0	13²	13	1	12	11	16.5	3.95	96	.277	.424	0	—	0	-0	-0	0	0.0
1962 Chi-A	6	5	.545	44	2	0	0	5	86¹	67	12	31	66	10.3	3.75	104	.214	.287	5	.278	2	2	1	2	0.6
1963 Chi-A	0	0	—	5	0	0	0	0	4¹	5	1	4	2	18.7	8.31	42	.294	.429	0	—	0	-2	-2	0	0.0
Cin-N	1	1	.500	31	0	0	0	5	43	39	2	21	40	13.4	4.19	80	.247	.350	1	.333	0	-4	-4	1	-0.2
1965 Cin-N	0	0	—	8	0	0	0	0	13¹	7	1	5	10	8.1	1.35	278	.159	.245	0	.000	-0	3	4	0	0.0
1966 Cin-N	0	0	—	5	0	0	0	0	7¹	5	0	3	5	11.0	0.00	—	.192	.300	1	1.000	0	3	3	-0	0.0
Total 7	9	6	.600	111	3	0	0	10	183	155	20	85	148	12.1	3.79	99	.233	.326	7	.280	2	-1	-1	4	0.6
● **JEFF ZASKE**				Zaske, Lloyd Jeffrey		b: 10/6/60, Seattle, Wash.			BR/TR, 6'5", 180 lbs.			Deb: 7/21/84													
1984 Pit-N	0	0	—	3	0	0	0	0	5	4	0	1	2	9.0	0.00	—	.211	.250	0	—	0	2	2	0	0.0
● **CLINT ZAVARAS**				Zavaras, Clinton Wayne		b: 1/4/67, Denver, Colo.			BR/TR, 6'1", 175 lbs.			Deb: 6/3/89													
1989 Sea-A	1	6	.143	10	10	0	0	0	52	49	4	30	31	14.0	5.19	78	.253	.358	0	—	0	-8	-7	0	-1.1
● **ZAY**				Zay		Deb: 10/7/1886 ♦																			
1886 Bal-a	0	1	.000	1	1	0	0	0	2	4	0	4	2	36.0	9.00	38	.333	.500	0	.000	-0	-1	-1	-0	-0.4
● **MATT ZEISER**				Zeiser, Matthew J.		b: 9/25/1888, Chicago, Ill.		d: 6/10/42, Norwood Park, Ill	BR/TR, 5'10", 170 lbs.			Deb: 4/27/14													
1914 Bos-A	0	0	—	2	0	0	0	0	10	9	0	8	0	16.2	1.80	150	.281	.439	0	.000	-0	1	1	-1	-0.1
● **BILL ZEPP**				Zepp, William Clinton		b: 7/22/46, Detroit, Mich.			BR/TR, 6'2", 185 lbs.			Deb: 8/12/69													
1969 Min-A	0	0	—	4	0	0	0	0	5¹	6	1	4	2	16.9	6.75	54	.286	.400	0	.000	-0	-2	-2	-0	0.0
1970 *Min-A	9	4	.692	43	20	1	1	2	151	154	9	51	64	12.8	3.22	116	.266	.335	6	.136	-1	8	8	-2	0.4
1971 Det-A	1	1	.500	16	4	0	0	2	31²	41	2	17	15	17.3	5.12	70	.328	.421	0	.000	-0	-6	-5	0	-0.4
Total 3	10	5	.667	63	24	1	1	4	188	201	12	72	81	13.6	3.64	102	.278	.353	6	.122	-2	1	1	-2	0.0
● **GEORGE ZETTLEIN**				Zettlein, George "Charmer"		b: 7/18/1844, Brooklyn, N.Y.		d: 5/23/05, Patchogue, N.Y.	BR/TR, 5'9", 162 lbs.			Deb: 5/8/1871													
1871 Chi-n	18	9	.667	28	28	25	0	0	240²	298	6	25	22	12.1	2.73	168	.267	.283	32	.250	-7	40	50		2.9
1872 Tro-n	14	8	.636	25	22	17	2	0	187²	209	2	6	17	10.4	2.54	146	.250	.257	29	.250	-0	25	24		1.8
Eck-n	1	8	.111	9	9	8	0	0	75¹	105	1	6	8	13.3	2.99	116	.298	.310	3	.088	-4	6	4		0.0
Yr	15	16	.484	34	31	25	2	0	263	314	3	14	25	11.2	2.67	136	.265	.273	32	.213	-5	31	28		1.8
1873 Phi-n	36	15	.706	51	51	49	0	0	460	593	3	41	28	12.4	2.70	122	.288	.297	50	.207	-8	28	31		1.6
1874 Chi-n	27	30	.474	57	57	57	3	0	515²	653	3	46		12.2	3.07	99	.280	.294	47	.193	-11	-4	-1		-0.9
1875 Chi-n	17	14	.548	31	31	29	6	0	282	269	0	6		8.8	1.82	138	.232	.236	29	.223	-3	20	22		1.6
Phi-n	12	8	.600	21	21	20	1	0	180¹	208	0	10		10.9	2.40	105	.263	.272	15	.179	-4	1	2		-0.1
Yr	29	22	.569	52	52	49	7	0	462¹	477	0	16		9.6	2.04	123	.245	.251	44	.206	-7	21	24		1.5
1876 Phi-N	4	20	.167	28	25	23	1	2	234	358	2	6	10	14.0	3.88	62	.331	.334	27	.211	-5	-41	-38	-1	-3.4
Total 5 n	125	92	.576	222	219	205	12	0	1941²	2335	15	142	75	11.5	2.64	123	.269	.281	205	.210	-37	116	130		6.9
● **BOB ZICK**				Zick, Robert George		b: 4/26/27, Chicago, Ill.			BL/TR, 6', 168 lbs.			Deb: 5/2/54													
1954 Chi-N	0	0	—	8	0	0	0	0	16¹	23	1	7	9	16.5	8.27	51	.343	.405	1	.250	0	-8	-7	-0	0.0
● **GEORGE ZIEGLER**				Ziegler, George J.		b: 1872, Chicago, Ill.		d: 7/22/16, Kankakee, Ill.				Deb: 6/19/1890													
1890 Pit-N	0	1	.000	1	1	0	0	0	6	12	0	0	1	18.0	10.50	31	.403	.403	0	.000	-0	-5	-5	-0	-0.5
● **STEVE ZIEM**				Ziem, Stephen Graeling		b: 10/24/61, Milwaukee, Wis.			BR/TR, 6'2", 210 lbs.			Deb: 4/30/87													
1987 Atl-N	0	1	.000	2	0	0	0	0	2¹	4	0	1	0	19.3	7.71	56	.364	.417	0	—	0	-1	-1	-0	-0.3
● **WALTER ZINK**				Zink, Walter Noble		b: 11/21/1899, Pittsfield, Mass.		d: 6/12/64, Quincy, Mass.	BR/TR, 6', 165 lbs.			Deb: 7/6/21													
1921 NY-N	0	0	—	2	0	0	0	0	4	4	0	3	1	15.8	2.25	163	.235	.350	0	.000	-0	1	1	-0	0.0
● **JIMMY ZINN**				Zinn, James Edward		b: 1/21/1895, Benton, Ark.		d: 2/26/91, Memphis, Tenn.	BL/TR, 6'0.5", 195 lbs.			Deb: 9/4/19													
1919 Phi-A	1	3	.250	5	3	2	0	0	25²	38	1	10	9	17.2	6.31	54	.365	.426	4	.308	2	-9	-8	-0	-0.9
1920 Pit-N	1	1	.500	6	3	2	0	0	31	32	2	5	18	11.0	3.48	92	.260	.295	3	.200	0	-1	-1	-0	0.0
1921 Pit-N	7	6	.538	32	9	5	1	4	127¹	159	3	30	49	13.5	3.68	104	.318	.359	11	.224	0	2	2	-2	0.0
1922 Pit-N	0	0	—	5	0	0	0	1	9²	11	1	2	3	12.1	1.86	219	.297	.333	0	.000	-0	2	2	0	0.0
1929 Cle-A	4	6	.400	18	11	6	1	2	105¹	150	8	33	29	15.9	5.04	88	.340	.390	16	.381	7	-9	-7	-0	0.0
Total 5	13	16	.448	66	26	15	2	7	299	390	15	80	108	14.4	4.30	92	.324	.369	34	.283	9	-15	-12	-3	-0.9
● **BILL ZINSER**				Zinser, William Francis		b: 1/6/18, Astoria, N.Y.			BR/TR, 6'1", 185 lbs.			Deb: 8/19/44													
1944 Was-A	0	0	—	2	0	0	0	0	0²	1	0	5	1	81.0	27.00	12	.333	.750	0	—	0	-2	-2	0	0.0
● **ED ZMICH**				Zmich, Edward Albert		b: 10/1/1884, Cleveland, Ohio		d: 8/20/50, Cleveland, Ohio	BL/TL, 6', 180 lbs.			Deb: 7/23/10													
1910 StL-N	0	5	.000	9	6	2	0	0	36	38	0	29	19	17.5	6.25	48	.304	.446	1	.077	-1	-13	-13	1	-1.6
1911 StL-N	1	0	1.000	4	0	0	0	0	12²	8	0	8	4	12.1	2.13	158	.182	.321	0	.000	-1	2	2	-1	0.0
Total 2	1	5	.167	13	6	2	0	0	48²	46	0	37	23	16.1	5.18	60	.272	.414	1	.059	-2	-11	-11	0	-1.6
● **SAM ZOLDAK**				Zoldak, Samuel Walter "Sad Sam"		b: 12/8/18, Brooklyn, N.Y.		d: 8/25/66, New Hyde Park, N.Y	BL/TL, 5'11.5", 185 lbs.			Deb: 5/13/44													
1944 StL-A	0	0	—	18	0	0	0	0	38²	49	1	19	15	15.8	3.72	97	.310	.384	2	.333	0	-1	-1	0	0.0
1945 StL-A	3	2	.600	26	1	1	0	0	69²	74	3	18	19	11.9	3.36	105	.267	.312	1	.050	-2	0	1	-1	-0.3
1946 StL-A	9	11	.450	35	21	9	2	2	170¹	166	11	57	51	11.8	3.43	109	.256	.317	9	.173	-0	1	6	1	0.7
1947 StL-A	9	10	.474	35	19	6	1	1	171	162	7	76	36	12.5	3.47	112	.254	.334	10	.172	-1	4	8	3	1.0
1948 StL-A	2	4	.333	11	9	0	0	0	54	64	4	19	13	14.0	4.67	98	.296	.356	0	.273	-0	-1	0	0	0.0
Cle-A	9	6	.600	23	12	4	1	0	105²	104	6	24	17	10.9	2.81	144	.261	.303	5	.139	-2	17	15	2	1.9
Yr	11	10	.524	34	21	4	1	0	159²	168	10	43	30	11.9	3.44	123	.273	.321	11	.190	-2	15	14	2	1.9
1949 Cle-A	1	2	.333	27	0	0	0	0	53	60	4	18	11	13.2	4.25	94	.291	.348	3	.375	-1	-0	-1	3	0.3
1950 Cle-A	4	2	.667	33	3	0	0	0	63²	64	6	21	15	12.2	3.96	109	.259	.320	3	.188	0	4	3	-0	0.2
1951 Phi-A	6	10	.375	26	18	8	1	0	128	127	9	24	18	10.6	3.16	135	.257	.292	7	.156	-3	14	16	-2	1.3
1952 Phi-A	0	6	.000	16	10	2	0	0	75¹	86	3	25	12	13.3	4.06	97	.290	.345	4	.174	-1	-3	-1	2	0.1
Total 9	43	53	.448	250	93	30	5	8	929¹	956	54	301	207	12.2	3.54	112	.267	.325	50	.175	-7	34	45	7	5.2

YEAR TM/L	W	L	PCT	G	GS	CG	SH	SV	IP	H	HR	BB	SO	RAT	ERA	ERA+	OAV	OOB	BH	AVG	PB	PR	/A	PD	TPI
● **BILL ZUBER**   Zuber, William Henry "Goober"   b: 3/26/13, Middle Amana, Iowa   d: 11/2/82, Cedar Rapids, Iowa   BR/TR, 6'2", 195 lbs.   Deb: 9/16/36
1936 Cle-A	1	1	.500	2	2	1	0	0	13²	14	0	15	5	19.1	6.59	76	.269	.433	1	.200	-0	-2	-2	-0	-0.3
1938 Cle-A	0	3	.000	15	0	0	0	1	28²	33	0	20	14	16.6	5.02	92	.295	.402	0	.000	-1	-1	-1	-0	-0.2
1939 Cle-A	2	0	1.000	16	1	0	0	0	31²	41	2	19	16	17.3	5.97	74	.323	.415	1	.200	1	-5	-6	1	-0.2
1940 Cle-A	1	1	.500	17	0	0	0	0	24	25	3	14	12	14.6	5.63	75	.260	.355	1	.333	0	-3	-4	-0	-0.3
1941 Was-A	6	4	.600	36	7	1	0	2	96¹	110	5	61	51	16.2	5.42	75	.291	.392	0	.000	-3	-14	-15	-1	-1.8
1942 Was-A	9	9	.500	37	7	3	1	1	126²	115	5	82	64	14.0	3.84	95	.243	.355	6	.154	0	-3	-3	-3	-0.5
1943 NY-A	8	4	.667	20	13	7	0	1	118	100	3	74	57	13.3	3.89	83	.234	.347	7	.184	2	-8	-9	-2	-0.8
1944 NY-A	5	7	.417	22	13	2	1	0	107	101	5	54	59	13.1	4.21	83	.255	.346	4	.129	-2	-9	-9	-1	-1.1
1945 NY-A	5	11	.313	21	14	7	0	1	127	121	6	56	50	12.5	3.19	109	.259	.338	7	.167	-1	2	4	-1	0.2
1946 NY-A	0	1	.000	3	0	0	0	0	5²	10	2	3	3	20.6	12.71	27	.385	.448	0	.000	-0	-6	-6	-0	-0.9
*Bos-A	5	1	.833	15	7	2	1	0	56²	37	4	39	29	12.1	2.54	144	.187	.321	2	.111	-1	6	7	0	0.6
Yr	5	2	.714	18	7	2	1	0	62¹	47	6	42	32	12.9	3.47	105	.210	.335	2	.100	-1	0	1	-0	-0.3
1947 Bos-A	1	0	1.000	20	1	0	0	0	50²	60	4	31	23	16.2	5.33	73	.311	.406	2	.154	-0	-9	-8	-0	-0.2
Total 11	43	42	.506	224	65	23	3	6	786	767	35	468	383	14.2	4.28	87	.260	.362	31	.135	-6	-51	-50	-8	-5.5
● **GEORGE ZUVERINK**   Zuverink, George   b: 8/20/24, Holland, Mich.   BR/TR, 6'4", 200 lbs.   Deb: 4/21/51
1951 Cle-A	0	0	—	16	0	0	0	0	25¹	24	2	13	14	13.5	5.33	71	.253	.349	0	—	0	-3	-4	0	0.0
1952 Cle-A	0	0	—	1	1	0	0	0	1¹	1	0	0	1	6.8	6.00	—	.200	.200	0	—	1	0	0	0	0.0
1954 Cin-N	0	0	—	2	0	0	0	0	6	10	1	1	2	16.5	9.00	47	.385	.407	1	.500	0	-3	-3	-0	0.0
Det-A	9	13	.409	35	25	9	2	4	203	201	22	62	70	12.0	3.59	103	.257	.318	8	.125	-3	3	2	3	0.2
1955 Det-A	0	5	.000	14	1	0	0	0	28¹	38	6	14	13	16.8	6.99	55	.309	.384	0	.000	-1	-10	-10	-0	-1.5
Bal-A	4	3	.571	28	5	0	0	4	86¹	80	5	17	31	10.5	2.19	174	.264	.312	5	.217	1	17	16	1	1.5
Yr	4	8	.333	42	6	0	0	4	114²	118	11	31	44	12.0	3.38	113	.276	.331	5	.185	0	7	6	1	0.0
1956 Bal-A	7	6	.538	**62**	0	0	0	**16**	97¹	112	9	34	33	13.8	4.16	94	.294	.356	2	.118	-1	-0	-3	-1	-0.4
1957 Bal-A	10	6	.625	**56**	0	0	0	9	112²	105	9	39	36	11.8	2.48	145	.257	.327	3	.130	-0	16	14	1	2.2
1958 Bal-A	2	2	.500	45	0	0	0	7	69	74	4	17	22	12.7	3.39	106	.286	.344	2	.222	1	3	2	1	0.4
1959 Bal-A	0	1	.000	6	0	0	0	0	13	15	1	6	1	14.5	4.15	91	.306	.382	0	—	1	-0	-1	0	0.0
Total 8	32	36	.471	265	31	9	2	40	642¹	660	56	203	223	12.5	3.54	105	.271	.334	21	.148	-2	23	13	7	2.4

The Situational Statistics Register

Baseball has been blessed over the years with a wealth of numbers. Its statistics make almost tangible the exploits of players long gone, and the accuracy and scope of these numbers are what makes meaningful comparisons of players from different eras possible. New to this edition of *Total Baseball* is this situational record of the past eleven years, for batters and for pitchers. The editors of this volume are grateful to Gary Gillette and The Baseball Workshop for this important contribution to baseball statistical analysis and scholarship.

Baseball encyclopedias have always contained batting and pitching statistics. This Situational Statistics Register marks the first time that extensive situational statistics have also been included. These situational statistics add depth and texture to the official batting and pitching statistics and give us another tool for understanding the way the game is played.

The familiar traditional stats—batting average, runs, home runs, runs batted in, wins, losses earned run average, and strikeouts—obviously have considerable merit, otherwise they wouldn't be universally known and discussed. In contrast to these traditional totals and averages, "situationals" are an attempt to break baseball statistics into *how* and *when* they happened.

The most important situational breakdowns are how batters perform against lefthanded and righthanded pitchers (and pitchers vs. their opposite-batting counterparts) and how players perform in their home park as opposed to when they are on the road. In reality, these situational stats have been part of the game for decades, as generations of fans have argued about the effect of Yankee Stadium on sluggers like Ruth and Maris, while generations of managers have platooned their hitters. Aside from these two key categories, several other types of breakdowns have become prominent, including performance with runners in scoring position and other ways of measuring "clutch" performance.

The biggest problem with situational statistics to date has been how to use the data. For example, when a manager chooses to start a righthanded batter (who would normally be platooned) against a righthanded pitcher, he can justify it statistically in any number of ways. He could base his decisions on that hitter's past performance against the opposing team, or by his performance against the opposing pitcher, or by his performance in day games, or by his performance against ground-ball pitchers, or even by his performance in the past week if he's been on a hot streak. All of these statistics (and many more) are available to teams on a daily basis. Of course, many of these numbers will be contradictory: a hitter might have done poorly against righthanded pitchers, but have done well against that team. He could also carry a pitiful average against that day's starting pitcher, but have done excellently in day games.

No one really knows if individual pitcher-batter matchups are more reliable predictors of performance than left/right breakdowns, and while everyone talks about "clutch" hitters, there are a dozen ways of measuring what might be called "clutch" hitting. Indeed, many studies have been done which fail to show any consistent, measurable effect which could be labeled as "clutch" hitting. Just what is true and what isn't?

Most of the statistics quoted and published are literally true. That is, they are accounts of events which actually happened on the field, and therefore must be true. Stating that a player batted .390 with runners in scoring position doesn't leave anything to argue over. What is manifestly false, however, are most of the claims made about these statistics. If one argues that batting .390 with runners in scoring position means that the player is a good "clutch" hitter, the validity of that statement depends not on the actual numbers, but on the interpretation of those numbers. The interpretation and misinterpretation of the numbers and the predictions that flow from them are what cause the arguments.

This Situational Statistics Register should elevate the level of debate. It includes year-by-year statistics and career totals (1984-1994) for men who have been regular players in the major leagues for at least a portion of the past eleven seasons. If a player qualified for the register, his statistics are shown for every year in which he played in the majors, whether he was a regular or not. In order to qualify for a listing in this register, a player needed to meet one of two criteria:

Players who were active in the major leagues in 1994 are included as long as they played regularly in 1994.

Players who did not play in the majors in 1994 had to have played regularly for a total of three seasons between 1984 and 1994.

Regular batters are defined as having played in 100 or more games during a season. Regular pitchers are defined as having pitched at least 150 innings *or* 50 or more games in a season. Six separate situations are shown for both batters and pitchers:

"Vs. Left" and "Vs. Right" break batters' statistics down

into how they batted against lefthanded pitchers and how they batted against righthanded pitchers. For pitchers, the breakdowns represent how opposing lefthanded and righthanded batters hit against them.

"At Home" and "On Road" break players' statistics into how they performed in games in their home ballpark and how they performed in games in all other ballparks. This is the only category in which the statistics shown for batters and pitchers are different.

"Scoring Position" statistics for both batters and pitchers show performance in situations with a runner on second base and/or third base—the traditional definition of scoring position.

The "Late and Close" statistics show performance when the score is close in the late innings of a game, a measure of a player's "clutch" performance. "Late and Close" situations are defined as at bats in the seventh inning or later when a player's team is ahead by only one run, or the score is tied, or his team is behind but the tying run is at bat, on base or on deck. While the definition of a "Late

and Close" situation does not change, "Late and Close" situations can change from one at bat to the next if the score or the runners on base change. The "close" part of the definition is similar to what is used in the official Save rule for pitchers.

Five statistics are shown for each situation: At Bats, Home Runs, Batting Average, On Base Percentage, and Slugging Percentage. For pitchers, the only variation from these categories occurs in Home/Road breakdowns, where Wins, Losses, Saves, Innings Pitched, and Earned Run Average are shown. The abbreviations used are the same as those used elsewhere in *Total Baseball*.

A player's seasonal totals in each category are also shown with the Situational Statistics. These totals are the same as those in the Batting and Pitching Registers and are shown simply for ease of use (avoiding excessive page-turning).

For a key to the team and league abbreviations used in the Situational Statistics Register, go to the last page of the book. For definitions of the terms found in the headings, consult the Glossary.

Kurt Abbott BR/TR

YEAR TM/L	TOTAL					HOME					AWAY					LEFT					RIGHT					ON-BASE					LATE/CLOSE				
	AB	HR	AVG	OBP	SLG	AB	HR	AVG	OBP	SLG	AB	HR	AVG	OBP	SLG	AB	HR	AVG	OBP	SLG	AB	HR	AVG	OBP	SLG	AB	HR	AVG	OBP	SLG	AB	HR	AVG	OBP	SLG
1993 Oak-A	61	3	.246	.281	.410	23	0	.087	.125	.087	38	3	.342	.375	.605	26	2	.231	.259	.462	35	1	.257	.297	.371	32	2	.313	.333	.500	9	0	.333	.333	.333
1994 Fla-N	345	9	.249	.291	.394	183	4	.257	.301	.404	162	5	.241	.279	.383	107	2	.262	.298	.411	238	7	.244	.287	.387	138	5	.210	.260	.362	58	2	.241	.262	.431
TOTALS	406	12	.249	.289	.397	206	4	.238	.282	.369	200	8	.260	.297	.425	133	4	.256	.291	.421	273	8	.245	.289	.385	170	7	.229	.273	.388	67	2	.254	.271	.418

Andy Allanson BR/TR

YEAR TM/L	TOTAL					HOME					AWAY					LEFT					RIGHT					ON-BASE					LATE/CLOSE				
	AB	HR	AVG	OBP	SLG	AB	HR	AVG	OBP	SLG	AB	HR	AVG	OBP	SLG	AB	HR	AVG	OBP	SLG	AB	HR	AVG	OBP	SLG	AB	HR	AVG	OBP	SLG	AB	HR	AVG	OBP	SLG
1986 Cle-A	293	1	.225	.260	.280	147	0	.238	.268	.286	146	1	.212	.252	.274	84	0	.274	.307	.333	209	1	.206	.241	.258	144	1	.264	.276	.354	41	0	.341	.357	.439
1987 Cle-A	154	1	.266	.298	.364	75	2	.200	.250	.320	79	1	.329	.345	.405	47	0	.277	.309	.362	107	1	.262	.292	.364	69	1	.217	.262	.304	23	0	.304	.304	.304
1988 Cle-A	434	5	.263	.305	.323	223	4	.274	.318	.354	211	1	.251	.290	.289	104	0	.269	.306	.308	330	5	.261	.304	.327	178	2	.303	.347	.376	76	1	.276	.345	.355
1989 Cle-A	323	3	.232	.289	.294	149	1	.208	.279	.248	174	2	.253	.298	.333	94	0	.287	.340	.351	229	3	.209	.268	.271	137	1	.204	.282	.241	47	2	.298	.327	.468
1991 Det-A	151	1	.232	.266	.318	63	0	.254	.299	.286	88	1	.216	.242	.341	115	0	.217	.244	.270	36	1	.278	.333	.444	55	1	.291	.316	.473	22	0	.273	.273	.318
1992 Mil-A	25	0	.320	.346	.360	12	0	.167	.231	.250	13	0	.462	.462	.462	7	0	.143	.143	.143	18	0	.389	.421	.444	11	0	.182	.250	.182	3	0	.333	.500	.333
1993 SF-N	24	0	.167	.200	.208	12	0	.083	.154	.167	12	0	.250	.250	.250	12	0	.167	.231	.167	12	0	.167	.167	.250	11	0	.273	.333	.364	3	0	.000	.000	.000
TOTALS	1404	13	.244	.286	.310	681	7	.236	.285	.301	723	6	.252	.287	.318	463	0	.257	.294	.313	941	13	.238	.282	.308	605	6	.258	.301	.337	215	3	.293	.330	.381

Roberto Alomar BB/TR

YEAR TM/L	TOTAL					HOME					AWAY					LEFT					RIGHT					ON-BASE					LATE/CLOSE				
	AB	HR	AVG	OBP	SLG	AB	HR	AVG	OBP	SLG	AB	HR	AVG	OBP	SLG	AB	HR	AVG	OBP	SLG	AB	HR	AVG	OBP	SLG	AB	HR	AVG	OBP	SLG	AB	HR	AVG	OBP	SLG
1988 SD-N	545	9	.266	.328	.382	279	5	.254	.309	.355	266	4	.278	.347	.410	178	4	.258	.330	.382	367	5	.270	.327	.381	203	1	.291	.351	.360	94	1	.266	.330	.351
1989 SD-N	623	7	.295	.347	.376	286	3	.329	.394	.399	337	4	.267	.306	.356	195	4	.256	.316	.369	428	3	.313	.362	.379	247	2	.296	.338	.364	94	1	.319	.390	.383
1990 SD-N	586	6	.287	.340	.381	298	4	.285	.334	.383	288	2	.288	.346	.378	204	3	.260	.330	.377	382	3	.301	.345	.382	264	3	.311	.362	.424	105	0	.229	.311	.286
1991 Tor-A	637	9	.295	.354	.436	313	6	.297	.367	.479	324	3	.293	.341	.395	191	4	.246	.295	.419	446	4	.316	.379	.444	247	2	.296	.358	.417	105	2	.286	.371	.419
1992 Tor-A	571	8	.310	.405	.427	268	5	.354	.444	.500	303	3	.271	.369	.363	156	3	.308	.414	.436	415	3	.311	.403	.424	245	6	.339	.438	.482	79	1	.430	.526	.557
1993 Tor-A	589	17	.326	.408	.492	289	8	.325	.409	.498	300	9	.327	.407	.487	166	4	.241	.297	.313	423	13	.359	.449	.539	251	7	.315	.404	.490	84	3	.274	.344	.440
1994 Tor-A	392	8	.306	.386	.452	185	4	.292	.379	.432	207	4	.319	.393	.469	114	4	.254	.331	.412	278	4	.327	.408	.468	161	5	.267	.349	.429	48	2	.229	.351	.438
TOTALS	3943	64	.298	.367	.419	1918	35	.306	.377	.435	2025	29	.290	.357	.404	1204	29	.260	.330	.394	2739	35	.314	.383	.431	1618	26	.304	.374	.425	609	10	.291	.374	.402

Moises Alou BR/TR

YEAR TM/L	TOTAL					HOME					AWAY					LEFT					RIGHT					ON-BASE					LATE/CLOSE				
	AB	HR	AVG	OBP	SLG	AB	HR	AVG	OBP	SLG	AB	HR	AVG	OBP	SLG	AB	HR	AVG	OBP	SLG	AB	HR	AVG	OBP	SLG	AB	HR	AVG	OBP	SLG	AB	HR	AVG	OBP	SLG
1990 Pit-N	5	0	.200	.200	.200	5	0	.200	.200	.200	0	0	—	—	—	5	0	.200	.200	.200	0	0	—	—	—	2	0	.000	.000	.000	0	0	—	—	—
1990 Mon-N	15	0	.200	.200	.333	13	0	.231	.231	.385	2	0	.000	.000	.000	12	0	.167	.167	.333	3	0	.333	.333	.333	4	0	.000	.000	.000	3	0	.000	.000	.000
1992 Mon-N	341	9	.282	.328	.455	143	6	.336	.376	.587	198	3	.242	.293	.359	136	2	.294	.329	.419	205	7	.273	.327	.478	162	6	.290	.330	.494	66	3	.273	.300	.500
1993 Mon-N	482	18	.286	.340	.483	222	10	.252	.310	.432	260	8	.315	.366	.527	164	5	.268	.320	.445	318	13	.296	.350	.503	234	6	.303	.366	.474	68	1	.250	.384	.353
1994 Mon-N	422	22	.339	.397	.592	186	9	.371	.444	.640	236	13	.314	.357	.555	104	5	.365	.426	.587	318	17	.330	.388	.594	187	9	.337	.419	.551	57	2	.333	.449	.544
TOTALS	1265	49	.301	.354	.509	569	25	.311	.369	.536	696	24	.293	.341	.487	421	12	.297	.344	.466	844	37	.303	.359	.531	589	21	.307	.370	.499	194	6	.278	.373	.454

Brady Anderson BL/TR

YEAR TM/L	TOTAL					HOME					AWAY					LEFT					RIGHT					ON-BASE					LATE/CLOSE				
	AB	HR	AVG	OBP	SLG	AB	HR	AVG	OBP	SLG	AB	HR	AVG	OBP	SLG	AB	HR	AVG	OBP	SLG	AB	HR	AVG	OBP	SLG	AB	HR	AVG	OBP	SLG	AB	HR	AVG	OBP	SLG
1988 Bos-A	148	0	.230	.315	.304	79	0	.253	.352	.316	69	0	.203	.273	.290	37	0	.297	.435	.378	111	0	.207	.270	.279	63	0	.270	.373	.333	19	0	.105	.227	.105
1988 Bal-A	177	1	.198	.232	.271	95	1	.147	.173	.221	82	0	.256	.299	.329	48	0	.125	.143	.146	129	1	.225	.265	.318	69	1	.174	.186	.246	35	0	.114	.114	.143
1989 Bal-A	266	4	.207	.324	.312	135	2	.222	.327	.333	131	2	.191	.321	.290	70	1	.129	.265	.243	196	3	.235	.345	.337	88	2	.239	.417	.341	30	0	.267	.389	.367
1990 Bal-A	234	3	.231	.327	.308	126	1	.175	.272	.238	108	2	.296	.391	.389	46	0	.152	.250	.174	188	3	.250	.347	.340	101	1	.307	.380	.406	31	0	.258	.324	.323
1991 Bal-A	256	2	.230	.338	.324	111	1	.225	.336	.306	145	1	.234	.339	.338	36	0	.139	.347	.194	220	2	.245	.336	.345	97	1	.227	.297	.320	53	1	.226	.328	.321
1992 Bal-A	623	21	.271	.373	.449	313	15	.262	.364	.463	310	6	.281	.383	.435	190	5	.226	.345	.368	433	16	.291	.386	.485	205	7	.278	.389	.454	89	1	.303	.390	.416
1993 Bal-A	560	13	.262	.363	.425	265	2	.242	.344	.343	295	11	.281	.381	.498	170	2	.259	.390	.353	390	11	.264	.350	.456	207	2	.266	.378	.406	85	2	.306	.396	.518
1994 Bal-A	453	12	.263	.356	.419	214	7	.257	.350	.425	239	5	.268	.362	.414	125	1	.248	.347	.344	328	11	.268	.360	.448	169	2	.254	.354	.379	54	0	.222	.328	.278
TOTALS	2717	56	.247	.345	.382	1338	29	.233	.330	.360	1379	27	.261	.359	.404	722	9	.216	.336	.313	1995	47	.259	.348	.408	999	16	.258	.361	.381	396	4	.250	.341	.356

Dave Anderson BR/TR

YEAR TM/L	TOTAL					HOME					AWAY					LEFT					RIGHT					ON-BASE					LATE/CLOSE				
	AB	HR	AVG	OBP	SLG	AB	HR	AVG	OBP	SLG	AB	HR	AVG	OBP	SLG	AB	HR	AVG	OBP	SLG	AB	HR	AVG	OBP	SLG	AB	HR	AVG	OBP	SLG	AB	HR	AVG	OBP	SLG
1984 LA-N	374	3	.251	.331	.329	178	2	.275	.342	.331	196	1	.230	.322	.327	120	1	.292	.394	.408	254	1	.232	.299	.291	155	0	.258	.306	.316	77	0	.169	.278	.208
1985 LA-N	221	4	.199	.310	.281	106	1	.189	.312	.236	115	3	.209	.308	.322	67	2	.194	.333	.313	154	2	.201	.299	.266	97	1	.165	.281	.206	31	1	.290	.389	.387
1986 LA-N	216	1	.245	.314	.301	97	0	.289	.355	.330	119	1	.210	.280	.277	75	0	.240	.313	.267	141	1	.248	.314	.319	89	1	.247	.299	.326	48	0	.292	.346	.396
1987 LA-N	265	1	.234	.299	.313	140	0	.250	.316	.321	125	1	.216	.279	.304	72	0	.250	.316	.333	193	1	.228	.292	.306	92	0	.293	.327	.380	42	0	.310	.348	.476
1988 LA-N	285	2	.249	.325	.319	132	1	.227	.301	.273	153	1	.268	.345	.359	117	0	.248	.331	.299	168	2	.250	.321	.333	122	0	.221	.297	.254	46	1	.261	.357	.413
1989 LA-N	140	1	.229	.310	.264	62	1	.290	.397	.355	78	0	.179	.235	.192	67	0	.209	.289	.209	73	1	.247	.329	.315	74	1	.368	.448	.439	36	0	.222	.317	.222
1990 SF-N	100	1	.350	.369	.450	51	0	.353	.377	.529	49	0	.347	.360	.367	54	1	.389	.411	.500	46	0	.304	.319	.391	41	0	.268	.302	.341	27	1	.519	.536	.704
1991 SF-N	226	2	.248	.286	.314	127	1	.197	.239	.268	99	1	.313	.346	.374	81	1	.148	.207	.210	145	1	.303	.331	.372	100	2	.260	.295	.350	62	0	.274	.318	.355
1992 LA-N	84	3	.286	.311	.440	37	0	.270	.317	.297	47	3	.298	.306	.553	64	2	.250	.286	.406	20	1	.400	.400	.550	38	1	.211	.220	.342	15	0	.267	.267	.400
TOTALS	1911	18	.246	.316	.321	930	7	.251	.321	.313	981	11	.243	.310	.329	717	8	.245	.323	.325	1194	10	.247	.311	.319	791	6	.250	.308	.317	384	3	.271	.340	.367

Tony Armas BR/TR

YEAR TM/L	TOTAL					HOME					AWAY					LEFT					RIGHT					ON-BASE					LATE/CLOSE				
	AB	HR	AVG	OBP	SLG	AB	HR	AVG	OBP	SLG	AB	HR	AVG	OBP	SLG	AB	HR	AVG	OBP	SLG	AB	HR	AVG	OBP	SLG	AB	HR	AVG	OBP	SLG	AB	HR	AVG	OBP	SLG
1984 Bos-A	639	43	.268	.300	.531	315	21	.289	.325	.552	324	22	.247	.276	.509	151	4	.245	.299	.377	488	39	.275	.301	.578	318	18	.274	.308	.516	91	7	.176	.219	.429
1985 Bos-A	385	23	.265	.298	.514	173	11	.289	.332	.555	212	12	.245	.268	.481	140	9	.336	.377	.636	245	14	.224	.251	.445	181	8	.232	.262	.459	69	1	.232	.232	.333
1986 Bos-A	425	11	.264	.305	.409	210	5	.271	.328	.429	215	6	.256	.281	.391	128	2	.289	.319	.430	297	9	.253	.299	.401	188	5	.282	.328	.447	55	0	.200	.228	.255
1987 Cal-A	81	3	.198	.205	.370	34	1	.176	.171	.324	47	2	.213	.229	.404	51	2	.216	.216	.412	30	1	.167	.188	.300	32	1	.219	.212	.438	17	0	.059	.059	.059
1988 Cal-A	368	13	.272	.311	.443	199	5	.241	.282	.387	169	8	.308	.346	.515	203	5	.261	.284	.384	165	8	.285	.345	.515	156	6	.276	.311	.449	66	4	.258	.329	.515
1989 Cal-A	202	11	.257	.280	.465	104	5	.221	.257	.404	98	6	.296	.304	.531	102	5	.235	.264	.422	100	6	.280	.295	.510	82	3	.268	.311	.415	41	2	.195	.195	.341
TOTALS	2100	104	.263	.297	.475	1035	48	.266	.307	.473	1065	56	.261	.287	.477	737	30	.278	.318	.475	1363	74	.255	.286	.475	957	41	.265	.302	.460	339	14	.204	.235	.369

Brad Ausmus BR/TR

YEAR TM/L	TOTAL					HOME					AWAY					LEFT					RIGHT					ON-BASE					LATE/CLOSE				
	AB	HR	AVG	OBP	SLG	AB	HR	AVG	OBP	SLG	AB	HR	AVG	OBP	SLG	AB	HR	AVG	OBP	SLG	AB	HR	AVG	OBP	SLG	AB	HR	AVG	OBP	SLG	AB	HR	AVG	OBP	SLG
1993 SD-N	160	5	.256	.283	.412	80	4	.325	.341	.575	80	1	.188	.226	.250	44	1	.295	.340	.477	116	4	.241	.261	.388	87	2	.228	.267	.404	21	0	.190	.227	.238
1994 SD-N	327	7	.251	.314	.358	159	6	.283	.352	.447	168	1	.220	.277	.274	86	1	.244	.309	.326	241	6	.253	.316	.369	142	3	.176	.283	.246	69	2	.246	.278	.348
TOTALS	487	12	.253	.304	.376	239	10	.297	.349	.490	248	2	.210	.261	.266	130	2	.262	.319	.377	357	10	.249	.298	.375	199	5	.191	.279	.291	90	2	.233	.266	.322

Wally Backman BB/TR

YEAR TM/L	TOTAL					HOME					AWAY					LEFT					RIGHT					ON-BASE					LATE/CLOSE				
	AB	HR	AVG	OBP	SLG	AB	HR	AVG	OBP	SLG	AB	HR	AVG	OBP	SLG	AB	HR	AVG	OBP	SLG	AB	HR	AVG	OBP	SLG	AB	HR	AVG	OBP	SLG	AB	HR	AVG	OBP	SLG
1984 NY-N	436	1	.280	.360	.339	203	0	.305	.399	.350	233	1	.258	.324	.330	37	0	.162	.340	.189	399	1	.291	.362	.353	138	1	.254	.352	.290	71	1	.296	.358	.394
1985 NY-N	520	1	.273	.320	.344	251	0	.259	.311	.335	269	1	.286	.328	.353	131	0	.122	.207	.153	389	1	.324	.359	.409	206	1	.306	.351	.383	78	0	.256	.306	.282
1986 NY-N	387	1	.320	.376	.385	180	1	.311	.377	.372	207	0	.329	.374	.396	52	0	.192	.259	.250	335	1	.340	.394	.406	149	0	.302	.363	.342	68	0	.368	.427	.412
1987 NY-N	300	1	.250	.307	.287	169	0	.284	.322	.314	131	1	.206	.288	.252	35	0	.086	.158	.086	265	1	.272	.326	.313	116	0	.328	.388	.345	35	0	.200	.349	.200
1988 NY-N	294	0	.303	.388	.344	144	0	.340	.424	.396	150	0	.267	.353	.293	35	0	.257	.341	.286	259	0	.309	.395	.351	106	0	.274	.378	.321	43	0	.256	.319	.279
1989 Min-A	299	1	.231	.306	.284	150	0	.247	.343	.293	149	1	.215	.267	.275	57	0	.281	.349	.351	242	1	.219	.296	.269	116	0	.259	.351	.319	33	0	.273	.400	.273
1990 Pit-N	315	2	.292	.374	.397	154	0	.279	.364	.370	161	2	.304	.384	.422	31	0	.194	.359	.226	284	2	.303	.376	.415	80	0	.350	.461	.463	37	0	.162	.295	.270
1991 Phi-N	185	0	.243	.344	.308	82	0	.280	.367	.390	103	0	.214	.325	.243	24	0	.083	.148	.125	161	0	.267	.372	.335	70	0	.243	.349	.329	50	0	.200	.300	.280
1992 Phi-N	48	0	.271	.352	.292	17	0	.412	.474	.471	31	0	.194	.286	.194	1	0	.000	.000	.000	47	0	.277	.358	.298	27	0	.370	.433	.407	21	0	.333	.391	.381
1993 Sea-A	29	0	.138	.167	.138	16	0	.188	.188	.188	13	0	.077	.143	.077	1	0	.000	.000	.000	28	0	.138	.167	.138	13	0	.077	.143	.077	5	0	.200	.333	.200
TOTALS	2813	7	.276	.345	.337	1366	1	.288	.361	.348	1447	6	.264	.330	.326	403	0	.169	.306	.206	2410	7	.293	.359	.359	1021	2	.290	.369	.346	441	1	.265	.350	.315

Carlos Baerga BB/TR

YEAR TM/L	TOTAL					HOME					AWAY					LEFT					RIGHT					ON-BASE					LATE/CLOSE				
	AB	HR	AVG	OBP	SLG	AB	HR	AVG	OBP	SLG	AB	HR	AVG	OBP	SLG	AB	HR	AVG	OBP	SLG	AB	HR	AVG	OBP	SLG	AB	HR	AVG	OBP	SLG	AB	HR	AVG	OBP	SLG
1990 Cle-A	312	7	.260	.300	.394	150	3	.300	.348	.440	162	4	.222	.254	.352	103	2	.243	.257	.340	209	5	.268	.320	.421	130	3	.262	.289	.431	60	1	.250	.333	.383
1991 Cle-A	593	11	.288	.328	.455	299	2	.291	.337	.368	294	9	.286	.355	.428	188	2	.329	.376	.416	405	9	.267	.305	.391	250	5	.312	.379	.436	107	2	.224	.284	.327
1992 Cle-A	657	20	.312	.354	.455	329	8	.353	.392	.486	328	11	.271	.318	.424	168	4	.375	.387	.500	489	16	.290	.343	.440	295	10	.339	.382	.485	126	2	.317	.370	.437
1993 Cle-A	624	21	.321	.355	.486	299	8	.331	.356	.468	325	13	.311	.353	.502	219	6	.315	.345	.447	405	15	.323	.360	.506	291	10	.340	.377	.509	96	3	.292	.358	.406
1994 Cle-A	442	19	.314	.333	.525	193	8	.290	.311	.503	249	11	.333	.350	.542	161	8	.261	.284	.472	281	11	.345	.360	.555	205	10	.298	.318	.537	68	2	.279	.324	.397
TOTALS	2628	78	.303	.342	.454	1270	30	.317	.353	.451	1358	48	.289	.333	.457	839	22	.300	.345	.459	1789	56	.300	.345	.483	1171	38	.318	.359	.483	457	10	.276	.336	.392

Jeff Bagwell BR/TR

YEAR TM/L	TOTAL					HOME					AWAY					LEFT					RIGHT					ON-BASE					LATE/CLOSE				
	AB	HR	AVG	OBP	SLG	AB	HR	AVG	OBP	SLG	AB	HR	AVG	OBP	SLG	AB	HR	AVG	OBP	SLG	AB	HR	AVG	OBP	SLG	AB	HR	AVG	OBP	SLG	AB	HR	AVG	OBP	SLG
1991 Hou-N	554	15	.294	.387	.437	274	6	.296	.392	.431	280	9	.293	.382	.443	206	7	.320	.417	.471	348	8	.279	.369	.417	252	10	.298	.391	.464	86	2	.360	.481	.547
1992 Hou-N	586	18	.273	.357	.432	294	8	.259	.355	.432	292	10	.288	.382	.455	210	10	.290	.394	.524	376	8	.263	.354	.399	268	7	.269	.380	.410	99	8	.354	.492	.677
1993 Hou-N	535	20	.320	.388	.516	267	9	.330	.409	.509	268	11	.310	.365	.522	179	10	.318	.408	.592	356	10	.320	.376	.478	241	7	.336	.409	.510	84	2	.226	.290	.357
1994 Hou-N	400	39	.368	.451	.750	201	23	.373	.459	.816	199	16	.362	.443	.683	105	18	.457	.544	1.095	295	21	.336	.418	.627	192	17	.344	.449	.698	50	2	.280	.429	.480
TOTALS	2075	92	.309	.394	.520	1036	46	.309	.399	.526	1039	46	.309	.390	.513	700	45	.331	.427	.611	1375	47	.297	.377	.473	953	41	.308	.404	.508	319	14	.310	.430	.527

Harold Baines BL/TL

YEAR TM/L	TOTAL					HOME					AWAY					LEFT					RIGHT					ON-BASE					LATE/CLOSE				
	AB	HR	AVG	OBP	SLG	AB	HR	AVG	OBP	SLG	AB	HR	AVG	OBP	SLG	AB	HR	AVG	OBP	SLG	AB	HR	AVG	OBP	SLG	AB	HR	AVG	OBP	SLG	AB	HR	AVG	OBP	SLG
1984 Chi-A	569	29	.304	.361	.541	261	16	.330	.385	.582	308	13	.282	.342	.506	198	10	.278	.318	.515	371	19	.318	.384	.555	256	16	.320	.383	.602	79	4	.215	.311	.405
1985 Chi-A	640	22	.309	.348	.467	315	13	.283	.324	.463	325	9	.335	.371	.471	217	6	.341	.368	.465	423	16	.293	.338	.468	309	13	.337	.370	.521	83	4	.349	.413	.590
1986 Chi-A	570	21	.296	.338	.465	275	8	.313	.372	.491	295	13	.264	.306	.441	206	2	.262	.297	.354	364	18	.316	.361	.527	202	8	.282	.317	.490	90	7	.311	.380	.567
1987 Chi-A	505	20	.293	.352	.479	253	12	.312	.353	.538	252	8	.274	.351	.421	181	6	.254	.308	.409	324	14	.315	.376	.519	216	13	.338	.396	.616	78	1	.308	.372	.410
1988 Chi-A	599	13	.277	.347	.411	295	5	.281	.369	.424	304	8	.273	.325	.398	190	2	.253	.316	.358	409	11	.289	.361	.435	251	5	.287	.372	.418	100	4	.340	.436	.560
1989 Chi-A	333	13	.321	.423	.505	165	4	.291	.411	.455	168	9	.351	.436	.554	120	3	.250	.348	.367	213	10	.362	.463	.582	154	4	.338	.459	.494	46	2	.261	.370	.457

YEAR	TM/L	TOT AB	HR	AVG	OBP	SLG	HOME AB	HR	AVG	OBP	SLG	AWAY AB	HR	AVG	OBP	SLG	LEFT AB	HR	AVG	OBP	SLG	RIGHT AB	HR	AVG	OBP	SLG	ON-BASE AB	HR	AVG	OBP	SLG	LATE/CLOSE AB	HR	AVG	OBP	SLG
1989	Tex-A	172	3	.285	.333	.390	82	1	.305	.360	.427	90	2	.267	.309	.356	36	1	.306	.342	.444	136	2	.279	.331	.375	81	2	.259	.307	.370	30	1	.167	.265	.300
1990	Tex-A	321	13	.290	.377	.449	157	6	.287	.363	.420	164	7	.293	.391	.476	83	3	.241	.332	.373	238	10	.307	.399	.475	146	2	.260	.369	.322	51	3	.353	.492	.569
1990	Oak-A	94	3	.266	.381	.415	43	3	.256	.345	.488	51	0	.275	.413	.353	8	0	.375	.462	.500	86	3	.256	.371	.407	52	0	.269	.354	.308	8	0	.500	.600	.750
1991	Oak-A	488	20	.295	.383	.473	227	11	.264	.358	.458	261	9	.322	.406	.487	83	4	.301	.348	.506	405	16	.294	.390	.467	226	11	.314	.412	.522	73	3	.205	.333	.370
1992	Oak-A	478	16	.253	.331	.391	231	10	.277	.346	.442	247	6	.231	.318	.344	53	1	.245	.311	.302	425	15	.254	.334	.402	205	12	.307	.373	.522	63	2	.206	.296	.317
1993	Bal-A	416	20	.313	.390	.510	197	12	.345	.431	.584	219	8	.283	.352	.443	96	4	.260	.330	.427	320	16	.328	.408	.534	188	9	.340	.427	.543	54	2	.278	.349	.463
1994	Bal-A	326	16	.294	.356	.485	152	11	.316	.377	.566	174	5	.276	.337	.414	51	1	.176	.208	.255	275	15	.316	.382	.527	159	4	.270	.333	.390	44	0	.295	.380	.364
TOTALS		5511	209	.294	.361	.466	2653	112	.300	.368	.489	2858	97	.288	.354	.444	1522	44	.271	.323	.411	3989	165	.302	.375	.487	2485	99	.312	.383	.493	799	33	.284	.375	.467

■ Steve Balboni BR/TR

YEAR	TM/L	TOT AB	HR	AVG	OBP	SLG	HOME AB	HR	AVG	OBP	SLG	AWAY AB	HR	AVG	OBP	SLG	LEFT AB	HR	AVG	OBP	SLG	RIGHT AB	HR	AVG	OBP	SLG	ON-BASE AB	HR	AVG	OBP	SLG	LATE/CLOSE AB	HR	AVG	OBP	SLG
1984	KC-A	438	28	.244	.320	.498	218	10	.216	.280	.431	220	18	.273	.357	.564	152	10	.270	.366	.507	286	18	.231	.294	.493	194	11	.268	.344	.510	64	4	.281	.370	.531
1985	KC-A	600	36	.243	.307	.477	304	17	.253	.308	.497	296	19	.233	.305	.456	164	8	.220	.312	.421	436	28	.252	.325	.485	260	15	.262	.325	.485	102	8	.284	.360	.598
1986	KC-A	512	29	.229	.286	.451	251	10	.203	.264	.386	261	19	.253	.309	.513	134	12	.276	.370	.590	378	17	.212	.255	.402	233	12	.227	.271	.425	96	4	.198	.218	.365
1987	KC-A	386	24	.207	.273	.427	190	8	.189	.255	.347	196	16	.224	.290	.505	103	6	.194	.265	.379	283	18	.212	.276	.445	190	11	.216	.262	.442	62	5	.161	.185	.403
1988	KC-A	63	2	.143	.156	.270	31	1	.194	.219	.355	32	1	.094	.094	.188	19	2	.158	.158	.474	21	0	.250	.250	.500	10	0	.300	.300	.300	10	0	.300	.300	.300
1988	Sea-A	350	21	.251	.298	.480	184	14	.245	.296	.527	166	7	.259	.299	.428	120	6	.225	.273	.433	230	15	.265	.310	.504	179	11	.246	.294	.486	53	3	.245	.322	.453
1989	NY-A	300	17	.237	.296	.460	127	7	.236	.296	.425	173	10	.237	.297	.486	194	13	.247	.296	.505	106	4	.217	.298	.377	170	10	.259	.313	.500	44	2	.273	.327	.432
1990	NY-A	266	17	.192	.291	.406	123	8	.211	.315	.447	143	9	.175	.270	.371	161	14	.211	.340	.497	105	3	.162	.205	.267	106	3	.226	.317	.349	64	4	.219	.329	.422
1993	Tex-A	5	0	.600	.600	.600	5	0	.600	.600	.600	0	0	—	—	—	4	0	.500	.500	.500	1	0	.000	.000	.000	1	0	.000	.000	.000	0	0	—	—	—
TOTALS		2920	174	.230	.295	.457	1433	75	.224	.286	.438	1487	99	.236	.302	.475	1072	69	.232	.315	.468	1848	105	.229	.283	.450	1353	73	.245	.302	.463	495	30	.238	.302	.461

■ Bret Barberie BB/TR

YEAR	TM/L	TOT AB	HR	AVG	OBP	SLG	HOME AB	HR	AVG	OBP	SLG	AWAY AB	HR	AVG	OBP	SLG	LEFT AB	HR	AVG	OBP	SLG	RIGHT AB	HR	AVG	OBP	SLG	ON-BASE AB	HR	AVG	OBP	SLG	LATE/CLOSE AB	HR	AVG	OBP	SLG
1991	Mon-N	136	2	.353	.435	.515	41	2	.268	.354	.415	95	0	.389	.469	.558	37	1	.270	.364	.432	99	1	.384	.462	.545	51	0	.294	.426	.431	35	1	.314	.385	.486
1992	Mon-N	285	1	.232	.354	.281	132	0	.288	.414	.318	153	1	.183	.300	.248	67	0	.164	.287	.209	218	1	.252	.374	.303	107	0	.252	.374	.299	62	0	.226	.324	.290
1993	Fla-N	375	5	.277	.344	.371	199	2	.226	.305	.307	176	3	.335	.391	.443	109	2	.312	.370	.422	266	3	.263	.334	.350	153	2	.281	.351	.366	75	0	.320	.378	.373
1994	Fla-N	372	5	.301	.356	.406	177	2	.299	.358	.435	195	3	.303	.355	.379	119	0	.319	.362	.395	253	5	.292	.354	.411	165	1	.291	.354	.345	73	2	.301	.354	.438
TOTALS		1168	13	.283	.362	.377	549	6	.268	.353	.359	619	7	.296	.369	.393	332	3	.280	.349	.370	836	10	.283	.366	.379	476	3	.279	.366	.351	245	3	.290	.358	.388

■ Jesse Barfield BR/TR

YEAR	TM/L	TOT AB	HR	AVG	OBP	SLG	HOME AB	HR	AVG	OBP	SLG	AWAY AB	HR	AVG	OBP	SLG	LEFT AB	HR	AVG	OBP	SLG	RIGHT AB	HR	AVG	OBP	SLG	ON-BASE AB	HR	AVG	OBP	SLG	LATE/CLOSE AB	HR	AVG	OBP	SLG
1984	Tor-A	320	14	.284	.357	.466	166	10	.289	.344	.536	154	4	.279	.369	.390	187	6	.310	.382	.460	133	8	.248	.320	.474	147	5	.306	.388	.476	56	2	.286	.349	.411
1985	Tor-A	539	27	.289	.369	.536	255	15	.286	.368	.565	284	12	.292	.371	.511	207	9	.309	.379	.541	332	18	.277	.363	.533	229	11	.279	.366	.507	90	4	.233	.310	.456
1986	Tor-A	589	40	.289	.368	.559	291	16	.278	.371	.526	298	24	.299	.365	.591	148	9	.284	.397	.527	441	31	.290	.358	.569	254	13	.291	.381	.520	101	6	.308	.377	.542
1987	Tor-A	590	28	.263	.331	.458	302	11	.305	.371	.487	288	17	.219	.288	.427	177	9	.299	.380	.525	413	19	.247	.309	.429	261	8	.257	.342	.410	101	2	.267	.333	.376
1988	Tor-A	468	18	.244	.302	.425	236	12	.250	.309	.483	232	6	.237	.296	.366	165	9	.212	.284	.406	303	9	.261	.312	.436	190	5	.242	.330	.379	63	1	.175	.264	.286
1989	Tor-A	80	5	.200	.256	.438	29	1	.138	.219	.276	51	4	.235	.278	.529	34	3	.176	.243	.441	46	2	.217	.265	.435	41	3	.122	.182	.366	15	0	.000	.118	.000
1989	NY-A	441	18	.240	.360	.410	232	6	.254	.367	.392	209	12	.225	.352	.431	126	5	.254	.432	.413	315	13	.235	.326	.410	194	9	.247	.392	.438	60	3	.167	.351	.350
1990	NY-A	476	25	.246	.359	.456	239	12	.218	.314	.410	237	13	.274	.403	.502	162	13	.259	.394	.543	314	12	.239	.341	.411	189	11	.270	.404	.508	90	3	.211	.333	.333
1991	NY-A	284	17	.225	.312	.447	130	11	.231	.331	.538	154	6	.221	.294	.370	108	9	.315	.408	.602	176	8	.170	.250	.352	131	7	.214	.302	.435	44	2	.273	.429	.500
1992	NY-A	95	2	.137	.210	.221	54	2	.148	.190	.278	41	0	.122	.234	.146	33	1	.152	.282	.242	62	1	.129	.167	.210	51	1	.118	.207	.196	17	0	.059	.105	.059
TOTALS		3882	194	.258	.342	.468	1934	96	.262	.344	.480	1948	98	.255	.340	.456	1347	73	.275	.375	.493	2535	121	.249	.324	.455	1687	73	.257	.357	.451	643	23	.233	.330	.392

■ Marty Barrett BR/TR

YEAR	TM/L	TOT AB	HR	AVG	OBP	SLG	HOME AB	HR	AVG	OBP	SLG	AWAY AB	HR	AVG	OBP	SLG	LEFT AB	HR	AVG	OBP	SLG	RIGHT AB	HR	AVG	OBP	SLG	ON-BASE AB	HR	AVG	OBP	SLG	LATE/CLOSE AB	HR	AVG	OBP	SLG
1984	Bos-A	475	3	.303	.358	.383	225	1	.311	.381	.409	250	2	.296	.337	.360	161	1	.323	.345	.398	314	2	.293	.365	.376	195	1	.287	.341	.385	63	0	.270	.333	.333
1985	Bos-A	534	5	.266	.336	.343	265	3	.275	.341	.366	269	2	.257	.330	.320	164	0	.274	.356	.341	370	5	.262	.326	.343	231	2	.251	.332	.325	92	2	.261	.346	.359
1986	Bos-A	625	4	.286	.353	.381	302	4	.278	.350	.377	323	0	.294	.355	.384	171	4	.322	.418	.485	454	0	.273	.326	.341	242	3	.289	.376	.405	82	0	.317	.398	.439
1987	Bos-A	559	3	.293	.351	.351	274	2	.292	.350	.369	285	1	.295	.351	.333	150	2	.347	.412	.420	409	1	.274	.327	.325	206	2	.345	.426	.417	71	0	.239	.341	.268
1988	Bos-A	612	1	.283	.330	.337	308	1	.295	.338	.370	304	0	.270	.321	.303	181	0	.254	.288	.298	431	1	.295	.347	.353	310	1	.303	.343	.358	84	0	.226	.301	.286
1989	Bos-A	336	1	.256	.320	.318	167	0	.263	.335	.341	169	1	.249	.304	.296	104	0	.260	.325	.346	232	1	.254	.318	.306	154	0	.253	.318	.305	58	0	.328	.385	.345
1990	Bos-A	159	0	.226	.294	.252	68	0	.250	.346	.265	91	0	.209	.253	.242	37	0	.243	.383	.297	122	0	.221	.262	.238	71	0	.282	.329	.324	26	0	.346	.393	.385
1991	SD-N	16	1	.188	.235	.438	5	1	.400	.400	1.000	11	0	.091	.167	.182	6	1	.167	.167	.667	10	0	.200	.273	.300	7	1	.143	.143	.571	5	1	.200	.200	.800
TOTALS		3316	18	.280	.339	.350	1614	12	.286	.349	.371	1702	6	.274	.330	.330	974	8	.295	.359	.381	2342	10	.273	.331	.336	1416	10	.289	.355	.367	481	3	.274	.351	.347

■ Kevin Bass BB/TR

YEAR	TM/L	TOT AB	HR	AVG	OBP	SLG	HOME AB	HR	AVG	OBP	SLG	AWAY AB	HR	AVG	OBP	SLG	LEFT AB	HR	AVG	OBP	SLG	RIGHT AB	HR	AVG	OBP	SLG	ON-BASE AB	HR	AVG	OBP	SLG	LATE/CLOSE AB	HR	AVG	OBP	SLG
1984	Hou-N	331	2	.260	.279	.360	161	1	.292	.321	.404	170	1	.229	.238	.318	158	2	.228	.261	.329	173	0	.289	.297	.387	122	0	.311	.339	.410	73	1	.301	.311	.438
1985	Hou-N	539	16	.269	.315	.427	264	9	.250	.307	.402	275	7	.287	.323	.451	219	10	.311	.359	.553	320	6	.241	.284	.341	224	8	.259	.317	.429	84	3	.310	.370	.464
1986	Hou-N	591	20	.311	.357	.486	296	5	.314	.361	.426	295	15	.308	.353	.546	248	12	.323	.345	.540	343	8	.303	.365	.446	256	5	.293	.360	.426	102	3	.324	.395	.451
1987	Hou-N	592	19	.284	.344	.449	302	10	.285	.348	.454	290	9	.283	.340	.445	227	10	.282	.315	.507	365	9	.285	.361	.414	259	10	.282	.350	.463	104	4	.284	.353	.471
1988	Hou-N	541	14	.255	.314	.390	249	6	.277	.347	.390	292	8	.236	.286	.390	193	6	.316	.354	.503	348	8	.221	.293	.328	231	7	.277	.366	.420	101	2	.257	.315	.327
1989	Hou-N	313	5	.300	.357	.435	168	2	.298	.344	.417	145	3	.303	.370	.455	83	2	.265	.315	.434	230	3	.313	.373	.435	129	2	.341	.414	.512	53	2	.264	.365	.453
1990	SF-N	214	7	.252	.303	.402	115	3	.226	.282	.339	99	4	.283	.327	.475	90	5	.256	.302	.467	124	2	.250	.304	.355	96	4	.323	.377	.510	38	1	.263	.317	.368
1991	SF-N	361	10	.233	.307	.366	167	5	.210	.298	.335	194	5	.253	.315	.392	113	6	.239	.276	.442	248	4	.230	.320	.331	123	3	.242	.299	.339	65	2	.338	.358	.508
1992	SF-N	265	7	.268	.310	.411	148	5	.284	.323	.453	117	2	.248	.294	.359	93	4	.194	.200	.376	172	3	.308	.365	.430	124	3	.242	.299	.339	34	1	.206	.243	.412
1992	NY-N	137	2	.270	.303	.431	68	2	.309	.342	.544	69	0	.232	.264	.319	51	0	.275	.302	.471	86	2	.267	.304	.407	58	0	.172	.246	.224	34	1	.206	.243	.412
1993	Hou-N	229	3	.284	.359	.402	100	2	.270	.336	.400	129	1	.295	.377	.403	80	2	.225	.303	.412	149	1	.315	.389	.396	104	2	.327	.397	.500	62	0	.226	.314	.258
1994	Hou-N	203	6	.310	.393	.483	89	3	.360	.453	.584	114	3	.272	.344	.404	69	3	.420	.481	.652	134	3	.254	.348	.396	97	3	.351	.458	.526	40	2	.350	.413	.575
TOTALS		4316	111	.275	.330	.423	2127	52	.279	.337	.419	2189	59	.272	.324	.426	1624	62	.283	.322	.483	2692	49	.271	.334	.387	1856	47	.282	.354	.427	822	23	.283	.344	.422

■ Don Baylor BR/TR

YEAR	TM/L	TOT AB	HR	AVG	OBP	SLG	HOME AB	HR	AVG	OBP	SLG	AWAY AB	HR	AVG	OBP	SLG	LEFT AB	HR	AVG	OBP	SLG	RIGHT AB	HR	AVG	OBP	SLG	ON-BASE AB	HR	AVG	OBP	SLG	LATE/CLOSE AB	HR	AVG	OBP	SLG
1984	NY-A	493	27	.262	.341	.489	223	10	.247	.325	.430	270	17	.274	.354	.537	188	9	.282	.366	.473	305	18	.249	.326	.498	272	13	.265	.343	.474	102	7	.275	.318	.569
1985	NY-A	477	23	.231	.300	.430	231	12	.216	.315	.433	246	11	.244	.345	.427	193	11	.254	.377	.492	284	12	.215	.265	.371	215	11	.265	.371	.493	81	6	.259	.295	.506
1986	Bos-A	585	31	.238	.344	.439	279	9	.233	.370	.376	306	22	.242	.317	.497	152	5	.230	.359	.388	433	26	.240	.338	.457	289	15	.221	.345	.422	79	5	.253	.352	.494
1987	Bos-A	339	16	.239	.355	.404	151	10	.272	.387	.483	188	6	.213	.327	.340	118	6	.237	.313	.390	221	10	.240	.375	.412	160	8	.262	.383	.450	59	1	.203	.338	.271
1987	Min-A	49	0	.286	.397	.306	32	0	.250	.314	.281	17	0	.353	.522	.353	17	0	.471	.591	.529	32	0	.188	.278	.188	22	0	.364	.462	.409	14	0	.214	.214	.214
1988	Oak-A	264	7	.220	.332	.326	110	2	.200	.268	.273	154	5	.234	.374	.364	123	1	.220	.305	.285	141	6	.220	.355	.362	105	3	.305	.424	.419	46	2	.217	.357	.370
TOTALS		2207	104	.241	.342	.426	1026	43	.235	.339	.403	1181	61	.246	.344	.447	791	32	.253	.356	.421	1416	72	.234	.334	.429	1063	50	.259	.366	.453	381	21	.247	.326	.457

■ Buddy Bell BR/TR

YEAR	TM/L	TOT AB	HR	AVG	OBP	SLG	HOME AB	HR	AVG	OBP	SLG	AWAY AB	HR	AVG	OBP	SLG	LEFT AB	HR	AVG	OBP	SLG	RIGHT AB	HR	AVG	OBP	SLG	ON-BASE AB	HR	AVG	OBP	SLG	LATE/CLOSE AB	HR	AVG	OBP	SLG
1984	Tex-A	553	11	.315	.382	.458	271	6	.310	.375	.458	282	5	.319	.389	.457	152	4	.336	.412	.513	401	7	.307	.370	.436	249	6	.357	.423	.474	92	2	.315	.389	.435
1985	Tex-A	313	4	.236	.308	.335	155	2	.226	.311	.310	158	2	.247	.305	.361	76	0	.289	.356	.382	237	4	.219	.292	.321	162	0	.247	.311	.321	50	1	.280	.333	.440
1985	Cin-N	247	6	.219	.311	.368	118	4	.246	.323	.466	129	2	.194	.300	.279	72	1	.250	.321	.361	175	5	.206	.307	.371	118	5	.246	.326	.492	43	0	.093	.149	.116
1986	Cin-N	568	20	.278	.362	.445	276	14	.308	.387	.525	292	6	.250	.339	.370	174	8	.270	.348	.471	394	12	.282	.368	.434	247	11	.283	.369	.486	97	2	.320	.417	.454
1987	Cin-N	522	17	.284	.369	.420	262	8	.298	.395	.435	260	9	.269	.342	.415	142	7	.261	.367	.430	380	10	.292	.370	.454	216	8	.282	.359	.454	82	3	.280	.352	.476
1988	Cin-N	54	0	.185	.270	.185	25	0	.200	.333	.200	29	0	.172	.212	.172	8	0	.125	.222	.125	46	0	.196	.278	.196	29	0	.172	.257	.172	7	0	.143	.222	.143
1988	Hou-N	269	7	.253	.301	.375	124	1	.234	.269	.315	145	6	.269	.327	.428	83	2	.253	.291	.386	186	5	.253	.306	.371	124	2	.274	.331	.379	56	2	.196	.224	.339
1989	Tex-A	82	0	.183	.247	.232	49	0	.224	.309	.265	33	0	.121	.147	.182	49	0	.163	.212	.224	33	0	.212	.297	.242	37	0	.108	.175	.108	10	0	.200	.200	.200
TOTALS		2608	65	.269	.345	.404	1280	35	.278	.356	.424	1328	30	.260	.334	.385	756	22	.271	.351	.423	1852	43	.268	.342	.396	1182	28	.281	.356	.425	437	10	.263	.333	.394

■ Derek Bell BR/TR

YEAR	TM/L	TOT AB	HR	AVG	OBP	SLG	HOME AB	HR	AVG	OBP	SLG	AWAY AB	HR	AVG	OBP	SLG	LEFT AB	HR	AVG	OBP	SLG	RIGHT AB	HR	AVG	OBP	SLG	ON-BASE AB	HR	AVG	OBP	SLG	LATE/CLOSE AB	HR	AVG	OBP	SLG
1991	Tor-A	28	0	.143	.314	.143	15	0	.067	.222	.067	13	0	.231	.412	.231	20	0	.150	.292	.150	8	0	.125	.364	.125	9	0	.111	.333	.111	7	0	.286	.500	.286
1992	Tor-A	161	2	.242	.324	.354	84	2	.167	.278	.298	77	0	.325	.376	.416	47	2	.255	.333	.489	114	0	.237	.320	.298	64	0	.281	.365	.391	21	1	.286	.360	.429
1993	SD-N	542	21	.262	.303	.417	274	12	.252	.309	.416	268	9	.272	.296	.418	177	11	.299	.342	.520	365	10	.244	.284	.367	236	11	.288	.341	.470	101	2	.218	.288	.297
1994	SD-N	434	14	.311	.354	.454	202	8	.317	.381	.480	232	6	.306	.329	.431	117	4	.299	.369	.427	317	10	.315	.348	.464	226	7	.305	.361	.442	71	2	.239	.284	.366
TOTALS		1165	37	.275	.325	.415	575	22	.257	.327	.412	590	15	.292	.323	.419	361	17	.285	.347	.465	804	20	.270	.315	.393	535	18	.292	.352	.443	200	5	.235	.305	.335

■ Jay Bell BR/TR

YEAR	TM/L	TOT AB	HR	AVG	OBP	SLG	HOME AB	HR	AVG	OBP	SLG	AWAY AB	HR	AVG	OBP	SLG	LEFT AB	HR	AVG	OBP	SLG	RIGHT AB	HR	AVG	OBP	SLG	ON-BASE AB	HR	AVG	OBP	SLG	LATE/CLOSE AB	HR	AVG	OBP	SLG
1986	Cle-A	14	1	.357	.438	.714	4	0	.250	.400	.500	10	1	.400	.455	.800	9	0	.444	.545	.667	5	1	.200	.200	.800	6	0	.500	.625	.833	2	0	.000	.000	.000
1987	Cle-A	125	2	.216	.269	.352	63	1	.222	.300	.381	62	1	.210	.234	.323	38	1	.289	.357	.500	87	1	.184	.228	.287	62	2	.242	.277	.387	14	0	.071	.133	.071
1988	Cle-A	211	2	.218	.289	.280	117	2	.197	.267	.291	94	0	.245	.317	.266	40	0	.350	.386	.425	171	2	.187	.267	.246	94	1	.234	.288	.298	26	0	.192	.276	.192
1989	Pit-N	271	2	.258	.307	.351	141	1	.255	.303	.340	130	1	.262	.312	.362	107	1	.271	.331	.355	164	1	.250	.291	.348	108	0	.306	.325	.435	48	0	.188	.231	.313
1990	Pit-N	583	7	.254	.329	.362	287	1	.261	.336	.366	296	6	.247	.321	.358	251	2	.255	.358	.342	332	5	.253	.307	.377	233	3	.292	.350	.425	78	0	.308	.374	.359
1991	Pit-N	608	16	.270	.330	.428	303	7	.281	.332	.446	305	9	.259	.327	.410	194	6	.289	.368	.500	414	10	.261	.311	.394	254	5	.315	.370	.469	92	3	.283	.365	.457
1992	Pit-N	632	9	.264	.326	.383	302	5	.278	.352	.411	330	4	.252	.301	.358	238	1	.324	.396	.450	394	8	.228	.282	.343	222	3	.333	.393	.477	115	2	.278	.336	.417
1993	Pit-N	604	9	.310	.392	.437	286	3	.322	.424	.441	318	6	.299	.362	.434	190	3	.342	.449	.484	414	6	.295	.364	.415	227	0	.300	.403	.379	97	0	.268	.383	.320

YEAR	TM/L	TOTAL AB	HR	AVG	OBP	SLG	HOME AB	HR	AVG	OBP	SLG	AWAY AB	HR	AVG	OBP	SLG	LEFT AB	HR	AVG	OBP	SLG	RIGHT AB	HR	AVG	OBP	SLG	ON-BASE AB	HR	AVG	OBP	SLG	LATE/CLOSE AB	HR	AVG	OBP	SLG
1994	Pit-N	424	9	.276	.353	.441	224	3	.277	.351	.415	200	6	.275	.355	.470	106	4	.377	.432	.660	318	5	.242	.327	.368	159	2	.327	.392	.459	71	2	.296	.370	.479
TOTALS		3472	57	.268	.337	.395	1727	23	.273	.347	.397	1745	34	.263	.327	.393	1173	18	.311	.390	.462	2299	39	.246	.309	.361	1365	16	.304	.367	.430	543	7	.265	.342	.376

■ George Bell BR/TR

YEAR	TM/L	TOTAL AB	HR	AVG	OBP	SLG	HOME AB	HR	AVG	OBP	SLG	AWAY AB	HR	AVG	OBP	SLG	LEFT AB	HR	AVG	OBP	SLG	RIGHT AB	HR	AVG	OBP	SLG	ON-BASE AB	HR	AVG	OBP	SLG	LATE/CLOSE AB	HR	AVG	OBP	SLG
1984	Tor-A	606	26	.292	.326	.498	294	12	.320	.353	.534	312	14	.266	.301	.465	210	11	.310	.348	.557	396	15	.283	.314	.467	286	9	.308	.330	.479	104	6	.346	.389	.577
1985	Tor-A	607	28	.275	.327	.479	286	10	.255	.321	.430	321	18	.293	.333	.523	214	11	.252	.314	.463	393	17	.288	.335	.489	281	11	.253	.297	.441	91	4	.330	.396	.549
1986	Tor-A	641	31	.309	.349	.532	300	15	.327	.375	.567	341	16	.293	.326	.501	179	10	.330	.363	.553	462	21	.301	.344	.524	306	11	.317	.356	.507	118	5	.263	.290	.466
1987	Tor-A	610	47	.308	.352	.605	302	19	.291	.346	.543	308	28	.325	.357	.666	175	16	.343	.385	.686	435	31	.294	.339	.572	300	21	.303	.355	.563	95	7	.305	.355	.579
1988	Tor-A	614	24	.269	.304	.446	304	9	.296	.329	.461	310	15	.242	.280	.432	196	10	.270	.296	.485	418	14	.268	.308	.428	289	12	.308	.333	.481	85	5	.259	.300	.471
1989	Tor-A	613	18	.297	.330	.458	281	8	.306	.350	.466	332	10	.289	.312	.452	178	9	.287	.323	.517	435	9	.301	.333	.434	280	7	.304	.328	.450	97	3	.330	.356	.515
1990	Tor-A	562	21	.265	.303	.422	274	11	.255	.299	.420	288	10	.274	.306	.424	149	5	.248	.315	.389	413	16	.271	.298	.433	255	8	.255	.302	.400	95	5	.191	.245	.382
1991	Chi-N	558	25	.285	.323	.468	288	9	.267	.294	.413	270	16	.304	.354	.526	208	15	.288	.341	.543	350	10	.283	.313	.423	255	8	.278	.301	.427	100	5	.260	.312	.460
1992	Chi-N	627	25	.255	.294	.418	326	16	.261	.293	.442	301	9	.249	.295	.392	142	7	.310	.355	.514	485	18	.239	.276	.390	355	14	.276	.310	.442	99	2	.232	.283	.323
1993	Chi-N	410	13	.217	.243	.363	201	7	.224	.249	.388	209	6	.211	.238	.340	109	3	.193	.217	.312	301	10	.226	.252	.382	197	7	.244	.258	.406	53	1	.226	.250	.321
TOTALS		5848	258	.279	.318	.473	2856	116	.282	.324	.477	2992	142	.277	.312	.477	1760	97	.286	.330	.511	4088	161	.276	.313	.457	2804	108	.286	.320	.463	931	43	.277	.321	.472

■ Albert Belle BR/TR

YEAR	TM/L	TOTAL AB	HR	AVG	OBP	SLG	HOME AB	HR	AVG	OBP	SLG	AWAY AB	HR	AVG	OBP	SLG	LEFT AB	HR	AVG	OBP	SLG	RIGHT AB	HR	AVG	OBP	SLG	ON-BASE AB	HR	AVG	OBP	SLG	LATE/CLOSE AB	HR	AVG	OBP	SLG
1989	Cle-A	218	7	.225	.269	.394	115	3	.243	.276	.391	103	4	.204	.261	.398	58	3	.259	.308	.448	160	4	.213	.254	.375	97	4	.268	.291	.485	39	1	.256	.286	.385
1990	Cle-A	23	1	.174	.208	.304	13	1	.231	.286	.462	10	0	.100	.100	.100	9	1	.222	.222	.556	14	0	.143	.200	.143	14	1	.143	.143	.357	2	0	.000	.333	.000
1991	Cle-A	461	28	.282	.323	.540	236	8	.254	.294	.419	225	20	.311	.352	.667	132	8	.288	.312	.568	329	20	.280	.327	.529	234	15	.321	.362	.598	66	2	.197	.280	.333
1992	Cle-A	585	34	.260	.320	.477	285	15	.267	.331	.481	300	19	.253	.310	.473	138	8	.254	.307	.500	447	26	.262	.325	.470	282	18	.252	.318	.486	106	5	.236	.267	.396
1993	Cle-A	594	38	.290	.370	.552	271	20	.306	.399	.583	323	18	.276	.344	.526	162	12	.327	.412	.617	432	26	.275	.353	.528	287	17	.300	.391	.547	81	7	.333	.444	.679
1994	Cle-A	412	36	.357	.438	.714	179	21	.413	.509	.894	233	15	.313	.381	.575	120	9	.367	.480	.675	292	27	.353	.419	.729	193	17	.321	.430	.648	67	6	.358	.450	.657
TOTALS		2293	144	.285	.350	.542	1099	68	.295	.366	.551	1194	76	.276	.336	.534	619	41	.302	.373	.575	1674	103	.279	.342	.530	1107	72	.291	.363	.552	361	21	.274	.349	.493

■ Rafael Belliard BR/TR

YEAR	TM/L	TOTAL AB	HR	AVG	OBP	SLG	HOME AB	HR	AVG	OBP	SLG	AWAY AB	HR	AVG	OBP	SLG	LEFT AB	HR	AVG	OBP	SLG	RIGHT AB	HR	AVG	OBP	SLG	ON-BASE AB	HR	AVG	OBP	SLG	LATE/CLOSE AB	HR	AVG	OBP	SLG
1984	Pit-N	22	0	.227	.227	.227	13	0	.231	.231	.231	9	0	.222	.222	.222	4	0	.000	.000	.000	18	0	.278	.278	.278	11	0	.182	.182	.182	6	0	.167	.167	.167
1985	Pit-N	20	0	.200	.200	.200	14	0	.143	.143	.143	6	0	.333	.333	.333	2	0	.000	.000	.000	18	0	.222	.222	.222	8	0	.250	.250	.250	1	0	1.000	1.000	1.000
1986	Pit-N	309	0	.233	.298	.262	144	0	.208	.278	.236	165	0	.255	.315	.285	122	0	.246	.298	.246	187	0	.225	.298	.273	138	0	.225	.285	.268	30	0	.167	.324	.200
1987	Pit-N	203	1	.207	.286	.271	91	0	.187	.299	.220	112	1	.223	.275	.313	75	0	.213	.306	.293	128	1	.203	.275	.258	92	1	.207	.302	.304	26	0	.231	.310	.231
1988	Pit-N	286	0	.213	.288	.241	136	0	.213	.272	.272	150	0	.213	.302	.213	89	0	.225	.303	.270	197	0	.208	.281	.228	119	0	.244	.318	.277	39	0	.205	.279	.256
1989	Pit-N	154	0	.214	.253	.240	72	0	.250	.250	.208	82	0	.220	.256	.268	36	0	.306	.306	.333	118	0	.186	.238	.212	66	0	.288	.319	.333	19	0	.421	.450	.421
1990	Pit-N	54	0	.204	.283	.259	31	0	.161	.257	.226	23	0	.261	.320	.304	21	0	.190	.261	.286	33	0	.212	.297	.242	20	0	.250	.318	.400	4	0	.000	.333	.000
1991	Atl-N	353	0	.249	.296	.286	173	0	.254	.299	.312	180	0	.244	.294	.261	95	0	.242	.287	.263	258	0	.252	.300	.295	148	0	.270	.310	.311	44	0	.227	.261	.227
1992	Atl-N	285	0	.211	.255	.239	125	0	.200	.259	.216	160	0	.219	.251	.256	61	0	.197	.210	.197	224	0	.214	.267	.250	120	0	.208	.252	.208	35	0	.229	.229	.257
1993	Atl-N	79	0	.228	.291	.291	38	0	.184	.244	.211	41	0	.268	.333	.366	17	0	.118	.167	.118	62	0	.258	.324	.339	41	0	.195	.267	.268	10	0	.100	.100	.100
1994	Atl-N	120	0	.242	.264	.317	38	0	.184	.225	.237	82	0	.268	.282	.354	31	0	.355	.355	.452	89	0	.202	.234	.270	45	0	.267	.306	.422	10	0	.200	.273	.200
TOTALS		1885	1	.224	.280	.263	875	0	.210	.272	.247	1010	1	.237	.288	.276	553	0	.233	.284	.266	1332	1	.221	.279	.261	808	1	.238	.294	.288	224	0	.223	.287	.241

■ Juan Beniquez BR/TR

YEAR	TM/L	TOTAL AB	HR	AVG	OBP	SLG	HOME AB	HR	AVG	OBP	SLG	AWAY AB	HR	AVG	OBP	SLG	LEFT AB	HR	AVG	OBP	SLG	RIGHT AB	HR	AVG	OBP	SLG	ON-BASE AB	HR	AVG	OBP	SLG	LATE/CLOSE AB	HR	AVG	OBP	SLG
1984	Cal-A	354	8	.336	.370	.452	203	5	.399	.433	.527	151	3	.252	.288	.351	163	3	.368	.386	.472	191	5	.309	.357	.435	136	4	.316	.347	.434	64	1	.313	.343	.375
1985	Cal-A	411	8	.304	.364	.418	214	6	.327	.386	.467	197	2	.279	.340	.365	174	6	.356	.414	.540	237	2	.266	.327	.329	179	6	.313	.380	.453	78	0	.231	.294	.269
1986	Bal-A	343	6	.300	.372	.397	154	4	.273	.349	.364	189	2	.323	.392	.423	128	3	.336	.412	.453	215	3	.279	.348	.365	160	2	.294	.360	.369	65	2	.415	.446	.538
1987	KC-A	174	3	.236	.282	.328	72	0	.250	.300	.292	102	3	.225	.269	.353	57	1	.228	.254	.351	117	2	.239	.295	.316	82	1	.280	.322	.378	25	0	.280	.296	.280
1987	Tor-A	81	5	.284	.330	.556	40	2	.200	.238	.475	41	3	.366	.413	.634	59	5	.305	.354	.627	22	0	.227	.261	.364	40	3	.300	.326	.650	23	1	.174	.231	.391
1988	Tor-A	58	1	.293	.373	.379	27	1	.370	.452	.519	31	0	.226	.306	.258	53	1	.302	.377	.396	5	0	.200	.333	.200	29	1	.379	.472	.483	8	0	.500	.636	.500
TOTALS		1421	31	.301	.356	.417	710	18	.323	.376	.446	711	13	.280	.336	.387	634	19	.334	.384	.484	787	12	.274	.334	.362	626	17	.307	.362	.431	263	4	.304	.352	.380

■ Todd Benzinger BB/TR

YEAR	TM/L	TOTAL AB	HR	AVG	OBP	SLG	HOME AB	HR	AVG	OBP	SLG	AWAY AB	HR	AVG	OBP	SLG	LEFT AB	HR	AVG	OBP	SLG	RIGHT AB	HR	AVG	OBP	SLG	ON-BASE AB	HR	AVG	OBP	SLG	LATE/CLOSE AB	HR	AVG	OBP	SLG
1987	Bos-A	223	8	.278	.344	.444	106	5	.311	.390	.528	117	3	.248	.299	.368	80	2	.325	.371	.450	143	6	.252	.329	.441	104	6	.250	.341	.481	35	1	.200	.282	.286
1988	Bos-A	405	13	.254	.293	.425	204	6	.270	.315	.446	201	7	.239	.270	.403	104	1	.212	.259	.308	301	12	.269	.305	.465	200	6	.245	.278	.420	63	3	.317	.358	.556
1989	Cin-N	628	17	.245	.293	.381	306	6	.278	.327	.418	322	11	.214	.261	.345	231	7	.242	.283	.377	397	10	.247	.299	.383	264	7	.208	.272	.341	96	2	.167	.264	.250
1990	Cin-N	376	5	.253	.291	.340	190	4	.258	.296	.374	186	1	.247	.285	.306	172	2	.285	.306	.360	204	3	.225	.279	.324	173	1	.266	.306	.358	62	1	.210	.242	.306
1991	Cin-N	123	1	.187	.244	.268	78	1	.167	.195	.256	45	0	.222	.321	.289	49	1	.224	.264	.327	74	0	.162	.232	.230	58	0	.103	.194	.172	27	1	.148	.233	.333
1991	KC-A	293	2	.294	.338	.386	138	1	.326	.367	.457	155	1	.265	.311	.323	94	0	.266	.289	.309	199	2	.307	.359	.422	139	1	.302	.347	.403	54	0	.259	.355	.315
1992	LA-N	293	4	.239	.272	.348	143	1	.238	.275	.336	150	3	.240	.269	.360	126	1	.270	.282	.349	167	3	.216	.264	.347	122	3	.238	.263	.377	69	1	.246	.280	.362
1993	SF-N	177	6	.288	.332	.452	72	0	.194	.218	.222	105	6	.352	.409	.610	37	2	.486	.512	.730	140	4	.236	.280	.379	82	3	.207	.277	.354	47	0	.213	.240	.277
1994	SF-N	328	9	.265	.304	.399	155	5	.290	.343	.452	173	4	.243	.267	.353	98	1	.245	.292	.337	230	8	.274	.309	.426	126	0	.206	.255	.270	60	3	.333	.375	.533
TOTALS		2846	65	.257	.301	.385	1392	29	.268	.314	.404	1454	36	.246	.288	.367	991	17	.267	.301	.369	1855	48	.251	.300	.394	1268	27	.233	.286	.364	513	12	.236	.295	.359

■ Dave Bergman BL/TL

YEAR	TM/L	TOTAL AB	HR	AVG	OBP	SLG	HOME AB	HR	AVG	OBP	SLG	AWAY AB	HR	AVG	OBP	SLG	LEFT AB	HR	AVG	OBP	SLG	RIGHT AB	HR	AVG	OBP	SLG	ON-BASE AB	HR	AVG	OBP	SLG	LATE/CLOSE AB	HR	AVG	OBP	SLG
1984	Det-A	271	7	.273	.351	.417	133	4	.248	.342	.414	138	3	.297	.361	.420	23	0	.217	.250	.217	248	7	.278	.360	.435	126	3	.294	.354	.444	40	3	.375	.426	.700
1985	Det-A	140	3	.179	.250	.257	78	2	.167	.221	.256	62	1	.194	.286	.258	5	0	.200	.333	.200	135	4	.178	.247	.259	57	0	.140	.227	.158	42	1	.214	.261	.333
1986	Det-A	130	1	.231	.338	.315	61	0	.213	.360	.295	69	1	.246	.316	.333	8	0	.250	.500	.625	122	1	.230	.324	.295	54	1	.204	.328	.296	28	1	.179	.233	.286
1987	Det-A	172	6	.273	.379	.453	85	4	.306	.394	.482	87	2	.241	.364	.425	19	0	.263	.263	.263	153	6	.275	.390	.477	72	2	.264	.378	.389	30	2	.233	.314	.433
1988	Det-A	289	5	.294	.372	.394	127	4	.283	.394	.425	162	1	.302	.352	.370	17	0	.235	.278	.294	272	5	.298	.377	.401	119	3	.286	.355	.395	12	1	.242	.329	.339
1989	Det-A	385	7	.268	.345	.361	173	6	.249	.325	.382	212	1	.283	.361	.344	60	0	.200	.250	.233	325	7	.280	.361	.385	161	0	.292	.388	.342	59	0	.203	.288	.203
1990	Det-A	205	2	.258	.375	.366	109	1	.248	.354	.367	96	1	.313	.398	.365	13	0	.231	.286	.385	192	2	.281	.381	.365	99	1	.273	.345	.343	36	0	.194	.333	.222
1991	Det-A	194	7	.237	.351	.407	87	2	.218	.346	.322	107	5	.252	.355	.477	19	0	.053	.182	.105	175	7	.257	.368	.440	75	1	.280	.423	.387	37	1	.243	.326	.378
1992	Det-A	181	1	.232	.305	.265	93	1	.204	.262	.247	88	0	.261	.350	.284	14	0	.143	.250	.214	167	1	.240	.310	.269	78	0	.231	.303	.256	26	1	.192	.300	.308
TOTALS		1967	39	.259	.346	.368	946	24	.242	.337	.365	1021	15	.274	.355	.370	178	0	.197	.267	.253	1789	39	.265	.353	.379	841	11	.264	.354	.350	360	10	.233	.316	.350

■ Tony Bernazard BB/TR

YEAR	TM/L	TOTAL AB	HR	AVG	OBP	SLG	HOME AB	HR	AVG	OBP	SLG	AWAY AB	HR	AVG	OBP	SLG	LEFT AB	HR	AVG	OBP	SLG	RIGHT AB	HR	AVG	OBP	SLG	ON-BASE AB	HR	AVG	OBP	SLG	LATE/CLOSE AB	HR	AVG	OBP	SLG
1984	Cle-A	439	2	.221	.290	.287	207	1	.246	.325	.343	232	1	.198	.257	.237	135	2	.237	.321	.341	304	0	.214	.275	.263	182	1	.225	.283	.302	62	0	.145	.250	.161
1985	Cle-A	500	11	.274	.361	.404	246	4	.301	.383	.431	254	7	.248	.339	.378	128	0	.258	.364	.313	372	11	.280	.359	.435	225	2	.280	.381	.364	83	2	.277	.365	.422
1986	Cle-A	562	17	.301	.362	.456	286	9	.329	.384	.486	276	8	.272	.341	.424	151	5	.338	.419	.510	411	12	.287	.341	.436	224	5	.313	.372	.442	80	0	.250	.330	.363
1987	Cle-A	293	11	.239	.300	.399	153	3	.229	.276	.346	140	8	.250	.325	.457	68	3	.250	.292	.441	225	8	.236	.302	.387	107	2	.215	.315	.308	40	1	.250	.302	.400
1987	Oak-A	214	3	.266	.354	.383	74	0	.257	.382	.324	140	3	.271	.338	.414	71	1	.211	.349	.324	143	2	.294	.356	.413	85	1	.282	.382	.376	29	0	.310	.444	.448
1991	Det-A	12	0	.167	.167	.167	5	0	.200	.200	.200	7	0	.143	.143	.143	1	0	1.000	1.000	1.000	11	0	.091	.091	.091	6	0	.167	.167	.167	4	0	.000	.000	.000
TOTALS		2020	44	.263	.336	.389	971	17	.282	.354	.406	1049	27	.246	.319	.373	554	11	.269	.359	.392	1466	33	.261	.326	.387	829	11	.268	.348	.364	298	3	.238	.327	.346

■ Sean Berry BR/TR

YEAR	TM/L	TOTAL AB	HR	AVG	OBP	SLG	HOME AB	HR	AVG	OBP	SLG	AWAY AB	HR	AVG	OBP	SLG	LEFT AB	HR	AVG	OBP	SLG	RIGHT AB	HR	AVG	OBP	SLG	ON-BASE AB	HR	AVG	OBP	SLG	LATE/CLOSE AB	HR	AVG	OBP	SLG
1990	KC-A	23	0	.217	.280	.348	0	0	—	—	—	23	0	.217	.280	.348	13	0	.231	.286	.385	10	0	.200	.273	.300	7	0	.286	.444	.571	4	0	.250	.250	.250
1991	KC-A	60	0	.133	.212	.183	22	0	.136	.240	.227	38	0	.132	.195	.158	30	0	.167	.219	.200	30	0	.100	.206	.167	28	0	.107	.167	.143	7	0	.000	.000	.000
1992	Mon-N	57	1	.333	.345	.404	22	0	.409	.435	.455	35	1	.286	.286	.371	3	0	.667	.667	.667	54	1	.315	.327	.389	26	0	.423	.444	.462	14	0	.429	.429	.429
1993	Mon-N	299	14	.261	.348	.465	134	5	.261	.362	.410	165	9	.261	.335	.509	95	3	.232	.348	.379	204	11	.275	.347	.505	131	4	.214	.310	.366	61	0	.197	.254	.197
1994	Mon-N	320	11	.278	.347	.453	138	4	.283	.344	.457	182	7	.275	.350	.451	76	6	.316	.409	.579	244	5	.266	.327	.414	144	4	.264	.345	.417	57	1	.175	.230	.333
TOTALS		759	26	.262	.335	.430	316	9	.272	.351	.424	443	17	.255	.323	.436	217	9	.258	.353	.429	542	17	.264	.327	.430	336	8	.244	.326	.391	143	1	.203	.248	.266

■ Dante Bichette BR/TR

YEAR	TM/L	TOTAL AB	HR	AVG	OBP	SLG	HOME AB	HR	AVG	OBP	SLG	AWAY AB	HR	AVG	OBP	SLG	LEFT AB	HR	AVG	OBP	SLG	RIGHT AB	HR	AVG	OBP	SLG	ON-BASE AB	HR	AVG	OBP	SLG	LATE/CLOSE AB	HR	AVG	OBP	SLG
1988	Cal-A	46	0	.261	.240	.304	21	0	.238	.227	.333	25	0	.280	.250	.280	27	0	.296	.276	.370	19	0	.211	.190	.211	17	0	.235	.190	.235	8	0	.250	.200	.250
1989	Cal-A	138	3	.210	.240	.326	68	2	.206	.203	.338	70	1	.214	.273	.314	86	3	.221	.253	.395	52	0	.192	.218	.212	58	1	.241	.233	.379	26	0	.192	.185	.192
1990	Cal-A	349	15	.255	.292	.433	159	8	.258	.296	.447	190	7	.253	.289	.421	146	5	.274	.312	.445	203	10	.241	.278	.424	171	6	.222	.250	.363	59	3	.237	.279	.576
1991	Mil-A	445	15	.238	.272	.393	213	6	.249	.296	.399	232	9	.228	.249	.388	154	6	.253	.299	.429	291	9	.230	.257	.375	206	7	.243	.274	.403	88	3	.273	.297	.409
1992	Mil-A	387	5	.287	.318	.406	219	2	.288	.324	.397	168	3	.286	.310	.417	119	2	.286	.336	.437	268	3	.287	.309	.392	176	2	.267	.298	.392	66	0	.258	.290	.273
1993	Col-N	538	21	.310	.348	.526	260	11	.373	.408	.650	278	10	.252	.291	.410	119	4	.286	.346	.496	419	17	.317	.348	.535	239	10	.322	.361	.536	83	8	.313	.352	.675
1994	Col-N	484	27	.304	.334	.548	241	15	.353	.387	.614	243	12	.255	.281	.481	105	10	.400	.413	.848	379	17	.277	.313	.464	224	12	.299	.318	.549	66	5	.318	.366	.621
TOTALS		2387	86	.277	.310	.457	1132	45	.297	.332	.500	1255	41	.259	.289	.418	756	30	.286	.324	.496	1631	56	.273	.303	.438	1091	38	.272	.299	.450	396	19	.288	.322	.485

■ Craig Biggio BR/TR

YEAR	TM/L	TOTAL AB	HR	AVG	OBP	SLG	HOME AB	HR	AVG	OBP	SLG	AWAY AB	HR	AVG	OBP	SLG	LEFT AB	HR	AVG	OBP	SLG	RIGHT AB	HR	AVG	OBP	SLG	ON-BASE AB	HR	AVG	OBP	SLG	LATE/CLOSE AB	HR	AVG	OBP	SLG
1988	Hou-N	123	3	.211	.254	.350	55	1	.164	.207	.291	68	2	.250	.292	.397	39	2	.231	.268	.385	84	1	.202	.247	.333	40	0	.075	.159	.125	19	2	.316	.316	.737
1989	Hou-N	443	13	.257	.336	.402	219	6	.233	.323	.379	224	7	.281	.349	.424	122	1	.270	.352	.336	321	12	.252	.330	.427	190	5	.253	.335	.389	90	3	.311	.380	.522
1990	Hou-N	555	4	.276	.342	.348	277	2	.274	.338	.343	278	2	.277	.345	.353	188	2	.229	.316	.293	367	2	.306	.356	.378	244	1	.291	.363	.344	109	0	.193	.241	.229
1991	Hou-N	546	4	.295	.358	.374	277	0	.343	.401	.437	269	4	.245	.313	.309	186	1	.274	.346	.366	360	3	.306	.364	.378	229	1	.332	.391	.389	97	0	.258	.351	.289
1992	Hou-N	613	6	.277	.378	.369	303	3	.281	.384	.386	310	3	.274	.373	.352	218	3	.275	.410	.372	395	3	.278	.359	.367	171	1	.269	.404	.351	95	0	.263	.402	.295

YEAR	TM/L	TOTAL AB	HR	AVG	OBP	SLG	HOME AB	HR	AVG	OBP	SLG	AWAY AB	HR	AVG	OBP	SLG	LEFT AB	HR	AVG	OBP	SLG	RIGHT AB	HR	AVG	OBP	SLG	ON-BASE AB	HR	AVG	OBP	SLG	LATE/CLOSE AB	HR	AVG	OBP	SLG
1993	Hou-N	610	21	.287	.373	.474	295	8	.285	.389	.444	315	13	.289	.358	.502	183	8	.295	.408	.508	427	13	.283	.357	.459	190	4	.316	.408	.463	86	2	.244	.387	.372
1994	Hou-N	437	6	.318	.411	.483	220	4	.332	.422	.514	217	2	.304	.398	.452	109	0	.294	.439	.422	328	6	.326	.400	.503	172	2	.366	.437	.564	58	1	.328	.429	.534
TOTALS		3327	57	.282	.363	.404	1646	24	.287	.372	.411	1681	33	.277	.353	.397	1075	17	.269	.373	.380	2252	40	.288	.357	.416	1236	14	.297	.381	.402	554	8	.262	.358	.370

■ Jeff Blauser BR/TR

YEAR	TM/L	TOTAL AB	HR	AVG	OBP	SLG	HOME AB	HR	AVG	OBP	SLG	AWAY AB	HR	AVG	OBP	SLG	LEFT AB	HR	AVG	OBP	SLG	RIGHT AB	HR	AVG	OBP	SLG	ON-BASE AB	HR	AVG	OBP	SLG	LATE/CLOSE AB	HR	AVG	OBP	SLG
1987	Atl-N	165	2	.242	.328	.352	78	1	.295	.382	.462	87	1	.195	.278	.253	47	2	.277	.346	.511	118	0	.229	.321	.288	76	1	.276	.360	.382	17	0	.176	.300	.294
1988	Atl-N	67	2	.239	.268	.403	28	2	.286	.286	.571	39	0	.205	.256	.282	26	1	.308	.321	.462	41	1	.195	.233	.366	22	0	.182	.240	.273	17	1	.294	.294	.529
1989	Atl-N	456	12	.270	.325	.410	229	5	.249	.308	.376	227	7	.291	.341	.445	197	4	.279	.342	.416	259	8	.263	.311	.405	149	1	.289	.360	.376	100	2	.260	.276	.400
1990	Atl-N	386	8	.269	.338	.409	172	3	.297	.373	.442	214	5	.248	.309	.383	136	3	.294	.373	.463	250	5	.256	.319	.380	157	3	.274	.360	.427	61	4	.180	.265	.459
1991	Atl-N	352	11	.259	.358	.409	174	7	.270	.382	.425	178	4	.247	.333	.393	128	4	.305	.416	.484	224	7	.232	.323	.366	161	4	.317	.418	.484	72	2	.236	.321	.347
1992	Atl-N	343	14	.262	.354	.458	162	5	.284	.380	.457	181	9	.243	.330	.459	142	9	.303	.402	.585	201	5	.234	.317	.368	126	6	.270	.387	.484	61	3	.164	.271	.344
1993	Atl-N	597	15	.305	.401	.436	282	4	.277	.396	.369	315	11	.330	.407	.495	145	5	.283	.374	.469	452	10	.312	.410	.425	257	6	.350	.431	.494	92	2	.272	.361	.359
1994	Atl-N	380	6	.258	.329	.382	187	3	.246	.316	.374	193	3	.269	.341	.389	116	1	.267	.326	.371	264	5	.254	.330	.386	158	3	.285	.346	.405	56	1	.304	.381	.464
TOTALS		2746	70	.271	.351	.414	1312	30	.271	.360	.409	1434	40	.271	.343	.418	937	29	.288	.369	.466	1809	41	.262	.342	.386	1106	24	.299	.384	.441	476	15	.239	.312	.393

■ Bruce Bochte BL/TL

YEAR	TM/L	TOTAL AB	HR	AVG	OBP	SLG	HOME AB	HR	AVG	OBP	SLG	AWAY AB	HR	AVG	OBP	SLG	LEFT AB	HR	AVG	OBP	SLG	RIGHT AB	HR	AVG	OBP	SLG	ON-BASE AB	HR	AVG	OBP	SLG	LATE/CLOSE AB	HR	AVG	OBP	SLG
1984	Oak-A	469	5	.264	.333	.345	223	1	.269	.356	.327	246	4	.260	.310	.362	112	0	.241	.277	.259	357	5	.272	.349	.373	194	3	.320	.367	.418	71	0	.268	.333	.282
1985	Oak-A	424	14	.295	.367	.439	204	6	.314	.378	.466	220	8	.277	.357	.414	54	4	.333	.438	.611	370	10	.289	.356	.414	184	11	.342	.396	.571	67	2	.328	.416	.478
1986	Oak-A	407	6	.256	.357	.337	198	3	.247	.362	.328	209	3	.263	.353	.344	49	0	.204	.278	.204	358	6	.263	.368	.355	172	1	.273	.382	.320	62	0	.258	.387	.290
TOTALS		1300	25	.272	.352	.373	625	10	.277	.365	.373	675	15	.267	.339	.373	215	4	.256	.321	.335	1085	21	.275	.358	.381	550	15	.313	.381	.438	200	2	.285	.378	.350

■ Wade Boggs BL/TR

YEAR	TM/L	TOTAL AB	HR	AVG	OBP	SLG	HOME AB	HR	AVG	OBP	SLG	AWAY AB	HR	AVG	OBP	SLG	LEFT AB	HR	AVG	OBP	SLG	RIGHT AB	HR	AVG	OBP	SLG	ON-BASE AB	HR	AVG	OBP	SLG	LATE/CLOSE AB	HR	AVG	OBP	SLG
1984	Bos-A	625	6	.325	.407	.416	318	5	.352	.436	.472	307	1	.296	.376	.358	167	2	.240	.335	.293	458	4	.356	.433	.461	236	2	.301	.388	.390	90	1	.311	.398	.356
1985	Bos-A	653	8	.368	.450	.478	311	6	.418	.503	.566	342	2	.322	.401	.398	213	2	.347	.418	.441	440	6	.377	.465	.495	285	2	.386	.476	.491	88	0	.398	.523	.420
1986	Bos-A	580	8	.357	.453	.486	277	3	.357	.456	.495	303	5	.356	.450	.479	182	3	.352	.420	.489	398	5	.359	.467	.485	227	4	.379	.502	.524	74	0	.405	.477	.500
1987	Bos-A	551	24	.363	.461	.588	282	10	.411	.500	.638	269	14	.312	.421	.535	169	7	.331	.403	.544	382	17	.377	.484	.590	229	11	.358	.480	.590	81	1	.272	.388	.383
1988	Bos-A	584	5	.366	.476	.490	285	4	.382	.512	.547	299	1	.351	.438	.435	172	2	.331	.458	.453	412	3	.381	.483	.505	239	1	.339	.455	.452	72	0	.250	.396	.319
1989	Bos-A	621	3	.330	.430	.449	300	3	.377	.475	.547	321	0	.287	.386	.358	210	0	.295	.377	.352	411	3	.348	.455	.499	228	0	.351	.469	.443	98	1	.276	.351	.378
1990	Bos-A	619	6	.302	.386	.418	309	3	.359	.449	.492	310	3	.245	.320	.345	230	1	.274	.332	.365	389	5	.319	.415	.450	253	2	.320	.416	.419	103	0	.291	.402	.359
1991	Bos-A	546	8	.332	.421	.460	252	6	.389	.482	.587	294	2	.282	.368	.350	166	2	.265	.333	.341	380	6	.361	.456	.503	188	3	.324	.453	.447	91	1	.290	.395	.377
1992	Bos-A	514	7	.259	.353	.358	251	4	.243	.366	.367	263	3	.274	.339	.350	158	1	.272	.326	.367	356	6	.253	.364	.354	203	2	.286	.412	.365	90	0	.322	.426	.411
1993	NY-A	560	2	.302	.378	.363	271	1	.314	.383	.373	289	1	.291	.373	.353	168	1	.262	.323	.339	392	1	.319	.401	.372	221	1	.339	.395	.394	74	1	.297	.372	.338
1994	NY-A	366	11	.342	.433	.489	181	6	.343	.441	.514	185	5	.324	.425	.465	108	1	.315	.409	.380	258	10	.353	.443	.535	175	3	.354	.445	.469	47	0	.319	.431	.383
TOTALS		6219	88	.332	.423	.453	3037	50	.362	.457	.510	3182	38	.303	.390	.399	1943	22	.299	.376	.399	4276	66	.347	.444	.478	2484	31	.341	.446	.454	886	4	.312	.414	.384

■ Barry Bonds BL/TL

YEAR	TM/L	TOTAL AB	HR	AVG	OBP	SLG	HOME AB	HR	AVG	OBP	SLG	AWAY AB	HR	AVG	OBP	SLG	LEFT AB	HR	AVG	OBP	SLG	RIGHT AB	HR	AVG	OBP	SLG	ON-BASE AB	HR	AVG	OBP	SLG	LATE/CLOSE AB	HR	AVG	OBP	SLG
1986	Pit-N	413	16	.233	.330	.416	211	9	.242	.355	.469	202	7	.203	.303	.361	151	3	.219	.348	.371	262	13	.225	.319	.443	140	4	.257	.350	.421	70	1	.200	.325	.329
1987	Pit-N	551	25	.261	.329	.492	268	12	.265	.324	.500	283	13	.258	.333	.484	206	8	.228	.303	.456	345	17	.281	.345	.513	196	10	.255	.338	.485	95	5	.274	.333	.537
1988	Pit-N	538	24	.283	.368	.491	256	14	.285	.374	.516	282	10	.280	.363	.468	162	9	.302	.383	.556	376	15	.274	.362	.463	161	5	.255	.396	.398	106	3	.236	.325	.358
1989	Pit-N	580	19	.248	.351	.426	280	7	.204	.309	.343	300	12	.290	.390	.503	178	4	.253	.399	.416	402	15	.241	.342	.423	202	9	.272	.421	.465	98	1	.214	.361	.327
1990	Pit-N	519	33	.301	.406	.565	239	14	.276	.401	.515	280	19	.321	.410	.607	240	17	.304	.386	.592	279	16	.297	.422	.541	221	14	.344	.445	.615	82	3	.293	.389	.451
1991	Pit-N	510	25	.292	.410	.514	261	12	.272	.384	.448	249	13	.313	.436	.582	201	7	.284	.385	.473	309	18	.298	.425	.540	251	17	.327	.448	.610	80	2	.338	.450	.538
1992	Pit-N	473	34	.311	.456	.624	210	15	.338	.498	.671	263	19	.289	.418	.586	222	13	.311	.445	.595	251	21	.311	.465	.645	222	18	.302	.476	.631	91	3	.253	.462	.440
1993	SF-N	539	46	.336	.458	.677	266	21	.312	.403	.613	273	25	.359	.507	.740	218	15	.326	.423	.619	321	31	.343	.481	.717	227	22	.374	.524	.744	81	11	.370	.436	.827
1994	SF-N	391	37	.312	.426	.647	195	15	.282	.410	.569	196	22	.342	.443	.724	117	11	.291	.400	.607	274	26	.321	.437	.664	162	13	.290	.435	.568	70	6	.257	.369	.543
TOTALS		4514	259	.285	.394	.537	2186	119	.274	.383	.511	2328	140	.296	.404	.561	1695	87	.283	.385	.526	2819	172	.286	.399	.543	1758	108	.301	.433	.559	773	35	.269	.383	.477

■ Bobby Bonilla BB/TR

YEAR	TM/L	TOTAL AB	HR	AVG	OBP	SLG	HOME AB	HR	AVG	OBP	SLG	AWAY AB	HR	AVG	OBP	SLG	LEFT AB	HR	AVG	OBP	SLG	RIGHT AB	HR	AVG	OBP	SLG	ON-BASE AB	HR	AVG	OBP	SLG	LATE/CLOSE AB	HR	AVG	OBP	SLG
1986	Chi-A	234	2	.269	.361	.355	108	2	.287	.381	.417	126	0	.254	.343	.302	93	0	.269	.330	.323	141	2	.270	.380	.376	96	2	.292	.361	.438	43	0	.256	.333	.302
1986	Pit-N	192	1	.240	.342	.307	92	0	.250	.349	.304	100	1	.230	.336	.310	89	0	.270	.375	.337	103	1	.214	.314	.282	74	0	.324	.419	.446	35	1	.171	.293	.286
1987	Pit-N	466	15	.300	.351	.481	223	7	.265	.327	.430	243	8	.333	.374	.527	234	7	.308	.345	.474	232	8	.293	.357	.487	241	6	.299	.352	.477	81	1	.321	.391	.506
1988	Pit-N	584	24	.274	.366	.476	286	15	.329	.411	.594	298	9	.221	.320	.363	212	6	.278	.366	.420	372	18	.272	.366	.508	260	12	.288	.406	.527	103	5	.282	.422	.437
1989	Pit-N	616	24	.281	.358	.490	296	13	.311	.393	.551	320	11	.253	.325	.434	221	8	.226	.310	.389	395	16	.311	.386	.547	278	6	.270	.372	.432	123	5	.220	.314	.374
1990	Pit-N	625	32	.280	.322	.518	310	13	.261	.295	.461	315	19	.298	.347	.575	280	16	.296	.338	.559	345	16	.265	.309	.483	302	12	.258	.315	.477	79	2	.241	.316	.342
1991	Pit-N	577	18	.302	.391	.492	285	9	.309	.408	.512	292	9	.295	.374	.473	232	14	.284	.349	.530	345	4	.313	.418	.467	293	11	.321	.412	.519	83	3	.265	.396	.458
1992	NY-N	438	19	.249	.348	.432	196	5	.214	.325	.347	242	14	.277	.367	.500	175	4	.240	.307	.349	263	15	.255	.373	.487	192	9	.271	.376	.469	74	6	.270	.400	.554
1993	NY-N	502	34	.265	.352	.522	240	18	.275	.341	.550	262	16	.256	.362	.496	155	10	.277	.325	.516	347	24	.259	.360	.524	210	13	.276	.360	.524	83	6	.241	.369	.494
1994	NY-N	403	20	.290	.374	.504	181	8	.293	.357	.481	222	12	.288	.387	.523	119	9	.261	.338	.538	284	11	.303	.388	.489	173	8	.335	.432	.549	69	6	.290	.432	.594
TOTALS		4637	189	.278	.357	.476	2217	84	.269	.349	.455	2420	105	.286	.365	.495	1810	72	.268	.332	.449	2827	117	.285	.373	.494	2119	79	.290	.377	.486	773	35	.259	.372	.444

■ Bret Boone BR/TR

YEAR	TM/L	TOTAL AB	HR	AVG	OBP	SLG	HOME AB	HR	AVG	OBP	SLG	AWAY AB	HR	AVG	OBP	SLG	LEFT AB	HR	AVG	OBP	SLG	RIGHT AB	HR	AVG	OBP	SLG	ON-BASE AB	HR	AVG	OBP	SLG	LATE/CLOSE AB	HR	AVG	OBP	SLG
1992	Sea-A	129	4	.194	.224	.318	56	1	.250	.276	.429	73	3	.151	.184	.233	40	0	.150	.190	.175	89	4	.213	.239	.382	58	0	.241	.241	.379	26	0	.077	.077	.115
1993	Sea-A	271	12	.251	.301	.443	135	7	.259	.301	.489	136	5	.243	.300	.397	79	4	.266	.337	.494	192	8	.245	.285	.422	109	6	.275	.325	.495	46	0	.326	.367	.435
1994	Cin-N	381	12	.320	.368	.491	195	5	.323	.369	.477	186	7	.317	.366	.505	89	2	.270	.316	.416	292	10	.336	.383	.514	176	5	.341	.387	.517	67	2	.254	.333	.388
TOTALS		781	28	.275	.322	.446	386	14	.290	.333	.474	395	14	.261	.311	.418	208	6	.245	.301	.399	573	22	.286	.329	.462	343	13	.303	.345	.487	139	2	.245	.300	.353

■ Bob Boone BR/TR

YEAR	TM/L	TOTAL AB	HR	AVG	OBP	SLG	HOME AB	HR	AVG	OBP	SLG	AWAY AB	HR	AVG	OBP	SLG	LEFT AB	HR	AVG	OBP	SLG	RIGHT AB	HR	AVG	OBP	SLG	ON-BASE AB	HR	AVG	OBP	SLG	LATE/CLOSE AB	HR	AVG	OBP	SLG
1984	Cal-A	450	3	.202	.242	.262	220	1	.200	.250	.250	230	2	.204	.234	.274	159	0	.176	.222	.214	291	3	.216	.252	.289	187	0	.150	.204	.182	72	2	.236	.276	.375
1985	Cal-A	460	5	.248	.306	.317	221	0	.235	.305	.258	239	5	.259	.306	.372	135	1	.259	.331	.326	325	4	.243	.295	.314	218	1	.257	.297	.307	73	0	.260	.341	.288
1986	Cal-A	442	7	.222	.287	.305	212	1	.189	.264	.250	230	6	.252	.310	.357	152	2	.217	.292	.276	290	5	.224	.284	.321	212	3	.236	.291	.307	73	3	.208	.256	.325
1987	Cal-A	389	3	.242	.304	.311	186	1	.242	.316	.296	203	2	.241	.292	.325	134	0	.284	.333	.321	255	3	.220	.288	.306	163	0	.264	.309	.344	57	1	.158	.250	.211
1988	Cal-A	352	5	.295	.352	.386	177	3	.282	.339	.390	175	2	.309	.366	.383	140	1	.264	.318	.336	212	4	.316	.375	.420	156	2	.333	.381	.417	60	1	.350	.435	.433
1989	KC-A	405	1	.274	.351	.323	199	1	.317	.392	.372	206	0	.233	.312	.277	97	0	.289	.400	.330	308	1	.269	.331	.321	176	1	.307	.371	.364	66	0	.379	.432	.409
1990	KC-A	117	0	.239	.336	.265	69	0	.290	.380	.333	48	0	.167	.273	.167	40	0	.250	.348	.275	77	0	.234	.330	.260	50	0	.240	.345	.260	19	0	.263	.300	.263
TOTALS		2615	24	.245	.306	.313	1284	7	.245	.313	.301	1331	17	.245	.300	.325	857	4	.244	.313	.295	1758	20	.245	.303	.321	1162	7	.254	.307	.313	424	7	.264	.330	.337

■ Pat Borders BR/TR

YEAR	TM/L	TOTAL AB	HR	AVG	OBP	SLG	HOME AB	HR	AVG	OBP	SLG	AWAY AB	HR	AVG	OBP	SLG	LEFT AB	HR	AVG	OBP	SLG	RIGHT AB	HR	AVG	OBP	SLG	ON-BASE AB	HR	AVG	OBP	SLG	LATE/CLOSE AB	HR	AVG	OBP	SLG
1988	Tor-A	154	5	.273	.285	.448	72	2	.292	.320	.472	82	3	.256	.253	.427	132	4	.280	.294	.455	22	1	.227	.227	.409	66	1	.197	.229	.333	34	1	.324	.343	.500
1989	Tor-A	241	3	.257	.290	.349	105	1	.248	.279	.352	136	2	.265	.299	.346	171	2	.281	.313	.374	70	1	.200	.233	.286	109	1	.284	.316	.376	46	1	.261	.277	.370
1990	Tor-A	346	15	.286	.319	.497	164	10	.274	.318	.549	182	5	.297	.319	.451	186	10	.285	.337	.554	160	5	.287	.297	.431	158	7	.253	.288	.443	67	2	.254	.282	.388
1991	Tor-A	291	5	.244	.271	.354	146	2	.247	.268	.356	145	3	.241	.275	.352	147	1	.238	.271	.320	144	4	.250	.272	.389	125	4	.312	.346	.480	59	1	.271	.323	.407
1992	Tor-A	480	13	.242	.290	.385	231	7	.242	.296	.398	249	6	.241	.285	.373	120	0	.233	.333	.300	360	13	.244	.274	.414	196	5	.245	.314	.357	82	2	.220	.281	.341
1993	Tor-A	488	9	.254	.285	.371	247	6	.239	.273	.352	241	3	.270	.296	.390	119	2	.244	.278	.361	369	7	.257	.287	.374	207	4	.232	.277	.357	71	1	.296	.338	.423
1994	Tor-A	295	3	.247	.284	.329	141	3	.255	.291	.362	154	0	.240	.278	.299	75	1	.253	.282	.307	220	2	.245	.284	.336	127	0	.307	.348	.362	59	0	.305	.328	.390
TOTALS		2295	53	.256	.290	.384	1106	31	.252	.290	.401	1189	22	.259	.290	.377	950	20	.262	.305	.396	1345	32	.251	.279	.383	988	20	.261	.305	.388	418	8	.270	.308	.395

■ Mike Bordick BR/TR

YEAR	TM/L	TOTAL AB	HR	AVG	OBP	SLG	HOME AB	HR	AVG	OBP	SLG	AWAY AB	HR	AVG	OBP	SLG	LEFT AB	HR	AVG	OBP	SLG	RIGHT AB	HR	AVG	OBP	SLG	ON-BASE AB	HR	AVG	OBP	SLG	LATE/CLOSE AB	HR	AVG	OBP	SLG
1990	Oak-A	14	0	.071	.133	.071	5	0	.000	.000	.000	9	0	.111	.200	.111	6	0	.000	.000	.000	8	0	.125	.222	.125	2	0	.000	.333	.000	3	0	.000	.000	.000
1991	Oak-A	235	0	.238	.289	.268	106	0	.226	.287	.264	129	0	.248	.290	.271	58	0	.224	.274	.241	177	0	.243	.293	.277	85	0	.294	.330	.329	17	0	.235	.350	.294
1992	Oak-A	504	3	.300	.358	.371	240	3	.296	.360	.396	264	0	.303	.357	.348	131	1	.336	.393	.427	373	2	.287	.346	.351	242	1	.302	.341	.364	69	0	.261	.308	.348
1993	Oak-A	546	3	.249	.332	.311	280	2	.250	.324	.314	266	1	.248	.341	.308	162	1	.265	.351	.346	384	2	.242	.324	.297	224	2	.259	.351	.330	87	0	.195	.339	.195
1994	Oak-A	391	2	.253	.332	.335	200	1	.230	.309	.335	191	1	.277	.356	.335	135	1	.252	.333	.348	256	1	.254	.313	.328	155	0	.245	.315	.316	49	0	.224	.316	.245
TOTALS		1690	8	.262	.330	.327	822	6	.254	.324	.335	868	2	.270	.335	.319	492	3	.272	.345	.352	1198	5	.258	.324	.316	708	3	.274	.337	.338	225	0	.222	.322	.258

■ Daryl Boston BL/TL

YEAR	TM/L	TOTAL AB	HR	AVG	OBP	SLG	HOME AB	HR	AVG	OBP	SLG	AWAY AB	HR	AVG	OBP	SLG	LEFT AB	HR	AVG	OBP	SLG	RIGHT AB	HR	AVG	OBP	SLG	ON-BASE AB	HR	AVG	OBP	SLG	LATE/CLOSE AB	HR	AVG	OBP	SLG
1984	Chi-A	83	0	.169	.207	.229	43	0	.163	.217	.256	40	0	.175	.195	.200	17	0	.059	.111	.059	66	0	.197	.232	.273	30	0	.133	.161	.133	12	0	.083	.083	.083
1985	Chi-A	232	3	.228	.271	.332	106	0	.175	.214	.237	126	3	.267	.313	.400	17	0	.118	.211	.118	215	3	.237	.276	.349	90	1	.244	.296	.322	42	1	.167	.205	.262
1986	Chi-A	199	5	.266	.335	.427	97	1	.309	.393	.454	102	4	.225	.275	.402	48	1	.125	.333	.417	151	4	.272	.335	.430	68	2	.250	.333	.471	26	0	.115	.258	.115
1987	Chi-A	337	10	.258	.307	.421	168	5	.321	.365	.488	169	5	.195	.250	.355	59	0	.305	.311	.373	278	10	.248	.306	.432	127	2	.213	.280	.315	56	0	.214	.290	.357
1988	Chi-A	281	15	.217	.273	.438	138	6	.181	.231	.362	143	9	.252	.311	.503	28	0	.250	.241	.393	253	15	.213	.279	.439	108	5	.194	.261	.361	53	0	.189	.254	.264
1989	Chi-A	218	5	.252	.325	.372	114	3	.289	.389	.444	104	2	.212	.311	.288	27	0	.111	.107	.185	191	5	.272	.353	.398	97	3	.247	.327	.381	41	0	.244	.367	.341
1990	Chi-A	1	0	.000	.000	.000	1	0	.000	.000	.000	0	0	—	—	—	27	0	.111	.107	.185	1	0	.000	.000	.000	0	0	—	—	—	0	0	—	—	—
1990	NY-N	366	12	.273	.338	.449	185	4	.270	.328	.470	181	8	.276	.348	.428	60	0	.250	.288	.350	306	12	.278	.349	.467	158	6	.272	.324	.456	61	1	.279	.313	.443
1991	NY-N	255	4	.275	.350	.416	135	1	.244	.338	.400	120	3	.308	.364	.433	31	1	.194	.194	.387	224	3	.286	.369	.420	88	1	.250	.337	.364	40	1	.275	.383	.500
1992	NY-N	289	11	.249	.338	.426	140	5	.229	.311	.386	149	6	.268	.364	.463	47	1	.319	.407	.447	242	10	.236	.325	.421	96	3	.281	.381	.438	61	4	.230	.373	.475

YEAR	TM/L	TOTAL AB	HR	AVG	OBP	SLG	HOME AB	HR	AVG	OBP	SLG	AWAY AB	HR	AVG	OBP	SLG	LEFT AB	HR	AVG	OBP	SLG	RIGHT AB	HR	AVG	OBP	SLG	ON-BASE AB	HR	AVG	OBP	SLG	LATE/CLOSE AB	HR	AVG	OBP	SLG
1993	Col-N	291	14	.261	.325	.464	136	3	.279	.359	.412	155	11	.245	.293	.510	13	1	.231	.286	.462	278	13	.263	.327	.464	140	4	.214	.255	.350	46	0	.174	.255	.217
1994	NY-A	77	4	.182	.250	.364	43	2	.116	.208	.256	34	2	.265	.306	.500	1	0	.000	.000	.000	76	4	.184	.253	.368	44	3	.205	.271	.432	19	2	.263	.364	.579
TOTALS		2629	83	.249	.312	.410	1297	32	.250	.315	.395	1332	51	.248	.308	.426	348	4	.236	.285	.336	2281	79	.251	.316	.422	1046	30	.235	.302	.378	457	9	.214	.302	.350

■ Phil Bradley BR/TR

YEAR	TM/L	TOTAL AB	HR	AVG	OBP	SLG	HOME AB	HR	AVG	OBP	SLG	AWAY AB	HR	AVG	OBP	SLG	LEFT AB	HR	AVG	OBP	SLG	RIGHT AB	HR	AVG	OBP	SLG	ON-BASE AB	HR	AVG	OBP	SLG	LATE/CLOSE AB	HR	AVG	OBP	SLG
1984	Sea-A	322	0	.301	.373	.363	163	0	.331	.404	.417	159	0	.270	.341	.308	112	0	.205	.270	.277	210	0	.352	.426	.410	145	0	.338	.404	.434	51	0	.294	.379	.333
1985	Sea-A	641	26	.300	.365	.498	321	15	.305	.376	.526	320	11	.294	.353	.469	176	9	.267	.337	.483	465	17	.312	.375	.503	273	9	.311	.387	.487	92	7	.337	.374	.641
1986	Sea-A	526	12	.310	.405	.445	287	5	.324	.417	.467	239	7	.293	.390	.418	126	2	.325	.418	.421	400	10	.305	.400	.452	192	1	.307	.410	.396	83	0	.313	.412	.422
1987	Sea-A	603	14	.297	.387	.463	304	12	.309	.398	.520	299	2	.284	.376	.405	176	11	.347	.426	.642	427	3	.276	.371	.389	247	3	.243	.358	.348	71	2	.268	.358	.408
1988	Phi-N	569	11	.264	.341	.392	284	8	.268	.339	.423	285	3	.261	.344	.361	169	4	.272	.342	.420	400	7	.260	.341	.380	208	3	.274	.346	.394	90	0	.222	.311	.311
1989	Bal-A	545	11	.277	.364	.417	255	5	.286	.378	.400	290	6	.269	.352	.431	192	8	.297	.379	.531	353	3	.266	.356	.354	197	2	.264	.404	.371	69	0	.188	.300	.203
1990	Bal-A	289	4	.270	.352	.349	142	4	.268	.348	.394	147	0	.272	.355	.306	95	2	.242	.314	.368	194	2	.284	.369	.340	100	2	.270	.388	.360	55	1	.309	.350	.436
1990	Chi-A	133	0	.226	.344	.278	48	0	.146	.305	.188	85	0	.271	.367	.329	66	0	.227	.370	.303	67	0	.224	.316	.254	38	0	.184	.340	.263	13	0	.308	.400	.308
TOTALS		3628	78	.287	.370	.424	1804	47	.295	.379	.452	1824	31	.278	.360	.395	1112	36	.281	.363	.459	2516	42	.289	.373	.408	1400	20	.283	.382	.399	524	10	.277	.356	.401

■ Scott Bradley BL/TR

YEAR	TM/L	TOTAL AB	HR	AVG	OBP	SLG	HOME AB	HR	AVG	OBP	SLG	AWAY AB	HR	AVG	OBP	SLG	LEFT AB	HR	AVG	OBP	SLG	RIGHT AB	HR	AVG	OBP	SLG	ON-BASE AB	HR	AVG	OBP	SLG	LATE/CLOSE AB	HR	AVG	OBP	SLG
1984	NY-A	21	0	.286	.318	.333	9	0	.444	.500	.444	12	0	.167	.167	.250	3	0	.000	.000	.000	18	0	.333	.368	.389	9	0	.222	.222	.222	0	0	—	—	—
1985	NY-A	49	1	.163	.196	.245	15	0	.067	.176	.067	34	0	.206	.206	.324	9	0	.111	.111	.222	40	1	.175	.214	.250	19	0	.158	.238	.211	12	0	.250	.250	.500
1986	Chi-A	21	0	.286	.375	.286	8	0	.375	.444	.375	13	0	.231	.333	.231	1	0	1.000	1.000	1.000	20	0	.250	.318	.250	9	0	.333	.400	.333	4	0	.500	.600	.500
1986	Sea-A	199	5	.302	.344	.447	110	4	.345	.395	.555	89	1	.247	.281	.315	13	0	.154	.154	.308	186	5	.312	.356	.457	91	3	.275	.333	.418	29	0	.379	.455	.414
1987	Sea-A	342	5	.278	.310	.371	145	5	.290	.329	.448	197	0	.269	.297	.315	54	1	.259	.273	.352	288	4	.281	.317	.375	170	3	.241	.289	.335	43	1	.302	.348	.442
1988	Sea-A	335	4	.257	.295	.349	170	3	.247	.281	.371	165	1	.267	.309	.327	46	0	.152	.152	.174	289	4	.273	.316	.377	139	2	.266	.307	.367	36	2	.278	.350	.556
1989	Sea-A	270	3	.274	.322	.367	131	1	.275	.329	.374	139	2	.273	.316	.360	14	0	.143	.250	.214	256	3	.281	.326	.375	113	2	.345	.385	.487	59	1	.271	.306	.407
1990	Sea-A	233	1	.223	.264	.275	112	1	.250	.290	.321	121	0	.198	.233	.231	25	0	.160	.233	.160	208	1	.231	.268	.288	100	1	.290	.330	.360	58	1	.259	.297	.345
1991	Sea-A	172	0	.203	.280	.244	84	0	.202	.277	.238	88	0	.205	.283	.250	11	0	.182	.308	.182	161	0	.205	.278	.248	69	0	.232	.313	.275	32	0	.156	.250	.188
1992	Sea-A	1	0	.000	.500	.000	1	0	.000	.500	.000	0	0	—	—	—	0	0	—	—	—	1	0	.000	.500	.000	1	0	.000	.000	.000	1	0	.000	.000	.000
1992	Cin-N	5	0	.400	.500	.400	2	0	.500	.667	.500	3	0	.333	.333	.333	0	0	—	—	—	5	0	.400	.500	.400	3	0	.333	.500	.333	2	0	.000	.000	.000
TOTALS		1648	18	.257	.302	.343	787	14	.269	.319	.385	861	4	.246	.286	.304	176	1	.188	.225	.244	1472	17	.266	.311	.355	723	11	.271	.321	.368	276	5	.272	.326	.395

■ Glenn Braggs BR/TR

YEAR	TM/L	TOTAL AB	HR	AVG	OBP	SLG	HOME AB	HR	AVG	OBP	SLG	AWAY AB	HR	AVG	OBP	SLG	LEFT AB	HR	AVG	OBP	SLG	RIGHT AB	HR	AVG	OBP	SLG	ON-BASE AB	HR	AVG	OBP	SLG	LATE/CLOSE AB	HR	AVG	OBP	SLG
1986	Mil-A	215	4	.237	.274	.349	86	2	.314	.368	.453	129	2	.186	.207	.279	58	3	.293	.313	.517	157	1	.217	.259	.287	86	1	.198	.242	.256	37	0	.216	.293	.243
1987	Mil-A	505	13	.269	.332	.430	253	4	.261	.323	.383	252	9	.278	.342	.476	168	2	.274	.349	.393	337	11	.267	.324	.448	232	3	.267	.332	.392	86	1	.256	.327	.395
1988	Mil-A	272	10	.261	.307	.423	143	6	.259	.305	.420	129	4	.264	.309	.426	85	5	.247	.283	.471	187	5	.267	.318	.401	104	5	.288	.333	.481	49	2	.245	.275	.469
1989	Mil-A	514	15	.247	.305	.370	275	8	.211	.279	.345	239	7	.289	.336	.397	142	6	.303	.365	.465	372	9	.226	.282	.333	230	6	.274	.312	.396	74	1	.243	.317	.324
1990	Mil-A	113	3	.248	.328	.372	46	1	.239	.321	.391	67	2	.254	.333	.358	34	1	.118	.279	.265	79	2	.304	.352	.418	44	0	.182	.264	.250	16	0	.313	.421	.375
1990	Cin-N	201	6	.299	.385	.443	115	4	.296	.388	.452	86	2	.302	.381	.430	115	5	.339	.437	.513	86	1	.244	.313	.349	76	2	.395	.478	.553	38	0	.289	.349	.316
1991	Cin-N	250	11	.260	.323	.432	120	8	.300	.346	.550	130	3	.223	.301	.323	124	5	.282	.352	.452	126	6	.238	.292	.413	120	3	.267	.313	.392	44	1	.205	.327	.295
1992	Cin-N	266	8	.237	.330	.410	117	4	.239	.350	.436	149	4	.235	.314	.389	145	5	.248	.343	.428	121	3	.223	.314	.388	128	5	.227	.336	.445	49	1	.388	.446	.592
TOTALS		2336	70	.257	.322	.405	1155	37	.257	.326	.414	1181	33	.257	.317	.395	871	32	.277	.351	.445	1465	38	.246	.303	.380	1020	25	.266	.327	.403	393	6	.265	.337	.382

■ Sid Bream BL/TL

YEAR	TM/L	TOTAL AB	HR	AVG	OBP	SLG	HOME AB	HR	AVG	OBP	SLG	AWAY AB	HR	AVG	OBP	SLG	LEFT AB	HR	AVG	OBP	SLG	RIGHT AB	HR	AVG	OBP	SLG	ON-BASE AB	HR	AVG	OBP	SLG	LATE/CLOSE AB	HR	AVG	OBP	SLG
1984	LA-N	49	0	.184	.263	.245	25	0	.160	.214	.200	24	0	.208	.310	.292	2	0	.000	.000	.000	47	0	.191	.273	.255	20	0	.200	.308	.300	11	0	.091	.267	.091
1985	LA-N	53	3	.132	.230	.302	24	2	.167	.250	.417	29	1	.103	.212	.207	18	1	.056	.150	.222	35	2	.171	.268	.343	23	1	.087	.214	.217	11	0	.000	.154	.000
1985	Pit-N	95	3	.284	.355	.453	32	0	.250	.342	.313	63	3	.302	.362	.524	23	0	.261	.320	.261	72	3	.292	.366	.514	49	0	.306	.417	.388	15	1	.333	.421	.667
1986	Pit-N	522	16	.268	.341	.450	262	5	.282	.348	.450	260	11	.254	.333	.450	152	2	.224	.268	.349	370	14	.286	.370	.492	241	8	.299	.378	.490	99	2	.232	.322	.384
1987	Pit-N	516	13	.275	.336	.411	259	10	.282	.347	.467	257	3	.268	.324	.354	193	8	.275	.314	.456	323	5	.276	.348	.384	245	6	.265	.345	.392	72	3	.264	.376	.458
1988	Pit-N	462	10	.264	.328	.409	226	6	.235	.292	.425	236	4	.292	.362	.394	116	3	.190	.220	.319	346	7	.289	.362	.439	205	5	.302	.371	.454	83	2	.277	.354	.446
1989	Pit-N	36	0	.222	.417	.306	8	0	.375	.615	.375	28	0	.179	.343	.286	10	0	.300	.500	.500	26	0	.192	.382	.231	14	0	.357	.609	.500	6	0	.167	.500	.167
1990	Pit-N	389	15	.270	.349	.455	181	8	.276	.356	.481	208	7	.264	.343	.433	96	2	.260	.308	.427	293	13	.273	.362	.464	184	9	.277	.364	.505	61	2	.295	.380	.475
1991	Atl-N	265	11	.253	.313	.423	115	3	.270	.310	.391	150	8	.240	.315	.447	40	1	.150	.150	.225	225	10	.271	.339	.458	115	5	.235	.313	.417	32	0	.219	.219	.219
1992	Atl-N	372	10	.261	.340	.414	178	4	.264	.353	.393	194	6	.258	.329	.433	33	1	.242	.265	.455	339	9	.263	.347	.410	165	3	.303	.383	.455	52	1	.212	.263	.365
1993	Atl-N	277	9	.260	.332	.415	125	5	.232	.309	.392	152	4	.283	.351	.434	29	0	.276	.290	.379	248	9	.258	.337	.419	115	4	.261	.331	.426	54	2	.185	.313	.352
1994	Hou-N	61	0	.344	.429	.426	33	0	.485	.541	.606	28	0	.179	.303	.214	6	0	.167	.375	.167	55	0	.364	.435	.455	31	0	.387	.486	.484	18	0	.389	.542	.556
TOTALS		3097	90	.264	.336	.420	1468	43	.267	.337	.432	1629	47	.261	.335	.410	718	18	.233	.276	.376	2379	72	.273	.353	.434	1407	41	.281	.364	.443	514	13	.243	.339	.397

■ Bob Brenly BR/TR

YEAR	TM/L	TOTAL AB	HR	AVG	OBP	SLG	HOME AB	HR	AVG	OBP	SLG	AWAY AB	HR	AVG	OBP	SLG	LEFT AB	HR	AVG	OBP	SLG	RIGHT AB	HR	AVG	OBP	SLG	ON-BASE AB	HR	AVG	OBP	SLG	LATE/CLOSE AB	HR	AVG	OBP	SLG
1984	SF-N	506	20	.291	.352	.464	249	6	.273	.342	.410	257	14	.307	.361	.518	125	3	.280	.352	.392	381	17	.294	.352	.488	252	13	.274	.323	.484	107	3	.243	.291	.364
1985	SF-N	440	19	.220	.311	.391	225	9	.227	.310	.400	215	10	.214	.313	.381	114	6	.193	.298	.377	326	13	.230	.316	.396	164	8	.238	.335	.427	106	6	.217	.308	.406
1986	SF-N	472	16	.246	.350	.403	235	8	.234	.331	.379	237	8	.257	.368	.426	157	6	.268	.378	.484	315	10	.235	.335	.362	201	7	.234	.335	.393	102	1	.206	.283	.304
1987	SF-N	375	18	.267	.348	.467	173	10	.301	.389	.532	202	8	.238	.311	.411	101	7	.238	.304	.535	274	11	.277	.364	.442	145	4	.269	.349	.407	76	3	.276	.353	.539
1988	SF-N	206	5	.189	.265	.296	96	2	.177	.259	.250	110	3	.200	.270	.336	58	1	.207	.273	.310	148	4	.182	.262	.291	86	3	.198	.268	.349	45	0	.222	.308	.289
1989	Tor-A	88	1	.170	.255	.261	45	0	.178	.275	.222	43	1	.163	.234	.302	79	0	.165	.250	.228	9	1	.222	.300	.556	39	0	.179	.289	.282	15	0	.267	.389	.400
1989	SF-N	22	0	.182	.208	.273	15	0	.200	.235	.267	7	0	.143	.143	.286	21	0	.143	.174	.190	1	0	1.000	1.000	2.000	7	0	.286	.333	.429	6	0	.167	.286	.167
TOTALS		2109	79	.246	.328	.409	1038	35	.245	.329	.396	1071	44	.246	.328	.421	655	23	.231	.317	.400	1454	56	.252	.334	.413	894	35	.246	.326	.418	457	15	.232	.309	.381

■ George Brett BL/TR

YEAR	TM/L	TOTAL AB	HR	AVG	OBP	SLG	HOME AB	HR	AVG	OBP	SLG	AWAY AB	HR	AVG	OBP	SLG	LEFT AB	HR	AVG	OBP	SLG	RIGHT AB	HR	AVG	OBP	SLG	ON-BASE AB	HR	AVG	OBP	SLG	LATE/CLOSE AB	HR	AVG	OBP	SLG
1984	KC-A	377	13	.284	.344	.459	172	6	.314	.385	.506	205	7	.259	.308	.420	137	8	.270	.325	.496	240	5	.292	.354	.438	177	8	.288	.354	.497	55	4	.327	.387	.673
1985	KC-A	550	30	.335	.436	.585	285	15	.368	.469	.628	265	15	.298	.400	.540	191	10	.330	.395	.550	359	20	.337	.456	.604	221	13	.367	.497	.615	77	2	.312	.481	.481
1986	KC-A	441	16	.290	.401	.481	205	8	.322	.418	.556	236	8	.263	.386	.415	148	5	.243	.329	.385	293	11	.314	.435	.529	206	7	.306	.424	.476	66	3	.273	.400	.439
1987	KC-A	427	22	.290	.388	.496	231	14	.268	.364	.494	196	8	.316	.415	.500	149	7	.268	.317	.430	278	15	.302	.422	.532	232	8	.284	.385	.435	61	3	.328	.432	.525
1988	KC-A	589	24	.306	.389	.509	290	13	.293	.377	.500	299	11	.318	.401	.518	198	10	.313	.379	.533	391	14	.302	.394	.499	270	12	.348	.445	.593	110	3	.273	.360	.418
1989	KC-A	457	12	.282	.362	.431	229	3	.275	.363	.389	228	9	.289	.360	.474	167	2	.222	.296	.323	290	10	.317	.398	.493	242	6	.285	.359	.413	65	1	.323	.450	.446
1990	KC-A	544	14	.329	.387	.515	288	3	.319	.373	.448	256	11	.340	.403	.590	187	5	.316	.366	.487	357	9	.336	.398	.529	245	4	.367	.443	.547	74	2	.257	.345	.405
1991	KC-A	505	10	.255	.327	.402	243	3	.247	.326	.379	262	7	.263	.327	.424	167	2	.234	.309	.353	338	8	.266	.337	.426	216	4	.250	.349	.380	76	2	.197	.326	.316
1992	KC-A	592	7	.285	.330	.397	312	6	.288	.328	.378	280	6	.282	.331	.418	184	0	.277	.320	.348	408	7	.289	.334	.419	258	2	.310	.361	.411	97	4	.227	.294	.371
1993	KC-A	560	19	.266	.312	.434	275	7	.269	.313	.439	285	12	.263	.311	.439	187	2	.209	.246	.299	373	17	.295	.344	.501	268	7	.250	.299	.381	100	5	.260	.321	.390
TOTALS		5042	167	.293	.369	.471	2530	73	.297	.372	.468	2512	94	.289	.365	.475	1715	51	.270	.330	.422	3327	116	.305	.388	.497	2335	71	.306	.394	.474	781	25	.273	.376	.434

■ Greg Briley BL/TR

YEAR	TM/L	TOTAL AB	HR	AVG	OBP	SLG	HOME AB	HR	AVG	OBP	SLG	AWAY AB	HR	AVG	OBP	SLG	LEFT AB	HR	AVG	OBP	SLG	RIGHT AB	HR	AVG	OBP	SLG	ON-BASE AB	HR	AVG	OBP	SLG	LATE/CLOSE AB	HR	AVG	OBP	SLG
1988	Sea-A	36	1	.250	.333	.389	24	0	.125	.276	.125	12	1	.500	.462	.917	4	0	.000	.000	.000	32	1	.281	.368	.438	12	0	.167	.313	.167	3	0	.000	.000	.000
1989	Sea-A	394	13	.266	.336	.442	164	5	.207	.281	.354	230	8	.309	.376	.504	53	1	.321	.400	.472	341	12	.258	.326	.437	175	4	.240	.303	.389	68	0	.221	.274	.294
1990	Sea-A	337	5	.246	.319	.356	166	4	.247	.312	.380	171	1	.246	.326	.333	33	0	.212	.297	.242	304	5	.250	.322	.368	135	3	.274	.350	.437	48	1	.313	.353	.479
1991	Sea-A	381	2	.260	.307	.336	185	2	.249	.310	.314	196	0	.270	.303	.357	39	0	.231	.250	.333	342	2	.263	.313	.336	150	2	.273	.317	.380	79	1	.266	.289	.392
1992	Sea-A	200	5	.275	.290	.400	95	1	.305	.316	.400	105	4	.248	.266	.400	5	0	.000	.000	.000	195	5	.282	.297	.410	74	0	.189	.225	.203	37	0	.351	.368	.405
1993	Fla-N	170	3	.194	.250	.282	85	2	.165	.234	.247	85	1	.224	.267	.318	14	1	.214	.214	.429	156	2	.192	.253	.269	74	2	.203	.259	.311	46	1	.152	.250	.261
TOTALS		1518	29	.253	.310	.372	719	14	.232	.294	.335	799	15	.272	.324	.404	148	2	.243	.300	.351	1370	29	.254	.311	.374	620	11	.244	.303	.361	281	3	.253	.297	.359

■ Greg Brock BL/TR

YEAR	TM/L	TOTAL AB	HR	AVG	OBP	SLG	HOME AB	HR	AVG	OBP	SLG	AWAY AB	HR	AVG	OBP	SLG	LEFT AB	HR	AVG	OBP	SLG	RIGHT AB	HR	AVG	OBP	SLG	ON-BASE AB	HR	AVG	OBP	SLG	LATE/CLOSE AB	HR	AVG	OBP	SLG
1984	LA-N	271	14	.225	.319	.402	145	8	.248	.319	.455	126	6	.198	.320	.341	77	6	.208	.244	.468	194	8	.232	.346	.376	117	4	.197	.326	.316	56	1	.196	.286	.268
1985	LA-N	438	21	.251	.332	.438	219	7	.251	.331	.388	219	14	.251	.333	.489	102	2	.176	.222	.255	336	19	.274	.368	.501	208	12	.288	.380	.510	66	2	.227	.301	.333
1986	LA-N	325	16	.234	.309	.422	140	5	.236	.306	.343	185	11	.232	.311	.481	59	0	.102	.221	.153	266	16	.263	.329	.481	148	8	.257	.333	.439	58	0	.069	.169	.086
1987	Mil-A	532	13	.299	.371	.438	270	5	.300	.370	.426	262	8	.298	.372	.450	157	3	.287	.351	.395	375	10	.304	.380	.456	262	7	.347	.416	.500	81	0	.284	.366	.358
1988	Mil-A	364	6	.212	.329	.310	195	4	.231	.335	.344	169	2	.189	.324	.272	103	1	.233	.316	.320	261	5	.203	.334	.307	165	3	.230	.370	.358	40	0	.250	.423	.275
1989	Mil-A	373	12	.265	.345	.405	176	7	.261	.350	.403	197	5	.269	.341	.406	90	2	.333	.388	.444	283	10	.244	.332	.392	176	6	.290	.373	.438	51	1	.216	.310	.314
1990	Mil-A	367	7	.248	.324	.368	176	3	.239	.319	.341	191	4	.257	.329	.393	86	2	.209	.283	.337	281	5	.260	.336	.377	165	3	.267	.338	.394	58	1	.190	.242	.276
1991	Mil-A	60	1	.283	.419	.400	18	0	.278	.480	.389	42	1	.286	.388	.405	15	1	.400	.471	.667	45	0	.244	.404	.311	26	0	.308	.438	.385	8	0	.375	.545	.375
TOTALS		2730	90	.253	.338	.401	1339	39	.256	.339	.388	1391	51	.249	.337	.413	689	17	.237	.303	.356	2041	73	.258	.349	.416	1267	43	.279	.370	.434	418	5	.211	.306	.280

■ Tom Brookens BR/TR

YEAR	TM/L	TOTAL AB	HR	AVG	OBP	SLG	HOME AB	HR	AVG	OBP	SLG	AWAY AB	HR	AVG	OBP	SLG	LEFT AB	HR	AVG	OBP	SLG	RIGHT AB	HR	AVG	OBP	SLG	ON-BASE AB	HR	AVG	OBP	SLG	LATE/CLOSE AB	HR	AVG	OBP	SLG
1984	Det-A	224	5	.246	.306	.397	110	4	.245	.333	.427	114	1	.246	.277	.368	138	3	.261	.313	.413	86	2	.221	.295	.372	96	1	.271	.336	.406	21	1	.429	.500	.762
1985	Det-A	485	7	.237	.277	.375	232	3	.233	.270	.379	253	4	.241	.283	.372	162	4	.290	.350	.483	323	3	.211	.238	.322	211	1	.223	.263	.308	65	0	.170	.179	.369
1986	Det-A	281	3	.270	.319	.356	144	2	.257	.299	.354	137	1	.285	.340	.358	171	2	.298	.337	.409	110	1	.227	.292	.273	111	2	.270	.308	.387	46	1	.261	.314	.326
1987	Det-A	444	13	.241	.295	.376	212	6	.226	.291	.325	232	7	.254	.300	.422	154	7	.240	.310	.422	290	6	.241	.287	.352	215	7	.242	.298	.381	54	1	.222	.250	.315
1988	Det-A	441	5	.243	.313	.351	221	4	.258	.331	.394	220	1	.227	.295	.309	177	2	.220	.310	.311	264	3	.258	.315	.379	186	2	.210	.274	.274	81	2	.272	.310	.420

	TOTAL					HOME					AWAY					LEFT					RIGHT					ON-BASE					LATE/CLOSE				
YEAR TM/L	AB	HR	AVG	OBP	SLG	AB	HR	AVG	OBP	SLG	AB	HR	AVG	OBP	SLG	AB	HR	AVG	OBP	SLG	AB	HR	AVG	OBP	SLG	AB	HR	AVG	OBP	SLG	AB	HR	AVG	OBP	SLG
1989 NY-A	168	4	.226	.272	.333	69	0	.246	.293	.290	99	4	.212	.257	.364	116	4	.267	.312	.422	52	0	.135	.182	.135	85	1	.306	.348	.400	26	0	.115	.115	.154
1990 Cle-A	154	1	.266	.322	.357	71	0	.225	.284	.282	83	1	.301	.356	.422	93	1	.258	.340	.376	61	0	.279	.292	.328	64	0	.328	.361	.406	26	1	.308	.379	.423
TOTALS	2197	38	.245	.299	.366	1059	19	.242	.300	.361	1138	19	.249	.298	.371	1011	23	.262	.324	.405	1186	15	.231	.277	.333	968	14	.249	.300	.351	319	6	.263	.307	.379
■ Hubie Brooks BR/TR																																			
1984 NY-N	561	16	.283	.341	.417	277	12	.321	.382	.516	284	4	.246	.301	.320	183	7	.290	.361	.459	378	9	.280	.331	.397	227	3	.269	.359	.366	92	4	.283	.359	.446
1985 Mon-N	605	13	.269	.310	.413	278	4	.281	.313	.428	327	9	.260	.307	.401	184	4	.310	.361	.476	418	9	.251	.287	.385	289	5	.294	.331	.433	108	1	.269	.304	.343
1986 Mon-N	306	14	.340	.388	.569	137	3	.350	.409	.504	169	11	.331	.370	.621	85	5	.365	.450	.682	221	9	.330	.361	.525	148	5	.318	.373	.493	65	3	.385	.437	.662
1987 Mon-N	430	14	.263	.301	.426	228	9	.289	.333	.478	202	5	.233	.263	.366	121	5	.331	.354	.554	309	9	.236	.280	.375	211	4	.299	.324	.450	65	4	.246	.254	.462
1988 Mon-N	588	20	.279	.318	.447	292	9	.260	.300	.411	296	11	.297	.337	.483	156	7	.314	.366	.538	432	13	.266	.300	.414	287	11	.293	.337	.463	128	6	.273	.299	.453
1989 Mon-N	542	14	.268	.317	.404	260	7	.288	.339	.438	282	7	.248	.297	.372	162	6	.284	.352	.463	380	8	.261	.302	.379	245	6	.265	.321	.392	93	2	.278	.311	.423
1990 LA-N	568	20	.266	.307	.424	275	9	.251	.303	.385	293	11	.280	.312	.461	217	9	.240	.294	.419	351	11	.282	.316	.427	261	8	.280	.337	.425	83	4	.301	.363	.506
1991 NY-N	357	16	.238	.324	.409	172	4	.238	.340	.355	185	12	.238	.309	.459	121	5	.248	.343	.413	236	11	.233	.315	.407	162	4	.210	.348	.327	57	2	.211	.328	.351
1992 Cal-A	306	8	.216	.247	.337	150	2	.247	.300	.333	156	6	.186	.215	.340	82	1	.220	.256	.280	224	7	.214	.244	.357	129	4	.225	.268	.364	56	2	.250	.311	.375
1993 KC-A	168	1	.286	.331	.375	84	0	.286	.330	.381	84	1	.286	.333	.369	110	1	.327	.368	.445	58	0	.207	.266	.241	88	1	.307	.361	.420	42	0	.286	.326	.310
1994 KC-A	61	1	.230	.239	.311	23	1	.304	.308	.478	38	0	.184	.195	.211	33	1	.273	.270	.394	28	0	.179	.200	.214	31	1	.258	.273	.387	22	0	.227	.261	.273
TOTALS	4492	137	.270	.317	.422	2176	60	.280	.331	.429	2316	77	.260	.303	.415	1457	51	.290	.347	.469	3035	86	.260	.302	.399	2078	52	.277	.335	.417	815	29	.277	.326	.432
■ Jerry Browne BB/TR																																			
1986 Tex-A	24	0	.417	.440	.500	22	0	.409	.435	.500	2	0	.500	.500	.500	5	0	.600	.600	.800	19	0	.368	.400	.421	12	0	.583	.583	.667	4	0	.500	.600	.500
1987 Tex-A	454	1	.271	.358	.339	245	1	.306	.390	.380	209	0	.230	.321	.292	119	1	.311	.403	.420	335	0	.257	.342	.310	138	0	.254	.364	.333	63	0	.317	.469	.365
1988 Tex-A	214	1	.229	.308	.304	121	1	.256	.341	.355	93	0	.194	.265	.237	70	0	.243	.289	.300	144	1	.222	.317	.306	87	0	.218	.303	.287	33	0	.303	.378	.455
1989 Cle-A	598	5	.299	.370	.390	316	1	.332	.399	.424	282	4	.262	.336	.351	175	2	.309	.349	.417	423	3	.296	.378	.378	198	1	.293	.382	.359	97	1	.299	.398	.381
1990 Cle-A	513	6	.267	.353	.372	250	2	.272	.369	.376	263	4	.262	.337	.369	139	0	.281	.392	.388	374	6	.262	.337	.366	161	2	.280	.371	.360	82	1	.244	.357	.305
1991 Cle-A	290	1	.228	.292	.269	135	1	.259	.313	.304	155	0	.200	.274	.239	78	0	.231	.310	.244	212	1	.226	.285	.278	123	1	.268	.319	.333	41	1	.313	.355	.373
1992 Oak-A	324	3	.287	.366	.364	146	1	.281	.369	.336	178	2	.292	.364	.388	49	0	.184	.226	.204	275	3	.305	.389	.393	140	2	.321	.392	.421	43	1	.465	.529	.605
1993 Oak-A	260	2	.250	.306	.323	112	1	.321	.372	.393	148	1	.196	.258	.270	60	1	.267	.302	.350	200	1	.245	.308	.315	104	0	.231	.274	.269	48	0	.167	.231	.188
1994 Fla-N	329	1	.295	.392	.398	162	0	.315	.395	.401	167	3	.275	.390	.395	104	2	.327	.413	.462	225	1	.280	.383	.369	114	0	.298	.442	.377	56	1	.321	.400	.500
TOTALS	3006	22	.272	.351	.355	1509	8	.299	.376	.380	1497	14	.246	.326	.329	799	6	.284	.356	.375	2207	16	.268	.349	.347	1077	6	.279	.365	.352	493	5	.300	.393	.385
■ Tom Brunansky BR/TR																																			
1984 Min-A	567	32	.254	.320	.460	273	14	.234	.310	.425	294	18	.272	.329	.493	163	15	.239	.342	.546	404	17	.260	.310	.426	255	10	.263	.331	.416	92	5	.293	.371	.467
1985 Min-A	567	27	.242	.320	.448	287	12	.254	.326	.439	280	15	.229	.313	.457	182	5	.214	.302	.379	385	22	.255	.328	.481	280	12	.232	.307	.418	85	7	.306	.375	.624
1986 Min-A	593	23	.256	.315	.423	296	15	.267	.324	.480	297	8	.246	.306	.367	167	11	.311	.354	.575	426	12	.235	.300	.364	282	15	.238	.302	.390	89	2	.180	.232	.315
1987 Min-A	532	32	.259	.352	.489	273	19	.300	.384	.574	259	13	.216	.318	.396	158	10	.228	.321	.481	374	22	.273	.366	.492	223	12	.269	.379	.502	78	3	.282	.371	.449
1988 Min-A	49	1	.184	.286	.265	26	0	.154	.214	.154	23	1	.217	.357	.391	21	0	.190	.227	.238	28	1	.179	.324	.286	25	0	.160	.276	.200	9	0	.111	.273	.111
1988 StL-N	523	22	.245	.345	.428	253	7	.225	.336	.364	270	15	.263	.354	.489	171	4	.281	.376	.421	352	18	.227	.329	.432	243	7	.226	.358	.362	98	3	.194	.316	.357
1989 StL-N	556	20	.239	.312	.410	263	4	.232	.300	.354	293	16	.246	.322	.461	220	11	.236	.320	.423	336	9	.241	.306	.402	264	12	.258	.328	.466	86	3	.209	.300	.372
1990 StL-N	57	1	.158	.310	.263	17	0	.235	.381	.294	40	1	.125	.280	.250	29	0	.172	.265	.241	28	1	.143	.351	.286	19	0	.105	.357	.158	10	0	.100	.357	.100
1990 Bos-A	461	15	.267	.342	.438	235	13	.340	.395	.626	226	2	.190	.289	.243	150	6	.307	.347	.527	311	9	.248	.340	.395	241	9	.257	.335	.452	76	0	.250	.360	.303
1991 Bos-A	459	16	.229	.303	.390	234	10	.256	.315	.453	225	6	.200	.289	.324	142	5	.254	.321	.423	317	11	.218	.294	.375	227	10	.242	.305	.436	68	0	.250	.333	.382
1992 Bos-A	458	15	.266	.354	.445	217	10	.323	.405	.576	241	5	.216	.308	.328	132	6	.227	.354	.439	326	9	.282	.354	.448	228	6	.276	.361	.443	90	4	.289	.394	.511
1993 Mil-A	224	6	.183	.265	.321	100	2	.180	.261	.310	124	4	.185	.268	.331	101	3	.178	.284	.347	123	3	.187	.248	.301	107	3	.187	.269	.308	30	2	.233	.343	.433
1994 Mil-A	28	0	.214	.241	.286	22	0	.227	.227	.318	6	0	.167	.286	.167	18	0	.167	.167	.278	10	0	.300	.364	.300	15	0	.200	.250	.267	9	0	.222	.300	.222
1994 Bos-A	177	10	.237	.319	.475	87	4	.184	.291	.402	90	6	.289	.347	.544	40	1	.200	.377	.350	137	9	.248	.298	.511	77	7	.299	.363	.623	25	3	.360	.485	.760
TOTALS	5251	220	.245	.325	.429	2587	110	.261	.338	.459	2664	110	.231	.312	.401	1694	77	.246	.330	.447	3557	143	.245	.322	.421	2486	99	.247	.330	.426	845	32	.249	.343	.422
■ Bill Buckner BL/TL																																			
1984 Chi-N	43	0	.209	.239	.209	22	0	.091	.125	.091	21	0	.333	.364	.333	12	0	.250	.286	.250	31	0	.194	.219	.194	25	0	.200	.250	.200	16	0	.313	.389	.313
1984 Bos-A	439	11	.278	.321	.410	230	6	.274	.327	.422	209	5	.282	.314	.397	137	5	.277	.338	.416	302	6	.278	.313	.407	191	5	.335	.387	.476	57	1	.386	.455	.474
1985 Bos-A	673	16	.299	.325	.447	328	6	.299	.322	.433	345	10	.299	.329	.461	230	4	.291	.311	.404	443	12	.302	.333	.470	334	11	.329	.356	.494	101	3	.386	.411	.564
1986 Bos-A	629	18	.267	.311	.421	299	8	.258	.303	.411	330	10	.276	.318	.430	202	4	.218	.257	.322	427	14	.290	.336	.468	341	7	.276	.332	.408	74	1	.311	.409	.432
1987 Bos-A	286	2	.273	.299	.322	148	0	.297	.329	.331	138	2	.246	.266	.312	76	0	.250	.259	.250	210	2	.281	.314	.348	123	2	.301	.326	.390	46	0	.196	.260	.196
1987 Cal-A	183	3	.306	.337	.432	90	2	.311	.340	.456	93	1	.301	.333	.409	43	0	.279	.295	.349	140	3	.314	.349	.457	86	1	.337	.370	.465	30	0	.400	.419	.533
1988 Cal-A	43	0	.209	.271	.209	21	0	.190	.217	.190	22	0	.227	.320	.227	1	0	.000	.000	.000	42	0	.214	.277	.214	17	0	.294	.381	.294	7	0	.286	.333	.286
1988 KC-A	242	3	.256	.290	.351	116	0	.284	.323	.336	126	3	.230	.259	.365	31	0	.290	.324	.387	211	3	.251	.284	.346	109	0	.367	.411	.468	59	0	.322	.358	.356
1989 KC-A	176	1	.216	.240	.267	84	0	.190	.225	.214	92	1	.239	.255	.315	23	0	.348	.375	.391	153	1	.196	.220	.248	80	0	.213	.247	.250	38	0	.263	.293	.316
1990 Bos-A	43	1	.186	.234	.256	26	1	.269	.333	.385	17	0	.059	.059	.059	1	0	.000	.000	.000	42	1	.190	.239	.262	23	0	.174	.259	.174	12	0	.167	.231	.167
TOTALS	2757	55	.272	.307	.391	1364	23	.273	.310	.385	1393	32	.272	.305	.397	756	13	.265	.297	.361	2001	42	.275	.311	.402	1329	26	.305	.347	.427	440	5	.325	.378	.416
■ Steve Buechele BR/TR																																			
1985 Tex-A	219	6	.219	.271	.356	110	5	.218	.256	.409	109	1	.220	.286	.303	75	3	.267	.304	.427	144	3	.194	.255	.319	90	5	.244	.296	.367	28	1	.286	.333	.429
1986 Tex-A	461	18	.243	.302	.410	224	6	.237	.292	.353	237	12	.249	.310	.464	139	5	.273	.346	.446	322	13	.230	.282	.394	169	3	.237	.294	.331	75	3	.267	.300	.440
1987 Tex-A	363	13	.237	.290	.399	188	6	.250	.316	.404	175	7	.223	.262	.394	177	8	.288	.333	.497	186	5	.188	.250	.306	168	3	.226	.280	.345	50	0	.300	.375	.380
1988 Tex-A	503	16	.250	.342	.404	246	8	.260	.352	.415	257	8	.241	.332	.393	153	5	.235	.335	.392	350	11	.257	.345	.409	222	4	.257	.353	.378	97	4	.237	.315	.381
1989 Tex-A	486	16	.235	.294	.387	227	7	.225	.296	.339	259	9	.244	.291	.429	148	6	.257	.322	.439	338	10	.225	.280	.362	213	4	.235	.302	.362	71	2	.239	.325	.366
1990 Tex-A	251	7	.215	.294	.339	136	5	.243	.316	.397	115	2	.183	.269	.270	80	4	.275	.372	.488	171	3	.187	.255	.269	124	4	.234	.322	.371	34	0	.235	.289	.265
1991 Tex-A	416	18	.267	.335	.447	190	7	.300	.368	.474	226	11	.239	.308	.425	97	6	.289	.391	.546	319	12	.260	.317	.417	178	9	.292	.366	.517	83	3	.277	.341	.434
1991 Pit-N	114	4	.246	.315	.412	61	2	.197	.265	.361	53	2	.302	.373	.472	34	3	.324	.439	.647	80	1	.213	.256	.313	61	3	.279	.348	.492	25	0	.160	.160	.200
1992 Pit-N	285	8	.249	.331	.389	149	3	.235	.318	.322	136	5	.265	.346	.463	113	4	.292	.375	.478	172	4	.221	.303	.331	123	3	.293	.390	.423	55	0	.200	.267	.309
1992 Chi-N	239	1	.276	.338	.351	127	1	.260	.314	.370	112	0	.295	.365	.330	94	1	.319	.369	.457	145	0	.248	.319	.283	101	0	.287	.365	.337	50	0	.220	.316	.220
1993 Chi-N	460	15	.272	.345	.437	224	8	.281	.359	.451	236	7	.263	.332	.424	128	5	.281	.378	.469	332	10	.268	.332	.425	199	5	.276	.344	.432	60	0	.242	.329	.306
1994 Chi-N	339	14	.242	.325	.404	173	7	.260	.342	.416	166	7	.223	.307	.392	85	2	.235	.330	.376	254	12	.244	.323	.413	160	7	.325	.366	.512	52	1	.173	.283	.250
TOTALS	4136	136	.247	.318	.400	2055	65	.252	.323	.396	2081	71	.243	.312	.404	1323	52	.274	.352	.461	2813	84	.235	.301	.371	1808	48	.264	.335	.404	682	14	.240	.311	.348
■ Jay Buhner BR/TR																																			
1987 NY-A	22	0	.227	.261	.318	15	0	.200	.250	.333	7	0	.286	.286	.286	20	0	.200	.200	.250	2	0	.500	.667	1.000	10	0	.100	.100	.100	3	0	.000	.000	.000
1988 NY-A	69	3	.188	.250	.319	29	1	.241	.281	.345	40	2	.150	.227	.300	28	1	.179	.200	.286	41	2	.195	.283	.341	34	2	.235	.289	.412	14	0	.071	.071	.071
1988 Sea-A	192	10	.224	.320	.458	97	7	.206	.284	.485	95	3	.242	.354	.432	61	3	.164	.212	.344	131	7	.252	.365	.511	80	4	.225	.312	.450	29	0	.103	.188	.172
1989 Sea-A	204	9	.275	.341	.490	104	7	.279	.342	.529	100	2	.270	.339	.450	60	2	.233	.299	.400	144	7	.292	.358	.528	88	5	.295	.351	.568	36	2	.278	.316	.444
1990 Sea-A	163	7	.276	.357	.479	68	2	.250	.378	.412	95	5	.295	.340	.526	56	4	.357	.438	.714	107	3	.234	.314	.355	88	5	.261	.340	.500	27	1	.259	.286	.407
1991 Sea-A	406	27	.244	.337	.498	212	14	.212	.321	.472	194	13	.278	.355	.526	146	9	.240	.371	.486	260	18	.246	.316	.504	199	12	.231	.320	.487	72	3	.222	.337	.389
1992 Sea-A	543	25	.243	.333	.422	308	11	.250	.352	.430	235	14	.234	.310	.413	148	10	.230	.347	.459	395	15	.248	.335	.408	235	11	.247	.344	.434	79	5	.224	.330	.429
1993 Sea-A	563	27	.272	.379	.476	275	13	.273	.402	.491	288	14	.271	.355	.462	172	9	.320	.435	.535	391	18	.251	.353	.450	256	13	.270	.398	.477	79	2	.304	.426	.468
1994 Sea-A	358	21	.279	.394	.542	159	8	.270	.390	.535	199	13	.286	.397	.548	110	8	.336	.439	.655	248	13	.254	.374	.492	169	10	.266	.397	.503	51	2	.294	.446	.490
TOTALS	2520	129	.256	.351	.471	1222	61	.251	.357	.473	1298	68	.261	.347	.470	801	46	.267	.366	.501	1719	83	.251	.345	.458	1159	62	.254	.356	.475	409	15	.240	.344	.403
■ Ellis Burks BR/TR																																			
1987 Bos-A	558	20	.272	.324	.441	256	11	.289	.365	.480	302	9	.258	.287	.407	151	4	.325	.380	.483	407	16	.253	.303	.425	177	8	.249	.333	.463	76	1	.184	.262	.263
1988 Bos-A	540	18	.294	.367	.481	246	8	.325	.402	.524	294	10	.269	.335	.446	142	5	.324	.410	.486	398	13	.284	.351	.480	267	10	.326	.396	.547	74	1	.297	.429	.419
1989 Bos-A	399	12	.303	.365	.471	205	6	.319	.376	.480	194	6	.287	.354	.462	104	2	.279	.351	.413	295	10	.312	.366	.492	200	6	.315	.368	.475	66	4	.242	.304	.561
1990 Bos-A	588	21	.296	.349	.486	297	10	.306	.357	.502	291	11	.285	.341	.471	188	5	.298	.365	.452	400	16	.295	.341	.503	294	9	.286	.331	.483	93	1	.280	.346	.398
1991 Bos-A	474	14	.251	.314	.422	232	8	.267	.328	.466	242	6	.236	.301	.380	135	5	.259	.313	.489	339	9	.248	.315	.395	225	4	.253	.308	.382	69	1	.217	.299	.348
1992 Bos-A	235	8	.255	.327	.417	108	3	.231	.309	.426	127	5	.276	.343	.409	66	3	.197	.299	.394	169	5	.278	.339	.430	123	3	.246	.328	.430	50	2	.240	.304	.380
1993 Chi-A	499	17	.275	.352	.441	238	7	.298	.383	.475	261	10	.253	.323	.410	153	5	.281	.380	.477	346	12	.272	.339	.426	209	6	.273	.350	.426	71	1	.268	.357	.380
1994 Col-N	149	13	.322	.388	.678	65	7	.369	.423	.815	84	6	.286	.362	.571	35	4	.343	.395	.771	114	9	.316	.386	.649	66	2	.242	.342	.424	19	2	.263	.333	.632
TOTALS	3442	123	.282	.346	.465	1646	61	.299	.367	.498	1796	62	.266	.326	.434	974	36	.291	.365	.474	2468	87	.278	.338	.461	1552	48	.281	.347	.462	518	13	.249	.335	.400
■ Randy Bush BL/TL																																			
1984 Min-A	311	11	.222	.292	.389	154	8	.227	.313	.455	157	3	.217	.272	.325	3	0	.000	.000	.000	308	11	.224	.295	.393	129	5	.279	.360	.465	51	1	.216	.283	.314
1985 Min-A	234	10	.239	.321	.449	136	5	.250	.335	.456	98	5	.224	.300	.439	12	0	.083	.214	.167	222	10	.247	.327	.464	112	4	.223	.299	.402	42	2	.190	.244	.357
1986 Min-A	357	7	.269	.347	.420	181	6	.304	.376	.525	176	1	.233	.317	.313	12	0	.167	.286	.250	345	7	.272	.349	.426	164	4	.293	.357	.470	57	1	.351	.456	.526
1987 Min-A	293	11	.253	.349	.413	128	3	.258	.380	.367	165	8	.248	.323	.448	9	0	.222	.417	.222	284	11	.254	.346	.419	128	4	.289	.385	.453	46	1	.239	.364	.391
1988 Min-A	394	14	.261	.365	.434	185	10	.243	.372	.492	209	4	.278	.358	.383	11	0	.182	.333	.364	383	14	.264	.366	.436	180	7	.283	.399	.444	54	2	.259	.397	.481

YEAR	TM/L	TOTAL AB	HR	AVG	OBP	SLG	HOME AB	HR	AVG	OBP	SLG	AWAY AB	HR	AVG	OBP	SLG	LEFT AB	HR	AVG	OBP	SLG	RIGHT AB	HR	AVG	OBP	SLG	ON-BASE AB	HR	AVG	OBP	SLG	LATE/CLOSE AB	HR	AVG	OBP	SLG
1989	Min-A	391	14	.263	.347	.435	181	6	.265	.368	.436	210	8	.262	.328	.433	20	0	.250	.250	.400	371	14	.264	.351	.437	160	7	.306	.405	.519	57	1	.228	.328	.316
1990	Min-A	181	6	.243	.338	.387	98	4	.296	.375	.490	83	2	.181	.296	.265	4	0	.250	.333	.500	177	6	.243	.338	.384	66	4	.212	.333	.439	31	2	.258	.378	.452
1991	Min-A	165	6	.303	.401	.485	64	2	.250	.377	.391	101	4	.337	.417	.545	2	0	.000	.000	.000	163	6	.307	.405	.491	78	2	.269	.394	.397	37	2	.378	.489	.622
1992	Min-A	182	2	.214	.263	.302	83	0	.217	.286	.253	99	2	.212	.243	.343	8	0	.000	.000	.000	174	2	.224	.274	.316	95	0	.221	.267	.253	48	0	.188	.235	.250
1993	Min-A	45	0	.156	.269	.200	20	0	.200	.333	.250	25	0	.120	.214	.160	1	0	.000	.000	.000	44	0	.159	.275	.205	23	0	.174	.296	.174	12	0	.167	.412	.167
TOTALS		2553	81	.251	.337	.412	1230	44	.258	.356	.441	1323	37	.245	.318	.385	82	0	.159	.253	.256	2471	81	.254	.340	.417	1135	37	.270	.362	.433	435	12	.253	.357	.400

■ Brett Butler BL/TL

YEAR	TM/L	TOTAL AB	HR	AVG	OBP	SLG	HOME AB	HR	AVG	OBP	SLG	AWAY AB	HR	AVG	OBP	SLG	LEFT AB	HR	AVG	OBP	SLG	RIGHT AB	HR	AVG	OBP	SLG	ON-BASE AB	HR	AVG	OBP	SLG	LATE/CLOSE AB	HR	AVG	OBP	SLG
1984	Cle-A	602	3	.269	.361	.355	297	1	.279	.360	.360	305	2	.259	.362	.351	190	0	.295	.400	.363	412	3	.257	.342	.352	179	1	.302	.410	.380	97	0	.237	.351	.278
1985	Cle-A	591	5	.311	.377	.431	289	1	.329	.382	.429	302	4	.295	.372	.434	193	1	.332	.378	.430	398	4	.302	.376	.432	198	3	.328	.390	.444	90	0	.211	.276	.244
1986	Cle-A	587	4	.278	.356	.375	276	0	.272	.360	.351	311	4	.283	.352	.395	160	1	.306	.390	.412	427	3	.267	.342	.361	228	0	.276	.370	.333	87	1	.356	.396	.414
1987	Cle-A	522	9	.295	.399	.425	246	4	.337	.443	.492	276	5	.257	.359	.366	146	2	.267	.397	.342	376	7	.306	.400	.457	165	2	.303	.432	.412	63	4	.254	.342	.492
1988	SF-N	568	6	.287	.393	.398	276	1	.290	.401	.366	292	5	.284	.387	.428	190	1	.253	.380	.332	378	5	.304	.400	.431	156	1	.256	.398	.340	90	0	.244	.346	.300
1989	SF-N	594	4	.283	.349	.354	296	2	.304	.370	.382	298	2	.262	.328	.327	200	1	.280	.353	.350	394	3	.284	.347	.355	171	0	.292	.367	.345	92	1	.293	.347	.359
1990	SF-N	622	3	.309	.397	.384	312	3	.337	.427	.410	310	0	.281	.367	.358	245	1	.302	.389	.355	377	2	.313	.403	.403	169	1	.320	.390	.414	98	1	.265	.342	.327
1991	LA-N	615	2	.296	.401	.343	295	2	.312	.425	.369	320	0	.281	.377	.319	256	0	.281	.397	.313	359	2	.306	.404	.365	174	1	.310	.427	.362	106	1	.302	.444	.387
1992	LA-N	553	3	.309	.413	.391	267	1	.303	.411	.375	286	2	.315	.414	.406	223	1	.296	.402	.345	330	2	.318	.420	.421	192	1	.307	.396	.396	92	0	.348	.455	.380
1993	LA-N	607	1	.298	.387	.371	291	0	.347	.441	.409	316	1	.253	.336	.335	206	0	.330	.407	.374	401	1	.282	.378	.369	191	0	.304	.396	.382	104	1	.337	.444	.500
1994	LA-N	417	8	.314	.411	.446	190	2	.274	.400	.379	227	6	.348	.421	.502	128	1	.281	.388	.367	289	7	.329	.421	.481	118	1	.314	.435	.390	72	1	.375	.483	.500
TOTALS		6278	48	.295	.385	.386	3035	17	.309	.402	.392	3243	31	.282	.369	.380	2137	9	.294	.389	.360	4141	39	.295	.383	.400	1941	11	.301	.400	.381	991	10	.293	.387	.375

■ Enos Cabell BR/TR

YEAR	TM/L	TOTAL AB	HR	AVG	OBP	SLG	HOME AB	HR	AVG	OBP	SLG	AWAY AB	HR	AVG	OBP	SLG	LEFT AB	HR	AVG	OBP	SLG	RIGHT AB	HR	AVG	OBP	SLG	ON-BASE AB	HR	AVG	OBP	SLG	LATE/CLOSE AB	HR	AVG	OBP	SLG
1984	Hou-N	436	8	.310	.341	.417	212	2	.269	.299	.373	224	6	.348	.380	.460	184	4	.332	.371	.435	252	4	.294	.318	.405	195	2	.277	.318	.354	93	1	.247	.278	.312
1985	Hou-N	143	2	.245	.321	.357	80	1	.250	.336	.363	63	1	.238	.314	.349	100	1	.270	.348	.400	43	1	.186	.255	.256	67	1	.209	.293	.358	32	0	.313	.371	.406
1985	LA-N	192	0	.292	.340	.349	102	0	.284	.342	.343	90	0	.300	.337	.356	81	0	.333	.400	.395	111	0	.261	.293	.315	75	0	.373	.434	.440	31	0	.290	.353	.323
1986	LA-N	277	2	.256	.294	.318	144	2	.271	.308	.361	133	0	.241	.279	.271	197	2	.284	.321	.371	80	0	.188	.230	.188	111	1	.261	.309	.324	51	1	.275	.333	.353
TOTALS		1048	12	.283	.325	.370	538	5	.270	.314	.362	510	7	.298	.338	.378	562	7	.304	.354	.400	486	5	.259	.292	.335	448	4	.279	.331	.362	207	2	.271	.318	.338

■ Ivan Calderon BR/TR

YEAR	TM/L	TOTAL AB	HR	AVG	OBP	SLG	HOME AB	HR	AVG	OBP	SLG	AWAY AB	HR	AVG	OBP	SLG	LEFT AB	HR	AVG	OBP	SLG	RIGHT AB	HR	AVG	OBP	SLG	ON-BASE AB	HR	AVG	OBP	SLG	LATE/CLOSE AB	HR	AVG	OBP	SLG
1984	Sea-A	24	1	.208	.269	.375	11	0	.091	.167	.091	13	1	.308	.357	.615	11	1	.273	.273	.636	13	0	.154	.267	.154	11	0	.091	.091	.091	7	0	.143	.143	.143
1985	Sea-A	210	8	.286	.349	.514	111	6	.297	.358	.550	99	2	.273	.339	.475	71	3	.296	.383	.535	139	5	.281	.331	.504	92	6	.261	.337	.446	33	3	.273	.385	.576
1986	Sea-A	131	2	.237	.275	.321	63	1	.206	.265	.270	68	1	.265	.286	.368	30	0	.167	.242	.233	101	2	.257	.286	.347	56	1	.250	.288	.339	22	0	.273	.273	.273
1986	Chi-A	33	0	.303	.361	.424	1	0	.000	.000	.000	32	0	.313	.371	.438	22	0	.318	.348	.455	11	0	.273	.385	.364	11	0	.364	.417	.455	8	0	.375	.375	.625
1987	Chi-A	542	28	.293	.362	.526	260	15	.315	.402	.573	282	13	.273	.324	.482	190	13	.279	.360	.542	352	15	.301	.364	.517	255	9	.263	.331	.424	79	2	.342	.426	.506
1988	Chi-A	264	14	.212	.299	.424	131	6	.191	.255	.374	133	8	.233	.340	.474	80	5	.237	.347	.488	184	9	.201	.277	.397	121	6	.174	.264	.347	41	1	.244	.333	.415
1989	Chi-A	622	14	.286	.332	.437	286	2	.248	.294	.364	336	12	.318	.364	.500	184	4	.332	.389	.495	438	10	.267	.308	.413	296	9	.284	.343	.473	100	1	.300	.355	.430
1990	Chi-A	607	14	.273	.327	.422	284	6	.306	.370	.468	323	8	.245	.287	.381	227	6	.295	.351	.476	380	8	.261	.313	.389	261	9	.287	.333	.475	88	1	.216	.293	.284
1991	Mon-N	470	19	.300	.368	.481	224	7	.308	.374	.455	246	12	.293	.362	.504	161	11	.354	.423	.627	309	8	.272	.339	.405	217	7	.323	.357	.488	90	5	.344	.435	.567
1992	Mon-N	170	3	.265	.323	.424	101	2	.257	.296	.416	69	1	.275	.359	.435	51	0	.333	.414	.510	119	3	.235	.281	.387	75	2	.267	.325	.413	29	1	.241	.258	.448
1993	Bos-A	213	1	.221	.291	.291	84	0	.202	.272	.310	129	1	.233	.303	.279	45	0	.156	.235	.178	168	1	.238	.306	.321	100	0	.230	.288	.290	36	0	.250	.308	.306
1993	Chi-A	26	0	.115	.115	.192	5	0	.000	.000	.000	21	0	.143	.143	.238	18	0	.056	.056	.111	8	0	.250	.250	.375	12	0	.167	.167	.250	6	0	.167	.167	.333
TOTALS		3312	104	.272	.333	.442	1561	45	.272	.336	.438	1751	59	.272	.330	.445	1090	43	.292	.361	.495	2222	61	.262	.318	.415	1507	45	.269	.326	.431	539	14	.284	.355	.432

■ Ken Caminiti BB/TR

YEAR	TM/L	TOTAL AB	HR	AVG	OBP	SLG	HOME AB	HR	AVG	OBP	SLG	AWAY AB	HR	AVG	OBP	SLG	LEFT AB	HR	AVG	OBP	SLG	RIGHT AB	HR	AVG	OBP	SLG	ON-BASE AB	HR	AVG	OBP	SLG	LATE/CLOSE AB	HR	AVG	OBP	SLG
1987	Hou-N	203	3	.246	.287	.335	90	2	.267	.313	.389	113	1	.230	.267	.292	100	2	.310	.349	.430	103	1	.184	.227	.243	97	1	.237	.272	.309	43	1	.349	.370	.465
1988	Hou-N	83	1	.181	.225	.241	40	0	.200	.233	.225	43	1	.163	.217	.256	24	1	.125	.222	.250	59	0	.203	.226	.237	36	1	.222	.256	.333	19	0	.158	.150	.211
1989	Hou-N	585	10	.255	.316	.369	293	3	.256	.313	.362	292	7	.253	.319	.377	165	4	.315	.363	.473	420	6	.231	.297	.329	271	3	.247	.304	.358	119	3	.210	.254	.319
1990	Hou-N	541	4	.242	.302	.309	285	2	.288	.348	.361	256	2	.191	.250	.250	240	2	.246	.280	.317	301	2	.239	.318	.302	242	2	.244	.310	.310	100	0	.280	.345	.340
1991	Hou-N	574	13	.253	.312	.383	289	9	.253	.307	.422	285	4	.253	.316	.344	232	9	.310	.347	.500	342	4	.213	.289	.301	278	9	.277	.341	.442	92	3	.272	.302	.380
1992	Hou-N	506	13	.294	.350	.441	246	7	.329	.389	.496	260	6	.262	.311	.388	208	7	.303	.357	.476	298	6	.289	.345	.416	223	6	.278	.353	.430	92	2	.283	.391	.424
1993	Hou-N	543	13	.262	.321	.390	288	5	.257	.308	.375	255	8	.267	.336	.408	187	5	.246	.319	.401	356	8	.270	.322	.385	269	5	.245	.300	.364	80	2	.287	.345	.438
1994	Hou-N	406	18	.283	.352	.495	204	6	.289	.350	.466	202	12	.277	.355	.525	128	5	.266	.331	.484	278	13	.291	.362	.500	209	7	.311	.385	.502	58	1	.207	.292	.310
TOTALS		3441	75	.260	.319	.386	1735	34	.273	.330	.403	1706	41	.246	.308	.368	1284	35	.280	.330	.433	2157	40	.248	.313	.357	1625	34	.268	.334	.391	603	12	.260	.320	.370

■ Casey Candaele BB/TR

YEAR	TM/L	TOTAL AB	HR	AVG	OBP	SLG	HOME AB	HR	AVG	OBP	SLG	AWAY AB	HR	AVG	OBP	SLG	LEFT AB	HR	AVG	OBP	SLG	RIGHT AB	HR	AVG	OBP	SLG	ON-BASE AB	HR	AVG	OBP	SLG	LATE/CLOSE AB	HR	AVG	OBP	SLG
1986	Mon-N	104	0	.231	.264	.288	62	0	.274	.308	.355	42	0	.167	.200	.190	41	0	.268	.286	.366	63	0	.206	.250	.238	31	0	.161	.156	.194	20	0	.200	.304	.200
1987	Mon-N	449	1	.272	.330	.347	244	1	.270	.321	.344	205	0	.273	.341	.351	113	0	.310	.352	.407	336	1	.259	.322	.327	137	0	.263	.322	.299	71	1	.296	.338	.423
1988	Mon-N	116	0	.172	.238	.233	55	0	.164	.258	.236	61	0	.180	.219	.230	47	0	.213	.260	.319	69	0	.145	.224	.174	48	0	.188	.264	.229	14	0	.214	.353	.357
1988	Hou-N	31	0	.161	.188	.258	20	0	.150	.150	.300	11	0	.182	.250	.182	16	0	.250	.250	.438	15	0	.067	.125	.067	9	0	.333	.400	.556	9	0	.111	.111	.111
1990	Hou-N	262	3	.286	.364	.397	126	1	.286	.375	.413	136	2	.287	.350	.382	126	2	.341	.407	.444	136	1	.235	.325	.353	107	1	.299	.375	.402	64	1	.250	.333	.406
1991	Hou-N	461	4	.262	.319	.362	235	1	.294	.361	.396	226	3	.230	.274	.327	158	1	.285	.347	.361	303	3	.251	.305	.363	206	1	.301	.347	.398	102	0	.265	.336	.324
1992	Hou-N	320	1	.213	.269	.266	159	1	.195	.267	.264	161	0	.230	.272	.267	128	1	.266	.326	.344	192	0	.177	.230	.214	118	0	.195	.246	.220	77	0	.312	.368	.403
1993	Hou-N	121	1	.240	.298	.331	56	0	.196	.262	.250	65	1	.277	.329	.400	41	1	.268	.333	.366	80	0	.225	.279	.313	45	0	.200	.234	.289	31	0	.323	.364	.419
TOTALS		1864	10	.249	.308	.331	957	4	.253	.318	.341	907	6	.245	.298	.321	670	5	.288	.343	.381	1194	5	.227	.289	.303	701	2	.255	.309	.324	388	2	.273	.339	.369

■ John Cangelosi BB/TL

YEAR	TM/L	TOTAL AB	HR	AVG	OBP	SLG	HOME AB	HR	AVG	OBP	SLG	AWAY AB	HR	AVG	OBP	SLG	LEFT AB	HR	AVG	OBP	SLG	RIGHT AB	HR	AVG	OBP	SLG	ON-BASE AB	HR	AVG	OBP	SLG	LATE/CLOSE AB	HR	AVG	OBP	SLG
1985	Chi-A	2	0	.000	.333	.000	2	0	.000	.000	.000	0	0	—	1.000	—	0	0	—	1.000	—	2	0	.000	.000	.000	0	0	—	1.000	—	0	0	—	—	—
1986	Chi-A	438	2	.235	.349	.299	202	1	.238	.384	.317	236	1	.233	.316	.284	134	2	.216	.350	.343	304	0	.243	.348	.280	140	1	.250	.410	.307	65	1	.262	.338	.415
1987	Pit-N	182	4	.275	.427	.418	102	2	.294	.411	.431	80	2	.250	.444	.400	103	4	.282	.400	.485	79	0	.266	.458	.329	45	1	.311	.467	.511	42	1	.238	.407	.310
1988	Pit-N	118	0	.254	.353	.305	61	0	.246	.352	.328	57	0	.263	.354	.281	60	0	.267	.353	.317	58	0	.241	.353	.293	34	0	.324	.452	.353	44	0	.273	.396	.364
1989	Pit-N	160	0	.219	.365	.269	78	0	.269	.430	.333	82	0	.171	.300	.207	82	0	.207	.327	.268	78	0	.231	.402	.269	44	0	.182	.377	.205	67	0	.194	.321	.224
1990	Pit-N	76	0	.197	.307	.224	43	0	.186	.286	.233	33	0	.212	.333	.212	42	0	.214	.283	.238	34	0	.176	.333	.206	16	0	.188	.278	.250	20	0	.250	.423	.250
1992	Tex-A	85	1	.188	.330	.247	37	0	.189	.318	.216	48	1	.188	.339	.271	19	0	.158	.385	.368	66	1	.197	.312	.212	29	1	.241	.389	.379	13	0	.231	.375	.308
1994	NY-N	111	0	.252	.371	.288	46	0	.217	.379	.239	65	0	.277	.365	.323	48	0	.229	.292	.292	63	0	.270	.395	.286	28	0	.321	.441	.321	36	0	.222	.333	.222
TOTALS		1172	7	.236	.362	.304	571	3	.243	.380	.320	601	4	.230	.344	.289	488	7	.234	.353	.344	684	2	.238	.369	.275	336	3	.259	.414	.330	287	2	.237	.361	.307

■ Jose Canseco BR/TR

YEAR	TM/L	TOTAL AB	HR	AVG	OBP	SLG	HOME AB	HR	AVG	OBP	SLG	AWAY AB	HR	AVG	OBP	SLG	LEFT AB	HR	AVG	OBP	SLG	RIGHT AB	HR	AVG	OBP	SLG	ON-BASE AB	HR	AVG	OBP	SLG	LATE/CLOSE AB	HR	AVG	OBP	SLG
1985	Oak-A	96	5	.302	.330	.490	45	4	.333	.375	.622	51	1	.275	.288	.373	28	1	.250	.276	.393	68	4	.324	.352	.529	42	1	.310	.341	.381	13	0	.385	.429	.385
1986	Oak-A	600	33	.240	.318	.457	301	14	.213	.296	.385	299	19	.268	.340	.528	185	8	.281	.323	.470	415	25	.222	.316	.451	271	22	.310	.368	.609	97	6	.289	.349	.557
1987	Oak-A	630	31	.257	.310	.470	298	16	.275	.332	.507	332	15	.241	.289	.437	204	15	.309	.356	.618	426	16	.232	.288	.399	292	12	.260	.326	.459	102	4	.265	.306	.451
1988	Oak-A	610	42	.307	.391	.569	288	16	.313	.407	.538	322	26	.301	.375	.596	150	10	.340	.412	.620	460	32	.296	.384	.552	291	26	.313	.391	.639	106	5	.274	.386	.462
1989	Oak-A	227	17	.269	.333	.542	104	8	.269	.328	.538	123	9	.268	.358	.545	50	7	.260	.381	.700	177	10	.271	.318	.497	119	9	.319	.374	.597	31	2	.290	.361	.516
1990	Oak-A	481	37	.274	.371	.543	217	18	.258	.386	.539	264	19	.288	.358	.545	123	12	.276	.357	.610	358	25	.274	.376	.520	231	18	.286	.362	.563	62	1	.161	.246	.242
1991	Oak-A	572	44	.266	.359	.556	267	16	.270	.371	.506	305	28	.262	.349	.600	136	8	.250	.370	.493	436	36	.271	.354	.576	254	20	.268	.362	.551	97	9	.237	.292	.588
1992	Oak-A	366	22	.246	.335	.456	170	12	.253	.340	.482	196	10	.240	.330	.434	81	7	.284	.392	.580	285	15	.235	.318	.421	185	8	.238	.341	.395	55	5	.291	.391	.582
1992	Tex-A	73	4	.233	.385	.452	34	3	.265	.405	.559	39	1	.205	.367	.359	13	0	.077	.250	.077	60	4	.267	.413	.533	40	3	.425	.413	.600	15	1	.267	.353	.533
1993	Tex-A	231	10	.255	.308	.455	110	6	.291	.331	.536	121	4	.223	.289	.380	38	3	.237	.302	.474	193	7	.259	.310	.451	99	6	.303	.345	.536	33	0	.182	.263	.242
1994	Tex-A	429	31	.282	.386	.552	223	17	.260	.370	.538	206	14	.306	.404	.568	92	7	.293	.426	.565	337	24	.279	.374	.549	215	14	.279	.387	.516	63	4	.349	.494	.587
TOTALS		4315	276	.267	.349	.512	2057	130	.267	.355	.505	2258	146	.266	.343	.518	1100	78	.285	.366	.556	3215	198	.261	.343	.496	2037	139	.287	.365	.542	674	37	.266	.349	.485

■ Chuck Carr BB/TR

YEAR	TM/L	TOTAL AB	HR	AVG	OBP	SLG	HOME AB	HR	AVG	OBP	SLG	AWAY AB	HR	AVG	OBP	SLG	LEFT AB	HR	AVG	OBP	SLG	RIGHT AB	HR	AVG	OBP	SLG	ON-BASE AB	HR	AVG	OBP	SLG	LATE/CLOSE AB	HR	AVG	OBP	SLG
1990	NY-N	2	0	.000	.000	.000	0	0	—	—	—	2	0	.000	.000	.000	1	0	.000	.000	.000	1	0	.000	.000	.000	1	0	.000	.000	.000	2	0	.000	.000	.000
1991	NY-N	11	0	.182	.182	.182	5	0	.000	.000	.000	6	0	.333	.333	.333	5	0	.400	.400	.400	6	0	.000	.000	.000	5	0	.200	.200	.200	2	0	.000	.000	.000
1992	StL-N	64	0	.219	.315	.266	23	0	.261	.370	.304	41	0	.195	.283	.244	24	0	.250	.280	.292	40	0	.200	.333	.250	19	0	.263	.333	.316	8	0	.125	.417	.250
1993	Fla-N	551	4	.267	.327	.330	271	3	.284	.349	.347	280	1	.250	.305	.314	173	2	.254	.309	.353	378	2	.272	.335	.320	166	2	.247	.325	.349	90	0	.356	.400	.400
1994	Fla-N	433	2	.263	.305	.330	221	1	.262	.301	.326	212	1	.264	.310	.335	136	1	.228	.267	.324	297	1	.279	.323	.333	158	2	.285	.335	.380	68	1	.324	.378	.426
TOTALS		1061	6	.261	.315	.324	520	4	.271	.327	.333	541	2	.251	.304	.316	339	3	.245	.290	.336	722	3	.269	.327	.319	349	6	.264	.327	.344	170	1	.324	.384	.394

■ Gary Carter BR/TR

YEAR	TM/L	TOTAL AB	HR	AVG	OBP	SLG	HOME AB	HR	AVG	OBP	SLG	AWAY AB	HR	AVG	OBP	SLG	LEFT AB	HR	AVG	OBP	SLG	RIGHT AB	HR	AVG	OBP	SLG	ON-BASE AB	HR	AVG	OBP	SLG	LATE/CLOSE AB	HR	AVG	OBP	SLG
1984	Mon-N	596	27	.294	.366	.487	286	14	.301	.396	.493	310	13	.287	.337	.481	156	7	.340	.406	.551	440	20	.277	.352	.464	275	12	.316	.401	.513	106	4	.264	.322	.425
1985	NY-N	555	32	.281	.365	.488	263	12	.266	.355	.437	292	20	.295	.373	.537	219	13	.329	.429	.566	336	19	.250	.320	.438	271	14	.288	.393	.483	104	4	.269	.350	.423
1986	NY-N	490	24	.255	.337	.439	228	13	.268	.352	.478	262	11	.244	.323	.405	171	10	.275	.397	.480	319	14	.245	.301	.417	262	14	.267	.347	.450	88	3	.318	.406	.443
1987	NY-N	523	20	.235	.290	.392	255	9	.231	.294	.376	268	11	.239	.286	.407	183	7	.240	.322	.404	340	13	.232	.271	.385	261	10	.241	.297	.450	87	5	.276	.337	.483
1988	NY-N	455	11	.242	.301	.358	228	5	.211	.258	.298	227	6	.273	.343	.419	164	5	.256	.295	.396	291	6	.234	.304	.337	176	4	.256	.335	.347	83	3	.265	.326	.398

YEAR	TM/L	TOTAL AB	HR	AVG	OBP	SLG	HOME AB	HR	AVG	OBP	SLG	AWAY AB	HR	AVG	OBP	SLG	LEFT AB	HR	AVG	OBP	SLG	RIGHT AB	HR	AVG	OBP	SLG	ON-BASE AB	HR	AVG	OBP	SLG	LATE/CLOSE AB	HR	AVG	OBP	SLG
1989	NY-N	153	2	.183	.241	.275	77	1	.143	.173	.234	76	1	.224	.306	.316	66	2	.167	.225	.273	87	0	.195	.253	.276	64	1	.172	.239	.250	30	1	.133	.161	.233
1990	SF-N	244	9	.254	.324	.406	127	6	.307	.350	.504	117	3	.197	.296	.299	127	3	.236	.322	.362	117	6	.274	.325	.453	107	2	.252	.311	.374	51	1	.255	.333	.353
1991	LA-N	248	6	.246	.323	.375	125	3	.216	.298	.304	123	3	.276	.348	.447	151	3	.252	.343	.371	97	3	.237	.288	.381	109	1	.248	.328	.339	54	1	.222	.300	.333
1992	Mon-N	285	5	.218	.299	.340	153	2	.242	.335	.353	132	3	.189	.257	.326	139	2	.230	.301	.367	146	3	.205	.298	.315	124	3	.242	.347	.387	47	0	.213	.260	.234
TOTALS		3549	136	.254	.326	.416	1742	65	.251	.327	.404	1807	71	.257	.325	.427	1376	52	.268	.352	.438	2173	84	.245	.309	.402	1649	61	.264	.347	.423	650	22	.260	.329	.395

■ Joe Carter BR/TR

YEAR	TM/L	TOTAL AB	HR	AVG	OBP	SLG	HOME AB	HR	AVG	OBP	SLG	AWAY AB	HR	AVG	OBP	SLG	LEFT AB	HR	AVG	OBP	SLG	RIGHT AB	HR	AVG	OBP	SLG	ON-BASE AB	HR	AVG	OBP	SLG	LATE/CLOSE AB	HR	AVG	OBP	SLG
1984	Cle-A	244	13	.275	.307	.467	125	9	.312	.344	.568	119	4	.235	.270	.361	85	8	.329	.352	.659	159	5	.245	.284	.365	106	4	.349	.369	.509	40	2	.300	.326	.450
1985	Cle-A	489	15	.262	.298	.409	247	5	.267	.320	.389	242	10	.256	.276	.430	161	5	.248	.303	.391	328	10	.268	.296	.418	220	5	.273	.314	.418	79	3	.342	.366	.468
1986	Cle-A	663	29	.302	.335	.514	324	14	.312	.350	.522	339	15	.292	.320	.507	181	7	.315	.354	.530	482	22	.297	.327	.508	319	14	.292	.322	.495	92	3	.315	.343	.511
1987	Cle-A	588	32	.264	.304	.480	279	15	.251	.298	.409	309	23	.275	.310	.544	153	7	.248	.287	.431	435	25	.269	.310	.497	303	11	.241	.278	.396	87	5	.264	.347	.471
1988	Cle-A	621	27	.271	.314	.478	299	16	.281	.336	.498	322	11	.261	.292	.460	132	7	.311	.348	.553	489	20	.260	.305	.458	281	11	.288	.338	.502	93	5	.215	.277	.462
1989	Cle-A	651	35	.243	.292	.465	329	16	.243	.294	.456	322	19	.242	.289	.475	186	8	.215	.267	.387	465	27	.254	.301	.497	322	15	.252	.315	.450	108	5	.185	.248	.352
1990	SD-N	634	24	.232	.290	.391	322	12	.220	.263	.366	312	12	.244	.316	.417	203	7	.197	.258	.335	431	17	.248	.305	.418	313	14	.252	.300	.441	123	4	.220	.267	.358
1991	Tor-A	638	33	.273	.330	.503	321	23	.290	.348	.583	317	10	.256	.311	.423	188	10	.335	.366	.569	450	23	.247	.315	.476	292	14	.274	.348	.479	107	1	.196	.295	.280
1992	Tor-A	622	34	.264	.309	.498	301	21	.259	.303	.538	321	13	.268	.315	.461	157	7	.312	.355	.535	465	27	.247	.294	.486	310	20	.258	.308	.519	86	3	.233	.269	.372
1993	Tor-A	603	33	.254	.312	.489	312	21	.250	.304	.529	291	12	.258	.321	.447	162	10	.296	.341	.531	441	23	.238	.302	.474	326	14	.252	.321	.445	88	3	.227	.284	.375
1994	Tor-A	435	27	.271	.317	.524	207	18	.300	.335	.628	228	9	.246	.300	.430	114	9	.298	.346	.596	321	18	.262	.306	.498	215	17	.293	.343	.605	64	4	.188	.222	.438
TOTALS		6188	302	.264	.310	.475	3066	164	.268	.316	.493	3122	138	.259	.305	.457	1722	85	.278	.321	.487	4466	217	.258	.306	.470	3007	139	.269	.323	.474	967	38	.239	.292	.404

■ Jack Clark BR/TR

YEAR	TM/L	TOTAL AB	HR	AVG	OBP	SLG	HOME AB	HR	AVG	OBP	SLG	AWAY AB	HR	AVG	OBP	SLG	LEFT AB	HR	AVG	OBP	SLG	RIGHT AB	HR	AVG	OBP	SLG	ON-BASE AB	HR	AVG	OBP	SLG	LATE/CLOSE AB	HR	AVG	OBP	SLG
1984	SF-N	203	11	.320	.434	.537	97	4	.278	.410	.443	106	7	.358	.457	.623	53	4	.283	.479	.528	150	7	.333	.415	.540	98	5	.286	.411	.490	45	2	.444	.554	.644
1985	StL-N	442	22	.281	.393	.502	225	8	.231	.335	.409	217	14	.332	.450	.599	139	9	.324	.467	.597	303	13	.261	.355	.459	233	11	.283	.379	.506	62	3	.306	.449	.548
1986	StL-N	232	9	.237	.362	.422	117	4	.239	.393	.453	115	5	.235	.331	.391	89	6	.303	.415	.596	143	3	.196	.329	.315	102	2	.206	.379	.324	53	1	.245	.365	.396
1987	StL-N	419	35	.286	.459	.597	202	17	.292	.457	.604	217	18	.281	.460	.590	138	10	.261	.480	.543	281	25	.299	.447	.623	227	20	.330	.500	.665	80	8	.287	.414	.650
1988	NY-A	496	27	.242	.381	.433	232	13	.233	.384	.422	264	14	.250	.380	.443	149	10	.248	.435	.483	347	17	.239	.356	.412	247	16	.239	.379	.457	73	5	.219	.341	.438
1989	SD-N	455	26	.242	.410	.459	211	11	.232	.406	.436	244	15	.250	.413	.480	125	4	.272	.474	.440	330	22	.233	.383	.467	230	18	.274	.445	.543	77	6	.221	.402	.468
1990	SD-N	334	25	.266	.441	.533	176	16	.256	.419	.568	158	9	.278	.465	.494	114	9	.377	.541	.667	220	16	.209	.386	.464	154	9	.286	.484	.532	60	4	.200	.442	.433
1991	Bos-A	481	28	.249	.374	.466	253	18	.281	.377	.542	228	10	.215	.372	.382	117	6	.325	.465	.530	364	22	.225	.342	.445	239	15	.264	.407	.510	88	5	.205	.278	.386
1992	Bos-A	257	5	.210	.350	.311	116	0	.259	.390	.310	141	5	.170	.316	.312	95	2	.295	.460	.421	162	3	.160	.278	.247	133	3	.188	.307	.301	62	0	.177	.268	.226
TOTALS		3319	188	.258	.402	.478	1629	91	.257	.396	.475	1690	97	.259	.408	.480	1019	60	.297	.469	.534	2300	128	.241	.369	.453	1663	99	.267	.417	.500	600	34	.248	.385	.463

■ Jerald Clark BR/TR

YEAR	TM/L	TOTAL AB	HR	AVG	OBP	SLG	HOME AB	HR	AVG	OBP	SLG	AWAY AB	HR	AVG	OBP	SLG	LEFT AB	HR	AVG	OBP	SLG	RIGHT AB	HR	AVG	OBP	SLG	ON-BASE AB	HR	AVG	OBP	SLG	LATE/CLOSE AB	HR	AVG	OBP	SLG
1988	SD-N	15	0	.200	.200	.267	4	0	.250	.250	.500	11	0	.182	.182	.182	8	0	.125	.125	.125	7	0	.286	.286	.429	5	0	.400	.400	.600	1	0	.000	.000	.000
1989	SD-N	41	1	.195	.250	.317	25	1	.160	.222	.360	16	0	.250	.294	.250	16	0	.250	.294	.250	25	1	.160	.222	.360	26	0	.154	.185	.231	3	0	.000	.000	.000
1990	SD-N	101	5	.267	.299	.475	41	2	.195	.233	.366	60	3	.317	.344	.550	53	2	.189	.218	.358	48	3	.354	.385	.604	41	3	.268	.311	.537	25	0	.200	.231	.240
1991	SD-N	369	10	.228	.295	.352	195	8	.210	.270	.379	174	2	.247	.323	.322	126	4	.175	.239	.294	243	6	.255	.324	.383	168	6	.262	.308	.417	71	2	.225	.263	.338
1992	SD-N	496	12	.242	.278	.383	247	9	.255	.292	.425	249	3	.229	.264	.341	152	6	.276	.306	.480	344	6	.227	.266	.340	202	7	.252	.303	.436	95	3	.211	.240	.358
1993	Col-N	478	13	.282	.324	.444	227	8	.322	.387	.524	251	5	.247	.262	.371	116	2	.276	.323	.422	362	11	.285	.325	.450	209	7	.316	.360	.493	74	4	.284	.289	.473
TOTALS		1500	41	.251	.297	.398	739	28	.257	.310	.438	761	13	.246	.283	.359	471	14	.236	.279	.389	1029	27	.259	.305	.402	651	23	.273	.319	.449	269	9	.230	.255	.368

■ Will Clark BL/TL

YEAR	TM/L	TOTAL AB	HR	AVG	OBP	SLG	HOME AB	HR	AVG	OBP	SLG	AWAY AB	HR	AVG	OBP	SLG	LEFT AB	HR	AVG	OBP	SLG	RIGHT AB	HR	AVG	OBP	SLG	ON-BASE AB	HR	AVG	OBP	SLG	LATE/CLOSE AB	HR	AVG	OBP	SLG
1986	SF-N	408	11	.287	.343	.444	220	7	.336	.388	.509	188	4	.229	.290	.367	130	2	.308	.348	.415	278	9	.277	.341	.457	158	4	.241	.337	.386	82	5	.402	.457	.659
1987	SF-N	529	35	.308	.371	.580	274	22	.339	.393	.657	255	13	.275	.347	.498	173	7	.318	.341	.555	356	28	.303	.385	.593	198	15	.338	.412	.641	96	3	.292	.370	.490
1988	SF-N	575	29	.282	.386	.508	283	14	.269	.364	.484	292	15	.295	.407	.531	221	7	.262	.331	.434	354	22	.294	.417	.554	268	15	.287	.419	.549	97	3	.237	.348	.392
1989	SF-N	588	23	.333	.407	.546	292	7	.325	.394	.516	296	11	.341	.420	.572	215	8	.321	.371	.512	373	15	.340	.428	.566	259	13	.355	.432	.629	90	5	.300	.379	.556
1990	SF-N	600	19	.295	.357	.448	296	8	.318	.384	.459	304	11	.273	.329	.438	249	9	.317	.372	.486	351	10	.279	.347	.422	286	9	.308	.370	.444	94	4	.266	.357	.426
1991	SF-N	565	29	.301	.359	.536	283	17	.283	.344	.558	282	12	.319	.373	.514	197	9	.239	.291	.452	368	20	.334	.394	.582	253	18	.332	.395	.640	89	3	.303	.382	.528
1992	SF-N	513	16	.300	.384	.476	270	11	.337	.422	.563	243	5	.259	.342	.379	205	2	.307	.366	.395	308	14	.295	.396	.529	210	8	.338	.436	.524	87	2	.264	.404	.402
1993	SF-N	491	14	.283	.367	.432	257	5	.249	.349	.362	234	9	.321	.389	.507	182	1	.269	.335	.330	309	13	.291	.386	.492	229	6	.284	.339	.441	69	3	.290	.364	.493
1994	Tex-A	389	13	.329	.431	.501	210	9	.338	.443	.533	179	4	.318	.417	.464	118	1	.314	.370	.449	271	12	.336	.455	.524	188	6	.324	.429	.505	61	2	.311	.456	.443
TOTALS		4658	189	.302	.378	.499	2370	102	.309	.386	.516	2288	87	.294	.371	.481	1690	46	.294	.347	.450	2968	143	.306	.395	.527	2049	94	.314	.399	.533	765	30	.294	.388	.486

■ Royce Clayton BR/TR

YEAR	TM/L	TOTAL AB	HR	AVG	OBP	SLG	HOME AB	HR	AVG	OBP	SLG	AWAY AB	HR	AVG	OBP	SLG	LEFT AB	HR	AVG	OBP	SLG	RIGHT AB	HR	AVG	OBP	SLG	ON-BASE AB	HR	AVG	OBP	SLG	LATE/CLOSE AB	HR	AVG	OBP	SLG
1991	SF-N	26	0	.115	.148	.154	13	0	.154	.154	.154	13	0	.077	.143	.154	5	0	.200	.200	.200	21	0	.095	.136	.143	11	0	.091	.091	.091	1	0	.000	.000	.000
1992	SF-N	321	4	.224	.281	.308	172	3	.250	.309	.343	149	1	.195	.248	.268	96	0	.250	.327	.333	225	4	.213	.260	.298	143	1	.224	.271	.315	61	0	.197	.279	.197
1993	SF-N	549	6	.282	.331	.372	266	5	.305	.346	.421	283	1	.261	.316	.325	170	2	.247	.286	.341	379	4	.298	.350	.385	259	1	.266	.309	.320	79	0	.177	.217	.203
1994	SF-N	385	2	.236	.295	.327	208	1	.240	.301	.341	177	2	.232	.288	.311	85	2	.176	.255	.341	300	1	.253	.307	.323	165	2	.242	.306	.345	66	0	.197	.250	.197
TOTALS		1281	13	.251	.304	.338	659	9	.267	.318	.370	622	4	.233	.289	.304	356	4	.230	.289	.337	925	9	.258	.310	.338	578	4	.246	.295	.322	207	0	.188	.246	.198

■ Alex Cole BL/TL

YEAR	TM/L	TOTAL AB	HR	AVG	OBP	SLG	HOME AB	HR	AVG	OBP	SLG	AWAY AB	HR	AVG	OBP	SLG	LEFT AB	HR	AVG	OBP	SLG	RIGHT AB	HR	AVG	OBP	SLG	ON-BASE AB	HR	AVG	OBP	SLG	LATE/CLOSE AB	HR	AVG	OBP	SLG
1990	Cle-A	227	0	.300	.379	.357	121	0	.306	.400	.372	106	0	.292	.353	.340	52	0	.269	.381	.288	175	0	.314	.378	.377	83	0	.289	.337	.349	22	0	.273	.385	.273
1991	Cle-A	387	0	.295	.386	.354	182	0	.291	.399	.341	205	0	.298	.374	.366	62	0	.387	.500	.500	325	0	.277	.362	.326	130	0	.262	.338	.308	77	0	.286	.360	.299
1992	Cle-A	97	0	.206	.284	.216	43	0	.302	.392	.302	54	0	.130	.190	.148	21	0	.333	.423	.333	76	0	.171	.241	.184	38	0	.158	.214	.158	20	0	.100	.217	.100
1992	Pit-N	205	0	.278	.335	.361	94	0	.298	.371	.426	111	0	.261	.303	.306	28	0	.250	.323	.393	177	0	.282	.337	.356	53	0	.245	.328	.377	40	0	.275	.356	.375
1993	Col-N	348	0	.256	.339	.305	179	0	.235	.315	.302	169	0	.278	.365	.308	21	0	.143	.182	.286	327	0	.263	.349	.306	122	0	.320	.397	.385	46	0	.239	.321	.283
1994	Min-A	345	4	.296	.375	.403	164	2	.317	.411	.463	181	2	.276	.342	.348	48	0	.104	.232	.104	297	4	.327	.399	.451	141	1	.255	.371	.362	44	1	.364	.408	.477
TOTALS		1609	4	.280	.360	.347	783	2	.287	.379	.370	826	2	.272	.341	.324	232	0	.254	.366	.323	1377	4	.284	.359	.351	567	1	.268	.350	.340	249	1	.273	.351	.321

■ Vince Coleman BB/TR

YEAR	TM/L	TOTAL AB	HR	AVG	OBP	SLG	HOME AB	HR	AVG	OBP	SLG	AWAY AB	HR	AVG	OBP	SLG	LEFT AB	HR	AVG	OBP	SLG	RIGHT AB	HR	AVG	OBP	SLG	ON-BASE AB	HR	AVG	OBP	SLG	LATE/CLOSE AB	HR	AVG	OBP	SLG
1985	StL-N	636	1	.267	.320	.335	315	1	.305	.356	.387	321	0	.231	.285	.283	211	0	.237	.284	.341	425	1	.282	.338	.332	194	0	.253	.301	.320	81	0	.222	.267	.309
1986	StL-N	600	0	.232	.301	.280	320	0	.269	.345	.316	280	0	.189	.250	.239	227	0	.238	.327	.278	373	0	.228	.285	.282	193	0	.212	.270	.264	115	0	.235	.313	.287
1987	StL-N	623	3	.289	.363	.358	287	3	.254	.384	.376	336	0	.301	.376	.342	209	3	.268	.361	.416	414	0	.300	.364	.329	217	1	.318	.371	.387	106	0	.368	.417	.406
1988	StL-N	616	3	.260	.313	.339	326	2	.276	.330	.374	290	1	.241	.294	.300	220	2	.273	.324	.395	396	1	.253	.307	.308	182	1	.264	.312	.368	109	0	.275	.344	.339
1989	StL-N	563	2	.254	.316	.334	277	1	.260	.316	.361	286	1	.248	.316	.308	264	2	.235	.285	.326	299	0	.271	.342	.341	168	0	.208	.270	.280	91	0	.209	.265	.242
1990	StL-N	497	6	.292	.340	.400	259	5	.297	.342	.440	238	1	.286	.337	.357	191	5	.262	.297	.450	306	1	.310	.366	.369	167	1	.269	.305	.335	67	1	.254	.324	.313
1991	NY-N	278	1	.255	.347	.327	107	0	.234	.364	.262	171	1	.269	.335	.368	105	1	.248	.307	.305	173	0	.260	.369	.341	85	0	.271	.361	.341	52	0	.308	.400	.385
1992	NY-N	229	2	.275	.355	.358	119	2	.277	.370	.353	110	0	.273	.339	.364	60	1	.283	.358	.433	169	1	.272	.354	.331	67	2	.284	.380	.463	41	1	.220	.304	.341
1993	NY-N	373	2	.279	.316	.379	190	2	.284	.328	.389	183	0	.273	.304	.366	100	1	.290	.333	.430	273	1	.275	.309	.355	114	0	.237	.276	.263	61	0	.197	.219	.279
1994	KC-A	438	2	.240	.285	.340	217	2	.300	.347	.438	221	0	.181	.224	.244	126	2	.262	.293	.389	312	0	.231	.282	.321	142	0	.268	.310	.380	59	0	.186	.235	.220
TOTALS		4853	22	.264	.324	.342	2417	17	.280	.343	.375	2436	5	.248	.304	.310	1713	17	.255	.314	.368	3140	5	.268	.329	.328	1529	5	.258	.312	.334	782	2	.253	.315	.313

■ Darnell Coles BR/TR

YEAR	TM/L	TOTAL AB	HR	AVG	OBP	SLG	HOME AB	HR	AVG	OBP	SLG	AWAY AB	HR	AVG	OBP	SLG	LEFT AB	HR	AVG	OBP	SLG	RIGHT AB	HR	AVG	OBP	SLG	ON-BASE AB	HR	AVG	OBP	SLG	LATE/CLOSE AB	HR	AVG	OBP	SLG
1984	Sea-A	143	0	.161	.259	.196	62	0	.177	.261	.194	81	0	.148	.258	.198	48	0	.146	.241	.146	95	0	.168	.269	.221	64	0	.172	.254	.188	26	0	.115	.233	.192
1985	Sea-A	59	1	.237	.338	.356	28	0	.250	.364	.321	31	1	.226	.316	.387	21	1	.095	.240	.238	38	0	.316	.391	.421	19	0	.158	.308	.158	12	0	.083	.200	.083
1986	Det-A	521	20	.273	.333	.453	252	12	.286	.346	.468	269	8	.260	.320	.439	170	3	.282	.346	.400	351	17	.268	.326	.479	222	8	.288	.322	.468	75	2	.227	.294	.320
1987	Det-A	149	4	.181	.263	.309	78	3	.192	.247	.333	71	1	.169	.280	.282	72	2	.208	.284	.347	77	2	.156	.244	.273	64	2	.172	.250	.328	17	0	.059	.238	.118
1987	Pit-N	119	6	.227	.333	.445	63	5	.286	.412	.603	56	1	.161	.230	.268	77	6	.247	.362	.545	42	0	.190	.277	.262	57	4	.298	.408	.614	19	0	.158	.304	.263
1988	Pit-N	211	5	.232	.299	.374	98	1	.184	.279	.286	113	4	.274	.315	.451	77	4	.260	.344	.506	134	1	.216	.272	.299	94	1	.255	.325	.362	36	1	.222	.326	.361
1988	Sea-A	195	10	.292	.356	.508	103	9	.301	.361	.621	92	1	.283	.350	.391	58	5	.328	.418	.638	137	5	.277	.329	.453	80	3	.275	.322	.463	27	1	.222	.300	.333
1989	Sea-A	535	10	.252	.294	.359	241	4	.286	.337	.394	294	6	.224	.258	.330	157	2	.242	.268	.350	378	8	.257	.305	.362	239	5	.230	.281	.343	83	3	.289	.348	.446
1990	Sea-A	107	2	.215	.248	.336	72	2	.250	.276	.389	35	0	.143	.189	.229	41	1	.220	.267	.390	66	1	.212	.235	.303	51	2	.275	.309	.471	15	0	.267	.250	.467
1990	Det-A	108	1	.204	.281	.250	52	1	.231	.322	.308	56	0	.179	.242	.196	80	1	.213	.297	.237	28	1	.179	.233	.286	51	0	.176	.218	.196	24	0	.167	.259	.167
1991	SF-N	14	0	.214	.214	.214	9	0	.333	.333	.333	5	0	.000	.000	.000	7	0	.429	.429	.429	7	0	.000	.000	.000	7	0	.143	.143	.143	5	0	.200	.200	.200
1992	Cin-N	141	3	.312	.322	.482	60	1	.250	.250	.400	81	2	.358	.372	.543	97	1	.320	.330	.485	44	2	.295	.304	.477	52	1	.250	.268	.365	27	0	.333	.333	.444
1993	Tor-A	194	4	.253	.319	.371	90	3	.300	.376	.467	104	1	.212	.260	.288	61	0	.213	.310	.230	133	4	.271	.323	.426	88	3	.261	.330	.420	29	0	.310	.412	.379
1994	Tor-A	143	4	.210	.263	.350	76	1	.171	.238	.342	67	3	.254	.292	.448	59	3	.203	.226	.424	84	1	.214	.287	.298	67	2	.209	.267	.328	24	0	.167	.200	.208
TOTALS		2639	70	.244	.305	.383	1284	42	.256	.322	.407	1355	28	.233	.288	.359	1030	28	.243	.309	.386	1609	42	.245	.303	.380	1155	31	.243	.300	.382	419	7	.224	.300	.325

■ Dave Collins BB/TL

YEAR	TM/L	TOTAL AB	HR	AVG	OBP	SLG	HOME AB	HR	AVG	OBP	SLG	AWAY AB	HR	AVG	OBP	SLG	LEFT AB	HR	AVG	OBP	SLG	RIGHT AB	HR	AVG	OBP	SLG	ON-BASE AB	HR	AVG	OBP	SLG	LATE/CLOSE AB	HR	AVG	OBP	SLG
1984	Tor-A	441	2	.308	.366	.444	210	2	.310	.366	.514	231	0	.307	.366	.381	63	0	.349	.391	.476	378	2	.302	.362	.439	170	1	.288	.344	.429	81	0	.346	.413	.444
1985	Oak-A	379	4	.251	.303	.346	190	1	.232	.300	.284	189	3	.270	.305	.407	87	1	.218	.260	.287	292	3	.260	.315	.363	130	1	.300	.354	.385	68	0	.279	.364	.294
1986	Det-A	419	1	.270	.340	.329	196	0	.250	.326	.311	223	1	.287	.354	.345	108	1	.231	.261	.343	311	0	.283	.366	.325	173	1	.260	.326	.324	76	1	.250	.301	.316
1987	Cin-N	85	0	.294	.388	.353	46	0	.239	.300	.283	39	0	.359	.479	.436	28	0	.321	.424	.393	57	0	.281	.369	.333	28	0	.250	.364	.321	27	0	.259	.310	.333

| | | TOTAL | | | | | HOME | | | | | AWAY | | | | | LEFT | | | | | RIGHT | | | | | ON-BASE | | | | | LATE/CLOSE | | | | |
YEAR	TM/L	AB	HR	AVG	OBP	SLG	AB	HR	AVG	OBP	SLG	AB	HR	AVG	OBP	SLG	AB	HR	AVG	OBP	SLG	AB	HR	AVG	OBP	SLG	AB	HR	AVG	OBP	SLG	AB	HR	AVG	OBP	SLG
1988	Cin-N	174	0	.236	.286	.293	90	0	.200	.232	.256	84	0	.274	.340	.333	60	0	.233	.277	.317	114	0	.237	.290	.281	68	0	.279	.354	.309	55	0	.145	.242	.145
1989	Cin-N	106	0	.236	.302	.274	49	0	.184	.216	.204	57	0	.281	.369	.333	62	0	.258	.313	.323	44	0	.205	.286	.205	41	0	.195	.250	.220	25	0	.240	.387	.280
1990	StL-N	58	0	.224	.366	.241	28	0	.179	.361	.179	30	0	.267	.371	.300	36	0	.194	.293	.222	22	0	.273	.467	.273	26	0	.308	.455	.308	18	0	.389	.577	.389
TOTALS		1662	7	.270	.334	.354	809	3	.248	.314	.339	853	4	.290	.353	.369	444	2	.252	.302	.338	1218	5	.276	.346	.360	636	3	.275	.343	.355	350	1	.269	.355	.317

■ Dave Concepcion BR/TR

YEAR	TM/L	AB	HR	AVG	OBP	SLG	AB	HR	AVG	OBP	SLG	AB	HR	AVG	OBP	SLG	AB	HR	AVG	OBP	SLG	AB	HR	AVG	OBP	SLG	AB	HR	AVG	OBP	SLG	AB	HR	AVG	OBP	SLG
1984	Cin-N	531	4	.245	.307	.320	283	3	.219	.289	.307	248	1	.274	.328	.335	191	3	.288	.352	.398	340	1	.221	.282	.276	209	1	.282	.356	.354	109	1	.174	.242	.248
1985	Cin-N	560	7	.252	.314	.330	273	1	.271	.342	.333	287	6	.233	.288	.328	156	4	.244	.322	.359	404	3	.255	.312	.319	236	3	.212	.275	.275	104	2	.212	.274	.288
1986	Cin-N	311	3	.260	.314	.344	135	0	.274	.331	.348	176	3	.250	.301	.341	101	1	.337	.384	.455	210	2	.224	.279	.290	127	0	.213	.278	.252	67	2	.313	.343	.493
1987	Cin-N	279	1	.319	.377	.384	133	1	.316	.361	.406	146	0	.322	.392	.363	150	1	.340	.392	.420	129	0	.295	.361	.341	130	0	.346	.397	.392	49	0	.367	.426	.429
1988	Cin-N	197	0	.198	.265	.244	104	0	.240	.313	.298	93	0	.151	.210	.183	114	0	.202	.278	.237	83	0	.193	.247	.253	81	0	.185	.290	.210	29	0	.172	.294	.172
TOTALS		1878	15	.256	.317	.329	928	5	.259	.324	.334	950	10	.253	.310	.323	712	9	.282	.346	.376	1166	6	.239	.298	.299	783	4	.250	.320	.305	358	5	.237	.299	.324

■ Jeff Conine BR/TR

YEAR	TM/L	AB	HR	AVG	OBP	SLG	AB	HR	AVG	OBP	SLG	AB	HR	AVG	OBP	SLG	AB	HR	AVG	OBP	SLG	AB	HR	AVG	OBP	SLG	AB	HR	AVG	OBP	SLG	AB	HR	AVG	OBP	SLG
1990	KC-A	20	0	.250	.318	.350	1	0	.000	.500	.000	19	0	.263	.300	.368	11	0	.364	.462	.455	9	0	.111	.111	.222	10	0	.400	.400	.600	4	0	.000	.200	.000
1992	KC-A	91	0	.253	.313	.352	31	0	.258	.343	.355	60	0	.250	.297	.350	23	0	.304	.429	.348	68	0	.235	.268	.353	45	0	.311	.380	.400	14	0	.214	.267	.214
1993	Fla-N	595	12	.292	.351	.403	307	5	.296	.340	.381	288	7	.288	.362	.427	167	5	.299	.366	.455	428	7	.290	.345	.383	271	9	.321	.367	.476	102	3	.225	.283	.353
1994	Fla-N	451	18	.319	.373	.525	230	8	.283	.345	.457	221	10	.357	.402	.597	136	6	.316	.375	.566	315	12	.321	.372	.508	214	8	.322	.399	.519	71	0	.324	.351	.423
TOTALS		1157	30	.299	.356	.446	569	13	.288	.343	.409	588	17	.310	.369	.481	337	11	.309	.378	.493	820	19	.295	.347	.427	540	17	.322	.382	.489	191	3	.257	.305	.361

■ Cecil Cooper BL/TL

YEAR	TM/L	AB	HR	AVG	OBP	SLG	AB	HR	AVG	OBP	SLG	AB	HR	AVG	OBP	SLG	AB	HR	AVG	OBP	SLG	AB	HR	AVG	OBP	SLG	AB	HR	AVG	OBP	SLG	AB	HR	AVG	OBP	SLG
1984	Mil-A	603	11	.275	.307	.386	272	3	.279	.315	.364	331	8	.272	.301	.405	215	1	.298	.336	.386	388	10	.263	.291	.387	291	5	.268	.305	.388	89	0	.236	.263	.292
1985	Mil-A	631	16	.293	.322	.456	309	6	.285	.315	.430	322	10	.301	.329	.481	209	6	.321	.360	.498	422	10	.280	.303	.436	307	8	.322	.349	.505	103	1	.359	.394	.437
1986	Mil-A	542	12	.258	.310	.373	255	6	.235	.294	.349	287	6	.279	.324	.394	137	3	.285	.342	.358	405	9	.249	.298	.378	264	7	.295	.345	.428	76	1	.316	.384	.408
1987	Mil-A	250	6	.248	.293	.372	108	4	.296	.342	.463	142	2	.211	.255	.303	81	1	.259	.308	.358	169	5	.243	.285	.379	108	3	.278	.341	.407	37	1	.405	.410	.541
TOTALS		2026	45	.273	.311	.403	944	19	.271	.312	.393	1082	26	.274	.309	.411	642	11	.298	.341	.413	1384	34	.262	.296	.398	970	23	.294	.334	.438	305	3	.318	.356	.400

■ Scott Cooper BL/TR

YEAR	TM/L	AB	HR	AVG	OBP	SLG	AB	HR	AVG	OBP	SLG	AB	HR	AVG	OBP	SLG	AB	HR	AVG	OBP	SLG	AB	HR	AVG	OBP	SLG	AB	HR	AVG	OBP	SLG	AB	HR	AVG	OBP	SLG
1990	Bos-A	1	0	.000	.000	.000	1	0	.000	.000	.000	0	0	—	—	—	81	1	.259	.308	.358	1	0	.000	.000	.000	0	0	—	—	—	0	0	—	—	—
1991	Bos-A	35	0	.457	.486	.686	25	0	.560	.577	.880	10	0	.200	.273	.200	6	0	.667	.714	1.000	29	0	.414	.433	.621	11	0	.545	.545	.818	6	0	.500	.571	.833
1992	Bos-A	337	5	.276	.346	.383	155	2	.290	.353	.368	182	3	.264	.340	.396	41	1	.268	.375	.415	296	4	.277	.341	.378	130	0	.269	.345	.406	76	0	.316	.366	.434
1993	Bos-A	526	9	.279	.355	.397	255	5	.325	.396	.443	271	6	.236	.316	.354	144	2	.257	.321	.361	382	7	.288	.367	.411	234	4	.308	.389	.436	78	0	.192	.319	.282
1994	Bos-A	369	13	.282	.333	.453	199	9	.296	.357	.503	170	4	.265	.304	.394	108	3	.194	.252	.278	261	10	.318	.367	.525	143	4	.266	.337	.413	65	0	.215	.224	.246
TOTALS		1268	27	.284	.349	.417	635	14	.317	.380	.460	633	13	.251	.319	.374	299	6	.244	.312	.351	969	21	.296	.361	.438	518	8	.292	.366	.403	225	0	.249	.316	.338

■ Wil Cordero BR/TR

YEAR	TM/L	AB	HR	AVG	OBP	SLG	AB	HR	AVG	OBP	SLG	AB	HR	AVG	OBP	SLG	AB	HR	AVG	OBP	SLG	AB	HR	AVG	OBP	SLG	AB	HR	AVG	OBP	SLG	AB	HR	AVG	OBP	SLG
1992	Mon-N	126	2	.302	.353	.397	62	1	.306	.348	.387	64	1	.297	.357	.406	34	0	.471	.514	.500	92	2	.239	.293	.359	49	1	.327	.377	.388	25	0	.240	.296	.240
1993	Mon-N	475	10	.248	.308	.387	213	8	.225	.288	.423	262	2	.267	.324	.359	148	1	.243	.315	.365	327	9	.251	.304	.398	188	6	.277	.363	.468	81	4	.235	.279	.444
1994	Mon-N	415	15	.294	.363	.456	180	5	.278	.351	.456	235	10	.306	.373	.515	101	5	.356	.440	.584	314	10	.274	.338	.459	197	6	.294	.369	.482	66	3	.318	.361	.530
TOTALS		1016	27	.274	.336	.430	455	14	.257	.321	.431	561	13	.287	.349	.430	283	6	.311	.384	.459	733	21	.259	.318	.419	434	13	.290	.367	.465	172	7	.267	.314	.448

■ Henry Cotto BR/TR

YEAR	TM/L	AB	HR	AVG	OBP	SLG	AB	HR	AVG	OBP	SLG	AB	HR	AVG	OBP	SLG	AB	HR	AVG	OBP	SLG	AB	HR	AVG	OBP	SLG	AB	HR	AVG	OBP	SLG	AB	HR	AVG	OBP	SLG
1984	Chi-N	146	0	.274	.325	.308	73	0	.329	.355	.356	73	0	.219	.296	.260	59	0	.271	.317	.322	87	0	.276	.330	.299	56	0	.250	.344	.304	26	0	.346	.452	.385
1985	NY-A	56	1	.304	.339	.375	37	0	.297	.333	.297	19	1	.316	.350	.526	52	0	.308	.333	.327	4	1	.250	.400	1.000	28	1	.321	.345	.429	8	0	.625	.625	.750
1986	NY-A	80	1	.213	.229	.287	41	0	.220	.214	.268	39	1	.205	.244	.308	57	0	.193	.203	.228	23	1	.261	.292	.435	40	1	.225	.238	.300	9	0	.000	.000	.000
1987	NY-A	149	5	.235	.269	.403	87	5	.253	.286	.506	62	0	.210	.246	.258	80	2	.200	.229	.325	69	3	.275	.315	.493	71	2	.239	.270	.394	20	0	.050	.174	.050
1988	Sea-A	386	8	.259	.302	.373	188	5	.255	.307	.383	198	3	.263	.297	.364	148	4	.277	.306	.412	238	4	.248	.300	.349	146	4	.267	.317	.390	49	1	.204	.278	.286
1989	Sea-A	295	9	.264	.300	.407	149	5	.248	.282	.376	146	4	.281	.318	.438	160	5	.262	.306	.412	135	4	.267	.293	.400	118	0	.331	.358	.500	53	2	.245	.273	.358
1990	Sea-A	355	4	.259	.307	.349	173	2	.260	.321	.358	182	2	.258	.294	.341	192	2	.260	.308	.349	163	2	.258	.307	.350	164	2	.274	.326	.366	65	1	.231	.311	.308
1991	Sea-A	177	6	.305	.347	.463	73	2	.301	.366	.438	104	4	.308	.333	.481	96	4	.323	.359	.490	81	2	.284	.333	.432	63	4	.302	.328	.619	32	0	.219	.242	.281
1992	Sea-A	294	5	.259	.294	.354	117	2	.248	.315	.350	177	3	.266	.278	.356	168	4	.321	.375	.446	126	1	.175	.175	.230	114	2	.298	.341	.404	51	1	.216	.245	.333
1993	Sea-A	105	2	.190	.213	.257	51	0	.235	.235	.255	54	2	.148	.193	.259	81	1	.210	.209	.259	24	1	.125	.160	.250	49	0	.184	.184	.184	18	1	.333	.333	.500
1993	Fla-N	135	3	.296	.312	.415	65	1	.277	.310	.400	70	2	.314	.314	.429	68	1	.368	.384	.471	67	2	.224	.235	.358	52	2	.308	.333	.462	29	0	.241	.303	.241
TOTALS		2178	44	.261	.299	.370	1054	22	.263	.307	.374	1124	22	.260	.292	.367	1161	23	.275	.312	.382	1017	21	.246	.285	.356	901	22	.277	.318	.403	359	6	.234	.290	.312

■ Jose Cruz BL/TL

YEAR	TM/L	AB	HR	AVG	OBP	SLG	AB	HR	AVG	OBP	SLG	AB	HR	AVG	OBP	SLG	AB	HR	AVG	OBP	SLG	AB	HR	AVG	OBP	SLG	AB	HR	AVG	OBP	SLG	AB	HR	AVG	OBP	SLG
1984	Hou-N	600	12	.312	.381	.462	286	0	.276	.367	.371	314	12	.344	.394	.545	223	4	.296	.357	.426	377	8	.321	.394	.483	270	5	.315	.389	.467	107	1	.280	.389	.374
1985	Hou-N	544	9	.300	.349	.426	255	1	.310	.355	.396	289	8	.291	.344	.453	220	5	.277	.306	.405	324	4	.315	.377	.441	254	3	.311	.369	.457	79	1	.291	.371	.380
1986	Hou-N	479	10	.278	.351	.403	245	5	.298	.378	.416	234	5	.256	.322	.389	194	2	.284	.325	.392	285	8	.274	.367	.411	206	6	.354	.426	.524	82	2	.244	.354	.341
1987	Hou-N	365	11	.241	.307	.400	180	6	.267	.320	.444	185	5	.216	.295	.357	128	4	.227	.270	.359	237	7	.249	.326	.422	160	2	.231	.311	.350	79	4	.241	.307	.456
1988	NY-A	80	1	.200	.273	.262	44	1	.182	.250	.273	36	0	.222	.300	.250	5	0	.600	.600	.800	75	1	.173	.253	.227	38	1	.211	.286	.316	19	0	.158	.158	.158
TOTALS		2068	43	.284	.349	.420	1010	13	.284	.354	.397	1058	30	.284	.344	.442	770	15	.278	.322	.403	1298	28	.287	.363	.431	928	18	.304	.374	.450	366	8	.260	.354	.374

■ Chad Curtis BR/TR

YEAR	TM/L	AB	HR	AVG	OBP	SLG	AB	HR	AVG	OBP	SLG	AB	HR	AVG	OBP	SLG	AB	HR	AVG	OBP	SLG	AB	HR	AVG	OBP	SLG	AB	HR	AVG	OBP	SLG	AB	HR	AVG	OBP	SLG
1992	Cal-A	441	10	.259	.341	.372	201	5	.264	.349	.378	240	5	.254	.333	.367	122	6	.270	.393	.484	319	4	.254	.318	.329	172	4	.250	.332	.372	76	2	.237	.348	.342
1993	Cal-A	583	6	.285	.361	.369	303	3	.310	.374	.402	280	3	.257	.349	.332	148	2	.324	.405	.446	435	4	.270	.347	.343	238	0	.256	.371	.298	95	0	.305	.383	.337
1994	Cal-A	453	11	.256	.317	.397	237	8	.253	.332	.418	216	3	.259	.299	.375	132	2	.280	.367	.432	321	9	.246	.295	.383	183	5	.251	.305	.399	68	1	.176	.263	.235
TOTALS		1477	27	.268	.342	.378	741	16	.279	.354	.401	736	11	.257	.330	.356	402	10	.294	.389	.453	1075	17	.259	.323	.351	593	9	.253	.315	.351	239	3	.247	.338	.310

■ Kal Daniels BL/TR

YEAR	TM/L	AB	HR	AVG	OBP	SLG	AB	HR	AVG	OBP	SLG	AB	HR	AVG	OBP	SLG	AB	HR	AVG	OBP	SLG	AB	HR	AVG	OBP	SLG	AB	HR	AVG	OBP	SLG	AB	HR	AVG	OBP	SLG
1986	Cin-N	181	6	.320	.398	.519	110	3	.309	.369	.482	71	3	.338	.440	.577	32	0	.188	.278	.219	149	6	.349	.424	.584	66	2	.303	.390	.485	33	2	.333	.439	.636
1987	Cin-N	368	26	.334	.429	.617	175	13	.309	.398	.600	193	13	.358	.456	.632	76	1	.197	.291	.289	292	25	.370	.464	.702	127	5	.307	.429	.520	56	1	.321	.479	.429
1988	Cin-N	495	18	.291	.397	.463	227	12	.330	.436	.555	268	6	.257	.363	.384	135	3	.267	.387	.363	360	15	.300	.401	.500	189	4	.296	.439	.423	77	2	.221	.365	.312
1989	Cin-N	133	2	.246	.390	.346	63	1	.222	.405	.381	70	1	.214	.375	.314	44	1	.227	.435	.364	89	1	.213	.364	.337	53	0	.189	.380	.245	25	0	.200	.400	.320
1989	LA-N	38	2	.342	.435	.553	6	1	.500	.571	1.167	32	1	.313	.410	.438	13	0	.077	.077	.077	25	2	.480	.576	.800	15	1	.200	.316	.467	4	0	.250	.250	.250
1990	LA-N	450	27	.296	.389	.531	231	12	.290	.379	.498	219	15	.301	.400	.566	151	6	.285	.379	.444	299	21	.301	.387	.575	218	16	.312	.407	.601	52	3	.308	.410	.538
1991	LA-N	461	17	.249	.337	.397	242	12	.248	.332	.426	219	5	.251	.343	.365	206	6	.252	.309	.379	255	11	.247	.359	.412	255	11	.247	.363	.466	76	1	.237	.318	.329
1992	LA-N	104	2	.231	.302	.337	56	1	.250	.295	.339	48	1	.208	.309	.333	37	1	.216	.293	.351	67	1	.239	.307	.328	50	1	.140	.228	.200	15	1	.267	.313	.467
1992	Chi-N	108	4	.250	.328	.417	45	2	.289	.389	.489	63	2	.222	.279	.365	28	0	.250	.300	.321	80	4	.250	.337	.450	51	2	.235	.298	.412	30	0	.233	.294	.233
TOTALS		2338	104	.285	.382	.479	1155	57	.289	.382	.497	1183	47	.281	.382	.461	722	18	.247	.343	.363	1616	86	.302	.399	.530	975	42	.278	.389	.468	368	10	.264	.382	.394

■ Doug Dascenzo BB/TL

YEAR	TM/L	AB	HR	AVG	OBP	SLG	AB	HR	AVG	OBP	SLG	AB	HR	AVG	OBP	SLG	AB	HR	AVG	OBP	SLG	AB	HR	AVG	OBP	SLG	AB	HR	AVG	OBP	SLG	AB	HR	AVG	OBP	SLG
1988	Chi-N	75	0	.213	.298	.253	41	0	.317	.378	.390	34	0	.088	.205	.088	19	0	.421	.476	.526	56	0	.143	.238	.161	21	0	.238	.360	.286	14	0	.143	.250	.143
1989	Chi-N	139	1	.165	.234	.194	74	0	.176	.237	.176	65	1	.154	.230	.215	61	0	.197	.242	.197	78	1	.141	.227	.192	46	1	.217	.309	.283	17	0	.176	.250	.176
1990	Chi-N	241	1	.253	.312	.344	119	1	.277	.336	.387	122	0	.230	.288	.303	136	1	.279	.322	.368	105	0	.219	.300	.314	84	1	.286	.323	.393	30	0	.267	.395	.467
1991	Chi-N	239	1	.255	.327	.314	125	0	.232	.309	.272	114	1	.281	.346	.360	87	0	.299	.340	.345	152	1	.230	.320	.296	96	0	.240	.315	.271	59	0	.339	.385	.424
1992	Chi-N	376	0	.255	.304	.311	202	0	.252	.301	.337	174	0	.259	.307	.282	169	0	.243	.275	.296	207	0	.266	.326	.324	134	0	.261	.294	.284	81	0	.259	.318	.272
1993	Tex-A	146	2	.199	.239	.288	65	0	.215	.261	.308	81	2	.185	.221	.272	59	0	.237	.233	.288	87	2	.172	.242	.287	55	0	.218	.254	.273	28	0	.250	.323	.286
TOTALS		1216	5	.235	.294	.299	626	1	.244	.303	.315	590	4	.225	.284	.281	531	1	.262	.297	.318	685	4	.215	.292	.283	436	2	.250	.304	.300	229	0	.266	.337	.323

■ Darren Daulton BL/TR

YEAR	TM/L	AB	HR	AVG	OBP	SLG	AB	HR	AVG	OBP	SLG	AB	HR	AVG	OBP	SLG	AB	HR	AVG	OBP	SLG	AB	HR	AVG	OBP	SLG	AB	HR	AVG	OBP	SLG	AB	HR	AVG	OBP	SLG
1985	Phi-N	103	4	.204	.311	.369	47	0	.191	.309	.255	56	4	.214	.313	.464	12	0	.083	.154	.083	91	4	.220	.330	.407	53	1	.189	.306	.245	17	0	.176	.300	.176
1986	Phi-N	138	8	.225	.391	.428	65	4	.231	.438	.462	73	4	.219	.344	.397	17	0	.235	.409	.294	121	8	.223	.385	.463	54	5	.255	.463	.491	25	0	.120	.241	.160
1987	Phi-N	129	3	.194	.281	.310	54	1	.259	.355	.389	75	2	.147	.226	.253	8	0	.125	.222	.250	121	3	.198	.285	.314	59	1	.169	.286	.254	22	2	.182	.357	.455
1988	Phi-N	144	1	.208	.288	.271	69	0	.217	.295	.275	75	1	.200	.282	.267	18	0	.111	.111	.111	126	1	.222	.310	.294	68	0	.221	.267	.235	41	0	.244	.262	.244
1989	Phi-N	368	8	.201	.303	.310	172	2	.163	.291	.250	196	6	.235	.314	.362	58	1	.241	.366	.328	310	7	.194	.290	.306	156	4	.263	.343	.404	69	0	.203	.267	.232
1990	Phi-N	459	12	.268	.367	.416	224	5	.250	.345	.384	235	7	.285	.388	.447	113	1	.257	.378	.354	346	11	.272	.363	.436	200	5	.310	.401	.500	85	3	.259	.319	.388
1991	Phi-N	285	12	.196	.298	.365	152	8	.211	.327	.401	133	4	.180	.271	.293	96	2	.146	.224	.250	189	10	.222	.332	.423	117	2	.231	.331	.325	60	2	.183	.271	.317
1992	Phi-N	485	27	.270	.385	.524	229	17	.319	.434	.651	256	10	.227	.363	.410	137	6	.255	.371	.500	348	21	.276	.389	.534	255	11	.247	.373	.427	81	4	.223	.318	.362
1993	Phi-N	510	24	.257	.392	.482	262	10	.260	.375	.458	248	14	.254	.409	.508	188	8	.213	.346	.404	322	16	.283	.418	.528	262	13	.252	.415	.481	81	4	.284	.473	.506
1994	Phi-N	257	15	.300	.380	.549	128	7	.305	.375	.531	129	8	.295	.385	.566	90	4	.289	.347	.478	167	11	.305	.397	.587	123	8	.317	.414	.585	44	0	.205	.300	.250
TOTALS		2878	114	.245	.353	.426	1402	54	.249	.361	.437	1476	60	.237	.346	.415	802	27	.228	.336	.390	2076	87	.249	.359	.440	1337	57	.266	.387	.464	538	13	.223	.346	.336

■ Alvin Davis BL/TR

YEAR	TM/L	AB	HR	AVG	OBP	SLG	AB	HR	AVG	OBP	SLG	AB	HR	AVG	OBP	SLG	AB	HR	AVG	OBP	SLG	AB	HR	AVG	OBP	SLG	AB	HR	AVG	OBP	SLG	AB	HR	AVG	OBP	SLG
1984	Sea-A	567	27	.284	.391	.497	277	15	.296	.409	.556	290	12	.272	.374	.441	206	5	.286	.389	.417	361	22	.283	.392	.543	261	17	.303	.417	.571	83	6	.277	.421	.578
1985	Sea-A	578	18	.287	.381	.441	297	11	.293	.393	.461	281	7	.281	.369	.420	176	4	.239	.340	.358	402	14	.308	.399	.478	254	7	.264	.372	.406	82	0	.232	.364	.280

YEAR	TM/L	TOTAL AB	HR	AVG	OBP	SLG	HOME AB	HR	AVG	OBP	SLG	AWAY AB	HR	AVG	OBP	SLG	LEFT AB	HR	AVG	OBP	SLG	RIGHT AB	HR	AVG	OBP	SLG	ON-BASE AB	HR	AVG	OBP	SLG	LATE/CLOSE AB	HR	AVG	OBP	SLG
1986	Sea-A	479	18	.271	.373	.426	249	14	.281	.385	.494	230	4	.261	.361	.352	122	0	.246	.376	.270	357	18	.280	.372	.479	230	5	.278	.387	.396	74	3	.230	.367	.365
1987	Sea-A	580	29	.295	.370	.516	277	18	.307	.402	.570	303	11	.284	.339	.465	208	5	.240	.301	.380	372	24	.325	.406	.591	269	17	.294	.381	.550	73	4	.274	.386	.507
1988	Sea-A	478	18	.295	.412	.462	228	12	.294	.423	.509	250	6	.296	.403	.420	137	3	.321	.428	.496	341	15	.284	.406	.449	215	6	.302	.424	.433	68	1	.309	.472	.412
1989	Sea-A	498	21	.305	.424	.496	249	13	.365	.453	.614	249	8	.245	.396	.378	154	6	.318	.416	.526	344	15	.299	.427	.483	217	9	.327	.445	.539	77	3	.208	.292	.351
1990	Sea-A	494	17	.283	.387	.429	252	12	.278	.392	.464	242	5	.289	.381	.393	168	6	.256	.360	.405	326	11	.298	.401	.442	256	10	.281	.404	.416	85	3	.271	.361	.447
1991	Sea-A	462	12	.221	.299	.335	226	6	.230	.313	.354	236	6	.212	.286	.318	101	4	.238	.339	.376	361	8	.216	.288	.324	190	10	.258	.357	.463	75	4	.213	.302	.387
1992	Cal-A	104	0	.250	.331	.327	46	0	.304	.418	.413	58	0	.207	.254	.259	12	0	.167	.231	.167	92	0	.261	.343	.348	41	0	.390	.469	.512	16	0	.563	.563	.688
TOTALS		4240	160	.280	.380	.450	2101	101	.294	.398	.503	2139	59	.267	.362	.398	1284	33	.267	.366	.403	2956	127	.286	.386	.471	1903	77	.293	.400	.475	633	24	.259	.376	.423

■ **Chili Davis** BB/TR

YEAR	TM/L	TOTAL AB	HR	AVG	OBP	SLG	HOME AB	HR	AVG	OBP	SLG	AWAY AB	HR	AVG	OBP	SLG	LEFT AB	HR	AVG	OBP	SLG	RIGHT AB	HR	AVG	OBP	SLG	ON-BASE AB	HR	AVG	OBP	SLG	LATE/CLOSE AB	HR	AVG	OBP	SLG
1984	SF-N	499	21	.315	.368	.507	229	7	.306	.351	.467	270	14	.322	.381	.541	112	2	.259	.300	.384	387	19	.331	.387	.543	213	8	.333	.379	.507	100	6	.280	.363	.540
1985	SF-N	481	13	.270	.349	.412	234	7	.265	.335	.406	247	6	.275	.363	.417	105	1	.248	.296	.314	376	12	.277	.363	.439	196	6	.240	.350	.398	83	3	.217	.365	.349
1986	SF-N	526	13	.278	.375	.416	258	7	.291	.389	.426	268	6	.265	.361	.407	148	5	.226	.267	.345	358	8	.302	.420	.450	218	6	.335	.453	.491	94	2	.245	.379	.394
1987	SF-N	500	24	.250	.344	.442	223	9	.242	.352	.404	277	15	.256	.338	.473	183	14	.262	.337	.536	317	10	.243	.349	.388	208	12	.274	.399	.495	87	4	.241	.393	.414
1988	Cal-A	600	21	.268	.326	.432	291	11	.251	.302	.405	309	10	.285	.348	.456	219	8	.256	.307	.429	381	13	.276	.336	.433	287	11	.293	.349	.481	105	4	.200	.280	.352
1989	Cal-A	560	22	.271	.340	.436	274	6	.248	.337	.354	286	16	.294	.343	.514	200	8	.245	.300	.415	360	14	.286	.361	.447	256	10	.281	.360	.426	87	2	.184	.287	.276
1990	Cal-A	412	12	.265	.357	.398	216	10	.306	.389	.495	196	2	.219	.323	.291	126	4	.254	.345	.389	286	8	.269	.363	.402	188	9	.250	.351	.431	54	0	.296	.403	.352
1991	Min-A	534	29	.277	.385	.507	267	14	.303	.420	.539	267	15	.251	.348	.476	174	11	.270	.358	.511	360	18	.281	.397	.506	248	14	.302	.433	.560	70	3	.343	.478	.571
1992	Min-A	444	12	.288	.386	.439	245	6	.273	.364	.437	199	6	.307	.412	.442	121	4	.256	.321	.397	323	8	.300	.408	.455	210	4	.276	.399	.395	81	2	.296	.372	.432
1993	Cal-A	573	27	.243	.327	.440	283	13	.269	.353	.466	290	14	.217	.302	.414	131	8	.260	.326	.496	442	19	.238	.327	.423	286	17	.294	.388	.545	90	3	.278	.409	.422
1994	Cal-A	392	26	.311	.410	.561	215	14	.270	.387	.502	177	12	.362	.440	.633	116	8	.319	.414	.578	276	18	.308	.409	.554	182	12	.319	.440	.560	49	2	.306	.485	.490
TOTALS		5521	220	.275	.359	.452	2735	104	.274	.361	.444	2786	116	.275	.356	.460	1655	73	.258	.324	.439	3866	147	.282	.373	.458	2492	109	.291	.391	.483	900	31	.257	.377	.414

■ **Eric Davis** BR/TR

YEAR	TM/L	TOTAL AB	HR	AVG	OBP	SLG	HOME AB	HR	AVG	OBP	SLG	AWAY AB	HR	AVG	OBP	SLG	LEFT AB	HR	AVG	OBP	SLG	RIGHT AB	HR	AVG	OBP	SLG	ON-BASE AB	HR	AVG	OBP	SLG	LATE/CLOSE AB	HR	AVG	OBP	SLG
1984	Cin-N	174	10	.224	.320	.466	78	3	.256	.389	.462	96	7	.198	.257	.469	81	5	.185	.283	.420	93	5	.258	.352	.505	76	7	.276	.356	.618	29	3	.207	.343	.517
1985	Cin-N	122	8	.246	.287	.516	48	1	.271	.314	.479	74	7	.230	.269	.541	53	5	.264	.316	.604	69	3	.232	.264	.449	43	1	.256	.273	.395	24	0	.208	.269	.208
1986	Cin-N	415	27	.277	.378	.523	197	12	.264	.368	.497	218	15	.289	.387	.546	144	11	.319	.422	.590	271	16	.255	.354	.487	175	13	.291	.398	.549	76	6	.316	.398	.566
1987	Cin-N	474	37	.293	.399	.593	232	17	.280	.394	.560	242	20	.306	.403	.624	147	17	.340	.440	.741	327	20	.272	.380	.526	203	15	.286	.410	.606	73	5	.205	.359	.452
1988	Cin-N	472	26	.273	.363	.489	212	14	.259	.377	.491	260	12	.285	.350	.488	120	7	.292	.390	.517	352	19	.267	.353	.480	223	14	.327	.425	.596	88	6	.341	.437	.625
1989	Cin-N	462	34	.281	.367	.541	204	15	.289	.380	.544	258	19	.275	.357	.539	156	10	.250	.369	.481	306	24	.297	.366	.572	207	21	.304	.399	.652	80	8	.325	.412	.663
1990	Cin-N	453	24	.260	.347	.486	193	13	.233	.344	.487	260	11	.281	.351	.485	150	8	.287	.365	.520	303	16	.248	.339	.469	221	10	.244	.349	.466	75	3	.240	.313	.413
1991	Cin-N	285	11	.235	.353	.386	140	5	.243	.376	.393	145	6	.228	.329	.379	105	3	.229	.359	.362	180	8	.239	.349	.400	129	5	.233	.365	.395	39	2	.154	.327	.333
1992	LA-N	267	5	.228	.325	.322	133	1	.233	.316	.301	134	4	.224	.333	.343	89	4	.236	.393	.416	178	1	.225	.286	.275	133	1	.233	.354	.308	45	0	.200	.294	.222
1993	LA-N	376	14	.234	.308	.391	191	7	.236	.326	.372	185	7	.232	.289	.411	106	3	.226	.328	.368	270	11	.237	.300	.400	166	3	.235	.325	.325	81	3	.210	.281	.346
1993	Det-A	75	6	.253	.371	.533	41	3	.317	.417	.561	34	3	.176	.317	.500	31	1	.194	.306	.290	44	5	.295	.415	.705	38	4	.289	.400	.684	10	1	.200	.385	.500
1994	Det-A	120	3	.183	.290	.292	67	3	.224	.342	.418	53	0	.132	.220	.132	24	0	.125	.323	.125	96	3	.198	.280	.333	66	2	.242	.351	.379	12	0	.083	.154	.083
TOTALS		3695	205	.259	.353	.477	1736	94	.257	.364	.468	1959	111	.260	.342	.484	1206	74	.265	.373	.498	2489	131	.256	.342	.466	1680	96	.273	.377	.507	632	37	.252	.353	.462

■ **Glenn Davis** BR/TR

YEAR	TM/L	TOTAL AB	HR	AVG	OBP	SLG	HOME AB	HR	AVG	OBP	SLG	AWAY AB	HR	AVG	OBP	SLG	LEFT AB	HR	AVG	OBP	SLG	RIGHT AB	HR	AVG	OBP	SLG	ON-BASE AB	HR	AVG	OBP	SLG	LATE/CLOSE AB	HR	AVG	OBP	SLG
1984	Hou-N	61	2	.213	.258	.393	40	1	.225	.256	.375	21	1	.190	.261	.429	33	0	.242	.286	.394	28	2	.179	.226	.393	27	0	.222	.267	.296	13	0	.077	.071	.154
1985	Hou-N	350	20	.271	.332	.474	164	8	.317	.367	.494	186	12	.231	.303	.457	144	12	.278	.346	.563	206	8	.267	.323	.413	152	7	.309	.374	.487	46	1	.174	.224	.283
1986	Hou-N	574	31	.265	.344	.493	285	17	.298	.372	.547	289	14	.232	.316	.439	211	12	.270	.359	.512	363	19	.262	.335	.482	265	15	.257	.352	.487	102	6	.294	.368	.520
1987	Hou-N	578	27	.251	.310	.458	285	12	.249	.312	.439	293	15	.253	.308	.478	193	10	.244	.323	.477	385	17	.255	.304	.449	278	11	.248	.327	.442	104	3	.192	.286	.356
1988	Hou-N	561	30	.271	.341	.478	290	15	.297	.363	.510	271	15	.244	.317	.443	167	7	.228	.322	.395	394	23	.289	.349	.513	294	20	.260	.354	.517	101	3	.287	.395	.436
1989	Hou-N	581	34	.269	.350	.492	291	15	.317	.402	.551	290	19	.221	.297	.435	146	14	.288	.392	.616	435	20	.262	.335	.451	248	13	.278	.393	.512	111	7	.252	.309	.468
1990	Hou-N	327	22	.251	.357	.523	175	4	.217	.315	.349	152	18	.289	.403	.724	123	11	.252	.378	.569	204	11	.250	.343	.495	153	10	.248	.382	.510	60	3	.267	.405	.500
1991	Bal-A	176	10	.227	.307	.460	73	3	.247	.304	.438	103	7	.214	.308	.476	47	5	.255	.314	.638	129	5	.217	.304	.395	82	3	.232	.316	.402	32	0	.219	.242	.250
1992	Bal-A	398	13	.276	.338	.422	200	5	.290	.330	.415	198	8	.263	.345	.429	107	4	.252	.287	.411	291	9	.285	.356	.426	188	6	.277	.343	.415	54	2	.185	.290	.315
1993	Bal-A	113	1	.177	.230	.230	51	1	.157	.214	.235	62	0	.194	.242	.226	36	0	.222	.282	.222	77	1	.156	.205	.234	49	0	.122	.170	.143	20	0	.050	.050	.050
TOTALS		3719	190	.259	.332	.467	1850	81	.279	.347	.471	1869	109	.240	.318	.464	1207	75	.257	.341	.499	2512	115	.261	.328	.452	1696	85	.259	.351	.466	643	25	.233	.316	.400

■ **Jody Davis** BR/TR

YEAR	TM/L	TOTAL AB	HR	AVG	OBP	SLG	HOME AB	HR	AVG	OBP	SLG	AWAY AB	HR	AVG	OBP	SLG	LEFT AB	HR	AVG	OBP	SLG	RIGHT AB	HR	AVG	OBP	SLG	ON-BASE AB	HR	AVG	OBP	SLG	LATE/CLOSE AB	HR	AVG	OBP	SLG
1984	Chi-N	523	19	.256	.315	.421	248	13	.282	.356	.496	275	6	.233	.276	.353	144	6	.271	.354	.493	379	13	.251	.300	.393	258	12	.271	.332	.484	82	1	.268	.360	.354
1985	Chi-N	482	17	.232	.300	.400	259	10	.255	.325	.429	223	7	.206	.269	.368	115	5	.235	.291	.470	367	12	.232	.302	.379	218	6	.206	.306	.358	84	1	.131	.215	.179
1986	Chi-N	528	21	.250	.300	.428	262	14	.267	.315	.481	266	7	.233	.285	.376	133	3	.233	.286	.353	395	18	.256	.305	.453	250	11	.264	.292	.452	99	5	.232	.275	.404
1987	Chi-N	428	19	.248	.331	.418	207	7	.256	.347	.411	221	12	.240	.315	.425	107	5	.252	.325	.430	321	14	.246	.332	.414	190	4	.205	.292	.305	64	5	.359	.406	.625
1988	Chi-N	249	6	.229	.309	.337	105	3	.181	.263	.295	144	3	.264	.341	.368	95	1	.179	.269	.221	154	5	.260	.333	.409	127	1	.244	.327	.323	35	1	.171	.333	.343
1988	Atl-N	8	1	.250	.250	.625	0	0	—	—	—	8	1	.250	.250	.625	7	1	.286	.286	.714	1	0	.000	.000	.000	1	0	1.500	.500	1.250	1	0	.000	.000	.000
1989	Atl-N	231	4	.169	.246	.242	105	1	.143	.224	.200	126	3	.190	.264	.278	93	1	.204	.286	.280	138	3	.145	.219	.217	88	2	.148	.224	.250	52	0	.135	.246	.135
1990	Atl-N	28	0	.071	.161	.071	15	0	.067	.125	.067	13	0	.077	.200	.077	19	0	.105	.227	.105	9	0	.000	.000	.000	11	0	.000	.154	.000	7	0	.000	.125	.000
TOTALS		2477	87	.236	.303	.390	1201	48	.245	.317	.415	1276	39	.227	.289	.366	713	22	.230	.303	.381	1764	65	.238	.303	.393	1146	37	.232	.302	.386	424	13	.217	.298	.337

■ **Mike Davis** BL/TL

YEAR	TM/L	TOTAL AB	HR	AVG	OBP	SLG	HOME AB	HR	AVG	OBP	SLG	AWAY AB	HR	AVG	OBP	SLG	LEFT AB	HR	AVG	OBP	SLG	RIGHT AB	HR	AVG	OBP	SLG	ON-BASE AB	HR	AVG	OBP	SLG	LATE/CLOSE AB	HR	AVG	OBP	SLG
1984	Oak-A	382	9	.230	.285	.364	177	4	.237	.291	.373	205	5	.224	.280	.356	73	1	.205	.262	.356	309	8	.236	.291	.366	168	4	.244	.287	.381	63	2	.317	.366	.476
1985	Oak-A	547	24	.287	.348	.484	246	12	.276	.349	.492	301	12	.296	.347	.478	155	8	.271	.335	.484	392	16	.293	.353	.485	236	9	.280	.348	.458	90	5	.256	.316	.467
1986	Oak-A	489	19	.268	.314	.454	244	11	.266	.338	.475	245	8	.269	.287	.433	117	4	.299	.339	.479	372	15	.258	.306	.447	196	4	.265	.317	.398	82	4	.171	.198	.366
1987	Oak-A	494	22	.265	.320	.468	234	9	.261	.318	.449	260	13	.269	.323	.485	126	6	.278	.326	.500	368	16	.261	.319	.457	212	8	.269	.332	.453	76	5	.329	.422	.618
1988	LA-N	281	2	.196	.260	.270	133	1	.150	.210	.203	148	1	.236	.303	.331	64	0	.172	.229	.297	217	2	.203	.269	.263	110	2	.191	.248	.300	53	0	.264	.291	.358
1989	LA-N	173	5	.229	.309	.387	88	2	.273	.333	.386	85	3	.224	.283	.388	17	0	.118	.118	.118	156	5	.263	.328	.417	66	1	.212	.239	.318	41	1	.195	.313	.341
TOTALS		2366	81	.256	.312	.423	1122	39	.250	.314	.418	1244	42	.261	.310	.427	552	19	.254	.305	.437	1814	62	.256	.314	.418	988	28	.254	.310	.405	405	17	.257	.319	.449

■ **Andre Dawson** BR/TR

YEAR	TM/L	TOTAL AB	HR	AVG	OBP	SLG	HOME AB	HR	AVG	OBP	SLG	AWAY AB	HR	AVG	OBP	SLG	LEFT AB	HR	AVG	OBP	SLG	RIGHT AB	HR	AVG	OBP	SLG	ON-BASE AB	HR	AVG	OBP	SLG	LATE/CLOSE AB	HR	AVG	OBP	SLG
1984	Mon-N	533	17	.248	.301	.409	252	6	.210	.268	.345	281	11	.281	.330	.466	146	7	.281	.354	.479	387	10	.235	.280	.382	257	11	.280	.346	.479	100	4	.210	.245	.370
1985	Mon-N	529	23	.255	.295	.444	253	11	.249	.297	.419	276	12	.261	.294	.467	167	10	.275	.303	.515	362	13	.246	.292	.412	252	14	.286	.342	.508	92	3	.239	.314	.402
1986	Mon-N	496	20	.284	.338	.478	243	11	.296	.356	.477	253	9	.273	.320	.478	160	11	.331	.384	.625	336	9	.262	.315	.408	242	6	.277	.349	.417	107	3	.290	.364	.430
1987	Chi-N	621	49	.287	.328	.568	292	27	.332	.373	.668	329	22	.246	.288	.480	141	9	.298	.348	.525	480	40	.283	.321	.581	310	23	.310	.341	.597	90	9	.289	.340	.611
1988	Chi-N	591	24	.303	.344	.504	293	12	.314	.360	.515	298	12	.292	.329	.493	159	4	.296	.346	.523	432	20	.306	.346	.523	258	8	.287	.346	.469	98	1	.337	.405	.418
1989	Chi-N	416	21	.252	.307	.476	218	6	.239	.293	.385	198	15	.268	.323	.576	114	8	.298	.364	.579	302	13	.235	.284	.437	201	9	.239	.325	.438	61	3	.164	.224	.361
1990	Chi-N	529	27	.310	.358	.535	266	14	.316	.374	.534	263	13	.304	.342	.536	181	8	.298	.343	.508	348	19	.316	.366	.549	265	11	.321	.384	.532	87	4	.310	.417	.483
1991	Chi-N	563	31	.272	.302	.488	280	22	.293	.328	.575	283	9	.251	.277	.403	223	16	.296	.319	.556	340	15	.256	.291	.444	265	19	.291	.319	.547	118	7	.220	.250	.424
1992	Chi-N	542	22	.277	.316	.456	252	13	.306	.357	.540	290	9	.252	.279	.383	195	7	.287	.321	.467	347	15	.271	.314	.450	282	9	.287	.321	.473	113	6	.336	.364	.531
1993	Bos-A	461	13	.273	.313	.425	247	8	.304	.340	.486	214	5	.238	.283	.355	125	7	.320	.356	.576	336	6	.256	.298	.369	224	6	.286	.321	.424	76	2	.303	.303	.434
1994	Bos-A	292	16	.240	.271	.456	146	7	.267	.291	.500	146	9	.212	.252	.432	80	6	.287	.329	.587	212	10	.222	.249	.420	153	8	.235	.267	.458	45	3	.222	.255	.489
TOTALS		5573	263	.275	.318	.480	2742	137	.287	.334	.500	2831	126	.264	.303	.461	1691	93	.297	.340	.529	3882	170	.266	.309	.459	2709	124	.285	.336	.487	987	45	.271	.324	.451

■ **Doug DeCinces** BR/TR

YEAR	TM/L	TOTAL AB	HR	AVG	OBP	SLG	HOME AB	HR	AVG	OBP	SLG	AWAY AB	HR	AVG	OBP	SLG	LEFT AB	HR	AVG	OBP	SLG	RIGHT AB	HR	AVG	OBP	SLG	ON-BASE AB	HR	AVG	OBP	SLG	LATE/CLOSE AB	HR	AVG	OBP	SLG
1984	Cal-A	547	20	.269	.327	.431	266	10	.256	.327	.406	281	10	.281	.327	.456	175	9	.309	.383	.514	372	11	.250	.299	.392	261	9	.261	.319	.414	96	3	.250	.292	.365
1985	Cal-A	427	20	.244	.317	.440	208	12	.264	.345	.505	219	8	.224	.290	.379	127	6	.244	.345	.449	300	14	.243	.304	.437	216	13	.245	.317	.472	67	1	.254	.351	.343
1986	Cal-A	512	26	.256	.325	.459	259	14	.263	.328	.456	253	12	.249	.322	.462	173	9	.272	.345	.486	339	17	.248	.314	.445	268	12	.272	.328	.451	90	5	.311	.347	.533
1987	Cal-A	453	16	.234	.337	.391	226	10	.274	.385	.451	227	6	.194	.287	.330	159	7	.283	.413	.459	294	9	.207	.292	.354	197	6	.228	.351	.365	70	2	.200	.341	.329
1987	StL-N	9	0	.222	.222	.444	0	0	—	—	—	9	0	.222	.222	.444	4	0	.250	.250	.500	5	0	.200	.200	.400	4	0	.250	.250	.500	3	0	.333	.333	.667
TOTALS		1948	82	.252	.326	.431	968	46	.263	.344	.451	980	36	.240	.308	.411	638	31	.279	.373	.480	1310	51	.238	.302	.408	946	40	.254	.328	.428	326	11	.258	.331	.402

■ **Rob Deer** BR/TR

YEAR	TM/L	TOTAL AB	HR	AVG	OBP	SLG	HOME AB	HR	AVG	OBP	SLG	AWAY AB	HR	AVG	OBP	SLG	LEFT AB	HR	AVG	OBP	SLG	RIGHT AB	HR	AVG	OBP	SLG	ON-BASE AB	HR	AVG	OBP	SLG	LATE/CLOSE AB	HR	AVG	OBP	SLG
1984	SF-N	24	3	.167	.375	.542	14	2	.143	.429	.571	10	1	.200	.273	.500	3	1	.333	.333	1.333	21	2	.143	.379	.429	10	0	.000	.231	.000	4	1	.500	.667	1.250
1985	SF-N	162	8	.185	.283	.377	82	5	.159	.271	.378	80	3	.213	.297	.375	33	1	.212	.333	.303	129	7	.178	.269	.395	74	3	.122	.239	.270	35	1	.086	.200	.171
1986	Mil-A	466	33	.232	.336	.494	238	19	.227	.345	.504	228	14	.237	.345	.482	129	11	.279	.416	.605	337	22	.214	.303	.451	228	18	.250	.351	.544	67	5	.209	.293	.418
1987	Mil-A	474	28	.238	.360	.456	232	11	.228	.332	.409	242	17	.248	.386	.500	152	8	.257	.394	.467	322	20	.230	.344	.450	235	14	.234	.351	.443	67	3	.269	.417	.448
1988	Mil-A	492	23	.252	.328	.441	260	10	.254	.344	.415	232	13	.248	.311	.427	130	7	.231	.316	.431	362	16	.258	.332	.445	226	12	.159	.216	.293	73	3	.233	.356	.425
1989	Mil-A	466	26	.210	.305	.425	234	15	.201	.310	.436	232	11	.220	.299	.414	134	8	.254	.341	.515	332	18	.193	.290	.407	219	11	.228	.316	.429	63	4	.222	.324	.524
1990	Mil-A	440	27	.209	.313	.432	214	11	.187	.310	.374	226	16	.230	.317	.487	140	16	.293	.399	.671	300	11	.170	.271	.320	192	14	.229	.371	.495	73	4	.233	.356	.425
1991	Det-A	448	25	.179	.314	.386	228	12	.193	.332	.399	220	13	.164	.295	.373	149	6	.154	.299	.315	299	19	.191	.322	.421	199	14	.196	.299	.312	65	3	.164	.299	.315
1992	Det-A	393	32	.247	.337	.547	173	13	.254	.352	.549	220	19	.241	.325	.545	99	14	.293	.369	.747	294	18	.231	.326	.480	179	10	.218	.322	.436	65	5	.262	.324	.554
1993	Det-A	323	14	.217	.302	.381	126	9	.238	.340	.492	197	5	.203	.276	.310	90	6	.267	.385	.511	233	8	.197	.267	.330	159	4	.233	.317	.346	49	3	.265	.379	.469

YEAR TM/L	TOTAL					HOME					AWAY					LEFT					RIGHT					ON-BASE					LATE/CLOSE				
	AB	HR	AVG	OBP	SLG	AB	HR	AVG	OBP	SLG	AB	HR	AVG	OBP	SLG	AB	HR	AVG	OBP	SLG	AB	HR	AVG	OBP	SLG	AB	HR	AVG	OBP	SLG	AB	HR	AVG	OBP	SLG
1993 Bos-A	143	7	.196	.303	.399	66	3	.167	.313	.333	77	4	.221	.294	.455	31	3	.323	.432	.774	112	4	.161	.266	.295	71	3	.183	.318	.366	30	4	.300	.382	.800
TOTALS	3831	226	.220	.323	.442	1843	112	.216	.328	.442	1988	114	.224	.319	.442	1120	90	.259	.372	.551	2711	136	.204	.302	.397	1792	103	.228	.334	.445	608	34	.217	.322	.433

■ Rick Dempsey BR/TR

YEAR TM/L	TOTAL					HOME					AWAY					LEFT					RIGHT					ON-BASE					LATE/CLOSE				
	AB	HR	AVG	OBP	SLG	AB	HR	AVG	OBP	SLG	AB	HR	AVG	OBP	SLG	AB	HR	AVG	OBP	SLG	AB	HR	AVG	OBP	SLG	AB	HR	AVG	OBP	SLG	AB	HR	AVG	OBP	SLG
1984 Bal-A	330	11	.230	.312	.364	145	6	.228	.315	.379	185	5	.232	.310	.351	85	5	.282	.392	.518	245	6	.212	.282	.310	157	4	.191	.268	.293	44	2	.273	.340	.455
1985 Bal-A	362	12	.254	.345	.406	179	4	.235	.346	.358	183	8	.273	.343	.454	157	7	.325	.403	.529	205	5	.200	.299	.312	167	8	.305	.366	.521	52	2	.250	.333	.385
1986 Bal-A	327	13	.208	.309	.379	158	7	.215	.326	.380	169	6	.201	.293	.379	138	6	.254	.356	.457	189	7	.175	.274	.323	147	3	.122	.228	.211	50	1	.160	.250	.220
1987 Cle-A	141	1	.177	.295	.270	71	1	.169	.250	.282	70	0	.186	.337	.257	42	1	.167	.286	.333	99	0	.182	.299	.242	55	0	.164	.277	.236	14	0	.000	.176	.000
1988 LA-N	167	7	.251	.338	.455	65	3	.277	.354	.492	102	4	.235	.328	.431	122	5	.246	.324	.434	45	2	.267	.375	.511	67	3	.313	.358	.567	44	2	.227	.320	.432
1989 LA-N	151	4	.179	.319	.305	72	3	.181	.306	.278	79	2	.177	.330	.329	117	1	.171	.307	.239	34	3	.206	.357	.529	70	1	.200	.364	.286	44	2	.182	.280	.318
1990 LA-N	128	2	.195	.318	.281	64	2	.234	.329	.391	64	0	.156	.308	.172	94	2	.170	.310	.266	34	0	.265	.342	.324	60	0	.217	.319	.267	24	0	.125	.222	.125
1991 Mil-A	147	4	.231	.329	.347	73	2	.260	.364	.384	74	2	.203	.294	.311	97	3	.237	.330	.371	50	1	.220	.328	.300	65	4	.277	.359	.508	25	1	.320	.469	.440
1992 Bal-A	9	0	.111	.273	.111	6	0	.167	.375	.167	3	0	.000	.000	.000	3	0	.000	.250	.000	6	0	.167	.286	.167	5	0	.000	.286	.000	6	0	.167	.286	.167
TOTALS	1762	54	.221	.322	.363	833	27	.224	.327	.366	929	27	.219	.317	.360	855	30	.241	.345	.405	907	24	.203	.299	.323	793	23	.219	.310	.358	303	10	.208	.307	.327

■ Bob Dernier BR/TR

YEAR TM/L	TOTAL					HOME					AWAY					LEFT					RIGHT					ON-BASE					LATE/CLOSE				
	AB	HR	AVG	OBP	SLG	AB	HR	AVG	OBP	SLG	AB	HR	AVG	OBP	SLG	AB	HR	AVG	OBP	SLG	AB	HR	AVG	OBP	SLG	AB	HR	AVG	OBP	SLG	AB	HR	AVG	OBP	SLG
1984 Chi-N	536	3	.278	.356	.362	254	2	.303	.377	.402	282	1	.255	.338	.326	123	0	.260	.355	.317	413	3	.283	.357	.375	143	0	.273	.354	.329	62	0	.226	.333	.323
1985 Chi-N	469	1	.254	.315	.316	230	1	.278	.328	.352	239	0	.230	.303	.280	118	0	.288	.351	.373	351	1	.242	.303	.296	133	0	.233	.320	.286	65	0	.277	.373	.308
1986 Chi-N	324	4	.225	.275	.312	157	2	.255	.299	.350	167	2	.198	.251	.275	105	2	.305	.360	.429	219	2	.187	.233	.256	106	2	.189	.232	.274	62	1	.194	.219	.306
1987 Chi-N	199	8	.317	.379	.497	99	4	.313	.364	.475	100	4	.320	.393	.520	141	7	.340	.408	.553	58	1	.259	.306	.362	65	1	.292	.361	.369	37	3	.432	.523	.676
1988 Phi-N	166	1	.289	.330	.337	72	0	.208	.240	.250	94	1	.351	.396	.404	131	1	.314	.361	.372	29	0	.172	.172	.172	60	0	.267	.290	.283	26	0	.308	.308	.308
1989 Phi-N	187	1	.171	.225	.214	97	1	.165	.210	.206	90	0	.178	.242	.222	132	1	.197	.253	.250	55	0	.109	.155	.127	61	1	.213	.271	.295	47	1	.234	.260	.319
TOTALS	1881	18	.257	.319	.339	909	10	.267	.322	.355	972	8	.248	.317	.324	756	11	.284	.348	.384	1125	7	.239	.300	.309	568	4	.243	.310	.305	299	5	.264	.332	.358

■ Delino De Shields BL/TR

YEAR TM/L	TOTAL					HOME					AWAY					LEFT					RIGHT					ON-BASE					LATE/CLOSE				
	AB	HR	AVG	OBP	SLG	AB	HR	AVG	OBP	SLG	AB	HR	AVG	OBP	SLG	AB	HR	AVG	OBP	SLG	AB	HR	AVG	OBP	SLG	AB	HR	AVG	OBP	SLG	AB	HR	AVG	OBP	SLG
1990 Mon-N	499	4	.289	.375	.393	226	3	.314	.402	.438	273	1	.267	.352	.355	193	2	.264	.356	.373	306	2	.304	.387	.405	161	0	.267	.378	.373	101	0	.228	.328	.277
1991 Mon-N	563	10	.238	.347	.332	238	3	.265	.379	.349	325	7	.218	.324	.320	189	3	.217	.338	.275	374	7	.249	.352	.361	180	3	.261	.358	.350	106	1	.245	.355	.330
1992 Mon-N	530	7	.292	.359	.398	271	1	.277	.338	.351	259	6	.309	.381	.448	185	2	.314	.389	.400	345	5	.281	.343	.397	177	2	.282	.366	.395	82	2	.293	.355	.439
1993 Mon-N	481	2	.295	.389	.372	234	2	.333	.435	.432	247	0	.259	.343	.316	161	2	.311	.407	.435	320	0	.287	.379	.341	159	0	.270	.382	.327	85	0	.318	.381	.353
1994 LA-N	320	2	.250	.357	.322	151	1	.285	.366	.351	169	1	.219	.350	.296	98	0	.276	.398	.337	222	2	.239	.339	.315	138	2	.246	.360	.362	50	1	.260	.431	.400
TOTALS	2393	25	.274	.365	.366	1120	10	.295	.385	.385	1273	15	.255	.348	.350	826	9	.275	.374	.364	1567	16	.273	.361	.367	815	7	.266	.369	.362	424	4	.267	.364	.351

■ Mike Devereaux BR/TR

YEAR TM/L	TOTAL					HOME					AWAY					LEFT					RIGHT					ON-BASE					LATE/CLOSE				
	AB	HR	AVG	OBP	SLG	AB	HR	AVG	OBP	SLG	AB	HR	AVG	OBP	SLG	AB	HR	AVG	OBP	SLG	AB	HR	AVG	OBP	SLG	AB	HR	AVG	OBP	SLG	AB	HR	AVG	OBP	SLG
1987 LA-N	54	0	.222	.263	.278	27	0	.296	.345	.296	27	0	.148	.179	.259	39	0	.205	.244	.256	15	0	.267	.313	.333	24	0	.250	.308	.333	15	0	.200	.200	.200
1988 LA-N	43	0	.116	.156	.140	22	0	.136	.136	.136	21	0	.095	.174	.143	24	0	.125	.192	.125	19	0	.105	.105	.158	20	0	.150	.190	.150	11	0	.182	.182	.182
1989 Bal-A	391	8	.266	.329	.379	191	4	.246	.327	.366	200	4	.285	.330	.390	189	3	.280	.351	.402	202	5	.252	.308	.356	158	5	.259	.341	.411	60	3	.233	.277	.433
1990 Bal-A	367	12	.240	.291	.392	150	6	.233	.304	.407	217	6	.244	.281	.387	160	7	.231	.273	.406	207	5	.246	.304	.382	169	5	.249	.288	.396	64	1	.297	.378	.375
1991 Bal-A	608	19	.260	.313	.431	305	10	.252	.302	.420	303	9	.267	.324	.442	167	6	.293	.350	.515	441	13	.247	.302	.418	194	6	.247	.302	.418	104	3	.260	.300	.365
1992 Bal-A	653	24	.276	.321	.464	334	14	.257	.301	.461	319	10	.295	.342	.467	168	9	.351	.383	.589	485	15	.249	.300	.421	281	9	.263	.305	.441	98	6	.214	.259	.429
1993 Bal-A	527	14	.250	.306	.400	247	8	.263	.331	.457	280	6	.239	.283	.350	156	5	.256	.352	.442	371	9	.246	.286	.383	251	8	.267	.309	.438	76	1	.197	.262	.276
1994 Bal-A	301	9	.203	.256	.332	124	5	.210	.286	.363	177	4	.198	.234	.311	81	2	.235	.267	.358	220	7	.191	.252	.323	136	1	.184	.243	.235	39	0	.103	.119	.179
TOTALS	2944	86	.251	.304	.404	1400	47	.248	.308	.415	1544	39	.255	.301	.394	984	32	.275	.329	.444	1960	54	.239	.291	.384	1233	34	.248	.299	.397	467	14	.225	.273	.349

■ Gary Disarcina BR/TR

YEAR TM/L	TOTAL					HOME					AWAY					LEFT					RIGHT					ON-BASE					LATE/CLOSE				
	AB	HR	AVG	OBP	SLG	AB	HR	AVG	OBP	SLG	AB	HR	AVG	OBP	SLG	AB	HR	AVG	OBP	SLG	AB	HR	AVG	OBP	SLG	AB	HR	AVG	OBP	SLG	AB	HR	AVG	OBP	SLG
1989 Cal-A	0	0	—	—	—	0	0	—	—	—	0	0	—	—	—	0	0	—	—	—	0	0	—	—	—	0	0	—	—	—	0	0	—	—	—
1990 Cal-A	57	0	.140	.183	.193	26	0	.038	.107	.038	31	0	.226	.250	.323	12	0	.000	.077	.000	45	0	.178	.213	.244	23	0	.130	.167	.130	9	0	.000	.182	.000
1991 Cal-A	57	0	.211	.274	.246	27	0	.148	.258	.185	30	0	.267	.290	.300	18	0	.222	.222	.278	39	0	.205	.295	.231	17	0	.235	.381	.235	8	0	.125	.222	.125
1992 Cal-A	518	3	.247	.283	.301	251	2	.235	.269	.295	267	1	.258	.296	.307	114	0	.228	.264	.263	404	3	.252	.288	.312	209	2	.220	.259	.273	91	1	.132	.194	.176
1993 Cal-A	416	3	.238	.273	.313	216	2	.250	.279	.324	200	1	.225	.265	.300	119	0	.210	.234	.244	297	3	.249	.288	.340	197	2	.244	.276	.320	74	0	.176	.218	.189
1994 Cal-A	389	3	.260	.294	.329	207	2	.261	.294	.329	182	1	.258	.295	.330	117	2	.274	.303	.376	272	1	.254	.291	.309	175	1	.291	.323	.354	74	0	.311	.320	.351
TOTALS	1437	9	.242	.279	.305	727	6	.237	.273	.300	710	3	.248	.285	.311	380	2	.229	.259	.284	1057	7	.247	.286	.313	621	5	.245	.283	.304	256	1	.191	.236	.223

■ Bill Doran BB/TR

YEAR TM/L	TOTAL					HOME					AWAY					LEFT					RIGHT					ON-BASE					LATE/CLOSE				
	AB	HR	AVG	OBP	SLG	AB	HR	AVG	OBP	SLG	AB	HR	AVG	OBP	SLG	AB	HR	AVG	OBP	SLG	AB	HR	AVG	OBP	SLG	AB	HR	AVG	OBP	SLG	AB	HR	AVG	OBP	SLG
1984 Hou-N	548	4	.261	.341	.356	267	2	.232	.311	.333	281	2	.288	.369	.377	176	2	.295	.375	.364	372	2	.245	.325	.352	186	0	.247	.335	.290	90	0	.300	.370	.344
1985 Hou-N	578	14	.287	.362	.434	269	5	.283	.372	.450	309	9	.291	.354	.421	217	5	.300	.383	.461	361	9	.280	.350	.418	195	5	.297	.383	.431	93	4	.258	.330	.430
1986 Hou-N	550	6	.276	.368	.373	270	3	.274	.379	.374	280	3	.279	.358	.371	214	3	.304	.391	.407	336	3	.259	.356	.351	157	0	.268	.375	.331	83	1	.217	.309	.325
1987 Hou-N	625	16	.283	.365	.406	292	7	.305	.412	.414	333	9	.264	.320	.399	223	7	.291	.395	.417	402	9	.279	.348	.400	256	7	.316	.385	.449	105	1	.314	.413	.371
1988 Hou-N	480	7	.248	.338	.333	229	2	.249	.351	.323	251	5	.247	.325	.343	156	2	.263	.372	.346	324	5	.241	.321	.327	187	3	.289	.372	.385	78	1	.179	.312	.218
1989 Hou-N	507	8	.219	.301	.323	250	3	.252	.332	.360	257	5	.187	.271	.288	167	4	.269	.357	.311	340	4	.271	.341	.414	203	4	.271	.341	.414	95	3	.189	.260	.305
1990 Hou-N	344	6	.288	.405	.413	169	3	.314	.420	.456	175	3	.263	.390	.371	135	2	.267	.409	.415	209	4	.301	.402	.411	119	3	.294	.418	.429	46	0	.217	.410	.261
1990 Cin-N	59	1	.373	.448	.559	30	1	.433	.500	.633	29	0	.310	.394	.483	7	0	.286	.375	.286	52	1	.385	.458	.596	29	0	.276	.344	.379	6	0	.500	.667	.500
1991 Cin-N	361	6	.280	.359	.374	169	3	.296	.390	.408	192	3	.266	.330	.344	80	2	.262	.362	.412	281	4	.285	.358	.363	141	1	.305	.365	.383	78	1	.244	.322	.346
1992 Cin-N	387	8	.235	.342	.349	197	6	.223	.338	.345	190	2	.247	.347	.353	125	2	.200	.353	.288	262	6	.252	.337	.378	187	4	.241	.357	.364	68	2	.235	.361	.382
1993 Mil-A	60	0	.217	.284	.283	27	0	.185	.267	.222	33	0	.242	.297	.333	40	0	.200	.267	.275	20	0	.250	.318	.300	25	0	.360	.414	.440	15	0	.133	.188	.200
TOTALS	4499	76	.266	.353	.376	2169	35	.270	.367	.385	2330	41	.261	.339	.367	1513	29	.272	.371	.387	2986	47	.262	.344	.370	1685	27	.282	.369	.389	757	13	.243	.342	.336

■ Brian Downing BR/TR

YEAR TM/L	TOTAL					HOME					AWAY					LEFT					RIGHT					ON-BASE					LATE/CLOSE				
	AB	HR	AVG	OBP	SLG	AB	HR	AVG	OBP	SLG	AB	HR	AVG	OBP	SLG	AB	HR	AVG	OBP	SLG	AB	HR	AVG	OBP	SLG	AB	HR	AVG	OBP	SLG	AB	HR	AVG	OBP	SLG
1984 Cal-A	539	23	.275	.360	.462	263	9	.255	.345	.403	276	14	.293	.374	.518	174	7	.293	.394	.471	365	16	.266	.344	.458	227	11	.286	.389	.493	79	3	.253	.380	.430
1985 Cal-A	520	20	.263	.371	.427	249	10	.241	.362	.406	271	10	.284	.379	.446	172	8	.262	.343	.483	348	12	.264	.384	.399	227	12	.300	.385	.515	83	3	.301	.385	.470
1986 Cal-A	513	20	.267	.389	.492	260	13	.277	.392	.488	253	7	.257	.385	.415	183	7	.290	.385	.443	330	13	.282	.390	.458	243	13	.276	.403	.506	71	4	.296	.451	.563
1987 Cal-A	567	29	.272	.400	.487	280	11	.279	.412	.475	287	18	.265	.388	.498	177	11	.299	.432	.554	390	18	.259	.384	.456	216	7	.269	.384	.407	98	3	.255	.357	.378
1988 Cal-A	484	25	.242	.362	.442	239	11	.238	.365	.423	245	14	.245	.360	.461	175	8	.223	.385	.383	309	17	.252	.349	.476	200	7	.275	.391	.420	93	7	.290	.380	.570
1989 Cal-A	544	14	.283	.354	.414	250	10	.296	.370	.464	294	4	.272	.340	.371	187	8	.299	.388	.476	357	6	.255	.336	.381	209	3	.287	.368	.383	87	3	.299	.396	.448
1990 Cal-A	330	14	.273	.374	.467	162	11	.302	.403	.562	168	3	.244	.347	.375	119	5	.345	.466	.555	211	9	.232	.318	.417	139	7	.317	.407	.547	65	3	.246	.319	.415
1991 Tex-A	407	17	.278	.377	.455	204	8	.255	.365	.431	203	9	.300	.389	.478	139	9	.281	.401	.511	268	8	.276	.364	.425	148	4	.291	.425	.419	75	2	.293	.365	.400
1992 Tex-A	320	10	.278	.407	.428	157	6	.248	.382	.401	163	4	.307	.430	.454	121	3	.281	.429	.421	199	7	.276	.392	.432	124	4	.258	.404	.403	49	1	.184	.322	.306
TOTALS	4224	172	.270	.376	.448	2070	87	.270	.381	.453	2154	85	.269	.372	.444	1447	66	.278	.400	.475	2777	106	.265	.364	.434	1733	68	.284	.394	.457	700	29	.273	.376	.449

■ Mariano Duncan BR/TR

YEAR TM/L	TOTAL					HOME					AWAY					LEFT					RIGHT					ON-BASE					LATE/CLOSE				
	AB	HR	AVG	OBP	SLG	AB	HR	AVG	OBP	SLG	AB	HR	AVG	OBP	SLG	AB	HR	AVG	OBP	SLG	AB	HR	AVG	OBP	SLG	AB	HR	AVG	OBP	SLG	AB	HR	AVG	OBP	SLG
1985 LA-N	562	6	.244	.293	.340	275	1	.240	.286	.313	287	5	.247	.300	.366	182	4	.286	.332	.429	380	2	.224	.275	.297	180	3	.250	.291	.367	69	3	.188	.269	.362
1986 LA-N	407	8	.229	.275	.259	205	2	.220	.275	.259	202	6	.238	.294	.351	173	4	.260	.295	.347	234	4	.205	.276	.274	162	2	.241	.287	.302	69	1	.319	.347	.377
1987 LA-N	261	6	.215	.267	.322	110	3	.227	.277	.336	151	3	.205	.259	.311	91	4	.275	.305	.451	170	2	.182	.247	.253	96	1	.208	.238	.292	43	0	.302	.400	.419
1989 LA-N	84	0	.250	.267	.333	62	0	.210	.222	.306	22	0	.364	.391	.409	45	0	.356	.356	.489	39	0	.128	.171	.154	31	0	.323	.344	.452	26	0	.346	.370	.423
1989 Cin-N	174	3	.247	.292	.368	68	2	.250	.311	.397	106	1	.245	.279	.349	54	2	.222	.300	.444	120	1	.258	.288	.333	55	1	.309	.345	.455	28	1	.214	.267	.321
1990 Cin-N	435	10	.306	.345	.476	230	5	.309	.346	.470	205	5	.302	.344	.483	188	4	.410	.437	.606	247	6	.227	.276	.377	191	4	.277	.314	.424	68	0	.250	.307	.279
1991 Cin-N	333	12	.258	.288	.411	167	10	.311	.333	.539	166	2	.205	.243	.283	140	5	.314	.347	.493	193	7	.218	.244	.352	127	4	.283	.293	.433	52	0	.231	.245	.269
1992 Phi-N	574	8	.267	.292	.389	276	3	.243	.277	.351	298	5	.289	.306	.423	231	4	.286	.308	.407	343	4	.254	.278	.376	235	4	.255	.278	.379	90	1	.267	.302	.344
1993 Phi-N	496	11	.282	.304	.417	211	5	.289	.315	.427	285	6	.277	.295	.411	198	6	.273	.291	.429	298	5	.289	.312	.409	250	5	.288	.294	.404	76	3	.276	.273	.474
1994 Phi-N	347	8	.268	.306	.406	190	6	.247	.285	.389	157	2	.293	.331	.427	111	4	.297	.345	.495	236	4	.254	.289	.364	179	8	.307	.333	.525	50	1	.340	.382	.480
TOTALS	3673	72	.259	.297	.383	1794	37	.259	.297	.380	1879	35	.261	.299	.386	1413	37	.300	.332	.454	2260	35	.235	.276	.338	1506	30	.270	.297	.400	571	10	.270	.312	.373

■ Shawon Dunston BR/TR

YEAR TM/L	TOTAL					HOME					AWAY					LEFT					RIGHT					ON-BASE					LATE/CLOSE				
	AB	HR	AVG	OBP	SLG	AB	HR	AVG	OBP	SLG	AB	HR	AVG	OBP	SLG	AB	HR	AVG	OBP	SLG	AB	HR	AVG	OBP	SLG	AB	HR	AVG	OBP	SLG	AB	HR	AVG	OBP	SLG
1985 Chi-N	250	4	.260	.310	.388	147	3	.299	.362	.449	103	1	.204	.231	.301	45	1	.222	.255	.356	205	3	.268	.321	.395	97	1	.268	.336	.330	23	0	.261	.280	.304
1986 Chi-N	581	17	.250	.278	.411	305	10	.262	.287	.443	276	7	.236	.269	.377	156	6	.231	.247	.423	425	11	.256	.290	.407	230	6	.278	.320	.457	110	4	.182	.204	.336
1987 Chi-N	346	5	.246	.267	.358	181	3	.221	.239	.337	165	2	.273	.298	.382	78	1	.231	.237	.321	268	4	.250	.276	.369	130	2	.231	.239	.338	64	0	.297	.324	.344
1988 Chi-N	575	9	.249	.271	.357	263	5	.278	.300	.407	312	4	.224	.245	.314	167	4	.234	.247	.371	408	5	.255	.280	.350	226	4	.252	.275	.363	105	0	.219	.243	.257
1989 Chi-N	471	9	.278	.320	.403	225	3	.307	.347	.404	246	6	.252	.295	.402	139	2	.338	.382	.489	332	7	.253	.294	.367	211	4	.280	.342	.417	75	2	.267	.313	.280
1990 Chi-N	545	17	.262	.283	.449	268	7	.250	.275	.403	277	10	.274	.291	.495	188	9	.287	.295	.505	357	8	.250	.277	.426	217	9	.240	.267	.438	92	3	.272	.306	.446
1991 Chi-N	492	12	.260	.292	.407	237	7	.295	.329	.451	255	5	.227	.258	.365	194	5	.232	.269	.366	298	7	.279	.308	.433	193	3	.249	.268	.383	112	3	.357	.395	.527
1992 Chi-N	73	0	.315	.342	.384	28	0	.321	.367	.429	45	0	.311	.326	.356	24	0	.417	.417	.417	49	0	.265	.308	.367	22	0	.273	.273	.364	14	0	.286	.286	.286
1993 Chi-N	10	0	.400	.400	.600	4	0	.667	.667	1.000	6	0	.286	.286	.333	4	0	.429	.429	.714	3	0	.333	.333	.333	4	0	.500	.500	.750	2	0	1.000	1.000	1.000
1994 Chi-N	331	11	.278	.313	.435	159	2	.220	.256	.308	172	9	.331	.366	.552	90	6	.267	.302	.556	241	5	.282	.318	.390	117	2	.274	.326	.368	51	3	.294	.333	.490
TOTALS	3674	84	.261	.291	.399	1816	40	.269	.301	.407	1858	44	.253	.281	.391	1088	34	.263	.286	.430	2586	50	.260	.293	.386	1447	31	.260	.294	.397	648	13	.269	.300	.380

Leon Durham BL/TL

YEAR	TM/L	TOTAL					HOME					AWAY					LEFT					RIGHT					ON-BASE					LATE/CLOSE				
		AB	HR	AVG	OBP	SLG	AB	HR	AVG	OBP	SLG	AB	HR	AVG	OBP	SLG	AB	HR	AVG	OBP	SLG	AB	HR	AVG	OBP	SLG	AB	HR	AVG	OBP	SLG	AB	HR	AVG	OBP	SLG
1984	Chi-N	473	23	.279	.369	.505	245	19	.327	.417	.645	228	4	.228	.315	.355	109	2	.257	.362	.385	364	21	.286	.371	.541	243	15	.300	.397	.572	69	0	.217	.341	.304
1985	Chi-N	542	21	.282	.357	.465	257	15	.331	.414	.595	285	6	.239	.304	.347	127	4	.268	.340	.425	415	17	.287	.363	.477	234	9	.274	.385	.449	90	4	.267	.340	.489
1986	Chi-N	484	20	.262	.350	.452	279	13	.283	.360	.505	205	7	.234	.338	.380	128	3	.227	.275	.367	356	17	.275	.375	.483	202	10	.282	.388	.475	84	7	.286	.434	.560
1987	Chi-N	439	27	.273	.348	.513	236	16	.297	.375	.551	203	11	.246	.316	.468	74	2	.257	.286	.378	365	25	.277	.359	.540	182	8	.247	.359	.429	57	2	.263	.323	.404
1988	Chi-N	73	3	.219	.305	.452	22	0	.091	.167	.227	51	3	.275	.362	.549	4	0	.250	.400	.250	69	3	.217	.299	.464	34	1	.147	.256	.265	11	1	.273	.429	.636
1988	Cin-N	51	1	.216	.286	.333	42	1	.190	.244	.333	9	0	.333	.455	.333	3	0	.333	.333	.333	48	1	.208	.283	.333	23	0	.174	.240	.261	9	0	.556	.556	.667
1989	StL-N	18	0	.056	.182	.111	7	0	.143	.364	.286	11	0	.000	.000	.000	5	0	.200	.333	.400	13	0	.000	.125	.000	10	0	.100	.167	.200	9	0	.111	.100	.222
TOTALS		2080	95	.269	.351	.475	1088	64	.299	.381	.554	992	31	.237	.318	.387	450	11	.251	.320	.389	1630	84	.274	.359	.498	928	43	.268	.373	.469	329	14	.264	.366	.456

Lenny Dykstra BL/TL

YEAR	TM/L	TOTAL					HOME					AWAY					LEFT					RIGHT					ON-BASE					LATE/CLOSE				
		AB	HR	AVG	OBP	SLG	AB	HR	AVG	OBP	SLG	AB	HR	AVG	OBP	SLG	AB	HR	AVG	OBP	SLG	AB	HR	AVG	OBP	SLG	AB	HR	AVG	OBP	SLG	AB	HR	AVG	OBP	SLG
1985	NY-N	236	1	.254	.338	.331	109	0	.239	.323	.294	127	1	.268	.352	.362	56	0	.268	.349	.321	180	1	.250	.335	.333	92	1	.228	.291	.337	33	0	.212	.270	.273
1986	NY-N	431	8	.295	.377	.445	211	4	.322	.397	.493	220	4	.268	.357	.400	103	0	.233	.336	.291	328	8	.314	.390	.494	124	2	.298	.386	.435	74	1	.324	.412	.459
1987	NY-N	431	10	.285	.352	.455	212	7	.292	.359	.481	219	3	.279	.344	.429	74	1	.203	.289	.324	357	9	.303	.365	.482	132	4	.303	.387	.485	57	1	.246	.348	.386
1988	NY-N	429	8	.270	.321	.385	201	3	.254	.306	.343	228	5	.285	.335	.421	74	1	.270	.321	.365	355	7	.270	.321	.389	136	3	.235	.307	.353	62	0	.290	.366	.339
1989	NY-N	159	3	.270	.362	.415	69	2	.275	.373	.449	90	1	.267	.352	.389	34	0	.294	.316	.412	125	3	.264	.373	.416	47	1	.255	.304	.404	22	0	.273	.419	.364
1989	Phi-N	352	4	.222	.297	.330	165	3	.242	.332	.376	187	1	.203	.265	.289	119	0	.202	.296	.261	233	4	.232	.297	.365	96	2	.208	.294	.323	65	0	.246	.319	.277
1990	Phi-N	590	9	.325	.418	.441	280	6	.339	.445	.464	310	3	.313	.392	.419	200	1	.290	.385	.345	390	8	.344	.434	.490	177	1	.418	.518	.508	83	1	.361	.480	.458
1991	Phi-N	246	3	.297	.391	.427	118	3	.322	.424	.492	128	0	.273	.359	.367	94	2	.309	.414	.500	152	1	.289	.376	.382	67	1	.269	.402	.433	51	1	.314	.435	.451
1992	Phi-N	345	6	.301	.375	.406	196	5	.306	.385	.423	149	1	.295	.361	.383	146	4	.322	.389	.452	199	2	.286	.364	.372	101	2	.366	.433	.505	58	1	.414	.446	.517
1993	Phi-N	637	19	.305	.420	.482	307	12	.300	.425	.518	330	7	.309	.416	.448	217	2	.281	.414	.390	420	17	.317	.424	.529	216	5	.282	.410	.417	84	5	.310	.463	.548
1994	Phi-N	315	5	.273	.404	.435	165	3	.291	.426	.497	150	2	.253	.379	.367	91	1	.231	.388	.330	224	4	.290	.411	.478	96	2	.271	.450	.417	44	1	.182	.419	.318
TOTALS		4171	76	.287	.375	.422	2033	48	.295	.389	.449	2138	28	.279	.362	.398	1208	12	.268	.368	.365	2963	64	.294	.379	.446	1284	24	.294	.395	.426	633	11	.299	.409	.415

Mike Easler BL/TR

YEAR	TM/L	TOTAL					HOME					AWAY					LEFT					RIGHT					ON-BASE					LATE/CLOSE				
		AB	HR	AVG	OBP	SLG	AB	HR	AVG	OBP	SLG	AB	HR	AVG	OBP	SLG	AB	HR	AVG	OBP	SLG	AB	HR	AVG	OBP	SLG	AB	HR	AVG	OBP	SLG	AB	HR	AVG	OBP	SLG
1984	Bos-A	601	27	.313	.376	.516	299	16	.375	.434	.612	302	11	.252	.317	.421	179	7	.240	.290	.425	422	20	.344	.411	.555	241	11	.315	.399	.539	90	6	.367	.412	.667
1985	Bos-A	568	16	.262	.325	.412	273	4	.249	.311	.377	295	12	.275	.337	.444	173	2	.277	.345	.364	395	14	.256	.316	.433	244	6	.258	.321	.426	104	1	.212	.259	.279
1986	NY-A	490	14	.302	.362	.449	233	6	.288	.349	.442	257	8	.315	.375	.455	106	1	.226	.252	.302	384	13	.323	.390	.490	241	5	.311	.380	.436	71	1	.268	.381	.380
1987	Phi-A	110	1	.282	.316	.345	69	1	.261	.288	.333	41	0	.317	.364	.366	15	0	.133	.188	.133	95	1	.305	.337	.379	45	0	.244	.271	.267	11	0	.182	.250	.273
1987	NY-A	167	4	.281	.337	.389	90	2	.356	.416	.478	77	2	.195	.241	.286	21	0	.190	.333	.190	146	4	.295	.338	.418	65	2	.308	.382	.462	29	1	.345	.406	.517
TOTALS		1936	62	.291	.351	.448	964	29	.308	.367	.472	972	33	.274	.335	.424	494	10	.245	.301	.358	1442	52	.307	.368	.479	836	24	.293	.363	.456	305	9	.282	.347	.439

Jim Eisenreich BL/TL

YEAR	TM/L	TOTAL					HOME					AWAY					LEFT					RIGHT					ON-BASE					LATE/CLOSE				
		AB	HR	AVG	OBP	SLG	AB	HR	AVG	OBP	SLG	AB	HR	AVG	OBP	SLG	AB	HR	AVG	OBP	SLG	AB	HR	AVG	OBP	SLG	AB	HR	AVG	OBP	SLG	AB	HR	AVG	OBP	SLG
1984	Min-A	32	0	.219	.250	.250	27	0	.222	.258	.259	5	0	.200	.200	.200	0	0	—	.000	—	32	0	.219	.257	.250	14	0	.071	.118	.071	8	0	.250	.333	.250
1987	KC-A	105	4	.238	.278	.467	53	3	.302	.350	.660	52	1	.173	.200	.269	3	0	.000	.000	.000	102	4	.245	.286	.480	51	2	.314	.367	.549	18	0	.167	.318	.278
1988	KC-A	202	1	.218	.236	.282	99	0	.222	.238	.283	103	1	.214	.234	.282	38	0	.368	.385	.421	164	1	.183	.202	.250	92	1	.239	.253	.337	45	0	.222	.239	.244
1989	KC-A	475	9	.293	.341	.448	228	4	.307	.359	.482	247	5	.279	.325	.417	107	2	.336	.360	.430	368	7	.280	.336	.454	193	5	.326	.382	.492	66	1	.288	.382	.439
1990	KC-A	496	5	.280	.335	.397	236	2	.258	.327	.377	260	3	.300	.343	.415	156	1	.224	.268	.327	340	4	.306	.365	.429	210	2	.267	.328	.352	82	2	.268	.310	.427
1991	KC-A	375	2	.301	.333	.392	193	2	.311	.337	.409	182	0	.291	.330	.374	87	1	.322	.351	.402	288	1	.295	.328	.389	171	1	.304	.339	.386	71	1	.254	.286	.408
1992	KC-A	353	2	.269	.313	.340	160	1	.244	.301	.313	193	1	.290	.324	.365	75	0	.240	.284	.320	278	2	.277	.321	.345	154	1	.208	.256	.260	79	1	.278	.330	.392
1993	Phi-N	362	7	.318	.363	.445	156	3	.327	.371	.455	206	4	.311	.357	.437	58	1	.293	.354	.414	304	6	.322	.365	.451	189	4	.323	.381	.444	71	0	.268	.321	.296
1994	Phi-N	290	4	.300	.337	.421	148	3	.372	.430	.534	142	1	.225	.311	.303	53	0	.264	.316	.321	237	4	.308	.383	.443	143	3	.315	.379	.483	61	1	.246	.303	.295
TOTALS		2690	34	.284	.330	.399	1300	18	.292	.341	.422	1390	16	.276	.320	.378	577	5	.281	.318	.369	2113	29	.285	.334	.407	1217	19	.286	.337	.401	501	6	.259	.315	.361

Kevin Elster BR/TR

YEAR	TM/L	TOTAL					HOME					AWAY					LEFT					RIGHT					ON-BASE					LATE/CLOSE				
		AB	HR	AVG	OBP	SLG	AB	HR	AVG	OBP	SLG	AB	HR	AVG	OBP	SLG	AB	HR	AVG	OBP	SLG	AB	HR	AVG	OBP	SLG	AB	HR	AVG	OBP	SLG	AB	HR	AVG	OBP	SLG
1986	NY-N	30	0	.167	.242	.200	20	0	.150	.261	.150	10	0	.200	.200	.300	8	0	.125	.300	.125	22	0	.182	.217	.227	11	0	.182	.308	.273	2	0	.000	.000	.000
1987	NY-N	10	0	.400	.400	.600	2	0	1.000	1.000	1.500	8	0	.250	.250	.375	4	0	.750	.750	1.000	6	0	.167	.167	.333	4	0	.250	.250	.500	1	0	1.000	1.000	1.000
1988	NY-N	406	9	.214	.282	.313	196	6	.194	.268	.306	210	3	.233	.312	.319	145	3	.228	.304	.324	261	6	.207	.269	.307	175	6	.251	.345	.389	63	2	.159	.232	.254
1989	NY-N	458	10	.231	.283	.360	235	5	.226	.281	.345	223	5	.238	.285	.377	159	2	.258	.314	.365	299	8	.217	.266	.358	196	4	.265	.327	.383	78	1	.256	.289	.372
1990	NY-N	314	9	.207	.274	.363	163	2	.196	.262	.313	151	7	.219	.286	.417	119	2	.227	.282	.336	195	7	.195	.268	.379	125	3	.264	.324	.448	48	1	.125	.204	.229
1991	NY-N	348	6	.241	.318	.351	181	3	.265	.335	.376	167	3	.216	.300	.323	159	1	.296	.362	.371	189	5	.196	.282	.333	157	2	.255	.324	.357	57	0	.140	.290	.140
1992	NY-N	18	0	.222	.222	.222	9	0	.222	.222	.222	9	0	.222	.222	.222	6	0	.167	.167	.167	12	0	.250	.250	.250	9	0	.222	.222	.222	2	0	.000	.000	.000
1994	NY-A	20	0	.000	.048	.000	17	0	.000	.056	.000	3	0	.000	.000	.000	10	0	.000	.091	.000	10	0	.000	.000	.000	7	0	.000	.000	.000	1	0	.000	.000	.000
TOTALS		1604	34	.221	.285	.339	823	16	.216	.278	.326	781	18	.227	.293	.353	610	8	.251	.316	.344	994	26	.203	.266	.336	684	15	.254	.326	.383	252	4	.179	.256	.258

Nick Esasky BR/TR

YEAR	TM/L	TOTAL					HOME					AWAY					LEFT					RIGHT					ON-BASE					LATE/CLOSE				
		AB	HR	AVG	OBP	SLG	AB	HR	AVG	OBP	SLG	AB	HR	AVG	OBP	SLG	AB	HR	AVG	OBP	SLG	AB	HR	AVG	OBP	SLG	AB	HR	AVG	OBP	SLG	AB	HR	AVG	OBP	SLG
1984	Cin-N	322	10	.193	.301	.348	168	5	.208	.323	.375	154	5	.175	.275	.318	143	6	.224	.339	.441	179	4	.168	.269	.274	144	5	.215	.314	.424	62	1	.210	.311	.323
1985	Cin-N	413	21	.262	.332	.465	196	7	.230	.276	.403	217	14	.290	.378	.521	141	7	.298	.375	.518	272	14	.243	.309	.438	180	10	.261	.327	.483	81	6	.235	.304	.469
1986	Cin-N	330	12	.230	.325	.403	159	9	.226	.306	.459	171	3	.234	.342	.351	118	5	.237	.331	.458	212	7	.226	.321	.373	143	8	.224	.339	.427	54	5	.185	.297	.352
1987	Cin-N	346	22	.272	.327	.529	191	10	.246	.313	.461	155	12	.303	.345	.613	91	6	.253	.370	.505	255	16	.278	.310	.537	148	12	.297	.367	.635	52	3	.231	.328	.404
1988	Cin-N	391	15	.243	.327	.412	213	7	.254	.331	.408	178	8	.230	.321	.416	116	3	.250	.357	.388	275	12	.240	.313	.422	177	5	.232	.325	.362	75	3	.240	.293	.427
1989	Bos-A	564	30	.277	.355	.500	283	15	.300	.379	.541	281	15	.253	.331	.459	172	11	.250	.345	.488	392	19	.288	.360	.505	284	21	.296	.390	.570	89	5	.303	.386	.573
1990	Atl-N	35	0	.171	.256	.171	23	0	.217	.308	.217	12	0	.083	.154	.083	10	0	.400	.455	.400	25	0	.080	.179	.080	14	0	.214	.353	.214	3	0	.000	.250	.000
TOTALS		2401	110	.249	.329	.445	1233	53	.249	.324	.444	1168	57	.248	.335	.446	791	38	.254	.353	.466	1610	72	.246	.317	.435	1090	61	.259	.349	.488	416	21	.238	.321	.435

Alvaro Espinoza BR/TR

YEAR	TM/L	TOTAL					HOME					AWAY					LEFT					RIGHT					ON-BASE					LATE/CLOSE				
		AB	HR	AVG	OBP	SLG	AB	HR	AVG	OBP	SLG	AB	HR	AVG	OBP	SLG	AB	HR	AVG	OBP	SLG	AB	HR	AVG	OBP	SLG	AB	HR	AVG	OBP	SLG	AB	HR	AVG	OBP	SLG
1985	Min-A	57	0	.263	.288	.298	36	0	.194	.216	.222	21	0	.381	.409	.429	17	0	.412	.444	.412	40	0	.200	.220	.250	25	0	.320	.370	.400	5	0	.400	.500	.400
1986	Min-A	42	0	.214	.233	.238	23	0	.217	.217	.217	19	0	.211	.250	.263	10	0	.500	.545	.500	32	0	.125	.125	.156	10	0	.300	.300	.300	3	0	.000	.250	.000
1988	NY-A	3	0	.000	.000	.000	3	0	.000	.000	.000						10	0	.500	.545	.500	3	0	.000	.000	.000	0		—	—	—	1	0	.000	.000	.000
1989	NY-A	503	0	.282	.301	.332	241	0	.299	.320	.357	262	0	.267	.284	.309	162	0	.383	.407	.426	341	0	.235	.249	.287	206	0	.325	.336	.364	70	0	.300	.329	.300
1990	NY-A	438	2	.224	.258	.274	219	0	.215	.251	.265	219	2	.233	.265	.283	144	1	.250	.294	.299	294	1	.211	.240	.262	170	0	.235	.258	.276	59	1	.254	.286	.390
1991	NY-A	480	5	.256	.282	.344	254	2	.228	.273	.327	226	3	.265	.292	.363	161	1	.261	.294	.342	319	4	.254	.276	.345	186	1	.274	.301	.349	75	0	.200	.231	.240
1993	Cle-A	263	4	.278	.298	.380	124	3	.218	.244	.331	139	1	.331	.347	.424	113	2	.345	.364	.478	150	2	.227	.248	.307	104	1	.308	.324	.413	46	1	.370	.367	.478
1994	Cle-A	231	1	.238	.258	.307	98	1	.327	.347	.429	133	0	.173	.194	.218	85	1	.271	.276	.376	146	0	.219	.248	.267	99	0	.273	.295	.313	37	0	.162	.158	.189
TOTALS		2017	12	.255	.280	.322	998	6	.254	.279	.324	1019	6	.257	.280	.321	692	5	.309	.337	.383	1325	7	.227	.249	.291	800	2	.285	.306	.343	296	2	.257	.282	.314

Cecil Espy BB/TR

YEAR	TM/L	TOTAL					HOME					AWAY					LEFT					RIGHT					ON-BASE					LATE/CLOSE				
		AB	HR	AVG	OBP	SLG	AB	HR	AVG	OBP	SLG	AB	HR	AVG	OBP	SLG	AB	HR	AVG	OBP	SLG	AB	HR	AVG	OBP	SLG	AB	HR	AVG	OBP	SLG	AB	HR	AVG	OBP	SLG
1987	Tex-A	8	0	.000	.111	.000	7	0	.000	.125	.000	1	0	.000	.000	.000	2	0	.000	.333	.000	6	0	.000	.000	.000	3	0	.000	.000	.000	1	0	.000	.000	.000
1988	Tex-A	347	2	.248	.288	.349	155	2	.297	.313	.445	192	0	.208	.269	.271	61	1	.328	.359	.508	286	1	.231	.274	.315	144	2	.313	.346	.424	65	1	.154	.240	.215
1989	Tex-A	475	3	.257	.313	.331	239	2	.272	.316	.364	236	1	.242	.310	.297	95	3	.242	.282	.347	380	0	.261	.321	.326	175	0	.206	.246	.229	65	0	.338	.427	.369
1990	Tex-A	71	0	.127	.235	.127	25	0	.160	.300	.160	46	0	.109	.196	.109	23	0	.174	.269	.174	48	0	.104	.218	.104	29	0	.138	.242	.138	11	0	.091	.231	.091
1991	Pit-N	82	1	.244	.281	.329	53	1	.245	.263	.358	29	0	.241	.313	.276	16	0	.188	.188	.188	66	1	.258	.301	.364	31	1	.290	.273	.419	20	0	.150	.250	.150
1992	Pit-N	194	1	.258	.310	.340	97	0	.278	.333	.340	97	1	.237	.284	.340	62	1	.210	.290	.290	132	0	.280	.319	.364	84	1	.262	.308	.357	65	0	.154	.247	.215
1993	Cin-N	60	0	.233	.368	.267	18	0	.278	.440	.333	42	0	.214	.333	.238	13	0	.231	.267	.231	47	0	.234	.393	.277	28	0	.214	.314	.286	26	0	.269	.345	.308
TOTALS		1237	7	.243	.301	.320	594	5	.269	.315	.367	643	2	.219	.288	.277	272	5	.243	.294	.338	965	2	.244	.303	.315	494	4	.247	.290	.316	253	1	.209	.300	.253

Darrell Evans BL/TR

YEAR	TM/L	TOTAL					HOME					AWAY					LEFT					RIGHT					ON-BASE					LATE/CLOSE				
		AB	HR	AVG	OBP	SLG	AB	HR	AVG	OBP	SLG	AB	HR	AVG	OBP	SLG	AB	HR	AVG	OBP	SLG	AB	HR	AVG	OBP	SLG	AB	HR	AVG	OBP	SLG	AB	HR	AVG	OBP	SLG
1984	Det-A	401	16	.232	.353	.384	188	6	.239	.351	.356	213	10	.225	.354	.408	90	1	.267	.404	.344	311	15	.222	.339	.395	173	7	.237	.387	.387	54	0	.148	.292	.167
1985	Det-A	505	40	.248	.356	.519	242	21	.244	.362	.533	263	19	.251	.350	.506	120	9	.208	.275	.467	385	31	.260	.379	.535	200	16	.290	.419	.580	85	8	.259	.351	.576
1986	Det-A	507	29	.241	.356*	.442	246	15	.236	.351	.451	261	14	.245	.361	.433	147	9	.272	.374	.483	360	20	.228	.349	.425	229	10	.253	.387	.424	77	8	.338	.433	.688
1987	Det-A	499	34	.257	.379	.501	265	19	.248	.359	.512	234	15	.265	.397	.490	148	5	.209	.312	.338	351	29	.276	.406	.570	234	16	.291	.401	.556	74	3	.257	.360	.405
1988	Det-A	437	22	.208	.337	.380	215	14	.223	.365	.442	222	8	.194	.309	.320	64	0	.156	.270	.188	373	22	.217	.348	.413	213	7	.211	.349	.338	80	5	.250	.333	.475
1989	Atl-N	276	11	.207	.303	.355	144	5	.229	.309	.382	132	6	.182	.298	.326	73	2	.247	.298	.384	203	9	.192	.305	.345	116	2	.276	.362	.388	63	0	.143	.200	.143
TOTALS		2625	152	.235	.351	.440	1281	80	.237	.353	.455	1344	72	.232	.350	.425	642	26	.231	.327	.386	1983	126	.236	.359	.457	1165	58	.259	.386	.452	433	24	.240	.335	.434

Dwight Evans BR/TR

YEAR	TM/L	TOTAL					HOME					AWAY					LEFT					RIGHT					ON-BASE					LATE/CLOSE				
		AB	HR	AVG	OBP	SLG	AB	HR	AVG	OBP	SLG	AB	HR	AVG	OBP	SLG	AB	HR	AVG	OBP	SLG	AB	HR	AVG	OBP	SLG	AB	HR	AVG	OBP	SLG	AB	HR	AVG	OBP	SLG
1984	Bos-A	630	32	.295	.388	.532	315	15	.330	.415	.587	315	17	.260	.361	.476	142	7	.331	.462	.585	488	25	.285	.364	.516	307	17	.306	.394	.537	99	7	.333	.397	.616
1985	Bos-A	617	29	.263	.378	.454	292	14	.277	.382	.483	325	15	.249	.375	.428	170	12	.271	.416	.518	447	17	.260	.363	.430	275	10	.255	.371	.418	103	8	.262	.373	.515
1986	Bos-A	529	26	.259	.376	.476	241	8	.253	.364	.436	288	18	.264	.386	.510	136	6	.228	.360	.412	393	20	.270	.381	.504	226	11	.281	.403	.526	87	5	.284	.429	.567
1987	Bos-A	541	34	.305	.417	.569	263	14	.304	.399	.572	278	20	.306	.433	.572	144	12	.368	.465	.688	397	22	.282	.400	.526	256	16	.324	.450	.582	67	4	.264	.381	.460
1988	Bos-A	559	21	.293	.375	.487	277	11	.318	.398	.542	282	10	.270	.352	.433	144	6	.333	.439	.521	415	15	.280	.351	.475	304	14	.316	.396	.549	78	5	.256	.337	.487
1989	Bos-A	520	20	.285	.397	.463	242	8	.273	.403	.430	278	12	.295	.392	.493	155	4	.303	.401	.452	365	16	.277	.396	.468	261	8	.284	.384	.460	92	1	.283	.356	.359
1990	Bos-A	445	13	.249	.349	.391	218	7	.252	.348	.413	227	6	.247	.349	.370	147	3	.265	.375	.422	298	10	.242	.335	.376	220	6	.241	.337	.373	85	8	.294	.365	.600

YEAR	TM/L	TOTAL					HOME					AWAY					LEFT					RIGHT					ON-BASE					LATE/CLOSE				
		AB	HR	AVG	OBP	SLG	AB	HR	AVG	OBP	SLG	AB	HR	AVG	OBP	SLG	AB	HR	AVG	OBP	SLG	AB	HR	AVG	OBP	SLG	AB	HR	AVG	OBP	SLG	AB	HR	AVG	OBP	SLG
1991	Bal-A	270	6	.270	.393	.378	135	4	.259	.373	.370	135	2	.281	.413	.385	107	1	.308	.468	.364	163	5	.245	.339	.387	119	3	.319	.450	.454	68	2	.221	.341	.324
TOTALS		4111	181	.279	.385	.478	1983	81	.287	.390	.491	2128	100	.271	.379	.465	1145	51	.300	.422	.498	2966	130	.270	.369	.470	1977	86	.290	.394	.493	679	40	.277	.373	.495

■ Mike Felder BB/TR

YEAR	TM/L	AB	HR	AVG	OBP	SLG	AB	HR	AVG	OBP	SLG	AB	HR	AVG	OBP	SLG	AB	HR	AVG	OBP	SLG	AB	HR	AVG	OBP	SLG	AB	HR	AVG	OBP	SLG	AB	HR	AVG	OBP	SLG
1985	Mil-A	56	0	.196	.262	.214	34	0	.235	.297	.265	22	0	.136	.208	.136	22	0	.091	.130	.091	34	0	.265	.342	.294	21	0	.143	.217	.143	13	0	.154	.154	.154
1986	Mil-A	155	1	.239	.289	.323	86	1	.267	.340	.384	69	0	.203	.224	.246	44	0	.409	.426	.500	111	1	.171	.238	.252	53	1	.245	.274	.340	30	0	.267	.281	.400
1987	Mil-A	289	2	.266	.329	.353	126	1	.302	.399	.421	163	1	.239	.269	.301	94	0	.309	.380	.372	195	2	.246	.303	.344	116	0	.293	.364	.414	50	0	.340	.411	.360
1988	Mil-A	81	0	.173	.183	.185	35	0	.086	.086	.086	46	0	.239	.255	.261	23	0	.043	.043	.043	58	0	.224	.237	.241	35	0	.143	.143	.143	14	0	.143	.143	.143
1989	Mil-A	315	3	.241	.293	.324	139	1	.180	.250	.230	176	2	.290	.328	.398	101	0	.277	.336	.297	214	3	.224	.272	.336	119	1	.269	.326	.361	55	2	.182	.286	.364
1990	Mil-A	237	3	.274	.330	.359	110	1	.264	.311	.336	127	2	.283	.345	.378	80	3	.275	.315	.463	157	0	.274	.337	.306	96	0	.250	.319	.302	50	0	.260	.291	.340
1991	SF-N	348	0	.264	.325	.328	168	0	.262	.337	.351	180	0	.244	.313	.306	107	0	.271	.316	.336	241	0	.261	.328	.324	102	0	.304	.393	.373	64	0	.203	.346	.219
1992	SF-N	322	4	.286	.330	.382	164	1	.262	.299	.335	158	3	.310	.362	.430	88	1	.307	.340	.398	234	3	.278	.327	.376	94	2	.298	.337	.436	90	1	.289	.350	.378
1993	Sea-A	342	1	.211	.262	.269	167	0	.234	.287	.293	175	1	.189	.237	.246	63	0	.190	.271	.238	279	1	.215	.259	.276	154	1	.214	.274	.273	75	0	.160	.220	.187
1994	Hou-N	117	0	.239	.264	.291	64	0	.234	.269	.328	53	0	.245	.259	.245	35	0	.257	.257	.371	82	0	.232	.267	.256	45	0	.244	.261	.311	21	0	.286	.286	.286
TOTALS		2262	14	.249	.301	.322	1093	5	.248	.306	.321	1169	9	.251	.297	.323	657	4	.269	.317	.344	1605	10	.241	.294	.313	835	6	.256	.314	.337	462	3	.236	.304	.301

■ Junior Felix BB/TR

YEAR	TM/L	AB	HR	AVG	OBP	SLG	AB	HR	AVG	OBP	SLG	AB	HR	AVG	OBP	SLG	AB	HR	AVG	OBP	SLG	AB	HR	AVG	OBP	SLG	AB	HR	AVG	OBP	SLG	AB	HR	AVG	OBP	SLG
1989	Tor-A	415	9	.258	.315	.395	199	4	.251	.326	.392	216	5	.264	.305	.398	129	2	.202	.291	.310	286	7	.283	.327	.434	169	5	.237	.294	.373	67	4	.224	.264	.433
1990	Tor-A	463	15	.263	.328	.441	236	7	.246	.316	.441	227	8	.282	.341	.441	152	6	.289	.351	.434	311	6	.250	.317	.444	190	6	.274	.332	.437	75	1	.160	.210	.267
1991	Cal-A	230	2	.283	.321	.370	105	2	.305	.351	.400	125	0	.264	.295	.344	55	0	.291	.286	.382	175	2	.280	.332	.366	100	0	.280	.308	.340	27	1	.296	.387	.444
1992	Cal-A	509	9	.246	.289	.361	251	5	.247	.292	.355	258	4	.244	.287	.368	118	3	.271	.285	.424	391	6	.238	.291	.343	223	2	.305	.339	.408	81	1	.185	.233	.235
1993	Fla-N	214	7	.238	.276	.397	83	3	.277	.348	.446	131	4	.214	.226	.366	68	4	.250	.271	.485	146	3	.233	.277	.356	91	5	.242	.274	.451	34	1	.324	.395	.529
1994	Det-A	301	13	.306	.372	.525	154	4	.279	.355	.455	147	9	.333	.389	.599	84	4	.298	.318	.512	217	9	.309	.390	.530	136	6	.324	.407	.522	48	1	.250	.308	.396
TOTALS		2132	55	.264	.317	.413	1028	25	.261	.324	.409	1104	30	.266	.310	.417	606	22	.244	.289	.422	1526	33	.271	.328	.409	909	24	.279	.331	.421	332	9	.220	.275	.352

■ Felix Fermin BR/TR

YEAR	TM/L	AB	HR	AVG	OBP	SLG	AB	HR	AVG	OBP	SLG	AB	HR	AVG	OBP	SLG	AB	HR	AVG	OBP	SLG	AB	HR	AVG	OBP	SLG	AB	HR	AVG	OBP	SLG	AB	HR	AVG	OBP	SLG
1987	Pit-N	68	0	.250	.301	.250	42	0	.286	.348	.286	26	0	.192	.222	.192	35	0	.171	.237	.171	33	0	.333	.371	.333	29	0	.241	.290	.241	10	0	.100	.308	.100
1988	Pit-N	87	0	.276	.354	.322	43	0	.279	.373	.326	44	0	.273	.333	.318	34	0	.294	.324	.353	53	0	.264	.371	.302	36	0	.222	.310	.222	15	0	.273	.273	.273
1989	Cle-A	484	0	.238	.302	.260	235	0	.226	.304	.255	249	0	.249	.300	.265	130	0	.246	.333	.277	354	0	.234	.290	.254	183	0	.197	.278	.213	66	0	.273	.360	.288
1990	Cle-A	414	1	.256	.297	.304	205	1	.278	.301	.361	209	0	.234	.293	.249	130	0	.262	.303	.285	284	1	.254	.294	.313	183	0	.273	.307	.322	36	0	.306	.359	.361
1991	Cle-A	424	0	.262	.307	.302	210	0	.290	.339	.348	214	0	.234	.274	.257	121	0	.281	.341	.314	303	0	.254	.293	.297	185	0	.276	.332	.324	81	0	.185	.233	.198
1992	Cle-A	215	0	.270	.326	.321	102	0	.294	.351	.363	113	0	.248	.304	.283	42	0	.333	.440	.357	173	0	.254	.296	.312	87	0	.276	.337	.299	37	0	.216	.310	.243
1993	Cle-A	480	2	.262	.303	.317	254	2	.280	.325	.358	226	0	.230	.277	.274	157	1	.293	.293	.395	323	1	.248	.305	.324	209	1	.316	.357	.364	65	1	.369	.446	.477
1994	Sea-A	379	1	.317	.338	.380	146	0	.329	.342	.397	233	1	.309	.336	.369	105	0	.400	.409	.467	274	1	.285	.311	.347	149	0	.302	.323	.362	72	1	.333	.355	.431
TOTALS		2551	4	.265	.311	.310	1209	4	.269	.317	.323	1342	3	.262	.306	.298	754	3	.289	.339	.338	1797	3	.255	.299	.298	1061	1	.270	.320	.310	378	2	.275	.339	.325

■ Tony Fernandez BB/TR

YEAR	TM/L	AB	HR	AVG	OBP	SLG	AB	HR	AVG	OBP	SLG	AB	HR	AVG	OBP	SLG	AB	HR	AVG	OBP	SLG	AB	HR	AVG	OBP	SLG	AB	HR	AVG	OBP	SLG	AB	HR	AVG	OBP	SLG
1984	Tor-A	233	3	.270	.317	.356	96	1	.229	.283	.313	137	2	.299	.342	.387	76	0	.250	.313	.303	157	3	.280	.320	.382	93	1	.215	.272	.269	51	0	.275	.309	.373
1985	Tor-A	564	2	.289	.340	.390	265	1	.306	.366	.445	299	1	.274	.318	.341	194	0	.294	.366	.412	370	2	.286	.327	.378	240	2	.283	.336	.371	98	1	.286	.357	.418
1986	Tor-A	687	10	.310	.338	.428	337	4	.320	.345	.427	350	6	.300	.332	.429	205	5	.317	.347	.468	482	5	.307	.334	.411	232	5	.328	.347	.491	111	2	.360	.372	.532
1987	Tor-A	578	5	.322	.379	.426	299	1	.301	.363	.399	279	4	.344	.397	.459	192	2	.297	.367	.380	386	3	.334	.385	.448	210	0	.324	.387	.419	86	1	.349	.396	.477
1988	Tor-A	648	5	.287	.335	.386	316	3	.285	.337	.399	332	2	.289	.333	.373	219	3	.279	.318	.374	429	2	.291	.344	.392	238	1	.319	.376	.450	84	1	.357	.402	.464
1989	Tor-A	573	11	.257	.291	.389	276	2	.239	.286	.341	297	9	.273	.296	.434	184	2	.272	.307	.380	389	9	.249	.284	.393	230	5	.248	.280	.370	82	1	.256	.311	.354
1990	Tor-A	635	4	.276	.352	.391	321	2	.308	.376	.455	314	2	.242	.328	.325	202	1	.238	.340	.302	433	3	.293	.358	.432	259	3	.309	.371	.463	85	0	.329	.414	.412
1991	SD-N	558	4	.272	.337	.360	271	1	.292	.362	.365	287	3	.254	.313	.355	184	2	.261	.323	.342	374	2	.278	.344	.369	212	1	.307	.362	.396	87	0	.276	.330	.322
1992	SD-N	622	4	.275	.337	.359	301	3	.282	.355	.372	321	1	.268	.320	.346	207	1	.280	.349	.338	415	3	.272	.331	.369	172	1	.267	.338	.320	103	0	.320	.377	.379
1993	NY-N	173	1	.225	.323	.295	91	0	.209	.311	.275	82	1	.244	.337	.317	49	0	.233	.382	.256	124	1	.223	.301	.308	68	0	.206	.341	.265	26	0	.154	.311	.192
1993	Tor-A	353	4	.306	.361	.442	164	1	.305	.374	.433	189	3	.307	.350	.450	122	0	.254	.321	.344	231	4	.333	.382	.494	184	2	.353	.420	.505	66	1	.348	.377	.439
1994	Cin-N	366	8	.279	.361	.426	184	3	.245	.332	.337	182	5	.313	.391	.516	100	3	.290	.348	.460	266	5	.274	.366	.414	145	4	.310	.418	.503	64	2	.266	.375	.375
TOTALS		5990	61	.285	.340	.392	2921	22	.286	.346	.392	3069	39	.284	.335	.393	1928	19	.276	.339	.372	4062	42	.289	.341	.402	2283	25	.298	.357	.417	943	9	.310	.367	.411

■ Cecil Fielder BR/TR

YEAR	TM/L	AB	HR	AVG	OBP	SLG	AB	HR	AVG	OBP	SLG	AB	HR	AVG	OBP	SLG	AB	HR	AVG	OBP	SLG	AB	HR	AVG	OBP	SLG	AB	HR	AVG	OBP	SLG	AB	HR	AVG	OBP	SLG
1985	Tor-A	74	4	.311	.358	.527	40	2	.300	.349	.525	34	2	.324	.368	.529	69	4	.319	.360	.551	5	0	.200	.333	.200	36	1	.222	.237	.361	9	0	.333	.455	.333
1986	Tor-A	83	4	.157	.222	.325	24	0	.083	.120	.083	59	4	.186	.262	.424	40	0	.150	.227	.175	43	4	.163	.217	.465	39	3	.231	.302	.513	19	0	.053	.182	.053
1987	Tor-A	175	14	.269	.345	.560	90	10	.344	.422	.756	85	4	.188	.263	.353	153	13	.268	.343	.582	22	1	.273	.360	.409	88	3	.261	.333	.420	26	2	.192	.323	.462
1988	Tor-A	174	9	.230	.289	.431	79	6	.190	.220	.430	95	3	.263	.343	.432	145	9	.228	.294	.462	29	0	.241	.267	.276	76	2	.250	.326	.395	31	0	.194	.286	.194
1990	Det-A	573	51	.277	.377	.592	271	25	.280	.396	.605	302	26	.275	.359	.579	178	25	.371	.479	.854	395	26	.235	.330	.473	278	25	.284	.405	.604	85	3	.224	.353	.353
1991	Det-A	624	44	.261	.347	.513	305	27	.256	.348	.561	319	17	.266	.345	.467	159	13	.296	.399	.597	465	31	.249	.328	.484	298	26	.289	.392	.601	99	3	.232	.339	.354
1992	Det-A	594	35	.244	.325	.458	296	18	.257	.339	.490	298	17	.232	.312	.426	134	9	.231	.352	.470	460	26	.248	.317	.454	295	21	.254	.346	.512	83	5	.349	.396	.542
1993	Det-A	573	30	.267	.368	.464	283	20	.283	.381	.537	290	10	.252	.354	.393	142	8	.324	.462	.570	431	22	.248	.333	.429	321	13	.259	.364	.421	70	2	.214	.333	.343
1994	Det-A	425	28	.259	.337	.504	204	12	.284	.369	.520	221	16	.235	.306	.489	77	6	.260	.387	.584	348	22	.259	.325	.486	202	13	.252	.326	.485	57	1	.246	.328	.316
TOTALS		3295	219	.259	.345	.501	1592	120	.263	.359	.542	1703	99	.256	.332	.462	1097	87	.284	.386	.581	2198	132	.246	.324	.461	1633	107	.265	.361	.509	479	16	.240	.341	.363

■ Steve Finley BL/TL

YEAR	TM/L	AB	HR	AVG	OBP	SLG	AB	HR	AVG	OBP	SLG	AB	HR	AVG	OBP	SLG	AB	HR	AVG	OBP	SLG	AB	HR	AVG	OBP	SLG	AB	HR	AVG	OBP	SLG	AB	HR	AVG	OBP	SLG
1989	Bal-A	217	2	.249	.298	.318	114	0	.219	.280	.254	103	2	.282	.318	.388	38	1	.158	.220	.263	179	1	.268	.314	.330	94	2	.223	.279	.362	29	0	.345	.406	.379
1990	Bal-A	464	3	.256	.304	.328	247	1	.231	.274	.304	217	2	.286	.338	.355	114	1	.193	.202	.237	350	2	.277	.336	.373	184	0	.266	.307	.293	69	1	.203	.250	.261
1991	Hou-N	596	8	.285	.331	.406	300	6	.273	.309	.377	296	2	.297	.353	.436	184	1	.250	.290	.310	412	7	.301	.350	.449	184	3	.261	.314	.380	89	1	.281	.327	.315
1992	Hou-N	607	5	.292	.355	.407	294	5	.303	.381	.439	313	0	.281	.329	.377	226	1	.279	.336	.372	381	4	.299	.366	.428	270	0	.307	.364	.422	102	2	.314	.377	.422
1993	Hou-N	545	8	.266	.304	.333	252	1	.246	.280	.333	293	7	.283	.325	.430	164	2	.268	.297	.378	381	6	.265	.307	.378	222	2	.297	.321	.405	85	3	.306	.348	.482
1994	Hou-N	373	11	.276	.329	.434	185	4	.270	.318	.400	188	7	.282	.340	.468	108	1	.204	.283	.250	265	10	.306	.349	.509	183	4	.284	.323	.399	56	2	.232	.295	.393
TOTALS		2802	37	.274	.324	.386	1392	11	.262	.313	.362	1410	26	.286	.335	.410	834	7	.243	.288	.320	1968	30	.287	.339	.414	1137	11	.281	.324	.383	430	8	.279	.332	.379

■ Carlton Fisk BR/TR

YEAR	TM/L	AB	HR	AVG	OBP	SLG	AB	HR	AVG	OBP	SLG	AB	HR	AVG	OBP	SLG	AB	HR	AVG	OBP	SLG	AB	HR	AVG	OBP	SLG	AB	HR	AVG	OBP	SLG	AB	HR	AVG	OBP	SLG
1984	Chi-A	359	21	.231	.289	.468	195	11	.231	.288	.477	164	10	.232	.291	.457	141	9	.241	.292	.475	218	12	.225	.287	.463	155	3	.187	.261	.290	62	4	.306	.328	.597
1985	Chi-A	543	37	.238	.320	.488	271	20	.203	.294	.465	272	17	.272	.346	.511	183	9	.251	.329	.464	360	28	.231	.316	.500	237	19	.287	.371	.603	77	4	.273	.374	.494
1986	Chi-A	457	14	.221	.263	.337	232	5	.207	.236	.289	225	9	.236	.290	.387	157	5	.223	.253	.350	300	9	.220	.268	.330	210	7	.248	.296	.367	87	3	.230	.274	.356
1987	Chi-A	454	23	.256	.321	.460	218	5	.266	.328	.394	236	18	.246	.316	.521	172	14	.256	.332	.477	282	9	.255	.314	.436	195	10	.231	.300	.425	79	4	.253	.344	.418
1988	Chi-A	253	19	.277	.377	.542	121	9	.273	.371	.537	132	10	.280	.382	.545	93	10	.290	.427	.667	160	9	.269	.344	.469	122	6	.270	.381	.459	55	3	.345	.554	.554
1989	Chi-A	375	13	.293	.356	.475	172	4	.343	.417	.500	203	9	.251	.300	.453	120	4	.325	.371	.508	255	9	.278	.348	.459	183	6	.333	.407	.519	70	2	.300	.354	.486
1990	Chi-A	452	18	.285	.378	.451	219	5	.288	.387	.416	233	13	.283	.370	.485	165	9	.315	.397	.539	287	9	.268	.367	.401	190	4	.247	.363	.395	70	3	.229	.325	.429
1991	Chi-A	460	18	.241	.299	.413	233	9	.236	.295	.408	227	9	.247	.304	.419	157	5	.229	.274	.376	303	13	.248	.312	.432	235	13	.247	.306	.468	91	6	.242	.317	.484
1992	Chi-A	188	3	.229	.313	.309	79	2	.228	.340	.329	109	1	.229	.292	.294	49	0	.204	.328	.204	139	3	.237	.308	.345	83	1	.241	.330	.337	33	0	.333	.450	.394
1993	Chi-A	53	1	.189	.228	.245	30	0	.133	.212	.133	23	1	.261	.250	.391	31	1	.290	.290	.387	22	0	.045	.154	.045	25	0	.160	.185	.160	9	0	.111	.200	.111
TOTALS		3594	167	.251	.321	.439	1770	70	.247	.321	.418	1824	97	.254	.322	.459	1278	61	.259	.329	.455	2316	106	.247	.319	.429	1635	69	.255	.333	.434	634	30	.263	.339	.461

■ Mike Fitzgerald BR/TR

YEAR	TM/L	AB	HR	AVG	OBP	SLG	AB	HR	AVG	OBP	SLG	AB	HR	AVG	OBP	SLG	AB	HR	AVG	OBP	SLG	AB	HR	AVG	OBP	SLG	AB	HR	AVG	OBP	SLG	AB	HR	AVG	OBP	SLG
1984	NY-N	360	2	.242	.288	.306	186	2	.215	.251	.285	174	0	.270	.326	.328	141	2	.241	.305	.305	219	0	.242	.277	.306	161	1	.267	.337	.354	64	0	.172	.243	.203
1985	Mon-N	295	5	.207	.297	.288	163	3	.166	.253	.245	132	2	.258	.351	.341	97	0	.237	.336	.268	198	5	.192	.278	.298	115	0	.217	.349	.252	49	1	.184	.259	.245
1986	Mon-N	209	6	.282	.364	.440	97	1	.278	.355	.351	112	5	.286	.372	.518	66	1	.227	.320	.333	143	5	.308	.384	.490	82	2	.305	.422	.463	52	2	.269	.339	.462
1987	Mon-N	287	3	.240	.338	.310	154	1	.253	.363	.325	133	2	.226	.309	.293	126	2	.214	.327	.294	161	1	.261	.348	.323	139	1	.237	.355	.302	43	0	.233	.340	.279
1988	Mon-N	155	1	.271	.347	.419	77	1	.260	.341	.455	78	2	.282	.352	.385	67	0	.254	.333	.313	88	1	.284	.361	.500	70	4	.271	.361	.561	41	2	.366	.386	.561
1989	Mon-N	290	7	.238	.322	.386	141	3	.284	.353	.440	149	4	.195	.295	.336	101	2	.267	.351	.406	189	5	.222	.307	.376	140	4	.257	.329	.429	70	0	.229	.316	.300
1990	Mon-N	313	9	.243	.365	.393	134	2	.246	.374	.366	179	7	.240	.358	.413	138	5	.225	.359	.362	175	4	.257	.370	.417	134	4	.291	.387	.440	88	0	.216	.330	.273
1991	Mon-N	198	4	.202	.278	.308	85	1	.141	.187	.212	113	3	.248	.341	.381	86	3	.233	.320	.395	112	1	.179	.260	.241	79	3	.228	.319	.392	44	1	.229	.296	.354
1992	Cal-A	189	6	.212	.294	.317	92	3	.207	.291	.304	97	3	.216	.296	.330	69	3	.304	.392	.464	120	3	.158	.235	.233	75	1	.253	.341	.320	40	1	.175	.250	.250
TOTALS		2296	47	.236	.321	.347	1129	19	.228	.309	.327	1167	28	.245	.333	.367	891	18	.241	.335	.343	1405	29	.233	.313	.349	995	20	.258	.355	.377	495	7	.226	.307	.315

■ Tim Flannery BL/TR

YEAR	TM/L	AB	HR	AVG	OBP	SLG	AB	HR	AVG	OBP	SLG	AB	HR	AVG	OBP	SLG	AB	HR	AVG	OBP	SLG	AB	HR	AVG	OBP	SLG	AB	HR	AVG	OBP	SLG	AB	HR	AVG	OBP	SLG
1984	SD-N	128	2	.273	.347	.391	59	2	.288	.373	.424	69	0	.261	.325	.362	13	0	.154	.154	.154	115	2	.287	.366	.417	39	0	.282	.341	.359	44	0	.182	.234	.205
1985	SD-N	384	1	.281	.386	.341	165	1	.273	.402	.333	219	0	.288	.373	.347	37	0	.162	.262	.243	347	1	.294	.399	.352	129	1	.349	.411	.457	76	0	.303	.386	.395
1986	SD-N	368	3	.280	.378	.345	183	2	.295	.392	.344	185	1	.265	.364	.346	56	1	.143	.200	.250	312	2	.304	.407	.362	133	2	.278	.351	.353	75	1	.173	.262	.213
1987	SD-N	276	0	.228	.332	.254	122	0	.246	.361	.270	154	0	.214	.309	.240	41	0	.244	.311	.268	235	0	.226	.336	.251	107	0	.308	.382	.346	49	0	.143	.276	.163
1988	SD-N	170	0	.265	.365	.341	77	0	.260	.367	.286	93	0	.269	.364	.387	16	0	.125	.300	.125	154	0	.279	.372	.364	79	0	.304	.380	.443	38	0	.211	.318	.289

YEAR	TM/L	AB	HR	AVG	OBP	SLG	AB	HR	AVG	OBP	SLG	AB	HR	AVG	OBP	SLG	AB	HR	AVG	OBP	SLG	AB	HR	AVG	OBP	SLG	AB	HR	AVG	OBP	SLG	AB	HR	AVG	OBP	SLG
		TOTAL					**HOME**					**AWAY**					**LEFT**					**RIGHT**					**ON-BASE**					**LATE/CLOSE**				
1989	SD-N	130	0	.231	.299	.269	45	0	.200	.260	.244	85	0	.247	.319	.282	8	0	.125	.300	.125	122	0	.238	.299	.279	54	0	.241	.276	.278	25	0	.400	.500	.400
TOTALS		1456	6	.264	.361	.323	651	4	.269	.375	.321	805	2	.260	.348	.325	171	1	.170	.253	.228	1285	5	.276	.374	.336	541	2	.301	.368	.383	307	1	.225	.319	.274

■ Scott Fletcher BR/TR

YEAR	TM/L	AB	HR	AVG	OBP	SLG	AB	HR	AVG	OBP	SLG	AB	HR	AVG	OBP	SLG	AB	HR	AVG	OBP	SLG	AB	HR	AVG	OBP	SLG	AB	HR	AVG	OBP	SLG	AB	HR	AVG	OBP	SLG
1984	Chi-A	456	3	.250	.328	.311	227	2	.282	.362	.361	229	1	.218	.294	.262	165	1	.230	.335	.267	291	2	.261	.324	.337	160	1	.275	.362	.325	56	0	.268	.293	.286
1985	Chi-A	301	2	.256	.332	.309	142	0	.225	.327	.246	159	2	.283	.337	.365	168	2	.298	.374	.381	133	0	.203	.279	.218	115	0	.287	.366	.313	39	0	.256	.326	.256
1986	Tex-A	530	3	.300	.360	.400	253	2	.308	.360	.415	277	1	.292	.359	.386	175	2	.291	.347	.423	355	1	.304	.365	.389	195	1	.308	.366	.405	80	0	.213	.264	.262
1987	Tex-A	588	5	.287	.358	.374	287	4	.341	.413	.463	301	1	.236	.305	.289	220	3	.318	.388	.409	368	2	.269	.341	.353	236	1	.322	.377	.403	89	0	.247	.352	.303
1988	Tex-A	515	0	.276	.364	.328	252	0	.286	.368	.341	263	0	.266	.359	.316	163	0	.337	.407	.399	352	0	.247	.345	.295	219	0	.311	.386	.374	81	0	.259	.380	.321
1989	Tex-A	314	0	.239	.323	.290	159	0	.233	.318	.289	155	0	.245	.328	.290	99	0	.293	.369	.384	215	0	.214	.302	.247	130	0	.238	.318	.292	39	0	.179	.238	.205
1989	Chi-A	232	1	.272	.344	.341	111	0	.288	.341	.324	121	1	.256	.345	.355	65	0	.262	.342	.354	167	1	.275	.344	.335	81	0	.259	.330	.296	45	0	.222	.308	.244
1990	Chi-A	509	4	.242	.304	.312	265	1	.242	.291	.294	244	3	.242	.319	.332	173	1	.283	.365	.324	336	3	.220	.271	.307	217	3	.323	.377	.429	83	1	.229	.323	.301
1991	Chi-A	248	1	.206	.262	.266	115	0	.200	.285	.252	133	1	.211	.241	.278	101	0	.188	.248	.218	147	1	.218	.272	.299	92	1	.250	.314	.380	58	0	.241	.297	.259
1992	Mil-A	386	3	.275	.335	.360	175	2	.314	.379	.423	211	1	.242	.297	.308	104	0	.308	.360	.375	282	3	.262	.326	.355	168	2	.315	.380	.417	63	1	.286	.352	.381
1993	Bos-A	480	5	.285	.341	.402	250	2	.284	.348	.380	230	3	.287	.333	.426	123	3	.268	.292	.423	357	2	.291	.357	.395	158	1	.259	.318	.354	71	0	.239	.299	.282
1994	Bos-A	185	3	.227	.296	.335	111	2	.216	.293	.324	74	1	.243	.300	.351	68	1	.206	.250	.353	117	2	.239	.321	.325	70	0	.229	.289	.300	21	1	.143	.333	.333
TOTALS		4744	30	.265	.335	.343	2347	15	.277	.347	.356	2397	15	.254	.322	.330	1624	13	.281	.350	.364	3120	17	.257	.327	.331	1841	10	.291	.357	.370	725	3	.239	.319	.290

■ Cliff Floyd BL/TL

YEAR	TM/L	AB	HR	AVG	OBP	SLG	AB	HR	AVG	OBP	SLG	AB	HR	AVG	OBP	SLG	AB	HR	AVG	OBP	SLG	AB	HR	AVG	OBP	SLG	AB	HR	AVG	OBP	SLG	AB	HR	AVG	OBP	SLG
1993	Mon-N	31	0	.226	.226	.323	13	0	.154	.154	.154	18	1	.278	.278	.444	2	0	.000	.000	.000	29	1	.241	.241	.345	6	1	.500	.500	1.000	3	0	.000	.000	.000
1994	Mon-N	334	4	.281	.332	.398	147	2	.265	.327	.381	187	2	.294	.337	.412	47	0	.319	.365	.340	287	4	.275	.327	.408	160	1	.363	.420	.469	51	2	.373	.429	.549
TOTALS		365	5	.277	.324	.392	160	2	.256	.315	.363	205	3	.293	.332	.415	49	0	.306	.352	.327	316	5	.272	.320	.402	166	2	.367	.422	.488	54	2	.352	.407	.519

■ Tom Foley BL/TR

YEAR	TM/L	AB	HR	AVG	OBP	SLG	AB	HR	AVG	OBP	SLG	AB	HR	AVG	OBP	SLG	AB	HR	AVG	OBP	SLG	AB	HR	AVG	OBP	SLG	AB	HR	AVG	OBP	SLG	AB	HR	AVG	OBP	SLG
1984	Cin-N	277	5	.253	.310	.357	120	2	.283	.338	.408	157	3	.229	.288	.318	59	0	.237	.297	.237	218	5	.257	.314	.390	113	3	.292	.359	.469	53	2	.245	.310	.377
1985	Cin-N	92	0	.196	.245	.272	46	0	.196	.275	.283	46	0	.196	.213	.261	12	0	.333	.385	.333	80	0	.175	.224	.262	39	0	.205	.279	.282	21	0	.143	.250	.238
1985	Phi-N	158	3	.266	.322	.373	69	2	.362	.429	.551	89	1	.191	.234	.236	28	0	.143	.172	.143	130	3	.292	.352	.423	61	2	.213	.304	.344	32	1	.313	.333	.406
1986	Phi-N	61	0	.295	.389	.361	27	0	.259	.364	.370	34	0	.324	.410	.353	8	0	.375	.444	.375	53	0	.283	.381	.358	28	0	.286	.382	.321	16	0	.375	.500	.375
1986	Mon-N	202	1	.257	.320	.356	93	1	.237	.324	.312	109	0	.275	.316	.394	23	0	.261	.308	.304	179	1	.257	.322	.363	81	0	.222	.290	.309	46	0	.217	.308	.326
1987	Mon-N	280	5	.293	.322	.432	121	3	.314	.346	.479	159	2	.277	.303	.396	21	0	.190	.190	.238	259	5	.301	.332	.448	117	2	.256	.256	.385	44	1	.409	.447	.614
1988	Mon-N	377	5	.265	.319	.377	193	3	.264	.319	.394	184	2	.266	.318	.359	20	0	.150	.143	.150	357	5	.272	.328	.389	160	1	.281	.341	.381	100	1	.240	.290	.350
1989	Mon-N	375	7	.229	.314	.347	203	4	.217	.281	.325	172	3	.244	.350	.372	23	0	.261	.292	.435	352	7	.227	.315	.341	149	4	.242	.328	.389	56	1	.250	.377	.393
1990	Mon-N	164	0	.213	.266	.238	84	0	.190	.225	.238	80	0	.237	.307	.237	18	0	.278	.278	.278	146	0	.205	.264	.233	70	0	.257	.321	.300	44	0	.182	.265	.182
1991	Mon-N	168	0	.208	.269	.286	80	0	.188	.280	.262	88	0	.227	.258	.307	20	0	.150	.217	.200	148	0	.216	.276	.297	64	0	.219	.312	.281	44	0	.273	.319	.386
1992	Mon-N	115	0	.174	.230	.217	64	0	.172	.194	.234	51	0	.176	.271	.196	19	0	.158	.190	.158	96	0	.177	.238	.229	51	0	.137	.207	.137	25	0	.120	.154	.120
1993	Pit-N	194	3	.253	.287	.366	81	1	.272	.299	.395	113	2	.239	.279	.345	12	0	.417	.417	.500	182	3	.242	.279	.357	87	2	.218	.250	.345	49	1	.245	.250	.388
1994	Pit-N	123	3	.236	.307	.366	69	2	.217	.276	.362	54	1	.259	.344	.370	15	1	.333	.375	.667	108	2	.222	.298	.324	51	0	.275	.356	.353	28	0	.250	.276	.357
TOTALS		2586	32	.246	.303	.347	1250	18	.247	.305	.362	1336	14	.245	.302	.334	278	1	.234	.269	.281	2308	31	.247	.307	.355	1071	14	.246	.310	.352	558	7	.251	.313	.358

■ Julio Franco BR/TR

YEAR	TM/L	AB	HR	AVG	OBP	SLG	AB	HR	AVG	OBP	SLG	AB	HR	AVG	OBP	SLG	AB	HR	AVG	OBP	SLG	AB	HR	AVG	OBP	SLG	AB	HR	AVG	OBP	SLG	AB	HR	AVG	OBP	SLG
1984	Cle-A	658	3	.286	.331	.348	318	1	.302	.357	.362	340	2	.271	.305	.335	188	3	.330	.381	.447	470	0	.268	.310	.309	286	2	.297	.334	.364	107	1	.252	.283	.336
1985	Cle-A	636	6	.288	.343	.381	307	3	.306	.354	.394	329	3	.271	.332	.368	196	4	.286	.340	.408	440	2	.289	.344	.368	292	4	.301	.355	.404	93	1	.204	.267	.290
1986	Cle-A	599	10	.306	.338	.422	302	4	.291	.318	.401	297	6	.320	.358	.444	164	6	.341	.370	.537	435	4	.292	.326	.379	278	4	.299	.331	.406	73	1	.274	.329	.384
1987	Cle-A	495	8	.319	.389	.428	242	5	.310	.383	.421	253	3	.328	.395	.435	130	4	.308	.389	.492	365	4	.323	.389	.405	212	4	.278	.365	.382	69	2	.435	.494	.609
1988	Cle-A	613	10	.303	.361	.409	286	3	.364	.416	.462	327	7	.251	.314	.364	133	5	.383	.461	.624	480	5	.281	.333	.350	208	2	.274	.340	.385	89	3	.337	.388	.483
1989	Tex-A	548	13	.316	.386	.462	267	9	.356	.430	.554	281	4	.278	.343	.374	161	5	.286	.361	.453	387	8	.328	.397	.465	252	5	.345	.428	.508	77	2	.325	.361	.468
1990	Tex-A	582	11	.296	.383	.402	303	4	.317	.399	.409	279	7	.272	.366	.394	179	3	.296	.398	.397	403	8	.295	.376	.404	250	9	.336	.432	.480	97	2	.340	.429	.443
1991	Tex-A	589	15	.341	.408	.474	294	7	.344	.409	.480	295	8	.339	.407	.468	155	8	.368	.424	.626	434	7	.332	.402	.419	262	7	.344	.416	.489	103	2	.330	.415	.437
1992	Tex-A	107	2	.234	.328	.355	64	2	.313	.397	.500	43	0	.116	.224	.140	39	1	.333	.409	.487	68	1	.176	.282	.279	38	1	.184	.354	.289	16	0	.125	.364	.125
1993	Tex-A	532	14	.289	.360	.438	264	6	.330	.400	.500	268	8	.250	.321	.377	102	3	.265	.330	.422	430	11	.295	.368	.442	223	6	.332	.405	.480	74	2	.243	.301	.419
1994	Chi-A	433	20	.319	.406	.510	198	10	.359	.427	.571	235	10	.285	.389	.460	99	7	.364	.496	.677	334	13	.305	.376	.461	246	8	.305	.380	.484	63	4	.333	.434	.556
TOTALS		5792	112	.304	.368	.422	2845	54	.326	.388	.450	2947	58	.283	.349	.395	1546	49	.321	.392	.497	4246	63	.298	.359	.395	2547	52	.310	.378	.435	861	20	.301	.368	.427

■ Travis Fryman BR/TR

YEAR	TM/L	AB	HR	AVG	OBP	SLG	AB	HR	AVG	OBP	SLG	AB	HR	AVG	OBP	SLG	AB	HR	AVG	OBP	SLG	AB	HR	AVG	OBP	SLG	AB	HR	AVG	OBP	SLG	AB	HR	AVG	OBP	SLG
1990	Det-A	232	9	.297	.348	.470	108	5	.259	.350	.426	124	4	.331	.346	.508	88	5	.318	.375	.568	144	4	.285	.331	.410	100	3	.260	.327	.420	22	0	.364	.364	.455
1991	Det-A	557	21	.259	.309	.447	261	8	.249	.303	.421	296	13	.267	.313	.470	152	5	.296	.349	.480	405	16	.244	.293	.435	292	10	.265	.304	.445	90	3	.233	.289	.400
1992	Det-A	659	20	.266	.316	.416	319	9	.232	.289	.357	340	11	.297	.341	.471	158	7	.285	.333	.475	501	13	.259	.310	.397	332	7	.277	.330	.410	85	4	.200	.271	.388
1993	Det-A	607	22	.300	.379	.486	285	13	.316	.402	.537	322	9	.286	.358	.441	166	9	.265	.349	.482	441	13	.313	.390	.488	319	13	.320	.401	.508	71	1	.324	.417	.437
1994	Det-A	464	18	.263	.326	.474	229	10	.262	.314	.502	235	8	.264	.338	.447	94	7	.255	.311	.574	370	11	.265	.330	.449	229	8	.297	.363	.507	70	1	.229	.253	.371
TOTALS		2519	90	.275	.335	.455	1202	45	.264	.330	.448	1317	45	.285	.339	.462	658	33	.283	.343	.505	1861	57	.272	.332	.438	1240	41	.288	.349	.465	338	9	.251	.310	.402

■ Gary Gaetti BR/TR

YEAR	TM/L	AB	HR	AVG	OBP	SLG	AB	HR	AVG	OBP	SLG	AB	HR	AVG	OBP	SLG	AB	HR	AVG	OBP	SLG	AB	HR	AVG	OBP	SLG	AB	HR	AVG	OBP	SLG	AB	HR	AVG	OBP	SLG
1984	Min-A	588	5	.262	.315	.350	294	2	.282	.331	.388	294	3	.241	.299	.313	179	2	.240	.294	.335	409	3	.271	.324	.357	239	5	.272	.317	.402	96	0	.208	.276	.250
1985	Min-A	560	20	.246	.301	.409	280	10	.261	.309	.421	280	10	.232	.293	.393	175	6	.206	.272	.349	385	14	.265	.314	.436	204	3	.235	.289	.375	73	2	.260	.365	.425
1986	Min-A	596	34	.287	.347	.518	296	16	.250	.311	.473	300	18	.323	.383	.563	151	11	.344	.409	.603	445	23	.267	.335	.490	267	16	.285	.352	.517	87	4	.253	.343	.448
1987	Min-A	584	31	.257	.303	.485	301	18	.306	.352	.575	283	13	.205	.250	.389	166	7	.235	.287	.422	418	24	.266	.309	.510	283	12	.276	.325	.481	78	4	.231	.302	.449
1988	Min-A	468	28	.301	.355	.551	219	9	.297	.363	.489	249	19	.305	.344	.606	130	8	.338	.400	.592	338	20	.287	.334	.536	233	12	.300	.363	.699	73	8	.301	.329	.699
1989	Min-A	498	19	.251	.286	.404	249	10	.249	.278	.398	249	9	.253	.294	.410	152	5	.230	.274	.368	346	14	.260	.291	.419	239	12	.251	.299	.427	82	6	.232	.264	.451
1990	Min-A	577	16	.229	.274	.376	286	7	.238	.279	.385	291	9	.220	.269	.368	166	5	.223	.283	.361	411	11	.231	.270	.382	268	9	.250	.310	.410	88	3	.227	.255	.375
1991	Cal-A	586	18	.246	.293	.379	280	12	.275	.331	.429	306	6	.219	.257	.333	159	6	.239	.303	.396	427	12	.248	.289	.372	241	5	.290	.336	.398	78	1	.179	.226	.244
1992	Cal-A	456	12	.226	.267	.342	231	8	.260	.289	.403	225	4	.191	.246	.280	124	5	.250	.299	.419	332	7	.217	.256	.313	195	5	.251	.304	.369	87	1	.230	.261	.333
1993	Cal-A	50	0	.180	.250	.220	26	0	.231	.286	.308	24	0	.125	.214	.125	26	0	.154	.281	.154	24	0	.208	.208	.292	27	0	.222	.313	.222	15	0	.133	.133	.133
1993	KC-A	281	14	.256	.309	.477	142	6	.296	.352	.528	139	8	.216	.263	.424	71	3	.324	.398	.718	210	7	.233	.276	.395	119	6	.261	.319	.479	55	2	.255	.317	.418
1994	KC-A	327	12	.287	.328	.462	154	6	.292	.325	.487	173	7	.283	.330	.439	95	5	.263	.317	.537	232	7	.297	.332	.431	164	7	.305	.343	.512	56	3	.357	.400	.643
TOTALS		5571	209	.257	.306	.427	2758	103	.271	.319	.447	2813	106	.244	.294	.407	1594	67	.255	.316	.437	3977	142	.258	.302	.423	2518	97	.270	.323	.440	868	34	.242	.297	.414

■ Greg Gagne BR/TR

YEAR	TM/L	AB	HR	AVG	OBP	SLG	AB	HR	AVG	OBP	SLG	AB	HR	AVG	OBP	SLG	AB	HR	AVG	OBP	SLG	AB	HR	AVG	OBP	SLG	AB	HR	AVG	OBP	SLG	AB	HR	AVG	OBP	SLG
1984	Min-A	1	0	.000	.000	.000	0	0	—	—	—	1	0	.000	.000	.000	0	0	—	—	—	1	0	.000	.000	.000	1	0	.000	.000	.000	0	0	—	—	—
1985	Min-A	293	2	.225	.279	.317	142	0	.232	.297	.331	151	2	.219	.261	.305	127	1	.244	.265	.354	166	1	.211	.289	.289	134	0	.239	.266	.299	28	0	.250	.400	.321
1986	Min-A	472	12	.250	.301	.398	238	10	.239	.295	.441	234	2	.261	.308	.355	126	6	.230	.277	.452	346	6	.257	.310	.379	191	4	.262	.311	.398	62	0	.242	.324	.306
1987	Min-A	437	10	.265	.310	.430	212	7	.241	.303	.434	225	3	.289	.316	.426	128	2	.266	.294	.367	309	10	.265	.316	.456	172	2	.250	.292	.384	48	1	.208	.269	.375
1988	Min-A	461	14	.236	.288	.397	225	5	.222	.279	.360	236	9	.250	.298	.432	111	2	.297	.354	.477	350	12	.217	.267	.370	208	6	.212	.283	.370	58	3	.254	.296	.448
1989	Min-A	460	9	.272	.298	.424	218	5	.298	.326	.477	242	4	.248	.272	.376	171	5	.292	.320	.515	289	4	.260	.284	.370	204	2	.216	.253	.299	60	0	.200	.210	.300
1990	Min-A	388	7	.235	.280	.361	182	3	.247	.298	.390	206	4	.223	.263	.335	124	3	.298	.353	.484	264	4	.205	.244	.303	168	3	.220	.265	.333	52	0	.385	.421	.519
1991	Min-A	408	8	.265	.310	.395	194	3	.263	.321	.376	214	5	.266	.300	.411	118	2	.280	.348	.322	290	6	.259	.294	.379	193	3	.259	.299	.373	42	0	.167	.239	.190
1992	Min-A	439	7	.246	.280	.346	219	1	.228	.265	.297	220	6	.264	.294	.395	105	1	.181	.225	.248	334	6	.266	.297	.377	180	5	.261	.298	.389	75	1	.267	.295	.333
1993	KC-A	540	10	.280	.319	.406	269	3	.305	.340	.420	271	7	.255	.298	.391	137	2	.314	.364	.445	403	8	.268	.303	.392	212	5	.278	.323	.415	114	2	.237	.256	.342
1994	KC-A	375	7	.259	.314	.392	176	2	.313	.395	.438	199	5	.211	.237	.352	90	1	.233	.289	.311	285	6	.267	.323	.418	168	4	.298	.335	.482	60	1	.233	.266	.350
TOTALS		4274	86	.255	.299	.390	2075	39	.260	.312	.399	2199	47	.250	.286	.381	1237	23	.267	.312	.417	3037	63	.250	.294	.379	1831	36	.249	.293	.375	608	8	.245	.291	.352

■ Andres Galarraga BR/TR

YEAR	TM/L	AB	HR	AVG	OBP	SLG	AB	HR	AVG	OBP	SLG	AB	HR	AVG	OBP	SLG	AB	HR	AVG	OBP	SLG	AB	HR	AVG	OBP	SLG	AB	HR	AVG	OBP	SLG	AB	HR	AVG	OBP	SLG
1985	Mon-N	75	2	.187	.228	.280	36	0	.167	.211	.194	39	2	.205	.244	.359	42	0	.190	.244	.214	33	2	.182	.206	.364	30	0	.200	.250	.200	10	1	.100	.100	.400
1986	Mon-N	321	10	.271	.338	.405	161	4	.286	.348	.410	160	6	.256	.328	.400	120	4	.333	.398	.475	201	6	.234	.302	.363	146	4	.281	.354	.390	76	2	.276	.360	.434
1987	Mon-N	551	13	.305	.361	.459	264	7	.314	.385	.492	287	6	.296	.339	.429	164	7	.323	.385	.543	387	6	.297	.351	.424	262	6	.344	.415	.515	77	2	.234	.302	.390
1988	Mon-N	609	29	.302	.352	.540	296	14	.314	.369	.588	313	15	.291	.336	.495	170	10	.310	.361	.539	439	19	.298	.348	.543	255	12	.290	.357	.562	121	8	.273	.355	.562
1989	Mon-N	572	23	.257	.327	.434	286	13	.241	.324	.448	286	10	.273	.330	.420	174	11	.385	.459	.672	398	12	.201	.273	.329	261	15	.257	.346	.464	118	6	.237	.302	.432
1990	Mon-N	579	20	.256	.306	.409	286	6	.266	.317	.399	293	14	.246	.294	.420	217	9	.226	.260	.392	362	11	.273	.332	.420	278	10	.266	.313	.410	119	2	.261	.321	.345
1991	Mon-N	375	9	.219	.268	.336	152	3	.224	.258	.336	223	6	.215	.274	.336	137	6	.350	.383	.573	258	3	.199	.258	.256	176	3	.199	.278	.324	72	1	.208	.278	.292
1992	StL-N	325	10	.243	.282	.391	159	4	.264	.298	.390	166	6	.223	.268	.392	125	6	.320	.348	.559	200	4	.195	.242	.300	144	2	.215	.270	.340	72	2	.236	.263	.375
1993	Col-N	470	22	.370	.403	.602	266	13	.402	.430	.647	204	9	.328	.368	.544	117	6	.350	.383	.573	353	16	.377	.410	.612	221	10	.421	.460	.665	53	0	.358	.414	.453
1994	Col-N	417	31	.319	.356	.592	204	16	.348	.390	.627	213	15	.291	.323	.559	88	12	.386	.406	.886	329	19	.301	.343	.514	190	17	.284	.338	.589	48	3	.271	.417	.479
TOTALS		4294	169	.283	.334	.466	2110	80	.297	.350	.489	2184	89	.270	.318	.444	1348	71	.300	.347	.526	2946	98	.276	.328	.439	1963	81	.288	.350	.472	766	27	.256	.327	.420

YEAR	TM/L	TOTAL					HOME					AWAY					LEFT					RIGHT					ON-BASE					LATE/CLOSE				
		AB	HR	AVG	OBP	SLG	AB	HR	AVG	OBP	SLG	AB	HR	AVG	OBP	SLG	AB	HR	AVG	OBP	SLG	AB	HR	AVG	OBP	SLG	AB	HR	AVG	OBP	SLG	AB	HR	AVG	OBP	SLG
■ Mike Gallego BR/TR																																				
1985	Oak-A	77	1	.208	.319	.338	37	0	.216	.356	.243	40	1	.200	.283	.425	24	0	.292	.357	.375	53	1	.170	.302	.321	35	0	.143	.225	.286	5	0	.200	.500	.200
1986	Oak-A	37	0	.270	.289	.324	25	0	.200	.231	.200	12	0	.417	.417	.583	18	0	.333	.333	.444	19	0	.211	.250	.211	14	0	.357	.357	.429	3	0	.000	.000	.000
1987	Oak-A	124	2	.250	.319	.347	73	0	.247	.309	.329	51	2	.255	.333	.373	60	2	.300	.348	.467	64	0	.203	.292	.234	55	1	.309	.361	.418	19	0	.211	.250	.211
1988	Oak-A	277	2	.209	.298	.260	142	2	.218	.302	.296	135	0	.200	.294	.222	103	1	.233	.336	.311	174	1	.195	.275	.230	108	0	.213	.286	.241	40	0	.100	.234	.125
1989	Oak-A	357	3	.252	.327	.328	178	2	.275	.351	.360	179	1	.229	.302	.296	125	0	.264	.333	.312	232	3	.246	.323	.336	154	1	.247	.300	.318	49	0	.184	.216	.224
1990	Oak-A	389	3	.206	.277	.272	187	1	.214	.305	.262	202	2	.198	.249	.282	128	1	.180	.234	.242	261	2	.218	.297	.287	182	1	.258	.308	.319	44	0	.250	.327	.273
1991	Oak-A	482	12	.247	.343	.369	230	6	.270	.378	.409	252	6	.226	.310	.333	122	5	.311	.408	.500	360	7	.225	.320	.325	182	4	.258	.358	.390	80	3	.313	.402	.488
1992	NY-A	173	3	.254	.343	.358	77	1	.221	.291	.338	96	2	.281	.384	.375	38	0	.237	.396	.342	135	3	.259	.327	.363	60	0	.300	.394	.400	39	1	.410	.425	.590
1993	NY-A	403	10	.283	.364	.412	192	5	.302	.394	.438	211	5	.265	.336	.389	151	5	.305	.376	.464	252	5	.270	.356	.381	184	3	.283	.360	.370	60	2	.217	.266	.333
1994	NY-A	306	6	.239	.327	.359	142	2	.239	.331	.366	164	4	.238	.323	.354	80	3	.275	.404	.475	226	3	.226	.312	.319	155	3	.200	.285	.310	40	1	.300	.364	.450
TOTALS		2625	42	.242	.325	.340	1283	19	.251	.340	.350	1342	23	.233	.311	.330	849	17	.266	.347	.388	1776	25	.230	.315	.317	1129	13	.251	.324	.339	379	7	.251	.321	.351
■ Ron Gant BR/TR																																				
1987	Atl-N	83	2	.265	.271	.386	38	1	.289	.308	.395	45	1	.244	.239	.378	24	0	.208	.240	.208	59	2	.288	.283	.458	38	1	.132	.150	.211	10	0	.300	.300	.400
1988	Atl-N	563	19	.259	.317	.439	267	7	.247	.316	.423	296	12	.270	.317	.453	193	9	.280	.355	.513	370	10	.249	.296	.400	178	5	.298	.358	.466	107	2	.252	.314	.393
1989	Atl-N	260	9	.177	.237	.335	135	5	.178	.240	.341	125	4	.176	.234	.328	79	1	.114	.205	.203	181	8	.204	.251	.392	95	0	.137	.168	.211	44	1	.091	.111	.159
1990	Atl-N	575	32	.303	.357	.539	288	18	.313	.362	.559	287	14	.293	.352	.519	204	10	.299	.361	.520	371	22	.305	.355	.550	245	10	.269	.325	.453	77	4	.234	.298	.429
1991	Atl-N	561	32	.251	.338	.496	258	18	.279	.370	.558	303	14	.228	.310	.442	164	10	.287	.383	.567	397	22	.237	.318	.466	281	14	.235	.331	.470	83	5	.169	.304	.313
1992	Atl-N	544	17	.259	.321	.415	257	10	.276	.336	.463	287	7	.244	.307	.373	177	5	.254	.322	.412	367	12	.262	.320	.417	247	4	.223	.298	.344	85	1	.259	.333	.353
1993	Atl-N	606	36	.274	.345	.510	301	17	.279	.352	.505	305	19	.269	.337	.515	149	8	.295	.385	.510	457	28	.267	.331	.510	287	14	.289	.357	.509	95	7	.253	.291	.547
TOTALS		3192	147	.262	.326	.466	1544	76	.271	.338	.486	1648	71	.254	.316	.448	990	43	.268	.346	.473	2202	104	.259	.317	.464	1371	48	.249	.318	.427	501	18	.224	.292	.387
■ Jim Gantner BL/TR																																				
1984	Mil-A	613	3	.282	.314	.344	296	0	.291	.325	.331	317	3	.274	.304	.356	204	0	.270	.315	.299	409	3	.289	.313	.367	257	2	.292	.314	.362	105	0	.276	.313	.295
1985	Mil-A	523	5	.254	.300	.327	261	4	.238	.274	.322	262	1	.271	.325	.332	164	0	.329	.368	.372	359	5	.220	.270	.306	219	2	.251	.309	.311	91	1	.242	.320	.319
1986	Mil-A	497	7	.274	.313	.370	247	4	.259	.301	.372	250	3	.288	.326	.368	128	0	.219	.268	.250	369	7	.293	.329	.412	193	1	.228	.284	.290	91	2	.341	.388	.440
1987	Mil-A	265	4	.272	.331	.370	121	0	.298	.370	.347	144	4	.250	.297	.389	86	0	.233	.280	.279	179	4	.291	.355	.413	124	3	.226	.287	.331	47	2	.277	.340	.447
1988	Mil-A	539	0	.276	.322	.336	275	0	.273	.311	.342	264	0	.280	.333	.330	146	0	.274	.318	.329	393	0	.277	.323	.338	213	0	.263	.318	.329	78	0	.269	.310	.359
1989	Mil-A	409	0	.274	.321	.333	189	0	.254	.321	.302	220	0	.291	.322	.359	113	0	.274	.320	.336	296	0	.274	.322	.331	150	0	.287	.333	.347	58	0	.328	.359	.379
1990	Mil-A	323	0	.263	.328	.319	158	0	.278	.356	.310	165	0	.248	.299	.327	88	0	.307	.390	.330	235	0	.247	.303	.315	134	0	.216	.286	.261	48	0	.208	.321	.229
1991	Mil-A	526	2	.283	.320	.361	254	1	.287	.328	.362	272	1	.279	.311	.360	139	0	.266	.304	.288	387	2	.289	.325	.388	215	0	.251	.298	.307	100	1	.310	.340	.430
1992	Mil-A	256	1	.246	.278	.313	136	1	.243	.278	.309	120	0	.250	.278	.317	34	0	.206	.300	.235	222	1	.252	.274	.324	119	0	.269	.294	.345	53	1	.226	.305	.358
TOTALS		3951	22	.271	.315	.343	1937	10	.269	.316	.336	2014	12	.274	.314	.350	1102	0	.271	.320	.309	2849	22	.271	.313	.356	1624	8	.256	.304	.321	671	7	.280	.333	.364
■ Damaso Garcia BR/TR																																				
1984	Tor-A	633	5	.284	.310	.374	313	2	.268	.303	.351	320	3	.300	.316	.397	202	3	.347	.377	.460	431	2	.255	.277	.334	192	1	.260	.295	.333	97	1	.258	.294	.330
1985	Tor-A	600	8	.282	.302	.377	300	4	.303	.334	.423	300	4	.260	.269	.330	219	2	.251	.276	.333	381	6	.299	.317	.402	226	2	.283	.301	.367	90	1	.267	.287	.367
1986	Tor-A	424	6	.281	.306	.375	174	3	.282	.300	.391	250	3	.280	.311	.364	139	2	.324	.336	.432	285	4	.260	.292	.347	171	3	.292	.315	.409	76	0	.263	.282	.303
1988	Atl-N	60	1	.117	.159	.183	37	0	.162	.184	.189	23	1	.043	.120	.174	19	0	.158	.200	.158	41	1	.098	.140	.195	24	1	.083	.154	.208	12	0	.167	.231	.250
1989	Mon-N	203	3	.271	.317	.369	109	3	.284	.322	.413	94	0	.255	.311	.319	131	3	.298	.343	.427	72	0	.222	.269	.264	78	1	.231	.276	.282	42	1	.286	.333	.381
TOTALS		1920	23	.276	.303	.369	933	12	.280	.310	.383	987	11	.273	.296	.356	710	10	.299	.327	.401	1210	13	.263	.288	.350	691	8	.266	.294	.353	317	3	.262	.292	.338
■ Phil Garner BR/TR																																				
1984	Hou-N	374	4	.278	.355	.388	195	1	.328	.394	.436	179	3	.223	.316	.335	177	2	.328	.396	.480	197	2	.234	.318	.305	172	1	.320	.383	.448	82	2	.280	.355	.402
1985	Hou-N	463	6	.268	.317	.400	232	2	.272	.325	.371	231	4	.264	.309	.429	220	1	.268	.318	.368	243	5	.267	.317	.428	202	2	.262	.322	.391	81	3	.296	.370	.481
1986	Hou-N	313	9	.265	.329	.415	151	2	.265	.335	.364	162	7	.265	.322	.463	192	6	.292	.356	.469	121	3	.223	.282	.331	144	2	.215	.293	.340	57	3	.263	.317	.491
1987	Hou-N	112	3	.223	.268	.348	52	0	.192	.246	.212	60	3	.250	.288	.467	72	1	.222	.275	.347	40	1	.225	.256	.350	45	1	.089	.100	.400	22	0	.318	.318	.364
1987	LA-N	126	2	.190	.299	.270	59	0	.203	.329	.237	67	2	.179	.273	.299	71	2	.239	.345	.366	55	0	.127	.238	.145	50	1	.140	.333	.220	25	0	.240	.345	.240
1988	SF-N	13	0	.154	.214	.154	10	0	.200	.200	.200	3	0	.000	.250	.000	8	0	.125	.125	.125	5	0	.200	.333	.200	3	0	.000	.000	.000	7	0	.143	.143	.143
TOTALS		1401	24	.258	.324	.382	699	5	.273	.339	.362	702	19	.244	.308	.402	740	13	.280	.344	.416	661	11	.234	.301	.343	616	8	.258	.330	.380	274	8	.277	.343	.420
■ Steve Garvey BR/TR																																				
1984	SD-N	617	8	.284	.307	.373	302	5	.278	.303	.381	315	3	.289	.310	.365	195	3	.292	.327	.390	422	5	.280	.297	.365	294	3	.323	.345	.401	95	0	.242	.275	.274
1985	SD-N	654	17	.281	.318	.430	313	10	.284	.331	.454	341	7	.279	.306	.408	209	9	.297	.345	.502	445	8	.274	.305	.396	315	5	.263	.306	.365	124	2	.298	.331	.387
1986	SD-N	557	21	.255	.284	.408	279	11	.244	.282	.398	278	10	.266	.287	.417	184	12	.283	.311	.527	373	9	.241	.271	.349	279	9	.244	.284	.391	113	1	.239	.287	.301
1987	SD-N	76	1	.211	.231	.276	33	0	.242	.265	.273	43	1	.186	.205	.279	31	1	.258	.258	.387	45	0	.178	.213	.200	32	1	.188	.188	.344	8	0	.250	.250	.250
TOTALS		1904	47	.272	.301	.399	927	26	.269	.305	.407	977	21	.274	.297	.391	619	25	.289	.325	.468	1285	22	.263	.289	.365	920	18	.274	.308	.384	340	3	.262	.299	.324
■ Rich Gedman BL/TR																																				
1984	Bos-A	449	24	.269	.312	.506	228	16	.320	.356	.627	221	8	.217	.266	.384	55	1	.255	.328	.382	394	23	.272	.310	.523	179	7	.263	.325	.475	73	5	.233	.278	.438
1985	Bos-A	498	18	.295	.362	.484	248	9	.335	.386	.540	250	9	.256	.338	.428	135	2	.244	.299	.348	363	16	.314	.384	.534	230	5	.317	.393	.491	82	5	.293	.376	.439
1986	Bos-A	462	16	.258	.315	.424	224	2	.214	.284	.299	238	14	.298	.345	.542	118	5	.186	.210	.347	344	11	.282	.349	.451	221	6	.262	.339	.434	76	4	.289	.357	.500
1987	Bos-A	151	1	.205	.250	.278	90	1	.222	.255	.333	61	0	.180	.242	.197	35	1	.286	.297	.400	116	0	.181	.237	.241	65	0	.215	.289	.262	23	0	.174	.296	.217
1988	Bos-A	299	9	.231	.279	.368	125	5	.256	.312	.432	174	4	.213	.254	.322	37	0	.243	.306	.378	262	9	.229	.271	.366	142	5	.232	.273	.387	49	2	.184	.246	.327
1989	Bos-A	260	4	.212	.273	.292	117	2	.222	.303	.299	143	2	.203	.247	.287	37	1	.270	.341	.405	223	3	.202	.261	.274	109	1	.202	.256	.266	44	0	.227	.292	.295
1990	Bos-A	15	0	.200	.429	.200	7	0	.143	.400	.143	8	0	.250	.455	.250	0	0				15	0	.200	.429	.200	6	0	.167	.375	.167	1	0	.000	.500	.000
1990	Hou-N	104	1	.202	.300	.298	49	0	.245	.383	.306	55	1	.164	.217	.291	9	0	.111	.111	.111	95	1	.211	.315	.316	43	1	.256	.400	.419	16	0	.188	.364	.250
1991	StL-N	94	3	.106	.140	.213	47	1	.064	.132	.128	47	2	.149	.149	.298	10	0	.000	.091	.000	84	3	.119	.146	.238	29	1	.138	.182	.276	17	1	.118	.118	.353
1992	StL-N	105	1	.219	.291	.286	64	1	.219	.311	.297	41	0	.220	.256	.268	11	0	.000	.083	.000	94	1	.245	.314	.319	39	0	.256	.348	.308	27	0	.111	.172	.111
TOTALS		2437	77	.246	.304	.400	1199	37	.260	.322	.420	1238	40	.232	.286	.381	447	10	.221	.272	.342	1990	67	.251	.311	.414	1063	26	.257	.328	.408	408	13	.230	.302	.375
■ Kirk Gibson BL/TL																																				
1984	Det-A	531	27	.282	.363	.516	262	11	.275	.349	.508	269	16	.290	.377	.524	168	9	.256	.333	.464	363	18	.295	.377	.540	253	11	.285	.357	.502	73	4	.205	.293	.438
1985	Det-A	581	29	.287	.364	.518	286	18	.311	.384	.580	295	11	.264	.345	.458	170	7	.224	.297	.424	411	22	.314	.392	.557	257	13	.319	.393	.518	94	6	.266	.364	.500
1986	Det-A	441	28	.268	.371	.492	216	15	.278	.378	.505	225	13	.258	.365	.480	164	7	.262	.360	.421	277	21	.271	.378	.534	205	19	.273	.386	.576	64	3	.281	.410	.438
1987	Det-A	487	24	.277	.372	.489	240	14	.242	.350	.471	247	10	.312	.394	.506	179	4	.268	.374	.385	308	20	.282	.371	.549	221	10	.290	.392	.462	60	3	.283	.419	.500
1988	LA-N	542	25	.290	.377	.483	256	14	.316	.389	.527	286	11	.266	.366	.444	204	11	.294	.344	.520	338	14	.287	.396	.462	221	10	.285	.391	.484	81	4	.321	.423	.556
1989	LA-N	253	9	.213	.312	.368	135	4	.222	.318	.378	118	5	.203	.304	.356	95	4	.126	.227	.263	158	5	.266	.363	.430	116	3	.207	.319	.345	49	1	.163	.241	.286
1990	LA-N	315	8	.260	.345	.400	157	2	.248	.339	.338	158	6	.272	.352	.462	102	3	.255	.347	.412	213	5	.263	.344	.394	146	5	.253	.339	.384	54	0	.315	.406	.389
1991	KC-A	462	16	.236	.341	.403	239	4	.222	.327	.343	223	12	.251	.356	.466	132	3	.197	.307	.331	330	13	.252	.355	.442	179	8	.251	.364	.475	79	2	.177	.309	.342
1992	Pit-N	56	2	.196	.237	.304	16	0	.188	.278	.188	40	2	.200	.220	.350	7	0	.000	.000	.000	49	2	.224	.269	.347	14	0	.143	.250	.357	8	0	.125	.222	.125
1993	Det-A	403	13	.261	.373	.432	197	5	.254	.326	.421	206	8	.267	.348	.442	40	0	.275	.326	.325	363	13	.259	.338	.444	191	2	.272	.343	.414	53	1	.226	.328	.321
1994	Det-A	330	23	.276	.358	.548	164	9	.305	.380	.530	166	14	.247	.337	.566	33	3	.273	.350	.576	297	20	.276	.359	.545	144	12	.306	.393	.618	50	5	.220	.322	.540
TOTALS		4401	204	.268	.356	.470	2168	96	.270	.356	.468	2233	108	.266	.356	.472	1294	50	.244	.329	.412	3107	154	.278	.367	.494	1947	90	.278	.371	.483	665	29	.254	.354	.435
■ Bernard Gilkey BR/TR																																				
1990	StL-N	64	1	.297	.375	.484	33	0	.152	.243	.242	31	1	.452	.514	.742	29	0	.276	.364	.483	35	1	.314	.385	.486	18	0	.333	.429	.500	6	0	.333	.500	.667
1991	StL-N	268	5	.216	.316	.313	149	2	.215	.316	.295	119	3	.218	.317	.336	137	2	.190	.297	.270	131	3	.244	.336	.359	112	0	.196	.324	.232	39	1	.256	.388	.359
1992	StL-N	384	7	.302	.364	.427	196	3	.296	.338	.418	188	4	.309	.391	.436	176	2	.352	.402	.449	208	5	.260	.333	.409	142	5	.338	.406	.521	94	3	.309	.371	.457
1993	StL-N	557	16	.305	.361	.481	265	7	.325	.380	.506	292	9	.288	.361	.459	137	4	.343	.396	.518	420	12	.293	.362	.469	216	6	.329	.390	.505	99	2	.293	.377	.444
1994	StL-N	380	6	.253	.336	.363	180	0	.189	.279	.233	200	6	.310	.388	.480	104	2	.279	.395	.385	276	4	.243	.313	.355	157	4	.255	.339	.389	58	3	.293	.373	.534
TOTALS		1653	35	.278	.352	.414	823	12	.261	.330	.377	830	23	.294	.373	.452	583	10	.295	.372	.413	1070	25	.268	.341	.415	645	15	.290	.370	.433	296	9	.294	.379	.459
■ Dan Gladden BR/TR																																				
1984	SF-N	342	4	.351	.410	.447	170	4	.371	.432	.482	172	0	.331	.388	.413	80	2	.375	.451	.525	262	2	.344	.397	.424	105	1	.352	.405	.457	66	0	.333	.362	.409
1985	SF-N	502	7	.243	.307	.347	254	6	.232	.306	.362	248	1	.254	.307	.331	135	3	.289	.335	.320	367	4	.223	.295	.358	158	1	.253	.318	.361	97	1	.227	.303	.351
1986	SF-N	351	4	.276	.357	.362	162	1	.272	.376	.321	189	3	.280	.340	.397	123	0	.276	.373	.325	228	4	.276	.348	.382	112	2	.295	.336	.393	71	1	.211	.325	.296
1987	Min-A	438	8	.249	.312	.361	203	4	.271	.342	.404	235	4	.230	.285	.323	163	2	.258	.307	.362	275	6	.244	.315	.360	161	2	.217	.285	.311	56	2	.196	.270	.357
1988	Min-A	576	11	.269	.325	.403	300	8	.317	.365	.473	276	3	.217	.282	.326	159	6	.321	.388	.509	417	5	.249	.300	.362	185	2	.297	.354	.427	89	2	.281	.343	.472
1989	Min-A	461	8	.295	.331	.410	222	1	.284	.331	.351	239	7	.305	.331	.464	157	3	.306	.345	.427	304	5	.289	.323	.401	179	2	.279	.299	.380	71	1	.348	.378	.470
1990	Min-A	534	5	.275	.314	.376	263	2	.300	.339	.418	271	3	.251	.290	.336	163	2	.270	.297	.356	371	3	.278	.322	.385	183	2	.273	.301	.366	82	0	.183	.261	.232
1991	Min-A	461	6	.247	.306	.356	244	3	.266	.333	.381	217	3	.226	.275	.327	118	1	.254	.341	.390	343	5	.245	.293	.344	171	2	.246	.300	.404	53	2	.189	.306	.377
1992	Det-A	417	7	.254	.304	.357	177	3	.226	.291	.339	240	4	.275	.314	.371	124	4	.282	.341	.460	293	3	.242	.288	.314	190	5	.279	.317	.405	65	1	.338	.389	.446

YEAR	TM/L	TOTAL					HOME					AWAY					LEFT					RIGHT					ON-BASE					LATE/CLOSE				
		AB	HR	AVG	OBP	SLG	AB	HR	AVG	OBP	SLG	AB	HR	AVG	OBP	SLG	AB	HR	AVG	OBP	SLG	AB	HR	AVG	OBP	SLG	AB	HR	AVG	OBP	SLG	AB	HR	AVG	OBP	SLG
1993	Det-A	356	13	.267	.312	.433	167	11	.251	.302	.497	189	2	.280	.320	.376	138	8	.261	.304	.478	218	5	.271	.316	.404	189	8	.302	.330	.466	31	2	.258	.294	.452
TOTALS		4438	73	.271	.325	.383	2162	43	.280	.341	.404	2276	30	.262	.310	.363	1372	29	.283	.343	.410	3066	44	.265	.317	.371	1633	27	.277	.321	.392	676	12	.256	.324	.380

■ Juan Gonzalez BR/TR

YEAR	TM/L	AB	HR	AVG	OBP	SLG	AB	HR	AVG	OBP	SLG	AB	HR	AVG	OBP	SLG	AB	HR	AVG	OBP	SLG	AB	HR	AVG	OBP	SLG	AB	HR	AVG	OBP	SLG	AB	HR	AVG	OBP	SLG
1989	Tex-A	60	1	.150	.227	.250	37	1	.135	.179	.216	23	0	.174	.296	.304	24	0	.125	.160	.125	36	1	.167	.268	.333	29	1	.207	.258	.345	5	0	.000	.000	.000
1990	Tex-A	90	4	.289	.316	.522	47	3	.340	.373	.660	43	1	.233	.250	.372	24	1	.292	.333	.542	66	3	.288	.309	.515	41	1	.244	.238	.415	21	1	.286	.286	.571
1991	Tex-A	545	27	.264	.321	.479	262	7	.267	.328	.408	283	20	.261	.315	.544	147	9	.299	.366	.531	398	18	.251	.304	.460	267	19	.296	.365	.562	93	7	.215	.306	.473
1992	Tex-A	584	43	.260	.304	.529	294	19	.265	.305	.534	290	24	.255	.303	.524	158	8	.253	.302	.443	426	35	.263	.304	.561	283	16	.247	.285	.452	93	6	.258	.327	.505
1993	Tex-A	536	46	.310	.368	.632	273	24	.330	.386	.656	263	22	.289	.349	.608	108	9	.333	.374	.657	428	37	.304	.367	.626	250	28	.332	.400	.728	74	6	.324	.359	.649
1994	Tex-A	422	19	.275	.330	.472	228	6	.272	.346	.425	194	13	.278	.311	.526	94	5	.298	.382	.521	328	14	.268	.314	.457	217	13	.304	.367	.544	73	3	.178	.286	.356
TOTALS		2237	140	.274	.327	.523	1141	60	.281	.337	.507	1096	80	.266	.317	.539	555	32	.285	.343	.512	1682	108	.271	.322	.530	1087	78	.289	.346	.557	359	23	.242	.313	.493

■ Luis Gonzalez BL/TR

YEAR	TM/L	AB	HR	AVG	OBP	SLG	AB	HR	AVG	OBP	SLG	AB	HR	AVG	OBP	SLG	AB	HR	AVG	OBP	SLG	AB	HR	AVG	OBP	SLG	AB	HR	AVG	OBP	SLG	AB	HR	AVG	OBP	SLG
1990	Hou-N	21	0	.190	.261	.286	7	0	.286	.444	.429	14	0	.143	.143	.214	1	0	.000	.000	.000	20	0	.200	.273	.300	3	0	.000	.250	.000	8	0	.250	.400	.375
1991	Hou-N	473	13	.254	.320	.433	227	4	.273	.339	.445	246	9	.236	.303	.423	122	1	.172	.257	.270	351	12	.282	.342	.490	246	5	.260	.331	.439	74	0	.284	.357	.365
1992	Hou-N	387	10	.243	.289	.385	204	4	.206	.255	.324	183	6	.284	.328	.454	80	1	.350	.404	.512	307	9	.215	.258	.352	188	4	.250	.296	.362	71	3	.310	.364	.507
1993	Hou-N	540	15	.300	.361	.457	265	8	.291	.341	.445	275	7	.309	.379	.469	172	3	.302	.369	.413	368	12	.299	.357	.478	247	6	.279	.349	.425	84	1	.310	.356	.417
1994	Hou-N	392	8	.273	.353	.429	204	3	.294	.365	.436	188	5	.250	.341	.420	101	1	.267	.347	.366	291	7	.275	.355	.450	189	3	.265	.344	.423	54	0	.315	.397	.463
TOTALS		1813	46	.269	.333	.427	907	19	.268	.328	.416	906	27	.269	.337	.439	476	6	.269	.341	.382	1337	40	.269	.330	.444	873	18	.263	.332	.414	291	4	.302	.367	.433

■ Mark Grace BL/TL

YEAR	TM/L	AB	HR	AVG	OBP	SLG	AB	HR	AVG	OBP	SLG	AB	HR	AVG	OBP	SLG	AB	HR	AVG	OBP	SLG	AB	HR	AVG	OBP	SLG	AB	HR	AVG	OBP	SLG	AB	HR	AVG	OBP	SLG
1988	Chi-N	486	7	.296	.371	.403	250	0	.296	.378	.340	236	7	.297	.364	.470	147	3	.286	.373	.429	339	4	.301	.370	.392	218	4	.317	.378	.431	73	0	.329	.427	.411
1989	Chi-N	510	13	.314	.405	.457	258	8	.337	.440	.504	252	5	.290	.367	.409	159	4	.264	.343	.421	351	9	.336	.431	.473	238	7	.349	.451	.500	69	3	.348	.471	.551
1990	Chi-N	589	9	.309	.372	.413	308	4	.331	.391	.429	281	5	.285	.352	.395	185	3	.308	.378	.422	404	6	.309	.369	.408	256	0	.293	.361	.348	98	1	.316	.407	.367
1991	Chi-N	619	8	.273	.346	.373	322	5	.289	.364	.398	297	3	.256	.327	.347	252	2	.270	.333	.345	367	6	.275	.355	.392	244	2	.307	.371	.426	118	1	.237	.345	.288
1992	Chi-N	603	9	.307	.380	.430	285	5	.281	.373	.393	318	4	.330	.387	.462	225	3	.280	.332	.378	378	6	.323	.407	.460	265	3	.317	.384	.445	108	2	.343	.430	.426
1993	Chi-N	594	14	.325	.393	.475	300	5	.353	.421	.480	294	9	.296	.364	.469	193	6	.352	.412	.528	401	8	.312	.383	.449	299	6	.328	.391	.478	86	5	.453	.529	.709
1994	Chi-N	403	6	.298	.370	.414	222	5	.270	.349	.369	181	1	.331	.396	.470	122	1	.295	.343	.393	281	5	.299	.381	.423	174	1	.316	.405	.425	76	4	.368	.448	.566
TOTALS		3804	66	.303	.376	.424	1945	32	.310	.389	.418	1859	34	.296	.364	.429	1283	22	.293	.358	.413	2521	44	.308	.386	.429	1694	23	.318	.391	.437	628	16	.336	.431	.459

■ Mike Greenwell BL/TR

YEAR	TM/L	AB	HR	AVG	OBP	SLG	AB	HR	AVG	OBP	SLG	AB	HR	AVG	OBP	SLG	AB	HR	AVG	OBP	SLG	AB	HR	AVG	OBP	SLG	AB	HR	AVG	OBP	SLG	AB	HR	AVG	OBP	SLG
1985	Bos-A	31	4	.323	.382	.742	10	1	.400	.455	.800	21	3	.286	.348	.714	6	2	.667	.714	1.833	25	2	.240	.296	.480	15	2	.333	.412	.800	7	2	.429	.500	1.286
1986	Bos-A	35	0	.314	.400	.371	12	0	.417	.462	.417	23	0	.261	.370	.348	3	0	.333	.333	.667	32	0	.313	.405	.344	18	0	.278	.350	.333	14	0	.286	.333	.357
1987	Bos-A	412	19	.328	.386	.570	217	8	.327	.387	.571	195	11	.328	.385	.569	74	1	.378	.420	.514	338	18	.317	.379	.583	234	10	.359	.405	.590	71	6	.366	.416	.803
1988	Bos-A	590	22	.325	.416	.531	305	12	.331	.417	.564	285	10	.319	.414	.495	197	4	.289	.332	.416	393	18	.344	.453	.588	316	15	.326	.418	.541	76	0	.224	.337	.276
1989	Bos-A	578	14	.308	.370	.443	286	6	.325	.387	.465	292	8	.291	.352	.421	202	2	.272	.339	.332	376	12	.327	.406	.503	306	4	.301	.375	.405	77	2	.364	.467	.506
1990	Bos-A	610	14	.297	.367	.434	306	6	.310	.379	.451	304	8	.283	.354	.418	202	3	.257	.326	.361	408	11	.316	.386	.471	282	5	.298	.376	.418	99	3	.232	.313	.404
1991	Bos-A	544	9	.300	.350	.419	255	5	.302	.365	.451	289	4	.298	.337	.391	168	4	.327	.357	.476	376	5	.287	.346	.394	267	4	.296	.343	.401	74	0	.284	.349	.365
1992	Bos-A	180	2	.233	.307	.278	83	0	.229	.313	.229	97	2	.237	.302	.320	58	0	.224	.308	.241	122	2	.238	.307	.289	90	2	.211	.277	.289	38	0	.395	.452	.395
1993	Bos-A	540	13	.315	.379	.480	247	6	.332	.401	.522	293	7	.300	.361	.444	161	5	.304	.362	.466	379	8	.319	.387	.485	236	9	.339	.420	.533	83	3	.386	.457	.530
1994	Bos-A	327	11	.269	.348	.453	180	10	.272	.350	.511	147	1	.265	.345	.381	104	5	.288	.313	.500	223	6	.260	.363	.430	136	5	.309	.385	.493	51	1	.275	.321	.373
TOTALS		3847	108	.304	.372	.465	1901	54	.314	.383	.492	1946	54	.295	.362	.439	1175	26	.293	.337	.420	2672	82	.309	.387	.485	1900	56	.312	.384	.471	590	17	.310	.386	.468

■ Ken Griffey BL/TL

YEAR	TM/L	AB	HR	AVG	OBP	SLG	AB	HR	AVG	OBP	SLG	AB	HR	AVG	OBP	SLG	AB	HR	AVG	OBP	SLG	AB	HR	AVG	OBP	SLG	AB	HR	AVG	OBP	SLG	AB	HR	AVG	OBP	SLG
1989	Sea-A	455	16	.264	.329	.420	218	10	.261	.335	.459	237	6	.266	.323	.384	118	3	.212	.271	.339	337	13	.282	.348	.448	202	4	.252	.326	.361	72	4	.222	.296	.403
1990	Sea-A	597	22	.300	.366	.481	305	8	.292	.364	.452	292	14	.308	.369	.510	219	5	.306	.357	.447	378	17	.296	.371	.500	252	9	.298	.382	.492	95	2	.221	.292	.337
1991	Sea-A	548	22	.327	.399	.527	282	16	.365	.432	.617	266	6	.286	.364	.432	159	5	.314	.386	.472	389	17	.332	.404	.550	265	11	.343	.425	.540	81	2	.284	.410	.444
1992	Sea-A	565	27	.308	.361	.535	277	16	.314	.369	.581	288	11	.302	.354	.490	173	12	.353	.413	.624	392	15	.286	.339	.495	278	17	.331	.443	.506	81	3	.333	.443	.506
1993	Sea-A	582	45	.309	.408	.617	274	21	.332	.455	.646	308	24	.289	.363	.591	211	13	.318	.394	.569	371	32	.305	.416	.644	249	16	.297	.419	.578	95	3	.305	.412	.474
1994	Sea-A	433	40	.323	.402	.674	166	18	.343	.441	.771	267	22	.311	.376	.614	162	16	.296	.343	.654	271	24	.339	.434	.686	190	17	.337	.431	.716	63	10	.317	.403	.873
TOTALS		3180	172	.306	.379	.541	1522	89	.318	.400	.577	1658	83	.294	.359	.508	1042	54	.306	.367	.525	2138	118	.305	.384	.549	1436	74	.315	.400	.552	487	24	.279	.377	.489

■ Ken Griffey BL/TL

YEAR	TM/L	AB	HR	AVG	OBP	SLG	AB	HR	AVG	OBP	SLG	AB	HR	AVG	OBP	SLG	AB	HR	AVG	OBP	SLG	AB	HR	AVG	OBP	SLG	AB	HR	AVG	OBP	SLG	AB	HR	AVG	OBP	SLG
1984	NY-A	399	7	.273	.321	.381	208	5	.279	.327	.409	191	2	.267	.314	.351	124	1	.274	.300	.387	275	6	.273	.330	.378	182	4	.280	.335	.412	83	1	.325	.378	.398
1985	NY-A	438	10	.274	.331	.425	195	6	.292	.359	.477	243	4	.259	.307	.383	107	2	.243	.278	.346	331	8	.284	.347	.450	210	6	.281	.340	.452	69	1	.217	.305	.304
1986	NY-A	198	9	.303	.349	.475	90	5	.244	.306	.444	108	4	.352	.383	.500	34	0	.235	.257	.294	164	9	.317	.366	.512	91	1	.275	.314	.352	39	1	.333	.350	.462
1986	Atl-N	292	12	.308	.351	.503	155	9	.342	.387	.587	137	3	.270	.310	.409	85	3	.259	.300	.447	207	9	.329	.372	.527	115	3	.243	.313	.374	57	4	.368	.400	.596
1987	Atl-N	399	14	.286	.358	.456	223	8	.291	.355	.475	176	6	.278	.362	.432	87	2	.253	.298	.345	312	12	.295	.374	.487	190	1	.242	.330	.342	84	1	.238	.264	.345
1988	Atl-N	193	2	.249	.307	.306	102	2	.255	.300	.343	91	0	.242	.314	.264	21	1	.190	.190	.381	172	1	.256	.319	.297	71	1	.221	.287	.299	43	0	.279	.326	.326
1988	Cin-N	50	2	.280	.308	.420	21	1	.333	.391	.524	29	1	.241	.241	.345	1	0	.667	.667	.667	47	2	.255	.286	.404	18	1	.278	.350	.444	11	0	.182	.182	.182
1989	Cin-N	236	8	.263	.346	.424	120	6	.267	.353	.375	116	6	.259	.338	.474	16	0	.313	.500	.500	220	8	.259	.332	.418	100	0	.240	.345	.380	49	0	.265	.333	.347
1990	Cin-N	63	1	.206	.235	.286	20	1	.200	.273	.350	43	0	.209	.217	.256	4	0	.250	.250	.250	59	1	.203	.234	.288	25	0	.200	.214	.240	22	0	.136	.167	.136
1990	Sea-A	77	3	.377	.443	.519	30	1	.300	.400	.400	47	2	.426	.472	.596	11	0	.273	.385	.273	66	3	.394	.453	.561	41	2	.415	.444	.610	10	0	.500	.500	.500
1991	Sea-A	85	1	.282	.380	.400	44	1	.318	.404	.500	41	0	.244	.354	.293	3	0	.333	.333	.667	82	1	.280	.381	.390	36	0	.278	.372	.361	16	0	.313	.333	.438
TOTALS		2430	69	.287	.340	.425	1208	41	.287	.349	.453	1222	34	.275	.331	.398	495	9	.259	.300	.378	1935	60	.287	.350	.437	1085	23	.263	.331	.390	483	8	.282	.326	.379

■ Alfredo Griffin BB/TR

YEAR	TM/L	AB	HR	AVG	OBP	SLG	AB	HR	AVG	OBP	SLG	AB	HR	AVG	OBP	SLG	AB	HR	AVG	OBP	SLG	AB	HR	AVG	OBP	SLG	AB	HR	AVG	OBP	SLG	AB	HR	AVG	OBP	SLG
1984	Tor-A	419	4	.241	.248	.298	203	1	.207	.210	.256	216	3	.273	.283	.338	131	1	.229	.235	.275	288	3	.247	.253	.309	178	1	.230	.230	.281	67	0	.194	.194	.194
1985	Oak-A	614	2	.270	.290	.332	292	0	.257	.277	.298	322	2	.283	.302	.363	187	1	.326	.337	.401	427	1	.246	.270	.302	247	2	.296	.296	.393	101	0	.198	.215	.228
1986	Oak-A	594	4	.285	.323	.364	302	1	.281	.319	.331	292	3	.288	.328	.397	205	0	.254	.282	.298	389	4	.301	.344	.398	246	1	.285	.313	.346	97	2	.289	.327	.454
1987	Oak-A	494	3	.263	.306	.348	233	2	.236	.278	.318	261	1	.287	.331	.375	188	1	.245	.292	.309	306	2	.275	.315	.373	215	3	.321	.346	.419	86	0	.314	.333	.372
1988	LA-N	316	1	.199	.259	.253	158	0	.184	.254	.209	158	1	.215	.265	.297	90	0	.167	.269	.222	226	1	.212	.255	.265	113	0	.221	.282	.301	46	1	.261	.333	.370
1989	LA-N	506	0	.247	.287	.308	250	0	.252	.289	.312	256	0	.242	.286	.305	177	0	.282	.323	.339	329	0	.228	.268	.292	113	0	.272	.294	.335	104	0	.221	.250	.240
1990	LA-N	461	1	.210	.258	.254	218	0	.220	.268	.248	243	1	.202	.249	.259	169	1	.207	.257	.237	292	0	.212	.259	.264	205	0	.229	.286	.263	63	0	.159	.232	.175
1991	LA-N	350	0	.243	.286	.271	158	0	.203	.247	.215	192	0	.276	.319	.318	148	0	.270	.319	.291	202	0	.223	.261	.257	120	0	.292	.342	.328	64	0	.328	.358	.359
1992	Tor-A	150	0	.233	.273	.280	70	0	.214	.269	.271	80	0	.250	.277	.287	29	0	.310	.394	.345	121	0	.254	.242	.264	59	0	.237	.288	.254	22	0	.273	.273	.409
1993	Tor-A	95	0	.211	.235	.242	46	0	.261	.292	.304	49	0	.163	.180	.184	27	0	.148	.148	.148	68	0	.235	.268	.279	42	0	.214	.233	.262	14	0	.214	.267	.286
TOTALS		3999	15	.248	.284	.308	1930	4	.236	.273	.282	2069	11	.259	.294	.331	1351	4	.253	.292	.301	2648	11	.245	.280	.311	1615	7	.269	.298	.334	664	3	.245	.277	.303

■ Marquis Grissom BR/TR

YEAR	TM/L	AB	HR	AVG	OBP	SLG	AB	HR	AVG	OBP	SLG	AB	HR	AVG	OBP	SLG	AB	HR	AVG	OBP	SLG	AB	HR	AVG	OBP	SLG	AB	HR	AVG	OBP	SLG	AB	HR	AVG	OBP	SLG
1989	Mon-N	74	1	.257	.360	.324	37	0	.324	.432	.378	37	1	.189	.286	.270	34	0	.265	.324	.294	40	1	.250	.388	.350	30	0	.200	.273	.233	14	0	.143	.250	.143
1990	Mon-N	288	3	.257	.320	.351	146	2	.247	.321	.349	142	1	.268	.318	.352	181	2	.243	.317	.359	107	1	.280	.325	.336	119	2	.286	.348	.378	66	2	.303	.361	.439
1991	Mon-N	558	6	.267	.310	.373	233	3	.279	.323	.373	325	3	.258	.301	.372	211	3	.284	.341	.389	347	3	.256	.291	.363	213	3	.296	.339	.385	110	2	.191	.239	.273
1992	Mon-N	653	14	.276	.322	.418	316	8	.266	.309	.430	337	6	.285	.335	.407	212	6	.269	.325	.458	441	8	.279	.321	.399	262	4	.275	.333	.397	109	2	.229	.288	.330
1993	Mon-N	630	19	.298	.351	.438	307	9	.319	.366	.450	323	10	.279	.336	.427	192	7	.307	.362	.495	438	12	.295	.346	.413	284	8	.271	.324	.415	98	1	.347	.398	.459
1994	Mon-N	475	11	.288	.344	.427	210	4	.295	.336	.429	265	7	.283	.349	.426	112	4	.250	.323	.420	363	7	.300	.350	.430	187	2	.273	.327	.358	70	2	.414	.468	.600
TOTALS		2678	54	.279	.331	.405	1249	26	.286	.336	.413	1429	28	.273	.328	.398	942	22	.273	.334	.420	1736	32	.282	.330	.397	1095	18	.277	.331	.386	467	9	.281	.337	.394

■ Kelly Gruber BR/TR

YEAR	TM/L	AB	HR	AVG	OBP	SLG	AB	HR	AVG	OBP	SLG	AB	HR	AVG	OBP	SLG	AB	HR	AVG	OBP	SLG	AB	HR	AVG	OBP	SLG	AB	HR	AVG	OBP	SLG	AB	HR	AVG	OBP	SLG
1984	Tor-A	16	1	.063	.063	.250	5	0	.000	.000	.000	11	1	.091	.091	.364	10	0	.000	.000	.000	6	1	.167	.167	.667	10	1	.100	.100	.400	3	0	.000	.000	.000
1985	Tor-A	13	0	.231	.231	.231	10	0	.200	.200	.200	3	0	.333	.333	.333	4	0	.250	.250	.250	9	0	.222	.222	.222	9	0	.333	.333	.333	3	0	.333	.333	.333
1986	Tor-A	143	5	.196	.220	.343	71	4	.183	.231	.394	72	1	.208	.208	.292	60	2	.217	.226	.350	83	3	.181	.216	.337	64	3	.234	.239	.391	23	0	.087	.125	.087
1987	Tor-A	341	12	.235	.283	.399	144	5	.222	.283	.396	197	7	.244	.284	.401	152	4	.230	.289	.395	189	8	.238	.279	.402	136	2	.250	.311	.368	54	5	.315	.387	.630
1988	Tor-A	569	16	.278	.328	.438	294	5	.269	.316	.384	275	11	.287	.341	.495	187	1	.251	.288	.364	382	15	.291	.348	.474	244	5	.336	.381	.525	84	4	.345	.387	.536
1989	Tor-A	545	18	.290	.328	.448	278	8	.295	.324	.453	267	10	.285	.331	.442	166	7	.325	.356	.500	379	11	.274	.315	.425	251	7	.287	.345	.455	81	2	.284	.337	.407
1990	Tor-A	592	31	.274	.330	.512	305	23	.292	.331	.587	287	8	.254	.328	.432	166	8	.295	.349	.536	426	23	.265	.322	.495	266	17	.289	.336	.549	97	3	.258	.298	.443
1991	Tor-A	429	20	.252	.308	.443	221	8	.262	.327	.398	208	12	.240	.288	.490	112	8	.277	.323	.527	317	12	.243	.303	.413	202	8	.252	.319	.431	76	3	.224	.268	.368
1992	Tor-A	446	11	.229	.275	.374	211	7	.242	.284	.408	235	4	.217	.267	.340	134	4	.217	.291	.393	312	7	.234	.270	.339	201	6	.244	.284	.393	72	1	.236	.278	.361
1993	Cal-A	65	3	.277	.309	.462	19	1	.158	.273	.316	46	2	.326	.326	.522	23	1	.304	.304	.478	42	2	.262	.311	.452	27	1	.296	.345	.444	9	1	.111	.111	.444
TOTALS		3159	117	.259	.307	.432	1558	61	.263	.309	.440	1601	56	.255	.305	.425	987	34	.266	.308	.443	2172	83	.256	.306	.427	1383	50	.281	.327	.460	502	19	.263	.310	.430

■ Pedro Guerrero BR/TR

YEAR	TM/L	AB	HR	AVG	OBP	SLG	AB	HR	AVG	OBP	SLG	AB	HR	AVG	OBP	SLG	AB	HR	AVG	OBP	SLG	AB	HR	AVG	OBP	SLG	AB	HR	AVG	OBP	SLG	AB	HR	AVG	OBP	SLG
1984	LA-N	535	16	.303	.358	.462	286	7	.322	.368	.462	249	9	.281	.346	.462	168	3	.298	.374	.387	367	13	.305	.349	.496	228	7	.285	.347	.434	93	5	.290	.350	.495
1985	LA-N	487	33	.320	.422	.577	257	13	.311	.416	.498	230	20	.330	.429	.665	135	9	.304	.412	.556	352	24	.327	.425	.585	224	12	.304	.423	.509	72	7	.319	.430	.681
1986	LA-N	61	5	.246	.281	.541	23	1	.217	.250	.348	38	4	.263	.300	.658	29	2	.345	.345	.621	32	3	.156	.229	.469	31	2	.129	.182	.323	11	0	.091	.091	.091

		TOTAL					HOME					AWAY					LEFT					RIGHT					ON-BASE					LATE/CLOSE			
YEAR	TM/L	AB	HR	AVG	OBP	SLG	AB	HR	AVG	OBP	SLG	AB	HR	AVG	OBP	SLG	AB	HR	AVG	OBP	SLG	AB	HR	AVG	OBP	SLG	AB	HR	AVG	OBP	SLG	AB	HR	AVG	OBP	SLG
1987	LA-N	545	27	.338	.416	.539	275	12	.324	.434	.495	270	15	.352	.434	.575	167	8	.365	.451	.524	378	19	.325	.400	.524	243	11	.337	.421	.514	81	2	.272	.412	.420
1988	LA-N	215	5	.298	.374	.409	118	3	.364	.412	.508	97	2	.216	.330	.289	71	2	.268	.354	.352	144	3	.313	.384	.438	99	2	.283	.327	.384	32	1	.313	.421	.406
1988	StL-N	149	5	.268	.358	.430	74	2	.230	.314	.365	75	3	.307	.400	.493	54	1	.296	.424	.444	95	4	.253	.318	.421	63	2	.397	.517	.587	19	0	.211	.385	.316
1989	StL-N	570	17	.311	.391	.477	281	3	.288	.372	.409	289	14	.332	.410	.543	218	8	.317	.402	.505	352	9	.307	.384	.460	267	10	.356	.449	.551	85	2	.282	.357	.388
1990	StL-N	498	13	.281	.334	.426	261	8	.276	.333	.437	237	5	.287	.335	.414	168	4	.274	.319	.446	330	9	.285	.341	.415	256	6	.266	.325	.398	72	1	.250	.364	.375
1991	StL-N	427	8	.272	.326	.361	216	4	.282	.340	.370	211	4	.261	.311	.351	160	0	.256	.312	.300	267	8	.281	.327	.397	206	4	.301	.341	.388	71	1	.254	.308	.310
1992	StL-N	146	1	.219	.270	.295	71	1	.254	.325	.338	75	0	.187	.215	.253	38	1	.211	.286	.316	108	0	.222	.265	.287	71	0	.169	.228	.211	25	0	.240	.323	.240
	TOTALS	3633	130	.299	.371	.465	1862	54	.300	.369	.443	1771	76	.298	.372	.488	1208	38	.299	.379	.454	2425	92	.299	.366	.470	1688	56	.302	.380	.454	561	19	.273	.368	.422

■ Ozzie Guillen BL/TR

YEAR	TM/L	AB	HR	AVG	OBP	SLG	AB	HR	AVG	OBP	SLG	AB	HR	AVG	OBP	SLG	AB	HR	AVG	OBP	SLG	AB	HR	AVG	OBP	SLG	AB	HR	AVG	OBP	SLG	AB	HR	AVG	OBP	SLG
1985	Chi-A	491	1	.273	.291	.358	244	1	.279	.298	.377	247	0	.267	.285	.340	90	0	.211	.228	.244	401	1	.287	.305	.384	194	0	.278	.295	.351	88	0	.375	.409	.432
1986	Chi-A	547	2	.250	.265	.311	272	1	.254	.264	.305	275	1	.247	.267	.316	167	1	.257	.283	.299	380	1	.247	.258	.316	229	0	.306	.311	.384	89	1	.236	.237	.292
1987	Chi-A	560	2	.279	.303	.354	269	2	.316	.352	.409	291	0	.244	.256	.302	164	0	.201	.227	.238	396	2	.311	.334	.402	209	2	.254	.278	.316	97	1	.278	.301	.351
1988	Chi-A	566	0	.261	.294	.314	280	0	.261	.303	.311	286	0	.262	.284	.318	171	0	.263	.285	.287	395	0	.261	.297	.327	217	0	.309	.326	.378	102	0	.255	.296	.314
1989	Chi-A	597	1	.253	.270	.318	292	0	.240	.246	.298	305	1	.266	.292	.338	209	0	.254	.264	.292	388	1	.253	.273	.332	269	0	.275	.290	.349	110	0	.300	.310	.391
1990	Chi-A	516	1	.279	.312	.341	247	1	.279	.318	.356	269	0	.279	.306	.327	206	0	.267	.288	.316	310	1	.287	.327	.358	226	0	.305	.341	.394	90	0	.300	.382	.356
1991	Chi-A	524	3	.273	.284	.340	247	1	.287	.291	.364	277	2	.260	.278	.318	161	1	.211	.213	.248	363	2	.300	.315	.380	217	3	.281	.285	.364	128	1	.273	.296	.344
1992	Chi-A	40	0	.200	.214	.300	17	0	.176	.222	.294	23	0	.217	.208	.304	19	0	.158	.158	.316	21	0	.238	.261	.286	19	0	.316	.300	.421	8	0	.000	.111	.000
1993	Chi-A	457	4	.280	.292	.374	212	3	.297	.309	.396	245	1	.265	.277	.355	130	0	.231	.241	.292	327	4	.300	.312	.407	196	4	.291	.289	.413	77	0	.273	.296	.312
1994	Chi-A	365	1	.288	.311	.348	164	0	.250	.277	.311	201	1	.318	.338	.378	115	1	.261	.298	.313	250	0	.300	.317	.364	176	1	.250	.269	.313	60	0	.250	.288	.350
	TOTALS	4663	15	.269	.290	.338	2244	9	.273	.295	.346	2419	6	.265	.285	.330	1432	3	.241	.259	.284	3231	12	.281	.303	.362	1952	10	.284	.299	.364	849	3	.280	.311	.346

■ Tony Gwynn BL/TL

YEAR	TM/L	AB	HR	AVG	OBP	SLG	AB	HR	AVG	OBP	SLG	AB	HR	AVG	OBP	SLG	AB	HR	AVG	OBP	SLG	AB	HR	AVG	OBP	SLG	AB	HR	AVG	OBP	SLG	AB	HR	AVG	OBP	SLG
1984	SD-N	606	5	.351	.410	.444	303	3	.376	.422	.492	303	2	.327	.398	.396	202	1	.312	.368	.356	404	4	.371	.430	.488	233	2	.403	.482	.515	86	1	.360	.471	.465
1985	SD-N	622	6	.317	.364	.408	316	3	.326	.368	.424	306	3	.307	.360	.392	205	2	.288	.354	.351	417	4	.331	.369	.436	255	3	.337	.384	.404	115	2	.313	.383	.417
1986	SD-N	642	14	.329	.381	.467	317	8	.341	.392	.486	325	6	.317	.369	.449	235	7	.328	.384	.523	407	7	.329	.379	.435	240	6	.313	.386	.433	117	3	.350	.411	.496
1987	SD-N	589	7	.370	.447	.511	282	5	.390	.473	.574	307	2	.352	.423	.453	249	3	.361	.433	.470	340	4	.376	.457	.541	231	0	.338	.447	.472	88	1	.341	.438	.466
1988	SD-N	521	7	.313	.373	.415	242	4	.310	.393	.393	279	4	.315	.355	.434	204	0	.314	.358	.358	317	7	.312	.382	.451	217	2	.382	.456	.516	94	0	.330	.364	.372
1989	SD-N	604	4	.336	.389	.424	288	3	.326	.384	.427	316	1	.345	.394	.421	200	0	.305	.355	.345	404	4	.351	.406	.463	248	1	.327	.396	.407	94	0	.351	.415	.404
1990	SD-N	573	4	.309	.357	.415	306	2	.310	.356	.422	267	2	.307	.358	.408	228	3	.281	.307	.373	345	1	.328	.388	.443	259	1	.347	.412	.479	106	1	.283	.345	.349
1991	SD-N	530	4	.317	.355	.432	244	1	.307	.348	.406	286	3	.325	.361	.455	211	2	.294	.332	.393	319	2	.332	.370	.458	231	2	.368	.410	.494	89	1	.348	.398	.438
1992	SD-N	520	6	.317	.371	.455	229	4	.306	.371	.393	291	2	.326	.371	.433	205	3	.327	.368	.420	315	3	.311	.372	.413	205	4	.322	.393	.459	75	2	.360	.437	.520
1993	SD-N	489	7	.358	.398	.497	254	4	.382	.421	.524	235	3	.332	.373	.468	192	3	.359	.393	.490	297	4	.357	.401	.502	200	3	.380	.415	.535	89	2	.371	.416	.539
1994	SD-N	419	12	.394	.454	.568	181	4	.403	.486	.558	238	8	.387	.427	.576	139	2	.374	.429	.504	280	10	.404	.466	.600	199	3	.342	.414	.467	76	1	.421	.482	.526
	TOTALS	6115	76	.336	.390	.451	2962	40	.342	.400	.462	3153	36	.330	.381	.441	2270	26	.321	.370	.416	3845	50	.345	.401	.472	2518	27	.350	.418	.469	1029	14	.345	.412	.450

■ Mel Hall BL/TL

YEAR	TM/L	AB	HR	AVG	OBP	SLG	AB	HR	AVG	OBP	SLG	AB	HR	AVG	OBP	SLG	AB	HR	AVG	OBP	SLG	AB	HR	AVG	OBP	SLG	AB	HR	AVG	OBP	SLG	AB	HR	AVG	OBP	SLG
1984	Chi-N	150	4	.280	.329	.473	67	3	.313	.365	.567	83	1	.253	.300	.398	9	0	.000	.100	.000	141	4	.298	.344	.504	71	1	.296	.350	.465	17	1	.294	.294	.471
1984	Cle-A	257	7	.257	.344	.397	139	4	.266	.344	.388	118	3	.246	.345	.407	26	0	.192	.371	.231	231	7	.264	.341	.416	105	3	.295	.392	.448	43	3	.302	.354	.581
1985	Cle-A	66	0	.318	.387	.409	30	0	.367	.394	.467	36	0	.278	.381	.361	4	0	.000	.000	.000	62	0	.339	.400	.435	39	0	.359	.409	.462	11	0	.273	.273	.364
1986	Cle-A	442	18	.296	.346	.493	206	8	.277	.318	.466	236	10	.314	.369	.517	26	0	.154	.241	.231	416	18	.305	.353	.510	209	9	.254	.312	.474	60	2	.317	.417	.517
1987	Cle-A	485	18	.280	.309	.439	222	8	.288	.319	.441	263	10	.274	.301	.437	33	1	.364	.417	.515	452	17	.274	.301	.434	210	5	.271	.308	.390	75	3	.280	.299	.453
1988	Cle-A	515	6	.280	.312	.392	249	3	.289	.322	.418	266	3	.271	.302	.368	46	1	.109	.163	.196	469	5	.296	.327	.412	220	2	.291	.339	.405	79	1	.291	.345	.380
1989	NY-A	361	17	.260	.295	.427	202	11	.282	.317	.465	159	6	.233	.267	.377	69	1	.159	.224	.217	292	16	.284	.312	.476	163	6	.258	.291	.393	51	2	.275	.316	.431
1990	NY-A	360	12	.258	.272	.433	187	3	.273	.287	.412	173	9	.243	.256	.457	58	1	.207	.203	.310	302	11	.268	.285	.457	165	5	.285	.297	.467	60	4	.267	.274	.567
1991	NY-A	492	19	.285	.321	.455	245	13	.273	.317	.478	247	6	.296	.324	.433	162	5	.309	.353	.444	330	14	.273	.305	.461	258	11	.275	.323	.446	75	5	.218	.252	.449
1992	NY-A	583	15	.280	.310	.429	285	7	.246	.292	.361	298	8	.312	.328	.493	179	2	.257	.284	.346	404	13	.290	.322	.465	292	4	.332	.352	.442	116	1	.284	.295	.431
	TOTALS	3711	116	.278	.316	.436	1832	60	.277	.316	.434	1879	56	.278	.315	.437	612	11	.237	.285	.335	3099	105	.286	.322	.456	1732	46	.287	.329	.435	590	22	.278	.318	.463

■ Bob Hamelin BL/TL

YEAR	TM/L	AB	HR	AVG	OBP	SLG	AB	HR	AVG	OBP	SLG	AB	HR	AVG	OBP	SLG	AB	HR	AVG	OBP	SLG	AB	HR	AVG	OBP	SLG	AB	HR	AVG	OBP	SLG	AB	HR	AVG	OBP	SLG
1993	KC-A	49	2	.224	.309	.408	17	1	.235	.350	.471	32	1	.219	.286	.375	5	0	.400	.400	.400	44	2	.205	.300	.409	18	0	.111	.238	.111	11	0	.182	.357	.273
1994	KC-A	312	24	.282	.388	.599	161	13	.311	.403	.646	151	11	.252	.372	.550	51	0	.255	.333	.353	261	24	.287	.397	.648	144	13	.257	.388	.590	39	3	.359	.490	.744
	TOTALS	361	26	.274	.378	.573	178	14	.303	.398	.629	183	12	.246	.358	.519	56	0	.268	.339	.357	305	26	.275	.384	.613	162	13	.241	.373	.537	50	3	.320	.462	.640

■ Darryl Hamilton BL/TR

YEAR	TM/L	AB	HR	AVG	OBP	SLG	AB	HR	AVG	OBP	SLG	AB	HR	AVG	OBP	SLG	AB	HR	AVG	OBP	SLG	AB	HR	AVG	OBP	SLG	AB	HR	AVG	OBP	SLG	AB	HR	AVG	OBP	SLG
1988	Mil-A	103	1	.184	.274	.252	34	1	.176	.293	.324	69	0	.188	.263	.217	30	0	.067	.152	.133	73	1	.233	.321	.301	39	0	.205	.256	.282	20	0	.250	.400	.300
1990	Mil-A	156	1	.295	.333	.346	72	1	.250	.280	.306	84	0	.333	.378	.381	9	0	.111	.273	.222	147	1	.306	.338	.354	62	1	.323	.364	.371	27	0	.333	.357	.370
1991	Mil-A	405	1	.311	.361	.385	195	0	.344	.406	.436	210	1	.281	.317	.338	87	0	.276	.308	.322	318	1	.321	.374	.403	189	1	.370	.405	.471	54	0	.389	.468	.407
1992	Mil-A	470	5	.298	.356	.402	233	1	.288	.356	.382	237	4	.308	.355	.418	89	0	.247	.323	.303	381	5	.310	.363	.423	207	2	.304	.368	.377	69	1	.362	.423	.522
1993	Mil-A	520	9	.310	.367	.406	262	6	.317	.388	.416	258	3	.302	.345	.395	182	1	.264	.316	.308	338	8	.334	.394	.459	201	0	.294	.373	.333	83	1	.349	.413	.470
1994	Mil-A	141	1	.262	.331	.369	72	0	.306	.378	.403	69	1	.217	.280	.333	31	0	.258	.324	.387	110	1	.264	.333	.364	50	0	.220	.298	.260	22	0	.227	.261	.318
	TOTALS	1795	18	.295	.351	.383	868	8	.303	.370	.397	927	10	.287	.333	.369	428	1	.245	.304	.301	1367	17	.310	.366	.408	748	4	.309	.368	.376	275	2	.342	.409	.436

■ Brian Harper BR/TR

YEAR	TM/L	AB	HR	AVG	OBP	SLG	AB	HR	AVG	OBP	SLG	AB	HR	AVG	OBP	SLG	AB	HR	AVG	OBP	SLG	AB	HR	AVG	OBP	SLG	AB	HR	AVG	OBP	SLG	AB	HR	AVG	OBP	SLG
1984	Pit-N	112	1	.259	.300	.348	65	1	.262	.284	.323	47	1	.255	.321	.383	74	2	.176	.235	.270	38	0	.421	.436	.500	53	1	.302	.321	.415	19	0	.158	.200	.211
1985	StL-N	52	0	.250	.273	.327	24	0	.292	.346	.417	28	0	.214	.207	.250	44	0	.250	.261	.341	8	0	.250	.333	.250	31	0	.226	.219	.290	18	0	.333	.350	.444
1986	Det-A	36	1	.139	.200	.167	17	0	.118	.211	.118	19	1	.158	.190	.211	30	1	.100	.176	.133	6	0	.333	.333	.333	15	0	.267	.294	.333	4	0	.500	.500	.500
1987	Oak-A	17	0	.235	.222	.294	7	0	.286	.286	.429	10	0	.200	.182	.200	16	0	.250	.235	.313	1	0	.000	.000	.000	8	0	.250	.222	.375	3	0	.333	.333	.333
1988	Min-A	166	3	.295	.344	.428	82	0	.293	.322	.378	84	3	.298	.366	.476	49	1	.286	.345	.408	117	2	.299	.344	.436	92	0	.304	.350	.402	22	2	.318	.348	.591
1989	Min-A	385	8	.325	.353	.449	181	4	.304	.333	.442	204	4	.343	.370	.456	155	3	.310	.339	.419	230	5	.335	.362	.470	187	4	.310	.348	.439	57	2	.316	.322	.491
1990	Min-A	479	6	.294	.328	.432	230	4	.283	.326	.391	249	5	.305	.331	.470	146	4	.315	.357	.541	333	2	.285	.315	.384	219	2	.297	.333	.425	78	1	.308	.349	.372
1991	Min-A	441	10	.311	.336	.447	217	4	.341	.364	.470	224	6	.281	.309	.424	114	2	.316	.344	.447	327	8	.309	.333	.446	210	9	.352	.374	.552	68	3	.324	.333	.515
1992	Min-A	502	9	.307	.343	.410	241	3	.324	.361	.402	261	6	.291	.326	.418	109	1	.275	.339	.358	393	8	.316	.344	.425	239	2	.301	.342	.372	84	1	.298	.365	.357
1993	Min-A	530	12	.304	.347	.425	255	6	.325	.374	.471	275	6	.284	.322	.382	123	5	.333	.373	.545	407	7	.295	.339	.388	217	3	.327	.376	.406	99	3	.306	.346	.439
1994	Mil-A	251	4	.291	.318	.398	115	2	.304	.336	.426	136	2	.279	.303	.375	49	1	.367	.415	.490	202	3	.272	.294	.376	115	1	.287	.306	.383	43	1	.372	.413	.512
	TOTALS	2971	54	.300	.334	.419	1434	21	.308	.345	.422	1537	33	.292	.325	.417	909	19	.290	.332	.428	2062	35	.304	.335	.424	1386	23	.310	.345	.424	494	12	.312	.347	.435

■ Lenny Harris BL/TR

YEAR	TM/L	AB	HR	AVG	OBP	SLG	AB	HR	AVG	OBP	SLG	AB	HR	AVG	OBP	SLG	AB	HR	AVG	OBP	SLG	AB	HR	AVG	OBP	SLG	AB	HR	AVG	OBP	SLG	AB	HR	AVG	OBP	SLG
1988	Cin-N	43	0	.372	.420	.395	22	0	.409	.462	.455	21	0	.333	.375	.333	3	0	.667	.667	.667	40	0	.350	.404	.375	19	0	.421	.480	.474	9	0	.222	.222	.333
1989	Cin-N	188	2	.223	.263	.277	91	0	.275	.298	.308	97	2	.175	.231	.247	55	0	.200	.254	.218	133	2	.233	.266	.301	64	2	.219	.242	.344	25	0	.160	.222	.160
1989	LA-N	147	1	.252	.308	.327	70	1	.229	.280	.329	77	0	.273	.333	.325	13	0	.154	.267	.231	134	1	.261	.313	.336	76	1	.250	.287	.329	32	0	.250	.333	.281
1990	LA-N	431	2	.304	.348	.374	217	0	.276	.322	.332	214	2	.332	.376	.416	42	0	.238	.304	.286	389	2	.311	.353	.383	128	0	.305	.338	.344	54	0	.259	.310	.259
1991	LA-N	429	3	.287	.349	.350	211	1	.275	.341	.318	218	2	.298	.357	.381	87	1	.241	.309	.276	342	2	.298	.359	.368	195	3	.287	.350	.374	73	0	.315	.414	.370
1992	LA-N	347	0	.271	.318	.303	177	0	.266	.307	.294	170	0	.276	.330	.312	36	0	.139	.205	.139	311	0	.286	.331	.322	157	0	.299	.341	.363	60	0	.283	.358	.283
1993	LA-N	160	2	.237	.303	.325	67	1	.284	.314	.343	93	2	.204	.295	.312	15	0	.333	.333	.400	145	2	.228	.300	.317	59	0	.322	.382	.340	50	0	.320	.382	.340
1994	Cin-N	100	0	.310	.340	.360	50	0	.300	.308	.320	50	0	.320	.370	.400	11	0	.545	.583	.545	89	0	.281	.309	.337	46	0	.370	.375	.457	33	0	.273	.273	.333
	TOTALS	1845	10	.278	.328	.337	905	2	.275	.320	.322	940	8	.280	.336	.351	262	1	.237	.297	.267	1583	9	.284	.334	.348	744	6	.292	.338	.364	336	0	.277	.344	.304

■ Mickey Hatcher BR/TR

YEAR	TM/L	AB	HR	AVG	OBP	SLG	AB	HR	AVG	OBP	SLG	AB	HR	AVG	OBP	SLG	AB	HR	AVG	OBP	SLG	AB	HR	AVG	OBP	SLG	AB	HR	AVG	OBP	SLG	AB	HR	AVG	OBP	SLG
1984	Min-A	576	5	.302	.342	.406	286	4	.297	.336	.448	290	1	.307	.348	.366	176	3	.330	.368	.449	400	2	.290	.330	.387	250	3	.336	.370	.436	79	3	.316	.386	.481
1985	Min-A	444	5	.282	.308	.365	244	3	.299	.325	.393	200	2	.260	.287	.330	132	3	.280	.312	.379	312	2	.282	.307	.359	209	2	.297	.320	.397	57	0	.263	.288	.298
1986	Min-A	317	3	.278	.315	.366	156	1	.314	.345	.417	161	2	.242	.285	.317	140	2	.364	.405	.493	177	1	.209	.241	.266	129	2	.287	.319	.403	46	0	.196	.224	.239
1987	LA-N	287	7	.282	.328	.429	137	4	.255	.301	.401	150	3	.307	.352	.453	125	4	.328	.384	.528	162	3	.247	.283	.352	119	3	.294	.345	.445	51	1	.196	.255	.255
1988	LA-N	191	1	.293	.322	.351	102	0	.284	.302	.333	89	1	.303	.344	.371	142	1	.261	.282	.324	49	0	.388	.434	.429	94	1	.319	.359	.372	41	1	.415	.455	.561
1989	LA-N	224	2	.295	.328	.379	116	0	.284	.323	.362	108	2	.306	.333	.398	131	2	.321	.352	.443	93	0	.258	.294	.290	106	1	.255	.286	.321	50	0	.260	.293	.320
1990	LA-N	132	0	.212	.248	.250	67	0	.239	.268	.299	65	0	.185	.229	.200	102	0	.225	.273	.265	30	0	.167	.161	.200	65	0	.246	.301	.323	27	0	.259	.364	.296
	TOTALS	2171	21	.285	.320	.378	1108	10	.289	.322	.397	1063	11	.280	.319	.357	948	13	.305	.343	.417	1223	8	.269	.303	.348	972	12	.299	.337	.398	351	5	.274	.324	.359

■ Billy Hatcher BR/TR

YEAR	TM/L	AB	HR	AVG	OBP	SLG	AB	HR	AVG	OBP	SLG	AB	HR	AVG	OBP	SLG	AB	HR	AVG	OBP	SLG	AB	HR	AVG	OBP	SLG	AB	HR	AVG	OBP	SLG	AB	HR	AVG	OBP	SLG
1984	Chi-N	9	0	.111	.200	.111	4	0	.000	.200	.000	5	0	.200	.200	.200	1	0	.000	.500	.000	8	0	.125	.125	.125	2	0	.000	.333	.000	1	0	.000	.000	.000
1985	Chi-N	163	2	.245	.290	.368	109	2	.229	.259	.339	40	0	.278	.350	.426	40	0	.225	.244	.250	123	2	.252	.304	.407	56	0	.179	.250	.214	18	0	.333	.400	.389
1986	Hou-N	419	6	.258	.302	.356	218	2	.257	.300	.339	201	4	.259	.304	.373	210	3	.286	.326	.390	209	3	.230	.278	.321	159	2	.239	.278	.321	67	2	.254	.286	.388
1987	Hou-N	564	11	.296	.352	.415	259	3	.305	.358	.382	305	8	.289	.346	.443	202	4	.277	.335	.406	362	7	.307	.361	.420	191	5	.314	.370	.455	90	1	.333	.400	.500
1988	Hou-N	530	7	.268	.321	.370	263	3	.243	.308	.342	267	4	.292	.333	.397	183	4	.284	.333	.415	347	3	.259	.314	.346	202	3	.292	.360	.416	100	1	.320	.389	.450

YEAR	TM/L	TOTAL AB	HR	AVG	OBP	SLG	HOME AB	HR	AVG	OBP	SLG	AWAY AB	HR	AVG	OBP	SLG	LEFT AB	HR	AVG	OBP	SLG	RIGHT AB	HR	AVG	OBP	SLG	ON-BASE AB	HR	AVG	OBP	SLG	LATE/CLOSE AB	HR	AVG	OBP	SLG
1989	Hou-N	395	3	.228	.281	.304	197	0	.234	.301	.299	198	3	.222	.261	.308	139	2	.281	.315	.374	256	1	.199	.263	.266	157	2	.274	.314	.357	70	1	.186	.219	.286
1989	Pit-N	86	1	.244	.253	.326	34	0	.235	.235	.294	52	1	.250	.264	.346	54	0	.241	.241	.278	32	1	.250	.273	.406	27	0	.185	.185	.259	11	0	.273	.273	.273
1990	Cin-N	504	5	.276	.327	.381	246	2	.264	.314	.378	258	3	.287	.339	.384	207	1	.246	.299	.319	297	4	.296	.347	.424	182	0	.258	.323	.308	76	0	.224	.306	.250
1991	Cin-N	442	4	.262	.312	.360	216	2	.269	.323	.380	226	2	.257	.300	.341	130	1	.277	.324	.369	312	3	.256	.307	.356	161	1	.298	.352	.404	77	0	.325	.361	.416
1992	Cin-N	94	2	.287	.314	.383	34	0	.294	.333	.353	60	2	.283	.303	.400	34	0	.294	.316	.324	60	2	.283	.313	.417	48	0	.271	.255	.292	21	0	.238	.261	.238
1992	Bos-A	315	1	.238	.283	.311	157	1	.268	.326	.350	158	0	.209	.238	.272	81	0	.210	.247	.284	234	1	.248	.295	.321	121	0	.264	.291	.339	60	1	.350	.371	.467
1993	Bos-A	508	9	.287	.336	.400	261	5	.295	.344	.418	247	4	.279	.327	.381	138	1	.232	.269	.304	370	8	.308	.360	.435	209	6	.316	.366	.469	68	2	.338	.378	.515
1994	Bos-A	164	1	.244	.292	.329	80	0	.338	.391	.450	84	1	.155	.198	.214	53	0	.189	.214	.208	111	1	.270	.328	.387	66	0	.288	.333	.429	21	0	.286	.333	.429
1994	Phi-N	134	2	.246	.271	.343	63	0	.238	.261	.286	71	2	.254	.280	.394	53	1	.208	.250	.302	81	1	.272	.286	.370	49	0	.224	.208	.265	25	0	.240	.259	.320
TOTALS		4327	54	.265	.313	.364	2141	20	.267	.319	.362	2186	34	.262	.307	.367	1551	19	.260	.303	.353	2776	35	.267	.318	.370	1630	19	.277	.325	.374	705	8	.289	.338	.400

■ Charlie Hayes BR/TR

YEAR	TM/L	TOTAL AB	HR	AVG	OBP	SLG	HOME AB	HR	AVG	OBP	SLG	AWAY AB	HR	AVG	OBP	SLG	LEFT AB	HR	AVG	OBP	SLG	RIGHT AB	HR	AVG	OBP	SLG	ON-BASE AB	HR	AVG	OBP	SLG	LATE/CLOSE AB	HR	AVG	OBP	SLG
1988	SF-N	11	0	.091	.091	.091	5	0	.000	.000	.000	6	0	.167	.167	.167	11	0	.091	.091	.091	0	0	—	—	—	4	0	.250	.250	.250	3	0	.000	.000	.000
1989	SF-N	5	0	.200	.200	.200	4	0	.250	.250	.250	1	0	.000	.000	.000	4	0	.000	.000	.000	1	0	1.000	1.000	1.000	3	0	.000	.000	.000	1	0	.000	.000	.000
1989	Phi-N	299	8	.258	.281	.395	152	3	.230	.262	.362	147	5	.286	.301	.429	101	1	.277	.306	.376	198	7	.247	.268	.404	122	3	.303	.318	.459	51	2	.196	.226	.353
1990	Phi-N	561	10	.258	.293	.348	282	3	.245	.272	.309	279	7	.272	.314	.387	193	5	.295	.324	.425	368	5	.239	.277	.307	248	5	.246	.277	.327	95	2	.274	.303	.358
1991	Phi-N	460	12	.230	.257	.363	248	6	.262	.292	.407	212	6	.193	.216	.311	190	4	.258	.283	.395	270	8	.211	.239	.341	218	5	.225	.251	.362	100	4	.320	.352	.530
1992	NY-A	509	18	.257	.297	.409	245	7	.220	.267	.351	264	11	.292	.325	.462	150	6	.213	.262	.353	359	12	.276	.312	.432	214	6	.276	.321	.407	91	3	.242	.271	.385
1993	Col-N	573	25	.305	.355	.522	296	17	.338	.387	.601	277	8	.271	.319	.437	142	5	.338	.367	.542	431	20	.295	.351	.515	256	14	.309	.353	.547	72	1	.319	.378	.472
1994	Col-N	423	10	.288	.348	.433	208	4	.317	.364	.481	215	6	.260	.332	.386	89	4	.270	.323	.494	334	6	.293	.354	.416	186	3	.301	.370	.398	59	0	.271	.313	.356
TOTALS		2841	83	.267	.307	.413	1440	40	.271	.310	.422	1401	43	.263	.303	.403	880	25	.272	.305	.420	1961	58	.265	.308	.409	1251	36	.273	.314	.414	472	12	.273	.310	.413

■ Von Hayes BL/TR

YEAR	TM/L	TOTAL AB	HR	AVG	OBP	SLG	HOME AB	HR	AVG	OBP	SLG	AWAY AB	HR	AVG	OBP	SLG	LEFT AB	HR	AVG	OBP	SLG	RIGHT AB	HR	AVG	OBP	SLG	ON-BASE AB	HR	AVG	OBP	SLG	LATE/CLOSE AB	HR	AVG	OBP	SLG
1984	Phi-N	561	16	.292	.359	.447	264	10	.292	.362	.473	297	6	.293	.356	.424	111	2	.234	.267	.333	450	14	.307	.379	.476	243	4	.284	.369	.383	96	5	.281	.330	.479
1985	Phi-N	570	13	.263	.332	.398	278	12	.288	.360	.493	292	1	.240	.306	.308	157	4	.229	.291	.338	413	9	.276	.348	.421	245	5	.265	.348	.376	102	1	.265	.342	.333
1986	Phi-N	610	19	.305	.379	.480	296	11	.314	.393	.503	314	8	.296	.365	.459	195	3	.231	.301	.328	415	16	.340	.414	.552	273	8	.333	.400	.487	112	3	.259	.311	.384
1987	Phi-N	556	21	.277	.404	.473	278	14	.252	.401	.475	278	7	.302	.407	.471	168	3	.232	.361	.345	388	18	.296	.422	.528	247	8	.300	.427	.514	88	3	.284	.418	.455
1988	Phi-N	367	6	.272	.355	.409	175	2	.229	.310	.354	192	4	.313	.396	.458	101	2	.129	.196	.238	266	4	.327	.413	.474	156	2	.308	.372	.455	67	1	.224	.325	.343
1989	Phi-N	540	26	.259	.376	.461	257	15	.249	.377	.479	283	11	.269	.375	.445	208	8	.245	.356	.404	332	18	.268	.388	.497	255	13	.282	.397	.486	89	4	.225	.386	.416
1990	Phi-N	467	17	.261	.375	.413	203	10	.276	.392	.478	264	7	.250	.362	.364	179	6	.274	.365	.419	288	11	.253	.381	.410	226	7	.310	.411	.465	72	3	.306	.441	.472
1991	Phi-N	284	0	.225	.303	.285	99	0	.202	.319	.242	185	0	.238	.294	.308	90	0	.267	.355	.333	194	0	.206	.278	.263	114	0	.193	.276	.246	51	0	.216	.344	.235
1992	Cal-A	307	4	.225	.305	.326	162	2	.241	.315	.346	145	2	.207	.294	.303	42	0	.119	.208	.143	265	4	.242	.321	.355	122	3	.213	.303	.352	46	2	.217	.302	.391
TOTALS		4262	122	.270	.361	.424	2012	76	.268	.367	.450	2250	46	.271	.355	.401	1251	28	.230	.317	.345	3011	94	.286	.379	.457	1881	50	.285	.378	.434	723	22	.257	.359	.397

■ Mike Heath BR/TR

YEAR	TM/L	TOTAL AB	HR	AVG	OBP	SLG	HOME AB	HR	AVG	OBP	SLG	AWAY AB	HR	AVG	OBP	SLG	LEFT AB	HR	AVG	OBP	SLG	RIGHT AB	HR	AVG	OBP	SLG	ON-BASE AB	HR	AVG	OBP	SLG	LATE/CLOSE AB	HR	AVG	OBP	SLG
1984	Oak-A	475	13	.248	.287	.396	210	8	.252	.287	.443	265	5	.245	.286	.358	170	5	.306	.346	.482	305	8	.216	.253	.348	211	4	.289	.328	.431	84	2	.262	.311	.440
1985	Oak-A	436	13	.250	.313	.408	209	8	.244	.301	.407	227	5	.256	.324	.410	151	5	.285	.341	.490	285	8	.232	.298	.365	178	5	.275	.348	.427	70	2	.200	.243	.286
1986	StL-N	190	4	.205	.293	.321	104	1	.212	.305	.298	86	3	.198	.278	.349	121	4	.215	.294	.380	69	0	.188	.291	.217	84	3	.226	.333	.405	39	0	.128	.261	.154
1986	Det-A	98	4	.265	.291	.418	55	3	.309	.316	.491	43	1	.209	.261	.326	57	2	.316	.333	.456	41	2	.195	.233	.366	47	2	.234	.275	.383	17	0	.235	.316	.353
1987	Det-A	270	8	.281	.339	.430	145	8	.297	.352	.531	125	0	.264	.324	.312	159	5	.302	.356	.465	111	3	.252	.314	.378	113	4	.301	.365	.451	42	0	.167	.250	.238
1988	Det-A	219	5	.247	.307	.365	95	4	.179	.264	.337	124	1	.298	.341	.387	148	5	.243	.300	.399	71	0	.254	.321	.296	89	0	.225	.289	.303	49	1	.122	.189	.204
1989	Det-A	396	10	.263	.308	.389	189	6	.238	.284	.365	207	5	.285	.330	.411	161	5	.317	.360	.472	235	5	.226	.273	.332	160	4	.231	.298	.363	85	5	.294	.344	.529
1990	Det-A	370	7	.270	.311	.386	169	3	.272	.321	.402	201	4	.269	.302	.373	149	3	.228	.264	.329	221	4	.299	.342	.425	164	3	.226	.257	.317	58	2	.207	.246	.310
1991	Atl-N	139	1	.209	.250	.266	75	1	.227	.256	.320	64	0	.188	.243	.203	64	1	.167	.182	.259	85	0	.235	.290	.271	63	0	.159	.250	.159	30	0	.167	.219	.233
TOTALS		2593	65	.253	.304	.385	1251	41	.249	.300	.404	1342	24	.256	.307	.367	1170	35	.271	.319	.427	1423	30	.238	.291	.350	1109	25	.251	.311	.376	474	12	.211	.271	.335

■ Dave Henderson BR/TR

YEAR	TM/L	TOTAL AB	HR	AVG	OBP	SLG	HOME AB	HR	AVG	OBP	SLG	AWAY AB	HR	AVG	OBP	SLG	LEFT AB	HR	AVG	OBP	SLG	RIGHT AB	HR	AVG	OBP	SLG	ON-BASE AB	HR	AVG	OBP	SLG	LATE/CLOSE AB	HR	AVG	OBP	SLG
1984	Sea-A	350	14	.280	.320	.466	188	8	.314	.355	.521	162	6	.241	.279	.401	134	5	.291	.324	.478	216	9	.273	.317	.458	147	2	.272	.312	.367	54	5	.296	.321	.648
1985	Sea-A	502	14	.241	.310	.388	253	8	.249	.330	.403	249	6	.233	.289	.373	132	3	.280	.345	.439	370	11	.227	.298	.370	236	6	.267	.319	.394	75	4	.280	.341	.467
1986	Sea-A	337	14	.276	.350	.481	168	10	.304	.369	.565	169	4	.249	.332	.396	86	6	.291	.361	.547	251	8	.271	.346	.458	141	5	.262	.335	.468	56	4	.250	.311	.518
1986	Bos-A	51	1	.196	.226	.314	38	0	.211	.231	.289	13	1	.154	.214	.385	15	0	.133	.188	.200	36	1	.222	.243	.361	24	0	.167	.200	.208	13	0	.077	.077	.077
1987	Bos-A	184	8	.234	.313	.418	107	4	.234	.320	.411	77	4	.234	.302	.429	66	4	.258	.319	.515	118	4	.220	.309	.364	86	4	.174	.247	.349	31	1	.226	.294	.323
1987	SF-N	21	0	.238	.448	.333	14	0	.214	.389	.357	7	0	.286	.545	.286	15	0	.333	.524	.467	6	0	.000	.250	.000	9	0	.333	.571	.556	4	0	.250	.571	.500
1988	Oak-A	507	24	.304	.363	.525	246	12	.293	.354	.512	261	12	.314	.371	.536	147	6	.306	.372	.524	360	18	.303	.359	.525	242	8	.322	.364	.512	81	6	.272	.337	.519
1989	Oak-A	579	15	.250	.315	.380	299	10	.280	.333	.423	280	5	.221	.297	.338	171	5	.287	.347	.427	408	10	.231	.301	.360	275	5	.255	.317	.360	79	4	.253	.302	.443
1990	Oak-A	450	20	.271	.331	.467	222	11	.302	.353	.514	228	9	.241	.310	.421	133	11	.353	.404	.654	317	9	.237	.300	.388	194	9	.268	.327	.474	69	1	.261	.282	.377
1991	Oak-A	572	25	.276	.346	.465	282	15	.259	.329	.450	290	10	.293	.362	.479	144	8	.354	.416	.618	428	17	.250	.322	.414	267	10	.292	.353	.468	96	1	.271	.327	.354
1992	Oak-A	63	0	.143	.169	.159	39	0	.128	.171	.128	24	0	.167	.167	.208	24	0	.208	.208	.250	39	0	.103	.146	.103	32	0	.125	.152	.156	10	0	.200	.273	.200
1993	Oak-A	382	20	.220	.275	.427	211	7	.194	.239	.336	171	13	.251	.318	.538	142	11	.225	.291	.500	240	9	.217	.265	.383	185	5	.189	.229	.314	74	2	.216	.286	.338
1994	KC-A	198	5	.247	.304	.404	97	2	.278	.330	.464	101	3	.218	.277	.347	84	3	.298	.362	.488	114	2	.211	.260	.342	86	2	.256	.305	.384	30	0	.133	.206	.133
TOTALS		4196	160	.260	.323	.437	2154	87	.267	.327	.449	2042	73	.253	.318	.425	1293	62	.293	.354	.508	2903	98	.245	.309	.406	1924	56	.260	.316	.410	672	28	.250	.306	.417

■ Rickey Henderson BR/TL

YEAR	TM/L	TOTAL AB	HR	AVG	OBP	SLG	HOME AB	HR	AVG	OBP	SLG	AWAY AB	HR	AVG	OBP	SLG	LEFT AB	HR	AVG	OBP	SLG	RIGHT AB	HR	AVG	OBP	SLG	ON-BASE AB	HR	AVG	OBP	SLG	LATE/CLOSE AB	HR	AVG	OBP	SLG
1984	Oak-A	502	16	.293	.399	.458	228	7	.285	.408	.447	274	9	.299	.392	.467	185	7	.286	.379	.465	317	9	.297	.411	.454	173	8	.324	.420	.503	84	2	.298	.388	.464
1985	NY-A	547	24	.314	.419	.516	246	8	.305	.416	.459	301	16	.322	.422	.561	180	12	.361	.487	.656	367	12	.292	.383	.447	190	8	.337	.433	.489	79	3	.329	.432	.456
1986	NY-A	608	28	.263	.358	.469	298	13	.235	.332	.440	310	15	.290	.383	.497	192	8	.234	.370	.443	416	20	.276	.352	.481	214	8	.248	.337	.444	88	7	.352	.442	.705
1987	NY-A	358	17	.291	.423	.497	161	10	.317	.453	.590	197	7	.269	.397	.421	118	9	.314	.445	.585	240	10	.279	.412	.454	119	4	.244	.423	.378	49	2	.408	.540	.633
1988	NY-A	554	6	.305	.394	.399	256	2	.297	.389	.391	298	4	.312	.398	.406	163	4	.368	.470	.521	391	2	.269	.360	.348	166	2	.289	.380	.373	71	1	.324	.414	.408
1989	NY-A	235	3	.247	.392	.349	126	1	.257	.401	.349	109	2	.238	.385	.349	89	0	.292	.427	.326	146	3	.219	.372	.363	85	2	.259	.429	.388	30	1	.200	.351	.333
1989	Oak-A	306	9	.294	.425	.438	144	6	.313	.466	.507	162	3	.278	.384	.377	84	1	.262	.398	.393	222	8	.306	.435	.455	106	2	.311	.465	.443	48	1	.292	.404	.396
1990	Oak-A	489	28	.325	.439	.577	220	8	.305	.425	.486	269	20	.342	.451	.651	134	9	.313	.421	.604	355	19	.330	.446	.566	153	8	.307	.449	.503	61	5	.426	.563	.754
1991	Oak-A	470	18	.268	.400	.423	248	8	.278	.401	.415	222	10	.257	.399	.432	114	8	.289	.401	.526	356	10	.261	.399	.390	159	5	.264	.431	.459	71	3	.239	.400	.408
1992	Oak-A	396	15	.283	.426	.457	200	10	.295	.441	.495	196	5	.270	.410	.418	105	5	.267	.398	.476	291	10	.289	.435	.450	142	4	.289	.455	.430	50	2	.280	.472	.480
1993	Oak-A	318	17	.327	.469	.553	168	8	.327	.475	.524	150	9	.327	.463	.587	74	10	.378	.535	.811	244	7	.311	.448	.475	126	3	.310	.480	.460	55	1	.236	.358	.382
1993	Tor-A	163	4	.215	.356	.319	83	2	.193	.306	.325	80	2	.237	.404	.313	56	2	.232	.348	.375	107	2	.206	.360	.290	59	0	.186	.286	.237	19	1	.263	.391	.526
1994	Oak-A	296	6	.260	.411	.365	132	4	.250	.415	.379	164	2	.268	.407	.354	105	3	.248	.407	.371	191	3	.267	.412	.361	86	1	.244	.407	.302	41	0	.220	.385	.220
TOTALS		5242	191	.289	.409	.460	2493	87	.284	.410	.452	2749	104	.292	.407	.467	1599	76	.299	.423	.510	3643	115	.284	.402	.438	1778	58	.285	.419	.434	746	29	.307	.431	.489

■ Keith Hernandez BL/TL

YEAR	TM/L	TOTAL AB	HR	AVG	OBP	SLG	HOME AB	HR	AVG	OBP	SLG	AWAY AB	HR	AVG	OBP	SLG	LEFT AB	HR	AVG	OBP	SLG	RIGHT AB	HR	AVG	OBP	SLG	ON-BASE AB	HR	AVG	OBP	SLG	LATE/CLOSE AB	HR	AVG	OBP	SLG
1984	NY-N	550	15	.311	.409	.449	268	10	.366	.461	.537	282	5	.259	.360	.365	196	3	.291	.371	.362	354	12	.322	.430	.497	238	11	.332	.431	.538	95	0	.284	.403	.358
1985	NY-N	593	10	.309	.384	.430	285	4	.284	.365	.375	308	6	.331	.402	.481	260	3	.315	.358	.415	333	7	.303	.403	.441	260	5	.315	.401	.462	103	1	.340	.430	.417
1986	NY-N	551	13	.310	.413	.446	239	6	.310	.422	.431	312	7	.311	.405	.458	218	4	.312	.409	.422	333	9	.309	.415	.462	276	6	.337	.445	.482	100	3	.283	.395	.424
1987	NY-N	587	18	.290	.377	.436	281	6	.288	.386	.406	306	12	.291	.369	.464	252	6	.254	.343	.373	335	12	.316	.403	.430	284	7	.299	.399	.430	100	2	.270	.360	.340
1988	NY-N	348	11	.276	.333	.417	146	2	.274	.348	.349	202	9	.277	.323	.465	135	4	.274	.333	.452	213	5	.277	.333	.394	172	8	.308	.356	.488	49	4	.306	.382	.551
1989	NY-N	215	4	.233	.324	.326	95	1	.263	.358	.358	120	2	.208	.296	.300	79	1	.291	.364	.354	136	3	.199	.301	.309	92	2	.272	.362	.370	45	0	.200	.294	.267
1990	Cle-A	130	1	.200	.283	.238	42	0	.167	.286	.190	88	1	.216	.281	.261	27	0	.148	.233	.148	103	1	.214	.296	.262	55	1	.218	.317	.291	24	0	.208	.296	.208
TOTALS		2974	72	.292	.379	.420	1356	29	.299	.394	.414	1618	42	.285	.365	.426	1167	21	.287	.361	.392	1807	49	.294	.390	.438	1377	40	.312	.404	.463	515	10	.283	.383	.383

■ Larry Herndon BR/TR

YEAR	TM/L	TOTAL AB	HR	AVG	OBP	SLG	HOME AB	HR	AVG	OBP	SLG	AWAY AB	HR	AVG	OBP	SLG	LEFT AB	HR	AVG	OBP	SLG	RIGHT AB	HR	AVG	OBP	SLG	ON-BASE AB	HR	AVG	OBP	SLG	LATE/CLOSE AB	HR	AVG	OBP	SLG
1984	Det-A	407	7	.280	.333	.400	204	3	.314	.355	.441	203	4	.246	.302	.360	223	4	.314	.360	.448	184	3	.239	.302	.342	189	1	.265	.327	.349	46	1	.326	.407	.413
1985	Det-A	442	12	.244	.298	.385	211	7	.256	.308	.417	231	5	.234	.288	.355	155	7	.265	.347	.484	287	5	.233	.269	.331	171	2	.211	.280	.281	45	1	.224	.290	.318
1986	Det-A	283	8	.247	.310	.385	137	4	.234	.289	.358	146	4	.260	.329	.411	189	6	.233	.302	.365	94	2	.277	.327	.426	136	6	.235	.292	.434	47	1	.255	.327	.404
1987	Det-A	225	9	.324	.378	.583	115	7	.313	.372	.583	110	2	.336	.384	.582	168	7	.333	.426	.593	57	2	.316	.351	.561	106	6	.302	.365	.500	32	0	.375	.400	.469
1988	Det-A	174	4	.224	.313	.322	91	2	.198	.302	.297	83	2	.253	.326	.349	157	4	.236	.328	.344	17	0	.118	.167	.118	76	1	.237	.307	.316	29	0	.276	.389	.345
TOTALS		1531	40	.264	.323	.402	758	23	.269	.329	.423	773	17	.259	.318	.380	901	29	.286	.353	.447	630	11	.232	.279	.337	678	16	.248	.313	.369	239	3	.276	.348	.377

■ Tom Herr BB/TR

YEAR	TM/L	TOTAL AB	HR	AVG	OBP	SLG	HOME AB	HR	AVG	OBP	SLG	AWAY AB	HR	AVG	OBP	SLG	LEFT AB	HR	AVG	OBP	SLG	RIGHT AB	HR	AVG	OBP	SLG	ON-BASE AB	HR	AVG	OBP	SLG	LATE/CLOSE AB	HR	AVG	OBP	SLG
1984	StL-N	558	4	.276	.335	.346	266	2	.281	.348	.366	292	2	.271	.321	.323	178	2	.287	.335	.388	380	2	.271	.335	.326	223	1	.265	.324	.323	80	1	.200	.273	.237
1985	StL-N	596	8	.302	.379	.416	287	4	.303	.375	.432	309	4	.301	.383	.401	212	3	.283	.354	.368	384	5	.313	.402	.443	295	3	.356	.410	.481	93	3	.312	.383	.441
1986	StL-N	559	2	.252	.342	.331	273	1	.260	.367	.322	286	1	.245	.315	.339	219	1	.315	.407	.402	340	1	.212	.299	.285	231	1	.277	.360	.364	117	1	.222	.289	.265
1987	StL-N	510	2	.263	.346	.331	246	1	.280	.368	.341	264	1	.246	.325	.322	191	2	.298	.386	.398	319	0	.241	.322	.279	266	2	.274	.357	.361	85	1	.306	.367	.388
1988	StL-N	50	1	.260	.393	.320	24	1	.231	.355	.346	26	0	.292	.433	.292	17	1	.412	.500	.588	33	0	.182	.341	.182	17	0	.294	.429	.294	7	0	.000	.125	.000
1988	Min-A	304	1	.263	.349	.326	167	0	.228	.314	.263	137	1	.307	.391	.401	76	1	.289	.349	.395	228	0	.254	.349	.303	120	0	.233	.324	.275	42	0	.238	.360	.238
1989	Phi-N	561	2	.287	.352	.364	270	0	.285	.360	.367	291	2	.289	.344	.361	229	1	.288	.353	.349	332	1	.286	.351	.373	206	1	.296	.350	.364	100	1	.260	.299	.380

		TOTAL					HOME					AWAY					LEFT					RIGHT					ON-BASE					LATE/CLOSE				
YEAR	TM/L	AB	HR	AVG	OBP	SLG	AB	HR	AVG	OBP	SLG	AB	HR	AVG	OBP	SLG	AB	HR	AVG	OBP	SLG	AB	HR	AVG	OBP	SLG	AB	HR	AVG	OBP	SLG	AB	HR	AVG	OBP	SLG
1990	Phi-N	447	4	.264	.320	.351	211	3	.265	.328	.384	236	1	.263	.314	.322	157	1	.268	.327	.331	290	3	.262	.316	.362	221	2	.290	.346	.398	79	1	.203	.241	.291
1990	NY-N	100	1	.250	.342	.330	54	1	.296	.377	.407	46	0	.196	.302	.239	51	0	.255	.333	.314	49	1	.245	.351	.347	42	0	.310	.370	.357	11	0	.273	.429	.364
1991	NY-N	155	1	.194	.328	.258	70	0	.157	.286	.200	85	1	.224	.362	.306	63	0	.190	.346	.238	92	1	.196	.315	.272	57	0	.175	.355	.193	37	0	.081	.209	.108
1991	SF-N	60	0	.250	.384	.300	30	0	.267	.405	.267	30	0	.233	.361	.333	20	0	.300	.391	.400	40	0	.225	.380	.250	35	0	.314	.415	.400	12	0	.583	.722	.833
TOTALS		3900	26	.269	.348	.349	1900	12	.269	.350	.347	2000	14	.270	.345	.352	1413	12	.287	.360	.369	2487	14	.260	.341	.338	1713	10	.288	.360	.371	663	7	.244	.319	.321

■ Donnie Hill BB/TR

YEAR	TM/L	AB	HR	AVG	OBP	SLG	AB	HR	AVG	OBP	SLG	AB	HR	AVG	OBP	SLG	AB	HR	AVG	OBP	SLG	AB	HR	AVG	OBP	SLG	AB	HR	AVG	OBP	SLG	AB	HR	AVG	OBP	SLG
1984	Oak-A	174	2	.230	.249	.299	94	0	.213	.227	.255	80	2	.250	.274	.350	47	0	.170	.170	.191	127	2	.252	.276	.339	83	1	.289	.282	.373	21	0	.333	.348	.381
1985	Oak-A	393	3	.285	.321	.351	190	0	.268	.309	.321	203	3	.300	.333	.379	88	0	.250	.306	.284	305	3	.295	.326	.370	160	1	.325	.356	.406	52	1	.269	.356	.327
1986	Oak-A	339	4	.283	.329	.378	157	0	.293	.339	.350	182	4	.275	.320	.401	138	1	.275	.324	.377	201	3	.289	.332	.383	160	3	.262	.314	.350	63	1	.286	.318	.397
1987	Chi-A	410	9	.239	.290	.368	201	1	.254	.303	.363	209	8	.225	.278	.373	130	5	.262	.319	.400	280	4	.229	.276	.354	174	3	.247	.301	.374	60	3	.300	.364	.467
1988	Chi-A	221	2	.217	.296	.281	89	1	.236	.346	.292	132	1	.205	.259	.273	61	0	.180	.311	.246	160	1	.231	.290	.294	88	0	.170	.276	.216	48	0	.229	.351	.229
1990	Cal-A	352	3	.264	.319	.352	169	0	.249	.319	.302	183	3	.279	.318	.399	98	1	.235	.315	.347	254	2	.276	.320	.354	154	2	.273	.333	.377	54	1	.296	.367	.444
1991	Cal-A	209	1	.239	.335	.301	102	1	.196	.281	.265	107	0	.280	.384	.336	35	0	.257	.395	.400	174	1	.236	.321	.282	85	1	.306	.422	.412	34	0	.176	.282	.176
1992	Min-A	51	0	.294	.368	.353	18	0	.278	.316	.389	33	0	.303	.395	.333	2	0	.000	.000	.000	49	0	.306	.382	.367	23	0	.304	.360	.348	8	0	.250	.333	.375
TOTALS		2149	24	.257	.310	.342	1020	3	.251	.308	.318	1129	21	.262	.313	.365	599	8	.242	.310	.334	1550	16	.263	.310	.346	927	11	.271	.327	.364	340	6	.271	.343	.359

■ Thomas Howard BB/TR

YEAR	TM/L	AB	HR	AVG	OBP	SLG	AB	HR	AVG	OBP	SLG	AB	HR	AVG	OBP	SLG	AB	HR	AVG	OBP	SLG	AB	HR	AVG	OBP	SLG	AB	HR	AVG	OBP	SLG	AB	HR	AVG	OBP	SLG
1990	SD-N	44	0	.273	.273	.318	22	0	.318	.318	.318	22	0	.227	.227	.318	16	0	.188	.188	.188	28	0	.321	.321	.393	18	0	.167	.167	.167	11	0	.182	.182	.273
1991	SD-N	281	4	.249	.309	.356	140	4	.257	.316	.386	141	0	.241	.303	.326	28	1	.286	.394	.464	253	3	.245	.299	.344	107	2	.271	.352	.393	61	1	.197	.246	.262
1992	SD-N	3	0	.333	.333	.333	2	0	.500	.500	.500	1	0	.000	.000	.000	0	0	—	—	—	3	0	.333	.333	.333	0	0	—	—	—	1	0	.000	.000	.000
1992	Cle-A	358	2	.277	.308	.346	179	1	.268	.302	.335	179	1	.285	.314	.358	104	2	.288	.321	.375	254	0	.272	.302	.335	145	1	.317	.340	.386	74	1	.284	.308	.378
1993	Cle-A	178	3	.236	.278	.326	82	3	.220	.280	.354	96	0	.250	.277	.302	75	1	.160	.224	.213	103	2	.291	.321	.408	78	1	.179	.236	.244	35	0	.229	.256	.314
1993	Cin-N	141	4	.277	.331	.461	61	2	.295	.377	.492	80	2	.262	.294	.438	34	0	.147	.189	.147	107	4	.318	.376	.561	56	2	.286	.339	.464	20	0	.100	.217	.100
1994	Cin-N	178	5	.264	.302	.410	88	4	.318	.365	.500	90	1	.211	.237	.322	28	0	.214	.267	.250	150	5	.273	.308	.440	75	3	.267	.309	.453	44	1	.341	.388	.455
TOTALS		1183	18	.262	.304	.368	574	14	.272	.321	.392	609	4	.253	.288	.345	285	4	.225	.274	.291	898	14	.274	.314	.392	479	9	.267	.314	.376	246	3	.244	.286	.325

■ Jack Howell BL/TR

YEAR	TM/L	AB	HR	AVG	OBP	SLG	AB	HR	AVG	OBP	SLG	AB	HR	AVG	OBP	SLG	AB	HR	AVG	OBP	SLG	AB	HR	AVG	OBP	SLG	AB	HR	AVG	OBP	SLG	AB	HR	AVG	OBP	SLG
1985	Cal-A	137	5	.197	.279	.336	69	2	.159	.272	.261	68	3	.235	.288	.412	40	1	.175	.244	.275	97	4	.206	.294	.361	52	2	.250	.344	.404	20	1	.150	.150	.300
1986	Cal-A	151	4	.272	.349	.470	67	1	.239	.320	.418	84	3	.298	.371	.512	24	0	.208	.240	.458	127	4	.283	.367	.472	56	1	.286	.373	.518	31	1	.161	.212	.290
1987	Cal-A	449	23	.245	.331	.461	230	15	.270	.344	.526	219	8	.219	.319	.393	73	1	.123	.200	.260	376	22	.269	.356	.500	196	10	.245	.339	.454	77	3	.260	.345	.468
1988	Cal-A	500	16	.254	.323	.422	244	9	.238	.318	.393	256	7	.270	.329	.449	156	4	.237	.296	.397	344	12	.262	.335	.433	220	8	.295	.379	.486	85	2	.200	.274	.306
1989	Cal-A	474	20	.228	.308	.411	225	9	.236	.309	.418	249	11	.221	.306	.406	136	2	.140	.220	.235	338	18	.263	.342	.482	207	9	.242	.333	.411	85	4	.259	.340	.459
1990	Cal-A	316	8	.228	.326	.370	156	3	.218	.305	.333	160	5	.237	.346	.406	62	0	.177	.292	.210	254	8	.240	.334	.409	135	3	.259	.363	.393	57	1	.211	.348	.351
1991	Cal-A	81	2	.210	.304	.309	41	0	.220	.289	.220	40	2	.200	.319	.400	13	0	.077	.077	.077	68	2	.235	.342	.353	41	1	.279	.326	.349	11	0	.273	.333	.364
1991	SD-N	160	6	.206	.287	.350	76	3	.197	.299	.342	84	3	.214	.275	.357	16	0	.125	.176	.188	144	6	.215	.298	.368	64	3	.234	.300	.391	28	2	.357	.419	.607
TOTALS		2268	84	.236	.318	.409	1108	42	.233	.314	.401	1160	42	.239	.321	.417	520	8	.175	.247	.292	1748	76	.254	.338	.444	973	37	.261	.350	.436	394	14	.234	.315	.398

■ Kent Hrbek BL/TR

YEAR	TM/L	AB	HR	AVG	OBP	SLG	AB	HR	AVG	OBP	SLG	AB	HR	AVG	OBP	SLG	AB	HR	AVG	OBP	SLG	AB	HR	AVG	OBP	SLG	AB	HR	AVG	OBP	SLG	AB	HR	AVG	OBP	SLG
1984	Min-A	559	27	.311	.383	.522	285	15	.358	.428	.596	274	12	.263	.337	.445	186	10	.296	.368	.495	373	17	.319	.391	.536	260	15	.335	.417	.573	82	0	.280	.388	.341
1985	Min-A	593	21	.278	.351	.444	314	10	.312	.378	.487	279	11	.240	.322	.394	199	4	.256	.324	.402	394	15	.289	.365	.464	267	11	.262	.358	.434	79	1	.291	.404	.354
1986	Min-A	550	29	.267	.353	.478	278	18	.273	.359	.529	272	11	.261	.347	.426	152	4	.270	.333	.382	398	25	.266	.361	.515	260	12	.292	.363	.485	85	3	.212	.302	.329
1987	Min-A	477	34	.285	.389	.545	234	20	.295	.413	.590	243	14	.276	.364	.498	138	6	.225	.290	.370	339	28	.310	.426	.617	225	16	.302	.417	.556	76	6	.329	.391	.618
1988	Min-A	510	25	.312	.387	.520	253	13	.304	.386	.526	257	12	.319	.388	.514	132	2	.250	.336	.379	378	23	.333	.405	.569	247	11	.271	.364	.441	78	5	.346	.429	.564
1989	Min-A	375	25	.272	.360	.517	191	17	.283	.371	.597	184	8	.261	.349	.435	109	6	.266	.374	.468	266	19	.274	.354	.538	184	11	.234	.335	.451	53	6	.302	.356	.717
1990	Min-A	492	22	.287	.377	.474	247	8	.279	.362	.437	245	14	.294	.391	.510	129	2	.287	.377	.357	363	20	.287	.377	.513	228	10	.307	.403	.482	77	1	.299	.400	.403
1991	Min-A	462	20	.284	.373	.461	236	11	.318	.407	.504	226	9	.248	.336	.416	128	6	.281	.357	.445	334	14	.284	.379	.467	238	15	.315	.398	.546	54	4	.389	.450	.630
1992	Min-A	394	15	.244	.357	.409	193	10	.259	.358	.466	201	5	.229	.355	.353	83	1	.265	.319	.361	311	14	.238	.366	.421	209	4	.230	.364	.335	64	1	.250	.355	.359
1993	Min-A	392	25	.242	.357	.467	193	12	.249	.364	.482	199	13	.236	.350	.452	58	3	.224	.352	.397	334	22	.246	.358	.479	196	15	.260	.384	.520	60	0	.333	.459	.417
1994	Min-A	274	10	.270	.353	.420	135	4	.274	.374	.422	139	6	.266	.331	.417	39	2	.282	.378	.462	235	8	.268	.349	.413	127	6	.323	.405	.512	47	0	.340	.418	.362
TOTALS		5078	253	.280	.368	.481	2559	138	.295	.383	.517	2519	115	.264	.353	.444	1353	48	.265	.344	.411	3725	205	.285	.377	.506	2441	126	.285	.383	.485	755	27	.302	.393	.454

■ Glenn Hubbard BR/TR

YEAR	TM/L	AB	HR	AVG	OBP	SLG	AB	HR	AVG	OBP	SLG	AB	HR	AVG	OBP	SLG	AB	HR	AVG	OBP	SLG	AB	HR	AVG	OBP	SLG	AB	HR	AVG	OBP	SLG	AB	HR	AVG	OBP	SLG
1984	Atl-N	397	9	.234	.331	.380	189	5	.254	.364	.397	208	4	.216	.299	.365	120	2	.225	.304	.367	277	7	.238	.343	.386	169	5	.272	.332	.361	70	1	.186	.284	.314
1985	Atl-N	439	5	.232	.321	.314	232	3	.250	.323	.328	207	2	.213	.318	.300	144	1	.229	.335	.278	295	4	.234	.313	.332	190	1	.216	.295	.268	58	1	.241	.380	.310
1986	Atl-N	408	4	.230	.340	.304	203	4	.246	.370	.355	205	0	.215	.309	.254	127	1	.220	.365	.291	281	3	.235	.328	.310	160	2	.250	.401	.338	59	0	.153	.275	.203
1987	Atl-N	443	5	.264	.378	.382	222	3	.252	.383	.365	221	2	.276	.373	.398	104	2	.288	.419	.433	339	3	.257	.365	.366	177	2	.277	.423	.367	71	1	.257	.321	.338
1988	Oak-A	294	3	.255	.334	.340	131	1	.267	.351	.374	163	2	.245	.321	.313	79	1	.278	.329	.342	215	2	.247	.336	.340	136	3	.294	.351	.426	54	0	.204	.246	.204
1989	Oak-A	131	3	.198	.296	.313	70	2	.171	.247	.314	61	1	.230	.347	.311	57	1	.228	.323	.316	74	2	.176	.276	.311	53	1	.151	.242	.226	15	0	.133	.316	.133
TOTALS		2112	29	.240	.339	.342	1047	18	.247	.352	.358	1065	11	.233	.326	.327	631	8	.242	.349	.334	1481	21	.239	.335	.346	885	14	.241	.354	.340	330	3	.206	.304	.273

■ Jeff Huson BL/TR

YEAR	TM/L	AB	HR	AVG	OBP	SLG	AB	HR	AVG	OBP	SLG	AB	HR	AVG	OBP	SLG	AB	HR	AVG	OBP	SLG	AB	HR	AVG	OBP	SLG	AB	HR	AVG	OBP	SLG	AB	HR	AVG	OBP	SLG
1988	Mon-N	42	0	.310	.370	.357	25	0	.280	.357	.320	17	0	.353	.389	.412	7	0	.143	.143	.143	35	0	.343	.410	.400	22	0	.227	.346	.227	7	0	.286	.444	.286
1989	Mon-N	74	0	.162	.225	.230	42	0	.214	.313	.286	32	0	.094	.094	.156	12	0	.167	.231	.250	62	0	.161	.224	.226	31	0	.097	.243	.129	13	0	.231	.231	.231
1990	Tex-A	396	0	.240	.320	.280	191	0	.220	.291	.272	205	0	.259	.346	.288	46	0	.261	.327	.283	350	0	.237	.319	.280	143	0	.266	.333	.315	65	0	.262	.355	.277
1991	Tex-A	268	2	.213	.312	.287	141	1	.177	.297	.234	127	1	.252	.329	.346	27	0	.074	.194	.074	241	2	.228	.325	.311	116	2	.233	.308	.345	37	0	.270	.386	.270
1992	Tex-A	318	4	.261	.342	.362	149	0	.255	.325	.309	169	4	.266	.355	.408	32	1	.281	.361	.438	286	3	.259	.339	.353	125	1	.224	.304	.328	54	0	.148	.258	.222
1993	Tex-A	45	0	.133	.133	.200	20	0	.050	.050	.050	25	0	.200	.200	.320	9	0	.222	.222	.556	36	0	.111	.111	.111	21	0	.143	.143	.190	8	0	.000	.000	.000
TOTALS		1143	6	.233	.313	.301	568	1	.215	.299	.268	575	5	.250	.328	.334	133	1	.211	.284	.286	1010	5	.236	.317	.303	458	3	.227	.305	.303	184	0	.217	.316	.245

■ Pete Incaviglia BR/TR

YEAR	TM/L	AB	HR	AVG	OBP	SLG	AB	HR	AVG	OBP	SLG	AB	HR	AVG	OBP	SLG	AB	HR	AVG	OBP	SLG	AB	HR	AVG	OBP	SLG	AB	HR	AVG	OBP	SLG	AB	HR	AVG	OBP	SLG
1986	Tex-A	540	30	.250	.320	.463	275	17	.287	.353	.527	265	13	.211	.286	.396	160	12	.306	.374	.600	380	18	.226	.297	.405	264	13	.231	.311	.420	74	4	.284	.379	.486
1987	Tex-A	509	27	.271	.332	.497	255	11	.259	.336	.451	254	16	.283	.328	.543	182	13	.341	.407	.632	327	14	.232	.290	.422	232	11	.259	.309	.453	70	4	.243	.313	.500
1988	Tex-A	418	22	.249	.321	.467	193	12	.249	.316	.492	225	10	.249	.325	.444	126	9	.254	.319	.524	292	13	.247	.322	.442	195	7	.231	.308	.379	59	1	.254	.343	.390
1989	Tex-A	453	21	.236	.293	.453	223	13	.251	.327	.480	230	8	.222	.257	.426	148	6	.209	.264	.412	305	15	.249	.307	.472	224	11	.237	.277	.446	79	4	.215	.253	.418
1990	Tex-A	529	24	.233	.302	.420	247	15	.247	.332	.433	282	9	.220	.272	.365	169	8	.249	.347	.444	360	16	.225	.275	.408	257	11	.245	.315	.432	100	4	.178	.215	.356
1991	Det-A	337	11	.214	.290	.353	171	6	.205	.283	.357	166	5	.223	.297	.349	97	0	.206	.264	.258	240	11	.217	.300	.392	159	6	.226	.298	.384	66	0	.152	.222	.212
1992	Hou-N	349	11	.266	.319	.430	189	6	.296	.338	.471	160	5	.231	.298	.381	170	7	.282	.344	.494	179	4	.251	.295	.369	169	5	.254	.323	.444	65	2	.277	.347	.446
1993	Phi-N	368	24	.274	.318	.530	205	15	.278	.324	.551	163	9	.270	.311	.503	162	13	.278	.318	.586	206	11	.272	.319	.485	182	12	.286	.325	.533	65	1	.154	.227	.215
1994	Phi-N	244	13	.230	.278	.439	115	6	.209	.276	.409	129	7	.248	.279	.465	103	4	.252	.319	.417	141	9	.213	.247	.454	115	5	.174	.260	.313	45	2	.200	.217	.400
TOTALS		3747	183	.248	.310	.453	1873	101	.257	.325	.476	1874	82	.239	.295	.430	1317	72	.270	.335	.501	2430	111	.236	.297	.426	1797	83	.241	.305	.428	624	22	.216	.280	.381

■ Garth Iorg BR/TR

YEAR	TM/L	AB	HR	AVG	OBP	SLG	AB	HR	AVG	OBP	SLG	AB	HR	AVG	OBP	SLG	AB	HR	AVG	OBP	SLG	AB	HR	AVG	OBP	SLG	AB	HR	AVG	OBP	SLG	AB	HR	AVG	OBP	SLG
1984	Tor-A	247	1	.227	.244	.304	134	1	.269	.288	.351	113	0	.177	.191	.248	180	1	.250	.269	.344	67	0	.164	.176	.194	120	1	.275	.296	.383	37	0	.324	.324	.459
1985	Tor-A	288	7	.313	.358	.469	119	5	.378	.417	.588	169	2	.266	.317	.385	200	5	.310	.361	.480	88	2	.318	.351	.443	138	5	.304	.374	.457	40	2	.375	.432	.600
1986	Tor-A	327	3	.260	.303	.352	167	1	.216	.251	.305	160	2	.306	.354	.400	166	3	.289	.335	.410	161	0	.230	.269	.292	154	2	.292	.327	.390	75	0	.280	.333	.333
1987	Tor-A	310	4	.210	.262	.284	148	1	.209	.267	.264	162	3	.210	.257	.302	138	1	.181	.238	.225	172	3	.233	.281	.331	135	1	.215	.283	.267	56	0	.268	.313	.321
TOTALS		1172	15	.253	.294	.352	568	8	.261	.299	.364	604	7	.245	.289	.341	684	10	.263	.306	.376	488	5	.238	.276	.320	547	9	.272	.322	.404	208	2	.303	.345	.404

■ Darrin Jackson BR/TR

YEAR	TM/L	AB	HR	AVG	OBP	SLG	AB	HR	AVG	OBP	SLG	AB	HR	AVG	OBP	SLG	AB	HR	AVG	OBP	SLG	AB	HR	AVG	OBP	SLG	AB	HR	AVG	OBP	SLG	AB	HR	AVG	OBP	SLG
1985	Chi-N	11	0	.091	.091	.091	0	0	—	—	—	11	0	.091	.091	.091	3	0	.000	.000	.000	8	0	.125	.125	.125	4	0	.000	.000	.000	0	0	—	—	—
1987	Chi-N	5	0	.800	.800	1.000	0	0	—	—	—	5	0	.800	.800	1.000	4	0	.750	.750	1.000	1	0	1.000	1.000	1.000	3	0	1.000	1.000	1.000	1	0	1.000	1.000	1.000
1988	Chi-N	188	6	.266	.287	.452	85	3	.329	.360	.518	103	3	.214	.226	.398	111	5	.315	.339	.568	77	1	.195	.213	.286	93	1	.226	.270	.323	31	1	.258	.303	.355
1989	Chi-N	83	1	.229	.281	.313	41	0	.220	.273	.268	42	1	.238	.289	.357	58	1	.259	.328	.379	25	0	.160	.160	.160	31	0	.258	.324	.355	23	0	.217	.217	.261
1989	SD-N	87	3	.207	.260	.345	47	1	.170	.204	.277	40	2	.250	.319	.425	27	1	.148	.219	.296	60	2	.233	.281	.367	36	1	.194	.279	.306	16	0	.125	.222	.188
1990	SD-N	113	3	.257	.286	.363	36	1	.222	.237	.333	77	2	.273	.309	.377	65	2	.277	.314	.385	48	1	.229	.245	.333	38	0	.184	.238	.237	17	0	.235	.300	.235
1991	SD-N	359	21	.262	.315	.476	174	12	.259	.317	.494	185	9	.265	.312	.459	163	11	.264	.311	.497	196	10	.260	.318	.459	124	6	.266	.333	.427	65	3	.169	.217	.323
1992	SD-N	587	17	.249	.283	.392	299	11	.288	.316	.451	288	6	.208	.252	.333	188	7	.202	.242	.388	399	10	.271	.302	.393	236	7	.254	.298	.398	140	3	.236	.280	.343
1993	Tor-A	176	5	.216	.250	.347	93	4	.237	.260	.419	83	1	.193	.239	.265	33	1	.212	.235	.364	143	4	.217	.253	.343	92	1	.217	.258	.326	21	1	.286	.348	.524
1993	NY-N	87	1	.195	.211	.241	42	0	.214	.244	.238	45	1	.178	.178	.244	36	0	.083	.083	.083	51	1	.275	.296	.353	21	0	.143	.174	.143	14	0	.214	.214	.214
1994	Chi-A	369	10	.312	.362	.455	162	4	.346	.380	.500	207	6	.285	.338	.420	123	5	.301	.368	.488	246	5	.309	.358	.439	177	5	.282	.335	.367	60	0	.283	.306	.367
TOTALS		2065	67	.257	.297	.406	979	36	.277	.314	.443	1086	31	.239	.282	.373	826	34	.262	.303	.443	1239	33	.254	.293	.382	855	21	.248	.300	.367	340	11	.244	.290	.385

■ Reggie Jackson BL/TL

YEAR	TM/L	AB	HR	AVG	OBP	SLG	AB	HR	AVG	OBP	SLG	AB	HR	AVG	OBP	SLG	AB	HR	AVG	OBP	SLG	AB	HR	AVG	OBP	SLG	AB	HR	AVG	OBP	SLG	AB	HR	AVG	OBP	SLG
1964	Cal-A	525	25	.223	.300	.406	246	15	.211	.287	.415	279	10	.233	.312	.398	146	10	.219	.265	.432	379	15	.224	.313	.396	243	16	.263	.332	.506	87	2	.218	.277	.322

YEAR	TM/L	TOTAL AB	HR	AVG	OBP	SLG	HOME AB	HR	AVG	OBP	SLG	AWAY AB	HR	AVG	OBP	SLG	LEFT AB	HR	AVG	OBP	SLG	RIGHT AB	HR	AVG	OBP	SLG	ON-BASE AB	HR	AVG	OBP	SLG	LATE/CLOSE AB	HR	AVG	OBP	SLG
1985	Cal-A	460	27	.252	.360	.487	225	15	.218	.328	.462	235	12	.285	.391	.511	113	4	.221	.355	.398	347	23	.262	.362	.516	218	15	.271	.376	.532	70	0	.157	.326	.171
1986	Cal-A	419	18	.241	.379	.408	195	11	.277	.426	.497	224	7	.210	.336	.330	71	0	.239	.349	.282	348	18	.241	.385	.434	216	9	.250	.398	.421	64	1	.188	.342	.250
1987	Oak-A	336	15	.220	.297	.402	165	7	.218	.303	.394	171	8	.222	.291	.409	48	2	.292	.333	.521	288	13	.208	.291	.382	143	10	.217	.289	.455	70	3	.200	.243	.371
TOTALS		1740	85	.234	.336	.427	831	48	.230	.337	.443	909	37	.239	.335	.413	378	16	.233	.319	.405	1362	69	.235	.341	.433	820	50	.254	.356	.482	291	6	.192	.298	.282
■ Bo Jackson BR/TR																																				
1986	KC-A	82	2	.207	.286	.329	44	1	.250	.298	.318	38	1	.158	.273	.342	21	0	.095	.174	.190	61	2	.246	.324	.377	33	1	.273	.385	.455	13	1	.077	.200	.308
1987	KC-A	396	22	.235	.296	.455	197	14	.284	.344	.579	199	8	.186	.247	.332	113	7	.248	.315	.496	283	15	.230	.288	.438	179	6	.207	.258	.363	56	2	.214	.308	.339
1988	KC-A	439	25	.246	.287	.472	211	10	.318	.362	.555	228	15	.180	.214	.395	123	8	.276	.315	.520	316	17	.234	.276	.453	185	8	.232	.280	.416	79	1	.253	.314	.329
1989	KC-A	515	32	.256	.310	.495	248	11	.234	.296	.431	267	21	.277	.324	.554	128	7	.266	.365	.492	387	25	.253	.291	.496	254	17	.248	.318	.508	83	5	.241	.300	.446
1990	KC-A	405	28	.272	.342	.523	192	12	.307	.370	.573	213	16	.239	.317	.479	143	10	.273	.348	.510	262	18	.271	.339	.531	193	16	.264	.358	.539	66	6	.288	.347	.561
1991	Chi-A	71	3	.225	.333	.408	40	3	.200	.267	.475	31	0	.258	.410	.323	26	2	.231	.323	.500	45	1	.222	.340	.356	32	2	.281	.385	.531	7	2	.429	.500	1.286
1993	Chi-A	284	16	.232	.289	.433	145	9	.228	.277	.448	139	7	.237	.301	.417	133	9	.203	.264	.414	151	7	.258	.311	.450	130	9	.269	.324	.492	30	0	.267	.313	.300
1994	Cal-A	201	13	.279	.344	.507	101	10	.287	.354	.604	100	3	.270	.333	.410	97	6	.289	.352	.515	104	7	.269	.336	.500	94	7	.319	.411	.585	38	4	.316	.350	.684
TOTALS		2393	141	.250	.309	.474	1178	70	.272	.330	.515	1215	71	.228	.289	.435	784	49	.253	.322	.482	1609	92	.249	.303	.470	1100	66	.252	.323	.478	372	21	.255	.319	.449
■ Brook Jacoby BR/TR																																				
1984	Cle-A	439	7	.264	.314	.369	222	2	.261	.320	.342	217	5	.267	.308	.396	139	3	.317	.378	.446	300	4	.240	.283	.333	202	1	.248	.315	.317	83	3	.241	.250	.373
1985	Cle-A	606	20	.274	.324	.426	303	9	.271	.323	.426	303	11	.277	.324	.426	185	9	.276	.335	.459	421	11	.273	.319	.411	272	11	.298	.351	.482	90	0	.256	.284	.278
1986	Cle-A	583	17	.288	.350	.441	274	10	.266	.338	.431	309	7	.307	.361	.450	161	5	.261	.339	.404	422	12	.299	.354	.455	270	8	.322	.378	.489	81	3	.370	.433	.556
1987	Cle-A	540	32	.300	.387	.541	280	21	.279	.366	.564	260	11	.323	.410	.515	142	5	.261	.382	.444	398	27	.314	.389	.575	219	5	.274	.383	.393	85	5	.282	.330	.518
1988	Cle-A	552	9	.241	.300	.335	264	3	.239	.307	.333	288	6	.243	.294	.337	129	3	.233	.277	.357	423	6	.243	.307	.329	225	2	.236	.311	.302	81	0	.173	.218	.210
1989	Cle-A	519	13	.272	.348	.416	248	7	.266	.353	.423	271	6	.277	.343	.410	152	6	.296	.363	.493	367	7	.262	.342	.384	222	7	.293	.368	.446	91	3	.264	.361	.418
1990	Cle-A	553	14	.293	.365	.427	261	10	.287	.374	.464	292	4	.298	.356	.394	158	3	.316	.383	.411	395	11	.284	.358	.433	258	6	.314	.380	.422	87	2	.253	.323	.368
1991	Cle-A	231	4	.234	.289	.333	102	2	.216	.279	.314	129	2	.248	.297	.349	62	1	.242	.347	.339	169	3	.231	.266	.331	102	1	.235	.304	.314	52	2	.212	.255	.346
1991	Oak-A	188	0	.213	.255	.277	88	0	.216	.273	.284	100	0	.210	.238	.270	54	0	.259	.300	.315	134	0	.194	.236	.261	89	0	.225	.263	.303	33	0	.152	.176	.152
1992	Cle-A	291	4	.261	.324	.326	126	3	.310	.362	.421	165	1	.224	.295	.255	97	2	.258	.311	.351	194	2	.263	.330	.314	134	1	.276	.348	.321	50	1	.320	.397	.400
TOTALS		4502	120	.271	.335	.406	2168	67	.265	.336	.417	2334	53	.275	.333	.396	1279	37	.276	.347	.417	3223	83	.268	.330	.402	1993	40	.280	.349	.397	733	19	.258	.312	.375
■ Dion James BL/TL																																				
1984	Mil-A	387	1	.295	.351	.377	179	1	.246	.308	.330	208	0	.337	.387	.418	56	0	.339	.393	.411	331	1	.287	.343	.372	159	1	.327	.375	.415	70	0	.200	.284	.229
1985	Mil-A	49	1	.224	.309	.245	18	0	.278	.350	.278	31	1	.194	.286	.226	8	0	.250	.400	.375	41	1	.220	.289	.220	28	0	.250	.250	.250	11	0	.273	.385	.364
1987	Atl-N	494	10	.312	.397	.472	237	5	.376	.466	.561	257	5	.253	.331	.389	89	1	.303	.442	.438	405	9	.314	.386	.479	173	4	.318	.415	.497	84	1	.250	.337	.310
1988	Atl-N	386	3	.256	.353	.350	188	1	.250	.357	.351	198	2	.263	.350	.348	35	0	.114	.205	.200	351	3	.271	.368	.365	133	0	.278	.406	.353	68	1	.235	.369	.368
1989	Atl-N	170	1	.259	.355	.318	81	0	.235	.333	.272	89	1	.281	.375	.360	25	0	.160	.300	.160	145	1	.276	.365	.345	64	0	.250	.364	.297	35	0	.200	.317	.229
1989	Cle-A	245	4	.306	.368	.400	119	1	.210	.288	.261	126	3	.397	.445	.532	27	0	.259	.333	.370	218	4	.312	.372	.404	111	3	.333	.388	.459	41	0	.268	.400	.317
1990	Cle-A	248	1	.274	.347	.363	123	0	.325	.400	.439	125	1	.224	.292	.288	9	0	.111	.200	.222	239	1	.280	.352	.368	101	1	.327	.389	.436	46	0	.174	.240	.196
1992	NY-A	145	3	.262	.359	.379	54	2	.315	.391	.481	91	1	.231	.340	.319	14	1	.214	.421	.429	131	2	.267	.351	.374	81	2	.259	.333	.370	30	0	.167	.219	.167
1993	NY-A	343	7	.332	.390	.466	181	5	.359	.394	.519	162	2	.302	.386	.407	26	0	.231	.310	.269	317	7	.341	.397	.483	155	0	.335	.402	.413	44	1	.318	.412	.318
TOTALS		2467	30	.291	.367	.398	1180	15	.297	.375	.415	1287	15	.284	.360	.383	289	2	.253	.364	.349	2178	28	.296	.368	.405	1005	11	.308	.386	.412	429	2	.231	.330	.280
■ Chris James BR/TR																																				
1986	Phi-N	46	1	.283	.298	.413	22	0	.318	.318	.409	24	1	.250	.280	.417	22	1	.227	.261	.409	24	0	.333	.333	.417	21	1	.286	.318	.476	5	1	.200	.200	.800
1987	Phi-N	358	17	.293	.344	.525	172	9	.302	.366	.552	186	8	.285	.322	.500	149	9	.282	.327	.570	209	8	.301	.355	.493	158	7	.247	.299	.462	53	1	.302	.373	.396
1988	Phi-N	566	19	.242	.283	.389	298	10	.262	.300	.419	268	9	.220	.264	.354	157	7	.229	.265	.408	409	12	.247	.289	.381	258	9	.225	.263	.360	109	3	.257	.308	.394
1989	Phi-N	179	2	.207	.243	.263	80	1	.225	.253	.287	99	1	.192	.198	.242	73	2	.219	.247	.301	106	0	.198	.206	.236	84	2	.238	.253	.321	25	0	.080	.080	.080
1989	SD-N	303	11	.264	.314	.429	130	6	.292	.343	.485	173	5	.243	.292	.387	95	5	.347	.400	.579	208	6	.226	.274	.361	155	4	.258	.312	.400	54	2	.278	.339	.407
1990	Cle-A	528	12	.299	.341	.443	234	6	.286	.333	.427	294	6	.310	.347	.456	162	4	.302	.361	.432	366	8	.298	.332	.448	247	2	.324	.366	.417	73	0	.274	.329	.315
1991	Cle-A	437	5	.238	.273	.318	221	1	.290	.328	.357	216	4	.185	.217	.278	131	2	.198	.239	.298	306	3	.255	.288	.327	182	3	.214	.253	.302	80	0	.188	.226	.225
1992	SF-N	248	5	.242	.285	.375	127	3	.213	.239	.370	121	2	.273	.331	.380	116	2	.302	.333	.431	132	3	.189	.243	.326	123	1	.252	.291	.358	41	1	.244	.319	.366
1993	Hou-N	129	6	.256	.333	.488	65	6	.277	.333	.662	64	0	.234	.333	.313	103	6	.243	.310	.524	26	0	.308	.419	.346	56	2	.304	.397	.518	29	2	.276	.400	.586
1993	Tex-A	31	0	.355	.412	.677	0	0	—	—	—	31	0	.355	.412	.677	15	2	.267	.313	.733	16	1	.438	.500	.625	13	1	.385	.429	.692	8	1	.500	.500	.875
1994	Tex-A	133	7	.256	.361	.534	60	4	.233	.351	.533	73	3	.274	.369	.534	63	5	.349	.434	.762	70	2	.171	.293	.329	57	1	.175	.319	.333	22	1	.182	.308	.364
TOTALS		2958	88	.261	.307	.414	1409	46	.272	.318	.437	1549	42	.251	.296	.393	1086	45	.270	.319	.467	1872	43	.256	.300	.384	1354	33	.255	.303	.387	499	12	.246	.307	.361
■ Stan Javier BB/TR																																				
1984	NY-A	7	0	.143	.143	.143	6	0	.000	.000	.000	1	0	1.000	1.000	1.000	5	0	.000	.000	.000	2	0	.500	.500	.500	2	0	.000	.000	.000	2	0	.000	.000	.000
1986	Oak-A	114	0	.202	.305	.272	56	0	.214	.371	.268	58	0	.190	.230	.276	50	0	.160	.250	.240	64	0	.234	.347	.297	43	0	.256	.396	.349	17	0	.176	.222	.235
1987	Oak-A	151	2	.185	.276	.258	87	1	.264	.354	.345	64	1	.078	.169	.141	85	1	.165	.253	.212	66	1	.212	.307	.318	66	1	.182	.280	.242	19	0	.158	.304	.263
1988	Oak-A	397	2	.257	.313	.320	176	0	.261	.323	.307	221	2	.253	.305	.330	91	1	.253	.277	.308	306	1	.258	.324	.324	182	0	.247	.307	.302	77	1	.260	.329	.351
1989	Oak-A	310	1	.248	.317	.316	138	1	.225	.319	.290	172	0	.267	.315	.337	74	1	.230	.278	.311	236	0	.254	.328	.318	144	1	.257	.335	.340	61	0	.295	.394	.393
1990	Oak-A	33	0	.242	.306	.364	23	0	.261	.346	.348	10	0	.200	.200	.400	5	0	.400	.400	.800	28	0	.214	.290	.286	14	0	.143	.250	.286	11	0	.091	.167	.273
1990	LA-N	276	3	.304	.364	.399	138	1	.290	.369	.348	138	2	.319	.399	.449	119	1	.311	.401	.387	157	2	.299	.371	.408	104	0	.317	.371	.365	52	0	.250	.339	.269
1991	LA-N	176	1	.205	.268	.284	83	0	.205	.292	.229	93	1	.204	.245	.333	97	1	.247	.315	.320	79	1	.152	.209	.241	75	0	.173	.264	.200	47	1	.170	.235	.277
1992	LA-N	58	1	.190	.277	.293	25	1	.160	.250	.320	33	0	.212	.297	.273	22	0	.227	.320	.273	36	1	.167	.250	.306	36	1	.167	.250	.306	23	0	.087	.160	.130
1992	Phi-N	276	0	.261	.338	.319	125	0	.296	.355	.376	151	0	.232	.324	.272	124	0	.218	.276	.290	152	0	.296	.384	.342	104	0	.298	.353	.394	41	0	.195	.286	.220
1993	Cal-A	237	3	.291	.362	.405	88	0	.318	.396	.375	149	3	.275	.341	.423	85	1	.271	.357	.376	152	2	.303	.365	.421	98	1	.286	.330	.439	53	0	.264	.365	.340
1994	Oak-A	419	10	.272	.349	.399	191	2	.267	.363	.330	228	9	.276	.336	.456	154	3	.318	.386	.461	265	7	.245	.328	.362	168	6	.284	.359	.443	51	1	.216	.311	.294
TOTALS		2454	23	.255	.328	.341	1136	5	.260	.344	.321	1318	18	.250	.314	.357	911	8	.251	.321	.337	1543	15	.257	.333	.343	1037	10	.258	.330	.351	454	3	.222	.310	.297
■ Gregg Jefferies BB/TR																																				
1987	NY-N	6	0	.500	.500	.667	4	0	.750	.750	1.000	2	0	.000	.000	.000	2	0	.500	.500	.500	4	0	.500	.500	.750	4	0	.500	.500	.750	2	0	.000	.000	.000
1988	NY-N	109	6	.321	.364	.596	67	3	.328	.352	.567	42	3	.310	.383	.643	36	4	.306	.342	.722	73	2	.329	.375	.534	48	2	.333	.377	.563	17	2	.412	.412	.765
1989	NY-N	508	12	.258	.314	.392	237	7	.287	.357	.464	271	5	.232	.274	.320	174	5	.253	.294	.402	334	7	.260	.324	.386	192	3	.245	.318	.365	80	0	.162	.212	.213
1990	NY-N	604	15	.283	.337	.434	311	9	.318	.380	.495	293	6	.246	.290	.369	222	5	.266	.308	.419	382	10	.293	.353	.442	252	4	.282	.327	.421	98	0	.286	.333	.327
1991	NY-N	486	9	.272	.336	.374	244	5	.295	.371	.406	242	4	.248	.300	.343	174	1	.293	.353	.379	312	8	.260	.328	.372	222	4	.288	.351	.387	85	2	.271	.380	.365
1992	KC-A	604	10	.285	.329	.404	280	4	.289	.346	.396	324	6	.281	.313	.410	179	3	.257	.282	.363	425	7	.296	.348	.421	262	3	.271	.308	.370	110	1	.282	.333	.355
1993	StL-N	544	16	.342	.408	.485	249	10	.341	.417	.518	295	6	.342	.401	.458	148	8	.351	.394	.568	396	8	.338	.414	.455	269	8	.346	.425	.461	87	2	.402	.465	.506
1994	StL-N	397	12	.325	.391	.489	201	7	.343	.414	.537	196	5	.306	.368	.439	123	2	.301	.350	.423	274	10	.336	.410	.518	178	7	.360	.443	.545	49	1	.204	.391	.367
TOTALS		3258	80	.294	.352	.434	1593	44	.313	.379	.473	1665	36	.276	.325	.397	1058	28	.284	.327	.435	2200	52	.299	.363	.435	1427	31	.300	.362	.427	528	8	.278	.353	.367
■ Steve Jeltz BB/TR																																				
1984	Phi-N	68	1	.206	.276	.279	36	0	.167	.244	.222	32	1	.250	.314	.344	19	1	.211	.273	.368	49	0	.204	.278	.245	24	0	.250	.345	.333	5	0	.000	.000	.000
1985	Phi-N	196	0	.189	.273	.219	99	0	.202	.273	.263	97	0	.175	.292	.175	62	0	.194	.324	.226	134	0	.187	.262	.216	91	0	.220	.364	.242	26	0	.154	.345	.192
1986	Phi-N	439	0	.219	.320	.272	226	0	.217	.301	.279	213	0	.221	.339	.244	140	0	.221	.314	.257	299	0	.217	.322	.264	189	0	.212	.320	.280	66	0	.242	.412	.273
1987	Phi-N	293	0	.232	.324	.304	163	0	.209	.303	.270	130	0	.262	.351	.346	80	0	.175	.258	.262	213	0	.254	.348	.319	128	0	.172	.274	.250	36	0	.222	.349	.361
1988	Phi-N	379	1	.187	.295	.237	184	0	.179	.288	.239	195	1	.195	.303	.236	79	0	.152	.287	.203	300	1	.197	.298	.247	166	0	.229	.326	.271	56	0	.143	.286	.196
1989	Phi-N	263	4	.243	.356	.358	130	1	.277	.377	.400	133	1	.211	.335	.278	71	0	.268	.409	.366	192	3	.234	.335	.328	106	3	.292	.385	.425	62	1	.194	.306	.242
1990	KC-A	103	0	.155	.200	.194	42	0	.190	.255	.214	61	0	.131	.159	.180	32	0	.250	.294	.313	71	0	.113	.158	.141	42	0	.238	.267	.310	15	0	.200	.250	.200
TOTALS		1741	5	.210	.308	.267	880	3	.211	.302	.280	861	2	.209	.314	.254	483	2	.207	.314	.269	1258	3	.211	.306	.266	746	3	.224	.322	.295	266	1	.192	.318	.244
■ Cliff Johnson BR/TR																																				
1984	Tor-A	359	16	.304	.390	.507	164	3	.311	.399	.433	195	13	.297	.383	.569	180	6	.317	.422	.511	179	10	.291	.355	.503	172	6	.308	.402	.459	78	2	.333	.429	.462
1985	Tex-A	296	12	.257	.330	.443	130	8	.254	.344	.492	166	4	.259	.319	.404	70	1	.329	.412	.457	226	11	.235	.304	.438	127	6	.307	.377	.535	44	1	.341	.388	.523
1985	Tor-A	73	1	.274	.349	.315	31	0	.323	.364	.323	42	1	.238	.340	.310	42	1	.333	.429	.405	31	0	.194	.235	.194	35	0	.400	.400	.400	13	0	.077	.077	.077
1986	Tor-A	336	15	.250	.355	.426	174	11	.270	.365	.494	162	4	.228	.346	.352	107	8	.290	.408	.579	229	7	.231	.330	.354	150	8	.273	.376	.467	73	3	.329	.405	.514
TOTALS		1064	44	.272	.360	.450	510	23	.276	.369	.459	554	21	.267	.352	.442	399	16	.313	.417	.509	665	28	.247	.324	.415	484	20	.304	.390	.477	205	6	.317	.392	.468
■ Howard Johnson BB/TR																																				
1984	Det-A	355	12	.248	.324	.394	180	4	.222	.316	.322	175	8	.274	.333	.469	97	2	.227	.269	.351	258	10	.256	.344	.411	157	7	.236	.330	.414	58	3	.172	.238	.362
1985	NY-N	389	11	.242	.300	.393	188	5	.229	.297	.367	201	6	.254	.303	.418	77	3	.156	.241	.299	312	8	.263	.315	.417	181	4	.227	.304	.348	71	4	.239	.333	.479
1986	NY-N	220	10	.245	.341	.445	92	5	.217	.345	.457	128	5	.266	.338	.438	47	2	.213	.339	.404	173	8	.254	.342	.457	95	5	.284	.398	.526	60	3	.217	.266	.383
1987	NY-N	554	36	.265	.364	.504	271	13	.262	.364	.450	283	23	.269	.365	.555	194	15	.289	.376	.552	360	21	.253	.358	.478	248	15	.306	.405	.548	91	7	.363	.450	.659
1988	NY-N	495	24	.230	.343	.422	221	9	.213	.339	.389	274	15	.245	.346	.449	142	6	.183	.304	.338	353	18	.249	.359	.456	210	7	.200	.341	.333	80	6	.262	.410	.525

YEAR	TM/L	TOTAL					HOME					AWAY					LEFT					RIGHT					ON-BASE					LATE/CLOSE				
		AB	HR	AVG	OBP	SLG	AB	HR	AVG	OBP	SLG	AB	HR	AVG	OBP	SLG	AB	HR	AVG	OBP	SLG	AB	HR	AVG	OBP	SLG	AB	HR	AVG	OBP	SLG	AB	HR	AVG	OBP	SLG
1989	NY-N	571	36	.287	.369	.559	276	19	.290	.371	.572	295	17	.285	.368	.546	194	7	.278	.383	.464	377	29	.292	.362	.607	233	16	.313	.403	.618	84	5	.250	.388	.488
1990	NY-N	590	23	.244	.319	.434	291	13	.234	.297	.416	299	10	.254	.339	.452	221	6	.208	.296	.344	369	17	.266	.333	.488	250	9	.272	.359	.472	111	4	.252	.300	.423
1991	NY-N	564	38	.259	.342	.535	280	21	.268	.347	.557	284	17	.250	.337	.514	217	14	.253	.320	.498	347	24	.262	.355	.559	266	15	.256	.334	.489	97	6	.247	.339	.515
1992	NY-N	350	7	.223	.309	.337	164	2	.189	.293	.274	186	5	.253	.361	.392	132	4	.227	.340	.379	218	3	.220	.323	.312	164	2	.226	.340	.335	49	1	.245	.415	.367
1993	NY-N	235	7	.238	.354	.379	116	3	.207	.313	.319	119	4	.269	.390	.437	68	0	.162	.269	.206	167	7	.269	.386	.449	47	0	.298	.370	.319					
1994	Col-N	227	10	.211	.323	.405	90	3	.278	.391	.489	137	7	.168	.277	.350	34	1	.176	.300	.353	193	9	.218	.328	.415	111	6	.243	.351	.486	55	2	.145	.254	.291
TOTALS		4550	214	.249	.339	.452	2169	97	.242	.334	.432	2381	117	.256	.344	.469	1423	60	.230	.323	.408	3127	154	.257	.346	.471	2020	88	.258	.358	.457	803	41	.250	.349	.457

■ Lance Johnson BL/TL

YEAR	TM/L	TOTAL					HOME					AWAY					LEFT					RIGHT					ON-BASE					LATE/CLOSE				
		AB	HR	AVG	OBP	SLG	AB	HR	AVG	OBP	SLG	AB	HR	AVG	OBP	SLG	AB	HR	AVG	OBP	SLG	AB	HR	AVG	OBP	SLG	AB	HR	AVG	OBP	SLG	AB	HR	AVG	OBP	SLG
1987	StL-N	59	0	.220	.270	.288	42	0	.262	.295	.333	17	0	.118	.211	.176	6	0	.167	.167	.167	53	0	.226	.281	.302	25	0	.240	.269	.320	12	0	.167	.231	.167
1988	Chi-A	124	0	.185	.223	.234	63	0	.143	.194	.175	61	0	.230	.254	.295	22	0	.091	.130	.091	102	0	.206	.243	.265	36	0	.167	.189	.194	16	0	.188	.278	.188
1989	Chi-A	180	0	.300	.360	.367	84	0	.274	.330	.369	96	0	.323	.387	.365	58	0	.259	.306	.328	122	0	.320	.385	.385	66	0	.364	.408	.424	34	0	.235	.297	.265
1990	Chi-A	541	1	.285	.325	.357	265	0	.302	.336	.381	276	1	.268	.314	.333	156	0	.321	.353	.378	385	1	.270	.313	.348	211	1	.318	.339	.412	85	0	.271	.330	.376
1991	Chi-A	588	0	.274	.304	.342	286	0	.266	.298	.325	302	0	.281	.310	.358	164	0	.244	.291	.274	424	0	.285	.309	.368	246	0	.252	.300	.301	113	0	.212	.244	.257
1992	Chi-A	567	3	.279	.318	.363	274	2	.263	.312	.339	293	1	.294	.324	.386	158	0	.266	.302	.310	409	3	.284	.324	.384	248	0	.258	.300	.339	94	0	.223	.286	.234
1993	Chi-A	540	0	.311	.354	.396	259	0	.320	.369	.386	281	0	.302	.340	.406	147	0	.272	.318	.333	393	0	.326	.368	.420	230	0	.339	.382	.430	84	0	.274	.337	.393
1994	Chi-A	412	3	.277	.321	.393	201	1	.254	.301	.353	211	2	.299	.339	.431	131	1	.298	.338	.382	281	2	.267	.312	.399	205	2	.278	.326	.385	63	1	.270	.333	.444
TOTALS		3011	7	.281	.321	.361	1474	3	.275	.318	.349	1537	4	.286	.325	.373	842	1	.272	.313	.325	2169	6	.284	.324	.375	1267	3	.287	.327	.368	501	1	.242	.298	.315

■ Felix Jose BB/TR

YEAR	TM/L	TOTAL					HOME					AWAY					LEFT					RIGHT					ON-BASE					LATE/CLOSE				
		AB	HR	AVG	OBP	SLG	AB	HR	AVG	OBP	SLG	AB	HR	AVG	OBP	SLG	AB	HR	AVG	OBP	SLG	AB	HR	AVG	OBP	SLG	AB	HR	AVG	OBP	SLG	AB	HR	AVG	OBP	SLG
1988	Oak-A	6	0	.333	.333	.500	2	0	.500	.500	1.000	4	0	.250	.250	.250	2	0	.000	.000	.000	4	0	.500	.500	.750	2	0	.000	.000	.000	3	0	.333	.333	.333
1989	Oak-A	57	0	.193	.246	.228	34	0	.235	.235	.294	23	0	.130	.259	.130	21	0	.333	.364	.429	36	0	.111	.179	.111	24	0	.250	.250	.333	7	0	.000	.000	.000
1990	Oak-A	341	8	.264	.306	.370	180	3	.228	.286	.371	161	5	.304	.329	.435	63	1	.317	.362	.413	278	7	.252	.293	.360	156	6	.308	.335	.462	41	1	.293	.326	.390
1990	StL-N	85	3	.271	.333	.447	30	2	.267	.353	.567	55	1	.273	.322	.382	40	1	.275	.326	.450	45	2	.267	.340	.444	47	1	.277	.292	.404	12	0	.083	.214	.083
1991	StL-N	568	8	.305	.360	.438	280	3	.296	.353	.421	288	5	.313	.367	.455	262	3	.294	.354	.405	306	6	.310	.365	.467	270	5	.322	.384	.489	91	3	.352	.417	.538
1992	StL-N	509	14	.295	.347	.432	255	12	.294	.354	.482	254	2	.295	.339	.382	182	6	.374	.419	.555	327	8	.251	.306	.364	224	4	.277	.340	.388	113	4	.319	.374	.478
1993	KC-A	499	6	.253	.303	.349	238	2	.269	.327	.370	261	4	.238	.281	.330	64	0	.094	.134	.109	435	6	.276	.327	.384	187	4	.257	.312	.369	81	1	.210	.273	.284
1994	KC-A	366	11	.303	.362	.475	200	1	.295	.360	.420	166	10	.313	.365	.542	105	3	.324	.363	.514	261	8	.295	.362	.460	166	5	.325	.377	.488	61	4	.361	.426	.639
TOTALS		2431	50	.282	.335	.410	1219	23	.278	.337	.409	1212	27	.286	.333	.412	739	13	.303	.352	.434	1692	37	.273	.328	.400	1076	25	.296	.347	.435	409	13	.296	.356	.447

■ Wally Joyner BL/TL

YEAR	TM/L	TOTAL					HOME					AWAY					LEFT					RIGHT					ON-BASE					LATE/CLOSE				
		AB	HR	AVG	OBP	SLG	AB	HR	AVG	OBP	SLG	AB	HR	AVG	OBP	SLG	AB	HR	AVG	OBP	SLG	AB	HR	AVG	OBP	SLG	AB	HR	AVG	OBP	SLG	AB	HR	AVG	OBP	SLG
1986	Cal-A	593	22	.290	.348	.457	294	11	.279	.347	.432	299	11	.301	.348	.482	192	6	.234	.289	.354	401	16	.317	.375	.506	275	9	.320	.382	.476	86	2	.314	.398	.488
1987	Cal-A	564	34	.285	.366	.528	307	19	.261	.336	.505	257	15	.315	.399	.556	201	8	.284	.347	.478	363	26	.287	.376	.556	265	13	.309	.401	.547	102	2	.186	.282	.304
1988	Cal-A	597	13	.295	.356	.419	290	6	.279	.339	.420	307	7	.309	.372	.433	212	1	.264	.309	.321	385	12	.312	.381	.473	281	9	.292	.369	.438	108	3	.343	.424	.472
1989	Cal-A	593	16	.282	.335	.420	286	8	.273	.332	.406	307	8	.290	.338	.433	206	6	.262	.305	.379	387	10	.292	.351	.442	259	5	.297	.362	.417	97	2	.247	.290	.340
1990	Cal-A	310	8	.268	.350	.394	135	5	.274	.367	.422	175	3	.263	.337	.371	106	2	.226	.291	.302	204	6	.289	.379	.441	125	2	.312	.372	.424	55	2	.236	.283	.436
1991	Cal-A	551	21	.301	.360	.488	268	10	.276	.343	.448	283	11	.325	.375	.527	189	5	.275	.308	.444	362	16	.315	.384	.511	243	9	.321	.382	.490	69	3	.304	.377	.507
1992	KC-A	572	9	.269	.336	.386	282	1	.266	.324	.358	290	8	.272	.349	.414	192	2	.240	.307	.339	380	7	.284	.352	.411	261	5	.287	.358	.418	105	3	.238	.298	.362
1993	KC-A	497	15	.292	.375	.467	256	4	.320	.389	.488	241	11	.261	.360	.444	166	2	.259	.340	.367	331	13	.308	.392	.517	219	4	.297	.398	.429	83	3	.325	.440	.494
1994	KC-A	363	8	.311	.386	.449	192	2	.359	.418	.484	171	6	.257	.349	.409	124	1	.306	.367	.379	239	7	.314	.395	.485	167	4	.341	.410	.455	50	0	.320	.414	.380
TOTALS		4640	146	.286	.356	.447	2310	66	.285	.351	.438	2330	80	.291	.360	.457	1588	33	.261	.317	.377	3052	113	.302	.375	.484	2095	60	.307	.381	.457	755	20	.277	.355	.416

■ David Justice BL/TL

YEAR	TM/L	TOTAL					HOME					AWAY					LEFT					RIGHT					ON-BASE					LATE/CLOSE				
		AB	HR	AVG	OBP	SLG	AB	HR	AVG	OBP	SLG	AB	HR	AVG	OBP	SLG	AB	HR	AVG	OBP	SLG	AB	HR	AVG	OBP	SLG	AB	HR	AVG	OBP	SLG	AB	HR	AVG	OBP	SLG
1989	Atl-N	51	1	.235	.291	.353	37	1	.243	.282	.405	14	0	.214	.313	.214	10	0	.100	.100	.100	41	1	.268	.333	.415	18	0	.278	.350	.389	8	0	.125	.125	.125
1990	Atl-N	439	28	.282	.373	.535	225	19	.320	.405	.662	214	9	.243	.340	.402	131	10	.366	.443	.656	308	18	.247	.344	.484	188	11	.351	.425	.601	62	4	.290	.371	.516
1991	Atl-N	396	21	.275	.377	.503	175	11	.269	.371	.537	221	10	.281	.382	.475	155	7	.277	.333	.465	241	14	.274	.403	.527	196	11	.316	.435	.556	58	2	.259	.386	.466
1992	Atl-N	484	21	.256	.359	.446	245	10	.229	.346	.420	239	11	.285	.373	.473	159	5	.283	.352	.447	325	16	.243	.362	.446	230	13	.291	.415	.526	77	3	.247	.314	.429
1993	Atl-N	585	40	.270	.357	.515	290	18	.272	.348	.486	295	22	.268	.365	.542	177	11	.294	.362	.508	408	29	.260	.354	.517	273	20	.297	.401	.553	91	7	.242	.343	.516
1994	Atl-N	352	19	.313	.427	.531	173	9	.335	.436	.549	179	10	.291	.418	.514	122	4	.287	.416	.451	230	15	.326	.433	.574	143	6	.336	.467	.524	49	4	.245	.356	.490
TOTALS		2307	130	.276	.374	.501	1145	68	.280	.374	.521	1162	62	.272	.373	.481	754	37	.297	.375	.497	1553	93	.266	.373	.503	1048	61	.314	.423	.550	345	20	.252	.347	.475

■ Eric Karros BR/TR

YEAR	TM/L	TOTAL					HOME					AWAY					LEFT					RIGHT					ON-BASE					LATE/CLOSE				
		AB	HR	AVG	OBP	SLG	AB	HR	AVG	OBP	SLG	AB	HR	AVG	OBP	SLG	AB	HR	AVG	OBP	SLG	AB	HR	AVG	OBP	SLG	AB	HR	AVG	OBP	SLG	AB	HR	AVG	OBP	SLG
1991	LA-N	14	0	.071	.133	.143	6	0	.167	.286	.333	8	0	.000	.000	.000	10	0	.000	.091	.000	4	0	.250	.250	.500	6	0	.167	.286	.333	2	0	.500	.667	1.000
1992	LA-N	545	20	.257	.304	.426	251	6	.259	.320	.394	294	14	.255	.289	.452	213	8	.277	.325	.437	332	12	.244	.291	.419	261	9	.245	.306	.428	98	4	.245	.308	.429
1993	LA-N	619	23	.247	.287	.409	303	13	.231	.279	.403	316	10	.263	.295	.415	170	5	.312	.343	.494	449	18	.223	.267	.376	297	9	.239	.282	.370	121	4	.182	.227	.306
1994	LA-N	406	14	.266	.310	.426	191	5	.267	.313	.377	215	9	.265	.308	.470	102	4	.265	.331	.412	304	10	.266	.303	.431	167	3	.246	.297	.335	72	2	.208	.241	.306
TOTALS		1584	57	.254	.298	.417	751	24	.249	.302	.393	833	33	.258	.294	.438	495	17	.281	.327	.442	1089	40	.242	.284	.405	731	21	.242	.294	.379	293	10	.212	.262	.352

■ Bobby Kelly BR/TR

YEAR	TM/L	TOTAL					HOME					AWAY					LEFT					RIGHT					ON-BASE					LATE/CLOSE				
		AB	HR	AVG	OBP	SLG	AB	HR	AVG	OBP	SLG	AB	HR	AVG	OBP	SLG	AB	HR	AVG	OBP	SLG	AB	HR	AVG	OBP	SLG	AB	HR	AVG	OBP	SLG	AB	HR	AVG	OBP	SLG
1987	NY-A	52	1	.269	.328	.385	29	0	.207	.303	.241	23	1	.348	.360	.565	33	1	.242	.333	.424	19	0	.316	.316	.316	21	1	.286	.304	.476	10	0	.300	.300	.400
1988	NY-A	77	1	.247	.272	.364	49	1	.245	.275	.388	28	0	.250	.267	.321	54	0	.241	.268	.296	23	1	.261	.280	.522	33	0	.242	.278	.303	8	0	.000	.100	.000
1989	NY-A*	441	9	.302	.369	.417	205	2	.317	.397	.405	236	7	.288	.344	.428	145	3	.372	.424	.497	296	6	.267	.342	.378	186	1	.306	.371	.392	79	2	.329	.398	.468
1990	NY-A	641	15	.285	.323	.418	315	5	.305	.334	.435	326	10	.267	.311	.402	181	5	.304	.352	.442	460	10	.278	.311	.409	220	5	.282	.314	.405	111	4	.261	.311	.432
1991	NY-A	486	20	.267	.333	.444	232	11	.310	.369	.500	254	9	.228	.301	.394	159	9	.296	.372	.503	327	11	.254	.313	.416	210	7	.295	.354	.467	81	6	.272	.352	.519
1992	NY-A	580	10	.272	.322	.384	296	6	.257	.309	.378	284	4	.289	.336	.391	184	4	.277	.344	.391	396	6	.270	.310	.381	254	4	.295	.360	.370	106	2	.236	.287	.340
1993	Cin-N	320	9	.319	.354	.475	152	4	.296	.337	.421	168	5	.339	.369	.524	96	3	.250	.280	.427	224	6	.348	.384	.496	136	1	.324	.371	.397	43	0	.256	.292	.279
1994	Cin-N	179	3	.302	.351	.397	77	1	.234	.294	.325	102	2	.353	.394	.451	41	0	.293	.341	.317	138	3	.304	.353	.420	82	1	.354	.386	.512	27	0	.296	.367	.407
1994	Atl-N	255	6	.286	.345	.439	128	3	.281	.340	.414	127	3	.291	.350	.465	67	2	.299	.373	.448	188	4	.282	.335	.436	88	3	.330	.378	.489	34	2	.441	.444	.735
TOTALS		3031	74	.286	.337	.420	1483	33	.287	.340	.415	1548	41	.284	.334	.425	960	27	.296	.354	.435	2071	47	.281	.328	.413	1230	22	.296	.342	.417	499	16	.279	.333	.431

■ Terry Kennedy BL/TR

YEAR	TM/L	TOTAL					HOME					AWAY					LEFT					RIGHT					ON-BASE					LATE/CLOSE				
		AB	HR	AVG	OBP	SLG	AB	HR	AVG	OBP	SLG	AB	HR	AVG	OBP	SLG	AB	HR	AVG	OBP	SLG	AB	HR	AVG	OBP	SLG	AB	HR	AVG	OBP	SLG	AB	HR	AVG	OBP	SLG
1984	SD-N	530	14	.240	.284	.353	272	8	.235	.275	.371	258	6	.244	.294	.334	160	4	.188	.206	.287	370	10	.262	.316	.381	236	4	.233	.287	.335	96	1	.240	.291	.292
1985	SD-N	532	10	.261	.301	.372	279	7	.233	.274	.358	253	3	.292	.331	.387	147	3	.259	.283	.374	385	7	.262	.308	.371	257	5	.288	.332	.401	97	1	.278	.346	.351
1986	SD-N	432	12	.264	.324	.403	214	7	.280	.346	.421	218	5	.248	.302	.385	96	3	.229	.288	.396	336	9	.274	.334	.405	166	5	.271	.358	.410	90	2	.289	.379	.422
1987	Bal-A	512	18	.250	.299	.385	240	11	.213	.279	.383	272	7	.283	.318	.386	183	6	.219	.255	.339	329	12	.267	.323	.410	218	6	.239	.308	.362	74	6	.243	.341	.527
1988	Bal-A	265	3	.226	.269	.298	136	2	.176	.211	.243	129	1	.279	.326	.357	39	1	.231	.268	.308	226	2	.226	.269	.296	100	0	.185	.231	.222	36	1	.167	.231	.278
1989	SF-N	355	5	.239	.306	.324	172	1	.267	.332	.326	183	4	.213	.282	.322	39	0	.154	.233	.205	316	5	.250	.315	.339	136	1	.250	.346	.309	51	1	.235	.371	.333
1990	SF-N	303	2	.277	.342	.370	148	2	.291	.369	.399	155	0	.265	.315	.342	32	0	.188	.257	.219	271	2	.288	.352	.387	119	2	.286	.360	.420	45	0	.378	.417	.422
1991	SF-N	171	2	.234	.283	.339	75	2	.240	.287	.413	96	1	.229	.279	.281	10	1	.300	.273	.800	161	2	.230	.283	.311	79	1	.215	.321	.392	28	1	.179	.226	.321
TOTALS		3100	67	.251	.302	.361	1536	40	.242	.297	.366	1564	27	.260	.308	.357	706	18	.218	.254	.334	2394	49	.253	.319	.361	1314	25	.253	.334	.369	517	13	.259	.336	.375

■ Jeff Kent BR/TR

YEAR	TM/L	TOTAL					HOME					AWAY					LEFT					RIGHT					ON-BASE					LATE/CLOSE				
		AB	HR	AVG	OBP	SLG	AB	HR	AVG	OBP	SLG	AB	HR	AVG	OBP	SLG	AB	HR	AVG	OBP	SLG	AB	HR	AVG	OBP	SLG	AB	HR	AVG	OBP	SLG	AB	HR	AVG	OBP	SLG
1992	Tor-A	192	2	.240	.324	.443	99	2	.232	.328	.394	93	0	.247	.321	.495	48	2	.250	.327	.438	144	6	.236	.323	.444	90	4	.211	.279	.422	28	1	.250	.276	.607
1992	NY-N	113	3	.239	.289	.407	68	2	.250	.301	.426	45	1	.222	.271	.378	44	1	.182	.250	.295	69	2	.275	.315	.478	20	2	.267	.302	.500	20	2	.400	.455	.750
1993	NY-N	496	21	.270	.320	.446	247	9	.275	.319	.437	249	12	.265	.320	.454	148	0	.230	.277	.291	348	21	.287	.338	.511	216	12	.296	.347	.500	101	4	.208	.252	.347
1994	NY-N	415	14	.292	.341	.475	188	10	.319	.360	.580	227	4	.269	.327	.388	110	4	.373	.434	.582	305	10	.262	.307	.436	170	7	.353	.411	.582	84	5	.274	.322	.500
TOTALS		1216	40	.270	.325	.451	602	23	.279	.331	.473	614	23	.261	.319	.430	350	7	.271	.331	.403	866	39	.269	.323	.471	536	25	.297	.351	.513	233	13	.253	.298	.468

■ Jeff King BR/TR

YEAR	TM/L	TOTAL					HOME					AWAY					LEFT					RIGHT					ON-BASE					LATE/CLOSE				
		AB	HR	AVG	OBP	SLG	AB	HR	AVG	OBP	SLG	AB	HR	AVG	OBP	SLG	AB	HR	AVG	OBP	SLG	AB	HR	AVG	OBP	SLG	AB	HR	AVG	OBP	SLG	AB	HR	AVG	OBP	SLG
1989	Pit-N	215	5	.195	.266	.353	119	3	.185	.252	.345	96	2	.208	.282	.365	112	0	.196	.279	.321	103	5	.194	.250	.388	97	1	.134	.200	.237	42	2	.262	.340	.524
1990	Pit-N	371	14	.245	.283	.410	179	9	.274	.304	.475	192	5	.219	.263	.349	231	9	.264	.303	.446	140	5	.214	.248	.350	158	6	.222	.274	.380	60	0	.117	.172	.133
1991	Pit-N	109	4	.239	.328	.376	63	3	.222	.310	.413	46	1	.261	.352	.326	31	1	.323	.500	.419	78	3	.205	.241	.359	47	3	.298	.382	.553	16	1	.250	.333	.438
1992	Pit-N	480	14	.231	.272	.371	247	6	.239	.280	.360	233	8	.223	.264	.382	216	6	.236	.277	.394	264	8	.227	.269	.352	227	2	.225	.273	.308	93	3	.215	.263	.333
1993	Pit-N	611	9	.295	.356	.406	297	4	.306	.366	.428	314	5	.283	.347	.385	188	4	.324	.383	.463	423	5	.281	.345	.381	308	5	.289	.351	.399	105	0	.257	.339	.295
1994	Pit-N	339	5	.263	.316	.375	184	2	.288	.338	.408	155	3	.232	.291	.335	86	2	.244	.323	.384	253	3	.269	.314	.372	146	1	.261	.308	.339	46	1	.261	.308	.320
TOTALS		2125	51	.254	.308	.387	1089	27	.264	.317	.407	1036	24	.242	.299	.366	864	22	.262	.322	.413	1261	29	.248	.299	.369	983	18	.242	.299	.361	362	7	.224	.289	.320

■ Mike Kingery BL/TL

YEAR	TM/L	TOTAL					HOME					AWAY					LEFT					RIGHT					ON-BASE					LATE/CLOSE				
		AB	HR	AVG	OBP	SLG	AB	HR	AVG	OBP	SLG	AB	HR	AVG	OBP	SLG	AB	HR	AVG	OBP	SLG	AB	HR	AVG	OBP	SLG	AB	HR	AVG	OBP	SLG	AB	HR	AVG	OBP	SLG
1986	KC-A	209	3	.258	.296	.388	115	1	.278	.309	.400	94	2	.234	.280	.372	30	0	.067	.121	.067	179	3	.291	.326	.441	85	1	.259	.293	.318	37	0	.216	.237	.378
1987	Sea-A	354	9	.280	.329	.449	174	5	.305	.349	.523	180	4	.256	.310	.378	39	1	.179	.200	.282	315	8	.292	.344	.470	151	4	.265	.313	.450	40	1	.250	.333	.450
1988	Sea-A	123	1	.203	.313	.276	62	1	.194	.296	.323	61	0	.213	.329	.230	3	0	.000	.400	.000	120	1	.208	.309	.283	53	0	.189	.267	.226	18	0	.167	.348	.167
1989	Sea-A	76	2	.224	.285	.342	47	2	.213	.255	.362	29	0	.241	.333	.310	2	0	.500	.500	.500	74	2	.216	.280	.338	28	0	.143	.219	.143	16	0	.188	.278	.250
1990	SF-N	207	0	.295	.335	.338	107	0	.271	.333	.318	100	0	.320	.337	.360	25	0	.400	.444	.440	182	0	.280	.320	.324	80	0	.338	.361	.463	11	0	.333	.361	.333
1991	SF-N	110	0	.182	.280	.236	53	0	.189	.283	.264	57	0	.175	.277	.211	13	0	.077	.143	.231	97	0	.196	.297	.237	57	0	.193	.281	.228	32	0	.219	.359	.281
1992	Oak-A	28	0	.107	.138	.107	8	0	.000	.111	.000	20	0	.150	.150	.150	1	0	.000	.000	.000	27	0	.111	.143	.111	13	0	.154	.214	.154	7	0	.143	.143	.143

YEAR	TM/L	TOTAL					HOME					AWAY					LEFT					RIGHT					ON-BASE					LATE/CLOSE				
		AB	HR	AVG	OBP	SLG	AB	HR	AVG	OBP	SLG	AB	HR	AVG	OBP	SLG	AB	HR	AVG	OBP	SLG	AB	HR	AVG	OBP	SLG	AB	HR	AVG	OBP	SLG	AB	HR	AVG	OBP	SLG
1994	Col-N	301	4	.349	.402	.532	138	0	.333	.381	.507	163	4	.362	.419	.552	37	1	.378	.415	.486	264	3	.345	.400	.538	132	2	.318	.364	.455	58	1	.310	.365	.534
TOTALS		1408	19	.273	.330	.397	704	9	.273	.328	.415	704	10	.273	.332	.379	150	2	.233	.282	.307	1258	17	.277	.335	.408	607	7	.282	.334	.381	241	2	.253	.327	.378

■ Dave Kingman BR/TR

YEAR	TM/L	TOTAL					HOME					AWAY					LEFT					RIGHT					ON-BASE					LATE/CLOSE				
		AB	HR	AVG	OBP	SLG	AB	HR	AVG	OBP	SLG	AB	HR	AVG	OBP	SLG	AB	HR	AVG	OBP	SLG	AB	HR	AVG	OBP	SLG	AB	HR	AVG	OBP	SLG	AB	HR	AVG	OBP	SLG
1984	Oak-A	549	35	.268	.321	.505	279	19	.272	.328	.509	270	16	.263	.315	.500	178	9	.270	.345	.472	371	26	.267	.310	.520	257	24	.307	.349	.638	86	6	.256	.298	.488
1985	Oak-A	592	30	.238	.309	.417	278	14	.223	.312	.410	314	16	.252	.305	.424	176	13	.244	.295	.483	416	17	.236	.302	.389	283	12	.226	.295	.385	77	6	.234	.348	.468
1986	Oak-A	561	35	.210	.255	.431	297	15	.212	.244	.391	264	20	.208	.266	.477	173	14	.220	.277	.509	388	21	.206	.245	.397	256	10	.223	.256	.375	85	4	.200	.250	.412
TOTALS		1702	100	.239	.296	.450	854	48	.235	.295	.436	848	52	.242	.296	.465	527	36	.245	.317	.488	1175	64	.236	.286	.433	796	46	.251	.301	.464	248	18	.230	.299	.456

■ Ron Kittle BR/TR

YEAR	TM/L	TOTAL					HOME					AWAY					LEFT					RIGHT					ON-BASE					LATE/CLOSE				
		AB	HR	AVG	OBP	SLG	AB	HR	AVG	OBP	SLG	AB	HR	AVG	OBP	SLG	AB	HR	AVG	OBP	SLG	AB	HR	AVG	OBP	SLG	AB	HR	AVG	OBP	SLG	AB	HR	AVG	OBP	SLG
1984	Chi-A	466	32	.215	.295	.453	236	17	.212	.296	.466	230	15	.217	.295	.439	179	12	.246	.332	.486	287	20	.195	.272	.432	200	17	.250	.319	.550	73	2	.137	.222	.233
1985	Chi-A	379	26	.230	.295	.467	199	12	.241	.300	.462	180	14	.217	.290	.472	148	10	.236	.323	.459	231	16	.225	.276	.472	161	10	.193	.250	.398	48	2	.188	.291	.313
1986	Chi-A	296	17	.213	.282	.422	143	5	.189	.280	.336	153	12	.235	.285	.503	113	3	.159	.262	.283	183	14	.246	.296	.508	143	8	.245	.301	.448	51	2	.216	.276	.373
1986	NY-A	80	4	.237	.292	.412	30	1	.200	.206	.300	50	3	.260	.328	.480	66	4	.197	.250	.409	14	0	.429	.471	.429	43	2	.163	.208	.326	11	1	.091	.091	.364
1987	NY-A	159	12	.277	.318	.535	73	7	.288	.337	.603	86	5	.267	.300	.477	94	6	.309	.368	.553	65	6	.231	.239	.508	68	4	.235	.276	.426	26	0	.231	.333	.231
1988	Cle-A	225	18	.258	.323	.533	85	7	.247	.340	.518	140	11	.264	.312	.543	89	9	.236	.333	.562	136	9	.272	.315	.515	105	6	.248	.317	.448	32	2	.281	.359	.531
1989	Chi-A	169	11	.302	.378	.556	70	6	.271	.338	.586	99	5	.323	.405	.535	55	4	.291	.403	.564	114	7	.307	.364	.553	80	6	.338	.400	.650	26	1	.462	.517	.654
1990	Chi-A	277	16	.245	.311	.469	153	7	.248	.311	.464	124	9	.242	.312	.476	113	11	.257	.333	.602	164	5	.238	.296	.378	117	5	.256	.338	.427	39	2	.205	.326	.385
1990	Bal-A	61	2	.164	.203	.295	32	1	.125	.176	.250	29	1	.207	.233	.345	38	2	.132	.154	.289	23	0	.217	.280	.304	25	0	.120	.120	.120	12	0	.167	.167	.167
1991	Chi-A	47	2	.191	.291	.319	30	0	.200	.273	.200	17	2	.176	.318	.529	16	1	.188	.316	.375	31	1	.194	.278	.290	27	2	.222	.267	.444	6	0	.333	.333	.333
TOTALS		2159	140	.236	.304	.467	1051	63	.228	.300	.450	1108	77	.243	.308	.483	911	62	.234	.318	.474	1248	78	.237	.294	.462	969	60	.238	.300	.459	324	12	.216	.297	.352

■ Ray Knight BR/TR

YEAR	TM/L	TOTAL					HOME					AWAY					LEFT					RIGHT					ON-BASE					LATE/CLOSE				
		AB	HR	AVG	OBP	SLG	AB	HR	AVG	OBP	SLG	AB	HR	AVG	OBP	SLG	AB	HR	AVG	OBP	SLG	AB	HR	AVG	OBP	SLG	AB	HR	AVG	OBP	SLG	AB	HR	AVG	OBP	SLG
1984	Hou-N	278	2	.223	.259	.281	134	1	.239	.278	.321	144	1	.208	.242	.243	101	1	.248	.274	.317	177	1	.209	.251	.260	125	1	.288	.311	.336	56	1	.161	.203	.232
1984	NY-N	93	1	.280	.337	.355	55	1	.236	.300	.327	38	0	.342	.390	.395	35	1	.257	.278	.400	58	0	.293	.369	.328	31	0	.161	.316	.194	15	0	.333	.412	.400
1985	NY-N	271	6	.218	.252	.328	127	4	.197	.234	.339	144	2	.236	.268	.319	170	6	.259	.285	.418	101	0	.149	.198	.178	124	5	.226	.246	.411	55	1	.164	.179	.255
1986	NY-N	486	11	.298	.351	.424	228	7	.289	.353	.452	258	4	.306	.350	.399	197	9	.381	.410	.604	289	2	.242	.314	.301	210	4	.329	.377	.433	83	2	.325	.345	.494
1987	Bal-A	563	14	.256	.310	.373	270	8	.274	.319	.411	293	6	.239	.302	.338	206	8	.218	.293	.354	357	6	.277	.321	.384	262	8	.286	.336	.431	85	2	.329	.376	.424
1988	Det-A	299	3	.217	.271	.301	154	3	.188	.242	.286	145	0	.248	.300	.317	169	3	.219	.256	.325	130	0	.215	.290	.269	139	2	.223	.270	.360	54	0	.241	.293	.296
TOTALS		1990	37	.252	.301	.355	968	24	.247	.298	.374	1022	13	.256	.304	.337	878	28	.268	.307	.415	1112	9	.239	.296	.308	891	20	.274	.319	.396	348	6	.261	.300	.362

■ Chuck Knoblauch BR/TR

YEAR	TM/L	TOTAL					HOME					AWAY					LEFT					RIGHT					ON-BASE					LATE/CLOSE				
		AB	HR	AVG	OBP	SLG	AB	HR	AVG	OBP	SLG	AB	HR	AVG	OBP	SLG	AB	HR	AVG	OBP	SLG	AB	HR	AVG	OBP	SLG	AB	HR	AVG	OBP	SLG	AB	HR	AVG	OBP	SLG
1991	Min-A	565	1	.281	.351	.350	287	1	.328	.391	.415	278	0	.234	.310	.284	148	0	.257	.325	.324	417	1	.290	.360	.360	214	0	.290	.372	.336	78	0	.269	.301	.321
1992	Min-A	600	2	.297	.384	.358	289	0	.287	.388	.318	311	2	.305	.381	.395	124	1	.315	.405	.419	476	1	.292	.379	.342	242	0	.293	.369	.355	95	0	.274	.360	.326
1993	Min-A	602	2	.277	.354	.346	312	2	.298	.369	.362	290	0	.255	.337	.328	156	0	.269	.321	.327	446	2	.280	.365	.352	227	0	.278	.376	.344	89	0	.236	.333	.270
1994	Min-A	445	5	.312	.381	.461	227	1	.344	.411	.485	218	4	.280	.349	.436	105	2	.286	.348	.438	340	3	.321	.391	.468	167	0	.353	.406	.491	58	1	.328	.394	.483
TOTALS		2212	10	.291	.367	.373	1115	4	.312	.388	.389	1097	6	.269	.345	.357	533	3	.280	.348	.370	1679	7	.294	.373	.375	850	0	.300	.379	.374	320	1	.272	.345	.338

■ John Kruk BL/TL

YEAR	TM/L	TOTAL					HOME					AWAY					LEFT					RIGHT					ON-BASE					LATE/CLOSE				
		AB	HR	AVG	OBP	SLG	AB	HR	AVG	OBP	SLG	AB	HR	AVG	OBP	SLG	AB	HR	AVG	OBP	SLG	AB	HR	AVG	OBP	SLG	AB	HR	AVG	OBP	SLG	AB	HR	AVG	OBP	SLG
1986	SD-N	278	4	.309	.403	.424	103	1	.311	.408	.447	175	3	.309	.400	.411	79	0	.304	.402	.342	199	4	.312	.403	.457	124	2	.387	.462	.500	52	0	.308	.390	.327
1987	SD-N	447	20	.313	.406	.488	215	8	.298	.416	.437	232	12	.328	.397	.534	137	4	.255	.329	.380	310	16	.339	.439	.535	207	10	.304	.406	.512	86	3	.372	.465	.512
1988	SD-N	378	9	.241	.369	.362	182	6	.253	.414	.429	196	1	.230	.321	.301	98	3	.194	.270	.337	280	6	.257	.401	.371	165	3	.248	.414	.370	65	1	.246	.367	.338
1989	SD-N	76	3	.184	.333	.303	44	0	.182	.308	.318	32	1	.188	.366	.281	10	0	.100	.250	.100	66	3	.197	.346	.333	37	2	.162	.295	.324	8	1	.250	.455	.625
1989	Phi-N	281	5	.331	.386	.473	148	4	.351	.409	.541	133	1	.308	.361	.383	91	0	.286	.323	.352	190	5	.353	.414	.532	133	3	.308	.367	.481	36	3	.139	.419	.611
1990	Phi-N	443	7	.291	.386	.431	220	4	.318	.401	.450	223	3	.265	.372	.413	117	2	.222	.303	.325	326	5	.316	.415	.469	215	4	.321	.417	.502	71	2	.268	.429	.408
1991	Phi-N	538	21	.294	.367	.483	276	8	.286	.363	.442	262	13	.302	.372	.527	202	4	.297	.350	.436	336	17	.292	.378	.512	244	10	.295	.376	.488	103	1	.282	.375	.359
1992	Phi-N	507	10	.323	.423	.458	248	7	.306	.409	.444	259	3	.340	.437	.471	210	1	.314	.414	.381	297	9	.330	.430	.512	242	4	.331	.442	.442	87	0	.322	.429	.379
1993	Phi-N	535	14	.316	.430	.475	257	6	.327	.441	.506	278	8	.306	.420	.446	185	5	.292	.377	.416	350	9	.329	.456	.506	261	7	.330	.455	.479	85	4	.329	.468	.541
1994	Phi-N	255	5	.302	.395	.427	124	3	.290	.399	.435	131	2	.313	.392	.420	73	1	.219	.321	.274	182	4	.335	.424	.489	125	1	.280	.373	.368	42	2	.310	.408	.476
TOTALS		3738	98	.300	.397	.448	1817	51	.301	.404	.456	1921	47	.299	.389	.440	1202	20	.272	.351	.373	2536	78	.313	.417	.484	1753	46	.309	.413	.462	635	16	.307	.420	.433

■ Lee Lacy BR/TR

YEAR	TM/L	TOTAL					HOME					AWAY					LEFT					RIGHT					ON-BASE					LATE/CLOSE				
		AB	HR	AVG	OBP	SLG	AB	HR	AVG	OBP	SLG	AB	HR	AVG	OBP	SLG	AB	HR	AVG	OBP	SLG	AB	HR	AVG	OBP	SLG	AB	HR	AVG	OBP	SLG	AB	HR	AVG	OBP	SLG
1984	Pit-N	474	12	.321	.362	.464	238	6	.332	.377	.492	236	6	.309	.347	.436	168	7	.345	.396	.548	306	5	.307	.344	.418	194	4	.361	.400	.521	86	2	.337	.387	.488
1985	Bal-A	492	9	.293	.343	.409	250	3	.308	.358	.396	242	6	.277	.328	.421	166	5	.313	.375	.470	326	4	.282	.327	.377	200	3	.310	.366	.405	68	3	.235	.329	.368
1986	Bal-A	491	11	.287	.334	.391	230	5	.304	.353	.404	261	6	.272	.317	.379	157	5	.280	.333	.408	334	6	.290	.334	.383	197	4	.259	.298	.345	80	1	.300	.341	.387
1987	Bal-A	258	7	.244	.326	.399	130	2	.231	.318	.346	128	5	.258	.336	.453	156	4	.237	.306	.404	102	3	.255	.356	.392	90	1	.200	.277	.333	38	1	.263	.364	.395
TOTALS		1715	39	.292	.343	.417	848	16	.302	.356	.417	867	23	.281	.331	.418	647	21	.295	.354	.459	1068	18	.289	.337	.392	681	12	.295	.344	.411	272	7	.290	.355	.415

■ Ken Landreaux BL/TR

YEAR	TM/L	TOTAL					HOME					AWAY					LEFT					RIGHT					ON-BASE					LATE/CLOSE				
		AB	HR	AVG	OBP	SLG	AB	HR	AVG	OBP	SLG	AB	HR	AVG	OBP	SLG	AB	HR	AVG	OBP	SLG	AB	HR	AVG	OBP	SLG	AB	HR	AVG	OBP	SLG	AB	HR	AVG	OBP	SLG
1984	LA-N	438	11	.251	.295	.374	231	5	.251	.310	.359	207	6	.251	.279	.391	57	1	.281	.373	.368	381	10	.247	.283	.375	174	2	.293	.332	.374	86	5	.256	.278	.500
1985	LA-N	482	12	.268	.311	.405	223	2	.247	.294	.318	259	10	.286	.326	.479	59	2	.186	.246	.339	423	10	.279	.320	.414	195	2	.241	.294	.354	71	1	.268	.316	.352
1986	LA-N	283	4	.261	.313	.364	127	1	.236	.308	.291	156	3	.282	.317	.423	45	0	.267	.313	.333	238	4	.261	.313	.370	111	1	.261	.333	.360	61	1	.213	.258	.328
1987	LA-N	182	6	.203	.269	.324	91	4	.297	.343	.462	91	2	.110	.196	.187	20	1	.200	.238	.250	162	6	.204	.272	.333	80	4	.262	.299	.438	46	0	.196	.275	.217
TOTALS		1385	33	.253	.301	.376	672	12	.256	.309	.347	713	21	.252	.293	.404	181	3	.238	.303	.337	1204	30	.255	.300	.382	560	9	.264	.304	.373	264	7	.239	.283	.371

■ Ray Lankford BL/TL

YEAR	TM/L	TOTAL					HOME					AWAY					LEFT					RIGHT					ON-BASE					LATE/CLOSE				
		AB	HR	AVG	OBP	SLG	AB	HR	AVG	OBP	SLG	AB	HR	AVG	OBP	SLG	AB	HR	AVG	OBP	SLG	AB	HR	AVG	OBP	SLG	AB	HR	AVG	OBP	SLG	AB	HR	AVG	OBP	SLG
1990	StL-N	126	3	.286	.353	.452	43	2	.256	.360	.512	83	1	.301	.348	.422	45	0	.311	.367	.422	81	3	.272	.344	.469	57	1	.281	.349	.439	20	0	.300	.364	.300
1991	StL-N	566	9	.251	.301	.392	283	4	.237	.294	.385	283	5	.265	.308	.399	220	0	.236	.290	.305	346	9	.260	.308	.451	228	3	.294	.357	.482	91	1	.253	.313	.352
1992	StL-N	598	20	.293	.371	.480	314	13	.309	.375	.510	284	7	.275	.366	.447	216	4	.255	.345	.380	382	16	.314	.385	.537	241	11	.320	.419	.556	131	5	.282	.381	.443
1993	StL-N	407	7	.238	.366	.346	197	6	.249	.375	.396	210	1	.229	.358	.300	116	0	.207	.357	.233	291	7	.251	.370	.392	191	3	.251	.389	.340	73	1	.205	.318	.356
1994	StL-N	416	19	.267	.354	.488	195	8	.318	.390	.559	221	11	.222	.322	.425	105	3	.190	.317	.324	311	16	.293	.374	.543	155	4	.258	.364	.413	52	3	.154	.297	.346
TOTALS		2113	58	.265	.349	.431	1032	33	.277	.356	.463	1081	25	.254	.342	.400	702	7	.235	.328	.340	1411	51	.281	.359	.476	872	22	.284	.383	.483	367	10	.243	.339	.381

■ Carney Lansford BR/TR

YEAR	TM/L	TOTAL					HOME					AWAY					LEFT					RIGHT					ON-BASE					LATE/CLOSE				
		AB	HR	AVG	OBP	SLG	AB	HR	AVG	OBP	SLG	AB	HR	AVG	OBP	SLG	AB	HR	AVG	OBP	SLG	AB	HR	AVG	OBP	SLG	AB	HR	AVG	OBP	SLG	AB	HR	AVG	OBP	SLG
1984	Oak-A	597	14	.300	.342	.439	280	7	.329	.360	.482	317	7	.274	.327	.401	202	4	.342	.373	.465	395	10	.278	.326	.425	262	5	.290	.339	.412	101	2	.307	.355	.426
1985	Oak-A	401	13	.277	.311	.429	205	7	.302	.321	.463	196	6	.250	.300	.393	131	3	.237	.266	.359	270	10	.296	.332	.463	150	7	.333	.364	.527	58	2	.190	.238	.328
1986	Oak-A	591	19	.284	.332	.421	298	10	.319	.368	.477	293	9	.249	.294	.365	187	6	.305	.363	.460	404	13	.275	.317	.403	241	7	.299	.352	.419	90	5	.233	.310	.467
1987	Oak-A	554	19	.289	.366	.455	271	9	.288	.371	.469	283	10	.290	.361	.442	175	8	.280	.352	.440	379	11	.293	.372	.462	230	8	.296	.380	.465	87	2	.218	.320	.322
1988	Oak-A	556	7	.279	.327	.360	277	1	.245	.299	.307	279	6	.312	.355	.412	153	0	.203	.244	.222	403	7	.308	.358	.412	223	3	.296	.346	.372	89	0	.247	.330	.292
1989	Oak-A	551	2	.336	.398	.405	259	1	.309	.372	.363	292	1	.360	.422	.442	149	1	.389	.465	.503	402	1	.316	.372	.368	243	0	.321	.403	.374	82	0	.280	.366	.317
1990	Oak-A	507	3	.268	.333	.320	215	1	.298	.376	.335	292	2	.247	.300	.308	119	1	.345	.443	.429	388	2	.245	.296	.286	239	0	.272	.353	.297	66	0	.152	.213	.167
1991	Oak-A	16	0	.063	.063	.063	11	0	.091	.091	.091	5	0	.000	.000	.000	9	0	.000	.000	.000	7	0	.143	.143	.143	7	0	.000	.000	.000	1	0	.000	.000	.000
1992	Oak-A	496	7	.262	.325	.369	218	4	.234	.301	.358	278	3	.284	.344	.378	132	1	.280	.342	.394	364	6	.255	.319	.360	228	5	.263	.338	.404	65	2	.246	.329	.369
TOTALS		4269	84	.287	.342	.399	2034	40	.291	.346	.408	2235	44	.284	.339	.391	1257	24	.297	.355	.411	3012	60	.283	.337	.394	1823	35	.293	.358	.403	639	13	.239	.313	.343

■ Mike Lansing BR/TR

YEAR	TM/L	TOTAL					HOME					AWAY					LEFT					RIGHT					ON-BASE					LATE/CLOSE				
		AB	HR	AVG	OBP	SLG	AB	HR	AVG	OBP	SLG	AB	HR	AVG	OBP	SLG	AB	HR	AVG	OBP	SLG	AB	HR	AVG	OBP	SLG	AB	HR	AVG	OBP	SLG	AB	HR	AVG	OBP	SLG
1993	Mon-N	491	3	.287	.352	.369	261	1	.261	.331	.337	230	2	.317	.376	.404	150	1	.247	.315	.307	341	2	.305	.369	.396	206	2	.296	.376	.357	80	0	.298	.368	.357
1994	Mon-N	394	5	.266	.328	.368	179	3	.313	.371	.453	215	2	.228	.292	.298	91	3	.308	.337	.495	303	2	.254	.325	.330	168	3	.280	.366	.393	58	0	.224	.281	.276
TOTALS		885	8	.278	.342	.368	440	4	.282	.347	.384	445	4	.274	.336	.353	241	4	.270	.323	.378	644	4	.281	.348	.365	374	5	.289	.371	.393	142	0	.268	.333	.324

■ Barry Larkin BR/TR

YEAR	TM/L	TOTAL					HOME					AWAY					LEFT					RIGHT					ON-BASE					LATE/CLOSE				
		AB	HR	AVG	OBP	SLG	AB	HR	AVG	OBP	SLG	AB	HR	AVG	OBP	SLG	AB	HR	AVG	OBP	SLG	AB	HR	AVG	OBP	SLG	AB	HR	AVG	OBP	SLG	AB	HR	AVG	OBP	SLG
1986	Cin-N	159	3	.283	.320	.403	82	3	.280	.310	.463	77	0	.286	.329	.338	50	2	.340	.382	.480	109	1	.257	.289	.367	58	1	.379	.422	.534	24	0	.458	.458	.500
1987	Cin-N	439	12	.244	.306	.371	241	6	.237	.306	.349	198	6	.253	.307	.399	131	5	.275	.349	.450	308	7	.231	.288	.338	183	6	.290	.354	.443	71	1	.282	.329	.338
1988	Cin-N	588	12	.296	.347	.429	303	9	.307	.353	.469	285	3	.284	.342	.386	145	5	.352	.421	.559	443	7	.278	.322	.386	182	3	.313	.366	.451	107	1	.318	.368	.374
1989	Cin-N	325	4	.342	.375	.446	156	1	.353	.376	.455	169	3	.331	.373	.438	121	2	.372	.421	.488	204	2	.324	.347	.422	117	1	.359	.394	.470	53	1	.358	.419	.528
1990	Cin-N	614	7	.301	.358	.396	286	4	.273	.349	.357	328	3	.326	.365	.430	203	4	.266	.344	.404	411	3	.319	.365	.392	194	3	.376	.418	.410	94	1	.309	.371	.426
1991	Cin-N	464	20	.302	.378	.506	242	16	.326	.404	.612	222	4	.275	.349	.392	135	8	.326	.433	.585	329	12	.292	.353	.474	192	8	.318	.414	.516	71	1	.254	.321	.352
1992	Cin-N	533	12	.304	.377	.454	254	8	.307	.393	.449	279	4	.301	.366	.437	200	6	.355	.443	.586	333	6	.273	.336	.375	188	4	.335	.414	.466	79	0	.291	.380	.380
1993	Cin-N	384	8	.315	.394	.445	195	4	.292	.379	.400	189	4	.339	.409	.492	95	3	.358	.448	.579	289	5	.301	.375	.401	188	6	.436	.438	.489	56	0	.286	.385	.321
1994	Cin-N	427	9	.279	.369	.419	219	6	.260	.365	.365	208	3	.298	.373	.476	102	3	.284	.382	.441	325	6	.277	.365	.412	178	3	.270	.363	.404	75	1	.227	.344	.333
TOTALS		3933	87	.296	.360	.431	1978	54	.292	.362	.436	1955	33	.300	.359	.425	1182	39	.322	.403	.508	2751	48	.285	.341	.397	1590	32	.319	.392	.457	630	6	.297	.367	.384

■ Gene Larkin BB/TR

YEAR	TM/L	TOTAL					HOME					AWAY					LEFT					RIGHT					ON-BASE					LATE/CLOSE				
		AB	HR	AVG	OBP	SLG	AB	HR	AVG	OBP	SLG	AB	HR	AVG	OBP	SLG	AB	HR	AVG	OBP	SLG	AB	HR	AVG	OBP	SLG	AB	HR	AVG	OBP	SLG	AB	HR	AVG	OBP	SLG
1987	Min-A	233	4	.266	.340	.382	112	0	.295	.367	.384	121	4	.240	.313	.380	77	1	.286	.375	.377	156	3	.256	.322	.385	107	0	.262	.347	.327	41	0	.390	.468	.512
1988	Min-A	505	8	.267	.368	.382	254	5	.283	.389	.421	251	3	.251	.346	.343	150	2	.307	.380	.440	355	6	.251	.363	.358	251	5	.267	.368	.398	76	1	.316	.413	.434
1989	Min-A	446	6	.267	.353	.368	239	3	.259	.336	.339	207	3	.275	.373	.401	156	1	.365	.436	.474	290	5	.214	.308	.310	208	3	.269	.355	.361	70	1	.257	.350	.314

YEAR	TM/L	TOTAL AB	HR	AVG	OBP	SLG	HOME AB	HR	AVG	OBP	SLG	AWAY AB	HR	AVG	OBP	SLG	LEFT AB	HR	AVG	OBP	SLG	RIGHT AB	HR	AVG	OBP	SLG	ON-BASE AB	HR	AVG	OBP	SLG	LATE/CLOSE AB	HR	AVG	OBP	SLG
1990	Min-A	401	5	.269	.343	.392	199	5	.286	.348	.462	202	0	.252	.338	.322	121	0	.248	.303	.331	280	5	.279	.359	.418	196	2	.240	.298	.352	63	0	.206	.280	.254
1991	Min-A	255	2	.286	.361	.373	131	0	.313	.387	.359	124	2	.258	.333	.387	88	1	.273	.363	.398	167	1	.293	.360	.359	115	1	.235	.313	.313	46	1	.179	.207	.286
1992	Min-A	337	6	.246	.308	.359	153	5	.261	.326	.418	184	1	.234	.294	.310	55	0	.218	.295	.327	282	6	.252	.311	.365	163	3	.270	.332	.393	63	0	.302	.389	.413
1993	Min-A	144	1	.235	.357	.347	81	1	.235	.330	.333	63	0	.302	.392	.365	38	0	.263	.310	.316	106	1	.281	.383	.375						29	1	.379	.419	.621
TOTALS		2321	32	.266	.348	.374	1169	19	.277	.357	.394	1152	13	.255	.339	.354	685	5	.293	.340	.400	1636	27	.255	.340	.364	1104	15	.260	.342	.365	388	3	.286	.369	.384

Tim Laudner BR/TR

YEAR	TM/L	TOTAL AB	HR	AVG	OBP	SLG	HOME AB	HR	AVG	OBP	SLG	AWAY AB	HR	AVG	OBP	SLG	LEFT AB	HR	AVG	OBP	SLG	RIGHT AB	HR	AVG	OBP	SLG	ON-BASE AB	HR	AVG	OBP	SLG	LATE/CLOSE AB	HR	AVG	OBP	SLG
1984	Min-A	262	10	.206	.258	.389	107	3	.224	.288	.411	155	7	.194	.236	.374	95	4	.274	.330	.505	167	6	.168	.217	.323	149	6	.215	.261	.389	37	2	.135	.200	.324
1985	Min-A	164	7	.238	.292	.396	68	5	.309	.377	.574	96	2	.188	.228	.271	115	7	.270	.341	.487	49	0	.163	.163	.184	69	1	.174	.205	.246	28	0	.179	.207	.286
1986	Min-A	193	10	.244	.333	.451	95	9	.232	.321	.558	98	1	.255	.345	.347	111	7	.261	.379	.514	82	3	.220	.267	.366	91	1	.220	.298	.330	23	0	.174	.310	.217
1987	Min-A	288	16	.191	.252	.389	151	7	.172	.247	.344	137	9	.212	.257	.438	98	7	.194	.279	.449	190	9	.189	.236	.358	113	9	.221	.302	.487	41	2	.171	.244	.341
1988	Min-A	375	13	.251	.316	.408	182	8	.231	.299	.429	193	5	.269	.332	.389	109	3	.321	.359	.495	266	10	.222	.299	.372	182	5	.220	.282	.341	54	2	.222	.300	.370
1989	Min-A	239	6	.222	.293	.351	132	2	.220	.288	.318	107	4	.224	.300	.393	91	2	.253	.324	.429	148	4	.203	.274	.304	110	2	.227	.326	.364	37	1	.162	.225	.270
TOTALS		1521	62	.225	.290	.396	735	34	.223	.295	.419	786	28	.226	.286	.375	619	30	.263	.337	.481	902	32	.198	.257	.338	714	24	.216	.283	.367	220	7	.177	.251	.314

Mike La Valliere BL/TR

YEAR	TM/L	TOTAL AB	HR	AVG	OBP	SLG	HOME AB	HR	AVG	OBP	SLG	AWAY AB	HR	AVG	OBP	SLG	LEFT AB	HR	AVG	OBP	SLG	RIGHT AB	HR	AVG	OBP	SLG	ON-BASE AB	HR	AVG	OBP	SLG	LATE/CLOSE AB	HR	AVG	OBP	SLG
1984	Phi-N	7	0	.000	.222	.000	3	0	.000	.400	.000	4	0	.000	.000	.000	0	0	—	1.000	—	7	0	.000	.125	.000	3	0	.000	.250	.000	2	0	.000	.000	.000
1985	StL-N	34	0	.147	.273	.176	20	0	.150	.296	.150	14	0	.143	.235	.214	2	0	.000	.000	.000	32	0	.156	.293	.188	17	0	.176	.261	.176	5	0	.400	.333	.600
1986	StL-N	303	3	.234	.318	.310	150	1	.220	.304	.280	153	2	.248	.331	.340	57	1	.211	.274	.333	246	2	.240	.327	.305	133	2	.241	.348	.323	59	1	.220	.303	.356
1987	Pit-N	340	1	.300	.377	.365	174	1	.305	.378	.368	166	0	.295	.377	.361	77	0	.221	.302	.273	263	1	.323	.399	.392	142	0	.289	.416	.338	51	0	.314	.364	.373
1988	Pit-N	352	2	.261	.353	.330	178	0	.258	.338	.320	174	2	.264	.368	.339	63	0	.159	.293	.190	289	2	.284	.366	.360	134	2	.306	.419	.433	65	0	.308	.370	.415
1989	Pit-N	190	2	.316	.406	.400	98	2	.378	.487	.490	92	0	.250	.310	.304	25	0	.280	.379	.320	165	2	.321	.411	.412	84	1	.298	.416	.369	26	1	.308	.419	.462
1990	Pit-N	279	3	.258	.362	.344	127	2	.276	.374	.378	152	1	.243	.352	.316	56	2	.375	.470	.536	223	1	.229	.335	.296	113	2	.301	.429	.407	35	0	.200	.378	.286
1991	Pit-N	336	3	.289	.351	.360	163	1	.331	.400	.393	173	2	.249	.304	.329	54	0	.222	.259	.296	282	3	.301	.368	.372	146	1	.240	.310	.315	37	0	.108	.277	.135
1992	Pit-N	293	2	.256	.350	.328	135	1	.259	.373	.311	158	1	.253	.328	.342	31	0	.161	.297	.226	262	2	.267	.356	.340	124	2	.258	.370	.355	47	2	.234	.419	.277
1993	Pit-N	5	0	.200	.200	.200	0	0	—	—	—	5	0	.200	.200	.200	1	0	1.000	1.000	1.000	4	0	.000	.000	.000	3	0	.000	.000	.000	0	0	—	—	—
1993	Chi-A	97	1	.258	.282	.278	52	0	.250	.286	.288	45	0	.267	.277	.267	13	0	.308	.308	.385	84	0	.250	.278	.262	44	0	.273	.277	.273	11	0	.091	.091	.091
1994	Chi-A	139	1	.281	.368	.331	61	0	.279	.353	.295	78	1	.282	.379	.359	23	0	.304	.414	.391	116	1	.276	.358	.319	65	1	.262	.354	.354	22	1	.409	.481	.545
TOTALS		2375	17	.269	.353	.338	1166	8	.280	.367	.345	1209	9	.258	.339	.332	402	3	.239	.328	.318	1973	14	.275	.358	.342	1008	11	.270	.375	.351	360	3	.253	.358	.342

Vance Law BR/TR

YEAR	TM/L	TOTAL AB	HR	AVG	OBP	SLG	HOME AB	HR	AVG	OBP	SLG	AWAY AB	HR	AVG	OBP	SLG	LEFT AB	HR	AVG	OBP	SLG	RIGHT AB	HR	AVG	OBP	SLG	ON-BASE AB	HR	AVG	OBP	SLG	LATE/CLOSE AB	HR	AVG	OBP	SLG
1984	Chi-A	481	17	.252	.309	.403	238	11	.269	.318	.458	243	6	.235	.301	.350	187	9	.241	.309	.422	294	8	.259	.309	.391	185	6	.276	.340	.411	66	1	.303	.356	.439
1985	Mon-N	519	10	.266	.369	.405	247	5	.263	.393	.409	272	5	.268	.344	.401	159	4	.245	.353	.384	360	6	.275	.376	.414	220	4	.250	.364	.405	89	1	.258	.356	.382
1986	Mon-N	360	5	.225	.298	.325	177	3	.260	.333	.384	183	2	.191	.262	.268	127	4	.252	.307	.417	233	1	.210	.292	.275	161	2	.273	.339	.373	79	1	.203	.325	.354
1987	Mon-N	436	12	.273	.347	.422	209	3	.268	.339	.397	227	9	.278	.354	.445	153	3	.288	.384	.412	283	9	.265	.326	.428	192	3	.266	.366	.375	74	2	.297	.366	.473
1988	Chi-N	556	11	.293	.358	.412	285	5	.302	.362	.411	271	6	.284	.354	.413	151	5	.291	.371	.464	405	6	.294	.353	.393	262	8	.294	.358	.431	96	0	.323	.377	.365
1989	Chi-N	408	7	.235	.296	.355	187	4	.235	.303	.364	221	3	.235	.289	.348	111	3	.297	.363	.441	297	4	.212	.271	.323	191	0	.209	.275	.288	61	0	.131	.167	.148
1991	Oak-A	134	0	.209	.303	.276	63	0	.206	.286	.286	71	0	.211	.317	.268	54	0	.259	.365	.352	80	0	.175	.258	.225	60	0	.267	.353	.333	18	0	.167	.318	.222
TOTALS		2894	62	.258	.332	.386	1406	31	.266	.343	.401	1488	31	.250	.321	.371	942	28	.266	.348	.418	1952	34	.254	.324	.370	1271	23	.263	.343	.382	483	5	.265	.333	.360

Manuel Lee BB/TR

YEAR	TM/L	TOTAL AB	HR	AVG	OBP	SLG	HOME AB	HR	AVG	OBP	SLG	AWAY AB	HR	AVG	OBP	SLG	LEFT AB	HR	AVG	OBP	SLG	RIGHT AB	HR	AVG	OBP	SLG	ON-BASE AB	HR	AVG	OBP	SLG	LATE/CLOSE AB	HR	AVG	OBP	SLG
1985	Tor-A	40	0	.200	.238	.200	26	0	.154	.214	.154	14	0	.286	.286	.286	13	0	.077	.077	.077	27	0	.259	.310	.259	13	0	.000	.071	.000	4	0	.000	.000	.000
1986	Tor-A	78	1	.205	.241	.269	41	1	.244	.262	.366	37	0	.162	.220	.162	19	0	.263	.300	.368	59	1	.186	.222	.237	36	0	.167	.184	.222	10	0	.100	.100	.100
1987	Tor-A	121	1	.256	.289	.347	60	0	.200	.269	.233	61	1	.311	.311	.459	48	0	.313	.340	.438	73	1	.219	.256	.288	48	1	.271	.308	.438	29	0	.310	.333	.379
1988	Tor-A	381	2	.291	.333	.365	196	2	.296	.338	.403	185	0	.286	.328	.324	131	2	.336	.365	.458	250	0	.268	.318	.316	169	0	.331	.354	.396	75	0	.280	.341	.280
1989	Tor-A	300	3	.260	.305	.333	126	0	.238	.289	.310	174	3	.276	.317	.351	139	1	.295	.344	.374	161	2	.230	.271	.298	135	2	.267	.324	.356	56	1	.232	.328	.304
1990	Tor-A	391	6	.243	.288	.340	190	2	.263	.302	.337	201	4	.224	.275	.343	178	6	.242	.265	.410	213	0	.244	.306	.282	171	1	.240	.253	.339	65	0	.215	.271	.262
1991	Tor-A	445	0	.234	.274	.288	213	0	.249	.306	.324	232	0	.220	.242	.254	144	0	.285	.333	.347	301	0	.209	.245	.259	177	0	.226	.262	.282	80	0	.200	.270	.237
1992	Tor-A	396	3	.263	.343	.316	184	2	.223	.321	.261	212	1	.297	.363	.363	118	0	.212	.299	.246	278	3	.284	.362	.345	157	1	.274	.346	.325	62	0	.210	.306	.210
1993	Tex-A	205	1	.220	.300	.259	76	1	.263	.352	.316	129	0	.194	.268	.225	43	0	.233	.298	.256	162	1	.216	.301	.259	86	1	.209	.310	.267	23	0	.217	.280	.217
1994	Tex-A	335	2	.278	.319	.361	171	1	.269	.330	.345	164	1	.287	.308	.378	71	0	.296	.351	.352	264	2	.273	.311	.364	157	2	.261	.291	.357	56	1	.286	.305	.375
TOTALS		2692	19	.254	.305	.323	1283	8	.253	.312	.323	1409	11	.256	.299	.323	904	9	.272	.318	.364	1788	10	.246	.299	.303	1149	8	.256	.299	.332	460	2	.235	.297	.272

Mark Lemke BB/TR

YEAR	TM/L	TOTAL AB	HR	AVG	OBP	SLG	HOME AB	HR	AVG	OBP	SLG	AWAY AB	HR	AVG	OBP	SLG	LEFT AB	HR	AVG	OBP	SLG	RIGHT AB	HR	AVG	OBP	SLG	ON-BASE AB	HR	AVG	OBP	SLG	LATE/CLOSE AB	HR	AVG	OBP	SLG
1988	Atl-N	58	0	.224	.274	.293	41	0	.220	.273	.268	17	0	.235	.278	.353	38	0	.158	.200	.211	20	0	.350	.409	.450	22	0	.273	.333	.364	17	0	.176	.222	.176
1989	Atl-N	55	2	.182	.250	.364	29	1	.241	.290	.483	26	1	.115	.207	.231	17	2	.412	.444	.941	38	0	.079	.167	.105	20	1	.300	.417	.600	14	0	.071	.071	.071
1990	Atl-N	239	0	.226	.286	.280	109	0	.211	.265	.275	130	0	.238	.303	.285	97	0	.268	.330	.351	142	0	.197	.256	.232	94	0	.309	.362	.372	44	0	.205	.217	.227
1991	Atl-N	269	2	.234	.305	.312	132	2	.280	.345	.386	137	0	.190	.266	.241	114	0	.254	.313	.333	155	2	.219	.299	.297	122	0	.221	.288	.262	53	0	.358	.426	.415
1992	Atl-N	427	6	.227	.307	.304	222	4	.225	.302	.302	205	2	.229	.312	.307	145	5	.228	.289	.352	282	1	.227	.316	.280	184	0	.223	.313	.272	69	1	.203	.325	.304
1993	Atl-N	493	7	.252	.335	.341	246	3	.256	.338	.341	247	4	.247	.332	.340	139	5	.309	.382	.482	354	2	.229	.317	.285	211	2	.270	.375	.351	89	4	.236	.313	.393
1994	Atl-N	350	3	.294	.363	.363	177	2	.316	.373	.384	173	1	.272	.354	.341	102	3	.294	.357	.431	248	0	.294	.366	.335	147	2	.320	.422	.408	67	2	.299	.338	.418
TOTALS		1891	20	.245	.319	.324	956	12	.256	.325	.340	935	8	.234	.314	.308	652	15	.267	.329	.396	1239	5	.234	.314	.287	800	5	.256	.355	.339	353	7	.246	.314	.340

Chet Lemon BR/TR

YEAR	TM/L	TOTAL AB	HR	AVG	OBP	SLG	HOME AB	HR	AVG	OBP	SLG	AWAY AB	HR	AVG	OBP	SLG	LEFT AB	HR	AVG	OBP	SLG	RIGHT AB	HR	AVG	OBP	SLG	ON-BASE AB	HR	AVG	OBP	SLG	LATE/CLOSE AB	HR	AVG	OBP	SLG
1984	Det-A	509	20	.287	.357	.495	256	12	.273	.350	.465	253	8	.300	.365	.526	198	9	.384	.441	.636	311	11	.225	.304	.405	248	8	.278	.349	.440	70	3	.286	.412	.486
1985	Det-A	517	18	.265	.334	.439	243	9	.288	.348	.473	274	9	.245	.321	.409	149	8	.322	.378	.564	368	10	.242	.316	.389	221	5	.253	.323	.439	91	2	.264	.327	.396
1986	Det-A	403	12	.251	.326	.407	190	7	.237	.318	.416	213	5	.263	.333	.399	162	7	.284	.346	.500	241	5	.228	.313	.344	187	6	.283	.358	.433	75	1	.240	.313	.307
1987	Det-A	470	20	.277	.376	.481	223	10	.260	.379	.471	247	10	.291	.373	.490	180	8	.272	.382	.494	290	12	.279	.372	.472	217	8	.295	.390	.498	63	1	.206	.286	.349
1988	Det-A	512	17	.264	.346	.436	245	12	.278	.349	.498	267	5	.251	.343	.378	165	9	.297	.370	.539	347	8	.248	.335	.386	222	8	.279	.363	.441	93	6	.280	.402	.559
1989	Det-A	414	7	.237	.323	.343	189	4	.228	.332	.365	225	3	.244	.316	.324	153	5	.275	.376	.438	261	2	.215	.291	.287	179	5	.279	.370	.441	79	0	.203	.259	.253
1990	Det-A	322	5	.258	.359	.379	133	2	.256	.380	.361	189	3	.259	.343	.392	138	3	.283	.375	.420	184	2	.239	.347	.348	138	0	.283	.384	.377	45	0	.156	.296	.244
TOTALS		3147	99	.264	.346	.431	1479	56	.262	.351	.444	1668	43	.265	.343	.419	1145	49	.305	.383	.519	2002	50	.240	.325	.381	1412	44	.278	.361	.442	516	13	.240	.334	.384

Jeffrey Leonard BR/TR

YEAR	TM/L	TOTAL AB	HR	AVG	OBP	SLG	HOME AB	HR	AVG	OBP	SLG	AWAY AB	HR	AVG	OBP	SLG	LEFT AB	HR	AVG	OBP	SLG	RIGHT AB	HR	AVG	OBP	SLG	ON-BASE AB	HR	AVG	OBP	SLG	LATE/CLOSE AB	HR	AVG	OBP	SLG
1984	SF-N	514	21	.302	.357	.484	260	13	.300	.364	.504	254	8	.303	.350	.465	166	13	.380	.419	.681	348	8	.264	.328	.391	257	11	.292	.353	.471	101	3	.198	.265	.307
1985	SF-N	507	17	.241	.272	.393	238	8	.239	.263	.370	269	9	.242	.279	.413	141	7	.255	.266	.489	366	10	.235	.274	.355	239	7	.243	.283	.393	92	2	.272	.323	.424
1986	SF-N	341	6	.279	.322	.381	168	2	.315	.350	.417	173	4	.243	.294	.347	119	3	.328	.350	.437	222	3	.252	.307	.351	175	4	.286	.330	.389	58	2	.276	.328	.448
1987	SF-N	503	19	.280	.309	.467	225	9	.280	.311	.471	278	10	.281	.307	.464	145	5	.283	.306	.462	358	14	.279	.310	.469	220	6	.259	.300	.386	88	2	.284	.330	.432
1988	SF-N	160	2	.256	.292	.356	79	0	.215	.247	.278	81	2	.296	.337	.432	55	1	.236	.295	.382	105	1	.267	.291	.343	71	1	.338	.355	.408	35	1	.371	.405	.543
1988	Mil-A	374	8	.235	.270	.350	188	5	.239	.286	.372	186	3	.231	.253	.328	111	3	.270	.317	.441	263	5	.221	.249	.312	187	5	.225	.259	.342	51	0	.255	.283	.294
1989	Sea-A	566	24	.254	.301	.420	258	9	.260	.307	.407	308	15	.250	.296	.432	157	8	.280	.326	.497	409	16	.244	.292	.391	289	10	.246	.292	.391	90	3	.233	.263	.344
1990	Sea-A	478	10	.251	.305	.356	234	7	.222	.295	.348	244	3	.279	.325	.348	175	6	.309	.361	.463	303	4	.218	.272	.294	252	7	.270	.327	.401	78	0	.141	.250	.154
TOTALS		3443	107	.263	.305	.409	1650	53	.262	.306	.410	1793	54	.264	.304	.408	1069	46	.299	.336	.496	2374	61	.247	.292	.370	1690	51	.263	.310	.402	593	13	.243	.297	.356

Darren Lewis BR/TR

YEAR	TM/L	TOTAL AB	HR	AVG	OBP	SLG	HOME AB	HR	AVG	OBP	SLG	AWAY AB	HR	AVG	OBP	SLG	LEFT AB	HR	AVG	OBP	SLG	RIGHT AB	HR	AVG	OBP	SLG	ON-BASE AB	HR	AVG	OBP	SLG	LATE/CLOSE AB	HR	AVG	OBP	SLG
1990	Oak-A	35	0	.229	.372	.229	18	0	.167	.250	.167	17	0	.294	.478	.294	8	0	.375	.500	.375	27	0	.185	.333	.185	20	0	.100	.182	.100	2	0	.500	.750	.500
1991	SF-N	222	1	.248	.358	.311	121	0	.231	.354	.248	101	1	.267	.362	.386	75	1	.280	.386	.400	147	0	.231	.343	.265	84	0	.298	.398	.333	34	0	.294	.415	.382
1992	SF-N	320	1	.231	.295	.272	142	1	.176	.248	.211	178	0	.275	.333	.320	125	0	.216	.285	.264	195	1	.241	.302	.277	83	0	.253	.297	.277	54	0	.222	.276	.259
1993	SF-N	522	2	.253	.302	.324	250	2	.256	.302	.344	272	0	.250	.301	.305	172	0	.267	.321	.343	350	2	.246	.292	.314	186	2	.306	.326	.403	66	0	.197	.254	.242
1994	SF-N	451	4	.257	.340	.357	228	4	.259	.339	.364	223	0	.256	.341	.350	115	1	.217	.297	.287	336	3	.271	.354	.381	153	1	.268	.347	.346	76	1	.276	.337	.382
TOTALS		1550	8	.248	.322	.319	759	7	.236	.311	.306	791	1	.260	.333	.331	495	3	.246	.320	.319	1055	5	.249	.323	.318	526	3	.278	.334	.344	232	1	.246	.319	.315

Jose Lind BR/TR

YEAR	TM/L	TOTAL AB	HR	AVG	OBP	SLG	HOME AB	HR	AVG	OBP	SLG	AWAY AB	HR	AVG	OBP	SLG	LEFT AB	HR	AVG	OBP	SLG	RIGHT AB	HR	AVG	OBP	SLG	ON-BASE AB	HR	AVG	OBP	SLG	LATE/CLOSE AB	HR	AVG	OBP	SLG
1987	Pit-N	143	0	.322	.358	.434	80	0	.313	.353	.425	63	0	.333	.364	.444	73	0	.342	.368	.507	70	0	.300	.347	.357	48	0	.375	.423	.521	22	0	.318	.400	.318
1988	Pit-N	611	2	.262	.308	.324	313	1	.300	.342	.377	298	1	.221	.272	.268	214	0	.248	.305	.304	397	2	.270	.310	.335	243	0	.251	.299	.313	115	1	.261	.298	.339
1989	Pit-N	578	2	.232	.280	.289	296	2	.220	.273	.277	282	0	.245	.288	.301	195	1	.256	.315	.318	383	1	.219	.262	.274	254	0	.252	.291	.311	107	0	.215	.274	.234
1990	Pit-N	514	1	.261	.305	.340	262	1	.282	.321	.347	252	0	.240	.288	.333	216	0	.260	.316	.335	298	1	.262	.297	.343	240	1	.275	.332	.342	80	0	.319	.356	.404
1991	Pit-N	502	3	.265	.306	.339	262	2	.244	.290	.332	240	1	.287	.323	.346	167	2	.269	.326	.429	335	1	.263	.295	.343	243	1	.267	.319	.358	80	0	.250	.274	.250
1992	Pit-N	468	0	.235	.275	.269	229	0	.253	.298	.293	239	0	.218	.251	.247	177	0	.237	.277	.282	291	0	.234	.273	.261	236	0	.246	.305	.271	90	0	.289	.326	.344
1993	KC-A	431	0	.248	.271	.288	207	0	.246	.267	.280	224	0	.250	.275	.295	105	0	.257	.274	.305	326	0	.245	.271	.283	181	0	.282	.299	.337	72	0	.167	.197	.167
1994	KC-A	290	1	.269	.306	.348	163	0	.313	.351	.399	127	1	.213	.248	.283	74	1	.257	.321	.432	216	0	.273	.301	.319	119	0	.277	.298	.345	45	1	.333	.354	.489
TOTALS		3537	9	.255	.296	.318	1795	6	.263	.303	.334	1742	3	.247	.287	.301	1221	5	.255	.304	.333	2316	4	.255	.291	.309	1564	2	.266	.311	.329	625	2	.261	.300	.310

Kenny Lofton BL/TL

YEAR	TM/L	TOTAL AB	HR	AVG	OBP	SLG	HOME AB	HR	AVG	OBP	SLG	AWAY AB	HR	AVG	OBP	SLG	LEFT AB	HR	AVG	OBP	SLG	RIGHT AB	HR	AVG	OBP	SLG	ON-BASE AB	HR	AVG	OBP	SLG	LATE/CLOSE AB	HR	AVG	OBP	SLG
1991	Hou-N	74	0	.203	.253	.216	34	0	.176	.222	.176	40	0	.225	.279	.250	20	0	.250	.318	.250	54	0	.185	.228	.204	13	0	.308	.357	.385	13	0	.385	.385	.462

YEAR	TM/L	TOTAL					HOME					AWAY					LEFT					RIGHT					ON-BASE					LATE/CLOSE				
		AB	HR	AVG	OBP	SLG	AB	HR	AVG	OBP	SLG	AB	HR	AVG	OBP	SLG	AB	HR	AVG	OBP	SLG	AB	HR	AVG	OBP	SLG	AB	HR	AVG	OBP	SLG	AB	HR	AVG	OBP	SLG
1992	Cle-A	576	5	.285	.362	.365	277	3	.292	.375	.379	299	2	.278	.349	.351	122	0	.369	.466	.434	454	5	.262	.331	.346	200	2	.285	.354	.385	102	1	.225	.331	.265
1993	Cle-A	569	1	.325	.408	.408	278	1	.313	.414	.410	291	0	.337	.401	.405	195	0	.292	.388	.349	374	1	.342	.418	.439	191	1	.298	.384	.361	89	0	.281	.381	.326
1994	Cle-A	459	12	.349	.412	.536	200	10	.365	.433	.625	259	2	.336	.395	.467	169	3	.331	.409	.503	290	9	.359	.414	.555	155	1	.316	.388	.452	71	2	.254	.325	.394
TOTALS		1678	18	.312	.387	.420	789	14	.313	.398	.444	889	4	.312	.377	.398	506	3	.322	.412	.417	1172	15	.308	.376	.421	559	4	.299	.374	.395	275	3	.258	.348	.327
■ Steve Lombardozzi BR/TR																																				
1985	Min-A	54	0	.370	.426	.481	29	0	.414	.455	.517	25	0	.320	.393	.440	20	0	.350	.409	.400	34	0	.382	.436	.529	20	0	.400	.458	.550	5	0	.400	.400	.400
1986	Min-A	453	8	.227	.308	.347	235	6	.251	.333	.413	218	2	.202	.281	.275	121	3	.207	.289	.347	332	5	.235	.315	.346	174	3	.213	.332	.316	56	1	.268	.317	.393
1987	Min-A	432	8	.238	.298	.352	213	3	.211	.272	.315	219	5	.265	.324	.388	139	2	.288	.333	.417	293	6	.215	.281	.321	160	3	.244	.303	.369	49	2	.245	.373	.388
1988	Min-A	287	3	.209	.295	.307	137	3	.204	.296	.350	150	0	.213	.294	.267	72	0	.250	.337	.319	215	3	.195	.280	.302	116	2	.241	.345	.362	31	0	.161	.257	.290
1989	Hou-N	37	1	.216	.293	.432	19	1	.211	.348	.526	18	0	.222	.222	.333	15	0	.200	.294	.333	22	1	.227	.292	.500	12	0	.250	.308	.500	6	0	.167	.286	.167
1990	Hou-N	1	0	.000	.500	.000	1	0	.000	.500	.000	0	0	—	—	—	0	0	—	1.000	—	1	0	.000	.000	.000	0	0	—	1.000	—	0	0	—	—	—
TOTALS		1264	20	.233	.307	.347	634	13	.233	.311	.374	630	7	.232	.302	.321	367	5	.253	.324	.371	897	15	.224	.300	.338	482	8	.239	.332	.359	147	3	.238	.325	.361
■ Fred Lynn BL/TL																																				
1984	Cal-A	517	23	.271	.366	.474	242	16	.240	.341	.492	275	7	.298	.389	.458	135	6	.222	.348	.430	382	17	.288	.373	.490	231	11	.273	.368	.476	78	3	.231	.378	.385
1985	Bal-A	448	23	.263	.339	.449	217	14	.272	.343	.502	231	9	.255	.335	.398	153	4	.242	.312	.379	295	19	.275	.352	.485	200	12	.260	.356	.450	63	4	.270	.378	.492
1986	Bal-A	397	23	.287	.371	.499	197	13	.284	.371	.513	200	10	.290	.370	.485	96	7	.271	.333	.521	301	16	.292	.382	.492	185	12	.297	.380	.519	61	3	.295	.377	.525
1987	Bal-A	396	23	.253	.320	.487	191	11	.241	.290	.461	205	12	.263	.346	.512	125	5	.224	.297	.400	271	18	.266	.330	.528	156	10	.256	.352	.500	77	4	.247	.310	.442
1988	Bal-A	301	18	.252	.312	.482	142	11	.275	.344	.563	159	7	.233	.282	.409	83	1	.157	.200	.277	218	17	.289	.354	.560	123	5	.179	.255	.341	49	0	.184	.250	.204
1988	Det-A	90	7	.222	.265	.467	52	2	.212	.241	.327	38	5	.237	.295	.658	26	3	.231	.222	.577	64	4	.219	.282	.422	39	2	.256	.295	.410	20	4	.250	.250	.850
1989	Det-A	353	11	.241	.328	.371	173	9	.214	.324	.405	180	2	.267	.332	.339	63	0	.175	.257	.190	290	11	.255	.342	.410	186	3	.258	.338	.344	57	1	.175	.319	.263
1990	SD-N	196	6	.240	.315	.357	112	2	.241	.315	.321	84	4	.238	.316	.405	20	0	.250	.348	.250	176	6	.239	.312	.369	77	1	.234	.319	.312	44	1	.295	.380	.364
TOTALS		2698	134	.265	.338	.454	1326	78	.263	.331	.468	1372	56	.267	.344	.441	701	26	.223	.300	.387	1997	108	.272	.351	.478	1197	56	.257	.344	.434	449	20	.243	.340	.412
■ Steve Lyons BL/TR																																				
1985	Bos-A	371	5	.264	.322	.358	193	4	.264	.322	.378	178	1	.264	.321	.337	67	1	.269	.338	.358	304	4	.263	.318	.359	158	3	.253	.316	.342	62	1	.274	.375	.387
1986	Bos-A	124	1	.250	.312	.363	56	1	.304	.365	.464	68	0	.206	.267	.279	17	0	.412	.421	.647	107	1	.224	.294	.318	61	0	.279	.333	.377	19	0	.263	.391	.263
1986	Chi-A	123	0	.203	.248	.236	68	0	.206	.276	.250	55	0	.200	.211	.218	16	0	.063	.063	.063	107	0	.224	.274	.262	47	0	.170	.212	.170	19	0	.158	.158	.158
1987	Chi-A	193	1	.280	.320	.363	107	0	.280	.316	.336	86	1	.279	.326	.395	25	0	.320	.320	.360	168	1	.274	.320	.363	87	1	.310	.351	.414	22	0	.182	.217	.182
1988	Chi-A	472	5	.269	.313	.373	227	1	.269	.321	.357	245	4	.269	.305	.384	139	3	.266	.305	.374	333	2	.270	.317	.372	191	2	.272	.319	.398	85	1	.271	.319	.341
1989	Chi-A	443	2	.264	.317	.339	207	0	.217	.255	.275	236	2	.305	.370	.394	94	0	.213	.253	.255	349	2	.278	.334	.361	210	2	.267	.302	.348	83	1	.301	.348	.398
1990	Chi-A	146	1	.192	.245	.267	68	0	.162	.230	.250	78	1	.218	.259	.282	25	0	.080	.143	.080	121	1	.215	.267	.306	57	0	.193	.250	.246	38	0	.211	.231	.289
1991	Bos-A	212	4	.241	.277	.354	120	2	.217	.246	.317	92	2	.272	.316	.402	12	1	.167	.231	.417	200	3	.245	.280	.350	97	1	.237	.257	.320	43	1	.163	.217	.209
1992	Atl-N	14	0	.071	.071	.214	3	0	.000	.000	.000	11	0	.091	.091	.273	2	0	.000	.000	.000	12	0	.083	.083	.250	6	0	.167	.167	.500	3	0	.000	.000	.000
1992	Mon-N	13	0	.231	.286	.231	7	0	.286	.375	.286	6	0	.167	.167	.167	4	0	.500	.500	.500	9	0	.111	.200	.111	6	0	.500	.500	.500	4	0	.250	.400	.250
1992	Bos-A	28	0	.250	.300	.321	13	0	.231	.286	.231	15	0	.267	.313	.400	0	0	—	—	—	28	0	.250	.300	.321	9	0	.222	.300	.222	10	0	.300	.364	.300
1993	Bos-A	23	0	.130	.200	.174	12	0	.083	.154	.167	11	0	.182	.250	.182	9	0	.111	.200	.111	14	0	.143	.200	.214	8	0	.000	.111	.000	4	0	.250	.400	.500
TOTALS		2162	19	.252	.301	.340	1081	8	.241	.291	.326	1081	11	.263	.311	.355	410	5	.239	.281	.320	1752	14	.255	.306	.345	937	9	.256	.301	.345	392	3	.247	.308	.316
■ Mike Macfarlane BR/TR																																				
1987	KC-A	19	0	.211	.286	.263	5	0	.200	.200	.200	14	0	.214	.313	.214	5	0	.000	.000	.000	14	0	.286	.375	.357	10	0	.300	.364	.400	3	0	.333	.500	.333
1988	KC-A	211	4	.265	.332	.393	106	2	.264	.328	.377	105	2	.267	.336	.410	84	1	.238	.250	.345	127	3	.283	.381	.425	86	3	.291	.357	.465	33	0	.091	.189	.121
1989	KC-A	157	2	.223	.263	.299	62	0	.290	.313	.371	95	2	.179	.233	.253	64	0	.172	.197	.203	93	2	.258	.307	.366	51	1	.292	.365	.354	31	1	.226	.250	.323
1990	KC-A	400	6	.255	.306	.380	191	1	.257	.307	.372	209	5	.254	.305	.388	147	2	.245	.300	.381	253	4	.261	.309	.379	185	2	.276	.330	.384	67	1	.313	.370	.493
1991	KC-A	267	13	.277	.330	.506	126	6	.286	.348	.516	141	7	.270	.314	.496	112	5	.321	.372	.563	155	8	.245	.301	.465	121	3	.289	.333	.438	48	1	.208	.309	.333
1992	KC-A	402	17	.234	.310	.445	184	7	.239	.319	.451	218	10	.229	.302	.440	138	7	.261	.331	.500	264	10	.220	.298	.417	168	6	.190	.285	.375	74	4	.243	.349	.500
1993	KC-A	388	20	.273	.360	.497	197	7	.284	.374	.487	191	13	.262	.344	.508	150	4	.233	.337	.373	238	16	.298	.375	.576	177	9	.266	.355	.480	83	5	.277	.344	.518
1994	KC-A	314	14	.255	.359	.462	161	9	.280	.380	.547	153	5	.229	.339	.373	104	3	.260	.350	.442	210	11	.252	.364	.471	143	9	.252	.364	.517	53	2	.170	.297	.302
TOTALS		2158	76	.255	.327	.435	1032	32	.268	.341	.453	1126	44	.243	.314	.418	804	22	.250	.315	.413	1354	54	.258	.334	.448	955	33	.260	.338	.432	392	14	.235	.320	.408
■ Shane Mack BR/TR																																				
1987	SD-N	238	4	.239	.299	.361	111	2	.225	.293	.396	127	2	.252	.304	.331	132	4	.265	.313	.417	106	0	.208	.282	.292	111	1	.297	.328	.441	43	0	.163	.234	.209
1988	SD-N	119	0	.244	.336	.269	50	0	.180	.268	.200	69	0	.290	.383	.319	55	0	.236	.354	.255	64	0	.250	.319	.281	54	0	.222	.306	.259	19	0	.316	.333	.316
1990	Min-A	313	8	.326	.392	.460	141	5	.369	.433	.560	172	3	.291	.358	.378	146	5	.370	.439	.548	167	3	.287	.350	.383	131	2	.344	.427	.450	47	1	.362	.423	.511
1991	Min-A	442	18	.310	.363	.529	213	4	.333	.383	.531	229	14	.288	.345	.528	137	9	.350	.412	.701	305	9	.292	.341	.452	197	10	.305	.360	.533	62	2	.194	.224	.306
1992	Min-A	600	16	.315	.394	.467	286	10	.304	.390	.493	314	6	.325	.397	.443	128	4	.297	.357	.516	472	12	.320	.403	.453	237	6	.325	.411	.477	94	0	.277	.352	.319
1993	Min-A	503	10	.276	.335	.412	218	3	.289	.350	.436	285	7	.267	.323	.393	118	2	.288	.317	.424	385	8	.273	.340	.408	194	7	.299	.364	.505	81	3	.235	.303	.432
1994	Min-A	303	15	.333	.402	.564	166	8	.331	.399	.554	137	7	.336	.405	.577	79	5	.418	.467	.734	224	10	.304	.379	.504	129	6	.326	.421	.550	40	2	.275	.347	.525
TOTALS		2518	71	.299	.366	.458	1185	32	.305	.374	.484	1333	39	.294	.359	.435	795	29	.321	.380	.527	1723	42	.290	.360	.427	1053	32	.311	.383	.483	386	8	.254	.316	.373
■ Bill Madlock BR/TR																																				
1984	Pit-N	403	4	.253	.297	.323	196	1	.270	.318	.332	207	3	.237	.277	.314	115	2	.270	.320	.391	288	2	.247	.288	.295	183	2	.284	.341	.344	80	2	.162	.236	.200
1985	Pit-N	399	10	.251	.323	.388	198	6	.273	.348	.429	201	4	.229	.297	.348	123	3	.252	.345	.382	276	7	.250	.313	.391	179	4	.251	.344	.380	79	1	.253	.314	.329
1985	LA-N	114	2	.360	.422	.447	52	0	.365	.460	.385	62	2	.355	.385	.500	35	1	.371	.439	.486	79	1	.354	.414	.430	47	1	.340	.396	.426	18	1	.556	.579	.722
1986	LA-N	379	10	.280	.336	.404	186	4	.263	.336	.360	193	6	.295	.335	.446	141	6	.312	.364	.482	238	4	.261	.320	.357	158	7	.291	.362	.449	61	1	.209	.280	.299
1987	LA-N	61	3	.180	.265	.344	28	1	.214	.313	.357	33	2	.152	.222	.333	21	1	.190	.320	.381	40	2	.175	.233	.325	27	1	.185	.290	.296	11	1	.182	.308	.455
1987	Det-A	326	14	.279	.351	.460	152	7	.270	.323	.447	174	7	.287	.373	.471	151	7	.278	.323	.477	175	7	.280	.373	.446	143	6	.308	.391	.476	34	1	.353	.405	.500
TOTALS		1682	43	.268	.330	.392	812	19	.273	.340	.388	870	24	.263	.320	.397	586	20	.282	.344	.429	1096	23	.261	.322	.368	737	19	.282	.358	.404	289	5	.246	.304	.329
■ Dave Magadan BL/TR																																				
1986	NY-N	18	0	.444	.524	.444	17	0	.471	.550	.471	1	0	.000	.000	.000	3	0	.000	.000	.000	15	0	.533	.611	.533	11	0	.636	.667	.636	2	0	.500	.500	.500
1987	NY-N	192	3	.318	.386	.443	89	2	.382	.451	.539	103	1	.262	.327	.359	48	2	.438	.481	.625	144	1	.278	.354	.382	90	0	.311	.388	.400	36	0	.306	.359	.389
1988	NY-N	314	1	.277	.393	.334	166	1	.301	.407	.361	148	0	.250	.378	.304	86	0	.279	.394	.314	228	1	.276	.393	.342	152	1	.316	.422	.395	61	0	.213	.360	.230
1989	NY-N	374	4	.286	.367	.393	183	3	.306	.378	.415	191	1	.267	.356	.372	92	0	.261	.327	.304	282	4	.294	.379	.422	163	1	.307	.387	.405	68	2	.250	.311	.368
1990	NY-N	451	6	.328	.417	.457	212	4	.278	.391	.373	239	2	.372	.442	.531	168	2	.256	.335	.351	283	4	.371	.462	.519	180	3	.406	.461	.550	69	1	.391	.468	.507
1991	NY-N	418	4	.258	.378	.342	202	2	.243	.358	.322	216	2	.273	.398	.361	151	0	.245	.347	.272	267	4	.266	.395	.382	184	2	.283	.388	.364	57	0	.179	.337	.209
1992	NY-N	321	3	.283	.390	.368	153	2	.314	.426	.399	168	1	.256	.356	.298	120	0	.308	.390	.333	201	3	.269	.390	.353	134	2	.306	.429	.426	47	2	.298	.476	.426
1993	Fla-N	227	4	.286	.400	.392	104	3	.317	.455	.471	123	1	.260	.348	.325	74	0	.243	.344	.311	153	4	.307	.427	.431	111	2	.297	.396	.396	43	2	.256	.373	.442
1993	Sea-A	228	1	.259	.356	.320	102	0	.255	.391	.333	126	1	.262	.324	.310	44	0	.227	.314	.273	184	1	.266	.366	.332	107	1	.243	.354	.299	32	0	.250	.306	.281
1994	Fla-N	211	1	.275	.386	.322	121	1	.306	.407	.372	90	0	.233	.358	.256	67	0	.269	.315	.313	144	1	.278	.414	.326	85	0	.247	.380	.329	35	0	.286	.409	.286
TOTALS		2754	27	.288	.388	.376	1349	16	.297	.403	.389	1405	11	.279	.374	.363	853	4	.272	.355	.329	1901	23	.295	.402	.397	1217	13	.311	.407	.401	460	7	.270	.381	.350
■ Candy Maldonado BR/TR																																				
1984	LA-N	254	5	.268	.318	.382	117	1	.265	.301	.342	137	4	.270	.331	.416	198	4	.303	.343	.429	56	1	.143	.234	.214	111	0	.288	.349	.351	50	2	.240	.264	.360
1985	LA-N	213	5	.225	.288	.359	103	2	.194	.270	.272	110	3	.255	.305	.400	168	5	.232	.301	.363	45	0	.200	.234	.244	97	0	.227	.309	.309	45	3	.222	.271	.422
1986	SF-N	405	18	.252	.289	.477	197	6	.228	.258	.411	208	12	.274	.318	.538	132	6	.235	.252	.477	273	12	.260	.307	.476	183	11	.311	.353	.612	96	6	.313	.350	.625
1987	SF-N	442	20	.292	.346	.509	228	14	.241	.288	.474	214	6	.346	.406	.547	132	6	.295	.371	.515	310	14	.290	.334	.506	217	6	.286	.336	.465	88	3	.338	.369	.550
1988	SF-N	499	12	.255	.311	.377	246	5	.236	.283	.346	253	7	.273	.338	.407	183	1	.251	.303	.311	316	11	.256	.316	.415	229	5	.258	.323	.371	88	0	.148	.200	.148
1989	SF-N	345	9	.217	.296	.362	156	1	.199	.256	.269	189	8	.233	.329	.439	147	2	.211	.310	.313	198	7	.222	.286	.399	165	1	.231	.296	.354	65	1	.231	.286	.354
1990	Cle-A	590	22	.273	.330	.446	298	12	.268	.307	.426	292	10	.277	.353	.466	175	10	.331	.387	.543	415	12	.248	.306	.405	272	9	.283	.355	.438	82	2	.293	.341	.427
1991	Mil-A	111	5	.207	.288	.396	50	3	.200	.317	.440	61	2	.213	.262	.344	27	0	.148	.351	.185	84	5	.226	.261	.464	61	5	.197	.286	.492	19	1	.053	.100	.211
1991	Tor-A	177	7	.277	.375	.446	77	4	.247	.355	.416	100	3	.300	.391	.470	49	3	.347	.429	.612	128	4	.250	.355	.383	81	3	.311	.436	.514	30	1	.167	.306	.267
1992	Tor-A	489	20	.272	.357	.462	219	8	.251	.343	.434	270	12	.289	.368	.485	117	4	.291	.400	.444	372	16	.266	.342	.468	232	10	.297	.399	.517	72	2	.284	.377	.388
1993	Chi-A	140	3	.186	.260	.286	69	1	.203	.236	.290	71	2	.169	.280	.282	70	2	.243	.312	.371	70	1	.129	.208	.200	69	2	.188	.309	.319	32	1	.125	.176	.250
1993	Cle-A	81	5	.247	.333	.457	36	4	.306	.381	.667	45	1	.200	.294	.289	35	3	.286	.375	.600	46	2	.217	.302	.348	54	4	.278	.344	.519	20	0	.250	.304	.300
1994	Cle-A	92	5	.196	.333	.435	35	4	.286	.444	.743	57	1	.140	.258	.246	76	5	.211	.362	.500	16	0	.125	.176	.125	36	2	.167	.348	.389	11	0	.091	.333	.091
TOTALS		3838	136	.255	.321	.424	1831	65	.240	.299	.399	2007	71	.269	.341	.447	1509	51	.266	.338	.429	2329	85	.248	.310	.422	1792	59	.270	.348	.444	685	22	.242	.300	.387
■ Fred Manrique BR/TR																																				
1984	Tor-A	9	0	.333	.333	.333	6	0	.333	.333	.333	3	0	.333	.333	.333	5	0	.200	.200	.200	4	0	.500	.500	.500	5	0	.400	.400	.400	2	0	.500	.500	.500
1985	Mon-N	13	1	.308	.357	.769	7	1	.429	.500	1.000	6	0	.167	.167	.500	10	1	.300	.364	.900	3	0	.333	.333	.333	2	0	.000	.333	.000	4	0	.250	.250	.750
1986	StL-N	17	1	.176	.222	.353	7	0	.000	.000	.000	10	1	.300	.364	.600	17	1	.176	.222	.353	0	0	—	—	—	4	0	.250	.250	.250	5	0	.000	.167	.000
1987	Chi-A	298	4	.258	.302	.362	141	2	.305	.359	.440	157	2	.217	.248	.293	144	2	.299	.361	.451	154	2	.221	.245	.279	118	2	.263	.333	.364	44	0	.227	.227	.273

		TOTAL					HOME					AWAY					LEFT					RIGHT					ON-BASE					LATE/CLOSE				
YEAR	TM/L	AB	HR	AVG	OBP	SLG	AB	HR	AVG	OBP	SLG	AB	HR	AVG	OBP	SLG	AB	HR	AVG	OBP	SLG	AB	HR	AVG	OBP	SLG	AB	HR	AVG	OBP	SLG	AB	HR	AVG	OBP	SLG
1988	Chi-A	345	5	.235	.283	.342	176	3	.222	.274	.330	169	2	.249	.293	.355	149	2	.248	.289	.329	196	3	.224	.278	.352	141	2	.234	.276	.348	64	1	.156	.217	.266
1989	Chi-A	187	2	.299	.333	.412	87	1	.299	.344	.425	100	1	.300	.324	.400	95	1	.337	.388	.432	92	1	.261	.274	.391	87	2	.414	.429	.609	30	0	.367	.424	.400
1989	Tex-A	191	2	.288	.318	.382	87	0	.333	.389	.414	104	2	.250	.255	.356	46	0	.239	.250	.304	145	2	.303	.340	.407	68	1	.309	.324	.412	30	1	.233	.281	.433
1990	Min-A	228	5	.237	.254	.346	100	3	.240	.274	.370	128	2	.234	.238	.328	61	1	.246	.254	.328	167	4	.234	.254	.353	101	4	.248	.250	.406	29	0	.241	.267	.276
1991	Oak-A	21	0	.143	.217	.143	12	0	.167	.231	.167	9	0	.111	.200	.111	10	0	.100	.100	.100	11	0	.182	.308	.182	8	0	.000	.111	.000	2	0	.000	.000	.000
TOTALS		1309	20	.257	.286	.364	623	10	.270	.319	.387	686	10	.245	.271	.344	537	8	.272	.315	.384	772	12	.246	.279	.351	534	11	.279	.314	.406	210	2	.224	.266	.314

■ Mike Marshall BR/TR

		TOTAL					HOME					AWAY					LEFT					RIGHT					ON-BASE					LATE/CLOSE				
YEAR	TM/L	AB	HR	AVG	OBP	SLG	AB	HR	AVG	OBP	SLG	AB	HR	AVG	OBP	SLG	AB	HR	AVG	OBP	SLG	AB	HR	AVG	OBP	SLG	AB	HR	AVG	OBP	SLG	AB	HR	AVG	OBP	SLG
1984	LA-N	495	21	.257	.315	.438	254	11	.260	.303	.437	241	10	.253	.327	.440	158	8	.278	.378	.500	337	13	.246	.282	.409	209	11	.263	.350	.464	90	2	.200	.242	.311
1985	LA-N	518	28	.293	.342	.515	261	15	.303	.345	.536	257	13	.284	.338	.490	157	8	.287	.349	.490	361	20	.296	.339	.526	248	11	.302	.352	.504	83	4	.289	.322	.434
1986	LA-N	330	19	.233	.298	.439	179	13	.240	.305	.497	151	6	.225	.291	.371	129	9	.248	.329	.512	201	10	.224	.278	.393	156	7	.256	.320	.442	59	3	.271	.343	.458
1987	LA-N	402	16	.294	.327	.460	183	5	.284	.327	.404	219	11	.301	.328	.507	125	5	.280	.313	.464	277	11	.300	.333	.458	210	10	.329	.358	.538	58	2	.224	.258	.362
1988	LA-N	542	20	.277	.314	.445	264	9	.261	.299	.432	278	11	.291	.328	.457	186	4	.231	.277	.366	356	16	.301	.333	.486	276	11	.286	.352	.475	89	5	.236	.284	.449
1989	LA-N	377	11	.260	.325	.408	177	6	.294	.352	.480	200	5	.230	.300	.345	130	7	.246	.340	.469	247	4	.267	.316	.377	179	7	.235	.299	.419	69	1	.203	.286	.319
1990	NY-N	163	6	.239	.278	.411	85	4	.235	.280	.435	78	2	.244	.277	.385	67	3	.224	.257	.418	96	3	.250	.292	.406	81	3	.210	.230	.395	27	1	.185	.233	.333
1990	Bos-A	112	4	.286	.316	.464	61	3	.279	.313	.475	51	1	.294	.321	.451	29	1	.207	.258	.379	83	3	.313	.337	.494	50	1	.300	.327	.420	16	0	.313	.313	.313
1991	Bos-A	62	1	.290	.290	.403	31	1	.290	.290	.452	31	0	.290	.290	.355	13	0	.385	.385	.462	49	1	.265	.265	.388	30	0	.300	.300	.400	10	0	.000	.000	.000
1991	Cal-A	7	0	.000	.000	.000	7	0	.000	.000	.000	0	0	—	—	—	3	0	.000	.000	.000	4	0	.000	.000	.000	3	0	.000	.000	.000	2	0	.000	.000	.000
TOTALS		3008	126	.270	.317	.450	1502	67	.271	.316	.461	1506	59	.268	.318	.438	997	45	.258	.324	.455	2011	81	.275	.314	.447	1442	61	.278	.329	.468	503	18	.231	.279	.374

■ Carmelo Martinez BR/TR

		TOTAL					HOME					AWAY					LEFT					RIGHT					ON-BASE					LATE/CLOSE				
YEAR	TM/L	AB	HR	AVG	OBP	SLG	AB	HR	AVG	OBP	SLG	AB	HR	AVG	OBP	SLG	AB	HR	AVG	OBP	SLG	AB	HR	AVG	OBP	SLG	AB	HR	AVG	OBP	SLG	AB	HR	AVG	OBP	SLG
1984	SD-N	488	13	.250	.340	.395	230	6	.252	.360	.391	258	7	.248	.322	.399	161	2	.267	.372	.410	327	11	.242	.325	.388	212	6	.283	.367	.443	89	0	.247	.342	.303
1985	SD-N	514	21	.253	.362	.434	256	15	.273	.390	.496	258	6	.233	.333	.372	166	8	.247	.379	.452	348	13	.256	.353	.425	243	9	.288	.366	.465	108	3	.250	.322	.380
1986	SD-N	244	9	.238	.333	.389	123	6	.179	.297	.358	121	3	.298	.372	.421	110	7	.282	.407	.518	134	2	.201	.265	.284	106	4	.217	.303	.368	64	3	.234	.306	.422
1987	SD-N	447	15	.273	.372	.430	216	10	.282	.390	.468	231	5	.264	.355	.394	184	9	.272	.395	.478	263	6	.274	.355	.395	229	4	.310	.415	.441	74	0	.216	.293	.270
1988	SD-N	365	18	.236	.301	.416	178	11	.258	.337	.489	187	7	.214	.266	.348	154	7	.234	.318	.390	211	11	.237	.288	.436	178	8	.247	.306	.438	77	3	.221	.294	.351
1989	SD-N	267	6	.221	.302	.348	121	2	.165	.257	.248	146	4	.267	.339	.432	118	2	.271	.348	.390	149	4	.181	.266	.315	145	4	.179	.267	.348	60	2	.200	.284	.367
1990	Phi-N	198	8	.242	.339	.404	107	4	.224	.297	.374	91	4	.264	.385	.440	79	3	.215	.333	.380	119	5	.261	.343	.420	94	3	.277	.382	.426	28	2	.250	.382	.500
1990	Pit-N	19	2	.211	.250	.579	15	2	.267	.313	.733	4	0	.000	.000	.000	11	2	.364	.417	1.000	8	0	.000	.000	.000	11	2	.182	.182	.727	5	0	.000	.000	.000
1991	Pit-N	16	0	.250	.294	.250	9	0	.286	.286	.286	7	0	.222	.300	.222	7	0	.143	.250	.143	9	0	.333	.333	.333	7	0	.000	.000	.000	3	0	.333	.333	.333
1991	KC-A	121	4	.207	.351	.355	57	3	.228	.371	.439	64	1	.188	.333	.281	51	2	.216	.375	.392	70	2	.200	.333	.329	55	1	.218	.317	.345	28	2	.179	.343	.464
1991	Cin-N	138	6	.232	.301	.399	66	2	.197	.247	.303	72	4	.264	.349	.486	73	0	.233	.313	.288	65	6	.231	.288	.523	53	1	.245	.295	.358	23	0	.174	.269	.217
TOTALS		2817	102	.245	.338	.405	1376	61	.242	.343	.419	1441	41	.248	.334	.391	1114	42	.254	.364	.426	1703	60	.239	.320	.391	1333	42	.260	.345	.420	559	15	.225	.312	.352

■ Dave Martinez BL/TL

		TOTAL					HOME					AWAY					LEFT					RIGHT					ON-BASE					LATE/CLOSE				
YEAR	TM/L	AB	HR	AVG	OBP	SLG	AB	HR	AVG	OBP	SLG	AB	HR	AVG	OBP	SLG	AB	HR	AVG	OBP	SLG	AB	HR	AVG	OBP	SLG	AB	HR	AVG	OBP	SLG	AB	HR	AVG	OBP	SLG
1986	Chi-N	108	1	.139	.190	.194	66	1	.136	.186	.212	42	0	.143	.196	.167	10	0	.200	.200	.200	98	1	.133	.189	.194	45	0	.200	.245	.222	18	0	.167	.211	.278
1987	Chi-N	459	8	.292	.372	.418	231	5	.281	.366	.433	228	3	.303	.377	.404	23	1	.261	.320	.391	436	7	.294	.374	.420	158	1	.278	.372	.354	68	1	.324	.403	.426
1988	Chi-N	256	4	.254	.311	.348	105	2	.295	.367	.390	151	2	.225	.270	.318	34	2	.206	.282	.412	222	2	.261	.316	.338	80	3	.287	.371	.488	39	0	.282	.333	.436
1988	Mon-N	191	2	.257	.316	.356	95	0	.221	.286	.316	96	2	.292	.346	.396	12	0	.167	.333	.167	179	2	.263	.314	.369	66	0	.227	.278	.227	36	0	.111	.250	.139
1989	Mon-N	361	3	.274	.324	.382	178	1	.208	.258	.264	183	2	.339	.387	.497	30	0	.133	.161	.133	331	3	.287	.338	.405	123	0	.276	.333	.382	65	0	.231	.254	.292
1990	Mon-N	391	11	.279	.321	.422	204	5	.275	.309	.382	187	6	.283	.333	.465	78	1	.244	.333	.308	313	10	.288	.317	.450	153	4	.275	.319	.444	67	2	.209	.260	.284
1991	Mon-N	396	7	.295	.332	.419	173	3	.283	.315	.410	223	4	.305	.345	.426	93	0	.237	.287	.323	303	7	.314	.346	.449	149	0	.302	.359	.389	78	0	.205	.259	.218
1992	Cin-N	393	3	.254	.323	.354	196	3	.291	.355	.423	197	0	.218	.292	.284	59	0	.271	.348	.356	334	3	.251	.319	.353	174	1	.236	.322	.322	52	0	.058	.169	.096
1993	SF-N	241	5	.241	.317	.361	117	1	.197	.254	.274	124	4	.282	.373	.444	27	0	.259	.394	.407	214	5	.238	.306	.355	99	1	.263	.365	.343	32	1	.250	.415	.375
1994	SF-N	235	4	.247	.314	.362	125	4	.200	.270	.256	110	3	.300	.364	.482	28	0	.250	.300	.321	207	4	.246	.316	.367	91	0	.275	.359	.352	42	1	.262	.354	.333
TOTALS		3031	48	.265	.324	.379	1490	22	.250	.309	.354	1541	26	.280	.339	.404	394	4	.234	.307	.320	2637	44	.270	.327	.388	1138	10	.267	.340	.365	497	3	.215	.292	.286

■ Edgar Martinez BR/TR

		TOTAL					HOME					AWAY					LEFT					RIGHT					ON-BASE					LATE/CLOSE				
YEAR	TM/L	AB	HR	AVG	OBP	SLG	AB	HR	AVG	OBP	SLG	AB	HR	AVG	OBP	SLG	AB	HR	AVG	OBP	SLG	AB	HR	AVG	OBP	SLG	AB	HR	AVG	OBP	SLG	AB	HR	AVG	OBP	SLG
1987	Sea-A	43	0	.372	.413	.581	13	0	.308	.400	.615	30	0	.400	.419	.567	14	0	.214	.313	.286	29	0	.448	.467	.724	20	0	.400	.400	.550	9	0	.111	.273	.222
1988	Sea-A	32	0	.281	.351	.406	10	0	.400	.400	.600	22	0	.227	.333	.318	8	0	.375	.500	.625	24	0	.250	.296	.333	10	0	.300	.333	.500	6	0	.333	.429	.500
1989	Sea-A	171	2	.240	.314	.304	77	0	.221	.291	.260	94	2	.255	.333	.340	69	1	.261	.288	.348	102	1	.225	.331	.275	81	1	.296	.348	.358	23	0	.174	.269	.174
1990	Sea-A	487	11	.302	.397	.433	244	3	.299	.401	.414	243	8	.305	.393	.453	156	6	.308	.412	.487	331	5	.299	.390	.408	213	6	.268	.393	.371	90	1	.344	.413	.500
1991	Sea-A	544	14	.307	.405	.452	250	8	.320	.427	.480	294	6	.296	.385	.429	156	2	.359	.442	.481	388	12	.286	.390	.441	216	5	.264	.385	.384	65	1	.354	.522	.462
1992	Sea-A	528	18	.343	.404	.544	268	11	.313	.377	.545	260	7	.373	.432	.542	141	4	.376	.444	.574	387	14	.331	.390	.532	227	9	.300	.364	.480	82	2	.390	.440	.573
1993	Sea-A	135	4	.237	.366	.378	57	1	.228	.371	.316	78	3	.244	.362	.423	36	0	.111	.298	.139	99	4	.283	.393	.465	59	1	.288	.456	.407	23	1	.261	.400	.435
1994	Sea-A	326	13	.285	.387	.482	119	4	.319	.427	.504	207	9	.266	.364	.469	82	4	.329	.471	.573	244	9	.270	.356	.451	135	6	.311	.451	.504	41	1	.366	.519	.634
TOTALS		2266	62	.303	.391	.460	1038	27	.302	.395	.461	1228	35	.304	.387	.458	662	17	.320	.414	.479	1604	45	.296	.381	.452	961	28	.287	.394	.425	339	9	.327	.447	.493

■ Don Mattingly BL/TL

		TOTAL					HOME					AWAY					LEFT					RIGHT					ON-BASE					LATE/CLOSE				
YEAR	TM/L	AB	HR	AVG	OBP	SLG	AB	HR	AVG	OBP	SLG	AB	HR	AVG	OBP	SLG	AB	HR	AVG	OBP	SLG	AB	HR	AVG	OBP	SLG	AB	HR	AVG	OBP	SLG	AB	HR	AVG	OBP	SLG
1984	NY-A	603	23	.343	.381	.537	282	12	.319	.357	.514	321	11	.364	.401	.558	184	5	.279	.373	.500	419	18	.351	.384	.554	276	11	.359	.410	.551	108	4	.352	.417	.546
1985	NY-A	652	35	.324	.371	.567	318	22	.336	.374	.616	334	13	.311	.368	.521	264	18	.288	.328	.568	388	17	.348	.400	.567	315	16	.321	.373	.549	102	6	.353	.391	.569
1986	NY-A	677	31	.352	.394	.573	320	17	.334	.383	.566	357	14	.367	.404	.580	243	5	.358	.398	.523	434	26	.348	.392	.601	317	12	.328	.377	.521	94	4	.351	.421	.521
1987	NY-A	569	30	.327	.378	.559	283	17	.330	.374	.573	286	13	.318	.373	.545	199	11	.302	.355	.523	370	19	.341	.391	.578	279	17	.337	.395	.591	77	2	.234	.348	.377
1988	NY-A	599	18	.311	.353	.462	296	11	.294	.334	.453	303	7	.327	.372	.472	221	3	.290	.316	.389	378	15	.323	.374	.505	291	10	.320	.360	.474	83	2	.265	.303	.386
1989	NY-A	631	23	.303	.351	.477	317	19	.334	.378	.577	314	4	.271	.323	.376	237	8	.338	.382	.532	394	15	.282	.332	.444	298	11	.319	.399	.490	89	4	.303	.392	.517
1990	NY-A	394	5	.256	.308	.335	183	4	.246	.308	.383	211	1	.265	.308	.336	126	0	.262	.301	.310	268	5	.254	.312	.347	167	3	.299	.372	.395	68	2	.206	.308	.353
1991	NY-A	587	9	.288	.339	.394	266	7	.305	.356	.462	321	2	.274	.325	.336	227	5	.264	.321	.383	360	4	.303	.350	.400	256	4	.301	.356	.406	89	4	.303	.402	.494
1992	NY-A	640	14	.287	.327	.416	303	6	.317	.371	.449	337	8	.261	.284	.386	204	2	.284	.318	.397	436	12	.289	.330	.424	282	8	.312	.355	.472	114	5	.263	.317	.447
1993	NY-A	530	17	.291	.364	.445	241	8	.336	.386	.481	289	9	.280	.345	.415	201	5	.264	.344	.388	329	12	.307	.377	.480	257	7	.350	.424	.502	75	2	.307	.342	.440
1994	NY-A	372	6	.304	.397	.411	173	3	.295	.377	.382	199	3	.312	.414	.437	134	1	.299	.382	.373	238	5	.307	.405	.433	184	5	.326	.431	.467	44	1	.364	.481	.500
TOTALS		6254	211	.310	.361	.479	2982	126	.315	.366	.504	3272	85	.306	.356	.456	2240	63	.300	.348	.455	4014	148	.316	.368	.492	2922	104	.325	.384	.499	943	36	.301	.373	.474

■ Derrick May BL/TR

		TOTAL					HOME					AWAY					LEFT					RIGHT					ON-BASE					LATE/CLOSE				
YEAR	TM/L	AB	HR	AVG	OBP	SLG	AB	HR	AVG	OBP	SLG	AB	HR	AVG	OBP	SLG	AB	HR	AVG	OBP	SLG	AB	HR	AVG	OBP	SLG	AB	HR	AVG	OBP	SLG	AB	HR	AVG	OBP	SLG
1990	Chi-N	61	1	.246	.270	.344	25	1	.280	.333	.440	36	0	.222	.222	.278	5	0	.400	.500	.400	56	1	.232	.246	.339	27	1	.296	.296	.519	7	1	.286	.286	.714
1991	Chi-N	22	1	.227	.280	.455	20	1	.250	.304	.500	2	0	.000	.000	.000	1	0	.000	.500	.000	21	1	.238	.261	.476	7	0	.286	.333	.429	7	0	.000	.000	.000
1992	Chi-N	351	8	.274	.306	.373	202	3	.292	.327	.376	149	5	.248	.277	.369	76	2	.250	.287	.355	275	6	.280	.311	.378	164	6	.287	.314	.433	64	3	.250	.290	.406
1993	Chi-N	465	10	.295	.336	.422	248	3	.319	.360	.427	217	7	.267	.309	.415	89	4	.247	.266	.438	376	6	.306	.352	.418	237	7	.325	.366	.498	83	2	.301	.310	.422
1994	Chi-N	345	8	.284	.340	.420	175	5	.280	.332	.423	170	3	.288	.348	.418	67	2	.313	.324	.448	278	6	.277	.343	.414	175	2	.286	.335	.371	59	1	.237	.297	.339
TOTALS		1244	28	.282	.325	.404	670	13	.297	.340	.413	574	15	.265	.307	.394	238	8	.269	.296	.412	1006	20	.285	.331	.403	610	16	.302	.340	.444	220	7	.259	.291	.391

■ Oddibe McDowell BL/TL

		TOTAL					HOME					AWAY					LEFT					RIGHT					ON-BASE					LATE/CLOSE				
YEAR	TM/L	AB	HR	AVG	OBP	SLG	AB	HR	AVG	OBP	SLG	AB	HR	AVG	OBP	SLG	AB	HR	AVG	OBP	SLG	AB	HR	AVG	OBP	SLG	AB	HR	AVG	OBP	SLG	AB	HR	AVG	OBP	SLG
1985	Tex-A	406	18	.239	.304	.431	203	10	.266	.323	.463	203	8	.212	.286	.399	123	3	.244	.311	.431	283	15	.237	.301	.431	146	4	.192	.259	.329	62	5	.194	.296	.452
1986	Tex-A	572	18	.266	.341	.427	290	8	.279	.340	.441	282	10	.252	.342	.411	128	3	.219	.296	.336	444	15	.279	.353	.453	182	3	.308	.379	.407	87	2	.287	.386	.414
1987	Tex-A	407	14	.241	.324	.428	196	5	.250	.315	.413	211	9	.232	.332	.441	71	2	.225	.371	.352	336	12	.244	.313	.443	168	4	.226	.323	.387	61	1	.246	.395	.344
1988	Tex-A	437	6	.247	.311	.355	211	4	.246	.301	.374	226	2	.248	.302	.336	96	2	.229	.288	.354	341	4	.252	.318	.355	165	0	.248	.303	.345	73	0	.301	.342	.370
1989	Cle-A	239	3	.222	.296	.297	96	1	.250	.348	.344	143	2	.203	.258	.266	70	0	.214	.304	.229	169	3	.225	.293	.325	98	1	.194	.264	.327	29	1	.172	.296	.276
1989	Atl-N	280	7	.304	.365	.471	136	2	.316	.380	.449	144	5	.292	.350	.493	100	0	.230	.280	.280	180	7	.344	.410	.578	88	2	.330	.404	.580	47	1	.277	.346	.426
1990	Atl-N	305	7	.243	.295	.357	150	4	.273	.321	.400	155	3	.213	.269	.316	39	0	.103	.222	.103	266	7	.263	.306	.395	87	3	.276	.340	.414	43	1	.186	.234	.279
1994	Tex-A	183	1	.262	.355	.317	104	1	.231	.344	.288	79	0	.304	.371	.354	26	0	.308	.444	.308	157	1	.255	.337	.318	73	0	.288	.382	.342	32	0	.406	.472	.438
TOTALS		2829	74	.253	.323	.395	1386	35	.266	.334	.408	1443	39	.240	.313	.383	653	10	.224	.308	.323	2176	64	.261	.328	.417	1007	19	.254	.328	.385	434	11	.260	.345	.382

■ Willie McGee BB/TR

		TOTAL					HOME					AWAY					LEFT					RIGHT					ON-BASE					LATE/CLOSE				
YEAR	TM/L	AB	HR	AVG	OBP	SLG	AB	HR	AVG	OBP	SLG	AB	HR	AVG	OBP	SLG	AB	HR	AVG	OBP	SLG	AB	HR	AVG	OBP	SLG	AB	HR	AVG	OBP	SLG	AB	HR	AVG	OBP	SLG
1984	StL-N	571	6	.291	.325	.394	263	2	.304	.338	.392	308	4	.279	.313	.396	164	5	.268	.297	.433	407	1	.300	.336	.378	224	3	.263	.309	.375	82	2	.256	.308	.415
1985	StL-N	612	10	.353	.384	.503	283	3	.353	.370	.473	329	7	.353	.395	.529	210	7	.348	.372	.571	402	3	.356	.390	.468	253	5	.360	.404	.510	85	2	.306	.337	.459
1986	StL-N	497	7	.256	.306	.370	264	7	.280	.325	.462	233	0	.227	.285	.266	199	5	.246	.301	.387	298	2	.262	.310	.359	203	2	.236	.303	.355	98	0	.214	.275	.255
1987	StL-N	620	11	.285	.312	.434	298	6	.297	.316	.457	322	5	.275	.308	.412	208	6	.288	.309	.500	412	5	.284	.313	.400	322	9	.295	.328	.463	114	0	.272	.292	.368
1988	StL-N	562	3	.292	.329	.372	283	1	.283	.322	.353	279	2	.301	.337	.391	197	0	.294	.322	.355	365	3	.290	.333	.381	249	1	.289	.326	.373	120	1	.275	.293	.317
1989	StL-N	199	3	.236	.275	.352	106	1	.255	.292	.349	93	2	.215	.255	.355	77	2	.156	.195	.273	122	1	.287	.326	.402	65	1	.262	.290	.354	40	0	.275	.310	.275
1990	StL-N	501	3	.335	.362	.447	304	3	.348	.388	.487	197	0	.320	.330	.391	197	2	.335	.362	.442	304	1	.335	.362	.451	235	0	.323	.378	.430	79	1	.380	.424	.506
1990	Oak-A	113	0	.274	.333	.336	55	0	.273	.333	.309	58	0	.276	.333	.362	28	0	.250	.276	.321	85	0	.282	.351	.341	60	0	.267	.302	.350	14	0	.357	.471	.500
1991	SF-N	497	4	.312	.357	.408	222	2	.270	.306	.351	275	2	.345	.397	.455	154	2	.338	.380	.448	343	2	.300	.347	.391	180	1	.339	.401	.417	85	1	.329	.370	.424
1992	SF-N	474	1	.297	.339	.354	224	0	.317	.361	.384	250	1	.280	.318	.328	159	1	.283	.305	.365	315	0	.305	.355	.349	171	0	.351	.407	.421	95	0	.274	.296	.316
1993	SF-N	475	4	.301	.353	.389	217	0	.318	.374	.382	258	4	.287	.335	.395	144	1	.319	.349	.403	331	3	.293	.354	.384	191	1	.325	.396	.408	75	1	.400	.438	.493

YEAR TM/L	TOTAL AB HR AVG OBP SLG	HOME AB HR AVG OBP SLG	AWAY AB HR AVG OBP SLG	LEFT AB HR AVG OBP SLG	RIGHT AB HR AVG OBP SLG	ON-BASE AB HR AVG OBP SLG	LATE/CLOSE AB HR AVG OBP SLG
1994 SF-N	156 5 .282 .337 .397	97 2 .299 .349 .381	59 3 .254 .318 .424	43 2 .279 .326 .442	113 3 .283 .341 .381	82 1 .268 .312 .329	35 0 .257 .325 .286
TOTALS	5277 57 .299 .340 .406	2587 25 .305 .342 .408	2690 32 .294 .338 .403	1780 33 .294 .326 .429	3497 24 .302 .347 .394	2235 24 .304 .353 .413	922 8 .292 .332 .379

■ Fred McGriff BL/TL

YEAR TM/L	TOTAL AB HR AVG OBP SLG	HOME AB HR AVG OBP SLG	AWAY AB HR AVG OBP SLG	LEFT AB HR AVG OBP SLG	RIGHT AB HR AVG OBP SLG	ON-BASE AB HR AVG OBP SLG	LATE/CLOSE AB HR AVG OBP SLG
1986 Tor-A	5 0 .200 .200 .200	1 0 1.000 1.000 1.000	4 0 .000 .000 .000	0 0 — — —	5 0 .200 .200 .200	1 0 .000 .000 .000	2 0 .000 .000 .000
1987 Tor-A	295 20 .247 .376 .505	156 13 .269 .384 .551	139 7 .223 .368 .453	26 1 .154 .241 .346	269 19 .257 .388 .520	129 6 .225 .363 .411	41 0 .146 .314 .195
1988 Tor-A	536 34 .282 .376 .552	250 18 .256 .363 .536	286 16 .304 .387 .566	151 5 .234 .307 .368	385 29 .304 .406 .638	236 15 .258 .362 .504	84 2 .286 .388 .488
1989 Tor-A	551 36 .269 .399 .525	273 18 .282 .406 .549	278 18 .255 .393 .500	189 5 .254 .360 .376	362 31 .276 .419 .602	241 15 .257 .420 .494	89 4 .292 .434 .472
1990 Tor-A	557 35 .300 .400 .530	264 14 .277 .399 .473	293 21 .321 .401 .580	202 8 .257 .324 .411	355 27 .324 .440 .597	226 11 .270 .383 .447	87 4 .230 .303 .448
1991 SD-N	528 31 .278 .396 .494	239 18 .280 .426 .536	289 13 .277 .369 .460	213 14 .272 .380 .512	315 17 .283 .406 .483	248 14 .302 .439 .524	72 2 .222 .412 .333
1992 SD-N	531 35 .286 .394 .556	273 21 .304 .406 .612	258 14 .267 .381 .496	205 13 .283 .369 .551	326 22 .288 .409 .558	235 16 .294 .444 .604	81 2 .321 .418 .494
1993 SD-N	302 18 .275 .361 .497	138 7 .225 .335 .391	164 11 .317 .384 .585	119 4 .252 .346 .378	183 14 .290 .371 .574	148 7 .257 .363 .419	45 5 .311 .429 .667
1993 Atl-N	255 19 .310 .392 .612	117 8 .350 .449 .624	138 11 .275 .340 .601	82 4 .305 .367 .549	173 15 .312 .403 .642	120 9 .342 .441 .650	36 2 .306 .375 .556
1994 Atl-N	424 34 .318 .389 .623	201 13 .284 .365 .547	223 21 .350 .411 .691	157 10 .293 .351 .522	267 24 .333 .411 .682	202 18 .347 .418 .668	55 3 .345 .439 .673
TOTALS	3984 262 .285 .389 .541	1895 124 .277 .393 .530	2089 138 .292 .385 .551	1364 64 .265 .349 .455	2620 198 .296 .409 .586	1786 111 .283 .404 .526	592 24 .274 .392 .475

■ Mark McGwire BR/TR

YEAR TM/L	TOTAL AB HR AVG OBP SLG	HOME AB HR AVG OBP SLG	AWAY AB HR AVG OBP SLG	LEFT AB HR AVG OBP SLG	RIGHT AB HR AVG OBP SLG	ON-BASE AB HR AVG OBP SLG	LATE/CLOSE AB HR AVG OBP SLG
1986 Oak-A	53 3 .189 .259 .377	21 1 .143 .250 .286	32 2 .219 .265 .438	36 2 .250 .325 .444	17 1 .059 .111 .235	20 1 .300 .333 .500	8 0 .125 .125 .125
1987 Oak-A	557 49 .289 .370 .618	278 21 .277 .366 .572	279 28 .301 .373 .663	171 16 .287 .400 .626	386 33 .290 .355 .614	242 17 .302 .383 .595	82 6 .276 .323 .529
1988 Oak-A	550 32 .260 .352 .478	256 12 .246 .347 .430	294 20 .272 .356 .520	150 11 .247 .358 .533	400 21 .265 .349 .458	240 17 .296 .403 .558	97 8 .258 .330 .515
1989 Oak-A	490 33 .231 .339 .467	246 12 .232 .321 .427	244 21 .230 .357 .508	132 6 .235 .344 .439	358 27 .229 .337 .478	224 16 .263 .346 .522	67 3 .239 .312 .388
1990 Oak-A	523 39 .235 .370 .489	245 14 .224 .369 .429	278 25 .245 .370 .543	132 11 .258 .387 .530	391 28 .228 .364 .476	245 19 .224 .360 .482	62 5 .339 .549 .613
1991 Oak-A	483 22 .201 .330 .383	243 15 .185 .329 .412	240 7 .217 .332 .354	130 5 .200 .316 .354	353 17 .201 .336 .394	239 14 .230 .355 .444	65 4 .169 .337 .385
1992 Oak-A	467 42 .268 .385 .585	218 24 .252 .398 .619	249 18 .281 .373 .554	97 14 .330 .447 .804	370 28 .251 .368 .527	200 15 .255 .378 .530	59 5 .237 .373 .508
1993 Oak-A	84 9 .333 .467 .726	41 5 .341 .491 .756	43 4 .326 .442 .698	22 3 .455 .556 1.000	62 6 .290 .438 .629	40 3 .275 .464 .575	12 2 .333 .500 .833
1994 Oak-A	135 9 .252 .413 .474	62 6 .210 .395 .516	73 3 .288 .429 .438	62 4 .194 .405 .403	73 5 .301 .420 .534	67 5 .254 .444 .507	21 1 .143 .250 .286
TOTALS	3342 238 .250 .362 .507	1610 110 .237 .359 .486	1732 128 .261 .364 .527	932 72 .258 .379 .539	2410 166 .246 .355 .495	1517 107 .262 .377 .522	478 34 .249 .367 .485

■ Mark McLemore BB/TR

YEAR TM/L	TOTAL AB HR AVG OBP SLG	HOME AB HR AVG OBP SLG	AWAY AB HR AVG OBP SLG	LEFT AB HR AVG OBP SLG	RIGHT AB HR AVG OBP SLG	ON-BASE AB HR AVG OBP SLG	LATE/CLOSE AB HR AVG OBP SLG
1986 Cal-A	4 0 .000 .200 .000	1 0 .000 .500 .000	3 0 .000 .000 .000	62 4 .194 .405 .403	4 0 .000 .200 .000	1 0 .000 .000 .000	1 0 .000 .000 .000
1987 Cal-A	433 3 .236 .310 .300	213 3 .235 .315 .319	220 0 .236 .305 .282	126 1 .222 .293 .294	307 2 .241 .317 .303	193 1 .238 .333 .316	77 1 .351 .438 .416
1988 Cal-A	233 2 .240 .312 .330	102 1 .216 .298 .294	131 1 .260 .322 .359	65 0 .200 .268 .246	168 2 .256 .328 .363	87 1 .161 .227 .230	51 0 .255 .283 .275
1989 Cal-A	103 0 .243 .295 .291	43 0 .302 .362 .372	60 0 .200 .246 .233	35 0 .314 .351 .400	68 0 .206 .267 .235	43 0 .326 .333 .395	18 0 .167 .211 .167
1990 Cal-A	48 0 .146 .212 .188	26 0 .154 .267 .192	22 0 .136 .136 .182	17 0 .235 .235 .294	31 0 .097 .200 .129	27 0 .074 .167 .074	7 0 .143 .333 .143
1990 Cle-A	12 0 .167 .167 .167	6 0 .333 .333 .333	6 0 .000 .000 .000	5 0 .200 .200 .200	7 0 .143 .143 .143	4 0 .250 .250 .250	3 0 .000 .000 .000
1991 Hou-N	61 0 .148 .221 .164	34 0 .088 .158 .088	27 0 .222 .300 .259	28 0 .179 .233 .214	33 0 .121 .211 .121	23 0 .130 .222 .130	11 0 .182 .333 .182
1992 Bal-A	228 0 .246 .308 .294	111 0 .198 .250 .252	117 0 .291 .362 .333	58 0 .276 .333 .310	170 0 .235 .299 .288	120 0 .267 .326 .333	52 0 .231 .298 .250
1993 Bal-A	581 4 .284 .353 .368	293 2 .314 .377 .399	288 2 .253 .328 .337	162 2 .216 .270 .253	419 4 .310 .383 .413	248 1 .278 .358 .363	87 1 .264 .340 .356
1994 Bal-A	343 3 .257 .354 .321	162 2 .272 .355 .340	181 1 .243 .352 .304	54 0 .167 .318 .185	289 3 .273 .361 .346	168 2 .262 .378 .339	59 0 .220 .324 .220
TOTALS	2046 12 .249 .323 .317	991 8 .254 .327 .327	1055 4 .245 .319 .308	550 1 .222 .289 .269	1496 11 .259 .335 .335	914 5 .246 .330 .318	366 2 .257 .336 .298

■ Brian McRae BB/TR

YEAR TM/L	TOTAL AB HR AVG OBP SLG	HOME AB HR AVG OBP SLG	AWAY AB HR AVG OBP SLG	LEFT AB HR AVG OBP SLG	RIGHT AB HR AVG OBP SLG	ON-BASE AB HR AVG OBP SLG	LATE/CLOSE AB HR AVG OBP SLG
1990 KC-A	168 2 .286 .318 .405	81 1 .309 .348 .469	87 1 .264 .289 .345	72 1 .361 .382 .458	96 1 .229 .272 .365	64 1 .297 .319 .438	21 0 .429 .455 .476
1991 KC-A	629 8 .261 .288 .372	318 3 .267 .305 .384	311 5 .254 .270 .360	204 2 .294 .326 .407	425 6 .245 .270 .355	230 5 .239 .274 .361	97 1 .247 .295 .351
1992 KC-A	533 4 .223 .285 .308	257 2 .245 .301 .346	276 2 .203 .271 .272	163 3 .233 .282 .362	370 1 .219 .287 .284	220 2 .241 .290 .345	100 0 .210 .281 .290
1993 KC-A	627 12 .282 .325 .413	321 5 .287 .322 .408	306 7 .278 .328 .418	199 5 .322 .340 .477	428 7 .264 .318 .383	235 6 .260 .300 .409	110 3 .300 .336 .473
1994 KC-A	436 4 .273 .359 .378	221 2 .285 .377 .389	215 2 .260 .339 .367	127 1 .307 .380 .425	309 3 .259 .350 .359	169 1 .266 .371 .361	70 0 .229 .316 .314
TOTALS	2393 30 .262 .313 .372	1198 13 .274 .326 .389	1195 17 .250 .299 .355	765 12 .297 .335 .424	1628 18 .246 .303 .348	918 16 .254 .307 .375	398 4 .259 .314 .369

■ Hal McRae BR/TR

YEAR TM/L	TOTAL AB HR AVG OBP SLG	HOME AB HR AVG OBP SLG	AWAY AB HR AVG OBP SLG	LEFT AB HR AVG OBP SLG	RIGHT AB HR AVG OBP SLG	ON-BASE AB HR AVG OBP SLG	LATE/CLOSE AB HR AVG OBP SLG
1984 KC-A	317 3 .303 .363 .397	173 2 .312 .371 .428	144 1 .292 .354 .361	157 3 .331 .388 .459	160 0 .275 .337 .338	157 2 .261 .317 .376	48 0 .375 .467 .479
1985 KC-A	320 14 .259 .349 .450	165 7 .267 .349 .461	155 7 .252 .348 .439	150 8 .233 .345 .467	170 6 .282 .353 .435	163 9 .307 .395 .540	50 3 .300 .403 .500
1986 KC-A	278 7 .252 .298 .378	125 1 .272 .331 .360	153 6 .235 .270 .392	153 5 .268 .325 .431	125 2 .232 .263 .312	141 4 .241 .306 .369	62 2 .242 .309 .339
1987 KC-A	32 1 .313 .405 .500	22 1 .227 .320 .455	10 0 .500 .583 .600	16 1 .438 .571 .750	16 0 .188 .188 .250	16 0 .500 .579 .688	10 0 .300 .364 .300
TOTALS	947 25 .273 .341 .413	485 11 .282 .351 .423	462 14 .264 .331 .403	476 17 .284 .362 .462	471 8 .263 .319 .363	477 15 .279 .350 .404	170 5 .300 .388 .424

■ Kevin McReynolds BR/TR

YEAR TM/L	TOTAL AB HR AVG OBP SLG	HOME AB HR AVG OBP SLG	AWAY AB HR AVG OBP SLG	LEFT AB HR AVG OBP SLG	RIGHT AB HR AVG OBP SLG	ON-BASE AB HR AVG OBP SLG	LATE/CLOSE AB HR AVG OBP SLG
1984 SD-N	525 20 .278 .317 .465	264 10 .299 .347 .496	261 10 .257 .286 .433	161 9 .267 .331 .509	364 11 .283 .310 .445	213 4 .300 .347 .423	102 5 .265 .280 .490
1985 SD-N	564 15 .234 .290 .371	264 6 .235 .282 .360	300 9 .233 .297 .380	173 3 .260 .340 .370	391 12 .223 .266 .371	260 7 .281 .348 .431	111 1 .198 .252 .279
1986 SD-N	560 26 .287 .358 .504	276 14 .293 .368 .514	284 12 .282 .349 .493	192 10 .339 .395 .589	368 16 .261 .339 .459	263 14 .289 .359 .525	111 5 .252 .325 .423
1987 NY-N	590 29 .276 .318 .495	298 18 .275 .324 .503	292 11 .277 .312 .486	221 12 .290 .325 .534	369 17 .268 .314 .472	279 11 .222 .274 .409	101 1 .228 .286 .277
1988 NY-N	552 27 .288 .336 .496	279 13 .276 .320 .470	273 14 .300 .351 .524	185 12 .270 .330 .541	367 15 .297 .349 .472	257 11 .311 .359 .502	90 2 .322 .354 .544
1989 NY-N	545 22 .272 .326 .450	274 12 .266 .330 .445	271 10 .277 .321 .454	189 10 .296 .377 .508	356 12 .258 .297 .419	217 7 .249 .331 .415	99 5 .313 .364 .505
1990 NY-N	521 24 .269 .353 .455	244 11 .258 .336 .426	277 13 .278 .368 .480	194 4 .232 .358 .351	327 20 .291 .350 .517	234 10 .286 .382 .479	97 4 .289 .369 .433
1991 NY-N	522 16 .259 .322 .416	236 7 .237 .289 .386	286 9 .276 .349 .441	189 6 .259 .311 .418	333 10 .258 .329 .414	220 9 .268 .350 .455	85 5 .259 .323 .541
1992 KC-A	373 13 .247 .357 .418	186 4 .253 .363 .398	187 9 .241 .351 .439	113 5 .345 .461 .575	260 8 .204 .309 .350	159 6 .258 .356 .421	72 4 .236 .353 .472
1993 KC-A	351 11 .245 .316 .425	194 8 .284 .340 .515	158 3 .197 .289 .312	126 2 .222 .333 .349	225 9 .258 .306 .467	140 2 .243 .339 .343	76 1 .263 .317 .421
1994 NY-N	180 4 .256 .308 .406	86 3 .291 .351 .477	94 1 .223 .266 .340	43 1 .279 .340 .488	137 3 .248 .296 .380	79 1 .253 .336 .367	30 1 .133 .188 .233
TOTALS	5283 207 .267 .329 .450	2601 106 .269 .330 .454	2682 101 .264 .328 .446	1786 74 .278 .353 .476	3497 133 .261 .317 .437	2321 82 .271 .343 .443	974 38 .258 .317 .427

■ Orlando Merced BB/TR

YEAR TM/L	TOTAL AB HR AVG OBP SLG	HOME AB HR AVG OBP SLG	AWAY AB HR AVG OBP SLG	LEFT AB HR AVG OBP SLG	RIGHT AB HR AVG OBP SLG	ON-BASE AB HR AVG OBP SLG	LATE/CLOSE AB HR AVG OBP SLG
1990 Pit-N	24 0 .208 .240 .250	12 0 .250 .308 .333	12 0 .167 .167 .167	8 0 .125 .125 .125	16 0 .250 .294 .313	10 0 .100 .100 .100	7 0 .429 .500 .571
1991 Pit-N	411 10 .275 .373 .399	192 5 .255 .370 .391	219 5 .292 .376 .406	53 0 .208 .263 .302	358 10 .285 .388 .507	150 6 .320 .383 .507	62 3 .210 .359 .403
1992 Pit-N	405 6 .247 .332 .385	199 4 .251 .345 .407	206 2 .243 .319 .364	84 0 .190 .306 .226	321 6 .262 .339 .427	179 4 .274 .372 .425	86 1 .233 .320 .372
1993 Pit-N	447 8 .313 .414 .443	205 3 .298 .401 .415	242 5 .326 .425 .467	111 0 .297 .389 .405	336 8 .318 .423 .455	235 6 .319 .417 .472	78 2 .321 .411 .449
1994 Pit-N	386 9 .272 .343 .412	201 4 .249 .338 .383	185 5 .297 .350 .443	96 3 .281 .361 .427	290 6 .269 .337 .407	176 5 .278 .368 .443	56 4 .339 .406 .607
TOTALS	1673 33 .277 .366 .408	809 16 .263 .363 .398	864 17 .289 .369 .418	352 3 .250 .337 .347	1321 30 .284 .374 .425	750 21 .296 .384 .456	289 10 .277 .374 .450

■ Randy Milligan BR/TR

YEAR TM/L	TOTAL AB HR AVG OBP SLG	HOME AB HR AVG OBP SLG	AWAY AB HR AVG OBP SLG	LEFT AB HR AVG OBP SLG	RIGHT AB HR AVG OBP SLG	ON-BASE AB HR AVG OBP SLG	LATE/CLOSE AB HR AVG OBP SLG
1987 NY-N	1 0 .000 .500 .000	1 0 .000 .500 .000	0 0 — 1.000 —	1 0 .000 .500 .000	0 0 — — —	1 0 .000 .500 .000	0 0 — 1.000 —
1988 Pit-N	82 3 .220 .379 .390	42 1 .190 .414 .357	40 2 .250 .333 .425	56 2 .196 .366 .375	26 1 .269 .406 .423	37 1 .216 .370 .351	19 0 .263 .417 .421
1989 Bal-A	365 12 .268 .394 .458	178 6 .287 .446 .461	187 6 .251 .338 .455	169 6 .225 .351 .396	196 6 .306 .430 .510	162 6 .278 .405 .469	46 2 .370 .516 .565
1990 Bal-A	362 20 .265 .408 .492	166 11 .265 .419 .536	196 9 .265 .398 .454	100 8 .330 .473 .680	262 12 .240 .382 .420	171 3 .287 .414 .409	60 4 .250 .438 .483
1991 Bal-A	483 16 .263 .373 .406	237 8 .249 .362 .388	246 8 .276 .384 .423	140 5 .229 .347 .371	343 11 .277 .384 .420	222 5 .252 .361 .369	86 2 .244 .363 .372
1992 Bal-A	462 11 .240 .383 .361	233 7 .193 .361 .313	229 4 .288 .406 .410	107 3 .280 .462 .421	355 8 .228 .356 .344	215 5 .247 .355 .353	75 2 .200 .307 .347
1993 Cin-N	234 6 .274 .394 .406	107 5 .280 .431 .449	127 1 .268 .359 .370	101 4 .337 .422 .545	133 2 .226 .373 .301	98 1 .306 .410 .388	31 0 .226 .385 .290
1993 Cle-A	47 0 .426 .557 .574	23 0 .435 .606 .609	24 0 .417 .500 .542	32 0 .531 .651 .719	15 0 .200 .333 .267	23 0 .304 .385 .391	12 0 .167 .375 .167
1994 Mon-N	82 2 .232 .337 .329	45 1 .244 .320 .333	37 1 .216 .354 .324	50 1 .260 .362 .360	32 1 .188 .300 .281	47 2 .234 .377 .383	21 1 .143 .310 .333
TOTALS	2118 70 .261 .391 .420	1032 39 .250 .400 .415	1086 31 .272 .381 .424	756 29 .275 .409 .462	1362 41 .253 .380 .396	976 23 .265 .384 .391	350 11 .243 .390 .397

■ Eddie Milner BL/TL

YEAR TM/L	TOTAL AB HR AVG OBP SLG	HOME AB HR AVG OBP SLG	AWAY AB HR AVG OBP SLG	LEFT AB HR AVG OBP SLG	RIGHT AB HR AVG OBP SLG	ON-BASE AB HR AVG OBP SLG	LATE/CLOSE AB HR AVG OBP SLG
1984 Cin-N	336 7 .232 .333 .342	148 5 .264 .373 .399	188 2 .207 .301 .298	77 1 .221 .304 .312	259 6 .236 .334 .351	113 3 .221 .343 .354	63 2 .270 .397 .413
1985 Cin-N	453 3 .254 .342 .347	223 1 .247 .336 .350	230 2 .261 .347 .343	47 0 .213 .327 .234	406 3 .259 .343 .360	155 1 .245 .326 .310	71 0 .254 .354 .282
1986 Cin-N	424 15 .259 .317 .446	208 8 .288 .346 .486	216 7 .231 .288 .407	58 0 .224 .262 .276	366 15 .265 .325 .473	140 3 .271 .348 .450	66 4 .212 .268 .455
1987 SF-N	214 4 .252 .328 .374	110 4 .236 .317 .400	104 0 .269 .340 .346	32 0 .156 .229 .156	182 4 .269 .345 .412	69 0 .290 .355 .377	40 0 .250 .348 .350
1988 Cin-N	51 0 .176 .236 .196	18 0 .111 .158 .167	33 0 .212 .278 .212	14 0 .214 .267 .214	37 0 .162 .225 .189	17 0 .235 .316 .235	7 0 .143 .250 .286
TOTALS	1478 29 .248 .327 .373	707 18 .257 .340 .403	771 11 .239 .316 .345	228 1 .211 .296 .259	1250 28 .254 .333 .394	494 7 .253 .340 .366	247 6 .243 .340 .372

■ Kevin Mitchell BR/TR

YEAR TM/L	TOTAL AB HR AVG OBP SLG	HOME AB HR AVG OBP SLG	AWAY AB HR AVG OBP SLG	LEFT AB HR AVG OBP SLG	RIGHT AB HR AVG OBP SLG	ON-BASE AB HR AVG OBP SLG	LATE/CLOSE AB HR AVG OBP SLG
1984 NY-N	14 0 .214 .214 .214	6 0 .167 .167 .167	8 0 .250 .250 .250	7 0 .286 .286 .286	7 0 .143 .143 .143	8 0 .250 .250 .250	1 0 .000 .000 .000
1986 NY-N	328 12 .277 .344 .466	162 4 .302 .370 .481	166 8 .253 .319 .452	199 7 .307 .358 .503	129 5 .233 .324 .411	136 5 .294 .370 .485	59 3 .288 .323 .492
1987 SD-N	196 7 .245 .313 .398	83 2 .241 .312 .398	113 5 .248 .315 .398	66 4 .258 .338 .515	130 3 .238 .301 .338	98 3 .276 .345 .398	33 1 .182 .289 .273
1987 SF-N	268 15 .306 .376 .530	144 7 .319 .387 .521	124 8 .290 .362 .540	73 6 .411 .488 .767	195 9 .267 .333 .446	115 8 .357 .417 .609	46 1 .239 .271 .326
1988 SF-N	505 19 .251 .319 .442	253 10 .265 .319 .470	252 9 .238 .318 .413	160 5 .200 .280 .338	345 14 .275 .337 .490	240 7 .275 .337 .438	80 5 .188 .267 .387
1989 SF-N	543 47 .291 .387 .635	255 22 .298 .403 .663	288 25 .285 .373 .611	171 19 .304 .426 .725	372 28 .285 .369 .594	288 22 .278 .404 .573	76 6 .303 .423 .605

YEAR	TM/L	TOTAL AB	HR	AVG	OBP	SLG	HOME AB	HR	AVG	OBP	SLG	AWAY AB	HR	AVG	OBP	SLG	LEFT AB	HR	AVG	OBP	SLG	RIGHT AB	HR	AVG	OBP	SLG	ON-BASE AB	HR	AVG	OBP	SLG	LATE/CLOSE AB	HR	AVG	OBP	SLG
1990	SF-N	524	35	.290	.360	.544	241	15	.278	.360	.515	283	20	.300	.360	.569	170	10	.306	.395	.547	354	25	.282	.342	.542	266	11	.241	.324	.421	88	8	.352	.414	.670
1991	SF-N	371	27	.256	.338	.515	190	9	.242	.307	.432	181	18	.271	.370	.602	114	7	.272	.370	.491	257	20	.249	.323	.525	179	12	.244	.330	.480	61	2	.148	.284	.279
1992	Sea-A	360	9	.286	.351	.428	207	5	.319	.368	.473	153	4	.242	.328	.366	92	5	.380	.438	.598	268	4	.254	.320	.369	180	5	.322	.373	.494	58	0	.293	.339	.328
1993	Cin-N	323	19	.341	.385	.601	186	10	.349	.386	.613	137	9	.328	.384	.584	94	8	.394	.424	.745	229	11	.319	.370	.541	165	6	.321	.376	.527	46	4	.283	.346	.609
1994	Cin-N	310	30	.326	.429	.681	170	18	.347	.462	.724	140	12	.300	.387	.629	78	9	.346	.441	.769	232	21	.319	.425	.651	148	11	.338	.459	.622	46	3	.217	.424	.457
TOTALS		3742	220	.286	.361	.529	1897	102	.296	.369	.536	1845	118	.275	.352	.522	1224	80	.307	.387	.575	2518	140	.276	.348	.506	1823	90	.287	.371	.501	594	33	.256	.345	.461

■ Paul Molitor BR/TR

YEAR	TM/L	TOTAL AB	HR	AVG	OBP	SLG	HOME AB	HR	AVG	OBP	SLG	AWAY AB	HR	AVG	OBP	SLG	LEFT AB	HR	AVG	OBP	SLG	RIGHT AB	HR	AVG	OBP	SLG	ON-BASE AB	HR	AVG	OBP	SLG	LATE/CLOSE AB	HR	AVG	OBP	SLG
1984	Mil-A	46	0	.217	.245	.239	21	0	.238	.273	.286	25	0	.200	.222	.200	24	0	.250	.280	.250	22	0	.182	.208	.227	19	0	.368	.409	.368	6	0	.167	.286	.167
1985	Mil-A	576	10	.297	.356	.408	257	6	.323	.382	.467	319	4	.276	.334	.361	179	5	.324	.384	.464	397	5	.285	.343	.383	180	1	.300	.375	.361	91	2	.352	.396	.495
1986	Mil-A	437	9	.281	.340	.426	213	5	.300	.345	.451	224	4	.263	.335	.402	100	1	.270	.318	.400	337	8	.285	.346	.433	155	5	.310	.385	.452	74	3	.324	.342	.541
1987	Mil-A	465	16	.353	.438	.566	231	7	.394	.470	.610	234	9	.312	.406	.521	145	3	.331	.426	.476	320	13	.363	.443	.606	166	8	.422	.495	.681	73	4	.425	.488	.685
1988	Mil-A	609	13	.312	.384	.452	316	9	.316	.382	.468	293	4	.307	.386	.433	196	4	.276	.353	.393	413	9	.329	.399	.479	185	5	.357	.438	.508	74	1	.297	.376	.419
1989	Mil-A	615	11	.315	.379	.439	296	6	.328	.399	.453	319	5	.304	.359	.426	157	4	.325	.413	.484	458	7	.312	.366	.424	199	2	.337	.397	.422	69	1	.319	.420	.406
1990	Mil-A	418	12	.285	.343	.464	185	6	.286	.343	.470	233	6	.283	.343	.459	112	5	.313	.364	.563	306	7	.275	.335	.428	144	5	.285	.375	.451	51	2	.196	.250	.353
1991	Mil-A	665	17	.325	.399	.489	315	7	.292	.374	.454	350	10	.354	.422	.520	174	5	.322	.405	.489	491	12	.326	.397	.489	234	4	.333	.431	.479	92	3	.293	.435	.424
1992	Mil-A	609	12	.320	.389	.461	286	4	.304	.390	.420	323	8	.334	.389	.498	132	6	.424	.464	.659	477	6	.291	.369	.407	268	6	.328	.403	.463	87	1	.322	.417	.402
1993	Tor-A	636	22	.332	.402	.509	316	13	.364	.431	.573	320	9	.300	.374	.447	171	7	.363	.446	.585	465	15	.320	.385	.482	314	8	.331	.411	.481	90	2	.411	.486	.544
1994	Tor-A	454	14	.341	.410	.518	230	8	.378	.430	.570	224	6	.304	.390	.464	110	5	.391	.481	.627	344	9	.326	.385	.483	212	9	.382	.465	.608	57	1	.246	.377	.386
TOTALS		5530	136	.316	.384	.470	2666	71	.328	.395	.490	2864	65	.305	.374	.451	1500	45	.331	.404	.503	4030	91	.311	.377	.458	2076	51	.339	.418	.488	764	20	.325	.407	.469

■ Raul Mondesi BR/TR

YEAR	TM/L	TOTAL AB	HR	AVG	OBP	SLG	HOME AB	HR	AVG	OBP	SLG	AWAY AB	HR	AVG	OBP	SLG	LEFT AB	HR	AVG	OBP	SLG	RIGHT AB	HR	AVG	OBP	SLG	ON-BASE AB	HR	AVG	OBP	SLG	LATE/CLOSE AB	HR	AVG	OBP	SLG
1993	LA-N	86	4	.291	.322	.488	43	2	.302	.318	.488	43	2	.279	.326	.488	54	2	.315	.339	.519	32	2	.250	.294	.438	43	3	.209	.244	.465	17	0	.235	.316	.235
1994	LA-N	434	16	.306	.333	.516	210	10	.281	.306	.486	224	6	.330	.357	.545	122	4	.262	.278	.434	312	12	.324	.354	.548	182	4	.341	.374	.489	75	3	.320	.346	.520
TOTALS		520	20	.304	.331	.512	253	12	.285	.308	.486	267	8	.322	.352	.536	176	6	.278	.297	.460	344	14	.317	.348	.538	225	7	.316	.350	.484	92	3	.304	.340	.467

■ Keith Moreland BR/TR

YEAR	TM/L	TOTAL AB	HR	AVG	OBP	SLG	HOME AB	HR	AVG	OBP	SLG	AWAY AB	HR	AVG	OBP	SLG	LEFT AB	HR	AVG	OBP	SLG	RIGHT AB	HR	AVG	OBP	SLG	ON-BASE AB	HR	AVG	OBP	SLG	LATE/CLOSE AB	HR	AVG	OBP	SLG
1984	Chi-N	495	16	.279	.326	.422	244	13	.262	.321	.463	251	3	.295	.331	.382	161	7	.298	.361	.497	334	9	.269	.308	.386	244	6	.283	.345	.414	81	2	.284	.376	.370
1985	Chi-N	587	14	.307	.374	.440	300	11	.340	.411	.517	287	3	.272	.336	.359	124	3	.315	.415	.460	463	11	.305	.363	.434	298	8	.329	.385	.477	97	2	.309	.364	.474
1986	Chi-N	586	12	.271	.326	.384	297	8	.293	.339	.438	289	4	.249	.314	.329	147	5	.306	.395	.449	439	7	.260	.301	.362	266	5	.244	.298	.357	106	5	.311	.380	.509
1987	Chi-N	563	27	.266	.309	.465	272	19	.290	.338	.548	291	8	.244	.282	.388	122	3	.295	.362	.451	441	24	.259	.294	.469	251	12	.263	.314	.458	76	2	.224	.272	.329
1988	SD-N	511	5	.256	.305	.331	235	3	.268	.327	.336	276	2	.246	.286	.326	179	2	.240	.303	.307	332	3	.265	.307	.343	255	1	.231	.276	.302	79	0	.203	.207	.241
1989	Det-N	318	5	.299	.357	.396	158	4	.278	.333	.361	160	1	.319	.381	.431	119	2	.328	.385	.437	199	3	.281	.341	.372	139	3	.266	.350	.403	55	0	.218	.283	.236
1989	Bal-A	107	1	.215	.243	.280	56	0	.214	.214	.250	51	1	.216	.273	.314	58	1	.207	.220	.241	49	1	.224	.269	.327	42	1	.238	.256	.381	17	0	.118	.211	.235
TOTALS		3167	80	.277	.330	.404	1562	56	.289	.344	.446	1605	24	.265	.316	.363	910	22	.288	.348	.416	2257	58	.272	.317	.399	1495	36	.270	.326	.403	511	11	.260	.320	.374

■ Hal Morris BL/TL

YEAR	TM/L	TOTAL AB	HR	AVG	OBP	SLG	HOME AB	HR	AVG	OBP	SLG	AWAY AB	HR	AVG	OBP	SLG	LEFT AB	HR	AVG	OBP	SLG	RIGHT AB	HR	AVG	OBP	SLG	ON-BASE AB	HR	AVG	OBP	SLG	LATE/CLOSE AB	HR	AVG	OBP	SLG
1988	NY-A	20	0	.100	.100	.100	9	0	.111	.111	.111	11	0	.091	.091	.091	7	0	.000	.000	.000	13	0	.154	.154	.154	6	0	.167	.167	.167	6	0	.000	.000	.000
1989	NY-A	18	0	.278	.316	.278	11	0	.182	.250	.182	7	0	.429	.429	.429	1	0	.000	.500	.000	17	0	.294	.294	.294	11	0	.273	.273	.273	8	0	.000	.000	.000
1990	Cin-N	309	7	.340	.381	.498	148	3	.338	.383	.493	161	4	.342	.380	.503	76	0	.224	.280	.224	233	7	.378	.414	.588	149	2	.302	.350	.396	53	0	.245	.273	.340
1991	Cin-N	478	14	.318	.374	.479	238	9	.319	.370	.525	240	5	.317	.378	.433	103	1	.252	.288	.379	375	13	.336	.397	.507	203	2	.296	.367	.404	72	1	.333	.400	.403
1992	Cin-N	395	6	.271	.347	.385	198	3	.273	.333	.389	197	3	.269	.360	.381	139	1	.252	.325	.309	256	5	.281	.359	.426	179	3	.291	.368	.402	62	1	.290	.353	.516
1993	Cin-N	379	7	.317	.371	.420	184	2	.321	.376	.418	195	5	.313	.366	.421	86	0	.244	.305	.291	293	7	.338	.390	.457	163	2	.319	.368	.399	60	1	.283	.338	.383
1994	Cin-N	436	10	.335	.385	.491	232	5	.328	.375	.496	204	5	.343	.396	.485	110	0	.255	.325	.327	326	10	.362	.405	.546	221	5	.353	.397	.529	70	3	.286	.358	.443
TOTALS		2035	44	.313	.368	.450	1020	22	.312	.364	.461	1015	22	.314	.373	.438	522	2	.243	.305	.307	1513	42	.337	.390	.499	932	14	.312	.369	.428	331	6	.278	.336	.402

■ Jim Morrison BR/TR

YEAR	TM/L	TOTAL AB	HR	AVG	OBP	SLG	HOME AB	HR	AVG	OBP	SLG	AWAY AB	HR	AVG	OBP	SLG	LEFT AB	HR	AVG	OBP	SLG	RIGHT AB	HR	AVG	OBP	SLG	ON-BASE AB	HR	AVG	OBP	SLG	LATE/CLOSE AB	HR	AVG	OBP	SLG
1984	Pit-N	304	11	.286	.328	.454	145	6	.283	.325	.469	159	5	.289	.331	.440	117	4	.308	.357	.462	187	7	.273	.310	.449	130	3	.285	.326	.423	61	2	.246	.258	.426
1985	Pit-N	244	4	.254	.277	.344	132	2	.258	.277	.348	112	2	.250	.277	.339	109	1	.266	.287	.349	135	3	.244	.270	.341	110	1	.282	.299	.336	52	1	.250	.304	.346
1986	Pit-N	537	23	.274	.334	.482	269	11	.297	.374	.506	268	12	.250	.292	.459	192	6	.266	.329	.438	345	17	.278	.337	.507	251	11	.291	.351	.498	104	4	.240	.313	.423
1987	Pit-N	348	9	.264	.315	.411	175	6	.303	.354	.486	173	3	.225	.275	.335	142	5	.289	.307	.472	206	4	.248	.273	.369	158	4	.278	.331	.411	60	2	.250	.328	.417
1987	Det-A	117	4	.205	.221	.333	41	1	.098	.136	.171	76	3	.263	.269	.421	48	1	.229	.255	.292	69	3	.188	.197	.362	59	1	.203	.210	.288	12	0	.000	.077	.000
1988	Det-A	74	0	.216	.216	.284	38	0	.237	.237	.263	36	0	.194	.194	.306	15	0	.200	.200	.267	59	0	.220	.220	.288	41	0	.268	.268	.366	13	0	.154	.154	.154
1988	Atl-N	92	2	.152	.229	.239	51	2	.137	.214	.255	41	0	.171	.245	.220	66	2	.152	.224	.273	26	0	.154	.241	.154	41	1	.171	.260	.268	32	1	.156	.216	.250
TOTALS		1716	53	.268	.303	.411	851	28	.268	.321	.429	865	25	.247	.286	.394	689	19	.263	.318	.405	1027	34	.254	.293	.416	790	21	.272	.317	.411	334	10	.225	.281	.368

■ Lloyd Moseby BL/TR

YEAR	TM/L	TOTAL AB	HR	AVG	OBP	SLG	HOME AB	HR	AVG	OBP	SLG	AWAY AB	HR	AVG	OBP	SLG	LEFT AB	HR	AVG	OBP	SLG	RIGHT AB	HR	AVG	OBP	SLG	ON-BASE AB	HR	AVG	OBP	SLG	LATE/CLOSE AB	HR	AVG	OBP	SLG
1984	Tor-A	592	18	.280	.368	.470	277	10	.296	.389	.534	315	8	.267	.349	.413	210	2	.252	.332	.371	382	16	.296	.387	.524	257	9	.261	.369	.471	91	2	.275	.377	.473
1985	Tor-A	584	18	.259	.345	.426	283	11	.258	.344	.466	301	7	.259	.347	.389	234	7	.256	.330	.393	350	11	.260	.355	.449	243	9	.309	.378	.519	90	1	.267	.343	.356
1986	Tor-A	589	21	.253	.329	.418	290	11	.248	.337	.410	299	10	.258	.320	.425	188	6	.229	.277	.378	401	15	.264	.354	.436	235	9	.289	.341	.472	94	4	.237	.327	.392
1987	Tor-A	592	26	.282	.358	.473	298	15	.292	.371	.503	294	11	.272	.345	.442	198	5	.278	.362	.419	394	21	.284	.357	.500	266	15	.274	.340	.492	94	4	.234	.333	.415
1988	Tor-A	472	10	.239	.343	.369	211	2	.232	.345	.336	261	8	.245	.341	.395	170	2	.253	.344	.359	302	8	.232	.343	.374	197	4	.203	.331	.310	61	1	.212	.329	.288
1989	Tor-A	502	11	.221	.306	.349	222	6	.180	.293	.293	280	5	.254	.317	.393	138	2	.196	.297	.268	364	9	.231	.310	.379	198	5	.242	.338	.359	88	1	.239	.343	.364
1990	Det-A	431	14	.248	.329	.406	221	8	.240	.341	.394	210	6	.257	.316	.419	132	2	.182	.264	.242	299	12	.278	.358	.478	191	4	.225	.309	.340	73	1	.274	.321	.384
1991	Det-A	260	6	.262	.321	.396	151	4	.272	.335	.417	109	2	.248	.299	.367	46	1	.239	.340	.391	214	5	.266	.316	.397	111	3	.270	.333	.423	44	0	.205	.286	.227
TOTALS		4022	124	.257	.340	.418	1953	65	.254	.347	.428	2069	59	.259	.333	.408	1316	27	.240	.320	.359	2706	97	.265	.349	.446	1698	58	.261	.345	.432	643	14	.246	.336	.375

■ John Moses BB/TL

YEAR	TM/L	TOTAL AB	HR	AVG	OBP	SLG	HOME AB	HR	AVG	OBP	SLG	AWAY AB	HR	AVG	OBP	SLG	LEFT AB	HR	AVG	OBP	SLG	RIGHT AB	HR	AVG	OBP	SLG	ON-BASE AB	HR	AVG	OBP	SLG	LATE/CLOSE AB	HR	AVG	OBP	SLG
1984	Sea-A	35	0	.343	.395	.429	16	0	.438	.526	.625	19	0	.263	.263	.263	9	0	.222	.300	.222	26	0	.385	.429	.500	13	0	.385	.500	.385	9	0	.444	.444	.444
1985	Sea-A	62	0	.194	.219	.194	25	0	.120	.154	.120	37	0	.243	.263	.243	12	0	.167	.231	.167	50	0	.200	.216	.200	19	0	.368	.368	.368	10	0	.300	.364	.300
1986	Sea-A	399	3	.256	.311	.333	220	2	.232	.298	.323	179	1	.285	.328	.346	110	2	.291	.361	.418	289	1	.242	.292	.301	130	0	.292	.349	.346	58	0	.241	.318	.276
1987	Sea-A	390	3	.246	.301	.331	214	2	.220	.286	.294	176	1	.278	.319	.375	129	1	.209	.277	.256	261	2	.264	.313	.368	141	2	.270	.325	.369	50	0	.280	.294	.340
1988	Min-A	206	2	.316	.366	.422	85	0	.259	.330	.376	121	2	.355	.392	.455	9	0	.222	.300	.444	197	2	.320	.369	.421	69	1	.319	.385	.449	35	1	.343	.361	.429
1989	Min-A	242	1	.281	.333	.368	97	0	.309	.370	.443	145	1	.262	.308	.317	63	0	.286	.333	.302	179	1	.279	.333	.391	105	1	.267	.331	.362	56	0	.250	.300	.339
1990	Min-A	172	1	.221	.303	.267	80	0	.237	.303	.287	92	1	.207	.302	.250	21	0	.381	.435	.381	151	1	.199	.285	.252	80	1	.225	.340	.300	31	0	.194	.278	.226
1991	Det-A	21	0	.048	.130	.095	4	0	.000	.000	.000	17	0	.059	.158	.118	3	0	.000	.000	.000	18	0	.056	.150	.111	6	0	.000	.000	.000	4	0	.000	.000	.000
1992	Sea-A	22	0	.136	.296	.182	10	0	.200	.385	.300	12	0	.083	.214	.083	3	0	.000	.000	.000	19	0	.158	.333	.211	10	0	.100	.250	.100	6	0	.167	.286	.167
TOTALS		1549	10	.256	.314	.334	751	4	.241	.309	.330	798	6	.271	.319	.337	359	3	.253	.317	.318	1190	7	.257	.313	.339	573	5	.274	.337	.354	259	1	.263	.311	.317

■ Rance Mulliniks BL/TR

YEAR	TM/L	TOTAL AB	HR	AVG	OBP	SLG	HOME AB	HR	AVG	OBP	SLG	AWAY AB	HR	AVG	OBP	SLG	LEFT AB	HR	AVG	OBP	SLG	RIGHT AB	HR	AVG	OBP	SLG	ON-BASE AB	HR	AVG	OBP	SLG	LATE/CLOSE AB	HR	AVG	OBP	SLG
1984	Tor-A	343	3	.324	.383	.440	159	1	.296	.362	.415	184	2	.348	.401	.462	7	0	.429	.500	.429	336	3	.321	.380	.440	144	1	.375	.432	.479	56	0	.357	.431	.482
1985	Tor-A	366	10	.295	.383	.454	174	4	.316	.407	.483	192	6	.276	.360	.427	22	0	.227	.393	.318	344	10	.299	.382	.462	138	3	.326	.387	.486	49	3	.224	.350	.469
1986	Tor-A	348	11	.259	.340	.417	176	5	.284	.373	.449	172	6	.233	.306	.384	20	0	.200	.238	.250	328	11	.262	.346	.427	145	5	.276	.371	.441	39	0	.179	.289	.231
1987	Tor-A	332	11	.310	.371	.500	162	6	.315	.364	.537	170	5	.306	.378	.471	18	1	.389	.450	.667	314	10	.306	.367	.490	129	5	.302	.376	.519	54	3	.315	.422	.537
1988	Tor-A	337	12	.300	.395	.475	165	7	.303	.382	.521	172	5	.297	.408	.430	15	1	.267	.389	.533	322	11	.301	.396	.472	135	5	.296	.428	.459	39	2	.333	.413	.564
1989	Tor-A	273	3	.238	.320	.326	117	1	.231	.316	.308	156	2	.244	.324	.340	16	0	.188	.316	.250	257	3	.241	.321	.331	128	2	.219	.320	.313	46	0	.239	.364	.261
1990	Tor-A	97	2	.289	.417	.392	44	1	.318	.444	.477	53	1	.264	.394	.321	7	0	.429	.636	.571	90	2	.278	.394	.378	50	0	.320	.462	.380	28	0	.357	.455	.429
1991	Tor-A	240	2	.250	.364	.333	120	1	.250	.355	.333	120	1	.250	.372	.333	12	0	.083	.083	.083	228	2	.259	.376	.346	97	0	.258	.378	.309	41	1	.220	.377	.317
1992	Tor-A	2	0	.500	.667	.500	2	0	.500	.667	.500	0	0	—	—	—	1	0	1.000	1.000	1.000	1	0	.000	.500	.000	1	0	.000	.000	.000	1	0	.000	.000	.000
TOTALS		2338	54	.285	.369	.426	1119	26	.290	.373	.446	1219	28	.281	.366	.408	118	2	.263	.370	.381	2220	52	.286	.369	.428	967	21	.297	.390	.432	353	9	.278	.386	.416

■ Jerry Mumphrey BB/TR

YEAR	TM/L	TOTAL AB	HR	AVG	OBP	SLG	HOME AB	HR	AVG	OBP	SLG	AWAY AB	HR	AVG	OBP	SLG	LEFT AB	HR	AVG	OBP	SLG	RIGHT AB	HR	AVG	OBP	SLG	ON-BASE AB	HR	AVG	OBP	SLG	LATE/CLOSE AB	HR	AVG	OBP	SLG
1984	Hou-N	524	9	.290	.355	.391	258	1	.302	.372	.376	266	8	.278	.339	.406	175	0	.246	.309	.280	349	9	.312	.378	.447	255	7	.306	.380	.435	99	0	.343	.416	.374
1985	Hou-N	444	8	.277	.329	.396	200	4	.305	.369	.445	244	4	.254	.294	.357	133	0	.241	.323	.293	311	8	.293	.331	.441	203	4	.310	.379	.438	72	0	.250	.304	.306
1986	Chi-N	309	5	.304	.355	.401	147	4	.361	.417	.517	162	1	.253	.297	.296	61	0	.197	.279	.213	248	5	.331	.374	.448	137	3	.277	.338	.365	77	2	.208	.281	.286
1987	Chi-N	309	13	.333	.400	.534	156	7	.288	.366	.487	153	6	.379	.435	.582	7	0	.143	.250	.286	302	13	.338	.404	.540	134	3	.284	.374	.410	49	3	.347	.439	.612
1988	Chi-N	66	0	.136	.219	.167	35	0	.143	.231	.143	31	0	.129	.206	.194	0	0	—	—	—	66	0	.136	.219	.167	35	0	.200	.300	.229	33	0	.121	.237	.152
TOTALS		1652	35	.291	.351	.412	796	16	.304	.372	.431	856	19	.279	.331	.395	376	0	.234	.308	.274	1276	35	.308	.364	.453	764	17	.293	.367	.410	330	5	.270	.346	.352

■ Dale Murphy BR/TR

YEAR	TM/L	TOTAL AB	HR	AVG	OBP	SLG	HOME AB	HR	AVG	OBP	SLG	AWAY AB	HR	AVG	OBP	SLG	LEFT AB	HR	AVG	OBP	SLG	RIGHT AB	HR	AVG	OBP	SLG	ON-BASE AB	HR	AVG	OBP	SLG	LATE/CLOSE AB	HR	AVG	OBP	SLG
1984	Atl-N	607	36	.290	.372	.547	300	18	.297	.376	.543	307	18	.283	.368	.550	169	15	.314	.415	.651	438	21	.281	.354	.507	272	18	.265	.375	.507	105	7	.333	.412	.629
1985	Atl-N	616	37	.300	.388	.539	308	19	.299	.401	.539	308	18	.302	.374	.539	183	10	.333	.440	.552	433	27	.286	.364	.533	278	19	.324	.401	.604	103	5	.272	.405	.466
1986	Atl-N	614	29	.265	.347	.467	298	17	.268	.366	.503	316	12	.263	.328	.433	193	9	.280	.382	.518	421	20	.259	.329	.442	263	16	.278	.372	.510	104	8	.288	.422	.606
1987	Atl-N	566	44	.295	.417	.580	269	25	.346	.493	.673	297	19	.249	.348	.495	150	14	.320	.512	.653	416	30	.286	.376	.553	259	19	.263	.422	.521	88	4	.205	.345	.386
1988	Atl-N	592	24	.226	.313	.421	283	14	.261	.358	.505	309	10	.194	.270	.343	180	9	.256	.379	.478	412	15	.214	.281	.396	263	7	.198	.327	.338	115	2	.209	.290	.330

YEAR	TM/L	AB	HR	AVG	OBP	SLG	AB	HR	AVG	OBP	SLG	AB	HR	AVG	OBP	SLG	AB	HR	AVG	OBP	SLG	AB	HR	AVG	OBP	SLG	AB	HR	AVG	OBP	SLG	AB	HR	AVG	OBP	SLG
		TOTAL					HOME					AWAY					LEFT					RIGHT					ON-BASE					LATE/CLOSE				
1989	Atl-N	574	20	.228	.306	.361	276	9	.257	.329	.380	298	11	.201	.285	.342	172	5	.244	.373	.355	402	15	.221	.274	.363	273	14	.249	.341	.432	95	3	.253	.318	.379
1990	Atl-N	349	17	.232	.312	.418	174	8	.218	.290	.385	175	9	.246	.333	.451	110	10	.309	.438	.645	239	7	.197	.245	.314	125	12	.320	.429	.656	48	0	.063	.207	.063
1990	Phi-N	214	7	.266	.328	.416	105	1	.248	.333	.333	109	6	.284	.322	.495	70	4	.314	.360	.571	144	3	.243	.313	.340	105	3	.295	.364	.429	37	0	.216	.341	.270
1991	Phi-N	544	18	.252	.309	.415	279	9	.280	.343	.452	265	9	.223	.272	.377	192	5	.297	.351	.443	352	13	.227	.286	.401	257	6	.245	.302	.381	108	7	.241	.291	.481
1992	Phi-N	62	2	.161	.175	.274	47	2	.149	.167	.277	15	0	.200	.200	.267	31	1	.194	.219	.323	31	1	.129	.129	.226	33	1	.242	.242	.364	13	0	.000	.000	.000
1993	Col-N	42	0	.143	.224	.167	23	0	.130	.259	.174	19	0	.158	.182	.158	28	0	.143	.235	.179	14	0	.143	.200	.143	23	0	.174	.276	.217	10	0	.000	.083	.000
TOTALS		4780	234	.261	.345	.466	2362	122	.276	.369	.488	2418	112	.246	.320	.444	1478	82	.289	.401	.518	3302	152	.248	.318	.442	2151	115	.265	.365	.476	826	36	.237	.338	.424

■ Eddie Murray BB/TR

YEAR	TM/L	AB	HR	AVG	OBP	SLG	AB	HR	AVG	OBP	SLG	AB	HR	AVG	OBP	SLG	AB	HR	AVG	OBP	SLG	AB	HR	AVG	OBP	SLG	AB	HR	AVG	OBP	SLG	AB	HR	AVG	OBP	SLG
1984	Bal-A	588	29	.306	.410	.509	283	18	.329	.437	.572	305	11	.285	.385	.449	150	5	.267	.392	.413	438	24	.320	.416	.541	285	16	.323	.431	.561	91	9	.374	.500	.736
1985	Bal-A	583	31	.297	.383	.523	291	15	.296	.396	.515	292	16	.298	.369	.531	203	10	.286	.384	.502	380	21	.303	.382	.534	266	16	.361	.438	.647	79	7	.380	.427	.747
1986	Bal-A	495	17	.305	.396	.463	242	9	.310	.387	.471	253	8	.300	.405	.455	136	6	.301	.360	.493	359	11	.306	.409	.451	245	11	.322	.394	.510	72	4	.250	.349	.458
1987	Bal-A	618	30	.277	.352	.477	300	14	.263	.347	.433	318	16	.289	.356	.519	221	11	.271	.336	.475	397	19	.280	.360	.478	288	15	.274	.367	.486	94	3	.255	.320	.404
1988	Bal-A	603	28	.284	.361	.474	297	14	.283	.368	.461	306	14	.284	.355	.487	213	7	.230	.288	.371	390	21	.313	.400	.531	276	15	.279	.365	.504	86	3	.256	.360	.430
1989	LA-N	594	20	.247	.342	.401	292	4	.253	.342	.346	302	16	.242	.342	.454	210	4	.210	.317	.329	384	16	.268	.356	.440	291	15	.258	.361	.471	111	4	.198	.321	.315
1990	LA-N	558	26	.330	.414	.520	271	12	.343	.444	.524	287	14	.317	.384	.516	206	8	.316	.385	.466	352	18	.338	.431	.551	284	14	.335	.439	.518	78	1	.321	.426	.397
1991	LA-N	576	19	.260	.321	.403	282	11	.270	.347	.426	294	8	.252	.295	.381	254	6	.217	.269	.327	322	13	.295	.361	.463	276	9	.272	.355	.424	97	3	.268	.357	.423
1992	NY-N	551	16	.261	.336	.423	266	7	.226	.303	.380	285	9	.295	.366	.463	202	3	.238	.286	.371	349	13	.275	.364	.453	250	8	.288	.380	.492	91	1	.209	.318	.330
1993	NY-N	610	27	.285	.325	.467	314	15	.290	.320	.475	296	12	.280	.329	.459	183	8	.311	.355	.497	427	19	.274	.312	.454	251	16	.307	.339	.538	102	4	.265	.312	.441
1994	Cle-A	433	17	.254	.302	.435	199	7	.266	.313	.437	234	10	.244	.292	.415	153	5	.216	.242	.366	280	12	.275	.333	.457	209	9	.311	.355	.512	67	4	.284	.329	.493
TOTALS		6209	260	.283	.360	.463	3037	126	.284	.366	.459	3172	134	.281	.354	.468	2131	73	.258	.327	.415	4078	187	.295	.376	.488	2921	144	.302	.386	.514	968	43	.275	.365	.464

■ Graig Nettles BL/TR

YEAR	TM/L	AB	HR	AVG	OBP	SLG	AB	HR	AVG	OBP	SLG	AB	HR	AVG	OBP	SLG	AB	HR	AVG	OBP	SLG	AB	HR	AVG	OBP	SLG	AB	HR	AVG	OBP	SLG	AB	HR	AVG	OBP	SLG
1984	SD-N	395	20	.228	.329	.413	195	11	.210	.313	.405	200	9	.245	.345	.420	77	1	.130	.216	.182	318	19	.252	.355	.469	186	10	.253	.342	.446	59	4	.254	.380	.525
1985	SD-N	440	15	.261	.363	.420	217	6	.258	.358	.387	223	9	.265	.368	.453	97	4	.216	.300	.433	343	11	.274	.380	.417	200	3	.280	.372	.400	80	4	.237	.344	.412
1986	SD-N	354	16	.218	.300	.379	166	13	.265	.374	.530	188	3	.176	.229	.245	53	3	.170	.224	.358	301	13	.226	.313	.382	164	10	.256	.335	.463	70	4	.214	.304	.414
1987	Atl-N	177	5	.209	.294	.350	82	2	.232	.330	.378	95	3	.189	.260	.326	48	0	.229	.291	.313	129	5	.202	.295	.364	91	4	.253	.352	.462	44	2	.227	.340	.409
1988	Mon-N	93	1	.172	.240	.247	42	1	.214	.267	.357	51	0	.137	.220	.157	5	0	.200	.333	.400	88	1	.170	.235	.239	53	0	.189	.262	.245	42	1	.214	.283	.357
TOTALS		1459	57	.230	.323	.389	702	33	.241	.341	.423	757	24	.219	.306	.357	280	8	.186	.262	.329	1179	49	.240	.337	.403	694	27	.256	.344	.424	295	15	.231	.333	.427

■ Al Newman BB/TR

YEAR	TM/L	AB	HR	AVG	OBP	SLG	AB	HR	AVG	OBP	SLG	AB	HR	AVG	OBP	SLG	AB	HR	AVG	OBP	SLG	AB	HR	AVG	OBP	SLG	AB	HR	AVG	OBP	SLG	AB	HR	AVG	OBP	SLG
1985	Mon-N	29	0	.172	.250	.207	16	0	.125	.222	.125	13	0	.231	.286	.308	9	0	.222	.300	.333	20	0	.150	.227	.150	7	0	.000	.000	.000	9	0	.222	.222	.333
1986	Mon-N	185	1	.200	.279	.232	84	0	.190	.278	.202	101	1	.208	.279	.257	41	1	.220	.327	.317	144	0	.194	.264	.208	63	1	.270	.333	.349	53	0	.189	.200	.226
1987	Min-A	307	0	.221	.298	.303	153	0	.235	.339	.327	154	0	.208	.255	.279	94	0	.319	.407	.489	213	0	.178	.248	.221	133	0	.241	.277	.346	36	0	.250	.325	.333
1988	Min-A	260	0	.223	.301	.250	128	0	.234	.319	.266	132	0	.212	.282	.235	69	0	.174	.260	.188	191	0	.241	.316	.272	99	0	.242	.306	.263	34	0	.235	.297	.265
1989	Min-A	446	0	.253	.341	.303	224	0	.259	.351	.295	222	0	.248	.329	.311	163	0	.252	.328	.319	283	0	.254	.348	.293	149	0	.301	.365	.349	70	0	.386	.436	.429
1990	Min-A	388	0	.242	.304	.278	199	0	.261	.338	.302	189	0	.222	.265	.254	123	0	.252	.333	.301	265	0	.238	.289	.268	165	0	.230	.303	.279	62	0	.161	.224	.210
1991	Min-A	246	0	.191	.260	.211	117	0	.179	.263	.205	129	0	.202	.257	.217	66	0	.242	.265	.303	180	0	.172	.259	.178	114	0	.219	.270	.254	43	0	.116	.283	.140
1992	Tex-A	246	0	.220	.317	.240	114	0	.202	.300	.228	132	0	.235	.331	.250	56	0	.268	.423	.286	190	0	.205	.281	.226	97	0	.247	.305	.278	30	0	.233	.343	.233
TOTALS		2107	1	.226	.304	.266	1035	0	.230	.320	.270	1072	1	.222	.289	.263	621	1	.251	.337	.322	1486	0	.215	.290	.243	844	1	.249	.308	.301	337	0	.231	.302	.273

⬛ Dave Nilsson BL/TR

YEAR	TM/L	AB	HR	AVG	OBP	SLG	AB	HR	AVG	OBP	SLG	AB	HR	AVG	OBP	SLG	AB	HR	AVG	OBP	SLG	AB	HR	AVG	OBP	SLG	AB	HR	AVG	OBP	SLG	AB	HR	AVG	OBP	SLG
1992	Mil-A	164	4	.232	.304	.354	55	1	.236	.373	.309	109	3	.229	.263	.376	27	0	.222	.276	.296	137	4	.234	.309	.365	86	2	.233	.313	.372	25	0	.160	.222	.160
1993	Mil-A	296	7	.257	.336	.375	164	5	.274	.344	.433	132	2	.235	.327	.303	81	2	.272	.358	.457	215	5	.251	.328	.344	139	3	.245	.333	.374	49	0	.245	.302	.265
1994	Mil-A	397	12	.275	.326	.451	195	4	.292	.335	.451	202	8	.257	.317	.450	92	2	.228	.232	.348	305	10	.289	.352	.482	183	6	.279	.336	.454	58	3	.259	.328	.483
TOTALS		857	23	.260	.325	.406	414	10	.278	.344	.425	443	13	.244	.307	.388	200	4	.245	.292	.385	657	19	.265	.335	.412	408	11	.257	.330	.409	132	3	.235	.299	.341

⬛ Otis Nixon BB/TR

YEAR	TM/L	AB	HR	AVG	OBP	SLG	AB	HR	AVG	OBP	SLG	AB	HR	AVG	OBP	SLG	AB	HR	AVG	OBP	SLG	AB	HR	AVG	OBP	SLG	AB	HR	AVG	OBP	SLG	AB	HR	AVG	OBP	SLG
1984	Cle-A	91	0	.154	.220	.154	40	0	.175	.267	.175	51	0	.137	.182	.137	27	0	.148	.226	.148	64	0	.156	.217	.156	32	0	.094	.118	.094	15	0	.267	.313	.267
1985	Cle-A	162	3	.235	.271	.315	69	1	.275	.315	.348	93	2	.204	.237	.290	50	1	.220	.235	.300	112	2	.241	.286	.321	58	1	.241	.241	.328	22	1	.273	.304	.409
1986	Cle-A	95	0	.263	.352	.326	45	0	.156	.255	.178	50	0	.360	.439	.460	37	0	.270	.357	.324	58	0	.259	.348	.328	41	0	.268	.333	.366	14	0	.286	.474	.357
1987	Cle-A	17	0	.059	.200	.059	6	0	.000	.250	.000	11	0	.091	.167	.091	2	0	.000	.333	.000	15	0	.067	.176	.067	9	0	.111	.200	.111	1	0	.000	.500	.000
1988	Mon-N	271	0	.244	.312	.288	145	0	.234	.321	.276	126	0	.254	.301	.302	93	0	.226	.308	.280	178	0	.253	.315	.292	71	0	.254	.267	.310	58	0	.293	.328	.345
1989	Mon-N	258	0	.217	.306	.260	132	0	.212	.302	.273	126	0	.222	.310	.246	150	0	.233	.299	.273	108	0	.194	.315	.241	95	0	.211	.292	.295	54	0	.259	.322	.296
1990	Mon-N	231	1	.251	.331	.307	108	0	.241	.322	.306	123	1	.260	.338	.309	151	0	.238	.307	.305	80	1	.275	.372	.313	89	0	.270	.298	.337	63	0	.349	.414	.381
1991	Atl-N	401	0	.297	.371	.327	207	0	.329	.404	.367	194	0	.263	.335	.284	95	0	.305	.405	.358	306	0	.294	.360	.317	120	0	.275	.348	.317	54	0	.352	.435	.444
1992	Atl-N	456	2	.294	.348	.346	221	1	.299	.366	.335	235	1	.289	.331	.357	178	2	.343	.379	.433	278	0	.263	.329	.291	134	2	.246	.295	.306	73	0	.288	.366	.315
1993	Atl-N	461	0	.269	.351	.315	216	0	.287	.379	.361	245	0	.253	.325	.273	152	0	.263	.335	.316	309	0	.272	.359	.314	151	0	.212	.291	.245	74	0	.230	.341	.270
1994	Bos-A	398	0	.274	.360	.317	216	0	.301	.386	.347	182	0	.242	.330	.280	108	0	.231	.303	.269	290	0	.290	.381	.334	134	0	.306	.379	.351	54	0	.259	.388	.352
TOTALS		2841	6	.262	.336	.307	1405	3	.272	.354	.321	1436	4	.252	.318	.294	1043	5	.261	.328	.318	1798	5	.263	.341	.301	934	3	.246	.304	.301	482	1	.286	.370	.340

■ Matt Nokes BL/TR

YEAR	TM/L	AB	HR	AVG	OBP	SLG	AB	HR	AVG	OBP	SLG	AB	HR	AVG	OBP	SLG	AB	HR	AVG	OBP	SLG	AB	HR	AVG	OBP	SLG	AB	HR	AVG	OBP	SLG	AB	HR	AVG	OBP	SLG
1985	SF-N	53	2	.208	.236	.358	24	1	.208	.240	.333	29	1	.207	.233	.379	3	0	.000	.000	.000	50	2	.220	.250	.380	28	2	.179	.233	.393	9	1	.333	.333	.667
1986	Det-A	24	1	.333	.360	.500	7	0	.143	.143	.286	17	1	.412	.444	.588	1	0	.000	.000	.000	23	1	.348	.375	.522	11	0	.273	.333	.273	3	0	.667	.750	.667
1987	Det-A	461	32	.289	.345	.536	214	14	.308	.374	.542	247	18	.271	.318	.530	87	4	.207	.278	.356	374	28	.307	.360	.578	245	12	.290	.324	.465	68	5	.250	.292	.471
1988	Det-A	382	16	.251	.313	.424	196	9	.250	.302	.413	186	7	.253	.324	.435	38	2	.263	.300	.500	344	14	.250	.314	.416	175	6	.263	.338	.406	59	3	.237	.292	.424
1989	Det-A	268	9	.250	.298	.388	127	7	.268	.316	.465	141	2	.234	.281	.319	43	2	.256	.283	.442	225	7	.249	.300	.378	124	7	.282	.336	.484	40	1	.250	.340	.350
1990	Det-A	111	3	.270	.305	.414	48	1	.292	.314	.375	63	2	.254	.299	.444	4	0	.000	.000	.000	107	3	.280	.316	.430	47	0	.234	.288	.255	14	1	.286	.333	.500
1990	NY-A	240	8	.237	.307	.354	109	3	.239	.303	.339	131	5	.237	.310	.366	10	0	.200	.273	.200	230	8	.239	.308	.361	103	3	.282	.345	.388	36	2	.278	.297	.472
1991	NY-A	456	24	.268	.308	.469	200	13	.260	.300	.495	256	11	.273	.315	.449	111	7	.261	.303	.459	345	17	.270	.310	.472	207	13	.280	.325	.522	75	2	.280	.353	.387
1992	NY-A	384	22	.224	.293	.424	177	18	.266	.347	.593	207	4	.188	.246	.280	71	5	.197	.275	.465	313	17	.230	.297	.415	180	12	.222	.295	.444	72	6	.194	.310	.458
1993	NY-A	217	10	.249	.303	.424	102	4	.245	.294	.402	115	6	.252	.310	.443	30	2	.100	.129	.300	187	8	.273	.329	.444	94	5	.245	.327	.436	28	2	.286	.333	.536
1994	NY-A	79	7	.291	.329	.595	46	6	.261	.286	.674	33	1	.333	.389	.485	10	1	.500	.545	.900	69	6	.261	.297	.551	42	4	.286	.311	.619	15	0	.200	.278	.200
TOTALS		2675	134	.257	.311	.445	1250	76	.265	.319	.478	1425	58	.250	.303	.417	408	23	.225	.278	.424	2267	111	.262	.317	.449	1256	64	.265	.321	.451	419	23	.253	.320	.437

■ Ken Oberkfell BL/TR

YEAR	TM/L	AB	HR	AVG	OBP	SLG	AB	HR	AVG	OBP	SLG	AB	HR	AVG	OBP	SLG	AB	HR	AVG	OBP	SLG	AB	HR	AVG	OBP	SLG	AB	HR	AVG	OBP	SLG	AB	HR	AVG	OBP	SLG
1984	StL-N	152	0	.309	.379	.395	72	0	.222	.273	.306	80	0	.387	.467	.475	22	0	.273	.318	.318	130	0	.315	.395	.408	65	0	.354	.455	.400	26	0	.269	.387	.346
1984	Atl-N	172	1	.233	.289	.308	90	1	.244	.290	.356	82	0	.220	.289	.256	38	0	.237	.268	.342	134	1	.231	.295	.299	69	1	.232	.263	.362	30	0	.200	.294	.267
1985	Atl-N	412	3	.272	.359	.359	209	2	.301	.402	.392	203	1	.241	.311	.325	115	0	.243	.323	.287	297	3	.283	.372	.387	176	2	.239	.340	.347	76	0	.197	.274	.211
1986	Atl-N	503	5	.270	.373	.360	268	2	.284	.382	.362	235	3	.255	.363	.357	129	2	.233	.333	.310	374	3	.283	.387	.377	201	2	.299	.387	.383	88	1	.261	.394	.330
1987	Atl-N	508	3	.280	.342	.362	259	2	.293	.363	.382	249	1	.265	.320	.341	142	0	.310	.349	.415	366	3	.268	.340	.342	211	1	.265	.347	.341	73	0	.274	.349	.356
1988	Atl-N	422	3	.277	.325	.365	201	1	.279	.323	.358	221	2	.276	.328	.371	88	0	.273	.296	.364	334	3	.278	.333	.365	145	1	.303	.363	.448	78	0	.231	.282	.295
1988	Pit-N	54	0	.222	.288	.259	23	0	.391	.440	.391	31	0	.097	.176	.161	12	0	.167	.231	.250	42	0	.238	.304	.262	21	0	.190	.261	.190	10	0	.100	.182	.100
1989	Pit-N	40	0	.125	.163	.150	18	0	.222	.286	.278	22	0	.045	.045	.045	4	0	.000	.000	.000	36	0	.139	.179	.167	16	0	.063	.111	.063	7	0	.143	.143	.143
1989	SF-N	116	2	.319	.367	.431	49	1	.306	.364	.388	67	1	.328	.370	.463	17	0	.118	.167	.118	99	2	.354	.400	.485	47	1	.298	.327	.383	16	0	.389	.436	.444
1990	Hou-N	150	1	.207	.281	.280	59	0	.136	.188	.186	91	1	.253	.340	.341	17	0	.059	.158	.059	133	1	.226	.297	.308	71	1	.155	.237	.254	33	0	.182	.243	.242
1991	Hou-N	70	0	.229	.357	.286	24	0	.250	.486	.292	46	0	.217	.265	.283	3	0	.333	.333	.333	67	0	.224	.358	.284	38	0	.237	.420	.316	29	0	.138	.242	.172
1992	Cal-A	91	0	.264	.317	.275	51	0	.235	.293	.235	40	0	.300	.349	.325	12	0	.083	.083	.083	79	0	.291	.348	.304	41	0	.220	.292	.220	19	0	.211	.370	.211
TOTALS		2690	18	.267	.341	.348	1323	9	.274	.351	.353	1367	9	.260	.330	.344	599	2	.247	.305	.321	2091	16	.273	.354	.352	1101	9	.261	.345	.352	505	1	.236	.324	.289

■ Pete O'Brien BL/TL

YEAR	TM/L	AB	HR	AVG	OBP	SLG	AB	HR	AVG	OBP	SLG	AB	HR	AVG	OBP	SLG	AB	HR	AVG	OBP	SLG	AB	HR	AVG	OBP	SLG	AB	HR	AVG	OBP	SLG	AB	HR	AVG	OBP	SLG
1984	Tex-A	520	18	.287	.348	.448	262	7	.317	.378	.462	258	11	.256	.318	.434	150	2	.213	.294	.293	370	16	.316	.371	.511	230	6	.300	.373	.452	103	2	.291	.351	.408
1985	Tex-A	573	22	.267	.342	.452	277	12	.292	.367	.487	296	10	.243	.318	.420	169	2	.225	.289	.296	404	20	.285	.363	.578	274	7	.255	.332	.409	82	2	.220	.327	.329
1986	Tex-A	551	23	.290	.385	.468	265	11	.268	.356	.442	286	12	.311	.411	.493	165	4	.309	.380	.448	386	19	.282	.387	.477	249	12	.301	.408	.510	86	3	.291	.396	.430
1987	Tex-A	569	23	.286	.348	.457	265	9	.272	.341	.426	304	14	.299	.354	.484	186	3	.247	.294	.339	383	20	.305	.373	.514	249	8	.309	.372	.466	88	7	.295	.370	.568
1988	Tex-A	547	16	.272	.342	.408	266	6	.286	.357	.402	281	10	.260	.327	.413	163	3	.252	.305	.350	384	13	.281	.351	.432	223	5	.265	.361	.390	92	6	.239	.311	.467
1989	Cle-A	554	12	.260	.356	.372	261	5	.287	.386	.398	293	7	.235	.327	.348	167	4	.293	.362	.425	387	8	.245	.353	.349	221	6	.253	.384	.348	86	0	.186	.327	.256
1990	Sea-A	366	5	.224	.308	.314	172	3	.262	.361	.372	194	2	.191	.257	.263	130	1	.200	.291	.238	236	4	.237	.317	.356	166	0	.157	.238	.175	64	0	.234	.338	.281
1991	Sea-A	560	17	.248	.332	.402	290	12	.238	.330	.402	270	5	.259	.334	.402	179	4	.257	.317	.346	381	13	.244	.340	.428	169	9	.278	.328	.438	98	5	.276	.369	.469
1992	Sea-A	396	14	.222	.289	.371	188	6	.218	.286	.372	208	8	.226	.292	.370	56	1	.214	.288	.339	340	13	.224	.289	.376	174	5	.259	.340	.397	76	5	.303	.380	.539
1993	Sea-A	210	7	.257	.335	.390	99	1	.222	.310	.283	111	6	.288	.357	.486	25	0	.200	.286	.200	185	7	.265	.341	.416	95	3	.232	.339	.347	34	2	.294	.385	.500
TOTALS		4846	157	.264	.339	.414	2345	72	.271	.347	.421	2501	85	.258	.332	.408	1390	24	.246	.311	.345	3456	133	.272	.350	.442	2147	59	.267	.352	.405	809	30	.253	.341	.409

		TOTAL					HOME					AWAY					LEFT					RIGHT					ON-BASE					LATE/CLOSE			
YEAR	TM/L	AB	HR	AVG	OBP	SLG	AB	HR	AVG	OBP	SLG	AB	HR	AVG	OBP	SLG	AB	HR	AVG	OBP	SLG	AB	HR	AVG	OBP	SLG	AB	HR	AVG	OBP	SLG	AB	HR	AVG	OBP	SLG

■ Ron Oester BB/TR

YEAR	TM/L	AB	HR	AVG	OBP	SLG	AB	HR	AVG	OBP	SLG	AB	HR	AVG	OBP	SLG	AB	HR	AVG	OBP	SLG	AB	HR	AVG	OBP	SLG	AB	HR	AVG	OBP	SLG	AB	HR	AVG	OBP	SLG
1984	Cin-N	553	3	.242	.295	.316	288	2	.247	.308	.326	265	1	.238	.281	.306	164	1	.232	.272	.287	389	2	.247	.305	.329	237	0	.232	.282	.295	103	1	.223	.286	.282
1985	Cin-N	526	1	.295	.354	.361	270	0	.304	.354	.378	256	1	.285	.354	.344	148	0	.277	.312	.338	378	1	.302	.369	.370	213	1	.305	.405	.385	99	0	.374	.426	.465
1986	Cin-N	523	8	.258	.325	.356	261	6	.280	.349	.410	262	2	.237	.300	.302	136	1	.184	.263	.243	387	7	.284	.347	.395	245	3	.261	.348	.339	103	3	.320	.383	.447
1987	Cin-N	237	2	.253	.317	.367	125	0	.232	.304	.296	112	2	.277	.331	.446	60	0	.200	.262	.217	177	2	.271	.335	.418	109	1	.266	.350	.394	43	1	.233	.267	.372
1988	Cin-N	150	0	.280	.319	.327	83	0	.253	.315	.277	67	0	.313	.324	.388	26	0	.231	.300	.308	124	0	.290	.323	.331	53	0	.283	.339	.358	30	0	.333	.355	.333
1989	Cin-N	305	1	.246	.318	.305	148	1	.270	.345	.358	157	0	.223	.291	.255	63	0	.175	.288	.175	242	1	.264	.326	.339	125	0	.304	.404	.336	58	0	.224	.250	.259
1990	Cin-N	154	0	.299	.339	.377	53	0	.321	.390	.396	101	0	.287	.311	.366	40	0	.300	.349	.375	114	0	.298	.336	.377	72	0	.264	.316	.347	29	0	.345	.406	.379
TOTALS		2448	15	.264	.323	.342	1228	9	.271	.335	.356	1220	6	.257	.311	.330	637	2	.228	.286	.278	1811	13	.277	.337	.365	1054	5	.270	.351	.345	465	5	.292	.344	.372

■ Ben Oglivie BL/TL

YEAR	TM/L	AB	HR	AVG	OBP	SLG	AB	HR	AVG	OBP	SLG	AB	HR	AVG	OBP	SLG	AB	HR	AVG	OBP	SLG	AB	HR	AVG	OBP	SLG	AB	HR	AVG	OBP	SLG	AB	HR	AVG	OBP	SLG
1984	Mil-A	461	12	.262	.327	.384	216	7	.264	.325	.412	245	5	.261	.328	.359	153	2	.235	.304	.307	308	10	.276	.338	.422	194	5	.273	.359	.402	77	2	.312	.430	.442
1985	Mil-A	341	10	.290	.354	.440	160	4	.319	.363	.488	181	6	.265	.346	.398	75	2	.213	.237	.387	266	8	.312	.384	.455	137	7	.328	.389	.555	60	3	.283	.377	.483
1986	Mil-A	346	5	.283	.334	.390	169	2	.290	.340	.402	177	3	.277	.328	.379	63	0	.254	.294	.349	283	5	.290	.343	.399	169	3	.284	.326	.420	52	1	.250	.333	.385
TOTALS		1148	27	.277	.337	.402	545	13	.288	.341	.431	603	14	.267	.334	.376	291	4	.234	.285	.337	857	23	.292	.354	.425	500	15	.292	.357	.450	189	6	.286	.387	.439

■ John Olerud BL/TL

YEAR	TM/L	AB	HR	AVG	OBP	SLG	AB	HR	AVG	OBP	SLG	AB	HR	AVG	OBP	SLG	AB	HR	AVG	OBP	SLG	AB	HR	AVG	OBP	SLG	AB	HR	AVG	OBP	SLG	AB	HR	AVG	OBP	SLG
1989	Tor-A	8	0	.375	.375	.375	7	0	.429	.429	.429	1	0	.000	.000	.000	1	0	.000	.000	.000	7	0	.429	.429	.429	5	0	.400	.400	.400	2	0	.000	.000	.000
1990	Tor-A	358	14	.265	.364	.430	187	11	.273	.372	.497	171	3	.257	.356	.357	73	3	.342	.444	.534	285	11	.246	.342	.404	173	6	.295	.382	.457	68	3	.324	.390	.500
1991	Tor-A	454	17	.256	.353	.438	226	7	.270	.374	.447	228	10	.241	.332	.430	83	3	.217	.358	.386	371	14	.264	.352	.450	194	5	.278	.383	.443	89	2	.258	.369	.427
1992	Tor-A	458	16	.284	.375	.450	231	4	.264	.368	.385	227	12	.304	.383	.515	97	3	.258	.393	.392	361	13	.291	.370	.465	218	7	.234	.323	.381	72	3	.361	.427	.569
1993	Tor-A	551	24	.363	.473	.599	269	9	.346	.464	.550	282	15	.379	.481	.645	172	4	.291	.413	.424	379	20	.396	.500	.678	232	9	.358	.495	.560	78	3	.308	.455	.474
1994	Tor-A	384	12	.297	.393	.477	190	6	.305	.412	.479	194	6	.289	.373	.474	121	3	.264	.353	.380	263	9	.312	.411	.521	174	6	.333	.427	.534	60	1	.300	.400	.450
TOTALS		2213	83	.297	.397	.486	1110	37	.295	.402	.473	1103	46	.300	.392	.499	547	16	.274	.392	.417	1666	67	.305	.399	.508	996	33	.300	.406	.475	369	12	.306	.406	.480

■ Joe Oliver BR/TR

YEAR	TM/L	AB	HR	AVG	OBP	SLG	AB	HR	AVG	OBP	SLG	AB	HR	AVG	OBP	SLG	AB	HR	AVG	OBP	SLG	AB	HR	AVG	OBP	SLG	AB	HR	AVG	OBP	SLG	AB	HR	AVG	OBP	SLG
1989	Cin-N	151	3	.272	.300	.384	79	1	.278	.280	.367	72	2	.264	.321	.403	78	1	.346	.369	.449	73	2	.192	.224	.315	66	1	.242	.278	.364	31	0	.355	.394	.419
1990	Cin-N	364	8	.231	.304	.360	172	3	.221	.306	.349	192	5	.240	.303	.370	180	5	.283	.350	.439	184	3	.179	.260	.283	173	4	.272	.349	.422	50	2	.220	.304	.440
1991	Cin-N	269	11	.216	.265	.379	145	7	.200	.256	.386	124	4	.234	.275	.371	131	8	.229	.308	.450	138	3	.203	.220	.312	112	8	.232	.289	.491	47	0	.234	.234	.234
1992	Cin-N	485	10	.270	.316	.388	245	7	.278	.320	.429	240	3	.262	.313	.346	176	4	.307	.359	.438	309	6	.249	.291	.359	220	6	.236	.316	.355	79	0	.253	.311	.304
1993	Cin-N	482	14	.239	.276	.384	232	7	.250	.283	.414	250	7	.228	.269	.356	134	6	.291	.338	.507	348	8	.218	.251	.336	228	9	.259	.288	.447	78	3	.269	.298	.436
1994	Cin-N	19	1	.211	.286	.368	16	1	.188	.278	.375	3	0	.333	.333	.333	5	1	.400	.400	1.000	14	0	.143	.250	.143	10	1	.300	.364	.600	1	0	.000	.500	.000
TOTALS		1770	47	.245	.293	.379	889	26	.245	.293	.396	881	21	.244	.294	.362	704	25	.288	.345	.459	1066	22	.216	.259	.326	809	29	.251	.309	.408	286	5	.259	.313	.364

■ Paul O'Neill BL/TL

YEAR	TM/L	AB	HR	AVG	OBP	SLG	AB	HR	AVG	OBP	SLG	AB	HR	AVG	OBP	SLG	AB	HR	AVG	OBP	SLG	AB	HR	AVG	OBP	SLG	AB	HR	AVG	OBP	SLG	AB	HR	AVG	OBP	SLG
1985	Cin-N	12	0	.333	.333	.417	1	0	.000	.000	.000	11	0	.364	.364	.455	0	0	—	—	—	12	0	.333	.333	.417	7	0	.429	.429	.429	3	0	.333	.333	.333
1986	Cin-N	2	0	.000	.000	.000	0	0	—	.000	—	2	0	.000	.333	.000	0	0	—	—	—	2	0	.000	.333	.000	2	0	.000	.333	.000	0	0	.000	.000	.000
1987	Cin-N	160	7	.256	.331	.488	83	4	.253	.347	.494	77	3	.260	.313	.481	11	0	.091	.167	.182	149	7	.268	.343	.510	77	1	.260	.360	.468	36	1	.250	.341	.472
1988	Cin-N	485	16	.252	.306	.414	237	12	.245	.297	.435	248	4	.258	.314	.395	86	1	.233	.280	.349	399	15	.256	.311	.429	223	8	.251	.309	.413	86	3	.186	.239	.349
1989	Cin-N	428	15	.276	.346	.446	231	11	.316	.373	.545	197	4	.228	.316	.330	152	4	.178	.246	.303	276	11	.330	.399	.525	195	9	.323	.409	.559	74	0	.284	.384	.338
1990	Cin-N	503	16	.270	.339	.421	241	10	.290	.357	.456	262	6	.252	.323	.389	143	3	.259	.310	.406	360	13	.275	.351	.428	237	9	.274	.356	.430	86	2	.267	.360	.407
1991	Cin-N	532	28	.256	.346	.481	268	20	.284	.361	.586	264	8	.227	.331	.375	169	3	.201	.254	.308	363	25	.281	.385	.562	252	16	.266	.380	.516	73	2	.192	.366	.329
1992	Cin-N	496	14	.246	.346	.373	245	6	.237	.354	.359	251	8	.255	.338	.386	173	2	.225	.279	.295	323	12	.257	.377	.415	232	2	.241	.368	.306	81	3	.222	.337	.370
1993	NY-A	498	20	.311	.367	.504	249	8	.325	.377	.498	249	12	.297	.358	.510	135	2	.230	.279	.319	363	18	.342	.400	.573	246	3	.289	.346	.407	62	3	.355	.425	.597
1994	NY-A	368	21	.359	.460	.603	176	10	.409	.490	.659	192	11	.313	.435	.552	105	7	.305	.439	.571	263	14	.380	.469	.616	177	11	.350	.471	.605	55	3	.418	.522	.691
TOTALS		3484	137	.277	.355	.460	1733	81	.294	.367	.499	1751	56	.261	.343	.420	974	22	.227	.293	.351	2510	115	.297	.378	.502	1648	61	.281	.374	.455	558	17	.263	.366	.425

■ Jose Oquendo BB/TR

YEAR	TM/L	AB	HR	AVG	OBP	SLG	AB	HR	AVG	OBP	SLG	AB	HR	AVG	OBP	SLG	AB	HR	AVG	OBP	SLG	AB	HR	AVG	OBP	SLG	AB	HR	AVG	OBP	SLG	AB	HR	AVG	OBP	SLG
1984	NY-N	189	0	.222	.284	.249	104	0	.231	.264	.260	85	0	.212	.306	.235	59	0	.237	.303	.271	130	0	.215	.275	.238	85	0	.271	.312	.318	17	0	.294	.429	.294
1986	StL-N	138	0	.297	.359	.341	61	0	.311	.386	.377	77	0	.286	.337	.312	44	0	.364	.408	.432	94	0	.266	.336	.298	60	0	.333	.403	.367	43	0	.256	.333	.256
1987	StL-N	248	1	.286	.408	.335	111	0	.297	.424	.342	137	1	.277	.395	.328	112	1	.277	.375	.339	136	0	.294	.435	.331	104	1	.298	.417	.375	67	1	.254	.405	.343
1988	StL-N	451	7	.277	.350	.350	228	4	.289	.362	.360	223	3	.265	.337	.341	154	4	.299	.343	.461	297	0	.266	.353	.293	190	4	.279	.340	.374	100	2	.240	.316	.330
1989	StL-N	556	1	.291	.375	.372	269	0	.301	.387	.409	287	1	.282	.364	.338	229	0	.266	.340	.354	327	1	.309	.398	.385	239	0	.285	.358	.331	91	0	.308	.417	.374
1990	StL-N	469	1	.252	.350	.316	238	1	.239	.330	.294	231	0	.264	.371	.338	164	1	.220	.319	.287	305	0	.269	.367	.331	181	0	.282	.381	.348	86	0	.279	.398	.314
1991	StL-N	366	1	.240	.357	.301	184	0	.261	.372	.299	182	1	.220	.342	.302	150	1	.240	.365	.327	216	0	.241	.352	.282	133	0	.256	.424	.301	64	1	.297	.395	.375
1992	StL-N	35	0	.257	.350	.400	12	0	.250	.357	.250	23	0	.261	.346	.478	12	0	.167	.333	.250	23	0	.304	.360	.478	12	0	.500	.400	.333	6	0	.333	.500	.667
1993	StL-N	73	0	.205	.314	.205	26	0	.192	.250	.192	47	0	.213	.345	.213	24	0	.125	.160	.125	49	0	.245	.377	.245	29	0	.241	.281	.241	11	0	.364	.462	.364
1994	StL-N	129	0	.264	.364	.310	58	0	.293	.425	.397	71	0	.239	.308	.239	35	0	.343	.385	.371	94	0	.234	.357	.287	50	0	.320	.426	.360	18	0	.333	.429	.333
TOTALS		2654	11	.266	.358	.327	1291	5	.273	.363	.338	1363	6	.258	.352	.318	983	10	.261	.343	.346	1671	1	.268	.366	.317	1083	5	.283	.375	.342	503	4	.278	.386	.340

■ Joe Orsulak BL/TL

YEAR	TM/L	AB	HR	AVG	OBP	SLG	AB	HR	AVG	OBP	SLG	AB	HR	AVG	OBP	SLG	AB	HR	AVG	OBP	SLG	AB	HR	AVG	OBP	SLG	AB	HR	AVG	OBP	SLG	AB	HR	AVG	OBP	SLG
1984	Pit-N	67	0	.254	.271	.328	43	0	.233	.261	.326	24	0	.292	.292	.333	13	0	.308	.357	.308	54	0	.241	.250	.333	25	0	.240	.259	.240	15	0	.467	.471	.467
1985	Pit-N	397	0	.300	.342	.365	184	0	.370	.410	.451	213	0	.239	.282	.291	65	0	.215	.224	.231	332	0	.316	.364	.392	127	0	.236	.286	.283	68	0	.235	.303	.294
1986	Pit-N	401	2	.249	.299	.342	183	0	.224	.285	.301	218	2	.271	.312	.376	50	0	.260	.288	.320	351	2	.248	.301	.345	122	0	.189	.259	.213	71	0	.254	.289	.282
1988	Bal-A	379	8	.288	.331	.422	174	3	.287	.326	.408	205	5	.288	.335	.434	68	0	.235	.321	.235	311	8	.299	.333	.463	115	2	.252	.299	.357	63	1	.302	.328	.444
1989	Bal-A	390	7	.285	.351	.421	194	0	.273	.339	.366	196	7	.296	.362	.474	84	0	.202	.244	.262	306	7	.307	.378	.464	182	2	.291	.360	.412	61	1	.230	.356	.361
1990	Bal-A	413	11	.269	.343	.397	202	9	.272	.348	.441	211	2	.265	.338	.355	72	0	.250	.325	.278	341	11	.273	.346	.422	190	6	.253	.353	.389	61	1	.213	.368	.295
1991	Bal-A	486	5	.278	.321	.358	235	3	.277	.322	.357	251	2	.279	.320	.359	64	0	.234	.286	.281	422	5	.284	.326	.370	223	3	.247	.290	.323	81	1	.222	.273	.296
1992	Bal-A	391	4	.289	.342	.381	180	2	.278	.347	.361	211	2	.299	.338	.398	80	0	.250	.307	.338	311	4	.299	.351	.392	173	2	.301	.368	.399	65	1	.323	.380	.431
1993	NY-N	409	8	.284	.331	.399	179	5	.285	.350	.413	230	3	.283	.315	.387	42	0	.357	.364	.429	367	8	.275	.327	.395	145	2	.276	.327	.317	78	1	.282	.341	.359
1994	NY-N	292	4	.260	.299	.353	132	4	.303	.349	.402	160	4	.225	.256	.313	42	0	.214	.261	.238	250	8	.268	.305	.372	131	5	.290	.329	.420	60	2	.300	.333	.400
TOTALS		3625	53	.278	.328	.381	1706	26	.283	.339	.386	1919	27	.273	.319	.376	580	0	.243	.291	.286	3045	53	.284	.336	.399	1433	20	.261	.322	.349	623	8	.266	.332	.352

■ Jorge Orta BL/TR

YEAR	TM/L	AB	HR	AVG	OBP	SLG	AB	HR	AVG	OBP	SLG	AB	HR	AVG	OBP	SLG	AB	HR	AVG	OBP	SLG	AB	HR	AVG	OBP	SLG	AB	HR	AVG	OBP	SLG	AB	HR	AVG	OBP	SLG
1984	KC-A	403	9	.298	.343	.457	196	3	.265	.315	.418	207	6	.329	.371	.493	20	0	.350	.435	.350	383	9	.295	.338	.462	188	4	.239	.297	.378	62	3	.387	.429	.629
1985	KC-A	300	4	.267	.317	.383	142	1	.275	.329	.373	158	3	.259	.306	.392	12	0	.083	.083	.083	288	4	.274	.326	.396	162	3	.241	.294	.377	44	2	.227	.308	.409
1986	KC-A	336	9	.277	.321	.411	188	5	.298	.343	.452	148	4	.250	.294	.358	19	0	.211	.250	.211	317	9	.281	.326	.423	181	5	.320	.352	.453	54	0	.315	.367	.389
1987	KC-A	50	2	.180	.226	.380	9	0	.000	.000	.000	41	2	.220	.273	.463	19	0	.211	.250	.211	50	2	.180	.226	.380	19	0	.158	.200	.263	11	0	.182	.182	.273
TOTALS		1089	24	.277	.324	.419	535	9	.275	.324	.411	554	15	.280	.324	.426	51	0	.235	.291	.235	1038	24	.279	.326	.428	550	12	.264	.311	.398	171	5	.310	.363	.474

■ Spike Owen BB/TR

YEAR	TM/L	AB	HR	AVG	OBP	SLG	AB	HR	AVG	OBP	SLG	AB	HR	AVG	OBP	SLG	AB	HR	AVG	OBP	SLG	AB	HR	AVG	OBP	SLG	AB	HR	AVG	OBP	SLG	AB	HR	AVG	OBP	SLG
1984	Sea-A	530	3	.245	.308	.326	261	2	.226	.285	.303	269	1	.264	.330	.349	158	1	.234	.297	.342	372	2	.250	.313	.320	223	2	.256	.328	.354	106	0	.255	.325	.330
1985	Sea-A	352	6	.259	.322	.372	201	3	.274	.338	.383	151	3	.238	.301	.358	90	1	.256	.302	.356	262	5	.260	.329	.378	140	2	.257	.303	.386	39	0	.128	.277	.128
1986	Sea-A	402	0	.246	.305	.331	203	0	.251	.317	.374	199	0	.241	.293	.286	86	0	.267	.337	.349	316	0	.241	.297	.326	166	0	.271	.320	.367	62	0	.161	.212	.210
1986	Bos-A	126	1	.183	.283	.238	65	0	.231	.359	.292	61	1	.131	.194	.180	35	1	.286	.350	.400	91	0	.143	.257	.176	55	0	.218	.343	.273	13	0	.154	.313	.154
1987	Bos-A	437	2	.259	.337	.343	224	2	.263	.341	.371	213	0	.254	.333	.315	134	2	.321	.393	.455	303	0	.231	.313	.294	186	1	.280	.352	.409	64	1	.203	.271	.281
1988	Bos-A	257	5	.249	.324	.370	104	2	.269	.348	.423	153	3	.229	.308	.333	98	4	.276	.324	.480	159	1	.233	.324	.302	97	1	.216	.330	.320	40	1	.275	.356	.400
1989	Mon-N	437	6	.233	.349	.332	201	5	.274	.383	.408	236	1	.199	.319	.267	131	2	.275	.371	.374	306	4	.216	.340	.314	181	5	.271	.410	.409	81	3	.231	.317	.363
1990	Mon-N	453	5	.234	.339	.342	215	2	.228	.332	.335	238	3	.239	.335	.349	201	2	.259	.330	.403	252	3	.214	.336	.294	175	0	.206	.333	.269	91	3	.242	.311	.429
1991	Mon-N	424	3	.255	.321	.366	161	1	.211	.291	.280	263	2	.281	.338	.418	200	1	.305	.350	.430	224	2	.210	.296	.308	164	1	.232	.309	.329	79	1	.278	.348	.354
1992	Mon-N	386	7	.269	.348	.381	173	3	.243	.332	.347	213	4	.291	.369	.408	161	4	.286	.346	.447	225	3	.258	.350	.333	157	1	.306	.372	.395	57	0	.368	.479	.439
1993	NY-A	334	2	.234	.294	.311	157	1	.210	.256	.280	177	1	.254	.327	.339	137	1	.248	.290	.328	197	1	.223	.297	.299	144	1	.188	.239	.243	45	0	.200	.294	.311
1994	Cal-A	268	3	.310	.418	.422	164	2	.311	.408	.451	104	1	.308	.433	.375	83	3	.289	.416	.494	185	0	.319	.419	.389	97	1	.402	.500	.526	32	0	.344	.500	.438
TOTALS		4406	43	.250	.330	.347	2129	23	.250	.330	.355	2277	20	.250	.329	.341	1514	23	.275	.341	.404	2892	20	.237	.324	.318	1785	15	.243	.343	.358	719	9	.242	.330	.337

■ Mike Pagliarulo BL/TR

YEAR	TM/L	AB	HR	AVG	OBP	SLG	AB	HR	AVG	OBP	SLG	AB	HR	AVG	OBP	SLG	AB	HR	AVG	OBP	SLG	AB	HR	AVG	OBP	SLG	AB	HR	AVG	OBP	SLG	AB	HR	AVG	OBP	SLG
1984	NY-A	201	7	.239	.288	.448	105	4	.257	.313	.457	96	3	.219	.260	.438	30	0	.233	.361	.367	171	7	.240	.273	.462	108	5	.296	.342	.546	21	0	.143	.231	.190
1985	NY-A	380	19	.239	.324	.442	178	8	.242	.320	.416	202	11	.238	.328	.465	51	2	.157	.267	.275	329	17	.252	.333	.468	160	11	.231	.326	.449	61	4	.246	.347	.459
1986	NY-A	504	28	.238	.316	.464	243	14	.230	.325	.469	261	14	.245	.307	.475	163	2	.196	.254	.288	341	26	.258	.344	.548	231	10	.238	.328	.420	78	4	.256	.316	.449
1987	NY-A	522	32	.234	.305	.479	243	17	.214	.308	.473	279	15	.251	.302	.484	152	4	.230	.283	.355	370	28	.235	.314	.530	215	14	.251	.333	.512	79	5	.152	.227	.354
1988	NY-A	444	15	.216	.276	.367	203	8	.192	.250	.355	241	7	.237	.298	.378	106	5	.170	.224	.358	338	10	.231	.289	.370	218	11	.251	.314	.385	84	4	.250	.289	.393
1989	NY-A	223	4	.197	.266	.296	113	3	.204	.268	.319	110	1	.191	.264	.273	33	0	.242	.306	.303	190	4	.189	.260	.295	91	0	.231	.286	.286	38	0	.289	.341	.395
1989	SD-N	148	3	.196	.287	.304	69	2	.188	.291	.290	79	1	.203	.284	.316	26	0	.154	.185	.192	122	3	.205	.307	.328	64	2	.266	.356	.406	25	0	.280	.333	.400
1990	SD-N	398	7	.254	.322	.374	169	1	.272	.354	.361	229	6	.240	.298	.384	101	4	.248	.353	.396	297	3	.256	.311	.367	158	1	.272	.339	.348	64	2	.234	.333	.422

YEAR	TM/L	TOTAL AB	HR	AVG	OBP	SLG	HOME AB	HR	AVG	OBP	SLG	AWAY AB	HR	AVG	OBP	SLG	LEFT AB	HR	AVG	OBP	SLG	RIGHT AB	HR	AVG	OBP	SLG	ON-BASE AB	HR	AVG	OBP	SLG	LATE/CLOSE AB	HR	AVG	OBP	SLG
1991	Min-A	365	6	.279	.322	.384	190	4	.284	.332	.405	175	2	.274	.312	.360	16	0	.188	.316	.250	349	6	.284	.323	.390	153	2	.255	.310	.346	53	0	.245	.298	.283
1992	Min-A	105	0	.200	.213	.238	46	0	.217	.229	.261	59	0	.186	.200	.220	6	0	.167	.167	.167	99	0	.202	.216	.242	43	0	.186	.200	.209	14	0	.143	.143	.143
1993	Min-A	253	3	.292	.350	.423	107	2	.336	.388	.533	146	1	.260	.323	.342	20	0	.450	.500	.500	233	3	.279	.337	.416	123	3	.309	.372	.455	45	0	.289	.327	.356
1993	Bal-A	117	6	.325	.373	.556	62	3	.355	.403	.581	55	3	.291	.339	.527	16	0	.375	.412	.438	101	6	.317	.367	.574	53	4	.377	.411	.698	16	0	.250	.333	.250
TOTALS		3660	130	.242	.307	.410	1728	66	.244	.315	.416	1932	64	.241	.300	.406	720	17	.217	.287	.335	2940	113	.248	.312	.429	1617	63	.262	.332	.438	562	15	.230	.303	.356

■ Rafael Palmeiro BL/TL

YEAR	TM/L	AB	HR	AVG	OBP	SLG	AB	HR	AVG	OBP	SLG	AB	HR	AVG	OBP	SLG	AB	HR	AVG	OBP	SLG	AB	HR	AVG	OBP	SLG	AB	HR	AVG	OBP	SLG	AB	HR	AVG	OBP	SLG
1986	Chi-N	73	3	.247	.295	.425	38	1	.211	.268	.342	35	2	.286	.324	.514	8	0	.125	.125	.250	65	3	.262	.314	.446	38	2	.211	.231	.447	7	1	.429	.429	1.000
1987	Chi-N	221	14	.276	.336	.543	88	5	.273	.333	.500	133	9	.278	.338	.571	26	1	.115	.226	.231	195	13	.297	.352	.585	94	5	.245	.330	.479	39	1	.333	.395	.487
1988	Chi-N	580	8	.307	.349	.436	290	8	.321	.362	.486	290	0	.293	.337	.386	171	2	.333	.364	.480	409	6	.296	.343	.418	245	2	.261	.327	.343	98	0	.296	.314	.378
1989	Tex-A	559	8	.275	.354	.374	263	4	.259	.348	.354	296	4	.291	.360	.392	165	2	.248	.302	.333	394	6	.287	.375	.391	250	4	.292	.378	.404	72	2	.278	.366	.431
1990	Tex-A	598	14	.319	.361	.468	295	9	.288	.354	.478	303	5	.350	.367	.459	189	5	.339	.361	.476	409	9	.311	.360	.465	271	6	.362	.403	.531	111	3	.288	.316	.441
1991	Tex-A	631	26	.322	.389	.532	298	12	.339	.408	.540	333	14	.306	.372	.526	186	9	.274	.333	.473	445	17	.342	.411	.557	279	12	.297	.375	.520	107	6	.243	.317	.477
1992	Tex-A	608	22	.268	.352	.434	297	8	.263	.354	.401	311	14	.273	.350	.466	178	5	.281	.365	.438	430	17	.263	.347	.433	259	9	.274	.372	.448	97	3	.196	.273	.330
1993	Tex-A	597	37	.295	.371	.554	294	22	.282	.360	.578	303	15	.307	.382	.531	149	2	.268	.323	.356	448	35	.304	.387	.621	246	16	.293	.396	.557	72	6	.292	.376	.583
1994	Bal-A	436	23	.319	.392	.550	209	11	.340	.401	.574	227	12	.300	.383	.529	145	10	.352	.424	.641	291	13	.302	.375	.505	199	8	.296	.387	.518	50	2	.340	.404	.560
TOTALS		4303	155	.298	.364	.480	2072	80	.295	.365	.484	2231	75	.301	.362	.476	1217	36	.294	.348	.449	3086	119	.300	.369	.492	1881	64	.293	.372	.474	653	24	.276	.335	.453

■ Dave Parker BL/TR

YEAR	TM/L	AB	HR	AVG	OBP	SLG	AB	HR	AVG	OBP	SLG	AB	HR	AVG	OBP	SLG	AB	HR	AVG	OBP	SLG	AB	HR	AVG	OBP	SLG	AB	HR	AVG	OBP	SLG	AB	HR	AVG	OBP	SLG
1984	Cin-N	607	16	.285	.328	.410	299	10	.308	.360	.458	308	6	.263	.296	.364	207	5	.285	.304	.391	400	11	.285	.340	.420	297	8	.310	.355	.431	116	4	.250	.323	.397
1985	Cin-N	635	34	.312	.365	.551	312	16	.308	.356	.535	323	18	.316	.373	.567	201	7	.279	.305	.443	434	27	.327	.390	.601	322	18	.339	.402	.575	109	4	.339	.410	.578
1986	Cin-N	637	31	.273	.330	.477	313	17	.268	.325	.505	324	14	.278	.335	.451	232	10	.302	.325	.513	405	21	.257	.333	.457	295	22	.329	.393	.617	110	6	.255	.331	.491
1987	Cin-N	589	26	.253	.311	.433	291	14	.282	.339	.478	298	12	.225	.284	.389	205	8	.239	.285	.410	384	18	.260	.324	.445	278	15	.281	.350	.489	90	2	.233	.268	.322
1988	Oak-A	377	12	.257	.314	.406	177	6	.271	.305	.405	200	6	.245	.305	.405	55	2	.182	.274	.309	322	10	.270	.321	.422	186	9	.290	.343	.489	69	1	.246	.297	.377
1989	Oak-A	553	22	.264	.308	.432	272	10	.279	.334	.426	281	12	.249	.282	.438	127	6	.228	.233	.409	426	16	.275	.329	.439	261	10	.284	.334	.464	77	3	.182	.267	.325
1990	Mil-A	610	21	.289	.330	.451	293	9	.273	.316	.427	317	12	.303	.344	.473	185	6	.259	.282	.389	425	15	.301	.350	.478	294	8	.289	.336	.422	82	0	.232	.316	.268
1991	Cal-A	466	11	.232	.279	.358	213	6	.202	.260	.333	253	5	.257	.296	.379	128	4	.234	.261	.383	338	7	.231	.286	.349	215	5	.237	.277	.349	59	4	.220	.258	.475
1991	Tor-A	36	0	.333	.400	.444	16	0	.375	.444	.563	20	0	.300	.364	.350	5	0	.200	.200	.400	31	0	.355	.429	.452	17	0	.412	.412	.471	10	0	.600	.636	.800
TOTALS		4510	173	.273	.324	.445	2186	88	.278	.330	.455	2324	85	.269	.317	.436	1345	48	.262	.289	.420	3165	125	.278	.337	.456	2165	95	.299	.354	.485	722	24	.255	.321	.417

■ Lance Parrish BR/TR

YEAR	TM/L	AB	HR	AVG	OBP	SLG	AB	HR	AVG	OBP	SLG	AB	HR	AVG	OBP	SLG	AB	HR	AVG	OBP	SLG	AB	HR	AVG	OBP	SLG	AB	HR	AVG	OBP	SLG	AB	HR	AVG	OBP	SLG
1984	Det-A	578	33	.237	.287	.443	271	13	.269	.317	.461	307	20	.208	.260	.427	209	14	.263	.339	.502	369	19	.222	.256	.409	299	16	.231	.278	.421	84	6	.250	.300	.476
1985	Det-A	549	28	.273	.323	.479	268	11	.280	.341	.463	281	17	.267	.306	.495	151	9	.305	.372	.563	398	19	.261	.304	.447	258	13	.295	.353	.492	92	5	.272	.316	.478
1986	Det-A	327	22	.257	.340	.483	158	8	.247	.341	.411	169	14	.266	.340	.550	122	5	.262	.328	.410	205	17	.254	.347	.527	158	8	.247	.330	.424	50	0	.180	.344	.180
1987	Phi-N	466	17	.245	.313	.399	234	5	.252	.322	.389	232	12	.237	.305	.409	138	6	.304	.391	.464	328	11	.220	.278	.372	236	11	.258	.310	.458	84	4	.214	.290	.369
1988	Phi-N	424	15	.215	.293	.370	213	11	.225	.294	.441	211	4	.204	.292	.299	131	4	.252	.336	.397	293	11	.198	.274	.358	189	9	.255	.347	.457	80	1	.188	.305	.262
1989	Cal-A	433	17	.238	.306	.388	215	8	.251	.305	.400	218	9	.225	.306	.376	144	7	.236	.317	.410	289	10	.239	.300	.377	199	6	.241	.320	.377	78	2	.218	.303	.333
1990	Cal-A	470	24	.268	.338	.451	235	14	.277	.346	.485	235	10	.260	.331	.417	125	7	.304	.370	.488	345	17	.255	.327	.438	226	13	.292	.367	.500	85	5	.235	.316	.412
1991	Cal-A	402	19	.216	.285	.380	216	9	.227	.280	.380	186	10	.204	.292	.398	105	3	.219	.297	.314	297	16	.215	.281	.414	164	7	.220	.288	.384	57	1	.105	.159	.175
1992	Sea-A	83	4	.229	.270	.398	43	1	.209	.222	.279	40	3	.250	.318	.525	17	0	.235	.263	.235	66	4	.227	.271	.439	32	2	.250	.286	.438	16	0	.125	.125	.125
1992	Cal-A	192	8	.234	.304	.427	92	6	.239	.301	.500	100	2	.230	.306	.360	78	4	.231	.326	.474	114	4	.237	.288	.395	91	2	.209	.282	.341	46	1	.152	.216	.239
1993	Cle-A	20	1	.200	.333	.400	5	1	.200	.429	.800	15	0	.200	.294	.267	5	0	.000	.000	.000	15	1	.267	.421	.533	9	1	.111	.273	.444	4	0	.000	.000	.000
1994	Pit-N	126	3	.270	.363	.381	64	3	.297	.395	.516	62	0	.242	.329	.242	34	1	.265	.286	.412	92	2	.272	.387	.370	53	0	.321	.439	.377	22	0	.227	.280	.227
TOTALS		4070	191	.244	.311	.424	2014	90	.255	.319	.435	2056	101	.234	.303	.414	1259	60	.265	.340	.448	2811	131	.235	.297	.414	1913	88	.255	.324	.436	698	25	.208	.286	.335

■ Larry Parrish BR/TR

YEAR	TM/L	AB	HR	AVG	OBP	SLG	AB	HR	AVG	OBP	SLG	AB	HR	AVG	OBP	SLG	AB	HR	AVG	OBP	SLG	AB	HR	AVG	OBP	SLG	AB	HR	AVG	OBP	SLG	AB	HR	AVG	OBP	SLG
1984	Tex-A	613	22	.285	.336	.465	310	11	.310	.367	.500	303	11	.261	.303	.429	178	8	.309	.364	.517	435	14	.276	.324	.444	291	11	.299	.361	.495	103	5	.272	.336	.476
1985	Tex-A	346	17	.249	.314	.434	188	8	.218	.285	.378	158	9	.285	.349	.500	94	8	.245	.321	.532	252	9	.250	.312	.397	173	7	.254	.332	.410	52	4	.250	.350	.538
1986	Tex-A	464	28	.276	.347	.509	225	14	.289	.354	.533	239	14	.264	.341	.486	130	11	.254	.351	.569	334	17	.284	.346	.505	206	10	.306	.374	.505	67	2	.224	.338	.373
1987	Tex-A	557	32	.268	.328	.483	277	16	.264	.335	.477	280	16	.271	.320	.489	190	14	.268	.346	.516	367	18	.267	.318	.466	258	19	.326	.388	.589	87	3	.241	.298	.356
1988	Tex-A	248	7	.190	.253	.319	137	4	.212	.262	.358	111	3	.162	.242	.270	84	2	.167	.220	.274	164	5	.201	.269	.341	105	1	.162	.235	.248	42	0	.119	.196	.119
1988	Bos-A	158	7	.259	.298	.424	98	3	.296	.320	.439	60	4	.200	.262	.400	42	1	.333	.378	.429	116	6	.233	.268	.422	77	3	.312	.341	.455	25	2	.280	.308	.560
TOTALS		2386	113	.262	.322	.455	1235	56	.270	.330	.462	1151	57	.255	.313	.448	718	44	.265	.335	.494	1668	69	.261	.316	.438	1110	51	.287	.352	.479	376	16	.237	.313	.404

■ Dan Pasqua BL/TL

YEAR	TM/L	AB	HR	AVG	OBP	SLG	AB	HR	AVG	OBP	SLG	AB	HR	AVG	OBP	SLG	AB	HR	AVG	OBP	SLG	AB	HR	AVG	OBP	SLG	AB	HR	AVG	OBP	SLG	AB	HR	AVG	OBP	SLG
1985	NY-A	148	9	.209	.289	.426	87	7	.218	.284	.471	61	2	.197	.296	.361	15	0	.133	.188	.133	133	9	.218	.300	.459	57	5	.228	.328	.544	17	0	.235	.462	.235
1986	NY-A	280	16	.293	.399	.525	140	9	.271	.384	.500	140	7	.314	.401	.514	51	3	.216	.322	.451	229	13	.310	.415	.541	141	4	.284	.404	.440	45	3	.156	.328	.400
1987	NY-A	318	17	.233	.319	.421	141	6	.277	.372	.411	177	11	.198	.276	.429	55	0	.164	.246	.200	263	17	.247	.334	.468	138	8	.210	.333	.399	51	2	.235	.333	.412
1988	Chi-A	422	20	.227	.307	.417	213	11	.225	.297	.432	209	9	.230	.316	.402	81	0	.123	.217	.160	341	20	.252	.328	.478	196	6	.194	.301	.311	85	4	.224	.305	.424
1989	Chi-A	246	11	.248	.315	.427	113	5	.257	.336	.434	133	6	.241	.297	.421	76	3	.224	.259	.355	170	8	.259	.338	.473	112	4	.295	.346	.473	41	1	.171	.261	.268
1990	Chi-A	325	13	.274	.347	.495	157	4	.318	.392	.529	168	9	.232	.303	.464	31	0	.194	.265	.290	294	13	.282	.355	.517	140	7	.307	.404	.564	49	3	.224	.309	.490
1991	Chi-A	417	18	.259	.358	.465	196	10	.291	.402	.531	221	8	.231	.317	.407	49	5	.265	.379	.531	368	15	.258	.355	.457	205	8	.259	.381	.468	78	5	.295	.382	.462
1992	Chi-A	265	6	.211	.305	.347	128	2	.188	.284	.273	137	4	.234	.325	.416	18	0	.111	.200	.111	247	6	.219	.312	.364	117	3	.222	.314	.368	34	1	.176	.222	.353
1993	Chi-A	176	5	.205	.302	.358	76	2	.263	.380	.395	100	3	.160	.239	.330	10	2	.400	.500	1.100	166	3	.193	.290	.313	79	5	.203	.313	.418	20	1	.250	.407	.450
1994	Chi-A	23	2	.217	.217	.565	7	1	.286	.286	.857	16	1	.188	.188	.438	10	2	.400	.500	1.100	23	2	.217	.217	.565	10	1	.100	.100	.400	7	0	.000	.000	.000
TOTALS		2620	117	.244	.330	.438	1258	57	.259	.352	.455	1362	60	.229	.310	.422	386	11	.192	.275	.321	2234	106	.252	.340	.458	1195	51	.244	.349	.433	427	18	.220	.325	.400

■ Tony Pena BR/TR

YEAR	TM/L	AB	HR	AVG	OBP	SLG	AB	HR	AVG	OBP	SLG	AB	HR	AVG	OBP	SLG	AB	HR	AVG	OBP	SLG	AB	HR	AVG	OBP	SLG	AB	HR	AVG	OBP	SLG	AB	HR	AVG	OBP	SLG
1984	Pit-N	546	15	.286	.333	.425	264	7	.280	.321	.417	282	8	.291	.344	.433	150	7	.320	.350	.520	396	8	.273	.327	.389	248	7	.310	.350	.448	117	1	.282	.346	.385
1985	Pit-N	546	10	.249	.284	.361	280	2	.246	.294	.336	266	8	.252	.274	.387	151	2	.258	.309	.344	395	8	.246	.275	.367	230	5	.239	.271	.352	97	3	.196	.236	.309
1986	Pit-N	510	10	.288	.356	.406	255	5	.298	.384	.404	255	5	.278	.326	.408	174	4	.333	.405	.471	336	6	.265	.330	.372	247	1	.263	.327	.328	114	0	.281	.328	.316
1987	StL-N	384	5	.214	.281	.307	187	1	.225	.274	.310	197	4	.203	.288	.305	137	3	.226	.280	.321	247	2	.206	.282	.300	162	4	.210	.290	.333	82	1	.207	.270	.305
1988	StL-N	505	10	.263	.308	.372	255	4	.259	.301	.349	250	6	.268	.314	.396	166	5	.331	.380	.512	339	5	.230	.272	.304	223	4	.265	.317	.359	106	3	.255	.296	.406
1989	StL-N	424	4	.259	.318	.337	201	3	.229	.304	.313	223	1	.287	.332	.359	170	1	.294	.366	.371	254	2	.236	.284	.315	203	0	.271	.352	.330	76	1	.197	.237	.263
1990	Bos-A	491	7	.263	.322	.348	247	3	.275	.344	.348	244	4	.250	.298	.348	155	5	.290	.341	.413	336	2	.250	.313	.318	239	2	.285	.318	.347	99	0	.293	.333	.343
1991	Bos-A	464	5	.231	.291	.321	230	2	.222	.290	.313	234	3	.239	.293	.329	106	4	.283	.336	.434	358	1	.215	.278	.288	223	2	.215	.261	.278	71	0	.127	.213	.155
1992	Bos-A	410	1	.241	.284	.305	203	1	.276	.316	.379	207	0	.208	.252	.232	111	1	.252	.270	.333	299	0	.237	.289	.294	190	0	.258	.285	.311	79	1	.304	.375	.392
1993	Bos-A	304	4	.181	.246	.257	155	2	.155	.227	.232	149	2	.208	.265	.282	83	2	.253	.264	.373	221	2	.154	.239	.213	125	1	.160	.229	.224	31	0	.258	.324	.355
1994	Cle-A	112	2	.295	.341	.438	40	1	.300	.349	.450	72	1	.292	.338	.431	54	2	.352	.390	.574	58	0	.241	.297	.310	43	0	.279	.340	.395	15	1	.133	.188	.333
TOTALS		4696	73	.252	.311	.348	2317	31	.252	.311	.348	2379	42	.253	.303	.358	1457	37	.291	.340	.421	3239	36	.236	.292	.322	2133	26	.254	.305	.339	887	11	.242	.296	.328

■ Terry Pendleton BB/TR

YEAR	TM/L	AB	HR	AVG	OBP	SLG	AB	HR	AVG	OBP	SLG	AB	HR	AVG	OBP	SLG	AB	HR	AVG	OBP	SLG	AB	HR	AVG	OBP	SLG	AB	HR	AVG	OBP	SLG	AB	HR	AVG	OBP	SLG
1984	StL-N	262	1	.324	.357	.420	141	0	.355	.389	.454	121	1	.289	.317	.380	88	0	.261	.280	.352	174	1	.356	.395	.454	125	1	.304	.343	.416	42	0	.333	.356	.357
1985	StL-N	559	5	.240	.285	.306	272	3	.228	.273	.313	287	2	.251	.297	.300	171	2	.228	.257	.298	388	3	.245	.298	.309	280	2	.250	.295	.311	94	1	.277	.333	.426
1986	StL-N	578	1	.239	.279	.306	286	0	.255	.294	.336	292	1	.223	.264	.277	209	0	.278	.325	.364	369	1	.217	.253	.274	257	0	.237	.290	.300	121	0	.215	.280	.273
1987	StL-N	583	12	.286	.360	.412	293	5	.266	.331	.375	290	7	.307	.388	.448	208	4	.337	.386	.447	375	8	.259	.346	.392	275	7	.320	.393	.476	101	4	.287	.368	.515
1988	StL-N	391	6	.253	.293	.361	207	4	.280	.326	.415	184	2	.223	.254	.299	119	2	.328	.349	.429	272	5	.221	.268	.331	185	1	.259	.300	.341	71	0	.211	.250	.268
1989	StL-N	613	13	.264	.313	.396	295	8	.271	.324	.437	318	5	.258	.302	.346	247	2	.279	.313	.377	366	11	.254	.313	.399	365	5	.260	.313	.379	97	2	.227	.299	.330
1990	StL-N	447	6	.230	.277	.324	251	6	.243	.289	.375	196	0	.214	.262	.260	158	4	.209	.235	.361	289	2	.242	.299	.304	210	3	.229	.279	.333	85	0	.200	.274	.259
1991	Atl-N	586	22	.319	.363	.517	285	13	.340	.377	.561	301	9	.299	.350	.475	177	4	.299	.350	.458	409	18	.328	.368	.543	280	9	.318	.361	.482	88	1	.341	.392	.466
1992	Atl-N	640	21	.311	.345	.473	306	13	.307	.353	.503	334	8	.314	.338	.446	207	8	.357	.390	.527	433	13	.289	.323	.448	278	10	.335	.377	.543	91	5	.286	.330	.473
1993	Atl-N	633	17	.272	.311	.408	310	9	.281	.314	.435	323	8	.263	.307	.381	175	4	.297	.326	.429	458	13	.262	.305	.400	306	8	.268	.308	.405	87	2	.276	.354	.402
1994	Atl-N	309	7	.252	.280	.398	150	3	.233	.263	.360	159	4	.270	.297	.434	97	1	.278	.286	.392	212	6	.241	.278	.401	134	1	.261	.293	.388	39	0	.154	.233	.154
TOTALS		5601	111	.272	.317	.395	2796	63	.277	.322	.417	2805	48	.267	.312	.372	1856	30	.290	.324	.407	3745	81	.264	.313	.389	2615	47	.278	.326	.398	916	15	.257	.319	.369

■ Gerald Perry BL/TR

YEAR	TM/L	AB	HR	AVG	OBP	SLG	AB	HR	AVG	OBP	SLG	AB	HR	AVG	OBP	SLG	AB	HR	AVG	OBP	SLG	AB	HR	AVG	OBP	SLG	AB	HR	AVG	OBP	SLG	AB	HR	AVG	OBP	SLG
1984	Atl-N	347	7	.265	.372	.372	170	3	.294	.410	.394	177	4	.237	.333	.350	74	1	.216	.310	.284	273	6	.278	.387	.396	147	2	.265	.388	.367	62	1	.290	.459	.371
1985	Atl-N	238	3	.214	.282	.273	137	3	.226	.282	.321	101	0	.198	.283	.208	41	0	.171	.190	.244	197	2	.223	.300	.279	103	2	.223	.289	.291	59	1	.271	.333	.339
1986	Atl-N	70	2	.271	.342	.386	32	2	.250	.300	.406	38	0	.289	.382	.342	3	1	1.000	1.000	2.000	67	1	.239	.313	.343	25	1	.240	.375	.440	15	0	.267	.389	.267
1987	Atl-N	533	12	.270	.329	.411	255	6	.259	.331	.369	278	6	.281	.327	.450	125	5	.256	.321	.440	408	7	.275	.331	.390	246	7	.280	.338	.435	84	1	.333	.380	.452
1988	Atl-N	547	8	.300	.338	.400	280	4	.314	.351	.429	267	4	.285	.325	.371	211	3	.270	.279	.346	336	5	.318	.373	.435	254	6	.358	.397	.492	108	1	.250	.314	.343
1989	Atl-N	266	4	.252	.318	.338	142	2	.289	.368	.380	124	2	.210	.300	.290	104	3	.337	.386	.471	162	1	.198	.307	.253	126	2	.254	.329	.365	39	1	.154	.304	.256
1990	KC-A	465	8	.254	.313	.361	238	6	.286	.333	.395	227	5	.220	.291	.326	134	5	.209	.252	.269	331	7	.272	.336	.399	220	5	.282	.340	.350	67	2	.224	.274	.373
1991	StL-N	242	6	.240	.300	.380	130	1	.185	.246	.277	112	5	.304	.360	.500	104	2	.240	.286	.365	138	4	.239	.310	.391	111	2	.306	.370	.477	61	2	.230	.319	.361

YEAR	TM/L	TOTAL AB	HR	AVG	OBP	SLG	HOME AB	HR	AVG	OBP	SLG	AWAY AB	HR	AVG	OBP	SLG	LEFT AB	HR	AVG	OBP	SLG	RIGHT AB	HR	AVG	OBP	SLG	ON-BASE AB	HR	AVG	OBP	SLG	LATE/CLOSE AB	HR	AVG	OBP	SLG
1992	StL-N	143	1	.238	.311	.315	73	1	.260	.329	.356	70	0	.214	.291	.271	25	0	.200	.310	.200	118	1	.246	.311	.339	80	1	.237	.315	.338	61	1	.230	.284	.328
1993	StL-N	98	4	.337	.440	.510	32	3	.281	.452	.594	66	1	.364	.432	.470	8	0	.250	.400	.250	90	4	.344	.443	.533	51	1	.353	.476	.490	30	1	.333	.535	.500
1994	StL-N	77	3	.325	.435	.532	27	1	.333	.471	.444	50	2	.320	.414	.580	4	0	.000	.333	.000	73	3	.342	.442	.562	46	0	.304	.418	.413	19	2	.263	.481	.632
TOTALS		3026	58	.266	.334	.378	1516	25	.272	.342	.383	1510	33	.260	.326	.374	833	17	.252	.300	.360	2193	41	.271	.347	.385	1409	24	.289	.360	.407	605	13	.260	.359	.374

■ Geno Petralli BL/TR

YEAR	TM/L	TOTAL AB	HR	AVG	OBP	SLG	HOME AB	HR	AVG	OBP	SLG	AWAY AB	HR	AVG	OBP	SLG	LEFT AB	HR	AVG	OBP	SLG	RIGHT AB	HR	AVG	OBP	SLG	ON-BASE AB	HR	AVG	OBP	SLG	LATE/CLOSE AB	HR	AVG	OBP	SLG
1984	Tor-A	3	0	.000	.000	.000	3	0	.000	.000	.000	0	0	—	—	—	4	0	.000	.333	.000	3	0	.000	.000	.000	3	0	.000	.000	.000	0	0	—	—	—
1985	Tex-A	100	0	.270	.319	.290	37	0	.297	.400	.324	63	0	.254	.265	.270	5	0	.000	.000	.000	95	0	.284	.333	.305	38	0	.395	.426	.421	12	0	.167	.231	.167
1986	Tex-A	137	2	.255	.282	.409	49	1	.184	.216	.265	88	1	.295	.319	.489	11	0	.182	.182	.182	126	2	.262	.290	.429	58	1	.293	.317	.466	27	2	.296	.321	.630
1987	Tex-A	202	7	.302	.388	.480	94	4	.319	.423	.532	108	3	.287	.355	.435	15	0	.267	.353	.267	187	7	.305	.391	.497	97	1	.258	.376	.340	43	3	.318	.392	.545
1988	Tex-A	351	7	.282	.356	.393	169	1	.272	.371	.343	182	6	.291	.342	.440	44	0	.182	.245	.205	307	7	.296	.371	.420	158	1	.234	.323	.316	61	1	.279	.389	.361
1989	Tex-A	184	4	.304	.368	.408	88	1	.193	.260	.239	96	3	.406	.463	.563	9	0	.111	.333	.111	175	4	.314	.370	.423	82	2	.280	.368	.390	26	0	.308	.379	.346
1990	Tex-A	325	0	.255	.357	.302	170	0	.265	.373	.306	155	0	.245	.339	.297	20	0	.300	.483	.300	305	0	.252	.347	.302	127	0	.252	.355	.299	58	0	.224	.343	.276
1991	Tex-A	199	2	.271	.339	.352	85	0	.235	.298	.282	114	2	.298	.370	.404	9	0	.111	.100	.111	190	2	.279	.351	.363	86	1	.291	.354	.395	29	0	.207	.258	.276
1992	Tex-A	192	1	.198	.274	.276	100	0	.220	.271	.280	92	1	.174	.276	.272	22	0	.136	.136	.136	170	1	.206	.289	.294	87	1	.195	.300	.287	50	1	.180	.293	.260
1993	Tex-A	133	1	.241	.348	.301	54	1	.185	.267	.259	79	0	.278	.400	.329	15	0	.267	.353	.333	118	1	.237	.348	.297	63	0	.238	.360	.270	23	0	.261	.433	.304
TOTALS		1826	24	.266	.342	.359	849	8	.247	.334	.320	977	16	.281	.350	.393	150	0	.193	.279	.207	1676	24	.272	.348	.373	799	7	.258	.347	.340	329	7	.252	.348	.358

■ Gary Pettis BB/TR

YEAR	TM/L	TOTAL AB	HR	AVG	OBP	SLG	HOME AB	HR	AVG	OBP	SLG	AWAY AB	HR	AVG	OBP	SLG	LEFT AB	HR	AVG	OBP	SLG	RIGHT AB	HR	AVG	OBP	SLG	ON-BASE AB	HR	AVG	OBP	SLG	LATE/CLOSE AB	HR	AVG	OBP	SLG
1984	Cal-A	397	2	.227	.332	.300	182	1	.242	.325	.308	215	1	.214	.337	.293	134	0	.246	.325	.299	263	2	.217	.335	.300	123	1	.220	.317	.325	51	0	.196	.317	.235
1985	Cal-A	443	1	.257	.347	.323	182	0	.231	.340	.302	261	1	.276	.353	.337	139	0	.281	.370	.333	304	1	.247	.336	.319	164	1	.262	.346	.323	57	0	.263	.344	.333
1986	Cal-A	539	5	.258	.339	.343	251	0	.235	.320	.283	288	4	.278	.356	.396	176	2	.278	.328	.369	363	3	.248	.344	.331	197	3	.294	.392	.406	69	0	.217	.291	.290
1987	Cal-A	394	1	.208	.302	.259	204	1	.221	.300	.284	190	0	.195	.305	.232	128	1	.172	.248	.250	266	0	.226	.327	.263	158	0	.177	.282	.209	65	0	.262	.324	.292
1988	Det-A	458	3	.210	.285	.277	210	0	.200	.282	.248	248	3	.218	.287	.302	168	0	.214	.258	.250	290	3	.207	.299	.293	175	2	.246	.316	.349	70	1	.155	.211	.169
1989	Det-A	444	1	.257	.375	.309	234	1	.265	.392	.342	210	0	.248	.355	.271	152	0	.263	.374	.316	292	1	.253	.375	.305	153	0	.268	.371	.294	68	0	.265	.432	.309
1990	Tex-A	423	3	.239	.333	.336	221	3	.253	.348	.362	202	0	.223	.316	.307	152	0	.217	.320	.250	271	3	.251	.340	.358	143	0	.266	.349	.378	65	1	.277	.329	.385
1991	Tex-A	282	0	.216	.341	.277	137	0	.212	.343	.299	145	0	.221	.339	.255	77	0	.195	.315	.234	205	0	.224	.351	.293	128	0	.219	.303	.273	53	0	.245	.322	.302
1992	SD-N	30	0	.200	.250	.233	12	0	.167	.286	.167	18	0	.222	.222	.278	5	0	.200	.429	.200	25	0	.200	.200	.240	12	0	.250	.308	.333	3	0	.000	.000	.000
1992	Det-A	129	1	.202	.338	.302	48	1	.271	.426	.375	81	0	.160	.281	.259	38	0	.316	.435	.553	91	1	.154	.297	.198	54	0	.222	.348	.352	16	0	.188	.316	.250
TOTALS		3539	17	.234	.332	.305	1681	8	.234	.335	.305	1858	9	.234	.329	.305	1169	3	.240	.344	.306	2370	14	.232	.336	.304	1307	7	.246	.338	.324	518	1	.232	.321	.286

■ Ken Phelps BL/TL

YEAR	TM/L	TOTAL AB	HR	AVG	OBP	SLG	HOME AB	HR	AVG	OBP	SLG	AWAY AB	HR	AVG	OBP	SLG	LEFT AB	HR	AVG	OBP	SLG	RIGHT AB	HR	AVG	OBP	SLG	ON-BASE AB	HR	AVG	OBP	SLG	LATE/CLOSE AB	HR	AVG	OBP	SLG
1984	Sea-A	290	24	.241	.378	.521	161	13	.248	.363	.528	129	11	.233	.395	.512	40	1	.200	.333	.300	250	23	.248	.385	.556	128	9	.219	.381	.461	41	5	.244	.404	.610
1985	Sea-A	116	9	.207	.343	.466	56	5	.214	.333	.500	60	4	.200	.351	.433	10	0	.100	.182	.200	106	9	.217	.357	.491	58	6	.207	.378	.552	30	1	.167	.324	.267
1986	Sea-A	344	24	.247	.406	.526	174	15	.287	.445	.626	170	9	.206	.364	.424	59	1	.237	.373	.390	285	23	.249	.413	.554	152	11	.257	.453	.559	53	5	.208	.408	.509
1987	Sea-A	332	27	.259	.410	.548	164	15	.232	.394	.555	168	12	.286	.427	.542	37	3	.270	.451	.622	295	24	.258	.405	.539	153	11	.255	.438	.516	32	1	.156	.372	.281
1988	Sea-A	190	14	.284	.434	.547	85	6	.282	.441	.565	105	8	.286	.429	.533	9	0	.000	.091	.000	181	14	.298	.451	.575	80	7	.313	.482	.613	33	3	.182	.325	.455
1988	NY-A	107	10	.224	.339	.551	51	6	.235	.344	.608	56	4	.214	.333	.500	11	1	.182	.250	.455	96	9	.229	.348	.563	52	5	.212	.354	.538	26	2	.154	.241	.423
1989	NY-A	185	7	.249	.340	.378	98	4	.276	.368	.408	87	3	.218	.306	.345	9	0	.222	.357	.222	176	7	.250	.338	.386	95	5	.242	.324	.421	34	2	.294	.400	.500
1989	Oak-A	9	0	.111	.385	.222	6	0	.000	.143	.000	3	0	.333	.667	.667	2	0	.000	.000	.000	7	0	.143	.455	.286	4	0	.000	.333	.000	3	0	.000	.250	.000
1990	Oak-A	59	1	.186	.319	.271	31	1	.161	.257	.258	28	0	.214	.378	.286	2	0	.000	.000	.000	57	1	.193	.329	.281	20	0	.250	.484	.250	10	0	.100	.182	.100
1990	Cle-A	61	0	.115	.239	.115	31	0	.097	.243	.097	30	0	.133	.235	.133	2	0	.000	.333	.000	59	0	.119	.235	.119	26	0	.077	.226	.077	9	0	.000	.182	.000
TOTALS		1693	116	.241	.382	.488	857	65	.246	.383	.517	836	51	.236	.380	.458	181	6	.204	.345	.370	1512	110	.245	.386	.502	768	54	.240	.409	.493	271	19	.192	.352	.417

■ Tony Phillips BB/TR

YEAR	TM/L	TOTAL AB	HR	AVG	OBP	SLG	HOME AB	HR	AVG	OBP	SLG	AWAY AB	HR	AVG	OBP	SLG	LEFT AB	HR	AVG	OBP	SLG	RIGHT AB	HR	AVG	OBP	SLG	ON-BASE AB	HR	AVG	OBP	SLG	LATE/CLOSE AB	HR	AVG	OBP	SLG
1984	Oak-A	451	4	.266	.325	.359	226	2	.226	.279	.301	225	2	.307	.371	.418	153	1	.307	.349	.405	298	3	.245	.313	.336	166	2	.295	.361	.380	73	1	.329	.430	.479
1985	Oak-A	161	4	.280	.331	.453	73	2	.288	.342	.507	88	2	.273	.323	.409	58	2	.362	.383	.517	103	2	.233	.304	.417	59	1	.186	.234	.356	24	0	.167	.222	.292
1986	Oak-A	441	5	.256	.367	.345	214	3	.234	.362	.322	227	2	.278	.373	.366	134	3	.321	.443	.455	307	2	.228	.331	.296	154	0	.318	.419	.416	65	0	.308	.432	.385
1987	Oak-A	379	10	.240	.337	.372	175	5	.251	.351	.383	204	5	.230	.325	.363	128	3	.289	.403	.383	251	7	.215	.302	.367	143	6	.287	.382	.490	56	5	.242	.342	.530
1988	Oak-A	212	2	.203	.320	.307	106	2	.217	.297	.377	106	0	.189	.341	.236	71	0	.282	.427	.423	141	2	.163	.261	.248	88	1	.239	.333	.398	39	0	.128	.209	.179
1989	Oak-A	451	4	.262	.345	.348	214	2	.271	.363	.327	237	2	.253	.328	.367	139	2	.259	.364	.360	312	4	.263	.336	.343	203	3	.286	.336	.409	73	1	.233	.337	.370
1990	Det-A	573	8	.251	.364	.351	286	4	.241	.360	.322	287	4	.261	.369	.380	202	2	.248	.343	.351	371	6	.253	.375	.350	216	5	.282	.391	.412	76	1	.263	.398	.368
1991	Det-A	564	17	.284	.371	.438	292	9	.295	.398	.438	272	8	.272	.341	.438	154	11	.357	.466	.617	410	6	.256	.333	.371	194	3	.309	.394	.423	81	3	.222	.347	.383
1992	Det-A	606	10	.276	.387	.388	289	3	.273	.398	.353	317	7	.278	.377	.420	174	5	.270	.401	.420	432	5	.278	.382	.375	226	3	.274	.396	.376	85	2	.271	.380	.412
1993	Det-A	566	7	.313	.443	.398	256	3	.309	.452	.391	310	4	.316	.436	.403	171	1	.316	.444	.380	395	6	.311	.443	.405	195	2	.282	.435	.344	91	1	.275	.419	.377
1994	Det-A	438	19	.281	.409	.468	218	12	.252	.399	.468	220	7	.309	.419	.468	108	4	.269	.429	.444	330	15	.285	.402	.476	152	5	.243	.372	.414	57	4	.351	.500	.596
TOTALS		4842	90	.269	.372	.385	2349	47	.262	.374	.372	2493	43	.275	.371	.396	1492	32	.294	.404	.425	3350	58	.257	.357	.367	1796	31	.281	.382	.402	708	18	.263	.381	.410

■ Mike Piazza BR/TR

YEAR	TM/L	TOTAL AB	HR	AVG	OBP	SLG	HOME AB	HR	AVG	OBP	SLG	AWAY AB	HR	AVG	OBP	SLG	LEFT AB	HR	AVG	OBP	SLG	RIGHT AB	HR	AVG	OBP	SLG	ON-BASE AB	HR	AVG	OBP	SLG	LATE/CLOSE AB	HR	AVG	OBP	SLG
1992	LA-N	69	1	.232	.284	.319	18	1	.278	.316	.444	51	0	.216	.273	.275	30	0	.267	.313	.333	39	1	.205	.262	.308	28	1	.179	.303	.286	14	0	.214	.313	.286
1993	LA-N	547	35	.318	.370	.561	281	21	.313	.370	.584	266	14	.323	.371	.538	142	13	.324	.377	.655	405	22	.316	.368	.528	235	12	.332	.387	.523	97	2	.237	.288	.361
1994	LA-N	405	24	.319	.370	.541	193	13	.275	.307	.508	212	11	.358	.424	.571	94	7	.351	.413	.638	311	17	.309	.356	.511	203	16	.350	.410	.635	77	5	.325	.366	.545
TOTALS		1021	60	.312	.364	.537	492	35	.297	.344	.549	529	25	.327	.383	.526	266	20	.327	.383	.613	755	40	.307	.358	.510	466	29	.330	.392	.558	188	7	.271	.322	.431

■ Luis Polonia BL/TL

YEAR	TM/L	TOTAL AB	HR	AVG	OBP	SLG	HOME AB	HR	AVG	OBP	SLG	AWAY AB	HR	AVG	OBP	SLG	LEFT AB	HR	AVG	OBP	SLG	RIGHT AB	HR	AVG	OBP	SLG	ON-BASE AB	HR	AVG	OBP	SLG	LATE/CLOSE AB	HR	AVG	OBP	SLG
1987	Oak-A	435	4	.287	.335	.398	217	1	.258	.312	.364	218	3	.317	.359	.431	89	0	.236	.292	.326	346	4	.301	.347	.416	171	2	.333	.354	.444	60	0	.300	.323	.367
1988	Oak-A	288	2	.292	.338	.378	152	1	.322	.387	.401	136	1	.257	.280	.353	18	0	.167	.158	.278	270	2	.300	.349	.385	103	1	.291	.336	.398	44	1	.341	.356	.455
1989	Oak-A	206	1	.286	.315	.369	90	0	.367	.400	.433	116	1	.224	.248	.319	26	0	.308	.333	.308	180	1	.283	.312	.378	79	1	.278	.310	.367	32	0	.375	.382	.500
1989	NY-A	227	2	.313	.359	.405	109	1	.376	.417	.477	118	1	.254	.305	.339	45	0	.311	.354	.356	182	2	.313	.360	.418	101	2	.307	.324	.416	39	1	.205	.244	.308
1990	NY-A	22	0	.318	.304	.318	12	0	.417	.417	.417	10	0	.200	.182	.200	26	0	.308	.333	.308	22	0	.318	.304	.318	9	0	.444	.400	.444	4	0	.250	.250	.250
1990	Cal-A	381	2	.336	.376	.417	195	2	.349	.376	.431	186	0	.323	.376	.403	51	0	.294	.345	.373	330	2	.342	.380	.424	128	1	.289	.329	.383	51	0	.255	.310	.275
1991	Cal-A	604	2	.296	.352	.379	303	1	.261	.329	.333	301	1	.332	.374	.425	168	0	.238	.283	.298	436	2	.319	.377	.411	236	0	.305	.343	.386	77	0	.299	.349	.325
1992	Cal-A	577	0	.286	.337	.329	266	0	.286	.340	.350	311	0	.286	.333	.312	132	0	.227	.240	.250	445	0	.303	.353	.353	182	0	.302	.351	.335	87	0	.287	.311	.333
1993	Cal-A	576	1	.271	.328	.326	288	0	.229	.282	.271	288	1	.313	.372	.382	112	0	.232	.248	.241	464	1	.280	.344	.357	191	0	.304	.367	.356	95	0	.253	.311	.316
1994	NY-A	350	1	.311	.383	.414	173	0	.295	.379	.393	177	1	.328	.387	.435	54	0	.185	.290	.222	296	1	.334	.400	.449	135	1	.385	.462	.504	45	0	.244	.370	.333
TOTALS		3666	15	.295	.346	.373	1805	6	.290	.345	.366	1861	9	.300	.347	.380	695	0	.240	.286	.286	2971	15	.308	.360	.393	1335	8	.313	.357	.396	534	2	.281	.326	.345

■ Jim Presley BR/TR

YEAR	TM/L	TOTAL AB	HR	AVG	OBP	SLG	HOME AB	HR	AVG	OBP	SLG	AWAY AB	HR	AVG	OBP	SLG	LEFT AB	HR	AVG	OBP	SLG	RIGHT AB	HR	AVG	OBP	SLG	ON-BASE AB	HR	AVG	OBP	SLG	LATE/CLOSE AB	HR	AVG	OBP	SLG
1984	Sea-A	251	10	.227	.247	.402	126	5	.214	.237	.381	125	5	.240	.258	.424	84	4	.167	.176	.333	167	6	.257	.282	.437	108	4	.222	.254	.407	38	3	.184	.225	.421
1985	Sea-A	570	28	.275	.324	.484	296	12	.264	.320	.449	274	16	.288	.328	.522	157	8	.344	.398	.573	413	20	.249	.295	.450	257	12	.261	.325	.463	83	5	.205	.283	.253
1986	Sea-A	616	27	.265	.303	.463	319	16	.307	.348	.549	297	11	.219	.254	.370	158	6	.323	.367	.506	458	21	.245	.281	.448	293	13	.276	.315	.474	89	7	.303	.347	.596
1987	Sea-A	575	24	.247	.296	.433	288	11	.257	.295	.455	287	13	.237	.297	.411	190	5	.268	.310	.426	385	19	.236	.289	.436	267	13	.251	.306	.468	76	5	.250	.313	.513
1988	Sea-A	544	14	.230	.280	.355	269	7	.245	.290	.394	275	7	.215	.271	.316	164	2	.232	.278	.323	380	12	.229	.281	.368	232	7	.224	.286	.353	96	2	.208	.267	.302
1989	Sea-A	390	12	.236	.275	.385	213	7	.258	.295	.423	177	5	.209	.253	.339	116	4	.328	.352	.491	274	8	.197	.243	.339	178	4	.258	.298	.388	65	4	.169	.206	.415
1990	Atl-N	541	19	.242	.282	.414	288	10	.260	.304	.427	253	9	.221	.257	.399	180	6	.267	.333	.450	361	13	.230	.255	.396	243	7	.342	.414	.527	58	0	.179	.211	.310
1991	SD-N	59	1	.136	.200	.186	39	0	.128	.209	.128	20	1	.150	.182	.300	23	1	.130	.167	.261	36	0	.139	.220	.139	24	1	.125	.241	.125	7	0	.143	.125	.143
TOTALS		3546	135	.247	.290	.420	1838	68	.260	.303	.441	1708	67	.232	.276	.397	1072	36	.277	.323	.444	2474	99	.234	.276	.409	1596	56	.251	.303	.421	538	24	.217	.269	.394

■ Kirby Puckett BR/TR

YEAR	TM/L	TOTAL AB	HR	AVG	OBP	SLG	HOME AB	HR	AVG	OBP	SLG	AWAY AB	HR	AVG	OBP	SLG	LEFT AB	HR	AVG	OBP	SLG	RIGHT AB	HR	AVG	OBP	SLG	ON-BASE AB	HR	AVG	OBP	SLG	LATE/CLOSE AB	HR	AVG	OBP	SLG
1984	Min-A	557	0	.296	.320	.336	276	0	.326	.347	.373	281	0	.267	.293	.299	179	0	.313	.335	.358	378	0	.289	.312	.325	183	0	.322	.344	.366	76	0	.263	.287	.289
1985	Min-A	691	4	.288	.330	.385	352	2	.324	.374	.429	339	2	.251	.283	.339	219	4	.356	.383	.525	472	0	.256	.306	.320	248	3	.323	.376	.460	89	1	.315	.367	.427
1986	Min-A	680	31	.328	.366	.537	346	14	.367	.405	.584	334	17	.287	.326	.488	166	6	.325	.364	.524	514	25	.329	.367	.541	234	13	.333	.366	.573	91	5	.308	.364	.484
1987	Min-A	624	28	.332	.367	.534	309	18	.301	.343	.533	315	10	.362	.390	.536	177	11	.339	.377	.627	447	17	.329	.363	.497	284	8	.317	.353	.479	77	6	.299	.344	.636
1988	Min-A	657	24	.356	.375	.545	323	13	.406	.436	.638	334	11	.308	.314	.455	166	8	.398	.425	.614	491	16	.342	.358	.521	308	8	.344	.364	.513	94	2	.309	.330	.468
1989	Min-A	635	9	.339	.379	.465	328	7	.390	.412	.552	307	2	.283	.344	.371	191	1	.304	.341	.403	444	8	.354	.395	.491	312	4	.343	.397	.468	91	3	.352	.398	.516
1990	Min-A	551	12	.298	.365	.446	278	6	.252	.308	.399	273	6	.344	.422	.414	164	4	.299	.382	.451	387	8	.297	.357	.444	243	7	.342	.414	.527	89	2	.225	.303	.360
1991	Min-A	611	15	.319	.352	.460	328	7	.326	.356	.463	283	8	.311	.348	.456	155	5	.406	.436	.658	456	8	.289	.324	.393	284	5	.299	.331	.398	74	3	.378	.439	.581
1992	Min-A	639	19	.329	.374	.490	325	9	.348	.392	.508	314	10	.309	.356	.471	125	3	.328	.381	.456	514	16	.329	.372	.498	328	10	.335	.391	.506	104	1	.317	.376	.423
1993	Min-A	622	22	.296	.349	.474	320	12	.322	.392	.522	302	10	.268	.302	.424	189	7	.295	.371	.518	433	15	.296	.340	.455	295	12	.305	.362	.542	81	5	.358	.398	.473
1994	Min-A	439	20	.317	.362	.540	232	12	.366	.419	.612	207	8	.261	.296	.459	103	3	.359	.389	.738	336	12	.304	.353	.479	228	13	.368	.417	.658	61	1	.344	.397	.492
TOTALS		6706	184	.318	.358	.474	3412	100	.347	.389	.521	3294	84	.288	.326	.424	1784	59	.338	.379	.525	4922	125	.311	.351	.455	2948	83	.328	.375	.493	941	25	.315	.363	.465

■ Terry Puhl BL/TR

YEAR	TM/L	TOTAL AB	HR	AVG	OBP	SLG	HOME AB	HR	AVG	OBP	SLG	AWAY AB	HR	AVG	OBP	SLG	LEFT AB	HR	AVG	OBP	SLG	RIGHT AB	HR	AVG	OBP	SLG	ON-BASE AB	HR	AVG	OBP	SLG	LATE/CLOSE AB	HR	AVG	OBP	SLG
1984	Hou-N	449	9	.301	.380	.434	221	2	.299	.387	.403	228	7	.303	.374	.465	139	1	.259	.321	.331	310	8	.319	.406	.481	186	2	.269	.352	.392	75	1	.307	.447	.400

YEAR	TM/L	TOTAL AB	HR	AVG	OBP	SLG	HOME AB	HR	AVG	OBP	SLG	AWAY AB	HR	AVG	OBP	SLG	LEFT AB	HR	AVG	OBP	SLG	RIGHT AB	HR	AVG	OBP	SLG	ON-BASE AB	HR	AVG	OBP	SLG	LATE/CLOSE AB	HR	AVG	OBP	SLG
1985	Hou-N	194	2	.284	.343	.418	123	1	.325	.375	.455	71	1	.211	.287	.352	68	0	.294	.342	.382	126	2	.278	.343	.437	77	0	.351	.404	.532	29	0	.379	.457	.448
1986	Hou-N	172	3	.244	.302	.355	70	1	.214	.257	.271	102	2	.265	.330	.412	23	0	.304	.333	.348	149	3	.235	.297	.356	66	2	.212	.308	.318	36	0	.222	.300	.250
1987	Hou-N	122	3	.230	.293	.320	71	1	.197	.250	.268	51	1	.275	.351	.392	9	0	.111	.200	.111	113	2	.239	.301	.336	58	0	.241	.313	.379	40	0	.275	.356	.350
1988	Hou-N	234	3	.303	.395	.389	106	2	.377	.464	.509	128	1	.242	.336	.289	19	0	.211	.250	.211	215	3	.312	.406	.405	89	0	.258	.368	.270	55	2	.345	.486	.491
1989	Hou-N	354	0	.271	.353	.364	190	0	.254	.330	.339	160	0	.291	.379	.394	57	0	.246	.338	.333	297	0	.276	.356	.370	139	0	.273	.356	.388	60	0	.283	.377	.317
1990	Hou-N	41	0	.293	.375	.317	19	0	.211	.375	.211	22	0	.364	.375	.409	3	0	.667	.667	.667	38	0	.263	.356	.289	17	0	.412	.450	.471	12	0	.417	.429	.500
1991	KC-A	18	0	.222	.333	.222	9	0	.111	.333	.111	9	0	.333	.333	.333	2	0	.000	.000	.000	16	0	.250	.368	.250	15	0	.267	.353	.267	11	0	.182	.308	.182
TOTALS		1584	19	.280	.356	.387	808	7	.282	.360	.379	776	12	.277	.353	.396	320	1	.262	.323	.331	1264	18	.284	.365	.401	647	6	.274	.356	.382	318	3	.302	.411	.377

■ Carlos Quintana BR/TR

YEAR	TM/L	AB	HR	AVG	OBP	SLG	AB	HR	AVG	OBP	SLG	AB	HR	AVG	OBP	SLG	AB	HR	AVG	OBP	SLG	AB	HR	AVG	OBP	SLG	AB	HR	AVG	OBP	SLG	AB	HR	AVG	OBP	SLG
1988	Bos-A	6	0	.333	.500	.333	1	0	.000	.500	.000	5	0	.400	.500	.400	4	0	.500	.500	.500	2	0	.000	.500	.000	2	0	1.000	1.000	1.000	1	0	.000	.000	.000
1989	Bos-A	77	0	.208	.274	.273	15	0	.133	.188	.200	62	0	.226	.294	.290	34	0	.235	.278	.324	43	0	.186	.271	.233	42	0	.143	.182	.214	16	0	.250	.333	.250
1990	Bos-A	512	7	.287	.354	.383	251	3	.299	.366	.378	261	4	.276	.340	.387	182	3	.352	.407	.467	330	4	.252	.325	.336	248	4	.298	.358	.407	82	1	.305	.353	.402
1991	Bos-A	478	11	.295	.375	.412	236	2	.292	.382	.360	242	9	.298	.368	.463	153	5	.340	.436	.484	325	6	.274	.345	.378	231	6	.281	.357	.420	66	1	.394	.459	.470
1993	Bos-A	303	1	.244	.317	.271	148	0	.264	.329	.291	155	1	.226	.305	.252	104	0	.250	.342	.260	199	1	.241	.303	.276	145	0	.207	.291	.228	46	0	.283	.340	.283
TOTALS		1376	19	.276	.350	.362	651	5	.284	.361	.347	725	14	.269	.339	.375	477	8	.319	.394	.417	899	11	.254	.326	.333	668	10	.265	.335	.362	211	2	.322	.374	.384

■ Tim Raines BB/TR

YEAR	TM/L	AB	HR	AVG	OBP	SLG	AB	HR	AVG	OBP	SLG	AB	HR	AVG	OBP	SLG	AB	HR	AVG	OBP	SLG	AB	HR	AVG	OBP	SLG	AB	HR	AVG	OBP	SLG	AB	HR	AVG	OBP	SLG
1984	Mon-N	622	8	.309	.393	.437	303	2	.281	.365	.376	319	6	.335	.420	.495	193	3	.306	.363	.446	429	5	.310	.406	.434	236	6	.301	.405	.424	103	1	.311	.403	.437
1985	Mon-N	575	11	.320	.405	.475	280	4	.346	.446	.529	295	7	.295	.364	.424	178	6	.275	.351	.438	397	5	.340	.428	.491	162	2	.290	.398	.401	104	1	.356	.429	.452
1986	Mon-N	580	9	.334	.413	.476	282	4	.326	.409	.450	298	5	.342	.417	.500	181	4	.315	.382	.453	399	5	.343	.427	.486	209	3	.335	.413	.450	115	2	.339	.441	.452
1987	Mon-N	530	18	.330	.429	.526	276	9	.337	.437	.525	254	9	.323	.420	.528	164	5	.396	.471	.616	366	13	.301	.411	.486	195	7	.323	.458	.503	67	4	.358	.494	.657
1988	Mon-N	429	12	.270	.350	.431	202	5	.282	.350	.436	227	7	.260	.351	.427	125	4	.264	.321	.408	304	8	.273	.362	.441	139	6	.317	.421	.532	81	2	.346	.448	.481
1989	Mon-N	517	9	.286	.395	.418	258	6	.271	.375	.419	259	3	.301	.415	.417	133	3	.286	.389	.406	384	6	.286	.397	.422	186	2	.306	.468	.425	97	1	.340	.448	.433
1990	Mon-N	457	9	.287	.379	.392	202	6	.307	.391	.446	255	3	.271	.370	.349	180	3	.289	.357	.361	277	6	.285	.393	.412	198	4	.323	.418	.429	91	2	.319	.400	.396
1991	Chi-A	609	5	.268	.359	.345	284	1	.254	.348	.303	325	4	.280	.368	.382	208	2	.279	.343	.346	401	3	.262	.366	.344	183	2	.240	.377	.344	120	2	.217	.331	.317
1992	Chi-A	551	7	.294	.380	.405	263	4	.319	.405	.445	288	3	.271	.356	.368	135	0	.252	.369	.304	416	7	.308	.383	.433	197	1	.330	.421	.442	87	3	.287	.417	.448
1993	Chi-A	415	16	.306	.401	.480	196	7	.291	.378	.434	219	9	.320	.421	.521	112	3	.348	.439	.473	303	13	.290	.386	.482	142	5	.324	.443	.486	61	1	.361	.480	.459
1994	Chi-A	384	10	.266	.365	.409	168	5	.262	.367	.405	216	5	.269	.364	.412	96	1	.208	.303	.260	288	9	.285	.385	.458	166	5	.313	.397	.482	60	2	.317	.394	.467
TOTALS		5669	114	.299	.389	.436	2714	53	.300	.390	.433	2955	61	.298	.388	.438	1705	34	.296	.373	.415	3964	80	.300	.396	.444	2013	43	.309	.421	.444	986	21	.318	.422	.444

■ Rafael Ramirez BR/TR

YEAR	TM/L	AB	HR	AVG	OBP	SLG	AB	HR	AVG	OBP	SLG	AB	HR	AVG	OBP	SLG	AB	HR	AVG	OBP	SLG	AB	HR	AVG	OBP	SLG	AB	HR	AVG	OBP	SLG	AB	HR	AVG	OBP	SLG
1984	Atl-N	591	2	.266	.295	.327	267	1	.255	.295	.311	324	1	.275	.295	.340	167	1	.263	.287	.329	424	1	.267	.298	.325	220	0	.277	.321	.332	101	0	.267	.306	.287
1985	Atl-N	568	5	.248	.272	.333	272	4	.294	.321	.401	296	1	.206	.225	.270	192	0	.240	.271	.323	376	5	.253	.272	.338	226	2	.279	.294	.403	93	1	.312	.343	.419
1986	Atl-N	496	8	.240	.273	.335	238	1	.235	.287	.311	258	7	.244	.260	.357	179	2	.207	.247	.263	317	6	.259	.288	.375	198	2	.177	.213	.242	88	2	.284	.306	.375
1987	Atl-N	179	1	.263	.300	.346	83	0	.253	.300	.325	96	1	.271	.300	.365	65	0	.323	.353	.400	114	1	.228	.270	.316	83	0	.253	.284	.325	35	0	.229	.300	.286
1988	Hou-N	566	6	.276	.298	.378	274	2	.255	.274	.336	292	4	.295	.321	.418	193	2	.306	.322	.440	373	4	.260	.287	.346	234	2	.295	.321	.406	118	1	.212	.244	.280
1989	Hou-N	537	6	.246	.283	.324	268	3	.246	.291	.328	269	3	.245	.275	.320	156	2	.269	.311	.353	381	4	.236	.271	.312	223	4	.260	.306	.372	98	1	.255	.339	.316
1990	Hou-N	445	2	.261	.299	.330	206	1	.267	.320	.350	239	1	.255	.281	.314	192	1	.260	.306	.333	253	1	.261	.294	.328	182	1	.319	.365	.418	78	0	.269	.326	.321
1991	Hou-N	233	1	.236	.274	.292	91	0	.242	.300	.308	142	1	.232	.257	.282	110	1	.245	.294	.309	123	0	.228	.256	.276	100	0	.230	.275	.280	72	0	.250	.276	.306
1992	Hou-N	176	1	.250	.283	.301	89	0	.225	.266	.258	87	1	.276	.300	.345	82	1	.329	.353	.427	94	0	.181	.222	.191	81	1	.247	.282	.309	49	1	.204	.235	.306
TOTALS		3791	32	.255	.286	.334	1788	12	.256	.296	.333	2003	20	.254	.278	.334	1336	10	.264	.300	.347	2455	22	.250	.280	.327	1547	13	.264	.300	.353	732	6	.253	.297	.324

■ Willie Randolph BR/TR

YEAR	TM/L	AB	HR	AVG	OBP	SLG	AB	HR	AVG	OBP	SLG	AB	HR	AVG	OBP	SLG	AB	HR	AVG	OBP	SLG	AB	HR	AVG	OBP	SLG	AB	HR	AVG	OBP	SLG	AB	HR	AVG	OBP	SLG
1984	NY-A	564	2	.287	.377	.348	278	1	.273	.371	.324	286	1	.301	.384	.371	189	1	.333	.423	.429	375	1	.264	.354	.307	179	1	.274	.354	.335	106	1	.283	.377	.377
1985	NY-A	497	5	.276	.382	.356	221	3	.262	.387	.367	276	2	.286	.377	.348	181	2	.315	.418	.414	316	3	.253	.361	.323	211	2	.246	.337	.303	89	0	.281	.354	.292
1986	NY-A	492	5	.276	.393	.346	241	2	.311	.451	.359	251	3	.243	.332	.303	183	4	.311	.392	.426	309	1	.256	.393	.298	199	0	.276	.396	.307	67	0	.299	.395	.343
1987	NY-A	449	7	.305	.411	.414	253	3	.292	.395	.399	196	4	.321	.430	.434	133	3	.331	.467	.459	316	4	.294	.385	.396	187	5	.326	.430	.492	63	0	.397	.519	.460
1988	NY-A	404	2	.230	.322	.300	206	1	.218	.318	.267	198	1	.242	.326	.333	125	1	.208	.318	.288	279	1	.240	.324	.305	163	2	.270	.398	.356	60	0	.150	.250	.167
1989	LA-N	549	2	.282	.366	.326	266	0	.305	.393	.338	283	2	.261	.340	.314	191	1	.298	.385	.356	358	1	.274	.355	.310	186	1	.301	.392	.360	101	1	.248	.350	.317
1990	LA-N	96	1	.271	.364	.344	37	0	.270	.341	.351	59	1	.271	.377	.339	34	0	.353	.450	.441	62	1	.226	.314	.290	30	0	.333	.429	.367	8	1	.375	.500	.750
1990	Oak-A	292	1	.257	.331	.318	127	1	.244	.322	.299	165	0	.267	.339	.333	82	0	.354	.376	.439	210	1	.219	.315	.271	147	0	.272	.325	.347	42	0	.286	.326	.333
1991	Mil-A	431	0	.327	.424	.374	220	0	.336	.410	.400	211	0	.318	.438	.346	148	0	.358	.457	.405	283	0	.311	.407	.357	207	0	.377	.480	.425	79	0	.291	.371	.367
1992	NY-N	286	2	.252	.352	.318	153	2	.255	.349	.359	133	0	.248	.355	.271	105	2	.276	.397	.371	181	0	.238	.324	.287	99	0	.232	.372	.273	43	1	.302	.444	.419
TOTALS		4060	27	.279	.376	.347	2002	13	.281	.383	.352	2058	14	.277	.370	.341	1371	14	.311	.408	.400	2689	13	.263	.360	.319	1608	11	.291	.392	.360	658	4	.281	.378	.345

■ Johnny Ray BB/TR

YEAR	TM/L	AB	HR	AVG	OBP	SLG	AB	HR	AVG	OBP	SLG	AB	HR	AVG	OBP	SLG	AB	HR	AVG	OBP	SLG	AB	HR	AVG	OBP	SLG	AB	HR	AVG	OBP	SLG	AB	HR	AVG	OBP	SLG
1984	Pit-N	555	6	.312	.354	.434	274	3	.252	.301	.347	281	3	.370	.407	.520	101	0	.317	.357	.406	454	6	.311	.354	.441	240	2	.321	.379	.433	115	2	.252	.310	.409
1985	Pit-N	594	7	.274	.325	.375	278	3	.291	.353	.406	316	4	.259	.299	.348	170	1	.253	.291	.335	424	6	.283	.338	.392	233	3	.266	.324	.386	111	1	.261	.333	.333
1986	Pit-N	579	7	.301	.363	.394	298	2	.285	.356	.366	281	5	.317	.371	.423	222	1	.261	.318	.311	357	6	.325	.390	.445	259	2	.301	.354	.390	110	2	.264	.341	.364
1987	Pit-N	472	5	.273	.358	.358	228	5	.303	.361	.412	244	0	.246	.297	.307	191	2	.257	.322	.319	281	3	.285	.382	.384	222	3	.266	.331	.369	77	2	.312	.357	.494
1987	Cal-A	127	0	.346	.359	.433	47	0	.298	.313	.362	80	0	.375	.386	.475	47	0	.298	.298	.362	80	0	.375	.393	.475	62	0	.387	.391	.484	24	0	.250	.280	.375
1988	Cal-A	602	6	.306	.345	.429	287	4	.296	.348	.418	315	2	.314	.341	.438	210	2	.281	.327	.395	392	4	.319	.354	.469	260	2	.342	.374	.469	99	1	.263	.286	.333
1989	Cal-A	530	5	.289	.357	.358	268	3	.265	.296	.340	262	2	.313	.357	.378	195	1	.262	.299	.318	335	4	.304	.343	.382	219	3	.311	.337	.411	75	0	.200	.250	.227
1990	Cal-A	404	5	.277	.308	.371	210	5	.271	.302	.386	194	0	.284	.314	.356	120	0	.300	.317	.342	284	5	.268	.304	.384	182	1	.264	.286	.335	76	2	.250	.296	.382
TOTALS		3863	41	.293	.338	.392	1890	25	.281	.332	.381	1973	16	.305	.344	.402	1256	7	.272	.316	.343	2607	34	.303	.348	.415	1677	16	.301	.345	.405	687	9	.258	.312	.364

■ Randy Ready BR/TR

YEAR	TM/L	AB	HR	AVG	OBP	SLG	AB	HR	AVG	OBP	SLG	AB	HR	AVG	OBP	SLG	AB	HR	AVG	OBP	SLG	AB	HR	AVG	OBP	SLG	AB	HR	AVG	OBP	SLG	AB	HR	AVG	OBP	SLG
1984	Mil-A	123	3	.187	.270	.325	50	3	.140	.232	.360	73	0	.219	.296	.301	61	2	.197	.300	.361	62	1	.177	.239	.290	39	1	.205	.295	.385	28	0	.143	.200	.179
1985	Mil-A	181	1	.265	.318	.387	83	0	.265	.319	.386	98	1	.265	.318	.388	84	1	.250	.289	.369	97	0	.278	.343	.402	79	1	.291	.333	.443	36	1	.194	.256	.306
1986	Mil-A	79	1	.190	.273	.278	37	0	.189	.286	.243	42	1	.190	.261	.310	32	0	.219	.306	.313	47	1	.170	.250	.255	36	0	.139	.162	.167	18	1	.167	.211	.389
1986	SD-N	3	0	.000	.000	.000	3	0	.000	.000	.000	0	0	—	—	—	3	0	.000	.000	.000	0	0	—	—	—	1	0	.000	.000	.000	0	0	—	—	—
1987	SD-N	350	12	.309	.423	.520	171	7	.339	.443	.579	179	5	.279	.404	.464	175	6	.331	.473	.566	175	6	.286	.367	.474	157	4	.344	.441	.522	56	1	.214	.389	.304
1988	SD-N	331	7	.266	.346	.390	147	3	.265	.353	.374	184	4	.266	.340	.402	147	5	.286	.361	.416	184	2	.250	.333	.370	143	3	.273	.367	.413	81	1	.210	.304	.259
1989	SD-N	67	0	.254	.354	.313	19	0	.263	.375	.316	48	0	.250	.345	.313	41	0	.317	.417	.415	26	0	.154	.258	.154	27	0	.185	.281	.185	6	0	.167	.444	.167
1989	Phi-N	187	8	.267	.372	.465	95	3	.263	.388	.442	92	5	.272	.355	.489	109	5	.269	.389	.468	78	3	.269	.389	.462	80	2	.225	.369	.338	29	1	.276	.400	.448
1990	Phi-N	217	1	.244	.332	.309	117	0	.265	.388	.299	100	1	.220	.325	.320	128	1	.250	.336	.352	89	0	.236	.327	.247	102	1	.324	.395	.392	54	1	.407	.484	.537
1991	Phi-N	205	1	.249	.385	.322	108	1	.250	.414	.333	97	0	.247	.350	.299	147	1	.265	.418	.367	58	0	.207	.294	.207	87	0	.253	.405	.322	44	0	.182	.383	.182
1992	Oak-A	125	3	.200	.329	.288	73	1	.151	.304	.205	52	2	.269	.367	.404	59	3	.271	.366	.424	66	0	.136	.296	.167	56	1	.196	.319	.339	21	1	.381	.500	.571
1993	Mon-N	134	1	.209	.329	.351	67	0	.209	.329	.313	67	1	.209	.328	.388	43	0	.186	.255	.209	91	1	.286	.414	.418	61	0	.230	.382	.311	14	0	.286	.474	.286
1994	Tex-A	42	1	.381	.480	.476	29	0	.414	.485	.448	13	1	.308	.471	.538	30	1	.433	.514	.567	12	0	.250	.400	.250	16	1	.438	.571	.500	7	0	.000	.300	.000
TOTALS		2044	39	.258	.358	.385	999	18	.258	.365	.382	1045	21	.258	.352	.388	1059	25	.274	.378	.422	985	14	.242	.337	.345	884	14	.270	.374	.388	394	7	.239	.364	.325

■ Gary Redus BR/TR

YEAR	TM/L	AB	HR	AVG	OBP	SLG	AB	HR	AVG	OBP	SLG	AB	HR	AVG	OBP	SLG	AB	HR	AVG	OBP	SLG	AB	HR	AVG	OBP	SLG	AB	HR	AVG	OBP	SLG	AB	HR	AVG	OBP	SLG
1984	Cin-N	394	7	.254	.338	.376	206	4	.262	.361	.388	188	3	.245	.313	.362	169	2	.272	.380	.385	225	5	.240	.306	.369	117	2	.274	.362	.385	72	2	.208	.324	.292
1985	Cin-N	246	6	.252	.366	.415	135	4	.289	.404	.481	111	2	.207	.321	.333	128	2	.242	.366	.367	118	4	.263	.367	.466	87	3	.230	.333	.414	48	0	.229	.373	.333
1986	Phi-N	340	11	.247	.343	.432	170	8	.288	.374	.553	170	3	.206	.311	.312	109	2	.248	.397	.385	231	9	.247	.314	.455	105	3	.238	.341	.400	55	1	.182	.286	.309
1987	Chi-A	475	12	.236	.338	.392	238	4	.244	.331	.374	237	8	.228	.346	.410	201	7	.269	.372	.473	274	5	.212	.295	.332	171	3	.228	.322	.327	70	2	.300	.383	.429
1988	Chi-A	262	6	.263	.342	.401	154	4	.286	.372	.409	108	2	.231	.298	.389	105	3	.248	.333	.390	157	3	.274	.348	.408	92	2	.228	.284	.391	43	1	.233	.365	.349
1988	Pit-N	71	2	.197	.341	.310	33	2	.152	.293	.364	38	0	.237	.383	.263	44	1	.250	.382	.364	27	1	.111	.273	.222	25	0	.080	.294	.080	21	1	.238	.333	.381
1989	Pit-N	279	6	.283	.372	.462	137	3	.277	.373	.445	142	3	.289	.370	.479	113	3	.292	.391	.558	166	3	.277	.358	.398	107	3	.271	.372	.574	63	1	.311	.377	.574
1990	Pit-N	227	6	.247	.341	.419	108	2	.204	.333	.343	119	4	.286	.348	.487	202	6	.262	.345	.455	25	0	.120	.313	.120	76	2	.197	.283	.382	36	0	.278	.333	.389
1991	Pit-N	252	7	.246	.324	.393	125	3	.280	.353	.448	127	4	.213	.297	.339	173	5	.249	.302	.399	79	2	.241	.368	.380	77	1	.208	.309	.273	51	1	.275	.373	.353
1992	Pit-N	176	3	.256	.321	.381	88	1	.284	.344	.409	88	2	.227	.299	.352	151	2	.258	.329	.371	25	1	.240	.269	.440	39	1	.256	.341	.333	24	1	.400	.483	.640
1993	Tex-A	222	6	.288	.361	.459	109	2	.275	.339	.385	113	4	.301	.362	.531	86	2	.302	.358	.500	136	4	.279	.346	.434	99	3	.303	.368	.475	43	1	.279	.311	.372
1994	Tex-A	33	0	.273	.351	.303	17	0	.353	.389	.412	16	0	.188	.316	.188	16	0	.375	.474	.375	17	0	.176	.222	.235	23	0	.217	.280	.261	13	0	.231	.375	.308
TOTALS		2977	72	.254	.342	.407	1520	34	.266	.357	.422	1457	38	.241	.326	.391	1497	35	.264	.358	.424	1480	37	.244	.326	.390	1018	24	.240	.331	.375	538	13	.260	.350	.390

■ Jody Reed BR/TR

YEAR	TM/L	AB	HR	AVG	OBP	SLG	AB	HR	AVG	OBP	SLG	AB	HR	AVG	OBP	SLG	AB	HR	AVG	OBP	SLG	AB	HR	AVG	OBP	SLG	AB	HR	AVG	OBP	SLG	AB	HR	AVG	OBP	SLG
1987	Bos-A	30	0	.300	.382	.400	4	0	.000	.000	.000	26	0	.346	.433	.462	10	0	.500	.615	.600	20	0	.200	.238	.300	14	0	.429	.467	.643	4	0	.250	.250	.250
1988	Bos-A	338	1	.293	.380	.376	188	0	.309	.399	.399	150	1	.273	.357	.347	84	0	.226	.301	.262	254	1	.315	.405	.413	138	0	.290	.383	.370	52	0	.346	.393	.404
1989	Bos-A	524	3	.288	.370	.393	270	2	.300	.384	.415	254	1	.276	.355	.370	140	1	.321	.401	.450	384	2	.276	.357	.372	236	1	.305	.401	.415	99	0	.283	.409	.315
1990	Bos-A	598	5	.289	.371	.390	311	3	.293	.365	.405	287	2	.286	.377	.373	184	0	.299	.376	.386	414	5	.285	.368	.391	247	2	.304	.390	.393	91	1	.297	.429	.396
1991	Bos-A	618	5	.283	.349	.382	312	3	.263	.336	.385	306	2	.304	.362	.379	165	0	.267	.328	.321	453	5	.289	.356	.404	267	3	.318	.395	.446	78	0	.256	.356	.282

YEAR	TM/L	TOTAL AB	HR	AVG	OBP	SLG	HOME AB	HR	AVG	OBP	SLG	AWAY AB	HR	AVG	OBP	SLG	LEFT AB	HR	AVG	OBP	SLG	RIGHT AB	HR	AVG	OBP	SLG	ON-BASE AB	HR	AVG	OBP	SLG	LATE/CLOSE AB	HR	AVG	OBP	SLG
1992	Bos-A	550	3	.247	.321	.316	279	2	.276	.364	.358	271	1	.218	.276	.273	154	1	.260	.345	.370	396	2	.242	.312	.295	204	0	.250	.359	.304	107	0	.196	.267	.243
1993	LA-N	445	2	.276	.333	.346	233	0	.292	.357	.348	212	2	.259	.306	.344	123	0	.325	.381	.390	322	2	.258	.314	.329	191	1	.325	.400	.408	83	0	.253	.300	.313
1994	Mil-A	399	2	.271	.362	.341	199	0	.246	.333	.296	200	1	.295	.391	.385	78	0	.218	.390	.269	321	2	.283	.355	.358	153	1	.255	.371	.320	59	1	.288	.354	.390
TOTALS		3502	21	.278	.355	.365	1796	12	.282	.361	.375	1706	9	.274	.350	.355	938	2	.283	.365	.364	2564	19	.277	.352	.365	1450	8	.297	.388	.388	547	2	.263	.345	.325

■ Kevin Reimer BL/TR

YEAR	TM/L	AB	HR	AVG	OBP	SLG	AB	HR	AVG	OBP	SLG	AB	HR	AVG	OBP	SLG	AB	HR	AVG	OBP	SLG	AB	HR	AVG	OBP	SLG	AB	HR	AVG	OBP	SLG	AB	HR	AVG	OBP	SLG
1988	Tex-A	25	1	.120	.115	.240	3	0	.000	.000	.000	22	1	.136	.130	.273	3	0	.333	.333	.333	22	1	.091	.087	.227	15	0	.067	.063	.067	6	0	.000	.000	.000
1989	Tex-A	5	0	.000	.000	.000	5	0	.000	.000	.000	0	0	—	—	—	3	0	.333	.333	.333	5	0	.000	.000	.000	4	0	.000	.000	.000	1	0	.000	.000	.000
1990	Tex-A	100	2	.260	.333	.430	46	0	.283	.353	.435	54	2	.241	.317	.426	5	0	.000	.000	.000	95	2	.274	.349	.453	58	1	.276	.333	.483	34	1	.324	.395	.559
1991	Tex-A	394	20	.269	.332	.477	184	13	.272	.335	.565	210	7	.267	.329	.400	36	1	.222	.275	.333	358	19	.274	.338	.492	191	12	.309	.378	.555	56	2	.357	.438	.500
1992	Tex-A	494	16	.267	.336	.437	239	10	.285	.356	.481	255	6	.251	.318	.396	89	2	.247	.356	.360	405	14	.272	.332	.454	212	6	.250	.355	.387	83	3	.289	.368	.506
1993	Mil-A	437	13	.249	.303	.394	217	8	.240	.310	.406	220	5	.259	.295	.382	106	1	.208	.277	.283	331	12	.263	.311	.429	208	5	.245	.297	.389	71	1	.225	.296	.310
TOTALS		1455	52	.258	.320	.430	694	31	.264	.332	.471	761	21	.254	.309	.392	239	4	.222	.303	.314	1216	48	.266	.324	.452	688	24	.262	.335	.433	251	7	.283	.357	.442

■ Craig Reynolds BL/TR

YEAR	TM/L	AB	HR	AVG	OBP	SLG	AB	HR	AVG	OBP	SLG	AB	HR	AVG	OBP	SLG	AB	HR	AVG	OBP	SLG	AB	HR	AVG	OBP	SLG	AB	HR	AVG	OBP	SLG	AB	HR	AVG	OBP	SLG
1984	Hou-N	527	6	.260	.286	.364	251	0	.263	.291	.355	276	6	.257	.282	.373	157	2	.223	.252	.293	370	4	.276	.301	.395	230	3	.291	.313	.426	87	1	.264	.275	.322
1985	Hou-N	379	4	.272	.293	.393	191	1	.230	.264	.319	188	3	.314	.323	.468	54	0	.315	.339	.407	325	4	.265	.285	.391	159	1	.270	.293	.377	66	0	.212	.268	.273
1986	Hou-N	313	6	.249	.274	.348	144	4	.319	.340	.438	169	2	.189	.219	.272	35	0	.143	.143	.171	278	6	.263	.290	.371	138	2	.326	.356	.442	58	2	.259	.295	.414
1987	Hou-N	374	4	.254	.303	.348	189	0	.259	.316	.323	185	4	.249	.291	.373	43	0	.140	.196	.140	331	4	.269	.317	.375	163	2	.209	.267	.288	67	1	.239	.292	.299
1988	Hou-N	161	1	.255	.290	.317	78	0	.231	.268	.256	83	1	.277	.310	.373	12	0	.333	.333	.333	149	1	.248	.287	.315	60	1	.250	.308	.350	39	0	.308	.386	.436
1989	Hou-N	189	2	.201	.274	.254	102	0	.196	.281	.206	87	2	.207	.266	.310	8	0	.125	.300	.125	181	2	.204	.273	.260	83	1	.217	.309	.277	43	1	.186	.300	.302
TOTALS		1943	23	.253	.288	.349	955	5	.254	.295	.330	988	18	.252	.281	.368	309	2	.220	.252	.275	1634	21	.259	.295	.364	833	10	.267	.306	.372	360	5	.244	.294	.333

■ Harold Reynolds BB/TR

YEAR	TM/L	AB	HR	AVG	OBP	SLG	AB	HR	AVG	OBP	SLG	AB	HR	AVG	OBP	SLG	AB	HR	AVG	OBP	SLG	AB	HR	AVG	OBP	SLG	AB	HR	AVG	OBP	SLG	AB	HR	AVG	OBP	SLG
1984	Sea-A	10	0	.300	.364	.300	6	0	.500	.571	.500	4	0	.000	.000	.000	8	0	.375	.444	.375	2	0	.000	.000	.000	2	0	.000	.000	.000	0	0	—	—	—
1985	Sea-A	104	0	.144	.264	.192	59	0	.136	.261	.203	45	0	.156	.269	.178	31	0	.129	.289	.161	73	0	.151	.253	.205	44	0	.205	.271	.273	9	0	.125	.300	.250
1986	Sea-A	445	1	.222	.275	.290	220	1	.227	.283	.332	225	0	.218	.267	.249	117	1	.205	.250	.274	328	0	.229	.283	.296	172	0	.203	.251	.250	61	0	.164	.261	.213
1987	Sea-A	530	1	.275	.325	.370	257	1	.233	.296	.319	273	0	.315	.353	.418	162	1	.278	.320	.370	368	0	.274	.327	.370	212	0	.259	.296	.330	75	0	.267	.317	.347
1988	Sea-A	598	4	.283	.340	.383	290	4	.286	.344	.417	308	0	.279	.336	.360	185	2	.314	.344	.411	413	2	.269	.338	.370	214	3	.313	.355	.421	86	1	.291	.337	.395
1989	Sea-A	613	0	.300	.359	.369	307	0	.300	.351	.375	306	0	.301	.367	.363	170	0	.324	.378	.388	443	0	.291	.352	.361	203	0	.320	.382	.360	77	0	.351	.440	.364
1990	Sea-A	642	5	.252	.336	.347	297	0	.253	.350	.310	345	5	.252	.324	.380	207	1	.285	.335	.391	435	4	.237	.337	.326	230	3	.274	.332	.391	105	1	.295	.367	.410
1991	Sea-A	631	3	.254	.332	.341	314	1	.299	.387	.404	317	2	.208	.276	.278	174	1	.264	.326	.322	457	2	.249	.334	.348	260	2	.292	.349	.385	97	1	.309	.352	.412
1992	Sea-A	458	3	.247	.316	.330	237	2	.262	.326	.376	221	1	.231	.305	.281	116	0	.250	.348	.302	342	3	.246	.304	.339	184	1	.261	.320	.359	84	1	.167	.228	.214
1993	Bal-A	485	4	.252	.343	.334	261	0	.249	.331	.345	224	4	.254	.356	.321	134	0	.179	.213	.209	351	4	.279	.387	.382	221	1	.262	.354	.348	76	1	.355	.425	.447
1994	Cal-A	207	0	.232	.310	.270	117	0	.205	.277	.291	90	0	.267	.353	.289	17	0	.235	.381	.235	190	0	.232	.303	.295	82	0	.207	.283	.256	39	0	.231	.302	.256
TOTALS		4723	21	.259	.328	.342	2365	11	.260	.333	.340	2358	10	.257	.324	.330	1321	6	.266	.321	.338	3402	15	.256	.331	.343	1824	10	.267	.339	.352	708	5	.274	.341	.350

■ R. J. Reynolds BB/TR

YEAR	TM/L	AB	HR	AVG	OBP	SLG	AB	HR	AVG	OBP	SLG	AB	HR	AVG	OBP	SLG	AB	HR	AVG	OBP	SLG	AB	HR	AVG	OBP	SLG	AB	HR	AVG	OBP	SLG	AB	HR	AVG	OBP	SLG
1984	LA-N	240	2	.258	.300	.350	120	2	.233	.264	.317	120	0	.283	.333	.383	73	1	.301	.320	.397	167	1	.240	.291	.329	91	1	.253	.293	.330	50	0	.280	.308	.360
1985	LA-N	207	0	.266	.308	.353	92	0	.293	.353	.391	115	0	.243	.270	.322	72	0	.264	.284	.375	135	0	.267	.320	.341	88	0	.295	.362	.386	40	0	.225	.262	.400
1985	Pit-N	130	3	.308	.357	.462	58	1	.310	.385	.483	72	2	.306	.333	.444	39	0	.256	.293	.359	91	3	.330	.384	.505	55	1	.327	.383	.436	28	1	.393	.414	.607
1986	Pit-N	402	9	.269	.335	.420	198	6	.283	.357	.485	204	3	.255	.312	.358	105	0	.219	.278	.286	297	9	.286	.355	.468	166	4	.259	.313	.422	88	0	.182	.250	.250
1987	Pit-N	335	7	.260	.323	.400	172	2	.267	.318	.401	163	5	.252	.328	.399	57	0	.351	.391	.386	278	7	.241	.309	.403	162	4	.265	.335	.420	57	1	.263	.348	.351
1988	Pit-N	323	6	.248	.288	.359	174	4	.213	.274	.333	149	2	.289	.306	.389	88	3	.318	.362	.489	235	3	.221	.261	.311	154	2	.266	.304	.377	90	1	.300	.347	.400
1989	Pit-N	363	6	.270	.331	.375	204	3	.299	.354	.426	159	3	.233	.301	.308	116	1	.284	.341	.336	247	5	.263	.326	.393	179	5	.268	.341	.391	86	0	.291	.365	.337
1990	Pit-N	215	0	.288	.354	.344	96	0	.292	.369	.385	119	0	.286	.341	.311	112	0	.295	.373	.330	103	0	.282	.333	.359	99	0	.273	.351	.323	50	0	.320	.390	.380
TOTALS		2215	33	.267	.323	.382	1114	18	.270	.330	.403	1101	16	.264	.315	.361	662	5	.284	.333	.364	1553	28	.260	.318	.390	994	17	.271	.328	.388	489	3	.272	.331	.362

■ Jim Rice BR/TR

YEAR	TM/L	AB	HR	AVG	OBP	SLG	AB	HR	AVG	OBP	SLG	AB	HR	AVG	OBP	SLG	AB	HR	AVG	OBP	SLG	AB	HR	AVG	OBP	SLG	AB	HR	AVG	OBP	SLG	AB	HR	AVG	OBP	SLG
1984	Bos-A	657	28	.280	.323	.467	330	17	.288	.334	.506	327	11	.272	.313	.428	153	8	.327	.394	.529	504	20	.266	.301	.448	359	19	.306	.349	.535	99	5	.182	.243	.374
1985	Bos-A	546	27	.291	.349	.487	274	11	.350	.391	.540	272	16	.232	.309	.434	151	7	.258	.363	.470	395	20	.294	.343	.494	191	10	.294	.351	.448	86	5	.259	.308	.506
1986	Bos-A	618	20	.324	.384	.490	312	10	.337	.387	.526	306	10	.310	.381	.454	168	7	.351	.413	.560	450	13	.313	.373	.464	307	11	.339	.403	.511	83	2	.337	.427	.506
1987	Bos-A	404	13	.277	.357	.408	190	7	.305	.391	.447	214	6	.252	.326	.374	123	4	.285	.371	.398	281	9	.274	.351	.413	215	4	.274	.356	.367	68	1	.265	.342	.324
1988	Bos-A	485	15	.264	.330	.406	225	9	.276	.362	.453	260	6	.254	.301	.365	155	6	.290	.349	.477	330	9	.252	.322	.373	231	9	.273	.343	.442	90	1	.225	.287	.287
1989	Bos-A	209	3	.234	.276	.344	110	1	.245	.283	.327	99	2	.222	.269	.364	63	1	.254	.294	.397	146	2	.226	.269	.322	106	2	.226	.256	.321	30	0	.200	.265	.200
TOTALS		2919	106	.285	.344	.449	1441	55	.307	.364	.487	1478	51	.263	.324	.411	813	33	.300	.373	.485	2106	73	.279	.332	.435	1517	55	.295	.355	.460	441	15	.247	.316	.388

■ Ernest Riles BL/TR

YEAR	TM/L	AB	HR	AVG	OBP	SLG	AB	HR	AVG	OBP	SLG	AB	HR	AVG	OBP	SLG	AB	HR	AVG	OBP	SLG	AB	HR	AVG	OBP	SLG	AB	HR	AVG	OBP	SLG	AB	HR	AVG	OBP	SLG
1985	Mil-A	448	5	.286	.339	.377	226	2	.332	.381	.425	222	3	.239	.298	.329	141	0	.241	.310	.290	307	5	.306	.353	.414	203	2	.296	.354	.374	72	0	.236	.313	.264
1986	Mil-A	524	9	.252	.321	.357	246	2	.260	.337	.337	278	7	.245	.307	.374	116	3	.207	.270	.319	408	6	.265	.336	.368	217	8	.253	.327	.396	89	2	.270	.333	.360
1987	Mil-A	276	4	.261	.329	.351	133	1	.286	.365	.376	143	3	.238	.293	.329	57	0	.175	.250	.192	219	4	.283	.349	.384	134	1	.269	.316	.306	52	0	.308	.321	.404
1988	Mil-A	127	1	.252	.291	.339	75	1	.307	.333	.440	52	0	.173	.232	.192	15	0	.200	.250	.200	112	1	.259	.297	.357	48	0	.292	.346	.375	19	0	.368	.368	.474
1988	SF-N	187	3	.294	.323	.401	84	3	.321	.367	.476	103	0	.272	.288	.340	23	1	.304	.333	.435	164	2	.293	.322	.396	83	2	.325	.355	.458	28	1	.286	.344	.464
1989	SF-N	302	7	.278	.339	.404	130	5	.246	.346	.438	172	2	.302	.333	.378	39	0	.179	.256	.282	263	7	.293	.352	.422	114	5	.263	.358	.456	46	1	.283	.377	.391
1990	SF-N	155	8	.200	.313	.381	72	7	.236	.353	.583	83	1	.169	.278	.205	8	1	.250	.455	.625	147	7	.197	.304	.367	71	2	.197	.318	.324	35	1	.143	.333	.321
1991	Oak-A	281	5	.214	.290	.324	148	3	.236	.319	.358	133	2	.188	.258	.286	21	0	.143	.143	.143	260	5	.219	.301	.338	117	4	.248	.343	.393	47	2	.277	.364	.511
1992	Hou-N	61	1	.262	.281	.328	24	0	.208	.269	.208	37	1	.297	.289	.405	6	0	.000	.000	.000	55	1	.291	.310	.364	25	0	.240	.286	.240	20	1	.250	.250	.400
1993	Bos-A	143	5	.189	.292	.350	59	2	.220	.324	.390	84	3	.167	.268	.321	6	1	.167	.333	.667	137	4	.190	.289	.336	70	1	.157	.295	.243	42	2	.190	.255	.429
TOTALS		2504	48	.254	.319	.365	1197	26	.275	.348	.403	1307	22	.236	.293	.330	432	6	.211	.278	.296	2072	42	.264	.328	.379	1082	25	.261	.335	.369	443	10	.260	.328	.386

■ Cal Ripken BR/TR

YEAR	TM/L	AB	HR	AVG	OBP	SLG	AB	HR	AVG	OBP	SLG	AB	HR	AVG	OBP	SLG	AB	HR	AVG	OBP	SLG	AB	HR	AVG	OBP	SLG	AB	HR	AVG	OBP	SLG	AB	HR	AVG	OBP	SLG
1984	Bal-A	641	27	.304	.374	.510	307	16	.287	.367	.508	334	11	.320	.381	.512	159	7	.308	.385	.547	482	20	.303	.371	.498	279	11	.315	.383	.538	107	3	.411	.466	.570
1985	Bal-A	642	26	.282	.347	.469	311	15	.289	.371	.482	331	11	.275	.323	.456	202	7	.272	.346	.436	440	20	.286	.347	.484	199	11	.291	.360	.465	89	6	.292	.360	.528
1986	Bal-A	627	25	.282	.355	.461	291	10	.265	.344	.430	336	15	.298	.365	.488	164	12	.360	.428	.683	463	13	.255	.329	.382	303	9	.231	.339	.409	95	6	.284	.337	.558
1987	Bal-A	624	27	.252	.333	.436	310	17	.248	.313	.465	314	10	.255	.352	.408	211	7	.242	.311	.431	413	20	.257	.344	.438	283	17	.265	.336	.498	93	2	.226	.263	.323
1988	Bal-A	575	23	.264	.372	.431	285	11	.253	.370	.414	290	12	.266	.373	.448	190	9	.316	.430	.500	385	14	.239	.342	.397	247	13	.255	.376	.443	81	1	.247	.378	.333
1989	Bal-A	646	21	.257	.317	.401	312	13	.247	.317	.413	334	8	.266	.318	.389	196	5	.235	.287	.372	450	16	.267	.331	.413	285	13	.277	.352	.463	87	5	.241	.316	.483
1990	Bal-A	600	21	.250	.341	.415	300	8	.213	.295	.350	300	13	.287	.386	.480	182	9	.264	.363	.473	418	12	.244	.332	.390	290	9	.238	.347	.348	98	4	.276	.330	.469
1991	Bal-A	650	34	.323	.374	.566	315	16	.286	.343	.505	335	18	.358	.403	.624	164	12	.348	.411	.677	486	22	.315	.361	.529	292	13	.332	.388	.555	101	4	.347	.432	.564
1992	Bal-A	637	14	.251	.323	.366	312	5	.237	.310	.346	325	9	.265	.335	.385	165	2	.230	.297	.315	472	12	.258	.332	.383	280	8	.246	.337	.384	77	0	.247	.372	.286
1993	Bal-A	641	24	.257	.329	.420	311	14	.273	.360	.437	330	10	.242	.297	.403	177	7	.282	.355	.441	464	17	.248	.318	.412	281	10	.299	.387	.470	92	4	.239	.374	.413
1994	Bal-A	444	13	.315	.364	.459	203	5	.305	.368	.433	241	8	.324	.359	.481	110	2	.345	.381	.427	334	11	.305	.358	.470	209	8	.373	.426	.550	55	1	.236	.328	.309
TOTALS		6727	255	.275	.348	.449	3257	130	.264	.341	.435	3470	125	.286	.354	.461	1920	78	.287	.361	.479	4807	177	.271	.342	.437	3022	113	.284	.364	.462	975	36	.282	.363	.451

■ Billy Ripken BR/TR

YEAR	TM/L	AB	HR	AVG	OBP	SLG	AB	HR	AVG	OBP	SLG	AB	HR	AVG	OBP	SLG	AB	HR	AVG	OBP	SLG	AB	HR	AVG	OBP	SLG	AB	HR	AVG	OBP	SLG	AB	HR	AVG	OBP	SLG
1987	Bal-A	234	2	.308	.363	.372	115	0	.287	.322	.313	119	2	.328	.400	.429	89	1	.348	.392	.427	145	1	.283	.346	.338	96	2	.323	.359	.406	29	0	.207	.233	.207
1988	Bal-A	512	2	.207	.260	.258	261	0	.222	.282	.264	251	2	.191	.238	.251	186	0	.220	.281	.263	326	2	.199	.249	.255	189	1	.185	.249	.222	66	0	.242	.301	.288
1989	Bal-A	318	2	.239	.284	.305	167	0	.234	.280	.275	151	2	.245	.288	.338	103	0	.272	.316	.330	215	2	.223	.268	.293	125	1	.256	.269	.304	39	0	.256	.302	.308
1990	Bal-A	406	3	.291	.342	.387	198	2	.278	.329	.394	208	1	.303	.354	.380	140	2	.314	.370	.421	266	1	.278	.326	.368	170	1	.335	.363	.412	58	0	.362	.431	.397
1991	Bal-A	287	0	.216	.253	.261	126	0	.214	.254	.270	161	0	.217	.253	.255	100	0	.270	.302	.310	187	0	.187	.227	.235	109	0	.193	.217	.239	31	0	.161	.212	.161
1992	Bal-A	330	4	.230	.275	.312	149	3	.255	.305	.349	181	1	.210	.250	.282	109	0	.229	.280	.294	221	4	.231	.272	.321	158	1	.272	.320	.354	24	1	.208	.296	.417
1993	Tex-A	132	0	.189	.270	.220	52	0	.192	.306	.212	80	0	.188	.244	.225	45	0	.222	.280	.267	87	0	.172	.265	.195	57	0	.193	.266	.228	14	0	.357	.500	.429
1994	Tex-A	81	0	.309	.333	.370	56	0	.393	.414	.464	25	0	.120	.154	.160	31	0	.387	.406	.452	50	0	.260	.288	.320	41	0	.317	.317	.317	11	0	.364	.417	.455
TOTALS		2300	13	.243	.293	.309	1124	5	.251	.304	.313	1176	8	.236	.282	.304	803	3	.271	.320	.335	1497	10	.228	.278	.295	945	6	.257	.295	.314	272	1	.265	.329	.316

■ Luis Rivera BR/TR

YEAR	TM/L	AB	HR	AVG	OBP	SLG	AB	HR	AVG	OBP	SLG	AB	HR	AVG	OBP	SLG	AB	HR	AVG	OBP	SLG	AB	HR	AVG	OBP	SLG	AB	HR	AVG	OBP	SLG	AB	HR	AVG	OBP	SLG
1986	Mon-N	166	0	.205	.285	.283	92	0	.207	.275	.293	74	0	.203	.298	.270	69	0	.246	.312	.333	97	0	.175	.266	.247	70	0	.229	.286	.300	31	0	.323	.364	.355
1987	Mon-N	32	0	.156	.182	.219	18	0	.111	.158	.167	14	0	.214	.214	.286	22	0	.227	.227	.318	10	0	.000	.091	.000	3	0	.333	.333	.333	3	0	.333	.333	.333
1988	Mon-N	371	4	.224	.271	.318	189	0	.243	.266	.328	182	4	.203	.275	.308	154	0	.221	.268	.331	217	4	.226	.272	.309	167	1	.240	.293	.358	87	1	.218	.233	.322
1989	Bos-A	323	5	.257	.301	.362	163	4	.294	.333	.442	160	1	.219	.269	.281	102	0	.275	.304	.363	221	5	.249	.298	.344	142	3	.246	.285	.380	41	1	.195	.244	.317
1990	Bos-A	346	7	.225	.279	.344	177	4	.232	.286	.367	169	3	.219	.271	.320	105	2	.172	.226	.267	241	5	.253	.305	.383	161	2	.236	.288	.373	55	1	.236	.288	.382
1991	Bos-A	414	8	.258	.318	.384	204	4	.255	.336	.377	210	4	.262	.300	.390	108	4	.315	.356	.537	306	4	.239	.305	.330	180	2	.233	.300	.328	52	1	.154	.228	.173
1992	Bos-A	288	0	.215	.287	.260	127	0	.173	.245	.213	161	0	.248	.320	.298	78	0	.179	.273	.218	210	0	.229	.293	.276	132	0	.258	.315	.311	53	0	.132	.233	.208
1993	Bos-A	130	1	.208	.273	.308	54	1	.241	.281	.352	76	0	.184	.267	.276	46	0	.239	.286	.304	84	1	.190	.266	.310	49	1	.163	.236	.245	9	0	.111	.273	.111

YEAR	TM/L	TOTAL AB	HR	AVG	OBP	SLG	HOME AB	HR	AVG	OBP	SLG	AWAY AB	HR	AVG	OBP	SLG	LEFT AB	HR	AVG	OBP	SLG	RIGHT AB	HR	AVG	OBP	SLG	ON-BASE AB	HR	AVG	OBP	SLG	LATE/CLOSE AB	HR	AVG	OBP	SLG
1994	NY-N	43	3	.279	.367	.581	26	2	.231	.310	.500	17	1	.353	.450	.706	23	1	.261	.292	.478	20	2	.300	.440	.700	18	1	.222	.263	.444	8	0	.375	.375	.500
TOTALS		2113	28	.232	.290	.335	1050	17	.237	.292	.348	1063	11	.228	.289	.322	718	11	.235	.286	.352	1395	17	.231	.293	.325	932	11	.236	.292	.338	339	3	.206	.260	.292

■ Bip Roberts BB/TR

YEAR	TM/L	TOTAL AB	HR	AVG	OBP	SLG	HOME AB	HR	AVG	OBP	SLG	AWAY AB	HR	AVG	OBP	SLG	LEFT AB	HR	AVG	OBP	SLG	RIGHT AB	HR	AVG	OBP	SLG	ON-BASE AB	HR	AVG	OBP	SLG	LATE/CLOSE AB	HR	AVG	OBP	SLG
1986	SD-N	241	1	.253	.293	.303	118	0	.237	.283	.271	123	1	.268	.302	.333	138	1	.203	.247	.268	103	0	.320	.355	.350	81	0	.272	.310	.333	30	0	.200	.294	.200
1988	SD-N	9	0	.333	.400	.333	7	0	.429	.500	.429	2	0	.000	.000	.000	1	0	.000	.000	.000	8	0	.375	.444	.375	3	0	.333	.333	.333	2	0	.000	.333	.000
1989	SD-N	329	3	.301	.391	.422	159	2	.302	.385	.434	170	1	.300	.397	.412	117	3	.325	.391	.453	212	0	.288	.388	.373	97	2	.340	.400	.495	48	0	.313	.431	.396
1990	SD-N	556	9	.309	.375	.433	287	4	.282	.334	.387	269	5	.338	.416	.483	221	4	.294	.350	.425	335	5	.319	.391	.439	177	6	.333	.371	.514	94	1	.266	.349	.309
1991	SD-N	424	3	.281	.342	.347	223	3	.287	.331	.354	201	0	.274	.354	.338	118	0	.254	.302	.297	306	3	.291	.357	.366	122	1	.295	.341	.410	68	1	.279	.329	.368
1992	Cin-N	532	4	.323	.393	.432	252	3	.353	.432	.500	280	1	.296	.357	.371	185	3	.292	.350	.378	347	1	.340	.416	.461	157	2	.344	.406	.529	84	1	.310	.363	.429
1993	Cin-N	292	1	.240	.330	.295	140	0	.221	.313	.250	152	1	.257	.347	.336	84	0	.179	.258	.238	208	1	.264	.368	.317	108	1	.194	.268	.259	41	0	.171	.327	.195
1994	SD-N	403	2	.320	.383	.397	198	1	.308	.367	.409	205	1	.332	.397	.385	126	2	.302	.385	.405	277	0	.329	.382	.394	118	1	.347	.428	.432	68	0	.338	.444	.338
TOTALS		2786	23	.296	.365	.387	1384	13	.293	.357	.387	1402	10	.300	.373	.387	990	13	.271	.332	.371	1796	10	.310	.383	.396	863	13	.309	.366	.439	435	3	.278	.367	.336

■ Henry Rodriguez BL/TL

YEAR	TM/L	TOTAL AB	HR	AVG	OBP	SLG	HOME AB	HR	AVG	OBP	SLG	AWAY AB	HR	AVG	OBP	SLG	LEFT AB	HR	AVG	OBP	SLG	RIGHT AB	HR	AVG	OBP	SLG	ON-BASE AB	HR	AVG	OBP	SLG	LATE/CLOSE AB	HR	AVG	OBP	SLG
1992	LA-N	146	3	.219	.258	.329	83	2	.253	.292	.361	63	1	.175	.212	.286	15	0	.400	.438	.400	131	3	.198	.237	.321	69	2	.261	.278	.406	27	0	.185	.214	.259
1993	LA-N	176	8	.222	.266	.415	97	5	.237	.288	.443	79	3	.203	.238	.380	6	0	.000	.000	.000	170	8	.229	.275	.429	74	6	.230	.301	.486	38	0	.211	.231	.289
1994	LA-N	306	8	.268	.307	.405	141	5	.298	.340	.447	165	3	.242	.278	.370	14	2	.357	.400	.857	292	6	.264	.303	.384	139	4	.331	.353	.511	48	1	.188	.281	.250
TOTALS		628	19	.244	.284	.390	321	12	.268	.312	.424	307	7	.218	.255	.355	35	2	.314	.351	.514	593	17	.239	.280	.383	282	12	.287	.321	.479	113	1	.195	.250	.265

■ Chris Sabo BR/TR

YEAR	TM/L	TOTAL AB	HR	AVG	OBP	SLG	HOME AB	HR	AVG	OBP	SLG	AWAY AB	HR	AVG	OBP	SLG	LEFT AB	HR	AVG	OBP	SLG	RIGHT AB	HR	AVG	OBP	SLG	ON-BASE AB	HR	AVG	OBP	SLG	LATE/CLOSE AB	HR	AVG	OBP	SLG
1988	Cin-N	538	11	.271	.314	.414	260	8	.296	.344	.473	278	3	.248	.285	.360	140	4	.286	.338	.450	398	7	.266	.305	.402	208	2	.250	.313	.346	99	3	.313	.358	.485
1989	Cin-N	304	6	.260	.316	.395	158	3	.234	.303	.386	146	3	.288	.331	.404	100	0	.290	.360	.390	204	6	.245	.294	.397	105	1	.267	.352	.381	40	1	.150	.255	.300
1990	Cin-N	567	25	.270	.343	.476	275	15	.280	.361	.509	292	10	.260	.326	.445	214	14	.327	.408	.589	353	11	.235	.303	.408	214	8	.257	.325	.435	90	5	.244	.333	.456
1991	Cin-N	582	26	.301	.354	.505	298	15	.339	.393	.584	284	11	.261	.314	.423	193	9	.358	.412	.596	389	17	.272	.325	.460	260	12	.312	.366	.527	88	3	.227	.289	.352
1992	Cin-N	344	12	.244	.302	.422	148	8	.236	.282	.473	196	4	.250	.317	.383	146	6	.247	.311	.438	198	6	.242	.295	.409	170	5	.218	.272	.324	42	0	.262	.353	.262
1993	Cin-N	552	21	.259	.315	.440	263	12	.281	.346	.498	289	9	.239	.286	.388	135	4	.252	.333	.407	417	17	.261	.309	.451	259	10	.274	.329	.459	86	2	.221	.277	.372
1994	Bal-A	258	11	.256	.320	.465	132	3	.227	.277	.379	126	8	.286	.364	.556	72	4	.278	.373	.514	186	7	.247	.299	.446	125	6	.264	.316	.488	38	3	.289	.325	.658
TOTALS		3145	112	.269	.326	.450	1534	64	.281	.341	.488	1611	48	.258	.312	.413	1000	41	.298	.368	.499	2145	71	.255	.307	.427	1341	44	.266	.326	.430	483	17	.248	.315	.414

■ Luis Salazar BR/TR

YEAR	TM/L	TOTAL AB	HR	AVG	OBP	SLG	HOME AB	HR	AVG	OBP	SLG	AWAY AB	HR	AVG	OBP	SLG	LEFT AB	HR	AVG	OBP	SLG	RIGHT AB	HR	AVG	OBP	SLG	ON-BASE AB	HR	AVG	OBP	SLG	LATE/CLOSE AB	HR	AVG	OBP	SLG
1984	SD-N	228	3	.241	.261	.329	99	1	.202	.218	.253	129	2	.271	.293	.388	143	3	.252	.272	.357	85	0	.224	.241	.282	86	1	.209	.244	.279	47	0	.319	.360	.362
1985	Chi-A	327	10	.245	.267	.404	150	4	.260	.298	.413	177	6	.232	.240	.395	171	4	.246	.268	.398	156	6	.244	.267	.410	149	6	.255	.293	.436	57	1	.246	.271	.404
1986	Chi-A	7	0	.143	.250	.143	6	0	.167	.286	.167	1	0	.000	.000	.000	3	0	.143	.250	.143	0	0	—	—	—	1	0	.000	.000	.000	3	0	.333	.333	.333
1987	SD-N	189	3	.254	.302	.328	95	1	.284	.310	.326	94	2	.223	.295	.330	97	2	.258	.287	.361	92	1	.250	.317	.293	87	2	.264	.313	.368	33	0	.182	.200	.212
1988	Det-A	452	12	.270	.305	.385	213	5	.254	.292	.357	239	7	.285	.316	.410	200	8	.320	.351	.500	252	4	.230	.269	.294	202	5	.272	.321	.376	72	1	.264	.321	.333
1989	Det-A	246	8	.268	.302	.411	138	5	.232	.274	.384	108	3	.315	.339	.444	92	4	.283	.320	.489	154	4	.260	.292	.364	97	3	.268	.311	.381	49	2	.327	.327	.490
1989	Chi-A	80	1	.325	.357	.425	36	1	.361	.395	.556	44	0	.295	.326	.318	33	1	.333	.389	.485	47	0	.319	.333	.383	33	1	.424	.457	.606	15	0	.467	.500	.600
1990	Chi-A	410	12	.254	.293	.388	218	7	.294	.333	.440	192	5	.208	.246	.328	157	6	.293	.319	.465	253	6	.229	.277	.340	181	5	.232	.289	.354	60	2	.333	.403	.467
1991	Chi-A	333	14	.258	.292	.432	165	8	.261	.278	.473	168	6	.256	.306	.393	166	10	.271	.309	.500	167	4	.246	.276	.365	138	5	.246	.288	.413	73	3	.329	.372	.507
1992	Chi-A	255	5	.208	.237	.310	119	3	.235	.271	.378	136	2	.184	.206	.250	156	4	.250	.273	.391	99	1	.141	.181	.182	111	1	.198	.231	.279	43	0	.140	.220	.163
TOTALS		2527	68	.254	.287	.380	1234	35	.259	.293	.394	1293	33	.248	.281	.367	1222	42	.274	.303	.436	1305	26	.234	.271	.328	1085	29	.251	.295	.374	452	9	.283	.326	.392

■ Tim Salmon BR/TR

YEAR	TM/L	TOTAL AB	HR	AVG	OBP	SLG	HOME AB	HR	AVG	OBP	SLG	AWAY AB	HR	AVG	OBP	SLG	LEFT AB	HR	AVG	OBP	SLG	RIGHT AB	HR	AVG	OBP	SLG	ON-BASE AB	HR	AVG	OBP	SLG	LATE/CLOSE AB	HR	AVG	OBP	SLG
1992	Cal-A	79	2	.177	.283	.266	32	1	.219	.359	.344	47	1	.149	.226	.213	13	1	.231	.375	.462	66	1	.167	.263	.227	30	0	.167	.350	.167	19	1	.105	.227	.263
1993	Cal-A	515	31	.283	.382	.536	258	23	.314	.406	.636	257	8	.253	.358	.436	122	7	.230	.368	.434	393	24	.300	.386	.567	233	14	.305	.406	.567	84	4	.286	.384	.476
1994	Cal-A	373	23	.287	.382	.531	196	12	.270	.364	.505	177	11	.305	.401	.559	85	5	.259	.387	.494	288	18	.295	.380	.542	171	8	.292	.398	.515	60	3	.317	.369	.517
TOTALS		967	56	.276	.374	.512	486	36	.290	.386	.564	481	20	.262	.362	.459	220	13	.241	.376	.459	747	43	.286	.373	.527	434	22	.290	.398	.518	163	8	.276	.360	.466

■ Juan Samuel BR/TR

YEAR	TM/L	TOTAL AB	HR	AVG	OBP	SLG	HOME AB	HR	AVG	OBP	SLG	AWAY AB	HR	AVG	OBP	SLG	LEFT AB	HR	AVG	OBP	SLG	RIGHT AB	HR	AVG	OBP	SLG	ON-BASE AB	HR	AVG	OBP	SLG	LATE/CLOSE AB	HR	AVG	OBP	SLG
1984	Phi-N	701	15	.272	.307	.442	331	8	.251	.287	.423	370	7	.292	.325	.459	192	1	.276	.287	.380	509	14	.271	.314	.466	251	6	.263	.298	.446	115	1	.209	.248	.304
1985	Phi-N	663	19	.264	.303	.436	327	8	.248	.298	.394	336	11	.280	.307	.476	197	5	.239	.266	.386	466	14	.275	.318	.457	259	10	.266	.291	.448	101	4	.267	.324	.455
1986	Phi-N	591	16	.266	.302	.448	286	10	.266	.313	.486	305	6	.266	.292	.413	180	5	.256	.283	.456	411	11	.270	.310	.445	263	9	.270	.314	.506	99	5	.283	.333	.485
1987	Phi-N	655	28	.272	.335	.502	320	15	.287	.367	.559	335	13	.257	.302	.448	181	9	.249	.344	.492	474	19	.281	.331	.506	251	11	.311	.358	.558	92	3	.272	.387	.467
1988	Phi-N	629	12	.243	.298	.380	320	7	.272	.339	.459	309	5	.214	.253	.298	168	2	.244	.319	.381	461	10	.243	.290	.380	247	6	.279	.339	.449	108	1	.204	.250	.333
1989	Phi-N	199	8	.246	.311	.392	96	3	.260	.324	.396	103	5	.233	.298	.388	80	4	.237	.299	.425	119	4	.252	.318	.378	77	1	.234	.286	.299	33	0	.273	.351	.364
1989	NY-N	333	3	.228	.299	.300	173	2	.214	.280	.277	160	1	.244	.318	.325	110	0	.273	.367	.355	223	3	.206	.262	.274	140	2	.243	.305	.329	40	1	.225	.311	.350
1990	LA-N	492	13	.242	.316	.382	224	6	.246	.329	.388	268	7	.239	.305	.377	187	10	.289	.350	.524	305	3	.213	.297	.295	201	6	.219	.308	.353	69	4	.290	.367	.551
1991	LA-N	594	12	.271	.328	.389	295	4	.254	.315	.342	299	8	.288	.342	.435	250	7	.252	.294	.396	344	5	.285	.352	.384	255	5	.286	.344	.408	96	1	.302	.382	.396
1992	LA-N	122	0	.262	.303	.303	57	0	.298	.344	.368	65	0	.231	.268	.246	76	0	.303	.354	.368	46	0	.196	.232	.196	51	0	.216	.311	.255	23	0	.478	.478	.522
1992	KC-A	102	0	.284	.336	.392	48	0	.292	.333	.354	54	0	.278	.339	.426	28	0	.250	.323	.393	74	0	.297	.342	.392	39	0	.256	.326	.308	17	0	.294	.333	.412
1993	Cin-N	261	4	.230	.298	.345	98	1	.224	.310	.316	163	3	.233	.290	.362	98	1	.265	.339	.418	163	3	.209	.272	.301	97	2	.268	.360	.412	44	1	.273	.347	.364
1994	Det-A	136	5	.309	.364	.559	55	4	.364	.379	.745	81	1	.272	.355	.420	52	1	.269	.322	.442	84	4	.333	.391	.631	65	1	.338	.375	.538	23	0	.304	.333	.391
TOTALS		5478	135	.260	.313	.415	2630	68	.260	.320	.425	2848	67	.259	.305	.405	1799	47	.260	.314	.421	3679	88	.259	.312	.412	2196	59	.269	.323	.435	860	21	.265	.330	.412

■ Ryne Sandberg BR/TR

YEAR	TM/L	TOTAL AB	HR	AVG	OBP	SLG	HOME AB	HR	AVG	OBP	SLG	AWAY AB	HR	AVG	OBP	SLG	LEFT AB	HR	AVG	OBP	SLG	RIGHT AB	HR	AVG	OBP	SLG	ON-BASE AB	HR	AVG	OBP	SLG	LATE/CLOSE AB	HR	AVG	OBP	SLG
1984	Chi-N	636	19	.314	.367	.520	313	11	.332	.397	.575	323	8	.297	.336	.467	162	3	.358	.399	.562	474	16	.300	.356	.506	266	4	.316	.382	.470	84	4	.286	.351	.560
1985	Chi-N	609	26	.305	.364	.504	293	17	.304	.371	.560	316	9	.307	.357	.453	152	5	.276	.339	.434	457	21	.315	.372	.527	252	12	.274	.344	.496	92	5	.370	.417	.630
1986	Chi-N	627	14	.284	.330	.411	321	8	.302	.344	.445	306	6	.265	.315	.376	159	4	.264	.314	.377	468	10	.291	.335	.423	267	6	.307	.353	.427	109	5	.257	.297	.330
1987	Chi-N	523	16	.294	.367	.442	257	8	.300	.357	.463	266	8	.289	.376	.421	114	2	.307	.412	.439	409	14	.291	.353	.443	214	4	.285	.362	.374	80	1	.287	.380	.350
1988	Chi-N	618	19	.264	.322	.419	312	10	.279	.342	.452	306	9	.248	.300	.386	164	7	.293	.363	.482	454	12	.253	.306	.396	221	7	.308	.375	.484	97	2	.227	.312	.351
1989	Chi-N	606	30	.290	.356	.497	303	16	.297	.351	.505	303	14	.284	.362	.488	172	7	.314	.414	.517	434	23	.281	.331	.488	244	8	.262	.350	.422	94	4	.277	.327	.436
1990	Chi-N	615	40	.306	.354	.559	305	25	.357	.405	.679	310	15	.255	.303	.439	214	10	.252	.316	.463	401	30	.334	.374	.616	237	16	.367	.418	.637	96	6	.323	.352	.563
1991	Chi-N	585	26	.291	.379	.485	291	15	.309	.394	.528	294	11	.272	.364	.446	209	8	.359	.456	.565	376	18	.253	.335	.441	254	14	.339	.436	.579	111	3	.252	.375	.387
1992	Chi-N	612	26	.304	.371	.510	300	16	.307	.386	.570	312	10	.301	.357	.452	206	4	.340	.403	.500	406	22	.286	.355	.515	262	6	.294	.350	.550	109	4	.312	.377	.450
1993	Chi-N	456	9	.309	.359	.412	243	5	.296	.352	.399	213	4	.324	.368	.427	147	1	.385	.427	.459	309	8	.272	.331	.430	212	1	.283	.331	.330	68	0	.250	.333	.279
1994	Chi-N	223	5	.238	.312	.390	111	3	.252	.325	.396	112	2	.223	.298	.384	65	2	.154	.267	.292	158	3	.272	.331	.430	90	3	.267	.340	.456	37	0	.216	.256	.270
TOTALS		6110	230	.294	.355	.475	3049	134	.307	.369	.516	3061	96	.281	.341	.434	1726	53	.307	.380	.476	4384	177	.289	.345	.474	2519	89	.303	.370	.479	977	29	.281	.351	.429

■ Reggie Sanders BR/TR

YEAR	TM/L	TOTAL AB	HR	AVG	OBP	SLG	HOME AB	HR	AVG	OBP	SLG	AWAY AB	HR	AVG	OBP	SLG	LEFT AB	HR	AVG	OBP	SLG	RIGHT AB	HR	AVG	OBP	SLG	ON-BASE AB	HR	AVG	OBP	SLG	LATE/CLOSE AB	HR	AVG	OBP	SLG
1991	Cin-N	40	1	.200	.200	.275	11	0	.000	.000	.000	29	1	.276	.276	.379	16	0	.125	.125	.125	24	1	.250	.250	.375	9	1	.333	.333	.667	5	0	.200	.200	.200
1992	Cin-N	385	12	.270	.356	.462	205	6	.244	.353	.429	180	6	.300	.360	.500	175	7	.314	.391	.566	210	5	.233	.328	.376	166	3	.229	.325	.343	65	2	.308	.392	.477
1993	Cin-N	496	20	.274	.343	.444	237	8	.287	.357	.447	259	12	.263	.330	.440	129	6	.310	.366	.496	367	14	.262	.335	.425	254	7	.268	.351	.409	70	2	.243	.341	.386
1994	Cin-N	400	17	.262	.332	.480	210	10	.281	.363	.500	190	7	.242	.297	.458	91	6	.330	.386	.659	309	11	.243	.316	.427	182	8	.253	.335	.473	72	2	.264	.346	.431
TOTALS		1321	50	.267	.340	.455	663	24	.267	.352	.451	658	26	.267	.326	.459	411	19	.309	.373	.547	910	31	.248	.325	.413	611	19	.254	.339	.414	212	6	.269	.355	.429

■ Rafael Santana BR/TR

YEAR	TM/L	TOTAL AB	HR	AVG	OBP	SLG	HOME AB	HR	AVG	OBP	SLG	AWAY AB	HR	AVG	OBP	SLG	LEFT AB	HR	AVG	OBP	SLG	RIGHT AB	HR	AVG	OBP	SLG	ON-BASE AB	HR	AVG	OBP	SLG	LATE/CLOSE AB	HR	AVG	OBP	SLG
1984	NY-N	152	1	.276	.317	.382	55	1	.345	.400	.527	97	0	.237	.267	.299	49	1	.347	.396	.490	103	0	.243	.278	.330	53	0	.208	.222	.264	22	0	.318	.423	.364
1985	NY-N	529	1	.257	.295	.302	264	0	.235	.262	.265	265	1	.279	.326	.340	196	0	.265	.313	.301	333	1	.252	.284	.303	220	1	.236	.277	.286	92	0	.239	.278	.261
1986	NY-N	394	1	.218	.285	.254	191	0	.188	.270	.220	203	1	.246	.300	.286	163	1	.245	.328	.288	231	0	.199	.254	.229	170	1	.224	.315	.265	70	0	.200	.243	.229
1987	NY-N	439	5	.255	.302	.346	221	2	.244	.297	.330	218	3	.266	.307	.362	168	3	.262	.322	.363	271	2	.251	.289	.336	188	2	.282	.346	.388	59	0	.153	.194	.220
1988	NY-N	480	4	.240	.289	.294	240	2	.217	.261	.271	240	2	.262	.317	.317	145	1	.234	.268	.290	335	3	.242	.298	.296	198	2	.242	.286	.303	61	0	.311	.333	.311
1990	Cle-A	13	1	.231	.231	.462	0	0	—	—	—	13	1	.231	.231	.462	3	1	.333	.333	1.333	10	0	.200	.200	.200	6	1	.500	.500	1.000	0	0	—	—	—
TOTALS		2007	13	.246	.294	.307	971	5	.230	.279	.287	1036	8	.262	.308	.326	724	7	.260	.316	.327	1283	6	.239	.282	.296	835	7	.246	.301	.313	304	0	.234	.276	.263

■ Benito Santiago BR/TR

YEAR	TM/L	TOTAL AB	HR	AVG	OBP	SLG	HOME AB	HR	AVG	OBP	SLG	AWAY AB	HR	AVG	OBP	SLG	LEFT AB	HR	AVG	OBP	SLG	RIGHT AB	HR	AVG	OBP	SLG	ON-BASE AB	HR	AVG	OBP	SLG	LATE/CLOSE AB	HR	AVG	OBP	SLG
1986	SD-N	62	3	.290	.308	.468	27	2	.259	.300	.556	35	1	.314	.314	.400	22	2	.364	.375	.636	40	1	.250	.268	.375	25	0	.200	.250	.240	11	1	.182	.250	.455
1987	SD-N	546	18	.300	.324	.467	274	11	.281	.307	.471	272	7	.320	.342	.463	182	8	.341	.363	.577	364	10	.280	.304	.412	256	11	.309	.332	.500	101	3	.396	.408	.564
1988	SD-N	492	10	.248	.282	.362	261	3	.230	.253	.326	231	7	.268	.313	.403	140	5	.257	.291	.407	352	5	.244	.278	.344	220	2	.195	.232	.295	96	2	.240	.275	.333
1989	SD-N	462	16	.236	.277	.387	212	8	.264	.302	.434	250	8	.212	.256	.348	117	2	.222	.253	.333	345	14	.241	.283	.403	222	8	.230	.270	.378	84	1	.226	.250	.298
1990	SD-N	344	11	.270	.323	.419	189	6	.286	.350	.429	155	5	.252	.287	.406	116	1	.276	.323	.328	228	10	.268	.323	.465	140	8	.271	.327	.493	67	3	.433	.493	.657
1991	SD-N	580	17	.267	.296	.403	287	6	.244	.267	.334	293	11	.290	.325	.471	204	8	.318	.354	.480	376	9	.258	.284	.362	290	7	.290	.294	.407	106	4	.330	.363	.500
1992	SD-N	386	10	.251	.287	.383	195	8	.308	.328	.482	191	2	.194	.246	.283	130	7	.292	.326	.508	256	3	.230	.267	.320	168	3	.220	.250	.298	66	3	.258	.315	.470
1993	Fla-N	469	13	.230	.291	.380	233	6	.227	.291	.386	236	7	.233	.292	.373	123	4	.276	.355	.488	346	9	.214	.268	.341	207	5	.222	.292	.362	88	2	.148	.202	.250

YEAR	TM/L	TOTAL AB	HR	AVG	OBP	SLG	HOME AB	HR	AVG	OBP	SLG	AWAY AB	HR	AVG	OBP	SLG	LEFT AB	HR	AVG	OBP	SLG	RIGHT AB	HR	AVG	OBP	SLG	ON-BASE AB	HR	AVG	OBP	SLG	LATE/CLOSE AB	HR	AVG	OBP	SLG
1994	Fla-N	337	11	.273	.322	.424	169	4	.284	.344	.420	168	7	.262	.298	.429	100	3	.340	.391	.490	237	8	.245	.292	.397	147	6	.265	.317	.422	52	1	.269	.316	.327
	TOTALS	3678	109	.260	.299	.405	1847	53	.263	.301	.408	1831	56	.258	.298	.401	1134	40	.289	.332	.462	2544	69	.248	.285	.379	1675	51	.249	.288	.392	671	20	.286	.325	.425

■ Steve Sax BR/TR

YEAR	TM/L	TOTAL AB	HR	AVG	OBP	SLG	HOME AB	HR	AVG	OBP	SLG	AWAY AB	HR	AVG	OBP	SLG	LEFT AB	HR	AVG	OBP	SLG	RIGHT AB	HR	AVG	OBP	SLG	ON-BASE AB	HR	AVG	OBP	SLG	LATE/CLOSE AB	HR	AVG	OBP	SLG
1984	LA-N	569	1	.243	.300	.304	269	1	.249	.297	.309	300	0	.237	.303	.300	207	0	.275	.324	.348	362	1	.224	.286	.279	165	0	.242	.304	.303	95	0	.274	.320	.316
1985	LA-N	488	1	.279	.352	.318	239	1	.226	.317	.255	249	0	.329	.386	.378	144	1	.215	.324	.278	344	0	.305	.365	.334	120	1	.281	.366	.329	73	1	.315	.363	.411
1986	LA-N	633	6	.332	.390	.441	306	1	.310	.377	.389	327	5	.352	.402	.489	225	3	.329	.374	.467	408	3	.333	.398	.426	174	2	.339	.422	.454	108	2	.370	.423	.500
1987	LA-N	610	6	.280	.331	.369	289	2	.260	.310	.325	321	4	.299	.351	.408	205	2	.278	.330	.376	405	4	.281	.332	.365	209	1	.263	.326	.335	100	1	.360	.423	.500
1988	LA-N	632	5	.277	.325	.343	311	2	.302	.348	.354	321	3	.252	.303	.333	200	3	.290	.352	.375	432	2	.271	.312	.329	198	2	.333	.402	.394	92	0	.348	.413	.380
1989	NY-A	651	5	.315	.364	.387	324	2	.324	.363	.401	327	3	.306	.365	.373	202	2	.381	.427	.470	449	3	.285	.335	.350	255	2	.318	.367	.376	92	1	.315	.360	.391
1990	NY-A	615	4	.260	.316	.325	294	3	.259	.327	.347	321	1	.262	.305	.305	177	0	.249	.305	.299	438	4	.265	.312	.336	227	1	.242	.302	.295	94	1	.330	.404	.436
1991	NY-A	652	10	.304	.345	.414	327	6	.291	.340	.413	325	4	.317	.350	.415	215	5	.344	.390	.507	437	5	.284	.322	.368	236	3	.288	.331	.381	103	1	.243	.252	.311
1992	Chi-A	567	4	.236	.290	.317	292	1	.226	.287	.312	275	3	.247	.293	.324	157	1	.229	.278	.299	410	3	.239	.294	.324	206	2	.238	.303	.335	89	0	.202	.273	.258
1993	Chi-A	119	1	.235	.283	.303	60	1	.250	.286	.333	59	0	.220	.281	.271	67	0	.239	.282	.299	52	1	.231	.286	.308	46	0	.196	.245	.239	20	0	.350	.350	.400
1994	Oak-A	24	0	.250	.250	.333	17	0	.294	.294	.412	7	0	.143	.143	.143	11	0	.455	.455	.455	13	0	.077	.077	.231	8	0	.125	.125	.375	3	0	.333	.333	.333
	TOTALS	5560	43	.281	.334	.359	2728	20	.274	.330	.349	2832	23	.287	.338	.368	1810	17	.292	.349	.386	3750	26	.275	.327	.346	1934	14	.280	.344	.353	869	8	.308	.362	.391

■ Mike Schmidt BR/TR

YEAR	TM/L	TOTAL AB	HR	AVG	OBP	SLG	HOME AB	HR	AVG	OBP	SLG	AWAY AB	HR	AVG	OBP	SLG	LEFT AB	HR	AVG	OBP	SLG	RIGHT AB	HR	AVG	OBP	SLG	ON-BASE AB	HR	AVG	OBP	SLG	LATE/CLOSE AB	HR	AVG	OBP	SLG
1984	Phi-N	528	36	.277	.383	.536	235	16	.268	.375	.523	293	20	.283	.389	.546	130	8	.246	.379	.462	398	28	.286	.384	.560	254	13	.276	.383	.492	88	4	.330	.459	.568
1985	Phi-N	549	33	.277	.375	.532	265	14	.279	.379	.513	284	19	.275	.372	.549	155	6	.284	.391	.484	394	27	.274	.369	.551	254	8	.264	.377	.429	90	7	.300	.400	.611
1986	Phi-N	552	37	.290	.390	.547	258	20	.298	.406	.597	294	17	.282	.374	.503	157	15	.357	.474	.707	395	22	.263	.354	.484	266	21	.305	.417	.586	93	6	.290	.411	.516
1987	Phi-N	522	35	.293	.388	.548	260	15	.342	.433	.585	262	20	.244	.343	.511	133	7	.331	.442	.556	389	28	.280	.368	.545	270	17	.296	.389	.548	88	4	.295	.415	.545
1988	Phi-N	390	12	.249	.337	.405	186	6	.290	.401	.468	204	6	.211	.272	.348	91	3	.330	.435	.516	299	9	.224	.306	.371	184	5	.299	.405	.484	71	0	.127	.213	.155
1989	Phi-N	148	6	.203	.297	.372	63	2	.222	.300	.365	85	4	.188	.290	.376	57	2	.263	.328	.404	91	4	.165	.278	.352	82	4	.207	.299	.390	21	1	.238	.360	.476
	TOTALS	2689	159	.274	.373	.512	1267	73	.293	.395	.533	1422	86	.258	.352	.493	723	41	.306	.418	.539	1966	118	.263	.355	.502	1310	68	.282	.388	.503	451	24	.273	.388	.492

■ Dick Schofield BR/TR

YEAR	TM/L	TOTAL AB	HR	AVG	OBP	SLG	HOME AB	HR	AVG	OBP	SLG	AWAY AB	HR	AVG	OBP	SLG	LEFT AB	HR	AVG	OBP	SLG	RIGHT AB	HR	AVG	OBP	SLG	ON-BASE AB	HR	AVG	OBP	SLG	LATE/CLOSE AB	HR	AVG	OBP	SLG
1984	Cal-A	400	4	.192	.264	.262	181	4	.149	.234	.193	219	4	.228	.290	.320	141	1	.191	.260	.270	259	3	.193	.267	.259	149	3	.134	.250	.221	39	1	.256	.293	.385
1985	Cal-A	438	8	.219	.287	.331	219	5	.219	.269	.333	219	3	.219	.305	.329	147	2	.259	.323	.354	291	6	.199	.269	.320	188	3	.218	.312	.356	51	2	.216	.273	.373
1986	Cal-A	458	13	.249	.321	.397	226	7	.230	.322	.363	232	6	.267	.321	.431	163	4	.294	.397	.454	295	9	.224	.276	.366	201	4	.224	.301	.338	80	2	.200	.270	.325
1987	Cal-A	479	9	.251	.305	.355	257	4	.257	.310	.335	222	5	.243	.300	.378	161	2	.267	.324	.379	318	7	.242	.296	.343	195	4	.251	.297	.349	74	0	.176	.213	.189
1988	Cal-A	527	6	.239	.303	.317	274	3	.230	.271	.303	253	3	.249	.336	.332	180	4	.228	.302	.344	347	2	.245	.303	.303	200	2	.240	.316	.310	91	0	.297	.369	.374
1989	Cal-A	302	4	.228	.299	.318	143	1	.203	.280	.273	159	3	.252	.316	.358	127	1	.260	.304	.346	175	3	.206	.295	.297	96	1	.198	.288	.323	39	0	.282	.404	.333
1990	Cal-A	310	1	.255	.363	.297	158	1	.272	.384	.329	152	0	.237	.341	.263	89	1	.281	.404	.337	221	0	.244	.346	.281	122	0	.279	.412	.303	50	0	.220	.350	.220
1991	Cal-A	427	4	.225	.310	.260	211	0	.209	.286	.237	216	4	.241	.333	.282	115	0	.183	.314	.191	312	4	.240	.309	.285	185	0	.286	.380	.314	65	0	.200	.297	.215
1992	Cal-A	3	0	.333	.500	.333	3	0	.333	.500	.333	0	0	—	—	—	0	0	—	—	—	3	0	.333	.500	.333	0	0	—	1.000	—	1	0	.000	.000	.000
1992	NY-A	420	4	.205	.309	.286	201	3	.214	.323	.303	219	1	.196	.296	.269	145	2	.200	.316	.310	275	2	.207	.306	.273	178	1	.236	.377	.326	80	1	.200	.261	.275
1993	Tor-A	110	0	.191	.294	.236	55	0	.255	.388	.345	55	0	.127	.186	.127	35	0	.171	.293	.171	75	0	.200	.294	.267	45	0	.200	.294	.222	14	0	.143	.294	.143
1994	Tor-A	325	4	.255	.332	.342	141	2	.241	.318	.333	184	2	.266	.341	.348	87	1	.253	.320	.368	238	3	.256	.336	.332	116	2	.216	.301	.302	56	0	.125	.210	.125
	TOTALS	4199	53	.231	.308	.316	2069	26	.224	.302	.304	2130	27	.237	.314	.328	1390	18	.240	.325	.335	2809	35	.226	.299	.306	1675	20	.230	.324	.315	640	6	.214	.291	.277

■ Mike Scioscia BL/TR

YEAR	TM/L	TOTAL AB	HR	AVG	OBP	SLG	HOME AB	HR	AVG	OBP	SLG	AWAY AB	HR	AVG	OBP	SLG	LEFT AB	HR	AVG	OBP	SLG	RIGHT AB	HR	AVG	OBP	SLG	ON-BASE AB	HR	AVG	OBP	SLG	LATE/CLOSE AB	HR	AVG	OBP	SLG
1984	LA-N	341	5	.273	.367	.370	145	0	.283	.397	.324	196	5	.265	.342	.403	39	1	.128	.227	.154	302	5	.291	.384	.397	137	2	.307	.396	.401	68	0	.162	.278	.191
1985	LA-N	429	7	.296	.407	.420	202	1	.297	.415	.366	227	6	.295	.399	.467	87	1	.253	.337	.345	342	6	.307	.424	.439	187	1	.348	.447	.439	66	1	.273	.377	.409
1986	LA-N	374	5	.251	.359	.345	169	2	.249	.350	.325	205	3	.254	.366	.361	107	2	.234	.341	.308	267	3	.258	.366	.360	149	1	.242	.361	.302	72	0	.250	.364	.292
1987	LA-N	461	6	.265	.343	.364	219	2	.260	.345	.315	242	4	.269	.341	.409	132	0	.273	.356	.348	329	6	.261	.338	.371	187	0	.257	.335	.294	86	2	.233	.305	.360
1988	LA-N	408	3	.257	.318	.324	208	1	.264	.313	.313	200	2	.250	.324	.335	78	0	.244	.289	.244	330	3	.261	.325	.342	165	2	.261	.351	.339	73	0	.274	.369	.301
1989	LA-N	408	10	.250	.338	.363	200	4	.235	.309	.305	208	6	.264	.347	.389	100	3	.230	.300	.330	308	7	.256	.350	.373	168	4	.250	.321	.333	78	1	.244	.337	.333
1990	LA-N	435	12	.264	.348	.405	208	5	.279	.363	.409	227	7	.251	.335	.401	119	2	.235	.295	.328	316	10	.275	.367	.434	189	2	.265	.373	.360	58	1	.207	.343	.345
1991	LA-N	345	8	.264	.353	.391	163	3	.288	.380	.399	182	5	.242	.329	.385	106	3	.189	.276	.292	239	5	.297	.388	.435	146	0	.274	.371	.342	63	2	.317	.429	.413
1992	LA-N	348	3	.221	.286	.282	178	1	.247	.297	.315	170	2	.194	.275	.247	81	1	.235	.297	.333	267	2	.217	.283	.266	135	2	.230	.318	.304	68	1	.265	.324	.324
	TOTALS	3549	59	.261	.348	.364	1692	19	.267	.354	.345	1857	40	.256	.342	.382	849	12	.232	.310	.311	2700	47	.270	.360	.381	1463	14	.269	.366	.347	632	8	.247	.347	.329

■ Kevin Seitzer BR/TR

YEAR	TM/L	TOTAL AB	HR	AVG	OBP	SLG	HOME AB	HR	AVG	OBP	SLG	AWAY AB	HR	AVG	OBP	SLG	LEFT AB	HR	AVG	OBP	SLG	RIGHT AB	HR	AVG	OBP	SLG	ON-BASE AB	HR	AVG	OBP	SLG	LATE/CLOSE AB	HR	AVG	OBP	SLG
1986	KC-A	96	2	.323	.440	.448	48	1	.458	.552	.646	48	1	.188	.328	.250	18	1	.278	.480	.444	78	1	.333	.429	.449	38	1	.289	.460	.395	14	0	.500	.563	.643
1987	KC-A	641	15	.323	.399	.470	319	7	.335	.413	.511	322	8	.311	.386	.429	175	2	.309	.386	.434	466	13	.328	.404	.483	264	7	.307	.391	.470	86	0	.337	.396	.419
1988	KC-A	559	5	.304	.387	.406	272	4	.320	.401	.441	287	1	.289	.374	.373	153	1	.353	.432	.477	406	4	.286	.371	.379	216	1	.324	.425	.407	87	0	.218	.314	.253
1989	KC-A	597	4	.281	.387	.337	299	2	.311	.405	.368	298	2	.252	.370	.305	175	3	.337	.387	.343	422	1	.291	.387	.334	231	0	.294	.416	.333	85	1	.318	.426	.412
1990	KC-A	622	6	.275	.346	.370	308	5	.312	.384	.451	314	1	.239	.308	.290	209	4	.278	.345	.455	413	2	.274	.347	.327	208	2	.293	.358	.404	84	0	.214	.272	.238
1991	KC-A	234	1	.265	.350	.350	117	0	.274	.344	.368	117	1	.256	.356	.333	66	1	.333	.429	.424	168	0	.238	.317	.321	102	0	.294	.381	.382	47	0	.319	.373	.426
1992	Mil-A	540	5	.270	.337	.367	259	2	.236	.315	.305	281	3	.302	.358	.423	128	2	.313	.404	.453	412	3	.257	.315	.340	231	1	.268	.338	.359	86	1	.349	.416	.453
1993	Oak-A	255	4	.255	.324	.357	121	2	.231	.331	.314	134	2	.276	.318	.396	65	0	.262	.359	.308	190	4	.253	.311	.374	113	0	.292	.359	.372	54	0	.315	.322	.389
1993	Mil-A	162	1	.290	.359	.457	86	4	.314	.406	.488	76	3	.263	.300	.421	78	4	.295	.353	.474	84	4	.295	.365	.440	75	3	.226	.273	.445	31	2	.226	.273	.484
1994	Mil-A	309	5	.314	.375	.453	143	4	.280	.358	.427	166	1	.343	.390	.476	60	1	.267	.413	.417	249	4	.325	.364	.462	145	2	.372	.444	.476	38	1	.342	.375	.526
	TOTALS	4015	54	.290	.369	.395	1972	31	.301	.383	.419	2043	23	.279	.356	.372	1127	19	.296	.389	.426	2888	35	.287	.361	.383	1623	18	.305	.392	.407	612	5	.297	.363	.389

■ Mike Sharperson BR/TR

YEAR	TM/L	TOTAL AB	HR	AVG	OBP	SLG	HOME AB	HR	AVG	OBP	SLG	AWAY AB	HR	AVG	OBP	SLG	LEFT AB	HR	AVG	OBP	SLG	RIGHT AB	HR	AVG	OBP	SLG	ON-BASE AB	HR	AVG	OBP	SLG	LATE/CLOSE AB	HR	AVG	OBP	SLG
1987	Tor-A	96	0	.208	.269	.271	44	0	.205	.255	.318	52	0	.212	.281	.231	27	0	.222	.222	.222	69	0	.203	.286	.290	42	0	.262	.326	.405	13	0	.000	.071	.000
1987	LA-N	33	0	.273	.351	.333	14	0	.357	.438	.357	19	0	.211	.286	.316	10	0	.300	.364	.300	23	0	.261	.346	.348	13	0	.231	.286	.308	3	0	.000	.000	.000
1988	LA-N	59	0	.271	.290	.288	27	0	.148	.200	.148	32	0	.375	.375	.406	22	0	.227	.250	.273	37	0	.297	.316	.297	20	0	.200	.227	.200	17	0	.235	.278	.235
1989	LA-N	28	0	.250	.333	.357	8	0	.125	.300	.125	20	0	.300	.348	.450	13	0	.231	.375	.308	15	0	.267	.294	.400	11	0	.273	.400	.273	10	0	.100	.231	.200
1990	LA-N	357	3	.297	.376	.373	195	1	.308	.373	.369	162	2	.284	.379	.377	208	1	.322	.396	.385	149	2	.262	.349	.356	149	1	.336	.430	.389	52	1	.250	.350	.385
1991	LA-N	216	2	.278	.355	.375	97	1	.330	.409	.402	119	1	.235	.311	.353	158	2	.323	.392	.449	58	0	.155	.258	.172	97	0	.278	.333	.361	45	0	.311	.380	.400
1992	LA-N	317	3	.300	.387	.394	159	2	.314	.382	.421	158	1	.285	.392	.367	199	3	.312	.388	.422	118	0	.280	.386	.347	175	2	.297	.376	.406	75	1	.267	.367	.387
1993	LA-N	90	2	.256	.299	.367	37	1	.243	.293	.324	53	1	.264	.304	.396	79	2	.253	.277	.367	11	0	.273	.429	.273	38	1	.211	.295	.316	31	1	.250	.250	.393
	TOTALS	1196	10	.281	.356	.365	581	5	.293	.361	.368	615	5	.270	.351	.361	716	8	.303	.369	.397	480	2	.248	.336	.317	545	4	.290	.368	.374	243	3	.243	.322	.346

■ Larry Sheets BL/TR

YEAR	TM/L	TOTAL AB	HR	AVG	OBP	SLG	HOME AB	HR	AVG	OBP	SLG	AWAY AB	HR	AVG	OBP	SLG	LEFT AB	HR	AVG	OBP	SLG	RIGHT AB	HR	AVG	OBP	SLG	ON-BASE AB	HR	AVG	OBP	SLG	LATE/CLOSE AB	HR	AVG	OBP	SLG
1984	Bal-A	16	1	.438	.471	.688	6	0	.500	.571	.667	10	1	.400	.400	.700	1	0	.000	.000	.000	15	1	.467	.500	.733	10	1	.700	.727	1.100	1	1	1.000	1.000	4.000
1985	Bal-A	328	17	.262	.323	.442	170	5	.276	.344	.394	158	12	.247	.300	.494	17	0	.118	.273	.176	311	17	.270	.326	.457	146	8	.274	.331	.452	55	3	.218	.259	.382
1986	Bal-A	338	18	.272	.317	.488	181	10	.276	.302	.497	157	8	.268	.333	.478	26	1	.154	.207	.308	312	17	.282	.326	.503	158	14	.278	.329	.595	49	1	.143	.250	.245
1987	Bal-A	469	31	.316	.358	.563	241	21	.324	.371	.627	228	10	.307	.344	.496	145	10	.303	.348	.538	324	21	.321	.363	.574	208	13	.298	.326	.538	77	4	.299	.333	.481
1988	Bal-A	452	10	.230	.302	.343	218	6	.206	.275	.339	234	4	.252	.327	.346	114	1	.202	.305	.237	338	9	.240	.300	.379	192	5	.260	.315	.391	72	1	.333	.402	.444
1989	Bal-A	304	7	.243	.305	.359	133	1	.233	.302	.301	171	6	.251	.307	.404	39	0	.154	.209	.179	265	7	.257	.319	.385	133	3	.248	.335	.346	49	0	.224	.309	.265
1990	Det-A	360	10	.261	.308	.403	179	7	.246	.288	.419	181	3	.276	.327	.387	17	0	.235	.278	.235	343	10	.262	.309	.411	183	5	.251	.284	.410	43	2	.326	.396	.581
1993	Sea-A	17	0	.118	.250	.176	7	0	.000	.300	.000	10	0	.200	.200	.300	0	0	—	—	—	17	0	.118	.250	.176	10	0	.200	.284	.410	2	0	.000	.333	.000
	TOTALS	2284	94	.266	.321	.437	1135	50	.263	.317	.441	1149	44	.269	.324	.432	359	12	.231	.301	.354	1925	82	.272	.324	.452	1040	49	.273	.322	.463	348	12	.264	.331	.414

■ Gary Sheffield BR/TR

YEAR	TM/L	TOTAL AB	HR	AVG	OBP	SLG	HOME AB	HR	AVG	OBP	SLG	AWAY AB	HR	AVG	OBP	SLG	LEFT AB	HR	AVG	OBP	SLG	RIGHT AB	HR	AVG	OBP	SLG	ON-BASE AB	HR	AVG	OBP	SLG	LATE/CLOSE AB	HR	AVG	OBP	SLG
1988	Mil-A	80	4	.237	.295	.400	32	1	.188	.289	.313	48	3	.271	.300	.458	23	1	.217	.302	.348	57	3	.246	.302	.421	34	3	.324	.351	.588	12	1	.417	.500	.667
1989	Mil-A	368	5	.247	.303	.337	198	2	.258	.307	.343	170	3	.235	.299	.329	113	2	.292	.336	.442	255	3	.227	.289	.290	170	1	.229	.287	.282	55	1	.255	.311	.345
1990	Mil-A	487	10	.294	.350	.421	239	3	.272	.338	.381	248	7	.315	.361	.460	135	3	.274	.338	.412	352	7	.301	.355	.412	217	4	.359	.403	.488	63	2	.397	.472	.556
1991	Mil-A	175	2	.194	.277	.320	74	2	.257	.368	.459	101	0	.149	.209	.218	43	0	.140	.264	.233	132	2	.212	.282	.348	75	1	.227	.333	.373	27	0	.222	.276	.333
1992	SD-N	557	33	.330	.385	.580	288	23	.365	.426	.684	269	10	.294	.340	.468	189	13	.365	.420	.640	368	20	.313	.367	.549	255	17	.337	.401	.584	78	4	.410	.467	.628
1993	SD-N	258	10	.295	.344	.473	117	6	.350	.397	.590	141	4	.248	.298	.376	72	3	.321	.360	.436	186	7	.283	.337	.489	111	6	.256	.338	.487	45	4	.289	.327	.578
1993	Fla-N	236	10	.292	.378	.479	124	4	.282	.369	.427	112	6	.304	.388	.536	57	2	.333	.449	.456	179	8	.279	.354	.486	111	7	.288	.402	.468	43	2	.366	.518	.488
1994	Fla-N	322	27	.276	.380	.584	167	15	.269	.382	.593	155	12	.284	.378	.574	104	8	.212	.299	.452	218	19	.307	.416	.647	160	18	.281	.409	.681	41	2	.195	.365	.390
	TOTALS	2483	101	.284	.350	.468	1239	56	.296	.369	.501	1244	45	.272	.332	.436	742	32	.291	.358	.480	1741	69	.281	.347	.464	1139	57	.295	.367	.503	362	14	.326	.411	.503

■ John Shelby BB/TR

YEAR	TM/L	TOTAL AB	HR	AVG	OBP	SLG	HOME AB	HR	AVG	OBP	SLG	AWAY AB	HR	AVG	OBP	SLG	LEFT AB	HR	AVG	OBP	SLG	RIGHT AB	HR	AVG	OBP	SLG	ON-BASE AB	HR	AVG	OBP	SLG	LATE/CLOSE AB	HR	AVG	OBP	SLG
1984	Bal-A	383	6	.209	.248	.313	184	2	.190	.232	.261	199	4	.226	.263	.362	158	4	.215	.257	.329	225	2	.204	.242	.302	158	0	.247	.283	.354	66	1	.152	.222	.242
1985	Bal-A	205	7	.283	.307	.434	102	4	.245	.267	.402	103	3	.320	.346	.466	82	2	.244	.262	.378	123	5	.309	.336	.472	75	4	.293	.329	.520	36	0	.167	.211	.250
1986	Bal-A	404	11	.228	.263	.364	186	5	.199	.226	.312	218	6	.252	.294	.408	134	5	.231	.264	.388	270	6	.226	.262	.352	165	2	.242	.270	.376	79	6	.241	.259	.329
1987	Bal-A	32	1	.188	.212	.281	21	0	.143	.182	.143	11	1	.273	.273	.545	17	1	.176	.222	.353	15	0	.200	.200	.200	19	1	.158	.158	.316	6	0	.167	.167	.167

YEAR TM/L	TOTAL AB HR AVG OBP SLG	HOME AB HR AVG OBP SLG	AWAY AB HR AVG OBP SLG	LEFT AB HR AVG OBP SLG	RIGHT AB HR AVG OBP SLG	ON-BASE AB HR AVG OBP SLG	LATE/CLOSE AB HR AVG OBP SLG
1987 LA-N	476 21 .277 .317 .464	239 8 .243 .284 .377	237 13 .312 .352 .553	158 10 .335 .366 .595	318 11 .248 .293 .399	209 8 .278 .301 .450	79 2 .190 .256 .316
1988 LA-N	494 10 .263 .320 .395	236 5 .309 .351 .445	258 5 .221 .291 .349	189 2 .238 .286 .323	305 8 .279 .340 .439	212 4 .283 .339 .415	82 4 .256 .337 .463
1989 LA-N	345 1 .183 .237 .229	186 0 .183 .221 .215	159 1 .182 .256 .245	125 0 .168 .206 .208	220 1 .191 .254 .241	136 1 .176 .236 .250	77 1 .143 .183 .195
1990 LA-N	24 0 .250 .250 .292	11 0 .182 .182 .273	13 0 .308 .308 .308	12 0 .167 .167 .167	12 0 .333 .333 .417	5 0 .400 .400 .600	8 0 .375 .375 .500
1990 Det-A	222 4 .248 .280 .369	103 3 .262 .303 .417	119 1 .235 .260 .328	66 2 .182 .217 .333	156 2 .276 .307 .385	98 3 .214 .274 .357	33 0 .212 .212 .273
1991 Det-A	143 3 .154 .204 .287	63 2 .159 .221 .317	80 1 .150 .190 .262	63 2 .175 .212 .349	80 1 .138 .198 .237	57 2 .140 .210 .281	28 1 .357 .400 .607
TOTALS	2728 64 .236 .279 .363	1331 29 .228 .267 .339	1397 35 .243 .290 .386	1004 28 .231 .268 .367	1724 36 .239 .285 .361	1134 27 .244 .287 .382	494 9 .209 .258 .324
■ Pat Sheridan BL/TR							
1984 KC-A	481 8 .283 .338 .399	233 3 .253 .319 .378	248 5 .310 .357 .419	58 1 .207 .246 .328	423 7 .293 .351 .409	203 4 .286 .348 .424	73 0 .301 .354 .384
1985 KC-A	206 3 .228 .307 .335	98 2 .286 .343 .418	108 1 .176 .276 .259	14 0 .071 .071 .143	192 3 .240 .323 .349	81 1 .185 .264 .284	43 0 .256 .340 .372
1986 Det-A	236 6 .237 .300 .360	111 3 .234 .303 .360	125 3 .240 .297 .360	26 0 .231 .286 .231	210 6 .238 .302 .376	106 1 .236 .297 .302	28 0 .179 .258 .250
1987 Det-A	421 6 .259 .327 .361	187 3 .278 .324 .396	234 3 .244 .330 .333	77 0 .195 .250 .234	344 6 .273 .344 .390	196 2 .270 .324 .367	55 1 .200 .262 .291
1988 Det-A	347 11 .254 .339 .417	163 7 .233 .321 .417	184 4 .272 .355 .391	26 1 .308 .379 .654	321 10 .249 .336 .383	147 5 .252 .313 .415	52 3 .327 .375 .538
1989 Det-A	120 3 .242 .333 .342	54 2 .241 .333 .389	66 1 .242 .333 .303	8 0 .125 .300 .125	112 3 .250 .336 .357	47 1 .255 .390 .340	18 0 .333 .368 .333
1989 SF-N	161 3 .205 .264 .329	81 1 .198 .278 .284	80 3 .213 .250 .375	13 0 .077 .077 .077	148 3 .216 .280 .351	65 0 .185 .221 .200	21 0 .143 .143 .143
1991 NY-A	113 4 .204 .286 .336	59 1 .288 .382 .424	54 2 .111 .172 .241	15 0 .200 .200 .200	98 4 .204 .297 .357	45 1 .222 .300 .311	23 1 .217 .357 .348
TOTALS	2085 44 .250 .320 .369	986 22 .253 .322 .385	1099 22 .247 .318 .355	237 2 .198 .248 .283	1848 42 .256 .329 .380	890 15 .249 .315 .356	313 5 .256 .319 .358
■ Ruben Sierra BB/TR							
1986 Tex-A	382 16 .264 .302 .476	172 8 .238 .256 .459	210 8 .286 .339 .490	99 4 .253 .269 .434	283 12 .269 .315 .491	169 6 .290 .335 .467	73 3 .329 .355 .603
1987 Tex-A	643 30 .263 .302 .470	315 15 .276 .323 .502	328 15 .250 .282 .439	237 12 .249 .267 .456	406 18 .271 .321 .478	316 15 .266 .295 .500	97 4 .227 .262 .392
1988 Tex-A	615 23 .254 .301 .424	299 15 .281 .336 .505	316 8 .228 .266 .348	193 8 .285 .305 .487	422 15 .239 .299 .396	301 13 .269 .321 .458	94 1 .223 .291 .277
1989 Tex-A	634 29 .306 .347 .543	309 21 .317 .356 .621	325 8 .295 .338 .468	205 10 .341 .378 .600	429 19 .289 .332 .515	319 15 .329 .364 .564	84 4 .310 .375 .548
1990 Tex-A	608 16 .280 .330 .426	301 10 .266 .317 .429	307 6 .293 .343 .423	216 3 .324 .361 .440	392 13 .255 .314 .418	279 8 .290 .362 .444	98 5 .296 .367 .510
1991 Tex-A	661 25 .307 .357 .502	328 12 .320 .353 .521	333 13 .294 .360 .483	188 7 .335 .393 .548	473 18 .296 .342 .484	341 14 .331 .366 .534	114 4 .289 .359 .456
1992 Tex-A	500 14 .278 .315 .446	239 8 .230 .267 .397	261 6 .322 .359 .490	145 3 .338 .376 .510	355 11 .254 .291 .420	248 8 .294 .337 .460	81 1 .198 .239 .272
1992 Oak-A	101 3 .277 .359 .426	55 2 .291 .361 .455	46 1 .261 .357 .391	26 2 .346 .433 .577	75 1 .253 .333 .373	45 3 .311 .421 .556	16 1 .313 .421 .563
1993 Oak-A	630 22 .233 .288 .390	306 9 .222 .280 .353	324 13 .244 .295 .426	199 8 .231 .297 .392	431 14 .234 .283 .390	309 16 .249 .318 .440	103 4 .252 .363 .398
1994 Oak-A	426 23 .268 .298 .484	208 11 .255 .303 .466	218 12 .280 .293 .500	156 10 .327 .374 .603	270 13 .233 .252 .415	207 14 .290 .307 .536	63 5 .302 .338 .571
TOTALS	5200 201 .273 .318 .461	2532 111 .271 .316 .476	2668 90 .275 .320 .447	1664 67 .299 .338 .497	3536 134 .261 .309 .444	2534 112 .291 .337 .492	823 32 .269 .332 .442
■ Don Slaught BR/TR							
1984 KC-A	409 4 .264 .297 .379	191 1 .304 .338 .429	218 3 .229 .259 .335	111 3 .324 .347 .523	298 1 .242 .278 .326	159 3 .252 .300 .371	65 1 .262 .282 .385
1985 Tex-A	343 8 .280 .331 .423	181 4 .293 .347 .436	162 4 .265 .312 .407	101 3 .287 .351 .426	242 5 .277 .322 .421	154 2 .279 .335 .390	62 1 .306 .338 .387
1986 Tex-A	314 13 .264 .308 .449	149 5 .302 .348 .477	165 8 .230 .271 .424	119 5 .303 .323 .504	195 8 .241 .299 .415	131 5 .313 .354 .481	48 4 .313 .365 .604
1987 Tex-A	237 8 .224 .298 .405	125 5 .256 .311 .432	112 3 .188 .283 .375	135 6 .237 .313 .459	102 2 .206 .277 .333	102 1 .186 .272 .275	49 1 .245 .315 .388
1988 NY-A	322 9 .283 .344 .450	172 7 .279 .330 .500	150 2 .287 .339 .393	116 3 .310 .377 .474	206 6 .267 .309 .437	140 1 .250 .288 .321	49 2 .265 .339 .449
1989 NY-A	350 5 .251 .315 .371	169 3 .278 .324 .420	181 2 .227 .307 .326	131 2 .237 .301 .405	219 3 .260 .324 .352	145 0 .255 .315 .324	66 0 .303 .361 .409
1990 Pit-N	230 4 .300 .375 .457	113 1 .274 .381 .425	117 3 .325 .369 .487	164 2 .317 .393 .457	66 2 .258 .329 .455	98 1 .306 .379 .418	42 1 .238 .333 .381
1991 Pit-N	220 1 .295 .363 .395	118 0 .322 .372 .415	102 1 .265 .353 .373	126 0 .262 .345 .341	94 1 .340 .388 .468	108 0 .241 .314 .324	39 1 .282 .391 .462
1992 Pit-N	255 4 .345 .384 .482	131 2 .336 .379 .511	124 2 .355 .388 .452	174 3 .322 .362 .437	81 1 .395 .429 .580	126 1 .349 .383 .460	52 0 .308 .356 .365
1993 Pit-N	377 10 .300 .356 .440	183 1 .284 .333 .388	194 9 .314 .377 .490	120 2 .333 .374 .458	257 8 .284 .347 .432	186 6 .355 .412 .516	81 3 .321 .396 .469
1994 Pit-N	240 2 .287 .381 .342	132 1 .258 .351 .318	108 1 .324 .417 .370	60 0 .367 .457 .433	180 2 .261 .356 .311	111 1 .270 .393 .306	40 0 .325 .391 .375
TOTALS	3297 68 .280 .337 .417	1664 30 .290 .345 .433	1633 38 .270 .329 .401	1357 29 .297 .355 .447	1940 39 .268 .324 .396	1460 21 .282 .342 .388	593 14 .290 .352 .425
■ Roy Smalley BB/TR							
1984 NY-A	209 7 .239 .286 .388	105 4 .238 .296 .371	104 3 .240 .277 .404	53 2 .170 .254 .302	156 5 .263 .298 .417	100 0 .180 .234 .220	53 2 .226 .288 .358
1984 Min-A	135 4 .170 .285 .289	68 4 .191 .309 .397	67 0 .149 .260 .179	31 0 .097 .152 .097	104 4 .192 .320 .346	52 2 .250 .365 .423	28 0 .107 .219 .143
1985 Min-A	388 12 .258 .357 .402	201 7 .249 .348 .408	187 5 .267 .367 .396	72 0 .236 .349 .333	316 12 .263 .359 .418	161 2 .286 .384 .398	60 1 .183 .286 .267
1986 Min-A	459 20 .246 .342 .438	222 9 .266 .368 .464	237 11 .228 .317 .414	58 2 .138 .250 .310	401 18 .262 .356 .456	196 5 .260 .377 .398	68 0 .176 .300 .265
1987 Min-A	309 8 .275 .352 .411	140 5 .271 .342 .436	169 3 .278 .359 .391	24 1 .250 .280 .375	285 7 .277 .357 .414	125 3 .240 .329 .376	58 0 .259 .306 .310
TOTALS	1500 51 .247 .335 .403	736 29 .251 .342 .424	764 22 .243 .329 .382	238 5 .181 .273 .294	1262 46 .260 .347 .423	634 12 .249 .347 .368	267 3 .199 .287 .281
■ Dwight Smith BL/TR							
1989 Chi-N	343 9 .324 .382 .493	157 5 .363 .423 .541	186 4 .290 .347 .452	29 1 .241 .324 .414	314 8 .331 .388 .500	162 5 .321 .366 .500	49 1 .245 .269 .388
1990 Chi-N	290 6 .262 .329 .376	131 3 .252 .317 .382	159 3 .270 .339 .371	36 1 .222 .263 .361	254 5 .268 .338 .378	122 0 .279 .353 .328	52 2 .288 .345 .462
1991 Chi-N	167 3 .228 .279 .347	95 2 .253 .297 .379	72 1 .194 .256 .306	5 0 .000 .167 .000	162 3 .235 .283 .358	71 2 .310 .380 .465	44 0 .182 .217 .273
1992 Chi-N	217 3 .276 .318 .392	100 3 .290 .339 .430	117 0 .265 .298 .359	20 1 .200 .200 .350	197 2 .284 .329 .396	93 0 .312 .359 .398	64 1 .250 .304 .344
1993 Chi-N	310 11 .300 .355 .494	146 6 .377 .440 .637	164 5 .232 .274 .366	11 0 .364 .462 .636	299 11 .298 .351 .488	98 3 .296 .339 .480	43 1 .279 .333 .372
1994 Cal-N	122 5 .262 .300 .443	66 2 .182 .229 .303	56 3 .357 .383 .607	5 0 .200 .375 .200	117 5 .265 .295 .453	50 1 .260 .309 .360	21 0 .190 .227 .238
1994 Bal-A	74 3 .311 .363 .486	32 0 .344 .400 .438	42 3 .286 .333 .524	3 0 .667 .750 .667	71 3 .296 .342 .479	39 2 .333 .366 .590	13 0 .385 .467 .385
TOTALS	1523 40 .284 .339 .436	727 21 .304 .362 .469	796 19 .266 .317 .406	109 3 .239 .309 .385	1414 37 .288 .341 .440	635 13 .302 .355 .439	286 5 .252 .300 .360
■ Lonnie Smith BR/TR							
1984 StL-N	504 6 .250 .349 .341	232 3 .241 .364 .345	272 3 .257 .336 .338	159 2 .245 .342 .352	345 4 .252 .352 .336	179 1 .268 .386 .369	66 0 .227 .427 .258
1985 StL-N	96 0 .260 .377 .323	49 0 .306 .414 .408	47 0 .213 .339 .234	34 0 .265 .405 .324	62 0 .258 .361 .323	39 0 .179 .256 .308	16 0 .188 .381 .188
1985 KC-A	448 6 .257 .321 .366	225 2 .231 .307 .338	223 4 .283 .336 .395	140 2 .293 .350 .414	308 4 .240 .308 .344	169 3 .249 .330 .402	66 0 .212 .297 .333
1986 KC-A	508 8 .287 .357 .411	243 2 .317 .390 .432	265 6 .260 .327 .392	149 2 .309 .360 .443	359 6 .279 .356 .398	187 2 .305 .374 .433	83 1 .277 .326 .349
1987 KC-A	167 3 .251 .355 .359	81 1 .259 .365 .346	86 2 .244 .347 .372	50 2 .280 .400 .380	117 1 .239 .336 .350	53 0 .226 .338 .283	22 0 .091 .231 .182
1988 Atl-N	114 3 .237 .296 .342	59 2 .237 .292 .373	55 1 .236 .300 .309	79 3 .253 .306 .405	35 0 .200 .275 .200	36 1 .278 .325 .361	13 0 .152 .222 .182
1989 Atl-N	482 21 .315 .415 .533	226 10 .358 .442 .597	256 11 .277 .392 .477	165 7 .321 .429 .564	317 14 .312 .408 .517	189 6 .407 .496 .630	67 3 .269 .398 .463
1990 Atl-N	466 9 .305 .384 .459	231 2 .312 .390 .442	235 7 .298 .379 .477	197 6 .294 .365 .487	269 3 .312 .397 .439	153 2 .281 .389 .405	61 2 .328 .425 .525
1991 Atl-N	353 7 .275 .377 .394	193 6 .290 .394 .435	160 1 .256 .356 .350	115 0 .339 .435 .435	238 7 .244 .348 .374	139 3 .288 .384 .403	56 2 .232 .368 .286
1992 Atl-N	158 6 .247 .324 .437	71 3 .239 .333 .437	87 3 .253 .316 .437	65 3 .277 .347 .508	93 3 .226 .308 .387	74 4 .297 .378 .554	42 2 .167 .288 .357
1993 Pit-N	199 6 .286 .422 .442	90 4 .300 .432 .467	109 2 .275 .413 .422	120 3 .300 .414 .417	79 3 .266 .433 .481	76 1 .250 .398 .355	45 2 .267 .459 .467
1993 Bal-A	24 2 .208 .406 .500	9 2 .444 .583 1.111	15 0 .067 .300 .133	12 1 .333 .529 .833	12 1 .083 .267 .167	12 0 .250 .471 .333	4 0 .250 .250 .500
1994 Bal-A	59 0 .203 .333 .254	39 0 .256 .408 .333	20 0 .100 .174 .100	42 0 .286 .404 .357	17 0 .000 .150 .000	30 0 .133 .229 .133	6 0 .167 .286 .167
TOTALS	3578 77 .275 .366 .411	1748 37 .287 .379 .428	1830 40 .264 .354 .394	1327 30 .293 .381 .444	2251 47 .265 .357 .391	1336 22 .287 .385 .425	567 10 .236 .360 .351
■ Ozzie Smith BB/TR							
1984 StL-N	412 1 .257 .347 .337	176 1 .244 .304 .313	236 0 .267 .376 .356	118 1 .305 .424 .415	294 0 .238 .313 .306	186 1 .258 .344 .339	63 1 .270 .338 .397
1985 StL-N	537 6 .276 .355 .361	258 2 .298 .389 .388	279 4 .254 .321 .337	161 6 .298 .407 .484	376 0 .266 .330 .309	227 2 .295 .386 .357	97 1 .268 .349 .340
1986 StL-N	514 0 .280 .376 .333	254 0 .287 .400 .346	260 0 .273 .352 .319	203 0 .276 .370 .315	311 0 .283 .380 .344	193 0 .295 .414 .363	104 0 .279 .400 .375
1987 StL-N	600 0 .303 .392 .383	286 0 .287 .375 .371	314 0 .318 .408 .395	220 0 .250 .346 .318	380 0 .334 .419 .421	260 0 .308 .385 .400	97 0 .294 .397 .353
1988 StL-N	575 3 .270 .350 .336	288 2 .278 .366 .344	287 1 .261 .334 .328	201 2 .259 .355 .343	374 1 .275 .348 .332	210 2 .314 .406 .405	107 2 .243 .308 .318
1989 StL-N	593 2 .273 .335 .361	297 1 .253 .323 .330	296 1 .294 .348 .392	248 1 .286 .346 .383	345 1 .264 .328 .345	239 0 .301 .366 .368	83 1 .361 .449 .506
1990 StL-N	512 1 .254 .330 .305	256 1 .266 .347 .332	256 0 .242 .313 .277	201 1 .289 .347 .373	311 0 .232 .319 .260	217 0 .258 .321 .290	81 0 .185 .263 .235
1991 StL-N	550 3 .285 .380 .367	291 3 .323 .416 .416	259 0 .243 .336 .313	248 3 .262 .356 .387	302 0 .305 .399 .351	217 2 .300 .381 .410	76 0 .237 .379 .276
1992 StL-N	518 0 .295 .367 .342	278 0 .335 .396 .378	240 0 .250 .333 .300	202 0 .272 .339 .332	316 0 .310 .384 .348	196 0 .265 .364 .296	113 0 .265 .349 .283
1993 StL-N	545 1 .288 .337 .356	288 1 .299 .357 .375	257 0 .276 .331 .334	150 1 .320 .354 .413	395 0 .276 .331 .334	248 1 .302 .326 .395	93 0 .323 .347 .441
1994 StL-N	381 3 .262 .326 .349	183 1 .284 .343 .377	198 2 .242 .311 .323	126 2 .262 .309 .389	255 1 .263 .335 .329	155 0 .265 .337 .329	54 1 .204 .290 .296
TOTALS	5737 20 .278 .355 .349	2855 10 .288 .368 .362	2882 10 .268 .343 .336	2078 17 .278 .358 .372	3659 3 .278 .354 .336	2348 8 .289 .367 .362	973 5 .269 .355 .347
■ Cory Snyder BR/TR							
1986 Cle-A	416 24 .272 .299 .500	186 12 .280 .309 .532	230 12 .265 .290 .474	118 6 .322 .333 .585	298 16 .252 .285 .466	190 11 .274 .296 .500	61 2 .262 .297 .426
1987 Cle-A	577 33 .236 .273 .456	276 17 .214 .255 .442	301 16 .256 .290 .468	163 5 .221 .271 .399	414 28 .242 .274 .478	232 10 .216 .266 .397	89 9 .292 .304 .652
1988 Cle-A	511 26 .272 .326 .483	270 11 .233 .283 .396	241 15 .315 .374 .581	111 9 .342 .400 .667	400 17 .253 .305 .433	218 12 .266 .328 .495	78 8 .256 .310 .603
1989 Cle-A	489 18 .215 .251 .360	246 6 .207 .244 .350	243 12 .222 .258 .370	135 4 .222 .291 .370	303 10 .238 .256 .419	216 8 .227 .260 .361	90 0 .141 .150 .162
1990 Cle-A	438 14 .233 .268 .404	196 3 .235 .287 .357	242 11 .231 .251 .442	135 4 .222 .291 .370	303 10 .238 .256 .419	219 7 .251 .295 .420	78 2 .218 .256 .410
1991 Chi-A	117 3 .188 .228 .299	56 2 .196 .237 .357	61 1 .180 .219 .246	93 3 .183 .208 .323	24 0 .208 .296 .208	55 0 .145 .203 .182	22 1 .318 .400 .500
1991 Tor-N	49 0 .143 .184 .184	16 0 .133 .188 .133	33 0 .147 .180 .206	23 0 .087 .125 .087	26 0 .192 .241 .269	21 0 .190 .182 .286	16 0 .188 .235 .188
1992 SF-N	390 14 .269 .311 .444	184 8 .299 .342 .505	206 6 .243 .283 .388	170 6 .294 .331 .471	220 8 .250 .295 .423	182 5 .264 .312 .407	79 2 .228 .271 .405
1993 LA-N	516 11 .266 .331 .397	256 5 .266 .335 .379	260 6 .265 .327 .415	151 3 .265 .333 .397	365 8 .266 .330 .397	218 4 .280 .355 .408	90 1 .267 .353 .389

		TOTAL					HOME					AWAY					LEFT					RIGHT					ON-BASE					LATE/CLOSE				
YEAR	TM/L	AB	HR	AVG	OBP	SLG	AB	HR	AVG	OBP	SLG	AB	HR	AVG	OBP	SLG	AB	HR	AVG	OBP	SLG	AB	HR	AVG	OBP	SLG	AB	HR	AVG	OBP	SLG	AB	HR	AVG	OBP	SLG
1994	LA-N	153	6	.235	.300	.392	64	1	.250	.351	.328	89	5	.225	.258	.438	100	5	.250	.300	.440	53	1	.208	.300	.302	67	5	.269	.363	.507	33	0	.152	.200	.182
TOTALS		3656	149	.247	.291	.425	1749	65	.242	.291	.407	1907	84	.251	.291	.441	1228	53	.258	.308	.448	2428	96	.241	.282	.413	1618	62	.249	.299	.419	645	25	.233	.276	.412

■ Sammy Sosa BR/TR

YEAR	TM/L	AB	HR	AVG	OBP	SLG	AB	HR	AVG	OBP	SLG	AB	HR	AVG	OBP	SLG	AB	HR	AVG	OBP	SLG	AB	HR	AVG	OBP	SLG	AB	HR	AVG	OBP	SLG	AB	HR	AVG	OBP	SLG
1989	Tex-A	84	1	.238	.238	.310	24	0	.375	.375	.375	60	1	.183	.183	.283	44	0	.318	.318	.364	40	1	.150	.150	.250	25	0	.280	.280	.280	13	0	.231	.231	.308
1989	Chi-A	99	3	.273	.351	.414	43	1	.233	.327	.349	56	2	.304	.371	.464	34	2	.382	.465	.647	65	1	.215	.282	.292	48	1	.250	.321	.375	13	0	.154	.313	.231
1990	Chi-A	532	15	.233	.282	.404	266	10	.256	.314	.477	266	5	.211	.251	.331	233	12	.262	.316	.502	299	3	.211	.255	.328	221	6	.240	.281	.425	82	0	.183	.256	.207
1991	Chi-A	316	10	.203	.240	.335	145	3	.186	.222	.297	171	7	.216	.256	.368	128	5	.227	.277	.383	188	5	.186	.214	.303	132	6	.235	.277	.409	69	3	.275	.296	.493
1992	Chi-N	262	8	.260	.317	.393	116	4	.267	.344	.440	146	4	.253	.295	.356	75	0	.280	.353	.320	187	8	.251	.302	.422	93	4	.258	.324	.441	51	1	.216	.298	.333
1993	Chi-N	598	33	.261	.309	.485	298	23	.272	.323	.557	300	10	.250	.295	.413	150	10	.287	.344	.567	448	23	.251	.312	.483	267	15	.251	.312	.483	103	2	.214	.264	.282
1994	Chi-N	426	25	.300	.339	.545	228	11	.285	.331	.518	198	14	.318	.349	.576	113	9	.336	.395	.619	313	16	.288	.318	.518	204	9	.275	.303	.486	72	4	.250	.282	.486
TOTALS		2317	95	.253	.300	.437	1120	52	.260	.313	.472	1197	43	.247	.287	.404	777	38	.282	.338	.493	1540	57	.239	.280	.409	990	41	.253	.299	.442	403	10	.223	.276	.345

■ Bill Spiers BL/TR

YEAR	TM/L	AB	HR	AVG	OBP	SLG	AB	HR	AVG	OBP	SLG	AB	HR	AVG	OBP	SLG	AB	HR	AVG	OBP	SLG	AB	HR	AVG	OBP	SLG	AB	HR	AVG	OBP	SLG	AB	HR	AVG	OBP	SLG
1989	Mil-A	345	4	.255	.298	.333	172	1	.273	.298	.343	173	3	.237	.298	.324	70	1	.271	.282	.371	275	3	.251	.302	.324	135	1	.267	.303	.370	50	0	.240	.309	.260
1990	Mil-A	363	2	.242	.274	.317	176	2	.267	.305	.375	187	0	.219	.245	.262	81	0	.235	.279	.296	282	2	.245	.273	.323	143	1	.231	.276	.322	69	0	.261	.264	.275
1991	Mil-A	414	8	.283	.337	.401	187	1	.299	.370	.369	227	7	.269	.309	.427	117	2	.222	.305	.282	297	6	.306	.350	.448	176	5	.318	.371	.466	72	1	.347	.415	.500
1992	Mil-A	16	0	.313	.353	.438	6	0	.667	.667	1.000	10	0	.100	.182	.100	3	0	.000	.000	.000	13	0	.385	.429	.538	4	0	.500	.500	1.000					
1993	Mil-A	340	2	.238	.302	.303	166	2	.277	.344	.367	174	0	.201	.262	.241	68	0	.176	.273	.235	272	2	.254	.310	.320	147	0	.231	.312	.286	56	0	.250	.311	.304
1994	Mil-A	214	0	.252	.316	.308	86	0	.291	.344	.326	128	0	.227	.298	.297	35	0	.114	.184	.114	179	0	.279	.342	.346	96	0	.271	.327	.313	40	0	.250	.268	.300
TOTALS		1692	16	.256	.306	.338	793	6	.284	.334	.364	899	10	.231	.281	.315	374	3	.214	.276	.275	1318	13	.268	.315	.350	701	7	.265	.320	.359	289	1	.277	.323	.343

■ Ed Sprague BR/TR

YEAR	TM/L	AB	HR	AVG	OBP	SLG	AB	HR	AVG	OBP	SLG	AB	HR	AVG	OBP	SLG	AB	HR	AVG	OBP	SLG	AB	HR	AVG	OBP	SLG	AB	HR	AVG	OBP	SLG	AB	HR	AVG	OBP	SLG
1991	Tor-A	160	4	.275	.361	.394	77	3	.286	.329	.429	83	1	.265	.386	.361	90	3	.267	.347	.400	70	1	.286	.378	.386	64	3	.313	.384	.500	14	0	.214	.450	.286
1992	Tor-A	47	1	.234	.280	.340	24	1	.167	.231	.292	23	0	.304	.333	.391	10	0	.400	.455	.500	37	1	.189	.231	.297	21	1	.238	.304	.429	8	1	.250	.250	.625
1993	Tor-A	546	12	.260	.310	.386	268	6	.291	.328	.463	278	4	.230	.293	.313	146	2	.247	.304	.363	400	10	.265	.312	.395	270	3	.241	.299	.326	70	0	.257	.303	.300
1994	Tor-A	405	11	.240	.296	.373	210	6	.243	.306	.367	195	5	.236	.285	.379	118	3	.288	.356	.441	287	8	.220	.270	.345	188	4	.218	.278	.340	63	1	.238	.258	.333
TOTALS		1158	28	.254	.311	.381	579	18	.268	.316	.416	579	10	.240	.306	.345	364	8	.269	.336	.401	794	20	.247	.300	.372	543	11	.241	.302	.355	155	2	.245	.300	.329

■ Terry Steinbach BR/TR

YEAR	TM/L	AB	HR	AVG	OBP	SLG	AB	HR	AVG	OBP	SLG	AB	HR	AVG	OBP	SLG	AB	HR	AVG	OBP	SLG	AB	HR	AVG	OBP	SLG	AB	HR	AVG	OBP	SLG	AB	HR	AVG	OBP	SLG
1986	Oak-A	15	2	.333	.375	.733	4	0	.250	.400	.250	11	2	.364	.364	.909	6	2	.500	.500	1.500	9	0	.222	.300	.222	5	1	.600	.600	1.200	4	1	.500	.500	1.250
1987	Oak-A	391	16	.284	.349	.463	175	6	.234	.308	.360	216	10	.324	.384	.546	137	5	.292	.359	.504	254	11	.280	.344	.441	171	6	.316	.368	.503	71	3	.282	.346	.423
1988	Oak-A	351	9	.265	.334	.402	171	6	.287	.347	.439	180	3	.244	.322	.367	114	2	.342	.400	.421	237	7	.228	.302	.392	153	4	.281	.347	.431	58	0	.138	.242	.172
1989	Oak-A	454	7	.273	.319	.352	216	5	.292	.328	.384	238	2	.256	.312	.324	159	3	.258	.298	.352	295	4	.281	.330	.353	189	3	.238	.283	.317	59	2	.237	.292	.356
1990	Oak-A	379	9	.251	.291	.372	185	4	.249	.302	.324	194	6	.253	.281	.418	109	3	.284	.336	.440	270	6	.237	.273	.344	178	5	.270	.300	.388	66	0	.242	.271	.273
1991	Oak-A	456	6	.274	.312	.386	220	1	.277	.314	.377	236	5	.271	.310	.394	139	2	.266	.302	.410	317	3	.278	.316	.375	217	3	.276	.317	.392	86	0	.291	.340	.326
1992	Oak-A	438	12	.279	.345	.411	214	3	.229	.301	.313	224	9	.326	.386	.504	110	5	.300	.361	.482	328	7	.271	.340	.387	209	4	.306	.368	.426	50	0	.180	.268	.180
1993	Oak-A	389	10	.285	.333	.416	184	4	.326	.377	.489	205	6	.249	.292	.351	108	6	.296	.350	.500	281	4	.281	.326	.384	170	5	.259	.328	.406	67	1	.209	.284	.299
1994	Oak-A	369	11	.285	.327	.442	172	6	.302	.340	.471	197	5	.269	.315	.416	140	6	.343	.394	.564	229	5	.249	.285	.367	163	5	.344	.386	.528	57	1	.211	.262	.298
TOTALS		3242	82	.275	.327	.406	1541	34	.274	.326	.391	1701	48	.276	.327	.419	1022	35	.297	.349	.463	2220	47	.264	.316	.379	1455	36	.287	.337	.423	518	8	.232	.294	.305

■ Kurt Stillwell BB/TR

YEAR	TM/L	AB	HR	AVG	OBP	SLG	AB	HR	AVG	OBP	SLG	AB	HR	AVG	OBP	SLG	AB	HR	AVG	OBP	SLG	AB	HR	AVG	OBP	SLG	AB	HR	AVG	OBP	SLG	AB	HR	AVG	OBP	SLG
1986	Cin-N	279	0	.229	.309	.258	151	0	.219	.298	.245	128	0	.242	.322	.273	86	0	.244	.363	.279	193	0	.223	.282	.249	119	0	.252	.310	.286	53	0	.189	.232	.226
1987	Cin-N	395	4	.258	.316	.375	150	3	.260	.323	.433	245	1	.257	.311	.339	97	0	.227	.286	.289	298	4	.268	.325	.403	157	3	.299	.353	.459	68	0	.250	.303	.309
1988	KC-A	459	10	.251	.322	.398	249	4	.257	.320	.398	210	6	.243	.325	.400	124	2	.226	.299	.323	335	8	.260	.331	.427	169	5	.308	.362	.491	68	0	.265	.290	.294
1989	KC-A	463	7	.261	.325	.380	217	6	.226	.293	.309	246	5	.293	.353	.443	121	1	.264	.336	.364	342	6	.260	.321	.386	201	3	.308	.345	.443	61	0	.197	.296	.230
1990	KC-A	506	3	.249	.304	.352	254	3	.268	.319	.413	252	0	.230	.289	.290	128	0	.211	.302	.313	378	3	.262	.305	.365	229	2	.284	.321	.410	81	1	.247	.287	.333
1991	KC-A	385	6	.265	.322	.361	183	1	.257	.324	.339	202	5	.272	.320	.381	109	1	.266	.304	.367	276	5	.264	.328	.359	190	4	.284	.343	.389	75	1	.187	.299	.213
1992	SD-N	379	2	.227	.274	.298	191	0	.220	.274	.277	188	1	.234	.275	.319	112	1	.250	.289	.321	267	1	.217	.268	.288	150	1	.220	.276	.267	71	0	.225	.282	.296
1993	SD-N	121	1	.215	.286	.273	56	1	.232	.328	.321	65	0	.200	.246	.231	21	0	.143	.280	.143	100	1	.230	.287	.300	55	0	.218	.295	.255	34	1	.088	.162	.176
1993	Cal-A	61	0	.262	.299	.361	28	0	.286	.323	.357	33	0	.242	.278	.364	4	0	.250	.250	.250	57	0	.263	.302	.368	20	0	.150	.240	.150	14	0	.214	.250	.214
TOTALS		3048	33	.249	.310	.349	1479	15	.245	.309	.349	1569	18	.252	.310	.349	802	5	.238	.309	.319	2246	28	.252	.310	.360	1290	18	.278	.330	.390	525	2	.215	.292	.242

■ Darryl Strawberry BL/TL

YEAR	TM/L	AB	HR	AVG	OBP	SLG	AB	HR	AVG	OBP	SLG	AB	HR	AVG	OBP	SLG	AB	HR	AVG	OBP	SLG	AB	HR	AVG	OBP	SLG	AB	HR	AVG	OBP	SLG	AB	HR	AVG	OBP	SLG
1984	NY-N	522	26	.251	.343	.467	242	8	.215	.309	.393	280	18	.282	.372	.532	167	6	.222	.278	.359	355	20	.265	.371	.518	249	14	.285	.391	.522	85	3	.259	.376	.400
1985	NY-N	393	29	.277	.389	.557	188	14	.298	.399	.585	205	15	.259	.381	.532	156	11	.256	.348	.506	237	18	.291	.414	.591	178	11	.303	.420	.545	66	6	.227	.358	.545
1986	NY-N	475	27	.259	.358	.507	211	11	.227	.324	.445	264	16	.284	.385	.557	187	5	.209	.296	.353	288	22	.292	.396	.608	240	14	.292	.383	.542	94	4	.255	.333	.447
1987	NY-N	532	39	.284	.398	.583	264	20	.322	.418	.629	268	19	.246	.380	.537	230	16	.248	.330	.517	302	23	.311	.446	.632	236	23	.314	.447	.695	84	3	.202	.340	.333
1988	NY-N	543	39	.269	.366	.545	253	21	.265	.375	.581	290	18	.272	.357	.514	216	20	.250	.318	.560	327	19	.281	.395	.535	256	20	.258	.376	.527	79	3	.190	.340	.329
1989	NY-N	476	29	.225	.312	.466	224	15	.272	.355	.549	252	14	.183	.274	.393	178	9	.219	.279	.438	298	20	.228	.331	.483	224	11	.232	.337	.464	82	3	.134	.228	.293
1990	NY-N	542	37	.277	.361	.518	268	18	.254	.332	.549	274	19	.299	.388	.489	217	9	.244	.300	.498	325	28	.298	.398	.594	262	18	.271	.378	.504	88	5	.239	.356	.432
1991	LA-N	505	28	.265	.361	.491	257	14	.284	.374	.510	248	14	.246	.347	.472	228	11	.276	.370	.478	277	17	.256	.353	.502	252	15	.302	.389	.540	91	3	.264	.346	.407
1992	LA-N	156	5	.237	.322	.385	72	3	.278	.366	.458	84	2	.202	.284	.321	66	2	.242	.324	.348	90	3	.233	.320	.411	78	5	.295	.391	.526	25	2	.200	.333	.440
1993	LA-N	100	5	.140	.267	.310	38	3	.158	.227	.421	62	2	.129	.289	.242	21	0	.143	.367	.190	79	5	.139	.233	.342	47	2	.106	.279	.234	15	0	.067	.333	.067
1994	SF-N	92	4	.239	.363	.424	44	2	.182	.307	.341	48	2	.292	.397	.500	29	1	.207	.310	.310	63	3	.254	.380	.476	34	1	.206	.396	.324	9	0	.000	.333	.000
TOTALS		4336	268	.259	.358	.505	2061	135	.264	.358	.523	2275	133	.255	.357	.490	1695	90	.240	.318	.446	2641	178	.271	.381	.531	2056	134	.277	.387	.531	717	32	.216	.335	.386

■ Franklin Stubbs BL/TL

YEAR	TM/L	AB	HR	AVG	OBP	SLG	AB	HR	AVG	OBP	SLG	AB	HR	AVG	OBP	SLG	AB	HR	AVG	OBP	SLG	AB	HR	AVG	OBP	SLG	AB	HR	AVG	OBP	SLG	AB	HR	AVG	OBP	SLG
1984	LA-N	217	8	.194	.273	.341	111	4	.216	.313	.351	106	4	.170	.228	.330	45	1	.200	.213	.267	172	7	.192	.287	.360	88	4	.170	.282	.352	35	1	.143	.318	.286
1985	LA-N	9	0	.222	.222	.222	5	0	.200	.200	.200	4	0	.250	.250	.250	2	0	.000	.000	.000	7	0	.286	.286	.286	6	0	.167	.167	.167	5	0	.400	.400	.400
1986	LA-N	420	23	.226	.291	.421	195	12	.262	.318	.482	225	11	.196	.267	.369	97	4	.227	.250	.381	323	19	.226	.302	.433	187	8	.225	.326	.390	66	3	.242	.359	.424
1987	LA-N	386	16	.233	.290	.415	209	6	.167	.221	.287	177	10	.311	.371	.565	86	0	.186	.205	.186	300	16	.247	.313	.480	159	8	.289	.350	.503	63	3	.175	.278	.349
1988	LA-N	242	8	.223	.288	.376	127	3	.220	.284	.323	115	5	.226	.292	.435	27	0	.185	.214	.222	215	8	.228	.296	.395	108	3	.213	.268	.343	47	2	.170	.264	.319
1989	LA-N	103	4	.291	.387	.466	63	1	.317	.394	.429	40	3	.250	.375	.525	14	1	.286	.333	.500	89	3	.292	.394	.461	53	4	.321	.410	.604	21	0	.238	.333	.238
1990	Hou-N	448	23	.261	.334	.475	229	9	.253	.327	.445	219	14	.269	.342	.507	159	9	.258	.300	.465	289	16	.263	.352	.481	204	12	.240	.326	.456	86	7	.360	.402	.686
1991	Mil-A	362	11	.213	.266	.368	183	8	.219	.304	.410	179	3	.207	.259	.307	87	2	.218	.236	.368	275	9	.211	.295	.356	167	4	.210	.302	.359	72	0	.181	.253	.222
1992	Mil-A	288	9	.229	.297	.368	101	3	.198	.268	.297	187	6	.246	.312	.406	43	1	.256	.356	.395	245	8	.227	.290	.363	118	4	.297	.400	.475	65	3	.200	.246	.369
TOTALS		2475	102	.232	.300	.404	1223	46	.226	.297	.383	1252	56	.236	.303	.425	560	16	.227	.253	.359	1915	86	.233	.313	.418	1090	47	.241	.327	.419	460	19	.226	.310	.393

■ Jim Sundberg BR/TR

YEAR	TM/L	AB	HR	AVG	OBP	SLG	AB	HR	AVG	OBP	SLG	AB	HR	AVG	OBP	SLG	AB	HR	AVG	OBP	SLG	AB	HR	AVG	OBP	SLG	AB	HR	AVG	OBP	SLG	AB	HR	AVG	OBP	SLG
1984	Mil-A	348	7	.261	.332	.399	174	4	.236	.302	.362	174	3	.287	.360	.437	121	2	.298	.386	.455	227	5	.242	.301	.370	140	4	.321	.376	.536	59	1	.254	.338	.356
1985	KC-A	367	10	.245	.308	.381	188	2	.250	.294	.340	179	8	.240	.322	.425	115	7	.217	.268	.452	252	3	.258	.325	.349	138	2	.254	.323	.348	61	2	.377	.381	.525
1986	KC-A	429	12	.212	.303	.322	209	5	.196	.278	.287	220	7	.227	.325	.355	141	6	.191	.272	.348	288	6	.222	.317	.309	184	6	.228	.322	.337	77	1	.260	.337	.351
1987	Chi-N	139	4	.201	.306	.302	68	2	.206	.310	.309	71	2	.197	.296	.296	23	1	.261	.414	.435	116	3	.190	.282	.276	58	2	.241	.343	.362	28	1	.214	.290	.357
1988	Chi-N	54	2	.241	.333	.370	20	1	.150	.250	.300	34	1	.294	.385	.412	4	1	.250	.250	1.000	50	1	.240	.346	.320	32	0	.250	.324	.281	10	0	.100	.182	.100
1988	Tex-A	91	4	.286	.323	.462	43	1	.209	.244	.302	48	3	.354	.392	.604	35	2	.314	.351	.514	56	2	.268	.305	.429	41	0	.244	.262	.268	21	2	.333	.364	.667
1989	Tex-A	147	2	.197	.304	.299	65	2	.108	.244	.231	82	0	.268	.355	.354	80	1	.262	.366	.412	67	1	.119	.231	.164	55	0	.145	.284	.164	22	0	.182	.217	.227
TOTALS		1575	41	.234	.313	.359	767	17	.211	.285	.316	808	24	.255	.339	.400	519	20	.245	.328	.426	1056	21	.228	.305	.326	648	14	.250	.329	.363	278	7	.273	.329	.396

■ B.J. Surhoff BL/TR

YEAR	TM/L	AB	HR	AVG	OBP	SLG	AB	HR	AVG	OBP	SLG	AB	HR	AVG	OBP	SLG	AB	HR	AVG	OBP	SLG	AB	HR	AVG	OBP	SLG	AB	HR	AVG	OBP	SLG	AB	HR	AVG	OBP	SLG
1987	Mil-A	395	7	.299	.350	.423	194	5	.314	.355	.464	201	2	.284	.345	.383	85	2	.318	.379	.424	310	5	.294	.342	.423	180	4	.333	.374	.467	72	2	.306	.381	.431
1988	Mil-A	493	5	.245	.292	.318	244	2	.225	.294	.319	249	3	.265	.291	.345	115	2	.191	.256	.270	378	3	.262	.304	.333	203	2	.276	.342	.350	75	0	.187	.274	.227
1989	Mil-A	436	5	.248	.287	.339	213	4	.239	.302	.333	223	1	.256	.272	.345	84	2	.310	.314	.452	352	3	.233	.281	.313	181	2	.260	.284	.354	70	1	.271	.289	.357
1990	Mil-A	474	6	.276	.331	.376	235	4	.306	.364	.417	239	2	.247	.298	.335	104	2	.317	.353	.433	370	4	.265	.324	.359	198	2	.288	.336	.404	69	0	.232	.289	.304
1991	Mil-A	505	5	.289	.319	.372	236	3	.267	.303	.364	269	2	.309	.332	.379	102	0	.255	.291	.294	403	5	.298	.326	.392	232	0	.323	.346	.384	88	2	.284	.323	.398
1992	Mil-A	480	4	.252	.314	.321	243	4	.280	.349	.383	237	1	.224	.278	.291	126	2	.270	.329	.357	354	2	.246	.309	.308	218	2	.280	.343	.362	93	2	.247	.297	.333
1993	Mil-A	552	7	.274	.318	.391	263	4	.289	.325	.422	289	3	.260	.311	.363	186	3	.274	.328	.403	366	4	.273	.312	.385	223	1	.283	.335	.390	91	1	.253	.300	.297
1994	Mil-A	134	5	.261	.336	.485	79	2	.253	.333	.468	55	3	.273	.342	.509	51	3	.392	.440	.618	83	2	.205	.280	.402	62	2	.306	.348	.500	24	2	.250	.357	.583
TOTALS		3469	44	.268	.318	.367	1707	26	.273	.328	.379	1762	18	.264	.305	.355	836	15	.275	.324	.384	2633	29	.266	.314	.362	1497	15	.293	.339	.391	582	10	.254	.310	.345

■ Pat Tabler BR/TR

YEAR	TM/L	AB	HR	AVG	OBP	SLG	AB	HR	AVG	OBP	SLG	AB	HR	AVG	OBP	SLG	AB	HR	AVG	OBP	SLG	AB	HR	AVG	OBP	SLG	AB	HR	AVG	OBP	SLG	AB	HR	AVG	OBP	SLG
1984	Cle-A	473	10	.290	.354	.410	223	5	.336	.405	.466	250	5	.248	.308	.360	159	3	.283	.370	.403	314	7	.293	.346	.414	235	0	.306	.366	.447	67	2	.254	.333	.373
1985	Cle-A	404	5	.275	.321	.371	218	5	.325	.369	.473	186	0	.215	.269	.285	154	3	.312	.352	.416	250	2	.252	.301	.344	179	3	.302	.382	.413	62	1	.290	.362	.484
1986	Cle-A	473	6	.326	.368	.433	227	5	.348	.389	.467	246	1	.305	.347	.402	150	2	.333	.387	.447	323	4	.322	.359	.427	204	5	.324	.379	.431	74	5	.284	.354	.419
1987	Cle-A	553	11	.307	.369	.439	285	5	.333	.394	.481	268	6	.280	.342	.396	172	6	.366	.412	.564	381	5	.281	.350	.383	270	5	.356	.421	.459	82	2	.293	.372	.378

YEAR TM/L	TOTAL AB	HR	AVG	OBP	SLG	HOME AB	HR	AVG	OBP	SLG	AWAY AB	HR	AVG	OBP	SLG	LEFT AB	HR	AVG	OBP	SLG	RIGHT AB	HR	AVG	OBP	SLG	ON-BASE AB	HR	AVG	OBP	SLG	LATE/CLOSE AB	HR	AVG	OBP	SLG
1988 Cle-A	143	1	.224	.333	.294	67	0	.239	.354	.284	76	1	.211	.315	.303	41	1	.220	.319	.341	102	0	.225	.339	.275	66	1	.258	.351	.364	18	0	.056	.261	.056
1988 KC-A	301	1	.309	.358	.389	147	0	.299	.360	.401	154	1	.318	.355	.377	98	0	.337	.402	.429	203	1	.296	.335	.369	145	1	.372	.414	.476	59	0	.254	.258	.288
1989 KC-A	390	2	.259	.325	.308	181	0	.271	.327	.343	209	0	.249	.323	.278	160	2	.350	.403	.412	230	0	.196	.271	.235	185	2	.270	.325	.341	66	1	.288	.342	.364
1990 KC-A	195	1	.272	.338	.359	98	0	.245	.327	.327	97	1	.299	.349	.392	81	1	.333	.396	.457	114	0	.228	.297	.289	106	0	.274	.328	.321	32	0	.281	.333	.375
1990 NY-N	43	1	.279	.340	.419	16	1	.250	.333	.438	27	0	.296	.345	.407	24	0	.333	.385	.417	19	1	.211	.286	.421	25	1	.320	.393	.480	6	0	.000	.143	.000
1991 Tor-A	185	1	.216	.318	.270	93	1	.215	.286	.290	92	0	.217	.348	.250	147	0	.190	.275	.238	38	1	.316	.469	.395	79	1	.215	.356	.304	31	1	.226	.390	.355
1992 Tor-A	135	0	.252	.306	.289	51	0	.196	.293	.235	84	0	.286	.315	.321	67	0	.284	.355	.313	68	0	.221	.254	.265	62	0	.274	.352	.323	13	0	.231	.333	.231
TOTALS	3295	39	.284	.345	.379	1606	24	.303	.364	.412	1689	15	.266	.327	.347	1253	18	.308	.370	.413	2042	21	.270	.330	.358	1556	23	.308	.370	.409	510	10	.263	.338	.363
■ Danny Tartabull BR/TR																																			
1984 Sea-A	20	2	.300	.375	.650	7	1	.286	.444	.714	13	1	.308	.333	.615	7	0	.000	.000	.000	13	2	.462	.529	1.000	10	1	.300	.333	.700	3	1	1.000	1.000	1.000
1985 Sea-A	61	1	.328	.406	.525	23	0	.348	.444	.478	38	1	.316	.381	.553	21	1	.476	.577	.810	40	0	.250	.302	.375	28	1	.321	.345	.500	11	0	.182	.308	.273
1986 Sea-A	511	25	.270	.347	.489	268	13	.272	.338	.500	243	12	.267	.357	.477	125	3	.304	.385	.464	386	22	.259	.335	.497	235	16	.302	.384	.596	87	2	.287	.347	.448
1987 KC-A	582	34	.309	.390	.541	282	15	.291	.381	.511	300	19	.327	.398	.570	149	7	.289	.389	.503	433	27	.316	.390	.554	288	16	.302	.378	.517	80	5	.300	.356	.550
1988 KC-A	507	26	.274	.369	.515	249	15	.289	.397	.562	258	11	.260	.341	.469	149	8	.289	.404	.537	358	18	.268	.354	.506	264	13	.303	.389	.545	91	2	.187	.283	.330
1989 KC-A	441	18	.268	.369	.440	214	9	.280	.388	.463	227	9	.256	.350	.419	125	8	.312	.420	.568	316	10	.250	.348	.389	197	5	.234	.352	.355	67	5	.403	.506	.701
1990 KC-A	313	15	.268	.341	.473	142	5	.232	.291	.366	171	10	.298	.381	.561	106	5	.321	.426	.509	207	10	.242	.291	.454	163	8	.276	.339	.485	44	3	.318	.362	.659
1991 KC-A	484	31	.316	.397	.593	226	13	.314	.395	.571	258	18	.318	.398	.612	142	8	.296	.408	.542	342	23	.325	.392	.614	217	14	.355	.451	.641	79	4	.316	.379	.557
1992 NY-A	421	25	.266	.409	.489	204	11	.289	.428	.500	217	14	.244	.390	.479	119	11	.286	.494	.613	302	14	.258	.368	.440	190	15	.295	.449	.589	84	4	.262	.392	.464
1993 NY-A	513	31	.250	.363	.503	229	11	.210	.343	.410	284	20	.282	.381	.577	175	7	.200	.341	.394	338	24	.275	.375	.559	256	12	.273	.397	.484	69	3	.348	.483	.609
1994 NY-A	399	19	.256	.360	.464	199	10	.246	.326	.472	200	9	.265	.391	.455	121	9	.339	.490	.645	278	10	.219	.294	.385	203	7	.241	.350	.424	55	1	.200	.318	.291
TOTALS	4252	227	.278	.374	.505	2043	103	.273	.370	.491	2209	124	.282	.377	.518	1239	67	.290	.416	.526	3013	160	.272	.355	.497	2051	108	.289	.389	.519	670	29	.290	.381	.501
■ Garry Templeton BB/TR																																			
1984 SD-N	493	2	.258	.312	.320	254	2	.240	.297	.307	239	0	.276	.328	.335	144	0	.250	.285	.313	349	2	.261	.323	.324	196	2	.260	.358	.327	89	0	.270	.330	.292
1985 SD-N	546	6	.282	.332	.377	267	4	.281	.319	.393	279	2	.283	.343	.362	177	1	.254	.291	.316	369	5	.295	.351	.407	204	2	.314	.389	.412	94	1	.234	.321	.309
1986 SD-N	510	2	.247	.296	.308	269	1	.230	.284	.294	241	1	.266	.309	.324	175	2	.257	.323	.343	335	0	.242	.281	.290	211	1	.242	.328	.318	119	0	.336	.397	.395
1987 SD-N	510	5	.222	.281	.296	250	2	.204	.267	.288	260	3	.238	.293	.304	189	2	.233	.284	.307	321	3	.215	.278	.290	222	3	.207	.275	.302	95	2	.232	.291	.326
1988 SD-N	362	3	.249	.286	.354	186	3	.253	.307	.398	176	0	.244	.262	.307	76	0	.237	.256	.289	286	3	.252	.293	.371	142	3	.282	.352	.437	69	2	.261	.278	.420
1989 SD-N	506	6	.255	.286	.354	255	5	.259	.292	.384	251	1	.251	.279	.323	145	1	.317	.353	.421	361	5	.230	.259	.327	202	1	.228	.287	.297	90	0	.200	.240	.233
1990 SD-N	505	9	.248	.280	.362	255	6	.247	.278	.380	250	3	.248	.281	.344	189	4	.246	.286	.370	316	5	.244	.275	.358	232	6	.284	.317	.414	104	2	.240	.277	.346
1991 SD-N	57	1	.193	.203	.298	31	1	.194	.219	.323	26	0	.192	.185	.269	13	1	.385	.385	.769	44	0	.136	.152	.159	23	1	.130	.125	.304	19	1	.105	.105	.316
1991 NY-N	219	2	.228	.257	.306	107	1	.271	.322	.374	112	1	.188	.191	.241	83	0	.337	.378	.410	136	2	.162	.179	.243	94	1	.213	.248	.319	42	0	.262	.304	.333
TOTALS	3708	36	.249	.293	.336	1874	25	.245	.292	.348	1834	11	.254	.294	.323	1191	11	.266	.306	.349	2517	25	.242	.287	.330	1526	20	.254	.350	.352	721	8	.252	.304	.331
■ Mickey Tettleton BB/TR																																			
1984 Oak-A	76	1	.263	.352	.355	47	1	.298	.404	.447	29	0	.207	.258	.207	34	1	.206	.300	.324	42	0	.310	.396	.381	30	0	.200	.286	.233	9	0	.000	.000	.000
1985 Oak-A	211	3	.251	.344	.351	110	1	.245	.336	.309	101	2	.257	.353	.396	61	1	.213	.304	.344	150	2	.267	.360	.353	102	0	.250	.359	.295	34	1	.265	.342	.412
1986 Oak-A	211	10	.204	.325	.389	106	4	.198	.326	.349	105	6	.210	.325	.429	84	6	.262	.370	.524	127	4	.165	.297	.299	102	2	.225	.356	.363	36	2	.222	.282	.389
1987 Oak-A	211	8	.194	.292	.322	105	5	.219	.311	.381	106	3	.170	.273	.264	84	2	.214	.323	.310	127	6	.181	.271	.331	87	4	.218	.346	.368	29	1	.207	.314	.310
1988 Bal-A	283	11	.261	.330	.424	135	4	.244	.305	.380	148	7	.277	.358	.474	147	9	.252	.313	.463	136	2	.272	.349	.382	125	5	.230	.340	.405	54	2	.222	.300	.370
1989 Bal-A	411	26	.258	.369	.509	203	15	.310	.401	.611	208	11	.207	.339	.409	139	10	.245	.342	.532	272	16	.265	.382	.496	170	9	.200	.382	.394	60	1	.283	.386	.383
1990 Bal-A	444	15	.223	.376	.381	215	8	.237	.394	.419	229	7	.210	.358	.345	128	5	.234	.351	.414	316	10	.218	.385	.367	197	6	.223	.408	.355	78	6	.179	.337	.423
1991 Det-A	501	31	.263	.387	.491	246	13	.264	.402	.498	255	18	.271	.408	.545	109	9	.248	.349	.532	392	22	.268	.397	.480	207	17	.275	.406	.541	100	6	.240	.303	.440
1992 Det-A	525	32	.238	.379	.469	255	18	.271	.408	.545	270	14	.207	.352	.396	135	8	.274	.377	.511	390	24	.226	.380	.454	236	13	.225	.386	.428	74	5	.257	.396	.486
1993 Det-A	522	32	.245	.372	.492	256	16	.230	.360	.480	266	16	.259	.384	.504	123	7	.260	.408	.520	399	25	.241	.360	.484	228	15	.289	.423	.570	75	5	.320	.422	.547
1994 Det-A	339	17	.248	.419	.463	167	9	.263	.431	.491	172	8	.233	.407	.436	81	3	.235	.376	.407	258	14	.252	.431	.481	144	9	.257	.450	.493	48	5	.250	.400	.604
TOTALS	3734	186	.242	.368	.443	1836	99	.257	.383	.475	1898	87	.229	.354	.413	1125	61	.245	.362	.463	2609	125	.241	.375	.435	1615	80	.241	.391	.436	597	34	.243	.349	.441
■ Tim Teufel BR/TR																																			
1984 Min-A	568	14	.262	.349	.400	290	9	.241	.319	.397	278	5	.284	.380	.403	168	5	.298	.392	.435	400	9	.248	.331	.385	257	4	.288	.368	.393	87	3	.333	.463	.471
1985 Min-A	434	10	.260	.335	.399	221	6	.276	.340	.421	213	4	.244	.331	.376	135	4	.200	.288	.267	299	9	.288	.357	.458	190	3	.263	.330	.395	71	1	.155	.221	.225
1986 NY-N	279	4	.247	.324	.369	140	2	.236	.308	.350	139	2	.259	.340	.388	196	3	.245	.318	.372	83	1	.253	.337	.361	129	2	.302	.363	.457	54	1	.222	.300	.352
1987 NY-N	299	14	.308	.398	.545	132	4	.326	.419	.538	167	10	.293	.380	.551	190	8	.321	.412	.563	109	6	.284	.373	.514	142	8	.289	.380	.563	49	2	.286	.435	.469
1988 NY-N	273	4	.234	.306	.352	130	1	.208	.246	.285	143	3	.259	.358	.413	165	3	.248	.323	.394	108	1	.213	.281	.287	120	3	.175	.264	.308	52	0	.212	.300	.250
1989 NY-N	219	2	.256	.350	.333	107	1	.215	.320	.252	112	1	.295	.380	.411	132	1	.273	.368	.333	87	1	.230	.323	.333	80	0	.250	.386	.313	33	1	.242	.333	.394
1990 NY-N	175	10	.246	.304	.480	64	4	.250	.324	.469	111	6	.243	.292	.486	108	5	.241	.317	.444	67	5	.254	.282	.537	84	3	.262	.315	.405	39	1	.231	.279	.385
1991 NY-N	34	1	.118	.167	.206	18	1	.056	.056	.222	16	0	.188	.278	.188	19	0	.158	.238	.158	15	1	.067	.067	.267	15	1	.067	.125	.267	7	0	.143	.333	.143
1991 SD-N	307	11	.228	.334	.388	144	5	.250	.374	.424	163	6	.209	.297	.356	113	7	.292	.400	.549	194	4	.191	.295	.294	132	8	.235	.335	.470	53	3	.246	.319	.446
1992 SD-N	246	6	.224	.312	.337	109	2	.257	.357	.367	137	4	.197	.275	.314	92	4	.239	.333	.435	154	2	.214	.299	.279	85	2	.231	.302	.346	55	1	.182	.338	.255
1993 SD-N	200	7	.250	.338	.430	99	5	.273	.366	.495	101	2	.228	.316	.366	133	6	.286	.381	.519	67	1	.179	.247	.254	93	4	.323	.407	.538	30	1	.233	.343	.367
TOTALS	3034	83	.252	.336	.400	1454	40	.251	.333	.396	1580	43	.253	.339	.404	1451	43	.265	.354	.427	1583	40	.240	.320	.375	1346	37	.262	.344	.412	542	14	.236	.341	.360
■ Andres Thomas BR/TR																																			
1985 Atl-N	18	0	.278	.278	.278	3	0	.333	.333	.333	15	0	.267	.267	.267	8	0	.250	.250	.250	10	0	.300	.300	.300	8	0	.250	.250	.250	5	0	.200	.200	.200
1986 Atl-N	323	6	.251	.267	.372	139	1	.200	.231	.274	184	5	.288	.295	.441	139	2	.266	.271	.388	184	4	.239	.264	.359	148	2	.257	.277	.351	55	1	.255	.317	.364
1987 Atl-N	324	5	.231	.268	.312	174	4	.259	.283	.351	150	1	.200	.250	.267	96	1	.229	.260	.302	228	4	.232	.271	.316	158	3	.253	.285	.348	48	0	.167	.231	.167
1988 Atl-N	606	13	.252	.268	.360	289	6	.263	.286	.367	317	7	.243	.251	.353	192	7	.240	.267	.380	414	6	.258	.268	.350	247	2	.247	.267	.308	120	1	.217	.234	.267
1989 Atl-N	554	13	.213	.228	.316	251	5	.195	.212	.287	303	8	.228	.242	.340	173	4	.208	.218	.318	381	9	.215	.224	.315	245	6	.220	.235	.314	107	4	.271	.282	.411
1990 Atl-N	278	5	.219	.248	.302	157	4	.229	.262	.274	121	1	.207	.230	.339	102	4	.225	.259	.363	176	1	.216	.242	.267	118	1	.229	.264	.288	46	1	.261	.277	.348
TOTALS	2103	42	.234	.255	.334	1009	17	.232	.256	.317	1094	25	.237	.254	.350	710	18	.234	.258	.352	1393	24	.235	.253	.325	924	14	.240	.263	.320	381	7	.236	.264	.318
■ Frank Thomas BR/TR																																			
1990 Chi-A	191	7	.330	.454	.529	73	2	.342	.510	.534	118	5	.322	.413	.525	71	5	.408	.538	.732	120	2	.283	.401	.408	87	2	.356	.478	.517	28	2	.357	.419	.714
1991 Chi-A	559	32	.318	.453	.553	267	24	.371	.509	.708	292	8	.271	.399	.411	170	11	.376	.500	.624	389	21	.293	.432	.522	263	14	.323	.461	.548	95	3	.295	.465	.442
1992 Chi-A	573	24	.323	.439	.536	292	10	.305	.430	.500	281	14	.342	.448	.573	140	8	.357	.456	.650	433	16	.312	.433	.499	287	8	.338	.454	.523	108	4	.296	.379	.491
1993 Chi-A	549	41	.317	.426	.607	270	26	.326	.432	.681	279	15	.307	.420	.530	151	14	.311	.419	.649	398	27	.319	.429	.590	256	22	.313	.446	.645	69	5	.304	.456	.580
1994 Chi-A	399	38	.353	.487	.729	179	22	.385	.519	.832	220	16	.327	.461	.645	104	12	.385	.504	.798	295	26	.342	.482	.705	187	13	.332	.482	.663	55	3	.236	.403	.473
TOTALS	2271	142	.326	.449	.590	1090	84	.342	.471	.654	1181	58	.312	.429	.532	636	50	.362	.476	.676	1635	92	.313	.439	.557	1080	59	.329	.461	.581	355	17	.293	.426	.510
■ Milt Thompson BL/TR																																			
1984 Atl-N	99	2	.303	.373	.374	43	0	.302	.375	.326	56	2	.304	.371	.411	17	0	.059	.059	.059	82	2	.354	.430	.439	32	0	.281	.378	.281	20	1	.300	.333	.450
1985 Atl-N	182	2	.302	.339	.363	95	0	.326	.354	.421	87	0	.276	.323	.299	14	0	.143	.143	.143	168	2	.315	.354	.381	58	0	.328	.350	.328	40	1	.400	.455	.500
1986 Phi-N	299	6	.251	.311	.341	154	4	.273	.331	.390	145	2	.228	.289	.290	50	0	.220	.264	.240	249	6	.257	.320	.361	101	1	.277	.336	.356	51	0	.255	.333	.275
1987 Phi-N	527	7	.302	.351	.425	279	3	.330	.382	.474	248	4	.272	.319	.374	84	0	.214	.283	.250	443	7	.318	.365	.458	176	2	.313	.371	.432	83	2	.313	.352	.458
1988 Phi-N	378	2	.288	.354	.357	173	1	.295	.377	.370	205	1	.283	.333	.346	20	0	.350	.462	.400	358	2	.285	.347	.355	133	0	.323	.404	.391	63	1	.381	.466	.476
1989 StL-N	545	4	.290	.340	.393	271	2	.303	.336	.432	274	2	.277	.344	.354	210	1	.267	.297	.381	335	3	.304	.366	.400	249	3	.337	.391	.466	85	1	.294	.347	.376
1990 StL-N	418	6	.218	.292	.328	221	3	.213	.290	.312	197	3	.223	.295	.345	120	0	.175	.227	.233	298	6	.235	.317	.366	168	3	.244	.317	.363	76	1	.224	.314	.342
1991 StL-N	326	6	.307	.368	.442	159	4	.283	.347	.447	167	2	.329	.388	.437	74	1	.216	.247	.297	252	5	.333	.401	.484	144	1	.257	.341	.347	71	1	.282	.342	.437
1992 StL-N	208	4	.293	.350	.404	105	4	.276	.327	.362	103	0	.311	.372	.447	22	0	.318	.375	.455	186	4	.290	.347	.398	69	0	.246	.316	.290	69	1	.304	.368	.449
1993 Phi-N	340	4	.262	.341	.350	159	2	.252	.341	.346	181	2	.271	.342	.354	57	0	.175	.250	.175	283	4	.279	.376	.382	165	2	.279	.358	.382	66	0	.242	.307	.242
1994 Phi-N	220	3	.273	.348	.345	103	3	.311	.399	.456	117	0	.239	.321	.248	33	0	.182	.250	.182	187	3	.289	.365	.374	98	2	.357	.448	.449	41	0	.244	.340	.268
1994 Hou-N	21	1	.286	.318	.429	21	1	.286	.318	.429	0	0	—	—	—	3	0	.333	.333	.333	18	1	.278	.316	.444	16	1	.188	.188	.375	2	0	.000	.000	.000
TOTALS	3563	45	.279	.344	.378	1774	24	.286	.346	.401	1789	21	.272	.333	.355	704	2	.222	.270	.286	2859	43	.293	.356	.401	1409	15	.296	.367	.392	667	7	.288	.357	.387
■ Robby Thompson BR/TR																																			
1986 SF-N	549	7	.271	.328	.370	255	4	.294	.364	.424	294	3	.252	.296	.323	168	3	.286	.344	.411	381	4	.265	.321	.352	212	2	.255	.329	.340	95	1	.295	.337	.358
1987 SF-N	420	10	.262	.338	.439	205	7	.263	.346	.449	215	3	.260	.329	.391	129	3	.310	.382	.465	291	7	.241	.318	.399	136	4	.287	.366	.426	69	1	.217	.325	.348
1988 SF-N	477	7	.264	.328	.384	214	3	.257	.326	.374	263	4	.270	.330	.392	144	2	.325	.385	.487	333	5	.238	.293	.343	195	3	.303	.373	.456	82	0	.305	.333	.402
1989 SF-N	547	13	.241	.321	.400	286	7	.266	.333	.434	261	6	.215	.307	.364	194	5	.304	.378	.505	353	8	.207	.289	.343	223	6	.256	.316	.435	86	3	.233	.298	.419
1990 SF-N	498	15	.245	.299	.392	248	8	.266	.333	.435	250	7	.224	.262	.348	183	4	.273	.325	.475	315	7	.229	.284	.343	216	6	.255	.308	.380	88	3	.239	.279	.386
1991 SF-N	492	19	.262	.352	.447	241	11	.295	.399	.519	251	8	.231	.305	.378	135	7	.281	.378	.511	357	12	.255	.342	.423	181	4	.227	.320	.398	86	2	.163	.223	.256
1992 SF-N	443	14	.260	.333	.415	236	8	.271	.342	.441	207	6	.246	.323	.386	164	5	.280	.357	.396	279	13	.247	.319	.427	186	6	.237	.311	.382	86	2	.163	.223	.256
1993 SF-N	494	19	.312	.375	.496	223	13	.309	.389	.561	271	6	.314	.362	.443	145	5	.352	.409	.538	349	14	.295	.361	.479	204	4	.358	.426	.500	71	1	.239	.263	.366

	TOTAL					HOME					AWAY					LEFT					RIGHT					ON-BASE					LATE/CLOSE				
YEAR TM/L	AB	HR	AVG	OBP	SLG	AB	HR	AVG	OBP	SLG	AB	HR	AVG	OBP	SLG	AB	HR	AVG	OBP	SLG	AB	HR	AVG	OBP	SLG	AB	HR	AVG	OBP	SLG	AB	HR	AVG	OBP	SLG
1994 SF-N	129	2	.209	.290	.349	68	1	.206	.286	.309	61	1	.213	.294	.393	42	2	.286	.348	.524	87	0	.172	.263	.264	50	0	.160	.232	.240	19	0	.263	.417	.316
TOTALS	4049	106	.263	.332	.412	1976	62	.275	.352	.449	2073	44	.251	.313	.378	1314	35	.300	.367	.474	2735	71	.245	.315	.383	1603	34	.268	.343	.403	678	12	.248	.312	.361

■ Dickie Thon BR/TR

YEAR TM/L	AB	HR	AVG	OBP	SLG	AB	HR	AVG	OBP	SLG	AB	HR	AVG	OBP	SLG	AB	HR	AVG	OBP	SLG	AB	HR	AVG	OBP	SLG	AB	HR	AVG	OBP	SLG	AB	HR	AVG	OBP	SLG
1984 Hou-N	17	0	.353	.389	.471	17	0	.353	.389	.471	0	0	—	—	—	1	0	1.000	1.000	1.000	16	0	.313	.353	.438	8	0	.250	.333	.500	2	0	.500	.500	.500
1985 Hou-N	251	6	.251	.299	.355	121	3	.190	.246	.298	130	3	.308	.348	.408	162	4	.272	.324	.383	89	2	.213	.253	.303	98	3	.286	.333	.429	31	1	.226	.294	.323
1986 Hou-N	278	3	.248	.318	.335	148	0	.250	.321	.324	130	3	.246	.315	.346	177	1	.243	.318	.305	101	2	.257	.318	.386	117	1	.197	.296	.282	45	1	.311	.404	.378
1987 Hou-N	66	1	.212	.366	.273	34	0	.176	.300	.206	32	1	.250	.429	.344	56	1	.196	.348	.250	10	0	.300	.462	.400	32	1	.188	.350	.313	20	0	.250	.348	.250
1988 SD-N	258	1	.264	.347	.337	112	0	.223	.331	.268	146	1	.295	.360	.390	139	1	.302	.391	.403	119	0	.218	.293	.261	93	0	.258	.336	.333	50	1	.140	.200	.200
1989 Phi-N	435	15	.271	.321	.434	208	8	.264	.292	.428	227	7	.278	.345	.441	176	6	.273	.328	.443	259	9	.270	.315	.429	174	8	.316	.378	.511	67	2	.269	.338	.418
1990 Phi-N	552	8	.255	.305	.350	254	3	.248	.316	.311	298	5	.262	.295	.383	202	5	.262	.310	.391	350	3	.251	.302	.326	265	3	.242	.290	.313	97	0	.320	.383	.361
1991 Phi-N	539	9	.252	.283	.351	270	4	.270	.299	.359	269	5	.234	.268	.342	205	2	.259	.306	.341	334	7	.249	.269	.356	214	3	.215	.249	.318	113	3	.248	.265	.372
1992 Tex-A	275	4	.247	.293	.367	142	2	.261	.306	.408	133	2	.233	.280	.323	99	3	.293	.360	.495	176	1	.222	.264	.295	121	2	.264	.314	.421	48	0	.292	.327	.354
1993 Mil-A	245	1	.269	.324	.331	118	0	.280	.333	.322	127	1	.260	.315	.339	122	1	.270	.336	.320	123	0	.268	.311	.341	111	0	.324	.380	.378	49	0	.184	.250	.224
TOTALS	2916	48	.257	.311	.359	1424	20	.251	.306	.344	1492	28	.262	.315	.374	1339	24	.267	.332	.375	1577	24	.249	.292	.346	1233	21	.256	.316	.367	522	8	.257	.313	.337

■ Andy Thornton BR/TR

YEAR TM/L	AB	HR	AVG	OBP	SLG	AB	HR	AVG	OBP	SLG	AB	HR	AVG	OBP	SLG	AB	HR	AVG	OBP	SLG	AB	HR	AVG	OBP	SLG	AB	HR	AVG	OBP	SLG	AB	HR	AVG	OBP	SLG
1984 Cle-A	587	33	.271	.366	.484	284	19	.320	.414	.577	303	14	.224	.319	.396	157	10	.274	.403	.510	430	23	.270	.351	.474	296	12	.284	.379	.459	87	4	.264	.394	.425
1985 Cle-A	461	22	.236	.304	.408	221	12	.231	.302	.421	240	10	.242	.305	.396	153	8	.268	.358	.451	308	14	.221	.275	.386	218	15	.266	.325	.518	70	7	.300	.375	.600
1986 Cle-A	401	17	.229	.333	.392	222	12	.279	.357	.477	179	5	.168	.305	.285	123	6	.236	.356	.407	278	11	.227	.322	.385	193	7	.244	.336	.389	55	3	.255	.373	.491
1987 Cle-A	85	0	.118	.206	.141	43	0	.163	.245	.186	42	0	.071	.167	.095	5	0	.075	.150	.094	32	0	.188	.297	.219	45	0	.067	.120	.089	16	0	.000	.105	.000
TOTALS	1534	72	.241	.337	.418	770	43	.274	.357	.492	764	29	.208	.303	.353	486	24	.241	.351	.420	1048	48	.241	.320	.417	752	34	.255	.338	.436	228	14	.254	.364	.465

■ Wayne Tolleson BB/TR

YEAR TM/L	AB	HR	AVG	OBP	SLG	AB	HR	AVG	OBP	SLG	AB	HR	AVG	OBP	SLG	AB	HR	AVG	OBP	SLG	AB	HR	AVG	OBP	SLG	AB	HR	AVG	OBP	SLG	AB	HR	AVG	OBP	SLG
1984 Tex-A	338	0	.213	.276	.251	180	0	.222	.289	.272	158	0	.203	.262	.228	96	0	.271	.358	.323	242	0	.190	.242	.223	132	0	.182	.243	.220	65	0	.246	.319	.246
1985 Tex-A	323	1	.313	.353	.381	178	0	.354	.394	.410	145	1	.262	.301	.345	87	0	.253	.275	.356	236	1	.335	.380	.390	133	1	.263	.296	.316	54	1	.315	.351	.426
1986 Chi-A	260	3	.250	.342	.335	127	1	.228	.327	.307	133	2	.271	.358	.361	102	3	.284	.370	.441	158	0	.228	.324	.266	98	2	.296	.390	.408	41	1	.244	.373	.366
1986 NY-A	215	0	.284	.332	.344	103	0	.301	.330	.369	112	0	.268	.333	.321	81	0	.284	.322	.321	134	0	.284	.338	.358	89	0	.236	.274	.326	36	0	.278	.316	.389
1987 NY-A	349	1	.221	.306	.241	152	1	.211	.314	.230	197	1	.228	.300	.249	106	0	.198	.315	.208	243	1	.230	.302	.255	133	0	.256	.340	.263	49	1	.286	.375	.347
1988 NY-A	59	0	.254	.338	.288	21	0	.238	.333	.286	38	0	.263	.341	.289	13	0	.538	.571	.538	46	0	.174	.278	.217	23	0	.304	.370	.391	10	0	.200	.200	.200
1989 NY-A	140	1	.164	.255	.250	71	0	.113	.241	.155	69	1	.217	.270	.348	48	1	.229	.315	.354	92	0	.130	.223	.196	59	0	.102	.221	.136	22	0	.182	.217	.227
1990 NY-A	74	0	.149	.210	.189	35	0	.114	.158	.171	39	0	.179	.256	.205	12	0	.167	.167	.167	62	0	.145	.217	.194	28	0	.071	.182	.071	17	0	.118	.118	.118
TOTALS	1758	6	.242	.310	.295	867	1	.245	.317	.296	891	5	.239	.304	.294	545	4	.259	.331	.332	1213	2	.234	.301	.279	695	3	.227	.297	.279	294	3	.255	.321	.320

■ Alan Trammell BR/TR

YEAR TM/L	AB	HR	AVG	OBP	SLG	AB	HR	AVG	OBP	SLG	AB	HR	AVG	OBP	SLG	AB	HR	AVG	OBP	SLG	AB	HR	AVG	OBP	SLG	AB	HR	AVG	OBP	SLG	AB	HR	AVG	OBP	SLG
1984 Det-A	555	14	.314	.382	.468	260	7	.304	.391	.454	295	7	.322	.374	.481	198	9	.318	.416	.540	357	5	.311	.362	.429	243	7	.329	.402	.506	76	2	.368	.417	.474
1985 Det-A	605	13	.258	.312	.380	296	7	.287	.347	.405	309	6	.230	.278	.356	184	4	.250	.324	.364	421	9	.261	.307	.387	246	4	.264	.321	.366	102	0	.186	.270	.206
1986 Det-A	574	21	.277	.347	.469	282	8	.262	.335	.415	292	13	.291	.359	.521	204	8	.279	.344	.505	370	13	.276	.349	.449	241	6	.249	.344	.382	82	1	.268	.375	.366
1987 Det-A	597	28	.343	.402	.551	296	13	.348	.404	.534	301	15	.339	.401	.568	214	11	.360	.419	.575	383	17	.334	.393	.538	298	10	.322	.388	.490	83	5	.410	.452	.639
1988 Det-A	466	15	.311	.373	.464	215	7	.312	.364	.465	251	8	.311	.380	.462	138	5	.348	.417	.522	328	10	.296	.354	.439	222	6	.311	.375	.450	82	5	.402	.462	.610
1989 Det-A	449	5	.243	.314	.334	236	2	.250	.326	.339	213	3	.235	.301	.329	161	1	.286	.341	.373	288	4	.219	.304	.313	198	1	.283	.344	.348	73	1	.301	.407	.397
1990 Det-A	559	14	.304	.377	.449	271	9	.339	.413	.513	288	5	.271	.342	.389	173	7	.289	.370	.486	386	7	.311	.380	.433	263	7	.335	.410	.487	73	1	.301	.393	.452
1991 Det-A	375	9	.248	.320	.373	218	6	.243	.318	.376	157	3	.255	.322	.369	113	4	.212	.268	.372	262	5	.263	.341	.374	192	5	.250	.335	.396	51	0	.157	.283	.196
1992 Det-A	102	1	.275	.370	.392	48	0	.229	.339	.333	54	1	.315	.397	.444	28	0	.357	.406	.500	74	1	.243	.356	.351	55	0	.327	.397	.418	14	0	.143	.200	.143
1993 Det-A	401	12	.329	.388	.496	203	6	.330	.396	.498	198	6	.328	.380	.495	135	7	.289	.386	.504	266	5	.350	.389	.492	197	6	.345	.405	.497	53	0	.245	.298	.264
1994 Det-A	292	8	.267	.307	.414	154	6	.299	.345	.481	138	2	.232	.264	.341	91	3	.297	.340	.462	201	5	.254	.292	.393	152	3	.270	.311	.375	56	0	.286	.310	.393
TOTALS	4975	140	.291	.356	.443	2479	71	.297	.365	.446	2496	69	.286	.346	.441	1639	59	.297	.369	.477	3336	81	.288	.349	.427	2307	55	.299	.368	.434	745	15	.294	.368	.403

■ Jeff Treadway BL/TR

YEAR TM/L	AB	HR	AVG	OBP	SLG	AB	HR	AVG	OBP	SLG	AB	HR	AVG	OBP	SLG	AB	HR	AVG	OBP	SLG	AB	HR	AVG	OBP	SLG	AB	HR	AVG	OBP	SLG	AB	HR	AVG	OBP	SLG
1987 Cin-N	84	2	.333	.356	.452	45	2	.311	.326	.467	39	0	.359	.390	.436	7	0	.143	.250	.143	77	2	.351	.367	.481	30	0	.300	.300	.300	14	0	.214	.214	.214
1988 Cin-N	301	2	.252	.315	.362	137	2	.299	.370	.438	164	0	.213	.268	.299	33	0	.242	.265	.333	268	2	.254	.320	.366	96	0	.271	.392	.417	58	0	.310	.359	.466
1989 Atl-N	473	8	.277	.317	.378	234	2	.261	.313	.338	239	6	.293	.321	.418	106	0	.198	.254	.208	367	8	.300	.335	.428	180	3	.267	.308	.367	94	2	.255	.290	.330
1990 Atl-N	474	11	.283	.320	.403	219	5	.301	.336	.416	255	6	.267	.307	.392	119	4	.303	.359	.445	355	7	.276	.307	.389	212	5	.325	.352	.443	62	1	.290	.338	.419
1991 Atl-N	306	3	.320	.368	.418	159	1	.264	.343	.340	147	2	.381	.399	.503	20	0	.250	.250	.250	286	3	.325	.376	.430	124	2	.339	.384	.460	37	0	.243	.275	.297
1992 Atl-N	126	0	.222	.274	.286	64	0	.234	.269	.313	62	0	.210	.279	.258	10	0	.100	.250	.100	116	0	.233	.276	.302	47	0	.213	.288	.319	18	0	.056	.105	.056
1993 Cle-A	221	2	.303	.347	.403	102	0	.265	.290	.314	119	2	.336	.394	.479	19	0	.105	.227	.105	202	2	.322	.359	.431	92	1	.348	.386	.478	45	1	.289	.347	.422
1994 LA-N	67	0	.299	.351	.343	25	0	.200	.250	.200	42	0	.357	.413	.429	14	0	.143	.200	.143	53	0	.340	.390	.396	24	0	.167	.250	.208	23	0	.348	.448	.391
TOTALS	2052	28	.284	.328	.386	985	12	.275	.325	.368	1067	16	.291	.332	.404	328	4	.232	.289	.296	1724	24	.294	.336	.404	805	11	.298	.348	.410	351	4	.268	.316	.362

■ Willie Upshaw BL/TL

YEAR TM/L	AB	HR	AVG	OBP	SLG	AB	HR	AVG	OBP	SLG	AB	HR	AVG	OBP	SLG	AB	HR	AVG	OBP	SLG	AB	HR	AVG	OBP	SLG	AB	HR	AVG	OBP	SLG	AB	HR	AVG	OBP	SLG
1984 Tor-A	569	19	.278	.345	.464	271	6	.284	.348	.472	298	13	.272	.342	.456	199	4	.266	.313	.432	370	15	.284	.361	.481	283	6	.265	.347	.431	96	3	.271	.364	.427
1985 Tor-A	501	15	.275	.342	.447	236	6	.297	.366	.479	265	9	.257	.320	.419	171	5	.295	.362	.462	330	10	.276	.357	.465	230	5	.291	.357	.465	79	1	.228	.299	.380
1986 Tor-A	573	9	.251	.341	.368	267	3	.247	.350	.363	306	6	.255	.332	.373	179	4	.223	.291	.341	394	5	.264	.362	.381	250	4	.248	.329	.364	100	4	.230	.322	.380
1987 Tor-A	512	15	.244	.324	.391	236	7	.225	.319	.369	276	8	.261	.329	.409	144	2	.208	.305	.319	368	13	.258	.332	.418	212	7	.255	.351	.425	77	0	.260	.387	.338
1988 Cle-A	493	11	.245	.330	.369	244	3	.238	.325	.336	249	8	.253	.335	.402	74	0	.203	.280	.216	419	11	.253	.338	.396	216	3	.231	.317	.333	76	0	.184	.276	.197
TOTALS	2648	69	.259	.337	.408	1254	25	.258	.342	.404	1394	44	.260	.332	.412	767	15	.241	.302	.375	1881	54	.266	.350	.422	1191	25	.259	.340	.405	428	8	.236	.331	.325

■ Jose Uribe BB/TR

YEAR TM/L	AB	HR	AVG	OBP	SLG	AB	HR	AVG	OBP	SLG	AB	HR	AVG	OBP	SLG	AB	HR	AVG	OBP	SLG	AB	HR	AVG	OBP	SLG	AB	HR	AVG	OBP	SLG	AB	HR	AVG	OBP	SLG
1984 StL-N	19	0	.211	.211	.211	10	0	.300	.300	.300	9	0	.111	.111	.111	6	0	.167	.167	.167	13	0	.231	.231	.231	10	0	.200	.200	.200	4	0	.250	.250	.250
1985 SF-N	476	3	.237	.285	.315	248	2	.214	.272	.306	228	1	.263	.300	.325	121	1	.256	.263	.296	355	2	.245	.293	.322	185	0	.265	.323	.324	100	0	.230	.280	.300
1986 SF-N	453	3	.223	.315	.280	219	1	.219	.332	.265	234	2	.226	.298	.295	145	3	.214	.287	.324	308	0	.227	.328	.260	196	1	.250	.344	.327	54	1	.185	.362	.259
1987 SF-N	309	5	.291	.343	.424	155	4	.316	.346	.503	154	1	.266	.341	.344	96	1	.260	.311	.406	213	4	.305	.358	.432	124	2	.306	.383	.476	55	1	.309	.377	.418
1988 SF-N	493	3	.252	.301	.318	224	1	.268	.308	.321	269	2	.238	.296	.316	152	2	.303	.350	.395	341	1	.229	.280	.284	200	1	.270	.333	.345	85	1	.247	.297	.294
1989 SF-N	453	1	.221	.273	.280	214	0	.224	.287	.285	239	1	.218	.260	.276	150	0	.213	.269	.253	303	1	.224	.275	.294	187	1	.235	.316	.267	56	0	.214	.302	.321
1990 SF-N	415	1	.248	.297	.304	197	0	.223	.285	.264	218	1	.271	.309	.339	142	0	.282	.325	.324	273	1	.231	.283	.293	186	0	.258	.327	.333	57	0	.211	.297	.211
1991 SF-N	231	1	.221	.283	.303	115	0	.235	.290	.296	116	1	.207	.276	.310	60	0	.250	.333	.317	171	1	.211	.266	.298	85	0	.259	.344	.353	29	0	.207	.324	.241
1992 SF-N	162	2	.241	.299	.346	69	0	.275	.311	.362	93	2	.215	.291	.333	53	1	.302	.333	.472	109	1	.211	.283	.284	66	0	.227	.307	.273	39	0	.256	.310	.333
1993 Hou-N	53	0	.245	.355	.264	15	0	.333	.444	.333	38	0	.211	.318	.237	17	0	.294	.400	.353	36	0	.222	.333	.222	18	0	.167	.375	.222	10	0	.100	.100	.100
TOTALS	3064	19	.241	.300	.314	1466	8	.243	.304	.317	1598	11	.239	.296	.312	946	10	.252	.306	.336	2118	9	.236	.297	.304	1257	7	.258	.334	.333	489	3	.231	.310	.294

■ Dave Valle BR/TR

YEAR TM/L	AB	HR	AVG	OBP	SLG	AB	HR	AVG	OBP	SLG	AB	HR	AVG	OBP	SLG	AB	HR	AVG	OBP	SLG	AB	HR	AVG	OBP	SLG	AB	HR	AVG	OBP	SLG	AB	HR	AVG	OBP	SLG
1984 Sea-A	27	1	.296	.321	.444	22	1	.273	.304	.409	5	0	.400	.400	.600	10	0	.100	.100	.100	17	1	.412	.444	.647	11	1	.455	.455	.818	2	0	.000	.000	.000
1985 Sea-A	70	0	.157	.181	.171	24	0	.167	.167	.208	46	0	.152	.188	.152	25	0	.280	.280	.320	45	0	.089	.128	.089	37	0	.216	.237	.243	10	0	.100	.100	.100
1986 Sea-A	53	5	.340	.417	.679	34	4	.324	.425	.706	19	1	.368	.400	.632	22	3	.318	.400	.636	31	3	.355	.429	.710	26	3	.346	.393	.731	13	2	.385	.429	.846
1987 Sea-A	324	12	.256	.292	.435	180	8	.244	.285	.433	144	4	.271	.301	.438	148	7	.304	.340	.554	176	5	.216	.251	.335	145	5	.297	.338	.441	53	3	.226	.241	.415
1988 Sea-A	290	10	.231	.295	.400	145	5	.241	.304	.428	145	5	.221	.285	.372	125	4	.264	.316	.416	165	6	.206	.279	.388	124	5	.298	.350	.548	59	1	.271	.328	.424
1989 Sea-A	316	7	.237	.311	.354	163	1	.252	.324	.325	153	6	.222	.297	.386	106	4	.236	.317	.396	210	3	.238	.308	.333	133	2	.271	.333	.368	55	1	.164	.270	.255
1990 Sea-A	308	7	.214	.339	.331	131	4	.198	.340	.290	177	3	.226	.338	.362	104	2	.202	.308	.298	204	5	.221	.338	.348	143	2	.217	.333	.294	49	0	.184	.322	.245
1991 Sea-A	324	8	.194	.286	.299	173	6	.162	.238	.197	151	2	.232	.339	.417	112	4	.232	.320	.420	212	2	.175	.269	.245	139	4	.165	.242	.273	56	2	.214	.241	.393
1992 Sea-A	367	3	.240	.352	.340	198	1	.247	.307	.424	169	2	.231	.303	.290	110	1	.245	.348	.417	241	1	.238	.334	.336	153	1	.209	.269	.261	47	0	.213	.302	.213
1993 Sea-A	423	13	.258	.354	.395	219	4	.265	.340	.365	204	9	.250	.368	.426	118	5	.280	.370	.508	305	8	.249	.347	.370	204	5	.255	.333	.377	75	2	.267	.341	.373
1994 Bos-A	76	1	.158	.256	.250	36	0	.167	.231	.278	40	1	.150	.277	.225	19	0	.158	.238	.316	57	1	.158	.262	.228	34	0	.147	.293	.206	10	0	.000	.091	.000
1994 Mil-A	36	1	.389	.522	.639	18	1	.389	.476	.778	18	0	.389	.560	.500	15	1	.400	.571	.733	21	0	.381	.480	.571	18	0	.333	.455	.611	1	0	1.000	1.000	2.000
TOTALS	2614	76	.235	.334	.371	1343	32	.235	.307	.366	1271	42	.235	.319	.377	924	35	.261	.333	.429	1690	39	.221	.302	.340	1167	28	.246	.317	.371	430	11	.221	.294	.342

■ Andy Van Slyke BL/TR

YEAR TM/L	AB	HR	AVG	OBP	SLG	AB	HR	AVG	OBP	SLG	AB	HR	AVG	OBP	SLG	AB	HR	AVG	OBP	SLG	AB	HR	AVG	OBP	SLG	AB	HR	AVG	OBP	SLG	AB	HR	AVG	OBP	SLG
1984 StL-N	361	7	.244	.354	.368	177	3	.232	.344	.345	184	4	.255	.364	.391	42	0	.262	.340	.405	319	7	.241	.356	.364	163	4	.294	.415	.460	62	2	.274	.405	.468
1985 StL-N	424	13	.259	.335	.419	193	5	.301	.386	.497	231	8	.225	.291	.390	54	0	.111	.158	.148	370	13	.281	.360	.481	204	6	.235	.363	.480	64	0	.172	.274	.219
1986 StL-N	418	13	.270	.343	.452	211	6	.280	.365	.474	207	7	.261	.320	.430	116	2	.207	.290	.353	302	12	.295	.364	.490	192	6	.286	.375	.464	91	2	.264	.368	.385
1987 Pit-N	564	21	.293	.359	.507	278	11	.273	.353	.475	286	10	.311	.365	.538	229	3	.231	.292	.354	335	18	.334	.403	.609	233	10	.288	.360	.498	93	8	.333	.347	.677
1988 Pit-N	587	25	.288	.345	.506	280	16	.293	.364	.575	307	9	.283	.327	.443	207	4	.184	.255	.319	380	21	.345	.405	.606	277	10	.300	.349	.513	115	4	.296	.336	.496
1989 Pit-N	476	9	.237	.308	.370	216	4	.213	.304	.347	260	5	.258	.311	.388	162	1	.247	.339	.370	314	8	.232	.291	.370	208	0	.245	.312	.399	96	1	.198	.274	.354
1990 Pit-N	493	17	.284	.367	.465	219	6	.288	.373	.447	274	11	.281	.362	.478	188	5	.261	.349	.378	305	12	.298	.378	.518	239	9	.289	.389	.481	77	3	.234	.277	.377
1991 Pit-N	491	17	.265	.355	.446	265	9	.226	.319	.392	226	8	.310	.397	.509	185	4	.195	.287	.330	306	13	.307	.396	.516	224	9	.290	.366	.500	71	2	.268	.321	.380

YEAR	TM/L	TOTAL AB	HR	AVG	OBP	SLG	HOME AB	HR	AVG	OBP	SLG	AWAY AB	HR	AVG	OBP	SLG	LEFT AB	HR	AVG	OBP	SLG	RIGHT AB	HR	AVG	OBP	SLG	ON-BASE AB	HR	AVG	OBP	SLG	LATE/CLOSE AB	HR	AVG	OBP	SLG
1992	Pit-N	614	14	.324	.381	.505	315	6	.321	.360	.492	299	8	.328	.402	.518	269	4	.297	.341	.454	345	10	.345	.411	.545	260	5	.331	.382	.538	111	1	.315	.389	.414
1993	Pit-N	323	8	.310	.357	.449	153	5	.255	.297	.412	170	3	.359	.410	.482	117	1	.308	.347	.376	206	7	.311	.362	.490	165	6	.339	.388	.527	62	2	.274	.328	.403
1994	Pit-N	374	6	.246	.340	.358	200	4	.265	.338	.390	174	2	.224	.341	.322	106	1	.255	.333	.377	268	5	.243	.342	.351	161	1	.273	.377	.348	54	0	.185	.343	.241
TOTALS		5125	150	.277	.351	.450	2507	75	.270	.347	.448	2618	75	.283	.354	.451	1672	23	.240	.307	.364	3453	127	.295	.371	.491	2326	68	.289	.366	.475	896	25	.262	.336	.415

■ Greg Vaughn BR/TR

YEAR	TM/L	TOTAL AB	HR	AVG	OBP	SLG	HOME AB	HR	AVG	OBP	SLG	AWAY AB	HR	AVG	OBP	SLG	LEFT AB	HR	AVG	OBP	SLG	RIGHT AB	HR	AVG	OBP	SLG	ON-BASE AB	HR	AVG	OBP	SLG	LATE/CLOSE AB	HR	AVG	OBP	SLG
1989	Mil-A	113	5	.265	.336	.425	50	1	.200	.286	.260	63	4	.317	.375	.556	22	0	.227	.367	.227	91	5	.275	.327	.473	42	4	.381	.440	.690	15	1	.333	.333	.533
1990	Mil-A	382	17	.220	.280	.432	193	9	.218	.277	.435	189	8	.222	.282	.429	127	4	.197	.254	.386	255	13	.231	.292	.455	172	7	.256	.330	.483	39	1	.128	.205	.256
1991	Mil-A	542	27	.244	.319	.456	256	16	.246	.332	.504	286	11	.241	.306	.413	154	5	.227	.307	.377	388	22	.250	.323	.487	241	13	.266	.345	.490	99	5	.212	.297	.384
1992	Mil-A	501	23	.228	.313	.409	244	11	.234	.330	.410	257	12	.222	.297	.409	105	6	.248	.370	.476	396	17	.222	.297	.391	229	12	.231	.317	.410	81	2	.210	.319	.296
1993	Mil-A	569	30	.267	.369	.482	271	12	.284	.389	.469	298	18	.252	.350	.493	166	7	.319	.443	.518	403	23	.246	.336	.467	274	10	.303	.405	.471	93	2	.226	.339	.333
1994	Mil-A	370	19	.254	.345	.478	178	9	.292	.377	.539	192	10	.219	.315	.422	64	7	.266	.390	.656	306	12	.252	.335	.441	176	7	.222	.337	.415	53	0	.094	.172	.113
TOTALS		2477	121	.245	.328	.451	1192	58	.253	.341	.461	1285	63	.237	.316	.441	638	29	.252	.356	.455	1839	92	.242	.319	.449	1134	53	.264	.354	.464	380	11	.195	.288	.308

■ Mo Vaughn BL/TR

YEAR	TM/L	TOTAL AB	HR	AVG	OBP	SLG	HOME AB	HR	AVG	OBP	SLG	AWAY AB	HR	AVG	OBP	SLG	LEFT AB	HR	AVG	OBP	SLG	RIGHT AB	HR	AVG	OBP	SLG	ON-BASE AB	HR	AVG	OBP	SLG	LATE/CLOSE AB	HR	AVG	OBP	SLG
1991	Bos-A	219	4	.260	.339	.370	100	1	.320	.421	.430	119	3	.210	.262	.319	33	0	.212	.257	.273	186	4	.269	.352	.387	102	1	.324	.392	.431	32	0	.156	.200	.188
1992	Bos-A	355	13	.234	.326	.400	202	8	.262	.343	.455	153	5	.196	.303	.327	79	5	.190	.281	.418	276	8	.246	.339	.395	174	6	.247	.340	.420	70	1	.257	.350	.329
1993	Bos-A	539	29	.297	.390	.525	277	13	.332	.418	.563	262	16	.260	.361	.485	112	12	.268	.351	.543	375	17	.309	.407	.517	230	14	.309	.430	.563	84	5	.262	.326	.500
1994	Bos-A	394	26	.310	.408	.576	215	15	.302	.411	.567	179	11	.318	.405	.587	126	11	.310	.386	.635	268	15	.310	.418	.549	184	14	.348	.470	.663	54	3	.278	.420	.500
TOTALS		1507	72	.280	.373	.486	794	37	.305	.398	.520	713	35	.252	.344	.449	402	28	.261	.341	.525	1105	44	.287	.384	.472	690	35	.306	.414	.530	240	9	.250	.341	.408

■ Robin Ventura BL/TR

YEAR	TM/L	TOTAL AB	HR	AVG	OBP	SLG	HOME AB	HR	AVG	OBP	SLG	AWAY AB	HR	AVG	OBP	SLG	LEFT AB	HR	AVG	OBP	SLG	RIGHT AB	HR	AVG	OBP	SLG	ON-BASE AB	HR	AVG	OBP	SLG	LATE/CLOSE AB	HR	AVG	OBP	SLG
1989	Chi-A	45	0	.178	.298	.244	23	0	.174	.300	.217	22	0	.182	.296	.273	7	0	.286	.500	.286	38	0	.158	.255	.237	22	0	.136	.241	.227	8	0	.000	.111	.000
1990	Chi-A	493	5	.249	.324	.318	238	2	.273	.348	.324	255	3	.227	.302	.314	154	0	.221	.318	.247	339	5	.263	.327	.351	188	3	.303	.365	.394	68	0	.250	.320	.250
1991	Chi-A	606	23	.284	.367	.442	304	16	.289	.368	.490	302	7	.278	.367	.394	192	5	.260	.364	.370	414	18	.295	.369	.476	267	12	.303	.375	.476	116	4	.284	.341	.457
1992	Chi-A	592	16	.282	.375	.431	285	7	.295	.392	.442	307	9	.270	.359	.420	182	2	.258	.348	.368	410	14	.293	.387	.459	256	6	.336	.435	.488	100	2	.260	.345	.390
1993	Chi-A	554	22	.262	.379	.433	254	12	.248	.386	.437	300	10	.273	.372	.430	176	5	.267	.361	.420	378	17	.259	.387	.439	264	10	.273	.389	.439	83	3	.289	.368	.446
1994	Chi-A	401	18	.282	.373	.459	182	8	.275	.372	.429	219	10	.288	.374	.484	122	4	.270	.311	.418	279	14	.287	.398	.477	213	8	.315	.417	.474	59	1	.186	.296	.254
TOTALS		2691	84	.271	.363	.414	1286	45	.275	.373	.425	1405	39	.266	.355	.405	833	16	.256	.345	.364	1858	68	.277	.372	.437	1210	39	.302	.395	.453	434	10	.256	.333	.371

■ Ozzie Virgil BR/TR

YEAR	TM/L	TOTAL AB	HR	AVG	OBP	SLG	HOME AB	HR	AVG	OBP	SLG	AWAY AB	HR	AVG	OBP	SLG	LEFT AB	HR	AVG	OBP	SLG	RIGHT AB	HR	AVG	OBP	SLG	ON-BASE AB	HR	AVG	OBP	SLG	LATE/CLOSE AB	HR	AVG	OBP	SLG
1984	Phi-N	456	18	.261	.331	.434	227	10	.291	.355	.498	229	8	.231	.308	.371	119	6	.252	.331	.427	337	12	.264	.331	.427	218	11	.252	.339	.454	73	1	.247	.349	.315
1985	Phi-N	426	19	.246	.330	.432	214	7	.252	.355	.425	212	12	.241	.303	.439	122	4	.238	.307	.385	304	15	.250	.339	.451	193	7	.218	.301	.378	91	2	.220	.308	.330
1986	Atl-N	359	15	.223	.343	.373	170	6	.265	.344	.406	189	9	.185	.342	.344	107	2	.262	.396	.355	252	13	.206	.319	.381	155	6	.245	.381	.374	67	1	.254	.378	.299
1987	Atl-N	429	27	.247	.331	.471	213	15	.258	.354	.516	216	12	.236	.307	.426	110	7	.218	.328	.427	319	20	.257	.331	.486	194	7	.247	.326	.397	72	4	.208	.287	.375
1988	Atl-N	320	9	.256	.313	.372	149	5	.315	.389	.470	171	4	.205	.243	.287	104	3	.279	.347	.404	216	6	.245	.297	.356	133	1	.278	.340	.338	77	0	.338	.393	.351
1989	Tor-A	11	1	.182	.400	.545	9	1	.111	.200	.444	2	0	.500	.800	1.000	1	0	.000	.000	.000	10	1	.200	.429	.600	6	1	.167	.444	.667	2	0	.000	.500	.000
1990	Tor-A	5	0	.000	.000	.000	4	0	.000	.000	.000	1	0	.000	.000	.000	0	0	.000	.000	.000	1	0	.000	.000	.000	2	0	.000	.000	.000	1	0	.000	.000	.000
TOTALS		2006	89	.246	.330	.420	986	44	.272	.355	.463	1020	45	.222	.305	.378	576	23	.247	.341	.406	1430	66	.246	.325	.426	901	33	.245	.337	.395	383	8	.251	.342	.332

■ Jose Vizcaino BB/TR

YEAR	TM/L	TOTAL AB	HR	AVG	OBP	SLG	HOME AB	HR	AVG	OBP	SLG	AWAY AB	HR	AVG	OBP	SLG	LEFT AB	HR	AVG	OBP	SLG	RIGHT AB	HR	AVG	OBP	SLG	ON-BASE AB	HR	AVG	OBP	SLG	LATE/CLOSE AB	HR	AVG	OBP	SLG
1989	LA-N	10	0	.200	.200	.200	3	0	.333	.333	.333	7	0	.143	.143	.143	1	0	.000	.000	.000	9	0	.222	.222	.222	4	0	.250	.250	.250	2	0	.000	.000	.000
1990	LA-N	51	0	.275	.327	.333	32	0	.281	.324	.375	19	0	.263	.333	.263	19	0	.368	.478	.368	32	0	.219	.219	.313	14	0	.143	.250	.143	6	0	.333	.429	.333
1991	Chi-N	145	0	.262	.283	.297	81	0	.235	.256	.284	64	0	.297	.318	.313	37	0	.216	.231	.216	108	0	.278	.301	.324	58	0	.345	.365	.397	38	0	.184	.220	.237
1992	Chi-N	285	1	.225	.260	.298	126	0	.230	.269	.278	159	1	.220	.253	.314	88	0	.216	.242	.318	197	1	.228	.268	.289	87	0	.253	.290	.310	52	0	.250	.298	.308
1993	Chi-N	551	4	.287	.340	.358	278	1	.338	.384	.399	273	3	.234	.296	.315	128	0	.297	.364	.328	423	4	.284	.333	.366	214	3	.304	.336	.402	86	1	.244	.298	.279
1994	NY-N	410	3	.256	.310	.324	184	1	.223	.291	.266	226	2	.283	.327	.372	107	0	.280	.325	.299	303	3	.248	.305	.333	133	2	.248	.303	.308	69	0	.362	.430	.420
TOTALS		1452	8	.262	.304	.329	704	2	.274	.322	.328	748	6	.251	.298	.329	380	0	.268	.319	.308	1072	8	.260	.306	.336	510	5	.280	.320	.353	253	1	.269	.325	.316

■ Omar Vizquel BB/TR

YEAR	TM/L	TOTAL AB	HR	AVG	OBP	SLG	HOME AB	HR	AVG	OBP	SLG	AWAY AB	HR	AVG	OBP	SLG	LEFT AB	HR	AVG	OBP	SLG	RIGHT AB	HR	AVG	OBP	SLG	ON-BASE AB	HR	AVG	OBP	SLG	LATE/CLOSE AB	HR	AVG	OBP	SLG
1989	Sea-A	387	1	.220	.273	.261	189	0	.228	.254	.296	198	1	.212	.290	.227	102	1	.196	.212	.265	285	0	.228	.293	.260	154	0	.234	.273	.266	52	0	.250	.291	.288
1990	Sea-A	255	2	.247	.295	.298	114	0	.237	.299	.254	141	2	.255	.291	.333	81	1	.235	.279	.296	174	1	.253	.302	.299	120	1	.200	.240	.258	43	0	.233	.283	.233
1991	Sea-A	426	1	.230	.302	.293	206	1	.252	.319	.359	220	0	.209	.286	.232	87	0	.230	.284	.276	339	1	.230	.306	.298	184	0	.261	.329	.315	74	0	.203	.262	.338
1992	Sea-A	483	0	.294	.340	.352	241	0	.286	.337	.357	242	0	.302	.342	.347	105	0	.229	.283	.267	378	0	.312	.356	.376	177	0	.316	.354	.379	87	0	.287	.319	.356
1993	Sea-A	560	2	.255	.319	.298	274	1	.266	.333	.303	286	1	.245	.306	.294	132	0	.197	.264	.242	428	2	.273	.336	.315	234	1	.261	.315	.303	101	0	.267	.351	.277
1994	Cle-A	286	1	.273	.325	.325	134	0	.284	.333	.313	152	1	.263	.317	.336	115	1	.226	.274	.287	171	0	.304	.358	.351	129	0	.333	.380	.364	40	0	.325	.372	.425
TOTALS		2397	7	.254	.311	.305	1158	3	.261	.316	.320	1239	4	.248	.306	.292	622	3	.217	.266	.270	1775	4	.267	.326	.318	998	2	.269	.318	.316	397	0	.259	.315	.317

■ Chico Walker BB/TR

YEAR	TM/L	TOTAL AB	HR	AVG	OBP	SLG	HOME AB	HR	AVG	OBP	SLG	AWAY AB	HR	AVG	OBP	SLG	LEFT AB	HR	AVG	OBP	SLG	RIGHT AB	HR	AVG	OBP	SLG	ON-BASE AB	HR	AVG	OBP	SLG	LATE/CLOSE AB	HR	AVG	OBP	SLG
1984	Bos-A	2	0	.000	.000	.000	1	0	.000	.000	.000	1	0	.000	.000	.000	0	0	—	—	—	2	0	.000	.000	.000	1	0	.000	.000	.000	1	0	.000	.000	.000
1985	Chi-N	12	0	.083	.083	.083	2	0	.000	.000	.000	10	0	.100	.100	.100	3	0	.000	.000	.000	9	0	.111	.111	.111	6	0	.000	.000	.000	6	0	.000	.000	.000
1986	Chi-N	101	1	.277	.339	.376	47	0	.277	.364	.362	54	1	.278	.316	.389	16	0	.313	.353	.375	85	1	.271	.337	.376	42	0	.238	.267	.286	14	0	.214	.267	.214
1987	Chi-N	105	0	.200	.277	.238	59	0	.153	.224	.169	46	0	.261	.346	.326	12	0	.167	.286	.167	93	0	.204	.276	.247	41	0	.171	.250	.171	18	0	.333	.368	.389
1988	Cal-A	78	0	.154	.214	.167	35	0	.229	.289	.257	43	0	.093	.152	.093	15	0	.133	.375	.400	63	0	.111	.176	.111	34	0	.206	.250	.235	20	0	.050	.136	.050
1991	Chi-N	374	6	.257	.315	.337	200	4	.270	.324	.365	174	2	.241	.304	.305	119	3	.210	.256	.319	255	3	.278	.342	.345	126	4	.278	.373	.397	95	1	.326	.398	.400
1992	Chi-N	26	0	.115	.200	.115	17	0	.176	.300	.176	9	0	.000	.000	.000	5	0	.000	.273	.000	21	0	.143	.250	.143	7	0	.000	.273	.000	7	0	.286	.400	.286
1992	NY-N	227	4	.308	.369	.423	87	0	.345	.406	.402	140	4	.286	.344	.436	85	0	.341	.363	.388	142	4	.289	.372	.444	102	2	.363	.430	.480	67	0	.239	.329	.284
1993	NY-N	213	5	.225	.271	.338	96	1	.208	.245	.260	117	4	.239	.291	.402	72	2	.319	.347	.514	141	3	.177	.234	.248	99	3	.242	.300	.384	74	1	.122	.198	.203
TOTALS		1138	16	.245	.304	.329	544	5	.252	.312	.316	594	11	.239	.296	.340	327	5	.272	.308	.373	811	11	.234	.302	.311	458	9	.262	.335	.358	302	2	.225	.301	.281

■ Greg Walker BL/TR

YEAR	TM/L	TOTAL AB	HR	AVG	OBP	SLG	HOME AB	HR	AVG	OBP	SLG	AWAY AB	HR	AVG	OBP	SLG	LEFT AB	HR	AVG	OBP	SLG	RIGHT AB	HR	AVG	OBP	SLG	ON-BASE AB	HR	AVG	OBP	SLG	LATE/CLOSE AB	HR	AVG	OBP	SLG
1984	Chi-A	442	24	.294	.346	.532	217	16	.318	.379	.618	225	8	.271	.314	.449	84	2	.190	.289	.294	358	22	.318	.361	.587	217	14	.281	.338	.539	65	2	.231	.271	.369
1985	Chi-A	601	24	.258	.309	.454	293	11	.266	.319	.481	308	13	.250	.300	.429	183	4	.230	.257	.388	418	20	.270	.331	.483	263	12	.285	.350	.513	91	7	.275	.313	.549
1986	Chi-A	282	13	.277	.349	.453	151	6	.278	.366	.517	131	7	.275	.319	.466	89	2	.236	.324	.360	193	11	.295	.355	.554	124	7	.274	.345	.508	41	0	.268	.279	.366
1987	Chi-A	566	27	.256	.346	.465	273	12	.249	.352	.465	293	15	.263	.339	.485	210	13	.238	.326	.467	356	14	.267	.357	.463	257	13	.272	.373	.506	81	3	.259	.384	.444
1988	Chi-A	377	8	.247	.304	.374	205	6	.229	.288	.327	172	2	.267	.323	.430	112	1	.232	.294	.321	265	7	.253	.318	.396	160	2	.306	.369	.425	66	1	.227	.301	.288
1989	Chi-A	233	5	.210	.286	.335	91	4	.165	.255	.319	142	1	.239	.306	.345	48	0	.188	.264	.208	185	5	.216	.292	.368	102	4	.216	.291	.284	36	0	.139	.250	.194
1990	Chi-A	5	0	.200	.200	.200	5	0	.200	.200	.200	0	0	—	—	—	0	0	—	—	—	5	0	.200	.200	.200	4	0	.250	.250	.250	0	0	—	—	—
1990	Bal-N	34	0	.147	.237	.147	18	0	.167	.250	.167	16	0	.125	.222	.125	3	0	.000	.000	.000	31	0	.161	.257	.161	19	0	.158	.238	.158	8	0	.000	.111	.000
TOTALS		2540	101	.258	.324	.447	1253	51	.258	.332	.458	1287	50	.259	.316	.436	729	22	.225	.291	.373	1811	79	.272	.337	.477	1146	48	.275	.348	.476	388	13	.237	.306	.389

■ Larry Walker BL/TR

YEAR	TM/L	TOTAL AB	HR	AVG	OBP	SLG	HOME AB	HR	AVG	OBP	SLG	AWAY AB	HR	AVG	OBP	SLG	LEFT AB	HR	AVG	OBP	SLG	RIGHT AB	HR	AVG	OBP	SLG	ON-BASE AB	HR	AVG	OBP	SLG	LATE/CLOSE AB	HR	AVG	OBP	SLG
1989	Mon-N	47	0	.170	.264	.170	37	0	.189	.286	.189	10	0	.100	.182	.100	4	0	.000	.000	.000	43	0	.186	.286	.186	21	0	.143	.217	.143	12	0	.167	.231	.167
1990	Mon-N	419	19	.241	.326	.434	196	9	.255	.338	.454	223	10	.229	.316	.417	116	6	.207	.264	.414	303	13	.254	.349	.442	188	7	.213	.309	.362	87	2	.241	.327	.368
1991	Mon-N	487	16	.290	.349	.458	187	5	.273	.330	.428	300	11	.300	.361	.477	160	4	.287	.352	.419	327	12	.291	.348	.477	196	9	.296	.357	.505	96	4	.292	.376	.521
1992	Mon-N	528	23	.301	.353	.506	257	13	.284	.349	.506	271	10	.317	.357	.506	209	10	.316	.354	.517	319	13	.292	.352	.499	253	10	.316	.360	.506	89	4	.281	.369	.438
1993	Mon-N	490	22	.265	.371	.469	241	13	.307	.410	.560	249	9	.225	.333	.382	185	7	.238	.336	.400	305	15	.282	.391	.511	236	7	.284	.417	.462	81	2	.235	.361	.383
1994	Mon-N	395	19	.322	.394	.587	169	7	.331	.401	.604	226	12	.314	.388	.575	115	4	.330	.410	.574	280	15	.318	.387	.593	189	10	.317	.375	.587	54	2	.296	.426	.537
TOTALS		2366	99	.281	.357	.483	1087	47	.286	.364	.500	1279	52	.278	.350	.468	789	31	.276	.344	.460	1577	68	.284	.363	.494	1083	43	.284	.368	.477	419	14	.265	.365	.437

■ Tim Wallach BR/TR

YEAR	TM/L	TOTAL AB	HR	AVG	OBP	SLG	HOME AB	HR	AVG	OBP	SLG	AWAY AB	HR	AVG	OBP	SLG	LEFT AB	HR	AVG	OBP	SLG	RIGHT AB	HR	AVG	OBP	SLG	ON-BASE AB	HR	AVG	OBP	SLG	LATE/CLOSE AB	HR	AVG	OBP	SLG
1984	Mon-N	582	18	.246	.311	.395	279	4	.251	.319	.355	303	14	.241	.303	.432	155	7	.265	.341	.471	427	11	.239	.300	.368	249	10	.261	.361	.434	103	4	.252	.330	.408
1985	Mon-N	569	22	.260	.310	.450	272	9	.257	.322	.430	297	13	.263	.297	.468	168	5	.256	.287	.423	401	17	.262	.319	.461	235	11	.264	.326	.464	93	3	.194	.269	.323
1986	Mon-N	480	18	.233	.308	.396	226	9	.226	.309	.348	254	12	.240	.307	.440	135	3	.215	.305	.356	345	15	.241	.309	.412	224	7	.250	.322	.411	99	3	.242	.345	.374
1987	Mon-N	593	26	.298	.343	.514	290	13	.300	.349	.552	303	13	.297	.337	.479	160	1	.306	.353	.444	433	25	.296	.340	.540	299	10	.288	.351	.485	80	7	.363	.386	.675
1988	Mon-N	592	12	.257	.302	.389	292	3	.253	.302	.346	300	9	.260	.301	.430	172	4	.262	.310	.413	420	8	.255	.298	.379	255	2	.243	.303	.333	134	2	.216	.259	.306
1989	Mon-N	573	13	.277	.341	.419	266	6	.318	.386	.479	307	7	.241	.303	.368	185	5	.274	.355	.500	388	8	.277	.333	.379	233	4	.274	.353	.399	99	3	.263	.388	.424
1990	Mon-N	626	21	.296	.339	.471	301	9	.276	.328	.452	325	12	.314	.350	.489	204	6	.289	.355	.456	422	15	.299	.331	.479	272	11	.309	.359	.515	129	3	.287	.348	.426
1991	Mon-N	577	13	.225	.290	.334	230	5	.213	.303	.317	347	8	.233	.285	.346	185	5	.222	.293	.346	392	8	.227	.292	.329	257	5	.222	.318	.319	116	1	.233	.336	.284
1992	Mon-N	537	9	.223	.296	.331	262	5	.263	.333	.393	275	4	.185	.259	.273	177	3	.263	.329	.429	360	6	.203	.280	.283	220	4	.245	.322	.364	98	2	.224	.290	.367
1993	LA-N	477	12	.222	.271	.342	217	4	.253	.297	.396	260	8	.196	.249	.298	139	5	.194	.223	.338	338	7	.234	.290	.343	198	2	.258	.307	.333	86	2	.174	.283	.279
1994	LA-N	414	23	.280	.356	.502	187	7	.235	.326	.401	227	16	.317	.382	.586	111	8	.279	.341	.577	303	15	.281	.362	.475	192	17	.286	.377	.625	70	3	.171	.262	.314
TOTALS		6020	187	.257	.315	.413	2846	71	.261	.326	.406	3174	116	.253	.305	.420	1787	59	.259	.319	.430	4233	128	.256	.314	.406	2656	87	.264	.338	.429	1107	33	.239	.318	.376

Situational Statistics: Player Register

Denny Walling BL/TR

	TOTAL					HOME					AWAY					LEFT					RIGHT					ON-BASE					LATE/CLOSE				
YEAR TM/L	AB	HR	AVG	OBP	SLG	AB	HR	AVG	OBP	SLG	AB	HR	AVG	OBP	SLG	AB	HR	AVG	OBP	SLG	AB	HR	AVG	OBP	SLG	AB	HR	AVG	OBP	SLG	AB	HR	AVG	OBP	SLG
1984 Hou-N	249	3	.281	.325	.402	122	0	.344	.364	.467	127	3	.220	.288	.339	32	0	.250	.273	.281	217	3	.286	.332	.419	131	2	.298	.352	.405	52	0	.212	.288	.231
1985 Hou-N	345	7	.270	.316	.394	181	2	.260	.306	.370	164	5	.280	.326	.421	45	0	.267	.298	.289	300	7	.270	.318	.410	136	4	.287	.331	.434	63	1	.190	.239	.270
1986 Hou-N	382	13	.312	.367	.479	190	5	.295	.349	.426	192	8	.328	.385	.531	58	0	.190	.266	.207	324	13	.333	.385	.528	170	7	.282	.373	.459	80	3	.300	.387	.450
1987 Hou-N	325	5	.283	.356	.418	156	2	.288	.364	.372	169	3	.278	.349	.462	35	1	.200	.222	.314	290	4	.293	.370	.431	151	4	.232	.306	.371	38	0	.316	.422	.368
1988 Hou-N	176	1	.244	.304	.341	85	0	.282	.322	.353	91	1	.209	.287	.330	12	0	.250	.357	.333	164	1	.244	.299	.341	73	0	.274	.361	.384	37	0	.243	.282	.324
1988 StL-N	58	0	.224	.250	.276	28	0	.107	.138	.179	30	0	.333	.355	.367	2	0	.000	.000	.000	56	0	.232	.259	.286	22	0	.182	.217	.182	8	0	.000	.000	.000
1989 StL-N	79	1	.304	.409	.430	30	0	.367	.486	.500	49	1	.265	.357	.388	9	0	.333	.455	.444	70	1	.300	.402	.429	36	1	.333	.478	.472	24	0	.375	.500	.458
1990 StL-N	127	1	.220	.265	.283	63	1	.254	.319	.381	64	0	.188	.209	.188	7	0	.000	.000	.000	120	1	.233	.279	.300	66	1	.288	.342	.394	38	0	.289	.317	.289
1991 Tex-A	44	0	.091	.184	.114	19	0	.000	.208	.000	25	0	.160	.160	.200	6	0	.000	.000	.000	38	0	.105	.209	.132	23	0	.130	.231	.174	16	0	.188	.235	.188
1992 Hou-N	3	0	.333	.333	.333	3	0	.333	.333	.333	0	0	—	—	—	6	0	.000	.000	.000	3	0	.333	.333	.333	0	0	—	—	—	1	0	.000	.000	.000
TOTALS	1788	31	.272	.330	.395	877	10	.279	.336	.385	911	21	.266	.324	.405	206	1	.214	.264	.257	1582	30	.280	.338	.413	808	19	.271	.344	.402	357	4	.255	.327	.325

Jerome Walton BR/TR

	TOTAL					HOME					AWAY					LEFT					RIGHT					ON-BASE					LATE/CLOSE				
YEAR TM/L	AB	HR	AVG	OBP	SLG	AB	HR	AVG	OBP	SLG	AB	HR	AVG	OBP	SLG	AB	HR	AVG	OBP	SLG	AB	HR	AVG	OBP	SLG	AB	HR	AVG	OBP	SLG	AB	HR	AVG	OBP	SLG
1989 Chi-N	475	5	.293	.335	.385	231	3	.303	.345	.403	244	2	.283	.326	.369	128	2	.320	.374	.438	347	3	.282	.321	.366	137	0	.314	.340	.409	66	0	.227	.312	.273
1990 Chi-N	392	2	.263	.350	.329	200	2	.290	.363	.365	192	0	.234	.338	.292	146	1	.288	.365	.370	246	1	.248	.342	.305	127	0	.276	.386	.331	57	0	.263	.323	.316
1991 Chi-N	270	5	.219	.275	.330	120	3	.225	.286	.350	150	2	.213	.265	.313	128	0	.195	.261	.242	142	5	.239	.288	.408	89	0	.191	.235	.225	56	1	.161	.213	.268
1992 Chi-N	55	0	.127	.273	.164	20	0	.150	.261	.250	35	0	.114	.279	.114	47	0	.149	.273	.191	8	0	.000	.273	.000	21	0	.048	.231	.048	7	0	.000	.300	.000
1993 Cal-A	2	0	.000	.333	.000	0	0	—	—	—	2	0	.000	.333	.000	1	0	.000	.500	.000	1	0	.000	.000	.000	1	0	.000	.000	.000	0	0	—	—	—
1994 Cin-N	68	1	.309	.347	.412	23	1	.304	.333	.522	45	0	.311	.354	.356	33	0	.394	.444	.515	35	1	.229	.250	.314	28	1	.250	.300	.500	19	1	.263	.333	.474
TOTALS	1262	13	.261	.325	.347	594	9	.278	.336	.379	668	4	.246	.315	.319	483	3	.265	.336	.346	779	10	.258	.318	.348	403	1	.256	.323	.330	205	2	.215	.290	.293

Gary Ward BR/TR

	TOTAL					HOME					AWAY					LEFT					RIGHT					ON-BASE					LATE/CLOSE				
YEAR TM/L	AB	HR	AVG	OBP	SLG	AB	HR	AVG	OBP	SLG	AB	HR	AVG	OBP	SLG	AB	HR	AVG	OBP	SLG	AB	HR	AVG	OBP	SLG	AB	HR	AVG	OBP	SLG	AB	HR	AVG	OBP	SLG
1984 Tex-A	602	21	.284	.343	.447	288	7	.285	.357	.424	314	14	.283	.330	.468	185	5	.270	.332	.427	417	16	.290	.349	.456	251	10	.299	.356	.490	101	4	.248	.321	.396
1985 Tex-A	593	15	.287	.329	.433	282	10	.344	.375	.539	311	5	.235	.288	.338	176	7	.301	.354	.511	417	8	.281	.318	.400	239	6	.289	.342	.431	92	1	.283	.333	.380
1986 Tex-A	380	5	.316	.372	.405	193	3	.321	.370	.420	187	2	.310	.373	.390	120	3	.317	.388	.467	260	2	.315	.364	.377	151	3	.338	.393	.477	65	0	.323	.362	.415
1987 NY-A	529	16	.248	.291	.384	259	7	.282	.320	.402	270	9	.215	.263	.367	197	4	.279	.321	.376	332	12	.229	.274	.389	244	6	.287	.326	.414	71	4	.268	.308	.479
1988 NY-A	231	4	.225	.302	.312	100	3	.230	.306	.360	131	1	.221	.299	.275	128	4	.227	.308	.375	103	0	.223	.296	.233	116	3	.207	.279	.319	37	2	.378	.452	.568
1989 NY-A	17	0	.294	.400	.353	10	0	.300	.417	.300	7	0	.286	.375	.429	17	0	.294	.400	.353	0	0	—	—	—	4	0	.500	.600	.500	0	0	—	—	—
1989 Det-A	275	9	.251	.300	.400	129	6	.256	.305	.465	146	3	.247	.296	.342	170	9	.276	.330	.500	105	0	.210	.252	.238	138	2	.225	.288	.304	62	1	.210	.254	.323
1990 Det-A	309	9	.256	.322	.392	131	8	.260	.331	.389	178	7	.253	.314	.393	152	5	.257	.315	.421	157	4	.255	.328	.363	131	4	.244	.344	.359	43	0	.256	.319	.326
TOTALS	2936	79	.271	.326	.406	1392	38	.292	.345	.438	1544	41	.253	.308	.378	1145	37	.276	.335	.438	1791	42	.269	.319	.385	1274	34	.278	.337	.414	471	12	.274	.329	.406

Turner Ward BB/TR

	TOTAL					HOME					AWAY					LEFT					RIGHT					ON-BASE					LATE/CLOSE				
YEAR TM/L	AB	HR	AVG	OBP	SLG	AB	HR	AVG	OBP	SLG	AB	HR	AVG	OBP	SLG	AB	HR	AVG	OBP	SLG	AB	HR	AVG	OBP	SLG	AB	HR	AVG	OBP	SLG	AB	HR	AVG	OBP	SLG
1990 Cle-A	46	1	.348	.388	.500	18	0	.278	.278	.333	28	1	.393	.452	.607	12	0	.333	.333	.333	34	1	.353	.405	.559	29	1	.345	.367	.552	4	0	.250	.400	.250
1991 Cle-A	100	0	.230	.300	.300	35	0	.114	.205	.200	65	0	.292	.352	.354	29	0	.241	.333	.310	71	0	.225	.286	.296	44	0	.273	.360	.364	13	0	.308	.400	.308
1991 Tor-A	13	0	.308	.357	.308	6	0	.333	.333	.333	7	0	.286	.375	.286	3	0	.333	.500	.333	10	0	.300	.300	.300	7	0	.429	.429	.429	6	0	.167	.167	.167
1992 Tor-A	29	1	.345	.424	.552	18	0	.278	.381	.333	11	1	.455	.500	.909	8	0	.625	.667	.875	21	1	.238	.333	.429	14	0	.286	.375	.429	7	0	.000	.000	.000
1993 Tor-A	167	4	.192	.287	.311	76	2	.132	.212	.276	91	2	.242	.345	.341	30	1	.367	.424	.600	137	3	.153	.259	.248	78	3	.205	.305	.385	33	1	.152	.275	.242
1994 Mil-A	367	9	.232	.328	.357	158	3	.259	.355	.380	209	6	.211	.307	.340	91	2	.198	.286	.319	276	7	.243	.342	.370	154	3	.253	.381	.396	53	4	.302	.418	.585
TOTALS	722	15	.235	.322	.355	311	5	.215	.301	.328	411	10	.251	.338	.375	173	3	.266	.342	.393	549	12	.226	.316	.342	326	5	.258	.360	.405	116	5	.233	.343	.388

Claudell Washington BL/TL

	TOTAL					HOME					AWAY					LEFT					RIGHT					ON-BASE					LATE/CLOSE				
YEAR TM/L	AB	HR	AVG	OBP	SLG	AB	HR	AVG	OBP	SLG	AB	HR	AVG	OBP	SLG	AB	HR	AVG	OBP	SLG	AB	HR	AVG	OBP	SLG	AB	HR	AVG	OBP	SLG	AB	HR	AVG	OBP	SLG
1984 Atl-N	416	17	.286	.374	.469	239	12	.293	.367	.515	177	5	.277	.383	.407	115	0	.304	.389	.443	301	14	.279	.368	.478	151	5	.252	.356	.417	77	2	.325	.398	.494
1985 Atl-N	398	15	.276	.342	.455	191	4	.277	.337	.398	207	11	.275	.348	.507	63	1	.206	.261	.365	335	14	.290	.358	.472	132	4	.273	.376	.417	83	3	.205	.287	.313
1986 Atl-N	137	5	.270	.336	.460	71	3	.239	.321	.408	66	2	.303	.352	.515	34	0	.265	.278	.353	103	5	.272	.353	.495	42	1	.262	.347	.381	26	2	.192	.250	.423
1986 NY-A	135	6	.237	.285	.407	55	4	.236	.263	.491	80	2	.237	.299	.350	14	0	.214	.267	.286	121	6	.240	.287	.421	53	1	.264	.316	.377	20	1	.200	.273	.350
1987 NY-A	312	9	.279	.336	.420	144	5	.299	.361	.451	168	4	.262	.315	.393	61	1	.361	.435	.475	251	8	.259	.311	.406	122	5	.352	.415	.541	49	0	.245	.275	.245
1988 NY-A	455	11	.308	.342	.442	218	6	.358	.397	.509	237	5	.262	.290	.380	48	1	.313	.333	.458	407	10	.307	.343	.440	214	4	.299	.333	.425	78	3	.321	.346	.462
1989 Cal-A	418	13	.273	.319	.428	210	9	.295	.344	.495	208	4	.250	.294	.361	102	0	.294	.333	.382	316	13	.266	.315	.443	157	2	.268	.310	.350	60	0	.250	.313	.333
1990 Cal-A	34	1	.176	.222	.294	13	0	.077	.200	.077	21	1	.238	.238	.429	3	0	.333	.333	.333	31	1	.161	.212	.290	10	0	.200	.273	.200	4	1	.500	.500	1.250
1990 NY-A	80	0	.162	.181	.200	41	0	.171	.209	.171	39	0	.154	.150	.231	9	0	.333	.300	.333	71	0	.141	.164	.183	33	0	.273	.286	.303	15	0	.000	.063	.000
TOTALS	2385	77	.276	.348	.432	1182	43	.291	.348	.459	1203	34	.261	.318	.406	449	6	.292	.346	.410	1936	71	.272	.330	.438	914	22	.283	.348	.414	412	12	.255	.313	.376

Mitch Webster BB/TL

	TOTAL					HOME					AWAY					LEFT					RIGHT					ON-BASE					LATE/CLOSE				
YEAR TM/L	AB	HR	AVG	OBP	SLG	AB	HR	AVG	OBP	SLG	AB	HR	AVG	OBP	SLG	AB	HR	AVG	OBP	SLG	AB	HR	AVG	OBP	SLG	AB	HR	AVG	OBP	SLG	AB	HR	AVG	OBP	SLG
1984 Tor-A	22	0	.227	.261	.409	13	0	.231	.231	.308	9	0	.222	.300	.556	16	0	.188	.188	.375	6	0	.333	.429	.500	15	0	.200	.250	.467	9	0	.222	.300	.444
1985 Tor-A	1	0	.000	.000	.000	1	0	.000	.000	.000	0	0	—	—	—	0	0	.188	.188	.375	1	0	.000	.000	.000	1	0	.000	.000	.000	0	0	—	—	—
1985 Mon-N	212	11	.274	.335	.486	81	3	.247	.287	.444	131	8	.290	.363	.511	90	6	.322	.361	.578	122	5	.238	.316	.418	87	3	.253	.320	.414	39	2	.179	.256	.385
1986 Mon-N	576	8	.290	.355	.431	283	2	.265	.329	.396	293	6	.314	.380	.464	199	5	.337	.376	.513	377	3	.265	.345	.387	238	2	.290	.370	.391	121	2	.231	.309	.322
1987 Mon-N	588	15	.281	.361	.435	285	9	.267	.353	.439	303	6	.294	.368	.432	200	7	.285	.344	.455	388	8	.278	.369	.425	250	6	.284	.371	.436	76	2	.289	.360	.434
1988 Mon-N	259	2	.255	.354	.313	122	0	.303	.415	.369	137	2	.212	.297	.263	95	0	.253	.318	.274	164	2	.256	.374	.335	104	0	.240	.347	.260	57	1	.158	.284	.211
1988 Chi-N	264	4	.265	.319	.398	151	3	.265	.329	.391	113	1	.265	.306	.407	73	0	.219	.250	.260	191	4	.283	.344	.450	85	3	.341	.383	.518	51	0	.294	.351	.392
1989 Chi-N	272	3	.257	.331	.364	132	1	.250	.315	.341	140	2	.264	.346	.386	61	1	.311	.364	.443	211	2	.242	.322	.341	108	2	.269	.362	.361	50	1	.160	.288	.220
1990 Cle-A	437	12	.252	.285	.407	231	6	.247	.284	.372	206	6	.257	.287	.447	192	8	.292	.320	.495	245	4	.220	.259	.339	181	7	.282	.313	.475	72	2	.222	.263	.375
1991 Cle-A	32	0	.125	.200	.125	12	0	.250	.308	.250	20	0	.050	.136	.050	20	0	.200	.304	.200	12	0	.000	.000	.000	11	0	.091	.231	.091	8	0	.250	.250	.250
1991 Pit-N	97	1	.175	.245	.320	32	1	.156	.300	.313	65	0	.185	.209	.323	35	1	.200	.282	.400	62	0	.161	.224	.274	42	0	.190	.244	.310	15	1	.267	.421	.667
1991 LA-N	74	1	.284	.361	.419	22	1	.227	.346	.500	52	0	.308	.368	.385	49	1	.286	.344	.429	25	0	.280	.400	.400	40	1	.275	.310	.400	28	1	.286	.412	.464
1992 LA-N	262	6	.267	.334	.420	125	1	.216	.308	.296	137	5	.314	.360	.533	130	3	.292	.361	.438	132	3	.242	.309	.402	122	2	.230	.298	.352	66	1	.318	.432	.439
1993 LA-N	172	2	.244	.293	.337	77	1	.221	.279	.299	95	1	.263	.304	.368	69	0	.275	.292	.391	103	2	.223	.293	.301	80	1	.225	.270	.313	62	2	.242	.277	.387
1994 LA-N	84	4	.274	.344	.464	38	1	.316	.350	.395	46	3	.239	.340	.522	61	3	.295	.343	.508	23	1	.217	.333	.348	39	1	.256	.310	.333	30	1	.333	.394	.500
TOTALS	3352	69	.265	.331	.403	1605	29	.255	.326	.381	1747	40	.274	.336	.424	1290	35	.288	.335	.443	2062	34	.251	.329	.378	1403	27	.267	.337	.393	684	16	.244	.327	.376

Walt Weiss BB/TR

	TOTAL					HOME					AWAY					LEFT					RIGHT					ON-BASE					LATE/CLOSE				
YEAR TM/L	AB	HR	AVG	OBP	SLG	AB	HR	AVG	OBP	SLG	AB	HR	AVG	OBP	SLG	AB	HR	AVG	OBP	SLG	AB	HR	AVG	OBP	SLG	AB	HR	AVG	OBP	SLG	AB	HR	AVG	OBP	SLG
1987 Oak-A	26	0	.462	.500	.615	14	0	.500	.563	.643	12	0	.417	.417	.583	10	0	.300	.300	.400	16	0	.563	.611	.750	7	0	.429	.500	.429	1	0	1.000	1.000	1.000
1988 Oak-A	452	3	.250	.312	.321	211	0	.237	.292	.289	241	3	.261	.330	.349	101	0	.208	.259	.257	351	3	.262	.329	.339	206	1	.272	.302	.345	66	0	.061	.125	.076
1989 Oak-A	236	3	.233	.298	.318	120	2	.200	.273	.283	116	1	.267	.325	.353	57	0	.228	.254	.281	179	3	.235	.312	.330	112	3	.232	.277	.330	33	0	.152	.222	.152
1990 Oak-A	445	2	.265	.337	.321	235	1	.247	.316	.281	210	1	.286	.360	.362	115	0	.261	.306	.304	330	2	.267	.347	.327	178	0	.287	.370	.315	74	0	.405	.457	.500
1991 Oak-A	133	0	.226	.286	.286	78	0	.167	.233	.192	55	0	.309	.361	.418	31	0	.194	.219	.258	102	0	.235	.304	.294	64	0	.203	.274	.246	17	0	.353	.368	.471
1992 Oak-A	316	0	.212	.305	.241	144	0	.174	.280	.208	172	0	.244	.327	.267	74	0	.135	.190	.162	242	0	.236	.337	.264	143	0	.217	.301	.245	40	0	.225	.377	.225
1993 Fla-N	500	1	.266	.367	.308	244	0	.250	.362	.283	256	1	.281	.372	.332	128	0	.234	.353	.281	372	1	.277	.372	.317	219	0	.297	.388	.342	106	0	.255	.370	.274
1994 Col-N	423	1	.251	.336	.303	214	1	.262	.331	.318	209	0	.239	.342	.287	96	1	.323	.400	.385	327	0	.229	.317	.278	147	0	.252	.311	.306	60	0	.233	.343	.267
TOTALS	2531	10	.250	.330	.306	1260	4	.233	.313	.279	1271	6	.268	.347	.333	612	1	.235	.301	.284	1919	9	.255	.339	.313	1076	4	.262	.330	.315	397	0	.242	.327	.277

Lou Whitaker BL/TR

	TOTAL					HOME					AWAY					LEFT					RIGHT					ON-BASE					LATE/CLOSE				
YEAR TM/L	AB	HR	AVG	OBP	SLG	AB	HR	AVG	OBP	SLG	AB	HR	AVG	OBP	SLG	AB	HR	AVG	OBP	SLG	AB	HR	AVG	OBP	SLG	AB	HR	AVG	OBP	SLG	AB	HR	AVG	OBP	SLG
1984 Det-A	558	13	.289	.357	.407	273	8	.300	.362	.436	285	5	.277	.352	.379	174	2	.230	.292	.305	384	11	.315	.386	.453	195	7	.282	.361	.441	71	2	.324	.449	.451
1985 Det-A	609	21	.279	.362	.456	303	11	.267	.352	.439	306	10	.291	.372	.474	145	2	.228	.323	.324	464	19	.295	.374	.498	205	9	.312	.399	.507	96	4	.292	.389	.458
1986 Det-A	584	20	.269	.338	.437	286	8	.248	.334	.406	298	12	.289	.341	.466	163	3	.221	.283	.325	421	17	.287	.359	.480	225	10	.298	.370	.489	90	2	.289	.359	.400
1987 Det-A	604	16	.265	.341	.435	283	10	.261	.341	.435	321	6	.268	.342	.421	226	4	.277	.279	.327	378	12	.294	.376	.487	213	7	.207	.282	.357	82	2	.293	.333	.463
1988 Det-A	403	12	.275	.376	.419	175	8	.269	.388	.457	228	4	.281	.366	.390	92	0	.228	.330	.272	311	12	.289	.390	.461	165	7	.279	.410	.461	59	0	.271	.403	.305
1989 Det-A	509	28	.251	.361	.462	235	17	.264	.377	.519	274	11	.241	.347	.412	149	5	.188	.305	.349	360	23	.278	.383	.508	220	12	.245	.357	.455	82	7	.220	.330	.500
1990 Det-A	472	18	.237	.338	.437	219	8	.215	.330	.384	253	10	.257	.356	.439	99	2	.162	.278	.253	373	16	.257	.353	.448	208	13	.231	.342	.447	67	0	.164	.273	.209
1991 Det-A	470	23	.279	.391	.489	237	15	.304	.442	.557	233	8	.253	.335	.421	97	2	.247	.354	.340	373	21	.287	.400	.528	214	12	.304	.421	.547	78	5	.231	.396	.462
1992 Det-A	453	19	.278	.386	.461	228	11	.320	.442	.548	225	8	.236	.326	.373	62	2	.355	.481	.548	391	17	.266	.370	.448	221	9	.294	.394	.462	67	3	.269	.387	.448
1993 Det-A	383	9	.290	.412	.449	193	5	.269	.388	.440	190	4	.311	.435	.458	49	0	.122	.254	.143	334	9	.314	.434	.494	212	6	.288	.385	.462	59	2	.271	.357	.424
1994 Det-A	322	12	.301	.377	.491	154	8	.318	.403	.545	168	4	.286	.352	.440	36	1	.278	.349	.417	286	11	.304	.380	.500	143	6	.259	.355	.427	46	1	.196	.309	.283
TOTALS	5367	191	.273	.365	.444	2586	109	.275	.375	.464	2781	82	.271	.354	.425	1292	23	.221	.310	.324	4075	168	.289	.382	.482	2221	98	.273	.369	.462	797	28	.260	.365	.410

Devon White BB/TR

	TOTAL					HOME					AWAY					LEFT					RIGHT					ON-BASE					LATE/CLOSE				
YEAR TM/L	AB	HR	AVG	OBP	SLG	AB	HR	AVG	OBP	SLG	AB	HR	AVG	OBP	SLG	AB	HR	AVG	OBP	SLG	AB	HR	AVG	OBP	SLG	AB	HR	AVG	OBP	SLG	AB	HR	AVG	OBP	SLG
1985 Cal-A	7	0	.143	.333	.143	2	0	.000	.500	.000	5	0	.200	.200	.200	0	0	—	1.000	—	7	0	.143	.250	.143	3	0	.333	.600	.333	2	0	.500	.500	.500
1986 Cal-A	51	1	.235	.316	.353	21	0	.190	.261	.286	30	1	.267	.353	.400	17	0	.294	.333	.294	34	1	.206	.308	.382	13	0	.231	.375	.385	14	0	.214	.313	.214
1987 Cal-A	639	24	.263	.306	.443	314	11	.248	.293	.417	325	13	.277	.320	.468	199	11	.246	.296	.477	440	13	.270	.311	.427	292	9	.250	.294	.397	118	7	.246	.288	.475
1988 Cal-A	455	11	.259	.297	.389	211	3	.237	.283	.341	244	8	.279	.310	.430	150	6	.247	.289	.420	305	5	.266	.301	.374	173	4	.266	.313	.399	76	1	.289	.341	.421
1989 Cal-A	636	12	.245	.282	.371	317	9	.243	.283	.394	319	3	.248	.281	.348	214	2	.248	.291	.355	422	10	.244	.277	.379	268	6	.235	.281	.343	85	0	.212	.287	.235
1990 Cal-A	443	11	.217	.290	.343	219	5	.215	.278	.352	224	6	.219	.302	.335	130	3	.246	.315	.354	313	8	.204	.280	.339	191	5	.215	.311	.330	87	3	.195	.286	.310

YEAR TM/L	TOTAL AB	HR	AVG	OBP	SLG	HOME AB	HR	AVG	OBP	SLG	AWAY AB	HR	AVG	OBP	SLG	LEFT AB	HR	AVG	OBP	SLG	RIGHT AB	HR	AVG	OBP	SLG	ON-BASE AB	HR	AVG	OBP	SLG	LATE/CLOSE AB	HR	AVG	OBP	SLG
1991 Tor-A	642	17	.282	.342	.455	326	9	.298	.355	.497	316	8	.266	.330	.411	199	8	.302	.350	.518	443	9	.273	.339	.427	224	3	.246	.319	.371	108	0	.306	.370	.370
1992 Tor-A	641	17	.248	.303	.390	306	7	.265	.321	.415	335	10	.233	.286	.367	179	5	.212	.272	.324	462	12	.262	.315	.416	242	7	.219	.286	.368	90	3	.222	.314	.400
1993 Tor-A	598	15	.273	.341	.438	307	10	.290	.361	.498	291	5	.254	.321	.375	185	3	.254	.324	.395	413	12	.281	.349	.458	214	4	.262	.343	.411	73	1	.247	.360	.397
1994 Tor-A	403	13	.270	.313	.457	193	5	.275	.311	.440	210	8	.267	.316	.471	124	4	.306	.328	.508	279	9	.254	.307	.434	141	4	.284	.327	.454	62	4	.274	.328	.597
TOTALS	4515	121	.258	.311	.411	2216	59	.260	.313	.423	2299	62	.255	.308	.399	1397	42	.257	.309	.417	3118	79	.258	.312	.408	1761	40	.245	.308	.380	715	19	.249	.321	.393

■ Frank White BR/TR

YEAR TM/L	AB	HR	AVG	OBP	SLG	AB	HR	AVG	OBP	SLG	AB	HR	AVG	OBP	SLG	AB	HR	AVG	OBP	SLG	AB	HR	AVG	OBP	SLG	AB	HR	AVG	OBP	SLG	AB	HR	AVG	OBP	SLG
1984 KC-A	479	17	.271	.311	.445	240	6	.258	.306	.412	239	11	.285	.316	.477	127	7	.299	.336	.520	352	10	.261	.302	.418	204	5	.289	.330	.441	75	3	.227	.284	.387
1985 KC-A	563	22	.249	.284	.414	297	9	.242	.277	.377	266	13	.256	.292	.455	166	9	.247	.277	.446	397	13	.249	.287	.401	221	4	.281	.314	.389	95	2	.284	.310	.389
1986 KC-A	566	22	.272	.322	.465	277	12	.282	.329	.491	289	10	.263	.315	.439	149	1	.268	.337	.349	417	21	.273	.316	.506	261	8	.276	.326	.437	102	8	.284	.327	.559
1987 KC-A	563	17	.245	.308	.400	256	6	.273	.355	.418	307	11	.221	.267	.384	148	5	.284	.352	.453	415	12	.231	.292	.381	264	6	.269	.334	.417	67	2	.164	.263	.284
1988 KC-A	537	8	.235	.266	.330	269	3	.242	.274	.338	268	5	.228	.257	.321	155	2	.265	.296	.368	382	6	.223	.254	.314	240	3	.221	.252	.317	100	1	.180	.224	.250
1989 KC-A	418	2	.256	.307	.328	210	1	.238	.277	.314	208	1	.274	.336	.341	125	0	.240	.307	.296	293	2	.263	.307	.341	105	0	.281	.337	.346	64	1	.281	.343	.375
1990 KC-A	241	2	.216	.253	.307	145	2	.248	.281	.366	96	0	.167	.212	.219	93	1	.194	.240	.280	148	1	.230	.261	.324	109	2	.229	.243	.339	33	0	.091	.114	.121
TOTALS	3367	90	.252	.296	.393	1694	39	.256	.302	.392	1673	51	.247	.290	.393	963	25	.260	.310	.394	2404	65	.248	.291	.392	1484	28	.265	.310	.389	536	17	.229	.280	.364

■ Mark Whiten BB/TR

YEAR TM/L	AB	HR	AVG	OBP	SLG	AB	HR	AVG	OBP	SLG	AB	HR	AVG	OBP	SLG	AB	HR	AVG	OBP	SLG	AB	HR	AVG	OBP	SLG	AB	HR	AVG	OBP	SLG	AB	HR	AVG	OBP	SLG
1990 Tor-A	88	2	.273	.323	.375	29	1	.241	.290	.379	59	1	.288	.338	.373	38	1	.316	.357	.474	50	1	.240	.296	.300	33	1	.212	.325	.333	15	0	.267	.389	.267
1991 Tor-A	149	2	.221	.274	.329	74	2	.203	.280	.378	75	0	.240	.268	.280	41	1	.146	.217	.244	108	1	.250	.297	.361	65	0	.215	.289	.323	25	1	.200	.231	.440
1991 Cle-A	258	7	.256	.310	.422	123	2	.276	.328	.415	135	5	.237	.293	.430	68	1	.324	.368	.515	190	6	.232	.288	.389	106	1	.245	.281	.358	54	1	.204	.241	.296
1992 Cle-A	508	9	.254	.347	.360	260	6	.269	.350	.404	248	3	.238	.344	.315	127	3	.283	.401	.409	381	6	.244	.330	.344	209	4	.244	.361	.340	91	3	.242	.373	.374
1993 StL-N	562	25	.253	.323	.423	262	12	.237	.302	.397	300	13	.267	.340	.447	160	8	.231	.296	.394	402	17	.261	.333	.435	259	15	.274	.358	.479	98	3	.204	.298	.316
1994 StL-N	334	14	.293	.364	.485	151	6	.272	.358	.417	183	8	.311	.368	.541	99	4	.293	.336	.444	235	10	.294	.375	.502	151	6	.278	.376	.464	49	2	.327	.382	.510
TOTALS	1899	59	.259	.331	.408	899	29	.255	.327	.403	1000	30	.263	.335	.412	533	18	.266	.337	.417	1366	41	.256	.329	.404	823	27	.256	.346	.407	332	10	.235	.323	.364

■ Ernie Whitt BL/TR

YEAR TM/L	AB	HR	AVG	OBP	SLG	AB	HR	AVG	OBP	SLG	AB	HR	AVG	OBP	SLG	AB	HR	AVG	OBP	SLG	AB	HR	AVG	OBP	SLG	AB	HR	AVG	OBP	SLG	AB	HR	AVG	OBP	SLG
1984 Tor-A	315	15	.238	.327	.425	144	5	.236	.343	.403	171	10	.240	.313	.444	25	0	.160	.222	.320	290	15	.245	.335	.434	139	7	.216	.333	.381	59	3	.288	.400	.475
1985 Tor-A	412	19	.245	.323	.444	197	7	.223	.319	.406	215	12	.265	.326	.479	75	2	.213	.318	.320	337	17	.252	.324	.472	184	8	.266	.363	.457	72	1	.222	.287	.347
1986 Tor-A	395	16	.268	.326	.448	189	7	.265	.341	.460	206	9	.272	.311	.437	46	3	.370	.396	.565	349	13	.255	.317	.433	193	6	.295	.353	.446	71	2	.324	.355	.437
1987 Tor-A	446	19	.269	.334	.455	214	11	.262	.339	.481	232	8	.276	.329	.431	63	0	.238	.314	.286	383	19	.274	.337	.483	212	10	.264	.335	.467	72	0	.222	.301	.306
1988 Tor-A	398	16	.251	.348	.410	194	9	.242	.359	.418	204	7	.260	.336	.402	39	2	.282	.408	.462	359	14	.248	.341	.404	171	7	.269	.355	.439	49	2	.224	.293	.367
1989 Tor-A	385	11	.262	.349	.416	184	8	.234	.346	.418	201	3	.289	.351	.413	44	1	.159	.240	.227	341	10	.276	.362	.440	168	7	.256	.352	.458	65	2	.246	.338	.369
1990 Atl-N	180	2	.172	.265	.250	86	2	.163	.284	.279	94	0	.181	.245	.223	17	0	.118	.167	.118	163	2	.178	.274	.264	71	0	.155	.274	.183	32	0	.281	.361	.344
1991 Bal-A	62	0	.242	.329	.274	29	0	.276	.344	.310	33	0	.212	.316	.242	5	0	.200	.200	.200	57	0	.246	.338	.281	28	0	.179	.281	.179	17	0	.294	.429	.353
TOTALS	2593	98	.250	.329	.417	1237	49	.239	.337	.420	1356	49	.260	.322	.415	314	8	.232	.313	.341	2279	90	.253	.332	.428	1166	45	.255	.342	.422	437	10	.259	.335	.378

■ Curtis Wilkerson BB/TR

YEAR TM/L	AB	HR	AVG	OBP	SLG	AB	HR	AVG	OBP	SLG	AB	HR	AVG	OBP	SLG	AB	HR	AVG	OBP	SLG	AB	HR	AVG	OBP	SLG	AB	HR	AVG	OBP	SLG	AB	HR	AVG	OBP	SLG
1984 Tex-A	484	1	.248	.282	.279	239	0	.255	.295	.276	245	1	.241	.270	.282	136	0	.221	.287	.243	348	1	.259	.281	.293	173	0	.243	.281	.260	84	0	.238	.264	.274
1985 Tex-A	360	0	.244	.293	.308	160	0	.225	.267	.262	200	0	.263	.313	.345	86	0	.279	.367	.395	274	0	.234	.268	.281	124	0	.234	.295	.298	57	0	.351	.383	.456
1986 Tex-A	236	0	.237	.273	.305	116	0	.233	.274	.319	120	0	.242	.272	.292	27	0	.111	.172	.111	209	0	.254	.286	.330	83	0	.253	.284	.349	25	0	.280	.308	.280
1987 Tex-A	138	2	.268	.308	.391	67	1	.269	.300	.373	71	1	.268	.316	.408	21	1	.286	.286	.476	117	1	.265	.312	.376	54	0	.278	.316	.407	17	0	.176	.222	.176
1988 Tex-A	338	0	.293	.345	.358	152	0	.289	.331	.368	186	0	.296	.356	.349	47	0	.255	.300	.277	291	0	.299	.352	.371	156	0	.288	.354	.353	60	0	.333	.394	.433
1989 Chi-N	160	1	.244	.278	.313	88	1	.284	.304	.375	72	0	.194	.247	.236	41	1	.171	.209	.268	119	0	.269	.302	.328	63	0	.143	.179	.175	36	1	.361	.389	.500
1990 Chi-N	186	0	.220	.249	.258	81	0	.296	.313	.370	105	0	.162	.200	.171	58	0	.241	.279	.293	128	0	.211	.235	.242	79	0	.241	.286	.278	29	0	.276	.344	.345
1991 Pit-N	191	2	.188	.243	.277	89	2	.180	.255	.326	102	0	.196	.232	.235	49	0	.224	.286	.306	142	2	.176	.227	.268	95	1	.211	.255	.274	50	1	.160	.192	.260
1992 KC-A	296	2	.250	.292	.311	160	2	.269	.326	.344	136	0	.228	.250	.272	68	1	.294	.351	.368	228	1	.237	.272	.294	112	1	.223	.283	.277	54	0	.241	.300	.259
1993 KC-A	28	0	.143	.172	.143	10	0	.100	.182	.100	18	0	.167	.167	.167	7	0	.000	.000	.000	21	0	.190	.227	.190	10	0	.100	.100	.100	7	0	.000	.000	.000
TOTALS	2417	8	.246	.287	.306	1162	6	.254	.296	.322	1255	2	.238	.279	.292	540	3	.235	.294	.298	1877	5	.249	.285	.308	949	2	.238	.287	.294	419	2	.267	.308	.334

■ Rick Wilkins BL/TR

YEAR TM/L	AB	HR	AVG	OBP	SLG	AB	HR	AVG	OBP	SLG	AB	HR	AVG	OBP	SLG	AB	HR	AVG	OBP	SLG	AB	HR	AVG	OBP	SLG	AB	HR	AVG	OBP	SLG	AB	HR	AVG	OBP	SLG
1991 Chi-N	203	6	.222	.307	.355	103	3	.175	.248	.291	100	4	.270	.365	.420	38	1	.237	.326	.342	165	5	.218	.303	.358	85	2	.200	.292	.318	46	1	.304	.385	.500
1992 Chi-N	244	8	.270	.344	.414	129	3	.264	.354	.357	115	5	.278	.333	.478	50	0	.280	.345	.340	194	8	.268	.344	.433	109	2	.211	.315	.303	49	2	.224	.333	.347
1993 Chi-N	446	30	.303	.376	.561	238	10	.256	.317	.429	208	20	.356	.440	.712	67	3	.224	.325	.403	379	27	.317	.385	.588	180	9	.322	.425	.528	78	6	.282	.371	.551
1994 Chi-N	313	7	.227	.317	.387	154	4	.227	.328	.377	159	3	.226	.306	.396	52	1	.154	.267	.269	261	6	.241	.327	.410	128	2	.234	.329	.367	54	1	.148	.281	.222
TOTALS	1206	51	.263	.342	.451	624	19	.237	.316	.378	582	32	.290	.370	.529	207	5	.222	.315	.343	999	46	.271	.348	.473	502	15	.255	.355	.402	227	10	.242	.344	.419

■ Bernie Williams BB/TR

YEAR TM/L	AB	HR	AVG	OBP	SLG	AB	HR	AVG	OBP	SLG	AB	HR	AVG	OBP	SLG	AB	HR	AVG	OBP	SLG	AB	HR	AVG	OBP	SLG	AB	HR	AVG	OBP	SLG	AB	HR	AVG	OBP	SLG
1991 NY-A	320	3	.237	.336	.350	159	1	.264	.355	.371	161	2	.211	.317	.329	104	2	.202	.309	.317	216	1	.255	.349	.366	122	0	.287	.366	.385	55	0	.218	.317	.273
1992 NY-A	261	5	.280	.354	.406	134	3	.291	.375	.433	127	2	.268	.331	.378	84	1	.298	.379	.429	177	4	.271	.342	.395	102	2	.275	.345	.422	46	0	.196	.260	.283
1993 NY-A	567	12	.268	.333	.400	256	5	.266	.339	.395	311	7	.270	.328	.405	191	7	.325	.402	.503	376	5	.239	.297	.348	245	5	.290	.340	.392	84	3	.262	.326	.381
1994 NY-A	408	12	.289	.384	.453	184	4	.261	.358	.391	224	8	.313	.405	.504	145	6	.366	.404	.600	263	6	.247	.362	.373	195	6	.287	.362	.446	57	0	.263	.368	.298
TOTALS	1556	32	.269	.351	.405	733	13	.269	.354	.398	823	19	.270	.348	.413	524	16	.307	.386	.481	1032	16	.250	.333	.366	664	13	.286	.352	.411	242	3	.240	.322	.318

■ Matt Williams BR/TR

YEAR TM/L	AB	HR	AVG	OBP	SLG	AB	HR	AVG	OBP	SLG	AB	HR	AVG	OBP	SLG	AB	HR	AVG	OBP	SLG	AB	HR	AVG	OBP	SLG	AB	HR	AVG	OBP	SLG	AB	HR	AVG	OBP	SLG
1987 SF-N	245	8	.188	.240	.339	112	5	.179	.227	.357	133	3	.195	.250	.323	78	4	.192	.241	.385	167	4	.186	.239	.317	101	2	.158	.225	.257	31	1	.161	.182	.355
1988 SF-N	156	8	.205	.251	.410	97	7	.227	.257	.474	59	1	.169	.242	.305	54	5	.167	.237	.463	102	3	.225	.259	.382	68	1	.147	.224	.206	25	1	.160	.222	.360
1989 SF-N	292	18	.202	.242	.455	144	10	.215	.248	.514	148	8	.189	.236	.399	87	9	.264	.330	.644	205	9	.176	.202	.376	134	10	.172	.231	.463	36	0	.194	.237	.306
1990 SF-N	617	33	.277	.319	.488	303	20	.271	.312	.521	314	13	.283	.325	.455	208	12	.284	.332	.500	409	21	.274	.312	.482	273	16	.330	.382	.571	100	3	.230	.267	.360
1991 SF-N	589	34	.268	.310	.499	289	17	.287	.327	.526	300	17	.250	.294	.473	165	7	.279	.315	.455	424	27	.264	.309	.517	279	15	.276	.308	.480	92	4	.217	.280	.391
1992 SF-N	529	20	.227	.286	.384	269	9	.230	.283	.387	260	11	.223	.290	.381	164	10	.226	.279	.445	365	10	.227	.290	.356	232	10	.211	.283	.401	107	2	.187	.281	.271
1993 SF-N	579	38	.294	.325	.561	287	19	.293	.330	.571	292	19	.295	.319	.551	186	17	.328	.363	.683	393	21	.277	.306	.504	275	17	.302	.341	.545	84	7	.262	.289	.548
1994 SF-N	445	43	.267	.319	.607	219	20	.265	.326	.584	226	23	.270	.311	.628	104	16	.298	.373	.788	341	27	.258	.301	.551	204	16	.245	.302	.534	76	2	.211	.274	.355
TOTALS	3452	202	.253	.298	.485	1720	107	.257	.301	.503	1732	95	.250	.295	.466	1046	80	.269	.319	.547	2406	122	.247	.289	.458	1566	87	.254	.307	.475	551	20	.212	.268	.372

■ Glenn Wilson BR/TR

YEAR TM/L	AB	HR	AVG	OBP	SLG	AB	HR	AVG	OBP	SLG	AB	HR	AVG	OBP	SLG	AB	HR	AVG	OBP	SLG	AB	HR	AVG	OBP	SLG	AB	HR	AVG	OBP	SLG	AB	HR	AVG	OBP	SLG
1984 Phi-N	341	6	.240	.276	.372	160	5	.244	.282	.394	181	1	.238	.271	.354	125	3	.264	.295	.408	216	3	.227	.265	.352	156	3	.224	.248	.346	63	0	.206	.265	.238
1985 Phi-N	608	14	.275	.311	.424	307	7	.257	.292	.397	301	7	.292	.329	.452	171	6	.287	.330	.485	437	8	.270	.303	.405	284	10	.268	.297	.465	106	5	.292	.321	.519
1986 Phi-N	584	15	.271	.319	.413	285	7	.302	.357	.467	299	8	.241	.283	.361	185	4	.222	.271	.335	399	11	.293	.341	.449	273	8	.282	.323	.421	103	1	.320	.379	.408
1987 Phi-N	569	14	.264	.308	.381	278	7	.252	.315	.342	291	9	.275	.300	.419	155	2	.271	.307	.355	414	12	.261	.308	.391	266	3	.244	.284	.316	99	2	.273	.345	.364
1988 Sea-A	284	3	.250	.286	.324	132	2	.273	.297	.371	152	1	.230	.276	.283	101	1	.317	.340	.396	183	2	.213	.256	.284	108	2	.176	.216	.259	53	0	.189	.214	.189
1988 Pit-N	126	0	.270	.288	.381	54	0	.259	.259	.370	72	2	.278	.284	.389	63	2	.254	.277	.429	63	0	.286	.299	.333	51	0	.235	.268	.294	31	0	.226	.273	.258
1989 Pit-N	330	9	.282	.342	.448	147	2	.259	.341	.367	183	7	.301	.343	.514	119	3	.319	.371	.513	211	6	.261	.326	.412	133	3	.308	.374	.459	67	1	.343	.430	.507
1989 Hou-N	102	2	.216	.250	.333	51	2	.275	.302	.490	51	0	.157	.200	.176	24	1	.333	.385	.542	78	1	.179	.207	.269	44	1	.205	.234	.341	20	1	.250	.250	.450
1990 Hou-N	368	10	.245	.293	.364	174	5	.259	.307	.402	194	5	.232	.281	.330	164	2	.262	.311	.360	204	8	.238	.279	.368	168	4	.238	.283	.351	62	2	.226	.286	.323
1993 Pit-N	14	0	.143	.143	.143	5	0	.000	.000	.000	9	0	.222	.222	.222	12	0	.167	.167	.167	2	0	.000	.000	.000	6	0	.000	.000	.000	4	0	.000	.000	.000
TOTALS	3326	75	.261	.304	.391	1587	35	.271	.320	.406	1739	40	.252	.289	.377	1119	24	.272	.313	.405	2207	51	.256	.300	.384	1489	34	.251	.291	.378	608	12	.268	.323	.377

■ Mookie Wilson BB/TR

YEAR TM/L	AB	HR	AVG	OBP	SLG	AB	HR	AVG	OBP	SLG	AB	HR	AVG	OBP	SLG	AB	HR	AVG	OBP	SLG	AB	HR	AVG	OBP	SLG	AB	HR	AVG	OBP	SLG	AB	HR	AVG	OBP	SLG
1984 NY-N	587	10	.276	.308	.409	309	7	.278	.308	.440	278	3	.273	.308	.374	199	4	.276	.306	.437	388	6	.276	.309	.394	244	5	.283	.303	.418	92	1	.250	.314	.370
1985 NY-N	337	6	.276	.331	.424	152	2	.329	.396	.441	185	4	.232	.274	.411	149	4	.295	.361	.490	188	2	.261	.305	.372	112	0	.214	.276	.286	64	4	.297	.384	.547
1986 NY-N	381	9	.289	.345	.430	173	4	.289	.351	.422	208	5	.288	.339	.438	196	3	.291	.341	.418	185	6	.286	.348	.443	129	4	.326	.397	.519	82	1	.268	.318	.378
1987 NY-N	385	9	.299	.359	.455	176	5	.267	.337	.415	209	4	.325	.379	.488	225	3	.271	.329	.404	160	6	.338	.401	.525	136	2	.265	.348	.397	71	1	.278	.350	.361
1988 NY-N	378	8	.296	.345	.431	185	1	.259	.292	.335	193	7	.332	.393	.523	195	4	.282	.335	.421	183	4	.311	.355	.443	145	4	.283	.321	.421	70	3	.314	.402	.500
1989 NY-N	249	3	.205	.237	.289	120	1	.192	.218	.267	129	2	.217	.254	.310	122	1	.164	.203	.221	127	2	.244	.269	.354	99	0	.182	.224	.222	50	0	.200	.208	.240
1989 Tor-A	238	2	.298	.311	.370	127	1	.252	.267	.323	111	1	.351	.363	.423	78	0	.346	.346	.397	160	2	.275	.294	.356	89	0	.247	.244	.292	37	0	.216	.237	.243
1990 Tor-A	588	3	.265	.300	.355	271	0	.247	.279	.321	317	3	.281	.318	.385	188	0	.245	.294	.351	400	1	.275	.303	.357	235	0	.268	.307	.357	97	1	.309	.346	.423
1991 Tor-A	241	2	.241	.277	.349	115	1	.270	.298	.383	126	1	.214	.259	.317	43	0	.209	.209	.256	198	2	.247	.291	.369	117	1	.282	.312	.393	53	0	.226	.281	.415
TOTALS	3384	52	.274	.316	.395	1628	22	.267	.308	.378	1756	30	.281	.324	.412	1395	21	.279	.318	.396	1989	31	.279	.318	.396	1306	16	.266	.309	.378	617	11	.269	.326	.397

■ Willie Wilson BB/TR

YEAR TM/L	AB	HR	AVG	OBP	SLG	AB	HR	AVG	OBP	SLG	AB	HR	AVG	OBP	SLG	AB	HR	AVG	OBP	SLG	AB	HR	AVG	OBP	SLG	AB	HR	AVG	OBP	SLG	AB	HR	AVG	OBP	SLG
1984 KC-A	541	2	.301	.350	.390	260	1	.304	.360	.381	281	1	.299	.340	.399	167	1	.341	.387	.449	374	1	.283	.333	.364	198	2	.323	.372	.424	78	0	.256	.306	.308
1985 KC-A	605	4	.278	.316	.408	303	1	.313	.351	.417	302	3	.243	.281	.399	144	1	.293	.316	.409	461	3	.272	.316	.408	193	1	.306	.348	.435	96	0	.302	.333	.385
1986 KC-A	631	9	.269	.313	.366	309	5	.265	.322	.379	322	4	.273	.303	.354	175	4	.309	.338	.429	456	5	.254	.307	.342	235	2	.268	.308	.345	103	0	.303	.337	.354
1987 KC-A	610	4	.279	.320	.377	321	4	.296	.334	.399	289	0	.260	.305	.353	170	1	.241	.270	.312	440	3	.293	.340	.402	199	0	.271	.318	.367	81	0	.358	.395	.519
1988 KC-A	591	1	.262	.289	.333	297	0	.283	.303	.364	294	1	.241	.274	.303	186	0	.258	.275	.366	405	1	.264	.295	.319	207	0	.295	.317	.357	93	0	.269	.292	.323

YEAR	TM/L	TOTAL AB	HR	AVG	OBP	SLG	HOME AB	HR	AVG	OBP	SLG	AWAY AB	HR	AVG	OBP	SLG	LEFT AB	HR	AVG	OBP	SLG	RIGHT AB	HR	AVG	OBP	SLG	ON-BASE AB	HR	AVG	OBP	SLG	LATE/CLOSE AB	HR	AVG	OBP	SLG
1989	KC-A	383	3	.253	.300	.358	197	1	.269	.318	.345	186	2	.237	.281	.371	123	1	.276	.306	.398	260	2	.242	.297	.338	156	1	.256	.287	.359	50	1	.200	.259	.320
1990	KC-A	307	2	.290	.354	.371	166	1	.331	.381	.422	141	1	.241	.323	.312	103	0	.272	.306	.350	204	2	.299	.377	.382	154	1	.331	.384	.435	53	1	.208	.300	.264
1991	Oak-A	294	0	.238	.290	.313	132	0	.250	.303	.341	162	0	.228	.280	.290	99	0	.253	.302	.293	195	0	.231	.284	.323	128	0	.258	.299	.359	42	0	.238	.333	.310
1992	Oak-A	396	0	.270	.329	.333	199	0	.271	.339	.322	197	0	.269	.318	.345	121	0	.248	.316	.306	275	0	.280	.334	.345	197	0	.269	.326	.335	63	0	.286	.348	.333
1993	Chi-A	221	1	.258	.301	.348	114	0	.289	.331	.395	107	1	.224	.270	.299	102	0	.235	.257	.275	119	1	.277	.336	.412	66	0	.227	.288	.242	56	0	.286	.322	.357
1994	Chi-A	21	0	.238	.273	.429	10	0	.100	.182	.100	11	0	.364	.364	.727	14	0	.214	.214	.500	7	0	.286	.375	.286	4	0	.000	.000	.000	4	0	.500	.500	.500
TOTALS		4600	26	.272	.316	.365	2307	9	.283	.329	.378	2293	17	.261	.304	.352	1424	8	.275	.307	.368	3176	18	.270	.320	.363	1737	7	.284	.327	.372	715	2	.280	.326	.355

■ Dave Winfield BR/TR

YEAR	TM/L	TOTAL AB	HR	AVG	OBP	SLG	HOME AB	HR	AVG	OBP	SLG	AWAY AB	HR	AVG	OBP	SLG	LEFT AB	HR	AVG	OBP	SLG	RIGHT AB	HR	AVG	OBP	SLG	ON-BASE AB	HR	AVG	OBP	SLG	LATE/CLOSE AB	HR	AVG	OBP	SLG
1984	NY-A	567	19	.340	.393	.515	260	9	.331	.401	.504	307	10	.349	.386	.524	170	5	.324	.395	.476	397	14	.348	.392	.531	295	10	.342	.399	.532	100	4	.310	.361	.500
1985	NY-A	633	26	.275	.328	.471	298	15	.285	.343	.507	335	11	.266	.315	.439	215	10	.251	.343	.470	418	16	.287	.320	.471	317	14	.281	.345	.473	93	4	.258	.310	.419
1986	NY-A	565	24	.262	.349	.462	279	12	.272	.362	.477	286	12	.252	.336	.448	197	12	.259	.373	.523	368	12	.264	.336	.429	293	14	.270	.355	.491	84	2	.238	.305	.345
1987	NY-A	575	27	.275	.358	.457	269	11	.283	.374	.450	306	16	.268	.343	.464	177	13	.345	.449	.621	398	14	.244	.314	.384	259	10	.320	.403	.486	87	5	.264	.340	.471
1988	NY-A	559	25	.322	.398	.530	274	12	.332	.405	.518	285	13	.312	.391	.540	175	11	.331	.426	.594	384	14	.318	.384	.500	268	13	.340	.418	.556	92	3	.315	.388	.457
1990	NY-A	61	2	.213	.269	.361	33	0	.091	.118	.152	28	2	.357	.424	.607	30	0	.200	.250	.300	31	2	.226	.286	.419	26	0	.115	.143	.154	13	0	.231	.286	.308
1990	Cal-A	414	19	.275	.348	.466	205	13	.288	.364	.537	209	6	.263	.330	.397	126	3	.246	.350	.508	288	16	.286	.348	.448	202	9	.282	.346	.475	69	4	.319	.360	.565
1991	Cal-A	568	28	.262	.326	.472	271	13	.244	.305	.432	297	15	.279	.345	.508	160	11	.300	.381	.575	408	17	.248	.304	.431	251	11	.279	.360	.482	74	5	.216	.275	.378
1992	Tor-A	583	26	.290	.377	.491	268	13	.302	.403	.500	315	13	.279	.353	.483	146	8	.301	.395	.527	437	18	.286	.370	.478	261	13	.303	.403	.529	70	4	.243	.386	.443
1993	Min-A	547	21	.271	.325	.442	278	12	.255	.313	.439	269	9	.286	.338	.446	137	4	.292	.345	.460	410	17	.263	.318	.437	246	13	.244	.278	.300	91	2	.242	.300	.352
1994	Min-A	294	10	.252	.321	.425	139	5	.281	.369	.460	155	5	.226	.275	.394	67	5	.343	.470	.657	227	5	.225	.270	.357	132	4	.227	.329	.364	43	1	.279	.333	.419
TOTALS		5366	227	.283	.353	.474	2574	115	.285	.361	.478	2792	112	.282	.346	.471	1600	84	.299	.390	.530	3766	143	.276	.337	.451	2550	111	.292	.369	.489	816	32	.268	.336	.434

■ Herm Winningham BL/TR

YEAR	TM/L	TOTAL AB	HR	AVG	OBP	SLG	HOME AB	HR	AVG	OBP	SLG	AWAY AB	HR	AVG	OBP	SLG	LEFT AB	HR	AVG	OBP	SLG	RIGHT AB	HR	AVG	OBP	SLG	ON-BASE AB	HR	AVG	OBP	SLG	LATE/CLOSE AB	HR	AVG	OBP	SLG
1984	NY-N	27	0	.407	.429	.519	13	0	.308	.357	.385	14	0	.500	.500	.643	2	0	1.000	1.000	1.000	25	0	.360	.385	.480	14	0	.500	.500	.714	5	0	.600	.600	.600
1985	Mon-N	312	3	.237	.297	.317	162	0	.191	.277	.247	150	3	.287	.319	.393	46	1	.217	.224	.283	266	2	.241	.308	.323	116	0	.233	.306	.276	55	1	.200	.254	.291
1986	Mon-N	185	4	.216	.286	.346	85	1	.153	.265	.247	100	3	.270	.305	.430	26	1	.308	.333	.423	159	3	.201	.278	.333	71	1	.183	.266	.282	49	0	.245	.339	.327
1987	Mon-N	347	4	.239	.304	.349	180	2	.272	.332	.367	167	2	.204	.275	.329	29	0	.345	.394	.448	318	4	.230	.295	.340	139	4	.281	.358	.446	64	1	.219	.315	.313
1988	Mon-N	90	0	.233	.320	.278	39	0	.333	.409	.410	51	0	.157	.254	.176	6	0	.167	.167	.167	84	0	.238	.330	.286	28	0	.393	.455	.464	24	0	.208	.310	.333
1988	Cin-N	113	0	.230	.261	.292	57	0	.228	.241	.316	56	0	.232	.279	.268	32	0	.250	.242	.375	81	0	.222	.267	.259	53	0	.264	.273	.377	22	0	.318	.318	.409
1989	Cin-N	251	3	.251	.316	.355	133	1	.248	.329	.346	118	2	.254	.302	.364	37	1	.216	.256	.351	214	2	.257	.326	.355	79	1	.253	.314	.304	47	1	.319	.373	.447
1990	Cin-N	160	3	.256	.314	.425	82	0	.195	.241	.207	78	3	.321	.386	.654	28	1	.143	.167	.286	132	2	.280	.345	.455	68	0	.250	.307	.368	30	1	.300	.323	.667
1991	Cin-N	169	1	.225	.272	.290	84	1	.238	.289	.321	85	0	.212	.256	.259	13	0	.154	.214	.154	156	1	.231	.277	.301	56	0	.161	.230	.196	36	0	.361	.361	.444
1992	Bos-A	234	1	.235	.266	.291	125	1	.240	.275	.328	109	0	.229	.257	.248	21	0	.143	.143	.190	213	1	.244	.278	.300	83	1	.241	.284	.313	58	0	.190	.230	.190
TOTALS		1888	19	.239	.296	.334	960	6	.231	.296	.309	928	13	.248	.297	.359	240	4	.233	.256	.329	1648	15	.240	.302	.334	707	7	.250	.313	.344	390	4	.256	.312	.359

■ George Wright BB/TR

YEAR	TM/L	TOTAL AB	HR	AVG	OBP	SLG	HOME AB	HR	AVG	OBP	SLG	AWAY AB	HR	AVG	OBP	SLG	LEFT AB	HR	AVG	OBP	SLG	RIGHT AB	HR	AVG	OBP	SLG	ON-BASE AB	HR	AVG	OBP	SLG	LATE/CLOSE AB	HR	AVG	OBP	SLG
1984	Tex-A	383	9	.243	.273	.384	201	6	.254	.282	.413	182	3	.231	.263	.352	122	3	.197	.244	.311	261	6	.264	.287	.418	163	5	.276	.305	.423	85	2	.306	.322	.400
1985	Tex-A	363	2	.190	.241	.242	158	2	.158	.213	.215	205	0	.215	.262	.263	122	0	.172	.231	.221	241	2	.199	.246	.253	151	0	.159	.241	.172	64	0	.234	.286	.266
1986	Tex-A	106	0	.217	.250	.321	43	1	.140	.178	.256	63	0	.270	.299	.365	25	0	.120	.179	.120	81	0	.247	.274	.383	40	0	.225	.273	.300	24	1	.125	.222	.333
1986	Mon-N	117	0	.188	.258	.265	50	0	.140	.224	.180	67	0	.224	.284	.328	26	0	.269	.321	.423	91	0	.165	.240	.220	47	0	.191	.226	.234	31	0	.161	.182	.226
TOTALS		969	13	.214	.257	.310	452	9	.197	.241	.303	517	3	.228	.270	.315	295	3	.186	.240	.268	674	10	.226	.264	.328	401	5	.217	.268	.294	204	3	.240	.276	.324

■ Marvell Wynne BL/TL

YEAR	TM/L	TOTAL AB	HR	AVG	OBP	SLG	HOME AB	HR	AVG	OBP	SLG	AWAY AB	HR	AVG	OBP	SLG	LEFT AB	HR	AVG	OBP	SLG	RIGHT AB	HR	AVG	OBP	SLG	ON-BASE AB	HR	AVG	OBP	SLG	LATE/CLOSE AB	HR	AVG	OBP	SLG
1984	Pit-N	653	0	.266	.310	.337	310	0	.271	.313	.348	343	0	.262	.307	.327	166	0	.259	.328	.337	487	0	.269	.304	.337	198	0	.253	.309	.298	122	0	.254	.295	.328
1985	Pit-N	337	2	.205	.247	.258	158	1	.234	.297	.297	179	1	.179	.201	.223	111	1	.252	.278	.306	226	1	.181	.232	.235	65	0	.200	.246	.231	65	0	.200	.244	.231
1986	SD-N	288	7	.264	.300	.417	177	5	.311	.328	.492	111	2	.189	.258	.297	70	2	.186	.230	.329	218	5	.289	.322	.445	125	0	.248	.292	.360	75	3	.280	.341	.493
1987	SD-N	188	2	.250	.321	.346	80	2	.162	.230	.300	108	0	.315	.385	.380	39	0	.231	.318	.256	149	2	.255	.321	.369	81	1	.284	.359	.407	49	0	.327	.382	.408
1988	SD-N	333	11	.264	.325	.426	164	6	.280	.343	.463	169	5	.249	.308	.391	55	1	.327	.413	.491	278	10	.252	.307	.414	116	6	.328	.370	.560	70	2	.214	.276	.371
1989	SD-N	294	6	.252	.282	.357	131	3	.244	.286	.351	163	3	.258	.280	.362	33	1	.424	.441	.606	261	5	.231	.263	.326	132	3	.280	.319	.417	48	0	.313	.313	.375
1989	Chi-N	48	1	.188	.220	.333	19	0	.316	.316	.421	29	1	.103	.161	.276	12	0	.167	.167	.250	36	1	.194	.237	.361	18	0	.167	.211	.333	9	0	.111	.111	.111
1990	Chi-N	186	4	.204	.264	.333	103	2	.233	.275	.369	83	2	.169	.250	.289	17	1	.176	.263	.353	169	3	.207	.264	.331	84	1	.238	.312	.381	46	1	.239	.314	.391
TOTALS		2327	33	.247	.294	.351	1142	19	.260	.305	.380	1185	14	.235	.283	.323	503	6	.258	.314	.356	1824	27	.244	.288	.350	885	11	.260	.313	.373	484	6	.254	.303	.362

■ Gerald Young BB/TR

YEAR	TM/L	TOTAL AB	HR	AVG	OBP	SLG	HOME AB	HR	AVG	OBP	SLG	AWAY AB	HR	AVG	OBP	SLG	LEFT AB	HR	AVG	OBP	SLG	RIGHT AB	HR	AVG	OBP	SLG	ON-BASE AB	HR	AVG	OBP	SLG	LATE/CLOSE AB	HR	AVG	OBP	SLG
1987	Hou-N	274	1	.321	.380	.380	145	0	.359	.423	.441	129	1	.279	.329	.310	105	1	.390	.425	.467	169	0	.278	.353	.325	78	0	.346	.411	.397	53	0	.340	.397	.415
1988	Hou-N	576	0	.257	.334	.325	288	0	.236	.302	.288	288	0	.278	.365	.361	205	0	.273	.339	.337	371	0	.248	.331	.318	165	0	.279	.361	.364	107	0	.355	.400	.467
1989	Hou-N	533	0	.233	.326	.276	267	0	.247	.336	.292	266	0	.218	.316	.259	147	0	.238	.335	.265	386	0	.231	.322	.280	180	0	.300	.376	.356	97	0	.216	.313	.247
1990	Hou-N	154	1	.175	.269	.234	93	1	.183	.267	.269	61	0	.164	.271	.180	46	1	.174	.264	.326	108	0	.176	.270	.194	49	0	.143	.259	.163	35	0	.086	.179	.086
1991	Hou-N	142	1	.218	.327	.275	74	0	.230	.333	.270	68	1	.206	.321	.279	78	1	.244	.326	.333	64	0	.188	.329	.203	53	0	.226	.394	.283	35	0	.143	.200	.171
1992	Hou-N	76	0	.184	.279	.224	35	0	.257	.350	.343	41	0	.122	.217	.122	35	0	.171	.293	.171	41	0	.200	.351	.200	30	0	.200	.300	.308	26	0	.192	.300	.308
1993	Col-N	19	0	.053	.217	.053	12	0	.083	.313	.083	7	0	.000	.000	.000	3	0	.000	.000	.000	16	0	.063	.250	.063	8	0	.000	.111	.000	7	0	.143	.143	.143
1994	StL-N	41	0	.317	.364	.488	24	0	.333	.385	.500	17	0	.294	.333	.471	18	0	.278	.278	.500	23	0	.348	.423	.478	10	0	.400	.455	.700	7	0	.143	.250	.143
TOTALS		1815	3	.246	.329	.304	938	1	.254	.333	.314	877	2	.237	.325	.292	637	3	.267	.339	.334	1178	0	.234	.324	.287	573	0	.272	.365	.333	367	0	.251	.321	.313

■ Mike Young BB/TR

YEAR	TM/L	TOTAL AB	HR	AVG	OBP	SLG	HOME AB	HR	AVG	OBP	SLG	AWAY AB	HR	AVG	OBP	SLG	LEFT AB	HR	AVG	OBP	SLG	RIGHT AB	HR	AVG	OBP	SLG	ON-BASE AB	HR	AVG	OBP	SLG	LATE/CLOSE AB	HR	AVG	OBP	SLG
1984	Bal-A	401	17	.252	.355	.431	187	9	.273	.374	.471	214	8	.234	.337	.397	118	3	.195	.304	.305	283	14	.276	.376	.484	158	6	.266	.389	.449	69	4	.174	.278	.391
1985	Bal-A	450	28	.273	.348	.513	216	15	.278	.377	.537	234	13	.269	.319	.491	181	12	.293	.335	.547	269	16	.260	.356	.491	196	13	.296	.377	.566	69	4	.246	.350	.478
1986	Bal-A	369	9	.252	.342	.411	167	5	.269	.359	.413	202	4	.238	.328	.357	125	3	.272	.357	.400	244	6	.242	.335	.357	195	2	.267	.348	.338	62	1	.274	.403	.355
1987	Bal-A	363	16	.240	.328	.405	190	11	.237	.327	.442	173	5	.243	.328	.364	144	5	.236	.341	.354	219	11	.242	.318	.438	155	8	.232	.326	.413	62	4	.290	.362	.516
1988	Phi-N	146	1	.226	.343	.342	56	1	.250	.368	.429	90	0	.211	.327	.289	69	1	.290	.364	.464	77	0	.169	.327	.234	71	0	.239	.378	.296	44	0	.250	.389	.409
1988	Mil-A	14	0	.000	.176	.000	14	0	.000	.176	.000	—	—	—	—	—	7	0	.000	.125	.000	7	0	.000	.222	.000	4	0	.000	.000	.000	4	0	.000	.000	.000
1989	Cle-A	59	1	.186	.273	.237	26	0	.231	.310	.231	33	1	.152	.243	.242	28	0	.179	.207	.179	31	1	.194	.324	.290	26	0	.192	.300	.192	27	0	.148	.233	.148
TOTALS		1802	72	.249	.340	.417	856	41	.258	.356	.452	946	31	.240	.325	.386	672	24	.251	.331	.406	1130	48	.247	.345	.424	808	29	.260	.359	.418	337	13	.234	.341	.404

■ Robin Yount BR/TR

YEAR	TM/L	TOTAL AB	HR	AVG	OBP	SLG	HOME AB	HR	AVG	OBP	SLG	AWAY AB	HR	AVG	OBP	SLG	LEFT AB	HR	AVG	OBP	SLG	RIGHT AB	HR	AVG	OBP	SLG	ON-BASE AB	HR	AVG	OBP	SLG	LATE/CLOSE AB	HR	AVG	OBP	SLG
1984	Mil-A	624	16	.298	.362	.441	303	8	.310	.360	.469	321	8	.287	.364	.414	207	5	.304	.374	.459	417	11	.295	.349	.432	269	10	.309	.375	.491	99	4	.343	.402	.495
1985	Mil-A	466	15	.277	.342	.442	243	11	.309	.382	.523	223	4	.242	.297	.354	150	4	.300	.357	.453	316	11	.266	.335	.437	218	7	.321	.379	.486	62	2	.226	.351	.355
1986	Mil-A	522	9	.312	.388	.450	259	4	.297	.370	.436	263	5	.327	.406	.464	121	3	.248	.343	.355	401	6	.332	.402	.479	196	2	.306	.403	.403	78	1	.346	.422	.487
1987	Mil-A	635	21	.312	.384	.479	311	12	.354	.422	.550	324	9	.272	.347	.410	195	2	.272	.336	.369	440	19	.330	.404	.527	290	12	.376	.448	.583	96	1	.281	.363	.323
1988	Mil-A	621	13	.306	.369	.465	300	7	.307	.374	.450	321	6	.305	.364	.480	183	7	.284	.381	.448	438	6	.315	.363	.473	293	4	.321	.378	.468	81	1	.333	.409	.481
1989	Mil-A	614	21	.318	.384	.511	300	14	.307	.383	.533	314	7	.328	.386	.490	167	6	.341	.398	.587	447	15	.309	.379	.483	285	7	.330	.402	.505	83	0	.337	.391	.446
1990	Mil-A	587	17	.247	.337	.380	293	8	.222	.310	.365	294	9	.272	.364	.395	156	5	.269	.359	.410	431	12	.239	.329	.369	251	10	.263	.334	.414	86	1	.233	.320	.291
1991	Mil-A	503	10	.260	.332	.376	250	8	.236	.311	.396	253	2	.285	.352	.356	129	2	.256	.377	.341	374	8	.262	.314	.388	246	6	.285	.373	.419	75	4	.240	.301	.467
1992	Mil-A	557	8	.264	.325	.390	269	3	.268	.327	.379	288	5	.260	.323	.399	125	2	.280	.359	.424	432	6	.259	.315	.380	265	4	.287	.347	.426	74	1	.257	.366	.351
1993	Mil-A	454	8	.258	.326	.379	234	1	.270	.359	.365	220	7	.259	.305	.427	122	2	.262	.362	.369	332	6	.255	.309	.383	202	0	.243	.318	.317	73	0	.233	.301	.233
TOTALS		5583	138	.287	.356	.434	2762	76	.288	.359	.447	2821	62	.285	.354	.422	1555	38	.284	.367	.427	4028	100	.288	.352	.437	2515	62	.307	.378	.458	807	15	.286	.364	.395

■ Todd Zeile BR/TR

YEAR	TM/L	TOTAL AB	HR	AVG	OBP	SLG	HOME AB	HR	AVG	OBP	SLG	AWAY AB	HR	AVG	OBP	SLG	LEFT AB	HR	AVG	OBP	SLG	RIGHT AB	HR	AVG	OBP	SLG	ON-BASE AB	HR	AVG	OBP	SLG	LATE/CLOSE AB	HR	AVG	OBP	SLG
1989	StL-N	82	1	.256	.326	.354	39	0	.231	.279	.282	43	1	.279	.367	.419	39	0	.282	.364	.308	43	1	.233	.292	.395	39	0	.308	.364	.359	17	0	.176	.263	.235
1990	StL-N	495	15	.244	.333	.398	233	8	.262	.358	.429	262	7	.229	.311	.370	173	6	.266	.347	.451	322	9	.233	.326	.370	213	5	.230	.341	.380	88	1	.205	.311	.273
1991	StL-N	565	11	.280	.353	.412	279	7	.297	.374	.459	286	4	.262	.331	.367	237	5	.304	.375	.439	328	6	.262	.337	.393	255	2	.294	.369	.404	104	1	.288	.375	.385
1992	StL-N	439	7	.257	.352	.364	226	4	.230	.337	.332	213	3	.286	.368	.399	133	1	.278	.394	.353	306	6	.248	.333	.369	201	2	.249	.350	.323	99	0	.212	.295	.263
1993	StL-N	571	17	.277	.352	.433	280	8	.304	.376	.454	291	9	.251	.329	.412	133	4	.271	.355	.434	438	13	.279	.352	.434	180	10	.276	.366	.445	96	1	.229	.306	.323
1994	StL-N	415	19	.267	.348	.470	199	9	.307	.372	.518	216	10	.231	.327	.426	107	7	.299	.389	.579	308	12	.256	.333	.432	200	13	.220	.321	.470	61	0	.246	.324	.311
TOTALS		2567	70	.266	.347	.413	1256	36	.279	.361	.433	1311	34	.252	.333	.394	822	23	.285	.370	.438	1745	47	.257	.336	.402	1191	32	.259	.352	.406	465	3	.234	.321	.310

● Jim Abbott BL/TL

YEAR TM/L	TOTAL					HOME					AWAY					LEFT					RIGHT					ON-BASE					LATE/CLOSE				
	W	L	SV	IP	ERA	W	L	SV	IP	ERA	W	L	SV	IP	ERA	AB	HR	AVG	OBP	SLG	AB	HR	AVG	OBP	SLG	AB	HR	AVG	OBP	SLG	AB	HR	AVG	OBP	SLG
1989 Cal-A	12	12	0	181	3.92	5	5	0	87	4.84	7	7	0	94	3.06	123	2	.325	.388	.463	571	11	.263	.335	.361	303	4	.261	.336	.343	40	0	.400	.489	.425
1990 Cal-A	10	14	0	212	4.51	4	7	0	110	4.75	6	7	0	102	4.25	110	3	.318	.398	.436	723	13	.292	.345	.396	359	6	.298	.363	.393	74	2	.257	.286	.365
1991 Cal-A	18	11	0	243	2.89	8	7	0	129	2.57	10	4	0	114	3.25	142	3	.303	.348	.430	767	11	.233	.293	.318	358	6	.240	.297	.341	90	2	.267	.320	.333
1992 Cal-A	7	15	0	211	2.77	2	8	0	95	3.32	5	7	0	116	2.33	128	0	.273	.343	.359	662	12	.261	.321	.347	338	6	.263	.316	.367	91	3	.363	.414	.516
1993 NY-A	11	14	0	214	4.37	8	6	0	112	3.12	3	8	0	102	5.75	102	0	.294	.376	.362	712	22	.268	.326	.406	340	14	.300	.355	.471	62	1	.355	.388	.468
1994 NY-A	9	8	0	160	4.55	5	5	0	93	3.86	4	3	0	67	5.51	102	3	.275	.308	.431	510	21	.273	.347	.461	272	10	.239	.309	.404	31	2	.290	.313	.645
TOTALS	67	74	0	1221	3.78	32	38	0	627	3.67	35	36	0	594	3.89	707	11	.298	.361	.414	3945	90	.264	.326	.378	1970	47	.268	.330	.386	388	10	.317	.365	.438

● Jim Acker BR/TR

YEAR TM/L	W	L	SV	IP	ERA	W	L	SV	IP	ERA	W	L	SV	IP	ERA	AB	HR	AVG	OBP	SLG	AB	HR	AVG	OBP	SLG	AB	HR	AVG	OBP	SLG	AB	HR	AVG	OBP	SLG
1984 Tor-A	3	5	1	72	4.38	1	1	0	29	4.71	2	4	1	43	4.15	132	1	.242	.318	.311	144	2	.326	.394	.438	127	0	.346	.408	.425	49	1	.327	.377	.469
1985 Tor-A	7	2	10	86	3.23	3	1	5	46	1.96	4	1	5	40	4.69	146	2	.308	.398	.390	175	5	.234	.323	.354	169	5	.260	.324	.373	116	2	.302	.374	.371
1986 Tor-A	2	4	0	60	4.35	1	1	0	30	5.76	1	3	0	30	2.97	106	6	.340	.407	.575	118	0	.229	.285	.288	102	4	.265	.339	.461	46	0	.283	.393	.304
1986 Atl-N	3	8	0	95	3.79	1	4	0	52	3.14	2	4	0	43	4.57	222	4	.302	.347	.396	143	5	.231	.279	.385	153	3	.268	.329	.386	25	0	.360	.407	.520
1987 Atl-N	4	9	14	115	4.16	4	1	7	60	4.50	0	8	7	55	3.79	231	3	.238	.317	.329	199	8	.271	.358	.447	208	3	.250	.332	.351	168	3	.280	.363	.405
1988 Atl-N	0	4	0	42	4.71	0	2	0	20	7.20	0	2	0	22	2.45	75	2	.280	.365	.427	86	4	.279	.309	.442	63	3	.333	.408	.540	34	1	.324	.400	.471
1989 Atl-N	0	6	2	98	2.67	0	3	0	46	2.76	0	3	2	52	2.60	183	2	.284	.333	.383	171	2	.187	.217	.275	150	1	.233	.289	.293	108	0	.287	.316	.352
1989 Tor-A	2	1	0	28	1.59	1	0	0	18	0.00	1	1	0	10	4.50	38	0	.289	.426	.421	64	1	.203	.250	.297	42	0	.238	.347	.310	59	0	.186	.294	.237
1990 Tor-A	4	4	1	92	3.83	2	3	1	53	3.76	2	1	0	39	3.92	149	2	.289	.355	.409	217	7	.276	.329	.424	172	6	.285	.347	.448	100	1	.320	.376	.410
1991 Tor-A	3	5	1	88	5.20	2	2	0	53	4.92	1	3	1	35	5.60	126	5	.294	.372	.460	197	11	.203	.276	.401	121	6	.322	.396	.595	93	2	.183	.267	.269
1992 Sea-A	0	0	0	31	5.28	0	0	0	16	3.31	0	0	0	14	7.53	59	2	.407	.435	.610	74	2	.284	.353	.432	64	2	.313	.387	.484	0	0	—	—	—
TOTALS	28	48	29	807	3.93	15	18	13	422	3.82	13	30	16	385	4.05	1467	28	.288	.357	.406	1588	47	.247	.309	.384	1371	36	.279	.348	.414	798	10	.278	.349	.370

● Juan Agosto BL/TL

YEAR TM/L	W	L	SV	IP	ERA	W	L	SV	IP	ERA	W	L	SV	IP	ERA	AB	HR	AVG	OBP	SLG	AB	HR	AVG	OBP	SLG	AB	HR	AVG	OBP	SLG	AB	HR	AVG	OBP	SLG
1984 Chi-A	2	1	7	55	3.09	2	1	2	33	3.00	0	0	5	22	3.22	96	1	.188	.297	.240	104	1	.346	.457	.481	112	1	.268	.394	.384	83	1	.265	.330	.361
1985 Chi-A	4	3	1	60	3.58	2	2	0	37	4.42	2	1	1	24	2.28	98	1	.214	.310	.316	116	2	.207	.277	.276	91	2	.253	.330	.385	76	2	.158	.267	.276
1986 Chi-A	0	2	0	5	7.71	0	1	0	4	8.31	0	1	0	0	0.00	12	0	.167	.333	.167	8	0	.500	.556	.750	10	0	.500	.615	.700	3	0	.333	.600	.333
1986 Min-A	1	2	1	20	8.85	0	1	0	10	6.30	1	2	0	10	11.32	28	0	.393	.500	.393	68	1	.471	.538	.603	59	1	.441	.535	.542	24	0	.375	.400	.417
1987 Hou-N	1	1	2	27	2.63	1	0	2	16	1.15	0	1	0	12	4.63	28	0	.214	.313	.214	77	1	.260	.313	.364	49	0	.286	.340	.327	41	1	.268	.318	.415
1988 Hou-N	10	2	4	92	2.26	5	0	4	53	1.03	5	2	0	39	3.92	107	1	.140	.184	.178	220	5	.268	.335	.400	133	1	.211	.299	.278	192	1	.224	.285	.297
1989 Hou-N	4	5	1	83	2.93	3	2	0	44	2.66	1	3	1	39	3.23	109	0	.220	.276	.266	207	3	.275	.348	.362	156	2	.237	.321	.308	80	1	.300	.344	.387
1990 Hou-N	9	8	4	92	4.29	6	4	3	44	2.47	3	4	1	49	5.92	110	1	.227	.303	.282	239	3	.276	.364	.381	166	4	.247	.349	.361	180	2	.283	.366	.356
1991 StL-N	5	3	2	86	4.81	3	2	2	47	4.21	2	1	0	39	5.54	96	0	.271	.393	.375	220	4	.300	.373	.423	164	3	.293	.383	.451	99	1	.242	.324	.293
1992 StL-N	2	4	0	32	6.25	2	2	0	20	8.10	0	2	0	12	3.09	36	0	.222	.317	.306	89	2	.348	.494	.494	60	2	.350	.391	.517	34	0	.265	.390	.294
1992 Sea-A	0	0	0	18	5.89	0	0	0	5	16.20	0	0	0	13	2.03	12	1	.519	.552	.704	51	0	.255	.264	.255	48	0	.396	.412	.500	11	0	.455	.500	.636
1993 Hou-N	0	0	0	6	6.00	0	0	0	0	0.00	0	0	0	6	10.80	12	1	.333	.333	.667	14	0	.286	.286	.286	16	1	.375	.375	.563	4	0	.250	.250	.250
TOTALS	38	31	22	577	3.95	24	14	14	315	3.49	14	17	8	262	4.49	759	5	.229	.314	.298	1413	22	.292	.363	.400	1064	17	.280	.365	.391	827	9	.256	.329	.336

● Rick Aguilera BR/TR

YEAR TM/L	W	L	SV	IP	ERA	W	L	SV	IP	ERA	W	L	SV	IP	ERA	AB	HR	AVG	OBP	SLG	AB	HR	AVG	OBP	SLG	AB	HR	AVG	OBP	SLG	AB	HR	AVG	OBP	SLG
1985 NY-N	10	7	0	122	3.24	3	2	0	46	2.14	7	5	0	76	3.91	224	3	.241	.310	.335	233	5	.275	.317	.408	180	2	.283	.338	.389	36	0	.167	.244	.167
1986 NY-N	10	7	0	142	3.88	5	5	0	68	3.72	5	5	0	74	4.01	269	4	.290	.341	.442	282	11	.238	.288	.408	227	8	.264	.309	.441	23	1	.391	.440	.565
1987 NY-N	11	3	0	115	3.60	6	2	0	68	3.82	5	1	0	47	3.28	219	6	.301	.361	.447	230	6	.232	.297	.396	198	6	.227	.286	.379	39	0	.282	.333	.308
1988 NY-N	0	4	0	25	6.93	0	1	0	13	4.72	0	3	0	11	9.53	45	0	.222	.286	.267	46	2	.358	.433	.528	46	2	.370	.442	.565	8	0	.250	.333	.250
1989 NY-N	6	6	7	69	2.34	5	3	3	37	1.72	1	3	4	33	3.03	133	1	.241	.301	.293	122	2	.221	.286	.303	102	2	.275	.364	.353	110	3	.264	.336	.382
1989 Min-A	3	5	0	76	3.21	1	2	0	36	3.53	2	3	0	40	2.93	142	2	.275	.318	.437	148	3	.216	.261	.345	110	1	.245	.303	.355	17	0	.176	.222	.235
1990 Min-A	5	3	32	65	2.76	3	2	16	34	3.44	2	1	16	31	2.01	114	0	.219	.299	.237	131	5	.229	.284	.397	133	3	.203	.284	.308	175	5	.223	.284	.343
1991 Min-A	4	5	42	69	2.35	2	2	23	36	1.00	2	3	19	33	3.82	136	2	.184	.285	.272	104	1	.183	.259	.279	113	1	.204	.295	.327	184	1	.185	.268	.261
1992 Min-A	2	6	41	67	2.83	1	3	17	30	4.25	1	3	24	37	1.70	129	3	.248	.310	.326	123	4	.228	.262	.382	133	5	.233	.283	.368	173	5	.214	.275	.318
1993 Min-A	4	3	34	72	3.11	2	1	15	36	2.97	2	2	19	36	3.25	145	3	.200	.247	.324	124	6	.250	.282	.444	99	4	.273	.318	.485	168	6	.250	.294	.417
1994 Min-A	1	4	23	45	3.63	0	2	13	25	3.65	1	2	10	20	3.60	95	3	.242	.301	.358	91	4	.374	.430	.538	96	2	.260	.294	.333	119	4	.294	.336	.420
TOTALS	56	53	179	867	3.29	28	20	87	429	3.13	28	33	92	438	3.45	1651	27	.250	.312	.340	1641	49	.249	.296	.395	1437	36	.251	.311	.385	1052	25	.235	.296	.344

● Doyle Alexander BR/TR

YEAR TM/L	W	L	SV	IP	ERA	W	L	SV	IP	ERA	W	L	SV	IP	ERA	AB	HR	AVG	OBP	SLG	AB	HR	AVG	OBP	SLG	AB	HR	AVG	OBP	SLG	AB	HR	AVG	OBP	SLG
1984 Tor-A	17	6	0	262	3.13	12	3	0	164	2.58	5	3	0	98	4.04	509	17	.261	.306	.420	474	4	.222	.259	.342	382	9	.212	.257	.353	127	5	.268	.306	.441
1985 Tor-A	17	10	0	261	3.45	11	5	0	162	2.83	6	5	0	98	4.48	515	16	.264	.310	.442	493	12	.268	.297	.375	394	9	.277	.324	.391	119	6	.311	.349	.504
1986 Tor-A	5	4	0	111	4.46	2	2	0	62	3.65	3	2	0	49	5.47	228	7	.268	.303	.417	212	11	.278	.314	.524	170	8	.294	.313	.524	53	2	.132	.132	.264
1986 Atl-N	6	6	0	117	3.84	4	2	0	62	4.09	2	4	0	56	3.56	217	4	.295	.339	.424	193	3	.280	.314	.383	163	5	.281	.286	.395	36	2	.444	.487	.778
1987 Atl-N	5	10	0	118	4.13	3	5	0	69	4.30	2	5	0	49	3.87	207	15	.300	.345	.565	241	6	.220	.261	.340	190	10	.300	.337	.507	39	5	.487	.545	.923
1987 Det-A	9	0	0	88	1.53	5	0	0	39	1.14	4	0	0	49	1.84	151	1	.199	.288	.258	162	2	.204	.237	.265	103	1	.214	.314	.291	29	0	.207	.303	.276
1988 Det-A	14	11	0	229	4.32	9	5	0	128	3.09	5	6	0	101	5.88	458	12	.293	.337	.476	352	13	.278	.326	.452						120	2	.225	.262	.325
1989 Det-A	6	18	0	223	4.44	3	9	0	120	4.44	3	9	0	103	4.44	490	14	.284	.330	.437	386	14	.271	.345	.430	377	9	.271	.330	.406	83	3	.301	.363	.458
TOTALS	79	65	0	1409	3.74	49	31	0	805	3.26	30	34	0	603	4.37	2775	86	.274	.324	.433	2685	72	.255	.291	.391	2121	61	.264	.312	.410	606	25	.282	.327	.460

● Wilson Alvarez BL/TL

YEAR TM/L	W	L	SV	IP	ERA	W	L	SV	IP	ERA	W	L	SV	IP	ERA	AB	HR	AVG	OBP	SLG	AB	HR	AVG	OBP	SLG	AB	HR	AVG	OBP	SLG	AB	HR	AVG	OBP	SLG
1989 Tex-A	0	1	0	0	∞	0	1	0	0	∞	0	0	0	0	—	0	0	—	1.000	—	3	2	1.000	1.000	3.000	1	1	1.000	1.000	4.000	0	0	—	—	—
1991 Chi-A	3	2	0	56	3.51	1	1	0	19	2.79	2	1	0	37	3.89	18	0	.222	.263	.222	186	9	.231	.330	.425	74	2	.216	.337	.311	0	0	—	—	—
1992 Chi-A	5	3	1	100	5.20	2	1	0	45	5.56	3	2	1	55	4.91	91	0	.220	.348	.286	288	12	.288	.391	.438	176	6	.273	.394	.415	32	1	.375	.474	.500
1993 Chi-A	15	8	0	208	2.95	7	5	0	107	3.38	8	3	0	101	2.50	89	1	.258	.432	.315	640	13	.227	.330	.331	311	6	.209	.321	.296	65	1	.215	.373	.277
1994 Chi-A	12	8	0	162	3.45	6	4	0	84	3.11	6	4	0	78	3.82	95	1	.232	.288	.305	516	15	.242	.313	.362	264	9	.231	.280	.375	50	2	.220	.316	.380
TOTALS	35	22	1	526	3.64	16	12	0	255	3.74	19	10	1	271	3.56	293	2	.235	.356	.297	1633	51	.244	.337	.375	826	24	.231	.328	.352	149	4	.255	.378	.362

● Larry Andersen BR/TR

YEAR TM/L	W	L	SV	IP	ERA	W	L	SV	IP	ERA	W	L	SV	IP	ERA	AB	HR	AVG	OBP	SLG	AB	HR	AVG	OBP	SLG	AB	HR	AVG	OBP	SLG	AB	HR	AVG	OBP	SLG
1984 Phi-N	3	7	4	91	2.38	1	2	2	37	2.17	2	5	2	53	2.53	163	3	.264	.330	.374	180	2	.233	.263	.306	152	3	.263	.329	.362	167	3	.251	.328	.329
1985 Phi-N	3	3	3	73	4.32	3	0	2	42	3.21	0	3	1	31	5.81	123	2	.309	.403	.415	162	3	.247	.287	.377	114	2	.264	.344	.396	114	2	.307	.336	.447
1986 Phi-N	0	0	0	13	4.26	0	0	0	8	1.17	0	0	0	5	9.00	20	0	.450	.500	.600	29	0	.345	.355	.483	37	0	.324	.333	.486	12	0	.250	.308	.250
1986 Hou-N	2	1	1	65	2.78	2	0	0	29	3.07	0	1	1	35	2.55	108	1	.278	.350	.343	124	1	.274	.329	.363	117	1	.265	.348	.342	51	1	.275	.345	.353
1987 Hou-N	9	5	5	102	3.45	4	4	1	52	2.56	5	1	4	49	4.41	191	3	.230	.323	.344	194	4	.263	.316	.392	167	3	.240	.338	.353	219	3	.237	.313	.342
1988 Hou-N	2	4	5	83	2.94	1	2	0	40	2.03	1	2	5	43	3.80	150	1	.293	.359	.360	173	2	.220	.239	.302	152	0	.270	.321	.322	184	2	.228	.278	.299
1989 Hou-N	4	4	3	88	1.54	2	3	2	52	1.22	2	1	1	36	2.00	160	2	.250	.305	.306	146	0	.146	.194	.184	137	0	.204	.260	.219	133	1	.218	.293	.263
1990 Hou-N	5	2	6	74	1.95	4	0	3	39	0.23	1	2	3	34	3.93	124	2	.282	.361	.371	142	0	.183	.224	.204	129	1	.171	.243	.256	161	1	.255	.320	.298
1990 Bos-A	0	0	1	22	1.23	0	0	0	14	1.93	0	0	1	8	0.00	42	0	.262	.295	.286	40	0	.175	.214	.200	45	0	.244	.277	.289	28	0	.214	.214	.250
1991 SD-N	3	4	13	47	2.30	3	0	8	25	2.19	0	4	5	22	2.42	89	0	.281	.340	.337	79	0	.177	.217	.190	69	0	.261	.303	.290	125	0	.224	.279	.256
1992 SD-N	1	2	2	35	3.34	1	0	1	19	3.26	0	1	1	16	3.45	69	1	.203	.295	.275	60	1	.200	.197	.250	47	0	.298	.333	.319	52	1	.231	.298	.288
1993 Phi-N	3	2	0	62	2.92	1	0	0	32	1.14	2	2	0	30	4.80	86	2	.291	.330	.395	104	1	.221	.283	.298						148	1	.223	.299	.270
1994 Phi-N	3	2	1	61	4.41	0	1	0	14	5.02	3	1	1	47	3.93	72	2	.306	.359	.444	57	0	.193	.303	.281	80	0	.175	.241	.188	53	0	.321	.410	.434
TOTALS	36	35	43	785	2.82	22	12	20	404	2.12	14	23	23	381	3.57	1397	19	.272	.342	.359	1544	15	.218	.264	.298	1380	12	.241	.307	.315	1447	15	.245	.309	.316

● Allan Anderson BL/TL

YEAR TM/L	W	L	SV	IP	ERA	W	L	SV	IP	ERA	W	L	SV	IP	ERA	AB	HR	AVG	OBP	SLG	AB	HR	AVG	OBP	SLG	AB	HR	AVG	OBP	SLG	AB	HR	AVG	OBP	SLG
1986 Min-A	3	6	0	84	5.55	1	4	0	48	6.52	2	2	0	36	4.25	89	3	.337	.392	.551	246	8	.309	.364	.484	147	3	.333	.388	.490	25	0	.200	.310	.200
1987 Min-A	1	0	0	12	10.95	1	0	0	9	11.57	0	0	0	3	9.00	16	1	.500	.556	.813	35	2	.343	.465	.600	30	1	.367	.457	.533	0	0	—	—	—
1988 Min-A	16	9	0	202	2.45	9	2	0	102	2.29	7	7	0	100	2.60	125	0	.320	.390	.368	638	14	.249	.290	.387	303	3	.257	.292	.317	40	0	.162	.205	.189
1989 Min-A	17	10	0	197	3.80	6	5	0	72	6.47	11	5	0	124	2.24	117	2	.274	.348	.368	660	13	.276	.321	.400	347	6	.288	.326	.412	19	1	.211	.250	.368
1990 Min-A	7	18	0	189	4.53	4	12	0	111	4.17	3	6	0	77	4.19	109	2	.257	.297	.330	632	18	.294	.330	.451	306	6	.307	.339	.431	53	2	.302	.351	.415
1991 Min-A	5	11	0	134	4.96	2	4	0	66	4.52	3	7	0	67	5.40	111	2	.225	.265	.315	416	22	.296	.334	.517	190	10	.289	.359	.516	43	2	.326	.396	.535
TOTALS	49	54	0	819	4.11	23	27	0	411	4.77	26	27	0	408	3.44	567	10	.287	.345	.392	2627	77	.281	.325	.433	1323	28	.293	.337	.421	214	5	.238	.297	.332

● Joaquin Andujar BB/TR

YEAR TM/L	W	L	SV	IP	ERA	W	L	SV	IP	ERA	W	L	SV	IP	ERA	AB	HR	AVG	OBP	SLG	AB	HR	AVG	OBP	SLG	AB	HR	AVG	OBP	SLG	AB	HR	AVG	OBP	SLG
1984 StL-N	20	14	0	261	3.34	8	11	0	139	3.70	12	3	0	123	2.93	463	10	.233	.300	.341	491	10	.224	.268	.348	355	11	.259	.311	.425	102	1	.206	.308	.324
1985 StL-N	21	12	0	270	3.40	13	3	0	144	3.06	8	9	0	125	3.81	545	9	.263	.300	.393	525	9	.223	.258	.337	433	7	.252	.316	.387	104	1	.240	.278	.337
1986 Oak-A	12	7	1	155	3.82	8	4	1	88	3.87	4	3	0	67	3.76	307	15	.254	.318	.453	275	8	.222	.297	.338	206	7	.238	.335	.388	71	2	.211	.313	.254
1987 Oak-A	3	5	0	61	6.08	1	4	0	40	6.02	2	1	0	20	6.20	116	3	.267	.356	.397	118	6	.271	.341	.500	95	7	.284	.378	.547	14	2	.357	.400	.786
1988 Hou-N	2	5	0	79	4.00	1	1	0	48	3.78	1	4	0	31	4.35	148	4	.284	.345	.439	169	5	.308	.346	.467	149	5	.295	.331	.463	37	3	.324	.390	.676
TOTALS	58	43	1	826	3.72	27	30	1	459	3.74	31	13	0	366	3.69	1528	38	.266	.331	.408	1578	40	.236	.293	.362	1238	37	.259	.325	.409	328	8	.238	.345	.372

		TOTAL					HOME					AWAY					LEFT					RIGHT					ON-BASE					LATE/CLOSE				
YEAR	TM/L	W	L	SV	IP	ERA	W	L	SV	IP	ERA	W	L	SV	IP	ERA	AB	HR	AVG	OBP	SLG	AB	HR	AVG	OBP	SLG	AB	HR	AVG	OBP	SLG	AB	HR	AVG	OBP	SLG

● Kevin Appier BR/TR

YEAR	TM/L	W	L	SV	IP	ERA	W	L	SV	IP	ERA	W	L	SV	IP	ERA	AB	HR	AVG	OBP	SLG	AB	HR	AVG	OBP	SLG	AB	HR	AVG	OBP	SLG	AB	HR	AVG	OBP	SLG
1989	KC-A	1	4	0	22	9.14	1	1	0	6	12.71	0	3	0	16	7.87	44	3	.386	.434	.614	47	0	.362	.434	.447	55	3	.345	.361	.545	0	0	—	—	—
1990	KC-A	12	8	0	186	2.76	7	4	0	84	2.77	5	4	0	101	2.75	311	7	.260	.331	.363	398	6	.246	.287	.312	292	4	.260	.308	.336	57	1	.246	.295	.316
1991	KC-A	13	10	0	208	3.42	5	5	0	97	2.79	8	5	0	111	3.97	403	8	.268	.327	.395	400	5	.243	.287	.320	321	7	.302	.352	.436	84	0	.226	.244	.274
1992	KC-A	15	8	0	208	2.46	8	5	0	104	2.60	7	3	0	104	2.33	370	7	.205	.283	.324	401	3	.227	.278	.314	329	5	.182	.242	.271	91	2	.110	.221	.198
1993	KC-A	18	8	0	239	2.56	8	5	0	117	2.39	10	3	0	122	2.73	439	5	.239	.311	.321	424	3	.184	.245	.262	324	2	.244	.309	.330	109	1	.248	.320	.312
1994	KC-A	7	6	0	155	3.83	4	2	0	76	4.01	3	4	0	79	3.66	290	3	.279	.370	.390	280	8	.200	.259	.325	253	5	.225	.307	.328	69	1	.217	.295	.333
TOTALS		66	44	0	1017	3.09	33	22	0	484	2.96	33	22	0	533	3.21	1857	33	.252	.325	.362	1950	25	.224	.276	.308	1574	26	.247	.305	.348	410	5	.207	.275	.283

● Jack Armstrong BR/TR

YEAR	TM/L	W	L	SV	IP	ERA	W	L	SV	IP	ERA	W	L	SV	IP	ERA	AB	HR	AVG	OBP	SLG	AB	HR	AVG	OBP	SLG	AB	HR	AVG	OBP	SLG	AB	HR	AVG	OBP	SLG
1988	Cin-N	4	7	0	65	5.79	2	3	0	29	7.14	2	4	0	36	4.71	129	5	.302	.422	.481	117	3	.205	.258	.376	116	4	.241	.321	.422	4	0	.250	.625	.500
1989	Cin-N	2	3	0	43	4.64	2	1	0	25	5.76	0	2	0	18	3.06	92	1	.283	.368	.402	71	4	.197	.278	.394	62	3	.306	.389	.565	5	0	.200	.333	.200
1990	Cin-N	12	9	0	166	3.42	6	4	0	71	3.93	6	5	0	95	3.03	387	6	.258	.329	.387	238	3	.214	.281	.307	256	6	.277	.343	.410	38	0	.211	.231	.316
1991	Cin-N	7	13	0	140	5.48	4	8	0	66	6.38	3	5	0	73	4.66	297	13	.279	.355	.481	243	12	.309	.352	.502	206	10	.335	.392	.563	18	0	.278	.316	.389
1992	Cle-N	6	15	0	167	4.64	5	5	0	73	4.54	1	10	0	93	4.72	277	10	.274	.366	.433	377	13	.265	.315	.427	274	10	.314	.367	.471	31	0	.290	.333	.419
1993	Fla-N	9	17	0	196	4.49	5	13	0	118	4.73	4	4	0	78	4.14	422	22	.284	.384	.505	354	7	.254	.300	.370	322	11	.264	.338	.441	50	0	.280	.357	.320
1994	Tex-A	0	1	0	10	3.60	0	1	0	4	4.50	0	0	0	6	3.00	18	0	.111	.158	.111	21	3	.333	.364	.857	11	1	.182	.250	.455	50	0	.280	.357	.320
TOTALS		40	65	0	787	4.58	24	35	0	387	5.07	16	30	0	400	4.10	1622	57	.275	.359	.446	1421	45	.254	.306	.420	1247	45	.289	.354	.466	146	0	.260	.329	.349

● Andy Ashby BR/TR

YEAR	TM/L	W	L	SV	IP	ERA	W	L	SV	IP	ERA	W	L	SV	IP	ERA	AB	HR	AVG	OBP	SLG	AB	HR	AVG	OBP	SLG	AB	HR	AVG	OBP	SLG	AB	HR	AVG	OBP	SLG
1991	Phi-N	1	5	0	42	6.00	1	3	0	26	6.49	0	2	0	16	5.17	93	3	.247	.317	.409	67	2	.269	.370	.463	71	3	.310	.358	.507	3	1	.333	.500	1.333
1992	Phi-N	1	3	0	37	7.54	1	1	0	21	6.00	0	2	0	16	9.56	85	4	.318	.406	.506	60	2	.250	.338	.467	66	2	.273	.383	.439	0	0	—	—	—
1993	Col-N	0	4	1	54	8.50	0	2	0	28	8.58	0	2	1	26	8.42	128	1	.352	.439	.422	108	4	.407	.468	.648	136	3	.397	.475	.566	21	0	.238	.304	.238
1993	SD-N	3	6	0	69	5.48	2	1	0	38	4.06	1	5	0	31	7.18	146	6	.267	.325	.425	122	8	.328	.380	.607	115	3	.296	.336	.426	3	0	.000	.000	.000
1994	SD-N	6	11	0	164	3.40	3	4	0	71	2.52	3	7	0	93	4.06	313	8	.249	.308	.393	309	8	.217	.261	.346	232	6	.233	.309	.379	82	1	.207	.217	.280
TOTALS		11	29	1	366	5.26	6	11	0	185	4.73	5	18	1	182	5.80	765	22	.277	.347	.418	666	24	.276	.337	.450	620	17	.294	.366	.450	109	2	.211	.239	.294

● Paul Assenmacher BL/TL

YEAR	TM/L	W	L	SV	IP	ERA	W	L	SV	IP	ERA	W	L	SV	IP	ERA	AB	HR	AVG	OBP	SLG	AB	HR	AVG	OBP	SLG	AB	HR	AVG	OBP	SLG	AB	HR	AVG	OBP	SLG
1986	Atl-N	7	3	7	68	2.50	4	1	5	39	1.15	3	2	2	29	4.30	82	1	.268	.348	.354	171	4	.228	.293	.322	116	0	.250	.328	.276	135	3	.252	.315	.348
1987	Atl-N	1	1	2	55	5.10	0	0	2	26	5.47	1	1	0	28	4.76	79	1	.177	.261	.253	144	7	.306	.373	.556	101	4	.317	.402	.545	58	2	.293	.379	.517
1988	Atl-N	8	7	5	79	3.06	7	5	3	41	4.87	1	2	2	39	1.16	91	2	.275	.320	.385	196	2	.240	.330	.321	148	2	.243	.331	.331	173	3	.254	.343	.347
1989	Atl-N	1	3	0	58	3.59	1	3	0	32	3.69	0	0	0	26	3.46	64	0	.234	.258	.250	157	2	.255	.316	.363	108	0	.222	.301	.269	83	0	.325	.360	.434
1989	Chi-N	2	1	0	19	5.21	2	0	0	10	4.35	0	1	0	9	6.23	21	0	.286	.423	.333	48	1	.271	.357	.375	34	1	.294	.419	.441	46	1	.304	.373	.435
1990	Chi-N	7	2	10	103	2.80	6	1	3	52	3.46	1	1	7	51	2.12	122	1	.221	.265	.279	254	9	.248	.324	.386	173	5	.214	.298	.341	190	5	.247	.324	.347
1991	Chi-N	7	8	15	103	3.24	4	2	8	61	2.07	3	6	7	42	4.97	134	1	.179	.247	.301	247	9	.247	.304	.409	164	3	.226	.314	.341	279	7	.219	.278	.344
1992	Chi-N	4	4	8	68	4.10	3	3	5	39	4.15	1	1	3	29	4.03	91	3	.220	.294	.374	175	3	.297	.364	.434	142	2	.246	.339	.352	176	2	.239	.322	.341
1993	Chi-N	2	1	0	39	3.49	1	0	0	23	3.09	1	1	0	15	4.11	65	4	.277	.309	.477	88	1	.295	.367	.398	67	3	.313	.361	.493	74	2	.311	.363	.405
1993	NY-A	2	2	0	17	3.12	1	1	0	9	4.00	1	1	0	8	2.16	26	0	.154	.333	.154	31	0	.194	.265	.258	30	0	.200	.351	.200	20	0	.200	.333	.250
1994	Chi-A	1	2	1	33	3.55	1	2	0	14	4.40	0	0	1	19	2.89	50	1	.200	.246	.280	66	1	.242	.342	.348	60	0	.200	.261	.217	58	0	.190	.269	.207
TOTALS		42	34	48	642	3.44	29	18	26	347	3.43	13	16	22	295	3.45	825	14	.224	.288	.314	1577	39	.258	.330	.389	1143	20	.244	.329	.347	1292	25	.251	.322	.358

● Keith Atherton BR/TR

YEAR	TM/L	W	L	SV	IP	ERA	W	L	SV	IP	ERA	W	L	SV	IP	ERA	AB	HR	AVG	OBP	SLG	AB	HR	AVG	OBP	SLG	AB	HR	AVG	OBP	SLG	AB	HR	AVG	OBP	SLG
1984	Oak-A	7	6	2	104	4.33	3	2	1	52	3.66	4	4	1	52	4.99	176	7	.290	.365	.472	226	6	.261	.313	.407	183	6	.290	.367	.464	137	5	.270	.329	.453
1985	Oak-A	4	7	3	105	4.30	2	2	2	57	3.92	2	5	1	47	4.75	163	6	.258	.349	.436	223	11	.211	.267	.417	186	9	.204	.290	.419	154	8	.247	.337	.468
1986	Oak-A	1	2	0	15	5.87	0	1	0	8	3.38	1	1	0	7	8.59	26	1	.346	.471	.538	35	1	.257	.325	.486	34	2	.294	.381	.529	7	1	.571	.667	1.143
1986	Min-A	5	8	10	82	3.75	4	2	6	43	3.74	1	6	4	38	3.76	156	7	.295	.379	.468	155	2	.232	.293	.335	172	3	.273	.342	.378	137	3	.234	.303	.328
1987	Min-A	7	5	2	79	4.54	5	1	1	37	2.89	2	4	1	42	6.00	162	6	.265	.339	.441	147	4	.259	.325	.401	167	4	.251	.323	.407	139	3	.237	.329	.381
1988	Min-A	7	5	3	74	3.41	3	1	2	41	3.32	4	4	1	33	3.51	128	7	.273	.340	.500	149	3	.201	.252	.295	122	6	.270	.333	.467	123	8	.276	.345	.520
1989	Cle-A	0	3	2	39	4.15	0	0	0	18	2.55	0	3	2	21	5.48	61	5	.246	.303	.525	103	2	.320	.369	.524	80	4	.325	.400	.587	43	2	.279	.367	.535
TOTALS		31	36	22	498	4.16	18	9	12	256	3.48	13	27	10	242	4.87	872	39	.276	.346	.470	1038	29	.243	.299	.396	944	34	.264	.339	.443	740	30	.257	.335	.442

● Steve Avery BL/TL

YEAR	TM/L	W	L	SV	IP	ERA	W	L	SV	IP	ERA	W	L	SV	IP	ERA	AB	HR	AVG	OBP	SLG	AB	HR	AVG	OBP	SLG	AB	HR	AVG	OBP	SLG	AB	HR	AVG	OBP	SLG
1990	Atl-N	3	11	0	99	5.64	3	4	0	59	4.10	0	7	0	40	7.94	61	1	.262	.318	.311	340	7	.309	.381	.453	206	6	.330	.374	.490	34	0	.294	.333	.382
1991	Atl-N	18	8	0	210	3.38	9	5	0	106	3.75	9	3	0	105	3.01	164	3	.183	.237	.287	624	18	.255	.315	.394	286	10	.269	.332	.416	35	0	.143	.211	.143
1992	Atl-N	11	11	0	234	3.20	6	4	0	108	2.51	5	7	0	126	3.79	155	3	.258	.341	.348	723	11	.243	.291	.342	338	5	.260	.314	.358	94	1	.287	.352	.362
1993	Atl-N	18	6	0	223	2.94	9	2	0	117	2.85	9	4	0	107	3.04	143	2	.245	.299	.329	684	12	.265	.294	.368	296	6	.274	.307	.372	95	2	.263	.300	.368
1994	Atl-N	8	3	0	152	4.04	5	1	0	75	3.70	3	2	0	76	4.36	80	1	.200	.293	.300	479	14	.232	.299	.380	193	5	.249	.329	.404	50	0	.220	.245	.260
TOTALS		58	39	0	918	3.58	32	16	0	465	3.27	26	23	0	453	3.89	603	9	.227	.299	.320	2850	62	.253	.301	.379	1319	32	.274	.328	.401	308	3	.253	.301	.325

● Floyd Bannister BL/TL

YEAR	TM/L	W	L	SV	IP	ERA	W	L	SV	IP	ERA	W	L	SV	IP	ERA	AB	HR	AVG	OBP	SLG	AB	HR	AVG	OBP	SLG	AB	HR	AVG	OBP	SLG	AB	HR	AVG	OBP	SLG
1984	Chi-A	14	11	0	218	4.83	6	4	0	105	4.47	8	7	0	113	5.16	150	6	.260	.335	.413	685	24	.251	.315	.423	334	12	.269	.332	.461	42	2	.333	.349	.571
1985	Chi-A	10	14	0	211	4.87	5	6	0	95	3.61	5	8	0	116	5.90	146	6	.301	.360	.568	660	24	.253	.339	.423	331	17	.269	.359	.489	58	3	.362	.479	.569
1986	Chi-A	10	14	0	165	3.54	5	6	0	98	2.84	5	8	0	67	4.57	98	2	.204	.255	.316	528	15	.269	.322	.413	235	6	.251	.327	.362	48	0	.229	.302	.271
1987	Chi-A	16	11	0	229	3.58	6	5	0	92	3.93	10	6	0	137	3.35	125	3	.240	.314	.376	753	35	.247	.280	.434	306	10	.248	.287	.389	72	3	.236	.276	.431
1988	KC-A	12	13	0	189	4.33	4	6	0	96	4.22	8	7	0	93	4.44	145	0	.214	.253	.276	588	22	.257	.330	.437	296	9	.277	.345	.446	25	0	.200	.310	.280
1989	KC-A	4	1	0	75	4.66	2	1	0	45	4.60	2	0	0	30	4.75	48	1	.354	.404	.500	252	7	.278	.316	.417	114	2	.289	.336	.421	16	0	.375	.421	.563
1991	Cal-A	0	0	0	25	3.96	0	0	0	12	2.25	0	0	0	13	5.54	31	2	.258	.343	.484	63	3	.270	.333	.508	33	2	.212	.366	.515	9	0	.222	.300	.222
1992	Tex-A	1	1	0	37	6.32	1	0	0	24	5.70	0	1	0	13	7.43	46	2	.174	.288	.391	93	1	.333	.414	.441	76	2	.237	.343	.368	19	0	.368	.458	.368
TOTALS		67	65	0	1149	4.34	29	28	0	566	3.93	38	37	0	583	4.74	789	22	.250	.314	.402	3622	131	.254	.319	.428	1725	60	.263	.333	.432	289	8	.287	.361	.436

● Jose Bautista BR/TR

YEAR	TM/L	W	L	SV	IP	ERA	W	L	SV	IP	ERA	W	L	SV	IP	ERA	AB	HR	AVG	OBP	SLG	AB	HR	AVG	OBP	SLG	AB	HR	AVG	OBP	SLG	AB	HR	AVG	OBP	SLG
1988	Bal-A	6	15	0	172	4.30	4	7	0	86	4.48	2	8	0	85	4.11	333	13	.258	.314	.432	331	8	.257	.306	.384	265	13	.249	.291	.449	53	1	.264	.291	.340
1989	Bal-A	3	4	0	78	5.31	2	3	0	49	5.36	1	1	0	29	5.22	157	6	.280	.307	.411	150	11	.267	.311	.513	102	11	.363	.383	.745	12	1	.250	.308	.667
1990	Bal-A	1	0	0	27	4.05	0	0	0	17	3.18	1	0	0	10	5.59	37	4	.405	.450	.919	66	0	.197	.239	.242	58	4	.276	.317	.569	19	1	.211	.286	.474
1991	Bal-A	0	1	0	5	16.88	0	0	0	1	9.00	0	1	0	4	18.69	15	0	.400	.500	.533	13	1	.538	.625	1.000	17	0	.529	.619	.647	2	1	.500	.500	2.000
1993	Chi-N	10	3	2	112	2.82	5	0	1	54	2.32	5	3	1	57	3.30	185	3	.232	.311	.324	235	8	.264	.293	.430	180	5	.239	.289	.350	106	2	.179	.269	.264
1994	Chi-N	4	5	1	69	3.89	2	0	0	42	3.64	2	5	1	27	4.28	108	5	.315	.375	.491	156	5	.263	.298	.391	111	6	.234	.321	.432	124	3	.306	.360	.395
TOTALS		24	28	3	463	4.18	14	12	1	249	3.97	10	16	2	213	4.43	835	31	.273	.330	.447	951	33	.261	.303	.415	733	39	.269	.318	.477	316	9	.250	.324	.367

● Steve Bedrosian BR/TR

YEAR	TM/L	W	L	SV	IP	ERA	W	L	SV	IP	ERA	W	L	SV	IP	ERA	AB	HR	AVG	OBP	SLG	AB	HR	AVG	OBP	SLG	AB	HR	AVG	OBP	SLG	AB	HR	AVG	OBP	SLG
1984	Atl-N	9	6	11	84	2.37	3	3	4	46	2.93	6	3	7	38	1.67	171	4	.240	.348	.386	138	1	.174	.219	.246	136	2	.184	.273	.272	130	3	.200	.266	.330
1985	Atl-N	7	15	0	207	3.83	4	5	0	96	3.46	3	10	0	110	4.16	386	13	.282	.386	.443	393	4	.226	.309	.303	319	9	.276	.383	.404	18	0	.556	.619	.611
1986	Phi-N	8	6	29	90	3.39	2	3	14	39	3.00	6	3	15	51	3.68	178	10	.213	.300	.410	163	2	.252	.297	.313	167	4	.234	.311	.347	263	10	.209	.281	.350
1987	Phi-N	5	3	40	89	2.83	2	2	17	43	3.38	3	1	23	46	2.33	193	8	.249	.315	.394	141	3	.220	.272	.319	150	2	.220	.293	.313	267	7	.251	.304	.352
1988	Phi-N	6	6	28	74	3.75	5	3	13	37	4.42	1	3	15	38	3.11	154	4	.292	.366	.461	138	2	.217	.259	.297	145	1	.276	.345	.372	223	4	.238	.302	.359
1989	Phi-N	2	3	6	34	3.21	2	1	4	20	3.66	0	2	2	14	2.57	66	5	.197	.313	.485	49	2	.163	.255	.306	47	4	.191	.322	.489	54	5	.222	.368	.556
1989	SF-N	1	4	17	51	2.65	0	1	10	26	0.68	1	3	7	25	4.74	98	3	.204	.316	.296	84	2	.179	.228	.262	80	3	.200	.283	.325	124	3	.202	.289	.282
1990	SF-N	9	9	17	79	4.20	8	4	11	48	3.54	1	5	6	31	5.23	165	4	.267	.373	.388	134	2	.209	.301	.284	153	3	.255	.358	.346	179	3	.229	.337	.324
1991	Min-A	5	3	6	77	4.42	3	0	1	33	2.97	2	3	5	44	5.52	123	4	.260	.365	.439	165	7	.230	.297	.406	135	4	.244	.342	.400	127	3	.244	.345	.378
1993	Atl-N	5	2	0	50	1.63	2	1	0	27	1.32	3	1	0	22	2.01	74	2	.203	.256	.311	101	2	.188	.267	.297	80	0	.188	.266	.237	30	1	.233	.294	.367
1994	Atl-N	0	2	0	46	3.33	0	1	0	21	1.71	0	1	0	25	4.68	69	2	.304	.364	.507	100	2	.200	.289	.307	84	2	.226	.302	.369	52	2	.212	.349	.365
TOTALS		57	59	154	881	3.38	30	26	75	447	3.28	27	33	79	434	3.49	1677	59	.254	.346	.414	1606	29	.214	.281	.305	1496	35	.238	.329	.355	1467	41	.230	.311	.355

● Tim Belcher BR/TR

YEAR	TM/L	W	L	SV	IP	ERA	W	L	SV	IP	ERA	W	L	SV	IP	ERA	AB	HR	AVG	OBP	SLG	AB	HR	AVG	OBP	SLG	AB	HR	AVG	OBP	SLG	AB	HR	AVG	OBP	SLG
1987	LA-N	4	2	0	34	2.38	4	1	0	29	2.17	0	1	0	5	3.60	63	1	.286	.343	.349	62	1	.194	.206	.290	47	1	.255	.280	.362	20	0	.300	.333	.300
1988	LA-N	12	6	4	180	2.91	6	3	2	78	2.90	6	3	2	102	2.91	340	5	.212	.271	.306	319	3	.223	.279	.285	240	4	.242	.312	.363	42	1	.214	.327	.310
1989	LA-N	15	12	1	230	2.82	10	4	0	124	2.10	5	8	1	106	3.66	473	13	.218	.298	.292	365	13	.216	.278	.362	312	7	.192	.287	.295	128	2	.195	.257	.273
1990	LA-N	9	9	0	153	4.00	6	3	0	75	2.77	3	6	0	78	5.17	298	8	.226	.293	.403	268	9	.254	.300	.407	199	7	.276	.339	.437	36	0	.194	.205	.222
1991	LA-N	10	9	0	209	2.62	7	4	0	121	2.67	3	5	0	88	2.56	445	4	.274	.343	.342	344	6	.195	.258	.288	342	4	.228	.303	.301	97	0	.268	.339	.351
1992	Cin-N	15	14	0	228	3.91	11	7	0	126	3.43	4	7	0	102	4.51	512	16	.277	.350	.410	320	6	.294	.356	.438						86	2	.302	.371	.453
1993	Cin-N	0	3	0	137	4.47	0	2	0	73	5.52	0	1	0	64	3.25	279	5	.262	.352	.387	248	6	.246	.285	.379	217	4	.304	.377	.463	15	0	.467	.467	.533
1993	Chi-A	3	5	0	72	4.40	2	2	0	41	3.32	1	3	0	31	5.81	117	3	.248	.313	.359	148	5	.236	.313	.447	94	4	.277	.330	.447	15	0	.467	.467	.533
1994	Det-A	7	15	0	162	5.89	3	6	0	73	5.79	4	9	0	89	5.97	347	8	.294	.366	.427	315	13	.286	.368	.511	318	8	.299	.383	.450	42	3	.476	.560	.833
TOTALS		84	78	5	1404	3.69	55	32	2	740	3.34	29	46	3	664	4.08	2874	50	.254	.326	.359	2400	64	.226	.285	.359	2089	45	.260	.334	.388	496	8	.272	.338	.381

Stan Belinda BR/TR

YEAR	TM/L	TOT W	L	SV	IP	ERA	HOME W	L	SV	IP	ERA	AWAY W	L	SV	IP	ERA	LEFT AB	HR	AVG	OBP	SLG	RIGHT AB	HR	AVG	OBP	SLG	ON-BASE AB	HR	AVG	OBP	SLG	LATE AB	HR	AVG	OBP	SLG
1989	Pit-N	0	1	0	10	6.10	0	1	0	7	9.00	0	0	0	3	0.00	19	0	.368	.429	.368	25	0	.240	.240	.240	22	0	.318	.348	.318	13	0	.154	.154	.154
1990	Pit-N	3	4	8	58	3.55	1	2	2	25	4.97	2	2	6	33	2.45	88	1	.182	.282	.273	123	3	.260	.350	.398	100	2	.260	.345	.380	124	1	.226	.329	.323
1991	Pit-N	7	5	16	78	3.45	2	1	13	42	1.94	5	4	3	37	5.15	149	6	.168	.272	.329	114	4	.219	.324	.360	159	5	.189	.282	.333					
1992	Pit-N	6	4	18	71	3.15	3	1	8	33	1.89	3	3	10	38	4.26	135	4	.193	.277	.326	125	4	.256	.314	.440	112	7	.250	.318	.509	196	6	.224	.300	.372
1993	Pit-N	3	1	19	42	3.61	3	1	8	22	5.40	0	0	11	21	1.74	75	3	.253	.325	.427	81	1	.198	.230	.296	79	2	.228	.276	.342	101	2	.208	.248	.337
1993	KC-A	1	0	0	27	4.28	1	0	0	13	3.46	0	1	0	14	5.02	44	2	.386	.426	.636	63	0	.206	.254	.222	51	1	.333	.382	.412	45	1	.267	.283	.400
1994	KC-A	2	2	1	49	5.14	0	0	1	23	3.47	2	2	0	26	6.66	62	1	.242	.367	.387	126	5	.254	.333	.468	88	4	.261	.364	.534	48	1	.208	.309	.333
TOTALS		22	18	62	337	3.82	9	6	32	165	3.48	13	12	30	172	4.14	546	15	.229	.316	.364	692	19	.225	.298	.370	566	20	.254	.332	.420	686	16	.214	.291	.344

Andy Benes BR/TR

YEAR	TM/L	TOT W	L	SV	IP	ERA	HOME W	L	SV	IP	ERA	AWAY W	L	SV	IP	ERA	LEFT AB	HR	AVG	OBP	SLG	RIGHT AB	HR	AVG	OBP	SLG	ON-BASE AB	HR	AVG	OBP	SLG	LATE AB	HR	AVG	OBP	SLG
1989	SD-N	6	3	0	67	3.51	2	0	0	39	4.38	3	1	0	28	2.28	131	4	.214	.333	.359	109	3	.211	.263	.339	99	3	.273	.295	.455	23	0	.304	.346	.348
1990	SD-N	10	11	0	192	3.60	6	4	0	89	3.93	4	7	0	103	3.32	436	9	.243	.306	.369	294	9	.241	.308	.381	281	4	.242	.324	.342	50	3	.320	.358	.560
1991	SD-N	15	11	0	223	3.03	6	5	0	111	3.73	9	6	0	112	2.33	466	13	.230	.281	.354	370	10	.235	.289	.362	301	9	.236	.301	.349	88	1	.239	.316	.284
1992	SD-N	13	14	0	231	3.35	7	6	0	117	3.55	6	8	0	115	3.14	533	10	.246	.283	.335	337	4	.246	.283	.335	356	6	.275	.327	.390	74	1	.284	.346	.419
1993	SD-N	15	15	0	231	3.78	8	8	0	104	3.47	7	7	0	127	4.04	433	10	.242	.327	.374	429	13	.221	.278	.368	339	9	.230	.315	.354	83	1	.301	.379	.398
1994	SD-N	6	14	0	172	3.86	5	7	0	94	4.60	1	7	0	78	2.99	322	5	.224	.292	.345	331	15	.251	.295	.456	252	7	.254	.315	.425	60	2	.267	.371	.467
TOTALS		65	68	0	1116	3.51	33	31	0	554	3.87	32	37	0	563	3.15	2321	51	.243	.311	.369	1870	54	.236	.288	.377	1628	38	.249	.316	.376	378	8	.280	.352	.405

Juan Berenguer BR/TR

YEAR	TM/L	TOT W	L	SV	IP	ERA	HOME W	L	SV	IP	ERA	AWAY W	L	SV	IP	ERA	LEFT AB	HR	AVG	OBP	SLG	RIGHT AB	HR	AVG	OBP	SLG	ON-BASE AB	HR	AVG	OBP	SLG	LATE AB	HR	AVG	OBP	SLG
1984	Det-A	11	10	0	168	3.48	6	5	0	97	3.24	5	5	0	71	3.80	342	10	.231	.333	.360	285	4	.235	.305	.323	261	8	.238	.323	.387	25	1	.240	.406	.360
1985	Det-A	5	6	0	95	5.59	3	4	0	48	7.82	2	2	0	47	3.28	203	6	.305	.389	.448	167	6	.204	.286	.383	150	5	.307	.400	.473	22	1	.273	.448	.409
1986	SF-N	2	3	4	73	2.70	1	2	3	34	2.94	1	1	1	40	2.50	134	2	.254	.359	.366	131	2	.229	.346	.321	112	2	.286	.396	.393	79	1	.215	.357	.266
1987	Min-A	8	1	4	112	3.94	5	0	1	62	2.31	3	1	3	50	5.98	223	8	.278	.360	.462	197	2	.193	.257	.274	177	4	.266	.343	.412	113	0	.230	.308	.310
1988	Min-A	8	4	2	100	3.96	5	0	0	50	3.40	3	4	2	50	4.53	184	6	.212	.344	.364	173	1	.202	.296	.283	172	5	.198	.317	.326	134	1	.254	.382	.373
1989	Min-A	9	3	3	106	3.48	8	2	2	70	3.36	1	1	1	36	3.72	164	7	.329	.407	.524	227	4	.185	.266	.269	186	5	.220	.299	.349	134	4	.216	.293	.321
1990	Min-A	8	5	0	100	3.41	4	2	0	48	3.54	4	3	0	52	3.29	159	3	.264	.361	.390	208	6	.207	.321	.313	180	4	.233	.330	.339	159	3	.220	.311	.333
1991	Atl-N	0	3	17	64	2.24	0	1	9	33	2.76	0	2	8	32	1.71	106	1	.198	.303	.255	122	4	.180	.221	.344	97	2	.206	.262	.320	116	3	.164	.269	.293
1992	Atl-N	3	1	1	33	5.13	2	1	0	15	7.36	1	0	1	19	3.38	68	1	.206	.260	.309	67	5	.269	.355	.537	43	3	.302	.388	.558					
1992	KC-A	1	4	0	45	5.64	1	0	0	25	5.33	0	1	0	19	6.05	73	2	.342	.417	.521	97	1	.175	.255	.258	85	3	.259	.340	.412	85	1	.273	.385	.500
TOTALS		55	40	31	897	3.82	35	20	15	483	3.82	20	20	16	415	3.82	1650	51	.266	.363	.420	1675	31	.204	.286	.307	1487	43	.245	.335	.385	847	18	.226	.331	.341

Mike Bielecki BR/TR

YEAR	TM/L	TOT W	L	SV	IP	ERA	HOME W	L	SV	IP	ERA	AWAY W	L	SV	IP	ERA	LEFT AB	HR	AVG	OBP	SLG	RIGHT AB	HR	AVG	OBP	SLG	ON-BASE AB	HR	AVG	OBP	SLG	LATE AB	HR	AVG	OBP	SLG
1984	Pit-N	0	0	0	4	0.00	0	0	0	1	0.00	0	0	0	3	0.00	9	0	.222	.222	.222	7	0	.286	.286	.286	7	0	.143	.143	.143	0	0	—	—	—
1985	Pit-N	2	3	0	46	4.53	1	2	0	23	6.65	1	1	0	23	2.38	109	3	.257	.341	.404	66	2	.258	.417	.394	84	1	.286	.406	.345	10	0	.400	.571	.400
1986	Pit-N	6	11	0	149	4.66	2	6	0	78	4.64	4	5	0	71	4.69	308	7	.260	.331	.409	261	3	.264	.381	.375	258	5	.271	.358	.411	14	0	.143	.333	.214
1987	Pit-N	2	3	0	48	4.73	2	0	0	27	3.67	0	3	0	22	6.27	95	3	.253	.305	.442	76	3	.250	.296	.461	61	3	.246	.294	.492	3	0	.000	.250	.000
1988	Chi-N	2	2	0	48	3.35	1	1	0	23	3.13	1	1	0	25	3.55	108	2	.296	.342	.380	86	2	.267	.319	.407	95	3	.263	.315	.400	35	0	.114	.205	.143
1989	Chi-N	18	7	0	212	3.14	9	3	0	114	2.83	9	4	0	98	3.49	420	10	.252	.338	.398	369	6	.220	.270	.322	301	4	.226	.318	.326	49	2	.265	.357	.469
1990	Chi-N	8	11	1	168	4.93	2	7	0	76	4.88	6	4	1	92	4.97	396	8	.275	.350	.412	258	5	.306	.373	.453	282	6	.291	.374	.433	42	2	.190	.244	.381
1991	Chi-N	13	11	0	172	4.50	6	8	0	95	4.74	5	4	0	77	4.21	343	10	.277	.343	.429	303	8	.244	.288	.409	264	5	.269	.330	.409	69	2	.290	.390	.449
1991	Atl-N	0	0	0	2	0.00	0	0	0	0	—	0	0	0	2	0.00	2	0	.000	.333	.000	5	0	.400	.500	.600	4	0	.250	.400	.250	3	0	.333	.600	.333
1992	Atl-N	2	4	0	81	2.57	1	2	0	39	2.54	1	2	0	42	2.59	178	0	.270	.333	.348	125	2	.232	.290	.376	130	0	.246	.301	.331	18	0	.111	.158	.111
1993	Cle-A	4	5	0	69	5.90	3	1	0	45	4.23	1	4	0	24	9.00	141	4	.312	.372	.447	149	4	.309	.354	.463	133	3	.286	.362	.376	10	3	.667	.667	.667
1994	Atl-N	2	0	0	27	4.00	2	0	0	16	4.96	0	0	0	11	2.53	49	1	.163	.241	.163	52	3	.385	.467	.577	49	2	.245	.327	.449	10	0	.000	.333	.200
TOTALS		59	57	1	1023	4.17	31	29	1	537	4.09	28	28	1	486	4.26	2158	47	.267	.338	.401	1757	37	.262	.331	.401	1668	32	.263	.341	.388	256	6	.227	.330	.348

Bud Black BL/TL

YEAR	TM/L	TOT W	L	SV	IP	ERA	HOME W	L	SV	IP	ERA	AWAY W	L	SV	IP	ERA	LEFT AB	HR	AVG	OBP	SLG	RIGHT AB	HR	AVG	OBP	SLG	ON-BASE AB	HR	AVG	OBP	SLG	LATE AB	HR	AVG	OBP	SLG
1984	KC-A	17	12	0	257	3.12	10	7	0	146	2.66	7	5	0	111	3.72	205	4	.205	.265	.298	764	18	.241	.288	.360	352	8	.244	.303	.366	120	7	.317	.354	.550
1985	KC-A	10	15	0	206	4.33	6	7	0	109	4.38	4	8	0	97	4.28	176	2	.267	.303	.364	629	15	.269	.328	.407	350	8	.274	.328	.391	77	0	.247	.314	.325
1986	KC-A	5	10	9	121	3.20	3	2	5	62	2.63	2	8	4	59	3.79	137	3	.219	.285	.308	308	11	.227	.307	.390	199	9	.206	.302	.367	137	6	.190	.293	.336
1987	KC-A	8	6	1	122	3.60	5	1	1	63	3.14	3	5	0	59	4.10	117	4	.231	.278	.393	358	12	.277	.334	.444	207	7	.227	.288	.353	40	1	.300	.378	.525
1988	KC-A	2	1	0	22	4.91	1	1	0	12	4.63	1	0	0	10	5.23	17	0	.176	.364	.176	69	2	.290	.347	.406	37	2	.324	.468	.514	23	0	.304	.484	.304
1988	Cle-A	2	3	1	59	5.03	0	1	1	30	6.37	2	2	0	29	3.68	52	1	.173	.274	.231	153	5	.289	.358	.422	95	3	.232	.339	.368	28	0	.321	.367	.321
1989	Cle-A	12	11	0	222	3.36	5	9	0	115	4.06	7	2	0	107	2.61	124	2	.158	.215	.233	724	12	.268	.308	.384	316	5	.253	.305	.351	104	2	.288	.309	.433
1990	Cle-A	11	10	0	191	3.53	7	5	0	102	3.10	4	5	0	89	4.03	131	6	.275	.329	.443	594	11	.227	.287	.330	264	5	.250	.321	.352	56	0	.179	.246	.196
1990	Tor-A	2	1	0	16	4.02	1	0	0	2	4.50	1	1	0	14	3.95	14	1	.214	.188	.429	39	1	.179	.256	.308	15	1	.267	.235	.600	13	1	.231	.313	.462
1991	SF-N	12	16	0	214	3.99	8	7	0	112	2.81	4	9	0	102	5.28	175	6	.274	.326	.406	625	19	.245	.309	.394	289	13	.273	.350	.481	64	0	.219	.296	.266
1992	SF-N	10	12	0	177	3.97	8	5	0	111	2.91	2	7	0	66	5.76	140	4	.229	.281	.364	537	19	.272	.332	.438	247	8	.243	.323	.393	42	3	.214	.298	.476
1993	SF-N	8	2	0	94	3.56	4	2	0	39	3.46	4	0	0	55	3.27	51	1	.294	.333	.392	296	12	.250	.319	.412	127	6	.220	.299	.378	6	0	.000	.143	.000
1994	SF-N	4	2	0	54	4.47	2	1	0	18	7.50	2	1	0	36	2.97	32	0	.313	.389	.313	172	9	.233	.291	.471	62	2	.323	.389	.516	2	0	.500	.750	.500
TOTALS		103	101	11	1755	3.73	60	48	7	920	3.46	43	53	4	836	4.02	1367	34	.235	.291	.350	5288	146	.254	.311	.390	2560	77	.250	.320	.389	712	20	.250	.321	.385

Bert Blyleven BR/TR

YEAR	TM/L	TOT W	L	SV	IP	ERA	HOME W	L	SV	IP	ERA	AWAY W	L	SV	IP	ERA	LEFT AB	HR	AVG	OBP	SLG	RIGHT AB	HR	AVG	OBP	SLG	ON-BASE AB	HR	AVG	OBP	SLG	LATE AB	HR	AVG	OBP	SLG
1984	Cle-A	19	7	0	245	2.87	10	2	0	123	3.23	9	5	0	122	2.50	475	7	.200	.269	.282	435	12	.251	.302	.382	350	8	.226	.290	.343	78	3	.269	.352	.410
1985	Cle-A	9	11	0	180	3.26	5	8	0	109	3.48	4	3	0	71	2.92	384	7	.263	.322	.380	295	7	.210	.262	.332	265	3	.264	.323	.362	57	0	.123	.242	.158
1985	Min-A	8	5	0	114	3.00	6	1	0	61	1.91	2	4	0	53	4.27	260	4	.250	.295	.335	167	5	.216	.258	.353	167	5	.216	.270	.347	64	1	.203	.246	.297
1986	Min-A	17	14	0	272	4.01	12	5	0	155	4.12	5	9	0	117	3.86	638	26	.282	.318	.499	411	24	.246	.318	.499	386	23	.246	.298	.469	100	6	.310	.340	.560
1987	Min-A	15	12	0	267	4.01	9	3	0	165	3.83	6	9	0	102	4.31	555	32	.234	.313	.447	447	14	.266	.331	.416	382	12	.246	.323	.385	86	1	.198	.314	.302
1988	Min-A	10	17	0	207	5.43	6	9	0	108	5.83	4	8	0	99	4.98	438	10	.304	.356	.441	378	11	.283	.333	.426	344	11	.343	.391	.497	45	1	.378	.404	.556
1989	Cal-A	17	5	0	241	2.73	8	1	0	119	2.64	9	4	0	122	2.81	485	4	.252	.290	.318	422	10	.244	.283	.358	351	4	.219	.272	.296	96	1	.240	.284	.292
1990	Cal-A	8	7	0	134	5.24	4	2	0	71	3.82	4	5	0	63	6.82	270	8	.311	.346	.470	268	7	.295	.331	.455	222	8	.333	.371	.509	12	0	.250	.412	.250
1992	Cal-A	8	12	0	133	4.74	4	6	0	65	4.31	4	6	0	68	5.14	253	6	.261	.305	.387	273	11	.308	.345	.487	208	5	.332	.368	.462	22	0	.318	.348	.409
TOTALS		111	90	0	1793	3.85	64	40	0	975	3.75	47	50	0	818	3.97	3758	104	.252	.305	.386	3096	101	.261	.310	.414	2675	79	.266	.321	.406	560	13	.248	.315	.370

Mike Boddicker BR/TR

YEAR	TM/L	TOT W	L	SV	IP	ERA	HOME W	L	SV	IP	ERA	AWAY W	L	SV	IP	ERA	LEFT AB	HR	AVG	OBP	SLG	RIGHT AB	HR	AVG	OBP	SLG	ON-BASE AB	HR	AVG	OBP	SLG	LATE AB	HR	AVG	OBP	SLG
1984	Bal-A	20	11	0	261	2.79	8	6	0	120	2.17	12	5	0	141	3.32	529	11	.238	.299	.340	427	12	.215	.278	.349	357	10	.221	.286	.342	103	2	.136	.224	.214
1985	Bal-A	12	17	0	203	4.07	5	9	0	103	3.40	7	8	0	100	4.77	452	8	.294	.375	.405	342	5	.275	.342	.360	379	5	.269	.347	.335	85	5	.224	.356	.412
1986	Bal-A	14	12	0	218	4.70	7	4	0	102	4.66	7	8	0	116	4.73	428	12	.243	.313	.415	412	18	.243	.313	.415	356	16	.275	.318	.458	65	2	.246	.319	.369
1987	Bal-A	10	12	0	226	4.18	5	6	0	117	4.24	5	6	0	109	4.12	485	18	.239	.303	.416	369	11	.240	.303	.409	331	10	.245	.321	.402	81	1	.284	.366	.395
1988	Bal-A	6	12	0	147	3.86	2	5	0	67	3.11	4	7	0	80	4.48	292	7	.288	.367	.397	271	7	.240	.295	.376	241	6	.261	.333	.390	53	3	.170	.214	.396
1988	Bos-A	7	3	0	89	2.63	5	1	0	40	3.38	2	2	0	49	2.02	167	1	.246	.292	.323	164	2	.268	.342	.341	126	2	.246	.308	.349	15	0	.333	.353	.400
1989	Bos-A	15	11	0	212	4.00	7	8	0	103	4.89	8	3	0	109	3.15	444	12	.279	.333	.421	369	7	.252	.325	.374	369	5	.259	.331	.354	59	1	.153	.231	.237
1990	Bos-A	17	8	0	228	3.36	11	5	0	136	2.97	6	3	0	92	3.93	464	7	.261	.317	.366	409	6	.254	.321	.369	354	5	.251	.353	.353	81	0	.185	.267	.198
1991	KC-A	12	12	0	181	4.08	7	8	0	111	4.07	5	4	0	70	4.11	355	7	.301	.365	.470	307	8	.257	.316	.394	307	8	.257	.316	.394	63	1	.270	.329	.333
1992	KC-A	1	4	3	87	4.98	1	2	0	36	5.70	0	2	3	50	4.47	168	2	.292	.355	.387	173	3	.249	.350	.393	173	2	.277	.358	.412	24	1	.292	.379	.417
1993	Mil-A	3	5	0	54	5.67	3	2	0	35	5.09	0	3	0	19	6.75	130	6	.392	.429	.592	98	0	.265	.333	.327	104	3	.375	.416	.500	0	0	—	—	—
TOTALS		117	107	3	1906	3.89	61	56	3	971	3.78	56	51	3	935	4.00	3914	91	.272	.335	.402	3371	80	.249	.318	.373	3068	73	.260	.328	.382	629	16	.213	.296	.320

Joe Boever BR/TR

YEAR	TM/L	TOT W	L	SV	IP	ERA	HOME W	L	SV	IP	ERA	AWAY W	L	SV	IP	ERA	LEFT AB	HR	AVG	OBP	SLG	RIGHT AB	HR	AVG	OBP	SLG	ON-BASE AB	HR	AVG	OBP	SLG	LATE AB	HR	AVG	OBP	SLG
1985	StL-N	0	0	0	16	4.41	0	0	0	7	2.57	0	0	0	9	5.79	21	0	.238	.273	.286	42	3	.286	.326	.548	26	1	.269	.333	.462	3	1	.667	.750	1.667
1986	StL-N	0	1	0	22	1.66	0	0	0	14	1.88	0	0	0	7	1.23	27	1	.296	.441	.407	55	1	.200	.254	.273	38	1	.263	.333	.368	9	0	.444	.500	.444
1987	Atl-N	1	0	0	18	7.36	0	0	0	10	7.20	1	0	0	8	7.56	43	1	.349	.431	.512	36	3	.389	.463	.722	46	0	.261	.340	.326	6	1	.500	.500	1.000
1988	Atl-N	0	2	1	20	1.77	0	1	1	15	0.60	0	1	0	5	5.40	35	0	.143	.167	.171	31	1	.226	.250	.323	21	0	.190	.190	.190	35	1	.189	.231	.216
1989	Atl-N	4	11	21	82	3.94	4	6	9	51	3.53	0	5	12	31	4.60	179	1	.251	.333	.307	130	5	.254	.322	.423	149	2	.228	.307	.302	202	5	.248	.333	.366
1990	Atl-N	1	3	8	42	4.68	1	2	2	12	6.45	0	1	6	30	3.64	85	1	.188	.343	.282	74	5	.324	.429	.608	75	1	.267	.430	.373	81	3	.222	.390	.420
1990	Phi-N	3	6	6	46	2.15	1	3	3	30	2.37	2	3	3	16	1.72	89	0	.180	.291	.202	89	3	.225	.271	.337	88	0	.193	.266	.261	109	0	.193	.267	.229
1991	Phi-N	3	5	0	98	3.84	2	1	0	54	3.17	1	4	0	44	4.67	171	4	.257	.361	.380	197	6	.234	.314	.386	162	3	.259	.373	.407	158	4	.228	.348	.335
1992	Hou-N	3	6	2	111	2.51	1	2	1	61	1.32	2	4	1	50	3.88	186	1	.242	.346	.310	230	2	.252	.306	.304	225	0	.213	.298	.249	141	1	.270	.352	.348
1993	Oak-A	4	2	0	79	3.86	4	2	0	37	3.89	0	0	0	42	3.83	141	3	.305	.379	.461	170	5	.259	.338	.406	170	5	.259	.338	.406	141	1	.396	.444	.583
1993	Det-A	2	1	3	23	2.74	1	0	1	11	0.84	1	1	2	12	4.38	31	1	.226	.306	.355	47	0	.149	.246	.234	30	0	.133	.268	.167	18	0	.167	.200	.167
1994	Det-A	9	2	3	81	3.98	7	0	1	46	3.15	2	2	2	36	5.05	140	3	.214	.296	.307	164	9	.305	.387	.518	153	7	.235	.339	.418	73	3	.247	.329	.397
TOTALS		29	36	44	641	3.51	21	16	18	359	2.99	8	20	26	282	4.18	1148	16	.243	.338	.335	1259	40	.260	.328	.407	1153	19	.234	.333	.338	885	19	.247	.340	.359

YEAR	TM/L	TOTAL W	L	SV	IP	ERA	HOME W	L	SV	IP	ERA	AWAY W	L	SV	IP	ERA	LEFT AB	HR	AVG	OBP	SLG	RIGHT AB	HR	AVG	OBP	SLG	ON-BASE AB	HR	AVG	OBP	SLG	LATE/CLOSE AB	HR	AVG	OBP	SLG

● Ricky Bones BR/TR
1991	SD-N	4	6	0	54	4.83	3	3	0	33	5.40	1	3	0	21	3.92	116	2	.267	.323	.345	96	1	.271	.317	.365	87	3	.333	.380	.506	2	0	.000	.000	.000
1992	Mil-A	9	10	0	163	4.57	6	4	0	100	3.25	3	6	0	64	6.64	302	9	.268	.321	.421	339	18	.260	.322	.472	241	9	.261	.309	.411	39	2	.205	.244	.410
1993	Mil-A	11	11	0	204	4.86	4	6	0	72	4.75	7	5	0	132	4.92	390	12	.256	.303	.433	410	16	.298	.363	.488	306	8	.301	.363	.441	46	0	.196	.213	.239
1994	Mil-A	10	9	0	171	3.43	4	5	0	82	3.51	6	4	0	89	3.35	321	8	.255	.309	.386	330	9	.255	.299	.424	246	6	.272	.316	.419	40	3	.225	.279	.500
TOTALS		34	36	0	592	4.37	17	18	0	287	3.95	17	18	0	305	4.76	1129	31	.260	.311	.407	1175	44	.272	.330	.455	880	26	.285	.337	.433	127	5	.205	.241	.370

● Chris Bosio BR/TR
1986	Mil-A	0	4	0	35	7.01	0	2	0	19	6.05	0	2	0	15	8.22	68	5	.324	.378	.662	72	4	.264	.329	.486	61	4	.361	.409	.705	0	0	—	—	—
1987	Mil-A	11	8	2	170	5.24	4	4	0	74	6.23	7	4	2	96	4.48	356	11	.264	.322	.424	321	7	.290	.329	.405	293	6	.290	.347	.406	122	2	.246	.287	.352
1988	Mil-A	7	15	6	182	3.36	5	6	3	92	2.73	2	9	3	90	4.01	405	7	.259	.294	.356	305	6	.279	.315	.390	300	4	.283	.311	.377	129	0	.178	.252	.209
1989	Mil-A	15	10	0	235	2.95	9	3	0	127	2.06	6	7	0	108	4.01	458	8	.247	.294	.325	447	8	.251	.285	.347	355	9	.259	.309	.380	77	1	.247	.284	.299
1990	Mil-A	4	9	0	133	4.00	2	7	0	81	5.11	2	2	0	52	2.26	273	10	.286	.336	.465	235	5	.226	.282	.349	198	6	.278	.338	.434	37	0	.189	.184	.270
1991	Mil-A	14	10	0	205	3.25	5	6	0	96	3.83	9	4	0	108	2.74	418	6	.251	.303	.347	348	9	.236	.300	.351	296	6	.253	.318	.351	64	2	.297	.384	.391
1992	Mil-A	16	6	0	231	3.62	9	3	0	128	3.03	7	3	0	104	4.34	421	10	.273	.310	.399	457	11	.236	.273	.354	338	9	.290	.319	.435	92	0	.261	.289	.348
1993	Sea-A	9	9	1	164	3.45	6	6	1	95	2.95	3	3	0	70	4.13	296	8	.260	.339	.402	306	6	.199	.266	.304	229	6	.236	.319	.384	59	4	.356	.397	.610
1994	Sea-A	4	10	0	125	4.32	3	2	0	67	2.83	1	8	0	58	6.02	279	5	.301	.344	.430	216	10	.245	.311	.449	220	8	.273	.314	.445	51	1	.216	.298	.314
TOTALS		80	81	9	1479	3.77	43	39	4	779	3.50	37	42	5	701	4.07	2974	70	.267	.316	.393	2707	66	.246	.294	.368	2290	58	.273	.324	.407	631	10	.244	.295	.336

● Oil Can Boyd BR/TR
1984	Bos-A	12	12	0	198	4.37	6	8	0	116	4.28	6	4	0	82	4.50	444	5	.252	.299	.349	325	13	.292	.334	.502	312	8	.298	.334	.458	70	1	.329	.356	.429
1985	Bos-A	15	13	0	272	3.70	11	8	0	158	3.76	4	5	0	114	3.62	589	10	.231	.272	.334	456	16	.300	.349	.478	418	12	.266	.294	.414	151	6	.311	.358	.470
1986	Bos-A	16	10	0	214	3.78	9	6	0	120	3.66	7	4	0	94	3.93	442	18	.278	.306	.452	395	14	.251	.298	.405	308	13	.253	.293	.425	71	1	.296	.324	.366
1987	Bos-A	1	3	0	37	5.89	1	1	0	19	5.79	0	2	0	18	6.00	86	2	.279	.312	.477	62	4	.371	.420	.629	61	1	.328	.353	.541	6	0	.667	.571	1.167
1988	Bos-A	9	7	0	130	5.34	4	2	0	54	5.96	5	5	0	75	4.90	250	9	.292	.328	.468	259	16	.286	.352	.560	197	6	.294	.335	.467	37	2	.297	.381	.486
1989	Bos-A	3	2	0	59	4.42	0	2	0	22	5.40	3	0	0	37	3.86	119	3	.235	.300	.319	106	5	.274	.319	.500	88	5	.261	.302	.466	16	0	.188	.278	.188
1990	Mon-N	10	6	0	191	2.93	6	3	0	90	2.91	4	3	0	101	2.94	430	9	.226	.280	.344	272	10	.246	.290	.426	281	7	.196	.258	.327	13	1	.231	.375	.462
1991	Mon-N	6	8	0	120	3.52	3	2	0	69	2.47	3	6	0	51	4.94	265	4	.253	.320	.411	185	5	.259	.305	.400	183	3	.235	.284	.377	33	0	.273	.273	.455
1991	Tex-A	2	7	0	62	6.68	2	3	0	31	4.94	0	4	0	31	8.42	102	1	.294	.327	.353	156	11	.327	.375	.628	103	7	.350	.402	.621	2	1	.500	.500	2.000
TOTALS		74	68	0	1283	4.09	42	35	0	679	3.93	32	33	0	604	4.28	2727	61	.253	.299	.382	2216	94	.281	.330	.481	1951	62	.265	.306	.430	399	12	.306	.349	.451

● Jeff Brantley BR/TR
1988	SF-N	0	1	1	21	5.66	0	1	0	7	5.14	0	1	1	14	5.93	26	1	.192	.323	.192	54	2	.315	.339	.537	38	2	.289	.341	.500	0	0	—	—	—
1989	SF-N	7	1	0	97	4.07	4	1	0	45	3.60	3	0	0	52	4.47	192	4	.302	.364	.422	181	6	.238	.308	.365	173	5	.277	.350	.405	85	0	.212	.284	.282
1990	SF-N	5	3	19	87	1.56	4	1	9	41	1.77	1	2	10	46	1.37	186	1	.274	.341	.328	135	2	.193	.278	.244	167	0	.228	.307	.251	221	2	.240	.321	.299
1991	SF-N	5	2	15	95	2.45	2	0	7	42	2.14	3	2	8	53	2.70	185	3	.205	.338	.286	161	5	.248	.324	.398	164	1	.183	.320	.238	235	5	.234	.348	.319
1992	SF-N	7	7	7	92	2.95	4	3	3	47	2.30	3	4	4	45	3.63	193	4	.181	.300	.280	130	4	.246	.320	.377	143	4	.231	.327	.357	111	3	.252	.363	.369
1993	SF-N	5	6	0	114	4.28	3	2	0	60	3.58	2	4	0	53	5.06	221	11	.285	.374	.511	212	8	.231	.295	.363	170	4	.282	.349	.406	61	3	.180	.286	.344
1994	Cin-N	6	6	15	65	2.48	4	4	6	38	3.29	2	2	9	27	1.33	97	1	.206	.300	.289	131	5	.198	.279	.336	101	3	.208	.289	.307	163	5	.227	.306	.362
TOTALS		35	26	57	571	3.15	21	12	25	280	2.89	14	14	32	290	3.41	1100	24	.245	.340	.359	1004	32	.232	.303	.361	956	19	.240	.327	.336	876	18	.231	.325	.326

● Billy Brewer BL/TL
1993	KC-A	2	2	0	39	3.46	1	2	0	20	3.10	1	0	0	19	3.86	60	3	.183	.286	.333	75	1	.267	.360	.467	69	1	.116	.235	.188	44	1	.136	.255	.205
1994	KC-A	4	1	3	39	2.56	2	0	2	19	2.37	2	1	1	20	2.75	57	4	.246	.313	.491	78	0	.179	.286	.256	73	2	.219	.289	.342	70	2	.214	.309	.314
TOTALS		6	3	3	78	3.01	3	2	2	39	2.75	3	1	1	38	3.29	117	7	.214	.299	.410	153	3	.222	.322	.359	142	3	.169	.262	.268	114	3	.184	.288	.272

● Kevin Brown BR/TR
1986	Tex-A	1	0	0	5	3.60	1	0	0	5	3.60	0	0	0	0	—	13	0	.308	.308	.385	6	0	.333	.333	.500	7	0	.286	.286	.286	0	0	—	—	—
1988	Tex-A	1	1	0	23	4.24	0	1	0	12	5.11	1	0	0	11	3.27	42	1	.405	.444	.595	58	1	.276	.344	.345	50	1	.320	.346	.400	8	0	.375	.375	.375
1989	Tex-A	12	9	0	191	3.35	6	3	0	80	3.25	6	6	0	111	3.42	351	5	.225	.294	.291	364	5	.242	.312	.332	295	4	.237	.298	.319	82	2	.183	.261	.280
1990	Tex-A	12	10	0	180	3.60	6	4	0	87	2.58	6	6	0	93	4.56	337	6	.249	.309	.362	348	7	.261	.301	.357	305	9	.256	.343	.527	93	5	.269	.343	.527
1991	Tex-A	9	12	0	211	4.40	4	5	0	111	4.14	5	7	0	100	4.70	410	8	.273	.349	.395	411	9	.294	.375	.414	385	6	.288	.367	.387	85	4	.353	.427	.600
1992	Tex-A	21	11	0	266	3.32	11	4	0	123	2.71	10	7	0	143	3.85	488	7	.268	.339	.365	519	4	.252	.294	.306	433	7	.286	.344	.379	133	1	.323	.359	.383
1993	Tex-A	15	12	0	233	3.59	9	5	0	124	2.46	6	7	0	109	4.89	509	9	.253	.324	.358	394	5	.251	.312	.348	370	6	.257	.340	.354	61	2	.197	.242	.361
1994	Tex-A	7	9	0	170	4.82	5	5	0	97	4.07	2	4	0	73	5.82	379	9	.332	.379	.485	316	9	.291	.341	.418	319	9	.313	.358	.464	78	1	.244	.298	.385
TOTALS		78	64	0	1279	3.81	42	27	0	641	3.22	36	37	0	638	4.40	2529	45	.270	.335	.380	2416	40	.265	.325	.360	2153	40	.274	.337	.378	540	15	.272	.331	.424

● Tom Browning BL/TL
1984	Cin-N	1	0	0	23	1.54	0	0	0	8	2.25	1	0	0	15	1.17	10	0	.600	.636	.600	79	0	.266	.301	.316	38	0	.184	.244	.211	14	0	.286	.333	.286
1985	Cin-N	20	9	0	261	3.55	10	6	0	131	4.11	10	3	0	130	2.98	148	1	.223	.282	.277	839	28	.249	.300	.403	375	12	.240	.300	.413	54	2	.222	.300	.370
1986	Cin-N	14	13	0	243	3.81	7	6	0	107	3.80	7	7	0	137	3.82	133	4	.241	.295	.353	785	22	.246	.291	.378	329	7	.271	.321	.392	79	1	.190	.235	.266
1987	Cin-N	10	13	0	183	5.02	5	6	0	101	4.92	4	7	0	82	5.14	116	4	.267	.351	.431	592	23	.287	.340	.480	298	10	.258	.327	.426	32	1	.313	.389	.469
1988	Cin-N	18	5	0	251	3.41	5	0	0	117	4.40	13	2	0	134	2.55	151	8	.285	.347	.536	765	28	.212	.263	.370	314	16	.239	.276	.452	104	3	.212	.259	.337
1989	Cin-N	15	12	0	250	3.39	7	8	0	126	4.14	8	4	0	124	2.62	132	6	.265	.327	.424	814	25	.253	.298	.405	344	8	.262	.310	.404	68	0	.162	.219	.221
1990	Cin-N	15	9	0	228	3.80	8	8	0	128	4.64	7	1	0	100	2.71	162	5	.253	.309	.395	720	19	.269	.309	.415	338	6	.269	.326	.414	101	2	.277	.330	.406
1991	Cin-N	14	14	0	230	4.18	10	4	0	121	3.50	4	10	0	109	4.94	212	4	.203	.269	.344	694	28	.285	.321	.452	350	10	.286	.326	.443	71	3	.324	.355	.507
1992	Cin-N	6	5	0	87	5.07	5	1	0	34	5.03	1	4	0	53	5.09	83	1	.325	.385	.470	264	5	.307	.355	.489	146	3	.329	.396	.507	9	0	.222	.222	.222
1993	Cin-N	7	7	0	114	4.74	4	2	0	51	4.84	3	5	0	63	6.25	78	2	.244	.302	.372	400	13	.301	.331	.533	223	6	.296	.329	.444	10	0	.200	.273	.200
1994	Cin-N	3	1	0	41	4.20	1	0	0	12	5.84	2	1	0	28	3.49	24	1	.083	.233	.208	129	7	.248	.295	.426	54	0	.222	.279	.222	6	0	.000	.000	.000
TOTALS		123	88	0	1911	3.92	63	44	0	935	4.17	60	44	0	976	3.68	1249	36	.250	.317	.393	6081	198	.264	.308	.422	2809	78	.265	.317	.420	548	12	.235	.287	.349

● Dave Burba BR/TR
1990	Sea-A	0	0	0	8	4.50	0	0	0	5	0.00	0	0	0	3	13.50	9	0	.111	.273	.111	0	0	.333	.364	.333	17	0	.118	.211	.118	1	0	1.000	1.000	1.000
1991	Sea-A	2	2	1	37	3.68	1	1	1	15	5.28	1	1	0	21	2.53	59	2	.288	.373	.441	80	4	.213	.267	.463	52	1	.231	.333	.365	16	0	.250	.368	.563
1992	SF-N	2	7	0	71	4.97	1	3	0	34	2.94	1	5	0	37	6.81	151	2	.318	.370	.424	183	3	.250	.344	.367	124	2	.323	.421	.460	10	0	.000	.083	.000
1993	SF-N	10	3	0	95	4.25	5	1	0	58	3.39	5	2	0	37	5.59	151	6	.318	.379	.464	208	8	.226	.305	.389	154	7	.286	.376	.474	49	1	.224	.298	.367
1994	SF-N	3	6	0	74	4.38	2	4	0	35	4.11	1	2	0	39	4.62	101	4	.178	.325	.267	166	4	.247	.357	.404	130	3	.238	.338	.415	116	3	.207	.361	.345
TOTALS		17	18	1	285	4.39	9	8	1	148	3.53	8	10	0	137	5.32	471	10	.280	.361	.399	603	19	.239	.326	.396	477	13	.270	.368	.430	192	4	.208	.338	.354

● Tim Burke BR/TR
1985	Mon-N	9	4	8	120	2.39	4	3	2	50	2.88	5	1	6	70	2.05	186	3	.253	.355	.360	235	6	.166	.233	.268	192	5	.188	.284	.276	190	4	.200	.293	.295
1986	Mon-N	9	7	4	101	2.93	4	2	2	47	1.74	5	5	2	55	3.95	205	5	.302	.391	.415	188	2	.218	.290	.319	183	2	.273	.381	.355	233	4	.266	.350	.361
1987	Mon-N	7	0	18	91	1.19	5	0	7	46	0.97	2	0	11	45	1.41	174	2	.213	.258	.282	153	1	.176	.206	.222	139	1	.180	.232	.223	199	1	.181	.207	.221
1988	Mon-N	3	5	18	82	3.40	3	2	5	48	4.50	0	3	13	34	1.85	147	5	.306	.385	.449	162	2	.241	.272	.346	137	3	.285	.383	.409	206	5	.252	.317	.374
1989	Mon-N	9	3	28	85	2.55	7	0	13	46	2.35	2	3	15	39	2.79	159	5	.239	.287	.371	143	1	.210	.258	.273	131	1	.229	.293	.305	222	4	.230	.274	.329
1990	Mon-N	3	3	20	75	2.52	2	2	8	31	2.87	1	1	12	44	2.27	144	3	.285	.331	.403	145	4	.262	.317	.379	204	5	.240	.290	.343	204	5	.240	.290	.343
1991	Mon-N	3	4	5	46	4.11	0	2	3	21	3.43	3	2	2	25	4.68	74	1	.351	.395	.514	95	2	.158	.252	.242	81	2	.272	.368	.432	123	2	.236	.309	.350
1991	NY-N	3	4	1	56	2.75	2	1	0	29	1.24	1	3	0	27	4.39	118	1	.263	.315	.356	98	4	.245	.262	.398	92	1	.217	.260	.272	85	1	.224	.253	.318
1992	NY-N	1	2	0	16	5.74	0	0	0	9	1.04	1	2	0	7	11.57	38	1	.289	.308	.368	36	0	.444	.462	.556	5	0	.000	.000	.000
1992	NY-A	2	2	0	28	3.25	1	1	0	15	4.80	1	1	0	13	1.42	40	0	.150	.244	.200	64	2	.313	.413	.547	55	0	.145	.319	.218	37	0	.270	.386	.405
TOTALS		49	33	102	699	2.72	28	12	41	342	2.55	21	21	61	357	2.87	1285	25	.268	.335	.378	1313	24	.235	.289	.312	1191	17	.238	.321	.329	1504	26	.230	.292	.325

● John Burkett BR/TR
1987	SF-N	0	0	0	6	4.50	0	0	0	4	6.75	0	0	0	2	0.00	11	0	.182	.182	.182	12	2	.417	.563	1.083	13	1	.154	.267	.385	0	0	—	—	—
1990	SF-N	14	7	1	204	3.79	6	2	0	104	3.98	8	5	1	100	3.60	454	11	.258	.312	.370	327	7	.257	.318	.370	315	8	.263	.327	.390	59	0	.305	.359	.373
1991	SF-N	12	11	0	207	4.18	6	6	0	109	3.54	6	5	0	97	4.90	467	14	.293	.347	.441	337	5	.255	.312	.323	368	6	.291	.334	.389	54	3	.222	.283	.389
1992	SF-N	13	9	0	190	3.84	10	2	0	102	3.09	3	7	0	88	4.72	466	11	.296	.334	.448	269	2	.208	.265	.268	293	5	.280	.343	.444	30	2	.300	.303	.567
1993	SF-N	22	7	0	232	3.65	9	3	0	122	2.66	13	4	0	111	4.72	464	8	.282	.321	.369	415	10	.224	.269	.345	328	12	.280	.324	.445	68	2	.250	.290	.394
1994	SF-N	6	8	0	159	3.62	2	6	0	92	4.87	4	2	0	67	1.88	321	4	.274	.325	.355	295	10	.298	.335	.485	253	4	.261	.314	.375	53	1	.208	.276	.321
TOTALS		67	42	1	997	3.83	33	19	0	533	3.59	34	23	1	464	4.09	2183	48	.281	.327	.404	1655	36	.249	.300	.363	1570	36	.275	.328	.410	262	8	.256	.303	.393

● Greg Cadaret BL/TL
1987	Oak-A	6	2	0	40	4.54	3	1	0	20	1.80	3	1	0	20	7.32	65	2	.231	.333	.323	82	4	.268	.374	.463	68	0	.265	.388	.382	30	1	.233	.333	.367
1988	Oak-A	5	2	3	72	2.89	3	1	2	39	2.52	2	1	1	32	3.34	106	0	.198	.309	.217	160	2	.244	.322	.325	138	2	.225	.313	.297	131	1	.206	.297	.267
1989	Oak-A	0	0	0	28	2.28	0	0	0	11	3.27	0	0	0	17	1.62	50	0	.200	.300	.240	48	0	.229	.373	.229	50	0	.280	.415	.300	9	0	.222	.533	.222

YEAR	TM/L	TOTAL					HOME					AWAY					LEFT					RIGHT					ON-BASE					LATE/CLOSE				
		W	L	SV	IP	ERA	W	L	SV	IP	ERA	W	L	SV	IP	ERA	AB	HR	AVG	OBP	SLG	AB	HR	AVG	OBP	SLG	AB	HR	AVG	OBP	SLG	AB	HR	AVG	OBP	SLG
1989	NY-A	5	5	0	92	4.58	4	2	0	52	4.64	1	3	0	40	4.50	73	1	.288	.333	.384	293	6	.300	.372	.427	172	3	.349	.413	.471	32	0	.406	.429	.531
1990	NY-A	5	4	0	121	4.15	3	0	0	58	2.78	2	4	3	63	5.43	119	3	.252	.333	.372	328	5	.274	.367	.418	215	2	.265	.352	.372	101	0	.277	.376	.376
1991	NY-A	8	6	3	122	3.62	4	3	0	61	4.72	4	3	3	61	2.52	118	0	.246	.311	.305	329	8	.246	.342	.386	205	5	.249	.335	.395	122	2	.230	.340	.320
1992	NY-A	4	8	1	104	4.25	4	3	0	66	3.29	0	5	1	38	5.92	88	3	.227	.340	.386	301	9	.279	.397	.422	205	2	.320	.353	.337	50	1	.320	.493	.480
1993	Cin-N	2	1	1	33	4.96	1	1	1	19	2.84	1	0	0	14	7.90	37	0	.324	.444	.324	94	3	.298	.400	.457	70	2	.329	.447	.471	42	1	.286	.434	.381
1993	KC-A	1	1	0	15	2.93	0	1	0	9	2.08	1	0	0	7	4.05	26	0	.346	.346	.423	27	0	.185	.371	.185	24	0	.292	.320	.375	15	0	.533	.563	.533
1994	Tor-A	0	1	0	20	5.85	0	0	0	12	4.50	0	1	0	8	7.87	27	0	.333	.455	.333	54	4	.268	.388	.500	43	2	.279	.415	.442	16	0	.313	.500	.313
1994	Det-A	1	0	2	20	3.60	0	0	1	10	4.66	1	0	1	10	2.61	28	0	.250	.400	.321	47	0	.213	.339	.298	42	0	.238	.385	.310	7	0	.143	.333	.143
TOTALS		37	30	13	666	3.99	22	12	4	357	3.50	15	18	9	309	4.54	737	9	.248	.339	.324	1765	41	.268	.367	.401	1232	23	.266	.367	.379	555	6	.265	.380	.353
● John Candelaria BL/TL																																				
1984	Pit-N	12	11	2	185	2.72	5	6	1	95	3.30	7	5	1	90	2.10	87	0	.195	.231	.230	613	19	.264	.297	.427	245	7	.249	.288	.404	61	2	.213	.286	.377
1985	Pit-N	2	4	9	54	3.64	2	2	6	28	2.57	0	2	3	26	4.78	49	0	.204	.200	.265	158	7	.297	.352	.525	100	4	.270	.330	.470	153	3	.242	.290	.379
1985	Cal-A	7	3	0	71	3.80	2	2	0	33	7.02	5	1	0	38	0.96	45	1	.156	.152	.244	222	6	.284	.359	.459	119	3	.269	.291	.395	7	1	.286	.250	1.000
1986	Cal-A	10	2	0	92	2.55	5	1	0	47	2.66	5	1	0	44	2.44	59	0	.186	.254	.271	271	4	.210	.271	.314	130	2	.215	.271	.338	13	0	.154	.294	.154
1987	Cal-A	8	6	0	117	4.71	6	3	0	74	4.72	2	3	0	42	4.68	71	2	.338	.377	.446	384	15	.268	.295	.440	169	10	.331	.355	.586	24	0	.167	.231	.167
1987	NY-N	2	0	0	12	5.84	1	0	0	6	4.50	1	0	0	6	7.11	3	0	.000	.000	.000	48	1	.354	.385	.604	26	0	.308	.321	.346	0	0	—	—	—
1988	NY-A	13	7	1	157	3.38	7	5	0	99	3.28	6	2	1	58	3.55	97	4	.144	.189	.268	508	14	.268	.292	.423	220	8	.259	.296	.436	45	0	.133	.133	.156
1989	NY-A	3	3	0	49	5.14	2	2	0	26	5.54	1	1	0	23	4.70	34	0	.147	.194	.147	156	8	.282	.321	.494	67	3	.343	.387	.567	17	1	.176	.222	.412
1989	Mon-N	0	2	0	16	3.31	0	1	0	7	3.86	0	1	0	9	2.89	16	0	.188	.211	.375	44	3	.318	.354	.659	21	0	.238	.296	.429	18	2	.278	.300	.778
1990	Min-A	7	3	4	58	3.39	2	2	4	33	3.86	5	1	0	26	2.81	51	0	.196	.222	.255	174	9	.259	.284	.466	88	5	.205	.247	.398	64	2	.203	.264	.313
1990	Tor-A	0	3	1	21	5.48	0	0	1	7	2.70	0	3	0	15	6.75	28	0	.357	.367	.464	62	2	.355	.447	.581	53	0	.264	.364	.321	26	0	.462	.500	.692
1991	LA-N	1	1	2	34	3.74	1	0	1	15	3.60	0	1	1	19	3.86	58	1	.138	.206	.207	65	2	.354	.392	.600	65	1	.215	.270	.323	90	1	.267	.324	.400
1992	LA-N	2	5	5	25	2.84	1	3	2	12	2.92	1	2	3	13	2.77	52	1	.269	.328	.385	39	0	.154	.292	.179	53	1	.226	.328	.321	74	0	.230	.314	.270
1993	Pit-N	0	3	1	20	8.24	0	3	1	11	8.74	0	0	0	8	7.56	31	0	.290	.333	.355	49	2	.327	.414	.592	41	1	.341	.452	.571	35	1	.343	.452	.571
TOTALS		67	53	25	912	3.66	34	30	16	494	3.95	33	23	9	418	3.32	681	9	.209	.247	.292	2793	92	.270	.313	.445	1397	45	.264	.310	.432	627	13	.239	.300	.376
● Tom Candiotti BR/TR																																				
1984	Mil-A	2	2	0	32	5.29	2	0	0	17	2.16	0	2	0	16	8.62	90	4	.344	.374	.533	47	1	.149	.231	.255	55	3	.364	.397	.618	12	1	.500	.538	.750
1986	Cle-A	16	12	0	252	3.57	10	6	0	137	3.35	6	6	0	115	3.82	497	15	.237	.311	.334	455	11	.255	.337	.382	415	4	.222	.318	.301	74	2	.257	.345	.378
1987	Cle-A	7	18	0	202	4.78	5	11	0	135	4.39	2	7	0	66	5.56	389	12	.237	.318	.365	384	16	.263	.341	.448	309	8	.239	.347	.366	90	3	.256	.356	.400
1988	Cle-A	14	8	0	217	3.28	10	2	0	123	2.63	4	6	0	93	4.15	457	7	.280	.333	.383	370	8	.262	.301	.359	346	7	.246	.302	.344	92	1	.261	.340	.370
1989	Cle-A	13	10	0	206	3.10	7	3	0	101	2.95	6	7	0	105	3.25	395	5	.246	.306	.327	383	5	.238	.280	.311	282	4	.259	.300	.351	70	0	.234	.310	.273
1990	Cle-A	15	11	0	202	3.65	7	6	0	112	4.10	8	5	0	90	3.10	403	9	.256	.311	.355	385	14	.270	.318	.423	316	10	.291	.336	.421	58	1	.310	.355	.431
1991	Cle-A	7	6	0	108	2.24	3	3	0	45	3.20	4	3	0	63	1.56	198	4	.237	.289	.354	206	2	.199	.247	.282	182	2	.216	.251	.284	40	0	.175	.267	.175
1991	Tor-A	6	7	0	130	2.98	3	3	0	65	3.05	3	4	0	65	2.92	251	2	.247	.300	.355	232	4	.224	.300	.348	186	2	.210	.291	.306	55	0	.218	.279	.327
1992	LA-N	11	15	0	204	3.00	6	6	0	89	2.33	5	9	0	115	3.53	408	4	.245	.321	.343	338	7	.228	.267	.352	289	6	.201	.284	.294	102	3	.255	.313	.382
1993	LA-N	8	10	0	214	3.12	5	3	0	116	1.95	3	7	0	98	4.50	410	5	.232	.304	.312	387	7	.251	.305	.364	319	4	.270	.333	.370	97	0	.155	.226	.196
1994	LA-N	7	7	0	153	4.12	3	4	0	64	5.46	4	3	0	89	3.15	282	4	.248	.316	.362	294	5	.269	.330	.391	252	3	.262	.322	.373	55	2	.291	.328	.491
TOTALS		106	106	0	1919	3.47	61	47	0	1004	3.28	45	59	0	915	3.68	3780	65	.249	.314	.352	3481	80	.248	.306	.370	2931	53	.246	.317	.349	752	13	.245	.316	.350
● Steve Carlton BL/TL																																				
1984	Phi-N	13	7	0	229	3.58	5	5	0	113	3.98	8	2	0	116	3.18	125	1	.224	.271	.320	745	13	.250	.313	.368	362	5	.249	.313	.356	62	1	.242	.304	.387
1985	Phi-N	1	8	0	92	3.33	1	3	0	44	1.22	0	5	0	48	5.29	43	0	.233	.298	.256	295	6	.251	.357	.373	164	3	.238	.333	.360	12	0	.167	.375	.167
1986	Phi-N	4	8	0	83	6.18	2	2	0	34	5.77	2	6	0	49	6.47	50	2	.280	.368	.460	293	13	.300	.377	.481	141	5	.291	.408	.454	15	0	.467	.500	.467
1986	SF-N	1	3	0	30	5.10	0	2	0	17	7.41	1	1	0	13	2.08	15	0	.333	.375	.467	104	4	.298	.392	.462	56	2	.339	.431	.518	0	0	—	—	—
1986	Chi-N	4	3	0	63	3.69	2	0	0	33	3.51	2	3	0	30	3.90	16	0	.188	.235	.188	214	6	.257	.337	.425	89	3	.276	.337	.425	29	0	.345	.406	.483
1987	Cle-A	5	9	1	109	5.37	2	5	0	56	5.59	3	4	1	53	5.13	82	2	.244	.315	.390	336	15	.271	.372	.461	180	8	.283	.395	.489	43	2	.349	.431	.581
1987	Min-A	1	5	0	43	6.70	1	2	0	28	3.86	0	3	0	15	12.00	31	0	.290	.389	.517	143	7	.315	.399	.517	83	3	.349	.432	.518	3	0	.000	.000	.000
1988	Min-A	0	1	0	10	16.76	0	1	0	9	18.69	0	0	0	1	0.00	12	0	.500	.500	.833	37	5	.378	.452	.919	21	1	.476	.542	1.000	0	0	—	—	—
TOTALS		29	44	1	659	4.64	13	20	0	335	4.57	16	24	1	324	4.72	374	5	.254	.317	.369	2167	69	.269	.351	.427	1094	30	.277	.374	.430	164	3	.299	.374	.439
● Don Carman BL/TL																																				
1984	Phi-N	0	1	0	13	5.40	0	0	0	9	5.00	0	1	0	4	6.23	17	0	.176	.263	.294	38	2	.289	.357	.500	23	2	.391	.481	.783	9	0	.333	.500	.444
1985	Phi-N	9	4	7	86	2.08	6	0	4	43	1.05	3	4	3	44	3.09	87	1	.218	.269	.299	205	5	.161	.275	.263	127	2	.181	.278	.283	199	3	.161	.254	.236
1986	Phi-N	10	5	1	134	3.22	6	2	1	67	3.90	4	3	0	67	2.54	90	3	.233	.289	.389	392	8	.235	.316	.352	183	6	.213	.316	.295	132	0	.288	.367	.371
1987	Phi-N	13	11	0	211	4.22	6	7	0	101	4.72	7	4	0	110	3.76	109	3	.312	.364	.468	687	31	.233	.297	.425	290	12	.279	.352	.455	43	0	.256	.333	.302
1988	Phi-N	10	14	0	201	4.29	7	6	0	111	3.58	3	8	0	91	5.16	145	5	.262	.319	.407	637	15	.272	.332	.407	318	6	.270	.350	.374	60	1	.250	.308	.333
1989	Phi-N	5	15	0	149	5.24	4	5	0	76	4.26	1	10	0	73	6.26	108	6	.222	.294	.435	476	15	.269	.369	.443	241	5	.257	.380	.382	61	1	.213	.333	.328
1990	Phi-N	6	2	1	87	4.15	5	0	0	44	3.50	1	2	1	43	4.81	103	7	.175	.250	.408	213	6	.239	.333	.390	137	8	.219	.331	.445	63	1	.175	.257	.222
1991	Cin-N	0	2	1	36	5.25	0	2	0	20	7.08	0	0	1	16	2.87	50	1	.300	.368	.420	90	7	.278	.370	.437	71	3	.296	.370	.437	12	0	.333	.467	.333
1992	Tex-A	0	0	0	2	7.71	0	0	0	2	7.71	0	0	0	0	—	3	0	.333	.333	.333	8	0	.375	.375	.375	3	0	.667	.667	.667	0	0	—	—	—
TOTALS		53	54	10	921	4.12	34	22	5	473	3.94	19	32	5	448	4.30	712	26	.243	.304	.403	2746	89	.246	.325	.404	1393	39	.253	.347	.391	579	6	.219	.311	.295
● Cris Carpenter BR/TR																																				
1988	StL-N	2	3	0	48	4.72	0	1	0	18	6.00	2	2	0	30	3.94	86	2	.360	.385	.523	82	1	.245	.279	.353	79	1	.304	.314	.456	10	0	.500	.500	.800
1989	StL-N	4	4	0	68	3.18	1	3	0	37	4.42	3	1	0	31	1.72	137	1	.277	.357	.372	130	3	.246	.297	.415	115	3	.261	.346	.443	46	0	.239	.333	.326
1990	StL-N	0	0	0	8	4.50	0	0	0	2	5.40	0	0	0	6	4.26	12	2	.250	.308	.750	18	0	.111	.158	.111	8	1	.250	.333	.625	4	1	.500	.600	1.250
1991	StL-N	10	4	0	66	4.23	5	1	0	35	3.38	5	3	0	31	5.17	123	0	.228	.304	.333	118	6	.212	.248	.398	94	3	.277	.369	.447	106	4	.217	.284	.396
1992	StL-N	5	4	1	88	2.97	1	1	1	43	3.59	4	3	0	45	2.38	162	6	.222	.287	.395	151	4	.219	.290	.344	154	3	.227	.303	.328	121	6	.256	.345	.504
1993	Fla-N	0	1	0	37	2.89	0	0	0	18	2.95	0	1	0	19	2.84	56	0	.304	.403	.446	81	1	.148	.198	.210	67	1	.209	.280	.328	41	1	.220	.298	.317
1993	Tex-A	4	1	1	32	4.22	3	1	1	20	5.31	1	0	0	12	2.31	55	3	.364	.397	.618	66	1	.227	.320	.303	62	0	.274	.368	.339	81	3	.284	.341	.469
1994	Tex-A	2	5	5	59	5.03	0	2	5	34	5.41	2	3	0	25	7.30	102	4	.363	.426	.529	135	3	.237	.276	.356	121	6	.298	.358	.512	93	2	.355	.408	.484
TOTALS		27	22	7	406	3.83	10	9	7	207	4.01	17	13	0	199	3.66	733	18	.286	.332	.441	801	19	.220	.272	.345	700	18	.263	.334	.416	502	17	.273	.343	.452
● Norm Charlton BB/TL																																				
1988	Cin-N	4	5	0	61	3.96	3	1	0	35	3.34	1	4	0	26	4.78	38	1	.184	.279	.289	196	5	.270	.326	.403	90	4	.278	.350	.433	13	1	.308	.308	.692
1989	Cin-N	8	3	0	95	2.93	2	1	0	46	2.93	6	2	0	49	2.92	81	1	.148	.258	.173	259	5	.212	.292	.324	138	3	.217	.286	.312	143	1	.182	.265	.252
1990	Cin-N	12	9	2	154	2.74	6	4	1	76	3.09	6	5	1	79	2.40	116	4	.224	.338	.379	451	6	.233	.314	.313	249	2	.245	.333	.289	123	3	.228	.307	.366
1991	Cin-N	3	5	1	108	2.91	0	4	0	42	4.01	3	1	0	66	2.19	87	0	.253	.359	.299	303	6	.231	.290	.349	153	4	.248	.329	.412	94	1	.234	.327	.309
1992	Cin-N	4	2	26	81	2.99	2	1	13	40	2.27	2	1	13	42	3.67	71	2	.296	.359	.465	231	5	.251	.313	.377	141	3	.284	.350	.426	189	4	.249	.333	.365
1993	Sea-A	1	3	18	35	2.34	1	1	10	20	0.90	0	2	8	14	4.30	21	0	.095	.269	.095	102	4	.196	.278	.343	50	3	.220	.333	.400	83	1	.181	.289	.313
TOTALS		32	27	47	535	2.96	14	12	25	259	2.95	18	15	22	276	2.96	414	7	.217	.322	.314	1542	31	.234	.304	.344	821	18	.250	.329	.362	645	13	.220	.306	.332
● Jim Clancy BR/TR																																				
1984	Tor-A	13	15	0	220	5.12	6	9	0	86	5.86	7	6	0	134	4.65	432	9	.310	.386	.433	435	16	.264	.320	.418	379	14	.301	.363	.470	97	2	.351	.422	.443
1985	Tor-A	9	6	0	129	3.78	4	1	0	46	2.53	5	5	0	82	4.48	255	5	.251	.316	.396	230	10	.230	.265	.435	187	7	.235	.264	.417	9	0	.444	.444	.556
1986	Tor-A	14	14	0	219	3.94	5	6	0	87	5.26	9	8	0	132	3.07	441	9	.229	.287	.373	391	15	.283	.321	.410	315	9	.283	.331	.410	62	2	.355	.414	.500
1987	Tor-A	15	11	0	241	3.54	7	5	0	120	3.00	8	6	0	121	4.08	508	12	.281	.335	.433	410	12	.222	.288	.361	366	7	.238	.298	.374	52	0	.327	.397	.404
1988	Tor-A	11	13	1	196	4.49	6	6	0	91	5.26	5	7	1	106	3.83	404	10	.280	.344	.415	356	16	.264	.317	.438	294	6	.286	.335	.398	34	1	.471	.486	.588
1989	Hou-N	7	14	0	147	5.08	4	5	0	62	5.66	3	9	0	85	4.66	313	10	.291	.377	.460	263	3	.243	.298	.376	255	5	.290	.375	.451	47	2	.191	.255	.319
1990	Hou-N	2	8	1	76	6.51	1	2	1	30	6.67	1	6	0	46	6.41	164	7	.366	.436	.488	147	3	.272	.331	.435	150	2	.353	.439	.513	31	1	.258	.361	.452
1991	Hou-N	0	3	5	55	2.78	0	3	3	30	3.00	0	0	2	25	4.01	95	1	.179	.269	.284	97	4	.206	.264	.351	82	3	.232	.286	.390	48	2	.208	.255	.438
1991	Atl-N	3	2	3	35	5.71	2	0	2	15	4.70	1	2	1	19	6.52	52	1	.308	.373	.519	42	1	.262	.333	.452	63	2	.333	.389	.556	51	0	.196	.283	.275
TOTALS		74	86	10	1318	4.40	35	37	4	562	4.69	39	49	6	756	4.19	2664	58	.277	.342	.413	2412	81	.248	.303	.406	2091	55	.280	.338	.429	431	10	.302	.365	.427
● Roger Clemens BR/TR																																				
1984	Bos-A	9	4	0	133	4.32	5	1	0	78	4.27	4	3	0	55	4.39	291	3	.261	.305	.372	247	10	.283	.314	.449	219	5	.301	.345	.420	39	1	.308	.308	.462
1985	Bos-A	7	5	0	98	3.29	4	2	0	51	3.73	3	3	0	48	2.83	202	1	.248	.308	.297	162	4	.204	.297	.302	142	3	.218	.296	.329	14	1	.571	.625	.786
1986	Bos-A	24	4	0	254	2.48	11	3	0	119	2.56	13	1	0	135	2.41	523	13	.210	.274	.317	393	13	.176	.221	.290	317	8	.202	.258	.312	118	0	.212	.266	.314
1987	Bos-A	20	9	0	282	2.97	11	6	0	160	2.75	9	3	0	121	3.26	603	6	.235	.299	.332	452	13	.235	.290	.369	444	9	.205	.289	.311	108	0	.241	.305	.380
1988	Bos-A	18	12	0	264	2.93	9	3	0	122	3.91	9	9	0	142	2.00	482	9	.256	.308	.361	482	8	.183	.228	.292	366	8	.238	.291	.361	140	1	.179	.243	.250
1989	Bos-A	17	11	0	253	3.13	9	3	0	106	2.90	8	8	0	148	3.29	503	7	.243	.320	.332	426	13	.218	.287	.345	339	2	.233	.331	.341	114	0	.246	.323	.360
1990	Bos-A	21	6	0	228	1.93	11	2	0	112	1.53	10	4	0	117	2.31	443	7	.242	.288	.343	404	0	.213	.267	.265	368	4	.190	.233	.272	120	1	.158	.223	.200

YEAR	TM/L	TOTAL					HOME					AWAY					LEFT					RIGHT					ON-BASE					LATE/CLOSE				
		W	L	SV	IP	ERA	W	L	SV	IP	ERA	W	L	SV	IP	ERA	AB	HR	AVG	OBP	SLG	AB	HR	AVG	OBP	SLG	AB	HR	AVG	OBP	SLG	AB	HR	AVG	OBP	SLG
1991	Bos-A	18	10	0	271	2.62	8	5	0	143	2.59	10	5	0	129	2.66	563	3	.218	.279	.302	430	12	.223	.258	.363	358	7	.243	.299	.366	125	0	.224	.312	.320
1992	Bos-A	18	11	0	247	2.41	8	6	0	128	2.88	10	5	0	118	1.90	447	6	.226	.277	.304	460	5	.222	.280	.311	354	3	.223	.295	.314	98	0	.214	.274	.245
1993	Bos-A	11	14	0	192	4.46	6	8	0	105	5.14	5	6	0	87	3.63	404	8	.260	.346	.381	314	9	.223	.273	.360	278	8	.277	.358	.428	63	1	.159	.221	.222
1994	Bos-A	9	7	0	171	2.85	5	3	0	79	2.75	4	4	0	92	2.93	319	7	.219	.315	.339	290	8	.186	.259	.310	234	5	.179	.257	.286	70	2	.157	.211	.257
TOTALS		172	93	0	2393	2.93	84	48	0	1202	3.09	88	45	0	1191	2.77	4802	64	.236	.300	.333	4060	96	.214	.267	.328	3419	63	.226	.294	.335	1009	17	.211	.275	.300
● Pat Clements BR/TL																																				
1985	Cal-A	5	0	1	62	3.34	4	0	1	39	1.37	1	0	0	23	6.75	100	3	.240	.327	.380	116	1	.198	.285	.250	95	3	.232	.318	.358	61	0	.246	.395	.279
1985	Pit-N	0	2	2	34	3.67	0	2	1	17	3.18	0	0	1	17	4.15	28	0	.321	.441	.357	107	2	.280	.333	.421	67	2	.328	.410	.478	52	0	.365	.443	.442
1986	Pit-N	0	4	2	61	2.80	0	0	1	31	2.90	0	4	1	30	2.70	67	1	.284	.412	.373	144	0	.236	.317	.271	103	0	.243	.364	.282	78	0	.359	.449	.436
1987	NY-A	3	3	7	80	4.95	1	1	5	42	3.46	2	2	2	38	6.57	84	1	.167	.255	.250	220	3	.350	.405	.455	161	1	.298	.364	.379	85	1	.306	.365	.424
1988	NY-A	0	0	0	8	6.48	0	0	0	1	13.50	0	0	0	7	5.14	10	0	.200	.217	.200	25	1	.400	.464	.600	19	1	.368	.364	.526	3	0	.667	.500	1.333
1989	SD-N	4	1	0	39	3.92	1	0	0	21	3.80	3	1	0	18	4.08	45	0	.178	.229	.222	101	4	.307	.377	.465	54	1	.278	.394	.389	35	2	.286	.306	.457
1990	SD-N	0	0	0	13	4.15	0	0	0	8	3.24	0	0	0	5	5.79	27	1	.296	.367	.556	29	0	.414	.485	.586	34	1	.265	.359	.500	0	0	—	—	—
1991	SD-N	1	0	0	14	3.77	0	0	0	7	1.23	1	0	0	7	6.43	23	0	.174	.240	.261	28	0	.321	.421	.357	29	0	.310	.410	.379	6	0	.333	.333	.333
1992	SD-N	2	1	0	24	2.66	0	0	0	18	2.00	2	1	0	6	4.76	39	0	.154	.250	.154	50	0	.380	.475	.460	49	0	.327	.459	.388	20	0	.250	.318	.250
1992	Bal-A	2	0	0	25	3.28	0	0	0	16	0.57	2	0	0	9	8.00	38	0	.316	.350	.395	51	0	.216	.349	.216	48	0	.250	.351	.271	16	0	.125	.263	.125
TOTALS		17	11	12	360	3.77	8	3	8	201	2.60	9	8	4	159	5.25	461	6	.230	.317	.321	871	11	.294	.369	.386	659	9	.281	.373	.375	356	3	.306	.390	.390
● David Cone BL/TR																																				
1986	KC-A	0	0	0	23	5.56	0	0	0	10	6.97	0	0	0	12	4.38	46	2	.413	.500	.674	48	0	.296	.296	.292	54	2	.315	.403	.500	2	0	.500	.667	1.500
1987	NY-N	5	6	1	99	3.71	3	3	0	46	3.94	2	3	1	54	3.52	192	5	.229	.333	.370	172	6	.250	.319	.407	150	5	.227	.328	.393	34	1	.294	.400	.471
1988	NY-N	20	3	0	231	2.22	10	1	0	118	1.29	10	2	0	113	3.19	436	5	.257	.335	.351	400	5	.165	.225	.230	318	4	.220	.301	.308	130	3	.200	.224	.300
1989	NY-N	14	8	0	220	3.52	8	2	0	114	2.61	6	6	0	106	4.50	449	9	.234	.309	.379	373	11	.209	.263	.335	306	8	.235	.312	.382	91	1	.286	.330	.341
1990	NY-N	14	10	0	212	3.23	7	6	0	108	3.85	7	4	0	104	2.60	467	14	.214	.274	.377	317	7	.243	.299	.344	296	8	.233	.287	.382	75	2	.200	.274	.373
1991	NY-N	14	14	0	233	3.29	6	7	0	115	3.91	8	7	0	118	2.68	545	7	.248	.311	.345	323	6	.214	.270	.303	354	9	.237	.297	.345	84	1	.226	.258	.333
1992	NY-N	13	7	0	197	2.88	6	3	0	85	3.40	7	4	0	112	2.49	410	9	.232	.328	.346	318	3	.211	.277	.296	317	6	.199	.297	.300	58	1	.224	.329	.328
1992	Tor-A	4	3	0	53	2.55	2	3	0	38	3.35	2	0	0	15	0.59	95	1	.221	.342	.305	93	2	.194	.294	.312	92	0	.174	.262	.217	25	0	.200	.355	.240
1993	KC-A	11	14	0	254	3.33	4	6	0	127	4.05	7	8	0	127	2.62	498	14	.227	.319	.355	422	6	.218	.304	.329	378	6	.220	.308	.323	140	4	.307	.386	.471
1994	KC-A	16	5	0	172	2.94	8	3	0	85	3.06	8	2	0	86	2.81	340	9	.238	.319	.376	283	6	.173	.224	.279	228	5	.189	.288	.311	50	1	.255	.333	.333
TOTALS		111	70	1	1693	3.12	54	34	0	845	3.26	57	36	1	848	2.98	3478	75	.237	.318	.364	2749	52	.207	.272	.309	2493	53	.221	.302	.339	690	13	.248	.315	.367
● Danny Cox BR/TR																																				
1984	StL-N	9	11	0	156	4.03	5	6	0	77	3.99	4	5	0	80	4.07	263	7	.312	.387	.468	329	2	.271	.324	.350	262	5	.298	.355	.420	38	1	.211	.231	.289
1985	StL-N	18	9	0	241	2.88	10	4	0	129	2.30	8	5	0	112	3.54	432	7	.264	.313	.382	469	12	.239	.288	.382	355	8	.234	.272	.363	82	1	.293	.330	.427
1986	StL-N	12	13	0	220	2.90	8	7	0	124	2.90	4	6	0	96	2.92	433	9	.233	.286	.351	375	5	.235	.290	.341	305	3	.252	.298	.351	99	0	.232	.296	.273
1987	StL-N	11	9	0	199	3.88	6	3	0	122	3.40	5	6	0	78	4.64	383	7	.313	.379	.446	389	10	.267	.321	.396	342	5	.275	.332	.365	66	2	.288	.347	.439
1988	StL-N	3	8	0	86	3.98	3	3	0	54	3.67	0	5	0	32	4.50	176	5	.341	.395	.545	151	1	.192	.236	.258	128	2	.273	.342	.422	23	2	.261	.292	.565
1991	Phi-N	4	6	0	102	4.57	2	4	0	49	4.41	2	2	0	53	4.72	189	7	.270	.346	.450	191	7	.246	.300	.403	153	5	.288	.318	.471	21	0	.238	.280	.333
1992	Phi-N	2	2	0	38	5.40	1	1	0	25	4.38	1	1	0	14	7.24	82	2	.329	.412	.488	72	1	.264	.321	.347	72	1	.333	.398	.444	0	0	—	—	—
1992	Pit-N	3	1	3	24	3.33	2	1	2	12	2.92	1	0	1	12	3.75	47	1	.213	.315	.298	42	1	.238	.250	.381	46	2	.217	.288	.435	54	0	.222	.295	.296
1993	Tor-A	7	6	2	84	3.12	3	1	0	42	3.21	4	5	2	42	3.02	137	5	.255	.344	.431	181	3	.210	.251	.276	123	4	.252	.354	.374	147	3	.231	.317	.327
1994	Tor-A	1	1	3	19	1.45	0	1	3	9	0.96	1	0	0	9	1.93	32	0	.094	.189	.125	30	0	.133	.235	.133	21	0	.095	.231	.095	38	0	.105	.190	.105
TOTALS		70	66	8	1170	3.52	38	30	5	643	3.23	32	36	3	527	3.88	2174	50	.277	.342	.418	2229	42	.242	.294	.353	1807	35	.265	.320	.386	568	9	.238	.300	.335
● Chuck Crim BR/TR																																				
1987	Mil-A	6	8	12	130	3.67	4	4	7	68	3.19	2	4	5	62	4.19	227	9	.286	.357	.436	273	6	.249	.292	.352	228	6	.259	.331	.377	147	1	.238	.291	.272
1988	Mil-A	7	6	9	105	2.91	5	4	4	53	3.38	2	2	5	52	2.44	174	5	.253	.320	.385	210	6	.243	.279	.381	169	4	.207	.271	.320	166	3	.259	.324	.373
1989	Mil-A	9	7	7	118	2.83	4	3	5	66	2.60	5	4	2	52	3.12	166	3	.271	.344	.367	274	4	.252	.295	.347	220	4	.263	.329	.353	208	4	.250	.332	.351
1990	Mil-A	3	5	11	86	3.47	0	3	6	41	3.10	3	2	5	45	3.80	131	1	.252	.288	.321	206	6	.267	.322	.403	148	3	.297	.349	.385	219	5	.251	.291	.361
1991	Mil-A	8	5	3	91	4.63	5	2	2	50	5.07	3	3	1	42	4.10	184	7	.293	.355	.389	193	2	.316	.347	.389	177	4	.339	.392	.435	164	2	.305	.361	.378
1992	Cal-A	7	6	1	87	5.17	4	1	0	41	5.31	3	5	1	46	5.05	137	2	.241	.286	.321	204	9	.328	.399	.520	155	4	.348	.426	.458	88	5	.318	.375	.523
1993	Cal-A	2	2	0	15	5.87	2	0	0	8	7.87	0	2	0	7	3.68	26	1	.308	.379	.423	31	1	.290	.361	.452	25	2	.320	.400	.640	12	1	.333	.429	.583
1994	Chi-N	5	4	2	64	4.48	3	3	1	34	4.81	2	1	1	31	4.11	101	3	.307	.364	.446	153	6	.248	.320	.405	107	3	.299	.405	.402	99	3	.283	.355	.424
TOTALS		47	43	45	696	3.83	27	20	25	359	3.86	20	23	20	337	3.79	1146	31	.273	.334	.394	1544	40	.271	.320	.396	1233	29	.285	.354	.392	1103	24	.267	.326	.373
● Ron Darling BR/TR																																				
1984	NY-N	12	9	0	206	3.81	7	2	0	102	3.01	5	7	0	104	4.59	365	4	.247	.337	.348	396	13	.225	.321	.366	319	10	.223	.326	.386	47	0	.128	.288	.149
1985	NY-N	16	6	0	248	2.90	9	5	0	148	3.09	7	1	0	100	2.62	461	8	.241	.323	.354	448	13	.230	.320	.366	384	5	.216	.302	.302	116	2	.293	.397	.414
1986	NY-N	15	6	0	237	2.81	10	2	0	118	2.36	5	4	0	119	3.25	503	12	.227	.288	.344	364	9	.245	.316	.369	329	4	.207	.280	.286	96	1	.198	.267	.281
1987	NY-N	12	8	0	208	4.29	4	4	0	89	3.86	8	4	0	119	4.61	447	10	.221	.297	.353	337	14	.249	.345	.415	329	10	.224	.324	.392	70	4	.343	.397	.557
1988	NY-N	17	9	0	241	3.25	14	1	0	149	2.29	3	8	0	91	4.83	452	12	.236	.304	.387	436	10	.236	.285	.378	326	9	.248	.305	.393	106	2	.198	.254	.274
1989	NY-N	14	14	0	217	3.52	8	6	0	121	3.04	6	8	0	96	4.13	481	9	.283	.338	.407	344	10	.224	.281	.353	322	9	.280	.341	.419	57	1	.263	.268	.386
1990	NY-N	7	9	0	126	4.50	4	2	0	54	3.52	3	7	0	72	5.23	283	10	.258	.333	.403	212	10	.292	.341	.514	196	6	.276	.364	.444	41	1	.220	.319	.390
1991	NY-N	5	6	0	102	3.87	1	4	0	40	6.30	4	2	0	62	2.31	213	1	.254	.302	.366	169	6	.249	.319	.432	157	4	.280	.324	.439	19	1	.368	.400	.632
1991	Mon-N	0	2	0	17	7.41	0	1	0	6	6.00	0	1	0	11	8.18	33	2	.273	.273	.485	42	4	.381	.458	.786	33	2	.212	.278	.394	0	0	—	—	—
1991	Oak-A	3	7	0	75	4.08	2	4	0	44	4.50	1	3	0	31	3.48	145	3	.207	.310	.317	125	4	.272	.357	.440	114	2	.263	.353	.395	26	1	.192	.344	.346
1992	Oak-A	15	10	0	206	3.66	8	6	0	106	3.57	7	4	0	100	3.77	371	6	.270	.348	.402	412	9	.238	.290	.359	314	5	.274	.342	.398	44	0	.136	.240	.136
1993	Oak-A	5	9	0	178	5.16	3	6	0	95	4.75	2	3	0	83	5.62	346	12	.275	.344	.440	359	10	.287	.348	.440	296	13	.267	.357	.446	27	0	.259	.310	.333
1994	Oak-A	10	11	0	160	4.50	4	7	0	83	4.25	6	4	0	77	4.77	298	12	.255	.330	.400	308	6	.279	.343	.416	237	12	.304	.377	.506	62	3	.306	.377	.532
TOTALS		131	106	0	2221	3.78	74	52	0	1155	3.42	57	54	0	1066	4.17	4398	103	.251	.321	.380	3956	120	.249	.320	.398	3356	91	.251	.328	.392	711	16	.242	.322	.361
● Danny Darwin BR/TR																																				
1984	Tex-A	8	12	0	224	3.94	4	6	0	104	3.89	4	6	0	120	3.99	470	14	.317	.367	.481	421	5	.238	.270	.314	374	6	.305	.354	.414	110	4	.264	.289	.400
1985	Mil-A	8	18	2	218	3.80	2	10	1	95	2.85	6	8	1	123	4.54	418	17	.270	.343	.459	416	17	.238	.270	.404	319	15	.285	.338	.480	111	3	.279	.344	.441
1986	Mil-A	6	8	0	130	3.52	2	6	0	74	3.75	4	2	0	56	3.21	243	8	.259	.332	.412	245	5	.233	.260	.339	196	6	.291	.348	.439	93	5	.269	.320	.484
1986	Hou-N	5	2	0	54	2.32	0	2	0	17	4.86	5	0	0	38	1.19	102	3	.304	.343	.471	107	0	.178	.195	.206	82	0	.195	.233	.220	18	0	.333	.333	.389
1987	Hou-N	9	10	0	196	3.59	4	6	0	99	3.09	5	4	0	97	4.10	372	11	.266	.342	.433	376	6	.226	.283	.316	304	4	.266	.331	.355	63	1	.317	.377	.492
1988	Hou-N	8	13	3	192	3.84	2	5	1	92	3.33	6	8	2	100	4.32	387	10	.264	.313	.401	343	10	.254	.301	.382	296	8	.270	.322	.402	108	2	.167	.262	.222
1989	Hou-N	11	4	7	122	2.36	7	0	4	73	1.98	4	4	3	49	2.92	240	3	.246	.295	.329	194	5	.170	.236	.260	193	3	.212	.270	.290	242	5	.198	.259	.289
1990	Hou-N	11	4	2	163	2.21	7	3	1	85	2.01	4	1	1	78	2.42	364	7	.264	.311	.382	241	4	.166	.198	.253	230	3	.213	.271	.304	111	2	.234	.267	.333
1991	Bos-A	3	6	0	68	5.16	2	4	0	45	4.84	1	2	0	23	5.79	139	3	.245	.301	.396	131	12	.282	.319	.611	94	5	.245	.305	.468	11	1	.364	.417	.909
1992	Bos-A	9	9	3	161	3.96	6	4	1	76	4.26	3	5	2	85	3.69	274	1	.281	.345	.387	344	10	.258	.297	.375	289	10	.225	.279	.377	144	3	.250	.327	.361
1993	Bos-A	15	11	0	229	3.26	8	3	0	101	3.38	7	8	0	128	3.16	469	19	.254	.298	.448	383	12	.201	.238	.339	289	10	.225	.279	.377	78	3	.256	.294	.449
1994	Bos-A	7	5	0	76	6.30	4	4	0	51	6.66	3	1	0	24	5.55	157	7	.369	.414	.592	162	6	.265	.309	.451	137	6	.314	.389	.518	12	0	.083	.083	.083
TOTALS		100	102	17	1833	3.60	48	50	8	905	3.54	52	52	9	928	3.66	3635	103	.275	.332	.430	3363	92	.226	.268	.351	2794	71	.263	.319	.395	1101	29	.240	.297	.368
● Storm Davis BR/TR																																				
1984	Bal-A	14	9	1	225	3.12	8	6	1	119	3.17	6	3	0	106	3.07	409	3	.254	.330	.330	422	4	.239	.282	.310	346	3	.275	.325	.367	98	2	.286	.360	.429
1985	Bal-A	10	8	0	175	4.53	5	5	0	89	4.53	5	3	0	86	4.52	360	6	.258	.346	.394	313	5	.252	.300	.355	284	6	.303	.378	.437	35	1	.229	.263	.343
1986	Bal-A	9	12	0	154	3.62	5	7	0	83	3.35	4	5	0	71	3.95	300	11	.293	.358	.453	303	5	.257	.298	.347	248	4	.302	.342	.399	55	3	.255	.305	.436
1987	SD-N	2	7	0	63	6.18	2	3	0	31	4.06	0	4	0	32	8.24	128	2	.313	.417	.461	122	3	.246	.324	.402	113	3	.292	.406	.478	10	2	.300	.417	1.000
1987	Oak-A	1	1	0	30	3.26	1	0	0	17	4.67	0	1	0	13	1.38	73	1	.274	.316	.342	43	2	.186	.286	.395	52	0	.212	.250	.269	5	0	.400	.400	.400
1988	Oak-A	16	7	0	202	3.70	7	3	0	97	3.71	9	4	0	105	3.70	396	4	.263	.320	.348	370	12	.287	.362	.442	325	8	.249	.340	.372	39	3	.385	.432	.641
1989	Oak-A	19	7	0	169	4.36	9	4	0	82	4.70	10	4	0	87	4.01	314	10	.264	.353	.414	335	9	.310	.356	.454	297	6	.269	.327	.364	33	2	.273	.306	.485
1990	KC-A	7	10	0	112	4.74	5	7	0	80	4.50	2	3	0	32	5.34	235	4	.294	.353	.421	224	5	.268	.305	.393	213	4	.272	.322	.376	12	0	.333	.467	.333
1991	KC-A	3	9	2	114	4.96	2	3	0	55	4.12	1	6	2	60	5.73	227	5	.277	.333	.377	210	3	.281	.340	.386	212	1	.296	.350	.403	81	3	.296	.370	.432
1992	Bal-A	7	3	4	89	3.43	5	1	1	47	2.85	2	3	3	42	4.07	137	2	.241	.338	.299	187	3	.246	.306	.337	154	2	.247	.330	.325	113	2	.221	.305	.283
1993	Oak-A	2	6	0	63	6.18	2	0	0	43	4.98	0	6	0	19	8.84	111	2	.267	.373	.402	98	4	.286	.355	.444	112	2	.321	.422	.402	19	1	.421	.560	.632
1993	Det-A	2	4	0	35	3.06	2	1	0	21	2.40	0	3	0	15	2.40	56	2	.250	.329	.304	70	2	.229	.280	.429	52	1	.091	.239	.182	38	1	.263	.317	.395
1994	Det-A	2	4	0	48	3.56	1	1	0	25	4.01	1	3	0	23	3.09	69	1	.116	.291	.217	105	4	.267	.366	.390	69	0	.159	.372	.203	62	1	.258	.370	.371
TOTALS		92	85	11	1480	4.12	50	44	5	790	3.95	42	41	6	690	4.31	2824	53	.269	.350	.386	2854	61	.265	.321	.384	2492	45	.272	.347	.379	600	21	.277	.353	.420

YEAR	TM/L	TOTAL W	L	SV	IP	ERA	HOME W	L	SV	IP	ERA	AWAY W	L	SV	IP	ERA	LEFT AB	HR	AVG	OBP	SLG	RIGHT AB	HR	AVG	OBP	SLG	ON-BASE AB	HR	AVG	OBP	SLG	LATE/CLOSE AB	HR	AVG	OBP	SLG
● Mark Davis BL/TL																																				
1984	SF-N	5	17	0	175	5.36	3	12	0	92	4.97	2	5	0	82	5.79	142	3	.211	.253	.310	544	22	.314	.368	.515	282	12	.298	.356	.489	66	3	.242	.311	.424
1985	SF-N	5	12	7	114	3.54	4	5	5	53	3.71	1	7	2	61	3.39	114	3	.184	.231	.316	293	10	.232	.317	.358	179	7	.279	.333	.441	214	9	.210	.302	.369
1986	SF-N	5	7	4	84	2.99	3	2	0	40	2.50	2	5	4	45	3.43	84	1	.131	.213	.190	213	5	.244	.321	.357	124	2	.250	.355	.347	95	1	.189	.266	.253
1987	SF-N	4	5	0	71	4.71	1	4	0	31	5.17	3	1	0	39	4.35	52	3	.308	.368	.500	212	6	.264	.344	.415	123	5	.252	.299	.431	11	2	.273	.385	.818
1987	SD-N	5	3	2	62	3.18	3	0	1	32	0.85	2	3	1	31	5.58	61	0	.148	.246	.213	167	5	.251	.349	.389	104	5	.240	.375	.394	103	2	.243	.371	.398
1988	SD-N	5	10	28	98	2.01	4	2	14	48	0.94	1	8	14	50	3.04	86	1	.209	.277	.302	266	1	.195	.286	.226	164	1	.207	.318	.262	283	1	.208	.300	.240
1989	SD-N	4	3	44	93	1.85	2	0	21	46	1.17	2	3	23	47	2.51	46	2	.239	.321	.457	284	4	.194	.261	.268	190	3	.174	.248	.263	258	5	.194	.260	.291
1990	KC-A	2	7	6	69	5.11	2	1	5	38	4.46	0	6	1	30	5.93	55	0	.182	.348	.236	219	9	.279	.392	.470	145	5	.283	.411	.448	106	4	.311	.407	.481
1991	KC-A	6	3	1	63	4.45	4	1	0	29	4.66	2	2	1	34	4.28	56	0	.304	.394	.393	173	6	.220	.332	.387	104	4	.240	.368	.404	22	1	.409	.567	.682
1992	KC-A	1	3	0	36	7.18	0	2	0	15	9.82	1	1	0	22	5.40	37	1	.243	.310	.378	106	5	.311	.429	.547	72	4	.319	.398	.542	0	0	—	—	—
1992	Atl-N	1	0	0	17	7.02	1	0	0	11	7.36	0	0	0	6	6.35	22	0	.409	.462	.455	48	3	.271	.407	.542	41	0	.317	.442	.439	2	0	.500	.500	.500
1993	Phi-N	1	2	0	31	5.17	1	1	0	14	3.29	0	1	0	18	6.62	31	0	.258	.410	.355	97	4	.278	.386	.464	76	2	.250	.367	.368	20	0	.350	.519	.400
1993	SD-N	0	3	4	38	3.52	0	2	2	23	4.63	0	1	2	15	1.80	64	5	.250	.304	.516	85	1	.329	.426	.447	82	1	.268	.344	.378	75	2	.267	.364	.400
1994	SD-N	0	1	0	16	8.82	0	0	0	8	10.80	0	1	0	8	6.75	23	0	.217	.379	.261	44	4	.341	.431	.636	36	1	.250	.357	.361	28	1	.286	.444	.393
TOTALS		44	76	96	968	4.07	28	32	48	481	3.78	16	44	48	487	4.36	873	19	.218	.296	.330	2751	85	.258	.344	.405	1722	50	.256	.346	.397	1283	31	.229	.323	.343
● Ron Davis BR/TR																																				
1984	Min-A	7	11	29	83	4.55	6	2	13	43	3.98	1	9	16	40	5.17	160	7	.262	.366	.438	152	4	.243	.306	.388	186	4	.274	.359	.419	236	10	.267	.351	.453
1985	Min-A	2	6	25	65	3.48	1	0	14	32	1.97	1	6	11	33	4.96	116	3	.233	.343	.379	123	4	.228	.324	.374	152	5	.217	.335	.349	158	6	.228	.326	.373
1986	Min-A	2	6	2	39	9.08	2	2	1	21	6.33	0	4	1	17	12.46	82	5	.390	.510	.707	84	3	.287	.383	.450	104	5	.317	.446	.548	50	4	.380	.537	.740
1986	Chi-N	0	2	0	20	7.65	0	1	0	8	10.80	0	1	0	12	5.40	33	1	.242	.257	.333	54	2	.426	.446	.593	39	1	.462	.476	.590	24	1	.375	.375	.542
1987	Chi-N	0	0	0	32	5.85	0	0	0	16	8.62	0	0	0	17	3.24	66	5	.348	.380	.652	65	3	.308	.384	.492	57	4	.368	.403	.632	7	0	.286	.375	.286
1987	LA-N	0	0	0	4	6.75	0	0	0	1	27.00	0	0	0	3	3.00	6	0	.500	.700	.500	10	1	.364	.467	.455	10	0	.400	.588	.500	0	0	—	—	—
1988	SF-N	1	1	0	17	4.67	0	1	0	8	6.48	1	0	0	9	3.00	27	0	.259	.310	.259	37	4	.216	.310	.541	23	3	.261	.346	.652	10	1	.500	.500	.800
TOTALS		12	26	56	260	5.40	9	6	28	130	5.21	3	20	28	130	5.59	490	21	.290	.384	.482	522	19	.274	.350	.441	571	22	.291	.386	.468	485	22	.276	.369	.466
● Ken Dayley BL/TL																																				
1984	Atl-N	0	3	0	19	5.30	0	3	0	19	5.30	0	0	0	0	—	17	0	.235	.350	.235	65	5	.369	.406	.662	38	2	.421	.463	.632	1	0	1.000	1.000	1.000
1984	StL-N	0	2	0	6	19.50	0	1	0	1	27.00	0	2	0	5	18.00	3	0	.667	.667	1.000	23	1	.609	.679	.826	21	1	.571	.609	.810	0	0	—	—	—
1985	StL-N	4	4	11	65	2.76	3	1	6	34	2.38	1	3	5	31	3.16	80	1	.313	.341	.400	167	1	.240	.297	.341	125	0	.280	.333	.368	146	1	.281	.327	.356
1986	StL-N	0	3	5	39	3.26	0	3	3	20	2.70	0	0	2	19	3.86	41	0	.341	.386	.439	112	1	.250	.303	.339	73	1	.301	.358	.438	117	1	.291	.346	.393
1987	StL-N	9	5	4	61	2.66	3	1	1	26	4.56	6	4	3	35	1.27	73	0	.247	.337	.301	149	2	.228	.337	.356	117	1	.222	.343	.316	170	1	.235	.338	.322
1988	StL-N	2	7	5	55	2.77	2	3	4	32	1.71	0	4	1	24	4.18	54	0	.278	.371	.333	147	2	.224	.281	.313	99	1	.283	.363	.354	141	0	.262	.335	.319
1989	StL-N	4	3	12	75	2.87	2	1	8	37	3.65	2	2	4	38	2.11	101	1	.188	.248	.287	175	2	.251	.333	.360	138	1	.217	.301	.304	187	3	.241	.324	.374
1990	StL-N	4	4	2	73	3.56	1	0	0	39	3.23	1	3	2	34	3.93	106	3	.283	.330	.396	164	2	.201	.289	.299	117	2	.316	.388	.444	124	4	.274	.308	.403
1991	Tor-A	0	0	0	4	6.23	0	0	0	2	0.00	0	0	0	2	13.50	10	0	.300	.467	.300	9	0	.444	.545	.444	14	0	.214	.333	.214	2	0	1.000	.833	1.000
1993	Tor-A	0	0	0	1	0.00	0	0	0	1	0.00	0	0	0	0	—	2	0	.000	.333	.000	1	0	1.000	1.000	2.000	2	0	.000	.600	.000	0	0	—	—	—
TOTALS		23	31	39	398	3.30	13	13	22	208	3.02	10	18	17	189	3.42	487	2	.267	.332	.351	1012	16	.252	.327	.370	744	9	.281	.359	.387	888	10	.264	.334	.363
● Jeff Dedmon BL/TR																																				
1984	Atl-N	4	3	4	81	3.78	1	0	2	45	2.58	3	3	2	36	5.30	160	4	.287	.378	.406	150	1	.267	.323	.313	149	3	.248	.349	.336	67	0	.328	.430	.373
1985	Atl-N	6	3	0	86	4.08	2	0	0	43	3.53	4	1	0	43	4.64	143	1	.231	.382	.322	174	4	.293	.347	.408	168	3	.262	.381	.369	96	0	.219	.359	.281
1986	Atl-N	6	6	3	100	2.98	4	3	1	56	3.67	2	3	2	43	2.08	165	5	.248	.321	.370	207	3	.237	.318	.324	181	2	.227	.324	.298	166	5	.259	.320	.373
1987	Atl-N	3	4	4	90	3.91	1	3	0	45	3.83	2	1	4	45	4.00	158	4	.222	.311	.323	176	4	.267	.342	.409	164	5	.268	.349	.439	89	1	.281	.377	.371
1988	Cle-A	1	0	1	34	4.54	1	0	0	17	3.71	0	0	1	17	5.40	42	2	.310	.392	.524	85	1	.259	.379	.376	80	3	.300	.404	.500	20	0	.300	.348	.300
TOTALS		20	16	12	390	3.74	10	6	3	207	3.44	10	10	6	183	4.07	668	16	.251	.351	.367	792	13	.264	.337	.365	742	16	.256	.356	.375	438	6	.267	.360	.349
● Jose DeLeon BR/TR																																				
1984	Pit-N	7	13	0	192	3.74	5	8	0	113	3.12	2	5	0	80	4.63	355	6	.256	.361	.377	331	4	.169	.245	.242	269	4	.234	.322	.349	59	2	.203	.254	.322
1985	Pit-N	2	19	3	163	4.70	2	9	1	93	3.97	0	10	2	70	5.68	285	7	.277	.389	.414	312	8	.189	.278	.304	267	9	.251	.322	.401	59	3	.339	.403	.593
1986	Pit-N	1	3	1	16	8.27	1	3	1	15	7.80	0	0	0	1	13.50	32	1	.375	.545	.625	32	1	.156	.289	.313	30	1	.233	.465	.500	26	0	.115	.343	.192
1986	Chi-A	4	5	0	79	2.96	2	3	0	32	3.94	2	2	0	47	2.30	136	4	.184	.306	.309	138	3	.174	.286	.261	124	5	.161	.250	.298	15	1	.267	.421	.600
1987	Chi-A	11	12	0	206	4.02	3	7	0	95	5.12	8	5	0	111	3.08	397	13	.254	.351	.393	373	11	.204	.290	.346	312	4	.234	.336	.321	70	2	.271	.381	.429
1988	StL-N	13	10	0	225	3.67	7	6	0	112	3.79	6	4	0	114	3.56	431	5	.260	.349	.355	404	8	.213	.259	.334	340	5	.244	.316	.341	61	0	.262	.333	.328
1989	StL-N	16	12	0	245	3.05	8	6	0	134	2.55	8	6	0	110	3.67	509	10	.234	.312	.360	369	6	.146	.204	.238	311	6	.248	.307	.386	99	1	.131	.225	.202
1990	StL-N	7	19	0	183	4.43	3	9	0	84	5.55	4	10	0	98	3.48	404	8	.285	.373	.423	279	7	.190	.268	.294	279	7	.272	.351	.395	45	1	.267	.358	.467
1991	StL-N	5	9	0	163	2.71	3	4	0	89	2.42	2	5	0	73	3.07	326	9	.252	.339	.408	277	6	.224	.281	.343	226	3	.230	.296	.323	37	1	.324	.375	.541
1992	StL-N	2	7	0	102	4.57	2	3	0	62	3.50	0	4	0	41	6.20	216	5	.278	.348	.435	171	2	.205	.284	.322	185	4	.243	.298	.378	7	0	.143	.364	.429
1992	Phi-N	1	0	0	15	3.00	0	0	0	6	1.50	1	0	0	9	4.15	29	0	.310	.375	.345	28	0	.250	.300	.250	27	0	.259	.310	.259	1	0	1.000	1.000	1.000
1993	Phi-N	3	0	0	47	3.26	1	0	0	28	3.18	2	0	0	19	3.38	85	3	.271	.382	.471	84	2	.190	.317	.274	72	3	.250	.378	.403	27	1	.222	.344	.407
1993	Chi-A	0	0	0	10	1.74	0	0	0	6	0.00	0	0	0	4	4.15	7	0	.143	.333	.143	26	2	.154	.214	.385	11	1	.091	.231	.364	12	1	.083	.154	.333
1994	Chi-A	3	2	2	67	3.36	0	2	0	29	4.40	3	0	2	38	2.58	92	2	.228	.339	.370	148	3	.182	.277	.277	120	1	.200	.294	.275	55	1	.218	.333	.327
TOTALS		74	112	6	1713	3.75	37	60	2	898	3.72	37	52	4	815	3.78	3304	73	.257	.352	.390	2972	63	.190	.266	.298	2588	53	.238	.319	.356	573	14	.230	.327	.377
● John Denny BR/TR																																				
1984	Phi-N	7	7	0	154	2.45	3	5	0	88	2.45	4	2	0	66	2.44	323	6	.223	.265	.331	247	5	.202	.244	.320	198	2	.217	.272	.293	57	2	.333	.381	.526
1985	Phi-N	11	14	0	231	3.82	4	10	0	123	4.02	7	4	0	108	3.59	456	6	.285	.356	.388	437	9	.279	.328	.396	401	7	.284	.343	.392	68	2	.235	.299	.382
1986	Cin-N	11	10	0	171	4.20	6	5	0	89	4.43	5	5	0	82	3.95	327	8	.318	.381	.486	331	7	.227	.281	.335	272	8	.265	.331	.430	59	1	.237	.318	.373
TOTALS		29	31	0	556	3.56	13	20	0	300	3.69	16	11	0	256	3.41	1106	20	.277	.338	.401	1015	21	.243	.292	.358	871	17	.263	.323	.381	184	5	.266	.330	.424
● Jim Deshaies BL/TL																																				
1984	NY-A	0	1	0	7	11.57	0	1	0	4	9.00	0	0	0	3	15.00	8	1	.500	.500	1.375	24	1	.417	.531	.417	15	1	.467	.550	.667	0	0	—	—	—
1985	Hou-N	0	0	0	3	0.00	0	0	0	0	0.00	0	0	0	3	0.00	4	0	.250	.250	.250	6	0	.000	.000	.000	4	0	.250	.250	.250	0	0	—	—	—
1986	Hou-N	12	5	0	144	3.25	6	0	0	85	3.39	6	2	0	59	3.05	87	3	.241	.333	.402	444	13	.232	.306	.374	205	6	.180	.266	.312	27	0	.222	.222	.222
1987	Hou-N	11	6	0	152	4.62	6	0	0	75	2.75	5	6	0	77	6.46	99	2	.263	.345	.404	480	20	.256	.314	.431	221	10	.262	.328	.457	13	0	.308	.308	.308
1988	Hou-N	11	14	0	207	3.00	7	8	0	111	2.91	4	6	0	96	3.10	129	6	.248	.310	.465	623	14	.212	.278	.345	294	8	.201	.255	.354	78	1	.192	.241	.295
1989	Hou-N	15	10	0	226	2.91	8	4	0	118	3.13	7	6	0	108	2.67	120	0	.258	.361	.317	709	15	.210	.273	.333	321	4	.227	.299	.336	75	2	.200	.247	.307
1990	Hou-N	7	12	0	209	3.78	4	3	0	98	2.75	3	9	0	111	4.70	115	1	.304	.429	.426	645	20	.234	.303	.378	292	4	.243	.338	.336	51	1	.157	.246	.216
1991	Hou-N	5	12	0	161	4.98	2	3	0	65	3.72	3	9	0	96	5.83	104	4	.279	.386	.471	498	15	.255	.324	.422	225	10	.316	.388	.569	52	0	.250	.333	.308
1992	SD-N	4	7	0	96	3.28	2	4	0	50	4.11	2	3	0	46	2.36	59	1	.356	.451	.458	297	5	.239	.293	.340	148	3	.270	.321	.372	20	0	.400	.478	.450
1993	Min-A	11	13	0	167	4.41	8	4	0	84	3.42	3	9	0	83	5.42	109	3	.229	.317	.349	516	21	.260	.313	.452	219	7	.274	.333	.447	35	1	.200	.293	.314
1993	SF-N	2	2	0	17	4.24	2	0	0	7	3.86	0	2	0	10	5.13	13	0	.231	.231	.385	56	2	.375	.444	.571	34	1	.324	.378	.559	0	0	—	—	—
1994	Min-A	6	12	0	130	7.39	4	5	0	71	6.85	2	7	0	59	8.04	68	4	.338	.422	.574	462	26	.318	.376	.584	225	9	.338	.396	.560	14	1	.286	.286	.571
TOTALS		84	94	0	1520	4.09	47	37	0	770	3.60	37	57	0	750	4.58	915	25	.274	.366	.428	4760	151	.245	.309	.404	2203	63	.256	.326	.414	365	6	.219	.278	.304
● Rob Dibble BL/TR																																				
1988	Cin-N	1	1	0	59	1.82	1	1	0	35	1.82	0	0	0	25	1.82	93	1	.215	.321	.323	115	2	.200	.242	.270	85	2	.188	.280	.341	68	1	.191	.243	.265
1989	Cin-N	10	5	2	99	2.09	4	2	0	45	1.00	6	3	2	54	3.00	172	1	.186	.286	.256	180	3	.167	.236	.244	174	2	.167	.262	.230	220	4	.200	.286	.295
1990	Cin-N	8	3	11	98	1.74	4	1	6	46	2.15	4	2	5	52	1.38	173	1	.185	.282	.254	166	2	.181	.225	.253	152	0	.197	.264	.257	224	1	.223	.286	.290
1991	Cin-N	3	5	31	82	3.17	1	4	18	39	5.26	2	1	13	43	1.26	173	2	.197	.255	.272	148	3	.258	.312	.391	146	3	.233	.286	.329	215	4	.247	.298	.349
1992	Cin-N	3	5	25	70	3.07	2	1	16	37	1.47	1	4	9	34	4.81	128	2	.180	.298	.258	121	1	.207	.271	.273	123	2	.236	.319	.325	163	3	.178	.261	.258
1993	Cin-N	1	4	19	42	6.48	0	0	9	21	8.71	1	4	10	21	4.29	72	5	.250	.481	.486	79	3	.203	.308	.367	83	4	.205	.389	.410	89	5	.225	.425	.438
TOTALS		26	23	88	451	2.74	12	9	49	222	2.91	14	14	39	228	2.56	811	12	.196	.306	.287	789	13	.199	.260	.290	763	13	.203	.293	.301	979	18	.213	.297	.311
● Frank Di Pino BL/TL																																				
1984	Hou-N	4	9	14	75	3.35	3	7	7	40	4.54	1	2	7	36	2.02	71	0	.211	.253	.225	214	3	.276	.369	.355	155	1	.226	.326	.277	208	2	.240	.322	.298
1985	Hou-N	3	7	6	76	4.03	2	3	2	32	4.26	1	4	4	44	3.83	64	2	.344	.442	.500	214	5	.220	.321	.346	126	5	.294	.406	.476	116	5	.310	.401	.491
1986	Hou-N	1	3	3	40	3.57	1	0	1	23	1.96	0	3	2	17	5.71	42	1	.167	.239	.262	94	0	.198	.293	.256	73	2	.219	.256	.370	69	2	.217	.316	.362
1986	Chi-N	2	4	0	40	5.17	1	2	0	18	5.50	1	2	0	22	4.91	51	2	.176	.241	.314	107	4	.355	.407	.561	69	1	.333	.392	.449	66	2	.318	.387	.470
1987	Chi-N	3	3	4	80	3.15	3	2	3	44	2.68	0	1	1	36	3.72	94	2	.245	.284	.340	203	5	.256	.346	.391	144	2	.264	.341	.361	131	2	.237	.306	.305
1988	Chi-N	2	3	6	90	4.98	2	1	2	48	3.72	0	2	4	42	6.43	125	0	.192	.228	.248	233	6	.335	.396	.472	185	4	.308	.356	.438	99	2	.232	.300	.293
1989	StL-N	9	0	0	88	2.45	4	0	0	46	1.58	5	0	0	43	3.38	129	0	.209	.241	.248	192	6	.240	.287	.417	139	3	.223	.276	.367	57	2	.228	.262	.333
1990	StL-N	5	2	3	81	4.56	3	2	3	41	3.92	2	0	0	40	5.22	133	2	.293	.349	.391	180	6	.294	.354	.489	155	6	.310	.367	.529	65	2	.338	.403	.538

YEAR	TM/L	TOTAL					HOME					AWAY					LEFT					RIGHT					ON-BASE					LATE/CLOSE				
		W	L	SV	IP	ERA	W	L	SV	IP	ERA	W	L	SV	IP	ERA	AB	HR	AVG	OBP	SLG	AB	HR	AVG	OBP	SLG	AB	HR	AVG	OBP	SLG	AB	HR	AVG	OBP	SLG
1992	StL-N	0	0	0	11	1.64	0	0	0	5	3.60	0	0	0	6	0.00	16	0	.188	.235	.250	25	4	.240	.296	.280	15	0	.267	.313	.400	6	0	.333	.500	.333
1993	KC-A	1	1	0	16	6.89	1	1	0	11	4.35	0	0	0	5	11.81	12	0	.333	.467	.583	52	2	.327	.373	.577	32	1	.344	.361	.594	1	0	1.000	1.000	1.000
	TOTALS	30	32	36	598	3.88	19	17	17	307	3.43	11	15	19	291	4.36	737	9	.235	.287	.316	1521	41	.274	.348	.419	1093	25	.274	.343	.414	818	19	.262	.339	.368

● John Dopson BL/TR

YEAR	TM/L	W	L	SV	IP	ERA	W	L	SV	IP	ERA	W	L	SV	IP	ERA	AB	HR	AVG	OBP	SLG	AB	HR	AVG	OBP	SLG	AB	HR	AVG	OBP	SLG	AB	HR	AVG	OBP	SLG
1985	Mon-N	0	2	0	13	11.08	0	1	0	1	54.00	0	1	0	12	8.76	31	2	.387	.406	.677	35	2	.371	.421	.600	29	2	.414	.469	.690	5	0	.400	.400	.600
1988	Mon-N	3	11	0	169	3.04	1	6	0	89	2.74	2	5	0	80	3.38	333	7	.258	.334	.363	305	8	.210	.258	.338	248	4	.222	.296	.319	40	1	.325	.341	.500
1989	Bos-A	12	8	0	169	3.99	6	5	0	104	4.07	6	3	0	65	3.86	316	5	.247	.315	.323	331	9	.266	.341	.405	285	6	.253	.309	.368	45	0	.244	.255	.267
1990	Bos-A	0	0	0	18	2.04	0	0	0	11	3.27	0	0	0	7	0.00	27	1	.148	.250	.259	38	1	.237	.326	.342	22	1	.182	.269	.318	0	0	—	—	—
1991	Bos-A	0	0	0	1	18.00	0	0	0	1	18.00	0	0	0	0	—	2	0	.500	.500	.500	2	0	.500	.500	1.000	4	0	.500	.400	.750	0	0	—	—	—
1992	Bos-A	7	11	0	141	4.08	5	5	0	84	2.69	2	6	0	58	6.09	257	5	.276	.324	.389	297	12	.296	.343	.478	228	7	.281	.317	.425	36	2	.444	.500	.722
1993	Bos-A	7	11	0	156	4.97	5	3	0	85	4.64	2	8	0	70	5.37	308	9	.302	.365	.474	296	7	.260	.320	.399	241	4	.282	.363	.415	20	1	.400	.455	.750
1994	Cal-A	1	4	1	59	6.14	0	2	0	36	5.94	1	2	1	22	6.45	105	1	.248	.310	.314	128	5	.320	.408	.516	104	4	.317	.400	.500	18	0	.333	.500	.500
	TOTALS	30	47	1	725	4.27	17	22	0	411	3.88	13	25	1	315	4.78	1379	30	.269	.333	.385	1432	44	.266	.328	.418	1161	28	.267	.331	.399	164	4	.341	.391	.518

● Richard Dotson BR/TR

YEAR	TM/L	W	L	SV	IP	ERA	W	L	SV	IP	ERA	W	L	SV	IP	ERA	AB	HR	AVG	OBP	SLG	AB	HR	AVG	OBP	SLG	AB	HR	AVG	OBP	SLG	AB	HR	AVG	OBP	SLG
1984	Chi-A	14	15	0	246	3.59	6	9	0	133	3.92	8	6	0	112	3.20	477	17	.237	.327	.394	430	7	.240	.306	.365	363	7	.220	.307	.325	146	6	.260	.317	.459
1985	Chi-A	3	4	0	52	4.47	3	1	0	39	2.75	0	3	0	13	9.69	107	4	.290	.372	.477	96	1	.229	.269	.281	78	1	.385	.425	.500	15	1	.533	.579	.733
1986	Chi-A	10	17	0	197	5.48	7	9	0	106	4.84	3	8	0	91	6.23	408	14	.265	.324	.407	374	10	.316	.371	.465	319	11	.298	.363	.464	53	1	.264	.291	.358
1987	Chi-A	11	12	0	211	4.17	6	8	0	108	4.35	5	4	0	104	3.99	430	15	.251	.326	.419	377	9	.247	.314	.377	333	9	.276	.339	.429	109	5	.312	.348	.523
1988	NY-A	12	9	0	171	5.00	6	3	0	79	3.99	6	6	0	92	5.87	347	11	.239	.306	.392	322	16	.295	.372	.522	274	10	.310	.370	.504	23	0	.304	.448	.304
1989	NY-A	2	5	0	52	5.57	1	3	0	16	10.91	1	2	0	36	3.25	105	4	.314	.357	.571	113	4	.319	.374	.478	95	5	.274	.355	.484	5	0	.200	.429	.200
1989	Chi-A	3	7	0	100	3.88	2	4	0	58	2.81	1	3	0	42	5.36	208	5	.279	.335	.433	189	3	.286	.362	.407	186	1	.274	.328	.376	29	0	.172	.250	.172
1990	KC-A	0	4	0	29	8.48	0	2	0	18	7.00	0	2	0	11	10.97	56	3	.357	.393	.643	65	0	.354	.423	.523	55	3	.418	.455	.709	1	0	1.000	1.000	2.000
	TOTALS	55	73	0	1057	4.59	31	39	0	557	4.28	24	34	0	501	4.93	2138	73	.259	.329	.424	1966	50	.277	.342	.424	1703	47	.283	.349	.435	381	13	.283	.341	.444

● Doug Drabek BR/TR

YEAR	TM/L	W	L	SV	IP	ERA	W	L	SV	IP	ERA	W	L	SV	IP	ERA	AB	HR	AVG	OBP	SLG	AB	HR	AVG	OBP	SLG	AB	HR	AVG	OBP	SLG	AB	HR	AVG	OBP	SLG
1986	NY-A	7	8	0	132	4.10	2	3	0	62	3.75	5	5	0	69	4.41	259	9	.278	.356	.456	242	4	.223	.284	.335	198	2	.253	.324	.364	25	2	.200	.375	.440
1987	Pit-N	11	12	0	176	3.88	6	5	0	79	3.66	5	7	0	98	4.05	345	15	.275	.332	.481	323	7	.217	.251	.344	248	11	.270	.291	.488	27	1	.481	.500	.630
1988	Pit-N	15	7	0	219	3.08	7	3	0	103	3.22	8	4	0	116	2.95	375	6	.237	.290	.325	437	15	.240	.283	.400	303	8	.244	.289	.370	72	2	.264	.329	.389
1989	Pit-N	14	12	0	244	2.80	8	5	0	136	1.85	6	7	0	108	3.99	492	7	.250	.311	.339	410	14	.224	.270	.363	329	8	.255	.319	.374	146	2	.212	.280	.281
1990	Pit-N	22	6	0	231	2.76	11	3	0	120	3.00	11	3	0	111	2.51	532	10	.244	.290	.370	314	5	.191	.248	.240	291	4	.241	.300	.340	72	1	.153	.208	.208
1991	Pit-N	15	14	0	235	3.07	9	8	0	131	2.40	6	6	0	104	3.91	530	8	.287	.337	.391	364	8	.255	.298	.376	368	5	.258	.306	.351	72	3	.319	.412	.444
1992	Pit-N	15	11	0	257	2.77	8	3	0	111	2.44	7	8	0	146	3.02	548	11	.261	.314	.370	397	6	.189	.217	.275	340	6	.215	.280	.312	131	0	.214	.272	.260
1993	Hou-N	9	18	0	238	3.79	5	8	0	142	3.04	4	10	0	95	4.91	459	11	.288	.337	.427	447	7	.246	.287	.333	348	8	.302	.363	.437	117	2	.248	.296	.308
1994	Hou-N	12	6	0	165	2.84	6	5	0	87	3.50	6	1	0	77	2.09	305	6	.220	.281	.318	294	8	.221	.266	.344	222	3	.194	.248	.270	53	2	.189	.246	.321
	TOTALS	120	94	0	1897	3.17	62	43	0	972	2.87	58	51	0	925	3.49	3845	83	.261	.316	.383	3228	74	.224	.268	.339	2647	55	.250	.305	.368	715	14	.236	.302	.323

● Dave Dravecky BR/TL

YEAR	TM/L	W	L	SV	IP	ERA	W	L	SV	IP	ERA	W	L	SV	IP	ERA	AB	HR	AVG	OBP	SLG	AB	HR	AVG	OBP	SLG	AB	HR	AVG	OBP	SLG	AB	HR	AVG	OBP	SLG
1984	SD-N	9	8	8	157	2.93	5	4	6	79	3.20	4	4	2	78	2.65	98	1	.204	.297	.265	465	11	.226	.288	.344	216	6	.199	.283	.315	143	5	.224	.297	.371
1985	SD-N	13	11	0	215	2.93	6	3	0	97	2.97	7	8	0	118	2.91	90	1	.267	.320	.322	712	17	.247	.296	.358	319	8	.238	.283	.348	67	6	.328	.384	.627
1986	SD-N	9	11	0	161	3.07	3	6	0	86	3.45	6	5	0	75	2.63	81	1	.222	.258	.321	524	16	.250	.314	.397	220	7	.227	.306	.377	50	1	.300	.339	.440
1987	SD-N	3	7	0	79	3.76	1	3	0	32	4.45	2	4	0	47	3.24	56	2	.107	.180	.232	240	8	.271	.346	.421	111	4	.288	.374	.441	27	2	.333	.419	.556
1987	SF-N	7	5	0	112	3.20	5	3	0	69	2.21	2	2	0	43	4.81	50	1	.180	.268	.260	373	7	.284	.333	.389	177	3	.254	.304	.339	10	0	.200	.385	.200
1988	SF-N	2	2	0	37	3.16	1	0	0	14	3.86	1	0	0	23	2.74	24	0	.083	.083	.083	112	4	.277	.317	.455	50	1	.240	.255	.420	7	0	.286	.286	.571
1989	SF-N	2	0	0	13	3.46	1	0	0	5	3.60	1	0	0	5	3.60	0	0	—	—	—	44	2	.182	.265	.364	12	1	.167	.286	.500	3	1	.333	.333	1.333
	TOTALS	45	44	8	774	3.10	22	21	6	385	3.15	23	23	2	389	3.06	399	6	.198	.263	.273	2470	65	.252	.309	.379	1105	30	.235	.299	.360	307	15	.270	.337	.463

● Dennis Eckersley BR/TR

YEAR	TM/L	W	L	SV	IP	ERA	W	L	SV	IP	ERA	W	L	SV	IP	ERA	AB	HR	AVG	OBP	SLG	AB	HR	AVG	OBP	SLG	AB	HR	AVG	OBP	SLG	AB	HR	AVG	OBP	SLG
1984	Bos-A	4	4	0	65	5.01	2	2	0	27	6.00	2	2	0	38	4.30	132	6	.288	.324	.515	118	4	.280	.312	.441	95	4	.274	.308	.453	12	1	.417	.417	.750
1984	Chi-N	10	8	0	160	3.03	7	5	0	84	3.23	3	3	0	77	2.82	319	5	.270	.318	.392	289	6	.228	.266	.329	238	2	.227	.288	.315	64	1	.188	.254	.328
1985	Chi-N	11	7	0	169	3.08	5	2	0	70	3.45	6	5	0	99	2.82	324	11	.256	.282	.414	310	4	.200	.224	.287	213	6	.202	.239	.347	56	1	.250	.271	.357
1986	Chi-N	6	11	0	201	4.57	4	5	0	83	5.18	2	6	0	118	4.13	425	9	.301	.347	.471	368	12	.266	.289	.438	333	12	.294	.340	.505	42	1	.214	.250	.381
1987	Oak-A	6	8	16	116	3.03	3	3	8	62	1.31	0	5	8	54	5.03	184	5	.272	.313	.429	250	6	.196	.220	.312	177	5	.198	.245	.322	173	6	.231	.256	.376
1988	Oak-A	4	2	45	73	2.35	3	1	22	39	2.33	1	1	23	34	2.38	126	3	.198	.229	.286	137	2	.197	.231	.255	103	3	.233	.274	.359	200	4	.205	.243	.285
1989	Oak-A	4	0	33	58	1.56	2	0	19	31	2.01	2	0	14	26	1.03	97	1	.206	.218	.258	101	4	.119	.133	.257	67	3	.194	.194	.343	146	5	.137	.150	.253
1990	Oak-A	4	2	48	73	0.61	3	2	22	35	1.02	1	0	26	38	0.24	119	1	.168	.180	.244	138	1	.152	.164	.210	97	1	.155	.178	.206	192	2	.167	.183	.240
1991	Oak-A	5	4	43	76	2.96	5	1	18	39	1.83	0	3	25	37	4.17	150	5	.227	.261	.353	138	6	.188	.206	.377	117	6	.171	.211	.333	220	7	.205	.232	.341
1992	Oak-A	7	1	51	80	1.91	7	0	21	42	2.76	0	1	30	38	0.96	149	3	.262	.299	.369	145	2	.159	.181	.241	132	1	.182	.223	.242	227	1	.172	.200	.225
1993	Oak-A	2	4	36	67	4.16	1	3	19	38	3.08	1	1	17	29	5.59	129	5	.326	.367	.543	124	2	.195	.230	.266	121	3	.298	.341	.463	195	6	.262	.301	.421
1994	Oak-A	5	4	19	44	4.26	4	3	7	23	3.57	1	1	12	22	4.98	87	2	.322	.398	.483	91	3	.231	.255	.429	90	2	.289	.366	.478	124	3	.274	.338	.444
	TOTALS	68	55	291	1182	3.18	49	27	136	574	3.07	19	28	155	608	3.27	2241	56	.265	.303	.409	2213	52	.209	.235	.328	1763	48	.231	.277	.373	1651	38	.207	.239	.323

● Mark Eichhorn BR/TR

YEAR	TM/L	W	L	SV	IP	ERA	W	L	SV	IP	ERA	W	L	SV	IP	ERA	AB	HR	AVG	OBP	SLG	AB	HR	AVG	OBP	SLG	AB	HR	AVG	OBP	SLG	AB	HR	AVG	OBP	SLG
1986	Tor-A	14	6	10	157	1.72	7	5	4	79	1.94	7	1	6	78	1.50	251	7	.259	.345	.434	297	5	.135	.186	.165	224	2	.183	.299	.246	285	2	.193	.267	.246
1987	Tor-A	10	6	4	128	3.17	6	1	2	67	2.27	4	5	2	60	4.18	183	6	.257	.350	.410	288	8	.219	.292	.351	204	7	.240	.354	.392	141	3	.227	.306	.355
1988	Tor-A	0	3	1	67	4.18	0	1	0	42	4.25	0	2	1	24	4.07	117	0	.299	.346	.333	143	3	.308	.407	.434	145	1	.303	.386	.379	36	1	.389	.488	.611
1989	Atl-N	5	5	0	68	4.35	1	3	0	32	5.40	4	2	0	37	3.44	123	2	.350	.410	.504	132	4	.205	.236	.318	121	6	.306	.358	.537	97	4	.258	.321	.423
1990	Cal-A	2	5	13	85	3.08	2	4	3	38	2.82	0	1	10	46	3.30	155	1	.290	.353	.348	184	1	.288	.332	.359	204	1	.275	.336	.324	160	1	.262	.316	.313
1991	Cal-A	3	3	1	82	1.98	2	2	1	42	1.30	1	1	0	40	2.70	126	2	.262	.280	.389	162	0	.185	.236	.247	124	0	.210	.257	.298	145	0	.207	.261	.290
1992	Cal-A	2	4	2	57	2.38	2	0	2	28	2.93	0	4	0	29	1.86	78	1	.308	.389	.397	136	1	.199	.234	.272	93	1	.269	.355	.355	112	1	.304	.381	.393
1992	Tor-A	2	0	0	31	4.35	1	0	0	13	5.68	1	0	0	18	3.44	51	1	.392	.418	.529	72	0	.208	.266	.264	62	0	.290	.333	.387	24	1	.333	.360	.458
1993	Tor-A	3	1	0	73	2.72	2	1	0	43	3.38	1	0	0	30	1.80	132	2	.326	.382	.417	147	1	.224	.284	.333	134	0	.284	.380	.351	55	1	.200	.302	.345
1994	Bal-A	6	5	1	71	2.15	2	2	1	38	2.11	4	3	0	33	2.20	94	0	.181	.255	.223	164	1	.274	.328	.366	126	1	.206	.288	.286	115	0	.252	.323	.287
	TOTALS	47	38	32	817	2.81	25	19	13	422	2.84	22	19	19	396	2.78	1310	22	.284	.350	.398	1725	20	.219	.276	.304	1437	19	.251	.334	.349	1170	14	.239	.309	.326

● Cal Eldred BR/TR

YEAR	TM/L	W	L	SV	IP	ERA	W	L	SV	IP	ERA	W	L	SV	IP	ERA	AB	HR	AVG	OBP	SLG	AB	HR	AVG	OBP	SLG	AB	HR	AVG	OBP	SLG	AB	HR	AVG	OBP	SLG
1991	Mil-A	2	0	0	16	4.50	1	0	0	10	6.52	1	0	0	6	1.42	36	1	.222	.243	.306	31	1	.387	.472	.516	29	0	.310	.355	.345	2	0	.500	.500	.500
1992	Mil-A	11	2	0	100	1.79	7	0	0	59	0.76	4	2	0	41	3.27	154	2	.188	.251	.240	213	2	.221	.262	.315	139	1	.158	.199	.216	48	0	.208	.240	.313
1993	Mil-A	16	16	0	258	4.01	11	6	0	149	2.91	5	10	0	109	5.52	507	12	.245	.320	.393	462	20	.234	.294	.411	367	14	.234	.317	.398	109	6	.239	.286	.450
1994	Mil-A	11	11	0	179	4.68	5	3	0	73	3.95	6	8	0	106	5.18	367	11	.221	.309	.360	302	12	.255	.337	.447	266	12	.233	.328	.410	48	4	.375	.436	.646
	TOTALS	40	29	0	553	3.84	24	9	0	290	2.85	16	20	0	263	4.93	1064	26	.227	.304	.356	1008	35	.242	.307	.405	801	27	.223	.303	.368	207	10	.266	.314	.464

● Scott Erickson BR/TR

YEAR	TM/L	W	L	SV	IP	ERA	W	L	SV	IP	ERA	W	L	SV	IP	ERA	AB	HR	AVG	OBP	SLG	AB	HR	AVG	OBP	SLG	AB	HR	AVG	OBP	SLG	AB	HR	AVG	OBP	SLG
1990	Min-A	8	4	0	113	2.87	7	2	0	78	3.45	1	2	0	35	1.56	224	4	.246	.329	.348	198	5	.268	.356	.389	182	3	.280	.364	.390	18	1	.167	.348	.333
1991	Min-A	20	8	0	204	3.18	10	3	0	97	3.53	10	5	0	107	2.86	417	8	.295	.363	.424	345	5	.191	.255	.290	325	7	.231	.286	.363	63	1	.254	.277	.397
1992	Min-A	13	12	0	212	3.40	9	6	0	123	3.43	4	6	0	89	3.35	410	7	.241	.311	.337	371	11	.264	.345	.410	336	7	.238	.304	.339	91	3	.308	.370	.484
1993	Min-A	8	19	0	219	5.19	4	11	0	127	5.30	4	8	0	91	5.03	474	7	.342	.392	.481	398	10	.261	.320	.372	410	7	.312	.359	.422	66	0	.333	.416	.409
1994	Min-A	8	11	0	144	5.44	6	3	0	70	4.13	2	8	0	74	6.66	308	10	.338	.415	.513	271	5	.255	.318	.376	259	5	.324	.399	.456	27	1	.296	.387	.556
	TOTALS	57	54	0	892	4.05	36	25	0	496	4.03	22	29	0	396	4.07	1833	36	.296	.364	.425	1583	36	.246	.316	.366	1512	29	.276	.339	.391	265	6	.291	.361	.442

● Steve Farr BR/TR

YEAR	TM/L	W	L	SV	IP	ERA	W	L	SV	IP	ERA	W	L	SV	IP	ERA	AB	HR	AVG	OBP	SLG	AB	HR	AVG	OBP	SLG	AB	HR	AVG	OBP	SLG	AB	HR	AVG	OBP	SLG
1984	Cle-A	3	11	1	116	4.58	1	5	1	61	4.84	2	6	0	55	4.28	226	9	.239	.328	.385	206	5	.252	.317	.374	172	6	.285	.337	.448	51	1	.294	.379	.353
1985	KC-A	2	1	1	38	3.11	2	1	0	29	3.41	0	0	1	9	2.08	62	1	.210	.355	.387	77	1	.273	.333	.325	71	1	.183	.294	.254	32	0	.313	.405	.344
1986	KC-A	8	4	8	109	3.13	7	0	4	61	2.23	1	4	4	49	4.25	203	2	.222	.300	.310	192	8	.234	.305	.411	173	3	.208	.308	.324	118	1	.186	.259	.245
1987	KC-A	4	3	1	91	4.15	2	1	1	45	4.37	2	2	0	46	3.94	146	4	.274	.369	.432	212	5	.269	.339	.406	197	4	.264	.327	.381	78	6	.282	.349	.526
1988	KC-A	5	4	20	83	2.50	1	2	11	41	1.54	1	9	4	42	3.46	155	2	.277	.349	.406	153	3	.203	.268	.327	161	1	.230	.296	.338	153	3	.265	.331	.404
1989	KC-A	2	5	18	63	4.12	2	1	14	36	3.46	0	4	4	27	5.60	125	0	.280	.333	.352	128	5	.313	.368	.508	112	3	.286	.362	.393	107	4	.290	.347	.458
1990	KC-A	13	7	1	127	1.98	9	2	1	66	1.37	4	5	0	61	2.64	204	2	.225	.319	.294	247	4	.215	.286	.296	204	5	.181	.288	.221	130	4	.254	.349	.292
1991	NY-A	5	5	23	70	2.19	3	1	12	39	2.56	2	4	11	31	1.72	116	2	.241	.333	.345	144	2	.215	.326	.292	115	3	.216	.302	.339	125	2	.224	.327	.336
1992	NY-A	2	2	30	52	1.56	1	1	16	31	1.16	1	1	14	21	2.11	100	1	.160	.190	.230	69	1	.145	.256	.203	125	2	.184	.268	.256
1993	NY-A	2	2	25	47	4.21	2	0	14	21	5.23	0	2	11	26	3.42	72	3	.292	.393	.500	102	5	.225	.331	.451	80	5	.313	.422	.575	125	2	.224	.327	.336
1994	Cle-A	1	1	4	15	5.28	1	0	0	6	11.12	0	1	4	10	1.86	31	1	.290	.421	.419	30	2	.267	.439	.533	36	1	.278	.438	.417	21	1	.333	.483	.524

YEAR	TM/L	TOTAL W	L	SV	IP	ERA	HOME W	L	SV	IP	ERA	AWAY W	L	SV	IP	ERA	LEFT AB	HR	AVG	OBP	SLG	RIGHT AB	HR	AVG	OBP	SLG	ON-BASE AB	HR	AVG	OBP	SLG	LATE/CLOSE AB	HR	AVG	OBP	SLG
1994	Bos-A	1	0	0	13	6.23	0	0	0	9	3.86	1	0	0	4	12.27	19	1	.474	.524	.737	39	1	.385	.400	.513	37	2	.351	.368	.514	19	0	.474	.500	.579
TOTALS		48	45	132	824	3.25	32	17	76	442	3.05	16	28	56	382	3.49	1442	28	.250	.340	.366	1630	42	.239	.307	.369	1425	32	.238	.324	.352	1112	24	.246	.328	.353
● Jeff Fassero BL/TL																																				
1991	Mon-N	2	5	8	55	2.44	2	2	3	29	2.17	0	3	5	26	2.73	70	0	.243	.293	.329	129	1	.171	.246	.233	102	1	.186	.252	.275	118	0	.212	.290	.237
1992	Mon-N	8	7	1	86	2.84	6	3	0	40	4.05	2	4	1	46	1.77	93	1	.269	.320	.344	232	0	.241	.323	.319	156	1	.263	.350	.346	157	1	.236	.311	.318
1993	Mon-N	12	5	1	150	2.29	7	1	1	68	2.00	5	4	0	82	2.52	114	1	.184	.275	.246	437	6	.224	.287	.302	217	5	.230	.313	.327	93	1	.237	.324	.290
1994	Mon-N	8	6	0	139	2.99	4	3	0	70	3.99	4	3	0	69	1.97	93	2	.204	.272	.312	426	11	.235	.288	.357	185	5	.265	.324	.378	46	1	.196	.229	.283
TOTALS		30	23	10	429	2.64	19	9	4	207	3.09	11	14	6	223	2.22	370	4	.222	.289	.303	1224	18	.225	.290	.317	660	12	.241	.316	.338	414	3	.225	.299	.285
● Alex Fernandez BR/TR																																				
1990	Chi-A	5	5	0	88	3.80	2	1	0	27	3.67	3	4	0	61	3.86	176	3	.273	.340	.369	160	3	.256	.335	.350	155	2	.297	.351	.387	27	0	.111	.172	.111
1991	Chi-A	9	13	0	192	4.51	5	7	0	96	4.48	4	6	0	95	4.53	330	4	.252	.331	.355	389	12	.265	.342	.416	298	8	.285	.362	.423	53	1	.226	.317	.302
1992	Chi-A	8	11	0	188	4.27	4	7	0	111	4.39	4	4	0	77	4.09	351	9	.251	.295	.385	385	12	.288	.346	.423	297	5	.290	.352	.394	76	3	.263	.273	.382
1993	Chi-A	18	9	0	247	3.13	9	4	0	119	2.79	9	5	0	128	3.45	437	15	.261	.313	.430	482	12	.222	.280	.336	365	9	.236	.281	.353	93	3	.258	.303	.430
1994	Chi-A	11	7	0	170	3.86	8	1	0	89	2.23	3	6	0	82	5.62	325	14	.240	.309	.418	326	11	.261	.295	.411	245	9	.245	.300	.416	55	2	.273	.317	.436
TOTALS		51	45	0	885	3.88	28	20	0	442	3.50	23	25	0	443	4.25	1619	45	.254	.315	.396	1742	50	.257	.317	.389	1360	33	.267	.327	.393	304	9	.243	.289	.368
● Sid Fernandez BL/TL																																				
1984	NY-N	6	6	0	90	3.50	3	3	0	40	3.57	3	3	0	50	3.44	65	1	.200	.246	.262	262	7	.233	.306	.397	119	1	.210	.298	.303	32	2	.250	.324	.594
1985	NY-N	9	9	0	170	2.80	5	4	0	71	2.67	4	5	0	100	2.89	97	2	.163	.222	.240	504	12	.185	.289	.298	214	2	.196	.300	.266	45	2	.178	.245	.356
1986	NY-N	16	6	1	204	3.52	8	3	1	108	2.17	8	3	0	97	5.03	97	1	.214	.292	.330	510	14	.214	.292	.330	310	7	.213	.297	.348	47	1	.298	.375	.447
1987	NY-N	12	8	0	156	3.81	9	3	0	94	2.98	3	5	0	62	5.05	71	2	.225	.291	.408	510	14	.224	.312	.357	234	6	.235	.320	.376	42	0	.167	.255	.190
1988	NY-N	12	10	0	187	3.03	8	4	0	98	1.83	4	6	0	89	4.36	72	1	.236	.325	.347	594	14	.185	.264	.300	243	6	.193	.270	.321	51	0	.235	.298	.353
1989	NY-N	14	5	0	219	2.83	7	2	0	130	2.78	7	3	0	90	2.91	117	2	.197	.258	.299	677	19	.198	.273	.340	270	10	.200	.296	.404	71	3	.268	.293	.465
1990	NY-N	9	14	0	179	3.46	8	5	0	105	2.41	1	9	0	75	4.94	124	3	.226	.322	.363	526	16	.194	.267	.335	241	9	.212	.285	.386	22	0	.318	.348	.409
1991	NY-N	1	3	0	44	2.86	1	1	0	19	1.42	0	2	0	25	3.96	35	1	.371	.389	.457	127	3	.181	.228	.291	55	3	.218	.290	.418	4	0	.250	.250	.250
1992	NY-N	14	11	0	215	2.73	7	4	0	99	2.17	7	7	0	115	3.20	152	0	.184	.267	.289	619	12	.216	.275	.338	257	3	.214	.302	.323	57	1	.316	.381	.421
1993	NY-N	5	6	0	120	2.93	2	2	0	58	3.24	3	4	0	61	2.64	81	2	.185	.298	.382	345	15	.194	.250	.351	123	4	.211	.315	.325	43	2	.186	.205	.372
1994	Bal-A	6	6	0	115	5.15	4	4	0	63	4.69	3	2	0	52	5.71	55	1	.255	.305	.382	384	26	.247	.323	.526	171	11	.222	.292	.480	32	3	.344	.400	.719
TOTALS		104	84	1	1700	3.28	61	35	1	885	2.67	43	49	0	815	3.93	961	16	.212	.292	.326	5197	149	.206	.282	.347	2237	62	.214	.296	.356	446	14	.253	.310	.422
● Chuck Finley BL/TL																																				
1986	Cal-A	3	1	0	46	3.30	1	0	0	26	4.50	2	1	0	20	1.77	78	0	.269	.360	.308	92	2	.207	.305	.304	88	0	.261	.330	.307	14	0	.214	.353	.286
1987	Cal-A	2	7	0	91	4.67	2	4	0	41	5.23	0	3	0	49	4.20	135	1	.259	.299	.356	220	6	.305	.405	.445	165	2	.303	.397	.436	64	1	.250	.304	.359
1988	Cal-A	9	15	0	194	4.17	5	8	0	95	4.44	4	7	0	99	3.91	135	1	.289	.374	.370	591	14	.257	.330	.387	295	5	.271	.342	.407	73	3	.301	.395	.479
1989	Cal-A	16	9	0	200	2.57	8	7	0	113	2.23	8	2	0	87	3.01	99	0	.172	.252	.192	634	13	.243	.320	.356	292	6	.226	.298	.336	91	3	.253	.333	.429
1990	Cal-A	18	9	0	236	2.40	11	4	0	132	1.63	7	5	0	104	3.39	121	0	.256	.333	.273	743	17	.241	.304	.363	348	2	.227	.290	.305	144	0	.285	.340	.347
1991	Cal-A	18	9	0	227	3.80	9	2	0	125	3.03	9	6	0	103	4.73	109	4	.257	.336	.422	730	19	.242	.329	.379	333	8	.249	.345	.369	95	3	.211	.292	.316
1992	Cal-A	7	12	0	204	3.96	3	5	0	105	3.93	4	7	0	99	4.00	87	1	.402	.441	.517	675	23	.262	.349	.413	347	10	.248	.309	.369	62	2	.242	.314	.371
1993	Cal-A	16	14	0	251	3.15	8	5	0	123	2.79	8	9	0	129	3.50	128	2	.313	.381	.414	831	20	.244	.303	.356	404	9	.248	.312	.351	102	0	.245	.306	.275
1994	Cal-A	10	10	0	183	4.32	4	6	0	106	4.50	6	4	0	77	4.07	111	5	.288	.360	.477	574	16	.254	.317	.401	282	5	.270	.335	.376	82	2	.216	.324	.330
TOTALS		99	86	0	1633	3.50	51	42	0	867	3.27	48	44	0	767	3.77	1003	14	.277	.351	.370	5090	130	.250	.320	.370	2554	47	.252	.324	.361	733	14	.251	.327	.356
● Brian Fisher BR/TR																																				
1985	NY-A	4	4	14	98	2.38	3	3	8	56	2.75	1	1	6	43	1.90	173	2	.225	.302	.289	184	2	.207	.245	.266	173	3	.214	.262	.301	160	3	.225	.299	.325
1986	NY-A	9	5	8	97	4.93	2	2	3	43	5.91	7	2	4	54	4.11	152	6	.316	.400	.493	227	8	.251	.300	.401	181	6	.287	.370	.453	153	5	.261	.347	.425
1987	Pit-N	11	9	0	185	4.52	4	5	0	82	5.79	7	4	0	103	3.50	376	6	.266	.350	.439	329	18	.258	.310	.480	289	9	.253	.318	.457	51	2	.275	.373	.471
1988	Pit-N	8	10	1	146	4.61	5	6	0	87	3.74	3	4	1	60	5.88	285	7	.326	.400	.502	282	6	.227	.287	.348	241	6	.270	.359	.436	40	0	.175	.277	.250
1989	Pit-N	0	3	1	17	7.94	0	1	0	9	6.00	0	2	1	8	10.13	37	2	.486	.587	.757	39	0	.179	.195	.308	44	1	.318	.392	.500	8	0	.500	.500	.875
1990	Hou-N	0	0	0	5	7.20	0	0	0	3	8.10	0	0	0	2	5.40	12	1	.500	.429	.917	10	0	.300	.300	.300	14	0	.286	.250	.286	0	0	—	—	—
1992	Sea-N	4	3	1	91	4.53	2	2	0	44	6.34	2	1	1	47	2.85	167	2	.234	.351	.311	175	7	.234	.298	.429	126	5	.246	.372	.444	39	0	.231	.412	.282
TOTALS		36	34	23	640	4.39	16	20	10	324	4.84	20	14	13	316	3.93	1202	29	.285	.370	.436	1246	41	.237	.288	.390	1068	30	.258	.337	.424	451	10	.244	.336	.375
● Mike Flanagan BL/TL																																				
1984	Bal-A	13	13	0	227	3.53	8	4	0	109	2.90	5	9	0	118	4.12	164	3	.207	.258	.293	687	21	.261	.327	.394	348	14	.270	.318	.443	71	1	.197	.296	.239
1985	Bal-A	4	5	0	86	5.13	2	3	0	32	6.40	2	3	0	54	4.36	49	0	.306	.346	.388	291	14	.296	.353	.502	143	9	.301	.325	.545	29	0	.207	.207	.276
1986	Bal-A	7	11	0	172	4.24	5	2	0	72	3.73	2	9	0	100	4.61	129	1	.248	.312	.349	535	14	.275	.339	.424	303	9	.277	.324	.436	49	1	.327	.417	.551
1987	Bal-A	3	6	0	95	4.94	2	2	0	49	4.01	1	4	0	45	5.96	50	0	.280	.357	.320	317	9	.271	.339	.421	156	3	.301	.333	.429	31	1	.290	.371	.484
1987	Tor-A	3	2	0	49	2.37	1	1	0	32	2.25	0	1	0	17	2.60	50	0	.220	.264	.220	144	3	.243	.301	.389	81	0	.185	.250	.222	27	1	.296	.321	.296
1988	Tor-A	13	13	0	211	4.18	6	6	0	108	3.76	7	7	0	103	4.62	115	3	.270	.320	.426	697	20	.271	.342	.423	344	3	.250	.307	.360	39	2	.205	.311	.359
1989	Tor-A	8	10	0	172	3.93	5	4	0	85	3.51	3	6	0	87	4.34	97	0	.206	.279	.237	561	10	.296	.341	.435	280	3	.296	.326	.396	41	0	.195	.267	.220
1990	Tor-A	2	2	0	20	5.31	2	1	0	16	5.06	0	1	0	4	6.23	10	1	.300	.364	.600	75	2	.333	.390	.453	41	0	.317	.349	.341	0	0	—	—	—
1991	Bal-A	2	7	3	98	2.38	2	5	0	45	3.18	0	2	3	53	1.70	127	2	.181	.221	.236	229	4	.266	.327	.371	164	3	.195	.266	.274	134	2	.254	.325	.343
1992	Bal-A	0	0	0	35	8.05	0	0	0	14	7.71	0	0	0	21	8.27	62	0	.274	.378	.274	86	3	.384	.481	.581	100	3	.340	.429	.490	19	1	.421	.500	.632
TOTALS		55	69	3	1165	4.06	33	27	0	562	3.73	22	42	3	602	4.38	853	10	.234	.293	.309	3622	100	.279	.341	.429	1960	47	.271	.319	.404	440	8	.252	.329	.355
● Ray Fontenot BL/TL																																				
1984	NY-A	8	9	0	169	3.61	4	5	0	82	2.96	4	4	0	87	4.24	120	3	.267	.331	.400	531	5	.296	.353	.386	296	6	.284	.335	.399	74	1	.257	.337	.378
1985	Chi-N	6	10	0	155	4.36	2	6	0	90	5.18	4	4	0	64	3.22	76	1	.184	.267	.250	526	22	.310	.353	.492	252	9	.306	.347	.460	61	3	.377	.424	.557
1986	Chi-N	3	5	2	56	3.86	2	3	1	31	2.90	1	2	1	25	5.04	73	2	.274	.329	.411	141	6	.262	.333	.411	94	3	.287	.356	.468	74	2	.270	.333	.432
1986	Min-A	0	0	0	16	9.92	0	0	0	9	12.00	0	0	0	7	7.36	24	1	.208	.269	.333	51	2	.431	.473	.667	41	3	.415	.455	.756	18	0	.556	.579	.611
TOTALS		17	24	2	396	4.20	8	14	1	212	4.28	9	10	1	184	4.11	293	7	.242	.309	.356	1249	32	.303	.356	.445	683	21	.300	.349	.452	227	6	.317	.378	.463
● Tony Fossas BL/TL																																				
1988	Tex-A	0	0	0	4	4.76	0	0	0	0	—	0	0	0	4	7.36	6	0	.167	.375	.167	20	0	.500	.500	.750	16	0	.438	.471	.625	0	0	—	—	—
1989	Mil-A	2	2	1	61	3.54	2	0	1	39	2.79	0	2	0	22	4.84	81	1	.183	.253	.220	141	2	.298	.361	.411	113	2	.283	.359	.354	37	0	.270	.400	.351
1990	Mil-A	2	3	0	29	6.44	0	0	0	16	4.50	2	3	0	13	8.77	40	1	.300	.349	.375	93	4	.344	.386	.559	77	4	.351	.393	.558	37	1	.297	.357	.486
1991	Bos-A	3	2	1	57	3.47	1	0	1	22	2.45	2	2	0	35	4.11	84	2	.190	.277	.298	124	1	.226	.372	.347	131	1	.229	.331	.290	63	1	.175	.307	.286
1992	Bos-A	1	2	2	30	2.43	1	2	1	19	1.40	0	0	1	10	5.06	56	0	.214	.254	.321	51	1	.345	.463	.509	72	0	.292	.354	.417	44	0	.295	.354	.341
1993	Bos-A	1	1	0	40	5.17	1	1	0	22	3.68	0	0	0	18	7.00	68	0	.132	.211	.162	89	4	.326	.394	.517	81	1	.272	.341	.370	62	2	.210	.310	.339
1994	Bos-A	2	0	1	34	4.76	1	0	0	17	3.12	1	0	1	17	6.48	55	1	.182	.286	.273	78	5	.321	.384	.615	74	4	.230	.321	.459	28	2	.214	.313	.500
TOTALS		11	10	5	257	4.17	6	3	3	139	3.04	5	7	2	118	5.51	391	5	.192	.270	.263	600	17	.317	.389	.483	564	12	.277	.352	.399	271	6	.236	.335	.365
● John Franco BL/TL																																				
1984	Cin-N	6	2	4	79	2.61	4	2	3	48	2.25	2	0	1	31	3.16	76	1	.237	.318	.289	213	2	.263	.346	.343	137	2	.263	.340	.343	144	1	.222	.290	.278
1985	Cin-N	12	3	12	99	2.18	7	0	5	58	1.25	5	3	7	41	3.48	85	1	.176	.222	.224	269	4	.253	.340	.353	147	2	.238	.327	.293	267	4	.240	.302	.330
1986	Cin-N	6	6	29	101	2.94	2	2	16	54	3.02	4	4	13	47	2.81	76	0	.211	.250	.263	295	7	.251	.341	.353	189	4	.238	.332	.349	286	6	.243	.335	.339
1987	Cin-N	8	5	32	82	2.52	4	2	16	37	4.14	4	3	16	45	1.20	46	0	.239	.280	.283	264	6	.246	.308	.321	140	1	.257	.338	.321	216	3	.245	.321	.324
1988	Cin-N	6	6	39	86	1.57	4	2	20	46	0.99	2	4	19	40	2.23	51	1	.137	.167	.235	210	2	.210	.282	.242	113	2	.205	.274	.265	240	2	.179	.241	.221
1989	Cin-N	4	8	32	81	3.12	4	4	17	41	3.92	0	4	15	39	2.29	50	0	.200	.245	.240	249	3	.269	.351	.325	142	3	.275	.361	.373	243	3	.247	.326	.309
1990	NY-N	5	3	33	68	2.53	4	2	17	38	2.82	1	1	16	29	2.15	57	0	.228	.323	.298	205	6	.259	.301	.361	136	0	.235	.295	.287	202	4	.248	.295	.332
1991	NY-N	5	9	30	55	2.93	1	4	18	27	3.00	4	5	12	28	2.86	63	0	.340	.397	.415	172	2	.250	.306	.343	131	1	.252	.329	.351	202	2	.272	.326	.371
1992	NY-N	6	2	15	33	1.64	1	1	9	20	0.92	5	1	6	13	2.51	28	0	.250	.389	.286	87	1	.195	.228	.310	46	0	.239	.327	.326	91	0	.220	.284	.297
1993	NY-N	4	3	10	36	5.20	1	0	6	19	3.31	3	3	4	17	7.34	41	2	.317	.378	.488	106	4	.311	.398	.453	76	3	.329	.409	.487	87	3	.322	.434	.460
1994	NY-N	1	4	30	50	2.70	1	2	15	25	2.55	0	2	15	25	2.84	49	0	.306	.340	.347	144	2	.222	.304	.313	92	0	.228	.308	.261	128	1	.266	.340	.328
TOTALS		63	51	266	770	2.63	36	21	141	409	2.51	27	30	125	361	2.77	612	5	.234	.293	.296	2256	37	.249	.322	.337	1368	18	.249	.329	.329	2100	29	.241	.313	.320
● George Frazier BR/TR																																				
1984	Cle-A	3	2	1	44	3.65	2	1	0	29	3.14	1	1	1	16	4.60	85	2	.271	.340	.400	89	1	.247	.287	.315	77	1	.351	.425	.442	49	0	.286	.352	.388
1984	Chi-N	6	3	0	40	4.46	3	1	0	36	4.46	3	2	0	27	3.62	127	2	.260	.336	.394	113	2	.177	.252	.257	97	2	.227	.328	.351	102	1	.167	.241	.235
1985	Chi-N	7	8	7	76	6.39	5	4	1	41	6.64	2	4	6	35	6.10	140	5	.307	.413	.486	154	6	.292	.404	.449	95	7	.326	.430	.589					
1986	Chi-N	2	4	0	52	5.40	1	2	0	21	5.14	1	2	0	31	5.58	89	0	.281	.379	.348	114	5	.333	.428	.588	103	3	.311	.398	.534	43	1	.349	.440	.512
1986	Min-A	1	1	6	27	4.39	1	0	3	14	3.21	0	1	3	13	5.68	41	0	.195	.352	.244	58	2	.259	.313	.414	44	0	.295	.393	.364	78	2	.256	.348	.385

YEAR TM/L	TOTAL W L SV IP ERA	HOME W L SV IP ERA	AWAY W L SV IP ERA	LEFT AB HR AVG OBP SLG	RIGHT AB HR AVG OBP SLG	ON-BASE AB HR AVG OBP SLG	LATE/CLOSE AB HR AVG OBP SLG
1987 Min-A	5 5 2 81 4.98	4 1 2 39 4.15	1 4 0 42 5.74	169 4 .249 .345 .402	130 4 .269 .377 .392	158 7 .272 .342 .462	81 0 .278 .366 .304
TOTALS	24 23 14 344 4.98	15 8 9 180 4.66	9 15 5 164 5.32	651 14 .267 .363 .401	658 20 .266 .355 .407	626 18 .288 .378 .444	446 11 .267 .355 .392

● Steve Frey BR/TL

YEAR TM/L	TOTAL	HOME	AWAY	LEFT	RIGHT	ON-BASE	LATE/CLOSE
1989 Mon-N	3 2 0 21 5.48	1 1 0 10 4.66	2 1 0 12 6.17	26 0 .308 .419 .423	62 4 .339 .394 .438	48 1 .292 .379 .438	18 1 .278 .409 .500
1990 Mon-N	8 2 9 56 2.10	4 0 7 30 0.59	4 2 2 25 3.91	62 2 .258 .347 .387	139 2 .201 .304 .288	93 1 .226 .315 .280	141 4 .220 .306 .326
1991 Mon-N	0 1 1 40 4.99	0 0 0 15 5.52	0 1 1 25 4.68	56 1 .268 .354 .357	97 2 .289 .386 .381	77 2 .377 .425 .494	37 0 .270 .396 .324
1992 Cal-A	4 2 4 45 3.57	2 1 2 21 3.00	2 1 2 24 4.07	53 5 .189 .271 .472	111 1 .261 .356 .324	91 2 .231 .311 .330	77 1 .234 .351 .312
1993 Cal-A	2 3 13 48 2.98	2 2 7 31 2.61	0 1 6 17 3.63	50 2 .231 .406 .346	126 1 .230 .302 .286	106 0 .198 .317 .226	103 1 .214 .344 .282
1994 SF-N	1 0 0 31 4.94	0 0 0 18 3.57	1 0 0 13 6.75	42 3 .238 .306 .476	73 3 .370 .448 .603	58 1 .241 .360 .362	27 1 .333 .424 .481
TOTALS	18 10 27 241 3.69	9 4 16 124 2.82	9 6 11 117 4.62	291 11 .244 .348 .405	608 13 .266 .354 .380	473 7 .254 .345 .338	403 8 .236 .346 .330

● Todd Frohwirth BR/TR

YEAR TM/L	TOTAL	HOME	AWAY	LEFT	RIGHT	ON-BASE	LATE/CLOSE
1987 Phi-N	1 0 0 11 0.00	1 0 0 7 0.00	0 0 0 4 0.00	15 0 .400 .400 .467	26 0 .231 .286 .231	20 0 .150 .227 .150	8 0 .500 .500 .625
1988 Phi-N	1 2 0 12 8.25	1 0 0 4 0.00	0 2 0 8 12.91	18 0 .278 .519 .389	31 2 .355 .382 .613	28 1 .357 .500 .607	10 0 .400 .533 .600
1989 Phi-N	1 0 0 63 3.59	0 0 0 36 3.96	1 0 0 26 3.08	100 3 .350 .409 .530	132 1 .159 .222 .212	97 2 .258 .365 .381	45 0 .244 .277 .289
1990 Phi-N	0 1 0 1 18.00	0 0 0 0 27.00	0 1 0 1 13.50	1 0 1.000 1.000 1.000	5 0 .400 .700 .400	4 0 .250 .667 .250	3 0 .667 .833 .667
1991 Bal-A	7 3 3 96 1.87	4 1 1 54 2.48	3 2 2 42 1.07	130 0 .223 .320 .315	207 2 .169 .211 .237	142 1 .197 .272 .275	144 1 .181 .248 .264
1992 Bal-A	4 3 4 106 2.46	2 1 2 59 1.84	2 2 2 47 3.23	125 1 .246 .341 .289	250 3 .248 .311 .332	203 2 .266 .333 .345	155 1 .226 .326 .284
1993 Bal-A	6 7 3 96 3.83	6 1 1 57 3.92	0 6 2 39 3.69	115 4 .270 .373 .417	240 3 .250 .326 .317	195 4 .262 .348 .349	139 1 .245 .350 .288
1994 Bos-A	0 3 1 27 10.80	0 1 1 15 5.28	0 2 0 11 18.26	48 0 .375 .444 .500	70 3 .314 .422 .486	65 3 .354 .468 .585	20 0 .400 .520 .500
TOTALS	20 19 11 412 3.50	14 4 5 233 3.01	6 15 6 179 4.13	569 8 .281 .373 .390	961 14 .228 .296 .309	754 13 .259 .351 .362	524 3 .237 .329 .302

● Gene Garber BR/TR

YEAR TM/L	TOTAL	HOME	AWAY	LEFT	RIGHT	ON-BASE	LATE/CLOSE
1984 Atl-N	3 6 11 106 3.06	2 3 4 58 4.50	1 3 7 48 1.31	193 6 .254 .293 .368	213 2 .254 .294 .338	171 3 .281 .333 .404	172 4 .262 .286 .366
1985 Atl-N	6 6 1 97 3.61	4 4 0 55 3.42	2 2 1 42 3.86	195 3 .246 .293 .349	176 5 .284 .335 .403	154 4 .247 .324 .377	139 3 .273 .350 .381
1986 Atl-N	5 5 24 78 2.54	3 3 9 35 2.55	2 2 15 43 2.53	154 3 .273 .302 .364	146 0 .253 .321 .295	161 4 .286 .359 .391	190 2 .253 .309 .326
1987 Atl-N	8 10 10 69 4.41	7 3 5 42 3.83	1 7 5 27 5.33	129 2 .279 .350 .380	151 5 .338 .391 .510	146 0 .250 .329 .301	206 4 .311 .377 .427
1987 KC-A	0 0 8 14 2.51	0 0 2 7 5.14	0 0 6 7 0.00	24 1 .250 .280 .417	29 0 .241 .267 .345	28 0 .179 .207 .250	24 0 .167 .200 .208
1988 KC-A	0 4 6 33 3.58	0 3 1 20 4.58	0 1 5 13 2.08	60 3 .233 .292 .417	62 1 .242 .347 .290	58 2 .241 .362 .345	72 3 .264 .346 .417
TOTALS	22 31 60 398 3.35	16 16 21 218 3.80	6 15 39 180 2.80	739 14 .253 .307 .357	785 16 .279 .327 .387	718 13 .262 .333 .362	803 16 .271 .330 .375

● Mark Gardner BR/TR

YEAR TM/L	TOTAL	HOME	AWAY	LEFT	RIGHT	ON-BASE	LATE/CLOSE
1989 Mon-N	0 3 0 26 5.13	0 1 0 10 2.70	0 2 0 16 6.61	66 0 .197 .293 .258	38 2 .342 .405 .579	34 0 .353 .500 .500	9 1 .444 .500 1.000
1990 Mon-N	7 9 0 153 3.42	5 3 0 80 1.91	2 6 0 73 5.08	318 8 .230 .327 .362	243 5 .230 .291 .337	206 5 .311 .394 .447	37 0 .297 .350 .324
1991 Mon-N	9 11 0 168 3.85	4 4 0 65 2.51	5 7 0 104 4.69	351 8 .228 .321 .363	223 7 .233 .313 .363	234 11 .265 .351 .462	51 1 .216 .322 .314
1992 Mon-N	12 10 0 180 4.36	6 5 0 105 4.80	6 5 0 75 3.74	397 7 .272 .330 .398	293 8 .242 .316 .369	282 4 .273 .348 .379	49 1 .286 .386 .429
1993 KC-A	4 6 0 92 6.19	3 2 0 40 6.30	1 4 0 52 6.10	164 7 .311 .376 .512	174 10 .236 .312 .511	114 4 .316 .406 .553	7 1 .429 .556 .857
1994 Fla-N	4 4 0 92 4.87	0 3 0 48 5.63	4 1 0 44 4.06	162 4 .327 .380 .506	189 10 .233 .288 .455	137 7 .270 .331 .511	10 1 .300 .364 .800
TOTALS	36 43 0 711 4.37	18 18 0 348 3.93	18 25 0 363 4.78	1488 36 .259 .336 .397	1160 42 .239 .308 .403	1007 31 .286 .369 .454	163 5 .282 .371 .442

● Scott Garrelts BR/TR

YEAR TM/L	TOTAL	HOME	AWAY	LEFT	RIGHT	ON-BASE	LATE/CLOSE
1984 SF-N	2 3 0 43 5.65	2 1 0 24 4.18	0 2 0 19 7.45	75 1 .320 .485 .360	89 5 .236 .314 .416	72 3 .361 .473 .486	31 0 .290 .410 .290
1985 SF-N	9 6 13 106 2.30	7 4 4 56 2.26	2 2 9 50 2.34	169 1 .231 .314 .302	215 1 .172 .300 .174	180 1 .206 .342 .256	226 0 .190 .303 .226
1986 SF-N	13 9 10 174 3.11	8 4 7 97 2.23	5 5 3 77 4.23	337 6 .237 .322 .320	287 11 .223 .298 .387	254 8 .220 .317 .343	188 4 .239 .336 .330
1987 SF-N	11 7 12 106 3.22	5 3 4 42 3.86	6 4 8 64 2.80	197 4 .183 .286 .284	167 6 .204 .309 .341	164 7 .201 .307 .354	265 6 .196 .300 .309
1988 SF-N	5 9 13 98 3.58	1 7 9 45 4.20	4 2 4 53 3.06	157 1 .217 .313 .287	197 2 .234 .320 .299	176 0 .256 .370 .313	189 1 .238 .318 .291
1989 SF-N	14 5 0 193 2.28	10 2 0 109 1.57	4 3 0 85 3.19	377 6 .236 .296 .353	327 5 .183 .211 .266	250 6 .224 .266 .360	53 1 .245 .286 .415
1990 SF-N	12 11 0 182 4.15	6 7 0 103 3.83	6 4 0 79 4.58	389 8 .296 .365 .427	309 8 .243 .306 .375	287 9 .279 .354 .422	66 2 .258 .300 .394
1991 SF-N	1 1 0 20 6.41	0 1 0 6 12.00	1 0 0 14 3.95	42 2 .405 .458 .643	38 3 .211 .286 .474	36 2 .250 .317 .500	0 0 — — —
TOTALS	67 51 48 922 3.30	39 29 24 481 2.97	28 22 24 440 3.66	1743 29 .244 .332 .352	1629 41 .212 .288 .326	1419 36 .241 .333 .359	1018 14 .200 .314 .302

● Tom Glavine BL/TL

YEAR TM/L	TOTAL	HOME	AWAY	LEFT	RIGHT	ON-BASE	LATE/CLOSE
1987 Atl-N	2 4 0 50 5.54	2 2 0 24 5.55	0 2 0 26 5.54	27 0 .259 .375 .333	170 5 .282 .387 .435	86 1 .302 .432 .384	10 0 .300 .462 .400
1988 Atl-N	7 17 0 195 4.56	2 7 0 86 5.00	5 10 0 109 4.21	133 2 .244 .343 .350	622 9 .275 .326 .376	309 3 .291 .365 .385	52 2 .269 .328 .462
1989 Atl-N	14 8 0 186 3.68	6 4 0 94 3.72	8 4 0 92 3.63	108 0 .204 .252 .269	601 20 .250 .289 .389	242 9 .260 .322 .409	60 3 .183 .234 .333
1990 Atl-N	10 12 0 214 4.28	5 8 0 104 4.86	5 4 0 111 3.74	154 2 .221 .310 .279	673 16 .294 .350 .440	341 3 .293 .379 .402	72 1 .417 .447 .583
1991 Atl-N	20 11 0 247 2.55	10 4 0 106 2.71	10 7 0 140 2.44	171 4 .292 .354 .433	734 13 .206 .259 .307	318 4 .242 .316 .343	91 0 .231 .268 .308
1992 Atl-N	20 8 0 225 2.76	13 4 0 140 2.31	7 4 0 85 3.19	176 1 .273 .353 .341	663 5 .225 .277 .302	343 2 .245 .303 .321	107 0 .224 .259 .280
1993 Atl-N	22 6 0 239 3.20	13 3 0 136 3.18	9 3 0 104 3.21	176 1 .271 .349 .341	744 15 .257 .322 .382	387 5 .240 .333 .346	91 2 .209 .273 .297
1994 Atl-N	13 9 0 165 3.97	5 5 0 74 3.89	8 4 0 91 4.04	125 1 .320 .393 .424	520 9 .256 .325 .365	286 3 .262 .352 .364	36 0 .222 .300 .250
TOTALS	108 75 0 1522 3.58	56 37 0 765 3.60	52 38 0 758 3.55	1050 12 .252 .330 .341	4727 92 .252 .309 .367	2312 30 .263 .341 .365	519 8 .250 .301 .355

● Dwight Gooden BR/TR

YEAR TM/L	TOTAL	HOME	AWAY	LEFT	RIGHT	ON-BASE	LATE/CLOSE
1984 NY-N	17 9 0 218 2.60	12 2 0 118 1.90	5 7 0 100 3.43	425 4 .228 .290 .311	374 3 .171 .246 .235	316 3 .218 .282 .285	123 1 .236 .275 .268
1985 NY-N	24 4 0 277 1.53	13 2 0 144 1.50	11 2 0 133 1.56	567 3 .203 .260 .249	419 10 .198 .246 .298	360 2 .181 .229 .219	166 2 .235 .289 .295
1986 NY-N	17 6 0 250 2.84	9 3 0 123 3.24	8 3 0 127 3.47	527 7 .211 .283 .306	390 10 .221 .273 .341	384 8 .203 .265 .297	124 2 .169 .252 .250
1987 NY-N	15 7 0 180 3.21	8 5 0 95 3.41	7 2 0 85 2.98	365 5 .241 .304 .321	300 6 .247 .293 .373	273 3 .231 .281 .311	84 2 .250 .319 .381
1988 NY-N	18 9 0 248 3.19	8 4 0 117 2.46	10 5 0 131 3.84	491 4 .236 .290 .308	453 4 .287 .313 .360	380 5 .276 .328 .376	80 1 .275 .330 .338
1989 NY-N	9 4 1 118 2.89	6 1 0 66 2.33	3 3 1 53 3.59	232 3 .181 .270 .259	209 6 .244 .309 .373	176 2 .199 .287 .267	62 1 .226 .279 .290
1990 NY-N	19 7 0 233 3.83	9 3 0 126 3.56	10 4 0 106 4.15	522 6 .259 .316 .354	366 4 .257 .313 .331	402 8 .254 .288 .361	73 1 .219 .284 .274
1991 NY-N	13 7 0 190 3.60	9 3 0 106 3.55	4 4 0 84 3.66	412 4 .252 .321 .345	309 8 .262 .298 .401	308 5 .253 .304 .357	62 1 .210 .234 .258
1992 NY-N	10 13 0 206 3.67	7 5 0 97 4.25	3 8 0 109 3.15	450 9 .267 .337 .380	323 2 .238 .288 .359	334 5 .263 .318 .380	70 2 .229 .267 .329
1993 NY-N	12 15 0 209 3.45	8 10 0 139 2.78	4 5 0 70 4.78	396 9 .247 .307 .366	382 4 .236 .296 .348	310 4 .248 .314 .345	85 2 .200 .292 .318
1994 NY-N	3 4 0 41 6.31	1 2 0 26 6.45	2 2 0 16 6.16	78 6 .256 .333 .526	85 3 .306 .359 .482	60 2 .300 .382 .467	7 1 .571 .571 1.000
TOTALS	157 85 1 2170 3.10	90 41 0 1154 2.81	67 44 1 1015 3.42	4465 60 .234 .298 .324	3610 63 .234 .288 .342	3303 47 .236 .291 .325	936 16 .226 .284 .294

● Tom Gordon BR/TR

YEAR TM/L	TOTAL	HOME	AWAY	LEFT	RIGHT	ON-BASE	LATE/CLOSE
1988 KC-A	0 2 0 16 5.17	0 1 0 6 8.53	0 1 0 9 2.89	30 0 .233 .303 .300	30 1 .300 .382 .433	30 1 .300 .382 .467	3 0 .000 .000 .000
1989 KC-A	17 9 1 163 3.64	11 5 0 99 3.38	6 4 1 64 4.06	307 4 .218 .322 .306	275 6 .200 .297 .305	241 4 .274 .381 .382	179 3 .184 .298 .285
1990 KC-A	12 11 0 195 3.73	7 5 0 93 3.10	5 6 0 102 4.31	365 6 .252 .352 .345	380 11 .263 .340 .426	350 5 .229 .313 .317	30 1 .300 .344 .433
1991 KC-A	9 14 1 158 3.87	2 8 1 92 4.00	7 6 0 66 3.70	302 4 .248 .340 .344	283 12 .191 .307 .371	252 5 .187 .322 .298	142 1 .261 .348 .310
1992 KC-A	6 10 0 118 4.59	5 4 0 59 3.36	1 6 0 59 5.83	202 3 .287 .352 .391	247 6 .235 .331 .368	215 5 .260 .332 .381	57 2 .316 .418 .526
1993 KC-A	12 6 1 156 3.58	6 1 1 72 2.38	6 5 0 84 4.63	293 6 .229 .320 .341	268 5 .216 .309 .340	243 6 .222 .316 .358	88 3 .273 .354 .466
1994 KC-A	11 7 0 155 4.35	4 4 0 79 4.33	7 3 0 76 4.36	282 6 .248 .346 .372	292 9 .226 .326 .370	231 9 .238 .359 .398	53 1 .226 .311 .377
TOTALS	67 59 3 961 3.94	35 28 2 500 3.51	32 31 1 460 4.42	1781 29 .245 .338 .346	1775 50 .225 .321 .368	1562 35 .235 .335 .354	552 11 .241 .334 .361

● Jim Gott BR/TR

YEAR TM/L	TOTAL	HOME	AWAY	LEFT	RIGHT	ON-BASE	LATE/CLOSE
1984 Tor-A	7 6 2 110 4.02	5 3 2 71 3.69	2 3 0 39 4.62	183 2 .219 .315 .333	216 5 .245 .320 .403	173 5 .243 .312 .410	71 1 .239 .357 .310
1985 SF-N	7 10 0 148 3.88	4 4 0 78 2.32	3 6 0 71 5.60	294 4 .245 .321 .357	273 6 .264 .307 .399	235 5 .268 .328 .396	25 1 .400 .464 .560
1986 SF-N	0 0 1 13 7.62	0 0 0 7 6.43	0 0 1 9 9.00	29 0 .345 .457 .414	22 0 .273 .433 .273	7 0 .370 .500 .407	7 0 .143 .333 .143
1987 SF-N	1 0 0 56 4.50	0 0 0 19 4.66	1 0 0 37 4.42	98 4 .306 .444 .500	119 0 .193 .256 .218	105 1 .276 .353 .371	14 1 .286 .412 .500
1987 Pit-N	0 2 13 31 1.45	0 1 8 21 1.74	0 1 5 10 0.87	63 0 .254 .309 .286	57 0 .211 .250 .228	69 0 .232 .284 .261	90 0 .233 .281 .267
1988 Pit-N	6 6 34 77 3.49	4 2 17 41 1.99	2 4 17 35 5.15	132 6 .220 .293 .394	148 3 .264 .306 .378	115 1 .296 .354 .400	196 6 .270 .335 .408
1989 Pit-N	0 0 0 1 0.00	0 0 0 1 0.00	0 0 0 0 —	0 0 — — —	3 0 .333 .500 .333	3 0 .333 .500 .333	3 0 .333 .500 .333
1990 LA-N	3 5 3 62 2.90	2 3 1 34 2.88	1 2 2 28 2.93	132 1 .288 .379 .379	98 4 .214 .304 .357	104 3 .269 .375 .375	98 3 .224 .327 .367
1991 LA-N	4 3 2 76 2.96	1 1 0 37 3.65	3 2 2 39 2.31	142 2 .190 .277 .268	140 5 .207 .331 .357	110 1 .200 .331 .364	68 0 .221 .346 .265
1992 LA-N	3 3 6 88 2.45	1 1 2 40 1.79	2 2 4 48 3.02	148 3 .264 .382 .365	172 1 .192 .249 .221	160 1 .200 .303 .244	165 3 .200 .309 .291
1993 LA-N	4 8 25 78 2.32	2 4 12 42 3.19	2 4 13 35 1.27	153 5 .222 .264 .346	175 1 .278 .322 .331	125 4 .264 .329 .368	224 6 .272 .315 .384
1994 LA-N	5 5 1 35 6.35	1 2 1 19 6.16	4 3 0 16 6.63	76 2 .224 .375 .408	81 3 .309 .387 .432	77 1 .373 .440 .467	154 3 .221 .326 .359
TOTALS	40 46 88 776 3.48	23 19 43 401 2.92	17 27 45 375 4.08	1440 28 .248 .336 .363	1458 25 .245 .307 .342	1307 26 .256 .337 .366	1028 22 .256 .335 .359

● Mark Grant BR/TR

YEAR TM/L	TOTAL	HOME	AWAY	LEFT	RIGHT	ON-BASE	LATE/CLOSE
1984 SF-N	1 4 1 54 6.37	1 0 0 20 4.95	0 4 1 34 7.22	97 4 .258 .345 .485	109 2 .284 .319 .431	79 5 .380 .409 .658	13 1 .154 .214 .385
1986 SF-N	0 1 0 10 3.60	0 0 0 2 9.00	0 1 0 8 2.25	22 0 .136 .136 .136	12 0 .250 .471 .250	13 0 .308 .438 .308	3 0 .000 .000 .000

YEAR	TM/L	TOTAL W	L	SV	IP	ERA	HOME W	L	SV	IP	ERA	AWAY W	L	SV	IP	ERA	LEFT AB	HR	AVG	OBP	SLG	RIGHT AB	HR	AVG	OBP	SLG	ON-BASE AB	HR	AVG	OBP	SLG	LATE/CLOSE AB	HR	AVG	OBP	SLG
1987	SF-N	1	2	1	61	3.54	0	2	0	35	3.89	1	0	1	26	3.08	127	3	.331	.403	.465	107	3	.224	.265	.355	97	4	.268	.357	.454	16	1	.438	.471	.750
1987	SD-N	6	7	0	102	4.66	4	3	0	59	3.97	2	4	0	43	5.61	237	4	.224	.313	.342	159	12	.321	.400	.597	19	0	.316	.409	.316
1988	SD-N	2	8	0	98	3.69	1	4	0	39	4.58	1	4	0	58	3.09	180	3	.261	.327	.378	182	11	.275	.342	.500	155	6	.232	.301	.374	56	2	.286	.375	.446
1989	SD-N	8	2	2	116	3.33	3	1	2	54	4.33	5	1	0	62	2.45	199	4	.246	.307	.347	225	7	.249	.300	.409	176	5	.256	.318	.415	96	2	.229	.295	.323
1990	SD-N	1	1	0	39	4.85	0	0	0	22	6.55	1	0	0	17	2.65	68	3	.294	.354	.500	26	0	.423	.483	.615
1990	Atl-N	1	2	3	52	4.64	1	2	0	25	4.97	0	2	1	27	4.33	111	2	.297	.355	.486	97	2	.289	.343	.361	102	4	.363	.422	.569	30	1	.300	.432	.400
1992	Sea-A	2	4	0	81	3.89	1	3	0	38	3.29	1	1	0	43	4.43	149	3	.336	.385	.456	173	3	.289	.333	.428	145	3	.310	.357	.448	23	2	.522	.522	.826
1993	Hou-N	0	0	0	11	0.82	0	0	0	7	0.00	0	0	0	4	2.25	12	0	.250	.286	.250	28	0	.286	.375	.429	21	0	.190	.308	.238	0	0	—	—	—
1993	Col-N	0	1	0	14	12.56	0	1	1	7	13.50	0	0	0	7	11.57	26	0	.462	.517	.538	35	4	.314	.359	.714	27	2	.481	.531	.778	6	0	.167	.375	.167
	TOTALS	22	32	8	639	4.31	11	14	5	306	4.59	11	18	3	333	4.06	1246	25	.276	.345	.406	1195	47	.278	.336	.457	1067	40	.286	.355	.462	288	9	.299	.373	.441

● **Kevin Gross** BR/TR

YEAR	TM/L	W	L	SV	IP	ERA	W	L	SV	IP	ERA	W	L	SV	IP	ERA	AB	HR	AVG	OBP	SLG	AB	HR	AVG	OBP	SLG	AB	HR	AVG	OBP	SLG	AB	HR	AVG	OBP	SLG
1984	Phi-N	8	5	1	129	4.12	5	4	0	71	4.29	3	1	1	58	3.90	251	6	.275	.351	.398	253	2	.281	.328	.372	221	1	.294	.361	.362	59	0	.390	.463	.475
1985	Phi-N	15	13	0	206	3.41	8	4	0	96	2.99	7	9	0	109	3.79	426	4	.242	.329	.354	347	7	.262	.322	.369	327	4	.245	.324	.361	84	0	.310	.398	.405
1986	Phi-N	12	12	0	242	4.02	7	7	0	134	3.56	5	5	0	108	4.60	530	16	.272	.360	.445	393	12	.244	.291	.379	390	7	.264	.338	.379	106	2	.264	.333	.377
1987	Phi-N	9	16	0	201	4.35	5	11	0	119	3.85	4	5	0	81	5.09	428	12	.280	.370	.432	339	14	.251	.316	.425	355	3	.245	.312	.341	52	3	.269	.345	.500
1988	Phi-N	12	14	0	232	3.69	6	6	0	114	3.64	6	8	0	118	3.74	491	10	.255	.349	.383	385	8	.218	.270	.325	357	4	.255	.335	.350	77	3	.234	.294	.390
1989	Mon-N	11	12	0	201	4.38	6	4	0	94	4.29	5	8	0	107	4.46	415	10	.241	.337	.378	345	10	.255	.319	.400	318	9	.242	.342	.409	50	1	.240	.269	.300
1990	Mon-N	9	12	0	163	4.57	3	5	0	69	4.43	6	7	0	94	4.67	369	7	.255	.373	.415	259	2	.239	.291	.301	270	3	.274	.357	.370	33	1	.364	.378	.515
1991	LA-N	10	11	3	116	3.58	7	3	1	61	2.79	3	8	2	54	4.47	233	4	.313	.398	.446	214	4	.234	.291	.308	181	2	.304	.387	.381	109	2	.294	.369	.385
1992	LA-N	8	13	0	205	3.17	4	5	0	113	3.35	4	8	0	92	2.95	409	5	.276	.356	.389	347	6	.199	.255	.277	319	5	.241	.309	.351	100	1	.270	.330	.340
1993	LA-N	13	13	0	202	4.14	8	5	0	109	3.29	5	8	0	93	5.13	394	7	.277	.363	.360	401	8	.287	.325	.397	369	3	.282	.339	.344	39	0	.282	.396	.359
1994	LA-N	9	7	1	157	3.60	4	3	1	76	3.07	5	4	0	81	4.11	323	4	.272	.344	.412	292	3	.253	.276	.325	261	6	.280	.327	.391	69	0	.319	.347	.333
	TOTALS	116	128	5	2053	3.91	64	61	2	1058	3.59	52	67	3	995	4.25	4269	91	.270	.356	.400	3575	76	.248	.299	.356	3368	47	.263	.336	.366	778	13	.289	.355	.389

● **Cecilio Guante** BR/TR

YEAR	TM/L	W	L	SV	IP	ERA	W	L	SV	IP	ERA	W	L	SV	IP	ERA	AB	HR	AVG	OBP	SLG	AB	HR	AVG	OBP	SLG	AB	HR	AVG	OBP	SLG	AB	HR	AVG	OBP	SLG
1984	Pit-N	2	3	2	41	2.61	1	0	0	15	1.76	1	3	2	26	3.12	63	2	.286	.343	.492	80	1	.175	.277	.262	53	2	.208	.286	.434	81	2	.259	.371	.420
1985	Pit-N	4	6	5	109	2.72	2	0	3	56	2.25	2	6	2	53	3.23	152	3	.289	.394	.447	241	2	.166	.222	.253	163	2	.196	.298	.313	186	3	.220	.310	.328
1986	Pit-N	5	2	4	78	3.35	1	1	3	43	3.35	4	1	1	35	3.34	119	2	.185	.292	.286	170	9	.253	.306	.476	138	7	.268	.322	.471	120	3	.175	.263	.300
1987	NY-A	3	2	1	44	5.73	3	0	1	30	4.15	0	2	0	14	9.22	76	4	.237	.337	.447	94	4	.255	.311	.468	90	4	.233	.291	.400	49	3	.224	.283	.429
1988	NY-A	5	6	11	75	2.88	4	1	5	37	2.68	1	5	6	38	3.08	126	3	.238	.319	.357	151	7	.192	.250	.391	136	4	.199	.276	.331	137	5	.168	.245	.307
1988	Tex-A	0	0	1	5	1.93	0	0	1	3	0.00	0	0	0	2	4.50	8	0	.125	.300	.125	12	1	.583	.643	.917	12	0	.333	.467	.417	8	0	.375	.444	.500
1989	Tex-A	6	6	2	69	3.91	5	3	1	40	2.95	1	3	1	29	5.22	86	5	.256	.414	.488	179	2	.246	.303	.335	132	2	.265	.369	.356	105	2	.248	.347	.362
1990	Cle-A	2	3	0	47	5.01	1	0	0	30	5.70	1	0	0	17	3.78	71	4	.183	.284	.394	102	6	.245	.313	.480	65	2	.277	.355	.446	37	2	.297	.357	.486
	TOTALS	27	28	26	468	3.52	17	8	14	254	3.19	10	20	12	214	3.92	701	23	.240	.344	.404	1029	32	.220	.281	.372	789	23	.234	.317	.381	723	20	.217	.305	.351

● **Mark Gubicza** BR/TR

YEAR	TM/L	W	L	SV	IP	ERA	W	L	SV	IP	ERA	W	L	SV	IP	ERA	AB	HR	AVG	OBP	SLG	AB	HR	AVG	OBP	SLG	AB	HR	AVG	OBP	SLG	AB	HR	AVG	OBP	SLG
1984	KC-A	10	14	0	189	4.05	8	8	0	134	3.01	2	6	0	55	6.59	364	9	.239	.323	.376	343	4	.248	.310	.338	306	6	.255	.319	.359	50	1	.260	.339	.380
1985	KC-A	14	10	0	177	4.06	7	5	0	86	3.47	7	5	0	92	4.61	379	9	.253	.329	.391	292	5	.219	.305	.339	270	4	.248	.330	.363	48	2	.271	.352	.438
1986	KC-A	12	6	0	181	3.64	8	4	0	118	2.91	4	2	0	63	5.00	352	4	.247	.345	.332	312	4	.218	.292	.317	296	2	.250	.324	.324	53	1	.226	.388	.358
1987	KC-A	13	18	0	242	3.98	7	10	0	122	3.75	6	8	0	119	4.22	512	10	.260	.350	.385	381	8	.257	.342	.383	380	11	.242	.334	.376	70	2	.329	.400	.457
1988	KC-A	20	8	0	270	2.70	8	4	0	141	2.99	12	3	0	128	2.38	523	7	.252	.318	.340	489	4	.215	.269	.299	426	4	.232	.275	.305	139	2	.252	.320	.381
1989	KC-A	15	11	0	255	3.04	8	6	0	142	3.17	7	5	0	113	2.87	513	4	.246	.299	.320	460	6	.274	.312	.370	394	5	.249	.309	.338	125	0	.240	.267	.312
1990	KC-A	4	7	0	94	4.50	3	2	0	38	5.45	1	5	0	56	3.86	158	3	.266	.371	.367	199	2	.246	.341	.407	174	3	.264	.330	.348	23	0	.261	.320	.348
1991	KC-A	9	12	0	133	5.68	4	6	0	66	5.21	5	6	0	67	6.15	258	3	.326	.394	.438	287	7	.293	.330	.411	251	5	.343	.384	.462	11	0	.091	.167	.091
1992	KC-A	7	6	0	111	3.72	5	2	0	69	2.88	2	4	0	43	5.06	215	5	.228	.285	.363	210	3	.290	.348	.386	172	2	.291	.346	.395	40	2	.250	.354	.425
1993	KC-A	5	8	2	104	4.66	4	4	2	61	5.02	1	4	0	43	4.15	190	1	.311	.382	.411	227	1	.304	.359	.379	217	2	.300	.363	.419	144	0	.292	.382	.354
1994	KC-A	7	9	0	130	4.50	5	3	0	75	4.34	2	6	0	55	4.72	261	4	.291	.326	.418	264	7	.311	.336	.451	209	5	.354	.383	.507	18	0	.389	.480	.389
	TOTALS	116	109	2	1886	3.86	67	55	2	1051	3.57	49	54	0	835	4.22	3725	59	.261	.334	.370	3464	51	.260	.317	.364	3095	49	.268	.330	.373	721	10	.266	.346	.370

● **Lee Guetterman** BL/TL

YEAR	TM/L	W	L	SV	IP	ERA	W	L	SV	IP	ERA	W	L	SV	IP	ERA	AB	HR	AVG	OBP	SLG	AB	HR	AVG	OBP	SLG	AB	HR	AVG	OBP	SLG	AB	HR	AVG	OBP	SLG
1984	Sea-A	0	0	0	4	4.15	0	0	0	2	7.71	0	0	0	2	0.00	6	0	.333	.333	.333	14	0	.500	.563	.500	15	0	.333	.375	.333	1	0	1.000	1.000	1.000
1986	Sea-A	0	4	0	76	7.34	0	3	0	40	8.26	0	1	0	36	6.31	102	2	.333	.404	.471	209	5	.354	.407	.498	164	7	.372	.429	.585	30	1	.433	.526	.567
1987	Sea-A	11	4	0	113	3.81	6	0	0	54	3.64	5	4	0	59	3.97	75	0	.160	.220	.213	364	13	.288	.341	.462	179	4	.268	.327	.408	6	0	.167	.250	.167
1988	NY-A	1	2	0	41	4.65	1	1	0	24	6.00	0	1	0	17	2.70	47	0	.277	.358	.340	113	2	.319	.366	.460	83	0	.265	.354	.349	28	1	.321	.367	.464
1989	NY-A	5	5	13	103	2.45	3	2	8	59	2.30	2	4	5	44	2.64	106	1	.236	.289	.283	274	5	.266	.310	.358	192	3	.260	.318	.349	171	3	.281	.320	.363
1990	NY-A	11	7	2	93	3.39	9	4	1	58	2.64	2	3	1	35	4.63	99	1	.242	.306	.354	240	5	.233	.281	.338	151	4	.225	.298	.351	211	5	.251	.310	.379
1991	NY-A	3	4	6	88	3.68	2	1	4	52	4.18	1	3	2	36	2.97	97	2	.175	.250	.289	243	4	.305	.348	.428	160	3	.250	.311	.356	120	4	.292	.331	.433
1992	NY-A	1	1	0	23	9.53	1	1	0	11	14.73	0	0	0	12	4.63	30	1	.233	.343	.333	69	1	.406	.456	.710	50	3	.400	.467	.740	22	2	.318	.400	.591
1992	NY-N	3	4	2	43	5.82	2	3	1	24	5.55	1	1	1	19	6.16	41	1	.300	.358	.367	116	4	.336	.378	.526	83	2	.289	.354	.446	89	5	.326	.376	.539
1993	StL-N	3	3	1	46	2.93	1	0	0	22	2.49	0	2	1	24	3.33	47	1	.234	.345	.298	124	0	.242	.294	.339	91	0	.253	.346	.330	79	1	.228	.291	.342
	TOTALS	38	34	24	630	4.27	27	15	14	346	4.47	11	19	10	284	4.02	669	8	.244	.314	.336	1766	43	.296	.344	.434	1168	26	.280	.346	.414	757	22	.283	.337	.415

● **Ron Guidry** BL/TL

YEAR	TM/L	W	L	SV	IP	ERA	W	L	SV	IP	ERA	W	L	SV	IP	ERA	AB	HR	AVG	OBP	SLG	AB	HR	AVG	OBP	SLG	AB	HR	AVG	OBP	SLG	AB	HR	AVG	OBP	SLG
1984	NY-A	10	11	0	196	4.51	8	2	0	101	2.93	2	9	0	94	6.20	131	2	.305	.313	.420	646	22	.283	.324	.461	348	10	.279	.303	.445	70	1	.386	.400	.514
1985	NY-A	22	6	0	259	3.27	13	2	0	137	2.82	9	4	0	122	3.77	184	8	.212	.241	.348	796	20	.256	.285	.402	361	12	.247	.271	.410	115	2	.287	.305	.391
1986	NY-A	9	12	0	192	3.98	6	8	0	121	4.39	3	4	0	71	3.28	137	4	.248	.290	.394	624	24	.269	.302	.431	290	9	.276	.312	.428	76	4	.263	.317	.487
1987	NY-A	5	8	0	118	3.67	2	4	0	59	2.58	3	4	0	58	4.78	86	3	.302	.362	.453	362	11	.235	.294	.409	176	3	.244	.289	.386	42	2	.333	.378	.571
1988	NY-A	2	3	0	56	4.18	1	1	0	17	2.65	1	2	0	39	4.85	49	2	.265	.294	.449	171	5	.257	.316	.456	94	4	.213	.272	.436	0	0	—	—	—
	TOTALS	48	40	0	821	3.85	30	17	0	436	3.24	18	23	0	385	4.54	587	19	.259	.291	.399	2599	82	.263	.302	.428	1269	38	.259	.292	.422	303	9	.310	.341	.469

● **Bill Gullickson** BR/TR

YEAR	TM/L	W	L	SV	IP	ERA	W	L	SV	IP	ERA	W	L	SV	IP	ERA	AB	HR	AVG	OBP	SLG	AB	HR	AVG	OBP	SLG	AB	HR	AVG	OBP	SLG	AB	HR	AVG	OBP	SLG
1984	Mon-N	12	9	0	227	3.61	7	3	0	123	3.15	5	6	0	104	4.17	445	13	.261	.291	.429	424	14	.269	.298	.443	293	8	.287	.328	.454	117	2	.256	.304	.342
1985	Mon-N	14	12	0	181	3.52	10	2	0	98	1.65	4	10	0	83	5.75	362	3	.282	.338	.362	329	5	.258	.288	.365	288	3	.267	.322	.372	55	0	.255	.328	.327
1986	Cin-N	15	12	0	245	3.38	9	6	0	124	3.70	6	6	0	121	3.06	484	10	.275	.329	.399	443	14	.253	.281	.384	365	7	.268	.295	.364	99	0	.192	.236	.232
1987	Cin-N	10	11	0	165	4.85	5	5	0	77	5.63	5	6	0	88	4.18	336	17	.262	.305	.479	309	14	.272	.311	.495	243	11	.272	.307	.494	30	0	.300	.323	.367
1987	NY-A	1	1	0	48	4.88	4	1	0	39	4.66	0	1	0	9	5.79	106	7	.283	.336	.528	76	0	.211	.237	.276	55	0	.327	.391	.418	9	1	.333	.409	.833
1990	Hou-N	10	14	0	193	3.82	8	7	0	114	3.94	2	7	0	79	3.65	468	11	.314	.337	.453	301	10	.246	.285	.422	330	8	.282	.332	.424	32	2	.375	.417	.594
1991	Det-A	20	9	0	226	3.90	10	4	0	104	4.95	10	5	0	123	3.01	487	15	.275	.312	.444	403	9	.303	.333	.424	347	9	.300	.341	.450	72	1	.306	.367	.431
1992	Det-A	14	13	0	222	4.34	6	9	0	130	4.28	8	4	0	91	4.43	414	18	.280	.322	.473	439	17	.255	.288	.421	313	16	.246	.284	.444	78	4	.308	.353	.487
1993	Det-A	13	9	0	159	5.37	7	7	0	95	5.02	6	2	0	64	5.88	316	13	.329	.373	.554	323	15	.254	.300	.440	265	8	.279	.329	.453	32	2	.333	.389	.576
1994	Det-A	4	5	0	115	5.93	3	2	0	67	4.01	1	3	0	48	8.63	245	10	.335	.379	.543	239	14	.310	.340	.561	205	15	.341	.387	.639	22	0	.273	.273	.273
	TOTALS	116	96	0	1782	4.18	69	46	0	971	4.00	47	50	0	810	4.39	3663	117	.287	.333	.454	3286	112	.266	.300	.429	2704	84	.281	.324	.445	544	12	.274	.323	.386

● **Mark Guthrie** BB/TR

YEAR	TM/L	W	L	SV	IP	ERA	W	L	SV	IP	ERA	W	L	SV	IP	ERA	AB	HR	AVG	OBP	SLG	AB	HR	AVG	OBP	SLG	AB	HR	AVG	OBP	SLG	AB	HR	AVG	OBP	SLG
1989	Min-A	2	4	0	57	4.55	2	1	0	33	3.03	0	3	0	25	6.57	44	2	.295	.333	.477	182	5	.291	.351	.434	98	5	.255	.304	.408	16	0	.500	.579	.563
1990	Min-A	7	9	0	145	3.79	2	4	0	69	3.93	5	5	0	76	3.67	99	1	.343	.363	.414	458	7	.262	.317	.360	226	5	.288	.329	.398	57	1	.351	.393	.544
1991	Min-A	7	5	2	98	4.32	1	4	1	45	6.25	6	1	1	53	2.70	86	4	.337	.383	.500	297	7	.293	.365	.455	186	5	.237	.303	.376	52	3	.288	.339	.519
1992	Min-A	2	3	5	75	2.88	1	2	3	36	2.02	1	1	2	39	3.66	88	0	.205	.242	.261	186	7	.220	.289	.349	125	2	.192	.280	.256	96	1	.208	.280	.292
1993	Min-A	2	1	0	21	4.71	1	0	0	12	5.11	1	1	0	9	4.15	27	0	.148	.233	.185	48	1	.333	.460	.521	44	1	.250	.364	.364	41	2	.244	.396	.415
1994	Min-A	4	2	1	51	6.14	3	1	0	22	3.68	1	1	1	29	7.98	67	1	.284	.363	.433	139	7	.331	.368	.640	113	4	.283	.336	.540	64	2	.313	.319	.547
	TOTALS	24	24	8	447	4.16	11	10	5	216	4.00	13	14	3	231	4.32	411	8	.285	.330	.394	1310	35	.277	.341	.426	792	20	.254	.315	.390	326	9	.285	.348	.451

● **Jose Guzman** BR/TR

YEAR	TM/L	W	L	SV	IP	ERA	W	L	SV	IP	ERA	W	L	SV	IP	ERA	AB	HR	AVG	OBP	SLG	AB	HR	AVG	OBP	SLG	AB	HR	AVG	OBP	SLG	AB	HR	AVG	OBP	SLG
1985	Tex-A	3	2	0	33	2.76	3	0	0	23	0.79	0	2	0	10	7.20	70	2	.229	.270	.357	56	1	.196	.318	.286	48	2	.167	.245	.313	10	0	.300	.364	.300
1986	Tex-A	9	15	0	172	4.54	6	7	0	103	3.92	3	8	0	69	5.48	374	15	.290	.367	.480	305	10	.272	.336	.403	272	9	.290	.377	.445	51	1	.311	.404	.444
1987	Tex-A	14	14	0	208	4.67	9	9	0	108	4.98	5	5	0	100	4.32	408	11	.240	.300	.363	373	19	.263	.344	.483	305	14	.285	.339	.469	42	1	.256	.291	.404
1988	Tex-A	11	13	0	207	3.70	6	7	0	115	3.14	5	6	0	92	4.40	375	8	.205	.286	.312	404	12	.255	.325	.403	307	9	.241	.319	.381	100	3	.210	.295	.350
1991	Tex-A	13	7	0	170	3.08	5	3	0	61	3.86	8	4	0	109	2.64	283	2	.214	.316	.304	349	8	.270	.336	.383	262	5	.282	.345	.393	67	1	.209	.274	.328
1992	Tex-A	16	11	0	224	3.66	4	5	0	103	4.28	12	6	0	121	3.12	399	4	.278	.323	.395	454	12	.260	.330	.390	360	2	.250	.301	.331	40	0	.313	.345	.325
1993	Chi-N	12	10	0	191	4.34	8	5	0	115	4.32	4	5	0	76	4.36	396	16	.273	.345	.475	333	9	.240	.295	.372	273	9	.286	.367	.458	40	2	.225	.333	.275
1994	Chi-N	2	2	0	20	9.15	1	1	0	8	9.72	1	1	0	11	8.74	32	0	.344	.523	.406	44	1	.250	.277	.409	32	1	.375	.512	.594	40	2	.225	.333	.275
	TOTALS	80	74	0	1224	4.05	44	39	0	636	4.05	36	35	0	588	4.05	2338	62	.259	.329	.401	2322	67	.253	.325	.394	1877	49	.260	.336	.396	394	6	.251	.320	.350

		TOTAL					HOME					AWAY					LEFT					RIGHT					ON-BASE					LATE/CLOSE				
YEAR	TM/L	W	L	SV	IP	ERA	W	L	SV	IP	ERA	W	L	SV	IP	ERA	AB	HR	AVG	OBP	SLG	AB	HR	AVG	OBP	SLG	AB	HR	AVG	OBP	SLG	AB	HR	AVG	OBP	SLG

● John Habyan BR/TR

YEAR	TM/L	W	L	SV	IP	ERA	W	L	SV	IP	ERA	W	L	SV	IP	ERA	AB	HR	AVG	OBP	SLG	AB	HR	AVG	OBP	SLG	AB	HR	AVG	OBP	SLG	AB	HR	AVG	OBP	SLG
1985	Bal-A	1	0	0	3	0.00	1	0	0	2	0.00	0	0	0	1	0.00	5	0	.200	.200	.200	7	0	.286	.286	.286	8	0	.125	.125	.125	1	0	.000	.000	.000
1986	Bal-A	1	3	0	26	4.44	1	0	0	20	3.60	0	3	0	6	7.11	42	0	.286	.412	.381	54	3	.222	.328	.444	37	1	.216	.388	.378	8	1	.250	.250	.625
1987	Bal-A	6	7	1	116	4.80	3	5	0	57	6.00	3	2	1	59	3.64	256	9	.254	.318	.441	187	11	.241	.301	.455	151	5	.238	.339	.397	31	2	.194	.188	.387
1988	Bal-A	1	0	0	15	4.30	0	0	0	5	5.06	1	0	0	9	3.86	28	1	.250	.267	.429	34	1	.441	.474	.647	39	1	.333	.364	.538	1	0	1.000	1.000	1.000
1990	NY-A	0	0	0	9	2.08	0	0	0	2	3.86	0	0	0	6	1.42	21	0	.333	.364	.524	13	0	.231	.333	.385	18	0	.222	.300	.444	3	0	.333	.600	1.000
1991	NY-A	4	2	2	90	2.30	3	0	2	47	1.33	1	2	0	43	3.38	114	0	.272	.306	.351	210	2	.200	.257	.295	144	1	.243	.295	.361	148	1	.250	.297	.324
1992	NY-A	5	6	7	73	3.84	5	3	3	37	4.17	0	3	4	36	3.50	118	2	.339	.388	.449	167	4	.263	.313	.395	139	3	.309	.365	.402	189	4	.296	.343	.402
1993	NY-A	2	1	1	42	4.04	2	0	1	21	2.11	0	1	0	21	6.00	57	3	.263	.313	.509	106	2	.283	.350	.396	82	4	.329	.394	.524	71	3	.296	.338	.493
1993	KC-A	0	0	0	14	4.50	0	0	0	7	3.86	0	0	0	7	5.14	21	0	.190	.190	.333	33	1	.303	.378	.455	26	1	.269	.321	.462	4	0	.250	.250	.500
1994	StL-N	1	0	1	47	3.23	1	0	1	26	2.08	0	0	0	21	4.64	67	1	.313	.403	.493	115	1	.252	.312	.365	99	2	.263	.371	.434	49	0	.265	.368	.306
TOTALS		21	19	12	435	3.74	16	8	7	225	3.52	5	11	5	210	3.99	729	16	.278	.336	.412	925	25	.251	.312	.394	743	18	.269	.347	.412	505	11	.273	.324	.390

● Erik Hanson BR/TR

YEAR	TM/L	W	L	SV	IP	ERA	W	L	SV	IP	ERA	W	L	SV	IP	ERA	AB	HR	AVG	OBP	SLG	AB	HR	AVG	OBP	SLG	AB	HR	AVG	OBP	SLG	AB	HR	AVG	OBP	SLG
1988	Sea-A	2	3	0	42	3.24	0	2	0	21	5.14	2	1	0	21	1.31	70	1	.271	.338	.357	82	3	.195	.250	.415	55	1	.255	.305	.382	18	0	.222	.263	.278
1989	Sea-A	9	5	0	113	3.18	5	2	0	58	3.57	4	3	0	55	2.77	226	2	.212	.267	.283	197	5	.279	.344	.396	156	2	.282	.351	.397	39	0	.231	.302	.282
1990	Sea-A	18	9	0	236	3.24	7	6	0	111	3.56	11	3	0	125	2.96	465	5	.222	.283	.308	418	10	.244	.291	.359	327	6	.251	.312	.367	78	1	.192	.229	.282
1991	Sea-A	8	8	0	175	3.81	4	5	0	89	4.25	4	3	0	86	3.36	355	10	.239	.275	.411	321	6	.302	.374	.417	277	6	.267	.324	.404	63	0	.238	.315	.302
1992	Sea-A	8	17	0	187	4.82	6	6	0	90	4.78	2	11	0	96	4.86	365	5	.241	.291	.329	363	9	.333	.390	.477	290	7	.328	.391	.479	53	2	.283	.333	.453
1993	Sea-A	11	12	0	215	3.47	6	5	0	119	2.79	5	7	0	96	4.33	425	4	.231	.285	.327	394	13	.297	.348	.482	313	8	.272	.333	.399	80	5	.325	.389	.650
1994	Cin-N	5	5	0	123	4.11	1	1	0	50	3.58	4	4	0	72	4.48	222	6	.275	.317	.419	262	3	.290	.318	.397	201	3	.303	.336	.398	18	0	.222	.263	.222
TOTALS		61	59	0	1090	3.74	29	27	0	539	3.77	32	32	0	551	3.71	2128	33	.236	.287	.343	2037	50	.287	.340	.424	1619	33	.281	.339	.407	349	8	.252	.310	.393

● Pete Harnisch BB/TR

YEAR	TM/L	W	L	SV	IP	ERA	W	L	SV	IP	ERA	W	L	SV	IP	ERA	AB	HR	AVG	OBP	SLG	AB	HR	AVG	OBP	SLG	AB	HR	AVG	OBP	SLG	AB	HR	AVG	OBP	SLG
1988	Bal-A	0	2	0	13	5.54	0	0	0	0	—	0	2	0	13	5.54	16	1	.188	.350	.313	34	1	.294	.385	.441	28	1	.286	.394	.464	0	0	—	—	—
1989	Bal-A	5	9	0	103	4.62	3	1	0	34	3.41	2	8	0	69	5.22	183	3	.257	.390	.377	207	7	.242	.328	.391	173	3	.254	.362	.376	25	1	.240	.345	.360
1990	Bal-A	11	11	0	189	4.34	7	6	0	89	4.63	4	5	0	99	4.08	435	10	.287	.358	.439	288	7	.222	.310	.326	306	9	.288	.354	.441	48	2	.250	.368	.458
1991	Hou-N	12	9	0	217	2.70	7	4	0	119	2.41	5	5	0	97	3.05	457	10	.234	.319	.352	339	4	.183	.247	.260	331	3	.202	.281	.272	83	0	.133	.232	.181
1992	Hou-N	9	10	0	207	3.70	7	4	0	138	2.75	2	6	0	69	5.61	466	10	.234	.300	.365	313	8	.233	.285	.380	295	8	.261	.322	.420	53	1	.245	.293	.396
1993	Hou-N	16	9	0	218	2.98	9	5	0	129	2.52	7	4	0	89	3.64	429	13	.238	.327	.375	369	7	.187	.241	.298	314	6	.229	.299	.344	48	2	.167	.231	.333
1994	Hou-N	8	5	0	95	5.40	5	3	0	59	5.49	3	2	0	36	5.25	168	4	.274	.349	.440	204	9	.265	.335	.441	155	5	.290	.367	.458	14	0	.071	.071	.071
TOTALS		61	55	0	1041	3.73	38	23	0	568	3.25	23	32	0	473	4.30	2154	50	.250	.333	.386	1754	43	.218	.286	.340	1602	35	.250	.325	.378	271	6	.188	.272	.310

● Greg Harris BB/TR

YEAR	TM/L	W	L	SV	IP	ERA	W	L	SV	IP	ERA	W	L	SV	IP	ERA	AB	HR	AVG	OBP	SLG	AB	HR	AVG	OBP	SLG	AB	HR	AVG	OBP	SLG	AB	HR	AVG	OBP	SLG
1984	Mon-N	0	1	2	18	2.04	0	1	0	5	1.69	0	0	2	12	2.19	26	0	.192	.344	.231	32	0	.156	.229	.188	24	0	.167	.286	.167	16	0	.125	.222	.188
1984	SD-N	2	1	1	37	2.70	0	0	0	11	3.27	2	1	1	26	2.45	59	2	.237	.313	.390	75	1	.187	.300	.307	58	3	.207	.290	.414	8	0	.125	.333	.125
1985	Tex-A	5	4	11	113	2.47	4	2	3	57	2.68	1	2	8	56	2.25	206	4	.175	.257	.286	191	3	.199	.290	.293	159	4	.214	.298	.352	173	5	.202	.287	.329
1986	Tex-A	10	8	20	111	2.83	9	4	13	65	2.64	1	4	7	47	3.09	179	5	.251	.335	.397	211	7	.251	.340	.407	214	7	.238	.307	.393	243	8	.226	.296	.383
1987	Tex-A	5	10	0	141	4.86	3	2	0	81	4.65	2	8	0	59	5.16	270	4	.256	.319	.363	289	14	.304	.377	.512	251	10	.303	.367	.498	72	4	.319	.405	.569
1988	Phi-N	4	6	1	107	2.36	1	6	1	58	2.18	3	0	0	49	2.55	182	3	.209	.316	.302	200	4	.210	.303	.300	181	1	.193	.315	.238	131	4	.214	.293	.336
1989	Phi-N	2	2	1	75	3.58	1	1	1	41	5.01	1	1	0	34	1.85	121	1	.190	.329	.281	153	6	.268	.349	.438	134	2	.246	.340	.328	30	0	.267	.405	.300
1989	Bos-A	2	2	0	28	2.57	1	1	0	9	1.00	1	2	0	19	3.32	56	1	.196	.297	.304	45	0	.222	.321	.267	40	0	.250	.354	.300	39	0	.256	.341	.308
1990	Bos-A	13	9	0	184	4.00	8	5	0	89	4.45	5	4	0	95	3.59	352	5	.239	.312	.338	351	8	.291	.364	.425	286	3	.280	.364	.360	50	0	.240	.304	.280
1991	Bos-A	11	12	2	173	3.85	4	2	1	71	3.80	7	6	0	102	3.88	303	5	.244	.322	.353	342	8	.243	.314	.377	271	7	.266	.330	.413	121	1	.190	.305	.264
1992	Bos-A	4	9	4	108	2.51	3	1	3	58	2.79	1	8	1	50	2.17	142	2	.211	.335	.303	240	4	.217	.317	.317	189	2	.217	.332	.312	164	2	.207	.330	.274
1993	Bos-A	6	7	8	112	3.77	3	5	5	55	4.77	3	2	3	58	2.81	198	2	.253	.353	.348	212	5	.212	.329	.311	216	5	.255	.370	.370	231	3	.260	.356	.355
1994	Bos-A	3	4	2	46	8.28	1	1	1	29	7.53	2	3	1	17	9.53	85	1	.282	.390	.380	102	7	.353	.402	.618	101	5	.376	.448	.604	80	1	.262	.344	.338
1994	NY-A	1	3	0	24	3.75	0	1	0	5	5.40	1	2	0	19	3.32	9	0	.333	.455	.444	9	1	.111	.308	.444	11	1	.273	.400	.636	4	1	.250	.400	1.000
TOTALS		67	76	52	1258	3.59	38	35	29	634	3.82	29	41	23	624	3.35	2188	35	.231	.322	.337	2472	68	.249	.331	.385	2135	50	.255	.343	.381	1362	29	.230	.322	.341

● Greg Harris BR/TR

YEAR	TM/L	W	L	SV	IP	ERA	W	L	SV	IP	ERA	W	L	SV	IP	ERA	AB	HR	AVG	OBP	SLG	AB	HR	AVG	OBP	SLG	AB	HR	AVG	OBP	SLG	AB	HR	AVG	OBP	SLG
1988	SD-N	2	0	0	18	1.50	1	0	0	9	1.00	1	0	0	9	2.00	42	0	.238	.256	.286	23	0	.130	.200	.174	25	0	.200	.231	.240	2	0	.000	.000	.000
1989	SD-N	8	9	6	135	2.60	6	4	1	61	2.36	2	5	5	74	2.80	281	2	.196	.276	.253	212	6	.241	.312	.358	173	2	.249	.365	.324	176	1	.210	.303	.256
1990	SD-N	8	8	9	117	2.30	4	4	3	56	2.10	4	4	6	62	2.48	220	2	.277	.355	.364	199	4	.156	.246	.251	196	1	.230	.319	.311	259	2	.216	.317	.286
1991	SD-N	9	5	0	133	2.23	5	2	0	73	1.85	4	3	0	60	2.70	309	12	.252	.288	.398	189	4	.201	.248	.307	170	6	.212	.265	.341	81	0	.148	.216	.185
1992	SD-N	4	8	0	118	4.12	2	3	0	62	3.36	2	5	0	56	4.95	287	11	.279	.330	.436	161	2	.255	.267	.292	166	7	.235	.319	.380	30	1	.200	.250	.300
1993	SD-N	10	9	0	152	3.67	5	3	0	82	2.95	5	6	0	70	4.52	317	9	.252	.305	.394	270	9	.263	.307	.430	215	5	.228	.309	.353	45	2	.267	.267	.444
1993	Col-N	1	8	0	73	6.50	1	4	0	38	5.26	0	4	0	36	7.82	148	7	.311	.382	.514	146	8	.288	.358	.575	150	6	.323	.400	.592	20	1	.350	.458	.600
1994	Col-N	3	12	1	130	6.65	1	7	0	70	7.20	2	5	1	60	6.00	259	15	.301	.372	.556	254	7	.299	.360	.488	212	15	.302	.377	.585	42	1	.310	.362	.452
TOTALS		45	59	16	877	3.80	25	27	4	450	3.46	20	32	12	426	4.16	1863	58	.262	.321	.406	1454	40	.237	.300	.384	1287	42	.251	.333	.405	655	8	.218	.302	.296

● Bryan Harvey BR/TR

YEAR	TM/L	W	L	SV	IP	ERA	W	L	SV	IP	ERA	W	L	SV	IP	ERA	AB	HR	AVG	OBP	SLG	AB	HR	AVG	OBP	SLG	AB	HR	AVG	OBP	SLG	AB	HR	AVG	OBP	SLG
1987	Cal-A	0	0	0	5	0.00	0	0	0	3	0.00	0	0	0	2	0.00	10	0	.400	.500	.500	10	0	.200	.200	.200	13	0	.231	.286	.308	0	0	—	—	—
1988	Cal-A	7	5	17	76	2.13	3	4	6	41	1.96	4	1	11	35	2.34	143	0	.147	.212	.217	133	2	.286	.326	.376	135	1	.200	.265	.274	195	4	.215	.274	.313
1989	Cal-A	3	3	25	55	3.44	2	0	16	32	2.56	1	3	9	23	4.63	100	1	.160	.303	.280	97	2	.206	.339	.320	104	2	.183	.351	.269	134	4	.194	.341	.299
1990	Cal-A	4	4	25	64	3.22	3	1	10	36	4.00	1	3	15	28	2.22	106	1	.208	.331	.292	118	3	.195	.278	.297	109	2	.211	.338	.339	135	3	.200	.309	.304
1991	Cal-A	2	4	46	79	1.60	2	2	22	39	2.06	0	2	24	39	1.14	164	1	.183	.233	.293	122	2	.172	.215	.230	136	2	.154	.220	.221	214	4	.187	.245	.271
1992	Cal-A	0	4	13	29	2.83	0	3	6	15	3.07	0	1	7	14	2.57	58	2	.172	.222	.293	48	2	.250	.333	.396	53	0	.151	.213	.170	81	2	.222	.283	.309
1993	Fla-N	1	5	45	69	1.70	1	1	24	41	1.11	0	4	21	28	2.54	121	4	.132	.191	.140	121	3	.240	.254	.339	114	2	.175	.200	.237	207	3	.174	.213	.222
1994	Fla-N	0	0	6	10	5.23	0	0	1	3	9.00	0	0	5	7	3.68	23	0	.348	.423	.391	20	1	.400	.471	.467	15	0	.400	.471	.467	24	0	.333	.360	.375
TOTALS		17	25	177	387	2.42	11	11	85	210	2.40	6	14	92	177	2.44	725	12	.175	.257	.257	669	17	.223	.284	.318	679	9	.187	.274	.264	990	20	.199	.273	.283

● Andy Hawkins BR/TR

YEAR	TM/L	W	L	SV	IP	ERA	W	L	SV	IP	ERA	W	L	SV	IP	ERA	AB	HR	AVG	OBP	SLG	AB	HR	AVG	OBP	SLG	AB	HR	AVG	OBP	SLG	AB	HR	AVG	OBP	SLG
1984	SD-N	8	9	0	146	4.68	5	5	0	92	4.03	3	4	0	54	5.80	262	10	.286	.381	.469	298	5	.228	.302	.299	244	6	.262	.370	.369	59	2	.203	.294	.356
1985	SD-N	18	8	0	229	3.15	10	6	0	126	3.14	8	2	0	103	3.16	414	4	.268	.331	.401	445	9	.265	.304	.389	330	4	.248	.318	.339	86	5	.302	.390	.535
1986	SD-N	10	8	0	209	4.30	6	2	0	108	3.07	4	6	0	101	5.61	405	11	.323	.384	.462	407	13	.214	.279	.361	336	13	.274	.349	.446	46	2	.348	.412	.565
1987	SD-N	3	10	0	118	5.05	1	5	0	58	5.55	2	5	0	59	4.55	231	7	.333	.414	.511	226	9	.239	.292	.425	202	5	.248	.320	.391	15	1	.267	.421	.600
1988	SD-N	14	11	0	218	3.35	8	6	0	132	2.53	6	5	0	86	4.60	421	4	.259	.355	.347	383	12	.267	.260	.352	297	6	.249	.324	.346	95	0	.263	.369	.337
1989	NY-A	15	15	0	208	4.80	9	10	0	125	4.54	6	5	0	83	5.18	436	14	.323	.397	.534	384	5	.253	.302	.375	327	7	.321	.394	.465	48	3	.479	.527	.854
1990	NY-A	5	12	0	158	5.37	2	8	0	89	5.44	3	4	0	68	5.27	313	8	.294	.398	.431	286	12	.224	.291	.409	251	10	.279	.369	.450	63	1	.143	.289	.206
1991	NY-A	0	2	0	13	9.95	0	0	0	0	13.50	0	2	0	9	8.68	36	2	.250	.325	.444	24	3	.583	.615	1.000	25	4	.440	.500	.960	0	0	—	—	—
1991	Oak-A	4	4	0	77	4.79	1	4	0	43	4.57	3	0	0	34	5.08	140	2	.243	.372	.357	147	3	.231	.283	.374	117	3	.299	.361	.487	5	0	.400	.500	.400
TOTALS		77	79	0	1375	4.34	42	46	0	777	3.93	35	33	0	598	4.88	2658	67	.293	.376	.442	2600	73	.240	.292	.377	2129	58	.274	.352	.416	417	14	.281	.377	.456

● Neal Heaton BL/TL

YEAR	TM/L	W	L	SV	IP	ERA	W	L	SV	IP	ERA	W	L	SV	IP	ERA	AB	HR	AVG	OBP	SLG	AB	HR	AVG	OBP	SLG	AB	HR	AVG	OBP	SLG	AB	HR	AVG	OBP	SLG
1984	Cle-A	12	15	0	199	5.21	6	7	0	106	4.77	6	8	0	93	5.71	142	3	.303	.361	.472	647	18	.290	.348	.434	336	8	.318	.376	.482	28	1	.429	.448	.679
1985	Cle-A	9	17	0	208	4.90	7	5	0	117	3.55	2	12	0	91	6.63	161	2	.304	.367	.435	658	17	.296	.361	.445	380	8	.263	.322	.392	70	3	.300	.367	.500
1986	Cle-A	3	6	0	74	4.24	2	3	0	35	3.06	1	3	0	39	5.31	53	1	.245	.322	.302	234	7	.256	.338	.389	124	6	.226	.342	.403	15	0	.200	.294	.267
1986	Min-A	4	9	1	124	3.98	2	5	1	67	3.38	2	4	0	58	4.68	91	5	.253	.281	.505	378	13	.278	.350	.455	191	6	.230	.309	.398	34	1	.235	.325	.441
1987	Mon-N	13	10	0	193	4.52	7	4	0	109	3.87	6	6	0	84	5.36	123	4	.244	.266	.415	633	21	.280	.316	.428	268	14	.306	.348	.515	46	0	.348	.400	.435
1988	Mon-N	3	10	2	97	4.99	1	4	0	58	5.35	2	6	2	40	4.47	90	4	.244	.306	.433	271	10	.280	.365	.480	130	2	.269	.372	.392	84	2	.262	.344	.357
1989	Pit-N	6	7	0	147	3.05	2	4	0	75	2.52	4	3	0	72	3.61	114	0	.132	.194	.158	430	12	.266	.339	.414	230	3	.243	.330	.348	49	1	.245	.315	.347
1990	Pit-N	12	9	0	146	3.45	6	5	0	80	3.02	6	4	0	66	3.97	90	3	.311	.376	.522	453	13	.254	.297	.391	199	6	.256	.303	.407	21	1	.429	.435	.714
1991	Pit-N	3	3	0	69	4.33	1	2	0	31	5.17	2	1	0	37	3.62	82	2	.354	.382	.463	180	4	.239	.313	.372	114	3	.316	.367	.447	42	1	.333	.404	.476
1992	KC-A	3	1	0	41	4.17	2	0	0	20	5.49	1	1	0	21	2.95	54	1	.222	.313	.296	103	4	.301	.387	.466	79	1	.253	.326	.316	73	1	.233	.333	.329
1992	Mil-A	0	0	0	1	0.00	0	0	0	1	0.00	0	0	0	0	—	91	5	.253	.281	.505	3	0	.000	.250	.000	92	5	.250	.278	.500	0	0	—	—	—
1993	NY-A	1	2	0	17	6.00	1	0	0	0	0.00	0	2	0	16	5.84	60	2	.350	.420	.517	62	1	.321	.458	.593	60	2	.350	.420	.517	7	1	.143	.333	.571
TOTALS		69	87	3	1327	4.38	37	39	1	690	3.83	32	48	2	636	4.96	1032	26	.264	.320	.404	4071	125	.277	.340	.423	2112	59	.275	.342	.423	469	12	.288	.360	.433

● Tom Henke BR/TR

YEAR	TM/L	W	L	SV	IP	ERA	W	L	SV	IP	ERA	W	L	SV	IP	ERA	AB	HR	AVG	OBP	SLG	AB	HR	AVG	OBP	SLG	AB	HR	AVG	OBP	SLG	AB	HR	AVG	OBP	SLG
1984	Tex-A	1	1	2	28	6.35	1	0	0	14	5.02	0	1	2	14	7.71	58	0	.310	.438	.362	57	0	.316	.373	.439	66	0	.333	.429	.439	44	0	.341	.415	.386
1985	Tor-A	3	3	13	40	2.03	3	2	6	21	2.61	0	1	7	19	1.40	80	4	.225	.262	.387	61	0	.180	.224	.213	59	3	.203	.258	.337	101	3	.218	.259	.337
1986	Tor-A	9	5	27	91	3.35	5	2	12	43	3.16	4	3	15	49	3.51	177	4	.220	.299	.322	152	6	.158	.216	.243	158	3	.222	.291	.323	223	6	.188	.272	.309
1987	Tor-A	0	6	34	94	2.49	0	2	17	50	1.62	0	4	17	44	3.48	163	3	.172	.225	.288	167	7	.204	.258	.371	139	7	.201	.275	.410	228	7	.184	.253	.325

		TOTAL					HOME					AWAY					LEFT					RIGHT					ON-BASE					LATE/CLOSE				
YEAR	TM/L	W	L	SV	IP	ERA	W	L	SV	IP	ERA	W	L	SV	IP	ERA	AB	HR	AVG	OBP	SLG	AB	HR	AVG	OBP	SLG	AB	HR	AVG	OBP	SLG	AB	HR	AVG	OBP	SLG
1988	Tor-A	4	4	25	68	2.91	2	1	11	33	2.48	2	3	14	35	3.31	134	4	.261	.322	.321	119	4	.210	.289	.412	118	2	.237	.324	.339	176	5	.239	.310	.398
1989	Tor-A	8	3	20	89	1.92	6	0	7	36	2.48	2	3	13	53	1.54	149	3	.195	.272	.315	173	2	.214	.257	.312	141	4	.191	.282	.328	198	5	.192	.250	.328
1990	Tor-A	2	4	32	75	2.17	2	0	16	38	2.39	0	4	16	37	1.95	138	4	.210	.267	.355	134	4	.216	.266	.328	124	4	.177	.231	.290	176	6	.222	.277	.375
1991	Tor-A	0	2	32	50	2.32	0	1	14	23	2.31	0	1	18	27	2.33	95	3	.179	.243	.347	84	1	.190	.218	.262	62	3	.194	.265	.387	118	2	.153	.187	.254
1992	Tor-A	3	2	34	56	2.26	2	0	19	29	2.48	1	2	15	27	2.03	105	2	.190	.279	.286	98	3	.204	.264	.347	79	2	.215	.301	.329	126	4	.222	.265	.373
1993	Tex-A	5	5	40	74	2.91	5	1	27	44	1.62	0	4	13	30	4.80	132	4	.205	.289	.303	136	4	.206	.267	.309	114	4	.228	.326	.368	205	6	.210	.290	.327
1994	Tex-A	3	6	15	38	3.79	1	2	9	20	2.21	2	4	6	18	5.60	72	4	.208	.293	.486	70	2	.257	.288	.400	62	4	.242	.314	.516	101	6	.238	.310	.505
TOTALS		38	41	274	704	2.75	24	11	139	351	2.41	14	30	135	352	3.09	1303	32	.211	.289	.332	1251	29	.208	.261	.328	1122	36	.217	.297	.364	1696	50	.208	.273	.348

● Mike Henneman BR/TR

YEAR	TM/L	W	L	SV	IP	ERA	W	L	SV	IP	ERA	W	L	SV	IP	ERA	AB	HR	AVG	OBP	SLG	AB	HR	AVG	OBP	SLG	AB	HR	AVG	OBP	SLG	AB	HR	AVG	OBP	SLG
1987	Det-A	11	3	7	97	2.98	7	0	4	49	1.65	4	3	3	48	4.34	170	6	.241	.328	.412	192	2	.234	.273	.297	176	3	.210	.284	.290	125	2	.176	.246	.272
1988	Det-A	9	6	22	91	1.87	7	3	9	43	2.28	2	3	13	48	1.50	142	2	.218	.293	.303	189	5	.217	.257	.312	151	6	.212	.297	.364	258	5	.224	.275	.307
1989	Det-A	11	4	8	90	3.70	8	0	5	49	3.65	3	4	3	41	3.76	155	1	.265	.377	.361	180	3	.239	.336	.317	155	1	.277	.401	.355	191	3	.267	.379	.361
1990	Det-A	8	6	22	94	3.05	5	3	8	48	3.72	3	3	14	46	2.35	144	0	.278	.364	.326	212	4	.236	.288	.340	166	2	.259	.335	.343	209	3	.249	.339	.330
1991	Det-A	10	2	21	84	2.88	7	0	15	51	1.95	3	2	6	34	4.38	127	0	.268	.373	.339	187	2	.251	.290	.348	168	2	.238	.314	.351	224	1	.232	.300	.286
1992	Det-A	2	6	24	77	3.96	1	4	14	42	3.19	1	2	10	35	4.89	144	2	.278	.314	.389	149	4	.235	.284	.349	125	2	.256	.315	.368	171	4	.269	.312	.404
1993	Det-A	5	3	24	72	2.64	3	1	7	32	3.41	2	2	17	40	2.03	129	3	.287	.380	.442	146	1	.219	.286	.281	155	1	.232	.331	.297	181	3	.271	.353	.370
1994	Det-A	1	3	8	35	5.19	1	1	4	18	8.15	0	2	4	17	2.12	64	2	.281	.397	.438	81	3	.309	.356	.481	72	4	.389	.464	.625	75	3	.267	.371	.467
TOTALS		57	33	136	640	3.12	39	12	66	332	3.09	18	21	70	308	3.16	1075	16	.262	.350	.372	1336	24	.238	.292	.331	1168	21	.249	.335	.354	1404	24	.244	.321	.340

● Pat Hentgen BR/TR

YEAR	TM/L	W	L	SV	IP	ERA	W	L	SV	IP	ERA	W	L	SV	IP	ERA	AB	HR	AVG	OBP	SLG	AB	HR	AVG	OBP	SLG	AB	HR	AVG	OBP	SLG	AB	HR	AVG	OBP	SLG
1991	Tor-A	0	0	0	7	2.45	0	0	0	2	3.86	0	0	0	5	1.80	6	1	.333	.500	.833	18	0	.167	.286	.278	7	0	.143	.333	.143	0	0	—	—	—
1992	Tor-A	5	2	0	50	5.36	3	1	0	29	4.91	2	1	0	21	6.00	87	1	.253	.383	.368	106	6	.255	.333	.481	92	2	.185	.300	.293	27	1	.222	.343	.444
1993	Tor-A	19	9	0	216	3.87	7	6	0	111	4.77	12	3	0	105	2.91	423	11	.286	.341	.430	411	16	.229	.302	.397	362	10	.251	.305	.365	62	1	.258	.370	.355
1994	Tor-A	13	8	0	175	3.40	7	4	0	92	2.05	6	4	0	82	4.92	346	11	.266	.321	.408	311	10	.212	.287	.347	270	10	.241	.302	.389	70	1	.143	.200	.200
TOTALS		37	19	0	449	3.83	17	11	0	235	3.71	20	8	0	213	3.97	862	24	.275	.339	.418	846	32	.225	.300	.387	731	22	.238	.303	.363	159	3	.201	.295	.302

● Willie Hernandez BL/TL

YEAR	TM/L	W	L	SV	IP	ERA	W	L	SV	IP	ERA	W	L	SV	IP	ERA	AB	HR	AVG	OBP	SLG	AB	HR	AVG	OBP	SLG	AB	HR	AVG	OBP	SLG	AB	HR	AVG	OBP	SLG
1984	Det-A	9	3	32	140	1.92	3	2	18	66	2.19	6	1	14	75	1.69	139	0	.173	.212	.194	357	6	.202	.267	.277	210	0	.176	.248	.195	298	2	.168	.228	.208
1985	Det-A	8	10	31	107	2.70	6	4	13	59	2.15	2	6	18	48	3.38	105	1	.171	.193	.229	286	12	.224	.252	.399	158	4	.241	.273	.373	260	11	.215	.240	.377
1986	Det-A	8	7	24	89	3.55	6	3	9	43	3.77	2	4	15	46	3.35	97	1	.206	.238	.268	249	12	.269	.325	.470	160	6	.256	.303	.412	190	10	.265	.309	.447
1987	Det-A	3	4	8	49	3.67	2	2	1	17	4.76	1	2	7	32	3.09	70	2	.243	.286	.386	122	6	.295	.370	.516	97	5	.330	.398	.526	94	3	.277	.373	.457
1988	Det-A	6	5	10	68	3.06	4	3	6	38	2.11	2	2	4	29	4.30	85	3	.224	.296	.365	155	5	.200	.311	.342	116	3	.224	.336	.353	109	4	.248	.359	.385
1989	Det-A	2	2	15	31	5.74	2	2	8	18	8.00	0	0	7	13	2.70	40	1	.200	.289	.275	83	3	.337	.421	.542	69	4	.333	.432	.580	76	1	.263	.349	.355
TOTALS		36	31	120	484	2.98	23	16	55	241	3.07	13	15	65	243	2.89	536	8	.198	.243	.292	1252	44	.238	.302	.392	810	22	.243	.311	.368	1056	31	.224	.285	.350

● Orel Hershiser BR/TR

YEAR	TM/L	W	L	SV	IP	ERA	W	L	SV	IP	ERA	W	L	SV	IP	ERA	AB	HR	AVG	OBP	SLG	AB	HR	AVG	OBP	SLG	AB	HR	AVG	OBP	SLG	AB	HR	AVG	OBP	SLG
1984	LA-N	11	8	2	190	2.66	5	5	0	101	3.40	6	3	2	89	1.82	343	2	.245	.296	.300	369	7	.206	.262	.293	276	4	.228	.296	.315	90	2	.233	.317	.311
1985	LA-N	19	3	0	240	2.03	11	0	0	133	1.08	8	3	0	106	3.22	477	3	.222	.281	.289	393	5	.186	.249	.252	328	4	.210	.281	.296	91	2	.165	.248	.264
1986	LA-N	14	14	0	231	3.85	10	5	0	129	3.07	4	9	0	102	4.84	469	7	.252	.320	.354	408	6	.233	.303	.321	352	4	.247	.342	.313	93	2	.237	.327	.366
1987	LA-N	16	16	1	265	3.06	9	6	0	134	2.42	7	10	1	131	3.71	589	10	.272	.330	.385	411	7	.212	.266	.304	397	6	.254	.317	.353	153	3	.301	.378	.444
1988	LA-N	23	8	1	267	2.26	11	5	0	125	2.31	12	3	1	142	2.21	533	13	.220	.294	.343	442	6	.206	.238	.269	343	5	.187	.273	.268	189	2	.212	.260	.302
1989	LA-N	15	15	0	257	2.31	9	8	0	126	2.71	6	7	0	131	1.93	519	6	.258	.323	.339	423	4	.217	.265	.288	392	4	.227	.299	.309	139	1	.223	.321	.302
1990	LA-N	1	1	0	25	4.26	1	1	0	19	4.19	0	0	0	6	4.50	53	1	.189	.218	.264	47	0	.340	.380	.404	40	0	.350	.381	.425	3	0	.667	.800	.667
1991	LA-N	7	2	0	112	3.46	3	2	0	63	3.27	4	0	0	49	3.70	208	2	.284	.345	.375	225	1	.236	.289	.289	197	2	.239	.314	.310	7	0	.143	.143	.143
1992	LA-N	10	15	0	211	3.67	7	5	0	118	2.75	3	10	0	93	4.86	455	11	.286	.366	.418	357	4	.221	.257	.314	343	3	.259	.332	.335	61	2	.262	.338	.393
1993	LA-N	12	14	0	216	3.59	4	8	0	99	3.17	8	6	0	116	3.95	436	5	.241	.319	.351	381	12	.252	.302	.402	315	4	.292	.371	.419	73	1	.219	.345	.342
1994	LA-N	6	6	0	135	3.79	3	4	0	80	3.59	3	2	0	55	4.09	273	9	.297	.368	.484	251	6	.259	.292	.390	234	5	.252	.305	.380	30	3	.300	.417	.633
TOTALS		134	102	4	2148	3.00	73	49	0	1128	2.71	61	53	4	1020	3.33	4355	68	.254	.320	.361	3707	57	.222	.272	.310	3217	41	.241	.314	.330	929	18	.236	.319	.349

● Joe Hesketh BR/TL

YEAR	TM/L	W	L	SV	IP	ERA	W	L	SV	IP	ERA	W	L	SV	IP	ERA	AB	HR	AVG	OBP	SLG	AB	HR	AVG	OBP	SLG	AB	HR	AVG	OBP	SLG	AB	HR	AVG	OBP	SLG
1984	Mon-N	2	2	1	45	1.80	1	1	0	23	1.93	1	1	1	22	1.66	26	0	.154	.185	.154	137	2	.248	.314	.365	66	0	.182	.243	.258	22	0	.227	.292	.273
1985	Mon-N	10	5	0	155	2.49	6	3	0	78	2.30	4	2	0	77	2.69	93	1	.215	.270	.269	469	9	.224	.281	.343	200	4	.260	.309	.410	48	0	.313	.389	.417
1986	Mon-N	6	5	0	83	5.01	3	2	0	43	5.61	3	3	0	39	4.35	281	11	.288	.346	.495	129	6	.310	.381	.535	33	0	.273	.314	.273					
1987	Mon-N	0	0	1	29	3.14	0	0	0	11	3.18	0	0	1	17	3.12	38	1	.237	.341	.342	71	1	.197	.305	.282	52	0	.212	.349	.231	18	0	.111	.238	.111
1988	Mon-N	4	3	9	73	2.85	2	0	4	33	3.58	2	3	5	40	2.25	78	0	.205	.300	.244	182	1	.258	.340	.357	118	0	.212	.322	.280	157	0	.248	.331	.325
1989	Mon-N	6	4	3	48	5.77	1	3	1	27	8.00	5	1	2	21	2.95	57	2	.298	.412	.456	128	3	.289	.359	.414	88	1	.330	.419	.443	73	2	.274	.374	.397
1990	Mon-N	1	0	0	3	0.00	1	0	0	3	0.00	0	0	0	0	—	5	0	.200	.333	.200	5	0	.200	.333	.200	4	0	.250	.400	.250	0	0	—	—	—
1990	Atl-N	0	2	5	31	5.81	0	1	2	16	6.19	0	1	3	16	5.40	41	3	.171	.267	.463	80	2	.287	.341	.450	66	4	.288	.351	.530	47	3	.277	.346	.511
1990	Bos-A	0	4	0	26	3.51	0	2	0	17	3.63	0	2	0	9	3.24	27	0	.407	.467	.407	84	2	.310	.370	.452	61	1	.279	.343	.377	4	0	.250	.400	.250
1991	Bos-A	12	4	0	153	3.29	7	1	0	71	2.04	5	3	0	83	4.35	87	2	.241	.327	.391	481	17	.252	.310	.430	235	7	.191	.261	.336	40	1	.175	.313	.275
1992	Bos-A	8	9	1	149	4.36	4	5	1	83	4.25	4	4	0	66	4.50	98	2	.255	.288	.367	490	13	.280	.349	.437	250	5	.276	.346	.412	27	1	.259	.333	.481
1993	Bos-A	3	4	1	53	5.06	2	1	1	29	2.17	1	3	0	24	8.51	68	1	.206	.267	.294	143	4	.336	.425	.483	104	2	.279	.369	.385	4	0	.250	.500	.250
1994	Bos-A	8	5	0	114	4.26	5	2	0	65	3.86	3	3	0	49	4.81	63	1	.222	.282	.286	375	8	.275	.343	.435	199	5	.271	.323	.452	11	0	.364	.462	.545
TOTALS		60	47	21	962	3.78	32	20	9	482	3.60	28	27	12	479	3.96	725	13	.234	.310	.331	2926	72	.266	.332	.416	1572	35	.256	.329	.396	484	6	.254	.343	.357

● Greg Hibbard BL/TL

YEAR	TM/L	W	L	SV	IP	ERA	W	L	SV	IP	ERA	W	L	SV	IP	ERA	AB	HR	AVG	OBP	SLG	AB	HR	AVG	OBP	SLG	AB	HR	AVG	OBP	SLG	AB	HR	AVG	OBP	SLG
1989	Chi-A	6	7	0	137	3.21	4	3	0	69	2.86	2	4	0	68	3.57	70	0	.314	.390	.400	459	5	.261	.310	.359	229	3	.258	.307	.371	31	0	.323	.382	.355
1990	Chi-A	14	9	0	211	3.16	8	5	0	121	2.98	6	4	0	90	3.39	91	0	.209	.270	.275	701	11	.261	.309	.365	294	3	.272	.321	.371	88	1	.239	.287	.318
1991	Chi-A	11	11	0	194	4.31	4	5	0	92	3.44	7	6	0	102	5.10	120	5	.250	.283	.392	617	18	.269	.326	.400	283	11	.300	.346	.481	64	1	.234	.290	.328
1992	Chi-A	10	7	1	176	4.40	7	3	1	97	3.44	3	4	0	79	5.56	85	1	.224	.302	.271	590	16	.285	.342	.424	276	5	.301	.354	.428	70	2	.300	.367	.429
1993	Chi-N	15	11	0	191	3.96	7	6	0	102	4.24	8	5	0	89	3.64	117	5	.274	.338	.436	614	14	.288	.325	.448	293	9	.276	.313	.457	39	1	.205	.262	.333
1994	Sea-A	1	5	0	81	6.69	1	3	0	49	5.33	0	2	0	32	8.91	75	4	.240	.310	.427	276	7	.351	.404	.500	173	5	.329	.395	.480	7	0	.143	.250	.143
TOTALS		57	50	1	990	4.05	30	24	1	513	3.76	27	26	0	477	4.37	558	15	.251	.313	.396	3257	71	.280	.330	.409	1548	36	.287	.336	.430	299	5	.254	.313	.348

● Teddy Higuera BB/TL

YEAR	TM/L	W	L	SV	IP	ERA	W	L	SV	IP	ERA	W	L	SV	IP	ERA	AB	HR	AVG	OBP	SLG	AB	HR	AVG	OBP	SLG	AB	HR	AVG	OBP	SLG	AB	HR	AVG	OBP	SLG
1985	Mil-A	15	8	0	212	3.90	7	4	0	89	5.44	8	4	0	123	2.78	127	3	.236	.293	.378	666	19	.234	.289	.372	290	7	.228	.282	.345	134	3	.269	.313	.343
1986	Mil-A	20	11	0	248	2.79	10	3	0	131	1.79	10	8	0	117	3.91	152	4	.243	.275	.382	784	22	.241	.300	.379	369	7	.238	.281	.352	123	0	.236	.294	.285
1987	Mil-A	18	10	0	262	3.85	12	4	0	149	3.50	6	6	0	112	4.33	163	4	.276	.310	.393	817	20	.234	.300	.364	401	6	.267	.316	.384	147	3	.190	.241	.286
1988	Mil-A	16	9	0	227	2.45	9	4	0	121	2.15	7	5	0	106	2.80	149	2	.208	.256	.315	664	12	.206	.265	.297	275	6	.247	.301	.360	118	2	.263	.333	.339
1989	Mil-A	9	6	0	135	3.46	6	3	0	83	2.94	3	3	0	53	4.27	93	2	.215	.245	.323	411	7	.255	.330	.350	205	3	.273	.336	.361	24	0	.250	.250	.292
1990	Mil-A	11	10	0	170	3.76	7	4	0	96	3.36	4	6	0	74	4.28	126	1	.238	.284	.286	527	15	.260	.316	.400	274	6	.281	.323	.398	76	1	.250	.322	.342
1991	Mil-A	3	2	0	36	4.46	2	0	0	20	4.50	1	2	0	16	4.41	32	1	.219	.242	.281	109	2	.275	.333	.385	66	1	.303	.329	.409	3	0	.000	.000	.000
1993	Mil-A	1	3	0	30	7.20	1	2	0	17	4.67	0	1	0	13	10.66	13	0	.385	.500	.538	116	4	.353	.432	.621	60	3	.367	.432	.700	0	0	—	—	—
1994	Mil-A	1	5	0	59	7.06	0	0	0	24	9.75	1	3	0	35	5.19	49	2	.224	.308	.388	189	11	.333	.423	.619	101	7	.327	.421	.634	8	0	.375	.500	.375
TOTALS		94	64	0	1380	3.61	55	26	0	731	3.38	39	38	0	649	3.87	904	19	.236	.280	.347	4283	112	.245	.308	.379	2041	46	.263	.316	.391	633	9	.240	.297	.314

● Ken Hill BR/TR

YEAR	TM/L	W	L	SV	IP	ERA	W	L	SV	IP	ERA	W	L	SV	IP	ERA	AB	HR	AVG	OBP	SLG	AB	HR	AVG	OBP	SLG	AB	HR	AVG	OBP	SLG	AB	HR	AVG	OBP	SLG
1988	StL-N	0	3	0	38	8.05	0	2	0	24	9.75	0	1	0	14	5.14	24	0	.250	.333	.333	32	0	.313	.371	.469	25	0	.400	.444	.560	0	0	—	—	—
1989	StL-N	7	15	0	197	3.80	2	5	0	97	3.80	5	10	0	100	3.80	395	3	.271	.372	.359	344	6	.230	.306	.331	336	4	.253	.344	.354	31	1	.516	.595	.645
1990	StL-N	5	6	0	79	5.49	2	2	0	28	6.75	3	4	0	51	4.80	184	4	.261	.344	.397	115	3	.270	.317	.435	126	2	.270	.331	.381	26	0	.423	.483	.577
1991	StL-N	11	10	0	181	3.57	6	4	0	88	3.18	5	6	0	92	3.94	367	8	.237	.307	.341	289	7	.208	.288	.353	254	6	.256	.317	.417	63	2	.222	.310	.397
1992	Mon-N	16	9	0	218	2.68	6	6	0	94	3.15	10	3	0	124	2.33	469	6	.222	.298	.318	343	7	.242	.295	.359	349	5	.212	.276	.292	62	4	.258	.338	.452
1993	Mon-N	9	7	0	184	3.23	4	4	0	101	3.12	5	3	0	83	3.38	376	4	.234	.322	.343	308	5	.244	.307	.328	296	5	.233	.318	.328	55	1	.236	.246	.400
1994	Mon-N	16	5	0	155	3.32	7	2	0	63	2.59	9	3	0	92	3.82	289	7	.270	.330	.409	289	7	.225	.277	.343	234	6	.261	.319	.380	33	1	.455	.472	.697
TOTALS		64	53	0	1027	3.50	27	23	0	471	3.42	37	30	0	556	3.56	2111	30	.246	.327	.354	1720	33	.234	.298	.351	1620	25	.246	.318	.355	270	9	.315	.375	.493

● Brian Holman BR/TR

YEAR	TM/L	W	L	SV	IP	ERA	W	L	SV	IP	ERA	W	L	SV	IP	ERA	AB	HR	AVG	OBP	SLG	AB	HR	AVG	OBP	SLG	AB	HR	AVG	OBP	SLG	AB	HR	AVG	OBP	SLG
1988	Mon-N	4	8	0	100	3.23	3	6	0	69	3.12	1	2	0	31	3.48	211	3	.270	.345	.379	171	1	.257	.297	.310	152	1	.289	.359	.388	26	0	.385	.407	.385
1989	Mon-N	1	2	0	32	4.83	1	1	0	13	5.90	0	1	0	19	4.02	59	1	.271	.380	.407	67	0	.239	.278	.328	69	2	.261	.333	.377	4	0	.500	.500	.500
1989	Sea-A	8	10	0	160	3.44	4	3	0	67	3.88	4	7	0	92	3.12	292	4	.257	.344	.366	321	5	.265	.323	.368	260	3	.258	.344	.358	58	2	.293	.388	.414
1990	Sea-A	11	11	0	190	4.03	4	6	0	105	4.04	7	5	0	85	4.02	379	10	.280	.346	.417	345	7	.238	.299	.345	286	5	.294	.369	.427	66	1	.333	.371	.439
1991	Sea-A	13	14	0	195	3.69	9	7	0	119	2.65	4	7	0	77	5.28	391	6	.284	.362	.394	352	10	.250	.322	.389	342	7	.246	.319	.365	53	1	.189	.259	.264
TOTALS		37	45	0	677	3.71	20	24	0	373	3.45	17	21	0	304	4.03	1332	24	.276	.354	.392	1256	23	.251	.310	.357	1109	18	.268	.344	.383	207	4	.295	.354	.382

● Rick Honeycutt BL/TL

YEAR	TM/L	TOTAL					HOME					AWAY					LEFT					RIGHT					ON-BASE					LATE/CLOSE				
		W	L	SV	IP	ERA	W	L	SV	IP	ERA	W	L	SV	IP	ERA	AB	HR	AVG	OBP	SLG	AB	HR	AVG	OBP	SLG	AB	HR	AVG	OBP	SLG	AB	HR	AVG	OBP	SLG
1984	LA-N	10	9	0	184	2.84	6	2	0	96	2.24	4	7	0	87	3.50	135	3	.185	.206	.252	563	8	.275	.332	.362	255	5	.282	.358	.373	80	1	.200	.247	.250
1985	LA-N	8	12	1	142	3.42	5	6	0	80	2.70	3	6	1	62	4.35	73	0	.219	.272	.329	468	9	.267	.329	.397	214	5	.271	.344	.425	24	0	.125	.192	.125
1986	LA-N	11	9	0	171	3.32	6	4	0	97	2.69	5	5	0	74	4.14	105	0	.238	.266	.343	553	9	.251	.306	.373	241	4	.282	.348	.425	49	0	.265	.308	.306
1987	LA-N	2	12	0	116	4.59	2	7	0	64	3.92	0	5	0	51	5.44	87	2	.218	.253	.333	391	8	.292	.362	.435	206	5	.291	.379	.447	8	0	.500	.600	.625
1987	Oak-A	1	4	0	24	5.32	0	2	0	13	6.07	1	2	0	10	4.35	25	0	.120	.233	.240	66	3	.333	.387	.561	41	0	.244	.292	.366	5	0	.400	.400	.400
1988	Oak-A	3	2	7	80	3.50	2	1	2	33	2.18	1	1	5	47	4.44	97	3	.227	.282	.371	196	3	.265	.327	.378	149	2	.221	.282	.336	127	4	.197	.259	.339
1989	Oak-A	2	2	12	77	2.35	0	2	6	41	2.85	2	0	6	36	1.77	90	1	.156	.248	.200	181	4	.232	.291	.315	123	2	.195	.279	.276	178	1	.202	.284	.230
1990	Oak-A	2	2	7	63	2.70	2	0	6	30	1.80	0	2	1	33	3.51	86	1	.163	.204	.221	139	1	.230	.311	.309	109	1	.239	.288	.303	149	1	.154	.216	.195
1991	Oak-A	2	4	0	38	3.58	0	2	0	21	2.14	2	2	0	17	5.40	54	1	.204	.306	.315	88	2	.295	.388	.443	75	3	.240	.348	.440	103	1	.252	.366	.369
1992	Oak-A	1	4	3	39	3.69	1	2	2	18	3.06	0	2	1	21	4.22	62	1	.258	.313	.339	91	1	.281	.337	.393	85	2	.294	.351	.424	88	2	.261	.305	.386
1993	Oak-A	1	4	1	42	2.81	0	2	1	21	2.14	1	2	0	21	3.48	54	1	.241	.317	.352	88	1	.193	.298	.261	67	2	.209	.305	.343	96	0	.240	.347	.281
1994	Tex-A	1	2	1	25	7.20	0	1	0	12	8.25	1	1	1	13	6.23	51	1	.412	.423	.608	55	3	.291	.400	.509	53	1	.340	.407	.453	40	1	.325	.460	.475
TOTALS		44	66	32	999	3.44	24	31	17	527	2.87	20	35	15	472	4.08	919	14	.217	.267	.316	2877	52	.266	.330	.388	1618	32	.263	.336	.388	947	11	.219	.296	.291

● Charlie Hough BR/TR

YEAR	TM/L	W	L	SV	IP	ERA	W	L	SV	IP	ERA	W	L	SV	IP	ERA	AB	HR	AVG	OBP	SLG	AB	HR	AVG	OBP	SLG	AB	HR	AVG	OBP	SLG	AB	HR	AVG	OBP	SLG
1984	Tex-A	16	14	0	266	3.76	8	5	0	129	2.94	8	9	0	137	4.52	541	14	.274	.342	.420	475	12	.236	.300	.381	419	10	.253	.332	.387	161	1	.230	.290	.298
1985	Tex-A	14	16	0	250	3.31	8	6	0	115	3.52	6	10	0	135	3.13	495	11	.226	.290	.343	425	12	.202	.275	.332	316	8	.225	.321	.345	105	2	.219	.284	.314
1986	Tex-A	17	10	0	230	3.79	8	5	0	106	3.99	9	5	0	124	3.62	436	13	.204	.282	.335	414	19	.239	.322	.425	295	10	.251	.335	.403	118	1	.195	.252	.263
1987	Tex-A	18	13	0	285	3.79	11	8	0	153	4.40	7	5	0	132	3.07	509	17	.240	.336	.375	560	19	.207	.288	.370	420	11	.205	.307	.314	127	6	.213	.281	.394
1988	Tex-A	15	16	0	252	3.32	9	8	0	126	3.63	6	8	0	126	3.01	451	9	.220	.321	.317	462	11	.223	.321	.335	336	6	.241	.363	.393	153	3	.216	.315	.281
1989	Tex-A	10	13	0	182	4.35	5	6	0	79	4.88	5	7	0	103	3.94	336	9	.238	.327	.366	349	19	.252	.351	.461	271	10	.255	.356	.406	41	5	.341	.426	.829
1990	Tex-A	12	12	0	219	4.07	5	8	0	97	4.47	7	4	0	122	3.76	349	7	.241	.345	.347	458	17	.231	.332	.386	342	6	.225	.340	.322	54	0	.222	.377	.278
1991	Chi-A	9	10	0	199	4.02	5	5	0	107	3.38	4	5	0	93	4.76	355	8	.237	.323	.375	374	13	.222	.317	.388	301	8	.233	.308	.382	72	3	.264	.368	.431
1992	Chi-A	7	12	0	176	3.93	6	4	0	101	3.49	1	8	0	76	4.52	267	7	.236	.304	.352	403	12	.241	.316	.387	260	8	.262	.336	.412	64	3	.266	.351	.469
1993	Fla-N	9	16	0	204	4.27	5	6	0	114	4.18	4	10	0	90	4.38	382	11	.251	.311	.387	397	9	.267	.338	.403	313	10	.262	.333	.422	65	1	.292	.329	.354
1994	Fla-N	5	9	0	114	5.15	1	5	0	45	7.94	4	4	0	68	3.29	189	3	.249	.319	.349	241	14	.295	.389	.564	151	3	.291	.423	.464	10	1	.300	.467	.600
TOTALS		132	141	0	2378	3.89	71	66	0	1172	4.02	61	75	0	1206	3.77	4310	109	.238	.319	.362	4558	157	.234	.319	.394	3424	90	.242	.337	.374	970	26	.234	.314	.355

● Jay Howell BR/TR

YEAR	TM/L	W	L	SV	IP	ERA	W	L	SV	IP	ERA	W	L	SV	IP	ERA	AB	HR	AVG	OBP	SLG	AB	HR	AVG	OBP	SLG	AB	HR	AVG	OBP	SLG	AB	HR	AVG	OBP	SLG
1984	NY-A	9	4	7	104	2.69	7	2	4	53	1.53	2	2	3	51	3.91	182	2	.220	.294	.291	204	3	.225	.275	.309	166	1	.229	.296	.283	196	2	.219	.265	.286
1985	Oak-A	9	8	29	98	2.85	9	3	14	59	2.61	0	5	15	39	3.20	201	1	.254	.318	.313	174	4	.270	.314	.374	193	2	.254	.321	.321	325	4	.255	.307	.329
1986	Oak-A	3	6	16	53	3.38	1	3	9	29	3.72	2	3	7	24	2.96	97	2	.330	.420	.464	105	1	.200	.261	.248	101	2	.287	.365	.396	154	2	.279	.356	.377
1987	Oak-A	3	4	16	44	5.89	1	1	8	20	5.03	2	3	8	25	6.57	83	1	.253	.340	.373	90	5	.300	.369	.567	97	3	.268	.330	.423	125	2	.272	.359	.424
1988	LA-N	5	3	21	65	2.08	3	0	8	28	1.61	2	3	13	37	2.43	124	1	.169	.232	.226	110	0	.209	.281	.255	106	1	.226	.292	.321	180	0	.161	.239	.200
1989	LA-N	5	3	28	80	1.58	4	3	16	47	1.16	1	0	12	33	2.18	159	1	.208	.282	.270	125	2	.216	.244	.312	117	1	.188	.265	.248	239	2	.209	.265	.276
1990	LA-N	5	5	16	66	2.18	4	3	8	34	2.91	1	2	8	32	1.41	149	3	.242	.307	.349	95	2	.242	.327	.337	108	0	.250	.341	.306	173	5	.272	.357	.405
1991	LA-N	6	5	16	51	3.18	6	2	8	32	2.84	0	3	8	19	3.72	97	1	.175	.234	.289	86	2	.256	.289	.372	74	1	.216	.277	.311	137	2	.182	.240	.263
1992	LA-N	1	3	4	47	1.54	1	2	0	23	1.57	0	1	4	24	1.52	91	2	.242	.310	.330	87	0	.218	.296	.230	79	0	.253	.333	.266	88	0	.295	.370	.318
1993	Atl-N	3	3	0	58	2.31	2	1	0	40	1.82	1	2	0	19	3.38	90	1	.233	.263	.256	120	3	.225	.289	.333	78	1	.269	.322	.359	50	0	.240	.273	.280
1994	Tex-A	4	1	2	43	5.44	1	0	0	22	2.82	3	1	2	21	8.27	72	7	.278	.358	.597	96	3	.250	.299	.417	73	3	.315	.384	.534	66	4	.258	.307	.515
TOTALS		53	45	155	709	2.83	36	20	75	386	2.33	17	25	80	323	3.42	1345	21	.233	.302	.326	1292	25	.237	.293	.337	1192	15	.247	.318	.333	1733	23	.236	.300	.322

● Ken Howell BR/TR

YEAR	TM/L	W	L	SV	IP	ERA	W	L	SV	IP	ERA	W	L	SV	IP	ERA	AB	HR	AVG	OBP	SLG	AB	HR	AVG	OBP	SLG	AB	HR	AVG	OBP	SLG	AB	HR	AVG	OBP	SLG
1984	LA-N	5	5	6	51	3.33	2	5	2	26	4.85	3	0	4	25	1.78	90	0	.356	.390	.422	101	1	.188	.210	.267	88	0	.284	.309	.352	124	0	.250	.289	.331
1985	LA-N	4	7	12	86	3.77	1	4	4	45	4.17	3	3	8	41	3.32	151	1	.185	.268	.245	166	7	.229	.304	.373	148	4	.230	.301	.338	194	5	.222	.314	.325
1986	LA-N	6	12	12	98	3.87	5	5	8	54	2.65	1	7	4	43	5.40	193	3	.238	.366	.332	167	4	.240	.340	.347	176	5	.227	.371	.375	291	7	.251	.360	.375
1987	LA-N	3	4	1	55	4.91	1	0	1	21	4.29	2	4	0	34	5.29	96	1	.271	.381	.375	108	6	.259	.333	.509	93	5	.269	.358	.495	72	2	.292	.378	.444
1988	LA-N	0	1	0	13	6.39	0	0	0	4	0.00	0	1	0	9	9.35	30	0	.433	.452	.500	20	0	.150	.261	.200	22	0	.455	.478	.591	7	0	.000	.000	.000
1989	Phi-N	12	12	0	204	3.44	4	5	0	102	3.19	8	7	0	102	3.69	413	6	.235	.321	.341	309	5	.188	.264	.275	288	7	.226	.297	.358	55	0	.255	.339	.291
1990	Phi-N	8	7	0	107	4.64	4	4	0	61	5.43	4	3	0	45	3.57	254	7	.299	.385	.469	154	5	.195	.271	.344	177	7	.237	.327	.441	34	2	.206	.250	.471
TOTALS		38	48	31	613	3.95	17	23	15	314	3.84	21	25	16	300	4.05	1227	18	.259	.348	.367	1025	28	.211	.287	.336	992	28	.243	.327	.390	777	16	.243	.333	.356

● La Marr Hoyt BR/TR

YEAR	TM/L	W	L	SV	IP	ERA	W	L	SV	IP	ERA	W	L	SV	IP	ERA	AB	HR	AVG	OBP	SLG	AB	HR	AVG	OBP	SLG	AB	HR	AVG	OBP	SLG	AB	HR	AVG	OBP	SLG
1984	Chi-A	13	18	0	236	4.47	9	9	0	122	4.93	4	9	0	113	3.97	515	23	.276	.321	.485	403	8	.253	.274	.390	310	7	.306	.353	.487	85	3	.224	.258	.376
1985	SD-N	16	8	0	210	3.47	9	5	0	117	4.08	7	3	0	93	2.70	432	11	.287	.304	.412	373	9	.231	.251	.357	273	8	.315	.333	.465	97	2	.227	.250	.340
1986	SD-N	8	11	0	159	5.15	5	3	0	87	3.95	3	8	0	72	6.59	308	10	.273	.365	.422	307	17	.280	.333	.511	262	13	.263	.353	.454	39	2	.256	.370	.462
TOTALS		37	37	0	605	4.30	23	17	0	326	4.36	14	20	0	279	4.23	1255	44	.279	.327	.445	1083	34	.253	.284	.413	845	28	.296	.347	.470	221	7	.231	.277	.376

● Charles Hudson BB/TR

YEAR	TM/L	W	L	SV	IP	ERA	W	L	SV	IP	ERA	W	L	SV	IP	ERA	AB	HR	AVG	OBP	SLG	AB	HR	AVG	OBP	SLG	AB	HR	AVG	OBP	SLG	AB	HR	AVG	OBP	SLG
1984	Phi-N	9	11	0	174	4.04	3	7	0	73	5.05	6	4	0	101	3.31	358	5	.285	.284	.394	324	7	.244	.284	.361	276	4	.279	.339	.388	38	1	.211	.250	.289
1985	Phi-N	8	13	0	193	3.78	3	5	0	93	3.86	5	8	0	100	3.70	377	9	.273	.344	.419	369	14	.230	.293	.404	308	8	.282	.350	.442	79	5	.304	.356	.532
1986	Phi-N	7	10	0	144	4.94	3	5	0	70	4.52	4	5	0	74	5.33	319	11	.282	.358	.436	248	9	.302	.352	.468	244	6	.320	.357	.451	17	0	.294	.333	.353
1987	NY-A	11	7	0	155	3.61	4	4	0	73	4.09	7	3	0	82	3.18	250	7	.268	.354	.424	323	12	.217	.270	.365	229	7	.236	.290	.367	50	1	.220	.264	.300
1988	NY-A	6	6	2	106	4.49	3	2	2	45	3.80	3	4	0	61	4.99	181	1	.215	.283	.298	214	8	.252	.316	.430	151	4	.278	.345	.417	63	2	.333	.386	.540
1989	Det-A	1	5	0	67	6.34	1	1	0	19	4.82	0	4	0	48	6.94	135	6	.222	.306	.387	125	8	.360	.433	.632	109	6	.321	.385	.587	29	1	.345	.424	.552
TOTALS		42	52	2	838	4.29	17	24	2	372	4.30	25	28	0	466	4.29	1620	39	.266	.338	.401	1603	58	.255	.310	.419	1317	35	.283	.341	.428	276	10	.286	.339	.449

● Bruce Hurst BL/TL

YEAR	TM/L	W	L	SV	IP	ERA	W	L	SV	IP	ERA	W	L	SV	IP	ERA	AB	HR	AVG	OBP	SLG	AB	HR	AVG	OBP	SLG	AB	HR	AVG	OBP	SLG	AB	HR	AVG	OBP	SLG
1984	Bos-A	12	12	0	218	3.92	6	6	0	108	4.67	6	6	0	110	3.19	153	1	.248	.303	.346	704	24	.276	.349	.449	381	8	.257	.322	.356	79	1	.190	.261	.278
1985	Bos-A	11	13	0	229	4.51	6	8	0	106	4.66	5	5	0	123	4.39	153	5	.281	.337	.425	737	26	.271	.325	.442	368	14	.293	.332	.476	99	4	.374	.415	.636
1986	Bos-A	13	8	0	174	2.99	8	3	0	102	2.37	5	5	0	72	3.88	86	4	.256	.312	.442	574	14	.256	.310	.385	277	2	.231	.275	.314	58	0	.259	.306	.328
1987	Bos-A	15	13	0	239	4.41	12	4	0	136	4.30	3	9	0	103	4.56	129	4	.248	.333	.419	782	31	.265	.314	.435	359	13	.270	.313	.443	100	6	.320	.369	.580
1988	Bos-A	18	6	0	217	3.66	13	2	0	130	3.33	5	4	0	87	4.14	147	2	.279	.327	.374	695	19	.260	.314	.391	347	10	.280	.324	.427	69	0	.217	.295	.246
1989	SD-N	15	11	0	245	2.69	9	6	0	140	2.58	6	5	0	105	2.83	144	5	.299	.357	.424	759	14	.225	.275	.323	343	4	.236	.301	.321	114	3	.202	.242	.298
1990	SD-N	11	9	0	224	3.14	7	3	0	122	2.66	4	6	0	102	3.72	165	7	.230	.302	.400	658	14	.228	.279	.347	315	7	.222	.281	.359	95	4	.305	.359	.474
1991	SD-N	15	8	0	222	3.29	7	5	0	127	3.34	8	3	0	95	3.22	136	1	.176	.247	.221	699	16	.253	.301	.363	326	4	.267	.310	.350	90	0	.211	.260	.267
1992	SD-N	14	9	0	217	3.85	5	4	0	101	4.38	9	5	0	117	3.39	157	8	.293	.335	.478	678	14	.261	.302	.370	325	9	.280	.302	.434	74	2	.297	.325	.432
1993	SD-N	0	1	0	4	12.46	0	1	0	1	6.75	0	0	0	3	15.00	3	0	.333	.500	.333	19	0	.421	.476	.474	17	0	.353	.389	.353	0	0	—	—	—
1993	Col-N	0	1	0	9	5.19	0	1	0	9	5.19	0	0	0	0	—	2	0	.000	.000	.000	29	1	.207	.281	.310	8	0	.375	.444	.375	0	0	—	—	—
1994	Tex-A	2	1	0	38	7.11	1	0	0	23	6.17	1	1	0	15	8.59	25	3	.280	.333	.720	130	5	.354	.405	.569	67	3	.358	.382	.597	4	1	.500	.500	1.500
TOTALS		126	92	0	2035	3.71	74	43	0	1105	3.63	52	49	0	931	3.81	1300	37	.258	.318	.397	6464	178	.257	.310	.394	3133	74	.264	.310	.398	782	21	.267	.317	.409

● Jeff Innis BR/TR

YEAR	TM/L	W	L	SV	IP	ERA	W	L	SV	IP	ERA	W	L	SV	IP	ERA	AB	HR	AVG	OBP	SLG	AB	HR	AVG	OBP	SLG	AB	HR	AVG	OBP	SLG	AB	HR	AVG	OBP	SLG
1987	NY-N	0	1	0	26	3.16	0	1	0	8	1.08	0	0	0	17	4.15	37	1	.378	.410	.676	67	2	.224	.257	.343	37	1	.216	.293	.297	12	1	.250	.308	.500
1988	NY-N	1	1	0	19	1.89	1	0	0	10	0.00	0	1	0	9	3.86	25	0	.320	.370	.400	51	0	.216	.212	.216	38	0	.237	.250	.263	10	0	.400	.364	.400
1989	NY-N	0	1	0	40	3.18	0	1	0	22	2.01	0	0	0	17	4.67	54	1	.315	.356	.463	95	1	.221	.260	.274	69	0	.261	.316	.319	21	1	.381	.381	.571
1990	NY-N	1	3	1	26	2.39	1	2	1	10	2.79	0	1	0	17	2.16	37	3	.270	.349	.541	51	1	.167	.246	.241	32	0	.125	.268	.156	46	2	.217	.321	.370
1991	NY-N	0	2	0	85	2.66	0	2	0	49	2.59	0	0	0	36	2.75	124	1	.250	.301	.331	178	1	.197	.247	.264	132	0	.227	.301	.273	80	0	.237	.307	.313
1992	NY-N	6	9	1	88	2.86	3	5	1	48	2.81	3	4	0	40	2.93	159	2	.289	.399	.390	160	2	.244	.291	.325	145	2	.269	.375	.366	182	2	.313	.399	.434
1993	NY-N	2	3	3	77	4.11	1	0	1	41	3.51	1	3	2	36	4.79	115	1	.296	.409	.357	150	2	.267	.347	.415	150	2	.253	.365	.360	89	3	.236	.340	.360
TOTALS		10	20	5	360	3.05	6	11	3	188	2.59	4	9	2	172	3.55	551	11	.290	.372	.407	781	11	.227	.279	.314	603	5	.242	.332	.315	440	9	.277	.358	.398

● Danny Jackson BR/TL

YEAR	TM/L	W	L	SV	IP	ERA	W	L	SV	IP	ERA	W	L	SV	IP	ERA	AB	HR	AVG	OBP	SLG	AB	HR	AVG	OBP	SLG	AB	HR	AVG	OBP	SLG	AB	HR	AVG	OBP	SLG
1984	KC-A	2	6	0	76	4.26	2	2	0	37	4.14	0	4	0	39	4.38	60	1	.217	.319	.350	235	3	.302	.383	.387	159	2	.302	.351	.396	17	2	.471	.571	.941
1985	KC-A	14	12	0	208	3.42	6	5	0	99	3.38	8	7	0	109	3.46	198	1	.272	.350	.367	643	6	.258	.322	.359	331	3	.266	.331	.375	104	0	.298	.348	.423
1986	KC-A	11	12	0	186	3.20	6	4	0	80	2.15	5	8	0	106	3.99	137	2	.292	.362	.409	555	11	.247	.327	.353	305	5	.262	.334	.364	97	1	.237	.333	.289
1987	KC-A	9	18	0	224	4.02	6	9	0	121	4.30	3	9	0	103	3.68	159	1	.277	.328	.346	690	10	.254	.348	.368	388	7	.265	.344	.387	96	2	.198	.250	.292
1988	Cin-N	23	8	0	261	2.73	12	3	0	134	2.63	11	5	0	127	2.83	115	3	.270	.299	.336	820	12	.211	.269	.308	444	8	.252	.316	.355	130	1	.162	.193	.254
1989	Cin-N	6	11	0	116	5.60	3	5	0	60	5.10	3	6	0	56	6.14	67	1	.269	.333	.373	384	9	.272	.354	.398	199	7	.312	.403	.477	21	1	.190	.292	.333
1990	Cin-N	6	6	0	117	3.61	4	3	0	54	3.83	2	3	0	63	3.41	85	2	.235	.330	.365	363	9	.273	.324	.391	179	0	.257	.327	.402	35	2	.286	.316	.457
1991	Chi-N	1	5	0	71	6.75	0	2	0	47	7.20	1	3	0	24	6.16	18	0	.311	.400	.456	150	5	.333	.417	.469	150	5	.333	.404	.469	19	2	.526	.557	1.000
1992	Chi-N	4	9	0	113	4.22	2	2	0	53	2.21	2	7	0	60	6.00	68	1	.279	.370	.353	366	4	.268	.337	.374	213	2	.272	.328	.352	20	1	.500	.524	.650
1992	Pit-N	4	4	0	88	3.36	4	2	0	64	3.39	0	2	0	25	3.28	51	1	.196	.276	.255	290	6	.290	.340	.366	157	0	.274	.328	.325	23	0	.348	.375	.348

YEAR	TM/L	TOTAL					HOME					AWAY					LEFT					RIGHT					ON-BASE					LATE/CLOSE				
		W	L	SV	IP	ERA	W	L	SV	IP	ERA	W	L	SV	IP	ERA	AB	HR	AVG	OBP	SLG	AB	HR	AVG	OBP	SLG	AB	HR	AVG	OBP	SLG	AB	HR	AVG	OBP	SLG
1993	Phi-N	12	11	0	210	3.77	8	5	0	110	3.86	4	6	0	101	3.67						671	8	.256	.319	.415	375	5	.269	.325	.500	38	1	.316	.400	.500
1994	Phi-N	14	6	0	179	3.26	8	4	0	110	3.10	6	2	0	69	3.52	96	4	.240	.260	.260	591	15	.271	.320	.401	307	6	.248	.290	.362	35	0	.229	.229	.314
TOTALS		106	108	1	1849	3.75	59	46	1	961	3.57	47	62	0	888	3.95	1217	15	.267	.337	.357	5825	93	.259	.328	.368	3104	53	.271	.336	.381	635	13	.258	.314	.381
● **Mike Jackson** BR/TR																																				
1986	Phi-N	0	0	0	13	3.38	0	0	0	8	4.50	0	0	0	5	1.69	25	0	.320	.414	.360	23	2	.174	.240	.478	24	1	.292	.370	.500	0	0	—	—	—
1987	Phi-N	3	10	1	109	4.20	2	3	1	55	2.13	1	7	0	54	6.29	189	6	.265	.397	.407	213	10	.178	.236	.352	176	10	.227	.317	.432	84	2	.274	.380	.393
1988	Sea-A	6	5	4	99	2.63	5	3	0	45	3.00	1	2	4	54	2.32	159	5	.258	.340	.421	195	5	.169	.249	.272	184	6	.179	.265	.310	152	6	.224	.309	.382
1989	Sea-A	4	6	7	99	3.17	2	2	4	54	3.50	2	4	3	45	2.78	158	5	.222	.344	.367	205	3	.224	.322	.317	169	2	.243	.384	.337	165	2	.224	.366	.315
1990	Sea-A	5	7	3	77	4.54	3	4	0	40	4.95	2	3	3	37	4.10	105	5	.257	.375	.438	174	3	.213	.307	.293	150	2	.233	.333	.327	169	2	.231	.337	.308
1991	Sea-A	7	7	14	89	3.25	3	2	6	48	2.64	4	5	8	41	3.95	119	2	.252	.355	.387	200	3	.170	.249	.245	144	1	.222	.345	.319	208	4	.221	.296	.346
1992	SF-N	6	6	2	82	3.73	3	0	1	40	3.15	3	6	1	42	4.29	162	3	.265	.363	.401	140	4	.236	.291	.371	120	1	.283	.405	.400	150	5	.240	.309	.387
1993	SF-N	6	6	1	77	3.03	3	4	1	33	4.32	3	2	0	44	2.05	126	3	.246	.317	.365	158	4	.171	.236	.272	132	6	.220	.291	.386	170	5	.218	.281	.347
1994	SF-N	3	2	4	42	1.49	2	1	2	25	1.44	1	1	2	17	1.56	67	2	.194	.267	.299	73	2	.137	.203	.233	55	3	.182	.258	.345	110	3	.164	.225	.255
TOTALS		40	49	36	689	3.37	23	19	15	348	3.18	17	30	21	341	3.56	1110	31	.250	.354	.391	1381	36	.190	.266	.301	1154	32	.226	.330	.360	1208	29	.224	.313	.341
● **Tommy John** BR/TL																																				
1984	Cal-A	7	13	0	181	4.52	1	4	0	55	6.02	6	9	0	126	3.86	150	1	.287	.352	.367	578	14	.311	.358	.452	326	5	.276	.328	.380	58	1	.328	.371	.448
1985	Cal-A	2	4	0	38	4.70	0	3	0	14	4.50	2	1	0	24	4.81	43	0	.302	.375	.349	112	3	.339	.392	.509	70	0	.343	.407	.414	13	0	.615	.600	.923
1985	Oak-A	2	6	0	48	6.19	1	2	0	24	3.75	1	4	0	24	8.63	41	1	.317	.326	.439	158	5	.335	.384	.519	80	3	.387	.427	.587	9	0	.000	.000	.000
1986	NY-A	5	3	0	71	2.93	2	2	0	41	3.76	3	1	0	30	1.80	42	2	.286	.354	.500	223	6	.274	.308	.372	110	4	.200	.254	.336	22	1	.273	.273	.409
1987	NY-A	13	6	0	188	4.03	6	3	0	90	4.38	7	3	0	97	3.70	123	1	.203	.258	.260	613	11	.305	.351	.413	307	4	.283	.348	.368	35	0	.343	.361	.400
1988	NY-A	9	8	0	176	4.49	3	5	0	86	4.19	6	3	0	90	4.78	146	3	.281	.335	.418	571	8	.315	.359	.424	313	2	.288	.359	.390	46	0	.348	.362	.391
1989	NY-A	2	7	0	64	5.80	0	3	0	26	7.01	2	4	0	38	4.97	36	2	.444	.487	.611	223	4	.318	.377	.417	115	3	.330	.397	.443	28	0	.500	.563	.536
TOTALS		40	47	0	766	4.46	13	22	0	336	4.69	27	25	0	430	4.29	581	10	.281	.336	.386	2478	51	.311	.357	.432	1321	21	.289	.350	.396	211	2	.355	.386	.445
● **Randy Johnson** BR/TL																																				
1988	Mon-N	3	0	0	26	2.42	2	0	0	17	3.18	1	0	0	9	1.00	8	0	.125	.125	.125	94	3	.234	.287	.383	42	0	.262	.311	.333	0	0	—	—	—
1989	Mon-N	0	4	0	30	6.67	0	1	0	15	1.80	0	3	0	15	11.66	29	1	.276	.323	.483	81	1	.259	.413	.321	61	2	.262	.338	.426	4	0	.250	.250	.250
1989	Sea-A	7	9	0	131	4.40	2	5	0	55	5.56	5	4	0	76	3.55	59	1	.169	.254	.271	424	10	.255	.349	.387	197	5	.254	.347	.386	38	0	.237	.286	.263
1990	Sea-A	14	11	0	220	3.65	8	4	0	102	2.90	6	7	0	117	4.30	82	0	.195	.256	.232	724	26	.218	.326	.369	342	6	.213	.309	.304	67	2	.149	.278	.239
1991	Sea-A	13	10	0	201	3.98	6	3	0	106	3.92	7	5	0	96	4.05	85	2	.212	.337	.306	623	13	.213	.361	.327	316	7	.244	.379	.361	61	0	.246	.352	.311
1992	Sea-A	12	14	0	210	3.77	8	6	0	117	2.76	4	8	0	93	5.03	75	1	.187	.303	.240	674	12	.208	.348	.315	352	9	.207	.336	.332	83	2	.181	.343	.301
1993	Sea-A	19	8	1	255	3.24	11	3	1	151	2.86	8	5	0	104	3.80	71	0	.183	.256	.239	842	22	.204	.293	.329	347	6	.225	.312	.320	107	3	.159	.266	.290
1994	Sea-A	13	6	0	172	3.19	5	3	0	69	3.39	8	3	0	103	3.06	51	0	.235	.316	.333	561	14	.214	.303	.339	214	3	.229	.333	.322	57	2	.211	.274	.368
TOTALS		81	62	1	1245	3.70	42	27	1	632	3.30	39	35	0	613	4.11	460	5	.200	.284	.278	4023	101	.217	.329	.342	1871	38	.228	.335	.337	417	9	.189	.300	.295
● **Barry Jones** BR/TR																																				
1986	Pit-N	3	4	3	37	2.89	1	2	1	22	2.49	2	2	2	16	3.45	56	2	.250	.317	.411	79	1	.190	.304	.304	55	1	.291	.403	.418	83	2	.289	.388	.458
1987	Pit-N	2	4	1	43	5.61	2	1	0	25	5.04	0	3	1	18	6.38	84	1	.286	.365	.393	91	5	.341	.413	.593	91	3	.319	.413	.527	62	1	.290	.357	.403
1988	Pit-N	1	1	2	56	3.04	1	1	0	27	5.40	0	0	2	30	0.91	81	1	.284	.375	.346	128	2	.266	.309	.367	102	3	.275	.345	.373	81	1	.284	.333	.383
1988	Chi-A	2	2	1	26	2.42	2	1	1	14	1.98	0	1	0	12	2.92	35	2	.200	.364	.400	53	1	.151	.258	.208	37	1	.135	.327	.216	47	2	.170	.264	.298
1989	Chi-A	3	2	1	30	2.37	0	1	0	13	3.46	3	1	1	17	1.56	47	1	.213	.302	.340	59	1	.203	.234	.254	60	1	.183	.239	.283	50	1	.240	.296	.300
1990	Chi-A	11	4	1	74	2.31	8	1	0	45	2.18	3	3	1	29	2.51	112	2	.304	.364	.402	152	0	.184	.282	.211	127	0	.260	.349	.299	227	0	.238	.328	.273
1991	Chi-A	4	9	13	89	3.35	1	2	6	40	2.70	3	7	7	49	3.88	141	2	.255	.348	.369	168	6	.238	.291	.369	144	6	.292	.356	.479	185	5	.286	.357	.427
1992	Phi-N	5	6	0	54	4.64	3	4	0	29	4.08	2	2	0	26	5.26	105	0	.343	.421	.419	108	3	.269	.333	.454	105	2	.371	.433	.533	108	2	.296	.376	.407
1992	NY-N	2	0	1	15	9.39	2	0	1	9	7.71	0	0	0	6	12.00	31	0	.323	.405	.387	32	0	.313	.421	.375	40	0	.325	.417	.400	15	0	.400	.438	.533
1993	Chi-A	0	1	0	7	8.59	0	1	0	6	7.50	0	1	0	1	13.50	11	2	.636	.667	1.182	23	0	.304	.360	.348	19	1	.421	.450	.632	9	1	.444	.444	.778
TOTALS		33	33	23	433	3.66	20	13	9	229	3.65	13	20	14	204	3.67						893	19	.286	.369	.398	780	17	.287	.369	.417	867	15	.270	.346	.373
● **Doug Jones** BR/TR																																				
1986	Cle-A	1	0	1	18	2.50	0	0	1	7	2.45	1	0	0	11	2.53	33	0	.273	.314	.303	37	0	.243	.326	.270	34	0	.235	.325	.265	42	0	.262	.319	.310
1987	Cle-A	6	5	8	91	3.15	5	1	0	53	3.76	1	4	8	39	2.33	186	1	.269	.310	.317	174	3	.293	.354	.393	189	3	.312	.372	.413	144	1	.313	.377	.375
1988	Cle-A	3	4	37	83	2.27	1	4	19	38	3.99	2	0	18	45	0.80	177	1	.203	.254	.266	140	0	.236	.267	.271	170	0	.229	.280	.276	254	0	.224	.273	.252
1989	Cle-A	7	10	32	81	2.34	6	4	15	46	2.15	1	6	17	35	2.60	160	4	.244	.281	.369	143	0	.259	.276	.301	159	3	.226	.250	.314	264	4	.254	.280	.348
1990	Cle-A	5	5	43	84	2.56	4	4	23	46	3.11	1	1	20	38	1.89	165	3	.200	.249	.315	138	2	.239	.303	.333	155	3	.219	.281	.329	229	2	.227	.278	.314
1991	Cle-A	4	8	7	63	5.54	1	4	1	27	6.41	3	4	6	37	4.91	132	4	.341	.380	.530	140	3	.300	.336	.464	136	3	.316	.358	.500	91	4	.407	.433	.725
1992	Hou-N	11	8	36	112	1.85	6	5	17	63	2.42	5	3	19	49	1.12	217	3	.253	.296	.355	192	2	.214	.249	.281	194	3	.175	.227	.263	322	5	.239	.282	.342
1993	Hou-N	4	10	26	85	4.54	3	4	8	36	5.00	1	6	18	49	4.20	177	5	.322	.353	.441	157	6	.350	.401	.497	195	5	.318	.374	.421					
1994	Phi-N	2	4	27	54	2.17	2	2	19	32	1.14	0	2	8	22	3.63	110	2	.327	.348	.409	106	0	.179	.202	.189	110	1	.227	.234	.273	179	2	.251	.272	.302
TOTALS		43	54	217	672	2.96	28	28	103	348	3.31	15	26	114	324	2.59	1345	20	.259	.298	.353	1247	25	.258	.298	.338	1304	22	.255	.304	.354	1720	23	.263	.307	.353
● **Bobby Jones** BR/TR																																				
1993	NY-N	2	4	0	62	3.65	0	3	0	28	3.54	2	1	0	34	3.74	125	1	.224	.317	.320	108	5	.306	.339	.546	96	2	.240	.321	.344	18	0	.222	.333	.278
1994	NY-N	12	7	0	160	3.15	4	6	0	89	4.25	8	1	0	71	1.77	330	5	.267	.332	.364	280	5	.246	.309	.336	258	9	.248	.315	.364	62	1	.242	.309	.306
TOTALS		14	11	0	222	3.29	4	9	0	117	4.08	10	2	0	105	2.41	455	6	.255	.328	.352	388	10	.263	.318	.394	354	9	.246	.317	.359	80	1	.237	.315	.300
● **Jimmy Key** BR/TL																																				
1984	Tor-A	4	5	10	62	4.65	1	2	3	26	5.13	3	3	7	36	4.29	95	2	.316	.394	.442	150	6	.267	.353	.447	132	5	.326	.434	.508	149	5	.309	.388	.483
1985	Tor-A	14	6	0	213	3.00	10	3	0	129	2.66	4	3	0	84	3.54	157	4	.178	.233	.306	637	18	.251	.295	.403	277	8	.224	.286	.372	72	0	.208	.284	.222
1986	Tor-A	14	11	0	232	3.57	7	9	0	114	4.50	7	2	0	118	2.67	190	1	.268	.319	.321	676	23	.253	.314	.426	340	14	.229	.282	.406	107	3	.280	.325	.393
1987	Tor-A	17	8	0	261	2.76	10	4	0	157	2.36	7	4	0	104	3.36	157	4	.248	.290	.382	794	20	.215	.268	.330	330	8	.264	.317	.409	96	5	.250	.330	.448
1988	Tor-A	12	5	0	131	3.29	4	3	0	55	4.45	8	2	0	77	2.47	75	1	.147	.200	.253	434	12	.267	.313	.408	187	4	.262	.305	.390	29	0	.138	.194	.138
1989	Tor-A	13	14	0	216	3.88	7	8	0	120	3.81	6	6	0	96	3.95	150	2	.227	.245	.327	688	16	.279	.302	.435	310	7	.284	.308	.432	67	1	.254	.246	.328
1990	Tor-A	13	7	0	155	4.25	7	3	0	89	4.47	6	4	0	66	3.95	131	2	.182	.213	.193	541	14	.280	.298	.420	232	8	.276	.296	.435	12	0	.250	.250	.333
1991	Tor-A	16	12	0	209	3.05	9	7	0	110	3.43	9	4	0	99	2.64	112	2	.286	.325	.357	703	10	.249	.288	.346	331	7	.287	.327	.417	67	2	.284	.324	.388
1992	Tor-A	13	13	0	217	3.53	7	5	0	105	3.35	6	8	0	112	3.70	131	2	.176	.216	.252	697	22	.261	.314	.418	300	9	.287	.336	.437	57	4	.316	.371	.614
1993	NY-A	18	6	0	237	3.00	8	2	0	105	2.75	10	4	0	132	3.20	131	6	.260	.292	.420	758	20	.244	.277	.376	321	7	.227	.264	.318	56	3	.268	.276	.482
1994	NY-A	17	4	0	168	3.27	7	4	0	91	3.86	10	0	0	77	2.57	126	1	.238	.273	.341	523	9	.281	.341	.382	277	5	.267	.326	.390	33	0	.242	.257	.273
TOTALS		151	91	10	2100	3.36	75	51	3	1100	3.48	76	40	7	1000	3.24	1412	25	.232	.275	.331	6574	176	.257	.302	.399	3037	82	.263	.311	.405	745	23	.267	.318	.403
● **Eric King** BR/TR																																				
1986	Det-A	11	4	3	138	3.51	6	0	1	68	2.00	5	4	2	71	4.97	247	8	.239	.326	.389	254	5	.193	.299	.272	220	6	.227	.308	.314	68	2	.191	.214	.294
1987	Det-A	6	9	9	116	4.89	2	2	2	56	5.95	4	5	7	60	3.90	229	6	.240	.332	.358	214	10	.262	.355	.430	196	6	.260	.365	.403	170	2	.282	.366	.359
1988	Det-A	4	1	3	69	3.41	2	1	3	38	2.82	2	0	0	30	4.15	108	2	.213	.331	.380	149	2	.248	.333	.342	135	2	.185	.268	.296	24	0	.292	.452	.333
1989	Chi-A	9	10	0	159	3.39	6	7	0	98	3.20	3	3	0	61	3.69	308	11	.231	.312	.373	303	8	.258	.308	.307	238	2	.248	.320	.298	52	0	.212	.288	.269
1990	Chi-A	12	4	0	151	3.28	5	1	0	76	3.93	7	3	0	75	2.63	268	5	.216	.286	.321	302	5	.255	.300	.344	213	6	.258	.314	.404	26	1	.192	.323	.423
1991	Cle-A	6	11	0	151	4.60	2	7	0	85	5.95	4	4	0	66	3.57	326	5	.285	.334	.393	268	2	.272	.321	.373	256	6	.301	.355	.406	25	0	.480	.567	.720
1992	Det-A	4	6	1	79	5.22	1	4	1	30	6.07	3	2	0	50	4.71	141	7	.291	.357	.482	175	5	.280	.332	.423	139	5	.324	.377	.460	2	1	.500	.667	2.000
TOTALS		52	45	16	863	3.97	24	26	7	431	4.08	28	19	9	431	3.87	1627	44	.246	.322	.376	1645	26	.259	.330	.367	1397	25	.259	.330	.367	367	6	.264	.349	.371
● **Bob Kipper** BR/TL																																				
1985	Cal-A	0	1	0	3	21.60	0	1	0	3	13.50	0	0	0	1	54.00	3	0	.333	.400	.667	12	1	.500	.533	.833	8	0	.500	.500	.750	0	0	—	—	—
1985	Pit-N	1	0	0	25	5.11	0	0	0	10	6.97	1	0	0	14	3.77	11	0	.364	.364	.455	84	4	.202	.261	.393	3	0	.333	.361	.630	1	0	1.000	1.000	1.000
1986	Pit-N	6	8	0	114	4.03	2	4	0	55	4.75	4	4	0	59	3.36	71	0	.268	.328	.331	382	17	.272	.331	.476	180	7	.272	.330	.467	33	1	.303	.343	.424
1987	Pit-N	5	9	0	111	5.94	2	5	0	65	5.57	3	4	0	46	6.46	79	1	.203	.241	.241	353	25	.286	.372	.578	177	11	.288	.355	.582	17	0	.176	.333	.235
1988	Pit-N	2	6	0	65	3.74	1	4	0	37	2.41	1	2	0	28	5.53	86	2	.244	.301	.326	205	5	.228	.320	.379	92	3	.272	.373	.402	76	1	.197	.307	.276
1989	Pit-N	3	4	4	83	2.93	2	0	1	39	1.85	1	4	3	44	3.89	94	0	.170	.257	.277	199	5	.196	.272	.342	117	2	.231	.316	.359	122	2	.156	.254	.270
1990	Pit-N	5	2	3	63	3.02	4	1	0	30	2.70	1	1	3	33	3.31	80	2	.225	.323	.275	146	7	.178	.261	.356	99	3	.162	.259	.303	59	1	.186	.282	.322
1991	Pit-N	2	4	2	60	4.65	1	1	1	30	3.00	1	3	1	29	2.45	78	3	.321	.341	.500	181	6	.255	.331	.398	104	4	.317	.376	.519	78	3	.269	.360	.462
1992	Min-A	3	3	0	39	4.42	1	2	0	24	5.55	2	1	0	14	2.51	44	3	.250	.313	.500	105	5	.276	.356	.448	70	2	.214	.295	.329	51	2	.235	.328	.353
TOTALS		27	37	11	562	4.34	13	20	2	294	4.47	14	17	9	268	4.20	546	9	.240	.294	.342	1587	72	.250	.325	.451	880	35	.262	.329	.453	437	10	.211	.305	.334
● **Bob Knepper** BL/TL																																				
1984	Hou-N	15	10	0	234	3.20	10	4	0	139	2.60	5	6	0	95	4.07	104	2	.269	.290	.375	783	24	.249	.295	.386	340	12	.238	.291	.400	62	1	.226	.273	.290

YEAR	TM/L	TOTAL					HOME					AWAY					LEFT					RIGHT					ON-BASE					LATE/CLOSE				
		W	L	SV	IP	ERA	W	L	SV	IP	ERA	W	L	SV	IP	ERA	AB	HR	AVG	OBP	SLG	AB	HR	AVG	OBP	SLG	AB	HR	AVG	OBP	SLG	AB	HR	AVG	OBP	SLG
1985	Hou-N	15	13	0	241	3.55	5	8	0	123	3.51	10	5	0	118	3.58	115	3	.261	.287	.409	820	18	.272	.313	.412	374	6	.275	.330	.404	70	1	.286	.333	.386
1986	Hou-N	17	12	0	258	3.14	9	6	0	132	3.62	8	6	0	126	2.64	154	4	.227	.255	.383	806	15	.244	.295	.364	348	7	.244	.315	.374	80	1	.237	.303	.363
1987	Hou-N	8	17	0	178	5.27	5	7	0	98	4.30	3	10	0	79	6.47	117	3	.282	.317	.419	606	23	.318	.370	.518	306	8	.330	.383	.497	49	0	.306	.370	.388
1988	Hou-N	14	5	0	175	3.14	9	3	0	103	2.36	5	2	0	72	4.25	92	1	.239	.273	.348	550	12	.244	.321	.364	270	5	.226	.287	.330	58	1	.172	.200	.276
1989	Hou-N	4	10	0	113	5.89	0	5	0	47	6.89	4	5	0	66	5.18	66	3	.318	.384	.530	379	9	.301	.387	.430	205	7	.337	.406	.522	9	1	.667	.727	1.111
1989	SF-N	3	2	0	52	3.46	0	2	0	24	5.92	3	0	0	28	1.30	34	0	.265	.324	.353	170	4	.271	.317	.418	93	2	.237	.302	.366	0	0	—	—	—
1990	SF-N	3	3	0	44	5.68	1	2	0	21	5.66	2	1	0	24	5.70	25	0	.200	.231	.240	155	7	.329	.398	.587	74	2	.284	.375	.473	7	1	.571	.571	1.286
	TOTALS	79	72	0	1295	3.86	39	37	0	687	3.67	40	35	0	608	4.07	707	16	.259	.293	.395	4269	112	.270	.326	.415	2010	49	.270	.332	.415	335	6	.263	.315	.382

● Bill Krueger BL/TL

YEAR	TM/L	W	L	SV	IP	ERA	W	L	SV	IP	ERA	W	L	SV	IP	ERA	AB	HR	AVG	OBP	SLG	AB	HR	AVG	OBP	SLG	AB	HR	AVG	OBP	SLG	AB	HR	AVG	OBP	SLG
1984	Oak-A	10	10	0	142	4.75	7	3	0	79	3.66	3	7	0	63	6.11	104	2	.260	.355	.337	444	7	.291	.383	.378	280	2	.286	.352	.350	34	0	.294	.351	.353
1985	Oak-A	9	10	0	151	4.52	4	6	0	79	4.56	5	4	0	72	4.48	123	3	.317	.390	.439	474	10	.266	.338	.401	275	6	.280	.343	.417	27	0	.148	.207	.185
1986	Oak-A	1	2	1	34	6.03	1	0	1	21	6.10	0	2	0	14	5.93	35	2	.257	.333	.571	98	2	.316	.367	.449	61	2	.328	.386	.541	9	0	.333	.400	.333
1987	Oak-A	0	3	0	6	9.53	0	2	0	4	9.82	0	1	0	2	9.00	9	0	.333	.500	.444	16	0	.375	.524	.563	15	0	.400	.591	.600	14	0	.286	.474	.429
1987	LA-N	0	0	0	2	0.00	0	0	0	2	0.00	0	0	0	0	0.00	2	0	.000	.333	.000	10	0	.300	.300	.400	8	0	.250	.250	.375	0	0	—	—	—
1988	LA-N	0	0	0	2	11.57	0	0	0	2	11.57	0	0	0	0	—	1	0	.000	.000	.000	10	0	.400	.538	.500	4	0	.500	.714	.500	0	0	—	—	—
1989	Mil-A	3	2	3	94	3.84	2	2	1	47	3.61	1	0	2	46	4.08	94	0	.223	.298	.245	270	9	.278	.333	.422	171	3	.275	.339	.374	33	0	.212	.278	.212
1990	Mil-A	6	8	0	129	3.98	4	6	0	77	4.23	2	2	0	52	3.61	93	1	.237	.265	.323	403	9	.285	.361	.419	231	3	.281	.351	.398	49	2	.204	.231	.347
1991	Sea-A	11	8	0	175	3.60	7	3	0	94	3.73	4	5	0	81	3.44	140	2	.307	.351	.414	532	13	.284	.345	.419	275	2	.276	.356	.378	50	1	.340	.389	.480
1992	Min-A	10	6	0	161	4.30	2	3	0	56	4.53	8	3	0	106	4.17	93	1	.312	.333	.452	537	17	.255	.313	.397	239	8	.293	.368	.452	47	1	.213	.302	.298
1992	Mon-N	0	2	0	17	6.75	0	1	0	10	6.30	0	1	0	7	7.36	11	0	.273	.429	.364	62	0	.323	.373	.403	30	0	.333	.444	.467	6	0	.000	.000	.000
1993	Det-A	6	4	0	82	3.40	4	0	0	43	1.69	2	4	0	39	5.26	72	3	.292	.308	.458	244	3	.283	.355	.373	147	3	.245	.341	.354	41	1	.341	.400	.463
1994	Det-A	0	2	0	20	9.61	0	1	0	10	6.97	0	1	0	9	12.54	26	1	.192	.364	.423	55	2	.382	.464	.564	44	2	.295	.433	.455	14	0	.286	.450	.357
1994	SD-N	3	2	0	41	4.83	1	1	0	18	4.00	2	1	0	23	5.48	31	1	.303	.343	.455	129	4	.248	.279	.411	59	3	.288	.328	.475	11	0	.182	.182	.182
	TOTALS	59	59	4	1057	4.38	32	28	2	541	4.09	27	31	2	516	4.67	836	16	.278	.343	.394	3284	76	.280	.349	.408	1839	34	.283	.359	.402	335	5	.254	.323	.340

● Mike Krukow BR/TR

YEAR	TM/L	W	L	SV	IP	ERA	W	L	SV	IP	ERA	W	L	SV	IP	ERA	AB	HR	AVG	OBP	SLG	AB	HR	AVG	OBP	SLG	AB	HR	AVG	OBP	SLG	AB	HR	AVG	OBP	SLG
1984	SF-N	11	12	1	199	4.56	6	4	0	103	3.66	5	8	1	96	5.53	408	16	.309	.376	.490	400	6	.270	.329	.387	362	10	.293	.354	.445	70	2	.257	.312	.429
1985	SF-N	8	11	0	195	3.38	6	5	0	116	2.24	2	6	0	78	5.06	387	10	.232	.301	.390	392	9	.218	.292	.356	106	1	.160	.239	.236
1986	SF-N	20	9	0	245	3.05	12	4	0	127	2.47	8	5	0	118	3.67	518	11	.226	.283	.349	395	13	.220	.250	.362	326	11	.227	.288	.368	112	1	.223	.248	.268
1987	SF-N	5	6	0	163	4.80	1	3	0	87	4.26	4	3	0	76	5.42	353	13	.309	.366	.479	280	11	.261	.292	.443	256	8	.301	.351	.457	42	4	.381	.386	.738
1988	SF-N	7	4	0	125	3.54	4	2	0	69	3.54	3	2	0	56	3.54	245	6	.261	.314	.412	225	7	.209	.262	.342	177	1	.226	.302	.316	29	1	.345	.472	.655
1989	SF-N	4	3	0	43	3.98	2	1	0	18	3.44	2	2	0	25	4.38	86	3	.233	.316	.360	71	2	.239	.325	.380	52	3	.288	.387	.538	5	1	.400	.333	1.000
	TOTALS	55	45	1	970	3.82	31	19	0	521	3.13	24	26	1	449	4.63	1997	59	.273	.332	.427	1723	48	.232	.278	.367	1457	42	.257	.322	.400	364	10	.242	.295	.385

● Mike La Coss BR/TR

YEAR	TM/L	W	L	SV	IP	ERA	W	L	SV	IP	ERA	W	L	SV	IP	ERA	AB	HR	AVG	OBP	SLG	AB	HR	AVG	OBP	SLG	AB	HR	AVG	OBP	SLG	AB	HR	AVG	OBP	SLG
1984	Hou-N	7	5	3	132	4.02	3	1	2	70	3.33	4	4	1	62	4.82	243	1	.255	.345	.300	261	2	.268	.322	.349	220	2	.286	.374	.368	58	0	.138	.219	.190
1985	KC-A	1	1	1	41	5.09	1	1	0	21	6.33	0	0	0	19	3.72	70	2	.229	.372	.286	91	2	.363	.442	.516	84	1	.333	.472	.464	37	0	.297	.409	.378
1986	SF-N	10	13	0	204	3.57	7	4	0	108	2.83	3	9	0	96	4.39	425	5	.228	.297	.322	322	9	.255	.324	.370	277	9	.282	.357	.433	60	0	.200	.273	.267
1987	SF-N	13	10	0	171	3.68	7	8	0	100	3.23	6	2	0	71	4.33	369	11	.301	.370	.463	282	5	.259	.314	.362	274	7	.270	.351	.409	71	4	.296	.427	.549
1988	SF-N	7	7	0	114	3.62	7	2	0	76	2.25	0	5	0	38	6.34	214	0	.224	.282	.276	209	5	.244	.300	.359	170	0	.241	.340	.276	36	1	.278	.333	.500
1989	SF-N	10	10	6	150	3.17	6	4	4	68	2.90	4	6	2	82	3.40	305	3	.266	.359	.331	255	0	.243	.309	.298	254	2	.264	.345	.331	103	2	.252	.373	.330
1990	SF-N	6	4	0	78	3.94	2	2	0	27	3.67	4	2	0	51	4.09	178	3	.242	.343	.331	112	2	.286	.341	.384	132	4	.280	.344	.432	21	0	.095	.174	.095
1991	SF-N	1	5	0	47	7.23	1	2	0	28	5.40	0	3	0	19	9.95	112	3	.330	.398	.482	82	1	.293	.383	.402	90	2	.322	.422	.456	39	3	.282	.417	.590
	TOTALS	55	55	10	938	3.88	34	24	7	500	3.24	21	31	3	438	4.60	1916	26	.258	.343	.352	1614	26	.265	.328	.363	1501	27	.278	.364	.387	425	10	.238	.345	.369

● Dennis Lamp BR/TR

YEAR	TM/L	W	L	SV	IP	ERA	W	L	SV	IP	ERA	W	L	SV	IP	ERA	AB	HR	AVG	OBP	SLG	AB	HR	AVG	OBP	SLG	AB	HR	AVG	OBP	SLG	AB	HR	AVG	OBP	SLG
1984	Tor-A	8	8	9	85	4.55	4	0	6	44	3.07	4	7	3	41	6.15	148	2	.311	.400	.378	192	7	.266	.324	.396	181	6	.315	.381	.442	130	3	.308	.401	.408
1985	Tor-A	11	0	2	106	3.32	6	0	0	42	3.02	5	0	2	64	3.52	172	3	.238	.292	.320	216	4	.255	.293	.352	183	5	.240	.286	.372	116	2	.207	.256	.284
1986	Tor-A	2	6	2	73	5.05	1	5	2	43	5.44	1	1	0	30	4.50	126	1	.349	.410	.405	175	4	.280	.317	.406	136	4	.382	.426	.544	41	2	.585	.638	.756
1987	Oak-A	1	3	0	57	5.08	0	1	0	26	4.15	1	2	0	31	5.87	95	1	.316	.405	.379	138	4	.333	.365	.507	116	3	.362	.412	.509	14	0	.286	.412	.286
1988	Bos-A	7	6	0	83	3.48	5	0	0	41	3.73	2	6	0	42	3.24	147	2	.313	.357	.422	177	1	.260	.300	.339	164	1	.280	.333	.360	67	1	.328	.403	.433
1989	Bos-A	4	2	2	112	2.32	3	1	2	74	2.93	1	1	0	39	1.16	180	2	.289	.352	.350	228	2	.193	.220	.254	167	2	.263	.312	.311	51	1	.314	.357	.412
1990	Bos-A	3	5	0	106	4.68	2	2	0	57	4.40	1	3	0	48	5.03	194	3	.299	.354	.418	214	7	.262	.302	.477	201	4	.348	.395	.488	83	4	.277	.315	.470
1991	Bos-A	6	3	0	92	4.70	3	3	0	41	6.59	3	0	0	51	3.18	129	2	.333	.419	.457	235	6	.243	.286	.400	183	4	.279	.343	.421	80	1	.262	.337	.350
1992	Pit-N	1	1	0	28	5.14	1	0	0	14	3.29	0	1	0	14	6.91	50	2	.280	.379	.420	63	1	.302	.333	.413	52	2	.250	.361	.423	38	1	.316	.381	.447
	TOTALS	43	34	15	741	4.07	25	13	10	381	4.04	18	21	5	360	4.10	1241	18	.301	.369	.390	1638	36	.258	.299	.380	1383	31	.303	.358	.426	620	15	.300	.367	.411

● Les Lancaster BR/TR

YEAR	TM/L	W	L	SV	IP	ERA	W	L	SV	IP	ERA	W	L	SV	IP	ERA	AB	HR	AVG	OBP	SLG	AB	HR	AVG	OBP	SLG	AB	HR	AVG	OBP	SLG	AB	HR	AVG	OBP	SLG
1987	Chi-N	8	3	0	132	4.90	6	2	0	70	4.78	2	1	0	63	5.03	265	6	.317	.375	.479	250	6	.216	.281	.328	220	8	.264	.333	.423	36	1	.278	.366	.389
1988	Chi-N	4	6	5	86	3.78	2	3	3	52	3.98	2	3	2	34	3.48	156	2	.282	.362	.404	170	2	.265	.314	.382	147	4	.293	.358	.435	135	4	.281	.377	.415
1989	Chi-N	4	2	8	73	1.36	3	1	3	36	1.75	1	1	5	37	0.98	130	3	.203	.250	.248	132	2	.250	.279	.326	125	0	.208	.243	.216	148	1	.236	.274	.297
1990	Chi-N	9	5	6	109	4.62	4	3	3	57	5.37	5	2	3	52	3.81	228	4	.285	.367	.390	199	7	.281	.313	.437	199	4	.312	.374	.422	136	3	.301	.377	.404
1991	Chi-N	9	7	3	156	3.52	7	2	1	83	3.46	2	5	2	73	3.59	310	6	.261	.337	.374	277	7	.249	.290	.379	237	7	.253	.330	.405	135	1	.289	.349	.370
1992	Det-A	3	4	0	87	6.33	1	2	0	54	5.47	2	2	0	32	7.79	120	2	.358	.490	.492	224	9	.299	.321	.429	187	7	.299	.395	.457	43	2	.372	.471	.558
1993	StL-N	4	1	0	61	2.93	0	0	0	25	5.04	4	1	0	36	1.49	97	1	.237	.321	.361	134	4	.246	.297	.388	111	4	.261	.331	.423	49	0	.204	.291	.245
	TOTALS	41	28	22	704	4.05	23	13	10	377	4.29	18	15	12	326	3.78	1309	23	.280	.360	.399	1386	37	.251	.299	.382	1226	33	.272	.343	.409	682	12	.277	.350	.374

● Bill Landrum BR/TR

YEAR	TM/L	W	L	SV	IP	ERA	W	L	SV	IP	ERA	W	L	SV	IP	ERA	AB	HR	AVG	OBP	SLG	AB	HR	AVG	OBP	SLG	AB	HR	AVG	OBP	SLG	AB	HR	AVG	OBP	SLG
1986	Cin-N	0	0	0	13	6.75	0	0	0	6	10.50	0	0	0	7	3.68	26	0	.269	.286	.308	33	0	.485	.528	.576	34	0	.353	.395	.412	0	0	—	—	—
1987	Cin-N	3	2	0	65	4.71	2	0	0	37	4.91	1	2	0	28	4.45	101	2	.277	.387	.386	132	1	.303	.373	.417	115	0	.296	.390	.417	55	0	.200	.333	.255
1988	Chi-N	1	0	0	12	5.84	1	0	0	6	1.50	0	0	0	6	9.95	22	0	.318	.348	.318	30	1	.400	.438	.767	29	1	.241	.313	.483	4	0	.250	.250	.250
1989	Pit-N	2	3	26	81	1.67	1	2	11	36	2.75	1	1	15	45	0.80	159	0	.176	.241	.214	133	2	.241	.311	.323	126	2	.222	.311	.302	199	1	.191	.267	.241
1990	Pit-N	7	3	13	72	2.13	4	2	7	37	1.93	3	1	6	34	2.36	137	2	.270	.329	.350	126	2	.254	.296	.333	131	1	.229	.278	.267	126	1	.270	.333	.333
1991	Pit-N	4	4	17	76	3.18	1	1	9	35	1.80	3	3	8	41	4.35	139	2	.273	.336	.360	162	2	.235	.260	.302	141	0	.262	.335	.312	175	3	.246	.305	.320
1992	Mon-N	1	1	0	20	7.20	1	1	0	14	10.54	0	0	0	6	0.00	44	3	.341	.396	.614	39	0	.308	.413	.385	39	2	.333	.447	.406	32	0	.281	.343	.406
1993	Cin-N	0	2	0	22	3.74	0	0	0	9	5.19	0	2	0	13	2.77	40	0	.225	.311	.375	38	0	.237	.256	.368	31	0	.258	.324	.387	27	0	.222	.276	.259
	TOTALS	18	15	58	361	3.39	10	6	28	179	3.76	8	9	30	182	3.02	668	9	.253	.321	.341	693	9	.276	.328	.375	646	7	.262	.339	.354	618	5	.230	.302	.293

● Mark Langston BR/TL

YEAR	TM/L	W	L	SV	IP	ERA	W	L	SV	IP	ERA	W	L	SV	IP	ERA	AB	HR	AVG	OBP	SLG	AB	HR	AVG	OBP	SLG	AB	HR	AVG	OBP	SLG	AB	HR	AVG	OBP	SLG
1984	Sea-A	17	10	0	225	3.40	10	3	0	122	2.52	7	7	0	103	4.44	140	2	.186	.301	.300	679	14	.239	.336	.364	342	5	.254	.333	.357	90	1	.189	.345	.300
1985	Sea-A	7	14	0	127	5.47	4	5	0	56	5.43	3	9	0	70	5.50	79	3	.228	.344	.392	400	19	.260	.380	.463	222	6	.257	.363	.410	20	1	.200	.360	.400
1986	Sea-A	12	14	0	239	4.85	5	7	0	120	5.39	7	7	0	119	4.31	163	4	.184	.260	.294	754	26	.271	.361	.454	405	14	.274	.352	.447	107	2	.355	.412	.486
1987	Sea-A	19	13	0	272	3.84	7	8	0	126	4.29	12	5	0	146	3.45	147	4	.197	.265	.323	868	26	.245	.325	.399	451	12	.255	.310	.403	94	2	.277	.313	.383
1988	Sea-A	15	11	0	261	3.34	8	6	0	137	3.48	7	5	0	124	3.18	154	2	.201	.271	.286	800	30	.239	.320	.409	358	10	.226	.288	.391	164	5	.268	.320	.415
1989	Sea-A	4	5	0	73	3.56	2	2	0	34	5.82	2	3	0	39	1.60	32	0	.031	.114	.094	239	3	.247	.302	.356	111	2	.234	.302	.360	34	0	.176	.194	.206
1989	Mon-N	12	9	0	177	2.39	6	3	0	79	2.62	6	6	0	98	2.21	81	1	.185	.283	.247	553	12	.222	.321	.331	271	4	.207	.300	.284	93	2	.215	.302	.323
1990	Cal-A	10	17	0	223	4.40	3	11	0	119	4.55	7	6	0	104	4.23	138	1	.246	.318	.348	691	12	.262	.348	.419	368	5	.277	.349	.397	67	4	.299	.360	.537
1991	Cal-A	19	8	0	246	3.00	9	3	0	127	3.33	10	5	0	119	2.64	129	1	.217	.294	.295	755	20	.215	.291	.371	326	12	.209	.267	.368	98	3	.224	.300	.337
1992	Cal-A	13	14	0	229	3.66	9	7	0	132	3.61	4	7	0	97	3.71	131	2	.252	.282	.312	742	12	.252	.313	.352	373	7	.275	.348	.380	115	2	.209	.283	.330
1993	Cal-A	16	11	0	256	3.20	9	5	0	135	3.66	7	6	0	121	2.68	135	2	.178	.235	.244	807	20	.243	.306	.364	373	7	.260	.299	.365	139	3	.230	.301	.309
1994	Cal-A	7	8	0	119	4.68	3	5	0	65	4.96	4	3	0	54	4.33	70	3	.214	.247	.357	382	16	.277	.357	.471	184	6	.266	.325	.408	52	2	.212	.293	.365
	TOTALS	151	134	0	2448	3.74	75	65	0	1253	3.94	76	69	0	1196	3.52	1378	25	.196	.274	.274	7670	219	.246	.328	.390	3742	89	.251	.319	.386	1073	27	.246	.319	.370

● Dave La Point BL/TL

YEAR	TM/L	W	L	SV	IP	ERA	W	L	SV	IP	ERA	W	L	SV	IP	ERA	AB	HR	AVG	OBP	SLG	AB	HR	AVG	OBP	SLG	AB	HR	AVG	OBP	SLG	AB	HR	AVG	OBP	SLG
1984	StL-N	12	10	0	193	3.96	8	3	0	95	3.79	4	8	0	94	4.13	131	4	.305	.350	.374	607	8	.272	.345	.379	309	5	.282	.353	.382	60	0	.250	.318	.300
1985	SF-N	7	17	0	207	3.57	2	10	0	111	3.09	5	7	0	96	4.13	106	4	.264	.284	.406	694	14	.269	.335	.396	340	6	.268	.333	.368	74	5	.311	.378	.527
1986	Det-A	3	6	0	68	5.72	1	3	0	37	4.06	2	5	0	30	7.12	61	0	.279	.361	.328	186	6	.301	.367	.473	122	7	.352	.437	.598	6	0	.333	.500	.333
1986	SD-N	1	4	0	61	4.26	0	0	0	30	3.00	1	4	0	30	5.46	57	2	.193	.258	.333	186	5	.301	.367	.473	103	2	.301	.384	.456	12	0	.250	.400	.250
1987	StL-N	1	1	0	16	6.75	1	0	0	9	6.75	0	1	0	7	6.75	8	0	.375	.444	.500	66	4	.348	.394	.591	38	0	.289	.308	.342	5	0	.200	.429	.400
1987	Chi-A	6	3	0	83	2.94	4	1	0	50	3.24	2	2	0	33	2.48	36	3	.201	.302	.237	270	7	.226	.296	.348	134	3	.201	.267	.299	16	2	.250	.250	.688
1988	Chi-A	10	11	0	161	3.40	5	6	0	84	3.32	5	5	0	77	3.49	85	1	.259	.293	.376	532	9	.242	.300	.336	245	6	.261	.316	.343	47	4	.362	.380	.617
1988	Pit-N	4	2	0	52	2.77	3	1	0	34	2.14	1	1	0	18	3.93	28	2	.321	.387	.571	171	2	.263	.291	.368	76	1	.250	.301	.342	21	0	.190	.292	.238
1989	NY-A	6	9	0	114	5.62	3	3	0	47	4.60	3	6	0	67	6.34	86	4	.326	.389	.535	384	5	.307	.366	.469	211	2	.336	.395	.464	22	0	.500	.560	.591

YEAR	TM/L	TOTAL W	L	SV	IP	ERA	HOME W	L	SV	IP	ERA	AWAY W	L	SV	IP	ERA	LEFT AB	HR	AVG	OBP	SLG	RIGHT AB	HR	AVG	OBP	SLG	ON-BASE AB	HR	AVG	OBP	SLG	LATE/CLOSE AB	HR	AVG	OBP	SLG
1990	NY-A	7	10	0	158	4.11	6	3	0	95	3.13	1	7	0	63	5.60	95	2	.284	.340	.400	522	9	.293	.348	.420	264	3	.261	.316	.356	50	1	.240	.296	.360
1991	Phi-N	0	1	0	5	16.20	0	1	0	4	40.50	0	0	0	4	7.36	95	2	.284	.344	.400	23	0	.435	.548	.565	109	2	.321	.384	.440	0	0	—	—	—
	TOTALS	57	74	0	1117	4.09	33	28	0	587	3.51	24	46	0	530	4.72	695	16	.278	.328	.397	3671	78	.276	.339	.406	1856	31	.281	.345	.392	313	10	.294	.360	.447

● Terry Leach BR/TR

YEAR	TM/L	TOTAL W	L	SV	IP	ERA	HOME W	L	SV	IP	ERA	AWAY W	L	SV	IP	ERA	LEFT AB	HR	AVG	OBP	SLG	RIGHT AB	HR	AVG	OBP	SLG	ON-BASE AB	HR	AVG	OBP	SLG	LATE/CLOSE AB	HR	AVG	OBP	SLG
1985	NY-N	3	4	1	56	2.91	2	1	0	30	2.97	1	3	1	25	2.84	79	1	.291	.352	.443	125	2	.200	.241	.280	82	1	.207	.256	.305	16	1	.438	.571	.625
1986	NY-N	0	0	0	7	2.70	0	0	0	2	0.00	0	0	0	5	3.60	11	0	.273	.333	.273	16	0	.188	.278	.188	12	0	.167	.286	.167	2	0	.500	.500	.500
1987	NY-N	11	1	0	131	3.22	3	0	0	41	4.61	8	1	0	90	2.59	244	6	.275	.322	.430	259	8	.251	.286	.378	204	1	.225	.284	.289	51	0	.275	.302	.314
1988	NY-N	7	2	3	92	2.54	1	1	3	39	3.49	6	1	0	53	1.86	137	2	.292	.355	.401	217	3	.253	.293	.327	170	0	.253	.309	.300	63	0	.317	.405	.333
1989	NY-N	0	0	0	21	4.22	0	0	0	8	2.16	0	0	0	13	5.54	36	1	.306	.375	.444	42	0	.190	.200	.286	26	1	.308	.333	.500	2	0	.500	.500	.500
1989	KC-A	5	6	0	74	4.15	3	0	0	40	2.70	2	6	0	34	5.88	137	2	.307	.391	.423	144	2	.250	.323	.340	136	2	.316	.390	.426	36	0	.111	.273	.139
1990	Min-A	2	5	2	82	3.20	0	0	1	43	3.53	2	5	1	38	2.82	126	0	.270	.331	.381	187	2	.267	.303	.353	151	1	.298	.353	.384	119	1	.311	.362	.429
1991	Min-A	1	2	0	67	3.61	0	0	0	39	2.54	1	2	0	28	5.08	128	1	.367	.388	.484	146	2	.240	.284	.329	134	2	.328	.359	.448	54	0	.296	.356	.370
1992	Chi-A	6	5	0	74	1.95	3	0	0	32	0.84	3	5	0	42	2.81	99	0	.263	.333	.313	166	2	.187	.246	.283	99	1	.192	.296	.283	114	1	.272	.325	.377
1993	Chi-A	1	0	0	16	2.81	0	0	0	7	2.70	0	0	1	9	2.89	22	0	.227	.227	.227	38	0	.263	.310	.342	26	0	.308	.345	.423	15	0	.267	.267	.333
	TOTALS	35	25	7	619	3.11	12	2	4	281	2.98	23	23	3	338	3.22	1019	13	.292	.349	.410	1340	21	.237	.282	.330	1040	9	.264	.324	.351	472	3	.286	.352	.367

● Tim Leary BR/TR

YEAR	TM/L	TOTAL W	L	SV	IP	ERA	HOME W	L	SV	IP	ERA	AWAY W	L	SV	IP	ERA	LEFT AB	HR	AVG	OBP	SLG	RIGHT AB	HR	AVG	OBP	SLG	ON-BASE AB	HR	AVG	OBP	SLG	LATE/CLOSE AB	HR	AVG	OBP	SLG
1984	NY-N	3	3	0	54	4.02	2	2	0	31	4.88	1	1	0	22	2.82	98	2	.327	.389	.408	116	0	.250	.305	.319	93	1	.344	.422	.398	30	1	.333	.375	.500
1985	Mil-A	1	4	0	33	4.05	1	1	0	13	2.84	0	3	0	21	4.79	81	3	.321	.368	.481	54	2	.259	.298	.481	54	0	.259	.298	.296	15	0	.533	.588	.667
1986	Mil-A	12	12	0	188	4.21	5	8	0	96	4.30	7	4	0	92	4.11	369	11	.282	.354	.423	378	9	.296	.324	.421	324	8	.296	.343	.417	48	1	.313	.353	.396
1987	LA-N	3	11	1	108	4.76	2	5	0	55	4.55	1	6	1	52	4.99	204	5	.289	.344	.451	220	10	.282	.343	.473	176	7	.313	.381	.506	48	1	.250	.321	.333
1988	LA-N	17	11	0	229	2.91	11	6	0	125	2.66	6	5	0	103	3.22	422	4	.237	.304	.320	438	9	.231	.265	.336	310	2	.242	.312	.303	84	0	.190	.274	.214
1989	LA-N	6	7	0	117	3.38	3	3	0	60	3.02	3	4	0	58	3.75	239	7	.285	.348	.427	195	2	.200	.254	.282	171	4	.234	.315	.386	63	0	.222	.310	.238
1989	Cin-N	2	7	0	90	3.71	1	5	0	58	3.86	1	2	0	31	3.45	167	3	.323	.376	.491	185	3	.238	.304	.335	153	2	.255	.333	.379	21	1	.429	.458	.810
1990	NY-A	9	19	0	208	4.11	1	9	0	84	4.73	8	10	0	124	3.69	408	10	.260	.338	.392	377	8	.255	.318	.363	324	8	.262	.340	.389	74	2	.270	.341	.365
1991	NY-A	4	10	0	121	6.49	1	4	0	56	5.75	3	6	0	64	7.13	267	9	.303	.371	.491	214	11	.322	.408	.521	209	8	.349	.425	.531	29	1	.241	.343	.414
1992	NY-A	5	6	0	97	5.57	5	2	0	62	5.66	0	4	0	35	5.40	160	4	.219	.321	.350	183	5	.268	.381	.404	145	4	.276	.369	.428	35	0	.171	.326	.229
1992	Sea-A	3	4	0	44	4.91	3	1	0	22	5.32	0	3	0	22	4.50	84	3	.262	.363	.476	84	0	.298	.425	.321	88	3	.284	.382	.455	7	0	.429	.500	.429
1993	Sea-A	11	9	0	169	5.05	5	3	0	67	4.97	6	6	0	102	5.10	340	9	.338	.399	.521	324	12	.260	.323	.419	290	5	.297	.371	.488	35	2	.371	.488	.657
1994	Tex-A	1	1	0	21	8.14	1	0	0	12	5.40	0	1	0	9	11.57	45	2	.333	.436	.600	40	2	.275	.311	.500	48	1	.250	.316	.354	35	2	.371	.488	.657
	TOTALS	77	104	1	1479	4.38	36	51	0	715	4.22	41	53	1	764	4.52	2884	74	.283	.353	.429	2818	73	.262	.322	.391	2385	53	.282	.354	.409	489	9	.272	.353	.374

● Craig Lefferts BL/TL

YEAR	TM/L	TOTAL W	L	SV	IP	ERA	HOME W	L	SV	IP	ERA	AWAY W	L	SV	IP	ERA	LEFT AB	HR	AVG	OBP	SLG	RIGHT AB	HR	AVG	OBP	SLG	ON-BASE AB	HR	AVG	OBP	SLG	LATE/CLOSE AB	HR	AVG	OBP	SLG
1984	SD-N	3	4	10	106	2.13	3	2	4	52	0.87	0	2	6	54	3.35	85	0	.200	.263	.212	300	4	.237	.274	.330	184	0	.190	.240	.217	173	2	.214	.257	.277
1985	SD-N	7	6	2	83	3.35	4	1	1	44	3.86	3	5	1	39	2.77	89	1	.191	.255	.270	218	6	.266	.333	.417	135	3	.252	.320	.385	133	2	.263	.327	.361
1986	SD-N	9	8	4	108	3.09	7	5	2	58	2.48	2	3	2	50	3.81	90	1	.222	.271	.289	297	6	.263	.343	.394	173	6	.266	.353	.353	216	5	.269	.339	.394
1987	SD-N	2	2	2	51	4.38	1	1	1	25	2.84	1	1	1	26	5.81	64	4	.313	.353	.594	142	5	.254	.316	.415	96	2	.229	.315	.354	74	2	.284	.321	.486
1987	SF-N	3	3	4	47	3.23	3	0	2	21	3.05	0	3	2	27	3.38	50	1	.120	.151	.180	117	3	.256	.343	.402	77	3	.260	.359	.442	100	4	.280	.321	.460
1988	SF-N	3	8	11	92	2.92	3	4	8	38	2.84	0	4	3	54	2.98	95	2	.242	.280	.368	234	5	.218	.273	.325	130	3	.200	.282	.323	153	3	.209	.274	.307
1989	SF-N	2	4	20	107	2.69	0	2	10	55	2.28	2	2	10	52	3.14	85	2	.200	.227	.282	314	9	.242	.284	.401	185	7	.200	.244	.357	229	5	.218	.262	.341
1990	SD-N	7	5	23	79	2.52	4	2	11	38	2.39	3	3	12	41	2.63	87	1	.207	.281	.241	211	9	.237	.283	.398	141	3	.241	.303	.312	235	8	.226	.277	.345
1991	SD-N	1	6	23	69	3.91	0	5	10	42	3.46	1	1	13	27	4.61	64	1	.281	.309	.422	196	4	.286	.321	.403	140	2	.257	.283	.364	186	4	.269	.310	.382
1992	SD-N	13	9	0	163	3.69	6	5	0	82	3.83	7	4	0	81	3.56	112	2	.250	.267	.366	520	14	.292	.331	.421	251	4	.279	.321	.406	46	1	.283	.277	.370
1992	Bal-A	1	3	0	33	4.09	1	1	0	13	2.70	0	2	0	20	5.03	11	0	.182	.231	.182	116	3	.276	.306	.388	52	3	.250	.286	.462	6	0	.333	.333	.333
1993	Tex-A	3	9	0	83	6.05	1	3	0	33	5.51	2	6	0	51	6.39	86	2	.256	.312	.360	249	15	.321	.372	.546	139	8	.367	.431	.583	58	1	.328	.381	.414
1994	Cal-A	1	1	3	35	4.67	1	0	1	14	3.29	0	1	2	21	5.57	44	2	.341	.380	.523	99	5	.354	.398	.596	72	1	.319	.373	.417	23	0	.478	.500	.478
	TOTALS	55	68	100	1057	3.45	33	30	46	515	2.99	22	38	54	542	3.88	962	19	.232	.277	.332	3013	88	.267	.318	.412	1775	40	.252	.312	.372	1632	37	.251	.301	.364

● Charlie Leibrandt BR/TL

YEAR	TM/L	TOTAL W	L	SV	IP	ERA	HOME W	L	SV	IP	ERA	AWAY W	L	SV	IP	ERA	LEFT AB	HR	AVG	OBP	SLG	RIGHT AB	HR	AVG	OBP	SLG	ON-BASE AB	HR	AVG	OBP	SLG	LATE/CLOSE AB	HR	AVG	OBP	SLG
1984	KC-A	11	7	0	144	3.63	3	3	0	62	3.50	8	4	0	82	3.73	108	2	.296	.336	.370	461	9	.273	.319	.393	236	4	.267	.321	.373	34	0	.294	.333	.412
1985	KC-A	17	9	0	238	2.69	9	2	0	105	2.56	8	7	0	132	2.79	204	4	.250	.294	.348	696	13	.247	.303	.358	365	7	.219	.277	.313	97	3	.247	.318	.392
1986	KC-A	14	11	0	231	4.09	7	7	0	108	4.25	7	4	0	123	3.94	178	3	.281	.342	.388	711	15	.264	.311	.401	355	7	.276	.342	.406	73	1	.274	.338	.397
1987	KC-A	16	11	0	240	3.41	8	4	0	113	3.28	8	7	0	128	3.52	155	2	.232	.273	.310	774	21	.257	.314	.408	362	6	.246	.322	.340	89	2	.202	.294	.348
1988	KC-A	13	12	0	243	3.19	8	3	0	110	2.94	5	9	0	133	3.39	150	2	.253	.290	.360	774	18	.266	.315	.385	345	5	.270	.331	.357	129	2	.209	.261	.295
1989	KC-A	5	11	0	161	5.14	3	3	0	68	3.71	2	8	0	93	6.19	130	0	.338	.365	.431	514	13	.296	.356	.442	292	6	.312	.355	.452	49	0	.265	.390	.306
1990	Atl-N	9	11	0	162	3.16	6	5	0	87	2.59	3	6	0	75	3.82	105	3	.210	.263	.314	523	6	.272	.309	.386	257	5	.265	.328	.381	45	0	.178	.213	.178
1991	Atl-N	15	13	0	230	3.49	6	8	0	101	4.35	9	5	0	128	2.81	190	2	.274	.319	.389	674	16	.237	.285	.356	318	10	.264	.316	.443	77	1	.260	.287	.312
1992	Atl-N	15	7	0	193	3.36	9	4	0	110	3.76	6	3	0	83	2.82	173	1	.225	.273	.266	568	8	.268	.309	.377	283	5	.244	.312	.367	45	0	.222	.286	.289
1993	Tex-A	9	10	0	150	4.55	1	6	0	68	4.74	8	4	0	82	4.39	86	2	.384	.418	.581	509	13	.267	.323	.417	251	7	.259	.333	.430	57	1	.344	.364	.531
	TOTALS	124	102	0	1992	3.60	60	45	0	933	3.53	64	57	0	1060	3.66	1479	21	.268	.312	.366	6204	132	.263	.313	.391	3064	62	.261	.323	.385	670	10	.240	.302	.339

● Derek Lilliquist BL/TL

YEAR	TM/L	TOTAL W	L	SV	IP	ERA	HOME W	L	SV	IP	ERA	AWAY W	L	SV	IP	ERA	LEFT AB	HR	AVG	OBP	SLG	RIGHT AB	HR	AVG	OBP	SLG	ON-BASE AB	HR	AVG	OBP	SLG	LATE/CLOSE AB	HR	AVG	OBP	SLG
1989	Atl-N	8	10	0	166	3.97	5	5	0	98	3.32	3	5	0	69	4.90	102	3	.265	.292	.412	569	13	.308	.343	.439	261	6	.349	.387	.471	33	1	.424	.429	.576
1990	Atl-N	2	8	0	62	6.28	2	5	0	44	4.26	0	3	0	17	11.42	36	0	.250	.289	.306	213	10	.310	.357	.512	111	6	.315	.360	.514	11	0	.273	.429	.455
1990	SD-N	3	3	0	60	4.33	0	1	0	13	6.23	3	2	0	47	3.80	56	3	.375	.453	.589	173	3	.231	.298	.324	95	2	.253	.327	.379	23	0	.217	.333	.261
1991	SD-N	0	2	0	14	8.79	0	1	0	6	11.12	0	1	0	9	7.27	18	1	.333	.368	.611	48	2	.396	.431	.604	31	0	.355	.412	.419	0	0	—	—	—
1992	Cle-A	5	3	6	62	1.75	2	2	5	32	2.25	3	1	1	30	1.21	91	1	.198	.242	.275	118	4	.178	.261	.331	91	2	.231	.295	.352	130	3	.231	.290	.338
1993	Cle-A	4	4	10	64	2.25	3	3	6	30	2.67	1	1	4	34	1.87	64	0	.266	.294	.297	178	5	.264	.327	.416	119	1	.261	.313	.345	114	1	.281	.341	.342
1994	Cle-A	1	3	1	29	4.91	0	0	0	16	3.31	1	3	1	13	6.92	39	1	.205	.273	.359	73	5	.356	.387	.603	57	3	.228	.299	.421	47	2	.277	.352	.489
	TOTALS	23	33	17	457	4.00	12	17	11	239	3.61	11	16	6	218	4.42	406	9	.261	.306	.382	1372	42	.287	.335	.438	765	20	.295	.347	.426	358	7	.271	.334	.380

● Greg Maddux BR/TR

YEAR	TM/L	TOTAL W	L	SV	IP	ERA	HOME W	L	SV	IP	ERA	AWAY W	L	SV	IP	ERA	LEFT AB	HR	AVG	OBP	SLG	RIGHT AB	HR	AVG	OBP	SLG	ON-BASE AB	HR	AVG	OBP	SLG	LATE/CLOSE AB	HR	AVG	OBP	SLG
1986	Chi-N	2	4	0	31	5.52	0	2	0	4	14.54	2	2	0	27	4.05	53	1	.321	.400	.434	78	2	.346	.386	.513	67	1	.313	.370	.388	4	1	.250	.250	1.000
1987	Chi-N	6	14	0	156	5.61	1	6	0	79	4.65	5	8	0	76	6.60	341	8	.323	.403	.487	274	9	.259	.336	.409	286	10	.301	.383	.486	45	2	.333	.400	.533
1988	Chi-N	18	8	0	249	3.18	8	6	0	133	3.66	10	2	0	116	2.63	498	7	.237	.293	.321	445	6	.252	.294	.335	384	5	.271	.338	.346	141	3	.191	.263	.234
1989	Chi-N	19	12	0	238	2.95	10	5	0	113	3.03	9	7	0	125	2.87	495	4	.279	.355	.366	395	9	.213	.263	.314	387	6	.248	.313	.357	81	0	.198	.278	.210
1990	Chi-N	15	15	0	237	3.46	8	6	0	116	3.58	7	9	0	121	3.34	562	6	.270	.352	.377	351	5	.222	.266	.316	380	6	.295	.353	.416	98	1	.286	.333	.337
1991	Chi-N	15	11	0	263	3.35	7	5	0	128	3.45	8	6	0	135	3.26	587	14	.252	.306	.378	392	4	.214	.262	.296	369	10	.266	.313	.412	111	2	.333	.385	.459
1992	Chi-N	20	11	0	268	2.18	12	4	0	137	1.91	8	7	0	131	2.47	566	6	.233	.304	.320	393	1	.176	.226	.249	350	2	.231	.320	.326	124	0	.210	.313	.234
1993	Atl-N	20	10	0	267	2.36	8	4	0	123	2.19	12	6	0	144	2.51	520	3	.235	.280	.304	464	9	.228	.264	.332	392	3	.219	.262	.273	135	4	.207	.270	.341
1994	Atl-N	16	6	0	202	1.56	6	4	0	97	1.76	10	2	0	105	1.37	374	4	.201	.249	.249	352	1	.213	.238	.270	257	1	.202	.247	.241	108	2	.287	.336	.361
	TOTALS	131	91	0	1911	3.02	60	42	0	930	3.03	71	49	0	981	3.01	3996	54	.256	.322	.349	3144	46	.225	.270	.314	2872	44	.256	.318	.358	847	13	.247	.313	.326

● Mike Maddux BL/TR

YEAR	TM/L	TOTAL W	L	SV	IP	ERA	HOME W	L	SV	IP	ERA	AWAY W	L	SV	IP	ERA	LEFT AB	HR	AVG	OBP	SLG	RIGHT AB	HR	AVG	OBP	SLG	ON-BASE AB	HR	AVG	OBP	SLG	LATE/CLOSE AB	HR	AVG	OBP	SLG
1986	Phi-N	3	7	0	78	5.42	3	3	0	38	5.02	0	4	0	40	5.80	189	3	.254	.347	.344	119	3	.336	.380	.479	141	5	.305	.369	.468	18	0	.333	.333	.389
1987	Phi-N	2	0	0	17	2.65	2	0	0	10	0.00	0	0	0	7	6.75	32	0	.250	.314	.281	35	0	.257	.297	.286	29	0	.276	.344	.276	3	0	.000	.000	.000
1988	Phi-N	4	3	0	89	3.76	2	0	0	46	2.93	2	3	0	43	4.64	176	4	.313	.393	.472	155	2	.232	.297	.316	141	3	.284	.373	.411	41	0	.171	.227	.195
1989	Phi-N	1	3	1	44	5.15	1	2	0	22	8.59	0	1	1	22	1.66	81	1	.272	.333	.321	90	2	.333	.388	.511	79	2	.342	.424	.494	13	1	.385	.438	.615
1990	LA-N	0	1	0	21	6.53	0	0	0	10	5.23	0	1	0	10	7.84	43	1	.279	.319	.395	39	2	.308	.341	.487	36	2	.278	.308	.500	3	0	.000	.250	.000
1991	SD-N	7	2	5	99	2.46	5	1	1	51	1.75	2	1	4	47	3.23	171	0	.246	.296	.298	182	4	.198	.259	.342	140	0	.221	.293	.264	102	0	.225	.292	.255
1992	SD-N	2	2	5	80	2.37	2	0	2	34	1.87	0	2	3	46	2.74	162	1	.235	.294	.290	139	1	.237	.284	.295	141	1	.206	.281	.270	101	1	.267	.348	.327
1993	NY-N	3	8	5	75	3.60	1	3	1	35	3.31	2	5	4	40	3.86	125	2	.264	.351	.392	151	5	.225	.279	.305	136	5	.250	.325	.368	127	2	.283	.358	.417
1994	NY-N	2	1	2	44	5.11	1	1	2	26	5.61	1	0	0	18	4.42	79	5	.291	.352	.570	92	2	.239	.276	.337	64	3	.297	.382	.516	51	2	.353	.433	.608
	TOTALS	24	27	18	545	3.83	19	10	5	272	3.60	5	17	13	273	4.05	1058	17	.266	.337	.371	1002	21	.251	.303	.353	907	19	.266	.341	.383	459	6	.266	.338	.362

● Joe Magrane BR/TL

YEAR	TM/L	TOTAL W	L	SV	IP	ERA	HOME W	L	SV	IP	ERA	AWAY W	L	SV	IP	ERA	LEFT AB	HR	AVG	OBP	SLG	RIGHT AB	HR	AVG	OBP	SLG	ON-BASE AB	HR	AVG	OBP	SLG	LATE/CLOSE AB	HR	AVG	OBP	SLG
1987	StL-N	9	7	0	170	3.54	5	2	0	86	2.81	4	5	0	84	4.29	93	1	.226	.301	.312	547	8	.249	.321	.342	255	4	.282	.361	.388	66	1	.258	.364	.333
1988	StL-N	5	9	0	165	2.18	1	4	0	88	1.95	4	3	0	78	2.43	113	2	.177	.232	.319	499	4	.226	.298	.309	241	1	.199	.278	.270	83	1	.241	.292	.313
1989	StL-N	18	9	0	235	2.91	9	5	0	119	3.09	9	4	0	115	2.73	128	0	.234	.319	.289	743	5	.254	.309	.345	336	2	.265	.339	.345	88	0	.193	.245	.227
1990	StL-N	10	17	0	203	3.59	4	10	0	116	4.27	6	7	0	87	2.68	153	1	.281	.357	.373	620	9	.260	.311	.373	329	4	.252	.308	.368	66	2	.364	.394	.591
1992	StL-N	1	2	0	31	4.02	0	0	0	7	2.57	1	2	0	24	4.44	15	0	.133	.278	.133	53	1	.245	.377	.421	11	0	.545	.615	.545	11	0	.545	.615	.545
1993	StL-N	8	10	0	116	4.97	3	3	0	46	4.27	5	7	0	70	5.43	71	3	.310	.417	.493	373	12	.282	.328	.440	177	6	.294	.340	.458	33	0	.242	.297	.242
1993	Cal-A	3	2	0	48	3.94	2	1	0	24	4.94	1	1	0	24	2.96	23	0	.174	.296	.174	158	4	.278	.343	.437	87	2	.276	.320	.414	10	0	.100	.182	.100

YEAR	TM/L	TOTAL W	L	SV	IP	ERA	HOME W	L	SV	IP	ERA	AWAY W	L	SV	IP	ERA	LEFT AB	HR	AVG	OBP	SLG	RIGHT AB	HR	AVG	OBP	SLG	ON-BASE AB	HR	AVG	OBP	SLG	LATE/CLOSE AB	HR	AVG	OBP	SLG
1994	Cal-A	2	6	0	74	7.30	1	3	0	47	7.04	1	3	0	27	7.76	54	4	.370	.460	.704	243	14	.284	.398	.510	142	11	.324	.421	.620	12	0	.333	.385	.583
TOTALS		56	62	0	1043	3.65	25	30	0	534	3.64	31	32	0	509	3.66	650	11	.249	.334	.360	3290	58	.258	.321	.374	1620	31	.264	.333	.385	369	3	.263	.323	.350

● **Rick Mahler** BR/TR

YEAR	TM/L	W	L	SV	IP	ERA	W	L	SV	IP	ERA	W	L	SV	IP	ERA	AB	HR	AVG	OBP	SLG	AB	HR	AVG	OBP	SLG	AB	HR	AVG	OBP	SLG	AB	HR	AVG	OBP	SLG
1984	Atl-N	13	10	0	222	3.12	5	6	0	93	4.06	8	4	0	129	2.44	454	12	.273	.327	.396	378	1	.225	.274	.275	331	2	.257	.321	.308	107	3	.280	.353	.374
1985	Atl-N	17	15	0	267	3.48	8	5	0	135	3.27	9	10	0	132	3.69	543	7	.262	.308	.372	471	17	.276	.335	.435	382	8	.319	.368	.466	73	2	.274	.354	.411
1986	Atl-N	14	18	0	238	4.88	8	6	0	118	4.56	6	12	0	119	5.20	520	14	.335	.398	.498	420	11	.260	.321	.367	381	10	.320	.401	.475	63	1	.333	.419	.397
1987	Atl-N	8	13	0	197	4.98	6	6	0	114	4.18	2	7	0	83	6.07	401	11	.314	.391	.469	349	13	.246	.314	.401	309	8	.301	.388	.456	72	3	.347	.434	.542
1988	Atl-N	9	16	0	249	3.69	4	6	0	114	3.96	5	10	0	135	3.46	560	7	.268	.301	.352	429	10	.301	.334	.441	382	8	.319	.368	.466	130	2	.223	.257	.292
1989	Cin-N	9	13	0	221	3.83	6	6	0	120	4.42	3	7	0	101	3.13	488	8	.305	.344	.451	371	7	.251	.307	.350	345	8	.290	.352	.420	45	1	.267	.327	.467
1990	Cin-N	7	6	4	135	4.28	3	1	1	57	4.45	4	5	3	78	4.15	299	9	.274	.325	.418	215	7	.242	.299	.381	190	4	.295	.367	.416	29	2	.241	.353	.517
1991	Mon-N	1	3	0	37	3.62	1	0	0	13	2.03	0	3	0	24	4.50	70	1	.257	.329	.400	68	1	.279	.347	.368	61	1	.262	.343	.393	2	0	.000	.333	.000
1991	Atl-N	1	1	0	29	5.65	1	1	0	18	5.89	0	0	0	10	5.23	62	0	.242	.309	.339	55	2	.327	.422	.491	66	2	.273	.346	.409	6	0	.000	.250	.000
TOTALS		79	95	4	1594	4.02	42	37	1	782	4.10	37	58	3	811	3.94	3397	69	.288	.341	.418	2756	69	.262	.317	.383	2452	53	.292	.361	.419	527	14	.273	.347	.395

● **Dennis Martinez** BR/TR

YEAR	TM/L	W	L	SV	IP	ERA	W	L	SV	IP	ERA	W	L	SV	IP	ERA	AB	HR	AVG	OBP	SLG	AB	HR	AVG	OBP	SLG	AB	HR	AVG	OBP	SLG	AB	HR	AVG	OBP	SLG
1984	Bal-A	6	9	0	142	5.02	3	6	0	75	5.04	3	3	0	67	4.99	291	13	.234	.288	.416	260	13	.296	.340	.523	191	8	.288	.335	.476	42	2	.238	.319	.452
1985	Bal-A	13	11	0	180	5.15	5	6	0	74	6.11	8	5	0	106	4.49	388	14	.273	.344	.459	318	15	.305	.354	.487	271	13	.299	.360	.506	61	1	.279	.318	.410
1986	Bal-A	0	0	0	7	6.75	0	0	0	1	40.50	0	0	0	6	3.00	8	0	.250	.250	.500	22	0	.409	.440	.591	16	0	.500	.471	.625	0	0	—	—	
1986	Mon-N	3	6	0	98	4.59	1	4	0	51	5.29	2	2	0	47	3.82	209	5	.244	.300	.359	167	6	.311	.365	.485	145	7	.255	.355	.448	28	0	.321	.387	.429
1987	Mon-N	11	4	0	145	3.30	6	1	0	81	2.44	5	3	0	64	4.38	342	5	.237	.293	.342	204	4	.255	.314	.377	217	4	.253	.318	.359	41	0	.171	.209	.220
1988	Mon-N	15	13	0	235	2.72	6	4	0	97	2.50	9	9	0	138	2.87	473	8	.233	.291	.347	426	13	.246	.280	.411	335	9	.239	.296	.376	99	2	.192	.221	.313
1989	Mon-N	16	7	0	232	3.18	7	4	0	116	2.79	9	3	0	116	3.58	492	12	.285	.330	.429	392	9	.222	.263	.342	333	7	.240	.296	.360	108	3	.259	.273	.389
1990	Mon-N	10	11	0	226	2.95	6	10	0	135	3.41	4	1	0	91	2.27	506	9	.223	.263	.322	333	7	.234	.291	.354	316	7	.218	.290	.342	90	6	.300	.364	.544
1991	Mon-N	14	11	0	222	2.39	7	4	0	96	2.16	7	7	0	126	2.57	489	4	.233	.304	.301	340	5	.215	.247	.326	318	3	.220	.305	.305	127	1	.205	.246	.268
1992	Mon-N	16	11	0	226	2.47	8	4	0	116	2.09	8	7	0	110	2.85	503	8	.211	.261	.288	311	4	.212	.288	.286	284	4	.222	.294	.292	81	3	.173	.264	.309
1993	Mon-N	15	9	1	225	3.85	9	2	1	110	3.51	6	7	0	114	4.17	434	13	.249	.312	.410	422	14	.244	.300	.410	339	10	.198	.287	.345	70	1	.286	.324	.386
1994	Cle-A	11	6	0	177	3.52	3	3	0	80	3.26	8	3	0	97	3.72	359	9	.273	.311	.398	312	5	.218	.285	.349	268	3	.228	.296	.313	82	0	.256	.295	.317
TOTALS		130	98	1	2114	3.42	61	48	1	1032	3.34	69	50	0	1082	3.49	4494	100	.244	.299	.366	3507	95	.247	.298	.391	3033	75	.239	.309	.368	829	19	.239	.285	.361

● **Ramon Martinez** BR/TR

YEAR	TM/L	W	L	SV	IP	ERA	W	L	SV	IP	ERA	W	L	SV	IP	ERA	AB	HR	AVG	OBP	SLG	AB	HR	AVG	OBP	SLG	AB	HR	AVG	OBP	SLG	AB	HR	AVG	OBP	SLG
1988	LA-N	1	3	0	36	3.79	0	3	0	26	5.26	1	0	0	10	0.00	58	0	.259	.403	.293	67	0	.179	.267	.239	52	0	.250	.371	.308	14	0	.071	.188	.071
1989	LA-N	6	4	0	99	3.19	3	3	0	50	2.17	3	1	0	49	4.22	203	6	.246	.343	.369	157	5	.185	.260	.318	145	4	.228	.304	.338	27	0	.296	.387	.296
1990	LA-N	20	6	0	234	2.92	12	2	0	130	2.71	8	4	0	105	3.15	508	13	.246	.319	.390	358	9	.184	.216	.310	328	6	.226	.277	.345	96	2	.208	.262	.323
1991	LA-N	17	13	0	220	3.27	9	4	0	105	2.91	8	9	0	115	3.59	453	7	.225	.302	.318	375	11	.235	.282	.360	323	9	.260	.319	.378	66	1	.121	.194	.182
1992	LA-N	8	11	0	151	4.00	4	7	0	92	4.29	4	4	0	58	3.55	316	9	.256	.367	.415	259	2	.232	.282	.297	254	5	.256	.349	.366	52	0	.231	.298	.308
1993	LA-N	10	12	0	212	3.44	5	8	0	111	4.14	5	4	0	101	2.68	414	9	.246	.362	.372	379	6	.264	.319	.359	352	5	.236	.332	.321	67	2	.254	.306	.358
1994	LA-N	12	7	0	170	3.97	5	3	0	85	3.59	7	4	0	85	4.36	305	10	.233	.300	.374	337	4	.264	.323	.392	258	4	.260	.325	.349	63	2	.254	.319	.397
TOTALS		74	56	0	1121	3.44	38	30	0	599	3.44	36	26	0	523	3.44	2257	54	.242	.333	.369	1932	41	.230	.282	.340	1712	33	.245	.320	.348	385	7	.213	.279	.304

● **Kirk McCaskill** BR/TR

YEAR	TM/L	W	L	SV	IP	ERA	W	L	SV	IP	ERA	W	L	SV	IP	ERA	AB	HR	AVG	OBP	SLG	AB	HR	AVG	OBP	SLG	AB	HR	AVG	OBP	SLG	AB	HR	AVG	OBP	SLG
1985	Cal-A	12	12	0	190	4.70	7	4	0	96	4.58	5	8	0	93	4.82	407	11	.278	.339	.420	325	12	.234	.295	.394	290	13	.300	.358	.500	54	2	.333	.357	.500
1986	Cal-A	17	10	0	246	3.36	6	5	0	114	2.93	11	5	0	133	3.73	504	11	.234	.311	.355	401	8	.222	.291	.324	358	11	.263	.317	.402	110	5	.191	.264	.382
1987	Cal-A	4	6	0	75	5.67	1	1	0	29	5.02	3	5	0	46	6.07	156	9	.314	.382	.532	138	5	.254	.342	.384	122	7	.295	.374	.484	6	0	.667	.667	.667
1988	Cal-A	8	6	0	146	4.31	5	5	0	83	3.90	3	1	0	63	4.88	288	3	.267	.336	.351	278	6	.281	.348	.417	255	2	.290	.355	.373	68	0	.265	.324	.279
1989	Cal-A	15	10	0	212	2.93	10	4	0	112	3.12	5	6	0	100	2.71	401	10	.252	.297	.369	394	6	.256	.316	.345	319	5	.235	.291	.301	77	2	.182	.241	.299
1990	Cal-A	12	11	0	174	3.25	7	3	0	81	2.77	5	8	0	93	3.68	334	6	.251	.322	.368	326	3	.236	.318	.294	287	4	.265	.327	.359	40	0	.275	.356	.375
1991	Cal-A	10	19	0	178	4.26	4	10	0	93	4.08	6	9	0	85	4.45	351	11	.313	.355	.467	330	8	.252	.338	.400	291	9	.296	.343	.464	35	2	.200	.263	.371
1992	Chi-A	12	13	0	209	4.18	6	7	0	109	3.54	6	6	0	100	4.84	379	6	.280	.358	.391	417	5	.209	.295	.300	351	7	.279	.350	.422	51	1	.255	.350	.451
1993	Chi-A	4	8	2	114	5.23	2	2	1	66	3.80	2	6	1	47	7.23	200	7	.350	.410	.545	260	5	.285	.324	.388	205	5	.337	.388	.473	54	0	.296	.350	.370
1994	Chi-A	1	4	3	53	3.42	1	1	0	22	2.01	0	3	2	30	4.45	77	3	.221	.330	.390	125	3	.272	.316	.416	89	3	.281	.350	.483	103	4	.291	.367	.476
TOTALS		95	99	5	1596	3.99	49	42	2	806	3.57	46	57	3	790	4.41	3097	77	.273	.338	.406	2994	61	.245	.315	.357	2567	66	.280	.341	.415	598	16	.254	.324	.393

● **Bob McClure** BR/TL

YEAR	TM/L	W	L	SV	IP	ERA	W	L	SV	IP	ERA	W	L	SV	IP	ERA	AB	HR	AVG	OBP	SLG	AB	HR	AVG	OBP	SLG	AB	HR	AVG	OBP	SLG	AB	HR	AVG	OBP	SLG
1984	Mil-A	4	8	1	140	4.38	2	3	0	69	3.52	2	5	1	71	5.22	119	1	.261	.328	.353	427	8	.288	.346	.417	236	5	.305	.375	.445	38	0	.342	.458	.500
1985	Mil-A	4	1	3	86	4.31	3	1	1	50	4.53	1	0	2	36	4.00	96	3	.240	.295	.365	236	7	.288	.355	.470	154	7	.260	.337	.487	66	0	.258	.279	.318
1986	Mil-A	2	1	0	16	3.86	2	0	0	5	1.80	0	1	0	11	4.76	17	0	.176	.318	.176	46	2	.326	.404	.500	33	0	.242	.381	.303	13	0	.462	.579	.615
1986	Mon-N	2	5	6	63	3.02	2	2	2	30	4.25	0	3	4	33	1.91	76	1	.184	.238	.329	152	1	.257	.335	.309	102	1	.255	.304	.343	150	2	.240	.325	.340
1987	Mon-N	6	1	5	52	3.44	4	0	3	30	3.26	2	1	2	22	3.68	80	3	.175	.230	.363	115	3	.252	.362	.478	89	5	.303	.385	.551	71	3	.211	.263	.394
1988	Mon-N	3	2	3	19	6.16	1	3	0	12	8.49	2	0	0	7	2.45	28	0	.286	.344	.393	47	3	.319	.365	.638	41	1	.220	.277	.390	15	0	.333	.444	.533
1988	NY-N	1	0	1	11	4.09	0	0	1	3	0.00	1	0	0	8	5.40	24	0	.208	.269	.292	19	1	.368	.400	.737	25	1	.200	.286	.360	17	0	.176	.222	.235
1989	Cal-A	6	1	3	52	1.55	4	0	1	24	1.88	2	1	2	28	1.27	65	1	.154	.237	.215	119	1	.244	.289	.319	88	2	.182	.262	.295	83	1	.157	.220	.217
1990	Cal-A	2	2	0	30	6.43	1	0	0	12	7.71	1	0	0	5	5.79	12	0	.333	.385	.333	14	0	.214	.313	.214	11	0	.364	.500	.364	21	0	.286	.348	.286
1991	Cal-A	0	0	0	10	9.31	0	0	0	5	3.60	0	0	0	5	15.43	18	0	.278	.409	.278	23	3	.348	.385	.739	16	1	.438	.524	.625	4	0	.500	.667	.500
1991	StL-N	1	1	0	23	3.13	1	0	0	14	3.77	0	1	0	9	2.08	43	1	.209	.280	.326	42	0	.357	.404	.429	45	0	.311	.370	.356	46	0	.239	.321	.304
1992	StL-N	2	2	0	54	3.17	1	0	0	28	2.22	1	2	0	26	4.21	91	4	.198	.272	.407	108	2	.315	.405	.426	97	2	.227	.361	.340	71	1	.247	.313	.370
1993	Fla-N	1	1	0	6	7.11	1	0	0	4	9.82	1	0	0	3	3.38	20	1	.450	.522	.700	11	1	.364	.462	.636	19	2	.474	.545	.842	10	2	.600	.692	1.300
TOTALS		32	24	21	539	3.86	21	10	8	276	3.75	11	14	13	263	3.96	689	15	.222	.291	.348	1359	34	.289	.354	.432	956	27	.271	.352	.423	607	9	.249	.326	.361

● **Lance McCullers** BB/TR

YEAR	TM/L	W	L	SV	IP	ERA	W	L	SV	IP	ERA	W	L	SV	IP	ERA	AB	HR	AVG	OBP	SLG	AB	HR	AVG	OBP	SLG	AB	HR	AVG	OBP	SLG	AB	HR	AVG	OBP	SLG
1985	SD-N	0	2	5	35	2.31	0	0	4	23	2.38	0	1		12	2.19	47	2	.234	.390	.426	71	1	.169	.224	.254	61	1	.197	.279	.311	74	1	.216	.333	.324
1986	SD-N	10	10	5	136	2.78	5	3	1	61	2.66	5	7	4	75	2.88	237	5	.278	.371	.388	240	7	.154	.236	.275	186	6	.188	.306	.317	187	5	.225	.338	.332
1987	SD-N	8	10	16	123	3.72	6	5	8	64	2.97	2	5	8	60	4.53	241	2	.232	.345	.307	230	9	.257	.312	.448	236	5	.242	.347	.356	266	7	.244	.344	.387
1988	SD-N	3	6	10	98	2.49	2	2	6	59	1.58	1	4	4	39	4.15	163	0	.153	.289	.190	179	8	.251	.335	.469	159	5	.208	.317	.333	216	6	.218	.312	.361
1989	NY-A	4	3	3	85	4.57	2	1	3	53	5.13	2	2	0	32	3.66	143	3	.252	.357	.392	182	6	.258	.312	.440	152	7	.283	.367	.480	94	2	.245	.342	.362
1990	NY-A	1	0	0	15	3.60	1	0	0	9	1.93	0	0	0	6	6.35	25	1	.160	.222	.280	33	1	.303	.368	.455	26	1	.269	.333	.423	12	1	.250	.308	.500
1990	Det-A	1	0	0	30	2.73	0	0	0	18	3.44	1	0	0	11	1.59	45	0	.222	.294	.289	61	2	.131	.229	.279	44	2	.227	.321	.409	9	0	.111	.200	.111
1992	Tex-A	1	0	0	5	5.40	0	0	0	3	10.13	1	0	0	2	0.00	8	0	.125	.300	.125	7	0	.000	.462	.000	8	0	.000	.333	.000	0	0	—	—	
TOTALS		28	31	39	526	3.25	16	11	22	289	2.99	12	20	17	237	3.56	909	13	.230	.340	.321	1003	34	.217	.290	.382	872	27	.226	.330	.364	858	22	.230	.332	.359

● **Ben McDonald** BR/TR

YEAR	TM/L	W	L	SV	IP	ERA	W	L	SV	IP	ERA	W	L	SV	IP	ERA	AB	HR	AVG	OBP	SLG	AB	HR	AVG	OBP	SLG	AB	HR	AVG	OBP	SLG	AB	HR	AVG	OBP	SLG
1989	Bal-A	1	0	0	7	8.59	0	0	0	4	13.50	1	0	0	3	2.70	13	0	.231	.375	.231	15	2	.333	.353	.800	14	1	.357	.412	.571	6	1	.167	.167	.667
1990	Bal-A	8	5	0	119	2.43	4	3	0	75	2.41	4	2	0	44	2.45	216	2	.181	.236	.236	213	7	.230	.289	.366	160	4	.200	.257	.313	75	3	.173	.235	.320
1991	Bal-A	6	8	0	126	4.84	2	4	0	73	3.70	4	4	0	53	6.41	256	8	.255	.313	.402	270	6	.272	.313	.348	227	8	.313	.362	.498	27	2	.259	.310	.556
1992	Bal-A	13	13	0	227	4.24	5	8	0	118	4.90	8	5	0	109	3.54	458	14	.235	.311	.398	458	18	.258	.314	.441	311	11	.273	.337	.450	58	3	.276	.338	.517
1993	Bal-A	13	14	0	220	3.39	10	4	0	132	2.72	3	10	0	88	4.40	434	5	.230	.307	.327	378	12	.225	.301	.360	296	7	.267	.358	.409	80	1	.287	.329	.350
1994	Bal-A	14	7	0	157	4.06	5	4	0	60	5.55	9	3	0	97	3.14	307	8	.244	.309	.365	285	6	.267	.330	.389	223	5	.256	.343	.345	29	0	.241	.324	.276
TOTALS		55	47	0	857	3.86	26	23	0	462	3.84	29	24	0	395	3.89	1631	37	.225	.296	.342	1576	53	.256	.317	.414	1180	35	.267	.341	.413	275	10	.244	.300	.396

● **Jack McDowell** BR/TR

YEAR	TM/L	W	L	SV	IP	ERA	W	L	SV	IP	ERA	W	L	SV	IP	ERA	AB	HR	AVG	OBP	SLG	AB	HR	AVG	OBP	SLG	AB	HR	AVG	OBP	SLG	AB	HR	AVG	OBP	SLG
1987	Chi-A	3	0	0	28	1.93	3	0	0	21	2.57	0	0	0	7	0.00	51	1	.157	.218	.216	44	0	.182	.250	.250	30	1	.167	.194	.300	10	0	.200	.200	.300
1988	Chi-A	5	10	0	159	3.97	2	3	0	87	3.01	3	7	0	72	5.13	306	6	.275	.357	.386	293	6	.215	.293	.331	249	7	.237	.323	.361	60	2	.250	.333	.433
1990	Chi-A	14	9	0	205	3.82	9	4	0	128	3.30	5	5	0	77	4.73	408	11	.243	.302	.380	368	9	.245	.330	.380	295	8	.258	.335	.407	58	0	.224	.274	.310
1991	Chi-A	17	10	0	254	3.41	10	6	0	139	3.89	7	4	0	115	2.82	485	7	.225	.289	.324	445	12	.231	.295	.373	353	10	.269	.325	.425	92	2	.228	.297	.359
1992	Chi-A	20	10	0	261	3.18	9	5	0	120	2.77	11	5	0	140	3.53	486	13	.263	.328	.409	497	8	.239	.287	.350	387	9	.235	.299	.367	101	0	.218	.270	.257
1993	Chi-A	22	10	0	257	3.37	9	6	0	126	3.52	13	4	0	131	3.20	491	8	.259	.302	.354	490	12	.273	.326	.404	414	8	.249	.299	.357	44	1	.244	.284	.362
1994	Chi-A	10	9	0	181	3.73	5	4	0	88	3.38	5	5	0	93	4.06	343	6	.268	.317	.388	357	6	.263	.303	.373	294	7	.259	.304	.374	99	3	.253	.279	.414
TOTALS		91	58	0	1344	3.50	47	29	0	714	3.44	44	29	0	630	3.56	2570	52	.252	.312	.368	2494	53	.245	.305	.368	2022	50	.250	.311	.380	547	11	.236	.286	.353

● **Roger McDowell** BR/TR

YEAR	TM/L	W	L	SV	IP	ERA	W	L	SV	IP	ERA	W	L	SV	IP	ERA	AB	HR	AVG	OBP	SLG	AB	HR	AVG	OBP	SLG	AB	HR	AVG	OBP	SLG	AB	HR	AVG	OBP	SLG
1985	NY-N	6	5	17	127	2.83	5	3	9	68	2.11	1	2	8	59	3.66	226	2	.235	.287	.319	244	7	.225	.286	.344	186	6	.226	.298	.387	263	5	.228	.288	.331
1986	NY-N	14	9	22	128	3.02	7	3	10	62	1.73	7	6	12	66	4.25	227	4	.247	.341	.366	242	0	.211	.246	.231	204	5	.265	.326	.373	310	4	.242	.309	.326
1987	NY-N	7	5	25	89	4.16	5	3	13	52	4.53	2	2	12	37	3.65	171	3	.246	.316	.322	173	4	.306	.344	.410	184	2	.283	.332	.342	228	6	.272	.316	.377
1988	NY-N	5	5	16	89	2.63	2	1	4	35	1.53	3	4	12	54	3.35	154	0	.260	.337	.301	182	1	.220	.275	.247	157	0	.229	.315	.255	209	1	.268	.340	.316

YEAR	TM/L	TOTAL W	L	SV	IP	ERA	HOME W	L	SV	IP	ERA	AWAY W	L	SV	IP	ERA	LEFT AB	HR	AVG	OBP	SLG	RIGHT AB	HR	AVG	OBP	SLG	ON-BASE AB	HR	AVG	OBP	SLG	LATE/CLOSE AB	HR	AVG	OBP	SLG
1989	NY-N	1	5	4	35	3.31	1	3	2	14	3.14	0	2	2	21	3.43	68	1	.324	.418	.426	66	0	.182	.257	.227	69	1	.290	.375	.406	60	0	.267	.362	.300
1989	Phi-N	3	3	19	57	1.11	3	2	8	25	0.36	0	1	11	32	1.69	117	2	.231	.323	.308	88	0	.205	.263	.261	130	2	.215	.306	.285					
1990	Phi-N	6	8	22	86	3.86	3	4	10	37	5.40	3	4	12	50	2.72	183	2	.328	.414	.415	139	0	.230	.270	.295	180	1	.317	.383	.389	186	1	.328	.398	.403
1991	Phi-N	3	6	3	59	3.20	1	3	1	28	3.18	2	3	2	31	3.23	128	0	.289	.399	.352	101	1	.238	.306	.327	121	0	.256	.385	.306	149	1	.302	.403	.383
1991	LA-N	6	3	7	42	2.55	4	2	3	23	3.86	2	1	4	19	0.95	69	2	.232	.349	.406	83	1	.277	.299	.361	68	0	.221	.313	.265	109	2	.229	.315	.330
1992	LA-N	6	10	14	84	4.09	2	2	8	37	2.92	4	8	6	47	5.01	154	3	.318	.428	.432	183	0	.295	.337	.333	183	3	.301	.394	.393	215	2	.279	.350	.344
1993	LA-N	5	3	2	68	2.25	2	1	0	33	2.45	3	2	2	35	2.06	125	1	.312	.399	.400	139	1	.266	.331	.324	139	2	.259	.354	.374	88	0	.216	.327	.250
1994	LA-N	0	3	0	41	5.23	0	1	0	18	3.57	0	2	0	24	6.46	72	1	.333	.404	.444	93	2	.280	.337	.419	90	3	.322	.430	.489	26	1	.500	.552	.692
TOTALS		62	65	151	906	3.17	35	28	68	433	2.83	27	37	83	473	3.48	1694	21	.274	.364	.364	1733	17	.245	.295	.295	1684	23	.264	.348	.353	1973	25	.264	.337	.343
● Chuck McElroy BL/TL																																				
1989	Phi-N	0	0	0	10	1.74	0	0	0	5	1.69	0	0	0	5	1.80	8	0	.375	.444	.500	34	1	.265	.324	.441	22	0	.273	.333	.318	3	0	.000	.250	.000
1990	Phi-N	0	1	0	14	7.71	0	1	0	10	10.24	0	0	0	4	2.08	21	0	.286	.360	.429	44	0	.409	.490	.500	45	0	.311	.385	.400	8	0	.375	.583	.625
1991	Chi-N	6	2	3	101	1.95	3	1	3	59	1.53	3	1	0	43	2.53	122	3	.172	.280	.270	225	4	.231	.337	.324	160	4	.213	.305	.319	147	3	.245	.343	.367
1992	Chi-N	4	7	6	84	3.55	3	4	1	42	3.64	1	3	5	42	3.46	102	2	.275	.345	.422	206	3	.218	.339	.340	149	1	.228	.365	.315	166	1	.253	.365	.373
1993	Chi-N	2	2	0	47	4.56	1	1	0	26	5.47	1	1	0	21	3.43	64	2	.313	.416	.438	118	2	.263	.341	.373	89	2	.303	.394	.449	28	0	.321	.387	.429
1994	Cin-N	1	2	5	58	2.34	1	0	4	38	1.67	0	2	1	20	3.60	76	0	.237	.318	.303	137	3	.248	.280	.358	85	2	.294	.362	.424	128	2	.273	.331	.375
TOTALS		13	14	14	314	3.09	8	7	8	180	3.11	5	7	6	135	3.07	393	7	.244	.334	.356	764	13	.247	.337	.357	550	9	.255	.352	.362	480	6	.260	.355	.377
● Andy McGaffigan BR/TR																																				
1984	Mon-N	3	4	1	46	2.54	1	2	1	17	3.78	2	2	0	29	1.84	78	0	.192	.281	.231	90	2	.244	.284	.411	73	0	.219	.284	.260	60	1	.217	.277	.333
1984	Cin-N	0	2	0	23	5.48	0	1	0	16	5.17	0	1	0	7	6.14	41	1	.317	.417	.537	47	1	.213	.229	.319	34	2	.324	.361	.647	5	0	.400	.400	.600
1985	Cin-N	3	3	0	94	3.72	3	2	0	59	3.36	0	1	0	35	4.33	207	2	.275	.342	.357	149	2	.208	.262	.329	144	2	.257	.340	.382	18	0	.111	.158	.167
1986	Mon-N	10	5	2	143	2.65	3	2	1	63	1.99	7	3	1	79	3.18	265	2	.204	.296	.268	246	7	.244	.301	.386	207	3	.203	.292	.275	77	0	.260	.359	.338
1987	Mon-N	5	2	12	120	2.39	3	0	3	57	3.00	2	2	9	63	1.85	243	4	.267	.339	.387	204	1	.196	.258	.240	203	1	.202	.283	.261	150	2	.200	.286	.293
1988	Mon-N	6	0	4	91	2.76	4	0	3	49	2.92	2	0	1	42	2.57	177	1	.192	.284	.243	170	3	.276	.337	.400	162	2	.247	.337	.352	158	2	.203	.293	.266
1989	Mon-N	3	5	2	75	4.68	3	2	0	37	4.66	0	3	2	38	4.70	140	0	.229	.331	.321	150	3	.353	.390	.460	151	2	.311	.361	.430	106	0	.264	.350	.311
1990	SF-N	0	0	0	5	17.36	0	0	0	1	0.00	0	0	0	4	22.09	11	1	.364	.462	.636	11	1	.545	.615	1.091	11	1	.636	.692	1.182	0	0	—	—	—
1990	KC-A	4	3	1	79	3.09	0	1	0	27	2.33	4	2	1	52	3.48	158	5	.259	.324	.405	145	1	.234	.302	.283	128	2	.305	.359	.406	21	0	.333	.417	.381
1991	KC-A	0	0	0	8	4.50	0	0	0	4	4.70	0	0	0	0	0.00	17	0	.471	.474	.647	19	0	.368	.381	.474	0	0	—	—	—					
TOTALS		34	24	22	684	3.25	17	10	8	333	3.16	17	14	14	351	3.34	1337	16	.242	.323	.336	1231	21	.251	.305	.359	1132	15	.254	.326	.355	595	5	.225	.310	.301
● Scott McGregor BB/TL																																				
1984	Bal-A	15	12	0	196	3.94	11	4	0	124	2.90	4	8	0	72	5.72	159	5	.245	.299	.384	613	13	.289	.337	.401	317	10	.287	.346	.438	86	1	.221	.280	.302
1985	Bal-A	14	14	0	204	4.81	8	6	0	100	4.14	6	8	0	104	5.45	177	12	.260	.286	.503	623	22	.289	.337	.447	318	12	.283	.341	.472	66	0	.318	.366	.379
1986	Bal-A	11	15	0	203	4.52	5	8	0	87	4.53	6	7	0	116	4.51	166	10	.223	.260	.452	633	25	.283	.334	.458	310	13	.265	.310	.442	66	3	.348	.386	.576
1987	Bal-A	2	7	0	85	6.64	0	5	0	42	6.43	2	2	0	43	6.85	62	2	.242	.324	.339	282	13	.344	.403	.546	156	9	.353	.404	.564	17	1	.588	.579	.824
1988	Bal-A	0	3	0	17	8.83	0	1	0	7	3.68	0	2	0	10	12.60	7	0	.429	.429	.714	66	3	.364	.413	.591	37	1	.324	.341	.541	6	1	.333	.333	1.000
TOTALS		42	51	0	706	4.81	24	24	0	361	4.07	18	27	0	345	5.58	571	29	.245	.288	.445	2217	76	.296	.346	.457	1138	45	.290	.343	.469	241	6	.311	.355	.452
● Greg McMichael BR/TR																																				
1993	Atl-N	2	3	19	92	2.06	0	2	8	45	1.61	2	1	11	47	2.49	155	1	.194	.269	.252	175	2	.217	.268	.269	140	0	.214	.268	.236	186	2	.237	.289	.290
1994	Atl-N	4	6	21	59	3.84	1	3	10	25	5.84	3	3	11	34	2.38	118	1	.288	.344	.373	118	0	.271	.320	.322	110	0	.273	.357	.345	149	1	.302	.364	.396
TOTALS		6	9	40	150	2.75	1	5	18	69	3.12	5	4	22	81	2.44	273	2	.234	.301	.304	293	2	.239	.289	.290	250	0	.240	.308	.284	335	3	.266	.322	.337
● Jose Mesa BR/TR																																				
1987	Bal-A	1	3	0	31	6.03	0	2	0	10	10.24	1	1	0	22	4.15	71	5	.324	.385	.606	57	2	.263	.354	.456	60	3	.233	.324	.450	16	1	.375	.375	.625
1990	Bal-A	3	2	0	47	3.86	2	1	0	27	4.33	1	1	0	20	3.20	91	0	.220	.339	.253	79	2	.215	.308	.367	72	2	.250	.341	.375	11	0	.091	.333	.091
1991	Bal-A	6	11	0	124	5.97	2	8	0	59	5.68	4	3	0	65	6.23	258	4	.302	.380	.407	234	7	.312	.390	.496	221	6	.335	.403	.516	12	0	.250	.357	.333
1992	Bal-A	3	8	0	68	5.19	0	4	0	26	5.81	3	4	0	41	4.79	148	5	.331	.377	.507	120	4	.233	.326	.381	113	1	.292	.346	.381	13	0	.462	.462	.615
1992	Cle-A	4	4	0	93	4.16	2	1	0	51	3.68	2	3	0	42	4.75	180	3	.283	.352	.378	171	2	.240	.337	.322	146	4	.322	.399	.452	24	1	.208	.296	.333
1993	Cle-A	10	12	0	209	4.92	7	5	0	101	4.63	3	7	0	108	5.18	375	7	.304	.363	.392	435	14	.271	.318	.422	351	10	.291	.338	.422	72	1	.278	.333	.361
1994	Cle-A	7	5	2	73	3.82	5	3	1	44	2.45	2	2	1	29	5.90	119	1	.269	.346	.328	160	2	.244	.301	.331	137	3	.299	.363	.394	160	2	.244	.318	.325
TOTALS		34	45	2	644	4.89	18	24	1	318	4.61	16	21	1	326	5.16	1242	25	.295	.364	.403	1256	33	.264	.334	.410	1100	29	.299	.363	.435	308	5	.260	.330	.354
● Greg Minton BB/TR																																				
1984	SF-N	4	9	19	124	3.76	2	3	7	57	5.05	2	6	12	67	2.67	218	4	.248	.319	.312	268	4	.284	.359	.366	249	2	.281	.353	.345	321	4	.280	.358	.349
1985	SF-N	5	4	4	97	3.54	3	2	3	40	1.80	2	2	1	57	4.76	139	1	.353	.462	.432	221	5	.222	.294	.335	184	2	.272	.378	.337	169	4	.260	.359	.373
1986	SF-N	4	4	5	69	3.93	1	2	3	31	3.16	3	2	2	37	4.58	126	3	.302	.396	.466	125	1	.200	.279	.272	127	0	.260	.366	.354	132	3	.242	.315	.348
1987	SF-N	1	0	1	23	3.47	0	0	0	5	5.06	1	0	1	18	3.00	44	0	.341	.408	.386	49	2	.306	.382	.551	52	1	.308	.390	.442	18	0	.278	.409	.333
1987	Cal-A	5	4	10	76	3.08	3	1	4	41	2.85	2	3	6	35	3.34	127	3	.268	.338	.378	111	1	.252	.326	.323	141	2	.284	.369	.355					
1988	Cal-A	4	5	7	79	2.85	1	2	4	39	3.03	3	2	5	40	2.68	133	1	.241	.305	.308	154	0	.227	.313	.260	138	0	.268	.377	.319	150	0	.213	.312	.253
1989	Cal-A	4	3	8	90	2.20	4	2	3	50	1.97	0	1	5	40	2.50	147	0	.211	.282	.272	184	4	.245	.332	.321	162	1	.278	.359	.340	161	3	.186	.294	.280
1990	Cal-A	1	1	0	15	2.35	0	0	0	9	0.00	1	1	0	6	6.00	18	0	.222	.333	.222	34	1	.206	.308	.294	22	0	.136	.296	.136	33	1	.212	.316	.303
TOTALS		28	30	54	573	3.23	14	13	22	273	3.00	14	17	32	300	3.45	952	10	.270	.354	.354	1184	18	.244	.323	.326	1061	7	.270	.361	.338	1125	17	.249	.339	.329
● Dale Mohorcic BR/TR																																				
1986	Tex-A	2	4	7	79	2.51	2	0	2	40	1.56	0	4	5	39	3.49	123	1	.285	.343	.358	185	4	.276	.295	.384	153	1	.268	.313	.353	133	1	.263	.300	.323
1987	Tex-A	7	6	16	99	2.99	4	3	7	51	3.53	3	3	9	48	2.42	151	5	.298	.335	.444	208	6	.207	.249	.313	185	7	.222	.270	.357	176	8	.295	.333	.483
1988	Tex-A	2	6	5	52	4.85	1	1	2	25	5.04	1	5	3	27	4.67	91	1	.330	.364	.495	119	5	.269	.362	.429	123	4	.293	.343	.463	70	2	.357	.397	.571
1988	NY-A	2	2	1	23	2.78	2	1	0	10	2.70	0	1	1	13	2.84	39	0	.282	.326	.333	49	1	.204	.328	.306	43	1	.233	.346	.326	68	1	.235	.312	.338
1989	NY-A	2	1	2	58	4.99	1	0	1	30	6.37	1	1	1	28	3.54	100	4	.320	.373	.520	127	4	.260	.336	.409	117	6	.299	.391	.513	36	1	.306	.395	.417
1990	Mon-N	1	2	2	53	3.23	1	0	0	21	2.95	0	2	2	32	3.41	97	5	.320	.368	.495	99	1	.253	.333	.323	92	2	.293	.352	.370	38	4	.395	.490	.737
TOTALS		16	21	33	364	3.49	11	5	12	177	3.65	5	16	21	186	3.33	601	16	.306	.352	.448	787	21	.247	.308	.363	713	21	.266	.328	.400	521	17	.296	.349	.449
● Jeff Montgomery BR/TR																																				
1987	Cin-N	2	2	0	19	6.52	2	1	0	8	4.50	0	1	0	11	7.94	42	1	.381	.469	.524	38	1	.237	.275	.342	42	0	.357	.413	.405	11	2	.273	.333	.818
1988	KC-A	7	2	1	63	3.45	6	0	1	32	2.78	1	2	0	30	4.15	101	2	.218	.316	.347	133	4	.241	.325	.391	108	3	.259	.359	.398	105	2	.267	.333	.419
1989	KC-A	7	3	18	92	1.37	6	3	9	48	1.32	1	0	9	44	1.42	152	2	.211	.264	.270	182	1	.187	.251	.236	152	1	.164	.220	.217	183	1	.213	.256	.262
1990	KC-A	6	5	24	94	2.39	3	1	14	53	1.20	3	4	10	42	3.89	176	4	.278	.357	.415	180	2	.178	.247	.250	170	4	.218	.311	.324	215	4	.237	.322	.358
1991	KC-A	4	4	33	90	2.90	3	3	15	50	3.44	1	1	18	40	2.23	168	4	.262	.323	.399	170	2	.229	.288	.312	178	3	.236	.289	.315	255	5	.243	.296	.345
1992	KC-A	1	6	39	83	2.18	1	2	24	49	1.89	0	2	15	34	2.65	146	2	.205	.293	.274	151	3	.205	.261	.265	133	2	.203	.265	.263	209	4	.244	.313	.325
1993	KC-A	7	5	45	87	2.27	5	4	16	43	2.49	2	1	29	44	2.05	158	1	.234	.297	.329	158	2	.177	.229	.253	143	1	.196	.275	.287	257	2	.210	.271	.276
1994	KC-A	2	3	27	45	4.03	2	2	12	23	5.09	0	1	15	22	2.91	96	3	.302	.364	.469	78	2	.244	.298	.385	87	3	.264	.323	.425	119	4	.277	.336	.454
TOTALS		36	30	187	573	2.64	28	18	91	305	2.42	8	12	96	268	2.89	1039	19	.249	.322	.361	1090	17	.222	.294	.313	1013	17	.222	.294	.313	1354	24	.237	.300	.339
● Mike Moore BR/TR																																				
1984	Sea-A	7	17	0	212	4.97	6	8	0	121	4.55	1	9	0	91	5.52	481	9	.297	.375	.414	355	7	.262	.314	.411	359	8	.315	.379	.454	69	0	.246	.288	.348
1985	Sea-A	17	10	0	247	3.46	8	5	0	133	3.18	9	5	0	114	3.79	514	9	.226	.285	.333	419	9	.272	.319	.388	361	7	.277	.313	.388	115	0	.226	.283	.278
1986	Sea-A	11	13	0	266	4.30	7	4	0	127	4.18	4	9	0	139	4.40	529	15	.282	.362	.405	494	17	.263	.314	.411	426	15	.275	.345	.427	113	4	.354	.447	.531
1987	Sea-A	9	19	0	231	4.71	4	8	0	109	4.12	5	11	0	122	5.25	547	15	.298	.353	.463	372	14	.282	.341	.457	403	10	.298	.353	.432	89	3	.236	.327	.393
1988	Sea-A	9	15	0	229	3.78	6	4	0	103	3.31	3	11	0	125	4.16	493	12	.233	.292	.365	353	12	.229	.301	.429	294	11	.252	.320	.429	99	5	.222	.280	.394
1989	Oak-A	19	11	0	242	2.61	9	4	0	125	2.02	10	7	0	117	3.23	426	3	.218	.296	.277	454	11	.220	.277	.335	326	7	.233	.306	.337	79	1	.215	.276	.354
1990	Oak-A	13	15	0	199	4.65	6	8	0	120	4.66	7	7	0	80	4.63	404	5	.260	.333	.374	360	9	.275	.346	.422	329	5	.277	.359	.413	47	1	.234	.302	.340
1991	Oak-A	17	8	0	210	2.96	11	3	0	118	2.14	6	5	0	92	4.00	394	4	.228	.322	.307	373	7	.230	.307	.329	320	1	.234	.331	.291	54	0	.296	.367	.389
1992	Oak-A	17	12	0	223	4.12	7	4	0	104	3.46	10	8	0	119	4.69	445	8	.261	.326	.364	407	12	.278	.373	.437	364	4	.253	.342	.341	63	2	.238	.300	.365
1993	Det-A	13	9	0	214	5.22	6	4	0	91	5.12	7	5	0	122	5.30	430	15	.270	.337	.437	408	20	.272	.336	.471	357	20	.272	.350	.501	34	1	.176	.222	.265
1994	Det-A	11	10	0	154	5.42	6	4	0	63	4.74	5	6	0	91	6.31	300	12	.260	.375	.440	279	15	.265	.383	.395	246	8	.268	.383	.395	39	3	.231	.286	.538
TOTALS		143	139	2	2427	4.14	78	58	2	1238	3.71	65	81	0	1189	4.59	4963	103	.259	.332	.380	4275	150	.259	.324	.410	3767	93	.270	.343	.403	801	20	.250	.318	.385
● Mike Morgan BR/TR																																				
1985	Sea-A	1	1	0	6	12.00	1	0	0	5	10.80	0	1	0	1	18.00	18	1	.444	.524	.667	10	1	.300	.417	.600	11	1	.545	.643	.818	0	0	—	—	—
1986	Sea-A	11	17	1	216	4.53	4	10	0	100	5.11	7	7	1	116	4.03	479	10	.274	.347	.390	410	14	.298	.359	.466	387	7	.269	.333	.370	53	1	.434	.483	.528
1987	Sea-A	12	17	0	207	4.65	7	10	0	128	4.79	5	7	0	79	4.42	447	13	.302	.345	.468	380	12	.289	.335	.435	369	9	.279	.317	.415	22	1	.273	.333	.455
1988	Bal-A	1	6	1	71	5.43	0	2	1	43	2.30	1	4	0	28	10.16	126	4	.317	.372	.492	148	2	.203	.267	.297	97	4	.381	.459	.598	15	0	.067	.125	.067

		TOTAL					HOME					AWAY					LEFT					RIGHT					ON-BASE					LATE/CLOSE				
YEAR	TM/L	W	L	SV	IP	ERA	W	L	SV	IP	ERA	W	L	SV	IP	ERA	AB	HR	AVG	OBP	SLG	AB	HR	AVG	OBP	SLG	AB	HR	AVG	OBP	SLG	AB	HR	AVG	OBP	SLG
1989	LA-N	8	11	0	153	2.53	4	6	0	87	2.27	4	5	0	65	2.89	299	5	.254	.310	.355	256	1	.211	.236	.277	208	2	.236	.292	.327	83	1	.193	.239	.277
1990	LA-N	11	15	0	211	3.75	5	6	0	105	3.77	6	9	0	106	3.74	455	9	.290	.341	.418	356	10	.236	.292	.360	318	7	.286	.346	.418	64	2	.344	.417	.469
1991	LA-N	14	10	1	236	2.78	6	5	1	119	3.32	8	5	0	117	2.23	495	9	.228	.290	.321	376	3	.223	.262	.287	301	1	.249	.327	.312	90	1	.256	.313	.367
1992	Chi-N	16	8	0	240	2.55	9	2	0	130	1.38	7	6	0	110	3.94	491	8	.248	.328	.354	377	6	.215	.257	.308	336	10	.238	.313	.372	57	0	.228	.274	.333
1993	Chi-N	10	15	0	208	4.03	5	6	0	104	3.12	5	9	0	104	4.95	424	7	.245	.330	.351	362	8	.282	.328	.395						60	2	.300	.333	.450
1994	Chi-N	2	10	0	81	6.69	0	5	0	38	6.69	2	5	0	43	6.70	145	6	.386	.450	.572	183	6	.301	.361	.470	172	5	.297	.365	.442	7	0	.286	.286	.429
TOTALS		86	110	3	1629	3.82	41	52	2	860	3.52	45	58	1	769	4.16	3341	72	.271	.336	.394	2858	63	.254	.303	.371	2518	54	.272	.337	.393	451	8	.275	.327	.386
● Jack Morris BR/TR																																				
1984	Det-A	19	11	0	240	3.60	11	7	0	139	3.81	8	4	0	101	3.30	491	13	.244	.310	.379	427	7	.237	.304	.323	373	10	.263	.322	.378	65	2	.262	.333	.369
1985	Det-A	16	11	0	257	3.33	5	5	0	106	4.49	11	6	0	151	2.51	533	11	.223	.310	.341	411	10	.226	.302	.338	395	8	.225	.297	.327	139	3	.245	.314	.367
1986	Det-A	21	8	0	267	3.27	10	3	0	111	2.76	11	5	0	156	3.63	529	13	.223	.281	.344	471	27	.236	.293	.469	371	9	.210	.267	.332	133	7	.248	.315	.444
1987	Det-A	18	11	0	266	3.38	8	7	0	157	3.15	10	4	0	109	3.73	533	28	.236	.313	.441	463	11	.218	.269	.333	363	12	.226	.308	.369	125	6	.248	.304	.432
1988	Det-A	15	13	0	235	3.94	6	6	0	106	4.82	9	7	0	129	3.2	487	9	.234	.306	.337	408	11	.272	.330	.422	377	9	.265	.324	.408	97	2	.227	.283	.309
1989	Det-A	6	14	0	170	4.86	4	6	0	85	4.75	2	8	0	85	4.98	307	11	.296	.358	.479	362	12	.271	.322	.425	277	3	.300	.356	.401	94	2	.255	.294	.362
1990	Det-A	15	18	0	250	4.51	8	8	0	113	4.06	7	10	0	137	4.87	466	13	.268	.350	.397	487	13	.218	.277	.353	409	16	.249	.327	.408	109	2	.275	.319	.358
1991	Min-A	18	12	0	247	3.43	13	3	0	133	3.31	5	9	0	113	3.57	456	9	.281	.359	.393	466	9	.210	.269	.303	366	10	.243	.323	.350	111	2	.243	.317	.351
1992	Tor-A	21	6	0	241	4.04	11	2	0	128	3.09	10	4	0	113	5.11	460	10	.263	.322	.389	442	8	.229	.302	.326	363	8	.284	.339	.419	106	2	.208	.250	.330
1993	Tor-A	7	12	0	153	6.19	3	6	0	76	7.34	4	6	0	77	5.05	321	9	.318	.385	.480	304	9	.286	.350	.434	299	11	.344	.393	.522	39	2	.256	.302	.436
1994	Cle-A	10	6	0	141	5.60	6	2	0	72	5.97	4	4	0	69	5.22	301	8	.302	.365	.468	258	6	.279	.373	.415	258	8	.279	.369	.434	26	0	.346	.433	.346
TOTALS		166	122	0	2467	4.02	85	55	0	1228	4.08	81	67	0	1238	3.97	4884	134	.257	.328	.396	4499	123	.240	.304	.372	3851	104	.259	.326	.391	1044	30	.248	.307	.375
● Jamie Moyer BL/TL																																				
1986	Chi-N	7	4	0	87	5.05	4	1	0	59	4.88	3	3	0	28	5.40	40	2	.300	.417	.575	304	8	.313	.384	.434	170	5	.312	.381	.447	28	1	.214	.267	.321
1987	Chi-N	12	15	0	201	5.10	7	8	0	108	4.82	5	7	0	93	5.44	108	5	.222	.336	.398	668	23	.278	.355	.433	341	14	.267	.357	.446	80	5	.313	.421	.575
1988	Chi-N	9	15	0	202	3.48	3	8	0	101	3.65	6	7	0	101	3.30	127	3	.228	.267	.331	651	17	.281	.333	.419	317	8	.256	.316	.382	51	2	.275	.315	.471
1989	Tex-A	4	9	0	76	4.86	3	4	0	48	4.34	1	5	0	28	5.72	42	1	.214	.377	.310	255	9	.294	.350	.459	123	4	.301	.371	.472	13	1	.308	.471	.615
1990	Tex-A	2	6	0	102	4.66	2	2	0	60	3.77	0	4	0	43	5.91	81	1	.222	.267	.333	315	5	.308	.376	.460	176	1	.295	.355	.403	23	1	.217	.308	.435
1991	StL-N	0	5	0	31	5.74	0	1	0	13	6.07	0	4	0	18	5.50	25	3	.520	.556	1.000	94	2	.266	.360	.404	49	2	.408	.456	.633	3	0	.333	.500	.333
1993	Bal-A	12	9	0	152	3.43	3	5	0	67	4.68	9	4	0	85	2.44	102	3	.304	.377	.471	480	8	.256	.302	.356	207	4	.285	.361	.406	33	1	.394	.412	.545
1994	Bal-A	5	7	0	149	4.77	2	3	0	71	4.71	3	4	0	78	4.83	84	5	.286	.347	.512	500	18	.268	.311	.450	210	9	.333	.380	.557	55	4	.273	.344	.509
TOTALS		51	70	0	1001	4.42	22	31	0	527	4.44	29	39	0	474	4.41	609	23	.263	.339	.433	3267	90	.281	.341	.425	1593	47	.291	.359	.446	286	15	.290	.368	.503
● Terry Mulholland BR/TL																																				
1986	SF-N	1	7	0	55	4.94	1	3	0	32	3.13	0	4	0	23	7.43	44	1	.273	.407	.432	159	2	.245	.349	.340	88	2	.273	.387	.398	18	0	.500	.526	.722
1988	SF-N	2	1	0	46	3.72	2	1	0	31	1.72	0	0	0	15	7.98	22	0	.227	.261	.273	156	3	.288	.319	.423	80	2	.275	.301	.412	15	1	.400	.400	1.000
1989	SF-N	0	0	0	11	4.09	0	0	0	6	3.00	0	0	0	5	5.40	12	0	.417	.500	.583	35	0	.286	.324	.371	26	0	.154	.241	.231	1	0	.000	.000	.000
1989	Phi-N	4	7	0	104	5.00	2	3	0	53	4.05	2	4	0	51	6.00	73	0	.178	.208	.233	345	8	.316	.376	.443	185	5	.297	.367	.470	25	0	.360	.407	.400
1990	Phi-N	9	10	0	181	3.34	3	4	0	71	2.66	6	6	0	110	3.74	101	2	.277	.299	.366	582	13	.247	.291	.392	271	3	.262	.300	.354	56	2	.286	.298	.536
1991	Phi-N	16	13	0	232	3.61	11	2	0	131	2.96	5	11	0	101	4.44	157	6	.255	.280	.414	730	9	.262	.303	.366	355	9	.287	.326	.414	113	3	.230	.263	.372
1992	Phi-N	13	11	0	229	3.81	9	6	0	146	3.63	4	5	0	83	4.14	161	4	.211	.263	.342	710	10	.272	.306	.370	336	6	.265	.319	.381	93	1	.280	.295	.398
1993	Phi-N	12	9	0	191	3.25	6	4	0	92	3.62	6	5	0	99	2.91	137	3	.212	.265	.343	597	17	.248	.285	.389	279	8	.251	.297	.401	89	2	.292	.326	.449
1994	NY-A	6	7	0	121	6.49	4	2	0	52	6.27	2	5	0	69	6.65	68	4	.338	.390	.588	427	20	.297	.346	.532	225	12	.320	.367	.564	20	2	.350	.350	.800
TOTALS		63	65	0	1169	4.04	38	25	0	614	3.50	25	40	0	555	4.64	775	20	.244	.291	.378	3741	82	.269	.314	.402	1845	47	.276	.327	.418	430	11	.291	.315	.472
● Mike Munoz BL/TL																																				
1989	LA-N	0	0	0	3	16.88	0	0	0	1	0.00	0	0	0	1	33.75	4	0	.250	.400	.250	8	1	.500	.556	1.000	5	0	.200	.429	.400	0	0	—	—	—
1990	LA-N	0	1	0	6	3.18	0	0	0	1	0.00	0	1	0	4	4.15	9	0	.333	.400	.333	11	0	.273	.385	.273	16	0	.250	.368	.250	4	0	.500	.500	.500
1991	Det-A	0	0	0	9	9.64	0	0	0	5	11.81	0	0	0	4	6.75	14	0	.357	.400	.500	26	0	.346	.419	.346	22	0	.409	.462	.500	4	0	.250	.250	.250
1992	Det-A	1	2	2	48	3.00	1	0	0	22	3.68	0	2	2	26	2.42	73	0	.192	.259	.219	106	3	.283	.384	.425	92	0	.174	.291	.196	55	2	.218	.302	.364
1993	Det-A	0	1	0	3	6.00	0	0	0	2	0.00	0	1	0	1	13.50	5	1	.400	.500	1.000						6	1	.500	.727	1.500	5	0	.600	.714	1.200
1993	Col-N	2	1	0	18	4.50	2	0	0	8	7.04	0	1	0	10	2.61	33	1	.303	.333	.485	35	0	.314	.419	.429	33	0	.364	.452	.515	25	1	.360	.433	.640
1994	Col-N	4	2	1	46	3.74	3	1	1	30	3.34	1	1	0	16	4.50	71	1	.225	.329	.338	95	2	.221	.353	.326	86	0	.186	.336	.233	57	0	.228	.353	.298
TOTALS		7	7	3	132	4.28	5	3	1	69	4.30	2	4	2	63	4.26	209	3	.244	.319	.344	289	6	.277	.391	.401	260	1	.235	.363	.312	150	3	.267	.364	.413
● Rob Murphy BL/TL																																				
1985	Cin-N	0	0	0	3	6.00	0	0	0	1	18.00	0	0	0	2	4.00	3	0	.000	.333	.000	8	1	.250	.333	.750	5	0	.200	.200	.400	0	0	—	—	—
1986	Cin-N	6	0	1	50	0.72	2	0	1	28	0.65	4	0	0	23	0.79	45	0	.133	.184	.156	123	0	.163	.266	.187	78	0	.128	.237	.141	66	0	.197	.286	.212
1987	Cin-N	8	5	3	101	3.04	5	3	1	55	3.93	3	2	2	46	1.97	121	1	.240	.292	.314	259	6	.239	.299	.375	151	0	.252	.320	.338	117	2	.308	.379	.427
1988	Cin-N	0	6	3	85	3.08	0	3	1	47	2.30	0	3	2	38	4.06	82	0	.207	.270	.320	313	6	.253	.306	.394	140	3	.243	.335	.350	143	2	.231	.306	.294
1989	Bos-A	5	7	9	105	2.74	2	2	2	47	3.26	3	5	7	58	2.33	114	2	.254	.280	.386	272	5	.250	.339	.353	197	4	.249	.332	.355	185	3	.254	.330	.319
1990	Bos-A	0	6	7	57	6.32	0	2	5	30	5.10	0	4	2	27	7.67	83	0	.241	.340	.289	161	10	.404	.462	.677	138	2	.333	.407	.464	122	5	.320	.403	.516
1991	Sea-A	0	1	4	48	3.00	0	0	0	26	1.40	0	1	1	22	4.94	74	2	.203	.224	.351	114	2	.281	.379	.447	100	2	.290	.355	.480	56	0	.268	.349	.304
1992	Hou-N	3	1	0	56	4.04	1	1	0	32	3.69	2	0	0	24	4.50	86	0	.256	.337	.270	129	2	.264	.312	.403	107	1	.299	.355	.393	65	2	.292	.390	.477
1993	StL-N	5	7	1	65	4.87	2	2	1	32	4.22	3	5	0	33	5.51	82	2	.293	.326	.402	170	6	.288	.349	.441	102	5	.275	.372	.382	149	5	.248	.313	.376
1994	StL-N	4	3	2	40	3.79	3	2	0	22	4.43	1	1	2	18	3.00	58	3	.241	.267	.448	94	4	.223	.305	.383	63	2	.270	.333	.429	63	5	.270	.313	.540
1994	NY-A	0	0	0	2	16.20	0	0	0	0	∞	0	0	0	2	10.80	3	0	.333	.333	.667	5	2	.400	.400	1.600	2	0	.000	.000	.000	1	0	1.000	1.000	2.000
TOTALS		31	36	30	611	3.49	15	15	11	319	3.33	16	21	19	292	3.67	750	10	.236	.288	.323	1554	41	.262	.339	.403	1083	17	.262	.341	.372	967	24	.266	.341	.381
● Mike Mussina BR/TR																																				
1991	Bal-A	4	5	0	88	2.87	3	1	0	43	2.74	1	4	0	45	3.00	140	4	.271	.304	.421	117	2	.265	.285	.368						42	1	.262	.311	.429
1992	Bal-A	18	5	0	241	2.54	7	3	0	116	2.65	11	2	0	125	2.44	422	1	.220	.269	.280	466	15	.255	.286	.410	330	8	.218	.250	.342	82	1	.256	.292	.341
1993	Bal-A	14	6	0	168	4.46	5	2	0	74	4.72	9	4	0	93	4.24	281	4	.256	.308	.352	355	16	.256	.304	.456	249	8	.261	.304	.410	52	0	.212	.281	.231
1994	Bal-A	16	5	0	176	3.06	8	4	0	93	3.98	8	1	0	83	2.04	361	7	.241	.283	.391	296	12	.257	.299	.453	233	4	.275	.318	.378	70	1	.186	.247	.286
TOTALS		52	21	0	673	3.20	23	10	0	325	3.51	29	11	0	347	2.90	1246	15	.241	.284	.283	1257	47	.258	.296	.434	929	22	.250	.286	.372	246	3	.228	.280	.317
● Randy Myers BL/TL																																				
1985	NY-N	0	0	0	2	0.00	0	0	0	2	0.00	0	0	0	0	—	0	0	—	—	—	6	0	.000	.143	.000	1	0	.000	.000	.000	6	0	.000	.143	.000
1986	NY-N	0	0	0	11	4.22	0	0	0	5	5.40	0	0	0	6	3.18	9	0	.111	.385	.111	34	1	.294	.400	.441	25	0	.160	.344	.160	4	0	.000	.200	.000
1987	NY-N	3	6	6	75	3.96	1	0	3	35	4.37	2	6	3	40	3.60	79	1	.177	.247	.304	192	5	.245	.317	.359	124	3	.210	.262	.306	74	2	.189	.307	.284
1988	NY-N	7	3	26	68	1.72	6	1	14	38	1.64	1	2	12	30	1.82	50	0	.180	.250	.220	187	5	.193	.248	.294	121	1	.149	.205	.198	181	3	.166	.219	.238
1989	NY-N	7	4	24	84	2.35	4	0	17	49	2.02	3	4	7	35	2.80	73	2	.164	.244	.315	228	2	.219	.314	.307	161	3	.211	.303	.342	250	4	.200	.291	.304
1990	Cin-N	4	6	31	87	2.08	2	2	15	43	0.62	2	4	16	43	3.53	72	2	.181	.294	.264	234	4	.197	.284	.286	137	2	.175	.294	.241	210	5	.181	.266	.271
1991	Cin-N	6	13	6	132	3.55	3	5	5	72	3.75	3	8	1	60	3.30	132	3	.287	.407	.426	358	5	.226	.326	.313	221	2	.258	.368	.344	169	2	.278	.396	.379
1992	SD-N	3	6	38	80	4.29	2	3	20	39	4.58	1	3	18	40	4.02	63	0	.270	.390	.365	238	7	.282	.337	.412	165	3	.267	.347	.382	244	6	.275	.343	.393
1993	Chi-N	2	4	53	75	3.11	1	2	25	37	3.16	1	2	28	38	3.05	45	1	.178	.302	.289	238	6	.239	.293	.378	136	2	.206	.267	.272	192	5	.245	.313	.375
1994	Chi-N	1	5	21	40	3.79	1	3	11	22	4.43	0	2	10	18	3.00	29	0	.138	.212	.172	125	2	.288	.355	.400	81	2	.284	.344	.407	111	1	.297	.373	.378
TOTALS		33	47	205	654	3.11	19	16	110	343	3.01	14	31	95	311	3.22	542	9	.208	.313	.315	1840	38	.234	.311	.340	1172	18	.220	.307	.310	1441	28	.226	.310	.327
● Charles Nagy BL/TR																																				
1990	Cle-A	2	4	0	46	5.91	2	3	0	38	5.21	0	1	0	8	9.39	106	3	.321	.392	.434	78	3	.308	.379	.538	74	3	.378	.460	.541	8	0	.125	.125	.125
1991	Cle-A	10	15	0	211	4.13	6	5	0	94	3.56	4	10	0	118	4.59	460	7	.289	.341	.417	368	8	.258	.316	.386	364	10	.264	.323	.409	72	0	.236	.291	.264
1992	Cle-A	17	10	0	252	2.96	8	4	0	134	2.34	9	6	0	118	3.67	424	5	.250	.292	.330	520	6	.255	.288	.360	378	3	.246	.290	.302	100	1	.320	.349	.400
1993	Cle-A	2	6	0	49	6.29	2	2	0	23	4.37	0	4	0	26	7.96	104	2	.288	.324	.385	101	4	.356	.409	.545	96	5	.313	.368	.510	8	1	.250	.333	.625
1994	Cle-A	10	8	0	169	3.45	5	2	0	73	3.22	5	6	0	97	3.63	330	5	.224	.285	.312	330	10	.306	.353	.427	266	8	.271	.338	.380	43	1	.256	.298	.372
TOTALS		41	43	0	727	3.83	23	16	0	361	3.26	18	27	0	366	4.38	1424	22	.265	.316	.366	1397	32	.283	.332	.406	1178	29	.271	.329	.385	231	3	.273	.313	.351
● Jaime Navarro BR/TR																																				
1989	Mil-A	7	8	0	110	3.12	6	4	0	67	2.82	1	4	0	43	3.59	194	2	.273	.327	.356	236	4	.280	.327	.381	182	3	.297	.340	.379	26	1	.385	.385	.577
1990	Mil-A	8	7	1	149	4.46	4	4	1	73	4.09	4	3	0	77	4.81	321	4	.299	.348	.374	279	5	.287	.330	.437	275	5	.305	.347	.422	47	1	.404	.442	.532
1991	Mil-A	15	12	0	234	3.92	9	3	0	113	3.58	6	9	0	121	4.24	480	13	.271	.318	.392	428	5	.250	.305	.346	380	8	.255	.311	.386	94	3	.234	.279	.383
1992	Mil-A	17	11	0	246	3.33	9	4	0	109	3.29	8	7	0	137	3.36	435	6	.257	.304	.370	477	8	.235	.288	.333	323	9	.263	.318	.353	102	1	.265	.300	.373
1993	Mil-A	11	12	0	214	5.33	5	5	0	98	5.03	6	7	0	116	5.59	448	11	.317	.367	.459	400	10	.280	.344	.400	354	19	.322	.382	.469	40	1	.300	.383	.450

YEAR	TM/L	TOTAL W	L	SV	IP	ERA	HOME W	L	SV	IP	ERA	AWAY W	L	SV	IP	ERA	LEFT AB	HR	AVG	OBP	SLG	RIGHT AB	HR	AVG	OBP	SLG	ON-BASE AB	HR	AVG	OBP	SLG	LATE/CLOSE AB	HR	AVG	OBP	SLG
1994	Mil-A	4	9	0	90	6.62	1	5	0	42	7.87	3	4	0	47	5.51	183	7	.344	.387	.546	183	3	.284	.367	.410	177	4	.356	.410	.531	34	1	.324	.410	.500
	TOTALS	62	59	1	1043	4.30	34	25	1	503	4.14	28	34	0	540	4.45	2061	43	.289	.340	.413	2003	37	.264	.321	.376	1691	32	.294	.348	.413	343	8	.294	.341	.434

● **Gene Nelson** BR/TR

YEAR	TM/L	W	L	SV	IP	ERA	W	L	SV	IP	ERA	W	L	SV	IP	ERA	AB	HR	AVG	OBP	SLG	AB	HR	AVG	OBP	SLG	AB	HR	AVG	OBP	SLG	AB	HR	AVG	OBP	SLG
1984	Chi-A	3	5	1	75	4.46	1	2	1	20	6.64	2	3	0	54	3.64	170	3	.241	.272	.353	113	6	.274	.333	.513	104	3	.308	.321	.510	44	1	.136	.191	.205
1985	Chi-A	10	10	2	146	4.26	7	6	1	81	3.46	3	4	1	65	5.26	257	10	.249	.334	.440	300	13	.267	.353	.470	237	6	.211	.315	.346	68	3	.191	.353	.368
1986	Chi-A	6	6	6	115	3.85	3	2	0	60	3.47	3	4	6	55	4.25	193	3	.285	.359	.430	243	4	.259	.318	.387	223	3	.260	.331	.377	143	1	.252	.344	.364
1987	Oak-A	6	5	3	124	3.93	4	2	1	70	3.36	2	3	2	54	4.67	239	4	.259	.300	.393	243	8	.239	.307	.428	216	8	.255	.314	.435	113	3	.230	.281	.389
1988	Oak-A	9	6	3	112	3.06	5	4	1	57	3.79	4	2	2	55	2.30	168	4	.232	.314	.339	240	5	.225	.282	.342	174	3	.247	.318	.322	129	2	.163	.265	.233
1989	Oak-A	3	5	3	80	3.26	3	2	0	40	3.18	0	3	3	40	3.35	112	3	.250	.331	.384	184	2	.174	.244	.239	126	1	.190	.293	.246	97	2	.227	.296	.309
1990	Oak-A	3	3	5	75	1.57	1	2	3	28	1.91	2	1	2	46	1.36	110	2	.236	.263	.327	155	3	.187	.256	.290	102	1	.186	.235	.265	114	2	.246	.293	.342
1991	Oak-A	1	5	0	49	6.84	0	1	0	27	5.27	1	4	0	21	8.86	76	3	.355	.453	.618	120	9	.275	.328	.550	106	8	.283	.370	.585	83	6	.325	.389	.639
1992	Oak-A	3	1	0	52	6.45	2	1	0	27	5.67	1	0	0	25	7.30	93	0	.333	.411	.430	110	5	.336	.373	.518	109	3	.312	.365	.486	15	1	.267	.368	.600
1993	Cal-A	0	0	4	53	3.08	0	2	3	25	2.49	0	3	1	27	3.62	63	1	.302	.432	.508	136	2	.228	.272	.294	99	0	.253	.322	.343	82	0	.305	.390	.390
1993	Tex-A	0	0	1	8	3.38	0	0	1	7	1.29	0	0	0	1	18.00	11	0	.455	.500	.455	22	0	.227	.227	.273	16	0	.375	.412	.438	16	0	.438	.471	.500
	TOTALS	44	51	28	886	3.90	26	24	11	442	3.67	18	27	17	444	4.14	1492	33	.266	.336	.409	1866	57	.243	.306	.395	1512	36	.249	.320	.386	904	21	.238	.319	.366

● **Tom Niedenfuer** BR/TR

YEAR	TM/L	W	L	SV	IP	ERA	W	L	SV	IP	ERA	W	L	SV	IP	ERA	AB	HR	AVG	OBP	SLG	AB	HR	AVG	OBP	SLG	AB	HR	AVG	OBP	SLG	AB	HR	AVG	OBP	SLG
1984	LA-N	2	5	11	47	2.47	1	2	8	26	2.10	1	3	3	22	2.91	95	2	.295	.407	.400	77	1	.143	.214	.195	91	1	.187	.275	.220	147	2	.224	.321	.286
1985	LA-N	7	9	19	106	2.71	2	3	11	59	2.75	5	6	8	47	2.66	201	5	.224	.284	.363	185	1	.222	.250	.276	155	5	.245	.290	.355	247	4	.243	.294	.352
1986	LA-N	6	6	11	80	3.71	4	4	5	46	3.33	2	2	6	34	4.24	155	4	.284	.371	.477	152	5	.276	.309	.428	152	5	.263	.347	.428	204	7	.284	.347	.456
1987	LA-N	1	0	1	16	2.76	1	0	0	6	0.00	0	0	1	10	4.50	28	1	.250	.389	.357	31	0	.194	.265	.226	24	1	.208	.394	.333	31	0	.258	.361	.258
1987	Bal-A	3	5	13	52	4.99	2	0	7	29	4.71	1	5	6	24	5.32	108	8	.306	.370	.602	98	3	.224	.301	.378	109	2	.266	.341	.385	129	7	.264	.340	.481
1988	Bal-A	3	4	18	59	3.51	1	1	7	31	4.06	1	3	11	28	2.89	110	4	.291	.371	.473	118	4	.229	.270	.356	119	3	.269	.323	.370	110	2	.245	.311	.327
1989	Sea-A	0	3	0	36	6.69	0	2	0	23	6.56	0	1	0	13	6.92	61	3	.328	.406	.557	88	4	.295	.347	.523	74	5	.351	.405	.649	24	2	.500	.600	.875
1990	StL-N	0	6	2	65	3.46	0	4	1	41	3.92	0	2	1	24	2.66	101	1	.337	.423	.455	144	2	.222	.257	.354	124	1	.202	.278	.282	90	0	.333	.386	.478
	TOTALS	22	38	75	463	3.64	12	16	39	261	3.62	10	22	36	201	3.67	859	30	.283	.365	.456	893	20	.232	.277	.352	848	21	.250	.322	.374	982	24	.267	.336	.399

● **Phil Niekro** BR/TR

YEAR	TM/L	W	L	SV	IP	ERA	W	L	SV	IP	ERA	W	L	SV	IP	ERA	AB	HR	AVG	OBP	SLG	AB	HR	AVG	OBP	SLG	AB	HR	AVG	OBP	SLG	AB	HR	AVG	OBP	SLG
1984	NY-A	16	8	0	216	3.09	7	4	0	106	3.49	9	4	0	110	2.70	449	11	.261	.329	.388	372	4	.274	.325	.363	353	6	.255	.312	.343	78	1	.231	.330	.333
1985	NY-A	16	12	0	220	4.09	9	5	0	110	3.85	7	7	0	110	4.34	440	17	.261	.366	.432	389	12	.226	.311	.383	348	10	.250	.355	.388	55	3	.291	.371	.491
1986	Cle-A	11	11	0	210	4.32	6	5	0	96	4.05	5	6	0	115	4.55	455	9	.284	.360	.404	386	15	.290	.365	.459	389	10	.275	.343	.406	66	5	.303	.403	.561
1987	Tor-A	0	2	0	12	8.25	0	1	0	6	11.37	0	1	0	6	4.76	31	2	.387	.472	.710	18	2	.167	.250	.611	21	2	.333	.417	.762	0	0	—	—	—
1987	Cle-A	7	11	0	124	5.89	2	5	0	46	7.29	5	6	0	78	5.08	273	9	.311	.382	.491	224	9	.254	.324	.442	197	5	.279	.385	.437	39	0	.154	.298	.179
1987	Atl-N	0	0	0	3	15.00	0	0	0	3	15.00	0	0	0	0	—	8	0	.500	.667	.500	6	0	.333	.500	.667	7	0	.429	.667	.429	0	0	—	—	—
	TOTALS	50	44	0	785	4.27	24	20	0	366	4.45	26	24	0	418	4.11	1656	48	.279	.361	.428	1395	42	.261	.332	.412	1315	33	.265	.351	.395	238	9	.252	.354	.408

● **Al Nipper** BR/TR

YEAR	TM/L	W	L	SV	IP	ERA	W	L	SV	IP	ERA	W	L	SV	IP	ERA	AB	HR	AVG	OBP	SLG	AB	HR	AVG	OBP	SLG	AB	HR	AVG	OBP	SLG	AB	HR	AVG	OBP	SLG
1984	Bos-A	11	6	0	183	3.89	5	2	0	93	3.19	6	4	0	90	4.62	396	5	.255	.313	.351	317	13	.259	.312	.435	301	11	.262	.317	.419	90	2	.333	.362	.456
1985	Bos-A	9	12	0	162	4.06	5	6	0	94	3.34	4	6	0	68	5.05	299	8	.274	.378	.421	315	6	.253	.340	.377	273	6	.253	.340	.377	50	2	.280	.315	.460
1986	Bos-A	10	12	0	159	5.38	5	5	0	78	5.17	7	7	0	81	5.58	348	8	.305	.358	.463	294	16	.272	.317	.500	269	12	.294	.340	.520	58	1	.241	.290	.328
1987	Bos-A	11	12	0	174	5.43	5	4	0	73	4.07	6	8	0	102	6.42	374	16	.267	.318	.471	317	14	.303	.375	.530	284	11	.278	.350	.454	45	3	.311	.333	.578
1988	Chi-N	2	4	1	80	3.04	2	2	1	46	3.33	0	2	0	34	2.65	158	4	.259	.339	.386	143	5	.217	.302	.350	127	3	.213	.299	.323	17	0	.118	.167	.235
1990	Cle-A	2	3	0	24	6.75	1	1	0	7	4.91	1	2	0	17	7.56	37	1	.351	.426	.459	62	1	.355	.462	.468	50	0	.380	.471	.460	4	0	.000	.000	.000
	TOTALS	45	49	1	782	4.57	21	20	1	392	3.83	24	29	0	390	5.31	1612	42	.275	.342	.422	1448	55	.267	.336	.448	1304	43	.270	.341	.431	264	8	.280	.314	.428

● **Bob Ojeda** BL/TL

YEAR	TM/L	W	L	SV	IP	ERA	W	L	SV	IP	ERA	W	L	SV	IP	ERA	AB	HR	AVG	OBP	SLG	AB	HR	AVG	OBP	SLG	AB	HR	AVG	OBP	SLG	AB	HR	AVG	OBP	SLG
1984	Bos-A	12	12	0	217	3.99	4	5	0	92	4.89	8	7	0	125	3.32	157	2	.248	.310	.318	659	15	.261	.342	.392	363	9	.234	.311	.377	73	1	.274	.369	.397
1985	Bos-A	9	11	1	158	4.00	4	7	0	98	3.50	5	4	1	60	4.80	127	2	.315	.346	.449	481	9	.262	.322	.383	247	5	.267	.348	.389	87	1	.264	.373	.356
1986	NY-N	18	5	0	217	2.57	9	2	0	107	2.86	9	3	0	110	2.28	107	1	.150	.207	.206	697	14	.242	.289	.349	324	4	.204	.252	.290	106	2	.274	.319	.340
1987	NY-N	3	5	0	46	3.88	2	2	0	27	2.70	1	3	0	20	5.49	45	1	.244	.277	.444	133	4	.256	.296	.406	75	3	.240	.256	.387	24	1	.250	.308	.500
1988	NY-N	10	13	0	190	2.88	6	9	0	109	3.15	4	4	0	82	2.53	127	2	.165	.195	.283	576	6	.238	.276	.325	245	2	.253	.303	.343	70	0	.257	.284	.314
1989	NY-N	13	11	0	192	3.47	6	4	0	85	2.95	7	7	0	107	3.88	161	3	.236	.324	.379	570	11	.247	.314	.354	304	5	.243	.321	.342	43	1	.209	.292	.302
1990	NY-N	7	6	0	118	3.66	4	2	0	64	3.50	3	4	0	54	3.86	113	1	.168	.230	.257	339	9	.307	.365	.466	201	3	.224	.277	.318	72	0	.181	.272	.264
1991	LA-N	12	9	0	189	3.18	6	4	0	99	3.01	6	5	0	91	3.38	136	1	.257	.301	.324	569	14	.257	.328	.388	292	3	.247	.316	.329	38	0	.316	.435	.421
1992	LA-N	6	9	0	166	3.63	4	2	0	83	2.40	2	7	0	84	4.84	116	1	.216	.290	.276	515	7	.280	.362	.392	269	1	.283	.379	.372	19	1	.368	.500	.526
1993	Cle-A	2	1	0	43	4.40	1	1	0	21	4.22	1	0	0	22	4.57	36	1	.278	.341	.472	130	4	.292	.369	.469	83	3	.217	.299	.349	2	1	.500	.500	2.000
1994	NY-A	0	0	0	3	24.00	0	0	0	2	15.43	0	0	0	1	54.00	2	0	.500	.500	.500	16	1	.625	.696	.875	12	0	.583	.667	.583	2	1	.500	.500	2.000
	TOTALS	92	82	1	1540	3.47	46	38	0	787	3.32	46	44	1	753	3.63	1127	17	.226	.285	.327	4685	92	.261	.324	.381	2415	38	.244	.314	.348	534	8	.258	.338	.360

● **Omar Olivares** BR/TR

YEAR	TM/L	W	L	SV	IP	ERA	W	L	SV	IP	ERA	W	L	SV	IP	ERA	AB	HR	AVG	OBP	SLG	AB	HR	AVG	OBP	SLG	AB	HR	AVG	OBP	SLG	AB	HR	AVG	OBP	SLG
1990	StL-N	1	1	0	49	2.92	0	0	0	13	2.13	1	1	0	37	3.19	88	0	.193	.304	.216	93	2	.301	.337	.441	77	0	.247	.301	.299	20	0	.150	.227	.200
1991	StL-N	11	7	1	167	3.71	7	5	1	97	3.33	4	2	0	70	4.24	345	5	.235	.321	.322	264	8	.254	.309	.402	232	5	.259	.331	.379	56	1	.232	.358	.357
1992	StL-N	9	9	0	197	3.84	5	6	0	120	3.96	4	3	0	77	3.64	428	13	.285	.345	.451	308	7	.218	.275	.315	286	10	.245	.305	.413	87	2	.287	.344	.425
1993	StL-N	5	3	1	119	4.17	2	3	1	63	4.71	3	0	0	56	3.56	232	6	.276	.361	.448	234	4	.299	.378	.397	239	4	.280	.365	.393	77	2	.273	.378	.442
1994	StL-N	3	4	1	74	5.54	1	2	1	35	6.17	2	2	0	39	5.35	140	5	.336	.423	.550	146	5	.253	.335	.399	143	4	.294	.342	.427	16	3	.313	.389	.938
	TOTALS	29	24	3	606	4.02	15	16	3	328	4.08	14	8	0	278	3.95	1233	29	.268	.348	.409	1045	26	.257	.321	.377	977	23	.264	.331	.393	256	8	.262	.352	.430

● **Gregg Olson** BR/TR

YEAR	TM/L	W	L	SV	IP	ERA	W	L	SV	IP	ERA	W	L	SV	IP	ERA	AB	HR	AVG	OBP	SLG	AB	HR	AVG	OBP	SLG	AB	HR	AVG	OBP	SLG	AB	HR	AVG	OBP	SLG
1988	Bal-A	1	1	0	11	3.27	0	0	0	4	2.08	1	1	0	7	4.05	18	0	.111	.333	.111	23	1	.348	.444	.522	25	0	.120	.353	.120	18	0	.222	.391	.278
1989	Bal-A	5	2	27	85	1.69	3	0	12	47	0.77	2	2	15	38	2.82	141	0	.135	.247	.149	163	1	.233	.337	.313	165	0	.164	.298	.200	195	0	.169	.289	.210
1990	Bal-A	6	5	37	74	2.42	5	0	13	31	2.93	1	5	24	44	2.06	145	1	.290	.298	.248	123	2	.228	.301	.309	128	2	.227	.313	.297	201	3	.214	.304	.284
1991	Bal-A	4	6	31	74	3.18	3	1	13	34	3.15	1	5	18	39	3.20	139	1	.230	.316	.266	143	0	.294	.348	.343	145	0	.276	.365	.303	194	1	.268	.341	.320
1992	Bal-A	1	5	36	61	2.05	1	1	17	33	1.38	0	4	19	28	2.89	110	0	.195	.262	.200	105	3	.229	.322	.419	106	1	.189	.261	.226	162	3	.228	.306	.321
1993	Bal-A	0	2	29	45	1.60	0	2	16	23	1.96	0	0	13	22	1.23	85	1	.212	.281	.294	81	0	.235	.311	.296	92	1	.228	.291	.293	123	1	.236	.304	.317
1994	Atl-N	0	2	1	15	9.20	0	0	0	7	8.59	0	2	1	7	9.82	23	1	.174	.321	.435	37	0	.405	.511	.568	25	0	.440	.571	.680	7	0	.429	.692	.571
	TOTALS	17	23	161	365	2.54	12	4	71	179	2.21	5	19	90	186	2.85	664	4	.190	.283	.236	675	7	.258	.342	.345	686	4	.220	.323	.271	900	8	.223	.316	.290

● **Jesse Orosco** BR/TL

YEAR	TM/L	W	L	SV	IP	ERA	W	L	SV	IP	ERA	W	L	SV	IP	ERA	AB	HR	AVG	OBP	SLG	AB	HR	AVG	OBP	SLG	AB	HR	AVG	OBP	SLG	AB	HR	AVG	OBP	SLG
1984	NY-N	10	6	31	87	2.59	5	4	15	43	3.53	5	2	16	44	1.65	67	0	.179	.230	.179	246	7	.187	.277	.329	157	3	.166	.247	.268	249	5	.201	.282	.313
1985	NY-N	8	6	17	79	2.73	3	3	7	37	2.45	5	3	10	42	2.98	60	0	.200	.238	.200	235	6	.230	.318	.345	164	3	.213	.293	.280	244	5	.217	.304	.311
1986	NY-N	8	6	21	81	2.33	4	4	7	35	4.15	4	2	14	46	0.97	75	1	.187	.235	.253	220	5	.227	.325	.323	153	4	.183	.277	.261	230	6	.239	.330	.352
1987	NY-N	3	9	16	77	4.44	2	4	8	41	2.83	1	5	8	36	6.31	74	0	.230	.275	.243	219	5	.279	.356	.397	160	3	.256	.335	.350	190	4	.258	.335	.347
1988	LA-N	3	2	9	53	2.72	1	0	2	20	2.75	2	2	7	33	2.70	62	1	.226	.338	.306	129	4	.209	.316	.326	95	1	.168	.305	.221	111	2	.225	.355	.315
1989	Cle-A	3	4	3	78	2.08	2	2	1	43	1.69	1	2	2	35	2.55	87	0	.138	.211	.184	186	7	.226	.297	.403	122	1	.156	.215	.246	163	4	.209	.264	.344
1990	Cle-A	5	4	2	65	3.90	3	3	2	39	3.00	2	1	0	26	5.26	67	2	.224	.338	.358	176	7	.244	.338	.426	124	3	.210	.322	.339	90	2	.222	.330	.344
1991	Cle-A	2	0	0	46	3.74	1	0	0	24	1.90	1	0	0	22	5.73	63	1	.286	.313	.381	119	3	.286	.351	.403	103	5	.320	.376	.437	40	0	.325	.370	.400
1992	Mil-A	3	1	1	39	3.23	3	1	1	23	3.52	0	0	0	16	2.81	55	2	.273	.348	.418	87	3	.207	.278	.333	73	4	.233	.275	.411	52	1	.192	.283	.250
1993	Mil-A	3	5	8	57	3.18	0	5	5	29	4.60	3	0	3	27	1.65	64	1	.313	.353	.438	146	1	.185	.262	.247	107	1	.224	.292	.308	143	2	.203	.275	.301
1994	Mil-A	3	1	0	39	5.08	1	0	0	22	4.50	2	1	0	17	5.82	57	1	.263	.344	.351	83	3	.195	.345	.333	73	4	.233	.356	.342	49	0	.245	.351	.306
	TOTALS	51	44	108	700	3.15	25	26	47	355	3.12	26	18	61	345	3.19	731	9	.224	.287	.294	1850	50	.216	.315	.354	1331	28	.212	.297	.308	1561	31	.224	.310	.327

● **Donn Pall** BR/TR

YEAR	TM/L	W	L	SV	IP	ERA	W	L	SV	IP	ERA	W	L	SV	IP	ERA	AB	HR	AVG	OBP	SLG	AB	HR	AVG	OBP	SLG	AB	HR	AVG	OBP	SLG	AB	HR	AVG	OBP	SLG
1988	Chi-A	0	2	0	29	3.45	0	0	0	13	2.77	0	2	0	16	4.02	49	1	.347	.360	.490	70	0	.314	.372	.357	67	1	.269	.324	.373	33	0	.303	.378	.364
1989	Chi-A	4	5	6	87	3.31	1	2	3	37	3.38	3	3	3	50	3.26	157	4	.255	.306	.389	176	5	.239	.339	.432	185	3	.265	.299	.368	148	6	.257	.313	.426
1990	Chi-A	3	5	2	76	3.32	0	3	0	39	4.50	3	2	2	37	2.16	115	0	.209	.279	.261	157	6	.197	.270	.350	132	3	.212	.293	.341	101	4	.248	.336	.426
1991	Chi-A	7	2	0	71	2.41	3	1	0	37	2.19	4	1	0	34	2.65	106	1	.189	.259	.245	149	6	.262	.321	.403	101	2	.287	.357	.376	101	2	.248	.321	.337
1992	Chi-A	5	2	1	73	4.93	4	0	1	39	5.26	1	2	0	34	4.54	103	2	.291	.373	.369	187	6	.281	.314	.433	128	6	.281	.362	.461	78	0	.269	.370	.321
1993	Chi-A	2	3	1	59	3.22	1	2	1	30	2.76	1	1	0	29	5.76	111	3	.270	.331	.378	114	1	.305	.339	.351	68	0	.279	.319	.324	51	0	.294	.333	.392
1993	Phi-N	1	0	0	18	2.55	1	0	0	9	4.15	0	0	0	9	4.15	31	0	.258	.273	.278	29	1	.241	.290	.379	26	0	.269	.321	.308	19	0	.158	.158	.211
1994	NY-A	1	2	0	35	3.60	0	0	0	17	2.60	1	2	0	18	4.58	47	1	.277	.320	.362	99	2	.303	.346	.434	61	2	.328	.400	.459	41	0	.341	.372	.390
1994	Chi-N	0	0	0	4	4.50	0	0	0	0	—	0	0	0	4	4.50	10	0	.714	.750	1.000	11	1	.273	.273	.545	7	1	.429	.429	1.000	19	0	.158	.158	.211
	TOTALS	23	21	10	451	3.43	12	7	6	226	3.82	11	14	4	225	3.04	735	12	.267	.322	.371	994	31	.264	.317	.402	812	19	.273	.333	.390	589	12	.263	.330	.370

YEAR	TM/L	TOTAL W	L	SV	IP	ERA	HOME W	L	SV	IP	ERA	AWAY W	L	SV	IP	ERA	LEFT AB	HR	AVG	OBP	SLG	RIGHT AB	HR	AVG	OBP	SLG	ON-BASE AB	HR	AVG	OBP	SLG	LATE/CLOSE AB	HR	AVG	OBP	SLG
● **Jeff Parrett** BR/TR																																				
1986	Mon-N	0	1	0	20	4.87	0	1	0	12	5.25	0	0	0	8	4.32	46	1	.239	.364	.370	31	2	.258	.333	.452	40	3	.275	.333	.550	1	1	1.000	1.000	4.000
1987	Mon-N	7	6	6	62	4.21	3	4	4	37	3.93	4	2	2	25	4.62	141	5	.255	.338	.411	90	3	.189	.284	.344	98	3	.245	.348	.408	94	3	.266	.358	.426
1988	Mon-N	12	4	6	92	2.65	5	3	4	48	2.08	7	1	2	44	3.27	138	4	.210	.319	.254	170	8	.218	.304	.412	123	3	.195	.314	.309	171	4	.216	.319	.345
1989	Phi-N	12	6	6	106	2.98	7	0	3	49	2.22	5	6	3	57	3.63	202	0	.218	.309	.292	186	6	.247	.304	.435	163	3	.245	.347	.368	189	4	.228	.317	.354
1990	Phi-N	4	9	1	82	5.18	2	4	1	44	5.15	2	5	0	38	5.21	159	6	.289	.390	.484	155	4	.297	.339	.452	152	5	.283	.364	.467	99	3	.313	.409	.455
1990	Atl-N	1	1	1	27	3.00	0	1	1	15	4.80	1	0	0	12	0.75	48	1	.229	.387	.354	48	0	.333	.397	.354	61	0	.230	.292	.295	50	0	.320	.403	.360
1991	Atl-N	1	2	1	21	6.33	1	2	0	16	8.04	0	0	1	6	1.59	47	0	.362	.434	.489	48	2	.292	.370	.417	62	0	.274	.348	.355	28	2	.393	.433	.607
1992	Oak-A	9	1	0	98	3.02	4	0	0	52	3.29	5	1	0	46	2.72	144	2	.278	.376	.375	214	5	.192	.258	.322	174	2	.236	.332	.339	145	2	.214	.292	.303
1993	Col-N	3	3	1	74	5.38	3	2	0	44	6.18	0	1	1	30	4.20	149	1	.295	.383	.362	136	5	.250	.358	.419	141	3	.312	.417	.426	73	1	.329	.390	.411
TOTALS		49	33	22	582	3.87	25	17	13	315	4.06	24	16	9	267	3.65	1074	16	.259	.357	.367	1078	35	.240	.314	.398	1014	22	.254	.349	.385	850	20	.258	.345	.381
● **Bob Patterson** BR/TL																																				
1985	SD-N	0	0	0	4	24.75	0	0	0	4	24.75	0	0	0	0	—	6	1	.833	.875	1.500	17	1	.471	.500	.765	14	2	.643	.688	1.143	0	0	—	—	—
1986	Pit-N	2	3	0	36	4.95	2	0	0	24	3.75	0	3	0	12	7.30	21	0	.286	.375	.429	131	0	.328	.336	.420	73	0	.370	.390	.466	23	0	.435	.480	.565
1987	Pit-N	1	4	0	43	6.70	1	2	0	29	5.34	0	2	0	14	9.42	41	1	.220	.319	.366	127	4	.315	.388	.512	84	3	.298	.386	.476	7	0	.000	.125	.000
1989	Pit-N	4	3	1	27	4.05	2	2	0	19	4.66	2	1	1	7	2.45	25	0	.120	.185	.160	73	3	.274	.325	.438	36	3	.250	.317	.500	7	0	.143	.300	.286
1990	Pit-N	8	5	5	95	2.95	4	1	3	53	2.70	4	4	2	41	3.27	103	1	.204	.252	.272	251	8	.267	.311	.414	147	3	.252	.289	.340	96	1	.229	.302	.313
1991	Pit-N	4	3	2	66	4.11	2	2	0	27	4.94	2	1	2	38	3.52	81	1	.181	.218	.265	168	6	.310	.348	.476	113	3	.301	.325	.434	77	4	.260	.296	.429
1992	Pit-N	6	3	9	65	2.92	4	2	6	36	3.47	2	1	3	28	2.22	78	1	.256	.330	.359	162	6	.245	.299	.420	104	5	.240	.325	.433	130	6	.269	.333	.485
1993	Tex-A	2	4	1	53	4.78	1	2	0	22	6.14	1	2	1	31	3.82	72	1	.250	.267	.347	137	7	.299	.345	.504	93	5	.312	.340	.495	53	3	.293	.339	.448
1994	Cal-A	2	3	1	42	4.07	1	2	0	23	3.47	1	1	1	19	4.82	70	1	.229	.289	.357	83	5	.229	.319	.458	72	4	.250	.341	.500	60	1	.167	.254	.217
TOTALS		29	28	19	430	4.27	17	13	9	238	4.42	12	15	10	191	4.09	499	7	.226	.284	.331	1149	40	.286	.335	.456	736	28	.289	.342	.454	458	14	.251	.314	.393
● **Alejandro Pena** BR/TR																																				
1984	LA-N	12	6	0	199	2.48	7	4	0	91	2.27	5	2	0	108	2.67	371	1	.248	.309	.318	385	6	.244	.274	.335	313	1	.243	.287	.310	100	0	.240	.283	.300
1985	LA-N	0	1	0	4	8.31	0	1	0	2	18.00	0	0	0	2	0.00	5	1	.200	.500	.500	15	0	.400	.400	.467	10	1	.300	.364	.700	0	0	—	—	—
1986	LA-N	1	2	1	70	4.89	1	1	1	36	2.25	0	1	0	34	7.68	145	6	.310	.390	.497	129	0	.225	.289	.279	132	1	.273	.345	.371	28	0	.286	.459	.357
1987	LA-N	2	7	11	87	3.50	1	4	6	54	2.52	1	3	5	34	5.08	177	2	.237	.320	.305	150	7	.267	.331	.473	141	4	.248	.333	.383	92	0	.196	.286	.239
1988	LA-N	6	7	12	94	1.91	2	4	6	44	1.64	4	3	6	50	2.15	167	0	.251	.326	.281	177	4	.186	.222	.277	138	0	.246	.310	.275	211	3	.204	.260	.275
1989	LA-N	4	3	5	76	2.13	1	0	2	35	2.80	3	3	3	41	1.55	151	4	.232	.280	.338	131	2	.206	.261	.305	114	0	.219	.268	.272	163	5	.252	.309	.399
1990	NY-N	3	3	5	76	3.20	1	0	2	31	3.19	2	3	3	45	3.20	131	1	.252	.322	.321	159	3	.239	.272	.352	126	1	.270	.324	.341	102	1	.206	.265	.284
1991	NY-N	6	1	4	63	2.71	3	1	2	34	3.44	3	0	2	29	1.86	116	2	.207	.268	.293	120	3	.325	.364	.458	97	3	.289	.336	.464	104	2	.288	.328	.385
1991	Atl-N	2	0	11	19	1.40	1	0	3	6	0.00	1	0	8	13	1.80	34	1	.147	.216	.235	32	0	.188	.188	.188	29	0	.103	.133	.103	43	0	.093	.152	.093
1992	Atl-N	1	6	15	42	4.07	0	2	5	18	4.42	1	4	10	24	3.80	78	5	.205	.262	.436	79	2	.304	.356	.405	58	3	.310	.397	.500	105	4	.267	.345	.419
1994	Pit-N	3	2	7	29	5.02	1	2	3	15	6.00	2	0	4	14	3.95	56	2	.179	.281	.357	51	2	.235	.278	.412	47	2	.191	.269	.362	64	2	.188	.268	.313
TOTALS		40	38	71	760	2.99	17	19	30	365	2.79	23	19	41	395	3.19	1431	25	.241	.311	.338	1428	29	.244	.286	.352	1205	16	.250	.310	.343	1012	17	.226	.292	.318
● **Melido Perez** BR/TR																																				
1987	KC-A	1	1	0	10	7.84	1	1	0	10	7.84	0	0	0	0	—	32	0	.375	.429	.500	16	2	.375	.444	.813	24	1	.458	.519	.708	2	0	.500	.500	.500
1988	Chi-A	12	10	0	197	3.79	6	2	0	92	3.52	6	8	0	105	4.03	397	12	.232	.299	.385	352	14	.267	.329	.435	306	8	.239	.291	.389	60	3	.300	.364	.533
1989	Chi-A	11	14	0	183	5.01	4	6	0	78	5.06	7	8	0	105	4.97	371	12	.264	.352	.445	337	11	.264	.344	.418	300	10	.286	.359	.461	41	1	.268	.318	.390
1990	Chi-A	13	14	0	197	4.61	5	6	0	81	5.11	8	8	0	116	4.27	380	6	.250	.322	.374	355	8	.231	.318	.361	297	3	.263	.334	.384	40	1	.225	.326	.400
1991	Chi-A	8	7	1	136	3.12	2	3	0	62	3.61	6	4	1	73	2.70	223	6	.202	.279	.332	272	9	.243	.315	.368	211	5	.223	.298	.327	152	5	.211	.277	.322
1992	NY-A	13	16	0	248	2.87	5	6	0	99	3.01	8	10	0	149	2.78	430	8	.247	.324	.344	411	6	.225	.293	.321	359	6	.223	.308	.309	87	1	.264	.337	.379
1993	NY-A	6	14	0	163	5.19	3	9	0	83	6.26	3	5	0	80	4.07	339	9	.277	.352	.407	308	13	.256	.312	.458	274	12	.310	.368	.504	69	0	.232	.293	.290
1994	NY-A	9	4	0	151	4.10	4	1	0	83	3.59	5	3	0	69	4.72	263	10	.247	.337	.418	300	6	.230	.287	.373	218	5	.275	.353	.468	44	0	.318	.388	.409
TOTALS		73	80	1	1285	4.09	30	34	0	589	4.34	43	46	1	697	3.88	2435	63	.249	.326	.389	2411	71	.245	.314	.389	1993	50	.261	.332	.406	495	11	.251	.319	.374
● **Pascual Perez** BR/TR																																				
1984	Atl-N	14	8	0	212	3.74	6	4	0	95	3.61	8	4	0	117	3.85	413	18	.264	.310	.441	387	8	.256	.300	.377	281	10	.263	.317	.423	83	3	.229	.323	.361
1985	Atl-N	1	13	0	95	6.14	1	8	0	46	6.99	0	5	0	49	5.33	212	6	.302	.400	.467	175	4	.291	.369	.440	183	5	.301	.407	.454	14	0	.429	.400	.500
1987	Mon-N	7	0	0	70	2.30	3	0	0	33	2.97	4	0	0	37	1.70	149	2	.221	.284	.289	103	3	.184	.213	.311	82	3	.244	.300	.378	32	1	.219	.219	.344
1988	Mon-N	12	8	0	188	2.44	6	3	0	102	1.68	6	5	0	86	3.34	363	9	.215	.275	.342	314	6	.175	.225	.258	229	3	.210	.278	.297	60	2	.167	.219	.283
1989	Mon-N	9	13	0	198	3.31	6	9	0	125	2.80	3	4	0	73	4.19	414	9	.237	.290	.362	337	6	.237	.273	.356	285	6	.242	.308	.375	67	0	.403	.467	.552
1990	NY-A	1	2	0	14	1.29	1	1	0	8	2.25	0	1	0	6	0.00	23	0	.130	.231	.174	26	0	.192	.192	.269	10	0	.100	.250	.200	0	0	—	—	—
1991	NY-A	2	4	0	74	3.18	1	3	0	43	3.53	1	1	0	30	2.67	140	5	.279	.344	.450	132	2	.220	.275	.288	101	5	.248	.327	.406	40	0	.333	.333	.333
TOTALS		46	48	0	851	3.41	24	28	0	453	3.22	22	20	0	399	3.63	1714	49	.247	.309	.388	1474	29	.229	.277	.340	1171	32	.249	.322	.385	262	6	.271	.330	.397
● **Dan Petry** BR/TR																																				
1984	Det-A	18	8	0	233	3.24	10	4	0	121	2.74	8	4	0	112	3.78	494	12	.249	.305	.370	397	9	.272	.321	.406	343	9	.289	.342	.449	56	1	.286	.333	.411
1985	Det-A	15	13	0	239	3.36	7	9	0	132	3.60	8	4	0	106	3.05	487	13	.222	.306	.347	388	11	.211	.258	.345	312	11	.250	.318	.397	103	1	.146	.228	.204
1986	Det-A	5	10	0	116	4.66	1	7	0	62	4.65	4	3	0	54	4.67	242	12	.231	.311	.442	214	3	.308	.389	.435	212	4	.250	.333	.387	28	0	.179	.281	.179
1987	Det-A	9	7	0	135	5.61	4	4	0	62	5.95	5	3	0	73	5.33	254	8	.272	.367	.433	277	14	.285	.383	.491	259	13	.274	.367	.483	36	3	.333	.442	.611
1988	Cal-A	3	9	0	140	4.38	3	6	0	87	3.92	0	3	0	52	5.16	264	7	.288	.377	.417	264	11	.239	.303	.432	219	9	.283	.343	.484	63	4	.270	.324	.492
1989	Cal-A	3	2	0	51	5.47	3	1	0	33	4.09	0	1	0	18	8.00	88	6	.352	.404	.602	105	2	.210	.301	.286	85	4	.235	.286	.400	15	0	.200	.400	.200
1990	Det-A	10	9	0	150	4.45	4	5	0	62	5.49	6	4	0	87	3.71	245	3	.249	.345	.351	318	11	.274	.353	.443	239	4	.259	.353	.368	41	1	.268	.400	.415
1991	Det-A	2	3	0	55	4.94	1	1	0	29	3.41	1	2	0	26	6.66	93	5	.312	.373	.538	127	4	.291	.343	.465	90	4	.344	.416	.567	20	1	.350	.409	.550
1991	Atl-N	0	0	0	24	5.55	0	0	0	18	7.64	0	0	0	7	0.00	48	2	.313	.377	.500	50	0	.280	.400	.360	57	1	.263	.344	.386	0	0	—	—	—
1991	Bos-A	0	0	0	22	4.43	0	0	0	15	4.80	0	0	1	7	3.68	27	0	.185	.303	.259	57	3	.281	.369	.491	47	3	.298	.370	.574	16	0	.313	.389	.375
TOTALS		65	61	1	1164	4.22	33	37	1	622	4.17	32	24	1	542	4.28	2242	68	.256	.334	.401	2197	68	.261	.331	.416	1863	62	.271	.344	.436	378	11	.241	.328	.368
● **Dan Plesac** BL/TL																																				
1986	Mil-A	10	7	14	91	2.97	6	3	6	50	3.58	4	4	8	41	2.21	79	1	.266	.333	.367	258	4	.233	.285	.333	167	3	.228	.287	.329	206	3	.243	.300	.350
1987	Mil-A	5	6	23	79	2.61	2	2	9	35	3.31	3	4	14	44	2.05	57	2	.140	.219	.281	239	6	.230	.288	.326	143	7	.252	.310	.427	216	7	.241	.308	.370
1988	Mil-A	1	2	30	52	2.41	0	0	16	27	1.69	1	2	14	26	3.16	40	0	.225	.262	.375	157	2	.236	.281	.306	109	2	.248	.299	.367	142	2	.246	.291	.352
1989	Mil-A	3	4	33	61	2.35	1	1	15	33	1.89	2	3	18	28	2.89	49	1	.224	.231	.306	172	5	.209	.274	.331	117	3	.205	.274	.299	165	6	.224	.286	.370
1990	Mil-A	3	7	24	69	4.43	2	3	11	31	6.03	1	4	13	38	3.11	62	0	.161	.254	.226	199	5	.286	.364	.413	138	2	.290	.363	.413	177	4	.288	.365	.429
1991	Mil-A	2	7	8	92	4.29	0	4	5	48	5.63	2	3	3	44	2.84	64	4	.297	.361	.516	286	8	.255	.330	.416	176	2	.233	.286	.358	61	4	.295	.380	.557
1992	Mil-A	5	4	1	79	2.96	2	2	0	29	2.48	3	2	1	50	3.24	67	2	.254	.342	.403	213	3	.221	.309	.324	132	4	.258	.346	.417	51	1	.275	.383	.333
1993	Chi-N	2	1	0	63	4.74	1	1	0	32	5.85	1	0	0	30	3.56	89	2	.258	.305	.393	159	8	.321	.373	.516	110	6	.318	.381	.527	54	2	.333	.415	.519
1994	Chi-N	2	3	1	54	4.61	0	1	0	28	4.23	2	2	1	27	5.00	69	1	.188	.243	.275	150	8	.320	.356	.547	103	6	.291	.321	.505	88	4	.307	.319	.511
TOTALS		33	41	134	642	3.48	15	17	62	314	3.96	18	24	72	328	3.02	576	6	.227	.290	.352	1833	49	.253	.317	.384	1195	35	.255	.313	.398	1160	33	.260	.324	.399
● **Eric Plunk** BR/TR																																				
1986	Oak-A	4	7	0	120	5.31	3	3	0	63	5.68	1	4	0	57	4.89	239	7	.226	.377	.339	186	7	.199	.362	.344	195	8	.241	.373	.395	29	2	.310	.429	.517
1987	Oak-A	4	6	2	95	4.74	2	3	2	46	4.86	2	3	0	49	4.62	192	2	.276	.371	.365	167	6	.228	.353	.371	185	4	.232	.329	.341	75	2	.160	.276	.267
1988	Oak-A	7	2	5	78	3.00	4	1	3	35	4.93	3	1	2	43	1.45	122	1	.205	.305	.279	164	5	.226	.316	.348	129	4	.209	.320	.326	109	3	.211	.317	.294
1989	Oak-A	1	1	0	29	2.20	0	0	0	14	1.29	1	1	1	15	3.04	39	1	.179	.304	.359	60	0	.167	.242	.217	46	0	.109	.196	.174	22	0	.227	.320	.273
1989	NY-A	7	5	0	76	3.69	3	4	0	40	3.02	4	1	0	36	2.72	136	3	.236	.367	.386	147	4	.238	.343	.361	124	4	.250	.349	.387	46	3	.239	.340	.457
1990	NY-A	6	3	0	73	2.72	4	0	0	27	3.71	2	3	0	46	2.15	91	1	.220	.404	.385	167	5	.192	.304	.317	125	3	.200	.351	.328	75	1	.280	.386	.373
1991	NY-A	2	5	0	112	4.76	2	2	0	62	4.35	0	3	0	50	5.26	223	10	.291	.385	.502	225	8	.280	.357	.453	219	7	.279	.365	.429	30	1	.300	.382	.467
1992	Cle-A	9	6	4	72	3.64	6	3	2	37	4.10	3	3	2	34	3.15	118	1	.237	.297	.314	148	4	.223	.343	.324	114	3	.237	.350	.351	165	5	.200	.295	.315
1993	Cle-A	4	5	15	71	2.79	3	1	7	36	2.25	1	4	8	35	3.34	105	2	.238	.333	.390	144	5	.215	.307	.299	161	4	.261	.342	.410	111	3	.243	.346	.414
1994	Cle-A	7	2	3	71	2.54	6	1	0	35	2.57	1	1	3	36	2.51	124	2	.242	.323	.387	140	1	.171	.255	.250	120	1	.217	.335	.295	123	4	.233	.346	.414
TOTALS		51	42	30	796	3.81	34	16	14	381	4.13	17	26	16	414	3.52	1380	32	.254	.363	.389	1569	43	.224	.324	.345	1413	36	.231	.340	.350	823	24	.233	.332	.365
● **Mark Portugal** BR/TR																																				
1985	Min-A	1	3	0	24	5.55	1	1	0	15	5.40	0	2	0	9	5.79	50	2	.340	.441	.540	39	1	.179	.261	.308	35	3	.286	.386	.600	4	1	.500	.600	1.250
1986	Min-A	6	10	1	113	4.31	3	4	1	44	4.09	3	7	0	69	4.46	206	3	.218	.334	.325	216	7	.313	.370	.454	143	7	.252	.330	.427	36	1	.417	.475	.556
1987	Min-A	1	3	0	44	7.77	0	2	0	18	11.29	1	1	0	26	5.26	106	6	.255	.339	.500	72	7	.431	.506	.792	78	5	.282	.367	.564	11	1	.182	.250	.455
1988	Min-A	3	3	0	58	4.53	2	2	1	30	5.40	1	1	2	28	3.58	118	8	.288	.339	.542	101	3	.257	.310	.416	105	3	.238	.278	.390	41	1	.293	.348	.439
1989	Hou-N	7	1	0	108	2.75	4	1	0	52	3.12	3	0	0	56	2.41	209	3	.220	.297	.321	183	4	.246	.305	.339	154	3	.214	.278	.318	39	0	.231	.250	.256
1990	Hou-N	11	10	0	197	3.62	8	2	0	101	1.78	3	8	0	95	5.57	427	10	.281	.331	.434	320	11	.246	.315	.382	309	11	.246	.315	.382	54	1	.315	.393	.407

YEAR	TM/L	TOTAL W	L	SV	IP	ERA	HOME W	L	SV	IP	ERA	AWAY W	L	SV	IP	ERA	LEFT AB	HR	AVG	OBP	SLG	RIGHT AB	HR	AVG	OBP	SLG	ON-BASE AB	HR	AVG	OBP	SLG	LATE/CLOSE AB	HR	AVG	OBP	SLG
1991	Hou-N	10	12	1	168	4.49	4	5	1	79	3.06	6	7	0	89	5.76	366	10	.243	.313	.380	271	9	.273	.326	.428	253	8	.265	.342	.427	58	2	.345	.415	.500
1992	Hou-N	6	3	0	101	2.66	4	0	0	58	1.86	2	3	0	43	3.74	205	5	.244	.328	.395	152	2	.171	.250	.243	133	1	.211	.289	.263	31	2	.194	.286	.419
1993	Hou-N	18	4	0	208	2.77	10	1	0	95	2.37	8	3	0	113	3.11	411	4	.234	.305	.294	370	6	.265	.332	.354	327	6	.260	.325	.352	47	1	.319	.353	.426
1994	SF-N	10	8	0	137	3.93	5	4	0	78	3.45	5	4	0	59	4.58	258	11	.244	.322	.399	261	6	.276	.326	.406	227	6	.233	.276	.335	41	3	.146	.186	.366
TOTALS		73	57	5	1158	3.78	41	21	3	571	3.18	32	36	2	587	4.35	2356	62	.239	.316	.365	1985	56	.270	.329	.403	1816	51	.245	.313	.372	362	13	.287	.347	.434
● Ted Power BR/TR																																					
1984	Cin-N	9	7	11	109	2.82	4	5	4	56	3.67	5	2	7	52	1.89	177	3	.271	.367	.384	216	1	.208	.262	.259	208	2	.236	.321	.308	163	3	.239	.325	.344
1985	Cin-N	8	6	27	80	2.70	4	3	16	46	2.15	4	3	11	34	3.44	125	1	.224	.346	.320	161	1	.230	.317	.280	152	1	.257	.354	.349	237	2	.253	.339	.338
1986	Cin-N	10	6	1	129	3.70	6	2	0	69	3.38	4	4	1	60	4.07	229	6	.262	.342	.402	240	7	.229	.294	.342	200	8	.240	.328	.410	85	4	.353	.424	.529
1987	Cin-N	10	13	0	204	4.50	3	5	0	85	5.72	7	8	0	119	3.63	425	11	.285	.347	.440	373	17	.247	.302	.437	341	12	.267	.332	.426	45	0	.289	.373	.356
1988	KC-A	5	6	0	80	5.94	3	3	0	49	4.81	2	3	0	32	7.67	144	3	.292	.354	.424	177	4	.316	.375	.497	146	5	.315	.370	.500	38	0	.211	.295	.263
1988	Det-A	1	1	0	19	5.79	0	0	0	7	3.86	1	1	0	12	6.94	32	1	.313	.421	.469	43	0	.302	.333	.302	34	1	.324	.410	.412	5	0	.600	.600	.600
1989	StL-N	7	7	0	97	3.71	3	2	0	40	2.95	4	5	0	57	4.24	207	3	.280	.324	.396	170	4	.224	.256	.371	158	5	.259	.306	.418	12	0	.333	.357	.500
1990	Pit-N	1	3	7	52	3.66	1	1	5	28	4.88	0	2	2	24	2.25	78	2	.256	.366	.372	118	3	.254	.270	.381	87	2	.299	.376	.414	76	2	.276	.325	.421
1991	Cin-N	5	3	3	87	3.62	5	0	2	50	3.04	0	3	1	37	4.42	171	4	.292	.378	.456	157	2	.236	.272	.313	140	2	.279	.352	.407	104	1	.260	.319	.346
1992	Cle-A	3	3	6	99	2.54	2	1	3	55	1.64	1	2	3	44	3.65	133	1	.226	.302	.301	222	6	.261	.324	.374	197	5	.213	.291	.310	151	2	.238	.308	.311
1993	Cle-A	0	2	0	20	7.20	0	0	0	7	7.36	0	2	0	13	7.11	31	1	.387	.441	.613	59	1	.305	.354	.441	51	0	.333	.397	.431	13	0	.462	.500	.692
1993	Sea-A	2	2	13	25	3.91	0	1	8	12	6.75	2	1	5	13	1.35	39	1	.256	.356	.359	55	0	.309	.339	.364	55	1	.255	.323	.364	75	1	.267	.341	.347
TOTALS		61	59	68	1001	3.86	31	23	38	504	3.80	30	36	30	497	3.91	1791	37	.273	.350	.405	1991	46	.249	.303	.368	1769	44	.262	.335	.392	1004	15	.266	.340	.365
● Dan Quisenberry BR/TR																																					
1984	KC-A	6	3	44	129	2.64	3	1	24	59	2.43	3	2	20	70	2.83	276	5	.264	.284	.359	213	5	.225	.237	.324	192	5	.266	.287	.391	334	5	.246	.263	.326
1985	KC-A	8	9	37	129	2.37	6	3	20	74	2.30	2	6	17	55	2.47	271	4	.317	.350	.425	237	4	.236	.244	.308	254	2	.268	.303	.335	360	5	.275	.301	.361
1986	KC-A	3	7	12	81	2.77	2	3	2	37	2.45	1	4	10	45	3.02	145	1	.310	.380	.379	171	1	.275	.308	.322	164	1	.299	.365	.354	142	0	.317	.383	.359
1987	KC-A	4	1	8	49	2.76	4	0	3	27	0.99	0	1	5	22	4.98	103	2	.320	.364	.466	99	1	.253	.279	.374	105	3	.343	.375	.543	91	2	.330	.358	.495
1988	KC-A	0	1	1	25	3.55	0	1	0	9	7.00	0	0	1	16	1.65	40	0	.400	.429	.475	65	0	.246	.279	.292	54	0	.278	.328	.315	11	0	.545	.545	.636
1988	StL-N	2	0	0	38	6.16	1	0	0	19	5.12	1	0	0	19	7.23	54	2	.278	.322	.426	103	2	.379	.387	.583	79	4	.367	.381	.646	22	1	.409	.435	.682
1989	StL-N	3	1	6	78	2.64	3	0	4	38	4.30	0	1	2	41	1.11	143	2	.238	.297	.336	156	0	.282	.289	.365	117	1	.291	.349	.385	72	0	.264	.312	.319
1990	SF-N	0	1	0	7	13.50	0	1	0	3	21.00	0	0	0	4	7.36	11	0	.727	.600	1.091	20	1	.250	.318	.400	15	0	.467	.476	.467	16	1	.438	.450	.750
TOTALS		26	23	108	537	3.03	19	9	53	267	3.07	7	14	55	270	3.00	1043	16	.297	.336	.405	1064	14	.263	.280	.355	980	16	.295	.335	.403	1048	14	.283	.314	.374
● Scott Radinsky BL/TL																																					
1990	Chi-A	6	1	4	52	4.82	2	1	3	26	4.50	4	0	1	26	5.13	62	0	.177	.268	.226	133	1	.271	.402	.331	106	0	.217	.380	.236	74	0	.162	.295	.230
1991	Chi-A	5	5	8	71	2.02	1	2	6	42	1.51	4	3	2	30	2.73	78	3	.205	.220	.346	179	1	.207	.299	.263	131	1	.160	.230	.221	157	2	.210	.282	.280
1992	Chi-A	3	7	15	59	2.73	3	2	9	31	1.17	0	5	6	29	4.40	66	2	.182	.280	.318	156	1	.269	.375	.365	133	2	.263	.349	.406	160	3	.231	.340	.338
1993	Chi-A	8	2	4	55	4.28	3	2	3	30	5.70	5	0	2	25	2.55	88	0	.239	.287	.261	140	3	.286	.351	.379	117	2	.256	.341	.333	113	1	.239	.295	.283
TOTALS		22	15	31	238	3.33	9	7	20	128	3.02	13	8	11	109	3.70	294	5	.204	.264	.289	608	6	.255	.352	.331	487	5	.224	.323	.302	504	6	.216	.306	.292
● Dennis Rasmussen BL/TL																																					
1984	NY-A	9	6	0	148	4.57	5	3	0	78	4.17	4	3	0	70	5.01	86	3	.279	.354	.430	456	13	.226	.304	.390	214	8	.248	.300	.425	37	1	.324	.359	.541
1985	NY-A	3	5	0	102	3.98	2	2	0	44	5.08	1	3	0	57	3.14	98	3	.255	.305	.408	282	7	.255	.334	.404	145	3	.324	.376	.462	29	0	.345	.387	.345
1986	NY-A	18	6	0	202	3.88	8	2	0	75	4.32	10	4	0	127	3.61	136	2	.184	.247	.250	601	26	.298		.393	247	12	.263	.322	.445	59	2	.237	.303	.356
1987	NY-A	9	7	0	146	4.75	6	3	0	64	4.06	3	4	0	82	5.29	99	5	.313	.370	.535	459	26	.248	.319	.497	215	7	.219	.285	.405	17	1	.235	.300	.529
1987	Cin-N	4	1	0	45	3.97	2	1	0	26	3.12	2	0	0	19	5.12	9	0	.111	.200	.222	161	5	.236	.287	.385	62	1	.274	.313	.403	7	0	.143	.143	.143
1988	Cin-N	2	6	0	56	5.75	1	3	0	29	3.99	1	3	0	27	7.67	36	1	.361	.405	.500	191	7	.288	.355	.476	89	4	.348	.417	.562	2	1	1.000	1.000	2.500
1988	SD-N	14	4	0	148	2.55	6	1	0	58	2.31	8	3	0	90	2.70	82	2	.268	.302	.427	469	7	.232	.283	.328	201	4	.239	.282	.333	66	1	.242	.292	.348
1989	SD-N	10	10	0	184	4.26	5	4	0	76	3.42	5	6	0	107	4.86	133	4	.248	.311	.391	571	14	.275	.341	.406	303	11	.294	.352	.446	41	1	.268	.400	.366
1990	SD-N	11	15	0	188	4.51	5	9	0	101	4.37	6	6	0	87	4.67	109	5	.330	.381	.532	633	23	.286	.342	.438	305	9	.285	.347	.416	32	1	.375	.444	.500
1991	SD-N	6	13	0	147	3.74	4	5	0	60	3.88	2	8	0	86	3.65	104	2	.231	.286	.327	468	10	.280	.337	.397	249	6	.265	.320	.382	36	0	.278	.350	.333
1992	Chi-N	0	0	0	5	10.80	0	0	0	4	6.75	0	0	0	1	27.00	8	0	.250	.400	.250	12	2	.417	.429	1.167	8	0	.375	.400	.750	1	1	1.000	1.000	4.000
1992	KC-A	4	1	0	38	1.43	2	1	0	22	2.49	2	0	0	16	0.00	12	0	.167	.167	.167	115	0	.200	.240	.226	35	0	.257	.333	.257	20	0	.100	.100	.100
1993	KC-A	1	2	0	29	7.45	1	0	0	15	6.14	0	2	0	14	8.79	19	0	.316	.333	.368	103	4	.330	.410	.544	59	3	.356	.435	.576	8	0	.250	.455	.250
TOTALS		91	76	0	1437	4.13	47	34	0	653	3.94	44	42	0	784	4.29	931	27	.262	.318	.402	4521	144	.256	.321	.410	2132	68	.273	.332	.424	355	9	.273	.341	.394
● Shane Rawley BR/TL																																					
1984	NY-A	2	3	0	42	6.21	1	2	0	33	5.73	1	1	0	9	8.00	31	0	.226	.333	.323	138	0	.283	.381	.370	74	0	.365	.466	.514	10	0	.200	.200	.200
1984	Phi-N	10	6	0	120	3.81	5	4	0	69	3.13	5	2	0	51	4.73	60	2	.267	.333	.400	396	11	.255	.293	.384	158	5	.253	.310	.405	31	1	.226	.265	.387
1985	Phi-N	13	8	0	199	3.31	6	6	0	99	3.44	7	2	0	99	3.17	91	2	.231	.322	.319	664	14	.252	.322	.364	318	7	.233	.310	.340	55	1	.255	.328	.345
1986	Phi-N	11	7	0	158	3.54	7	3	0	69	3.91	4	4	0	89	3.25	81	1	.287	.313	.425	535	12	.267	.326	.402	252	2	.270	.336	.312	77	2	.195	.235	.312
1987	Phi-N	17	11	0	230	4.39	8	4	0	111	4.38	9	7	0	119	4.40	102	3	.294	.357	.471	793	20	.277	.341	.422	389	11	.270	.336	.427	83	5	.337	.391	.554
1988	Phi-N	8	16	0	198	4.18	4	7	0	94	4.90	4	9	0	104	3.54	136	3	.265	.299	.368	632	24	.291	.362	.464	332	12	.259	.337	.425	38	2	.316	.400	.605
1989	Min-A	5	12	0	145	5.21	2	7	0	79	6.18	3	5	0	66	4.07	116	4	.362	.393	.543	453	15	.276	.350	.448	257	8	.284	.336	.416	45	0	.378	.420	.511
TOTALS		66	63	0	1091	4.15	33	33	0	554	4.42	33	30	0	538	3.87	616	15	.284	.336	.419	3611	96	.271	.337	.413	1780	45	.266	.334	.403	339	11	.280	.335	.440
● Jeff Reardon BR/TR																																					
1984	Mon-N	7	7	23	87	2.90	4	5	10	40	3.79	3	2	13	47	2.12	157	4	.280	.375	.395	161	1	.161	.233	.217	156	3	.212	.317	.314	222	5	.221	.308	.324
1985	Mon-N	2	8	41	88	3.18	2	5	21	41	3.27	0	3	20	46	3.11	181	4	.210	.274	.287	144	3	.208	.263	.306	132	3	.242	.322	.348	249	4	.213	.284	.277
1986	Mon-N	7	9	35	89	3.94	5	6	14	46	4.73	2	3	21	43	3.12	172	5	.250	.330	.390	159	7	.252	.279	.447	151	2	.219	.287	.311	298	10	.252	.304	.406
1987	Min-A	8	8	31	80	4.48	5	2	19	44	3.48	3	6	12	36	5.70	156	3	.301	.364	.532	146	5	.158	.231	.295	142	10	.254	.319	.500	229	11	.258	.325	.445
1988	Min-A	2	4	42	73	2.47	1	4	23	38	2.58	1	0	19	35	2.34	148	2	.264	.313	.380	129	4	.225	.259	.380	142	3	.225	.279	.362	203	5	.241	.286	.355
1989	Min-A	5	4	31	73	4.07	2	1	19	39	4.12	3	3	12	34	4.01	129	5	.248	.286	.434	147	3	.245	.276	.340	136	5	.272	.293	.441	179	6	.246	.287	.402
1990	Bos-A	5	3	21	51	3.16	5	1	12	27	2.03	0	2	9	25	4.38	91	1	.143	.243	.209	98	2	.265	.321	.469	79	2	.278	.367	.430	139	4	.216	.301	.353
1991	Bos-A	1	4	40	59	3.03	1	3	19	32	3.62	0	1	21	27	2.33	72	1	.299	.348	.528	102	2	.157	.209	.284	94	2	.234	.321	.351	175	6	.223	.279	.394
1992	Bos-A	2	2	27	42	4.25	1	1	18	27	3.95	1	1	9	15	4.80	80	5	.250	.306	.575	92	1	.315	.337	.413	83	2	.313	.344	.458	132	5	.295	.321	.477
1992	Atl-N	3	0	3	16	1.15	2	0	1	8	2.35	1	0	2	8	0.00	28	0	.321	.367	.321	30	0	.167	.194	.167	24	0	.333	.360	.333	35	0	.229	.270	.229
1993	Cin-N	4	6	8	62	4.09	4	3	5	30	3.34	0	3	3	32	4.78	118	0	.297	.351	.390	126	4	.246	.265	.405	110	2	.318	.363	.505	145	4	.303	.325	.455
1994	NY-A	1	0	2	10	8.38	1	0	0	5	5.06	0	0	2	4	12.46	17	2	.412	.412	.824	27	1	.370	.433	.593	20	1	.450	.500	.600	10	0	.400	.455	.400
TOTALS		47	55	304	730	3.55	35	31	161	378	3.55	12	24	143	352	3.55	1404	44	.263	.326	.407	1361	35	.221	.266	.350	1269	35	.256	.320	.393	2016	60	.245	.302	.380
● Steve Reed BR/TR																																					
1992	SF-N	1	0	0	16	2.30	0	0	0	8	2.35	1	0	0	8	2.25	22	0	.273	.304	.409	37	2	.189	.250	.378	34	2	.235	.278	.500	19	1	.316	.409	.526
1993	Col-N	9	5	3	84	4.48	7	3	1	51	6.39	2	2	2	34	1.60	122	7	.336	.410	.607	187	6	.209	.272	.332	109	5	.275	.369	.468	100	2	.180	.265	.300
1994	Col-N	3	2	3	64	3.94	1	2	1	33	5.94	2	0	2	31	1.76	95	5	.379	.456	.600	163	4	.264	.322	.460	126	4	.302	.375	.484	97	2	.237	.304	.381
TOTALS		13	7	6	164	4.06	8	5	2	92	5.89	5	2	4	72	1.74	239	12	.347	.420	.586	387	12	.230	.291	.390	269	11	.283	.362	.480	216	5	.218	.296	.356
● Rick Reuschel BR/TR																																					
1984	Chi-N	5	5	0	92	5.17	4	1	0	54	5.67	1	4	0	38	4.46	178	1	.326	.362	.421	185	6	.351	.387	.546	157	4	.389	.413	.541	23	0	.261	.346	.304
1985	Pit-N	14	8	1	194	2.27	13	3	0	113	2.14	1	5	1	81	2.45	323	5	.226	.284	.310	387	4	.207	.260	.279	255	2	.224	.312	.298	100	2	.270	.330	.390
1986	Pit-N	9	16	0	216	3.96	5	8	0	104	3.28	4	8	0	111	4.61	465	9	.305	.359	.441	463	10	.237	.277	.368	380	11	.237	.277	.409	60	2	.367	.409	.583
1987	Pit-N	8	6	0	177	2.75	4	3	0	81	3.22	4	3	0	96	2.34	386	7	.262	.299	.396	277	5	.224	.271	.296	264	5	.239	.273	.333	77	2	.221	.291	.338
1987	SF-N	5	3	0	50	4.32	3	1	0	27	4.00	2	2	0	23	4.70	103	0	.233	.266	.359	88	1	.227	.261	.307	73	1	.315	.354	.479	7	0	.000	.000	.000
1988	SF-N	19	11	0	245	3.12	8	5	0	113	2.63	11	6	0	132	3.55	510	4	.284	.313	.369	348	2	.259	.310	.342	95	1	.284	.317	.368					
1989	SF-N	17	8	0	208	2.94	9	5	0	110	2.79	8	3	0	99	3.10	445	5	.261	.309	.364	345	13	.229	.275	.400	298	5	.262	.304	.376	85	0	.247	.273	.318
1990	SF-N	3	6	1	87	3.93	2	1	0	43	3.14	1	5	1	44	4.70	206	6	.325	.384	.505	137	2	.255	.304	.343	143	3	.301	.375	.427	27	1	.222	.353	.333
1991	SF-N	0	2	0	14	6.40	0	0	0	4	6.50	0	2	0	9	4.50	24	0	.417	.517	.583	22	0	.318	.375	.364	31	0	.355	.412	.452	12	0	.333	.429	.500
TOTALS		80	65	2	1280	3.31	47	28	0	650	3.10	37	37	2	630	3.53	2640	35	.279	.324	.392	2239	46	.259	.282	.352	1937	29	.270	.323	.377	486	8	.267	.322	.379
● Rick Rhoden BR/TR																																					
1984	Pit-N	14	9	0	238	2.72	8	3	0	129	1.88	6	6	0	109	3.72	475	4	.251	.301	.318	413	9	.235	.282	.349	326	5	.218	.296	.304	114	0	.316	.358	.351
1985	Pit-N	10	15	0	213	4.47	7	9	0	118	4.42	3	6	0	95	4.53	431	6	.302	.345	.424	426	12	.285	.345	.435	376	5	.293	.364	.460	60	1	.350	.426	.533
1986	Pit-N	15	12	0	254	2.84	9	6	0	140	2.76	6	6	0	114	2.93	509	4	.230	.294	.303	417	13	.225	.277	.400	332	3	.226	.296	.328	100	2	.210	.282	.310
1987	NY-A	16	10	0	182	3.86	10	3	0	93	3.29	6	7	0	89	4.47	363	14	.275	.342	.455	324	8	.259	.311	.380	263	9	.259	.324	.399	49	2	.163	.196	.327
1988	NY-A	12	12	0	197	4.29	8	8	0	125	3.90	4	4	0	72	4.98	411	10	.280	.340	.409	356	10	.256	.300	.402	299	12	.274	.340	.448	50	1	.280	.333	.440

YEAR	TM/L	TOTAL W	L	SV	IP	ERA	HOME W	L	SV	IP	ERA	AWAY W	L	SV	IP	ERA	LEFT AB	HR	AVG	OBP	SLG	RIGHT AB	HR	AVG	OBP	SLG	ON-BASE AB	HR	AVG	OBP	SLG	LATE/CLOSE AB	HR	AVG	OBP	SLG
1989	Hou-N	2	6	0	97	4.28	1	6	0	57	4.42	1	0	0	40	4.08	221	4	.271	.344	.403	153	3	.314	.385	.431	158	4	.297	.390	.437	9	0	.222	.300	.222
TOTALS		69	64	0	1181	3.63	43	35	0	662	3.32	26	29	0	519	4.03	2410	42	.267	.327	.378	2091	55	.256	.309	.398	1754	38	.258	.331	.381	382	6	.267	.325	.374
● Dave Righetti BL/TL																																				
1984	NY-A	5	6	31	96	2.34	3	1	16	50	1.80	2	5	15	46	2.91	75	1	.173	.295	.240	280	4	.236	.292	.307	176	3	.244	.332	.341	313	4	.224	.296	.291
1985	NY-A	12	7	29	107	2.78	9	1	17	56	2.24	3	6	12	51	3.38	112	1	.196	.308	.277	286	4	.259	.320	.346	211	1	.261	.329	.332	286	3	.252	.324	.325
1986	NY-A	8	8	46	107	2.45	5	5	18	50	1.99	3	3	28	57	2.84	91	1	.304	.387	.391	320	3	.209	.269	.275	199	3	.226	.301	.322	295	4	.237	.306	.322
1987	NY-A	8	6	31	95	3.51	5	2	17	48	2.79	3	4	14	47	4.24	96	3	.271	.324	.396	266	6	.259	.348	.350	201	5	.279	.356	.383	280	7	.257	.341	.346
1988	NY-A	5	4	25	87	3.52	4	1	11	47	2.66	1	3	14	40	4.54	86	2	.279	.347	.442	249	3	.249	.327	.329	176	2	.284	.360	.358	278	4	.248	.321	.349
1989	NY-A	2	6	25	69	3.00	0	1	10	31	3.16	2	5	15	38	2.87	62	1	.274	.343	.355	202	2	.277	.341	.366	139	1	.266	.338	.367	180	3	.261	.332	.367
1990	NY-A	1	1	36	53	3.57	1	1	21	28	2.60	0	0	15	25	4.62	41	2	.244	.295	.415	164	6	.232	.332	.396	109	5	.239	.300	.431	146	7	.212	.294	.377
1991	SF-N	2	7	24	72	3.39	1	4	14	37	4.14	1	3	10	35	2.60	72	0	.167	.197	.167	195	4	.267	.357	.390	129	4	.264	.340	.341	187	4	.241	.321	.342
1992	SF-N	2	7	3	78	5.06	1	3	3	45	2.82	1	4	0	34	8.02	89	0	.236	.330	.337	205	4	.283	.351	.390	122	2	.303	.395	.426	98	1	.296	.391	.367
1993	SF-N	1	1	1	47	5.70	1	1	1	23	3.57	1	0	0	25	7.66	59	4	.288	.311	.576	131	7	.313	.388	.511	91	6	.286	.323	.516	41	3	.268	.333	.585
1994	Oak-A	0	0	0	7	16.71	0	0	0	1	13.50	0	0	0	6	17.47	16	3	.438	.550	1.063	15	0	.400	.545	.400	17	3	.529	.609	1.059	4	1	.500	.500	1.250
1994	Tor-A	0	1	0	13	6.75	0	1	0	8	5.87	0	0	0	6	7.94	12	0	.167	.286	.250	36	2	.194	.333	.444	19	0	.263	.348	.421	9	0	.333	.600	.556
TOTALS		46	54	251	832	3.53	29	21	128	424	2.76	17	33	123	408	4.33	789	18	.243	.321	.364	2349	45	.254	.328	.354	1589	32	.266	.341	.374	2117	41	.246	.323	.344
● Jose Rijo BR/TR																																				
1984	NY-A	2	8	2	62	4.76	1	2	0	19	4.82	1	6	2	44	4.74	102	4	.353	.450	.510	146	1	.260	.331	.336	131	2	.252	.327	.328	48	1	.313	.421	.417
1985	Oak-A	6	4	0	64	3.53	2	1	0	25	3.65	4	3	0	39	3.46	125	5	.280	.379	.488	113	1	.195	.254	.265	100	1	.238	.328	.314	27	1	.259	.333	.407
1986	Oak-A	9	11	1	194	4.65	3	4	1	90	3.90	6	7	0	104	5.30	395	11	.241	.354	.403	330	13	.233	.312	.409	299	12	.274	.374	.468	77	1	.286	.375	.429
1987	Oak-A	2	7	0	82	5.90	2	3	0	41	4.35	0	4	0	41	7.46	175	6	.303	.387	.491	172	4	.308	.370	.419	172	4	.279	.365	.413	10	1	.400	.571	.800
1988	Cin-N	13	8	0	162	2.39	6	7	0	92	3.12	7	1	0	70	1.42	308	6	.231	.307	.347	266	1	.184	.241	.244	214	1	.206	.330	.271	114	3	.193	.292	.316
1989	Cin-N	7	6	0	111	2.84	2	2	0	43	3.16	5	4	0	68	2.63	242	5	.273	.372	.384	163	1	.215	.256	.270	172	1	.227	.305	.262	25	0	.360	.448	.440
1990	Cin-N	14	8	0	197	2.70	8	4	0	108	2.24	6	4	0	89	3.25	409	7	.218	.316	.318	303	3	.205	.255	.307	266	3	.237	.322	.331	49	0	.265	.345	.367
1991	Cin-N	15	6	0	204	2.51	9	0	0	99	2.99	6	6	0	105	2.06	437	5	.252	.311	.352	318	3	.173	.215	.239	272	1	.250	.309	.305	36	0	.222	.282	.278
1992	Cin-N	15	10	0	211	2.56	9	4	0	89	2.74	6	6	0	122	2.43	429	6	.266	.317	.368	347	9	.205	.234	.305	303	3	.211	.261	.297	62	5	.258	.266	.500
1993	Cin-N	14	9	0	257	2.48	8	6	0	135	2.60	6	3	0	122	2.35	523	10	.241	.296	.359	426	9	.216	.254	.322	360	1	.192	.259	.247	75	1	.200	.231	.267
1994	Cin-N	9	6	0	172	3.08	6	3	0	103	3.58	3	3	0	69	2.34	316	7	.275	.354	.405	351	9	.256	.290	.387	288	5	.240	.307	.326	33	1	.333	.371	.455
TOTALS		106	83	3	1717	3.12	53	36	1	844	3.12	53	47	2	873	3.12	3461	72	.255	.336	.380	2935	54	.219	.269	.321	2582	34	.234	.313	.323	556	14	.255	.330	.383
● Don Robinson BR/TR																																				
1984	Pit-N	5	6	10	122	3.02	3	2	3	56	3.21	2	4	7	66	2.86	178	3	.213	.319	.326	260	3	.235	.283	.323	195	4	.226	.301	.333	248	3	.194	.277	.282
1985	Pit-N	5	11	3	95	3.87	3	2	2	44	3.07	2	9	1	51	4.56	206	6	.241	.337	.289	267	3	.235	.289	.372	229	3	.258	.314	.336	107	2	.243	.336	.336
1986	Pit-N	3	4	14	69	3.38	2	1	6	37	3.19	1	3	8	33	3.58	113	0	.186	.282	.212	144	5	.278	.333	.444	125	3	.240	.303	.360	159	3	.226	.300	.314
1987	Pit-N	6	6	12	65	3.86	4	1	8	34	2.94	2	5	4	32	4.83	126	1	.270	.333	.357	121	5	.264	.318	.430	123	3	.285	.336	.423	154	5	.312	.367	.468
1987	SF-N	5	1	7	43	2.74	2	1	4	15	5.52	3	0	3	28	1.29	91	1	.206	.304	.299	66	0	.288	.324	.439	75	0	.253	.333	.377	97	1	.247	.315	.361
1988	SF-N	10	5	6	177	2.45	4	3	0	66	2.47	6	5	3	111	2.43	324	6	.216	.272	.324	334	5	.246	.296	.362	256	8	.238	.312	.375	126	2	.246	.312	.397
1989	SF-N	12	11	0	197	3.43	9	4	0	120	2.10	3	7	0	77	5.49	434	13	.260	.301	.412	309	9	.230	.258	.372	255	6	.239	.284	.361	69	1	.203	.243	.275
1990	SF-N	10	7	0	158	4.57	4	1	0	61	5.04	6	6	0	97	4.27	365	12	.285	.343	.455	263	6	.273	.295	.399	236	9	.314	.363	.496	77	0	.260	.313	.338
1991	SF-N	5	9	1	121	4.38	3	2	0	62	2.77	2	7	1	60	6.03	251	5	.279	.371	.422	214	7	.248	.286	.411	191	3	.293	.367	.403	36	1	.306	.350	.444
1992	Cal-A	1	0	0	16	2.20	1	0	0	6	0.00	0	0	0	10	3.60	33	0	.273	.273	.303	32	1	.313	.371	.469	31	0	.129	.182	.129	3	0	.667	.667	.667
1992	Phi-N	1	4	0	44	6.18	1	0	0	12	3.75	0	4	0	32	7.11	95	2	.326	.323	.463	74	4	.243	.272	.473	68	3	.309	.293	.500	3	0	.000	.000	.000
TOTALS		63	64	53	1107	3.62	37	16	26	511	3.03	26	48	27	596	4.12	2182	43	.252	.318	.373	2013	51	.253	.297	.393	1723	43	.263	.326	.393	1079	18	.241	.310	.348
● Jeff Robinson BR/TR																																				
1984	SF-N	7	15	0	172	4.56	4	4	0	74	3.91	3	11	0	98	5.05	375	9	.320	.380	.475	302	3	.248	.293	.321	289	4	.301	.350	.401	37	1	.162	.184	.243
1985	SF-N	0	0	0	12	5.11	0	0	0	9	5.19	0	0	0	4	4.91	13	1	.231	.313	.462	30	2	.333	.432	.533	0	0	—	—	—	0	0	—	—	—
1986	SF-N	6	3	8	104	3.36	2	1	5	54	3.19	4	2	3	51	3.55	180	4	.278	.337	.394	214	4	.196	.251	.280	145	4	.269	.369	.428	145	4	.269	.312	.386
1987	SF-N	6	8	10	97	2.79	3	3	4	46	2.93	3	5	6	51	2.66	185	6	.243	.340	.405	148	4	.162	.263	.270	137	4	.204	.331	.314	186	6	.220	.316	.371
1987	Pit-N	2	1	4	27	3.04	1	0	2	14	0.63	1	1	2	12	5.84	50	1	.182	.237	.218	38	1	.263	.300	.421	40	0	.225	.279	.325	67	1	.164	.211	.209
1988	Pit-N	11	5	9	125	3.03	2	4	3	59	3.64	9	1	6	65	2.48	235	3	.247	.277	.328	228	3	.241	.328	.342	193	3	.269	.344	.373	279	3	.237	.308	.301
1989	Pit-N	7	13	4	141	4.58	3	6	2	63	4.16	4	7	2	79	4.92	302	5	.258	.328	.384	267	9	.311	.369	.476	249	6	.273	.367	.390	119	3	.311	.373	.513
1990	NY-A	3	6	0	89	3.45	1	3	0	45	3.02	2	3	0	44	3.89	140	3	.221	.273	.314	191	5	.267	.350	.424	150	3	.227	.308	.327	90	1	.244	.370	.333
1991	Cal-A	0	3	3	57	5.37	0	1	1	31	2.30	0	2	2	26	9.12	98	4	.276	.327	.459	118	5	.246	.366	.432	115	6	.235	.338	.426	68	1	.221	.308	.324
1992	Chi-N	4	3	1	78	3.00	1	2	1	36	3.25	3	1	0	42	2.79	155	2	.290	.351	.394	134	3	.231	.358	.381	131	2	.244	.357	.359	106	2	.264	.328	.377
TOTALS		46	57	39	901	3.79	17	24	18	430	3.37	29	33	21	471	4.18	1738	37	.269	.330	.394	1675	38	.247	.324	.368	1479	34	.263	.348	.381	1097	22	.242	.315	.351
● Ron Robinson BR/TR																																				
1984	Cin-N	1	2	0	40	2.72	1	2	0	25	4.32	0	0	0	15	0.00	67	1	.224	.293	.299	84	2	.238	.289	.393	58	0	.224	.292	.362	8	0	.000	.000	.000
1985	Cin-N	7	7	1	108	3.99	4	4	0	54	3.86	3	3	1	55	4.12	215	5	.302	.353	.447	198	6	.212	.266	.354	174	6	.264	.313	.414	34	0	.294	.351	.382
1986	Cin-N	10	3	14	117	3.24	3	1	8	66	3.55	7	2	6	51	2.84	194	3	.294	.304	.407	241	7	.220	.257	.365	177	5	.243	.338	.379	285	6	.281	.347	.396
1987	Cin-N	7	5	4	154	3.68	2	5	1	75	4.56	5	0	3	79	2.85	276	5	.290	.339	.453	303	9	.224	.273	.373	221	4	.276	.343	.448	107	5	.252	.322	.449
1988	Cin-N	3	7	0	79	4.12	2	3	0	34	5.35	1	4	0	45	3.20	163	4	.331	.402	.485	146	1	.233	.266	.288	125	2	.336	.397	.448	11	1	.545	.615	.909
1989	Cin-N	5	3	0	83	3.35	2	1	0	27	3.04	3	2	0	57	3.49	175	3	.274	.339	.383	142	5	.225	.288	.387	123	1	.252	.326	.309	5	0	.400	.400	.400
1990	Cin-N	2	2	0	31	4.88	0	1	0	17	3.24	2	1	0	15	6.70	74	2	.284	.361	.432	40	0	.313	.377	.396	60	0	.283	.306	.333	3	0	.000	.400	.000
1990	Mil-A	12	5	0	148	2.91	6	2	0	70	2.20	6	3	0	79	3.55	296	2	.260	.309	.324	278	3	.291	.336	.381	251	5	.275	.320	.347	39	1	.256	.341	.385
1991	Mil-A	0	2	0	21	3.86	0	1	0	17	3.24	0	1	0	4	6.23	14	0	.357	.438	.571	11	0	.182	.357	.273	11	0	.187	.412	.538	0	0	—	—	—
1992	Mil-A	1	4	0	35	5.86	0	1	0	13	5.68	1	3	0	23	5.96	79	1	.316	.368	.405	80	1	.387	.412	.538	0	0	—	—	—	0	0	—	—	—
TOTALS		48	39	19	800	3.63	20	20	9	379	3.78	28	19	10	421	3.51	1549	27	.289	.353	.416	1522	34	.244	.292	.368	1280	22	.277	.338	.395	492	13	.274	.344	.409
● Rich Rodriguez BL/TL																																				
1990	SD-N	1	1	1	48	2.83	1	0	0	28	2.57	0	1	1	20	3.20	66	0	.242	.306	.348	115	2	.313	.370	.443	91	1	.264	.333	.363	63	0	.222	.300	.238
1991	SD-N	3	1	0	80	3.26	1	0	0	37	4.58	2	1	0	43	2.11	96	3	.219	.336	.354	186	5	.242	.335	.371	139	1	.223	.337	.309	82	4	.195	.330	.366
1992	SD-N	6	3	0	91	2.37	4	1	0	51	1.93	2	2	0	40	2.95	104	2	.231	.302	.327	232	2	.228	.283	.306	150	2	.247	.294	.327	51	0	.216	.333	.235
1993	SD-N	2	3	2	30	3.30	2	1	1	13	2.13	0	2	1	17	4.15	36	1	.389	.436	.556	85	1	.235	.293	.294	55	1	.236	.323	.309	73	2	.315	.367	.423
1993	Fla-N	0	1	1	46	4.11	0	0	1	23	4.24	0	1	0	23	3.97	63	2	.190	.301	.317	107	6	.252	.344	.467	78	5	.295	.382	.538	43	3	.209	.370	.442
1994	StL-N	3	5	0	60	4.03	1	2	0	29	5.90	2	3	0	31	2.30	60	1	.183	.269	.250	170	5	.300	.372	.488	107	4	.290	.389	.477	81	3	.284	.348	.432
TOTALS		15	14	4	355	3.22	9	5	2	182	3.52	6	9	2	173	2.91	425	9	.231	.317	.329	895	21	.259	.331	.390	620	14	.256	.340	.379	393	12	.244	.341	.361
● Kenny Rogers BL/TL																																				
1989	Tex-A	3	4	2	74	2.93	3	3	1	46	3.33	0	1	1	28	2.24	90	0	.169	.303	.217	176	2	.261	.364	.341	152	0	.263	.358	.349	109	1	.220	.315	.284
1990	Tex-A	10	6	15	98	3.13	9	1	8	54	2.01	1	5	7	44	4.50	96	1	.219	.272	.333	278	5	.259	.340	.385	204	5	.230	.321	.353	198	3	.242	.323	.354
1991	Tex-A	10	10	5	110	5.42	6	5	3	47	5.59	4	5	2	63	5.29	98	3	.224	.342	.357	322	11	.298	.385	.470	204	7	.275	.390	.426	124	4	.210	.322	.355
1992	Tex-A	3	6	6	79	3.09	1	4	2	43	3.53	2	2	4	35	2.55	92	1	.261	.284	.348	214	6	.262	.332	.411	160	5	.281	.348	.438	180	4	.289	.350	.444
1993	Tex-A	16	10	0	208	4.10	9	4	0	94	5.00	7	6	0	115	3.38	90	0	.222	.271	.333	708	18	.268	.331	.415	315	6	.308	.374	.451	39	0	.179	.220	.179
1994	Tex-A	11	8	0	167	4.46	6	5	0	102	3.72	5	3	0	66	5.62	90	8	.311	.344	.644	560	16	.252	.311	.409	257	8	.284	.354	.455	54	1	.204	.246	.352
TOTALS		53	44	28	735	4.03	34	22	14	385	3.95	19	22	14	350	4.11	549	13	.235	.304	.373	2268	58	.266	.338	.412	1292	30	.277	.359	.419	704	13	.239	.317	.357
● Mel Rojas BR/TR																																				
1990	Mon-N	3	1	1	40	3.60	0	0	1	14	6.59	3	1	0	26	2.05	92	3	.207	.342	.348	53	2	.283	.367	.453	81	3	.148	.281	.284	39	1	.205	.354	.308
1991	Mon-N	3	3	6	48	3.75	1	2	2	17	3.12	2	1	4	31	4.11	89	2	.247	.310	.449	95	2	.211	.250	.305	87	2	.195	.258	.345	78	1	.167	.244	.256
1992	Mon-N	7	1	10	101	1.43	5	0	3	52	1.72	2	1	7	48	1.12	199	1	.196	.268	.246	158	1	.203	.274	.297	175	0	.143	.236	.160	151	0	.238	.318	.265
1993	Mon-N	5	8	10	88	2.95	4	4	6	44	3.07	1	4	4	44	2.84	185	4	.270	.338	.427	145	2	.207	.269	.324	155	2	.219	.302	.348	184	4	.239	.307	.386
1994	Mon-N	3	2	16	84	3.32	2	1	6	33	3.78	1	1	10	51	3.02	169	7	.225	.294	.373	144	4	.229	.270	.333	148	4	.250	.273	.358	179	6	.218	.269	.335
TOTALS		21	15	43	361	2.79	12	6	16	161	3.08	9	9	27	200	2.56	734	17	.229	.307	.376	595	11	.218	.277	.328	646	11	.193	.269	.291	631	12	.222	.295	.322
● Bruce Ruffin BB/TL																																				
1986	Phi-N	9	4	0	146	2.46	6	2	0	88	2.16	3	2	0	59	2.91	80	2	.138	.216	.250	469	4	.271	.322	.362	224	5	.250	.304	.353	64	1	.281	.314	.391
1987	Phi-N	11	14	0	205	4.35	7	3	0	88	5.13	4	11	0	117	3.77	134	2	.269	.333	.351	656	15	.305	.360	.441	337	7	.279	.348	.392	48	2	.313	.340	.479
1988	Phi-N	6	10	3	144	4.43	3	8	2	82	3.75	3	2	1	63	5.31	124	0	.274	.412	.338	426	7	.275	.354	.387	264	4	.291	.394	.394	92	1	.272	.417	.370
1989	Phi-N	6	10	0	126	4.44	4	7	0	75	4.90	2	3	0	50	3.75	64	1	.281	.427	.438	441	9	.304	.368	.431	251	2	.295	.375	.398	18	0	.222	.263	.278
1990	Phi-N	6	13	0	149	5.38	5	7	0	78	5.40	1	6	0	71	5.35	120	0	.292	.351	.358	479	14	.299	.363	.480	269	6	.342	.398	.509	17	0	.294	.500	.353

YEAR	TM/L	TOTAL W	L	SV	IP	ERA	HOME W	L	SV	IP	ERA	AWAY W	L	SV	IP	ERA	LEFT AB	HR	AVG	OBP	SLG	RIGHT AB	HR	AVG	OBP	SLG	ON-BASE AB	HR	AVG	OBP	SLG	LATE/CLOSE AB	HR	AVG	OBP	SLG
1991	Phi-N	4	7	0	119	3.78	3	3	0	76	3.21	1	4	0	43	4.78	111	1	.252	.291	.333	348	5	.279	.309	.358	212	3	.250	.309	.358	55	0	.327	.383	.400
1992	Mil-A	1	6	0	58	6.67	1	3	0	16	7.87	0	3	0	42	6.21	68	1	.221	.354	.294	157	6	.325	.417	.522	108	4	.324	.424	.519	32	0	.281	.361	.375
1993	Col-N	6	5	2	140	3.87	3	3	1	80	3.81	3	2	1	59	3.94	120	3	.233	.360	.350	419	7	.279	.347	.389	257	7	.272	.366	.409	66	1	.182	.260	.227
1994	Col-N	4	5	16	56	4.04	2	0	7	25	5.11	2	5	9	31	3.19	49	2	.286	.417	.429	168	4	.244	.319	.363	125	3	.232	.293	.336	121	5	.248	.373	.413
TOTALS		53	74	21	1142	4.25	34	33	10	607	4.18	19	41	11	535	4.32	870	12	.252	.350	.345	3563	71	.288	.353	.418	2037	39	.283	.358	.406	513	10	.265	.360	.374

● Johnny Ruffin BR/TR

YEAR	TM/L	W	L	SV	IP	ERA	W	L	SV	IP	ERA	W	L	SV	IP	ERA	AB	HR	AVG	OBP	SLG	AB	HR	AVG	OBP	SLG	AB	HR	AVG	OBP	SLG	AB	HR	AVG	OBP	SLG
1993	Cin-N	2	1	2	38	3.58	0	0	1	19	1.86	2	1	1	18	5.40	77	1	.286	.329	.468	69	3	.203	.276	.391	63	3	.270	.324	.524	36	0	.278	.316	.417
1994	Cin-N	7	2	1	70	3.09	4	1	1	37	2.89	3	1	0	33	3.31	100	3	.240	.330	.390	156	4	.212	.271	.340	103	1	.204	.276	.320	128	3	.258	.340	.367
TOTALS		9	3	3	108	3.26	4	1	2	57	2.54	5	2	1	51	4.06	177	4	.260	.330	.424	225	7	.209	.272	.356	166	4	.229	.293	.398	164	3	.262	.335	.378

● Scott Ruskin BR/TL

YEAR	TM/L	W	L	SV	IP	ERA	W	L	SV	IP	ERA	W	L	SV	IP	ERA	AB	HR	AVG	OBP	SLG	AB	HR	AVG	OBP	SLG	AB	HR	AVG	OBP	SLG	AB	HR	AVG	OBP	SLG
1990	Pit-N	2	2	2	48	3.02	1	0	2	25	2.16	1	2	0	23	3.97	70	1	.243	.354	.314	116	1	.284	.375	.379	106	2	.274	.352	.377	91	1	.297	.393	.363
1990	Mon-N	1	0	0	28	2.28	1	0	0	16	0.00	0	0	0	11	5.56	44	2	.341	.366	.477	59	0	.169	.279	.220	41	1	.244	.340	.317	50	2	.320	.358	.480
1991	Mon-N	4	4	6	64	4.24	3	2	2	38	1.93	1	2	4	36	6.06	91	0	.275	.347	.363	146	4	.219	.325	.377	99	2	.253	.373	.414	114	1	.254	.341	.368
1992	Cin-N	4	3	0	54	5.03	2	2	0	26	4.10	2	1	0	27	5.93	68	1	.250	.333	.353	136	5	.287	.342	.441	93	5	.344	.411	.559	77	3	.299	.360	.468
1993	Cin-N	0	0	0	1	18.00	0	0	0	0	27.00	0	0	0	1	13.50	2	1	.500	.500	2.000	4	0	.500	.667	.750	2	0	.500	.667	.500	2	0	1.000	1.000	1.500
TOTALS		11	9	8	194	3.95	7	4	4	96	2.34	4	5	4	98	5.53	275	5	.273	.347	.378	461	10	.252	.341	.380	341	10	.284	.375	.431	334	7	.290	.368	.413

● Jeff Russell BR/TR

YEAR	TM/L	W	L	SV	IP	ERA	W	L	SV	IP	ERA	W	L	SV	IP	ERA	AB	HR	AVG	OBP	SLG	AB	HR	AVG	OBP	SLG	AB	HR	AVG	OBP	SLG	AB	HR	AVG	OBP	SLG
1984	Cin-N	6	18	0	182	4.26	5	3	0	84	3.76	1	15	0	98	4.68	316	6	.282	.351	.411	391	9	.248	.308	.368	299	9	.284	.346	.435	87	0	.207	.296	.241
1985	Tex-A	3	6	0	62	7.55	1	4	0	36	8.33	2	2	0	26	6.49	146	5	.322	.390	.534	116	5	.328	.385	.517	124	5	.306	.378	.532	12	0	.167	.231	.250
1986	Tex-A	5	2	2	82	3.40	2	0	1	30	3.30	3	2	1	52	3.46	124	5	.290	.376	.452	179	6	.212	.270	.358	138	3	.275	.346	.391	59	2	.119	.212	.254
1987	Tex-A	5	4	3	97	4.44	1	2	2	41	5.71	4	2	1	56	3.51	182	7	.291	.362	.467	201	2	.279	.374	.373	192	4	.260	.366	.380	77	2	.286	.385	.429
1988	Tex-A	10	9	0	189	3.82	6	6	0	110	3.75	4	3	0	78	3.91	370	10	.292	.370	.411	343	5	.219	.273	.297	290	9	.314	.375	.441	95	0	.242	.314	.295
1989	Tex-A	6	4	38	73	1.98	2	1	24	38	1.64	4	3	14	34	2.36	112	0	.205	.289	.241	135	4	.163	.235	.311	126	3	.222	.308	.365	176	3	.205	.290	.318
1990	Tex-A	1	5	10	25	4.26	0	4	6	13	5.54	1	1	4	12	2.92	39	1	.128	.209	.231	52	0	.346	.462	.462	54	1	.315	.406	.463	63	1	.286	.387	.444
1991	Tex-A	6	4	30	79	3.29	2	1	18	39	3.00	4	3	12	40	3.57	145	2	.241	.317	.297	156	9	.231	.273	.429	153	7	.248	.312	.418	226	8	.208	.277	.327
1992	Tex-A	2	3	28	57	1.91	0	1	14	30	1.21	2	2	14	27	2.67	99	1	.253	.353	.364	115	2	.226	.274	.304	126	1	.206	.271	.278	172	2	.238	.311	.320
1992	Oak-A	2	0	2	10	0.00	2	0	2	9	0.00	0	0	0	1	0.00	11	0	.182	.182	.273	21	0	.095	.208	.095	11	0	.182	.308	.273	19	0	.158	.200	.211
1993	Bos-A	1	4	33	47	2.70	0	1	15	23	1.99	1	3	18	24	3.38	92	0	.261	.300	.359	77	1	.195	.273	.260	74	1	.311	.368	.405	124	1	.210	.261	.290
1994	Bos-A	0	5	12	28	5.14	0	2	7	13	4.05	0	3	5	16	6.14	48	1	.292	.393	.417	63	2	.254	.310	.397	52	3	.309	.365	.491	73	3	.260	.364	.438
1994	Cle-A	1	1	5	13	4.97	0	1	2	5	10.80	1	0	3	8	1.17	21	1	.333	.364	.524	28	1	.214	.267	.321	21	1	.286	.348	.429	27	2	.296	.367	.519
TOTALS		48	65	163	943	3.85	21	26	91	470	3.83	27	39	72	472	3.87	1705	39	.274	.349	.401	1877	46	.237	.302	.356	1663	46	.276	.348	.415	1210	24	.223	.302	.330

● Nolan Ryan BR/TR

YEAR	TM/L	W	L	SV	IP	ERA	W	L	SV	IP	ERA	W	L	SV	IP	ERA	AB	HR	AVG	OBP	SLG	AB	HR	AVG	OBP	SLG	AB	HR	AVG	OBP	SLG	AB	HR	AVG	OBP	SLG
1984	Hou-N	12	11	0	184	3.04	5	5	0	79	2.16	7	6	0	105	3.70	324	4	.188	.272	.256	352	8	.233	.299	.349	276	8	.239	.319	.370	61	1	.148	.175	.197
1985	Hou-N	10	12	0	232	3.80	7	3	0	135	3.14	3	9	0	97	4.72	415	5	.246	.317	.337	441	7	.234	.319	.340	367	6	.245	.326	.365	107	4	.262	.299	.430
1986	Hou-N	12	8	0	178	3.34	9	4	0	109	2.56	3	4	0	69	4.57	311	4	.186	.298	.283	324	10	.188	.267	.343	230	9	.213	.325	.383	56	2	.232	.348	.393
1987	Hou-N	8	16	0	212	2.76	5	7	0	114	2.21	3	9	0	98	3.41	408	6	.213	.301	.289	363	8	.185	.265	.295	303	7	.215	.295	.327	58	0	.155	.246	.172
1988	Hou-N	12	11	0	220	3.52	7	4	0	105	2.91	5	7	0	115	4.08	438	8	.215	.301	.315	380	10	.242	.308	.384	365	5	.219	.291	.304	74	1	.189	.277	.311
1989	Tex-A	16	10	0	239	3.20	9	6	0	139	3.68	7	4	0	100	2.52	446	8	.177	.261	.262	421	9	.197	.289	.304	308	6	.260	.344	.354	108	2	.213	.286	.315
1990	Tex-A	13	9	0	204	3.44	8	5	0	130	3.32	5	4	0	74	3.65	362	8	.218	.305	.356	367	10	.158	.230	.289	237	6	.203	.300	.350	76	1	.158	.314	.224
1991	Tex-A	12	6	0	173	2.91	10	4	0	132	3.08	2	2	0	41	2.40	345	5	.183	.257	.281	249	7	.157	.271	.289	190	4	.226	.307	.342	49	1	.143	.222	.245
1992	Tex-A	5	9	0	157	3.72	3	6	0	93	3.40	2	3	0	65	4.18	294	5	.245	.339	.364	286	4	.231	.316	.318	250	4	.248	.339	.344	34	0	.294	.314	.412
1993	Tex-A	5	5	0	66	4.88	4	2	0	39	4.12	1	3	0	27	6.00	133	2	.188	.339	.278	113	3	.257	.315	.416	107	3	.252	.339	.393	5	0	.400	.500	.400
TOTALS		105	97	0	1865	3.36	67	46	0	1075	3.03	38	51	0	790	3.81	3476	55	.207	.296	.303	3296	76	.206	.287	.328	2633	58	.232	.317	.349	628	12	.202	.269	.306

● Bret Saberhagen BR/TR

YEAR	TM/L	W	L	SV	IP	ERA	W	L	SV	IP	ERA	W	L	SV	IP	ERA	AB	HR	AVG	OBP	SLG	AB	HR	AVG	OBP	SLG	AB	HR	AVG	OBP	SLG	AB	HR	AVG	OBP	SLG
1984	KC-A	10	11	1	158	3.48	4	5	1	78	2.20	6	6	0	80	4.72	289	10	.256	.304	.429	294	3	.218	.259	.299	223	10	.256	.299	.475	73	1	.151	.205	.192
1985	KC-A	20	6	0	235	2.87	10	3	0	129	2.80	10	3	0	107	2.95	501	14	.242	.280	.363	375	5	.240	.260	.349	313	4	.217	.248	.304	102	6	.235	.278	.422
1986	KC-A	7	12	0	156	4.15	2	5	0	76	3.67	5	7	0	80	4.61	368	8	.253	.288	.394	247	7	.291	.323	.413	243	4	.276	.312	.424	51	1	.216	.245	.314
1987	KC-A	18	10	0	257	3.36	11	4	0	138	3.58	7	6	0	119	3.11	512	14	.242	.290	.391	463	13	.263	.298	.410	363	8	.234	.287	.361	108	4	.269	.296	.444
1988	KC-A	14	16	0	261	3.80	6	9	0	130	4.36	8	7	0	131	3.24	530	6	.245	.299	.343	478	12	.295	.330	.462	398	6	.296	.333	.422	118	2	.229	.242	.381
1989	KC-A	23	6	0	262	2.16	11	1	0	131	1.71	12	5	0	131	2.61	524	4	.195	.236	.290	437	5	.245	.270	.350	336	4	.208	.259	.304	128	3	.227	.277	.352
1990	KC-A	5	9	0	135	3.27	3	5	0	74	3.42	2	4	0	61	3.08	222	5	.275	.318	.405	302	4	.281	.311	.374	217	5	.281	.313	.401	53	2	.283	.316	.453
1991	KC-A	13	8	0	196	3.07	7	3	0	95	2.76	6	5	0	102	3.36	354	9	.215	.270	.333	370	3	.241	.290	.335	275	3	.247	.298	.335	59	2	.254	.279	.390
1992	NY-N	3	5	0	98	3.50	1	2	0	60	2.41	2	3	0	38	5.21	212	3	.226	.292	.344	148	3	.243	.291	.345	135	2	.244	.323	.393	59	2	.254	.279	.390
1993	NY-N	7	7	0	139	3.29	3	3	0	60	2.41	4	4	0	80	3.95	250	7	.264	.298	.412	274	4	.237	.253	.325	175	5	.269	.295	.417	65	0	.338	.375	.415
1994	NY-N	14	4	0	177	2.74	4	2	0	61	2.93	10	2	0	116	2.64	366	6	.238	.256	.379	299	7	.274	.299	.375	228	3	.259	.284	.375	99	1	.273	.291	.374
TOTALS		134	94	1	2075	3.19	62	42	1	1031	2.99	72	52	0	1044	3.40	4128	90	.238	.281	.365	3687	66	.258	.288	.374	2906	54	.252	.294	.375	958	24	.243	.278	.372

● Scott Sanderson BR/TR

YEAR	TM/L	W	L	SV	IP	ERA	W	L	SV	IP	ERA	W	L	SV	IP	ERA	AB	HR	AVG	OBP	SLG	AB	HR	AVG	OBP	SLG	AB	HR	AVG	OBP	SLG	AB	HR	AVG	OBP	SLG
1984	Chi-N	8	5	0	141	3.14	3	2	0	54	3.17	5	3	0	87	3.12	282	2	.227	.266	.309	249	3	.305	.326	.406	202	2	.270	.297	.365	26	1	.346	.357	.462
1985	Chi-N	5	6	0	121	3.12	3	2	0	69	3.25	2	3	0	52	2.96	251	10	.243	.296	.478	188	3	.207	.231	.319	149	3	.228	.269	.356	42	0	.143	.143	.143
1986	Chi-N	9	11	0	170	4.19	7	5	0	94	3.54	2	6	1	76	5.00	358	13	.260	.296	.439	289	8	.249	.295	.398	243	9	.255	.295	.432	51	2	.255	.321	.392
1987	Chi-N	8	9	2	145	4.29	3	4	1	58	4.99	5	5	1	87	3.83	325	11	.292	.364	.471	244	12	.250	.290	.467	229	7	.249	.327	.415	61	3	.230	.314	.410
1988	Chi-N	1	2	0	15	5.28	0	2	0	7	8.87	1	0	0	7	2.45	27	0	.259	.367	.333	29	1	.207	.250	.414	21	1	.381	.385	.619	51	1	.280	.321	.480
1989	Chi-N	11	9	0	146	3.94	6	3	0	70	3.75	5	6	0	77	4.11	341	8	.293	.335	.422	225	8	.244	.277	.400	219	6	.301	.350	.461	51	1	.275	.351	.412
1990	Oak-A	17	11	0	206	3.88	6	7	0	97	3.17	11	4	0	110	4.51	402	13	.234	.300	.391	401	14	.277	.325	.454	311	12	.277	.334	.466	20	0	.150	.190	.150
1991	NY-A	16	10	0	208	3.81	7	6	0	93	4.66	9	4	0	115	3.12	437	15	.261	.290	.437	358	7	.240	.265	.386	287	9	.244	.277	.404	32	0	.188	.212	.219
1992	NY-A	12	11	0	193	4.93	5	6	0	97	5.47	7	5	0	96	4.39	367	13	.300	.362	.466	402	15	.274	.319	.463	338	12	.260	.326	.423	17	0	.294	.455	.353
1993	Cal-A	7	11	0	135	4.46	3	3	0	55	5.43	4	8	0	81	3.79	259	8	.270	.318	.417	271	7	.306	.331	.465	206	9	.316	.361	.510	35	1	.429	.444	.571
1993	SF-N	3	3	0	49	3.51	2	2	0	31	3.82	2	0	0	18	3.00	97	9	.231	.245	.352	93	3	.270	.294	.365	63	2	.270	.299	.365	0	0	—	—	—
1994	Chi-A	8	4	0	92	5.09	4	1	0	35	3.34	4	3	0	57	6.16	173	10	.324	.361	.578	198	10	.273	.286	.483	143	6	.287	.318	.483	11	0	.182	.250	.273
TOTALS		106	91	3	1621	4.07	49	44	1	759	4.14	57	47	2	862	4.01	3319	112	.268	.317	.437	2945	91	.263	.296	.423	2409	78	.269	.316	.432	371	9	.253	.309	.364

● Dan Schatzeder BL/TL

YEAR	TM/L	W	L	SV	IP	ERA	W	L	SV	IP	ERA	W	L	SV	IP	ERA	AB	HR	AVG	OBP	SLG	AB	HR	AVG	OBP	SLG	AB	HR	AVG	OBP	SLG	AB	HR	AVG	OBP	SLG
1984	Mon-N	7	7	1	136	2.71	6	3	0	77	2.09	1	4	1	59	3.53	113	0	.212	.239	.274	388	13	.227	.286	.366	178	5	.230	.258	.343	70	2	.186	.250	.314
1985	Mon-N	3	5	0	104	3.80	2	2	0	61	3.08	1	3	0	43	4.81	59	0	.220	.266	.237	331	13	.266	.319	.459	159	3	.220	.266	.327	31	1	.226	.273	.355
1986	Mon-N	3	2	1	59	3.20	1	1	0	34	1.59	2	1	1	25	5.40	55	1	.273	.322	.382	166	5	.229	.290	.380	88	4	.284	.330	.511	47	2	.234	.294	.404
1986	Phi-N	3	3	1	29	3.38	3	1	1	17	2.08	0	2	0	12	5.25	35	0	.343	.400	.371	76	3	.211	.318	.434	48	1	.208	.361	.313	55	1	.255	.382	.364
1987	Phi-N	0	0	0	38	4.06	0	0	0	22	2.45	3	1	0	16	6.32	50	1	.240	.264	.320	94	4	.298	.367	.511	65	1	.262	.342	.385	19	1	.421	.500	.632
1987	Min-A	3	1	0	44	6.39	1	1	0	16	6.89	1	0	0	28	6.11	68	2	.353	.405	.515	119	6	.336	.396	.563	111	6	.342	.380	.586	18	1	.667	.750	1.222
1988	Cle-A	0	2	3	16	9.56	0	2	1	7	13.50	0	0	2	9	6.23	23	2	.348	.375	.652	51	4	.353	.377	.627	37	3	.432	.432	.730	18	0	.444	.444	.444
1988	Min-A	0	0	0	10	1.74	0	0	0	8	2.25	0	0	0	2	0.00	13	0	.231	.286	.231	24	1	.250	.368	.250	16	0	.250	.357	.250	24	0	.250	.357	.250
1989	Hou-N	4	1	0	57	4.45	1	0	0	31	3.73	1	1	0	25	5.33	80	1	.287	.345	.338	143	2	.287	.389	.448	120	1	.333	.420	.483	65	0	.154	.247	.169
1990	Hou-N	1	3	0	64	2.39	1	2	0	33	3.55	0	1	0	31	1.16	78	1	.269	.330	.372	156	1	.256	.316	.321	112	1	.313	.344	.393	29	1	.276	.343	.483
1990	NY-N	0	0	0	6	0.00	0	0	0	3	0.00	0	0	0	3	0.00	10	0	.200	.200	.200	9	0	.333	.333	.333	6	0	.222	.222	.222	6	0	.250	.250	.250
1991	KC-A	0	0	0	7	9.45	0	0	0	5	9.64	0	0	0	1	9.00	11	2	.455	.500	.545	22	0	.316	.480	.421	22	2	.409	.500	.500	2	0	.500	.500	1.000
TOTALS		27	26	7	569	3.73	15	14	2	315	3.17	12	12	5	254	4.42	595	6	.272	.318	.355	1576	52	.261	.328	.425	965	26	.282	.336	.423	373	9	.249	.330	.367

● Curt Schilling BR/TR

YEAR	TM/L	W	L	SV	IP	ERA	W	L	SV	IP	ERA	W	L	SV	IP	ERA	AB	HR	AVG	OBP	SLG	AB	HR	AVG	OBP	SLG	AB	HR	AVG	OBP	SLG	AB	HR	AVG	OBP	SLG
1988	Bal-A	0	3	0	15	9.82	0	1	0	11	6.55	0	2	0	4	19.64	30	2	.367	.400	.767	32	1	.344	.463	.531	28	1	.429	.486	.750	0	0	—	—	—
1989	Bal-A	0	1	0	9	6.23	0	1	0	9	9.53	0	0	0	0	0.00	15	1	.267	.267	.533	12	2	.500	.538	1.000	12	0	.333	.391	.450	0	0	—	—	—
1990	Bal-A	1	2	3	46	2.54	1	2	2	29	1.24	0	0	1	18	1.47	65	0	.308	.378	.369	101	1	.178	.252	.257	82	1	.244	.313	.341	48	1	.208	.291	.292
1991	Hou-N	3	5	8	76	3.81	3	3	3	47	3.64	0	2	5	29	4.08	149	1	.255	.367	.342	142	1	.289	.344	.387	158	0	.272	.366	.361	138	1	.283	.365	.384
1992	Phi-N	14	11	2	226	2.35	8	6	0	130	2.21	6	5	2	96	2.53	456	7	.197	.259	.289	363	6	.207	.247	.287	298	5	.195	.253	.292	102	3	.216	.261	.382
1993	Phi-N	16	7	0	235	4.02	9	4	0	113	3.90	7	3	0	122	4.13	495	13	.257	.307	.398	410	10	.261	.298	.377	334	7	.284	.310	.404	27	1	.260	.301	.404
1994	Phi-N	2	8	0	82	4.48	1	4	0	42	3.67	1	4	0	41	5.31	161	3	.248	.299	.360	161	7	.292	.367	.460	131	4	.305	.378	.443	19	1	.368	.480	.632
TOTALS		36	37	13	689	3.55	22	20	5	376	3.37	14	17	8	313	3.77	1371	27	.241	.302	.360	1229	25	.248	.301	.360	1043	20	.263	.328	.384	411	9	.255	.322	.389

● Calvin Schiraldi BR/TR

YEAR	TM/L	W	L	SV	IP	ERA	W	L	SV	IP	ERA	W	L	SV	IP	ERA	AB	HR	AVG	OBP	SLG	AB	HR	AVG	OBP	SLG	AB	HR	AVG	OBP	SLG	AB	HR	AVG	OBP	SLG
1984	NY-N	0	2	0	17	5.71	0	0	0	3	10.80	0	2	0	14	4.50	29	3	.241	.333	.621	41	0	.317	.404	.390	24	2	.250	.357	.500	0	0	—	—	—

YEAR	TM/L	TOTAL W	L	SV	IP	ERA	HOME W	L	SV	IP	ERA	AWAY W	L	SV	IP	ERA	LEFT AB	HR	AVG	OBP	SLG	RIGHT AB	HR	AVG	OBP	SLG	ON-BASE AB	HR	AVG	OBP	SLG	LATE/CLOSE AB	HR	AVG	OBP	SLG
1985	NY-N	2	1	0	26	8.89	0	1	0	4	12.27	2	0	0	23	8.34	60	3	.383	.413	.533	57	1	.351	.456	.632	60	3	.383	.456	.667	2	0	.500	.500	.500
1986	Bos-A	4	2	9	51	1.41	1	1	7	28	0.95	3	1	2	23	1.99	94	2	.170	.248	.277	85	3	.235	.286	.365	73	1	.164	.250	.219	80	4	.200	.253	.387
1987	Bos-A	8	5	6	84	4.41	4	0	5	44	3.27	4	5	1	40	5.67	142	9	.282	.392	.514	171	6	.205	.265	.345	170	13	.247	.316	.524	149	8	.215	.320	.396
1988	Chi-N	9	13	1	166	4.38	3	7	1	75	5.18	6	6	0	92	3.73	362	8	.298	.368	.439	284	5	.204	.265	.306	258	7	.291	.355	.465	39	0	.231	.268	.282
1989	Chi-N	3	6	4	79	3.78	2	3	1	45	3.83	1	3	3	34	3.71	146	2	.219	.354	.322	141	5	.199	.296	.340	132	6	.220	.340	.394	132	5	.220	.333	.386
1989	SD-N	3	1	0	21	2.53	1	1	0	8	4.32	2	0	0	13	1.38	55	1	.164	.292	.218	19	0	.158	.273	.263	29	0	.138	.265	.172	8	0	.250	.333	.375
1990	SD-N	3	8	1	104	4.41	2	5	1	64	4.24	1	3	0	40	4.69	201	7	.259	.380	.428	196	4	.270	.338	.418	198	5	.258	.342	.404	65	1	.262	.364	.385
1991	Tex-A	0	1	0	5	11.57	0	1	0	5	11.57	0	0	0	0	∞	12	2	.286	.286	.714	12	2	.250	.471	.750	7	2	.429	.556	1.286	6	0	.167	.286	.167
TOTALS		32	39	21	553	4.28	15	18	10	265	4.31	17	21	11	288	4.25	1096	36	.264	.359	.418	1006	26	.232	.306	.371	963	39	.258	.340	.445	481	18	.222	.316	.378

● Ken Schrom BR/TR

YEAR	TM/L	W	L	SV	IP	ERA	W	L	SV	IP	ERA	W	L	SV	IP	ERA	AB	HR	AVG	OBP	SLG	AB	HR	AVG	OBP	SLG	AB	HR	AVG	OBP	SLG	AB	HR	AVG	OBP	SLG
1984	Min-A	5	11	0	137	4.47	4	6	0	75	3.86	1	5	0	62	5.20	305	9	.311	.364	.452	243	6	.251	.293	.391	220	5	.318	.364	.441	30	0	.467	.500	.600
1985	Min-A	9	12	0	161	4.99	7	7	0	108	5.42	2	5	0	53	4.10	321	15	.283	.359	.470	282	13	.259	.313	.482	217	9	.281	.333	.465	45	1	.111	.184	.178
1986	Cle-A	14	7	0	206	4.54	9	4	0	118	3.88	5	3	0	88	5.44	447	17	.293	.335	.472	355	17	.242	.297	.434	318	10	.242	.289	.390	63	3	.270	.338	.444
1987	Cle-A	6	13	0	154	6.50	3	8	0	97	6.70	3	5	0	57	6.16	323	17	.316	.363	.548	297	12	.279	.350	.465	252	11	.333	.400	.544	50	1	.280	.339	.400
TOTALS		34	43	0	657	5.09	23	25	0	398	4.98	11	18	0	260	5.27	1396	58	.300	.351	.485	1177	48	.257	.314	.444	1007	35	.290	.343	.456	188	5	.266	.329	.394

● Mike Scott BR/TR

YEAR	TM/L	W	L	SV	IP	ERA	W	L	SV	IP	ERA	W	L	SV	IP	ERA	AB	HR	AVG	OBP	SLG	AB	HR	AVG	OBP	SLG	AB	HR	AVG	OBP	SLG	AB	HR	AVG	OBP	SLG
1984	Hou-N	5	11	0	154	4.68	4	5	0	79	3.89	1	6	0	75	5.50	291	2	.289	.339	.395	318	5	.299	.337	.390	248	3	.355	.402	.464	21	0	.333	.400	.476
1985	Hou-N	18	8	0	222	3.29	11	2	0	120	2.18	7	6	0	102	4.60	429	3	.217	.289	.289	398	17	.254	.317	.442	316	7	.241	.315	.351	71	1	.113	.203	.169
1986	Hou-N	18	10	0	275	2.22	10	8	0	151	2.20	8	2	0	124	2.25	508	6	.215	.282	.307	468	11	.156	.198	.274	331	6	.181	.243	.287	110	3	.218	.301	.364
1987	Hou-N	16	13	0	248	3.23	10	3	0	123	2.20	6	10	0	125	4.16	513	9	.234	.299	.333	403	12	.196	.259	.328	329	7	.264	.347	.374	92	1	.261	.289	.337
1988	Hou-N	14	8	0	219	2.92	7	3	0	99	2.09	7	5	0	120	3.61	405	10	.185	.260	.311	388	9	.224	.260	.340	285	8	.207	.260	.347	113	1	.177	.248	.257
1989	Hou-N	20	10	0	229	3.10	12	6	0	134	3.03	8	4	0	95	3.21	482	14	.247	.298	.392	366	9	.167	.227	.281	309	7	.217	.289	.359	78	1	.179	.304	.256
1990	Hou-N	9	13	0	206	3.81	5	4	0	130	2.42	4	9	0	76	6.19	445	10	.238	.302	.366	344	17	.256	.302	.451	306	10	.245	.301	.389	63	0	.159	.197	.222
1991	Hou-N	0	2	0	7	12.86	0	1	0	3	15.00	0	1	0	4	11.25	12	0	.417	.500	.583	18	2	.333	.429	.722	15	1	.400	.526	.733	0	0	—	—	—
TOTALS		100	75	0	1559	3.26	59	32	0	839	2.55	41	43	0	720	4.09	3085	54	.230	.294	.341	2703	82	.218	.269	.356	2139	49	.242	.308	.367	548	7	.195	.269	.285

● Tom Seaver BR/TR

YEAR	TM/L	W	L	SV	IP	ERA	W	L	SV	IP	ERA	W	L	SV	IP	ERA	AB	HR	AVG	OBP	SLG	AB	HR	AVG	OBP	SLG	AB	HR	AVG	OBP	SLG	AB	HR	AVG	OBP	SLG
1984	Chi-A	15	11	0	237	3.95	9	4	0	126	3.64	6	7	0	111	4.31	473	15	.220	.275	.368	427	12	.262	.302	.403	343	9	.245	.293	.376	117	3	.231	.274	.342
1985	Chi-A	16	11	0	239	3.17	5	6	0	103	4.35	11	5	0	135	2.26	466	10	.249	.314	.363	435	12	.246	.293	.386	331	6	.272	.340	.384	127	3	.252	.338	.378
1986	Chi-A	2	6	0	72	4.38	1	4	0	42	5.10	1	2	0	30	3.54	129	4	.264	.345	.473	144	5	.222	.296	.354	96	5	.292	.375	.531	23	0	.348	.400	.478
1986	Bos-A	5	7	0	104	3.80	2	3	0	39	4.15	3	4	0	65	3.58	219	4	.288	.336	.416	191	4	.267	.314	.372	175	2	.246	.313	.326	34	0	.353	.395	.500
TOTALS		38	35	0	652	3.69	17	17	0	311	4.14	21	18	0	341	3.27	1287	33	.246	.307	.385	1197	33	.252	.300	.386	945	22	.259	.322	.385	301	5	.262	.325	.385

● Eric Show BR/TR

YEAR	TM/L	W	L	SV	IP	ERA	W	L	SV	IP	ERA	W	L	SV	IP	ERA	AB	HR	AVG	OBP	SLG	AB	HR	AVG	OBP	SLG	AB	HR	AVG	OBP	SLG	AB	HR	AVG	OBP	SLG
1984	SD-N	15	9	0	207	3.40	6	5	0	91	3.77	9	4	0	116	3.10	373	6	.273	.368	.386	375	10	.195	.262	.312	293	7	.229	.318	.334	80	3	.300	.391	.438
1985	SD-N	12	11	0	233	3.09	6	5	0	107	3.52	6	6	0	126	2.72	464	16	.287	.362	.453	407	11	.194	.259	.312	345	6	.223	.298	.345	83	2	.205	.280	.337
1986	SD-N	9	5	0	136	2.97	5	3	0	78	2.78	4	2	0	59	3.22	272	4	.250	.357	.342	212	7	.193	.285	.311	191	4	.188	.288	.272	36	2	.278	.333	.472
1987	SD-N	8	16	0	206	3.84	5	6	0	112	2.73	3	10	0	94	5.15	430	13	.247	.327	.405	348	13	.236	.315	.402	287	5	.230	.343	.355	44	2	.227	.292	.386
1988	SD-N	16	11	0	235	3.26	8	5	0	126	2.85	8	6	0	108	3.74	462	10	.253	.316	.392	407	12	.206	.234	.324	293	6	.232	.320	.358	97	3	.247	.311	.392
1989	SD-N	8	6	0	106	4.23	4	3	0	56	4.37	4	3	0	51	4.09	234	4	.269	.345	.427	178	5	.281	.325	.444	164	7	.299	.368	.500	54	0	.241	.317	.259
1990	SD-N	6	8	1	106	5.76	3	5	0	51	6.22	3	3	1	56	5.34	232	8	.310	.389	.474	196	8	.301	.344	.469	176	7	.324	.414	.483	44	1	.227	.292	.318
1991	Oak-A	1	2	0	52	5.92	0	2	0	26	6.84	1	0	0	25	4.97	95	4	.358	.436	.621	112	1	.250	.263	.330	88	2	.330	.364	.477	17	0	.176	.263	.235
TOTALS		75	68	1	1281	3.71	37	34	0	647	3.62	38	34	1	635	3.80	2562	67	.271	.352	.420	2235	67	.222	.279	.353	1837	46	.244	.332	.373	455	13	.244	.317	.367

● Doug Sisk BR/TR

YEAR	TM/L	W	L	SV	IP	ERA	W	L	SV	IP	ERA	W	L	SV	IP	ERA	AB	HR	AVG	OBP	SLG	AB	HR	AVG	OBP	SLG	AB	HR	AVG	OBP	SLG	AB	HR	AVG	OBP	SLG
1984	NY-N	1	3	15	78	2.09	0	2	7	42	2.38	1	1	8	36	1.75	127	1	.197	.358	.268	138	0	.232	.350	.254	134	1	.194	.341	.254	167	1	.168	.312	.204
1985	NY-N	4	5	2	73	5.30	1	1	1	30	5.04	3	4	1	43	5.48	135	2	.304	.390	.400	161	0	.280	.370	.379	163	3	.313	.398	.442	111	0	.279	.375	.306
1986	NY-N	4	2	1	71	3.06	1	2	0	34	1.57	3	0	1	36	4.46	117	0	.265	.363	.316	156	0	.295	.368	.327	144	0	.299	.380	.326	98	0	.286	.381	.316
1987	NY-N	3	1	3	78	3.46	0	0	2	36	3.79	3	1	1	42	3.19	137	0	.270	.327	.343	170	5	.271	.321	.406	141	5	.319	.376	.489	96	2	.271	.320	.365
1988	Bal-A	3	3	0	94	3.72	3	2	0	47	3.83	0	1	0	47	3.61	159	1	.358	.450	.415	197	2	.264	.329	.330	190	2	.337	.413	.440	51	0	.490	.565	.549
1990	Atl-N	0	0	0	2	3.86	0	0	0	0	4.50	0	0	0	2	4.50	2	0	.000	.429	.000	5	0	.200	.333	.200	4	0	.000	.250	.000	0	0	—	—	—
1991	Atl-N	2	1	0	14	5.02	1	0	0	10	4.50	1	1	0	4	6.23	33	1	.394	.488	.667	30	0	.267	.290	.267	35	1	.343	.429	.514	28	0	.321	.429	.393
TOTALS		17	15	21	410	3.58	6	7	10	201	3.36	11	8	11	209	3.78	710	5	.287	.387	.366	857	8	.268	.344	.338	811	12	.297	.385	.390	551	3	.267	.369	.314

● Heathcliff Slocumb BR/TR

YEAR	TM/L	W	L	SV	IP	ERA	W	L	SV	IP	ERA	W	L	SV	IP	ERA	AB	HR	AVG	OBP	SLG	AB	HR	AVG	OBP	SLG	AB	HR	AVG	OBP	SLG	AB	HR	AVG	OBP	SLG
1991	Chi-N	2	1	1	63	3.45	2	0	1	33	3.00	0	1	0	30	3.94	107	3	.290	.361	.439	122	0	.180	.288	.221	125	3	.256	.340	.392	55	1	.182	.338	.291
1992	Chi-N	0	3	1	36	6.50	0	2	1	20	4.58	0	1	0	16	8.82	75	3	.413	.506	.533	73	0	.288	.349	.329	75	2	.440	.506	.547	31	1	.419	.513	.516
1993	Chi-N	1	0	0	11	3.38	0	0	0	4	9.00	1	0	0	7	0.00	16	0	.188	.235	.188	21	0	.190	.280	.238	19	0	.105	.250	.105	7	0	.429	.600	.429
1993	Cle-A	3	1	0	27	4.28	1	0	0	18	1.02	2	1	0	10	10.24	29	1	.276	.436	.379	74	2	.270	.329	.378	56	2	.286	.382	.411	32	1	.344	.421	.469
1994	Phi-N	5	1	0	72	2.86	1	0	0	35	3.12	4	1	0	38	2.63	128	0	.242	.326	.266	158	0	.278	.330	.354	141	0	.291	.362	.355	151	0	.265	.345	.311
TOTALS		11	6	2	209	3.88	4	2	2	109	3.22	7	4	0	100	4.59	355	7	.293	.382	.380	448	2	.248	.318	.313	416	7	.279	.379	.397	276	3	.279	.380	.351

● John Smiley BL/TL

YEAR	TM/L	W	L	SV	IP	ERA	W	L	SV	IP	ERA	W	L	SV	IP	ERA	AB	HR	AVG	OBP	SLG	AB	HR	AVG	OBP	SLG	AB	HR	AVG	OBP	SLG	AB	HR	AVG	OBP	SLG
1986	Pit-N	1	0	0	12	3.86	0	0	0	6	1.42	1	0	0	5	6.75	13	1	.154	.214	.154	25	2	.080	.179	.320	15	1	.133	.133	.333	7	0	.000	.125	.000
1987	Pit-N	5	5	4	75	5.76	5	3	2	49	2.77	0	2	2	26	11.28	87	1	.195	.287	.299	196	6	.265	.383	.429	126	3	.278	.397	.421	123	1	.228	.366	.333
1988	Pit-N	13	11	0	205	3.25	5	6	0	87	3.61	8	5	0	118	2.98	107	2	.159	.252	.243	660	13	.255	.290	.373	297	6	.276	.312	.404	82	2	.220	.235	.341
1989	Pit-N	12	8	0	205	2.81	8	4	0	109	2.64	4	4	0	96	2.99	103	1	.243	.291	.320	667	21	.223	.271	.354	279	9	.211	.261	.341	103	5	.233	.292	.427
1990	Pit-N	9	10	0	149	4.64	3	4	0	64	3.80	6	6	0	85	5.27	93	3	.301	.350	.484	492	12	.200	.250	.311	222	5	.300	.333	.464	40	2	.200	.233	.375
1991	Pit-N	20	8	0	208	3.08	10	5	0	100	2.98	10	3	0	108	3.17	153	3	.196	.220	.320	621	14	.264	.309	.396	283	8	.261	.295	.413	62	1	.226	.313	.258
1992	Min-A	16	9	0	241	3.21	10	4	0	137	2.83	6	5	0	104	3.71	139	1	.259	.316	.367	747	16	.226	.280	.353	334	6	.225	.282	.326	81	1	.185	.241	.272
1993	Cin-N	3	9	0	106	5.62	1	5	0	49	4.81	2	4	0	57	6.32	51	1	.275	.383	.412	538	14	.288	.330	.458	151	6	.344	.404	.530	22	2	.273	.273	.545
1994	Cin-N	11	10	0	159	3.86	7	4	0	86	3.77	4	6	0	73	3.96	109	3	.248	.322	.358	506	15	.281	.320	.435	231	10	.303	.356	.494	34	2	.294	.351	.559
TOTALS		90	70	4	1359	3.70	49	35	2	686	3.25	41	35	2	673	4.16	855	15	.229	.293	.342	4272	113	.253	.301	.390	1951	55	.267	.317	.411	552	15	.223	.294	.357

● Bryn Smith BR/TR

YEAR	TM/L	W	L	SV	IP	ERA	W	L	SV	IP	ERA	W	L	SV	IP	ERA	AB	HR	AVG	OBP	SLG	AB	HR	AVG	OBP	SLG	AB	HR	AVG	OBP	SLG	AB	HR	AVG	OBP	SLG
1984	Mon-N	12	13	0	179	3.32	4	8	0	94	3.06	8	5	0	85	3.60	348	8	.273	.334	.402	340	7	.244	.288	.368	281	8	.242	.293	.377	61	3	.262	.328	.525
1985	Mon-N	18	5	0	222	2.91	11	2	0	112	2.32	7	3	0	110	3.52	417	1	.240	.267	.312	414	11	.225	.269	.348	324	5	.235	.272	.324	60	1	.183	.284	.267
1986	Mon-N	10	8	0	187	3.94	5	3	0	86	3.75	5	5	0	101	4.10	409	8	.286	.354	.421	314	7	.207	.265	.328	313	8	.259	.325	.390	33	0	.394	.429	.576
1987	Mon-N	10	9	0	150	4.37	6	3	0	82	4.50	4	6	0	68	4.21	347	8	.259	.293	.372	251	8	.295	.333	.462	242	8	.293	.328	.475	3	0	.000	.000	.000
1988	Mon-N	12	10	0	198	3.00	7	2	0	87	2.37	5	8	0	111	3.50	378	6	.259	.300	.360	358	9	.265	.263	.352	273	7	.245	.281	.374	32	1	.344	.364	.469
1989	Mon-N	10	11	0	216	2.84	5	5	0	125	2.73	5	6	0	90	2.99	446	6	.215	.265	.305	348	10	.233	.286	.374	291	6	.234	.283	.388	58	2	.276	.300	.397
1990	StL-N	9	8	0	141	4.27	6	4	0	84	3.84	3	4	0	57	4.89	339	3	.301	.339	.392	220	8	.264	.302	.414	236	3	.322	.355	.428	22	0	.318	.375	.318
1991	StL-N	12	9	0	199	3.85	5	4	0	107	3.52	7	5	0	91	4.24	441	7	.272	.319	.401	308	9	.221	.266	.351	276	10	.261	.324	.442	25	0	.280	.280	.480
1992	StL-N	4	2	0	21	4.64	2	2	0	12	5.11	2	0	0	9	4.00	37	0	.270	.341	.324	44	3	.227	.292	.432	26	1	.231	.333	.346	30	2	.333	.394	.567
1993	Col-N	2	4	0	52	8.49	1	3	0	23	4.63	1	1	0	29	22.74	70	1	.371	.392	.471	60	1	.350	.435	.433	71	1	.366	.410	.423	5	1	.400	.400	1.000
TOTALS		99	79	0	1544	3.60	52	34	0	815	3.27	47	45	0	729	3.98	3232	48	.264	.310	.371	2657	73	.239	.285	.372	2333	57	.262	.310	.406	329	10	.283	.324	.444

● Dave Smith BR/TR

YEAR	TM/L	W	L	SV	IP	ERA	W	L	SV	IP	ERA	W	L	SV	IP	ERA	AB	HR	AVG	OBP	SLG	AB	HR	AVG	OBP	SLG	AB	HR	AVG	OBP	SLG	AB	HR	AVG	OBP	SLG
1984	Hou-N	5	4	5	77	2.21	5	2	2	37	1.70	0	2	3	40	2.68	132	1	.152	.221	.212	148	4	.270	.312	.399	109	2	.220	.271	.321	142	3	.246	.310	.366
1985	Hou-N	9	5	27	79	2.27	7	4	16	51	2.65	2	1	11	28	1.59	131	2	.183	.280	.259	166	2	.229	.267	.313	133	2	.238	.278	.314	223	3	.238	.278	.314
1986	Hou-N	4	7	33	56	2.73	3	1	14	25	2.92	1	6	19	31	2.59	102	2	.167	.234	.235	93	3	.237	.333	.355	97	3	.196	.262	.299	163	5	.215	.291	.325
1987	Hou-N	2	3	24	60	1.65	1	2	13	37	1.47	1	1	11	23	1.93	114	0	.202	.295	.237	100	1	.160	.213	.220	98	0	.204	.307	.235	158	0	.196	.269	.241
1988	Hou-N	4	5	27	57	2.67	3	3	17	30	2.70	1	2	10	27	2.63	98	0	.306	.367	.357	126	1	.238	.294	.333	120	1	.275	.338	.358	188	1	.250	.311	.324
1989	Hou-N	3	4	25	58	2.64	3	1	12	28	3.81	0	3	13	30	1.52	118	1	.237	.302	.322	92	0	.228	.294	.261	92	1	.228	.308	.315	157	1	.210	.269	.287
1990	Hou-N	6	6	23	60	2.39	3	4	13	32	2.25	3	2	10	28	2.54	111	1	.234	.298	.288	103	3	.184	.254	.330	100	3	.210	.266	.360	152	3	.211	.298	.322
1991	Chi-N	0	6	17	33	6.00	0	3	10	18	5.60	0	3	7	15	6.46	74	4	.378	.459	.676	55	2	.236	.333	.345	64	3	.324	.410	.632	99	5	.333	.426	.576
1992	Chi-N	0	0	0	14	2.51	0	0	0	7	1.35	0	0	0	8	3.52	27	0	.333	.400	.444	28	0	.214	.233	.214	33	0	.273	.324	.364	15	0	.200	.200	.267
TOTALS		33	40	181	496	2.60	25	20	97	264	2.63	8	20	84	232	2.56	892	11	.233	.303	.315	922	16	.225	.284	.319	883	16	.234	.299	.342	1297	21	.233	.299	.331

● Lee Smith BR/TR

YEAR	TM/L	W	L	SV	IP	ERA	W	L	SV	IP	ERA	W	L	SV	IP	ERA	AB	HR	AVG	OBP	SLG	AB	HR	AVG	OBP	SLG	AB	HR	AVG	OBP	SLG	AB	HR	AVG	OBP	SLG
1984	Chi-N	9	7	33	101	3.65	5	3	14	53	4.05	4	4	19	48	3.21	218	1	.273	.345	.344	166	5	.235	.298	.305	193	1	.233	.298	.301	277	4	.245	.311	.354
1985	Chi-N	7	4	33	98	3.04	3	3	17	55	4.09	4	1	16	43	1.69	192	4	.266	.324	.401	168	5	.214	.283	.357	183	5	.230	.294	.388	289	8	.242	.306	.388
1986	Chi-N	9	9	31	90	3.09	6	3	20	56	2.75	3	6	11	35	3.63	172	5	.221	.343	.349	149	2	.208	.252	.296	152	3	.191	.308	.296	277	7	.217	.297	.329

		TOTAL					HOME					AWAY					LEFT					RIGHT					ON-BASE					LATE/CLOSE				
YEAR	TM/L	W	L	SV	IP	ERA	W	L	SV	IP	ERA	W	L	SV	IP	ERA	AB	HR	AVG	OBP	SLG	AB	HR	AVG	OBP	SLG	AB	HR	AVG	OBP	SLG	AB	HR	AVG	OBP	SLG
1987	Chi-N	4	10	36	84	3.12	3	5	16	38	3.79	1	5	20	46	2.56	179	3	.268	.358	.397	145	1	.248	.283	.310	170	0	.253	.339	.312	259	3	.270	.339	.367
1988	Bos-A	4	5	29	84	2.80	3	2	19	47	2.66	1	3	10	36	2.97	164	3	.232	.321	.317	156	4	.218	.289	.359	174	7	.247	.311	.414	206	5	.228	.315	.359
1989	Bos-A	6	1	25	71	3.57	6	0	12	38	4.06	0	1	13	33	3.00	121	5	.223	.317	.364	132	1	.197	.282	.250	129	2	.233	.331	.318	156	5	.224	.301	.359
1990	Bos-A	2	1	4	14	1.88	1	0	3	10	1.86	1	1	1	5	1.93	26	0	.192	.382	.269	29	0	.276	.300	.310	29	0	.207	.324	.241	51	0	.255	.356	.314
1990	StL-N	3	4	27	69	2.10	2	3	9	37	2.65	1	1	18	31	1.44	152	3	.237	.306	.349	103	0	.214	.241	.282	120	2	.242	.299	.333	205	3	.234	.295	.332
1991	StL-N	6	3	47	73	2.34	6	1	26	46	1.38	0	2	21	27	3.95	165	3	.255	.301	.364	116	2	.241	.252	.336	128	3	.250	.287	.344	230	5	.252	.288	.357
1992	StL-N	4	9	43	75	3.12	3	8	18	44	3.25	1	1	25	31	2.93	164	2	.220	.303	.335	117	2	.222	.260	.299	115	2	.261	.344	.383	240	2	.204	.274	.262
1993	StL-N	2	4	43	50	4.50	1	3	21	24	4.81	1	1	22	26	4.21	108	6	.250	.278	.463	87	5	.253	.286	.529	74	6	.243	.293	.514	157	11	.255	.292	.516
1993	NY-A	0	0	3	8	0.00	0	0	2	4	0.00	0	0	1	4	0.00	11	0	.000	.267	.000	16	0	.250	.278	.313	19	0	.105	.182	.105	12	0	.250	.250	.250
1994	Bal-A	1	4	33	38	3.29	0	2	15	18	3.00	1	2	18	20	3.54	72	4	.306	.366	.542	70	2	.171	.205	.271	68	2	.206	.233	.324	119	5	.218	.280	.370
TOTALS		57	61	387	854	3.07	39	33	192	470	3.22	18	28	195	384	2.88	1744	39	.246	.325	.369	1454	39	.223	.268	.331	1554	33	.234	.306	.346	2478	58	.237	.303	.356

● **Zane Smith** BL/TL

		TOTAL					HOME					AWAY					LEFT					RIGHT					ON-BASE					LATE/CLOSE				
YEAR	TM/L	W	L	SV	IP	ERA	W	L	SV	IP	ERA	W	L	SV	IP	ERA	AB	HR	AVG	OBP	SLG	AB	HR	AVG	OBP	SLG	AB	HR	AVG	OBP	SLG	AB	HR	AVG	OBP	SLG
1984	Atl-N	1	0	0	20	2.25	0	0	0	7	3.86	1	0	0	13	1.38	18	1	.167	.167	.389	55	0	.236	.382	.327	34	0	.176	.300	.206	7	0	.143	.400	.143
1985	Atl-N	9	10	0	147	3.80	2	5	0	73	4.46	7	5	0	74	3.15	81	0	.284	.348	.309	450	4	.249	.356	.362	251	2	.251	.346	.351	54	0	.148	.270	.148
1986	Atl-N	8	16	1	205	4.05	7	7	1	127	3.41	1	9	0	78	5.08	115	0	.226	.274	.304	645	8	.284	.379	.394	354	5	.274	.350	.387	72	0	.319	.424	.417
1987	Atl-N	15	10	0	242	4.09	6	6	0	111	5.69	9	4	0	131	2.74	105	1	.257	.310	.314	817	18	.267	.336	.386	392	13	.276	.346	.421	68	2	.309	.338	.441
1988	Atl-N	5	10	0	140	4.30	2	5	0	75	3.46	3	5	0	65	5.26	84	0	.238	.297	.262	461	8	.302	.356	.395	249	4	.301	.351	.394	68	0	.279	.329	.309
1989	Atl-N	1	12	0	99	4.45	1	4	0	54	3.15	0	8	0	45	6.04	78	0	.141	.181	.179	304	5	.299	.360	.418	174	3	.259	.330	.379	17	0	.471	.471	.647
1989	Mon-N	0	1	2	48	1.50	0	1	1	23	1.99	0	0	1	25	1.07	59	1	.136	.215	.203	118	1	.263	.341	.339	75	2	.200	.318	.293	122	2	.230	.314	.311
1990	Mon-N	6	7	0	139	3.23	4	2	0	72	2.51	2	5	0	68	3.99	71	1	.183	.266	.254	459	10	.279	.330	.394	210	5	.271	.332	.386	42	2	.238	.273	.405
1990	Pit-N	6	2	0	76	1.30	5	1	0	47	1.35	1	1	0	29	1.23	45	0	.133	.170	.200	226	4	.217	.239	.319	81	0	.210	.235	.272	46	0	.196	.208	.196
1991	Pit-N	16	10	0	228	3.20	11	3	0	129	2.78	5	7	0	99	3.74	146	1	.267	.291	.315	727	14	.268	.292	.381	319	7	.288	.320	.404	76	1	.263	.273	.316
1992	Pit-N	8	8	0	141	3.06	4	4	0	64	3.25	4	4	0	77	2.91	93	2	.215	.232	.312	436	6	.271	.298	.376	189	4	.307	.332	.439	69	1	.246	.278	.333
1993	Pit-N	3	7	0	83	4.55	1	3	0	44	3.48	2	4	0	39	5.77	57	0	.211	.262	.246	268	5	.317	.360	.493	134	2	.321	.368	.515	26	0	.231	.310	.269
1994	Pit-N	10	8	0	157	3.27	5	3	0	99	2.73	5	5	0	58	4.19	92	2	.217	.245	.337	509	16	.279	.319	.422	231	5	.247	.300	.364	61	0	.262	.297	.311
TOTALS		88	101	3	1725	3.56	48	44	2	924	3.38	40	57	1	802	3.76	1044	9	.218	.264	.283	5475	99	.275	.334	.391	2693	52	.272	.335	.390	728	8	.255	.313	.327

● **Mike Smithson** BL/TR

		TOTAL					HOME					AWAY					LEFT					RIGHT					ON-BASE					LATE/CLOSE				
YEAR	TM/L	W	L	SV	IP	ERA	W	L	SV	IP	ERA	W	L	SV	IP	ERA	AB	HR	AVG	OBP	SLG	AB	HR	AVG	OBP	SLG	AB	HR	AVG	OBP	SLG	AB	HR	AVG	OBP	SLG
1984	Min-A	15	13	0	252	3.68	7	5	0	116	3.88	8	8	0	136	3.51	582	23	.265	.310	.447	395	12	.233	.284	.357	356	15	.230	.284	.402	93	6	.269	.313	.484
1985	Min-A	15	14	0	257	4.34	8	6	0	120	4.34	7	8	0	137	4.35	570	19	.288	.333	.467	408	6	.245	.329	.350	389	13	.283	.336	.455	73	1	.288	.369	.452
1986	Min-A	13	14	0	198	4.77	9	6	0	110	4.34	4	8	0	88	5.32	485	18	.315	.368	.501	311	8	.260	.318	.402	354	9	.302	.343	.435	55	1	.345	.393	.455
1987	Min-A	4	7	0	109	5.94	2	1	0	50	4.71	2	6	0	59	6.98	253	17	.320	.371	.593	188	0	.239	.326	.303	188	10	.346	.396	.617	16	0	.250	.368	.313
1988	Bos-A	9	6	0	127	5.97	7	2	0	73	5.89	2	4	0	53	6.07	282	11	.291	.338	.472	229	14	.293	.353	.511	200	11	.325	.384	.535	16	2	.375	.375	.875
1989	Bos-A	7	14	2	144	4.95	5	6	1	79	4.88	2	8	1	64	5.04	289	13	.311	.341	.519	284	8	.282	.328	.415	248	9	.286	.343	.440	39	3	.308	.349	.590
TOTALS		63	68	2	1086	4.70	38	26	1	549	4.56	25	42	1	538	4.84	2461	101	.294	.342	.488	1815	48	.256	.318	.386	1735	67	.288	.340	.465	292	13	.298	.354	.497

● **John Smoltz** BR/TR

		TOTAL					HOME					AWAY					LEFT					RIGHT					ON-BASE					LATE/CLOSE				
YEAR	TM/L	W	L	SV	IP	ERA	W	L	SV	IP	ERA	W	L	SV	IP	ERA	AB	HR	AVG	OBP	SLG	AB	HR	AVG	OBP	SLG	AB	HR	AVG	OBP	SLG	AB	HR	AVG	OBP	SLG
1988	Atl-N	2	7	0	64	5.48	1	4	0	35	6.11	1	3	0	29	4.71	156	4	.314	.409	.487	104	6	.240	.307	.452	113	4	.292	.407	.487	32	3	.344	.400	.750
1989	Atl-N	12	11	0	208	2.94	6	4	0	99	2.63	6	7	0	109	3.23	454	6	.214	.289	.317	302	9	.209	.266	.321	301	7	.239	.293	.355	105	1	.181	.250	.257
1990	Atl-N	14	11	0	231	3.85	9	4	0	124	2.76	5	7	0	107	5.11	506	10	.269	.347	.383	352	10	.199	.255	.321	331	11	.254	.330	.408	67	0	.179	.263	.224
1991	Atl-N	14	13	0	230	3.80	9	7	0	136	4.10	5	6	0	94	3.36	486	10	.288	.363	.422	363	8	.182	.221	.278	350	5	.243	.303	.366	42	0	.214	.233	.238
1992	Atl-N	15	12	0	247	2.85	5	6	0	103	2.87	10	6	0	143	2.83	544	9	.246	.309	.338	377	8	.191	.254	.324	369	7	.220	.292	.309	110	3	.182	.224	.318
1993	Atl-N	15	11	0	244	3.62	4	5	0	101	3.92	11	6	0	143	3.41	459	10	.261	.346	.412	446	13	.197	.271	.325	370	10	.222	.316	.375	115	3	.330	.421	.513
1994	Atl-N	6	10	0	135	4.14	2	7	0	79	5.01	4	3	0	56	2.91	240	6	.271	.347	.408	263	9	.209	.256	.350	196	8	.260	.338	.439	40	1	.300	.333	.425
TOTALS		78	75	0	1358	3.59	36	37	0	678	3.64	42	38	0	680	3.53	2845	55	.260	.338	.383	2207	61	.199	.257	.325	2030	52	.240	.316	.375	511	11	.237	.301	.366

● **Bob Stanley** BR/TR

		TOTAL					HOME					AWAY					LEFT					RIGHT					ON-BASE					LATE/CLOSE				
YEAR	TM/L	W	L	SV	IP	ERA	W	L	SV	IP	ERA	W	L	SV	IP	ERA	AB	HR	AVG	OBP	SLG	AB	HR	AVG	OBP	SLG	AB	HR	AVG	OBP	SLG	AB	HR	AVG	OBP	SLG
1984	Bos-A	9	10	22	107	3.54	5	8	8	57	4.55	4	2	14	49	2.37	221	4	.253	.320	.389	202	4	.282	.293	.376	207	8	.329	.369	.493	260	6	.250	.300	.377
1985	Bos-A	6	6	10	88	2.87	3	2	5	42	3.21	3	4	5	46	2.56	161	3	.248	.324	.354	160	3	.225	.279	.356	146	1	.281	.370	.377	218	6	.234	.290	.362
1986	Bos-A	6	6	16	82	4.37	3	1	9	39	6.00	3	5	7	43	2.91	154	3	.338	.392	.442	184	4	.310	.332	.478	179	4	.324	.375	.441	151	4	.311	.369	.424
1987	Bos-A	4	15	0	153	5.01	3	5	0	74	4.28	1	10	0	79	5.70	299	8	.358	.413	.522	317	9	.287	.314	.416	294	9	.286	.333	.429	76	2	.382	.435	.539
1988	Bos-A	6	4	5	102	3.19	3	2	3	55	2.28	3	2	2	46	4.27	171	4	.263	.332	.330	201	5	.224	.281	.333	183	4	.246	.311	.355	133	1	.248	.313	.316
1989	Bos-A	5	2	4	79	4.88	3	0	3	42	4.32	2	2	1	38	5.50	141	2	.348	.415	.489	177	2	.299	.326	.373	169	2	.361	.401	.462	96	2	.271	.327	.385
TOTALS		36	43	57	610	4.04	20	18	28	309	4.05	16	25	29	301	4.03	1147	23	.304	.368	.431	1241	29	.273	.305	.392	1178	28	.303	.357	.429	934	21	.269	.325	.387

● **Mike Stanton** BL/TL

		TOTAL					HOME					AWAY					LEFT					RIGHT					ON-BASE					LATE/CLOSE				
YEAR	TM/L	W	L	SV	IP	ERA	W	L	SV	IP	ERA	W	L	SV	IP	ERA	AB	HR	AVG	OBP	SLG	AB	HR	AVG	OBP	SLG	AB	HR	AVG	OBP	SLG	AB	HR	AVG	OBP	SLG
1989	Atl-N	0	1	7	24	1.50	0	1	3	14	2.63	0	0	4	10	0.00	14	0	.214	.313	.357	68	0	.206	.270	.250	44	0	.205	.300	.318	61	0	.230	.299	.311
1990	Atl-N	0	3	2	7	18.00	0	1	1	5	19.29	0	2	1	2	15.43	8	0	.250	.400	.250	28	1	.500	.548	.643	26	1	.500	.567	.615	23	0	.391	.481	.435
1991	Atl-N	5	5	7	78	2.88	1	1	4	41	2.21	4	4	3	37	3.62	103	1	.194	.252	.233	183	5	.230	.284	.377	122	3	.205	.292	.328	162	1	.198	.257	.278
1992	Atl-N	5	4	8	64	4.10	2	1	3	30	3.00	3	3	5	34	5.08	74	6	.237	.344	.434	163	2	.252	.289	.337	109	2	.211	.279	.330	139	4	.245	.303	.374
1993	Atl-N	4	6	27	52	4.67	4	3	14	28	2.25	0	3	13	24	7.50	55	1	.218	.357	.309	145	3	.269	.342	.393	102	2	.284	.359	.402	130	4	.277	.371	.423
1994	Atl-N	3	1	3	46	3.55	3	1	1	31	2.93	0	0	2	15	4.90	60	1	.200	.300	.267	105	1	.276	.392	.352	79	2	.266	.372	.392	68	1	.279	.375	.368
TOTALS		17	20	54	270	3.90	10	8	26	148	3.11	7	12	28	123	4.84	316	7	.212	.311	.307	692	12	.259	.325	.366	482	10	.249	.333	.369	583	10	.247	.322	.353

● **Dave Stewart** BR/TR

		TOTAL					HOME					AWAY					LEFT					RIGHT					ON-BASE					LATE/CLOSE				
YEAR	TM/L	W	L	SV	IP	ERA	W	L	SV	IP	ERA	W	L	SV	IP	ERA	AB	HR	AVG	OBP	SLG	AB	HR	AVG	OBP	SLG	AB	HR	AVG	OBP	SLG	AB	HR	AVG	OBP	SLG
1984	Tex-A	7	14	0	192	4.73	3	9	0	122	4.51	4	5	0	71	5.09	394	13	.269	.355	.421	353	13	.246	.316	.422	296	8	.274	.368	.409	104	3	.212	.291	.356
1985	Tex-A	0	6	4	81	5.42	0	2	1	36	7.43	0	4	3	45	3.80	164	4	.323	.408	.524	151	7	.219	.285	.424	148	8	.236	.339	.480	67	3	.254	.354	.418
1985	Phi-N	0	0	0	4	6.23	0	0	0	3	8.10	0	0	0	1	0.00	9	0	.444	.583	.444	9	0	.111	.200	.111	7	0	.571	.700	.571	0	0	—	—	—
1986	Phi-N	0	0	0	12	6.57	0	0	0	7	7.36	0	0	0	5	5.40	10	1	.300	.429	.900	39	0	.308	.310	.410	20	0	.300	.320	.400	0	0	—	—	—
1986	Oak-A	9	5	0	149	3.74	5	3	0	85	2.86	4	2	0	64	4.90	284	7	.236	.318	.366	283	8	.247	.324	.368	238	4	.214	.305	.303	52	0	.231	.328	.269
1987	Oak-A	20	13	0	261	3.68	11	6	0	133	2.84	9	7	0	128	4.56	554	13	.233	.314	.357	426	11	.223	.294	.357	385	8	.231	.321	.348	100	4	.240	.330	.400
1988	Oak-A	21	12	0	276	3.23	9	5	0	127	3.25	12	7	0	148	3.22	563	9	.224	.305	.323	464	5	.246	.310	.345	431	7	.239	.315	.343	91	0	.165	.257	.220
1989	Oak-A	21	9	0	258	3.32	11	4	0	133	2.77	10	5	0	124	3.91	522	12	.264	.315	.387	464	11	.263	.310	.403	407	7	.243	.304	.378	90	0	.289	.330	.378
1990	Oak-A	22	11	0	267	2.56	11	4	0	145	1.68	11	7	0	122	3.61	478	9	.253	.303	.345	502	8	.253	.280	.345	403	9	.228	.280	.340	99	2	.232	.294	.323
1991	Oak-A	11	11	0	226	5.18	8	3	0	115	4.21	3	8	0	111	6.18	444	8	.302	.361	.428	436	16	.255	.350	.429	380	11	.295	.373	.458	45	1	.311	.475	.378
1992	Oak-A	12	10	0	199	3.66	5	5	0	101	3.73	7	5	0	98	3.58	340	11	.262	.351	.415	397	14	.217	.282	.375	283	9	.272	.333	.439	69	4	.304	.395	.507
1993	Tor-A	12	8	0	162	4.44	6	4	0	85	4.01	6	4	0	77	4.93	266	8	.248	.336	.414	338	15	.237	.316	.423	248	10	.254	.325	.427	24	2	.250	.240	.500
1994	Tor-A	7	8	0	133	5.87	4	3	0	78	4.38	3	5	0	55	7.97	250	12	.284	.378	.484	280	14	.286	.346	.500	235	9	.332	.406	.498	30	0	.133	.235	.167
TOTALS		142	107	4	2222	3.97	72	48	1	1172	3.49	70	59	3	1050	4.49	4278	108	.254	.331	.388	4142	122	.246	.313	.393	3481	89	.256	.331	.391	771	19	.239	.324	.355

● **Dave Stieb** BR/TR

		TOTAL					HOME					AWAY					LEFT					RIGHT					ON-BASE					LATE/CLOSE				
YEAR	TM/L	W	L	SV	IP	ERA	W	L	SV	IP	ERA	W	L	SV	IP	ERA	AB	HR	AVG	OBP	SLG	AB	HR	AVG	OBP	SLG	AB	HR	AVG	OBP	SLG	AB	HR	AVG	OBP	SLG
1984	Tor-A	16	8	0	267	2.83	9	4	0	116	2.71	7	4	0	151	2.93	511	11	.225	.290	.335	461	8	.217	.294	.328	400	5	.203	.261	.283	164	6	.268	.315	.421
1985	Tor-A	14	13	0	265	2.48	8	6	0	112	2.96	6	7	0	153	2.12	560	10	.198	.281	.286	406	12	.234	.302	.367	389	5	.229	.294	.306	123	2	.293	.383	.415
1986	Tor-A	7	12	1	205	4.74	5	5	0	131	3.93	2	7	1	74	6.17	416	17	.329	.410	.546	389	12	.262	.333	.401	356	13	.317	.385	.475	40	4	.450	.511	.875
1987	Tor-A	13	9	0	185	4.09	5	4	0	78	4.98	8	5	0	107	3.44	364	10	.242	.338	.390	321	6	.237	.319	.361	280	4	.271	.355	.386	36	0	.056	.105	.056
1988	Tor-A	16	8	0	207	3.04	12	5	0	127	2.70	4	3	0	81	3.57	400	8	.218	.293	.315	348	7	.201	.298	.316	292	4	.229	.298	.308	45	0	.267	.340	.378
1989	Tor-A	17	8	0	207	3.35	7	4	0	94	3.34	10	4	0	112	3.36	387	7	.248	.319	.346	361	5	.188	.283	.293	311	4	.260	.317	.354	38	0	.211	.302	.289
1990	Tor-A	18	6	0	209	2.93	9	5	0	103	3.15	9	1	0	106	2.73	403	8	.253	.326	.357	375	3	.205	.263	.280	298	2	.255	.316	.329	72	0	.194	.266	.250
1991	Tor-A	4	3	0	60	3.17	1	2	0	18	5.50	3	1	0	42	2.16	117	2	.239	.334	.333	94	2	.247	.324	.361	96	3	.229	.286	.365	15	0	.133	.278	.133
1992	Tor-A	4	6	0	96	5.04	2	4	0	57	5.53	2	2	0	39	4.35	172	4	.279	.354	.419	185	5	.270	.355	.422	159	4	.289	.348	.453	22	2	.227	.346	.500
1993	Chi-A	1	3	0	22	6.04	1	2	0	16	6.06	0	1	0	6	6.00	45	0	.222	.357	.244	45	1	.378	.429	.489	44	0	.364	.453	.432	0	0	—	—	—
TOTALS		110	76	1	1723	3.42	59	41	0	852	3.57	51	35	1	871	3.27	3375	77	.244	.322	.363	2988	61	.227	.305	.343	2625	44	.254	.320	.358	555	14	.254	.327	.389

● **Tim Stoddard** BR/TR

		TOTAL					HOME					AWAY					LEFT					RIGHT					ON-BASE					LATE/CLOSE				
YEAR	TM/L	W	L	SV	IP	ERA	W	L	SV	IP	ERA	W	L	SV	IP	ERA	AB	HR	AVG	OBP	SLG	AB	HR	AVG	OBP	SLG	AB	HR	AVG	OBP	SLG	AB	HR	AVG	OBP	SLG
1984	Chi-N	10	6	7	92	3.82	8	3	3	44	4.70	2	3	4	48	3.00	173	6	.231	.328	.445	153	7	.242	.306	.340	158	2	.222	.352	.342	172	4	.215	.332	.360
1985	SD-N	1	6	1	60	4.65	1	3	0	29	2.48	0	3	1	31	6.68	98	1	.286	.395	.367	136	2	.257	.344	.390	120	3	.267	.379	.408	64	1	.391	.474	.531
1986	SD-N	1	3	0	45	3.77	1	1	0	26	3.16	0	2	0	20	4.58	51	2	.176	.408	.392	114	4	.211	.297	.342	77	2	.234	.398	.390	32	3	.156	.289	.438
1986	NY-A	4	1	0	49	3.83	3	0	0	23	2.80	1	1	0	26	4.18	65	1	.308	.387	.385	112	5	.188	.276	.357	90	3	.211	.294	.344	37	1	.270	.333	.378
1987	NY-A	4	3	8	93	3.50	3	1	4	53	2.91	1	2	4	40	4.28	145	6	.276	.340	.447	208	7	.260	.320	.404	152	5	.230	.302	.375	124	4	.234	.292	.363
1988	NY-A	2	2	0	55	6.38	1	2	1	28	4.76	1	0	0	27	8.10	84	2	.238	.343	.381	133	3	.316	.373	.451	97	2	.309	.407	.443	46	0	.217	.260	.283
1989	Cle-A	0	0	0	2	2.95	0	0	0	9	5.19	0	0	0	13	1.42	26	0	.269	.286	.269	54	1	.333	.387	.519	38	0	.342	.364	.447	3	0	.333	.333	.333
TOTALS		22	21	19	416	4.16	16	10	9	216	3.74	6	11	10	199	4.61	642	18	.255	.355	.434	910	25	.240	.322	.379	732	17	.249	.353	.384	478	13	.245	.332	.383

		TOTAL					HOME					AWAY					LEFT					RIGHT					ON-BASE					LATE/CLOSE				
YEAR	TM/L	W	L	SV	IP	ERA	W	L	SV	IP	ERA	W	L	SV	IP	ERA	AB	HR	AVG	OBP	SLG	AB	HR	AVG	OBP	SLG	AB	HR	AVG	OBP	SLG	AB	HR	AVG	OBP	SLG

● Todd Stottlemyre BL/TR

YEAR	TM/L	W	L	SV	IP	ERA	W	L	SV	IP	ERA	W	L	SV	IP	ERA	AB	HR	AVG	OBP	SLG	AB	HR	AVG	OBP	SLG	AB	HR	AVG	OBP	SLG	AB	HR	AVG	OBP	SLG
1988	Tor-A	4	8	0	98	5.69	1	4	0	39	7.22	3	4	0	59	4.70	198	7	.369	.442	.551	187	8	.193	.280	.353	174	6	.287	.386	.454	26	0	.269	.321	.385
1989	Tor-A	7	7	0	128	3.88	4	3	0	79	3.53	3	4	0	49	4.44	223	7	.314	.362	.480	263	4	.255	.328	.376	219	4	.228	.282	.329	43	0	.372	.449	.465
1990	Tor-A	13	17	0	203	4.34	7	8	0	103	4.28	6	9	0	100	4.41	393	8	.300	.365	.443	388	10	.247	.309	.376	321	11	.280	.353	.452	35	0	.143	.211	.143
1991	Tor-A	15	8	0	219	3.78	9	3	0	116	3.96	6	5	0	103	3.58	422	11	.242	.310	.355	404	10	.228	.300	.356	339	12	.242	.301	.395	58	1	.293	.339	.414
1992	Tor-A	12	11	0	174	4.50	7	5	0	83	4.79	5	6	0	91	4.24	284	6	.282	.355	.394	385	14	.247	.310	.400	275	10	.295	.371	.447	43	1	.209	.261	.302
1993	Tor-A	11	12	0	177	4.84	6	5	0	93	4.18	5	7	0	84	5.57	374	7	.305	.375	.452	324	4	.278	.328	.392	337	6	.285	.351	.407	25	0	.200	.259	.240
1994	Tor-A	7	7	1	141	4.22	4	3	1	68	3.82	3	4	0	72	4.60	274	10	.288	.356	.464	266	9	.263	.323	.451	212	7	.283	.369	.439	57	1	.351	.449	.509
TOTALS		69	70	1	1139	4.39	38	31	1	580	4.31	31	39	0	559	4.46	2168	56	.293	.361	.450	2217	59	.246	.312	.386	1877	56	.271	.343	.417	287	3	.275	.345	.373

● Rick Sutcliffe BL/TR

YEAR	TM/L	W	L	SV	IP	ERA	W	L	SV	IP	ERA	W	L	SV	IP	ERA	AB	HR	AVG	OBP	SLG	AB	HR	AVG	OBP	SLG	AB	HR	AVG	OBP	SLG	AB	HR	AVG	OBP	SLG
1984	Cle-A	4	5	0	94	5.15	2	2	0	41	4.43	2	3	0	54	5.70	203	4	.300	.372	.453	170	3	.294	.378	.406	172	4	.314	.389	.471	24	0	.292	.370	.458
1984	Chi-N	16	1	0	150	2.69	8	0	0	68	2.77	8	1	0	82	2.63	304	3	.217	.289	.316	256	6	.223	.286	.367	207	4	.237	.300	.372	60	1	.267	.302	.383
1985	Chi-N	8	8	0	130	3.18	4	2	0	55	3.44	4	6	0	75	3.00	244	5	.270	.331	.410	251	7	.211	.279	.319	194	5	.237	.321	.356	58	2	.241	.254	.379
1986	Chi-N	5	14	0	177	4.64	3	6	0	99	4.35	2	8	0	77	5.00	372	8	.245	.339	.368	287	10	.261	.357	.425	267	10	.266	.381	.431	61	1	.262	.370	.393
1987	Chi-N	18	10	0	237	3.68	10	5	0	124	3.49	8	5	0	114	3.88	503	13	.260	.355	.417	381	11	.241	.301	.381	340	7	.265	.361	.403	73	1	.288	.404	.425
1988	Chi-N	13	14	0	226	3.86	5	10	0	102	3.19	8	9	0	124	4.42	456	7	.263	.329	.371	408	11	.275	.317	.407	330	5	.288	.368	.397	107	1	.252	.316	.327
1989	Chi-N	16	11	0	229	3.66	5	7	0	99	4.80	11	4	0	130	2.78	503	11	.245	.305	.362	339	7	.233	.283	.342	309	6	.243	.311	.353	53	2	.340	.345	.491
1990	Chi-N	0	2	0	21	5.91	0	1	0	10	9.58	0	1	0	11	2.45	47	0	.298	.414	.362	35	2	.314	.342	.543	38	0	.316	.404	.421	1	0	1.000	1.000	1.000
1991	Chi-N	6	5	0	97	4.10	3	1	0	57	3.18	3	4	0	40	5.40	218	4	.289	.366	.436	146	0	.226	.294	.295	158	1	.266	.340	.361	7	0	.286	.375	.429
1992	Bal-N	16	15	0	237	4.47	9	8	0	132	4.17	7	7	0	106	4.85	431	13	.265	.320	.418	489	7	.280	.335	.372	404	10	.255	.305	.381	101	2	.248	.291	.337
1993	Bal-A	10	10	0	166	5.75	6	6	0	100	4.50	4	4	0	66	7.64	338	12	.320	.382	.512	306	14	.327	.399	.546						33	1	.303	.361	.394
1994	StL-N	6	4	0	38	6.52						3	2	0	30	5.76	127	6	.354	.431	.583	154	5	.312	.378	.487	113	5	.381	.474	.602	7	0	.143	.333	.143
TOTALS		118	99	0	1833	4.19	58	45	0	925	4.08	60	54	0	908	4.31	3746	85	.266	.339	.404	3254	81	.263	.325	.395	2838	71	.275	.354	.416	585	11	.270	.332	.383

● Don Sutton BR/TR

YEAR	TM/L	W	L	SV	IP	ERA	W	L	SV	IP	ERA	W	L	SV	IP	ERA	AB	HR	AVG	OBP	SLG	AB	HR	AVG	OBP	SLG	AB	HR	AVG	OBP	SLG	AB	HR	AVG	OBP	SLG
1984	Mil-A	14	12	0	213	3.77	7	9	0	126	4.00	7	3	0	87	3.43	441	12	.283	.331	.420	402	12	.246	.278	.376	336	13	.280	.325	.432	51	4	.373	.396	.686
1985	Oak-A	13	8	0	194	3.89	7	2	0	101	3.20	6	6	0	93	4.65	384	11	.242	.288	.367	375	8	.269	.313	.384	296	6	.274	.321	.385	55	1	.309	.321	.382
1985	Cal-A	2	2	0	32	3.69	1	1	0	13	4.15	1	1	0	19	3.38	58	2	.259	.328	.414	58	4	.207	.233	.483	38	2	.158	.158	.316	4	0	.250	.250	.500
1986	Cal-A	15	11	0	207	3.74	10	6	0	128	3.23	5	5	0	79	4.58	407	11	.224	.260	.293	388	20	.260	.293	.479	275	17	.291	.322	.524	42	3	.238	.304	.476
1987	Cal-A	11	11	0	192	4.70	6	6	0	95	4.28	5	5	0	97	5.10	369	16	.233	.286	.398	371	22	.305	.338	.518	275	17	.291	.322	.524	29	3	.207	.207	.552
1988	LA-N	3	6	0	87	3.92	2	3	0	41	3.27	1	3	0	46	4.50	172	4	.291	.367	.401	165	3	.248	.282	.345	149	3	.228	.298	.315	0	0	—	—	—
TOTALS		58	50	0	925	3.99	30	27	0	505	3.64	28	23	0	420	4.41	1831	56	.251	.306	.386	1759	69	.265	.300	.431	1361	50	.270	.315	.425	181	11	.293	.319	.519

● Bill Swift BR/TR

YEAR	TM/L	W	L	SV	IP	ERA	W	L	SV	IP	ERA	W	L	SV	IP	ERA	AB	HR	AVG	OBP	SLG	AB	HR	AVG	OBP	SLG	AB	HR	AVG	OBP	SLG	AB	HR	AVG	OBP	SLG
1985	Sea-A	6	10	0	121	4.77	2	6	0	60	5.67	4	4	0	60	3.88	260	7	.308	.383	.485	210	1	.243	.307	.290	198	2	.278	.376	.374	38	1	.237	.326	.368
1986	Sea-A	2	9	0	115	5.46	2	3	0	62	4.23	0	6	0	54	6.88	255	2	.384	.463	.486	209	3	.239	.313	.330	228	3	.333	.399	.439	42	1	.310	.370	.429
1988	Sea-A	8	12	0	175	4.59	5	4	0	92	3.53	3	8	0	83	5.75	332	5	.307	.371	.410	343	5	.283	.353	.376	306	5	.327	.392	.448	50	2	.220	.278	.360
1989	Sea-A	7	3	1	130	4.43	3	2	0	73	4.93	4	1	1	57	3.79	231	3	.316	.368	.411	273	4	.245	.296	.337	233	5	.305	.350	.438	37	1	.162	.244	.270
1990	Sea-A	6	4	6	128	2.39	3	1	2	54	1.34	3	3	4	74	3.15	216	4	.287	.317	.398	280	0	.261	.302	.314	229	2	.288	.332	.376	129	2	.279	.350	.349
1991	Sea-A	1	2	17	90	1.99	1	2	7	44	1.65	0	0	10	47	2.31	123	1	.236	.288	.276	207	2	.217	.280	.275	173	1	.197	.257	.225	169	1	.254	.304	.302
1992	SF-N	10	4	1	165	2.08	4	3	1	85	2.55	6	1	0	80	1.58	384	5	.263	.331	.359	218	1	.197	.219	.234	241	4	.224	.270	.308	69	2	.232	.254	.333
1993	SF-N	21	8	0	233	2.82	11	4	0	111	2.35	10	4	0	122	3.25	470	12	.268	.331	.387	391	6	.176	.208	.253	327	5	.226	.280	.324	74	1	.216	.247	.311
1994	SF-N	8	7	0	109	3.38	3	2	0	45	5.32	5	5	0	64	1.98	228	5	.268	.324	.382	188	5	.255	.300	.351	160	1	.287	.345	.356	40	1	.225	.244	.325
TOTALS		69	59	25	1266	3.51	36	27	10	643	3.16	33	32	15	622	3.86	2499	44	.293	.356	.403	2319	27	.236	.286	.307	2095	28	.275	.335	.372	648	12	.245	.298	.332

● Greg Swindell BR/TL

YEAR	TM/L	W	L	SV	IP	ERA	W	L	SV	IP	ERA	W	L	SV	IP	ERA	AB	HR	AVG	OBP	SLG	AB	HR	AVG	OBP	SLG	AB	HR	AVG	OBP	SLG	AB	HR	AVG	OBP	SLG
1986	Cle-A	5	2	0	62	4.23	3	1	0	33	4.09	2	1	0	29	4.40	26	0	.154	.185	.192	209	9	.254	.302	.416	84	3	.262	.315	.393	26	1	.308	.333	.423
1987	Cle-A	3	8	0	102	5.10	2	3	0	47	3.80	1	5	0	55	6.22	68	4	.309	.333	.574	328	14	.277	.345	.445	161	9	.304	.358	.540	54	2	.315	.403	.481
1988	Cle-A	18	14	0	242	3.20	9	5	0	113	2.88	9	9	0	129	3.48	164	3	.274	.301	.372	764	15	.247	.283	.361	343	8	.274	.312	.411	116	2	.319	.336	.457
1989	Cle-A	13	6	0	184	3.37	6	4	0	94	3.34	7	2	0	90	3.40	109	1	.220	.265	.284	581	15	.251	.303	.384	251	4	.247	.306	.347	69	0	.232	.274	.290
1990	Cle-A	12	9	0	215	4.40	7	4	0	114	4.67	5	5	0	101	4.10	106	4	.286	.318	.421	724	23	.289	.325	.456	338	7	.324	.353	.466	59	2	.288	.382	.475
1991	Cle-A	9	16	0	238	3.48	7	9	0	153	2.52	2	7	0	85	5.21	153	1	.275	.309	.373	763	20	.261	.283	.397	338	13	.290	.317	.476	139	1	.252	.271	.331
1992	Cin-N	12	8	0	214	2.70	7	2	0	109	2.31	5	6	0	105	3.10	168	2	.244	.285	.345	640	12	.264	.297	.370	302	4	.228	.264	.301	65	3	.292	.329	.462
1993	Hou-N	12	13	0	190	4.16	3	9	0	83	4.90	9	4	0	108	3.59	127	3	.315	.353	.520	634	21	.276	.311	.442	316	12	.285	.324	.465	49	0	.327	.340	.388
1994	Hou-N	8	9	0	148	4.37	5	4	0	76	3.30	3	5	0	72	5.50	100	2	.350	.398	.470	480	18	.292	.314	.467	231	8	.273	.306	.424	39	2	.256	.293	.436
TOTALS		92	85	0	1595	3.74	49	41	0	822	3.38	43	44	0	773	4.12	1041	20	.277	.313	.401	5123	147	.268	.304	.411	2362	68	.278	.316	.421	616	13	.284	.323	.406

● Frank Tanana BL/TL

YEAR	TM/L	W	L	SV	IP	ERA	W	L	SV	IP	ERA	W	L	SV	IP	ERA	AB	HR	AVG	OBP	SLG	AB	HR	AVG	OBP	SLG	AB	HR	AVG	OBP	SLG	AB	HR	AVG	OBP	SLG
1984	Tex-A	15	15	0	246	3.25	6	8	0	113	3.75	9	7	0	134	2.83	172	3	.267	.337	.401	784	27	.240	.300	.395	376	11	.263	.325	.410	37	4	.324	.405	.703
1985	Tex-A	2	7	0	78	5.91	2	4	0	44	6.70	0	3	0	33	4.86	67	5	.313	.324	.657	243	10	.280	.337	.461	120	7	.342	.394	.600	22	3	.318	.375	.682
1985	Det-A	10	7	0	137	3.34	6	4	0	65	3.58	4	3	0	72	3.13	83	2	.157	.195	.277	441	11	.268	.314	.408	183	2	.240	.322	.355	38	1	.289	.349	.395
1986	Det-A	12	9	0	188	4.16	8	6	0	112	3.87	4	3	0	77	4.58	123	2	.317	.354	.447	608	21	.253	.323	.428	290	10	.248	.330	.403	64	0	.250	.333	.313
1987	Det-A	15	10	0	219	3.91	10	5	0	109	3.06	5	5	0	110	4.76	140	2	.236	.296	.364	704	23	.260	.304	.419	332	6	.268	.315	.367	75	0	.253	.269	.320
1988	Det-A	14	11	0	203	4.21	7	5	0	108	4.08	7	6	0	95	4.36	119	2	.210	.248	.286	680	23	.276	.336	.440	310	12	.300	.375	.474	83	4	.241	.337	.470
1989	Det-A	10	14	0	224	3.58	4	6	0	119	3.48	6	8	0	105	3.70	125	2	.304	.374	.400	791	13	.259	.318	.376	352	10	.253	.319	.369	76	3	.276	.353	.461
1990	Det-A	9	8	1	176	5.31	4	6	0	99	6.00	5	2	1	77	4.42	113	1	.230	.290	.292	565	24	.290	.360	.485	263	11	.297	.387	.483	62	2	.200	.329	.333
1991	Det-A	13	12	0	217	3.77	7	5	0	121	4.10	6	7	0	97	3.35	159	5	.233	.282	.371	659	21	.273	.338	.422	332	6	.235	.308	.337	38	0	.395	.479	.421
1992	Det-A	13	11	0	187	4.39	7	5	0	78	4.98	6	6	0	109	3.96	102	2	.225	.282	.333	602	20	.274	.362	.429	303	7	.264	.342	.396	46	2	.217	.368	.457
1993	NY-N	7	15	0	183	4.48	3	7	0	86	4.71	4	8	0	97	4.27	148	4	.250	.300	.378	563	22	.286	.338	.469	262	10	.279	.365	.447	42	1	.357	.386	.476
1993	NY-A	0	2	0	20	3.20	0	1	0	13	4.05	0	1	0	6	1.42	11	0	.182	.182	.273	70	2	.229	.299	.371	30	1	.267	.353	.400	5	1	.600	.600	1.200
TOTALS		120	121	1	2078	4.08	64	62	0	1067	4.23	56	59	1	1011	3.92	1362	32	.250	.301	.375	6650	223	.267	.328	.426	3153	93	.268	.340	.411	586	20	.275	.354	.439

● Kevin Tapani BR/TR

YEAR	TM/L	W	L	SV	IP	ERA	W	L	SV	IP	ERA	W	L	SV	IP	ERA	AB	HR	AVG	OBP	SLG	AB	HR	AVG	OBP	SLG	AB	HR	AVG	OBP	SLG	AB	HR	AVG	OBP	SLG
1989	NY-N	0	0	0	7	3.68	0	0	0	1	9.00	0	0	0	6	2.84	9	1	.333	.500	.889	17	0	.118	.158	.118	12	0	.167	.214	.333	0	0	—	—	—
1989	Min-A	2	2	0	33	3.86	1	2	0	17	5.71	1	0	0	15	1.76	81	1	.284	.326	.395	47	1	.234	.275	.319	42	1	.333	.408	.476	18	0	.389	.421	.389
1990	Min-A	12	8	0	159	4.07	8	2	0	75	3.38	4	6	0	85	4.68	317	6	.284	.328	.435	304	6	.243	.263	.349	218	5	.321	.359	.454	37	0	.324	.342	.432
1991	Min-A	16	9	0	244	2.99	10	5	0	132	2.79	6	4	0	112	3.22	520	8	.235	.257	.342	397	15	.259	.302	.433	335	5	.224	.251	.316	74	2	.257	.300	.378
1992	Min-A	16	11	0	220	3.97	11	4	0	127	3.48	5	7	0	93	4.63	434	12	.279	.313	.452	405	5	.259	.304	.356	325	4	.277	.305	.403	65	2	.200	.288	.369
1993	Min-A	12	15	0	226	4.43	3	9	0	98	4.39	9	6	0	127	4.45	525	12	.280	.320	.432	368	9	.261	.317	.399	370	7	.276	.323	.424	72	1	.264	.321	.389
1994	Min-A	11	7	0	156	4.62	8	3	0	95	3.33	3	4	0	61	6.60	325	5	.271	.311	.400	296	8	.314	.361	.486	261	6	.307	.356	.464	68	1	.294	.360	.412
TOTALS		69	52	0	1045	3.94	41	25	0	545	3.52	28	27	0	500	4.41	2211	45	.269	.305	.411	1834	44	.264	.307	.398	1563	28	.277	.316	.408	334	6	.269	.325	.392

● Kent Tekulve BR/TR

YEAR	TM/L	W	L	SV	IP	ERA	W	L	SV	IP	ERA	W	L	SV	IP	ERA	AB	HR	AVG	OBP	SLG	AB	HR	AVG	OBP	SLG	AB	HR	AVG	OBP	SLG	AB	HR	AVG	OBP	SLG
1984	Pit-N	3	9	13	88	2.66	1	5	6	51	3.00	2	4	7	37	2.19	113	1	.292	.400	.398	215	3	.247	.288	.350	162	3	.265	.363	.352	208	4	.293	.370	.428
1985	Pit-N	0	0	0	3	16.20	0	0	0	3	18.00	0	0	0	0	—	9	0	.444	.583	.556	6	1	.500	.625	1.167	12	1	.333	.500	.667	0	0	—	—	—
1985	Phi-N	4	10	14	72	2.99	3	4	5	36	2.97	1	6	9	36	3.00	119	2	.286	.346	.387	153	2	.216	.287	.294	125	2	.240	.331	.352	190	6	.274	.347	.384
1986	Phi-N	11	5	4	110	2.54	6	2	2	54	2.35	5	3	2	56	2.72	197	1	.254	.302	.305	216	1	.257	.261	.296	183	0	.230	.296	.262	190	2	.274	.329	.368
1987	Phi-N	6	4	3	105	3.09	2	2	2	57	3.47	4	2	1	48	2.63	166	5	.307	.375	.464	229	3	.197	.230	.266	179	3	.212	.284	.302	205	5	.210	.256	.310
1988	Phi-N	3	7	4	80	3.60	3	2	2	43	4.15	0	5	2	37	2.94	151	1	.225	.298	.278	164	2	.323	.353	.445	169	1	.249	.332	.325	183	5	.290	.328	.377
1989	Cin-N	0	3	1	52	5.02	0	2	0	30	5.76	0	1	1	22	4.03	105	4	.362	.442	.543	101	1	.178	.234	.248	99	3	.333	.398	.465	47	0	.340	.404	.383
TOTALS		27	38	39	511	3.24	15	17	17	274	3.61	12	21	22	237	2.81	860	14	.286	.356	.386	1084	13	.234	.277	.320	929	13	.250	.331	.354	1018	17	.271	.330	.374

● Walt Terrell BL/TR

YEAR	TM/L	W	L	SV	IP	ERA	W	L	SV	IP	ERA	W	L	SV	IP	ERA	AB	HR	AVG	OBP	SLG	AB	HR	AVG	OBP	SLG	AB	HR	AVG	OBP	SLG	AB	HR	AVG	OBP	SLG
1984	NY-N	11	12	0	215	3.52	3	7	0	102	4.15	8	5	0	113	2.95	392	4	.268	.336	.347	431	12	.295	.354	.425	366	6	.281	.339	.383	60	1	.317	.388	.500
1985	Det-A	15	10	0	229	3.85	9	2	0	120	2.86	6	8	0	109	4.94	500	2	.267	.357	.388	393	7	.267	.357	.388	358	7	.283	.333	.357	83	3	.313	.387	.446
1986	Det-A	15	12	0	217	4.56	10	3	0	116	3.35	5	9	0	102	5.93	422	11	.242	.324	.389	390	19	.249	.331	.444	338	10	.275	.346	.444	81	3	.198	.278	.346
1987	Det-A	17	10	0	245	4.05	13	2	0	138	2.47	4	8	0	106	6.09	475	15	.257	.326	.419	472	15	.280	.340	.430	386	11	.256	.331	.415	107	5	.299	.358	.495
1988	Det-A	7	16	0	206	3.97	4	5	0	84	3.76	3	11	0	121	4.11	410	8	.260	.333	.401	503	15	.260	.333	.401	266	3	.269	.340	.377	112	6	.277	.331	.473
1989	SD-N	5	13	0	123	4.01	2	6	0	71	3.78	3	7	0	52	4.38	234	5	.291	.334	.398	240	9	.262	.294	.463	190	6	.305	.320	.447	29	1	.304	.304	.571
1989	NY-A	6	5	0	83	5.20	2	3	0	31	6.32	4	2	0	52	4.53	171	4	.333	.392	.556	161	2	.280	.316	.379	154	2	.292	.319	.390	20	2	.350	.350	.750
1990	Pit-N	2	7	0	83	5.88	2	0	0	38	5.68	0	5	0	45	6.04	189	11	.320	.408	.582	162	7	.252	.308	.371	147	6	.299	.379	.524	17	1	.294	.400	.529
1990	Det-A	6	4	0	75	4.54	4	2	0	41	3.54	2	2	0	34	5.64	153	5	.314	.380	.471	144	2	.264	.346	.368	131	4	.290	.361	.435	20	0	.182	.250	.227
1991	Det-A	12	14	0	219	4.24	9	7	0	112	4.84	3	7	0	107	3.62	461	9	.306	.371	.440	392	7	.296	.343	.423	366	6	.303	.376	.402	76	1	.303	.349	.408

YEAR	TM/L	TOTAL W	L	SV	IP	ERA	HOME W	L	SV	IP	ERA	AWAY W	L	SV	IP	ERA	LEFT AB	HR	AVG	OBP	SLG	RIGHT AB	HR	AVG	OBP	SLG	ON-BASE AB	HR	AVG	OBP	SLG	LATE/CLOSE AB	HR	AVG	OBP	SLG
1992	Det-A	7	10	0	137	5.20	4	3	0	62	4.76	3	7	0	74	5.57	235	3	.285	.342	.387	312	11	.308	.362	.465	241	7	.365	.420	.515	71	3	.282	.338	.451
TOTALS		103	113	0	1832	4.27	61	42	0	896	3.80	42	71	0	936	4.73	3657	81	.275	.340	.405	3406	97	.276	.339	.421	3013	67	.288	.350	.416	705	29	.284	.341	.461

● **Scott Terry** BR/TR

YEAR	TM/L	W	L	SV	IP	ERA	W	L	SV	IP	ERA	W	L	SV	IP	ERA	AB	HR	AVG	OBP	SLG	AB	HR	AVG	OBP	SLG	AB	HR	AVG	OBP	SLG	AB	HR	AVG	OBP	SLG
1986	Cin-N	1	2	0	56	6.14	1	1	0	31	4.88	0	1	0	24	7.77	108	3	.343	.410	.500	112	5	.259	.366	.411	111	7	.333	.409	.577	27	0	.296	.375	.333
1987	StL-N	0	0	0	13	3.38	0	0	0	5	1.80	0	0	0	8	4.32	19	0	.368	.500	.474	31	0	.194	.265	.226	30	0	.200	.294	.200	14	0	.286	.444	.286
1988	StL-N	9	6	3	129	2.92	5	3	1	73	3.10	4	3	2	57	2.70	231	4	.251	.298	.355	250	1	.244	.293	.328	191	3	.314	.359	.429	110	2	.255	.331	.355
1989	StL-N	8	10	2	149	3.57	6	4	1	88	3.08	2	6	1	61	4.28	280	6	.261	.331	.400	281	8	.246	.283	.409	226	8	.257	.312	.425	54	1	.241	.293	.333
1990	StL-N	2	6	2	72	4.75	1	3	1	36	4.04	1	3	1	36	5.45	127	4	.260	.336	.433	157	3	.268	.328	.401	129	5	.341	.408	.543	43	1	.302	.377	.442
1991	StL-N	4	4	1	80	2.80	4	1	0	45	1.19	0	3	1	35	4.89	171	1	.240	.330	.304	134	0	.261	.308	.313	145	1	.234	.339	.303	132	1	.265	.336	.333
TOTALS		24	28	8	499	3.73	17	12	3	278	3.08	7	16	5	222	4.55	936	18	.266	.337	.389	965	17	.251	.306	.368	832	24	.287	.355	.435	380	5	.266	.341	.350

● **Bob Tewksbury** BR/TR

YEAR	TM/L	W	L	SV	IP	ERA	W	L	SV	IP	ERA	W	L	SV	IP	ERA	AB	HR	AVG	OBP	SLG	AB	HR	AVG	OBP	SLG	AB	HR	AVG	OBP	SLG	AB	HR	AVG	OBP	SLG
1986	NY-A	9	5	0	130	3.31	4	1	0	60	2.56	5	4	0	71	3.95	266	6	.252	.286	.380	245	2	.314	.365	.416	218	2	.280	.322	.349	34	0	.265	.297	.353
1987	NY-A	1	4	0	33	6.75	1	2	0	21	5.48	0	2	0	12	9.00	66	0	.348	.386	.394	73	5	.329	.364	.562	54	3	.407	.448	.630	7	2	.429	.500	1.286
1987	Chi-N	0	4	0	18	6.50	0	1	0	5	5.40	0	3	0	13	6.92	43	1	.395	.458	.581	33	0	.455	.548	.485	42	0	.429	.500	.476	8	0	.750	.800	.875
1988	Chi-N	1	2	0	25	5.84	1	2	0	21	5.48	0	0	0	3	8.10	7	1	.714	.750	1.143	8	0	.125	.200	.125	7	0	.286	.333	.286	0	0	—		—
1989	StL-N	1	0	0	30	3.30	0	0	0	19	3.32	1	0	0	11	3.27	55	1	.255	.333	.345	56	1	.196	.262	.321	43	1	.233	.320	.372	4	1	.250	.500	1.000
1990	StL-N	10	9	1	145	3.47	4	5	0	66	3.66	6	4	1	79	3.30	334	4	.278	.302	.383	231	3	.251	.263	.372	209	4	.321	.338	.450	24	0	.167	.167	.250
1991	StL-N	11	12	0	191	3.25	6	3	0	94	3.24	5	9	0	97	3.26	406	4	.278	.326	.392	327	9	.284	.305	.440	291	5	.271	.313	.399	43	1	.233	.313	.372
1992	StL-N	16	5	0	233	2.16	10	2	0	124	1.52	6	3	0	109	2.90	517	10	.242	.250	.344	359	5	.256	.286	.365	309	4	.223	.235	.298	81	2	.210	.229	.321
1993	StL-N	17	10	0	214	3.83	11	7	0	132	3.35	6	3	0	82	4.61	426	9	.289	.311	.406	361	4	.288	.311	.402	361	6	.313	.338	.391	64	0	.313	.338	.391
1994	StL-N	12	10	0	156	5.32	4	6	0	66	6.00	8	6	0	90	4.82	329	8	.295	.316	.450	297	11	.313	.342	.515	248	9	.367	.390	.569	50	1	.180	.180	.260
TOTALS		77	59	1	1154	3.62	40	25	0	588	3.29	37	34	1	566	3.96	2454	41	.281	.307	.396	2055	45	.286	.316	.421	1782	32	.293	.323	.413	315	7	.251	.287	.375

● **Bobby Thigpen** BR/TR

YEAR	TM/L	W	L	SV	IP	ERA	W	L	SV	IP	ERA	W	L	SV	IP	ERA	AB	HR	AVG	OBP	SLG	AB	HR	AVG	OBP	SLG	AB	HR	AVG	OBP	SLG	AB	HR	AVG	OBP	SLG
1986	Chi-A	2	0	7	36	1.77	1	0	5	17	1.08	1	0	2	19	2.37	53	0	.170	.254	.189	74	1	.230	.293	.324	62	0	.226	.310	.258	83	1	.205	.230	.301
1987	Chi-A	7	5	16	89	2.73	4	2	10	55	2.78	3	3	6	34	2.65	177	4	.277	.340	.367	159	6	.233	.278	.377	158	4	.228	.307	.323	210	6	.238	.295	.348
1988	Chi-A	5	8	34	90	3.30	5	4	15	55	3.27	0	4	19	35	3.34	165	1	.315	.384	.345	187	5	.235	.294	.337	203	3	.261	.332	.320	275	3	.265	.337	.316
1989	Chi-A	2	6	34	79	3.76	1	2	18	40	3.60	1	4	16	39	3.92	136	5	.191	.311	.338	149	5	.242	.311	.396	162	7	.204	.256	.377	206	7	.214	.303	.359
1990	Chi-A	4	6	57	89	1.83	3	3	27	46	1.94	1	3	30	42	1.70	158	3	.215	.294	.310	149	2	.174	.247	.255	146	4	.185	.233	.274	253	5	.186	.269	.277
1991	Chi-A	7	5	30	70	3.49	5	2	12	33	4.59	2	3	18	36	2.48	124	6	.258	.363	.468	133	4	.233	.333	.353	144	5	.229	.349	.389	189	8	.265	.385	.444
1992	Chi-A	1	3	22	55	4.75	1	2	9	29	3.77	0	1	13	26	5.81	80	1	.338	.429	.400	131	6	.237	.340	.359	113	2	.301	.415	.407	143	2	.252	.351	.343
1993	Chi-A	0	0	1	35	5.71	0	0	0	14	5.79	0	0	1	21	5.66	71	3	.324	.380	.521	75	2	.373	.437	.507	77	2	.416	.448	.584	3	0	.000	.000	.000
1993	Phi-N	3	1	0	19	6.05	1	1	0	9	8.31	2	0	0	11	4.22	35	1	.343	.442	.543	40	1	.275	.326	.375	33	1	.303	.385	.485	35	0	.257	.341	.286
1994	Sea-A	0	2	0	8	9.39	0	0	0	3	13.50	0	2	0	6	6.23	11	0	.273	.333	.455	23	3	.391	.481	.870	14	2	.286	.444	.786	12	1	.333	.429	.583
TOTALS		31	36	201	569	3.43	21	16	96	301	3.47	10	20	105	268	3.40	1010	24	.241	.349	.374	1120	32	.241	.313	.367	1112	30	.248	.327	.366	1409	33	.234	.317	.340

● **Jay Tibbs** BR/TR

YEAR	TM/L	W	L	SV	IP	ERA	W	L	SV	IP	ERA	W	L	SV	IP	ERA	AB	HR	AVG	OBP	SLG	AB	HR	AVG	OBP	SLG	AB	HR	AVG	OBP	SLG	AB	HR	AVG	OBP	SLG
1984	Cin-N	6	2	0	101	2.86	4	1	0	60	2.55	2	1	0	41	3.32	195	4	.267	.325	.385	170	0	.206	.274	.271	142	0	.239	.299	.296	48	0	.250	.321	.292
1985	Cin-N	10	16	0	218	3.92	5	7	0	108	3.66	5	9	0	110	4.19	431	5	.267	.336	.390	395	9	.256	.315	.362	360	6	.283	.333	.389	49	1	.286	.397	.429
1986	Mon-N	7	9	0	190	3.97	3	6	0	108	3.93	4	3	0	83	4.03	383	4	.274	.338	.379	323	8	.235	.308	.372	273	6	.289	.363	.429	55	0	.218	.306	.218
1987	Mon-N	4	5	0	83	4.99	2	2	0	35	4.11	2	3	0	48	5.63	167	4	.287	.362	.467	162	6	.290	.347	.432	139	5	.317	.381	.489	11	2	.273	.385	.909
1988	Bal-A	4	15	0	159	5.39	4	8	0	104	4.59	0	7	0	55	6.91	334	9	.299	.367	.461	295	9	.285	.344	.431	262	8	.347	.399	.531	42	1	.286	.388	.381
1989	Bal-A	5	0	0	54	2.82	2	0	0	35	3.57	3	0	0	19	1.42	120	1	.283	.356	.350	96	1	.292	.330	.354	96	1	.260	.318	.333	4	0	.500	.600	.500
1990	Bal-A	2	7	0	51	5.68	2	5	0	30	6.37	0	2	0	21	4.71	98	3	.265	.324	.408	99	5	.293	.345	.485	66	3	.348	.392	.545	7	1	.429	.500	.857
1990	Pit-N	1	0	0	7	2.57	0	0	0	0	—	1	0	0	7	2.57	14	0	.286	.286	.286	13	0	.231	.333	.385	14	0	.214	.267	.214	0	0	—		—
TOTALS		39	54	0	863	4.20	20	29	0	480	3.97	19	25	0	383	4.49	1742	30	.278	.344	.405	1553	38	.259	.319	.382	1352	29	.297	.355	.427	216	5	.269	.363	.375

● **John Tudor** BL/TL

YEAR	TM/L	W	L	SV	IP	ERA	W	L	SV	IP	ERA	W	L	SV	IP	ERA	AB	HR	AVG	OBP	SLG	AB	HR	AVG	OBP	SLG	AB	HR	AVG	OBP	SLG	AB	HR	AVG	OBP	SLG
1984	Pit-N	12	11	0	212	3.27	6	5	0	102	2.73	6	6	0	110	3.78	111	3	.243	.287	.351	697	16	.248	.296	.374	301	5	.252	.308	.352	62	1	.403	.457	.484
1985	StL-N	21	8	0	275	1.93	14	2	0	151	1.49	7	6	0	124	2.47	148	2	.203	.244	.264	853	12	.210	.249	.288	326	4	.212	.272	.279	111	2	.225	.259	.315
1986	StL-N	13	7	0	219	2.92	9	2	0	127	2.48	4	5	0	92	3.52	141	1	.191	.223	.277	666	21	.255	.302	.411	269	9	.283	.328	.439	147	4	.245	.296	.374
1987	StL-N	10	2	0	96	3.84	5	1	0	50	2.88	5	1	0	46	4.89	65	2	.246	.310	.446	302	9	.278	.335	.457	142	4	.232	.315	.380	16	0	.375	.444	.563
1988	StL-N	6	5	0	145	2.29	3	2	0	77	2.70	3	3	0	69	1.83	88	4	.273	.305	.500	443	1	.242	.283	.318	196	3	.230	.297	.347	85	1	.271	.319	.365
1988	LA-N	4	3	0	52	2.41	2	2	0	29	3.07	2	1	0	23	1.57	30	1	.300	.300	.433	174	4	.282	.321	.379	78	1	.231	.286	.295	9	0	.333	.333	.333
1989	LA-N	0	0	0	14	3.14	0	0	0	13	1.35	0	0	0	1	27.00	10	0	.200	.273	.200	45	1	.333	.400	.422	23	0	.348	.400	.391	1	0	1.000	1.000	1.000
1990	StL-N	12	4	0	146	2.40	4	1	0	75	2.52	8	3	0	71	2.27	128	1	.211	.241	.273	406	9	.229	.276	.350	185	2	.222	.268	.308	36	0	.250	.357	.278
TOTALS		78	40	0	1160	2.66	43	15	0	625	2.35	35	25	0	535	3.03	721	14	.225	.274	.333	3586	73	.243	.289	.359	1520	28	.241	.299	.346	467	8	.274	.326	.373

● **Fernando Valenzuela** BL/TL

YEAR	TM/L	W	L	SV	IP	ERA	W	L	SV	IP	ERA	W	L	SV	IP	ERA	AB	HR	AVG	OBP	SLG	AB	HR	AVG	OBP	SLG	AB	HR	AVG	OBP	SLG	AB	HR	AVG	OBP	SLG
1984	LA-N	12	17	0	261	3.03	6	8	0	135	2.94	6	9	0	126	3.13	209	5	.244	.305	.354	743	25	.225	.305	.318	365	6	.258	.341	.367	159	2	.208	.301	.283
1985	LA-N	17	10	0	272	2.45	7	5	0	134	2.09	10	5	0	139	2.79	163	3	.233	.291	.344	823	11	.210	.285	.282	387	7	.251	.313	.341	145	1	.166	.241	.207
1986	LA-N	21	11	0	269	3.14	11	3	0	131	2.27	10	8	0	139	3.96	187	0	.246	.286	.321	811	18	.222	.287	.326	400	8	.255	.311	.355	148	1	.291	.331	.351
1987	LA-N	14	14	0	251	3.98	8	7	0	121	3.50	6	7	0	130	4.43	167	4	.228	.283	.377	801	21	.270	.361	.409	479	11	.255	.328	.386	142	1	.218	.302	.296
1988	LA-N	5	8	1	142	4.24	1	5	1	64	5.34	4	3	0	78	3.33	96	3	.313	.391	.448	434	8	.258	.349	.357	240	5	.283	.359	.396	44	1	.318	.464	.455
1989	LA-N	10	13	0	197	3.43	4	6	0	99	3.26	6	7	0	97	3.61	125	1	.256	.324	.352	613	10	.250	.340	.351	311	5	.264	.364	.370	46	1	.370	.408	.522
1990	LA-N	13	13	0	204	4.59	6	5	0	118	3.75	7	8	0	86	5.73	130	4	.315	.381	.454	678	15	.268	.329	.400	368	11	.296	.359	.459	54	0	.259	.333	.296
1991	Cal-A	0	2	0	7	12.15	0	2	0	7	12.15	0	0	0	0	—	6	1	.500	.500	1.000	25	2	.440	.483	.800	13	1	.308	.412	.615	0	0	—		—
1993	Bal-A	8	10	0	179	4.94	5	3	0	88	4.40	3	7	0	91	5.46	120	4	.283	.379	.483	554	14	.262	.335	.417	282	9	.301	.368	.479	34	0	.235	.366	.294
1994	Phi-N	1	2	0	45	3.00	1	0	0	33	2.76	0	2	0	12	3.65	33	1	.212	.206	.333	137	7	.255	.290	.460	51	1	.275	.316	.392	8	0	.250	.333	.375
TOTALS		101	100	1	1827	3.62	49	44	1	899	3.30	52	56	0	899	3.96	1236	26	.259	.321	.383	5619	115	.245	.321	.359	2896	64	.268	.340	.392	780	7	.238	.317	.310

● **Ed Vande Berg** BR/TL

YEAR	TM/L	W	L	SV	IP	ERA	W	L	SV	IP	ERA	W	L	SV	IP	ERA	AB	HR	AVG	OBP	SLG	AB	HR	AVG	OBP	SLG	AB	HR	AVG	OBP	SLG	AB	HR	AVG	OBP	SLG
1984	Sea-A	8	12	7	130	4.76	4	6	4	59	5.19	4	6	3	71	4.42	111	4	.225	.331	.342	415	15	.337	.379	.525	248	8	.327	.390	.484	68	4	.324	.429	.529
1985	Sea-A	2	1	3	68	3.52	0	1	1	31	4.31	2	0	2	36	3.22	118	1	.246	.333	.331	141	3	.298	.365	.447	151	3	.272	.354	.391	56	1	.339	.471	.482
1986	LA-N	1	5	0	71	3.41	1	2	0	33	3.00	0	3	0	38	3.76	80	0	.275	.348	.375	206	8	.296	.371	.447	153	4	.261	.345	.392	76	3	.368	.442	.553
1987	Cle-A	1	0	0	72	5.10	1	0	0	40	6.25	0	0	0	32	3.66	136	4	.257	.322	.324	159	9	.365	.400	.591	164	4	.317	.354	.427	45	0	.311	.415	.378
1988	Tex-A	2	2	2	37	4.14	2	0	2	26	2.77	0	2	0	11	7.36	52	0	.269	.286	.327	91	2	.330	.390	.462	73	0	.247	.305	.329	47	0	.362	.404	.404
TOTALS		14	20	12	379	4.33	8	9	7	190	4.56	6	11	5	189	4.10	497	9	.258	.327	.338	1012	37	.327	.380	.503	789	19	.294	.359	.422	292	8	.342	.435	.483

● **Frank Viola** BL/TL

YEAR	TM/L	W	L	SV	IP	ERA	W	L	SV	IP	ERA	W	L	SV	IP	ERA	AB	HR	AVG	OBP	SLG	AB	HR	AVG	OBP	SLG	AB	HR	AVG	OBP	SLG	AB	HR	AVG	OBP	SLG
1984	Min-A	18	12	0	258	3.21	8	2	0	105	2.40	10	10	0	153	3.77	160	3	.262	.326	.381	804	25	.228	.281	.372	353	11	.269	.315	.416	86	3	.198	.255	.326
1985	Min-A	18	14	0	251	4.09	9	6	0	125	3.68	9	8	0	126	4.50	216	7	.287	.325	.463	763	19	.262	.312	.397	396	13	.290	.332	.447	61	1	.230	.277	.328
1986	Min-A	16	13	0	246	4.51	6	6	0	124	4.58	10	7	0	122	4.43	154	5	.273	.311	.409	804	32	.267	.330	.448	393	15	.247	.306	.420	95	3	.347	.390	.558
1987	Min-A	17	10	0	252	2.90	11	5	0	137	2.69	6	5	0	115	3.14	163	5	.245	.305	.374	792	26	.240	.291	.379	366	11	.232	.286	.369	120	1	.250	.286	.317
1988	Min-A	24	7	0	255	2.64	14	2	0	132	2.18	10	5	0	123	3.14	163	4	.233	.280	.368	799	16	.248	.287	.354	369	9	.236	.269	.347	116	4	.190	.254	.319
1989	Min-A	8	12	0	176	3.79	4	6	0	96	3.09	4	6	0	80	4.63	118	3	.280	.323	.475	550	14	.251	.303	.382	268	6	.250	.305	.381	68	1	.221	.254	.294
1989	NY-N	5	5	0	85	3.38	2	3	0	32	4.78	3	2	0	53	2.53	54	0	.241	.268	.259	264	5	.235	.301	.330	137	4	.241	.312	.372	31	0	.065	.121	.065
1990	NY-N	20	12	0	250	2.67	12	5	0	126	2.44	8	7	0	124	2.90	183	1	.257	.317	.388	755	14	.238	.307	.354	374	4	.235	.283	.303	63	1	.222	.290	.302
1991	NY-N	13	15	0	231	3.97	8	8	0	123	4.26	5	7	0	109	3.64	193	5	.233	.279	.363	712	20	.301	.339	.440	374	8	.297	.333	.412	92	3	.315	.360	.435
1992	Bos-A	13	12	0	238	3.44	8	7	0	117	4.08	5	5	0	121	2.83	109	1	.211	.281	.294	777	12	.246	.317	.336	369	7	.241	.319	.352	121	2	.190	.244	.256
1993	Bos-A	11	8	0	184	3.14	5	3	0	92	4.01	6	5	0	92	2.26	114	1	.272	.341	.400	580	11	.257	.329	.366	294	1	.241	.313	.316	62	0	.210	.246	.226
1994	Bos-A	1	1	0	31	4.65	1	0	0	18	6.87	0	1	0	13	1.42	18	0	.222	.227	.278	97	2	.309	.405	.485	52	0	.327	.383	.500	3	0	.333	.500	1.000
TOTALS		164	121	0	2456	3.44	87	52	0	1226	3.28	77	69	0	1230	3.59	1645	35	.255	.306	.381	7697	194	.253	.308	.380	3745	89	.255	.308	.380	918	19	.232	.282	.332

● **Bob Walk** BR/TR

YEAR	TM/L	W	L	SV	IP	ERA	W	L	SV	IP	ERA	W	L	SV	IP	ERA	AB	HR	AVG	OBP	SLG	AB	HR	AVG	OBP	SLG	AB	HR	AVG	OBP	SLG	AB	HR	AVG	OBP	SLG
1984	Pit-N	1	1	0	10	2.61	1	1	0	10	2.61	0	0	0	0	—	19	0	.263	.364	.316	21	1	.143	.182	.333	14	0	.286	.412	.429	3	0	.000	.250	.000
1985	Pit-N	2	3	0	59	3.68	0	2	0	10	7.84	2	1	0	48	2.79	128	1	.281	.326	.367	98	2	.245	.308	.378	85	1	.282	.340	.376	20	0	.550	.571	.600
1986	Pit-N	7	8	2	142	3.75	2	5	0	66	3.68	5	3	2	76	3.81	260	6	.254	.308	.381	254	5	.248	.319	.394	206	7	.248	.347	.403	83	5	.253	.366	.458
1987	Pit-N	8	2	0	117	3.31	6	0	0	74	3.05	2	2	0	43	3.74	230	4	.257	.333	.383	205	7	.234	.322	.371	195	5	.262	.330	.385	25	1	.320	.393	.560
1988	Pit-N	12	10	0	213	2.71	6	4	0	110	3.12	6	6	0	103	2.27	419	2	.202	.250	.285	376	4	.202	.250	.285	324	3	.222	.290	.318	80	1	.213	.284	.300
1989	Pit-N	13	10	0	196	4.41	7	4	0	91	3.18	6	6	0	105	5.47	431	9	.285	.343	.406	337	6	.252	.313	.371	309	8	.307	.365	.466	49	2	.286	.364	.469
1990	Pit-N	7	5	1	130	3.75	3	3	0	60	3.90	4	2	1	70	3.62	297	9	.263	.326	.394	206	8	.282	.317	.456	200	9	.250	.305	.415	24	0	.167	.200	.208

YEAR	TM/L	W	L	SV	IP	ERA	W	L	SV	IP	ERA	W	L	SV	IP	ERA	AB	HR	AVG	OBP	SLG	AB	HR	AVG	OBP	SLG	AB	HR	AVG	OBP	SLG	AB	HR	AVG	OBP	SLG
			TOTAL					HOME					AWAY					LEFT					RIGHT					ON-BASE					LATE/CLOSE				
1991	Pit-N	9	2	0	115	3.60	4	2	0	62	3.48	5	0	0	53	3.74	244	5	.258	.323	.385	189	5	.217	.274	.333	170	5	.288	.328	.435	17	0	.294	.294	.353
1992	Pit-N	10	6	2	135	3.20	8	3	1	77	2.82	2	3	1	58	3.70	287	6	.289	.359	.425	225	4	.218	.273	.320	207	3	.256	.346	.357	66	1	.348	.403	.455
1993	Pit-N	13	14	0	187	5.68	9	6	0	101	5.35	4	8	0	86	6.07	385	12	.275	.348	.449	343	11	.315	.365	.455	305	11	.321	.383	.502	45	1	.378	.417	.556
TOTALS		82	61	5	1303	3.83	46	30	3	660	3.65	36	31	2	643	4.02	2700	54	.269	.338	.397	2254	56	.246	.304	.371	2015	52	.271	.339	.430	412	11	.291	.359	.430

● **Duane Ward** BR/TR

YEAR	TM/L	W	L	SV	IP	ERA	W	L	SV	IP	ERA	W	L	SV	IP	ERA	AB	HR	AVG	OBP	SLG	AB	HR	AVG	OBP	SLG	AB	HR	AVG	OBP	SLG	AB	HR	AVG	OBP	SLG
1986	Atl-N	0	1	0	16	7.31	0	1	0	7	5.40	0	0	0	9	8.68	28	2	.357	.455	.679	35	0	.343	.395	.457	36	0	.361	.439	.417	9	2	.222	.222	.889
1986	Tor-A	0	1	0	2	13.50	0	0	0	1	0.00	0	1	0	1	27.00	5	0	.200	.500	.400	7	0	.143	.455	.286	0	0	—	—	—					
1987	Tor-A	1	0	0	12	6.94	0	0	0	8	9.00	1	0	0	4	2.45	15	0	.200	.455	.333	28	0	.393	.471	.500	28	0	.393	.500	.536	7	0	.143	.417	.143
1988	Tor-A	9	3	15	112	3.30	5	1	8	59	2.29	4	2	7	53	4.44	173	3	.231	.332	.312	240	2	.254	.352	.338	218	2	.239	.321	.307	190	1	.232	.329	.295
1989	Tor-A	4	10	15	115	3.77	2	6	8	54	3.81	2	4	7	60	3.73	172	2	.262	.383	.300	236	2	.208	.280	.263	214	3	.229	.331	.290	245	3	.237	.337	.322
1990	Tor-A	2	8	11	128	3.45	0	4	5	66	3.02	2	4	6	62	3.92	189	5	.259	.372	.386	268	4	.194	.219	.276	168	5	.280	.363	.429	229	5	.258	.320	.380
1991	Tor-A	7	6	23	107	2.77	5	4	14	63	3.14	2	2	9	44	2.23	187	3	.193	.275	.278	199	0	.221	.266	.246	154	2	.234	.333	.299	237	2	.211	.283	.266
1992	Tor-A	7	4	12	101	1.95	6	1	6	52	1.57	1	3	6	50	2.36	183	5	.197	.289	.322	184	0	.217	.275	.250	176	3	.182	.260	.284	231	4	.199	.278	.286
1993	Tor-A	2	3	45	72	2.13	1	2	21	33	2.73	1	1	24	39	1.63	123	2	.211	.310	.285	131	2	.176	.221	.244	109	1	.229	.301	.284	154	2	.156	.237	.208
TOTALS		32	36	121	664	3.19	19	19	62	342	2.97	13	17	59	322	3.41	1075	22	.229	.335	.336	1326	10	.222	.283	.284	1110	16	.240	.329	.324	1302	19	.218	.301	.301

● **Bill Wegman** BR/TR

YEAR	TM/L	W	L	SV	IP	ERA	W	L	SV	IP	ERA	W	L	SV	IP	ERA	AB	HR	AVG	OBP	SLG	AB	HR	AVG	OBP	SLG	AB	HR	AVG	OBP	SLG	AB	HR	AVG	OBP	SLG
1985	Mil-A	2	0	0	18	3.57	1	0	0	12	3.75	1	0	0	6	3.18	37	2	.297	.325	.486	32	1	.188	.212	.344	27	1	.222	.267	.370	1	1	1.000	1.000	4.000
1986	Mil-A	5	12	0	198	5.13	2	5	0	110	5.06	3	7	0	88	5.22	437	19	.268	.313	.446	340	13	.294	.331	.485	296	10	.307	.340	.480	66	1	.273	.304	.424
1987	Mil-A	12	11	0	225	4.24	7	5	0	143	3.66	5	6	0	82	5.25	467	16	.257	.308	.420	398	15	.274	.311	.432	325	14	.262	.303	.443	75	1	.307	.354	.427
1988	Mil-A	13	13	0	199	4.12	8	6	0	112	4.50	5	7	0	87	3.62	403	11	.273	.313	.407	377	13	.257	.306	.419	286	6	.301	.348	.430	46	1	.239	.286	.326
1989	Mil-A	2	6	0	51	6.71	1	2	0	20	7.20	2	4	0	31	6.39	114	5	.360	.394	.588	101	1	.277	.354	.386	99	4	.364	.412	.576	9	1	.556	.556	1.000
1990	Mil-A	2	2	0	30	4.85	1	0	0	11	0.00	1	2	0	19	7.71	56	2	.286	.310	.464	68	4	.309	.342	.559	50	5	.280	.327	.580	6	0	.333	.429	.333
1991	Mil-A	15	7	0	193	2.84	7	4	0	103	2.62	8	3	0	90	3.09	384	6	.221	.271	.307	344	10	.265	.303	.410	262	4	.229	.275	.302	73	4	.219	.260	.411
1992	Mil-A	13	14	0	262	3.20	9	5	0	144	2.26	4	9	0	118	4.35	469	7	.209	.247	.296	535	21	.286	.334	.467	372	9	.255	.315	.387	128	3	.281	.336	.438
1993	Mil-A	4	14	0	121	4.48	3	6	0	63	3.88	1	8	0	58	5.12	221	5	.326	.358	.493	243	8	.259	.313	.453	194	6	.278	.307	.454	43	0	.465	.519	.558
1994	Mil-A	8	4	0	116	4.51	5	2	0	68	4.08	3	2	0	47	5.13	218	8	.307	.340	.486	244	6	.299	.337	.471	200	5	.290	.315	.460	7	0	.429	.500	.571
TOTALS		76	83	0	1412	4.10	43	35	0	786	3.68	33	48	0	626	4.63	2806	81	.263	.305	.406	2682	92	.276	.320	.447	2111	64	.277	.320	.430	454	12	.297	.346	.449

● **Bob Welch** BR/TR

YEAR	TM/L	W	L	SV	IP	ERA	W	L	SV	IP	ERA	W	L	SV	IP	ERA	AB	HR	AVG	OBP	SLG	AB	HR	AVG	OBP	SLG	AB	HR	AVG	OBP	SLG	AB	HR	AVG	OBP	SLG
1984	LA-N	13	13	0	179	3.78	6	6	0	88	3.67	7	7	0	90	3.89	319	2	.245	.313	.348	380	9	.297	.345	.424	302	5	.268	.354	.391	58	1	.328	.361	.466
1985	LA-N	14	4	0	167	2.31	9	3	0	97	2.70	5	1	0	71	1.78	327	3	.214	.254	.291	299	13	.237	.291	.435	228	2	.193	.268	.272	52	0	.173	.204	.250
1986	LA-N	7	13	0	236	3.28	5	6	0	132	2.66	2	7	0	104	4.04	483	7	.265	.308	.371	421	7	.235	.284	.342	361	3	.244	.310	.321	119	7	.235	.272	.445
1987	LA-N	15	9	0	252	3.22	7	6	0	136	3.24	8	3	0	116	3.19	529	10	.236	.301	.346	392	11	.202	.273	.337	317	11	.249	.332	.404	96	1	.271	.330	.344
1988	Oak-A	17	9	0	245	3.64	13	4	0	148	2.56	4	5	0	97	5.29	459	12	.248	.318	.386	464	10	.205	.275	.304	321	9	.236	.328	.348	97	0	.237	.267	.258
1989	Oak-A	17	8	0	210	3.00	10	2	0	107	2.77	7	6	0	102	3.25	418	3	.211	.300	.304	374	10	.275	.327	.417	321	6	.221	.310	.336	51	1	.255	.333	.353
1990	Oak-A	27	6	0	238	2.95	14	2	0	117	1.92	13	4	0	121	3.94	465	12	.258	.325	.404	421	14	.223	.281	.375	322	10	.236	.312	.379	76	1	.158	.247	.211
1991	Oak-A	12	13	0	220	4.58	8	7	0	125	3.60	4	6	0	95	5.87	430	8	.272	.348	.377	405	17	.254	.334	.432	351	10	.279	.359	.433	86	3	.244	.309	.419
1992	Oak-A	11	7	0	124	3.27	4	3	0	52	2.94	7	4	0	72	3.52	241	6	.266	.325	.373	220	7	.227	.299	.345	182	4	.247	.296	.324	22	0	.136	.174	.136
1993	Oak-A	9	11	0	167	5.29	5	6	0	85	5.61	4	5	0	82	4.96	369	11	.309	.362	.477	301	14	.312	.375	.508	287	6	.296	.357	.460	23	0	.348	.348	.348
1994	Oak-A	3	6	0	69	7.08	0	1	0	26	7.86	3	5	0	42	6.59	139	5	.331	.435	.547	133	5	.248	.329	.414	130	3	.323	.429	.508	26	1	.269	.441	.462
TOTALS		145	99	0	2105	3.63	81	46	0	1113	3.36	64	53	0	991	4.04	4179	79	.255	.320	.374	3810	117	.241	.313	.398	3152	71	.251	.330	.376	706	15	.239	.295	.346

● **David Wells** BL/TL

YEAR	TM/L	W	L	SV	IP	ERA	W	L	SV	IP	ERA	W	L	SV	IP	ERA	AB	HR	AVG	OBP	SLG	AB	HR	AVG	OBP	SLG	AB	HR	AVG	OBP	SLG	AB	HR	AVG	OBP	SLG
1987	Tor-A	4	3	1	29	3.99	2	1	0	13	3.38	2	2	1	16	4.50	44	0	.318	.375	.318	75	0	.307	.373	.400	66	0	.273	.333	.303	43	0	.140	.213	.186
1988	Tor-A	3	5	4	64	4.62	1	3	2	32	3.66	2	2	2	32	5.57	68	0	.265	.351	.324	174	12	.270	.355	.557	116	7	.259	.353	.517	134	8	.291	.368	.560
1989	Tor-A	7	4	2	86	2.40	5	2	1	49	2.40	2	2	1	38	2.39	78	1	.231	.294	.346	241	4	.199	.261	.282	138	1	.196	.266	.275	155	4	.252	.322	.381
1990	Tor-A	11	6	3	189	3.14	3	2	2	83	2.61	8	4	1	106	3.55	110	2	.264	.319	.436	591	12	.230	.276	.359	277	7	.235	.277	.401	83	2	.253	.295	.410
1991	Tor-A	15	10	1	198	3.72	6	5	0	86	4.81	9	5	1	112	2.88	130	3	.208	.246	.315	617	21	.261	.308	.421	284	12	.246	.283	.430	98	2	.255	.284	.337
1992	Tor-A	7	9	2	120	5.40	4	3	1	60	3.60	3	6	1	60	7.20	92	3	.293	.363	.446	386	13	.288	.342	.477	201	5	.328	.398	.507	67	1	.313	.356	.388
1993	Det-A	11	9	0	187	4.19	8	3	0	108	2.74	3	6	0	79	6.18	108	2	.250	.328	.361	613	24	.254	.295	.426	273	13	.245	.301	.447	59	3	.390	.431	.678
1994	Det-A	5	7	0	111	3.96	3	2	0	58	3.43	2	5	0	54	4.53	75	2	.253	.253	.347	359	11	.262	.311	.426	159	6	.289	.360	.491	20	1	.300	.300	.500
TOTALS		63	53	13	986	3.88	32	21	6	489	3.32	31	32	7	497	4.44	705	13	.254	.311	.366	3056	97	.254	.305	.414	1514	51	.257	.316	.431	659	21	.273	.329	.432

● **John Wetteland** BR/TR

YEAR	TM/L	W	L	SV	IP	ERA	W	L	SV	IP	ERA	W	L	SV	IP	ERA	AB	HR	AVG	OBP	SLG	AB	HR	AVG	OBP	SLG	AB	HR	AVG	OBP	SLG	AB	HR	AVG	OBP	SLG
1989	LA-N	5	8	1	103	3.77	4	3	1	47	3.45	1	5	0	56	4.04	193	3	.212	.269	.295	178	5	.225	.296	.365	155	4	.232	.280	.361	64	0	.234	.300	.313
1990	LA-N	2	4	0	43	4.81	1	2	0	17	4.32	1	2	0	26	5.13	88	3	.295	.392	.432	79	3	.228	.287	.380	68	2	.309	.400	.471	25	2	.360	.407	.640
1991	LA-N	1	0	0	9	0.00	1	0	0	2	0.00	0	0	0	7	0.00	16	0	.188	.263	.250	15	0	.133	.235	.133	18	0	.167	.167	.167	0	0	—	1.000	—
1992	Mon-N	4	4	37	83	2.92	2	3	21	45	3.83	2	1	16	39	1.86	175	3	.200	.288	.297	230	3	.230	.326	.325	158	3	.209	.308	.297	207	6	.227	.315	.343
1993	Mon-N	9	3	43	85	1.37	6	1	22	44	1.44	3	2	21	42	1.30	177	3	.175	.254	.266	131	0	.206	.268	.290	151	1	.166	.237	.242	268	3	.183	.254	.272
1994	Mon-N	4	6	25	64	2.83	3	3	10	29	4.30	1	3	15	34	1.57	132	4	.205	.284	.341	96	1	.198	.259	.281	97	1	.206	.296	.278	169	4	.207	.294	.320
TOTALS		25	25	106	387	2.93	17	12	54	183	3.24	8	13	52	204	2.65	781	16	.209	.287	.310	625	12	.216	.288	.325	653	11	.213	.290	.311	733	15	.211	.291	.319

● **Ed Whitson** BR/TR

YEAR	TM/L	W	L	SV	IP	ERA	W	L	SV	IP	ERA	W	L	SV	IP	ERA	AB	HR	AVG	OBP	SLG	AB	HR	AVG	OBP	SLG	AB	HR	AVG	OBP	SLG	AB	HR	AVG	OBP	SLG
1984	SD-N	14	8	0	189	3.24	9	4	0	104	2.94	5	4	0	85	3.60	356	9	.267	.318	.382	354	7	.243	.275	.353	284	6	.239	.274	.352	51	1	.255	.283	.373
1985	NY-A	10	8	0	159	4.88	4	2	0	68	4.08	6	6	0	90	5.48	376	11	.311	.342	.481	274	8	.307	.362	.453	289	11	.346	.364	.540	22	1	.182	.217	.364
1986	NY-A	5	2	0	37	7.54	2	2	0	20	7.52	3	0	0	17	7.56	61	3	.361	.494	.656	100	2	.320	.355	.470	88	3	.330	.410	.545	6	0	.167	.545	.167
1986	SD-N	1	7	0	76	5.59	1	3	0	38	4.30	0	4	0	38	6.89	176	4	.244	.307	.347	120	4	.350	.419	.575	129	3	.310	.397	.450	0	0	—	—	—
1987	SD-N	10	13	0	206	4.73	5	7	0	107	4.96	5	6	0	99	4.47	429	14	.284	.350	.441	355	22	.211	.260	.445	293	14	.276	.310	.505	60	6	.350	.381	.667
1988	SD-N	13	11	0	205	3.77	9	5	0	109	3.46	4	6	0	96	4.13	399	7	.266	.312	.383	380	10	.253	.283	.374	306	8	.258	.296	.412	74	2	.311	.333	.419
1989	SD-N	16	11	0	227	2.66	9	6	0	124	2.98	7	5	0	103	2.27	497	16	.262	.305	.408	344	6	.198	.238	.291	301	6	.219	.275	.326	88	2	.216	.242	.330
1990	SD-N	14	9	0	229	2.60	5	6	0	126	2.65	9	3	0	103	2.53	522	6	.270	.309	.383	333	7	.222	.259	.330	325	4	.262	.299	.345	70	2	.329	.380	.500
1991	SD-N	4	6	0	79	5.03	0	3	0	33	5.18	4	3	0	46	4.93	180	5	.283	.326	.439	117	8	.321	.341	.534	117	9	.316	.352	.598	16	0	.188	.235	.250
TOTALS		87	75	0	1406	3.86	44	38	0	729	3.68	43	37	0	676	4.06	2996	75	.276	.326	.410	2391	74	.251	.291	.395	2132	64	.274	.316	.430	387	14	.276	.318	.432

● **Bob Wickman** BR/TR

YEAR	TM/L	W	L	SV	IP	ERA	W	L	SV	IP	ERA	W	L	SV	IP	ERA	AB	HR	AVG	OBP	SLG	AB	HR	AVG	OBP	SLG	AB	HR	AVG	OBP	SLG	AB	HR	AVG	OBP	SLG
1992	NY-A	6	1	0	50	4.11	2	1	0	23	5.09	4	0	0	27	3.29	89	1	.281	.347	.427	98	1	.265	.342	.347	92	0	.250	.273	.359	13	0	.385	.500	.462
1993	NY-A	14	4	4	140	4.63	9	0	1	69	2.75	5	4	3	71	6.43	244	6	.279	.374	.426	306	7	.288	.363	.425	259	5	.263	.360	.405	61	2	.344	.394	.525
1994	NY-A	5	4	6	70	3.09	4	1	2	37	2.45	1	3	4	33	3.78	89	1	.236	.355	.371	164	2	.201	.246	.268	118	1	.178	.261	.263	157	2	.223	.298	.331
TOTALS		25	9	10	260	4.11	15	2	3	128	3.09	10	7	7	132	5.11	422	8	.270	.364	.415	568	10	.259	.326	.366	469	6	.239	.318	.360	231	4	.264	.335	.390

● **Frank Williams** BR/TR

YEAR	TM/L	W	L	SV	IP	ERA	W	L	SV	IP	ERA	W	L	SV	IP	ERA	AB	HR	AVG	OBP	SLG	AB	HR	AVG	OBP	SLG	AB	HR	AVG	OBP	SLG	AB	HR	AVG	OBP	SLG
1984	SF-N	9	4	3	106	3.55	3	2	2	53	3.59	6	2	1	54	3.52	178	1	.298	.383	.388	211	1	.166	.264	.199	200	1	.200	.299	.255	143	0	.245	.321	.280
1985	SF-N	2	4	0	73	4.19	1	2	0	40	1.82	1	2	0	33	7.02	172	3	.342	.436	.504	152	3	.164	.259	.230	113	3	.248	.364	.381	85	1	.200	.324	.259
1986	SF-N	3	1	1	52	1.20	1	0	0	23	1.16	2	1	1	29	1.24	69	0	.232	.338	.246	96	0	.198	.297	.198	71	0	.197	.318	.197	24	0	.292	.452	.292
1987	Cin-N	4	0	2	106	2.30	0	0	1	60	1.50	4	0	1	46	3.35	170	0	.235	.318	.271	227	5	.269	.325	.427	162	1	.272	.360	.383	133	2	.241	.309	.346
1988	Cin-N	3	2	1	63	2.59	2	2	0	35	4.08	1	0	1	27	0.66	91	3	.286	.404	.429	143	3	.231	.321	.343	108	3	.241	.354	.352	60	1	.233	.378	.383
1989	Det-A	3	3	1	72	3.64	1	1	0	36	4.00	2	2	1	36	3.28	123	3	.260	.392	.382	153	2	.248	.335	.320	152	3	.237	.362	.329	52	1	.288	.431	.423
TOTALS		24	14	8	472	3.00	8	7	3	247	2.70	16	7	5	225	3.32	748	9	.277	.377	.370	982	14	.215	.300	.296	806	11	.233	.342	.320	497	5	.241	.345	.322

● **Mitch Williams** BL/TL

YEAR	TM/L	W	L	SV	IP	ERA	W	L	SV	IP	ERA	W	L	SV	IP	ERA	AB	HR	AVG	OBP	SLG	AB	HR	AVG	OBP	SLG	AB	HR	AVG	OBP	SLG	AB	HR	AVG	OBP	SLG
1986	Tex-A	8	6	8	98	3.58	3	3	5	52	3.46	5	3	3	46	3.72	118	3	.203	.331	.322	223	5	.202	.384	.336	183	4	.219	.371	.344	174	3	.213	.365	.316
1987	Tex-A	8	6	6	109	3.23	6	2	1	57	2.84	2	4	5	52	3.66	123	3	.146	.309	.244	238	6	.189	.374	.298	183	5	.180	.373	.290	166	3	.175	.308	.241
1988	Tex-A	2	7	18	68	4.63	1	3	10	35	5.71	1	4	8	33	3.51	65	0	.185	.345	.231	171	4	.211	.344	.333	142	5	.218	.350	.345	154	5	.201	.317	.325
1989	Chi-N	4	4	36	82	2.76	3	2	15	37	3.65	1	2	21	45	2.01	76	0	.254	.352	.296	185	2	.233	.361	.378	124	5	.218	.358	.324	225	5	.218	.338	.324
1990	Chi-N	1	8	16	66	3.93	1	1	4	33	3.78	0	7	12	33	4.09	66	2	.227	.369	.424	185	2	.243	.362	.378	145	4	.269	.381	.476	105	1	.238	.380	.371
1991	Phi-N	12	5	30	88	2.34	9	2	17	47	2.11	3	3	13	41	2.61	68	0	.191	.353	.279	240	4	.179	.323	.262	175	1	.143	.280	.211	245	4	.180	.337	.269
1992	Phi-N	5	8	29	81	3.78	3	5	16	52	4.29	2	3	13	30	2.65	49	0	.265	.379	.286	212	3	.250	.388	.363	128	2	.250	.386	.352	212	3	.250	.388	.363
1993	Phi-N	3	7	43	62	3.34	1	3	19	28	4.18	2	4	24	34	2.65	49	0	.250	.340	.250	177	5	.243	.374	.350	122	2	.238	.362	.320	169	2	.260	.392	.320
1994	Hou-N	1	4	6	20	7.65	0	3	0	12	6.94	1	1	3	8	8.64	27	1	.148	.303	.259	51	3	.333	.507	.549	40	2	.350	.500	.550	38	2	.289	.471	.474
TOTALS		44	55	192	674	3.53	27	23	90	343	3.73	17	32	102	331	3.31	627	6	.203	.340	.290	1762	37	.219	.369	.339	1316	26	.216	.358	.336	1488	26	.218	.356	.317

● **Mark Williamson** BR/TR

YEAR	TM/L	W	L	SV	IP	ERA	W	L	SV	IP	ERA	W	L	SV	IP	ERA	AB	HR	AVG	OBP	SLG	AB	HR	AVG	OBP	SLG	AB	HR	AVG	OBP	SLG	AB	HR	AVG	OBP	SLG
1987	Bal-A	8	9	3	125	4.03	5	5	2	61	4.43	3	4	1	64	3.66	210	5	.271	.338	.395	258	7	.252	.310	.380	213	5	.282	.358	.385	162	5	.340	.417	.494

YEAR	TM/L	TOTAL W	L	SV	IP	ERA	HOME W	L	SV	IP	ERA	AWAY W	L	SV	IP	ERA	LEFT AB	HR	AVG	OBP	SLG	RIGHT AB	HR	AVG	OBP	SLG	ON-BASE AB	HR	AVG	OBP	SLG	LATE/CLOSE AB	HR	AVG	OBP	SLG
1988	Bal-A	5	8	2	118	4.90	2	4	2	65	3.20	3	4	0	53	6.96	223	7	.265	.337	.426	236	7	.280	.327	.436	189	8	.344	.408	.550	80	2	.313	.389	.475
1989	Bal-A	10	5	9	107	2.93	7	2	4	59	2.61	3	3	5	49	3.33	177	0	.260	.296	.305	226	4	.261	.325	.376	193	4	.290	.369	.409	196	4	.301	.368	.439
1990	Bal-A	8	2	1	85	2.21	5	0	0	47	1.35	3	2	1	39	3.26	139	6	.223	.257	.410	163	2	.209	.291	.301	144	4	.201	.265	.333	146	4	.212	.293	.342
1991	Bal-A	5	5	4	80	4.48	3	4	1	44	2.66	2	1	3	36	6.69	121	2	.248	.326	.347	195	7	.292	.353	.472	159	4	.296	.368	.459	150	4	.240	.326	.380
1992	Bal-A	0	0	1	19	0.96	0	0	0	8	0.00	0	0	1	10	1.74	32	0	.188	.257	.188	35	1	.286	.405	.457	38	0	.263	.349	.289	2	0	.500	.500	.500
1993	Bal-A	7	5	0	88	4.91	5	1	0	34	4.76	2	4	0	54	5.00	138	3	.254	.333	.370	211	2	.336	.365	.450	159	2	.346	.389	.453	110	2	.300	.358	.427
1994	Bal-A	3	1	1	67	4.01	1	0	0	39	4.12	2	1	1	28	3.86	101	3	.257	.296	.386	169	6	.290	.339	.485	117	3	.256	.315	.419	27	2	.259	.310	.519
TOTALS		46	35	21	690	3.86	28	16	9	357	3.18	18	19	12	333	4.59	1141	26	.254	.312	.374	1493	36	.275	.332	.415	1212	30	.290	.357	.427	873	23	.283	.357	.427

● Mike Witt BR/TR

YEAR	TM/L	W	L	SV	IP	ERA	W	L	SV	IP	ERA	W	L	SV	IP	ERA	AB	HR	AVG	OBP	SLG	AB	HR	AVG	OBP	SLG	AB	HR	AVG	OBP	SLG	AB	HR	AVG	OBP	SLG
1984	Cal-A	15	11	0	247	3.47	8	5	0	120	2.69	7	6	0	126	4.20	542	9	.258	.320	.367	387	8	.225	.291	.341	359	4	.245	.315	.345	103	2	.204	.305	.301
1985	Cal-A	15	9	0	250	3.56	8	5	0	123	3.38	7	4	0	127	3.75	520	11	.263	.332	.375	418	11	.218	.296	.342	389	11	.247	.320	.388	114	5	.219	.321	.377
1986	Cal-A	18	10	0	269	2.84	11	5	0	141	2.62	7	5	0	128	3.09	578	15	.215	.270	.339	409	7	.230	.282	.330	364	12	.239	.295	.387	157	4	.223	.281	.331
1987	Cal-A	16	14	0	247	4.01	9	8	0	138	4.05	7	6	0	109	3.95	525	22	.272	.338	.463	440	12	.248	.300	.402	413	19	.247	.314	.429	110	4	.255	.339	.400
1988	Cal-A	13	16	0	250	4.15	6	7	0	133	2.77	7	9	0	117	5.71	524	7	.261	.324	.357	442	7	.285	.343	.398	390	4	.300	.363	.397	128	1	.281	.329	.367
1989	Cal-A	9	15	0	220	4.54	5	7	0	108	4.85	4	8	0	112	4.25	434	12	.295	.326	.424	430	14	.288	.325	.442	336	9	.321	.347	.449	75	1	.360	.377	.427
1990	Cal-A	0	3	1	20	1.77	0	2	1	11	2.45	0	1	0	9	0.96	28	0	.250	.400	.250	48	1	.303	.455	.455	39	1	.256	.302	.359					
1990	NY-A	5	6	0	97	4.47	2	3	0	41	3.51	3	3	0	56	5.17	189	3	.270	.329	.381	174	5	.207	.286	.356	145	4	.248	.321	.407	25	2	.280	.296	.600
1991	NY-A	0	1	0	5	10.13	0	0	0	5	5.40	0	0	0	0	81.00	13	0	.385	.385	.538	12	1	.250	.308	.500	9	1	.444	.500	.889	0	0	—	—	—
1993	NY-A	3	2	0	41	5.27	2	2	0	32	4.78	1	0	0	9	7.00	75	2	.213	.359	.320	82	5	.280	.344	.500	76	3	.224	.298	.408	4	0	.250	.250	.250
TOTALS		94	87	1	1646	3.81	51	44	1	851	3.41	43	43	0	794	4.24	3428	81	.259	.320	.383	2842	71	.260	.307	.380	2514	68	.265	.327	.403	755	20	.252	.317	.370

● Bobby Witt BR/TR

YEAR	TM/L	W	L	SV	IP	ERA	W	L	SV	IP	ERA	W	L	SV	IP	ERA	AB	HR	AVG	OBP	SLG	AB	HR	AVG	OBP	SLG	AB	HR	AVG	OBP	SLG	AB	HR	AVG	OBP	SLG
1986	Tex-A	11	9	0	158	5.48	6	3	0	90	4.00	5	6	0	68	7.45	314	7	.248	.409	.382	269	11	.193	.330	.353	281	8	.231	.380	.374	20	0	.400	.409	.500
1987	Tex-A	8	10	0	143	4.91	4	3	0	81	3.89	4	7	0	62	6.24	292	6	.229	.387	.332	228	4	.206	.382	.316	281	5	.228	.351	.331	38	0	.211	.423	.263
1988	Tex-A	8	10	0	174	3.92	4	3	0	66	3.70	4	7	0	109	4.06	345	4	.223	.331	.301	276	9	.207	.315	.341	259	5	.228	.333	.324	22	2	.170	.270	.295
1989	Tex-A	12	13	0	194	5.14	5	7	0	89	4.74	7	6	0	105	5.49	349	10	.249	.364	.387	384	4	.247	.332	.326	331	5	.290	.379	.411	47	0	.191	.321	.191
1990	Tex-A	17	10	0	222	3.36	9	5	0	101	3.40	10	5	0	121	3.34	396	5	.232	.323	.321	433	7	.242	.332	.330	356	4	.253	.337	.340	40	4	.226	.323	.310
1991	Tex-A	3	7	0	89	6.09	0	5	0	40	6.30	3	2	0	49	5.92	151	2	.232	.381	.331	180	2	.272	.394	.378	167	2	.257	.376	.371	11	0	.182	.500	.182
1992	Tex-A	9	13	0	161	4.46	6	8	0	99	4.17	3	5	0	62	4.94	249	4	.245	.374	.361	349	10	.261	.338	.390	259	3	.236	.346	.320	54	2	.241	.359	.370
1992	Oak-A	1	1	0	32	3.41	1	0	0	25	2.16	0	1	0	7	8.10	43	0	.233	.365	.233	74	2	.284	.360	.392	52	1	.250	.359	.327	5	0	.200	.333	.200
1993	Oak-A	14	13	0	220	4.21	7	6	0	125	3.30	7	7	0	95	5.42	426	7	.279	.350	.418	413	9	.259	.330	.366	371	7	.283	.346	.418	91	1	.231	.278	.308
1994	Oak-A	8	10	0	136	5.04	6	3	0	76	4.04	2	7	0	60	6.30	294	12	.310	.395	.507	240	10	.250	.331	.408	223	11	.314	.403	.507	16	1	.250	.294	.438
TOTALS		91	96	0	1529	4.56	46	43	0	792	3.94	45	53	0	737	5.23	2859	57	.251	.366	.371	2846	68	.240	.340	.355	2580	51	.258	.359	.376	454	6	.220	.328	.306

● Mark Wohlers BR/TR

YEAR	TM/L	W	L	SV	IP	ERA	W	L	SV	IP	ERA	W	L	SV	IP	ERA	AB	HR	AVG	OBP	SLG	AB	HR	AVG	OBP	SLG	AB	HR	AVG	OBP	SLG	AB	HR	AVG	OBP	SLG
1991	Atl-N	3	1	2	20	3.20	1	0	1	11	1.64	2	1	1	9	5.19	28	1	.321	.457	.536	43	0	.186	.308	.279	43	0	.256	.353	.372	33	1	.273	.375	.394
1992	Atl-N	1	2	4	35	2.55	0	1	2	16	3.38	1	1	2	19	1.86	65	0	.231	.342	.246	54	0	.241	.288	.278	58	0	.207	.309	.241	62	0	.290	.380	.323
1993	Atl-N	6	2	0	48	4.50	4	2	0	29	4.91	2	0	0	19	3.86	71	1	.225	.337	.282	99	1	.212	.288	.303	79	1	.278	.356	.380	93	1	.204	.302	.269
1994	Atl-N	7	2	1	51	4.59	3	2	0	28	5.08	4	0	1	23	3.97	86	1	.314	.419	.477	107	0	.224	.315	.290	106	0	.292	.396	.377	76	1	.276	.400	.395
TOTALS		17	7	7	154	3.92	8	5	3	85	4.25	9	2	4	69	3.50	250	3	.268	.381	.368	303	1	.218	.301	.290	286	1	.266	.362	.350	264	3	.254	.359	.333

● Todd Worrell BR/TR

YEAR	TM/L	W	L	SV	IP	ERA	W	L	SV	IP	ERA	W	L	SV	IP	ERA	AB	HR	AVG	OBP	SLG	AB	HR	AVG	OBP	SLG	AB	HR	AVG	OBP	SLG	AB	HR	AVG	OBP	SLG
1985	StL-N	3	0	5	22	2.91	2	0	3	12	4.38	1	0	2	9	0.96	31	1	.194	.219	.419	48	1	.229	.304	.396	37	0	.189	.256	.297	40	1	.225	.250	.400
1986	StL-N	9	10	36	104	2.08	6	5	17	55	1.65	3	5	19	49	2.57	181	7	.265	.352	.425	194	0	.196	.254	.284	200	5	.185	.275	.280	319	7	.226	.297	.335
1987	StL-N	8	6	33	95	2.66	5	3	12	44	3.25	3	3	21	50	2.15	147	3	.231	.331	.313	208	5	.250	.288	.404	190	3	.200	.277	.274	285	7	.235	.308	.372
1988	StL-N	5	9	32	90	3.00	3	6	15	49	2.76	2	3	17	41	3.29	141	5	.213	.305	.397	182	2	.214	.271	.291	150	5	.240	.328	.380	250	7	.216	.293	.356
1989	StL-N	3	5	20	52	2.96	3	4	12	26	3.08	0	1	8	25	2.84	88	3	.250	.350	.455	101	1	.198	.283	.287	95	2	.221	.348	.358	140	2	.214	.317	.336
1992	StL-N	5	3	3	64	2.11	1	0	2	35	0.76	4	3	1	29	3.77	121	3	.174	.254	.264	106	1	.226	.311	.302	93	2	.183	.262	.269	169	3	.189	.259	.278
1993	LA-N	1	1	5	39	6.05	0	1	0	19	7.23	1	0	5	20	4.95	80	4	.313	.359	.433	67	2	.313	.333	.433	71	4	.296	.325	.507	73	0	.315	.357	.370
1994	LA-N	6	5	11	42	4.29	4	2	5	25	2.19	2	3	6	17	7.27	87	3	.230	.287	.379	70	1	.243	.295	.386	67	1	.284	.333	.418	119	3	.227	.299	.345
TOTALS		40	39	145	506	2.97	24	21	66	265	2.71	16	18	79	241	3.25	876	29	.235	.318	.388	976	15	.227	.284	.336	903	22	.217	.298	.331	1395	30	.225	.298	.344

● Curt Young BR/TL

YEAR	TM/L	W	L	SV	IP	ERA	W	L	SV	IP	ERA	W	L	SV	IP	ERA	AB	HR	AVG	OBP	SLG	AB	HR	AVG	OBP	SLG	AB	HR	AVG	OBP	SLG	AB	HR	AVG	OBP	SLG
1984	Oak-A	9	4	0	109	4.06	3	2	0	50	4.89	6	2	0	59	3.36	90	1	.256	.309	.322	341	6	.279	.337	.431	189	4	.270	.336	.407	28	0	.179	.233	.214
1985	Oak-A	0	4	0	46	7.24	0	3	0	30	6.30	0	1	0	16	9.00	48	2	.208	.269	.354	142	13	.331	.407	.690	72	5	.319	.405	.611	1	0	1.000	1.000	1.000
1986	Oak-A	13	9	0	198	3.45	9	2	0	122	2.37	4	7	0	76	5.19	146	1	.219	.286	.260	599	18	.240	.295	.391	293	10	.256	.310	.403	65	1	.185	.254	.292
1987	Oak-A	13	7	0	203	4.08	5	3	0	91	3.67	8	4	0	112	4.41	147	5	.218	.243	.361	624	33	.260	.304	.474	277	15	.260	.292	.484	61	3	.262	.324	.410
1988	Oak-A	11	8	0	156	4.14	2	5	0	75	4.32	9	3	0	81	3.98	97	3	.258	.287	.392	492	20	.278	.342	.443	209	7	.282	.349	.421	38	3	.184	.279	.421
1989	Oak-A	5	9	0	111	3.73	3	4	0	60	4.05	2	5	0	51	3.35	80	0	.213	.278	.250	364	10	.275	.351	.431	183	3	.284	.364	.388	21	1	.286	.400	.476
1990	Oak-A	9	6	0	124	4.85	5	2	0	71	3.18	4	4	0	54	7.04	96	1	.260	.311	.333	370	16	.268	.350	.441	186	7	.296	.361	.457	18	0	.111	.273	.111
1991	Oak-A	4	2	0	68	5.00	1	1	0	30	4.55	3	1	0	39	5.35	109	2	.229	.298	.321	157	6	.312	.407	.497	126	2	.230	.347	.302	31	0	.290	.410	.387
1992	KC-A	1	2	0	24	5.18	1	1	0	10	9.31	0	1	0	15	2.45	23	0	.174	.174	.261	76	1	.329	.381	.461	48	1	.313	.346	.500	6	0	.167	.167	.167
1992	NY-A	3	0	0	43	3.32	2	0	0	31	3.48	1	0	0	12	2.92	28	0	.571	.567	.643	143	1	.245	.297	.343	75	0	.333	.366	.400	6	0	.333	.375	.500
1993	Oak-A	1	1	0	15	4.30	1	1	0	11	3.38	0	0	0	4	6.75	12	0	.333	.385	.417	46	5	.217	.294	.543	18	1	.167	.250	.333	0	0	—	—	—
TOTALS		69	52	0	1098	4.21	32	24	0	579	3.83	37	28	0	519	4.64	876	15	.243	.291	.332	3354	131	.269	.333	.447	1676	55	.274	.337	.427	275	8	.222	.307	.345

● Matt Young BL/TL

YEAR	TM/L	W	L	SV	IP	ERA	W	L	SV	IP	ERA	W	L	SV	IP	ERA	AB	HR	AVG	OBP	SLG	AB	HR	AVG	OBP	SLG	AB	HR	AVG	OBP	SLG	AB	HR	AVG	OBP	SLG
1984	Sea-A	6	8	0	113	5.72	5	4	0	64	4.64	1	4	0	49	7.11	78	1	.269	.352	.359	382	10	.314	.386	.455	213	3	.338	.404	.432	15	0	.267	.353	.333
1985	Sea-A	12	19	1	218	4.91	8	8	0	133	3.85	4	11	1	85	6.56	148	1	.264	.335	.304	710	22	.286	.346	.439	352	12	.304	.378	.449	98	1	.286	.358	.347
1986	Sea-A	8	6	13	104	3.82	6	2	8	64	3.52	2	4	5	40	4.31	129	2	.209	.306	.310	268	7	.302	.381	.448	236	3	.254	.332	.364	189	3	.291	.357	.413
1987	LA-N	5	8	11	54	4.47	4	2	6	30	2.10	1	6	5	24	7.40	64	1	.234	.279	.313	151	2	.311	.364	.411	125	2	.312	.374	.416	141	1	.319	.362	.390
1989	Oak-A	1	4	0	37	6.75	1	3	0	17	8.83	0	1	0	20	4.95	46	0	.239	.364	.283	101	2	.307	.427	.465	88	0	.273	.381	.375	18	0	.222	.263	.278
1990	Sea-A	8	18	0	225	3.51	4	10	0	134	2.69	4	8	0	91	4.73	101	0	.149	.209	.158	735	15	.249	.340	.351	357	7	.238	.323	.325	73	4	.370	.446	.644
1991	Bos-A	3	7	0	89	5.18	2	3	0	46	4.53	1	4	0	43	5.86	51	1	.255	.356	.353	295	3	.268	.366	.332	158	2	.266	.379	.342	22	0	.318	.483	.364
1992	Bos-A	0	4	0	71	4.58	0	2	0	31	5.23	0	2	0	40	4.08	52	1	.269	.409	.385	217	6	.253	.347	.378	131	3	.275	.380	.412	17	0	.118	.211	.118
1993	Cle-A	1	6	0	74	5.21	0	3	0	30	5.04	1	3	0	44	5.32	55	1	.236	.364	.291	227	7	.273	.401	.414	135	3	.259	.395	.378	2	0	1.000	1.000	1.000
TOTALS		44	80	25	986	4.64	30	37	14	550	3.88	14	43	11	436	5.59	724	8	.232	.322	.298	3086	74	.279	.363	.404	1795	35	.279	.366	.388	575	9	.303	.372	.410

The Annual Record

This section contains the season-by-season standings and records for all teams since 1871, plus 28 statistical categories for each team's batting and baserunning, and 26 categories for its pitching and fielding. In those years in which major league play consisted of more than one league, the statistics are presented in the order of the leagues' founding: that is, the National Association comes first; the National League record precedes those of all its rivals; the American Association precedes the Union Association and Players League; and the American League follows the National League but precedes the Federal League.

The figure for the leading team in a given category is displayed in boldface. Where data are unavailable, the statistical column is blank. In the case of the National Association, much of the data that had been missing from the records for the five years of its existence, 1871–1875, are at last available. A research project of the Society for American Baseball Research to reconstruct all data from this period, based on original box scores and play-by-plays collected over decades by Michael Stagno of New York, is still in progress, though. It is hoped that additional, authoritative records can be developed for the next edition of *Total Baseball*.

Also presented here are the top three to five players/pitchers in up to 48 categories per season. When fewer than 48 categories are shown, it means that official records are lacking; that data is not reconstructible at present, which is the case for records of stolen bases before 1886 (with the exception, to date, being 1871-73); or that available data is not meaningful, such as for Relief Runs or Relief Ranking in the early years of this century. When fewer than five individuals appear in a given category, credible standouts are lacking, as in the case of Stolen Base Wins in most years. The criterion used for identifying pitching leaders is a minimum of one inning pitched per scheduled game; for batters the criterion employed is the one officially in place at the time or, in the absence of any known practice, 3.1 plate appearances per scheduled game.

Ties in counting stats are common, and occasionally they are so numerous that space does not permit listing all the players by name; ties for fifth place are not shown. Highly uncommon are ties in stats based on a large array of data, as with batting averages, on base percentages, earned run averages, and sabermetric stats such as Runs Created, Total Average, or the various Linear Weights measures. Where rounding off has created the appearance of a tie, the true leader—as extra decimal places for a complete calculation would have revealed—is listed first. An example is the AL batting race of 1949, in which

George Kell and Ted Williams are both shown as hitting .343; Kell in fact hit .3429 and Williams .3428. Both men are credited with batting averages of .343, but Kell, the actual leader, is listed first. (This procedure does not hold for calculated stats based on pitchers' won-lost percentages, where the narrow array of data frequently produces actual ties.)

For additional useful information about a team in a given year, we refer the reader to the home/road section, the preceding registers, the rosters, and the appendix on game scores. Team abbreviations used in the Annual Record are to be found on the last page of this book.

The abbreviations employed in the team statistical reviews of the Annual Record, plus brief descriptions of what the less common statistics measure, follow. For fuller explanations, see "The History of Major League Baseball Statistics," and for more technical information about formulas and computation, see the Glossary. Also included below are descriptions of statistics computed for league-leading players shown in the Annual Record.

Batting and Baserunning

G	Games played
W	Wins
L	Losses
PCT	Percentage of games won
GB	Games Behind the league or division leader
R	Runs scored
OR	Opponents' Runs scored
AB	At-Bats
H	Hits
2B	Doubles
3B	Triples
HR	Home Runs
BB	Bases on Balls
SO	Strikeouts
AVG	Batting Average (note that league-awarded championships are reflected by the champion's top ranking, even though his AVG may have been lower than that of a rival)
OBP	On Base Percentage
SLG	Slugging Average

PRO   Production (On Base Percentage plus Slugging Average)

PRO+   Normalized and park-adjusted Production. A figure of 100 is a league-average performance.

BR   Batting Runs (Linear Weights measure of runs contributed *beyond* what a league-average batter or team might have contributed, defined as zero.)

/A   Adjusted (Signifies that the stat to the immediate left, in this instance Batting Runs, is here normalized to league average and adjusted for home-park factor. A mark of 100 is a league-average performance. Pitcher batting is removed from all league batting statistics before normalization for a variety of reasons expanded upon in the Glossary.)

PF   Park Factor (Calculated separately for batters and pitchers: above 100 signifies a park favorable to hitters, below 100 signifies a park favorable to pitchers; see Glossary for further data and technical information.)

CHI   Clutch Hitting Index (Calculated for individuals, actual RBIs over expected RBIs, adjusted for league average and position in batting order; calculated for teams, actual runs scored divided by Batting Runs. Marks above the median of 100 are superior. See Glossary for precise formula.)

RC   Runs Created (Bill James's formulation for run contribution from a variety of batting and baserunning events; many different formulas are applied, depending on data available; see Glossary.)

SB   Stolen Bases (1886 to the present.)

CS   Caught Stealing (Available 1915, 1916 for players with more than 20 steals, 1920–1925, 1951–1990 NL; 1914–1915, 1916 for players with more than 20 steals, 1920–1990 AL.)

SBA   Stolen Base Average (Stolen bases divided by attempts; availability dependent upon CS, as shown above.)

SBR   Stolen Base Runs (Linear Weights measure of runs contributed *beyond* what a league-average base stealer or team might have gained, defined as zero; individual SBRs are calculated on the basis of a 66.7 percent success rate, the rate necessary to produce benefit, while team SBRs are normalized to the success rate for the league in that season; availability dependent upon CS.)

Pitching and Fielding

CG   Complete Games

SH   Shutouts (Individual and combined when calculated for teams; individual only for top five leaders.)

SV   Saves (Employing definition in force at the time, and 1969 definition for years prior to 1969.)

IP   Innings Pitched (Fractional innings given for teams; rounded-off whole innings for individuals.)

H   Hits allowed

H/G   Hits allowed per Game (Game defined as nine innings.)

HR   Home Runs allowed

BB   Bases on Balls allowed

SO   Strikeouts

RAT   Hits allowed plus walks allowed per nine innings.

ERA   Earned Run Average

ERA+   Normalized and park-adjusted ERA. A mark of 100 is a league-average performance, while marks over 100 are superior to league average and those below 100 indicate poor pitching performance.

OAV   Opponents' Batting Average

OOB   Opponents' On Base Percentage

PR   Pitching Runs (Linear Weights measure of runs saved *beyond* what a league-average pitcher or team might have saved, defined as zero.)

/A   Adjusted (Signifies that the stat to the immediate left, in this instance Pitching Runs, is here normalized to league average and adjusted for home-park factor.)

PF   Park Factor (Calculated separately for batters and pitchers; above 100 signifies a park favorable to hitters, below 100 signifies a park favorable to pitchers; see Glossary for further data and technical information.)

CPI   Clutch Pitching Index (Expected runs over actual runs, with 100 being a league-average performance and marks above 100 indicating better than expected results. See Glossary.)

FA   Fielding Average

E   Errors

DP   Double Plays

FW   Fielding Wins (Fielding Runs divided by the number of runs required to create an additional win beyond average; average is defined as a team record of .500 because a league won-lost average must be .500. For more technical data about Runs Per Win and Fielding Run formulas, see Glossary.)

PW   Pitching Wins (Adjusted Pitching Runs divided by the number of runs required to create an additional win beyond average; average is defined as a team record of .500 because a league won-lost average must be .500. For more technical data about Runs Per Win and Pitching Run formulas, see Glossary.)

BW   Batting Wins (Adjusted Batting Runs divided by the number of runs required to create an additional win beyond average; average is defined as a team record of .500 because a league won-lost average must be .500. For more technical data about Runs Per Win and Batting Run formulas, see Glossary.)

SBW   Stolen Base Wins (Stolen Base Runs divided by the number of runs required to create an additional win beyond average; average is defined as a team record of .500 because a league won-lost average must be .500. For more technical data about Runs Per Win and Stolen Base Run formulas, see Glossary.)

DIF   Differential (Difference between the team's actual won-lost record and that predicted by the total of its Pitching Wins, Batting Wins, Fielding Wins, and Stolen Base Wins; indicates the extent to which a team outperformed or underperformed its talent.)

Other stats carried only on an individual basis in the Annual Record portion of *Total Baseball* are as follows:

Total Average   Tom Boswell's formulation for offensive contribution from a variety of batting and baserunning events; calculated to make use of the maximum available data.

Fielding Runs   The Linear Weights measure of runs saved *beyond* what a league-average player at that position might have saved, defined as zero; calculated to take into account the particular demands of the different positions. See Glossary for formulas.

Total Player Rating   The sum of a player's Adjusted Batting Runs, Fielding Runs, and Base Stealing Runs, minus his positional adjustment, all divided by the Runs Per Win factor for that year (generally around 10, historically in the 9–11 range).

Bases on Balls Per Game   Game defined as nine innings; league leaders calculated on the basis of fewest walks per nine innings.

Strikeouts Per Game   Game defined as nine innings; league leaders calculated on the basis of most strikeouts per nine innings.

Starter Runs   Identical to Pitching Runs but confined to starting pitchers, defined as pitchers who average more than three innings per appearance.

Relief Runs   Identical to Pitching Runs but confined to relief pitchers.

Relief Ranking   Adjusted Relief Runs, weighted for the greater value of a bullpen "closer" who limits his opponents' scoring in the late innings; see Glossary for formula. Relief Runs will tend to benefit long and middle relievers, who are effective over many innings, while Relief Ranking will tend to benefit relievers with perhaps fewer innings but more saves and decisions.

Total Pitcher Index   The sum of a pitcher's Pitching Runs, Batting Runs (in the AL since 1973, zero), and Fielding Runs, all divided by the Runs Per Win factor for that year (generally around 10, historically in the 9–11 range).

Total Baseball Ranking   The "MVP" of statistics, this ranks pitchers and position players by the total runs contributed in all their endeavors, revealing the most valuable performers in a given year. For rare individuals like Babe Ruth in his Red Sox years, or Bob Caruthers, both of whom played a position in the field when they were not pitching, the TPR will sum up their records in both endeavors.

How to Read a Team Line

TEAM	G	W	L	PCT	GB	R	OR	AB	H	2B	3B	HR	BB	SO	AVG	OBP	SLG	PRO	PRO+	BR	/A	PF	CHI	RC	SB	CS	SBA	SBR
EAST																												
NY	160	100	60	.625		703	532	5408	1387	251	24	152	544	842	.256	.328	.396	.724	120	95	131	95	97	717	140	51	73	11
PIT	160	85	75	.531	15	651	616	5379	1327	240	45	110	553	947	.247	.321	.369	.690	105	33	42	99	99	648	119	60	66	0
MON	163	81	81	.500	20	628	592	5573	1400	260	48	107	454	1053	.251	.311	.373	.684	98	12	-18	105	97	636	189	89	68	3
CHI	163	77	85	.475	24	660	694	5675	1481	262	46	113	403	910	.261	.312	.383	.695	100	31	1	105	99	673	120	46	72	8
STL	162	76	86	.469	25	578	633	5518	1373	207	33	71	484	827	.249	.312	.337	.649	92	-47	-53	101	98	601	234	64	79	32
PHI	162	65	96	.404	35.5	597	734	5403	1294	246	31	106	489	981	.239	.308	.355	.663	94	-22	-35	102	100	599	112	49	70	4
WEST																												
LA	162	94	67	.584		628	544	5431	1346	217	25	99	437	947	.248	.308	.352	.660	99	-32	-14	97	107	590	131	46	74	12
CIN	161	87	74	.540	7	641	596	5426	1334	246	25	122	479	922	.246	.311	.368	.679	97	6	-19	104	102	639	207	56	79	29
SD	161	83	78	.516	11	594	583	5366	1325	205	35	94	494	892	.247	.313	.351	.664	99	-19	-8	98	99	594	123	50	71	7
SF	162	83	79	.512	11.5	670	626	5450	1353	227	44	113	550	1023	.248	.321	.368	.689	109	32	61	96	101	650	121	78	61	-11
HOU	162	82	80	.506	12.5	617	631	5494	1338	239	31	96	474	840	.244	.308	.351	.659	99	-32	-9	96	103	604	198	71	74	17
ATL	160	54	106	.338	39.5	555	741	5440	1319	228	28	96	432	848	.242	.301	.348	.649	88	-56	-84	105	99	549	95	69	58	-13
TOT	969					7522		65563	16277	2828	415	1279	5793	11032	.248	.313	.363	.675							1789	729	71	99

TEAM	CG	SH	SV	IP	H	H/G	HR	BB	SO	RAT	ERA	ERA+	OAV	OOB	PR	/A	PF	CPI	FA	E	DP	FW	PW	BW	SBW	DIF
EAST																										
NY	31	22	46	1439	1253	7.8	78	404	1100	10.6	2.91	111	.235	.293	86	50	93	97	.981	115	127	.9	5.4	14.1	.3	-.7
PIT	12	11	46	1440²	1349	8.4	108	469	790	11.6	3.47	98	.250	.314	-3	-10	99	101	.980	125	128	.3	-1.1	4.5	-.9	2.1
MON	18	12	43	1482²	1310	8.0	122	476	923	11.1	3.08	117	.238	.303	60	84	104	105	.978	142	145	-.5	9.1	-1.9	-.6	-6.0
CHI	30	10	29	1464¹	1494	9.2	115	490	897	12.4	3.84	94	.265	.327	-64	-38	105	102	.980	125	128	.5	-4.1	.1	-.0	-.4
STL	17	14	42	1470²	1387	8.5	91	486	881	11.6	3.47	100	.252	.314	-4	1	101	99	.981	121	131	.6	.1	-5.7	2.6	-2.6
PHI	16	6	36	1433	1447	9.1	118	628	859	13.3	4.14	86	.265	.344	-110	-92	103	102	.976	145	139	-.7	-9.9	-3.8	-.5	-.6
WEST																										
LA	32	24	49	1463¹	1291	7.9	84	473	1029	11.0	2.96	112	.237	.301	78	59	97	102	.977	142	126	-.5	6.4	-1.5	.4	8.8
CIN	24	13	43	1455	1271	7.9	121	504	934	11.1	3.35	107	.237	.306	16	38	104	98	.980	125	131	.4	4.1	-2.0	2.2	1.9
SD	30	9	39	1449	1332	8.3	112	439	885	11.1	3.28	104	.247	.306	27	19	99	102	.981	120	147	.6	2.0	-.9	-.1	.8
SF	25	13	42	1462¹	1323	8.1	99	422	875	10.9	3.39	96	.242	.300	10	-20	95	93	.980	129	145	.2	-2.2	6.6	-2.1	-.5
HOU	21	15	40	1474²	1339	8.2	123	478	1049	11.3	3.41	97	.242	.307	7	-14	96	99	.978	138	124	-.3	-1.5	-1.0	.9	2.9
ATL	14	4	25	1446	1481	9.2	108	524	810	12.7	4.09	90	.268	.336	-103	-67	107	100	.976	151	138	-1.1	-7.2	-9.1	-2.3	-6.3
TOT	270	153	480	17480²		8.4				11.6	3.45		.248	.313					.979	1578	1609					

The Los Angeles Dodgers had a miracle season in 1988, winning the National League pennant and the World Series against seemingly far superior opponents, the New York Mets and the Oakland Athletics, respectively. But their first miracle was to win the National League's Western Division title after finishing 73-89 in each of the previous two seasons. How did they win the West so easily? With mirrors, mostly, for they had below-average fielding and hitting that should have partially negated their outstanding pitching.

Let's just track the Dodgers' performance in some of the key categories to show how illuminating a close examination of team data in the Annual Record can be. The Dodgers' on base percentage (OBP) and slugging average (SLG) reveal them to have been a weak hitting club, though their Adjusted Production (PRO+) is a bit better, for they scored more runs in their park than might have been expected from the total run-scoring picture at Chavez Ravine (Park Factor 97). However, their Clutch Hitting Index (CHI) was the best in their division, testifying to their character, their good fortune, or both. Their Stolen Base Average was above average, but still only accounted for 12 extra runs over the course of the season, so this wasn't the secret of their success.

The pitching numbers are superlative—fewest runs allowed in the West and lowest ERA—despite the fact that Cincinnati held opponents to the same batting average (OAV) and San Francisco to the same on base percentage (OOB). Their Clutch Pitching Index (CPI) suggests that Dodger hurlers pulled their belts a notch tighter when men were on base, and their Home Runs allowed (HR) gives another tip that they knew how to stay away from the big inning. And maybe all those Shutouts (SH) are indicative of the many games they won while scoring few runs themselves.

Look at their batting (which cost them 1.5 wins in the BW, or Batting Wins, column) and baserunning and fielding (which are a virtual wash at +0.4 and −0.5, respectively, in the SBW and FW columns), and notice that their pitching, good as it was, only supplied 6.4 wins beyond average (.500). On balance, then, their offense and defense combined to produce only five wins beyond average. They should have finished with a record of 86–76, or five games beyond the 81–81 league average. Instead they finished 94–67, eight wins beyond their expectations, as indicated in the Differential (DIF) column. Maybe it was manager Tommy Lasorda's doing after all.

TEAM	G	W	L	PCT	GB	R	OR	AB	H	2B	3B	HR	BB	SO	AVG	OBP	SLG	PRO	PRO+	BR	/A	PF	CHI	RC	SB	CS SBA	SBR
ATH	28	21	7	.750		376	266	1281	410	66	27	9	46	23	.320	.344	.435	.779	125	38	42	99	107	216	56		
BOS	31	20	10	.667	2	401	303	1372	426	70	37	3	60	19	.310	.339	.422	.761	115	33	21	103	108	227	73		
CHI	28	19	9	.679	2	302	241	1196	323	52	21	10	60	22	.270	.305	.374	.679	86	-7	-38	111	104	161	69		
MUT	33	16	17	.485	7.5	302	313	1404	403	43	21	1	33	15	.287	.303	.350	.653	97	-20	-8	91	94	167	46		
OLY	32	15	15	.500	7	310	303	1353	375	54	26	6	48	13	.277	.302	.369	.671	98	-12	4	95	97	169	48		
TRO	29	13	15	.464	8	351	362	1248	384	51	34	6	49	19	.308	.334	.417	.751	114	25	20	101	106	199	62		
CLE	29	10	19	.345	11.5	249	341	1186	328	35	40	7	26	25	.277	.292	.391	.683	102	-7	8	95	89	144	18		
KEK	19	7	12	.368	9.5	137	243	746	178	19	8	2	33	9	.239	.271	.294	.565	63	-34	-37	102	91	65	16		
ROK	25	4	21	.160	15.5	231	287	1036	274	44	25	3	38	30	.264	.291	.364	.655	92	-16	-5	96	97	128	53		
TOT	127					2659		10822	3101	434	239	47	393	175	.287	.312	.384	.695						441			

TEAM	CG	SH	SV	IP	H	H/G	HR	BB	SO	RAT	ERA	ERA+	OAV	OOB	PR	/A	PF	CPI	FA	E	DP	FW	PW	BW	SBW	DIF
ATH	27	0	0	249	329	11.9	3	53	16	13.8	4.95	81	.284	.315	-20	-26	95	85	.845	194	13	1.1	-1.7	2.7		4.8
BOS	22	1	3	276	367	12.0	2	42	23	13.3	3.55	117	.273	.296	20	18	99	101	.834	243	24	-.3	1.2	1.4		2.7
CHI	25	0	1	251	308	11.0	6	28	22	12.0	2.76	166	.264	.281	41	51	109	121	.829	229	16	-.8	3.3	-2.5		4.9
MUT	32	1	0	293	373	11.5	7	42	22	12.7	3.72	102	.271	.292	16	2	90	98	.840	235	14	1.0	.1	.5		-2.1
OLY	32	0	0	282	371	11.8	4	45	13	13.3	4.37	95	.281	.305	-5	-6	99	90	.850	218	20	1.5	-.4	.3		-1.4
TRO	28	0	0	250	431	15.5	4	75	12	18.2	5.51	76	.342	.378	-36	-36	100	118	.845	198	22	1.3	-2.3	1.3		-1.3
CLE	23	0	0	254	346	12.3	13	53	34	14.1	4.11	100	.283	.312	3	0	98	107	.818	234	15	-.6	.0	.5		-4.4
KEK	19	1	0	169	261	13.9	5	21	17	15.0	5.17	88	.305	.322	-18	-11	108	93	.803	163	8	-.9	-.7	-2.4		1.5
ROK	23	1	0	226	315	12.5	3	34	16	13.9	4.30	95	.282	.303	-2	-5	97	91	.821	220	14	-1.5	-.3	-.3		-6.3
TOT	231	4	4	2250		12.4				14.0	4.22		.287	.312					.833	1934	146					

Runs		Hits		Doubles		Triples		Home Runs		Total Bases	
Barnes-Bos	66	McVey-Bos	66	Anson-Rok	11	Bass-Cle	10	Treacey-Chi	4	Meyerle-Ath	91
Birdsall-Bos	51	Meyerle-Ath	64			Wolters-Mut	9	Pike-Tro	4	Barnes-Bos	91
Radcliff-Ath	47	Barnes-Bos	63			Barnes-Bos	9	Meyerle-Ath	4	Pike-Tro	85
Cuthbert-Ath	47	Start-Mut	58			Pratt-Cle	8			McVey-Bos	85
Waterman-Oly	46	King-Tro	57							King-Tro	79

Runs Batted In		Runs Produced		Bases On Balls		Batting Average		On Base Percentage		Slugging Average	
Wolters-Mut	44	Barnes-Bos	100	Pinkham-Chi	18	Meyerle-Ath	.492	Meyerle-Ath	.500	Meyerle-Ath	.700
McVey-Bos	43	McVey-Bos	86	H.Wright-Bos	13	McVey-Bos	.431	G.Wright-Bos	.453	Pike-Tro	.654
Meyerle-Ath	40	Meyerle-Ath	81	Barnes-Bos	13	G.Wright-Bos	.412	Barnes-Bos	.447	Bass-Cle	.640
Pike-Tro	39	King-Tro	79	Wood-Chi	11	Barnes-Bos	.401	McVey-Bos	.435	G.Wright-Bos	.625
		Pike-Tro	78			King-Tro	.396	Wood-Chi	.425	Barnes-Bos	.580

Production		Adjusted Production		Batter Runs		Adjusted Batter Runs		Clutch Hitting Index		Runs Created	
Meyerle-Ath	1.200	Meyerle-Ath	243	Meyerle-Ath	22.6	Meyerle-Ath	23.2	Goldsmith-Kek	169	Meyerle-Ath	49
G.Wright-Bos	1.078	G.Wright-Bos	199	Barnes-Bos	18.9	Wolters-Mut	19.4	Barrows-Bos	150	Barnes-Bos	47
Pike-Tro	1.054	Pike-Tro	194	Pike-Tro	15.5	Barnes-Bos	17.0	McMullin-Tro	149	Wood-Chi	41
Barnes-Bos	1.027	Wolters-Mut	188	McVey-Bos	15.5	Pike-Tro	14.9	Brainard-Oly	143	McVey-Bos	41
McVey-Bos	.991	Barnes-Bos	186	Wolters-Mut	14.8	McVey-Bos	13.9	Fisher-Rok	137	Pike-Tro	36

Total Average		Stolen Bases		Stolen Base Average		Stolen Base Runs		Fielding Runs		Total Player Rating	
Meyerle-Ath	1.470	McGeary-Tro	20							Meyerle-Ath	1.4
G.Wright-Bos	1.383	Wood-Chi	18							Barnes-Bos	1.0
Wood-Chi	1.250	Cuthbert-Ath	16							Pike-Tro	1.0
Barnes-Bos	1.223	Leonard-Oly	14							McVey-Bos	.9
Pike-Tro	1.148	Eggler-Mut	14							King-Tro	.8

Wins		Win Percentage		Games		Complete Games		Shutouts		Saves	
Spalding-Bos	19	McBride-Ath	.783	Wolters-Mut	32	Wolters-Mut	31	Wolters-Mut	1	H.Wright-Bos	3
Zettlein-Chi	18	Zettlein-Chi	.667	Spalding-Bos	31	Brainard-Oly	30	Spalding-Bos	1	Pinkham-Chi	1
McBride-Ath	18	Spalding-Bos	.655	Brainard-Oly	30	McMullin-Tro	28	Mathews-Kek	1		
Wolters-Mut	16	Wolters-Mut	.500	McMullin-Tro	29	Zettlein-Chi	25	Fisher-Rok	1		
						McBride-Ath	25				

Innings Pitched		Fewest Hits/Game		Fewest BB/Game		Strikeouts		Strikeouts/Game		Ratio	
Wolters-Mut	283.0	Wolters-Mut	10.97	Zettlein-Chi	.93	Pratt-Cle	34	Pratt-Cle	1.36	Zettlein-Chi	12.08
Brainard-Oly	264.0	Zettlein-Chi	11.14	Mathews-Kek	1.12	Spalding-Bos	23	Mathews-Kek	.91	Wolters-Mut	12.21
Spalding-Bos	257.1	McBride-Ath	11.55	Wolters-Mut	1.24	Zettlein-Chi	22	Zettlein-Chi	.82	Spalding-Bos	12.98
McMullin-Tro	249.0	Spalding-Bos	11.65	Brainard-Oly	1.26	Wolters-Mut	22	Spalding-Bos	.80	McBride-Ath	13.18
Zettlein-Chi	240.2	Pratt-Cle	11.86	Fisher-Rok	1.31	Mathews-Kek	17	Wolters-Mut	.70	Brainard-Oly	13.57

Earned Run Average		Adjusted ERA		Opponents' Batting Avg.		Opponents' On Base Pct.		Starter Runs		Adjusted Starter Runs	
Zettlein-Chi	2.73	Zettlein-Chi	168	Wolters-Mut	.263	Zettlein-Chi	.283	Zettlein-Chi	39.8	Zettlein-Chi	49.7
Spalding-Bos	3.36	Spalding-Bos	124	Zettlein-Chi	.267	Wolters-Mut	.285	Wolters-Mut	24.7	Spalding-Bos	22.9
Wolters-Mut	3.43	Wolters-Mut	110	Spalding-Bos	.268	Spalding-Bos	.290	Spalding-Bos	24.7	Wolters-Mut	11.2
Pratt-Cle	3.77	Pratt-Cle	110	Pratt-Cle	.277	Fisher-Rok	.302	Pratt-Cle	11.3	Pratt-Cle	9.0
Fisher-Rok	4.35	Fisher-Rok	94	McBride-Ath	.280	McBride-Ath	.307	Stearns-Oly	3.4	Stearns-Oly	3.3

Clutch Pitching Index		Relief Runs		Adjusted Relief Runs		Relief Ranking		Total Pitcher Index		Total Baseball Ranking	
Zettlein-Chi	124	Pinkham-Chi	.8	Pinkham-Chi	1.3	Pinkham-Chi	1.4	Zettlein-Chi	2.9	Zettlein-Chi	3.1
McMullin-Tro	118							Wolters-Mut	2.0	Wolters-Mut	2.0
Pratt-Cle	110							Spalding-Bos	1.6	Spalding-Bos	1.9
Spalding-Bos	101							Pratt-Cle	.8	Meyerle-Ath	1.4
Wolters-Mut	99							Stearns-Oly	.1	Pratt-Cle	1.1

TEAM	G	W	L	PCT	GB	R	OR	AB	H	2B	3B	HR	BB	SO	AVG	OBP	SLG	PRO	PRO+	BR	/A	PF	CHI	RC	SB	CS	SBA	SBR
BOS	48	39	8	.830		521	236	2137	677	114	31	7	28	26	.317	.326	.409	.735	122	65	37	105	99	301	47	14	77	6
BAL	58	35	19	.648	7.5	617	434	2576	747	94	35	14	27	28	.290	.297	.370	.667	102	19	-7	105	108	295	35	15	70	2
MUT	56	34	20	.630	8.5	523	362	2423	668	86	13	4	55	52	.276	.292	.327	.619	99	-19	13	94	103	246	56	21	73	4
ATH	47	30	14	.682	7.5	539	349	2140	678	77	23	4	69	47	.317	.338	.380	.718	124	59	57	100	102	289	58	32	64	-2
TRO	25	15	10	.600	13	273	191	1124	329	56	11	5	7	14	.293	.297	.375	.672	107	10	6	101	109	129	9	7	56	-2
ATL	37	9	28	.243	25	237	473	1466	370	46	10	0	19	24	.252	.262	.297	.559	63	-42	-90	117	87	117	17	14	55	-3
CLE	22	6	16	.273	20.5	174	254	935	272	37	6	0	17	13	.291	.304	.343	.647	107	2	13	95	85	103	12	3	80	2
MAN	24	5	19	.208	22.5	220	348	1014	305	31	8	1	5	12	.301	.304	.350	.654	109	4	17	94	100	111	5	3	63	0
ECK	29	3	26	.103	27	152	413	1075	235	26	6	0	14	29	.219	.229	.254	.483	59	-59	-35	85	88	65	8	4	67	0
OLY	9	2	7	.222	18	54	140	363	93	12	3	0	4	4	.256	.264	.306	.570	81	-9	-6	95	78	29	0	3	0	-2
NAT	11	0	11	.0	21	80	190	460	105	3	2	0	1	3	.228	.230	.243	.473	41	-27	-39	117	113	26				
TOT	183					3390		15713	4479	582	148	35	246	252	.285	.296	.348	.644							247	116	68	5

TEAM	CG	SH	SV	IP	H	H/G	HR	BB	SO	RAT	ERA	ERA+	OAV	OOB	PR	/A	PF	CPI	FA	E	DP	FW	PW	BW	SBW	DIF
BOS	41	3	1	430¹	438	9.2	0	27		9.7	1.99	188	.240	.251	83	83	100	118					5.8	2.6	.4	6.8
BAL	48	1	1	515²	566	9.9	3	63		11.0	3.02	124	.243	.263	40	42	101	84					2.9	-.5	.1	5.5
MUT	54	3	0	512	618	10.9	2	32		11.4	2.55	135	.269	.279	66	51	93	125					3.6	.9	.2	2.3
ATH	47	1	0	419	513	11.0	3	26		11.6	3.01	121	.268	.278	33	29	98	104					2.0	4.0	-.2	2.2
TRO	17	2	0	225	282	11.3	2	10		11.7	3.08	120	.272	.279	16	16	100	105					1.1	.4	-.2	1.1
ATL	37	0	0	336	561	15.0	6	19		15.5	5.06	91	.323	.331	-50	-17	124	100					-1.2	-6.3	-.2	-1.8
CLE	15	0	0	199	289	13.1	6	24		14.2	4.57	80	.291	.307	-19	-21	98	91					-1.5	.9	.1	-4.6
MAN	22	0	0	211	368	15.7	5	13		16.3	5.97	61	.320	.328	-53	-54	99	84					-3.8	1.2	-.0	-4.4
ECK	28	0	0	259¹	503	17.5	6	24		18.3	5.73	61	.355	.365	-58	-65	93	112					-4.5	-2.4	-.0	-4.5
OLY	9	0	0	79	147	16.7	0	5		17.3	6.38	58	.332	.339	-23	-24	99	84					-1.7	-.4	-.2	-.2
NAT	11	0	0	99	194	17.6	2	3		17.9	6.91	68	.339	.343	-35	-24	127	83					-1.7	-2.7	-.0	-1.1
TOT	329	10	2	3285¹		12.3				12.9	3.72		.285	.296												

Runs		Hits		Doubles		Triples		Home Runs		Total Bases	
Eggler-Mut	95	Eggler-Mut	97	Barnes-Bos	28	Hall-Bal	8	Pike-Bal	6	Barnes-Bos	132
G.Wright-Bos	87	Barnes-Bos	97	Eggler-Mut	20	Gould-Bos	8	Gedney-Tro-Eck	3	Pike-Bal	120
Cuthbert-Ath	82	Force-Tro-Bal	93	G.Wright-Bos	16	Anson-Ath	7			G.Wright-Bos	119
Barnes-Bos	81	Hatfield-Mut	91	Hall-Bal	14	Meyerle-Ath	6			Eggler-Mut	117
Hatfield-Mut	75	Cuthbert-Ath	90	Fisler-Ath	14					Hall-Bal	115

Runs Batted In		Runs Produced		Bases On Balls		Batting Average		On Base Percentage		Slugging Average	
Pike-Bal	62	Cuthbert-Ath	128	Mack-Ath	23	Barnes-Bos	.422	Anson-Ath	.455	Barnes-Bos	.574
Anson-Ath	50	Pike-Bal	124	Anson-Ath	16	Anson-Ath	.414	Barnes-Bos	.444	Anson-Ath	.521
Start-Mut	49	Barnes-Bos	124	McMullin-Mut	11	Force-Tro-Bal	.406	Force-Tro-Bal	.411	Meyerle-Ath	.479
Spalding-Bos	48	Hatfield-Mut	119			McCarton-Man	.373	Hastings-Cle-Bal	.374	Force-Tro-Bal	.476
Fisler-Ath	48	G.Wright-Bos	118			Hastings-Cle-Bal	.360	White-Cle	.366	G.Wright-Bos	.467

Production		Adjusted Production		Batter Runs		Adjusted Batter Runs		Clutch Hitting Index		Runs Created	
Barnes-Bos	1.017	Barnes-Bos	200	Barnes-Bos	29.2	Anson-Ath	25.2	Start-Mut	164	Barnes-Bos	64
Anson-Ath	.975	Anson-Ath	199	Anson-Ath	25.5	Barnes-Bos	25.1	Zettlein-Tro-Eck	160	Anson-Ath	52
Force-Tro-Bal	.887	Force-Tro-Bal	168	Force-Tro-Bal	18.6	Force-Tro-Bal	16.8	White-Cle	145	Force-Tro-Bal	47
G.Wright-Bos	.816	Hastings-Cle-Bal	147	G.Wright-Bos	13.9	Eggler-Mut	16.2	Tipper-Man	145	Eggler-Mut	47
Spalding-Bos	.815	White-Cle	146	Spalding-Bos	13.5	Hatfield-Mut	11.8	McBride-Ath	137	G.Wright-Bos	45

Total Average		Stolen Bases		Stolen Base Average		Stolen Base Runs		Fielding Runs		Total Player Rating	
Barnes-Bos	1.119	Eggler-Mut	17	Eggler-Mut	77.3	Barnes-Bos	2.4			Barnes-Bos	1.6
Anson-Ath	.970	G.Wright-Bos	14			Eggler-Mut	2.1			Eggler-Mut	1.4
Force-Tro-Bal	.826	Cuthbert-Ath	14			Bechtel-Mut	2.1			Anson-Ath	1.4
G.Wright-Bos	.767	McGeary-Ath	13							Force-Tro-Bal	1.0
Wood-Tro-Eck	.765	Barnes-Bos	12							Cuthbert-Ath	.9

Wins		Win Percentage		Games		Complete Games		Shutouts		Saves	
Spalding-Bos	38	Spalding-Bos	.826	Cummings-Mut	55	Cummings-Mut	53	Spalding-Bos	3	H.Wright-Bos	1
Cummings-Mut	33	McBride-Ath	.682	Mathews-Bal	49	McBride-Ath	47	Cummings-Mut	3	Fisher-Bal	1
McBride-Ath	30	Cummings-Mut	.623	Spalding-Bos	48	Spalding-Bos	41	Zettlein-Tro-Eck	2		
Mathews-Bal	25	Mathews-Bal	.581	McBride-Ath	47	Mathews-Bal	39	McBride-Ath	1		
Zettlein-Tro-Eck	15	Zettlein-Tro-Eck	.484	Britt-Atl	37	Britt-Atl	37	Fisher-Bal	1		

Innings Pitched		Fewest Hits/Game		Fewest BB/Game		Strikeouts		Strikeouts/Game		Ratio	
Cummings-Mut	497.0	Fisher-Bal	7.26	Buttery-Man	.18	Mathews-Bal	55	Fisher-Bal	1.63	Fisher-Bal	8.16
McBride-Ath	419.0	Spalding-Bos	9.16	Stearns-Nat	.27	McBride-Ath	44	Mathews-Bal	1.22	Spalding-Bos	9.76
Mathews-Bal	405.1	Mathews-Bal	10.59	P.Martin-Tro-Eck	.44	Cummings-Mut	43	McBride-Ath	.95	Zettlein-Tro-Eck	11.22
Spalding-Bos	404.2	Zettlein-Tro-Eck	10.75	Zettlein-Tro-Eck	.48	Spalding-Bos	27	Zettlein-Tro-Eck	.86	Cummings-Mut	11.41
Britt-Atl	336.0	Cummings-Mut	10.87	Britt-Atl	.51	Zettlein-Tro-Eck	25	Cummings-Mut	.78	McBride-Ath	11.58

Earned Run Average		Adjusted ERA		Opponents' Batting Avg.		Opponents' On Base Pct.		Starter Runs		Adjusted Starter Runs	
Spalding-Bos	1.98	Spalding-Bos	188	Fisher-Bal	.189	Fisher-Bal	.207	Spalding-Bos	78.1	Spalding-Bos	78.6
Cummings-Mut	2.52	Fisher-Bal	148	Spalding-Bos	.240	Spalding-Bos	.252	Cummings-Mut	66.3	Cummings-Mut	51.1
Fisher-Bal	2.53	Cummings-Mut	137	Mathews-Bal	.256	Zettlein-Tro-Eck	.273	McBride-Ath	33.1	McBride-Ath	28.7
Zettlein-Tro-Eck	2.67	Zettlein-Tro-Eck	136	Zettlein-Tro-Eck	.265	Mathews-Bal	.277	Zettlein-Tro-Eck	30.6	Zettlein-Tro-Eck	28.4
McBride-Ath	3.01	McBride-Ath	121	McBride-Ath	.268	McBride-Ath	.278	Mathews-Bal	25.4	Mathews-Bal	26.8

Clutch Pitching Index		Relief Runs		Adjusted Relief Runs		Relief Ranking		Total Pitcher Index		Total Baseball Ranking	
Cummings-Mut	127	H.Wright-Bos	4.6	H.Wright-Bos	4.6	H.Wright-Bos	2.0	Spalding-Bos	7.1	Spalding-Bos	7.7
Spalding-Bos	119							Cummings-Mut	3.1	Cummings-Mut	3.7
Zettlein-Tro-Eck	114							McBride-Ath	2.1	Zettlein-Tro-Eck	2.2
P.Martin-Tro-Eck	109							Zettlein-Tro-Eck	1.9	McBride-Ath	2.1
McBride-Ath	104							Mathews-Bal	1.2	Mathews-Bal	1.7

TEAM	G	W	L	PCT	GB	R	OR	AB	H	2B	3B	HR	BB	SO	AVG	OBP	SLG	PRO	PRO+	BR	/A	PF	CHI	RC	SB	CS	SBA	SBR
BOS	60	43	16	.729		739	460	2755	930	137	46	13	62	24	.338	.352	.435	.787	126	117	60	108	106	434	39	27	59	-5
PHI	53	36	17	.679	4	526	396	2325	645	83	20	8	62	39	.277	.296	.341	.637	89	-21	-39	104	111	249	44	14	76	5
BAL	57	34	22	.607	7.5	644	451	2563	810	119	39	12	40	25	.316	.327	.407	.734	121	59	62	100	108	352	21	10	68	0
MUT	53	29	24	.547	11	424	385	2214	622	67	41	5	42	22	.281	.294	.355	.649	96	-13	-10	99	93	240	15	5	75	2
ATH	52	28	23	.549	11	474	403	2266	683	76	22	4	35	32	.301	.312	.360	.672	95	6	-30	108	98	261	29	24	55	-6
ATL	55	17	37	.315	23.5	366	549	2210	588	60	27	6	53	43	.266	.283	.326	.609	93	-42	3	89	86	211	18	9	67	0
WAS	39	8	31	.205	25	283	485	1563	408	45	25	3	19	33	.261	.270	.328	.598	83	-38	-29	97	98	141	5	5	50	-2
RES	23	2	21	.87	23	98	299	868	204	21	8	0	8	22	.235	.242	.278	.520	62	-44	-34	92	71	60	2	1	67	0
MAR	6	0	6	.0	16.5	26	152	211	33	5	0	0	0	0	.156	.156	.180	.336	1	-24	-21	77	132	6				
TOT	199					3580		16975	4923	613	228	51	321	240	.290	.303	.362	.665							173	95	65	-5

TEAM	CG	SH	SV	IP	H	H/G	HR	BB	SO	RAT	ERA	ERA+	OAV	OOB	PR	/A	PF	CPI	FA	E	DP	FW	PW	BW	SBW	DIF
BOS	48	1	3	536	708	11.9	5	35	31	12.5	2.59	128	.287	.297	40	44	102	118	.838	465	45	.4	3.1	4.2	-.3	6.0
PHI	50	0	0	481	627	11.7	3	44	28	12.6	2.77	119	.284	.298	26	28	101	109	.848	379	43	2.0	2.0	-2.8	.4	7.9
BAL	55	1	0	508²	680	12.0	4	42	34	12.8	3.01	108	.285	.297	14	14	100	100	.859	353	33	5.0	1.0	4.4	.0	-4.4
MUT	48	2	0	477	539	10.2	5	69	76	11.5	2.62	121	.254	.278	33	29	97	87	.820	424	28	-.3	2.1	-.7	.2	1.3
ATH	44	3	1	475	553	10.5	4	58	41	11.6	3.03	113	.257	.276	12	20	105	75	.842	383	30	1.4	1.4	-2.1	-.4	2.2
ATL	52	1	0	500	737	13.3	8	42	15	14.0	3.98	76	.303	.315	-40	-52	93	93	.830	471	30	-1.9	-3.7	.2	.0	-4.6
WAS	39	0	0	346	593	15.4	11	22	7	16.0	4.71	71	.335	.343	-56	-52	103	104	.817	337	27	-1.5	-3.7	-2.1	-.1	-4.1
RES	22	0	0	207	342	14.9	7	9	8	15.3	3.22	104	.310	.316	1	3	103	124	.790	243	9	-3.2	.2	-2.4	.0	-4.1
MAR	6	0	0	54	144	24.0	4	0	0	24.0	8.00	40	.392	.392	-28	-29	100	102	.781	66	7	-1.0	-2.1	-1.5	.0	1.5
TOT	364	8	4	3584²		12.4				13.2	3.25		.290	.303					.833	3121	247					

Runs
Barnes-Bos 125
G.Wright-Bos 99
Spalding-Bos 83
Eggler-Mut 82
Leonard-Bos 81

Hits
Barnes-Bos 137
G.Wright-Bos 126
White-Bos 121
Spalding-Bos 106
Anson-Ath 101

Doubles
Barnes-Bos 28
O'Rourke-Bos 22
White-Bos 20
Pike-Bal 18
Carey-Bal 18

Triples
Barnes-Bos 10
White-Bos 8
Pike-Bal 8
Holdsworth-Mut ... 8

Home Runs
Pike-Bal 4
G.Wright-Bos 3
Meyerle-Phi 3
McVey-Bal 3
Barnes-Bos 3

Total Bases
Barnes-Bos 194
G.Wright-Bos 162
White-Bos 157
Pike-Bal 136
O'Rourke-Bos 129

Runs Batted In
White-Bos 64
Barnes-Bos 61
Spalding-Bos 59
Leonard-Bos 58
Mills-Bal 57

Runs Produced
Barnes-Bos 183
G.Wright-Bos 144
White-Bos 143
Spalding-Bos 141
Leonard-Bos 139

Bases On Balls
Barnes-Bos 18
Mack-Phi 15
O'Rourke-Bos 14
Malone-Phi 14

Batting Average
Barnes-Bos .... .425
Anson-Ath .... .398
White-Bos .... .390
G.Wright-Bos ..... .388
McVey-Bal .... .380

On Base Percentage
Barnes-Bos ...... .456
Anson-Ath .... .409
G.Wright-Bos .... .402
Force-Bal .... .391
White-Bos .... .390

Slugging Average
Barnes-Bos ...... .602
McVey-Bal .... .521
White-Bos .... .506
G.Wright-Bos .... .498
Meyerle-Phi ..... .479

Production
Barnes-Bos 1.058
McVey-Bal .... .911
G.Wright-Bos .... .901
White-Bos .... .897
Anson-Ath .... .858

Adjusted Production
Barnes-Bos 193
McVey-Bal 166
Pabor-Atl 151
G.Wright-Bos 151
White-Bos 149

Batter Runs
Barnes-Bos 43.2
G.Wright-Bos 25.0
White-Bos 22.6
Anson-Ath 16.3
O'Rourke-Bos 16.3

Adjusted Batter Runs
Barnes-Bos 34.0
G.Wright-Bos 17.4
Pabor-Atl 16.3
White-Bos 15.5
McVey-Bal 15.3

Clutch Hitting Index
Cummings-Bal 177
McBride-Ath 163
Addy-Phi-Bal 134
Mills-Bal 133
Malone-Phi 133

Runs Created
Barnes-Bos 94
G.Wright-Bos 64
White-Bos 64
O'Rourke-Bos 51
Pike-Bal 48

Total Average
Barnes-Bos 1.169
McVey-Bal .... .874
White-Bos .... .843
G.Wright-Bos .... .824
O'Rourke-Bos .... .788

Stolen Bases
Cuthbert-Phi 13
Barnes-Bos 13
McMullin-Ath 9
Wood-Phi 8

Stolen Base Average

Stolen Base Runs
Cuthbert-Phi 2.7
McMullin-Ath 2.1

Fielding Runs

Total Player Rating
Barnes-Bos 2.2
Pabor-Atl 1.3
White-Bos 1.2
McVey-Bal 1.1
Pike-Bal 1.0

Wins
Spalding-Bos 41
Zettlein-Phi 36
Mathews-Mut 29
Cummings-Bal 28
McBride-Ath 24

Win Percentage
Spalding-Bos .... .745
Zettlein-Phi .... .706
Cummings-Bal .... .667
McBride-Ath ..... .558
Mathews-Mut ..... .558

Games
Spalding-Bos 60
Britt-Atl 54
Mathews-Mut 52
Zettlein-Phi 51
McBride-Ath 46

Complete Games
Britt-Atl 51
Zettlein-Phi 49
Spalding-Bos 48
Mathews-Mut 47
Cummings-Bal 42

Shutouts
McBride-Ath 3
Mathews-Mut 2
Spalding-Bos 1
Cummings-Bal 1
Britt-Atl 1

Saves
Spalding-Bos 2
H.Wright-Bos 1
Fisher-Ath 1

Innings Pitched
Spalding-Bos 497.2
Britt-Atl 480.2
Zettlein-Phi 460.0
Mathews-Mut 443.0
McBride-Ath 382.2

Fewest Hits/Game
Fisher-Ath 9.60
Mathews-Mut 9.93
McBride-Ath 10.65
Cummings-Bal ... 11.19
Zettlein-Phi ... 11.60

Fewest BB/Game
H.Campbell-Res ... .38
Stearns-Was ..... .48
Spalding-Bos .... .51
Brainard-Bal .... .75
Britt-Atl .... .75

Strikeouts
Mathews-Mut 75
Spalding-Bos 31
Cummings-Bal 31
Zettlein-Phi 28
McBride-Ath 25

Strikeouts/Game
Mathews-Mut 1.52
Fisher-Ath 1.49
Cummings-Bal .... .73
McBride-Ath ..... .59
Spalding-Bos .... .56

Ratio
Fisher-Ath 10.67
Mathews-Mut 11.19
McBride-Ath 11.76
Cummings-Bal ... 11.97
Spalding-Bos ... 12.13

Earned Run Average
Fisher-Ath 1.81
Spalding-Bos 2.46
Mathews-Mut 2.56
Cummings-Bal 2.66
Zettlein-Phi 2.70

Adjusted ERA
Fisher-Ath 188
Spalding-Bos 135
Mathews-Mut 124
Cummings-Bal 122
Zettlein-Phi 122

Opponents' Batting Avg.
Fisher-Ath ...... .227
Mathews-Mut ..... .251
McBride-Ath ..... .263
Cummings-Bal .... .274
Zettlein-Phi .... .283

Opponents' On Base Pct.
Fisher-Ath .... .246
Mathews-Mut ..... .274
McBride-Ath ..... .282
Cummings-Bal .... .287
Spalding-Bos .... .292

Starter Runs
Spalding-Bos 43.8
Mathews-Mut 34.0
Zettlein-Phi ... 28.2
Cummings-Bal ... 25.0
Fisher-Ath 13.5

Adjusted Starter Runs
Spalding-Bos 47.4
Zettlein-Phi 30.5
Mathews-Mut 29.7
Cummings-Bal 25.0
Fisher-Ath 15.0

Clutch Pitching Index
H.Campbell-Res ... 124
Spalding-Bos 118
Zettlein-Phi 110
Greyson -Was 108
Brainard-Bal 103

Relief Runs

Adjusted Relief Runs

Relief Ranking

Total Pitcher Index
Spalding-Bos 4.3
Mathews-Mut 2.0
Cummings-Bal 1.9
Zettlein-Phi 1.6
Fisher-Ath 8

Total Baseball Ranking
Spalding-Bos 5.1
Mathews-Mut 2.6
Zettlein-Phi 2.2
Barnes-Bos 2.2
Cummings-Bal 1.9

TEAM	G	W	L	PCT	GB	R	OR	AB	H	2B	3B	HR	BB	SO	AVG	OBP	SLG	PRO	PRO+	BR	/A	PF	CHI	RC	SB	CS	SBA	SBR
BOS	71	52	18	.743		735	415	3122	981	130	57	18	32		.314	.321	.410	.731	128	114	76	106	108	421				
MUT	65	42	23	.646	7.5	500	377	2719	709	100	31	8	38		.261	.271	.329	.600	90	-19	-34	103	105	249				
ATH	55	33	22	.600	11.5	441	344	2260	646	87	17	6	24		.286	.293	.347	.640	98	15	-21	109	104	236				
PHI	58	29	29	.500	17	476	428	2432	690	74	51	3	28		.284	.292	.360	.652	106	25	9	104	102	262				
CHI	59	28	31	.475	18.5	418	480	2457	690	89	3	3	34		.281	.291	.323	.614	98	-4	-8	101	94	237				
ATL	56	22	33	.400	22.5	301	449	2165	497	50	11	1	32		.230	.241	.264	.505	71	-83	-48	88	97	141				
HAR	53	16	37	.302	27.5	371	471	2140	587	92	19	2	26		.274	.283	.338	.621	95	0	-19	105	95	210				
BAL	47	9	38	.191	31.5	227	505	1781	435	53	8	1	24		.244	.254	.285	.539	75	-48	-46	99	82	132				
TOT	232					3469		19076	5235	675	197	42	238	0	.274	.283	.337	.620										

TEAM	CG	SH	SV	IP	H	H/G	HR	BB	SO	RAT	ERA	ERA+	OAV	OOB	PR	/A	PF	CPI	FA	E	DP	FW	PW	BW	SBW	DIF
BOS	65	4	3	633	777	11.0	1	27		11.4	2.36	126	.274	.281	45	42	99	123				3.3	5.9			7.9
MUT	62	4	0	586	658	10.1	3	40		10.7	2.30	133	.259	.271	45	50	103	111				3.9	-2.6			8.3
ATH	55	0	0	487	514	9.5	5	29		10.0	2.55	124	.241	.251	24	33	106	80				2.6	-1.6			4.6
PHI	56	3	0	524	666	11.4	4	21		11.8	2.95	103	.275	.281	3	5	101	100				.4	.7			-1.1
CHI	58	3	0	533²	696	11.7	7	48		12.5	3.25	94	.285	.299	-15	-12	102	106				-.9	-.6			.0
ATL	56	1	0	506	621	11.0	16	13		11.3	3.20	88	.268	.272	-11	-22	94	90				-1.7	-3.7			-.0
HAR	45	0	1	481	660	12.3	2	23		12.8	3.54	89	.288	.295	-29	-20	105	94				-1.6	-1.5			-7.5
BAL	43	0	0	420	643	13.8	4	37		14.6	4.31	71	.306	.319	-61	-59	102	96				-4.6	-3.6			-6.4
TOT	440	15	4	4170²		11.3				11.8	3.00		.274	.283												

Runs		Hits		Doubles		Triples		Home Runs		Total Bases	
McVey-Bos	91	McVey-Bos	124	Pike-Har	24	G.Wright-Bos	15	O'Rourke-Bos	5	McVey-Bos	166
O'Rourke-Bos	82	Spalding-Bos	119	McVey-Bos	22	Craver-Phi	11	McVey-Bos	4	G.Wright-Bos	153
Spalding-Bos	80	Leonard-Bos	109	Meyerle-Chi	20	Holdsworth-Phi	9	White-Bos	3	O'Rourke-Bos	144
G.Wright-Bos	76	G.Wright-Bos	106	Leonard-Bos	18	York-Phi	8	Clapp-Ath	3	Spalding-Bos	136
White-Bos	75	White-Bos	106	Burdock-Mut	16					Leonard-Bos	135

Runs Batted In	Runs Produced		Bases On Balls		Batting Average		On Base Percentage		Slugging Average	
	McVey-Bos	87	Nelson-Mut	9	Meyerle-Chi	.403	Meyerle-Chi	.410	Pike-Har	.496
	Spalding-Bos	80	Stearns-Har	8	McVey-Bos	.364	McVey-Bos	.364	Meyerle-Chi	.494
	O'Rourke-Bos	77	Hatfield-Mut	8	Craver-Phi	.352	Barnes-Bos	.363	G.Wright-Bos	.489
	G.Wright-Bos	74	Barnes-Bos	8	Manning-Bal-Har	.347	Craver-Phi	.362	McVey-Bos	.487
					Barnes-Bos	.344	McMullin-Ath	.357	Craver-Phi	.483

Production		Adjusted Production		Batter Runs		Adjusted Batter Runs		Clutch Hitting Index	Runs Created	
Meyerle-Chi	.904	Meyerle-Chi	185	McVey-Bos	24.7	Meyerle-Chi	22.9		McVey-Bos	62
McVey-Bos	.850	Craver-Phi	161	Meyerle-Chi	23.6	McVey-Bos	19.9		G.Wright-Bos	55
Craver-Phi	.845	McVey-Bos	159	G.Wright-Bos	22.1	G.Wright-Bos	17.7		Meyerle-Chi	53
G.Wright-Bos	.842	G.Wright-Bos	156	Spalding-Bos	20.8	Craver-Phi	16.7		Craver-Phi	48
Pike-Har	.836	Pike-Har	155	Craver-Phi	19.1	Spalding-Bos	16.0		O'Rourke-Bos	47

Total Average		Stolen Bases	Stolen Base Average	Stolen Base Runs	Fielding Runs	Total Player Rating	
Meyerle-Chi	.848					Meyerle-Chi	1.7
G.Wright-Bos	.773					McVey-Bos	1.6
Craver-Phi	.769					G.Wright-Bos	1.2
McVey-Bos	.765					Craver-Phi	1.1
Pike-Har	.752					Pike-Har	1.0

Wins		Win Percentage		Games		Complete Games		Shutouts		Saves	
Spalding-Bos	52	Spalding-Bos	.765	Spalding-Bos	71	Spalding-Bos	65	Spalding-Bos	4	H.Wright-Bos	3
Mathews-Mut	42	Mathews-Mut	.656	Mathews-Mut	65	Mathews-Mut	62	Mathews-Mut	4	Stearns-Har	1
McBride-Ath	33	McBride-Ath	.600	Zettlein-Chi	57	Zettlein-Chi	57	Zettlein-Chi	3		
Cummings-Phi	28	Cummings-Phi	.519	McBride-Ath	55	McBride-Ath	55	Cummings-Phi	3		
Zettlein-Chi	27	Zettlein-Chi	.474	Bond-Atl	55	Bond-Atl	55	Bond-Atl	1		

Innings Pitched		Fewest Hits/Game		Fewest BB/Game		Strikeouts	Strikeouts/Game	Ratio	
Spalding-Bos	616.1	McBride-Ath	9.50	Bond-Atl	.18			McBride-Ath	10.03
Mathews-Mut	578.0	Mathews-Mut	10.07	Fisher-Har	.28			Mathews-Mut	10.68
Zettlein-Chi	515.2	Spalding-Bos	11.00	Spalding-Bos	.34			Bond-Atl	11.21
Bond-Atl	497.0	Bond-Atl	11.03	Cummings-Phi	.39			Spalding-Bos	11.33
McBride-Ath	487.0	Cummings-Phi	11.24	McBride-Ath	.54			Cummings-Phi	11.63

Earned Run Average		Adjusted ERA		Opponents' Batting Avg.		Opponents' On Base Pct.		Starter Runs		Adjusted Starter Runs	
Mathews-Mut	2.30	Mathews-Mut	133	McBride-Ath	.241	McBride-Ath	.251	Mathews-Mut	44.5	Mathews-Mut	49.5
Spalding-Bos	2.35	Spalding-Bos	126	Mathews-Mut	.258	Mathews-Mut	.270	Spalding-Bos	44.3	Spalding-Bos	42.0
McBride-Ath	2.55	McBride-Ath	124	Bond-Atl	.268	Bond-Atl	.271	McBride-Ath	24.2	McBride-Ath	33.3
Cummings-Phi	2.88	Cummings-Phi	106	Cummings-Phi	.271	Cummings-Phi	.278	Cummings-Phi	6.5	Cummings-Phi	8.6
Fisher-Har	3.04	Fisher-Har	104	Spalding-Bos	.273	Spalding-Bos	.279			Fisher-Har	4.2

Clutch Pitching Index		Relief Runs	Adjusted Relief Runs	Relief Ranking	Total Pitcher Index		Total Baseball Ranking	
Spalding-Bos	120				Spalding-Bos	4.6	Spalding-Bos	4.6
Mathews-Mut	110				Mathews-Mut	3.6	Mathews-Mut	3.6
Zettlein-Chi	105				McBride-Ath	1.9	McBride-Ath	1.9
Cummings-Phi	99				Cummings-Phi	.5	Meyerle-Chi	1.7
Brainard-Bal	99				H.Wright-Bos	.0	McVey-Bos	1.6

TEAM	G	W	L	PCT	GB	R	OR	AB	H	2B	3B	HR	BB	SO	AVG	OBP	SLG	PRO	PRO+	BR	/A	PF	CHI	RC	SB	CS	SBA	SBR
BOS	82	71	8	.899		831	343	3516	1124	157	54	14	31		.320	.326	.407	.733	151	184	158	104	112	478				
HAR	86	54	28	.659	18.5	557	343	3342	873	98	34	2	40		.261	.270	.313	.583	99	12	-15	105	103	289				
ATH	77	53	20	.726	15	699	402	3245	940	126	61	10	40		.290	.298	.375	.673	122	107	39	111	112	372				
STL	70	39	29	.574	26.5	386	369	2679	641	84	27	0	33		.239	.249	.291	.540	98	-29	7	91	97	198				
PHI	70	37	31	.544	28.5	470	376	2717	681	65	28	5	22		.251	.257	.301	.558	91	-13	-29	104	113	215				
MUT	71	30	38	.441	35.5	328	425	2683	626	84	24	7	21		.233	.239	.290	.529	81	-38	-59	105	85	191				
CHI	69	30	37	.448	35	379	416	2658	697	85	13	0	24		.262	.269	.304	.573	100	1	-3	101	90	223				
NH	47	7	40	.149	48	170	397	1708	374	42	12	2	13		.219	.225	.261	.486	80	-48	-21	87	77	103				
WAS	28	5	23	.179	40.5	107	338	997	194	12	11	0	5		.195	.199	.229	.428	52	-48	-44	96	98	46				
RS	19	4	15	.211	37	60	161	688	138	20	1	0	14		.201	.217	.233	.450	64	-27	-19	90	72	36				
CEN	14	2	12	.143	36.5	70	138	529	126	19	3	0	8		.238	.250	.285	.535	95	-6	0	92	90	39				
ATL	44	2	42	.45	51.5	132	438	1547	304	32	9	2	10		.197	.202	.233	.435	60	-70	-49	87	76	74				
WES	13	1	12	.77	37	45	88	449	81	9	6	0	1		.180	.182	.227	.409	41	-24	-27	105	97	19				
TOT	345					4234		26758	6799	833	283	42	262	0	.254	.261	.311	.572										

TEAM	CG	SH	SV	IP	H	H/G	HR	BB	SO	RAT	ERA	ERA+	OAV	OOB	PR	/A	PF	CPI	FA	E	DP	FW	PW	BW	SBW	DIF
BOS	60	10	17	732	751	9.2	2	29		9.6	1.70	140	.249	.256	62	55	96	135					4.7	13.5		13.3
HAR	83	13	0	771	706	8.2	4	16		8.4	1.61	161	.228	.231	73	84	105	106					7.2	-1.3		7.1
ATH	75	6	0	687	775	10.2	4	40		10.7	2.11	125	.268	.278	27	41	107	137					3.5	3.3		9.7
STL	67	5	1	630	634	9.1	3	20		9.3	2.11	105	.240	.245	24	8	90	96					.7	.6		3.7
PHI	64	5	0	627	650	9.3	6	30		9.8	2.15	117	.244	.252	21	25	102	103					2.1	-2.5		3.3
MUT	70	2	0	637²	716	10.1	3	24		10.4	2.40	107	.258	.264	4	13	105	106					1.1	-5.0		-.0
CHI	65	7	0	625	652	9.4	0	28		9.8	2.40	104	.244	.252	4	7	102	89					.6	-.3		-3.8
NH	40	0	0	426	500	10.6	5	22		11.0	3.34	69	.255	.263	-42	-49	93	76					-4.2	-1.8		-10.5
WAS	23	0	0	250²	397	14.3	6	11		14.6	4.85	54	.312	.318	-66	-62	107	93					-5.3	-3.8		.0
RS	16	2	0	171	207	10.9	0	3		11.1	3.37	72	.264	.267	-17	-18	98	78					-1.5	-1.6		-2.3
CEN	14	0	0	126	170	12.1	0	3		12.4	3.93	61	.277	.281	-21	-21	98	78					-1.8	.0		-3.2
ATL	31	0	0	396	531	12.1	9	22		12.6	3.95	58	.285	.293	-66	-73	94	90					-6.2	-4.2		-9.6
WES	13	0	0	112	110	8.8	0	14		10.0	2.81	96	.225	.247	-4	-1	110	65					-.0	-2.3		-3.1
TOT	621	50	18	6191¹		9.9				10.3	2.46		.254	.261												

Runs		Hits		Doubles		Triples		Home Runs		Total Bases	
Barnes-Bos	114	Barnes-Bos	142	McVey-Bos	33	Craver-Cen-Ath	13	O'Rourke-Bos	6	McVey-Bos	197
G.Wright-Bos	105	McVey-Bos	137	Barnes-Bos	22	Hall-Ath	13	Hall-Ath	5	Barnes-Bos	179
O'Rourke-Bos	98	White-Bos	136	Pike-StL	21	Pike-StL	10	Start-Mut	4	G.Wright-Bos	170
McVey-Bos	88	G.Wright-Bos	135	Force-Ath	21	Meyerle-Phi	9	Hallinan-Wes-Mut	3	White-Bos	167
Leonard-Bos	87	Leonard-Bos	127	White-Bos	20	McVey-Bos	9	McVey-Bos	3	Hall-Ath	160

Runs Batted In		Runs Produced		Bases On Balls		Batting Average		On Base Percentage		Slugging Average	
		Barnes-Bos	113	Harbidge-Har	12	White-Bos	.366	Barnes-Bos	.373	McVey-Bos	.506
		G.Wright-Bos	104	Dehlman-StL	11	Barnes-Bos	.361	White-Bos	.369	Pike-StL	.474
		O'Rourke-Bos	92	O'Rourke-Bos	10	McVey-Bos	.352	McVey-Bos	.354	Craver-Cen-Ath	.458
		Leonard-Bos	86	Nelson-Mut	10	Pike-StL	.343	Pike-StL	.349	Barnes-Bos	.455
		McVey-Bos	85	Hastings-Chi	9	G.Wright-Bos	.333	Anson-Ath	.336	White-Bos	.449

Production		Adjusted Production		Batter Runs		Adjusted Batter Runs		Clutch Hitting Index		Runs Created	
McVey-Bos	.860	Pike-StL	200	McVey-Bos	35.0	Pike-StL	31.6			McVey-Bos	71
Barnes-Bos	.828	McVey-Bos	187	Barnes-Bos	32.3	McVey-Bos	31.6			Barnes-Bos	68
Pike-StL	.824	Barnes-Bos	178	White-Bos	28.9	Barnes-Bos	28.9			White-Bos	63
White-Bos	.818	White-Bos	175	Pike-StL	24.7	White-Bos	25.8			G.Wright-Bos	59
Craver-Cen-Ath	.778	Luff-NH	158	G.Wright-Bos	23.0	G.Wright-Bos	19.9			Pike-StL	53

Total Average		Stolen Bases		Stolen Base Average		Stolen Base Runs		Fielding Runs		Total Player Rating	
McVey-Bos	.786									Pike-StL	2.7
Barnes-Bos	.741									McVey-Bos	2.7
Pike-StL	.737									White-Bos	2.4
White-Bos	.716									Barnes-Bos	2.3
Craver-Cen-Ath	.683									G.Wright-Bos	1.4

Wins		Win Percentage		Games		Complete Games		Shutouts		Saves	
Spalding-Bos	55	Spalding-Bos	.917	Spalding-Bos	72	Mathews-Mut	69	Zettlein-Chi-Phi	7	Spalding-Bos	8
McBride-Ath	44	Manning-Bos	.882	Mathews-Mut	70	McBride-Ath	59	Spalding-Bos	7	Manning-Bos	7
Cummings-Har	35	McBride-Ath	.759	McBride-Ath	60	Bradley-StL	57	Cummings-Har	7	McVey-Bos	1
Bradley-StL	33	Cummings-Har	.745	Bradley-StL	60	Spalding-Bos	52	McBride-Ath	6	Heifer-Bos	1
		Zettlein-Chi-Phi	.569	Zettlein-Chi-Phi	52	Zettlein-Chi-Phi	49	Bond-Har	6	Galvin-StL	1

Innings Pitched		Fewest Hits/Game		Fewest BB/Game		Strikeouts		Strikeouts/Game		Ratio	
Mathews-Mut	626.2	Borden-Phi	6.41	Cummings-Har	.13					Borden-Phi	7.36
Spalding-Bos	575.0	Galvin-StL	7.69	Blong-RS	.14					Galvin-StL	7.84
McBride-Ath	538.0	Bond-Har	7.70	Galvin-StL	.15					Bond-Har	7.95
Bradley-StL	535.2	Cummings-Har	8.55	Spalding-Bos	.22					Cummings-Har	8.68
Zettlein-Chi-Phi	462.1	Fisher-Phi	8.71	Fisher-Phi	.23					Fisher-Phi	8.93

Earned Run Average		Adjusted ERA		Opponents' Batting Avg.		Opponents' On Base Pct.		Starter Runs		Adjusted Starter Runs	
Spalding-Bos	1.52	Bond-Har	166	Borden-Phi	.181	Borden-Phi	.203	Spalding-Bos	60.2	Spalding-Bos	54.4
Bond-Har	1.56	Cummings-Har	162	Galvin-StL	.209	Galvin-StL	.213	Cummings-Har	40.0	Cummings-Har	46.1
Cummings-Har	1.60	Spalding-Bos	156	Bond-Har	.215	Bond-Har	.220	Bond-Har	35.3	Bond-Har	40.4
Borden-Phi	1.64	Borden-Phi	154	Fisher-Phi	.232	Fisher-Phi	.237	McBride-Ath	29.1	McBride-Ath	40.0
Fisher-Phi	1.92	McBride-Ath	134	Cummings-Har	.235	Cummings-Har	.237	Bradley-StL	24.5	Zettlein-Chi-Phi	24.0

Clutch Pitching Index		Relief Runs		Adjusted Relief Runs		Relief Ranking		Total Pitcher Index		Total Baseball Ranking	
McBride-Ath	142							Spalding-Bos	6.0	Spalding-Bos	6.7
Spalding-Bos	140							Cummings-Har	3.7	Cummings-Har	4.0
Manning-Bos	124							McBride-Ath	3.6	Bond-Har	3.9
Cummings-Har	114							Bond-Har	3.5	McBride-Ath	3.6
Knight-Ath	113							Fisher-Phi	2.0	Pike-StL	2.7

TEAM	G	W	L	PCT	GB	R	OR	AB	H	2B	3B	HR	BB	SO	AVG	OBP	SLG	PRO	PRO+	BR	/A	PF	CHI	RC	SB	CS	SBA	SBR
CHI	66	52	14	.788		624	257	2748	926	131	32	8	70	45	.337	.353	.417	.770	140	160	93	112	107	415				
STL	64	45	19	.703	6	386	229	2478	642	73	27	2	59	63	.259	.276	.313	.589	102	-6	14	95	103	219				
HAR	69	47	21	.691	6	429	261	2664	711	96	22	2	39	78	.267	.277	.322	.599	92	1	-33	108	106	244				
BOS	70	39	31	.557	15	471	450	2722	723	96	24	9	58	98	.266	.281	.328	.609	102	11	4	102	110	257				
LOU	69	30	36	.455	22	280	344	2570	641	68	14	6	24	98	.249	.256	.294	.550	71	-42	-105	118	81	198				
NY	57	21	35	.375	26	260	412	2180	494	39	15	2	18	35	.227	.233	.261	.494	75	-76	-45	87	103	136				
PHI	60	14	45	.237	34.5	378	534	2387	646	79	35	7	27	36	.271	.279	.342	.621	108	16	19	99	100	233				
CIN	65	9	56	.138	42.5	238	579	2372	555	51	12	4	41	136	.234	.247	.271	.518	86	-63	-22	86	80	163				
TOT	260					3066		20121	5338	633	181	40	336	589	.265	.277	.321	.598										

TEAM	CG	SH	SV	IP	H	H/G	HR	BB	SO	RAT	ERA	ERA+	OAV	OOB	PR	/A	PF	CPI	FA	E	DP	FW	PW	BW	SBW	DIF
CHI	59	9	4	592¹	608	9.2	6	29	51	9.7	1.76	139	.247	.256	36	45	106	100	.899	282	33	6.0	4.0	8.2		.9
STL	63	16	0	577	472	7.4	3	39	103	8.0	1.22	175	.210	.224	70	59	93	74	.902	268	33	6.1	5.2	1.2		.5
HAR	69	11	0	624	570	8.2	2	27	114	8.6	1.67	142	.227	.235	44	49	103	72	.888	337	27	4.0	4.3	-2.9		7.6
BOS	49	3	7	632	732	10.4	7	104	77	11.9	2.51	90	.268	.295	-14	-18	98	106	.860	442	42	-1.1	-1.6	.4		6.3
LOU	67	5	0	643	605	8.5	3	38	125	9.0	1.69	160	.229	.240	44	73	118	75	.875	397	44	.9	6.4	-9.2		-1.1
NY	56	2	0	530	718	12.2	8	24	37	12.6	2.94	73	.302	.309	-37	-47	93	114	.825	473	18	-6.8	-4.1	-4.0		7.9
PHI	53	1	2	550	783	12.8	2	41	22	13.5	3.22	75	.310	.321	-56	-49	105	112	.839	456	32	-5.0	-4.3	1.7		-7.9
CIN	57	0	0	591	850	12.9	9	34	60	13.5	3.62	61	.313	.322	-86	-94	95	103	.841	469	45	-4.1	-8.3	-1.9		-9.2
TOT	473	47	13	4739¹		10.1				10.8	2.31		.265	.277					.866	3124	274					

Runs
Barnes-Chi 126
G.Wright-Bos . . 72
Peters-Chi 70
White-Chi 66
Burdock-Har 66

Hits
Barnes-Chi 138
Peters-Chi 111
Anson-Chi 110
McVey-Chi 107
White-Chi 104

Doubles
Hines-Chi 21
Higham-Har 21
Barnes-Chi 21
Pike-StL 19

Triples
Barnes-Chi 14
Hall-Phi 13
Pike-StL 10
Meyerle-Phi 8

Home Runs
Hall-Phi 5
Jones-Cin 4

Total Bases
Barnes-Chi 190
Hall-Phi 146
Anson-Chi 139
Hines-Chi 134

Runs Batted In
White-Chi 60
Hines-Chi 59
Barnes-Chi 59
Anson-Chi 59
McVey-Chi 53

Runs Produced
Barnes-Chi 184
White-Chi 125
Anson-Chi 120
Hines-Chi 119
Peters-Chi 116

Bases On Balls
Barnes-Chi 20
O'Rourke-Bos 15
Burdock-Har 13
Glenn-Chi 12
Anson-Chi 12

Batting Average
Barnes-Chi 429
Hall-Phi 366
Anson-Chi 356
Peters-Chi 351
McVey-Chi 347

On Base Percentage
Barnes-Chi 462
Hall-Phi 384
Anson-Chi 380
White-Chi 358
O'Rourke-Bos 358

Slugging Average
Barnes-Chi 590
Hall-Phi 545
Pike-StL 472
Anson-Chi 450
Meyerle-Phi 449

Production
Barnes-Chi 1.052
Hall-Phi 929
Anson-Chi 830
Pike-StL 813
Meyerle-Phi 797

Adjusted Production
Barnes-Chi 222
Hall-Phi 208
Pike-StL 178
Meyerle-Phi 165
Jones-Cin 162

Batter Runs
Barnes-Chi 50.0
Hall-Phi 29.1
Anson-Chi 24.2
Pike-StL 19.7
O'Rourke-Bos 19.1

Adjusted Batter Runs
Barnes-Chi 38.7
Hall-Phi 29.7
Pike-StL 23.1
Jones-Cin 18.9
O'Rourke-Bos . . . 18.1

Clutch Hitting Index
Battin-StL 150
White-Chi 142
McVey-Chi 140
Anson-Chi 138
McGeary-StL 135

Runs Created
Barnes-Chi 90
Hall-Phi 57
Anson-Chi 54
Peters-Chi 48
O'Rourke-Bos 48

Total Average
Barnes-Chi 1.141
Hall-Phi 906
Anson-Chi 759
Pike-StL 738
Meyerle-Phi 698

Stolen Bases

Stolen Base Average

Stolen Base Runs

Fielding Runs
Somerville-Lou . . . 29.7
Force-Phi-NY . . . 21.3
Battin-StL 13.6
G.Wright-Bos . . . 13.1
Anson-Chi 12.8

Total Player Rating
Barnes-Chi 3.7
Anson-Chi 2.6
Hall-Phi 2.4
Battin-StL 2.2
G.Wright-Bos 2.1

Wins
Spalding-Chi 47
Bradley-StL 45
Bond-Har 31
Devlin-Lou 30
Mathews-NY 21

Win Percentage
Spalding-Chi 797
Manning-Bos 783
Bond-Har 705
Bradley-StL 703
Cummings-Har 667

Games
Devlin-Lou 68
Bradley-StL 64
Spalding-Chi 61
Mathews-NY 56
Bond-Har 45

Complete Games
Devlin-Lou 66
Bradley-StL 63
Mathews-NY 55
Spalding-Chi 53
Bond-Har 45

Shutouts
Bradley-StL 16
Spalding-Chi 8
Bond-Har 6
Devlin-Lou 5
Cummings-Har 5

Saves
Manning-Bos 5
Zettlein-Phi 2
McVey-Chi 2

Innings Pitched
Devlin-Lou 622.0
Bradley-StL 573.0
Spalding-Chi 528.2
Mathews-NY 516.0
Bond-Har 408.0

Fewest Hits/Game
Bradley-StL 7.38
Bond-Har 7.83
Devlin-Lou 8.19
Cummings-Har . . . 8.96
Spalding-Chi 9.23

Fewest BB/Game
Zettlein-Phi 23
Fisher-Cin 24
Bond-Har 29
Mathews-NY 42
Williams-Cin 43

Strikeouts
Devlin-Lou 122
Bradley-StL 103
Bond-Har 88
Spalding-Chi 39
Mathews-NY 37

Strikeouts/Game
Bond-Har 1.94
Devlin-Lou 1.77
Bradley-StL 1.62
Borden-Bos 1.40
Fisher-Cin 1.14

Ratio
Bradley-StL 7.98
Bond-Har 8.12
Devlin-Lou 8.73
Cummings-Har . . . 9.54
Spalding-Chi 9.67

Earned Run Average
Bradley-StL 1.23
Devlin-Lou 1.56
Cummings-Har . . . 1.67
Bond-Har 1.68
Spalding-Chi 1.75

Adjusted ERA
Bradley-StL 174
Devlin-Lou 174
Cummings-Har . . . 142
Bond-Har 141
Spalding-Chi 139

Opponents' Batting Avg.
Bradley-StL 211
Bond-Har 220
Devlin-Lou 224
Cummings-Har 239
Spalding-Chi 247

Opponents' On Base Pct.
Bradley-StL 224
Bond-Har 227
Devlin-Lou 235
Cummings-Har 251
Spalding-Chi 256

Starter Runs
Bradley-StL 68.9
Devlin-Lou 51.5
Spalding-Chi 32.5
Bond-Har 28.6
Cummings-Har . . . 15.4

Adjusted Starter Runs
Devlin-Lou 79.8
Bradley-StL 57.9
Spalding-Chi 40.5
Bond-Har 31.5
Cummings-Har . . . 16.9

Clutch Pitching Index
Knight-Phi 126
Mathews-NY 116
Borden-Bos 108
Dean-Cin 108
Zettlein-Phi 107

Relief Runs

Adjusted Relief Runs

Relief Ranking

Total Pitcher Index
Devlin-Lou 7.3
Bradley-StL 5.8
Spalding-Chi 4.6
Bond-Har 3.2
McVey-Chi 8

Total Baseball Ranking
Devlin-Lou 7.3
Bradley-StL 5.8
Spalding-Chi 4.4
Barnes-Chi 3.7
Bond-Har 3.2

TEAM	G	W	L	PCT	GB	R	OR	AB	H	2B	3B	HR	BB	SO	AVG	OBP	SLG	PRO	PRO+	BR	/A	PF	CHI	RC	SB	CS	SBA	SBR
BOS	61	42	18	.700		419	263	2368	700	91	37	4	65	121	.296	.314	.370	.684	114	47	33	104	104	283				
LOU	61	35	25	.583	7	339	288	2355	659	75	36	9	58	140	.280	.297	.354	.651	92	19	-47	118	92	254				
HAR	60	31	27	.534	10	341	311	2358	637	63	31	4	30	97	.270	.279	.328	.607	105	-17	18	89	103	222				
STL	60	28	32	.467	14	284	318	2178	531	51	36	1	57	147	.244	.263	.302	.565	84	-46	-31	95	102	177				
CHI	60	26	33	.441	15.5	366	375	2273	633	79	30	0	57	111	.278	.296	.340	.636	92	8	-33	112	105	234				
CIN	58	15	42	.263	25.5	291	485	2135	545	72	34	6	78	110	.255	.282	.329	.611	107	-11	24	89	94	203				
TOT	180					2040		13667	3705	431	204	24	345	726	.271	.289	.338	.627										

TEAM	CG	SH	SV	IP	H	H/G	HR	BB	SO	RAT	ERA	ERA+	OAV	OOB	PR	/A	PF	CPI	FA	E	DP	FW	PW	BW	SBW	DIF
BOS	61	7	0	548	557	9.1	5	38	177	9.8	2.15	130	.249	.261	40	40	100	98	.889	290	36	1.2	3.6	2.9		4.3
LOU	61	4	0	559	617	9.9	4	41	141	10.6	2.25	147	.270	.283	34	65	118	119	.904	267	37	2.4	5.8	-4.2		1.0
HAR	59	4	0	544	572	9.5	2	56	99	10.4	2.32	105	.253	.271	30	7	87	97	.885	313	32	-.2	.6	1.6		-.0
STL	52	1	0	541	582	9.7	2	92	132	11.2	2.66	98	.262	.291	9	-4	93	102	.892	281	29	1.4	-.4	-2.8		-.3
CHI	45	3	3	534	630	10.6	7	58	92	11.6	3.37	88	.274	.292	-33	-24	106	87	.883	313	43	-.2	-2.1	-2.9		1.7
CIN	48	1	1	515	747	13.1	4	61	85	14.1	4.19	63	.318	.335	-79	-89	94	102	.851	394	33	-4.7	-7.9	2.1		-3.0
TOT	326	20	4	3241		10.3				11.2	2.81		.271	.289					.884	1858	210					

Runs
O'Rourke-Bos 68
G.Wright-Bos 58
McVey-Chi 58
Start-Har 55

Hits
D.White-Bos 103
McVey-Chi 98
O'Rourke-Bos 96
Cassidy-Har 95
Start-Har 90

Doubles
Anson-Chi 19
York-Har 16
Manning-Cin 16
G.Wright-Bos 15
Hall-Lou 15

Triples
D.White-Bos 11
Jones-Cin-Chi-Cin 10
Hall-Lou 8
Brown-Bos 8

Home Runs
Pike-Cin 4
Shaffer-Lou 3
Jones-Cin-Chi-Cin 2
D.White-Bos 2
Snyder-Lou 2

Total Bases
D.White-Bos 145
McVey-Chi 121
O'Rourke-Bos 118
Hall-Lou 118
Cassidy-Har 115

Runs Batted In
D.White-Bos 49
Peters-Chi 41
Sutton-Bos 39
Jones-Cin-Chi-Cin 38
York-Har 37

Runs Produced
D.White-Bos 98
McVey-Chi 94
G.Wright-Bos 93
O'Rourke-Bos 91
Jones-Cin-Chi-Cin 89

Bases On Balls
O'Rourke-Bos 20
Jones-Cin-Chi-Cin 15
Hall-Lou 12
Booth-Cin.......... 12
Force-StL 11

Batting Average
D.White-Bos 387
Cassidy-Har 378
McVey-Chi 368
O'Rourke-Bos 362
Anson-Chi.........337

On Base Percentage
O'Rourke-Bos 407
D.White-Bos 405
McVey-Chi 387
Cassidy-Har 386
Anson-Chi 360

Slugging Average
D.White-Bos 545
Jones-Cin-Chi-Cin 471
Cassidy-Har 458
McVey-Chi 455
O'Rourke-Bos 445

Production
D.White-Bos 950
O'Rourke-Bos 852
Cassidy-Har 844
McVey-Chi 842
Jones-Cin-Chi-Cin 824

Adjusted Production
D.White-Bos 190
Cassidy-Har 184
Jones-Cin-Chi-Cin ...175
O'Rourke-Bos 162
Manning-Cin 157

Batter Runs
D.White-Bos 28.2
O'Rourke-Bos 21.2
McVey-Chi 18.9
Cassidy-Har 17.6
Jones-Cin-Chi-Cin 15.6

Adjusted Batter Runs
D.White-Bos 25.8
Cassidy-Har 23.7
Jones-Cin-Chi-Cin 21.2
O'Rourke-Bos 18.9
Manning-Cin 16.4

Clutch Hitting Index
Ferguson-Har 142
Peters-Chi 139
Bond-Bos 139
Croft-StL 139
Addy-Cin 138

Runs Created
D.White-Bos 60
O'Rourke-Bos 49
McVey-Chi 48
Cassidy-Har 45
Hall-Lou 43

Total Average
D.White-Bos 939
O'Rourke-Bos 817
Jones-Cin-Chi-Cin 776
McVey-Chi 768
Cassidy-Har 756

Stolen Bases

Stolen Base Average

Stolen Base Runs

Fielding Runs
Gerhardt-Lou 19.8
Peters-Chi 19.1
Ferguson-Har 17.2
Brown-Bos 15.4
Snyder-Lou 15.2

Total Player Rating
Jones-Cin-Chi-Cin 2.7
D.White-Bos 2.3
Peters-Chi 1.8
Gerhardt-Lou 1.7
Brown-Bos 1.6

Wins
Bond-Bos 40
Devlin-Lou 35
Larkin-Har 29
Nichols-StL 18
Bradley-Chi 18

Win Percentage
Bond-Bos .... .702
Devlin-Lou .... .583
Larkin-Har .... .537
Nichols-StL .... .439
Bradley-Chi .... .439

Games
Devlin-Lou 61
Bond-Bos 58
Larkin-Har 56
Bradley-Chi 50
Nichols-StL 42

Complete Games
Devlin-Lou......... 61
Bond-Bos 58
Larkin-Har 55
Nichols-StL 35
Bradley-Chi........ 35

Shutouts
Bond-Bos 6
Larkin-Har 4
Devlin-Lou 4
Bradley-Chi 2

Saves
McVey-Chi 2
Spalding-Chi 1
Manning-Cin 1

Innings Pitched
Devlin-Lou 559.0
Bond-Bos 521.0
Larkin-Har 501.0
Bradley-Chi...... 394.0
Nichols-StL 350.0

Fewest Hits/Game
Bond-Bos 9.16
Larkin-Har 9.16
Nichols-StL 9.67
Blong-StL 9.75
Devlin-Lou 9.93

Fewest BB/Game
Bond-Bos .... .62
Devlin-Lou .... .66
Cummings-Cin ...... .75
Bradley-Chi .... .89
Larkin-Har .... .95

Strikeouts
Bond-Bos 170
Devlin-Lou 141
Larkin-Har 96
Nichols-StL 80
Bradley-Chi 59

Strikeouts/Game
Mitchell-Cin 3.69
Bond-Bos 2.94
Blong-StL 2.45
Devlin-Lou 2.27
Nichols-StL 2.06

Ratio
Bond-Bos 9.78
Larkin-Har 10.11
Devlin-Lou 10.59
Nichols-StL 11.03
Bradley-Chi 11.22

Earned Run Average
Bond-Bos 2.11
Larkin-Har 2.14
Devlin-Lou 2.25
Nichols-StL 2.60
Blong-StL 2.74

Adjusted ERA
Devlin-Lou 147
Bond-Bos 133
Larkin-Har 114
Nichols-StL 100
Blong-StL 95

Opponents' Batting Avg.
Larkin-Har .... .245
Bond-Bos .... .249
Blong-StL .... .262
Nichols-StL .... .263
Bradley-Chi .... .269

Opponents' On Base Pct.
Bond-Bos .... .261
Larkin-Har .... .264
Devlin-Lou .... .283
Bradley-Chi .... .286
Nichols-StL .... .289

Starter Runs
Bond-Bos 40.5
Larkin-Har 37.3
Devlin-Lou 34.4
Reis-Chi 8.2
Nichols-StL 8.2

Adjusted Starter Runs
Devlin-Lou 65.4
Bond-Bos 40.5
Larkin-Har 16.3
Reis-Chi 8.9

Clutch Pitching Index
Mathews-Cin 123
Devlin-Lou 119
Booth-Cin 104
Nichols-StL....... 104
Blong-StL 101

Relief Runs

Adjusted Relief Runs

Relief Ranking

Total Pitcher Index
Devlin-Lou 5.9
Bond-Bos 3.5
Larkin-Har 1.8
Reis-Chi 7
Spalding-Chi 0

Total Baseball Ranking
Devlin-Lou 5.9
Bond-Bos 3.4
Jones-Cin-Chi-Cin 2.7
D.White-Bos 2.3
Peters-Chi 1.8

TEAM	G	W	L	PCT	GB	R	OR	AB	H	2B	3B	HR	BB	SO	AVG	OBP	SLG	PRO	PRO+	BR	/A	PF	CHI	RC	SB	CS	SBA	SBR
BOS	60	41	19	.683		298	241	2220	535	75	25	2	35	154	.241	.253	.300	.553	79	-35	-56	108	110	173				
CIN	61	37	23	.617	4	333	281	2281	629	67	22	5	58	141	.276	.294	.331	.625	120	21	53	91	98	227				
PRO	62	33	27	.550	8	353	337	2298	604	107	30	8	50	218	.263	.279	.346	.625	109	19	20	100	104	227				
CHI	61	30	30	.500	11	371	331	2333	677	91	20	3	88	157	.290	.316	.350	.666	115	56	31	107	96	265				
IND	63	24	36	.400	17	293	328	2300	542	76	15	3	64	197	.236	.256	.286	.542	95	-43	-6	87	105	173				
MIL	61	15	45	.250	26	256	386	2212	552	65	20	2	69	214	.250	.272	.300	.572	86	-18	-38	107	88	185				
TOT	184					1904		13644	3539	481	132	23	364	1081	.259	.279	.319	.598										

TEAM	CG	SH	SV	IP	H	H/G	HR	BB	SO	RAT	ERA	ERA+	OAV	OOB	PR	/A	PF	CPI	FA	E	DP	FW	PW	BW	SBW	DIF
BOS	58	9	0	544	595	9.8	6	38	184	10.5	2.32	102	.272	.284	-1	2	102	111	.914	228	48	3.5	.2	-5.2		12.5
CIN	61	6	0	548	546	9.0	2	63	220	10.0	1.84	116	.248	.269	28	17	92	108	.900	269	37	1.5	1.6	5.0		-1.1
PRO	59	6	0	556	609	9.9	5	86	173	11.3	2.38	93	.265	.291	-5	-11	96	108	.892	311	42	-.5	-1.0	1.9		2.7
CHI	61	1	0	551	577	9.4	4	35	175	10.0	2.37	102	.253	.265	-4	3	105	85	.891	304	37	-.4	.3	2.9		-2.8
IND	59	2	1	578	621	9.7	3	87	182	11.0	2.32	87	.262	.288	-1	-19	88	106	.898	290	37	.9	-1.8	-.6		-4.6
MIL	54	1	0	547	589	9.7	3	55	147	10.5	2.60	101	.255	.272	-18	1	114	82	.866	376	32	-4.4	.0	-3.6		-7.1
TOT	352	25	1	3324		9.6				10.6	2.30		.259	.279					.893	1778	233					

Runs
Higham-Pro 60
Start-Chi 58
York-Pro 56
Anson-Chi 55
Dalrymple-Mil 52

Hits
Start-Chi 100
Dalrymple-Mil 96
Hines-Pro 92
Ferguson-Chi 91

Doubles
Higham-Pro 22
Brown-Pro 21
York-Pro 19
Shaffer-Ind 19
O'Rourke-Bos 17

Triples
York-Pro 10
O'Rourke-Bos 7
Jones-Cin 7

Home Runs
Hines-Pro 4
Jones-Cin 3
McVey-Cin 2
McKelvy-Ind 2

Total Bases
York-Pro 125
Start-Chi 125
Hines-Pro 125
Shaffer-Ind 121
Higham-Pro 117

Runs Batted In
Hines-Pro 50
Brown-Pro 43
Anson-Chi 40
Jones-Cin 39
Ferguson-Chi 39

Runs Produced
Anson-Chi 95
Hines-Pro 88
Higham-Pro 88
Jones-Cin 86
Brown-Pro 86

Bases On Balls
Remsen-Chi 17
Larkin-Chi 17
Shaffer-Ind 13
Clapp-Ind 13
Anson-Chi 13

Batting Average
Dalrymple-Mil 354
Hines-Pro 358
Ferguson-Chi 351
Start-Chi 351
Anson-Chi 341

On Base Percentage
Ferguson-Chi 375
Anson-Chi 372
Shaffer-Ind 369
Dalrymple-Mil 368
Hines-Pro 363

Slugging Average
Hines-Pro 486
York-Pro 465
Shaffer-Ind 455
Brown-Pro 453
Jones-Cin 441

Production
Hines-Pro 849
Shaffer-Ind 824
Start-Chi 794
York-Pro 793
Dalrymple-Mil 789

Adjusted Production
Shaffer-Ind 196
Hines-Pro 177
Jones-Cin 163
York-Pro 159
Brown-Pro 153

Batter Runs
Hines-Pro 20.0
Shaffer-Ind 19.6
Start-Chi 17.2
Dalrymple-Mil 16.4
York-Pro 16.1

Adjusted Batter Runs
Shaffer-Ind 27.8
Hines-Pro 20.2
Jones-Cin 17.4
York-Pro 16.3
Clapp-Ind 14.5

Clutch Hitting Index
McClellan-Chi 165
Harbidge-Chi 151
Hague-Pro 142
McKelvy-Ind 140
Bond-Bos 131

Runs Created
Hines-Pro 47
Shaffer-Ind 46
Start-Chi 46
Dalrymple-Mil 43
York-Pro 42

Total Average
Hines-Pro 770
Shaffer-Ind 761
York-Pro 715
Brown-Pro 692
Start-Chi 686

Stolen Bases

Stolen Base Average

Stolen Base Runs

Fielding Runs
Burdock-Bos 21.3
Hague-Pro 18.7
Ferguson-Chi 15.9
Kelly-Cin 11.1
Wright-Bos 10.5

Total Player Rating
Shaffer-Ind 2.9
Ferguson-Chi 2.8
Burdock-Bos 2.2
Jones-Cin 1.9
Hines-Pro 1.8

Wins
Bond-Bos 40
W.White-Cin 30
Larkin-Chi 29
Ward-Pro 22
Nolan-Ind 13

Win Percentage
Bond-Bos 678
Ward-Pro 629
W.White-Cin 588
Larkin-Chi 527

Games
Bond-Bos 59
Larkin-Chi 56
W.White-Cin 52
Weaver-Mil 45
Nolan-Ind 38

Complete Games
Bond-Bos 57
Larkin-Chi 56
W.White-Cin 52
Weaver-Mil 39

Shutouts
Bond-Bos 9
Ward-Pro 6
W.White-Cin 5

Saves
Healey-Pro-Ind 1

Innings Pitched
Bond-Bos 532.2
Larkin-Chi 506.0
W.White-Cin 468.0
Weaver-Mil 383.0
Nolan-Ind 347.0

Fewest Hits/Game
Mitchell-Cin 7.76
Ward-Pro 8.30
Weaver-Mil 8.72
Larkin-Chi 9.09
W.White-Cin 9.17

Fewest BB/Game
Weaver-Mil .... .49
Larkin-Chi .... .55
Bond-Bos .... .56
Nichols-Pro .... .73
W.White-Cin .... .87

Strikeouts
Bond-Bos 182
W.White-Cin 169
Larkin-Chi 163
Nolan-Ind 125
Ward-Pro 116

Strikeouts/Game
Mitchell-Cin 5.74
Wheeler-Pro 3.63
W.White-Cin 3.25
Nolan-Ind 3.24
Ward-Pro 3.13

Ratio
Weaver-Mil 9.21
Ward-Pro 9.22
Larkin-Chi 9.64
Mitchell-Cin 9.79
W.White-Cin 10.04

Earned Run Average
Ward-Pro 1.51
McCormick-Ind ...1.69
W.White-Cin 1.79
Weaver-Mil 1.95
Bond-Bos 2.06

Adjusted ERA
Ward-Pro 146
Weaver-Mil 134
McCormick-Ind 120
W.White-Cin 119
Bond-Bos 114

Opponents' Batting Avg.
Mitchell-Cin 223
Ward-Pro 231
Weaver-Mil 237
Larkin-Chi 246
W.White-Cin 252

Opponents' On Base Pct.
Weaver-Mil 247
Ward-Pro 251
Larkin-Chi 257
Mitchell-Cin 265
W.White-Cin 269

Starter Runs
Ward-Pro 29.5
W.White-Cin 26.8
Weaver-Mil 15.1
Bond-Bos 14.4
McCormick-Ind 8.0

Adjusted Starter Runs
Weaver-Mil 28.6
Ward-Pro 25.7
Bond-Bos 17.6
W.White-Cin 17.6
Larkin-Chi 10.2

Clutch Pitching Index
McCormick-Ind ... 152
Healey-Pro-Ind ... 122
Bond-Bos 119
W.White-Cin 114
Nichols-Pro 112

Relief Runs

Adjusted Relief Runs

Relief Ranking

Total Pitcher Index
Weaver-Mil 2.7
Ward-Pro 2.6
Larkin-Chi 1.8
Bond-Bos 1.3
W.White-Cin 7

Total Baseball Ranking
Shaffer-Ind 2.9
Ferguson-Chi 2.8
Ward-Pro 2.6
Weaver-Mil 2.4
Burdock-Bos 2.2

TEAM	G	W	L	PCT	GB	R	OR	AB	H	2B	3B	HR	BB	SO	AVG	OBP	SLG	PRO	PRO+	BR	/A	PF	CHI	RC	SB	CS	SBA	SBR
PRO	85	59	25	.702		612	355	3392	1003	142	55	12	91	172	.296	.314	.381	.695	134	110	119	98	103	416				
BOS	84	54	30	.643	5	562	348	3217	883	138	51	20	90	222	.274	.294	.368	.662	118	68	56	102	107	357				
BUF	79	46	32	.590	10	394	365	2906	733	105	54	2	78	314	.252	.272	.328	.600	98	1	-9	102	95	265				
CHI	83	46	33	.582	10.5	437	411	3116	808	167	32	3	73	294	.259	.276	.336	.612	98	-14	-13	106	96	297				
CIN	81	43	37	.538	14	485	464	3085	813	127	53	8	66	207	.264	.279	.347	.626	115	27	50	95	105	306				
CLE	82	27	55	.329	31	322	461	2987	666	116	29	4	37	214	.223	.232	.285	.517	73	-83	-80	99	96	203				
SYR	71	22	48	.314	30	276	462	2611	592	61	19	5	28	238	.227	.235	.270	.505	78	-82	-51	89	98	170				
TRO	77	19	56	.253	35.5	321	543	2841	673	102	24	4	45	182	.237	.249	.294	.543	87	-54	-31	93	93	213				
TOT	321					3409		24155	6171	958	317	58	508	1843	.255	.271	.329	.599										

TEAM	CG	SH	SV	IP	H	H/G	HR	BB	SO	RAT	ERA	ERA+	OAV	OOB	PR	/A	PF	CPI	FA	E	DP	FW	PW	BW	SBW	DIF
PRO	73	3	2	776	765	8.9	9	62	329	9.6	2.18	108	.243	.258	27	15	94	99	.902	382	41	1.8	1.4	11.0		2.8
BOS	80	13	0	753	757	9.0	9	46	230	9.6	2.19	114	.251	.262	26	25	100	107	.913	319	58	4.9	2.3	5.2		-.3
BUF	78	8	0	713	698	8.8	3	47	198	9.4	2.34	112	.242	.254	13	22	105	87	.906	331	62	2.9	2.0	-.8		2.9
CHI	82	6	0	744	762	9.2	5	57	211	9.9	2.46	105	.244	.258	3	9	103	86	.900	381	52	1.3	.8	-1.2		5.5
CIN	79	4	0	726	756	9.4	11	81	246	10.4	2.29	102	.248	.267	16	4	93	104	.877	454	48	-3.1	.4	4.6		1.1
CLE	79	3	0	741	818	9.9	4	116	287	11.3	2.65	95	.265	.292	-12	-12	100	111	.889	406	42	-.3	-1.1	-7.4		-5.3
SYR	64	5	0	649	775	10.7	4	52	132	11.5	3.19	74	.277	.290	-50	-59	95	96	.873	398	37	-2.7	-5.4	-4.7		-.2
TRO	75	3	0	695	840	10.9	13	47	210	11.5	2.80	89	.275	.286	-23	-22	100	110	.875	460	44	-4.4	-2.0	-2.9		-9.2
TOT	610	45	2	5797		9.6				10.4	2.50		.255	.271					.892	3131	384					

Runs
Jones-Bos 85
Hines-Pro 81
Wright-Pro 79
Kelly-Cin 78
Dickerson-Cin 73

Hits
Hines-Pro 146
O'Rourke-Pro 126
Kelly-Cin 120
Jones-Bos 112
D.White-Cin 110

Doubles
Eden-Cle 31
York-Pro 25
Hines-Pro 25
Dalrymple-Chi 25
Houck-Bos 24

Triples
Dickerson-Cin 14
Williamson-Chi 13
Kelly-Cin 12
O'Rourke-Bos 11

Home Runs
Jones-Bos 9
O'Rourke-Bos 6
Brouthers-Tro 4
Eden-Cle 3

Total Bases
Hines-Pro 197
Jones-Bos 181
Kelly-Cin 170
O'Rourke-Pro 166
O'Rourke-Bos 165

Runs Batted In
O'Rourke-Bos 62
Jones-Bos 62
Dickerson-Cin 57
McVey-Cin 55

Runs Produced
Jones-Bos 138
Hines-Pro 131
Dickerson-Cin 128
O'Rourke-Bos 125
Kelly-Cin 123

Bases On Balls
Jones-Bos 29
Williamson-Chi 24
York-Pro 19
Richardson-Buf ... 16
Barnes-Cin 16

Batting Average
Anson-Chi .... .317
Hines-Pro .... .357
O'Rourke-Pro ..... .348
Kelly-Cin .... .348
O'Rourke-Bos ...... .341

On Base Percentage
O'Rourke-Pro ..... .371
Hines-Pro .... .369
Jones-Bos .... .367
Kelly-Cin .... .363
O'Rourke-Bos ...... .357

Slugging Average
O'Rourke-Bos ..... .521
Jones-Bos .... .510
Kelly-Cin .... .493
Hines-Pro .... .482
O'Rourke-Pro ..... .459

Production
O'Rourke-Bos ..... .877
Jones-Bos .... .877
Kelly-Cin .... .855
Hines-Pro .... .851
O'Rourke-Pro ..... .829

Adjusted Production
Kelly-Cin 188
Jones-Bos 182
O'Rourke-Bos 181
Hines-Pro 181
O'Rourke-Pro 174

Batter Runs
Jones-Bos 33.1
Hines-Pro 32.9
Kelly-Cin 28.1
O'Rourke-Bos 28.0
O'Rourke-Pro 27.2

Adjusted Batter Runs
Hines-Pro 34.3
Kelly-Cin 32.1
Jones-Bos 31.2
O'Rourke-Pro 28.4
O'Rourke-Bos 26.4

Clutch Hitting Index
Gerhardt-Cin 150
McVey-Cin 143
Brown-Pro-Chi 137
Morrill-Bos 124
W.White-Cin 122

Runs Created
Hines-Pro 75
Jones-Bos 68
Kelly-Cin 63
O'Rourke-Pro 63
O'Rourke-Bos 60

Total Average
Jones-Bos .... .864
O'Rourke-Bos .... .828
Kelly-Cin .... .791
Hines-Pro .... .779
O'Rourke-Pro ..... .758

Stolen Bases

Stolen Base Average

Stolen Base Runs

Fielding Runs
Snyder-Bos 23.9
Wright-Pro 20.5
Shaffer-Chi 20.3
Evans-Tro 17.7
Fulmer-Buf 17.4

Total Player Rating
Kelly-Cin 3.9
Jones-Bos 3.5
Hines-Pro 3.3
Williamson-Chi 3.2
Wright-Pro 3.2

Wins
Ward-Pro 47
W.White-Cin 43
Bond-Bos 43
Galvin-Buf 37
Larkin-Chi 31

Win Percentage
Ward-Pro .... .712
Bond-Bos .... .694
Hankinson-Chi ..... .600
W.White-Cin ..... .581
Galvin-Buf .... .578

Games
W.White-Cin 76
Ward-Pro 70
Galvin-Buf 66
Bond-Bos 64
McCormick-Cle 62

Complete Games
W.White-Cin 75
Galvin-Buf 65
McCormick-Cle 59
Bond-Bos 59
Ward-Pro 58

Shutouts
Bond-Bos 11
Galvin-Buf 6
McCormick-Syr 5
W.White-Cin 4
Larkin-Chi 4

Saves
Ward-Pro 1
Mathews-Pro 1

Innings Pitched
W.White-Cin 680.0
Galvin-Buf 593.0
Ward-Pro 587.0
Bond-Bos 555.1
McCormick-Cle 546.1

Fewest Hits/Game
McGunnigle-Buf .. 8.48
Ward-Pro 8.75
Bond-Bos 8.80
Galvin-Buf 8.88
W.White-Cin 8.95

Fewest BB/Game
Bond-Bos .... .39
Galvin-Buf .... .47
Bradley-Tro .... .48
Larkin-Chi .... .53
Ward-Pro .... .55

Strikeouts
Ward-Pro 239
W.White-Cin 232
McCormick-Cle ... 197
Bond-Bos 155
Larkin-Chi 142

Strikeouts/Game
McGunnigle-Buf .. 4.65
Mathews-Pro 4.29
Mitchell-Cle 4.16
Ward-Pro 3.66
McCormick-Cle ... 3.25

Ratio
Bond-Bos 9.19
Ward-Pro 9.31
Galvin-Buf 9.35
Larkin-Chi 9.54
McGunnigle-Buf ... 9.68

Earned Run Average
Bond-Bos 1.96
W.White-Cin 1.99
Ward-Pro 2.15
Salisbury-Tro 2.22
Galvin-Buf 2.28

Adjusted ERA
Bond-Bos 127
W.White-Cin 117
Galvin-Buf 115
Salisbury-Tro 112
Ward-Pro 110

Opponents' Batting Avg.
McGunnigle-Buf ... .235
W.White-Cin ...... .238
Ward-Pro .... .239
Larkin-Chi .... .240
Galvin-Buf .... .243

Opponents' On Base Pct.
Larkin-Chi .... .250
Ward-Pro .... .250
Galvin-Buf .... .253
W.White-Cin ...... .256
Bond-Bos .... .259

Starter Runs
W.White-Cin 38.6
Bond-Bos 33.0
Ward-Pro 22.8
Galvin-Buf 14.5
Goldsmith-Tro 6.5

Adjusted Starter Runs
Bond-Bos 32.3
W.White-Cin 26.2
Galvin-Buf 22.2
Ward-Pro 13.7
Larkin-Chi 7.4

Clutch Pitching Index
Salisbury-Tro 125
Mathews-Pro 122
Bond-Bos 117
McCormick-Cle ... 111
Mitchell-Cle 109

Relief Runs

Adjusted Relief Runs

Relief Ranking

Total Pitcher Index
Bond-Bos 3.8
Ward-Pro 2.9
Galvin-Buf 2.8
McCormick-Cle 7
Goldsmith-Tro 6

Total Baseball Ranking
Kelly-Cin 3.9
Bond-Bos 3.6
Jones-Bos 3.5
Hines-Pro 3.3
Williamson-Chi 3.2

TEAM	G	W	L	PCT	GB	R	OR	AB	H	2B	3B	HR	BB	SO	AVG	OBP	SLG	PRO	PRO+	BR	/A	PF	CHI	RC	SB	CS	SBA	SBR
CHI	86	67	17	.798		538	317	3135	876	164	39	4	104	217	.279	.303	.360	.663	119	81	52	106	109	350				
PRO	87	52	32	.619	15	419	299	3196	793	114	34	8	89	186	.248	.268	.313	.581	101	-6	7	97	102	275				
CLE	85	47	37	.560	20	387	337	3002	726	130	52	7	76	237	.242	.261	.327	.588	102	-1	-1	98	99	262				
TRO	83	41	42	.494	25.5	392	438	3007	755	114	37	5	120	260	.251	.280	.319	.599	100	15	-6	105	95	275				
WOR	85	40	43	.482	26.5	412	370	3024	699	129	52	8	81	278	.231	.251	.316	.567	86	-21	-54	109	110	246				
BOS	86	40	44	.476	27	416	456	3080	779	134	41	20	105	221	.253	.278	.343	.621	115	34	48	97	95	300				
BUF	85	24	58	.293	42	331	502	2962	669	104	37	3	90	221	.226	.249	.289	.538	82	-48	-54	102	97	218				
CIN	83	21	59	.263	44	296	472	2895	649	91	36	7	75	267	.224	.244	.288	.532	82	-54	-50	99	91	208				
TOT	340					3191		24301	5946	980	328	62	740	1993	.245	.267	.320	.587										

TEAM	CG	SH	SV	IP	H	H/G	HR	BB	SO	RAT	ERA	ERA+	OAV	OOB	PR	/A	PF	CPI	FA	E	DP	FW	PW	BW	SBW	DIF
CHI	80	8	3	775	622	7.2	8	129	367	8.7	1.93	126	.209	.242	38	43	102	83	.913	329	41	2.3	4.2	5.1		13.4
PRO	75	13	2	799	663	7.5	7	51	286	8.0	1.64	134	.215	.228	65	49	93	87	.910	357	53	1.1	4.8	.7		3.5
CLE	83	7	1	759²	685	8.1	4	98	289	9.3	1.90	124	.228	.253	40	39	99	101	.910	330	52	2.0	3.8	.7		-1.5
TRO	81	4	0	738	763	9.3	8	113	173	10.7	2.74	92	.256	.283	-30	-18	106	101	.900	366	58	-.3	-1.7	-.6		2.2
WOR	68	7	5	762²	709	8.4	13	97	297	9.5	2.27	115	.233	.257	9	28	109	94	.906	355	49	.7	2.7	-5.2		.3
BOS	70	4	0	744²	840	10.2	2	86	187	11.2	3.08	74	.276	.296	-59	-67	96	102	.901	367	54	.3	-6.5	4.7		-.5
BUF	72	6	1	739	879	10.7	10	78	186	11.7	3.09	79	.279	.297	-59	-52	104	108	.891	408	55	-2.1	-5.1	-5.2		-4.6
CIN	79	3	0	713¹	785	9.9	10	88	208	11.0	2.44	102	.259	.280	-5	5	105	116	.877	437	49	-4.1	.5	-4.9		-10.6
TOT	608	52	12	6031¹		8.9				10.0	2.37		.245	.267					.901	2949	411					

Runs		Hits		Doubles		Triples		Home Runs		Total Bases	
Dalrymple-Chi	91	Dalrymple-Chi	126	Dunlap-Cle	27	Stovey-Wor	14	Stovey-Wor	6	Dalrymple-Chi	175
Stovey-Wor	76	Anson-Chi	120	Dalrymple-Chi	25	Dalrymple-Chi	12	J.O'Rourke-Bos	6	Stovey-Wor	161
Kelly-Chi	72	Gore-Chi	116	Anson-Chi	24	J.O'Rourke-Bos	11	Jones-Bos	5	J.O'Rourke-Bos	160
J.O'Rourke-Bos	71	Hines-Pro	115	Gore-Chi	23	Hornung-Buf	11	Dunlap-Cle	4	Dunlap-Cle	160
Gore-Chi	70	Connor-Tro	113	J.O'Rourke-Bos	22	Phillips-Cle	10			Connor-Tro	156

Runs Batted In		Runs Produced		Bases On Balls		Batting Average		On Base Percentage		Slugging Average	
Anson-Chi	74	Kelly-Chi	131	Ferguson-Tro	24	Gore-Chi	.360	Gore-Chi	.399	Gore-Chi	.463
Kelly-Chi	60	Dalrymple-Chi	127	J.O'Rourke-Bos	21	Anson-Chi	.337	Anson-Chi	.362	Connor-Tro	.459
Gore-Chi	47	Anson-Chi	127	Gore-Chi	21	Connor-Tro	.332	Connor-Tro	.357	Dalrymple-Chi	.458
Connor-Tro	47	Gore-Chi	115	Clapp-Cin	21	Dalrymple-Chi	.330	Dalrymple-Chi	.335	Stovey-Wor	.454
J.O'Rourke-Bos	45	J.O'Rourke-Bos	110	Crowley-Buf	19	Burns-Chi	.309	Burns-Chi	.333	J.O'Rourke-Bos	.441

Production		Adjusted Production		Batter Runs		Adjusted Batter Runs		Clutch Hitting Index		Runs Created	
Gore-Chi	.862	Gore-Chi	180	Gore-Chi	30.4	Gore-Chi	26.0	Anson-Chi	178	Gore-Chi	61
Connor-Tro	.816	Connor-Tro	166	Connor-Tro	25.4	J.O'Rourke-Bos	22.2	Hotaling-Cle	147	Dalrymple-Chi	60
Dalrymple-Chi	.793	Jones-Bos	159	Dalrymple-Chi	24.5	Connor-Tro	21.8	Kelly-Chi	141	Connor-Tro	57
Anson-Chi	.781	J.O'Rourke-Bos	158	Anson-Chi	22.9	Dalrymple-Chi	20.2	Richmond-Wor	131	Anson-Chi	55
J.O'Rourke-Bos	.756	Dalrymple-Chi	156	J.O'Rourke-Bos	19.9	Hines-Pro	19.1	Creamer-Wor	127	J.O'Rourke-Bos	52

Total Average		Stolen Bases		Stolen Base Average		Stolen Base Runs		Fielding Runs		Total Player Rating	
Gore-Chi	.825							Irwin-Wor	31.2	Irwin-Wor	3.4
Connor-Tro	.744							Force-Buf	30.9	Clapp-Cin	2.9
Dalrymple-Chi	.695							Bradley-Pro	19.2	Gore-Chi	2.8
Anson-Chi	.691							Shaffer-Cle	17.2	Dunlap-Cle	2.7
J.O'Rourke-Bos	.688							Clapp-Cin	17.2	Hines-Pro	2.4

Wins		Win Percentage		Games		Complete Games		Shutouts		Saves	
McCormick-Cle	45	Goldsmith-Chi	.875	Richmond-Wor	74	McCormick-Cle	72	Ward-Pro	8	Richmond-Wor	3
Corcoran-Chi	43	Corcoran-Chi	.754	McCormick-Cle	74	Welch-Tro	64	McCormick-Cle	7	Corey-Wor	2
Ward-Pro	39	Ward-Pro	.619	Ward-Pro	70	Ward-Pro	59	Richmond-Wor	5	Corcoran-Chi	2
Welch-Tro	34	McCormick-Cle	.616	Welch-Tro	65	W.White-Cin	58	Galvin-Buf	5		
Richmond-Wor	32	Welch-Tro	.531								

Innings Pitched		Fewest Hits/Game		Fewest BB/Game		Strikeouts		Strikeouts/Game		Ratio	
McCormick-Cle	657.2	Keefe-Tro	6.09	Bradley-Pro	.28	Corcoran-Chi	268	Corcoran-Chi	4.50	Bradley-Pro	7.53
Ward-Pro	595.0	Corcoran-Chi	6.78	Galvin-Buf	.63	McCormick-Cle	260	Goldsmith-Chi	3.85	Keefe-Tro	7.54
Richmond-Wor	590.2	Bradley-Pro	7.26	Ward-Pro	.68	Richmond-Wor	243	Richmond-Wor	3.70	Ward-Pro	8.26
Welch-Tro	574.0	Ward-Pro	7.58	Weidman-Buf	.71	Ward-Pro	230	Keefe-Tro	3.69	Corcoran-Chi	8.44
Corcoran-Chi	536.1	Corey-Wor	7.95	Goldsmith-Chi	.77	W.White-Cin	161	McCormick-Cle	3.56	Goldsmith-Chi	8.86

Earned Run Average		Adjusted ERA		Opponents' Batting Avg.		Opponents' On Base Pct.		Starter Runs		Adjusted Starter Runs	
Keefe-Tro	.86	Keefe-Tro	294	Keefe-Tro	.187	Bradley-Pro	.217	Ward-Pro	42.0	McCormick-Cle	36.8
Bradley-Pro	1.38	Bradley-Pro	160	Corcoran-Chi	.199	Keefe-Tro	.222	McCormick-Cle	38.5	Ward-Pro	30.8
Ward-Pro	1.74	Goldsmith-Chi	138	Bradley-Pro	.210	Ward-Pro	.232	Corcoran-Chi	25.5	Richmond-Wor	29.5
Goldsmith-Chi	1.75	McCormick-Cle	127	Ward-Pro	.217	Corcoran-Chi	.236	Bradley-Pro	21.7	Corcoran-Chi	28.3
McCormick-Cle	1.85	Ward-Pro	127	Corey-Wor	.219	Corey-Wor	.239	Keefe-Tro	17.7	W.White-Cin	19.6

Clutch Pitching Index		Relief Runs		Adjusted Relief Runs		Relief Ranking		Total Pitcher Index		Total Baseball Ranking	
W.White-Cin	124							McCormick-Cle	4.0	Ward-Pro	4.1
Keefe-Tro	120							Ward-Pro	3.4	McCormick-Cle	3.7
Bond-Bos	114							Corcoran-Chi	3.1	Irwin-Wor	3.4
Poorman-Buf-Chi	112							Keefe-Tro	2.2	Bradley-Pro	3.4
Galvin-Buf	111							Goldsmith-Chi	1.9	Clapp-Cin	2.9

1881 National League

TEAM	G	W	L	PCT	GB	R	OR	AB	H	2B	3B	HR	BB	SO	AVG	OBP	SLG	PRO	PRO+	BR	/A	PF	CHI	RC	SB	CS	SBA	SBR
CHI	84	56	28	.667		550	379	3114	918	157	36	12	140	224	.295	.325	.380	.705	119	85	60	105	105	394				
PRO	85	47	37	.560	9	447	426	3077	780	144	37	11	146	214	.253	.287	.335	.622	100	-4	3	98	104	304				
BUF	83	45	38	.542	10.5	440	447	3019	797	157	50	12	108	270	.264	.289	.361	.650	109	22	28	99	99	323				
DET	84	41	43	.488	15	439	429	2995	780	131	53	17	136	250	.260	.293	.357	.650	103	22	4	104	99	320				
TRO	85	39	45	.464	17	399	429	3046	754	124	31	5	140	240	.248	.281	.314	.595	86	-32	-53	105	100	275				
BOS	83	38	45	.458	17.5	349	410	2916	733	121	27	5	110	193	.251	.279	.317	.596	94	-31	-14	95	93	264				
CLE	85	36	48	.429	20	392	414	3117	796	120	39	7	132	224	.255	.286	.326	.612	100	-16	6	95	93	297				
WOR	83	32	50	.390	23	410	492	3093	781	114	31	7	121	169	.253	.281	.316	.597	86	-31	-54	106	102	281				
TOT	336					3426		24377	6339	1068	304	76	1033	1784	.260	.289	.338	.627										

TEAM	CG	SH	SV	IP	H	H/G	HR	BB	SO	RAT	ERA	ERA+	OAV	OOB	PR	/A	PF	CPI	FA	E	DP	FW	PW	BW	SBW	DIF
CHI	81	9	0	744²	722	8.7	14	122	228	10.2	2.43	113	.243	.273	29	26	99	97	.916	309	54	2.1	2.4	5.6		3.9
PRO	76	7	0	757²	756	9.0	5	138	264	10.6	2.40	111	.243	.275	32	22	96	94	.896	390	66	-2.0	2.1	.3		4.7
BUF	72	5	0	742¹	881	10.7	9	89	185	11.8	2.84	98	.281	.301	-5	-5	100	114	.892	408	48	-3.4	-.5	2.6		4.8
DET	83	10	0	744²	785	9.5	8	137	265	11.1	2.65	110	.257	.289	11	22	105	102	.906	338	80	.5	2.1	.4		-3.9
TRO	85	8	0	770	813	9.5	11	159	207	11.4	2.97	99	.265	.301	-17	-2	106	102	.917	311	70	2.2	-.2	-5.0		-.0
BOS	72	6	3	730²	763	9.4	9	143	199	11.2	2.71	98	.258	.292	5	-4	96	103	.909	325	54	1.0	-.4	-1.3		-2.8
CLE	82	2	0	760	737	8.7	9	126	240	10.2	2.68	98	.244	.274	8	-5	94	87	.904	348	68	.2	-.5	.6		-6.3
WOR	80	5	0	737¹	882	10.8	11	120	196	12.2	3.54	85	.288	.315	-63	-43	109	101	.903	353	50	-.5	-4.0	-5.0		.6
TOT	631	52	3	5987¹		9.5				11.1	2.77		.260	.289					.905	2782	490					

Runs		Hits		Doubles		Triples		Home Runs		Total Bases	
Gore-Chi	86	Anson-Chi	137	Kelly-Chi	27	Rowe-Buf	11	Brouthers-Buf	8	Anson-Chi	175
Kelly-Chi	84	Dalrymple-Chi	117	Hines-Pro	27	Phillips-Cle	10	Bennett-Det	7	Dunlap-Cle	156
Dalrymple-Chi	72	Dickerson-Wor	116	Stovey-Wor	25			Farrell-Pro	5	Kelly-Chi	153
O'Rourke-Buf	71			Dunlap-Cle	25			Burns-Chi	4	Dalrymple-Chi	150
Farrell-Pro	69			White-Buf	24					Dickerson-Wor	149

Runs Batted In		Runs Produced		Bases On Balls		Batting Average		On Base Percentage		Slugging Average	
Anson-Chi	82	Anson-Chi	148	Clapp-Cle	35	Anson-Chi	.399	Anson-Chi	.442	Brouthers-Buf	.541
Bennett-Det	64	Kelly-Chi	137	York-Pro	29	Powell-Det	.338	York-Pro	.362	Anson-Chi	.510
Kelly-Chi	55	Gore-Chi	129	Ferguson-Tro	29	Rowe-Buf	.333	Brouthers-Buf	.361	Rowe-Buf	.480
		Knight-Det	118	Farrell-Pro	29	Start-Pro	.328	Dunlap-Cle	.358	Bennett-Det	.478
		Richardson-Buf	113			Dunlap-Cle	.325	Gore-Chi	.354	Dunlap-Cle	.444

Production		Adjusted Production		Batter Runs		Adjusted Batter Runs		Clutch Hitting Index		Runs Created	
Anson-Chi	.952	Anson-Chi	189	Anson-Chi	38.9	Anson-Chi	34.7	Knight-Det	164	Anson-Chi	79
Brouthers-Buf	.902	Brouthers-Buf	182	Brouthers-Buf	24.1	Brouthers-Buf	25.0	Anson-Chi	145	Dunlap-Cle	57
Bennett-Det	.819	Dunlap-Cle	159	Dunlap-Cle	20.0	Dunlap-Cle	23.8	Ward-Pro	143	Kelly-Chi	55
Dunlap-Cle	.802	York-Pro	150	Bennett-Det	18.3	York-Pro	18.9	Radbourn-Pro	135	Brouthers-Buf	54
York-Pro	.790	Bennett-Det	149	Kelly-Chi	18.0	O'Rourke-Buf	16.0	White-Buf	128	Dalrymple-Chi	54

Total Average		Stolen Bases	Stolen Base Average	Stolen Base Runs	Fielding Runs		Total Player Rating	
Anson-Chi	.976				Ewing-Tro	25.3	Bennett-Det	3.3
Brouthers-Buf	.891				Richardson-Buf	24.6	Anson-Chi	3.1
Bennett-Det	.770				Force-Buf	24.3	Richardson-Buf	3.1
York-Pro	.745				Williamson-Chi	22.2	Dunlap-Cle	3.0
Dunlap-Cle	.734				Bennett-Det	18.3	Ewing-Tro	2.2

Wins		Win Percentage		Games		Complete Games		Shutouts		Saves	
Whitney-Bos	31	Radbourn-Pro	.694	Whitney-Bos	66	Whitney-Bos	57	Derby-Det	9	Mathews-Pro-Bos	2
Corcoran-Chi	31	Corcoran-Chi	.689	McCormick-Cle	59	McCormick-Cle	57	Whitney-Bos	6	Morrill-Bos	1
Derby-Det	29	Goldsmith-Chi	.649	Galvin-Buf	56	Derby-Det	55	Goldsmith-Chi	5		
Galvin-Buf	28	Welch-Tro	.538	Derby-Det	56	Richmond-Wor	50	Galvin-Buf	5		
McCormick-Cle	26	Galvin-Buf	.538	Richmond-Wor	53	Galvin-Buf	48				

Innings Pitched		Fewest Hits/Game		Fewest BB/Game		Strikeouts		Strikeouts/Game		Ratio	
Whitney-Bos	552.1	McCormick-Cle	8.28	Galvin-Buf	.87	Derby-Det	212	Derby-Det	3.86	Weidman-Det	9.39
McCormick-Cle	526.0	Weidman-Det	8.45	Weidman-Det	.94	McCormick-Cle	178	Corcoran-Chi	3.40	McCormick-Cle	9.72
Derby-Det	494.2	Radbourn-Pro	8.55	Goldsmith-Chi	1.20	Whitney-Bos	162	Ward-Pro	3.25	Goldsmith-Chi	10.15
Galvin-Buf	474.0	Corcoran-Chi	8.62	Richmond-Wor	1.32	Richmond-Wor	156	Radbourn-Pro	3.24	Radbourn-Pro	10.32
Richmond-Wor	462.1	Ward-Pro	8.89	McCormick-Cle	1.44	Corcoran-Chi	150	McCormick-Cle	3.05	Ward-Pro	10.34

Earned Run Average		Adjusted ERA		Opponents' Batting Avg.		Opponents' On Base Pct.		Starter Runs		Adjusted Starter Runs	
Weidman-Det	1.80	Weidman-Det	162	Radbourn-Pro	.235	Weidman-Det	.258	Derby-Det	31.5	Derby-Det	39.3
Ward-Pro	2.13	Derby-Det	132	McCormick-Cle	.235	McCormick-Cle	.265	Ward-Pro	23.7	Galvin-Buf	21.3
Derby-Det	2.20	Ward-Pro	125	Weidman-Det	.238	Radbourn-Pro	.270	Galvin-Buf	21.1	Ward-Pro	19.4
Corcoran-Chi	2.31	Corcoran-Chi	118	Corcoran-Chi	.242	Goldsmith-Chi	.271	Corcoran-Chi	20.3	Corcoran-Chi	18.7
Galvin-Buf	2.37	Galvin-Buf	117	Ward-Pro	.242	Ward-Pro	.271	McCormick-Cle	19.2	Weidman-Det	14.3

Clutch Pitching Index		Relief Runs	Adjusted Relief Runs	Relief Ranking	Total Pitcher Index		Total Baseball Ranking	
Galvin-Buf	123				Derby-Det	3.0	Bennett-Det	3.3
Derby-Det	112				Galvin-Buf	2.6	Anson-Chi	3.1
Weidman-Det	109				Ward-Pro	2.5	Richardson-Buf	3.1
Fox-Bos	108				Whitney-Bos	1.9	Dunlap-Cle	3.0
Lynch-Buf	106				Corcoran-Chi	1.4	Derby-Det	2.8

TEAM	G	W	L	PCT	GB	R	OR	AB	H	2B	3B	HR	BB	SO	AVG	OBP	SLG	PRO	PRO+	BR	/A	PF	CHI	RC	SB	CS	SBA	SBR
CHI	84	55	29	.655		604	353	3225	892	209	54	15	142	262	.277	.307	.389	.696	119	82	56	105	108	395				
PRO	84	52	32	.619	3	463	356	3104	776	121	53	11	102	255	.250	.274	.334	.608	96	-16	-15	100	105	291				
BUF	84	45	39	.536	10	500	461	3128	858	146	47	18	116	228	.274	.300	.368	.668	113	50	41	102	98	355				
BOS	85	45	39	.536	10	472	414	3118	823	114	50	15	134	244	.264	.294	.347	.641	107	23	22	100	97	326				
CLE	84	42	40	.512	12	402	411	3009	716	139	40	20	122	261	.238	.268	.331	.599	96	-24	-10	97	95	273				
DET	86	42	41	.506	12.5	407	488	3144	724	117	44	19	122	308	.230	.259	.314	.573	84	-53	-52	100	99	262				
TRO	85	35	48	.422	19.5	430	522	3057	747	116	59	19	109	298	.244	.270	.333	.603	99	-20	1	95	100	282				
WOR	84	18	66	.214	37	379	652	2984	689	109	57	16	113	303	.231	.259	.322	.581	85	-43	-53	102	95	255				
TOT	338					3657		24769	6225	1071	404	126	960	2159	.251	.279	.342	.622										

TEAM	CG	SH	SV	IP	H	H/G	HR	BB	SO	RAT	ERA	ERA+	OAV	OOB	PR	/A	PF	CPI	FA	E	DP	FW	PW	BW	SBW	DIF
CHI	83	7	0	763²	667	7.9	13	102	279	9.1	2.22	129	.221	.246	57	51	99	87	.898	376	54	.1	4.6	5.1		3.1
PRO	80	10	1	752	690	8.3	12	87	273	9.3	2.27	123	.228	.250	51	47	97	94	.901	371	67	.4	4.3	-1.4		6.7
BUF	79	3	0	737	778	9.5	16	114	287	10.9	3.25	90	.254	.280	-30	-30	101	89	.910	315	42	3.3	-2.7	3.7		-1.3
BOS	81	4	0	749	738	8.9	10	77	352	9.8	2.80	102	.239	.258	7	4	99	83	.910	314	37	3.6	.4	2.0		-2.9
CLE	81	4	0	751²	743	8.9	22	132	232	10.5	2.75	101	.249	.280	11	1	97	106	.905	358	71	1.1	.0	-.9		.7
DET	82	7	0	793	808	9.2	19	129	354	10.6	2.98	98	.248	.277	-9	-8	101	94	.893	396	44	-.4	-.7	-4.7		6.4
TRO	81	6	0	757	837	10.0	13	168	189	11.9	3.08	91	.268	.305	-16	-24	98	113	.887	432	70	-2.5	-2.2	.0		-1.9
WOR	75	0	0	738¹	964	11.8	21	151	195	13.6	3.75	83	.294	.325	-71	-54	107	115	.878	468	66	-4.6	-4.9	-4.8		-9.7
TOT	642	41	1	6041²		9.3				10.7	2.89		.251	.279					.897	3030	451					

Runs
Gore-Chi 99
Dalrymple-Chi 96
Stovey-Wor 90
Kelly-Chi 81
Purcell-Buf 79

Hits
Brouthers-Buf 129
Anson-Chi 126

Doubles
Kelly-Chi 37
Anson-Chi 29
Hines-Pro 28
Williamson-Chi 27
Glasscock-Cle 27

Triples
Connor-Tro 18
Wood-Det 12
Corey-Wor 12

Home Runs
Wood-Det 7
Muldoon-Cle 6
Brouthers-Buf 6

Total Bases
Brouthers-Buf 192
Connor-Tro 185
Hines-Pro 177
Anson-Chi 174
Dalrymple-Chi 167

Runs Batted In
Anson-Chi 83
Brouthers-Buf 63
Williamson-Chi 60
Richardson-Buf 57
Kelly-Chi 55

Runs Produced
Anson-Chi 151
Gore-Chi 147
Kelly-Chi 135
Dalrymple-Chi 131
Brouthers-Buf 128

Bases On Balls
Gore-Chi 29
Williamson-Chi 27
Shaffer-Cle 27
Hanlon-Det 26

Batting Average
Brouthers-Buf .... .368
Anson-Chi .... .362
Connor-Tro ...... .330
Start-Pro .... .329
Whitney-Bos ..... .323

On Base Percentage
Brouthers-Buf .... .403
Anson-Chi .... .397
Whitney-Bos ..... .382
Gore-Chi .... .369
Connor-Tro ...... .354

Slugging Average
Brouthers-Buf .... .547
Connor-Tro .... .530
Whitney-Bos ..... .510
Anson-Chi .... .500
Hines-Pro .... .467

Production
Brouthers-Buf ..... .950
Anson-Chi .... .897
Whitney-Bos ..... .892
Connor-Tro ...... .884
Hines-Pro .... .793

Adjusted Production
Brouthers-Buf 198
Connor-Tro 188
Whitney-Bos 183
Anson-Chi 177
Hines-Pro 151

Batter Runs
Brouthers-Buf 39.1
Anson-Chi 32.7
Connor-Tro 29.7
Whitney-Bos 23.7
Gore-Chi 22.2

Adjusted Batter Runs
Brouthers-Buf 37.5
Connor-Tro 33.6
Anson-Chi 28.9
Whitney-Bos 23.5
Hines-Pro 20.7

Clutch Hitting Index
Pfeffer-Tro 147
Holbert-Tro 146
Anson-Chi 143
Rowen-Bos 129
Hayes-Wor 128

Runs Created
Brouthers-Buf 79
Anson-Chi 71
Connor-Tro 67
Hines-Pro 59
Gore-Chi 59

Total Average
Brouthers-Buf ..... .959
Whitney-Bos ..... .894
Anson-Chi .... .874
Connor-Tro .... .846
Gore-Chi .... .736

Stolen Bases

Stolen Base Average

Stolen Base Runs

Fielding Runs
Glasscock-Cle 24.0
A.Irwin-Wor 20.5
Evans-Wor 19.8
Dunlap-Cle 17.6
Williamson-Chi ... 16.2

Total Player Rating
Glasscock-Cle 4.1
Connor-Tro 2.9
Williamson-Chi ... 2.6
Brouthers-Buf 2.6
Dunlap-Cle 2.6

Wins
McCormick-Cle 36
Radbourn-Pro 33
Goldsmith-Chi 28
Galvin-Buf 28
Corcoran-Chi 27

Win Percentage
Corcoran-Chi ..... .692
Radbourn-Pro ..... .623
Goldsmith-Chi .... .622
Ward-Pro .... .613
Mathews-Bos .... .559

Games
McCormick-Cle 68
Radbourn-Pro 55
Galvin-Buf 52
Whitney-Bos 49
Richmond-Wor 48

Complete Games
McCormick-Cle 65
Radbourn-Pro 51
Galvin-Buf 48
Whitney-Bos 46
Goldsmith-Chi 45

Shutouts
Radbourn-Pro 6
Welch-Tro 5

Saves
Ward-Pro 1

Innings Pitched
McCormick-Cle ... 595.2
Radbourn-Pro 474.0
Galvin-Buf 445.1
Whitney-Bos 420.0

Fewest Hits/Game
Corcoran-Chi 7.11
Radbourn-Pro 8.15
McCormick-Cle 8.31
Goldsmith-Chi 8.38
Ward-Pro 8.45

Fewest BB/Game
Mathews-Bos ..... .69
Galvin-Buf .... .81
Goldsmith-Chi .... .84
Weidman-Det ..... .85
Whitney-Bos ...... .88

Strikeouts
Radbourn-Pro 201
McCormick-Cle 200
Derby-Det 182
Whitney-Bos 180
Corcoran-Chi 170

Strikeouts/Game
Mathews-Bos 4.83
Derby-Det 4.52
Corcoran-Chi 4.30
Daily-Buf 4.08
Whitney-Bos 3.86

Ratio
Corcoran-Chi 8.70
Radbourn-Pro 9.11
Goldsmith-Chi ... 9.22
Weidman-Det 9.42
Mathews-Bos 9.47

Earned Run Average
Corcoran-Chi 1.95
Radbourn-Pro 2.09
McCormick-Cle 2.37
Goldsmith-Chi 2.42
Keefe-Tro 2.50

Adjusted ERA
Corcoran-Chi 147
Radbourn-Pro 134
Goldsmith-Chi 118
McCormick-Cle 118
Keefe-Tro 113

Opponents' Batting Avg.
Corcoran-Chi ..... .200
Radbourn-Pro ..... .226
Mathews-Bos ..... .232
Ward-Pro .... .232
Daily-Buf .... .234

Opponents' On Base Pct.
Corcoran-Chi ..... .234
Mathews-Bos ..... .246
Radbourn-Pro ..... .246
Weidman-Det ..... .253
Goldsmith-Chi .... .254

Starter Runs
Radbourn-Pro 42.0
Corcoran-Chi 37.0
McCormick-Cle 34.0
Goldsmith-Chi 20.8
Keefe-Tro 16.2

Adjusted Starter Runs
Radbourn-Pro 37.6
Corcoran-Chi 35.9
McCormick-Cle 27.5
Goldsmith-Chi 19.5
Weidman-Det 13.5

Clutch Pitching Index
Egan-Tro 120
Richmond-Wor 116
F.Mountain-Wor-Wor ... 115
Welch-Tro 113
Corey-Wor 112

Relief Runs

Adjusted Relief Runs

Relief Ranking

Total Pitcher Index
Radbourn-Pro 3.4
Corcoran-Chi 3.1
Whitney-Bos 3.1
Keefe-Tro 2.2
McCormick-Cle ... 2.0

Total Baseball Ranking
Glasscock-Cle 4.1
Radbourn-Pro 3.3
Corcoran-Chi 3.1
Whitney-Bos 3.1
Connor-Tro 2.9

TEAM	G	W	L	PCT	GB	R	OR	AB	H	2B	3B	HR	BB	SO	AVG	OBP	SLG	PRO	PRO+	BR	/A	PF	CHI	RC	SB	CS	SBA	SBR
CIN	80	55	25	.688		489	268	3007	795	95	47	5	102	204	.264	.289	.332	.621	107	38	12	106	104	295				
PHI	75	41	34	.547	11.5	406	389	2707	660	89	21	5	125	164	.244	.277	.298	.575	88	-4	-50	112	104	229				
LOU	80	42	38	.525	13	443	352	2806	728	110	28	9	128	193	.259	.292	.328	.620	120	37	62	95	99	275				
PIT	79	39	39	.500	15	428	418	2904	730	110	59	18	90	183	.251	.274	.348	.622	118	35	56	95	95	284				
STL	80	37	43	.463	18	399	496	2865	663	87	41	11	112	226	.231	.260	.302	.562	90	-19	-34	104	101	231				
BAL	74	19	54	.260	32.5	273	515	2583	535	60	24	4	72	215	.207	.229	.254	.483	72	-87	-66	92	97	153				
TOT	234					2438		16872	4111	551	220	52	629	1185	.244	.271	.312	.582										

TEAM	CG	SH	SV	IP	H	H/G	HR	BB	SO	RAT	ERA	ERA+	OAV	OOB	PR	/A	PF	CPI	FA	E	DP	FW	PW	BW	SBW	DIF
CIN	77	11	0	721¹	609	7.6	7	125	165	9.2	1.65	160	.214	.247	83	79	98	119	.907	332	41	3.7	7.3	1.1		2.9
PHI	72	2	0	663	682	9.3	13	99	190	10.6	2.97	100	.249	.275	-21	0	111	97	.895	361	36	1.2	.0	-4.6		6.9
LOU	73	6	0	693¹	637	8.3	6	112	240	9.7	2.03	122	.229	.259	51	34	92	113	.893	385	57	1.3	3.1	5.7		-8.1
PIT	77	2	0	696²	694	10.0	4	82	252	10.0	2.79	93	.243	.264	-8	-14	97	90	.889	397	40	.5	-1.3	5.1		-4.3
STL	75	3	1	688¹	729	9.5	7	103	225	10.9	2.92	96	.254	.280	-18	-9	105	101	.875	446	41	-1.6	-.8	-3.1		2.5
BAL	64	1	0	646¹	760	10.6	15	108	113	12.1	3.88	71	.275	.302	-86	-82	102	94	.859	490	41	-5.0	-7.5	-6.1		1.1
TOT	438	25	1	4109		9.0				10.4	2.68		.244	.271					.886	2411	256					

Runs		Hits		Doubles		Triples		Home Runs		Total Bases	
Swartwood-Pit	86	Carpenter-Cin	120	Swartwood-Pit	18	Mansell-Pit	16	Walker-StL	7	Swartwood-Pit	159
Sommer-Cin	82	Browning-Lou	109	Mansell-Pit	18	Taylor-Pit	13	Browning-Lou	5	Mansell-Pit	152
Carpenter-Cin	78	Swartwood-Pit	107	Browning-Lou	17	Wheeler-Cin	11	Swartwood-Pit	4	Carpenter-Cin	148
Browning-Lou	67	Sommer-Cin	102	Taylor-Pit	16	Swartwood-Pit	11			Browning-Lou	147
Birchall-Phi	65	B.Gleason-StL	100	Cuthbert-StL	16	Wolf-Lou	8			Taylor-Pit	135

Runs Batted In		Runs Produced		Bases On Balls		Batting Average		On Base Percentage		Slugging Average	
		Swartwood-Pit	82	J.Gleason-StL	27	Browning-Lou	.378	Browning-Lou	.430	Browning-Lou	.510
		Sommer-Cin	81	Browning-Lou	26	Carpenter-Cin	.342	Swartwood-Pit	.370	Swartwood-Pit	.489
		Carpenter-Cin	77	Sommer-Cin	24	Swartwood-Pit	.329	Carpenter-Cin	.360	Taylor-Pit	.452
		Birchall-Phi	65	J.Reccius-Lou	23	O'Brien-Phi	.303	O'Brien-Phi	.339	Mansell-Pit	.438
				Swartwood-Pit	21	Wolf-Lou	.299	Sommer-Cin	.333	Carpenter-Cin	.422

Production		Adjusted Production		Batter Runs		Adjusted Batter Runs		Clutch Hitting Index		Runs Created	
Browning-Lou	.940	Browning-Lou	228	Browning-Lou	35.3	Browning-Lou	39.7			Browning-Lou	65
Swartwood-Pit	.859	Swartwood-Pit	197	Swartwood-Pit	29.3	Swartwood-Pit	33.0			Swartwood-Pit	60
Carpenter-Cin	.782	Taylor-Pit	157	Carpenter-Cin	22.0	Carpenter-Cin	18.1			Carpenter-Cin	55
O'Brien-Phi	.758	Carpenter-Cin	154	Taylor-Pit	14.5	Mansell-Pit	17.4			Mansell-Pit	45
Taylor-Pit	.749	Mansell-Pit	150	Mansell-Pit	14.5	Taylor-Pit	17.1			Sommer-Cin	44

Total Average		Stolen Bases		Stolen Base Average		Stolen Base Runs		Fielding Runs		Total Player Rating	
Browning-Lou	.966							Stricker-Phi	22.5	Browning-Lou	4.7
Swartwood-Pit	.826							Snyder-Cin	19.4	Snyder-Cin	2.3
Carpenter-Cin	.684							White-Cin	12.0	Swartwood-Pit	2.2
O'Brien-Phi	.679							Browning-Lou	11.8	O'Brien-Phi	1.9
Taylor-Pit	.660							O'Brien-Phi	11.4	Mansell-Pit	1.8

Wins		Win Percentage		Games		Complete Games		Shutouts		Saves	
White-Cin	40	White-Cin	.769	Mullane-Lou	55	White-Cin	52	White-Cin	8	Fusselback-StL	1
Mullane-Lou	30	Weaver-Phi	.634	White-Cin	54	Mullane-Lou	51	Mullane-Lou	5		
Weaver-Phi	26	McGinnis-StL	.581	McGinnis-StL	45	McGinnis-StL	43	McGinnis-StL	3		
McGinnis-StL	25	Mullane-Lou	.556	Landis-Phi-Bal	44	Weaver-Phi	41	McCormick-Cin	3		
Salisbury-Pit	20	Salisbury-Pit	.526	Weaver-Phi	42	Salisbury-Pit	38	Weaver-Phi	2		

Innings Pitched		Fewest Hits/Game		Fewest BB/Game		Strikeouts		Strikeouts/Game		Ratio	
White-Cin	480.0	Hecker-Lou	6.49	Hecker-Lou	.43	Mullane-Lou	170	Salisbury-Pit	3.63	Hecker-Lou	6.92
Mullane-Lou	460.1	McCormick-Cin	7.25	Driscoll-Pit	.54	Salisbury-Pit	135	Arundel-Pit	3.53	Driscoll-Pit	7.79
McGinnis-StL	388.1	Driscoll-Pit	7.25	Weaver-Phi	.85	McGinnis-StL	134	Mullane-Lou	3.32	McCormick-Cin	8.97
Weaver-Phi	371.0	White-Cin	7.71	Salisbury-Pit	.99	White-Cin	122	McGinnis-StL	3.11	White-Cin	9.04
Landis-Phi-Bal	358.0	Geis-Bal	7.90	Landis-Phi-Bal	1.18	Weaver-Phi	104	J.Reccius-Lou	2.94	Salisbury-Pit	9.46

Earned Run Average		Adjusted ERA		Opponents' Batting Avg.		Opponents' On Base Pct.		Starter Runs		Adjusted Starter Runs	
Driscoll-Pit	1.21	Driscoll-Pit	216	Hecker-Lou	.188	Hecker-Lou	.199	White-Cin	61.1	White-Cin	58.7
Hecker-Lou	1.30	Hecker-Lou	191	McCormick-Cin	.206	Driscoll-Pit	.218	Mullane-Lou	41.2	Driscoll-Pit	31.2
McCormick-Cin	1.52	McCormick-Cin	174	Driscoll-Pit	.206	McCormick-Cin	.243	Driscoll-Pit	32.9	Mullane-Lou	30.7
White-Cin	1.54	White-Cin	172	White-Cin	.216	White-Cin	.244	McCormick-Cin	28.5	McCormick-Cin	27.4
Mullane-Lou	1.88	Mullane-Lou	132	Geis-Bal	.220	Salisbury-Pit	.253	Hecker-Lou	16.0	Hecker-Lou	13.6

Clutch Pitching Index		Relief Runs		Adjusted Relief Runs		Relief Ranking		Total Pitcher Index		Total Baseball Ranking	
White-Cin	124							White-Cin	7.3	White-Cin	7.2
McCormick-Cin	124							Mullane-Lou	5.1	Mullane-Lou	5.0
Mullane-Lou	120							Driscoll-Pit	2.4	Browning-Lou	4.7
J.Reccius-Lou	119							McCormick-Cin	2.1	Driscoll-Pit	2.4
Driscoll-Pit	113							Hecker-Lou	2.1	Snyder-Cin	2.3

TEAM	G	W	L	PCT	GB	R	OR	AB	H	2B	3B	HR	BB	SO	AVG	OBP	SLG	PRO	PRO+	BR	/A	PF	CHI	RC	SB	CS	SBA	SBR
BOS	98	63	35	.643		669	456	3657	1010	209	86	34	123	423	.276	.300	.408	.708	114	68	53	102	104	459				
CHI	98	59	39	.602	4	679	540	3658	1000	277	61	13	129	399	.273	.298	.393	.691	106	49	13	106	109	439				
PRO	98	58	40	.592	5	636	436	3685	1001	189	59	21	149	309	.272	.300	.372	.672	104	29	13	103	104	422				
CLE	100	55	42	.567	7.5	476	443	3457	852	184	38	8	139	374	.246	.276	.329	.605	88	-53	-47	99	97	321				
BUF	98	52	45	.536	10.5	614	576	3729	1058	184	59	8	147	342	.284	.311	.371	.682	108	44	30	102	97	441				
NY	98	46	50	.479	16	530	577	3524	900	139	69	24	127	297	.255	.281	.354	.635	96	-18	-12	99	99	360				
DET	101	40	58	.408	23	524	650	3726	931	164	48	13	166	378	.250	.282	.330	.612	93	-46	-21	95	96	355				
PHI	99	17	81	.173	46	437	887	3576	859	181	48	3	141	355	.240	.269	.320	.589	90	-74	-32	91	89	316				
TOT	395					4565		29012	7611	1527	468	124	1121	2877	.262	.290	.360	.650										

TEAM	CG	SH	SV	IP	H	H/G	HR	BB	SO	RAT	ERA	ERA+	OAV	OOB	PR	/A	PF	CPI	FA	E	DP	FW	PW	BW	SBW	DIF
BOS	89	6	3	860	853	8.9	11	90	538	9.9	2.55	121	.245	.264	56	52	99	96	.901	409	58	3.1	4.5	4.6		1.7
CHI	91	5	1	862	942	9.8	21	123	299	11.1	2.78	115	.260	.284	34	37	102	109	.879	543	76	-3.5	3.2	1.1		9.1
PRO	88	4	1	871	827	8.5	12	111	376	9.7	2.37	130	.238	.262	75	68	98	99	.903	419	75	2.7	5.9	1.1		-.7
CLE	92	5	2	879	818	8.4	7	217	402	10.6	2.22	142	.237	.282	89	92	100	118	.909	389	69	4.6	8.0	-4.1		-2.0
BUF	90	5	2	859¹	971	10.2	12	101	362	11.2	3.32	96	.268	.288	-17	-8	101	97	.896	445	52	1.4	-.7	2.6		.2
NY	87	5	0	866	907	9.4	19	170	323	11.2	2.94	105	.253	.287	19	11	99	101	.889	468	52	.2	1.0	-1.0		-2.1
DET	89	5	2	894¹	1026	10.3	22	184	324	12.2	3.58	87	.270	.303	-44	-49	99	98	.893	470	77	.9	-4.3	-1.8		-3.7
PHI	91	3	0	864²	1267	13.2	20	125	253	14.5	5.34	58	.318	.338	-212	-216	98	92	.858	639	62	-8.0	-18.9	-2.8		-2.4
TOT	717	38	11	6956¹		9.8				11.3	3.14		.262	.290					.891	3782	521					

Runs
Hornung-Bos 107
Gore-Chi 105
O'Rourke-Buf 102
Sutton-Bos 101
Hines-Pro 94

Hits
Brouthers-Buf 159
Connor-NY 146
O'Rourke-Buf 143
Sutton-Bos 134
Wood-Det 133

Doubles
Williamson-Chi ... 49
Brouthers-Buf 41
Burns-Chi 37
Anson-Chi 36

Triples
Brouthers-Buf 17
Morrill-Bos 16
Sutton-Bos 15
Connor-NY 15

Home Runs
Ewing-NY 10
Hornung-Bos 8
Denny-Pro 8
Ward-NY 7
Morrill-Bos 6

Total Bases
Brouthers-Buf 243
Morrill-Bos 212
Connor-NY 207
Sutton-Bos 201
Hornung-Bos 199

Runs Batted In
Brouthers-Buf 97
Burdock-Bos 88
Sutton-Bos 73
Morrill-Bos 68
Anson-Chi 68

Runs Produced
Brouthers-Buf 179
Sutton-Bos 171
Hornung-Bos 165
Burdock-Bos 163
Gore-Chi 155

Bases On Balls
York-Cle 37
Hanlon-Det 34
Powell-Det 28
Shaffer-Buf 27
Gore-Chi 27

Batting Average
Brouthers-Buf 374
Connor-NY 357
Gore-Chi 334
Burdock-Bos 330
O'Rourke-Buf 328

On Base Percentage
Brouthers-Buf 397
Connor-NY 394
Gore-Chi 377
Dunlap-Cle 361
Burdock-Bos 353

Slugging Average
Brouthers-Buf 572
Morrill-Bos 525
Connor-NY 506
Sutton-Bos 486
Ewing-NY 481

Production
Brouthers-Buf.....969
Connor-NY 900
Morrill-Bos 868
Gore-Chi 849
Sutton-Bos 836

Adjusted Production
Brouthers-Buf 186
Connor-NY 173
Morrill-Bos 155
Bennett-Det 155
Gore-Chi 148

Batter Runs
Brouthers-Buf 44.4
Connor-NY 34.6
Morrill-Bos 27.6
Gore-Chi 26.5
Sutton-Bos 24.4

Adjusted Batter Runs
Brouthers-Buf 41.9
Connor-NY 35.7
Morrill-Bos 25.4
Bennett-Det 25.0
Wood-Det 22.9

Clutch Hitting Index
Start-Pro 140
Burdock-Bos 134
Kelly-Chi 131
Sutton-Bos 131
Anson-Chi 123

Runs Created
Brouthers-Buf 99
Connor-NY 84
Morrill-Bos 75
Sutton-Bos 72
Gore-Chi 72

Total Average
Brouthers-Buf.....974
Connor-NY 882
Morrill-Bos.......825
Gore-Chi 812
Bennett-Det 783

Stolen Bases

Stolen Base Average

Stolen Base Runs

Fielding Runs
Farrell-Pro 24.9
Shaffer-Buf 20.0
Ward-NY 19.3
Richardson-Buf ... 18.7
Williamson-Chi ... 17.8

Total Player Rating
Farrell-Pro 3.3
Richardson-Buf 3.1
Brouthers-Buf 2.9
Gore-Chi 2.7
Dunlap-Cle 2.7

Wins
Radbourn-Pro 48
Galvin-Buf 46
Whitney-Bos 37
Corcoran-Chi 34
McCormick-Cle 28

Win Percentage
McCormick-Cle ... .700
Radbourn-Pro .... .658
Buffinton-Bos 641
Whitney-Bos 638
Corcoran-Chi 630

Games
Radbourn-Pro 76
Galvin-Buf 76
Coleman-Phi 65
Whitney-Bos 62
Corcoran-Chi 56

Complete Games
Galvin-Buf 72
Radbourn-Pro 66
Coleman-Phi 59
Whitney-Bos 54
Corcoran-Chi 51

Shutouts
Galvin-Buf 5
Welch-NY 4
Radbourn-Pro 4
Daily-Cle 4
Buffinton-Bos 4

Saves
Whitney-Bos 2
Weidman-Det 2

Innings Pitched
Galvin-Buf 656.1
Radbourn-Pro 632.1
Coleman-Phi 538.1
Whitney-Bos 514.0
Corcoran-Chi 473.2

Fewest Hits/Game
Sawyer-Cle 7.60
Radbourn-Pro 8.01
McCormick-Cle... 8.32
Daily-Cle 8.56
Whitney-Bos 8.61

Fewest BB/Game
Whitney-Bos 61
Galvin-Buf 69
Radbourn-Pro 80
Coleman-Phi 80
Goldsmith-Chi 92

Strikeouts
Whitney-Bos 345
Radbourn-Pro 315
Galvin-Buf 279
Corcoran-Chi 216
Buffinton-Bos 188

Strikeouts/Game
Whitney-Bos 6.04
Buffinton-Bos 5.08
Sawyer-Cle 4.85
Radbourn-Pro 4.48
Corcoran-Chi 4.10

Ratio
Radbourn-Pro 8.81
Whitney-Bos 9.23
Galvin-Buf 9.96
McCormick-Cle .. 10.03
Ward-NY 10.04

Earned Run Average
McCormick-Cle ...1.84
Radbourn-Pro 2.05
Whitney-Bos......2.24
Sawyer-Cle 2.36
Daily-Cle 2.42

Adjusted ERA
McCormick-Cle 171
Radbourn-Pro 150
Whitney-Bos 138
Sawyer-Cle 133
Daily-Cle 130

Opponents' Batting Avg.
Sawyer-Cle ...... .217
Radbourn-Pro .... .227
McCormick-Cle ...233
Sweeney-Pro 237
Whitney-Bos 238

Opponents' On Base Pct.
Radbourn-Pro 244
Whitney-Bos 251
Galvin-Buf 265
Ward-NY 267
McCormick-Cle ...268

Starter Runs
Radbourn-Pro 76.4
Whitney-Bos 51.2
McCormick-Cle ... 49.2
Corcoran-Chi 34.1
Galvin-Buf 30.8

Adjusted Starter Runs
Radbourn-Pro 72.7
McCormick-Cle ... 49.7
Whitney-Bos 49.0
Corcoran-Chi 36.8
Galvin-Buf 33.5

Clutch Pitching Index
McCormick-Cle ... 125
Shaw-Det 121
Daily-Cle 119
O'Neill-NY 118
Goldsmith-Chi 113

Relief Runs

Adjusted Relief Runs

Relief Ranking

Total Pitcher Index
Radbourn-Pro 8.4
Whitney-Bos 6.0
McCormick-Cle ... 5.4
Corcoran-Chi 3.3
Galvin-Buf 2.6

Total Baseball Ranking
Radbourn-Pro 8.1
Whitney-Bos 6.1
McCormick-Cle ... 5.3
Farrell-Pro 3.3
Ward-NY 3.1

TEAM	G	W	L	PCT	GB	R	OR	AB	H	2B	3B	HR	BB	SO	AVG	OBP	SLG	PRO	PRO+	BR	/A	PF	CHI	RC	SB	CS	SBA	SBR
PHI	98	66	32	.673		720	547	3712	974	149	50	20	200	268	.262	.300	.346	.646	103	45	-5	108	114	395				
STL	98	65	33	.663	1	549	409	3495	891	118	46	7	124	240	.255	.280	.321	.601	91	-14	-44	106	104	323				
CIN	98	61	37	.622	5	662	413	3669	961	122	74	34	139	261	.262	.289	.363	.652	106	46	12	106	108	395				
NY	97	54	42	.563	11	498	534	3534	883	111	58	6	140	259	.250	.279	.319	.598	91	-17	-40	104	93	322				
LOU	98	52	45	.536	13.5	564	562	3553	892	114	64	14	141	304	.251	.280	.331	.611	107	-3	38	93	103	337				
COL	97	32	65	.330	33.5	476	659	3553	854	101	79	15	134	409	.240	.268	.326	.594	102	-25	17	92	90	318				
PIT	98	31	67	.316	35	525	728	3607	892	120	58	13	164	345	.247	.280	.324	.604	102	-10	15	95	95	335				
BAL	96	28	68	.292	37	471	742	3532	870	125	49	5	164	331	.246	.280	.314	.594	91	-21	-37	103	89	318				
TOT	390					4465		28655	7217	960	478	114	1208	2417	.252	.282	.331	.613										

TEAM	CG	SH	SV	IP	H	H/G	HR	BB	SO	RAT	ERA	ERA+	OAV	OOB	PR	/A	PF	CPI	FA	E	DP	FW	PW	BW	SBW	DIF
PHI	92	1	0	873	921	9.5	22	95	347	10.5	2.88	121	.254	.273	41	57	105	113	.865	584	40	-4.1	5.0	-.4		16.5
STL	93	9	1	879¹	729	7.5	7	150	325	9.0	2.23	156	.211	.244	104	122	106	97	.909	388	62	4.5	10.7	-3.9		4.6
CIN	96	8	0	866²	766	8.0	17	168	215	9.7	2.26	143	.222	.258	100	94	98	114	.905	383	57	4.7	8.3	1.1		-2.0
NY	97	6	0	874	751	7.7	12	123	490	9.0	2.90	115	.218	.244	-38	41	101	78	.905	391	45	4.1	3.6	-3.5		1.8
LOU	96	7	0	873²	987	10.2	7	110	269	11.3	3.50	85	.267	.288	-20	-50	91	101	.886	478	67	.6	-4.4	3.3		4.0
COL	90	4	0	840¹	980	10.5	16	211	222	12.8	3.96	78	.274	.314	-62	-83	93	105	.874	535	69	-2.1	-7.3	1.5		-8.5
PIT	82	1	1	867²	1140	11.8	21	151	271	13.4	4.62	69	.298	.325	-127	-137	97	102	.884	504	55	-.6	-12.1	1.3		-6.7
BAL	86	1	0	844²	943	10.0	12	190	290	12.1	4.08	85	.265	.303	-74	-58	105	93	.855	624	44	-6.3	-5.1	-3.3		-5.4
TOT	732	37	2	6919¹		9.4				10.9	3.30		.252	.282					.885	3887	439					

Runs
Stovey-Phi 110
Reilly-Cin 103
Carpenter-Cin 99
Knight-Phi 98

Hits
Swartwood-Pit 147
Reilly-Cin 136
Carpenter-Cin 130
Stovey-Phi 128
Nelson-NY 127

Doubles
Stovey-Phi 31
Swartwood-Pit 24
Knight-Phi 23
Hayes-Pit 23

Triples
Smith-Col 17
Reilly-Cin 14
Kuehne-Col 14
Mansell-Pit 13
Mann-Col 13

Home Runs
Stovey-Phi 14
Jones-Cin 10
Reilly-Cin 9
Fulmer-Cin 5
Brown-Col 5

Total Bases
Stovey-Phi 213
Reilly-Cin 212
Swartwood-Pit 196
Jones-Cin 184
B.Gleason-StL 167

Runs Batted In
Knight-Phi 97
Stovey-Phi 96
Carpenter-Cin 96
Reilly-Cin 94
Birchall-Phi 94

Runs Produced

Bases On Balls
Stearns-Bal 34
Nelson-NY 31
Moynahan-Phi 31
J.Gleason-StL-Lou . 29

Batting Average
Swartwood-Pit . . .357
Browning-Lou 338
Clinton-Bal 313
Rowe-Bal 313
Reilly-Cin 311

On Base Percentage
Swartwood-Pit 394
Browning-Lou 378
Moynahan-Phi 360
Clinton-Bal 357
Nelson-NY 353

Slugging Average
Stovey-Phi 506
Reilly-Cin 485
Swartwood-Pit 476
Jones-Cin 471
Browning-Lou 464

Production
Swartwood-Pit 869
Stovey-Phi 852
Browning-Lou 842
Reilly-Cin 810
Jones-Cin 799

Adjusted Production
Swartwood-Pit . . . 187
Browning-Lou 183
Stovey-Phi 158
Reilly-Cin 149
Jones-Cin 146

Batter Runs
Swartwood-Pit . . . 35.5
Stovey-Phi 32.4
Browning-Lou 27.4
Reilly-Cin 26.1
Jones-Cin 22.8

Adjusted Batter Runs
Swartwood-Pit 40.2
Stovey-Phi 33.8
Browning-Lou 24.7
Reilly-Cin 21.0
Jones-Cin 18.2

Clutch Hitting Index

Runs Created
Swartwood-Pit 79
Stovey-Phi 76
Reilly-Cin 71
Browning-Lou 64
Jones-Cin 62

Total Average
Swartwood-Pit 834
Stovey-Phi 819
Browning-Lou 797
Jones-Cin 739
Reilly-Cin 734

Stolen Bases

Stolen Base Average

Stolen Base Runs

Fielding Runs
Holbert-NY 35.4
Battin-Pit 29.0
Richmond-Col 25.5
Latham-StL 21.9
Gerhardt-Lou 20.4

Total Player Rating
Richmond-Col 3.5
Smith-Col 3.1
Swartwood-Pit 3.1
Gerhardt-Lou 2.4
Holbert-NY 2.3

Wins
White-Cin 43
Keefe-NY 41
Mullane-StL 35
Mathews-Phi 30
McGinnis-StL 28

Win Percentage
Mullane-StL 700
Mathews-Phi 698
Bradley-Phi 696
White-Cin 662
McGinnis-StL 636

Games
Keefe-NY 68
White-Cin 65
Mountain-Col 59
Mullane-StL 53
Hecker-Lou 51

Complete Games
Keefe-NY 68
White-Cin 64
Mountain-Col 57
Mullane-StL 49
Hecker-Lou 49

Shutouts
White-Cin 6
McGinnis-StL 5
Keefe-NY 5
Weaver-Lou 4
Mountain-Col 4

Saves
Mullane-StL 1
Barr-Pit 1

Innings Pitched
Keefe-NY 619.0
White-Cin 577.0
Mountain-Col 503.0
Mullane-StL 460.2
Hecker-Lou 451.0

Fewest Hits/Game
Keefe-NY 7.10
Mullane-StL 7.27
White-Cin 7.38
McGinnis-StL 7.64
Deagle-Cin 8.27

Fewest BB/Game
Mathews-Phi 73
Weaver-Lou 82
Lynch-NY 88
Bradley-Phi 92
Driscoll-Pit 1.04

Strikeouts
Keefe-NY 359
Mathews-Phi 203
Mullane-StL 191
Mountain-Col 159
Hecker-Lou 153

Strikeouts/Game
Keefe-NY 5.22
Mathews-Phi 4.80
Lynch-NY 4.20
Mullane-StL 3.73
Henderson-Bal 3.64

Ratio
Keefe-NY 8.67
Mullane-StL 8.71
White-Cin 9.00
McGinnis-StL 9.27
Bradley-Phi 9.95

Earned Run Average
White-Cin 2.09
Mullane-StL 2.19
Deagle-Cin 2.31
McGinnis-StL 2.33
Keefe-NY 2.41

Adjusted ERA
Mullane-StL 159
White-Cin 155
McGinnis-StL 149
Mathews-Phi 141
Deagle-Cin 140

Opponents' Batting Avg.
Keefe-NY 203
Mullane-StL 207
White-Cin 209
McGinnis-StL 215
Deagle-Cin 229

Opponents' On Base Pct.
Keefe-NY 237
Mullane-StL 238
White-Cin 244
McGinnis-StL 249
Bradley-Phi 263

Starter Runs
White-Cin 77.4
Keefe-NY 60.8
Mullane-StL 56.8
McGinnis-StL 41.2
Mathews-Phi 35.6

Adjusted Starter Runs
White-Cin 73.8
Mullane-StL 66.1
Keefe-NY 63.5
McGinnis-StL 48.9
Mathews-Phi 42.8

Clutch Pitching Index
Mathews-Phi 127
Corey-Phi 124
McCormick-Cin . . . 123
Valentine-Col 122
Deagle-Cin 117

Relief Runs

Adjusted Relief Runs

Relief Ranking

Total Pitcher Index
White-Cin 6.6
Keefe-NY 6.6
Mullane-StL 6.2
McGinnis-StL 4.2
Mathews-Phi 3.2

Total Baseball Ranking
White-Cin 6.6
Keefe-NY 6.6
Mullane-StL 5.9
McGinnis-StL 4.0
Richmond-Col 3.5

TEAM	G	W	L	PCT	GB	R	OR	AB	H	2B	3B	HR	BB	SO	AVG	OBP	SLG	PRO	PRO+	BR	/A	PF	CHI	RC	SB	CS	SBA	SBR
PRO	114	84	28	.750		665	388	4093	987	153	43	21	300	469	.241	.293	.315	.608	97	-18	-2	98	107	387				
BOS	116	73	38	.658	10.5	684	468	4189	1063	179	60	36	207	660	.254	.289	.351	.640	105	17	20	100	104	435				
BUF	115	64	47	.577	19.5	700	626	4197	1099	163	69	39	215	458	.262	.298	.361	.659	106	46	23	103	102	463				
NY	116	62	50	.554	22	693	623	4124	1053	149	67	23	249	492	.255	.298	.341	.639	102	20	4	102	105	429				
CHI	113	62	50	.554	22	834	647	4182	1176	162	50	142	264	469	.281	.324	.446	.770	133	201	133	108	98	619				
PHI	113	39	73	.348	45	549	824	3998	934	149	39	14	209	512	.234	.272	.301	.573	88	-72	-47	95	101	335				
CLE	113	35	77	.313	49	458	716	3934	934	147	49	16	170	576	.237	.269	.312	.581	83	-63	-81	103	86	338				
DET	114	28	84	.250	56	445	736	3970	825	114	47	31	207	699	.208	.247	.284	.531	74	-132	-104	94	93	285				
TOT	457					5028		32687	8071	1216	424	322	1821	4335	.247	.287	.340	.626										

TEAM	CG	SH	SV	IP	H	H/G	HR	BB	SO	RAT	ERA	ERA+	OAV	OOB	PR	/A	PF	CPI	FA	E	DP	FW	PW	BW	SBW	DIF
PRO	107	16	2	1036[1]	825	7.2	26	172	639	8.7	1.61	176	.209	.242	158	141	95	110	.918	398	50	5.1	12.6	-.2		10.4
BOS	109	14	2	1037	932	8.1	30	135	742	9.3	2.47	117	.226	.250	58	49	97	84	.922	384	46	6.3	4.4	1.8		5.0
BUF	108	14	1	1001	1041	9.4	46	189	534	11.1	2.95	107	.254	.286	3	21	106	105	.905	462	71	1.9	1.9	2.1		2.6
NY	111	4	0	1014	1011	9.0	28	326	567	11.9	3.12	95	.245	.300	-16	-19	100	98	.895	514	69	-.6	-1.7	.4		8.0
CHI	106	9	0	997[1]	1028	9.3	83	231	472	11.4	3.03	103	.250	.290	-6	11	105	112	.886	595	107	-5.6	1.0	11.9		-1.2
PHI	106	3	1	981	1090	10.0	38	254	411	12.3	3.93	76	.261	.304	-103	-106	100	87	.888	536	67	-2.5	-9.5	-4.2		-.8
CLE	107	7	0	994[2]	1046	9.5	35	269	482	11.9	3.43	92	.256	.302	-50	-32	106	97	.897	512	75	-1.2	-2.9	-7.2		-9.7
DET	109	3	0	984[2]	1097	10.0	36	245	488	12.3	3.38	86	.262	.302	-44	-54	97	100	.886	550	62	-3.0	-4.8	-9.3		-10.9
TOT	863	70	6	8046		9.0				11.1	2.98		.247	.287					.899	3951	547					

Runs
Kelly-Chi 120
O'Rourke-Buf 119
Hornung-Bos 119
Dalrymple-Chi 111
Anson-Chi 108

Hits
Sutton-Bos 162
O'Rourke-Buf 162
Dalrymple-Chi 161
Kelly-Chi 160
Anson-Chi 159

Doubles
Hines-Pro 36
O'Rourke-Buf 33
Anson-Chi 30
Manning-Phi 29

Triples
Ewing-NY 20
Brouthers-Buf 15
Rowe-Buf 14
Phillips-Cle 12
McKinnon-NY 12

Home Runs
Williamson-Chi 27
Pfeffer-Chi 25
Dalrymple-Chi 22
Anson-Chi 21
Brouthers-Buf 14

Total Bases
Dalrymple-Chi 263
Anson-Chi 258
Pfeffer-Chi 240
Kelly-Chi 237
Williamson-Chi 231

Runs Batted In
Anson-Chi 102
Pfeffer-Chi 101
Kelly-Chi 95
Williamson-Chi 84
Connor-NY 82

Runs Produced
Kelly-Chi 202
Anson-Chi 189
Pfeffer-Chi 181
O'Rourke-Buf 177
Connor-NY 176

Bases On Balls
Gore-Chi 61
Kelly-Chi 46
Hines-Pro 44
Williamson-Chi 42

Batting Average
O'Rourke-Buf 347
Kelly-Chi 354
Sutton-Bos 346
Anson-Chi 335
Brouthers-Buf 327

On Base Percentage
Kelly-Chi 414
Gore-Chi 404
O'Rourke-Buf 392
Sutton-Bos 384
Brouthers-Buf 378

Slugging Average
Brouthers-Buf 563
Williamson-Chi 554
Anson-Chi 543
Kelly-Chi 524
Pfeffer-Chi 514

Production
Brouthers-Buf 941
Kelly-Chi 938
Anson-Chi 916
Williamson-Chi 898
O'Rourke-Buf 872

Adjusted Production
Brouthers-Buf 186
Kelly-Chi 178
Anson-Chi 170
O'Rourke-Buf 167
Williamson-Chi 164

Batter Runs
Kelly-Chi 48.8
Anson-Chi 44.6
Brouthers-Buf 41.2
O'Rourke-Buf 38.8
Williamson-Chi 36.7

Adjusted Batter Runs
Kelly-Chi 39.2
Brouthers-Buf 37.8
Anson-Chi 35.2
O'Rourke-Buf 35.0
Sutton-Bos 33.9

Clutch Hitting Index
Connor-NY 148
Radbourn-Pro 132
Caskin-NY 132
Kelly-Chi 131
Dorgan-NY 124

Runs Created
Kelly-Chi 100
Anson-Chi 99
O'Rourke-Buf 90
Dalrymple-Chi 88
Brouthers-Buf 87

Total Average
Kelly-Chi 969
Brouthers-Buf 959
Anson-Chi 908
Williamson-Chi 907
O'Rourke-Buf 849

Stolen Bases

Stolen Base Average

Stolen Base Runs

Fielding Runs
Pfeffer-Chi 45.5
Williamson-Chi . . 23.8
Gilligan-Pro 17.2
Lillie-Buf 16.0
Hanlon-Det 13.3

Total Player Rating
Pfeffer-Chi 6.1
Williamson-Chi . . . 4.7
Kelly-Chi 3.1
Sutton-Bos 2.7
Hines-Pro 2.6

Wins
Radbourn-Pro 59
Buffinton-Bos 48
Galvin-Buf 46
Welch-NY 39
L.Corcoran-Chi . . . 35

Win Percentage
Radbourn-Pro 831
Buffinton-Bos 750
Sweeney-Pro 680
Galvin-Buf 676
Welch-NY 650

Games
Radbourn-Pro 75
Galvin-Buf 72
Buffinton-Bos 67
Welch-NY 65
L.Corcoran-Chi 60

Complete Games
Radbourn-Pro 73
Galvin-Buf 71
Buffinton-Bos 63
Welch-NY 62
L.Corcoran-Chi 57

Shutouts
Galvin-Buf 12
Radbourn-Pro 11
Buffinton-Bos 8
L.Corcoran-Chi . . . 7
Whitney-Bos 6

Saves
Morrill-Bos 2
Sweeney-Pro 1
Radbourn-Pro 1
O'Rourke-Buf 1
Ferguson-Phi 1

Innings Pitched
Radbourn-Pro . . .678.2
Galvin-Buf 636.1
Buffinton-Bos 587.0
Welch-NY 557.1
L.Corcoran-Chi . .516.2

Fewest Hits/Game
Sweeney-Pro 6.23
Radbourn-Pro . . . 7.00
Clarkson-Chi 7.17
Getzien-Det 7.21
Whitney-Bos 7.29

Fewest BB/Game
Whitney-Bos 72
Galvin-Buf 89
Buffinton-Bos 1.17
Sweeney-Pro 1.18
Coleman-Phi 1.28

Strikeouts
Radbourn-Pro 441
Buffinton-Bos 417
Galvin-Buf 369
Welch-NY 345
L.Corcoran-Chi . . . 272

Strikeouts/Game
Clarkson-Chi 7.78
Whitney-Bos 7.23
Getzien-Det 6.54
Buffinton-Bos 6.39
Sweeney-Pro 5.90

Ratio
Sweeney-Pro 7.41
Whitney-Bos 8.01
Radbourn-Pro . . . 8.30
Getzien-Det 8.74
Galvin-Buf 8.90

Earned Run Average
Radbourn-Pro 1.38
Sweeney-Pro 1.55
Getzien-Det 1.95
Galvin-Buf 1.99
Whitney-Bos 2.09

Adjusted ERA
Radbourn-Pro 204
Sweeney-Pro 182
Galvin-Buf 158
Getzien-Det 148
Clarkson-Chi 147

Opponents' Batting Avg.
Sweeney-Pro 187
Getzien-Det 204
Radbourn-Pro 205
Whitney-Bos 207
Clarkson-Chi 208

Opponents' On Base Pct.
Sweeney-Pro 215
Whitney-Bos 223
Radbourn-Pro 234
Getzien-Det 237
Buffinton-Bos 244

Starter Runs
Radbourn-Pro . . . 120.5
Galvin-Buf 69.5
Buffinton-Bos 54.2
Sweeney-Pro 35.1
Whitney-Bos 33.2

Adjusted Starter Runs
Radbourn-Pro . . . 108.6
Galvin-Buf 81.5
Buffinton-Bos 48.2
L.Corcoran-Chi . . . 41.7
Sweeney-Pro 31.2

Clutch Pitching Index
Radbourn-Pro 117
Meinke-Det 116
L.Corcoran-Chi . . . 113
Moffett-Cle 110
Welch-NY 107

Relief Runs

Adjusted Relief Runs

Relief Ranking

Total Pitcher Index
Radbourn-Pro 9.8
Galvin-Buf 6.8
Buffinton-Bos 5.7
L.Corcoran-Chi . . . 4.6
Whitney-Bos 4.0

Total Baseball Ranking
Radbourn-Pro 9.5
Galvin-Buf 6.8
Pfeffer-Chi 6.1
Buffinton-Bos 5.2
Williamson-Chi . . . 4.7

TEAM	G	W	L	PCT	GB	R	OR	AB	H	2B	3B	HR	BB	SO	AVG	OBP	SLG	PRO	PRO+	BR	/A	PF	CHI	RC	SB	CS	SBA	SBR
NY	112	75	32	.701		734	423	4012	1052	155	64	22	203	315	.262	.304	.349	.653	120	70	87	98	109	436				
COL	110	69	39	.639	6.5	585	459	3759	901	107	96	40	196	404	.240	.288	.351	.639	121	47	97	92	95	390				
LOU	110	68	40	.630	7.5	573	425	3957	1004	152	69	17	146	408	.254	.286	.340	.626	112	29	57	96	93	395				
STL	110	67	40	.626	8	658	539	3952	986	151	60	11	174	339	.249	.288	.326	.614	100	16	-5	104	109	381				
CIN	112	68	41	.624	8	754	512	4090	1037	109	96	36	154	404	.254	.289	.354	.643	108	53	21	105	114	429				
BAL	108	63	43	.594	11.5	636	515	3845	896	133	84	32	211	545	.233	.284	.336	.620	101	25	1	104	105	377				
PHI	108	61	46	.570	14	700	546	3959	1057	167	100	26	153	425	.267	.301	.379	.680	117	100	56	106	102	463				
TOL	110	46	58	.442	27.5	463	571	3712	859	153	48	8	157	541	.231	.268	.305	.573	87	-39	-57	104	90	310				
BRO	109	40	64	.385	33.5	476	644	3763	845	112	47	16	179	417	.225	.263	.292	.555	83	-61	-64	101	95	296				
RIC	46	12	30	.286	30.5	194	284	1469	325	40	33	7	53	284	.221	.260	.308	.568	89	-18	-16	99	97	120				
PIT	110	30	78	.278	45.5	406	725	3689	777	105	50	2	143	411	.211	.248	.268	.516	71	-109	-116	102	92	251				
IND	110	29	78	.271	46	462	755	3813	890	129	62	20	125	560	.233	.262	.315	.577	93	-38	-24	97	88	323				
WAS	63	12	51	.190	41	248	481	2166	434	61	24	6	102	377	.200	.242	.259	.501	76	-75	-47	88	100	139				
TOT	659					6889		46186	11063	1574	833	243	1996	5430	.240	.278	.325	.604										

TEAM	CG	SH	SV	IP	H	H/G	HR	BB	SO	RAT	ERA	ERA+	OAV	OOB	PR	/A	PF	CPI	FA	E	DP	FW	PW	BW	SBW	DIF
NY	111	9	0	984²	800	7.3	15	119	611	8.6	2.46	127	.209	.237	86	72	96	90	.907	441	42	2.3	6.6	7.9		4.6
COL	102	8	1	962¹	815	7.6	22	172	526	9.5	2.68	113	.217	.256	60	36	93	98	.908	433	74	2.3	3.3	8.9		.5
LOU	101	6	0	989²	836	7.6	9	97	470	8.8	2.17	142	.216	.241	118	100	95	106	.912	426	84	2.6	9.1	5.2		-2.9
STL	99	8	0	987	881	8.0	16	172	477	10.0	2.67	122	.226	.266	63	63	100	106	.900	490	65	-.2	5.8	-.5		8.4
CIN	111	11	0	983²	956	8.7	27	181	308	11.1	3.33	100	.243	.290	-10	-1	103	106	.909	430	82	2.8	-.0	1.9		8.9
BAL	105	8	1	955²	869	8.2	16	219	635	10.5	2.71	128	.224	.271	56	79	107	107	.899	461	61	.7	7.2	.0		2.0
PHI	105	5	0	948²	920	8.7	16	127	530	10.3	3.42	99	.237	.269	-18	-4	104	89	.901	457	63	.9	-.4	5.1		1.9
TOL	103	9	1	946	885	8.4	12	169	501	10.5	3.06	111	.233	.275	19	35	105	99	.900	469	67	.7	3.2	-5.2		-4.7
BRO	105	6	0	948²	996	9.4	20	163	378	11.2	3.79	87	.254	.288	-58	-51	102	94	.889	520	68	-1.6	-4.7	-5.8		.2
RIC	45	1	0	370¹	402	9.8	14	52	167	11.4	4.52	73	.257	.288	-53	-50	102	83	.874	239	27	-1.5	-4.6	-1.5		-1.4
PIT	108	4	0	943¹	1059	10.1	25	216	338	12.7	4.35	77	.265	.312	-116	-104	104	96	.889	523	71	-1.6	-9.5	-10.6		-2.3
IND	107	2	0	937²	1001	9.6	30	199	479	11.8	4.20	78	.255	.295	-100	-97	101	90	.889	515	45	-1.2	-8.9	-2.2		-12.2
WAS	62	3	0	543²	643	10.6	21	110	235	12.8	4.01	76	.273	.311	-46	-59	93	109	.858	400	40	-5.3	-5.4	-4.3		-4.6
TOT	1264	80	3	11501¹		8.7				10.6	3.24		.240	.278					.897	5804	789					

Runs		Hits		Doubles		Triples		Home Runs		Total Bases	
Stovey-Phi	124	Orr-NY	162	Barkley-Tol	39	Stovey-Phi	23	Reilly-Cin	11	Reilly-Cin	247
Jones-Cin	117	Reilly-Cin	152	Browning-Lou	33	Reilly-Cin	19	Stovey-Phi	10	Orr-NY	247
Latham-StL	115	Esterbrook-NY	150	Orr-NY	32	Mann-Col	18	Orr-NY	9	Stovey-Phi	244
Reilly-Cin	114	Browning-Lou	150	Esterbrook-NY	29	Peltz-Ind	17	Mann-Col	7	Jones-Cin	222
Nelson-NY	114	Jones-Cin	148	Lewis-StL	25	Jones-Cin	17	Jones-Cin	7	Browning-Lou	211

Runs Batted In		Runs Produced		Bases On Balls		Batting Average		On Base Percentage		Slugging Average	
Stovey-Phi	114			Nelson-NY	74	Esterbrook-NY	.314	Jones-Cin	.376	Reilly-Cin	.551
Latham-StL	114			Geer-Bro	38	Orr-NY	.354	Nelson-NY	.375	Stovey-Phi	.545
Nelson-NY	113			Jones-Cin	37	Reilly-Cin	.339	Stovey-Phi	.368	Orr-NY	.539
Jones-Cin	110			Macullar-Bal	36	Browning-Lou	.336	Fennelly-Was-Cin	.367	Fennelly-Was-Cin	.480
Esterbrook-NY	109			Richmond-Col	35	Stovey-Phi	.326	Reilly-Cin	.366	Browning-Lou	.472

Production		Adjusted Production		Batter Runs		Adjusted Batter Runs		Clutch Hitting Index		Runs Created	
Reilly-Cin	.918	Orr-NY	195	Stovey-Phi	44.8	Orr-NY	44.9			Reilly-Cin	93
Stovey-Phi	.913	Reilly-Cin	186	Reilly-Cin	44.6	Reilly-Cin	39.4			Stovey-Phi	92
Orr-NY	.901	Fennelly-Was-Cin	186	Orr-NY	42.1	Stovey-Phi	37.8			Orr-NY	92
Fennelly-Was-Cin	.847	Stovey-Phi	182	Jones-Cin	39.0	Fennelly-Was-Cin	36.6			Jones-Cin	85
Jones-Cin	.846	Browning-Lou	176	Browning-Lou	31.6	Browning-Lou	36.1			Browning-Lou	77

Total Average		Stolen Bases		Stolen Base Average		Stolen Base Runs		Fielding Runs		Total Player Rating	
Stovey-Phi	.907							Latham-StL	39.5	Barkley-Tol	4.4
Reilly-Cin	.899							Smith-Col	29.1	Latham-StL	4.3
Orr-NY	.855							Snyder-Cin	27.4	Fennelly-Was-Cin	4.0
Jones-Cin	.830							Gerhardt-Lou	27.3	Smith-Col	3.9
Fennelly-Was-Cin	.824							Barkley-Tol	24.6	Esterbrook-NY	3.4

Wins		Win Percentage		Games		Complete Games		Shutouts		Saves	
Hecker-Lou	52	Morris-Col	.723	Hecker-Lou	75	Hecker-Lou	72	White-Cin	7	O'Day-Tol	1
Lynch-NY	37	Hecker-Lou	.722	Mullane-Tol	67	Mullane-Tol	64	Mullane-Tol	7	Mountain-Col	1
Keefe-NY	37	Foutz-StL	.714	McKeon-Ind	61	McKeon-Ind	59	Hecker-Lou	6	O.Burns-Bal	1
Mullane-Tol	36	Lynch-NY	.712	Keefe-NY	57	Keefe-NY	56				
		Keefe-NY	.685	Terry-Bro	56						

Innings Pitched		Fewest Hits/Game		Fewest BB/Game		Strikeouts		Strikeouts/Game		Ratio	
Hecker-Lou	670.2	Morris-Col	7.02	Driscoll-Lou	.62	Hecker-Lou	385	Henderson-Bal	7.09	Hecker-Lou	8.02
Mullane-Tol	567.0	Keefe-NY	7.05	Mullane-Tol	.75	Henderson-Bal	346	Davis-StL	6.49	Morris-Col	8.36
McKeon-Ind	512.0	Hecker-Lou	7.06	Lynch-NY	.76	Mullane-Tol	325	Morris-Col	6.33	Lynch-NY	8.56
Lynch-NY	496.0	Mountain-Col	7.21	E.Dugan-Ric	.81	Keefe-NY	317	Mathews-Phi	5.98	Keefe-NY	8.73
Keefe-NY	482.2	Foutz-StL	7.27	McGinnis-StL	.89	McKeon-Ind	308	Keefe-NY	5.91	Foutz-StL	9.23

Earned Run Average		Adjusted ERA		Opponents' Batting Avg.		Opponents' On Base Pct.		Starter Runs		Adjusted Starter Runs	
Hecker-Lou	1.80	Hecker-Lou	171	Keefe-NY	.203	Hecker-Lou	.226	Hecker-Lou	107.6	Hecker-Lou	95.6
Foutz-StL	2.18	Foutz-StL	149	Hecker-Lou	.204	Morris-Col	.234	Keefe-NY	52.9	Mullane-Tol	55.7
Morris-Col	2.18	Morris-Col	139	Morris-Col	.204	Lynch-NY	.236	Morris-Col	50.8	Keefe-NY	46.1
Keefe-NY	2.26	Keefe-NY	138	Mountain-Col	.209	Keefe-NY	.240	Mullane-Tol	45.3	Henderson-Bal	40.9
Mountain-Col	2.45	Mullane-Tol	135	Foutz-StL	.212	Foutz-StL	.255	Mountain-Col	32.0	Morris-Col	40.3

Clutch Pitching Index		Relief Runs		Adjusted Relief Runs		Relief Ranking		Total Pitcher Index		Total Baseball Ranking	
Comiskey-StL	127							Hecker-Lou	12.6	Hecker-Lou	12.5
Foutz-StL	122							Mullane-Tol	7.7	Mullane-Tol	7.7
Davis-StL	120							Keefe-NY	5.5	Keefe-NY	5.6
O'Neill-StL	118							Henderson-Bal	4.4	Barkley-Tol	4.4
White-Cin	116							Morris-Col	4.2	Henderson-Bal	4.3

TEAM	G	W	L	PCT	GB	R	OR	AB	H	2B	3B	HR	BB	SO	AVG	OBP	SLG	PRO	PRO+	BR	/A	PF	CHI	RC	SB	CS	SBA	SBR
STL	114	94	19	.832		887	429	4285	1251	259	41	32	181	542	.292	.321	.394	.715	92	-33	-56	104	103	555				
MIL	12	8	4	.667	35.5	53	34	395	88	25	0	0	20	70	.223	.260	.286	.546	92	-27	-21	54	91	30				
CIN	105	69	36	.657	21	703	466	3786	1027	118	63	26	147	482	.271	.298	.356	.654	73	-111	-150	108	102	413				
BAL	106	58	47	.552	32	662	627	3883	952	150	26	17	144	652	.245	.272	.310	.582	53	-215	-259	110	109	336				
BOS	111	58	51	.532	34	636	558	3940	928	168	32	19	128	787	.236	.260	.309	.569	56	-242	-236	98	107	324				
CP	93	41	50	.451	42	438	482	3212	742	127	26	10	119	505	.231	.258	.296	.554	51	-211	-209	99	93	252				
WAS	114	47	65	.420	46.5	572	679	3926	931	120	26	4	118	558	.237	.259	.284	.543	51	-271	-260	97	102	296				
PHI	67	21	46	.313	50	414	545	2518	618	108	35	7	103	405	.245	.275	.324	.599	69	-125	-105	93	101	230				
STP	9	2	6	.250	39.5	24	57	272	49	13	1	0	7	47	.180	.201	.235	.436	35	-30	-36	54	84	13				
ALT	25	6	19	.240	44	90	216	899	223	30	6	2	22	130	.248	.266	.301	.567	54	-55	-56	101	67	74				
KC	82	16	63	.203	61	311	618	2802	557	104	15	6	123	529	.199	.232	.253	.485	38	-255	-235	87	88	169				
WIL	18	2	16	.111	44.5	35	114	521	91	8	8	2	22	123	.175	.208	.232	.440	19	-56	-57	103	61	26				
TOT	428					4825		30439	7457	1230	279	125	1134	4830	.245	.272	.316	.588										

TEAM	CG	SH	SV	IP	H	H/G	HR	BB	SO	RAT	ERA	ERA+	OAV	OOB	PR	/A	PF	CPI	FA	E	DP	FW	PW	BW	SBW	DIF
STL	104	8	6	993	838	7.6	9	110	550	8.6	1.96	122	.214	.235	53	47	98	106	.888	554	79	3.7	4.1	-4.9		34.6
MIL	12	3	0	104	49	4.2	1	13	139	5.4	2.25	59	.132	.161	2	-11	54	12	.892	53	4	.6	-1.0	-1.8		4.2
CIN	95	11	1	914¹	831	8.2	17	90	503	9.1	2.38	107	.226	.245	6	18	105	102	.882	532	45	2.5	1.6	-13.1		25.5
BAL	92	4	0	946²	1002	9.5	24	177	628	11.2	3.01	89	.254	.286	-61	-36	110	115	.872	616	53	-.8	-3.2	-22.7		32.1
BOS	100	5	1	953¹	885	8.4	17	110	753	9.4	2.70	88	.231	.252	-28	-35	98	95	.868	633	39	-.3	-3.1	-20.7		27.6
CP	86	6	0	803²	743	8.3	12	137	679	9.9	2.72	90	.230	.261	-25	-26	100	98	.882	459	38	2.7	-2.3	-18.3		13.3
WAS	94	5	0	953²	992	9.4	16	168	684	10.9	3.44	70	.251	.282	-106	-110	98	95	.869	625	55	.7	-9.6	-22.8		22.7
PHI	64	1	0	593¹	726	11.0	7	105	310	12.6	4.63	50	.283	.311	-144	-152	95	89	.841	501	36	-5.2	-13.3	-9.2		15.2
STP	7	1	0	71	72	9.1	1	27	44	12.5	3.17	42	.248	.312	-6	-15	54	117	.872	47	6	.2	-1.3	-3.2		2.3
ALT	20	0	0	219¹	292	12.0	3	52	93	14.1	4.67	57	.300	.335	-55	-49	109	104	.862	156	4	-.6	-4.3	-4.9		3.3
KC	70	0	0	702²	862	11.0	14	127	334	12.7	4.07	55	.283	.312	-128	-144	92	104	.861	520	51	-2.5	-12.6	-20.6		12.1
WIL	15	0	0	142	165	10.5	4	18	113	11.6	3.04	87	.273	.294	-10	-6	109	126	.860	104	10	-.1	-.5	-5.0		-1.4
TOT	759	44	8	7397¹		9.1				10.5	3.05		.245	.272					.872	4800	420					

Runs
Dunlap-StL 160
Shaffer-StL 130
Seery-Bal-KC 115
Robinson-Bal 101
Rowe-StL 95

Hits
Dunlap-StL 185
Shaffer-StL 168
Moore-Was 155
Seery-Bal-KC 146
Rowe-StL 142

Doubles
Shaffer-StL 40
Dunlap-StL 39
Rowe-StL 32
O'Brien-Bos 31
Gleason-StL 30

Triples
Burns-Cin 12
Rowe-StL 11
Shaffer-StL 10

Home Runs
Dunlap-StL 13
Crane-Bos 12
Levis-Bal-Was 6

Total Bases
Dunlap-StL 279
Shaffer-StL 234
Rowe-StL 208
Crane-Bos 193
Seery-Bal-KC 192

Runs Batted In / Runs Produced
Dunlap-StL 147
Shaffer-StL 128
Seery-Bal-KC 113
Robinson-Bal 99
Rowe-StL 91

Bases On Balls
Robinson-Bal 37
Shaffer-StL 30
Dunlap-StL 29
Harbidge-Cin 25
Gleason-StL 23

Batting Average
Dunlap-StL .... .412
Taylor-StL .... .366
Dickerson-StL .... .365
Hoover-Phi .... .364
Shaffer-StL ...... .360

On Base Percentage
Dunlap-StL .... .448
Shaffer-StL ...... .398
Hoover-Phi .... .390
Moore-Was .... .363
Gleason-StL ...... .361

Slugging Average
Dunlap-StL .... .621
Taylor-StL .... .548
Shaffer-StL ...... .501
Hoover-Phi .... .495
Burns-Cin .... .457

Production
Dunlap-StL 1.069
Shaffer-StL ...... .899
Hoover-Phi .... .885
Gleason-StL ...... .802
Moore-Was .... .777

Adjusted Production
Dunlap-StL 181
Hoover-Phi 150
Shaffer-StL 138
Moore-Was 114
Gleason-StL 113

Batter Runs
Dunlap-StL 53.4
Shaffer-StL 27.6
Glasscock-Cin 16.9
Hoover-Phi 14.4
Taylor-StL 12.6

Adjusted Batter Runs
Dunlap-StL 49.1
Shaffer-StL 24.0
Hoover-Phi 18.8
Glasscock-Cin 13.5
Taylor-StL 11.2

Clutch Hitting Index

Runs Created
Dunlap-StL 128
Shaffer-StL 96
Moore-Was 71
Seery-Bal-KC 67
Rowe-StL 65

Total Average
Dunlap-StL 1.167
Shaffer-StL ...... .883
Hoover-Phi .... .846
Gleason-StL ...... .738
Moore-Was .... .686

Stolen Bases

Stolen Base Average

Stolen Base Runs

Fielding Runs
Dunlap-StL 30.5
Fusselback-Bal ... 19.3
Baker-StL 16.3
Robinson-Bal 16.1
Krieg-CP 14.9

Total Player Rating
Dunlap-StL 6.9
Shaffer-StL 1.7
Briody-Cin 1.5
Hoover-Phi 1.5
Glasscock-Cin 1.3

Wins
B.Sweeney-Bal 40
Daily-CP-Was 28
Taylor-StL 25
Bradley-Cin 25
Sweeney-StL 24

Win Percentage
McCormick-Cin .... .875
Taylor-StL .... .862
Boyle-StL .... .833
Sweeney-StL ...... .774
B.Sweeney-Bal .... .656

Games
B.Sweeney-Bal 62
Daily-CP-Was 58
Wise-Was 50
Bakely-Phi-Wil-KC ... 46
Bradley-Cin 41

Complete Games
B.Sweeney-Bal 58
Daily-CP-Was 56
Bakely-Phi-Wil-KC ... 43
Bradley-Cin 36
Shaw-Bos 35

Shutouts
McCormick-Cin 7
Daily-CP-Was 5
Shaw-Bos 5
Wise-Was 4
B.Sweeney-Bal 4

Saves
Taylor-StL 4
Sylvester-Cin 1
Dunlap-StL 1
Brown-Bos 1
Boyle-StL 1

Innings Pitched
B.Sweeney-Bal 538.0
Daily-CP-Was 500.2
Bakely-Phi-Wil-KC ... 394.2
Wise-Was 364.1
Bradley-Cin 342.0

Fewest Hits/Game
McCormick-Cin 6.47
Shaw-Bos 6.47
Sweeney-StL 6.87
Boyle-StL 7.08
Werden-StL 7.20

Fewest BB/Game
Sweeney-StL ...... .43
McCormick-Cin .... .60
Boyle-StL .... .60
Bradley-Cin ...... .61
Murphy-Wil-Alt ... .62

Strikeouts
Daily-CP-Was 483
B.Sweeney-Bal 374
Shaw-Bos 309
Wise-Was 268
Burke-Bos 255

Strikeouts/Game
Shaw-Bos 8.81
Daily-CP-Was 8.68
Gagus-Was 7.92
Robinson-Bal 7.32
Burke-Bos 7.13

Ratio
McCormick-Cin 7.07
Sweeney-StL 7.31
Shaw-Bos 7.53
Boyle-StL 7.68
Werden-StL 8.60

Earned Run Average
McCormick-Cin 1.54
Taylor-StL 1.68
Boyle-StL 1.74
Shaw-Bos 1.77
Sweeney-StL 1.83

Adjusted ERA
McCormick-Cin 166
Taylor-StL 143
Boyle-StL 137
Shaw-Bos 134
Sweeney-StL 131

Opponents' Batting Avg.
McCormick-Cin .... .188
Shaw-Bos .... .188
Sweeney-StL ...... .197
Boyle-StL .... .202
Werden-StL .... .205

Opponents' On Base Pct.
McCormick-Cin .... .202
Sweeney-StL ...... .207
Shaw-Bos .... .212
Boyle-StL .... .215
Werden-StL .... .235

Starter Runs
Shaw-Bos 23.5
Taylor-StL 22.2
McCormick-Cin 20.9
Sweeney-StL 18.4
Boyle-StL 11.6

Adjusted Starter Runs
McCormick-Cin 23.7
Shaw-Bos 21.3
Taylor-StL 20.9
Sweeney-StL 17.0
Boyle-StL 10.8

Clutch Pitching Index
Hodnett-StL 140
Robinson-Bal 132
Taylor-StL 129
B.Sweeney-Bal 111
Murphy-Wil-Alt ... 110

Relief Runs

Adjusted Relief Runs

Relief Ranking

Total Pitcher Index
Taylor-StL 2.8
Sweeney-StL 2.4
McCormick-Cin 1.8
Shaw-Bos 1.5
Boyle-StL 8

Total Baseball Ranking
Dunlap-StL 6.7
Taylor-StL 3.2
Sweeney-StL 2.4
McCormick-Cin 1.8
Shaffer-StL 1.7

TEAM	G	W	L	PCT	GB	R	OR	AB	H	2B	3B	HR	BB	SO	AVG	OBP	SLG	PRO	PRO+	BR	/A	PF	CHI	RC	SB	CS	SBA	SBR
CHI	113	87	25	.777		834	470	4093	1079	184	75	54	340	429	.264	.320	.385	.705	115	143	36	115	113	517				
NY	112	85	27	.759	2	691	370	4029	1085	150	82	16	221	312	.269	.307	.359	.666	122	82	91	99	106	456				
PHI	111	56	54	.509	30	513	511	3893	891	156	35	20	220	401	.229	.270	.302	.572	91	-45	-35	98	102	326				
PRO	110	53	57	.482	33	442	531	3727	820	114	30	6	265	430	.220	.272	.272	.544	83	-74	-56	96	96	282				
BOS	113	46	66	.411	41	528	589	3950	915	144	53	22	190	522	.232	.267	.312	.579	94	-41	-23	96	103	337				
DET	108	41	67	.380	44	514	582	3773	917	149	66	25	216	451	.243	.284	.337	.621	105	17	16	100	93	371				
BUF	112	38	74	.339	49	495	761	3900	980	149	50	23	179	380	.251	.284	.333	.617	100	11	-8	103	89	378				
STL	111	36	72	.333	49	390	593	3758	829	121	21	8	214	412	.221	.263	.270	.533	81	-92	-64	94	89	273				
TOT	445					4407		31123	7516	1167	412	174	1845	3337	.241	.284	.322	.606										

TEAM	CG	SH	SV	IP	H	H/G	HR	BB	SO	RAT	ERA	ERA+	OAV	OOB	PR	/A	PF	CPI	FA	E	DP	FW	PW	BW	SBW	DIF
CHI	108	14	4	1015²	868	7.7	37	202	458	9.5	2.23	136	.221	.259	66	89	108	102	.903	496	80	-2.4	8.4	3.4		21.6
NY	109	16	1	994	758	6.9	11	265	516	9.3	1.72	155	.205	.258	121	106	95	114	.929	331	85	6.0	10.0	8.6		4.5
PHI	108	10	0	976	860	7.9	18	218	378	9.9	2.39	117	.224	.266	46	41	99	96	.905	447	66	-.3	3.9	-3.3		.7
PRO	108	8	0	960²	912	8.5	18	235	371	10.7	2.71	98	.235	.278	12	-7	94	96	.903	459	70	-1.1	-.7	-5.3		5.0
BOS	111	10	0	981	1045	9.6	26	188	480	11.3	3.03	89	.261	.294	-23	-38	95	107	.901	478	79	-1.5	-3.6	-2.2		-2.8
DET	105	6	1	954¹	966	9.1	18	224	475	11.2	2.88	99	.249	.290	-6	-2	101	104	.901	463	61	-1.7	-.2	1.5		-12.6
BUF	107	4	1	956	1175	11.1	31	234	320	13.3	4.29	69	.289	.328	-157	-140	106	99	.901	464	65	-.9	-13.2	-.8		-3.1
STL	107	4	0	965¹	935	8.7	15	278	337	11.3	3.37	82	.245	.296	-59	-68	97	89	.916	398	67	2.3	-6.4	-6.0		-7.9
TOT	863	72	7	7803		8.7				10.8	2.82		.241	.284					.908	3536	573					

Runs
Kelly-Chi 124
O'Rourke-NY ... 119
Gore-Chi 115
Dalrymple-Chi 109
Connor-NY 102

Hits
Connor-NY 169
Brouthers-Buf 146
Anson-Chi 144
Sutton-Bos 143
O'Rourke-NY 143

Doubles
Anson-Chi 35
Brouthers-Buf 32
Rowe-Buf 28
Dalrymple-Chi ... 27
Mulvey-Phi 25

Triples
O'Rourke-NY 16
Connor-NY 15
Gore-Chi 13
Bennett-Det 13

Home Runs
Dalrymple-Chi 11
Kelly-Chi 9

Total Bases
Connor-NY 225
Brouthers-Buf ... 221
Dalrymple-Chi 219
Anson-Chi 214
O'Rourke-NY 211

Runs Batted In
Anson-Chi 108
Kelly-Chi 75
Pfeffer-Chi 73
Burns-Chi 71

Runs Produced
Anson-Chi 201
Kelly-Chi 190
Gore-Chi 167
Connor-NY 166
Dalrymple-Chi 159

Bases On Balls
Williamson-Chi 75
Gore-Chi 68
Morrill-Bos 64
Connor-NY 51

Batting Average
Connor-NY .... .371
Brouthers-Buf ..... .359
Dorgan-NY .... .326
Richardson-Buf ... .319
Gore-Chi .... .313

On Base Percentage
Connor-NY .... .435
Brouthers-Buf ..... .408
Gore-Chi .... .405
Hanlon-Det .... .372
Anson-Chi .... .357

Slugging Average
Brouthers-Buf .... .543
Connor-NY .... .495
Ewing-NY .... .471
Anson-Chi .... .461
Richardson-Buf ... .458

Production
Brouthers-Buf .... .951
Connor-NY .... .929
Gore-Chi .... .858
Anson-Chi .... .819
Bennett-Det ...... .812

Adjusted Production
Connor-NY 203
Brouthers-Buf 199
Bennett-Det 161
Ewing-NY 159
O'Rourke-NY 158

Batter Runs
Connor-NY 51.7
Brouthers-Buf 46.8
Gore-Chi 40.6
Anson-Chi 31.7
O'Rourke-NY 29.5

Adjusted Batter Runs
Connor-NY 53.3
Brouthers-Buf 43.2
O'Rourke-NY 30.9
Gore-Chi 25.2
Sutton-Bos 24.5

Clutch Hitting Index
White-Buf 146
Williamson-Chi ... 146
Anson-Chi 145
Gerhardt-NY 139
Pfeffer-Chi 136

Runs Created
Connor-NY 100
Brouthers-Buf 92
Gore-Chi 83
Anson-Chi 78
O'Rourke-NY 77

Total Average
Brouthers-Buf ..... .977
Connor-NY .... .965
Gore-Chi .... .884
Bennett-Det ...... .808
Anson-Chi .... .775

Stolen Bases

Stolen Base Average

Stolen Base Runs

Fielding Runs
Dunlap-StL 25.8
Pfeffer-Chi 25.4
Fogarty-Phi 24.8
Glasscock-StL 19.4
Richardson-Buf ... 13.1

Total Player Rating
Connor-NY 4.0
Dunlap-StL 4.0
Richardson-Buf ... 3.4
Ewing-NY 3.2
Glasscock-StL 3.1

Wins
Clarkson-Chi 53
Welch-NY 44
Keefe-NY 32
Radbourn-Pro ... 28

Win Percentage
Welch-NY .... .800
Clarkson-Chi ..... .768
McCormick-Pro-Chi ... .750
Keefe-NY .... .711
Radbourn-Pro .... .571

Games
Clarkson-Chi 70
Welch-NY 56
Whitney-Bos 51
Buffinton-Bos 51
Daily-Phi 50

Complete Games
Clarkson-Chi 68
Welch-NY 55
Whitney-Bos 50

Shutouts
Clarkson-Chi 10
Welch-NY 7
Keefe-NY 7
Shaw-Pro 6
Buffinton-Bos 6

Saves
Williamson-Chi 2
Pfeffer-Chi 2
Welch-NY 1
Galvin-Buf 1
Baldwin-Det 1

Innings Pitched
Clarkson-Chi 623.0
Welch-NY 492.0
Radbourn-Pro ...445.2
Whitney-Bos.....441.1
Daily-Phi 440.0

Fewest Hits/Game
Keefe-NY 6.75
Welch-NY 6.80
Baldwin-Det 6.88
Clarkson-Chi 7.18
Daily-Phi 7.57

Fewest BB/Game
Whitney-Bos .... .75
Galvin-Buf 1.17
Clarkson-Chi 1.40
Baldwin-Det 1.41
C.Sweeney-StL ... 1.64

Strikeouts
Clarkson-Chi 308
Welch-NY 258
Buffinton-Bos 242
Keefe-NY 227
Whitney-Bos 200

Strikeouts/Game
Baldwin-Det 6.78
Keefe-NY 5.11
Buffinton-Bos 5.01
Welch-NY 4.72
Clarkson-Chi 4.45

Ratio
Baldwin-Det 8.28
Clarkson-Chi 8.58
Keefe-NY 9.05
Welch-NY 9.20
Daily-Phi 9.41

Earned Run Average
Keefe-NY 1.58
Welch-NY 1.66
Clarkson-Chi 1.85
Baldwin-Det 1.86
Radbourn-Pro ... 2.20

Adjusted ERA
Keefe-NY 169
Clarkson-Chi 164
Welch-NY 160
Baldwin-Det 153
Daily-Phi 126

Opponents' Batting Avg.
Baldwin-Det .... .197
Welch-NY .... .203
Keefe-NY .... .203
Clarkson-Chi ..... .208
Shaw-Pro .... .209

Opponents' On Base Pct.
Baldwin-Det ...... .228
Clarkson-Chi ..... .239
Shaw-Pro .... .254
Keefe-NY .... .255
Daily-Phi .... .256

Starter Runs
Clarkson-Chi 67.0
Welch-NY 63.0
Keefe-NY 55.2
Radbourn-Pro ... 30.5
Daily-Phi 29.7

Adjusted Starter Runs
Clarkson-Chi 82.0
Welch-NY 54.7
Keefe-NY 48.4
Daily-Phi 28.2
Ferguson-Phi 25.4

Clutch Pitching Index
Keefe-NY 121
Getzien-Det 118
Radbourn-Pro ... 116
Welch-NY 112
Whitney-Bos 111

Relief Runs

Adjusted Relief Runs

Relief Ranking

Total Pitcher Index
Clarkson-Chi 8.9
Welch-NY 5.0
Keefe-NY 4.7
Ferguson-Phi 4.3
Radbourn-Pro 3.5

Total Baseball Ranking
Clarkson-Chi 8.8
Welch-NY 5.0
Keefe-NY 4.7
Ferguson-Phi 4.5
Connor-NY 4.0

TEAM	G	W	L	PCT	GB	R	OR	AB	H	2B	3B	HR	BB	SO	AVG	OBP	SLG	PRO	PRO+	BR	/A	PF	CHI	RC	SB	CS	SBA	SBR
STL	112	79	33	.705		677	461	3972	979	132	57	17	234	282	.246	.297	.321	.618	96	1	-27	105	109	388				
CIN	112	63	49	.563	16	642	575	4050	1046	108	77	26	153	420	.258	.294	.342	.636	103	18	6	102	101	417				
PIT	111	56	55	.505	22.5	547	539	3975	955	123	79	5	189	537	.240	.282	.315	.597	94	-32	-24	99	94	362				
PHI	113	55	57	.491	24	764	691	4142	1099	169	76	30	223	410	.265	.310	.365	.675	111	77	34	106	106	480				
LOU	112	53	59	.473	26	564	598	3969	986	126	83	19	152	448	.248	.281	.336	.617	99	-11	-10	100	95	384				
BRO	112	53	59	.473	26	624	650	3943	966	121	65	14	238	324	.245	.295	.319	.614	97	-4	-8	101	102	381				
NY	108	44	64	.407	33	526	688	3731	921	123	57	21	217	428	.247	.295	.327	.622	110	4	50	92	90	369				
BAL	110	41	68	.376	36.5	541	683	3820	837	124	59	17	279	529	.219	.280	.296	.576	87	-53	-45	99	99	324				
TOT	445					4885		31602	7789	1026	553	149	1685	3378	.246	.292	.328	.620										

TEAM	CG	SH	SV	IP	H	H/G	HR	BB	SO	RAT	ERA	ERA+	OAV	OOB	PR	/A	PF	CPI	FA	E	DP	FW	PW	BW	SBW	DIF
STL	111	11	0	1002	879	7.9	12	168	378	9.8	2.44	134	.228	.268	89	91	101	106	.920	381	64	3.0	8.2	-2.4		14.2
CIN	102	7	1	999¹	998	9.0	24	250	330	11.9	3.26	100	.253	.309	-2	-1	100	112	.911	423	86	.8	-.0	.5		5.8
PIT	104	8	0	1011	918	8.2	14	201	454	10.3	2.92	110	.232	.275	36	32	99	95	.912	422	77	.6	2.9	-2.2		-.9
PHI	105	5	0	1003¹	1038	9.3	11	212	506	11.6	3.23	106	.254	.298	2	23	106	104	.901	483	79	-2.2	2.1	3.1		-4.0
LOU	109	3	1	1002	927	8.3	13	217	462	10.6	2.68	120	.232	.278	63	60	99	104	.905	460	75	-1.2	5.4	-.9		-6.3
BRO	110	3	1	991²	955	8.7	27	211	436	10.8	3.46	95	.240	.283	-24	-19	102	89	.910	434	56	.2	-1.7	-.7		-.8
NY	103	2	0	937	1015	9.7	36	204	408	11.9	4.15	71	.262	.303	-94	-125	91	91	.901	452	62	-1.6	-11.3	4.5		-1.7
BAL	103	2	4	971	1059	9.8	12	222	395	12.3	3.90	83	.269	.316	-71	-71	100	100	.910	418	71	.6	-6.4	-4.1		-3.7
TOT	847	41	7	7917¹		8.9				11.1	3.24		.246	.292					.909	3473	570					

Runs
Stovey-Phi 130
Larkin-Phi 114
Jones-Cin 108
Nelson-NY 98
Browning-Lou 98

Hits
Browning-Lou 174
Jones-Cin 157
Stovey-Phi 153
Orr-NY 152
Larkin-Phi 149

Doubles
Larkin-Phi 37
Browning-Lou 34
Orr-NY 29
Stovey-Phi 27

Triples
Orr-NY 21
Kuehne-Pit 19
Wolf-Lou 17
Jones-Cin 17
Fennelly-Cin 17

Home Runs
Stovey-Phi 13
Fennelly-Cin 10
Browning-Lou 9
Larkin-Phi 8
Orr-NY 6

Total Bases
Browning-Lou 255
Orr-NY 241
Larkin-Phi 238
Stovey-Phi 237
Jones-Cin 225

Runs Batted In
Stovey-Phi 117
Larkin-Phi 106
Jones-Cin 103
Nelson-NY 97
Browning-Lou 89

Runs Produced
Orr-NY 197
Browning-Lou 190
Larkin-Phi 171
Stovey-Phi 160
Jones-Cin 156

Bases On Balls
Nelson-NY 61
Macullar-Bal 49
Hotaling-Bro 49
Stovey-Phi 39

Batting Average
Browning-Lou 362
Orr-NY 342
Larkin-Phi 329
Jones-Cin 322
Stovey-Phi 315

On Base Percentage
Browning-Lou 393
Larkin-Phi 372
Stovey-Phi 371
Brown-Pit 366
Phillips-Bro 364

Slugging Average
Orr-NY 543
Browning-Lou 530
Larkin-Phi 525
Stovey-Phi 488
Jones-Cin 462

Production
Browning-Lou 923
Orr-NY 901
Larkin-Phi 897
Stovey-Phi 858
Jones-Cin 824

Adjusted Production
Orr-NY 197
Browning-Lou 190
Larkin-Phi 171
Stovey-Phi 160
Jones-Cin 156

Batter Runs
Browning-Lou 47.0
Larkin-Phi 40.3
Orr-NY 38.1
Stovey-Phi 37.9
Jones-Cin 31.5

Adjusted Batter Runs
Browning-Lou 47.3
Orr-NY 46.6
Larkin-Phi 33.8
Stovey-Phi 31.2
Jones-Cin 29.5

Clutch Hitting Index

Runs Created
Browning-Lou 103
Larkin-Phi 91
Stovey-Phi 90
Orr-NY 88
Jones-Cin 83

Total Average
Browning-Lou 912
Larkin-Phi 885
Orr-NY 863
Stovey-Phi 841
Jones-Cin 773

Stolen Bases

Stolen Base Average

Stolen Base Runs

Fielding Runs
G.Smith-Bro 39.9
Smith-Pit 33.2
Houck-Phi 21.8
Hankinson-NY 18.0
Corkhill-Cin 17.1

Total Player Rating
Browning-Lou 4.3
Larkin-Phi 3.8
G.Smith-Bro 3.7
Jones-Cin 3.4
Smith-Pit 3.2

Wins
Caruthers-StL 40
Morris-Pit 39
Porter-Bro 33
Foutz-StL 33

Win Percentage
Caruthers-StL 755
Foutz-StL 702
Mathews-Phi 638
Morris-Pit 619
Porter-Bro 611

Games
Morris-Pit 63
Henderson-Bal 61
Porter-Bro 54
Hecker-Lou 53
Caruthers-StL 53

Complete Games
Morris-Pit 63
Henderson-Bal 59
Porter-Bro 53
Caruthers-StL 53
Hecker-Lou 51

Shutouts
Morris-Pit 7
Caruthers-StL 6
McGinnis-StL 3

Saves
Burns-Bal 3
Terry-Bro 1
Sommer-Bal 1
Reccius-Lou 1
Corkhill-Cin 1

Innings Pitched
Morris-Pit 581.0
Henderson-Bal . . .539.1
Caruthers-StL 482.1
Porter-Bro 481.2
Hecker-Lou 480.0

Fewest Hits/Game
Morris-Pit 7.11
Mays-Lou 7.74
Foutz-StL 7.75
McGinnis-StL 7.87
Porter-Bro 7.98

Fewest BB/Game
Lynch-NY 1.00
Hecker-Lou 1.01
Caruthers-StL 1.06
Mathews-Phi 1.21
McGinnis-StL 1.53

Strikeouts
Morris-Pit 298
Mathews-Phi 286
Henderson-Bal 263
Hecker-Lou 209
Porter-Bro 197

Strikeouts/Game
Mathews-Phi 6.09
Cushman-Phi-NY . 5.50
Morris-Pit 4.62
Henderson-Bal . . . 4.39
Harkins-Bro 4.33

Ratio
Morris-Pit 8.89
Caruthers-StL 9.44
Hecker-Lou 9.86
McGinnis-StL 9.88
Mathews-Phi 10.04

Earned Run Average
Caruthers-StL 2.07
Hecker-Lou 2.17
Morris-Pit 2.35
Mathews-Phi 2.43
Foutz-StL 2.63

Adjusted ERA
Caruthers-StL 158
Hecker-Lou 148
Mathews-Phi 141
Morris-Pit 137
Foutz-StL 124

Opponents' Batting Avg.
Morris-Pit 208
Mays-Lou 219
Porter-Bro 223
McGinnis-StL 225
Foutz-StL 227

Opponents' On Base Pct.
Morris-Pit 247
Caruthers-StL 260
Hecker-Lou 265
Cushman-Phi-NY .266
Mathews-Phi 267

Starter Runs
Caruthers-StL 62.9
Morris-Pit 57.4
Hecker-Lou 57.0
Mathews-Phi 38.2
Foutz-StL 28.0

Adjusted Starter Runs
Caruthers-StL 64.1
Hecker-Lou 55.8
Morris-Pit 55.6
Mathews-Phi 47.2
Foutz-StL 29.0

Clutch Pitching Index
Knight-Phi 283
Hecker-Lou 121
Caruthers-StL 118
Mountjoy-Cin-Bal . . 111
Foutz-StL 107

Relief Runs

Adjusted Relief Runs

Relief Ranking

Total Pitcher Index
Hecker-Lou 6.6
Caruthers-StL 6.6
Morris-Pit 4.5
Foutz-StL 3.8
Mathews-Phi 3.8

Total Baseball Ranking
Caruthers-StL 6.5
Hecker-Lou 6.3
Morris-Pit 4.5
Browning-Lou 4.3
Larkin-Phi 3.8

1886 National League

TEAM	G	W	L	PCT	GB	R	OR	AB	H	2B	3B	HR	BB	SO	AVG	OBP	SLG	PRO	PRO+	BR	/A	PF	CHI	RC	SB	CS	SBA	SBR
CHI	126	90	34	.726		900	555	4378	1223	198	87	53	460	513	.279	.348	.401	.749	115	176	48	115	104	701	213			
DET	126	87	36	.707	2.5	829	538	4501	1260	176	81	53	374	426	.280	.335	.390	.725	122	137	113	103	100	670	194			
NY	124	75	44	.630	12.5	692	558	4298	1156	175	68	21	237	410	.269	.307	.356	.663	106	29	22	101	102	531	155			
PHI	119	71	43	.623	14	621	498	4072	976	145	66	26	282	516	.240	.289	.327	.616	91	-37	-42	101	106	461	226			
BOS	118	56	61	.479	30.5	657	661	4180	1085	151	59	24	250	537	.260	.301	.341	.642	104	0	23	96	104	489	156			
STL	126	43	79	.352	46	547	712	4250	1001	183	46	30	235	656	.236	.276	.321	.597	92	-71	-35	94	96	430	156			
KC	126	30	91	.248	58.5	494	872	4236	967	177	48	19	269	608	.228	.274	.306	.580	76	-92	-128	106	90	392	96			
WAS	125	28	92	.233	60	445	791	4082	856	135	51	23	265	582	.210	.258	.285	.543	73	-143	-116	94	93	345	143			
TOT	495					5185		33997	8524	1340	506	249	2372	4248	.251	.300	.342	.641							1339			

TEAM	CG	SH	SV	IP	H	H/G	HR	BB	SO	RAT	ERA	ERA+	OAV	OOB	PR	/A	PF	CPI	FA	E	DP	FW	PW	BW	SBW	DIF
CHI	116	8	3	1097²	988	8.1	49	262	647	10.2	2.54	142	.232	.277	91	131	110	111	.912	475	82	-1.8	11.9	4.4		13.5
DET	122	8	0	1103²	995	8.1	20	270	592	10.3	2.85	115	.231	.276	53	52	100	90	.928	373	82	3.8	4.7	10.2		6.8
NY	119	3	1	1062	1029	8.7	23	280	588	11.1	2.86	111	.247	.294	50	26	97	104	.927	359	70	4.2	2.4	2.0		7.0
PHI	110	10	2	1045²	923	7.9	29	264	540	10.2	2.45	134	.224	.271	97	94	100	101	.921	393	46	1.4	8.5	-3.8		7.9
BOS	116	3	0	1029	1049	9.2	33	298	511	11.8	3.24	98	.252	.302	5	-7	97	104	.905	465	63	-2.7	-.6	2.1		-1.2
STL	118	6	0	1077¹	1050	8.8	34	392	501	12.0	3.24	99	.246	.309	5	-7	97	105	.914	452	92	-.5	-.6	-3.2		-13.7
KC	117	4	0	1066²	1345	11.3	27	246	442	13.4	4.84	77	.295	.331	-184	-132	114	90	.910	482	79	-2.1	-12.0	-11.6		-4.8
WAS	116	4	0	1041	1147	9.9	34	379	500	13.2	4.30	76	.271	.331	-117	-124	99	95	.910	458	69	-1.0	-11.2	-10.5		-9.2
TOT	934	46	6	8523		9.0				11.5	3.29		.251	.300					.916	3457	583					

Runs
Kelly-Chi 155
Gore-Chi 150
Brouthers-Det 139
Richardson-Det . . . 125
Anson-Chi 117

Hits
Richardson-Det 189
Anson-Chi 187
Brouthers-Det 181
Kelly-Chi 175
Connor-NY 172

Doubles
Brouthers-Det 40
Anson-Chi 35
Kelly-Chi 32
Hines-Was 30

Triples
Connor-NY 20
Wood-Phi 15
Brouthers-Det 15
Thompson-Det . . . 13

Home Runs
Richardson-Det . . . 11
Brouthers-Det 11
Anson-Chi 10
Hines-Was 9
Denny-StL 9

Total Bases
Brouthers-Det 284
Anson-Chi 274
Richardson-Det . . . 271
Connor-NY 262
Kelly-Chi 241

Runs Batted In
Anson-Chi 147
Pfeffer-Chi 95
Thompson-Det 89
Rowe-Det 87
Ward-NY 81

Runs Produced
Anson-Chi 254
Kelly-Chi 230
Gore-Chi 207
Brouthers-Det 200
Thompson-Det . . . 182

Bases On Balls
Gore-Chi 102
Kelly-Chi 83
Williamson-Chi 80
Brouthers-Det 66
Radford-KC 58

Batting Average
Kelly-Chi 388
Anson-Chi 371
Brouthers-Det 370
Connor-NY 355
Richardson-Det 351

On Base Percentage
Kelly-Chi 483
Brouthers-Det 445
Gore-Chi 434
Anson-Chi 433
Connor-NY 405

Slugging Average
Brouthers-Det 581
Anson-Chi 544
Connor-NY 540
Kelly-Chi 534
Richardson-Det 504

Production
Brouthers-Det 1.026
Kelly-Chi 1.018
Anson-Chi 977
Connor-NY 945
Richardson-Det 906

Adjusted Production
Brouthers-Det 204
Connor-NY 183
Kelly-Chi 182
Anson-Chi 170
Richardson-Det . . . 169

Batter Runs
Brouthers-Det . . . 65.9
Kelly-Chi 64.3
Anson-Chi 58.3
Connor-NY 48.7
Richardson-Det . . . 47.4

Adjusted Batter Runs
Brouthers-Det 61.7
Connor-NY 47.5
Kelly-Chi 44.3
Richardson-Det . . . 43.7
Anson-Chi 38.5

Clutch Hitting Index
Anson-Chi 158
Ward-NY 153
Pfeffer-Chi 141
Dorgan-NY 139
Gillespie-NY 138

Runs Created
Kelly-Chi 146
Brouthers-Det 139
Anson-Chi 134
Richardson-Det . . . 129
Connor-NY 116

Total Average
Kelly-Chi 1.366
Brouthers-Det . . . 1.205
Anson-Chi 1.129
Gore-Chi 1.042
Richardson-Det . . . 1.029

Stolen Bases
Andrews-Phi 56
Kelly-Chi 53
Hanlon-Det 50
Richardson-Det 42
Radford-KC 39

Stolen Base Average

Stolen Base Runs

Fielding Runs
Knowles-Was 27.7
Denny-StL 22.7
Dunlap-StL-Det . . . 19.3
Johnston-Bos 16.6
Glasscock-StL 13.8

Total Player Rating
Richardson-Det 4.8
Kelly-Chi 4.5
Glasscock-StL 4.2
Connor-NY 3.9
Brouthers-Det 3.5

Wins
Keefe-NY 42
Baldwin-Det 42
Clarkson-Chi 36
Welch-NY 33
McCormick-Chi 31

Win Percentage
Flynn-Chi 793
Ferguson-Phi 769
Baldwin-Det 764
McCormick-Chi 738
Getzien-Det 732

Games
Keefe-NY 64
Welch-NY 59
Radbourn-Bos 58
Baldwin-Det 56
Clarkson-Chi 55

Complete Games
Keefe-NY 62
Radbourn-Bos 57
Welch-NY 56
Baldwin-Det 55
Clarkson-Chi 50

Shutouts
Baldwin-Det 7
Ferguson-Phi 4
Casey-Phi 4

Saves
Ferguson-Phi 2
Williamson-Chi 1
Ryan-Chi 1
Flynn-Chi 1
Devlin-NY 1

Innings Pitched
Keefe-NY 535.0
Radbourn-Bos . . . 509.1
Welch-NY 500.0
Baldwin-Det 487.0
Clarkson-Chi 466.2

Fewest Hits/Game
Baldwin-Det 6.86
Ferguson-Phi 7.21
Flynn-Chi 7.25
Stemmeyer-Bos . . 7.74
Boyle-StL 7.84

Fewest BB/Game
Whitney-KC 1.26
Ferguson-Phi 1.57
Clarkson-Chi 1.66
Keefe-NY 1.72
Baldwin-Det 1.85

Strikeouts
Baldwin-Det 323
Clarkson-Chi 313
Keefe-NY 297
Welch-NY 272
Stemmeyer-Bos . . . 239

Strikeouts/Game
Stemmeyer-Bos . . . 6.17
Clarkson-Chi 6.04
Baldwin-Det 5.97
Healy-StL 5.42
Flynn-Chi 5.11

Ratio
Baldwin-Det 8.70
Ferguson-Phi 8.78
Flynn-Chi 9.46
Clarkson-Chi 9.74
Keefe-NY 9.77

Earned Run Average
Boyle-StL 1.76
Ferguson-Phi 1.98
Baldwin-Det 2.24
Flynn-Chi 2.24
Clarkson-Chi 2.41

Adjusted ERA
Boyle-StL 182
Ferguson-Phi 166
Flynn-Chi 161
Clarkson-Chi 150
Baldwin-Det 147

Opponents' Batting Avg.
Baldwin-Det 202
Ferguson-Phi 210
Flynn-Chi 210
Stemmeyer-Bos 218
Boyle-StL 220

Opponents' On Base Pct.
Baldwin-Det 243
Ferguson-Phi 244
Flynn-Chi 257
Boyle-StL 261
Clarkson-Chi 264

Starter Runs
Ferguson-Phi 57.5
Baldwin-Det 56.9
Clarkson-Chi 45.4
Keefe-NY 43.4
Casey-Phi 35.8

Adjusted Starter Runs
Clarkson-Chi 62.7
Ferguson-Phi 57.1
Baldwin-Det 57.1
Flynn-Chi 39.3
Keefe-NY 37.5

Clutch Pitching Index
Boyle-StL 127
McCormick-Chi . . . 126
Welch-NY 121
Kirby-StL 112
Radbourn-Bos 108

Relief Runs

Adjusted Relief Runs

Relief Ranking

Total Pitcher Index
Ferguson-Phi 6.5
Clarkson-Chi 6.5
Baldwin-Det 6.1
Flynn-Chi 4.1
Boyle-StL 3.9

Total Baseball Ranking
Ferguson-Phi 6.4
Clarkson-Chi 6.3
Baldwin-Det 6.0
Kelly-Chi 4.5
Richardson-Det . . . 4.5

TEAM	G	W	L	PCT	GB	R	OR	AB	H	2B	3B	HR	BB	SO	AVG	OBP	SLG	PRO	PRO+	BR	/A	PF	CHI	RC	SB	CS	SBA	SBR
STL	139	93	46	.669		944	592	5009	1365	206	85	20	400	425	.273	.333	.360	.693	116	114	71	105	102	729	336			
PIT	140	80	57	.584	12	810	647	4854	1171	186	96	16	478	713	.241	.314	.329	.643	106	31	35	100	97	598	260			
BRO	141	76	61	.555	16	832	832	5053	1261	196	80	16	433	523	.250	.311	.330	.641	103	22	14	101	99	610	248			
LOU	138	66	70	.485	25.5	833	805	4921	1294	182	88	20	410	558	.263	.323	.348	.671	108	74	24	106	95	634	202			
CIN	141	65	73	.471	27.5	883	865	4915	1225	145	95	45	374	633	.249	.311	.345	.656	106	45	18	103	105	599	185			
PHI	139	63	72	.467	28	772	942	4856	1142	192	82	21	378	697	.235	.296	.321	.617	95	-22	-30	101	101	560	284			
NY	137	53	82	.393	38	628	766	4683	1047	108	72	18	330	578	.224	.279	.289	.568	85	-101	-73	96	96	422	120			
BAL	139	48	83	.366	41	625	878	4639	945	124	51	8	379	603	.204	.269	.258	.527	70	-163	-148	98	106	404	269			
TOT	557					6327		38930	9450	1339	649	164	3182	4730	.243	.305	.323	.628						1904				

TEAM	CG	SH	SV	IP	H	H/G	HR	BB	SO	RAT	ERA	ERA+	OAV	OOB	PR	/A	PF	CPI	FA	E	DP	FW	PW	BW	SBW	DIF
STL	134	14	2	1229¹	1087	8.0	13	329	583	10.6	2.49	138	.227	.281	130	128	100	113	.915	494	96	3.3	11.2	6.2		2.7
PIT	137	15	1	1226	1130	8.3	10	299	515	10.7	2.83	120	.235	.285	84	74	98	104	.917	487	90	3.9	6.5	3.1		-1.9
BRO	138	6	0	1234²	1202	8.8	17	464	540	12.4	3.42	102	.243	.312	3	9	101	104	.900	610	87	-2.2	.8	1.2		7.7
LOU	131	5	2	1209²	1109	8.3	16	432	720	11.7	3.07	118	.230	.297	51	75	106	101	.901	593	89	-2.0	6.6	2.1		-8.7
CIN	129	3	0	1247²	1267	9.1	25	481	495	13.0	4.18	84	.255	.327	-103	-94	102	95	.905	582	122	-.8	-8.3	1.6		3.4
PHI	134	4	0	1218²	1308	9.7	35	388	513	13.0	3.97	88	.259	.319	-72	-66	102	100	.894	637	99	-4.0	-5.8	-2.6		7.9
NY	134	5	0	1186¹	1148	8.7	23	386	559	11.8	3.50	97	.243	.304	-8	-14	99	98	.907	544	81	.3	-1.2	-6.4		-7.2
BAL	134	5	0	1206²	1197	8.9	25	403	805	12.3	4.08	84	.244	.308	-85	-90	99	87	.910	523	59	1.8	-7.9	-13.0		1.6
TOT	1071	57	5	9759		8.7				11.9	3.44		.243	.305					.906	4470	723					

Runs
Latham-StL	152
McPhee-Cin	139'
Larkin-Phi	133
McClellan-Bro	131
Pinkney-Bro	119

Hits
Orr-NY	193
O'Neill-StL	190
Larkin-Phi	180
Latham-StL	174
Phillips-Bro	160

Doubles
Larkin-Phi	36
McClellan-Bro	33
Welch-StL	31
Barkley-Pit	31
Browning-Lou	29

Triples
Orr-NY	31
Coleman-Phi-Pit	17
Kuehne-Pit	17
Fennelly-Cin	17
Larkin-Phi	16

Home Runs
McPhee-Cin	8
Stovey-Phi	7
Orr-NY	7

Total Bases
Orr-NY	301
O'Neill-StL	255
Larkin-Phi	254
Welch-StL	221
McPhee-Cin	221

Runs Batted In

Runs Produced
Latham-StL	151
McPhee-Cin	131
Larkin-Phi	131
McClellan-Bro	130
Pinkney-Bro	119

Bases On Balls
Swartwood-Bro	70
Pinkney-Bro	70
Mack-Lou	68
Kerins-Lou	66

Batting Average
Orr-NY	.338
Hecker-Lou	.341
Browning-Lou	.340
Caruthers-StL	.334
O'Neill-StL	.328

On Base Percentage
Larkin-Phi	.390
Browning-Lou	.389
O'Neill-StL	.385
Stovey-Phi	.377
Swartwood-Bro	.377

Slugging Average
Orr-NY	.527
Caruthers-StL	.527
Larkin-Phi	.450
Hecker-Lou	.446
Browning-Lou	.441

Production
Orr-NY	.890
Larkin-Phi	.839
Browning-Lou	.830
O'Neill-StL	.826
Stovey-Phi	.817

Adjusted Production
Orr-NY	186
Larkin-Phi	161
Stovey-Phi	154
O'Neill-StL	151
Browning-Lou	151

Batter Runs
Orr-NY	45.9
Caruthers-StL	41.4
Larkin-Phi	41.3
O'Neill-StL	38.6
Stovey-Phi	32.1

Adjusted Batter Runs
Orr-NY	51.9
Larkin-Phi	39.9
Caruthers-StL	36.8
O'Neill-StL	32.4
Stovey-Phi	31.0

Clutch Hitting Index

Runs Created
Orr-NY	118
Larkin-Phi	114
Stovey-Phi	109
O'Neill-StL	104
Latham-StL	104

Total Average
Stovey-Phi	1.009
Larkin-Phi	.914
Robinson-StL	.903
Orr-NY	.897
Browning-Lou	.873

Stolen Bases
Stovey-Phi	68
Latham-StL	60
Welch-StL	59
Robinson-StL	51
McClellan-Bro	43

Stolen Base Average

Stolen Base Runs

Fielding Runs
Kerins-Lou	39.0
McPhee-Cin	30.5
Hankinson-NY	25.4
Smith-Pit	21.0
Peoples-Bro	18.5

Total Player Rating
Kerins-Lou	4.6
McPhee-Cin	4.6
Larkin-Phi	3.6
Carroll-Pit	3.6
O'Neill-StL	3.2

Wins
Morris-Pit	41
Foutz-StL	41
Ramsey-Lou	38
Mullane-Cin	33
Caruthers-StL	30

Win Percentage
Foutz-StL	.719
Caruthers-StL	.682
Morris-Pit	.672
Hudson-StL	.615
Atkinson-Phi	.595

Games
Kilroy-Bal	68
Ramsey-Lou	67
Morris-Pit	64
Mullane-Cin	63
Foutz-StL	59

Complete Games
Ramsey-Lou	66
Kilroy-Bal	66
Morris-Pit	63
Mullane-Cin	55
Foutz-StL	55

Shutouts
Morris-Pit	12
Foutz-StL	11
Terry-Bro	5
Kilroy-Bal	5
Ramsey-Lou	3

Saves
Morris-Pit	1
Hudson-StL	1
Foutz-StL	1
Ely-Lou	1

Innings Pitched
Ramsey-Lou	588.2
Kilroy-Bal	583.0
Morris-Pit	555.1
Mullane-Cin	529.2
Foutz-StL	504.0

Fewest Hits/Game
Ramsey-Lou	6.83
Kilroy-Bal	7.35
Morris-Pit	7.37
Foutz-StL	7.46
Caruthers-StL	7.51

Fewest BB/Game
Galvin-Pit	1.55
Morris-Pit	1.91
Caruthers-StL	2.00
McGinnis-StL-Bal	2.27
Atkinson-Phi	2.29

Strikeouts
Kilroy-Bal	513
Ramsey-Lou	499
Morris-Pit	326
Foutz-StL	283
Mullane-Cin	250

Strikeouts/Game
Kilroy-Bal	7.92
Ramsey-Lou	7.63
Morris-Pit	5.28
Miller-Phi	5.25
Terry-Bro	5.06

Ratio
Morris-Pit	9.40
Caruthers-StL	9.67
Ramsey-Lou	10.18
Foutz-StL	10.21
Cushman-NY	10.45

Earned Run Average
Foutz-StL	2.11
Caruthers-StL	2.32
Ramsey-Lou	2.45
Morris-Pit	2.45
Galvin-Pit	2.67

Adjusted ERA
Foutz-StL	163
Ramsey-Lou	148
Caruthers-StL	148
Morris-Pit	138
Hecker-Lou	127

Opponents' Batting Avg.
Ramsey-Lou	.198
Kilroy-Bal	.210
Morris-Pit	.214
Foutz-StL	.216
Caruthers-StL	.217

Opponents' On Base Pct.
Morris-Pit	.258
Caruthers-StL	.263
Ramsey-Lou	.269
Foutz-StL	.274
Kilroy-Bal	.274

Starter Runs
Foutz-StL	74.8
Ramsey-Lou	65.2
Morris-Pit	61.4
Caruthers-StL	48.2
Galvin-Pit	37.3

Adjusted Starter Runs
Ramsey-Lou	77.6
Foutz-StL	74.2
Morris-Pit	57.6
Caruthers-StL	47.7
Hecker-Lou	35.8

Clutch Pitching Index
Galvin-Pit	130
McGinnis-StL-Bal	127
Foutz-StL	122
Miller-Phi	119
Mays-NY	107

Relief Runs

Adjusted Relief Runs

Relief Ranking

Total Pitcher Index
Foutz-StL	8.1
Caruthers-StL	6.8
Ramsey-Lou	6.5
Hecker-Lou	5.2
Morris-Pit	4.4

Total Baseball Ranking
Foutz-StL	8.1
Caruthers-StL	7.9
Ramsey-Lou	6.5
Hecker-Lou	5.2
Kerins-Lou	4.6

TEAM	G	W	L	PCT	GB	R	OR	AB	H	2B	3B	HR	BB	SO	AVG	OBP	SLG	PRO	PRO+	BR	/A	PF	CHI	RC	SB	CS	SBA	SBR
DET	127	79	45	.637		969	714	4689	1404	213	126	55	352	258	.299	.353	.434	.787	118	134	104	103	103	833	267			
PHI	128	75	48	.610	3.5	901	702	4630	1269	213	89	47	385	346	.274	.337	.389	.726	99	35	-13	106	107	744	355			
CHI	127	71	50	.587	6.5	813	716	4350	1177	178	98	80	407	400	.271	.336	.412	.748	98	62	-44	113	99	748	382			
NY	129	68	55	.553	10.5	816	723	4516	1259	167	93	48	361	326	.279	.339	.389	.728	111	37	76	95	100	753	415			
BOS	127	61	60	.504	16.5	831	792	4531	1255	185	94	53	340	392	.277	.333	.394	.727	106	32	31	100	102	736	373			
PIT	125	55	69	.444	24	621	750	4414	1141	183	78	20	319	381	.258	.314	.349	.663	94	-69	-27	94	90	567	221			
WAS	126	46	76	.377	32	601	818	4314	1039	149	63	47	269	339	.241	.292	.337	.629	82	-126	-95	95	99	535	334			
IND	127	37	89	.294	43	628	965	4368	1080	162	70	33	300	379	.247	.302	.339	.641	85	-105	-82	96	97	562	334			
TOT	508					6180		35812	9624	1450	711	383	2733	2821	.269	.326	.381	.707						2681				

TEAM	CG	SH	SV	IP	H	H/G	HR	BB	SO	RAT	ERA	ERA+	OAV	OOB	PR	/A	PF	CPI	FA	E	DP	FW	PW	BW	SBW	DIF
DET	122	3	1	1116¹	1172	9.4	52	344	337	12.5	3.95	102	.264	.322	12	-3	99	97	.925	394	92	3.3	-.3	8.8		5.1
PHI	119	7	1	1132²	1173	9.3	48	305	435	12.0	3.47	121	.259	.311	72	89	104	104	.912	471	76	-.4	7.5	-1.1		7.5
CHI	117	4	3	1126	1156	9.2	55	338	510	12.4	3.46	129	.257	.317	73	120	110	108	.914	472	99	-.6	10.2	-3.7		4.7
NY	123	5	1	1113²	1096	8.9	27	373	415	12.2	3.57	105	.250	.314	59	18	93	96	.920	431	83	1.8	1.5	6.4		-3.3
BOS	123	4	1	1100²	1226	10.0	55	396	254	13.6	4.41	91	.273	.338	-44	-46	100	99	.905	522	94	-3.1	-3.9	2.6		4.9
PIT	123	4	0	1108²	1287	10.4	39	246	248	12.7	4.12	94	.281	.322	-9	-32	95	99	.921	425	70	1.4	-2.7	-2.3		-3.4
WAS	124	3	0	1090¹	1216	10.0	47	299	396	12.9	4.19	96	.272	.323	-18	-21	100	96	.909	483	77	-1.4	-1.8	-8.1		-3.8
IND	118	4	1	1088	1289	10.7	60	431	245	14.6	5.24	79	.284	.352	-145	-139	102	92	.912	479	105	-1.0	-11.8	-6.9		-6.3
TOT	969	34	8	8876¹		9.7				12.8	4.05		.269	.326					.915	3677	696					

Runs
Brouthers-Det..... 153
Rowe-Det........ 135
Richardson-Det ... 131
Kelly-Bos 120

Hits
Thompson-Det ... 203
Ward-NY 184
Richardson-Det ... 178
Rowe-Det 171
Brouthers-Det 169

Doubles
Brouthers-Det 36
Kelly-Bos 34
Denny-Ind 34
Anson-Chi 33

Triples
Thompson-Det 23
Connor-NY 22
Johnston-Bos 20
Brouthers-Det 20
Wood-Phi 19

Home Runs
B.O'Brien-Was 19
Connor-NY 17
Pfeffer-Chi 16
Wood-Phi 14

Total Bases
Thompson-Det 311
Brouthers-Det 281
Richardson-Det 263
Denny-Ind........ 256
Connor-NY 255

Runs Batted In
Thompson-Det 166
Connor-NY 104
Anson-Chi 102
Brouthers-Det.... 101
Denny-Ind......... 97

Runs Produced
Thompson-Det 273
Brouthers-Det 242
Rowe-Det 225
Richardson-Det ... 217
Anson-Chi 202

Bases On Balls
Fogarty-Phi 82
Connor-NY 75
Williamson-Chi.... 73
Seery-Ind 71
Brouthers-Det 71

Batting Average
Thompson-Det....372
Anson-Chi.........347
Brouthers-Det 338
Ward-NY 338
Wise-Bos 334

On Base Percentage
Brouthers-Det ..... .426
Anson-Chi .... .422
Thompson-Det .... .416
Schomberg-Ind .... .397
Kelly-Bos .... .393

Slugging Average
Thompson-Det 571
Brouthers-Det 562
Connor-NY 541
Wise-Bos 522
Anson-Chi 517

Production
Brouthers-Det.....988
Thompson-Det 987
Anson-Chi........939
Connor-NY 933
Wise-Bos 913

Adjusted Production
Brouthers-Det 167
Thompson-Det 166
Connor-NY 164
Carroll-Pit 152
Wise-Bos 151

Batter Runs
Thompson-Det.... 51.2
Brouthers-Det 50.5
Anson-Chi 39.3
Connor-NY 37.1
Wise-Bos 31.7

Adjusted Batter Runs
Thompson-Det 46.6
Brouthers-Det 46.0
Connor-NY 43.1
Wise-Bos 31.6
Carroll-Pit 30.1

Clutch Hitting Index
Thompson-Det 149
O'Rourke-NY 143
Nash-Bos 129
Rowe-Det 125
Schomberg-Ind ... 122

Runs Created
Thompson-Det 142
Brouthers-Det 138
Kelly-Bos 129
Ward-NY 125
Connor-NY 120

Total Average
Brouthers-Det....1.184
Kelly-Bos 1.146
Connor-NY 1.131
Thompson-Det ...1.094
Fogarty-Phi.....1.085

Stolen Bases
Ward-NY 111
Fogarty-Phi 102
Kelly-Bos 84
Hanlon-Det 69
Glasscock-Ind..... 62

Stolen Base Average

Stolen Base Runs

Fielding Runs
Glasscock-Ind 35.0
Fogarty-Phi 31.7
Ward-NY 29.8
Johnston-Bos 25.3
Pfeffer-Chi 24.6

Total Player Rating
Thompson-Det 4.3
Denny-Ind........ 4.0
Ward-NY 3.9
Glasscock-Ind 3.5
Fogarty-Phi....... 3.3

Wins
Clarkson-Chi 38
Keefe-NY 35
Getzien-Det 29
Galvin-Pit 28
Casey-Phi 28

Win Percentage
Getzien-Det ...... .690
Ferguson-Phi...... .688
Casey-Phi .... .683
Keefe-NY .... .648
Clarkson-Chi ..... .644

Games
Clarkson-Chi 60
Keefe-NY 56
Radbourn-Bos ... 50
Galvin-Pit 49
Whitney-Was 47

Complete Games
Clarkson-Chi 56
Keefe-NY 54
Radbourn-Bos 48
Galvin-Pit 47
Whitney-Was 46

Shutouts
Casey-Phi 4
Madden-Bos 3
Healy-Ind 3
Galvin-Pit 3

Saves
VanHaltren-Chi ... 1
Twitchell-Det 1
Tiernan-NY 1
Stemmeyer-Bos ... 1
Pettit-Chi 1
Ferguson-Phi 1
Fast -Ind 1
Baldwin-Chi 1

Innings Pitched
Clarkson-Chi 523.0
Keefe-NY 476.2
Galvin-Pit 440.2
Radbourn-Bos 425.0
Whitney-Was 404.2

Fewest Hits/Game
Keefe-NY 8.08
Conway-Det 8.14
Casey-Phi 8.69
Welch-NY 8.82
Clarkson-Chi 8.83

Fewest BB/Game
Whitney-Was .... .93
Galvin-Pit 1.37
Ferguson-Phi 1.42
Clarkson-Chi 1.58
Boyle-Ind 1.89

Strikeouts
Clarkson-Chi 237
Keefe-NY 189
Baldwin-Chi 164
Buffinton-Phi 160
Whitney-Was 146

Strikeouts/Game
Baldwin-Chi 4.42
Gilmore-Was 4.37
Buffinton-Phi 4.33
VanHaltren-Chi ... 4.25
Clarkson-Chi 4.08

Ratio
Keefe-NY 10.33
Clarkson-Chi 10.55
Ferguson-Phi 10.75
Whitney-Was 10.85
Welch-NY 11.32

Earned Run Average
Casey-Phi 2.86
Conway-Det 2.90
Ferguson-Phi 3.00
Clarkson-Chi 3.08
Keefe-NY 3.12

Adjusted ERA
Casey-Phi 147
Clarkson-Chi 145
Ferguson-Phi..... 140
Conway-Det 139
Baldwin-Chi...... 131

Opponents' Batting Avg.
Keefe-NY .... .230
Conway-Det ..... .235
Casey-Phi....... .246
Clarkson-Chi .... .246
Baldwin-Chi ..... .248

Opponents' On Base Pct.
Keefe-NY .... .276
Clarkson-Chi..... .281
Whitney-Was ... .284
Ferguson-Phi .... .289
Galvin-Pit ...... .299

Starter Runs
Clarkson-Chi 56.1
Casey-Phi 51.5
Keefe-NY 49.3
Galvin-Pit 37.1
Whitney-Was ... 36.9

Adjusted Starter Runs
Clarkson-Chi 80.1
Casey-Phi 58.3
Ferguson-Phi ... 39.9
Baldwin-Chi 39.5
Whitney-Was ... 36.4

Clutch Pitching Index
VanHaltren-Chi ... 123
Casey-Phi 117
Baldwin-Chi 114
Ferguson-Phi 108
Madden-Bos 105

Relief Runs

Adjusted Relief Runs

Relief Ranking

Total Pitcher Index
Clarkson-Chi 8.3
Ferguson-Phi 4.7
Whitney-Was 4.7
Keefe-NY 3.8
Casey-Phi 3.7

Total Baseball Ranking
Clarkson-Chi 8.1
Ferguson-Phi 4.7
Whitney-Was 4.5
Thompson-Det.... 4.3
Denny-Ind........ 4.0

TEAM	G	W	L	PCT	GB	R	OR	AB	H	2B	3B	HR	BB	SO	AVG	OBP	SLG	PRO	PRO+	BR	/A	PF	CHI	RC	SB	CS	SBA	SBR
STL	138	95	40	.704		1131	761	5048	1550	261	78	39	442	340	.307	.371	.413	.784	111	151	37	111	103	1012	581			
CIN	136	81	54	.600	14	892	745	4797	1285	179	102	37	382	366	.268	.329	.371	.700	97	-11	-31	102	102	778	527			
BAL	141	77	58	.570	18	975	861	4825	1337	202	100	31	469	334	.277	.349	.380	.729	114	50	106	94	102	852	545			
LOU	139	76	60	.559	19.5	956	854	4916	1420	194	98	27	436	356	.289	.352	.385	.737	107	61	42	102	98	850	466			
PHI	137	64	69	.481	30	893	890	4954	1370	231	84	29	321	388	.277	.327	.375	.702	99	-13	-14	100	100	782	476			
BRO	138	60	74	.448	34.5	904	918	4913	1281	200	82	25	456	365	.261	.330	.350	.680	92	-40	-51	101	103	720	409			
NY	138	44	89	.331	50	754	1093	4820	1197	193	66	21	439	463	.248	.318	.329	.647	88	-98	-63	96	94	615	305			
CLE	133	39	92	.298	54	729	1112	4649	1170	178	77	14	375	463	.252	.314	.332	.646	87	-99	-77	97	96	611	355			
TOT	550					7234		38922	10610	1638	687	223	3320	3075	.273	.337	.367	.704							3664			

TEAM	CG	SH	SV	IP	H	H/G	HR	BB	SO	RAT	ERA	ERA+	OAV	OOB	PR	/A	PF	CPI	FA	E	DP	FW	PW	BW	SBW	DIF
STL	132	7	2	1199¹	1254	9.4	19	323	334	12.2	3.77	120	.258	.311	69	100	106	94	.916	481	86	3.6	8.1	3.0		12.8
CIN	129	11	1	1182²	1202	9.1	28	396	330	12.6	3.58	121	.257	.322	93	99	101	107	.916	484	106	3.0	8.0	-2.5		5.0
BAL	132	8	0	1220	1288	9.5	16	418	470	13.0	3.87	106	.262	.326	58	30	95	100	.907	549	66	.8	2.4	8.6		-2.3
LOU	133	3	1	1205²	1274	9.5	31	357	544	12.5	3.82	115	.260	.316	63	75	102	98	.903	574	83	-.9	6.1	3.4		-.6
PHI	131	5	1	1186¹	1227	9.3	29	433	417	13.1	4.59	94	.260	.331	-39	-41	100	88	.907	528	95	1.0	-3.3	-1.1		.9
BRO	132	3	3	1185¹	1348	10.2	27	454	332	14.0	4.47	96	.281	.348	-24	-24	100	103	.905	562	88	-.5	-1.9	-4.1		-.4
NY	132	1	0	1180¹	1545	11.8	39	406	316	15.3	5.28	80	.308	.365	-130	-138	99	102	.894	632	102	-4.0	-11.2	-5.1		-2.2
CLE	127	2	1	1136	1472	11.7	34	533	332	16.4	4.99	87	.308	.384	-88	-84	101	115	.898	576	97	-2.2	-6.8	-6.2		-11.3
TOT	1048	40	9	9495²		10.1				13.6	4.29		.273	.337					.906	4386	723					

Runs
O'Neill-StL 167
Latham-StL 163
Griffin-Bal 142
Poorman-Phi 140
Comiskey-StL 139

Hits
O'Neill-StL 225
Browning-Lou 220
Lyons-Phi 209
Latham-StL 198
Burns-Bal 188

Doubles
O'Neill-StL 52
Lyons-Phi 43
Reilly-Cin 35
Latham-StL 35
Browning-Lou 35

Triples
Poorman-Phi 19
O'Neill-StL 19
McPhee-Cin 19
Kerins-Lou 19
Davis-Bal 19
Burns-Bal 19

Home Runs
O'Neill-StL 14
Reilly-Cin 10
Burns-Bal 9

Total Bases
O'Neill-StL 357
Browning-Lou 299
Lyons-Phi 298
Burns-Bal 286
Reilly-Cin 263

Runs Batted In

Runs Produced
Latham-StL 161
O'Neill-StL 153
Griffin-Bal 139
Poorman-Phi 136

Bases On Balls
Radford-NY 106
Robinson-StL 92
Nicol-Cin 86
Mack-Lou 83
Fennelly-Cin 82

Batting Average
O'Neill-StL 435
Browning-Lou 402
Orr-NY 368
Lyons-Phi 367
Caruthers-StL 357

On Base Percentage
O'Neill-StL 490
Browning-Lou 464
Caruthers-StL 463
Robinson-StL 445
Lyons-Phi 421

Slugging Average
O'Neill-StL 691
Caruthers-StL 547
Browning-Lou 547
Lyons-Phi 523
Burns-Bal 519

Production
O'Neill-StL 1.180
Browning-Lou . . . 1.011
Caruthers-StL . . 1.010
Lyons-Phi 943
Burns-Bal 933

Adjusted Production
O'Neill-StL 205
Browning-Lou 178
Burns-Bal 169
Caruthers-StL 164
Lyons-Phi 162

Batter Runs
O'Neill-StL 86.4
Browning-Lou . . . 60.9
Lyons-Phi 46.7
Burns-Bal 43.7
Caruthers-StL . . 42.9

Adjusted Batter Runs
O'Neill-StL 67.9
Browning-Lou . . . 57.6
Burns-Bal 52.5
Lyons-Phi 46.5
Caruthers-StL . . 30.9

Clutch Hitting Index

Runs Created
O'Neill-StL 194
Browning-Lou . . . 191
Lyons-Phi 160
Burns-Bal 146
Latham-StL 146

Total Average
O'Neill-StL 1.514
Browning-Lou . . . 1.422
Caruthers-StL . . 1.368
Robinson-StL . . . 1.197
Lyons-Phi 1.175

Stolen Bases
Nicol-Cin 138
Latham-StL 129
Comiskey-StL 117
Browning-Lou 103
McPhee-Cin 95

Stolen Base Average

Stolen Base Runs

Fielding Runs
Smith-Bro 32.0
McPhee-Cin 26.2
Kerins-Lou 24.8
White-Lou 21.5
Welch-StL 19.4

Total Player Rating
O'Neill-StL 4.7
Browning-Lou 4.2
Lyons-Phi 3.5
McPhee-Cin 3.0
Burns-Bal 2.8

Wins
Kilroy-Bal 46
Ramsey-Lou 37
Smith-Cin 34
King-StL 32
Mullane-Cin 31

Win Percentage
Caruthers-StL 763
King-StL 727
Kilroy-Bal 708
Foutz-StL 676
Smith-Cin 667

Games
Kilroy-Bal 69
Ramsey-Lou 65
Smith-Bal 58
Weyhing-Phi 55
Seward-Phi 55

Complete Games
Kilroy-Bal 66
Ramsey-Lou 61
Smith-Bal 54
Weyhing-Phi 53
Seward-Phi 52

Shutouts
Mullane-Cin 6
Kilroy-Bal 6
Smith-Cin 3
Seward-Phi 3

Saves
Terry-Bro 3

Innings Pitched
Kilroy-Bal 589.1
Ramsey-Lou 561.0
Smith-Bal 491.1
Seward-Phi 470.2
Weyhing-Phi 466.1

Fewest Hits/Game
Smith-Cin 8.05
Seward-Phi 8.51
Toole-Bro 8.63
Ramsey-Lou 8.73
Caruthers-StL . . . 8.89

Fewest BB/Game
Hecker-Lou 1.58
Caruthers-StL . . . 1.61
Lynch-NY 1.73
Foutz-StL 2.39
Kilroy-Bal 2.40

Strikeouts
Ramsey-Lou 355
Kilroy-Bal 217
Smith-Bal 206
Weyhing-Phi 193
Smith-Cin 176

Strikeouts/Game
Ramsey-Lou 5.70
Morrison-Cle 4.49
Terry-Bro 3.91
Smith-Bal 3.77
Weyhing-Phi 3.72

Ratio
Smith-Cin 10.76
Caruthers-StL . . . 10.93
Kilroy-Bal 11.64
Seward-Phi 11.65
Ramsey-Lou 11.66

Earned Run Average
Smith-Cin 2.94
Kilroy-Bal 3.07
Mullane-Cin 3.24
Caruthers-StL . . . 3.30
Ramsey-Lou 3.43

Adjusted ERA
Smith-Cin 148
Caruthers-StL . . . 137
Mullane-Cin 134
Kilroy-Bal 133
Ramsey-Lou 128

Opponents' Batting Avg.
Smith-Cin 230
Ramsey-Lou 242
Seward-Phi 244
Caruthers-StL . . .247
Kilroy-Bal 253

Opponents' On Base Pct.
Smith-Cin 286
Caruthers-StL . . .287
Ramsey-Lou 299
Kilroy-Bal 306
Foutz-StL 306

Starter Runs
Kilroy-Bal 80.0
Smith-Cin 67.3
Ramsey-Lou 53.5
Mullane-Cin 48.5
Caruthers-StL . . . 37.6

Adjusted Starter Runs
Smith-Cin 69.6
Kilroy-Bal 67.0
Ramsey-Lou 59.3
Mullane-Cin 50.7
Caruthers-StL . . . 46.7

Clutch Pitching Index
Daily-Cle 140
Crowell-Cle 122
Morrison-Cle 121
Mullane-Cin 119
Chamberlain-Lou . . 117

Relief Runs

Adjusted Relief Runs

Relief Ranking

Total Pitcher Index
Kilroy-Bal 7.3
Caruthers-StL . . . 6.2
Smith-Cin 6.0
Mullane-Cin 4.5
Ramsey-Lou 3.5

Total Baseball Ranking
Caruthers-StL . . . 7.7
Kilroy-Bal 7.1
Smith-Cin 5.9
O'Neill-StL 4.7
Mullane-Cin 4.3

TEAM	G	W	L	PCT	GB	R	OR	AB	H	2B	3B	HR	BB	SO	AVG	OBP	SLG	PRO	PRO+	BR	/A	PF	CHI	RC	SB	CS	SBA	SBR
NY	138	84	47	.641		659	479	4747	1149	130	76	55	270	456	.242	.287	.336	.623	105	21	29	99	102	562	314			
CHI	136	77	58	.570	9	734	659	4616	1201	147	95	77	290	563	.260	.308	.383	.691	118	127	74	107	99	649	287			
PHI	132	69	61	.531	14.5	535	509	4528	1021	151	46	16	268	485	.225	.276	.290	.566	82	-63	-91	105	100	441	246			
BOS	137	70	64	.522	15.5	669	619	4834	1183	167	69	56	282	524	.245	.291	.351	.642	97	51	39	102	97	593	293			
DET	134	68	63	.519	16	721	629	4849	1275	177	72	51	307	396	.263	.313	.361	.674	121	110	111	100	96	623	193			
PIT	139	66	68	.493	19.5	534	580	4713	1070	150	49	14	194	583	.227	.264	.289	.553	89	-93	-54	92	103	446	287			
IND	136	50	85	.370	36	603	731	4623	1100	180	33	34	236	492	.238	.281	.313	.594	93	-24	-35	102	103	518	350			
WAS	136	48	86	.358	37.5	482	731	4546	944	98	49	30	246	499	.208	.255	.271	.526	77	-129	-103	94	103	408	331			
TOT	544					4937		37456	8943	1200	509	333	2093	3998	.239	.285	.325	.609						2301				

TEAM	CG	SH	SV	IP	H	H/G	HR	BB	SO	RAT	ERA	ERA+	OAV	OOB	PR	/A	PF	CPI	FA	E	DP	FW	PW	BW	SBW	DIF
NY	133	20	1	1208	907	6.8	27	307	726	9.3	1.96	139	.199	.255	117	103	96	95	.924	432	76	1.2	10.1	2.9		4.3
CHI	123	13	1	1186¹	1139	8.6	63	308	588	11.4	2.96	102	.246	.301	-17	6	106	112	.927	417	112	1.7	.6	7.3		-.0
PHI	125	16	3	1167	1072	8.3	26	196	519	10.0	2.38	124	.236	.271	58	69	104	103	.923	424	70	.6	6.8	-9.0		5.6
BOS	134	7	0	1225¹	1104	8.1	36	269	484	10.4	2.61	109	.232	.280	30	27	100	100	.917	494	91	-2.2	2.7	3.8		-1.3
DET	130	10	1	1199	1115	8.4	44	183	522	10.0	2.74	100	.234	.266	12	-2	97	90	.919	463	83	-1.1	-.2	10.9		-7.1
PIT	135	13	0	1203¹	1190	8.9	23	223	367	10.8	2.67	99	.249	.287	22	-4	94	107	.927	416	88	2.3	-.4	-5.3		2.5
IND	132	6	0	1187²	1260	9.5	64	308	388	12.2	3.81	77	.263	.313	-129	-117	104	98	.921	449	84	-.0	-11.5	-3.4		-2.5
WAS	133	6	0	1179¹	1157	8.8	50	298	406	11.5	3.54	79	.248	.300	-93	-104	98	91	.912	494	69	-2.4	-10.2	-10.1		3.8
TOT	1045	91	6	9556		8.4				10.7	2.83		.239	.285					.921	3589	673					

Runs
Brouthers-Det	118
Ryan-Chi	115
Johnston-Bos	102
Anson-Chi	101
Connor-NY	98

Hits
Ryan-Chi	182
Anson-Chi	177
Johnston-Bos	173
Brouthers-Det	160
White-Det	157

Doubles
Ryan-Chi	33
Brouthers-Det	33
Johnston-Bos	31
Denny-Ind	27
Hines-Ind	26

Triples
Johnston-Bos	18
Connor-NY	17
Nash-Bos	15
Ewing-NY	15

Home Runs
Ryan-Chi	16
Connor-NY	14
Johnston-Bos	12
Denny-Ind	12
Anson-Chi	12

Total Bases
Ryan-Chi	283
Johnston-Bos	276
Anson-Chi	257
Brouthers-Det	242
Connor-NY	231

Runs Batted In
Anson-Chi	84
Nash-Bos	75
Rowe-Det	74
Williamson-Chi	73

Runs Produced
Brouthers-Det	175
Anson-Chi	173
Ryan-Chi	163
Johnston-Bos	158
Connor-NY	155

Bases On Balls
Connor-NY	73
Hoy-Was	69
Brouthers-Det	68
Williamson-Chi	65
Seery-Ind	64

Batting Average
Anson-Chi	.344
Ryan-Chi	.332
Kelly-Bos	.318
Brouthers-Det	.307
Ewing-NY	.306

On Base Percentage
Anson-Chi	.400
Brouthers-Det	.399
Connor-NY	.389
Ryan-Chi	.377
Hoy-Was	.374

Slugging Average
Ryan-Chi	.515
Anson-Chi	.499
Connor-NY	.480
Kelly-Bos	.480
Johnston-Bos	.472

Production
Anson-Chi	.899
Ryan-Chi	.892
Connor-NY	.869
Brouthers-Det	.862
Kelly-Bos	.848

Adjusted Production
Connor-NY	178
Brouthers-Det	174
Anson-Chi	173
Ryan-Chi	170
Kelly-Bos	166

Batter Runs
Ryan-Chi	49.4
Anson-Chi	49.3
Brouthers-Det	46.6
Connor-NY	43.7
Kelly-Bos	33.4

Adjusted Batter Runs
Brouthers-Det	46.8
Connor-NY	45.0
Anson-Chi	41.0
Ryan-Chi	40.8
Kelly-Bos	31.8

Clutch Hitting Index
Rowe-Det	153
Burns-Chi	150
Bassett-Ind	126
Wood-Phi	122
Nash-Bos	121

Runs Created
Ryan-Chi	133
Anson-Chi	117
Brouthers-Det	113
Connor-NY	103
Kelly-Bos	101

Total Average
Ryan-Chi	1.044
Kelly-Bos	1.007
Anson-Chi	.985
Brouthers-Det	.983
Connor-NY	.982

Stolen Bases
Hoy-Was	82
Seery-Ind	80
Sunday-Pit	71
Pfeffer-Chi	64
Ryan-Chi	60

Stolen Base Average

Stolen Base Runs

Fielding Runs
Pfeffer-Chi	38.3
Nash-Bos	25.6
Denny-Ind	24.5
Burns-Chi	17.1
Sunday-Pit	16.6

Total Player Rating
Nash-Bos	4.9
Pfeffer-Chi	4.4
Ewing-NY	3.9
Ryan-Chi	3.8
Anson-Chi	3.6

Wins
Keefe-NY	35
Clarkson-Bos	33
Conway-Det	30
Morris-Pit	29
Buffinton-Phi	28

Win Percentage
Keefe-NY	.745
Conway-Det	.682
Sanders-Phi	.655
Krock-Chi	.641
Clarkson-Bos	.623

Games
Morris-Pit	55
Clarkson-Bos	54
Keefe-NY	51
Galvin-Pit	50
Welch-NY	47

Complete Games
Morris-Pit	54
Clarkson-Bos	53
Galvin-Pit	49
Keefe-NY	48
Welch-NY	47

Shutouts
Sanders-Phi	8
Keefe-NY	8
Galvin-Pit	6
Buffinton-Phi	6

Saves
Wood-Phi	2
VanHaltren-Chi	1
Tyng-Phi	1
Twitchell-Det	1
Crane-NY	1

Innings Pitched
Clarkson-Bos	483.1
Morris-Pit	480.0
Galvin-Pit	437.1
Keefe-NY	434.1
Welch-NY	425.1

Fewest Hits/Game
Keefe-NY	6.57
Titcomb-NY	6.81
Welch-NY	6.94
Conway-Det	7.25
Buffinton-Phi	7.28

Fewest BB/Game
Sanders-Phi	1.08
Galvin-Pit	1.09
Krock-Chi	1.19
Getzien-Det	1.20
Madden-Bos	1.31

Strikeouts
Keefe-NY	335
Clarkson-Bos	223
Getzien-Det	202
Buffinton-Phi	199
O'Day-Was	186

Strikeouts/Game
Keefe-NY	6.94
Titcomb-NY	5.89
Baldwin-Chi	5.63
VanHaltren-Chi	5.09
Getzien-Det	4.50

Ratio
Keefe-NY	8.68
Buffinton-Phi	8.70
Conway-Det	8.86
Sanders-Phi	9.02
Gruber-Det	9.04

Earned Run Average
Keefe-NY	1.74
Sanders-Phi	1.90
Buffinton-Phi	1.91
Welch-NY	1.93
Sowders-Bos	2.07

Adjusted ERA
Keefe-NY	156
Sanders-Phi	156
Buffinton-Phi	154
Welch-NY	141
Sowders-Bos	137

Opponents' Batting Avg.
Keefe-NY	.196
Titcomb-NY	.201
Welch-NY	.207
Conway-Det	.208
Buffinton-Phi	.213

Opponents' On Base Pct.
Conway-Det	.243
Keefe-NY	.243
Buffinton-Phi	.244
Gruber-Det	.249
Titcomb-NY	.253

Starter Runs
Keefe-NY	52.6
Welch-NY	42.8
Buffinton-Phi	40.9
Sanders-Phi	28.6
Morris-Pit	28.0

Adjusted Starter Runs
Keefe-NY	47.3
Buffinton-Phi	46.2
Welch-NY	37.6
Sanders-Phi	32.2
Sowders-Bos	26.7

Clutch Pitching Index
Baldwin-Chi	137
Gleason-Phi	125
Burdick-Ind	116
Sowders-Bos	113
Morris-Pit	112

Relief Runs

Adjusted Relief Runs

Relief Ranking

Total Pitcher Index
Buffinton-Phi	5.8
Sanders-Phi	4.2
Keefe-NY	4.2
Conway-Det	3.9
Welch-NY	3.3

Total Baseball Ranking
Buffinton-Phi	5.7
Nash-Bos	4.9
Pfeffer-Chi	4.4
Keefe-NY	4.1
Ryan-Chi	4.0

TEAM	G	W	L	PCT	GB	R	OR	AB	H	2B	3B	HR	BB	SO	AVG	OBP	SLG	PRO	PRO+	BR	/A	PF	CHI	RC	SB	CS	SBA	SBR
STL	137	92	43	.681		789	**501**	4755	1189	149	47	**36**	**410**	521	.250	**.316**	.324	.640	98	54	-30	111	102	651	468			
BRO	143	88	52	.629	6.5	758	584	4871	1177	172	70	25	353	439	.242	.300	.321	.621	103	17	19	100	101	584	334			
PHI	136	81	52	.609	10	**827**	594	4828	**1209**	183	**89**	31	303	473	.250	.305	**.344**	**.649**	113	60	65	99	106	656	434			
CIN	137	80	54	.597	11.5	745	628	4801	1161	132	82	32	345	555	.242	.301	.323	.624	99	21	-18	105	100	623	**469**			
BAL	137	57	80	.416	36	653	779	4656	1068	162	70	19	298	479	.229	.284	.306	.590	96	-37	-19	97	99	511	326			
CLE	135	50	82	.379	40.5	651	839	4603	1076	128	59	12	315	559	.234	.294	.295	.589	96	-32	-13	97	99	516	353			
LOU	139	48	87	.356	44	689	870	4881	1177	**183**	67	14	322	604	.241	.297	.315	.612	102	1	16	98	94	565	318			
KC	132	43	89	.326	47.5	579	896	4588	1000	142	61	19	288	604	.218	.273	.288	.561	78	-84	-122	106	97	441	257			
TOT	548					5691		37983	9057	1251	545	188	2634	4234	.238	.297	.315	.612							2959			

TEAM	CG	SH	SV	IP	H	H/G	HR	BB	SO	RAT	ERA	ERA+	OAV	OOB	PR	/A	PF	CPI	FA	E	DP	FW	PW	BW	SBW	DIF
STL	132	12	0	1212²	**939**	7.0	19	225	517	9.1	2.09	156	.206	.254	130	156	107	96	**.924**	430	73	3.4	14.4	-2.8		9.4
BRO	**138**	9	0	1286¹	1059	7.4	15	285	577	9.7	2.33	128	.217	.266	104	92	97	97	.918	502	88	.6	8.5	1.8		7.2
PHI	133	**13**	0	1208²	988	7.4	**14**	324	596	10.4	2.41	124	.216	.279	87	76	98	102	.919	475	73	.7	7.0	**6.0**		.8
CIN	132	10	2	1237²	1103	8.0	19	310	539	10.8	2.73	116	.230	.288	46	60	104	102	.923	456	**100**	2.0	5.5	-1.7		7.2
BAL	130	3	0	1200¹	1162	8.7	23	419	525	12.5	3.78	79	.245	.318	-96	-108	97	93	.920	461	88	1.7	-10.0	-1.8		-1.5
CLE	131	6	1	1171	1235	9.5	38	389	500	12.9	3.72	83	.261	.324	-86	-82	101	105	.915	488	87	-.2	-7.6	-1.2		-7.0
LOU	133	6	0	1231¹	1264	9.2	28	281	**599**	11.7	3.25	95	.256	.304	-26	-24	100	105	.900	609	75	-6.2	-2.2	1.5		-12.5
KC	128	4	0	1157²	1306	10.2	32	401	381	13.8	4.29	80	.275	.340	-159	-112	112	101	.914	507	95	-1.9	-10.3	-11.3		.5
TOT	1057	63	3	9705²		8.4				11.3	3.06		.238	.297					.917	3928	679					

Runs		Hits		Doubles		Triples		Home Runs		Total Bases	
Pinkney-Bro	134	O'Neill-StL	177	Collins-Lou-Bro	31	Stovey-Phi	20	Reilly-Cin	13	Reilly-Cin	264
Collins-Lou-Bro	133	Reilly-Cin	169	Wolf-Lou	28	Burns-Bal-Bro	15	Stovey-Phi	9	Stovey-Phi	244
Stovey-Phi	127	McKean-Cle	164	Reilly-Cin	28	McKean-Cle	15	Larkin-Phi	7	O'Neill-StL	236
Welch-Phi	125	Collins-Lou-Bro	162	Larkin-Phi	28	Reilly-Cin	14			McKean-Cle	233
Latham-StL	119	Corkhill-Cin-Bro	160			Foutz-Bro	13			Burns-Bal-Bro	230

Runs Batted In		Runs Produced		Bases On Balls		Batting Average		On Base Percentage		Slugging Average	
Reilly-Cin	103	Reilly-Cin	202	Robinson-StL	116	O'Neill-StL	.335	Robinson-StL	.400	Reilly-Cin	.501
Larkin-Phi	101	O'Neill-StL	189	Fennelly-Cin-Phi	72	Reilly-Cin	.321	O'Neill-StL	.390	Stovey-Phi	.460
Foutz-Bro	99	Foutz-Bro	187	Nicol-Cin	67	Browning-Lou	.313	Browning-Lou	.380	O'Neill-StL	.446
O'Neill-StL	98	Larkin-Phi	186	McTamany-KC	67	Collins-Lou-Bro	.307	Collins-Lou-Bro	.373	Browning-Lou	.436
Corkhill-Cin-Bro	93	Welch-Phi	185	Pinkney-Bro	66	Orr-Bro	.305	Stovey-Phi	.365	Burns-Bal-Bro	.435

Production		Adjusted Production		Batter Runs		Adjusted Batter Runs		Clutch Hitting Index		Runs Created	
Reilly-Cin	.864	Reilly-Cin	167	Reilly-Cin	41.7	Stovey-Phi	38.6	Hotaling-Cle	153	Reilly-Cin	129
O'Neill-StL	.836	Stovey-Phi	165	O'Neill-StL	39.7	Reilly-Cin	35.5	Foutz-Bro	135	Stovey-Phi	124
Stovey-Phi	.825	Browning-Lou	164	Stovey-Phi	37.8	Collins-Lou-Bro	34.8	Lyons-Phi	133	Collins-Lou-Bro	112
Browning-Lou	.816	Collins-Lou-Bro	158	Collins-Lou-Bro	32.6	Burns-Bal-Bro	29.5	Gleason-Phi	132	Welch-Phi	106
Collins-Lou-Bro	.796	Burns-Bal-Bro	152	Burns-Bal-Bro	27.7	McKean-Cle	28.5	Smith-Bro	130	O'Neill-StL	105

Total Average		Stolen Bases		Stolen Base Average	Stolen Base Runs	Fielding Runs		Total Player Rating	
Reilly-Cin	1.064	Latham-StL	109			Shindle-Bal	36.8	Collins-Lou-Bro	4.0
Stovey-Phi	1.048	Nicol-Cin	103			McPhee-Cin	31.3	Stovey-Phi	3.5
Collins-Lou-Bro	.956	Welch-Phi	95			Davis-KC	29.8	McPhee-Cin	3.3
Robinson-StL	.934	McCarthy-StL	93			McCarthy-StL	29.8	Davis-KC	3.0
Browning-Lou	.928	Stovey-Phi	87			Easterday-KC	26.4	McKean-Cle	3.0

Wins		Win Percentage		Games		Complete Games		Shutouts		Saves	
King-StL	45	Hudson-StL	.714	King-StL	66	King-StL	64	Seward-Phi	6	Mullane-Cin	1
Seward-Phi	35	Chamberlain-Lou-SL	.694	Bakely-Cle	61	Bakely-Cle	60	King-StL	6	Gilks-Cle	1
Caruthers-Bro	29	King-StL	.682	Seward-Phi	57	Seward-Phi	57	Smith-Cin	5		
Weyhing-Phi	28	Caruthers-Bro	.659	Porter-KC	55	Porter-KC	53	Hudson-StL	5		
Viau-Cin	27	Viau-Cin	.659	Cunningham-Bal	51	Cunningham-Bal	50				

Innings Pitched		Fewest Hits/Game		Fewest BB/Game		Strikeouts		Strikeouts/Game		Ratio	
King-StL	585.2	Terry-Bro	6.69	King-StL	1.17	Seward-Phi	272	Terry-Bro	6.37	King-StL	8.34
Bakely-Cle	532.2	King-StL	6.72	Caruthers-Bro	1.22	King-StL	258	Ramsey-Lou	5.99	Caruthers-Bro	9.19
Seward-Phi	518.2	Seward-Phi	6.73	Hudson-StL	1.59	Ramsey-Lou	228	Chamberlain-Lou-SL	5.14	Seward-Phi	9.32
Porter-KC	474.0	Chamberlain-Lou-SL	6.95	Ewing-Lou	1.60	Bakely-Cle	212	Smith-Bal-Phi	4.90	Foutz-Bro	9.51
Cunningham-Bal	453.1	Hughes-Bro	6.97	Hecker-Lou	1.73	Weyhing-Phi	204	Seward-Phi	4.72	Hughes-Bro	9.55

Earned Run Average		Adjusted ERA		Opponents' Batting Avg.		Opponents' On Base Pct.		Starter Runs		Adjusted Starter Runs	
King-StL	1.64	King-StL	198	Terry-Bro	.200	King-StL	.237	King-StL	92.0	King-StL	104.9
Seward-Phi	2.01	Seward-Phi	148	King-StL	.200	Caruthers-Bro	.255	Seward-Phi	60.2	Seward-Phi	56.0
Terry-Bro	2.03	Terry-Bro	147	Seward-Phi	.201	Seward-Phi	.258	Hughes-Bro	37.3	Hughes-Bro	34.1
Hughes-Bro	2.13	Chamberlain-Lou-SL	143	Chamberlain-Lou-SL	.206	Foutz-Bro	.262	Weyhing-Phi	36.3	Weyhing-Phi	33.0
Chamberlain-Lou-SL	2.19	Hughes-Bro	140	Hughes-Bro	.206	Hughes-Bro	.262	Chamberlain-Lou-SL	29.7	Chamberlain-Lou-SL	32.4

Clutch Pitching Index		Relief Runs	Adjusted Relief Runs	Relief Ranking	Total Pitcher Index		Total Baseball Ranking	
Sullivan-KC	115				King-StL	11.4	King-StL	11.3
Hecker-Lou	112				Seward-Phi	4.9	Seward-Phi	4.8
Terry-Bro	110				Weyhing-Phi	3.7	Collins-Lou-Bro	4.0
Ramsey-Lou	106				Caruthers-Bro	3.5	Weyhing-Phi	3.6
Bakely-Cle	106				Chamberlain-Lou-SL	3.1	Caruthers-Bro	3.6

TEAM	G	W	L	PCT	GB	R	OR	AB	H	2B	3B	HR	BB	SO	AVG	OBP	SLG	PRO	PRO+	BR	/A	PF	CHI	RC	SB	CS	SBA	SBR
NY	131	83	43	.659		935	708	4671	1319	208	77	52	538	386	.282	.360	.393	.753	117	108	106	100	105	785	292			
BOS	133	83	45	.648	1	826	626	4628	1251	196	54	42	471	450	.270	.343	.363	.706	98	26	-22	106	104	707	331			
CHI	136	67	65	.508	19	867	814	4849	1274	184	66	79	518	516	.263	.338	.377	.715	101	36	-6	105	103	716	243			
PHI	130	63	64	.496	20.5	742	748	4695	1248	215	52	44	393	353	.266	.327	.362	.689	91	-12	-78	109	98	660	269			
PIT	134	61	71	.462	25	726	801	4748	1202	209	65	42	420	467	.253	.320	.351	.671	104	-44	26	90	99	622	231			
CLE	136	61	72	.459	25.5	656	720	4673	1167	131	59	25	429	417	.250	.318	.319	.637	86	-93	-80	98	97	563	237			
IND	135	59	75	.440	28	819	894	4879	1356	228	35	62	377	447	.278	.335	.377	.712	103	27	11	102	100	719	252			
WAS	127	41	83	.331	41	632	892	4395	1105	151	57	25	466	456	.251	.329	.329	.658	96	-49	-7	94	92	566	232			
TOT	531					6203		37538	9922	1522	465	371	3612	3492	.264	.334	.359	.693						2087				

TEAM	CG	SH	SV	IP	H	H/G	HR	BB	SO	RAT	ERA	ERA+	OAV	OOB	PR	/A	PF	CPI	FA	E	DP	FW	PW	BW	SBW	DIF
NY	118	6	3	1151	1073	8.4	38	523	558	12.9	3.47	114	.241	.327	71	56	98	102	.919	437	90	-.3	4.9	9.2		6.3
BOS	121	10	4	1166	1152	8.9	41	413	497	12.4	3.36	124	.250	.317	86	106	104	105	.926	413	105	1.2	9.2	-1.9		10.5
CHI	123	6	2	1237	1313	9.6	71	408	434	12.8	3.73	112	.262	.323	41	64	104	106	.923	463	91	-.8	5.5	-.5		-3.2
PHI	106	4	2	1153¹	1288	10.1	33	428	443	13.6	4.00	109	.275	.339	3	42	108	103	.915	466	92	-2.0	3.6	-6.8		4.6
PIT	125	5	1	1130²	1296	10.3	42	374	345	13.5	4.51	83	.272	.329	-60	-78	93	92	.931	385	94	2.8	-6.8	2.3		-3.3
CLE	132	6	1	1191²	1182	8.9	36	519	435	13.2	3.66	110	.251	.332	48	47	100	102	.936	365	108	4.2	4.1	-6.9		-6.8
IND	109	3	2	1174¹	1365	10.5	73	420	408	14.0	4.85	86	.282	.344	-108	-88	104	95	.926	420	102	1.2	-7.6	1.0		-2.5
WAS	113	1	0	1103	1261	10.3	37	527	388	14.9	4.68	85	.279	.359	-80	-90	98	99	.904	519	91	-5.2	-7.8	-.6		-7.4
TOT	947	41	15	9307		9.6				13.4	4.02		.264	.334					.923	3468	773					

Runs
Tiernan-NY 147
Duffy-Chi 144
Ryan-Chi 140
Gore-NY 132
Glasscock-Ind 128

Hits
Glasscock-Ind 205
Brouthers-Bos 181
Ryan-Chi 177
Duffy-Chi 172
VanHaltren-Chi 168

Doubles
Kelly-Ind 41
Glasscock-Ind 40
Thompson-Phi 36
O'Rourke-NY 36
Richardson-Bos 33

Triples
Wilmot-Was 19
Fogarty-Phi 17
Connor-NY 17
Tiernan-NY 14
Ryan-Chi 14

Home Runs
Thompson-Phi 20
Denny-Ind 18
Ryan-Chi 17
Connor-NY 13
Duffy-Chi 12

Total Bases
Ryan-Chi 287
Glasscock-Ind 272
Thompson-Phi 262
Connor-NY 262
Tiernan-NY 248

Runs Batted In
Connor-NY 130
Brouthers-Bos 118
Anson-Chi 117
Denny-Ind 112
Thompson-Phi 111

Runs Produced
Connor-NY 234
Duffy-Chi 221
Brouthers-Bos 216
Tiernan-NY 210
Anson-Chi 210

Bases On Balls
Tiernan-NY 96
Connor-NY 93
Radford-Cle 91
Anson-Chi 86
Carroll-Pit 85

Batting Average
Brouthers-Bos 373
Glasscock-Ind 352
Tiernan-NY 335
Carroll-Pit 330
Ewing-NY 327

On Base Percentage
Carroll-Pit 486
Brouthers-Bos 462
Tiernan-NY 447
Connor-NY 426
Gore-NY 416

Slugging Average
Connor-NY 528
Brouthers-Bos 507
Ryan-Chi 498
Tiernan-NY 497
Thompson-Phi 492

Production
Carroll-Pit 970
Brouthers-Bos 969
Connor-NY 955
Tiernan-NY 944
Ryan-Chi 886

Adjusted Production
Carroll-Pit 190
Connor-NY 166
Tiernan-NY 163
Brouthers-Bos 161
Wilmot-Was 146

Batter Runs
Brouthers-Bos 49.6
Tiernan-NY 47.0
Connor-NY 46.1
Carroll-Pit 37.9
Ryan-Chi 35.3

Adjusted Batter Runs
Carroll-Pit 47.9
Tiernan-NY 46.8
Connor-NY 45.8
Brouthers-Bos 41.7
Ryan-Chi 28.7

Clutch Hitting Index
Anson-Chi 140
Dunlap-Pit 133
Twitchell-Cle 133
Whitney-NY 133
Brouthers-Bos 132

Runs Created
Ryan-Chi 132
Glasscock-Ind 132
Tiernan-NY 129
Brouthers-Bos 127
Connor-NY 124

Total Average
Carroll-Pit 1.263
Tiernan-NY 1.151
Brouthers-Bos 1.145
Connor-NY 1.115
Ryan-Chi 1.023

Stolen Bases
Fogarty-Phi 99
Kelly-Bos 68
Brown-Bos 63
Ward-NY 62
Glasscock-Ind 57

Stolen Base Average

Stolen Base Runs

Fielding Runs
Glasscock-Ind 35.5
Fogarty-Phi 19.4
Pfeffer-Chi 19.3
Ewing-NY 15.5
Wilmot-Was 14.5

Total Player Rating
Glasscock-Ind 5.9
Ewing-NY 3.8
Tiernan-NY 3.5
Carroll-Pit 3.2
Wilmot-Was 3.2

Wins
Clarkson-Bos 49
Keefe-NY 28
Buffinton-Phi 28
Welch-NY 27
Galvin-Pit 23

Win Percentage
Clarkson-Bos 721
Welch-NY 692
Keefe-NY 683
Radbourn-Bos 645
Buffinton-Phi 636

Games
Clarkson-Bos 73
Staley-Pit 49
Keefe-NY 47
Buffinton-Phi 47
Boyle-Ind 46

Complete Games
Clarkson-Bos 68
Staley-Pit 46
Welch-NY 39
O'Brien-Cle 39
Keefe-NY 39

Shutouts
Clarkson-Bos 8
Galvin-Pit 4

Saves
Sowders-Bos-Pit 2
Welch-NY 2
Bishop-Chi 2

Innings Pitched
Clarkson-Bos 620.0
Staley-Pit 420.0
Buffinton-Phi 380.0
Boyle-Ind 378.2
Welch-NY 375.0

Fewest Hits/Game
Keefe-NY 7.89
Welch-NY 8.16
Clarkson-Bos 8.55
Crane-NY 8.65
Hutchison-Chi 8.66

Fewest BB/Game
Galvin-Pit 2.06
Boyle-Ind 2.26
Radbourn-Bos 2.34
Dwyer-Chi 2.35
Sanders-Phi 2.47

Strikeouts
Clarkson-Bos 284
Keefe-NY 225
Staley-Pit 159
Buffinton-Phi 153
Getzien-Ind 139

Strikeouts/Game
Keefe-NY 5.56
Crane-NY 5.09
Rusie-Ind 4.36
Healy-Was-Chi 4.35
Clarkson-Bos 4.12

Ratio
Clarkson-Bos 11.74
Radbourn-Bos . . . 11.76
Staley-Pit 11.94
Welch-NY 11.98
Keefe-NY 12.07

Earned Run Average
Clarkson-Bos 2.73
Bakely-Cle 2.96
Welch-NY 3.02
Buffinton-Phi 3.24
Keefe-NY 3.31

Adjusted ERA
Clarkson-Bos 153
Bakely-Cle 136
Buffinton-Phi 134
Welch-NY 131
Sanders-Phi 123

Opponents' Batting Avg.
Keefe-NY 228
Welch-NY 234
Clarkson-Bos 243
Crane-NY 245
Hutchison-Chi 245

Opponents' On Base Pct.
Clarkson-Bos 305
Radbourn-Bos 306
Staley-Pit 309
Welch-NY 310
Keefe-NY 311

Starter Runs
Clarkson-Bos 89.2
Welch-NY 41.7
Bakely-Cle 36.1
Buffinton-Phi 32.9
Keefe-NY 28.7

Adjusted Starter Runs
Clarkson-Bos 99.4
Buffinton-Phi 47.0
Welch-NY 38.5
Bakely-Cle 36.5
Sanders-Phi 31.3

Clutch Pitching Index
Casey-Phi 118
Clarkson-Bos 116
Bakely-Cle 113
Sanders-Phi 113
Crane-NY 112

Relief Runs

Adjusted Relief Runs

Relief Ranking

Total Pitcher Index
Clarkson-Bos 10.1
Buffinton-Phi 4.3
Bakely-Cle 3.4
Sanders-Phi 3.0
Welch-NY 2.8

Total Baseball Ranking
Clarkson-Bos 10.1
Glasscock-Ind 5.9
Buffinton-Phi 4.3
Ewing-NY 3.8
Tiernan-NY 3.5

TEAM	G	W	L	PCT	GB	R	OR	AB	H	2B	3B	HR	BB	SO	AVG	OBP	SLG	PRO	PRO+	BR	/A	PF	CHI	RC	SB	CS	SBA	SBR
BRO	140	93	44	.679		995	706	4815	1265	188	79	47	550	401	.263	.344	.364	.708	106	43	40	100	111	756	389			
STL	141	90	45	.667	2	957	680	4939	1312	211	64	58	493	477	.266	.339	.370	.709	94	38	-79	113	106	751	336			
PHI	138	75	58	.564	16	880	787	4868	1339	239	65	43	534	496	.275	.354	.377	.731	114	85	97	99	93	758	252			
CIN	141	76	63	.547	18	897	769	4844	1307	197	96	52	452	511	.270	.340	.382	.722	107	57	30	103	100	806	462			
BAL	139	70	65	.519	22	791	795	4756	1209	155	68	20	418	536	.254	.325	.328	.653	88	-56	-69	102	103	624	311			
COL	140	60	78	.435	33.5	779	924	4816	1247	171	95	36	507	609	.259	.335	.356	.691	106	8	51	95	91	693	304			
KC	139	55	82	.401	38	852	1031	4947	1256	162	76	18	430	626	.254	.322	.328	.650	84	-66	-112	106	108	692	472			
LOU	140	27	111	.196	66.5	632	1091	4955	1249	170	75	22	320	521	.252	.303	.330	.633	86	-109	-95	98	87	571	203			
TOT	559					6783		38940	10184	1493	618	296	3704	4177	.262	.333	.354	.687						2729				

TEAM	CG	SH	SV	IP	H	H/G	HR	BB	SO	RAT	ERA	ERA+	OAV	OOB	PR	/A	PF	CPI	FA	E	DP	FW	PW	BW	SBW	DIF
BRO	120	10	1	1212²	1205	8.9	33	400	471	12.2	3.61	103	.251	.315	31	14	97	93	.928	421	92	4.6	1.2	3.4		15.4
STL	121	7	3	1237²	1166	8.5	39	413	617	11.9	3.00	141	.242	.309	116	167	110	106	.925	438	100	3.8	14.1	-6.7		11.2
PHI	130	9	1	1199¹	1200	9.0	35	509	479	13.4	3.53	107	.253	.335	42	33	98	107	.920	465	120	1.7	2.8	8.2		-4.2
CIN	114	3	8	1243	1270	9.2	35	475	562	13.0	3.50	111	.257	.328	47	54	102	105	.926	440	121	3.7	4.6	2.5		-4.3
BAL	128	10	1	1192	1168	8.8	27	424	540	12.6	3.56	111	.249	.322	38	49	103	97	.907	536	104	-2.1	4.1	-5.8		6.3
COL	114	4		1199	1274	9.6	33	551	610	14.1	4.39	82	.264	.346	-73	-103	94	93	.915	497	92	.3	-8.7	4.3		-4.9
KC	128	0	2	1204¹	1373	10.3	51	457	447	14.1	4.36	96	.278	.347	-69	-25	109	101	.899	611	109	-6.3	-2.1	-9.5		4.3
LOU	127	2	1	1226¹	1529	11.2	43	475	451	15.1	4.81	80	.297	.362	-132	-133	100	101	.906	584	117	-4.5	-11.3	-8.0		-18.2
TOT	982	50	21	9714¹		9.4				13.3	3.84		.262	.333					.916	3992	855					

Runs		Hits		Doubles		Triples		Home Runs		Total Bases	
Stovey-Phi	152	Tucker-Bal	196	Welch-Phi	39	Marr-Col	15	Stovey-Phi	19	Stovey-Phi	292
Griffin-Bal	152	Orr-Col	183	Stovey-Phi	38	Griffin-Bal	14	Holliday-Cin	19	Holliday-Cin	280
O'Brien-Bro	146	Holliday-Cin	181	Lyons-Phi	36	Beard-Cin	14	Duffee-StL	16	Tucker-Bal	255
Hamilton-KC	144	O'Neill-StL	179	O'Neill-StL	33			Milligan-StL	12	O'Neill-StL	255
Collins-Bro	139	Shindle-Bal	178	Long-KC	32					Orr-Col	250

Runs Batted In		Runs Produced		Bases On Balls		Batting Average		On Base Percentage		Slugging Average	
Stovey-Phi	119	Stovey-Phi	252	Robinson-Cin	118	Tucker-Bal	.372	Tucker-Bal	.450	Stovey-Phi	.525
Foutz-Bro	113	Foutz-Bro	225	McTamany-Col	116	O'Neill-StL	.335	Larkin-Phi	.428	Holliday-Cin	.497
O'Neill-StL	110	O'Neill-StL	224	Griffin-Bal	91	Lyons-Phi	.329	Lyons-Phi	.426	Tucker-Bal	.484
Bierbauer-Phi	105	O'Brien-Bro	221	Marr-Col	87	Orr-Col	.327	O'Neill-StL	.419	O'Neill-StL	.478
Holliday-Cin	104	Hamilton-KC	218	Hamilton-KC	87	Holliday-Cin	.321	Hamilton-KC	.413	Lyons-Phi	.469

Production		Adjusted Production		Batter Runs		Adjusted Batter Runs		Clutch Hitting Index		Runs Created	
Tucker-Bal	.934	Tucker-Bal	163	Tucker-Bal	48.2	Tucker-Bal	45.8	Mack-Bal	147	Tucker-Bal	147
Stovey-Phi	.918	Stovey-Phi	162	Stovey-Phi	42.6	Stovey-Phi	44.5	Foutz-Bro	145	Stovey-Phi	143
O'Neill-StL	.897	Lyons-Phi	157	O'Neill-StL	39.9	Lyons-Phi	41.0	Johnson-Col	128	Hamilton-KC	136
Lyons-Phi	.895	Larkin-Phi	145	Lyons-Phi	39.3	Larkin-Phi	35.9	Hornung-Bal	127	O'Brien-Bro	129
Holliday-Cin	.869	Holliday-Cin	142	Larkin-Phi	34.2	Marr-Col	34.2	Collins-Bro	126	Holliday-Cin	124

Total Average		Stolen Bases		Stolen Base Average	Stolen Base Runs	Fielding Runs		Total Player Rating	
Tucker-Bal	1.187	Hamilton-KC	111			McPhee-Cin	41.1	Stovey-Phi	4.9
Hamilton-KC	1.134	O'Brien-Bro	91			Bierbauer-Phi	36.6	Bierbauer-Phi	4.5
Stovey-Phi	1.125	Long-KC	89			Long-KC	32.2	Lyons-Phi	4.5
O'Brien-Bro	1.020	Nicol-Cin	80			Tomney-Lou	26.7	Marr-Col	4.1
O'Neill-StL	1.014	Latham-StL	69			Shindle-Bal	20.3	McPhee-Cin	4.0

Wins		Win Percentage		Games		Complete Games		Shutouts		Saves	
Caruthers-Bro	40	Caruthers-Bro	.784	Baldwin-Col	63	Kilroy-Bal	55	Caruthers-Bro	7	Mullane-Cin	5
King-StL	35	King-StL	.686	Kilroy-Bal	59	Baldwin-Col	54	Baldwin-Col	6		
Duryea-Cin	32	Chamberlain-StL	.681	King-StL	56	Weyhing-Phi	50	Kilroy-Bal	5		
Chamberlain-StL	32	Lovett-Bro	.630	Caruthers-Bro	56	King-StL	47	Foreman-Bal	5		
Weyhing-Phi	30	Duryea-Cin	.627	Weyhing-Phi	54	Caruthers-Bro	46	Weyhing-Phi	4		

Innings Pitched		Fewest Hits/Game		Fewest BB/Game		Strikeouts		Strikeouts/Game		Ratio	
Baldwin-Col	513.2	Stivetts-StL	7.18	Caruthers-Bro	2.10	Baldwin-Col	368	Stivetts-StL	6.71	Stivetts-StL	10.61
Kilroy-Bal	480.2	Weyhing-Phi	7.66	Conway-KC	2.42	Kilroy-Bal	217	Baldwin-Col	6.45	Caruthers-Bro	11.35
King-StL	458.0	Terry-Bro	7.87	King-StL	2.46	Weyhing-Phi	213	Terry-Bro	5.13	Duryea-Cin	11.56
Weyhing-Phi	449.0	Foreman-Bal	7.91	Lovett-Bro	2.55	Chamberlain-StL	202	Sowders-KC	5.06	Foreman-Bal	11.76
Caruthers-Bro	445.0	Baldwin-Col	8.02	Swartzel-KC	2.57	King-StL	188	Gastright-Col	4.65	Conway-KC	11.77

Earned Run Average		Adjusted ERA		Opponents' Batting Avg.		Opponents' On Base Pct.		Starter Runs		Adjusted Starter Runs	
Stivetts-StL	2.25	Stivetts-StL	187	Stivetts-StL	.212	Stivetts-StL	.285	Duryea-Cin	57.3	Duryea-Cin	59.8
Duryea-Cin	2.56	Duryea-Cin	152	Weyhing-Phi	.223	Caruthers-Bro	.299	Kilroy-Bal	53.3	Chamberlain-StL	58.7
Kilroy-Bal	2.85	Chamberlain-StL	142	Terry-Bro	.228	Duryea-Cin	.303	Weyhing-Phi	44.8	Kilroy-Bal	58.4
Weyhing-Phi	2.95	Kilroy-Bal	138	Foreman-Bal	.229	Foreman-Bal	.306	Chamberlain-StL	41.1	King-StL	54.8
Chamberlain-StL	2.97	King-StL	134	Baldwin-Col	.231	Conway-KC	.306	King-StL	35.6	Stivetts-StL	41.9

Clutch Pitching Index		Relief Runs	Adjusted Relief Runs	Relief Ranking	Total Pitcher Index		Total Baseball Ranking	
Mullane-Cin	119				Kilroy-Bal	6.9	Kilroy-Bal	6.9
Duryea-Cin	116				Duryea-Cin	6.7	Duryea-Cin	6.6
Kilroy-Bal	114				Chamberlain-StL	4.7	Stovey-Phi	4.9
Hughes-Bro	110				King-StL	4.5	Chamberlain-StL	4.7
Weyhing-Phi	109				Caruthers-Bro	4.2	Bierbauer-Phi	4.5

TEAM	G	W	L	PCT	GB	R	OR	AB	H	2B	3B	HR	BB	SO	AVG	OBP	SLG	PRO	PRO+	BR	/A	PF	CHI	RC	SB	CS	SBA	SBR
BRO	129	86	43	.667		884	620	4419	1166	184	75	43	517	361	.264	.346	.369	.715	113	74	71	100	112	702	349			
CHI	139	84	53	.613	6	847	692	4891	1271	147	60	67	516	514	.260	.336	.356	.692	102	37	4	104	103	713	329			
PHI	133	78	54	.591	9.5	823	707	4707	1267	220	78	23	522	403	.269	.350	.364	.714	110	79	58	103	98	735	335			
CIN	134	77	55	.583	10.5	753	633	4644	1203	150	120	27	433	377	.259	.329	.360	.689	106	25	29	100	99	670	312			
BOS	134	76	57	.571	12	763	593	4722	1220	175	62	31	530	515	.258	.342	.341	.683	96	30	-33	108	96	665	285			
NY	135	63	68	.481	24	713	698	4832	1250	208	89	25	350	479	.259	.315	.354	.669	99	-16	-17	100	97	647	289			
CLE	136	44	88	.333	43.5	630	832	4633	1073	132	59	21	497	474	.232	.312	.299	.611	84	-96	-84	98	97	491	152			
PIT	138	23	113	.169	66.5	597	1235	4739	1088	160	43	20	408	458	.230	.300	.294	.594	87	-134	-65	88	97	492	208			
TOT	539					6010		37587	9538	1376	586	257	3773	3581	.254	.329	.342	.671							2259			

TEAM	CG	SH	SV	IP	H	H/G	HR	BB	SO	RAT	ERA	ERA+	OAV	OOB	PR	/A	PF	CPI	FA	E	DP	FW	PW	BW	SBW	DIF
BRO	115	6	2	1145	1102	8.7	27	401	403	12.2	3.06	112	.246	.315	64	47	96	104	.940	320	92	4.5	4.2	6.3		6.5
CHI	126	6	3	1237¹	1103	8.0	41	481	504	11.9	3.24	113	.234	.311	44	50	103	93	.940	344	89	4.9	4.4	.4		5.8
PHI	122	9	2	1194²	1210	9.1	22	486	507	13.2	3.32	110	.255	.331	32	43	102	107	.929	398	122	.4	3.8	5.2		2.6
CIN	124	9	1	1190²	1097	8.3	41	407	488	11.8	2.79	127	.238	.307	102	100	100	109	.932	382	106	1.6	8.9	2.6		-2.1
BOS	132	13	1	1187	1132	8.6	27	354	506	11.5	2.93	128	.245	.303	83	104	105	101	.935	359	77	3.0	9.2	-2.9		.2
NY	115	6	1	1177	1029	7.9	14	607	612	13.0	3.06	114	.230	.331	66	52	98	104	.921	449	104	-2.3	4.6	-1.5		-3.3
CLE	129	2	0	1184¹	1322	10.0	33	462	306	14.0	4.13	86	.273	.342	-75	-70	100	99	.930	405	108	.6	-6.2	-7.5		-8.9
PIT	119	3	0	1176¹	1520	11.6	52	573	381	16.6	5.97	55	.304	.384	-315	-350	92	91	.897	607	94	-11.5	-31.1	-5.8		3.3
TOT	982	54	10	9492¹		9.0				13.0	3.56		.254	.329					.928	3264	792					

Runs
Collins-Bro 148
Carroll-Chi 134
Hamilton-Phi 133
Tiernan-NY 132
McPhee-Cin 125

Hits
Thompson-Phi 172
Glasscock-NY 172
Tiernan-NY 168
Reilly-Cin 166
Carroll-Chi 166

Doubles
Thompson-Phi 41
Glasscock-NY 32
Collins-Bro 32
Myers-Phi 29
O'Brien-Bro 28

Triples
Reilly-Cin 26
McPhee-Cin 22
Tiernan-NY 21
Beard-Cin 15

Home Runs
Wilmot-Chi 13
Tiernan-NY 13
Burns-Bro 13
Long-Bos 8

Total Bases
Tiernan-NY 274
Reilly-Cin 261
Thompson-Phi 243
Wilmot-Chi 239
Glasscock-NY 225

Runs Batted In
Burns-Bro 128
Anson-Chi 107
Thompson-Phi 102
Wilmot-Chi 99
Foutz-Bro 98

Runs Produced
Burns-Bro 217
Thompson-Phi 214
Collins-Bro 214
Wilmot-Chi 200
Foutz-Bro 199

Bases On Balls
Anson-Chi 113
McKean-Cle 87
Allen-Phi 87
Collins-Bro 85
Hamilton-Phi 83

Batting Average
Glasscock-NY 336
Hamilton-Phi 325
Clements-Phi 315
O'Brien-Bro 314
Thompson-Phi 313

On Base Percentage
Anson-Chi .... .443
Hamilton-Phi 430
Pinkney-Bro 411
McKean-Cle 401
Glasscock-NY 395

Slugging Average
Tiernan-NY 495
Clements-Phi 472
Reilly-Cin 472
Burns-Bro 464
Burkett-NY 461

Production
Tiernan-NY 880
Clements-Phi 864
Anson-Chi 844
Pinkney-Bro 842
Glasscock-NY 834

Adjusted Production
Tiernan-NY 156
Clements-Phi 148
Pinkney-Bro 145
Glasscock-NY 143
McKean-Cle 141

Batter Runs
Tiernan-NY 37.9
Anson-Chi 37.6
Hamilton-Phi 31.7
Pinkney-Bro 30.8
McKean-Cle 28.9

Adjusted Batter Runs
Tiernan-NY 37.7
Anson-Chi 32.6
McKean-Cle 31.2
Pinkney-Bro 30.4
Hamilton-Phi 28.8

Clutch Hitting Index
Burns-Bro 150
Anson-Chi 145
Myers-Phi 140
Hines-Pit-Bos 138
Bassett-NY 129

Runs Created
Hamilton-Phi 132
Tiernan-NY 130
Wilmot-Chi 114
Glasscock-NY 113
Collins-Bro 111

Total Average
Hamilton-Phi 1.170
Tiernan-NY 1.047
Pinkney-Bro 1.015
Anson-Chi 1.009
Collins-Bro 1.005

Stolen Bases
Hamilton-Phi 102
Collins-Bro 85
Sunday-Pit-Phi ... 84
Wilmot-Chi 76
Tiernan-NY 56

Stolen Base Average

Stolen Base Runs

Fielding Runs
Allen-Phi 38.6
McPhee-Cin 30.0
Glasscock-NY 22.0
Smalley-Cle 16.6
Carroll-Chi 14.5

Total Player Rating
Glasscock-NY 4.9
McPhee-Cin 4.5
Allen-Phi 4.0
Clements-Phi 2.9
Collins-Bro 2.7

Wins
Hutchison-Chi 42
Gleason-Phi 38
Lovett-Bro 30
Rusie-NY 29
Rhines-Cin 28

Win Percentage
Lovett-Bro .... .732
Gleason-Phi ..... .691
Luby-Chi .... .690
Caruthers-Bro .... .676
Hutchison-Chi .... .627

Games
Hutchison-Chi 71
Rusie-NY 67
Gleason-Phi 60
Beatin-Cle 54
Nichols-Bos 48

Complete Games
Hutchison-Chi 65
Rusie-NY 56
Gleason-Phi 54
Beatin-Cle 53
Nichols-Bos 47

Shutouts
Nichols-Bos 7
Rhines-Cin 6
Gleason-Phi 6
Hutchison-Chi 5

Saves
Hutchison-Chi 2
Gleason-Phi 2
Foutz-Bro 2

Innings Pitched
Hutchison-Chi ..603.0
Rusie-NY 548.2
Gleason-Phi 506.0
Beatin-Cle 474.1
Nichols-Bos 424.0

Fewest Hits/Game
Rusie-NY 7.15
Mullane-Cin 7.54
Hutchison-Chi ... 7.54
Rhines-Cin 7.56
Luby-Chi 7.60

Fewest BB/Game
Young-Cle 1.83
Duryea-Cin 1.97
Getzien-Bos 2.11
Nichols-Bos 2.38
Rhines-Cin 2.53

Strikeouts
Rusie-NY 341
Hutchison-Chi ... 289
Nichols-Bos 222
Gleason-Phi 222
Terry-Bro 185

Strikeouts/Game
Rusie-NY 5.59
Nichols-Bos 4.71
Terry-Bro 4.50
Hutchison-Chi ... 4.31
Sharrott-NY 4.11

Ratio
Rhines-Cin 10.43
Nichols-Bos 10.55
Hutchison-Chi .. 10.70
Getzien-Bos 10.98
Duryea-Cin 11.10

Earned Run Average
Rhines-Cin 1.95
Nichols-Bos 2.23
Mullane-Cin 2.24
Rusie-NY 2.56
Gleason-Phi 2.63

Adjusted ERA
Rhines-Cin 182
Nichols-Bos 168
Mullane-Cin 159
Gleason-Phi 139
Rusie-NY 137

Opponents' Batting Avg.
Rusie-NY 212
Mullane-Cin 221
Hutchison-Chi 221
Rhines-Cin 221
Luby-Chi 222

Opponents' On Base Pct.
Rhines-Cin 282
Nichols-Bos 284
Hutchison-Chi 287
Getzien-Bos 292
Duryea-Cin 295

Starter Runs
Rhines-Cin 71.8
Nichols-Bos 62.8
Rusie-NY 61.1
Hutchison-Chi ... 57.6
Gleason-Phi 52.2

Adjusted Starter Runs
Nichols-Bos 71.3
Rhines-Cin 71.3
Hutchison-Chi ... 63.6
Gleason-Phi 57.0
Rusie-NY 57.0

Clutch Pitching Index
Mullane-Cin 131
Vickery-Phi 120
Rhines-Cin 118
Gleason-Phi 112
Nichols-Bos 110

Relief Runs

Adjusted Relief Runs

Relief Ranking

Total Pitcher Index
Rusie-NY 6.9
Nichols-Bos 6.7
Rhines-Cin 6.5
Hutchison-Chi 5.9
Gleason-Phi 4.6

Total Baseball Ranking
Rusie-NY 6.7
Nichols-Bos 6.6
Rhines-Cin 6.5
Hutchison-Chi 5.9
Glasscock-NY 4.9

TEAM	G	W	L	PCT	GB	R	OR	AB	H	2B	3B	HR	BB	SO	AVG	OBP	SLG	PRO	PRO+	BR	/A	PF	CHI	RC	SB	CS	SBA	SBR
LOU	136	88	44	.667		819	**588**	4687	1310	156	65	15	410	**460**	**.279**	.344	.350	.694	**113**	53	72	98	101	699	341			
COL	140	79	55	.590	10	831	617	4741	1225	159	77	16	**545**	557	.258	.341	.335	.676	112	29	**85**	93	**103**	677	353			
STL	139	78	58	.574	12	**870**	736	4800	1308	178	73	**48**	474	490	.273	**.350**	**.370**	**.720**	103	**100**	-23	114	98	**746**	307			
TOL	134	68	64	.515	20	739	689	4575	1152	152	**108**	24	486	558	.252	.333	.348	.681	103	31	9	103	94	687	**421**			
ROC	133	63	63	.500	22	709	711	4553	1088	131	64	31	446	538	.239	.315	.316	.631	98	-53	-2	93	**103**	564	310			
BAL	38	15	19	.441	24	182	192	1213	278	34	16	2	125	152	.229	.316	.289	.605	79	-23	-31	105	**103**	146	101			
SYR	128	55	72	.433	30.5	698	831	4469	1158	151	59	14	457	482	.259	.333	.329	.662	112	1	77	90	96	600	292			
PHI	132	54	78	.409	34	702	945	4490	1057	**181**	51	24	475	540	.235	.320	.314	.634	94	-41	-25	98	100	564	305			
BRO	100	26	73	.263	45.5	492	733	3475	769	116	47	13	328	456	.221	.294	.293	.587	80	-98	-82	97	106	362	182			
TOT	540					6042		37003	9345	1258	560	187	3746	4233	.253	.330	.332	.662						2612				

TEAM	CG	SH	SV	IP	H	H/G	HR	BB	SO	RAT	ERA	ERA+	OAV	OOB	PR	/A	PF	CPI	FA	E	DP	FW	PW	BW	SBW	DIF
LOU	114	13	**7**	1206	1120	8.4	18	**293**	587	10.9	**2.57**	149	.239	**.291**	**173**	**169**	100	**117**	**.934**	380	79	2.8	**14.9**	6.3		-2.0
COL	120	**14**	3	1214²	**976**	**7.2**	20	471	624	11.2	2.99	120	**.214**	.297	118	80	93	95	.932	396	**101**	2.6	7.0	**7.5**		-5.1
STL	118	4	1	1195¹	1127	8.5	38	447	**733**	12.3	3.67	117	.242	.316	25	82	112	98	.916	478	93	-1.8	7.2	-2.0		6.6
TOL	**122**	4	2	1159¹	1122	8.7	23	429	533	12.6	3.56	111	.247	.321	39	49	102	102	.925	419	75	.4	4.3	.8		-3.5
ROC	**122**	5	2	1161²	1115	8.6	19	530	477	13.2	3.56	100	.246	.331	39	-2	92	106	.926	416	95	.4	-.2	-.2		-.0
BAL	36	1	0	315¹	307	8.8	3	123	134	13.0	4.00	101	.248	.328	-5	2	105	92	.928	109	21	.6	.2	-2.7		-.0
SYR	115	5	0	1089²	1158	9.6	28	518	454	14.4	4.98	71	.265	.351	-135	-176	91	89	.925	391	90	.9	-15.5	6.8		-.7
PHI	119	3	2	1132	1405	11.2	**17**	514	461	15.8	5.22	73	.296	.373	-171	-176	99	99	.918	452	93	-1.6	-15.5	-2.2		7.3
BRO	96	0	0	879	1011	10.4	21	421	230	15.2	4.71	83	.281	.365	-83	-81	101	104	.909	404	92	-4.4	-7.1	-7.2		-4.8
TOT	962	49	17	9353		9.0				13.1	3.86		.253	.330					.923	3445	739					

Runs	Hits	Doubles	Triples	Home Runs	Total Bases
McTamany-Col 140	Wolf-Lou 197	Childs-Syr 33	Werden-Tol 20	Campau-StL 9	Wolf-Lou 260
McCarthy-StL 137	McCarthy-StL 192	Wolf-Lou 29	Johnson-Col 18	Cartwright-StL 8	McCarthy-StL 256
Fuller-StL 118	Johnson-Col 186	Lyons-Phi 29	Alvord-Tol 16	Stivetts-StL 7	Johnson-Col 248
Sneed-Tol-Col 117	Childs-Syr 170		Sneed-Tol-Col 15	Lyons-Phi 7	Childs-Syr 237
Welch-Phi-Bal 116	Taylor-Lou 169				Werden-Tol 227

Runs Batted In	Runs Produced	Bases On Balls	Batting Average	On Base Percentage	Slugging Average
	McTamany-Col ... 139	McTamany-Col ... 112	Wolf-Lou 363	Lyons-Phi 461	Lyons-Phi 531
	McCarthy-StL 131	Crooks-Col 96	Lyons-Phi 354	Swartwood-Tol .... .444	Campau-StL 513
	Fuller-StL 117	Swartwood-Tol 80	McCarthy-StL 350	Childs-Syr 434	Childs-Syr 481
	Sneed-Tol-Col 115	Werden-Tol 78	Johnson-Col 346	McCarthy-StL 430	Wolf-Lou 479
	Taylor-Lou 115	Scheffler-Roc 78	Childs-Syr 345	Wright-Syr 428	McCarthy-StL 467

Production	Adjusted Production	Batter Runs	Adjusted Batter Runs	Clutch Hitting Index	Runs Created
Lyons-Phi 992	Lyons-Phi 197	McCarthy-StL 45.6	Childs-Syr 58.5		McCarthy-StL..... 150
Childs-Syr 915	Childs-Syr 189	Childs-Syr 44.7	Wolf-Lou 46.3		Wolf-Lou 132
Wolf-Lou 900	Wolf-Lou 169	Wolf-Lou 43.3	Johnson-Col 46.0		Childs-Syr........ 130
McCarthy-StL......898	Johnson-Col 168	Lyons-Phi 41.4	Lyons-Phi 43.7		Johnson-Col 122
Swartwood-Tol 887	Swartwood-Tol 157	Swartwood-Tol ... 40.6	Swartwood-Tol ...37.2		Werden-Tol 118

Total Average	Stolen Bases	Stolen Base Average	Stolen Base Runs	Fielding Runs	Total Player Rating
Lyons-Phi 1.224	McCarthy-StL 83			Gerhardt-Bro-StL . 41.5	Childs-Syr 6.7
McCarthy-StL 1.169	Scheffler-Roc 77			Reilly-Col 28.2	Lyons-Phi 4.8
Childs-Syr 1.149	VanDyke-Tol 73			Ely-Syr 19.3	O'Connor-Col 3.7
Swartwood-Tol ...1.141	Welch-Phi-Bal 72			Tomney-Lou 17.6	Wolf-Lou 3.6
Werden-Tol 1.074				Welch-Phi-Bal 15.7	Swartwood-Tol.....3.5

Wins	Win Percentage	Games	Complete Games	Shutouts	Saves
McMahon-Phi-Bal .. 36	Stratton-Lou ..... .708	McMahon-Phi-Bal .. 60	McMahon-Phi-Bal .. 55	Chamberlain-SL-Col .. 6	Goodall-Lou 4
Stratton-Lou 34	Chamberlain-SL-Col .. .682	Barr-Roc........... 57	Barr-Roc 52	Stratton-Lou 4	Knauss-Col 2
Gastright-Col 30	Gastright-Col .... .682	Stivetts-StL 54	Stratton-Lou 44	Gastright-Col 4	Ehret-Lou 2
Barr-Roc 28	Ehret-Lou .... .641	Stratton-Lou....... 50	Healy-Tol 44	Ehret-Lou 4	
Stivetts-StL........ 27	McMahon-Phi-Bal .632	Gastright-Col 48			

Innings Pitched	Fewest Hits/Game	Fewest BB/Game	Strikeouts	Strikeouts/Game	Ratio
McMahon-Phi-Bal .. 509.0	Knauss-Col 6.73	Stratton-Lou 1.27	McMahon-Phi-Bal .. 291	Ramsey-StL 6.63	Stratton-Lou 9.86
Barr-Roc 493.1	Gastright-Col 7.00	Ehret-Lou 1.98	Stivetts-StL 289	Stivetts-StL 6.20	Gastright-Col 10.43
Stratton-Lou 431.0	Easton-Col 7.50	Ramsey-StL 2.63	Ramsey-StL 257	Meakim-Lou 5.77	Knauss-Col 10.87
Stivetts-StL...... 419.1	Chamberlain-SL-Col .. 7.50	Smith-Tol 2.83	Healy-Tol 225	Chamberlain-SL-Col ... 5.49	Healy-Tol 11.04
Gastright-Col 401.1	Healy-Tol 7.54	McMahon-Phi-Bal . 2.94	Barr-Roc 209	Healy-Tol 5.21	Ehret-Lou 11.21

Earned Run Average	Adjusted ERA	Opponents' Batting Avg.	Opponents' On Base Pct.	Starter Runs	Adjusted Starter Runs
Stratton-Lou 2.36	Stratton-Lou 163	Knauss-Col 202	Stratton-Lou 270	Stratton-Lou 72.0	Stratton-Lou 71.1
Ehret-Lou 2.53	Ehret-Lou........ 152	Gastright-Col 208	Gastright-Col 282	Ehret-Lou 53.1	Ehret-Lou 52.3
Knauss-Col......2.81	Healy-Tol 136	Knauss-Col 220	Knauss-Col 290	Healy-Tol 42.0	Healy-Tol 45.5
Chamberlain-SL-Col .. 2.83	Meakim-Lou 132	Chamberlain-SL-Col ..220	Healy-Tol 293	Gastright-Col..... 41.3	Stivetts-StL 36.7
Healy-Tol 2.89	Chamberlain-SL-Col .. 131	Healy-Tol 221	Ehret-Lou 296	Barr-Roc 33.8	McMahon-Phi-Bal .. 33.8

Clutch Pitching Index	Relief Runs	Adjusted Relief Runs	Relief Ranking	Total Pitcher Index	Total Baseball Ranking
Ehret-Lou 126				Stratton-Lou 8.9	Stratton-Lou 8.9
Titcomb-Roc 121				Stivetts-StL 4.9	Childs-Syr......... 6.7
Daily-Bro-Lou 113				Healy-Tol 4.7	Stivetts-StL 5.0
Stratton-Lou 110				Ehret-Lou 4.3	Lyons-Phi 4.8
Chamberlain-SL-Col .. 110				McMahon-Phi-Bal .. 4.0	Healy-Tol......... 4.6

TEAM	G	W	L	PCT	GB	R	OR	AB	H	2B	3B	HR	BB	SO	AVG	OBP	SLG	PRO	PRO+	BR	/A	PF	CHI	RC	SB	CS	SBA	SBR
BOS	130	81	48	.628		992	767	4626	1306	223	76	54	652	435	.282	.376	.398	.774	105	90	24	107	100	869	412			
BRO	133	76	56	.576	6.5	964	893	4887	1354	186	93	34	502	369	.277	.349	.374	.723	92	-12	-67	106	106	752	272			
NY	132	74	57	.565	8	1018	875	4913	1393	204	97	66	486	364	.284	.352	.405	.757	98	40	-44	109	106	800	231			
CHI	138	75	62	.547	10	886	770	4968	1311	200	95	31	492	410	.264	.335	.361	.696	87	-66	-102	104	102	712	276			
PHI	132	68	63	.519	14	941	855	4855	1348	187	113	49	431	321	.278	.343	.393	.736	100	0	-21	102	104	742	203			
PIT	128	60	68	.469	20.5	835	892	4577	1192	168	113	35	569	375	.260	.349	.369	.718	106	-15	56	92	97	694	249			
CLE	131	55	75	.423	26.5	849	1027	4804	1373	213	94	27	509	345	.286	.360	.386	.746	114	32	109	92	90	751	180			
BUF	134	36	96	.273	46.5	793	1199	4795	1249	180	64	20	541	367	.260	.347	.337	.684	96	-69	1	92	93	632	160			
TOT	529					7278		38425	10526	1561	745	316	4182	2986	.274	.351	.378	.729							1983			

TEAM	CG	SH	SV	IP	H	H/G	HR	BB	SO	RAT	ERA	ERA+	OAV	OOB	PR	/A	PF	CPI	FA	E	DP	FW	PW	BW	SBW	DIF
BOS	105	6	2	1137¹	1291	10.2	49	467	345	14.3	3.79	116	.274	.346	55	76	104	111	.918	460	109	1.7	6.1	1.9		6.8
BRO	111	4	7	1184	1334	10.1	26	570	377	14.9	3.95	113	.273	.356	37	65	105	106	.909	531	114	-1.8	5.2	-5.3		11.9
NY	111	3	6	1172¹	1219	9.4	37	569	449	14.1	4.17	109	.257	.343	8	47	107	92	.921	450	94	2.8	3.8	-3.5		5.5
CHI	124	5	2	1219¹	1238	9.1	27	503	460	13.2	3.39	128	.252	.327	114	128	103	100	.918	492	107	1.6	10.2	-8.1		2.8
PHI	118	4	2	1154¹	1292	10.1	33	495	361	14.4	4.05	105	.271	.347	22	27	101	100	.910	510	118	-.7	2.2	-1.7		2.8
PIT	121	7	0	1116²	1267	10.2	32	334	318	13.2	4.22	93	.274	.328	2	-39	92	89	.907	512	80	-1.7	-3.1	4.5		-3.6
CLE	115	1	0	1143²	1386	10.9	45	571	325	15.8	4.23	94	.287	.369	0	-33	94	114	.907	533	103	-2.3	-2.6	8.7		-13.8
BUF	125	2	0	1141	1499	11.8	67	673	351	17.5	6.11	67	.304	.393	-239	-257	97	93	.914	491	116	.8	-20.5	.0		-10.4
TOT	930	32	19	9268²		10.2				14.7	4.23		.274	.351					.913	3979	841					

Runs
- Duffy-Chi 161
- Brown-Bos 146
- Stovey-Bos 142
- Ward-Bro 134
- Connor-NY 133

Hits
- Duffy-Chi 191
- Ward-Bro 189
- Shindle-Phi 188
- Browning-Cle 184
- Richardson-Bos ... 181

Doubles
- Browning-Cle 40
- Beckley-Pit 38
- O'Rourke-NY 37
- Duffy-Chi 36
- Brouthers-Bos 36

Triples
- Visner-Pit 22
- Beckley-Pit 22
- Shindle-Phi 21
- Fields-Pit 20
- Joyce-Bro 18

Home Runs
- Connor-NY 14
- Richardson-Bos ... 13
- Stovey-Bos 12
- Shindle-Phi 10
- Gore-NY 10

Total Bases
- Shindle-Phi 281
- Duffy-Chi 280
- Beckley-Pit 276
- Richardson-Bos ... 274
- Connor-NY 265

Runs Batted In
- Richardson-Bos ... 146
- Orr-Bro 124
- Beckley-Pit 120
- O'Rourke-NY 115
- Larkin-Cle 112

Runs Produced
- Richardson-Bos ... 259
- Duffy-Chi 236
- Connor-NY 222
- Bierbauer-Bro 220
- Beckley-Pit 220

Bases On Balls
- Joyce-Bro 123
- Robinson-Pit 101
- Brouthers-Bos 99
- Hoy-Buf 94

Batting Average
- Browning-Cle .... .373
- Orr-Bro .... .373
- O'Rourke-NY .... .360
- Connor-NY .... .349
- Ryan-Chi .... .340

On Base Percentage
- Brouthers-Bos .... .466
- Browning-Cle .... .459
- Connor-NY .... .450
- Robinson-Pit .... .434
- Gore-NY .... .432

Slugging Average
- Connor-NY .... .548
- B.Ewing-NY .... .545
- Orr-Bro .... .537
- Beckley-Pit .... .535
- Browning-Cle .... .517

Production
- Connor-NY .... .998
- Browning-Cle .... .976
- Orr-Bro .... .952
- Gore-NY .... .931
- O'Rourke-NY .... .925

Adjusted Production
- Browning-Cle 175
- Beckley-Pit 156
- Larkin-Cle 154
- Connor-NY 152
- Orr-Bro 145

Batter Runs
- Connor-NY 47.6
- Browning-Cle 45.2
- Brouthers-Bos ... 38.1
- Orr-Bro 33.0
- Larkin-Cle 31.0

Adjusted Batter Runs
- Browning-Cle 57.1
- Larkin-Cle 41.8
- Beckley-Pit 38.7
- Connor-NY 35.2
- Brouthers-Bos ... 29.2

Clutch Hitting Index
- Richardson-Bos ... 128
- Orr-Bro 127
- Brouthers-Bos 125
- Wise-Buf 119
- Larkin-Cle 118

Runs Created
- Duffy-Chi 141
- Browning-Cle 136
- Stovey-Bos 134
- Connor-NY 132
- Shindle-Phi 126

Total Average
- Stovey-Bos 1.210
- Connor-NY 1.194
- Browning-Cle 1.191
- Brouthers-Bos 1.149
- Gore-NY 1.129

Stolen Bases
- Stovey-Bos 97
- Brown-Bos 79
- Duffy-Chi 78
- Hanlon-Pit 65
- Ward-Bro 63

Stolen Base Average

Stolen Base Runs

Fielding Runs
- Farrell-Chi 26.5
- Richardson-NY ... 25.3
- Bierbauer-Bro 24.8
- Pfeffer-Chi 24.1
- Ward-Bro 21.3

Total Player Rating
- Browning-Cle 4.5
- Connor-NY 3.1
- B.Ewing-NY 3.0
- Ward-Bro 2.9
- Beckley-Pit 2.5

Wins
- Baldwin-Chi 34
- Weyhing-Bro 30
- King-Chi 30
- Radbourn-Bos 27
- Gumbert-Bos 23

Win Percentage
- Daley-Bos .... .720
- Radbourn-Bos ... .692
- Knell-Phi .... .667
- Gumbert-Bos .... .657
- Weyhing-Bro .... .652

Games
- Baldwin-Chi 59
- King-Chi 56
- Weyhing-Bro 49
- Gruber-Cle 48
- Staley-Pit 46

Complete Games
- Baldwin-Chi 54
- King-Chi 48
- Staley-Pit 44
- Gruber-Cle 39
- Weyhing-Bro 38

Shutouts
- King-Chi 4
- Weyhing-Bro 3
- Staley-Pit 3

Saves
- Hemming-Cle-Bro ... 3
- O'Day-NY 3

Innings Pitched
- Baldwin-Chi 501.0
- King-Chi 461.0
- Weyhing-Bro 390.0
- Staley-Pit 387.2
- Gruber-Cle 383.1

Fewest Hits/Game
- King-Chi 8.20
- Crane-NY 8.80
- Hemming-Cle-Bro ... 8.88
- Baldwin-Chi 8.95
- Keefe-NY 8.96

Fewest BB/Game
- Staley-Pit 1.72
- Sanders-Phi 1.79
- Galvin-Pit 2.03
- Morris-Pit 2.18
- Radbourn-Bos 2.62

Strikeouts
- Baldwin-Chi 211
- King-Chi 185
- Weyhing-Bro 177
- Staley-Pit 145
- J.Ewing-NY 145

Strikeouts/Game
- J.Ewing-NY 4.88
- Daley-Bos 4.21
- Weyhing-Bro 4.08
- McGill-Cle 4.02
- Haddock-Buf 3.81

Ratio
- Staley-Pit 11.07
- King-Chi 11.67
- Radbourn-Bos ... 12.15
- Keefe-NY 12.62
- Sanders-Phi 12.75

Earned Run Average
- King-Chi 2.69
- Staley-Pit 3.23
- Baldwin-Chi 3.31
- Radbourn-Bos 3.31
- Keefe-NY 3.38

Adjusted ERA
- King-Chi 161
- Keefe-NY 134
- Radbourn-Bos ... 133
- Baldwin-Chi 131
- Weyhing-Bro 124

Opponents' Batting Avg.
- King-Chi .... .232
- Crane-NY .... .245
- Hemming-Cle-Bro ... .247
- Baldwin-Chi .... .248
- Keefe-NY .... .249

Opponents' On Base Pct.
- Staley-Pit .... .290
- King-Chi .... .301
- Radbourn-Bos .... .310
- Keefe-NY .... .318
- Sanders-Phi .... .320

Starter Runs
- King-Chi 78.6
- Baldwin-Chi 51.4
- Staley-Pit 43.2
- Radbourn-Bos 35.2
- Weyhing-Bro 27.2

Adjusted Starter Runs
- King-Chi 84.2
- Baldwin-Chi 57.5
- Radbourn-Bos ... 41.4
- Weyhing-Bro 37.0
- Keefe-NY 29.5

Clutch Pitching Index
- O'Brien-Cle 126
- Daley-Bos 124
- McGill-Cle 117
- Kilroy-Bos 114
- Gruber-Cle 114

Relief Runs

Adjusted Relief Runs

Relief Ranking

Total Pitcher Index
- King-Chi 7.1
- Baldwin-Chi 5.2
- Radbourn-Bos 3.7
- Staley-Pit 2.5
- Sanders-Phi 2.4

Total Baseball Ranking
- King-Chi 7.1
- Baldwin-Chi 5.2
- Browning-Cle 4.5
- Radbourn-Bos 3.5
- Connor-NY 3.1

TEAM	G	W	L	PCT	GB	R	OR	AB	H	2B	3B	HR	BB	SO	AVG	OBP	SLG	PRO	PRO+	BR	/A	PF	CHI	RC	SB	CS	SBA	SBR
BOS	140	87	51	.630		**847**	**658**	4956	1264	181	81	53	**532**	538	.255	**.337**	.356	**.693**	97	**52**	-47	112	101	**710**	289			
CHI	137	82	53	.607	3.5	832	730	4873	1233	159	88	**60**	526	457	.253	.332	.359	.691	107	42	43	100	102	676	238			
NY	136	71	61	.538	13	754	711	4833	1271	189	72	46	438	394	**.263**	.329	**.360**	.689	**111**	34	**66**	96	96	663	224			
PHI	138	68	69	.496	18.5	756	773	4929	1244	180	51	21	482	412	.252	.326	.322	.648	92	-27	-46	103	101	609	232			
CLE	141	65	74	.468	22.5	835	888	5074	**1294**	183	88	22	519	464	.255	.330	.339	.669	97	6	-27	104	**104**	663	242			
BRO	137	61	76	.445	25.5	765	820	4748	1233	**200**	69	23	464	435	.260	.330	.345	.675	103	15	20	99	101	669	**337**			
CIN	138	56	81	.409	30.5	646	790	4791	1158	148	90	40	414	439	.242	.308	.335	.643	92	-49	-54	101	93	584	244			
PIT	137	55	80	.407	30.5	679	744	4794	1148	148	71	29	427	503	.239	.308	.318	.626	90	-73	-56	98	101	547	205			
TOT	552					6114		38998	9845	1388	610	294	3802	3642	.252	.325	.342	.667							2011			

TEAM	CG	SH	SV	IP	H	H/G	HR	BB	SO	RAT	ERA	ERA+	OAV	OOB	PR	/A	PF	CPI	FA	E	DP	FW	PW	BW	SBW	DIF
BOS	**126**	9	6	1241²	1223	8.9	51	364	525	11.8	**2.76**	132	.248	.305	80	122	109	109	**.938**	358	96	4.7	10.9	-4.2		6.6
CHI	114	6	3	1220²	1207	8.9	53	475	477	12.7	3.47	96	.249	.322	-17	-21	100	96	.932	397	**119**	1.5	-1.9	3.8		11.0
NY	117	**11**	3	1204	**1098**	8.2	26	593	**651**	13.1	2.99	107	**.234**	.327	47	28	96	104	.933	384	104	2.2	2.5	**5.9**		-5.5
PHI	105	3	5	1229¹	1280	9.4	29	505	343	13.4	3.73	91	.259	.333	-53	-46	102	94	.925	443	108	-1.3	-4.1	-4.1		9.0
CLE	118	1	3	1244	1371	9.9	**24**	466	400	13.6	3.50	99	.270	.336	-22	-7	103	105	.920	485	86	-3.5	-.6	-2.4		2.0
BRO	121	8	3	1204²	1272	9.5	40	459	407	13.4	3.86	86	.261	.332	-68	-75	99	93	.924	432	73	-.8	-6.7	1.8		-1.8
CIN	125	6	1	1218²	1234	9.1	40	465	393	13.0	3.55	95	.253	.326	-28	-25	101	96	.931	409	101	.9	-2.2	-4.8		-6.4
PIT	122	7	2	1197²	1160	8.7	31	465	446	12.7	2.89	114	.245	.320	61	51	98	**109**	.917	475	76	-3.6	4.6	-5.0		-8.4
TOT	948	51	26	9760²		9.1				12.9	3.34		.252	.325					.928	3383	763					

Runs
Hamilton-Phi 141
Long-Bos 129
Childs-Cle 120
Latham-Cin 119
Stovey-Bos 118

Hits
Hamilton-Phi 179
McKean-Cle 170
Tiernan-NY 166
Davis-Cle 165
O'Rourke-NY 164

Doubles
Griffin-Bro 36
Davis-Cle 35
Stovey-Bos 31
Tiernan-NY 30

Triples
Stovey-Bos 20
Beckley-Pit 19
McPhee-Cin 16
Ryan-Chi 15
Virtue-Cle 14

Home Runs
Tiernan-NY 16
Stovey-Bos 16
Wilmot-Chi 11

Total Bases
Stovey-Bos 271
Tiernan-NY 268
Long-Bos 235
Davis-Cle 233
Beckley-Pit 232

Runs Batted In
Anson-Chi 120
Stovey-Bos 95
O'Rourke-NY 95
Nash-Bos 95
Connor-NY 94

Runs Produced
Davis-Cle 201
Childs-Cle 201
Hamilton-Phi 199
Connor-NY 199
Stovey-Bos 197

Bases On Balls
Hamilton-Phi 102
Childs-Cle 97
Connor-NY 83
Long-Bos 80
Pfeffer-Chi 79

Batting Average
Hamilton-Phi 340
Holliday-Cin 319
Browning-Pit-Cin . .317
Clements-Phi 310
Tiernan-NY 306

On Base Percentage
Hamilton-Phi . .453
Connor-NY 399
Childs-Cle 395
Browning-Pit-Cin .395
Tiernan-NY 388

Slugging Average
Stovey-Bos 498
Tiernan-NY 494
Holliday-Cin 473
Connor-NY 449
Ryan-Chi 434

Production
Tiernan-NY 882
Hamilton-Phi 874
Stovey-Bos 870
Holliday-Cin 848
Connor-NY 848

Adjusted Production
Tiernan-NY 163
Connor-NY 153
Hamilton-Phi 151
Holliday-Cin 145
Browning-Pit-Cin . . 139

Batter Runs
Hamilton-Phi 44.1
Tiernan-NY 37.8
Stovey-Bos 34.9
Connor-NY 30.7
Holliday-Cin 24.3

Adjusted Batter Runs
Tiernan-NY 42.9
Hamilton-Phi 40.8
Connor-NY 35.3
Holliday-Cin 23.7
Browning-Pit-Cin . . 22.0

Clutch Hitting Index
Anson-Chi 130
Delahanty-Phi 126
Brodie-Bos 119
Zimmer-Cle 119
Allen-Phi 119

Runs Created
Hamilton-Phi 155
Tiernan-NY 128
Stovey-Bos 125
Long-Bos 114
Latham-Cin 112

Total Average
Hamilton-Phi 1.270
Tiernan-NY 1.045
Stovey-Bos 1.041
Latham-Cin 974
Connor-NY 968

Stolen Bases
Hamilton-Phi 111
Latham-Cin 87
Griffin-Bro 65
Long-Bos 60

Stolen Base Average

Stolen Base Runs

Fielding Runs
Richardson-NY . . . 49.1
Griffin-Bro 25.7
Pfeffer-Chi 25.0
McPhee-Cin 23.3
Latham-Cin 20.4

Total Player Rating
Richardson-NY 4.5
Latham-Cin 3.7
Hamilton-Phi 3.7
Pfeffer-Chi 3.2
McPhee-Cin 3.1

Wins
Hutchison-Chi 44
Rusie-NY 33
Clarkson-Bos 33
Nichols-Bos 30
Young-Cle 27

Win Percentage
J.Ewing-NY 724
Hutchison-Chi 698
Staley-Pit-Bos 649
Nichols-Bos 638
Clarkson-Bos 635

Games
Hutchison-Chi 66
Rusie-NY 61
Young-Cle 55
Clarkson-Bos 55

Complete Games
Hutchison-Chi 56
Rusie-NY 52
Baldwin-Pit 48
Clarkson-Bos 47
Nichols-Bos 45

Shutouts
Rusie-NY 6
Nichols-Bos 5
J.Ewing-NY 5
Hutchison-Chi 4

Saves
Nichols-Bos 3
Clarkson-Bos 3
Young-Cle 2
Thornton-Phi 2

Innings Pitched
Hutchison-Chi . . . 561.0
Rusie-NY 500.1
Clarkson-Bos 460.2
Baldwin-Pit 437.2
Mullane-Cin 426.1

Fewest Hits/Game
Rusie-NY 7.03
Baldwin-Pit 7.92
J.Ewing-NY 7.92
Hutchison-Chi 8.15
Mullane-Cin 8.23

Fewest BB/Game
Nichols-Bos 2.18
Staley-Pit-Bos 2.22
Galvin-Pit 2.26
Radbourn-Cin 2.56
Hutchison-Chi 2.86

Strikeouts
Rusie-NY 337
Hutchison-Chi 261
Nichols-Bos 240
Baldwin-Pit 197
King-Pit 160

Strikeouts/Game
Rusie-NY 6.06
Nichols-Bos 5.08
J.Ewing-NY 4.61
Hutchison-Chi 4.19
Baldwin-Pit 4.05

Ratio
Staley-Pit-Bos 11.08
Hutchison-Chi 11.12
Nichols-Bos 11.28
J.Ewing-NY 11.80
Clarkson-Bos 11.80

Earned Run Average
J.Ewing-NY 2.27
Nichols-Bos 2.39
Rusie-NY 2.55
Staley-Pit-Bos . . . 2.58
Baldwin-Pit 2.76

Adjusted ERA
Nichols-Bos 153
J.Ewing-NY 141
Staley-Pit-Bos 138
Clarkson-Bos 131
Rusie-NY 125

Opponents' Batting Avg.
Rusie-NY 207
Baldwin-Pit 228
J.Ewing-NY 228
Hutchison-Chi 233
Mullane-Cin 234

Opponents' On Base Pct.
Staley-Pit-Bos 292
Hutchison-Chi 293
Nichols-Bos 296
J.Ewing-NY 305
Clarkson-Bos 305

Starter Runs
Nichols-Bos 45.1
Rusie-NY 43.9
Hutchison-Chi 33.5
J.Ewing-NY 32.1
Baldwin-Pit 28.6

Adjusted Starter Runs
Nichols-Bos 59.6
Clarkson-Bos 43.9
Rusie-NY 35.7
Staley-Pit-Bos 35.5
Hutchison-Chi 32.4

Clutch Pitching Index
Viau-Cle 117
Nichols-Bos 116
Caruthers-Bro 116
Galvin-Pit 112
J.Ewing-NY 111

Relief Runs

Adjusted Relief Runs

Relief Ranking

Total Pitcher Index
Nichols-Bos 5.8
Clarkson-Bos 4.8
Rusie-NY 3.7
Staley-Pit-Bos 3.1
Hutchison-Chi 2.7

Total Baseball Ranking
Nichols-Bos 5.8
Clarkson-Bos 4.7
Richardson-NY 4.5
Latham-Cin 3.7
Hamilton-Phi 3.7

TEAM	G	W	L	PCT	GB	R	OR	AB	H	2B	3B	HR	BB	SO	AVG	OBP	SLG	PRO	PRO+	BR	/A	PF	CHI	RC	SB	CS	SBA	SBR
BOS	139	93	42	.689		1028	675	4889	1341	163	100	52	651	499	.274	.367	.380	.747	121	127	142	99	106	868	447			
STL	141	86	52	.623	8.5	976	753	5005	1330	169	51	58	625	440	.266	.357	.355	.712	95	65	-72	115	106	753	283			
MIL	36	21	15	.583	22.5	227	156	1271	332	58	15	13	107	114	.261	.333	.361	.694	86	3	-40	120	106	173	47			
BAL	139	71	64	.526	22	850	798	4771	1217	142	99	30	551	553	.255	.346	.345	.691	102	22	13	101	101	705	342			
PHI	143	73	66	.525	22	817	794	5039	1301	182	123	55	447	548	.258	.328	.376	.704	103	23	-3	103	95	686	149			
COL	138	61	76	.445	33	702	777	4697	1113	154	61	20	529	530	.237	.319	.308	.627	89	-93	-54	94	101	565	280			
CIN	102	43	57	.430	32.5	549	643	3574	838	105	58	28	428	385	.234	.322	.320	.642	81	-52	-101	109	99	432	164			
LOU	141	55	84	.396	40	713	890	4833	1247	130	69	17	443	473	.258	.329	.324	.653	93	-52	-42	99	95	606	230			
WAS	139	44	91	.326	49	691	1067	4715	1183	147	84	19	468	485	.251	.328	.330	.658	97	-43	-9	96	93	597	219			
TOT	559					6553		38794	9902	1250	660	292	4249	4027	.255	.338	.344	.682							2161			

TEAM	CG	SH	SV	IP	H	H/G	HR	BB	SO	RAT	ERA	ERA+	OAV	OOB	PR	/A	PF	CPI	FA	E	DP	FW	PW	BW	SBW	DIF
BOS	108	9	7	1219²	1158	8.5	42	497	524	12.6	3.03	115	.242	.321	94	62	94	109	.934	392	115	4.0	5.3	12.2		4.0
STL	103	8	5	1222²	1106	8.1	50	576	621	12.9	3.27	129	.234	.325	61	126	113	102	.920	468	91	-.2	10.9	-6.2		12.5
MIL	35	3	0	309²	291	8.5	6	120	137	12.2	2.50	176	.241	.314	42	65	118	122	.922	116	20	.2	5.6	-3.4		.7
BAL	118	6	2	1217	1238	9.2	33	472	408	13.1	3.43	109	.255	.329	39	40	100	103	.915	503	103	-2.6	3.4	1.1		1.6
PHI	135	3	0	1233²	1274	9.3	35	520	533	13.6	4.01	95	.258	.338	-40	-27	103	93	.933	389	109	4.9	-2.3	-.3		1.2
COL	118	6	0	1213¹	1141	8.5	29	588	502	13.5	3.75	92	.241	.336	-4	-39	93	93	.935	379	126	4.5	-3.4	-4.7		-4.0
CIN	86	2	1	902	921	9.2	20	446	331	14.2	3.43	120	.256	.347	29	68	111	112	.913	389	68	-3.1	5.9	-8.7		-1.1
LOU	128	9	1	1226	1353	9.9	33	464	485	13.8	4.27	85	.271	.341	-75	-85	98	92	.922	458	113	.4	-7.3	-3.6		-4.0
WAS	123	2	2	1181	1420	10.8	44	566	486	15.9	4.83	77	.288	.374	-146	-144	101	101	.900	589	95	-7.7	-12.4	-.8		-2.6
TOT	954	48	18	9725		9.2				13.6	3.72		.255	.338					.922	3683	840					

Runs
Brown-Bos 177
VanHaltren-Bal 136
Hoy-StL 136
Duffy-Bos 134
McCarthy-StL 127

Hits
Brown-Bos 189
VanHaltren-Bal 180
Duffy-Bos 180
McCarthy-StL 179
Brouthers-Bos 170

Doubles
Milligan-Phi 35
Brown-Bos 30
O'Neill-StL 28
Duffee-Col 28
Larkin-Phi 27

Triples
Brown-Bos 21
Brouthers-Bos 19
Canavan-Cin-Mil ... 18
Werden-Bal 18

Home Runs
Farrell-Bos 12
Milligan-Phi 11
Lyons-StL 11

Total Bases
Brown-Bos 276
VanHaltren-Bal 251
Brouthers-Bos 249
Duffy-Bos 243
McCarthy-StL 236

Runs Batted In
Farrell-Bos 110
Duffy-Bos 110
Brouthers-Bos 109
Milligan-Phi 106
Werden-Bal 104

Runs Produced
Brown-Bos 244
Duffy-Bos 235
Brouthers-Bos 221
McCarthy-StL 214
VanHaltren-Bal 210

Bases On Balls
Hoy-StL 119
Crooks-Col 103
McTamany-Col-Phi 101
Radford-Bos 96
Johnson-Bal 89

Batting Average
Brouthers-Bos 350
Duffy-Bos 336
Brown-Bos 321
O'Neill-StL 321
VanHaltren-Bal 318

On Base Percentage
Brouthers-Bos 471
Lyons-StL 445
Hoy-StL 424
Seery-Cin 423
Duffy-Bos 408

Slugging Average
Brouthers-Bos 512
Milligan-Phi 505
Farrell-Bos 474
Brown-Bos 469
Cross-Phi 458

Production
Brouthers-Bos 983
Milligan-Phi 903
Lyons-StL 900
Brown-Bos 865
Duffy-Bos 861

Adjusted Production
Brouthers-Bos 184
Milligan-Phi 153
Brown-Bos 150
Duffy-Bos 149
Farrell-Bos 147

Batter Runs
Brouthers-Bos 57.0
Lyons-StL 39.2
Brown-Bos 35.2
Milligan-Phi 33.3
Duffy-Bos 32.1

Adjusted Batter Runs
Brouthers-Bos 59.2
Brown-Bos 37.2
Duffy-Bos 34.0
Milligan-Phi 30.0
Joyce-Bos 28.9

Clutch Hitting Index
Sneed-Col 132
Comiskey-StL 128
Duffy-Bos 128
Ray-Bal 128
Radford-Bos 127

Runs Created
Brown-Bos 155
Duffy-Bos 137
Brouthers-Bos 135
VanHaltren-Bal 133
Hoy-StL 114

Total Average
Brouthers-Bos ...1.237
Brown-Bos 1.140
Duffy-Bos 1.104
VanHaltren-Bal ...1.039
Lyons-StL 1.036

Stolen Bases
Brown-Bos 106
Duffy-Bos 85
VanHaltren-Bal ... 75
Hoy-StL 59
Radford-Bos 55

Stolen Base Average

Stolen Base Runs

Fielding Runs
Stricker-Bos 24.2
Radford-Bos 19.9
Crooks-Col 19.6
Eagan-StL 19.5
Farrell-Bos 19.0

Total Player Rating
Farrell-Bos 4.4
Brouthers-Bos 3.8
Crooks-Col 3.3
Milligan-Phi 3.1
Radford-Bos 2.9

Wins
McMahon-Bal 35
Haddock-Bos 34
Stivetts-StL 33
Weyhing-Phi 31
Buffinton-Bos 29

Win Percentage
Buffinton-Bos ..... .763
Haddock-Bos .... .756
Weyhing-Phi ..... .608
Stivetts-StL .... .600
McMahon-Bal .... .593

Games
Stivetts-StL 64
McMahon-Bal 61
Knell-Col 58
Carsey-Was 54
Weyhing-Phi 52

Complete Games
McMahon-Bal 53
Weyhing-Phi 51
Knell-Col 47
Carsey-Was 46
Chamberlain-Phi ... 44

Shutouts
McMahon-Bal 5
Knell-Col 5
Haddock-Bos 5

Saves
O'Brien-Bos 2
Daley-Bos 2

Innings Pitched
McMahon-Bal 503.0
Knell-Col 462.0
Weyhing-Phi 450.0
Stivetts-StL 440.0
Carsey-Was 415.0

Fewest Hits/Game
Knell-Col 7.07
Stivetts-StL 7.30
Buffinton-Bos 7.50
Crane-Cin 7.78
Haddock-Bos 7.82

Fewest BB/Game
Stratton-Lou 1.78
Sanders-Phi 2.30
McMahon-Bal 2.67
Ehret-Lou 2.85
Griffith-StL-Bos ... 2.90

Strikeouts
Stivetts-StL 259
Knell-Col 228
Weyhing-Phi 219
McMahon-Bal 219
Chamberlain-Phi .. 204

Strikeouts/Game
Meekin-Lou 5.68
Stivetts-StL 5.30
McGill-Cin-StL 4.96
Daley-Bos 4.83
Chamberlain-Phi .. 4.53

Ratio
Buffinton-Bos ... 10.64
Haddock-Bos 11.40
McMahon-Bal ...11.79
Weyhing-Phi 12.40
Stivetts-StL 12.42

Earned Run Average
Crane-Cin 2.45
Haddock-Bos 2.49
Buffinton-Bos 2.55
McMahon-Bal 2.81
Stivetts-StL 2.86

Adjusted ERA
Crane-Cin 168
Stivetts-StL 147
Haddock-Bos 140
Buffinton-Bos 137
Mains-Cin-Mil 134

Opponents' Batting Avg.
Knell-Col .... .209
Stivetts-StL .... .215
Buffinton-Bos .... .219
Crane-Cin .... .225
Haddock-Bos .... .226

Opponents' On Base Pct.
Buffinton-Bos ..... .285
Haddock-Bos .... .299
McMahon-Bal .... .306
Weyhing-Phi ..... .317
Stivetts-StL .... .317

Starter Runs
Haddock-Bos 51.9
McMahon-Bal ... 50.9
Buffinton-Bos 47.3
Stivetts-StL 41.8
Knell-Col 40.9

Adjusted Starter Runs
Stivetts-StL 65.5
McMahon-Bal 51.7
Crane-Cin 46.3
Haddock-Bos 42.0
Buffinton-Bos 37.8

Clutch Pitching Index
Daley-Bos 134
Crane-Cin 128
O'Brien-Bos 123
Mains-Cin-Mil 122
Foreman-Was 113

Relief Runs

Adjusted Relief Runs

Relief Ranking

Total Pitcher Index
Stivetts-StL 7.7
Haddock-Bos 5.3
McMahon-Bal 5.0
Buffinton-Bos 3.6
Crane-Cin 3.5

Total Baseball Ranking
Stivetts-StL 7.5
Haddock-Bos 5.0
McMahon-Bal 4.9
Farrell-Bos 4.4
Brouthers-Bos 3.8

TEAM	G	W	L	PCT	GB	R	OR	AB	H	2B	3B	HR	BB	SO	AVG	OBP	SLG	PRO	PRO+	BR	/A	PF	CHI	RC	SB	CS	SBA	SBR
BOS	152	102	48	.680		862	649	5301	1324	203	51	34	526	488	.250	.325	.327	.652	93	18	-55	109	108	689	338			
CLE	153	93	56	.624	8.5	855	613	5412	1375	196	96	26	552	536	.254	.328	.340	.668	103	48	14	104	101	694	225			
BRO	158	95	59	.617	9	935	733	5485	1439	183	105	30	629	506	.262	.344	.350	.694	120	109	144	96	101	822	409			
PHI	155	87	66	.569	16.5	860	690	5413	1420	225	95	50	528	515	.262	.334	.367	.701	118	107	110	100	95	753	216			
CIN	155	82	68	.547	20	766	731	5349	1288	155	75	44	503	474	.241	.311	.322	.633	98	-23	-12	99	101	635	270			
PIT	155	80	73	.523	23.5	802	796	5469	1288	143	108	38	435	453	.236	.297	.322	.619	92	-59	-62	100	110	604	222			
CHI	147	70	76	.479	30	635	735	5063	1188	149	92	26	427	482	.235	.299	.316	.615	90	-60	-67	101	94	561	233			
NY	153	71	80	.470	31.5	811	826	5291	1326	173	85	39	510	469	.251	.320	.338	.658	106	25	38	98	101	686	301			
LOU	154	63	89	.414	40	649	804	5334	1208	133	61	18	433	508	.226	.290	.284	.574	85	-135	-85	92	102	533	275			
WAS	153	58	93	.384	44.5	731	869	5204	1245	149	78	37	529	553	.239	.314	.319	.633	100	-18	4	97	98	624	276			
STL	155	56	94	.373	46	703	922	5259	1187	138	53	46	607	491	.226	.312	.298	.610	95	-55	-19	95	96	568	209			
BAL	152	46	101	.313	54.5	779	1020	5296	1342	160	111	30	499	480	.253	.325	.343	.668	104	44	22	103	95	680	227			
TOT	921					9388		63876	15630	2007	1010	417	6178	5955	.245	.317	.327	.644						3201				

TEAM	CG	SH	SV	IP	H	H/G	HR	BB	SO	RAT	ERA	ERA+	OAV	OOB	PR	/A	PF	CPI	FA	E	DP	FW	PW	BW	SBW	DIF
BOS	142	15	1	1336	1156	7.8	41	460	509	11.1	2.86	123	.224	.292	64	96	107	93	.929	454	127	.5	8.9	-5.1		22.7
CLE	140	11	2	1336	1178	7.9	28	413	472	10.9	2.41	140	.228	.289	130	143	103	107	.935	407	95	3.4	13.2	1.3		.6
BRO	132	12	5	1405²	1285	8.2	26	600	597	12.4	3.25	97	.234	.315	6	-14	96	95	.940	398	98	4.8	-1.3	13.3		1.2
PHI	131	10	5	1359	1297	8.5	24	492	502	12.0	2.93	111	.239	.309	54	47	99	103	.939	393	128	4.5	4.4	10.2		-8.6
CIN	130	8	2	1377¹	1327	8.7	39	535	437	12.5	3.17	103	.243	.317	18	15	99	104	.939	402	140	4.0	1.4	-1.1		2.7
PIT	130	3	1	1347¹	1300	8.7	28	537	455	12.7	3.10	106	.244	.320	28	27	100	106	.927	483	113	-.7	2.5	-5.7		7.4
CHI	133	6	1	1298	1269	8.8	35	424	518	12.0	3.16	105	.246	.308	18	22	101	100	.932	424	85	1.3	2.0	-6.2		-.2
NY	139	5	1	1322²	1165	7.9	32	635	641	12.6	3.29	98	.227	.318	-1	-11	98	94	.912	565	97	-5.8	-1.0	3.5		-1.2
LOU	147	9	0	1346	1358	9.1	26	447	430	12.3	3.34	92	.252	.313	-8	-41	93	97	.928	471	133	-.2	-3.8	-7.9		-1.2
WAS	129	5	3	1315¹	1293	8.8	40	556	479	13.1	3.46	94	.247	.327	-26	-32	99	102	.916	547	122	-4.8	-3.0	.4		-10.1
STL	139	4	2	1344²	1466	9.8	47	543	478	13.8	4.20	76	.267	.339	-137	-151	97	96	.929	452	100	1.1	-14.0	-1.8		-4.4
BAL	131	2	2	1298²	1537	10.7	51	536	437	14.7	4.28	80	.284	.353	-144	-124	104	106	.910	584	100	-7.1	-11.5	2.0		-10.9
TOT	1623	90	24	16106²		8.7				12.5	3.28		.245	.317					.928	5580	1338					

Split Season: First-half winner BOS (52-22); second-half winner CLE (53-23)

Runs		Hits		Doubles		Triples		Home Runs		Total Bases	
Childs-Cle	136	Brouthers-Bro	197	Connor-Phi	37	Delahanty-Phi	21	Holliday-Cin	13	Brouthers-Bro	282
Hamilton-Phi	132	Thompson-Phi	186	Long-Bos	33	Virtue-Cle	20	Connor-Phi	12	Holliday-Cin	270
Duffy-Bos	125	Duffy-Bos	184	Delahanty-Phi	30	Brouthers-Bro	20	Ryan-Chi	10	Thompson-Phi	263
Connor-Phi	123	Hamilton-Phi	183	Brouthers-Bro	30	Dahlen-Chi	19	Beckley-Pit	10	Connor-Phi	261
Brouthers-Bro	121	Long-Bos	181	Zimmer-Cle	29	Beckley-Pit	19	Thompson-Phi	9	Duffy-Bos	251

Runs Batted In		Runs Produced		Bases On Balls		Batting Average		On Base Percentage		Slugging Average	
Brouthers-Bro	124	Brouthers-Bro	240	Crooks-StL	136	Brouthers-Bro	.335	Childs-Cle	.443	Delahanty-Phi	.495
Thompson-Phi	104	Thompson-Phi	204	Childs-Cle	117	Hamilton-Phi	.330	Brouthers-Bro	.432	Brouthers-Bro	.480
Larkin-Was	96	Duffy-Bos	201	Connor-Phi	116	Childs-Cle	.317	Hamilton-Phi	.423	Ewing-NY	.473
Burns-Bro	96	Holliday-Cin	192	McCarthy-Bos	93	Burns-Bro	.315	Connor-Phi	.420	Connor-Phi	.463
Beckley-Pit	96					Ewing-NY	.310	Crooks-StL	.400	Burns-Bro	.454

Production		Adjusted Production		Batter Runs		Adjusted Batter Runs		Clutch Hitting Index		Runs Created	
Brouthers-Bro	.911	Brouthers-Bro	182	Brouthers-Bro	56.9	Brouthers-Bro	62.5	McKean-Cle	165	Brouthers-Bro	138
Connor-Phi	.883	Connor-Phi	167	Connor-Phi	50.6	Connor-Phi	51.0	Pfeffer-Lou	142	Hamilton-Phi	123
Delahanty-Phi	.855	Burns-Bro	163	Childs-Cle	45.5	Burns-Bro	41.8	Nash-Bos	135	Connor-Phi	122
Burns-Bro	.849	Delahanty-Phi	158	Hamilton-Phi	39.0	Childs-Cle	40.1	Larkin-Was	131	VanHaltren-Bal-Pit	117
Childs-Cle	.841	Hamilton-Phi	153	Burns-Bro	37.3	Hamilton-Phi	39.3	Brouthers-Bro	128	Holliday-Cin	114

Total Average		Stolen Bases		Stolen Base Average	Stolen Base Runs	Fielding Runs		Total Player Rating	
Brouthers-Bro	1.056	Ward-Bro	88			D.Richardson-Was	57.6	Brouthers-Bro	6.1
Connor-Phi	1.018	Brown-Lou	78			Shindle-Bal	35.5	Dahlen-Chi	4.6
Hamilton-Phi	1.005	Latham-Cin	66			Bierbauer-Pit	31.7	McPhee-Cin	4.5
Childs-Cle	.982	Hoy-Was	60			McPhee-Cin	25.3	Hamilton-Phi	4.3
Burns-Bro	.943	Dahlen-Chi	60			Dahlen-Chi	25.2	D.Richardson-Was	4.0

Wins		Win Percentage		Games		Complete Games		Shutouts		Saves	
Hutchison-Chi	37	Young-Cle	.750	Hutchison-Chi	75	Hutchison-Chi	67	Young-Cle	9	Weyhing-Phi	3
Young-Cle	36	Terry-Bal-Pit	.692	Rusie-NY	64	Rusie-NY	58	Weyhing-Phi	6	Duryea-Cin-Was	2
Stivetts-Bos	35	Haddock-Bro	.690	Killen-Was	60	Nichols-Bos	49	Stein-Bro	6		
Nichols-Bos	35	Staley-Bos	.688	Weyhing-Phi	59	Young-Cle	48				
Weyhing-Phi	32			Baldwin-Pit	56						

Innings Pitched		Fewest Hits/Game		Fewest BB/Game		Strikeouts		Strikeouts/Game		Ratio	
Hutchison-Chi	627.0	Mullane-Cin	6.77	Stratton-Lou	1.79	Hutchison-Chi	316	Kennedy-Bro	5.09	Young-Cle	9.77
Rusie-NY	532.0	Rusie-NY	6.85	Dwyer-StL-Cin	2.03	Rusie-NY	288	Rusie-NY	4.87	Nichols-Bos	10.63
Weyhing-Phi	469.2	Terry-Bal-Pit	6.94	Sanders-Lou	2.08	Weyhing-Phi	202	Hutchison-Chi	4.54	Stratton-Lou	10.77
Killen-Was	459.2	Young-Cle	7.21	Young-Cle	2.34	Stein-Bro	190	Stein-Bro	4.53	Keefe-Phi	10.83
		Duryea-Cin-Was	7.25	Ehret-Pit	2.36	Nichols-Bos	187	Crane-NY	4.30	Mullane-Cin	11.01

Earned Run Average		Adjusted ERA		Opponents' Batting Avg.		Opponents' On Base Pct.		Starter Runs		Adjusted Starter Runs	
Young-Cle	1.93	Young-Cle	176	Mullane-Cin	.201	Young-Cle	.266	Young-Cle	68.3	Young-Cle	73.4
Keefe-Phi	2.36	J.Clarkson-Bos-Cle	139	Rusie-NY	.203	Nichols-Bos	.283	Hutchison-Chi	37.8	J.Clarkson-Bos-Cle	41.3
J.Clarkson-Bos-Cle	2.48	Keefe-Phi	138	Terry-Bal-Pit	.205	Stratton-Lou	.286	J.Clarkson-Bos-Cle	35.0	Hutchison-Chi	40.3
Cuppy-Cle	2.51	Cuppy-Cle	135	Young-Cle	.211	Keefe-Phi	.287	Weyhing-Phi	32.4	Cuppy-Cle	36.5
Terry-Bal-Pit	2.57	Davies-Cle	131	Duryea-Cin-Was	.212	Mullane-Cin	.290	Keefe-Phi	32.3	Nichols-Bos	33.6

Clutch Pitching Index		Relief Runs	Adjusted Relief Runs	Relief Ranking	Total Pitcher Index		Total Baseball Ranking	
Sullivan-Cin	136				Young-Cle	6.6	Young-Cle	6.6
Galvin-Pit-StL	122				Hutchison-Chi	4.8	Brouthers-Bro	6.1
Luby-Chi	117				Cuppy-Cle	3.8	Hutchison-Chi	4.7
Vickery-Bal	116				Stivetts-Bos	3.7	Dahlen-Chi	4.6
McMahon-Bal	115				J.Clarkson-Bos-Cle	3.3	McPhee-Cin	4.5

TEAM	G	W	L	PCT	GB	R	OR	AB	H	2B	3B	HR	BB	SO	AVG	OBP	SLG	PRO	PRO+	BR	/A	PF	CHI	RC	SB	CS	SBA	SBR
BOS	131	86	43	.667		1008	795	4678	1358	178	50	65	**561**	292	.290	.372	.391	.763	99	54	-18	108	**111**	790	243			
PIT	131	81	48	.628	5	970	**766**	4834	1447	176	**127**	37	537	273	.299	**.377**	.411	.788	116	96	**115**	98	99	848	210			
CLE	129	73	55	.570	12.5	976	839	4747	1425	222	98	32	532	**229**	.300	.374	.408	.782	106	84	28	106	103	841	252			
PHI	133	72	57	.558	14	**1011**	841	5151	**1553**	**246**	90	**80**	468	335	**.301**	.368	**.431**	**.799**	**117**	**108**	111	100	100	860	202			
NY	136	68	64	.515	19.5	941	845	4858	1424	182	101	61	504	279	.293	.366	.410	.776	111	68	65	100	100	860	**299**			
CIN	131	65	63	.508	20.5	759	814	4617	1195	161	65	29	532	256	.259	.342	.341	.683	84	-88	-106	102	101	634	238			
BRO	130	65	63	.508	20.5	775	845	4511	1200	173	83	45	473	296	.266	.341	.371	.712	97	-46	-11	95	101	659	213			
BAL	130	60	70	.462	26.5	820	893	4651	1281	164	86	27	537	323	.275	.359	.365	.724	95	-13	-26	102	98	711	233			
CHI	128	56	71	.441	29	829	874	4664	1299	186	93	32	465	262	.279	.348	.379	.727	99	-20	-8	99	102	722	255			
STL	135	57	75	.432	30.5	745	829	4879	1288	152	98	10	524	251	.264	.343	.341	.684	86	-89	-91	100	94	674	250			
LOU	126	50	75	.400	34	759	942	4566	1185	177	73	19	485	306	.260	.338	.343	.681	92	-94	-37	92	104	612	203			
WAS	130	40	89	.310	46	722	1032	4742	1260	180	83	23	524	237	.266	.347	.353	.700	92	-61	-39	97	90	650	154			
TOT	785					10315		56898	15915	2197	1047	460	6142	3339	.280	.356	.379	.736							2752			

TEAM	CG	SH	SV	IP	H	H/G	HR	BB	SO	RAT	ERA	ERA+	OAV	OOB	PR	/A	PF	CPI	FA	E	DP	FW	PW	BW	SBW	DIF
BOS	**114**	2	2	1163²	1314	10.2	66	402	253	**13.6**	4.43	111	.277	**.339**	30	64	106	100	.936	353	118	1.8	5.2	-1.5		16.0
PIT	104	**8**	2	1167	**1232**	9.5	29	504	280	13.8	4.08	112	.263	.342	75	60	98	101	.938	347	112	2.1	4.9	**9.4**		.0
CLE	110	2	2	1140¹	1361	10.7	35	**356**	242	13.8	4.20	**116**	.288	.342	59	86	105	**106**	.929	395	92	-.9	7.1	2.3		.6
PHI	107	4	2	1189	1359	10.3	30	521	283	14.8	4.68	98	.279	.358	-2	-14	98	99	**.944**	**318**	121	**4.1**	-1.1	9.1		-4.5
NY	111	6	4	1211¹	1271	**9.4**	36	581	**395**	14.2	4.29	108	**.262**	.347	49	48	100	99	.927	432	95	-1.8	3.9	5.3		-5.4
CIN	97	4	**5**	1172	1305	10.0	38	549	258	14.8	4.55	105	.274	.357	15	30	103	101	.943	321	**138**	3.6	2.5	-8.7		3.7
BRO	109	3	3	1154	1262	9.8	41	547	297	14.4	4.55	97	.270	.352	15	-16	95	98	.930	385	88	-.2	-1.3	-.9		3.4
BAL	104	1	2	1123²	1325	10.6	29	534	275	15.2	4.97	95	.285	.364	-39	-30	102	97	.929	384	95	-.1	-2.5	-2.1		-.3
CHI	101	4	**5**	1117¹	1278	10.3	**26**	553	273	15.3	4.99	86	.279	.365	-18	-24	99	99	.922	421	92	-2.5	-2.0	-.7		-2.3
STL	**114**	3	4	1207	1292	9.6	38	542	301	14.1	**4.06**	**116**	.266	.346	80	88	101	100	.930	398	110	-.0	**7.2**	-7.5		-8.7
LOU	113	4	1	1080	1431	11.9	38	479	190	16.3	5.90	74	.310	.380	-149	-181	94	94	.937	330	111	2.2	-14.8	-3.0		3.1
WAS	110	2	0	1139	1485	11.7	54	574	292	16.7	5.56	83	.306	.387	-114	-120	99	103	.912	497	96	-6.5	-9.8	-3.2		-5.0
TOT	1294	43	32	13864¹		10.3				14.7	4.66		.280	.356					.931	4581	1268					

Runs
Long-Bos 149
Duffy-Bos 147
Delahanty-Phi 145
Childs-Cle 145
Burkett-Cle 145

Hits
Thompson-Phi 222
Delahanty-Phi 219
Duffy-Bos 203
Davis-NY 195
Ward-NY 193

Doubles
Thompson-Phi 37
Delahanty-Phi 35
Tebeau-Cle 32
Beckley-Pit 32

Triples
Werden-StL 29
Davis-NY 27
McKean-Cle 24
Smith-Pit 23
Beckley-Pit 19

Home Runs
Delahanty-Phi 19
Clements-Phi 17
Tiernan-NY 14
Lowe-Bos 14

Total Bases
Delahanty-Phi 347
Thompson-Phi 318
Davis-NY 304
Smith-Pit 272

Runs Batted In
Delahanty-Phi 146
McKean-Cle 133
Thompson-Phi 126
Nash-Bos 123
Ewing-Cle 122

Runs Produced
Delahanty-Phi 272
Duffy-Bos 259
Thompson-Phi 245
Ewing-Cle 233
McKean-Cle 232

Bases On Balls
Crooks-StL 121
Childs-Cle 120
Radford-Was 105
McGraw-Bal 101
Burkett-Cle 98

Batting Average
Duffy-Bos .... .363
Hamilton-Phi ..... .380
Thompson-Phi ..... .370
Delahanty-Phi .... .368
Davis-NY .... .355

On Base Percentage
Hamilton-Phi ..... .490
Childs-Cle .... .463
Burkett-Cle ...... .459
McGraw-Bal .... .454
Smith-Pit .... .435

Slugging Average
Delahanty-Phi .... .583
Davis-NY .... .554
Thompson-Phi ..... .530
Smith-Pit .... .525
Hamilton-Phi ..... .524

Production
Hamilton-Phi 1.014
Delahanty-Phi ... 1.007
Davis-NY .... .964
Smith-Pit .... .960
Thompson-Phi ..... .954

Adjusted Production
Hamilton-Phi 170
Delahanty-Phi 167
Smith-Pit 158
Davis-NY 155
Thompson-Phi 153

Batter Runs
Delahanty-Phi 52.7
Burkett-Cle 43.6
Thompson-Phi 43.3
Smith-Pit 41.4
Davis-NY 40.0

Adjusted Batter Runs
Delahanty-Phi 53.2
Smith-Pit 44.0
Thompson-Phi 43.8
Hamilton-Phi 40.2
Davis-NY 39.6

Clutch Hitting Index
Anson-Chi 148
Vaughn-Cin 147
McKean-Cle 135
Glasscock-StL-Pit . 132
O'Rourke-Was 129

Runs Created
Delahanty-Phi 167
Thompson-Phi 146
Davis-NY 143
Burkett-Cle 137
Smith-Pit 133

Total Average
Hamilton-Phi 1.386
Burkett-Cle 1.186
Delahanty-Phi ... 1.173
Smith-Pit 1.121
Davis-NY 1.107

Stolen Bases
T.Brown-Lou 66
Dowd-StL 59
Latham-Cin 57
Burke-NY 54
Brodie-StL-Bal ... 49

Stolen Base Average

Stolen Base Runs

Fielding Runs
McPhee-Cin 34.0
Delahanty-Phi 30.8
T.Brown-Lou 27.1
G.Smith-Cin 19.5
Allen-Phi 18.4

Total Player Rating
Delahanty-Phi 6.3
McPhee-Cin 3.5
Davis-NY 3.4
Smith-Pit 3.3
Hamilton-Phi 3.3

Wins
Killen-Pit 36
Young-Cle 34
Nichols-Bos 34
Rusie-NY 33
Kennedy-Bro 25

Win Percentage
Gastright-Pit-Bos . .750
Killen-Pit .... .720
Nichols-Bos ...... .708
Young-Cle .... .680
Staley-Bos .... .643

Games
Rusie-NY 56
Killen-Pit 55
Young-Cle 53
Nichols-Bos 52
Mullane-Cin-Bal .. 49

Complete Games
Rusie-NY 50
Nichols-Bos 43
Young-Cle 42
Kennedy-Bro 40

Shutouts
Rusie-NY 4
Ehret-Pit 4

Saves
Mullane-Cin-Bal .. 2
Baldwin-Pit-NY ... 2
Dwyer-Cin 2
Donnelly-Chi 2
Colcolough-Pit ... 2

Innings Pitched
Rusie-NY 482.0
Nichols-Bos 425.0
Young-Cle 422.2
Killen-Pit 415.0

Fewest Hits/Game
Rusie-NY 8.42
Breitenstein-StL .. 8.44
Killen-Pit 8.70
Kennedy-Bro 8.84
Stein-Bro 8.87

Fewest BB/Game
Young-Cle 2.19
Nichols-Bos 2.50
Cuppy-Cle 2.77
Staley-Bos 2.77
Stratton-Lou 2.86

Strikeouts
Rusie-NY 208
Kennedy-Bro 107
Young-Cle 102
Breitenstein-StL .. 102
Weyhing-Phi 101

Strikeouts/Game
Rusie-NY 3.88
Meekin-Was 3.34
Hawley-StL 2.89
Terry-Pit 2.75
Hawke-StL-Bal 2.74

Ratio
Young-Cle 11.82
Nichols-Bos 11.84
Killen-Pit 12.06
Breitenstein-StL .. 12.30
Stein-Bro 12.70

Earned Run Average
Breitenstein-StL .. 3.18
Rusie-NY 3.23
Young-Cle 3.36
Ehret-Pit 3.44
Clarkson-StL 3.48

Adjusted ERA
Breitenstein-StL .. 149
Young-Cle 145
Rusie-NY 144
Nichols-Bos 140
Clarkson-StL 136

Opponents' Batting Avg.
Rusie-NY .... .240
Breitenstein-StL .. .241
Killen-Pit .... .246
Kennedy-Bro ...... .249
Stein-Bro .... .250

Opponents' On Base Pct.
Young-Cle .... .308
Nichols-Bos ...... .308
Killen-Pit .... .312
Breitenstein-StL .. .316
Stein-Bro .... .323

Starter Runs
Rusie-NY 76.6
Breitenstein-StL .. 63.2
Young-Cle 60.9
Nichols-Bos 54.1
Killen-Pit 46.9

Adjusted Starter Runs
Rusie-NY 76.1
Young-Cle 71.2
Nichols-Bos 66.9
Breitenstein-StL .. 65.9
Killen-Pit 41.8

Clutch Pitching Index
Esper-Was 120
Clarkson-StL 117
McNabb-Bal 113
Cuppy-Cle 111
Rusie-NY 111

Relief Runs

Adjusted Relief Runs

Relief Ranking

Total Pitcher Index
Rusie-NY 7.2
Young-Cle 6.4
Breitenstein-StL .. 5.5
Nichols-Bos 5.5
Killen-Pit 5.2

Total Baseball Ranking
Rusie-NY 7.2
Young-Cle 6.4
Delahanty-Phi 6.3
Breitenstein-StL .. 5.5
Nichols-Bos 5.4

TEAM	G	W	L	PCT	GB	R	OR	AB	H	2B	3B	HR	BB	SO	AVG	OBP	SLG	PRO	PRO+	BR	/A	PF	CHI	RC	SB	CS	SBA	SBR
BAL	129	89	39	.695		1171	819	4799	1647	271	**150**	33	516	**200**	.343	**.418**	.483	**.901**	116	**173**	122	104	99	**1146**	324			
NY	137	88	44	.667	3	940	**789**	4806	1446	197	96	43	476	217	.301	.368	.409	.777	92	-68	-61	99	104	869	319			
BOS	133	83	49	.629	8	**1220**	1002	5011	1658	**272**	94	**103**	535	261	.331	.401	**.484**	.885	108	135	44	108	**106**	1102	241			
PHI	129	71	57	.555	18	1143	966	4967	**1732**	252	131	40	496	245	**.349**	.414	.476	.890	**122**	156	**187**	97	97	1132	273			
BRO	134	70	61	.534	20.5	1021	1007	4816	1507	228	130	42	466	294	.313	.378	.440	.818	109	5	75	93	104	941	282			
CLE	130	68	61	.527	21.5	932	896	4764	1442	241	90	37	471	301	.303	.368	.414	.782	89	-57	-92	104	103	837	220			
PIT	132	65	65	.500	25	955	972	4676	1458	222	124	48	434	280	.312	.379	.443	.822	103	11	21	99	98	921	256			
CHI	135	57	75	.432	34	1041	1066	4960	1555	265	86	65	496	298	.314	.380	.441	.821	97	12	-43	105	102	987	**327**			
STL	133	56	76	.424	35	771	953	4610	1320	171	113	54	442	289	.286	.354	.408	.762	87	-100	-100	100	92	763	190			
CIN	132	55	75	.423	35	910	1085	4671	1374	224	67	61	508	252	.294	.368	.410	.778	88	-62	-96	104	102	812	215			
WAS	132	45	87	.341	46	882	1122	4581	1317	218	118	59	**617**	375	.287	.381	.425	.806	101	-7	24	97	92	864	249			
LOU	130	36	94	.277	54	692	1001	4482	1206	173	88	42	350	364	.269	.330	.375	.705	78	-199	-152	93	99	652	217			
TOT	793					11678		57143	17662	2734	1287	627	5807	3304	.309	.379	.435	.814						3113				

TEAM	CG	SH	SV	IP	H	H/G	HR	BB	SO	RAT	ERA	ERA+	OAV	OOB	PR	/A	PF	CPI	FA	E	DP	FW	PW	BW	SBW	DIF
BAL	97	1	**11**	1116[1]	1371	11.1	**31**	472	275	15.2	5.00	109	.299	.371	39	55	103	98	**.944**	293	105	**5.6**	4.2	9.4		5.8
NY	111	5	5	1212	**1292**	9.6	37	539	395	13.8	3.83	137	.271	.349	200	187	99	107	.924	443	101	-1.6	**14.3**	-4.7		13.9
BOS	108	3	1	1166	1529	11.8	89	**411**	262	15.3	5.41	105	.314	.372	-12	33	107	101	.925	415	120	-.7	2.5	3.4		11.8
PHI	102	3	4	1125[2]	1482	11.8	62	469	262	16.1	5.63	90	.314	.384	-39	-68	96	99	.935	338	111	3.0	-5.2	**14.3**		-5.2
BRO	105	3	5	1162[1]	1447	11.2	41	555	285	16.0	5.51	90	.302	.382	-25	-75	93	95	.928	390	85	.9	-5.8	5.8		3.6
CLE	106	**6**	1	1124[1]	1390	11.1	54	435	254	14.9	4.97	110	.301	.366	43	59	103	100	.935	344	107	2.9	4.5	-7.1		3.2
PIT	106	2	0	1164[2]	1552	12.0	39	457	304	16.5	6.60	93	.317	.380	-37	-50	98	96	.936	354	106	2.6	-3.8	1.6		-.4
CHI	**117**	0	0	1148	1561	12.2	43	557	281	17.1	5.68	99	.322	.398	-47	-11	106	103	.918	452	113	-2.4	-.8	-3.3		-2.4
STL	114	2	0	1161	1418	11.0	48	500	319	15.2	5.29	102	.299	.371	4	14	102	94	.923	426	109	-1.3	1.1	-7.7		-2.1
CIN	110	4	3	1147[1]	1585	12.4	85	491	219	16.7	5.99	93	.325	.393	-85	-56	104	101	.925	423	119	-1.3	-4.3	-7.4		2.9
WAS	101	0	4	1107	1573	12.8	59	446	190	16.9	5.51	95	.331	.396	-24	-32	99	**110**	.908	499	81	-5.6	-2.5	1.8		-14.8
LOU	113	2	1	1096[2]	1462	12.0	39	475	258	16.3	5.45	93	.317	.386	-16	-44	96	101	.920	428	**130**	-1.9	-3.4	-11.7		-12.1
TOT	1290	31	35	13731[1]		11.6				15.8	5.32		.309	.379					.927	4805	1287					

Runs		Hits		Doubles		Triples		Home Runs		Total Bases	
Hamilton-Phi	192	Duffy-Bos	237	Duffy-Bos	51	Reitz-Bal	31	Duffy-Bos	18	Duffy-Bos	374
Kelley-Bal	165	Hamilton-Phi	220	Kelley-Bal	48	Thompson-Phi	27	Lowe-Bos	17	Lowe-Bos	319
Keeler-Bal	165	Keeler-Bal	219	Wilmot-Chi	45	Treadway-Bro	26	Joyce-Was	17	Kelley-Bal	305
Duffy-Bos	160	Lowe-Bos	212			Connor-NY-StL	25	Dahlen-Chi	15	Keeler-Bal	305
Lowe-Bos	158	Brodie-Bal	210			Brouthers-Bal	23			Stenzel-Pit	303

Runs Batted In		Runs Produced		Bases On Balls		Batting Average		On Base Percentage		Slugging Average	
Duffy-Bos	145	Duffy-Bos	287	Hamilton-Phi	126	Duffy-Bos	.440	Hamilton-Phi	.523	Duffy-Bos	.694
Thompson-Phi	141	Hamilton-Phi	275	Kelley-Bal	107	Turner-Phi	.416	Kelley-Bal	.502	Thompson-Phi	.686
E.Delahanty-Phi	131	E.Delahanty-Phi	274	Childs-Cle	107	Thompson-Phi	.407	Duffy-Bos	.502	Joyce-Was	.648
Wilmot-Chi	130	Kelley-Bal	270	Nash-Bos	91	E.Delahanty-Phi	.407	Joyce-Was	.496	Kelley-Bal	.602
		Wilmot-Chi	259	McGraw-Bal	91	Hamilton-Phi	.404	E.Delahanty-Phi	.478	E.Delahanty-Phi	.585

Production		Adjusted Production		Batter Runs		Adjusted Batter Runs		Clutch Hitting Index		Runs Created	
Duffy-Bos	1.196	Joyce-Was	180	Duffy-Bos	75.7	Hamilton-Phi	64.7	Robinson-Bal	141	Duffy-Bos	217
Thompson-Phi	1.145	Thompson-Phi	177	Kelley-Bal	60.2	Duffy-Bos	61.4	Wilmot-Chi	132	Hamilton-Phi	207
Joyce-Was	1.143	Duffy-Bos	172	Hamilton-Phi	59.9	Thompson-Phi	52.9	McGraw-Bal	122	Kelley-Bal	182
Kelley-Bal	1.104	E.Delahanty-Phi	159	Thompson-Phi	49.3	Kelley-Bal	52.6	Bierbauer-Pit	121	Stenzel-Pit	165
E.Delahanty-Phi	1.063	Kelley-Bal	158	Joyce-Was	47.1	Joyce-Was	51.3	Reitz-Bal	118	Thompson-Phi	152

Total Average		Stolen Bases		Stolen Base Average		Stolen Base Runs		Fielding Runs		Total Player Rating	
Duffy-Bos	1.619	Hamilton-Phi	98					Jennings-Bal	33.1	Dahlen-Chi	4.8
Hamilton-Phi	1.605	McGraw-Bal	78					Dahlen-Chi	31.6	E.Delahanty-Phi	4.7
Joyce-Was	1.528	Wilmot-Chi	74					McPhee-Cin	31.2	Hamilton-Phi	4.6
Kelley-Bal	1.503	T.Brown-Lou	66					Farrell-NY	29.4	Duffy-Bos	4.3
Thompson-Phi	1.409	Lange-Chi	65					Reitz-Bal	26.9	Joyce-Was	3.7

Wins		Win Percentage		Games		Complete Games		Shutouts		Saves	
Rusie-NY	36	Meekin-NY	.786	Breitenstein-StL	56	Breitenstein-StL	46	Rusie-NY	3	Mullane-Bal-Cle	4
Meekin-NY	33	McMahon-Bal	.758	Rusie-NY	54	Rusie-NY	45	Nichols-Bos	3	Mercer-Was	3
Nichols-Bos	32	Rusie-NY	.735	Hawley-StL	53	Young-Cle	44	Cuppy-Cle	3	Hawke-Bal	3
Breitenstein-StL	27	Nichols-Bos	.711	Young-Cle	52	Nichols-Bos	40				
				Meekin-NY	52	Meekin-NY	40				

Innings Pitched		Fewest Hits/Game		Fewest BB/Game		Strikeouts		Strikeouts/Game		Ratio	
Breitenstein-StL	447.1	Young-Cle	8.64	Rusie-NY	2.33	Rusie-NY	195	Rusie-NY	3.95	Rusie-NY	12.79
Rusie-NY	444.0	Meekin-NY	8.89	Menefee-Lou-Pit	2.48	Breitenstein-StL	140	Hawke-Bal	2.97	Meekin-NY	12.89
Meekin-NY	409.0	Stein-Bro	9.98	Gleason-StL-Bal	2.54	Meekin-NY	133	Wadsworth-Lou	2.97	Clarkson-Cle	13.08
Young-Cle	408.2	Breitenstein-StL	10.00	Staley-Bos	2.63	Hawley-StL	120	Meekin-NY	2.93	Young-Cle	13.19
Nichols-Bos	407.0	Clarkson-Cle	10.33	Nichols-Bos	2.68	Nichols-Bos	113	Chamberlain-Cin	2.89	Nichols-Bos	13.67

Earned Run Average		Adjusted ERA		Opponents' Batting Avg.		Opponents' On Base Pct.		Starter Runs		Adjusted Starter Runs	
Rusie-NY	2.78	Rusie-NY	189	Rusie-NY	.250	Rusie-NY	.331	Rusie-NY	125.3	Rusie-NY	121.3
Meekin-NY	3.70	Meekin-NY	142	Meekin-NY	.256	Meekin-NY	.333	Meekin-NY	73.6	Meekin-NY	70.0
Mercer-Was	3.85	Young-Cle	138	Stein-Bro	.278	Clarkson-Cle	.336	Young-Cle	62.4	Young-Cle	68.7
Young-Cle	3.94	Mercer-Was	136	Breitenstein-StL	.279	Young-Cle	.338	Mercer-Was	54.7	Mercer-Was	52.5
Taylor-Phi	4.08	McMahon-Bal	129	Clarkson-Cle	.285	Nichols-Bos	.346	Taylor-Phi	41.0	Nichols-Bos	41.5

Clutch Pitching Index		Relief Runs		Adjusted Relief Runs		Relief Ranking		Total Pitcher Index		Total Baseball Ranking	
Mercer-Was	134							Rusie-NY	11.0	Rusie-NY	11.0
Rusie-NY	125							Young-Cle	5.6	Young-Cle	5.6
Terry-Pit-Chi	121							Meekin-NY	5.5	Meekin-NY	5.5
Hemming-Lou-Bal	112							Mercer-Was	5.0	Mercer-Was	5.0
Killen-Pit	111							Taylor-Phi	3.7	Dahlen-Chi	4.8

TEAM	G	W	L	PCT	GB	R	OR	AB	H	2B	3B	HR	BB	SO	AVG	OBP	SLG	PRO	PRO+	BR	/A	PF	CHI	RC	SB	CS	SBA	SBR
BAL	132	87	43	.669		1009	**646**	4725	1530	235	89	25	355	243	.324	.384	.427	.811	110	92	65	103	104	930	310			
CLE	131	84	46	.646	3	917	720	4658	1423	194	67	29	472	361	.305	.375	.395	.770	97	26	-26	106	102	790	187			
PHI	133	78	53	.595	9.5	**1068**	957	5037	**1664**	272	73	61	463	262	**.330**	**.394**	**.450**	**.844**	122	161	157	100	97	**1040**	276			
CHI	133	72	58	.554	15	866	854	4708	1401	171	85	55	422	344	.298	.361	.405	.766	95	6	-49	106	99	810	260			
BRO	133	71	60	.542	16.5	867	834	4717	1330	189	77	39	397	318	.282	.346	.379	.725	99	-66	-2	92	108	707	183			
BOS	132	71	60	.542	16.5	907	826	4715	1369	197	57	54	500	**236**	.290	.365	.391	.756	92	-4	-73	108	102	778	199			
PIT	134	71	61	.538	17	811	787	4645	1349	190	89	26	376	299	.290	.352	.386	.738	99	-41	3	95	99	753	257			
CIN	132	66	64	.508	21	903	834	4684	1395	235	**105**	36	414	249	.298	.359	.416	.775	99	18	-18	104	103	844	**326**			
NY	132	66	65	.504	21.5	852	834	4605	1324	191	90	32	454	292	.288	.355	.389	.744	98	-29	-9	98	104	763	292			
WAS	132	43	85	.336	43	837	1048	4577	1314	207	101	55	**518**	396	.287	.366	.412	.778	105	31	43	99	94	805	237			
STL	135	39	92	.298	48.5	747	1032	4781	1344	155	88	38	384	279	.281	.338	.374	.712	88	-94	-84	99	96	699	205			
LOU	133	35	96	.267	52.5	698	1090	4724	1320	171	73	34	346	323	.279	.339	.368	.707	92	-100	-52	94	92	665	156			
TOT	796					10482		56576	16763	2407	994	484	5101	3602	.296	.361	.400	.761							2888			

TEAM	CG	SH	SV	IP	H	H/G	HR	BB	SO	RAT	ERA	ERA+	OAV	OOB	PR	/A	PF	CPI	FA	E	DP	FW	PW	BW	SBW	DIF
BAL	104	**10**	4	1134[1]	**1216**	**9.6**	31	430	244	13.4	3.80	125	**.271**	.340	**123**	118	100	105	**.946**	288	108	**5.4**	9.6	5.3		1.8
CLE	108	6	3	1143[2]	1272	10.0	33	**346**	326	**13.0**	3.91	**127**	.278	**.333**	110	135	104	101	.936	348	77	1.8	**10.9**	-2.1		8.3
PHI	106	2	**7**	1161	1467	11.4	36	485	330	15.6	5.47	88	.304	.375	-89	-88	100	94	.933	369	93	1.0	-7.1	**12.7**		5.9
CHI	**119**	3	1	1150[2]	1422	11.1	38	432	297	15.0	4.67	109	.300	.366	14	52	106	105	.928	401	**113**	-.8	4.2	-4.0		7.6
BRO	103	5	6	1150[2]	1360	10.6	41	395	216	14.1	4.94	89	.290	.351	-21	-71	92	91	.941	325	96	3.5	-5.8	-.2		8.0
BOS	116	4	4	1175[1]	1364	10.4	56	363	370	13.6	4.27	119	.286	.343	66	107	107	103	.934	364	104	1.1	8.7	-5.9		1.6
PIT	106	4	6	1171[2]	1263	9.7	**17**	500	382	14.2	4.05	112	.272	.353	95	60	95	102	.930	392	95	-.1	4.9	.2		.0
CIN	97	2	6	1147[1]	1451	11.4	39	362	245	14.7	4.81	103	.304	.361	-4	19	104	101	.931	377	112	.4	1.5	-1.5		.5
NY	115	6	1	1147[1]	1359	10.7	34	415	**409**	14.3	4.51	103	.291	.354	34	16	97	100	.922	438	106	-3.0	1.3	-.7		3.0
WAS	99	0	5	1101[2]	1507	12.3	55	465	258	16.7	5.28	91	.321	.391	-61	-60	100	**110**	.917	447	96	-3.5	-4.9	3.5		-16.1
STL	105	1	1	1152[1]	1562	12.2	64	439	280	16.0	5.76	84	.319	.381	-126	-120	101	98	.930	380	94	.7	-9.7	-6.8		-10.7
LOU	104	3	1	1117[1]	1520	12.2	40	470	245	16.5	5.90	78	.320	.389	-139	-158	97	96	.913	477	104	-5.1	-12.8	-4.2		-8.4
TOT	1282	46	45	13753[1]		11.0				14.7	4.78		.296	.361					.930	4606	1198					

Runs
Hamilton-Phi 166
Keeler-Bal 162
Jennings-Bal 159
Burkett-Cle 153
Delahanty-Phi 149

Hits
Burkett-Cle 225
Keeler-Bal 213
Thompson-Phi 211
Jennings-Bal 204
Hamilton-Phi 201

Doubles
Delahanty-Phi 49
Thompson-Phi 45
Jennings-Bal 41
Stenzel-Pit 38
Griffin-Bro 38

Triples
Selbach-Was 22
Tiernan-NY 21
Thompson-Phi 21
Cooley-StL 20

Home Runs
Thompson-Phi 18
Joyce-Was 17
Clements-Phi 13
Delahanty-Phi 11

Total Bases
Thompson-Phi 352
Delahanty-Phi 296
Burkett-Cle 288
McKean-Cle 283
Kelley-Bal 283

Runs Batted In
Thompson-Phi 165
Kelley-Bal 134
Brodie-Bal 134
Jennings-Bal 125
McKean-Cle 119

Runs Produced
Jennings-Bal 280
Thompson-Phi 278
Kelley-Bal 272
Delahanty-Phi 244
McKean-Cle 242

Bases On Balls
Joyce-Was 96
Hamilton-Phi 96
Griffin-Bro 93
Delahanty-Phi 86
Kelley-Bal 77

Batting Average
Burkett-Cle .... .409
Delahanty-Phi ..... .404
Clements-Phi ...... .394
Thompson-Phi ..... .392
Lange-Chi .... .389

On Base Percentage
Delahanty-Phi ..... .500
Hamilton-Phi ...... .490
Burkett-Cle .... .486
McGraw-Bal ...... .459
Lange-Chi .... .456

Slugging Average
Thompson-Phi ..... .654
Delahanty-Phi ..... .617
Clements-Phi ...... .612
Lange-Chi .... .575
Kelley-Bal .... .546

Production
Delahanty-Phi 1.117
Thompson-Phi ... 1.085
Lange-Chi 1.032
Burkett-Cle 1.009
Kelley-Bal 1.003

Adjusted Production
Delahanty-Phi 186
Thompson-Phi 177
Stenzel-Pit 162
Lange-Chi 155
Hamilton-Phi 154

Batter Runs
Delahanty-Phi 66.4
Thompson-Phi 56.9
Burkett-Cle 54.2
Hamilton-Phi 49.6
Kelley-Bal 47.3

Adjusted Batter Runs
Delahanty-Phi ... 65.8
Thompson-Phi ... 56.3
Stenzel-Pit 49.7
Hamilton-Phi ... 49.0
Burkett-Cle 45.1

Clutch Hitting Index
Childs-Cle 141
Brodie-Bal 140
Kelley-Bal 130
Cross-Phi 128
Jennings-Bal 124

Runs Created
Hamilton-Phi 178
Delahanty-Phi ... 176
Thompson-Phi 167
Burkett-Cle 165
Lange-Chi 160

Total Average
Delahanty-Phi 1.517
Hamilton-Phi 1.443
Lange-Chi 1.373
Kelley-Bal 1.289
Thompson-Phi ... 1.269

Stolen Bases
Hamilton-Phi 97
Lange-Chi 67
McGraw-Bal 61
Kelley-Bal 54

Stolen Base Average

Stolen Base Runs

Fielding Runs
Jennings-Bal 35.7
Dahlen-Chi 35.6
Fuller-NY 34.0
Cross-Phi 33.5
Collins-Bos-Lou .. 18.9

Total Player Rating
Jennings-Bal 6.0
Thompson-Phi 4.7
Delahanty-Phi 4.7
Griffin-Bro 3.6
Kelley-Bal 3.5

Wins
Young-Cle 35
Hoffer-Bal 31
Hawley-Pit 31

Win Percentage
Hoffer-Bal .... .838
Young-Cle .... .778
Rhines-Cin .... .655

Games
Hawley-Pit 56
Breitenstein-StL.... 54
Rusie-NY 49

Complete Games
Breitenstein-StL 46
Hawley-Pit 44
Rusie-NY 42
Nichols-Bos 42
Griffith-Chi 39

Shutouts
Young-Cle 4
Rusie-NY 4
McMahon-Bal 4
Hoffer-Bal 4
Hawley-Pit 4

Saves
Parrott-Cin 3
Nichols-Bos 3
Beam-Phi 3

Innings Pitched
Hawley-Pit 444.1
Breitenstein-StL .. 429.2
Rusie-NY 393.1
Nichols-Bos 379.2
Young-Cle 369.2

Fewest Hits/Game
Foreman-Pit 8.44
Hoffer-Bal 8.48
Rusie-NY 8.79
Young-Cle 8.84
Maul-Was 9.02

Fewest BB/Game
Young-Cle 1.83
Clarke-NY 1.92
Nichols-Bos 2.04
Staley-StL 2.21
Taylor-Phi 2.23

Strikeouts
Rusie-NY 201
Hawley-Pit 142
Nichols-Bos 140
Breitenstein-StL ... 127
Young-Cle 121

Strikeouts/Game
Rusie-NY 4.60
McGill-Phi 4.32
Foreman-Pit 3.48
Stivetts-Bos 3.43
Nichols-Bos 3.32

Ratio
Young-Cle....... 10.86
Maul-Was 11.68
Nichols-Bos 12.04
Hawley-Pit 12.23
Cuppy-Cle 12.42

Earned Run Average
Maul-Was 2.45
Hawley-Pit 3.18
Hoffer-Bal 3.21
Foreman-Pit 3.22
Young-Cle 3.26

Adjusted ERA
Maul-Was 195
Young-Cle 153
Nichols-Bos...... 149
Hoffer-Bal 148
Hawley-Pit 142

Opponents' Batting Avg.
Foreman-Pit ..... .245
Hoffer-Bal ...... .246
Rusie-NY .... .252
Young-Cle ...... .253
Maul-Was ...... .257

Opponents' On Base Pct.
Young-Cle .... .294
Maul-Was .... .309
Nichols-Bos ..... .316
Hawley-Pit ...... .320
Cuppy-Cle ...... .323

Starter Runs
Hawley-Pit 78.8
Young-Cle 62.2
Nichols-Bos 57.5
Hoffer-Bal 54.6
Cuppy-Cle 48.3

Adjusted Starter Runs
Nichols-Bos 71.0
Young-Cle 70.6
Hawley-Pit 65.8
Cuppy-Cle 56.4
Hoffer-Bal 53.8

Clutch Pitching Index
Maul-Was 137
Mercer-Was 126
Clarke-NY 119
Foreman-Cin 116
Griffith-Chi 115

Relief Runs

Adjusted Relief Runs

Relief Ranking

Total Pitcher Index
Hawley-Pit 7.4
Young-Cle 7.0
Cuppy-Cle 5.8
Nichols-Bos...... 5.7
Griffith-Chi 4.5

Total Baseball Ranking
Hawley-Pit 7.4
Young-Cle 7.0
Jennings-Bal 6.0
Cuppy-Cle 5.8
Nichols-Bos 5.7

TEAM	G	W	L	PCT	GB	R	OR	AB	H	2B	3B	HR	BB	SO	AVG	OBP	SLG	PRO	PRO+	BR	/A	PF	CHI	RC	SB	CS	SBA	SBR
BAL	132	90	39	.698		995	662	4719	1548	207	100	23	386	201	.328	.393	.429	.822	120	151	137	101	103	1003	441			
CLE	135	80	48	.625	9.5	840	650	4856	1463	207	72	28	436	316	.301	.363	.391	.754	97	26	-23	106	98	785	175			
CIN	128	77	50	.606	12	783	620	4360	1283	204	73	20	382	226	.294	.357	.388	.745	95	7	-43	107	103	761	350			
BOS	132	74	57	.565	17	860	761	4717	1416	175	74	34	414	274	.300	.363	.390	.755	98	26	-23	106	102	791	241			
CHI	132	71	57	.555	18.5	815	799	4582	1311	182	97	34	409	290	.286	.349	.390	.739	95	-7	-37	104	105	769	332			
PIT	131	66	63	.512	24	787	741	4701	1371	169	94	27	387	286	.292	.353	.385	.738	103	-7	25	96	98	746	217			
NY	133	64	67	.489	27	829	821	4661	1383	159	87	40	439	271	.297	.364	.394	.758	108	32	55	97	99	795	274			
PHI	130	62	68	.477	28.5	890	891	4680	1382	234	84	49	438	297	.295	.363	.413	.776	110	58	68	99	103	801	191			
WAS	133	58	73	.443	33	818	920	4639	1328	179	79	45	516	365	.286	.365	.388	.753	103	29	30	100	97	783	258			
BRO	133	58	73	.443	33	692	764	4548	1292	174	87	28	344	269	.284	.340	.379	.719	100	-45	-4	94	95	680	198			
STL	131	40	90	.308	50.5	593	929	4520	1162	134	78	37	332	300	.257	.313	.346	.659	81	-149	-125	96	96	572	185			
LOU	134	38	93	.290	53	653	997	4588	1197	142	80	37	371	427	.261	.322	.351	.673	85	-123	-98	96	100	603	195			
TOT	792					9555		55571	16136	2166	1005	404	4854	3522	.290	.354	.387	.741						3057				

TEAM	CG	SH	SV	IP	H	H/G	HR	BB	SO	RAT	ERA	ERA+	OAV	OOB	PR	/A	PF	CPI	FA	E	DP	FW	PW	BW	SBW	DIF
BAL	115	9	1	1168¹	1281	9.9	22	339	302	12.7	3.67	116	.277	.331	89	77	98	100	.945	296	114	2.6	6.5	11.6		4.7
CLE	113	9	5	1195²	1363	10.3	27	280	336	12.6	3.46	131	.285	.329	119	141	104	109	.949	288	117	3.6	12.0	-2.0		2.4
CIN	105	12	4	1108	1240	10.1	27	310	219	13.0	3.67	125	.281	.335	84	114	106	105	.951	252	107	4.7	9.7	-3.6		2.8
BOS	110	6	3	1155²	1254	9.8	57	397	277	13.1	3.78	120	.275	.337	74	97	104	106	.934	368	94	-1.7	8.2	-2.0		3.9
CHI	118	2	1	1161	1302	10.1	30	467	353	14.3	4.41	103	.282	.358	-7	15	104	97	.934	366	115	-1.6	1.3	-3.1		10.4
PIT	108	8	1	1159¹	1286	10.0	18	439	362	13.9	4.30	98	.280	.351	7	-15	96	94	.941	317	103	1.2	-1.3	2.1		-.6
NY	104	1	2	1136²	1303	10.3	33	403	312	14.0	4.54	92	.286	.352	-24	-45	96	94	.933	365	90	-1.3	-3.8	4.7		-1.0
PHI	107	3	2	1117	1473	11.9	39	387	243	15.4	5.20	83	.316	.375	-104	-112	99	99	.941	313	112	1.3	-9.5	5.8		-.6
WAS	106	2	3	1136²	1435	11.4	24	435	292	15.2	4.61	95	.306	.372	-32	-28	101	105	.927	398	99	-3.3	-2.4	2.5		-4.3
BRO	97	3	1	1144	1353	10.6	39	400	259	14.1	4.25	97	.292	.354	14	-17	95	104	.945	297	104	2.7	-1.4	-.3		-8.5
STL	115	1	1	1130²	1448	11.5	40	456	279	15.5	5.33	82	.309	.376	-122	-124	100	95	.936	345	73	-.5	-10.5	-10.6		-3.4
LOU	108	1	4	1148²	1398	11.0	48	541	288	15.9	5.12	84	.298	.381	-98	-103	99	99	.916	475	110	-7.8	-8.7	-8.3		-2.6
TOT	1306	57	28	13761¹		10.6				14.1	4.36		.290	.354					.938	4080	1238					

Runs		Hits		Doubles		Triples		Home Runs		Total Bases	
Burkett-Cle	160	Burkett-Cle	240	Delahanty-Phi	44	VanHaltren-NY	21	Joyce-Was-NY	13	Burkett-Cle	317
Keeler-Bal	153	Keeler-Bal	210	Miller-Cin	38	McCreery-Lou	21	Delahanty-Phi	13	Delahanty-Phi	315
Hamilton-Bos	152	Jennings-Bal	209	Kelley-Bal	31	Kelley-Bal	19	Thompson-Phi	12	Kelley-Bal	282
Kelley-Bal	148	Delahanty-Phi	198	Dahlen-Chi	30	Dahlen-Chi	19	Connor-StL	11	VanHaltren-NY	272
Dahlen-Chi	137	VanHaltren-NY	197			Clarke-Lou	18			Keeler-Bal	270

Runs Batted In		Runs Produced		Bases On Balls		Batting Average		On Base Percentage		Slugging Average	
Delahanty-Phi	126	Jennings-Bal	246	Hamilton-Bos	110	Burkett-Cle	.410	Hamilton-Bos	.477	Delahanty-Phi	.631
Jennings-Bal	121	Delahanty-Phi	244	Joyce-Was-NY	101	Jennings-Bal	.401	Jennings-Bal	.472	Dahlen-Chi	.553
Duffy-Bos	113	Kelley-Bal	240	Childs-Cle	100	Delahanty-Phi	.397	Delahanty-Phi	.472	McCreery-Lou	.546
McKean-Cle	112	Keeler-Bal	231	Kelley-Bal	91	Keeler-Bal	.386	Joyce-Was-NY	.470	Kelley-Bal	.543
		Burkett-Cle	226	Tiernan-NY	77	Tiernan-NY	.369	Kelley-Bal	.469	Burkett-Cle	.541

Production		Adjusted Production		Batter Runs		Adjusted Batter Runs		Clutch Hitting Index		Runs Created	
Delahanty-Phi	1.103	Delahanty-Phi	192	Delahanty-Phi	64.7	Delahanty-Phi	66.6	Reitz-Bal	151	Kelley-Bal	178
Kelley-Bal	1.013	Kelley-Bal	164	Kelley-Bal	54.6	Kelley-Bal	52.5	Duffy-Bos	148	Delahanty-Phi	170
Burkett-Cle	1.002	Joyce-Was-NY	162	Burkett-Cle	54.5	Joyce-Was-NY	50.0	Anson-Chi	141	Burkett-Cle	166
Dahlen-Chi	.990	Tiernan-NY	159	Joyce-Was-NY	48.4	Tiernan-NY	47.8	Doyle-Bal	140	Hamilton-Bos	160
Joyce-Was-NY	.988	E.Smith-Pit	158	Hamilton-Bos	44.8	Burkett-Cle	45.9	Cross-Phi	139	Jennings-Bal	158

Total Average		Stolen Bases		Stolen Base Average	Stolen Base Runs	Fielding Runs		Total Player Rating	
Kelley-Bal	1.430	Kelley-Bal	87			Childs-Cle	42.4	Jennings-Bal	6.7
Delahanty-Phi	1.405	Lange-Chi	84			Jennings-Bal	34.2	Childs-Cle	6.6
Hamilton-Bos	1.316	Hamilton-Bos	83			Dahlen-Chi	24.5	Delahanty-Phi	6.0
Joyce-Was-NY	1.306	Miller-Cin	76			Clingman-Lou	23.7	Dahlen-Chi	5.5
Jennings-Bal	1.263	Doyle-Bal	73			Corcoran-Bro	23.5	Joyce-Was-NY	4.0

Wins		Win Percentage		Games		Complete Games		Shutouts		Saves	
Nichols-Bos	30	Hoffer-Bal	.781	Killen-Pit	52	Killen-Pit	44	Young-Cle	5	Young-Cle	3
Killen-Pit	30	Hemming-Bal	.714	Young-Cle	51	Young-Cle	42	Killen-Pit	5	Hill-Lou	2
Young-Cle	28	Dwyer-Cin	.686	Nichols-Bos	49	Mercer-Was	38			Fisher-Cin	2
Meekin-NY	26	Nichols-Bos	.682	Hawley-Pit	49						
		Griffith-Chi	.676	Clarke-NY	48						

Innings Pitched		Fewest Hits/Game		Fewest BB/Game		Strikeouts		Strikeouts/Game		Ratio	
Killen-Pit	432.1	Rhines-Cin	8.06	Young-Cle	1.35	Young-Cle	140	Briggs-Chi	3.90	Rhines-Cin	11.64
Young-Cle	414.1	Hawley-Pit	9.10	Clarke-NY	1.54	Hawley-Pit	137	Pond-Bal	3.36	Cuppy-Cle	11.82
Hawley-Pit	378.0	Sullivan-NY	9.13	Dwyer-Cin	1.87	Killen-Pit	134	McJames-Was	3.31	Young-Cle	11.95
Nichols-Bos	372.1	Friend-Chi	9.23	Cuppy-Cle	1.89	Breitenstein-StL	114	Hawley-Pit	3.26	Nichols-Bos	11.97
Mercer-Was	366.1	Hoffer-Bal	9.23	Griffith-Chi	1.98	Meekin-NY	110	Young-Cle	3.04	Esper-Bal	12.08

Earned Run Average		Adjusted ERA		Opponents' Batting Avg.		Opponents' On Base Pct.		Starter Runs		Adjusted Starter Runs	
Rhines-Cin	2.45	Rhines-Cin	188	Rhines-Cin	.238	Rhines-Cin	.311	Nichols-Bos	63.2	Nichols-Bos	70.6
Nichols-Bos	2.83	Nichols-Bos	160	Hawley-Pit	.261	Cuppy-Cle	.314	Young-Cle	51.5	Young-Cle	59.6
Cuppy-Cin	3.12	Dwyer-Cin	146	Sullivan-NY	.261	Young-Cle	.317	Cuppy-Cle	49.3	Cuppy-Cle	56.2
Dwyer-Cin	3.15	Cuppy-Cle	145	Friend-Chi	.264	Nichols-Bos	.317	Killen-Pit	45.3	Dwyer-Cin	46.7
Young-Cle	3.24	Young-Cle	140	Hoffer-Bal	.264	Esper-Bal	.319	Dwyer-Cin	38.7	Killen-Pit	37.5

Clutch Pitching Index		Relief Runs	Adjusted Relief Runs	Relief Ranking	Total Pitcher Index		Total Baseball Ranking	
Nichols-Bos	122				Nichols-Bos	6.6	Jennings-Bal	6.7
Wallace-Cle	120				Young-Cle	6.4	Childs-Cle	6.6
Payne-Bro	116				Cuppy-Cle	5.8	Nichols-Bos	6.5
Dwyer-Cin	115				Dwyer-Cin	4.7	Young-Cle	6.4
Rhines-Cin	114				Killen-Pit	4.2	Delahanty-Phi	6.0

TEAM	G	W	L	PCT	GB	R	OR	AB	H	2B	3B	HR	BB	SO	AVG	OBP	SLG	PRO	PRO+	BR	/A	PF	CHI	RC	SB	CS	SBA	SBR
BOS	135	93	39	.705		1025	665	4937	1574	230	83	45	423	262	.319	.378	.426	.804	110	117	59	106	108	919	233			
BAL	136	90	40	.692	2	964	674	4872	1584	243	66	19	437	256	.325	.394	.414	.808	118	138	138	100	100	984	401			
NY	137	83	48	.634	9.5	895	695	4844	1449	188	84	31	404	327	.299	.361	.392	.753	106	25	48	97	107	829	328			
CIN	134	76	56	.576	17	763	705	4524	1311	219	69	22	380	218	.290	.353	.383	.736	93	-6	-56	107	100	715	194			
CLE	132	69	62	.527	23.5	773	680	4604	1374	192	88	16	435	344	.298	.364	.389	.753	104	25	-18	105	96	747	181			
WAS	135	61	71	.462	32	781	793	4636	1376	194	77	36	374	348	.297	.357	.395	.752	104	18	22	100	98	755	208			
BRO	136	61	71	.462	32	802	845	4810	1343	202	72	24	351	255	.279	.336	.366	.702	95	-74	-34	95	110	684	187			
PIT	135	60	71	.458	32.5	676	835	4590	1266	140	108	25	359	334	.276	.337	.370	.707	95	-61	-34	96	95	657	170			
CHI	138	59	73	.447	34	832	894	4803	1356	189	97	38	430	317	.282	.347	.386	.733	94	-16	-46	104	105	766	264			
PHI	134	55	77	.417	38	752	792	4756	1392	213	83	40	399	299	.293	.353	.398	.751	106	13	34	97	93	754	163			
LOU	134	52	78	.400	40	669	859	4520	1197	160	70	40	370	453	.265	.329	.358	.687	89	-94	-71	97	100	624	195			
STL	132	29	102	.221	63.5	588	1083	4642	1277	149	67	31	354	314	.275	.336	.356	.692	89	-84	-70	98	85	639	172			
TOT	809					9520		56538	16499	2319	964	367	4716	3727	.292	.354	.386	.741							2696			

TEAM	CG	SH	SV	IP	H	H/G	HR	BB	SO	RAT	ERA	ERA+	OAV	OOB	PR	/A	PF	CPI	FA	E	DP	FW	PW	BW	SBW	DIF
BOS	115	8	7	1194¹	1273	9.6	39	393	329	12.9	3.65	122	.271	.333	87	107	104	102	.951	272	80	3.9	9.2	5.1		8.8
BAL	118	3	0	1197²	1296	9.7	18	382	361	13.2	3.55	117	.274	.338	100	81	97	104	.951	277	110	3.8	6.9	11.8		2.4
NY	118	8	3	1187¹	1214	9.2	26	486	456	13.4	3.47	120	.263	.342	110	89	96	100	.930	397	109	-3.3	7.6	4.1		9.1
CIN	100	4	2	1156²	1375	10.7	18	329	270	13.7	4.09	111	.294	.347	29	58	106	101	.948	273	100	3.7	5.0	-4.8		6.1
CLE	111	6	0	1119¹	1297	10.4	32	289	277	13.1	3.95	114	.288	.337	45	67	104	100	.950	261	74	4.2	5.7	-1.5		-4.9
WAS	102	7	6	1148	1383	10.8	27	400	348	14.6	4.01	108	.296	.362	37	40	101	112	.933	369	103	-1.9	3.4	1.9		-8.4
BRO	114	4	2	1194²	1417	10.7	34	410	256	14.2	4.60	89	.293	.355	-39	-68	95	94	.936	364	99	-1.5	-5.8	-2.9		5.2
PIT	112	2	2	1153¹	1397	10.9	22	318	342	13.9	4.67	89	.297	.350	-47	-66	97	91	.936	346	70	-.5	-5.7	-2.9		3.6
CHI	131	2	1	1197	1485	11.2	30	433	361	14.9	4.53	98	.303	.367	-30	-12	104	103	.932	393	111	-2.9	-1.0	-3.9		.9
PHI	115	4	2	1155¹	1415	11.0	28	364	253	14.3	4.60	91	.300	.356	-38	-53	97	96	.944	296	72	2.3	-4.5	2.9		-11.7
LOU	114	2	0	1138	1363	10.8	39	459	267	15.1	4.42	96	.295	.369	-14	-22	99	106	.929	395	84	-3.6	-1.9	-6.1		-1.4
STL	109	1	1	1127¹	1584	12.6	54	453	207	16.8	6.21	71	.329	.395	-239	-228	102	93	.933	375	84	-2.7	-19.5	-6.0		-8.2
TOT	1359	51	26	13969		10.6				14.1	4.31		.292	.354					.939	4018	1096					

Runs
Hamilton-Bos 152
Keeler-Bal 145
Griffin-Bro 136
Jones-Bro 134
Jennings-Bal 133

Hits
Keeler-Bal 239
F.Clarke-Lou 202
Delahanty-Phi 200
Burkett-Cle 198
Lajoie-Phi 197

Doubles
Stenzel-Bal 43
Lajoie-Phi 40
Delahanty-Phi 40
Wallace-Cle 33
Ryan-Chi 33

Triples
Davis-Pit 28
Lajoie-Phi 23
Wallace-Cle 21
Keeler-Bal 19

Home Runs
Duffy-Bos 11
Davis-NY 10
Lajoie-Phi 9
Beckley-NY-Cin 8

Total Bases
Lajoie-Phi 310
Keeler-Bal 304
Delahanty-Phi 285
F.Clarke-Lou 276
Duffy-Bos 265

Runs Batted In
Davis-NY 136
Collins-Bos 132
Duffy-Bos 129
Lajoie-Phi 127
Kelley-Bal 118

Runs Produced
Duffy-Bos 248
Davis-NY 238
Collins-Bos 229
Kelley-Bal 226

Bases On Balls
Hamilton-Bos 105
McGraw-Bal 99
Griffin-Bro 81
Selbach-Was 80
Joyce-NY 78

Batting Average
McGraw-Bal 424
F.Clarke-Lou 390
Burkett-Cle 383
Delahanty-Phi 377
Kelley-Bal 362

On Base Percentage
McGraw-Bal 471
Burkett-Cle 468
Keeler-Bal 464
Jennings-Bal 463
F.Clarke-Lou 462

Slugging Average
Lajoie-Phi 569
Keeler-Bal 539
Delahanty-Phi 538
F.Clarke-Lou 533
Davis-NY 509

Production
Keeler-Bal 1.003
F.Clarke-Lou 994
Delahanty-Phi 981
Lajoie-Phi 960
Burkett-Cle 944

Adjusted Production
F.Clarke-Lou 168
Keeler-Bal 164
Delahanty-Phi 162
Lajoie-Phi 156
Kelley-Bal 147

Batter Runs
Keeler-Bal 52.1
F.Clarke-Lou 48.5
Delahanty-Phi 45.1
Burkett-Cle 42.0
Kelley-Bal 37.2

Adjusted Batter Runs
F.Clarke-Lou 53.2
Keeler-Bal 52.1
Delahanty-Phi 48.6
Lajoie-Phi 39.3
Kelley-Bal 37.2

Clutch Hitting Index
Gleason-NY 139
Shindle-Bro 138
Collins-Bos 133
Reitz-Bal 131
Tenney-Bos 128

Runs Created
Keeler-Bal 176
F.Clarke-Lou 158
Delahanty-Phi 142
Davis-NY 138
Stenzel-Bal 136

Total Average
F.Clarke-Lou 1.272
Keeler-Bal 1.262
Jennings-Bal 1.251
Hamilton-Bos 1.162
Kelley-Bal 1.143

Stolen Bases
Lange-Chi 73
Stenzel-Bal 69
Hamilton-Bos 66
Davis-NY 65
Keeler-Bal 64

Fielding Runs
Clingman-Lou 28.9
Cross-StL 27.9
Jennings-Bal 27.2
Davis-NY 21.8
Reitz-Bal 21.5

Total Player Rating
Jennings-Bal 5.4
Davis-NY 4.9
F.Clarke-Lou 4.2
Delahanty-Phi 4.0
Collins-Bos 3.5

Wins
Nichols-Bos 31
Rusie-NY 28
Klobedanz-Bos 26
Corbett-Bal 24
Breitenstein-Cin . . . 23

Win Percentage
Klobedanz-Bos 788
Nops-Bal 769
Corbett-Bal 750
Nichols-Bos 738
Rusie-NY 737

Games
Young-Cle 46
Nichols-Bos 46
Mercer-Was 46
Donahue-StL 46

Complete Games
Killen-Pit 38
Griffith-Chi 38
Donahue-StL 38
Nichols-Bos 37
Kennedy-Bro 36

Shutouts
Mercer-Was 3
McJames-Was 3

Saves
Nichols-Bos 3
Mercer-Was 3

Innings Pitched
Nichols-Bos 368.0
Donahue-StL 348.0
Griffith-Chi 343.2
Kennedy-Bro 343.1
Killen-Pit 337.1

Fewest Hits/Game
Seymour-NY 8.23
Rusie-NY 8.77
Nichols-Bos 8.85
Hill-Lou 9.45
Corbett-Bal 9.49

Fewest BB/Game
Young-Cle 1.31
Tannehill-Pit 1.52
Nichols-Bos 1.66
Cuppy-Cle 1.70
Killen-Pit 2.03

Strikeouts
McJames-Was 156
Seymour-NY 149
Corbett-Bal 149
Rusie-NY 135
Nichols-Bos 127

Strikeouts/Game
Seymour-NY 4.83
McJames-Was 4.34
Corbett-Bal 4.28
Rusie-NY 3.77
Nichols-Bos 3.11

Ratio
Nichols-Bos 10.59
Rusie-NY 11.48
Cuppy-Cle 11.80
Young-Cle 12.04
Nops-Bal 12.07

Earned Run Average
Rusie-NY 2.54
Nichols-Bos 2.64
Nops-Bal 2.81
Corbett-Bal 3.11
Powell-Cle 3.16

Adjusted ERA
Nichols-Bos 169
Rusie-NY 163
Nops-Bal 148
Powell-Cle 142
Cuppy-Cle 140

Opponents' Batting Avg.
Seymour-NY 242
Rusie-NY 254
Nichols-Bos 256
Hill-Lou 268
Corbett-Bal 269

Opponents' On Base Pct.
Nichols-Bos 291
Rusie-NY 308
Cuppy-Cle 314
Young-Cle 318
Nops-Bal 319

Starter Runs
Nichols-Bos 68.1
Rusie-NY 63.3
Corbett-Bal 41.8
Mercer-Was 39.4
Nops-Bal 36.6

Adjusted Starter Runs
Nichols-Bos 74.6
Rusie-NY 57.7
Mercer-Was 40.5
Corbett-Bal 36.8
Powell-Cle 33.2

Clutch Pitching Index
Mercer-Was 132
Nops-Bal 120
Corbett-Bal 117
Rusie-NY 117
McJames-Was 117

Relief Ranking

Total Pitcher Index
Nichols-Bos 7.3
Rusie-NY 6.1
Mercer-Was 4.7
Corbett-Bal 3.1
Breitenstein-Cin . . . 3.1

Total Baseball Ranking
Nichols-Bos 7.3
Rusie-NY 6.1
Jennings-Bal 5.4
Davis-NY 4.9
Mercer-Was 4.7

TEAM	G	W	L	PCT	GB	R	OR	AB	H	2B	3B	HR	BB	SO	AVG	OBP	SLG	PRO	PRO+	BR	/A	PF	CHI	RC	SB	CS	SBA	SBR
BOS	152	102	47	.685		872	**614**	5276	1531	190	55	**53**	405	303	.290	.344	**.377**	.721	106	72	28	105	104	780	172			
BAL	154	96	53	.644	6	**933**	623	5242	**1584**	154	77	12	519	316	**.302**	**.382**	.368	**.750**	**118**	157	140	102	99	**864**	250			
CIN	157	92	60	.605	11.5	831	740	5334	1448	207	**101**	19	455	**300**	.271	.335	.359	.694	97	24	-31	107	103	732	165			
CHI	152	85	65	.567	17.5	828	679	5219	1431	175	84	18	476	394	.274	.343	.350	.693	104	29	31	100	104	735	220			
CLE	156	81	68	.544	21	730	683	5246	1379	162	56	18	**545**	306	.263	.338	.325	.663	96	-23	-13	99	97	641	93			
PHI	150	78	71	.523	24	823	784	5118	1431	**238**	31	15	472	382	.280	.348	**.377**	.725	**118**	84	120	96	98	769	182			
NY	157	77	73	.513	25.5	837	800	5349	1422	190	86	34	428	372	.266	.328	.353	.681	103	-5	19	97	**109**	714	214			
PIT	152	72	76	.486	29.5	634	694	5087	1313	140	88	14	336	343	.258	.313	.328	.641	90	-78	-65	98	96	589	107			
LOU	154	70	81	.464	33	728	833	5193	1389	150	71	32	375	429	.267	.325	.342	.667	98	-31	-19	98	101	687	235			
BRO	149	54	91	.372	46	638	811	5126	1314	156	66	17	328	314	.256	.309	.322	.631	85	-98	-95	100	101	577	130			
WAS	155	51	101	.336	52.5	704	939	5257	1423	177	80	36	370	386	.271	.327	.355	.682	100	-5	-3	100	94	703	197			
STL	154	39	111	.260	63.5	571	929	5214	1290	149	55	13	383	402	.247	.309	.305	.614	78	-127	-142	102	91	552	104			
TOT	921					9129		62661	16955	2088	900	299	5092	4247	.271	.334	.347	.681						2069				

TEAM	CG	SH	SV	IP	H	H/G	HR	BB	SO	RAT	ERA	ERA+	OAV	OOB	PR	/A	PF	CPI	FA	E	DP	FW	PW	BW	SBW	DIF
BOS	127	9	8	1340	**1186**	8.0	37	470	432	11.6	2.98	124	**.236**	**.310**	93	105	102	97	.950	310	102	3.1	9.8	2.6		12.0
BAL	138	12	0	1323	1236	8.4	17	400	422	**11.5**	2.90	123	.246	**.310**	104	98	99	99	.947	326	105	2.5	9.2	**13.1**		-3.2
CIN	131	10	2	1385[1]	1484	9.6	16	449	294	13.0	3.50	110	.272	.336	17	51	106	103	.950	325	128	2.9	4.8	-2.9		11.2
CHI	137	**13**	0	1342[2]	1357	9.1	17	364	323	12.1	**2.83**	**126**	.261	.319	**115**	111	99	**113**	.936	412	**149**	-2.9	**10.4**	2.9		-.4
CLE	**142**	9	0	1334	1429	9.6	26	**309**	339	12.1	3.20	113	.272	.320	59	60	100	105	**.952**	**301**	95	**4.2**	5.6	-1.2		-2.1
PHI	129	10	0	1288[1]	1440	10.1	23	399	325	13.4	3.72	92	.281	.342	-17	-42	95	104	.937	379	113	-1.2	-3.9	11.2		-2.6
NY	141	9	1	1353[2]	1359	9.0	21	587	**558**	13.5	3.44	101	.260	.344	25	4	96	106	.932	447	113	-4.2	.4	1.8		4.0
PIT	131	10	3	1323[2]	1400	9.5	**14**	346	330	12.3	3.41	104	.270	.323	29	21	99	98	.946	340	105	1.4	2.0	-6.1		.8
LOU	137	4	0	1334	1457	9.8	33	470	271	13.6	4.24	84	.276	.346	-95	-101	99	93	.939	382	114	-.8	-9.4	-1.8		6.5
BRO	134	1	0	1298[2]	1446	10.0	34	476	294	13.7	4.01	89	.280	.348	-59	-63	99	100	.947	334	125	1.3	-5.9	-8.9		-5.0
WAS	129	0	1	1307	1577	10.9	29	450	371	14.5	4.52	81	.297	.360	-134	-127	102	98	.929	443	119	-4.2	-11.9	-.3		-8.6
STL	133	0	2	1324[1]	1584	10.8	32	372	288	13.9	4.53	83	.295	.350	-137	-111	105	93	.939	388	97	-1.2	-10.4	-13.3		-11.2
TOT	1609	87	17	15954[2]		9.6				12.9	3.60		.271	.334					.942	4387	1354					

Runs	Hits	Doubles	Triples	Home Runs	Total Bases
McGraw-Bal 143	Keeler-Bal 216	Lajoie-Phi 43	Anderson-Br-Ws-Br . . 22	Collins-Bos 15	Collins-Bos 286
Jennings-Bal 135	Burkett-Cle 213	Delahanty-Phi 36	VanHaltren-NY 16	Wagner-Lou 10	Lajoie-Phi 280
VanHaltren-NY . . . 129	VanHaltren-NY 204	Dahlen-Chi 35	Hoy-Lou 16	Joyce-NY 10	VanHaltren-NY 270
Keeler-Bal 126	Lajoie-Phi 197	Collins-Bos 35		Anderson-Br-Ws-Br . . 9	Anderson-Br-Ws-Br . . 257
Cooley-Phi 123		Anderson-Br-Ws-Br . . 33		McKean-Cle 9	Cooley-Phi 256

Runs Batted In	Runs Produced	Bases On Balls	Batting Average	On Base Percentage	Slugging Average
Lajoie-Phi 127	Lajoie-Phi 234	McGraw-Bal 112	Keeler-Bal 385	Hamilton-Bos 480	Anderson-Br-Ws-Br . .494
Collins-Bos 111	Jennings-Bal 221	Joyce-NY 88	Hamilton-Bos 369	McGraw-Bal 475	Collins-Bos 479
Kelley-Bal 110	Delahanty-Phi 203	Hamilton-Bos 87	McGraw-Bal 342	Jennings-Bal 454	Lajoie-Phi 461
Duffy-Bos 108	Collins-Bos 203	Flick-Phi 86	Smith-Cin 342	Flick-Phi 430	Delahanty-Phi 454
McGann-Bal 106	McGann-Bal 200	Jennings-Bal 78	Burkett-Cle 341	Delahanty-Phi 426	Hamilton-Bos 453

Production	Adjusted Production	Batter Runs	Adjusted Batter Runs	Clutch Hitting Index	Runs Created
Hamilton-Bos 933	Hamilton-Bos 159	McGraw-Bal 45.1	Delahanty-Phi 45.6	Kelley-Bal 145	Delahanty-Phi 135
Delahanty-Phi 880	Delahanty-Phi 159	Jennings-Bal 44.2	McGraw-Bal 42.8	Grey-Pit 137	McGraw-Bal 121
Flick-Phi 878	Flick-Phi 158	Hamilton-Bos 43.4	Jennings-Bal 41.9	Davis-NY 136	Hamilton-Bos 120
Jennings-Bal 876	Jennings-Bal 149	Delahanty-Phi 40.2	Flick-Phi 39.9	Connor-Chi 136	Jennings-Bal 119
McGraw-Bal 871	McGraw-Bal 148	Flick-Phi 35.2	Hamilton-Bos 37.7	Hartman-NY 135	Ryan-Chi 119

Total Average	Stolen Bases	Stolen Base Average	Stolen Base Runs	Fielding Runs	Total Player Rating
Hamilton-Bos 1.262	Delahanty-Phi 58			Davis-NY 34.6	Dahlen-Chi 4.6
McGraw-Bal 1.115	Hamilton-Bos 54			Dahlen-Chi 25.5	Jennings-Bal 4.5
Delahanty-Phi . . . 1.082	DeMontreville-Bal . . . 49			Gleason-NY 20.5	Davis-NY 4.4
Jennings-Bal 1.050	Dexter-Lou 44			Selbach-Was 19.9	Collins-Bos 3.8
Flick-Phi 1.035	McGraw-Bal 43			Cross-StL 18.4	Delahanty-Phi 3.7

Wins	Win Percentage	Games	Complete Games	Shutouts	Saves
Nichols-Bos 31	Lewis-Bos 765	Taylor-StL 50	Taylor-StL 42	Powell-Cle 6	Nichols-Bos 4
Cunningham-Lou . . 28	Maul-Bal 741	Nichols-Bos 50	Cunningham-Lou . . 41	Piatt-Phi 6	Tannehill-Pit 2
McJames-Bal 27	Nichols-Bos 721	Young-Cle 46	Young-Cle 40	Tannehill-Pit 5	Lewis-Bos 2
Hawley-Cin 27	Hawley-Cin 711		Nichols-Bos 40	Nichols-Bos 5	Hickman-Bos 2
Lewis-Bos 26	Griffith-Chi 706		McJames-Bal 40	Hughes-Bal 5	Dammann-Cin 2

Innings Pitched	Fewest Hits/Game	Fewest BB/Game	Strikeouts	Strikeouts/Game	Ratio
Taylor-StL 397.1	Nichols-Bos 7.33	Young-Cle 98	Seymour-NY 239	Seymour-NY 6.03	Nichols-Bos 9.63
Nichols-Bos . . .388.0	Willis-Bos 7.64	Dwyer-Cin 1.58	McJames-Bal . . . 178	Willis-Bos 4.63	Maul-Bal 9.76
Young-Cle 377.2	Lewis-Bos 7.67	Cunningham-Lou . . 1.62	Willis-Bos 160	McJames-Bal 4.28	Young-Cle 10.41
McJames-Bal . .374.0	Maul-Bal 7.77	Tannehill-Pit 1.74	Nichols-Bos 138	Doheny-NY 4.06	Griffith-Chi 10.75
Cunningham-Lou .362.0	McJames-Bal 7.87	Griffith-Chi 1.77	Piatt-Phi 121	Piatt-Phi 3.56	McJames-Bal 10.88

Earned Run Average	Adjusted ERA	Opponents' Batting Avg.	Opponents' On Base Pct.	Starter Runs	Adjusted Starter Runs
Griffith-Chi 1.88	Griffith-Chi 190	Nichols-Bos 221	Nichols-Bos 272	Nichols-Bos 63.3	Nichols-Bos 67.1
Maul-Bal 2.10	Nichols-Bos 173	Willis-Bos 229	Maul-Bal 275	Griffith-Chi 62.4	Griffith-Chi 61.5
Nichols-Bos 2.13	Maul-Bal 170	Lewis-Bos 229	Young-Cle 288	McJames-Bal 51.7	McJames-Bal 50.5
McJames-Bal 2.36	McJames-Bal 152	Maul-Bal 232	Griffith-Chi 294	Young-Cle 45.2	Young-Cle 45.6
Callahan-Chi 2.46	Callahan-Chi 145	McJames-Bal 234	McJames-Bal 297	Maul-Bal 39.9	Maul-Bal 39.2

Clutch Pitching Index	Relief Runs	Adjusted Relief Runs	Relief Ranking	Total Pitcher Index	Total Baseball Ranking
Griffith-Chi 135				Nichols-Bos 6.9	Nichols-Bos 6.9
Orth-Phi 120				Griffith-Chi 5.8	Griffith-Chi 5.8
Dammann-Cin 118				Young-Cle 5.3	Young-Cle 5.3
Doheny-NY 117				McJames-Bal 4.3	Dahlen-Chi 4.6
Callahan-Chi 116				Callahan-Chi 3.9	Jennings-Bal 4.5

TEAM	G	W	L	PCT	GB	R	OR	AB	H	2B	3B	HR	BB	SO	AVG	OBP	SLG	PRO	PRO+	BR	/A	PF	CHI	RC	SB	CS	SBA	SBR
BRO	150	101	47	.682		892	658	4937	1436	178	97	27	477	263	.291	**.368**	.383	.751	110	87	68	102	103	824	271			
BOS	153	95	57	.625	8	858	**645**	5290	1517	178	90	39	431	269	.287	.345	.377	.722	94	21	-59	110	103	787	185			
PHI	154	94	58	.618	9	**916**	743	5353	**1613**	241	83	31	441	341	**.301**	.363	**.395**	**.758**	**118**	**96**	**128**	97	99	**879**	212			
BAL	152	86	62	.581	15	827	691	5073	1509	204	71	17	418	383	.297	.365	.376	.741	104	68	24	105	97	861	**364**			
STL	155	84	67	.556	18.5	819	739	5304	1514	172	88	**47**	468	262	.285	.347	.378	.725	102	28	9	102	97	801	210			
CIN	156	83	67	.553	19	856	770	5225	1439	194	105	13	**485**	295	.275	.345	.360	.705	97	-5	-20	102	**106**	762	228			
PIT	154	76	73	.510	25.5	834	765	5450	1574	196	**121**	27	384	345	.289	.343	.384	.727	105	26	29	100	97	815	179			
CHI	152	75	73	.507	26	812	763	5148	1428	173	82	27	406	342	.277	.338	.359	.697	99	-26	-5	97	105	743	247			
LOU	155	75	77	.493	28	827	775	5307	1484	192	68	40	436	375	.280	.343	.364	.707	99	-3	9	100	101	781	233			
NY	152	60	90	.400	42	734	863	5092	1431	161	65	23	387	360	.281	.337	.352	.689	97	-39	-13	97	100	708	234			
WAS	155	54	98	.355	49	743	983	5256	1429	162	87	**47**	350	341	.272	.328	.363	.691	96	-45	-37	99	99	710	176			
CLE	154	20	134	.130	84	529	1252	5279	1333	142	50	12	289	280	.253	.299	.305	.604	76	-209	-168	93	92	541	127			
TOT	921					9647		62714	17707	2193	1007	350	4972	3856	.282	.343	.366	.710							2666			

TEAM	CG	SH	SV	IP	H	H/G	HR	BB	SO	RAT	ERA	ERA+	OAV	OOB	PR	/A	PF	CPI	FA	E	DP	FW	PW	BW	SBW	DIF
BRO	121	9	**9**	1269¹	1320	9.4	32	463	331	13.0	**3.25**	120	.268	.337	85	92	102	**111**	.948	314	125	2.9	8.3	6.2		9.6
BOS	138	13	4	1348	**1273**	**8.5**	44	432	385	**11.8**	3.26	**127**	**.250**	.317	88	**133**	108	95	**.952**	**303**	124	**4.0**	**12.1**	-5.3		8.3
PHI	129	**15**	2	1333¹	1398	9.4	17	370	281	12.5	3.47	106	.270	.328	56	30	96	97	.940	379	110	-.4	2.7	**11.6**		4.0
BAL	132	10	4	1304¹	1403	9.7	**13**	349	294	12.6	3.31	119	.275	.330	78	93	103	103	.949	308	96	3.5	8.4	2.2		-2.1
STL	134	7	1	1340²	1476	9.9	41	**321**	331	12.4	3.36	118	.280	.327	73	91	103	107	.939	397	117	-1.3	8.2	.8		.7
CIN	130	8	5	1361	1484	9.8	26	370	360	12.8	3.70	106	.278	.333	23	32	102	97	.947	339	111	2.3	2.9	-1.8		4.6
PIT	117	9	4	1364	1464	9.7	27	437	334	13.0	3.60	106	.274	.337	39	55	97	99	.935	361	98	.7	2.9	2.6		-4.7
CHI	**147**	8	1	1331¹	1433	9.7	20	330	313	12.5	3.37	111	.275	.328	71	55	97	102	.935	428	**145**	-3.5	5.0	-.5		-.0
LOU	134	5	2	1351²	1509	10.0	33	323	287	12.6	3.45	112	.282	.331	60	60	100	106	.939	394	101	-1.1	5.4	-.2		-5.2
NY	138	4	0	1278¹	1454	10.2	19	628	**397**	15.3	4.29	87	.286	.375	-63	-78	97	103	.932	433	140	-3.8	-7.1	-1.2		-3.0
WAS	131	3	0	1300¹	1649	11.4	35	422	328	14.9	4.93	79	.309	.368	-157	-149	102	95	.935	403	99	-1.6	-13.5	-3.4		-3.5
CLE	138	0	0	1264	1844	13.1	43	527	215	17.7	6.37	58	.340	.409	-353	-378	96	94	.937	388	121	-.9	-34.3	-15.2		-6.6
TOT	1589	91	32	15846¹		10.1				13.4	3.85		.282	.343					.942	4447	1387					

Runs
McGraw-Bal 140
Keeler-Bro 140
Thomas-Phi 137
Delahanty-Phi 135
Williams-Pit 126

Hits
Delahanty-Phi 238
Burkett-StL 221
Williams-Pit 219
Keeler-Bro 216
Tenney-Bos 209

Doubles
Delahanty-Phi 55
Wagner-Lou 43
Holmes-Bal 31
Long-Bos 30
Duffy-Bos 29

Triples
Williams-Pit 27
Freeman-Was 25
Stahl-Bos 19
Tenney-Bos 17
McCarthy-Pit 17

Home Runs
Freeman-Was 25
Wallace-StL 12
Williams-Pit 9
Mertes-Chi 9
Delahanty-Phi 9

Total Bases
Delahanty-Phi 338
Freeman-Was 331
Williams-Pit 328
Stahl-Bos 284
Wagner-Lou 282

Runs Batted In
Delahanty-Phi 137
Freeman-Was 122
Williams-Pit 116
Wagner-Lou 113
Wallace-StL 108

Runs Produced
Delahanty-Phi 263
Williams-Pit 233
Wagner-Lou 204
Freeman-Was 204

Bases On Balls
McGraw-Bal 124
Thomas-Phi 115
VanHaltren-NY 74
Childs-StL 74

Batting Average
Delahanty-Phi 410
Burkett-StL 396
McGraw-Bal 391
Keeler-Bro 379
Williams-Pit 355

On Base Percentage
McGraw-Bal 547
Delahanty-Phi 464
Burkett-StL 463
Thomas-Phi 457
Stahl-Bos 426

Slugging Average
Delahanty-Phi 582
Freeman-Was 563
Williams-Pit 532
Burkett-StL 500
Wagner-Lou 494

Production
Delahanty-Phi 1.046
McGraw-Bal 994
Burkett-StL 963
Williams-Pit 949
Freeman-Was 925

Adjusted Production
Delahanty-Phi 193
McGraw-Bal 165
Burkett-StL 160
Williams-Pit 160
Freeman-Was 154

Batter Runs
Delahanty-Phi 67.9
McGraw-Bal 56.8
Burkett-StL 51.6
Williams-Pit 49.0
Stahl-Bos 42.2

Adjusted Batter Runs
Delahanty-Phi 73.5
McGraw-Bal 50.2
Williams-Pit 49.5
Burkett-StL 48.4
Freeman-Was 37.6

Clutch Hitting Index
Brodie-Bal 139
Long-Bos 131
Magoon-Bal-Chi . . . 129
Lauder-Phi 128
Corcoran-Cin 128

Runs Created
Delahanty-Phi 175
Williams-Pit 152
Burkett-StL 145
McGraw-Bal 141
Stahl-Bos 139

Total Average
McGraw-Bal 1.601
Delahanty-Phi 1.245
Burkett-StL 1.107
Williams-Pit 1.055
Stahl-Bos 1.051

Stolen Bases
Sheckard-Bal 77
McGraw-Bal 73
Heidrick-StL 55
Holmes-Bal 50
Clarke-Lou 49

Stolen Base Average

Stolen Base Runs

Fielding Runs
G.Davis-NY 46.3
Wallace-StL 38.8
Cross-Cle-StL 32.7
Gleason-NY 25.7
Collins-Bos 20.9

Total Player Rating
G.Davis-NY 6.2
Delahanty-Phi 5.6
Wallace-StL 5.3
Williams-Pit 5.2
Lajoie-Phi 4.9

Wins
McGinnity-Bal 28
Hughes-Bro 28
Willis-Bos 27
Young-StL 26
Tannehill-Pit 24

Win Percentage
Hughes-Bro 824
Willis-Bos 771
Hahn-Cin 742
Donahue-Phi 724
Kennedy-Bro 710

Games
Leever-Pit 51
Powell-StL 48
McGinnity-Bal 48
Young-StL 44
Carrick-NY 44

Complete Games
Young-StL 40
Powell-StL 40
Carrick-NY 40
Taylor-Chi 39
McGinnity-Bal 38

Shutouts
Willis-Bos 5

Saves
Leever-Pit 3

Innings Pitched
Leever-Pit 379.0
Powell-StL 373.0
Young-StL 369.1
McGinnity-Bal . . . 366.1
Carrick-NY 361.2

Fewest Hits/Game
Willis-Bos 7.28
Hughes-Bro 7.71
Hahn-Cin 8.16
Seymour-NY 8.28
Leever-Pit 8.38

Fewest BB/Game
Young-StL 1.07
Cuppy-StL 1.36
Tannehill-Pit 1.47
Kitson-Bal 1.79
Woods-Lou 1.79

Strikeouts
Hahn-Cin 145
Seymour-NY 142
Leever-Pit 121
Willis-Bos 120
Doheny-NY 115

Strikeouts/Game
Seymour-NY 4.76
Hahn-Cin 4.22
Doheny-NY 3.90
McJames-Bro 3.43
Willis-Bos 3.15

Ratio
Young-StL 10.19
Hahn-Cin 10.43
Nichols-Bos 10.85
Willis-Bos 11.14
Kitson-Bal 11.15

Earned Run Average
Willis-Bos 2.50
Young-StL 2.58
McGinnity-Bal 2.68
Hahn-Cin 2.68
Hughes-Bro 2.68

Adjusted ERA
Willis-Bos 166
Young-StL 154
McGinnity-Bal 148
Hahn-Cin 146
Hughes-Bro 146

Opponents' Batting Avg.
Willis-Bos 222
Hughes-Bro 232
Hahn-Cin 242
Seymour-NY 245
Leever-Pit 247

Opponents' On Base Pct.
Young-StL 285
Hahn-Cin 290
Nichols-Bos 298
Willis-Bos 303
Kitson-Bal 304

Starter Runs
Young-StL 52.0
Willis-Bos 51.6
McGinnity-Bal 47.7
Hahn-Cin 40.2
Kitson-Bal 39.2

Adjusted Starter Runs
Willis-Bos 63.1
Young-StL 57.2
McGinnity-Bal 52.1
Nichols-Bos 44.5
Kitson-Bal 43.1

Clutch Pitching Index
Kennedy-Bro 130
Tannehill-Pit 124
Dowling-Lou 121
Callahan-Chi 121
Woods-Lou 118

Relief Runs

Adjusted Relief Runs

Relief Ranking

Total Pitcher Index
Young-StL 6.2
Willis-Bos 5.3
McGinnity-Bal 5.0
Tannehill-Pit 4.8
Hughes-Bro 4.7

Total Baseball Ranking
G.Davis-NY 6.2
Young-StL 6.2
Delahanty-Phi 5.6
Willis-Bos 5.3
Wallace-StL 5.3

TEAM	G	W	L	PCT	GB	R	OR	AB	H	2B	3B	HR	BB	SO	AVG	OBP	SLG	PRO	PRO+	BR	/A	PF	CHI	RC	SB	CS	SBA	SBR
BRO	142	82	54	.603		816	722	4860	1423	199	81	26	421	272	.293	.359	.383	.742	104	72	23	106	100	795	274			
PIT	140	79	60	.568	4.5	733	612	4817	1312	185	100	26	327	321	.272	.327	.368	.695	96	-25	-30	101	105	666	174			
PHI	141	75	63	.543	8	810	792	4969	1439	187	82	29	440	374	.290	.356	.378	.734	109	58	65	99	99	774	205			
BOS	142	66	72	.478	17	778	739	4952	1403	163	68	48	395	278	.283	.342	.373	.715	92	16	-78	112	102	724	182			
STL	142	65	75	.464	19	744	748	4877	1420	141	81	36	406	318	.291	.356	.375	.731	108	52	58	99	94	766	243			
CHI	146	65	75	.464	19	635	751	4907	1276	202	51	33	343	383	.260	.317	.342	.659	90	-87	-63	98	97	622	189			
CIN	144	62	77	.446	21.5	703	745	5026	1335	178	83	33	333	408	.266	.318	.354	.672	92	-71	-54	98	103	651	183			
NY	141	60	78	.435	23	713	823	4724	1317	177	61	23	369	343	.279	.338	.357	.695	102	-16	16	95	102	676	236			
TOT	569					5932		39132	10925	1432	607	254	3034	2697	.279	.339	.366	.705						1686				

TEAM	CG	SH	SV	IP	H	H/G	HR	BB	SO	RAT	ERA	ERA+	OAV	OOB	PR	/A	PF	CPI	FA	E	DP	FW	PW	BW	SBW	DIF
BRO	104	8	4	1225²	1370	10.1	30	405	300	13.6	3.89	99	.282	.346	-27	-8	104	99	.948	303	102	2.6	-.7	2.1		10.1
PIT	114	11	1	1229	1232	9.0	24	295	415	11.7	3.06	119	.261	.313	87	77	98	97	.945	322	106	1.1	7.0	-2.7		4.1
PHI	116	7	3	1248²	1506	10.9	29	402	284	14.2	4.12	88	.298	.357	-59	-71	98	103	.945	330	125	.8	-6.5	5.9		5.8
BOS	116	8	2	1240¹	1263	9.2	59	463	340	12.9	3.72	111	.264	.335	-4	55	112	97	.953	273	86	4.4	5.0	-7.1		-5.3
STL	117	12	0	1217¹	1373	10.2	37	299	325	12.7	3.75	97	.284	.331	-7	-16	98	97	.943	331	73	.8	-1.5	5.3		-9.7
CHI	137	9	1	1271	1375	9.7	21	324	357	12.6	3.23	112	.276	.330	66	52	98	106	.933	418	98	-3.9	4.8	-5.8		-.0
CIN	118	9	1	1274²	1383	9.8	28	404	399	13.0	3.83	96	.276	.338	-20	-24	99	94	.945	341	120	.5	-2.2	-4.9		-.9
NY	113	4	0	1207¹	1423	10.6	26	442	277	14.6	3.96	91	.293	.363	-35	-47	98	108	.928	439	124	-6.0	-4.3	1.5		-.2
TOT	935	68	12	9914		9.9				13.2	3.69		.279	.339					.942	2757	834					

Runs
Thomas-Phi 132
Slagle-Phi 115
VanHaltren-NY 114
Barrett-Cin 114
Wagner-Pit 107

Hits
Keeler-Bro 204
Burkett-StL 203
Wagner-Pit 201
Flick-Phi.......... 200
Beckley-Cin 190

Doubles
Wagner-Pit 45
Lajoie-Phi 33
Flick-Phi 32
Delahanty-Phi 32
VanHaltren-NY 30

Triples
Wagner-Pit 22
Kelley-Bro 17
Hickman-NY 17
Stahl-Bos 16
Flick-Phi 16

Home Runs
Long-Bos 12
Flick-Phi........... 11
Donlin-StL 10
Hickman-NY 9
Sullivan-Bos 8

Total Bases
Wagner-Pit 302
Flick-Phi 297
Burkett-StL 265
Keeler-Bro 253
Beckley-Cin 242

Runs Batted In
Flick-Phi 110
Delahanty-Phi 109
Wagner-Pit 100
Collins-Bos 95
Beckley-Cin 94

Runs Produced
Flick-Phi 205
Wagner-Pit 203
Collins-Bos 193
Beckley-Cin 190
Delahanty-Phi 189

Bases On Balls
Thomas-Phi 115
Hamilton-Bos 107
McGraw-StL 85
Dahlen-Bro 73

Batting Average
Wagner-Pit .... .381
Flick-Phi .... .367
Burkett-StL .... .363
Keeler-Bro .... .362
McGraw-StL .... .344

On Base Percentage
McGraw-StL ...... .505
Thomas-Phi ...... .451
Hamilton-Bos ..... .449
Flick-Phi .... .441
Wagner-Pit .... .434

Slugging Average
Wagner-Pit .... .573
Flick-Phi .... .545
Lajoie-Phi .... .510
Kelley-Bro .... .485
Hickman-NY .... .482

Production
Wagner-Pit 1.007
Flick-Phi .... .986
McGraw-StL ...... .921
Burkett-StL ...... .904
Selbach-NY ...... .885

Adjusted Production
Wagner-Pit 175
Flick-Phi.......... 172
McGraw-StL 157
Selbach-NY 151
Burkett-StL 150

Batter Runs
Flick-Phi 53.5
Wagner-Pit 53.2
Burkett-StL 39.0
McGraw-StL 36.0
Selbach-NY 34.3

Adjusted Batter Runs
Flick-Phi 54.7
Wagner-Pit 52.3
Burkett-StL 40.0
Selbach-NY 39.8
McGraw-StL 36.8

Clutch Hitting Index
Delahanty-Phi 143
Cross-Phi 142
Jennings-Bro 138
Lowe-Bos 122
Collins-Bos 119

Runs Created
Wagner-Pit 152
Flick-Phi 151
Burkett-StL 133
Keeler-Bro 123
Selbach-NY 121

Total Average
McGraw-StL 1.260
Wagner-Pit 1.193
Flick-Phi 1.171
Selbach-NY 1.029
Burkett-StL 1.017

Stolen Bases
VanHaltren-NY 45
Donovan-StL 45
Barrett-Cin 44
Keeler-Bro 41

Stolen Base Average

Stolen Base Runs

Fielding Runs
Steinfeldt-Cin ... 35.6
Lajoie-Phi 29.5
Davis-NY 29.3
Dahlen-Bro 19.8
Bradley-Chi 16.8

Total Player Rating
Lajoie-Phi 5.0
Davis-NY 4.6
Flick-Phi 4.3
Selbach-NY 3.5
Wagner-Pit 3.3

Wins
McGinnity-Bro 28
Tannehill-Pit 20
Phillippe-Pit 20
Kennedy-Bro 20
Dinneen-Bos 20

Win Percentage
McGinnity-Bro ..... .778
Tannehill-Pit ...... .769
Fraser-Phi .... .625
Phillippe-Pit ...... .606
Kennedy-Bro ..... .606

Games
Carrick-NY 45
McGinnity-Bro 44
Scott-Cin 42
Kennedy-Bro 42

Complete Games
Hawley-NY 34
Dinneen-Bos 33

Shutouts
Young-StL 4
Nichols-Bos 4
Hahn-Cin 4
Griffith-Chi 4

Saves
Kitson-Bro 4
Bernhard-Phi 2

Innings Pitched
McGinnity-Bro ...343.0
Carrick-NY 341.2
Hawley-NY 329.1
Young-StL 321.1
Dinneen-Bos 320.2

Fewest Hits/Game
Waddell-Pit 7.59
Garvin-Chi 8.22
Nichols-Bos 8.36
Dinneen-Bos 8.53
Phillippe-Pit 8.84

Fewest BB/Game
Young-StL 1.01
Phillippe-Pit 1.35
Tannehill-Pit 1.65
Griffith-Chi 1.85
Leever-Pit........ 1.86

Strikeouts
Hahn-Cin 132
Waddell-Pit 130
Young-StL 115
Garvin-Chi........ 107
Dinneen-Bos 107

Strikeouts/Game
Waddell-Pit 5.61
Garvin-Chi 3.91
Hahn-Cin 3.82
Newton-Cin 3.38
Leever-Pit 3.25

Ratio
Phillippe-Pit 10.42
Waddell-Pit 10.52
Young-StL 10.53
Garvin-Chi 11.18
Leever-Pit 11.30

Earned Run Average
Waddell-Pit 2.37
Garvin-Chi 2.41
Taylor-Chi 2.55
Leever-Pit 2.71
Phillippe-Pit 2.84

Adjusted ERA
Waddell-Pit 153
Garvin-Chi 149
Taylor-Chi 141
Nichols-Bos 134
Leever-Pit 134

Opponents' Batting Avg.
Waddell-Pit .... .229
Garvin-Chi .... .243
Nichols-Bos ...... .246
Dinneen-Bos ...... .250
Phillippe-Pit ...... .257

Opponents' On Base Pct.
Phillippe-Pit ...... .289
Waddell-Pit ...... .291
Young-StL .... .291
Garvin-Chi........ .304
Leever-Pit .... .306

Starter Runs
Garvin-Chi 35.1
Waddell-Pit 30.7
McGinnity-Bro 28.8
Taylor-Chi 28.3
Phillippe-Pit 26.5

Adjusted Starter Runs
Dinneen-Bos 35.9
McGinnity-Bro 34.2
Garvin-Chi 32.6
Waddell-Pit....... 29.1
Nichols-Bos 27.0

Clutch Pitching Index
Fraser-Phi 131
Taylor-Chi 119
McGinnity-Bro 118
Carrick-NY 115
Donahue-Phi 113

Relief Runs

Adjusted Relief Runs

Relief Ranking

Total Pitcher Index
Dinneen-Bos 3.6
Garvin-Chi 3.1
Taylor-Chi 2.7
Tannehill-Pit 2.7
Nichols-Bos 2.6

Total Baseball Ranking
Lajoie-Phi 5.0
Davis-NY 4.6
Flick-Phi 4.3
Dinneen-Bos 3.6
Selbach-NY 3.5

TEAM	G	W	L	PCT	GB	R	OR	AB	H	2B	3B	HR	BB	SO	AVG	OBP	SLG	PRO	PRO+	BR	/A	PF	CHI	RC	SB	CS	SBA	SBR
PIT	140	90	49	.647		776	534	4913	1407	182	92	29	386	493	.286	.345	.379	.724	113	99	76	103	102	743	203			
PHI	140	83	57	.593	7.5	668	543	4793	1275	194	58	24	430	549	.266	.334	.346	.680	101	29	15	102	98	652	199			
BRO	137	79	57	.581	9.5	744	600	4879	1399	206	93	32	312	449	.287	.335	.387	.722	112	86	66	103	102	718	178			
STL	142	76	64	.543	14.5	792	689	5039	1430	187	94	39	314	540	.284	.337	.381	.718	120	87	125	95	104	744	190			
BOS	140	69	69	.500	20.5	531	556	4746	1180	135	36	28	303	519	.249	.298	.310	.608	75	-104	-153	109	101	515	158			
CHI	140	53	86	.381	37	578	649	4844	1250	153	61	18	314	532	.258	.310	.326	.636	94	-57	-35	96	99	575	204			
NY	141	52	85	.380	37	544	755	4839	1225	167	46	19	303	575	.253	.303	.318	.621	89	-83	-62	96	98	529	133			
CIN	142	52	87	.374	38	561	818	4914	1232	173	70	38	323	584	.251	.303	.338	.641	97	-56	-17	93	94	570	137			
TOT	561					5194		38967	10398	1397	550	227	2685	4241	.267	.321	.348	.669						1402				

TEAM	CG	SH	SV	IP	H	H/G	HR	BB	SO	RAT	ERA	ERA+	OAV	OOB	PR	/A	PF	CPI	FA	E	DP	FW	PW	BW	SBW	DIF
PIT	119	15	4	1244²	1198	8.7	20	244	505	10.9	2.58	126	.252	.297	102	94	98	104	.950	287	97	1.2	9.2	7.4		2.6
PHI	125	15	2	1246²	1221	8.8	19	259	480	11.0	2.87	119	.255	.300	63	73	102	97	.954	262	65	2.7	7.2	1.5		1.7
BRO	111	7	5	1213²	1244	9.2	18	435	583	12.8	3.14	107	.264	.333	24	27	101	109	.950	281	99	1.2	2.6	6.5		.7
STL	118	5	5	1269²	1333	9.4	39	332	445	12.2	3.68	86	.268	.321	-51	-71	96	93	.949	305	108	.4	-7.0	12.3		.3
BOS	128	11	0	1263	1196	8.5	29	349	558	11.3	2.90	125	.249	.305	59	99	109	98	.952	282	89	1.5	9.7	-15.0		3.8
CHI	131	2	0	1241²	1348	9.8	27	324	586	12.5	3.33	97	.275	.327	-2	-14	97	105	.943	336	87	-1.8	-1.4	-3.4		-9.9
NY	118	11	1	1232	1389	10.1	24	377	542	13.4	3.87	85	.283	.342	-75	-78	100	99	.941	348	81	-2.3	-7.6	-6.1		-.4
CIN	126	4	0	1265²	1469	10.4	51	365	542	13.5	4.17	77	.289	.345	-120	-138	96	99	.940	355	102	-2.6	-13.5	-1.7		.3
TOT	976	70	17	9977		9.4				12.2	3.32		.267	.321					.947	2456	728					

Runs
Burkett-StL 142
Keeler-Bro 123
Beaumont-Pit 120
Clarke-Pit 118
Sheckard-Bro 116

Hits
Burkett-StL 226
Keeler-Bro 202
Sheckard-Bro 196
Wagner-Pit 194
Delahanty-Phi 192

Doubles
Delahanty-Phi 38
Daly-Bro 38
Wagner-Pit 37
Beckley-Cin 36
Wallace-StL 34

Triples
Sheckard-Bro 19
Flick-Phi 17

Home Runs
Crawford-Cin 16
Sheckard-Bro 11
Burkett-StL 10

Total Bases
Burkett-StL 306
Sheckard-Bro 296
Delahanty-Phi 286
Wagner-Pit 271

Runs Batted In
Wagner-Pit 126
Delahanty-Phi 108
Sheckard-Bro 104
Crawford-Cin 104

Runs Produced
Wagner-Pit 221
Sheckard-Bro 209
Burkett-StL 207
Delahanty-Phi 206
Flick-Phi 192

Bases On Balls
Thomas-Phi 100
Hartsel-Chi 74
Davis-Bro-Pit 66
Delahanty-Phi 65
Hamilton-Bos 64

Batting Average
Burkett-StL 376
Delahanty-Phi 354
Sheckard-Bro 354
Wagner-Pit 353
Keeler-Bro 339

On Base Percentage
Burkett-StL .... .440
Thomas-Phi 437
Delahanty-Phi 427
Wagner-Pit 417
Hartsel-Chi ...... .414

Slugging Average
Sheckard-Bro 534
Delahanty-Phi 528
Crawford-Cin 524
Burkett-StL 509
Flick-Phi 500

Production
Delahanty-Phi 955
Burkett-StL 949
Sheckard-Bro 944
Wagner-Pit 911
Crawford-Cin 903

Adjusted Production
Burkett-StL 184
Delahanty-Phi 173
Crawford-Cin 172
Sheckard-Bro 168
Hartsel-Chi 163

Batter Runs
Burkett-StL 58.7
Delahanty-Phi 53.3
Sheckard-Bro 49.8
Wagner-Pit 44.9
Hartsel-Chi 42.6

Adjusted Batter Runs
Burkett-StL 65.9
Delahanty-Phi 50.7
Hartsel-Chi 47.2
Sheckard-Bro 46.5
Crawford-Cin 44.2

Clutch Hitting Index
Ganzel-NY 139
Dexter-Chi 136
Wagner-Pit 133
Long-Bos 133
Krueger-StL 128

Runs Created
Burkett-StL 151
Sheckard-Bro 139
Delahanty-Phi 139
Wagner-Pit 138
Hartsel-Chi 130

Total Average
Delahanty-Phi 1.097
Burkett-StL 1.072
Wagner-Pit 1.070
Sheckard-Bro 1.070
Hartsel-Chi 1.027

Stolen Bases
Wagner-Pit 49
Hartsel-Chi 41
Strang-NY 40
Harley-Cin 37
Beaumont-Pit 36

Fielding Runs
Wallace-StL 29.6
Davis-NY 23.1
Flick-Phi 14.9
Dahlen-Bro 13.7
Kittridge-Bos 12.0

Total Player Rating
Wallace-StL 6.2
Burkett-StL 5.2
Wagner-Pit 5.1
Davis-NY 4.9
Sheckard-Bro 4.3

Wins
Donovan-Bro 25
Harper-StL 23
Phillippe-Pit 22
Hahn-Cin 22

Win Percentage
Chesbro-Pit ...... .677
Phillippe-Pit ...... .647
Tannehill-Pit...... .643
Harper-StL .... .639
Kitson-Bro .... .633

Games
Taylor-NY 45
Powell-StL 45
Donovan-Bro 45
Hahn-Cin 42
Mathewson-NY 40

Complete Games
Hahn-Cin 41
Taylor-NY 37
Mathewson-NY 36
Donovan-Bro 36
Donahue-Phi 34

Shutouts
Willis-Bos 6
Orth-Phi 6
Chesbro-Pit 6

Saves
Powell-StL 3
Donovan-Bro 3
Sudhoff-StL 2
Phillippe-Pit 2
Kitson-Bro 2

Innings Pitched
Hahn-Cin 375.1
Taylor-NY 353.1
Donovan-Bro 351.0
Powell-StL 338.1
Mathewson-NY ..336.0

Fewest Hits/Game
Townsend-Phi 7.39
Mathewson-NY 7.71
Willis-Bos 7.72
Orth-Phi 7.99
Chesbro-Pit 8.17

Fewest BB/Game
Orth-Phi 1.02
Phillippe-Pit 1.16
Tannehill-Pit 1.28
Duggleby-Phi 1.31
Powell-StL 1.33

Strikeouts
Hahn-Cin 239
Donovan-Bro 226
Hughes-Chi....... 225
Mathewson-NY ... 221
Waddell-Pit-Chi .. 172

Strikeouts/Game
Hughes-Chi 6.57
Waddell-Pit-Chi .. 6.16
Mathewson-NY ... 5.92
Donovan-Bro 5.79
Hahn-Cin 5.73

Ratio
Orth-Phi 9.27
Phillippe-Pit 9.79
Tannehill-Pit 10.20
Chesbro-Pit 10.23
Willis-Bos 10.35

Earned Run Average
Tannehill-Pit 2.18
Phillippe-Pit 2.22
Orth-Phi 2.27
Willis-Bos 2.36
Chesbro-Pit 2.38

Adjusted ERA
Willis-Bos 153
Tannehill-Pit 150
Orth-Phi 150
Phillippe-Pit 147
Chesbro-Pit 137

Opponents' Batting Avg.
Townsend-Phi 223
Mathewson-NY 230
Willis-Bos .... .231
Orth-Phi 237
Chesbro-Pit ...... .241

Opponents' On Base Pct.
Orth-Phi .... .264
Phillippe-Pit ...... .275
Tannehill-Pit ..... .284
Chesbro-Pit ...... .284
Willis-Bos .... .286

Starter Runs
Phillippe-Pit 36.2
Mathewson-NY ... 34.0
Orth-Phi 32.9
Willis-Bos 32.7
Tannehill-Pit 32.1

Adjusted Starter Runs
Willis-Bos 42.6
Orth-Phi 35.3
Phillippe-Pit 34.4
Mathewson-NY ... 33.3
Tannehill-Pit 30.5

Clutch Pitching Index
Kitson-Bro 122
Taylor-Chi 116
Hughes-Bro 114
Taylor-NY 113
Duggleby-Phi 110

Total Pitcher Index
Orth-Phi 4.8
Willis-Bos 4.6
Phillippe-Pit 4.4
Mathewson-NY ... 4.1
Tannehill-Pit 3.2

Total Baseball Ranking
Wallace-StL 6.2
Burkett-StL 5.2
Wagner-Pit 5.1
Davis-NY 4.9
Willis-Bos 4.6

TEAM	G	W	L	PCT	GB	R	OR	AB	H	2B	3B	HR	BB	SO	AVG	OBP	SLG	PRO	PRO+	BR	/A	PF	CHI	RC	SB	CS	SBA	SBR
CHI	137	83	53	.610		819	631	4725	1303	173	89	32	475	337	.276	.350	.370	.720	108	41	62	97	103	744	280			
BOS	138	79	57	.581	4	759	608	4866	1353	183	104	37	331	282	.278	.330	.381	.711	104	9	23	98	101	693	157			
DET	136	74	61	.548	8.5	741	694	4676	1303	180	80	29	380	346	.279	.340	.370	.710	98	15	-19	105	99	690	204			
PHI	137	74	62	.544	9	805	761	4882	1409	239	87	35	301	344	.289	.337	.395	.732	103	42	8	104	103	734	173			
BAL	135	68	65	.511	13.5	760	750	4589	1348	179	111	24	369	377	.294	.353	.397	.750	108	80	45	104	96	746	207			
WAS	138	61	72	.459	20.5	682	771	4772	1282	191	83	33	356	340	.269	.326	.364	.690	97	-24	-13	99	96	633	127			
CLE	138	54	82	.397	29	667	831	4833	1311	197	68	12	243	326	.271	.313	.348	.661	92	-82	-56	96	104	588	125			
MIL	139	48	89	.350	35.5	641	828	4795	1250	192	66	26	325	384	.261	.314	.345	.659	91	-81	-49	95	98	602	176			
TOT	549					5874		38138	10559	1534	688	228	2780	2736	.277	.333	.371	.704						1449				

TEAM	CG	SH	SV	IP	H	H/G	HR	BB	SO	RAT	ERA	ERA+	OAV	OOB	PR	/A	PF	CPI	FA	E	DP	FW	PW	BW	SBW	DIF
CHI	110	11	2	1218¹	1250	9.2	27	312	394	11.9	2.98	117	.263	.315	93	68	95	106	.941	345	100	.9	6.1	5.6		2.4
BOS	123	7	1	1217	1178	8.7	33	294	396	11.2	3.04	116	.251	.301	84	66	96	93	.943	337	104	1.6	6.0	2.1		1.4
DET	118	8	2	1188²	1328	10.1	22	313	307	12.8	3.30	116	.280	.330	48	71	105	109	.930	410	127	-3.3	6.4	-1.7		5.1
PHI	124	6	1	1200²	1346	10.1	20	374	350	13.3	4.00	94	.280	.339	-45	-32	103	94	.942	337	93	1.4	-2.9	.7		6.8
BAL	115	4	3	1158	1313	10.2	21	344	271	13.3	3.73	104	.282	.338	-9	17	106	101	.926	401	76	-2.9	1.5	4.1		-1.2
WAS	118	8	2	1183	1396	10.6	51	284	308	13.3	4.09	89	.291	.339	-57	-58	100	100	.943	323	97	2.4	-5.2	-1.2		-1.5
CLE	122	7	4	1182¹	1365	10.4	22	464	334	14.5	4.12	86	.286	.358	-60	-75	97	102	.942	329	99	2.1	-6.8	-5.1		-4.2
MIL	107	3	4	1218	1383	10.2	32	395	376	13.6	4.06	89	.283	.344	-53	-63	98	98	.934	393	106	-1.8	-5.7	-4.4		-8.6
TOT	937	54	19	9566		9.9				13.0	3.66		.277	.333					.938	2875	802					

Runs		Hits		Doubles		Triples		Home Runs		Total Bases	
Lajoie-Phi	145	Lajoie-Phi	232	Lajoie-Phi	48	Williams-Bal	21	Lajoie-Phi	14	Lajoie-Phi	350
Jones-Chi	120	Anderson-Mil	190	Anderson-Mil	46	Keister-Bal	21	Freeman-Bos	12	Collins-Bos	279
Williams-Bal	113	Collins-Bos	187	Collins-Bos	42	Mertes-Chi	17	Grady-Was	9	Anderson-Mil	274
Hoy-Chi	112	Waldron-Mil-Was	186	Farrell-Was	32	Stahl-Bos	16			Freeman-Bos	255
Barrett-Det	110	Dungan-Was	179			Collins-Bos	16			Williams-Bal	248

Runs Batted In		Runs Produced		Bases On Balls		Batting Average		On Base Percentage		Slugging Average	
Lajoie-Phi	125	Lajoie-Phi	256	Hoy-Chi	86	Lajoie-Phi	.426	Lajoie-Phi	.463	Lajoie-Phi	.643
Freeman-Bos	114	Williams-Bal	202	Jones-Chi	84	Donlin-Bal	.340	Jones-Chi	.412	Freeman-Bos	.520
Anderson-Mil	99	Collins-Bos	196	Barrett-Det	76	Freeman-Bos	.339	Donlin-Bal	.409	Seybold-Phi	.503
Mertes-Chi	98	Freeman-Bos	190	McFarland-Chi	75	Seybold-Phi	.334	Hoy-Chi	.407	Williams-Bal	.495
Williams-Bal	96	Mertes-Chi	187	McGraw-Bal	61	Collins-Bos	.332	Freeman-Bos	.400	Collins-Bos	.495

Production		Adjusted Production		Batter Runs		Adjusted Batter Runs		Clutch Hitting Index		Runs Created	
Lajoie-Phi	1.106	Lajoie-Phi	196	Lajoie-Phi	74.1	Lajoie-Phi	67.4	Burke-Mil-Chi	140	Lajoie-Phi	179
Freeman-Bos	.920	Freeman-Bos	157	Freeman-Bos	34.9	Freeman-Bos	36.9	Mertes-Chi	134	Collins-Bos	116
Seybold-Phi	.901	Seybold-Phi	142	McGraw-Bal	31.1	Collins-Bos	30.3	Keister-Bal	122	Anderson-Mil	114
Donlin-Bal	.883	Collins-Bos	142	Donlin-Bal	29.5	McGraw-Bal	27.9	Hartman-Chi	120	Freeman-Bos	112
Williams-Bal	.883	Donlin-Bal	138	Williams-Bal	29.3	Anderson-Mil	26.3	Seymour-Bal	117	Donlin-Bal	109

Total Average		Stolen Bases		Stolen Base Average		Stolen Base Runs		Fielding Runs		Total Player Rating	
Lajoie-Phi	1.327	Isbell-Chi	52					Lajoie-Phi	28.7	Lajoie-Phi	8.9
Donlin-Bal	1.000	Mertes-Chi	46					Elberfeld-Det	22.0	Elberfeld-Det	4.2
Freeman-Bos	.994	Seymour-Bal	38					Conroy-Mil	19.4	Collins-Bos	4.0
Seybold-Phi	.963	Jones-Chi	38					Clingman-Was	17.8	Freeman-Bos	2.7
Williams-Bal	.956							Farrell-Was	16.6	Anderson-Mil	2.6

Wins		Win Percentage		Games		Complete Games		Shutouts		Saves	
Young-Bos	33	Griffith-Chi	.774	McGinnity-Bal	48	McGinnity-Bal	39	Young-Bos	5	Hoffer-Cle	3
McGinnity-Bal	26	Young-Bos	.767	Dowling-Mil-Cle	43	Young-Bos	38	Griffith-Chi	5	Garvin-Mil	2
Griffith-Chi	24	Callahan-Chi	.652	Young-Bos	43	Miller-Det	35	Patterson-Chi	4		
Miller-Det	23	Patten-Was	.643	Carrick-Was	42	Fraser-Phi	35	Patten-Was	4		
Fraser-Phi	22	Miller-Det	.639	Patterson-Chi	41	Carrick-Was	34	Moore-Cle	4		

Innings Pitched		Fewest Hits/Game		Fewest BB/Game		Strikeouts		Strikeouts/Game		Ratio	
McGinnity-Bal	382.0	Young-Bos	7.85	Young-Bos	.90	Young-Bos	158	Garvin-Mil	4.27	Young-Bos	8.92
Young-Bos	371.1	Callahan-Chi	8.15	Gear-Was	1.21	Patterson-Chi	127	Patten-Was	3.86	Callahan-Chi	10.62
Miller-Det	332.0	Moore-Cle	8.38	Lee-Was	1.55	Dowling-Mil-Cle	124	Young-Bos	3.83	Griffith-Chi	11.10
Fraser-Phi	331.0	Lewis-Bos	8.51	Griffith-Chi	1.69	Garvin-Mil	122	Patterson-Chi	3.66	Lewis-Bos	11.32
Carrick-Was	324.0	Winter-Bos	8.74	Cronin-Det	1.72	Fraser-Phi	110	Dowling-Mil-Cle	3.65	Winter-Bos	11.35

Earned Run Average		Adjusted ERA		Opponents' Batting Avg.		Opponents' On Base Pct.		Starter Runs		Adjusted Starter Runs	
Young-Bos	1.62	Young-Bos	217	Young-Bos	.232	Young-Bos	.256	Young-Bos	84.1	Young-Bos	78.5
Callahan-Chi	2.42	Yeager-Det	147	Callahan-Chi	.239	Callahan-Chi	.290	Callahan-Chi	29.6	Miller-Det	32.8
Yeager-Det	2.61	Callahan-Chi	143	Moore-Cle	.244	Griffith-Chi	.300	Griffith-Chi	29.5	Yeager-Det	27.3
Griffith-Chi	2.67	Griffith-Chi	130	Lewis-Bos	.247	Lewis-Bos	.304	Miller-Det	26.1	Callahan-Chi	25.2
Winter-Bos	2.80	Miller-Det	130	Winter-Bos	.252	Winter-Bos	.304	Yeager-Det	23.2	Griffith-Chi	24.1

Clutch Pitching Index		Relief Runs		Adjusted Relief Runs		Relief Ranking		Total Pitcher Index		Total Baseball Ranking	
Katoll-Chi	126							Young-Bos	8.3	Lajoie-Phi	8.9
Yeager-Det	121							Callahan-Chi	3.9	Young-Bos	8.3
Siever-Det	116							Griffith-Chi	3.7	Elberfeld-Det	4.2
Sparks-Mil	116							Yeager-Det	3.5	Collins-Bos	4.0
Young-Bos	113							Miller-Det	3.5	Callahan-Chi	3.9

TEAM	G	W	L	PCT	GB	R	OR	AB	H	2B	3B	HR	BB	SO	AVG	OBP	SLG	PRO	PRO+	BR	/A	PF	CHI	RC	SB	CS	SBA	SBR
PIT	142	103	36	.741		775	440	4926	1410	189	95	18	372	446	.286	.344	.374	.718	123	152	126	104	105	743	222			
BRO	141	75	63	.543	27.5	564	519	4845	1242	147	49	19	319	489	.256	.311	.319	.630	99	-4	-8	101	100	553	145			
BOS	142	73	64	.533	29	572	516	4728	1178	142	39	14	398	481	.249	.313	.305	.618	95	-16	-21	101	104	540	189			
CIN	141	70	70	.500	33.5	633	566	4908	1383	188	77	18	297	465	.282	.328	.362	.690	109	95	33	110	95	654	131			
CHI	141	68	69	.496	34	530	501	4802	1200	131	40	6	353	565	.250	.307	.298	.605	95	-41	-26	97	100	539	222			
STL	140	56	78	.418	44.5	517	695	4751	1226	116	37	10	273	438	.258	.306	.304	.610	97	-37	-16	96	101	516	158			
PHI	138	56	81	.409	46	484	649	4615	1139	110	43	5	356	481	.247	.305	.293	.598	90	-50	-50	100	98	473	108			
NY	139	48	88	.353	53.5	401	590	4571	1088	147	34	8	252	530	.238	.283	.290	.573	83	-98	-95	99	93	452	187			
TOT	562					4476		38146	9866	1170	414	98	2620	3895	.259	.313	.319	.631							1362			

TEAM	CG	SH	SV	IP	H	H/G	HR	BB	SO	RAT	ERA	ERA+	OAV	OOB	PR	/A	PF	CPI	FA	E	DP	FW	PW	BW	SBW	DIF
PIT	131	21	3	1264²	1142	8.1	4	250	564	10.3	2.30	119	.241	.288	67	61	98	94	.958	247	87	3.4	6.4	13.3		10.4
BRO	132	14	3	1256	1113	8.0	10	363	536	10.8	2.69	102	.238	.298	12	9	99	86	.952	275	79	1.5	.9	-.8		4.4
BOS	124	14	4	1259²	1233	8.8	16	372	523	11.8	2.61	108	.257	.316	24	29	102	109	.959	240	90	3.8	3.1	-2.2		-.2
CIN	130	9	1	1239	1228	8.9	15	352	430	11.9	2.67	112	.259	.318	14	43	108	108	.945	322	118	-1.4	4.5	3.5		-6.6
CHI	132	17	2	1275¹	1235	8.7	9	279	437	11.0	2.21	122	.254	.301	81	69	97	114	.946	327	111	-1.7	7.3	-2.7		-3.4
STL	112	7	4	1227²	1399	10.3	16	338	400	13.0	3.47	79	.287	.338	-95	-101	99	102	.944	336	107	-2.4	-10.7	-1.7		3.7
PHI	118	8	3	1211	1323	9.8	12	334	504	12.7	3.50	80	.278	.333	-97	-93	101	95	.946	305	81	-.7	-9.8	-5.3		3.3
NY	118	11	1	1226¹	1193	8.8	16	332	501	11.6	2.82	99	.255	.312	-5	-3	101	98	.943	330	104	-2.1	-.3	-10.0		-7.5
TOT	997	101	21	9959²		8.9				11.6	2.78		.259	.313					.949	2382	777					

Runs
Wagner-Pit 105
Clarke-Pit 103
Beaumont-Pit 100
Leach-Pit 97
Crawford-Cin 92

Hits
Beaumont-Pit 193
Keeler-Bro 186
Crawford-Cin 185
Wagner-Pit 176
Beckley-Cin 175

Doubles
Wagner-Pit 30
Clarke-Pit 27
Cooley-Bos 26
Dahlen-Bro 25
Beckley-Cin 23

Triples
Leach-Pit 22
Crawford-Cin 22
Wagner-Pit 16
Clarke-Pit 14
Gremminger-Bos ... 12

Home Runs
Leach-Pit 6
Beckley-Cin 5
Sheckard-Bro 4
McCreery-Bro 4

Total Bases
Crawford-Cin 256
Wagner-Pit 247
Beckley-Cin 227
Beaumont-Pit 226
Leach-Pit 219

Runs Batted In
Wagner-Pit 91
Leach-Pit 85
Crawford-Cin 78
Dahlen-Bro 74

Runs Produced
Wagner-Pit 193
Leach-Pit 176
Crawford-Cin 167
Beaumont-Pit 167
Clarke-Pit 154

Bases On Balls
R.Thomas-Phi 107
Lush-Bos 76
Tenney-Bos 73
Sheckard-Bro 57

Batting Average
Beaumont-Pit 357
Crawford-Cin 333
Keeler-Bro 333
Wagner-Pit 330
Beckley-Cin 330

On Base Percentage
R.Thomas-Phi 414
Tenney-Bos 409
Beaumont-Pit 404
Clarke-Pit 401
Wagner-Pit 394

Slugging Average
Wagner-Pit 463
Crawford-Cin 461
Clarke-Pit 449
Beckley-Cin 427
Leach-Pit 426

Production
Wagner-Pit 857
Clarke-Pit 850
Crawford-Cin 848
Beaumont-Pit 822
Beckley-Cin 804

Adjusted Production
Wagner-Pit 159
Clarke-Pit 156
Beaumont-Pit 148
Crawford-Cin 147
Tenney-Bos 141

Batter Runs
Wagner-Pit 39.9
Crawford-Cin 38.6
Clarke-Pit 34.9
Beaumont-Pit 34.1
Beckley-Cin 28.7

Adjusted Batter Runs
Wagner-Pit 36.3
Clarke-Pit 31.7
Beaumont-Pit 30.7
Crawford-Cin 29.1
Tenney-Bos 27.8

Clutch Hitting Index
Hartman-StL 160
Bransfield-Pit 133
Ritchey-Pit 124
McCreery-Bro 124
Wagner-Pit 123

Runs Created
Wagner-Pit 118
Beaumont-Pit 109
Crawford-Cin 108
Clarke-Pit 97
Beckley-Cin 94

Total Average
Wagner-Pit 966
Clarke-Pit 955
Beaumont-Pit 868
Crawford-Cin 865
Tenney-Bos 845

Stolen Bases
Wagner-Pit 42
Slagle-Chi 40
Donovan-StL 34
Beaumont-Pit 33
Smith-NY 32

Stolen Base Average

Stolen Base Runs

Fielding Runs
Farrell-StL 33.5
Lowe-Chi 26.0
H.Long-Bos 22.9
Steinfeldt-Cin ... 21.8
Leach-Pit 12.7

Total Player Rating
Wagner-Pit 4.4
Tenney-Bos 3.9
Farrell-StL 3.3
Leach-Pit 3.3
Crawford-Cin 2.5

Wins
Chesbro-Pit 28
Willis-Bos 27
Pittinger-Bos 27
Taylor-Chi 23
Hahn-Cin 23

Win Percentage
Chesbro-Pit 824
Doheny-Pit 800
Tannehill-Pit.......769
Phillippe-Pit 690
Leever-Pit 682

Games
Willis-Bos 51
Pittinger-Bos 46
Yerkes-StL 39

Complete Games
Willis-Bos 45
Pittinger-Bos 36
Hahn-Cin 35
White-Phi 34
Taylor-Chi 33

Shutouts
Mathewson-NY 8
Chesbro-Pit 8
Taylor-Chi 7
Pittinger-Bos 7
Hahn-Cin 6

Saves
Willis-Bos 3
M.O'Neill-StL 2
Newton-Bro 2
Leever-Pit 2

Innings Pitched
Willis-Bos 410.0
Pittinger-Bos 389.1
Taylor-Chi 324.2
Hahn-Cin 321.0
White-Phi 306.0

Fewest Hits/Game
Newton-Bro 7.08
McGinnity-NY ... 7.18
Taylor-Chi 7.51
Donovan-Bro 7.56
Chesbro-Pit 7.61

Fewest BB/Game
Phillippe-Pit 86
Tannehill-Pit 97
Menefee-Chi 1.19
Taylor-Chi 1.19
Leever-Pit 1.26

Strikeouts
Willis-Bos 225
White-Phi 185
Pittinger-Bos 174
Donovan-Bro 170
Mathewson-NY ... 159

Strikeouts/Game
White-Phi 5.44
Mathewson-NY ... 5.17
Donovan-Bro 5.14
Willis-Bos 4.94
Wicker-StL 4.61

Ratio
Taylor-Chi 8.98
Tannehill-Pit 9.27
McGinnity-NY 9.59
Hahn-Cin 9.70
Phillippe-Pit 9.76

Earned Run Average
Taylor-Chi 1.33
Hahn-Cin 1.77
Tannehill-Pit 1.95
Lundgren-Chi 1.97
Phillippe-Pit 2.05

Adjusted ERA
Taylor-Chi 203
Hahn-Cin 169
Poole-Pit-Cin 142
Tannehill-Pit.......140
Lundgren-Chi 137

Opponents' Batting Avg.
Newton-Bro 217
McGinnity-NY 219
Taylor-Chi 227
Donovan-Bro 228
Chesbro-Pit 229

Opponents' On Base Pct.
Taylor-Chi 260
Tannehill-Pit.......266
McGinnity-NY 273
Hahn-Cin 275
Phillippe-Pit 276

Starter Runs
Taylor-Chi 52.2
Hahn-Cin 36.1
Willis-Bos 26.5
Phillippe-Pit 22.0
Tannehill-Pit.......21.3

Adjusted Starter Runs
Taylor-Chi 49.3
Hahn-Cin 43.7
Willis-Bos 28.4
Mathewson-NY ... 21.2
Phillippe-Pit 20.6

Clutch Pitching Index
Lundgren-Chi 144
Eason-Chi-Bos.... 141
Poole-Pit-Cin 140
Taylor-NY 126
Taylor-Chi 122

Relief Runs

Adjusted Relief Runs

Relief Ranking

Total Pitcher Index
Taylor-Chi 6.3
Hahn-Cin 4.6
Tannehill-Pit 3.1
Willis-Bos 3.1
Phillips-Cin 3.1

Total Baseball Ranking
Taylor-Chi 6.0
Hahn-Cin 4.5
Wagner-Pit 4.4
Tenney-Bos 3.9
Farrell-StL 3.3

TEAM	G	W	L	PCT	GB	R	OR	AB	H	2B	3B	HR	BB	SO	AVG	OBP	SLG	PRO	PRO+	BR	/A	PF	CHI	RC	SB	CS	SBA	SBR
PHI	137	83	53	.610		775	636	4762	1369	235	67	38	343	293	.287	.340	.389	.729	104	50	20	104	107	729	201			
STL	140	78	58	.574	5	619	607	4736	1254	208	61	29	373	327	.265	.323	.353	.676	94	-38	-29	99	97	612	137			
BOS	138	77	60	.562	6.5	664	600	4875	1356	195	95	42	275	375	.278	.322	.383	.705	98	0	-19	103	98	671	132			
CHI	138	74	60	.552	8	675	602	4654	1248	170	50	14	411	381	.268	.332	.335	.667	95	-43	-15	96	107	641	265			
CLE	137	69	67	.507	14	686	667	4840	1401	248	68	33	308	356	.289	.336	.389	.725	111	41	70	96	95	712	140			
WAS	138	61	75	.449	22	707	790	4734	1338	261	66	47	329	296	.283	.335	.395	.730	107	48	42	101	99	694	121			
DET	137	52	83	.385	30.5	566	657	4644	1167	141	55	22	359	287	.251	.312	.320	.632	79	-109	-120	102	103	527	130			
BAL	141	50	88	.362	34	715	848	4760	1318	202	107	33	417	429	.277	.342	.385	.727	103	51	19	104	97	723	189			
TOT	553					5407		38005	10451	1660	569	258	2815	2744	.275	.331	.369	.700						1315				

TEAM	CG	SH	SV	IP	H	H/G	HR	BB	SO	RAT	ERA	ERA+	OAV	OOB	PR	/A	PF	CPI	FA	E	DP	FW	PW	BW	SBW	DIF
PHI	114	5	2	1216[1]	1292	9.6	33	368	455	12.7	3.29	111	.273	.334	39	51	103	110	.953	270	75	1.4	4.8	1.9		6.9
STL	120	7	2	1244	1273	9.2	36	343	348	12.0	3.34	106	.266	.321	32	26	99	99	.953	274	122	1.5	2.5	-2.8		8.7
BOS	123	6	1	1238	1217	8.8	27	326	431	11.5	3.02	118	.258	.311	75	75	100	99	.955	263	101	2.0	7.1	-1.8		1.2
CHI	116	11	0	1221[2]	1269	9.3	30	331	346	12.1	3.41	99	.269	.323	22	-5	95	98	.955	257	125	2.3	-.5	-1.4		6.6
CLE	116	16	3	1204[1]	1199	9.0	26	411	361	12.4	3.28	105	.260	.327	39	21	96	101	.950	287	96	.3	2.0	6.6		-8.0
WAS	130	2	1	1207[2]	1403	10.5	56	312	300	13.2	4.36	85	.291	.341	-106	-88	104	94	.945	316	70	-1.3	-8.3	4.0		-1.3
DET	116	9	3	1190[2]	1267	9.6	20	370	245	12.7	3.56	102	.274	.333	1	10	102	99	.943	332	111	-2.5	.9	-11.4		-2.6
BAL	119	3	1	1210[1]	1531	11.4	30	354	258	14.3	4.33	87	.309	.360	-102	-77	106	104	.938	357	109	-3.5	-7.3	1.8		-10.0
TOT	954	59	13	9733		9.7				12.6	3.57		.275	.331					.949	2356	809					

Runs
Hartsel-Phi 109
Fultz-Phi 109
Strang-Chi 108
Bradley-Cle 104
Delahanty-Was 103

Hits
Hickman-Bos-Cle .. 193
L.Cross-Phi 191
Bradley-Cle 187
Delahanty-Was 178
Freeman-Bos 174

Doubles
Delahanty-Was ... 43
Davis-Phi 43
L.Cross-Phi 39
Bradley-Cle 39
Freeman-Bos 38

Triples
Williams-Bal 21
Freeman-Bos 19
Ferris-Bos 14
Delahanty-Was 14
Hickman-Bos-Cle ... 13

Home Runs
Seybold-Phi 16
Hickman-Bos-Cle ... 11
Freeman-Bos 11
Bradley-Cle 11
Delahanty-Was 10

Total Bases
Hickman-Bos-Cle . 288
Freeman-Bos 283
Bradley-Cle 283
Delahanty-Was 279
Seybold-Phi 264

Runs Batted In
Freeman-Bos 121
Hickman-Bos-Cle . 110
L.Cross-Phi 108
Seybold-Phi 97

Runs Produced
L.Cross-Phi 198
Delahanty-Was 186
Freeman-Bos 185
Davis-Phi 175
Hickman-Bos-Cle .. 173

Bases On Balls
Hartsel-Phi 87
Strang-Chi 76
Barrett-Det 74
Burkett-StL 71
Davis-Chi 65

Batting Average
Lajoie-Phi-Cle 378
Delahanty-Was 376
Hickman-Bos-Cle ...361
Dougherty-Bos 342
L.Cross-Phi 342

On Base Percentage
Delahanty-Was 453
Dougherty-Bos 407
Barrett-Det 397
Selbach-Bal 393
Jones-Chi 390

Slugging Average
Delahanty-Was 590
Lajoie-Phi-Cle 565
Hickman-Bos-Cle ...539
Bradley-Cle 515
Seybold-Phi 506

Production
Delahanty-Was ...1.043
Hickman-Bos-Cle .926
Bradley-Cle........890
Seybold-Phi 881
Williams-Bal 861

Adjusted Production
Delahanty-Was 186
Hickman-Bos-Cle .. 159
Bradley-Cle........ 151
Seybold-Phi 137
Freeman-Bos 131

Batter Runs
Delahanty-Was ... 57.0
Hickman-Bos-Cle . 36.3
Lajoie-Phi-Cle 32.5
Bradley-Cle 30.7
Seybold-Phi 28.5

Adjusted Batter Runs
Delahanty-Was ...56.0
Hickman-Bos-Cle .39.1
Lajoie-Phi-Cle 35.7
Bradley-Cle 35.1
Seybold-Phi 24.2

Clutch Hitting Index
Davis-Chi 136
L.Cross-Phi 131
Anderson-StL 131
Elberfeld-Det 130
Mertes-Chi 129

Runs Created
Delahanty-Was ... 137
Hickman-Bos-Cle . 118
Bradley-Cle 114
Freeman-Bos 109
L.Cross-Phi 105

Total Average
Delahanty-Was ...1.224
Hickman-Bos-Cle .935
Bradley-Cle........895
Seybold-Phi 894
Hartsel-Phi 893

Stolen Bases
Hartsel-Phi 47
Mertes-Chi 46
Fultz-Phi 44

Stolen Base Average

Stolen Base Runs

Fielding Runs
Ferris-Bos 26.6
Schreck-Cle-Phi .. 20.4
Padden-StL 18.3
Jones-Chi 12.5
Coughlin-Was 11.8

Total Player Rating
Lajoie-Phi-Cle 6.2
Delahanty-Was 4.7
Bradley-Cle 4.4
Hickman-Bos-Cle .. 2.8
Schreck-Cle-Phi.... 2.7

Wins
Young-Bos 32
Waddell-Phi 24
Powell-StL 22
R.Donahue-StL ... 22
Dinneen-Bos 21

Win Percentage
Bernhard-Phi-Cle ..783
Waddell-Phi 774
Young-Bos 744
R.Donahue-StL 667
Griffith-Chi 625

Games
Young-Bos 45
Powell-StL 42
Dinneen-Bos 42
Wiltse-Phi-Bal 38
Orth-Was 38

Complete Games
Young-Bos 41
Dinneen-Bos 39
Powell-StL 36
Orth-Was 36

Shutouts
Joss-Cle 5
Siever-Det 4
Moore-Cle 4
Mercer-Det 4

Saves
Powell-StL 2

Innings Pitched
Young-Bos 384.2
Dinneen-Bos 371.1
Powell-StL 328.1
Orth-Was 324.0
R.Donahue-StL ..316.1

Fewest Hits/Game
Bernhard-Phi-Cle . 7.01
Waddell-Phi 7.30
Joss-Cle 7.52
Siever-Det 7.93
Winter-Bos 7.97

Fewest BB/Game
Orth-Was 1.11
Young-Bos 1.24
Bernhard-Phi-Cle . 1.47
Siever-Det 1.53
Plank-Phi 1.83

Strikeouts
Waddell-Phi 210
Young-Bos 160
Powell-StL 137
Dinneen-Bos 136
Plank-Phi 107

Strikeouts/Game
Waddell-Phi 6.84
Powell-StL 3.76
Young-Bos 3.74
Joss-Cle 3.54
Piatt-Chi 3.51

Ratio
Bernhard-Phi-Cle .. 8.68
Siever-Det 9.56
Waddell-Phi 9.71
Young-Bos 9.73
Joss-Cle 10.46

Earned Run Average
Siever-Det........ 1.91
Waddell-Phi 2.05
Bernhard-Phi-Cle . 2.15
Young-Bos 2.15
Garvin-Chi 2.21

Adjusted ERA
Siever-Det 191
Waddell-Phi 179
Young-Bos 166
Bernhard-Phi-Cle . 160
Garvin-Chi 153

Opponents' Batting Avg.
Bernhard-Phi-Cle ..216
Waddell-Phi 223
Joss-Cle 228
Siever-Det 237
Winter-Bos 238

Opponents' On Base Pct.
Bernhard-Phi-Cle ..254
Siever-Det 273
Waddell-Phi 276
Young-Bos 276
Joss-Cle 291

Starter Runs
Young-Bos 60.6
Waddell-Phi 46.6
Bernhard-Phi-Cle . 35.7
Siever-Det 34.7
R.Donahue-StL ... 28.5

Adjusted Starter Runs
Young-Bos 60.6
Waddell-Phi 49.5
Siever-Det 36.2
Bernhard-Phi-Cle.. 32.6
R.Donahue-StL ... 26.9

Clutch Pitching Index
Garvin-Chi 129
Shields-Bal-StL ... 123
Husting-Bos-Phi .. 120
Moore-Cle........ 119
Sudhoff-StL 110

Relief Runs

Adjusted Relief Runs

Relief Ranking

Total Pitcher Index
Waddell-Phi 5.9
Young-Bos 5.8
Bernhard-Phi-Cle . 2.9
Siever-Det 2.6
Garvin-Chi 2.4

Total Baseball Ranking
Lajoie-Phi-Cle 6.2
Waddell-Phi 5.9
Young-Bos 5.8
Delahanty-Was..... 4.7
Bradley-Cle 4.4

TEAM	G	W	L	PCT	GB	R	OR	AB	H	2B	3B	HR	BB	SO	AVG	OBP	SLG	PRO	PRO+	BR	/A	PF	CHI	RC	SB	CS	SBA	SBR
PIT	141	91	49	.650		**793**	613	4988	**1429**	208	**110**	**34**	364		.286	.341	**.393**	.734	**113**	89	65	103	101	**758**	172			
NY	142	84	55	.604	6.5	729	**567**	4741	1290	181	49	20	379		.272	.338	.344	.682	97	9	-17	104	**106**	678	264			
CHI	139	82	56	.594	8	695	599	4733	1300	191	62	9	422		.275	.340	.347	.687	105	19	38	97	101	678	259			
CIN	141	74	65	.532	16.5	765	656	4857	1399	**228**	92	28	403		**.288**	.346	.390	**.736**	104	**95**	10	111	99	735	144			
BRO	139	70	66	.515	19	667	682	4534	1201	177	56	15	**522**		.265	**.348**	.339	.687	105	27	47	97	97	661	**273**			
BOS	140	58	80	.420	32	578	699	4682	1145	176	47	25	398		.245	.312	.318	.630	90	-83	-60	96	100	540	159			
PHI	139	49	86	.363	39.5	617	738	4781	1283	186	62	12	338		.268	.322	.341	.663	98	-33	-12	97	97	596	120			
STL	139	43	94	.314	46.5	505	795	4689	1176	138	65	8	277		.251	.297	.313	.610	83	-124	-108	97	98	511	171			
TOT	560					5349		38005	10223	1485	543	151	3103	3767	.269	.331	.349	.679						1562				

TEAM	CG	SH	SV	IP	H	H/G	HR	BB	SO	RAT	ERA	ERA+	OAV	OOB	PR	/A	PF	CPI	FA	E	DP	FW	PW	BW	SBW	DIF
PIT	117	**16**	5	1251[1]	1215	8.7	**9**	384	454	11.8	2.91	111	.255	.316	48	44	99	95	**.951**	295	100	1.6	4.2	**6.2**		8.9
NY	115	8	**8**	1262[2]	1257	9.0	20	371	**628**	11.9	2.95	113	.258	.316	43	56	102	98	**.951**	287	87	2.3	5.4	-1.6		8.5
CHI	117	6	6	1240[1]	**1182**	8.6	14	**354**	451	11.4	**2.77**	113	**.250**	**.307**	67	46	96	93	.942	338	78	-1.6	4.4	3.6		6.5
CIN	**126**	11	1	1230	1277	9.3	14	378	480	12.6	3.07	116	.268	.331	26	**65**	109	105	.946	312	84	.4	**6.2**	1.0		-3.1
BRO	118	11	4	1221[1]	1276	9.4	18	377	438	12.7	3.44	92	.275	.339	-25	-38	98	100	**.951**	**284**	98	2.0	-3.6	4.5		-.9
BOS	125	8	1	1228[2]	1310	9.6	30	460	516	13.4	3.34	96	.278	.348	-11	-21	98	**112**	.939	361	89	-3.0	-2.0	-5.8		-.2
PHI	**126**	5	3	1212[1]	1347	10.0	21	425	381	13.6	3.96	82	.285	.352	-95	-97	100	97	.947	300	76	1.0	-9.3	-1.2		-9.0
STL	111	4	2	1212[1]	1353	10.0	25	430	419	13.6	3.67	89	.284	.350	-55	-56	100	104	.940	354	**111**	-2.7	-5.4	-10.4		-7.1
TOT	955	69	30	9859		9.3				12.6	3.26		.269	.331					.946	2531	723					

Runs		Hits		Doubles		Triples		Home Runs		Total Bases	
Beaumont-Pit	137	Beaumont-Pit	209	Steinfeldt-Cin	32	Wagner-Pit	19	Sheckard-Bro	9	Beaumont-Pit	272
Donlin-Cin	110	Seymour-Cin	191	Mertes-NY	32	Donlin-Cin	18			Seymour-Cin	267
Browne-NY	105	Browne-NY	185	Clarke-Pit	32	Leach-Pit	17			Wagner-Pit	265
Slagle-Chi	104	Wagner-Pit	182							Donlin-Cin	256
Strang-Bro	101	Donlin-Cin	174							Sheckard-Bro	245

Runs Batted In		Runs Produced		Bases On Balls		Batting Average		On Base Percentage		Slugging Average	
Mertes-NY	104	Beaumont-Pit	198	Thomas-Phi	107	Wagner-Pit	.355	Thomas-Phi	.453	Clarke-Pit	.532
Wagner-Pit	101	Mertes-NY	197	Dahlen-Bro	82	Clarke-Pit	.351	Bresnahan-NY	.443	Wagner-Pit	.518
Doyle-Bro	91	Wagner-Pit	193	Slagle-Chi	81	Donlin-Cin	.351	Chance-Chi	.439	Donlin-Cin	.516
Leach-Pit	87	Leach-Pit	177	Chance-Chi	78	Bresnahan-NY	.350	Sheckard-Bro	.423	Bresnahan-NY	.493
Steinfeldt-Cin	83	Doyle-Bro	175			Seymour-Cin	.342	Donlin-Cin	.420	Steinfeldt-Cin	.481

Production		Adjusted Production		Batter Runs		Adjusted Batter Runs		Clutch Hitting Index		Runs Created	
Clarke-Pit	.946	Clarke-Pit	164	Donlin-Cin	42.6	Sheckard-Bro	43.3	Corcoran-Cin	141	Sheckard-Bro	137
Donlin-Cin	.936	Sheckard-Bro	160	Wagner-Pit	42.1	Wagner-Pit	38.6	Doyle-Bro	131	Wagner-Pit	133
Bresnahan-NY	.936	Bresnahan-NY	160	Sheckard-Bro	39.8	Chance-Chi	36.8	Mertes-NY	123	Donlin-Cin	122
Wagner-Pit	.931	Wagner-Pit	160	Bresnahan-NY	37.8	Clarke-Pit	34.3	Chance-Chi	118	Beaumont-Pit	119
Sheckard-Bro	.899	Chance-Chi	155	Clarke-Pit	37.3	Bresnahan-NY	34.1	Dobbs-Chi-Bro	118	Chance-Chi	118

Total Average		Stolen Bases		Stolen Base Average	Stolen Base Runs	Fielding Runs		Total Player Rating	
Chance-Chi	1.175	Sheckard-Bro	67			Farrell-StL	28.1	Wagner-Pit	6.3
Bresnahan-NY	1.144	Chance-Chi	67			Wagner-Pit	24.6	Sheckard-Bro	5.4
Sheckard-Bro	1.142	Wagner-Pit	46			Sheckard-Bro	23.4	Thomas-Phi	3.8
Wagner-Pit	1.097	Strang-Bro	46			Moran-Bos	19.3	Moran-Bos	3.5
Clarke-Pit	1.061	Mertes-NY	45			Ritchey-Pit	19.0	Tenney-Bos	3.1

Wins		Win Percentage		Games		Complete Games		Shutouts		Saves	
McGinnity-NY	31	Leever-Pit	.781	McGinnity-NY	55	McGinnity-NY	44	Leever-Pit	7	Miller-NY	3
Mathewson-NY	30	Phillippe-Pit	.735	Mathewson-NY	45	Mathewson-NY	37	Schmidt-Bro	5	Lundgren-Chi	3
Phillippe-Pit	25	Weimer-Chi	.714	Pittinger-Bos	44	Pittinger-Bos	35	Hahn-Cin	5		
Leever-Pit	25	Mathewson-NY	.698	Schmidt-Bro	40	Hahn-Cin	34	Phillippe-Pit	4		
		Wicker-StL-Chi	.690			Taylor-Chi	33	Jones-Bro	4		

Innings Pitched		Fewest Hits/Game		Fewest BB/Game		Strikeouts		Strikeouts/Game		Ratio	
McGinnity-NY	434.0	Weimer-Chi	7.69	Phillippe-Pit	.90	Mathewson-NY	267	Mathewson-NY	6.56	Phillippe-Pit	9.39
Mathewson-NY	366.1	Mathewson-NY	7.89	Hahn-Cin	1.43	McGinnity-NY	171	Piatt-Bos	4.97	Taylor-Chi	9.77
Pittinger-Bos	351.2	Taylor-Chi	7.98	Taylor-Chi	1.64	Garvin-Bro	154	Garvin-Bro	4.65	Leever-Pit	10.13
Jones-Bro	324.1	Leever-Pit	8.07	McFarland-StL	1.89	Pittinger-Bos	140	Weimer-Chi	4.09	Mathewson-NY	10.59
Taylor-Chi	312.1	McGinnity-NY	8.11	Leever-Pit	1.90	Weimer-Chi	128	Willis-Bos	4.05	Hahn-Cin	10.70

Earned Run Average		Adjusted ERA		Opponents' Batting Avg.		Opponents' On Base Pct.		Starter Runs		Adjusted Starter Runs	
Leever-Pit	2.06	Leever-Pit	157	Weimer-Chi	.225	Phillippe-Pit	.263	Mathewson-NY	40.7	McGinnity-NY	44.0
Mathewson-NY	2.26	Mathewson-NY	148	Mathewson-NY	.231	Taylor-Chi	.273	McGinnity-NY	40.2	Mathewson-NY	43.9
Weimer-Chi	2.30	Hahn-Cin	141	Taylor-Chi	.235	Leever-Pit	.282	Leever-Pit	38.0	Leever-Pit	37.0
Phillippe-Pit	2.43	McGinnity-NY	138	McGinnity-NY	.236	Mathewson-NY	.287	Weimer-Chi	30.2	Hahn-Cin	33.8
McGinnity-NY	2.43	Weimer-Chi	136	Leever-Pit	.238	McGinnity-NY	.291	Taylor-Chi	28.2	Weimer-Chi	26.0

Clutch Pitching Index		Relief Runs	Adjusted Relief Runs	Relief Ranking	Total Pitcher Index		Total Baseball Ranking	
Brown-StL	153				Mathewson-NY	5.3	Wagner-Pit	6.3
Pittinger-Bos	126				McGinnity-NY	4.0	Sheckard-Bro	5.4
Malarkey-Bos	115				Leever-Pit	3.4	Mathewson-NY	5.3
Piatt-Bos	115				Hahn-Cin	3.2	McGinnity-NY	4.0
Poole-Cin	113				Taylor-Chi	2.9	Thomas-Phi	3.8

TEAM	G	W	L	PCT	GB	R	OR	AB	H	2B	3B	HR	BB	SO	AVG	OBP	SLG	PRO	PRO+	BR	/A	PF	CHI	RC	SB	CS	SBA	SBR
BOS	141	91	47	.659		708	504	4919	1336	222	113	48	262	561	.272	.313	.392	.705	111	91	55	105	103	680	141			
PHI	137	75	60	.556	14.5	597	519	4673	1236	227	68	32	268	513	.264	.309	.363	.672	102	36	9	105	100	598	157			
CLE	140	77	63	.550	15	639	573	4773	1265	231	95	31	259	595	.265	.308	.373	.681	112	51	62	98	102	634	175			
NY	136	72	62	.537	17	579	573	4565	1136	193	62	18	332	465	.249	.309	.330	.639	92	-6	-41	106	104	544	160			
DET	137	65	71	.478	25	567	539	4582	1229	162	91	12	292	526	.268	.318	.351	.669	110	39	56	97	94	587	128			
STL	139	65	74	.468	26.5	500	525	4639	1133	166	68	12	271	539	.244	.290	.317	.607	90	-66	-53	97	102	480	101			
CHI	138	60	77	.438	30.5	516	613	4670	1152	176	49	14	325	537	.247	.301	.314	.615	94	-46	-23	96	98	526	180			
WAS	140	43	94	.314	47.5	437	691	4613	1066	172	71	17	257	463	.231	.277	.310	.587	79	-99	-108	102	96	454	131			
TOT	554					4543		37434	9553	1549	617	184	2266	4199	.255	.303	.344	.648						1173				

TEAM	CG	SH	SV	IP	H	H/G	HR	BB	SO	RAT	ERA	ERA+	OAV	OOB	PR	/A	PF	CPI	FA	E	DP	FW	PW	BW	SBW	DIF
BOS	123	20	4	1255	1142	8.2	23	269	579	10.4	2.57	118	.242	.288	55	64	102	100	.959	239	86	2.3	6.6	5.7		7.4
PHI	112	10	1	1207	1124	8.4	20	315	728	11.3	2.98	103	.246	.305	-2	10	103	97	.960	217	66	3.2	1.0	.9		2.4
CLE	125	20	1	1243²	1161	8.4	16	271	521	10.6	2.73	105	.247	.293	32	17	96	97	.946	322	99	-3.2	1.8	6.4		2.0
NY	111	7	2	1201¹	1171	8.8	19	245	463	10.9	3.08	101	.255	.299	-16	5	105	93	.953	264	87	.0	.5	-4.3		8.7
DET	123	15	2	1196	1169	8.8	19	336	554	11.5	2.75	106	.256	.310	28	20	98	111	.950	281	82	-.9	2.1	5.8		-10.0
STL	124	12	3	1222¹	1220	9.0	26	237	511	11.0	2.77	105	.260	.300	26	19	98	98	.953	268	94	.2	2.0	-5.5		-1.1
CHI	114	9	4	1235	1233	9.0	23	287	391	11.5	3.02	93	.260	.309	-8	-29	95	103	.949	297	85	-1.8	-3.0	-2.4		-1.3
WAS	122	6	3	1223²	1333	9.8	38	306	452	12.4	3.82	82	.277	.325	-116	-94	106	96	.954	260	86	.8	-9.8	-11.2		-5.3
TOT	954	99	20	9784		8.8				11.2	2.96		.255	.303					.953	2148	685					

Runs		Hits		Doubles		Triples		Home Runs		Total Bases	
Dougherty-Bos	107	Dougherty-Bos	195	Seybold-Phi	45	Crawford-Det	25	Freeman-Bos	13	Freeman-Bos	281
Bradley-Cle	101	Crawford-Det	184	Lajoie-Cle	41	Bradley-Cle	22	Hickman-Cle	12	Crawford-Det	269
Keeler-NY	95	Parent-Bos	170	Freeman-Bos	39	Freeman-Bos	20	Ferris-Bos	9	Bradley-Cle	266
Barrett-Det	95	Bay-Cle	169	Bradley-Cle	36	Parent-Bos	17	Seybold-Phi	8	Lajoie-Cle	251
Bay-Cle	94	Bradley-Cle	168	Anderson-StL	34	Collins-Cle	17			Dougherty-Bos	250

Runs Batted In		Runs Produced		Bases On Balls		Batting Average		On Base Percentage		Slugging Average	
Freeman-Bos	104	Lajoie-Cle	176	Barrett-Det	74	Lajoie-Cle	.344	Barrett-Det	.407	Lajoie-Cle	.518
Hickman-Cle	97	Crawford-Det	173	Lush-Det	70	Crawford-Det	.335	Hartsel-Phi	.391	Bradley-Cle	.496
Lajoie-Cle	93	Freeman-Bos	165	Pickering-Phi	53	Dougherty-Bos	.331	Lajoie-Cle	.379	Freeman-Bos	.496
L.Cross-Phi	90	Bradley-Cle	163	Burkett-StL	52	Barrett-Det	.315	Lush-Det	.379	Crawford-Det	.489
Crawford-Det	89	Dougherty-Bos	162	Flick-Cle	51	Bradley-Cle	.313	Green-Chi	.375	Hartsel-Phi	.477

Production		Adjusted Production		Batter Runs		Adjusted Batter Runs		Clutch Hitting Index		Runs Created	
Lajoie-Cle	.896	Lajoie-Cle	170	Lajoie-Cle	37.6	Lajoie-Cle	39.3	Gochnauer-Cle	155	Dougherty-Bos	111
Hartsel-Phi	.868	Crawford-Det	159	Crawford-Det	34.5	Crawford-Det	37.5	L.Cross-Phi	144	Crawford-Det	110
Crawford-Det	.855	Bradley-Cle	154	Bradley-Cle	30.8	Bradley-Cle	32.6	Carr-Det	135	Lajoie-Cle	107
Bradley-Cle	.844	Hartsel-Phi	152	Barrett-Det	29.6	Barrett-Det	32.5	Williams-NY	130	Bradley-Cle	104
Freeman-Bos	.823	Green-Chi	146	Hartsel-Phi	28.0	Green-Chi	29.0	Anderson-StL	129	Barrett-Det	98

Total Average		Stolen Bases		Stolen Base Average		Stolen Base Runs		Fielding Runs		Total Player Rating	
Lajoie-Cle	.940	Bay-Cle	45					Lajoie-Cle	40.1	Lajoie-Cle	8.4
Hartsel-Phi	.934	Pickering-Phi	40					Criger-Bos	22.8	Bradley-Cle	4.7
Barrett-Det	.873	Holmes-Was-Chi	35					Schreckengost-Phi	18.2	Crawford-Det	3.3
Crawford-Det	.858	Dougherty-Bos	35					Wallace-StL	18.1	Elberfeld-Det-NY	3.2
Bradley-Cle	.856	Conroy-NY	33					Williams-NY	15.6	Barrett-Det	3.2

Wins		Win Percentage		Games		Complete Games		Shutouts		Saves	
Young-Bos	28	Young-Bos	.757	Plank-Phi	43	Young-Bos	34	Young-Bos	7	Young-Bos	2
Plank-Phi	23	Hughes-Bos	.741	Mullin-Det	41	Waddell-Phi	34	Mullin-Det	6	Powell-StL	2
		Moore-Cle	.679	Young-Bos	40	Donovan-Det	34	Dinneen-Bos	6	Orth-Was	2
		Dinneen-Bos	.618	Flaherty-Chi	40			Sudhoff-StL	5	Mullin-Det	2
		Plank-Phi	.590	Chesbro-NY	40			Hughes-Bos	5	Dinneen-Bos	2

Innings Pitched		Fewest Hits/Game		Fewest BB/Game		Strikeouts		Strikeouts/Game		Ratio	
Young-Bos	341.2	Young-Bos	7.12	Young-Bos	.97	Waddell-Phi	302	Waddell-Phi	8.39	Joss-Cle	8.82
Plank-Phi	336.0	Donovan-Det	7.24	Bernhard-Cle	1.14	Donovan-Det	187	Donovan-Det	5.48	Young-Bos	8.96
Chesbro-NY	324.2	Joss-Cle	7.36	Donahue-StL-Cle	1.14	Young-Bos	176	Moore-Cle	5.38	Bernhard-Cle	9.34
Waddell-Phi	324.0	Waddell-Phi	7.61	Joss-Cle	1.17	Plank-Phi	176	Powell-StL	4.97	Moore-Cle	9.56
Mullin-Det	320.2	Dinneen-Bos	7.68	Tannehill-NY	1.28	Mullin-Det	170	Mullin-Det	4.77	Dinneen-Bos	9.78

Earned Run Average		Adjusted ERA		Opponents' Batting Avg.		Opponents' On Base Pct.		Starter Runs		Adjusted Starter Runs	
Moore-Cle	1.74	Moore-Cle	164	Moore-Cle	.217	Joss-Cle	.256	Moore-Cle	33.5	Young-Bos	36.1
Young-Bos	2.08	Young-Bos	146	Donovan-Det	.220	Young-Bos	.259	Young-Bos	33.4	Moore-Cle	30.5
Bernhard-Cle	2.12	Bernhard-Cle	135	Joss-Cle	.223	Bernhard-Cle	.267	White-Chi	27.7	Dinneen-Bos	25.8
White-Chi	2.13	Dinneen-Bos	134	Waddell-Phi	.229	Moore-Cle	.271	Mullin-Det	25.5	Plank-Phi	24.9
Joss-Cle	2.19	White-Chi	132	Dinneen-Bos	.230	Dinneen-Bos	.276	Joss-Cle	24.4	Mullin-Det	23.6

Clutch Pitching Index		Relief Runs	Adjusted Relief Runs	Relief Ranking	Total Pitcher Index		Total Baseball Ranking	
Kitson-Det	127				Young-Bos	4.9	Lajoie-Cle	8.4
Mullin-Det	121				Mullin-Det	4.1	Young-Bos	4.9
Donahue-StL-Cle	119				White-Chi	3.3	Bradley-Cle	4.7
Plank-Phi	116				Sudhoff-StL	2.7	Mullin-Det	4.1
White-Chi	111				Joss-Cle	2.7	Crawford-Det	3.3

TEAM	G	W	L	PCT	GB	R	OR	AB	H	2B	3B	HR	BB	SO	AVG	OBP	SLG	PRO	PRO+	BR	/A	PF	CHI	RC	SB	CS	SBA	SBR
NY	158	106	47	.693		744	476	5150	1347	202	65	31	434		.262	.328	.344	.672	109	87	57	104	104	712	283			
CHI	156	93	60	.608	13	599	517	5210	1294	157	62	22	298		.248	.295	.315	.610	94	-38	-39	100	104	582	227			
CIN	157	88	65	.575	18	695	547	5231	1332	189	92	21	399		.255	.313	.338	.651	98	42	-17	109	104	642	179			
PIT	156	87	66	.569	19	675	592	5160	1333	164	102	15	391		.258	.316	.338	.654	105	48	30	103	102	639	178			
STL	155	75	79	.487	31.5	602	595	5104	1292	175	66	24	343		.253	.306	.327	.633	106	7	34	96	99	602	199			
BRO	154	56	97	.366	50	497	614	4917	1142	159	53	15	411		.232	.297	.295	.592	91	-57	-44	98	93	521	205			
BOS	155	55	98	.359	51	491	749	5135	1217	153	50	24	316		.237	.287	.300	.587	90	-78	-59	96	94	508	143			
PHI	155	52	100	.342	53.5	571	784	5103	1268	170	54	23	377		.248	.305	.316	.621	102	-11	10	96	96	570	159			
TOT	623					4874		41010	10225	1369	544	175	2969	4277	.249	.306	.322	.628						1573				

TEAM	CG	SH	SV	IP	H	H/G	HR	BB	SO	RAT	ERA	ERA+	OAV	OOB	PR	/A	PF	CPI	FA	E	DP	FW	PW	BW	SBW	DIF
NY	127	21	15	1396²	1151	7.4	36	349	707	9.9	2.17	125	.222	.276	86	83	100	93	.956	294	93	2.3	8.8	6.0		12.4
CHI	139	18	6	1383²	1150	7.5	16	402	618	10.3	2.30	115	.224	.285	65	53	97	90	.954	298	89	1.8	5.6	-4.1		13.2
CIN	142	12	2	1392²	1256	8.1	13	343	502	10.7	2.34	125	.241	.295	60	88	107	102	.954	301	81	1.7	9.3	-1.8		2.3
PIT	133	15	1	1348¹	1273	8.5	13	379	455	11.4	2.89	95	.248	.306	-24	-24	100	92	.955	291	93	2.2	-2.5	3.2		7.6
STL	146	7	2	1368	1286	8.5	23	319	529	10.8	2.64	102	.239	.286	13	5	99	85	.952	307	83	1.1	.5	3.6		-7.2
BRO	135	12	2	1337¹	1281	8.6	27	414	453	11.8	2.70	101	.255	.319	4	4	100	112	.945	343	87	-1.4	.4	-4.7		-14.9
BOS	136	13	0	1348¹	1405	9.4	25	500	544	13.1	3.43	80	.272	.343	-105	-105	101	105	.945	353	91	-1.9	-11.1	-6.2		-2.3
PHI	131	10	2	1339¹	1418	9.5	22	425	469	12.9	3.39	79	.270	.332	-99	-110	96	100	.937	403	93	-5.1	-11.6	1.1		-8.3
TOT	1089	108	30	10914¹		8.4				11.3	2.73		.249	.306					.950	2590	710					

Runs		Hits		Doubles		Triples		Home Runs		Total Bases	
Browne-NY	99	Beaumont-Pit	185	Wagner-Pit	44	Lumley-Bro	18	Lumley-Bro	9	Wagner-Pit	255
Wagner-Pit	97	Beckley-StL	179	Mertes-NY	28	Wagner-Pit	14	Brain-StL	7	Lumley-Bro	247
Beaumont-Pit	97	Wagner-Pit	171	Delahanty-Bos	27	Tinker-Chi	13			Seymour-Cin	233
Huggins-Cin	96	Browne-NY	169	Seymour-Cin	26	Seymour-Cin	13			Beaumont-Pit	230
		Seymour-Cin	166	Dahlen-NY	26	Kelley-Cin	13			Beckley-StL	222

Runs Batted In		Runs Produced		Bases On Balls		Batting Average		On Base Percentage		Slugging Average	
Dahlen-NY	80	Wagner-Pit	168	Thomas-Phi	102	Wagner-Pit	.349	Wagner-Pit	.423	Wagner-Pit	.520
Mertes-NY	78	Mertes-NY	157	Huggins-Cin	88	Donlin-Cin-NY	.329	Thomas-Phi	.416	Grady-StL	.474
Lumley-Bro	78	Lumley-Bro	148	Devlin-NY	62	Beckley-StL	.325	Chance-Chi	.382	Donlin-Cin-NY	.457
Wagner-Pit	75	Dahlen-NY	148	Wagner-Pit	59	Grady-StL	.313	Huggins-Cin	.377	Seymour-Cin	.439
Corcoran-Cin	74	Beaumont-Pit	148	Ritchey-Pit	59	Seymour-Cin	.313	Beckley-StL	.375	Chance-Chi	.430

Production		Adjusted Production		Batter Runs		Adjusted Batter Runs		Clutch Hitting Index		Runs Created	
Wagner-Pit	.944	Wagner-Pit	186	Wagner-Pit	52.7	Wagner-Pit	49.7	Devlin-NY	154	Wagner-Pit	134
Chance-Chi	.812	Chance-Chi	150	Thomas-Phi	28.4	Thomas-Phi	31.8	Dahlen-NY	146	Lumley-Bro	95
Seymour-Cin	.790	Beckley-StL	147	Chance-Chi	27.2	Beckley-StL	29.8	Corcoran-Cin	137	Beckley-StL	94
Beckley-StL	.778	Thomas-Phi	141	Beckley-StL	25.7	Chance-Chi	27.2	Bransfield-Pit	132	Chance-Chi	93
Thomas-Phi	.761	Lumley-Bro	137	Seymour-Cin	24.9	Grady-StL	25.7	Gilbert-NY	128	Mertes-NY	93

Total Average		Stolen Bases		Stolen Base Average		Stolen Base Runs		Fielding Runs		Total Player Rating	
Wagner-Pit	1.163	Wagner-Pit	53					Leach-Pit	35.8	Wagner-Pit	4.8
Chance-Chi	.926	Mertes-NY	47					Evers-Chi	31.3	Leach-Pit	4.1
Thomas-Phi	.869	Dahlen-NY	47					Dahlen-NY	27.6	Thomas-Phi	4.0
Mertes-NY	.813	McGann-NY	42					Tinker-Chi	19.3	Chance-Chi	3.7
McGann-NY	.802	Chance-Chi	42					Farrell-StL	16.3	Dahlen-NY	3.3

Wins		Win Percentage		Games		Complete Games		Shutouts		Saves	
McGinnity-NY	35	McGinnity-NY	.814	McGinnity-NY	51	Willis-Bos	39	McGinnity-NY	9	McGinnity-NY	5
Mathewson-NY	33	Mathewson-NY	.733	Mathewson-NY	48	Taylor-StL	39	Harper-Cin	6	Wiltse-NY	3
Harper-Cin	23	Harper-Cin	.719	Jones-Bro	46	McGinnity-NY	38			Briggs-Chi	3
Taylor-NY	21	Flaherty-Pit	.679	Willis-Bos	43	Jones-Bro	38			Ames-NY	3
Nichols-StL	21			Fraser-Phi	42						

Innings Pitched		Fewest Hits/Game		Fewest BB/Game		Strikeouts		Strikeouts/Game		Ratio	
McGinnity-NY	408.0	Brown-Chi	6.57	Hahn-Cin	1.06	Mathewson-NY	212	Wiltse-NY	5.74	Brown-Chi	8.94
Jones-Bro	377.0	Weimer-Chi	6.71	Phillippe-Pit	1.40	Willis-Bos	196	Mathewson-NY	5.19	McGinnity-NY	8.96
Mathewson-NY	367.2	McGinnity-NY	6.77	Nichols-StL	1.42	Weimer-Chi	177	Weimer-Chi	5.19	Hahn-Cin	9.07
Taylor-StL	352.0	Garvin-Bro	6.99	Kellum-Cin	1.84	Pittinger-Bos	146	Willis-Bos	5.04	Nichols-StL	9.17
Willis-Bos	350.0	Taylor-NY	7.02	McFarland-StL	1.87	McGinnity-NY	144	Phillippe-Pit	4.43	Mathewson-NY	9.50

Earned Run Average		Adjusted ERA		Opponents' Batting Avg.		Opponents' On Base Pct.		Starter Runs		Adjusted Starter Runs	
McGinnity-NY	1.61	McGinnity-NY	169	Brown-Chi	.199	Brown-Chi	.253	McGinnity-NY	50.6	McGinnity-NY	50.1
Garvin-Bro	1.68	Garvin-Bro	162	Weimer-Chi	.204	Nichols-StL	.256	Mathewson-NY	28.4	Hahn-Cin	28.5
Brown-Chi	1.86	Brown-Chi	142	McGinnity-NY	.206	McGinnity-NY	.256	Weimer-Chi	28.0	Mathewson-NY	28.0
Weimer-Chi	1.91	Hahn-Cin	142	Taylor-NY	.214	Hahn-Cin	.262	Nichols-StL	25.0	Weimer-Chi	25.6
Nichols-StL	2.02	Weimer-Chi	139	Garvin-Bro	.218	Mathewson-NY	.270	Hahn-Cin	22.2	Nichols-StL	23.6

Clutch Pitching Index		Relief Runs		Adjusted Relief Runs		Relief Ranking		Total Pitcher Index		Total Baseball Ranking	
Garvin-Bro	153							McGinnity-NY	5.6	McGinnity-NY	5.6
O'Neill-StL	131							Mathewson-NY	4.7	Wagner-Pit	4.8
Briggs-Chi	128							Flaherty-Pit	3.4	Mathewson-NY	4.7
Jones-Bro	117							Hahn-Cin	3.3	Leach-Pit	4.1
Mitchell-Phi-Bro	116							Weimer-Chi	2.9	Thomas-Phi	4.0

TEAM	G	W	L	PCT	GB	R	OR	AB	H	2B	3B	HR	BB	SO	AVG	OBP	SLG	PRO	PRO+	BR	/A	PF	CHI	RC	SB	CS	SBA	SBR
BOS	157	95	59	.617		608	466	5231	1294	194	105	26	347	570	.247	.301	.340	.641	102	42	8	106	101	597	101			
NY	155	92	59	.609	1.5	598	526	5220	1354	195	91	27	312	548	.259	.308	.347	.655	107	69	40	105	96	640	163			
CHI	156	89	65	.578	6	600	482	5027	1217	193	68	14	373	586	.242	.300	.316	.616	104	4	26	96	109	578	216			
CLE	154	86	65	.570	7.5	647	482	5152	1340	225	90	27	307	714	.260	.308	.354	.662	116	78	84	99	103	650	178			
PHI	155	81	70	.536	12.5	557	503	5088	1266	197	77	31	313	605	.249	.298	.336	.634	101	28	-1	105	98	579	137			
STL	156	65	87	.428	29	481	604	5291	1266	153	53	10	332	609	.239	.291	.294	.585	96	-52	-20	94	94	526	150			
DET	162	62	90	.408	32	505	627	5321	1231	154	69	11	344	635	.231	.282	.292	.574	90	-75	-60	97	102	502	112			
WAS	157	38	113	.252	55.5	437	743	5149	1170	171	57	10	283	759	.227	.275	.288	.563	84	-94	-87	98	97	475	150			
TOT	626					4433		41479	10138	1482	610	156	2611	5026	.244	.295	.321	.616						1207				

TEAM	CG	SH	SV	IP	H	H/G	HR	BB	SO	RAT	ERA	ERA+	OAV	OOB	PR	/A	PF	CPI	FA	E	DP	FW	PW	BW	SBW	DIF
BOS	148	21	1	1406	1208	7.7	31	233	612	9.4	2.12	126	.233	.270	75	86	103	101	.962	242	83	1.6	9.6	.9		5.9
NY	123	15	1	1380²	1180	7.7	29	311	684	10.0	2.57	106	.232	.282	4	22	104	90	.958	275	90	-.8	2.5	4.5		10.4
CHI	134	26	3	1380	1161	7.6	13	303	550	9.8	2.30	107	.229	.279	45	23	95	93	.964	238	95	1.7	2.6	2.9		4.8
CLE	141	20	0	1356²	1273	8.4	10	285	627	10.6	2.22	114	.249	.294	56	47	98	116	.959	255	86	.4	5.3	9.4		-4.5
PHI	136	26	0	1361¹	1149	7.6	13	366	887	10.4	2.35	114	.230	.291	38	50	103	100	.959	250	67	.8	5.6	-.1		-.8
STL	135	13	1	1410	1335	8.5	25	333	577	11.0	2.83	88	.251	.303	-36	-55	96	100	.960	267	78	-.2	-6.1	-2.2		-2.4
DET	143	15	2	1430	1345	8.5	16	433	556	11.6	2.77	92	.250	.314	-27	-35	98	106	.959	273	92	.0	-3.9	-6.7		-3.5
WAS	137	7	4	1359²	1487	9.8	19	347	533	12.5	3.62	73	.279	.330	-155	-145	102	99	.951	314	97	-3.1	-16.2	-9.7		-8.4
TOT	1097	143	12	11084¹		8.2				10.7	2.60		.244	.295					.959	2114	688					

Runs
Dougherty-Bos-NY 113
Flick-Cle 97
Bradley-Cle 94
Lajoie-Cle 92

Hits
Lajoie-Cle 208
Keeler-NY 186
Bradley-Cle 183
Dougherty-Bos-NY . 181
Flick-Cle 177

Doubles
Lajoie-Cle 49
Collins-Bos 33
Bradley-Cle 32

Triples
Stahl-Bos 19
Freeman-Bos 19
Cassidy-Was 19
Murphy-Phi 17
Flick-Cle 17

Home Runs
Davis-Phi 10
Murphy-Phi 7
Freeman-Bos 7

Total Bases
Flick-Cle 305
Flick-Cle 260
Freeman-Bos 246
Bradley-Cle 246

Runs Batted In
Lajoie-Cle 102
Freeman-Bos 84
Bradley-Cle 83
Anderson-NY 82

Runs Produced
Lajoie-Cle 188
Bradley-Cle 172
Parent-Bos 156
Collins-Bos 149
Murphy-Phi 148

Bases On Balls
Barrett-Det 79
Burkett-StL 78
Hartsel-Phi 75
Selbach-Was-Bos . . 72
Lush-Cle 72

Batting Average
Lajoie-Cle 376
Keeler-NY 343
Davis-Phi 309
Flick-Cle 306
Bradley-Cle 300

On Base Percentage
Lajoie-Cle 413
Keeler-NY 390
Flick-Cle 371
Stahl-Bos 366
Burkett-StL 363

Slugging Average
Lajoie-Cle 552
Davis-Phi 490
Flick-Cle 449
Murphy-Phi 440
Hickman-Cle-Det . .437

Production
Lajoie-Cle 965
Flick-Cle 820
Keeler-NY 799
Stahl-Bos 782
Murphy-Phi 760

Adjusted Production
Lajoie-Cle 205
Flick-Cle 160
Keeler-NY 146
Stahl-Bos 139
Hickman-Cle-Det . . 137

Batter Runs
Lajoie-Cle 62.4
Flick-Cle 38.7
Keeler-NY 32.7
Stahl-Bos 32.7
Davis-Phi 27.5

Adjusted Batter Runs
Lajoie-Cle 63.5
Flick-Cle 39.6
Keeler-NY 28.5
Stahl-Bos 27.3
Burkett-StL 24.4

Clutch Hitting Index
Callahan-Chi 132
Wallace-StL 130
Bradley-Cle 129
Tannehill-Chi 129
Anderson-NY 124

Runs Created
Lajoie-Cle 142
Flick-Cle 115
Keeler-NY 100
Stahl-Bos 99
Bradley-Cle 95

Total Average
Lajoie-Cle 1.070
Flick-Cle 891
Keeler-NY 798
Stahl-Bos 782
Murphy-Phi 741

Stolen Bases
Flick-Cle 38
Bay-Cle 38
Heidrick-StL 35
Davis-Chi 32
Conroy-NY 30

Fielding Runs
Tannehill-Chi 27.8
Davis-Chi 16.8
Williams-NY 16.8
Carr-Det-Cle 15.8
Elberfeld-NY 15.3

Total Player Rating
Lajoie-Cle 7.2
Flick-Cle 4.5
Murphy-Phi 3.9
Bradley-Cle 3.9
Davis-Chi 3.4

Wins
Chesbro-NY 41
Young-Bos 26
Plank-Phi 26
Waddell-Phi 25

Win Percentage
Chesbro-NY 774
Tannehill-Bos 656
Smith-Chi 640
Bernhard-Cle 639
Dinneen-Bos 622

Games
Chesbro-NY 55
Powell-NY 47
Waddell-Phi 46
Patten-Was 45
Mullin-Det 45

Complete Games
Chesbro-NY 48
Mullin-Det 42
Young-Bos 40
Waddell-Phi 39
Powell-NY 38

Shutouts
Young-Bos 10
Waddell-Phi 8
White-Chi 7
Plank-Phi 7
Mullin-Det 7

Saves
Patten-Was. 3

Innings Pitched
Chesbro-NY 454.2
Powell-NY 390.1
Waddell-Phi 383.0
Mullin-Det 382.1
Young-Bos 380.0

Fewest Hits/Game
Chesbro-NY 6.69
Owen-Chi 6.94
Smith-Chi 6.98
Gibson-Bos 7.12
Waddell-Phi 7.21

Fewest BB/Game
Young-Bos 69
Tannehill-Bos 1.05
Patterson-Chi 1.31
Joss-Cle 1.40
Altrock-Chi 1.41

Strikeouts
Waddell-Phi 349
Chesbro-NY 239
Powell-NY 202
Plank-Phi 201
Young-Bos 200

Strikeouts/Game
Waddell-Phi 8.20
Bender-Phi 6.58
Moore-Cle 5.49
Plank-Phi 5.06
Glade-StL 4.86

Ratio
Young-Bos 8.53
Chesbro-NY 8.57
Owen-Chi 9.00
Joss-Cle 9.22
Dinneen-Bos 9.33

Earned Run Average
Joss-Cle 1.59
Waddell-Phi 1.62
White-Chi 1.78
Chesbro-NY 1.82
Owen-Chi 1.94

Adjusted ERA
Waddell-Phi 165
Joss-Cle 159
Chesbro-NY 149
White-Chi 138
Young-Bos 136

Opponents' Batting Avg.
Chesbro-NY 208
Owen-Chi 214
Smith-Chi 215
Gibson-Bos 219
Waddell-Phi 221

Opponents' On Base Pct.
Young-Bos 251
Chesbro-NY 252
Owen-Chi 261
Joss-Cle 266
Dinneen-Bos 268

Starter Runs
Waddell-Phi 41.5
Chesbro-NY 39.2
Young-Bos 26.6
Owen-Chi 22.9
Joss-Cle 21.5

Adjusted Starter Runs
Chesbro-NY 45.0
Waddell-Phi 44.9
Young-Bos 29.8
Plank-Phi 20.3
Joss-Cle 20.2

Clutch Pitching Index
White-Chi 153
Siever-StL 134
Bernhard-Cle 130
Waddell-Phi 126
Donahue-Cle 118

Relief Runs

Adjusted Relief Runs

Relief Ranking

Total Pitcher Index
Chesbro-NY 6.9
Waddell-Phi 4.9
Owen-Chi 3.5
Mullin-Det 3.2
Young-Bos 3.1

Total Baseball Ranking
Lajoie-Cle 7.2
Chesbro-NY 6.9
Waddell-Phi 4.9
Flick-Cle 4.5
Murphy-Phi 3.9

TEAM	G	W	L	PCT	GB	R	OR	AB	H	2B	3B	HR	BB	SO	AVG	OBP	SLG	PRO	PRO+	BR	/A	PF	CHI	RC	SB	CS	SBA	SBR
NY	155	105	48	.686		780	505	5094	1392	191	88	39	517		.273	.351	.368	.719	119	143	126	102	99	796	291			
PIT	155	96	57	.627	9	692	570	5213	1385	190	91	22	382		.266	.320	.350	.670	104	38	21	103	102	683	202			
CHI	155	92	61	.601	13	667	442	5108	1249	157	82	12	448		.245	.313	.314	.627	90	-30	-54	104	109	625	267			
PHI	155	83	69	.546	21.5	708	602	5243	1362	187	82	16	406		.260	.318	.336	.654	106	13	38	96	107	655	180			
CIN	155	79	74	.516	26	735	698	5205	1401	160	101	27	434		.269	.332	.354	.686	101	74	-3	111	102	710	181			
STL	154	58	96	.377	47.5	535	734	5066	1254	140	85	20	391		.248	.307	.321	.628	97	-36	-18	97	92	576	162			
BOS	156	51	103	.331	54.5	468	733	5190	1217	148	52	17	302		.234	.284	.293	.577	80	-135	-124	98	96	491	132			
BRO	155	48	104	.316	56.5	506	807	5100	1255	154	60	29	327		.246	.297	.317	.614	97	-66	-25	93	91	564	186			
TOT	620					5091		41219	10515	1327	641	182	3207	4462	.255	.315	.332	.647							1601			

TEAM	CG	SH	SV	IP	H	H/G	HR	BB	SO	RAT	ERA	ERA+	OAV	OOB	PR	/A	PF	CPI	FA	E	DP	FW	PW	BW	SBW	DIF
NY	117	18	15	1370	1160	7.6	25	364	760	10.2	2.39	122	.229	.284	91	80	98	92	.960	258	93	2.3	8.3	13.1		4.8
PIT	113	12	6	1382²	1270	8.3	12	389	512	11.2	2.86	104	.248	.308	20	16	100	95	.961	255	112	2.5	1.7	2.2		13.2
CHI	133	23	2	1407¹	1135	7.3	14	385	627	10.0	2.04	146	.224	.286	149	144	99	105	.962	248	99	2.9	15.0	-5.6		3.2
PHI	119	12	5	1398²	1303	8.4	21	411	516	11.5	2.81	104	.253	.316	28	12	97	105	.957	275	99	1.2	1.2	4.0		.6
CIN	119	10	2	1365²	1409	9.3	22	439	547	12.5	3.01	109	.272	.335	-3	41	110	116	.953	310	122	-1.0	4.3	-.3		-.4
STL	135	10	2	1347²	1431	9.6	28	367	411	12.3	3.59	83	.276	.329	-89	-93	99	97	.957	274	83	1.2	-9.7	-1.9		-8.6
BOS	139	14	0	1383	1390	9.0	36	433	533	12.1	3.52	88	.265	.326	-81	-68	103	95	.951	325	89	-1.8	-7.1	-12.9		-4.2
BRO	125	7	3	1347	1416	9.5	24	476	556	13.1	3.76	77	.274	.343	-114	-132	96	98	.937	408	101	-7.2	-13.7	-2.6		-4.5
TOT	1000	106	35	11002		8.6				11.6	2.99		.255	.315					.954	2353	798					

Runs		Hits		Doubles		Triples		Home Runs		Total Bases	
Donlin-NY	124	Seymour-Cin	219	Seymour-Cin	40	Seymour-Cin	21	Odwell-Cin	9	Seymour-Cin	325
Thomas-Phi	118	Donlin-NY	216	Titus-Phi	36	Mertes-NY	17	Seymour-Cin	8	Donlin-NY	300
Huggins-Cin	117	Wagner-Pit	199	Wagner-Pit	32	Magee-Phi	17	Lumley-Bro	7	Wagner-Pit	277
Wagner-Pit	114	Barry-Chi-Cin	182	Donlin-NY	31	Smoot-StL	16	Donlin-NY	7	Magee-Phi	253
		Magee-Phi	180	Ritchey-Pit	29	Donlin-NY	16	Dahlen-NY	7	Titus-Phi	239

Runs Batted In		Runs Produced		Bases On Balls		Batting Average		On Base Percentage		Slugging Average	
Seymour-Cin	121	Wagner-Pit	209	Huggins-Cin	103	Seymour-Cin	.377	Chance-Chi	.450	Seymour-Cin	.559
Mertes-NY	108	Seymour-Cin	208	Slagle-Chi	97	Wagner-Pit	.363	Seymour-Cin	.429	Wagner-Pit	.505
Wagner-Pit	101	Donlin-NY	197	Thomas-Phi	93	Donlin-NY	.356	Wagner-Pit	.427	Donlin-NY	.495
Magee-Phi	98	Magee-Phi	193	Chance-Chi	78	Beaumont-Pit	.328	Thomas-Phi	.417	Titus-Phi	.436
Titus-Phi	89	Titus-Phi	186	Titus-Phi	69	Thomas-Phi	.317	Donlin-NY	.413	Grady-StL	.434

Production		Adjusted Production		Batter Runs		Adjusted Batter Runs		Clutch Hitting Index		Runs Created	
Seymour-Cin	.988	Seymour-Cin	175	Seymour-Cin	64.8	Seymour-Cin	50.8	Mertes-NY	139	Seymour-Cin	153
Wagner-Pit	.932	Wagner-Pit	173	Wagner-Pit	52.3	Wagner-Pit	49.3	Dahlen-NY	136	Wagner-Pit	147
Donlin-NY	.908	Donlin-NY	166	Donlin-NY	51.3	Donlin-NY	48.7	Wolverton-Bos	132	Donlin-NY	142
Chance-Chi	.883	Chance-Chi	157	Chance-Chi	37.2	Titus-Phi	38.6	Corcoran-Cin	131	Magee-Phi	111
Titus-Phi	.834	Titus-Phi	154	Titus-Phi	34.7	Chance-Chi	33.7	Courtney-Phi	131	Mertes-NY	103

Total Average		Stolen Bases		Stolen Base Average	Stolen Base Runs	Fielding Runs		Total Player Rating	
Wagner-Pit	1.132	Maloney-Chi	59			Huggins-Cin	36.2	Wagner-Pit	7.3
Chance-Chi	1.131	Devlin-NY	59			Gilbert-NY	25.4	Seymour-Cin	5.7
Seymour-Cin	1.102	Wagner-Pit	57			Tenney-Bos	22.2	Huggins-Cin	4.5
Donlin-NY	1.003	Mertes-NY	52			Wagner-Pit	20.3	Thomas-Phi	4.5
McGann-NY	.898	Magee-Phi	48			Dahlen-NY	19.8	Titus-Phi	4.1

Wins		Win Percentage		Games		Complete Games		Shutouts		Saves	
Mathewson-NY	31	Leever-Pit	.800	Pittinger-Phi	46	Young-Bos	41	Mathewson-NY	8	Elliott-NY	6
Pittinger-Phi	23	Mathewson-NY	.775	McGinnity-NY	46	Willis-Bos	36	Young-Bos	7	Wiltse-NY	4
Ames-NY	22	Ames-NY	.733	Young-Bos	43	Fraser-Bos	35	Reulbach-Chi	5	McGinnity-NY	3
McGinnity-NY	21	Wiltse-NY	.714	Mathewson-NY	43	Taylor-StL	34	Phillippe-Pit	5		
		Lynch-Pit	.680	Overall-Cin	42			Briggs-Chi	5		

Innings Pitched		Fewest Hits/Game		Fewest BB/Game		Strikeouts		Strikeouts/Game		Ratio	
Young-Bos	378.0	Reulbach-Chi	6.42	Phillippe-Pit	1.55	Mathewson-NY	206	Ames-NY	6.78	Mathewson-NY	8.42
Willis-Bos	342.0	Mathewson-NY	6.70	Brown-Chi	1.59	Ames-NY	198	Wiltse-NY	5.48	Reulbach-Chi	9.23
Mathewson-NY	338.2	Lundgren-Chi	7.02	Young-Bos	1.69	Overall-Cin	173	Mathewson-NY	5.47	Phillippe-Pit	9.45
Pittinger-Phi	337.1	Wicker-Chi	7.03	Mathewson-NY	1.70	Ewing-Cin	164	Overall-Cin	4.90	Wicker-Chi	9.46
Fraser-Bos	334.1	Wiltse-NY	7.22	McGinnity-NY	1.99	Young-Bos	156	Scanlan-Bro	4.87	Brown-Chi	9.54

Earned Run Average		Adjusted ERA		Opponents' Batting Avg.		Opponents' On Base Pct.		Starter Runs		Adjusted Starter Runs	
Mathewson-NY	1.28	Mathewson-NY	229	Reulbach-Chi	.201	Mathewson-NY	.245	Mathewson-NY	64.6	Mathewson-NY	61.9
Reulbach-Chi	1.42	Reulbach-Chi	209	Mathewson-NY	.205	Reulbach-Chi	.266	Reulbach-Chi	50.9	Reulbach-Chi	50.3
Wicker-Chi	2.02	Wicker-Chi	147	Wiltse-NY	.219	Brown-Chi	.271	Phillippe-Pit	24.7	Ewing-Cin	27.1
Briggs-Chi	2.14	Briggs-Chi	139	Lundgren-Chi	.220	Phillippe-Pit	.274	Sparks-Phi	23.3	Phillippe-Pit	24.7
Brown-Chi	2.17	Brown-Chi	137	Wicker-Chi	.221	Wicker-Chi	.276	Brown-Chi	22.8	Brown-Chi	22.2

Clutch Pitching Index		Relief Runs	Adjusted Relief Runs	Relief Ranking	Total Pitcher Index		Total Baseball Ranking	
Chech-Cin	133				Mathewson-NY	9.6	Mathewson-NY	9.6
Duggleby-Phi	126				Reulbach-Chi	4.8	Wagner-Pit	7.3
Overall-Cin	119				Ewing-Cin	2.7	Seymour-Cin	5.7
Briggs-Chi	119				Brown-Chi	2.4	Reulbach-Chi	4.8
Case-Pit	115				Wiltse-NY	2.4	Huggins-Cin	4.5

TEAM	G	W	L	PCT	GB	R	OR	AB	H	2B	3B	HR	BB	SO	AVG	OBP	SLG	PRO	PRO+	BR	/A	PF	CHI	RC	SB	CS	SBA	SBR
PHI	152	92	56	.622		623	492	5146	1310	256	51	24	376		.255	.310	.338	.648	109	60	49	102	98	632	190			
CHI	158	92	60	.605	2	612	451	5114	1213	200	55	11	439		.237	.305	.304	.609	103	0	24	96	104	577	194			
DET	154	79	74	.516	15.5	512	602	4971	1209	190	54	13	375		.243	.302	.311	.613	99	1	-3	101	92	540	129			
BOS	153	78	74	.513	16	579	564	5049	1179	165	69	29	486		.234	.305	.311	.616	100	14	8	101	99	550	131			
CLE	155	76	78	.494	19	567	587	5166	1318	211	72	18	286		.255	.301	.334	.635	106	33	25	101	94	608	188			
NY	152	71	78	.477	21.5	586	622	4957	1228	163	61	23	360		.248	.307	.319	.626	93	26	-40	111	101	580	200			
WAS	154	64	87	.424	29.5	559	623	5015	1121	193	68	22	298		.224	.274	.302	.576	92	-70	-51	96	115	492	169			
STL	156	54	99	.353	40.5	511	608	5204	1205	153	49	16	362		.232	.288	.289	.577	93	-64	-37	95	99	502	130			
TOT	617					4549		40622	9783	1531	479	156	2982	5107	.241	.299	.314	.613						1331				

TEAM	CG	SH	SV	IP	H	H/G	HR	BB	SO	RAT	ERA	ERA+	OAV	OOB	PR	/A	PF	CPI	FA	E	DP	FW	PW	BW	SBW	DIF
PHI	117	19	0	1383¹	1137	7.4	21	409	895	10.5	2.19	121	.227	.294	70	68	100	110	.957	265	64	.2	7.5	5.4		4.9
CHI	131	15	0	1427	1163	7.3	11	329	613	9.6	1.99	124	.226	.277	105	72	93	105	.968	217	95	4.1	7.9	2.6		1.3
DET	124	17	1	1348	1226	8.2	11	474	578	11.7	2.83	96	.246	.318	-27	-19	103	104	.957	265	80	.5	-2.1	-.3		4.5
BOS	124	14	1	1356¹	1198	7.9	33	292	652	10.2	2.84	95	.241	.289	-29	-26	102	89	.953	294	75	-1.6	-2.9	.9		5.6
CLE	140	16	0	1363¹	1251	8.3	23	334	555	10.9	2.85	92	.246	.301	-30	-34	99	97	.963	229	84	3.0	-3.7	2.7		-3.0
NY	88	16	4	1353²	1235	8.2	26	396	642	11.1	2.93	100	.246	.307	-42	-2	111	97	.952	293	88	-1.6	-.2	-4.4		2.7
WAS	118	12	1	1362¹	1250	8.3	12	385	539	11.2	2.87	92	.247	.308	-33	-35	100	98	.951	318	76	-3.1	-3.8	-5.6		1.0
STL	134	10	2	1384²	1245	8.1	19	389	633	11.0	2.74	93	.243	.304	-14	-33	96	100	.955	295	78	-1.3	-3.6	-4.1		-13.5
TOT	976	119	9	10978²		8.0				10.8	2.65		.241	.299					.957	2176	640					

Runs		Hits		Doubles		Triples		Home Runs		Total Bases	
Davis-Phi	93	Stone-StL	187	Davis-Phi	47	Flick-Cle	18	Davis-Phi	8	Stone-StL	259
Jones-Chi	91	Davis-Phi	173	Crawford-Det	38	Ferris-Bos	16	Stone-StL	7	Davis-Phi	256
Bay-Cle	90	Crawford-Det	171	Hickman-Det-Was	37	Turner-Cle	14			Crawford-Det	247
Hartsel-Phi	88	Keeler-NY	169	Seybold-Phi	37	Stone-StL	13			Hickman-Det-Was	232
Keeler-NY	81	Bay-Cle	166			Burkett-Bos	13			Flick-Cle	231

Runs Batted In		Runs Produced		Bases On Balls		Batting Average		On Base Percentage		Slugging Average	
Davis-Phi	83	Davis-Phi	168	Hartsel-Phi	121	Flick-Cle	.308	Hartsel-Phi	.409	Flick-Cle	.462
L.Cross-Phi	77	Donahue-Chi	146	Jones-Chi	73	Keeler-NY	.302	Flick-Cle	.383	Isbell-Chi	.440
Donahue-Chi	76	L.Cross-Phi	146	Selbach-Bos	67	Bay-Cle	.301	Keeler-NY	.357	Crawford-Det	.430
Crawford-Det	75	Crawford-Det	142	Burkett-Bos	67	Crawford-Det	.297	Crawford-Det	.357	Davis-Phi	.422
Turner-Cle	72	Murphy-Phi	136	Davis-Chi	60	Isbell-Chi	.296	Selbach-Bos	.355	Stone-StL	.410

Production		Adjusted Production		Batter Runs		Adjusted Batter Runs		Clutch Hitting Index		Runs Created	
Flick-Cle	.845	Flick-Cle	165	Flick-Cle	38.6	Flick-Cle	37.3	Gleason-StL	134	Flick-Cle	106
Crawford-Det	.786	Crawford-Det	148	Hartsel-Phi	32.9	Stone-StL	32.1	Donahue-Chi	131	Stone-StL	102
Stone-StL	.756	Stone-StL	147	Crawford-Det	31.0	Hartsel-Phi	31.2	L.Cross-Phi	128	Davis-Phi	101
Davis-Phi	.756	Hartsel-Phi	138	Stone-StL	26.9	Crawford-Det	30.3	Fultz-NY	121	Crawford-Det	99
Hartsel-Phi	.755	Davis-Phi	137	Davis-Phi	24.9	Davis-Phi	23.4	Collins-Bos	116	Hartsel-Phi	96

Total Average		Stolen Bases		Stolen Base Average	Stolen Base Runs	Fielding Runs		Total Player Rating	
Flick-Cle	.945	Hoffman-Phi	46			Cassidy-Was	33.1	Davis-Chi	4.0
Hartsel-Phi	.885	Fultz-NY	44			Tannehill-Chi	27.8	Crawford-Det	3.8
Crawford-Det	.797	Stahl-Was	41			Wallace-StL	19.0	Wallace-StL	3.8
Davis-Phi	.776	Hartsel-Phi	37			McIntyre-Det	16.4	Flick-Cle	3.3
Stone-StL	.751					Jones-Was	16.1	Stone-StL	2.8

Wins		Win Percentage		Games		Complete Games		Shutouts		Saves	
Waddell-Phi	27	Waddell-Phi	.730	Waddell-Phi	46	Plank-Phi	35	Killian-Det	8	Buchanan-StL	2
Plank-Phi	24	Tannehill-Bos	.710	Mullin-Det	44	Mullin-Det	35	Waddell-Phi	7		
Killian-Det	23	Coakley-Phi	.692	Patten-Was	42	Howell-StL	35	Tannehill-Bos	6		
Altrock-Chi	23	Plank-Phi	.667	Owen-Chi	42	Killian-Det	33	Orth-NY	6		
Tannehill-Bos	22	Altrock-Chi	.657			Owen-Chi	32	Hughes-Was	6		

Innings Pitched		Fewest Hits/Game		Fewest BB/Game		Strikeouts		Strikeouts/Game		Ratio	
Mullin-Det	347.2	Waddell-Phi	6.33	Young-Bos	.84	Waddell-Phi	287	Waddell-Phi	7.86	Young-Bos	8.03
Plank-Phi	346.2	Smith-Chi	6.63	Joss-Cle	1.45	Young-Bos	210	Young-Bos	5.89	Waddell-Phi	9.06
Owen-Chi	334.0	Young-Bos	6.96	Owen-Chi	1.51	Plank-Phi	210	Bender-Phi	5.58	Owen-Chi	9.19
Waddell-Phi	328.2	Howell-StL	7.02	Bernhard-Cle	1.76	Howell-StL	198	Howell-StL	5.52	White-Chi	9.37
Howell-StL	323.0	White-Chi	7.05	Altrock-Chi	1.80	Smith-Chi	171	Hogg-NY	5.49	Joss-Cle	9.53

Earned Run Average		Adjusted ERA		Opponents' Batting Avg.		Opponents' On Base Pct.		Starter Runs		Adjusted Starter Runs	
Waddell-Phi	1.48	Waddell-Phi	179	Waddell-Phi	.200	Young-Bos	.241	Waddell-Phi	42.7	Waddell-Phi	42.8
White-Chi	1.76	Young-Bos	147	Smith-Chi	.208	Waddell-Phi	.264	Young-Bos	29.3	Young-Bos	30.9
Young-Bos	1.82	Coakley-Phi	144	Young-Bos	.216	Owen-Chi	.267	Altrock-Chi	26.9	Chesbro-NY	24.6
Coakley-Phi	1.84	White-Chi	140	Howell-StL	.217	White-Chi	.270	White-Chi	25.6	Coakley-Phi	23.1
Altrock-Chi	1.88	Chesbro-NY	133	White-Chi	.218	Joss-Cle	.274	Howell-StL	24.0	Altrock-Chi	20.3

Clutch Pitching Index		Relief Runs	Adjusted Relief Runs	Relief Ranking	Total Pitcher Index		Total Baseball Ranking	
Coakley-Phi	142				Howell-StL	4.9	Waddell-Phi	4.9
Altrock-Chi	118				Waddell-Phi	4.9	Howell-StL	4.8
Waddell-Phi	116				Young-Bos	3.3	Davis-Chi	4.0
Townsend-Was	115				Chesbro-NY	3.0	Crawford-Det	3.8
Mullin-Det	113				Altrock-Chi	2.9	Wallace-StL	3.8

1906 National League

TEAM	G	W	L	PCT	GB	R	OR	AB	H	2B	3B	HR	BB	SO	AVG	OBP	SLG	PRO	PRO+	BR	/A	PF	CHI	RC	SB	CS	SBA	SBR
CHI	155	116	36	.763		705	381	5018	1316	181	71	20	448		.262	.328	.339	.667	109	83	46	106	109	695	283			
NY	153	96	56	.632	20	625	510	4768	1217	162	53	15	563		.255	.343	.321	.664	112	92	78	102	98	659	288			
PIT	154	93	60	.608	23.5	623	470	5030	1313	164	67	12	424		.261	.324	.327	.651	105	55	28	104	102	625	162			
PHI	154	71	82	.464	45.5	528	564	4911	1183	197	47	12	432		.241	.307	.307	.614	98	-10	-11	100	99	550	180			
BRO	153	66	86	.434	50	496	625	4897	1156	141	68	25	388		.236	.297	.308	.605	103	-31	8	92	98	532	175			
CIN	155	64	87	.424	51.5	533	582	5025	1198	140	71	16	395		.238	.301	.304	.605	91	-28	-51	104	101	545	170			
STL	154	52	98	.347	63	470	607	5075	1195	137	69	10	361		.235	.291	.296	.587	93	-66	-46	96	97	498	110			
BOS	152	49	102	.325	66.5	408	649	4925	1115	136	43	16	356		.226	.286	.281	.567	85	-96	-84	97	93	448	93			
TOT	615					4388		39649	9693	1258	489	126	3367	4537	.244	.310	.310	.620							1461			

TEAM	CG	SH	SV	IP	H	H/G	HR	BB	SO	RAT	ERA	ERA+	OAV	OOB	PR	/A	PF	CPI	FA	E	DP	FW	PW	BW	SBW	DIF
CHI	125	30	10	1388[1]	1018	6.6	12	446	702	9.8	1.75	150	.207	.280	135	135	100	100	.969	194	100	4.5	15.0	5.1		15.3
NY	105	19	18	1334[1]	1207	8.1	13	394	639	11.0	2.49	105	.241	.300	20	15	99	96	.963	233	84	1.8	1.7	8.7		7.9
PIT	116	27	2	1358	1234	8.2	13	309	532	10.5	2.21	120	.245	.294	62	70	102	107	.964	228	109	2.2	7.8	3.1		3.4
PHI	108	21	5	1354[1]	1201	8.0	18	436	500	11.3	2.58	101	.235	.304	7	0	99	94	.956	271	83	-.6	.0	-1.2		-3.7
BRO	119	22	11	1348[2]	1255	8.4	15	453	476	11.7	3.13	80	.249	.316	-76	-93	96	88	.955	283	73	-1.5	-10.3	.9		1.0
CIN	126	12	5	1369[2]	1248	8.2	14	470	567	11.6	2.69	102	.250	.320	-10	6	105	105	.959	262	97	.0	.7	-5.7		-6.6
STL	118	4	2	1354	1246	8.3	17	479	559	11.9	3.04	86	.246	.318	-63	-65	100	91	.957	272	92	-.7	-7.2	-5.1		-10.0
BOS	137	10	0	1334[1]	1291	8.7	24	436	562	12.0	3.14	85	.261	.328	-76	-70	102	100	.947	337	102	-5.2	-7.8	-9.3		-4.2
TOT	954	145	53	10841[2]		8.1				11.2	2.62		.244	.310					.959	2080	740					

Runs		Hits		Doubles		Triples		Home Runs		Total Bases	
Wagner-Pit	103	Steinfeldt-Chi	176	Wagner-Pit	38	Schulte-Chi	13	Jordan-Bro	12	Wagner-Pit	237
Chance-Chi	103	Wagner-Pit	175	Magee-Phi	36	Clarke-Pit	13	Lumley-Bro	9	Steinfeldt-Chi	232
Sheckard-Chi	90	Seymour-Cin-NY	165	Bransfield-Phi	28	Nealon-Pit	12	Seymour-Cin-NY	8	Lumley-Bro	231
Nealon-Pit	82	Magee-Phi	159	Steinfeldt-Chi	27	Lumley-Bro	12	Schulte-Chi	7	Magee-Phi	229
		Huggins-Cin	159	Sheckard-Chi	27					Schulte-Chi	223

Runs Batted In		Runs Produced		Bases On Balls		Batting Average		On Base Percentage		Slugging Average	
Steinfeldt-Chi	83	Wagner-Pit	172	Thomas-Phi	107	Wagner-Pit	.339	Bresnahan-NY	.419	Lumley-Bro	.477
Nealon-Pit	83	Chance-Chi	171	Bresnahan-NY	81	Steinfeldt-Chi	.327	Chance-Chi	.419	Wagner-Pit	.459
Seymour-Cin-NY	80	Nealon-Pit	162	Titus-Phi	78	Lumley-Bro	.324	Wagner-Pit	.416	Strang-NY	.435
Jordan-Bro	78	Steinfeldt-Chi	161	Dahlen-NY	76	Strang-NY	.319	Devlin-NY	.396	Steinfeldt-Chi	.430
		Seymour-Cin-NY	142	Devlin-NY	74	Chance-Chi	.319	Steinfeldt-Chi	.395	Chance-Chi	.430

Production		Adjusted Production		Batter Runs		Adjusted Batter Runs		Clutch Hitting Index		Runs Created	
Wagner-Pit	.875	Lumley-Bro	184	Wagner-Pit	44.7	Lumley-Bro	44.6	Tinker-Chi	138	Wagner-Pit	124
Lumley-Bro	.864	Wagner-Pit	166	Chance-Chi	39.1	Wagner-Pit	40.2	Nealon-Pit	134	Chance-Chi	114
Chance-Chi	.849	Chance-Chi	156	Lumley-Bro	37.2	Chance-Chi	33.6	Ritchey-Pit	128	Steinfeldt-Chi	109
Steinfeldt-Chi	.825	Jordan-Bro	153	Steinfeldt-Chi	36.1	Steinfeldt-Chi	30.6	Kelley-Cin	126	Lumley-Bro	107
Devlin-NY	.786	Steinfeldt-Chi	149	Devlin-NY	29.1	Devlin-NY	27.2	Shannon-StL-NY	125	Magee-Phi	102

Total Average		Stolen Bases		Stolen Base Average		Stolen Base Runs		Fielding Runs		Total Player Rating	
Chance-Chi	1.062	Chance-Chi	57					Devlin-NY	28.0	Wagner-Pit	7.3
Wagner-Pit	1.050	Magee-Phi	55					Brain-Bos	25.7	Devlin-NY	6.5
Lumley-Bro	.963	Devlin-NY	54					Wagner-Pit	23.8	Lumley-Bro	4.3
Devlin-NY	.940	Wagner-Pit	53					Gilbert-NY	22.6	Huggins-Cin	4.0
Bresnahan-NY	.911	Evers-Chi	49					Huggins-Cin	21.5	Bresnahan-NY	3.9

Wins		Win Percentage		Games		Complete Games		Shutouts		Saves	
McGinnity-NY	27	Reulbach-Chi	.826	McGinnity-NY	45	Young-Bos	37	Brown-Chi	9	Ferguson-NY	7
Brown-Chi	26	Brown-Chi	.813	Young-Bos	43	Pfeffer-Bos	33	Leifield-Pit	8	Wiltse-NY	6
Willis-Pit	23	Leever-Pit	.759	Sparks-Phi	42					Stricklett-Bro	5
Mathewson-NY	22	Lundgren-Chi	.739	Duggleby-Phi	42						
Leever-Pit	22	Pfiester-Chi	.714								

Innings Pitched		Fewest Hits/Game		Fewest BB/Game		Strikeouts		Strikeouts/Game		Ratio	
Young-Bos	358.1	Reulbach-Chi	5.33	Phillippe-Pit	1.07	Beebe-Chi-StL	171	Ames-NY	6.90	Brown-Chi	8.53
McGinnity-NY	339.2	Pfiester-Chi	6.21	Leever-Pit	1.66	Beebe-Chi-StL	158	Beebe-Chi-StL	6.67	Pfiester-Chi	8.94
Willis-Pit	322.0	Brown-Chi	6.43	Sparks-Phi	1.76	Ames-NY	156	Pfiester-Chi	5.49	Sparks-Phi	8.98
Sparks-Phi	316.2	Beebe-Chi-StL	6.67	Ewing-Cin	1.88	Pfiester-Chi	153	Overall-Cin-Chi	5.05	Reulbach-Chi	9.66
Lindaman-Bos	307.1	Lundgren-Chi	6.93	McGinnity-NY	1.88			Lush-Phi	4.84	Ewing-Cin	9.70

Earned Run Average		Adjusted ERA		Opponents' Batting Avg.		Opponents' On Base Pct.		Starter Runs		Adjusted Starter Runs	
Brown-Chi	1.04	Brown-Chi	253	Reulbach-Chi	.175	Brown-Chi	.252	Brown-Chi	48.9	Brown-Chi	49.0
Pfiester-Chi	1.51	Pfiester-Chi	174	Pfiester-Chi	.194	Sparks-Phi	.257	Willis-Pit	31.9	Willis-Pit	33.3
Reulbach-Chi	1.65	Reulbach-Chi	159	Brown-Chi	.202	Pfiester-Chi	.258	Pfiester-Chi	31.1	Pfiester-Chi	31.3
Willis-Pit	1.73	Willis-Pit	154	Beebe-Chi-StL	.209	Phillippe-Pit	.276	Reulbach-Chi	23.6	Reulbach-Chi	23.7
Leifield-Pit	1.87	Leifield-Pit	143	Sparks-Phi	.211	Reulbach-Chi	.278	Leifield-Pit	21.6	Leifield-Pit	22.7

Clutch Pitching Index		Relief Runs		Adjusted Relief Runs		Relief Ranking		Total Pitcher Index		Total Baseball Ranking	
Willis-Pit	139	Ferguson-NY	3	Ferguson-NY	1	Ferguson-NY	0	Brown-Chi	6.8	Wagner-Pit	7.3
Lindaman-Bos	126							Willis-Pit	4.5	Brown-Chi	6.8
Brown-Chi	122							Taylor-StL-Chi	2.9	Devlin-NY	6.5
Leifield-Pit	120							Weimer-Cin	2.9	Willis-Pit	4.5
Lush-Phi	114							Reulbach-Chi	2.8	Lumley-Bro	4.3

TEAM	G	W	L	PCT	GB	R	OR	AB	H	2B	3B	HR	BB	SO	AVG	OBP	SLG	PRO	PRO+	BR	/A	PF	CHI	RC	SB	CS	SBA	SBR
CHI	154	93	58	.616		570	460	4925	1133	152	52	7	453		.230	.301	.286	.587	91	-47	-33	97	110	531	214			
NY	155	90	61	.596	3	644	543	5095	1354	166	77	17	331		.266	.316	.339	.655	101	58	-5	110	103	644	192			
CLE	157	89	64	.582	5	663	482	5426	1516	240	73	12	330		.279	.326	.357	.683	122	112	122	99	93	737	203			
PHI	149	78	67	.538	12	561	543	4883	1206	213	49	32	385		.247	.308	.330	.638	102	30	12	103	97	581	165			
STL	154	76	73	.510	16	558	498	5030	1244	145	60	20	366		.247	.304	.312	.616	102	-6	18	96	101	579	221			
DET	151	71	78	.477	21	518	599	4930	1195	154	64	10	333		.242	.295	.306	.601	91	-37	-51	103	102	539	206			
WAS	151	55	95	.367	37.5	518	664	4956	1180	144	65	26	306		.238	.289	.309	.598	97	-44	-20	95	103	539	233			
BOS	155	49	105	.318	45.5	463	706	5168	1223	160	75	13	298		.237	.284	.304	.588	89	-66	-65	100	93	503	99			
TOT	613					4495		40413	10051	1374	515	137	2802	4561	.249	.303	.318	.621							1533			

TEAM	CG	SH	SV	IP	H	H/G	HR	BB	SO	RAT	ERA	ERA+	OAV	OOB	PR	/A	PF	CPI	FA	E	DP	FW	PW	BW	SBW	DIF
CHI	117	32	3	1375[1]	1212	7.9	11	255	543	9.8	2.13	119	.239	.280	85	63	94	103	.963	243	80	1.8	6.9	-3.6		12.4
NY	99	18	5	1357[2]	1236	8.2	21	351	605	10.8	2.78	107	.246	.301	-13	28	110	95	.957	272	69	.1	3.1	-.5		11.9
CLE	133	27	4	1412[2]	1197	7.6	16	365	530	10.3	2.09	125	.232	.289	94	83	97	110	.967	216	111	3.9	9.1	13.4		-13.9
PHI	107	19	4	1322	1135	7.7	9	425	749	11.0	2.60	105	.236	.306	13	17	101	98	.956	267	86	-.2	1.9	1.3		2.6
STL	133	17	5	1357[2]	1132	7.5	14	314	558	10.0	2.23	116	.230	.284	70	54	96	98	.954	290	80	-1.1	5.9	2.0		-5.3
DET	128	7	4	1334[1]	1398	9.4	14	389	469	12.4	3.06	90	.272	.330	-55	-43	103	111	.959	260	86	.4	-4.7	-5.6		6.4
WAS	115	13	1	1322[2]	1331	9.1	15	451	558	12.4	3.25	81	.264	.330	-83	-90	98	102	.955	279	78	-.8	-9.9	-2.2		-7.1
BOS	124	6	6	1382	1360	8.9	37	285	549	11.0	3.41	81	.262	.306	-111	-106	102	87	.949	335	84	-3.9	-11.7	-7.1		-5.3
TOT	956	139	32	10864[1]		8.3				11.0	2.69		.249	.303					.958	2162	674					

Runs
Flick-Cle 98
Keeler-NY 96
Hartsel-Phi 96
Davis-Phi 94
Stone-StL 91

Hits
Lajoie-Cle 214
Stone-StL 208
Flick-Cle 194
Chase-NY 193
Keeler-NY 180

Doubles
Lajoie-Cle 48
Davis-Phi 42
Flick-Cle 34
Murphy-Phi . . . 28
Turner-Cle 27

Triples
Flick-Cle 22
Stone-StL 20
Crawford-Det . . 16
Ferris-Bos 13

Home Runs
Davis-Phi 12
Hickman-Was . . 9
Stone-StL 6
Seybold-Phi . . . 5

Total Bases
Stone-StL 291
Lajoie-Cle 280
Flick-Cle 275
Davis-Phi 253
Chase-NY 236

Runs Batted In
Davis-Phi 96
Lajoie-Cle 91
Davis-Chi 80
Williams-NY . . . 77
Chase-NY 76

Runs Produced
Lajoie-Cle 179
Davis-Phi 178
Chase-NY 160
Flick-Cle 159
Stone-StL 156

Bases On Balls
Hartsel-Phi 88
Jones-Chi 83
E.Hahn-NY-Chi . . 72
Wallace-StL . . . 58
McIntyre-Det . . . 56

Batting Average
Stone-StL 358
Lajoie-Cle 355
Chase-NY 323
Congalton-Cle . . .320
Seybold-Phi 316

On Base Percentage
Stone-StL 417
Lajoie-Cle 392
Flick-Cle 372
Hartsel-Phi 363
Davis-Phi 355

Slugging Average
Stone-StL 501
Lajoie-Cle 465
Davis-Phi 459
Flick-Cle 441
Hickman-Was . . .421

Production
Stone-StL 918
Lajoie-Cle 857
Davis-Phi 815
Flick-Cle 813
Crawford-Det . . .747

Adjusted Production
Stone-StL 195
Lajoie-Cle 170
Flick-Cle 156
Davis-Phi 150
Hickman-Was . . 135

Batter Runs
Stone-StL 57.8
Lajoie-Cle 44.8
Flick-Cle 38.4
Davis-Phi 33.1
Seybold-Phi . . . 21.1

Adjusted Batter Runs
Stone-StL 63.2
Lajoie-Cle 46.4
Flick-Cle 39.9
Davis-Phi 30.2
Hemphill-StL . . 19.7

Clutch Hitting Index
Davis-Phi 154
Coughlin-Det . . 134
Stahl-Was 133
Wallace-StL . . . 131
Williams-NY . . . 130

Runs Created
Stone-StL 141
Lajoie-Cle 122
Flick-Cle 121
Davis-Phi 101
Chase-NY 95

Total Average
Stone-StL 1.032
Flick-Cle 872
Lajoie-Cle 866
Davis-Phi 846
Hartsel-Phi 753

Stolen Bases
Flick-Cle 39
Anderson-Was . . 39
Isbell-Chi 37
Altizer-Was . . . 37
Donahue-Chi . . . 36

Stolen Base Average

Stolen Base Runs

Fielding Runs
Tannehill-Chi . . 39.6
Lajoie-Cle 31.9
Turner-Cle 23.6
Schlafly-Was . . 14.0
McIntyre-Det . . . 11.9

Total Player Rating
Lajoie-Cle 8.5
Stone-StL 5.8
Turner-Cle 4.7
Davis-Chi 2.8
Davis-Phi 2.8

Wins
Orth-NY 27
Chesbro-NY . . . 23
Rhoads-Cle . . . 22
Owen-Chi 22

Win Percentage
Plank-Phi 760
White-Chi 750
Joss-Cle 700
Rhoads-Cle 688
Owen-Chi 629

Games
Chesbro-NY . . . 49
Orth-NY 45
Waddell-Phi . . . 43
Hess-Cle 43
Owen-Chi 42

Complete Games
Orth-NY 36
Mullin-Det 35
Hess-Cle 33
Rhoads-Cle . . . 31

Shutouts
Walsh-Chi 10
Joss-Cle 9
Waddell-Phi . . . 8

Saves
Hess-Cle 3
Bender-Phi 3

Innings Pitched
Orth-NY 338.2
Hess-Cle 333.2
Mullin-Det 330.0
Chesbro-NY . . . 325.0
Rhoads-Cle . . . 315.0

Fewest Hits/Game
Pelty-StL 6.53
White-Chi 6.57
Walsh-Chi 6.95
Joss-Cle 7.02
Powell-StL 7.23

Fewest BB/Game
Young-Bos 78
Altrock-Chi 1.31
Joss-Cle 1.37
White-Chi 1.56
Jacobson-StL . . 1.57

Strikeouts
Waddell-Phi . . . 196
Falkenberg-Was . 178
Walsh-Chi 171
Hess-Cle 167
Bender-Phi 159

Strikeouts/Game
Waddell-Phi . . . 6.47
Bender-Phi 6.00
Walsh-Chi 5.53
Falkenberg-Was . 5.36
Powell-StL 4.87

Ratio
White-Chi 8.33
Joss-Cle 8.49
Walsh-Chi 9.05
Pelty-StL 9.18
Powell-StL 9.55

Earned Run Average
White-Chi 1.52
Pelty-StL 1.59
Joss-Cle 1.72
Powell-StL 1.77
Rhoads-Cle . . . 1.80

Adjusted ERA
White-Chi 167
Pelty-StL 163
Joss-Cle 152
Powell-StL 146
Rhoads-Cle . . . 145

Opponents' Batting Avg.
Pelty-StL 206
White-Chi 207
Walsh-Chi 217
Joss-Cle 218
Powell-StL 223

Opponents' On Base Pct.
White-Chi 249
Joss-Cle 252
Walsh-Chi 265
Pelty-StL 267
Powell-StL 275

Starter Runs
Pelty-StL 31.9
Hess-Cle 31.7
Rhoads-Cle . . . 31.1
Joss-Cle 30.3
White-Chi 28.6

Adjusted Starter Runs
Hess-Cle 29.0
Pelty-StL 28.8
Rhoads-Cle . . . 28.6
Joss-Cle 28.0
White-Chi 24.9

Clutch Pitching Index
Rhoads-Cle . . . 126
Siever-Det 125
Hess-Cle 124
Smith-Was 121
Donahue-Det . . 121

Relief Runs

Adjusted Relief Runs

Relief Ranking

Total Pitcher Index
Orth-NY 3.7
Joss-Cle 3.7
White-Chi 3.6
Pelty-StL 3.5
Hess-Cle 3.3

Total Baseball Ranking
Lajoie-Cle 8.5
Stone-StL 5.8
Turner-Cle 4.7
Orth-NY 3.9
Joss-Cle 3.7

TEAM	G	W	L	PCT	GB	R	OR	AB	H	2B	3B	HR	BB	SO	AVG	OBP	SLG	PRO	PRO+	BR	/A	PF	CHI	RC	SB	CS	SBA	SBR
CHI	155	107	45	.704		574	390	4892	1224	162	48	13	435		.250	.318	.311	.629	98	25	-10	106	104	596	235			
PIT	157	91	63	.591	17	634	510	4957	1261	133	78	19	469		.254	.325	.324	.649	109	62	54	101	106	645	264			
PHI	149	83	64	.565	21.5	512	476	4725	1113	162	65	12	424		.236	.304	.305	.609	99	-11	-4	99	104	514	154			
NY	155	82	71	.536	25.5	574	510	4874	1222	160	45	23	516		.251	.331	.317	.648	107	68	49	103	96	617	205			
BRO	153	65	83	.439	40	446	522	4895	1135	142	63	18	336		.232	.287	.298	.585	98	-62	-26	92	98	488	121			
CIN	156	66	87	.431	41.5	526	519	4966	1226	126	90	15	372		.247	.304	.318	.622	98	3	-19	104	99	564	158			
BOS	152	58	90	.392	47	502	652	5020	1222	142	61	22	413		.243	.308	.309	.617	100	2	4	100	94	545	118			
STL	155	52	101	.340	55.5	419	608	5008	1163	121	51	19	312		.232	.283	.288	.571	88	-87	-73	97	97	474	125			
TOT	616					4187		39337	9566	1148	504	141	3277	4217	.243	.308	.309	.616						1380				

TEAM	CG	SH	SV	IP	H	H/G	HR	BB	SO	RAT	ERA	ERA+	OAV	OOB	PR	/A	PF	CPI	FA	E	DP	FW	PW	BW	SBW	DIF
CHI	114	32	8	1373¹	1054	6.9	11	402	586	9.8	1.73	144	.216	.281	112	115	101	101	.967	211	110	3.1	13.1	-1.1		16.0
PIT	111	24	5	1363	1207	8.0	12	368	497	10.7	2.30	106	.241	.299	25	19	99	99	.959	256	75	.2	2.2	6.1		5.5
PHI	110	21	4	1299¹	1095	7.6	13	422	499	10.9	2.43	99	.233	.304	5	-3	98	94	.957	256	104	-.7	-.3	-.5		11.0
NY	109	22	13	1371	1219	8.0	25	369	655	10.7	2.45	101	.238	.294	2	1	100	90	.963	232	75	1.6	.1	5.6		-1.8
BRO	125	20	1	1356¹	1218	8.1	16	463	479	11.4	2.38	98	.249	.319	12	-9	95	113	.959	262	94	-.7	-1.0	-3.0		-4.4
CIN	118	10	2	1351¹	1223	8.1	16	444	481	11.5	2.41	107	.251	.322	8	25	105	114	.963	227	118	2.1	2.8	-2.2		-13.3
BOS	121	9	2	1338²	1324	8.9	28	458	426	12.4	3.33	76	.268	.339	-129	-119	103	98	.961	249	128	.1	-13.5	.5		-3.1
STL	127	19	2	1365²	1212	8.0	20	500	594	11.6	2.70	93	.243	.318	-35	-32	101	97	.948	340	105	-5.8	-3.6	-8.3		-6.8
TOT	935	157	37	10818²		7.9				11.1	2.46		.243	.308					.960	2033	809					

Runs
Shannon-NY 104
Leach-Pit 102
Wagner-Pit 98
Clarke-Pit 97
Tenney-Bos 83

Hits
Beaumont-Bos ... 187
Wagner-Pit 180
Leach-Pit 166
Magee-Phi 165
Mitchell-Cin 163

Doubles
Wagner-Pit 38
Magee-Phi 28
Steinfeldt-Chi 25
Seymour-NY 25
Brain-Bos 24

Triples
Ganzel-Cin 16
Alperman-Bro 16
Wagner-Pit 14
Beaumont-Bos 14
Clarke-Pit 13

Home Runs
Brain-Bos 10
Lumley-Bro 9
Murray-StL 7
Wagner-Pit 6
Browne-NY 5

Total Bases
Wagner-Pit 264
Beaumont-Bos 246
Magee-Phi 229
Leach-Pit 221
Brain-Bos 214

Runs Batted In
Magee-Phi 85
Wagner-Pit 82
Abbaticchio-Pit ... 82
Seymour-NY 75
Steinfeldt-Chi 70

Runs Produced
Magee-Phi 174
Magee-Phi 156
Clarke-Pit 154
Abbaticchio-Pit ... 143
Leach-Pit 141

Bases On Balls
Thomas-Phi 83
Huggins-Cin 83
Tenney-Bos 82
Shannon-NY 82
Anderson-Pit 80

Batting Average
Wagner-Pit .... .350
Magee-Phi .... .328
Beaumont-Bos .... .322
Leach-Pit .... .303
Seymour-NY ...... .294

On Base Percentage
Wagner-Pit .... .408
Magee-Phi .... .396
Clarke-Pit .... .383
Devlin-NY .... .376
Thomas-Phi ...... .374

Slugging Average
Wagner-Pit .... .513
Magee-Phi .... .455
Lumley-Bro .... .425
Beaumont-Bos .... .424
Brain-Bos .... .420

Production
Wagner-Pit .... .921
Magee-Phi .... .852
Beaumont-Bos .... .790
Clarke-Pit .... .772
Leach-Pit .... .756

Adjusted Production
Wagner-Pit 186
Magee-Phi 169
Beaumont-Bos 148
Lumley-Bro 144
Jordan-Bro 141

Batter Runs
Wagner-Pit 50.5
Magee-Phi 38.4
Beaumont-Bos ... 29.5
Clarke-Pit 26.5
Leach-Pit 21.4

Adjusted Batter Runs
Wagner-Pit 49.1
Magee-Phi 39.8
Beaumont-Bos ... 29.8
Clarke-Pit 25.4
Jordan-Bro 25.3

Clutch Hitting Index
Abbaticchio-Pit ... 166
Seymour-NY 130
Steinfeldt-Chi 130
Devlin-NY 126
Magee-Phi 121

Runs Created
Wagner-Pit 137
Magee-Phi 113
Beaumont-Bos 103
Leach-Pit 98
Clarke-Pit 93

Total Average
Wagner-Pit 1.122
Magee-Phi .... .982
Clarke-Pit .... .865
Leach-Pit .... .801
Beaumont-Bos .... .791

Stolen Bases
Wagner-Pit 61
Magee-Phi 46
Evers-Chi 46
Leach-Pit 43
Devlin-NY 38

Stolen Base Average

Stolen Base Runs

Fielding Runs
Evers-Chi 27.7
Brain-Bos 24.8
Mitchell-Cin 22.2
Byrne-StL 22.1
Tinker-Chi 15.7

Total Player Rating
Wagner-Pit 6.3
Brain-Bos 5.0
Magee-Phi 4.6
Beaumont-Bos 3.2
Mitchell-Cin 3.2

Wins
Mathewson-NY 24
Overall-Chi 23
Sparks-Phi 22
Willis-Pit 21

Win Percentage
Reulbach-Chi ..... .810
Brown-Chi .... .769
Overall-Chi .... .767
Sparks-Phi .... .733
Lundgren-Chi .... .720

Games
McGinnity-NY 47
McGlynn-StL 45
Mathewson-NY 41
Ewing-Cin 41

Complete Games
McGlynn-StL 33
Ewing-Cin 32
Mathewson-NY 31
Karger-StL 29
Willis-Pit 27

Shutouts
Overall-Chi 8
Mathewson-NY 8
Lundgren-Chi 7

Saves
McGinnity-NY 4
Overall-Chi 3
Brown-Chi 3

Innings Pitched
McGlynn-StL 352.1
Ewing-Cin 332.2
Mathewson-NY ..315.0
Karger-StL 314.0
McGinnity-NY 310.1

Fewest Hits/Game
Lundgren-Chi 5.65
Pfiester-Chi 6.60
Overall-Chi 6.74
Camnitz-Pit 6.75
Reulbach-Chi 6.89

Fewest BB/Game
Phillippe-Pit 1.51
Mathewson-NY ... 1.51
Brown-Chi 1.55
McGinnity-NY 1.68
Sparks-Phi 1.73

Strikeouts
Mathewson-NY ... 178
Ewing-Cin 147
Ames-NY 146
Overall-Chi 141
Beebe-StL 141

Strikeouts/Game
Ames-NY 5.63
Beebe-StL 5.32
Mathewson-NY ... 5.09
Overall-Chi 4.73
Reulbach-Chi 4.50

Ratio
Mathewson-NY ... 8.71
Brown-Chi 8.73
Pfiester-Chi 9.05
Overall-Chi 9.42
Sparks-Phi 9.48

Earned Run Average
Pfiester-Chi 1.15
Lundgren-Chi 1.17
Brown-Chi 1.39
Leever-Pit 1.66
Overall-Chi 1.68

Adjusted ERA
Pfiester-Chi 215
Lundgren-Chi 212
Brown-Chi 179
Ewing-Cin 149
Overall-Chi 148

Opponents' Batting Avg.
Lundgren-Chi ..... .185
Pfiester-Chi ...... .207
Overall-Chi .... .208
Camnitz-Pit ...... .211
Mathewson-NY ... .212

Opponents' On Base Pct.
Mathewson-NY ... .247
Brown-Chi .... .262
Pfiester-Chi ...... .263
Overall-Chi .... .268
Karger-StL .... .270

Starter Runs
Lundgren-Chi 29.7
Pfiester-Chi 28.4
Brown-Chi 27.8
Ewing-Cin 27.1
Overall-Chi 23.5

Adjusted Starter Runs
Ewing-Cin 31.6
Lundgren-Chi 30.2
Pfiester-Chi 28.9
Brown-Chi 28.4
Overall-Chi 24.1

Clutch Pitching Index
Coakley-Cin 133
Pastorius-Bro 129
Brown-StL-Phi 126
McIntire-Bro 125
Leifield-Pit 122

Relief Runs

Adjusted Relief Runs

Relief Ranking

Total Pitcher Index
Brown-Chi 4.0
Lundgren-Chi 3.6
Overall-Chi 3.5
Pfiester-Chi 3.1
Ewing-Cin 2.9

Total Baseball Ranking
Wagner-Pit 6.3
Brain-Bos 5.0
Magee-Phi 4.6
Brown-Chi 3.9
Lundgren-Chi 3.6

TEAM	G	W	L	PCT	GB	R	OR	AB	H	2B	3B	HR	BB	SO	AVG	OBP	SLG	PRO	PRO+	BR	/A	PF	CHI	RC	SB	CS	SBA	SBR
DET	153	92	58	.613		694	532	5204	1383	179	75	11	315		.266	.313	.335	.648	108	63	40	104	110	641	192			
PHI	150	88	57	.607	1.5	582	511	5008	1274	223	43	22	384		.254	.311	.329	.640	106	51	36	102	96	591	137			
CHI	157	87	64	.576	5.5	588	474	5070	1205	149	33	5	421		.238	.302	.283	.585	95	-37	-19	97	111	523	175			
CLE	158	85	67	.559	8	530	525	5068	1221	182	68	11	335		.241	.295	.310	.605	97	-12	-16	101	97	555	193			
NY	152	70	78	.473	21	605	665	5044	1258	150	67	15	304		.249	.299	.315	.614	93	1	-44	108	110	565	206			
STL	155	69	83	.454	24	542	555	5224	1324	154	63	10	370		.253	.308	.313	.621	103	18	20	100	91	580	144			
BOS	155	59	90	.396	32.5	464	558	5235	1224	154	48	18	305		.234	.281	.292	.573	88	-76	-72	99	94	493	125			
WAS	154	49	102	.325	43.5	506	691	5112	1243	134	58	12	390		.243	.304	.299	.603	105	-8	35	92	91	564	223			
TOT	617					4511		40965	10132	1325	455	104	2824	4479	.247	.302	.310	.611						1395				

TEAM	CG	SH	SV	IP	H	H/G	HR	BB	SO	RAT	ERA	ERA+	OAV	OOB	PR	/A	PF	CPI	FA	E	DP	FW	PW	BW	SBW	DIF
DET	120	15	7	1370²	1281	8.4	8	380	512	11.2	2.33	112	.251	.309	32	40	102	114	.959	260	79	1.0	4.4	4.4		7.2
PHI	106	27	6	1354²	1106	7.3	13	378	789	10.3	2.35	111	.226	.290	29	38	102	91	.958	263	67	.4	4.2	4.0		6.9
CHI	112	17	9	1406¹	1279	8.2	13	305	604	10.3	2.22	108	.245	.290	50	26	94	105	.966	233	101	3.4	2.9	-2.1		7.3
CLE	127	20	5	1392²	1253	8.1	8	362	513	10.8	2.26	111	.244	.300	43	36	99	108	.960	264	137	1.3	4.0	-1.8		5.5
NY	93	10	5	1333²	1327	9.0	13	428	511	12.2	3.03	92	.264	.328	-73	-40	110	103	.947	334	79	-4.4	-4.4	-4.9		9.6
STL	129	15	9	1381¹	1254	8.2	17	352	463	10.8	2.61	96	.245	.300	-10	-16	99	96	.959	266	97	.8	-1.8	2.2		-8.2
BOS	100	17	7	1414	1222	7.8	22	337	517	10.2	2.45	105	.238	.290	14	15	101	93	.959	274	100	.2	1.7	-8.0		-9.4
WAS	106	12	5	1351¹	1383	9.2	10	344	570	11.8	3.11	78	.268	.320	-86	-106	95	97	.951	311	69	-2.5	-11.7	3.9		-16.2
TOT	893	133	53	11004²		8.3				10.9	2.54		.247	.302					.957	2205	729					

Runs
Crawford-Det 102
D.Jones-Det 101
Cobb-Det 97
Hartsel-Phi 93
Hahn-Chi 87

Hits
Cobb-Det 212
Stone-StL 191
Crawford-Det 188
Ganley-Was 167
Flick-Cle 166

Doubles
Davis-Phi 37
Crawford-Det 34
J.Collins-Bos-Phi ... 30
Lajoie-Cle 30
Seybold-Phi 29

Triples
Flick-Cle 18
Crawford-Det 17
Cobb-Det 14
Unglaub-Bos 13

Home Runs
Davis-Phi 8
Seybold-Phi 5
Hoffman-NY 5
Cobb-Det 5

Total Bases
Cobb-Det 283
Crawford-Det 268
Stone-StL 238
Davis-Phi 232
Flick-Cle 226

Runs Batted In
Cobb-Det 119
Seybold-Phi 92
Davis-Phi 87
Crawford-Det 81
Wallace-StL 70

Runs Produced
Cobb-Det 211
Crawford-Det 179
Davis-Phi 163
Seybold-Phi 145
Donahue-Chi 143

Bases On Balls
Hartsel-Phi 106
Hahn-Chi 84
Jones-Chi 67
Flick-Cle 64
D.Jones-Det 60

Batting Average
Cobb-Det .... .350
Crawford-Det ...... .323
Stone-StL .... .320
Flick-Cle .... .302
Nicholls-Phi .... .302

On Base Percentage
Hartsel-Phi .... .405
Stone-StL .... .387
Flick-Cle .... .386
Cobb-Det .... .380
Crawford-Det ...... .366

Slugging Average
Cobb-Det .... .468
Crawford-Det ...... .460
Flick-Cle .... .412
Stone-StL .... .399
Davis-Phi .... .399

Production
Cobb-Det .... .848
Crawford-Det ...... .826
Flick-Cle .... .798
Stone-StL .... .787
Hartsel-Phi .... .771

Adjusted Production
Cobb-Det 164
Crawford-Det 157
Flick-Cle 153
Stone-StL 151
Hartsel-Phi 143

Batter Runs
Cobb-Det 44.2
Crawford-Det 38.6
Flick-Cle 35.7
Stone-StL 35.4
Hartsel-Phi 33.0

Adjusted Batter Runs
Cobb-Det 40.4
Stone-StL 35.7
Crawford-Det 35.0
Flick-Cle 34.9
Hartsel-Phi 30.7

Clutch Hitting Index
Seybold-Phi 150
Cobb-Det 143
Donahue-Chi 134
Chase-NY 133
Wallace-StL 133

Runs Created
Cobb-Det 130
Crawford-Det 108
Flick-Cle 107
Stone-StL 105
Hartsel-Phi 87

Total Average
Cobb-Det .... .919
Flick-Cle .... .893
Hartsel-Phi .... .855
Crawford-Det ...... .825
Stone-StL .... .805

Stolen Bases
Cobb-Det 49
Flick-Cle 41
Conroy-NY 41
Ganley-Was 40
Altizer-Was 38

Fielding Runs
Lajoie-Cle 45.0
Donahue-Chi 20.7
Ferris-Bos 14.6
D.Jones-Det 13.0
Murphy-Phi 12.7

Total Player Rating
Lajoie-Cle 6.6
Cobb-Det 5.0
Crawford-Det 4.0
Flick-Cle 3.3
Stone-StL 2.9

Wins
White-Chi 27
Joss-Cle 27
Killian-Det 25
Donovan-Det 25

Win Percentage
Donovan-Det ..... .862
Dygert-Phi .... .724
Joss-Cle .... .711
Smith-Chi .... .697
White-Chi .... .675

Games
Walsh-Chi 56
White-Chi 46
Mullin-Det 46
Waddell-Phi 44

Complete Games
Walsh-Chi 37
Mullin-Det 35
Joss-Cle 34
Young-Bos 33
Plank-Phi 33

Shutouts
Plank-Phi 8
Waddell-Phi 6
Young-Bos 6
White-Chi 6
Joss-Cle 6

Saves
Dinneen-Bos-StL 4
Walsh-Chi 4
Hughes-Was 4

Innings Pitched
Walsh-Chi 422.1
Mullin-Det 357.1
Plank-Phi 343.2
Young-Bos 343.1
Joss-Cle 338.2

Fewest Hits/Game
Dygert-Phi 6.88
Winter-Bos 6.94
Walsh-Chi 7.27
Howell-StL 7.34
Donovan-Det 7.37

Fewest BB/Game
White-Chi 1.18
Altrock-Chi 1.31
Young-Bos 1.34
Bender-Phi 1.40
Joss-Cle 1.44

Strikeouts
Waddell-Phi 232
Walsh-Chi 206
Plank-Phi 183
Dygert-Phi 151
Young-Bos 147

Strikeouts/Game
Waddell-Phi 7.33
Dygert-Phi 5.19
Plank-Phi 4.79
Bender-Phi 4.60
Walsh-Chi 4.39

Ratio
Young-Bos 9.02
Joss-Cle 9.04
Bender-Phi 9.11
Winter-Bos 9.19
Walsh-Chi 9.29

Earned Run Average
Walsh-Chi 1.60
Killian-Det 1.78
Joss-Cle 1.83
Howell-StL 1.93
Young-Bos 1.99

Adjusted ERA
Walsh-Chi 150
Killian-Det 146
Joss-Cle 136
Howell-StL 130
Young-Bos 129

Opponents' Batting Avg.
Dygert-Phi .... .214
Winter-Bos .... .216
Walsh-Chi .... .224
Howell-StL .... .225
Donovan-Det ...... .226

Opponents' On Base Pct.
Young-Bos .... .263
Joss-Cle .... .264
Bender-Phi .... .265
Winter-Bos .... .267
Walsh-Chi .... .269

Starter Runs
Walsh-Chi 44.2
Killian-Det 26.6
Joss-Cle 26.6
Howell-StL 21.3
Young-Bos 20.9

Adjusted Starter Runs
Walsh-Chi 37.3
Killian-Det 28.8
Joss-Cle 25.2
Young-Bos 22.1
Howell-StL 20.2

Clutch Pitching Index
Killian-Det 144
Hogg-NY 125
Liebhardt-Cle 125
Rhoads-Cle 120
Walsh-Chi 112

Total Pitcher Index
Walsh-Chi 6.4
Killian-Det 4.7
Howell-StL 3.7
Joss-Cle 3.4
Plank-Phi 1.9

Total Baseball Ranking
Lajoie-Cle 6.6
Walsh-Chi 6.4
Cobb-Det 5.0
Killian-Det 4.8
Crawford-Det 4.0

TEAM	G	W	L	PCT	GB	R	OR	AB	H	2B	3B	HR	BB	SO	AVG	OBP	SLG	PRO	PRO+	BR	/A	PF	CHI	RC	SB	CS	SBA	SBR
CHI	158	99	55	.643		624	461	5085	1267	196	56	19	418		.249	.311	.321	.632	105	49	25	104	107	584	212			
PIT	155	98	56	.636	1	585	469	5109	1263	162	98	25	420		.247	.309	.332	.641	112	63	63	100	99	582	186			
NY	157	98	56	.636	1	652	456	5006	1339	182	43	20	494		.267	.342	.333	.675	117	138	106	105	97	646	181			
PHI	155	83	71	.539	16	504	445	5012	1223	194	68	11	334		.244	.298	.316	.614	100	12	-6	103	96	535	200			
CIN	155	73	81	.474	26	489	544	4879	1108	129	77	14	372		.227	.288	.294	.582	95	-41	-28	97	105	474	196			
BOS	156	63	91	.409	36	537	622	5131	1228	137	43	17	414		.239	.303	.293	.596	99	-12	-4	98	104	501	134			
BRO	154	53	101	.344	46	377	516	4897	1044	110	60	28	323		.213	.266	.277	.543	82	-112	-97	96	98	391	113			
STL	154	49	105	.318	50	371	626	4959	1105	134	57	17	282		.223	.271	.283	.554	87	-96	-77	95	92	420	150			
TOT	622					4139		40078	9577	1244	502	151	3057	4180	.239	.299	.306	.605						1372				

TEAM	CG	SH	SV	IP	H	H/G	HR	BB	SO	RAT	ERA	ERA+	OAV	OOB	PR	/A	PF	CPI	FA	E	DP	FW	PW	BW	SBW	DIF
CHI	108	29	12	1433²	1137	7.1	20	437	668	10.1	2.14	109	.221	.287	33	30	100	93	.969	205	76	3.7	3.5	2.9		11.9
PIT	100	24	9	1402¹	1142	7.3	16	406	468	10.3	2.12	108	.223	.287	34	24	97	92	.964	226	74	1.9	2.8	7.3		9.0
NY	95	25	18	1411	1214	7.7	26	288	656	10.3	2.14	112	.233	.277	32	39	102	92	.962	250	79	.4	4.5	12.3		3.7
PHI	116	22	6	1393	1167	7.5	8	379	476	10.3	2.10	115	.234	.294	38	46	103	103	.963	238	75	1.0	5.3	-.7		.3
CIN	110	17	8	1384	1218	7.9	19	415	433	10.9	2.37	96	.243	.307	-4	-19	98	104	.959	255	72	-.2	-2.2	-3.3		1.6
BOS	92	14	1	1404²	1262	8.1	29	423	416	11.2	2.79	86	.245	.310	-70	-68	102	93	.962	253	90	.0	-7.9	-.5		-5.7
BRO	118	20	4	1369	1165	7.7	17	444	535	11.0	2.47	94	.235	.306	-18	-24	99	97	.961	247	66	.3	-2.8	-11.3		-10.2
STL	97	13	4	1368	1217	8.0	16	430	528	11.1	2.64	89	.232	.296	-44	-51	100	82	.946	348	68	-6.8	-5.9	-8.9		-6.3
TOT	836	164	62	11165²		7.7				10.6	2.35		.239	.299					.961	2022	600					

Runs
Tenney-NY 101
Wagner-Pit 100
Leach-Pit 93
Evers-Chi 83
Clarke-Pit 83

Hits
Wagner-Pit 201
Donlin-NY 198
Murray-StL 167
Lobert-Cin 167
Bransfield-Phi 160

Doubles
Wagner-Pit 39
Magee-Phi 30
Chance-Chi 27
Knabe-Phi 26
Donlin-NY 26

Triples
Wagner-Pit 19
Lobert-Cin 18
Magee-Phi 16
Leach-Pit 16

Home Runs
Jordan-Bro 12
Wagner-Pit 10
Murray-StL 7
Tinker-Chi 6
Donlin-NY 6

Total Bases
Wagner-Pit 308
Donlin-NY 268
Murray-StL 237
Lobert-Cin 232
Leach-Pit 222

Runs Batted In
Wagner-Pit 109
Donlin-NY 106
Seymour-NY 92
Bransfield-Phi 71
Tinker-Chi 68

Runs Produced
Wagner-Pit 199
Donlin-NY 171
Tenney-NY 148
Seymour-NY 147

Bases On Balls
Bresnahan-NY 83
Tenney-NY 72
Evers-Chi 66
Clarke-Pit 65

Batting Average
Wagner-Pit 354
Donlin-NY 334
Doyle-NY 308
Evers-Chi 300

On Base Percentage
Wagner-Pit 415
Evers-Chi 402
Bresnahan-NY 401
Titus-Phi 365
Donlin-NY 364

Slugging Average
Wagner-Pit 542
Donlin-NY 452
Magee-Phi 417
Lobert-Cin 407
Murray-StL 400

Production
Wagner-Pit 957
Donlin-NY 816
Evers-Chi 777
Magee-Phi 776
Bresnahan-NY 760

Adjusted Production
Wagner-Pit 205
Donlin-NY 153
Lobert-Cin 145
Magee-Phi 143
Evers-Chi 143

Batter Runs
Wagner-Pit 65.2
Donlin-NY 36.6
Magee-Phi 27.3
Bresnahan-NY 27.0
Evers-Chi 26.4

Adjusted Batter Runs
Wagner-Pit 65.2
Donlin-NY 32.0
Lobert-Cin 27.3
Magee-Phi 24.6
Murray-StL 24.3

Clutch Hitting Index
Seymour-NY 150
McGann-Bos 133
Abbaticchio-Pit 132
Donlin-NY 129
Steinfeldt-Chi 129

Runs Created
Wagner-Pit 148
Donlin-NY 108
Lobert-Cin 97
Murray-StL 92
Magee-Phi 90

Total Average
Wagner-Pit 1.144
Evers-Chi 904
Magee-Phi 857
Donlin-NY 825
Bresnahan-NY 820

Stolen Bases
Wagner-Pit 53
Murray-StL 48
Lobert-Cin 47
Magee-Phi 40
Evers-Chi 36

Stolen Base Average

Stolen Base Runs

Fielding Runs
Dahlen-Bos 37.5
Tinker-Chi 30.4
Ritchey-Bos 15.6
Devlin-NY 12.8
Burch-Bro 12.6

Total Player Rating
Wagner-Pit 7.0
Tinker-Chi 4.8
Dahlen-Bos 4.2
Ritchey-Bos 3.1
Donlin-NY 3.0

Wins
Mathewson-NY . . . 37
Brown-Chi 29
Reulbach-Chi 24

Win Percentage
Reulbach-Chi 774
Mathewson-NY 771
Brown-Chi 763
Maddox-Pit 742
Leever-Pit 682

Games
Mathewson-NY 56
Raymond-StL 48
McQuillan-Phi 48
Reulbach-Chi 46

Complete Games
Mathewson-NY 34
Wilhelm-Bro 33
McQuillan-Phi 32
Wiltse-NY 30
Rucker-Bro 30

Shutouts
Mathewson-NY 11
Brown-Chi 9

Saves
McGinnity-NY 5
Mathewson-NY 5
Brown-Chi 5
Overall-Chi 4
Ewing-Cin 3

Innings Pitched
Mathewson-NY . .390.2
McQuillan-Phi 359.2
Rucker-Bro 333.1
Wilhelm-Bro 332.0
Wiltse-NY 330.0

Fewest Hits/Game
Brown-Chi 6.17
Raymond-StL 6.55
Mathewson-NY 6.57
McQuillan-Phi 6.58
Overall-Chi 6.60

Fewest BB/Game
Mathewson-NY 97
Brown-Chi 1.41
Sparks-Phi 1.74
Ewing-Cin 1.75
Campbell-Cin 1.79

Strikeouts
Mathewson-NY . . . 259
Rucker-Bro 199
Overall-Chi 167
Raymond-StL 145
Reulbach-Chi 133

Strikeouts/Game
Overall-Chi 6.68
Mathewson-NY 5.97
Rucker-Bro 5.37
Camnitz-Pit 4.49
Ferguson-Bos 4.24

Ratio
Mathewson-NY . . .7.60
Brown-Chi 7.72
McQuillan-Phi 9.01
Willis-Pit 9.28
Ewing-Cin 9.47

Earned Run Average
Mathewson-NY . . .1.43
Brown-Chi 1.47
McQuillan-Phi 1.53
Camnitz-Pit 1.56
Coakley-Cin-Chi . . .1.78

Adjusted ERA
Mathewson-NY 168
Brown-Chi 159
McQuillan-Phi 158
Camnitz-Pit 147
Richie-Phi 132

Opponents' Batting Avg.
Beebe-StL 193
Brown-Chi 195
Mathewson-NY 200
McQuillan-Phi 207
Raymond-StL 207

Opponents' On Base Pct.
Mathewson-NY 225
Brown-Chi 232
Willis-Pit 262
McQuillan-Phi 263
Beebe-StL 267

Starter Runs
Mathewson-NY . . . 39.8
McQuillan-Phi 32.7
Brown-Chi 30.4
Camnitz-Pit 20.7
Wilhelm-Bro 17.5

Adjusted Starter Runs
Mathewson-NY . . . 42.1
McQuillan-Phi 35.2
Brown-Chi 30.1
Camnitz-Pit 19.1
Wilhelm-Bro 16.8

Clutch Pitching Index
Coakley-Cin-Chi . . . 134
McGinnity-NY 134
Richie-Phi 126
Fraser-Chi 126
Rucker-Bro 118

Relief Runs

Adjusted Relief Runs

Relief Ranking

Total Pitcher Index
Mathewson-NY 7.3
Brown-Chi 4.1
McQuillan-Phi 3.9
Raymond-StL 2.1
Wilhelm-Bro 1.9

Total Baseball Ranking
Mathewson-NY 7.3
Wagner-Pit 7.0
Tinker-Chi 4.8
Dahlen-Bos 4.2
Brown-Chi 4.1

TEAM	G	W	L	PCT	GB	R	OR	AB	H	2B	3B	HR	BB	SO	AVG	OBP	SLG	PRO	PRO+	BR	/A	PF	CHI	RC	SB	CS	SBA	SBR
DET	154	90	63	.588		647	547	5115	1347	199	86	19	320		.263	.312	.347	.659	115	102	75	104	102	604	165			
CLE	157	90	64	.584	0.5	568	457	5108	1221	188	58	18	364		.239	.297	.309	.606	103	14	12	100	102	528	177			
CHI	156	88	64	.579	1.5	537	470	5027	1127	145	41	3	463		.224	.298	.271	.569	91	-38	-30	98	106	479	209			
STL	155	83	69	.546	6.5	544	483	5151	1261	173	52	20	343		.245	.296	.310	.606	102	13	10	101	98	514	126			
BOS	155	75	79	.487	15.5	564	513	5048	1239	117	88	14	289		.245	.295	.312	.607	100	13	-2	103	104	513	167			
PHI	157	68	85	.444	22	486	562	5065	1131	183	50	21	368		.223	.281	.292	.573	86	-46	-79	107	100	450	116			
WAS	155	67	85	.441	22.5	479	539	5041	1186	132	74	8	368		.235	.293	.296	.589	106	-15	28	92	92	490	170			
NY	155	51	103	.331	39.5	459	713	5046	1190	142	50	13	288		.236	.283	.292	.575	91	-44	-49	101	96	478	231			
TOT	622					4284		40601	9702	1279	499	116	2803	4930	.239	.294	.304	.598						1361				

TEAM	CG	SH	SV	IP	H	H/G	HR	BB	SO	RAT	ERA	ERA+	OAV	OOB	PR	/A	PF	CPI	FA	E	DP	FW	PW	BW	SBW	DIF
DET	119	15	5	1374¹	1313	8.6	12	318	553	11.1	2.40	100	.255	.306	-3	2	101	113	.953	305	95	-2.1	.2	8.6		6.8
CLE	108	18	5	1424¹	1172	7.4	16	328	548	9.7	2.02	118	.229	.280	59	56	100	102	.962	257	95	1.6	6.4	1.4		3.7
CHI	107	23	10	1414	1170	7.4	11	284	623	9.4	2.22	104	.226	.270	26	13	97	83	.966	232	82	3.2	1.5	-3.4		10.8
STL	107	15	5	1397	1151	7.4	7	387	607	10.3	2.15	111	.230	.294	37	36	100	105	.964	237	97	2.7	4.1	1.1		-1.0
BOS	102	12	7	1380¹	1200	7.8	18	364	624	10.5	2.28	108	.238	.295	17	27	103	105	.955	297	71	-1.4	3.1	-.2		-3.4
PHI	102	23	4	1400¹	1194	7.7	10	410	741	10.6	2.56	100	.235	.298	-27	-4	107	92	.957	272	68	.6	-.5	-9.0		.4
WAS	106	15	7	1391²	1236	8.0	16	348	649	10.5	2.34	97	.241	.294	7	-14	96	102	.958	275	89	.1	-1.6	3.2		.4
NY	90	11	3	1366	1288	8.5	26	458	585	12.0	3.16	78	.251	.322	-117	-106	104	95	.947	337	78	-4.1	-12.1	-5.6		-10.7
TOT	841	132	46	11148		7.9				10.5	2.39		.239	.294					.958	2212	675					

Runs
McIntyre-Det 105
Crawford-Det 102
Schaefer-Det 96
Jones-Chi 92
Stone-StL 89

Hits
Cobb-Det 188
Crawford-Det 184
McIntyre-Det 168
Lajoie-Cle 168
Stone-StL 165

Doubles
Cobb-Det 36
Rossman-Det 33
Crawford-Det 33
Lajoie-Cle 32
Stovall-Cle 29

Triples
Cobb-Det 20
Stahl-NY-Bos 16
Crawford-Det 16
Gessler-Bos 14

Home Runs
Crawford-Det 7
Hinchman-Cle 6
Niles-NY-Bos 5
Stone-StL 5
Davis-Phi 5

Total Bases
Cobb-Det 276
Crawford-Det 270
Rossman-Det 219
McIntyre-Det 218
Lajoie-Cle 218

Runs Batted In
Cobb-Det 108
Crawford-Det 80
Lajoie-Cle 74
Ferris-StL 74
Rossman-Det 71

Runs Produced
Cobb-Det 192
Crawford-Det 175
Lajoie-Cle 149
Schaefer-Det 145
Jones-Chi 141

Bases On Balls
Hartsel-Phi 93
Jones-Chi 86
McIntyre-Det 83
J.Clarke-Cle 76
Davis-Phi 61

Batting Average
Cobb-Det .... .324
Crawford-Det ..... .311
Gessler-Bos .... .308
Hemphill-NY ...... .297
McIntyre-Det ...... .295

On Base Percentage
Gessler-Bos .... .394
McIntyre-Det ..... .392
Hemphill-NY ...... .374
Hartsel-Phi .... .371
Dougherty-Chi .... .367

Slugging Average
Cobb-Det .... .475
Crawford-Det ..... .457
Gessler-Bos .... .423
Rossman-Det ...... .418
McIntyre-Det ...... .383

Production
Cobb-Det .... .842
Gessler-Bos .... .817
Crawford-Det ..... .812
McIntyre-Det ..... .775
Rossman-Det ...... .748

Adjusted Production
Cobb-Det 166
Gessler-Bos 161
Crawford-Det 157
McIntyre-Det 146
Rossman-Det 137

Batter Runs
Cobb-Det 43.8
Crawford-Det 38.3
McIntyre-Det 36.5
Gessler-Bos 33.2
Lajoie-Cle 23.3

Adjusted Batter Runs
Cobb-Det 39.6
Crawford-Det 34.2
McIntyre-Det 32.3
Gessler-Bos 31.0
Lajoie-Cle 23.0

Clutch Hitting Index
Cobb-Det 141
Wallace-StL 127
Ferris-StL 125
Lajoie-Cle 124
Jones-Chi 124

Runs Created
Cobb-Det 114
Crawford-Det 100
McIntyre-Det 93
Lajoie-Cle 83
Hemphill-NY 83

Total Average
Cobb-Det .... .903
Gessler-Bos .... .880
McIntyre-Det ..... .818
Hemphill-NY ...... .800
Crawford-Det ..... .799

Stolen Bases
Dougherty-Chi 47
Hemphill-NY 42
Schaefer-Det 40
Cobb-Det 39
J.Clarke-Cle 37

Stolen Base Average

Stolen Base Runs

Fielding Runs
Lajoie-Cle 49.3
McBride-Was 32.8
Wagner-Bos 31.7
Tannehill-Chi 18.0
Wallace-StL 18.0

Total Player Rating
Lajoie-Cle 7.8
McIntyre-Det 4.7
Cobb-Det 4.2
McBride-Was 3.5
Wallace-StL 3.1

Wins
Walsh-Chi 40
Summers-Det 24
Joss-Cle 24
Young-Bos 21
Waddell-StL 19

Win Percentage
Walsh-Chi .... .727
Donovan-Det ...... .720
Joss-Cle .... .686
Summers-Det ..... .667
Young-Bos .... .656

Games
Walsh-Chi 66
Vickers-Phi 53
Chesbro-NY 45
Waddell-StL 43
Hughes-Was 43

Complete Games
Walsh-Chi 42
Young-Bos 30
Joss-Cle 29
Howell-StL 27
Mullin-Det 26

Shutouts
Walsh-Chi 11
Joss-Cle 9
Vickers-Phi 6
Johnson-Was 6
Donovan-Det 6

Saves
Walsh-Chi 6
Hughes-Was 4
Waddell-StL 3

Innings Pitched
Walsh-Chi 464.0
Joss-Cle 325.0
Howell-StL 324.1
Vickers-Phi 317.0
Summers-Det 301.0

Fewest Hits/Game
Joss-Cle 6.42
Smith-Chi 6.44
Walsh-Chi 6.65
Johnson-Was 6.81
Berger-Cle 6.86

Fewest BB/Game
Joss-Cle .... .83
Burns-Was .... .98
Walsh-Chi 1.09
Young-Bos 1.11
Summers-Det 1.64

Strikeouts
Walsh-Chi 269
Waddell-StL 232
Hughes-Was 165
Dygert-Phi 164
Johnson-Was 160

Strikeouts/Game
Waddell-StL 7.31
Dygert-Phi 6.18
Johnson-Was 5.62
Hughes-Was 5.37
Donovan-Det 5.23

Ratio
Joss-Cle 7.31
Walsh-Chi 7.91
Young-Bos 8.07
Burns-Was 8.56
Smith-Chi 8.71

Earned Run Average
Joss-Cle 1.16
Young-Bos 1.26
Walsh-Chi 1.42
Summers-Det 1.64
Johnson-Was 1.65

Adjusted ERA
Joss-Cle 205
Young-Bos 194
Walsh-Chi 163
Summers-Det 147
Johnson-Was 138

Opponents' Batting Avg.
Joss-Cle .... .197
Smith-Chi .... .203
Walsh-Chi .... .203
Johnson-Was ...... .211
Young-Bos .... .213

Opponents' On Base Pct.
Joss-Cle .... .218
Walsh-Chi .... .232
Young-Bos .... .240
Smith-Chi .... .256
Burns-Was .... .257

Starter Runs
Walsh-Chi 50.0
Joss-Cle 44.2
Young-Bos 37.3
Summers-Det 24.8
Johnson-Was 21.0

Adjusted Starter Runs
Walsh-Chi 46.0
Joss-Cle 44.0
Young-Bos 39.5
Summers-Det 25.6
Rhoads-Cle 18.4

Clutch Pitching Index
Summers-Det 142
Willett-Det 140
Rhoads-Cle 137
Cicotte-Bos 122
Howell-StL 122

Relief Runs

Adjusted Relief Runs

Relief Ranking

Total Pitcher Index
Walsh-Chi 8.1
Joss-Cle 5.9
Young-Bos 4.1
Rhoads-Cle 2.9
Summers-Det 2.4

Total Baseball Ranking
Walsh-Chi 8.1
Lajoie-Cle 7.8
Joss-Cle 5.9
McIntyre-Det 4.7
Cobb-Det 4.2

TEAM	G	W	L	PCT	GB	R	OR	AB	H	2B	3B	HR	BB	SO	AVG	OBP	SLG	PRO	PRO+	BR	/A	PF	CHI	RC	SB	CS	SBA	SBR
PIT	153	110	42	.724		699	447	5129	1332	218	92	25	479		.260	.327	.353	.680	109	100	44	108	103	656	185			
CHI	155	104	49	.680	6.5	635	390	4999	1227	203	60	20	420		.245	.308	.322	.630	100	7	-7	102	112	562	187			
NY	158	92	61	.601	18.5	623	546	5218	1327	173	68	26	530		.254	.329	.328	.657	109	70	60	102	95	640	234			
CIN	156	77	76	.503	33.5	606	599	5088	1273	159	72	22	478		.250	.319	.323	.642	107	35	40	99	100	618	280			
PHI	154	74	79	.484	36.5	516	518	5034	1228	185	53	12	369		.244	.303	.309	.612	95	-26	-30	101	96	534	185			
BRO	155	55	98	.359	55.5	444	627	5056	1157	176	59	16	330		.229	.279	.296	.575	87	-98	-82	96	98	456	141			
STL	154	54	98	.355	56	583	731	5108	1242	148	56	15	568		.243	.326	.303	.629	109	25	62	94	97	556	161			
BOS	155	45	108	.294	65.5	435	683	5017	1121	124	43	15	400		.223	.285	.274	.559	76	-116	-136	105	99	435	135			
TOT	620					4541		40649	9907	1386	503	151	3574	4437	.244	.310	.314	.624						1508				

TEAM	CG	SH	SV	IP	H	H/G	HR	BB	SO	RAT	ERA	ERA+	OAV	OOB	PR	/A	PF	CPI	FA	E	DP	FW	PW	BW	SBW	DIF
PIT	93	21	11	1401²	1174	7.5	12	320	490	9.9	2.07	131	.232	.284	81	100	105	97	.964	228	100	3.4	11.1	4.9		14.6
CHI	111	32	11	1399¹	1094	7.0	6	364	680	9.6	1.75	145	.215	.272	131	124	98	94	.962	244	95	2.6	13.8	-.8		11.9
NY	105	17	15	1440²	1248	7.8	28	397	735	10.5	2.27	112	.238	.295	51	42	98	102	.954	307	99	-1.1	4.7	6.7		5.3
CIN	91	10	8	1407	1233	7.9	5	510	477	11.4	2.52	103	.240	.314	11	9	100	100	.952	309	120	-1.5	1.0	4.4		-3.5
PHI	89	17	6	1391	1190	7.7	23	472	612	11.0	2.44	106	.235	.304	23	20	100	99	.962	241	97	2.7	2.2	-3.3		-4.1
BRO	126	18	3	1384¹	1277	8.3	32	528	594	12.1	3.10	83	.256	.333	-79	-84	100	101	.955	282	86	.2	-9.3	-9.1		-3.2
STL	84	5	4	1379²	1368	8.9	22	483	435	12.4	3.41	74	.263	.331	-126	-139	97	92	.950	322	90	-2.5	-15.4	6.9		-10.9
BOS	98	13	6	1370²	1329	8.7	23	543	414	12.6	3.20	88	.263	.339	-93	-60	109	103	.948	342	101	-3.7	-6.7	-15.1		-6.0
TOT	797	133	64	11174¹		8.0				11.2	2.59		.244	.310					.956	2275	788					

Runs
Leach-Pit 126
Clarke-Pit 97
Byrne-StL-Pit 92
Wagner-Pit 92

Hits
Doyle-NY 172
Grant-Phi 170
Wagner-Pit 168
Konetchy-StL 165
Burch-Bro 163

Doubles
Wagner-Pit 39
Magee-Phi 33
D.Miller-Pit 31
Sheckard-Chi 29
Leach-Pit 29

Triples
Mitchell-Cin 17
Magee-Phi 14
Konetchy-StL 14
D.Miller-Pit 13

Home Runs
Murray-NY 7
Leach-Pit 6
Doyle-NY 6
Becker-Bos 6
Wagner-Pit......... 5

Total Bases
Wagner-Pit 242
Doyle-NY 239
Konetchy-StL 228
Mitchell-Cin 225
D.Miller-Pit 222

Runs Batted In
Wagner-Pit 100
Murray-NY 91
D.Miller-Pit 87
Mitchell-Cin 86
Konetchy-StL 80

Runs Produced
Wagner-Pit 187
Mitchell-Cin 165
Konetchy-StL 164
Leach-Pit 163
Clarke-Pit 162

Bases On Balls
Clarke-Pit 80
Byrne-StL-Pit 78
Evers-Chi 73
Sheckard-Chi 72
Bridwell-NY 67

Batting Average
Wagner-Pit 339
Mitchell-Cin 310
Hoblitzel-Cin 308
Doyle-NY 302
Bridwell-NY 294

On Base Percentage
Wagner-Pit 420
Bridwell-NY 386
Clarke-Pit 384
Mitchell-Cin 378
Evers-Chi 369

Slugging Average
Wagner-Pit 489
Mitchell-Cin 430
Doyle-NY 419
Hoblitzel-Cin 418
McCormick-NY ...402

Production
Wagner-Pit 909
Mitchell-Cin 808
Hoblitzel-Cin 782
Doyle-NY 779
Konetchy-StL 762

Adjusted Production
Wagner-Pit 168
Mitchell-Cin 152
Konetchy-StL 145
Hoblitzel-Cin 144
Doyle-NY 140

Batter Runs
Wagner-Pit 48.1
Mitchell-Cin 30.3
Doyle-NY 26.2
Clarke-Pit 25.4
Konetchy-StL 24.9

Adjusted Batter Runs
Wagner-Pit 39.6
Mitchell-Cin 31.1
Konetchy-StL 30.6
Hoblitzel-Cin 25.0
Doyle-NY 24.9

Clutch Hitting Index
Murray-NY 130
Abstein-Pit 129
Wagner-Pit 129
Lobert-Cin 125
D.Miller-Pit 124

Runs Created
Wagner-Pit 117
Mitchell-Cin 98
Doyle-NY 96
Clarke-Pit 92
Konetchy-StL 92

Total Average
Wagner-Pit 1.058
Mitchell-Cin 884
Clarke-Pit 821
Doyle-NY 809
Konetchy-StL 791

Stolen Bases
Bescher-Cin 54
Murray-NY 48
Egan-Cin 39
Magee-Phi 38
Burch-Bro 38

Stolen Base Average

Stolen Base Runs

Fielding Runs
Doolan-Phi 24.4
Egan-Cin 24.0
Byrne-StL-Pit 22.7
Bergen-Bro 22.0
Tinker-Chi 19.6

Total Player Rating
Wagner-Pit 5.2
Konetchy-StL 3.7
Devlin-NY 3.7
Mitchell-Cin 3.4
Byrne-StL-Pit 2.9

Wins
M.Brown-Chi 27
Mathewson-NY ... 25
H.Camnitz-Pit 25
Willis-Pit 22

Win Percentage
Mathewson-NY ... .806
H.Camnitz-Pit .... .806
M.Brown-Chi ..... .750
Pfiester-Chi ...... .739
Leifield-Pit .... .704

Games
M.Brown-Chi 50
Mattern-Bos 47
Gaspar-Cin 44
Beebe-StL 44

Complete Games
M.Brown-Chi 32
Bell-Bro 29
Rucker-Bro 28
Mathewson-NY 26

Shutouts
Overall-Chi......... 9
Mathewson-NY 8
M.Brown-Chi 8

Saves
M.Brown-Chi 7
Crandall-NY 6

Innings Pitched
M.Brown-Chi 342.2
Mattern-Bos 316.1
Rucker-Bro 309.1
Moore-Phi 299.2
Willis-Pit 289.2

Fewest Hits/Game
Mathewson-NY 6.28
Fromme-Cin 6.28
Overall-Chi 6.44
M.Brown-Chi 6.46
H.Camnitz-Pit 6.58

Fewest BB/Game
Mathewson-NY ... 1.18
M.Brown-Chi 1.39
Wiltse-NY 1.70
Maddox-Pit 1.73
McQuillan-Phi 1.96

Strikeouts
Overall-Chi 205
Rucker-Bro 201
Moore-Phi 173
M.Brown-Chi 172
Ames-NY 156

Strikeouts/Game
Overall-Chi....... 6.47
Rucker-Bro 5.85
Ames-NY 5.75
Marquard-NY 5.67
Moore-Phi 5.20

Ratio
Mathewson-NY .. 7.45
M.Brown-Chi 8.04
H.Camnitz-Pit..... 8.97
Overall-Chi 9.22
McQuillan-Phi 9.34

Earned Run Average
Mathewson-NY ... 1.14
M.Brown-Chi 1.31
Overall-Chi 1.42
H.Camnitz-Pit..... 1.62
Reulbach-Chi 1.78

Adjusted ERA
Mathewson-NY 223
M.Brown-Chi 193
Overall-Chi 178
H.Camnitz-Pit 167
Reulbach-Chi 142

Opponents' Batting Avg.
Overall-Chi .... .198
Mathewson-NY .... .200
Fromme-Cin ...... .201
M.Brown-Chi ..... .202
Moore-Phi .... .210

Opponents' On Base Pct.
Mathewson-NY ... .228
M.Brown-Chi ..... .239
Overall-Chi ...... .262
H.Camnitz-Pit .... .267
McQuillan-Phi..... .271

Starter Runs
M.Brown-Chi 48.6
Mathewson-NY ... 44.2
Overall-Chi 37.0
H.Camnitz-Pit 30.4
Reulbach-Chi 23.6

Adjusted Starter Runs
M.Brown-Chi 46.5
Mathewson-NY ... 43.0
Overall-Chi 35.2
H.Camnitz-Pit 34.3
Adams-Pit 23.2

Clutch Pitching Index
Richie-Phi-Bos ... 126
Corridon-Phi 123
Sallee-StL 119
Wilhelm-Bro 117
Marquard-NY 117

Relief Runs

Adjusted Relief Runs

Relief Ranking

Total Pitcher Index
Mathewson-NY 7.0
M.Brown-Chi 5.4
Overall-Chi 5.1
H.Camnitz-Pit 3.7
Fromme-Cin 3.1

Total Baseball Ranking
Mathewson-NY 7.0
M.Brown-Chi 5.4
Wagner-Pit 5.2
Overall-Chi 5.1
Konetchy-StL 3.7

TEAM	G	W	L	PCT	GB	R	OR	AB	H	2B	3B	HR	BB	SO	AVG	OBP	SLG	PRO	PRO+	BR	/A	PF	CHI	RC	SB	CS	SBA	SBR
DET	158	98	54	.645		666	493	5095	1360	209	58	19	397		.267	.325	.342	.667	113	98	70	104	103	660	280			
PHI	153	95	58	.621	3.5	605	408	4905	1257	186	88	21	403		.256	.321	.343	.664	115	91	79	102	97	613	205			
BOS	152	88	63	.583	9.5	597	550	4979	1307	151	69	20	348		.263	.321	.333	.654	112	73	60	102	99	599	215			
CHI	159	78	74	.513	20	492	463	5017	1110	145	56	4	441		.221	.292	.275	.567	90	-72	-52	96	104	474	211			
NY	153	74	77	.490	23.5	590	587	4981	1234	143	61	16	407		.248	.313	.311	.624	103	25	21	101	105	547	187			
CLE	155	71	82	.464	27.5	493	532	5048	1216	173	81	10	283		.241	.288	.313	.601	93	-28	-48	104	99	501	174			
STL	154	61	89	.407	36	441	575	4964	1151	116	45	10	331		.232	.287	.279	.566	91	-79	-48	93	100	436	136			
WAS	156	42	110	.276	56	380	656	4983	1112	149	41	9	321		.223	.276	.275	.551	84	-109	-90	95	91	419	136			
TOT	620					4264		39972	9747	1272	499	109	2931	4918	.244	.303	.309	.611						1544				

TEAM	CG	SH	SV	IP	H	H/G	HR	BB	SO	RAT	ERA	ERA+	OAV	OOB	PR	/A	PF	CPI	FA	E	DP	FW	PW	BW	SBW	DIF
DET	117	17	12	1420¹	1254	7.9	16	359	528	10.6	2.26	111	.238	.293	33	40	102	100	.959	276	87	.4	4.5	8.0		9.1
PHI	110	27	3	1378	1069	7.0	9	386	728	9.9	1.93	124	.217	.282	82	72	97	96	.961	245	92	1.8	8.2	9.0		-.5
BOS	75	11	15	1360¹	1214	8.0	18	384	555	10.9	2.59	96	.243	.303	-19	-16	101	96	.955	292	95	-1.3	-1.8	6.8		8.8
CHI	115	26	4	1430¹	1182	7.4	8	340	669	9.9	2.05	114	.229	.283	67	44	95	96	.964	246	101	2.4	5.0	-5.9		.5
NY	94	18	8	1350¹	1223	8.2	21	422	597	11.4	2.65	95	.248	.316	-26	-22	102	104	.948	329	94	-3.6	-2.5	2.4		2.2
CLE	110	15	3	1361	1212	8.0	9	348	568	10.6	2.40	104	.250	.307	11	21	103	107	.957	278	110	-.0	2.4	-5.5		-2.3
STL	105	21	4	1354²	1287	8.6	16	383	620	11.4	2.88	84	.261	.319	-61	-72	98	101	.958	267	107	.5	-8.2	-5.5		-.9
WAS	99	11	2	1374²	1288	8.4	12	424	653	11.6	3.04	80	.248	.312	-87	-96	98	87	.957	280	100	-.1	-10.9	-10.2		-12.7
TOT	825	146	51	11029²		7.9				10.8	2.47		.244	.303					.957	2213	786					

Runs
Cobb-Det ... 116
Bush-Det ... 114
Collins-Phi ... 104
Lord-Bos ... 86
Crawford-Det ... 83

Hits
Cobb-Det ... 216
Collins-Phi ... 198
Crawford-Det ... 185
Speaker-Bos ... 168
Lord-Bos ... 166

Doubles
Crawford-Det ... 35
Lajoie-Cle ... 33
Cobb-Det ... 33
Collins-Phi ... 30
Murphy-Phi ... 28

Triples
Baker-Phi ... 19
Murphy-Phi ... 14
Crawford-Det ... 14

Home Runs
Cobb-Det ... 9
Speaker-Bos ... 7
Stahl-Bos ... 6
Crawford-Det ... 6
Murphy-Phi ... 5

Total Bases
Cobb-Det ... 296
Crawford-Det ... 266
Collins-Phi ... 257
Baker-Phi ... 242
Speaker-Bos ... 241

Runs Batted In
Cobb-Det ... 107
Crawford-Det ... 97
Baker-Phi ... 85
Speaker-Bos ... 77
Davis-Phi ... 75

Runs Produced
Cobb-Det ... 214
Crawford-Det ... 174
Collins-Phi ... 157
Baker-Phi ... 154
Bush-Det ... 147

Bases On Balls
Bush-Det ... 88
Collins-Phi ... 62
Demmitt-NY ... 55
McIntyre-Det ... 54

Batting Average
Cobb-Det ... .377
Collins-Phi ... .346
Lajoie-Cle ... .324
Crawford-Det ... .314
Lord-Bos ... .311

On Base Percentage
Cobb-Det ... .431
Collins-Phi ... .416
Bush-Det ... .380
Lajoie-Cle ... .378
Stahl-Bos ... .377

Slugging Average
Cobb-Det ... .517
Crawford-Det ... .452
Collins-Phi ... .449
Baker-Phi ... .447
Speaker-Bos ... .443

Production
Cobb-Det ... .947
Collins-Phi ... .865
Crawford-Det ... .817
Stahl-Bos ... .812
Lajoie-Cle ... .809

Adjusted Production
Cobb-Det ... 190
Collins-Phi ... 170
Stahl-Bos ... 153
Crawford-Det ... 151
Speaker-Bos ... 151

Batter Runs
Cobb-Det ... 63.3
Collins-Phi ... 48.9
Crawford-Det ... 36.7
Speaker-Bos ... 31.5
Lajoie-Cle ... 28.8

Adjusted Batter Runs
Cobb-Det ... 57.9
Collins-Phi ... 46.7
Crawford-Det ... 32.4
Speaker-Bos ... 29.6
Stahl-Bos ... 26.8

Clutch Hitting Index
Chase-NY ... 143
Engle-NY ... 132
Crawford-Det ... 129
Cobb-Det ... 125
Davis-Phi ... 122

Runs Created
Cobb-Det ... 159
Collins-Phi ... 134
Crawford-Det ... 108
Speaker-Bos ... 99
Baker-Phi ... 90

Total Average
Cobb-Det ... 1.193
Collins-Phi ... 1.048
Stahl-Bos ... .857
Speaker-Bos ... .854
Crawford-Det ... .851

Stolen Bases
Cobb-Det ... 76
Collins-Phi ... 67
Bush-Det ... 53
Lord-Bos ... 36
Dougherty-Chi ... 36

Stolen Base Average

Stolen Base Runs

Fielding Runs
Speaker-Bos ... 22.9
Lajoie-Cle ... 18.6
Parent-Chi ... 16.5
McConnell-Bos ... 14.4
Engle-NY ... 14.0

Total Player Rating
Cobb-Det ... 6.1
Collins-Phi ... 5.7
Speaker-Bos ... 5.2
Lajoie-Cle ... 4.6
Baker-Phi ... 2.5

Wins
Mullin-Det ... 29
Smith-Chi ... 25
Willett-Det ... 21

Win Percentage
Mullin-Det ... .784
Krause-Phi ... .692
Bender-Phi ... .692
Summers-Det ... .679
Willett-Det ... .677

Games
Smith-Chi ... 51
Arellanes-Bos ... 45
Groom-Was ... 44
Willett-Det ... 41

Complete Games
Smith-Chi ... 37
Young-Cle ... 30
Mullin-Det ... 29
Johnson-Was ... 27
Morgan-Bos-Phi ... 26

Shutouts
Walsh-Chi ... 8
Smith-Chi ... 7
Krause-Phi ... 7
Coombs-Phi ... 6

Saves
Arellanes-Bos ... 8
Powell-StL ... 3

Innings Pitched
Smith-Chi ... 365.0
Mullin-Det ... 303.2
Johnson-Was ... 296.1
Young-Cle ... 295.0
Morgan-Bos-Phi ... 293.1

Fewest Hits/Game
Morgan-Bos-Phi ... 6.26
Krause-Phi ... 6.38
Walsh-Chi ... 6.49
Cicotte-Bos ... 6.59
Wood-Bos ... 6.78

Fewest BB/Game
Joss-Cle ... 1.15
White-Chi ... 1.57
Powell-StL ... 1.58
Bender-Phi ... 1.62
Summers-Det ... 1.66

Strikeouts
Smith-Chi ... 177
Johnson-Was ... 164
Berger-Cle ... 162
Bender-Phi ... 161
Waddell-StL ... 141

Strikeouts/Game
Berger-Cle ... 5.90
Krause-Phi ... 5.87
Bender-Phi ... 5.80
Waddell-StL ... 5.76
Bailey-StL ... 5.16

Ratio
Walsh-Chi ... 8.60
Joss-Cle ... 8.64
Smith-Chi ... 8.73
Bender-Phi ... 8.86
Krause-Phi ... 9.00

Earned Run Average
Krause-Phi ... 1.39
Walsh-Chi ... 1.41
Bender-Phi ... 1.66
Joss-Cle ... 1.71
Killian-Det ... 1.71

Adjusted ERA
Krause-Phi ... 172
Walsh-Chi ... 166
Joss-Cle ... 149
Killian-Det ... 147
Bender-Phi ... 145

Opponents' Batting Avg.
Morgan-Bos-Phi ... .202
Walsh-Chi ... .203
Krause-Phi ... .204
Wood-Bos ... .209
Cicotte-Bos ... .210

Opponents' On Base Pct.
Walsh-Chi ... .253
Bender-Phi ... .254
Joss-Cle ... .255
Smith-Chi ... .257
Krause-Phi ... .266

Starter Runs
Walsh-Chi ... 27.2
Smith-Chi ... 27.2
Krause-Phi ... 25.5
Bender-Phi ... 22.6
Morgan-Bos-Phi ... 21.5

Adjusted Starter Runs
Krause-Phi ... 23.8
Walsh-Chi ... 23.8
Joss-Cle ... 22.8
Smith-Chi ... 21.7
Bender-Phi ... 20.6

Clutch Pitching Index
Burns-Was-Chi ... 142
Killian-Det ... 132
Brockett-NY ... 132
Waddell-StL ... 125
Bailey-StL ... 117

Relief Runs

Adjusted Relief Runs

Relief Ranking

Total Pitcher Index
Smith-Chi ... 4.6
Walsh-Chi ... 4.4
Bender-Phi ... 2.9
Lake-NY ... 2.7
Plank-Phi ... 2.7

Total Baseball Ranking
Cobb-Det ... 6.1
Collins-Phi ... 5.7
Speaker-Bos ... 5.2
Lajoie-Cle ... 4.6
Smith-Chi ... 4.6

TEAM	G	W	L	PCT	GB	R	OR	AB	H	2B	3B	HR	BB	SO	AVG	OBP	SLG	PRO	PRO+	BR	/A	PF	CHI	RC	SB	CS	SBA	SBR
CHI	154	104	50	.675		712	499	4977	1333	219	84	34	542	501	.268	.344	.366	.710	114	81	87	99	101	696	173			
NY	155	91	63	.591	13	715	567	5061	1391	204	83	31	562	489	.275	.354	.366	.720	116	106	105	100	97	759	282			
PIT	154	86	67	.562	17.5	655	576	5125	1364	214	83	33	437	524	.266	.328	.360	.688	100	30	-8	106	100	655	148			
PHI	157	78	75	.510	25.5	674	639	5171	1319	223	71	22	506	559	.255	.327	.338	.665	97	-4	-25	103	106	641	199			
CIN	156	75	79	.487	29	620	684	5121	1326	150	79	23	529	515	.259	.332	.333	.665	105	0	28	96	98	669	310			
BRO	156	64	90	.416	40	497	623	5125	1174	166	73	25	434	706	.229	.294	.305	.599	82	-132	-117	97	101	506	151			
STL	153	63	90	.412	40.5	639	718	4912	1217	167	70	15	655	581	.248	.345	.319	.664	103	19	43	96	99	609	179			
BOS	157	53	100	.346	50.5	495	701	5123	1260	173	49	31	359	540	.246	.301	.317	.618	81	-99	-122	105	96	536	152			
TOT	621					5007		40615	10384	1516	592	214	4024	4415	.256	.328	.338	.666						1594				

TEAM	CG	SH	SV	IP	H	H/G	HR	BB	SO	RAT	ERA	ERA+	OAV	OOB	PR	/A	PF	CPI	FA	E	DP	FW	PW	BW	SBW	DIF
CHI	100	25	13	1378²	1171	7.6	18	474	609	11.0	2.51	115	.235	.307	79	54	95	95	.963	230	110	2.1	5.7	9.2		10.1
NY	96	9	10	1391²	1290	8.3	30	397	717	11.2	2.68	110	.250	.308	54	44	98	99	.955	291	117	-1.7	4.6	11.1		.0
PIT	73	13	12	1376	1254	8.2	20	392	479	11.1	2.83	109	.250	.311	29	38	102	93	.961	245	102	1.1	4.0	-.8		5.2
PHI	84	17	9	1411¹	1297	8.3	36	547	657	12.1	3.05	102	.253	.330	-5	9	103	101	.960	258	132	.6	.9	-2.6		2.6
CIN	86	16	11	1386²	1334	8.7	27	528	497	12.5	3.08	94	.261	.338	-9	-29	96	105	.955	291	103	-1.6	-3.1	2.9		-.3
BRO	103	15	5	1420¹	1331	8.4	17	545	555	12.1	3.07	99	.259	.335	-7	-9	100	101	.964	235	125	2.0	-.9	-12.3		-1.7
STL	81	4	14	1337¹	1396	9.4	30	541	466	13.3	3.78	79	.275	.350	-112	-120	98	96	.954	261	109	.0	-12.6	4.5		-5.4
BOS	72	12	9	1390¹	1328	8.6	36	599	531	12.8	3.22	103	.265	.349	-30	14	110	110	.954	305	137	-2.4	1.5	-12.8		-9.8
TOT	695	111	83	11092¹		8.4				12.0	3.02		.256	.328					.959	2116	935					

Runs
Magee-Phi 110
Huggins-StL 101
Byrne-Pit 101
Doyle-NY 97
Bescher-Cin 95

Hits
Wagner-Pit 178
Byrne-Pit 178
Wheat-Bro 172
Magee-Phi 172
Hoblitzel-Cin 170

Doubles
Byrne-Pit 43
Magee-Phi 39
Wheat-Bro 36
Merkle-NY 35
Wagner-Pit 34

Triples
Mitchell-Cin 18
Magee-Phi 17
Konetchy-StL 16
Hofman-Chi 16

Home Runs
Schulte-Chi 10
Beck-Bos 10
Doyle-NY 8
Daubert-Bro 8

Total Bases
Magee-Phi 263
Schulte-Chi 257
Byrne-Pit 251
Wheat-Bro 244
Wagner-Pit 240

Runs Batted In
Magee-Phi 123
Mitchell-Cin 88
Murray-NY 87
Hofman-Chi 86
Wagner-Pit 81

Runs Produced
Magee-Phi 227
Wagner-Pit 167
Hofman-Chi 166
Mitchell-Cin 162
Konetchy-StL 162

Bases On Balls
Huggins-StL 116
Evers-Chi 108
Magee-Phi 94
Titus-Phi 93
Sheckard-Chi 83

Batting Average
Magee-Phi 331
Campbell-Pit 326
Hofman-Chi 325
Snodgrass-NY 321
Wagner-Pit 320

On Base Percentage
Magee-Phi 445
Snodgrass-NY 440
Evers-Chi 413
Hofman-Chi 406
Huggins-StL 399

Slugging Average
Magee-Phi 507
Hofman-Chi 461
Schulte-Chi 460
Merkle-NY 441
Campbell-Pit 436

Production
Magee-Phi 952
Snodgrass-NY 871
Hofman-Chi 867
Konetchy-StL 822
Wagner-Pit 822

Adjusted Production
Magee-Phi 172
Snodgrass-NY . . . 154
Hofman-Chi 154
Konetchy-StL 145
Schulte-Chi 137

Batter Runs
Magee-Phi 54.9
Hofman-Chi 32.4
Snodgrass-NY . . . 31.9
Konetchy-StL 28.0
Wagner-Pit 27.9

Adjusted Batter Runs
Magee-Phi 50.9
Hofman-Chi 33.2
Snodgrass-NY . . . 31.8
Konetchy-StL 31.5
Wagner-Pit 22.4

Clutch Hitting Index
Magee-Phi 139
Evans-Chi 135
Devlin-NY 132
Murray-NY 125
Steinfeldt-Chi 124

Runs Created
Magee-Phi 139
Byrne-Pit 104
Wagner-Pit 103
Hofman-Chi 102
Doyle-NY 101

Total Average
Magee-Phi 1.205
Snodgrass-NY . . 1.071
Hofman-Chi 975
Konetchy-StL 884
Paskert-Cin 884

Stolen Bases
Bescher-Cin 70
Murray-NY 57
Paskert-Cin 51
Magee-Phi 49
Devore-NY 43

Stolen Base Average

Stolen Base Runs

Fielding Runs
Shean-Bos 42.5
Doolan-Phi 20.7
Tinker-Chi 15.5
Paskert-Cin 14.1
Knabe-Phi 13.9

Total Player Rating
Konetchy-StL 4.1
Hofman-Chi 3.4
Wagner-Pit 3.2
Mowrey-StL 3.2
Magee-Phi 3.2

Wins
Mathewson-NY . . 27
Brown-Chi 25
Moore-Phi 22
Suggs-Cin 20
Cole-Chi 20

Win Percentage
Cole-Chi 833
Crandall-NY 810
Mathewson-NY 750
Adams-Pit 667
Brown-Chi 641

Games
Mattern-Bos 51
Gaspar-Cin 48

Complete Games
Rucker-Bro 27
Mathewson-NY 27
Brown-Chi 27
Bell-Bro 25
Barger-Bro 25

Shutouts
Rucker-Bro 6
Moore-Phi 6
Mattern-Bos 6
Brown-Chi 6

Saves
Gaspar-Cin 7
Brown-Chi 7
Crandall-NY 5
Richie-Bos-Chi 4
Phillippe-Pit 4

Innings Pitched
Rucker-Bro 320.1
Mathewson-NY . . 318.1
Bell-Bro 310.0
Mattern-Bos 305.0
Brown-Chi 295.1

Fewest Hits/Game
Cole-Chi 6.53
Scanlan-Bro 7.25
Moore-Phi 7.25
Drucke-NY 7.27
Ames-NY 7.61

Fewest BB/Game
Suggs-Cin 1.62
Mathewson-NY . . 1.70
Crandall-NY 1.86
Brown-Chi 1.95
Wiltse-NY 1.99

Strikeouts
Moore-Phi 185
Mathewson-NY . . . 184
Frock-Pit-Bos . . . 171
Drucke-NY 151
Rucker-Bro 147

Strikeouts/Game
Drucke-NY 6.31
Frock-Pit-Bos . . . 5.98
Moore-Phi 5.88
Mathewson-NY . . 5.20
Ames-NY 4.44

Ratio
Brown-Chi 9.87
Mathewson-NY . . 10.04
Bell-Bro 10.25
Adams-Pit 10.40
Crandall-NY 10.44

Earned Run Average
Cole-Chi 1.80
Brown-Chi 1.86
Mathewson-NY . . 1.89
Ames-NY 2.22
Adams-Pit 2.24

Adjusted ERA
Cole-Chi 159
Mathewson-NY . . 156
Brown-Chi 155
Adams-Pit 138
Ames-NY 133

Opponents' Batting Avg.
Cole-Chi 211
Drucke-NY 228
Moore-Phi 228
Brown-Chi 232
Scanlan-Bro 234

Opponents' On Base Pct.
Brown-Chi 277
Mathewson-NY . . .286
Crandall-NY 289
Adams-Pit 291
Bell-Bro 296

Starter Runs
Mathewson-NY . . 40.0
Brown-Chi 38.2
Cole-Chi 32.5
McQuillan-Phi . . . 24.2
Adams-Pit 21.3

Adjusted Starter Runs
Mathewson-NY . . 37.6
Brown-Chi 33.3
Cole-Chi 28.5
McQuillan-Phi . . . 25.8
Adams-Pit 23.1

Clutch Pitching Index
Cole-Chi 136
Brown-Bos 122
Barger-Bro 122
Mathewson-NY . . 117
Curtis-Bos 116

Relief Runs

Adjusted Relief Runs

Relief Ranking

Total Pitcher Index
Mathewson-NY . . . 6.0
Brown-Chi 4.9
Cole-Chi 3.0
Brown-Bos 2.5
McQuillan-Phi 2.4

Total Baseball Ranking
Mathewson-NY . . . 6.0
Brown-Chi 4.9
Konetchy-StL 4.1
Hofman-Chi 3.4
Wagner-Pit 3.2

TEAM	G	W	L	PCT	GB	R	OR	AB	H	2B	3B	HR	BB	SO	AVG	OBP	SLG	PRO	PRO+	BR	/A	PF	CHI	RC	SB	CS	SBA	SBR
PHI	155	102	48	.680		673	441	5156	1373	191	105	19	409		.266	.326	.355	.681	120	104	111	99	99	665	207			
NY	156	88	63	.583	14.5	626	557	5051	1254	164	75	20	464		.248	.320	.322	.642	101	44	9	106	102	614	288			
DET	155	86	68	.558	18	679	582	5039	1317	190	72	28	459		.261	.329	.344	.673	110	96	52	107	102	655	249			
BOS	158	81	72	.529	22.5	638	564	5204	1350	175	87	43	430		.259	.323	.351	.674	114	94	78	102	94	656	194			
CLE	161	71	81	.467	32	548	657	5385	1316	188	64	9	366		.244	.297	.308	.605	94	-37	-44	101	99	549	189			
CHI	156	68	85	.444	35.5	457	479	5024	1058	115	58	7	403		.211	.275	.261	.536	76	-150	-133	96	112	415	183			
WAS	157	66	85	.437	36.5	501	550	4989	1145	145	46	9	449		.236	.309	.288	.597	97	-32	-7	95	94	508	192			
STL	158	47	107	.305	57	451	743	5077	1105	131	60	12	415		.218	.281	.274	.555	84	-117	-90	94	102	438	169			
TOT	628					4573		40925	9948	1299	567	147	3395	5278	.243	.308	.313	.621						1671				

TEAM	CG	SH	SV	IP	H	H/G	HR	BB	SO	RAT	ERA	ERA+	OAV	OOB	PR	/A	PF	CPI	FA	E	DP	FW	PW	BW	SBW	DIF
PHI	123	24	5	1421²	1103	7.0	8	450	789	10.2	1.79	133	.221	.292	116	91	94	111	.965	230	117	3.8	10.1	12.3		.7
NY	110	14	8	1399	1238	8.0	16	364	654	10.7	2.61	102	.243	.300	-15	4	106	91	.956	285	95	.2	.4	1.0		10.8
DET	108	17	5	1380¹	1257	8.2	34	460	532	11.6	2.82	93	.248	.319	-47	-28	104	101	.956	288	79	-.0	-3.1	5.8		6.4
BOS	100	12	6	1430	1236	7.8	30	414	670	10.7	2.45	104	.235	.297	10	14	101	94	.954	309	80	-1.1	1.6	8.7		-4.6
CLE	92	13	5	1467	1392	8.5	10	488	617	11.9	2.88	90	.261	.330	-60	-51	103	104	.964	247	112	3.4	-5.7	-4.9		2.1
CHI	103	23	7	1421	1130	7.2	16	381	785	9.8	2.03	118	.222	.281	77	56	95	92	.954	314	100	-1.7	6.2	-14.8		1.8
WAS	119	19	3	1373¹	1215	8.0	19	375	674	10.8	2.46	101	.244	.304	8	5	99	101	.959	264	99	1.8	.6	-.8		-11.1
STL	101	9	3	1391	1356	8.8	14	532	557	12.6	3.09	80	.265	.341	-89	-95	98	106	.943	385	113	-6.3	-10.6	-10.0		-3.2
TOT	856	131	42	11283¹		7.9				11.0	2.52		.243	.308					.956	2322	795					

Runs
Cobb-Det 106
Lajoie-Cle 94
Speaker-Bos 92
Bush-Det 90
Milan-Was.......... 89

Hits
Lajoie-Cle 227
Cobb-Det 194
Collins-Phi 188
Speaker-Bos 183
Crawford-Det 170

Doubles
Lajoie-Cle 51
Cobb-Det 35
Lewis-Bos 29
Murphy-Phi 28
Oldring-Phi........ 27

Triples
Crawford-Det 19
Lord-Cle-Phi 18
Murphy-Phi........ 18
Stahl-Bos 16
Cree-NY 16

Home Runs
Stahl-Bos.......... 10
Lewis-Bos 8
Cobb-Det 8
Speaker-Bos 7
Crawford-Det....... 5

Total Bases
Lajoie-Cle 304
Cobb-Det 279
Speaker-Bos 252
Crawford-Det 249
Murphy-Phi........ 244

Runs Batted In
Crawford-Det 120
Cobb-Det 91
Collins-Phi 81
Stahl-Bos 77
Lajoie-Cle 76

Runs Produced
Crawford-Det 198
Cobb-Det 189
Lajoie-Cle 166
Collins-Phi 159
Baker-Phi.......... 155

Bases On Balls
Bush-Det 78
Milan-Was 71
Wolter-NY 66
Cobb-Det 64

Batting Average
Cobb-Det .... .383
Lajoie-Cle .... .384
Speaker-Bos ..... .340
Collins-Phi .... .322
Knight-NY .... .312

On Base Percentage
Cobb-Det .... .456
Lajoie-Cle .... .445
Speaker-Bos ...... .404
Collins-Phi .... .381
Milan-Was .... .379

Slugging Average
Cobb-Det .... .551
Lajoie-Cle .... .514
Speaker-Bos ...... .468
Murphy-Phi .... .436
Oldring-Phi .... .430

Production
Cobb-Det 1.008
Lajoie-Cle .... .960
Speaker-Bos ..... .873
Collins-Phi .... .798
Cree-NY .... .775

Adjusted Production
Cobb-Det 202
Lajoie-Cle 198
Speaker-Bos 169
Collins-Phi 151
Murphy-Phi 143

Batter Runs
Lajoie-Cle 68.2
Cobb-Det 67.9
Speaker-Bos 44.9
Collins-Phi 33.0
Murphy-Phi 23.6

Adjusted Batter Runs
Lajoie-Cle 66.5
Cobb-Det 59.7
Speaker-Bos 42.4
Collins-Phi 33.9
Murphy-Phi 24.5

Clutch Hitting Index
LaPorte-NY 154
Crawford-Det 153
Chase-NY 135
Moriarty-Det 127
McBride-Was 122

Runs Created
Cobb-Det 156
Lajoie-Cle 147
Collins-Phi 122
Speaker-Bos 115
Crawford-Det 89

Total Average
Cobb-Det 1.321
Lajoie-Cle 1.085
Speaker-Bos ..... .972
Collins-Phi ...... .959
Cree-NY .... .820

Stolen Bases
Collins-Phi 81
Cobb-Det 65
Zeider-Chi 49
Bush-Det 49
Milan-Was 44

Stolen Base Average

Stolen Base Runs

Fielding Runs
Collins-Phi 33.7
McBride-Was 26.6
Wallace-StL 21.9
Lajoie-Cle 15.1
Speaker-Bos 15.0

Total Player Rating
Lajoie-Cle 8.5
Collins-Phi 7.0
Cobb-Det 6.7
Speaker-Bos 5.5
Wallace-StL 3.6

Wins
Coombs-Phi 31
Ford-NY 26
Johnson-Was 25
Bender-Phi 23
Mullin-Det 21

Win Percentage
Bender-Phi .... .821
Ford-NY .... .813
Coombs-Phi ...... .775
Donovan-Det ..... .708
Mullin-Det .... .636

Games
Walsh-Chi.......... 45
Johnson-Was....... 45
Coombs-Phi 45
Scott-Chi 41

Complete Games
Johnson-Was 38
Coombs-Phi 35
Walsh-Chi 33
Ford-NY 29
Mullin-Det 27

Shutouts
Coombs-Phi 13
Johnson-Was 8
Ford-NY 8
Walsh-Chi 7

Saves
Walsh-Chi 5
Browning-Det....... 3

Innings Pitched
Johnson-Was 370.0
Walsh-Chi 369.2
Coombs-Phi 353.0
Ford-NY 299.2
Morgan-Phi 290.2

Fewest Hits/Game
Ford-NY 5.83
Walsh-Chi 5.89
Coombs-Phi 6.32
Johnson-Was 6.37
Bender-Phi 6.55

Fewest BB/Game
Walsh-Chi 1.49
Young-Cle 1.49
Collins-Bos 1.51
Bender-Phi 1.69
Johnson-Was 1.85

Strikeouts
Johnson-Was 313
Walsh-Chi 258
Coombs-Phi 224
Ford-NY 209
Bender-Phi 155

Strikeouts/Game
Johnson-Was 7.61
Wood-Bos 6.57
Walsh-Chi 6.28
Ford-NY 6.28
Coombs-Phi 5.71

Ratio
Walsh-Chi 7.47
Ford-NY 8.17
Johnson-Was 8.54
Bender-Phi 8.60
Collins-Bos 9.09

Earned Run Average
Walsh-Chi 1.27
Coombs-Phi 1.30
Johnson-Was 1.36
Morgan-Phi 1.55
Bender-Phi 1.58

Adjusted ERA
Walsh-Chi 189
Johnson-Was 183
Coombs-Phi 182
Ford-NY 161
Collins-Bos 158

Opponents' Batting Avg.
Walsh-Chi .... .187
Ford-NY .... .188
Coombs-Phi ..... .201
Johnson-Was .... .205
Hall-Bos .... .207

Opponents' On Base Pct.
Walsh-Chi .... .226
Ford-NY .... .245
Bender-Phi ...... .255
Johnson-Was .... .257
Collins-Bos ...... .264

Starter Runs
Walsh-Chi 51.4
Coombs-Phi 47.7
Johnson-Was 47.5
Morgan-Phi 31.3
Ford-NY 28.8

Adjusted Starter Runs
Johnson-Was 46.3
Walsh-Chi 46.3
Coombs-Phi 42.0
Ford-NY 33.4
Morgan-Phi 26.6

Clutch Pitching Index
Morgan-Phi 142
Olmstead-Chi 142
Vaughn-NY 122
Wood-Bos 118
Coombs-Phi 114

Relief Runs

Adjusted Relief Runs

Relief Ranking

Total Pitcher Index
Walsh-Chi 7.1
Johnson-Was 5.8
Coombs-Phi 4.8
Ford-NY 4.0
Bender-Phi 3.8

Total Baseball Ranking
Lajoie-Cle 8.5
Walsh-Chi 7.1
Collins-Phi 7.0
Cobb-Det 6.7
Johnson-Was...... 5.8

TEAM	G	W	L	PCT	GB	R	OR	AB	H	2B	3B	HR	BB	SO	AVG	OBP	SLG	PRO	PRO+	BR	/A	PF	CHI	RC	SB	CS	SBA	SBR
NY	154	99	54	.647		756	542	5006	1399	225	103	41	530	506	.279	.358	.390	.748	113	109	85	103	96	820	347			
CHI	157	92	62	.597	7.5	757	607	5130	1335	218	101	54	585	617	.260	.341	.374	.715	107	44	43	100	102	729	214			
PIT	155	85	69	.552	14.5	744	557	5137	1345	206	106	49	525	583	.262	.336	.372	.708	101	28	1	104	104	698	160			
PHI	153	79	73	.520	19.5	658	669	5044	1307	214	56	60	490	588	.259	.328	.359	.687	98	-11	-19	101	100	647	153			
STL	158	75	74	.503	22	671	745	5132	1295	199	86	26	592	650	.252	.337	.340	.677	99	-18	0	97	99	651	175			
CIN	159	70	83	.458	29	682	706	5291	1379	180	105	21	578	594	.261	.337	.346	.683	102	-10	15	96	97	716	289			
BRO	154	64	86	.427	33.5	539	659	5059	1198	151	71	28	425	683	.237	.301	.311	.612	80	-152	-131	96	106	528	184			
BOS	156	44	107	.291	54	699	1021	5308	1417	249	54	37	554	577	.267	.340	.355	.695	93	10	-48	108	98	696	169			
TOT	623					5506		41107	10675	1642	682	316	4279	4798	.260	.335	.356	.691						1691				

TEAM	CG	SH	SV	IP	H	H/G	HR	BB	SO	RAT	ERA	ERA+	OAV	OOB	PR	/A	PF	CPI	FA	E	DP	FW	PW	BW	SBW	DIF
NY	95	19	13	1368	1267	8.3	33	369	771	11.0	2.69	125	.246	.300	106	100	99	97	.959	256	86	.5	10.0	8.5		3.4
CHI	85	12	16	1411	1270	8.1	26	525	582	11.7	2.90	114	.245	.320	78	62	97	100	.960	260	114	.6	6.2	4.3		3.9
PIT	91	13	11	1380¹	1249	8.1	36	375	605	10.8	2.84	121	.248	.306	85	87	101	97	.963	232	131	2.1	8.7	.1		-2.9
PHI	90	20	10	1373¹	1285	8.4	43	598	697	12.7	3.30	104	.255	.340	14	19	101	104	.963	231	113	1.9	1.9	-1.9		1.1
STL	88	6	10	1402¹	1296	8.3	39	701	561	13.2	3.68	91	.254	.350	-46	-52	99	97	.960	261	106	.6	-5.2	.0		5.1
CIN	77	4	12	1425	1410	8.9	36	476	557	12.3	3.26	101	.265	.332	21	5	97	103	.955	295	108	-1.4	.5	1.5		-7.1
BRO	81	13	10	1371²	1310	8.6	27	566	533	12.6	3.39	98	.263	.344	0	-12	98	103	.962	241	112	1.4	-1.2	-13.2		1.9
BOS	73	5	7	1374	1570	10.3	76	672	486	15.1	5.08	75	.296	.381	-258	-195	113	96	.947	347	110	-5.0	-19.6	-4.8		-2.1
TOT	680	92	89	11105²		8.6				12.4	3.39		.260	.335					.958	2123	880					

Runs
Sheckard-Chi 121
Huggins-StL 106
Bescher-Cin 106
Schulte-Chi 105
Doyle-NY 102

Hits
Miller-Bos 192
Hoblitzel-Cin 180
Daubert-Bro 176
Schulte-Chi 173
Luderus-Phi 166

Doubles
Konetchy-StL 38
Miller-Bos 36
Wilson-Pit 34
Herzog-Bos-NY 33
Sweeney-Bos 33

Triples
Doyle-NY 25
Mitchell-Cin 22
Schulte-Chi 21
Zimmerman-Chi 17
Byrne-Pit 17

Home Runs
Schulte-Chi 21
Luderus-Phi 16
Magee-Phi 15
Doyle-NY 13

Total Bases
Schulte-Chi 308
Doyle-NY 277
Luderus-Phi 260
Hoblitzel-Cin 258
Wilson-Pit 257

Runs Batted In
Wilson-Pit 107
Schulte-Chi 107
Luderus-Phi 99
Magee-Phi 94

Runs Produced
Schulte-Chi 191
Konetchy-StL 172
Wilson-Pit 167
Wagner-Pit 167
Sheckard-Chi 167

Bases On Balls
Sheckard-Chi 147
Bates-Cin 103
Bescher-Cin 102
Huggins-StL 96
Knabe-Phi 94

Batting Average
Wagner-Pit ..... .334
Miller-Bos ..... .333
Meyers-NY ..... .332
Clarke-Pit ..... .324
Fletcher-NY ..... .319

On Base Percentage
Sheckard-Chi ..... .434
Wagner-Pit ..... .423
Bates-Cin ..... .415
Sweeney-Bos ..... .404
Doyle-NY ..... .397

Slugging Average
Schulte-Chi ..... .534
Doyle-NY ..... .527
Wagner-Pit ..... .507
Clarke-Pit ..... .492
Magee-Phi ..... .483

Production
Wagner-Pit ..... .930
Doyle-NY ..... .924
Schulte-Chi ..... .918
Magee-Phi ..... .849
Wilson-Pit ..... .826

Adjusted Production
Schulte-Chi 155
Wagner-Pit 154
Doyle-NY 153
Magee-Phi 135
Konetchy-StL 132

Batter Runs
Schulte-Chi 40.6
Doyle-NY 39.3
Wagner-Pit 38.8
Sheckard-Chi 31.7
Clarke-Pit 27.0

Adjusted Batter Runs
Schulte-Chi 40.3
Doyle-NY 35.9
Wagner-Pit 35.0
Sheckard-Chi 31.5
Bates-Cin 27.5

Clutch Hitting Index
Hofman-Chi 133
Miller-Pit 128
Grant-Cin 126
Snodgrass-NY 124
Wilson-Pit 117

Runs Created
Schulte-Chi 127
Doyle-NY 124
Bescher-Cin 114
Wagner-Pit 109
Miller-Bos 107

Total Average
Doyle-NY 1.077
Wagner-Pit 1.057
Schulte-Chi 1.015
Sheckard-Chi 1.003
Bates-Cin ..... .943

Stolen Bases
Bescher-Cin 80
Devore-NY 61
Snodgrass-NY 51
Merkle-NY 49

Stolen Base Average

Stolen Base Runs

Fielding Runs
Tinker-Chi 23.4
Doolan-Phi 20.3
Ingerton-Bos 18.2
Herzog-Bos-NY 17.8
Merkle-NY 15.3

Total Player Rating
Wagner-Pit 4.5
Sheckard-Chi 3.8
Herzog-Bos-NY 3.2
Tinker-Chi 3.1
Schulte-Chi 2.7

Wins
Alexander-Phi 28
Mathewson-NY 26
Marquard-NY 24
Harmon-StL 23

Win Percentage
Marquard-NY ..... .774
Crandall-NY ..... .750
Cole-Chi ..... .720
Alexander-Phi ..... .683
Mathewson-NY ..... .667

Games
Brown-Chi 53
Harmon-StL 51
Rucker-Bro 48
Alexander-Phi 48

Complete Games
Alexander-Phi 31
Mathewson-NY 29
Harmon-StL 28
Leifield-Pit 26
Adams-Pit 24

Shutouts
Alexander-Phi 7
Adams-Pit 6

Saves
Brown-Chi 13
Crandall-NY 5

Innings Pitched
Alexander-Phi 367.0
Harmon-StL 348.0
Leifield-Pit 318.0
Rucker-Bro 315.2
Moore-Phi 308.1

Fewest Hits/Game
Alexander-Phi 6.99
Marquard-NY 7.16
Rucker-Bro 7.27
Ames-NY 7.46
Harmon-StL 7.50

Fewest BB/Game
Mathewson-NY 1.11
Adams-Pit 1.29
Steele-Pit-Bro 1.71
Brown-Chi 1.83
Wiltse-NY 1.87

Strikeouts
Marquard-NY 237
Alexander-Phi 227
Rucker-Bro 190
Moore-Phi 174
Harmon-StL 144

Strikeouts/Game
Marquard-NY 7.68
Alexander-Phi 5.57
Rucker-Bro 5.42
Ames-NY 5.18
Moore-Phi 5.08

Ratio
Adams-Pit 9.30
Ames-NY 10.01
Mathewson-NY 10.03
Steele-Pit-Bro 10.33
Alexander-Phi 10.35

Earned Run Average
Mathewson-NY 1.99
Richie-Chi 2.31
Adams-Pit 2.33
Marquard-NY 2.50
Alexander-Phi 2.57

Adjusted ERA
Mathewson-NY 168
Adams-Pit 147
Richie-Chi 143
Marquard-NY 134
Alexander-Phi 133

Opponents' Batting Avg.
Alexander-Phi ..... .219
Marquard-NY ..... .219
Ames-NY ..... .223
Rucker-Bro ..... .226
Keefe-Cin ..... .229

Opponents' On Base Pct.
Adams-Pit ..... .271
Ames-NY ..... .277
Mathewson-NY ..... .283
Wiltse-NY ..... .292
Alexander-Phi ..... .293

Starter Runs
Mathewson-NY 47.7
Adams-Pit 34.5
Alexander-Phi 33.3
Richie-Chi 30.3
Marquard-NY 27.6

Adjusted Starter Runs
Mathewson-NY 46.4
Adams-Pit 35.5
Alexander-Phi 34.9
Leifield-Pit 27.9
Richie-Chi 27.8

Clutch Pitching Index
Moore-Phi 130
Mathewson-NY 122
Richie-Chi 119
Leifield-Pit 117
Gaspar-Cin 115

Relief Runs
Richter-Chi 1.6

Adjusted Relief Runs
Richter-Chi 1.1

Relief Ranking
Richter-Chi 8

Total Pitcher Index
Mathewson-NY 6.7
Alexander-Phi 3.6
Adams-Pit 3.5
Leifield-Pit 3.2
Rucker-Bro 3.0

Total Baseball Ranking
Mathewson-NY 6.7
Wagner-Pit 4.5
Sheckard-Chi 3.8
Alexander-Phi 3.6
Adams-Pit 3.5

TEAM	G	W	L	PCT	GB	R	OR	AB	H	2B	3B	HR	BB	SO	AVG	OBP	SLG	PRO	PRO+	BR	/A	PF	CHI	RC	SB	CS	SBA	SBR
PHI	152	101	50	.669		861	601	5199	1540	237	93	35	424		.296	.357	.398	.755	119	108	123	98	104	821	226			
DET	154	89	65	.578	13.5	831	776	5294	1544	230	96	30	471		.292	.355	.388	.743	108	91	50	105	102	825	276			
CLE	156	80	73	.523	22	691	712	5321	1501	238	81	20	354		.282	.333	.369	.702	101	1	-7	101	97	716	209			
CHI	154	77	74	.510	24	719	624	5213	1401	179	92	20	385		.269	.325	.350	.675	97	-46	-25	97	108	659	201			
BOS	153	78	75	.510	24	680	643	5014	1379	203	66	35	506		.275	.350	.363	.713	106	39	46	99	91	710	190			
NY	153	76	76	.500	25.5	684	724	5052	1374	190	96	25	493		.272	.344	.362	.706	97	24	-23	107	94	724	269			
WAS	154	64	90	.416	38.5	625	766	5065	1308	159	54	16	466		.258	.330	.320	.650	89	-75	-63	98	100	607	215			
STL	152	45	107	.296	56.5	567	812	4996	1192	187	63	17	460		.239	.307	.311	.618	81	-142	-121	96	105	515	125			
TOT	614					5658		41154	11239	1623	641	198	3559	5093	.273	.338	.358	.696							1711			

TEAM	CG	SH	SV	IP	H	H/G	HR	BB	SO	RAT	ERA	ERA+	OAV	OOB	PR	/A	PF	CPI	FA	E	DP	FW	PW	BW	SBW	DIF
PHI	97	13	13	1375²	1343	8.8	17	487	739	12.5	3.01	105	.264	.338	50	21	94	106	.964	225	100	4.9	2.1	12.1		6.5
DET	108	8	3	1387²	1514	9.8	28	460	538	13.3	3.73	93	.283	.348	-60	-45	104	97	.951	318	78	-1.0	-4.4	4.9		12.5
CLE	93	6	6	1390²	1382	8.9	17	552	675	12.9	3.36	101	.267	.345	-3	7	102	100	.954	302	108	.3	.7	-.7		3.2
CHI	85	17	11	1386¹	1349	8.8	22	384	752	11.5	2.97	108	.255	.310	57	38	96	88	.961	252	98	3.4	3.7	-2.5		-3.1
BOS	87	10	8	1351²	1309	8.7	21	473	711	12.2	2.74	119	.262	.332	89	78	98	113	.949	323	93	-1.4	7.7	4.5		-9.3
NY	90	5	3	1360²	1404	9.3	26	406	667	12.3	3.54	101	.270	.329	-30	9	108	89	.949	328	99	-1.7	.9	-2.3		3.1
WAS	106	13	3	1353¹	1471	9.8	39	410	628	12.8	3.52	93	.277	.334	-27	-38	98	96	.953	305	90	-.1	-3.7	-6.2		-3.0
STL	92	8	1	1332¹	1465	9.9	28	463	383	13.4	3.86	87	.278	.342	-77	-73	101	90	.945	358	104	-3.8	-7.2	-11.9		-8.1
TOT	758	80	48	10938¹		9.2				12.6	3.34		.273	.338					.953	2411	770					

Runs
Cobb-Det 147
Jackson-Cle 126
Bush-Det 126
Milan-Was........ 109
Crawford-Det 109

Hits
Cobb-Det 248
Jackson-Cle 233
Crawford-Det 217
Baker-Phi 198
Milan-Was 194

Doubles
Cobb-Det 47
Jackson-Cle 45
Baker-Phi 42
Lord-Phi 37
LaPorte-StL 37

Triples
Cobb-Det 24
Cree-NY 22
Jackson-Cle 19
Lord-Chi 18
Wolter-NY 15

Home Runs
Baker-Phi 11
Speaker-Bos 8
Cobb-Det......... 8

Total Bases
Cobb-Det 367
Jackson-Cle 337
Crawford-Det 302
Baker-Phi 301
Cree-NY 267

Runs Batted In
Cobb-Det 127
Crawford-Det 115
Baker-Phi 115
Bodie-Chi 97
Delahanty-Det ... 94

Runs Produced
Cobb-Det 266
Crawford-Det 217
Jackson-Cle 202
Baker-Phi........ 200

Bases On Balls
Bush-Det 98
Milan-Was 74
Gessler-Was 74
Hooper-Bos 73
Austin-StL 69

Batting Average
Cobb-Det .... .420
Jackson-Cle ..... .408
Crawford-Det .... .378
Collins-Phi ..... .365
Cree-NY .... .348

On Base Percentage
Jackson-Cle ..... .468
Cobb-Det .... .467
Collins-Phi ..... .451
Crawford-Det..... .438
Speaker-Bos ..... .418

Slugging Average
Cobb-Det .... .621
Jackson-Cle ..... .590
Crawford-Det .... .526
Cree-NY .... .513
Baker-Phi .... .508

Production
Cobb-Det 1.088
Jackson-Cle 1.058
Crawford-Det 964
Collins-Phi 932
Cree-NY 928

Adjusted Production
Cobb-Det 193
Jackson-Cle 192
Collins-Phi 163
Crawford-Det 160
Speaker-Bos 158

Batter Runs
Cobb-Det 78.4
Jackson-Cle 71.8
Crawford-Det ... 52.4
Collins-Phi 43.0
Cree-NY 39.9

Adjusted Batter Runs
Cobb-Det 70.7
Jackson-Cle 70.1
Crawford-Det ... 45.9
Collins-Phi 45.0
Speaker-Bos 39.3

Clutch Hitting Index
Stovall-Cle 163
Gessler-Was 147
Hartzell-NY 131
Barry-Phi 130
Moriarty-Det 128

Runs Created
Cobb-Det 207
Jackson-Cle 175
Crawford-Det 147
Cree-NY 129
Baker-Phi 127

Total Average
Cobb-Det 1.464
Jackson-Cle 1.308
Collins-Phi 1.125
Crawford-Det ...1.120
Cree-NY 1.103

Stolen Bases
Cobb-Det 83
Milan-Was 58
Cree-NY 48
Callahan-Chi 45
Lord-Chi 43

Fielding Runs
Tannehill-Chi ... 42.5
Gardner-Bos 23.6
McBride-Was 23.5
Bush-Det 16.7
Austin-StL 16.3

Total Player Rating
Cobb-Det 7.1
Jackson-Cle 6.8
Collins-Phi 4.4
Speaker-Bos 3.7
Baker-Phi 3.6

Wins
Coombs-Phi 28
Walsh-Chi 27
Johnson-Was 25

Win Percentage
Bender-Phi ...... .773
Gregg-Cle .... .767
Plank-Phi .... .742
Coombs-Phi ...... .700
Morgan-Phi ...... .682

Games
Walsh-Chi........ 56
Coombs-Phi 47
Wood-Bos 44
Caldwell-NY 41

Complete Games
Johnson-Was 36
Walsh-Chi 33
Ford-NY 26
Coombs-Phi 26

Shutouts
Plank-Phi 6
Johnson-Was 6
Wood-Bos 5
Walsh-Chi 5
Gregg-Cle 5

Saves
Walsh-Chi........ 4
Plank-Phi 4
Hall-Bos 4
Wood-Bos 3
Bender-Phi 3

Innings Pitched
Walsh-Chi 368.2
Coombs-Phi 336.2
Johnson-Was 322.1
Ford-NY 281.1
Wood-Bos 275.2

Fewest Hits/Game
Gregg-Cle 6.33
Wood-Bos 7.38
Krapp-Cle 7.62
Morgan-Phi 7.82
Scott-Chi 7.91

Fewest BB/Game
White-Chi 1.47
Lake-StL......... 1.67
Walsh-Chi 1.76
Warhop-NY 1.89
Powell-StL 1.91

Strikeouts
Walsh-Chi 255
Wood-Bos 231
Johnson-Was 207
Coombs-Phi 185
Ford-NY 158

Strikeouts/Game
Wood-Bos 7.54
Walsh-Chi 6.23
Lange-Chi 5.79
Johnson-Was 5.78
Kahler-Cle 5.66

Ratio
Gregg-Cle 9.86
Walsh-Chi 9.91
Wood-Bos 10.22
Johnson-Was 10.33
Ford-NY 10.59

Earned Run Average
Gregg-Cle 1.80
Johnson-Was 1.90
Wood-Bos 2.02
Plank-Phi 2.10
Bender-Phi 2.16

Adjusted ERA
Gregg-Cle 189
Johnson-Was 173
Wood-Bos 162
Ford-NY 158
Plank-Phi 150

Opponents' Batting Avg.
Gregg-Cle .... .205
Wood-Bos .... .223
Krapp-Cle .... .232
Ford-NY .... .237
Johnson-Was ..... .238

Opponents' On Base Pct.
Walsh-Chi .... .280
Johnson-Was ..... .283
Wood-Bos .... .284
Gregg-Cle .... .286
Ford-NY .... .291

Starter Runs
Johnson-Was 51.6
Walsh-Chi 45.8
Gregg-Cle 41.8
Wood-Bos 40.3
Plank-Phi 35.2

Adjusted Starter Runs
Johnson-Was 49.4
Gregg-Cle 43.6
Ford-NY 41.2
Walsh-Chi 40.8
Wood-Bos 38.2

Clutch Pitching Index
Plank-Phi 133
Pape-Bos 130
Cicotte-Bos 122
Bender-Phi 117
Willett-Det...... 111

Total Pitcher Index
Wood-Bos 6.5
Johnson-Was 6.4
Walsh-Chi 6.2
Gregg-Cle 4.7
Ford-NY 4.3

Total Baseball Ranking
Cobb-Det 7.1
Jackson-Cle 6.8
Wood-Bos 6.5
Johnson-Was 6.4
Walsh-Chi 6.2

TEAM	G	W	L	PCT	GB	R	OR	AB	H	2B	3B	HR	BB	SO	AVG	OBP	SLG	PRO	PRO+	BR	/A	PF	CHI	RC	SB	CS	SBA	SBR
NY	154	103	48	.682		823	571	5067	1451	231	89	47	514	497	.286	.360	.395	.755	110	89	65	103	104	830	319			
PIT	152	93	58	.616	10	751	565	5252	1493	222	129	39	420	514	.284	.340	.398	.738	110	44	56	98	99	767	177			
CHI	152	91	59	.607	11.5	756	668	5048	1398	245	90	43	560	615	.277	.354	.387	.741	109	62	64	100	98	750	164			
CIN	155	75	78	.490	29	656	722	5115	1310	183	89	21	479	492	.256	.323	.339	.662	90	-90	-72	97	107	639	248			
PHI	152	73	79	.480	30.5	670	688	5077	1354	244	68	43	464	615	.267	.332	.367	.699	91	-23	-68	107	99	671	159			
STL	153	63	90	.412	41	659	830	5092	1366	190	77	27	508	620	.268	.340	.352	.692	97	-27	-11	98	97	675	193			
BRO	153	58	95	.379	46	651	754	5141	1377	220	73	32	490	584	.268	.336	.358	.694	100	-28	-2	96	96	677	179			
BOS	155	52	101	.340	52	693	861	5361	1465	227	68	35	454	690	.273	.335	.361	.696	94	-28	-40	102	99	693	137			
TOT	613					5659		41153	11214	1762	683	287	3889	4627	.272	.340	.369	.710						1576				

TEAM	CG	SH	SV	IP	H	H/G	HR	BB	SO	RAT	ERA	ERA+	OAV	OOB	PR	/A	PF	CPI	FA	E	DP	FW	PW	BW	SBW	DIF
NY	93	8	15	1369²	1352	8.9	36	338	652	11.3	2.58	130	.259	.307	124	118	99	103	.956	280	123	-2.1	11.6	6.4		11.6
PIT	94	18	7	1385	1268	8.2	28	497	664	11.8	2.85	114	.251	.324	84	60	96	99	.972	169	125	6.0	5.9	5.5		.1
CHI	80	15	9	1358²	1307	8.7	33	493	554	12.2	3.42	97	.259	.331	-4	-19	98	89	.960	249	125	-.0	-1.9	6.3		11.6
CIN	86	13	10	1377²	1455	9.5	28	452	561	12.9	3.42	98	.279	.344	-4	-14	99	102	.963	231	98	1.3	5.3	-6.7		-3.0
PHI	81	10	9	1355	1381	9.2	43	515	616	12.9	3.25	111	.272	.344	23	54	106	107	.960	249	102	.4	-1.4	-7.1		6.6
STL	61	6	12	1353	1466	9.8	31	560	487	13.7	3.85	89	.286	.361	-68	-63	101	102	.957	274	113	-1.8	-6.2	-1.1		-4.5
BRO	71	10	8	1357	1399	9.3	45	510	553	12.9	3.64	92	.273	.343	-37	-49	98	96	.959	255	96	-.3	-4.8	-.2		-13.1
BOS	88	5	5	1390²	1544	10.0	43	521	542	13.6	4.17	86	.291	.359	-119	-98	105	95	.954	297	129	-3.2	-9.6	-3.9		-7.7
TOT	654	85	75	10946²		9.2				12.7	3.40		.272	.340					.960	2004	911					

Runs
Bescher-Cin 120
Carey-Pit 114
Paskert-Phi 102
Campbell-Bos 102

Hits
Zimmerman-Chi . . . 207
Sweeney-Bos 204
Campbell-Bos 185
Doyle-NY 184
Wagner-Pit 181

Doubles
Zimmerman-Chi 41
Paskert-Phi 37
Wagner-Pit 35
Miller-Pit 33
Doyle-NY 33

Triples
Wilson-Pit 36
Wagner-Pit 20
Murray-NY 20
Daubert-Bro 16

Home Runs
Zimmerman-Chi 14
Schulte-Chi 12
Wilson-Pit 11
Merkle-NY 11
Cravath-Phi 11

Total Bases
Zimmerman-Chi . . . 318
Wilson-Pit 299
Wagner-Pit 277
Sweeney-Bos 264
Doyle-NY 263

Runs Batted In
Wagner-Pit 102
Sweeney-Bos 100
Zimmerman-Chi . . . 99
Wilson-Pit 95
Murray-NY 92

Runs Produced
Wagner-Pit 186
Sweeney-Bos 183
Zimmerman-Chi . . . 180
Doyle-NY 178
Carey-Pit 175

Bases On Balls
Sheckard-Chi 122
Paskert-Phi 91
Huggins-StL 87
Bescher-Cin 83
Titus-Phi-Bos 82

Batting Average
Zimmerman-Chi . . .372
Meyers-NY 358
Sweeney-Bos 344
Evers-Chi 341
Doyle-NY 330

On Base Percentage
Evers-Chi 431
Huggins-StL 422
Paskert-Phi 420
Zimmerman-Chi 418
Sweeney-Bos 416

Slugging Average
Zimmerman-Chi . . .571
Wilson-Pit 513
Wagner-Pit 496
Meyers-NY 477
Doyle-NY 471

Production
Zimmerman-Chi . . .989
Wagner-Pit 891
Evers-Chi 873
Doyle-NY 864
Titus-Phi-Bos 862

Adjusted Production
Zimmerman-Chi . . . 169
Wagner-Pit 145
Evers-Chi 139
Wilson-Pit 134
Konetchy-StL 134

Batter Runs
Zimmerman-Chi . . . 49.8
Wagner-Pit 32.1
Sweeney-Bos 30.9
Evers-Chi 29.1
Meyers-NY 28.2

Adjusted Batter Runs
Zimmerman-Chi . . . 50.2
Wagner-Pit 33.8
Evers-Chi 29.4
Sweeney-Bos 29.0
Meyers-NY 25.8

Clutch Hitting Index
Sweeney-Bos 138
Tinker-Chi 131
Hoblitzel-Cin 124
Murray-NY 119
Snodgrass-NY 114

Runs Created
Zimmerman-Chi . . . 141
Sweeney-Bos 123
Wagner-Pit 118
Doyle-NY 116
Paskert-Phi 108

Total Average
Zimmerman-Chi . . 1.100
Wagner-Pit 976
Paskert-Phi 965
Evers-Chi 962
Doyle-NY 955

Stolen Bases
Bescher-Cin 67
Carey-Pit 45
Snodgrass-NY 43
Murray-NY 38

Stolen Base Average

Stolen Base Runs

Fielding Runs
Sweeney-Bos 26.9
Tinker-Chi 24.7
Wagner-Pit 22.9
Herzog-NY 19.2
Fletcher-NY 15.8

Total Player Rating
Wagner-Pit 6.6
Zimmerman-Chi . . . 5.1
Sweeney-Bos 5.0
Evers-Chi 3.1
Konetchy-StL 2.8

Wins
Marquard-NY 26
Cheney-Chi 26
Hendrix-Pit 24
Mathewson-NY 23
Camnitz-Pit 22

Win Percentage
Hendrix-Pit 727
Cheney-Chi 722
Tesreau-NY 708
Marquard-NY 703
Richie-Chi 667

Games
Benton-Cin 50
Sallee-StL 48
Alexander-Phi 46
Rucker-Bro 45
Seaton-Phi 44

Complete Games
Cheney-Chi 28
Mathewson-NY 27
Suggs-Cin 25
Hendrix-Pit 25
Alexander-Phi 25

Shutouts
Rucker-Bro 6
Suggs-Cin 5
O'Toole-Pit 5

Saves
Sallee-StL 6
Rucker-Bro 4
Reulbach-Chi 4
Mathewson-NY 4

Innings Pitched
Alexander-Phi 310.1
Mathewson-NY 310.0
Cheney-Chi 303.1
Suggs-Cin 303.0
Benton-Cin 302.0

Fewest Hits/Game
Tesreau-NY 6.56
Robinson-Pit 7.51
O'Toole-Pit 7.75
Cheney-Chi 7.77
Brown-Bos 7.81

Fewest BB/Game
Mathewson-NY 99
Robinson-Pit 1.54
Suggs-Cin 1.66
Ames-NY 1.76
Adams-Pit 1.85

Strikeouts
Alexander-Phi 195
Hendrix-Pit 176
Marquard-NY 175
Benton-Cin 162
Rucker-Bro 151

Strikeouts/Game
Alexander-Phi 5.66
Hendrix-Pit 5.49
Marquard-NY 5.35
Tyler-Bos 5.06
O'Toole-Pit 4.90

Ratio
Robinson-Pit 9.57
Mathewson-NY . . . 10.07
Rucker-Bro 10.49
Tesreau-NY 10.85
Adams-Pit 10.94

Earned Run Average
Tesreau-NY 1.96
Mathewson-NY 2.12
Rucker-Bro 2.21
Robinson-Pit 2.26
Ames-NY 2.46

Adjusted ERA
Tesreau-NY 172
Mathewson-NY 159
Rucker-Bro 151
Rixey-Phi 145
Robinson-Pit 144

Opponents' Batting Avg.
Tesreau-NY 204
Cheney-Chi 234
Robinson-Pit 237
Brown-Bos 239
O'Toole-Pit 241

Opponents' On Base Pct.
Mathewson-NY 281
Robinson-Pit 284
Rucker-Bro 298
Tesreau-NY 298
Adams-Pit 303

Starter Runs
Mathewson-NY 44.1
Rucker-Bro 39.4
Tesreau-NY 38.8
Marquard-NY 27.3
Sallee-StL 26.0

Adjusted Starter Runs
Mathewson-NY 43.0
Tesreau-NY 37.9
Rucker-Bro 37.4
Alexander-Phi 27.7
Sallee-StL 26.6

Clutch Pitching Index
Ames-NY 125
Geyer-StL 125
Benton-Cin 116
Dickson-Bos 116
Yingling-Bro 114

Relief Runs

Adjusted Relief Runs

Relief Ranking

Total Pitcher Index
Rucker-Bro 5.2
Mathewson-NY 5.2
Hendrix-Pit 4.3
Tesreau-NY 3.3
Alexander-Phi 3.1

Total Baseball Ranking
Wagner-Pit 6.6
Rucker-Bro 5.2
Mathewson-NY 5.2
Zimmerman-Chi . . . 5.1
Sweeney-Bos 5.0

TEAM	G	W	L	PCT	GB	R	OR	AB	H	2B	3B	HR	BB	SO	AVG	OBP	SLG	PRO	PRO+	BR	/A	PF	CHI	RC	SB	CS	SBA	SBR
BOS	154	105	47	.691		799	544	5071	1404	269	84	29	565		.277	.355	.380	.735	110	104	64	105	100	752	185			
WAS	154	91	61	.599	14	699	581	5075	1298	202	86	20	472		.256	.324	.341	.665	94	-32	-37	101	108	645	274			
PHI	153	90	62	.592	15	779	658	5111	1442	204	108	22	485		.282	.349	.377	.726	117	83	111	96	101	763	258			
CHI	158	78	76	.506	28	639	648	5182	1321	174	80	17	423		.255	.317	.329	.646	93	-68	-48	97	102	610	205			
CLE	155	75	78	.490	30.5	677	681	5133	1403	219	77	12	407		.273	.333	.353	.686	98	5	-16	103	98	671	194			
DET	154	69	84	.451	36.5	720	777	5143	1376	189	86	19	530		.268	.343	.349	.692	106	26	49	97	100	705	270			
STL	157	53	101	.344	53	552	764	5080	1262	166	71	19	449		.248	.315	.320	.635	90	-86	-65	96	94	565	176			
NY	153	50	102	.329	55	630	842	5092	1320	168	79	18	463		.259	.329	.334	.663	90	-31	-70	106	97	638	247			
TOT	619					5495		40887	10826	1591	671	156	3794	5157	.265	.333	.348	.681						1809				

TEAM	CG	SH	SV	IP	H	H/G	HR	BB	SO	RAT	ERA	ERA+	OAV	OOB	PR	/A	PF	CPI	FA	E	DP	FW	PW	BW	SBW	DIF
BOS	108	18	6	1362	1243	8.2	18	385	712	11.0	2.76	124	.248	.306	88	104	103	98	.957	267	88	2.4	10.4	6.4		9.8
WAS	98	11	7	1376²	1219	8.0	24	525	828	11.8	2.69	125	.242	.320	99	105	101	108	.954	297	92	.7	10.5	-3.7		7.6
PHI	95	11	9	1357	1273	8.4	12	518	601	12.3	3.32	93	.258	.336	2	-31	93	99	.959	263	115	2.5	-3.1	11.1		3.5
CHI	85	14	16	1413	1398	8.9	26	426	698	11.8	3.16	105	.264	.322	44	26	96	104	.956	291	102	1.5	2.6	-4.8		1.7
CLE	94	7	7	1352²	1367	9.1	15	523	622	12.9	3.30	104	.272	.346	6	21	103	110	.954	287	124	1.4	2.1	-1.6		-3.4
DET	107	7	5	1367¹	1438	9.5	16	521	512	13.3	3.77	87	.277	.350	-66	-71	98	100	.950	338	91	-1.7	-7.1	4.9		-3.6
STL	85	8	5	1369²	1433	9.4	17	442	547	12.7	3.71	90	.277	.341	-56	-55	100	97	.947	341	127	-1.6	-5.5	-6.5		-10.5
NY	105	5	3	1335	1448	9.8	28	436	637	13.0	4.13	88	.282	.344	-117	-71	108	92	.940	382	77	-4.4	-7.1	-7.0		-7.5
TOT	777	81	58	10933¹		8.9				12.3	3.34		.265	.333					.952	2466	816					

Runs		Hits		Doubles		Triples		Home Runs		Total Bases	
Collins-Phi	137	Jackson-Cle	226	Speaker-Bos	53	Jackson-Cle	26	Speaker-Bos	10	Jackson-Cle	331
Speaker-Bos	136	Cobb-Det	226	Jackson-Cle	44	Cobb-Det	23	Baker-Phi	10	Speaker-Bos	329
Jackson-Cle	121	Speaker-Bos	222	Baker-Phi	40	Crawford-Det	21	Cobb-Det	7	Cobb-Det	323
Cobb-Det	120	Baker-Phi	200	Lewis-Bos	36	Baker-Phi	21			Baker-Phi	312
Baker-Phi	116					Gardner-Bos	18			Crawford-Det	273

Runs Batted In		Runs Produced		Bases On Balls		Batting Average		On Base Percentage		Slugging Average	
Baker-Phi	130	Baker-Phi	236	Bush-Det	117	Cobb-Det	.409	Speaker-Bos	.464	Cobb-Det	.584
Lewis-Bos	109	Speaker-Bos	216	Collins-Phi	101	Jackson-Cle	.395	Jackson-Cle	.458	Jackson-Cle	.579
Crawford-Det	109	Jackson-Cle	208	Rath-Phi	95	Speaker-Bos	.383	Cobb-Det	.456	Speaker-Bos	.567
McInnis-Phi	101	Collins-Phi	201	Shotton-StL	86	Lajoie-Cle	.368	Collins-Phi	.450	Baker-Phi	.541
		Cobb-Det	196	Speaker-Bos	82	Collins-Phi	.348	Lajoie-Cle	.414	Crawford-Det	.470

Production		Adjusted Production		Batter Runs		Adjusted Batter Runs		Clutch Hitting Index		Runs Created	
Cobb-Det	1.040	Cobb-Det	203	Speaker-Bos	72.8	Cobb-Det	71.7	Lajoie-Cle	145	Speaker-Bos	175
Jackson-Cle	1.036	Jackson-Cle	190	Jackson-Cle	70.3	Jackson-Cle	65.8	Lewis-Bos	130	Cobb-Det	173
Speaker-Bos	1.031	Speaker-Bos	185	Cobb-Det	67.1	Speaker-Bos	65.3	Gandil-Was	125	Jackson-Cle	166
Baker-Phi	.945	Baker-Phi	176	Baker-Phi	49.2	Baker-Phi	53.8	Milan-Was	124	Baker-Phi	140
Collins-Phi	.885	Collins-Phi	159	Collins-Phi	43.7	Collins-Phi	48.2	McInnis-Phi	120	Collins-Phi	136

Total Average		Stolen Bases		Stolen Base Average		Stolen Base Runs		Fielding Runs		Total Player Rating	
Cobb-Det	1.321	Milan-Was	88					McBride-Was	31.1	Speaker-Bos	7.7
Speaker-Bos	1.310	Collins-Phi	63					Bush-Det	29.4	Jackson-Cle	6.9
Jackson-Cle	1.249	Cobb-Det	61					Louden-Det	22.8	Cobb-Det	6.4
Collins-Phi	1.130	Speaker-Bos	52					Speaker-Bos	21.6	Baker-Phi	6.3
Baker-Phi	1.082	Zeider-Chi	47					Rath-Chi	18.3	Collins-Phi	5.8

Wins		Win Percentage		Games		Complete Games		Shutouts		Saves	
Wood-Bos	34	Wood-Bos	.872	Walsh-Chi	62	Wood-Bos	35	Wood-Bos	10	Walsh-Chi	10
Johnson-Was	33	Plank-Phi	.813	Johnson-Was	50	Johnson-Was	34	Johnson-Was	7	Warhop-NY	3
Walsh-Chi	27	Johnson-Was	.733	Wood-Bos	43	Walsh-Chi	32	Walsh-Chi	6	Mogridge-Chi	3
Plank-Phi	26	Bedient-Bos	.690	Groom-Was	43	Ford-NY	30	Plank-Phi	5	Lange-Chi	3
Groom-Was	24	Coombs-Phi	.677	Benz-Chi	42			Collins-Bos	4	Dubuc-Det	3

Innings Pitched		Fewest Hits/Game		Fewest BB/Game		Strikeouts		Strikeouts/Game		Ratio	
Walsh-Chi	393.0	Johnson-Was	6.32	Bender-Phi	1.74	Johnson-Was	303	Johnson-Was	7.39	Johnson-Was	8.56
Johnson-Was	369.0	Wood-Bos	6.99	Johnson-Was	1.85	Wood-Bos	258	Wood-Bos	6.75	Wood-Bos	9.44
Wood-Bos	344.0	Houck-Phi	7.37	Collins-Bos	1.90	Walsh-Chi	254	Gregg-Cle	6.10	Walsh-Chi	9.78
Groom-Was	316.0	Walsh-Chi	7.60	Powell-StL	1.99	Gregg-Cle	184	Walsh-Chi	5.82	Bedient-Bos	10.29
Ford-NY	291.2	O'Brien-Bos	7.74	Warhop-NY	2.06	Groom-Was	179	Lange-Chi	5.23	Collins-Bos	10.66

Earned Run Average		Adjusted ERA		Opponents' Batting Avg.		Opponents' On Base Pct.		Starter Runs		Adjusted Starter Runs	
Johnson-Was	1.39	Johnson-Was	241	Johnson-Was	.196	Johnson-Was	.248	Johnson-Was	79.9	Johnson-Was	80.5
Wood-Bos	1.91	Wood-Bos	179	Wood-Bos	.216	Wood-Bos	.272	Wood-Bos	54.6	Wood-Bos	57.8
Walsh-Chi	2.15	Walsh-Chi	149	Walsh-Chi	.231	Walsh-Chi	.279	Walsh-Chi	51.8	Walsh-Chi	46.5
Plank-Phi	2.22	Plank-Phi	140	Houck-Phi	.234	Bedient-Bos	.288	Plank-Phi	32.3	O'Brien-Bos	25.8
Collins-Bos	2.53	Collins-Bos	135	Dubuc-Det	.235	Collins-Bos	.297	Groom-Was	25.2	Groom-Was	25.8

Clutch Pitching Index		Relief Runs		Adjusted Relief Runs		Relief Ranking		Total Pitcher Index		Total Baseball Ranking	
Hughes-Was	129							Johnson-Was	11.2	Johnson-Was	11.2
McConnell-NY	121							Wood-Bos	8.6	Wood-Bos	8.6
Cashion-Was	120							Walsh-Chi	6.6	Speaker-Bos	7.7
Kahler-Cle	120							Plank-Phi	3.2	Jackson-Cle	6.9
Plank-Phi	119							McConnell-NY	2.9	Walsh-Chi	6.6

TEAM	G	W	L	PCT	GB	R	OR	AB	H	2B	3B	HR	BB	SO	AVG	OBP	SLG	PRO	PRO+	BR	/A	PF	CHI	RC	SB	CS	SBA	SBR
NY	156	101	51	.664		684	515	5218	1427	226	71	30	444	501	.273	.338	.361	.699	105	43	38	101	99	700	296			
PHI	159	88	63	.583	12.5	693	636	5400	1433	257	78	73	383	578	.265	.318	.382	.700	102	29	1	104	100	683	156			
CHI	155	88	65	.575	13.5	720	630	5022	1289	195	96	59	554	634	.257	.335	.369	.704	107	52	51	100	104	661	181			
PIT	155	78	71	.523	21.5	673	585	5252	1383	210	86	35	391	545	.263	.319	.356	.675	104	-13	15	96	106	629	181			
BOS	154	69	82	.457	31.5	641	690	5145	1318	191	60	32	488	640	.256	.326	.335	.661	93	-26	-38	102	103	603	177			
BRO	152	65	84	.436	34.5	595	613	5165	1394	193	86	39	361	555	.270	.321	.363	.684	98	4	-13	103	94	637	188			
CIN	156	64	89	.418	37.5	607	717	5132	1339	170	96	27	458	579	.261	.325	.347	.672	98	-10	-7	100	96	630	226			
STL	153	51	99	.340	49	528	755	4967	1229	152	72	15	451	573	.247	.316	.316	.632	88	-78	-70	99	97	534	171			
TOT	620					5141		41301	10812	1594	645	310	3530	4605	.262	.325	.354	.679						1576				

TEAM	CG	SH	SV	IP	H	H/G	HR	BB	SO	RAT	ERA	ERA+	OAV	OOB	PR	/A	PF	CPI	FA	E	DP	FW	PW	BW	SBW	DIF
NY	82	12	17	1422	1276	8.1	38	315	651	10.2	2.42	128	.243	.289	122	107	97	99	.961	254	107	-.6	11.1	4.0		10.5
PHI	77	20	11	1455[1]	1407	8.7	40	512	667	12.1	3.15	106	.261	.330	7	27	104	103	.968	214	112	2.2	2.8	.1		7.4
CHI	89	12	15	1372[1]	1330	8.7	39	478	556	12.1	3.13	101	.260	.328	9	6	99	103	.959	260	106	-1.1	.6	5.3		6.7
PIT	74	9	7	1400	1344	8.6	26	434	590	11.6	2.90	104	.260	.320	46	16	94	104	.964	226	94	1.1	1.7	1.6		-.8
BOS	105	13	3	1373	1343	8.8	37	419	597	11.8	3.19	103	.263	.324	1	12	103	100	.957	273	82	-2.0	1.2	-4.0		-1.8
BRO	71	9	7	1373	1287	8.4	33	439	548	11.6	3.13	105	.255	.321	11	23	103	97	.961	243	125	-.3	2.4	-1.4		-10.2
CIN	71	10	10	1380	1398	9.1	40	456	522	12.4	3.46	94	.273	.338	-40	-36	101	102	.961	251	104	-.4	-3.7	-.7		-7.6
STL	74	6	11	1351[2]	1426	9.5	57	477	465	13.0	4.23	76	.280	.348	-156	-152	101	92	.965	219	113	1.3	-15.8	-7.3		-2.2
TOT	643	91	81	11127[2]		8.7				11.9	3.20		.262	.325					.962	1940	843					

Runs		Hits		Doubles		Triples		Home Runs		Total Bases	
Leach-Chi	99	Cravath-Phi	179	Smith-Bro	40	Saier-Chi	21	Cravath-Phi	19	Cravath-Phi	298
Carey-Pit	99	Daubert-Bro	178	Burns-NY	37	Miller-Pit	20	Luderus-Phi	18	Luderus-Phi	254
Lobert-Phi	98	Burns-NY	173	Magee-Phi	36	Konetchy-StL	17	Saier-Chi	14	Saier-Chi	249
Saier-Chi	94	Lobert-Phi	172	Cravath-Phi	34	Wilson-Pit	14	Magee-Phi	11	Miller-Pit	243
Magee-Phi	92	Carey-Pit	172			Cravath-Phi	14	Wilson-Pit	10	Lobert-Phi	243

Runs Batted In		Runs Produced		Bases On Balls		Batting Average		On Base Percentage		Slugging Average	
Cravath-Phi	128	Cravath-Phi	187	Bescher-Cin	94	Daubert-Bro	.350	Huggins-StL	.432	Cravath-Phi	.568
Zimmerman-Chi	95	Saier-Chi	172	Huggins-StL	92	Cravath-Phi	.341	Cravath-Phi	.407	Becker-Cin-Phi	.502
Saier-Chi	92	Miller-Pit	158	Leach-Chi	77	Viox-Pit	.317	Daubert-Bro	.405	Zimmerman-Chi	.490
Miller-Pit	90	Zimmerman-Chi	155	Bridwell-Chi	74	Tinker-Cin	.317	Viox-Pit	.399	Saier-Chi	.480
Luderus-Phi	86	Magee-Phi	151			Becker-Cin-Phi	.316	Leach-Chi	.391	Magee-Phi	.479

Production		Adjusted Production		Batter Runs		Adjusted Batter Runs		Clutch Hitting Index		Runs Created	
Cravath-Phi	.974	Cravath-Phi	169	Cravath-Phi	50.5	Cravath-Phi	45.8	Zimmerman-Chi	132	Cravath-Phi	120
Zimmerman-Chi	.868	Zimmerman-Chi	147	Saier-Chi	27.5	Viox-Pit	28.8	Cutshaw-Bro	127	Saier-Chi	97
Saier-Chi	.850	Viox-Pit	142	Zimmerman-Chi	26.3	Saier-Chi	27.3	Cravath-Phi	123	Lobert-Phi	96
Magee-Phi	.848	Saier-Chi	141	Daubert-Bro	25.2	Zimmerman-Chi	26.1	Doyle-NY	119	Daubert-Bro	94
Daubert-Bro	.829	Magee-Phi	136	Viox-Pit	24.8	Daubert-Bro	22.9	Fletcher-NY	116	Carey-Pit	92

Total Average		Stolen Bases		Stolen Base Average	Stolen Base Runs	Fielding Runs		Total Player Rating	
Cravath-Phi	1.058	Carey-Pit	61			Evers-Chi	29.9	Tinker-Cin	3.9
Saier-Chi	.927	Myers-Bos	57			Paskert-Phi	17.7	Cravath-Phi	3.7
Zimmerman-Chi	.925	Lobert-Phi	41			Cutshaw-Bro	17.5	Evers-Chi	3.5
Magee-Phi	.905	Burns-NY	40			Tinker-Cin	17.3	Zimmerman-Chi	3.4
Leach-Phi	.895	Cutshaw-Bro	39			Doolan-Phi	17.2	Wagner-Pit	3.1

Wins		Win Percentage		Games		Complete Games		Shutouts		Saves	
Seaton-Phi	27	Humphries-Chi	.800	Cheney-Chi	54	Tyler-Bos	28	Alexander-Phi	9	Cheney-Chi	11
Mathewson-NY	25	Alexander-Phi	.733	Seaton-Phi	52	Mathewson-NY	25	Seaton-Phi	5	Crandall-NY	6
Marquard-NY	23	Marquard-NY	.697	Sallee-StL	50	Cheney-Chi	25			Brown-Cin	6
Tesreau-NY	22	Mathewson-NY	.694	Alexander-Phi	47	Adams-Pit	24			Sallee-StL	5
Alexander-Phi	22	Seaton-Phi	.692	Camnitz-Pit-Phi	45	Alexander-Phi	23				

Innings Pitched		Fewest Hits/Game		Fewest BB/Game		Strikeouts		Strikeouts/Game		Ratio	
Seaton-Phi	322.1	Tesreau-NY	7.09	Mathewson-NY	.62	Seaton-Phi	168	Tesreau-NY	5.33	Mathewson-NY	9.18
Adams-Pit	313.2	Seaton-Phi	7.32	Humphries-Chi	1.19	Tesreau-NY	167	Hendrix-Pit	5.15	Adams-Pit	9.18
Alexander-Phi	306.1	Allen-Bro	7.42	Adams-Pit	1.41	Alexander-Phi	159	Marquard-NY	4.72	Marquard-NY	9.38
Mathewson-NY	306.0	Pearce-Chi	7.55	Marquard-NY	1.53	Marquard-NY	151	Seaton-Phi	4.69	Humphries-Chi	9.70
Cheney-Chi	305.0	Tyler-Bos	7.59	Suggs-Cin	1.58	Adams-Pit	144	Alexander-Phi	4.67	Demaree-NY	9.87

Earned Run Average		Adjusted ERA		Opponents' Batting Avg.		Opponents' On Base Pct.		Starter Runs		Adjusted Starter Runs	
Mathewson-NY	2.06	Mathewson-NY	151	Tesreau-NY	.220	Mathewson-NY	.266	Mathewson-NY	38.7	Mathewson-NY	35.9
Adams-Pit	2.15	Tesreau-NY	143	Seaton-Phi	.226	Adams-Pit	.267	Adams-Pit	36.4	Adams-Pit	29.8
Tesreau-NY	2.17	Demaree-NY	141	Allen-Bro	.231	Marquard-NY	.273	Tesreau-NY	32.2	Tesreau-NY	29.5
Demaree-NY	2.21	Adams-Pit	140	Pearce-Chi	.234	Humphries-Chi	.277	Marquard-NY	22.3	Seaton-Phi	26.2
Pearce-Chi	2.31	Brennan-Phi	139	Tyler-Bos	.235	Demaree-NY	.286	Demaree-NY	21.9	Brennan-Phi	21.5

Clutch Pitching Index		Relief Runs		Adjusted Relief Runs		Relief Ranking		Total Pitcher Index		Total Baseball Ranking	
Brennan-Phi	128	Crandall-NY	3.7	Crandall-NY	2.8	Crandall-NY	2.4	Mathewson-NY	4.6	Mathewson-NY	4.6
Packard-Cin	127							Tesreau-NY	3.9	Tinker-Cin	3.9
Brown-Cin	119							Adams-Pit	3.7	Tesreau-NY	3.9
Ames-NY-Cin	119							Tyler-Bos	2.9	Adams-Pit	3.7
Pearce-Chi	112							Seaton-Phi	2.7	Cravath-Phi	3.7

TEAM	G	W	L	PCT	GB	R	OR	AB	H	2B	3B	HR	BB	SO	AVG	OBP	SLG	PRO	PRO+	BR	/A	PF	CHI	RC	SB	CS	SBA	SBR
PHI	153	96	57	.627		794	592	5044	1412	223	80	33	534	547	.280	.356	.375	.731	124	135	152	98	105	732	221			
WAS	155	90	64	.584	6.5	596	561	5074	1281	156	81	19	440	595	.252	.317	.326	.643	92	-35	-47	102	105	585	287			
CLE	155	86	66	.566	9.5	633	536	5031	1349	206	74	16	420	557	.268	.331	.348	.679	102	29	11	103	99	630	191			
BOS	151	79	71	.527	15.5	631	610	4965	1334	220	101	17	466	534	.269	.336	.364	.700	109	66	49	103	95	652	189			
CHI	153	78	74	.513	17.5	488	498	4822	1139	157	66	24	398	550	.236	.299	.311	.610	85	-94	-89	99	100	487	156			
DET	153	66	87	.431	30	624	716	5064	1344	180	101	24	496	501	.265	.336	.355	.691	111	56	66	99	93	655	218			
NY	153	57	94	.377	38	529	668	4880	1157	155	45	8	534	617	.237	.320	.292	.612	85	-75	-77	100	101	505	203			
STL	155	57	96	.373	39	528	642	5031	1193	179	73	18	455	769	.237	.306	.312	.618	90	-80	-65	97	101	524	209			
TOT	614					4823		39911	10209	1476	621	159	3743	4670	.256	.325	.336	.661						1674				

TEAM	CG	SH	SV	IP	H	H/G	HR	BB	SO	RAT	ERA	ERA+	OAV	OOB	PR	/A	PF	CPI	FA	E	DP	FW	PW	BW	SBW	DIF
PHI	69	17	22	1351¹	1200	8.0	24	532	630	11.8	3.19	87	.229	.304	-39	-65	94	70	.966	212	108	3.2	-6.9	16.2		7.0
WAS	78	23	20	1396¹	1177	7.6	35	465	758	11.0	2.73	108	.225	.297	31	34	101	80	.960	261	122	.3	3.6	-5.0		14.1
CLE	93	18	5	1386²	1278	8.3	19	502	689	11.8	2.54	119	.249	.321	59	74	104	108	.962	242	124	1.5	7.9	1.2		-.6
BOS	83	12	10	1358¹	1323	8.6	6	442	710	11.9	2.94	100	.260	.323	-2	-3	100	96	.961	237	84	1.4	-.3	5.2		-2.3
CHI	84	17	8	1360¹	1190	7.9	10	438	602	11.0	2.33	125	.237	.302	91	89	100	97	.960	255	104	.5	9.5	-9.5		1.5
DET	90	4	7	1360	1359	9.0	13	504	468	12.6	3.38	86	.265	.336	-68	-71	100	94	.954	300	105	-2.4	-7.6	7.0		-7.6
NY	75	8	7	1344	1318	8.8	31	455	530	12.2	3.27	91	.260	.327	-51	-42	102	94	.954	293	94	-1.9	-4.5	-8.2		-3.9
STL	104	14	5	1382¹	1369	8.9	21	454	476	12.2	3.06	96	.266	.332	-20	-22	100	103	.954	301	125	-2.2	-2.3	-6.9		-8.0
TOT	676	113	84	10939¹		8.4				11.8	2.93		.256	.325					.959	2101	866					

Runs
Collins-Phi 125
Baker-Phi 116
Jackson-Cle 109
Shotton-StL 105
E.Murphy-Phi 105

Hits
Jackson-Cle 197
Crawford-Det 193
Baker-Phi 190
Speaker-Bos 189
Collins-Phi 184

Doubles
Jackson-Cle 39
Speaker-Bos 35
Baker-Phi 34
Crawford-Det 32

Triples
Crawford-Det 23
Speaker-Bos 22
Jackson-Cle 17
Williams-StL 16
Cobb-Det 16

Home Runs
Baker-Phi 12
Crawford-Det 9
Bodie-Chi 8
Jackson-Cle 7

Total Bases
Crawford-Det 298
Jackson-Cle 291
Baker-Phi 278
Speaker-Bos 277
Collins-Phi 242

Runs Batted In
Baker-Phi 117
McInnis-Phi 90
Lewis-Bos 90
Pratt-StL 87
Barry-Phi 85

Runs Produced
Baker-Phi 221
Collins-Phi 195
Jackson-Cle 173
Oldring-Phi 167
McInnis-Phi 165

Bases On Balls
Shotton-StL 99
Collins-Phi 85
Wolter-NY 80
Jackson-Cle 80
Bush-Det 80

Batting Average
Cobb-Det 390
Jackson-Cle 373
Speaker-Bos 363
Collins-Phi 345
Baker-Phi 337

On Base Percentage
Cobb-Det 467
Jackson-Cle 460
Collins-Phi 441
Speaker-Bos 441
Baker-Phi 413

Slugging Average
Jackson-Cle 551
Cobb-Det 535
Speaker-Bos 533
Baker-Phi 493
Crawford-Det 489

Production
Jackson-Cle 1.011
Cobb-Det 1.002
Speaker-Bos 974
Baker-Phi 906
Collins-Phi 894

Adjusted Production
Cobb-Det 196
Jackson-Cle 190
Speaker-Bos 180
Baker-Phi 168
Collins-Phi 165

Batter Runs
Jackson-Cle 65.5
Speaker-Bos 55.9
Cobb-Det 51.8
Baker-Phi 45.9
Collins-Phi 45.7

Adjusted Batter Runs
Jackson-Cle 61.8
Cobb-Det 53.4
Speaker-Bos 52.9
Baker-Phi 48.5
Collins-Phi 48.3

Clutch Hitting Index
Barry-Phi 163
Lewis-Bos 133
Pratt-StL 127
McInnis-Phi 122
Turner-Cle 121

Runs Created
Jackson-Cle 140
Speaker-Bos 136
Collins-Phi 126
Cobb-Det 124
Baker-Phi 122

Total Average
Cobb-Det 1.310
Jackson-Cle 1.215
Speaker-Bos 1.193
Collins-Phi 1.111
Baker-Phi 1.029

Stolen Bases
Milan-Was 75
Moeller-Was 62
Collins-Phi 55
Cobb-Det 51
Speaker-Bos 46

Stolen Base Average

Stolen Base Runs

Fielding Runs
Weaver-Chi 33.6
Speaker-Bos 23.7
Turner-Cle 16.3
Collins-Phi 15.6
Shotton-StL 12.8

Total Player Rating
Speaker-Bos 7.3
Collins-Phi 6.4
Baker-Phi 6.1
Jackson-Cle 6.0
Cobb-Det 5.3

Wins
Johnson-Was 36
Falkenberg-Cle 23
Russell-Chi 22
Bender-Phi 21

Win Percentage
Johnson-Was 837
Bush-Phi 714
Boehling-Was 708
Collins-Bos 704
Falkenberg-Cle 697

Games
Russell-Chi 52
Scott-Chi 48
Johnson-Was 48
Bender-Phi 48
V.Gregg-Cle 44

Complete Games
Johnson-Was 29
Russell-Chi 26
Scott-Chi 25

Shutouts
Johnson-Was 11
Russell-Chi 8
Plank-Phi 7
Falkenberg-Cle 6

Saves
Bender-Phi 13
Hughes-Was 6
Bedient-Bos 5

Innings Pitched
Johnson-Was 346.0
Russell-Chi 316.2
Scott-Chi 312.1
V.Gregg-Cle 285.2
Falkenberg-Cle . . . 276.0

Fewest Hits/Game
Johnson-Was 6.03
Mitchell-Cle 6.35
Engel-Was 6.78
Leverenz-StL 7.06
Russell-Chi 7.11

Fewest BB/Game
Johnson-Was 99
Collins-Bos 1.35
Mitchell-StL 1.72
Plank-Phi 2.11
Weilman-StL 2.15

Strikeouts
Johnson-Was 243
V.Gregg-Cle 166
Falkenberg-Cle . . . 166
Scott-Chi 158
Groom-Was 156

Strikeouts/Game
Johnson-Was 6.32
Mitchell-Cle 5.85
Plank-Phi 5.60
Falkenberg-Cle . . . 5.41
Groom-Was 5.31

Ratio
Johnson-Was 7.26
Russell-Chi 9.55
Scott-Chi 10.00
Cicotte-Chi 10.07
Plank-Phi 10.13

Earned Run Average
Johnson-Was 1.14
Cicotte-Chi 1.58
Scott-Chi 1.90
Russell-Chi 1.90
Mitchell-Cle 1.91

Adjusted ERA
Johnson-Was 258
Cicotte-Chi 185
Mitchell-Cle 159
Scott-Chi 154
Russell-Chi 153

Opponents' Batting Avg.
Johnson-Was 187
Mitchell-Cle 199
Engel-Was 207
Houck-Phi 214
Russell-Chi 219

Opponents' On Base Pct.
Johnson-Was 217
Russell-Chi 273
Bender-Phi 277
Cicotte-Chi 281
Scott-Chi 281

Starter Runs
Johnson-Was 68.6
Cicotte-Chi 40.2
Russell-Chi 36.1
Scott-Chi 35.7
Mitchell-Cle 24.6

Adjusted Starter Runs
Johnson-Was 69.4
Cicotte-Chi 40.0
Russell-Chi 35.8
Scott-Chi 35.4
Mitchell-Cle 27.1

Clutch Pitching Index
Blanding-Cle 141
V.Gregg-Cle 130
Ford-NY 123
Baumgardner-StL . . 118
Cicotte-Chi 114

Relief Runs

Adjusted Relief Runs

Relief Ranking

Total Pitcher Index
Johnson-Was 10.9
Cicotte-Chi 5.2
Russell-Chi 4.2
Scott-Chi 3.8
Boehling-Was 2.6

Total Baseball Ranking
Johnson-Was 10.9
Speaker-Bos 7.3
Collins-Phi 6.4
Baker-Phi 6.1
Jackson-Cle 6.0

TEAM	G	W	L	PCT	GB	R	OR	AB	H	2B	3B	HR	BB	SO	AVG	OBP	SLG	PRO	PRO+	BR	/A	PF	CHI	RC	SB	CS	SBA	SBR
BOS	158	94	59	.614		657	548	5206	1307	213	60	35	502	617	.251	.323	.335	.658	103	17	21	99	103	602	139			
NY	156	84	70	.545	10.5	672	576	5146	1363	222	59	30	447	479	.265	.330	.348	.678	112	53	75	97	103	644	239			
STL	157	81	72	.529	13	558	540	5046	1249	203	65	33	445	618	.248	.314	.333	.647	100	-9	-2	99	95	576	204			
CHI	156	78	76	.506	16.5	605	638	5050	1229	199	74	42	501	577	.243	.317	.337	.654	101	7	9	100	100	579	164			
BRO	154	75	79	.487	19.5	622	618	5152	1386	172	90	31	376	559	.269	.323	.355	.678	106	43	29	102	97	629	173			
PHI	154	74	80	.481	20.5	651	687	5110	1345	211	52	62	472	570	.263	.329	.361	.690	105	69	26	107	97	636	145			
PIT	158	69	85	.448	25.5	503	540	5145	1197	148	79	18	416	608	.233	.295	.303	.598	88	-101	-80	96	101	488	147			
CIN	157	60	94	.390	34.5	530	651	4991	1178	142	64	16	441	627	.236	.305	.300	.605	83	-79	-94	103	105	506	224			
TOT	625					4798		40846	10254	1510	543	267	3600	4655	.251	.317	.334	.651							1435			

TEAM	CG	SH	SV	IP	H	H/G	HR	BB	SO	RAT	ERA	ERA+	OAV	OOB	PR	/A	PF	CPI	FA	E	DP	FW	PW	BW	SBW	DIF
BOS	104	19	6	1421	1272	8.1	38	477	606	11.4	2.74	100	.249	.319	7	1	99	102	.963	246	143	1.8	.1	2.3		13.3
NY	88	20	9	1390²	1298	8.4	47	367	563	11.0	2.94	90	.253	.306	-25	-46	95	92	.961	254	119	1.1	-5.0	8.1		2.8
STL	84	16	12	1424²	1279	8.1	26	422	531	11.1	2.38	117	.250	.313	64	64	100	112	.964	239	109	2.2	6.9	-.2		-4.4
CHI	70	14	11	1389¹	1169	7.6	37	528	651	11.2	2.71	103	.233	.311	12	9	100	92	.951	310	87	-2.7	1.0	1.0		1.8
BRO	80	11	11	1368¹	1282	8.4	36	466	605	11.8	2.82	101	.255	.323	-5	7	103	105	.961	248	112	1.2	.8	3.1		-7.1
PHI	85	14	7	1379¹	1403	9.2	26	452	650	12.4	3.06	96	.270	.335	-42	-21	105	106	.950	324	81	-3.9	-2.3	2.8		.3
PIT	86	10	11	1405	1272	8.1	27	392	488	10.9	2.70	98	.249	.308	13	-9	95	95	.966	223	96	3.4	-1.0	-8.6		-1.8
CIN	74	15	15	1387¹	1259	8.2	30	489	607	11.7	2.94	100	.248	.320	-24	-3	105	95	.952	314	113	-2.9	-.3	-10.1		-3.7
TOT	671	119	82	11165²		8.2				11.4	2.78		.251	.317					.958	2158	860					

Runs
Burns-NY 100
Magee-Phi 96
Daubert-Bro 89
Saier-Chi 87
Doyle-NY 87

Hits
Magee-Phi 171
Wheat-Bro 170
Burns-NY 170
Zimmerman-Chi ... 167
Becker-Phi 167

Doubles
Magee-Phi 39
Zimmerman-Chi.... 36
Burns-NY 35
Connolly-Bos 28

Triples
Carey-Pit 17
Zimmerman-Chi 12
Wilson-StL 12
Cutshaw-Bro 12

Home Runs
Cravath-Phi 19
Saier-Chi 18
Magee-Phi 15
Luderus-Phi 12

Total Bases
Magee-Phi 277
Cravath-Phi 249
Wheat-Bro 241
Zimmerman-Chi ... 239
Burns-NY 234

Runs Batted In
Magee-Phi 103
Cravath-Phi 100
Wheat-Bro 89
D.Miller-StL 88
Zimmerman-Chi ... 87

Runs Produced
Magee-Phi 184
Zimmerman-Chi ... 158
Cravath-Phi 157
Burns-NY 157
D.Miller-StL 151

Bases On Balls
Huggins-StL 105
Saier-Chi 94
Burns-NY 89
Evers-Bos 87
Cravath-Phi 83

Batting Average
Daubert-Bro 329
Becker-Phi 325
Dalton-Bro 319
Wheat-Bro 319
Stengel-Bro 316

On Base Percentage
Stengel-Bro 404
Burns-NY 403
Cravath-Phi 402
Huggins-StL 396
Dalton-Bro 396

Slugging Average
Magee-Phi 509
Cravath-Phi 499
Connolly-Bos 494
Wheat-Bro 452
Becker-Phi 446

Production
Cravath-Phi 901
Magee-Phi 890
Wheat-Bro 830
Stengel-Bro 829
Burns-NY 820

Adjusted Production
Cravath-Phi 157
Magee-Phi 154
Burns-NY 149
Stengel-Bro 143
Wheat-Bro 143

Batter Runs
Cravath-Phi 42.7
Magee-Phi 40.7
Burns-NY 34.0
Connolly-Bos 31.0
Wheat-Bro 29.3

Adjusted Batter Runs
Burns-NY 37.5
Cravath-Phi 36.0
Magee-Phi 34.0
Connolly-Bos 31.5
Wheat-Bro 27.3

Clutch Hitting Index
Fletcher-NY 129
Maranville-Bos ...127
Cutshaw-Bro 123
D.Miller-StL 122
Schmidt-Bos 121

Runs Created
Burns-NY 113
Magee-Phi 110
Cravath-Phi 103
Wheat-Bro 95
Becker-Phi 87

Total Average
Burns-NY 997
Cravath-Phi 997
Magee-Phi 965
Stengel-Bro 904
Wheat-Bro 857

Stolen Bases
Burns-NY 62
Herzog-Cin 46
Dolan-StL 42
Carey-Pit 38

Stolen Base Average

Stolen Base Runs

Fielding Runs
Maranville-Bos ... 51.8
Herzog-Cin 30.6
Cutshaw-Bro 27.5
Smith-Bro-Bos ... 22.6
Wheat-Bro 18.2

Total Player Rating
Maranville-Bos ... 5.9
Herzog-Cin 4.8
Magee-Phi 4.5
Smith-Bro-Bos ... 4.3
Wheat-Bro 4.2

Wins
Alexander-Phi ... 27
Tesreau-NY 26
Rudolph-Bos 26
James-Bos 26
Mathewson-NY ... 24

Win Percentage
James-Bos .... .788
Doak-StL .... .760
Tesreau-NY ...... .722
Rudolph-Bos ..... .722
Pfeffer-Bro .... .657

Games
Cheney-Chi 50
Mayer-Phi 48
Ames-Cin 47

Complete Games
Alexander-Phi 32
Rudolph-Bos 31
James-Bos 30
Mathewson-NY ... 29
Pfeffer-Bro 27

Shutouts
Tesreau-NY 8
Doak-StL 7
Rudolph-Bos 6
Cheney-Chi 6
Alexander-Phi 6

Saves
Sallee-StL 6
Ames-Cin 6
Cheney-Chi 5
Pfeffer-Bro 4
McQuillan-Pit 4

Innings Pitched
Alexander-Phi 355.0
Rudolph-Bos 336.1
James-Bos 332.1
Tesreau-NY 322.1
Mayer-Phi 321.0

Fewest Hits/Game
Tesreau-NY 6.65
Doak-StL 6.79
Cheney-Chi 6.91
Douglas-Cin 6.99
James-Bos 7.07

Fewest BB/Game
Mathewson-NY ... .66
Adams-Pit 1.24
Marquard-NY 1.58
Rudolph-Bos 1.63
Alexander-Phi ... 1.93

Strikeouts
Alexander-Phi 214
Tesreau-NY 189
Vaughn-Chi 165
Cheney-Chi 157
James-Bos 156

Strikeouts/Game
Alexander-Phi 5.43
Tesreau-NY 5.28
Vaughn-Chi 5.06
L.Tyler-Bos 4.64
Ragan-Bro 4.58

Ratio
Rudolph-Bos 9.45
Adams-Pit 9.51
Mathewson-NY ... 9.78
Doak-StL 10.09
Pfeffer-Bro 10.34

Earned Run Average
Doak-StL 1.72
James-Bos 1.90
Pfeffer-Bro 1.97
Vaughn-Chi 2.05
Sallee-StL 2.10

Adjusted ERA
Doak-StL 162
James-Bos 145
Pfeffer-Bro 145
Vaughn-Chi 135
Sallee-StL 133

Opponents' Batting Avg.
Tesreau-NY .... .209
Cheney-Chi ...... .215
Doak-StL .... .216
Vaughn-Chi ...... .222
Douglas-Cin ...... .223

Opponents' On Base Pct.
Adams-Pit 276
Rudolph-Bos 276
Mathewson-NY ...278
Alexander-Phi 290
Doak-StL..........290

Starter Runs
James-Bos 32.8
Doak-StL 30.2
Pfeffer-Bro 28.5
Vaughn-Chi 23.9
Sallee-StL 21.4

Adjusted Starter Runs
James-Bos 31.6
Pfeffer-Bro 30.9
Doak-StL 30.4
Vaughn-Chi 23.6
Alexander-Phi 21.8

Clutch Pitching Index
Cooper-Pit 126
James-Bos 121
Crutcher-Bos 120
Perritt-StL 116
Sallee-StL 116

Relief Runs

Adjusted Relief Runs

Relief Ranking

Total Pitcher Index
James-Bos 3.6
Alexander-Phi 3.3
Doak-StL 3.2
Pfeffer-Bro 3.1
Sallee-StL 2.9

Total Baseball Ranking
Maranville-Bos 5.9
Herzog-Cin 4.8
Magee-Phi 4.5
Smith-Bro-Bos 4.3
Wheat-Bro 4.2

TEAM	G	W	L	PCT	GB	R	OR	AB	H	2B	3B	HR	BB	SO	AVG	OBP	SLG	PRO	PRO+	BR	/A	PF	CHI	RC	SB	CS	SBA	SBR
PHI	158	99	53	.651	—	749	529	5126	1392	165	80	29	545	517	.272	.348	.352	.700	123	112	140	96	107	662	231	188	55	-44
BOS	159	91	62	.595	8.5	589	510	5117	1278	226	85	18	490	549	.250	.320	.338	.658	105	26	26	100	98	567	177	176	50	-53
WAS	158	81	73	.526	19	572	519	5108	1245	176	81	18	470	640	.244	.313	.320	.633	93	-17	-39	104	102	544	220	163	57	-32
DET	157	80	73	.523	19.5	615	618	5102	1318	195	84	25	557	537	.258	.336	.344	.680	109	76	56	103	93	630	211	154	58	-29
STL	159	71	82	.464	28.5	523	615	5101	1241	185	75	17	423	863	.243	.306	.319	.625	99	-38	-18	96	99	516	233	189	55	-44
NY	157	70	84	.455	30	537	550	4992	1144	149	52	12	577	711	.229	.315	.287	.602	88	-60	-58	100	105	484	251	191	57	-39
CHI	157	70	84	.455	30	487	560	5040	1205	161	71	19	408	609	.239	.302	.311	.613	92	-59	-52	99	96	497	167	152	52	-41
CLE	157	51	102	.333	48.5	538	709	5157	1262	178	70	10	450	685	.245	.310	.312	.622	90	-39	-60	104	100	517	167	157	52	-44
TOT	631					4610		40743	10085	1435	598	148	3920	5111	.248	.319	.323	.642							1657	1370	55	-325

TEAM	CG	SH	SV	IP	H	H/G	HR	BB	SO	RAT	ERA	ERA+	OAV	OOB	PR	/A	PF	CPI	FA	E	DP	FW	PW	BW	SBW	DIF
PHI	89	24	17	1404	1264	8.1	18	521	720	11.6	2.78	94	.249	.322	-6	-27	95	100	.966	213	116	3.5	-3.0	15.5	-.4	7.4
BOS	88	24	8	1427¹	1207	7.6	18	393	602	10.3	2.36	114	.236	.295	59	50	98	94	.963	242	99	1.8	5.5	2.9	-1.4	5.6
WAS	75	25	20	1420²	1170	7.4	20	520	784	11.0	2.54	111	.233	.311	31	41	103	97	.961	254	116	1.0	4.5	-4.3	1.0	1.8
DET	81	14	12	1412	1285	8.2	17	498	567	11.8	2.86	98	.249	.322	-19	-10	103	97	.958	286	101	-1.1	-1.1	6.2	1.3	-1.8
STL	81	15	11	1410²	1309	8.4	20	540	553	12.1	2.85	95	.251	.327	-17	-22	99	103	.952	317	114	-2.7	-2.4	-2.0	-.4	2.0
NY	98	9	5	1397¹	1277	8.2	30	390	563	10.9	2.81	98	.250	.308	-12	-10	101	94	.963	238	93	1.9	-1.1	-6.4	.2	-1.5
CHI	74	17	11	1398²	1207	7.8	15	401	660	10.5	2.48	108	.239	.298	40	30	98	92	.955	299	90	-1.9	3.3	-5.7	-.0	-2.7
CLE	69	9	3	1391²	1365	8.8	10	666	688	13.4	3.21	90	.267	.357	-74	-55	105	110	.953	300	119	-1.9	-6.1	-6.6	-.4	-10.5
TOT	655	137	87	11262¹		8.1				11.5	2.73		.248	.319					.959	2149	848					

Runs		Hits		Doubles		Triples		Home Runs		Total Bases	
Collins-Phi	122	Speaker-Bos	193	Speaker-Bos	46	Crawford-Det	26	Baker-Phi	9	Speaker-Bos	287
Speaker-Bos	101	Crawford-Det	183	Lewis-Bos	37	Gardner-Bos	19	Crawford-Det	8	Crawford-Det	281
Murphy-Phi	101	Baker-Phi	182	Pratt-StL	34	Speaker-Bos	18	T.Walker-StL	6	Baker-Phi	252
Bush-Det	97	McInnis-Phi	181	Collins-Chi	34	T.Walker-StL	16	Fournier-Chi	6	Pratt-StL	240
		Collins-Phi	181	Leary-StL	28	Hooper-Bos	15			Collins-Phi	238

Runs Batted In		Runs Produced		Bases On Balls		Batting Average		On Base Percentage		Slugging Average	
Crawford-Det	104	Collins-Phi	205	Bush-Det	112	Cobb-Det	.368	Collins-Phi	.452	Cobb-Det	.513
McInnis-Phi	95	Speaker-Bos	187	Collins-Phi	97	Collins-Phi	.344	Speaker-Bos	.423	Speaker-Bos	.503
Speaker-Bos	90	Crawford-Det	170	Murphy-Phi	87	Speaker-Bos	.338	Jackson-Cle	.399	Crawford-Det	.483
Baker-Phi	89	McInnis-Phi	168	Speaker-Bos	77	Jackson-Cle	.338	Crawford-Det	.388	Jackson-Cle	.464
Collins-Phi	85	Baker-Phi	164	Maisel-NY	76	Baker-Phi	.319	Baker-Phi	.380	Collins-Phi	.452

Production		Adjusted Production		Batter Runs		Adjusted Batter Runs		Clutch Hitting Index		Runs Created	
Speaker-Bos	.926	Collins-Phi	179	Speaker-Bos	54.9	Collins-Phi	56.4	McInnis-Phi	147	Speaker-Bos	124
Collins-Phi	.904	Speaker-Bos	178	Collins-Phi	51.6	Speaker-Bos	54.9	Gandil-Was	138	Collins-Phi	120
Crawford-Det	.871	Crawford-Det	157	Cobb-Det	42.3	Cobb-Det	39.7	Collins-Phi	127	Crawford-Det	113
Jackson-Cle	.862	Baker-Phi	153	Crawford-Det	42.1	Crawford-Det	38.7	Lewis-Bos	125	Baker-Phi	95
Baker-Phi	.822	Jackson-Cle	153	Jackson-Cle	31.6	Baker-Phi	35.0	Crawford-Det	125	Cobb-Det	89

Total Average		Stolen Bases		Stolen Base Average		Stolen Base Runs		Fielding Runs		Total Player Rating	
Collins-Phi	.984	Maisel-NY	74	Maisel-NY	81.3	Maisel-NY	12.0	Bush-Det	33.5	Speaker-Bos	7.6
Speaker-Bos	.943	Collins-Phi	58	Sweeney-NY	76.0	Sweeney-NY	2.1	Speaker-Bos	27.7	Collins-Phi	6.0
Crawford-Det	.867	Speaker-Bos	42	Chapman-Cle	72.7	Kopf-Phi	1.8	Gandil-Was	23.7	Bush-Det	5.0
Jackson-Cle	.835	Shotton-StL	40	Moriarty-Det	69.4	Chapman-Cle	1.8	Boone-NY	22.7	Baker-Phi	4.7
T.Walker-StL	.776			Peckinpaugh-NY	69.1			Turner-Cle	21.3	T.Walker-StL	3.9

Wins		Win Percentage		Games		Complete Games		Shutouts		Saves	
Johnson-Was	28	Bender-Phi	.850	Johnson-Was	51	Johnson-Was	33	Johnson-Was	9	Shaw-Was	4
Coveleski-Det	22	Leonard-Bos	.792	Ayers-Was	49	Coveleski-Det	23	Leonard-Bos	7	Mitchell-StL	4
Collins-Bos	20	Plank-Phi	.682	Shaw-Was	48	Dauss-Det	22	Bender-Phi	7	Faber-Chi	4
Leonard-Bos	19	Shawkey-Phi	.667	Benz-Chi	48	Caldwell-NY	22	Collins-Bos	6	Dauss-Det	4
		Caldwell-NY	.654							Bentley-Was	4

Innings Pitched		Fewest Hits/Game		Fewest BB/Game		Strikeouts		Strikeouts/Game		Ratio	
Johnson-Was	371.2	Leonard-Bos	5.57	McHale-NY	1.55	Johnson-Was	225	Leonard-Bos	7.05	Leonard-Bos	8.29
Coveleski-Det	303.1	Caldwell-NY	6.46	Russell-Chi	1.77	Mitchell-Cle	179	Mitchell-Cle	6.27	Caldwell-NY	8.79
Hamilton-StL	302.1	Shaw-Was	6.93	Johnson-Was	1.79	Leonard-Bos	176	Shaw-Was	5.74	Johnson-Was	9.01
Dauss-Det	302.0	Johnson-Was	6.95	Warhop-NY	1.83	Shaw-Was	164	Johnson-Was	5.45	Foster-Bos	9.48
Weilman-StL	299.0	Foster-Bos	6.97	Ayers-Was	1.83	Dauss-Det	150	Bender-Phi	5.38	Ayers-Was	9.60

Earned Run Average		Adjusted ERA		Opponents' Batting Avg.		Opponents' On Base Pct.		Starter Runs		Adjusted Starter Runs	
Leonard-Bos	.96	Leonard-Bos	279	Leonard-Bos	.180	Leonard-Bos	.246	Leonard-Bos	44.3	Johnson-Was	45.0
Foster-Bos	1.70	Johnson-Was	163	Caldwell-NY	.205	Caldwell-NY	.260	Johnson-Was	41.9	Leonard-Bos	43.0
Johnson-Was	1.72	Foster-Bos	158	Shaw-Was	.216	Johnson-Was	.265	Foster-Bos	24.3	Foster-Bos	23.2
Caldwell-NY	1.94	Caldwell-NY	142	Johnson-Was	.217	Foster-Bos	.274	Weilman-StL	21.8	Weilman-StL	20.7
Cicotte-Chi	2.04	Cicotte-Chi	131	Foster-Bos	.218	Benz-Chi	.282	Cicotte-Chi	20.8	Caldwell-NY	19.2

Clutch Pitching Index		Relief Runs		Adjusted Relief Runs		Relief Ranking		Total Pitcher Index		Total Baseball Ranking	
Hagerman-Cle	126							Johnson-Was	7.3	Speaker-Bos	7.6
Steen-Cle	123							Leonard-Bos	4.6	Johnson-Was	7.2
Shawkey-Phi	109							Cicotte-Chi	2.7	Collins-Phi	6.0
James-StL	106							Foster-Bos	2.6	Bush-Det	5.0
Bender-Phi	106							Caldwell-NY	2.5	Baker-Phi	4.7

TEAM	G	W	L	PCT	GB	R	OR	AB	H	2B	3B	HR	BB	SO	AVG	OBP	SLG	PRO	PRO+	BR	/A	PF	CHI	RC	SB	CS	SBA	SBR
IND	157	88	65	.575		762	622	5176	1474	230	90	33	470	668	.285	.349	.383	.732	86	-36	-103	111	100	765	273			
CHI	157	87	67	.565	1.5	621	517	5098	1314	227	50	52	520	645	.258	.331	.352	.683	87	-125	-95	94	94	634	171			
BAL	160	84	70	.545	4.5	645	628	5120	1374	222	67	32	487	589	.268	.337	.357	.694	82	-105	-122	103	94	652	152			
BUF	155	80	71	.530	7	620	602	5064	1264	177	74	37	430	761	.250	.311	.336	.647	71	-202	-211	102	109	574	228			
BRO	157	77	77	.500	11.5	662	677	5221	1402	225	85	42	404	665	.269	.326	.368	.694	86	-117	-113	99	99	669	220			
KC	154	67	84	.444	20	644	683	5127	1369	226	77	39	399	621	.267	.324	.364	.688	87	-127	-106	96	99	637	171			
PIT	154	64	86	.427	22.5	605	698	5114	1339	180	90	34	410	575	.262	.321	.352	.673	81	-152	-148	99	96	613	153			
STL	154	62	89	.411	25	565	697	5078	1254	193	65	26	503	662	.247	.319	.326	.645	68	-198	-222	105	96	554	113			
TOT	624					5124		40998	10790	1680	598	295	3623	5186	.263	.323	.355	.678						1481				

TEAM	CG	SH	SV	IP	H	H/G	HR	BB	SO	RAT	ERA	ERA+	OAV	OOB	PR	/A	PF	CPI	FA	E	DP	FW	PW	BW	SBW	DIF
IND	104	15	9	1397²	1352	8.7	29	476	664	12.1	3.06	102	.258	.325	-27	9	108	100	.956	289	113	-1.2	.9	-10.7		22.5
CHI	93	17	8	1420¹	1204	7.6	43	393	650	10.3	2.44	109	.233	.291	70	33	92	94	.962	249	114	1.1	3.4	-9.9		15.4
BAL	88	15	13	1392	1389	9.0	34	392	732	11.7	3.13	97	.268	.323	-38	-16	105	101	.960	263	105	.6	-1.7	-12.7		20.8
BUF	89	15	16	1387	1249	8.1	45	505	662	11.7	3.16	94	.245	.318	-42	-31	103	91	.962	242	109	1.3	-3.2	-21.9		28.4
BRO	91	11	9	1385¹	1375	8.9	31	559	636	12.9	3.33	86	.264	.341	-69	-71	100	102	.956	283	120	-.9	-7.4	-11.8		20.0
KC	82	10	12	1361	1387	9.2	37	445	600	12.4	3.41	82	.268	.331	-79	-95	96	98	.957	279	135	-.9	-9.9	-11.0		13.3
PIT	97	9	6	1370	1416	9.3	38	444	510	12.4	3.56	80	.273	.333	-103	-107	99	96	.960	253	92	.6	-11.1	-15.4		14.9
STL	97	9	6	1367²	1418	9.3	38	409	661	12.3	3.59	85	.267	.324	-107	-83	105	89	.957	273	94	-.6	-8.6	-23.1		18.8
TOT	741	101	79	11081		8.8				12.0	3.20		.263	.323					.959	2131	882					

Runs
Kauff-Ind 120
McKechnie-Ind 107
Duncan-Bal 99
Kenworthy-KC 93
Evans-Bro 93

Hits
Kauff-Ind 211
Zwilling-Chi 185
Evans-Bro 179
Oakes-Pit 178
Hanford-Buf 174

Doubles
Kauff-Ind 44
Evans-Bro 41
Kenworthy-KC 40
Zwilling-Chi 38

Triples
Evans-Bro 15
Esmond-Ind 15
Kenworthy-KC 14

Home Runs
Zwilling-Chi 16
Kenworthy-KC 15
Hanford-Buf 12
Evans-Bro 12

Total Bases
Kauff-Ind 305
Zwilling-Chi 287
Kenworthy-KC 286
Evans-Bro 286
Hanford-Buf 264

Runs Batted In
LaPorte-Ind 107
Evans-Bro 96
Zwilling-Chi 95
Kauff-Ind 95
Kenworthy-KC 91

Runs Produced
Kauff-Ind 207
LaPorte-Ind 189
Evans-Bro 177
Zwilling-Chi 170
Kenworthy-KC 169

Bases On Balls
Wickland-Chi 81
Agler-Buf 77
Kauff-Ind 72

Batting Average
Kauff-Ind 370
Evans-Bro 348
Easterly-KC 335
Shaw-Bro 324
Campbell-Ind 318

On Base Percentage
Kauff-Ind 447
Evans-Bro 416
Lennox-Pit 414
Meyer-Bal 395
Wilson-Chi 394

Slugging Average
Evans-Bro 556
Kauff-Ind 534
Kenworthy-KC 525
Lennox-Pit 493
Zwilling-Chi 485

Production
Kauff-Ind 981
Evans-Bro 973
Lennox-Pit 907
Kenworthy-KC 896
Wilson-Chi 860

Adjusted Production
Evans-Bro 152
Kauff-Ind 138
Kenworthy-KC 136
Lennox-Pit 135
Wilson-Chi 130

Batter Runs
Kauff-Ind 47.0
Evans-Bro 37.2
Lennox-Pit 23.2
Kenworthy-KC 21.3
Wilson-Chi 15.3

Adjusted Batter Runs
Evans-Bro 38.0
Kauff-Ind 34.5
Kenworthy-KC 25.0
Lennox-Pit 23.9
Wilson-Chi 19.8

Clutch Hitting Index
LaPorte-Ind 151
Swacina-Bal 137
Wisterzil-Bro 128
Stovall-KC 128
Carr-Ind 127

Runs Created
Kauff-Ind 160
Evans-Bro 121
Kenworthy-KC 114
Zwilling-Chi 106
McKechnie-Ind 94

Total Average
Kauff-Ind 1.278
Evans-Bro 1.087
Lennox-Pit 1.034
Kenworthy-KC 995
Wilson-Chi 939

Stolen Bases
Kauff-Ind 75
McKechnie-Ind 47
Myers-Bro 43
Chadbourne-KC 42

Stolen Base Average

Stolen Base Runs

Fielding Runs
Doolan-Bal 29.3
McKechnie-Ind 22.9
Kenworthy-KC 20.8
Rariden-Ind 20.1
Tinker-Chi 19.1

Total Player Rating
Wilson-Chi 4.6
Kenworthy-KC 4.6
Kauff-Ind 4.4
Evans-Bro 2.9
McKechnie-Ind 1.6

Wins
Hendrix-Chi 29
Quinn-Bal 26
Seaton-Bro 25
Falkenberg-Ind 25
Suggs-Bal 24

Win Percentage
Ford-Buf 778
Hendrix-Chi 744
Quinn-Bal 650
Seaton-Bro 641
Suggs-Bal 632

Games
Hendrix-Chi 49
Falkenberg-Ind 49
Wilhelm-Bal 47
Suggs-Bal 46
Quinn-Bal 46

Complete Games
Hendrix-Chi 34
Falkenberg-Ind 33
Moseley-Ind 29
Quinn-Bal 27

Shutouts
Falkenberg-Ind 9
Seaton-Bro 7
Suggs-Bal 6
Hendrix-Chi 6

Saves
Ford-Buf 6
Wilhelm-Bal 5
Packard-KC 5
Hendrix-Chi 5

Innings Pitched
Falkenberg-Ind . . . 377.1
Hendrix-Chi 362.0
Quinn-Bal 342.2
Suggs-Bal 319.1
Moseley-Ind 316.2

Fewest Hits/Game
Hendrix-Chi 6.51
Ford-Buf 6.91
Krapp-Buf 7.05
Fiske-Chi 7.32
Watson-Chi-StL . . . 7.34

Fewest BB/Game
Ford-Buf 1.49
Suggs-Bal 1.61
Quinn-Bal 1.71
Hendrix-Chi 1.91
Keupper-StL 2.07

Strikeouts
Falkenberg-Ind 236
Moseley-Ind 205
Hendrix-Chi 189
Seaton-Bro 172
Groom-StL 167

Strikeouts/Game
Davenport-StL 5.93
Moseley-Ind 5.83
Falkenberg-Ind 5.63
Groom-StL 5.36
Seaton-Bro 5.11

Ratio
Hendrix-Chi 8.55
Ford-Buf 8.66
Falkenberg-Ind . . . 10.16
Fiske-Chi 10.32
Lange-Chi 10.42

Earned Run Average
Hendrix-Chi 1.69
Ford-Buf 1.82
Watson-Chi-StL . . . 2.01
Falkenberg-Ind . . . 2.22
Lange-Chi 2.23

Adjusted ERA
Ford-Buf 163
Hendrix-Chi 157
Falkenberg-Ind 141
Watson-Chi-StL . . . 137
Lange-Chi 119

Opponents' Batting Avg.
Hendrix-Chi 203
Krapp-Buf 210
Ford-Buf 214
Lange-Chi 224
Watson-Chi-StL 230

Opponents' On Base Pct.
Hendrix-Chi 251
Ford-Buf 254
Lange-Chi 282
Falkenberg-Ind 284
Anderson-Buf 297

Starter Runs
Hendrix-Chi 48.0
Ford-Buf 29.3
Falkenberg-Ind 27.9
Watson-Chi-StL . . . 22.1
Cullop-KC 17.8

Adjusted Starter Runs
Hendrix-Chi 38.7
Falkenberg-Ind 37.7
Ford-Buf 31.3
Watson-Chi-StL . . . 18.6
Quinn-Bal 16.4

Clutch Pitching Index
Mullin-Ind 128
Lafitte-Bro 122
Watson-Chi-StL . . . 114
Kaiserling-Ind 109
Quinn-Bal 106

Relief Runs

Adjusted Relief Runs

Relief Ranking

Total Pitcher Index
Hendrix-Chi 5.4
Falkenberg-Ind 3.8
Ford-Buf 3.1
Quinn-Bal 2.7
Krapp-Buf 1.8

Total Baseball Ranking
Hendrix-Chi 5.4
Wilson-Chi 4.6
Kenworthy-KC 4.6
Kauff-Ind 4.4
Falkenberg-Ind 3.8

TEAM	G	W	L	PCT	GB	R	OR	AB	H	2B	3B	HR	BB	SO	AVG	OBP	SLG	PRO	PRO+	BR	/A	PF	CHI	RC	SB	CS	SBA	SBR
PHI	153	90	62	.592		589	463	4916	1216	202	39	58	460	600	.247	.316	.340	.656	104	31	25	101	101	550	121	113	52	-32
BOS	157	83	69	.546	7	582	545	5070	1219	231	57	17	549	620	.240	.321	.319	.640	105	15	42	96	98	554	121	98	55	-23
BRO	154	80	72	.526	10	536	560	5120	1268	165	75	14	313	496	.248	.295	.317	.612	89	-56	-65	102	107	496	131	126	51	-36
CHI	156	73	80	.477	17.5	570	620	5114	1246	212	66	53	393	639	.244	.303	.342	.645	102	4	3	100	100	555	166	124	57	-25
PIT	156	73	81	.474	18	557	520	5113	1259	197	91	24	419	656	.246	.309	.334	.643	102	8	16	99	97	563	182	111	62	-12
STL	157	72	81	.471	18.5	590	601	5106	1297	159	92	20	457	658	.254	.320	.333	.653	104	30	29	100	98	568	162	144	53	-38
CIN	160	71	83	.461	20	516	585	5231	1323	194	84	15	360	512	.253	.308	.331	.639	98	-5	-15	102	91	553	156	142	53	-38
NY	155	69	83	.454	21	582	628	5218	1312	195	68	24	315	547	.251	.300	.329	.629	103	-27	4	94	109	526	155	137	53	-36
TOT	624					4522		40888	10140	1555	572	225	3266	4728	.248	.309	.331	.640							1194	995	55	-239

TEAM	CG	SH	SV	IP	H	H/G	HR	BB	SO	RAT	ERA	ERA+	OAV	OOB	PR	/A	PF	CPI	FA	E	DP	FW	PW	BW	SBW	DIF
PHI	98	20	8	1374[1]	1161	7.6	26	342	652	10.0	2.17	126	.234	.288	87	85	100	103	.966	216	99	.8	9.4	2.8	-.2	1.2
BOS	95	17	13	1405[2]	1257	8.0	23	366	630	10.7	2.57	100	.246	.302	27	1	94	100	.966	213	115	1.4	.1	4.7	.8	.0
BRO	87	16	8	1389[2]	1252	8.1	29	473	499	11.6	2.66	104	.245	.318	14	17	101	108	.963	238	96	-.5	1.9	-7.2	-.7	10.6
CHI	71	18	8	1399	1272	8.2	28	480	657	11.6	3.11	89	.247	.316	-57	-54	101	91	.958	268	94	-2.3	-6.0	.3	.5	4.0
PIT	91	18	11	1380	1229	8.0	21	384	544	10.8	2.60	105	.246	.304	23	19	99	100	.966	214	100	1.2	2.1	1.8	2.0	-11.1
STL	79	13	9	1400[2]	1320	8.5	30	402	538	11.3	2.89	96	.256	.314	-22	-17	101	101	.964	235	109	-.0	-1.9	3.2	-.9	-4.9
CIN	80	19	12	1432[1]	1304	8.2	28	497	572	11.6	2.84	101	.250	.321	-15	2	104	104	.966	222	148	1.1	.2	-1.7	-.9	-4.8
NY	78	15	9	1385	1350	8.8	40	325	637	11.2	3.11	82	.260	.308	-57	-86	93	94	.960	256	119	-1.6	-9.6	.4	-.7	4.4
TOT	679	136	78	11166[2]		8.2				11.1	2.75		.248	.309					.964	1862	880					

Runs
Cravath-Phi 89
Doyle-NY 86
Bancroft-Phi 85
Burns-NY 83
O'Mara-Bro 77

Hits
Doyle-NY 189
Griffith-Cin 179
Hinchman-Pit 177
Groh-Cin 170
Burns-NY 169

Doubles
Doyle-NY 40
Luderus-Phi 36
Saier-Chi 35
Smith-Bos 34
Magee-Bos 34

Triples
Long-StL 25
H.Wagner-Pit 17
Griffith-Cin 16
Hinchman-Pit 14
Burns-NY 14

Home Runs
Cravath-Phi 24
Williams-Chi 13
Schulte-Chi 12
Saier-Chi 11
Becker-Phi 11

Total Bases
Cravath-Phi 266
Doyle-NY 261
Griffith-Cin 254
Hinchman-Pit 253
H.Wagner-Pit 239

Runs Batted In
Cravath-Phi 115
Magee-Bos 87
Griffith-Cin 85
H.Wagner-Pit 78
Hinchman-Pit 77

Runs Produced
Cravath-Phi 180
Magee-Bos 157
Doyle-NY 152
Hinchman-Pit 144
Miller-StL 143

Bases On Balls
Cravath-Phi 86
Bancroft-Phi 77
Viox-Pit 75
Huggins-StL 74
Smith-Bos 67

Batting Average
Doyle-NY 320
Luderus-Phi 315
Griffith-Cin 307
Hinchman-Pit 307
Daubert-Bro 301

On Base Percentage
Cravath-Phi 393
Luderus-Phi 376
Daubert-Bro 369
Hinchman-Pit 368
Doyle-NY 358

Slugging Average
Cravath-Phi 510
Luderus-Phi 457
Long-StL 446
Saier-Chi 445
Doyle-NY 442

Production
Cravath-Phi 902
Luderus-Phi 833
Hinchman-Pit 807
Doyle-NY 799
Saier-Chi 795

Adjusted Production
Cravath-Phi 170
Doyle-NY 150
Luderus-Phi 150
Hinchman-Pit 146
Saier-Chi 140

Batter Runs
Cravath-Phi 46.8
Luderus-Phi 30.3
Hinchman-Pit 29.7
Doyle-NY 27.1
Griffith-Cin 25.4

Adjusted Batter Runs
Cravath-Phi 45.6
Doyle-NY 32.5
Hinchman-Pit 31.0
Luderus-Phi 29.3
Griffith-Cin 23.8

Clutch Hitting Index
Fletcher-NY 134
Magee-Bos 131
Miller-StL 128
Schmidt-Bos 125
Cutshaw-Bro 123

Runs Created
Cravath-Phi 105
Doyle-NY 94
Hinchman-Pit 94
Luderus-Phi 87
Griffith-Cin 85

Total Average
Cravath-Phi 942
Saier-Chi 819
Luderus-Phi 799
Hinchman-Pit 741
Doyle-NY 714

Stolen Bases
Carey-Pit 36
Herzog-Cin 35
Saier-Chi 29
Baird-Pit 29
Cutshaw-Bro 28

Stolen Base Average
Bresnahan-Chi 86.4
Saier-Chi 76.3
Baird-Pit 70.7
Robertson-NY 68.8
Herzog-Cin 68.6

Stolen Base Runs
Bresnahan-Chi 3.9
Saier-Chi 3.3
Costello-Pit 1.5
Baird-Pit 1.5
Gerber-Pit 1.2

Fielding Runs
Fletcher-NY 34.1
Herzog-Cin 30.9
Maranville-Bos . . . 20.9
Cutshaw-Bro 16.8
Magee-Bos 15.4

Total Player Rating
Cravath-Phi 4.9
Herzog-Cin 4.2
Luderus-Phi 3.8
Snyder-StL 3.1
Fletcher-NY 3.1

Wins
Alexander-Phi 31
Rudolph-Bos 22
Mayer-Phi 21
Mamaux-Pit 21
Vaughn-Chi 20

Win Percentage
Alexander-Phi 756
Toney-Cin 739
Mamaux-Pit 724
Vaughn-Chi 625
Coombs-Bro 600

Games
Hughes-Bos 50
Dale-Cin 49
Alexander-Phi 49
Schneider-Cin 48
Sallee-StL 46

Complete Games
Alexander-Phi 36
Rudolph-Bos 30
Pfeffer-Bro 26
Harmon-Pit 25
Tesreau-NY 24

Shutouts
Alexander-Phi 12
Tesreau-NY 8
Mamaux-Pit 8
Toney-Cin 6
Pfeffer-Bro 6

Saves
Hughes-Bos 9
Benton-Cin-NY 5
Lavender-Chi 4
Cooper-Pit 4

Innings Pitched
Alexander-Phi 376.1
Rudolph-Bos 341.1
Tesreau-NY 306.0
Dale-Cin 296.2
Pfeffer-Bro 291.2

Fewest Hits/Game
Alexander-Phi 6.05
Toney-Cin 6.47
Mamaux-Pit 6.51
Hughes-Bos 6.68
Zabel-Chi 6.85

Fewest BB/Game
Mathewson-NY 97
Humphries-Chi 1.21
Adams-Pit 1.25
Alexander-Phi 1.53
Rudolph-Bos 1.69

Strikeouts
Alexander-Phi 241
Tesreau-NY 176
Hughes-Bos 171
Mamaux-Pit 152
Vaughn-Chi 148

Strikeouts/Game
Alexander-Phi 5.76
Hughes-Bos 5.49
Mamaux-Pit 5.44
Douglas-Cin-Br-Chi . 5.26
Tesreau-NY 5.18

Ratio
Alexander-Phi 7.82
Hughes-Bos 8.89
Tesreau-NY 9.26
Toney-Cin 9.54
Adams-Pit 9.73

Earned Run Average
Alexander-Phi 1.22
Toney-Cin 1.58
Mamaux-Pit 2.04
Pfeffer-Bro 2.10
Hughes-Bos 2.12

Adjusted ERA
Alexander-Phi 224
Toney-Cin 181
Mamaux-Pit 134
Pfeffer-Bro 132
Hughes-Bos 122

Opponents' Batting Avg.
Alexander-Phi 191
Toney-Cin 207
Mamaux-Pit 208
Hughes-Bos 213
Tesreau-NY 215

Opponents' On Base Pct.
Alexander-Phi 234
Hughes-Bos 265
Tesreau-NY 269
Toney-Cin 278
Adams-Pit 280

Starter Runs
Alexander-Phi 63.8
Toney-Cin 28.9
Pfeffer-Bro 21.0
Mamaux-Pit 19.8
Hughes-Bos 19.5

Adjusted Starter Runs
Alexander-Phi 63.4
Toney-Cin 31.6
Pfeffer-Bro 21.9
Mamaux-Pit 19.2
Hughes-Bos 14.5

Clutch Pitching Index
Humphries-Chi 139
Perritt-NY 122
Schneider-Cin 121
Rixey-Phi 120
Stroud-NY 118

Relief Runs

Adjusted Relief Runs

Relief Ranking

Total Pitcher Index
Alexander-Phi 8.6
Toney-Cin 3.1
Pfeffer-Bro 2.6
Mayer-Phi 2.2
Schneider-Cin 2.0

Total Baseball Ranking
Alexander-Phi 8.6
Cravath-Phi 4.9
Herzog-Cin 4.2
Luderus-Phi 3.8
Snyder-StL 3.1

TEAM	G	W	L	PCT	GB	R	OR	AB	H	2B	3B	HR	BB	SO	AVG	OBP	SLG	PRO	PRO+	BR	/A	PF	CHI	RC	SB	CS	SBA	SBR
BOS	155	101	50	.669		669	499	5024	1308	202	76	14	527	**476**	.260	.336	.339	.675	110	46	67	97	100	611	118	117	50	-35
DET	156	100	54	.649	2.5	**778**	597	5128	**1372**	**207**	94	23	**681**	527	**.268**	**.357**	**.358**	**.715**	**114**	**131**	**93**	105	101	**711**	**241**	146	62	-15
CHI	155	93	61	.604	9.5	717	509	4914	1269	163	**102**	25	583	575	.258	.345	.348	.693	110	83	62	103	102	637	233	**183**	56	-40
WAS	155	85	68	.556	17	569	**491**	5029	1225	152	79	12	458	541	.244	.312	.312	.624	99	-52	-63	102	**103**	535	186	106	**64**	**-8**
NY	154	69	83	.454	32.5	584	588	4982	1162	167	50	**31**	570	669	.233	.317	.305	.622	91	-46	-45	100	**103**	523	198	133	60	-20
STL	159	63	91	.409	39.5	521	680	5112	1255	166	65	19	472	765	.246	.315	.315	.630	98	-44	-22	96	91	535	202	160	56	-35
CLE	154	57	95	.375	44.5	539	670	5034	1210	169	79	20	490	681	.240	.312	.317	.629	91	-43	-54	102	95	526	138	117	54	-29
PHI	154	43	109	.283	58.5	545	888	5081	1204	183	72	16	436	634	.237	.304	.311	.615	92	-74	-56	97	**103**	507	127	89	59	-15
TOT	621					4922		40304	10005	1409	617	160	4217	4868	.248	.325	.326	.651							1443	1051	58	-198

TEAM	CG	SH	SV	IP	H	H/G	HR	BB	SO	RAT	ERA	ERA+	OAV	OOB	PR	/A	PF	CPI	FA	E	DP	FW	PW	BW	SBW	DIF
BOS	81	19	15	1397	1164	**7.5**	18	446	634	10.7	2.39	116	**.231**	.300	84	59	95	97	.964	226	95	2.5	6.3	7.1	-1.1	10.8
DET	86	10	**19**	1413¹	1259	8.0	14	492	550	11.5	2.86	106	.243	.316	11	25	103	94	.965	258	107	.5	2.7	**9.9**	1.0	9.0
CHI	91	16	9	1401	1242	8.0	14	**350**	635	10.4	2.43	122	.241	**.294**	78	84	101	95	.965	222	95	2.7	8.9	6.6	-1.6	-.6
WAS	87	**21**	13	1393²	**1161**	**7.5**	**12**	455	**715**	10.7	**2.31**	**129**	.232	.302	97	**102**	101	102	.964	230	101	2.2	**10.8**	-6.7	**1.8**	.4
NY	**101**	12	2	1382²	1272	8.3	41	517	559	12.0	3.06	96	.254	.329	-20	-20	100	**104**	**.966**	217	118	**2.9**	-2.1	-4.8	.5	-3.5
STL	76	6	7	1403	1256	8.1	21	612	566	12.4	3.04	94	.249	.338	-17	-31	98	103	.949	336	**144**	-4.3	-3.3	-2.3	-1.1	-3.0
CLE	62	11	10	1372	1287	8.4	18	518	610	12.0	3.13	91	.256	.329	-30	-13	104	98	.957	280	82	-1.2	-1.4	-5.7	-.5	-10.2
PHI	78	6	2	1348¹	1358	9.1	22	827	588	15.0	4.29	68	.278	.388	-204	-206	100	102	.947	338	118	-5.0	-21.9	-5.9	1.0	-1.2
TOT	662	101	77	11111		8.1				11.8	2.93		.248	.325					.959	2107	860					

Runs
Cobb-Det 144
E.Collins-Chi 118
Vitt-Det 116
Speaker-Bos 108
Chapman-Cle 101

Hits
Cobb-Det 208
Crawford-Det 183
Veach-Det 178
Speaker-Bos 176
Pratt-StL 175

Doubles
Veach-Det 40
Pratt-StL 31
Lewis-Bos 31
Crawford-Det 31
Cobb-Det 31

Triples
Crawford-Det 19
Fournier-Chi 18
Roth-Chi-Cle 17
S.Collins-Chi 17
Chapman-Cle 17

Home Runs
Roth-Chi-Cle 7
Oldring-Phi 6

Total Bases
Cobb-Det 274
Crawford-Det 264
Veach-Det 247
Pratt-StL 237
E.Collins-Chi 227

Runs Batted In
Veach-Det 112
Crawford-Det 112
Cobb-Det 99
S.Collins-Chi 85
J.Jackson-Cle-Chi . . 81

Runs Produced
Cobb-Det 240
E.Collins-Chi 191
Veach-Det 190
Crawford-Det 189
Speaker-Bos 177

Bases On Balls
E.Collins-Chi 119
Shotton-StL 118
Cobb-Det 118
Bush-Det 118
Hooper-Bos 89

Batting Average
Cobb-Det 369
E.Collins-Chi 332
Fournier-Chi 322
Speaker-Bos 322
McInnis-Phi 314

On Base Percentage
Cobb-Det 486
E.Collins-Chi 460
Fournier-Chi 429
Speaker-Bos 416
Shotton-StL 409

Slugging Average
Fournier-Chi 491
Cobb-Det 487
Kavanagh-Det 452
J.Jackson-Cle-Chi . . .445
Roth-Chi-Cle 438

Production
Cobb-Det 973
Fournier-Chi 920
E.Collins-Chi 896
J.Jackson-Cle-Chi . . .830
Speaker-Bos 827

Adjusted Production
Cobb-Det 182
Fournier-Chi 170
E.Collins-Chi 163
Speaker-Bos 152
J.Jackson-Cle-Chi . . 145

Batter Runs
Cobb-Det 71.6
E.Collins-Chi 51.9
Fournier-Chi 40.9
Speaker-Bos 35.0
Veach-Det 32.3

Adjusted Batter Runs
Cobb-Det 64.5
E.Collins-Chi 48.2
Speaker-Bos 38.3
Fournier-Chi 38.1
Shotton-StL 31.2

Clutch Hitting Index
Crawford-Det 138
Veach-Det 135
Schalk-Chi 128
Gardner-Bos 123
S.Collins-Chi 120

Runs Created
Cobb-Det 155
E.Collins-Chi 116
Crawford-Det 101
Speaker-Bos 97
Veach-Det 97

Total Average
Cobb-Det 1.170
E.Collins-Chi 971
Fournier-Chi 964
Speaker-Bos 801
Veach-Det 771

Stolen Bases
Cobb-Det 96
Maisel-NY 51
E.Collins-Chi 46
Shotton-StL 43
C.Milan-Was 40

Stolen Base Average
Schang-Phi 85.7
Maisel-NY 81.0
Foster-Was 76.9
Moeller-Was 76.2
Roth-Chi-Cle 72.2

Stolen Base Runs
Maisel-NY 8.1
Cobb-Det 6.0
Schang-Phi 3.6
Moeller-Was 3.6
Williams-StL 2.7

Fielding Runs
Boone-NY 20.8
T.Walker-StL 14.8
Vitt-Det 14.4
Lajoie-Phi 14.1
Speaker-Bos 13.4

Total Player Rating
Cobb-Det 6.2
E.Collins-Chi 6.1
Speaker-Bos 4.0
Fournier-Chi 3.5
Chapman-Cle 3.5

Wins
Johnson-Was 27
Scott-Chi 24
Faber-Chi 24
Dauss-Det 24
Coveleski-Det 22

Win Percentage
Wood-Bos 750
Shore-Bos 704
Foster-Bos 704
Ruth-Bos 692
Scott-Chi 686

Games
Faber-Chi 50
Coveleski-Det 50
Scott-Chi 48
Jones-Cle 48

Complete Games
Johnson-Was 35
Caldwell-NY 31
Dauss-Det 27
Scott-Chi 23
Dubuc-Det 22

Shutouts
Scott-Chi 7
Johnson-Was 7
Morton-Cle 6
Foster-Bos 5
Dubuc-Det 5

Saves
Mays-Bos 7

Innings Pitched
Johnson-Was 336.2
Coveleski-Det 312.2
Dauss-Det 309.2
Caldwell-NY 305.0
Faber-Chi 299.2

Fewest Hits/Game
Leonard-Bos 6.38
Ruth-Bos 6.86
Wood-Bos 6.86
Johnson-Was 6.90
Morton-Cle 7.09

Fewest BB/Game
Johnson-Was 1.50
Ayers-Was 1.62
Benz-Chi 1.62
Russell-Chi 1.84
Cicotte-Chi 1.93

Strikeouts
Johnson-Was 203
Faber-Chi 182
Wyckoff-Phi 157
Coveleski-Det 150
Mitchell-Cle 149

Strikeouts/Game
Leonard-Bos 5.69
Mitchell-Cle 5.68
Faber-Chi 5.47
Johnson-Was 5.43
Lowdermilk-StL-Det . . 5.32

Ratio
Johnson-Was 8.90
Morton-Cle 9.41
Wood-Bos 9.44
Ayers-Was 9.50
Benz-Chi 9.63

Earned Run Average
Wood-Bos 1.49
Johnson-Was 1.55
Shore-Bos 1.64
Scott-Chi 2.03
Fisher-NY 2.11

Adjusted ERA
Johnson-Was 191
Wood-Bos 186
Shore-Bos 169
Scott-Chi 146
Morton-Cle 142

Opponents' Batting Avg.
Leonard-Bos 208
Ruth-Bos 212
Johnson-Was 214
Morton-Cle 216
Wood-Bos 216

Opponents' On Base Pct.
Johnson-Was 260
Morton-Cle 268
Wood-Bos 275
Benz-Chi 276
Ayers-Was 276

Starter Runs
Johnson-Was 51.7
Shore-Bos 35.5
Scott-Chi 29.5
Wood-Bos 25.2
Foster-Bos 23.2

Adjusted Starter Runs
Johnson-Was 52.9
Shore-Bos 31.1
Scott-Chi 30.9
Morton-Cle 24.1
Benz-Chi 22.7

Clutch Pitching Index
Hamilton-StL 125
Shore-Bos 122
Foster-Bos 121
Fisher-NY 119
Wood-Bos 118

Relief Runs

Adjusted Relief Runs

Relief Ranking

Total Pitcher Index
Johnson-Was 7.7
Wood-Bos 3.6
Shore-Bos 3.5
Scott-Chi 3.4
Dauss-Det 3.2

Total Baseball Ranking
Johnson-Was 7.6
Cobb-Det 6.2
E.Collins-Chi 6.1
Speaker-Bos 4.0
Wood-Bos 3.6

TEAM	G	W	L	PCT	GB	R	OR	AB	H	2B	3B	HR	BB	SO	AVG	OBP	SLG	PRO	PRO+	BR	/A	PF	CHI	RC	SB	CS	SBA	SBR
CHI	155	86	66	.566		640	538	5133	1320	185	77	50	444	590	.257	.320	.352	.672	90	-110	-81	94	102	650	161			
STL	159	87	67	.565		634	527	5145	1344	199	81	23	576	502	.261	.340	.345	.685	85	-71	-100	105	92	698	195			
PIT	156	86	67	.562	0.5	592	524	5040	1318	180	80	20	448	561	.262	.326	.341	.667	85	-110	-106	99	95	655	224			
KC	153	81	72	.529	5.5	547	551	4937	1206	200	66	28	368	503	.244	.303	.329	.632	77	-182	-166	96	103	559	144			
NEW	155	80	72	.526	6	585	562	5097	1283	210	80	17	438	550	.252	.315	.334	.649	84	-148	-122	94	99	618	184			
BUF	153	74	78	.487	12	574	634	5065	1261	193	68	40	420	587	.249	.309	.338	.647	76	-158	-167	102	102	594	184			
BRO	153	70	82	.461	16	647	673	5035	1348	205	75	36	473	654	.268	.336	.360	.696	93	-56	-52	99	97	704	249			
BAL	154	47	107	.305	40	550	760	5060	1235	196	53	36	470	641	.244	.313	.325	.638	74	-167	-180	103	97	578	128			
TOT	619					4769		40512	10315	1568	580	250	3637	4588	.255	.316	.340	.656						1469				

TEAM	CG	SH	SV	IP	H	H/G	HR	BB	SO	RAT	ERA	ERA+	OAV	OOB	PR	/A	PF	CPI	FA	E	DP	FW	PW	BW	SBW	DIF
CHI	97	21	10	1397²	1232	7.9	33	402	576	10.7	2.64	95	.240	.299	14	-21	92	95	.964	233	102	.4	-2.3	-8.7		20.6
STL	94	24	9	1426	1267	8.0	22	396	698	10.7	2.73	105	.243	.300	-1	22	105	92	.967	212	111	2.0	2.4	-10.8		16.4
PIT	88	16	12	1382¹	1273	8.3	37	441	517	11.4	2.79	97	.253	.317	-10	-13	99	107	.971	182	98	3.5	-1.4	-11.4		18.8
KC	95	16	11	1359	1210	8.0	29	390	526	11.6	2.82	93	.242	.301	-14	-30	96	91	.962	246	96	-.5	-3.2	-17.9		26.1
NEW	100	16	7	1406²	1308	8.4	15	453	581	11.6	2.60	98	.253	.319	19	-7	94	111	.963	239	124	.0	-.8	-13.1		17.8
BUF	79	14	11	1360	1271	8.4	35	553	594	12.3	3.38	83	.254	.331	-99	-88	103	95	.964	232	112	.3	-9.5	-18.0		25.2
BRO	78	10	16	1355²	1299	8.6	27	536	467	12.3	3.37	81	.258	.332	-96	-98	100	97	.955	290	103	-3.1	-10.5	-5.6		13.3
BAL	85	5	7	1360¹	1455	9.6	52	466	570	13.0	3.96	72	.284	.349	-186	-165	105	100	.957	273	140	-2.0	-17.8	-19.4		9.2
TOT	716	122	83	11047²		8.4				11.6	3.03		.255	.316					.963	1907	886					

Runs
Borton-StL 97
Berghammer-Pit 96
Evans-Bro-Bal 94
Tobin-StL 92
Kauff-Bro 92

Hits
Tobin-StL 184
Konetchy-Pit 181
Evans-Bro-Bal 171
Kauff-Bro 165
Chase-Buf 165

Doubles
Evans-Bro-Bal 34
Zwilling-Chi 32
Konetchy-Pit 31
Chase-Buf 31

Triples
Mann-Chi 19
Konetchy-Pit 18
Kelly-Pit 17
Gilmore-KC 15

Home Runs
Chase-Buf 17
Zwilling-Chi 13
Kauff-Bro 12
Konetchy-Pit 10
Walsh-Bal-StL 9

Total Bases
Konetchy-Pit 278
Chase-Buf 267
Tobin-StL 254
Kauff-Bro 246
Zwilling-Chi 242

Runs Batted In
Zwilling-Chi 94
Konetchy-Pit 93
Chase-Buf 89
Kauff-Bro 83
Borton-StL 83

Runs Produced
Borton-StL 177
Kauff-Bro 163
Konetchy-Pit 162
Evans-Bro-Bal 157
Chase-Buf 157

Bases On Balls
Borton-StL 92
Kauff-Bro 85
Berghammer-Pit 83
W.Miller-StL 79

Batting Average
Kauff-Bro .... .342
Fischer-Chi .... .329
Magee-Bro .... .323
Konetchy-Pit ...... .314
Flack-Chi .... .314

On Base Percentage
Kauff-Bro .... .446
W.Miller-StL .... .400
Borton-StL .... .395
Evans-Bro-Bal .... .392
Cooper-Bro .... .388

Slugging Average
Kauff-Bro .... .509
Konetchy-Pit ...... .483
Chase-Buf .... .471
Fischer-Chi .... .449
Zwilling-Chi .... .442

Production
Kauff-Bro .... .955
Konetchy-Pit ...... .846
Evans-Bro-Bal .... .818
Zwilling-Chi .... .808
Mann-Chi .... .795

Adjusted Production
Kauff-Bro 156
Konetchy-Pit 126
Zwilling-Chi 123
Mann-Chi 119
Flack-Chi 117

Batter Runs
Kauff-Bro 41.3
Konetchy-Pit 17.5
Wilson-Chi 17.5
Evans-Bro-Bal 16.3
Crandall-StL 13.9

Adjusted Batter Runs
Kauff-Bro 42.1
Wilson-Chi 20.7
Konetchy-Pit 18.3
Zwilling-Chi 16.0
Evans-Bro-Bal 15.1

Clutch Hitting Index
Oakes-Pit 152
Engle-Buf 129
F.Smith-Buf-Bro ... 123
Borton-StL 122
Halt-Bro 118

Runs Created
Kauff-Bro 132
Konetchy-Pit 111
Tobin-StL 106
Zwilling-Chi 99
Evans-Bro-Bal 99

Total Average
Kauff-Bro 1.233
Konetchy-Pit ...... .884
Cooper-Bro .... .868
W.Miller-StL .... .863
Zwilling-Chi .... .857

Stolen Bases
Kauff-Bro 55
Mowrey-Pit 40
Kelly-Pit 38
Flack-Chi 37
Magee-Bro 34

Stolen Base Average

Stolen Base Runs

Fielding Runs
Doolan-Bal-Chi 33.0
Rariden-New 23.0
Cooper-Bro 18.3
Johnson-StL 17.7
Perring-KC 14.8

Total Player Rating
Kauff-Bro 5.3
Rariden-New 3.8
Cooper-Bro 2.5
Wilson-Chi 2.1
Zwilling-Chi 1.8

Wins
McConnell-Chi 25
Allen-Pit 23
Davenport-StL 22
Cullop-KC 22

Win Percentage
McConnell-Chi .... .714
Brown-Chi .... .680
Reulbach-New .... .677
Cullop-KC .... .667
Plank-StL .... .656

Games
Davenport-StL 55
Bedient-Buf 53
Crandall-StL 51
Johnson-KC 46

Complete Games
Davenport-StL 30
Hendrix-Chi 26
Schulz-Buf 25
Allen-Pit 24

Shutouts
Davenport-StL 10
Plank-StL 6
Allen-Pit 6

Saves
Bedient-Buf 10
Barger-Pit 6
Wiltse-Bro 5
Upham-Bro 5

Innings Pitched
Davenport-StL ... 392.2
Crandall-StL 312.2
Schulz-Buf 309.2
McConnell-Chi ... 303.0
Cullop-KC 302.1

Fewest Hits/Game
Davenport-StL ... 6.88
Main-KC 7.08
Plank-StL 7.11
Brown-Chi 7.20
Anderson-Buf 7.20

Fewest BB/Game
Plank-StL 1.81
Bender-Bal 1.87
Hearn-Pit 1.90
Cullop-KC 1.99
Quinn-Bal 2.07

Strikeouts
Davenport-StL 229
Schulz-Buf 160
McConnell-Chi 151
Plank-StL 147

Strikeouts/Game
Anderson-Buf 5.33
Davenport-StL 5.25
Plank-StL 4.93
Bailey-Bal-Chi 4.91
Groom-StL 4.78

Ratio
Plank-StL 9.02
Davenport-StL 9.19
Brown-Chi 9.90
Anderson-Buf 10.01
Reulbach-New ... 10.17

Earned Run Average
Moseley-New 1.91
Plank-StL 2.08
Brown-Chi 2.09
McConnell-Chi 2.20
Davenport-StL 2.20

Adjusted ERA
Plank-StL 138
Moseley-New 134
Davenport-StL ... 131
Brown-Chi 120
Reulbach-New 115

Opponents' Batting Avg.
Davenport-StL .... .215
Plank-StL .... .218
Brown-Chi .... .220
Main-KC .... .222
Anderson-Buf ..... .222

Opponents' On Base Pct.
Plank-StL .... .262
Davenport-StL .... .268
Brown-Chi .... .279
Anderson-Buf ..... .285
Reulbach-New .... .287

Starter Runs
Moseley-New 24.2
Davenport-StL 23.0
Plank-StL 19.3
McConnell-Chi 17.8
Brown-Chi 16.6

Adjusted Starter Runs
Davenport-StL 29.5
Plank-StL 23.7
Moseley-New 19.2
Brown-Chi 10.9
McConnell-Chi 10.5

Clutch Pitching Index
Moran-New 129
Kaiserling-New 127
Rogge-Pit 127
Moseley-New 122
Suggs-Bal 117

Relief Runs

Adjusted Relief Runs

Relief Ranking

Total Pitcher Index
Plank-StL 2.9
Crandall-StL 2.6
McConnell-Chi 2.0
Brown-Chi 2.0
Moseley-New 1.3

Total Baseball Ranking
Kauff-Bro 5.3
Rariden-New 3.8
Plank-StL 2.9
Crandall-StL 2.6
Cooper-Bro 2.5

TEAM	G	W	L	PCT	GB	R	OR	AB	H	2B	3B	HR	BB	SO	AVG	OBP	SLG	PRO	PRO+	BR	/A	PF	CHI	RC	SB	CS	SBA	SBR
BRO	156	94	60	.610		585	471	5234	1366	195	80	28	355	550	.261	.313	.345	.658	105	46	30	103	99	645	187			
PHI	154	91	62	.595	2.5	581	489	4985	1244	223	53	42	399	571	.250	.310	.341	.651	102	34	14	104	104	593	149			
BOS	158	89	63	.586	4	542	453	5075	1181	166	73	22	437	646	.233	.299	.307	.606	96	-38	-16	96	108	535	141			
NY	155	86	66	.566	7	597	504	5152	1305	188	74	42	356	558	.253	.307	.343	.650	112	31	61	95	106	617	206			
CHI	156	67	86	.438	26.5	520	541	5179	1237	194	56	46	399	662	.239	.298	.325	.623	88	-18	-74	111	99	559	133			
PIT	157	65	89	.422	29	484	586	5181	1246	147	91	20	372	618	.240	.298	.316	.614	94	-32	-37	101	95	556	173			
STL	153	60	93	.392	33.5	476	629	5030	1223	155	74	25	335	651	.243	.295	.318	.613	95	-35	-32	99	99	535	182			
CIN	155	60	93	.392	33.5	505	617	5254	1336	187	88	14	362	573	.254	.307	.331	.638	105	13	26	98	91	596	157			
TOT	622					4290		41090	10138	1455	589	239	3015	4829	.247	.303	.328	.632						1328				

TEAM	CG	SH	SV	IP	H	H/G	HR	BB	SO	RAT	ERA	ERA+	OAV	OOB	PR	/A	PF	CPI	FA	E	DP	FW	PW	BW	SBW	DIF
BRO	96	22	9	1427¹	1201	7.6	24	372	634	10.2	2.12	126	.232	.289	78	86	102	103	.965	224	90	1.2	9.8	3.4		2.5
PHI	97	25	9	1382¹	1238	8.1	28	295	601	10.3	2.36	112	.244	.292	39	44	101	101	.963	234	119	.4	5.0	1.6		7.5
BOS	97	23	11	1415²	1206	7.7	24	325	644	9.9	2.19	113	.235	.285	66	45	95	99	.967	212	124	2.1	5.1	-1.8		7.5
NY	88	22	12	1397¹	1267	8.2	41	310	638	10.4	2.60	93	.245	.293	2	-28	93	95	.966	217	108	1.5	-3.2	7.0		4.7
CHI	72	17	13	1416²	1265	8.0	32	365	616	10.6	2.65	110	.244	.298	-6	39	111	94	.957	286	104	-2.6	4.5	-8.5		-2.9
PIT	88	11	7	1419²	1277	8.1	24	443	596	11.1	2.76	97	.247	.311	-24	-14	103	97	.959	260	97	-.9	-1.6	-4.2		-5.3
STL	58	13	15	1355	1331	8.8	31	445	529	12.1	3.14	84	.265	.330	-80	-77	101	104	.957	278	124	-2.4	-8.8	-3.7		-1.7
CIN	86	7	6	1408	1356	8.7	35	461	569	11.9	3.10	84	.261	.326	-76	-82	99	102	.965	228	126	.9	-9.4	3.0		-11.0
TOT	682	140	82	11222		8.1				10.8	2.61		.247	.303					.963	1939	892					

Runs
Burns-NY 105
Carey-Pit 90
Robertson-NY 88
Groh-Cin 85
Paskert-Phi 82

Hits
Chase-Cin 184
Robertson-NY 180
Z.Wheat-Bro 177
Hinchman-Pit 175
Burns-NY 174

Doubles
Niehoff-Phi 42
Z.Wheat-Bro 32
Paskert-Phi 30

Triples
Hinchman-Pit 16
Roush-NY-Cin 15
Kauff-NY 15
Hornsby-StL 15

Home Runs
Williams-Chi 12
Robertson-NY 12
Cravath-Phi 11
Z.Wheat-Bro 9
Kauff-NY 9

Total Bases
Z.Wheat-Bro 262
Robertson-NY 250
Chase-Cin 249
Hinchman-Pit 237
Burns-NY 229

Runs Batted In
Zimmerman-Chi-NY .. 83
Chase-Cin 82
Hinchman-Pit 76
Kauff-NY 74
Z.Wheat-Bro 73

Runs Produced
Zimmerman-Chi-NY ... 153
Robertson-NY 145
Chase-Cin 144
Konetchy-Bos 143
Burns-NY 141

Bases On Balls
Groh-Cin 84
Saier-Chi 79
Bancroft-Phi 74
Kauff-NY 68
Cravath-Phi 64

Batting Average
Chase-Cin .... .339
Daubert-Bro ...... .316
Hinchman-Pit .... .315
Hornsby-StL ...... .313
Z.Wheat-Bro ..... .312

On Base Percentage
Cravath-Phi ...... .379
Hinchman-Pit .... .378
Williams-Chi ..... .372
Daubert-Bro ...... .371
Groh-Cin .... .370

Slugging Average
Z.Wheat-Bro ...... .461
Chase-Cin .... .459
Williams-Chi ..... .459
Hornsby-StL ...... .444
Cravath-Phi ...... .440

Production
Williams-Chi ...... .831
Z.Wheat-Bro ...... .828
Chase-Cin .... .822
Cravath-Phi ...... .819
Hornsby-StL ...... .814

Adjusted Production
Chase-Cin 155
Hornsby-StL 150
Z.Wheat-Bro 149
Cravath-Phi 146
Hinchman-Pit 146

Batter Runs
Z.Wheat-Bro 34.5
Hinchman-Pit 31.1
Chase-Cin 30.2
Cravath-Phi 28.7
Hornsby-StL 28.2

Adjusted Batter Runs
Chase-Cin 32.2
Z.Wheat-Bro 32.0
Hinchman-Pit 30.3
Hornsby-StL 28.7
Cravath-Phi 25.9

Clutch Hitting Index
Mowrey-Bro 145
Zimmerman-Chi-NY .. 134
Magee-Bos 133
Smith-Bos 121
Fletcher-NY 119

Runs Created
Z.Wheat-Bro 103
Hinchman-Pit 96
Chase-Cin 93
Hornsby-StL 88
Carey-Pit 87

Total Average
Williams-Chi ...... .863
Cravath-Phi ...... .857
Z.Wheat-Bro ...... .844
Hornsby-StL ...... .826
Hinchman-Pit ..... .797

Stolen Bases
Carey-Pit 63
Kauff-NY 40
Bescher-StL 39
Burns-NY 37
Herzog-Cin-NY 34

Stolen Base Average
Carey-Pit 76.8
Bescher-StL 76.5
Daubert-Bro 75.0
Maranville-Bos ... 68.1
Chase-Cin 66.7

Stolen Base Runs
Carey-Pit 7.5
Bescher-StL 4.5
Daubert-Bro 2.1
Maranville-Bos 6

Fielding Runs
Carey-Pit 29.9
Betzel-StL 28.4
Bancroft-Phi 24.5
Maranville-Bos ... 21.5
Doyle-NY-Chi 20.0

Total Player Rating
Groh-Cin 5.4
Carey-Pit 4.7
Fletcher-NY 4.3
Doyle-NY-Chi 4.2
Z.Wheat-Bro 3.8

Wins
Alexander-Phi 33
Pfeffer-Bro 25
Rixey-Phi 22
Mamaux-Pit 21

Win Percentage
Hughes-Bos ...... .842
Alexander-Phi .... .733
Pfeffer-Bro ...... .694
Rixey-Phi .... .688
Benton-NY .... .667

Games
Meadows-StL 51
Alexander-Phi 48
Mamaux-Pit 45
Ames-StL 45

Complete Games
Alexander-Phi 38
Pfeffer-Bro 30
Rudolph-Bos 27
Mamaux-Pit 26
Demaree-Phi 25

Shutouts
Alexander-Phi 16
Tyler-Bos 6
Pfeffer-Bro 6

Saves
Ames-StL 8
Packard-Chi 5
Marquard-Bro 5
Hughes-Bos 5

Innings Pitched
Alexander-Phi ... 389.0
Pfeffer-Bro 328.2
Rudolph-Bos ... 312.0
Mamaux-Pit 310.0
Toney-Cin 300.0

Fewest Hits/Game
Cheney-Bro 6.33
Hughes-Bos 6.76
Cooper-Pit 6.91
Miller-Pit 7.02
Ragan-Bos 7.07

Fewest BB/Game
Rudolph-Bos 1.10
Alexander-Phi ... 1.16
Demaree-Phi 1.52
Sallee-StL-NY ... 1.63
Marquard-Bro ... 1.67

Strikeouts
Alexander-Phi 167
Cheney-Bro 166
Mamaux-Pit 163
Toney-Cin 146
Vaughn-Chi 144

Strikeouts/Game
Cheney-Bro 5.91
Hughes-Bos 5.42
Hendrix-Chi 4.83
Mamaux-Pit 4.73
Marquard-Bro ... 4.70

Ratio
Rudolph-Bos 8.86
Alexander-Phi ... 8.86
Marquard-Bro ... 9.09
McConnell-Chi ... 9.30
Ragan-Bos 9.40

Earned Run Average
Alexander-Phi 1.55
Marquard-Bro ... 1.58
Rixey-Phi 1.85
Cooper-Pit 1.87
Pfeffer-Bro 1.92

Adjusted ERA
Alexander-Phi 171
Marquard-Bro ... 169
Cooper-Pit 144
Rixey-Phi 143
Pfeffer-Bro 140

Opponents' Batting Avg.
Cheney-Bro ...... .198
Cooper-Pit ...... .215
Hughes-Bos ..... .215
Ragan-Bos ...... .218
McConnell-Chi ... .223

Opponents' On Base Pct.
Rudolph-Bos .... .261
Alexander-Phi ... .262
Marquard-Bro ... .267
Ragan-Bos ...... .270
McConnell-Chi ... .271

Starter Runs
Alexander-Phi ... 45.9
Schupp-NY 26.7
Pfeffer-Bro 25.4
Rixey-Phi 24.3
Marquard-Bro ... 23.5

Adjusted Starter Runs
Alexander-Phi ... 47.4
Pfeffer-Bro 27.7
Rixey-Phi 25.4
Marquard-Bro ... 24.9
Schupp-NY 23.8

Clutch Pitching Index
Dell-Bro 124
Sallee-StL-NY 117
Meadows-StL 116
Schulz-Cin 114
Alexander-Phi 114

Relief Runs

Adjusted Relief Runs

Relief Ranking

Total Pitcher Index
Alexander-Phi 7.3
Pfeffer-Bro 3.6
Rixey-Phi 3.2
Tyler-Bos 2.5
Cheney-Bro 2.3

Total Baseball Ranking
Alexander-Phi 7.3
Groh-Cin 5.4
Carey-Pit 4.7
Fletcher-NY 4.3
Doyle-NY-Chi 4.2

TEAM	G	W	L	PCT	GB	R	OR	AB	H	2B	3B	HR	BB	SO	AVG	OBP	SLG	PRO	PRO+	BR	/A	PF	CHI	RC	SB	CS	SBA	SBR
BOS	156	91	63	.591		550	480	5018	1246	197	56	14	464	482	.248	.317	.318	.635	97	-20	-22	100	101	580	129			
CHI	155	89	65	.578	2	601	497	5081	1277	194	100	17	545	591	.251	.319	.339	.658	103	18	12	101	102	638	197			
DET	155	87	67	.565	4	670	595	5193	1371	202	96	17	545	529	.264	.337	.350	.687	109	78	55	104	101	700	190			
NY	156	80	74	.519	11	577	561	5198	1277	194	59	35	516	632	.246	.318	.326	.644	98	-4	-16	102	100	613	179			
STL	158	79	75	.513	12	588	545	5159	1262	181	50	14	627	640	.245	.331	.307	.638	103	2	30	95	99	620	234			
CLE	157	77	77	.500	14	630	602	5064	1264	233	66	16	522	605	.250	.324	.331	.655	97	17	-18	106	106	625	160			
WAS	159	76	77	.497	14.5	536	543	5114	1238	170	60	12	535	597	.242	.320	.306	.626	95	-30	-25	99	98	579	185			
PHI	154	36	117	.235	54.5	447	776	5010	1212	169	65	19	406	631	.242	.303	.313	.616	96	-61	-38	95	91	538	151			
TOT	625					4599		40837	10147	1540	552	144	4062	4707	.248	.321	.324	.645						1425				

TEAM	CG	SH	SV	IP	H	H/G	HR	BB	SO	RAT	ERA	ERA+	OAV	OOB	PR	/A	PF	CPI	FA	E	DP	FW	PW	BW	SBW	DIF
BOS	76	24	16	1410²	1221	7.8	10	463	584	11.0	2.48	112	.239	.307	55	44	98	99	.972	183	108	3.0	4.9	-2.4		8.5
CHI	73	20	15	1412¹	1189	7.6	14	405	644	10.3	2.36	117	.236	.296	72	61	98	96	.968	205	134	1.5	6.8	1.3		2.4
DET	81	8	13	1410	1254	8.0	12	578	531	12.1	2.97	96	.248	.333	-23	-18	101	100	.968	211	110	1.1	-2.0	6.1		4.8
NY	84	12	17	1428	1249	7.9	37	476	616	11.2	2.77	104	.244	.314	8	17	102	100	.967	219	119	.7	1.9	-1.8		2.2
STL	74	9	13	1443²	1292	8.1	15	478	505	11.3	2.58	106	.248	.316	39	26	97	105	.963	248	120	-.9	2.9	3.3		-3.3
CLE	65	9	16	1410	1383	8.8	16	467	537	12.0	2.90	103	.264	.328	-13	16	106	107	.965	232	130	.0	1.8	-2.0		.2
WAS	85	11	7	1430²	1271	8.0	14	490	706	11.3	2.67	104	.244	.314	25	17	99	99	.964	232	119	.2	1.9	-2.8		.2
PHI	94	11	3	1343²	1311	8.8	26	715	575	13.8	3.92	73	.267	.364	-163	-160	101	97	.951	314	126	-5.5	-17.7	-4.2		-13.1
TOT	632	104	100	11289		8.1				11.6	2.82		.248	.321					.965	1844	966					

Runs		Hits		Doubles		Triples		Home Runs		Total Bases	
Cobb-Det	113	Speaker-Cle	211	Speaker-Cle	41	Jackson-Chi	21	Pipp-NY	12	Jackson-Chi	293
Graney-Cle	106	Jackson-Chi	202	Graney-Cle	41	E.Collins-Chi	17	Baker-NY	10	Speaker-Cle	274
Speaker-Cle	102	Cobb-Det	201	Jackson-Chi	40	Witt-Phi	15	Schang-Phi	7	Cobb-Det	267
Shotton-StL	97	Sisler-StL	177	Pratt-StL	35	Veach-Det	15	Felsch-Chi	7	Veach-Det	245
Veach-Det	92	Shotton-StL	174	Veach-Det	33						

Runs Batted In		Runs Produced		Bases On Balls		Batting Average		On Base Percentage		Slugging Average	
Pratt-StL	103	Veach-Det	180	Shotton-StL	111	Speaker-Cle	.386	Speaker-Cle	.470	Speaker-Cle	.502
Pipp-NY	93	Speaker-Cle	179	Graney-Cle	102	Cobb-Det	.371	Cobb-Det	.452	Jackson-Chi	.495
Veach-Det	91	Cobb-Det	176	E.Collins-Chi	86	Jackson-Chi	.341	E.Collins-Chi	.405	Cobb-Det	.493
Speaker-Cle	79	Jackson-Chi	166	Speaker-Cle	82	Strunk-Phi	.316	Jackson-Chi	.393	Veach-Det	.433
Jackson-Chi	78	Pratt-StL	162	Hooper-Bos	80	Gardner-Bos	.308	Strunk-Phi	.393	Baker-NY	.428

Production		Adjusted Production		Batter Runs		Adjusted Batter Runs		Clutch Hitting Index		Runs Created	
Speaker-Cle	.972	Speaker-Cle	181	Speaker-Cle	64.6	Speaker-Cle	57.2	Pratt-StL	136	Cobb-Det	136
Cobb-Det	.944	Cobb-Det	177	Cobb-Det	57.5	Cobb-Det	53.4	Heilmann-Det	132	Speaker-Cle	132
Jackson-Chi	.888	Jackson-Chi	165	Jackson-Chi	44.9	Jackson-Chi	43.7	Marsans-StL	132	Jackson-Chi	119
Strunk-Phi	.814	Strunk-Phi	152	E.Collins-Chi	30.5	Strunk-Phi	34.7	Gandil-Cle	129	E.Collins-Chi	99
E.Collins-Chi	.802	E.Collins-Chi	139	Strunk-Phi	30.2	E.Collins-Chi	29.5	Burns-Det	127	Veach-Det	94

Total Average		Stolen Bases		Stolen Base Average		Stolen Base Runs		Fielding Runs		Total Player Rating	
Cobb-Det	1.071	Cobb-Det	68	Cobb-Det	73.9	Cobb-Det	6.0	Lavan-StL	34.2	Speaker-Cle	5.7
Speaker-Cle	1.017	Marsans-StL	46	Hooper-Bos	71.1	Hooper-Bos	1.5	Lajoie-Phi	30.4	Cobb-Det	5.5
Jackson-Chi	.876	Shotton-StL	41	Schalk-Chi	69.8	Schalk-Chi	1.2	Vitt-Det	27.6	Pratt-StL	4.2
E.Collins-Chi	.814	E.Collins-Chi	40	Roth-Cle	67.4	Roth-Cle	.3	Pratt-StL	22.4	Jackson-Chi	3.6
Graney-Cle	.761	Speaker-Cle	35	Shanks-Was	65.7			Milan-Was	16.5	Lavan-StL	3.4

Wins		Win Percentage		Games		Complete Games		Shutouts		Saves	
Johnson-Was	25	Cicotte-Chi	.682	Davenport-StL	59	Johnson-Was	36	Ruth-Bos	9	Shawkey-NY	8
Shawkey-NY	24	Ruth-Bos	.657	Russell-Chi	56	Myers-Phi	31	Bush-Phi	8	Russell-NY	6
Ruth-Bos	23	Coveleski-Det	.656	Shawkey-NY	53	Bush-Phi	25	Leonard-Bos	6	Leonard-Bos	6
Coveleski-Det	21	Faber-Chi	.654	Gallia-Was	49	Ruth-Bos	23	Russell-Chi	5	Cicotte-Chi	5
Dauss-Det	19	Shawkey-NY	.632			Coveleski-Det	22			Bagby-Cle	5

Innings Pitched		Fewest Hits/Game		Fewest BB/Game		Strikeouts		Strikeouts/Game		Ratio	
Johnson-Was	369.2	Ruth-Bos	6.40	Russell-Chi	1.43	Johnson-Was	228	Johnson-Was	5.55	Russell-Chi	8.51
Coveleski-Det	324.1	Shawkey-NY	6.64	Cullop-NY	1.72	Myers-Phi	182	Williams-Chi	5.54	Johnson-Was	9.28
Ruth-Bos	323.2	Cicotte-Chi	6.64	Coveleski-Det	1.75	Ruth-Bos	170	Russell-NY	5.46	Shawkey-NY	9.47
Myers-Phi	315.0	Bush-Phi	6.97	Shore-Bos	1.95	Bush-Phi	157	Harper-Was	5.37	Coveleski-Det	9.77
Davenport-StL	290.2	Russell-Chi	7.05	Johnson-Was	2.00	Harper-Was	149	Myers-Phi	5.20	Ruth-Bos	9.90

Earned Run Average		Adjusted ERA		Opponents' Batting Avg.		Opponents' On Base Pct.		Starter Runs		Adjusted Starter Runs	
Ruth-Bos	1.75	Ruth-Bos	158	Ruth-Bos	.201	Russell-Chi	.254	Ruth-Bos	38.6	Johnson-Was	36.5
Cicotte-Chi	1.78	Cicotte-Chi	155	Shawkey-NY	.209	Johnson-Was	.270	Johnson-Was	38.0	Ruth-Bos	36.4
Johnson-Was	1.90	Johnson-Was	147	Cicotte-Chi	.218	Shawkey-NY	.273	Coveleski-Det	30.8	Coveleski-Det	32.1
Coveleski-Det	1.97	Coveleski-Det	145	Bush-Phi	.219	Ruth-Bos	.280	Cicotte-Chi	21.7	Shawkey-NY	20.7
Faber-Chi	2.02	Cullop-NY	141	Johnson-Was	.220	Coveleski-Det	.282	Weilman-StL	20.6	Cicotte-Chi	20.3

Clutch Pitching Index		Relief Runs		Adjusted Relief Runs		Relief Ranking		Total Pitcher Index		Total Baseball Ranking	
Cicotte-Chi	117							Ruth-Bos	5.9	Ruth-Bos	5.9
Gallia-Was	117							Johnson-Was	5.1	Speaker-Cle	5.7
Mogridge-NY	113							Coveleski-Det	3.9	Cobb-Det	5.5
Fisher-NY	113							Mays-Bos	3.2	Johnson-Was	5.1
Weilman-StL	113							Shawkey-NY	2.9	Pratt-StL	4.2

TEAM	G	W	L	PCT	GB	R	OR	AB	H	2B	3B	HR	BB	SO	AVG	OBP	SLG	PRO	PRO+	BR	/A	PF	CHI	RC	SB	CS	SBA	SBR
NY	158	98	56	.636		635	457	5211	1360	170	71	39	373	533	.261	.317	.343	.660	113	50	69	97	105	597	162			
PHI	154	87	65	.572	10	578	500	5084	1262	225	60	38	435	533	.248	.310	.339	.649	101	29	5	104	100	556	109			
STL	154	82	70	.539	15	531	567	5083	1271	159	93	26	359	652	.250	.303	.333	.636	104	2	17	97	98	542	159			
CIN	157	78	76	.506	20	601	611	5251	1385	196	100	26	312	477	.264	.309	.354	.663	114	48	73	96	101	596	153			
CHI	157	74	80	.481	24	552	567	5135	1229	194	67	17	415	599	.239	.299	.313	.612	86	-35	-76	108	107	511	127			
BOS	157	72	81	.471	25.5	536	552	5201	1280	169	75	22	427	587	.246	.309	.320	.629	105	-2	30	94	96	549	155			
BRO	156	70	81	.464	26.5	511	559	5251	1299	159	78	25	334	527	.247	.296	.322	.618	93	-32	-46	103	98	522	130			
PIT	157	51	103	.331	47	464	595	5169	1230	160	61	9	399	580	.238	.298	.298	.596	86	-61	-78	103	94	493	150			
TOT	625					4408		41385	10316	1432	605	202	3054	4488	.249	.305	.328	.633						1145				

TEAM	CG	SH	SV	IP	H	H/G	HR	BB	SO	RAT	ERA	ERA+	OAV	OOB	PR	/A	PF	CPI	FA	E	DP	FW	PW	BW	SBW	DIF
NY	92	18	14	1426²	1221	7.7	29	327	551	9.9	2.27	112	.234	.283	69	43	94	97	.968	208	122	1.8	4.9	7.8		6.5
PHI	102	22	5	1389	1258	8.2	25	325	616	10.5	2.46	114	.246	.295	38	53	104	102	.967	212	112	1.2	6.0	.6		3.2
STL	66	16	10	1392²	1257	8.1	29	421	502	11.1	3.03	89	.248	.311	-51	-55	99	92	.967	221	153	.6	-6.2	1.9		9.7
CIN	94	12	6	1397¹	1358	8.7	20	402	488	11.5	2.70	97	.260	.317	1	-15	97	110	.962	247	120	-.7	-1.7	8.3		-4.9
CHI	79	16	9	1404	1303	8.4	34	374	654	10.9	2.62	110	.253	.307	14	40	107	108	.959	267	121	-1.9	4.5	-8.6		3.0
BOS	105	22	3	1424²	1309	8.3	19	371	593	10.8	2.77	92	.251	.304	-10	-38	94	96	.966	224	122	.7	-4.3	3.4		-4.3
BRO	99	8	9	1421¹	1288	8.2	32	405	582	11.0	2.78	100	.247	.307	-12	0	103	98	.962	245	102	-.7	.0	-5.2		.4
PIT	84	17	6	1417²	1318	8.4	14	432	509	11.3	3.01	94	.253	.314	-48	-29	105	94	.961	251	119	-.9	-3.3	-8.8		-13.0
TOT	721	131	62	11273¹		8.2				10.9	2.70		.249	.305					.964	1875	971					

Runs
Burns-NY ... 103
Groh-Cin ... 91
Kauff-NY ... 89
Hornsby-StL ... 86

Hits
Groh-Cin ... 182
Burns-NY ... 180
Roush-Cin ... 178
Zimmerman-NY ... 174
Carey-Pit ... 174

Doubles
Groh-Cin ... 39
Merkle-Bro-Chi ... 31
Smith-Bos ... 31
Cravath-Phi ... 29
Chase-Cin ... 28

Triples
Hornsby-StL ... 17
Cravath-Phi ... 16
Chase-Cin ... 15
Roush-Cin ... 14
Long-StL ... 14

Home Runs
Robertson-NY ... 12
Cravath-Phi ... 12
Hornsby-StL ... 8

Total Bases
Hornsby-StL ... 253
Groh-Cin ... 246
Burns-NY ... 246
Cravath-Phi ... 238

Runs Batted In
Zimmerman-NY ... 102
Chase-Cin ... 86
Cravath-Phi ... 83
Stengel-Bro ... 73
Luderus-Phi ... 72

Runs Produced
Zimmerman-NY ... 158
Chase-Cin ... 153
Kauff-NY ... 152
Roush-Cin ... 145
Hornsby-StL ... 144

Bases On Balls
Burns-NY ... 75
Groh-Cin ... 71
Cravath-Phi ... 70
Luderus-Phi ... 65
Paskert-Phi ... 62

Batting Average
Roush-Cin ... .341
Hornsby-StL ... .327
Z.Wheat-Bro ... .312
Kauff-NY ... .308
Groh-Cin ... .304

On Base Percentage
Groh-Cin ... .385
Hornsby-StL ... .385
Burns-NY ... .380
Roush-Cin ... .379
Kauff-NY ... .379

Slugging Average
Hornsby-StL ... .484
Cravath-Phi ... .473
Roush-Cin ... .454
Z.Wheat-Bro ... .423
Burns-NY ... .412

Production
Hornsby-StL ... .868
Cravath-Phi ... .842
Roush-Cin ... .833
Groh-Cin ... .796
Burns-NY ... .792

Adjusted Production
Hornsby-StL ... 170
Roush-Cin ... 162
Cravath-Phi ... 151
Groh-Cin ... 150
Burns-NY ... 148

Batter Runs
Hornsby-StL ... 39.6
Cravath-Phi ... 34.7
Groh-Cin ... 33.5
Roush-Cin ... 32.3
Burns-NY ... 32.2

Adjusted Batter Runs
Hornsby-StL ... 42.3
Groh-Cin ... 37.7
Roush-Cin ... 36.0
Burns-NY ... 35.4
Cravath-Phi ... 30.9

Clutch Hitting Index
Zimmerman-NY ... 146
Ward-Pit ... 133
Luderus-Phi ... 132
Deal-Chi ... 130
Chase-Cin ... 121

Runs Created
Burns-NY ... 102
Hornsby-StL ... 100
Groh-Cin ... 96
Roush-Cin ... 94
Carey-Pit ... 94

Total Average
Hornsby-StL ... .906
Cravath-Phi ... .870
Burns-NY ... .868
Roush-Cin ... .843
Groh-Cin ... .815

Stolen Bases
Carey-Pit ... 46
Burns-NY ... 40
Kauff-NY ... 30
Maranville-Bos ... 27
Baird-Pit-StL ... 26

Fielding Runs
Bancroft-Phi ... 27.9
Fletcher-NY ... 27.4
Carey-Pit ... 24.5
Hornsby-StL ... 21.3
Miller-StL ... 18.6

Total Player Rating
Hornsby-StL ... 7.7
Groh-Cin ... 5.3
Fletcher-NY ... 4.1
Carey-Pit ... 3.9
Burns-NY ... 3.5

Wins
Alexander-Phi ... 30
Toney-Cin ... 24
Vaughn-Chi ... 23
Schupp-NY ... 21
Schneider-Cin ... 20

Win Percentage
Schupp-NY ... .750
Sallee-NY ... .720
Perritt-NY ... .708
Alexander-Phi ... .698
Nehf-Bos ... .680

Games
Douglas-Chi ... 51
Barnes-Bos ... 50
Schneider-Cin ... 46
Alexander-Phi ... 45
Doak-StL ... 44

Complete Games
Alexander-Phi ... 34
Toney-Cin ... 31
Vaughn-Chi ... 27
Barnes-Bos ... 27
Schupp-NY ... 25

Shutouts
Alexander-Phi ... 8
Toney-Cin ... 7
Cooper-Pit ... 7
Schupp-NY ... 6

Saves
Sallee-NY ... 4

Innings Pitched
Alexander-Phi ... 388.0
Toney-Cin ... 339.2
Schneider-Cin ... 333.2
Cooper-Pit ... 297.2
Vaughn-Chi ... 295.2

Fewest Hits/Game
Schupp-NY ... 6.68
Anderson-NY ... 6.78
Nehf-Bos ... 7.60
Pfeffer-Bro ... 7.61
Tyler-Bos ... 7.64

Fewest BB/Game
Alexander-Phi ... 1.30
Sallee-NY ... 1.42
Nehf-Bos ... 1.50
Barnes-Bos ... 1.53
Douglas-Chi ... 1.53

Strikeouts
Alexander-Phi ... 200
Vaughn-Chi ... 195
Douglas-Chi ... 151
Schupp-NY ... 147
Schneider-Cin ... 138

Strikeouts/Game
Vaughn-Chi ... 5.94
Schupp-NY ... 4.86
Alexander-Phi ... 4.64
Douglas-Chi ... 4.63
Marquard-Bro ... 4.53

Ratio
Anderson-NY ... 8.78
Schupp-NY ... 9.13
Alexander-Phi ... 9.23
Nehf-Bos ... 9.26
Barnes-Bos ... 9.58

Earned Run Average
Anderson-NY ... 1.44
Alexander-Phi ... 1.83
Perritt-NY ... 1.88
Schupp-NY ... 1.95
Vaughn-Chi ... 2.01

Adjusted ERA
Anderson-NY ... 176
Alexander-Phi ... 153
Vaughn-Chi ... 144
Perritt-NY ... 135
Schupp-NY ... 130

Opponents' Batting Avg.
Schupp-NY ... .209
Anderson-NY ... .209
Nehf-Bos ... .231
Marquard-Bro ... .232
Pfeffer-Bro ... .234

Opponents' On Base Pct.
Anderson-NY ... .255
Schupp-NY ... .265
Alexander-Phi ... .266
Nehf-Bos ... .268
Barnes-Bos ... .277

Starter Runs
Alexander-Phi ... 37.5
Vaughn-Chi ... 22.8
Schupp-NY ... 22.7
Anderson-NY ... 22.7
Schneider-Cin ... 22.2

Adjusted Starter Runs
Alexander-Phi ... 41.7
Vaughn-Chi ... 28.8
Anderson-NY ... 19.8
Schneider-Cin ... 18.7
Schupp-NY ... 17.9

Clutch Pitching Index
Schneider-Cin ... 145
Vaughn-Chi ... 120
Perritt-NY ... 118
Hendrix-Chi ... 117
Mayer-Phi ... 114

Relief Runs

Adjusted Relief Runs

Relief Ranking

Total Pitcher Index
Alexander-Phi ... 5.9
Vaughn-Chi ... 4.1
Rixey-Phi ... 2.6
Schneider-Cin ... 1.8
Anderson-NY ... 1.7

Total Baseball Ranking
Hornsby-StL ... 7.7
Alexander-Phi ... 5.9
Groh-Cin ... 5.3
Vaughn-Chi ... 4.1
Fletcher-NY ... 4.1

TEAM	G	W	L	PCT	GB	R	OR	AB	H	2B	3B	HR	BB	SO	AVG	OBP	SLG	PRO	PRO+	BR	/A	PF	CHI	RC	SB	CS	SBA	SBR
CHI	156	100	54	.649		656	464	5057	1281	152	81	18	522	479	.253	.329	.326	.655	103	36	23	102	108	607	219			
BOS	157	90	62	.592	9	555	454	5048	1243	198	64	14	466	473	.246	.314	.319	.633	100	-10	-4	99	99	550	105			
CLE	156	88	66	.571	12	584	543	4994	1224	218	64	13	549	596	.245	.324	.322	.646	96	21	-23	107	99	588	210			
DET	154	78	75	.510	21.5	639	577	5093	1317	204	77	25	483	476	.259	.328	.344	.672	111	61	64	100	102	615	163			
WAS	157	74	79	.484	25.5	543	566	5142	1238	173	70	4	500	574	.241	.313	.304	.617	95	-34	-28	99	101	531	166			
NY	155	71	82	.464	28.5	524	558	5136	1226	172	52	27	496	535	.239	.310	.308	.618	93	-34	-39	101	98	526	136			
STL	155	57	97	.370	43	510	687	5091	1250	183	63	15	405	540	.246	.305	.315	.620	98	-39	-20	96	99	523	157			
PHI	154	55	98	.359	44.5	529	691	5109	1296	177	62	17	435	519	.254	.316	.323	.639	101	-1	7	99	94	551	112			
TOT	622					4540		40670	10075	1477	533	133	3856	4192	.248	.318	.320	.638						1268				

TEAM	CG	SH	SV	IP	H	H/G	HR	BB	SO	RAT	ERA	ERA+	OAV	OOB	PR	/A	PF	CPI	FA	E	DP	FW	PW	BW	SBW	DIF
CHI	78	22	21	1424[1]	1236	7.8	10	413	517	10.6	2.16	123	.238	.298	79	76	100	102	.967	204	117	2.3	8.5	2.6		9.7
BOS	115	15	7	1421[1]	1197	7.6	12	413	509	10.5	2.20	117	.231	.295	73	60	97	95	.972	183	116	3.9	6.7	-.4		3.9
CLE	73	20	22	1412[2]	1270	8.1	17	438	451	11.1	2.52	112	.247	.310	22	48	106	101	.964	242	136	-.5	5.3	-2.6		8.7
DET	78	20	15	1396[1]	1209	7.8	12	504	516	11.4	2.56	103	.240	.316	16	13	99	99	.964	234	95	-.1	1.4	7.1		-6.9
WAS	84	21	10	1413	1217	7.8	12	537	637	11.4	2.75	95	.239	.316	-14	-19	99	91	.961	251	127	-1.0	-2.1	-3.1		3.7
NY	87	10	6	1411[1]	1280	8.2	28	427	571	11.1	2.66	101	.252	.314	0	3	101	102	.965	225	129	.6	.3	-4.3		-2.1
STL	66	12	12	1385[1]	1320	8.6	19	537	429	12.3	3.20	81	.257	.332	-83	-96	98	94	.957	281	139	-3.4	-10.7	-2.2		-3.7
PHI	80	8	8	1365[2]	1310	8.6	23	562	516	12.5	3.27	84	.261	.338	-92	-79	103	97	.961	251	106	-1.4	-8.8	.8		-12.1
TOT	661	128	101	11230		8.0				11.4	2.66		.248	.318					.964	1871	965					

Runs
Bush-Det 112
Cobb-Det 107
Chapman-Cle 98
Jackson-Chi 91
E.Collins-Chi 91

Hits
Cobb-Det 225
Sisler-StL 190
Speaker-Cle 184
Veach-Det 182

Doubles
Cobb-Det 44
Speaker-Cle 42
Veach-Det 31
Sisler-StL 30
Roth-Cle 30

Triples
Cobb-Det 24
Jackson-Chi 17
Judge-Was 15
Chapman-Cle 13

Home Runs
Pipp-NY 9
Veach-Det 8
Bodie-Phi 7

Total Bases
Cobb-Det 335
Veach-Det 261
Speaker-Cle 254
Sisler-StL 244
Bodie-Phi 233

Runs Batted In
Veach-Det 103
Felsch-Chi 102
Cobb-Det 102
Heilmann-Det 86
Jackson-Chi 75

Runs Produced
Cobb-Det 203
Veach-Det 174
Felsch-Chi 171
Jackson-Chi 161
E.Collins-Chi 158

Bases On Balls
Graney-Cle 94
E.Collins-Chi 89
Hooper-Bos 80
Bush-Det 80
Leibold-Chi 74

Batting Average
Cobb-Det .... .383
Sisler-StL .... .353
Speaker-Cle ...... .352
Veach-Det .... .319
Felsch-Chi .... .308

On Base Percentage
Cobb-Det .... .444
Speaker-Cle ...... .432
Veach-Det .... .393
Sisler-StL .... .390
E.Collins-Chi ..... .389

Slugging Average
Cobb-Det .... .570
Speaker-Cle ...... .486
Veach-Det .... .457
Sisler-StL .... .453
Jackson-Chi ...... .429

Production
Cobb-Det 1.014
Speaker-Cle ..... .918
Veach-Det .... .850
Sisler-StL .... .843
Jackson-Chi ..... .805

Adjusted Production
Cobb-Det 210
Speaker-Cle 168
Sisler-StL 163
Veach-Det 160
Jackson-Chi 142

Batter Runs
Cobb-Det 74.4
Speaker-Cle 51.2
Veach-Det 40.1
Sisler-StL 34.0
Jackson-Chi 28.8

Adjusted Batter Runs
Cobb-Det 75.0
Speaker-Cle 43.3
Veach-Det 40.5
Sisler-StL 37.4
Jackson-Chi 26.9

Clutch Hitting Index
Schalk-Chi 135
Bates-Phi 134
Felsch-Chi 133
Veach-Det 130
E.Collins-Chi 128

Runs Created
Cobb-Det 164
Speaker-Cle 118
Veach-Det 108
Chapman-Cle 105
Sisler-StL 104

Total Average
Cobb-Det 1.253
Speaker-Cle 1.056
Veach-Det .... .905
Sisler-StL .... .900
E.Collins-Chi .... .873

Stolen Bases
Cobb-Det 55
E.Collins-Chi 53
Chapman-Cle 52
Roth-Cle 51
Sisler-StL 37

Fielding Runs
Chapman-Cle 24.4
Felsch-Chi 18.9
Wambsganss-Cle . 15.3
Ainsmith-Was 14.9
Pratt-StL 14.8

Total Player Rating
Cobb-Det 8.5
Chapman-Cle 5.4
Speaker-Cle 4.7
Veach-Det 4.0
Sisler-StL 4.0

Wins
Cicotte-Chi 28
Ruth-Bos 24
Johnson-Was 23
Bagby-Cle 23
Mays-Bos 22

Win Percentage
Russell-Chi ...... .750
Mays-Bos .... .710
Cicotte-Chi ...... .700
Williams-Chi ..... .680
Ruth-Bos .... .649

Games
Danforth-Chi 50
Cicotte-Chi 49
Bagby-Cle 49
Sothoron-StL 48

Complete Games
Ruth-Bos 35
Johnson-Was 30
Cicotte-Chi 29
Mays-Bos 27

Shutouts
Coveleski-Cle 9
Johnson-Was 8
Bagby-Cle 8
Cicotte-Chi 7

Saves
Danforth-Chi 9
Bagby-Cle 7
Boland-Det 6
Coumbe-Cle 5

Innings Pitched
Cicotte-Chi 346.2
Ruth-Bos 326.1
Johnson-Was 326.0
Bagby-Cle 320.2
Coveleski-Cle .. 298.1

Fewest Hits/Game
Coveleski-Cle 6.09
Cicotte-Chi 6.39
Ruth-Bos 6.73
Johnson-Was 6.85
Mays-Bos 7.16

Fewest BB/Game
Russell-Chi 1.52
Mogridge-NY 1.79
Cicotte-Chi 1.82
Johnson-Was 1.88
Bagby-Cle 2.05

Strikeouts
Johnson-Was 188
Cicotte-Chi 150
Leonard-Bos 144
Coveleski-Cle 133
Ruth-Bos 128

Strikeouts/Game
Johnson-Was 5.19
Harper-Was 4.97
Bush-Phi 4.67
Leonard-Bos 4.40
Danforth-Chi 4.11

Ratio
Cicotte-Chi 8.28
Coveleski-Cle ... 8.96
Johnson-Was 9.11
Russell-Chi 9.65
Mays-Bos 9.90

Earned Run Average
Cicotte-Chi 1.53
Mays-Bos 1.74
Coveleski-Cle ... 1.81
Faber-Chi 1.92
Russell-Chi 1.95

Adjusted ERA
Cicotte-Chi 173
Coveleski-Cle 156
Mays-Bos 148
Bagby-Cle 144
Faber-Chi 138

Opponents' Batting Avg.
Coveleski-Cle .... .194
Cicotte-Chi ..... .203
Ruth-Bos .... .211
Johnson-Was .... .211
Mays-Bos .... .221

Opponents' On Base Pct.
Cicotte-Chi ..... .248
Coveleski-Cle ... .261
Johnson-Was .... .263
Russell-Chi ..... .279
Mays-Bos .... .282

Starter Runs
Cicotte-Chi 43.5
Mays-Bos 29.4
Coveleski-Cle ... 28.2
Bagby-Cle 24.8
Ruth-Bos 23.5

Adjusted Starter Runs
Cicotte-Chi 43.3
Coveleski-Cle ... 33.8
Bagby-Cle 30.9
Mays-Bos 26.8
Ruth-Bos 20.5

Clutch Pitching Index
Faber-Chi 136
Ayers-Was 128
James-Det 127
Morton-Cle 117
Mitchell-Det 116

Relief Runs

Adjusted Relief Runs

Relief Ranking

Total Pitcher Index
Cicotte-Chi 5.4
Mays-Bos 4.8
Ruth-Bos 4.8
Bagby-Cle 3.8
Coveleski-Cle 3.1

Total Baseball Ranking
Cobb-Det 8.5
Chapman-Cle 5.4
Cicotte-Chi 5.4
Mays-Bos 4.8
Ruth-Bos 4.8

TEAM	G	W	L	PCT	GB	R	OR	AB	H	2B	3B	HR	BB	SO	AVG	OBP	SLG	PRO	PRO+	BR	/A	PF	CHI	RC	SB	CS	SBA	SBR
CHI	131	84	45	.651		**538**	393	4325	1147	164	53	21	358	343	.265	.325	.342	.667	106	48	35	102	102	524	159			
NY	124	71	53	.573	10.5	480	415	4164	1081	150	53	13	271	365	.260	.310	.330	.640	103	1	10	98	**107**	451	130			
CIN	129	68	60	.531	15.5	530	496	4265	**1185**	165	84	15	304	303	**.278**	**.330**	**.366**	**.696**	120	86	96	98	96	**545**	128			
PIT	126	65	60	.520	17	466	412	4091	1016	107	72	15	**371**	285	.248	.315	.321	.636	96	1	-15	104	102	466	**200**			
BRO	126	57	69	.452	25.5	360	463	4212	1052	121	62	10	212	326	.250	.291	.315	.606	90	-53	-51	100	91	405	113			
PHI	125	55	68	.447	26	430	507	4192	1022	158	28	25	346	400	.244	.305	.314	.618	88	-29	-58	107	101	417	97			
BOS	124	53	71	.427	28.5	424	469	4162	1014	107	59	13	350	438	.244	.307	.307	.614	97	-32	-14	96	100	412	83			
STL	131	51	78	.395	33	454	527	4369	1066	147	64	**27**	329	461	.244	.301	.325	.626	99	-21	-5	97	100	450	119			
TOT	508					3682		33780	8583	1119	475	139	2541	2921	.254	.311	.328	.638						1029				

TEAM	CG	SH	SV	IP	H	H/G	HR	BB	SO	RAT	ERA	ERA+	OAV	OOB	PR	/A	PF	CPI	FA	E	DP	FW	PW	BW	SBW	DIF
CHI	92	**23**	8	1197	1050	**7.9**	13	296	**472**	10.3	**2.18**	128	**.239**	.291	77	80	101	104	.966	188	91	.5	**8.9**	3.9		6.2
NY	74	18	**11**	1111[2]	**1002**	8.1	20	**228**	330	**10.1**	2.64	100	.243	**.287**	15	-1	95	87	**.971**	152	78	**2.1**	-.1	1.1		5.9
CIN	84	14	6	1142[1]	1136	9.0	19	381	321	12.1	3.00	89	.268	.332	-30	-42	97	**109**	.964	192	**127**	.0	-4.7	**10.7**		-2.1
PIT	85	10	7	1140[1]	1005	**7.9**	13	299	367	10.5	2.48	116	.243	.300	36	51	104	99	.966	179	108	.6	5.7	-1.7		-2.1
BRO	85	17	2	1131[1]	1024	8.1	22	320	395	10.9	2.81	99	.248	.307	-6	-4	101	95	.963	193	74	-.3	-.4	-5.7		.4
PHI	78	10	6	1139[2]	1086	8.6	22	369	312	11.7	3.15	95	.258	.323	-49	-20	109	96	.961	211	91	-1.5	-2.2	-6.5		3.7
BOS	**96**	13	0	1117[1]	1111	8.9	14	277	340	11.4	2.90	93	.266	.316	-17	-27	97	102	.965	184	89	.0	-3.0	-1.6		-4.5
STL	72	3	5	1193	1148	8.7	16	352	361	11.6	2.96	91	.261	.321	-27	-34	98	101	.962	220	116	-1.5	-3.8	-.6		-7.6
TOT	666	108	45	9172[2]		8.4				11.1	2.76		.254	.311					.965	1519	774					

Runs
Groh-Cin 86
Burns-NY 80
Flack-Chi 74
Hollocher-Chi 72

Hits
Hollocher-Chi 161
Groh-Cin 158
Roush-Cin 145
Youngs-NY 143
Merkle-Chi 143

Doubles
Groh-Cin 28
Mann-Chi 27
Cravath-Phi 27
Meusel-Phi 25
Merkle-Chi 25

Triples
Daubert-Bro 15
Wickland-Bos 13
S.Magee-Cin 13
L.Magee-Cin 13

Home Runs
Cravath-Phi 8
Williams-Phi 6
Cruise-StL 6

Total Bases
Hollocher-Chi 202
Roush-Cin 198
Groh-Cin 195
Mann-Chi 188
Merkle-Chi 187

Runs Batted In
S.Magee-Cin 76
Cutshaw-Pit 68
Luderus-Phi 67
R.Smith-Bos 65
Merkle-Chi 65

Runs Produced
Burns-NY 127
Paskert-Chi 125
Mann-Chi 122
Groh-Cin 122
S.Magee-Cin 120

Bases On Balls
Carey-Pit 62
Flack-Chi 56
Groh-Cin 54
Cravath-Phi 54
Bancroft-Phi 54

Batting Average
Z.Wheat-Bro ...... .335
Roush-Cin .... .333
Groh-Cin .... .320
Hollocher-Chi ..... .316
Daubert-Bro ...... .308

On Base Percentage
Groh-Cin .... .395
Hollocher-Chi ..... .379
R.Smith-Bos ...... .373
S.Magee-Cin ...... .370
Z.Wheat-Bro ...... .369

Slugging Average
Roush-Cin .... .455
Daubert-Bro ...... .429
Hornsby-StL ...... .416
S.Magee-Cin ...... .415
Wickland-Bos ...... .398

Production
Roush-Cin .... .823
Groh-Cin .... .791
Daubert-Bro ...... .789
S.Magee-Cin ...... .785
Hollocher-Chi ..... .775

Adjusted Production
Roush-Cin 153
Groh-Cin 144
S.Magee-Cin 142
Daubert-Bro 141
Wickland-Bos 139

Batter Runs
Groh-Cin 26.4
Roush-Cin 24.3
Hollocher-Chi 23.0
S.Magee-Cin 19.2
Daubert-Bro 18.2

Adjusted Batter Runs
Groh-Cin 27.9
Roush-Cin 25.6
Hollocher-Chi 21.0
S.Magee-Cin 20.3
Daubert-Bro 18.4

Clutch Hitting Index
S.Magee-Cin 158
Konetchy-Bos 137
R.Smith-Bos 135
Z.Wheat-Bro 122
Paulette-StL 122

Runs Created
Hollocher-Chi 85
Roush-Cin 80
Groh-Cin 79
Carey-Pit 76
Burns-NY 74

Total Average
Roush-Cin .... .848
Carey-Pit .... .844
Wickland-Bos ..... .812
Burns-NY .... .809
S.Magee-Cin ...... .804

Stolen Bases
Carey-Pit 58
Burns-NY 40
Hollocher-Chi ... 26
Cutshaw-Pit 25
Baird-StL 25

Stolen Base Average

Stolen Base Runs

Fielding Runs
Fletcher-NY 22.3
Carey-Pit 18.6
Bancroft-Phi 17.9
Schmidt-Pit 15.8
Myers-Bro 13.0

Total Player Rating
Groh-Cin 3.6
Hornsby-StL 3.6
Fisher-StL 3.5
Roush-Cin 3.0
L.Magee-Cin 3.0

Wins
Vaughn-Chi 22
Hendrix-Chi 20
Tyler-Chi 19
Grimes-Bro 19
Cooper-Pit 19

Win Percentage
Hendrix-Chi .... .741
Tyler-Chi .... .704
Mayer-Phi-Pit ..... .696
Vaughn-Chi .... .688
Grimes-Bro ...... .679

Games
Grimes-Bro 40
Cooper-Pit 38
Eller-Cin 37

Complete Games
Nehf-Bos 28
Vaughn-Chi 27
Cooper-Pit 26
Tyler-Chi 22
Hendrix-Chi 21

Shutouts
Vaughn-Chi 8
Grimes-Bro 7
Tyler-Chi 6
Perritt-NY 6

Saves
Toney-Cin-NY 3
Oeschger-Phi 3
Cooper-Pit 3
Anderson-NY 3

Innings Pitched
Vaughn-Chi 290.1
Nehf-Bos 284.1
Cooper-Pit 273.1
Grimes-Bro 269.2
Tyler-Chi 269.1

Fewest Hits/Game
Vaughn-Chi 6.70
Grimes-Bro 7.01
Cooper-Pit 7.21
Tyler-Chi 7.28
Jacobs-Pit-Phi 7.50

Fewest BB/Game
Sallee-NY .... .82
Perritt-NY 1.47
G.Smith-Cin-NY-Bro .. 1.50
Toney-Cin-NY 1.54
Demaree-NY 1.58

Strikeouts
Vaughn-Chi 148
Cooper-Pit 117
Grimes-Bro 113
Tyler-Chi 102
Nehf-Bos 96

Strikeouts/Game
Vaughn-Chi 4.59
Cooper-Pit 3.85
Grimes-Bro 3.77
Cheney-Bro 3.72
May-StL 3.60

Ratio
Sallee-NY 9.14
Vaughn-Chi 9.27
Grimes-Bro 9.68
Cooper-Pit 9.68
Tyler-Chi 9.69

Earned Run Average
Vaughn-Chi 1.74
Tyler-Chi 2.00
Cooper-Pit 2.11
Douglas-Chi 2.13
Grimes-Bro 2.14

Adjusted ERA
Vaughn-Chi 160
Tyler-Chi 139
Cooper-Pit 136
Douglas-Chi 131
Grimes-Bro 130

Opponents' Batting Avg.
Vaughn-Chi .... .208
Grimes-Bro ...... .216
Cooper-Pit ...... .223
Tyler-Chi .... .226
Jacobs-Pit-Phi .... .233

Opponents' On Base Pct.
Sallee-NY .... .259
Vaughn-Chi ...... .266
Grimes-Bro ...... .276
Perritt-NY .... .278
Cooper-Pit ...... .279

Starter Runs
Vaughn-Chi 33.1
Tyler-Chi 22.7
Cooper-Pit 19.9
Grimes-Bro 18.8
Hamilton-Pit 11.6

Adjusted Starter Runs
Vaughn-Chi 33.8
Cooper-Pit 23.3
Tyler-Chi 23.3
Grimes-Bro 19.4
Hamilton-Pit 12.2

Clutch Pitching Index
Bressler-Cin 123
Mayer-Phi-Pit 117
Schneider-Cin 113
Eller-Cin 112
Demaree-NY 112

Relief Runs

Adjusted Relief Runs

Relief Ranking

Total Pitcher Index
Vaughn-Chi 4.4
Cooper-Pit 3.1
Tyler-Chi 3.0
Grimes-Bro 2.6
Hogg-Phi 2.0

Total Baseball Ranking
Vaughn-Chi 4.4
Groh-Cin 3.6
Hornsby-StL 3.6
Fisher-StL 3.5
Cooper-Pit 3.1

TEAM	G	W	L	PCT	GB	R	OR	AB	H	2B	3B	HR	BB	SO	AVG	OBP	SLG	PRO	PRO+	BR	/A	PF	CHI	RC	SB	CS	SBA	SBR
BOS	126	75	51	.595		474	380	3982	990	159	54	15	406	324	.249	.322	.327	.649	103	5	13	98	105	455	110			
CLE	129	73	54	.575	2.5	504	447	4166	1084	176	67	9	491	386	.260	.344	.341	.685	102	68	17	110	93	537	165			
WAS	130	72	56	.563	4	461	412	4472	1144	156	49	4	376	361	.256	.318	.315	.633	98	-21	-13	98	99	479	137			
NY	126	60	63	.488	13.5	493	475	4224	1085	160	45	20	367	370	.257	.320	.330	.650	99	2	-8	102	106	469	88			
STL	123	58	64	.475	15	426	448	4019	1040	152	40	5	397	340	.259	.331	.320	.651	105	11	25	97	93	467	138			
CHI	124	57	67	.460	17	457	446	4132	1057	136	55	8	375	358	.256	.322	.321	.643	98	-5	-9	101	102	458	116			
DET	128	55	71	.437	20	476	557	4262	1063	141	56	13	452	380	.249	.325	.318	.643	103	-2	17	96	101	470	123			
PHI	130	52	76	.406	24	412	538	4278	1039	124	44	22	343	485	.243	.303	.308	.611	88	-59	-63	101	102	415	83			
TOT	508					3703		33535	8502	1204	410	96	3207	3004	.254	.323	.322	.646						960				

TEAM	CG	SH	SV	IP	H	H/G	HR	BB	SO	RAT	ERA	ERA+	OAV	OOB	PR	/A	PF	CPI	FA	E	DP	FW	PW	BW	SBW	DIF
BOS	105	26	2	1120	931	7.5	9	380	392	10.8	2.31	116	.231	.302	58	47	97	95	.971	152	89	2.5	5.2	1.5		2.8
CLE	78	5	13	1161	1126	8.7	9	343	364	11.5	2.64	114	.262	.319	18	46	108	105	.962	207	82	-.7	5.1	1.9		3.1
WAS	75	19	8	1228	1021	7.5	10	395	505	10.6	2.14	127	.231	.298	86	80	98	99	.960	226	95	-1.8	8.9	-1.5		2.3
NY	59	8	13	1157¹	1103	8.6	25	463	370	12.5	3.00	94	.261	.340	-30	-24	102	107	.970	161	137	1.9	-2.7	-.9		.2
STL	67	8	8	1111¹	993	8.0	11	402	346	11.5	2.75	99	.246	.319	2	-2	99	95	.963	190	86	-.2	-.2	2.8		-5.4
CHI	76	9	8	1126	1092	8.7	9	300	349	11.3	2.73	100	.261	.314	5	-3	99	97	.967	169	98	1.2	-.3	-1.0		-4.9
DET	74	8	7	1160²	1130	8.8	10	437	374	12.4	3.40	78	.263	.335	-81	-99	96	89	.960	212	77	-1.1	-11.0	1.9		2.2
PHI	80	13	9	1156	1106	8.6	13	486	277	12.7	3.22	91	.266	.348	-58	-39	106	103	.959	228	136	-1.9	-4.4	-7.0		1.3
TOT	614	96	68	9220¹		8.3				11.7	2.77		.254	.323					.964	1545	800					

Runs
Chapman-Cle 84
T.Cobb-Det 83
Hooper-Bos 81
Bush-Det 74
Speaker-Cle 73

Hits
Burns-Phi 178
T.Cobb-Det 161
Sisler-StL 154
Baker-NY 154
Speaker-Cle 150

Doubles
Speaker-Cle 33
Ruth-Bos 26
Hooper-Bos 26
Baker-NY 24

Triples
T.Cobb 14
Veach-Det 13
Hooper-Bos 13
Roth-Cle 12

Home Runs
Walker-Phi 11
Ruth-Bos 11
Burns-Phi 6
Baker-NY 6

Total Bases
Burns-Phi 236
T.Cobb-Det 217
Baker-NY 206
Speaker-Cle 205
Sisler-StL 199

Runs Batted In
Veach-Det 78
Burns-Phi 70
Wood-Cle 66
Ruth-Bos 66
T.Cobb-Det 64

Runs Produced
T.Cobb-Det 144
Veach-Det 134
Speaker-Cle 134
Burns-Phi 125
Hooper-Bos 124

Bases On Balls
Chapman-Cle 84
Bush-Det 79
Hooper-Bos 75
E.Collins-Chi 73
Shotton-Was 67

Batting Average
T.Cobb-Det 382
Burns-Phi 352
Sisler-StL 341
Speaker-Cle 318
Baker-NY 306

On Base Percentage
T.Cobb-Det 440
E.Collins-Chi 407
Speaker-Cle 403
Sisler-StL 400
Hooper-Bos 391

Slugging Average
Ruth-Bos 555
T.Cobb-Det 515
Burns-Phi 467
Sisler-StL 440
Speaker-Cle 435

Production
T.Cobb-Det 955
Burns-Phi 857
Sisler-StL 841
Speaker-Cle 839
Hooper-Bos 796

Adjusted Production
T.Cobb-Det 196
Sisler-StL 159
Burns-Phi 157
Hooper-Bos 142
Speaker-Cle 140

Batter Runs
T.Cobb-Det 44.0
Ruth-Bos 34.8
Burns-Phi 32.8
Speaker-Cle 31.3
Sisler-StL 28.8

Adjusted Batter Runs
T.Cobb-Det 47.8
Ruth-Bos 36.0
Burns-Phi 31.9
Sisler-StL 31.3
Hooper-Bos 26.5

Clutch Hitting Index
Veach-Det 140
Demmitt-StL 137
McInnis-Bos 136
Shanks-Was 133
S.Collins-Chi 132

Runs Created
T.Cobb-Det 105
Sisler-StL 92
Burns-Phi 91
Speaker-Cle 90
Hooper-Bos 82

Total Average
T.Cobb-Det 1.131
Sisler-StL 970
Speaker-Cle 931
Roth-Cle 929
Hooper-Bos 875

Stolen Bases
Sisler-StL 45
Roth-Cle 35
T.Cobb-Det 34
Chapman-Cle 30
Speaker-Cle 27

Stolen Base Average

Stolen Base Runs

Fielding Runs
Peckinpaugh-NY . . 25.0
Scott-StL 17.5
Dugan-Phi 17.0
Gedeon-StL 15.8
S.Collins-Chi 14.1

Total Player Rating
T.Cobb-Det 4.8
Sisler-StL 3.8
Burns-Phi 3.6
Baker-NY 3.2
Speaker-Cle 3.0

Wins
Johnson-Was 23
Coveleski-Cle 22
Mays-Bos 21
Perry-Phi 20
Bagby-Cle 17

Win Percentage
Jones-Bos 762
Johnson-Was 639
Coveleski-Cle 629
Mays-Bos 618
Shaw-Was 571

Games
Mogridge-NY 45
Bagby-Cle 45
Perry-Phi 44
Shaw-Was 41
Ayers-Was 40

Complete Games
Perry-Phi 30
Mays-Bos 30
Johnson-Was 29
Bush-Bos 26
Coveleski-Cle 25

Shutouts
Mays-Bos 8
Johnson-Was 8
Bush-Bos 7
Jones-Bos 5

Saves
Mogridge-NY 7
Bagby-Cle 6
Russell-NY 4
Geary-Phi 4

Innings Pitched
Perry-Phi 332.1
Johnson-Was 326.0
Coveleski-Cle 311.0
Mays-Bos 293.1
Bush-Bos 272.2

Fewest Hits/Game
Sothoron-StL 6.55
Johnson-Was 6.65
Harper-Was 6.71
Ruth-Bos 6.76
Mays-Bos 7.06

Fewest BB/Game
Cicotte-Chi 1.35
Mogridge-NY 1.62
Benz-Chi 1.64
Enzmann-Cle 1.91
Johnson-Was 1.93

Strikeouts
Johnson-Was 162
Shaw-Was 129
Bush-Bos 125
Morton-Cle 123
Mays-Bos 114

Strikeouts/Game
Morton-Cle 5.16
Shaw-Was 4.81
Johnson-Was 4.47
Bush-Bos 4.13
Love-NY 3.74

Ratio
Johnson-Was 8.81
Ruth-Bos 9.52
Sothoron-StL 9.56
Coveleski-Cle 9.87
Mays-Bos 9.88

Earned Run Average
Johnson-Was 1.27
Coveleski-Cle 1.82
Sothoron-StL 1.94
Perry-Phi 1.98
Bush-Bos 2.11

Adjusted ERA
Johnson-Was 214
Coveleski-Cle 164
Perry-Phi 148
Sothoron-StL 141
Mogridge-NY 129

Opponents' Batting Avg.
Sothoron-StL 205
Johnson-Was 210
Harper-Was 212
Ruth-Bos 214
Mays-Bos 221

Opponents' On Base Pct.
Johnson-Was 260
Sothoron-StL 274
Ruth-Bos 277
Coveleski-Cle 279
Mays-Bos 284

Starter Runs
Johnson-Was 54.4
Coveleski-Cle 32.8
Perry-Phi 29.4
Bush-Bos 20.0
Sothoron-StL 19.4

Adjusted Starter Runs
Johnson-Was 52.6
Coveleski-Cle 40.6
Perry-Phi 35.1
Sothoron-StL 18.5
Bush-Bos 17.1

Clutch Pitching Index
Perry-Phi 124
Mogridge-NY 123
Coumbe-Cle 119
Russell-NY 119
Shellenback-Chi . . . 116

Relief Runs
Houck-StL 3.1

Adjusted Relief Runs
Houck-StL 2.8

Relief Ranking
Houck-StL 2.3

Total Pitcher Index
Johnson-Was 7.6
Coveleski-Cle 4.6
Mays-Bos 4.1
Perry-Phi 3.9
Bush-Bos 3.1

Total Baseball Ranking
Johnson-Was 7.6
Ruth-Bos 5.6
T.Cobb-Det 4.8
Coveleski-Cle 4.6
Mays-Bos 4.1

1919 National League

TEAM	G	W	L	PCT	GB	R	OR	AB	H	2B	3B	HR	BB	SO	AVG	OBP	SLG	PRO	PRO+	BR	/A	PF	CHI	RC	SB	CS	SBA	SBR
CIN	140	96	44	.686		577	401	4577	1204	135	83	20	405	368	.263	.327	.342	.669	110	43	57	97	104	552	143			
NY	140	87	53	.621	9	605	470	4664	1254	204	64	40	328	407	.269	.322	.366	.688	113	64	70	99	106	576	157			
CHI	140	75	65	.536	21	454	407	4581	1174	166	58	21	298	359	.256	.308	.332	.640	98	-14	-16	101	93	500	150			
PIT	139	71	68	.511	24.5	472	466	4538	1132	130	82	17	344	381	.249	.306	.325	.631	91	-25	-44	104	100	493	196			
BRO	141	69	71	.493	27	525	513	4844	1272	167	66	25	258	405	.263	.304	.340	.644	97	-13	-24	102	104	518	112			
BOS	140	57	82	.410	38.5	465	563	4746	1201	142	62	24	355	481	.253	.311	.324	.635	100	-17	4	96	92	509	145			
STL	138	54	83	.394	40.5	463	552	4588	1175	163	52	18	304	418	.256	.305	.326	.631	101	-28	1	94	99	485	148			
PHI	138	47	90	.343	47.5	510	699	4746	1191	208	50	42	323	469	.251	.303	.342	.645	92	-9	-45	107	101	506	114			
TOT	558					4071		37284	9603	1315	517	207	2615	3288	.258	.311	.337	.648							1165			

TEAM	CG	SH	SV	IP	H	H/G	HR	BB	SO	RAT	ERA	ERA+	OAV	OOB	PR	/A	PF	CPI	FA	E	DP	FW	PW	BW	SBW	DIF
CIN	89	23	9	1274	1104	7.8	21	298	407	10.0	2.23	124	.239	.288	96	75	95	104	.974	151	98	2.7	8.3	6.3		8.6
NY	72	11	13	1256	1153	8.3	34	305	340	10.6	2.70	104	.247	.296	29	14	96	96	.964	216	96	-1.0	1.6	7.8		8.7
CHI	80	21	5	1265	1127	8.0	14	294	495	10.3	2.21	130	.242	.291	98	93	99	106	.969	185	87	.7	10.3	-1.8		-4.3
PIT	91	17	4	1249	1113	8.0	23	263	391	10.2	2.88	105	.244	.290	4	19	104	84	.970	165	89	1.8	2.1	-4.9		2.5
BRO	98	12	1	1281	1256	8.8	21	292	476	11.1	2.73	109	.262	.309	25	33	102	106	.963	219	84	-1.1	3.7	-2.7		-.9
BOS	79	5	9	1270[1]	1313	9.3	29	337	374	11.8	3.17	90	.276	.327	-36	-45	98	107	.966	204	111	-.4	-5.0	.4		-7.6
STL	55	6	8	1217[1]	1146	8.5	25	415	414	11.9	3.23	86	.256	.326	-44	-60	96	97	.963	214	112	-1.1	-6.7	.1		-6.8
PHI	93	6	2	1252	1391	10.0	40	408	397	13.3	4.14	78	.294	.356	-171	-129	111	100	.963	218	112	-1.3	-14.3	-5.0		-.8
TOT	657	101	51	10064[2]		8.6				11.2	2.91		.258	.311					.967	1572	789					

Runs		Hits		Doubles		Triples		Home Runs		Total Bases	
Burns-NY	86	Olson-Bro	164	Youngs-NY	31	Southworth-Pit	14	Cravath-Phi	12	Myers-Bro	223
Groh-Cin	79	Hornsby-StL	163	Luderus-Phi	30	Myers-Bro	14	Kauff-NY	10	Hornsby-StL	220
Daubert-Cin	79	Roush-Cin	162	Burns-NY	30			Williams-Phi	9	Z.Wheat-Bro	219
Rath-Cin	77	Burns-NY	162	Kauff-NY	27			Hornsby-StL	8	Roush-Cin	217
				Meusel-Phi	26			Doyle-NY	7	Burns-NY	216

Runs Batted In		Runs Produced		Bases On Balls		Batting Average		On Base Percentage		Slugging Average	
Myers-Bro	73	Roush-Cin	140	Burns-NY	82	Cravath-Phi	.341	Burns-NY	.396	Cravath-Phi	.640
Roush-Cin	71	Groh-Cin	137	Rath-Cin	64	Roush-Cin	.321	Groh-Cin	.392	Myers-Bro	.436
Hornsby-StL	71	Hornsby-StL	131	Groh-Cin	56	Hornsby-StL	.318	Hornsby-StL	.384	Doyle-NY	.433
Kauff-NY	67			Luderus-Phi	54	Youngs-NY	.311	Youngs-NY	.384	Groh-Cin	.431
Groh-Cin	63			Boeckel-Pit-Bos	53	Groh-Cin	.310	Roush-Cin	.380	Roush-Cin	.431

Production		Adjusted Production		Batter Runs		Adjusted Batter Runs		Clutch Hitting Index		Runs Created	
Groh-Cin	.823	Hornsby-StL	154	Cravath-Phi	32.2	Hornsby-StL	33.8	Kopf-Cin	125	Burns-NY	96
Hornsby-StL	.814	Groh-Cin	151	Burns-NY	31.1	Burns-NY	31.1	Southworth-Pit	123	Roush-Cin	88
Roush-Cin	.811	Roush-Cin	147	Hornsby-StL	28.5	Groh-Cin	29.4	Zimmerman-NY	121	Hornsby-StL	87
Burns-NY	.801	Burns-NY	142	Groh-Cin	27.4	Roush-Cin	29.1	Roush-Cin	121	Youngs-NY	84
Youngs-NY	.799	Youngs-NY	142	Roush-Cin	26.9	Cravath-Phi	28.3	Merkle-Chi	120	Groh-Cin	81

Total Average		Stolen Bases		Stolen Base Average		Stolen Base Runs		Fielding Runs		Total Player Rating	
Burns-NY	.909	Burns-NY	40					Maranville-Bos	28.7	Maranville-Bos	4.7
Groh-Cin	.887	Cutshaw-Pit	36					Fletcher-NY	24.0	Hornsby-StL	4.5
Youngs-NY	.846	Bigbee-Pit	31					Bigbee-Pit	17.9	Stock-StL	4.3
Hornsby-StL	.837	Smith-StL	30					Killefer-Chi	17.4	Groh-Cin	3.5
Roush-Cin	.833							Stock-StL	16.8	Roush-Cin	3.3

Wins		Win Percentage		Games		Complete Games		Shutouts		Saves	
J.Barnes-NY	25	Ruether-Cin	.760	Tuero-StL	45	Cooper-Pit	27	Alexander-Chi	9	Tuero-StL	4
Vaughn-Chi	21	Sallee-Cin	.750	Meadows-StL-Phi	40	Pfeffer-Bro	26	Eller-Cin	7		
Sallee-Cin	21	J.Barnes-NY	.735	Vaughn-Chi	38	Vaughn-Chi	25	Adams-Pit	6		
		Eller-Cin	.679	Eller-Cin	38	Rudolph-Bos	24	Fisher-Cin	5		
		Adams-Pit	.630	J.Barnes-NY	38						

Innings Pitched		Fewest Hits/Game		Fewest BB/Game		Strikeouts		Strikeouts/Game		Ratio	
Vaughn-Chi	306.2	Alexander-Chi	6.89	Adams-Pit	.79	Vaughn-Chi	141	Eller-Cin	4.97	Adams-Pit	8.17
J.Barnes-NY	295.2	Cooper-Pit	7.19	Sallee-Cin	.79	Eller-Cin	137	Alexander-Chi	4.63	Alexander-Chi	8.35
Cooper-Pit	286.2	Ruether-Cin	7.23	J.Barnes-NY	1.07	Alexander-Chi	121	Meadows-StL-Phi	4.17	J.Barnes-NY	9.13
Rudolph-Bos	273.2	Carlson-Pit	7.28	Cadore-Bro	1.40	Meadows-StL-Phi	116	Vaughn-Chi	4.14	Fisher-Cin	9.29
Nehf-Bos-NY	270.2	Fisher-Cin	7.28	Alexander-Chi	1.46	Cooper-Pit	106	Grimes-Bro	4.07	Miller-Pit	9.33

Earned Run Average		Adjusted ERA		Opponents' Batting Avg.		Opponents' On Base Pct.		Starter Runs		Adjusted Starter Runs	
Alexander-Chi	1.72	Alexander-Chi	167	Alexander-Chi	.211	Adams-Pit	.241	Vaughn-Chi	38.1	Vaughn-Chi	37.0
Vaughn-Chi	1.79	Vaughn-Chi	161	Adams-Pit	.220	Alexander-Chi	.245	Alexander-Chi	31.0	Adams-Pit	30.3
Ruether-Cin	1.82	Ruether-Cin	152	Ruether-Cin	.223	J.Barnes-NY	.260	Ruether-Cin	29.4	Alexander-Chi	30.1
Toney-NY	1.84	Toney-NY	152	Cooper-Pit	.225	Fisher-Cin	.271	Adams-Pit	27.1	Ruether-Cin	25.7
Adams-Pit	1.98	Adams-Pit	152	Nehf-Bos-NY	.225	Miller-Pit	.272	Rudolph-Bos	22.5	Rudolph-Bos	20.8

Clutch Pitching Index		Relief Runs		Adjusted Relief Runs		Relief Ranking		Total Pitcher Index		Total Baseball Ranking	
Rudolph-Bos	141							Alexander-Chi	4.4	Maranville-Bos	4.7
Smith-Bro	141							Vaughn-Chi	4.2	Hornsby-StL	4.5
Martin-Chi	122							Ruether-Cin	3.1	Alexander-Chi	4.4
Jacobs-Phi-StL	122							Rudolph-Bos	2.9	Stock-StL	4.3
Toney-NY	120							Adams-Pit	2.7	Vaughn-Chi	4.2

TEAM	G	W	L	PCT	GB	R	OR	AB	H	2B	3B	HR	BB	SO	AVG	OBP	SLG	PRO	PRO+	BR	/A	PF	CHI	RC	SB	CS	SBA	SBR
CHI	140	88	52	.629		667	534	4675	1343	218	70	25	427	358	.287	.351	.380	.731	111	69	66	100	103	668	150			
CLE	139	84	55	.604	3.5	636	537	4565	1268	254	72	24	498	367	.278	.354	.381	.735	107	78	39	106	98	651	113			
NY	141	80	59	.576	7.5	578	506	4775	1275	193	49	45	386	479	.267	.326	.356	.682	96	-20	-24	101	104	575	101			
DET	140	80	60	.571	8	618	578	4665	1319	222	84	23	429	427	.283	.346	.381	.727	113	60	75	98	97	649	121			
STL	140	67	72	.482	20.5	533	567	4672	1234	187	73	31	391	443	.264	.326	.355	.681	95	-22	-36	103	97	560	74			
BOS	138	66	71	.482	20.5	564	552	4548	1188	181	49	33	471	411	.261	.336	.344	.680	103	-11	21	94	102	559	108			
WAS	142	56	84	.400	32	533	570	4757	1238	177	63	24	416	511	.260	.325	.339	.664	93	-47	-42	99	100	558	142			
PHI	140	36	104	.257	52	457	742	4730	1156	175	71	35	349	565	.244	.300	.334	.634	82	-108	-113	101	100	487	103			
TOT	560					4586		37387	10021	1607	531	240	3367	3561	.268	.333	.359	.692						912				

TEAM	CG	SH	SV	IP	H	H/G	HR	BB	SO	RAT	ERA	ERA+	OAV	OOB	PR	/A	PF	CPI	FA	E	DP	FW	PW	BW	SBW	DIF
CHI	88	14	3	1265²	1245	8.9	24	342	468	11.5	3.04	105	.262	.315	26	19	99	92	.969	176	116	1.6	2.0	6.9		7.5
CLE	80	10	10	1245	1242	9.0	19	362	432	11.8	2.94	114	.264	.321	39	53	104	98	.965	201	102	-.0	5.5	4.1		4.9
NY	85	14	7	1287	1143	8.0	47	433	500	11.3	2.82	113	.240	.309	58	53	99	92	.968	193	108	.7	5.5	-2.5		6.8
DET	85	10	4	1256	1254	9.0	35	436	428	12.4	3.30	97	.266	.333	-11	-14	99	98	.964	205	81	-.2	-1.5	7.8		3.8
STL	78	14	4	1256	1255	9.0	35	421	415	12.3	3.13	106	.264	.328	13	24	103	99	.963	215	98	-.8	2.5	-3.8		-.4
BOS	89	15	8	1224¹	1251	9.2	16	421	381	11.5	3.31	91	.275	.341	-12	-41	94	101	.975	140	118	3.8	-4.3	2.2		-4.2
WAS	68	13	10	1274¹	1237	8.7	20	451	536	12.2	3.01	106	.259	.328	30	28	99	99	.960	227	86	-1.4	2.9	-4.4		-11.1
PHI	72	1	3	1239¹	1371	10.0	44	503	417	13.8	4.26	80	.292	.364	-143	-118	106	96	.956	257	96	-3.5	-12.4	-11.8		-6.3
TOT	645	91	49	10047²		9.0				12.2	3.22		.268	.333					.965	1614	805					

Runs
Ruth-Bos 103
Sisler-StL 96
Cobb-Det 92
Weaver-Chi 89
Peckinpaugh-NY ... 89

Hits
Veach-Det 191
Cobb-Det 191
Jackson-Chi 181
Sisler-StL 180
Rice-Was 179

Doubles
Veach-Det 45
Speaker-Cle 38
Cobb-Det 36
O'Neill-Cle 35

Triples
Veach-Det 17
Sisler-StL 15
Heilmann-Det 15
Jackson-Chi 14
Cobb-Det 13

Home Runs
Ruth-Bos 29
T.Walker-Phi 10
Sisler-StL 10
Baker-NY 10
Smith-Cle 9

Total Bases
Ruth-Bos 284
Veach-Det 279
Sisler-StL 271
Jackson-Chi 261

Runs Batted In
Ruth-Bos 114
Veach-Det 101
Jackson-Chi 96
Heilmann-Det 93
Lewis-NY 89

Runs Produced
Ruth-Bos 188
Veach-Det 185
Sisler-StL 169
Jackson-Chi 168
E.Collins-Chi 163

Bases On Balls
Graney-Cle 105
Ruth-Bos 101
Judge-Was 81
Hooper-Bos 79
Bush-Det 75

Batting Average
Cobb-Det .... .384
Veach-Det .... .355
Sisler-StL .... .352
Jackson-Chi ...... .351
Flagstead-Det ..... .331

On Base Percentage
Ruth-Bos .... .456
Cobb-Det .... .429
Jackson-Chi ...... .422
Leibold-Chi .... .404
E.Collins-Chi ..... .400

Slugging Average
Ruth-Bos .... .657
Sisler-StL .... .530
Veach-Det .... .519
Cobb-Det .... .515
Jackson-Chi ...... .506

Production
Ruth-Bos 1.114
Cobb-Det 944
Jackson-Chi 928
Sisler-StL 921
Veach-Det 916

Adjusted Production
Ruth-Bos 224
Cobb-Det 168
Veach-Det 160
Jackson-Chi 159
Sisler-StL 153

Batter Runs
Ruth-Bos 66.5
Jackson-Chi 41.7
Cobb-Det 41.6
Veach-Det 37.7
Sisler-StL 35.8

Adjusted Batter Runs
Ruth-Bos 74.0
Cobb-Det 44.0
Jackson-Chi 41.3
Veach-Det 40.1
Sisler-StL 33.4

Clutch Hitting Index
E.Collins-Chi 143
Lewis-NY 131
Jones-Det 130
Shanks-Was 123
Gardner-Cle 123

Runs Created
Ruth-Bos 128
Cobb-Det 116
Veach-Det 115
Sisler-StL 112
Jackson-Chi 111

Total Average
Ruth-Bos 1.358
Cobb-Det 1.056
Sisler-StL 1.000
Jackson-Chi 997
Veach-Det 968

Stolen Bases
E.Collins-Chi 33
Sisler-StL 28
Cobb-Det 28
Rice-Was 26

Stolen Base Average

Stolen Base Runs

Fielding Runs
Pratt-NY 28.0
Peckinpaugh-NY .. 27.7
Felsch-Chi 21.4
Speaker-Cle 19.1
Young-Det 17.3

Total Player Rating
Ruth-Bos 6.3
Peckinpaugh-NY ... 5.1
Sisler-StL 4.3
Veach-Det 4.3
Pratt-NY 3.8

Wins
Cicotte-Chi 29
Coveleski-Cle 24
Williams-Chi 23
Dauss-Det 21

Win Percentage
Cicotte-Chi .... .806
Dauss-Det ...... .700
Williams-Chi ..... .676
Pennock-Bos .... .667
Coveleski-Cle .... .667

Games
Shaw-Was 45
Russell-NY-Bos 44
Kinney-Phi 43
Coveleski-Cle...... 43

Complete Games
Cicotte-Chi 30
Williams-Chi 27
Johnson-Was 27
Mays-Bos-NY ... 26
Coveleski-Cle 24

Shutouts
Johnson-Was 7

Saves
Russell-NY-Bos 5
Shawkey-NY 5
Shaw-Was 5
Coveleski-Cle 4

Innings Pitched
Shaw-Was 306.2
Cicotte-Chi 306.2
Williams-Chi 297.0
Johnson-Was 290.1
Coveleski-Cle ... 286.0

Fewest Hits/Game
Johnson-Was 7.28
Thormahlen-NY ... 7.39
Shawkey-NY 7.51
Cicotte-Chi 7.51
Mays-Bos-NY ... 7.68

Fewest BB/Game
Cicotte-Chi....... 1.44
Johnson-Was 1.58
Bagby-Cle 1.64
Williams-Chi 1.76
Coveleski-Cle 1.89

Strikeouts
Johnson-Was 147
Shaw-Was 128
Williams-Chi 125
Shawkey-NY 122
Coveleski-Cle 118

Strikeouts/Game
Erickson-Det-Was . 5.52
Russell-NY-Bos .. 4.80
Johnson-Was 4.56
Kinney-Phi 4.31
Leonard-Det 4.22

Ratio
Cicotte-Chi....... 9.01
Johnson-Was 9.08
Williams-Chi 10.12
Thormahlen-NY ... 10.49
Quinn-NY 10.59

Earned Run Average
Johnson-Was 1.49
Cicotte-Chi 1.82
Weilman-StL 2.07
Mays-Bos-NY 2.10
Sothoron-StL 2.20

Adjusted ERA
Johnson-Was 215
Cicotte-Chi 175
Weilman-StL 160
Sothoron-StL 151
Mays-Bos-NY 147

Opponents' Batting Avg.
Johnson-Was ...... .219
Cicotte-Chi .... .228
Thormahlen-NY ... .228
Shawkey-NY ..... .231
Mays-Bos-NY .... .233

Opponents' On Base Pct.
Johnson-Was ..... .259
Cicotte-Chi .... .261
Williams-Chi ..... .289
Morton-Cle .... .293
Quinn-NY .... .295

Starter Runs
Johnson-Was 56.0
Cicotte-Chi 47.8
Mays-Bos-NY 33.3
Sothoron-StL 30.7
Coveleski-Cle 19.4

Adjusted Starter Runs
Johnson-Was 55.3
Cicotte-Chi 46.3
Sothoron-StL 33.4
Mays-Bos-NY 29.4
Coveleski-Cle..... 23.2

Clutch Pitching Index
Weilman-StL 119
Sothoron-StL 114
Ehmke-Det 113
Harper-Was 107
Pennock-Bos 107

Relief Runs
Phillips-Cle 1.7

Adjusted Relief Runs
Phillips-Cle 2.4

Relief Ranking
Phillips-Cle 2.0

Total Pitcher Index
Johnson-Was 7.2
Cicotte-Chi 5.2
Mays-Bos-NY ... 3.8
Coveleski-Cle 3.6
Sothoron-StL 3.1

Total Baseball Ranking
Ruth-Bos 7.9
Johnson-Was 7.1
Cicotte-Chi 5.2
Peckinpaugh-NY ... 5.1
Sisler-StL 4.3

TEAM	G	W	L	PCT	GB	R	OR	AB	H	2B	3B	HR	BB	SO	AVG	OBP	SLG	PRO	PRO+	BR	/A	PF	CHI	RC	SB	CS	SBA	SBR
BRO	155	93	61	.604		660	528	5399	1493	205	99	28	359	391	.277	.324	.367	.691	100	19	-2	103	103	637	70	80	47	-27
NY	155	86	68	.558	7	682	543	5309	1427	210	76	46	432	545	.269	.327	.363	.690	104	23	30	99	107	628	131	113	54	-29
CIN	154	82	71	.536	10.5	639	569	5176	1432	169	76	18	382	367	.277	.332	.349	.681	102	11	20	99	104	602	158	128	55	-29
PIT	155	79	75	.513	14	530	552	5219	1342	162	90	16	374	405	.257	.310	.332	.642	86	-67	-84	103	99	544	181	117	61	-16
STL	155	75	79	.487	18	675	682	5495	1589	238	96	32	373	484	.289	.337	.385	.722	117	83	110	96	94	704	126	114	53	-31
CHI	154	75	79	.487	18	619	635	5117	1350	223	67	34	428	421	.264	.326	.354	.680	98	7	-5	102	101	589	115	129	47	-43
BOS	153	62	90	.408	30	523	670	5218	1358	168	86	23	385	488	.260	.315	.339	.654	97	-45	-21	96	93	557	88	98	47	-32
PHI	153	62	91	.405	30.5	565	714	5264	1385	229	54	64	283	531	.263	.305	.305	.669	93	-30	-57	105	99	577	100	83	55	-20
TOT	617					4893		42197	11376	1604	644	261	3016	3632	.270	.322	.357	.679							969	862	53	-227

TEAM	CG	SH	SV	IP	H	H/G	HR	BB	SO	RAT	ERA	ERA+	OAV	OOB	PR	/A	PF	CPI	FA	E	DP	FW	PW	BW	SBW	DIF
BRO	89	17	10	1427¹	1381	8.7	25	327	553	10.9	2.62	122	.259	.304	81	91	102	102	.966	226	118	-.2	9.7	-.2	.1	6.5
NY	86	18	9	1408²	1379	8.8	44	297	380	10.8	2.80	107	.261	.303	51	30	96	99	.969	210	127	.8	3.2	3.2	-.0	1.9
CIN	90	12	9	1391²	1327	8.6	26	393	435	11.3	2.90	105	.256	.313	36	22	97	97	.968	200	125	1.3	2.4	2.1	-.0	-.2
PIT	92	17	10	1415¹	1389	8.8	25	280	444	10.8	2.89	111	.261	.301	39	51	103	91	.971	186	119	2.2	5.5	-9.0	1.3	2.0
STL	72	9	12	1426²	1488	9.4	30	479	529	12.8	3.43	87	.277	.343	-47	-72	95	103	.961	256	136	-2.0	-7.7	11.8	-.3	-3.8
CHI	95	13	9	1388²	1459	9.5	37	382	508	12.1	3.27	98	.276	.328	-21	-10	102	102	.965	225	112	-.2	-1.1	-.5	-1.6	1.4
BOS	93	14	6	1386¹	1464	9.5	39	415	368	12.4	3.54	86	.280	.337	-62	-75	97	100	.964	239	125	-1.1	-8.0	-2.2	-.4	-2.2
PHI	77	8	11	1380²	1480	9.6	35	444	419	12.8	3.63	94	.284	.345	-76	-35	109	102	.964	232	135	-.7	-3.7	-6.1	.9	-4.8
TOT	694	108	76	11225¹		9.1				11.7	3.13		.270	.322					.966	1774	1007					

Runs		Hits		Doubles		Triples		Home Runs		Total Bases	
Burns-NY	115	Hornsby-StL	218	Hornsby-StL	44	Myers-Bro	22	Williams-Phi	15	Hornsby-StL	329
Bancroft-Phi-NY	102	Youngs-NY	204	Bancroft-Phi-NY	36	Hornsby-StL	20	Meusel-Phi	14	Williams-Phi	293
Daubert-Cin	97	Stock-StL	204	Williams-Phi	36	Roush-Cin	16	Kelly-NY	11	Youngs-NY	277
Hornsby-StL	96	Roush-Cin	196	Myers-Bro	36	Maranville-Bos	15	Robertson-Chi	10	Wheat-Bro	270
Youngs-NY	92	Williams-Phi	192	Burns-NY	35	Bigbee-Pit	15	McHenry-StL	10	Myers-Bro	269

Runs Batted In		Runs Produced		Bases On Balls		Batting Average		On Base Percentage		Slugging Average	
Kelly-NY	94	Hornsby-StL	181	Burns-NY	76	Hornsby-StL	.370	Hornsby-StL	.431	Hornsby-StL	.559
Hornsby-StL	94	Roush-Cin	167	Youngs-NY	75	Nicholson-Pit	.360	Youngs-NY	.427	Nicholson-Pit	.530
Roush-Cin	90	Youngs-NY	164	Paskert-Chi	64	Youngs-NY	.351	Roush-Cin	.386	Williams-Phi	.497
Duncan-Cin	83	Stock-StL	161	Hornsby-StL	60	Roush-Cin	.339	Wheat-Bro	.385	Youngs-NY	.477
Myers-Bro	80	Myers-Bro	159	Groh-Cin	60	Wheat-Bro	.328	Groh-Cin	.375	Meusel-Phi	.473

Production		Adjusted Production		Batter Runs		Adjusted Batter Runs		Clutch Hitting Index		Runs Created	
Hornsby-StL	.990	Hornsby-StL	190	Hornsby-StL	62.6	Hornsby-StL	67.6	Whitted-Pit	151	Hornsby-StL	138
Youngs-NY	.904	Youngs-NY	161	Youngs-NY	47.1	Youngs-NY	48.4	Kopf-Cin	147	Youngs-NY	118
Williams-Phi	.861	Roush-Cin	142	Williams-Phi	32.1	Roush-Cin	31.1	Duncan-Cin	131	Williams-Phi	103
Wheat-Bro	.848	Williams-Phi	139	Wheat-Bro	31.9	Wheat-Bro	28.8	Roush-Cin	126	Wheat-Bro	102
Roush-Cin	.839	Wheat-Bro	138	Roush-Cin	29.7	Williams-Phi	27.5	Kelly-NY	122	Roush-Cin	98

Total Average		Stolen Bases		Stolen Base Average		Stolen Base Runs		Fielding Runs		Total Player Rating	
Hornsby-StL	1.008	Carey-Pit	52	Carey-Pit	83.9	Carey-Pit	9.6	Bancroft-Phi-NY	39.0	Hornsby-StL	8.1
Youngs-NY	.896	Roush-Cin	36	Frisch-NY	75.6	Frisch-NY	3.6	Lavan-StL	16.2	Bancroft-Phi-NY	5.7
Williams-Phi	.817	Frisch-NY	34	Neale-Cin	70.7	Neale-Cin	1.5	Roush-Cin	15.7	Youngs-NY	3.6
Wheat-Bro	.801	Bigbee-Pit	31	Bigbee-Pit	67.4	Tragesser-Phi	1.2	Maranville-Bos	14.3	Roush-Cin	3.4
Roush-Cin	.784	Neale-Cin	29	Meusel-Phi	60.7	Gowdy-Bos	1.2	Neale-Cin	14.3	Hollocher-Chi	2.7

Wins		Win Percentage		Games		Complete Games		Shutouts		Saves	
Alexander-Chi	27	Grimes-Bro	.676	Haines-StL	47	Alexander-Chi	33	Adams-Pit	8	Sherdel-StL	6
Cooper-Pit	24	Alexander-Chi	.659	Douglas-NY	46	Cooper-Pit	28	Alexander-Chi	7	McQuillan-Bos	5
Grimes-Bro	23	Toney-NY	.656	Alexander-Chi	46	Rixey-Phi	25			Alexander-Chi	5
Toney-NY	21	Pfeffer-Bro	.640	Scott-Bos	44	Grimes-Bro	25			Hubbell-NY-Phi	4
Nehf-NY	21	Nehf-NY	.636	Cooper-Pit	44	Vaughn-Chi	24			Mamaux-Bro	4

Innings Pitched		Fewest Hits/Game		Fewest BB/Game		Strikeouts		Strikeouts/Game		Ratio	
Alexander-Chi	363.1	Luque-Cin	7.28	Adams-Pit	.62	Alexander-Chi	173	Mamaux-Bro	4.77	Adams-Pit	8.86
Cooper-Pit	327.0	Ruether-Cin	7.96	Cooper-Pit	1.43	Vaughn-Chi	131	Alexander-Chi	4.29	Alexander-Chi	10.03
Grimes-Bro	303.2	Grimes-Bro	8.03	Nehf-NY	1.44	Grimes-Bro	131	Schupp-StL	4.27	Luque-Cin	10.05
Haines-StL	301.2	Mamaux-Bro	8.12	Benton-NY	1.44	Haines-StL	120	Marquard-Bro	4.22	J.Barnes-NY	10.12
Vaughn-Chi	301.0	Adams-Pit	8.21	Marquard-Bro	1.66	Schupp-StL	119	Sherdel-StL	3.92	Grimes-Bro	10.14

Earned Run Average		Adjusted ERA		Opponents' Batting Avg.		Opponents' On Base Pct.		Starter Runs		Adjusted Starter Runs	
Alexander-Chi	1.91	Alexander-Chi	168	Luque-Cin	.225	Adams-Pit	.259	Alexander-Chi	49.5	Alexander-Chi	52.4
Adams-Pit	2.16	Adams-Pit	149	Grimes-Bro	.238	Grimes-Bro	.282	Grimes-Bro	30.7	Grimes-Bro	33.0
Grimes-Bro	2.22	Grimes-Bro	144	Adams-Pit	.244	Alexander-Chi	.285	Adams-Pit	28.5	Adams-Pit	30.9
Cooper-Pit	2.39	Cooper-Pit	134	Ponder-Pit	.246	Luque-Cin	.286	Cooper-Pit	26.8	Cooper-Pit	29.8
Ruether-Cin	2.47	Vaughn-Chi	126	Ruether-Cin	.247	Ponder-Pit	.286	Vaughn-Chi	19.8	Vaughn-Chi	22.2

Clutch Pitching Index		Relief Runs		Adjusted Relief Runs		Relief Ranking		Total Pitcher Index		Total Baseball Ranking	
Meadows-Phi	121							Alexander-Chi	7.1	Hornsby-StL	8.1
Alexander-Chi	120							Grimes-Bro	5.4	Alexander-Chi	7.1
Vaughn-Chi	119							Smith-Bro	4.0	Bancroft-Phi-NY	5.7
Fillingim-Bos	118							Cooper-Pit	3.2	Grimes-Bro	5.4
Benton-NY	115							Adams-Pit	2.8	Smith-Bro	4.0

TEAM	G	W	L	PCT	GB	R	OR	AB	H	2B	3B	HR	BB	SO	AVG	OBP	SLG	PRO	PRO+	BR	/A	PF	CHI	RC	SB	CS	SBA	SBR
CLE	154	98	56	.636		857	642	5196	1574	300	95	35	576	379	.303	.376	.417	.793	113	125	98	103	98	827	73	93	44	-34
CHI	154	96	58	.623	2	794	665	5328	1574	263	98	37	471	355	.295	.357	.402	.759	107	49	49	100	100	769	109	96	53	-25
NY	154	95	59	.617	3	838	629	5176	1448	268	71	115	539	626	.280	.350	.426	.776	107	71	43	104	105	773	64	82	44	-30
STL	154	76	77	.497	21.5	797	766	5358	1651	279	83	50	427	339	.308	.363	.419	.782	110	93	68	103	95	822	121	79	61	-11
BOS	154	72	81	.471	25.5	650	698	5199	1397	216	71	22	533	429	.269	.342	.350	.692	93	-70	-41	96	97	637	98	111	47	-37
WAS	153	68	84	.447	29	723	802	5251	1526	233	81	36	433	543	.291	.351	.386	.737	104	7	27	97	98	718	160	114	58	-20
DET	155	61	93	.396	37	652	833	5215	1408	228	72	30	479	391	.270	.334	.359	.693	91	-80	-64	98	100	639	76	68	53	-18
PHI	156	48	106	.312	50	558	834	5256	1324	220	49	44	353	593	.252	.305	.338	.643	74	-188	-193	101	106	543	50	67	43	-25
TOT	617					5869		41979	11902	2007	620	369	3811	3655	.284	.347	.387	.734							751	710	51	-201

TEAM	CG	SH	SV	IP	H	H/G	HR	BB	SO	RAT	ERA	ERA+	OAV	OOB	PR	/A	PF	CPI	FA	E	DP	FW	PW	BW	SBW	DIF
CLE	94	11	7	1377	1448	9.5	31	401	466	12.3	3.41	111	.276	.331	57	58	100	98	.971	184	124	2.1	5.6	9.5	-.9	4.6
CHI	109	9	10	1386²	1467	9.5	45	405	438	12.3	3.59	105	.280	.335	31	24	99	98	.968	198	142	1.2	2.3	4.8	.0	10.7
NY	88	15	11	1368	1414	9.3	48	420	480	12.3	3.32	115	.270	.328	72	75	101	99	.969	194	129	1.4	7.3	4.2	-.5	5.6
STL	84	9	14	1378²	1481	9.7	53	578	444	13.7	4.03	97	.283	.359	-38	-23	103	99	.963	233	119	-1.2	-2.2	6.6	1.4	-5.0
BOS	92	11	6	1395¹	1481	9.7	39	456	481	12.7	3.82	95	.279	.339	-5	-30	96	93	.972	183	131	2.2	-2.9	-4.0	-1.2	1.3
WAS	81	10	10	1367	1521	10.0	51	520	418	13.7	4.17	89	.288	.357	-58	-70	98	97	.963	232	95	-1.3	-6.8	2.6	.5	-3.1
DET	74	9	7	1385	1487	9.7	46	561	483	13.7	4.04	92	.284	.359	-38	-51	98	99	.964	230	95	-.9	-4.9	-6.2	.7	-4.6
PHI	79	6	2	1380¹	1612	10.5	56	461	423	13.8	3.93	102	.302	.362	-21	12	106	110	.959	266	125	-3.3	1.2	-18.7	.0	-8.1
TOT	701	80	67	11038		9.7				13.1	3.79		.284	.347					.966	1720	960					

Runs
Ruth-NY 158
Speaker-Cle 137
Sisler-StL 137
E.Collins-Chi 117

Hits
Sisler-StL 257
E.Collins-Chi 224
Jackson-Chi 218
Jacobson-StL 216
Speaker-Cle 214

Doubles
Speaker-Cle 50
Sisler-StL 49
Jackson-Chi 42

Triples
Jackson-Chi 20
Sisler-StL 18
Hooper-Bos 17

Home Runs
Ruth-NY 54
Sisler-StL 19
T.Walker-Phi 17
Felsch-Chi 14

Total Bases
Sisler-StL 399
Ruth-NY 388
Jackson-Chi 336
Speaker-Cle 310
Jacobson-StL 305

Runs Batted In
Ruth-NY 137
Sisler-StL 122
Jacobson-StL 122
Jackson-Chi 121
Gardner-Cle 118

Runs Produced
Ruth-NY 241
Sisler-StL 240
Speaker-Cle 236
Jackson-Chi 214
Jacobson-StL 210

Bases On Balls
Ruth-NY 148
Speaker-Cle 97
Hooper-Bos 88
Young-Det 85
Roth-Was 75

Batting Average
Sisler-StL .... .407
Speaker-Cle 388
Jackson-Chi 382
Ruth-NY 376
E.Collins-Chi 372

On Base Percentage
Ruth-NY .... .530
Speaker-Cle 483
Sisler-StL .... .449
Jackson-Chi ...... .444
E.Collins-Chi ..... .438

Slugging Average
Ruth-NY .... .847
Sisler-StL 632
Jackson-Chi 589
Speaker-Cle 562
Felsch-Chi 540

Production
Ruth-NY 1.378
Sisler-StL 1.082
Speaker-Cle 1.045
Jackson-Chi 1.033
E.Collins-Chi 932

Adjusted Production
Ruth-NY 252
Sisler-StL 179
Jackson-Chi 172
Speaker-Cle 171
E.Collins-Chi 146

Batter Runs
Ruth-NY 113.2
Sisler-StL 73.2
Speaker-Cle 65.7
Jackson-Chi 58.4
E.Collins-Chi 42.3

Adjusted Batter Runs
Ruth-NY 106.7
Sisler-StL 68.5
Speaker-Cle 61.2
Jackson-Chi 58.4
E.Collins-Chi 42.3

Clutch Hitting Index
Gardner-Cle 144
Roth-Was 131
Smith-Cle 123
Risberg-Chi 121
Pratt-NY 118

Runs Created
Ruth-NY 211
Sisler-StL 176
Speaker-Cle 152
Jackson-Chi 145
E.Collins-Chi 134

Total Average
Ruth-NY 1.797
Sisler-StL 1.207
Speaker-Cle 1.165
Jackson-Chi 1.088
E.Collins-Chi ...... .984

Stolen Bases
Rice-Was 63
Sisler-StL 42
Roth-Was 24
Menosky-Bos 23
Tobin-StL 21

Stolen Base Average
E.Collins-Chi 71.4
Sisler-StL 71.2
Williams-StL 69.2
Rice-Was 67.7
Roth-Was 66.7

Stolen Base Runs
Sisler-StL 2.4
Burns-Phi-Cle 1.5
E.Collins-Chi 1.2
Smith-StL 9
Rice-Was 9

Fielding Runs
Perkins-Phi 22.8
Ward-NY 21.8
Rice-Was 21.4
Pinelli-Det 19.9
Felsch-Chi 17.7

Total Player Rating
Ruth-NY 8.6
Sisler-StL 7.8
E.Collins-Chi 5.6
Speaker-Cle 5.2
Jackson-Chi 4.0

Wins
Bagby-Cle 31
Mays-NY 26
Coveleski-Cle 24
Faber-Chi 23
Williams-Chi 22

Win Percentage
Bagby-Cle .... .721
Mays-NY .... .703
Kerr-Chi .... .700
Cicotte-Chi .... .677

Games
Bagby-Cle 48
Ayers-Det 46
Mays-NY 45
Kerr-Chi 45
Zachary-Was 44

Complete Games
Bagby-Cle 30
Faber-Chi 28
Cicotte-Chi 28
Mays-NY 26
Coveleski-Cle 26

Shutouts
Mays-NY 6
Shocker-StL 5
Shawkey-NY 5

Saves
Shocker-StL 5
Kerr-Chi 5
Burwell-StL 4

Innings Pitched
Bagby-Cle 339.2
Faber-Chi 319.0
Coveleski-Cle ... 315.0
Mays-NY 312.0
Cicotte-Chi 303.1

Fewest Hits/Game
Coveleski-Cle 8.11
Shocker-StL 8.21
Collins-NY 8.22
Shawkey-NY 8.27
Davis-StL 8.35

Fewest BB/Game
Quinn-NY 1.71
Coveleski-Cle 1.86
Bagby-Cle 2.09
Cicotte-Chi 2.20
Perry-Phi 2.22

Strikeouts
Coveleski-Cle 133
Williams-Chi 128
Shawkey-NY 126
Faber-Chi 108
Shocker-StL 107

Strikeouts/Game
Ayers-Det 4.44
Shawkey-NY 4.24
Harper-Bos 3.93
Shocker-StL 3.92
Williams-Chi 3.85

Ratio
Coveleski-Cle ... 10.09
Shocker-StL 10.92
Rommel-Phi 10.99
Shawkey-NY ... 11.16
Bagby-Cle 11.18

Earned Run Average
Shawkey-NY 2.45
Coveleski-Cle 2.49
Shocker-StL 2.71
Rommel-Phi 2.85
Bagby-Cle 2.89

Adjusted ERA
Shawkey-NY 155
Coveleski-Cle 153
Shocker-StL 144
Rommel-Phi 141
Bagby-Cle 131

Opponents' Batting Avg.
Coveleski-Cle ..... .243
Collins-NY .... .247
Shawkey-NY ..... .248
Shocker-StL ...... .248
Ehmke-Det .... .253

Opponents' On Base Pct.
Coveleski-Cle ..... .285
Shocker-StL ...... .305
Shawkey-NY ..... .308
Quinn-NY .... .308
Rommel-Phi ...... .309

Starter Runs
Coveleski-Cle 45.6
Shawkey-NY 39.6
Bagby-Cle 33.9
Shocker-StL 29.4
Faber-Chi 28.2

Adjusted Starter Runs
Coveleski-Cle 45.7
Shawkey-NY 40.3
Bagby-Cle 34.1
Shocker-StL 32.7
Faber-Chi 27.2

Clutch Pitching Index
Naylor-Phi 130
Harper-Bos 128
Davis-StL 117
Oldham-Det 116
Perry-Phi 113

Relief Runs

Adjusted Relief Runs

Relief Ranking

Total Pitcher Index
Coveleski-Cle 5.9
Shawkey-NY 4.3
Shocker-StL 4.0
Bagby-Cle 3.8
Mays-NY 3.7

Total Baseball Ranking
Ruth-NY 8.6
Sisler-StL 7.9
Coveleski-Cle 5.9
E.Collins-Chi 5.6
Speaker-Cle 5.2

1921 National League

TEAM	G	W	L	PCT	GB	R	OR	AB	H	2B	3B	HR	BB	SO	AVG	OBP	SLG	PRO	PRO+	BR	/A	PF	CHI	RC	SB	CS	SBA	SBR
NY	153	94	59	.614		840	637	5278	1575	237	93	75	469	390	.298	.359	.421	.780	112	94	92	100	104	795	137	114	55	-27
PIT	154	90	63	.588	4	692	595	5379	1533	231	104	37	341	371	.285	.330	.387	.717	93	-37	-55	103	102	684	134	93	59	-16
STL	154	87	66	.569	7	809	681	5309	1635	260	88	83	382	452	.308	.358	.437	.795	118	114	131	98	98	816	94	94	50	-28
BOS	153	79	74	.516	15	721	697	5385	1561	209	100	61	377	470	.290	.339	.400	.739	107	6	46	95	100	718	94	100	48	-32
BRO	152	77	75	.507	16.5	667	681	5263	1476	209	85	59	325	400	.280	.325	.386	.711	90	-52	-75	104	104	655	91	73	55	-17
CIN	153	70	83	.458	24	618	649	5112	1421	221	94	20	375	308	.278	.333	.370	.703	96	-56	-27	95	98	623	117	120	49	-37
CHI	153	64	89	.418	30	668	773	5321	1553	234	56	37	343	374	.292	.339	.378	.717	95	-31	-32	100	99	671	70	97	42	-37
PHI	154	51	103	.331	43.5	617	919	5329	1512	238	50	88	294	615	.284	.324	.397	.721	89	-37	-89	108	94	668	66	80	45	-28
TOT	613					5632		42376	12266	1839	670	460	2906	3380	.289	.338	.397	.736							803	771	51	-222

TEAM	CG	SH	SV	IP	H	H/G	HR	BB	SO	RAT	ERA	ERA+	OAV	OOB	PR	/A	PF	CPI	FA	E	DP	FW	PW	BW	SBW	DIF
NY	71	9	18	1372¹	1497	9.8	79	295	357	11.9	3.55	103	.286	.326	34	16	97	102	.971	187	155	1.3	1.6	9.1	.0	5.5
PIT	88	10	10	1415²	1448	9.2	37	322	500	11.5	3.17	121	.271	.316	96	104	101	96	.973	172	129	2.3	10.3	-5.4	1.2	5.3
STL	70	10	16	1371²	1486	9.8	61	399	464	12.6	3.62	101	.282	.337	24	5	97	102	.965	219	130	-.6	.5	12.9	-.0	-2.3
BOS	74	11	12	1385	1488	9.7	54	420	382	12.6	3.90	94	.280	.337	-18	-38	97	93	.969	199	122	.5	-3.8	4.5	-.4	1.6
BRO	82	8	12	1363¹	1556	10.3	46	361	471	12.9	3.70	105	.293	.342	13	28	103	103	.964	232	142	-1.5	2.8	-7.4	1.1	6.1
CIN	83	7	9	1363	1500	9.9	37	305	408	12.0	3.46	103	.287	.328	48	17	95	100	.969	193	139	.9	1.7	-2.7	-.9	-5.5
CHI	73	7	7	1363	1605	10.6	67	409	441	13.6	4.39	87	.303	.357	-93	-88	101	99	.974	166	129	2.5	-8.7	-3.2	-.9	-2.3
PHI	82	5	8	1348²	1665	11.1	79	371	333	13.8	4.48	94	.308	.356	-105	-39	112	99	.955	295	127	-5.2	-3.9	-8.8	-.0	-8.1
TOT	623	67	92	10982²		10.0				12.6	3.78		.289	.338					.967	1663	1073					

Runs
Hornsby-StL 131
Frisch-NY 121
Bancroft-NY 121
Powell-Bos 114
Burns-NY 111

Hits
Hornsby-StL 235
Frisch-NY 211
C.Bigbee-Pit 204
Johnston-Bro 203

Doubles
Hornsby-StL 44
Kelly-NY 42
Johnston-Bro 41
Grimes-Chi 38
McHenry-StL 37

Triples
Powell-Bos 18
Hornsby-StL 18
Grimm-Pit 17
Frisch-NY 17
C.Bigbee-Pit 17

Home Runs
Kelly-NY 23
Hornsby-StL 21
Williams-Phi 18
McHenry-StL 17
Fournier-StL 16

Total Bases
Hornsby-StL 378
Kelly-NY 310
McHenry-StL 305
Meusel-Phi-NY 302
Frisch-NY 300

Runs Batted In
Hornsby-StL 126
Kelly-NY 122
Youngs-NY 102
McHenry-StL 102
Frisch-NY 100

Runs Produced
Hornsby-StL 236
Frisch-NY 213
Kelly-NY 194
Youngs-NY 189
Bancroft-NY 182

Bases On Balls
Burns-NY 80
Youngs-NY 71
Grimes-Chi 70
Carey-Pit 70
Bancroft-NY 66

Batting Average
Hornsby-StL 397
Roush-Cin 352
McHenry-StL 350
Cruise-Bos 346
Fournier-StL 343

On Base Percentage
Hornsby-StL 458
Youngs-NY 411
Fournier-StL 409
Grimes-Chi 406
Carey-Pit 395

Slugging Average
Hornsby-StL 639
McHenry-StL 531
Kelly-NY 528
Meusel-Phi-NY 515
Mann-StL 512

Production
Hornsby-StL . . . 1.097
McHenry-StL 924
Fournier-StL 914
Meusel-Phi-NY 895
Kelly-NY 884

Adjusted Production
Hornsby-StL 191
McHenry-StL 145
Fournier-StL 144
Kelly-NY 131
Youngs-NY 129

Batter Runs
Hornsby-StL 74.4
Fournier-StL 34.5
McHenry-StL 33.5
Meusel-Phi-NY 27.6
Frisch-NY 24.8

Adjusted Batter Runs
Hornsby-StL 77.7
Fournier-StL 36.9
McHenry-StL 35.8
Cruise-Bos 28.5
Roush-Cin 26.7

Clutch Hitting Index
Youngs-NY 142
Stock-StL 142
Lavan-StL 140
Barnhart-Pit 123
Konetchy-Bro-Phi . . 115

Runs Created
Hornsby-StL 169
Frisch-NY 118
Fournier-StL 114
McHenry-StL 111
Meusel-Phi-NY 110

Total Average
Hornsby-StL . . . 1.203
Frisch-NY 902
Fournier-StL 882
Carey-Pit 868
Youngs-NY 860

Stolen Bases
Frisch-NY 49
Carey-Pit 37
Johnston-Bro 28
Bohne-Cin 26
Maranville-Pit 25

Stolen Base Average
Frisch-NY 79.0
Carey-Pit 75.5
Maisel-Chi 70.8
Maranville-Pit 67.6
Johnston-Bro 63.6

Stolen Base Runs
Frisch-NY 6.9
Carey-Pit 3.9
Stock-StL 1.5
Cutshaw-Pit 1.2

Fielding Runs
Lavan-StL 18.5
Bancroft-NY 17.4
Williams-Phi 16.3
C.Bigbee-Pit 16.2
Carey-Pit 16.1

Total Player Rating
Hornsby-StL 7.1
Bancroft-NY 4.8
Frisch-NY 4.3
Johnston-Bro 3.0
Kelly-NY 2.5

Wins
Grimes-Bro 22
Cooper-Pit 22
Oeschger-Bos 20
Nehf-NY 20
Rixey-Cin 19

Win Percentage
Doak-StL 714
Nehf-NY 667
Grimes-Bro 629
Barnes-NY 625
Toney-NY 621

Games
Scott-Bos 47
Oeschger-Bos 46
McQuillan-Bos 45
Watson-Bos 44
Fillingim-Bos 44

Complete Games
Grimes-Bro 30
Cooper-Pit 29
Luque-Cin 25

Shutouts
Oeschger-Bos 3
J.Morrison-Pit 3
Mitchell-Bro 3
Luque-Cin 3
Haines-StL 3
Fillingim-Bos 3
Douglas-NY 3
Alexander-Chi 3

Saves
North-StL 7
Barnes-NY 6
McQuillan-Bos 5

Innings Pitched
Cooper-Pit 327.0
Luque-Cin 304.0
Grimes-Bro 302.1
Rixey-Cin 301.0
Oeschger-Bos . . . 299.0

Fewest Hits/Game
Glazner-Pit 8.23
Adams-Pit 8.72
Oeschger-Bos 9.12
Pertica-StL 9.16
Nehf-NY 9.18

Fewest BB/Game
Adams-Pit 1.01
Alexander-Chi 1.18
Barnes-NY 1.53
Hubbell-Phi 1.55
Doak-StL 1.60

Strikeouts
Grimes-Bro 136
Cooper-Pit 134
Luque-Cin 102
McQuillan-Bos 94

Strikeouts/Game
Grimes-Bro 4.05
Cooper-Pit 3.69
Doak-StL 3.58
Martin-Chi 3.56
Glazner-Pit 3.38

Ratio
Adams-Pit 9.73
Glazner-Pit 10.92
Nehf-NY 11.15
Luque-Cin 11.34
Alexander-Chi 11.43

Earned Run Average
Doak-StL 2.59
Adams-Pit 2.64
Glazner-Pit 2.77
Rixey-Cin 2.78
Grimes-Bro 2.83

Adjusted ERA
Adams-Pit 145
Doak-StL 142
Glazner-Pit 138
Grimes-Bro 137
Mitchell-Bro 134

Opponents' Batting Avg.
Glazner-Pit 250
Adams-Pit 251
Pertica-StL 267
Watson-Bos 270
Nehf-NY 271

Opponents' On Base Pct.
Adams-Pit 272
Glazner-Pit 306
Nehf-NY 311
Luque-Cin 312
Doak-StL 313

Starter Runs
Rixey-Cin 33.4
Grimes-Bro 32.0
Doak-StL 27.6
Glazner-Pit 26.3
Adams-Pit 20.2

Adjusted Starter Runs
Grimes-Bro 35.5
Glazner-Pit 27.6
Rixey-Cin 26.6
Doak-StL 24.9
Cooper-Pit 21.2

Clutch Pitching Index
Barnes-NY 124
Mitchell-Bro 118
Doak-StL 116
Rixey-Cin 113
Grimes-Bro 112

Relief Runs
North-StL 2.3
Sallee-NY 1.5

Adjusted Relief Runs
North-StL 1.1
Sallee-NY 2

Relief Ranking
North-StL 1.1
Sallee-NY 2

Total Pitcher Index
Grimes-Bro 4.5
Rixey-Cin 2.8
Mitchell-Bro 2.8
Adams-Pit 2.5
Doak-StL 2.2

Total Baseball Ranking
Hornsby-StL 7.1
Bancroft-NY 4.8
Grimes-Bro 4.5
Frisch-NY 4.3
Johnston-Bro 3.0

TEAM	G	W	L	PCT	GB	R	OR	AB	H	2B	3B	HR	BB	SO	AVG	OBP	SLG	PRO	PRO+	BR	/A	PF	CHI	RC	SB	CS	SBA	SBR
NY	153	98	55	.641		948	708	5249	1576	285	87	134	588	569	.300	.375	.464	.839	116	142	122	102	102	929	89	64	58	-12
CLE	154	94	60	.610	4.5	925	712	5383	1656	355	90	42	623	376	.308	.383	.430	.813	111	112	98	102	100	916	51	42	55	-10
STL	154	81	73	.526	17.5	835	845	5442	1655	246	106	67	413	407	.304	.357	.425	.782	98	28	-20	106	102	827	91	71	56	-15
WAS	154	80	73	.523	18	704	738	5294	1468	240	96	42	462	472	.277	.342	.383	.725	95	-80	-47	95	101	712	112	66	63	-6
BOS	154	75	79	.487	23.5	668	696	5206	1440	248	69	17	428	344	.277	.335	.361	.696	84	-133	-116	97	107	642	83	65	56	-14
DET	154	71	82	.464	27	883	852	5461	1724	268	100	58	582	376	.316	.385	.433	.818	115	120	129	99	99	921	95	89	52	-25
CHI	154	62	92	.403	36.5	683	858	5329	1509	242	82	35	445	474	.283	.343	.379	.722	90	-86	-77	99	99	695	94	93	50	-28
PHI	155	53	100	.346	45	657	894	5465	1497	256	64	82	424	565	.274	.331	.389	.720	88	-102	-105	101	96	710	69	56	55	-13
TOT	616					6303		42829	12525	2140	694	477	3965	3583	.292	.356	.408	.765							684	546	56	-122

TEAM	CG	SH	SV	IP	H	H/G	HR	BB	SO	RAT	ERA	ERA+	OAV	OOB	PR	/A	PF	CPI	FA	E	DP	FW	PW	BW	SBW	DIF
NY	92	8	15	1364	1461	9.6	51	470	481	13.1	3.82	111	.277	.342	70	62	99	99	.965	222	138	-.3	5.8	11.4	.3	4.3
CLE	81	11	14	1377	1534	10.0	43	431	475	13.0	3.90	109	.288	.344	58	55	100	100	.967	204	124	.8	5.1	9.2	.5	1.4
STL	77	9	9	1379	1541	10.1	71	556	477	13.9	4.61	97	.288	.360	-51	-22	105	94	.964	224	127	-.3	-2.1	-1.9	.0	8.2
WAS	80	10	10	1383²	1568	10.2	51	442	452	13.3	3.97	104	.291	.349	47	22	96	102	.963	235	153	-.9	2.1	-4.4	.9	5.9
BOS	88	9	5	1364¹	1521	10.0	53	452	446	13.3	3.98	106	.291	.352	45	37	99	104	.975	157	151	3.5	3.5	-10.8	.1	1.8
DET	73	4	16	1386¹	1634	10.6	71	495	452	14.2	4.40	97	.297	.361	-18	-20	100	100	.963	232	107	-.8	-1.9	12.1	-.9	-14.0
CHI	84	7	9	1365¹	1603	10.6	52	549	392	14.4	4.94	86	.303	.372	-99	-107	99	94	.969	200	155	1.0	-10.0	-7.2	-1.2	2.3
PHI	75	2	7	1400¹	1645	10.6	85	548	431	14.3	4.61	97	.300	.367	-52	-25	104	102	.958	274	144	-3.1	-2.3	-9.8	.2	-8.5
TOT	650	60	85	11020		10.2				13.7	4.28		.292	.356					.965	1748	1099					

Runs
Ruth-NY 177
Tobin-StL 132
Peckinpaugh-NY .. 128
Sisler-StL 125
Cobb-Det 124

Hits
Heilmann-Det 237
Tobin-StL 236
Sisler-StL 216
Jacobson-StL 211
Veach-Det 207

Doubles
Speaker-Cle 52
Ruth-NY 44
Veach-Det 43
Heilmann-Det 43
Meusel-NY 40

Triples
Tobin-StL 18
Sisler-StL 18
Shanks-Was 18

Home Runs
Ruth-NY 59
Williams-StL 24
Meusel-NY 24
T.Walker-Phi 23
Heilmann-Det 19

Total Bases
Ruth-NY 457
Heilmann-Det 365
Meusel-NY 334
Tobin-StL 327
Sisler-StL 326

Runs Batted In
Ruth-NY 171
Heilmann-Det 139
Meusel-NY 135
Veach-Det 128
Gardner-Cle 120

Runs Produced
Ruth-NY 289
Heilmann-Det 234
Veach-Det 222
Gardner-Cle 218
Sisler-StL 217

Bases On Balls
Ruth-NY 144
Blue-Det 103
Peckinpaugh-NY ... 84
J.Sewell-Cle 80
Schang-NY 78

Batting Average
Heilmann-Det ..... .394
Cobb-Det .... .389
Ruth-NY .... .378
Sisler-StL .... .371
Speaker-Cle ...... .362

On Base Percentage
Ruth-NY .... .512
Cobb-Det .... .452
Heilmann-Det ..... .444
Speaker-Cle ...... .439
Williams-StL ...... .429

Slugging Average
Ruth-NY .... .846
Heilmann-Det ..... .606
Cobb-Det .... .596
Williams-StL ...... .561
Sisler-StL .... .560

Production
Ruth-NY 1.358
Heilmann-Det 1.051
Cobb-Det 1.048
Williams-StL ...... .990
Speaker-Cle ...... .977

Adjusted Production
Ruth-NY 236
Heilmann-Det 167
Cobb-Det 167
Speaker-Cle 146
Williams-StL 142

Batter Runs
Ruth-NY 119.2
Heilmann-Det 58.4
Cobb-Det 50.3
Williams-StL 42.5
Speaker-Cle 38.2

Adjusted Batter Runs
Ruth-NY 114.7
Heilmann-Det 59.9
Cobb-Det 51.5
Speaker-Cle 36.5
Williams-StL 35.2

Clutch Hitting Index
Gardner-Cle 141
Severeid-StL 127
Pratt-Bos 124
O'Rourke-Was 113
Sheely-Chi 112

Runs Created
Ruth-NY 238
Heilmann-Det 159
Cobb-Det 134
Sisler-StL 133
Williams-StL 130

Total Average
Ruth-NY 1.745
Cobb-Det 1.132
Heilmann-Det 1.121
Speaker-Cle 1.040
Williams-StL 1.037

Stolen Bases
Sisler-StL 35
Harris-Was 29
Rice-Was 26
Johnson-Chi 22
Cobb-Det 22

Stolen Base Average
Judge-Was 77.8
Harris-Was 76.3
Sisler-StL 76.1
Meusel-NY 73.9
Rice-Was 68.4

Stolen Base Runs
Sisler-StL 3.9
Harris-Was 3.3
Judge-Was 2.7
Welch-Phi 1.8

Fielding Runs
Scott-Bos 38.1
Collins-Chi 27.1
Dykes-Phi 25.0
Ward-NY 18.8
Johnson-Chi 18.0

Total Player Rating
Ruth-NY 9.4
Cobb-Det 4.9
Collins-Chi 4.0
Sisler-StL 3.6
Speaker-Cle 3.3

Wins
Shocker-StL 27
Mays-NY 27
Faber-Chi 25
Jones-Bos 23
Coveleski-Cle 23

Win Percentage
Mays-NY .... .750
Shocker-StL ...... .692
Bush-Bos .... .640
Coveleski-Cle ..... .639
Faber-Chi .... .625

Games
Mays-NY 49
Shocker-StL 47
Bayne-StL 47
Rommel-Phi 46

Complete Games
Faber-Chi 32
Shocker-StL 30
Mays-NY 30
Coveleski-Cle 28

Shutouts
Jones-Bos 5
Shocker-StL 4
Mogridge-Was 4
Faber-Chi 4

Saves
Middleton-Det 7
Mays-NY 7

Innings Pitched
Mays-NY 336.2
Faber-Chi 330.2
Shocker-StL 326.2
Coveleski-Cle 315.0
Kerr-Chi 308.2

Fewest Hits/Game
Faber-Chi 7.97
Bush-Bos 8.63
Mays-NY 8.88
Shawkey-NY 9.00
Johnson-Was 9.03

Fewest BB/Game
Hasty-Phi 2.01
Mays-NY 2.03
Mogridge-Was 2.06
Bagby-Cle 2.07
Zachary-Was 2.12

Strikeouts
Johnson-Was 143
Shocker-StL 132
Shawkey-NY 126
Faber-Chi 124
Leonard-Det 120

Strikeouts/Game
Johnson-Was 4.88
Shawkey-NY 4.63
Bayne-StL 4.50
Leonard-Det 4.41
Mails-Cle 4.03

Ratio
Faber-Chi 10.53
Mays-NY 11.15
Mogridge-Was 11.69
Shocker-StL 12.04
Jones-Bos 12.11

Earned Run Average
Faber-Chi 2.48
Mogridge-Was 3.00
Mays-NY 3.05
Hoyt-NY 3.09
Jones-Bos 3.22

Adjusted ERA
Faber-Chi 171
Mays-NY 139
Mogridge-Was 137
Hoyt-NY 137
Jones-Bos 131

Opponents' Batting Avg.
Faber-Chi .... .242
Mays-NY .... .257
Bush-Bos .... .260
Shawkey-NY .... .263
Johnson-Was ...... .263

Opponents' On Base Pct.
Faber-Chi .... .297
Mays-NY .... .303
Mogridge-Was ..... .313
Shocker-StL ...... .319
Johnson-Was ...... .326

Starter Runs
Faber-Chi 66.3
Mays-NY 46.2
Mogridge-Was 41.0
Hoyt-NY 37.3
Jones-Bos 35.1

Adjusted Starter Runs
Faber-Chi 64.6
Mays-NY 44.4
Hoyt-NY 35.8
Mogridge-Was 35.7
Shocker-StL 33.6

Clutch Pitching Index
Russell-Bos 122
Zachary-Was 118
Keefe-Phi 114
Uhle-Cle 108
Sothoron-SL-Bs-Cle .. 108

Relief Runs

Adjusted Relief Runs

Relief Ranking

Total Pitcher Index
Faber-Chi 7.0
Mays-NY 5.8
Shocker-StL 4.3
Jones-Bos 4.0
Hoyt-NY 3.3

Total Baseball Ranking
Ruth-NY 8.7
Faber-Chi 7.0
Mays-NY 5.8
Cobb-Det 4.9
Shocker-StL 4.3

TEAM	G	W	L	PCT	GB	R	OR	AB	H	2B	3B	HR	BB	SO	AVG	OBP	SLG	PRO	PRO+	BR	/A	PF	CHI	RC	SB	CS	SBA	SBR
NY	156	93	61	.604		852	**658**	5454	1661	253	90	80	448	421	.305	**.363**	.428	.791	109	77	70	101	99	848	116	83	58	-15
CIN	156	86	68	.558	7	766	677	5282	1561	226	99	45	436	381	.296	.353	.401	.754	102	8	23	98	99	737	130	136	49	-43
STL	154	85	69	.552	8	863	819	5425	1634	**280**	88	107	447	425	.301	.357	**.444**	**.801**	**118**	91	132	95	99	**860**	73	63	54	-16
PIT	155	85	69	.552	8	**865**	736	5521	**1698**	239	**110**	52	423	326	**.308**	.360	.419	.779	106	56	46	101	102	848	**145**	59	**71**	**8**
CHI	156	80	74	.519	13	771	808	5335	1564	248	71	42	**525**	447	.293	.359	.390	.749	97	7	-8	102	98	752	97	108	47	-36
BRO	155	76	78	.494	17	743	754	5413	1569	235	76	56	339	318	.290	.335	.392	.727	94	-58	-52	99	105	709	79	60	57	-12
PHI	154	57	96	.373	35.5	738	920	5459	1537	268	55	**116**	450	611	.282	.341	.415	.756	92	-3	-77	110	95	771	48	60	44	-22
BOS	154	53	100	.346	39.5	596	822	5161	1355	162	73	32	387	451	.263	.317	.341	.658	78	-179	-155	96	**106**	566	67	65	51	-19
TOT	620					6194		43050	12579	1911	662	530	3455	3380	.292	.348	.404	.753							755	634	54	-154

TEAM	CG	SH	SV	IP	H	H/G	HR	BB	SO	RAT	ERA	ERA+	OAV	OOB	PR	/A	PF	CPI	FA	E	DP	FW	PW	BW	SBW	DIF
NY	76	7	**15**	1396[1]	**1454**	9.4	71	393	388	12.0	**3.45**	116	**.272**	.324	**100**	83	98	99	**.970**	194	145	1.1	**7.8**	6.6	.4	.0
CIN	**88**	8	3	1385[2]	1481	9.6	**49**	**326**	357	11.9	3.53	113	.278	**.322**	87	69	97	95	.968	205	147	.4	6.5	2.2	-2.2	2.2
STL	60	8	12	1362[2]	1609	10.6	61	447	465	13.9	4.44	87	.299	.358	-52	-87	94	98	.961	239	122	-2.0	-8.2	**12.5**	.3	5.5
PIT	**88**	**15**	7	1387[1]	1613	10.5	52	358	490	13.0	3.98	102	.296	.343	18	13	99	99	**.970**	**187**	126	**1.5**	1.2	4.3	**2.6**	-1.6
CHI	74	8	12	1397[2]	1579	10.2	77	475	402	13.6	4.34	97	.292	.356	-38	-24	102	99	.968	204	**154**	.5	-2.3	-.8	-1.6	7.1
BRO	82	12	8	1385[2]	1574	10.2	74	490	**499**	13.6	4.05	100	.293	.356	8	2	99	**106**	.967	208	139	.1	.2	-4.9	.7	2.9
PHI	73	6	5	1372	1692	11.1	89	460	394	14.4	4.64	101	.307	.365	-82	7	114	102	.965	225	152	-1.1	.7	-7.3	-.3	-11.5
BOS	63	7	6	1348	1565	10.4	57	489	360	13.9	4.37	91	.298	.361	-41	-57	98	100	.965	215	121	-.4	-5.4	-14.6	.0	-3.1
TOT	604	71	68	11035[1]		10.2				13.3	4.10		.292	.348					.967	1677	1106					

Runs
Hornsby-StL 141
Carey-Pit 140
Smith-StL 117
Bancroft-NY 117
Maranville-Pit 115

Hits
Hornsby-StL 250
Bigbee-Pit 215
Bancroft-NY 209
Carey-Pit 207
Daubert-Cin 205

Doubles
Hornsby-StL 46
Grimes-Chi 45
Duncan-Cin 44
Bancroft-NY 41
Hollocher-Chi 37

Triples
Daubert-Cin 22
Meusel-NY 17
Maranville-Pit 15
Bigbee-Pit 15

Home Runs
Hornsby-StL 42
Williams-Phi 26
Lee-Phi 17
Kelly-NY 17

Total Bases
Hornsby-StL 450
Meusel-NY 314
Wheat-Bro 302
Williams-Phi 300
Daubert-Cin 300

Runs Batted In
Hornsby-StL 152
Meusel-NY 132
Wheat-Bro 112
Kelly-NY 107

Runs Produced
Hornsby-StL 251
Meusel-NY 216
Bigbee-Pit 207
Carey-Pit 200
Wheat-Bro 188

Bases On Balls
Carey-Pit 80
O'Farrell-Chi 79
Bancroft-NY 79
Burns-Cin 78
Grimes-Chi 75

Batting Average
Hornsby-StL 401
Grimes-Chi 354
Miller-Chi 352
Bigbee-Pit 350
Tierney-Pit 345

On Base Percentage
Hornsby-StL 459
Grimes-Chi 442
O'Farrell-Chi 439
Carey-Pit 408
Bigbee-Pit 405

Slugging Average
Hornsby-StL 722
Grimes-Chi 572
Lee-Phi 540
Tierney-Pit 515
Williams-Phi 514

Production
Hornsby-StL 1.181
Grimes-Chi 1.014
Williams-Phi 905
Miller-Chi 899
Walker-Phi 899

Adjusted Production
Hornsby-StL 210
Grimes-Chi 157
Daubert-Cin 130
Wheat-Bro 129
Miller-Chi 128

Batter Runs
Hornsby-StL 90.0
Grimes-Chi 47.1
Williams-Phi 27.5
Walker-Phi 26.3
Daubert-Cin 24.7

Adjusted Batter Runs
Hornsby-StL 98.7
Grimes-Chi 44.8
Daubert-Cin 26.8
Wheat-Bro 25.2
Russell-Phi 23.4

Clutch Hitting Index
Terry-Chi 125
Harper-Cin 117
Meusel-NY 116
Pinelli-Cin 115
Tierney-Pit 114

Runs Created
Hornsby-StL 200
Carey-Pit 131
Grimes-Chi 130
Walker-Phi 118
Bigbee-Pit 116

Total Average
Hornsby-StL 1.353
Grimes-Chi 1.107
Carey-Pit 995
O'Farrell-Chi 951
Walker-Phi 918

Stolen Bases
Carey-Pit 51
Frisch-NY 31
Burns-Cin 30
Maranville-Pit 24
Bigbee-Pit 24

Stolen Base Average
Carey-Pit 96.2
Traynor-Pit 85.0
Smith-StL 72.0
Johnston-Bro 66.7
Youngs-NY 65.4

Stolen Base Runs
Carey-Pit 14.1
Traynor-Pit 3.3
Kelly-NY 1.8
T.Griffith-Bro 1.5
Smith-StL 1.2

Fielding Runs
Parkinson-Phi 31.0
Bancroft-NY 21.9
Pinelli-Cin 21.1
Carey-Pit 19.5
Bigbee-Pit 17.4

Total Player Rating
Hornsby-StL 8.5
Bancroft-NY 4.5
Carey-Pit 4.2
O'Farrell-Chi 3.8
Grimes-Chi 3.3

Wins
Rixey-Cin 25
Cooper-Pit 23
Ruether-Bro 21
Pfeffer-StL 19
Nehf-NY 19

Win Percentage
Donohue-Cin 667
Rixey-Cin 658
Couch-Cin 640
Ruether-Bro 636
Cooper-Pit 622

Games
North-StL 53
Sherdel-StL 47
Ryan-NY 46
Oeschger-Bos 46
Morrison-Pit 45

Complete Games
Cooper-Pit 27
Ruether-Bro 26
Rixey-Cin 26

Shutouts
Vance-Bro 5
Morrison-Pit 5
Cooper-Pit 4
Adams-Pit 4
Sherdel-StL 3

Saves
Jonnard-NY 5
North-StL 4

Innings Pitched
Rixey-Cin 313.1
Cooper-Pit 294.2
Morrison-Pit 286.1
Nehf-NY 268.1
Ruether-Bro 267.1

Fewest Hits/Game
Douglas-NY 8.79
Osborne-Chi 8.95
Ryan-NY 9.11
Luque-Cin 9.17
Vance-Bro 9.49

Fewest BB/Game
Adams-Pit 79
Alexander-Chi 1.25
Rixey-Cin 1.29
Donohue-Cin 1.60
J.Barnes-NY 1.61

Strikeouts
Vance-Bro 134
Cooper-Pit 129
Ring-Phi 116
Morrison-Pit 104
Grimes-Bro 99

Strikeouts/Game
Vance-Bro 4.91
Ring-Phi 4.19
Osborne-Chi 3.96
Cooper-Pit 3.94
Doak-StL 3.64

Ratio
Douglas-NY 11.02
Adams-Pit 11.03
Rixey-Cin 11.09
Donohue-Cin 11.34
Luque-Cin 11.69

Earned Run Average
Douglas-NY 2.63
Ryan-NY 3.01
Donohue-Cin 3.12
Cooper-Pit 3.18
Nehf-NY 3.29

Adjusted ERA
Douglas-NY 152
Weinert-Phi 137
Ryan-NY 133
Cooper-Pit 128
Donohue-Cin 128

Opponents' Batting Avg.
Douglas-NY 257
Luque-Cin 268
Ryan-NY 269
Osborne-Chi 271
Rixey-Cin 275

Opponents' On Base Pct.
Douglas-NY 302
Rixey-Cin 303
Adams-Pit 307
J.Barnes-NY 311
Donohue-Cin 312

Starter Runs
Cooper-Pit 30.2
Donohue-Cin 26.2
Douglas-NY 25.8
Nehf-NY 24.2
Ryan-NY 23.3

Adjusted Starter Runs
Cooper-Pit 29.4
Douglas-NY 24.1
Weinert-Phi 23.4
Donohue-Cin 23.2
Nehf-NY 21.3

Clutch Pitching Index
Weinert-Phi 129
Ryan-NY 116
Cooper-Pit 113
Morrison-Pit 111
McQuillan-Bos-NY . . 110

Relief Runs
McNamara-Bos . . . 13.2
Causey-NY 7.2
Braxton-Bos 5.4
Mamaux-Bro 3.9
V.Barnes-NY 3.5

Adjusted Relief Runs
McNamara-Bos . . . 12.4
Causey-NY 6.4
Braxton-Bos 4.6
Mamaux-Bro 3.6
V.Barnes-NY 3.0

Relief Ranking
McNamara-Bos . . . 11.0
Causey-NY 5.9
Mamaux-Bro 2.1
Braxton-Bos 1.9
Jonnard-NY 1.3

Total Pitcher Index
Cooper-Pit 4.0
Ryan-NY 2.8
Meadows-Phi 2.6
Luque-Cin 2.6
Nehf-NY 2.5

Total Baseball Ranking
Hornsby-StL 8.5
Bancroft-NY 4.5
Carey-Pit 4.2
Cooper-Pit 4.0
O'Farrell-Chi 3.8

TEAM	G	W	L	PCT	GB	R	OR	AB	H	2B	3B	HR	BB	SO	AVG	OBP	SLG	PRO	PRO+	BR	/A	PF	CHI	RC	SB	CS	SBA	SBR
NY	154	94	60	.610		758	618	5245	1504	220	75	95	497	532	.287	.353	.412	.765	103	36	19	102	99	774	62	59	51	-17
STL	154	93	61	.604		867	643	5416	1693	291	94	98	473	381	.313	.372	.455	.827	117	157	125	104	96	923	136	76	64	-5
DET	155	79	75	.513	15	828	791	5360	1641	250	87	54	530	378	.306	.372	.415	.787	115	94	121	97	98	847	78	62	56	-14
CLE	155	78	76	.506	16	768	817	5293	1544	320	73	32	554	331	.292	.364	.398	.762	104	43	37	101	97	792	90	58	61	-8
CHI	155	77	77	.500	17	691	691	5267	1463	243	62	45	482	463	.278	.343	.373	.716	92	-52	-49	100	101	690	109	84	56	-18
WAS	154	69	85	.448	25	650	706	5201	1395	229	76	45	458	442	.268	.334	.367	.701	93	-84	-53	95	103	656	97	63	61	-9
PHI	155	65	89	.422	29	705	830	5211	1409	229	63	111	437	591	.270	.331	.402	.733	94	-36	-54	103	104	695	60	69	47	-23
BOS	154	61	93	.396	33	598	769	5288	1392	250	55	45	366	455	.263	.316	.357	.673	82	-149	-144	99	105	599	64	67	49	-21
TOT	618					5865		42281	12041	2032	585	525	3797	3573	.285	.348	.398	.746							696	538	56	-114

TEAM	CG	SH	SV	IP	H	H/G	HR	BB	SO	RAT	ERA	ERA+	OAV	OOB	PR	/A	PF	CPI	FA	E	DP	FW	PW	BW	SBW	DIF
NY	100	7	14	1393²	1402	9.1	73	423	458	11.9	3.39	118	.268	.325	99	91	99	101	.975	157	124	2.0	8.8	1.8	-.3	4.5
STL	79	8	22	1392	1412	9.1	71	419	534	12.1	3.38	122	.268	.327	101	115	103	103	.968	201	158	-.5	11.2	12.1	.9	-7.7
DET	67	7	15	1391	1554	10.1	62	473	461	13.7	4.27	91	.288	.354	-37	-64	96	97	.970	191	133	.2	-6.2	11.8	.0	-3.7
CLE	76	14	7	1383²	1605	10.4	58	464	489	13.7	4.59	87	.296	.356	-85	-92	99	93	.968	202	147	-.5	-8.9	3.6	.6	6.2
CHI	86	13	6	1403²	1472	9.4	57	529	484	13.0	3.94	103	.278	.346	15	15	101	98	.975	155	143	2.2	1.5	-4.8	-.4	1.4
WAS	84	13	10	1362¹	1485	9.8	49	500	422	13.4	3.81	101	.286	.354	33	5	96	107	.969	196	168	-.2	.5	-5.1	.5	-3.7
PHI	73	4	6	1362¹	1573	10.4	107	469	373	13.7	4.59	92	.297	.357	-85	-55	105	99	.966	215	118	-1.2	-5.3	-5.2	-.8	.6
BOS	71	10	6	1373¹	1508	9.9	48	503	359	13.5	4.30	95	.287	.354	-41	-32	102	94	.965	224	145	-1.8	-3.1	-14.0	-.7	3.5
TOT	636	76	88	11062		9.8				13.1	4.03		.285	.348					.969	1541	1136					

Runs
Sisler-StL 134
Blue-Det 131
Williams-StL 128
Tobin-StL 122

Hits
Sisler-StL 246
Cobb-Det 211
Tobin-StL 207
Veach-Det 202

Doubles
Speaker-Cle 48
Pratt-Bos 44
Sisler-StL 42
Cobb-Det 42

Triples
Sisler-StL 18
Jacobson-StL 16
Cobb-Det 16
Judge-Was 15
Mostil-Chi 14

Home Runs
Williams-StL 39
Walker-Phi 37
Ruth-NY 35
Miller-Phi 21
Heilmann-Det 21

Total Bases
Williams-StL 367
Sisler-StL 348
Walker-Phi 310
Cobb-Det 297
Tobin-StL 296

Runs Batted In
Williams-StL 155
Veach-Det 126
McManus-StL 109
Sisler-StL 105
Jacobson-StL 102

Runs Produced
Williams-StL 244
Sisler-StL 231
Veach-Det 213
Cobb-Det 194
McManus-StL 186

Bases On Balls
Witt-NY 89
Ruth-NY 84
Blue-Det 82
Speaker-Cle 77
Williams-StL 74

Batting Average
Sisler-StL .... .420
Cobb-Det .... .401
Speaker-Cle ...... .378
Heilmann-Det .... .356
Miller-Phi .... .335

On Base Percentage
Speaker-Cle ...... .474
Sisler-StL .... .467
Cobb-Det .... .462
Ruth-NY .... .434
Heilmann-Det .... .432

Slugging Average
Ruth-NY .... .672
Williams-StL ..... .627
Speaker-Cle ...... .606
Heilmann-Det .... .598
Sisler-StL .... .594

Production
Ruth-NY 1.106
Speaker-Cle 1.080
Sisler-StL 1.061
Williams-StL 1.040
Heilmann-Det 1.030

Adjusted Production
Ruth-NY 181
Speaker-Cle 178
Cobb-Det 172
Heilmann-Det 172
Sisler-StL 169

Batter Runs
Sisler-StL 64.4
Williams-StL 56.1
Speaker-Cle 52.8
Cobb-Det 52.4
Ruth-NY 50.5

Adjusted Batter Runs
Sisler-StL 59.4
Cobb-Det 56.5
Speaker-Cle 52.0
Williams-StL 51.3
Ruth-NY 48.1

Clutch Hitting Index
Veach-Det 143
O'Neill-Cle 132
Johnson-Chi 127
Wood-Cle 126
Gardner-Cle 125

Runs Created
Sisler-StL 162
Williams-StL 149
Cobb-Det 133
Speaker-Cle 127
Ruth-NY 120

Total Average
Speaker-Cle 1.272
Ruth-NY 1.254
Sisler-StL 1.203
Heilmann-Det 1.135
Williams-StL 1.131

Stolen Bases
Sisler-StL 51
Williams-StL 37
Harris-Was 25
Johnson-Chi 21

Stolen Base Average
Jacobson-StL 76.0
Sisler-StL 72.9
Harris-Was 69.4
Rice-Was 69.0
Rigney-Det 68.0

Stolen Base Runs
Sisler-StL 3.9
Veach-Det 2.1
Jacobson-StL 2.1
Evans-Cle 2.1
Shanks-Was 1.8

Fielding Runs
Harris-Was 26.4
Peckinpaugh-Was . 20.4
Schalk-Chi 20.2
Scott-NY 17.3
Sisler-StL 12.1

Total Player Rating
Sisler-StL 6.6
Speaker-Cle 5.0
Williams-StL 4.4
Cobb-Det 4.3
Ruth-NY 3.7

Wins
Rommel-Phi 27
Bush-NY 26
Shocker-StL 24
Uhle-Cle 22
Faber-Chi 21

Win Percentage
Bush-NY .... .788
Rommel-Phi ..... .675
Shawkey-NY ..... .625
Pillette-Det ...... .613
Hoyt-NY .... .613

Games
Rommel-Phi 51
Uhle-Cle 50
Shocker-StL 48
Harriss-Phi 47

Complete Games
Faber-Chi 31
Shocker-StL 29
Uhle-Cle 23
Johnson-Was 23

Shutouts
Uhle-Cle 5

Saves
Jones-NY 8
Pruett-StL 7
Wright-StL 5

Innings Pitched
Faber-Chi 352.0
Shocker-StL 348.0
Shawkey-NY 299.2
Rommel-Phi 294.0
Uhle-Cle 287.1

Fewest Hits/Game
Davis-StL 8.36
Bush-NY 8.46
Faber-Chi 8.54
Shawkey-NY 8.59
Wright-StL 8.65

Fewest BB/Game
Shocker-StL 1.47
Vangilder-StL 1.76
Mays-NY 1.88
Kolp-StL 1.91
Hasty-Phi 1.92

Strikeouts
Shocker-StL 149
Faber-Chi 148
Shawkey-NY 130
Ehmke-Det 108
Johnson-Was 105

Strikeouts/Game
Morton-Cle 4.53
Harriss-Phi 4.00
Shawkey-NY 3.90
Shocker-StL 3.85
Faber-Chi 3.78

Ratio
Faber-Chi 10.82
Shocker-StL 11.02
Rommel-Phi 11.08
Vangilder-StL 11.09
Quinn-Bos 11.43

Earned Run Average
Faber-Chi 2.81
Pillette-Det 2.85
Shawkey-NY 2.91
Wright-StL 2.92
Shocker-StL 2.97

Adjusted ERA
Faber-Chi 144
Wright-StL 141
Shocker-StL 139
Shawkey-NY 137
Pillette-Det 136

Opponents' Batting Avg.
Davis-StL .... .250
Bush-NY .... .252
Faber-Chi .... .252
Shawkey-NY ..... .256
Pillette-Det ...... .258

Opponents' On Base Pct.
Faber-Chi .... .299
Shocker-StL ...... .304
Rommel-Phi ..... .309
Vangilder-StL ..... .310
Quinn-Bos .... .311

Starter Runs
Faber-Chi 47.7
Shocker-StL 40.9
Shawkey-NY 37.2
Pillette-Det 36.0
Johnson-Was 32.4

Adjusted Starter Runs
Faber-Chi 48.8
Shocker-StL 44.8
Shawkey-NY 36.0
Rommel-Phi 31.5
Pillette-Det 31.1

Clutch Pitching Index
Mogridge-Was 124
Wright-StL 118
Johnson-Was 114
Pillette-Det 110
Shawkey-NY 109

Relief Runs
Murray-NY 0.4

Adjusted Relief Runs
Murray-NY 0.2

Relief Ranking
Murray-NY 0.1

Total Pitcher Index
Faber-Chi 4.9
Shocker-StL 4.8
Rommel-Phi 4.0
Vangilder-StL 3.4
Pillette-Det 3.2

Total Baseball Ranking
Sisler-StL 6.6
Speaker-Cle 5.0
Faber-Chi 4.9
Shocker-StL 4.8
Williams-StL 4.4

TEAM	G	W	L	PCT	GB	R	OR	AB	H	2B	3B	HR	BB	SO	AVG	OBP	SLG	PRO	PRO+	BR	/A	PF	CHI	RC	SB	CS	SBA	SBR
NY	153	95	58	.621		854	679	5452	1610	248	76	85	487	406	.295	.356	.415	.771	110	72	83	99	103	816	106	70	60	-10
CIN	154	91	63	.591	4.5	708	629	5278	1506	237	95	45	439	367	.285	.344	.392	.736	102	-1	14	98	96	707	96	105	48	-34
PIT	154	87	67	.565	8.5	786	696	5405	1592	224	111	49	407	362	.295	.347	.404	.751	102	26	9	102	103	766	154	75	67	1
CHI	154	83	71	.539	12.5	756	704	5259	1516	243	52	90	455	485	.288	.348	.406	.754	104	33	32	100	99	735	181	143	56	-32
STL	154	79	74	.516	16	746	732	5526	1582	274	76	63	438	446	.286	.343	.398	.741	103	5	21	98	97	761	89	61	59	-10
BRO	155	76	78	.494	19.5	753	741	5476	1559	214	81	62	425	382	.285	.340	.387	.727	100	-20	1	97	102	730	71	50	59	-9
BOS	155	54	100	.351	41.5	636	798	5329	1455	213	58	32	429	404	.273	.331	.353	.684	90	-99	-73	96	99	625	57	80	42	-31
PHI	155	50	104	.325	45.5	748	1008	5491	1528	259	39	112	414	556	.278	.333	.401	.734	89	-15	-100	112	101	729	70	73	49	-23
TOT	617					5987		43216	12348	1912	588	538	3494	3408	.286	.343	.395	.737							824	657	56	-147

TEAM	CG	SH	SV	IP	H	H/G	HR	BB	SO	RAT	ERA	ERA+	OAV	OOB	PR	/A	PF	CPI	FA	E	DP	FW	PW	BW	SBW	DIF
NY	62	10	18	1378	1440	9.4	82	424	453	12.3	3.90	98	.271	.328	15	-13	96	93	.972	176	141	2.4	-1.3	8.0	.8	8.6
CIN	88	11	9	1391[1]	1465	9.5	28	359	450	12.0	3.21	120	.273	.322	121	99	97	101	.969	202	144	.9	9.5	1.3	-1.5	3.7
PIT	92	5	9	1376[1]	1513	9.9	53	402	414	12.7	3.87	103	.284	.337	19	19	100	96	.971	179	157	2.3	1.8	.9	1.9	3.2
CHI	80	8	11	1366[2]	1419	9.3	86	435	408	12.4	3.82	105	.269	.329	27	25	100	96	.967	208	144	.5	2.4	3.1	-1.3	1.3
STL	77	9	7	1398[1]	1539	9.9	70	456	398	13.1	3.87	101	.284	.344	20	5	98	104	.963	232	141	-.9	.5	2.0	.8	.0
BRO	94	8	5	1396[2]	1503	9.7	55	476	548	13.0	3.74	103	.277	.340	39	20	97	100	.955	293	137	-4.4	1.9	.9		.5
BOS	54	13	7	1392[2]	1662	10.7	64	394	351	13.5	4.21	94	.302	.352	-34	-41	100	102	.964	230	157	-.7	-3.9	-7.0	-1.2	-10.1
PHI	68	3	8	1376[1]	1801	11.8	100	549	384	15.6	5.34	86	.322	.386	-205	-115	115	102	.966	217	172	.0	-11.1	-9.6	-.4	-6.0
TOT	615	67	74	11076[1]		10.0				13.1	3.99		.286	.343					.966	1737	1193					

Runs
Youngs-NY 121
Carey-Pit 120
Frisch-NY 116
Johnston-Bro 111
Statz-Chi 110

Hits
Frisch-NY 223
Statz-Chi 209
Traynor-Pit 208
Johnston-Bro 203
Youngs-NY 200

Doubles
Roush-Cin 41
Tierney-Pit-Phi . 36
Grantham-Chi 36
Bottomley-StL ... 34

Triples
Traynor-Pit 19
Carey-Pit 19
Roush-Cin 18
Southworth-Bos .. 16

Home Runs
Williams-Phi 41
Fournier-Bro 22
Miller-Chi 20
Meusel-NY 19
Hornsby-StL 17

Total Bases
Frisch-NY 311
Williams-Phi 308
Fournier-Bro 303
Traynor-Pit 301
Statz-Chi 288

Runs Batted In
Meusel-NY 125
Williams-Phi 114
Frisch-NY 111
Kelly-NY 103
Fournier-Bro 102

Runs Produced
Frisch-NY 215
Meusel-NY 208
Youngs-NY 205
Traynor-Pit 197
Carey-Pit 177

Bases On Balls
Burns-Cin 101
Sand-Phi 82
Youngs-NY 73
Carey-Pit 73
Grantham-Chi 71

Batting Average
Hornsby-StL ..... .384
Wheat-Bro .... .375
Bottomley-StL ... .371
Fournier-Bro .... .351
Roush-Cin .... .351

On Base Percentage
Hornsby-StL ..... .459
Bottomley-StL ... .425
Youngs-NY .... .412
Fournier-Bro .... .411
O'Farrell-Chi ... .408

Slugging Average
Hornsby-StL ..... .627
Fournier-Bro .... .588
Williams-Phi .... .576
Barnhart-Pit .... .563
Bottomley-StL ... .535

Production
Hornsby-StL ... 1.086
Fournier-Bro .... .999
Bottomley-StL ... .960
Williams-Phi .... .947
Roush-Cin .... .938

Adjusted Production
Hornsby-StL 188
Fournier-Bro 165
Bottomley-StL ... 155
Roush-Cin 149
Frisch-NY 133

Batter Runs
Hornsby-StL 52.1
Fournier-Bro 43.7
Bottomley-StL ... 39.2
Roush-Cin 34.0
Williams-Phi 33.2

Adjusted Batter Runs
Hornsby-StL 54.4
Fournier-Bro 47.0
Bottomley-StL ... 41.5
Roush-Cin 36.2
Frisch-NY 29.8

Clutch Hitting Index
Stock-StL 136
McInnis-Bos 124
Frisch-NY 123
Meusel-NY 117
Bigbee-Pit 114

Runs Created
Fournier-Bro 125
Frisch-NY 123
Hornsby-StL 120
Bottomley-StL ... 117
Carey-Pit 117

Total Average
Hornsby-StL ... 1.194
Fournier-Bro ... 1.071
Bottomley-StL ... .976
Williams-Phi .... .966
Carey-Pit .... .928

Stolen Bases
Carey-Pit 51
Grantham-Chi 43
Smith-StL 32
Heathcote-Chi ... 32

Stolen Base Average
Carey-Pit 86.4
Smith-StL 74.4
Frisch-NY 70.7
Traynor-Pit 68.3
Heathcote-Chi ... 65.3

Stolen Base Runs
Carey-Pit 10.5
Smith-StL 3.0
Rawlings-Pit 2.7

Fielding Runs
Bancroft-NY 21.3
Carey-Pit 19.7
Johnston-Bro 19.4
Statz-Chi 17.7
Tierney-Pit-Phi . 14.4

Total Player Rating
Fournier-Bro 4.3
Traynor-Pit 4.0
Carey-Pit 3.6
Bancroft-NY 3.6
Johnston-Bro 3.6

Wins
Luque-Cin 27
Morrison-Pit 25
Alexander-Chi ... 22
Grimes-Bro 21
Donohue-Cin 21

Win Percentage
Luque-Cin .... .771
Ryan-NY .... .762
Scott-NY .... .696
Morrison-Pit .... .658
Alexander-Chi ... .647

Games
Ryan-NY 45
Jonnard-NY 45
Oeschger-Bos 44
J.Barnes-NY-Bos . 43
Genewich-Bos 43

Complete Games
Grimes-Bro 33
Luque-Cin 28
Morrison-Pit 27
Cooper-Pit 26
Alexander-Chi ... 26

Shutouts
Luque-Cin 6
J.Barnes-NY-Bos . 5
McQuillan-NY 5

Saves
Jonnard-NY 5
Ryan-NY 4

Innings Pitched
Grimes-Bro 327.0
Luque-Cin 322.0
Rixey-Cin 309.0
Alexander-Chi .. 305.0
Ring-Phi 304.1

Fewest Hits/Game
Luque-Cin 7.80
Vance-Bro 8.44
Morrison-Pit 8.56
Keen-Chi 8.59
Aldridge-Chi 8.67

Fewest BB/Game
Alexander-Chi ... .89
B.Adams-Pit 1.42
Genewich-Bos ... 1.82
Rixey-Cin 1.89
Meadows-Phi-Pit 2.15

Strikeouts
Vance-Bro 197
Luque-Cin 151
Grimes-Bro 119
Morrison-Pit 114
Ring-Phi 112

Strikeouts/Game
Vance-Bro 6.32
Luque-Cin 4.22
Bentley-NY 3.93
Osborne-Chi 3.46
Morrison-Pit 3.40

Ratio
Alexander-Chi ... 9.97
Luque-Cin 10.40
Ryan-NY 11.31
Aldridge-Chi ... 11.49
McQuillan-NY ... 11.56

Earned Run Average
Luque-Cin 1.93
Rixey-Cin 2.80
Keen-Chi 3.00
Kaufmann-Chi 3.10
Haines-StL 3.11

Adjusted ERA
Luque-Cin 200
Rixey-Cin 138
Keen-Chi 133
Kaufmann-Chi 129
Alexander-Chi ... 125

Opponents' Batting Avg.
Luque-Cin .... .235
Vance-Bro .... .250
Aldridge-Chi .... .251
Morrison-Pit .... .253
Osborne-Chi ..... .255

Opponents' On Base Pct.
Alexander-Chi ... .277
Luque-Cin .... .291
Aldridge-Chi .... .307
Ryan-NY .... .308
McQuillan-NY .... .315

Starter Runs
Luque-Cin 73.9
Rixey-Cin 41.1
Alexander-Chi ... 27.4
Haines-StL 26.1
Kaufmann-Chi 20.6

Adjusted Starter Runs
Luque-Cin 69.1
Rixey-Cin 36.5
Alexander-Chi ... 27.4
Ring-Phi 24.3
Haines-StL 23.2

Clutch Pitching Index
Kaufmann-Chi 118
Rixey-Cin 116
Genewich-Bos 116
Doak-StL 116
Luque-Cin 115

Relief Runs
Decatur-Bro 15.3
Jonnard-NY 7.6
Keck-Cin 2.6
V.Barnes-NY 5

Adjusted Relief Runs
Decatur-Bro 14.0
Jonnard-NY 5.7
Keck-Cin 1.3

Relief Ranking
Decatur-Bro 8.7
Jonnard-NY 4.4
Keck-Cin 1.3

Total Pitcher Index
Luque-Cin 7.4
Rixey-Cin 3.4
Alexander-Chi ... 3.2
Kaufmann-Chi 2.4
Haines-StL 2.4

Total Baseball Ranking
Luque-Cin 7.4
Fournier-Bro 4.3
Traynor-Pit 4.0
Carey-Pit 3.6
Bancroft-NY 3.6

TEAM	G	W	L	PCT	GB	R	OR	AB	H	2B	3B	HR	BB	SO	AVG	OBP	SLG	PRO	PRO+	BR	/A	PF	CHI	RC	SB	CS	SBA	SBR
NY	152	98	54	.645		823	**622**	5347	1554	231	79	**105**	521	516	.291	.357	**.422**	.779	108	73	59	102	101	811	69	74	48	-24
DET	155	83	71	.539	16	831	741	5266	1579	270	69	41	596	385	.300	.377	.401	.778	113	91	108	98	98	827	87	62	58	-11
CLE	153	82	71	.536	16.5	**888**	746	5290	**1594**	**301**	75	59	**633**	384	**.301**	**.381**	.420	**.801**	**117**	**135**	**137**	100	100	**868**	79	79	50	-24
WAS	155	75	78	.490	23.5	720	747	5244	1436	224	**93**	26	532	448	.274	.346	.367	.713	98	-46	-11	95	**104**	693	102	68	60	**-10**
STL	154	74	78	.487	24	688	720	5298	1489	248	62	82	442	423	.281	.339	.398	.737	94	-15	-55	106	96	724	64	54	54	-13
PHI	153	69	83	.454	29	661	761	5196	1407	229	64	53	445	517	.271	.333	.370	.703	89	-74	-82	101	103	653	72	62	54	-16
CHI	156	69	85	.448	30	692	741	5246	1463	254	57	42	532	458	.279	.350	.351	.723	97	-26	-17	99	97	707	**191**	118	**62**	-14
BOS	154	61	91	.401	37	584	809	5181	1354	253	54	34	391	480	.261	.318	.351	.669	81	-143	-146	101	104	579	79	91	46	-31
TOT	616					5887		42068	11876	2010	553	442	4092	3611	.282	.351	.388	.739							743	608	55	-142

TEAM	CG	SH	SV	IP	H	H/G	HR	BB	SO	RAT	ERA	ERA+	OAV	OOB	PR	/A	PF	CPI	FA	E	DP	FW	PW	BW	SBW	DIF
NY	101	9	10	1380²	**1365**	8.9	68	491	**506**	12.3	3.62	109	.263	.330	55	49	99	96	**.977**	144	131	3.3	4.7	5.7	-.6	8.9
DET	61	9	12	1373²	1502	9.8	58	447	447	13.1	4.09	94	.283	.345	-16	-34	97	96	.968	200	103	.0	-3.3	10.4	.7	-1.9
CLE	77	**10**	11	1376	1517	9.9	**36**	465	407	13.2	3.91	101	.285	.346	11	4	100	97	.964	226	143	-1.7	.4	**13.2**	-.6	-5.9
WAS	71	8	**16**	1374²	1527	10.0	56	563	474	14.0	3.98	95	.291	.364	0	-30	95	**109**	.966	216	**182**	-.9	-2.9	-1.1	.7	2.6
STL	83	10	10	1373¹	1430	9.4	59	528	488	13.2	3.93	106	.275	.348	9	37	105	98	.971	177	145	1.4	3.6	-5.3	.5	-2.1
PHI	65	7	12	1364²	1465	9.7	68	550	400	13.5	4.08	101	.280	.352	-15	1	103	99	.965	221	127	-1.4	.0	-7.9	.2	2.0
CHI	74	5	11	1397	1512	9.7	49	534	467	13.4	4.05	98	.283	.353	-10	-13	99	99	.971	184	138	1.1	-1.3	-1.6	.4	-6.6
BOS	77	3	11	1372	1534	10.1	48	520	412	13.9	4.20	98	.294	.366	-33	-15	103	104	.963	232	126	-2.0	-1.5	-14.1	-1.3	3.8
TOT	609	61	93	11012		9.7				13.3	3.98		.282	.351					.968	1600	1095					

Runs		Hits		Doubles		Triples		Home Runs		Total Bases	
Ruth-NY	151	Jamieson-Cle	222	Speaker-Cle	59	Rice-Was	18	Ruth-NY	41	Ruth-NY	399
Speaker-Cle	133	Speaker-Cle	218	Burns-Bos	47	Goslin-Was	18	Williams-StL	29	Speaker-Cle	350
Jamieson-Cle	130	Heilmann-Det	211	Ruth-NY	45	Tobin-StL	15	Heilmann-Det	18	Williams-StL	346
Heilmann-Det	121	Ruth-NY	205	Heilmann-Det	44	Mostil-Chi	15	Speaker-Cle	17	Heilmann-Det	331
Rice-Was	117	Tobin-StL	202	J.Sewell-Cle	41			Hauser-Phi	17	Tobin-StL	303

Runs Batted In		Runs Produced		Bases On Balls		Batting Average		On Base Percentage		Slugging Average	
Ruth-NY	131	Speaker-Cle	246	Ruth-NY	170	Heilmann-Det	.403	Ruth-NY	.545	Ruth-NY	.764
Speaker-Cle	130	Ruth-NY	241	J.Sewell-Cle	98	Ruth-NY	.393	Heilmann-Det	.481	Heilmann-Det	.632
Heilmann-Det	115	Heilmann-Det	218	Blue-Det	96	Speaker-Cle	.380	Speaker-Cle	.469	Williams-StL	.623
J.Sewell-Cle	109	J.Sewell-Cle	204	Speaker-Cle	93	Collins-Chi	.360	J.Sewell-Cle	.456	Speaker-Cle	.610
Pipp-NY	108	Rice-Was	189	Collins-Chi	84	Williams-StL	.357	Collins-Chi	.455	Harris-Bos	.520

Production		Adjusted Production		Batter Runs		Adjusted Batter Runs		Clutch Hitting Index		Runs Created	
Ruth-NY	1.309	Ruth-NY	238	Ruth-NY	119.1	Ruth-NY	115.7	Pipp-NY	137	Ruth-NY	223
Heilmann-Det	1.113	Heilmann-Det	195	Speaker-Cle	70.9	Heilmann-Det	73.7	J.Sewell-Cle	123	Speaker-Cle	166
Speaker-Cle	1.079	Speaker-Cle	183	Heilmann-Det	70.7	Speaker-Cle	71.2	Bassler-Det	122	Heilmann-Det	160
Williams-StL	1.062	Williams-StL	168	Williams-StL	61.2	Williams-StL	53.5	Sheely-Chi	122	Williams-StL	148
J.Sewell-Cle	.935	J.Sewell-Cle	147	J.Sewell-Cle	42.8	J.Sewell-Cle	43.0	Meusel-NY	121	J.Sewell-Cle	128

Total Average		Stolen Bases		Stolen Base Average		Stolen Base Runs		Fielding Runs		Total Player Rating	
Ruth-NY	1.683	Collins-Chi	48	Mostil-Chi	71.9	Mostil-Chi	2.7	Peckinpaugh-Was	22.8	Ruth-NY	10.6
Heilmann-Det	1.288	Mostil-Chi	41	Rice-Was	71.4	Barrett-Chi	1.8	Mostil-Chi	22.0	Speaker-Cle	6.4
Speaker-Cle	1.222	Harris-Was	23	Elsh-Chi	66.7	Veach-Det	1.2	Lutzke-Cle	20.4	Heilmann-Det	6.2
Williams-StL	1.144	Rice-Was	20	Collins-Chi	62.3	Rice-Was	1.2	Harris-Was	19.7	J.Sewell-Cle	5.9
J.Sewell-Cle	1.025			Harris-Was	59.0	Pratt-Det	1.2	Flagstead-Det-Bos	18.7	Williams-StL	4.7

Wins		Win Percentage		Games		Complete Games		Shutouts		Saves	
Uhle-Cle	26	Pennock-NY	.760	Rommel-Phi	56	Uhle-Cle	29	Coveleski-Cle	5	Russell-Was	9
Jones-NY	21	Jones-NY	.724	Uhle-Cle	54	Ehmke-Bos	28	Vangilder-StL	4	Quinn-Bos	7
Dauss-Det	21	Hoyt-NY	.654	Russell-Was	52	Shocker-StL	24	Dauss-Det	4	Harriss-Phi	6
Shocker-StL	20	Shocker-StL	.625	Cole-Det	52	Dauss-Det	22				
Ehmke-Bos	20	Uhle-Cle	.619	Dauss-Det	50	Bush-NY	22				

Innings Pitched		Fewest Hits/Game		Fewest BB/Game		Strikeouts		Strikeouts/Game		Ratio	
Uhle-Cle	357.2	Shawkey-NY	8.07	Shocker-StL	1.59	Johnson-Was	130	Johnson-Det	4.75	Shocker-StL	11.16
Ehmke-Bos	316.2	Hoyt-NY	8.56	Coveleski-Cle	1.66	Shawkey-NY	125	Johnson-Was	4.48	Hoyt-NY	11.20
Dauss-Det	316.0	Bush-NY	8.59	Thurston-StL-Chi	1.75	Bush-NY	125	Shawkey-NY	4.35	Pennock-NY	11.52
Rommel-Phi	297.2	Russell-Was	8.78	Quinn-Bos	1.96	Ehmke-Bos	121	Bush-NY	4.08	Jones-NY	11.63
Vangilder-StL	282.1	Danforth-StL	8.79	Dauss-Det	2.22			Harriss-Phi	3.83	Coveleski-Cle	11.64

Earned Run Average		Adjusted ERA		Opponents' Batting Avg.		Opponents' On Base Pct.		Starter Runs		Adjusted Starter Runs	
Coveleski-Cle	2.76	Coveleski-Cle	143	Shawkey-NY	.246	Shocker-StL	.306	Coveleski-Cle	30.9	Vangilder-StL	34.8
Hoyt-NY	3.02	Vangilder-StL	136	Hoyt-NY	.253	Hoyt-NY	.307	Vangilder-StL	28.9	Coveleski-Cle	30.4
Russell-Was	3.03	Hoyt-NY	131	Jones-NY	.257	Faber-Chi	.311	Hoyt-NY	25.6	Rommel-Phi	27.8
Vangilder-StL	3.06	Thurston-StL-Chi	127	Faber-Chi	.259	Jones-NY	.312	Rommel-Phi	23.7	Hoyt-NY	24.4
Mogridge-Was	3.11	Rommel-Phi	126	Bush-NY	.260	Pennock-NY	.314	Pennock-NY	22.4	Shocker-StL	23.5

Clutch Pitching Index		Relief Runs		Adjusted Relief Runs		Relief Ranking		Total Pitcher Index		Total Baseball Ranking	
Thurston-StL-Chi	139							Rommel-Phi	4.0	Ruth-NY	10.6
Russell-Was	128							Vangilder-StL	3.3	Speaker-Cle	6.4
Mogridge-Was	122							Coveleski-Cle	2.9	Heilmann-Det	6.2
Vangilder-StL	121							Bush-NY	2.6	J.Sewell-Cle	5.9
Coveleski-Cle	121							Uhle-Cle	2.4	Williams-StL	4.7

TEAM	G	W	L	PCT	GB	R	OR	AB	H	2B	3B	HR	BB	SO	AVG	OBP	SLG	PRO	PRO+	BR	/A	PF	CHI	RC	SB	CS	SBA	SBR
NY	154	93	60	.608		857	641	5445	1634	269	81	95	467	479	.300	.358	.432	.790	120	124	148	97	102	849	82	53	61	-7
BRO	154	92	62	.597	1.5	717	675	5339	1534	227	54	72	447	357	.287	.345	.391	.736	105	19	42	97	99	725	34	46	43	-17
PIT	153	90	63	.588	3	724	588	5288	1517	222	122	44	366	396	.287	.336	.400	.736	100	11	0	102	103	715	181	92	66	-1
CIN	153	83	70	.542	10	649	579	5134	1539	236	111	34	349	334	.290	.337	.397	.734	103	8	19	99	93	698	103	98	51	-28
CHI	154	81	72	.529	12	698	699	5134	1419	207	59	66	469	521	.276	.340	.378	.718	96	-10	-16	101	103	652	137	149	48	-48
STL	154	65	89	.422	28.5	740	750	5349	1552	270	87	67	382	418	.290	.341	.411	.752	108	42	55	98	100	740	86	86	50	-26
PHI	152	55	96	.364	37	676	849	5306	1459	256	56	94	382	452	.275	.328	.397	.725	88	-13	-96	112	99	687	57	67	46	-23
BOS	154	53	100	.346	40	520	800	5283	1355	194	52	25	354	451	.256	.306	.327	.633	77	-181	-160	96	103	532	74	68	52	-19
TOT	614					5581		42445	12009	1881	622	499	3216	3408	.283	.337	.392	.729							754	659	53	-169

TEAM	CG	SH	SV	IP	H	H/G	HR	BB	SO	RAT	ERA	ERA+	OAV	OOB	PR	/A	PF	CPI	FA	E	DP	FW	PW	BW	SBW	DIF
NY	71	4	21	1378²	1464	9.6	77	392	406	12.2	3.62	101	.274	.326	38	7	95	100	.971	186	160	.4	.7	14.7	1.4	-.7
BRO	97	10	5	1376¹	1432	9.4	58	403	638	12.2	3.64	103	.270	.326	35	16	97	96	.968	196	121	-.2	1.6	4.2	.4	9.0
PIT	85	15	5	1382	1387	9.0	42	323	364	11.3	3.27	117	.267	.313	92	88	99	97	.971	183	161	.5	8.7	.0	2.0	2.3
CIN	77	14	9	1378	1408	9.2	30	293	451	11.3	3.12	121	.267	.309	115	99	97	97	.966	217	142	-1.4	9.8	1.9	-.7	-3.1
CHI	85	4	6	1380²	1459	9.5	89	438	416	12.5	3.83	102	.275	.333	6	11	101	101	.966	218	153	-1.4	1.1	-1.6	-2.7	9.1
STL	79	7	6	1364²	1528	10.1	70	486	393	13.5	4.15	91	.290	.354	-43	-57	98	104	.969	188	162	.3	-5.7	5.5	-.5	-11.6
PHI	59	7	10	1354¹	1689	11.2	84	469	349	14.5	4.87	92	.313	.372	-151	-60	115	103	.972	175	168	.8	-6.0	-9.5	-.2	-5.7
BOS	66	10	4	1379¹	1607	10.5	49	402	364	13.3	4.46	86	.301	.353	-92	-100	99	96	.973	168	154	1.4	-9.9	-15.9	.2	.7
TOT	619	71	66	10994		9.8				12.6	3.87		.283	.337					.970	1531	1221					

Runs
Hornsby-StL 121
Frisch-NY 121
Carey-Pit 113
Youngs-NY 112
Williams-Phi 101

Hits
Hornsby-StL 227
Wheat-Bro 212
Frisch-NY 198
High-Bro 191
Fournier-Bro 188

Doubles
Hornsby-StL 43
Wheat-Bro 41
Kelly-NY 37

Triples
Roush-Cin 21
Maranville-Pit ... 20
Wright-Pit 18
Cuyler-Pit 16
Frisch-NY 15

Home Runs
Fournier-Bro 27
Hornsby-StL 25
Williams-Phi 24
Kelly-NY 21

Total Bases
Hornsby-StL 373
Wheat-Bro 311
Williams-Phi 308
Kelly-NY 303
Fournier-Bro 302

Runs Batted In
Kelly-NY 136
Fournier-Bro 116
Wright-Pit 111
Bottomley-StL 111
Meusel-NY 102

Runs Produced
Kelly-NY 206
Hornsby-StL 190
Wright-Pit 184
Bottomley-StL..... 184
Frisch-NY 183

Bases On Balls
Hornsby-StL 89
Fournier-Bro 83
Youngs-NY 77
Williams-Phi 67
Friberg-Chi 66

Batting Average
Hornsby-StL 424
Wheat-Bro 375
Youngs-NY 356
Cuyler-Pit 354
Roush-Cin 348

On Base Percentage
Hornsby-StL ...... .507
Youngs-NY .... .441
Fournier-Bro ..... .428
Wheat-Bro .... .428
Williams-Phi...... .403

Slugging Average
Hornsby-StL 696
Williams-Phi 552
Wheat-Bro 549
Cuyler-Pit 539
Fournier-Bro 536

Production
Hornsby-StL 1.203
Wheat-Bro 978
Fournier-Bro 965
Youngs-NY 962
Williams-Phi 955

Adjusted Production
Hornsby-StL 223
Wheat-Bro 165
Fournier-Bro 162
Youngs-NY 161
Cuyler-Pit 147

Batter Runs
Hornsby-StL 94.1
Wheat-Bro 48.2
Fournier-Bro 48.1
Youngs-NY 45.3
Williams-Phi 42.0

Adjusted Batter Runs
Hornsby-StL 97.2
Fournier-Bro 52.2
Wheat-Bro 52.1
Youngs-NY 48.6
Kelly-NY 32.3

Clutch Hitting Index
Friberg-Chi........141
Griffith-NY........140
Meusel-NY 135
Wright-Pit........130
Pinelli-Cin 129

Runs Created
Hornsby-StL 186
Fournier-Bro 133
Wheat-Bro 132
Youngs-NY 123
Williams-Phi 121

Total Average
Hornsby-StL 1.424
Fournier-Bro 1.045
Youngs-NY 1.023
Wheat-Bro 1.014
Cuyler-Pit 990

Stolen Bases
Carey-Pit 49
Cuyler-Pit 32
Heathcote-Chi.... 26
Traynor-Pit 24
Smith-StL 24

Stolen Base Average
Carey-Pit 79.0
Cuyler-Pit 74.4
Frisch-NY 71.0
Critz-Cin 63.3
Smith-StL 60.0

Stolen Base Runs
Carey-Pit 6.9
Cuyler-Pit 3.0
Hartnett-Chi 1.8

Fielding Runs
Pinelli-Cin 26.7
Frisch-NY 24.9
Statz-Chi 14.5
Ford-Phi 11.9
Wright-Pit 10.7

Total Player Rating
Hornsby-StL 8.5
Frisch-NY 5.4
Fournier-Bro 4.7
Wheat-Bro 4.5
Youngs-NY 3.6

Wins
Vance-Bro 28
Grimes-Bro 22
Mays-Cin 20
Cooper-Pit 20
Kremer-Pit 18

Win Percentage
Yde-Pit .... .842
Vance-Bro .... .824
Bentley-NY .... .762
Mays-Cin .... .690
Kremer-Pit .... .643

Games
Morrison-Pit 41
Kremer-Pit 41
Keen-Chi 40
Sheehan-Cin 39

Complete Games
Vance-Bro 30
Grimes-Bro 30
Cooper-Pit 25
Barnes-Bos 21
Aldridge-Chi 20

Shutouts
Yde-Pit 4
Sothoron-StL 4
Rixey-Cin 4
Kremer-Pit 4
Cooper-Pit 4
Barnes-Bos 4

Saves
May-Cin 6
Ryan-NY 5
Jonnard-NY 5

Innings Pitched
Grimes-Bro 310.2
Vance-Bro 308.1
Cooper-Pit 268.2
Barnes-Bos 267.2
Kremer-Pit 259.1

Fewest Hits/Game
Vance-Bro 6.95
Yde-Pit........... 7.93
Morrison-Pit 8.07
Doak-StL-Bro ... 8.14
Rixey-Cin........ 8.27

Fewest BB/Game
Benton-Cin 1.33
Alexander-Chi 1.33
Cooper-Pit 1.34
Mays-Cin 1.43
Donohue-Cin 1.46

Strikeouts
Vance-Bro 262
Grimes-Bro 135
Luque-Cin 86
Morrison-Pit 85
Kaufmann-Chi 79

Strikeouts/Game
Vance-Bro 7.65
Grimes-Bro 3.91
Nehf-NY 3.77
Luque-Cin 3.53
Kaufmann-Chi 3.41

Ratio
Vance-Bro 9.46
Rixey-Cin 10.12
Benton-Cin 10.73
Doak-StL-Bro ... 10.87
McQuillan-NY 10.96

Earned Run Average
Vance-Bro 2.16
McQuillan-NY 2.69
Rixey-Cin 2.76
Benton-Cin 2.77
Yde-Pit 2.83

Adjusted ERA
Vance-Bro 173
Rixey-Cin 137
McQuillan-NY 136
Benton-Cin 136
Yde-Pit 136

Opponents' Batting Avg.
Vance-Bro .... .213
Yde-Pit .... .244
Morrison-Pit ..... .245
Rixey-Cin .... .246
Doak-StL-Bro .... .249

Opponents' On Base Pct.
Vance-Bro .... .269
Rixey-Cin .... .285
Benton-Cin ...... .297
Alexander-Chi.... .299
Nehf-NY .... .301

Starter Runs
Vance-Bro 58.4
Rixey-Cin 29.4
McQuillan-NY 24.0
Yde-Pit 22.3
Barnes-NY 20.5

Adjusted Starter Runs
Vance-Bro 54.3
Rixey-Cin 26.7
Yde-Pit 21.7
McQuillan-NY 19.9
Kremer-Pit 18.6

Clutch Pitching Index
Sherdel-StL 117
Sothoron-StL 115
Ring-Phi 113
McQuillan-NY 113
Aldridge-Chi 110

Relief Runs
Jonnard-NY 14.5
May-Cin 9.5
Stone-Pit 6.5

Adjusted Relief Runs
Jonnard-NY 12.5
May-Cin 8.4
Stone-Pit 6.3

Relief Ranking
Jonnard-NY 12.9
May-Cin 5.7
Stone-Pit 5.3

Total Pitcher Index
Vance-Bro 5.7
Mays-Cin 3.4
Rixey-Cin 3.1
Cooper-Pit 2.5
Yde-Pit 2.3

Total Baseball Ranking
Hornsby-StL 8.5
Vance-Bro 5.7
Frisch-NY 5.4
Fournier-Bro 4.7
Wheat-Bro 4.5

TEAM	G	W	L	PCT	GB	R	OR	AB	H	2B	3B	HR	BB	SO	AVG	OBP	SLG	PRO	PRO+	BR	/A	PF	CHI	RC	SB	CS	SBA	SBR
WAS	156	92	62	.597		755	613	5304	1558	255	88	22	513	392	.294	.361	.387	.748	101	-8	16	97	98	762	116	85	58	-16
NY	153	89	63	.586	2	798	667	5240	1516	248	86	98	478	420	.289	.352	.426	.778	106	29	31	100	102	789	69	67	51	-20
DET	156	86	68	.558	6	849	796	5389	1604	315	76	35	607	400	.298	.373	.404	.777	108	53	67	98	100	837	100	77	56	-16
STL	153	74	78	.487	17	769	809	5236	1543	266	62	67	465	349	.295	.356	.408	.764	96	9	-38	106	101	762	85	85	50	-26
PHI	152	71	81	.467	20	685	778	5184	1459	251	59	63	374	484	.281	.334	.389	.723	90	-77	-83	101	105	674	77	68	53	-18
CLE	153	67	86	.438	24.5	755	814	5332	1580	306	59	41	492	371	.296	.361	.399	.760	100	8	-2	101	97	784	85	57	60	-9
BOS	157	67	87	.435	25	737	806	5340	1481	302	63	30	603	417	.277	.356	.374	.730	94	-42	-43	100	99	741	78	61	56	-13
CHI	154	66	87	.431	25.5	793	858	5255	1512	254	58	41	604	421	.288	.365	.382	.747	101	-6	18	97	103	761	137	92	60	-14
TOT	617					6141		42280	12253	2197	551	397	4136	3254	.290	.358	.397	.755							747	592	56	-131

TEAM	CG	SH	SV	IP	H	H/G	HR	BB	SO	RAT	ERA	ERA+	OAV	OOB	PR	/A	PF	CPI	FA	E	DP	FW	PW	BW	SBW	DIF
WAS	74	13	25	1383	1329	8.6	34	505	469	12.2	3.34	121	.259	.330	136	106	95	99	.972	171	149	1.3	10.0	1.5	.0	2.1
NY	76	13	13	1359¹	1483	9.8	59	522	487	13.4	3.86	108	.284	.353	56	44	98	107	.974	156	131	2.0	4.2	2.9	-.3	4.2
DET	60	5	20	1394²	1586	10.2	55	467	441	13.5	4.19	98	.293	.354	5	-12	97	101	.971	187	142	.4	-1.1	6.3	.0	3.4
STL	65	11	7	1353¹	1511	10.0	68	517	386	13.8	4.57	99	.289	.358	-51	-9	107	95	.969	184	142	.3	-.8	-3.6	-.9	3.0
PHI	68	8	10	1345	1527	10.2	43	597	371	14.4	4.39	98	.292	.368	-24	-15	101	101	.971	180	157	.5	-1.4	-7.8	-.2	3.9
CLE	87	7	7	1349	1603	10.7	43	503	315	14.3	4.40	97	.300	.365	-25	-20	101	101	.967	205	130	-1.0	-1.9	-.2	.7	-7.1
BOS	73	8	16	1391¹	1563	10.1	43	523	414	13.9	4.35	100	.290	.359	-19	2	103	97	.967	210	126	-1.0	.2	-4.1	.3	-5.5
CHI	76	1	11	1370²	1635	10.7	52	512	360	14.3	4.74	87	.305	.368	-78	-95	97	98	.963	229	136	-2.4	-9.0	1.7	.2	-1.1
TOT	579	66	109	10946¹		10.1				13.7	4.23		.290	.358					.969	1522	1113					

Runs		Hits		Doubles		Triples		Home Runs		Total Bases	
Ruth-NY	143	Rice-Was	216	J.Sewell-Cle	45	Pipp-NY	19	Ruth-NY	46	Ruth-NY	391
Cobb-Det	115	Jamieson-Cle	213	Heilmann-Det	45	Goslin-Was	17	Hauser-Phi	27	Jacobson-StL	306
Collins-Chi	108	Cobb-Det	211	Wambsganss-Bos	41	Heilmann-Det	16	Jacobson-StL	19	Heilmann-Det	304
Hooper-Chi	107	Ruth-NY	200	Jacobson-StL	41	Rice-Was	14	Williams-StL	18	Goslin-Was	299
Heilmann-Det	107	Goslin-Was	199	Meusel-NY	40	Jacobson-StL	12	Boone-Bos	13	Hauser-Phi	290

Runs Batted In		Runs Produced		Bases On Balls		Batting Average		On Base Percentage		Slugging Average	
Goslin-Was	129	Ruth-NY	218	Ruth-NY	142	Ruth-NY	.378	Ruth-NY	.513	Ruth-NY	.739
Ruth-NY	121	Goslin-Was	217	Rigney-Det	102	Jamieson-Cle	.359	Collins-Chi	.441	Heilmann-Det	.533
Meusel-NY	120	Heilmann-Det	211	Sheely-Chi	95	Falk-Chi	.352	Speaker-Cle	.432	Williams-StL	.533
Hauser-Phi	115	J.Sewell-Cle	201	Collins-Chi	89	Collins-Chi	.349	Heilmann-Det	.428	Jacobson-StL	.528
		Meusel-NY	201	Cobb-Det	85	Bassler-Det	.346	Sheely-Chi	.426	Myatt-Cle	.518

Production		Adjusted Production		Batter Runs		Adjusted Batter Runs		Clutch Hitting Index		Runs Created	
Ruth-NY	1.252	Ruth-NY	221	Ruth-NY	100.8	Ruth-NY	101.1	Sheely-Chi	149	Ruth-NY	205
Heilmann-Det	.961	Heilmann-Det	149	Heilmann-Det	40.4	Heilmann-Det	42.4	Kamm-Chi	138	Heilmann-Det	134
Williams-StL	.958	Goslin-Was	145	Goslin-Was	35.6	Goslin-Was	39.3	Pratt-Det	138	Goslin-Was	125
Speaker-Cle	.943	Speaker-Cle	141	Speaker-Cle	32.4	Collins-Chi	34.1	Rigney-Det	137	Cobb-Det	121
Goslin-Was	.937	Williams-StL	137	Collins-Chi	30.5	Speaker-Cle	31.1	Veach-Bos	131	Collins-Chi	119

Total Average		Stolen Bases		Stolen Base Average		Stolen Base Runs		Fielding Runs		Total Player Rating	
Ruth-NY	1.558	Collins-Chi	42	Collins-Chi	71.2	Collins-Chi	2.4	J.Sewell-Cle	21.4	Ruth-NY	8.5
Heilmann-Det	1.042	Meusel-NY	26	Harris-Was	66.7			Lutzke-Cle	19.4	J.Sewell-Cle	4.3
Williams-StL	1.039	Rice-Was	24	Meusel-NY	65.0			Dykes-Phi	15.9	Heilmann-Det	3.9
Speaker-Cle	.988	Cobb-Det	23	Rice-Was	64.9			Jacobson-StL	15.8	Rigney-Det	3.4
Collins-Chi	.976	Jamieson-Cle	21	Williams-StL	64.5			Wambsganss-Bos	14.4	Collins-Chi	2.9

Wins		Win Percentage		Games		Complete Games		Shutouts		Saves	
Johnson-Was	23	Johnson-Was	.767	Marberry-Was	50	Thurston-Chi	28	Johnson-Was	6	Marberry-Was	15
Pennock-NY	21	Pennock-NY	.700	Holloway-Det	49	Ehmke-Bos	26	Davis-StL	5	Russell-Was	8
Thurston-Chi	20	Whitehill-Det	.654	Shaute-Cle	46	Pennock-NY	25	Shocker-StL	4	Quinn-Bos	7
Shaute-Cle	20	Zachary-Was	.625	Hoyt-NY	46	Shaute-Cle	21	Pennock-NY	4	Dauss-Det	6
Ehmke-Bos	19			Ehmke-Bos	45	Rommel-Phi	21	Ehmke-Bos	4	Connally-Chi	6

Innings Pitched		Fewest Hits/Game		Fewest BB/Game		Strikeouts		Strikeouts/Game		Ratio	
Ehmke-Bos	315.0	Johnson-Was	7.55	Smith-Cle	1.53	Johnson-Was	158	Johnson-Was	5.12	Johnson-Was	10.37
Thurston-Chi	291.0	Collins-Det	8.29	Thurston-Chi	1.86	Ehmke-Bos	119	Shawkey-NY	4.94	Collins-Det	11.08
Pennock-NY	286.1	Marberry-Was	8.75	Shocker-StL	1.90	Shawkey-NY	114	Ehmke-Bos	3.40	Zachary-Was	11.28
Shaute-Cle	283.0	Zachary-Was	8.79	Pennock-NY	2.01	Pennock-NY	101	Shocker-StL	3.22	Smith-Cle	11.48
Rommel-Phi	278.0	Wingard-StL	8.88	Quinn-Bos	2.05	Shocker-StL	88	Pennock-NY	3.17	Pennock-NY	11.54

Earned Run Average		Adjusted ERA		Opponents' Batting Avg.		Opponents' On Base Pct.		Starter Runs		Adjusted Starter Runs	
Johnson-Was	2.72	Baumgartner-Phi	149	Johnson-Was	.224	Johnson-Was	.284	Johnson-Was	46.5	Pennock-NY	42.3
Zachary-Was	2.75	Johnson-Was	148	Collins-Det	.249	Collins-Det	.307	Pennock-NY	44.6	Johnson-Was	40.5
Pennock-NY	2.83	Pennock-NY	147	Marberry-Was	.262	Smith-Cle	.312	Smith-Cle	33.4	Smith-Cle	34.5
Baumgartner-Phi	2.88	Zachary-Was	147	Wingard-StL	.262	Pennock-NY	.314	Zachary-Was	33.2	Ehmke-Bos	31.9
Smith-Cle	3.02	Smith-Cle	142	Davis-StL	.263	Zachary-Was	.315	Baumgartner-Phi	27.1	Zachary-Was	28.9

Clutch Pitching Index		Relief Runs		Adjusted Relief Runs		Relief Ranking		Total Pitcher Index		Total Baseball Ranking	
Baumgartner-Phi	132	Speece-Was	9.5	Speece-Was	8.4	Speece-Was	4.2	Johnson-Was	4.5	Ruth-NY	8.5
Pennock-NY	117							Pennock-NY	3.8	Johnson-Was	4.5
Zachary-Was	113							Zachary-Was	3.7	J.Sewell-Cle	4.3
Ferguson-Bos	113							Bush-NY	3.4	Heilmann-Det	3.9
Hoyt-NY	112							Smith-Cle	3.4	Pennock-NY	3.8

TEAM	G	W	L	PCT	GB	R	OR	AB	H	2B	3B	HR	BB	SO	AVG	OBP	SLG	PRO	PRO+	BR	/A	PF	CHI	RC	SB	CS	SBA	SBR
PIT	153	95	58	.621		912	715	5372	1651	316	105	78	499	363	.307	.369	.449	.818	108	116	55	107	101	909	159	63	72	10
NY	152	86	66	.566	8.5	736	702	5327	1507	239	61	114	411	494	.283	.337	.415	.752	101	-26	3	96	100	742	79	65	55	-15
CIN	153	80	73	.523	15	690	643	5233	1490	221	90	44	409	327	.285	.339	.387	.726	93	-66	-49	98	100	680	108	107	50	-32
STL	153	77	76	.503	18	828	764	5329	1592	292	80	109	446	414	.299	.356	.445	.801	108	72	53	102	98	846	70	51	58	-10
BOS	153	70	83	.458	25	708	802	5365	1567	260	70	41	405	380	.292	.345	.390	.735	102	-48	15	91	98	722	77	72	52	-20
PHI	153	68	85	.444	27	812	930	5412	1598	288	58	100	456	542	.295	.354	.425	.779	96	35	-37	109	99	814	48	59	45	-21
BRO	153	68	85	.444	27	786	866	5468	1617	250	80	64	437	383	.296	.351	.406	.757	102	-6	15	97	101	787	37	30	55	-7
CHI	154	68	86	.442	27.5	723	773	5353	1473	254	70	86	397	470	.275	.329	.397	.726	89	-77	-87	102	104	700	94	70	57	-14
TOT	612					6195		42859	12495	2120	614	636	3460	3373	.292	.348	.414	.762							672	517	57	-109

TEAM	CG	SH	SV	IP	H	H/G	HR	BB	SO	RAT	ERA	ERA+	OAV	OOB	PR	/A	PF	CPI	FA	E	DP	FW	PW	BW	SBW	DIF
PIT	77	2	13	1354²	1526	10.1	81	387	386	12.9	3.87	115	.287	.339	59	88	105	105	.964	224	171	-.9	8.2	5.1	2.2	3.8
NY	80	6	8	1354	1532	10.2	73	408	446	13.0	3.94	102	.289	.342	49	17	95	104	.968	199	129	.5	1.6	.3	-.1	7.8
CIN	92	11	12	1375¹	1447	9.5	35	324	437	11.8	3.38	121	.272	.317	135	110	96	95	.968	203	161	.3	10.3	-4.6	-1.7	-4.4
STL	82	8	7	1335²	1480	10.0	86	470	428	13.4	4.36	99	.283	.347	-14	-7	101	96	.966	204	156	.3	-.7	5.0	.3	-1.2
BOS	77	5	4	1366²	1567	10.3	67	458	351	13.4	4.39	91	.291	.348	-19	-58	94	96	.964	221	145	-.7	-5.4	1.4	-.6	-.6
PHI	69	8	9	1350²	1753	11.7	117	444	371	14.8	5.02	95	.315	.368	-114	-39	112	103	.966	211	147	-.1	-3.7	-3.5	-.7	-.6
BRO	82	4	4	1350²	1608	10.7	75	477	518	14.1	4.77	88	.301	.362	-76	-90	98	97	.966	210	130	-.0	-8.4	1.4	.6	-2.0
CHI	75	5	10	1370	1575	10.3	102	485	435	13.7	4.41	98	.292	.353	-21	-14	101	102	.969	198	161	.7	-1.3	-8.1	-.0	-.2
TOT	634	49	67	10857²		10.4				13.4	4.27		.292	.348					.966	1670	1200					

Runs		Hits		Doubles		Triples		Home Runs		Total Bases	
Cuyler-Pit	144	Bottomley-StL	227	Bottomley-StL	44	Cuyler-Pit	26	Hornsby-StL	39	Hornsby-StL	381
Hornsby-StL	133	Wheat-Bro	221	Cuyler-Pit	43	Walker-Cin	16	Hartnett-Chi	24	Cuyler-Pit	369
Wheat-Bro	125	Cuyler-Pit	220	Wheat-Bro	42	Roush-Cin	16	Fournier-Bro	22	Bottomley-StL	358
Traynor-Pit	114	Hornsby-StL	203	Hornsby-StL	41	Fournier-Bro	16	Meusel-NY	21	Wheat-Bro	333
Blades-StL	112	Stock-Bro	202	Burrus-Bos	41			Bottomley-StL	21	Fournier-Bro	310

Runs Batted In		Runs Produced		Bases On Balls		Batting Average		On Base Percentage		Slugging Average	
Hornsby-StL	143	Hornsby-StL	237	Fournier-Bro	86	Hornsby-StL	.403	Hornsby-StL	.489	Hornsby-StL	.756
Fournier-Bro	130	Cuyler-Pit	228	Hornsby-StL	83	Bottomley-StL	.367	Fournier-Bro	.446	Cuyler-Pit	.598
Bottomley-StL	128	Wheat-Bro	214	Moore-Pit	73	Wheat-Bro	.359	Blades-StL	.423	Wrightstone-Phi	.591
Wright-Pit	121	Traynor-Pit	214	Youngs-NY	66	Cuyler-Pit	.357	Cuyler-Pit	.423	Bottomley-StL	.578
Barnhart-Pit	114	Fournier-Bro	207	Carey-Pit	66	Fournier-Bro	.350	Carey-Pit	.418	Fournier-Bro	.569

Production		Adjusted Production		Batter Runs		Adjusted Batter Runs		Clutch Hitting Index		Runs Created	
Hornsby-StL	1.245	Hornsby-StL	208	Hornsby-StL	87.1	Hornsby-StL	83.3	Barnhart-Pit	146	Hornsby-StL	187
Cuyler-Pit	1.021	Fournier-Bro	162	Cuyler-Pit	53.1	Fournier-Bro	53.8	Traynor-Pit	117	Cuyler-Pit	158
Fournier-Bro	1.015	Cuyler-Pit	148	Fournier-Bro	50.1	Cuyler-Pit	43.5	Felix-Bos	115	Bottomley-StL	145
Bottomley-StL	.992	Bottomley-StL	147	Bottomley-StL	45.5	Bottomley-StL	42.4	E.Brown-Bro	114	Fournier-Bro	141
Blades-StL	.958	Wheat-Bro	143	Wheat-Bro	35.0	Wheat-Bro	38.3	Moore-Pit	112	Wheat-Bro	134

Total Average		Stolen Bases		Stolen Base Average		Stolen Base Runs		Fielding Runs		Total Player Rating	
Hornsby-StL	1.539	Carey-Pit	46	Smith-StL	90.9	Carey-Pit	7.2	Adams-Chi	28.1	Hornsby-StL	6.0
Cuyler-Pit	1.141	Cuyler-Pit	41	Carey-Pit	80.7	Smith-StL	4.8	Traynor-Pit	22.9	Fournier-Bro	4.2
Fournier-Bro	1.117	Adams-Chi	26	Cuyler-Pit	75.9	Cuyler-Pit	4.5	Critz-Cin	21.6	Cuyler-Pit	4.1
Bottomley-StL	1.025	Roush-Cin	22	Moore-Pit	73.1	Stock-Bro	1.8	Pinelli-Cin	20.8	Bancroft-Bos	3.8
Carey-Pit	1.011	Frisch-NY	21	Adams-Chi	68.4	Grantham-Pit	1.8	Kelly-NY	17.8	Traynor-Pit	3.5

Wins		Win Percentage		Games		Complete Games		Shutouts		Saves	
Vance-Bro	22	Sherdel-StL	.714	Morrison-Pit	44	Donohue-Cin	27	Vance-Bro	4	Morrison-Pit	4
Rixey-Cin	21	Vance-Bro	.710	Donohue-Cin	42	Vance-Bro	26	Luque-Cin	4	Bush-Chi	4
Donohue-Cin	21	Aldridge-Pit	.682	Bush-Chi	42	Rixey-Cin	22	Carlson-Phi	4		
Meadows-Pit	19	Kremer-Pit	.680	Osborne-Bro	41	Luque-Cin	22	Donohue-Cin	3		
		Rixey-Cin	.656	Kremer-Pit	40	Ring-Phi	21				

Innings Pitched		Fewest Hits/Game		Fewest BB/Game		Strikeouts		Strikeouts/Game		Ratio	
Donohue-Cin	301.0	Luque-Cin	8.13	Alexander-Chi	1.11	Vance-Bro	221	Vance-Bro	7.50	Luque-Cin	10.61
Luque-Cin	291.0	Benton-Bos	8.35	Donohue-Cin	1.47	Luque-Cin	140	Luque-Cin	4.33	Donohue-Cin	10.79
Rixey-Cin	287.1	Vance-Bro	8.38	Rixey-Cin	1.47	Ring-Phi	93	Sothoron-StL	3.87	Vance-Bro	10.96
Ring-Phi	270.0	Aldridge-Pit	9.20	Cooney-Bos	1.83	Blake-Chi	93	Bush-Chi	3.76	Rixey-Cin	11.15
Vance-Bro	265.1	Donohue-Cin	9.27	Sherdel-StL	1.89	Aldridge-Pit	88	Aldridge-Pit	3.71	Alexander-Chi	11.52

Earned Run Average		Adjusted ERA		Opponents' Batting Avg.		Opponents' On Base Pct.		Starter Runs		Adjusted Starter Runs	
Luque-Cin	2.63	Luque-Cin	156	Luque-Cin	.239	Luque-Cin	.291	Luque-Cin	53.0	Luque-Cin	47.9
Rixey-Cin	2.88	Rixey-Cin	143	Benton-Bos	.249	Donohue-Cin	.299	Rixey-Cin	44.2	Rixey-Cin	39.2
Donohue-Cin	3.08	Sherdel-StL	139	Vance-Bro	.250	Vance-Bro	.304	Donohue-Cin	39.7	Donohue-Cin	34.4
Benton-Bos	3.09	Donohue-Cin	133	Donohue-Cin	.268	Rixey-Cin	.307	Scott-NY	29.6	Sherdel-StL	27.0
Sherdel-StL	3.11	Benton-Bos	130	Scott-NY	.269	Cooney-Bos	.312	Sherdel-StL	25.8	Alexander-Chi	24.4

Clutch Pitching Index		Relief Runs		Adjusted Relief Runs		Relief Ranking		Total Pitcher Index		Total Baseball Ranking	
Nehf-NY	122	Huntzinger-NY	5.5	Huntzinger-NY	3.9	Huntzinger-NY	3.2	Luque-Cin	6.1	Luque-Cin	6.1
Yde-Pit	117							Donohue-Cin	4.0	Hornsby-StL	6.0
Sherdel-StL	109							Rixey-Cin	3.6	Fournier-Bro	4.2
Rixey-Cin	108							Scott-NY	3.3	Cuyler-Pit	4.1
Morrison-Pit	107							Sherdel-StL	2.6	Donohue-Cin	4.0

TEAM	G	W	L	PCT	GB	R	OR	AB	H	2B	3B	HR	BB	SO	AVG	OBP	SLG	PRO	PRO+	BR	/A	PF	CHI	RC	SB	CS	SBA	SBR
WAS	152	96	55	.636		829	670	5206	1577	251	71	56	533	427	.303	.373	.411	.784	106	39	56	98	100	815	135	92	59	-15
PHI	153	88	64	.579	8.5	831	713	5399	1659	298	79	76	453	432	.307	.364	.434	.798	101	54	-2	107	97	856	67	60	53	-16
STL	154	82	71	.536	15	900	906	5440	1620	304	68	110	498	375	.298	.360	.439	.799	103	52	8	105	105	859	85	78	52	-21
DET	156	81	73	.526	16.5	903	829	5371	1621	277	84	50	640	386	.302	.362	.413	.796	109	63	76	99	102	872	97	63	61	-9
CHI	154	79	75	.513	18.5	811	770	5224	1482	299	59	38	662	405	.284	.370	.385	.755	102	-7	36	95	101	782	131	87	60	-13
CLE	155	70	84	.455	27.5	782	817	5436	1613	285	58	52	520	379	.297	.361	.399	.760	97	-12	-18	101	98	795	90	77	54	-19
NY	156	69	85	.448	28.5	706	774	5353	1471	247	74	110	470	482	.275	.336	.410	.746	96	-61	-48	98	97	739	69	73	49	-23
BOS	152	47	105	.309	49.5	639	922	5166	1375	257	64	41	513	422	.266	.336	.364	.700	83	-131	-130	100	100	647	42	56	43	-21
TOT	616					6401		42595	12418	2218	557	533	4289	3308	.292	.360	.408	.768							716	586	55	-137

TEAM	CG	SH	SV	IP	H	H/G	HR	BB	SO	RAT	ERA	ERA+	OAV	OOB	PR	/A	PF	CPI	FA	E	DP	FW	PW	BW	SBW	DIF
WAS	69	10	21	1358¹	1434	9.5	49	543	463	13.3	3.70	114	.278	.351	105	79	96	107	.972	170	166	1.8	7.3	5.2	.2	6.0
PHI	61	8	18	1381²	1468	9.6	60	544	495	13.3	3.87	120	.276	.347	81	119	106	101	.966	211	148	-.6	11.0	-.2	.1	1.6
STL	67	7	10	1379²	1588	10.4	99	675	419	15.0	4.92	95	.298	.380	-80	-39	106	102	.964	226	164	-1.4	-3.6	.7	-.4	10.1
DET	66	2	18	1383²	1582	10.3	70	556	419	14.2	4.61	94	.296	.366	-32	-46	99	99	.972	173	143	1.9	-4.3	7.0	.8	-1.4
CHI	71	12	13	1385²	1579	10.3	69	489	374	13.6	4.29	97	.295	.356	17	-21	95	102	.968	200	162	.2	-1.9	3.3	.4	.0
CLE	93	6	9	1372¹	1604	10.5	41	493	345	14.0	4.49	98	.296	.359	-15	-9	101	95	.967	210	146	-.4	-.8	-1.7	-.2	-4.0
NY	80	8	13	1387²	1560	10.1	78	505	492	13.6	4.33	98	.289	.353	10	-11	97	99	.974	160	150	2.7	-1.0	-4.4	-.5	-4.7
BOS	68	6	6	1326²	1615	11.0	67	510	310	14.7	4.97	92	.308	.374	-84	-62	103	98	.957	271	150	-4.2	-5.7	-12.0	-.4	-6.6
TOT	575	59	108	10975²		10.2				14.0	4.39		.292	.360					.968	1621	1229					

Runs		Hits		Doubles		Triples		Home Runs		Total Bases	
Mostil-Chi	135	Simmons-Phi	253	McManus-StL	44	Goslin-Was	20	Meusel-NY	33	Simmons-Phi	392
Simmons-Phi	122	Rice-Was	227	Simmons-Phi	43	Mostil-Chi	16	Williams-StL	25	Meusel-NY	338
Combs-NY	117	Heilmann-Det	225	Sheely-Chi	43	Sisler-StL	15	Ruth-NY	25	Goslin-Was	329
Goslin-Was	116	Sisler-StL	224	Burns-Cle	41			Simmons-Phi	24	Heilmann-Det	326
Rice-Was	111	J.Sewell-Cle	204					Gehrig-NY	20	Sisler-StL	311

Runs Batted In		Runs Produced		Bases On Balls		Batting Average		On Base Percentage		Slugging Average	
Meusel-NY	138	Simmons-Phi	227	Mostil-Chi	90	Heilmann-Det	.393	Speaker-Cle	.479	Williams-StL	.613
Heilmann-Det	134	Heilmann-Det	218	Kamm-Chi	90	Speaker-Cle	.389	Cobb-Det	.468	Simmons-Phi	.599
Simmons-Phi	129	Goslin-Was	211	Collins-Chi	87	Simmons-Phi	.387	Collins-Chi	.461	Cobb-Det	.598
Goslin-Was	113	Meusel-NY	206	Bishop-Phi	87	Cobb-Det	.378	Heilmann-Det	.457	Speaker-Cle	.578
Sheely-Chi	111	Rice-Was	197	Blue-Det	83	Wingo-Det	.370	Wingo-Det	.456	Heilmann-Det	.569

Production		Adjusted Production		Batter Runs		Adjusted Batter Runs		Clutch Hitting Index		Runs Created	
Cobb-Det	1.066	Cobb-Det	171	Heilmann-Det	52.5	Heilmann-Det	54.6	Galloway-Phi	149	Simmons-Phi	155
Speaker-Cle	1.057	Speaker-Cle	166	Simmons-Phi	51.4	Cobb-Det	47.0	Blue-Det	136	Heilmann-Det	149
Heilmann-Det	1.026	Heilmann-Det	161	Speaker-Cle	47.0	Speaker-Cle	46.1	Sheely-Chi	127	Goslin-Was	131
Simmons-Phi	1.018	Wingo-Det	151	Cobb-Det	45.3	Simmons-Phi	42.1	Collins-Chi	123	Speaker-Cle	123
Wingo-Det	.983	Simmons-Phi	146	Wingo-Det	35.3	Wingo-Det	36.8	B.Harris-Was	120	Cobb-Det	118

Total Average		Stolen Bases		Stolen Base Average		Stolen Base Runs		Fielding Runs		Total Player Rating	
Speaker-Cle	1.231	Mostil-Chi	43	Blue-Det	79.2	Goslin-Was	3.3	Flagstead-Bos	19.9	Speaker-Cle	4.5
Cobb-Det	1.206	Goslin-Was	27	Goslin-Was	77.1	Haney-Det	2.7	J.Sewell-Cle	16.3	J.Sewell-Cle	3.8
Heilmann-Det	1.113	Rice-Was	26	Collins-Chi	76.0	Blue-Det	2.7	O'Rourke-Det	14.6	Heilmann-Det	3.7
Wingo-Det	1.041			Rice-Was	70.3	Collins-Chi	2.1	Goslin-Was	13.6	Goslin-Was	3.7
Collins-Chi	1.028			Mostil-Chi	68.3	Peckinpaugh-Was	1.5	Ruel-Was	11.5	Cobb-Det	3.3

Wins		Win Percentage		Games		Complete Games		Shutouts		Saves	
Rommel-Phi	21	Coveleski-Was	.800	Marberry-Was	55	Smith-Cle	22	Lyons-Chi	5	Marberry-Was	15
Lyons-Chi	21	Johnson-Was	.741	Walberg-Phi	53	Ehmke-Bos	22	Gray-Phi	4	Doyle-Det	8
Johnson-Was	20	Ruether-Was	.720	Vangilder-StL	52	Pennock-NY	21	Giard-StL	4	Connally-Chi	8
Coveleski-Was	20	Blankenship-Chi	.680	Rommel-Phi	52	Lyons-Chi	19			Walberg-Phi	7
Harriss-Phi	19	Rommel-Phi	.677	Pennock-NY	47	Wingfield-Bos	18				

Innings Pitched		Fewest Hits/Game		Fewest BB/Game		Strikeouts		Strikeouts/Game		Ratio	
Pennock-NY	277.0	Blankenship-Chi	8.46	Smith-Cle	1.82	Grove-Phi	116	Grove-Phi	5.30	Pennock-NY	11.05
Lyons-Chi	262.2	Johnson-Was	8.53	Quinn-Phi	1.85	Johnson-Was	108	Johnson-Was	4.24	Blankenship-Chi	11.13
Rommel-Phi	261.0	Coveleski-Was	8.59	Shocker-NY	2.14	Harriss-Phi	95	Shawkey-NY	3.92	Coveleski-Was	11.39
Ehmke-Bos	260.2	Pennock-NY	8.68	Faber-Chi	2.23	Ehmke-Bos	95	Walberg-Phi	3.85	Gray-Phi	11.71
Wingfield-Bos	254.1	Gray-Phi	8.79	Pennock-NY	2.31	Jones-NY	92	Gray-Phi	3.54	Johnson-Was	11.87

Earned Run Average		Adjusted ERA		Opponents' Batting Avg.		Opponents' On Base Pct.		Starter Runs		Adjusted Starter Runs	
Coveleski-Was	2.84	Coveleski-Was	149	Johnson-Was	.250	Pennock-NY	.303	Pennock-NY	44.2	Pennock-NY	40.2
Pennock-NY	2.96	Pennock-NY	144	Blankenship-Chi	.253	Blankenship-Chi	.308	Coveleski-Was	41.7	Coveleski-Was	37.2
Blankenship-Chi	3.03	Gray-Phi	142	Pennock-NY	.254	Coveleski-Was	.312	Blankenship-Chi	35.3	Harriss-Phi	32.5
Johnson-Was	3.07	Johnson-Was	138	Coveleski-Was	.255	Johnson-Was	.317	Johnson-Was	33.8	Gray-Phi	31.2
Dauss-Det	3.16	Blankenship-Chi	137	Gray-Phi	.260	Gray-Phi	.319	Lyons-Chi	33.3	Johnson-Was	29.6

Clutch Pitching Index		Relief Runs		Adjusted Relief Runs		Relief Ranking		Total Pitcher Index		Total Baseball Ranking	
Dauss-Det	119	Marberry-Was	9.6	Marberry-Was	7.8	Marberry-Was	13.4	Johnson-Was	4.3	Speaker-Cle	4.5
Shocker-NY	114	Gregg-Was	2.3	Gregg-Was	0.9	Gregg-Was	0.5	Pennock-NY	3.6	Johnson-Was	4.3
Zachary-Was	113							Harriss-Phi	3.4	J.Sewell-Cle	3.8
Lyons-Chi	111							Rommel-Phi	3.3	Heilmann-Det	3.7
Shawkey-NY	110							Dauss-Det	3.0	Goslin-Was	3.7

TEAM	G	W	L	PCT	GB	R	OR	AB	H	2B	3B	HR	BB	SO	AVG	OBP	SLG	PRO	PRO+	BR	/A	PF	CHI	RC	SB	CS	SBA	SBR
STL	156	89	65	.578		817	678	5381	1541	259	82	90	478	518	.286	.348	.415	.763	107	76	46	104	102	770	83			
CIN	157	87	67	.565	2	747	651	5320	1541	242	120	35	454	333	.290	.349	.400	.749	110	52	72	97	97	738	51			
PIT	157	84	69	.549	4.5	769	689	5312	1514	243	106	44	434	350	.285	.343	.396	.739	99	28	-11	105	104	713	91			
CHI	155	82	72	.532	7	682	602	5229	1453	291	49	66	445	447	.278	.338	.390	.728	100	7	-2	101	96	685	85			
NY	151	74	77	.490	13.5	663	668	5167	1435	214	58	73	339	420	.278	.325	.384	.709	97	-36	-28	99	104	631	94			
BRO	155	71	82	.464	17.5	623	705	5130	1348	246	62	40	475	464	.263	.328	.358	.686	91	-65	-56	99	100	607	76			
BOS	153	66	86	.434	22	624	719	5216	1444	209	62	16	426	348	.277	.335	.350	.685	99	-66	-10	91	99	612	81			
PHI	152	58	93	.384	29.5	687	900	5254	1479	244	50	75	422	479	.281	.337	.390	.727	96	5	-31	105	98	683	47			
TOT	618					5612		42009	11755	1948	589	439	3473	3359	.280	.338	.386	.724							608			

TEAM	CG	SH	SV	IP	H	H/G	HR	BB	SO	RAT	ERA	ERA+	OAV	OOB	PR	/A	PF	CPI	FA	E	DP	FW	PW	BW	SBW	DIF
STL	90	10	6	1398²	1423	9.2	76	397	365	11.8	3.67	106	.269	.322	24	36	102	96	.969	198	141	.3	3.6	4.5		3.6
CIN	88	14	8	1408²	1449	9.3	40	324	424	11.5	3.42	108	.271	.316	64	42	97	95	.972	183	160	1.3	4.2	7.1		-2.6
PIT	83	12	18	1379¹	1422	9.3	50	455	387	12.5	3.67	107	.272	.334	24	42	103	99	.965	220	161	-.9	4.2	-1.1		5.3
CHI	77	13	14	1378¹	1407	9.2	39	486	508	12.6	3.26	118	.273	.340	87	89	101	113	.974	162	174	2.4	8.8	-.2		-6.0
NY	61	4	15	1341²	1370	9.2	70	427	419	12.2	3.77	100	.269	.328	8	-3	98	96	.970	186	150	.7	-.3	-2.8		.9
BRO	83	5	9	1361²	1440	9.5	50	472	517	12.8	3.82	100	.276	.339	-1	0	100	98	.963	229	95	-1.5	.0	-5.5		1.6
BOS	60	9	9	1365¹	1536	10.1	46	455	408	13.4	4.01	88	.294	.354	-28	-71	93	105	.967	208	150	-.5	-7.0	-1.0		-1.5
PHI	68	5	5	1334¹	1699	11.5	68	454	331	14.7	5.03	82	.315	.371	-179	-133	108	98	.964	224	153	-1.5	-13.1	-3.1		.2
TOT	610	72	84	10968		9.6				12.7	3.82		.280	.338					.968	1610	1184					

Runs		Hits		Doubles		Triples		Home Runs		Total Bases	
Cuyler-Pit	113	Brown-Bos	201	Bottomley-StL	40	Waner-Pit	22	Wilson-Chi	21	Bottomley-StL	305
Waner-Pit	101	Cuyler-Pit	197	Roush-Cin	37	Walker-Cin	20	Bottomley-StL	19	L.Bell-StL	301
Southworth-NY-StL	99	Adams-Chi	193	Wilson-Chi	36	Traynor-Pit	17	Williams-Phi	18	Wilson-Chi	285
Sand-Phi	99	L.Bell-StL	189					L.Bell-StL	17	Waner-Pit	283
								Southworth-NY-StL	16	Cuyler-Pit	282

Runs Batted In		Runs Produced		Bases On Balls		Batting Average		On Base Percentage		Slugging Average	
Bottomley-StL	120	Bottomley-StL	199	Wilson-Chi	69	Hargrave-Cin	.353	Waner-Pit	.413	Williams-Phi	.568
Wilson-Chi	109	Cuyler-Pit	197	Waner-Pit	66	Christensen-Cin	.350	Blades-StL	.409	Wilson-Chi	.539
L.Bell-StL	100	Wilson-Chi	185	Sand-Phi	66	Smith-Pit	.346	Wilson-Chi	.406	Waner-Pit	.528
Southworth-NY-StL	99	Southworth-NY-StL	182	Bancroft-Bos	64	Williams-Phi	.345	Grantham-Pit	.400	Hargrave-Cin	.525
Pipp-Cin	99	Hornsby-StL	178	Blades-StL	62	Waner-Pit	.336	Bancroft-Bos	.399	L.Bell-StL	.518

Production		Adjusted Production		Batter Runs		Adjusted Batter Runs		Clutch Hitting Index		Runs Created	
Wilson-Chi	.944	Wilson-Chi	150	Waner-Pit	39.5	Wilson-Chi	37.9	Butler-Bro	125	Waner-Pit	115
Waner-Pit	.941	Waner-Pit	144	Wilson-Chi	39.2	Waner-Pit	33.6	Pipp-Cin	122	Wilson-Chi	115
L.Bell-StL	.901	Herman-Bro	136	L.Bell-StL	31.6	L.Bell-StL	27.4	Hornsby-StL	116	L.Bell-StL	112
Grantham-Pit	.890	L.Bell-StL	135	Williams-Phi	29.8	Williams-Phi	26.0	Thevenow-StL	116	Bottomley-StL	109
Herman-Bro	.875	Grantham-Pit	131	Bottomley-StL	25.2	Herman-Bro	23.7	Burrus-Bos	116	Cuyler-Pit	105

Total Average		Stolen Bases		Stolen Base Average		Stolen Base Runs		Fielding Runs		Total Player Rating	
Wilson-Chi	1.031	Cuyler-Pit	35					Critz-Cin	24.0	Waner-Pit	3.1
Waner-Pit	1.022	Adams-Chi	27					Friberg-Phi	22.4	Wilson-Chi	3.0
Grantham-Pit	.938	Frisch-NY	23					Cooney-Chi	19.4	Bancroft-Bos	2.7
Blades-StL	.938	Douthit-StL	23					Thevenow-StL	18.4	O'Farrell-StL	2.7
L.Bell-StL	.929	Youngs-NY	21					Douthit-StL	17.8	Jackson-NY	2.6

Wins		Win Percentage		Games		Complete Games		Shutouts		Saves	
Rhem-StL	20	Kremer-Pit	.769	Scott-NY	50	Mays-Cin	24	Donohue-Cin	5	Davies-NY	6
Meadows-Pit	20	Rhem-StL	.741	Willoughby-Phi	47	Petty-Bro	23	B.Smith-Bos	4	Scott-NY	5
Kremer-Pit	20	Meadows-Pit	.690	Donohue-Cin	47	Root-Chi	21	Blake-Chi	4	Kremer-Pit	5
Donohue-Cin	20	Mays-Cin	.613	Ulrich-Phi	45	Rhem-StL	20			Ehrhardt-Bro	4
Mays-Cin	19	Donohue-Cin	.588	May-Cin	45	Carlson-Phi	20				

Innings Pitched		Fewest Hits/Game		Fewest BB/Game		Strikeouts		Strikeouts/Game		Ratio	
Donohue-Cin	285.2	Petty-Bro	8.03	Donohue-Cin	1.23	Vance-Bro	140	Vance-Bro	7.46	Alexander-Chi-StL	10.06
Mays-Cin	281.0	Greenfield-NY	8.33	Alexander-Chi-StL	1.39	Root-Chi	127	May-Cin	5.53	Petty-Bro	10.71
Petty-Bro	275.2	Rhem-StL	8.41	Carlson-Phi	1.58	May-Cin	103	Jones-Chi	4.49	Kremer-Pit	10.74
Root-Chi	271.1	Jones-Chi	8.48	Mays-Cin	1.70	Benton-Bos	103	Blake-Chi	4.33	Donohue-Cin	10.90
Carlson-Phi	267.1	Bush-Chi	8.52	Lucas-Cin	1.75	Petty-Bro	101	Root-Chi	4.21	Mays-Cin	10.99

Earned Run Average		Adjusted ERA		Opponents' Batting Avg.		Opponents' On Base Pct.		Starter Runs		Adjusted Starter Runs	
Kremer-Pit	2.61	Kremer-Pit	151	Petty-Bro	.240	Alexander-Chi-StL	.281	Kremer-Pit	31.3	Kremer-Pit	34.1
Root-Chi	2.82	Root-Chi	136	Alexander-Chi-StL	.250	Petty-Bro	.296	Root-Chi	30.3	Root-Chi	30.9
Petty-Bro	2.84	Petty-Bro	134	Rhem-StL	.250	Kremer-Pit	.296	Petty-Bro	30.1	Petty-Bro	30.0
Bush-Chi	2.86	Bush-Chi	134	Greenfield-NY	.251	Donohue-Cin	.298	Fitzsimmons-NY	23.0	Carlson-Phi	27.0
Barnes-NY	2.87	Barnes-NY	131	Kremer-Pit	.252	Rhem-StL	.305	Mays-Cin	21.4	Fitzsimmons-NY	21.3

Clutch Pitching Index		Relief Runs		Adjusted Relief Runs		Relief Ranking		Total Pitcher Index		Total Baseball Ranking	
Jones-Chi	122	Hallahan-StL	1.1	Hallahan-StL	1.6	Hallahan-StL	1.3	Kremer-Pit	3.7	Kremer-Pit	3.7
Blake-Chi	119							Root-Chi	3.2	Root-Chi	3.2
Fitzsimmons-NY	118							Mays-Cin	3.1	Waner-Pit	3.1
Werts-Bos	117							Petty-Bro	2.7	Mays-Cin	3.1
Root-Chi	111							Carlson-Phi	2.6	Wilson-Chi	3.0

TEAM	G	W	L	PCT	GB	R	OR	AB	H	2B	3B	HR	BB	SO	AVG	OBP	SLG	PRO	PRO+	BR	/A	PF	CHI	RC	SB	CS	SBA	SBR
NY	155	91	63	.591		**847**	713	5221	1508	262	75	121	**642**	580	.289	**.369**	.437	**.806**	119	**123**	**137**	98	98	**866**	79	62	56	-14
CLE	134	88	66	.571	3	738	612	5293	1529	**333**	49	27	455	332	.289	.349	.386	.735	97	-17	-23	101	**103**	735	88	42	**68**	1
PHI	150	83	67	.553	6	677	**570**	5046	1359	259	65	61	523	452	.269	.341	.383	.724	90	-39	-77	106	101	682	56	45	55	-10
WAS	152	81	69	.540	8	802	761	5223	1525	244	**97**	43	555	369	**.292**	.364	.401	.765	109	48	68	98	**103**	779	117	91	56	-20
CHI	155	81	72	.529	9.5	730	665	5220	1508	314	60	32	556	381	.289	.361	.390	.751	106	24	51	96	96	761	**123**	78	61	-10
DET	157	79	75	.513	12	793	830	5315	**1547**	281	90	36	599	423	.291	.367	.398	.765	105	52	42	101	99	801	88	71	55	-16
STL	155	62	92	.403	29	682	845	5259	1449	253	78	72	437	472	.276	.335	.394	.729	92	-38	-70	105	100	700	64	66	49	-20
BOS	154	46	107	.301	44.5	562	835	5185	1325	249	54	32	465	454	.256	.321	.343	.664	82	-156	-138	97	101	588	52	48	52	-13
TOT	616					5831		41762	11750	2195	568	424	4232	3463	.281	.351	.392	.743							667	503	57	-102

TEAM	CG	SH	SV	IP	H	H/G	HR	BB	SO	RAT	ERA	ERA+	OAV	OOB	PR	/A	PF	CPI	FA	E	DP	FW	PW	BW	SBW	DIF
NY	63	4	20	1372[1]	1442	9.5	56	478	486	12.8	3.86	100	.274	.337	24	-1	96	96	.966	210	117	-1.1	-.0	**13.3**	-.1	2.0
CLE	**96**	**11**	4	1374	1412	9.2	49	**450**	381	12.5	3.40	119	.271	.334	94	101	101	105	.972	173	153	1.1	9.8	-2.2	**1.3**	1.1
PHI	62	10	16	1346	**1362**	**9.1**	38	451	571	12.3	3.00	139	**.268**	.331	153	174	104	114	.972	171	131	.9	**16.9**	-7.5	.3	-2.5
WAS	65	5	**26**	1348[1]	1489	9.9	45	566	418	14.0	4.34	89	.287	.361	-48	-71	96	98	.969	184	129	.2	-6.9	6.6	-.7	6.8
CHI	85	**11**	12	1380	1426	9.3	47	506	458	12.7	3.74	103	.271	.356	43	16	96	96	**.973**	165	122	**1.6**	1.6	4.9	.3	-3.9
DET	57	10	18	1394[2]	1570	10.1	58	555	469	14.0	4.41	92	.292	.363	-61	-54	101	99	.969	193	151	.0	-5.2	4.1	-.3	3.4
STL	64	5	9	1368	1549	10.2	86	654	337	14.7	4.66	92	.297	.379	-98	-59	107	105	.963	235	**167**	-2.6	-5.7	-6.8	-.7	.8
BOS	53	6	5	1362	1520	10.0	45	546	336	13.9	4.72	86	.294	.365	-107	-101	101	92	.970	193	143	-.2	-9.8	-13.4	-.0	-7.2
TOT	545	62	110	10945[1]		9.7				13.3	4.02		.281	.351					.969	1524	1113					

Runs
Ruth-NY 139
Gehrig-NY 135
Mostil-Chi 120
Combs-NY 113
Goslin-Was 105

Hits
Rice-Was 216
Burns-Cle 216
Goslin-Was 201
Simmons-Phi 199
Mostil-Chi 197

Doubles
Burns-Cle 64
Simmons-Phi 53
Speaker-Cle 52
Jacobson-StL-Bos . 51
Gehrig-NY 47

Triples
Gehrig-NY 20
Gehringer-Det 17
Mostil-Chi 15
Goslin-Was 15

Home Runs
Ruth-NY 47
Simmons-Phi 19
Lazzeri-NY 18
Williams-StL 17
Goslin-Was 17

Total Bases
Ruth-NY 365
Simmons-Phi 329
Gehrig-NY 314
Goslin-Was 308
Burns-Cle 298

Runs Batted In
Ruth-NY 146
Lazzeri-NY 114
Burns-Cle 114
Gehrig-NY 112
Simmons-Phi 109

Runs Produced
Ruth-NY 238
Gehrig-NY 231
Burns-Cle 207
Goslin-Was 196
Falk-Chi 186

Bases On Balls
Ruth-NY 144
Bishop-Phi 116
Rigney-Bos 108
Gehrig-NY 105
Speaker-Cle 94

Batting Average
Manush-Det 378
Ruth-NY 372
Fothergill-Det 367
Heilmann-Det 367
Burns-Cle 358

On Base Percentage
Ruth-NY 516
Heilmann-Det 445
Bishop-Phi 431
Goslin-Was 425
Manush-Det 421

Slugging Average
Ruth-NY 737
Simmons-Phi 564
Manush-Det 564
Gehrig-NY 549
Goslin-Was 542

Production
Ruth-NY 1.253
Manush-Det 985
Heilmann-Det 979
Gehrig-NY 969
Goslin-Was 967

Adjusted Production
Ruth-NY 228
Goslin-Was 155
Gehrig-NY 154
Manush-Det 153
Heilmann-Det 152

Batter Runs
Ruth-NY 97.4
Gehrig-NY 44.2
Goslin-Was 42.3
Heilmann-Det 41.7
Manush-Det 38.2

Adjusted Batter Runs
Ruth-NY 100.3
Gehrig-NY 46.2
Goslin-Was 45.3
Heilmann-Det 40.3
Manush-Det 36.8

Clutch Hitting Index
Judge-Was 134
Dugan-NY 131
Haney-Bos 127
Myer-Was 121
Lutzke-Cle 118

Runs Created
Ruth-NY 196
Gehrig-NY 137
Goslin-Was 131
Simmons-Phi 129
Mostil-Chi 122

Total Average
Ruth-NY 1.606
Gehrig-NY 1.058
Heilmann-Det 1.040
Manush-Det 1.029
Goslin-Was 1.008

Stolen Bases
Mostil-Chi 35
Rice-Was 24
Hunnefield-Chi . . . 24
McNeely-Was 18
J.Sewell-Cle 17

Stolen Base Average
McNeely-Was 75.0
Hunnefield-Chi . . . 72.7
Mostil-Chi 71.4
J.Sewell-Cle 70.8
Lazzeri-NY 69.6

Stolen Base Runs
Mostil-Chi 2.1
McNeely-Was 1.8
Hunnefield-Chi . . . 1.8
Simmons-Phi 1.5

Fielding Runs
Dykes-Phi 26.4
Rigney-Bos 19.6
Goslin-Was 18.5
Regan-Bos 17.4
Mostil-Chi 17.1

Total Player Rating
Ruth-NY 8.4
Goslin-Was 4.9
Mostil-Chi 4.0
Rigney-Bos 3.9
J.Sewell-Cle 3.3

Wins
Uhle-Cle 27
Pennock-NY 23
Shocker-NY 19
Lyons-Chi 18

Win Percentage
Uhle-Cle 711
Pennock-NY 676
Shocker-NY 633
Faber-Chi 625
Hoyt-NY 571

Games
Marberry-Was 64
Pate-Phi 47
Grove-Phi 45
Thomas-Chi 44

Complete Games
Uhle-Cle 32
Lyons-Chi 24
Johnson-Was 22
Grove-Phi 20
Pennock-NY 19

Shutouts
Wells-Det 4

Saves
Marberry-Was 22
Dauss-Det 9
Pate-Phi 6
Grove-Phi 6
Jones-NY 5

Innings Pitched
Uhle-Cle 318.1
Lyons-Chi 283.2
Pennock-NY 266.1
Johnson-Was 260.2
Shocker-NY 258.1

Fewest Hits/Game
Grove-Phi 7.92
Thomas-Chi 8.13
Uhle-Cle 8.48
Lyons-Chi 8.50
Buckeye-Cle 8.69

Fewest BB/Game
Pennock-NY 1.45
Smith-Cle 1.48
Quinn-Phi 1.98
Rommel-Phi 2.22
Wingfield-Bos 2.36

Strikeouts
Grove-Phi 194
Uhle-Cle 159
Thomas-Chi 127
Johnson-Was 125
Whitehill-Det 109

Strikeouts/Game
Grove-Phi 6.77
Thomas-Chi 4.59
Uhle-Cle 4.50
Johnson-Was 4.32
Whitehill-Det 3.89

Ratio
Pennock-NY 11.52
Rommel-Phi 11.55
Johnson-Was 11.64
Grove-Phi 11.65
Lyons-Chi 11.90

Earned Run Average
Grove-Phi 2.51
Uhle-Cle 2.83
Lyons-Chi 3.01
Rommel-Phi 3.08
Buckeye-Cle 3.10

Adjusted ERA
Grove-Phi 166
Uhle-Cle 143
Rommel-Phi 135
Buckeye-Cle 131
Lyons-Chi 128

Opponents' Batting Avg.
Thomas-Chi 244
Grove-Phi 244
Lyons-Chi 252
Uhle-Cle 253
Levsen-Cle 261

Opponents' On Base Pct.
Pennock-NY 313
Rommel-Phi 314
Hoyt-NY 316
Johnson-Was 317
Shocker-NY 318

Starter Runs
Grove-Phi 43.1
Uhle-Cle 42.1
Lyons-Chi 31.6
Coveleski-Was 24.5
Rommel-Phi 22.7

Adjusted Starter Runs
Grove-Phi 47.4
Uhle-Cle 43.4
Lyons-Chi 26.7
Rommel-Phi 26.4
Walberg-Phi 22.9

Clutch Pitching Index
Wingard-StL 128
Zachary-StL 122
Grove-Phi 119
Coveleski-Was 117
Buckeye-Cle 114

Relief Runs
Pate-Phi 16.4
Marberry-Was 15.6
Braxton-NY 10.1
Russell-Bos 4.7

Adjusted Relief Runs
Pate-Phi 18.3
Marberry-Was 13.3
Braxton-NY 8.8
Russell-Bos 5.3

Relief Ranking
Marberry-Was 21.2
Pate-Phi 15.3
Braxton-NY 7.7
Russell-Bos 2.4

Total Pitcher Index
Uhle-Cle 5.2
Grove-Phi 4.0
Lyons-Chi 3.3
Walberg-Phi 2.8
Zachary-StL 2.7

Total Baseball Ranking
Ruth-NY 8.4
Uhle-Cle 5.2
Goslin-Was 4.9
Grove-Phi 4.0
Mostil-Chi 4.0

TEAM	G	W	L	PCT	GB	R	OR	AB	H	2B	3B	HR	BB	SO	AVG	OBP	SLG	PRO	PRO+	BR	/A	PF	CHI	RC	SB	CS	SBA	SBR
PIT	156	94	60	.610		817	659	5397	1648	258	78	54	437	355	.305	.361	.412	.773	106	99	42	107	99	791	65			
STL	153	92	61	.601	1.5	754	665	5207	1450	264	79	84	484	511	.278	.343	.408	.751	104	47	24	103	101	723	110			
NY	155	92	62	.597	2	817	720	5372	1594	251	62	109	461	462	.297	.356	.427	.783	116	113	115	100	98	805	73			
CHI	153	85	68	.556	8.5	750	661	5303	1505	266	63	74	481	492	.284	.346	.400	.746	106	43	41	100	99	730	65			
CIN	153	75	78	.490	18.5	643	653	5185	1439	222	77	29	402	332	.278	.332	.367	.699	96	-47	-27	97	100	628	62			
BRO	154	65	88	.425	28.5	541	619	5193	1314	195	74	39	368	494	.253	.306	.342	.648	79	-152	-154	100	102	539	106			
BOS	155	60	94	.390	34	651	771	5370	1498	216	61	37	346	363	.279	.326	.363	.689	98	-73	-24	92	103	626	100			
PHI	155	51	103	.331	43	678	903	5317	1487	216	46	57	434	482	.280	.337	.370	.707	94	-30	-39	101	100	660	68			
TOT	617					5651		42344	11935	1888	540	483	3413	3491	.282	.339	.386	.725						649				

TEAM	CG	SH	SV	IP	H	H/G	HR	BB	SO	RAT	ERA	ERA+	OAV	OOB	PR	/A	PF	CPI	FA	E	DP	FW	PW	BW	SBW	DIF
PIT	90	10	10	1385	1400	9.1	58	418	435	12.0	3.66	112	.267	.324	39	68	105	95	.969	187	130	.6	6.7	4.1		5.5
STL	89	14	11	1367[1]	1416	9.3	72	363	394	11.8	3.57	110	.271	.320	52	57	101	99	.966	213	170	-1.0	5.6	2.4		8.5
NY	65	7	16	1381[2]	1520	9.9	77	453	442	13.0	3.97	97	.283	.341	-8	-17	98	102	.969	195	160	.1	-1.7	11.3		5.2
CHI	75	11	5	1385	1439	9.4	50	514	465	12.9	3.65	106	.273	.342	40	31	99	104	.971	181	152	.8	3.1	4.0		.6
CIN	87	12	12	1368	1472	9.7	36	316	407	11.9	3.54	107	.281	.281	57	36	97	100	.973	165	160	1.6	3.6	-2.7		-4.0
BRO	74	7	10	1375[1]	1382	9.0	63	418	574	11.9	3.36	118	.265	.323	85	90	101	100	.963	229	117	-1.8	8.9	-15.2		-3.4
BOS	52	3	11	1390	1602	10.4	43	468	402	13.6	4.22	88	.296	.356	-48	-79	95	102	.963	231	130	-1.8	-7.8	-2.4		-5.0
PHI	81	5	6	1355[1]	1710	11.4	84	462	377	14.7	5.36	77	.317	.374	-218	-187	106	96	.972	169	152	1.5	-18.5	-3.8		-5.2
TOT	613	69	81	11007[2]		9.8				12.7	3.91		.282	.339					.969	1570	1171					

Runs		Hits		Doubles		Triples		Home Runs		Total Bases	
L.Waner-Pit	133	P.Waner-Pit	237	Stephenson-Chi	46	P.Waner-Pit	18	Wilson-Chi	30	P.Waner-Pit	342
Hornsby-NY	133	L.Waner-Pit	223	P.Waner-Pit	42	Bottomley-StL	15	Williams-Phi	30	Hornsby-NY	333
Wilson-Chi	119	Frisch-StL	208	Lindstrom-NY	36	Thompson-Phi	14	Hornsby-NY	26	Wilson-Chi	319
P.Waner-Pit	114	Hornsby-NY	205	Dressen-Cin	36	Terry-NY	13	Terry-NY	20	Terry-NY	307
Frisch-StL	112	Stephenson-Chi	199	Brown-Bos	35	Wilson-Chi	12	Bottomley-StL	19	Bottomley-StL	292

Runs Batted In		Runs Produced		Bases On Balls		Batting Average		On Base Percentage		Slugging Average	
P.Waner-Pit	131	P.Waner-Pit	236	Hornsby-NY	86	P.Waner-Pit	.380	Hornsby-NY	.448	Hafey-StL	.590
Wilson-Chi	129	Hornsby-NY	232	Harper-NY	84	Hornsby-NY	.361	P.Waner-Pit	.437	Hornsby-NY	.586
Hornsby-NY	125	Wilson-Chi	218	Grantham-Pit	74	L.Waner-Pit	.355	Harper-NY	.435	Wilson-Chi	.579
Bottomley-StL	124	Terry-NY	202	Bottomley-StL	74	Stephenson-Chi	.344	Stephenson-Chi	.415	P.Waner-Pit	.549
Terry-NY	121	Bottomley-StL	200			Traynor-Pit	.342	Harris-Pit	.402	Terry-NY	.529

Production		Adjusted Production		Batter Runs		Adjusted Batter Runs		Clutch Hitting Index		Runs Created	
Hornsby-NY	1.035	Hornsby-NY	175	Hornsby-NY	62.5	Hornsby-NY	62.8	P.Waner-Pit	135	Hornsby-NY	148
P.Waner-Pit	.986	Wilson-Chi	159	P.Waner-Pit	55.6	P.Waner-Pit	46.1	Wright-Pit	134	P.Waner-Pit	145
Wilson-Chi	.980	P.Waner-Pit	152	Wilson-Chi	45.7	Wilson-Chi	45.5	Bressler-Cin	133	Wilson-Chi	126
Harper-NY	.930	Harper-NY	149	Harper-NY	37.1	Harper-NY	37.3	Farrell-NY-Bos	131	Stephenson-Chi	117
Terry-NY	.907	Stephenson-Chi	141	Stephenson-Chi	35.7	Stephenson-Chi	35.5	Bottomley-StL	124	Bottomley-StL	112

Total Average		Stolen Bases		Stolen Base Average		Stolen Base Runs		Fielding Runs		Total Player Rating	
Hornsby-NY	1.190	Frisch-StL	48					Frisch-StL	48.6	Frisch-StL	7.3
Wilson-Chi	1.088	Carey-Bro	32					Jackson-NY	27.9	Hornsby-NY	6.9
P.Waner-Pit	1.062	Hendrick-Bro	29					Friberg-Phi	25.3	Jackson-NY	5.4
Harper-NY	1.037	Adams-Chi	26					Beck-Chi	22.0	P.Waner-Pit	4.2
Stephenson-Chi	.955	Richbourg-Bos	24					Statz-Bro	15.2	Wilson-Chi	3.5

Wins		Win Percentage		Games		Complete Games		Shutouts		Saves	
Root-Chi	26	Benton-Bos-NY	.708	Scott-Phi	48	Vance-Bro	25	Haines-StL	6	Sherdel-StL	6
Haines-StL	24	Haines-StL	.706	Root-Chi	48	Meadows-Pit	25	Root-Chi	4	Nehf-Cin-Chi	5
Hill-Pit	22	Kremer-Pit	.704	Ehrhardt-Bro	46	Haines-StL	25	Lucas-Cin	4	Mogridge-Bos	5
Alexander-StL	21	Grimes-NY	.704	Henry-NY	45	Hill-Pit	22	Kremer-Pit	3	Henry-NY	4
		Alexander-StL	.677	May-Cin	44	Alexander-StL	22				

Innings Pitched		Fewest Hits/Game		Fewest BB/Game		Strikeouts		Strikeouts/Game		Ratio	
Root-Chi	309.0	Vance-Bro	7.97	Alexander-StL	1.28	Vance-Bro	184	Vance-Bro	6.06	Alexander-StL	10.07
Haines-StL	300.2	Kremer-Pit	8.16	Lucas-Cin	1.46	Root-Chi	145	Elliott-Bro	4.73	Lucas-Cin	10.14
Meadows-Pit	299.1	Haines-StL	8.17	Donohue-Cin	1.51	May-Cin	121	May-Cin	4.62	Kremer-Pit	10.27
Hill-Pit	277.2	Bush-Chi	8.24	Carlson-Phi-Chi	1.63	Grimes-NY	102	Pruett-Phi	4.35	Vance-Bro	10.44
Vance-Bro	273.1	Hill-Pit	8.43	Henry-NY	1.70	Petty-Bro	101	Root-Chi	4.22	Petty-Bro	10.60

Earned Run Average		Adjusted ERA		Opponents' Batting Avg.		Opponents' On Base Pct.		Starter Runs		Adjusted Starter Runs	
Kremer-Pit	2.47	Kremer-Pit	166	Vance-Bro	.239	Alexander-StL	.286	Alexander-StL	41.5	Alexander-StL	42.5
Alexander-StL	2.52	Alexander-StL	157	Kremer-Pit	.244	Lucas-Cin	.287	Haines-StL	39.8	Kremer-Pit	41.1
Vance-Bro	2.70	Vance-Bro	147	Haines-StL	.245	Kremer-Pit	.289	Vance-Bro	36.9	Haines-StL	40.8
Haines-StL	2.72	Haines-StL	145	Hill-Pit	.249	Vance-Bro	.291	Kremer-Pit	36.3	Vance-Bro	38.2
Petty-Bro	2.98	Petty-Bro	133	Bush-Chi	.250	Petty-Bro	.293	Petty-Bro	28.1	Petty-Bro	29.4

Clutch Pitching Index		Relief Runs		Adjusted Relief Runs		Relief Ranking		Total Pitcher Index		Total Baseball Ranking	
Blake-Chi	117	Clark-Bro	13.0	Clark-Bro	13.4	Clark-Bro	15.5	Alexander-StL	5.2	Frisch-StL	7.3
McWeeny-Bro	116	Ehrhardt-Bro	3.6	Cvengros-Pit	4.5	Ehrhardt-Bro	4.0	Haines-StL	4.3	Hornsby-NY	6.9
B.Smith-Bos	114	Cvengros-Pit	3.3	Ehrhardt-Bro	4.1	Cvengros-Pit	2.4	Kremer-Pit	4.3	Jackson-NY	5.4
Donohue-Cin	111	Songer-Pit-NY	1.9	Songer-Pit-NY	1.7	Songer-Pit-NY	2.3	Vance-Bro	3.8	Alexander-StL	5.2
Alexander-StL	109			H.Bell-StL	0.1	H.Bell-StL	0	Hill-Pit	3.2	Haines-StL	4.3

TEAM	G	W	L	PCT	GB	R	OR	AB	H	2B	3B	HR	BB	SO	AVG	OBP	SLG	PRO	PRO+	BR	/A	PF	CHI	RC	SB	CS	SBA	SBR
NY	155	110	44	.714		975	599	5347	1644	291	103	158	635	605	.307	.383	.489	.872	135	235	266	97	95	1016	90	64	58	-11
PHI	155	91	63	.591	19	841	726	5296	1606	281	70	56	551	326	.303	.372	.414	.786	103	79	32	106	99	839	101	63	62	-8
WAS	157	85	69	.552	25	782	730	5389	1549	268	87	29	498	359	.287	.351	.386	.737	97	-25	-16	99	104	758	133	52	72	9
DET	156	82	71	.536	27.5	845	805	5299	1533	282	100	51	587	420	.289	.363	.409	.772	105	47	35	101	103	813	139	73	66	-2
CHI	153	70	83	.458	39.5	662	708	5157	1433	285	61	36	493	389	.278	.344	.378	.722	94	-54	-37	98	95	685	89	75	54	-18
CLE	153	66	87	.431	43.5	668	766	5202	1471	321	52	26	381	366	.283	.337	.379	.716	90	-70	-75	101	100	669	65	72	47	-24
STL	155	59	94	.386	50.5	724	904	5220	1440	262	59	55	443	420	.276	.338	.380	.718	88	-68	-91	103	106	683	90	66	58	-13
BOS	154	51	103	.331	59	597	856	5207	1348	271	78	28	430	456	.259	.320	.357	.677	82	-149	-137	98	100	614	81	46	64	-3
TOT	619					6094		42117	12024	2261	610	439	4018	3341	.285	.352	.399	.751							788	511	61	-70

TEAM	CG	SH	SV	IP	H	H/G	HR	BB	SO	RAT	ERA	ERA+	OAV	OOB	PR	/A	PF	CPI	FA	E	DP	FW	PW	BW	SBW	DIF
NY	82	11	20	1389²	1403	9.1	42	409	431	11.9	3.20	120	.267	.323	145	100	93	104	.969	195	123	.7	9.5	25.3	-.2	-2.3
PHI	66	8	25	1384	1467	9.5	65	442	553	12.6	3.97	107	.278	.338	26	45	103	97	.970	190	124	1.0	4.3	3.0	.0	5.6
WAS	62	10	23	1402	1434	9.2	53	491	497	12.6	3.97	102	.269	.335	26	14	98	91	.969	195	125	.8	1.3	-1.5	1.7	5.7
DET	75	5	17	1387²	1542	10.0	52	577	421	14.0	4.14	102	.290	.364	0	9	102	106	.968	206	173	.1	.9	3.3	.6	.6
CHI	85	10	8	1367	1467	9.7	55	440	365	12.7	3.91	103	.283	.342	34	19	98	101	.971	178	131	1.6	1.8	-3.5	-.9	-5.5
CLE	72	5	8	1353¹	1542	10.3	37	508	366	13.9	4.27	98	.295	.361	-20	-11	102	102	.968	201	146	.2	-1.0	-7.1	-1.4	-1.0
STL	80	4	8	1353¹	1592	10.6	79	604	385	14.7	4.95	88	.304	.378	-122	-91	105	101	.960	248	166	-2.5	-8.6	-8.6	-.4	2.7
BOS	63	6	7	1366¹	1603	10.6	56	558	381	14.5	4.72	89	.305	.376	-88	-77	102	102	.964	228	167	-1.4	-7.3	-13.0	.5	-4.8
TOT	585	59	116	11003¹		9.9				13.4	4.14		.285	.352					.967	1641	1155					

Runs		Hits		Doubles		Triples		Home Runs		Total Bases	
Ruth-NY	158	Combs-NY	231	Gehrig-NY	52	Combs-NY	23	Ruth-NY	60	Gehrig-NY	447
Gehrig-NY	149	Gehrig-NY	218	Burns-Cle	51	Manush-Det	18	Gehrig-NY	47	Ruth-NY	417
Combs-NY	137	Sisler-StL	201	Heilmann-Det	50	Gehrig-NY	18	Lazzeri-NY	18	Combs-NY	331
Gehringer-Det	110	Heilmann-Det	201	J.Sewell-Cle	48	Goslin-Was	15	Williams-StL	17	Heilmann-Det	311
Heilmann-Det	106	Goslin-Was	194	Meusel-NY	47	Rice-Was	14	Simmons-Phi	15	Goslin-Was	300

Runs Batted In		Runs Produced		Bases On Balls		Batting Average		On Base Percentage		Slugging Average	
Gehrig-NY	175	Gehrig-NY	277	Ruth-NY	138	Heilmann-Det	.398	Ruth-NY	.487	Ruth-NY	.772
Ruth-NY	164	Ruth-NY	262	Gehrig-NY	109	Simmons-Phi	.392	Heilmann-Det	.475	Gehrig-NY	.765
Heilmann-Det	120	Heilmann-Det	212	Bishop-Phi	105	Gehrig-NY	.373	Gehrig-NY	.474	Simmons-Phi	.645
Goslin-Was	120	Goslin-Was	203	Heilmann-Det	72	Fothergill-Det	.359	Bishop-Phi	.442	Heilmann-Det	.616
Fothergill-Det	114	Fothergill-Det	198	Blue-Det	71	Cobb-Phi	.357	Cobb-Phi	.440	Williams-StL	.525

Production		Adjusted Production		Batter Runs		Adjusted Batter Runs		Clutch Hitting Index		Runs Created	
Ruth-NY	1.259	Ruth-NY	229	Gehrig-NY	100.8	Gehrig-NY	106.6	Fothergill-Det	119	Gehrig-NY	212
Gehrig-NY	1.240	Gehrig-NY	224	Ruth-NY	100.7	Ruth-NY	106.4	Goslin-Was	118	Ruth-NY	208
Heilmann-Det	1.091	Heilmann-Det	179	Heilmann-Det	62.3	Heilmann-Det	60.4	Sisler-StL	116	Heilmann-Det	150
Fothergill-Det	.929	Combs-NY	143	Simmons-Phi	44.1	Combs-NY	41.0	Harris-Was	115	Combs-NY	138
Williams-StL	.928	Fothergill-Det	138	Combs-NY	37.1	Simmons-Phi	38.5	J.Sewell-Cle	114	Goslin-Was	119

Total Average		Stolen Bases		Stolen Base Average		Stolen Base Runs		Fielding Runs		Total Player Rating	
Ruth-NY	1.571	Sisler-StL	27	Harris-Was	85.7	Sisler-StL	3.9	Gehringer-Det	19.8	Ruth-NY	9.2
Gehrig-NY	1.500	Meusel-NY	24	Sisler-StL	79.4	Harris-Was	3.6	Falk-Chi	18.2	Gehrig-NY	8.1
Heilmann-Det	1.265	Neun-Det	22	Goslin-Was	77.8	Goslin-Was	2.7	Metzler-Chi	15.7	Heilmann-Det	4.2
Williams-StL	.959	Lazzeri-NY	22	Rice-Was	76.0			Bluege-Was	15.0	Simmons-Phi	3.4
Combs-NY	.955	Cobb-Phi	22	Neun-Det	75.9			Koenig-NY	13.8	Combs-NY	3.2

Wins		Win Percentage		Games		Complete Games		Shutouts		Saves	
Lyons-Chi	22	Hoyt-NY	.759	Braxton-Was	58	Lyons-Chi	30	Lisenbee-Was	4	Moore-NY	13
Hoyt-NY	22	Shocker-NY	.750	Marberry-Was	56	Thomas-Chi	24			Braxton-Was	13
Grove-Phi	20	Moore-NY	.731	Grove-Phi	51	Hoyt-NY	23			Marberry-Was	9
		Pennock-NY	.704	Moore-NY	50	Gaston-StL	21			Grove-Phi	9
		Lisenbee-Was	.667	Walberg-Phi	46						

Innings Pitched		Fewest Hits/Game		Fewest BB/Game		Strikeouts		Strikeouts/Game		Ratio	
Thomas-Chi	307.2	Moore-NY	7.82	Quinn-Phi	1.65	Grove-Phi	174	Grove-Phi	5.97	Moore-NY	10.35
Lyons-Chi	307.2	Thomas-Chi	7.93	Shocker-NY	1.85	Walberg-Phi	136	Braxton-Was	5.56	Braxton-Was	10.37
Hudlin-Cle	264.2	Pipgras-NY	8.01	Hoyt-NY	1.90	Thomas-Chi	107	Walberg-Phi	4.91	Lyons-Chi	10.47
Grove-Phi	262.1	Hadley-Was	8.02	Braxton-Was	1.91	Lisenbee-Was	105	Pipgras-NY	4.38	Hoyt-NY	10.53
Hoyt-NY	256.1	Lisenbee-Was	8.22	Lyons-Chi	1.96	Braxton-Was	96	Ruffing-Bos	4.38	Thomas-Chi	10.71

Earned Run Average		Adjusted ERA		Opponents' Batting Avg.		Opponents' On Base Pct.		Starter Runs		Adjusted Starter Runs	
Moore-NY	2.28	Moore-NY	169	Moore-NY	.234	Moore-NY	.289	Lyons-Chi	44.4	Lyons-Chi	41.3
Hoyt-NY	2.63	Hoyt-NY	146	Thomas-Chi	.244	Braxton-Was	.289	Moore-NY	43.9	Moore-NY	37.1
Shocker-NY	2.84	Lyons-Chi	143	Hadley-Was	.244	Lyons-Chi	.292	Hoyt-NY	42.8	Thomas-Chi	36.3
Lyons-Chi	2.84	Hadley-Was	142	Lisenbee-Was	.245	Hoyt-NY	.294	Thomas-Chi	39.4	Hoyt-NY	34.7
Hadley-Was	2.85	Braxton-Was	137	Braxton-Was	.246	Thomas-Chi	.303	Shocker-NY	28.9	Grove-Phi	31.2

Clutch Pitching Index		Relief Runs		Adjusted Relief Runs		Relief Ranking		Total Pitcher Index		Total Baseball Ranking	
Ruether-NY	119	Braxton-Was	20.4	Braxton-Was	19.1	Braxton-Was	24.6	Lyons-Chi	5.1	Ruth-NY	9.2
Gibson-Det	119	Burke-Was	1.9	G.Smith-Det	2.3	G.Smith-Det	1.5	Moore-NY	4.8	Gehrig-NY	8.1
Pennock-NY	118	G.Smith-Det	1.8	Burke-Was	1.1	Burke-Was	.5	Hoyt-NY	3.5	Lyons-Chi	5.1
Zachary-StL-Was	115							Grove-Phi	3.3	Moore-NY	4.8
Stoner-Det	114							Thomas-Chi	2.9	Heilmann-Det	4.2

TEAM	G	W	L	PCT	GB	R	OR	AB	H	2B	3B	HR	BB	SO	AVG	OBP	SLG	PRO	PRO+	BR	/A	PF	CHI	RC	SB	CS	SBA	SBR
STL	154	95	59	.617		807	636	5357	1505	292	70	113	568	438	.281	.353	.425	.778	108	73	58	102	99	802	82			
NY	155	93	61	.604	2	807	653	5459	1600	276	59	118	508	376	.293	.349	.430	.779	110	68	65	100	100	805	62			
CHI	154	91	63	.591	4	714	615	5260	1460	251	64	92	508	517	.278	.345	.402	.747	103	11	21	99	97	728	83			
PIT	152	85	67	.559	9	837	704	5371	1659	246	100	52	435	352	.309	.364	.421	.785	108	89	56	104	103	809	64			
CIN	153	78	74	.513	16	648	686	5184	1449	229	67	32	386	330	.280	.333	.368	.701	91	-76	-66	98	104	630	83			
BRO	155	77	76	.503	17.5	665	640	5243	1393	229	70	66	557	510	.266	.340	.374	.714	94	-46	-37	99	98	673	81			
BOS	153	50	103	.327	44.5	631	878	5228	1439	241	41	52	447	377	.275	.335	.367	.702	95	-70	-37	95	99	643	60			
PHI	152	43	109	.283	51	660	957	5234	1396	257	47	85	503	510	.267	.333	.382	.715	90	-49	-72	103	99	667	53			
TOT	614					5769		42336	11901	2021	518	610	3848	3410	.281	.344	.397	.741						568				

TEAM	CG	SH	SV	IP	H	H/G	HR	BB	SO	RAT	ERA	ERA+	OAV	OOB	PR	/A	PF	CPI	FA	E	DP	FW	PW	BW	SBW	DIF
STL	83	4	21	1415[1]	1470	9.3	86	399	422	12.1	3.38	118	.270	.323	96	97	100	105	.974	160	134	1.3	9.5	5.7		1.5
NY	79	7	16	1394	1454	9.4	77	405	399	12.1	3.67	107	.273	.327	49	37	98	98	.972	178	175	.3	3.6	6.4		5.7
CHI	75	12	14	1380[2]	1383	9.0	56	508	531	12.5	3.40	113	.267	.336	91	68	96	105	.975	156	176	1.6	6.6	2.1		3.7
PIT	82	8	11	1354	1422	9.5	66	446	385	12.6	3.95	103	.274	.335	6	15	102	93	.967	201	123	-1.3	1.5	5.5		3.3
CIN	68	11	11	1371[2]	1516	9.9	54	410	355	12.7	3.94	100	.289	.342	8	2	99	100	.974	162	194	1.1	.2	-6.5		7.1
BRO	75	16	15	1396	1378	8.9	59	468	551	12.1	3.25	122	.261	.324	114	112	100	101	.965	217	113	-2.0	10.9	-3.6		-4.8
BOS	54	1	6	1360	1596	10.6	100	524	343	14.2	4.83	81	.298	.363	-128	-140	98	97	.969	193	141	-.7	-13.7	-3.6		-8.5
PHI	42	4	11	1352[2]	1660	11.0	108	675	404	15.8	5.56	77	.315	.397	-236	-198	107	100	.971	181	171	-.0	-19.4	-7.0		-6.5
TOT	558	63	105	11024[1]		9.7				13.0	3.99		.281	.344					.971	1448	1227					

Runs
P.Waner-Pit 142
Bottomley-StL 123
L.Waner-Pit 121
Douthit-StL 111
Frisch-StL 107

Hits
Lindstrom-NY 231
P.Waner-Pit 223
L.Waner-Pit 221
Richbourg-Bos 206
Traynor-Pit 192

Doubles
P.Waner-Pit 50
Hafey-StL 46
Hornsby-Bos 42
Bottomley-StL 42
Lindstrom-NY 39

Triples
Bottomley-StL 20
P.Waner-Pit 19
L.Waner-Pit 14
Bressler-Bro 13
Bissonette-Bro 13

Home Runs
Wilson-Chi 31
Bottomley-StL 31
Hafey-StL 27
Bissonette-Bro 25
Hornsby-Bos 21

Total Bases
Bottomley-StL 362
Lindstrom-NY 330
P.Waner-Pit 329
Bissonette-Bro 319
Hafey-StL 314

Runs Batted In
Bottomley-StL 136
Traynor-Pit 124
Wilson-Chi 120
Hafey-StL 111
Lindstrom-NY 107

Runs Produced
Bottomley-StL 228
P.Waner-Pit 222
Traynor-Pit 212
Lindstrom-NY 192
Hafey-StL 185

Bases On Balls
Hornsby-Bos 107
Douthit-StL 84
Bressler-Bro 80
Wilson-Chi 77
P.Waner-Pit 77

Batting Average
Hornsby-Bos 387
P.Waner-Pit 370
Lindstrom-NY 358
Sisler-Bos 340
Herman-Bro 340

On Base Percentage
Hornsby-Bos 498
P.Waner-Pit 446
Grantham-Pit 408
Stephenson-Chi ...407
Wilson-Chi 404

Slugging Average
Hornsby-Bos 632
Bottomley-StL 628
Hafey-StL 604
Wilson-Chi 588
P.Waner-Pit 547

Production
Hornsby-Bos 1.130
Bottomley-StL 1.030
Wilson-Chi 992
P.Waner-Pit 992
Hafey-StL 990

Adjusted Production
Hornsby-Bos 204
Bottomley-StL 163
Wilson-Chi 159
Hafey-StL 152
P.Waner-Pit 152

Batter Runs
Hornsby-Bos 72.5
P.Waner-Pit 53.4
Bottomley-StL ... 52.5
Wilson-Chi 42.1
Hafey-StL 38.5

Adjusted Batter Runs
Hornsby-Bos 80.3
Bottomley-StL 50.1
P.Waner-Pit 48.0
Wilson-Chi 43.7
Bissonette-Bro 38.1

Clutch Hitting Index
Traynor-Pit 147
Walker-Cin 126
Whitney-Phi 124
Ford-Cin 123
Wilson-Phi-StL 121

Runs Created
Hornsby-Bos 154
P.Waner-Pit 145
Bottomley-StL 142
Bissonette-Bro 125
Wilson-Chi 122

Total Average
Hornsby-Bos 1.409
Bottomley-StL 1.147
P.Waner-Pit 1.100
Wilson-Chi 1.090
Hafey-StL 1.055

Stolen Bases
Cuyler-Chi 37
Frisch-StL 29
Walker-Cin 19
Thompson-Phi 19

Stolen Base Average

Stolen Base Runs

Fielding Runs
Maguire-Chi 50.5
Jackson-NY 28.3
Douthit-StL 24.3
Lindstrom-NY 15.1
Ford-Cin 11.9

Total Player Rating
Hornsby-Bos 5.8
Lindstrom-NY 4.8
Jackson-NY 4.3
Hartnett-Chi 4.2
P.Waner-Pit 4.0

Wins
Grimes-Pit 25
Benton-NY 25
Vance-Bro 22
Sherdel-StL 21

Win Percentage
Benton-NY .... .735
Haines-StL .... .714
Bush-Chi .... .714
Fitzsimmons-NY .. .690
Vance-Bro .... .688

Games
Grimes-Pit 48
Kolp-Cin 44
Rixey-Cin 43

Complete Games
Grimes-Pit 28
Benton-NY 28
Vance-Bro 24
Sherdel-StL 20
Haines-StL 20

Shutouts
Vance-Bro 4
McWeeny-Bro 4
Lucas-Cin 4
Grimes-Pit 4
Blake-Chi 4

Saves
Sherdel-StL 5
Haid-StL 5
Carlson-Chi 4
Benton-NY 4

Innings Pitched
Grimes-Pit 330.2
Benton-NY 310.1
Rixey-Cin 291.1
Vance-Bro 280.1
Fitzsimmons-NY . 261.1

Fewest Hits/Game
Vance-Bro 7.26
Blake-Chi 7.82
Malone-Chi 7.83
McWeeny-Bro ... 8.04
Root-Chi 8.13

Fewest BB/Game
Alexander-StL ... 1.37
Sherdel-StL 2.03
Benton-NY 2.06
Rixey-Cin 2.07
Grimes-Pit 2.10

Strikeouts
Vance-Bro 200
Malone-Chi 155
Root-Chi 122
Grimes-Pit 97
Benton-NY 90

Strikeouts/Game
Vance-Bro 6.42
Malone-Chi 5.57
Root-Chi 4.63
Clark-Bro 3.93
Ring-Phi 3.75

Ratio
Vance-Bro 9.79
Benton-NY 10.73
Grimes-Pit 10.81
Lucas-Cin 11.08
Alexander-StL .. 11.12

Earned Run Average
Vance-Bro 2.09
Blake-Chi 2.47
Nehf-Chi 2.65
Clark-Bro 2.68
Benton-NY 2.73

Adjusted ERA
Vance-Bro 190
Blake-Chi 156
Clark-Bro 148
Nehf-Chi 145
Benton-NY 143

Opponents' Batting Avg.
Vance-Bro .... .221
McWeeny-Bro ... .235
Malone-Chi ...... .236
Blake-Chi .... .240
Root-Chi .... .242

Opponents' On Base Pct.
Vance-Bro .... .277
Grimes-Pit .... .297
Benton-NY .... .300
Sherdel-StL ...... .303
Lucas-Cin .... .304

Starter Runs
Vance-Bro 59.2
Benton-NY 43.5
Blake-Chi 40.6
Grimes-Pit 36.5
Malone-Chi 32.0

Adjusted Starter Runs
Vance-Bro 58.7
Benton-NY 40.7
Grimes-Pit 39.0
Blake-Chi 36.8
Sherdel-StL 31.4

Clutch Pitching Index
Nehf-Chi 133
Bush-Chi 117
Blake-Chi 115
Kolp-Cin 114
Rhem-StL 114

Relief Runs

Adjusted Relief Runs

Relief Ranking

Total Pitcher Index
Vance-Bro 7.0
Grimes-Pit 6.1
Benton-NY 3.9
Blake-Chi 3.8
Sherdel-StL 3.7

Total Baseball Ranking
Vance-Bro 7.0
Grimes-Pit 6.1
Hornsby-Bos 5.8
Lindstrom-NY 4.8
Jackson-NY 4.3

TEAM	G	W	L	PCT	GB	R	OR	AB	H	2B	3B	HR	BB	SO	AVG	OBP	SLG	PRO	PRO+	BR	/A	PF	CHI	RC	SB	CS	SBA	SBR
NY	154	101	53	.656		894	685	5337	1578	269	79	133	562	544	.296	.365	.450	.815	124	146	175	97	100	888	51	51	50	-15
PHI	153	98	55	.641	2.5	829	615	5226	1540	323	75	89	533	442	.295	.363	.436	.799	112	115	92	103	97	843	59	48	55	-11
STL	154	82	72	.532	19	772	742	5217	1431	276	76	63	548	479	.274	.346	.393	.739	97	2	-21	103	104	736	76	43	64	-3
WAS	155	75	79	.487	26	718	705	5320	1510	277	93	40	481	390	.284	.346	.393	.739	101	1	6	99	97	743	110	59	65	-2
CHI	155	72	82	.468	29	656	725	5207	1405	231	77	24	469	488	.270	.334	.358	.692	88	-88	-79	99	102	641	139	82	63	-8
DET	154	68	86	.442	33	744	804	5292	1476	265	97	62	469	438	.279	.340	.401	.741	99	-2	-13	102	102	730	113	77	59	-12
CLE	155	62	92	.403	39	674	830	5386	1535	299	61	34	377	426	.285	.335	.382	.717	93	-49	-56	101	98	693	50	52	49	-16
BOS	154	57	96	.373	43.5	589	770	5132	1356	260	62	38	389	512	.264	.319	.361	.680	86	-119	-108	98	100	602	99	64	61	-9
TOT	617					5876		42117	11831	2200	620	483	3828	3719	.281	.344	.397	.741							697	476	59	-77

TEAM	CG	SH	SV	IP	H	H/G	HR	BB	SO	RAT	ERA	ERA+	OAV	OOB	PR	/A	PF	CPI	FA	E	DP	FW	PW	BW	SBW	DIF
NY	82	13	21	1375¹	1466	9.6	59	452	487	12.7	3.74	101	.276	.335	46	3	93	102	.968	194	136	-.0	.3	16.9	-.5	7.4
PHI	81	15	16	1367²	1349	8.9	66	424	607	11.8	3.36	119	.259	.318	103	97	99	99	.970	181	124	.6	9.4	8.9	-.1	2.7
STL	80	6	15	1374¹	1487	9.7	93	454	456	12.8	4.17	101	.282	.340	-20	3	104	100	.969	189	146	.2	.3	-2.0	.6	5.9
WAS	77	15	10	1384	1420	9.2	40	466	462	12.5	3.88	103	.272	.335	25	19	99	94	.972	178	146	1.0	1.8	.6	.7	-6.1
CHI	88	6	11	1378	1518	9.9	66	501	418	13.4	3.98	102	.287	.352	8	8	100	108	.970	186	149	.5	.8	-7.6	.2	1.2
DET	65	5	16	1372	1481	9.7	58	567	451	13.7	4.32	95	.281	.355	-42	-34	102	97	.965	218	140	-1.5	-3.3	-1.3	-.2	-2.7
CLE	71	4	15	1378	1615	10.5	52	511	416	14.2	4.47	93	.303	.369	-66	-52	103	105	.965	221	187	-1.6	-5.0	-5.4	-.6	-2.4
BOS	70	5	9	1352	1492	9.9	49	452	407	13.2	4.39	93	.288	.349	-53	-44	102	94	.971	178	139	.9	-4.3	-10.4	.0	-5.8
TOT	614	69	113	10981¹		9.7				13.0	4.04		.281	.344					.969	1545	1167					

Runs
Ruth-NY 163
Gehrig-NY 139
Combs-NY 118
Blue-StL 116
Gehringer-Det 108

Hits
Manush-StL 241
Gehrig-NY 210
Rice-Was 202
Combs-NY 194
Gehringer-Det 193

Doubles
Manush-StL 47
Gehrig-NY 47
Meusel-NY 45
Schulte-StL 44
Lind-Cle 42

Triples
Combs-NY 21
Manush-StL 20
Gehringer-Det 16

Home Runs
Ruth-NY 54
Gehrig-NY 27
Goslin-Was 17
Hauser-Phi 16
Simmons-Phi 15

Total Bases
Ruth-NY 380
Manush-StL 367
Gehrig-NY 364
Combs-NY 290
Heilmann-Det 283

Runs Batted In
Ruth-NY 142
Gehrig-NY 142
Meusel-NY 113
Manush-StL 108

Runs Produced
Gehrig-NY 254
Ruth-NY 251
Manush-StL 199
Blue-StL 182
Meusel-NY 179

Bases On Balls
Ruth-NY 135
Blue-StL 105
Bishop-Phi 97
Gehrig-NY 95
Judge-Was 80

Batting Average
Goslin-Was 379
Manush-StL 378
Gehrig-NY 374
Simmons-Phi 351
Lazzeri-NY 332

On Base Percentage
Gehrig-NY 467
Ruth-NY 461
Goslin-Was 442
Bishop-Phi 435
Manush-StL 414

Slugging Average
Ruth-NY 709
Gehrig-NY 648
Goslin-Was 614
Manush-StL 575
Simmons-Phi 558

Production
Ruth-NY 1.170
Gehrig-NY 1.115
Goslin-Was ...1.056
Manush-StL 989
Simmons-Phi 954

Adjusted Production
Ruth-NY 210
Gehrig-NY 196
Goslin-Was 176
Manush-StL 153
Simmons-Phi 144

Batter Runs
Ruth-NY 83.9
Gehrig-NY 76.0
Manush-StL 50.3
Goslin-Was 49.0
Foxx-Phi 30.5

Adjusted Batter Runs
Ruth-NY 89.4
Gehrig-NY 81.2
Goslin-Was 49.8
Manush-StL 46.2
Foxx-Phi 28.1

Clutch Hitting Index
Cissell-Chi 130
Meusel-NY 128
Judge-Was 123
Hodapp-Cle 118
Boley-Phi 117

Runs Created
Ruth-NY 182
Gehrig-NY 169
Manush-StL 150
Goslin-Was 125
Combs-NY 114

Total Average
Ruth-NY 1.405
Gehrig-NY 1.256
Goslin-Was ...1.203
Manush-StL ...1.040
Simmons-Phi 951

Stolen Bases
Myer-Bos 30
Mostil-Chi 23
Rice-Det 20
Cissell-Chi 18
Bluege-Was 18

Stolen Base Average
Rice-Was 84.2
Goslin-Was 84.2
Judge-Was 80.0
Manush-StL 77.3

Stolen Base Runs
Rice-Was 3.0
Goslin-Was 3.0
Reynolds-Chi 2.7
Judge-Was 2.4
Manush-StL 2.1

Fielding Runs
Gerber-StL-Bos ..32.0
J.Sewell-Cle 27.0
Jamieson-Cle 19.9
Mostil-Chi 17.8
Schulte-StL 17.3

Total Player Rating
Ruth-NY 7.0
J.Sewell-Cle 5.4
Gehrig-NY 5.1
Goslin-Was 4.5
Manush-StL 3.8

Wins
Pipgras-NY 24
Grove-Phi 24
Hoyt-NY 23
Crowder-StL 21
Gray-StL 20

Win Percentage
Crowder-StL 808
Hoyt-NY 767
Grove-Phi 750
Pennock-NY 739
Quinn-Phi 720

Games
Marberry-Was 48
Morris-Bos 47
Pipgras-NY 46
Rommel-Phi 43

Complete Games
Ruffing-Bos 25
Thomas-Chi 24
Grove-Phi 24
Pipgras-NY 22

Shutouts
Pennock-NY 5
Quinn-Phi 4
Pipgras-NY 4
Jones-Was 4
Grove-Phi 4

Saves
Hoyt-NY 8
Hudlin-Cle 7
Lyons-Chi 6
Braxton-Was 6

Innings Pitched
Pipgras-NY 300.2
Ruffing-Bos 289.1
Thomas-Chi 283.0
Hoyt-NY 273.0
Gray-StL 262.2

Fewest Hits/Game
Braxton-Was 7.30
Grove-Phi 7.84
Earnshaw-Phi 8.13
Jones-Was 8.37
Johnson-NY 8.50

Fewest BB/Game
Rommel-Phi 1.35
Quinn-Phi 1.45
Pennock-NY 1.71
Braxton-Was 1.81
Russell-Bos 1.83

Strikeouts
Grove-Phi 183
Pipgras-NY 139
Thomas-Chi 129
Ruffing-Bos 118
Earnshaw-Phi 117

Strikeouts/Game
Earnshaw-Phi 6.65
Grove-Phi 6.29
Johnson-NY 4.97
Walberg-Phi 4.28
Whitehill-Det 4.26

Ratio
Braxton-Was 9.32
Grove-Phi 10.08
Rommel-Phi 10.62
Pennock-NY 10.88
Hoyt-NY 11.21

Earned Run Average
Braxton-Was 2.51
Pennock-NY 2.56
Grove-Phi 2.58
Jones-Was 2.84
Quinn-Phi 2.90

Adjusted ERA
Braxton-Was 159
Grove-Phi 155
Pennock-NY 147
Jones-Was 141
Quinn-Phi 138

Opponents' Batting Avg.
Braxton-Was 222
Grove-Phi 229
Earnshaw-Phi 240
Johnson-NY 250
Jones-Was 252

Opponents' On Base Pct.
Braxton-Was 267
Grove-Phi 277
Rommel-Phi 295
Pennock-NY 302
Thomas-Chi 310

Starter Runs
Grove-Phi 42.4
Braxton-Was 37.0
Pennock-NY 34.7
Thomas-Chi 30.0
Jones-Was 29.8

Adjusted Starter Runs
Grove-Phi 41.5
Braxton-Was 36.2
Thomas-Chi 30.2
Gray-StL 29.4
Jones-Was 29.0

Clutch Pitching Index
Miller-Cle 119
Quinn-Phi 119
Blankenship-Chi ..114
Pennock-NY 113
Adkins-Chi 113

Relief Runs

Adjusted Relief Runs
Simmons-Bos 0.5

Relief Ranking
Simmons-Bos......0.1

Total Pitcher Index
Grove-Phi 4.6
Jones-Was 3.5
Gray-StL 3.5
Braxton-Was 3.5
Thomas-Chi 3.3

Total Baseball Ranking
Ruth-NY 7.0
J.Sewell-Cle 5.4
Gehrig-NY 5.1
Grove-Phi 4.6
Goslin-Was 4.5

TEAM	G	W	L	PCT	GB	R	OR	AB	H	2B	3B	HR	BB	SO	AVG	OBP	SLG	PRO	PRO+	BR	/A	PF	CHI	RC	SB	CS	SBA	SBR
CHI	156	98	54	.645		982	758	5471	1655	310	46	139	589	567	.303	.373	.452	.825	111	92	90	100	104	916	103			
PIT	154	88	65	.575	10.5	904	780	5490	1663	285	60	136	503	335	.303	.364	.430	.794	101	28	7	102	104	850	94			
NY	152	84	67	.556	13.5	897	709	5388	1594	251	47	136	482	405	.296	.358	.436	.794	103	18	21	100	106	827	85			
STL	154	78	74	.513	20	831	806	5364	1569	310	84	100	490	455	.293	.354	.438	.792	101	12	4	101	100	819	72			
PHI	154	71	82	.464	27.5	897	1032	5484	1693	305	51	153	573	470	.309	.377	.467	.844	108	125	62	101	92	951	59			
BRO	153	70	83	.458	28.5	755	888	5273	1535	282	69	99	504	454	.291	.355	.427	.782	102	-1	15	98	93	792	80			
CIN	155	66	88	.429	33	686	760	5269	1478	258	79	34	412	347	.281	.336	.379	.715	87	-133	-102	95	103	664	134			
BOS	154	56	98	.364	43	657	876	5291	1481	252	77	33	408	432	.280	.335	.375	.710	85	-142	-116	96	99	659	65			
TOT	616					6609		43030	12668	2253	569	754	3961	3465	.294	.357	.426	.783						692				

TEAM	CG	SH	SV	IP	H	H/G	HR	BB	SO	RAT	ERA	ERA+	OAV	OOB	PR	/A	PF	CPI	FA	E	DP	FW	PW	BW	SBW	DIF
CHI	79	14	21	1398²	1542	9.9	77	537	548	13.5	4.16	111	.284	.350	86	70	98	104	.975	154	169	1.4	6.4	8.2		6.0
PIT	79	5	13	1379	1530	10.0	96	439	409	13.0	4.36	109	.284	.340	54	62	101	98	.970	181	136	-.2	5.6	.6		5.5
NY	68	9	13	1372	1536	10.1	102	387	431	12.7	3.97	115	.287	.337	113	93	97	109	.975	158	163	.9	8.5	1.9		-2.8
STL	83	6	8	1359²	1604	10.6	101	474	453	13.9	4.66	100	.297	.357	8	-1	99	102	.971	174	149	.2	-.0	.4		1.6
PHI	45	5	24	1348	1743	11.6	122	616	369	16.0	6.13	85	.319	.391	-212	-142	110	94	.969	191	153	-.8	-12.9	5.6		2.6
BRO	59	8	16	1358	1553	10.3	92	549	549	14.2	4.92	94	.290	.360	-32	-48	98	95	.968	192	113	-.9	-4.4	1.4		-2.6
CIN	75	5	8	1369¹	1558	10.2	61	413	347	13.1	4.41	103	.292	.345	46	22	97	97	.974	162	148	.9	2.0	-9.3		-4.6
BOS	78	4	12	1352²	1604	10.7	103	530	366	14.4	5.12	91	.302	.367	-62	-68	99	99	.967	204	146	-1.5	-6.2	-10.6		-2.7
TOT	566	56	115	10937¹		10.4				13.8	4.71		.294	.357					.971	1416	1177					

Runs
Hornsby-Chi 156
O'Doul-Phi 152
Ott-NY 138
Wilson-Chi 135
L.Waner-Pit 134

Hits
O'Doul-Phi 254
L.Waner-Pit 234
Hornsby-Chi 229
Terry-NY 226
Klein-Phi 219

Doubles
Frederick-Bro 52
Hornsby-Chi 47
Hafey-StL 47
Klein-Phi 45
Kelly-Cin 45

Triples
L.Waner-Pit 20
P.Waner-Pit 15
Walker-Cin 15
Whitney-Phi 14

Home Runs
Klein-Phi 43
Ott-NY 42
Wilson-Chi 39
Hornsby-Chi 39
O'Doul-Phi 32

Total Bases
Hornsby-Chi 409
Klein-Phi 405
O'Doul-Phi 397
Wilson-Chi 355
Herman-Bro 348

Runs Batted In
Wilson-Chi 159
Ott-NY 151
Hornsby-Chi 149
Klein-Phi 145
Bottomley-StL 137

Runs Produced
Hornsby-Chi 266
Wilson-Chi 255
Ott-NY 247
O'Doul-Phi 242
Klein-Phi 228

Bases On Balls
Ott-NY 113
Grantham-Pit 93
P.Waner-Pit 89
Hornsby-Chi 87
Walker-Cin 85

Batting Average
O'Doul-Phi .... .398
Herman-Bro ...... .381
Hornsby-Chi ...... .380
Terry-NY .... .372
Stephenson-Chi ... .362

On Base Percentage
O'Doul-Phi .... .465
Hornsby-Chi ...... .459
Ott-NY .... .449
Stephenson-Chi ... .445
Cuyler-Chi .... .438

Slugging Average
Hornsby-Chi ...... .679
Klein-Phi .... .657
Ott-NY .... .635
Hafey-StL .... .632
O'Doul-Phi .... .622

Production
Hornsby-Chi 1.139
O'Doul-Phi 1.087
Ott-NY 1.084
Klein-Phi 1.065
Herman-Bro 1.047

Adjusted Production
Hornsby-Chi 178
Ott-NY 166
Herman-Bro 160
O'Doul-Phi 157
Wilson-Chi 155

Batter Runs
Hornsby-Chi 74.1
O'Doul-Phi 68.5
Ott-NY 58.4
Klein-Phi 53.3
Herman-Bro 49.6

Adjusted Batter Runs
Hornsby-Chi 73.8
Ott-NY 58.9
O'Doul-Phi 57.8
Herman-Bro 52.4
Wilson-Chi 48.7

Clutch Hitting Index
Traynor-Pit 139
Sheely-Pit 137
Comorosky-Pit 133
Grimm-Chi 127
Kelly-Cin 122

Runs Created
Hornsby-Chi 183
O'Doul-Phi 180
Klein-Phi 158
Ott-NY 157
Wilson-Chi 148

Total Average
Hornsby-Chi 1.338
Ott-NY 1.287
O'Doul-Phi 1.247
Herman-Bro 1.205
Cuyler-Chi 1.181

Stolen Bases
Cuyler-Chi 43
Swanson-Cin 33
Frisch-StL 24
Herman-Bro 21
Allen-Cin 21

Fielding Runs
Whitney-Phi 21.3
Maranville-Bos ... 19.5
Jackson-NY 19.2
L.Waner-Pit 15.7
English-Chi 15.4

Total Player Rating
Hornsby-Chi 7.2
Ott-NY 5.2
O'Doul-Phi 4.7
Jackson-NY 4.1
Wilson-Chi 3.2

Wins
Malone-Chi 22
Root-Chi 19
Lucas-Cin 19

Win Percentage
Root-Chi .... .760
Bush-Chi .... .720
Grimes-Pit .... .708
Malone-Chi .... .688
Kremer-Pit .... .643

Games
Bush-Chi 50
Willoughby-Phi ... 49
Sweetland-Phi 43
Root-Chi 43
Collins-Phi 43

Complete Games
Lucas-Cin 28

Shutouts
Malone-Chi 5
Root-Chi 4
Fitzsimmons-NY ... 4

Saves
Morrison-Bro 8
Bush-Chi 8
Koupal-Bro-Phi ... 6

Innings Pitched
Clark-Bro 279.0
Root-Chi 272.0
Bush-Chi 270.2
Lucas-Cin 270.0
Hubbell-NY 268.0

Fewest Hits/Game
Lucas-Cin 8.90
Hubbell-NY 9.17
Kremer-Pit 9.18
Johnson-StL 9.18
Bush-Chi 9.21

Fewest BB/Game
Vance-Bro 1.83
Lucas-Cin 1.93
Petty-Pit 2.05
Hubbell-NY 2.25
Clark-Bro 2.29

Strikeouts
Malone-Chi 166
Clark-Bro 140
Vance-Bro 126
Root-Chi 124
Hubbell-NY 106

Strikeouts/Game
Malone-Chi 5.60
Vance-Bro 4.90
Clark-Bro 4.52
May-Cin 4.16
Root-Chi 4.10

Ratio
Lucas-Cin 10.87
Hubbell-NY 11.62
Kremer-Pit 11.65
Petty-Pit 11.67
Vance-Bro 11.67

Earned Run Average
Walker-NY 3.09
Grimes-Pit 3.13
Root-Chi 3.47
Malone-Chi 3.57
Lucas-Cin 3.60

Adjusted ERA
Grimes-Pit 152
Walker-NY 148
Root-Chi 133
Johnson-StL 129
Malone-Chi 129

Opponents' Batting Avg.
Lucas-Cin .... .257
Johnson-StL ...... .265
Hubbell-NY .... .265
Bush-Chi .... .265
Grimes-Pit .... .269

Opponents' On Base Pct.
Lucas-Cin .... .297
Hubbell-NY .... .313
Clark-Bro .... .316
Vance-Bro .... .316
Petty-Pit .... .317

Starter Runs
Grimes-Pit 40.8
Root-Chi 37.4
Malone-Chi 33.8
Lucas-Cin 33.3
Walker-NY 32.0

Adjusted Starter Runs
Grimes-Pit 42.2
Root-Chi 34.4
Malone-Chi 30.8
Walker-NY 29.4
Lucas-Cin 28.8

Clutch Pitching Index
Mitchell-StL 129
Walker-NY 129
Sweetland-Phi 116
Grimes-Pit 116
Malone-Chi 115

Relief Runs
Hill-Pit-StL 2.9
Cvengros-Chi 5

Adjusted Relief Runs
Hill-Pit-StL 3.3

Relief Ranking
Hill-Pit-StL 2.0

Total Pitcher Index
Grimes-Pit 4.7
Lucas-Cin 4.0
Malone-Chi 3.0
Clark-Bro 2.5
Root-Chi 2.4

Total Baseball Ranking
Hornsby-Chi 7.2
Ott-NY 5.2
Grimes-Pit 4.7
O'Doul-Phi 4.7
Jackson-NY 4.1

TEAM	G	W	L	PCT	GB	R	OR	AB	H	2B	3B	HR	BB	SO	AVG	OBP	SLG	PRO	PRO+	BR	/A	PF	CHI	RC	SB	CS	SBA	SBR
PHI	151	104	46	.693		901	615	5204	1539	288	76	122	543	440	.296	.365	.451	.816	111	113	81	104	102	875	61	38	62	-5
NY	154	88	66	.571	18	899	775	5379	1587	262	74	142	554	518	.295	.364	.450	.814	123	111	171	93	101	892	51	44	54	-11
CLE	152	81	71	.533	24	717	736	5187	1525	294	79	62	453	363	.294	.354	.417	.771	100	26	-2	104	92	763	75	85	47	-29
STL	154	79	73	.520	26	733	713	5174	1426	277	64	46	589	431	.276	.352	.381	.733	91	-33	-61	104	100	723	72	46	61	-6
WAS	153	71	81	.467	34	730	776	5237	1445	244	66	48	556	400	.276	.347	.375	.722	90	-56	-61	101	102	706	86	61	59	-11
DET	155	70	84	.455	36	926	928	5592	1671	339	97	110	521	496	.299	.360	.453	.813	114	110	106	100	101	914	95	72	57	-15
CHI	152	59	93	.388	46	627	792	5248	1406	240	74	37	425	436	.268	.325	.363	.688	83	-134	-127	99	102	633	109	65	63	-6
BOS	155	58	96	.377	48	605	803	5160	1377	285	69	28	413	494	.267	.325	.365	.690	85	-130	-115	98	99	616	85	80	52	-23
TOT	613					6138		42181	11976	2229	599	595	4054	3578	.284	.349	.407	.756							634	491	56	-104

TEAM	CG	SH	SV	IP	H	H/G	HR	BB	SO	RAT	ERA	ERA+	OAV	OOB	PR	/A	PF	CPI	FA	E	DP	FW	PW	BW	SBW	DIF
PHI	70	9	24	1357	1371	9.1	73	487	573	12.4	3.44	123	.264	.329	121	119	100	105	.975	146	117	2.6	11.2	7.6	.8	6.8
NY	64	12	18	1366²	1475	9.7	83	485	484	13.1	4.19	92	.278	.341	7	-52	91	96	.971	178	153	-.8	-4.9	16.1	.2	-1.2
CLE	80	8	10	1352	1570	10.5	56	488	389	13.9	4.05	109	.295	.357	28	57	105	109	.968	198	162	-.6	5.4	-.2	-1.5	1.9
STL	83	15	10	1371	1469	9.6	100	462	415	12.8	4.08	108	.279	.340	25	51	104	102	.975	156	148	2.2	4.8	-5.8	.7	1.1
WAS	62	3	17	1354²	1429	9.5	48	496	494	12.9	4.34	98	.276	.342	-15	-16	100	89	.968	195	156	-.3	-1.5	-5.8	.2	2.4
DET	82	5	9	1390¹	1641	10.6	73	646	467	15.0	4.96	86	.301	.377	-111	-105	101	101	.961	242	149	-3.0	-9.9	10.0	-.2	-3.9
CHI	78	5	7	1357²	1481	9.8	84	505	328	13.4	4.41	97	.284	.351	-26	-22	101	98	.970	188	153	.0	-2.1	-12.0	.7	-3.7
BOS	84	9	5	1366²	1537	10.1	78	496	416	13.6	4.43	96	.291	.355	-28	-25	101	100	.965	218	159	-1.6	-2.4	-10.8	-.9	-3.3
TOT	603	66	100	10916		9.9				13.4	4.24		.284	.349					.969	1521	1197					

Runs
Gehringer-Det 131
Johnson-Det 128
Gehrig-NY 127
Foxx-Phi 123
Ruth-NY 121

Hits
Gehringer-Det 215
Alexander-Det 215
Simmons-Phi 212
Fonseca-Cle 209
Manush-StL 204

Doubles
Manush-StL 45
Johnson-Det 45
Gehringer-Det 45
Fonseca-Cle 44

Triples
Gehringer-Det 19
Scarritt-Bos 17
B.Miller-Phi 16

Home Runs
Ruth-NY 46
Gehrig-NY 35
Simmons-Phi 34
Foxx-Phi 33
Alexander-Det 25

Total Bases
Simmons-Phi 373
Alexander-Det 363
Ruth-NY 348
Gehringer-Det 337

Runs Batted In
Simmons-Phi 157
Ruth-NY 154
Alexander-Det 137
Gehrig-NY 126
Heilmann-Det 120

Runs Produced
Simmons-Phi 237
Ruth-NY 229
Gehringer-Det 224
Alexander-Det 222
Gehrig-NY 218

Bases On Balls
Bishop-Phi 128
Blue-StL 126
Gehrig-NY 122
Foxx-Phi 103
Cronin-Was 85

Batting Average
Fonseca-Cle 369
Simmons-Phi 365
Manush-StL 355
Lazzeri-NY 354
Foxx-Phi 354

On Base Percentage
Foxx-Phi 463
Gehrig-NY 431
Ruth-NY 430
Lazzeri-NY 429
Fonseca-Cle 427

Slugging Average
Ruth-NY 697
Simmons-Phi 642
Foxx-Phi 625
Gehrig-NY 584
Alexander-Det 580

Production
Ruth-NY 1.128
Foxx-Phi 1.088
Simmons-Phi 1.040
Gehrig-NY 1.015
Lazzeri-NY 991

Adjusted Production
Ruth-NY 199
Foxx-Phi 171
Gehrig-NY 170
Lazzeri-NY 164
Simmons-Phi 158

Batter Runs
Foxx-Phi 63.1
Ruth-NY 61.9
Gehrig-NY 51.6
Simmons-Phi 50.3
Lazzeri-NY 43.9

Adjusted Batter Runs
Ruth-NY 71.2
Gehrig-NY 61.1
Foxx-Phi 58.0
Lazzeri-NY 52.4
Simmons-Phi 45.6

Clutch Hitting Index
West-Was 130
Heilmann-Det 129
Kress-StL..... 123
Myer-Was 119
Falk-Cle 118

Runs Created
Foxx-Phi 154
Ruth-NY 150
Gehrig-NY 146
Simmons-Phi 145
Alexander-Det 140

Total Average
Ruth-NY 1.288
Foxx-Phi 1.261
Gehrig-NY 1.151
Simmons-Phi 1.097
Lazzeri-NY 1.041

Stolen Bases
Gehringer-Det 27
Cissell-Chi 25
B.Miller-Phi 24
Rothrock-Bos 23
Johnson-Det 20

Stolen Base Average
Gehringer-Det 75.0
B.Miller-Phi 72.7
Myer-Was 72.0
Reynolds-Chi 67.9
Rice-Was 66.7

Stolen Base Runs
Gehringer-Det 2.7
B.Miller-Phi 1.8
Myer-Was 1.2
Goslin-Was 1.2
Berg-Chi 9

Fielding Runs
Durocher-NY 26.2
Kerr-Chi 24.0
Melillo-StL 22.5
Simmons-Phi 17.3
West-Was 15.0

Total Player Rating
Ruth-NY 4.9
Simmons-Phi 4.9
Lazzeri-NY 4.8
Gehringer-Det 3.9
Gehrig-NY 3.7

Wins
Earnshaw-Phi 24
Ferrell-Cle 21
Grove-Phi 20
Marberry-Was 19

Win Percentage
Grove-Phi 769
Earnshaw-Phi ... .750
Ferrell-Cle 677
Walberg-Phi 621
Marberry-Was 613

Games
Marberry-Was 49
Earnshaw-Phi 44
Gray-StL 43
Ferrell-Cle........ 43

Complete Games
Thomas-Chi 24
Uhle-Det 23
Gray-StL 23
Hudlin-Cle 22
Lyons-Chi 21

Shutouts
MacFayden-Bos 4
Gray-StL 4
Crowder-StL 4
Blaeholder-StL 4

Saves
Marberry-Was 11
Moore-NY 8
Shores-Phi 7
Ferrell-Cle......... 5

Innings Pitched
Gray-StL 305.0
Hudlin-Cle.......280.1
Grove-Phi 275.1
Walberg-Phi 267.2
Crowder-StL.....266.2

Fewest Hits/Game
Earnshaw-Phi 8.23
Wells-NY 8.33
Marberry-Was 8.38
Walberg-Phi 8.61
McKain-Chi 9.00

Fewest BB/Game
Russell-Bos 1.58
Pennock-NY 1.60
Thomas-Chi 2.08
Uhle-Det 2.10
Quinn-Phi 2.18

Strikeouts
Grove-Phi 170
Earnshaw-Phi 149
Pipgras-NY 125
Marberry-Was..... 121

Strikeouts/Game
Grove-Phi 5.56
Earnshaw-Phi 5.27
Pipgras-NY 4.99
Hadley-Was 4.52
Marberry-Was 4.35

Ratio
Marberry-Was 11.07
Thomas-Chi 11.44
Grove-Phi 11.83
Walberg-Phi 11.94
Faber-Chi 11.96

Earned Run Average
Grove-Phi 2.81
Marberry-Was 3.06
Thomas-Chi 3.19
Earnshaw-Phi 3.29
Hudlin-Cle.......3.34

Adjusted ERA
Grove-Phi 150
Marberry-Was 139
Thomas-Chi 134
Hudlin-Cle 133
Earnshaw-Phi 129

Opponents' Batting Avg.
Earnshaw-Phi 241
Wells-NY 248
Marberry-Was 252
Walberg-Phi 254
Grove-Phi 262

Opponents' On Base Pct.
Marberry-Was 308
Thomas-Chi 310
Grove-Phi 316
Hudlin-Cle 318
Walberg-Phi 320

Starter Runs
Grove-Phi 43.7
Marberry-Was 32.9
Thomas-Chi 30.3
Hudlin-Cle 28.1
Earnshaw-Phi 27.0

Adjusted Starter Runs
Grove-Phi 43.3
Hudlin-Cle 34.3
Marberry-Was 32.8
Thomas-Chi 31.4
Earnshaw-Phi 26.6

Clutch Pitching Index
McKain-Chi...... 130
M.Gaston-Bos 116
Shaute-Cle 116
Ferrell-Cle 116
Collins-StL 113

Relief Runs
Moore-NY 0.7

Adjusted Relief Runs

Relief Ranking

Total Pitcher Index
Hudlin-Cle 3.9
Marberry-Was 3.8
Grove-Phi 3.5
Thomas-Chi 3.4
Ferrell-Cle 3.4

Total Baseball Ranking
Ruth-NY 4.9
Simmons-Phi 4.9
Lazzeri-NY 4.8
Gehringer-Det 3.9
Hudlin-Cle 3.9

1930 National League

TEAM	G	W	L	PCT	GB	R	OR	AB	H	2B	3B	HR	BB	SO	AVG	OBP	SLG	PRO	PRO+	BR	/A	PF	CHI	RC	SB	CS	SBA	SBR
STL	154	92	62	.597		1004	784	5512	1732	373	89	104	479	496	.314	.372	.471	.843	105	72	40	103	104	944	72			
CHI	156	90	64	.584	2	998	870	5581	1722	305	72	171	588	635	.309	.378	.481	.859	111	110	103	101	98	1001	70			
NY	154	87	67	.565	5	959	814	5553	1769	264	83	143	422	382	.319	.369	.473	.842	110	67	87	98	101	941	59			
BRO	154	86	68	.558	6	871	738	5433	1654	303	73	122	481	541	.304	.364	.454	.818	103	21	32	99	97	881	53			
PIT	154	80	74	.519	12	891	928	5346	1622	285	119	86	494	449	.303	.365	.449	.814	101	15	12	100	101	862	76			
BOS	154	70	84	.455	22	693	835	5356	1503	246	78	66	332	397	.281	.326	.393	.719	81	-186	-164	97	105	669	69			
CIN	154	59	95	.383	33	665	857	5245	1475	265	67	74	445	489	.281	.339	.400	.739	87	-135	-100	95	94	703	48			
PHI	156	52	102	.338	40	944	1199	5667	1783	345	44	126	450	459	.315	.367	.458	.825	97	37	-31	107	100	929	34			
TOT	618					7025		43693	13260	2386	625	892	3691	3848	.303	.360	.448	.808							481			

TEAM	CG	SH	SV	IP	H	H/G	HR	BB	SO	RAT	ERA	ERA+	OAV	OOB	PR	/A	PF	CPI	FA	E	DP	FW	PW	BW	SBW	DIF
STL	63	5	21	1380²	1596	10.4	87	476	639	13.7	4.39	114	.294	.353	89	95	101	104	.970	183	176	.2	8.4	3.5		2.9
CHI	67	6	12	1403²	1642	10.5	111	528	601	14.1	4.80	102	.294	.357	26	14	98	99	.973	170	167	1.0	1.2	9.1		1.6
NY	64	6	19	1363¹	1546	10.2	117	439	522	13.3	4.61	103	.290	.348	54	18	95	99	.974	164	144	1.3	1.6	7.7		-.5
BRO	74	13	15	1372	1480	9.7	115	394	526	12.4	4.03	122	.278	.330	144	135	99	102	.972	174	167	.7	11.9	2.8		-6.4
PIT	80	7	13	1361¹	1730	11.4	128	438	393	14.5	5.24	95	.313	.367	-41	-40	100	101	.965	216	164	-1.8	-3.5	1.1		7.2
BOS	71	6	11	1361	1624	10.7	117	475	424	14.0	4.91	100	.302	.360	9	3	99	102	.971	178	167	.4	.3	-14.5		6.8
CIN	61	6	11	1335	1650	11.1	75	394	361	13.9	5.08	95	.310	.361	-15	-37	97	96	.973	161	164	1.4	-3.3	-8.8		-7.3
PHI	54	3	7	1372²	1993	13.1	142	543	384	16.8	6.71	81	.346	.405	-266	-189	110	99	.962	239	169	-3.0	-16.7	-2.7		-2.6
TOT	534	52	109	10949²		10.9				14.1	4.97		.303	.360					.970	1485	1318					

Runs
Klein-Phi 158
Cuyler-Chi 155
English-Chi 152
Wilson-Chi 146
Herman-Bro 143

Hits
Terry-NY 254
Klein-Phi 250
Herman-Bro 241
Lindstrom-NY 231
Cuyler-Chi 228

Doubles
Klein-Phi 59
Cuyler-Chi 50
Herman-Bro 48
Comorosky-Pit 47
Frisch-StL 46

Triples
Comorosky-Pit 23
P.Waner-Pit 18
English-Chi 17
Cuyler-Chi 17
Terry-NY 15

Home Runs
Wilson-Chi 56
Klein-Phi 40
Berger-Bos 38
Hartnett-Chi 37
Herman-Bro 35

Total Bases
Klein-Phi 445
Wilson-Chi 423
Herman-Bro 416
Terry-NY 392
Cuyler-Chi 351

Runs Batted In
Wilson-Chi 190
Klein-Phi 170
Cuyler-Chi 134
Herman-Bro 130
Terry-NY 129

Runs Produced
Klein-Phi 288
Wilson-Chi 280
Cuyler-Chi 276
Terry-NY 245
Herman-Bro 238

Bases On Balls
Wilson-Chi 105
Ott-NY 103
English-Chi 100
Grantham-Pit 81
Suhr-Pit 80

Batting Average
Terry-NY 401
Herman-Bro 393
Klein-Phi 386
O'Doul-Phi 383
Lindstrom-NY 379

On Base Percentage
Ott-NY 458
Herman-Bro 455
Wilson-Chi 454
O'Doul-Phi 453
Terry-NY 452

Slugging Average
Wilson-Chi 723
Klein-Phi 687
Herman-Bro 678
Hafey-StL 652
Hartnett-Chi 630

Production
Wilson-Chi 1.177
Herman-Bro 1.132
Klein-Phi 1.123
Terry-NY 1.071
Hafey-StL 1.059

Adjusted Production
Wilson-Chi 177
Herman-Bro 171
Terry-NY 159
Klein-Phi 155
Ott-NY 152

Batter Runs
Wilson-Chi 75.4
Herman-Bro 68.7
Klein-Phi 67.3
Terry-NY 57.6
O'Doul-Phi 46.9

Adjusted Batter Runs
Wilson-Chi 74.2
Herman-Bro 70.7
Terry-NY 61.0
Klein-Phi 55.3
Ott-NY 48.3

Clutch Hitting Index
Thevenow-Phi 138
Traynor-Pit 133
Cuyler-Chi 129
Frisch-StL 126
Whitney-Phi 120

Runs Created
Wilson-Chi 189
Klein-Phi 186
Herman-Bro 183
Terry-NY 170
Cuyler-Chi 148

Total Average
Wilson-Chi 1.411
Herman-Bro 1.351
Klein-Phi 1.274
Ott-NY 1.224
Terry-NY 1.208

Stolen Bases
Cuyler-Chi 37
P.Waner-Pit 18
Herman-Bro 18

Fielding Runs
Frisch-StL 27.5
Klein-Phi 23.0
Whitney-Phi 20.3
Terry-NY 12.6
Cuyler-Chi 12.2

Total Player Rating
Klein-Phi 5.8
Terry-NY 5.0
Wilson-Chi 4.8
Lindstrom-NY 4.8
Frisch-StL 4.4

Wins
Malone-Chi 20
Kremer-Pit 20
Fitzsimmons-NY . . . 19

Win Percentage
Fitzsimmons-NY . . .731
Malone-Chi 690
Brame-Pit 680
Kremer-Pit 625
Hallahan-StL 625

Games
Elliott-Phi 48
Collins-Phi 47
Bush-Chi 46
Pruett-NY 45
Malone-Chi 45

Complete Games
Malone-Chi 22
Brame-Pit 22
French-Pit 21
Vance-Bro 20
Seibold-Bos 20

Shutouts
Vance-Bro 4
Root-Chi 4
Hubbell-NY 3
French-Pit 3

Saves
Bell-StL 8
Heving-NY 6
Clark-Bro 6

Innings Pitched
Kremer-Pit 276.0
French-Pit 274.2
Malone-Chi 271.2
Vance-Bro 258.2
Seibold-Bos 251.0

Fewest Hits/Game
Vance-Bro 8.39
Hallahan-StL 8.84
Fitzsimmons-NY . 9.23
Elliott-Bro 9.26
Clark-Bro 9.41

Fewest BB/Game
Clark-Bro 1.71
Kolp-Cin 1.82
Johnson-StL 1.82
Lucas-Cin 1.88
Vance-Bro 1.91

Strikeouts
Hallahan-StL 177
Vance-Bro 173
Malone-Chi 142
Root-Chi 124
Hubbell-NY 117

Strikeouts/Game
Hallahan-StL 6.71
Vance-Bro 6.02
Root-Chi 5.07
Malone-Chi 4.70
Johnson-StL 4.41

Ratio
Vance-Bro 10.47
Clark-Bro 11.11
Kolp-Cin 11.44
Fitzsimmons-NY .11.63
Johnson-StL 12.33

Earned Run Average
Vance-Bro 2.61
Hubbell-NY 3.87
Walker-NY 3.93
Malone-Chi 3.94
Elliott-Bro 3.95

Adjusted ERA
Vance-Bro 188
Elliott-Bro 124
Malone-Chi 124
Grimes-Bos-StL . . 123
Hubbell-NY 122

Opponents' Batting Avg.
Vance-Bro 246
Hallahan-StL 260
Fitzsimmons-NY . .266
Walker-NY 268
Malone-Chi 271

Opponents' On Base Pct.
Vance-Bro 289
Clark-Bro 306
Fitzsimmons-NY . . .314
Kolp-Cin 314
Hubbell-NY 327

Starter Runs
Vance-Bro 67.9
Malone-Chi 31.1
Hubbell-NY 29.5
Walker-NY 28.5
Seibold-Bos 23.7

Adjusted Starter Runs
Vance-Bro 66.2
Malone-Chi 28.5
Hubbell-NY 23.1
Seibold-Bos 22.7
Walker-NY 22.0

Clutch Pitching Index
Grimes-Bos-StL . . . 119
Smith-Bos 117
Haines-StL 109
Vance-Bro 108
Seibold-Bos 107

Relief Runs
Bell-StL 13.7
Lindsey-StL 6.4
Johnson-Cin 0.3

Adjusted Relief Runs
Bell-StL 14.3
Lindsey-StL 6.9

Relief Ranking
Bell-StL 10.0
Lindsey-StL 7.8

Total Pitcher Index
Vance-Bro 6.6
Malone-Chi 2.8
Grimes-Bos-StL . . . 2.6
Fitzsimmons-NY . . . 2.2
Walker-NY 2.1

Total Baseball Ranking
Vance-Bro 6.6
Klein-Phi 5.8
Terry-NY 5.0
Wilson-Chi 4.8
Lindstrom-NY 4.8

TEAM	G	W	L	PCT	GB	R	OR	AB	H	2B	3B	HR	BB	SO	AVG	OBP	SLG	PRO	PRO+	BR	/A	PF	CHI	RC	SB	CS	SBA	SBR
PHI	154	102	52	.662		951	751	5345	1573	319	74	125	599	531	.294	.369	.452	.821	108	102	60	104	100	913	48	33	59	-5
WAS	154	94	60	.610	8	892	689	5370	1620	300	98	57	537	438	.302	.369	.426	.795	106	59	55	100	99	860	101	67	60	-10
NY	154	86	68	.558	16	1062	898	5448	1683	298	110	152	644	569	.309	.384	.488	.872	131	206	255	104	99	1035	91	60	60	-9
CLE	154	81	73	.526	21	890	915	5439	1654	358	59	72	490	461	.304	.364	.431	.795	102	54	20	104	99	863	51	47	52	-13
DET	154	75	79	.487	27	783	833	5297	1504	298	90	82	461	508	.284	.344	.421	.765	96	-18	-33	102	98	771	98	70	58	-13
STL	154	64	90	.416	38	751	886	5278	1415	289	67	75	497	550	.268	.333	.391	.724	85	-96	-121	103	104	696	93	71	57	-15
CHI	154	62	92	.403	40	729	884	5419	1496	256	90	63	389	479	.276	.328	.391	.719	89	-111	-87	97	102	706	74	40	65	-2
BOS	154	52	102	.338	50	612	814	5286	1393	257	68	47	358	552	.264	.313	.365	.678	79	-192	-169	96	100	608	42	35	55	-8
TOT	616					6670		42882	12338	2375	656	673	3975	4088	.288	.351	.421	.772							598	423	59	-74

TEAM	CG	SH	SV	IP	H	H/G	HR	BB	SO	RAT	ERA	ERA+	OAV	OOB	PR	/A	PF	CPI	FA	E	DP	FW	PW	BW	SBW	DIF
PHI	72	8	21	1371	1457	9.6	84	488	672	12.9	4.28	109	.274	.337	56	58	101	98	.975	145	121	3.0	5.2	5.4	.4	11.0
WAS	78	6	14	1369	1367	9.0	52	504	524	12.5	3.96	116	.264	.332	104	96	99	97	.974	157	150	2.3	8.7	5.0	.0	1.1
NY	65	7	15	1367²	1566	10.3	93	524	572	13.9	4.88	88	.287	.352	-36	-90	93	96	.965	207	132	-.7	-8.1	23.1	.0	-5.2
CLE	68	5	14	1360	1663	11.0	85	528	441	14.6	4.88	99	.305	.368	-36	-9	104	107	.962	237	156	-2.5	-.8	1.8	-.3	5.9
DET	68	4	17	1351²	1507	10.0	86	570	574	14.0	4.70	102	.286	.359	-8	13	103	102	.967	192	156	.2	1.2	-3.0	-.3	-.0
STL	68	5	10	1371²	1639	10.8	124	449	470	13.9	5.07	96	.300	.356	-65	-31	105	101	.970	188	152	.4	-2.8	-10.9	-.5	.9
CHI	63	2	10	1361	1629	10.8	74	407	471	13.6	4.71	98	.300	.352	-10	-15	99	101	.962	235	136	-2.4	-1.4	-7.9	.7	-4.0
BOS	78	4	5	1360¹	1515	10.0	75	488	356	13.4	4.68	98	.286	.348	-6	-12	99	97	.968	196	161	-.0	-1.1	-15.3	.1	-8.7
TOT	560	41	106	10912¹		10.2				13.6	4.65		.288	.351					.968	1557	1164					

Runs
Simmons-Phi 152
Ruth-NY 150
Gehringer-Det 144
Gehrig-NY 143
Combs-NY 129

Hits
Hodapp-Cle 225
Gehrig-NY 220
Simmons-Phi 211
Rice-Was 207
Morgan-Cle 204

Doubles
Hodapp-Cle 51
Manush-StL-Was . . 49
Morgan-Cle 47
Gehringer-Det 47

Triples
Combs-NY 22
Reynolds-Chi 18
Gehrig-NY 17
Simmons-Phi 16

Home Runs
Ruth-NY 49
Gehrig-NY 41
Goslin-Was-StL . . 37
Foxx-Phi 37
Simmons-Phi 36

Total Bases
Gehrig-NY 419
Simmons-Phi 392
Ruth-NY 379
Foxx-Phi 358

Runs Batted In
Gehrig-NY 174
Simmons-Phi 165
Foxx-Phi 156
Ruth-NY 153
Goslin-Was-StL . . . 138

Runs Produced
Simmons-Phi 281
Gehrig-NY 276
Ruth-NY 254
Foxx-Phi 246
Cronin-Was 240

Bases On Balls
Ruth-NY 136
Bishop-Phi 128
Gehrig-NY 101
Foxx-Phi 93
Blue-StL 81

Batting Average
Simmons-Phi 381
Gehrig-NY 379
Ruth-NY 359
Reynolds-Chi 359
Cochrane-Phi 357

On Base Percentage
Ruth-NY 493
Gehrig-NY 473
Foxx-Phi 429
Bishop-Phi 426
Combs-NY 424

Slugging Average
Ruth-NY 732
Gehrig-NY 721
Simmons-Phi 708
Foxx-Phi 637

Production
Ruth-NY 1.225
Gehrig-NY 1.194
Simmons-Phi 1.130
Foxx-Phi 1.066
Morgan-Cle 1.014

Adjusted Production
Ruth-NY 216
Gehrig-NY 207
Simmons-Phi 173
Foxx-Phi 159
Morgan-Cle 148

Batter Runs
Ruth-NY 89.5
Gehrig-NY 88.4
Simmons-Phi 64.2
Foxx-Phi 57.0
Morgan-Cle 46.3

Adjusted Batter Runs
Ruth-NY 97.9
Gehrig-NY 96.9
Simmons-Phi 57.8
Foxx-Phi 50.5
Morgan-Cle 41.1

Clutch Hitting Index
Rice-Det-NY 137
Lazzeri-NY 125
Dykes-Phi 113
Cronin-Was 112
Alexander-Det 112

Runs Created
Gehrig-NY 195
Ruth-NY 191
Simmons-Phi 163
Foxx-Phi 154
Morgan-Cle 144

Total Average
Ruth-NY 1.509
Gehrig-NY 1.389
Simmons-Phi 1.272
Foxx-Phi 1.184
Morgan-Cle 1.089

Stolen Bases
McManus-Det 23
Gehringer-Det 19
Goslin-Was-StL . . 17
Johnson-Det 17
Cronin-Was 17

Stolen Base Average
Reynolds-Chi 80.0
McManus-Det 74.2
Cissell-StL 64.0
Johnson-Det 63.0
Cronin-Was 63.0

Stolen Base Runs
Lary-NY 3.0
Reynolds-Chi 2.4
McManus-Det 2.1

Fielding Runs
Melillo-StL 26.8
Cronin-Was 26.2
Goldman-Cle 20.7
Oliver-Bos 15.2
Kamm-Chi 14.9

Total Player Rating
Ruth-NY 7.3
Gehrig-NY 6.9
Cronin-Was 6.7
Simmons-Phi 4.9
Cochrane-Phi 4.0

Wins
Grove-Phi 28
Ferrell-Cle 25
Lyons-Chi 22
Earnshaw-Phi 22
Stewart-StL 20

Win Percentage
Grove-Phi 848
Marberry-Was 750
Jones-Was 682
Ferrell-Cle 658
Ruffing-Bos-NY . . .652

Games
Grove-Phi 50
Earnshaw-Phi 49
Pipgras-NY 44
Johnson-NY 44
Ferrell-Cle 43

Complete Games
Lyons-Chi 29
Crowder-StL-Was . . 25
Ferrell-Cle 25
Stewart-StL 23
Grove-Phi 22

Shutouts
Pipgras-NY 3
Earnshaw-Phi 3
Brown-Cle 3

Saves
Grove-Phi 9
Braxton-Was-Chi . . 6
Quinn-Phi 6
Sullivan-Det 5
McKain-Chi 5

Innings Pitched
Lyons-Chi 297.2
Ferrell-Cle 296.2
Earnshaw-Phi 296.0
Grove-Phi 291.0
Crowder-StL-Was . . .279.2

Fewest Hits/Game
Hadley-Was 8.37
Grove-Phi 8.44
Collins-StL 8.81
Crowder-StL-Was . . 8.88
Gaston-Bos 8.97

Fewest BB/Game
Pennock-NY 1.15
Lyons-Chi 1.72
Grove-Phi 1.86
Russell-Bos 2.08
Brown-Cle 2.15

Strikeouts
Grove-Phi 209
Earnshaw-Phi 193
Hadley-Was 162
Ferrell-Cle 143
Ruffing-Bos-NY . . . 131

Strikeouts/Game
Grove-Phi 6.46
Johnson-NY 5.90
Earnshaw-Phi 5.87
Hadley-Was 5.60
Ruffing-Bos-NY . . . 5.32

Ratio
Grove-Phi 10.45
Stewart-StL 11.69
Lyons-Chi 11.79
Marberry-Was 11.82
Caraway-Chi 11.82

Earned Run Average
Grove-Phi 2.54
Ferrell-Cle 3.31
Stewart-StL 3.45
Uhle-Det 3.65
Hadley-Was 3.73

Adjusted ERA
Grove-Phi 184
Ferrell-Cle 146
Stewart-StL 141
Uhle-Det 131
Sorrell-Det 124

Opponents' Batting Avg.
Grove-Phi 247
Hadley-Was 247
Crowder-StL-Was . .259
Collins-StL 259
Gaston-Bos 259

Opponents' On Base Pct.
Grove-Phi 288
Stewart-StL 315
Lyons-Chi 319
Marberry-Was 321
Crowder-StL-Was . .321

Starter Runs
Grove-Phi 68.3
Ferrell-Cle 44.2
Stewart-StL 35.9
Lyons-Chi 28.7
Hadley-Was 26.4

Adjusted Starter Runs
Grove-Phi 69.0
Ferrell-Cle 50.0
Stewart-StL 42.7
Uhle-Det 30.4
Lyons-Chi 27.8

Clutch Pitching Index
Henry-Chi 122
Harder-Cle 115
Sorrell-Det 115
Hoyt-NY-Det 113
Ferrell-Cle 113

Relief Runs
Quinn-Phi 2.3

Adjusted Relief Runs
Quinn-Phi 2.5

Relief Ranking
Quinn-Phi 4.5

Total Pitcher Index
Grove-Phi 7.3
Ferrell-Cle 6.2
Stewart-StL 4.7
Lyons-Chi 4.1
Uhle-Det 3.2

Total Baseball Ranking
Ruth-NY 7.6
Grove-Phi 7.3
Gehrig-NY 6.9
Cronin-Was 6.7
Ferrell-Cle 6.2

TEAM	G	W	L	PCT	GB	R	OR	AB	H	2B	3B	HR	BB	SO	AVG	OBP	SLG	PRO	PRO+	BR	/A	PF	CHI	RC	SB	CS	SBA	SBR
STL	154	101	53	.656		815	614	5435	1554	353	74	60	432	475	.286	.342	.411	.753	105	61	31	104	107	787	114			
NY	153	87	65	.572	13	768	599	5372	1554	251	64	101	383	395	.289	.360	.422	.782	115	131	117	102	97	865	83			
CHI	156	84	70	.545	17	828	710	5451	1578	340	66	84	577	641	.289	.360	.422	.782	115	-3	2	99	101	705	45			
BRO	153	79	73	.520	21	681	673	5309	1464	240	77	71	409	512	.276	.331	.390	.721	101	-3	2	99	101	705	59			
PIT	155	75	79	.487	26	636	691	5360	1425	243	70	41	493	454	.266	.330	.360	.690	93	-54	-48	99	98	667	59			
PHI	155	66	88	.429	35	684	828	5375	1502	299	52	81	437	492	.279	.336	.400	.736	96	-137	-118	96	98	745	42			
BOS	156	64	90	.416	37	533	680	5296	1367	221	59	34	368	430	.258	.309	.341	.650	84	-85	-49	94	99	580	46			
CIN	154	58	96	.377	43	592	742	5343	1439	241	70	21	403	463	.269	.323	.352	.675	94					631	24			
TOT	618					5537		42941	11883	2188	532	493	3502	3862	.277	.334	.387	.721							462			

TEAM	CG	SH	SV	IP	H	H/G	HR	BB	SO	RAT	ERA	ERA+	OAV	OOB	PR	/A	PF	CPI	FA	E	DP	FW	PW	BW	SBW	DIF
STL	80	17	20	1384²	1470	9.6	65	449	626	12.6	3.45	114	.273	.332	63	74	102	110	.974	160	169	1.0	7.4	3.1		12.6
NY	90	17	12	1360²	1341	8.9	71	422	570	11.8	3.30	112	.255	.313	85	58	96	100	.974	159	126	1.0	5.8	8.0		-3.7
CHI	80	8	8	1385²	1448	9.4	54	524	541	13.0	3.97	97	.268	.337	-17	-19	100	94	.973	169	141	.6	-1.9	11.6		-3.3
BRO	64	9	18	1356	1520	10.1	56	351	546	12.5	3.84	99	.283	.329	3	-5	99	100	.969	187	154	-.7	-.5	.2		4.0
PIT	89	9	5	1390	1489	9.6	55	442	345	12.6	3.66	105	.274	.331	32	28	100	102	.968	194	167	-.9	2.8	-4.8		.9
PHI	60	6	16	1360¹	1603	10.6	75	511	499	14.2	4.58	93	.293	.358	-108	-51	110	100	.966	210	149	-1.9	-5.1	-3.0		-1.1
BOS	78	12	9	1380¹	1465	9.6	66	406	419	12.3	3.90	97	.272	.325	-5	-18	98	94	.973	170	141	.5	-1.8	-11.7		.0
CIN	70	7	6	1345	1545	10.3	51	399	317	13.1	4.22	89	.294	.346	-53	-72	97	101	.973	165	194	.7	-7.2	-4.9		-7.6
TOT	611	85	94	10962²		9.8				12.8	3.86		.277	.334					.971	1414	1241					

Runs
Terry-NY 121
Klein-Phi 121
English-Chi 117
Ott-NY 104
Cuyler-Chi 100

Hits
L.Waner-Pit 214
Terry-NY 213
English-Chi 202
Cuyler-Chi 202
Klein-Phi 200

Doubles
Adams-StL 46
Berger-Bos 44
Terry-NY 43
Herman-Bro 43
Bartell-Phi 43

Triples
Terry-NY 20
Herman-Bro 16
Traynor-Pit 15
Bissonette-Bro ... 14

Home Runs
Klein-Phi 31
Ott-NY 29
Berger-Bos 19
Herman-Bro 18
Arlett-Phi 18

Total Bases
Klein-Phi 347
Terry-NY 323
Herman-Bro 320
Berger-Bos 316
Cuyler-Chi 290

Runs Batted In
Klein-Phi 121
Ott-NY 115
Terry-NY 112
Traynor-Pit 103
Herman-Bro 97

Runs Produced
Terry-NY 224
Klein-Phi 211
Ott-NY 190
Traynor-Pit 182
Cuyler-Chi 179

Bases On Balls
Ott-NY 80
P.Waner-Pit 73
Cuyler-Chi 72
Grantham-Pit 71
English-Chi 68

Batting Average
Hafey-StL .... .349
Terry-NY .... .349
Bottomley-StL .... .348
Klein-Phi .... .337
O'Doul-Bro .... .336

On Base Percentage
Hafey-StL .... .404
Cuyler-Chi .... .404
P.Waner-Pit ...... .404
Grantham-Pit ..... .400
Klein-Phi .... .398

Slugging Average
Klein-Phi .... .584
Hornsby-Chi ...... .574
Hafey-StL .... .569
Ott-NY .... .545
Arlett-Phi .... .538

Production
Klein-Phi .... .982
Hafey-StL .... .973
Ott-NY .... .937
Terry-NY .... .926
Berger-Bos .... .892

Adjusted Production
Ott-NY 153
Hafey-StL 153
Terry-NY 150
Klein-Phi 149
Berger-Bos 143

Batter Runs
Klein-Phi 48.9
Terry-NY 39.0
Hafey-StL 36.2
Ott-NY 35.0
Hornsby-Chi 33.5

Adjusted Batter Runs
Terry-NY 42.0
Klein-Phi 39.3
Ott-NY 37.6
Berger-Bos 35.6
Hafey-StL 32.6

Clutch Hitting Index
Sheely-Bos 150
Traynor-Pit 127
Frisch-StL 122
Gelbert-StL 122
Hendrick-Bro-Cin .. 120

Runs Created
Klein-Phi 140
Terry-NY 130
Cuyler-Chi 122
Berger-Bos 122
Herman-Bro 118

Total Average
Hafey-StL 1.055
Klein-Phi 1.051
Ott-NY 1.031
Terry-NY .... .955
Cuyler-Chi .... .925

Stolen Bases
Frisch-StL 28
Herman-Bro 17
Martin-StL 16
Adams-StL 16
Watkins-StL 15

Stolen Base Average

Stolen Base Runs

Fielding Runs
L.Waner-Pit 18.3
Frisch-StL 16.3
P.Waner-Pit 14.6
Gelbert-StL 12.9
Hurst-Phi 11.4

Total Player Rating
Ott-NY 3.6
Terry-NY 3.6
Berger-Bos 3.5
Cuccinello-Cin ... 3.3
P.Waner-Pit 3.1

Wins
Meine-Pit 19
Hallahan-StL 19
J.Elliott-Phi 19

Win Percentage
Derringer-StL ..... .692
Hallahan-StL ...... .679
Bush-Chi .... .667
Grimes-StL .... .654

Games
J.Elliott-Phi 52
Johnson-Cin 42
Collins-Phi 42

Complete Games
Lucas-Cin 24
Brandt-Bos 23
Meine-Pit 22
Hubbell-NY 21
French-Pit 20

Shutouts
Walker-NY 6
Hubbell-NY 4
Fitzsimmons-NY ... 4
Derringer-StL 4

Saves
Quinn-Bro 15
Lindsey-StL 7
J.Elliott-Phi 5
Hallahan-StL 4
Collins-Phi 4

Innings Pitched
Meine-Pit 284.0
French-Pit 275.2
Johnson-Cin 262.1
Fitzsimmons-NY .. 253.2
Root-Chi 251.0

Fewest Hits/Game
Hubbell-NY 7.66
Walker-NY 7.97
Brandt-Bos 8.21
Fitzsimmons-NY .. 8.59
Root-Chi 8.61

Fewest BB/Game
Johnson-StL 1.40
Lucas-Cin 1.47
Cantwell-Bos 1.96
Clark-Bro 2.01
Zachary-Bos 2.08

Strikeouts
Hallahan-StL 159
Hubbell-NY 155
Vance-Bro 150
Derringer-StL 134
Root-Chi 131

Strikeouts/Game
Vance-Bro 6.17
Hallahan-StL 5.75
Derringer-StL 5.70
Hubbell-NY 5.63
Root-Chi 4.70

Ratio
Hubbell-NY 10.23
Walker-NY 10.49
Johnson-StL 10.50
Fitzsimmons-NY .. 10.79
Brandt-Bos 11.12

Earned Run Average
Walker-NY 2.26
Hubbell-NY 2.65
Brandt-Bos 2.92
Meine-Pit 2.98
Johnson-StL 3.00

Adjusted ERA
Walker-NY 164
Hubbell-NY 139
Benge-Phi 134
Johnson-StL 131
Brandt-Bos 130

Opponents' Batting Avg.
Hubbell-NY ...... .227
Walker-NY .... .231
Brandt-Bos ...... .244
Fitzsimmons-NY .. .251
Root-Chi .... .252

Opponents' On Base Pct.
Hubbell-NY ...... .282
Walker-NY .... .283
Johnson-StL ..... .286
Fitzsimmons-NY .. .296
Cantwell-Bos .... .301

Starter Runs
Walker-NY 42.7
Hubbell-NY 33.5
Meine-Pit 27.9
Brandt-Bos 26.3
Fitzsimmons-NY .. 22.9

Adjusted Starter Runs
Walker-NY 38.1
Benge-Phi 29.4
Hubbell-NY 28.7
Meine-Pit 27.3
Brandt-Bos 24.2

Clutch Pitching Index
Benton-Cin 125
Dudley-Phi 120
Grimes-StL 114
Hallahan-StL 113
Derringer-StL 112

Relief Runs
Lindsey-StL 9.1
Quinn-Bro 8.6
Moore-Bro 0.5

Adjusted Relief Runs
Lindsey-StL 9.6
Quinn-Bro 8.2
Moore-Bro 0.1

Relief Ranking
Quinn-Bro 14.7
Lindsey-StL 13.6
Moore-Bro 0

Total Pitcher Index
Fitzsimmons-NY .. 3.7
Brandt-Bos 3.6
Benge-Phi 3.3
Hubbell-NY 3.1
Walker-NY 2.8

Total Baseball Ranking
Fitzsimmons-NY .. 3.7
Ott-NY 3.6
Terry-NY 3.6
Brandt-Bos 3.6
Berger-Bos 3.5

TEAM	G	W	L	PCT	GB	R	OR	AB	H	2B	3B	HR	BB	SO	AVG	OBP	SLG	PRO	PRO+	BR	/A	PF	CHI	RC	SB	CS	SBA	SBR
PHI	153	107	45	.704		858	626	5377	1544	311	64	118	528	543	.287	.355	.435	.790	107	93	40	106	98	843	25	23	52	-6
NY	155	94	59	.614	13.5	1067	760	5608	1667	277	78	155	748	554	.297	.383	.457	.840	135	220	280	94	100	1016	138	68	67	1
WAS	156	92	62	.597	16	843	691	5576	1588	308	93	49	481	459	.285	.345	.400	.745	100	8	4	101	103	774	72	64	53	-17
CLE	155	78	76	.506	30	885	833	5445	1612	321	69	71	555	433	.296	.363	.419	.745	105	91	41	106	100	840	63	60	51	-17
STL	154	63	91	.409	45	722	870	5374	1455	287	62	76	488	580	.271	.333	.390	.723	92	-40	-66	104	98	696	73	80	48	-26
BOS	153	62	90	.408	45	625	800	5379	1409	289	34	37	405	565	.262	.315	.349	.664	85	-154	-121	95	102	596	42	43	49	-13
DET	154	61	93	.396	47	651	836	5430	1456	292	69	43	480	468	.268	.330	.371	.701	87	-79	-103	103	93	675	117	75	61	-10
CHI	156	56	97	.366	51.5	704	939	5481	1423	238	69	27	483	445	.260	.323	.343	.666	86	-146	-108	94	108	632	94	39	71	5
TOT	618					6355		43670	12154	2323	538	576	4168	4047	.278	.344	.396	.740							624	452	58	-84

TEAM	CG	SH	SV	IP	H	H/G	HR	BB	SO	RAT	ERA	ERA+	OAV	OOB	PR	/A	PF	CPI	FA	E	DP	FW	PW	BW	SBW	DIF
PHI	97	12	16	1365^1	1342	8.8	73	457	574	11.9	3.47	130	.256	.316	138	155	103	105	.976	141	151	3.2	14.4	3.7	.4	9.3
NY	78	4	17	1410^1	1461	9.3	67	543	686	12.9	4.20	94	.263	.332	28	-37	91	94	.972	169	131	1.7	-3.4	26.1	1.1	-7.9
WAS	60	7	24	1394^1	1434	9.3	73	498	582	12.6	3.76	114	.264	.327	95	82	98	104	.976	142	148	3.3	7.6	.4	-.6	4.3
CLE	76	6	9	1354^2	1577	10.5	64	561	470	14.4	4.63	100	.286	.355	-38	-2	106	100	.963	232	143	-2.0	-.2	3.8	-.6	.0
STL	65	4	10	1362	1623	10.7	84	444	436	13.8	4.76	97	.293	.348	-57	-18	106	99	.963	232	160	-2.1	-1.7	-6.1	-1.4	-2.6
BOS	61	5	10	1366^2	1559	10.3	54	473	365	13.5	4.60	94	.285	.344	-33	-44	98	95	.970	188	127	.4	-4.1	-11.3	-.2	1.2
DET	86	5	6	1384^1	1549	10.1	79	597	511	14.1	4.59	100	.282	.355	-32	-1	105	102	.964	220	139	-1.4	-.0	-9.6	.0	-5.0
CHI	54	6	10	1390^1	1613	10.4	82	588	421	14.5	5.04	85	.287	.358	-101	-122	97	96	.961	245	131	-2.7	-11.4	-10.1	1.4	2.2
TOT	577	49	102	11028		9.9				13.5	4.38		.278	.344					.968	1569	1130					2.2

Runs
Gehrig-NY 163
Ruth-NY 149
Averill-Cle 140
Combs-NY 120
Chapman-NY 120

Hits
Gehrig-NY 211
Averill-Cle 209
Simmons-Phi 200
Ruth-NY 199
Webb-Bos 196

Doubles
Webb-Bos 67
Alexander-Det 47
Kress-StL 46
Cronin-Was 44

Triples
Johnson-Det 19
Gehrig-NY 15
Blue-Chi 15
Vosmik-Cle 14
Reynolds-Chi 14

Home Runs
Ruth-NY 46
Gehrig-NY 46
Averill-Cle 32
Foxx-Phi 30
Goslin-StL 24

Total Bases
Gehrig-NY 410
Ruth-NY 374
Averill-Cle 361
Simmons-Phi 329
Goslin-StL 328

Runs Batted In
Gehrig-NY 184
Ruth-NY 163
Averill-Cle 143
Simmons-Phi 128
Cronin-Was 126

Runs Produced
Gehrig-NY 301
Ruth-NY 266
Averill-Cle 251
Chapman-NY 225
Cronin-Was 217

Bases On Balls
Ruth-NY 128
Blue-Chi 127
Gehrig-NY 117
Bishop-Phi 112
Lary-NY 88

Batting Average
Simmons-Phi .390
Ruth-NY .373
Morgan-Cle .351
Cochrane-Phi .349
Gehrig-NY .341

On Base Percentage
Ruth-NY .495
Morgan-Cle .451
Gehrig-NY .446
Simmons-Phi .444
Blue-Chi .430

Slugging Average
Ruth-NY .700
Gehrig-NY .662
Simmons-Phi .641
Averill-Cle .576
Foxx-Phi .567

Production
Ruth-NY 1.195
Gehrig-NY 1.108
Simmons-Phi 1.085
Averill-Cle .979
Cochrane-Phi .976

Adjusted Production
Ruth-NY 223
Gehrig-NY 199
Simmons-Phi 172
Webb-Bos 151
Goslin-StL 147

Batter Runs
Ruth-NY 91.5
Gehrig-NY 79.9
Simmons-Phi 59.6
Averill-Cle 48.2
Goslin-StL 44.7

Adjusted Batter Runs
Ruth-NY 101.8
Gehrig-NY 90.0
Simmons-Phi 51.6
Webb-Bos 43.4
Averill-Cle 40.5

Clutch Hitting Index
Bluege-Was 126
Kamm-Chi-Cle 124
Vosmik-Cle 119
Lazzeri-NY 118
Spencer-Was 118

Runs Created
Ruth-NY 192
Gehrig-NY 185
Simmons-Phi 145
Averill-Cle 144
Goslin-StL 137

Total Average
Ruth-NY 1.487
Gehrig-NY 1.267
Simmons-Phi 1.199
Morgan-Cle 1.046
Cochrane-Phi 1.033

Stolen Bases
Chapman-NY 61
Johnson-Det 33
Burns-StL 19
Lazzeri-NY 18
Cissell-Chi 18

Stolen Base Average
Cissell-Chi 75.0
Reynolds-Chi 73.9
Chapman-NY 72.6
Lazzeri-NY 66.7
Bluege-Was 61.5

Stolen Base Runs
Chapman-NY 4.5
H.Walker-Det 2.4
Blue-Chi 2.1
Cissell-Chi 1.8

Fielding Runs
Melillo-StL 33.1
McManus-Det-Bos 21.1
West-Was 21.0
Burns-StL 18.4
Rhyne-Bos 16.9

Total Player Rating
Ruth-NY 7.3
Gehrig-NY 5.8
Cronin-Was 4.6
Simmons-Phi 4.6
Cochrane-Phi 4.3

Wins
Grove-Phi 31
Ferrell-Cle 22
Gomez-NY 21
Earnshaw-Phi 21
Walberg-Phi 20

Win Percentage
Grove-Phi .886
Marberry-Was .800
Mahaffey-Phi .789
Earnshaw-Phi .750
Gomez-NY .700

Games
Hadley-Was 55
Moore-Bos 53
Caraway-Chi 51
Frasier-Chi 46
Fischer-Was 46

Complete Games
Grove-Phi 27
Ferrell-Cle 27
Earnshaw-Phi 23
Whitehill-Det 22
Stewart-StL 20

Shutouts
Grove-Phi 4
Earnshaw-Phi 3

Saves
Moore-Bos 10
Hadley-Was 8
Marberry-Was 7
Kimsey-StL 7
Earnshaw-Phi 6

Innings Pitched
Walberg-Phi 291.0
Grove-Phi 288.2
Earnshaw-Phi 281.2
Ferrell-Cle 276.1
Whitehill-Det 271.1

Fewest Hits/Game
Hadley-Was 7.26
Gomez-NY 7.63
Grove-Phi 7.76
Johnson-NY 8.07
Earnshaw-Phi 8.15

Fewest BB/Game
Pennock-NY 1.43
Gray-Chi 1.88
Grove-Phi 1.93
Brown-Cle 2.12
Blaeholder-StL 2.23

Strikeouts
Grove-Phi 175
Earnshaw-Phi 152
Gomez-NY 150
Ruffing-NY 132
Hadley-Was 124

Strikeouts/Game
Hadley-Was 6.21
Gomez-NY 5.56
Bridges-Det 5.46
Grove-Phi 5.46
Ruffing-NY 5.01

Ratio
Grove-Phi 9.73
Earnshaw-Phi 10.64
Gomez-NY 10.93
Coffman-StL 11.27
Uhle-Det 11.33

Earned Run Average
Grove-Phi 2.06
Gomez-NY 2.67
Hadley-Was 3.06
Brown-Was 3.20
Marberry-Was 3.45

Adjusted ERA
Grove-Phi 218
Gomez-NY 149
Hadley-Was 140
Brown-Was 134
Uhle-Det 131

Opponents' Batting Avg.
Hadley-Was .218
Gomez-NY .226
Grove-Phi .229
Johnson-NY .234
Earnshaw-Phi .236

Opponents' On Base Pct.
Grove-Phi .271
Earnshaw-Phi .288
Gomez-NY .295
Coffman-StL .298
Uhle-Det .304

Starter Runs
Grove-Phi 74.5
Gomez-NY 46.2
Brown-Was 33.9
Hadley-Was 26.4
Marberry-Was 22.6

Adjusted Starter Runs
Grove-Phi 78.1
Gomez-NY 35.1
Brown-Was 31.3
Ferrell-Cle 26.9
Earnshaw-Phi 25.6

Clutch Pitching Index
Grove-Phi 118
Faber-Chi 116
Whitehill-Det 115
Pennock-NY 110
Brown-Was 110

Relief Runs

Adjusted Relief Runs
Kimsey-StL 2.6

Relief Ranking
Kimsey-StL 2.9

Total Pitcher Index
Grove-Phi 8.7
Ferrell-Cle 5.2
Gomez-NY 3.5
Brown-Was 3.4
Earnshaw-Phi 2.9

Total Baseball Ranking
Grove-Phi 8.7
Ruth-NY 7.3
Gehrig-NY 5.8
Ferrell-Cle 5.2
Cronin-Was 4.6

TEAM	G	W	L	PCT	GB	R	OR	AB	H	2B	3B	HR	BB	SO	AVG	OBP	SLG	PRO	PRO+	BR	/A	PF	CHI	RC	SB	CS	SBA	SBR
CHI	154	90	64	.584		720	633	5462	1519	296	60	69	398	514	.278	.330	.392	.722	101	0	7	99	101	728	48			
PIT	154	86	68	.558	4	701	711	5421	1543	274	90	48	358	385	.285	.333	.395	.728	103	9	22	98	99	729	71			
BRO	154	81	73	.526	9	752	747	5433	1538	296	59	110	388	574	.283	.334	.420	.754	110	55	71	98	99	778	61			
PHI	154	78	76	.506	12	844	796	5510	1608	330	67	122	446	547	.292	.348	.442	.790	105	132	32	112	98	870	71			
BOS	155	77	77	.500	13	649	655	5506	1460	262	53	63	347	496	.265	.311	.366	.677	90	-94	-71	96	105	643	36			
STL	156	72	82	.468	18	684	717	5458	1467	307	51	76	420	514	.269	.324	.385	.709	93	-27	-47	103	100	702	92			
NY	154	72	82	.468	18	755	706	5530	1527	263	54	116	348	391	.276	.322	.406	.728	103	1	16	98	107	735	31			
CIN	155	60	94	.390	30	575	715	5443	1429	265	68	47	436	436	.263	.320	.362	.682	92	-77	-56	97	91	654	35			
TOT	618					5680		43763	12091	2293	502	651	3141	3857	.276	.328	.396	.724							445			

TEAM	CG	SH	SV	IP	H	H/G	HR	BB	SO	RAT	ERA	ERA+	OAV	OOB	PR	/A	PF	CPI	FA	E	DP	FW	PW	BW	SBW	DIF
CHI	79	9	7	1401	1444	9.3	68	409	527	12.1	3.44	109	.264	.319	68	50	97	102	.973	173	146	.4	4.9	.7		7.0
PIT	71	12	12	1377	1472	9.6	86	338	377	11.9	3.75	102	.270	.314	20	10	98	96	.969	185	124	-.4	1.0	2.2		6.2
BRO	61	7	16	1379²	1538	10.0	72	403	497	12.8	4.27	89	.282	.334	-60	-68	98	94	.971	183	169	-.3	-6.7	7.0		4.0
PHI	59	4	17	1384	1589	10.3	107	450	459	13.5	4.47	99	.287	.344	-91	-9	114	100	.968	194	133	-.9	-.9	3.2		-.3
BOS	72	8	8	1414	1483	9.4	61	420	440	12.3	3.53	107	.272	.328	55	36	97	105	.976	152	145	1.7	3.6	-7.0		1.7
STL	70	13	9	1396	1533	9.9	76	455	681	13.0	3.97	99	.282	.340	-14	-6	101	104	.971	175	155	.4	-.6	-4.7		-.1
NY	57	3	16	1375¹	1533	10.0	112	387	506	12.7	3.83	97	.280	.330	8	-18	96	108	.969	191	143	-.7	-1.8	1.6		-4.1
CIN	83	6	6	1394²	1505	9.7	69	276	359	11.6	3.79	102	.274	.311	14	10	99	92	.971	178	129	.1	1.0	-5.5		-12.6
TOT	552	62	91	11121²		9.8				12.5	3.88		.276	.328					.971	1431	1144					

Runs
Klein-Phi 152
Terry-NY 124
O'Doul-Bro 120
Ott-NY 119
Bartell-Phi 118

Hits
Klein-Phi 226
Terry-NY 225
O'Doul-Bro 219
P.Waner-Pit 215
Herman-Chi 206

Doubles
P.Waner-Pit 62
Klein-Phi 50
Stephenson-Chi . . . 49
Bartell-Phi 48

Triples
Herman-Cin 19
Suhr-Pit 16
Klein-Phi 15

Home Runs
Ott-NY 38
Klein-Phi 38
Terry-NY 28
Hurst-Phi 24
Wilson-Bro 23

Total Bases
Klein-Phi 420
Terry-NY 373
Ott-NY 340
O'Doul-Bro 330
P.Waner-Pit 321

Runs Batted In
Hurst-Phi 143
Klein-Phi 137
Whitney-Phi 124
Wilson-Bro 123
Ott-NY 123

Runs Produced
Klein-Phi 251
Hurst-Phi 228
Terry-NY 213
Whitney-Phi 204
Ott-NY 204

Bases On Balls
Ott-NY 100
Hurst-Phi 65
Bartell-Phi 64
Suhr-Pit 63

Batting Average
O'Doul-Bro 368
Terry-NY 350
Klein-Phi 348
P.Waner-Pit 341
Hurst-Phi 339

On Base Percentage
Ott-NY 424
O'Doul-Bro 423
Hurst-Phi 412
Klein-Phi 404
P.Waner-Pit 397

Slugging Average
Klein-Phi 646
Ott-NY 601
Terry-NY 580
O'Doul-Bro 555
Hurst-Phi 547

Production
Klein-Phi 1.050
Ott-NY 1.025
O'Doul-Bro 978
Terry-NY 962
Hurst-Phi 959

Adjusted Production
Ott-NY 175
O'Doul-Bro 164
Klein-Phi 158
Terry-NY 158
Herman-Cin 152

Batter Runs
Klein-Phi 68.2
Ott-NY 59.8
O'Doul-Bro 51.2
Terry-NY 46.4
Hurst-Phi 46.2

Adjusted Batter Runs
Ott-NY 62.8
O'Doul-Bro 53.9
Klein-Phi 50.9
Terry-NY 49.1
Herman-Cin 41.8

Clutch Hitting Index
Wilson-Bro 132
Whitney-Phi 131
Hogan-NY 129
Cuyler-Chi 126
Hurst-Phi 124

Runs Created
Klein-Phi 171
Ott-NY 151
O'Doul-Bro 142
Terry-NY 142
Hurst-Phi 134

Total Average
Klein-Phi 1.182
Ott-NY 1.166
O'Doul-Bro 1.059
Hurst-Phi 1.042
Terry-NY 981

Stolen Bases
Klein-Phi 20
Piet-Pit 19
Watkins-StL 18
Frisch-StL 18
K.Davis-Phi 16

Stolen Base Average

Stolen Base Runs

Fielding Runs
Jurges-Chi 31.7
Cuccinello-Bro . . . 19.0
Herman-Chi 16.8
Frisch-StL 16.4
Stripp-Bro 15.9

Total Player Rating
Ott-NY 5.3
Klein-Phi 4.9
Terry-NY 4.9
Herman-Cin 4.7
O'Doul-Bro 3.9

Wins
Warneke-Chi 22
Clark-Bro 20
Bush-Chi 19

Win Percentage
Warneke-Chi 786
Bush-Chi 633
Rhem-StL-Phi 625
Clark-Bro 625
Hubbell-NY 621

Games
French-Pit 47
Dean-StL 46
Carleton-StL 44
Collins-Phi 43

Complete Games
Lucas-Cin 28
Warneke-Chi 25
Hubbell-NY 22

Shutouts
Warneke-Chi 4
Swetonic-Pit 4
Dean-StL 4

Saves
Quinn-Bro 8
Benge-Phi 6
Luque-NY 5
Cantwell-Bos 5

Innings Pitched
Dean-StL 286.0
Hubbell-NY 284.0
Warneke-Chi 277.0
French-Pit 274.1
Clark-Bro 273.0

Fewest Hits/Game
Swetonic-Pit 7.41
Brown-Bos 7.90
Warneke-Chi 8.03
Hubbell-NY 8.24
Malone-Chi 8.43

Fewest BB/Game
Swift-Pit 1.09
Lucas-Cin 1.17
Hubbell-NY 1.27
Benton-Cin 1.35
Betts-Bos 1.42

Strikeouts
Dean-StL 191
Hubbell-NY 137
Malone-Chi 120
Carleton-StL 113
Brown-Bos 110

Strikeouts/Game
Dean-StL 6.01
Hallahan-StL 5.51
Vance-Bro 5.28
Carleton-StL 5.18
Brown-Bos 4.65

Ratio
Hubbell-NY 9.63
Swift-Pit 9.78
Lucas-Cin 9.92
Warneke-Chi 10.17
Swetonic-Pit 10.46

Earned Run Average
Warneke-Chi 2.37
Hubbell-NY 2.50
Betts-Bos 2.80
Swetonic-Pit 2.82
Lucas-Cin 2.94

Adjusted ERA
Warneke-Chi 159
Hubbell-NY 148
Swetonic-Pit 135
Betts-Bos 134
Lucas-Cin 131

Opponents' Batting Avg.
Swetonic-Pit 221
Warneke-Chi 237
Hubbell-NY 238
Brown-Bos 238
Malone-Chi 244

Opponents' On Base Pct.
Hubbell-NY 268
Swift-Pit 272
Lucas-Cin 274
Warneke-Chi 283
Swetonic-Pit 286

Starter Runs
Warneke-Chi 46.4
Hubbell-NY 43.4
Lucas-Cin 28.1
Betts-Bos 26.5
French-Pit 26.2

Adjusted Starter Runs
Warneke-Chi 42.9
Hubbell-NY 38.1
Lucas-Cin 27.4
French-Pit 24.2
Betts-Bos 23.6

Clutch Pitching Index
Bush-Chi 123
French-Pit 123
Zachary-Bos 117
Hallahan-StL 113
Derringer-StL 113

Relief Runs
Quinn-Bro 5.6
Frankhouse-Bos . . . 3.8

Adjusted Relief Runs
Quinn-Bro 5.0
Frankhouse-Bos . . . 2.4

Relief Ranking
Quinn-Bro 6.2
Frankhouse-Bos . . . 2.0

Total Pitcher Index
Hubbell-NY 4.8
Lucas-Cin 4.4
Warneke-Chi 4.1
Cantwell-Bos 2.6
French-Pit 2.5

Total Baseball Ranking
Ott-NY 5.3
Klein-Phi 4.9
Terry-NY 4.9
Hubbell-NY 4.8
Herman-Cin 4.7

TEAM	G	W	L	PCT	GB	R	OR	AB	H	2B	3B	HR	BB	SO	AVG	OBP	SLG	PRO	PRO+	BR	/A	PF	CHI	RC	SB	CS	SBA	SBR
NY	156	107	47	.695		1002	724	5477	1564	279	82	160	766	527	.286	.376	.454	.830	128	172	225	95	99	961	77	66	54	-17
PHI	154	94	60	.610	13	981	752	5537	1606	303	52	172	647	630	.290	.366	.457	.823	115	148	113	104	100	951	38	23	62	-2
WAS	154	93	61	.604	14	840	716	5515	1565	303	100	61	505	442	.284	.347	.408	.755	102	8	19	99	103	793	70	47	60	-7
CLE	153	87	65	.572	19	845	747	5412	1544	310	74	78	566	454	.285	.357	.413	.770	99	44	-11	107	99	811	52	54	49	-17
DET	153	76	75	.503	29.5	799	787	5409	1479	291	80	80	486	523	.273	.335	.401	.736	92	-35	-65	104	106	741	103	49	68	2
STL	154	63	91	.409	44	736	898	5449	1502	274	69	67	507	528	.276	.339	.388	.727	89	-45	-88	106	97	726	69	62	53	-17
CHI	152	49	102	.325	56.5	667	897	5336	1426	274	56	36	459	386	.267	.327	.360	.687	90	-122	-80	94	101	642	89	58	61	-8
BOS	154	43	111	.279	64	566	915	5295	1331	253	57	53	469	539	.251	.314	.351	.665	80	-171	-154	97	94	593	46	46	50	-14
TOT	615					6436		43430	12017	2287	570	707	4405	4029	.277	.346	.404	.750							544	405	57	-80

TEAM	CG	SH	SV	IP	H	H/G	HR	BB	SO	RAT	ERA	ERA+	OAV	OOB	PR	/A	PF	CPI	FA	E	DP	FW	PW	BW	SBW	DIF
NY	96	11	15	1408	1425	9.1	93	561	780	12.8	3.98	102	.260	.331	78	15	91	101	.969	188	124	.2	1.4	20.8	-.6	8.3
PHI	95	10	10	1386	1477	9.6	112	511	595	13.0	4.45	102	.271	.336	4	11	101	98	.979	124	142	3.8	1.0	10.4	.7	1.0
WAS	66	11	22	1383[1]	1463	9.5	73	526	437	13.0	4.16	104	.271	.337	49	24	96	100	.979	125	157	3.8	2.2	1.8	.3	8.0
CLE	94	6	8	1377[1]	1506	9.8	70	446	439	12.8	4.12	115	.273	.329	55	96	106	98	.969	191	129	-.2	8.9	-1.0	-.6	4.0
DET	67	9	17	1362[2]	1421	9.4	89	592	521	13.5	4.30	109	.269	.346	27	61	105	102	.969	187	154	.0	5.6	-6.0	1.1	-.3
STL	63	7	11	1376[2]	1592	10.4	103	574	496	14.3	5.01	97	.290	.359	-81	-24	108	100	.969	188	156	.0	-2.2	-8.1	-.6	-3.0
CHI	50	2	12	1348[2]	1551	10.4	88	580	379	14.4	4.82	90	.287	.359	-52	-75	97	101	.958	264	170	-4.6	-6.9	-7.4	.2	-7.8
BOS	42	3	7	1362	1574	10.4	79	612	365	14.6	5.02	90	.289	.364	-81	-79	100	99	.963	233	165	-2.6	-7.3	-14.2	-.4	-9.5
TOT	573	59	102	11004[2]		9.8				13.6	4.48		.277	.346					.969	1500	1197					

Runs
Foxx-Phi 151
Simmons-Phi 144
Combs-NY 143
Gehrig-NY 138
Manush-Was 121

Hits
Simmons-Phi 216
Manush-Was 214
Foxx-Phi 213
Gehrig-NY 208
Averill-Cle 198

Doubles
McNair-Phi 47
Gehringer-Det 44
Cronin-Was 43

Triples
Cronin-Was 18
Myer-Was 16
Lazzeri-NY 16
Chapman-NY 15

Home Runs
Foxx-Phi 58
Ruth-NY 41
Simmons-Phi 35
Gehrig-NY 34
Averill-Cle 32

Total Bases
Foxx-Phi 438
Gehrig-NY 370
Simmons-Phi 367
Averill-Cle 359
Manush-Was 325

Runs Batted In
Foxx-Phi 169
Simmons-Phi 151
Gehrig-NY 151
Ruth-NY 137
Averill-Cle 124

Runs Produced
Foxx-Phi 262
Simmons-Phi 260
Gehrig-NY 255
Manush-Was 223
Ruth-NY 216

Bases On Balls
Ruth-NY 130
Foxx-Phi 116
Bishop-Phi 110
Gehrig-NY 108
Cochrane-Phi 100

Batting Average
Alexander-Det-Bos 367
Foxx-Phi 364
Gehrig-NY 349
Manush-Was 342
Ruth-NY 341

On Base Percentage
Ruth-NY 489
Foxx-Phi 469
Gehrig-NY 451
Bishop-Phi 412
Cochrane-Phi 412

Slugging Average
Foxx-Phi 749
Ruth-NY 661
Gehrig-NY 621
Averill-Cle 569
Simmons-Phi 548

Production
Foxx-Phi 1.218
Ruth-NY 1.150
Gehrig-NY 1.072
Averill-Cle 961
Cochrane-Phi 921

Adjusted Production
Ruth-NY 206
Foxx-Phi 203
Gehrig-NY 184
Lazzeri-NY 140
Averill-Cle 137

Batter Runs
Foxx-Phi 96.7
Ruth-NY 71.2
Gehrig-NY 68.6
Averill-Cle 41.1
Alexander-Det-Bos . . 31.8

Adjusted Batter Runs
Foxx-Phi 90.0
Ruth-NY 79.2
Gehrig-NY 77.2
Alexander-Det-Bos . . 33.3
Averill-Cle 32.5

Clutch Hitting Index
Dykes-Phi 124
Cronin-Was 121
Kamm-Phi 119
Lazzeri-NY 118
Davis-Det 114

Runs Created
Foxx-Phi 207
Gehrig-NY 168
Ruth-NY 157
Averill-Cle 140
Simmons-Phi 134

Total Average
Foxx-Phi 1.451
Ruth-NY 1.432
Gehrig-NY 1.188
Cochrane-Phi 1.000
Averill-Cle 991

Stolen Bases
Chapman-NY 38
Walker-Det 30
Johnson-Det-Bos . . 20
Cissell-Chi-Cle . . . 18

Stolen Base Average
Walker-Det 83.3
Johnson-Det-Bos . . 76.9
Blue-Chi 73.9
Chapman-NY 67.9
Burns-StL 60.7

Stolen Base Runs
Walker-Det 5.4
Johnson-Det-Bos . . 2.4
Blue-Chi 1.5

Fielding Runs
Warstler-Bos 27.9
Vosmik-Cle 23.8
West-Was 19.3
Appling-Chi 18.1
Kress-StL-Chi 12.8

Total Player Rating
Foxx-Phi 6.5
Ruth-NY 5.8
Gehrig-NY 4.9
Cochrane-Phi 4.1
Cronin-Was 3.9

Wins
Crowder-Was 26
Grove-Phi 25
Gomez-NY 24
Ferrell-Cle 23
Weaver-Was 22

Win Percentage
Allen-NY 810
Gomez-NY 774
Ruffing-NY 720
Grove-Phi 714
Weaver-Was 688

Games
Marberry-Was 54
Gray-StL 52
Crowder-Was 50

Complete Games
Grove-Phi 27
Ferrell-Cle 26
Ruffing-NY 22

Shutouts
Grove-Phi 4
Bridges-Det 4

Saves
Marberry-Was 13
Moore-Bos-NY 8
Hogsett-Det 7
Grove-Phi 7
Faber-Chi 6

Innings Pitched
Crowder-Was 327.0
Grove-Phi 291.2
Ferrell-Cle 287.2
Walberg-Phi 272.0
Gomez-NY 265.1

Fewest Hits/Game
Allen-NY 7.59
Ruffing-NY 7.61
Bridges-Det 7.79
Grove-Phi 8.30
Crowder-Was 8.78

Fewest BB/Game
Brown-Cle 1.71
Crowder-Was 2.12
Gray-StL 2.31
Harder-Cle 2.40
Grove-Phi 2.44

Strikeouts
Ruffing-NY 190
Grove-Phi 188
Gomez-NY 176
Hadley-Chi-StL . . . 145
Pipgras-NY 111

Strikeouts/Game
Ruffing-NY 6.60
Gomez-NY 5.97
Grove-Phi 5.80
Hadley-Chi-StL . . . 5.26
Allen-NY 5.11

Ratio
Grove-Phi 10.77
Crowder-Was 10.90
Allen-NY 11.39
Ruffing-NY 11.71
Sorrell-Det 12.06

Earned Run Average
Grove-Phi 2.84
Ruffing-NY 3.09
Lyons-Chi 3.28
Crowder-Was 3.33
Bridges-Det 3.36

Adjusted ERA
Grove-Phi 159
Bridges-Det 140
Hogsett-Det 133
Lyons-Chi 132
Ruffing-NY 132

Opponents' Batting Avg.
Ruffing-NY 226
Allen-NY 228
Bridges-Det 233
Grove-Phi 241
Crowder-Was 252

Opponents' On Base Pct.
Grove-Phi 292
Crowder-Was 295
Allen-NY 306
Ruffing-NY 311
Brown-Cle 314

Starter Runs
Grove-Phi 53.2
Crowder-Was 41.7
Ruffing-NY 39.9
Lyons-Chi 30.8
Ferrell-Cle 26.2

Adjusted Starter Runs
Grove-Phi 54.6
Crowder-Was 35.7
Ferrell-Cle 34.6
Bridges-Det 30.0
Ruffing-NY 28.3

Clutch Pitching Index
Hogsett-Det 129
Lyons-Chi 120
Weiland-Bos 117
Bridges-Det 116
Gaston-Chi 115

Relief Runs
Faber-Chi 8.8
Kimsey-StL-Chi . . . 6.5

Adjusted Relief Runs
Kimsey-StL-Chi . . . 9.5
Faber-Chi 7.0

Relief Ranking
Kimsey-StL-Chi . . . 8.9
Faber-Chi 8.6

Total Pitcher Index
Grove-Phi 5.9
Ferrell-Cle 4.3
Ruffing-NY 3.5
Crowder-Was 3.5
Bridges-Det 3.2

Total Baseball Ranking
Foxx-Phi 6.5
Grove-Phi 5.9
Ruth-NY 5.8
Gehrig-NY 4.9
Ferrell-Cle 4.3

TEAM	G	W	L	PCT	GB	R	OR	AB	H	2B	3B	HR	BB	SO	AVG	OBP	SLG	PRO	PRO+	BR	/A	PF	CHI	RC	SB	CS	SBA	SBR
NY	156	91	61	.599		636	515	5461	1437	204	41	82	377	477	.263	.312	.361	.673	100	-14	-4	98	104	667	31			
PIT	154	87	67	.565	5	667	619	5429	1548	249	84	39	366	334	.285	.333	.383	.716	111	71	72	100	96	750	34			
CHI	154	86	68	.558	6	646	536	5255	1422	256	51	72	392	475	.271	.325	.380	.705	107	47	49	100	99	705	52			
BOS	156	83	71	.539	9	552	531	5243	1320	217	56	54	326	428	.252	.299	.345	.644	98	-70	-27	92	104	588	25			
STL	154	82	71	.536	9.5	687	609	5387	1486	256	61	57	391	528	.276	.329	.378	.707	103	53	18	96	102	726	99			
BRO	157	65	88	.425	26.5	617	695	5367	1413	224	51	62	397	453	.263	.316	.359	.675	103	-8	18	96	101	662	82			
PHI	152	60	92	.395	31	607	760	5261	1439	240	41	60	381	479	.274	.326	.369	.695	93	32	-49	113	95	689	55			
CIN	153	58	94	.382	33	496	643	5156	1267	208	37	34	349	354	.246	.298	.320	.618	83	-111	-104	99	103	540	30			
TOT	618					4908		42559	11332	1854	422	460	2979	3528	.266	.317	.362	.679							408			

TEAM	CG	SH	SV	IP	H	H/G	HR	BB	SO	RAT	ERA	ERA+	OAV	OOB	PR	/A	PF	CPI	FA	E	DP	FW	PW	BW	SBW	DIF
NY	75	23	15	1408²	1280	8.2	61	400	555	10.9	2.71	118	.242	.299	98	78	96	102	.973	178	156	-.5	8.3	-.4		7.6
PIT	70	16	12	1373¹	1417	9.3	54	313	401	11.5	3.27	101	.264	.308	10	7	99	95	.972	166	133	.2	.7	7.6		1.5
CHI	95	16	9	1362	1316	8.7	51	413	488	11.6	2.93	112	.254	.312	62	52	98	105	.973	168	163	.0	5.5	5.2		-1.7
BOS	85	15	16	1403	1391	8.9	54	355	383	11.3	2.96	103	.261	.309	58	14	92	105	.978	138	148	2.1	1.5	-2.9		5.2
STL	73	11	16	1382²	1391	9.1	55	452	635	12.1	3.37	103	.261	.321	-5	16	104	98	.973	162	119	.4	1.7	1.9		1.5
BRO	71	9	10	1386¹	1502	9.8	51	374	415	12.4	3.73	86	.275	.326	-60	-79	96	95	.971	177	120	-.3	-8.4	1.9		-4.7
PHI	52	10	13	1336²	1563	10.5	87	410	341	13.6	4.34	88	.293	.348	-150	-79	114	101	.970	183	156	-1.1	-8.4	-5.2		-1.4
CIN	74	13	8	1352	1470	9.8	47	257	310	11.6	3.42	99	.279	.314	-13	-5	102	99	.971	177	139	-.6	-.5	-11.0		-5.8
TOT	595	113	99	11004²		9.3				11.9	3.34		.266	.317					.973	1349	1134					

Runs		Hits		Doubles		Triples		Home Runs		Total Bases	
Martin-StL	122	Klein-Phi	223	Klein-Phi	44	Vaughan-Pit	19	Klein-Phi	28	Klein-Phi	365
P.Waner-Pit	101	Fullis-Phi	200	Medwick-StL	40	P.Waner-Pit	16	Berger-Bos	27	Berger-Bos	299
Klein-Phi	101	P.Waner-Pit	191	Lindstrom-Pit	39	Martin-StL	12	Ott-NY	23	Medwick-StL	296
Ott-NY	98	Traynor-Pit	190	P.Waner-Pit	38	B.Herman-Chi	12	Medwick-StL	18	P.Waner-Pit	282
Medwick-StL	92	Martin-StL	189	Berger-Bos	37					Vaughan-Pit	274

Runs Batted In		Runs Produced		Bases On Balls		Batting Average		On Base Percentage		Slugging Average	
Klein-Phi	120	Klein-Phi	193	Ott-NY	75	Klein-Phi	.368	Klein-Phi	.422	Klein-Phi	.602
Berger-Bos	106	Ott-NY	178	Suhr-Pit	72	Davis-Phi	.349	Davis-Phi	.395	Berger-Bos	.566
Ott-NY	103	Vaughan-Pit	173	Martin-StL	67	Stephenson-Chi	.329	Vaughan-Pit	.388	B.Herman-Chi	.502
Medwick-StL	98	Medwick-StL	172	Vaughan-Pit	64	Piet-Pit	.323	Martin-StL	.387	Medwick-StL	.497
Vaughan-Pit	97	Martin-StL	171	P.Waner-Pit	60	Terry-NY	.322	Terry-NY	.375	Vaughan-Pit	.478

Production		Adjusted Production		Batter Runs		Adjusted Batter Runs		Clutch Hitting Index		Runs Created	
Klein-Phi	1.025	Berger-Bos	177	Klein-Phi	69.1	Klein-Phi	52.4	Hartnett-Chi	120	Klein-Phi	162
Berger-Bos	.932	Klein-Phi	168	Berger-Bos	40.5	Berger-Bos	49.0	Traynor-Pit	119	Berger-Bos	113
Davis-Phi	.867	Vaughan-Pit	146	Vaughan-Pit	35.2	Vaughan-Pit	35.4	Rice-Cin	117	Vaughan-Pit	112
Vaughan-Pit	.866	B.Herman-Chi	142	Martin-StL	32.3	Ott-NY	29.9	Ott-NY	114	Martin-StL	111
B.Herman-Chi	.855	Ott-NY	139	Davis-Phi	29.8	P.Waner-Pit	28.9	Bottomley-Cin	111	P.Waner-Pit	109

Total Average		Stolen Bases		Stolen Base Average	Stolen Base Runs	Fielding Runs		Total Player Rating	
Klein-Phi	1.132	Martin-StL	26			Critz-NY	46.5	Klein-Phi	5.5
Berger-Bos	.935	Fullis-Phi	18			B.Herman-Chi	29.1	Berger-Bos	4.7
Martin-StL	.881	Frisch-StL	18			Jurges-Chi	20.1	Vaughan-Pit	3.8
Vaughan-Pit	.861	Klein-Phi	15			Lopez-Bro	18.4	B.Herman-Chi	3.5
B.Herman-Chi	.827	Orsatti-StL	14			Ryan-NY	17.4	Martin-StL	3.5

Wins		Win Percentage		Games		Complete Games		Shutouts		Saves	
Hubbell-NY	23	Cantwell-Bos	.667	Dean-StL	48	Warneke-Chi	26	Hubbell-NY	10	Collins-Phi	6
Dean-StL	20	Hubbell-NY	.657	French-Pit	47	Dean-StL	26	Schumacher-NY	7	Hubbell-NY	5
Cantwell-Bos	20	Meine-Pit	.652	Liska-Pit	45	Brandt-Bos	23	French-Pit	5	Harris-Pit	5
Bush-Chi	20	Bush-Chi	.625	Hubbell-NY	45	Hubbell-NY	22			Bell-NY	5
Schumacher-NY	19	Schumacher-NY	.613	Carleton-StL	44						

Innings Pitched		Fewest Hits/Game		Fewest BB/Game		Strikeouts		Strikeouts/Game		Ratio	
Hubbell-NY	308.2	Schumacher-NY	6.92	Lucas-Cin	.74	Dean-StL	199	Dean-StL	6.11	Hubbell-NY	8.92
Dean-StL	293.0	Hubbell-NY	7.46	Hubbell-NY	1.37	Hubbell-NY	156	Parmelee-NY	5.44	Schumacher-NY	9.88
French-Pit	291.1	Parmelee-NY	7.87	Swift-Pit	1.48	Carleton-StL	147	Carleton-StL	4.78	Betts-Bos	10.41
Brandt-Bos	287.2	Brandt-Bos	8.01	Hansen-Phi	1.60	Warneke-Chi	133	Hubbell-NY	4.55	Swift-Pit	10.47
Warneke-Chi	287.1	Mungo-Bro	8.09	French-Pit	1.70	Parmelee-NY	132	Warneke-Chi	4.17	Brandt-Bos	10.51

Earned Run Average		Adjusted ERA		Opponents' Batting Avg.		Opponents' On Base Pct.		Starter Runs		Adjusted Starter Runs	
Hubbell-NY	1.66	Hubbell-NY	193	Schumacher-NY	.214	Hubbell-NY	.260	Hubbell-NY	57.4	Hubbell-NY	53.1
Warneke-Chi	2.00	Warneke-Chi	163	Hubbell-NY	.227	Schumacher-NY	.280	Warneke-Chi	42.5	Warneke-Chi	40.4
Schumacher-NY	2.16	Schumacher-NY	149	Parmelee-NY	.232	Swift-Pit	.285	Schumacher-NY	33.9	Schumacher-NY	30.2
Brandt-Bos	2.60	Root-Chi	126	Mungo-Bro	.236	Betts-Bos	.290	Brandt-Bos	23.6	French-Pit	19.3
Root-Chi	2.60	French-Pit	122	Warneke-Chi	.244	Cantwell-Bos	.291	Cantwell-Bos	20.4	Root-Chi	18.0

Clutch Pitching Index		Relief Runs		Adjusted Relief Runs		Relief Ranking		Total Pitcher Index		Total Baseball Ranking	
Warneke-Chi	131	Bell-NY	15.0	Bell-NY	13.6	Bell-NY	14.2	Hubbell-NY	7.5	Hubbell-NY	7.5
Root-Chi	120	Luque-NY	5.8	Luque-NY	4.6	Luque-NY	5.7	Warneke-Chi	6.2	Warneke-Chi	6.2
Walker-StL	117	Harris-Pit	.7	Harris-Pit	.6	Harris-Pit	.9	Schumacher-NY	4.2	Klein-Phi	5.5
Holley-Phi	115							Brandt-Bos	2.7	Berger-Bos	4.7
Hubbell-NY	112							Bush-Chi	2.1	Schumacher-NY	4.2

TEAM	G	W	L	PCT	GB	R	OR	AB	H	2B	3B	HR	BB	SO	AVG	OBP	SLG	PRO	PRO+	BR	/A	PF	CHI	RC	SB	CS	SBA	SBR
WAS	153	99	53	.651		850	665	5524	1586	281	86	60	539	395	.287	.353	.402	.755	107	47	56	99	102	798	65	50	57	-11
NY	152	91	59	.607	7	927	768	5274	1495	241	75	144	700		.283	.369	.440	.809	129	155	211	94	100	880	76	59	56	-13
PHI	152	79	72	.523	19.5	875	853	5330	1519	297	57	139	625	618	.285	.362	.440	.802	118	135	126	101	97	868	34	34	50	-10
CLE	151	75	76	.497	23.5	654	669	5240	1366	218	77	50	448	426	.261	.321	.360	.681	82	-103	-132	105	103	616	36	40	47	-13
DET	155	75	79	.487	25	722	733	5502	1479	283	78	57	475	523	.269	.329	.380	.709	92	-54	-68	102	101	698	68	50	58	-10
CHI	151	67	83	.447	31	683	814	5318	1448	231	53	43	538	416	.272	.342	.360	.702	96	-50	-20	96	96	674	43	46	48	-15
BOS	149	63	86	.423	34.5	700	758	5201	1407	294	56	50	525	464	.271	.339	.377	.716	97	-29	-22	99	98	687	58	37	61	-5
STL	153	55	96	.364	43.5	669	820	5285	1337	244	64	64	520	556	.253	.322	.360	.682	81	-102	-143	106	103	625	72	60	55	-14
TOT	608					6080		42674	11637	2089	546	607	4370	3904	.273	.342	.390	.732							452	376	55	-90

TEAM	CG	SH	SV	IP	H	H/G	HR	BB	SO	RAT	ERA	ERA+	OAV	OOB	PR	/A	PF	CPI	FA	E	DP	FW	PW	BW	SBW	DIF
WAS	68	5	26	1389²	1415	9.2	64	452	447	12.2	3.82	109	.263	.322	71	56	98	98	.979	131	149	2.6	5.3	5.3	.0	9.8
NY	70	8	22	1354²	1426	9.5	66	612	711	13.6	4.36	89	.267	.344	-13	-72	91	96	.972	165	122	.4	-6.8	20.0	-.2	2.6
PHI	69	6	14	1343²	1523	10.2	77	644	423	14.6	4.81	89	.283	.361	-79	-78	100	99	.966	203	121	-1.9	-7.4	11.9	.1	.8
CLE	74	12	7	1350	1382	9.2	60	465	437	12.4	3.71	120	.264	.325	86	111	104	102	.974	156	127	.9	10.5	-12.5	-.2	.8
DET	69	6	17	1398	1415	9.1	84	561	575	12.9	3.95	109	.263	.335	52	57	101	103	.971	178	167	-.2	5.4	-6.4	.1	-.9
CHI	53	8	13	1371¹	1505	9.9	85	519	423	13.5	4.45	95	.277	.343	-26	-32	99	99	.970	186	143	-1.0	-3.0	-1.9	-.4	-1.8
BOS	60	4	14	1327²	1396	9.5	75	591	467	13.6	4.35	101	.271	.348	-10	4	102	100	.966	204	133	-2.2	.4	-2.1	.6	-8.2
STL	55	7	10	1360²	1574	10.4	96	531	426	14.0	4.82	97	.289	.354	-82	-25	109	100	.976	149	162	1.5	-2.4	-13.5	-.3	-5.8
TOT	518	56	123	10895²		9.6				13.3	4.28		.273	.342					.972	1372	1124					

Runs
Gehrig-NY 138
Foxx-Phi 125
Manush-Was 115
Chapman-NY 112
Cramer-Phi 109

Hits
Manush-Was 221
Gehringer-Det 204
Foxx-Phi 204
Simmons-Chi 200
Gehrig-NY 198

Doubles
Cronin-Was 45
Johnson-Phi 44
Burns-StL 43
Rogell-Det 42
Gehringer-Det 42

Triples
Manush-Was 17
Combs-NY 16
Averill-Cle 16
Myer-Was 15
Reynolds-StL 14

Home Runs
Foxx-Phi 48
Ruth-NY 34
Gehrig-NY 32
Johnson-Phi 21
Lazzeri-NY 18

Total Bases
Foxx-Phi 403
Gehrig-NY 359
Manush-Was 302
Gehringer-Det 294
Simmons-Chi 291

Runs Batted In
Foxx-Phi 163
Gehrig-NY 139
Simmons-Chi 119
Cronin-Was 118
Kuhel-Was 107

Runs Produced
Gehrig-NY 245
Foxx-Phi 240
Manush-Was 205
Cronin-Was 202
Chapman-NY 201

Bases On Balls
Ruth-NY 114
Cochrane-Phi 106
Bishop-Phi 106
Foxx-Phi 96
Swanson-Chi 93

Batting Average
Foxx-Phi 356
Manush-Was 336
Gehrig-NY 334
Simmons-Chi 331
Gehringer-Det 325

On Base Percentage
Cochrane-Phi 459
Foxx-Phi 449
Bishop-Phi 446
Ruth-NY 442
Gehrig-NY 424

Slugging Average
Foxx-Phi 703
Gehrig-NY 605
Ruth-NY 582
Cochrane-Phi 515
Johnson-Phi 505

Production
Foxx-Phi 1.153
Gehrig-NY 1.030
Ruth-NY 1.023
Cochrane-Phi 974
Johnson-Phi 892

Adjusted Production
Foxx-Phi 199
Gehrig-NY 181
Ruth-NY 180
Cochrane-Phi 156
Dickey-NY 138

Batter Runs
Foxx-Phi 82.7
Gehrig-NY 59.5
Ruth-NY 49.5
Cochrane-Phi 41.6
Johnson-Phi 26.8

Adjusted Batter Runs
Foxx-Phi 81.0
Gehrig-NY 68.5
Ruth-NY 57.1
Cochrane-Phi 40.5
Lazzeri-NY 27.7

Clutch Hitting Index
Cronin-Was 126
Melillo-StL 125
Ferrell-StL-Bos 124
Bluege-Was 123
Kress-Chi 121

Runs Created
Foxx-Phi 184
Gehrig-NY 151
Ruth-NY 124
Gehringer-Det 117
Manush-Was 111

Total Average
Foxx-Phi 1.348
Ruth-NY 1.172
Cochrane-Phi 1.118
Gehrig-NY 1.098
Johnson-Phi 940

Stolen Bases
Chapman-NY 27
Walker-Det 26
Swanson-Chi 19
Kuhel-Was 17

Stolen Base Average
Walker-Det 74.3
Kuhel-Was 68.0
Swanson-Chi 63.3
Chapman-NY 60.0

Stolen Base Runs
Walker-Det 2.4
Werber-NY-Bos . . . 1.5
Stumpf-Bos 1.2

Fielding Runs
Melillo-StL 23.3
Rogell-Det 19.5
Schulte-Was 15.8
Simmons-Chi 14.3
Scharein-StL 14.0

Total Player Rating
Foxx-Phi 6.7
Gehrig-NY 4.3
Cronin-Was 4.0
Ruth-NY 3.8
Cochrane-Phi 3.7

Wins
Grove-Phi 24
Crowder-Was 24
Whitehill-Was 22

Win Percentage
Grove-Phi 750
Whitehill-Was 733
Stewart-Was 714
Allen-NY 682

Games
Crowder-Was 52
Russell-Was 50
Welch-Bos 47
Kline-Bos 46

Complete Games
Grove-Phi 21
Whitehill-Was 19
Hadley-StL 19
Ruffing-NY 18

Shutouts
Hildebrand-Cle 6
Gomez-NY 4
Blaeholder-StL 3

Saves
Russell-Was 13
Hogsett-Det 9
Moore-NY 8
Heving-Chi 6
Grove-Phi 6

Innings Pitched
Hadley-StL 316.2
Crowder-Was 299.1
Grove-Phi 275.1
Whitehill-Was 270.0
Blaeholder-StL . . . 255.2

Fewest Hits/Game
Bridges-Det 7.42
Weiland-Bos 8.20
Allen-NY 8.33
Gomez-NY 8.36
Hildebrand-Cle . . . 8.37

Fewest BB/Game
Brown-Cle 1.65
Marberry-Det 2.30
Stewart-Was 2.34
Harder-Cle 2.38
Blaeholder-StL 2.43

Strikeouts
Gomez-NY 163
Hadley-StL 149
Ruffing-NY 122
Bridges-Det 120
Allen-NY 119

Strikeouts/Game
Gomez-NY 6.25
Allen-NY 5.80
Ruffing-NY 4.67
Bridges-Det 4.64
Fischer-Det 4.58

Ratio
Marberry-Det 11.10
Stewart-Was 11.24
Harder-Cle 11.53
Brown-Cle 11.58
Weaver-Was 11.88

Earned Run Average
Harder-Cle 2.95
Bridges-Det 3.09
Gomez-NY 3.18
Grove-Phi 3.20
Weaver-Was 3.25

Adjusted ERA
Harder-Cle 151
Bridges-Det 140
Grove-Phi 134
Marberry-Det 131
Brown-Cle 130

Opponents' Batting Avg.
Bridges-Det 226
Gomez-NY 240
Allen-NY 242
Weiland-Bos 244
Hildebrand-Cle 245

Opponents' On Base Pct.
Marberry-Det 302
Stewart-Was 304
Harder-Cle 309
Brown-Cle 310
Grove-Phi 316

Starter Runs
Harder-Cle 37.4
Grove-Phi 33.0
Bridges-Det 30.8
Pearson-Cle 29.4
Gomez-NY 28.6

Adjusted Starter Runs
Harder-Cle 41.9
Grove-Phi 33.1
Pearson-Cle 31.8
Bridges-Det 31.6
Marberry-Det 27.2

Clutch Pitching Index
Cain-Phi 125
Jones-Chi 124
Harder-Cle 115
Whitehill-Was 112
Grove-Phi 111

Relief Runs
Russell-Was 22.0
Heving-Chi 21.1
Faber-Chi 8.1
Burke-Was 7.4
Herring-Det 3.0

Adjusted Relief Runs
Russell-Was 20.6
Heving-Chi 20.6
Faber-Chi 7.7
Gray-StL 6.9
Burke-Was 6.7

Relief Ranking
Russell-Was 31.8
Heving-Chi 21.2
Gray-StL 6.7
Burke-Was 6.6
Faber-Chi 6.6

Total Pitcher Index
Harder-Cle 5.7
Bridges-Det 3.5
Russell-Was 3.4
Pearson-Cle 3.3
Grove-Phi 2.9

Total Baseball Ranking
Foxx-Phi 6.7
Harder-Cle 5.7
Gehrig-NY 4.3
Cronin-Was 4.0
Ruth-NY 3.8

TEAM	G	W	L	PCT	GB	R	OR	AB	H	2B	3B	HR	BB	SO	AVG	OBP	SLG	PRO	PRO+	BR	/A	PF	CHI	RC	SB	CS	SBA	SBR
STL	154	95	58	.621		**799**	656	5502	**1582**	294	75	104	392	535	**.288**	.337	**.425**	**.762**	102	63	12	107	101	**796**	69			
NY	153	93	60	.608	2	760	**583**	5396	1485	240	41	**126**	406	526	.275	.329	.405	.734	105	8	25	98	**105**	736	19			
CHI	152	86	65	.570	8	705	639	5347	1494	263	44	101	375	630	.279	.330	.402	.732	103	5	19	98	99	719	59			
BOS	152	78	73	.517	16	683	714	5370	1460	233	44	83	375	440	.272	.323	.378	.701	101	-52	-3	93	104	660	30			
PIT	151	74	76	.493	19.5	735	713	5361	1541	281	**77**	52	440	**398**	.287	.344	.398	.742	102	34	17	102	99	742	44			
BRO	153	71	81	.467	23.5	748	795	5427	1526	284	52	79	**548**	555	.281	**.350**	.396	.746	**112**	51	**90**	95	95	782	55			
PHI	149	56	93	.376	37	675	794	5218	1480	286	35	56	398	534	.284	.338	.384	.722	87	-3	-95	113	98	685	52			
CIN	152	52	99	.344	42	590	801	5361	1428	227	65	55	313	532	.266	.311	.364	.675	88	-105	-91	98	99	603	34			
TOT	608					5695		42982	11996	2108	433	656	3247	4150	.279	.333	.394	.727							362			

TEAM	CG	SH	SV	IP	H	H/G	HR	BB	SO	RAT	ERA	ERA+	OAV	OOB	PR	/A	PF	CPI	FA	E	DP	FW	PW	BW	SBW	DIF
STL	**78**	**15**	16	1386²	1463	9.5	77	411	**689**	12.4	3.69	115	.268	.323	58	83	104	101	.972	166	**141**	.3	8.1	1.2		8.9
NY	68	13	**30**	1370	**1384**	**9.1**	75	351	499	11.5	**3.19**	121	**.260**	**.308**	132	102	95	105	.972	179	**141**	-.5	9.9	2.4		4.6
CHI	73	11	9	1361¹	1432	9.5	80	417	633	12.3	3.76	103	.269	.325	46	18	95	101	**.977**	**137**	135	**1.9**	1.8	1.9		5.0
BOS	62	12	20	1359²	1512	10.0	78	405	462	12.8	4.11	93	.279	.331	-7	-44	94	97	.972	169	120	.0	-4.3	-.3		7.1
PIT	63	8	8	1329¹	1523	10.3	78	354	487	12.9	4.20	98	.284	.332	-20	-13	101	98	.975	145	118	1.4	-1.3	1.7		-2.8
BRO	66	6	12	1354¹	1540	10.2	81	475	520	13.6	4.48	87	.285	.346	-63	-87	96	97	.970	180	**141**	-.6	-8.5	**8.8**		-4.7
PHI	52	8	15	1297	1501	10.4	126	437	416	13.6	4.76	99	.288	.347	-101	-4	116	99	.966	197	140	-1.8	-.4	-9.3		-7.0
CIN	51	3	19	1347²	1645	11.0	**61**	389	438	13.8	4.37	93	.299	.348	-46	-43	101	102	.970	181	136	-.7	-4.2	-8.9		-9.8
TOT	513	76	129	10806¹		10.0				12.9	4.06		.279	.333					.972	1354	1072					

Runs		Hits		Doubles		Triples		Home Runs		Total Bases	
P.Waner-Pit	122	P.Waner-Pit	217	Cuyler-Chi	42	Medwick-StL	18	Ott-NY	35	Collins-StL	369
Ott-NY	119	Terry-NY	213	Allen-Phi	42	P.Waner-Pit	16	Collins-StL	35	Ott-NY	344
Collins-StL	116	Collins-StL	200	Vaughan-Pit	41	Suhr-Pit	13	Berger-Bos	34	Berger-Bos	336
Vaughan-Pit	115	Medwick-StL	198	Medwick-StL	40	Collins-StL	12	Hartnett-Chi	22	Medwick-StL	328
Medwick-StL	110			Collins-StL	40			Klein-Chi	20	P.Waner-Pit	323

Runs Batted In		Runs Produced		Bases On Balls		Batting Average		On Base Percentage		Slugging Average	
Ott-NY	135	Ott-NY	219	Vaughan-Pit	94	P.Waner-Pit	.362	Vaughan-Pit	.431	Collins-StL	.615
Collins-StL	128	Collins-StL	209	Ott-NY	85	Terry-NY	.354	P.Waner-Pit	.429	Ott-NY	.591
Berger-Bos	121	P.Waner-Pit	198	Koenecke-Bro	70	Cuyler-Chi	.338	Ott-NY	.415	DeLancey-StL	.565
Medwick-StL	106	Medwick-StL	198	Leslie-Bro	69	Vaughan-Pit	.333	Terry-NY	.414	Berger-Bos	.546
Suhr-Pit	103	Vaughan-Pit	197	P.Waner-Pit	68	Collins-StL	.333	Koenecke-Bro	.411	P.Waner-Pit	.539

Production		Adjusted Production		Batter Runs		Adjusted Batter Runs		Clutch Hitting Index		Runs Created	
Collins-StL	1.008	Ott-NY	170	Ott-NY	55.2	Ott-NY	58.5	Thevenow-Pit	133	Ott-NY	150
Ott-NY	1.006	Collins-StL	155	Collins-StL	53.3	P.Waner-Pit	47.2	Durocher-StL	132	Collins-StL	148
P.Waner-Pit	.968	P.Waner-Pit	154	P.Waner-Pit	50.2	Collins-StL	44.9	Leslie-Bro	126	P.Waner-Pit	142
Vaughan-Pit	.942	Koenecke-Bro	152	Vaughan-Pit	44.3	Vaughan-Pit	41.5	Jackson-NY	124	Vaughan-Pit	135
Koenecke-Bro	.919	Berger-Bos	148	Terry-NY	31.5	Berger-Bos	37.7	Cuccinello-Bro	124	Terry-NY	122

Total Average		Stolen Bases		Stolen Base Average		Stolen Base Runs		Fielding Runs		Total Player Rating	
Ott-NY	1.075	Martin-StL	23					Critz-NY	25.0	Vaughan-Pit	5.1
Collins-StL	1.046	Cuyler-Chi	15					K.Davis-StL-Phi	17.8	P.Waner-Pit	4.6
Vaughan-Pit	1.043	Bartell-Phi	13					B.Herman-Chi	15.6	Ott-NY	4.1
P.Waner-Pit	1.010	Taylor-Bro	12					Bartell-Phi	13.5	Collins-StL	3.8
Koenecke-Bro	.981							Hartnett-Chi	13.5	Hartnett-Chi	3.5

Wins		Win Percentage		Games		Complete Games		Shutouts		Saves	
D.Dean-StL	30	D.Dean-StL	.811	C.Davis-Phi	51	Hubbell-NY	25	D.Dean-StL	7	Hubbell-NY	8
Schumacher-NY	23	Hoyt-Pit	.714	Hansen-Phi	50	D.Dean-StL	24	Hubbell-NY	5	Luque-NY	7
Warneke-Chi	22	Schumacher-NY	.697	D.Dean-StL	50	Warneke-Chi	23	P.Dean-StL	5	D.Dean-StL	7
Hubbell-NY	21	Warneke-Chi	.688	Hubbell-NY	49	Mungo-Bro	22	Lee-Chi	4	Bell-NY	6
		Frankhouse-Bos	.654	French-Pit	49	Brandt-Bos	20				

Innings Pitched		Fewest Hits/Game		Fewest BB/Game		Strikeouts		Strikeouts/Game		Ratio	
Mungo-Bro	315.1	Parmelee-NY	7.90	Hubbell-NY	1.06	D.Dean-StL	195	P.Dean-StL	5.79	Hubbell-NY	9.35
Hubbell-NY	313.0	Hubbell-NY	8.22	Freitas-Cin	1.47	Mungo-Bro	184	D.Dean-StL	5.63	Warneke-Chi	10.53
D.Dean-StL	311.2	D.Dean-StL	8.32	Frey-Cin	1.54	P.Dean-StL	150	Weaver-Chi	5.55	D.Dean-StL	10.66
Schumacher-NY	297.0	Warneke-Chi	8.43	Leonard-Bro	1.62	Warneke-Chi	143	Mungo-Bro	5.25	Hoyt-Pit	10.81
Warneke-Chi	291.1	Mungo-Bro	8.56	Fitzsimmons-NY	1.74	Derringer-Cin	122	Malone-Chi	5.23	Fitzsimmons-NY	10.87

Earned Run Average		Adjusted ERA		Opponents' Batting Avg.		Opponents' On Base Pct.		Starter Runs		Adjusted Starter Runs	
Hubbell-NY	2.30	Hubbell-NY	168	Parmelee-NY	.238	Hubbell-NY	.263	Hubbell-NY	61.3	Hubbell-NY	54.5
D.Dean-StL	2.66	C.Davis-Phi	160	Hubbell-NY	.239	Warneke-Chi	.287	D.Dean-StL	48.7	D.Dean-StL	54.3
Hoyt-Pit	2.93	D.Dean-StL	159	D.Dean-StL	.241	D.Dean-StL	.289	C.Davis-Phi	33.8	C.Davis-Phi	54.0
C.Davis-Phi	2.95	Hoyt-Pit	141	Warneke-Chi	.244	P.Dean-StL	.292	Fitzsimmons-NY	29.8	Hoyt-Pit	25.2
Fitzsimmons-NY	3.04	Walker-StL	135	P.Dean-StL	.248	Hoyt-Pit	.296	Schumacher-NY	29.0	Fitzsimmons-NY	24.1

Clutch Pitching Index		Relief Runs		Adjusted Relief Runs		Relief Ranking		Total Pitcher Index		Total Baseball Ranking	
Walker-StL	137	Haines-StL	5.6	Haines-StL	7.2	Haines-StL	6.0	C.Davis-Phi	7.8	C.Davis-Phi	7.8
Leonard-Bro	121	Bell-NY	2.4	Brennan-Cin	2.4	Brennan-Cin	2.1	D.Dean-StL	6.4	D.Dean-StL	6.4
C.Davis-Phi	120	Brennan-Cin	2.2	Bell-NY	1.2	Bell-NY	1.7	Hubbell-NY	6.0	Hubbell-NY	6.0
Freitas-Cin	111							Fitzsimmons-NY	3.7	Vaughan-Pit	5.1
Frankhouse-Bos	110							Schumacher-NY	3.5	P.Waner-Pit	4.6

TEAM	G	W	L	PCT	GB	R	OR	AB	H	2B	3B	HR	BB	SO	AVG	OBP	SLG	PRO	PRO+	BR	/A	PF	CHI	RC	SB	CS	SBA	SBR
DET	154	101	53	.656		958	708	5475	1644	349	53	74	639	528	.300	.376	.424	.800	113	112	110	100	104	905	125	55	69	5
NY	154	94	60	.610	7	842	669	5368	1494	226	61	135	700	597	.278	.364	.419	.783	117	70	130	93	96	848	71	46	61	-6
CLE	154	85	69	.552	16	814	763	5396	1550	340	46	100	526	433	.287	.353	.423	.776	105	44	32	102	98	820	52	32	62	-4
BOS	153	76	76	.500	24	820	775	5339	1465	287	70	51	610	535	.274	.350	.383	.733	90	-28	-48	107	108	748	116	47	71	7
PHI	153	68	82	.453	31	764	838	5317	1491	236	50	144	491	584	.280	.343	.425	.768	108	20	49	96	97	785	57	35	62	-4
STL	154	67	85	.441	33	674	800	5288	1417	252	59	62	514	631	.268	.335	.373	.708	82	-84	-142	108	98	680	43	31	58	-6
WAS	155	66	86	.434	34	729	806	5448	1512	278	70	51	570	447	.278	.348	.382	.730	99	-35	-6	96	95	747	47	42	53	-11
CHI	153	53	99	.349	47	704	946	5301	1395	237	40	71	565	524	.263	.336	.363	.699	84	-97	-118	103	103	672	36	27	57	-5
TOT	615					6305		42932	11968	2205	449	688	4615	4279	.279	.351	.399	.750							547	315	63	-25

TEAM	CG	SH	SV	IP	H	H/G	HR	BB	SO	RAT	ERA	ERA+	OAV	OOB	PR	/A	PF	CPI	FA	E	DP	FW	PW	BW	SBW	DIF
DET	74	13	14	1370²	1467	9.6	86	488	640	12.9	4.06	108	.273	.335	67	50	98	102	.974	159	150	1.2	4.6	10.2	.8	7.2
NY	83	13	10	1382²	1349	8.8	71	542	656	12.4	3.76	108	.254	.324	114	48	90	97	.973	157	151	1.3	4.5	12.1	-.3	-.5
CLE	72	8	19	1367	1476	9.7	70	582	554	13.7	4.28	106	.275	.349	33	40	101	101	.972	172	164	.4	3.7	3.0	-.0	1.0
BOS	68	9	9	1361	1527	10.1	70	543	538	13.8	4.32	111	.283	.351	27	73	107	103	.969	188	141	-.5	6.8	-7.6	.9	.4
PHI	68	8	8	1337	1429	9.6	84	693	480	14.4	5.01	87	.275	.363	-77	-94	97	94	.967	196	166	-1.0	-8.7	4.6	-.0	-1.8
STL	50	6	20	1350	1499	10.0	94	632	499	14.3	4.69	111	.283	.361	1	75	111	107	.969	187	160	-.4	7.0	-13.2	-.3	-2.1
WAS	61	4	12	1381¹	1622	10.6	74	503	412	13.9	4.48	92	.295	.355	-28	-55	96	101	.974	162	167	1.0	-5.1	-.6	-.7	-4.6
CHI	72	5	8	1355	1599	10.6	139	628	506	14.9	5.41	88	.292	.367	-137	-101	105	97	.966	207	126	-1.6	-9.4	-11.0	-.2	-.9
TOT	548	66	100	10904²		9.9				13.8	4.50		.279	.351					.970	1428	1225					

Runs
Gehringer-Det 134
Werber-Bos 129
Gehrig-NY 128
Averill-Cle 128
Foxx-Phi 120

Hits
Gehringer-Det 214
Gehrig-NY 210
Trosky-Cle 206
Cramer-Phi 202
Greenberg-Det 201

Doubles
Greenberg-Det 63
Gehringer-Det 50
Averill-Cle 48
Trosky-Cle 45
Hale-Cle 44

Triples
Chapman-NY 13
Manush-Was 11

Home Runs
Gehrig-NY 49
Foxx-Phi 44
Trosky-Cle 35
Johnson-Phi 34
Averill-Cle 31

Total Bases
Gehrig-NY 409
Trosky-Cle 374
Greenberg-Det 356
Foxx-Phi 352
Averill-Cle 340

Runs Batted In
Gehrig-NY 165
Trosky-Cle 142
Greenberg-Det 139
Foxx-Phi 130
Gehringer-Det 127

Runs Produced
Gehringer-Det 250
Gehrig-NY 244
Greenberg-Det 231
Trosky-Cle 224
Rogell-Det 211

Bases On Balls
Foxx-Phi 111
Gehrig-NY 109
Ruth-NY 103
Myer-Was 102

Batting Average
Gehrig-NY .... .363
Gehringer-Det .... .356
Manush-Was ...... .349
Simmons-Chi ..... .344
Vosmik-Cle ...... .341

On Base Percentage
Gehrig-NY .... .465
Gehringer-Det .... .450
Foxx-Phi .... .449
Cochrane-Det ..... .428
Myer-Was .... .419

Slugging Average
Gehrig-NY .... .706
Foxx-Phi .... .653
Greenberg-Det .... .600
Trosky-Cle .... .598
Averill-Cle .... .569

Production
Gehrig-NY 1.172
Foxx-Phi 1.102
Greenberg-Det .. 1.005
Trosky-Cle .... .987
Averill-Cle ...... .982

Adjusted Production
Gehrig-NY 213
Foxx-Phi 188
Greenberg-Det 156
Trosky-Cle 149
Averill-Cle 149

Batter Runs
Gehrig-NY 85.6
Foxx-Phi 66.4
Gehringer-Det 47.8
Greenberg-Det 46.7
Averill-Cle 45.6

Adjusted Batter Runs
Gehrig-NY 98.0
Foxx-Phi 72.1
Gehringer-Det 47.5
Greenberg-Det 46.4
Averill-Cle 43.6

Clutch Hitting Index
Dykes-Chi 137
Cronin-Was 131
Pepper-StL 129
Cochrane-Det 129
Rogell-Det 126

Runs Created
Gehrig-NY 195
Foxx-Phi 165
Averill-Cle 145
Trosky-Cle 145
Gehringer-Det 144

Total Average
Gehrig-NY 1.401
Foxx-Phi 1.310
Averill-Cle 1.075
Greenberg-Det .. 1.071
Gehringer-Det .. 1.053

Stolen Bases
Werber-Bos 40
White-Det 28
Chapman-NY 26
Fox-Det 25
Walker-Det 20

Stolen Base Average
White-Det 82.4
Werber-Bos 72.7
Fox-Det 71.4
Walker-Det 69.0
Chapman-NY 61.9

Stolen Base Runs
White-Det 4.8
Werber-Bos 3.0
Lazzeri-NY 2.7
Cronin-Was 2.4

Fielding Runs
Hale-Cle 25.7
Hemsley-StL 23.3
Werber-Bos 20.3
Cronin-Was 18.4
Melillo-StL 18.1

Total Player Rating
Gehrig-NY 7.8
Foxx-Phi 6.1
Gehringer-Det 5.7
Averill-Cle 4.2
Werber-Bos 4.0

Wins
Gomez-NY 26
Rowe-Det 24
Bridges-Det 22
Harder-Cle 20
Ruffing-NY 19

Win Percentage
Gomez-NY .... .839
Rowe-Det .... .750
Marberry-Det .... .750
Auker-Det .... .682
Bridges-Det ..... .667

Games
Russell-Was 54
Newsom-StL 47
Rowe-Det 45
Knott-StL 45

Complete Games
Gomez-NY 25
Bridges-Det 23
Lyons-Chi 21
Rowe-Det 20

Shutouts
Harder-Cle 6
Gomez-NY 6
Ruffing-NY 5
Dietrich-Phi 4

Saves
Russell-Was 7
L.Brown-Cle 6
Newsom-StL 5

Innings Pitched
Gomez-NY 281.2
Bridges-Det 275.0
Rowe-Det 266.0
Newsom-StL ... 262.1
Ruffing-NY 256.1

Fewest Hits/Game
Gomez-NY 7.13
Ruffing-NY 8.15
Bridges-Det 8.15
Burke-Was 8.30
Murphy-NY 8.36

Fewest BB/Game
W.Ferrell-Bos ... 2.44
Auker-Det 2.46
Blaeholder-StL .. 2.61
Rowe-Det 2.74
Weaver-Was 2.77

Strikeouts
Gomez-NY 158
Bridges-Det 151
Ruffing-NY 149
Rowe-Det 149
Pearson-Cle 140

Strikeouts/Game
Ruffing-NY 5.23
Gomez-NY 5.05
Rowe-Det 5.04
Pearson-Cle 4.95
Bridges-Det 4.94

Ratio
Gomez-NY 10.19
Rowe-Det 11.54
Bridges-Det 11.65
Murphy-NY 11.66
Harder-Cle 11.77

Earned Run Average
Gomez-NY 2.33
Harder-Cle 2.61
Murphy-NY 3.12
Burke-Was 3.21
Auker-Det 3.42

Adjusted ERA
Harder-Cle 174
Gomez-NY 174
Ostermueller-Bos .. 138
Burke-Was 134
W.Ferrell-Bos 132

Opponents' Batting Avg.
Gomez-NY ...... .215
Ruffing-NY ..... .236
Bridges-Det .... .241
Burke-Was ..... .245
Benton-Phi ..... .249

Opponents' On Base Pct.
Gomez-NY ...... .282
Ruffing-NY ..... .310
Rowe-Det ...... .312
Bridges-Det .... .312
Harder-Cle ..... .316

Starter Runs
Gomez-NY 67.7
Harder-Cle 53.6
Murphy-NY 31.8
Rowe-Det 30.9
Bridges-Det 25.4

Adjusted Starter Runs
Harder-Cle 55.0
Gomez-NY 54.2
Ostermueller-Bos .. 29.0
Newsom-StL 28.6
Rowe-Det 27.7

Clutch Pitching Index
Harder-Cle 127
Auker-Det 123
Ostermueller-Bos .. 116
Murphy-NY 113
Coffman-StL 109

Relief Runs
Pennock-Bos 10.0
McColl-Was 8.0
Russell-Was 5.8
Bean-Cle 3.7

Adjusted Relief Runs
Pennock-Bos 12.1
McColl-Was 5.7
Bean-Cle 3.9
Russell-Was 2.6
Wells-StL 2.1

Relief Ranking
Bean-Cle 4.1
Pennock-Bos 3.9
McColl-Was 3.3
Russell-Was 2.5
Wells-StL 1.7

Total Pitcher Index
Harder-Cle 6.4
Gomez-NY 4.8
Rowe-Det 4.0
Newsom-StL 3.2
Ostermueller-Bos .. 3.1

Total Baseball Ranking
Gehrig-NY 7.8
Harder-Cle 6.4
Foxx-Phi 6.1
Gehringer-Det 5.7
Gomez-NY 4.8

TEAM	G	W	L	PCT	GB	R	OR	AB	H	2B	3B	HR	BB	SO	AVG	OBP	SLG	PRO	PRO+	BR	/A	PF	CHI	RC	SB	CS	SBA	SBR
CHI	154	100	54	.649		**847**	597	5486	1581	**303**	62	88	**464**	471	**.288**	.347	.414	**.761**	110	81	76	101	102	812	66			
STL	154	96	58	.623	4	829	625	5457	1548	286	59	86	404	521	.284	.335	.405	.740	101	33	3	104	**109**	759	71			
NY	156	91	62	.595	8.5	770	675	5623	**1608**	248	56	123	392	479	.286	.336	**.416**	.752	110	54	68	98	96	797	32			
PIT	153	86	67	.562	13.5	743	647	5415	1543	255	**90**	66	457	437	.285	.343	.402	.745	103	49	24	103	96	758	30			
BRO	154	70	83	.458	29.5	711	767	5410	1496	235	62	59	430	520	.277	.333	.376	.709	99	-21	-6	98	101	691	60			
CIN	154	68	85	.444	31.5	646	772	5296	1403	244	68	73	392	547	.265	.319	.378	.697	96	-51	-31	97	99	658	**72**			
PHI	156	64	89	.418	35.5	685	871	5442	1466	249	32	92	392	661	.269	.322	.378	.700	85	-47	-116	110	101	681	52			
BOS	153	38	115	.248	61.5	575	852	5309	1396	233	33	75	353	**436**	.263	.311	.362	.673	93	-98	-50	92	95	596	20			
TOT	617					5806		43438	12041	2053	462	662	3284	4072	.277	.331	.391	.722						403				

TEAM	CG	SH	SV	IP	H	H/G	HR	BB	SO	RAT	ERA	ERA+	OAV	OOB	PR	/A	PF	CPI	FA	E	DP	FW	PW	BW	SBW	DIF
CHI	81	12	14	1394[1]	**1417**	9.1	85	400	589	11.9	**3.26**	121	.263	.317	118	103	98	111	.970	186	**163**	.3	10.0	7.4		5.3
STL	73	10	18	1384[2]	1445	9.4	68	377	**602**	12.0	3.52	116	.267	.318	76	89	102	101	**.972**	164	133	1.6	8.6	.3		8.5
NY	76	10	11	1403[2]	1433	9.2	106	411	524	12.0	3.78	102	**.262**	.318	37	11	96	98	**.972**	174	129	1.1	1.1	6.6		5.7
PIT	76	**15**	11	1365[2]	1428	9.4	**63**	**312**	549	**11.6**	3.42	120	.265	**.307**	91	**103**	102	98	.968	190	94	.0	10.0	2.3		-2.8
BRO	62	11	**20**	1358	1519	10.1	88	436	480	13.1	4.22	94	.281	.337	-31	-37	99	100	.969	188	146	.2	-3.6	-.6		-2.5
CIN	59	9	13	1356	1490	9.9	65	438	500	13.0	4.30	93	.278	.336	-43	-49	99	94	.966	204	139	-.7	-4.8	-3.0		.0
PHI	53	8	15	1374[2]	1652	10.8	106	505	475	14.4	4.76	95	.295	.358	-113	-35	113	102	.963	228	145	-2.0	-3.4	-11.3		4.1
BOS	54	6	5	1330	1645	11.1	81	404	355	14.0	4.93	77	.303	.354	-135	-169	94	96	.967	197	101	-.4	-16.4	-4.9		-16.8
TOT	534	81	107	10967		9.9				12.7	4.02		.277	.331					.968	1531	1050					

Runs
Galan-Chi 133
Medwick-StL 132
Martin-StL 121
Ott-NY 113
Herman-Chi 113

Hits
Herman-Chi 227
Medwick-StL 224

Doubles
Herman-Chi 57
Medwick-StL 46
Allen-Phi 46
Martin-StL 41
Galan-Chi 41

Triples
Goodman-Cin 18
L.Waner-Pit 14
Medwick-StL 13

Home Runs
Berger-Bos 34
Ott-NY 31
Camilli-Phi 25
Medwick-StL 23
R.Collins-StL 23

Total Bases
Medwick-StL . . . 365
Ott-NY 329
Berger-Bos 323
Herman-Chi 317
Leiber-NY 314

Runs Batted In
Berger-Bos 130
Medwick-StL 126
R.Collins-StL 122
Ott-NY 114
Leiber-NY 107

Runs Produced
Medwick-StL 235
R.Collins-StL 208
Galan-Chi 200
Ott-NY 196
Leiber-NY 195

Bases On Balls
Vaughan-Pit 97
Galan-Chi 87
Ott-NY 82
Suhr-Pit 70
Frey-Bro 66

Batting Average
Vaughan-Pit 385
Medwick-StL 353
Hartnett-Chi 344
Lombardi-Cin 343
Herman-Chi 341

On Base Percentage
Vaughan-Pit 491
Ott-NY 407
Hack-Chi 406
Galan-Chi 399
P.Waner-Pit 392

Slugging Average
Vaughan-Pit 607
Medwick-StL 576
Ott-NY 555
Berger-Bos 548
Hartnett-Chi 545

Production
Vaughan-Pit 1.098
Medwick-StL 962
Ott-NY 962
R.Collins-StL 915
Berger-Bos 903

Adjusted Production
Vaughan-Pit 187
Ott-NY 159
Berger-Bos 151
Medwick-StL 149
Leiber-NY 143

Batter Runs
Vaughan-Pit 71.9
Ott-NY 47.6
Medwick-StL 46.0
R.Collins-StL 35.0
Leiber-NY 34.3

Adjusted Batter Runs
Vaughan-Pit 67.3
Ott-NY 50.0
Medwick-StL 41.0
Berger-Bos 38.7
Leiber-NY 36.4

Clutch Hitting Index
Leslie-Bro 135
Young-Pit 128
Durocher-StL 125
Jurges-Chi 121
Whitney-Bos 113

Runs Created
Vaughan-Pit 163
Ott-NY 144
Medwick-StL 139
Galan-Chi 133
R.Collins-StL 125

Total Average
Vaughan-Pit 1.317
Ott-NY 1.037
Medwick-StL 948
Galan-Chi 937
R.Collins-StL 930

Stolen Bases
Galan-Chi 22
Martin-StL 20
Bordagaray-Bro . . . 18
Hack-Chi 14
Goodman-Cin 14

Stolen Base Average

Stolen Base Runs

Fielding Runs
Jurges-Chi 30.2
Herman-Chi 18.9
Allen-Phi 16.5
Hartnett-Chi 14.5
T.Moore-StL 13.8

Total Player Rating
Vaughan-Pit 6.1
Herman-Chi 5.4
Ott-NY 4.9
Hartnett-Chi 4.8
Berger-Bos 4.0

Wins
D.Dean-StL 28
Hubbell-NY 23
Derringer-Cin 22
Warneke-Chi 20
Lee-Chi 20

Win Percentage
Lee-Chi 769
Castleman-NY 714
D.Dean-StL 700
Schumacher-NY . .679
Hubbell-NY 657

Games
Jorgens-Phi 53
D.Dean-StL 50
Bivin-Phi 47
Smith-Bos 46
P.Dean-StL 46

Complete Games
D.Dean-StL 29
Hubbell-NY 24
Blanton-Pit 23
Warneke-Chi 20
Derringer-Cin 20

Shutouts
Weaver-Pit 4
Mungo-Bro 4
French-Chi 4
Fitzsimmons-NY . . . 4
Blanton-Pit 4

Saves
Leonard-Bro 8
Johnson-Phi 6
Hoyt-Pit 6

Innings Pitched
D.Dean-StL 325.1
Hubbell-NY 302.2
Derringer-Cin . . . 276.2
P.Dean-StL 269.2

Fewest Hits/Game
Blanton-Pit 7.79
Schumacher-NY . . 8.08
Parmelee-NY 8.52
Swift-Pit 8.53
Hollingsworth-Cin . 8.57

Fewest BB/Game
Clark-Bro 1.22
Hubbell-NY 1.46
Hoyt-Pit 1.48
Derringer-Cin . . . 1.59
Johnson-Phi 1.60

Strikeouts
D.Dean-StL 190
Hubbell-NY 150
Mungo-Bro 143
P.Dean-StL 143
Blanton-Pit 142

Strikeouts/Game
Mungo-Bro 6.00
D.Dean-StL 5.26
Blanton-Pit 5.02
P.Dean-StL 4.77
Hollingsworth-Cin . 4.62

Ratio
Blanton-Pit 9.80
Swift-Pit 10.21
Clark-Bro 10.61
Warneke-Chi 10.66
Schumacher-NY . 10.66

Earned Run Average
Blanton-Pit 2.58
Swift-Pit 2.70
Schumacher-NY . . 2.89
French-Chi 2.96
Lee-Chi 2.96

Adjusted ERA
Blanton-Pit 159
Swift-Pit 152
D.Dean-StL 135
Schumacher-NY . . 133
French-Chi 133

Opponents' Batting Avg.
Blanton-Pit 229
Schumacher-NY . . .238
Hollingsworth-Cin . .243
Swift-Pit 247
P.Dean-StL 249

Opponents' On Base Pct.
Blanton-Pit 272
Swift-Pit 282
Clark-Bro 289
Schumacher-NY . . .292
P.Dean-StL 292

Starter Runs
Blanton-Pit 40.6
D.Dean-StL 35.3
Schumacher-NY . . 32.8
Swift-Pit 29.9
Lee-Chi 29.5

Adjusted Starter Runs
Blanton-Pit 43.0
D.Dean-StL 38.2
Swift-Pit 31.9
Schumacher-NY . . 28.0
Lee-Chi 27.0

Clutch Pitching Index
French-Chi 126
Zachary-Bro 121
Walker-StL 116
Lee-Chi 111
Hallahan-StL 111

Relief Runs

Adjusted Relief Runs

Relief Ranking

Total Pitcher Index
Blanton-Pit 4.7
D.Dean-StL 4.3
Schumacher-NY . . 3.7
Swift-Pit 3.2
Warneke-Chi 3.0

Total Baseball Ranking
Vaughan-Pit 6.1
Herman-Chi 5.4
Ott-NY 4.9
Hartnett-Chi 4.8
Blanton-Pit 4.7

TEAM	G	W	L	PCT	GB	R	OR	AB	H	2B	3B	HR	BB	SO	AVG	OBP	SLG	PRO	PRO+	BR	/A	PF	CHI	RC	SB	CS	SBA	SBR
DET	152	93	58	.616		919	665	5423	1573	301	83	106	627	456	.290	.366	.435	.801	116	95	126	97	104	885	70	45	61	-6
NY	149	89	60	.597	3	818	632	5214	1462	255	70	104	604	469	.280	.358	.416	.774	111	42	87	94	102	799	68	46	60	-7
CLE	156	82	71	.536	12	776	739	5534	1573	324	77	93	460	567	.284	.341	.421	.762	100	3	-11	102	99	796	63	54	54	-14
BOS	154	78	75	.510	16	718	732	5288	1458	281	63	69	609	470	.276	.353	.392	.745	92	-11	-62	107	94	757	91	59	61	-8
CHI	153	74	78	.487	19.5	738	750	5314	1460	262	42	74	580	405	.275	.348	.382	.730	92	-41	-59	103	101	733	46	28	62	-3
WAS	154	67	86	.438	27	823	903	5592	1591	255	95	32	596	406	.285	.357	.381	.738	99	-18	8	97	104	788	54	37	59	-6
STL	155	65	87	.428	28.5	718	930	5365	1446	291	51	73	593	561	.270	.344	.384	.728	90	-49	-83	105	98	735	45	25	64	-2
PHI	149	58	91	.389	34	710	869	5269	1470	243	44	112	475	602	.279	.341	.406	.747	99	-23	-17	99	98	738	43	35	55	-8
TOT	611					6220		42999	12033	2212	525	663	4544	3936	.280	.351	.402	.753							480	329	59	-53

TEAM	CG	SH	SV	IP	H	H/G	HR	BB	SO	RAT	ERA	ERA+	OAV	OOB	PR	/A	PF	CPI	FA	E	DP	FW	PW	BW	SBW	DIF
DET	87	16	11	1364	1440	9.5	78	522	584	13.1	3.82	109	.271	.339	96	53	94	107	.978	128	154	2.3	5.0	11.8	.0	-1.6
NY	76	12	13	1331	1276	8.6	91	516	594	12.2	3.60	112	.251	.321	126	66	91	101	.974	151	114	.8	6.2	8.1	-.0	-.6
CLE	67	12	21	1396	1527	9.8	68	457	498	12.9	4.15	108	.278	.335	47	55	101	97	.972	177	147	-.3	5.2	-1.0	-.7	2.3
BOS	82	6	11	1376	1520	9.9	67	520	470	13.5	4.05	117	.280	.346	62	106	107	105	.969	194	136	-1.4	9.9	-5.8	-.1	-1.1
CHI	80	8	8	1360²	1443	9.5	105	574	436	13.5	4.38	106	.272	.346	12	36	104	100	.976	146	133	1.3	3.4	-5.5	.3	-1.5
WAS	67	5	12	1378²	1672	10.9	89	613	456	15.1	5.25	82	.302	.371	-122	-142	97	99	.972	171	186	-.0	-13.3	.7	.0	3.0
STL	42	4	15	1380¹	1667	10.9	92	641	435	15.2	5.26	91	.297	.371	-124	-72	108	97	.970	187	138	-.9	-6.7	-7.8	.4	4.0
PHI	58	7	10	1326¹	1486	10.1	73	704	469	15.0	5.12	89	.285	.372	-97	-84	102	96	.968	190	150	-1.4	-7.9	-1.6	-.1	-5.5
TOT	559	70	101	10913		9.9				13.8	4.46		.280	.351					.972	1344	1158					

Runs		Hits		Doubles		Triples		Home Runs		Total Bases	
Gehrig-NY	125	Vosmik-Cle	216	Vosmik-Cle	47	Vosmik-Cle	20	Greenberg-Det	36	Greenberg-Det	389
Gehringer-Det	123	Myer-Was	215	Greenberg-Det	46	Stone-Was	18	Foxx-Phi	36	Foxx-Phi	340
Greenberg-Det	121	Cramer-Phi	214	Solters-Bos-StL	45	Greenberg-Det	16	Gehrig-NY	30	Vosmik-Cle	333
Foxx-Phi	118	Greenberg-Det	203	Fox-Det	38	Cronin-Bos	14	Johnson-Phi	28	Solters-Bos-StL	314
Chapman-NY	118			Chapman-NY	38	Averill-Cle	13	Trosky-Cle	26	Gehrig-NY	312

Runs Batted In		Runs Produced		Bases On Balls		Batting Average		On Base Percentage		Slugging Average	
Greenberg-Det	170	Greenberg-Det	255	Gehrig-NY	132	Myer-Was	.349	Gehrig-NY	.466	Foxx-Phi	.636
Gehrig-NY	119	Gehrig-NY	214	Appling-Chi	122	Vosmik-Cle	.348	Foxx-Phi	.461	Greenberg-Det	.628
Foxx-Phi	115	Gehringer-Det	212	Foxx-Phi	114	Foxx-Phi	.346	Cochrane-Det	.452	Gehrig-NY	.583
Trosky-Cle	113	Myer-Was	210	Myer-Was	96	Cramer-Phi	.332	Myer-Was	.440	Vosmik-Cle	.537
Solters-Bos-StL	112	Foxx-Phi	197	Cochrane-Det	96	Gehringer-Det	.330	Appling-Chi	.437	Fox-Det	.513

Production		Adjusted Production		Batter Runs		Adjusted Batter Runs		Clutch Hitting Index		Runs Created	
Foxx-Phi	1.096	Foxx-Phi	182	Foxx-Phi	67.2	Gehrig-NY	70.1	Owen-Det	134	Foxx-Phi	163
Gehrig-NY	1.049	Gehrig-NY	180	Gehrig-NY	61.6	Foxx-Phi	68.4	Kuhel-Was	124	Greenberg-Det	161
Greenberg-Det	1.039	Greenberg-Det	171	Greenberg-Det	57.5	Greenberg-Det	62.7	Goslin-Det	124	Gehrig-NY	154
Vosmik-Cle	.946	Vosmik-Cle	140	Vosmik-Cle	38.3	Myer-Was	40.8	Powell-Was	124	Vosmik-Cle	137
Gehringer-Det	.911	Myer-Was	139	Myer-Was	36.5	Gehringer-Det	36.3	Myer-Was	122	Myer-Was	132

Total Average		Stolen Bases		Stolen Base Average		Stolen Base Runs		Fielding Runs		Total Player Rating	
Foxx-Phi	1.288	Werber-Bos	29	Lary-Was-StL	87.5	Lary-Was-StL	6.0	Appling-Chi	21.3	Foxx-Phi	5.7
Gehrig-NY	1.230	Lary-Was-StL	28	Werber-Bos	80.6	Werber-Bos	4.5	Travis-Was	21.3	Myer-Was	5.4
Greenberg-Det	1.138	Almada-Bos	20	Almada-Bos	69.0	Solters-Bos-StL	2.1	Solters-Bos-StL	18.6	Gehrig-NY	4.8
Cochrane-Det	1.000	White-Det	19	White-Det	65.5	Hughes-Cle	2.1	Melillo-StL-Bos	18.6	Greenberg-Det	4.7
Vosmik-Cle	.980	Chapman-NY	17	Chapman-NY	63.0			Werber-Bos	17.2	Gehringer-Det	4.7

Wins		Win Percentage		Games		Complete Games		Shutouts		Saves	
W.Ferrell-Bos	25	Auker-Det	.720	VanAtta-NY-StL	58	W.Ferrell-Bos	31	Rowe-Det	6	Knott-StL	7
Harder-Cle	22	Broaca-NY	.682	Walkup-StL	55	Grove-Bos	23	Harder-Cle	4		
Bridges-Det	21	Bridges-Det	.677	Andrews-StL	50	Bridges-Det	23	Bridges-Det	4		
Grove-Bos	20	Harder-Cle	.667	Thomas-StL	49	Rowe-Det	21				
Rowe-Det	19	Lyons-Chi	.652	Knott-StL	48						

Innings Pitched		Fewest Hits/Game		Fewest BB/Game		Strikeouts		Strikeouts/Game		Ratio	
W.Ferrell-Bos	322.1	Allen-NY	8.03	Harder-Cle	1.66	Bridges-Det	163	Allen-NY	6.09	Grove-Bos	11.11
Harder-Cle	287.1	Ruffing-NY	8.15	Grove-Bos	2.14	Rowe-Det	140	Bridges-Det	5.35	Rowe-Det	11.17
Whitehill-Was	279.1	Gomez-NY	8.16	Rowe-Det	2.22	Gomez-NY	138	Gomez-NY	5.05	Ruffing-NY	11.27
Rowe-Det	275.2	Whitehead-Chi	8.46	Andrews-StL	2.24	Grove-Bos	121	VanAtta-NY-StL	4.63	Allen-NY	11.37
Bridges-Det	274.1	Grove-Bos	8.87	Hudlin-Cle	2.37	Allen-NY	113	Rowe-Det	4.57	Gomez-NY	11.38

Earned Run Average		Adjusted ERA		Opponents' Batting Avg.		Opponents' On Base Pct.		Starter Runs		Adjusted Starter Runs	
Grove-Bos	2.70	Grove-Bos	176	Allen-NY	.238	Rowe-Det	.301	Grove-Bos	53.1	Grove-Bos	61.9
Lyons-Chi	3.02	Lyons-Chi	153	Ruffing-NY	.239	Grove-Bos	.302	Harder-Cle	37.2	W.Ferrell-Bos	43.9
Ruffing-NY	3.12	Harder-Cle	137	Gomez-NY	.242	Ruffing-NY	.303	Gomez-NY	34.8	Harder-Cle	38.8
Gomez-NY	3.18	Andrews-StL	135	Whitehead-Chi	.250	Allen-NY	.307	W.Ferrell-Bos	33.6	Lyons-Chi	33.9
Harder-Cle	3.29	W.Ferrell-Bos	135	Broaca-NY	.254	Harder-Cle	.307	Ruffing-NY	32.9	Andrews-StL	29.6

Clutch Pitching Index		Relief Runs		Adjusted Relief Runs		Relief Ranking		Total Pitcher Index		Total Baseball Ranking	
Lyons-Chi	124	L.Brown-Cle	11.4	L.Brown-Cle	12.1	L.Brown-Cle	14.2	W.Ferrell-Bos	7.2	W.Ferrell-Bos	7.2
Bridges-Det	113	Hogsett-Det	9.9	Hogsett-Det	6.8	Hogsett-Det	8.4	Grove-Bos	6.4	Grove-Bos	6.4
Auker-Det	112	DeShong-NY	9.2	DeShong-NY	6.0	DeShong-NY	4.5	Harder-Cle	4.4	Foxx-Phi	5.7
Grove-Bos	112	Murphy-NY	4.9	Wilson-Bos	3.7	Wilson-Bos	3.8	Lyons-Chi	3.6	Myer-Was	5.4
Tietje-Chi	110	Wilson-Bos	1.7					Ruffing-NY	3.5	Gehrig-NY	4.8

TEAM	G	W	L	PCT	GB	R	OR	AB	H	2B	3B	HR	BB	SO	AVG	OBP	SLG	PRO	PRO+	BR	/A	PF	CHI	RC	SB	CS	SBA	SBR
NY	154	92	62	.597		742	621	5449	1529	237	48	97	431	452	.281	.337	.395	.732	104	19	27	99	99	744	31			
STL	155	87	67	.565	5	795	794	5537	1554	332	60	88	442	577	.281	.336	.410	.746	106	40	43	100	103	772	69			
CHI	154	87	67	.565	5	755	603	5409	1545	275	36	76	491	462	.286	.349	.392	.741	104	44	27	102	97	757	68			
PIT	156	84	70	.545	8	804	718	5586	1596	283	80	60	517	502	.286	.349	.397	.746	105	56	38	102	100	798	37			
CIN	154	74	80	.481	18	722	760	5393	1476	224	73	82	410	584	.274	.329	.388	.717	106	-14	30	94	104	699	68			
BOS	157	71	83	.461	21	631	715	5478	1450	207	45	67	433	582	.265	.322	.356	.678	94	-86	-45	94	98	635	23			
BRO	156	67	87	.435	25	662	752	5574	1518	263	43	33	390	458	.272	.323	.353	.676	87	-92	-98	101	104	649	55			
PHI	154	54	100	.351	38	726	874	5465	1538	250	46	103	451	586	.281	.339	.401	.740	95	32	-44	110	96	757	50			
TOT	620					5837		43891	12206	2071	431	606	3565	4203	.278	.335	.386	.722						401				

TEAM	CG	SH	SV	IP	H	H/G	HR	BB	SO	RAT	ERA	ERA+	OAV	OOB	PR	/A	PF	CPI	FA	E	DP	FW	PW	BW	SBW	DIF
NY	60	12	22	1385²	1458	9.5	75	401	500	12.2	3.46	113	.273	.327	86	67	97	110	.974	168	164	1.1	6.5	2.6		4.7
STL	65	5	24	1398	1610	10.4	89	434	559	13.4	4.47	88	.289	.344	-71	-84	98	98	.974	156	134	1.9	-8.2	4.2		12.1
CHI	77	18	10	1382¹	1413	9.2	77	434	597	12.2	3.54	113	.265	.324	74	68	99	104	.976	146	156	2.4	6.6	2.6		-1.6
PIT	67	5	12	1395¹	1475	9.5	74	379	559	12.1	3.89	104	.269	.319	20	25	101	92	.967	199	113	-.5	2.4	3.7		1.4
CIN	50	6	23	1367¹	1576	10.4	51	418	459	13.3	4.22	91	.287	.341	-31	-61	95	97	.969	191	150	-.2	-6.0	2.9		.2
BOS	61	7	13	1413¹	1566	10.0	69	451	421	13.0	3.94	97	.281	.337	12	-18	95	103	.971	189	175	.1	-1.8	-4.4		.0
BRO	59	7	18	1403	1466	9.4	84	528	651	13.0	3.98	104	.266	.333	5	22	103	97	.966	208	107	-1.0	2.1	-9.6		-1.6
PHI	51	7	14	1365¹	1630	10.7	87	515	454	14.4	4.64	98	.292	.356	-95	-17	113	100	.959	252	144	-3.7	-1.7	-4.3		-13.4
TOT	490	67	136	11110¹		9.9				12.9	4.02		.278	.335					.969	1509	1143					

Runs
Vaughan-Pit 122
P.Martin-StL 121
Ott-NY 120
Medwick-StL 115
Suhr-Pit 111

Hits
Medwick-StL 223
P.Waner-Pit 218
Demaree-Chi 212
Herman-Chi 211
Moore-NY 205

Doubles
Medwick-StL 64
Herman-Chi 57
P.Waner-Pit 53
Moore-StL 39
Moore-Bos 38

Triples
Goodman-Cin 14
Medwick-StL 13
Camilli-Phi 13

Home Runs
Ott-NY 33
Camilli-Phi 28
Klein-Chi-Phi 25
Berger-Bos 25
Mize-StL 19

Total Bases
Medwick-StL 367
Ott-NY 314
Klein-Chi-Phi 308
Camilli-Phi 306
P.Waner-Pit 304

Runs Batted In
Medwick-StL 138
Ott-NY 135
Suhr-Pit 118
Klein-Chi-Phi 104

Runs Produced
Medwick-StL 235
Ott-NY 222
Suhr-Pit 218
P.Waner-Pit 196
Vaughan-Pit 191

Bases On Balls
Vaughan-Pit 118
Camilli-Phi 116
Ott-NY 111
Suhr-Pit 95
Hack-Chi 89

Batting Average
P.Waner-Pit .... .373
Phelps-Bro .... .367
Medwick-StL ...... .351
Demaree-Chi ...... .350
Vaughan-Pit ...... .335

On Base Percentage
Vaughan-Pit ...... .453
Ott-NY .... .448
P.Waner-Pit ...... .446
Camilli-Phi ...... .441
Suhr-Pit .... .410

Slugging Average
Ott-NY .... .588
Camilli-Phi ...... .577
Mize-StL .... .577
Medwick-StL ...... .577
P.Waner-Pit ...... .520

Production
Ott-NY 1.036
Camilli-Phi 1.018
P.Waner-Pit ...... .965
Medwick-StL ...... .964
Vaughan-Pit ...... .927

Adjusted Production
Ott-NY 179
Medwick-StL 157
Camilli-Phi 156
P.Waner-Pit 156
Vaughan-Pit 146

Batter Runs
Ott-NY 61.9
Camilli-Phi 58.0
P.Waner-Pit 51.4
Vaughan-Pit 47.3
Medwick-StL 46.9

Adjusted Batter Runs
Ott-NY 63.5
P.Waner-Pit 48.4
Medwick-StL 47.4
Camilli-Phi 44.9
Vaughan-Pit 44.3

Clutch Hitting Index
Brubaker-Pit 147
Young-Pit 131
Suhr-Pit 124
Herman-Chi 115
Whitney-Bos-Phi ... 114

Runs Created
Ott-NY 153
Camilli-Phi 148
Medwick-StL 141
P.Waner-Pit 140
Vaughan-Pit 137

Total Average
Ott-NY 1.188
Camilli-Phi 1.162
Vaughan-Pit 1.034
P.Waner-Pit 1.016
Medwick-StL ...... .956

Stolen Bases
P.Martin-StL 23
S.Martin-StL 17
Hack-Chi 17
Chiozza-Phi 17

Stolen Base Average

Stolen Base Runs

Fielding Runs
Bartell-NY 44.8
Whitehead-NY 29.2
Kampouris-Cin 28.0
Berres-Bro 23.0

Total Player Rating
Bartell-NY 5.7
Medwick-StL 5.3
Ott-NY 5.2
Herman-Chi 5.0
P.Waner-Pit 4.9

Wins
Hubbell-NY 26
D.Dean-StL 24
Derringer-Cin 19

Win Percentage
Hubbell-NY .... .813
Lucas-Pit .... .789
French-Chi .... .667
D.Dean-StL .... .649
Lee-Chi .... .621

Games
Derringer-Cin 51
D.Dean-StL 51
Passeau-Phi 49
Brown-Pit 47

Complete Games
D.Dean-StL 28
Hubbell-NY 25
Mungo-Bro 22
MacFayden-Bos 21
Lee-Chi 20

Shutouts
Warneke-Chi 4
Walters-Phi 4
Smith-NY 4
Lee-Chi 4
French-Chi 4
Carleton-Chi 4
Blanton-Pit 4

Saves
D.Dean-StL 11
Brennan-Cin 9
Smith-Bos 8
Johnson-Phi 7
Coffman-NY 7

Innings Pitched
D.Dean-StL 315.0
Mungo-Bro 311.2
Hubbell-NY 304.0
Derringer-Cin 282.1
MacFayden-Bos .. 266.2

Fewest Hits/Game
Hubbell-NY 7.85
Mungo-Bro 7.94
Lee-Chi 8.28
D.Dean-StL 8.86
Blanton-Pit 8.97

Fewest BB/Game
Lucas-Pit 1.33
Derringer-Cin 1.34
D.Dean-StL 1.51
Hubbell-NY 1.69
Gabler-NY 1.89

Strikeouts
Mungo-Bro 238
D.Dean-StL 195
Blanton-Pit 127
Hubbell-NY 123
Derringer-Cin 121

Strikeouts/Game
Mungo-Bro 6.87
D.Dean-StL 5.57
Blanton-Pit 4.85
Weaver-Pit 4.31
Warneke-Chi 4.23

Ratio
Hubbell-NY 9.68
D.Dean-StL 10.46
Lucas-Pit 10.61
Blanton-Pit 11.19
Davis-Phi-Chi ... 11.35

Earned Run Average
Hubbell-NY 2.31
MacFayden-Bos ... 2.87
Gabler-NY 3.12
D.Dean-StL 3.17
Lucas-Pit 3.18

Adjusted ERA
Hubbell-NY 169
MacFayden-Bos ... 134
Passeau-Phi 130
Lucas-Pit 128
Gabler-NY 125

Opponents' Batting Avg.
Mungo-Bro .... .234
Hubbell-NY .... .236
Lee-Chi .... .246
D.Dean-StL .... .253
Blanton-Pit ...... .257

Opponents' On Base Pct.
Hubbell-NY .... .276
D.Dean-StL .... .285
Lucas-Pit .... .287
Blanton-Pit ...... .301
Mungo-Bro .... .305

Starter Runs
Hubbell-NY 57.7
MacFayden-Bos ... 34.0
D.Dean-StL 29.6
Mungo-Bro 23.1
Lee-Chi 20.4

Adjusted Starter Runs
Hubbell-NY 53.5
MacFayden-Bos .. 28.5
Mungo-Bro 27.0
D.Dean-StL 26.9
Passeau-Phi 25.4

Clutch Pitching Index
Schumacher-NY ... 120
Gabler-NY 119
Chaplin-Bos 111
Smith-NY 110
Carleton-Chi 109

Relief Runs
Bryant-Chi 4.6
Coffman-NY 1.4

Adjusted Relief Runs
Bryant-Chi 4.4
Johnson-Phi 2.9

Relief Ranking
Johnson-Phi 3.2
Bryant-Chi 2.1

Total Pitcher Index
Hubbell-NY 5.5
Passeau-Phi 3.3
D.Dean-StL 2.8
Mungo-Bro 2.8
MacFayden-Bos ... 2.7

Total Baseball Ranking
Bartell-NY 5.7
Hubbell-NY 5.5
Medwick-StL 5.3
Ott-NY 5.2
Herman-Chi 5.0

TEAM	G	W	L	PCT	GB	R	OR	AB	H	2B	3B	HR	BB	SO	AVG	OBP	SLG	PRO	PRO+	BR	/A	PF	CHI	RC	SB	CS	SBA	SBR
NY	155	102	51	.667		1065	731	5591	1676	315	83	182	700	594	.300	.381	.483	.864	124	162	200	97	100	1056	77	40	66	-1
DET	154	83	71	.539	19.5	921	871	5464	1638	326	55	94	640	462	.300	.377	.431	.808	106	57	54	100	98	912	73	49	60	-8
CHI	153	81	70	.536	20	920	873	5466	1597	282	56	60	684	417	.292	.374	.397	.771	94	-9	-41	104	104	851	66	29	69	2
WAS	153	82	71	.536	20	889	799	5433	1601	293	84	62	576	398	.295	.365	.414	.779	105	-7	41	94	104	847	104	42	71	6
CLE	157	80	74	.519	22.5	921	862	5646	1715	357	82	123	514	470	.304	.364	.461	.825	109	70	62	101	96	948	66	53	55	-12
BOS	155	74	80	.481	25.5	775	764	5383	1485	288	62	86	584	465	.276	.349	.400	.749	86	-72	-117	106	98	773	55	44	56	-10
STL	155	57	95	.375	44.5	804	1064	5391	1502	299	66	79	625	627	.279	.356	.403	.759	91	-51	-74	103	99	804	62	20	76	7
PHI	154	53	100	.346	49	714	1045	5373	1443	240	60	72	524	590	.269	.336	.376	.712	84	-151	-137	98	102	694	59	43	58	-8
TOT	618					7009		43747	12657	2400	548	758	4847	4023	.289	.363	.421	.784							562	320	64	-23

TEAM	CG	SH	SV	IP	H	H/G	HR	BB	SO	RAT	ERA	ERA+	OAV	OOB	PR	/A	PF	CPI	FA	E	DP	FW	PW	BW	SBW	DIF
NY	77	6	21	1400[1]	1474	9.5	84	663	624	13.8	4.17	112	.271	.351	135	75	92	108	.973	163	148	.8	6.6	17.7	.2	.3
DET	76	13	13	1360	1568	10.4	100	562	526	14.2	5.00	99	.289	.358	6	-7	98	100	.975	153	159	1.3	-.6	4.8	-.4	1.0
CHI	80	5	8	1365	1603	10.6	104	578	414	14.5	5.06	103	.293	.363	-4	21	103	102	.973	168	174	.4	1.9	-3.6	.4	6.5
WAS	78	8	14	1345[2]	1484	9.9	73	588	462	14.0	4.58	104	.279	.353	68	29	95	101	.970	182	163	-.4	2.6	3.6	.8	-1.1
CLE	74	6	12	1389[1]	1604	10.4	73	607	619	14.5	4.83	104	.289	.362	32	32	100	102	.971	178	154	.0	2.8	5.5	-.8	-4.6
BOS	78	11	9	1372[1]	1501	9.8	78	552	584	13.6	4.39	121	.277	.346	99	142	106	102	.972	165	139	.7	12.5	-10.3	-.6	-5.2
STL	54	3	13	1348[1]	1776	11.9	115	609	399	16.2	6.24	86	.314	.385	-180	-130	107	95	.969	188	143	-.6	-11.5	-6.5	.9	-1.2
PHI	68	3	12	1352[1]	1645	10.9	131	696	405	15.7	6.08	84	.300	.381	-156	-146	101	94	.965	209	152	-1.9	-12.9	-12.1	-.4	3.8
TOT	585	55	102	10933[1]		10.4				14.6	5.04		.289	.363					.971	1406	1232					

Runs		Hits		Doubles		Triples		Home Runs		Total Bases	
Gehrig-NY	167	Averill-Cle	232	Gehringer-Det	60	Rolfe-NY	15	Gehrig-NY	49	Trosky-Cle	405
Clift-StL	145	Gehringer-Det	227	Walker-Det	55	DiMaggio-NY	15	Trosky-Cle	42	Gehrig-NY	403
Gehringer-Det	144	Trosky-Cle	216	Chapman-NY-Was	50	Averill-Cle	15	Foxx-Bos	41	Averill-Cle	385
Crosetti-NY	137	Bell-StL	212	Hale-Cle	50	B.Johnson-Phi	14	DiMaggio-NY	29	Foxx-Bos	369
Averill-Cle	136	Radcliff-Chi	207					Averill-Cle	28	DiMaggio-NY	367

Runs Batted In		Runs Produced		Bases On Balls		Batting Average		On Base Percentage		Slugging Average	
Trosky-Cle	162	Gehrig-NY	270	Gehrig-NY	130	Appling-Chi	.388	Gehrig-NY	.478	Gehrig-NY	.696
Gehrig-NY	152	Bonura-Chi	246	Lary-StL	117	Averill-Cle	.378	Appling-Chi	.474	Trosky-Cle	.644
Foxx-Bos	143	Gehringer-Det	245	Clift-StL	115	Dickey-NY	.362	Foxx-Bos	.440	Foxx-Bos	.631
Bonura-Chi	138	Trosky-Cle	244	Foxx-Bos	105	Gehringer-Det	.354	Averill-Cle	.438	Averill-Cle	.627
Solters-StL	134	Averill-Cle	234	Lazzeri-NY	97	Gehrig-NY	.354	Gehringer-Det	.431	Dickey-NY	.617

Production		Adjusted Production		Batter Runs		Adjusted Batter Runs		Clutch Hitting Index		Runs Created	
Gehrig-NY	1.174	Gehrig-NY	193	Gehrig-NY	82.2	Gehrig-NY	88.8	Appling-Chi	132	Gehrig-NY	199
Foxx-Bos	1.071	Averill-Cle	159	Foxx-Bos	56.8	Averill-Cle	55.2	Sewell-Chi	131	Averill-Cle	168
Averill-Cle	1.065	Foxx-Bos	153	Averill-Cle	56.4	Foxx-Bos	48.2	Bonura-Chi	127	Foxx-Bos	168
Trosky-Cle	1.026	Trosky-Cle	148	Gehringer-Det	43.0	Gehringer-Det	42.6	Owen-Det	126	Gehringer-Det	157
Gehringer-Det	.987	Stone-Was	145	Trosky-Cle	41.9	Trosky-Cle	40.8	Vosmik-Cle	125	Trosky-Cle	150

Total Average		Stolen Bases		Stolen Base Average		Stolen Base Runs		Fielding Runs		Total Player Rating	
Gehrig-NY	1.426	Lary-StL	37	Lary-StL	80.4	Lary-StL	5.7	Hayes-Chi	17.1	Gehrig-NY	6.4
Foxx-Bos	1.238	Powell-Was-NY	26	Crosetti-NY	72.0	Hill-Was	3.3	Hale-Cle	16.5	Gehringer-Det	6.1
Averill-Cle	1.171	Werber-Bos	23	Powell-Was-NY	70.3	Stone-Was	2.4	Cramer-Bos	16.3	Appling-Chi	5.1
Appling-Chi	1.088	Chapman-NY-Was	20	Chapman-NY-Was	69.0	Sewell-Chi	2.1	Gehringer-Det	15.7	Averill-Cle	3.9
Gehringer-Det	1.075	Hughes-Cle	20	Hughes-Cle	69.0			Appling-Chi	15.2	Dickey-NY	3.8

Wins		Win Percentage		Games		Complete Games		Shutouts		Saves	
Bridges-Det	23	Pearson-NY	.731	VanAtta-StL	52	W.Ferrell-Bos	28	Grove-Bos	6	Malone-NY	9
Kennedy-Chi	21	Kennedy-Chi	.700	Knott-StL	47	Bridges-Det	26	Bridges-Det	5	Knott-StL	6
Ruffing-NY	20	Bridges-Det	.676			Ruffing-NY	25	Rowe-Det	4	Murphy-NY	5
W.Ferrell-Bos	20	Allen-Cle	.667			Newsom-Was	24	Newsom-Was	4	Brown-Chi	5
Allen-Cle	20	Rowe-Det	.655			Grove-Bos	22	Allen-Cle	4	Hildebrand-Cle	4

Innings Pitched		Fewest Hits/Game		Fewest BB/Game		Strikeouts		Strikeouts/Game		Ratio	
W.Ferrell-Bos	301.0	Pearson-NY	7.71	Lyons-Chi	2.23	Bridges-Det	175	Allen-Cle	6.11	Grove-Bos	10.87
Bridges-Det	294.2	Grove-Bos	8.42	Grove-Bos	2.31	Allen-Cle	165	Bridges-Det	5.35	Rowe-Det	12.18
Newsom-Was	285.2	Allen-Cle	8.67	Rowe-Det	2.35	Newsom-Was	156	Gomez-NY	5.01	Ruffing-NY	12.19
Kennedy-Chi	274.1	Gomez-NY	8.78	Andrews-StL	2.35	Grove-Bos	130	Newsom-Was	4.91	Allen-Cle	12.30
Ruffing-NY	271.0	Bridges-Det	8.83	Marcum-Bos	2.69	Pearson-NY	118	Pearson-NY	4.76	Appleton-Was	12.45

Earned Run Average		Adjusted ERA		Opponents' Batting Avg.		Opponents' On Base Pct.		Starter Runs		Adjusted Starter Runs	
Grove-Bos	2.81	Grove-Bos	189	Pearson-NY	.233	Grove-Bos	.297	Grove-Bos	62.8	Grove-Bos	70.6
Allen-Cle	3.44	Allen-Cle	146	Grove-Bos	.246	Rowe-Det	.321	Bridges-Det	46.9	Bridges-Det	44.1
Appleton-Was	3.53	Bridges-Det	137	Gomez-NY	.254	Ruffing-NY	.323	Allen-Cle	43.0	Allen-Cle	43.0
Bridges-Det	3.60	Appleton-Was	135	Appleton-Was	.254	Appleton-Was	.324	Ruffing-NY	35.7	W.Ferrell-Bos	37.8
Pearson-NY	3.71	Kelley-Phi	132	Bridges-Det	.255	Bridges-Det	.326	Appleton-Was	33.9	Kelley-Phi	32.4

Clutch Pitching Index		Relief Runs		Adjusted Relief Runs		Relief Ranking		Total Pitcher Index		Total Baseball Ranking	
Hadley-NY	116	Lee-Cle	2.1	Gumpert-Phi	2.3	Brown-Chi	2.0	Grove-Bos	7.0	Grove-Bos	7.0
Kelley-Phi	115	Gumpert-Phi	1.9	Lee-Cle	2.1	Lee-Cle	1.3	W.Ferrell-Bos	4.5	Gehrig-NY	6.4
Grove-Bos	115	Kimsey-Det	1.1	Brown-Chi	1.9	Gumpert-Phi	1.2	Allen-Cle	4.5	Gehringer-Det	6.1
Bridges-Det	109	Brown-Chi	.5	Kimsey-Det	.6	Kimsey-Det	.6	Bridges-Det	4.4	Appling-Chi	5.1
Thomas-StL	107							Ruffing-NY	3.9	W.Ferrell-Bos	4.5

TEAM	G	W	L	PCT	GB	R	OR	AB	H	2B	3B	HR	BB	SO	AVG	OBP	SLG	PRO	PRO+	BR	/A	PF	CHI	RC	SB	CS	SBA	SBR
NY	152	95	57	.625		732	602	5329	1484	251	41	111	412	492	.278	.334	.403	.737	105	40	31	101	100	734	45			
CHI	154	93	61	.604	3	811	682	5349	1537	253	74	96	538	496	.287	.355	.416	.771	111	117	83	104	98	816	71			
PIT	154	86	68	.558	10	704	646	5433	1550	223	86	47	463	480	.285	.343	.384	.727	104	30	30	100	96	734	32			
STL	157	81	73	.526	15	789	733	5476	1543	264	67	94	385	569	.282	.331	.406	.737	104	36	21	102	107	744	78			
BOS	152	79	73	.520	16	579	556	5124	1265	200	41	63	485	707	.247	.314	.339	.653	91	-109	-59	91	102	565	45			
BRO	155	62	91	.405	33.5	616	772	5295	1401	258	53	37	469	583	.265	.327	.354	.681	90	-57	-67	102	97	629	69			
PHI	155	61	92	.399	34.5	724	869	5424	1482	258	37	103	478	640	.273	.334	.391	.725	95	21	-38	108	100	730	66			
CIN	155	56	98	.364	40	612	707	5230	1329	215	59	73	437	586	.254	.315	.360	.675	94	-78	-49	95	102	599	53			
TOT	617					5567		42660	11591	1922	458	624	3667	4553	.272	.332	.382	.714							459			

TEAM	CG	SH	SV	IP	H	H/G	HR	BB	SO	RAT	ERA	ERA+	OAV	OOB	PR	/A	PF	CPI	FA	E	DP	FW	PW	BW	SBW	DIF
NY	67	11	17	1361	1341	8.9	85	404	653	11.7	3.43	113	.258	.314	73	69	99	102	.974	159	143	.9	6.8	3.1		8.2
CHI	73	11	13	1381¹	1434	9.3	91	502	596	12.8	3.97	100	.267	.332	-10	0	102	99	.975	151	141	1.5	.0	8.2		6.3
PIT	67	12	17	1366¹	1398	9.2	71	428	643	12.2	3.56	108	.264	.321	53	45	99	101	.970	181	135	-.2	4.5	3.0		1.8
STL	81	10	4	1392	1546	10.0	95	448	571	13.0	3.98	100	.281	.331	-10	-1	102	105	.973	164	127	1.0	-.0	2.1		1.1
BOS	85	16	10	1359¹	1344	8.9	60	372	387	11.4	3.22	111	.259	.310	105	55	92	103	.975	157	128	1.0	5.5	-5.9		2.4
BRO	63	5	8	1362²	1470	9.7	68	476	592	13.0	4.13	98	.274	.336	-33	-14	103	96	.964	217	127	-2.2	-1.4	-6.6		-4.3
PHI	59	6	15	1373²	1629	10.7	116	501	529	14.2	5.05	86	.297	.359	-174	-114	111	97	.970	184	157	-.3	-11.3	-3.8		-.1
CIN	64	10	18	1358¹	1428	9.5	38	533	581	13.1	3.94	95	.270	.339	-4	-32	95	97	.966	208	139	-1.6	-3.2	-4.9		-11.3
TOT	559	81	102	10954²		9.5				12.7	3.91		.272	.332					.971	1421	1097					

Runs		Hits		Doubles		Triples		Home Runs		Total Bases	
Medwick-StL	111	Medwick-StL	237	Medwick-StL	56	Vaughan-Pit	17	Ott-NY	31	Medwick-StL	406
Herman-Chi	106	P.Waner-Pit	219	Mize-StL	40	Suhr-Pit	14	Medwick-StL	31	Mize-StL	333
Hack-Chi	106	Mize-StL	204	Bartell-NY	38	Handley-Pit	12	Camilli-Phi	27	Demaree-Chi	298
Galan-Chi	104	Demaree-Chi	199	Phelps-Bro	37	Goodman-Cin	12	Mize-StL	25	Ott-NY	285
Demaree-Chi	104	Herman-Chi	189	Moore-NY	37	Herman-Chi	11	Galan-Chi	18	Camilli-Phi	279

Runs Batted In		Runs Produced		Bases On Balls		Batting Average		On Base Percentage		Slugging Average	
Medwick-StL	154	Medwick-StL	234	Ott-NY	102	Medwick-StL	.374	Camilli-Phi	.446	Medwick-StL	.641
Demaree-Chi	115	Demaree-Chi	202	Camilli-Phi	90	Mize-StL	.364	Mize-StL	.427	Mize-StL	.595
Mize-StL	113	Mize-StL	191	Suhr-Pit	83	Hartnett-Chi	.354	Medwick-StL	.414	Camilli-Phi	.587
Suhr-Pit	97	Hack-Chi	167	Hack-Chi	83	P.Waner-Pit	.354	P.Waner-Pit	.413	Hartnett-Chi	.548
Ott-NY	95	P.Waner-Pit	166	Galan-Chi	79	Whitney-Phi	.341	Ott-NY	.408	Ott-NY	.523

Production		Adjusted Production		Batter Runs		Adjusted Batter Runs		Clutch Hitting Index		Runs Created	
Medwick-StL	1.056	Medwick-StL	179	Medwick-StL	68.8	Medwick-StL	65.9	Scharein-Phi	136	Medwick-StL	170
Camilli-Phi	1.034	Mize-StL	171	Mize-StL	57.4	Mize-StL	54.9	Durocher-StL	133	Mize-StL	150
Mize-StL	1.021	Camilli-Phi	165	Camilli-Phi	54.9	Camilli-Phi	45.4	Suhr-Pit	129	Camilli-Phi	137
Ott-NY	.931	Ott-NY	149	Ott-NY	41.2	Ott-NY	39.8	Jurges-Chi	124	Ott-NY	128
Herman-Chi	.875	P.Waner-Pit	132	Hartnett-Chi	31.1	P.Waner-Pit	29.8	Todd-Pit	120	P.Waner-Pit	118

Total Average		Stolen Bases		Stolen Base Average	Stolen Base Runs	Fielding Runs		Total Player Rating	
Camilli-Phi	1.189	Galan-Chi	23			Bartell-NY	37.5	Medwick-StL	6.2
Medwick-StL	1.113	Hack-Chi	16			Whitehead-NY	26.1	Bartell-NY	6.1
Mize-StL	1.097					Riggs-Cin	19.5	Herman-Chi	5.2
Ott-NY	1.021					Herman-Chi	18.6	Ott-NY	3.7
Vaughan-Pit	.864					Young-Pit	18.1	Camilli-Phi	3.4

Wins		Win Percentage		Games		Complete Games		Shutouts		Saves	
Hubbell-NY	22	Hubbell-NY	.733	Mulcahy-Phi	56	Turner-Bos	24	Turner-Bos	5	Melton-NY	7
Turner-Bos	20	Melton-NY	.690	Jorgens-Phi	52	Fette-Bos	23	Grissom-Cin	5	Brown-Pit	7
Melton-NY	20	Fette-Bos	.667			Weiland-StL	21	Fette-Bos	5	Grissom-Cin	6
Fette-Bos	20	Carleton-Chi	.667							Root-Chi	5
Warneke-StL	18	Turner-Bos	.645							Hollingsworth-Cin	5

Innings Pitched		Fewest Hits/Game		Fewest BB/Game		Strikeouts		Strikeouts/Game		Ratio	
Passeau-Phi	292.1	Mungo-Bro	7.60	D.Dean-StL	1.51	Hubbell-NY	159	Mungo-Bro	6.82	Turner-Bos	9.82
Lee-Chi	272.1	Grissom-Cin	7.77	Root-Chi	1.61	Grissom-Cin	149	Grissom-Cin	6.00	Melton-NY	10.05
Weiland-StL	264.1	Melton-NY	7.84	Hoyt-Pit-Bro	1.66	Blanton-Pit	143	Bauers-Pit	5.66	Castleman-NY	10.16
Hubbell-NY	261.2	Carleton-Chi	7.91	Turner-Bos	1.82	Melton-NY	142	Henshaw-Bro	5.64	Root-Chi	10.53
Fette-Bos	259.0	Turner-Bos	7.99	Castleman-NY	1.85			LaMaster-Phi	5.51	D.Dean-StL	10.72

Earned Run Average		Adjusted ERA		Opponents' Batting Avg.		Opponents' On Base Pct.		Starter Runs		Adjusted Starter Runs	
Turner-Bos	2.38	Turner-Bos	150	Mungo-Bro	.229	Turner-Bos	.274	Turner-Bos	43.5	Melton-NY	35.0
Melton-NY	2.61	Melton-NY	149	Grissom-Cin	.232	Melton-NY	.280	Melton-NY	35.8	Turner-Bos	34.2
D.Dean-StL	2.69	D.Dean-StL	148	Melton-NY	.233	Castleman-NY	.287	Fette-Bos	29.5	D.Dean-StL	28.2
Bauers-Pit	2.88	Mungo-Bro	139	Turner-Bos	.235	Root-Chi	.290	MacFayden-Bos	26.9	Bauers-Pit	20.5
Fette-Bos	2.88	Bauers-Pit	134	Carleton-Chi	.236	D.Dean-StL	.291	D.Dean-StL	26.7	Mungo-Bro	20.1

Clutch Pitching Index		Relief Runs		Adjusted Relief Runs		Relief Ranking		Total Pitcher Index		Total Baseball Ranking	
Johnson-StL	128	Coffman-NY	7.8	Coffman-NY	7.5	Coffman-NY	9.9	Turner-Bos	4.5	Medwick-StL	6.2
Brandt-Pit	124	Hutchinson-Bos	1.8					Melton-NY	3.9	Bartell-NY	6.1
Weiland-StL	115							Mungo-Bro	3.0	Herman-Chi	5.2
Frankhouse-Bro	113							D.Dean-StL	3.0	Turner-Bos	4.5
MacFayden-Bos	112							Fette-Bos	2.5	Melton-NY	3.9

TEAM	G	W	L	PCT	GB	R	OR	AB	H	2B	3B	HR	BB	SO	AVG	OBP	SLG	PRO	PRO+	BR	/A	PF	CHI	RC	SB	CS	SBA	SBR
NY	157	102	52	.662		979	671	5487	1554	282	73	174	709	607	.283	.369	.456	.825	113	112	106	101	103	952	60	36	63	-4
DET	155	89	65	.578	13	935	841	5516	1611	309	62	150	656	711	.292	.370	.452	.822	111	106	85	102	100	947	89	45	66	0
CHI	154	86	68	.558	16	780	730	5277	1478	280	76	67	549	447	.280	.350	.400	.750	95	-38	-37	100	103	763	70	34	67	1
CLE	156	83	71	.539	19	817	768	5353	1499	304	76	103	570	551	.280	.352	.423	.775	100	4	-1	101	101	813	78	51	60	-7
BOS	154	80	72	.526	21	821	775	5354	1506	269	64	100	601	557	.281	.357	.411	.768	96	-1	-32	104	102	804	79	61	56	-13
WAS	158	73	80	.477	28.5	757	841	5578	1559	245	84	47	591	503	.279	.351	.379	.730	94	-74	-40	96	100	767	61	35	64	-3
PHI	154	54	97	.358	46.5	699	854	5228	1398	278	60	94	583	557	.267	.341	.397	.738	93	-63	-52	98	97	732	95	48	66	0
STL	156	46	108	.299	56	715	1023	5510	1573	327	44	71	514	510	.285	.348	.399	.747	93	-47	-52	101	93	780	30	27	53	-7
TOT	622					6503		43303	12178	2294	539	806	4773	4443	.281	.355	.415	.770							562	337	63	-34

TEAM	CG	SH	SV	IP	H	H/G	HR	BB	SO	RAT	ERA	ERA+	OAV	OOB	PR	/A	PF	CPI	FA	E	DP	FW	PW	BW	SBW	DIF
NY	82	15	21	1396	1417	9.1	92	506	652	12.5	3.65	122	.261	.325	151	124	96	103	.972	170	134	.2	11.4	9.7	.0	3.7
DET	70	6	11	1378	1521	9.9	102	635	485	14.2	4.87	96	.279	.357	-38	-30	101	95	.976	147	149	1.4	-2.8	7.8	.4	5.2
CHI	70	15	21	1351¹	1435	9.6	115	532	533	13.2	4.17	110	.273	.341	68	65	100	104	.971	174	173	-.2	6.0	-3.4	.5	6.2
CLE	64	4	15	1364²	1529	10.1	61	566	630	14.0	4.39	105	.285	.356	35	33	100	102	.974	159	153	.8	3.0	-.0	-.3	2.5
BOS	74	6	14	1366	1518	10.0	92	597	682	14.0	4.48	106	.279	.352	21	41	103	100	.970	177	139	-.4	3.8	-2.9	-.8	4.4
WAS	75	5	14	1398²	1498	9.6	96	671	524	14.1	4.58	97	.275	.357	7	-23	96	99	.972	170	181	.3	-2.1	-3.7	.1	1.9
PHI	65	6	9	1335	1490	10.0	105	613	469	14.3	4.85	97	.281	.358	-35	-21	102	97	.967	198	150	-1.7	-1.9	-4.8	.4	-13.5
STL	55	2	8	1363	1768	11.7	143	653	468	16.2	6.00	80	.315	.390	-209	-178	105	100	.972	173	166	-.0	-16.3	-4.8	-.3	-9.6
TOT	555	59	113	10952²		10.0				14.1	4.62		.281	.355					.972	1368	1245					

Runs		Hits		Doubles		Triples		Home Runs		Total Bases	
DiMaggio-NY	151	Bell-StL	218	Bell-StL	51	Walker-Det	16	DiMaggio-NY	46	DiMaggio-NY	418
Rolfe-NY	143	DiMaggio-NY	215	Greenberg-Det	49	Kreevich-Chi	16	Greenberg-Det	40	Greenberg-Det	397
Gehrig-NY	138	Walker-Det	213	Moses-Phi	48	Stone-Was	15	Gehrig-NY	37	Gehrig-NY	366
Greenberg-Det	137	Lewis-Was	210	Vosmik-StL	47	DiMaggio-NY	15	Foxx-Bos	36	Moses-Phi	357
Gehringer-Det	133	Gehringer-Det	209	Lary-Cle	46	Greenberg-Det	14	York-Det	35	Trosky-Cle	329

Runs Batted In		Runs Produced		Bases On Balls		Batting Average		On Base Percentage		Slugging Average	
Greenberg-Det	183	Greenberg-Det	280	Gehrig-NY	127	Gehringer-Det	.371	Gehringer-Det	.473	DiMaggio-NY	.673
DiMaggio-NY	167	DiMaggio-NY	272	Greenberg-Det	102	Gehrig-NY	.351	Gehrig-NY	.458	Greenberg-Det	.668
Gehrig-NY	159	Gehrig-NY	260	Foxx-Bos	99	DiMaggio-NY	.346	Greenberg-Det	.436	York-Det	.651
Dickey-NY	133	Gehringer-Det	215	Johnson-Phi	98	Bonura-Chi	.345	Johnson-Phi	.425	Gehrig-NY	.643
Trosky-Cle	128	Foxx-Bos	202	Clift-StL	98	Travis-Was	.344	Dickey-NY	.417	Bonura-Chi	.573

Production		Adjusted Production		Batter Runs		Adjusted Batter Runs		Clutch Hitting Index		Runs Created	
Gehrig-NY	1.116	Gehrig-NY	177	Gehrig-NY	73.3	Gehrig-NY	72.3	Hayes-Chi	152	Gehrig-NY	181
Greenberg-Det	1.105	Greenberg-Det	171	Greenberg-Det	67.2	Greenberg-Det	63.7	Higgins-Bos	127	Greenberg-Det	178
DiMaggio-NY	1.085	DiMaggio-NY	168	DiMaggio-NY	61.3	DiMaggio-NY	60.4	Myer-Was	125	DiMaggio-NY	173
Dickey-NY	.987	Johnson-Phi	147	Gehringer-Det	44.0	Gehringer-Det	41.1	Hale-Cle	117	Gehringer-Det	140
Bonura-Chi	.984	Bonura-Chi	146	Dickey-NY	37.5	Johnson-Phi	36.8	Werber-Phi	116	Clift-StL	134

Total Average		Stolen Bases		Stolen Base Average		Stolen Base Runs		Fielding Runs		Total Player Rating	
Gehrig-NY	1.339	Chapman-Was-Bos	35	Hill-Was-Phi	81.8	Chapman-Was-Bos	3.3	Clift-StL	41.0	Clift-StL	7.2
Greenberg-Det	1.277	Werber-Phi	35	Walker-Det	76.7	Hill-Was	3.0	Hale-Cle	25.9	DiMaggio-NY	6.0
DiMaggio-NY	1.207	Walker-Det	23	Pytlak-Cle	76.2	Werber-Phi	2.7	Hayes-Chi	20.5	Gehringer-Det	5.2
Gehringer-Det	1.089			Chapman-Was-Bos	74.5	Walker-Det	2.7	Appling-Chi	13.8	Dickey-NY	5.1
Johnson-Phi	1.083			Werber-Phi	72.9	Kreevich-Chi	2.4	Dickey-NY	12.3	Greenberg-Det	4.7

Wins		Win Percentage		Games		Complete Games		Shutouts		Saves	
Gomez-NY	21	Allen-Cle	.938	Brown-Chi	53	W.Ferrell-Bos-Was	26	Gomez-NY	6	Brown-Chi	18
Ruffing-NY	20	Stratton-Chi	.750	Wilson-Bos	51	Gomez-NY	25	Stratton-Chi	5	Murphy-NY	10
Lawson-Det	18	Ruffing-NY	.741	Newsom-Was-Bos	41	Ruffing-NY	22	Whitehead-Chi	4	Wilson-Bos	7
Grove-Bos	17	Lawson-Det	.720	Kelley-Phi	41	Grove-Bos	21	Ruffing-NY	4	Malone-NY	6
Auker-Det	17	Gomez-NY	.656	Heving-Cle	40	DeShong-Was	20	Appleton-Was	4		

Innings Pitched		Fewest Hits/Game		Fewest BB/Game		Strikeouts		Strikeouts/Game		Ratio	
W.Ferrell-Bos-Was	281.0	Gomez-NY	7.53	Stratton-Chi	2.02	Gomez-NY	194	Gomez-NY	6.27	Stratton-Chi	9.89
Gomez-NY	278.1	Stratton-Chi	7.76	Hudlin-Cle	2.20	Newsom-Was-Bos	166	Wilson-Bos	5.57	Gomez-NY	10.57
Newsom-Was-Bos	275.1	Smith-Phi	8.15	Marcum-Bos	2.30	Grove-Bos	153	Newsom-Was-Bos	5.43	Ruffing-NY	10.92
DeShong-Was	264.1	Allen-Cle	8.17	Ruffing-NY	2.39	Feller-Cle	150	Grove-Bos	5.26	Allen-Cle	11.55
Grove-Bos	262.0	Ruffing-NY	8.50	Lyons-Chi	2.39	Bridges-Det	138	Bridges-Det	5.06	Lee-Chi	11.87

Earned Run Average		Adjusted ERA		Opponents' Batting Avg.		Opponents' On Base Pct.		Starter Runs		Adjusted Starter Runs	
Gomez-NY	2.33	Stratton-Chi	191	Gomez-NY	.223	Stratton-Chi	.280	Gomez-NY	70.9	Gomez-NY	65.5
Stratton-Chi	2.40	Gomez-NY	191	Stratton-Chi	.234	Gomez-NY	.287	Ruffing-NY	46.6	Grove-Bos	50.2
Allen-Cle	2.55	Allen-Cle	181	Smith-Phi	.242	Ruffing-NY	.296	Grove-Bos	46.5	Ruffing-NY	41.6
Ruffing-NY	2.98	Grove-Bos	157	Allen-Cle	.244	Lee-Chi	.312	Stratton-Chi	40.6	Stratton-Chi	40.2
Grove-Bos	3.02	Ruffing-NY	149	Ruffing-NY	.247	Allen-Cle	.313	Allen-Cle	39.8	Allen-Cle	39.6

Clutch Pitching Index		Relief Runs		Adjusted Relief Runs		Relief Ranking		Total Pitcher Index		Total Baseball Ranking	
Allen-Cle	120	Brown-Chi	13.3	Brown-Chi	13.1	Brown-Chi	21.9	Gomez-NY	6.5	Clift-StL	7.2
Whitehead-Chi	119	Cohen-Was	9.2	Cohen-Was	8.1	Cohen-Was	9.2	Stratton-Chi	4.5	Gomez-NY	6.5
Knott-StL	112	Murphy-NY	5.5	Fink-Phi	5.9	Murphy-NY	5.3	Grove-Bos	4.0	DiMaggio-NY	6.0
Grove-Bos	111	Fink-Phi	5.1	Murphy-NY	3.3	Fink-Phi	2.2	Ruffing-NY	3.7	Gehringer-Det	5.2
Galehouse-Cle	110	Wyatt-Cle	1.5	Wyatt-Cle	1.4	Wyatt-Cle	.8	Auker-Det	2.9	Dickey-NY	5.1

TEAM	G	W	L	PCT	GB	R	OR	AB	H	2B	3B	HR	BB	SO	AVG	OBP	SLG	PRO	PRO+	BR	/A	PF	CHI	RC	SB	CS	SBA	SBR
CHI	154	89	63	.586		713	598	5333	1435	242	70	65	522	476	.269	.338	.377	.715	100	25	6	103	101	689	49			
PIT	152	86	64	.573	2	707	630	5422	1511	265	66	65	485	409	.279	.340	.388	.728	106	48	43	101	96	727	47			
NY	152	83	67	.553	5	705	637	5255	1424	210	36	125	465	528	.271	.334	.396	.730	106	45	39	101	99	715	31			
CIN	151	82	68	.547	6	723	634	5391	1495	251	57	110	366	518	.277	.327	.406	.733	110	43	62	97	101	720	19			
BOS	153	77	75	.507	12	561	618	5250	1311	199	39	54	424	548	.250	.309	.333	.642	91	-119	-66	90	104	549	49			
STL	156	71	80	.470	17.5	725	721	5528	1542	288	74	91	412	492	.279	.331	.407	.738	103	56	14	106	97	752	55			
BRO	151	69	80	.463	18.5	704	710	5142	1322	225	79	61	611	615	.257	.338	.367	.705	98	13	-3	102	103	671	66			
PHI	151	45	105	.300	43	550	840	5192	1318	233	29	40	425	507	.254	.312	.333	.645	85	-111	-96	97	101	549	38			
TOT	610					5388		42513	11358	1913	450	611	3708	4093	.267	.329	.376	.705							354			

TEAM	CG	SH	SV	IP	H	H/G	HR	BB	SO	RAT	ERA	ERA+	OAV	OOB	PR	/A	PF	CPI	FA	E	DP	FW	PW	BW	SBW	DIF
CHI	67	16	18	1396²	1414	9.1	71	454	583	12.1	3.37	113	.262	.322	64	66	101	105	.978	135	151	2.3	6.6	.6		3.5
PIT	57	8	15	1379²	1406	9.2	71	432	557	12.2	3.46	109	.266	.324	49	50	100	106	.974	163	168	.5	5.0	4.3		1.2
NY	59	8	18	1349	1370	9.1	87	389	497	11.9	3.62	104	.261	.314	24	20	99	97	.973	168	147	.2	2.0	3.9		1.9
CIN	72	11	16	1362	1329	8.8	75	463	542	11.9	3.62	101	.254	.316	25	3	96	94	.971	172	133	-.1	.3	6.2		.6
BOS	83	15	12	1380	1375	9.0	66	465	413	12.2	3.40	101	.258	.322	58	3	91	103	.972	173	136	-.0	.3	-6.6		7.4
STL	58	10	16	1384²	1482	9.6	77	474	534	12.8	3.84	103	.272	.333	-9	17	104	102	.967	199	145	-1.4	1.7	1.4		-6.2
BRO	56	12	14	1332	1464	9.9	88	446	469	13.1	4.07	96	.278	.338	-42	-26	103	102	.973	157	148	.8	-2.6	-.3		-3.3
PHI	68	3	6	1329¹	1516	10.3	76	582	492	14.4	4.93	79	.285	.358	-169	-155	103	92	.966	201	135	-1.8	-15.6	-9.7		-2.9
TOT	520	83	115	10913¹		9.4				12.6	3.78		.267	.329					.972	1368	1163					

Runs		Hits		Doubles		Triples		Home Runs		Total Bases	
Ott-NY	116	McCormick-Cin	209	Medwick-StL	47	Mize-StL	16	Ott-NY	36	Mize-StL	326
Hack-Chi	109	Hack-Chi	195	McCormick-Cin	40	Gutteridge-StL	15	Goodman-Cin	30	Medwick-StL	316
Camilli-Bro	106	L.Waner-Pit	194	Young-Pit	36	Suhr-Pit	14	Mize-StL	27	Ott-NY	307
Goodman-Cin	103	Medwick-StL	190	Martin-Phi	36	Riggs-Cin	13	Camilli-Bro	24	Goodman-Cin	303
Medwick-StL	100	Mize-StL	179			Koy-Bro	13	Rizzo-Pit	23	Rizzo-Pit	285

Runs Batted In		Runs Produced		Bases On Balls		Batting Average		On Base Percentage		Slugging Average	
Medwick-StL	122	Medwick-StL	201	Camilli-Bro	119	Lombardi-Cin	.342	Ott-NY	.442	Mize-StL	.614
Ott-NY	116	Ott-NY	196	Ott-NY	118	Mize-StL	.337	Vaughan-Pit	.433	Ott-NY	.583
Rizzo-Pit	111	McCormick-Cin	190	Vaughan-Pit	104	McCormick-Cin	.327	Mize-StL	.422	Medwick-StL	.536
McCormick-Cin	106	Rizzo-Pit	185	Hack-Chi	94	Medwick-StL	.322	Hack-Chi	.411	Goodman-Cin	.533
Mize-StL	102	Camilli-Bro	182	Suhr-Pit	87	Vaughan-Pit	.322	Suhr-Pit	.394	Lombardi-Cin	.524

Production		Adjusted Production		Batter Runs		Adjusted Batter Runs		Clutch Hitting Index		Runs Created	
Mize-StL	1.036	Ott-NY	178	Ott-NY	61.9	Ott-NY	60.8	Durocher-Bro	140	Ott-NY	149
Ott-NY	1.024	Mize-StL	172	Mize-StL	59.2	Mize-StL	52.2	McCormick-Cin	134	Mize-StL	141
Lombardi-Cin	.915	Lombardi-Cin	154	Vaughan-Pit	36.4	Goodman-Cin	36.4	Arnovich-Phi	128	Hack-Chi	119
Medwick-StL	.905	Goodman-Cin	149	Medwick-StL	34.4	Vaughan-Pit	35.6	Todd-Pit	127	Goodman-Cin	116
Goodman-Cin	.901	Vaughan-Pit	140	Goodman-Cin	33.5	Lombardi-Cin	34.4	Lavagetto-Bro	125	Vaughan-Pit	115

Total Average		Stolen Bases		Stolen Base Average		Stolen Base Runs		Fielding Runs		Total Player Rating	
Ott-NY	1.164	Hack-Chi	16					Young-Pit	31.8	Vaughan-Pit	6.4
Mize-StL	1.104	Lavagetto-Bro	15					Herman-Chi	24.8	Ott-NY	6.1
Camilli-Bro	.964	Koy-Bro	15					Bartell-NY	22.4	Lombardi-Cin	3.8
Vaughan-Pit	.960	Vaughan-Pit	14					Vaughan-Pit	18.3	Goodman-Cin	3.7
Goodman-Cin	.908	Gutteridge-StL	14					Arnovich-Phi	16.7	Hack-Chi	3.6

Wins		Win Percentage		Games		Complete Games		Shutouts		Saves	
Lee-Chi	22	Lee-Chi	.710	Coffman-NY	51	Derringer-Cin	26	Lee-Chi	9	Coffman-NY	12
Derringer-Cin	21	Bryant-Chi	.633	Brown-Pit	51	Turner-Bos	22	MacFayden-Bos	5	Root-Chi	8
Bryant-Chi	19	Brown-Pit	.625	McGee-StL	47	Walters-Phi-Cin	20	Warneke-StL	4	Hamlin-Bro	6
Weiland-StL	16	VanderMeer-Cin	.600	Mulcahy-Phi	46	MacFayden-Bos	19	Derringer-Cin	4	Errickson-Bos	6
		Derringer-Cin	.600			Lee-Chi	19				

Innings Pitched		Fewest Hits/Game		Fewest BB/Game		Strikeouts		Strikeouts/Game		Ratio	
Derringer-Cin	307.0	VanderMeer-Cin	7.07	Davis-StL	1.40	Bryant-Chi	135	Hubbell-NY	5.23	Hubbell-NY	10.36
Lee-Chi	291.0	Bauers-Pit	7.67	Derringer-Cin	1.44	Derringer-Cin	132	VanderMeer-Cin	4.99	Derringer-Cin	10.67
Bryant-Chi	270.1	Bryant-Chi	7.82	Hubbell-NY	1.66	VanderMeer-Cin	125	Weiland-StL	4.61	Root-Chi	10.92
Turner-Bos	268.0	MacFayden-Bos	8.52	Root-Chi	1.68	Lee-Chi	121	Bryant-Chi	4.49	Turner-Bos	10.95
Mulcahy-Phi	267.1	Klinger-Pit	8.59	Turner-Bos	1.81					Lee-Chi	11.04

Earned Run Average		Adjusted ERA		Opponents' Batting Avg.		Opponents' On Base Pct.		Starter Runs		Adjusted Starter Runs	
Lee-Chi	2.66	Lee-Chi	144	VanderMeer-Cin	.213	Hubbell-NY	.285	Lee-Chi	36.3	Lee-Chi	37.6
Root-Chi	2.86	Root-Chi	134	Bauers-Pit	.233	Derringer-Cin	.291	Derringer-Cin	29.1	Derringer-Cin	24.3
Derringer-Cin	2.93	Fitzsimmons-Bro	129	Bryant-Chi	.235	Root-Chi	.294	Bryant-Chi	20.6	Bryant-Chi	21.8
MacFayden-Bos	2.95	Klinger-Pit	127	MacFayden-Bos	.247	Lohrman-NY	.294	MacFayden-Bos	20.3	Fitzsimmons-Bro	19.8
Klinger-Pit	2.99	Derringer-Cin	124	Schumacher-NY	.248	Schumacher-NY	.299	Bauers-Pit	19.2	Bauers-Pit	19.4

Clutch Pitching Index		Relief Runs		Adjusted Relief Runs		Relief Ranking		Total Pitcher Index		Total Baseball Ranking	
Lee-Chi	119	Brown-NY	19.8	Brown-NY	19.6	Brown-NY	18.1	Lee-Chi	4.0	Vaughan-Pit	6.4
Pressnell-Bro	111	Russell-Chi	5.0	Russell-Chi	5.5	Coffman-NY	4.3	Bryant-Chi	2.4	Ott-NY	6.1
Blanton-Pit	111	Coffman-NY	3.8	Coffman-NY	3.5	Russell-Chi	3.7	Derringer-Cin	2.4	Lee-Chi	4.0
Tamulis-Bro	110							Fitzsimmons-Bro	2.3	Lombardi-Cin	3.8
Fette-Bos	110							Bauers-Pit	2.1	Goodman-Cin	3.7

TEAM	G	W	L	PCT	GB	R	OR	AB	H	2B	3B	HR	BB	SO	AVG	OBP	SLG	PRO	PRO+	BR	/A	PF	CHI	RC	SB	CS	SBA	SBR
NY	157	99	53	.651		966	710	5410	1480	283	63	174	749	616	.274	.366	.446	.812	111	77	82	100	104	926	91	28	76	11
BOS	150	88	61	.591	9.5	902	751	5229	1566	298	56	98	650	463	.299	.378	.434	.812	105	87	46	105	100	881	55	51	52	-14
CLE	153	86	66	.566	13	847	782	5356	1506	300	89	113	550	605	.281	.350	.434	.784	104	9	26	98	102	832	83	36	70	3
DET	155	84	70	.545	16	862	795	5270	1434	219	52	137	693	581	.272	.359	.411	.770	94	0	-47	106	104	812	76	41	65	-2
WAS	152	75	76	.497	23.5	814	873	5474	1602	278	72	85	573	379	.293	.362	.416	.778	108	12	71	93	96	845	65	37	64	-3
CHI	149	65	83	.439	32	709	752	5199	1439	239	55	67	514	489	.277	.343	.383	.726	86	-91	-107	102	101	700	56	39	59	-7
STL	156	55	97	.362	44	755	962	5333	1498	273	36	92	590	528	.281	.355	.397	.752	95	-38	-36	100	96	774	51	40	56	-9
PHI	154	53	99	.349	46	726	956	5229	1410	243	62	98	605	590	.270	.348	.396	.744	95	-57	-37	97	97	741	65	53	55	-12
TOT	613					6581		42500	11935	2133	485	864	4924	4251	.281	.358	.415	.773							542	325	63	-32

TEAM	CG	SH	SV	IP	H	H/G	HR	BB	SO	RAT	ERA	ERA+	OAV	OOB	PR	/A	PF	CPI	FA	E	DP	FW	PW	BW	SBW	DIF
NY	91	11	13	1382	1436	9.4	85	566	567	13.1	3.91	116	.268	.339	134	95	95	106	.973	169	177	.5	8.6	7.4	1.4	5.2
BOS	67	10	15	1316¹	1472	10.1	102	528	484	13.8	4.46	111	.281	.349	48	70	103	103	.968	190	172	-1.1	6.3	4.2	-.9	5.1
CLE	68	5	17	1353	1416	9.4	100	681	717	14.1	4.60	101	.268	.355	29	7	97	99	.974	151	145	1.2	.6	2.3	.6	5.1
DET	75	3	11	1348¹	1532	10.2	110	608	435	14.4	4.79	104	.287	.361	1	32	104	103	.976	147	172	1.6	2.9	-4.2	.2	6.6
WAS	59	6	11	1360¹	1472	9.7	92	655	515	14.3	4.94	91	.276	.358	-22	-64	94	94	.970	180	179	-.5	-5.8	6.4	.0	-.8
CHI	83	5	9	1316¹	1449	9.9	101	550	432	13.8	4.36	112	.279	.350	62	78	102	106	.967	196	155	-1.6	7.0	-9.7	-.3	-4.6
STL	71	3	7	1344²	1584	10.6	132	737	632	15.7	5.80	86	.295	.382	-151	-124	104	96	.975	145	163	1.8	-11.2	-3.3	-.4	-7.9
PHI	56	4	12	1324	1573	10.7	142	599	473	14.9	5.48	88	.292	.365	-101	-95	101	96	.965	206	119	-1.8	-8.6	-3.3	-.7	-8.6
TOT	570	47	95	10745		10.0				14.3	4.79		.281	.358					.971	1384	1282					

Runs
Greenberg-Det 144
Foxx-Bos 139
Gehringer-Det 133
Rolfe-NY 132
DiMaggio-NY 129

Hits
Vosmik-Bos 201
Cramer-Bos 198
Almada-Was-StL .. 197
Foxx-Bos 197
Rolfe-NY 196

Doubles
Cronin-Bos 51
McQuinn-StL 42
Trosky-Cle 40
Chapman-Bos 40
Vosmik-Bos 37

Triples
Heath-Cle 18
Averill-Cle 15
DiMaggio-NY 13

Home Runs
Greenberg-Det 58
Foxx-Bos 50
Clift-StL 34
York-Det 33
DiMaggio-NY 32

Total Bases
Foxx-Bos 398
Greenberg-Det 380
DiMaggio-NY 348
Johnson-Phi 311
Heath-Cle 302

Runs Batted In
Foxx-Bos 175
Greenberg-Det 146
DiMaggio-NY 140
York-Det 127
Clift-StL 118

Runs Produced
Foxx-Bos 264
DiMaggio-NY 237
Greenberg-Det 232
Gehringer-Det 220
Clift-StL 203

Bases On Balls
Greenberg-Det 119
Foxx-Bos 119
Clift-StL 118
Gehringer-Det 113
Gehrig-NY 107

Batting Average
Foxx-Bos .... .349
Heath-Cle .... .343
Chapman-Bos .... .340
Myer-Was .... .336
Travis-Was .... .335

On Base Percentage
Foxx-Bos .... .462
Myer-Was .... .454
Greenberg-Det ..... .438
Averill-Cle .... .429
Cronin-Bos .... .428

Slugging Average
Foxx-Bos .... .704
Greenberg-Det ..... .683
Heath-Cle .... .602
DiMaggio-NY .... .581
York-Det .... .579

Production
Foxx-Bos 1.166
Greenberg-Det .. 1.122
York-Det .... .995
Heath-Cle .... .985
Dickey-NY .... .981

Adjusted Production
Foxx-Bos 180
Greenberg-Det 167
Heath-Cle 146
Dickey-NY 144
Clift-StL 143

Batter Runs
Foxx-Bos 78.2
Greenberg-Det 66.0
Clift-StL 37.7
Cronin-Bos 34.8
York-Det 33.9

Adjusted Batter Runs
Foxx-Bos 70.4
Greenberg-Det 57.1
Clift-StL 38.0
Johnson-Phi 35.8
Averill-Cle 33.9

Clutch Hitting Index
Higgins-Bos 140
Heffner-Bos 138
R.Ferrell-Was 116
Doerr-Bos 116
Bonura-Was 111

Runs Created
Foxx-Bos 189
Greenberg-Det 172
DiMaggio-NY 136
Clift-StL 133
Gehrig-NY 131

Total Average
Foxx-Bos 1.392
Greenberg-Det .. 1.306
Clift-StL 1.104
York-Det 1.104
Dickey-NY 1.083

Stolen Bases
Crosetti-NY 27
Lary-Cle 23
Werber-Phi 19
Lewis-Was 17
Fox-Det 16

Stolen Base Average
Lary-Cle 79.3
Fox-Det 69.6
Crosetti-NY 69.2
Lewis-Was 65.4
Werber-Phi 55.9

Stolen Base Runs
Gehringer-Det 3.6
Rolfe-NY 3.3
Lary-Cle 3.3
Hale-Cle 1.8

Fielding Runs
Gordon-NY 23.7
Crosetti-NY 17.6
Clift-StL 14.0
Johnson-Phi 10.3
Cramer-Bos 8.7

Total Player Rating
Foxx-Bos 5.2
Clift-StL 4.8
Cronin-Bos 4.2
Greenberg-Det 4.0
Dickey-NY 3.7

Wins
Ruffing-NY 21
Newsom-StL 20
Gomez-NY 18
Harder-Cle 17
Feller-Cle 17

Win Percentage
Ruffing-NY .... .750
Pearson-NY .... .696
Harder-Cle .... .630
Stratton-Chi ..... .625
Feller-Cle .... .607

Games
Humphries-Cle 45
Newsom-StL 44
E.Smith-Phi 43
Bagby-Bos 43
Appleton-Was 43

Complete Games
Newsom-StL 31
Ruffing-NY 22
Gomez-NY 20
Feller-Cle 20
Caster-Phi 20

Shutouts
Gomez-NY 4
Wilson-Bos 3
Ruffing-NY 3
Leonard-Was 3

Saves
Murphy-NY 11
McKain-Bos 6
Humphries-Cle 6
Potter-Phi 5
Appleton-Was 5

Innings Pitched
Newsom-StL 329.2
Caster-Phi 281.1
Feller-Cle 277.2
Ruffing-NY 247.1
Lee-Chi 245.1

Fewest Hits/Game
Feller-Cle 7.29
Allen-Cle 8.51
Pearson-NY 8.82
Rigney-Chi 8.84
Hadley-NY 8.87

Fewest BB/Game
Leonard-Was 2.14
Harder-Cle 2.33
Lyons-Chi 2.40
Chandler-NY 2.46
Thomas-Phi 2.63

Strikeouts
Feller-Cle 240
Newsom-StL 226
L.Mills-StL 134
Gomez-NY 129
Ruffing-NY 127

Strikeouts/Game
Feller-Cle 7.78
Newsom-StL 6.17
L.Mills-StL 5.73
Grove-Bos 5.44
Allen-Cle 5.04

Ratio
Leonard-Was 11.32
Ruffing-NY 11.94
Stratton-Chi 12.03
Chandler-NY 12.14
Harder-Cle 12.15

Earned Run Average
Grove-Bos 3.08
Ruffing-NY 3.31
Gomez-NY 3.35
Leonard-Was 3.43
Lee-Chi 3.49

Adjusted ERA
Grove-Bos 160
Lee-Chi 140
Rigney-Chi 138
Ruffing-NY 137
Gomez-NY 135

Opponents' Batting Avg.
Feller-Cle .... .220
Allen-Cle .... .246
Hadley-NY .... .254
Stratton-Chi ..... .255
Rigney-Chi .... .256

Opponents' On Base Pct.
Leonard-Was ...... .305
Stratton-Chi ..... .315
Ruffing-NY .... .317
Harder-Cle .... .319
Grove-Bos .... .319

Starter Runs
Ruffing-NY 40.6
Gomez-NY 38.2
Lee-Chi 35.6
Leonard-Was 33.8
Grove-Bos 31.1

Adjusted Starter Runs
Lee-Chi 38.4
Grove-Bos 33.7
Ruffing-NY 33.6
Gomez-NY 31.4
Leonard-Was 27.0

Clutch Pitching Index
Lyons-Chi 125
Gill-Det 119
Grove-Bos 118
Rigney-Chi 117
Ruffing-NY 110

Relief Runs
Murphy-NY 5.6
McKain-Bos 3.0

Adjusted Relief Runs
McKain-Bos 4.6
Murphy-NY 3.0

Relief Ranking
McKain-Bos 4.4
Murphy-NY 3.8

Total Pitcher Index
Ruffing-NY 4.0
Lee-Chi 3.8
Gomez-NY 3.3
Leonard-Was 3.1
Grove-Bos 3.1

Total Baseball Ranking
Foxx-Bos 5.2
Clift-StL 4.8
Cronin-Bos 4.2
Greenberg-Det 4.0
Ruffing-NY 4.0

TEAM	G	W	L	PCT	GB	R	OR	AB	H	2B	3B	HR	BB	SO	AVG	OBP	SLG	PRO	PRO+	BR	/A	PF	CHI	RC	SB	CS	SBA	SBR
CIN	156	97	57	.630		767	595	5378	1493	269	60	98	500	538	.278	.343	.405	.748	106	51	47	101	102	759	46			
STL	155	92	61	.601	4.5	779	633	5447	1601	332	62	98	475	566	.294	.354	.432	.786	110	122	72	106	94	834	44			
BRO	157	84	69	.549	12.5	708	645	5350	1420	265	57	78	564	639	.265	.338	.380	.718	96	0	-25	104	102	697	59			
CHI	156	84	70	.545	13	724	678	5293	1407	263	62	91	523	553	.266	.336	.391	.727	99	10	-2	102	103	702	61			
NY	151	77	74	.510	18.5	703	685	5129	1395	211	38	116	498	499	.272	.340	.396	.736	103	28	22	101	101	683	26			
PIT	153	68	85	.444	28.5	666	721	5269	1453	261	60	63	477	420	.276	.338	.384	.722	102	4	15	98	97	687	44			
BOS	152	63	88	.417	32.5	572	659	5286	1395	199	39	56	366	494	.264	.314	.348	.662	91	-117	-78	93	104	575	41			
PHI	152	45	106	.298	50.5	553	856	5133	1341	232	40	49	421	486	.261	.318	.351	.669	89	-98	-82	97	99	570	47			
TOT	616					5472		42285	11505	2032	418	649	3824	4195	.272	.335	.386	.721						368				

TEAM	CG	SH	SV	IP	H	H/G	HR	BB	SO	RAT	ERA	ERA+	OAV	OOB	PR	/A	PF	CPI	FA	E	DP	FW	PW	BW	SBW	DIF
CIN	86	13	9	1403²	1340	8.6	81	499	637	12.0	3.27	117	.255	.322	101	87	98	107	.974	162	170	.6	8.7	4.7		6.0
STL	45	18	32	1384²	1377	9.0	76	498	603	12.3	3.59	115	.260	.326	50	80	105	100	.971	177	140	-.2	8.0	7.2		.5
BRO	69	9	13	1410¹	1431	9.1	93	399	528	11.9	3.64	110	.263	.317	43	60	103	97	.972	176	157	-.0	6.0	-2.5		4.0
CHI	72	8	13	1392¹	1504	9.7	74	430	584	12.6	3.80	104	.276	.331	18	21	101	101	.970	186	126	-.6	2.1	-.2		5.7
NY	55	6	20	1319	1412	9.6	86	477	505	13.1	4.07	96	.275	.340	-22	-20	100	100	.975	153	151	.8	-2.0	2.2		.5
PIT	53	10	15	1354	1537	10.2	70	423	464	13.2	4.15	92	.287	.342	-36	-49	98	100	.972	168	153	.1	-4.9	1.5		-5.2
BOS	68	11	15	1358¹	1400	9.3	63	513	430	12.8	3.71	100	.271	.339	31	-3	94	104	.971	181	178	-.6	-.3	-7.8		-3.8
PHI	67	3	12	1326²	1502	10.2	106	579	447	14.4	5.17	77	.289	.365	-185	-171	102	93	.970	171	136	-.0	-17.1	-8.2		-5.1
TOT	515	78	129	10949		9.5				12.8	3.92		.272	.335					.972	1374	1211					

Runs		Hits		Doubles		Triples		Home Runs		Total Bases	
Werber-Cin	115	McCormick-Cin	209	Slaughter-StL	52	Herman-Chi	18	Mize-StL	28	Mize-StL	353
Hack-Chi	112	Medwick-StL	201	Medwick-StL	48	Goodman-Cin	16	Ott-NY	27	McCormick-Cin	312
Herman-Chi	111	Mize-StL	197	Mize-StL	44	Mize-StL	14	Camilli-Bro	26	Medwick-StL	307
Camilli-Bro	105	Slaughter-StL	193	McCormick-Cin	41	Camilli-Bro	12	Leiber-Chi	24	Camilli-Bro	296
		Brown-StL	192					Lombardi-Cin	20	Slaughter-StL	291

Runs Batted In		Runs Produced		Bases On Balls		Batting Average		On Base Percentage		Slugging Average	
McCormick-Cin	128	McCormick-Cin	209	Camilli-Bro	110	Padgett-StL	.399	Ott-NY	.449	Mize-StL	.626
Medwick-StL	117	Medwick-StL	201	Ott-NY	100	Mize-StL	.349	Mize-StL	.444	Ott-NY	.581
Mize-StL	108	Mize-StL	184	Mize-StL	92	McCormick-Cin	.332	Camilli-Bro	.409	Leiber-Chi	.556
Camilli-Bro	104	Camilli-Bro	183	Werber-Cin	91	Medwick-StL	.332	Goodman-Cin	.401	Padgett-StL	.554
Leiber-Chi	88	Herman-Chi	174	Lavagetto-Bro	78	P.Waner-Pit	.328	Arnovich-Phi	.397	Camilli-Bro	.524

Production		Adjusted Production		Batter Runs		Adjusted Batter Runs		Clutch Hitting Index		Runs Created	
Mize-StL	1.070	Mize-StL	174	Mize-StL	68.7	Mize-StL	60.0	May-Phi	120	Mize-StL	162
Ott-NY	1.030	Ott-NY	173	Ott-NY	45.9	Ott-NY	45.1	Lavagetto-Bro	116	Camilli-Bro	128
Camilli-Bro	.933	Camilli-Bro	144	Camilli-Bro	41.8	Camilli-Bro	37.6	McCormick-Cin	116	Medwick-StL	114
Goodman-Cin	.916	Goodman-Cin	144	Leiber-Chi	30.5	Goodman-Cin	29.4	R.Russell-Chi	116	Ott-NY	112
Medwick-StL	.886	West-Bos	139	Goodman-Cin	29.8	Leiber-Chi	29.1	Bonura-NY	113	McCormick-Cin	110

Total Average		Stolen Bases		Stolen Base Average		Stolen Base Runs		Fielding Runs		Total Player Rating	
Mize-StL	1.194	Handley-Pit	17					Slaughter-StL	15.8	Frey-Cin	4.0
Ott-NY	1.194	Hack-Chi	17					Frey-Cin	15.1	Mize-StL	3.9
Camilli-Bro	.995	Werber-Cin	15					Arnovich-Phi	14.9	Vaughan-Pit	3.9
Goodman-Cin	.941	Lavagetto-Bro	14					Jurges-NY	14.9	Ott-NY	3.6
Frey-Cin	.860	Hassett-Bos	13					Werber-Cin	12.6	Goodman-Cin	3.1

Wins		Win Percentage		Games		Complete Games		Shutouts		Saves	
Walters-Cin	27	Derringer-Cin	.781	Shoun-StL	53	Walters-Cin	31	Fette-Bos	6	Shoun-StL	9
Derringer-Cin	25	Walters-Cin	.711	Sewell-Pit	52	Derringer-Cin	28	Posedel-Bos	5	Bowman-StL	9
Davis-StL	22	French-Chi	.652	Bowman-StL	51	Lee-Chi	20	Derringer-Cin	5	Davis-StL	7
Hamlin-Bro	20	Gumbert-NY	.621	Davis-StL	49	Hamlin-Bro	19	McGee-StL	4	Brown-NY	7
Lee-Chi	19	Hamlin-Bro	.606	Brown-Pit	47	Posedel-Bos	18			Brown-Pit	7

Innings Pitched		Fewest Hits/Game		Fewest BB/Game		Strikeouts		Strikeouts/Game		Ratio	
Walters-Cin	319.0	Walters-Cin	7.05	Derringer-Cin	1.05	Passeau-Phi-Chi	137	Cooper-StL	5.55	Hubbell-NY	10.29
Derringer-Cin	301.0	Bowman-StL	7.49	Hubbell-NY	1.40	Walters-Cin	137	Tamulis-Bro	4.71	Walters-Cin	10.30
Lee-Chi	282.1	Moore-Cin	8.49	Davis-StL	1.74	Cooper-StL	130	French-Chi	4.55	Hamlin-Bro	10.31
Passeau-Phi-Chi	274.1	Hamlin-Bro	8.51	Hamlin-Bro	1.80	Derringer-Cin	128	Passeau-Phi-Chi	4.49	Derringer-Cin	10.73
Hamlin-Bro	269.2	Hubbell-NY	8.77	Root-Chi	1.83	Lee-Chi	105	Bowman-StL	4.15	Bowman-StL	10.74

Earned Run Average		Adjusted ERA		Opponents' Batting Avg.		Opponents' On Base Pct.		Starter Runs		Adjusted Starter Runs	
Walters-Cin	2.29	Walters-Cin	168	Walters-Cin	.220	Hubbell-NY	.280	Walters-Cin	57.8	Walters-Cin	54.7
Bowman-StL	2.60	Bowman-StL	158	Bowman-StL	.232	Hamlin-Bro	.285	Derringer-Cin	33.0	Derringer-Cin	30.1
Hubbell-NY	2.75	Hubbell-NY	143	Hamlin-Bro	.248	Walters-Cin	.291	Casey-Bro	24.9	Bowman-StL	28.4
Casey-Bro	2.93	Casey-Bro	137	Hubbell-NY	.249	Derringer-Cin	.295	Bowman-StL	24.7	Casey-Bro	27.7
Derringer-Cin	2.93	Derringer-Cin	131	Moore-Cin	.254	Bowman-StL	.302	Thompson-Cin	23.3	Thompson-Cin	21.8

Clutch Pitching Index		Relief Runs		Adjusted Relief Runs		Relief Ranking		Total Pitcher Index		Total Baseball Ranking	
Brown-Pit	120	J.Russell-Chi	1.9	Shoun-StL	4.1	Shoun-StL	2.2	Walters-Cin	8.5	Walters-Cin	8.5
Shoffner-Bos-Cin	115	Shoun-StL	1.8	J.Russell-Chi	2.0	J.Russell-Chi	2.1	Davis-StL	3.3	Frey-Cin	4.0
Casey-Bro	113							Casey-Bro	3.1	Mize-StL	3.9
Cooper-StL	113							Bowman-StL	2.7	Vaughan-Pit	3.9
Moore-Cin	113							Derringer-Cin	2.7	Ott-NY	3.6

TEAM	G	W	L	PCT	GB	R	OR	AB	H	2B	3B	HR	BB	SO	AVG	OBP	SLG	PRO	PRO+	BR	/A	PF	CHI	RC	SB	CS	SBA	SBR
NY	152	106	45	.702		967	556	5300	1521	259	55	166	701	543	.287	.374	.451	.825	119	134	149	98	102	923	72	37	66	-1
BOS	152	89	62	.589	17	890	795	5308	1543	287	57	124	591	505	.291	.363	.436	.799	106	78	45	104	101	831	42	44	49	-14
CLE	154	87	67	.565	20.5	797	700	5316	1490	291	79	85	557	574	.280	.350	.413	.763	105	4	32	97	100	775	72	46	61	-6
CHI	155	85	69	.552	22.5	755	737	5279	1451	220	56	64	579	502	.275	.349	.374	.723	89	-62	-81	103	103	708	113	61	65	-3
DET	155	81	73	.526	26.5	849	762	5326	1487	277	67	124	620	592	.279	.356	.426	.782	99	43	-21	108	100	821	88	38	70	4
WAS	153	65	87	.428	41.5	702	797	5334	1483	249	79	44	547	460	.278	.346	.379	.725	98	-62	-8	93	96	718	94	47	67	0
PHI	153	55	97	.362	51.5	711	1022	5309	1438	282	55	98	503	532	.271	.336	.400	.736	96	-55	-40	98	97	713	60	34	64	-2
STL	156	43	111	.279	64.5	733	1035	5422	1453	242	50	91	559	606	.268	.339	.381	.720	88	-79	-94	102	100	706	48	38	56	-8
TOT	615					6404		42594	11866	2107	498	796	4657	4314	.279	.352	.407	.759							589	345	63	-30

TEAM	CG	SH	SV	IP	H	H/G	HR	BB	SO	RAT	ERA	ERA+	OAV	OOB	PR	/A	PF	CPI	FA	E	DP	FW	PW	BW	SBW	DIF
NY	87	15	26	1348²	1208	8.1	85	567	565	11.9	3.31	132	.241	.319	196	157	94	107	.978	126	159	2.9	14.5	13.7	.3	-.8
BOS	52	4	20	1350²	1533	10.2	77	543	539	14.0	4.56	104	.287	.355	9	25	102	102	.970	180	147	.0	2.3	4.1	-.9	7.9
CLE	69	10	13	1364²	1394	9.2	75	602	614	13.3	4.08	108	.267	.344	81	49	95	103	.970	180	148	.2	4.5	2.9	-.2	2.5
CHI	62	5	21	1377	1470	9.6	99	454	535	12.7	4.31	110	.275	.333	48	65	102	98	.972	167	140	1.0	6.0	-7.5	.0	8.4
DET	64	8	16	1367¹	1430	9.4	104	574	633	13.3	4.29	114	.268	.341	50	91	106	100	.967	198	147	-.6	8.4	-1.9	.7	-2.5
WAS	72	4	10	1354²	1420	9.4	75	602	521	13.6	4.60	94	.271	.348	2	-39	94	94	.966	205	167	-1.1	-3.6	-.7	.3	-5.9
PHI	50	6	12	1342²	1687	11.3	148	579	397	15.3	5.79	81	.307	.375	-175	-162	102	99	.964	210	131	-1.4	-14.9	-3.7	.2	-1.2
STL	56	3	3	1371¹	1724	11.3	133	739	516	16.4	6.01	81	.310	.393	-212	-175	105	100	.968	199	144	-.6	-16.1	-8.7	-.4	-8.2
TOT	512	55	121	10877		9.8				13.8	4.62		.279	.352					.969	1465	1183					

Runs		Hits		Doubles		Triples		Home Runs		Total Bases	
Rolfe-NY	139	Rolfe-NY	213	Rolfe-NY	46	Lewis-Was	16	Foxx-Bos	35	Williams-Bos	344
Williams-Bos	131	McQuinn-StL	195	Williams-Bos	44	McCosky-Det	14	Greenberg-Det	33	Foxx-Bos	324
Foxx-Bos	130	Keltner-Cle	191	Greenberg-Det	42	McQuinn-StL	13	Williams-Bos	31	Rolfe-NY	321
McCosky-Det	120	McCosky-Det	190	McQuinn-StL	37	Campbell-Cle	13	DiMaggio-NY	30	McQuinn-StL	318
Johnson-Phi	115	Williams-Bos	185	Keltner-Cle	35			Gordon-NY	28	Greenberg-Det	311

Runs Batted In		Runs Produced		Bases On Balls		Batting Average		On Base Percentage		Slugging Average	
Williams-Bos	145	Williams-Bos	245	Clift-StL	111	DiMaggio-NY	.381	Foxx-Bos	.464	Foxx-Bos	.694
DiMaggio-NY	126	Johnson-Phi	206	Williams-Bos	107	Foxx-Bos	.360	Selkirk-NY	.452	DiMaggio-NY	.671
Johnson-Phi	114	Rolfe-NY	205	Appling-Chi	105	Johnson-Phi	.338	DiMaggio-NY	.448	Greenberg-Det	.622
Greenberg-Det	112	DiMaggio-NY	204	Selkirk-NY	103	Trosky-Cle	.335	Keller-NY	.447	Williams-Bos	.609
		Foxx-Bos	200	Johnson-Phi	99	Rolfe-NY	.329	Johnson-Phi	.440	Trosky-Cle	.589

Production		Adjusted Production		Batter Runs		Adjusted Batter Runs		Clutch Hitting Index		Runs Created	
Foxx-Bos	1.158	DiMaggio-NY	185	Foxx-Bos	66.1	Foxx-Bos	60.8	Wright-Was	129	Williams-Bos	157
DiMaggio-NY	1.119	Foxx-Bos	185	Williams-Bos	56.3	DiMaggio-NY	58.1	McNair-Chi	116	Foxx-Bos	150
Williams-Bos	1.045	Williams-Bos	158	DiMaggio-NY	56.0	Williams-Bos	50.9	Dahlgren-NY	116	DiMaggio-NY	139
Greenberg-Det	1.042	Trosky-Cle	157	Greenberg-Det	47.3	Johnson-Phi	48.5	Selkirk-NY	115	Johnson-Phi	138
Trosky-Cle	.994	Johnson-Phi	156	Johnson-Phi	45.7	Greenberg-Det	38.0	Higgins-Det	115	Greenberg-Det	136

Total Average		Stolen Bases		Stolen Base Average		Stolen Base Runs		Fielding Runs		Total Player Rating	
Foxx-Bos	1.304	Case-Was	51	McCosky-Det	83.3	Case-Was	5.1	Doerr-Bos	27.3	DiMaggio-NY	5.7
DiMaggio-NY	1.242	Kreevich-Chi	23	Kuhel-Chi	78.3	McCosky-Det	3.6	Kreevich-Chi	16.1	Foxx-Bos	4.9
Williams-Bos	1.161	Fox-Det	23	Chapman-Cle	75.0	Welaj-Was	2.7	Tebbetts-Det	14.5	Johnson-Phi	4.7
Greenberg-Det	1.152	McCosky-Det	20	Case-Was	75.0	Kuhel-Chi	2.4	Lewis-Was	13.6	Williams-Bos	4.3
Selkirk-NY	1.121			Walker-Chi	73.9	Henrich-NY	2.1	Clift-StL	12.0	Dickey-NY	3.9

Wins		Win Percentage		Games		Complete Games		Shutouts		Saves	
Feller-Cle	24	Grove-Bos	.789	Brown-Chi	61	Newsom-StL-Det	24	Ruffing-NY	5	Murphy-NY	19
Ruffing-NY	21	Ruffing-NY	.750	Dean-Phi	54	Feller-Cle	24	Feller-Cle	4	Brown-Chi	18
Newsom-StL-Det	20	Feller-Cle	.727	Dickman-Bos	48	Ruffing-NY	22	Newsom-StL-Det	3	Heving-Bos	7
Leonard-Was	20	Leonard-Was	.714	Heving-Bos	46	Leonard-Was	21			Dean-Phi	7
Bridges-Det	17	Bridges-Det	.708			Grove-Bos	17			Appleton-Was	6

Innings Pitched		Fewest Hits/Game		Fewest BB/Game		Strikeouts		Strikeouts/Game		Ratio	
Feller-Cle	296.2	Feller-Cle	6.89	Lyons-Chi	1.36	Feller-Cle	246	Feller-Cle	7.46	Lyons-Chi	9.85
Newsom-StL-Det	291.2	Hadley-NY	7.71	Leonard-Was	1.97	Newsom-StL-Det	192	Newsom-StL-Det	5.92	Ruffing-NY	11.11
Leonard-Was	269.1	Gomez-NY	7.86	Beckmann-Phi	2.38	Bridges-Det	129	Bridges-Det	5.86	Leonard-Was	11.26
Lee-Chi	235.0	Ruffing-NY	8.14	Lee-Chi	2.68	Rigney-Chi	119	Rigney-Chi	4.90	Grove-Bos	11.26
Ruffing-NY	233.1	Chase-Was	8.34	Grove-Bos	2.73	Chase-Was	118	Gomez-NY	4.64	Feller-Cle	11.29

Earned Run Average		Adjusted ERA		Opponents' Batting Avg.		Opponents' On Base Pct.		Starter Runs		Adjusted Starter Runs	
Grove-Bos	2.54	Grove-Bos	186	Feller-Cle	.210	Lyons-Chi	.276	Feller-Cle	58.3	Feller-Cle	51.1
Lyons-Chi	2.76	Lyons-Chi	171	Gomez-NY	.235	Ruffing-NY	.301	Grove-Bos	44.0	Grove-Bos	46.3
Feller-Cle	2.85	Feller-Cle	154	Hadley-NY	.237	Feller-Cle	.303	Ruffing-NY	43.8	Newsom-StL-Det	42.3
Ruffing-NY	2.93	Ruffing-NY	149	Ruffing-NY	.240	Bridges-Det	.304	Lyons-Chi	35.6	Lyons-Chi	37.8
Hadley-NY	2.98	Hadley-NY	146	Bridges-Det	.243	Leonard-Was	.305	Newsom-StL-Det	33.7	Ruffing-NY	36.9

Clutch Pitching Index		Relief Runs		Adjusted Relief Runs		Relief Ranking		Total Pitcher Index		Total Baseball Ranking	
Hadley-NY	132	Heving-Bos	10.9	Heving-Bos	12.2	Brown-Chi	21.7	Feller-Cle	5.6	DiMaggio-NY	5.7
Grove-Bos	126	Brown-Chi	9.7	Brown-Chi	11.2	Heving-Bos	16.1	Ruffing-NY	4.7	Feller-Cle	5.6
Trout-Det	116	Dickman-Bos	2.3	Dickman-Bos	3.7	Dickman-Bos	3.6	Lyons-Chi	4.3	Foxx-Bos	4.9
Harder-Cle	116	Murphy-NY	1.5					Grove-Bos	3.7	Johnson-Phi	4.7
Milnar-Cle	110	Appleton-Was	.7					Newsom-StL-Det	3.5	Ruffing-NY	4.7

TEAM	G	W	L	PCT	GB	R	OR	AB	H	2B	3B	HR	BB	SO	AVG	OBP	SLG	PRO	PRO+	BR	/A	PF	CHI	RC	SB	CS	SBA	SBR
CIN	155	100	53	.654		707	**528**	5372	1427	264	38	89	453	503	.266	.327	.379	.706	100	6	-1	101	103	672	72			
BRO	156	88	65	.575	12	697	621	5470	1421	256	70	93	522	570	.260	.327	.383	.710	96	15	-28	106	98	692	56			
STL	156	84	69	.549	16	747	699	5499	**1514**	266	61	**119**	479	610	.275	.336	**.411**	**.747**	106	83	39	106	96	**764**	97			
PIT	156	78	76	.506	22.5	**809**	783	5466	1511	**276**	68	76	**553**	494	**.276**	**.346**	.394	.740	112	84	**90**	99	104	757	69			
CHI	154	75	79	.487	25.5	681	636	5389	1441	272	48	86	482	566	.267	.331	.384	.715	106	25	39	98	97	691	63			
NY	152	72	80	.474	27.5	663	659	5324	1423	201	46	91	453	**478**	.267	.329	.374	.703	99	3	-2	101	98	653	45			
BOS	152	65	87	.428	34.5	623	745	5329	1366	219	50	59	402	581	.256	.311	.349	.660	93	-83	-51	95	**108**	581	48			
PHI	153	50	103	.327	50	494	750	5137	1225	180	35	75	435	527	.238	.300	.331	.631	83	-133	-113	96	96	512	25			
TOT	617					5421		42986	11328	1934	416	688	3779	4329	.264	.326	.376	.702						475				

TEAM	CG	SH	SV	IP	H	H/G	HR	BB	SO	RAT	ERA	ERA+	OAV	OOB	PR	/A	PF	CPI	FA	E	DP	FW	PW	BW	SBW	DIF
CIN	91	10	11	1407²	**1263**	8.1	73	445	557	11.0	3.05	124	**.240**	.302	125	115	98	102	**.981**	117	158	2.9	11.6	-.1		9.1
BRO	65	**17**	14	1433	1366	8.6	101	**393**	**639**	11.2	3.50	114	.248	.302	56	79	104	95	.970	183	110	-.3	8.0	-2.8		6.7
STL	71	10	14	1396	1457	9.4	83	488	550	12.7	3.83	104	.266	.329	3	24	104	102	.971	174	134	.1	2.4	3.9		1.0
PIT	49	8	**24**	1388²	1569	10.2	**72**	492	491	13.6	4.36	87	.283	.345	-79	-85	99	99	.966	217	161	-2.0	-8.6	**9.1**		2.5
CHI	69	12	14	1392	1418	9.2	74	430	564	12.1	3.54	106	.262	.319	47	32	97	103	.968	199	143	-1.2	3.2	3.9		-8.0
NY	57	11	18	1360¹	1383	9.1	110	473	606	12.4	3.79	102	.262	.325	9	14	101	**104**	.977	139	132	1.6	1.4	-.2		-6.8
BOS	76	9	12	1359	1444	9.6	83	573	435	13.6	4.36	85	.274	.349	-77	-97	97	100	.970	184	**169**	-.6	-9.8	-5.2		4.6
PHI	66	5	8	1357	1429	9.5	92	475	485	12.8	4.40	89	.270	.333	-83	-75	101	93	.970	181	136	-.4	-7.6	-11.4		-7.1
TOT	544	82	115	11093²		9.2				12.4	3.85		.264	.326					.972	1394	1143					

Runs
Vaughan-Pit 113
Mize-StL 111
Werber-Cin 105
Frey-Cin 102
Hack-Chi 101

Hits
F.McCormick-Cin . . 191
Hack-Chi 191
Mize-StL 182
Vaughan-Pit 178
Medwick-StL-Bro . . 175

Doubles
F.McCormick-Cin . . 44
Vaughan-Pit 40
Gleeson-Chi 39
Hack-Chi 38
Walker-Bro 37

Triples
Vaughan-Pit 15
Ross-Bos 14
Slaughter-StL 13
Mize-StL 13
Camilli-Bro 13

Home Runs
Mize-StL 43
Nicholson-Chi 25
Rizzo-Pit-Cin-Phi . . 24
Camilli-Bro 23

Total Bases
Mize-StL 368
F.McCormick-Cin . . 298
Medwick-StL-Bro . . 280
Camilli-Bro 271
Vaughan-Pit 269

Runs Batted In
Mize-StL 137
F.McCormick-Cin . . 127
VanRobays-Pit 116
Fletcher-Pit 104
Young-NY 101

Runs Produced
Mize-StL 205
Vaughan-Pit 201
F.McCormick-Cin . . 201
VanRobays-Pit 187
Fletcher-Pit 182

Bases On Balls
Fletcher-Pit 119
Ott-NY 100
Camilli-Bro 89
Vaughan-Pit 88
Mize-StL 82

Batting Average
Garms-Pit 355
Davis-Pit 326
Lombardi-Cin 319
Cooney-Bos 318
Hack-Chi 317

On Base Percentage
Fletcher-Pit 418
Ott-NY 407
Mize-StL 404
Camilli-Bro 397
Hack-Chi 395

Slugging Average
Mize-StL 636
Nicholson-Chi 534
Camilli-Bro 529
DiMaggio-Cin-Pit . . .519
Slaughter-StL 504

Production
Mize-StL 1.039
Camilli-Bro 926
Nicholson-Chi 899
Slaughter-StL 874
Ott-NY 864

Adjusted Production
Mize-StL 173
Nicholson-Chi 148
Camilli-Bro 144
Gleeson-Chi 139
Fletcher-Pit 137

Batter Runs
Mize-StL 63.9
Camilli-Bro 38.7
Fletcher-Pit 31.8
Ott-NY 31.7
Vaughan-Pit 28.8

Adjusted Batter Runs
Mize-StL 56.2
Fletcher-Pit 32.6
Camilli-Bro 32.3
Ott-NY 30.8
Nicholson-Chi 30.5

Clutch Hitting Index
VanRobays-Pit 154
Fletcher-Pit 129
F.McCormick-Cin . . 121
Young-NY 115
Danning-NY 115

Runs Created
Mize-StL 152
Camilli-Bro 114
Vaughan-Pit 113
Hack-Chi 112
Ott-NY 107

Total Average
Mize-StL 1.135
Camilli-Bro 1.005
Fletcher-Pit 930
Ott-NY 915
Nicholson-Chi 901

Stolen Bases
Frey-Cin 22
Hack-Chi 21
Moore-StL 18
Werber-Cin 16
Reese-Bro 15

Stolen Base Average

Stolen Base Runs

Fielding Runs
Witek-NY 19.0
Herman-Chi 18.9
Frey-Cin 18.2
Moore-StL 16.8
Miller-Bos 14.7

Total Player Rating
Vaughan-Pit 5.1
Hack-Chi 4.5
Miller-Bos 3.5
Mize-StL 3.4
Frey-Cin 3.1

Wins
Walters-Cin 22
Passeau-Chi 20
Derringer-Cin 20

Win Percentage
Fitzsimmons-Bro . .889
Sewell-Pit 762
Walters-Cin 688
Thompson-Cin 640
Derringer-Cin 625

Games
Shoun-StL 54
Brown-Pit 48
Passeau-Chi 46
Casey-Bro 44
Raffensberger-Chi . 43

Complete Games
Walters-Cin 29
Derringer-Cin 26
Mulcahy-Phi 21
Passeau-Chi 20
Higbe-Phi 20

Shutouts
Wyatt-Bro 5
Salvo-Bos 5

Saves
Brown-NY 7
Brown-Pit 7
Beggs-Cin 7
Shoun-StL 5
Passeau-Chi 5

Innings Pitched
Walters-Cin 305.0
Derringer-Cin 296.2
Higbe-Phi 283.0
Passeau-Chi 280.2
Mulcahy-Phi 280.0

Fewest Hits/Game
Walters-Cin 7.11
Higbe-Phi 7.70
Thompson-Cin . . . 7.87
Casey-Bro 7.95
Sullivan-Bos 7.97

Fewest BB/Game
Derringer-Cin 1.46
Turner-Cin 1.54
Hamlin-Bro 1.68
Davis-StL-Bro 1.79
Warneke-StL 1.82

Strikeouts
Higbe-Phi 137
Wyatt-Bro 124
Passeau-Chi 124
Schumacher-NY . . . 123

Strikeouts/Game
Melton-NY 4.91
Schumacher-NY . . 4.88
Wyatt-Bro 4.66
Hamlin-Bro 4.49
Higbe-Phi 4.36

Ratio
Derringer-Cin 9.95
Walters-Cin 9.97
Passeau-Chi 10.33
Turner-Cin 10.54
Tamulis-Bro 10.73

Earned Run Average
Walters-Cin 2.48
Passeau-Chi 2.50
Sewell-Pit 2.80
Turner-Cin 2.89
Olsen-Chi 2.97

Adjusted ERA
Walters-Cin 153
Passeau-Chi 150
Sewell-Pit 136
Turner-Cin 131
Hamlin-Bro 131

Opponents' Batting Avg.
Walters-Cin 220
Higbe-Phi 232
Thompson-Cin 233
Passeau-Chi 237
Casey-Bro 237

Opponents' On Base Pct.
Derringer-Cin 276
Passeau-Chi 278
Walters-Cin 283
Tamulis-Bro 288
Hamlin-Bro 292

Starter Runs
Walters-Cin 46.4
Passeau-Chi 42.0
Derringer-Cin 25.8
Sewell-Pit 22.1
Turner-Cin 20.0

Adjusted Starter Runs
Walters-Cin 44.3
Passeau-Chi 38.9
Derringer-Cin 23.8
Warneke-StL 21.8
Sewell-Pit 21.3

Clutch Pitching Index
Errickson-Bos 124
Olsen-Chi 119
Schumacher-NY . . . 113
Turner-Cin 113
Hamlin-Bro 111

Relief Runs
Beggs-Cin 15.8
Russell-StL 8.1
Raffensberger-Chi . 6.0
MacFayden-Pit 3.0
Joiner-NY 2.7

Adjusted Relief Runs
Beggs-Cin 15.3
Russell-StL 8.9
Raffensberger-Chi . 4.8
Brown-NY 2.9
Joiner-NY 2.9

Relief Ranking
Beggs-Cin 30.0
Russell-StL 10.8
Raffensberger-Chi . 6.2
Brown-NY 3.6
Pressnell-Bro 3.6

Total Pitcher Index
Passeau-Chi 5.3
Walters-Cin 4.7
Beggs-Cin 3.3
Sewell-Pit 2.7
Warneke-StL 2.6

Total Baseball Ranking
Passeau-Chi 5.3
Vaughan-Pit 5.1
Walters-Cin 4.7
Hack-Chi 4.5
Miller-Bos 3.5

TEAM	G	W	L	PCT	GB	R	OR	AB	H	2B	3B	HR	BB	SO	AVG	OBP	SLG	PRO	PRO+	BR	/A	PF	CHI	RC	SB	CS	SBA	SBR
DET	155	90	64	.584		888	717	5418	1549	312	65	134	664	556	.286	.366	.442	.808	105	124	38	110	97	913	66	39	63	-4
CLE	155	89	65	.578	1	710	637	5361	1422	287	61	101	519	597	.265	.332	.398	.730	98	-43	-22	97	99	724	53	36	60	-6
NY	155	88	66	.571	2	817	671	5286	1371	243	66	155	648	606	.259	.344	.418	.762	107	25	57	96	103	789	59	56	62	-4
CHI	155	82	72	.532	8	735	672	5386	1499	238	63	73	496	569	.278	.340	.387	.727	93	-41	-50	101	102	713	52	60	46	-20
BOS	154	82	72	.532	8	872	825	5481	1566	301	80	145	590	597	.286	.356	.449	.805	110	109	73	104	97	889	55	49	53	-13
STL	156	67	87	.435	23	757	882	5416	1423	278	58	118	556	642	.263	.333	.401	.734	94	-35	-50	102	103	744	51	40	56	-9
WAS	154	64	90	.416	26	665	811	5365	1453	266	67	52	468	504	.271	.331	.374	.705	95	-85	-42	94	100	690	94	40	70	4
PHI	154	54	100	.351	36	703	932	5304	1391	242	53	105	556	656	.262	.334	.387	.721	95	-53	-38	98	100	704	48	33	59	-5
TOT	619					6147		43017	11674	2167	513	883	4497	4727	.271	.342	.407	.750							478	333	59	-56

TEAM	CG	SH	SV	IP	H	H/G	HR	BB	SO	RAT	ERA	ERA+	OAV	OOB	PR	/A	PF	CPI	FA	E	DP	FW	PW	BW	SBW	DIF
DET	59	10	23	1375[1]	1425	9.3	102	570	752	13.2	4.01	119	.266	.338	57	114	109	105	.968	194	116	-.7	10.8	3.6	.3	-1.0
CLE	72	13	22	1375	1328	8.7	86	512	686	12.2	3.63	116	.254	.324	115	89	96	102	.975	149	164	1.7	8.4	-2.1	.0	3.9
NY	76	10	14	1373	1389	9.1	119	511	559	12.6	3.89	104	.261	.328	76	22	92	104	.975	152	158	1.6	2.1	5.4	.3	1.7
CHI	83	10	18	1386[2]	1335	8.7	111	480	574	11.9	3.74	118	.250	.313	99	105	101	96	.969	185	125	-.2	9.9	-4.7	-1.2	1.2
BOS	51	4	16	1379[2]	1568	10.2	124	625	613	14.5	4.89	92	.284	.359	-77	-60	103	101	.972	173	156	.4	-5.7	6.9	-.6	3.9
STL	64	4	9	1373[1]	1592	10.4	113	646	439	14.8	5.12	89	.290	.367	-113	-82	105	100	.974	158	179	1.3	-7.7	-4.7	-.2	1.3
WAS	74	6	7	1350	1494	10.0	93	618	618	14.2	4.59	91	.281	.359	-31	-64	95	103	.968	194	166	-.7	-6.0	-4.0	1.0	-3.3
PHI	72	4	12	1345	1543	10.3	135	534	488	14.5	5.22	85	.283	.348	-125	-116	101	91	.960	238	131	-3.1	-11.0	-3.6	.2	-5.6
TOT	551	61	121	10958		9.6				13.4	4.38		.271	.342					.970	1443	1195					

Runs		Hits		Doubles		Triples		Home Runs		Total Bases	
Williams-Bos	134	Radcliff-StL	200	Greenberg-Det	50	McCosky-Det	19	Greenberg-Det	41	Greenberg-Det	384
Greenberg-Det	129	McCosky-Det	200	York-Det	46	Keller-NY	15	Foxx-Bos	36	York-Det	343
McCosky-Det	123	Cramer-Bos	200	Boudreau-Cle	46	Finney-Bos	15	York-Det	33	Williams-Bos	333
Gordon-NY	112	Appling-Chi	197	Williams-Bos	43	Williams-Bos	14	Johnson-Phi	31	DiMaggio-NY	318
Kuhel-Chi	111	Wright-Chi	196	Moses-Phi	41	Appling-Chi	13	DiMaggio-NY	31	Gordon-NY	315

Runs Batted In		Runs Produced		Bases On Balls		Batting Average		On Base Percentage		Slugging Average	
Greenberg-Det	150	Greenberg-Det	238	Keller-NY	106	DiMaggio-NY	.352	Williams-Bos	.442	Greenberg-Det	.670
York-Det	134	Williams-Bos	224	Clift-StL	104	Appling-Chi	.348	Greenberg-Det	.433	DiMaggio-NY	.626
DiMaggio-NY	133	York-Det	206	Gehringer-Det	101	Williams-Bos	.344	Gehringer-Det	.428	Williams-Bos	.594
Foxx-Bos	119	DiMaggio-NY	195	Foxx-Bos	101	Radcliff-StL	.342	DiMaggio-NY	.425	York-Det	.583
Williams-Bos	113	Cronin-Bos	191	Williams-Bos	96	Greenberg-Det	.340	Appling-Chi	.420	Foxx-Bos	.581

Production		Adjusted Production		Batter Runs		Adjusted Batter Runs		Clutch Hitting Index		Runs Created	
Greenberg-Det	1.103	DiMaggio-NY	176	Greenberg-Det	68.8	DiMaggio-NY	55.9	Tresh-Chi	131	Greenberg-Det	171
DiMaggio-NY	1.051	Greenberg-Det	166	Williams-Bos	57.2	Greenberg-Det	54.7	Boudreau-Cle	130	Williams-Bos	154
Williams-Bos	1.036	Williams-Bos	159	DiMaggio-NY	50.8	Williams-Bos	51.6	Walker-Was	117	York-Det	147
York-Det	.993	Foxx-Bos	148	York-Det	47.3	Foxx-Bos	37.8	Bell-Cle	114	DiMaggio-NY	135
Foxx-Bos	.993	Keller-NY	142	Foxx-Bos	42.6	York-Det	34.9	Cronin-Bos	109	Foxx-Bos	124

Total Average		Stolen Bases		Stolen Base Average		Stolen Base Runs		Fielding Runs		Total Player Rating	
Greenberg-Det	1.215	Case-Was	35	Walker-Was	84.0	Case-Was	4.5	Heffner-StL	19.1	DiMaggio-NY	4.5
Williams-Bos	1.122	Walker-Was	21	Case-Was	77.8	Walker-Was	3.9	Doerr-Bos	18.3	Greenberg-Det	4.4
DiMaggio-NY	1.098	Gordon-NY	18	Gordon-NY	69.2	Gehringer-Det	3.0	Tebbetts-Det	18.2	Williams-Bos	4.0
York-Det	1.050	Lewis-Was	15			Bartell-Det	2.4	Travis-Was	15.7	Gordon-NY	3.9
Foxx-Bos	1.026	Kreevich-Chi	15			Rosar-NY	1.5	Gordon-NY	14.0	Doerr-Bos	3.6

Wins		Win Percentage		Games		Complete Games		Shutouts		Saves	
Feller-Cle	27	Rowe-Det	.842	Feller-Cle	43	Feller-Cle	31	Milnar-Cle	4	Benton-Det	17
Newsom-Det	21	Newsom-Det	.808	Benton-Det	42	Lee-Chi	24	Lyons-Chi	4	Brown-Chi	10
Milnar-Cle	18	Feller-Cle	.711	Wilson-Bos	41	Leonard-Was	23	Feller-Cle	4	Murphy-NY	9
Hudson-Was	17	Smith-Cle	.682	Heusser-Phi	41						
		Milnar-Cle	.643	Dobson-Cle	40						

Innings Pitched		Fewest Hits/Game		Fewest BB/Game		Strikeouts		Strikeouts/Game		Ratio	
Feller-Cle	320.1	Feller-Cle	6.88	Lyons-Chi	1.79	Feller-Cle	261	Feller-Cle	7.33	Feller-Cle	10.34
Leonard-Was	289.0	Rigney-Chi	7.70	Lee-Chi	2.21	Newsom-Det	164	Bridges-Det	6.06	Rigney-Chi	10.65
Rigney-Chi	280.2	Smith-Chi	7.77	Rowe-Det	2.29	Rigney-Chi	141	Wilson-Bos	5.82	Lyons-Chi	10.87
Newsom-Det	264.0	Bridges-Det	7.79	Leonard-Was	2.43	Bridges-Det	133	Newsom-Det	5.59	Lee-Chi	11.09
Auker-StL	263.2	Newsom-Det	8.01	Russo-NY	2.61	Chase-Was	129	Smith-Chi	5.17	Russo-NY	11.27

Earned Run Average		Adjusted ERA		Opponents' Batting Avg.		Opponents' On Base Pct.		Starter Runs		Adjusted Starter Runs	
Feller-Cle	2.61	Newsom-Det	168	Feller-Cle	.210	Feller-Cle	.285	Feller-Cle	63.0	Feller-Cle	57.1
Newsom-Det	2.83	Feller-Cle	161	Smith-Chi	.228	Lyons-Chi	.287	Newsom-Det	45.6	Newsom-Det	56.5
Rigney-Chi	3.11	Rigney-Chi	142	Bridges-Det	.229	Rigney-Chi	.292	Rigney-Chi	39.7	Rigney-Chi	40.9
Smith-Chi	3.21	Bridges-Det	141	Rigney-Chi	.230	Lee-Chi	.300	Chase-Was	33.4	Bridges-Det	30.5
Chase-Was	3.23	Smith-Chi	138	Newsom-Det	.238	Russo-NY	.303	Milnar-Cle	30.0	Smith-Chi	27.9

Clutch Pitching Index		Relief Runs		Adjusted Relief Runs		Relief Ranking		Total Pitcher Index		Total Baseball Ranking	
Chase-Was	134	Eisenstat-Cle	9.9	Trotter-StL	8.9	Trotter-StL	11.1	Feller-Cle	6.1	Feller-Cle	6.1
Leonard-Was	122	Trotter-StL	6.7	Eisenstat-Cle	8.6	Brown-Chi	9.3	Newsom-Det	4.6	Newsom-Det	4.6
Newsom-Det	119	Brown-Chi	5.1	Brown-Chi	5.4	Benton-Det	6.7	Rigney-Chi	4.2	DiMaggio-NY	4.5
Smith-Cle	117	Murphy-NY	4.8	Benton-Det	2.9	Eisenstat-Cle	6.5	Smith-Chi	2.9	Greenberg-Det	4.4
Milnar-Cle	115			Murphy-NY	2.4	Murphy-NY	4.8	Rowe-Det	2.9	Rigney-Chi	4.2

TEAM	G	W	L	PCT	GB	R	OR	AB	H	2B	3B	HR	BB	SO	AVG	OBP	SLG	PRO	PRO+	BR	/A	PF	CHI	RC	SB	CS	SBA	SBR
BRO	157	100	54	.649		800	581	5485	1494	286	69	101	600	535	.272	.347	.405	.752	113	128	93	104	98	792	36			
STL	155	97	56	.634	2.5	734	589	5457	1482	254	56	70	540	543	.272	.340	.377	.717	102	62	13	107	99	719	47			
CIN	154	88	66	.571	12	616	564	5218	1288	213	33	64	477	428	.247	.313	.337	.650	89	-72	-74	100	108	556	68			
PIT	156	81	73	.526	19	690	643	5297	1417	233	65	56	547	516	.268	.338	.368	.706	105	39	42	100	99	670	59			
NY	156	74	79	.484	25.5	667	706	5395	1401	248	35	95	504	518	.260	.326	.371	.697	101	15	1	102	98	659	36			
CHI	155	70	84	.455	30	666	670	5230	1323	239	25	99	559	670	.253	.327	.365	.692	105	9	33	96	101	642	39			
BOS	156	62	92	.403	38	592	720	5414	1357	231	38	48	471	608	.251	.312	.334	.646	92	-82	-58	96	103	568	61			
PHI	155	43	111	.279	57	501	793	5233	1277	188	38	64	451	596	.244	.307	.331	.638	89	-97	-77	96	93	528	65			
TOT	622					5266		42729	11039	1892	359	597	4149	4414	.258	.326	.361	.688						411				

TEAM	CG	SH	SV	IP	H	H/G	HR	BB	SO	RAT	ERA	ERA+	OAV	OOB	PR	/A	PF	CPI	FA	E	DP	FW	PW	BW	SBW	DIF
BRO	66	17	22	1421	1236	7.8	81	495	603	11.1	3.14	117	.233	.300	78	83	101	93	.974	162	125	.9	8.5	9.6		4.0
STL	64	15	20	1416¹	1289	8.2	85	502	659	11.5	3.19	118	.242	.310	70	90	104	101	.973	172	146	.2	9.2	1.3		9.7
CIN	89	19	10	1386²	1300	8.4	61	510	627	11.9	3.17	114	.250	.319	72	66	99	106	.975	152	147	1.3	6.8	-7.6		10.6
PIT	71	8	12	1374¹	1392	9.1	66	492	410	12.4	3.48	104	.260	.323	23	19	99	102	.968	196	130	-1.1	2.0	4.3		-1.1
NY	55	12	18	1391²	1455	9.4	90	539	566	13.0	3.94	94	.269	.337	-48	-39	102	102	.974	160	144	.9	-4.0	.1		.5
CHI	74	8	9	1364²	1431	9.4	60	449	548	12.5	3.72	94	.267	.327	-13	-32	97	98	.970	180	139	-.3	-3.3	3.4		-6.8
BOS	62	10	9	1385²	1440	9.4	75	554	446	13.2	3.95	90	.269	.341	-49	-58	98	102	.969	191	174	-.9	-6.0	-6.0		-2.2
PHI	35	4	9	1372¹	1499	9.8	79	606	552	14.0	4.50	82	.279	.355	-132	-121	102	98	.969	187	147	-.7	-12.4	-7.9		-13.0
TOT	516	93	109	11112²		8.9				12.4	3.63		.258	.326					.972	1400	1152					

Runs		Hits		Doubles		Triples		Home Runs		Total Bases	
Reiser-Bro	117	Hack-Chi	186	Reiser-Bro	39	Reiser-Bro	17	Camilli-Bro	34	Reiser-Bro	299
Hack-Chi	111	Reiser-Bro	184	Mize-StL	39	Fletcher-Pit	13	Ott-NY	27	Camilli-Bro	294
Medwick-Bro	100	Litwhiler-Phi	180	Rucker-NY	38	Hopp-StL	11	Nicholson-Chi	26	Medwick-Bro	278
Rucker-NY	95	Rucker-NY	179	Dallessandro-Chi	36	Medwick-Bro	10	Young-NY	25	Litwhiler-Phi	275
Fletcher-Pit	95	Medwick-Bro	171			Elliott-Pit	10	Dahlgren-Bos-Chi	23	Young-NY	265

Runs Batted In		Runs Produced		Bases On Balls		Batting Average		On Base Percentage		Slugging Average	
Camilli-Bro	120	Reiser-Bro	179	Fletcher-Pit	118	Reiser-Bro	.343	Fletcher-Pit	.421	Reiser-Bro	.558
Young-NY	104	Camilli-Bro	178	Camilli-Bro	104	Cooney-Bos	.319	Hack-Chi	.417	Camilli-Bro	.556
Mize-StL	100	Medwick-Bro	170	Ott-NY	100	Medwick-Bro	.318	Camilli-Bro	.407	Mize-StL	.535
DiMaggio-Pit	100	Young-NY	169	Hack-Chi	99	Hack-Chi	.317	Reiser-Bro	.406	Medwick-Bro	.517
Nicholson-Chi	98	Fletcher-Pit	158			Mize-StL	.317	Mize-StL	.406	Slaughter-StL	.496

Production		Adjusted Production		Batter Runs		Adjusted Batter Runs		Clutch Hitting Index		Runs Created	
Reiser-Bro	.964	Reiser-Bro	163	Camilli-Bro	50.2	Camilli-Bro	45.1	Lavagetto-Bro	160	Camilli-Bro	128
Camilli-Bro	.962	Camilli-Bro	162	Reiser-Bro	48.0	Reiser-Bro	43.1	VanRobays-Pit	143	Reiser-Bro	124
Mize-StL	.941	Mize-StL	153	Mize-StL	40.2	Fletcher-Pit	38.6	Dallessandro-Chi	139	Ott-NY	115
Ott-NY	.898	Ott-NY	149	Ott-NY	38.7	Hack-Chi	37.9	Bragan-Phi	124	Hack-Chi	114
Slaughter-StL	.886	Fletcher-Pit	148	Fletcher-Pit	38.2	Ott-NY	36.5	Elliott-Pit	121	Fletcher-Pit	111

Total Average		Stolen Bases		Stolen Base Average		Stolen Base Runs		Fielding Runs		Total Player Rating	
Camilli-Bro	1.057	Murtaugh-Phi	18					May-Phi	25.2	Reiser-Bro	4.7
Reiser-Bro	1.006	Benjamin-Phi	17					Stringer-Chi	20.1	Camilli-Bro	3.7
Mize-StL	.991	Handley-Pit	16					Litwhiler-Phi	17.1	Fletcher-Pit	3.7
Ott-NY	.976	Frey-Cin	16					Werber-Cin	12.5	Ott-NY	3.3
Fletcher-Pit	.965	Hopp-StL	15					Miller-Bos	12.2	Litwhiler-Phi	3.2

Wins		Win Percentage		Games		Complete Games		Shutouts		Saves	
Wyatt-Bro	22	E.Riddle-Cin	.826	Higbe-Bro	48	Walters-Cin	27	Wyatt-Bro	7	Brown-NY	8
Higbe-Bro	22	Higbe-Bro	.710	Pearson-Phi	46	Wyatt-Bro	23	VanderMeer-Cin	6	Crouch-Phi-StL	7
Walters-Cin	19	White-StL	.708	Casey-Bro	45	Tobin-Bos	20	Walters-Cin	5	Casey-Bro	7
E.Riddle-Cin	19	Wyatt-Bro	.688	Hutchings-Cin-Bos	44	Passeau-Chi	20	Davis-Bro	5	Pearson-Phi	6
		Warneke-StL	.654	Johnson-Bos	43						

Innings Pitched		Fewest Hits/Game		Fewest BB/Game		Strikeouts		Strikeouts/Game		Ratio	
Walters-Cin	302.0	VanderMeer-Cin	6.84	Passeau-Chi	2.03	VanderMeer-Cin	202	VanderMeer-Cin	8.03	Wyatt-Bro	9.58
Higbe-Bro	298.0	Wyatt-Bro	6.96	Derringer-Cin	2.13	Wyatt-Bro	176	M.Cooper-StL	5.69	E.Riddle-Cin	10.14
Wyatt-Bro	288.1	White-StL	7.24	Lohrman-NY	2.26	Walters-Cin	129	Wyatt-Bro	5.49	White-StL	10.50
Sewell-Pit	249.0	Higbe-Bro	7.37	Tobin-Bos	2.27	Higbe-Bro	121	White-StL	5.01	Tobin-Bos	10.93
Warneke-StL	246.0	E.Riddle-Cin	7.48	Lee-Chi	2.31	M.Cooper-StL	118	Melton-NY	4.63	Sewell-Pit	11.28

Earned Run Average		Adjusted ERA		Opponents' Batting Avg.		Opponents' On Base Pct.		Starter Runs		Adjusted Starter Runs	
E.Riddle-Cin	2.24	E.Riddle-Cin	160	Wyatt-Bro	.212	Wyatt-Bro	.270	Wyatt-Bro	41.4	Wyatt-Bro	42.4
Wyatt-Bro	2.34	White-StL	157	VanderMeer-Cin	.214	E.Riddle-Cin	.282	E.Riddle-Cin	33.5	E.Riddle-Cin	32.6
White-StL	2.40	Wyatt-Bro	157	White-StL	.217	White-StL	.287	White-StL	28.8	White-StL	31.8
VanderMeer-Cin	2.82	VanderMeer-Cin	127	Higbe-Bro	.220	Sewell-Pit	.299	Walters-Cin	26.9	Walters-Cin	25.7
Walters-Cin	2.83	Walters-Cin	127	E.Riddle-Cin	.224	Tobin-Bos	.300	VanderMeer-Cin	20.4	VanderMeer-Cin	19.5

Clutch Pitching Index		Relief Runs		Adjusted Relief Runs		Relief Ranking		Total Pitcher Index		Total Baseball Ranking	
V.Olsen-Chi	120	Pressnell-Chi	4.3	Pressnell-Chi	3.3	Pressnell-Chi	3.5	Wyatt-Bro	5.3	Wyatt-Bro	5.3
Heintzelman-Pit	117	Brown-NY	2.0	Brown-NY	2.4	Brown-NY	3.0	E.Riddle-Cin	3.6	Reiser-Bro	4.7
Butcher-Pit	112	Pearson-Phi	.9	Pearson-Phi	1.9	Pearson-Phi	2.5	Walters-Cin	3.3	Camilli-Bro	3.7
Johnson-Bos	111	Sullivan-Bos-Pit	.0					White-StL	3.3	Fletcher-Pit	3.7
Walters-Cin	111							Gumbert-NY-StL	2.3	E.Riddle-Cin	3.6

TEAM	G	W	L	PCT	GB	R	OR	AB	H	2B	3B	HR	BB	SO	AVG	OBP	SLG	PRO	PRO+	BR	/A	PF	CHI	RC	SB	CS	SBA	SBR
NY	156	101	53	.656		830	631	5444	1464	243	60	151	616	565	.269	.346	.419	.765	111	64	75	99	103	822	51	33	61	-5
BOS	155	84	70	.545	17	865	750	5359	1517	304	55	124	683	567	.283	.366	.430	.796	115	136	115	102	98	872	67	51	57	-11
CHI	156	77	77	.500	24	638	649	5404	1376	245	47	47	510	476	.255	.322	.343	.665	84	-128	-120	99	106	612	91	53	63	-5
DET	155	75	79	.487	26	686	743	5370	1412	247	55	81	602	584	.263	.340	.375	.715	87	-27	-98	110	97	713	43	28	61	-4
CLE	155	75	79	.487	26	677	668	5283	1350	249	84	103	512	605	.256	.323	.393	.716	101	-40	-7	95	100	691	63	47	57	-9
WAS	156	70	84	.455	31	728	798	5521	1502	257	80	52	470	488	.272	.331	.376	.707	99	-53	-21	95	107	702	79	36	69	2
STL	157	70	84	.455	31	765	823	5408	1440	281	58	91	775	552	.266	.360	.390	.750	103	56	29	103	93	804	50	39	56	-8
PHI	154	64	90	.416	37	713	840	5336	1431	240	69	85	574	588	.268	.340	.387	.727	102	-7	11	98	99	711	27	36	43	-14
TOT	622					5902		43125	11492	2066	508	734	4742	4425	.266	.341	.389	.730							471	323	59	-53

TEAM	CG	SH	SV	IP	H	H/G	HR	BB	SO	RAT	ERA	ERA+	OAV	OOB	PR	/A	PF	CPI	FA	E	DP	FW	PW	BW	SBW	DIF
NY	75	13	26	1396[1]	1309	8.4	81	598	589	12.4	3.53	112	.248	.325	96	63	95	102	.973	165	196	.5	6.1	7.3	.2	10.0
BOS	70	8	11	1372	1453	9.5	88	611	574	13.7	4.19	100	.270	.347	-6	-3	101	102	.972	172	139	.0	-.3	11.1	-.4	-3.5
CHI	106	14	4	1416	1362	8.7	89	521	564	12.1	3.52	116	.252	.320	99	91	99	102	.971	180	145	-.3	8.8	-11.6	.2	3.0
DET	52	8	16	1381[2]	1399	9.1	80	645	697	13.4	4.18	109	.260	.341	-4	57	110	96	.969	186	129	-.7	5.5	-9.5	.2	2.5
CLE	68	10	19	1377	1366	8.9	71	660	617	13.4	3.90	101	.259	.344	39	7	95	103	.976	142	158	1.7	.7	-.7	-.2	-3.5
WAS	69	8	7	1389[1]	1524	9.9	69	603	544	13.9	4.35	93	.279	.353	-32	-48	98	101	.969	187	169	-.7	-4.7	-2.0	.8	-.4
STL	65	7	10	1389	1563	10.1	120	549	454	13.8	4.72	91	.283	.350	-88	-64	104	99	.975	151	156	1.3	-6.2	2.8	-.1	-4.8
PHI	64	3	18	1365[1]	1516	10.0	136	557	386	13.8	4.83	87	.279	.348	-104	-98	101	97	.967	200	150	-1.6	-9.5	1.1	-.7	-2.3
TOT	569	71	111	11086[2]		9.3				13.3	4.15		.266	.341					.972	1383	1242					

Runs		Hits		Doubles		Triples		Home Runs		Total Bases	
Williams-Bos	135	Travis-Was	218	Boudreau-Cle	45	Heath-Cle	20	Williams-Bos	37	DiMaggio-NY	348
DiMaggio-NY	122	Heath-Cle	199	DiMaggio-NY	43	Travis-Was	19	Keller-NY	33	Heath-Cle	343
DiMaggio-Bos	117	DiMaggio-NY	193	Judnich-StL	40	Keltner-Cle	13	Henrich-NY	31	Williams-Bos	335
Clift-StL	108	Appling-Chi	186	Travis-Was	39			DiMaggio-NY	30	Travis-Was	316
		Williams-Bos	185	Kuhel-Chi	39			York-Det	27	S.Chapman-Phi	300

Runs Batted In		Runs Produced		Bases On Balls		Batting Average		On Base Percentage		Slugging Average	
DiMaggio-NY	125	Williams-Bos	218	Williams-Bos	145	Williams-Bos	.406	Williams-Bos	.551	Williams-Bos	.735
Heath-Cle	123	DiMaggio-NY	217	Cullenbine-StL	121	Travis-Was	.359	Cullenbine-StL	.452	DiMaggio-NY	.643
Keller-NY	122	Travis-Was	200	Clift-StL	113	DiMaggio-NY	.357	DiMaggio-NY	.440	Heath-Cle	.586
Williams-Bos	120	Keller-NY	191	Keller-NY	102	Heath-Cle	.340	Keller-NY	.416	Keller-NY	.580
York-Det	111	Heath-Cle	188			Siebert-Phi	.334	Foxx-Bos	.412	S.Chapman-Phi	.543

Production		Adjusted Production		Batter Runs		Adjusted Batter Runs		Clutch Hitting Index		Runs Created	
Williams-Bos	1.286	Williams-Bos	232	Williams-Bos	102.0	Williams-Bos	97.9	Berardino-StL	152	Williams-Bos	202
DiMaggio-NY	1.083	DiMaggio-NY	186	DiMaggio-NY	64.3	DiMaggio-NY	66.3	Cullenbine-StL	126	DiMaggio-NY	162
Keller-NY	.996	Heath-Cle	165	Keller-NY	45.7	Heath-Cle	51.0	Tabor-Bos	125	Heath-Cle	138
Heath-Cle	.982	Keller-NY	163	Heath-Cle	44.8	Keller-NY	47.4	Foxx-Bos	116	Keller-NY	134
Travis-Was	.930	Travis-Was	152	Cullenbine-StL	38.3	Travis-Was	43.7	Wright-Chi	116	Travis-Was	131

Total Average		Stolen Bases		Stolen Base Average		Stolen Base Runs		Fielding Runs		Total Player Rating	
Williams-Bos	1.688	Case-Was	33	Kuhel-Chi	80.0	Case-Was	4.5	Bloodworth-Was	34.7	Williams-Bos	7.9
DiMaggio-NY	1.208	Kuhel-Chi	20	Case-Was	78.6	Kuhel-Chi	3.0	Keltner-Cle	22.5	DiMaggio-NY	6.4
Keller-NY	1.099	Heath-Cle	18	Kreevich-Chi	77.3	Kreevich-Chi	2.1	Rizzuto-NY	15.6	Travis-Was	5.3
Cullenbine-StL	1.023	Tabor-Bos	17	Tabor-Bos	65.4	Fox-Bos	1.5	Case-Was	15.2	Keller-NY	4.1
Heath-Cle	1.000	Kreevich-Chi	17	Heath-Cle	60.0			S.Chapman-Phi	14.4	Keltner-Cle	3.5

Wins		Win Percentage		Games		Complete Games		Shutouts		Saves	
Feller-Cle	25	Gomez-NY	.750	Feller-Cle	44	Lee-Chi	30	Feller-Cle	6	Murphy-NY	15
Lee-Chi	22	Ruffing-NY	.714	Newsom-Det	43	Feller-Cle	28	Leonard-Was	4	Ferrick-Phi	7
D.Newsome-Bos	19	Benton-Det	.714	Brown-Cle	41	Smith-Chi	21	Humphries-Chi	4	Benton-Det	7
Leonard-Was	18	Lee-Chi	.667	Ryba-Bos	40	Lyons-Chi	19	Chandler-NY	4	Ryba-Bos	6
		Feller-Cle	.658	Benton-Det	38	Leonard-Was	19				

Innings Pitched		Fewest Hits/Game		Fewest BB/Game		Strikeouts		Strikeouts/Game		Ratio	
Feller-Cle	343.0	Benton-Det	7.42	Lyons-Chi	1.78	Feller-Cle	260	Feller-Cle	6.82	Lee-Chi	10.61
Lee-Chi	300.1	Feller-Cle	7.45	Leonard-Was	1.90	Newsom-Det	175	Newsom-Det	6.29	Ruffing-NY	11.25
Smith-Chi	263.1	Lee-Chi	7.73	Muncrief-StL	2.23	Lee-Chi	130	Newhouser-Det	5.51	Benton-Det	11.30
Leonard-Was	256.0	Donald-NY	7.98	Ruffing-NY	2.62	Rigney-Chi	119	Harris-Bos	5.15	Chandler-NY	11.33
Newsom-Det	250.1	Chandler-NY	8.03	Lee-Chi	2.76			Rigney-Chi	4.52	Lyons-Chi	11.53

Earned Run Average		Adjusted ERA		Opponents' Batting Avg.		Opponents' On Base Pct.		Starter Runs		Adjusted Starter Runs	
Lee-Chi	2.37	Lee-Chi	173	Benton-Det	.221	Lee-Chi	.293	Lee-Chi	59.4	Lee-Chi	57.7
Benton-Det	2.97	Benton-Det	153	Feller-Cle	.226	Benton-Det	.302	Feller-Cle	38.1	Feller-Cle	30.2
Wagner-Bos	3.07	Wagner-Bos	136	Lee-Chi	.232	Ruffing-NY	.306	Smith-Chi	28.4	Benton-Det	27.6
Russo-NY	3.09	Smith-Chi	129	Donald-NY	.237	Chandler-NY	.307	Russo-NY	24.6	Smith-Chi	26.9
Feller-Cle	3.15	Harris-Bos	128	Chandler-NY	.239	Lyons-Chi	.308	Wagner-Bos	22.3	Wagner-Bos	22.8

Clutch Pitching Index		Relief Runs		Adjusted Relief Runs		Relief Ranking		Total Pitcher Index		Total Baseball Ranking	
Lee-Chi	122	Murphy-NY	18.6	Murphy-NY	16.8	Murphy-NY	28.8	Lee-Chi	6.6	Williams-Bos	7.9
Wagner-Bos	120	Heving-Cle	14.6	Heving-Cle	12.9	Heving-Cle	13.6	Smith-Chi	3.2	Lee-Chi	6.6
Gomez-NY	115	Carrasquel-Was	7.5	Carrasquel-Was	6.4	Carrasquel-Was	5.1	Feller-Cle	3.2	DiMaggio-NY	6.4
Marchildon-Phi	115	Brown-Cle	7.3	Brown-Cle	5.5	Brown-Cle	4.9	Benton-Det	3.1	Travis-Was	5.3
Smith-Chi	112			Thomas-Det	2.7	Thomas-Det	1.5	Murphy-NY	2.7	Keller-NY	4.1

TEAM	G	W	L	PCT	GB	R	OR	AB	H	2B	3B	HR	BB	SO	AVG	OBP	SLG	PRO	PRO+	BR	/A	PF	CHI	RC	SB	CS	SBA	SBR
STL	156	106	48	.688		755	482	5421	1454	282	69	60	551	507	.268	.338	.379	.717	109	109	54	108	103	718	71			
BRO	155	104	50	.675	2	742	510	5285	1398	263	34	62	572	484	.265	.338	.362	.700	110	80	69	102	107	671	81			
NY	154	85	67	.559	20	675	600	5210	1323	162	35	109	558	511	.254	.330	.361	.691	108	59	56	101	102	627	39			
CIN	154	76	76	.500	29	527	545	5260	1216	198	39	66	483	549	.231	.299	.321	.620	88	-81	-80	100	102	519	42			
PIT	151	66	81	.449	36.5	585	631	5104	1250	173	49	54	537	536	.245	.320	.330	.650	95	-15	-29	103	102	556	41			
CHI	155	68	86	.442	38	591	665	5352	1360	224	41	75	509	607	.254	.321	.353	.674	108	23	47	96	93	619	63			
BOS	150	59	89	.399	44	515	645	5077	1216	210	19	68	474	507	.240	.307	.329	.636	94	-48	-37	98	97	520	49			
PHI	151	42	109	.278	62.5	394	706	5060	1174	168	37	44	392	488	.232	.289	.306	.595	84	-125	-103	95	89	451	37			
TOT	613					4784		41769	10391	1680	323	538	4076	4189	.249	.318	.343	.661							423			

TEAM	CG	SH	SV	IP	H	H/G	HR	BB	SO	RAT	ERA	ERA+	OAV	OOB	PR	/A	PF	CPI	FA	E	DP	FW	PW	BW	SBW	DIF
STL	70	18	15	1410[1]	1192	7.6	49	473	651	10.7	2.55	134	.228	.294	120	137	103	102	.972	169	137	-.1	14.7	5.8		8.6
BRO	67	16	24	1398[2]	1205	7.8	73	493	612	11.1	2.84	115	.231	.302	73	64	98	101	.977	138	150	1.7	6.9	7.4		11.1
NY	70	12	13	1370	1299	8.5	94	493	497	11.1	3.31	101	.250	.316	0	7	101	104	.977	138	128	1.6	.8	6.0		.6
CIN	80	12	8	1411[2]	1213	7.7	47	526	616	11.2	2.82	117	.230	.302	78	73	99	97	.971	177	158	-.7	7.8	-8.6		1.5
PIT	64	13	11	1351[1]	1376	9.2	62	435	426	12.1	3.58	94	.262	.320	-41	-30	102	97	.969	184	128	-1.3	-3.2	-3.1		.1
CHI	71	10	14	1400[2]	1447	9.3	70	525	507	12.8	3.60	89	.267	.334	-44	-62	97	105	.973	170	136	-.2	-6.7	5.0		-7.2
BOS	68	9	8	1334	1326	8.9	82	518	414	12.6	3.76	89	.260	.331	-66	-62	101	100	.976	142	138	1.1	-6.7	-4.0		-5.5
PHI	51	2	6	1341	1328	8.9	61	605	472	13.1	4.12	80	.260	.342	-120	-122	100	93	.968	194	147	-1.9	-13.1	-11.1		-7.4
TOT	541	92	99	11017[2]		8.5				11.9	3.31		.249	.318					.973	1312	1122					

Runs
Ott-NY 118
Slaughter-StL 100
Mize-NY 97
Hack-Chi 91

Hits
Slaughter-StL 188
Nicholson-Chi 174
Medwick-Bro 166
Hack-Chi 166
Elliott-Pit 166

Doubles
Marion-StL 38
Medwick-Bro 37
Hack-Chi 36
Herman-Bro 34
Reiser-Bro 33

Triples
Slaughter-StL 17
Nicholson-Chi 11
Musial-StL 10
Litwhiler-Phi 9

Home Runs
Ott-NY 30
Mize-NY 26
Camilli-Bro 26
Nicholson-Chi 21
West-Bos 16

Total Bases
Slaughter-StL 292
Mize-NY 282
Nicholson-Chi 280
Ott-NY 273
Camilli-Bro 247

Runs Batted In
Mize-NY 110
Camilli-Bro 109
Slaughter-StL 98
Medwick-Bro 96
Ott-NY 93

Runs Produced
Slaughter-StL 185
Ott-NY 181
Mize-NY 181
Camilli-Bro 172
Medwick-Bro 161

Bases On Balls
Ott-NY 109
Fletcher-Pit 105
Camilli-Bro 97
Hack-Chi 94
Slaughter-StL 88

Batting Average
Lombardi-Bos 330
Slaughter-StL 318
Musial-StL 315
Reiser-Bro 310
Mize-NY 305

On Base Percentage
Fletcher-Pit 417
Ott-NY 415
Slaughter-StL 412
Hack-Chi 402
Musial-StL 397

Slugging Average
Mize-NY 521
Ott-NY 497
Slaughter-StL 494
Musial-StL 490
Lombardi-Bos 482

Production
Ott-NY 912
Slaughter-StL 906
Mize-NY 901
Musial-StL 888
Nicholson-Chi 859

Adjusted Production
Ott-NY 165
Mize-NY 161
Nicholson-Chi 156
Slaughter-StL 153
Musial-StL 148

Batter Runs
Slaughter-StL 49.8
Ott-NY 49.3
Mize-NY 40.8
Nicholson-Chi 37.6
Musial-StL 35.0

Adjusted Batter Runs
Ott-NY 48.7
Nicholson-Chi 41.7
Slaughter-StL 41.1
Mize-NY 40.2
Hack-Chi 33.5

Clutch Hitting Index
Brown-StL 146
Medwick-Bro 143
Owen-Bro 120
Camilli-Bro 117
F.McCormick-Cin . . 116

Runs Created
Slaughter-StL 128
Ott-NY 122
Nicholson-Chi 112
Mize-NY 110
Hack-Chi 100

Total Average
Ott-NY 990
Slaughter-StL 966
Musial-StL 926
Mize-NY 911
Camilli-Bro 888

Stolen Bases
Reiser-Bro 20
Reese-Bro 15
Fernandez-Bos 15
Merullo-Chi 14
Hopp-StL 14

Stolen Base Average

Stolen Base Runs

Fielding Runs
DiMaggio-Pit 19.8
Reese-Bro 17.4
May-Phi 17.2
Holmes-Bos 14.8
Fletcher-Pit 11.5

Total Player Rating
Nicholson-Chi 4.8
Ott-NY 4.2
Slaughter-StL 3.9
Fletcher-Pit 3.2
Mize-NY 3.0

Wins
M.Cooper-StL 22
Beazley-StL 21
Wyatt-Bro 19
Passeau-Chi 19
VanderMeer-Cin 18

Win Percentage
French-Bro 789
Beazley-StL 778
M.Cooper-StL 759
Wyatt-Bro 731
Davis-Bro 714

Games
Adams-NY 61
Casey-Bro 50
Podgajny-Phi 43
Beazley-StL 43

Complete Games
Tobin-Bos 28
Passeau-Chi 24
M.Cooper-StL 22
Walters-Cin 21
VanderMeer-Cin 21

Shutouts
M.Cooper-StL 10
Sewell-Pit 5
Javery-Bos 5
Davis-Bro 5

Saves
Casey-Bro 13
Adams-NY 11
Beggs-Cin 8
Sain-Bos 6
Gumbert-StL 5

Innings Pitched
Tobin-Bos 287.2
M.Cooper-StL . . . 278.2
Passeau-Chi 278.1
Starr-Cin 276.2
Javery-Bos 261.0

Fewest Hits/Game
M.Cooper-StL 6.69
VanderMeer-Cin . . . 6.93
Higbe-Bro 7.31
Starr-Cin 7.42
Beazley-StL 7.57

Fewest BB/Game
Warneke-StL-Chi . . 1.79
Lohrman-StL-NY . . 1.85
Hubbell-NY 1.94
Derringer-Cin 2.11
M.Cooper-StL 2.20

Strikeouts
VanderMeer-Cin . . . 186
M.Cooper-StL 152
Higbe-Bro 115
Walters-Cin 109
Melton-Phi 107

Strikeouts/Game
VanderMeer-Cin . . . 6.86
Lanier-StL 5.20
M.Cooper-StL 4.91
Higbe-Bro 4.67
Melton-Phi 4.60

Ratio
M.Cooper-StL 9.04
Lohrman-StL-NY . 10.07
Davis-Bro 10.35
Warneke-StL-Chi . 10.39
Wyatt-Bro 10.56

Earned Run Average
M.Cooper-StL 1.78
Beazley-StL 2.13
Davis-Bro 2.36
VanderMeer-Cin . . . 2.43
Lohrman-StL-NY . . 2.48

Adjusted ERA
M.Cooper-StL 193
Beazley-StL 161
Davis-Bro 138
Lohrman-StL-NY . . 136
VanderMeer-Cin . . . 135

Opponents' Batting Avg.
M.Cooper-StL 204
VanderMeer-Cin . . .208
Higbe-Bro 223
Wyatt-Bro 225
Starr-Cin 226

Opponents' On Base Pct.
M.Cooper-StL 258
Lohrman-StL-NY . . .281
Wyatt-Bro 286
Warneke-StL-Chi . . .286
Davis-Bro 287

Starter Runs
M.Cooper-StL 47.6
Beazley-StL 28.3
French-Bro 24.4
VanderMeer-Cin . . . 23.8
Davis-Bro 21.8

Adjusted Starter Runs
M.Cooper-StL 51.0
Beazley-StL 30.9
French-Bro 23.5
VanderMeer-Cin . . . 23.0
Davis-Bro 20.6

Clutch Pitching Index
Bithorn-Chi 130
Passeau-Chi 121
Beazley-StL 113
Schumacher-NY . . 113
Carpenter-NY 112

Relief Runs
Adams-NY 14.4
Casey-Bro 13.2
Beggs-Cin 11.6
Shoun-StL-Cin 9.4
Webber-Bro 2.0

Adjusted Relief Runs
Adams-NY 14.8
Casey-Bro 12.6
Beggs-Cin 11.3
Shoun-StL-Cin 9.1
Webber-Bro 1.7

Relief Ranking
Adams-NY 20.9
Beggs-Cin 15.0
Casey-Bro 12.4
Shoun-StL-Cin 4.4
Webber-Bro 1.6

Total Pitcher Index
M.Cooper-StL 5.0
Beazley-StL 4.0
French-Bro 3.4
Walters-Cin 3.0
VanderMeer-Cin . . . 2.9

Total Baseball Ranking
M.Cooper-StL 5.0
Nicholson-Chi 4.8
Ott-NY 4.2
Beazley-StL 4.0
Slaughter-StL 3.9

TEAM	G	W	L	PCT	GB	R	OR	AB	H	2B	3B	HR	BB	SO	AVG	OBP	SLG	PRO	PRO+	BR	/A	PF	CHI	RC	SB	CS	SBA	SBR
NY	154	103	51	.669		801	507	5305	1429	223	57	108	591	556	.269	.346	.394	.740	118	104	120	98	104	759	69	33	68	1
BOS	152	93	59	.612	9	761	594	5248	1451	244	55	103	591	508	.276	.352	.403	.755	116	132	105	103	96	774	68	61	53	-16
STL	151	82	69	.543	19.5	730	637	5229	1354	239	62	98	609	607	.259	.338	.385	.723	109	68	57	102	101	703	37	38	49	-12
CLE	156	75	79	.487	28	590	659	5317	1344	223	58	50	500	544	.253	.320	.345	.665	100	-43	-7	94	96	596	69	74	48	-24
DET	156	73	81	.474	30	589	587	5327	1313	217	37	76	509	476	.246	.314	.344	.658	85	-57	-106	108	98	582	39	40	49	-12
CHI	148	66	82	.446	34	538	609	4949	1215	214	36	25	497	427	.246	.316	.318	.634	87	-87	-75	98	102	520	114	70	62	-8
WAS	151	62	89	.411	39.5	653	817	5295	1364	224	49	40	581	536	.258	.333	.341	.674	98	-14	-8	99	101	641	98	29	77	12
PHI	154	55	99	.357	48	549	801	5285	1315	213	46	33	440	490	.249	.309	.325	.634	86	-101	-98	99	101	536	44	45	49	-14
TOT	611					5211		41955	10785	1797	400	533	4318	4144	.257	.329	.357	.686							538	390	58	-73

TEAM	CG	SH	SV	IP	H	H/G	HR	BB	SO	RAT	ERA	ERA+	OAV	OOB	PR	/A	PF	CPI	FA	E	DP	FW	PW	BW	SBW	DIF
NY	88	18	17	1375	1259	8.2	71	431	558	11.2	2.91	118	.244	.304	115	82	94	108	.976	142	190	2.0	8.4	12.3	1.0	2.3
BOS	84	11	17	1358²	1260	8.3	65	553	500	12.1	3.44	108	.247	.322	32	43	102	99	.974	157	156	1.0	4.4	10.8	-.7	1.5
STL	68	12	13	1363	1387	9.2	63	505	488	12.7	3.59	103	.262	.330	10	17	101	103	.972	167	143	.4	1.7	5.8	-.3	-1.2
CLE	61	12	11	1402²	1353	8.7	61	560	448	12.4	3.59	96	.254	.327	10	-23	94	99	.974	163	175	1.0	-2.4	-.7	-1.5	1.6
DET	65	12	14	1399¹	1321	8.5	60	598	671	12.5	3.13	126	.248	.326	82	127	108	111	.969	194	142	-.8	13.0	-10.9	-.3	-5.1
CHI	86	8	8	1314¹	1304	8.9	74	473	432	12.3	3.58	100	.258	.325	11	3	98	102	.970	173	144	-.1	.3	-7.7	.1	-.6
WAS	68	12	11	1346²	1496	10.0	50	558	496	13.8	4.58	80	.279	.349	-139	-139	100	91	.962	222	133	-2.7	-14.2	-.8	2.2	2.1
PHI	67	5	9	1374²	1404	9.2	89	639	546	13.5	4.45	85	.263	.344	-120	-102	103	93	.969	188	124	-.6	-10.4	-10.0	-.5	-.5
TOT	587	90	100	10934¹		8.9				12.6	3.66		.257	.329					.971	1406	1207					

Runs
Williams-Bos 141
DiMaggio-NY 123
DiMaggio-Bos 110
Clift-StL 108
Keller-NY 106

Hits
Pesky-Bos 205
Spence-Was 203
Williams-Bos 186
DiMaggio-NY 186
Keltner-Cle 179

Doubles
Kolloway-Chi 40
Clift-StL 39
Heath-Cle 37
DiMaggio-Bos 36

Triples
Spence-Was 15
Heath-Cle 13
DiMaggio-NY 13
McQuillen-StL 12

Home Runs
Williams-Bos 36
Laabs-StL 27
Keller-NY 26
York-Det 21
DiMaggio-NY 21

Total Bases
Williams-Bos 338
DiMaggio-NY 304
Keller-NY 279
Spence-Was 272
DiMaggio-Bos 272

Runs Batted In
Williams-Bos 137
DiMaggio-NY 114
Keller-NY 108
Gordon-NY 103
Doerr-Bos 102

Runs Produced
Williams-Bos 242
DiMaggio-NY 216
Keller-NY 188
Gordon-NY 173
Spence-Was 169

Bases On Balls
Williams-Bos 145
Keller-NY 114
Fleming-Cle 106
Clift-StL 106
Cullenbine-SL-W-NY 92

Batting Average
Williams-Bos .356
Pesky-Bos .331
Spence-Was .323
Gordon-NY .322
Case-Was .320

On Base Percentage
Williams-Bos .499
Keller-NY .417
Judnich-StL .413
Fleming-Cle .412
Gordon-NY .409

Slugging Average
Williams-Bos .648
Keller-NY .513
Judnich-StL .499
DiMaggio-NY .498
Laabs-StL .498

Production
Williams-Bos 1.147
Keller-NY .930
Judnich-StL .912
Gordon-NY .900
Laabs-StL .878

Adjusted Production
Williams-Bos 214
Keller-NY 164
Gordon-NY 156
Judnich-StL 153
DiMaggio-NY 148

Batter Runs
Williams-Bos 92.6
Keller-NY 46.9
Gordon-NY 38.6
Judnich-StL 35.4
DiMaggio-NY 34.5

Adjusted Batter Runs
Williams-Bos 87.0
Keller-NY 49.4
Gordon-NY 40.8
Fleming-Cle 38.3
DiMaggio-NY 36.8

Clutch Hitting Index
Lupien-Bos 124
Cullenbine-SL-W-NY 116
Vernon-Was 113
Siebert-Phi 113
Tabor-Bos 112

Runs Created
Williams-Bos 185
Keller-NY 131
DiMaggio-NY 120
Spence-Was 111
Gordon-NY 108

Total Average
Williams-Bos 1.394
Keller-NY 1.038
Judnich-StL .950
Gordon-NY .891
Laabs-StL .878

Stolen Bases
Case-Was 44
Vernon-Was 25
Rizzuto-NY 22
Kuhel-Chi 22

Stolen Base Average
Case-Was 88.0
Vernon-Was 80.6
Rizzuto-NY 78.6
Appling-Chi 77.3
Kuhel-Chi 71.0

Stolen Base Runs
Case-Was 9.6
Vernon-Was 3.9
Rizzuto-NY 3.0
Keller-NY 3.0
Appling-Chi 2.1

Fielding Runs
Rizzuto-NY 25.0
Pesky-Bos 17.7
DiMaggio-Bos 16.9
Keltner-Cle 15.6
York-Det 15.4

Total Player Rating
Williams-Bos 8.1
Gordon-NY 5.4
Keller-NY 4.4
Pesky-Bos 4.1
Rizzuto-NY 4.0

Wins
Hughson-Bos 22
Bonham-NY 21
Marchildon-Phi 17
Bagby-Cle 17
Chandler-NY 16

Win Percentage
Bonham-NY .808
Borowy-NY .789
Hughson-Bos .786
Chandler-NY .762
Bagby-Cle .654

Games
Haynes-Chi 40
Caster-StL 39

Complete Games
Hughson-Bos 22
Bonham-NY 22
Lyons-Chi 20
Hudson-Was 19

Shutouts
Bonham-NY 6

Saves
Murphy-NY 11
Haynes-Chi 6
Brown-Bos 6
Newhouser-Det 5
Caster-StL 5

Innings Pitched
Hughson-Bos 281.0
Bagby-Cle 270.2
Auker-StL 249.0
Marchildon-Phi 244.0
Hudson-Was 239.1

Fewest Hits/Game
Newhouser-Det 6.71
Niggeling-StL 7.55
Dobson-Bos 7.64
Trucks-Det 7.89
Chandler-NY 7.89

Fewest BB/Game
Bonham-NY .96
Lyons-Chi 1.30
Ruffing-NY 1.91
Breuer-NY 2.03
Bagby-Cle 2.13

Strikeouts
Newsom-Was 113
Hughson-Bos 113
Marchildon-Phi 110
Benton-Det 110
Niggeling-StL 107

Strikeouts/Game
Newhouser-Det 5.05
Bridges-Det 5.02
Trucks-Det 4.88
Newsom-Was 4.76
Niggeling-StL 4.67

Ratio
Bonham-NY 8.92
Lyons-Chi 9.73
Ruffing-NY 10.55
Breuer-NY 10.68
Hughson-Bos 10.70

Earned Run Average
Lyons-Chi 2.10
Bonham-NY 2.27
Chandler-NY 2.38
Newhouser-Det 2.45
Borowy-NY 2.52

Adjusted ERA
Lyons-Chi 172
Newhouser-Det 161
Bonham-NY 152
Chandler-NY 145
Trucks-Det 144

Opponents' Batting Avg.
Newhouser-Det .207
Niggeling-StL .226
Dobson-Bos .231
Trucks-Det .231
Borowy-NY .233

Opponents' On Base Pct.
Bonham-NY .259
Lyons-Chi .275
Ruffing-NY .292
Breuer-NY .295
Hughson-Bos .296

Starter Runs
Bonham-NY 34.8
Hughson-Bos 33.2
Lyons-Chi 31.3
Chandler-NY 28.5
Humphries-Chi 24.8

Adjusted Starter Runs
Hughson-Bos 35.5
Newhouser-Det 30.6
Lyons-Chi 30.1
Bonham-NY 29.4
Benton-Det 26.5

Clutch Pitching Index
Chandler-NY 136
Lyons-Chi 131
Hollingsworth-StL 123
Humphries-Chi 121
Niggeling-StL 119

Relief Runs
Ferrick-Cle 15.0
Haynes-Chi 11.9
Caster-StL 7.5
Murphy-NY 1.6
Brown-Bos 1.5

Adjusted Relief Runs
Ferrick-Cle 13.2
Haynes-Chi 11.2
Caster-StL 7.9
Brown-Bos 2.0
Murphy-NY .2

Relief Ranking
Haynes-Chi 14.2
Caster-StL 10.0
Ferrick-Cle 8.4
Brown-Bos 4.0
Murphy-NY .5

Total Pitcher Index
Lyons-Chi 4.0
Newhouser-Det 4.0
Hughson-Bos 3.8
Chandler-NY 3.2
Humphries-Chi 2.7

Total Baseball Ranking
Williams-Bos 8.1
Gordon-NY 5.4
Keller-NY 4.4
Pesky-Bos 4.1
Lyons-Chi 4.0

TEAM	G	W	L	PCT	GB	R	OR	AB	H	2B	3B	HR	BB	SO	AVG	OBP	SLG	PRO	PRO+	BR	/A	PF	CHI	RC	SB	CS	SBA	SBR
STL	157	105	49	.682		679	475	5438	1515	259	72	70	428	438	.279	.333	.391	.724	110	92	61	104	95	720	40			
CIN	155	87	67	.565	18	608	543	5329	1362	229	47	43	445	476	.256	.315	.340	.655	96	-35	-27	99	106	581	49			
BRO	153	81	72	.529	23.5	716	674	5309	1444	263	35	39	580	422	.272	.335	.357	.703	110	70	69	100	104	675	58			
PIT	157	80	74	.519	25	669	605	5353	1401	240	73	42	573	566	.262	.335	.357	.692	103	45	22	103	100	657	64			
CHI	154	74	79	.484	30.5	632	600	5279	1380	207	56	52	574	522	.261	.336	.351	.687	107	38	48	99	97	641	53			
BOS	153	68	85	.444	36.5	465	612	5196	1213	202	36	39	469	609	.233	.299	.309	.608	82	-121	-114	99	98	491	56			
PHI	157	64	90	.416	41	571	676	5297	1321	186	36	66	499	556	.249	.316	.335	.651	98	-38	-15	96	100	565	29			
NY	156	55	98	.359	49.5	558	713	5290	1309	153	33	81	480	470	.247	.313	.335	.648	92	-48	-52	101	100	552	35			
TOT	621					4898		42491	10945	1739	388	432	4048	4059	.258	.324	.347	.672							384			

TEAM	CG	SH	SV	IP	H	H/G	HR	BB	SO	RAT	ERA	ERA+	OAV	OOB	PR	/A	PF	CPI	FA	E	DP	FW	PW	BW	SBW	DIF
STL	94	21	15	1427	1246	7.9	33	477	639	11.0	2.57	131	.237	.303	129	126	99	105	.976	151	183	.9	13.5	6.5		7.2
CIN	78	18	17	1404	1299	8.3	38	579	498	12.1	3.13	106	.251	.328	39	28	98	105	.980	125	193	2.2	3.0	-2.9		7.7
BRO	50	13	22	1369²	1326	8.7	59	637	588	13.1	3.88	86	.254	.338	-76	-80	99	93	.972	168	137	-.3	-8.5	7.4		6.0
PIT	74	11	12	1404	1424	9.1	44	422	396	11.9	3.08	113	.264	.319	47	60	103	107	.973	170	159	-.2	6.4	2.3		-5.5
CHI	67	13	14	1386	1379	9.0	53	394	513	11.6	3.31	101	.254	.311	11	3	99	95	.973	168	138	-.3	.3	5.1		-7.7
BOS	87	13	4	1397²	1361	8.8	66	441	409	11.8	3.25	105	.255	.314	20	25	101	100	.972	176	139	-.8	2.7	-12.2		1.8
PHI	66	10	14	1392²	1436	9.3	59	451	431	12.3	3.79	89	.267	.326	-62	-64	100	93	.969	189	143	-1.3	-6.8	-1.6		-3.3
NY	35	6	19	1394²	1474	9.5	80	626	588	13.7	4.08	84	.272	.350	-108	-99	102	101	.973	166	140	-.0	-10.6	-5.6		-5.3
TOT	551	105	117	11175²		8.8				12.2	3.38		.258	.324					.974	1313	1232					

Runs
Vaughan-Bro 112
Musial-StL 108
Nicholson-Chi 95
Cavarretta-Chi 93
Stanky-Chi 92

Hits
Musial-StL 220
Witek-NY 195
Herman-Bro 193
Nicholson-Chi 188
Vaughan-Bro 186

Doubles
Musial-StL 48
Herman-Bro 41
DiMaggio-Pit 41
Vaughan-Bro 39
Holmes-Bos 33

Triples
Musial-StL 20
Klein-StL 14
Lowrey-Chi 12
Elliott-Pit 12

Home Runs
Nicholson-Chi 29
Ott-NY 18
Northey-Phi 16
Triplett-StL-Phi ... 15
DiMaggio-Pit 15

Total Bases
Musial-StL 347
Nicholson-Chi 323
Elliott-Pit 258
Klein-StL 257

Runs Batted In
Nicholson-Chi 128
Elliott-Pit 101
Herman-Bro 100
DiMaggio-Pit 88

Runs Produced
Nicholson-Chi 194
Musial-StL 176
Elliott-Pit 176
Herman-Bro 174
Vaughan-Bro 173

Bases On Balls
Galan-Bro 103
Ott-NY 95
Fletcher-Pit 95
Stanky-Chi 92
Tipton-Cin 85

Batting Average
Musial-StL .... .357
Herman-Bro ...... .330
W.Cooper-StL .... .318
Elliott-Pit .... .315
Witek-NY .... .314

On Base Percentage
Musial-StL .... .425
Galan-Bro .... .412
Herman-Bro ...... .398
Fletcher-Pit .... .395
Tipton-Cin .... .395

Slugging Average
Musial-StL .... .562
Nicholson-Chi .... .531
W.Cooper-StL .... .463
Elliott-Pit .... .444
Triplett-StL-Phi ... .439

Production
Musial-StL 988
Nicholson-Chi 917
Elliott-Pit 820
Tipton-Cin 819
Galan-Bro 818

Adjusted Production
Musial-StL 176
Nicholson-Chi 166
Tipton-Cin 138
Galan-Bro 136
Herman-Bro 135

Batter Runs
Musial-StL 65.5
Nicholson-Chi 47.7
Galan-Bro 28.5
Herman-Bro 28.0
Elliott-Pit 26.5

Adjusted Batter Runs
Musial-StL 59.6
Nicholson-Chi 49.5
Galan-Bro 28.3
Herman-Bro 27.8
Tipton-Cin 27.1

Clutch Hitting Index
Miller-Cin 138
Herman-Bro 131
Elliott-Pit 123
Wasdell-Pit-Phi ... 121
Medwick-Bro-NY .. 117

Runs Created
Musial-StL 147
Nicholson-Chi 129
Herman-Bro 97
Vaughan-Bro 96
Elliott-Pit 96

Total Average
Musial-StL 1.039
Nicholson-Chi 944
Ott-NY 895
Galan-Bro 876
Tipton-Cin 825

Stolen Bases
Vaughan-Bro 20
Lowrey-Chi 13
Workman-Bos 12
Russell-Pit 12
Gustine-Pit 12

Stolen Base Average

Stolen Base Runs

Fielding Runs
Miller-Cin 26.6
Marion-StL 25.3
Mueller-Cin 20.2
Wietelmann-Bos .. 20.0
Galan-Bro 16.1

Total Player Rating
Musial-StL 6.4
Nicholson-Chi 4.9
Galan-Bro 3.9
Mueller-Cin 3.8
Witek-NY 3.3

Wins
Sewell-Pit 21
Riddle-Cin 21
M.Cooper-StL 21
Bithorn-Chi 18
Javery-Bos 17

Win Percentage
M.Cooper-StL .... .724
Sewell-Pit .... .700
Lanier-StL .... .682
Riddle-Cin .... .656
Bithorn-Chi .... .600

Games
Adams-NY 70
Webber-Bro 54
Head-Bro 47
Shoun-Cin 45
Mungo-NY 45

Complete Games
Sewell-Pit 25
Tobin-Bos 24
M.Cooper-StL 24
Andrews-Bos 23

Shutouts
Bithorn-Chi 7
M.Cooper-StL 6

Saves
Webber-Bro 10
Adams-NY 9
Shoun-Cin 7
Head-Bro 6
Beggs-Cin 6

Innings Pitched
Javery-Bos 303.0
VanderMeer-Cin .. 289.0
Andrews-Bos 283.2
M.Cooper-StL 274.0
Sewell-Pit 265.1

Fewest Hits/Game
Wyatt-Bro 6.92
VanderMeer-Cin ... 7.10
M.Cooper-StL 7.49
Krist-StL 7.72
Barrett-Chi-Phi ... 7.94

Fewest BB/Game
Rowe-Chi 1.31
Wyse-Chi 1.96
Derringer-Chi 2.02
Davis-Bro 2.14
Wyatt-Bro 2.14

Strikeouts
VanderMeer-Cin ... 174
M.Cooper-StL 141
Javery-Bos 134
Lanier-StL 123
Higbe-Bro 108

Strikeouts/Game
VanderMeer-Cin .. 5.42
Higbe-Bro 5.25
Lanier-StL 5.19
M.Cooper-StL 4.63
Head-Bro 4.40

Ratio
Wyatt-Bro 9.07
M.Cooper-StL ... 10.25
Rowe-Phi 10.31
Andrews-Bos 10.60
Bithorn-Chi...... 10.60

Earned Run Average
Lanier-StL 1.90
M.Cooper-StL 2.30
Wyatt-Bro 2.49
Sewell-Pit 2.54
Andrews-Bos 2.57

Adjusted ERA
Lanier-StL 177
M.Cooper-StL 146
Sewell-Pit 137
Wyatt-Bro 135
Butcher-Pit 134

Opponents' Batting Avg.
Wyatt-Bro .... .207
VanderMeer-Cin .. .224
M.Cooper-StL .... .226
Krist-StL .... .233
Barrett-Chi-Phi ... .237

Opponents' On Base Pct.
Wyatt-Bro .... .255
Rowe-Phi .... .279
M.Cooper-StL .... .286
Andrews-Bos ..... .291
Bithorn-Chi .... .294

Starter Runs
Lanier-StL 35.2
M.Cooper-StL 33.0
Andrews-Bos 25.6
Sewell-Pit 24.7
Riddle-Cin 21.9

Adjusted Starter Runs
Lanier-StL 34.7
M.Cooper-StL 32.4
Sewell-Pit 27.5
Andrews-Bos 26.6
Pollet-StL 21.2

Clutch Pitching Index
Lanier-StL 151
Butcher-Pit 122
Sewell-Pit 121
Riddle-Cin 118
Tobin-Bos 113

Relief Runs
Beggs-Cin 13.4
Adams-NY 8.8
Prim-Chi 5.6
Brandt-Pit 1.6

Adjusted Relief Runs
Beggs-Cin 12.5
Adams-NY 9.7
Prim-Chi 5.2
Brandt-Pit 2.2

Relief Ranking
Beggs-Cin........14.1
Adams-NY 12.6
Prim-Chi 5.7
Brandt-Pit 1.7

Total Pitcher Index
Sewell-Pit 4.0
Tobin-Bos 3.5
Lanier-StL 3.5
Andrews-Bos..... 3.4
M.Cooper-StL 3.2

Total Baseball Ranking
Musial-StL 6.4
Nicholson-Chi 4.9
Sewell-Pit 4.0
Galan-Bro 3.9
Mueller-Cin........ 3.8

TEAM	G	W	L	PCT	GB	R	OR	AB	H	2B	3B	HR	BB	SO	AVG	OBP	SLG	PRO	PRO+	BR	/A	PF	CHI	RC	SB	CS	SBA	SBR
NY	155	98	56	.636		669	542	5282	1350	218	59	100	624	562	.256	.337	.376	.713	114	97	92	101	95	683	46	60	43	-22
WAS	153	84	69	.549	13.5	666	595	5233	1328	245	50	47	605	579	.254	.336	.347	.683	110	45	69	96	103	656	142	55	72	10
CLE	153	82	71	.536	15.5	600	577	5269	1344	246	45	55	567	521	.255	.329	.350	.679	112	32	71	94	95	626	47	58	45	-21
CHI	155	82	72	.532	16	573	594	5254	1297	193	46	33	561	581	.247	.322	.320	.642	94	-33	-32	100	102	570	173	87	67	0
DET	155	78	76	.506	20	632	560	5364	1401	200	47	77	483	553	.261	.324	.359	.683	98	32	-17	108	99	620	40	43	48	-14
STL	153	72	80	.474	25	596	604	5175	1269	229	36	78	569	564	.245	.322	.349	.671	100	14	1	102	98	603	37	43	46	-15
BOS	155	68	84	.447	29	563	607	5392	1314	223	42	57	486	591	.244	.308	.332	.640	92	-48	-57	102	101	570	86	61	59	-11
PHI	155	49	105	.318	49	497	717	5244	1219	174	44	26	430	465	.232	.294	.297	.591	78	-137	-135	100	111	466	55	42	57	-9
TOT	617					4796		42213	10522	1728	369	473	4325	4498	.249	.322	.341	.663							626	449	58	-82

TEAM	CG	SH	SV	IP	H	H/G	HR	BB	SO	RAT	ERA	ERA+	OAV	OOB	PR	/A	PF	CPI	FA	E	DP	FW	PW	BW	SBW	DIF
NY	83	14	13	1415¹	1229	7.8	60	489	653	11.0	2.93	110	.234	.301	58	46	98	95	.974	160	166	.2	5.0	10.0	-1.3	7.1
WAS	61	16	21	1388	1293	8.4	48	540	495	12.0	3.18	101	.246	.318	17	3	97	99	.971	179	145	-1.0	.3	7.5	2.2	-1.5
CLE	64	14	20	1406¹	1234	7.9	52	606	585	11.9	3.15	99	.239	.322	23	-6	94	100	.975	157	183	.3	-.6	7.7	-1.2	-.7
CHI	70	12	19	1400¹	1352	8.7	54	501	476	12.1	3.20	104	.255	.324	15	21	101	105	.973	166	167	-.0	2.3	-3.5	1.1	5.2
DET	67	18	20	1411²	1226	7.8	51	549	706	11.4	3.00	117	.234	.308	46	81	107	95	.974	177	130	-.7	8.8	-1.8	-.4	-4.8
STL	64	10	14	1385	1397	9.1	74	488	572	12.6	3.41	97	.263	.327	-18	-13	101	106	.975	152	127	.6	-1.4	.1	-.5	-2.8
BOS	62	13	16	1426¹	1369	8.6	61	615	513	12.6	3.45	96	.257	.335	-25	-22	101	105	.976	153	179	.6	-2.4	-6.2	-.0	.0
PHI	73	5	13	1394	1421	9.2	73	536	503	12.9	4.05	84	.265	.336	-117	-101	103	94	.973	162	148	.1	-10.9	-14.6	.1	-2.7
TOT	544	102	136	11227		8.4				12.0	3.30		.249	.322					.973	1306	1245					

Runs
Case-Was 102
Keller-NY 97
Wakefield-Det 91
York-Det 90
Vernon-Was 89

Hits
Wakefield-Det 200
Appling-Chi 192
Cramer-Det 182
Case-Was 180

Doubles
Wakefield-Det 38
Case-Was 36
Gutteridge-StL 35
Etten-NY 35

Triples
Moses-Chi 12
Lindell-NY 12
York-Det 11
Keller-NY 11
Spence-Was 10

Home Runs
York-Det 34
Keller-NY 31
Stephens-StL 22
Heath-Cle 18

Total Bases
York-Det 301
Wakefield-Det 275
Keller-NY 269
Doerr-Bos 249
Stephens-StL 247

Runs Batted In
York-Det 118
Etten-NY 107
Johnson-NY 94
Stephens-StL 91
Spence-Was 88

Runs Produced
York-Det 174
Etten-NY 171
Wakefield-Det 163
Johnson-NY 159
Case-Was 153

Bases On Balls
Keller-NY 106
Gordon-NY 98
Cullenbine-Cle 96
Boudreau-Cle 90
Appling-Chi 90

Batting Average
Appling-Chi .... .328
Wakefield-Det ...... .316
Hodgin-Chi .... .314
Cramer-Det .... .300
Case-Was .... .294

On Base Percentage
Appling-Chi .... .419
Cullenbine-Cle .... .407
Keller-NY .... .396
Boudreau-Cle ...... .388
Curtright-Chi ...... .382

Slugging Average
York-Det .... .527
Keller-NY .... .525
Stephens-StL ...... .482
Heath-Cle .... .481
Wakefield-Det ..... .434

Production
Keller-NY .... .922
York-Det .... .893
Heath-Cle .... .850
Stephens-StL ...... .839
Appling-Chi .... .825

Adjusted Production
Keller-NY 167
Heath-Cle 157
York-Det 148
Cullenbine-Cle 146
Appling-Chi 142

Batter Runs
Keller-NY 45.8
York-Det 41.0
Appling-Chi 35.0
Wakefield-Det 28.8
Cullenbine-Cle 27.4

Adjusted Batter Runs
Keller-NY 45.0
Appling-Chi 35.1
York-Det 33.0
Cullenbine-Cle 32.9
Heath-Cle 29.7

Clutch Hitting Index
Sullivan-Was 162
Johnson-NY 134
Siebert-Phi 128
Early-Was 125
McQuinn-StL 125

Runs Created
Keller-NY 116
Appling-Chi 109
York-Det 108
Wakefield-Det 101
Spence-Was 93

Total Average
Keller-NY .... .979
York-Det .... .871
Appling-Chi .... .841
Heath-Cle .... .828
Cullenbine-Cle .... .816

Stolen Bases
Case-Was 61
Moses-Chi 56
Tucker-Chi 29
Appling-Chi 27
Vernon-Was 24

Stolen Base Average
Case-Was 81.3
Moses-Chi 80.0
Appling-Chi 77.1
Vernon-Was 75.0
Fox-Bos 73.3

Stolen Base Runs
Case-Was 9.9
Moses-Chi 8.4
Culberson-Bos 4.2
Appling-Chi 3.3
Vernon-Was 2.4

Fielding Runs
Boudreau-Cle 28.4
Gordon-NY 25.7
Clift-StL-Was 18.3
York-Det 17.6
Bloodworth-Det 17.2

Total Player Rating
Boudreau-Cle 6.7
Appling-Chi 6.0
Gordon-NY 5.4
York-Det 4.3
Keller-NY 4.3

Wins
Trout-Det 20
Chandler-NY 20
Wynn-Was 18
Smith-Cle 17
Bagby-Cle 17

Win Percentage
Chandler-NY ...... .833
Smith-Cle .... .708
Bonham-NY ...... .652
Trout-Det .... .625
Grove-Chi .... .625

Games
Brown-Bos 49
Trout-Det 44
Wolff-Phi 41
Ryba-Bos 40
Carrasquel-Was 39

Complete Games
Hughson-Bos 20
Chandler-NY 20
Wensloff-NY 18
Trout-Det 18
Grove-Chi 18

Shutouts
Trout-Det 5
Chandler-NY 5
Hughson-Bos 4
Bonham-NY 4

Saves
Maltzberger-Chi 14
Heving-Cle 9
Brown-Bos 9
Murphy-NY 8
Caster-StL 8

Innings Pitched
Bagby-Cle 273.0
Hughson-Bos 266.0
Wynn-Was 256.2
Chandler-NY 253.0
Trout-Det 246.2

Fewest Hits/Game
Reynolds-Cle 6.34
Niggeling-StL-Was .. 6.66
Haefner-Was 6.86
Chandler-NY 7.01
Wensloff-NY 7.21

Fewest BB/Game
Leonard-Was 1.88
Chandler-NY 1.92
Bonham-NY 2.07
Muncrief-StL 2.11
Trucks-Det 2.31

Strikeouts
Reynolds-Cle 151
Newhouser-Det ... 144
Chandler-NY 134
Bridges-Det 124
Trucks-Det 118

Strikeouts/Game
Reynolds-Cle 6.84
Newhouser-Det ... 6.62
Bridges-Det 5.82
Trucks-Det 5.24
Chandler-NY 4.77

Ratio
Chandler-NY 9.07
Trucks-Det 9.90
Bonham-NY 9.97
Wensloff-NY 10.07
Niggeling-StL-Was . 10.24

Earned Run Average
Chandler-NY 1.64
Bonham-NY 2.27
Haefner-Was 2.29
Bridges-Det 2.39
Trout-Det 2.48

Adjusted ERA
Chandler-NY 197
Bridges-Det 147
Trout-Det 142
Bonham-NY 141
Haefner-Was 140

Opponents' Batting Avg.
Reynolds-Cle ...... .202
Niggeling-StL-Was . .204
Haefner-Was ..... .208
Chandler-NY ..... .215
Wensloff-NY ...... .219

Opponents' On Base Pct.
Chandler-NY ...... .261
Trucks-Det .... .276
Wensloff-NY ...... .282
Bonham-NY ...... .282
Niggeling-StL-Was . .282

Starter Runs
Chandler-NY 46.6
Bonham-NY 25.6
Trout-Det 22.3
Hughson-Bos 19.4
Bridges-Det 19.2

Adjusted Starter Runs
Chandler-NY 44.4
Trout-Det 28.5
Bridges-Det 24.0
Bonham-NY 23.6
Hughson-Bos 19.9

Clutch Pitching Index
Hughson-Bos 124
Muncrief-StL 120
Bonham-NY 116
Galehouse-StL 115
Candini-Was 115

Relief Runs
Brown-Bos 12.2
Caster-StL 10.0
Maltzberger-Chi 9.1
Naymick-Cle 6.9
Murphy-NY 5.9

Adjusted Relief Runs
Brown-Bos 10.2
Caster-StL 10.2
Maltzberger-Chi 9.6
Naymick-Cle 5.6
Murphy-NY 5.3

Relief Ranking
Caster-StL 19.2
Brown-Bos 17.0
Maltzberger-Chi ... 12.7
Murphy-NY 12.6
Naymick-Cle 6.9

Total Pitcher Index
Chandler-NY 5.7
Trout-Det 4.7
Bridges-Det 2.6
Caster-StL 2.1
Bonham-NY 2.0

Total Baseball Ranking
Boudreau-Cle 6.7
Appling-Chi 6.0
Chandler-NY 5.7
Gordon-NY 5.4
Trout-Det 4.7

TEAM	G	W	L	PCT	GB	R	OR	AB	H	2B	3B	HR	BB	SO	AVG	OBP	SLG	PRO	PRO+	BR	/A	PF	CHI	RC	SB	CS	SBA	SBR
STL	157	105	49	.682		772	490	5475	1507	274	59	100	544	473	.275	.344	.402	.746	114	110	96	102	98	775	37			
PIT	158	90	63	.588	14.5	744	662	5428	1441	248	80	70	573	616	.265	.338	.379	.717	104	58	27	104	102	707	87			
CIN	155	89	65	.578	16	573	537	5271	1340	229	31	51	423	391	.254	.313	.338	.651	92	-74	-53	96	101	558	51			
CHI	157	75	79	.487	30	702	669	5462	1425	236	46	71	520	521	.261	.328	.360	.688	101	-2	2	99	104	658	53			
NY	155	67	87	.435	38	682	773	5306	1398	191	47	93	512	480	.263	.331	.370	.701	103	22	24	100	100	656	39			
BOS	155	65	89	.422	40	593	674	5282	1299	250	39	79	456	509	.246	.308	.353	.661	88	-61	-85	104	101	586	37			
BRO	155	63	91	.409	42	690	832	5393	1450	255	51	56	486	451	.269	.331	.366	.697	91	16	28	98	101	664	45			
PHI	154	61	92	.399	43.5	539	658	5301	1331	199	42	55	470	500	.251	.316	.336	.652	92	-70	-51	97	92	571	32			
TOT	623					5295		42918	11191	1882	395	575	3984	3941	.261	.326	.363	.689							381			

TEAM	CG	SH	SV	IP	H	H/G	HR	BB	SO	RAT	ERA	ERA+	OAV	OOB	PR	/A	PF	CPI	FA	E	DP	FW	PW	BW	SBW	DIF
STL	89	26	12	1427	1228	7.7	55	468	637	10.8	2.67	132	.233	.298	148	134	98	103	.982	112	162	3.7	13.8	9.9		.7
PIT	77	10	19	1414¹	1466	9.3	65	435	452	12.2	3.44	108	.265	.321	27	45	103	103	.970	191	122	-1.1	4.6	2.5		7.2
CIN	93	17	12	1398¹	1292	8.3	60	390	369	10.9	2.97	117	.246	.300	99	80	97	99	.978	137	153	2.0	8.2	-5.4		7.2
CHI	70	11	13	1400²	1484	9.5	75	458	545	12.5	3.59	98	.274	.331	4	-8	98	108	.970	186	151	-.8	-.8	.2		-.5
NY	47	4	21	1363²	1413	9.3	116	587	499	13.4	4.29	85	.265	.342	-103	-94	102	98	.971	179	128	-.5	-9.6	2.5		-2.3
BOS	70	13	12	1388¹	1430	9.3	80	527	454	12.8	3.67	104	.267	.335	-9	23	106	106	.971	182	160	-.7	2.4	-8.7		-4.9
BRO	50	4	13	1367²	1471	9.7	75	660	487	14.3	4.68	76	.274	.357	-162	-172	98	93	.966	197	112	-1.7	-17.7	2.9		2.4
PHI	66	11	6	1395¹	1407	9.1	49	459	496	12.2	3.64	99	.261	.321	-4	-5	100	93	.972	177	138	-.5	-.5	-5.2		-9.3
TOT	562	96	108	11155¹		9.0				12.4	3.61		.261	.326					.972	1361	1126					

Runs		Hits		Doubles		Triples		Home Runs		Total Bases	
Nicholson-Chi	116	Musial-StL	197	Musial-StL	51	Barrett-Pit	19	Nicholson-Chi	33	Nicholson-Chi	317
Musial-StL	112	Cavarretta-Chi	197	Galan-Bro	43	Elliott-Pit	16	Ott-NY	26	Musial-StL	312
Russell-Pit	109	Holmes-Bos	195	Holmes-Bos	42	Cavarretta-Chi	15	Northey-Phi	22	Holmes-Bos	288
Hopp-StL	106	Walker-Bro	191			Russell-Pit	14	McCormick-Cin	20	Walker-Bro	283
Cavarretta-Chi	106	Russell-Pit	181			Musial-StL	14	Kurowski-StL	20	Northey-Phi	283

Runs Batted In		Runs Produced		Bases On Balls		Batting Average		On Base Percentage		Slugging Average	
Nicholson-Chi	122	Nicholson-Chi	205	Galan-Bro	101	Walker-Bro	.357	Musial-StL	.440	Musial-StL	.549
Elliott-Pit	108	Musial-StL	194	Nicholson-Chi	93	Musial-StL	.347	Walker-Bro	.434	Nicholson-Chi	.545
Northey-Phi	104	Elliott-Pit	183	Ott-NY	90	Medwick-NY	.337	Galan-Bro	.426	Ott-NY	.544
Sanders-StL	102	Cavarretta-Chi	183	Musial-StL	90	Hopp-StL	.336	Ott-NY	.423	Walker-Bro	.529
McCormick-Cin	102			Barrett-Pit	86	Cavarretta-Chi	.321	Hopp-StL	.404	Weintraub-NY	.524

Production		Adjusted Production		Batter Runs		Adjusted Batter Runs		Clutch Hitting Index		Runs Created	
Musial-StL	.990	Musial-StL	174	Musial-StL	60.9	Musial-StL	58.5	Olmo-Bro	132	Musial-StL	145
Ott-NY	.967	Walker-Bro	173	Walker-Bro	51.2	Walker-Bro	53.4	Elliott-Pit	126	Nicholson-Chi	132
Walker-Bro	.963	Ott-NY	171	Nicholson-Chi	47.4	Galan-Bro	48.7	Dahlgren-Pit	119	Walker-Bro	128
Nicholson-Chi	.935	Nicholson-Chi	162	Galan-Bro	46.5	Nicholson-Chi	48.2	Schultz-Bro	118	Galan-Bro	123
Galan-Bro	.922	Galan-Bro	162	Ott-NY	40.4	Ott-NY	40.7	Medwick-NY	117	Russell-Pit	112

Total Average		Stolen Bases		Stolen Base Average	Stolen Base Runs	Fielding Runs		Total Player Rating	
Musial-StL	1.095	Barrett-Pit	28			Kerr-NY	16.8	Musial-StL	5.4
Ott-NY	1.087	Lupien-Phi	18			Luby-NY	16.4	Walker-Bro	4.4
Walker-Bro	1.034	Hughes-Chi	16			Williams-Cin	15.0	Nicholson-Chi	4.2
Nicholson-Chi	1.002	Hopp-StL	15			Pafko-Chi	14.7	Galan-Bro	4.0
Galan-Bro	.992	Kerr-NY	14			Russell-Pit	13.3	McCormick-Cin	3.7

Wins		Win Percentage		Games		Complete Games		Shutouts		Saves	
Walters-Cin	23	Wilks-StL	.810	Adams-NY	65	Tobin-Bos	28	M.Cooper-StL	7	Adams-NY	13
M.Cooper-StL	22	Brecheen-StL	.762	Webber-Bro	48	Walters-Cin	27	Walters-Cin	6	Schmidt-StL	5
Voiselle-NY	21	M.Cooper-StL	.759	Rescigno-Pit	48	Voiselle-NY	25	Tobin-Bos	5	Rescigno-Pit	5
Sewell-Pit	21	Walters-Cin	.742	Voiselle-NY	43	Sewell-Pit	24	Lanier-StL	5	Davis-Bro	4
Tobin-Bos	18	Sewell-Pit	.636	Tobin-Bos	43	M.Cooper-StL	22	Butcher-Pit	5	Cuccurullo-Pit	4

Innings Pitched		Fewest Hits/Game		Fewest BB/Game		Strikeouts		Strikeouts/Game		Ratio	
Voiselle-NY	312.2	Walters-Cin	7.36	Raffensberger-Phi	1.57	Voiselle-NY	161	Lanier-StL	5.66	Wilks-StL	9.66
Tobin-Bos	299.1	Wilks-StL	7.50	Strincevich-Pit	1.75	Lanier-StL	141	Javery-Bos	4.85	Heusser-Cin	9.72
Sewell-Pit	286.0	Lanier-StL	7.70	Davis-Bro	1.81	Javery-Bos	137	Raffensberger-Phi	4.73	De LaCruz-Cin	10.16
Walters-Cin	285.0	Heusser-Cin	7.71	Shoun-Cin	1.87	Raffensberger-Phi	136	Voiselle-NY	4.63	Walters-Cin	10.23
Raffensberger-Phi	258.2	Voiselle-NY	7.94	Derringer-Chi	1.95			Melton-Bro	4.37	M.Cooper-StL	10.41

Earned Run Average		Adjusted ERA		Opponents' Batting Avg.		Opponents' On Base Pct.		Starter Runs		Adjusted Starter Runs	
Heusser-Cin	2.38	Heusser-Cin	146	Walters-Cin	.219	Wilks-StL	.275	Walters-Cin	38.3	Walters-Cin	34.4
Walters-Cin	2.40	Walters-Cin	145	Wilks-StL	.227	Heusser-Cin	.275	M.Cooper-StL	32.2	M.Cooper-StL	29.8
M.Cooper-StL	2.46	M.Cooper-StL	143	Heusser-Cin	.231	Walters-Cin	.281	Munger-StL	30.5	Munger-StL	29.4
Wilks-StL	2.64	Wilks-StL	133	Voiselle-NY	.232	De LaCruz-Cin	.284	Heusser-Cin	26.3	Tobin-Bos	27.0
Lanier-StL	2.65	Lanier-StL	133	Lanier-StL	.234	Raffensberger-Phi	.285	Lanier-StL	24.0	Ostermueller-Br-Pt	23.9

Clutch Pitching Index		Relief Runs		Adjusted Relief Runs		Relief Ranking		Total Pitcher Index		Total Baseball Ranking	
Fleming-Chi	121	Karl-Phi	12.7	Karl-Phi	12.7	Karl-Phi	7.1	Walters-Cin	4.7	Musial-StL	5.4
Ostermueller-Br-Pt	120	Donnelly-StL	12.6	Donnelly-StL	11.9	Donnelly-StL	4.9	Tobin-Bos	4.7	Walters-Cin	4.7
Chipman-Bro-Chi	119							Munger-StL	3.6	Tobin-Bos	4.7
Wyse-Chi	113							M.Cooper-StL	3.0	Walker-Bro	4.4
Javery-Bos	111							Heusser-Cin	2.9	Nicholson-Chi	4.2

TEAM	G	W	L	PCT	GB	R	OR	AB	H	2B	3B	HR	BB	SO	AVG	OBP	SLG	PRO	PRO+	BR	/A	PF	CHI	RC	SB	CS	SBA	SBR
STL	154	89	65	.578		684	587	5269	1328	223	45	72	531	604	.252	.323	.352	.675	94	-4	-40	106	110	629	44	33	57	-7
DET	156	88	66	.571	1	658	581	5344	1405	220	44	60	532	500	.263	.332	.354	.686	97	21	-15	106	100	641	61	55	53	-15
NY	154	83	71	.539	6	674	617	5331	1410	216	74	96	523	627	.264	.333	.387	.720	108	75	52	103	95	707	91	31	75	9
BOS	156	77	77	.500	12	739	676	5400	1456	277	56	69	522	505	.270	.336	.380	.716	112	73	82	99	103	710	60	40	60	-6
PHI	155	72	82	.468	17	525	594	5312	1364	169	47	36	422	490	.257	.314	.327	.641	90	-73	-65	99	96	547	42	32	57	-7
CLE	155	72	82	.468	17	643	677	5481	1458	270	50	70	512	593	.266	.331	.372	.703	111	46	72	96	93	684	48	42	53	-11
CHI	154	71	83	.461	18	543	662	5292	1307	210	55	23	439	448	.247	.307	.320	.627	86	-97	-90	99	104	533	66	47	58	-8
WAS	154	64	90	.416	25	592	664	5319	1386	186	42	33	470	477	.261	.324	.330	.654	97	-41	-15	96	101	594	127	59	68	3
TOT	619					5058		42748	11114	1771	413	459	3951	4244	.260	.325	.353	.678							539	339	61	-42

TEAM	CG	SH	SV	IP	H	H/G	HR	BB	SO	RAT	ERA	ERA+	OAV	OOB	PR	/A	PF	CPI	FA	E	DP	FW	PW	BW	SBW	DIF
STL	71	16	17	1397¹	1392	9.0	58	469	581	12.1	3.17	114	.259	.320	41	66	105	105	.972	171	142	.5	6.9	-4.2	-.2	9.0
DET	87	20	8	1400	1373	8.8	39	452	568	11.9	3.09	116	.257	.318	54	75	104	103	.970	190	184	-.5	7.9	-1.6	-1.0	6.2
NY	78	9	13	1390¹	1351	8.7	82	532	529	12.3	3.39	103	.257	.326	7	15	102	105	.974	156	170	1.3	1.6	5.5	1.5	-3.9
BOS	58	7	17	1394¹	1404	9.1	66	592	524	13.0	3.82	89	.263	.339	-60	-65	99	98	.972	171	154	.6	-6.8	8.6	-.0	-2.3
PHI	72	10	14	1397¹	1345	8.7	58	390	534	11.4	3.26	107	.252	.307	27	35	102	93	.971	176	127	.2	3.7	-6.8	-.2	-1.9
CLE	48	7	18	1419¹	1428	9.1	40	621	524	13.2	3.65	90	.265	.344	-35	-56	96	102	.974	165	192	.9	-5.9	7.6	-.6	-6.9
CHI	64	5	17	1390²	1411	9.1	68	420	481	12.0	3.58	96	.264	.320	-23	-23	100	97	.970	183	154	-.2	-2.4	-9.5	-.3	6.4
WAS	83	13	11	1381	1410	9.1	48	475	503	12.4	3.49	93	.264	.327	-10	-36	95	99	.964	218	156	-2.3	-3.8	-1.6	.9	-6.2
TOT	561	87	115	11170¹		9.0				12.3	3.43		.260	.325					.971	1430	1279					

Runs	Hits	Doubles	Triples	Home Runs	Total Bases
Stirnweiss-NY 125	Stirnweiss-NY 205	Boudreau-Cle 45	Stirnweiss-NY...... 16	Etten-NY 22	Lindell-NY 297
B.Johnson-Bos ... 106	Boudreau-Cle 191	Keltner-Cle 41	Lindell-NY 16	Stephens-StL 20	Stirnweiss-NY 296
Cullenbine-Cle 98	Spence-Was 187	B.Johnson-Bos 40	Gutteridge-StL 11	York-Det 18	Spence-Was 288
Doerr-Bos 95	Lindell-NY 178	Fox-Bos 37	Doerr-Bos 10	Spence-Was 18	B.Johnson-Bos 277
Metkovich-Bos..... 94	Rocco-Cle 174	Stirnweiss-NY 35		Lindell-NY 18	

Runs Batted In	Runs Produced	Bases On Balls	Batting Average	On Base Percentage	Slugging Average
Stephens-StL 109	B.Johnson-Bos ... 195	Etten-NY 97	Boudreau-Cle 327	B.Johnson-Bos ... .431	Doerr-Bos 528
B.Johnson-Bos 106	Stephens-StL 180	B.Johnson-Bos 95	Doerr-Bos 325	Boudreau-Cle .... .406	B.Johnson-Bos 528
Lindell-NY 103	Lindell-NY 176	Cullenbine-Cle 87	B.Johnson-Bos 324	Doerr-Bos .... .399	Lindell-NY 500
Spence-Was 100	Spence-Was 165	McQuinn-StL 85	Stirnweiss-NY 319	Etten-NY .... .399	Spence-Was 486
York-Det 98	Cullenbine-Cle 162	Higgins-Det 81	Spence-Was 316	Byrnes-StL ...... .396	

Production	Adjusted Production	Batter Runs	Adjusted Batter Runs	Clutch Hitting Index	Runs Created
B.Johnson-Bos ...959	B.Johnson-Bos ... 175	B.Johnson-Bos ... 52.9	B.Johnson-Bos ...54.4	Christman-StL.....134	Stirnweiss-NY 128
Doerr-Bos 927	Doerr-Bos 166	Spence-Was 38.1	Spence-Was 43.1	Carnett-Chi 123	B.Johnson-Bos ... 124
Spence-Was 877	Spence-Was 157	Doerr-Bos 38.0	Doerr-Bos 39.2	Mayo-Det........ 121	Spence-Was 118
Etten-NY.........865	Boudreau-Cle 146	Etten-NY......... 37.3	Boudreau-Cle 37.2	Torres-Was 115	Etten-NY 114
Lindell-NY........851	Etten-NY 142	Wakefield-Det 36.7	Etten-NY 33.7	Stephens-StL 112	Boudreau-Cle..... 112

Total Average	Stolen Bases	Stolen Base Average	Stolen Base Runs	Fielding Runs	Total Player Rating
B.Johnson-Bos ...987	Stirnweiss-NY 55	Stirnweiss-NY 83.3	Stirnweiss-NY......9.9	Mayo-Det 29.4	Boudreau-Cle 7.8
Doerr-Bos 945	Case-Was 49	Moses-Chi 75.0	Case-Was 3.9	Boudreau-Cle 25.8	Stirnweiss-NY 7.1
Stirnweiss-NY 910	Myatt-Was 26	Case-Was 73.1	Moses-Chi 2.1	Stirnweiss-NY 18.9	Spence-Was 5.2
Etten-NY.........879	Moses-Chi........ 21	Myatt-Was 72.2	Myatt-Was 1.8	Spence-Was 18.6	Doerr-Bos 5.2
Spence-Was......856	Gutteridge-StL 20	Gutteridge-StL 71.4	Grimes-NY 1.8	Tucker-Chi 17.7	B.Johnson-Bos ... 4.9

Wins	Win Percentage	Games	Complete Games	Shutouts	Saves
Newhouser-Det ... 29	Hughson-Bos .... .783	Heving-Cle 63	Trout-Det 33	Trout-Det 7	Maltzberger-Chi ... 12
Trout-Det......... 27	Newhouser-Det... .763	Berry-Phi 53	Newhouser-Det 25	Newhouser-Det 6	Caster-StL 12
Potter-StL........ 19	Potter-StL....... .731	Trout-Det 49		Jakucki-StL 4	Berry-Phi 12
Hughson-Bos 18	Trout-Det........ .659	Newhouser-Det ... 47			Heving-Cle 10
	Borowy-NY ...... .586	Klieman-Cle 47			Barrett-Bos 8

Innings Pitched	Fewest Hits/Game	Fewest BB/Game	Strikeouts	Strikeouts/Game	Ratio
Trout-Det........352.1	Gromek-Cle 7.07	Harris-Phi 1.34	Newhouser-Det ... 187	Newhouser-Det ... 5.39	Hughson-Bos 9.52
Newhouser-Det ..312.1	Niggeling-Was.... 7.17	Leonard-Was 1.45	Trout-Det 144	Niggeling-Was ... 5.29	Trout-Det 10.24
Newsom-Phi 265.0	Newhouser-Det ... 7.61	Bonham-NY 1.73	Newsom-Phi 142	Gromek-Cle 5.08	Leonard-Was 10.28
Kramer-StL 257.0	Hughson-Bos 7.61	Gorsica-Det 1.78	Kramer-StL 124	Hughson-Bos 4.96	Gromek-Cle 10.30
Borowy-NY 252.2	Borowy-NY 7.98	Hamlin-Phi 1.80	Niggeling-Was 121	Newsom-Phi 4.82	Newhouser-Det .. 10.58

Earned Run Average	Adjusted ERA	Opponents' Batting Avg.	Opponents' On Base Pct.	Starter Runs	Adjusted Starter Runs
Trout-Det.........2.12	Trout-Det 168	Gromek-Cle 219	Hughson-Bos 267	Trout-Det 51.3	Trout-Det 56.7
Newhouser-Det ...2.22	Newhouser-Det ... 161	Niggeling-Was 221	Leonard-Was 284	Newhouser-Det .. 42.1	Newhouser-Det .. 46.8
Hughson-Bos 2.26	Hughson-Bos 151	Hughson-Bos 225	Trout-Det 284	Kramer-StL 27.0	Kramer-StL 31.8
Niggeling-Was 2.32	Kramer-StL 145	Newhouser-Det ...230	Gromek-Cle 290	Hughson-Bos 26.5	Hughson-Bos 25.8
Kramer-StL.......2.49	Niggeling-Was 141	Borowy-NY 236	Newhouser-Det ...293	Niggeling-Was ... 25.5	Borowy-NY 23.9

Clutch Pitching Index	Relief Runs	Adjusted Relief Runs	Relief Ranking	Total Pitcher Index	Total Baseball Ranking
Donald-NY 129	Heving-Cle 19.6	Berry-Phi 19.1	Berry-Phi 32.4	Trout-Det 9.1	Trout-Det 9.1
Woods-Bos....... 122	Berry-Phi 18.4	Heving-Cle 17.9	Heving-Cle 18.2	Newhouser-Det ... 6.5	Boudreau-Cle 7.8
Smith-Cle 116	Caster-StL 8.9	Caster-StL 10.4	Caster-StL 17.3	Kramer-StL 4.3	Stirnweiss-NY 7.1
Haynes-Chi 116	Maltzberger-Chi ... 4.8	Maltzberger-Chi ... 4.8	Maltzberger-Chi ...8.5	Berry-Phi 3.6	Newhouser-Det ... 6.5
Bonham-NY 115				Hughson-Bos 3.0	Spence-Was.......5.2

TEAM	G	W	L	PCT	GB	R	OR	AB	H	2B	3B	HR	BB	SO	AVG	OBP	SLG	PRO	PRO+	BR	/A	PF	CHI	RC	SB	CS	SBA	SBR
CHI	155	98	56	.636		735	532	5298	1465	229	52	57	554	462	.277	.349	.372	.721	109	53	69	98	99	714	69			
STL	155	95	59	.617	3	756	583	5487	1498	256	44	64	515	488	.273	.338	.371	.709	102	25	7	102	103	716	55			
BRO	155	87	67	.565	11	795	724	5418	1468	257	71	57	629	434	.271	.349	.376	.725	109	66	72	99	102	746	75			
PIT	155	82	72	.532	16	753	686	5343	1425	259	56	72	590	480	.267	.342	.377	.719	102	45	16	104	102	701	81			
NY	154	78	74	.513	19	668	700	5350	1439	175	35	114	501	457	.269	.336	.379	.715	103	33	22	102	93	692	38			
BOS	154	67	85	.441	30	721	728	5441	1453	229	25	101	520	510	.267	.334	.374	.708	102	20	16	101	100	692	82			
CIN	154	61	93	.396	37	536	694	5283	1317	221	26	56	392	532	.249	.304	.333	.637	85	-122	-110	98	99	537	71			
PHI	154	46	108	.299	52	548	865	5203	1278	197	27	56	449	501	.246	.307	.326	.633	84	-122	-107	97	102	527	54			
TOT	618					5512		42823	11343	1823	336	577	4150	3864	.265	.333	.364	.696							525			

TEAM	CG	SH	SV	IP	H	H/G	HR	BB	SO	RAT	ERA	ERA+	OAV	OOB	PR	/A	PF	CPI	FA	E	DP	FW	PW	BW	SBW	DIF
CHI	86	15	14	1366¹	1301	8.6	57	385	541	11.3	2.98	123	.249	.304	125	102	96	102	.980	121	124	3.4	10.2	6.9		.5
STL	77	18	9	1408²	1351	8.6	70	497	510	12.0	3.24	116	.253	.320	88	79	99	106	.977	137	150	2.4	7.9	.7		7.0
BRO	61	7	18	1392¹	1357	8.8	74	586	557	12.8	3.70	101	.253	.331	15	7	99	98	.962	230	144	-3.2	.7	7.2		5.3
PIT	73	8	16	1387¹	1477	9.6	61	455	518	12.7	3.76	105	.272	.331	6	27	104	100	.971	178	141	-.0	2.7	1.6		.8
NY	53	13	21	1374²	1401	9.2	85	528	530	12.8	4.06	96	.263	.332	-40	-23	103	95	.973	166	112	.6	-2.3	2.2		1.5
BOS	57	7	13	1391²	1474	9.5	99	557	404	13.3	4.04	95	.272	.342	-37	-32	101	104	.969	193	160	-1.1	-3.2	1.6		-6.3
CIN	77	11	6	1365²	1438	9.5	70	534	372	13.3	4.00	94	.271	.340	-31	-36	99	100	.976	146	138	1.8	-3.6	-11.0		-3.2
PHI	31	4	26	1352²	1544	10.3	61	608	432	14.5	4.64	83	.285	.360	-126	-123	101	97	.962	234	150	-3.5	-12.3	-10.7		-4.4
TOT	515	83	123	11039¹		9.2				12.8	3.80		.265	.333					.971	1405	1119					

Runs
Stanky-Bro 128
Rosen-Bro 126
Holmes-Bos 125
Galan-Bro 114
Hack-Chi 110

Hits
Holmes-Bos 224
Rosen-Bro 197
Hack-Chi 193
Clay-Cin 184

Doubles
Holmes-Bos 47
Walker-Bro 42
Galan-Bro 36
Elliott-Pit 36
Cavarretta-Chi 34

Triples
Olmo-Bro 13
Pafko-Chi 12
Rucker-NY 11
Rosen-Bro 11
Cavarretta-Chi 10

Home Runs
Holmes-Bos 28
Workman-Bos 25
Adams-Phi-StL 22
Ott-NY 21
Kurowski-StL 21

Total Bases
Holmes-Bos 367
Adams-Phi-StL 279
Rosen-Bro 279
Walker-Bro 266
Kurowski-StL 261

Runs Batted In
Walker-Bro 124
Holmes-Bos 117
Pafko-Chi 110
Olmo-Bro 110
Adams-Phi-StL 109

Runs Produced
Walker-Bro 218
Holmes-Bos 214
Galan-Bro 197
Adams-Phi-StL 191
Rosen-Bro 189

Bases On Balls
Stanky-Bro 148
Galan-Bro 114
Hack-Chi 99
Nicholson-Chi 92
Sanders-StL 83

Batting Average
Cavarretta-Chi .... .355
Holmes-Bos .... .352
Rosen-Bro .... .325
Hack-Chi .... .323
Kurowski-StL .... .323

On Base Percentage
Cavarretta-Chi .... .449
Galan-Bro .... .423
Hack-Chi .... .420
Holmes-Bos .... .420
Stanky-Bro .... .417

Slugging Average
Holmes-Bos .... .577
Kurowski-StL .... .511
Cavarretta-Chi .... .500
Ott-NY .... .499
Olmo-Bro .... .462

Production
Holmes-Bos .... .997
Cavarretta-Chi .... .949
Ott-NY .... .910
Kurowski-StL .... .894
Galan-Bro .... .864

Adjusted Production
Holmes-Bos 175
Cavarretta-Chi 167
Ott-NY 150
Kurowski-StL 144
Galan-Bro 142

Batter Runs
Holmes-Bos 62.9
Cavarretta-Chi 46.4
Galan-Bro 36.8
Ott-NY 33.4
Kurowski-StL 30.7

Adjusted Batter Runs
Holmes-Bos 62.1
Cavarretta-Chi 48.8
Galan-Bro 37.7
Ott-NY 32.0
Hack-Chi 31.7

Clutch Hitting Index
Walker-Bro 135
Elliott-Pit 135
Lowrey-Chi 129
Cavarretta-Chi 126
Olmo-Bro 125

Runs Created
Holmes-Bos 156
Cavarretta-Chi 119
Galan-Bro 116
Hack-Chi 111
Rosen-Bro 110

Total Average
Holmes-Bos 1.078
Cavarretta-Chi ... 1.037
Ott-NY .... .959
Galan-Bro .... .936
Kurowski-StL .... .876

Stolen Bases
Schoendienst-StL 26
Barrett-Pit 25
Clay-Cin 19

Stolen Base Average

Stolen Base Runs

Fielding Runs
Kerr-NY 28.3
Gillenwater-Bos 23.8
Coscarart-Pit 21.1
Hack-Chi 18.0
Walker-Bro 12.4

Total Player Rating
Holmes-Bos 5.4
Hack-Chi 5.2
Cavarretta-Chi 3.8
Stanky-Bro 3.6
Kurowski-StL 3.3

Wins
Barrett-Bos-StL 23
Wyse-Chi 22
Gregg-Bro 18
Burkhart-StL 18
Passeau-Chi 17

Win Percentage
Brecheen-StL ..... .789
Burkhart-StL .... .692
Wyse-Chi .... .688
Barrett-Bos-StL ..... .657
Passeau-Chi .... .654

Games
Karl-Phi 67
Adams-NY 65
Hutchings-Bos 57
Barrett-Bos-StL 45
Fox-Cin 45

Complete Games
Barrett-Bos-StL 24
Wyse-Chi 23
Passeau-Chi 19
Strincevich-Pit 18
Heusser-Cin 18

Shutouts
Passeau-Chi 5
Voiselle-NY 4
Heusser-Cin 4
Donnelly-StL 4
Burkhart-StL 4

Saves
Karl-Phi 15
Adams-NY 15
Rescigno-Pit 9

Innings Pitched
Barrett-Bos-StL .. 284.2
Wyse-Chi 278.1
Gregg-Bro 254.1
Roe-Pit 235.0
Voiselle-NY 232.1

Fewest Hits/Game
Prim-Chi 7.73
Brecheen-StL 7.78
Gregg-Bro 7.82
Mungo-NY 7.92
Passeau-Chi 8.13

Fewest BB/Game
Prim-Chi 1.25
Barrett-Bos-StL 1.71
Roe-Pit 1.76
Wyse-Chi 1.78
Strincevich-Pit 1.93

Strikeouts
Roe-Pit 148
Gregg-Bro 139
Voiselle-NY 115
Mungo-NY 101
Hutchings-Bos 99

Strikeouts/Game
Roe-Pit 5.67
Mungo-NY 4.97
Gregg-Bro 4.92
Hutchings-Bos 4.82
Prim-Chi 4.79

Ratio
Prim-Chi 9.04
Roe-Pit 10.53
Passeau-Chi 10.55
Brecheen-StL 10.58
Wyse-Chi 10.74

Earned Run Average
Prim-Chi 2.40
Passeau-Chi 2.46
Brecheen-StL 2.52
Walters-Cin 2.68
Wyse-Chi 2.68

Adjusted ERA
Prim-Chi 152
Brecheen-StL 149
Passeau-Chi 149
Walters-Cin 140
Roe-Pit 137

Opponents' Batting Avg.
Prim-Chi .... .228
Gregg-Bro .... .232
Brecheen-StL .... .238
Mungo-NY .... .238
Passeau-Chi .... .238

Opponents' On Base Pct.
Prim-Chi .... .256
Passeau-Chi .... .289
Barrett-Bos-StL .... .295
Wyse-Chi .... .296
Roe-Pit .... .296

Starter Runs
Wyse-Chi 34.5
Passeau-Chi 33.8
Prim-Chi 25.8
Barrett-Bos-StL 25.2
Roe-Pit 24.2

Adjusted Starter Runs
Passeau-Chi 30.1
Wyse-Chi 29.9
Roe-Pit 28.0
Barrett-Bos-StL 23.7
Prim-Chi 23.1

Clutch Pitching Index
Butcher-Pit 124
Logan-Bos 124
Walters-Cin 124
Lee-Phi-Bos 123
Wyse-Chi 117

Relief Runs
Karl-Phi 16.3
Buker-Bro 4.9
Adams-NY 4.7
Chipman-Chi 2.4

Adjusted Relief Runs
Karl-Phi 16.9
Adams-NY 6.1
Buker-Bro 4.4
Chipman-Chi 1.2

Relief Ranking
Karl-Phi 16.6
Adams-NY 11.5
Buker-Bro 4.7
Chipman-Chi 1.4

Total Pitcher Index
Passeau-Chi 3.8
Wyse-Chi 3.2
Prim-Chi 3.0
Walters-Cin 2.9
Roe-Pit 2.8

Total Baseball Ranking
Holmes-Bos 5.4
Hack-Chi 5.2
Cavarretta-Chi 3.8
Passeau-Chi 3.8
Stanky-Bro 3.6

TEAM	G	W	L	PCT	GB	R	OR	AB	H	2B	3B	HR	BB	SO	AVG	OBP	SLG	PRO	PRO+	BR	/A	PF	CHI	RC	SB	CS	SBA	SBR
DET	155	88	65	.575		633	565	5257	1345	227	47	77	517	533	.256	.324	.361	.685	98	20	-20	106	102	627	60	54	53	-14
WAS	156	87	67	.565	1.5	622	562	5326	1375	197	63	27	545	489	.258	.330	.334	.664	107	-8	43	92	103	612	110	65	63	-6
STL	154	81	70	.536	6	597	548	5227	1302	215	37	63	500	555	.249	.316	.341	.657	91	-29	-58	105	105	584	25	31	45	-11
NY	152	81	71	.533	6.5	676	606	5176	1343	189	61	93	618	567	.259	.343	.373	.716	108	90	58	105	97	698	64	43	60	-7
CLE	147	73	72	.503	11	557	548	4898	1249	216	48	65	505	578	.255	.326	.359	.685	109	23	48	96	95	588	19	31	38	-13
CHI	150	71	78	.477	15	596	633	5077	1330	204	55	22	470	467	.262	.326	.337	.663	101	-13	2	97	105	571	78	54	59	-9
BOS	157	71	83	.461	17.5	599	674	5367	1393	225	44	50	541	534	.260	.330	.346	.676	100	12	-2	102	96	634	72	50	59	-8
PHI	153	52	98	.347	34.5	494	638	5296	1297	201	37	33	449	463	.245	.306	.316	.622	86	-96	-94	100	98	523	25	45	36	-20
TOT	612					4774		41624	10634	1674	392	430	4145	4186	.255	.325	.346	.671							453	373	55	-88

TEAM	CG	SH	SV	IP	H	H/G	HR	BB	SO	RAT	ERA	ERA+	OAV	OOB	PR	/A	PF	CPI	FA	E	DP	FW	PW	BW	SBW	DIF
DET	78	19	16	1393²	1305	8.4	48	538	588	12.1	2.99	118	.250	.322	58	81	105	108	.975	158	173	.4	8.7	-2.1	-.3	4.9
WAS	82	19	11	1412¹	1307	8.3	42	440	550	11.2	2.92	106	.242	.301	69	28	92	93	.970	183	124	-1.0	3.0	4.6	.5	2.8
STL	91	10	8	1382²	1307	8.5	59	506	570	11.8	3.14	112	.249	.316	34	58	105	101	.976	143	123	1.2	6.2	-6.2	.0	4.3
NY	78	9	14	1355	1277	8.5	66	485	474	11.8	3.45	100	.250	.316	-13	1	103	93	.971	175	170	-.7	.1	6.2	.4	-1.0
CLE	76	14	12	1302¹	1269	8.8	39	501	497	12.4	3.31	98	.251	.328	8	-9	97	102	.977	126	149	1.7	-1.0	5.1	-.2	-5.2
CHI	84	13	13	1330²	1400	9.5	63	448	486	12.7	3.69	90	.270	.332	-49	-55	99	100	.970	180	139	-1.1	-5.9	-.2	.3	3.1
BOS	71	15	13	1390²	1389	9.0	58	656	490	13.4	3.80	90	.264	.348	-67	-61	101	102	.973	169	198	-.1	-6.5	-.2	.3	.5
PHI	65	11	8	1381	1380	9.0	55	571	531	12.9	3.62	95	.262	.337	-40	-29	102	101	.973	168	160	-.3	-3.1	-10.1	-1.0	-8.6
TOT	625	110	95	10948¹		8.7				12.3	3.36		.255	.325					.973	1302	1236					

Runs
Stirnweiss-NY 107
Stephens-StL 90
Cullenbine-Cle-Det 83

Hits
Stirnweiss-NY 195
Moses-Chi 168
Stephens-StL 165
Hall-Phi 161
Etten-NY 161

Doubles
Moses-Chi 35
Stirnweiss-NY 32
Binks-Was 32
McQuinn-StL 31

Triples
Stirnweiss-NY 22
Moses-Chi 15
Kuhel-Was 13
Dickshot-Phi 10
Peck-Phi 9

Home Runs
Stephens-StL 24
Cullenbine-Cle-Det .. 18
York-Det 18
Etten-NY 18
Heath-Cle 15

Total Bases
Stirnweiss-NY 301
Stephens-StL 270
Etten-NY 247
York-Det 246
Moses-Chi 239

Runs Batted In
Etten-NY 111
Cullenbine-Cle-Det ... 93
Stephens-StL 89
York-Det 87
Binks-Was 81

Runs Produced
Etten-NY 170
Stirnweiss-NY 161
Cullenbine-Cle-Det . 158
Stephens-StL 155
Kuhel-Was 146

Bases On Balls
Cullenbine-Cle-Det ... 113
Lake-Bos 106
Grimes-NY 97
Etten-NY 90
Kuhel-Was 79

Batting Average
Stirnweiss-NY 309
Cuccinello-Chi 308
Dickshot-Chi 302
Estalella-Phi 299
Myatt-Was 296

On Base Percentage
Lake-Bos 412
Cullenbine-Cle-Det ..402
Estalella-Phi 399
Grimes-NY 395
Etten-NY 387

Slugging Average
Stirnweiss-NY 476
Stephens-StL 473
Cullenbine-Cle-Det ..444
Etten-NY 437
Estalella-Phi 435

Production
Stirnweiss-NY 862
Cullenbine-Cle-Det ..846
Estalella-Phi 834
Stephens-StL 825
Etten-NY 824

Adjusted Production
Stirnweiss-NY 143
Estalella-Phi 142
Kuhel-Was 137
Cullenbine-Cle-Det . 137
Lake-Bos 136

Batter Runs
Stirnweiss-NY 39.1
Cullenbine-Cle-Det . 35.1
Etten-NY 29.9
Heath-Cle 29.4
Lake-Bos 28.7

Adjusted Batter Runs
Stirnweiss-NY 34.0
Heath-Cle 32.6
Cullenbine-Cle-Det .29.2
Lake-Bos 26.7
Kuhel-Was 26.5

Clutch Hitting Index
Schalk-Chi 135
Michaels-Chi 132
Tresh-Chi 130
Etten-NY 121
Binks-Was 119

Runs Created
Stirnweiss-NY 121
Cullenbine-Cle-Det . 106
Etten-NY 98
Stephens-StL 98
Moses-Chi 97

Total Average
Cullenbine-Cle-Det ...888
Stirnweiss-NY 855
Lake-Bos 849
Etten-NY 794
Estalella-Phi 789

Stolen Bases
Stirnweiss-NY 33
Myatt-Was 30
Case-Was 30
Metkovich-Bos 19
Dickshot-Chi 18

Stolen Base Average
Dickshot-Chi 85.7
Metkovich-Bos 76.0
Myatt-Was 73.2
Stirnweiss-NY 66.0
Case-Was 65.2

Stolen Base Runs
Dickshot-Chi 3.6
Myatt-Was 2.4
Metkovich-Bos 2.1
Crosetti-NY 1.5
Richards-Det 1.2

Fielding Runs
Hall-Phi 26.1
Stirnweiss-NY 25.5
Webb-Det 23.0
Newsome-Bos 22.2
Kell-Phi 21.7

Total Player Rating
Stirnweiss-NY 7.2
Lake-Bos 5.7
Cullenbine-Cle-Det 3.4
Mayo-Det 3.1
Newsome-Bos 2.9

Wins
Newhouser-Det 25
Ferriss-Bos 21
Wolff-Was 20
Gromek-Cle 19

Win Percentage
Newhouser-Det 735
Leonard-Was 708
Gromek-Cle 679
Ferriss-Bos 677
Wolff-Was 667

Games
Berry-Phi 52
Reynolds-Cle 44
Pieretti-Was 44
Trout-Det 41
Newhouser-Det 40

Complete Games
Newhouser-Det 29
Ferriss-Bos 26
Wolff-Was 21
Potter-StL 21
Gromek-Cle 21

Shutouts
Newhouser-Det 8
Ferriss-Bos 5
Benton-Det 5

Saves
Turner-NY 10
Berry-Phi 5

Innings Pitched
Newhouser-Det 313.1
Ferriss-Bos 264.2
Newsom-Phi 257.1
Potter-StL 255.1
Gromek-Cle 251.0

Fewest Hits/Game
Newhouser-Det 6.86
Wolff-Was 7.20
Potter-StL 7.47
Lee-Chi 8.20
Niggeling-Was 8.20

Fewest BB/Game
Bonham-NY 1.10
Leonard-Was 1.46
Wolff-Was 1.91
Overmire-Det 2.33
Gromek-Cle 2.37

Strikeouts
Newhouser-Det 212
Potter-StL 129
Newsom-Phi 127
Reynolds-Cle 112

Strikeouts/Game
Newhouser-Det 6.09
Kramer-StL 4.62
Niggeling-Was 4.58
Potter-StL 4.55
Newsom-Phi 4.44

Ratio
Wolff-Was 9.14
Potter-StL 9.90
Newhouser-Det .. 10.02
Leonard-Was 10.21
Bonham-NY 10.41

Earned Run Average
Newhouser-Det ... 1.81
Benton-Det 2.02
Wolff-Was 2.12
Leonard-Was 2.13
Lee-Chi 2.44

Adjusted ERA
Newhouser-Det 194
Benton-Det 174
Wolff-Was 146
Leonard-Was 146
Potter-StL 143

Opponents' Batting Avg.
Newhouser-Det 211
Wolff-Was 215
Potter-StL 226
Niggeling-Was 240
Benton-Det 241

Opponents' On Base Pct.
Wolff-Was 258
Potter-StL 279
Leonard-Was 279
Newhouser-Det 281
Bonham-NY 288

Starter Runs
Newhouser-Det 54.1
Wolff-Was 34.5
Leonard-Was 29.8
Benton-Det 28.7
Potter-StL 25.5

Adjusted Starter Runs
Newhouser-Det 59.4
Benton-Det 31.9
Potter-StL 29.8
Wolff-Was 27.2
Leonard-Was 23.5

Clutch Pitching Index
Benton-Det 139
Lee-Chi 121
Shirley-StL 116
Hollingsworth-StL . 116
Ferriss-Bos 114

Relief Runs
Berry-Phi 14.7
Holcombe-NY 9.7
Barrett-Bos 7.2
Zoldak-StL 0

Adjusted Relief Runs
Berry-Phi 15.7
Holcombe-NY 10.3
Barrett-Bos 7.5
Zoldak-StL 1.2

Relief Ranking
Berry-Phi 17.6
Holcombe-NY 10.0
Barrett-Bos 6.1
Zoldak-StL 8

Total Pitcher Index
Newhouser-Det 7.8
Potter-StL 3.5
Ferriss-Bos 3.3
Benton-Det 3.2
Leonard-Was 2.8

Total Baseball Ranking
Newhouser-Det 7.8
Stirnweiss-NY 7.2
Lake-Bos 5.7
Potter-StL 3.5
Cullenbine-Cle-Det .3.4

TEAM	G	W	L	PCT	GB	R	OR	AB	H	2B	3B	HR	BB	SO	AVG	OBP	SLG	PRO	PRO+	BR	/A	PF	CHI	RC	SB	CS	SBA	SBR
STL	156	98	58	.628		**712**	545	5372	**1426**	**265**	56	81	530	537	**.265**	.334	**.381**	**.715**	105	54	25	104	**105**	**702**	58			
BRO	157	96	60	.615	2	701	570	5285	1376	233	**66**	55	**691**	575	.260	**.348**	.361	.709	106	**60**	**53**	101	101	699	**100**			
CHI	155	82	71	.536	14.5	626	581	5298	1344	223	50	56	586	599	.254	.331	.346	.677	100	-9	3	98	102	622	43			
BOS	154	81	72	.529	15.5	630	592	5225	1377	238	48	44	558	**468**	.264	.337	.353	.690	101	16	8	101	100	641	60			
PHI	155	69	85	.448	28	560	705	5233	1351	209	40	80	417	590	.258	.315	.359	.674	100	-30	-14	97	99	598	41			
CIN	156	67	87	.435	30	523	570	5291	1262	206	33	65	493	604	.239	.307	.327	.634	88	-101	-82	96	102	546	82			
PIT	155	63	91	.409	34	552	668	5199	1300	202	52	60	592	555	.250	.328	.344	.672	95	-18	-33	103	93	602	48			
NY	154	61	93	.396	36	612	685	5191	1326	176	37	**121**	532	546	.255	.328	.374	.702	104	27	23	101	97	644	46			
TOT	621					4916		42094	10762	1752	382	562	4399	4474	.256	.329	.355	.684							478			

TEAM	CG	SH	SV	IP	H	H/G	HR	BB	SO	RAT	ERA	ERA+	OAV	OOB	PR	/A	PF	CPI	FA	E	DP	FW	PW	BW	SBW	DIF
STL	**75**	**18**	15	1397	1326	8.5	63	493	607	11.9	**3.01**	115	.254	.322	63	70	101	108	**.980**	**124**	167	2.1	7.4	2.7		7.8
BRO	52	14	**28**	1418	1280	8.1	58	671	**647**	12.5	3.05	111	**.243**	.331	58	52	99	107	.972	174	154	-.9	5.5	**5.6**		7.7
CHI	59	15	11	1393	1370	8.9	58	527	619	12.4	3.24	104	.256	.325	26	15	97	102	.976	146	119	.7	1.6	.3		2.9
BOS	73	10	12	1371	1291	8.5	76	478	566	11.7	3.35	102	.249	**.314**	10	13	101	93	.972	169	129	-.8	1.4	.8		3.0
PHI	55	11	23	1369	1442	9.5	73	542	490	13.3	3.99	86	.273	.344	-88	-85	101	98	.975	148	144	.6	-9.0	-1.5		1.9
CIN	69	17	11	1413¹	1334	8.5	70	**467**	506	**11.6**	3.08	109	.252	**.314**	53	42	98	101	.975	155	**192**	.2	4.5	-8.7		-6.0
PIT	61	10	6	1370	1406	9.2	**50**	561	458	13.1	3.72	95	.269	.342	-46	-29	103	99	.970	184	127	-1.6	-3.1	-3.5		-5.8
NY	47	8	13	1353¹	1313	8.7	114	660	581	13.2	3.92	88	.256	.343	-76	-71	101	100	.973	159	121	-.2	-7.5	2.4		-10.7
TOT	491	103	119	11084²		8.7				12.5	3.41		.256	.329					.974	1259	1153					

Runs		Hits		Doubles		Triples		Home Runs		Total Bases	
Musial-StL	124	Musial-StL	228	Musial-StL	50	Musial-StL	20	Kiner-Pit	23	Musial-StL	366
Slaughter-StL	100	Walker-Bro	184	Holmes-Bos	35	Reese-Bro	10	Mize-NY	22	Slaughter-StL	283
Stanky-Bro	98	Slaughter-StL	183	Kurowski-StL	32	Cavarretta-Chi	10	Slaughter-StL	18	Ennis-Phi	262
Schoendienst-StL	94	Holmes-Bos	176	Herman-Bro-Bos	31	Walker-Bro	9	Ennis-Phi	17	Walker-Bro	258
Cavarretta-Chi	89	Schoendienst-StL	170							Holmes-Bos	241

Runs Batted In		Runs Produced		Bases On Balls		Batting Average		On Base Percentage		Slugging Average	
Slaughter-StL	130	Slaughter-StL	212	Stanky-Bro	137	Musial-StL	.365	Stanky-Bro	.436	Musial-StL	.587
Walker-Bro	116	Musial-StL	211	Fletcher-Pit	111	Hopp-Bos	.333	Musial-StL	.434	Ennis-Phi	.485
Musial-StL	103	Walker-Bro	187	Cavarretta-Chi	88	Walker-Bro	.319	Cavarretta-Chi	.401	Slaughter-StL	.465
Kurowski-StL	89	Cavarretta-Chi	159	Reese-Bro	87	Ennis-Phi	.313	Herman-Bro-Bos	.391	Kurowski-StL	.462
Kiner-Pit	81	Holmes-Bos	153	Hack-Chi	83	Holmes-Bos	.310	Walker-Bro	.391	Walker-Bro	.448

Production		Adjusted Production		Batter Runs		Adjusted Batter Runs		Clutch Hitting Index		Runs Created	
Musial-StL	1.021	Musial-StL	180	Musial-StL	70.9	Musial-StL	64.8	Walker-Bro	138	Musial-StL	164
Kurowski-StL	.853	Ennis-Phi	144	Mize-NY	43.6	Mize-NY	43.0	Slaughter-StL	131	Slaughter-StL	110
Ennis-Phi	.849	Cavarretta-Chi	140	Kurowski-StL	29.1	Cavarretta-Chi	29.5	Elliott-Pit	127	Walker-Bro	104
Walker-Bro	.839	Walker-Bro	136	Walker-Bro	28.9	Walker-Bro	27.9	Fletcher-Pit	123	Mize-NY	100
Slaughter-StL	.838	Kurowski-StL	136	Slaughter-StL	28.6	Ennis-Phi	27.9	Reiser-Bro	120	Kurowski-StL	97

Total Average		Stolen Bases		Stolen Base Average		Stolen Base Runs		Fielding Runs		Total Player Rating	
Musial-StL	1.114	Reiser-Bro	34					Marion-StL	18.8	Musial-StL	5.7
Stanky-Bro	.890	Haas-Cin	22					Wyrostek-Phi	17.2	Mize-NY	4.4
Reiser-Bro	.877	Hopp-Bos	21					Ennis-Phi	13.6	Ennis-Phi	3.7
Kurowski-StL	.855	Adams-Cin	16					Handley-Pit	13.2	Stanky-Bro	3.1
Walker-Bro	.848	Walker-Bro	14					Mueller-Cin	9.8	Kurowski-StL	2.9

Wins		Win Percentage		Games		Complete Games		Shutouts		Saves	
Pollet-StL	21	Dickson-StL	.714	Trinkle-NY	48	Sain-Bos	24	Brecheen-StL	5	Raffensberger-Phi	6
Sain-Bos	20	Higbe-Bro	.680	Dickson-StL	47	Pollet-StL	22	Blackwell-Cin	5	Pollet-StL	5
Higbe-Bro	17	Pollet-StL	.677	Behrman-Bro	47	Koslo-NY	17	VanderMeer-Cin	4	Karl-Phi	5
Dickson-StL	15	Sain-Bos	.588	Casey-Bro	46	Ostermueller-Pit	16	Pollet-StL	4	Herring-Bro	5
Brecheen-StL	15	Brecheen-StL	.500			Cooper-Bos	15	Cooper-Bos	4	Casey-Bro	5

Innings Pitched		Fewest Hits/Game		Fewest BB/Game		Strikeouts		Strikeouts/Game		Ratio	
Pollet-StL	266.0	Kennedy-NY	7.38	Cooper-Bos	1.76	Schmitz-Chi	135	Higbe-Bro	5.72	Cooper-Bos	9.95
Koslo-NY	265.1	Schmitz-Chi	7.38	Raffensberger-Phi	1.79	Higbe-Bro	134	Schmitz-Chi	5.42	Beggs-Cin	10.18
Sain-Bos	265.0	Blackwell-Cin	7.41	Beggs-Cin	1.85	Sain-Bos	129	Blackwell-Cin	4.63	Sain-Bos	10.66
Brecheen-StL	231.1	Higbe-Bro	7.60	Heusser-Cin	2.09	Koslo-NY	121	Brecheen-StL	4.55	Dickson-StL	10.74
Schmitz-Chi	224.1	Sain-Bos	7.64	Strincevich-Pit	2.25	Brecheen-StL	117	Voiselle-NY	4.50	Pollet-StL	10.79

Earned Run Average		Adjusted ERA		Opponents' Batting Avg.		Opponents' On Base Pct.		Starter Runs		Adjusted Starter Runs	
Pollet-StL	2.10	Pollet-StL	165	Schmitz-Chi	.221	Cooper-Bos	.276	Pollet-StL	38.9	Pollet-StL	40.1
Sain-Bos	2.21	Sain-Bos	155	Kennedy-NY	.224	Beggs-Cin	.287	Sain-Bos	35.5	Sain-Bos	36.0
Beggs-Cin	2.32	Beggs-Cin	144	Blackwell-Cin	.226	Sain-Bos	.294	Brecheen-StL	23.7	Brecheen-StL	24.8
Blackwell-Cin	2.45	Brecheen-StL	139	Higbe-Bro	.229	Dickson-StL	.295	Beggs-Cin	23.1	Beggs-Cin	21.6
Brecheen-StL	2.49	Blackwell-Cin	136	Sain-Bos	.230	Pollet-StL	.300	Blackwell-Cin	20.7	Rowe-Phi	19.9

Clutch Pitching Index		Relief Runs		Adjusted Relief Runs		Relief Ranking		Total Pitcher Index		Total Baseball Ranking	
Hatten-Bro	129	Casey-Bro	15.8	Casey-Bro	15.5	Casey-Bro	24.1	Sain-Bos	5.9	Sain-Bos	5.9
Pollet-StL	127	Thompson-NY	14.8	Thompson-NY	15.0	Thompson-NY	23.7	Pollet-StL	5.1	Musial-StL	5.7
Beggs-Cin	124	Malloy-Cin	5.3	Malloy-Cin	4.8	Malloy-Cin	4.5	Brecheen-StL	3.1	Pollet-StL	5.1
Wyse-Chi	117	Budnick-NY	2.5	Budnick-NY	2.8	Budnick-NY	1.6	Beggs-Cin	2.9	Mize-NY	4.4
Ostermueller-Pit	110	Herring-Bro	.6	Wilks-StL	.5	Wilks-StL	.4	Casey-Bro	2.9	Ennis-Phi	3.7

TEAM	G	W	L	PCT	GB	R	OR	AB	H	2B	3B	HR	BB	SO	AVG	OBP	SLG	PRO	PRO+	BR	/A	PF	CHI	RC	SB	CS	SBA	SBR
BOS	156	104	50	.675		**792**	594	5318	**1441**	268	50	109	687	661	**.271**	.356	.402	.758	113	136	92	106	101	790	45	36	56	-8
DET	155	92	62	.597	12	704	567	5318	1373	212	41	108	622	616	.258	.337	.374	.711	100	42	0	106	103	698	65	41	**61**	**-5**
NY	154	87	67	.565	17	684	547	5139	1275	208	50	**136**	627	706	.248	.334	.387	.721	107	55	46	101	101	695	48	35	58	-7
WAS	155	76	78	.494	28	608	706	5337	1388	260	**63**	60	511	641	.260	.324	.333	.656	106	1	39	94	96	653	51	50	50	-15
CHI	155	74	80	.481	30	562	595	5312	1364	206	44	37	501	600	.257	.323	.333	.656	94	-64	-43	96	100	579	**78**	64	55	-15
CLE	156	68	86	.442	36	537	638	5242	1285	233	56	79	506	697	.245	.313	.356	.669	99	-49	-12	94	94	596	57	49	54	-12
STL	156	66	88	.429	38	621	710	5373	1350	220	46	84	465	713	.251	.313	.356	.669	89	-53	-82	105	**108**	601	23	35	40	-14
PHI	155	49	105	.318	55	529	680	5200	1317	220	51	40	482	**594**	.253	.318	.338	.656	91	-68	-65	99	97	574	39	30	57	-6
TOT	621					5037		42239	10793	1827	401	653	4401	5228	.256	.328	.364	.692							406	340	54	-82

TEAM	CG	SH	SV	IP	H	H/G	HR	BB	SO	RAT	ERA	ERA+	OAV	OOB	PR	/A	PF	CPI	FA	E	DP	FW	PW	BW	SBW	DIF
BOS	79	15	**20**	1396^2	1359	8.8	89	501	667	12.1	3.38	108	.254	.319	19	44	105	100	**.977**	139	163	**1.5**	4.6	**9.6**	.2	11.0
DET	**94**	**18**	15	1402	1277	8.2	97	**497**	**896**	11.5	3.22	**114**	**.241**	**.307**	45	**68**	104	95	.974	155	138	.5	**7.1**	.0	.6	6.9
NY	68	17	17	1361	**1232**	**8.1**	66	552	653	11.9	3.13	110	.243	.319	56	48	99	100	.975	150	**174**	.7	5.0	4.8	.3	-.9
WAS	71	8	10	1396^1	1459	9.4	81	547	537	13.1	3.74	89	.269	.339	-36	-61	96	103	.966	211	162	-2.8	-6.4	4.1	-.5	4.6
CHI	62	9	16	1392^1	1348	8.7	80	508	550	12.1	**3.10**	110	.255	.323	63	49	97	**110**	.972	175	170	-.7	5.1	-4.5	-.5	-2.4
CLE	63	16	13	1388^2	1282	8.3	84	649	789	12.6	3.62	91	.245	.331	-17	-48	94	96	.975	147	147	1.0	-5.0	-1.3	-.2	-3.5
STL	63	13	12	1382^1	1465	9.5	73	573	574	13.3	3.95	94	.272	.343	-69	-34	107	99	.974	159	157	.3	-3.6	-8.6	-.4	1.3
PHI	61	10	5	1342^2	1371	9.2	83	577	562	13.2	3.90	91	.264	.340	-59	-53	101	98	.971	167	141	-.2	-5.6	-6.8	.4	-15.8
TOT	561	106	108	11062		8.8				12.5	3.50		.256	.328					.973	1303	1252					

Runs		Hits		Doubles		Triples		Home Runs		Total Bases	
Williams-Bos	142	Pesky-Bos	208	Vernon-Was	51	Edwards-Cle	16	Greenberg-Det	44	Williams-Bos	343
Pesky-Bos	115	Vernon-Was	207	Spence-Was	50	Lewis-Was	13	Williams-Bos	38	Greenberg-Det	316
Lake-Det	105	Appling-Chi	180	Pesky-Bos	43	Kell-Phi-Det	10	Keller-NY	30	Vernon-Was	298
Keller-NY	98	Williams-Bos	176	Williams-Bos	37	Spence-Was	10	Seerey-Cle	26	Spence-Was	287
Doerr-Bos	95	Lewis-Was	170	Doerr-Bos	34	Keller-NY	10	DiMaggio-NY	25	Keller-NY	287

Runs Batted In		Runs Produced		Bases On Balls		Batting Average		On Base Percentage		Slugging Average	
Greenberg-Det	127	Williams-Bos	227	Williams-Bos	156	Vernon-Was	.353	Williams-Bos	.497	Williams-Bos	.667
Williams-Bos	123	Doerr-Bos	193	Keller-NY	113	Williams-Bos	.342	Keller-NY	.405	Greenberg-Det	.604
York-Bos	119	York-Bos	180	Lake-Det	103	Pesky-Bos	.335	Vernon-Was	.403	Keller-NY	.533
Doerr-Bos	116	Greenberg-Det	174	Cullenbine-Det	88	Kell-Phi-Det	.322	Pesky-Bos	.401	DiMaggio-NY	.511
Keller-NY	101	Keller-NY	169	Henrich-NY	87	DiMaggio-Bos	.316	DiMaggio-Bos	.393	Edwards-Cle	.509

Production		Adjusted Production		Batter Runs		Adjusted Batter Runs		Clutch Hitting Index		Runs Created	
Williams-Bos	1.164	Williams-Bos	211	Williams-Bos	94.2	Williams-Bos	85.2	Travis-Was	136	Williams-Bos	188
Greenberg-Det	.977	Vernon-Was	163	Greenberg-Det	46.1	Vernon-Was	46.9	York-Bos	135	Keller-NY	127
Keller-NY	.938	Greenberg-Det	160	Keller-NY	45.9	Keller-NY	44.4	Doerr-Bos	126	Vernon-Was	120
Vernon-Was	.910	Keller-NY	158	Cullenbine-Det	42.2	Greenberg-Det	39.6	Henrich-NY	119	Greenberg-Det	119
DiMaggio-NY	.878	Edwards-Cle	151	Vernon-Was	40.3	Cullenbine-Det	37.0	Heath-Was-StL	109	Pesky-Bos	111

Total Average		Stolen Bases		Stolen Base Average		Stolen Base Runs		Fielding Runs		Total Player Rating	
Williams-Bos	1.431	Case-Cle	28	Stirnweiss-NY	75.0	Stirnweiss-NY	1.8	Doerr-Bos	26.8	Williams-Bos	7.9
Greenberg-Det	1.010	Stirnweiss-NY	18	Case-Cle	71.8	Dillinger-StL	1.8	Gordon-NY	21.5	Doerr-Bos	4.8
Keller-NY	1.005	Lake-Det	15			Case-Cle	1.8	Boudreau-Cle	16.2	Pesky-Bos	4.2
Vernon-Was	.873					Philley-Chi	1.5	Rizzuto-NY	13.1	Vernon-Was	3.6
DiMaggio-NY	.862					Evers-Det	1.5	Pesky-Bos	12.0	Greenberg-Det	3.5

Wins		Win Percentage		Games		Complete Games		Shutouts		Saves	
Newhouser-Det	26	Ferriss-Bos	.806	Feller-Cle	48	Feller-Cle	36	Feller-Cle	10	Klinger-Bos	9
Feller-Cle	26	Newhouser-Det	.743	Savage-Phi	40	Newhouser-Det	29	Newhouser-Det	6	Caldwell-Chi	8
Ferriss-Bos	25	Chandler-NY	.714	Ferriss-Bos	40	Ferriss-Bos	26	Hughson-Bos	6	Murphy-NY	7
Hughson-Bos	20	Harris-Bos	.654	Hughson-Bos	39	Trout-Det	23	Ferriss-Bos	6	Ferrick-Cle-StL	6
Chandler-NY	20	Hughson-Bos	.645	Caldwell-Chi	39	Hughson-Bos	21	Chandler-NY	6		

Innings Pitched		Fewest Hits/Game		Fewest BB/Game		Strikeouts		Strikeouts/Game		Ratio	
Feller-Cle	371.1	Newhouser-Det	6.61	Hughson-Bos	1.65	Feller-Cle	348	Newhouser-Det	8.46	Newhouser-Det	9.66
Newhouser-Det	292.2	Feller-Cle	6.71	Lopat-Chi	1.87	Newhouser-Det	275	Feller-Cle	8.43	Hughson-Bos	9.87
Hughson-Bos	278.0	Chandler-NY	6.99	Leonard-Was	2.00	Hughson-Bos	172	Trucks-Det	6.12	Chandler-NY	10.18
Trout-Det	276.1	Embree-Cle	7.65	Flores-Phi	2.21	Trucks-Det	161	Hutchinson-Det	6.00	Lopat-Chi	10.32
Ferriss-Bos	274.0	Bevens-NY	7.68	Ferriss-Bos	2.33	Trout-Det	151	Hughson-Bos	5.57	Feller-Cle	10.49

Earned Run Average		Adjusted ERA		Opponents' Batting Avg.		Opponents' On Base Pct.		Starter Runs		Adjusted Starter Runs	
Newhouser-Det	1.94	Newhouser-Det	189	Newhouser-Det	.201	Newhouser-Det	.269	Feller-Cle	54.5	Newhouser-Det	55.8
Chandler-NY	2.10	Chandler-NY	164	Feller-Cle	.208	Hughson-Bos	.274	Newhouser-Det	50.9	Feller-Cle	46.5
Feller-Cle	2.18	Trout-Det	156	Chandler-NY	.218	Chandler-NY	.288	Chandler-NY	40.2	Trout-Det	40.2
Bevens-NY	2.23	Bevens-NY	154	Embree-Cle	.227	Lopat-Chi	.288	Trout-Det	35.6	Chandler-NY	38.7
Flores-Phi	2.32	Flores-Phi	153	Bevens-NY	.232	Feller-Cle	.291	Bevens-NY	35.2	Bevens-NY	33.7

Clutch Pitching Index		Relief Runs		Adjusted Relief Runs		Relief Ranking		Total Pitcher Index		Total Baseball Ranking	
Grove-Chi	126	Caldwell-Chi	14.3	Caldwell-Chi	13.4	Caldwell-Chi	25.2	Newhouser-Det	7.1	Williams-Bos	7.9
Flores-Phi	121	Lemon-Cle	10.6	Lemon-Cle	8.5	Klinger-Bos	9.4	Trout-Det	5.3	Newhouser-Det	7.1
Trout-Det	119	Klinger-Bos	7.2	Klinger-Bos	8.2	Lemon-Cle	7.6	Feller-Cle	4.9	Trout-Det	5.3
Haynes-Chi	118	Kinder-StL	1.7	Kinder-StL	3.9	Kinder-StL	2.5	Chandler-NY	4.8	Feller-Cle	4.9
Bevens-NY	115							Bevens-NY	3.0	Chandler-NY	4.8

TEAM	G	W	L	PCT	GB	R	OR	AB	H	2B	3B	HR	BB	SO	AVG	OBP	SLG	PRO	PRO+	BR	/A	PF	CHI	RC	SB	CS	SBA	SBR
BRO	155	94	60	.610		774	668	5249	1428	241	50	83	732	561	.272	.364	.384	.748	102	62	32	104	98	781	88			
STL	156	89	65	.578	5	780	634	5422	1462	235	65	115	612	511	.270	.347	.401	.748	101	41	7	104	102	762	28			
BOS	154	86	68	.558	8	701	622	5253	1444	265	42	85	558	500	.275	.346	.390	.736	105	19	36	98	97	717	58			
NY	155	81	73	.526	13	830	761	5343	1446	220	48	221	494	568	.271	.335	.454	.789	114	95	90	101	104	809	29			
CIN	154	73	81	.474	21	681	755	5299	1372	242	43	95	539	530	.259	.330	.375	.705	95	-48	-43	99	103	672	46			
CHI	155	69	85	.448	25	567	722	5305	1373	231	48	71	471	578	.259	.321	.361	.682	91	-93	-69	96	94	620	22			
PIT	156	62	92	.403	32	744	817	5307	1385	216	44	156	607	687	.261	.340	.406	.746	102	31	10	103	100	738	30			
PHI	155	62	92	.403	32	589	687	5256	1354	210	52	60	464	594	.258	.321	.352	.673	88	-108	-87	96	101	597	60			
TOT	620					5666		42434	11264	1860	392	886	4477	4529	.265	.338	.390	.729							361			

TEAM	CG	SH	SV	IP	H	H/G	HR	BB	SO	RAT	ERA	ERA+	OAV	OOB	PR	/A	PF	CPI	FA	E	DP	FW	PW	BW	SBW	DIF
BRO	47	14	34	1375	1299	8.5	104	626	592	12.8	3.82	108	.251	.336	37	49	102	100	.978	129	169	.9	4.8	3.1		8.1
STL	65	12	20	1397²	1417	9.1	106	495	642	12.4	3.53	117	.266	.330	83	94	102	110	.979	128	169	1.1	9.2	.7		1.0
BOS	74	14	13	1362²	1342	8.9	93	453	494	11.9	3.62	108	.255	.316	67	41	96	95	.974	153	124	-.6	4.0	3.5		2.0
NY	58	6	14	1363²	1428	9.4	122	590	553	13.4	4.44	92	.267	.342	-58	-56	100	94	.974	155	136	-.7	-5.5	8.9		1.3
CIN	54	13	13	1365¹	1442	9.5	102	589	633	13.5	4.41	93	.274	.349	-53	-46	101	98	.977	138	134	-.3	-4.5	-4.2		4.4
CHI	46	8	15	1367	1449	9.5	106	618	571	13.7	4.04	98	.274	.353	4	-13	97	109	.975	150	159	-.4	-1.3	-6.8		.4
PIT	44	9	13	1374	1488	9.7	155	592	530	13.9	4.68	90	.278	.354	-95	-71	104	101	.975	149	131	-.2	-7.0	1.0		-8.8
PHI	70	8	14	1362	1399	9.2	98	513	514	12.8	3.96	101	.276	.346	15	7	99	108	.974	152	140	-.5	.7	-8.6		-6.7
TOT	458	84	136	10967¹		9.2				13.1	4.06		.265	.338					.976	1154	1162					

Runs
Mize-NY	137
Robinson-Bro	125
Kiner-Pit	118
Musial-StL	113
Kurowski-StL	108

Hits
Holmes-Bos	191
Walker-StL-Phi	186
Musial-StL	183
Gustine-Pit	183
Baumholtz-Cin	182

Doubles
Miller-Cin	38
B.Elliott-Bos	35
Ryan-Bos	33
Holmes-Bos	33
Baumholtz-Cin	32

Triples
Walker-StL-Phi	16
Slaughter-StL	13
Musial-StL	13
Schoendienst-StL	9
Baumholtz-Cin	9

Home Runs
Mize-NY	51
Kiner-Pit	51
Marshall-NY	36
W.Cooper-NY	35
Thomson-NY	29

Total Bases
Kiner-Pit	361
Mize-NY	360
Marshall-NY	310
W.Cooper-NY	302
Musial-StL	296

Runs Batted In
Mize-NY	138
Kiner-Pit	127
W.Cooper-NY	122
B.Elliott-Bos	113
Marshall-NY	107

Runs Produced
Mize-NY	224
Kiner-Pit	194
Musial-StL	189
Kurowski-StL	185
B.Elliott-Bos	184

Bases On Balls
Reese-Bro	104
Greenberg-Pit	104
Stanky-Bro	103
Kiner-Pit	98
Walker-Bro	97

Batting Average
Walker-StL-Phi	.363
B.Elliott-Bos	.317
Cavarretta-Chi	.314
Kiner-Pit	.313
Musial-StL	.312

On Base Percentage
Galan-Cin	.449
Walker-StL-Phi	.436
Kurowski-StL	.420
Kiner-Pit	.417
Walker-Bro	.415

Slugging Average
Kiner-Pit	.639
Mize-NY	.614
W.Cooper-NY	.586
Kurowski-StL	.544
Marshall-NY	.528

Production
Kiner-Pit	1.055
Mize-NY	.998
Kurowski-StL	.964
B.Elliott-Bos	.927
W.Cooper-NY	.926

Adjusted Production
Kiner-Pit	172
Mize-NY	160
Walker-StL-Phi	150
B.Elliott-Bos	148
Kurowski-StL	148

Batter Runs
Kiner-Pit	61.4
Mize-NY	48.3
Kurowski-StL	41.8
B.Elliott-Bos	36.8
Walker-StL-Phi	35.4

Adjusted Batter Runs
Kiner-Pit	57.5
Mize-NY	47.5
B.Elliott-Bos	39.5
Walker-StL-Phi	38.8
Kurowski-StL	36.8

Clutch Hitting Index
Marion-StL	128
Haas-Cin	125
Walker-Bro	125
Edwards-Bro	125
Jorgensen-Bro	122

Runs Created
Kiner-Pit	154
Mize-NY	143
B.Elliott-Bos	120
Kurowski-StL	118
Musial-StL	118

Total Average
Kiner-Pit	1.155
Mize-NY	1.060
Kurowski-StL	1.019
Walker-StL-Phi	.979
Torgeson-Bos	.973

Stolen Bases
Robinson-Bro	29
Reiser-Bro	14
Walker-StL-Phi	13
Hopp-Bos	13
Torgeson-Bos	11

Stolen Base Average

Stolen Base Runs

Fielding Runs
Marion-StL	20.1
Verban-Phi	16.9
Gustine-Pit	14.8
Kiner-Pit	13.2
Kerr-NY	12.1

Total Player Rating
Kiner-Pit	6.0
Mize-NY	4.9
Walker-StL-Phi	4.2
B.Elliott-Bos	3.7
Marshall-NY	2.9

Wins
Blackwell-Cin	22
Spahn-Bos	21
Sain-Bos	21
Jansen-NY	21
Branca-Bro	21

Win Percentage
Jansen-NY	.808
Munger-StL	.762
Blackwell-Cin	.733
Hatten-Bro	.680
Spahn-Bos	.677

Games
Trinkle-NY	62
Higbe-Bro-Pit	50
Behrman-Bro-Pt-Bro	50
Kush-Chi	47
Dickson-StL	47

Complete Games
Blackwell-Cin	23
Spahn-Bos	22
Sain-Bos	22
Jansen-NY	20
Leonard-Phi	19

Shutouts
Spahn-Bos	7
Munger-StL	6
Blackwell-Cin	6
Dickson-StL	4
Branca-Bro	4

Saves
Casey-Bro	18
Trinkle-NY	10
Gumbert-Cin	10
Behrman-Bro-Pt-Bro	8

Innings Pitched
Spahn-Bos	289.2
Branca-Bro	280.0
Blackwell-Cin	273.0
Sain-Bos	266.0
Jansen-NY	248.0

Fewest Hits/Game
Taylor-Bro	7.22
Blackwell-Cin	7.48
Spahn-Bos	7.61
Lombardi-Bro	8.04
Branca-Bro	8.07

Fewest BB/Game
Jansen-NY	2.07
Rowe-Phi	2.07
Leonard-Phi	2.18
Barrett-Bos	2.26
Brazle-StL	2.57

Strikeouts
Blackwell-Cin	193
Branca-Bro	148
Sain-Bos	132
Spahn-Bos	123
Munger-StL	123

Strikeouts/Game
Blackwell-Cin	6.36
Munger-StL	4.93
Branca-Bro	4.76
Brazle-StL	4.55
Sain-Bos	4.47

Ratio
Spahn-Bos	10.25
Blackwell-Cin	10.75
Leonard-Phi	10.84
Jansen-NY	10.85
Barrett-Bos	10.89

Earned Run Average
Spahn-Bos	2.33
Blackwell-Cin	2.47
Branca-Bro	2.67
Leonard-Phi	2.68
Brazle-StL	2.84

Adjusted ERA
Spahn-Bos	167
Blackwell-Cin	166
Branca-Bro	155
Leonard-Phi	149
Brazle-StL	146

Opponents' Batting Avg.
Taylor-Bro	.225
Spahn-Bos	.226
Blackwell-Cin	.234
Branca-Bro	.240
Lombardi-Bro	.241

Opponents' On Base Pct.
Spahn-Bos	.283
Barrett-Bos	.292
Blackwell-Cin	.304
Leonard-Phi	.306
Jansen-NY	.306

Starter Runs
Spahn-Bos	55.7
Blackwell-Cin	48.2
Branca-Bro	43.3
Leonard-Phi	36.0
Dickson-StL	25.5

Adjusted Starter Runs
Spahn-Bos	50.3
Blackwell-Cin	49.5
Branca-Bro	45.6
Leonard-Phi	34.6
Dickson-StL	27.4

Clutch Pitching Index
Brazle-StL	139
Leonard-Phi	123
Branca-Bro	122
Blackwell-Cin	115
Jansen-NY	114

Relief Runs
Lanfranconi-Bos	7.9
Kush-Chi	7.1
Trinkle-NY	3.3
Gumbert-Cin	1.8
Casey-Bro	.6

Adjusted Relief Runs
Lanfranconi-Bos	6.7
Kush-Chi	5.9
Trinkle-NY	3.4
Gumbert-Cin	2.2
Casey-Bro	1.2

Relief Ranking
Lanfranconi-Bos	7.8
Kush-Chi	7.2
Gumbert-Cin	4.9
Trinkle-NY	4.7
Casey-Bro	2.6

Total Pitcher Index
Blackwell-Cin	5.2
Spahn-Bos	5.1
Branca-Bro	4.4
Leonard-Phi	4.3
Brazle-StL	3.4

Total Baseball Ranking
Kiner-Pit	6.0
Blackwell-Cin	5.2
Spahn-Bos	5.1
Mize-NY	4.9
Branca-Bro	4.4

TEAM	G	W	L	PCT	GB	R	OR	AB	H	2B	3B	HR	BB	SO	AVG	OBP	SLG	PRO	PRO+	BR	/A	PF	CHI	RC	SB	CS	SBA	SBR
NY	155	97	57	.630		794	568	5308	1439	230	72	115	610	581	.271	.349	.407	.756	117	110	118	99	104	780	27	23	54	-6
DET	158	85	69	.552	12	714	642	5276	1363	234	42	103	762	565	.258	.353	.377	.730	106	77	55	103	96	735	52	60	46	-20
BOS	157	83	71	.539	14	720	669	5322	1412	206	54	103	666	590	.265	.349	.382	.731	102	71	17	107	98	734	41	35	54	-9
CLE	157	80	74	.519	17	687	588	5367	1392	234	51	112	502	609	.259	.324	.385	.709	106	9	27	97	105	687	29	25	54	-6
PHI	156	78	76	.506	19	633	614	5198	1311	218	52	61	605	563	.252	.333	.349	.682	94	-24	-36	102	102	635	37	33	53	-9
CHI	155	70	84	.455	27	553	661	5274	1350	211	41	53	492	527	.256	.321	.342	.663	93	-69	-48	96	98	584	91	57	61	-7
WAS	154	64	90	.416	33	496	675	5112	1234	186	48	42	525	534	.241	.313	.321	.634	84	-118	-105	97	99	523	53	51	51	-15
STL	154	59	95	.383	38	564	744	5145	1238	189	52	90	583	664	.241	.320	.350	.670	90	-55	-66	102	98	596	69	49	58	-9
TOT	623					5161		42002	10739	1708	412	679	4745	4633	.256	.333	.364	.698							399	333	55	-80

TEAM	CG	SH	SV	IP	H	H/G	HR	BB	SO	RAT	ERA	ERA+	OAV	OOB	PR	/A	PF	CPI	FA	E	DP	FW	PW	BW	SBW	DIF
NY	73	14	21	1374¹	1221	8.0	95	628	691	12.2	3.39	104	.238	.323	48	22	95	100	.981	109	151	1.5	2.3	12.2	.4	3.6
DET	77	15	18	1398²	1382	8.9	79	531	648	12.4	3.57	106	.258	.326	21	31	102	100	.975	155	142	-1.0	3.2	5.7	-1.0	1.1
BOS	64	13	19	1391¹	1383	8.9	84	575	586	12.8	3.81	102	.261	.335	-16	12	105	100	.977	137	172	-.0	1.2	1.8	.1	2.9
CLE	55	13	29	1402¹	1244	8.0	94	628	590	12.2	3.44	101	.240	.325	41	7	94	100	.983	104	178	1.9	.7	2.8	.4	-2.8
PHI	70	12	15	1391¹	1291	8.4	85	597	493	12.3	3.51	109	.247	.326	30	46	103	99	.976	143	161	-.4	4.8	-3.7	.1	-3
CHI	47	11	27	1391	1384	9.0	76	603	522	13.0	3.64	104	.261	.339	11	3	99	105	.975	155	180	-1.2	.3	-5.0	.3	-1.5
WAS	67	15	12	1362	1408	9.3	63	579	551	13.2	3.97	94	.267	.342	-40	-37	101	98	.976	143	151	-.5	-3.8	-10.9	-.5	2.7
STL	50	7	13	1365	1426	9.4	103	604	552	13.4	4.33	90	.272	.348	-94	-68	105	98	.977	134	169	.0	-7.0	-6.8	.1	-4.2
TOT	503	100	154	11076		8.7				12.7	3.71		.256	.333					.977	1080	1304					

Runs
Williams-Bos 125
Henrich-NY 109
Pesky-Bos 106
Stirnweiss-NY ... 102
DiMaggio-NY 97

Hits
Pesky-Bos 207
Kell-Det 188
Williams-Bos 181
McCosky-Phi 179

Doubles
Boudreau-Cle 45
Williams-Bos 40
Henrich-NY 35
DiMaggio-NY 31

Triples
Henrich-NY 13
Vernon-Was 12
Philley-Chi 11

Home Runs
Williams-Bos 32
Gordon-Cle 29
Heath-StL 27
Cullenbine-Det 24
York-Bos-Chi 21

Total Bases
Williams-Bos 335
Gordon-Cle 279
DiMaggio-NY 279
Henrich-NY 267
Pesky-Bos 250

Runs Batted In
Williams-Bos 114
Henrich-NY 98
DiMaggio-NY 97
Jones-Chi-Bos 96

Runs Produced
Williams-Bos 207
Henrich-NY 191
DiMaggio-NY 174
Kell-Det 163
Doerr-Bos 157

Bases On Balls
Williams-Bos 162
Cullenbine-Det 137
Lake-Det.......... 120
Joost-Phi 114
Fain-Phi 95

Batting Average
Williams-Bos 343
McCosky-Phi 328
Pesky-Bos 324
Wright-Chi 324
Kell-Det .... .320

On Base Percentage
Williams-Bos 499
Fain-Phi 414
Cullenbine-Det 401
McCosky-Phi ..... .395
McQuinn-NY ..... .395

Slugging Average
Williams-Bos 634
DiMaggio-NY 522
Gordon-Cle 496
Henrich-NY.......485
Heath-StL.........485

Production
Williams-Bos 1.133
DiMaggio-NY 913
Henrich-NY.......857
Heath-StL.........850
Gordon-Cle........842

Adjusted Production
Williams-Bos 199
DiMaggio-NY 154
Henrich-NY 139
Gordon-Cle 136
Heath-StL 133

Batter Runs
Williams-Bos 91.1
DiMaggio-NY 36.5
Henrich-NY 26.4
Fain-Phi 24.7
Cullenbine-Det ... 23.8

Adjusted Batter Runs
Williams-Bos.......79.3
DiMaggio-NY 37.5
Henrich-NY......27.4
McQuinn-NY......24.2
Gordon-Cle......23.8

Clutch Hitting Index
B.Johnson-NY.....140
Kell-Det 121
Jones-Chi-Bos ... 119
Joost-Phi 118
Majeski-Phi 115

Runs Created
DiMaggio-NY 186
DiMaggio-NY 112
Henrich-NY....... 104
Pesky-Bos 103
McQuinn-NY 97

Total Average
Williams-Bos 1.391
DiMaggio-NY 918
Cullenbine-Det 898
Heath-StL 856
Henrich-NY.......849

Stolen Bases
Dillinger-StL 34
Philley-Chi 21
Vernon-Was...... 12
Pesky-Bos 12

Stolen Base Average
Dillinger-StL 72.3
Philley-Chi 56.8

Stolen Base Runs
Dillinger-StL 2.4
Valo-Phi 1.5
Binks-Phi 1.2

Fielding Runs
Doerr-Bos 23.8
DiMaggio-Bos 19.0
Baker-Chi 18.3
Kell-Det 17.9
Boudreau-Cle 16.7

Total Player Rating
Williams-Bos 7.2
Boudreau-Cle 4.8
Doerr-Bos......... 3.3
Cullenbine-Det ... 3.3
Gordon-Cle 3.1

Wins
Feller-Cle 20
Reynolds-NY 19
Marchildon-Phi.... 19
Hutchinson-Det ... 18
Dobson-Bos 18

Win Percentage
Reynolds-NY ..... .704
Dobson-Bos ..... .692
Marchildon-Phi ... .679
Feller-Cle .... .645
Hutchinson-Det ... .643

Games
Klieman-Cle 58
Page-NY 56
Johnson-Bos 45
Savage-Phi 44
Christopher-Phi 44

Complete Games
Newhouser-Det 24
Wynn-Was 22
Lopat-Chi 22
Marchildon-Phi.... 21
Feller-Cle......... 20

Shutouts
Feller-Cle 5
Reynolds-NY 4
Masterson-Was 4
Haefner-Was 4

Saves
Page-NY 17
Klieman-Cle 17
Christopher-Phi 12
Ferrick-Was 9

Innings Pitched
Feller-Cle 299.0
Newhouser-Det ..285.0
Marchildon-Phi...276.2
Masterson-Was ..253.0
Lopat-Chi 252.2

Fewest Hits/Game
Shea-NY 6.40
Feller-Cle 6.92
Marchildon-Phi ... 7.42
Embree-Cle 7.58
Masterson-Was ... 7.65

Fewest BB/Game
Galehouse-StL-Bos .. 2.48
Hutchinson-Det ... 2.50
Lopat-Chi 2.60
Muncrief-StL 2.60
Dobson-Bos...... 2.87

Strikeouts
Feller-Cle 196
Newhouser-Det ... 176
Masterson-Was ... 135
Reynolds-NY 129
Marchildon-Phi.... 128

Strikeouts/Game
Feller-Cle 5.90
Hughson-Bos 5.66
Newhouser-Det ... 5.56
Trucks-Det 5.38
Kinder-StL 5.09

Ratio
Feller-Cle 10.87
Dobson-Bos 10.90
Shea-NY 11.08
Masterson-Was ..11.17
Hutchinson-Det ..11.23

Earned Run Average
Haynes-Chi.......2.42
Feller-Cle........2.68
Fowler-Phi 2.81
Lopat-Chi 2.81
Newhouser-Det....2.87

Adjusted ERA
Haynes-Chi.......151
Fowler-Phi 136
Dobson-Bos 132
Newhouser-Det....131
Feller-Cle.........130

Opponents' Batting Avg.
Shea-NY..........200
Feller-Cle.........215
Marchildon-Phi ...224
Reynolds-NY 227
Embree-Cle 233

Opponents' On Base Pct.
Dobson-Bos......299
Feller-Cle.........300
Shea-NY..........303
Hutchinson-Det ...304
Lopat-Chi 307

Starter Runs
Feller-Cle 34.1
Newhouser-Det ... 26.3
Haynes-Chi 25.9
Lopat-Chi 25.0
Fowler-Phi 22.6

Adjusted Starter Runs
Newhouser-Det ... 28.3
Feller-Cle 26.7
Fowler-Phi 25.3
Haynes-Chi 24.9
Dobson-Bos 23.8

Clutch Pitching Index
Haynes-Chi....... 124
Fowler-Phi 119
Lopat-Chi 116
Ferriss-Bos 114
Newsom-Was-NY . 112

Relief Runs
Page-NY 19.2
Christopher-Phi ... 7.2
Klieman-Cle 6.9
Murphy-Bos 5.5
Ferrick-Was 3.7

Adjusted Relief Runs
Page-NY 16.5
Christopher-Phi ... 8.2
Murphy-Bos 6.6
Klieman-Cle 4.6
Ferrick-Was...... 3.8

Relief Ranking
Page-NY 27.6
Christopher-Phi ..18.2
Klieman-Cle 6.0
Ferrick-Was 5.9
Maltzberger-Chi ... 1.6

Total Pitcher Index
Newhouser-Det ... 3.9
Hutchinson-Det ... 3.7
Feller-Cle 3.1
Page-NY 3.0
Haynes-Chi 2.9

Total Baseball Ranking
Williams-Bos 7.2
Boudreau-Cle 4.8
Newhouser-Det ... 3.9
Hutchinson-Det ... 3.7
Doerr-Bos 3.3

TEAM	G	W	L	PCT	GB	R	OR	AB	H	2B	3B	HR	BB	SO	AVG	OBP	SLG	PRO	PRO+	BR	/A	PF	CHI	RC	SB	CS	SBA	SBR
BOS	154	91	62	.595		739	**584**	5297	**1458**	**272**	49	95	**671**	536	**.275**	**.359**	.399	**.758**	114	**95**	**109**	98	92	**784**	43			
STL	155	85	69	.552	6.5	742	646	5302	1396	238	**58**	105	594	**521**	.263	.340	.389	.729	98	31	-10	106	103	713	24			
BRO	155	84	70	.545	7.5	744	667	5328	1393	256	54	91	601	684	.261	.338	.381	.719	98	13	-11	103	105	709	**114**			
PIT	156	83	71	.539	8.5	706	699	5286	1388	191	54	108	580	578	.263	.338	.380	.718	99	10	-4	102	101	698	68			
NY	155	78	76	.506	13.5	**780**	704	5277	1352	210	49	**164**	599	648	.256	.334	**.408**	.742	106	46	42	101	**106**	731	51			
PHI	155	66	88	.429	25.5	591	729	5287	1367	227	39	91	440	598	.259	.318	.368	.686	94	-63	-52	98	97	625	68			
CIN	153	64	89	.418	27	588	752	5127	1266	221	37	104	478	586	.247	.313	.365	.678	92	-76	-56	97	101	587	42			
CHI	155	64	90	.416	27.5	597	706	5352	1402	225	44	87	443	578	.262	.322	.369	.691	97	-52	-27	96	95	641	39			
TOT	619					5487		42256	11022	1840	384	845	4406	4729	.261	.333	.383	.715							449			

TEAM	CG	SH	SV	IP	H	H/G	HR	BB	SO	RAT	ERA	ERA+	OAV	OOB	PR	/A	PF	CPI	FA	E	DP	FW	PW	BW	SBW	DIF
BOS	**70**	10	17	1389[1]	1354	8.8	93	430	579	11.6	**3.37**	114	.249	.306	89	71	97	96	.976	143	132	.7	7.1	10.9		-4.2
STL	60	13	18	1368	1392	9.2	103	476	625	12.4	3.91	105	.262	.324	7	28	103	97	**.980**	119	138	**2.1**	2.8	-1.0		4.1
BRO	52	9	**22**	1392[2]	**1328**	8.6	119	633	670	12.9	3.75	106	.253	.337	31	37	101	107	.973	161	151	-.2	3.7	-1.1		4.6
PIT	65	5	19	1371[2]	1373	9.0	120	564	543	12.9	4.15	98	.261	.335	-29	-12	103	98	.977	137	150	1.2	-1.2	-.4		6.4
NY	54	**15**	21	1373	1425	9.3	122	556	527	13.2	3.93	100	.269	.342	4	0	100	**109**	.974	156	134	.1	.0	4.2		-3.3
PHI	61	6	15	1362[1]	1385	9.1	95	556	550	13.0	4.08	97	.262	.335	-18	-20	100	97	.964	210	126	-2.8	-2.0	-5.2		-1.0
CIN	40	8	20	1343[1]	1410	9.4	104	572	599	13.4	4.47	87	.270	.344	-77	-85	99	95	.973	158	135	-.1	-8.5	-5.6		1.7
CHI	51	7	10	1355[1]	1355	9.0	**89**	619	636	13.2	4.00	97	.261	.342	-7	-15	99	101	.972	172	**152**	-.7	-1.5	-2.7		-8.1
TOT	453	73	142	10955[2]		9.1				12.8	3.95		.261	.333					.974	1256	1118					

Runs
Musial-StL 135
Lockman-NY 117
Mize-NY 110
Robinson-Bro 108
Kiner-Pit 104

Hits
Musial-StL 230
Holmes-Bos ... 190
Rojek-Pit 186
Slaughter-StL ... 176
Dark-Bos 175

Doubles
Musial-StL 46
Ennis-Phi 40
Dark-Bos 39
Robinson-Bro 38
Holmes-Bos 35

Triples
Musial-StL 18
Hopp-Pit 12
Slaughter-StL 11
Waitkus-Chi 10
Lockman-NY 10

Home Runs
Mize-NY 40
Kiner-Pit 40
Musial-StL 39
Sauer-Cin 35

Total Bases
Musial-StL 429
Mize-NY 316
Ennis-Phi 309
Kiner-Pit 296
Pafko-Chi 283

Runs Batted In
Musial-StL 131
Mize-NY 125
Kiner-Pit 123
Gordon-NY 107
Pafko-Chi 101

Runs Produced
Musial-StL 227
Mize-NY 195
Kiner-Pit 187
Robinson-Bro 181
Gordon-NY 177

Bases On Balls
B.Elliott-Bos 131
Kiner-Pit 112
Mize-NY 94

Batting Average
Musial-StL 376
Ashburn-Phi 333
Holmes-Bos 325
Dark-Bos 322
Slaughter-StL 321

On Base Percentage
Musial-StL 450
B.Elliott-Bos 423
Ashburn-Phi 410
Slaughter-StL 409
Mize-NY 395

Slugging Average
Musial-StL 702
Mize-NY 564
Gordon-NY 537
Kiner-Pit 533
Ennis-Phi 525

Production
Musial-StL 1.152
Mize-NY 959
Gordon-NY 927
Kiner-Pit 924
B.Elliott-Bos 897

Adjusted Production
Musial-StL 196
Mize-NY 156
Gordon-NY 148
Kiner-Pit 145
B.Elliott-Bos 145

Batter Runs
Musial-StL 90.2
Mize-NY 44.6
Kiner-Pit 38.5
B.Elliott-Bos 37.8
Gordon-NY 35.1

Adjusted Batter Runs
Musial-StL 80.8
Mize-NY 43.9
B.Elliott-Bos 39.8
Kiner-Pit 36.2
Gordon-NY 34.4

Clutch Hitting Index
Murtaugh-Pit 135
Jones-StL 129
Stallcup-Cin 128
Lowrey-Chi 123
Torgeson-Bos 118

Runs Created
Musial-StL 191
Mize-NY 131
Kiner-Pit 120
B.Elliott-Bos 117
Slaughter-StL 110

Total Average
Musial-StL 1.298
Mize-NY 1.032
B.Elliott-Bos 980
Kiner-Pit 974
Gordon-NY 953

Stolen Bases
Ashburn-Phi 32
Reese-Bro 25
Rojek-Pit 24
Robinson-Bro 22
Torgeson-Bos 19

Stolen Base Average

Stolen Base Runs

Fielding Runs
Ashburn-Phi 17.8
Pafko-Chi 12.8
Reese-Bro 10.3
Marion-StL 9.4
Gustine-Pit 9.0

Total Player Rating
Musial-StL 6.3
Mize-NY 4.6
Pafko-Chi 4.3
Kiner-Pit 3.4
B.Elliott-Bos 2.8

Wins
Sain-Bos 24
Brecheen-StL 20
Schmitz-Chi 18
Jansen-NY 18
VanderMeer-Cin ... 17

Win Percentage
Brecheen-StL ..... .741
Jones-NY .... .667
Sain-Bos .... .615
Jansen-NY .... .600
Schmitz-Chi ...... .581

Games
Gumbert-Cin 61
Wilks-StL 57
Higbe-Pit 56
Jones-NY 55
Dobernic-Chi 54

Complete Games
Sain-Bos 28
Brecheen-StL 21
Schmitz-Chi 18
Spahn-Bos 16
Leonard-Phi 16

Shutouts
Brecheen-StL 7
Sain-Bos 4
Raffensberger-Cin ... 4
Jansen-NY 4
Barney-Bro 4

Saves
Gumbert-Cin 17
Wilks-StL 13
Higbe-Pit 10
Trinkle-NY 7
Behrman-Bro 7

Innings Pitched
Sain-Bos 314.2
Jansen-NY 277.0
Spahn-Bos 257.0
Dickson-StL 252.1
Barney-Bro 246.2

Fewest Hits/Game
Schmitz-Chi 6.92
Barney-Bro 7.04
Brecheen-StL 7.44
Branca-Bro 7.89
Roe-Bro 7.90

Fewest BB/Game
Roe-Bro 1.67
Jansen-NY 1.75
Raffensberger-Cin . 1.85
Brecheen-StL 1.89
Leonard-Phi 2.15

Strikeouts
Brecheen-StL 149
Barney-Bro 138
Sain-Bos 137
Jansen-NY 126
Branca-Bro 122

Strikeouts/Game
Brecheen-StL 5.75
Branca-Bro 5.09
Barney-Bro 5.04
Higbe-Pit 4.90
Meyer-Chi 4.86

Ratio
Brecheen-StL 9.41
Roe-Bro 9.68
Schmitz-Chi 10.60
Sain-Bos 11.01
Spahn-Bos 11.03

Earned Run Average
Brecheen-StL 2.24
Leonard-Phi 2.51
Sain-Bos 2.60
Roe-Bro 2.63
Schmitz-Chi 2.64

Adjusted ERA
Brecheen-StL 183
Leonard-Phi 157
Roe-Bro 152
Schmitz-Chi 148
Sain-Bos 147

Opponents' Batting Avg.
Schmitz-Chi 215
Barney-Bro 217
Brecheen-StL 222
Branca-Bro 232
Roe-Bro 233

Opponents' On Base Pct.
Brecheen-StL 265
Roe-Bro 271
Schmitz-Chi 295
Sain-Bos 296
Raffensberger-Cin .296

Starter Runs
Sain-Bos 47.3
Brecheen-StL 44.5
Leonard-Phi 36.2
Schmitz-Chi 35.3
Roe-Bro 26.1

Adjusted Starter Runs
Brecheen-StL 48.0
Sain-Bos 43.0
Leonard-Phi 35.9
Schmitz-Chi 34.0
Roe-Bro 26.8

Clutch Pitching Index
Leonard-Phi 134
Jones-NY 126
Hatten-Bro 124
Voiselle-Bos 120
Sain-Bos 115

Relief Runs
Wilks-StL 19.4
Hansen-NY 10.9
Minner-Bro 10.5
Higbe-Pit 10.4
Dobernic-Chi 7.6

Adjusted Relief Runs
Wilks-StL 21.4
Higbe-Pit 12.4
Minner-Bro 10.8
Hansen-NY 10.7
Dobernic-Chi 7.2

Relief Ranking
Wilks-StL 22.4
Higbe-Pit 12.4
Minner-Bro 11.3
Gumbert-Cin 9.7
Trinkle-NY 8.1

Total Pitcher Index
Brecheen-StL 5.5
Sain-Bos 5.3
Schmitz-Chi 4.6
Leonard-Phi 4.6
Roe-Bro 2.6

Total Baseball Ranking
Musial-StL 6.3
Brecheen-StL 5.5
Sain-Bos 5.3
Schmitz-Chi 4.6
Leonard-Phi 4.6

TEAM	G	W	L	PCT	GB	R	OR	AB	H	2B	3B	HR	BB	SO	AVG	OBP	SLG	PRO	PRO+	BR	/A	PF	CHI	RC	SB	CS	SBA	SBR
CLE	156	97	58	.626		840	568	5446	1534	242	54	155	646	575	.282	.360	.431	.791	119	112	134	97	97	868	54	44	55	-10
BOS	155	96	59	.619	1	907	720	5363	1471	277	40	121	823	552	.274	.374	.409	.783	109	116	72	105	104	869	38	17	69	1
NY	154	94	60	.610	2.5	857	633	5324	1480	251	75	139	623	478	.278	.356	.432	.788	116	99	107	99	103	838	24	24	50	-7
PHI	154	84	70	.545	12.5	729	735	5181	1345	231	47	68	726	523	.260	.353	.362	.715	96	-20	-21	100	102	699	40	32	56	-7
DET	154	78	76	.506	18.5	700	726	5235	1396	219	58	78	671	504	.267	.353	.375	.728	96	0	-20	103	95	723	22	32	41	-13
STL	155	59	94	.386	37	671	849	5303	1438	251	62	63	578	572	.271	.345	.378	.723	96	-21	-39	103	95	711	63	44	59	-8
WAS	154	56	97	.366	40	578	796	5111	1245	203	75	31	568	572	.244	.322	.331	.653	81	-151	-135	97	105	566	76	48	61	-6
CHI	154	51	101	.336	44.5	559	814	5192	1303	172	39	55	595	528	.251	.329	.331	.660	84	-134	-115	97	97	588	46	47	49	-14
TOT	618					5841		42155	11212	1846	450	710	5230	4304	.266	.349	.382	.731							363	288	56	-64

TEAM	CG	SH	SV	IP	H	H/G	HR	BB	SO	RAT	ERA	ERA+	OAV	OOB	PR	/A	PF	CPI	FA	E	DP	FW	PW	BW	SBW	DIF
CLE	66	26	30	1409¹	1246	8.0	82	628	595	12.1	3.22	126	.239	.323	167	130	95	108	.982	114	183	1.4	12.6	13.0	-.2	-7.3
BOS	70	11	13	1379¹	1445	9.4	83	592	513	13.4	4.26	103	.270	.345	4	21	102	99	.981	116	174	1.2	2.0	7.0	.9	7.4
NY	62	16	24	1365²	1289	8.5	94	641	654	12.9	3.75	109	.250	.336	82	51	95	104	.979	120	161	.9	4.9	10.4	.0	.6
PHI	74	7	18	1368²	1456	9.6	86	638	486	13.9	4.43	97	.275	.355	-21	-20	100	101	.981	113	180	1.3	-1.9	-2.0	.0	9.6
DET	60	5	22	1377	1367	8.9	92	589	678	12.9	4.15	105	.259	.335	21	33	102	95	.974	155	143	.9	3.2	-1.9	-.5	1.2
STL	35	4	20	1373¹	1513	9.9	103	737	531	14.9	5.01	91	.281	.371	-109	-69	106	99	.972	168	190	-1.6	-6.7	-3.8	.0	-5.4
WAS	42	4	22	1357¹	1439	9.5	81	734	446	14.6	4.65	93	.273	.364	-55	-47	101	99	.974	154	144	-.9	-4.6	-13.1	.2	-2.2
CHI	35	2	23	1345²	1454	9.7	89	673	403	14.4	4.89	87	.280	.365	-90	-94	99	97	.974	160	176	-1.2	-9.1	-11.1	-.6	-3.0
TOT	444	75	172	10976¹		9.2				13.6	4.29		.266	.349					.977	1100	1351					

Runs
Henrich-NY	138
DiMaggio-Bos	127
Williams-Bos	124
Pesky-Bos	124
Boudreau-Cle	116

Hits
Dillinger-StL	207
Mitchell-Cle	204
DiMaggio-Bos	199
DiMaggio-NY	190
Williams-Bos	188

Doubles
Williams-Bos	44
Henrich-NY	42
Majeski-Phi	41
Priddy-StL	40
DiMaggio-Bos	40

Triples
Henrich-NY	14
Stewart-NY-Was	13
Yost-Was	11
Mullin-Det	11
DiMaggio-NY	11

Home Runs
DiMaggio-NY	39
Gordon-Cle	32
Keltner-Cle	31
Stephens-Bos	29
Doerr-Bos	27

Total Bases
DiMaggio-NY	355
Henrich-NY	326
Williams-Bos	313
Stephens-Bos	299
Boudreau-Cle	299

Runs Batted In
DiMaggio-NY	155
Stephens-Bos	137
Williams-Bos	127
Gordon-Cle	124
Majeski-Phi	120

Runs Produced
Williams-Bos	226
DiMaggio-NY	226
Stephens-Bos	222
Henrich-NY	213
DiMaggio-Bos	205

Bases On Balls
Williams-Bos	126
Joost-Phi	119
Fain-Phi	113
DiMaggio-Bos	101
Pesky-Bos	99

Batting Average
Williams-Bos	.369
Boudreau-Cle	.355
Mitchell-Cle	.336
Zarilla-StL	.329
McCosky-Phi	.326

On Base Percentage
Williams-Bos	.497
Boudreau-Cle	.453
Appling-Chi	.423
Goodman-Bos	.414
Fain-Phi	.412

Slugging Average
Williams-Bos	.615
DiMaggio-NY	.598
Henrich-NY	.554
Boudreau-Cle	.534
Keltner-Cle	.522

Production
Williams-Bos	1.112
DiMaggio-NY	.994
Boudreau-Cle	.987
Henrich-NY	.945
Keltner-Cle	.917

Adjusted Production
Williams-Bos	185
Boudreau-Cle	166
DiMaggio-NY	164
Henrich-NY	151
Keltner-Cle	146

Batter Runs
Williams-Bos	75.7
Boudreau-Cle	52.7
DiMaggio-NY	48.6
Henrich-NY	38.9
Keltner-Cle	33.0

Adjusted Batter Runs
Williams-Bos	68.2
Boudreau-Cle	56.2
DiMaggio-NY	49.9
Henrich-NY	40.1
Keltner-Cle	36.0

Clutch Hitting Index
Platt-StL	126
Majeski-Phi	121
Goodman-Bos	120
Stephens-Bos	120
Tebbetts-Bos	119

Runs Created
Williams-Bos	172
Boudreau-Cle	143
DiMaggio-NY	140
Henrich-NY	130
Keltner-Cle	116

Total Average
Williams-Bos	1.347
Boudreau-Cle	1.058
DiMaggio-NY	1.012
Henrich-NY	.955
Keltner-Cle	.918

Stolen Bases
Dillinger-StL	28
Coan-Was	23
Vernon-Was	15
Mitchell-Cle	13

Stolen Base Average
Coan-Was	71.9
Dillinger-StL	71.8

Stolen Base Runs
Robertson-Was	2.4
Tucker-Cle	2.1
DiMaggio-Bos	1.8
Dillinger-StL	1.8

Fielding Runs
Pellagrini-StL	24.0
Priddy-StL	23.5
Hegan-Cle	21.3
DiMaggio-Bos	15.8
Philley-Chi	15.1

Total Player Rating
Boudreau-Cle	6.9
Williams-Bos	5.8
Priddy-StL	4.4
DiMaggio-NY	4.3
Doerr-Bos	3.6

Wins
Newhouser-Det	21
Lemon-Cle	20
Bearden-Cle	20
Raschi-NY	19
Feller-Cle	19

Win Percentage
Kramer-Bos	.783
Bearden-Cle	.741
Raschi-NY	.704
Reynolds-NY	.696

Games
Page-NY	55
Widmar-StL	49
Biscan-StL	47
Thompson-Was	46

Complete Games
Lemon-Cle	20
Newhouser-Det	19
Raschi-NY	18
Feller-Cle	18

Shutouts
Lemon-Cle	10
Raschi-NY	6
Bearden-Cle	6
Dobson-Bos	5

Saves
Christopher-Cle	17
Page-NY	16
Houtteman-Det	10
Ferrick-Was	10
Judson-Chi	8

Innings Pitched
Lemon-Cle	293.2
Feller-Cle	280.1
Newhouser-Det	272.1
Dobson-Bos	245.1
Reynolds-NY	236.1

Fewest Hits/Game
Shea-NY	6.76
Lemon-Cle	7.08
Bearden-Cle	7.33
Scarborough-Was	8.06
Trucks-Det	8.08

Fewest BB/Game
Hutchinson-Det	1.95
Zoldak-StL-Cle	2.42
Lopat-NY	2.62
Kramer-Bos	2.81
Houtteman-Det	2.85

Strikeouts
Feller-Cle	164
Lemon-Cle	147
Newhouser-Det	143
Brissie-Phi	127
Raschi-NY	124

Strikeouts/Game
Brissie-Phi	5.89
Feller-Cle	5.27
Trucks-Det	5.23
Raschi-NY	5.01
Newhouser-Det	4.73

Ratio
Hutchinson-Det	11.08
Lemon-Cle	11.12
Raschi-NY	11.52
Newhouser-Det	11.53
Bearden-Cle	11.60

Earned Run Average
Bearden-Cle	2.43
Scarborough-Was	2.82
Lemon-Cle	2.82
Newhouser-Det	3.01
Parnell-Bos	3.14

Adjusted ERA
Bearden-Cle	167
Scarborough-Was	154
Newhouser-Det	145
Lemon-Cle	144
Parnell-Bos	140

Opponents' Batting Avg.
Shea-NY	.208
Lemon-Cle	.216
Bearden-Cle	.229
Scarborough-Was	.233
Trucks-Det	.240

Opponents' On Base Pct.
Hutchinson-Det	.297
Lemon-Cle	.302
Scarborough-Was	.307
Newhouser-Det	.309
Raschi-NY	.310

Starter Runs
Lemon-Cle	48.0
Bearden-Cle	47.5
Newhouser-Det	38.8
Scarborough-Was	30.3
Parnell-Bos	27.1

Adjusted Starter Runs
Bearden-Cle	41.6
Newhouser-Det	41.1
Lemon-Cle	40.4
Scarborough-Was	31.5
Parnell-Bos	29.5

Clutch Pitching Index
Bearden-Cle	132
Garver-StL	129
Fowler-Phi	119
Lopat-NY	118
Reynolds-NY	117

Relief Runs
Klieman-Cle	15.0
Christopher-Cle	9.1
Thompson-Was	6.6
Hiller-NY	1.7
Harris-Phi	1.6

Adjusted Relief Runs
Klieman-Cle	12.9
Christopher-Cle	7.6
Thompson-Was	7.4
Harris-Phi	1.6
Ferrick-Was	1.6

Relief Ranking
Christopher-Cle	10.7
Klieman-Cle	8.8
Thompson-Was	8.6
Ferrick-Was	1.8
Harris-Phi	1.3

Total Pitcher Index
Lemon-Cle	6.8
Bearden-Cle	5.5
Newhouser-Det	4.9
Scarborough-Was	3.8
Garver-StL	2.7

Total Baseball Ranking
Boudreau-Cle	6.9
Lemon-Cle	6.8
Williams-Bos	5.8
Bearden-Cle	5.5
Newhouser-Det	4.9

TEAM	G	W	L	PCT	GB	R	OR	AB	H	2B	3B	HR	BB	SO	AVG	OBP	SLG	PRO	PRO+	BR	/A	PF	CHI	RC	SB	CS	SBA	SBR
BRO	156	97	57	.630		879	651	5400	1477	236	47	152	638	570	.274	.354	.419	.773	110	103	69	104	106	815	117			
STL	157	96	58	.623	1	766	616	5463	1513	281	54	102	569	482	.277	.348	.404	.752	103	61	25	105	98	777	17			
PHI	154	81	73	.526	16	662	668	5307	1349	232	55	122	528	670	.254	.325	.388	.713	100	-27	-9	97	99	674	27			
BOS	157	75	79	.487	22	706	719	5336	1376	246	33	103	684	656	.258	.345	.374	.719	105	6	45	95	97	710	28			
NY	156	73	81	.474	24	736	693	5308	1383	203	52	147	613	523	.261	.340	.401	.741	105	36	37	100	99	735	43			
PIT	154	71	83	.461	26	681	760	5214	1350	191	41	126	548	554	.259	.332	.384	.716	96	-14	-32	101	101	682	48			
CIN	156	62	92	.403	35	627	770	5469	1423	264	35	86	429	559	.260	.316	.368	.684	88	-84	-91	101	101	636	31			
CHI	154	61	93	.396	36	593	773	5214	1336	212	53	97	396	573	.256	.312	.373	.685	91	-83	-67	97	100	601	53			
TOT	622					5650		42711	11207	1865	370	935	4405	4587	.262	.334	.389	.723						364				

TEAM	CG	SH	SV	IP	H	H/G	HR	BB	SO	RAT	ERA	ERA+	OAV	OOB	PR	/A	PF	CPI	FA	E	DP	FW	PW	BW	SBW	DIF
BRO	62	15	17	1408²	1306	8.3	132	582	743	12.2	3.80	108	.246	.324	37	46	102	99	.980	122	162	1.5	4.6	6.8		7.1
STL	64	13	19	1407²	1356	8.7	87	507	606	12.1	3.44	121	.252	.319	94	113	103	101	.976	146	149	.3	11.2	2.5		5.1
PHI	58	12	15	1391²	1389	9.0	104	502	495	12.4	3.89	101	.268	.335	23	8	98	105	.974	156	141	-.5	.8	-.9		4.6
BOS	68	12	11	1400	1466	9.4	110	520	589	12.9	3.99	95	.268	.334	8	-32	94	102	.976	148	144	.1	-3.2	4.5		-3.4
NY	68	10	9	1374¹	1328	8.7	132	544	516	12.4	3.82	104	.249	.321	33	24	99	97	.973	161	134	-.6	2.4	3.7		-9.4
PIT	53	9	15	1356	1452	9.6	142	535	556	13.4	4.57	92	.274	.344	-79	-55	104	99	.978	132	173	.9	-5.5	-3.2		1.7
CIN	55	10	6	1401²	1423	9.1	124	640	538	13.4	4.34	96	.264	.345	-47	-24	104	99	.977	138	150	.6	-2.4	-9.0		-4.2
CHI	44	8	17	1357²	1487	9.9	104	575	544	13.8	4.50	90	.279	.351	-70	-71	100	100	.970	186	160	-2.1	-7.0	-6.6		-.2
TOT	472	89	109	11097²		9.1				12.8	4.04		.262	.334					.975	1189	1213					

Runs
Reese-Bro	132
Musial-StL	128
Robinson-Bro	122
Kiner-Pit	116
Schoendienst-StL	102

Hits
Musial-StL	207
Robinson-Bro	203
Thomson-NY	198
Slaughter-StL	191
Schoendienst-StL	190

Doubles
Musial-StL	41
Ennis-Phi	39
Robinson-Bro	38
Hatton-Cin	38

Triples
Slaughter-StL	13
Musial-StL	13
Robinson-Bro	12
Ennis-Phi	11
Ashburn-Phi	11

Home Runs
Kiner-Pit	54
Musial-StL	36
Sauer-Cin-Chi	31
Thomson-NY	27
Gordon-NY	26

Total Bases
Musial-StL	382
Kiner-Pit	361
Thomson-NY	332
Ennis-Phi	320
Robinson-Bro	313

Runs Batted In
Kiner-Pit	127
Robinson-Bro	124
Musial-StL	123
Hodges-Bro	115
Ennis-Phi	110

Runs Produced
Robinson-Bro	230
Musial-StL	215
Reese-Bro	189
Kiner-Pit	189
Hodges-Bro	186

Bases On Balls
Kiner-Pit	117
Reese-Bro	116
Stanky-Bos	113
Musial-StL	107
Gordon-NY	95

Batting Average
Robinson-Bro	.342
Musial-StL	.338
Slaughter-StL	.336
Furillo-Bro	.322
Kiner-Pit	.310

On Base Percentage
Musial-StL	.438
Robinson-Bro	.432
Kiner-Pit	.432
Slaughter-StL	.418
Stanky-Bos	.417

Slugging Average
Kiner-Pit	.658
Musial-StL	.624
Robinson-Bro	.528
Ennis-Phi	.525
Thomson-NY	.518

Production
Kiner-Pit	1.089
Musial-StL	1.062
Robinson-Bro	.960
Slaughter-StL	.929
Gordon-NY	.909

Adjusted Production
Kiner-Pit	183
Musial-StL	174
Robinson-Bro	150
Gordon-NY	142
Slaughter-StL	141

Batter Runs
Musial-StL	72.4
Kiner-Pit	70.0
Robinson-Bro	49.9
Slaughter-StL	40.1
Gordon-NY	31.6

Adjusted Batter Runs
Kiner-Pit	66.2
Musial-StL	65.3
Robinson-Bro	44.5
Slaughter-StL	34.8
Ennis-Phi	32.3

Clutch Hitting Index
Robinson-Bro	130
Marion-StL	117
Russell-Bos	116
Hodges-Bro	116
Cooper-NY-Cin	114

Runs Created
Musial-StL	173
Kiner-Pit	163
Robinson-Bro	135
Slaughter-StL	127
Ennis-Phi	118

Total Average
Kiner-Pit	1.247
Musial-StL	1.185
Robinson-Bro	1.078
Slaughter-StL	.971
Gordon-NY	.925

Stolen Bases
Robinson-Bro	37
Reese-Bro	26

Stolen Base Average

Stolen Base Runs

Fielding Runs
Ashburn-Phi	24.7
Schoendienst-StL	24.0
Thomson-NY	19.5
Marion-StL	16.6
Reich-Chi	14.1

Total Player Rating
Kiner-Pit	5.6
Robinson-Bro	4.9
Musial-StL	3.8
Thomson-NY	3.6
B.Elliott-Bos	3.5

Wins
Spahn-Bos	21
Pollet-StL	20
Raffensberger-Cin	18

Win Percentage
Roe-Bro	.714
Pollet-StL	.690
Newcombe-Bro	.680
Meyer-Phi	.680
Munger-StL	.652

Games
Wilks-StL	59
Konstanty-Phi	53
Palica-Bro	49
Banta-Bro	48
Muncrief-Pit-Chi	47

Complete Games
Spahn-Bos	25
Raffensberger-Cin	20
Newcombe-Bro	19
Pollet-StL	17
Jansen-NY	17

Shutouts
Raffensberger-Cin	5
Pollet-StL	5
Newcombe-Bro	5
Heintzelman-Phi	5

Saves
Wilks-StL	9
Potter-Bos	7
Konstanty-Phi	7
Staley-StL	6
Palica-Bro	6

Innings Pitched
Spahn-Bos	302.1
Raffensberger-Cin	284.0
Jansen-NY	259.2
Heintzelman-Phi	250.0
Newcombe-Bro	244.1

Fewest Hits/Game
Staley-StL	8.09
Koslo-NY	8.19
Newcombe-Bro	8.21
Kennedy-NY	8.38
Meyer-Phi	8.41

Fewest BB/Game
Koslo-NY	1.83
Roe-Bro	1.86
Werle-Pit	2.08
Jansen-NY	2.15
Leonard-Chi	2.15

Strikeouts
Spahn-Bos	151
Newcombe-Bro	149
Jansen-NY	113
Roe-Bro	109
Branca-Bro	109

Strikeouts/Game
Newcombe-Bro	5.49
Branca-Bro	5.26
Chambers-Pit	4.72
Roe-Bro	4.61
Spahn-Bos	4.50

Ratio
Koslo-NY	10.02
Staley-StL	10.40
Roe-Bro	10.45
Newcombe-Bro	11.01
Spahn-Bos	11.07

Earned Run Average
Koslo-NY	2.50
Staley-StL	2.73
Pollet-StL	2.77
Roe-Bro	2.79
Heintzelman-Phi	3.02

Adjusted ERA
Koslo-NY	159
Staley-StL	152
Pollet-StL	150
Roe-Bro	147
Brazle-StL	131

Opponents' Batting Avg.
Staley-StL	.238
Koslo-NY	.239
Kennedy-NY	.242
Newcombe-Bro	.243
Spahn-Bos	.245

Opponents' On Base Pct.
Koslo-NY	.278
Staley-StL	.286
Roe-Bro	.293
Spahn-Bos	.299
Newcombe-Bro	.301

Starter Runs
Koslo-NY	36.2
Spahn-Bos	32.7
Pollet-StL	32.6
Roe-Bro	29.5
Heintzelman-Phi	28.2

Adjusted Starter Runs
Pollet-StL	35.7
Koslo-NY	34.8
Roe-Bro	30.9
Staley-StL	27.2
Heintzelman-Phi	25.5

Clutch Pitching Index
Roe-Bro	126
Heintzelman-Phi	123
Brazle-StL	121
Jones-NY	116
Dickson-Pit	113

Relief Runs
Erautt-Cin	8.6
Konstanty-Phi	8.5
Hogue-Bos	7.3
Palica-Bro	4.5
Wilks-StL	4.1

Adjusted Relief Runs
Erautt-Cin	10.3
Konstanty-Phi	7.5
Wilks-StL	5.7
Hogue-Bos	5.2
Palica-Bro	5.2

Relief Ranking
Erautt-Cin	12.6
Konstanty-Phi	11.0
Palica-Bro	8.9
Wilks-StL	6.6
Hogue-Bos	3.1

Total Pitcher Index
Pollet-StL	4.2
Koslo-NY	4.2
Staley-StL	3.5
Dickson-Pit	3.0
Newcombe-Bro	2.8

Total Baseball Ranking
Kiner-Pit	5.6
Robinson-Bro	4.9
Pollet-StL	4.2
Koslo-NY	4.2
Musial-StL	3.8

TEAM	G	W	L	PCT	GB	R	OR	AB	H	2B	3B	HR	BB	SO	AVG	OBP	SLG	PRO	PRO+	BR	/A	PF	CHI	RC	SB	CS	SBA	SBR
NY	155	97	57	.630		829	637	5196	1396	215	60	115	731	539	.269	.362	.400	.762	108	58	58	100	**106**	790	58	30	**66**	-1
BOS	155	96	58	.623	1	**896**	667	5320	**1500**	272	36	**131**	**835**	510	**.282**	**.381**	**.420**	**.801**	111	147	83	107	100	**890**	43	25	63	-2
CLE	154	89	65	.578	8	675	**574**	5221	1358	194	58	112	601	534	.260	.339	.384	.723	99	-30	-16	98	99	696	44	40	52	-11
DET	155	87	67	.565	10	751	655	5259	1405	215	51	88	751	502	.267	.361	.378	.739	102	20	18	100	99	739	39	52	43	-20
PHI	154	81	73	.526	16	726	725	5123	1331	214	49	82	783	**493**	.260	.361	.369	.730	104	6	31	97	99	719	36	25	59	-4
CHI	154	63	91	.409	34	648	589	5204	1340	207	**66**	43	702	596	.257	.347	.347	.694	93	-66	-45	97	99	657	**62**	55	53	-14
STL	155	53	101	.344	44	667	913	5112	1301	213	30	117	631	700	.254	.339	.377	.716	92	-41	-69	104	101	670	38	39	49	-12
WAS	154	50	104	.325	47	584	868	5234	1330	207	41	81	593	495	.254	.333	.356	.689	90	-93	-80	98	95	640	46	43	58	-6
TOT	618					5776		41669	10961	1737	391	769	5627	4369	.263	.353	.379	.732							366	299	55	-70

TEAM	CG	SH	SV	IP	H	H/G	HR	BB	SO	RAT	ERA	ERA+	OAV	OOB	PR	/A	PF	CPI	FA	E	DP	FW	PW	BW	SBW	DIF
NY	59	12	**36**	1371¹	**1231**	**8.1**	98	812	**671**	13.6	3.69	110	**.242**	.351	77	54	96	**107**	.977	138	195	.0	5.3	5.6	**.7**	8.3
BOS	84	16	16	1377	1375	9.0	82	661	598	13.5	3.97	104	.262	.347	34	59	104	101	.980	120	207	1.1	5.7	**8.1**	**.7**	3.4
CLE	65	10	19	1383²	1275	8.3	82	**611**	594	12.4	3.36	119	.247	**.329**	129	98	95	104	**.983**	103	192	**2.1**	**9.5**	-1.6	-.2	2.2
DET	70	**19**	12	1393²	1338	8.6	102	628	631	12.8	3.77	110	.254	.335	66	60	99	100	.978	131	174	.4	5.8	1.8	-1.1	3.1
PHI	**85**	9	11	1365	1359	9.0	105	758	490	14.1	4.23	97	.263	.360	-5	-19	99	103	.976	140	217	-.1	-1.8	3.0	.5	2.5
CHI	57	10	17	1363¹	1362	9.0	108	693	502	13.7	4.30	97	.264	.353	-15	-19	99	99	.977	141	180	-.2	-1.8	-4.4	-.5	-7.0
STL	43	3	16	1341¹	1583	10.6	113	685	432	15.4	5.21	87	.294	.377	-151	-102	108	98	.971	166	154	-1.6	-9.9	-6.7	-.3	-5.4
WAS	44	9	9	1345²	1438	9.6	**79**	779	451	15.0	5.10	84	.276	.373	-134	-126	101	91	.973	161	168	-1.4	-12.3	-7.8	.3	-5.8
TOT	507	88	136	10941		9.0				13.8	4.20		.263	.353					.977	1100	1487					

Runs
Williams-Bos 150
Joost-Phi 128
DiMaggio-Bos ... 126
Stephens-Bos 113
Pesky-Bos 111

Hits
Mitchell-Cle 203
Williams-Bos 194
DiMaggio-Bos 186
Wertz-Det 185
Pesky-Bos 185

Doubles
Williams-Bos 39
Kell-Det 38
DiMaggio-Bos 34
Zarilla-StL-Bos ... 33
Stephens-Bos 31

Triples
Mitchell-Cle 23
Dillinger-StL 13
Valo-Phi 12

Home Runs
Williams-Bos 43
Stephens-Bos 39

Total Bases
Williams-Bos 368
Stephens-Bos 329
Wertz-Det 283
Mitchell-Cle 274
Doerr-Bos 269

Runs Batted In
Williams-Bos 159
Stephens-Bos 159
Wertz-Det 133
Doerr-Bos 109
Chapman-Phi 108

Runs Produced
Williams-Bos 266
Stephens-Bos 233
Wertz-Det 209
Joost-Phi 186
Doerr-Bos 182

Bases On Balls
Williams-Bos 162
Joost-Phi 149
Fain-Phi 136
Appling-Chi 121
Valo-Phi 119

Batting Average
Kell-Det 343
Williams-Bos 343
Dillinger-StL 324
Mitchell-Cle 317
Doerr-Bos 309

On Base Percentage
Williams-Bos 490
Appling-Chi 439
Joost-Phi 429
Kell-Det 424
Michaels-Chi 417

Slugging Average
Williams-Bos 650
Stephens-Bos 539
Henrich-NY.......526
Doerr-Bos 497
Berra-NY 480

Production
Williams-Bos ... 1.141
Henrich-NY.......942
Stephens-Bos 930
Kell-Det 892
Doerr-Bos 890

Adjusted Production
Williams-Bos 187
Henrich-NY 148
Joost-Phi 138
Kell-Det 136
Stephens-Bos 135

Batter Runs
Williams-Bos 88.9
Stephens-Bos ... 36.9
Joost-Phi 31.9
DiMaggio-NY ... 31.7
Henrich-NY 29.7

Adjusted Batter Runs
Williams-Bos 76.6
Joost-Phi 35.8
DiMaggio-NY ...31.7
Henrich-NY 29.7
Stephens-Bos....28.3

Clutch Hitting Index
Fain-Phi 143
Lipon-Det 124
Valo-Phi 124
Wertz-Det 121
Williams-Bos 120

Runs Created
Williams-Bos 193
Stephens-Bos ... 132
Joost-Phi 119
DiMaggio-Bos ... 110
Wertz-Det 110

Total Average
Williams-Bos ... 1.347
Henrich-NY......1.017
Joost-Phi 995
Stephens-Bos 947
Kell-Det 877

Stolen Bases
Dillinger-StL 20
Rizzuto-NY 18
Valo-Phi 14
Philley-Chi 13

Stolen Base Average
Rizzuto-NY 75.0
Dillinger-StL 58.8

Stolen Base Runs
Tebbetts-Bos 1.8
Rizzuto-NY 1.8
Mapes-NY 1.8
Fain-Phi 1.8
Philley-Chi.......1.5

Fielding Runs
Doerr-Bos 27.8
Pesky-Bos 21.4
Vernon-Cle....... 18.8
DiMaggio-Bos ... 14.3
Baker-Chi 11.8

Total Player Rating
Williams-Bos 6.7
Joost-Phi 5.2
Doerr-Bos 5.0
Stephens-Bos 4.1
Michaels-Chi 3.9

Wins
Parnell-Bos 25
Kinder-Bos 23
Lemon-Cle 22
Raschi-NY 21
Kellner-Phi 20

Win Percentage
Kinder-Bos .... .793
Parnell-Bos .... .781
Reynolds-NY ...... .739
Lemon-Cle........ .688

Games
Page-NY 60
Welteroth-Was 52
Ferrick-StL 50
Kennedy-StL 48
Surkont-Chi 44

Complete Games
Parnell-Bos 27
Newhouser-Det 22
Lemon-Cle 22
Raschi-NY 21

Shutouts
Trucks-Det 6
Kinder-Bos 6
Garcia-Cle 5

Saves
Page-NY 27
Benton-Cle 10
Ferrick-StL 6
Paige-Cle 5

Innings Pitched
Parnell-Bos.......295.1
Newhouser-Det .. 292.0
Lemon-Cle 279.2
Trucks-Det 275.0
Raschi-NY 274.2

Fewest Hits/Game
Byrne-NY 5.74
Lemon-Cle 6.79
Trucks-Det 6.84
Gray-Det 7.52
Pierce-Chi 7.60

Fewest BB/Game
Hutchinson-Det .. 2.48
Houtteman-Det ... 2.61
Lopat-NY 2.88
Garcia-Cle 3.07
Wynn-Cle 3.12

Strikeouts
Trucks-Det 153
Newhouser-Det ... 144
Lemon-Cle 138
Kinder-Bos 138
Byrne-NY 129

Strikeouts/Game
Byrne-NY 5.92
Trucks-Det 5.01
Pierce-Chi 4.98
Kinder-Bos 4.93
Garcia-Cle 4.82

Ratio
Hutchinson-Det .. 10.49
Trucks-Det 11.03
Garcia-Cle 11.07
Lemon-Cle 11.39
Gumpert-Chi 11.81

Earned Run Average
Garcia-Cle 2.36
Parnell-Bos.......2.77
Trucks-Det 2.81
Hutchinson-Det .. 2.96
Lemon-Cle 2.99

Adjusted ERA
Garcia-Cle 169
Parnell-Bos 157
Trucks-Det 148
Hutchinson-Det 141
Lemon-Cle 133

Opponents' Batting Avg.
Byrne-NY 183
Lemon-Cle 211
Trucks-Det 211
Gray-Det.........227
Pierce-Chi 228

Opponents' On Base Pct.
Hutchinson-Det 290
Trucks-Det 301
Garcia-Cle 308
Lemon-Cle 309
Gumpert-Chi.......318

Starter Runs
Parnell-Bos 46.7
Trucks-Det 42.3
Lemon-Cle 37.4
Garcia-Cle 35.9
Benton-Cle 31.3

Adjusted Starter Runs
Parnell-Bos....... 52.1
Trucks-Det 41.1
Garcia-Cle 31.9
Lemon-Cle 31.0
Benton-Cle....... 28.2

Clutch Pitching Index
Garcia-Cle 123
Lopat-NY 122
Wight-Chi 118
Houtteman-Det ... 115
Kinder-Bos 114

Relief Runs
Page-NY 24.1
Paige-Cle 10.7
Papish-Cle....... 6.9
Ferrick-StL 3.7

Adjusted Relief Runs
Page-NY......... 21.8
Paige-Cle 8.8
Ferrick-StL 7.5
Papish-Cle 5.5
Starr-StL.......... 1.9

Relief Ranking
Page-NY 40.3
Paige-Cle 11.7
Ferrick-StL 7.4
Starr-StL 1.7
Papish-Cle 1.0

Total Pitcher Index
Lemon-Cle........ 5.7
Parnell-Bos 5.5
Page-NY 3.8
Garcia-Cle 3.6
Hutchinson-Det 3.4

Total Baseball Ranking
Williams-Bos 6.7
Lemon-Cle 5.7
Parnell-Bos....... 5.5
Joost-Phi 5.2
Doerr-Bos 5.0

TEAM	G	W	L	PCT	GB	R	OR	AB	H	2B	3B	HR	BB	SO	AVG	OBP	SLG	PRO	PRO+	BR	/A	PF	CHI	RC	SB	CS	SBA	SBR
PHI	157	91	63	.591		722	**624**	5426	1440	225	55	125	535	569	.265	.334	.396	.730	100	-14	-2	98	101	714	33			
BRO	155	89	65	.578	2	**847**	724	5364	**1461**	247	46	**194**	607	632	**.272**	**.349**	**.444**	**.793**	**113**	107	90	102	101	**833**	**77**			
NY	154	86	68	.558	5	735	643	5238	1352	204	50	133	**627**	629	.258	.342	.392	.734	100	4	0	101	101	726	42			
BOS	156	83	71	.539	8	785	736	5363	1411	246	36	148	615	616	.263	.342	.405	.747	110	24	73	94	**104**	750	71			
STL	153	78	75	.510	12.5	693	670	5215	1353	255	50	102	606	604	.259	.339	.386	.725	93	-15	-49	105	99	696	23			
CIN	153	66	87	.431	24.5	654	734	5253	1366	**257**	27	99	504	**497**	.260	.327	.376	.703	91	-65	-67	100	102	643	37			
CHI	154	64	89	.418	26.5	643	772	5230	1298	224	47	161	479	767	.248	.315	.401	.716	95	-53	-45	99	100	658	46			
PIT	154	57	96	.373	33.5	681	857	5327	1404	227	**59**	138	564	693	.264	.338	.406	.744	99	13	-11	103	93	729	43			
TOT	618					5760		42416	11085	1885	370	1100	4537	5007	.261	.336	.401	.737							372			

TEAM	CG	SH	SV	IP	H	H/G	HR	BB	SO	RAT	ERA	ERA+	OAV	OOB	PR	/A	PF	CPI	FA	E	DP	FW	PW	BW	SBW	DIF
PHI	57	13	**27**	1406	1324	8.5	122	**530**	620	12.0	3.50	116	.250	**.320**	101	86	98	**105**	.975	151	155	.1	8.4	-.2		5.7
BRO	62	10	21	1389²	1397	9.0	163	591	**772**	13.0	4.28	96	.263	.339	-22	-29	99	102	**.979**	**127**	**183**	**1.4**	-2.8	**8.8**		4.7
NY	70	**19**	15	1375	**1268**	8.3	140	536	596	12.0	3.71	110	**.246**	**.320**	66	59	99	100	.977	137	181	.8	5.8	.0		2.5
BOS	**88**	7	10	1385¹	1411	9.2	129	554	615	13.0	4.14	93	.263	.336	0	-45	93	99	.970	182	146	-1.7	-4.4	7.1		4.9
STL	57	10	14	1356	1398	9.3	**119**	535	603	13.0	3.97	108	.268	.339	26	49	104	**105**	.978	130	172	1.1	4.8	-4.8		.4
CIN	67	7	13	1357²	1363	9.0	145	582	686	13.2	4.32	98	.259	.338	-26	-13	102	97	.976	140	132	.5	-1.3	-6.5		-3.2
CHI	55	9	19	1371¹	1452	9.5	130	593	559	13.6	4.28	98	.271	.347	-21	-11	101	103	.968	201	169	-2.8	-1.1	-4.4		-4.2
PIT	42	6	16	1368²	1472	9.7	152	616	556	13.9	4.96	88	.275	.353	-124	-88	106	95	.977	136	165	.8	-8.6	-1.1		-10.6
TOT	498	81	135	11009²		9.1				13.0	4.14		.261	.336					.975	1204	1303					

Runs
Torgeson-Bos 120
Stanky-NY 115
Kiner-Pit 112
Snider-Bro 109
Musial-StL 105

Hits
Snider-Bro 199
Musial-StL 192
Furillo-Bro 189
Ennis-Phi 185
Waitkus-Phi 182

Doubles
Schoendienst-StL .. 43
Musial-StL 41
Robinson-Bro 39
Kluszewski-Cin ... 37
Dark-NY 36

Triples
Ashburn-Phi 14
Bell-Pit 11
Snider-Bro 10
Smalley-Chi 9
Schoendienst-StL ... 9

Home Runs
Kiner-Pit 47
Pafko-Chi 36
Sauer-Chi 32
Hodges-Bro 32

Total Bases
Snider-Bro 343
Musial-StL 331
Ennis-Phi 328
Kiner-Pit 323
Pafko-Chi 304

Runs Batted In
Ennis-Phi 126
Kiner-Pit 118
Hodges-Bro 113
Kluszewski-Cin ... 111
Musial-StL 109

Runs Produced
Furillo-Bro 187
Ennis-Phi 187
Musial-StL 186
Snider-Bro 185
Torgeson-Bos 184

Bases On Balls
Stanky-NY 144
Kiner-Pit 122
Torgeson-Bos 119
Westrum-NY 92
Reese-Bro 91

Batting Average
Musial-StL .... .346
Robinson-Bro ..... .328
Snider-Bro .... .321
Ennis-Phi .... .311
Kluszewski-Cin .... .307

On Base Percentage
Stanky-NY .... .460
Musial-StL .... .437
Robinson-Bro ..... .423
Glaviano-StL ...... .421
Torgeson-Bos ..... .412

Slugging Average
Musial-StL .... .596
Pafko-Chi .... .591
Kiner-Pit .... .590
Gordon-Bos .... .557
Snider-Bro .... .553

Production
Musial-StL 1.034
Kiner-Pit .... .998
Pafko-Chi .... .989
Gordon-Bos ...... .960
Snider-Bro .... .932

Adjusted Production
Musial-StL 161
Gordon-Bos 160
Pafko-Chi 158
Kiner-Pit 154
Elliott-Bos 143

Batter Runs
Musial-StL 57.3
Kiner-Pit 48.7
Pafko-Chi 41.5
Snider-Bro 35.6
Gordon-Bos 35.3

Adjusted Batter Runs
Musial-StL 50.9
Kiner-Pit 44.5
Pafko-Chi 42.8
Gordon-Bos 42.1
Torgeson-Bos 38.7

Clutch Hitting Index
D.Mueller-NY 138
Slaughter-StL 136
Westlake-Pit 115
Wyrostek-Cin 112
Thompson-NY 111

Runs Created
Musial-StL 149
Kiner-Pit 133
Snider-Bro 131
Pafko-Chi 124
Torgeson-Bos 121

Total Average
Musial-StL 1.139
Kiner-Pit 1.071
Pafko-Chi 1.057
Stanky-NY 1.013
Gordon-Bos 1.003

Stolen Bases
Jethroe-Bos 35
Reese-Bro 17
Snider-Bro 16
Torgeson-Bos 15
Ashburn-Phi 14

Stolen Base Average

Stolen Base Runs

Fielding Runs
Smalley-Chi 21.3
Cox-Bro 12.0
Ryan-Bos-Cin 11.6
Robinson-Bro 10.6
Westrum-NY 10.4

Total Player Rating
Robinson-Bro 4.7
Stanky-NY 4.1
Gordon-Bos 4.1
Pafko-Chi 3.5
Seminick-Phi 3.5

Wins
Spahn-Bos 21
Sain-Bos 20
Roberts-Phi 20

Win Percentage
Maglie-NY .... .818
Konstanty-Phi ..... .696
Simmons-Phi ...... .680
Roberts-Phi .... .645

Games
Konstanty-Phi 74
Dickson-Pit 51
Werle-Pit 48
Maglie-NY 47
Brazle-StL 46

Complete Games
Bickford-Bos 27
Spahn-Bos 25
Sain-Bos 25
Roberts-Phi 21
Jansen-NY 21

Shutouts
Hearn-StL-NY 5
Roberts-Phi 5
Maglie-NY 5
Jansen-NY 5

Saves
Konstanty-Phi 22
Werle-Pit 8
Hogue-Bos 7
Branca-Bro 7

Innings Pitched
Bickford-Bos ... 311.2
Roberts-Phi 304.1
Spahn-Bos 293.0
Sain-Bos 278.1
Jansen-NY 275.0

Fewest Hits/Game
Blackwell-Cin 7.00
Maglie-NY 7.38
Simmons-Phi 7.46
Spahn-Bos 7.62
Jansen-NY 7.79

Fewest BB/Game
Raffensberger-Cin . 1.51
Jansen-NY 1.80
Sain-Bos 2.26
Roberts-Phi 2.28
Roe-Bro 2.37

Strikeouts
Spahn-Bos 191
Blackwell-Cin 188
Jansen-NY 161
Simmons-Phi 146
Roberts-Phi 146

Strikeouts/Game
Blackwell-Cin 6.48
Simmons-Phi 6.12
Spahn-Bos 5.87
Palica-Bro 5.86
Jansen-NY 5.27

Ratio
Jansen-NY 9.62
Roberts-Phi 10.68
Brecheen-StL ... 10.97
Spahn-Bos 11.06
Simmons-Phi ... 11.24

Earned Run Average
Maglie-NY 2.71
Blackwell-Cin 2.97
Jansen-NY 3.01
Roberts-Phi 3.02
Lanier-StL 3.13

Adjusted ERA
Maglie-NY 151
Blackwell-Cin 143
Lanier-StL 137
Jansen-NY 136
Roberts-Phi 134

Opponents' Batting Avg.
Blackwell-Cin ..... .210
Simmons-Phi ...... .223
Maglie-NY .... .226
Spahn-Bos .... .227
Jansen-NY .... .232

Opponents' On Base Pct.
Jansen-NY .... .271
Roberts-Phi ...... .297
Brecheen-StL ..... .298
Spahn-Bos .... .299
Blackwell-Cin ..... .301

Starter Runs
Roberts-Phi 38.0
Jansen-NY 34.5
Blackwell-Cin 34.1
Maglie-NY 32.8
Spahn-Bos 31.8

Adjusted Starter Runs
Blackwell-Cin 36.7
Roberts-Phi 34.8
Jansen-NY 33.1
Maglie-NY 31.7
Pollet-StL 25.9

Clutch Pitching Index
Brazle-StL 125
Roe-Bro 118
Maglie-NY 116
Ramsdell-Bro-Cin . 115
Minner-Chi 113

Relief Runs
Konstanty-Phi 24.9
Kramer-NY 5.9
Leonard-Chi 3.1
VanderMeer-Chi ... 2.9
Smith-Cin 2.7

Adjusted Relief Runs
Konstanty-Phi 23.3
Kramer-NY 5.4
Smith-Cin 3.6
Leonard-Chi 3.5
VanderMeer-Chi ... 3.4

Relief Ranking
Konstanty-Phi 39.4
Kramer-NY 5.2
Smith-Cin 3.5
Leonard-Chi 3.2
VanderMeer-Chi ... 3.0

Total Pitcher Index
Blackwell-Cin 4.3
Jansen-NY 3.8
Konstanty-Phi 3.6
Maglie-NY 3.3
Spahn-Bos 3.1

Total Baseball Ranking
Robinson-Bro 4.7
Blackwell-Cin 4.3
Stanky-NY 4.1
Gordon-Bos 4.1
Jansen-NY 3.8

TEAM	G	W	L	PCT	GB	R	OR	AB	H	2B	3B	HR	BB	SO	AVG	OBP	SLG	PRO	PRO+	BR	/A	PF	CHI	RC	SB	CS	SBA	SBR
NY	155	98	56	.636		914	691	5361	1511	234	70	159	687	463	.282	.367	.441	.808	116	92	118	97	104	902	41	28	59	-5
DET	157	95	59	.617	3	837	713	5381	1518	285	50	114	722	480	.282	.369	.417	.786	104	60	33	103	97	846	23	40	37	-17
BOS	154	94	60	.610	4	1027	804	5516	1665	287	61	161	719	582	.302	.385	.464	.849	112	185	90	110	103	1014	32	17	65	-1
CLE	155	92	62	.597	6	806	654	5263	1417	222	46	164	693	624	.269	.358	.422	.780	109	38	66	97	98	820	40	34	54	-8
WAS	155	67	87	.435	31	690	813	5251	1365	190	53	76	671	606	.260	.347	.360	.707	91	-93	-61	95	101	690	42	25	63	-2
CHI	156	60	94	.390	38	625	749	5260	1368	172	47	93	551	566	.260	.333	.364	.697	86	-125	-107	97	98	648	19	22	46	-8
STL	154	58	96	.377	40	684	916	5163	1269	235	43	106	690	744	.246	.337	.370	.707	84	-102	-127	104	103	667	39	40	49	-12
PHI	154	52	102	.338	46	670	913	5212	1361	204	53	100	685	493	.261	.349	.378	.727	94	-56	-42	98	94	708	42	25	63	-2
TOT	620					6253		42407	11474	1829	423	973	5418	4558	.271	.356	.402	.759							278	231	55	-55

TEAM	CG	SH	SV	IP	H	H/G	HR	BB	SO	RAT	ERA	ERA+	OAV	OOB	PR	/A	PF	CPI	FA	E	DP	FW	PW	BW	SBW	DIF
NY	66	12	31	1372²	1322	8.7	118	708	712	13.5	4.15	103	.255	.348	65	22	94	102	.980	119	188	1.3	2.1	11.0	.2	6.4
DET	72	9	20	1407¹	1444	9.2	141	553	576	13.0	4.12	114	.267	.339	71	88	102	105	.981	120	194	1.3	8.2	3.1	-.9	6.3
BOS	66	6	28	1362¹	1413	9.3	121	748	630	14.4	4.88	100	.270	.364	-46	3	107	97	.981	111	181	1.7	.3	8.4	.6	6.1
CLE	69	11	16	1378²	1289	8.4	120	647	674	12.8	3.75	115	.248	.333	126	88	95	103	.978	129	160	.7	8.2	6.2	-.1	-.0
WAS	59	7	18	1364²	1479	9.8	99	648	486	14.2	4.66	96	.278	.359	-12	-25	98	99	.972	167	181	-1.4	-2.3	-5.7	.5	-1.0
CHI	62	7	9	1365²	1370	9.0	107	734	566	14.0	4.41	102	.263	.356	26	12	98	100	.977	140	181	.2	1.1	-10.0	-.1	-8.2
STL	56	7	14	1365¹	1629	10.7	129	651	448	15.2	5.20	85	.295	.372	-94	-38	108	100	.967	196	155	-3.1	-3.6	-11.9	-.5	-.0
PHI	50	3	18	1346¹	1528	10.2	138	729	466	15.3	5.49	83	.287	.376	-136	-140	99	96	.974	155	208	-.8	-13.1	-3.9	.5	-7.7
TOT	500	62	154	10963		9.4				14.0	4.58		.271	.356					.976	1137	1448					

Runs		Hits		Doubles		Triples		Home Runs		Total Bases	
DiMaggio-Bos	131	Kell-Det	218	Kell-Det	56	Evers-Det	11	Rosen-Cle	37	Dropo-Bos	326
Stephens-Bos	125	Rizzuto-NY	200	Wertz-Det	37	Doerr-Bos	11	Dropo-Bos	34	Stephens-Bos	321
Rizzuto-NY	125	DiMaggio-Bos	193	Rizzuto-NY	36	DiMaggio-Bos	11	DiMaggio-NY	32	Berra-NY	318
Berra-NY	116	Berra-NY	192	Evers-Det	35			Stephens-Bos	30	Kell-Det	310
		Stephens-Bos	185	Stephens-Bos	34			Zernial-Chi	29	DiMaggio-NY	307

Runs Batted In		Runs Produced		Bases On Balls		Batting Average		On Base Percentage		Slugging Average	
Stephens-Bos	144	Stephens-Bos	239	Yost-Was	141	Goodman-Bos	.354	Doby-Cle	.442	DiMaggio-NY	.585
Dropo-Bos	144	Berra-NY	212	Fain-Phi	133	Kell-Det	.340	Yost-Was	.440	Dropo-Bos	.583
Berra-NY	124	Dropo-Bos	211	Pesky-Bos	104	DiMaggio-Bos	.328	Pesky-Bos	.437	Evers-Det	.551
Wertz-Det	123	Kell-Det	207	Joost-Phi	103	Doby-Cle	.326	Fain-Phi	.430	Doby-Cle	.545
DiMaggio-NY	122	DiMaggio-NY	204	Rosen-Cle	100	Zarilla-Bos	.325	Goodman-Bos	.427	Rosen-Cle	.543

Production		Adjusted Production		Batter Runs		Adjusted Batter Runs		Clutch Hitting Index		Runs Created	
Doby-Cle	.986	Doby-Cle	156	Doby-Cle	41.7	Doby-Cle	45.7	Vernon-Cle-Was	126	Doby-Cle	130
DiMaggio-NY	.979	DiMaggio-NY	152	Williams-Bos	40.9	DiMaggio-NY	38.8	Mele-Was	125	Wertz-Det	128
Dropo-Bos	.961	Rosen-Cle	146	DiMaggio-NY	35.4	Rosen-Cle	38.3	Noren-Was	116	DiMaggio-NY	125
Evers-Det	.959	Evers-Det	139	Rosen-Cle	34.3	Williams-Bos	32.1	Stephens-Bos	110	Berra-NY	125
Rosen-Cle	.948	Berra-NY	136	Evers-Det	33.5	Evers-Det	30.0	Fain-Phi	108	Rizzuto-NY	124

Total Average		Stolen Bases		Stolen Base Average		Stolen Base Runs		Fielding Runs		Total Player Rating	
Doby-Cle	1.073	DiMaggio-Bos	15			DiMaggio-Cle-Bos	2.1	Priddy-Det	31.3	Rizzuto-NY	4.1
DiMaggio-NY	1.018	Valo-Phi	12			Vernon-Cle-Was	1.8	Hegan-Cle	24.2	Berra-NY	3.4
Wertz-Det	.978	Rizzuto-NY	12			Collins-NY	1.5	Pesky-Bos	21.5	DiMaggio-NY	3.1
Zarilla-Bos	.954	Coan-Was	10			Avila-Cle	1.5	Noren-Was	15.9	Rosen-Cle	3.1
Rosen-Cle	.953	Lipon-Det	9			Jensen-NY	1.2	Carrasquel-Chi	11.2	Doby-Cle	3.1

Wins		Win Percentage		Games		Complete Games		Shutouts		Saves	
B.Lemon-Cle	23	Raschi-NY	.724	Harris-Was	53	B.Lemon-Cle	22	Houtteman-Det	4	Harris-Was	15
Raschi-NY	21	Wynn-Cle	.692	Kinder-Bos	48	Garver-StL	22			Page-NY	13
Houtteman-Det	19	Lopat-NY	.692	Ferrick-StL-NY	46	Parnell-Bos	21			Ferrick-StL-NY	11
		Hutchinson-Det	.680	Judson-Chi	46	Houtteman-Det	21			Kinder-Bos	9
		B.Lemon-Cle	.676	Brissie-Phi	46					Brissie-Phi	8

Innings Pitched		Fewest Hits/Game		Fewest BB/Game		Strikeouts		Strikeouts/Game		Ratio	
B.Lemon-Cle	288.0	Wynn-Cle	6.99	Hutchinson-Det	1.86	B.Lemon-Cle	170	Wynn-Cle	6.02	Wynn-Cle	11.41
Houtteman-Det	274.2	Pierce-Chi	7.76	Lopat-NY	2.48	Reynolds-NY	160	Reynolds-NY	5.98	Lopat-NY	11.92
Garver-StL	260.0	Cain-Chi	8.02	Overmire-StL	2.52	Raschi-NY	155	Raschi-NY	5.44	Houtteman-Det	11.93
Raschi-NY	256.2	Reynolds-NY	8.04	Trout-Det	3.12	Wynn-Cle	143	B.Lemon-Cle	5.31	Raschi-NY	12.31
Parnell-Bos	249.0	Raschi-NY	8.14	Houtteman-Det	3.24	Feller-Cle	119	Byrne-NY	5.22	Feller-Cle	12.32

Earned Run Average		Adjusted ERA		Opponents' Batting Avg.		Opponents' On Base Pct.		Starter Runs		Adjusted Starter Runs	
Wynn-Cle	3.20	Garver-StL	146	Wynn-Cle	.212	Wynn-Cle	.305	Garver-StL	34.3	Garver-StL	45.0
Garver-StL	3.39	Parnell-Bos	136	Pierce-Chi	.228	Lopat-NY	.317	Wynn-Cle	32.7	Parnell-Bos	35.5
Feller-Cle	3.43	Wynn-Cle	135	Reynolds-NY	.242	Houtteman-Det	.322	Houtteman-Det	31.7	Houtteman-Det	35.1
Lopat-NY	3.47	Houtteman-Det	132	Raschi-NY	.243	Feller-Cle	.325	Feller-Cle	31.7	Wynn-Cle	26.8
Houtteman-Det	3.54	Feller-Cle	126	Cain-Chi	.244	Raschi-NY	.327	Lopat-NY	29.2	Feller-Cle	24.9

Clutch Pitching Index		Relief Runs		Adjusted Relief Runs		Relief Ranking		Total Pitcher Index		Total Baseball Ranking	
Garver-StL	119	Judson-Chi	8.0	Judson-Chi	6.8	Ferrick-StL-NY	13.0	Garver-StL	5.7	Garver-StL	5.7
Hudson-Was	113	Aloma-Chi	7.6	Aloma-Chi	6.7	Aloma-Chi	6.9	Parnell-Bos	3.9	Rizzuto-NY	4.1
B.Lemon-Cle	111	Benton-Cle	7.0	Ferrick-StL-NY	6.2	Benton-Cle	5.3	B.Lemon-Cle	3.7	Parnell-Bos	3.9
Houtteman-Det	110	Ferrick-StL-NY	7.0	Benton-Cle	5.3	Flores-Cle	4.2	Wynn-Cle	3.6	B.Lemon-Cle	3.7
Parnell-Bos	110	Flores-Cle	5.0	Flores-Cle	3.5	Judson-Chi	2.7	Houtteman-Det	3.5	Wynn-Cle	3.6

1951 National League

TEAM	G	W	L	PCT	GB	R	OR	AB	H	2B	3B	HR	BB	SO	AVG	OBP	SLG	PRO	PRO+	BR	/A	PF	CHI	RC	SB	CS	SBA	SBR
NY	157	98	59	.624		781	**641**	5360	1396	201	53	179	**671**	624	.260	.347	.418	.765	111	91	85	101	97	812	55	34	62	-4
BRO	158	97	60	.618	1	**855**	672	5492	**1511**	249	37	**184**	603	649	**.275**	**.352**	**.434**	**.786**	116	130	113	102	101	**843**	**89**	70	56	-15
STL	155	81	73	.526	15.5	683	671	5317	1404	230	**57**	95	569	492	.264	.339	.382	.721	99	7	3	101	97	705	30	30	50	-9
BOS	155	76	78	.494	20.5	723	662	5293	1385	234	37	130	565	617	.262	.336	.394	.730	111	20	70	93	102	719	80	34	**70**	4
PHI	154	73	81	.474	23.5	648	644	5332	1384	199	47	108	505	525	.260	.326	.375	.701	96	-38	-28	99	99	676	63	28	69	2
CIN	155	68	86	.442	28.5	559	667	5285	1309	215	33	88	415	577	.248	.304	.351	.655	81	-134	-142	102	**104**	562	44	40	52	-11
PIT	155	64	90	.416	32.5	689	845	5318	1372	218	56	137	557	615	.258	.331	.397	.728	99	11	-9	103	98	712	29	27	52	-8
CHI	155	62	92	.403	34.5	614	750	5307	1327	200	47	103	477	647	.250	.315	.364	.679	86	-86	-97	102	103	613	63	30	68	1
TOT	622					5552		42704	11088	1746	367	1024	4362	4746	.260	.331	.390	.721							453	293	61	-40

TEAM	CG	SH	SV	IP	H	H/G	HR	BB	SO	RAT	ERA	ERA+	OAV	OOB	PR	/A	PF	CPI	FA	E	DP	FW	PW	BW	SBW	DIF
NY	64	9	18	1412²	**1334**	8.5	148	482	625	11.7	3.48	113	.248	.313	75	69	99	104	.972	171	175	-1.0	**6.9**	8.5	.0	5.0
BRO	64	10	13	1423¹	1360	8.6	150	549	**693**	12.2	3.88	101	.253	.326	13	8	99	101	.979	129	**192**	1.3	.8	11.3	-1.0	6.1
STL	58	9	**23**	1387²	1391	9.0	119	568	546	12.8	3.95	100	.264	.338	1	2	100	103	**.980**	125	187	1.3	.2	.3	-.4	2.6
BOS	**73**	16	12	1389	1378	8.9	**96**	595	604	13.0	3.75	98	.259	.337	33	-11	93	104	.976	145	157	.3	-1.1	7.0	**.9**	-8.1
PHI	57	**19**	15	1384²	1373	8.9	110	497	570	12.3	3.81	101	.258	.324	23	6	97	98	.977	138	146	.6	.6	-2.8	.7	-3.1
CIN	55	14	**23**	1390²	1357	8.8	119	490	584	12.2	3.70	110	.255	.323	40	58	103	100	.977	140	141	.5	5.8	-14.2	-.6	-.5
PIT	40	9	22	1380¹	1479	9.6	157	609	580	13.8	4.79	88	.274	.350	-128	-88	107	97	.972	170	178	-1.1	-8.8	-.9	-.3	-1.9
CHI	48	10	10	1385²	1416	9.2	125	572	544	13.1	4.34	94	.265	.340	-58	-38	103	96	.971	181	161	-1.7	-3.8	-9.7	.6	-.4
TOT	459	96	136	11154		8.9				12.6	3.96		.260	.331					.975	1199	1337					

Runs
Musial-StL 124
Kiner-Pit 124
Hodges-Bro 118
Dark-NY 114
Robinson-Bro 106

Hits
Ashburn-Phi 221
Musial-StL 205
Furillo-Bro 197
Dark-NY 196
Robinson-Bro 185

Doubles
Dark-NY 41
Kluszewski-Cin 35
Robinson-Bro 33
Campanella-Bro ... 33

Triples
Musial-StL......... 12
Bell-Pit............ 12
Irvin-NY 11
Jethroe-Bos 10
Baumholtz-Chi 10

Home Runs
Kiner-Pit 42
Hodges-Bro 40
Campanella-Bro ... 33
Thomson-NY 32
Musial-StL 32

Total Bases
Musial-StL 355
Kiner-Pit 333
Hodges-Bro 307
Campanella-Bro ... 298

Runs Batted In
Irvin-NY 121
Kiner-Pit 109
Gordon-Bos 109
Musial-StL 108
Campanella-Bro ... 108

Runs Produced
Musial-StL 200
Kiner-Pit........... 191
Irvin-NY 191
Hodges-Bro 181
Gordon-Bos 176

Bases On Balls
Kiner-Pit 137
Stanky-NY 127
Westrum-NY 104
Torgeson-Bos 102
Musial-StL 98

Batting Average
Musial-StL........ .355
Ashburn-Phi ...... .344
Robinson-Bro ..... .338
Campanella-Bro ... .325
Irvin-NY .... .312

On Base Percentage
Kiner-Pit .... .452
Musial-StL .... .449
Robinson-Bro ..... .429
Irvin-NY .... .415
Stanky-NY .... .401

Slugging Average
Kiner-Pit .... .627
Musial-StL .... .614
Campanella-Bro ... .590
Thomson-NY ...... .562
Hodges-Bro .... .527

Production
Kiner-Pit 1.079
Musial-StL 1.063
Campanella-Bro ... .983
Robinson-Bro ..... .957
Thomson-NY ...... .947

Adjusted Production
Musial-StL 182
Kiner-Pit 182
Campanella-Bro ... 158
Robinson-Bro 153
Thomson-NY 150

Batter Runs
Kiner-Pit 70.8
Musial-StL 70.1
Robinson-Bro ... 45.8
Campanella-Bro ... 41.7
Irvin-NY 40.7

Adjusted Batter Runs
Musial-StL........ 69.2
Kiner-Pit 66.5
Robinson-Bro ... 43.4
Irvin-NY 39.7
Campanella-Bro ... 39.6

Clutch Hitting Index
Slaughter-StL 136
Reese-Bro 130
Irvin-NY 118
Westlake-Pit-StL ... 112
Torgeson-Bos 109

Runs Created
Musial-StL 169
Kiner-Pit 165
Robinson-Bro 133
Irvin-NY.......... 127
Hodges-Bro 119

Total Average
Kiner-Pit 1.251
Musial-StL 1.180
Robinson-Bro ...1.034
Irvin-NY........... .985
Campanella-Bro ... .978

Stolen Bases
Jethroe-Bos 35
Ashburn-Phi 29
Robinson-Bro 25
Torgeson-Bos 20
Reese-Bro 20

Stolen Base Average
Jethroe-Bos 87.5
Ashburn-Phi 82.9
Robinson-Bro ... 75.8
Torgeson-Bos 64.5
Reese-Bro 58.8

Stolen Base Runs
Jethroe-Bos 7.5
Ashburn-Phi 5.1
Robinson-Bro 2.7
Jackson-Chi 2.4
Irvin-NY 2.4

Fielding Runs
Ashburn-Phi 32.3
Robinson-Bro 16.5
Furillo-Bro 16.1
Schoendienst-StL . 15.5
Hemus-StL 13.4

Total Player Rating
Robinson-Bro 6.8
Musial-StL 6.4
Kiner-Pit 5.4
Campanella-Bro ... 5.2
Ashburn-Phi 5.2

Wins
Maglie-NY 23
Jansen-NY 23
Spahn-Bos 22
Roe-Bro 22
Roberts-Phi 21

Win Percentage
Roe-Bro .... .880
Maglie-NY .... .793
Newcombe-Bro ... .690
Jansen-NY .... .676
Hearn-NY .... .654

Games
Wilks-StL-Pit 65
Werle-Pit 59
Konstanty-Phi 58
Spencer-NY 57
Brazle-StL 56

Complete Games
Spahn-Bos 26
Roberts-Phi 22
Maglie-NY 22
Roe-Bro 19
Dickson-Pit 19

Shutouts
Spahn-Bos 7
Roberts-Phi 6
Raffensberger-Cin .. 5

Saves
Wilks-StL-Pit 13
Smith-Cin 11
Konstanty-Phi 9
Brazle-StL 7

Innings Pitched
Roberts-Phi 315.0
Spahn-Bos 310.2
Maglie-NY 298.0
Dickson-Pit 288.2
Jansen-NY 278.2

Fewest Hits/Game
Maglie-NY 7.67
Newcombe-Bro ... 7.78
Blackwell-Cin 7.89
Branca-Bro 7.94
Queen-Pit 7.97

Fewest BB/Game
Raffensberger-Cin . 1.38
Jansen-NY 1.81
Roberts-Phi 1.83
Roe-Bro 2.24
Sain-Bos 2.53

Strikeouts
Spahn-Bos 164
Newcombe-Bro ... 164
Maglie-NY 146
Jansen-NY 145
Rush-Chi 129

Strikeouts/Game
Queen-Pit 6.58
Rush-Chi 5.49
Newcombe-Bro ... 5.43
Branca-Bro 5.21
Spahn-Bos 4.75

Ratio
Raffensberger-Cin . 9.99
Roberts-Phi 10.03
Jansen-NY 10.11
Maglie-NY 10.45
Roe-Bro 10.86

Earned Run Average
Nichols-Bos 2.88
Maglie-NY 2.93
Spahn-Bos 2.98
Roberts-Phi 3.03
Jansen-NY 3.04

Adjusted ERA
Maglie-NY 134
Roe-Bro 129
Jansen-NY 129
Nichols-Bos 127
Roberts-Phi 127

Opponents' Batting Avg.
Maglie-NY .... .230
Newcombe-Bro ... .230
Blackwell-Cin ..... .233
Queen-Pit .... .233
Branca-Bro .... .237

Opponents' On Base Pct.
Roberts-Phi ...... .278
Jansen-NY .... .279
Raffensberger-Cin . .279
Maglie-NY .... .289
Newcombe-Bro ... .297

Starter Runs
Maglie-NY 34.1
Spahn-Bos 33.7
Roberts-Phi 32.6
Jansen-NY 28.6
Roe-Bro 26.4

Adjusted Starter Runs
Maglie-NY 32.7
Roberts-Phi 28.7
Jansen-NY 27.2
Roe-Bro 25.3
Spahn-Bos 23.8

Clutch Pitching Index
Roe-Bro 122
Sain-Bos 113
Nichols-Bos 112
Minner-Chi 111
Bickford-Bos 108

Relief Runs
Brazle-StL 14.9
Kennedy-NY 12.9
Perkowski-Cin 12.9
Wilks-StL-Pit 12.3
Leonard-Chi 11.9

Adjusted Relief Runs
Brazle-StL 15.0
Wilks-StL-Pit 14.7
Perkowski-Cin 14.2
Leonard-Chi 13.1
Kennedy-NY 12.6

Relief Ranking
Leonard-Chi 24.3
Wilks-StL-Pit 14.8
Perkowski-Cin 11.6
Smith-Cin 11.2
Brazle-StL........ 11.1

Total Pitcher Index
Roberts-Phi 3.4
Maglie-NY 2.9
Blackwell-Cin 2.9
Jansen-NY 2.9
Spahn-Bos 2.9

Total Baseball Ranking
Robinson-Bro 6.8
Musial-StL 6.4
Kiner-Pit 5.4
Campanella-Bro ... 5.2
Ashburn-Phi 5.2

TEAM	G	W	L	PCT	GB	R	OR	AB	H	2B	3B	HR	BB	SO	AVG	OBP	SLG	PRO	PRO+	BR	/A	PF	CHI	RC	SB	CS	SBA	SBR
NY	154	98	56	.636		798	621	5194	1395	208	48	140	605	547	.269	.349	.408	.757	113	62	90	96	104	762	78	39	67	0
CLE	155	93	61	.604	5	696	594	5250	1346	208	35	140	606	632	.256	.336	.389	.725	106	0	40	94	98	710	52	35	60	-5
BOS	154	87	67	.565	11	804	725	5378	1428	233	32	127	756	594	.266	.358	.392	.750	98	64	-13	110	100	778	20	21	49	-7
CHI	155	81	73	.526	17	714	644	5378	1453	229	64	86	596	524	.270	.349	.385	.734	105	73	39	98	95	745	99	70	59	-12
DET	154	73	81	.474	25	685	741	5336	1413	231	35	104	568	525	.265	.338	.380	.718	99	-14	-17	100	98	697	37	34	52	-9
PHI	154	70	84	.455	28	736	745	5277	1381	262	43	102	677	565	.262	.349	.386	.735	101	29	13	102	98	745	47	36	57	-9
WAS	154	62	92	.403	36	672	764	5329	1399	242	45	54	560	515	.263	.336	.355	.691	93	-60	-48	98	103	648	45	38	54	-9
STL	154	52	102	.338	46	611	882	5219	1288	223	47	86	521	693	.247	.317	.357	.674	84	-102	-119	103	103	592	35	38	48	-12
TOT	617					5716		42361	11103	1836	349	839	4889	4595	.262	.342	.381	.723							413	311	57	-63

TEAM	CG	SH	SV	IP	H	H/G	HR	BB	SO	RAT	ERA	ERA+	OAV	OOB	PR	/A	PF	CPI	FA	E	DP	FW	PW	BW	SBW	DIF
NY	66	24	22	1367	1290	8.5	92	562	664	12.4	3.56	107	.250	.328	85	41	93	103	.975	144	190	.3	4.0	8.9	.8	7.0
CLE	76	10	19	1391¹	1287	8.3	86	577	642	12.2	3.38	112	.245	.323	114	63	92	103	.978	134	151	.9	6.2	3.9	.3	4.7
BOS	46	7	24	1399	1413	9.1	100	599	658	13.2	4.14	108	.264	.342	-2	50	108	100	.977	141	184	.5	4.9	-1.3	.0	5.8
CHI	74	11	14	1418¹	1353	8.6	109	549	572	12.2	3.50	115	.252	.323	97	84	98	105	.975	151	176	.0	8.3	3.8	-.4	-7.7
DET	51	8	17	1384	1385	9.0	102	602	597	13.2	4.29	97	.262	.342	-26	-18	101	96	.973	163	166	-.7	-1.8	-1.7	-.1	.2
PHI	52	7	22	1358	1421	9.4	109	569	437	13.4	4.47	96	.272	.347	-52	-29	104	98	.978	136	204	.8	-2.9	1.3	-.0	-6.2
WAS	58	6	13	1366¹	1429	9.4	110	630	475	13.7	4.49	91	.269	.348	-55	-59	99	97	.973	160	148	-.5	-5.8	-4.7	-.1	-3.8
STL	56	5	9	1370¹	1525	10.0	131	801	550	15.5	5.18	85	.282	.379	-160	-119	107	101	.971	172	179	-1.2	-11.7	-11.7	-.4	-.0
TOT	479	78	140	11054¹		9.0				13.2	4.12		.262	.342					.975	1201	1398					

Runs		Hits		Doubles		Triples		Home Runs		Total Bases	
DiMaggio-Bos	113	Kell-Det	191	Yost-Was	36	Minoso-Cle-Chi	14	Zernial-Chi-Phi	33	Williams-Bos	295
Minoso-Cle-Chi	112	Fox-Chi	189	Mele-Was	36	Coleman-StL-Chi	12	Williams-Bos	30	Zernial-Chi-Phi	292
Yost-Was	109	DiMaggio-Bos	189	Kell-Det	36	Fox-Chi	12	Robinson-Chi	29	Robinson-Chi	279
Williams-Bos	109	Minoso-Cle-Chi	173			Young-StL	9			Berra-NY	269
Joost-Phi	107	Williams-Bos	169							DiMaggio-Bos	267

Runs Batted In		Runs Produced		Bases On Balls		Batting Average		On Base Percentage		Slugging Average	
Zernial-Chi-Phi	129	Minoso-Cle	205	Williams-Bos	144	Fain-Phi	.344	Williams-Bos	.464	Williams-Bos	.556
Williams-Bos	126	Zernial-Chi-Phi	188	Yost-Was	126	Minoso-Cle-Chi	.326	Fain-Phi	.451	Doby-Cle	.512
Robinson-Chi	117	Minoso-Cle-Chi	178	Joost-Phi	106	Kell-Det	.319	Doby-Cle	.428	Zernial-Chi-Phi	.511
Easter-Cle	103	Robinson-Chi	173	Doby-Cle	101	Williams-Bos	.318	Yost-Was	.423	Wertz-Det	.511
Rosen-Cle	102	DiMaggio-Bos	173	Rosen-Cle	85	Fox-Chi	.313	Minoso-Cle-Chi	.422	Minoso-Cle-Chi	.500

Production		Adjusted Production		Batter Runs		Adjusted Batter Runs		Clutch Hitting Index		Runs Created	
Williams-Bos	1.019	Doby-Cle	163	Williams-Bos	62.8	Williams-Bos	49.5	Mele-Was	136	Williams-Bos	152
Doby-Cle	.941	Williams-Bos	159	Minoso-Cle-Chi	38.2	Doby-Cle	42.9	Busby-Chi	127	Minoso-Cle-Chi	120
Minoso-Cle-Chi	.922	Minoso-Cle-Chi	152	Doby-Cle	37.0	Minoso-Cle-Chi	40.8	Noren-Was	120	Yost-Was	117
Fain-Phi	.921	Fain-Phi	146	Fain-Phi	33.8	Yost-Was	32.2	Zernial-Chi-Phi	118	Joost-Phi	115
Wertz-Det	.894	Wertz-Det	140	Joost-Phi	30.5	Fain-Phi	31.8	DiMaggio-NY	113	Doby-Cle	108

Total Average		Stolen Bases		Stolen Base Average		Stolen Base Runs		Fielding Runs		Total Player Rating	
Williams-Bos	1.177	Minoso-Cle-Chi	31	Rizzuto-NY	85.7	Rizzuto-NY	3.6	Coan-Was	22.0	Williams-Bos	4.5
Doby-Cle	1.031	Busby-Chi	26	Minoso-Cle-Chi	75.6	Minoso-Cle-Chi	3.3	Noren-Was	14.7	Joost-Phi	3.9
Minoso-Cle-Chi	.987	Rizzuto-NY	18	Busby-Chi	70.3	Carrasquel-Chi	1.8	Stephens-Bos	14.1	Doby-Cle	3.6
Fain-Phi	.959							Fain-Phi	12.6	Fain-Phi	3.6
Yost-Was	.909							Carrasquel-Chi	12.5	Berra-NY	3.3

Wins		Win Percentage		Games		Complete Games		Shutouts		Saves	
Feller-Cle	22	Feller-Cle	.733	Kinder-Bos	63	Garver-StL	24	Reynolds-NY	7	Kinder-Bos	14
Raschi-NY	21	Lopat-NY	.700	Brissie-Phi-Cle	56	Wynn-Cle	21	Raschi-NY	4	Scheib-Phi	10
Lopat-NY	21	Reynolds-NY	.680	Garcia-Cle	47	Lopat-NY	20	Lopat-NY	4	Brissie-Phi-Cle	9
		Raschi-NY	.677	Scheib-Phi	46	Pierce-Chi	18	Feller-Cle	4	Reynolds-NY	7
		Shantz-Phi	.643							Garcia-Cle	6

Innings Pitched		Fewest Hits/Game		Fewest BB/Game		Strikeouts		Strikeouts/Game		Ratio	
Wynn-Cle	274.1	Reynolds-NY	6.96	Hutchinson-Det	1.29	Raschi-NY	164	McDermott-Bos	6.65	Lopat-NY	10.85
Lemon-Cle	263.1	McDermott-Bos	7.38	Lopat-NY	2.72	Wynn-Cle	133	Gray-Det	5.97	Rogovin-Det-Chi	10.97
Raschi-NY	258.1	Wynn-Cle	7.45	Pierce-Chi	2.73	Lemon-Cle	132	Raschi-NY	5.71	Wynn-Cle	11.06
Garcia-Cle	254.0	Rogovin-Det-Chi	7.85	Hooper-Phi	2.90	Gray-Det	131	Reynolds-NY	5.13	Hutchinson-Det	11.13
Feller-Cle	249.2	Lopat-NY	8.02	Garcia-Cle	2.91	McDermott-Bos	127	Lemon-Cle	4.51	Reynolds-NY	11.24

Earned Run Average		Adjusted ERA		Opponents' Batting Avg.		Opponents' On Base Pct.		Starter Runs		Adjusted Starter Runs	
Rogovin-Det-Chi	2.78	Rogovin-Det-Chi	146	Reynolds-NY	.213	Lopat-NY	.298	Wynn-Cle	33.6	Rogovin-Det-Chi	30.5
Lopat-NY	2.91	Parnell-Bos	137	Wynn-Cle	.225	Rogovin-Det-Chi	.301	Rogovin-Det-Chi	32.2	Parnell-Bos	29.5
Wynn-Cle	3.02	McDermott-Bos	133	McDermott-Bos	.226	Wynn-Cle	.301	Lopat-NY	31.5	Pierce-Chi	26.7
Pierce-Chi	3.03	Pierce-Chi	133	Rogovin-Det-Chi	.235	Hutchinson-Det	.302	Pierce-Chi	29.1	Lopat-NY	23.8
Reynolds-NY	3.05	Lopat-NY	131	Lopat-NY	.239	Reynolds-NY	.304	Garcia-Cle	27.3	Wynn-Cle	23.4

Clutch Pitching Index		Relief Runs		Adjusted Relief Runs		Relief Ranking		Total Pitcher Index		Total Baseball Ranking	
Parnell-Bos	119	Kinder-Bos	22.2	Kinder-Bos	26.9	Kinder-Bos	31.5	Parnell-Bos	4.1	Williams-Bos	4.5
Pierce-Chi	113	Aloma-Chi	17.7	Aloma-Chi	17.1	Aloma-Chi	15.0	Garver-StL	3.1	Parnell-Bos	4.1
Rogovin-Det-Chi	111	Brissie-Phi-Cle	7.5	Masterson-Bos	7.4	Harris-Was	4.3	Lopat-NY	3.0	Joost-Phi	3.9
Feller-Cle	109	Ostrowski-NY	6.7	Brissie-Phi-Cle	3.6	Masterson-Bos	3.9	Pierce-Chi	2.9	Doby-Cle	3.6
Raschi-NY	108	Masterson-Bos	5.2	Ostrowski-NY	3.6	Ostrowski-NY	3.8	Kinder-Bos	2.7	Fain-Phi	3.6

TEAM	G	W	L	PCT	GB	R	OR	AB	H	2B	3B	HR	BB	SO	AVG	OBP	SLG	PRO	PRO+	BR	/A	PF	CHI	RC	SB	CS	SBA	SBR
BRO	155	96	57	.627		**775**	603	5266	1380	199	32	**153**	**663**	699	.262	**.348**	**.399**	**.747**	113	107	98	101	100	**754**	90	49	**65**	-2
NY	154	92	62	.597	4.5	722	639	5229	1337	186	**56**	151	536	672	.256	.329	**.399**	.728	107	56	51	101	103	712	30	31	49	-10
STL	154	88	66	.571	8.5	677	630	5200	1386	**247**	54	97	537	**479**	**.267**	.340	.391	.731	110	68	67	100	95	708	33	32	51	-9
PHI	154	87	67	.565	9.5	657	**552**	5205	1353	237	45	93	540	534	.260	.332	.376	.708	104	26	33	99	98	671	60	41	59	-7
CHI	155	77	77	.500	19.5	628	631	5330	**1408**	223	45	107	422	712	.264	.321	.383	.704	101	5	-3	101	97	652	50	40	56	-9
CIN	154	69	85	.448	27.5	615	659	5234	1303	212	45	104	480	709	.249	.314	.366	.680	95	-36	-34	100	102	610	32	42	43	-16
BOS	155	64	89	.418	32	569	651	5221	1214	187	31	110	483	711	.233	.301	.343	.644	88	-102	-83	97	**106**	555	58	34	63	-3
PIT	155	42	112	.273	54.5	515	793	5193	1201	181	30	92	486	724	.231	.300	.331	.631	79	-125	-139	103	101	530	43	41	51	-12
TOT	618					5158		41878	10582	1672	338	907	4147	5240	.253	.323	.374	.697		396	310	56	-67					

TEAM	CG	SH	SV	IP	H	H/G	HR	BB	SO	RAT	ERA	ERA+	OAV	OOB	PR	/A	PF	CPI	FA	E	DP	FW	PW	BW	SBW	DIF
BRO	45	11	24	1399[1]	1295	8.3	121	544	**773**	12.0	3.53	103	.247	.321	31	17	98	103	**.982**	106	169	2.0	1.8	10.1	.7	4.9
NY	49	12	**31**	1371	1282	8.4	121	538	655	12.2	3.59	103	.248	.323	22	17	99	103	.974	158	175	-.8	1.8	5.3	-.2	8.9
STL	49	12	27	1361[1]	1274	8.4	119	501	712	11.9	3.66	101	.247	.317	11	8	100	98	.977	141	159	.1	.8	6.9	-.0	3.2
PHI	**80**	**17**	16	1386[2]	1306	8.5	**95**	373	609	11.0	**3.07**	**119**	.249	**.301**	102	90	98	104	.975	150	145	-.4	**9.3**	3.4	.1	-2.5
CHI	59	15	15	1386[1]	**1265**	**8.2**	101	534	661	11.9	3.58	107	**.240**	.314	23	41	103	94	.976	146	123	-.1	4.2	-.3	-.0	-3.8
CIN	56	11	12	1363[1]	1377	9.1	111	517	579	12.8	4.01	94	.267	.338	-43	-36	101	103	**.982**	107	145	1.9	-3.7	-3.5	-.8	-1.9
BOS	63	11	13	1396	1388	8.9	106	525	687	12.5	3.78	96	.259	.329	-7	-26	97	102	.975	154	143	-.5	-2.7	-8.6	.6	-1.3
PIT	43	5	8	1363[2]	1395	9.2	133	615	564	13.4	4.65	86	.265	.345	-139	-99	107	94	.970	182	167	-2.0	-10.2	-14.4	-.4	-8.0
TOT	444	94	146	11027[2]		8.6				12.2	3.73		.253	.323					.976	1144	1226					

Runs
Musial-StL 105
Hemus-StL 105
Robinson-Bro 104
Lockman-NY 99
Reese-Bro 94

Hits
Musial-StL 194
Schoendienst-StL .. 188
Adams-Cin 180
Dark-NY 177
Lockman-NY 176

Doubles
Musial-StL 42
Schoendienst-StL .. 40
McMillan-Cin 32
Sauer-Chi 31
Ashburn-Phi 31

Triples
Thomson-NY 14
Slaughter-StL 12
Kluszewski-Cin 11
Ennis-Phi 10

Home Runs
Sauer-Chi 37
Kiner-Pit 37
Hodges-Bro 32
Mathews-Bos 25
Gordon-Bos 25

Total Bases
Musial-StL 311
Sauer-Chi 301
Thomson-NY 293
Ennis-Phi 281
Snider-Bro 264

Runs Batted In
Sauer-Chi 121
Thomson-NY 108
Ennis-Phi 107
Hodges-Bro 102
Slaughter-StL 101

Runs Produced
Ennis-Phi 177
Musial-StL 175
Thomson-NY 173
Sauer-Chi 173
Slaughter-StL 163

Bases On Balls
Kiner-Pit 110
Hodges-Bro 107
Robinson-Bro 106
Musial-StL 96
Hemus-StL 96

Batting Average
Musial-StL .... .336
Baumholtz-Chi .... .325
Kluszewski-Cin .... .320
Robinson-Bro ..... .308
Snider-Bro .... .303

On Base Percentage
Robinson-Bro ..... .440
Musial-StL .... .432
Hemus-StL .... .392
Hodges-Bro .... .386
Slaughter-StL ..... .386

Slugging Average
Musial-StL .... .538
Sauer-Chi .... .531
Kluszewski-Cin .... .509
Kiner-Pit .... .500
Hodges-Bro .... .500

Production
Musial-StL .... .970
Robinson-Bro ..... .904
Kluszewski-Cin .... .892
Sauer-Chi .... .892
Hodges-Bro .... .886

Adjusted Production
Musial-StL 167
Robinson-Bro 149
Kluszewski-Cin 146
Gordon-Bos 144
Sauer-Chi 143

Batter Runs
Musial-StL 55.7
Robinson-Bro 41.9
Sauer-Chi 32.8
Kiner-Pit 32.7
Hodges-Bro 32.4

Adjusted Batter Runs
Musial-StL 55.6
Robinson-Bro 40.7
Gordon-Bos 31.8
Sauer-Chi 31.5
Hodges-Bro 31.3

Clutch Hitting Index
Slaughter-StL 138
Hatton-Cin 129
Campanella-Bro ... 128
Sauer-Chi 115
Wyrostek-Cin-Phi .. 112

Runs Created
Musial-StL 141
Robinson-Bro 116
Sauer-Chi 111
Kiner-Pit 111
Hodges-Bro 106

Total Average
Musial-StL 1.017
Robinson-Bro ..... .995
Kiner-Pit .... .955
Hodges-Bro .... .921
Sauer-Chi .... .886

Stolen Bases
Reese-Bro 30
Jethroe-Bos 28
Robinson-Bro 24
Ashburn-Phi 16

Stolen Base Average
Reese-Bro 85.7
Robinson-Bro 77.4
Jethroe-Bos 75.7
Ashburn-Phi 59.3

Stolen Base Runs
Reese-Bro 6.0
Robinson-Bro 3.0
Jethroe-Bos 3.0
Davis-Pit 1.5
Slaughter-StL 1.2

Fielding Runs
Schoendienst-StL . 32.9
Logan-Bos 17.6
Sauer-Chi 16.6
Ashburn-Phi 15.1
McMillan-Cin 10.6

Total Player Rating
Robinson-Bro 5.6
Schoendienst-StL . 4.9
Sauer-Chi 4.2
Musial-StL 4.2
Hemus-StL 3.8

Wins
Roberts-Phi 28
Maglie-NY 18
Staley-StL 17
Rush-Chi 17
Raffensberger-Cin . 17

Win Percentage
Wilhelm-NY ...... .833
Roberts-Phi .... .800
Black-Bro .... .789
Maglie-NY .... .692
Hacker-Chi .... .625

Games
Wilhelm-NY 71
Dickson-Pit 56
Yuhas-StL 54
Smith-Cin 53
Main-Pit 48

Complete Games
Roberts-Phi 30
Dickson-Pit 21
Spahn-Bos 19
Raffensberger-Cin . 18
Rush-Chi 17

Shutouts
Simmons-Phi 6
Raffensberger-Cin . 6

Saves
Brazle-StL 16
Black-Bro 15
Wilhelm-NY 11
Leonard-Chi 11

Innings Pitched
Roberts-Phi 330.0
Spahn-Bos 290.0
Dickson-Pit 277.2
Rush-Chi 250.1
Raffensberger-Cin . 247.0

Fewest Hits/Game
Hacker-Chi 7.01
Wilhelm-NY 7.17
Erskine-Bro 7.27
Rush-Chi 7.37
Loes-Bro 7.40

Fewest BB/Game
Roberts-Phi 1.23
Hacker-Chi 1.51
Raffensberger-Cin . 1.64
Staley-StL 1.95
Drews-Phi 2.05

Strikeouts
Spahn-Bos 183
Rush-Chi 157
Roberts-Phi 148
Mizell-StL 146
Simmons-Phi 141

Strikeouts/Game
Mizell-StL 6.92
Simmons-Phi 6.30
Wilhelm-NY 6.10
Wade-Bro 5.90
Erskine-Bro 5.70

Ratio
Hacker-Chi 8.56
Roberts-Phi 9.33
Erskine-Bro 10.45
Rush-Chi 10.50
Drews-Phi 10.59

Earned Run Average
Wilhelm-NY 2.43
Hacker-Chi 2.58
Roberts-Phi 2.59
Loes-Bro 2.69
Rush-Chi 2.70

Adjusted ERA
Wilhelm-NY 152
Hacker-Chi 149
Rush-Chi 143
Roberts-Phi 141
Loes-Bro 135

Opponents' Batting Avg.
Hacker-Chi .... .212
Rush-Chi .... .216
Wilhelm-NY ...... .220
Erskine-Bro .... .220
Loes-Bro .... .224

Opponents' On Base Pct.
Hacker-Chi .... .247
Roberts-Phi .... .263
Rush-Chi .... .282
Erskine-Bro .... .289
Spahn-Bos .... .291

Starter Runs
Roberts-Phi 41.8
Rush-Chi 28.8
Drews-Phi 25.8
Raffensberger-Cin . 25.4
Spahn-Bos 24.3

Adjusted Starter Runs
Roberts-Phi 39.0
Rush-Chi 32.1
Raffensberger-Cin . 26.6
Hacker-Chi 26.2
Drews-Phi 23.8

Clutch Pitching Index
Roe-Bro 127
Church-Phi-Cin ... 119
Wilhelm-NY 119
Raffensberger-Cin . 117
Maglie-NY 116

Relief Runs
Black-Bro 25.0
Wilhelm-NY 23.1
Brazle-StL 12.3
Leonard-Chi 11.6
Yuhas-StL 11.2

Adjusted Relief Runs
Black-Bro 23.5
Wilhelm-NY 22.5
Leonard-Chi 12.5
Brazle-StL 12.1
Yuhas-StL 11.0

Relief Ranking
Black-Bro 33.9
Wilhelm-NY 26.4
Brazle-StL 20.9
Yuhas-StL 15.4
Leonard-Chi 11.4

Total Pitcher Index
Rush-Chi 5.0
Roberts-Phi 4.0
Black-Bro 3.3
Wilhelm-NY 2.9
Drews-Phi 2.8

Total Baseball Ranking
Robinson-Bro 5.6
Rush-Chi 5.0
Schoendienst-StL . 4.9
Sauer-Chi 4.2
Musial-StL 4.2

TEAM	G	W	L	PCT	GB	R	OR	AB	H	2B	3B	HR	BB	SO	AVG	OBP	SLG	PRO	PRO+	BR	/A	PF	CHI	RC	SB	CS	SBA	SBR
NY	154	95	59	.617		727	557	5294	1411	221	56	129	566	652	.267	.341	.403	.744	121	89	134	94	99	758	52	42	55	-10
CLE	155	93	61	.604	2	763	606	5330	1399	211	49	148	626	749	.262	.342	.404	.746	122	95	144	94	102	759	46	39	54	-10
CHI	156	81	73	.526	14	610	568	5316	1337	199	38	80	541	521	.252	.327	.348	.675	93	-35	-40	101	99	633	61	38	62	-5
PHI	155	79	75	.513	16	664	723	5163	1305	212	35	89	683	561	.253	.343	.359	.702	96	26	-16	106	99	659	52	43	55	-10
WAS	157	78	76	.506	17	598	608	5357	1282	225	44	50	580	607	.239	.317	.326	.643	88	-98	-79	97	107	572	48	37	56	-8
BOS	154	76	78	.494	19	668	658	5246	1338	233	34	113	542	739	.255	.328	.377	.705	96	14	-37	108	103	659	59	47	56	-11
STL	155	64	90	.416	31	604	733	5353	1340	225	46	82	540	720	.250	.322	.356	.678	92	-39	-56	103	99	631	30	34	47	-11
DET	156	50	104	.325	45	557	738	5258	1278	190	37	103	553	605	.243	.318	.352	.670	92	-52	-57	101	95	594	27	38	42	-15
TOT	621					5191		42317	10690	1716	339	794	4631	5154	.253	.330	.365	.695							375	318	54	-78

TEAM	CG	SH	SV	IP	H	H/G	HR	BB	SO	RAT	ERA	ERA+	OAV	OOB	PR	/A	PF	CPI	FA	E	DP	FW	PW	BW	SBW	DIF
NY	72	21	27	1381	1240	8.1	94	581	666	12.1	3.14	106	.243	.324	82	28	90	110	.979	127	199	.8	2.9	13.9	-.0	.5
CLE	80	19	18	1407	1278	8.2	94	556	671	11.9	3.32	101	.241	.316	55	4	91	99	.975	155	141	-.8	.4	14.9	-.0	1.5
CHI	53	15	28	1416²	1251	7.9	86	578	774	11.7	3.25	112	.238	.316	66	62	99	98	.980	123	158	1.1	6.4	-4.2	.5	.1
PHI	73	11	16	1384¹	1402	9.1	113	526	562	12.8	4.15	95	.263	.333	-74	-30	108	94	.977	140	148	.0	-3.1	-1.7	-.0	6.7
WAS	75	10	15	1429²	1405	8.8	78	577	574	12.7	3.37	105	.258	.332	48	29	97	108	.978	132	152	.6	3.0	-8.2	.2	5.4
BOS	53	7	24	1372¹	1332	8.7	107	623	624	13.1	3.80	104	.256	.340	-20	21	107	104	.976	145	181	-.3	2.2	-3.8	-.1	1.1
STL	48	6	18	1399	1388	8.9	111	598	581	13.0	4.12	95	.260	.339	-69	-32	107	97	.974	155	155	-.8	-3.3	-5.8	-.1	-2.9
DET	51	10	14	1388¹	1394	9.0	111	591	702	13.0	4.25	90	.262	.338	-89	-69	104	94	.975	152	145	-.6	-7.2	-5.9	-.5	-12.8
TOT	505	99	160	11178¹		8.6				12.5	3.67		.253	.330					.977	1129	1300					

Runs
Doby-Cle 104
Avila-Cle 102
Rosen-Cle 101
Berra-NY 97
Minoso-Chi 96

Hits
Fox-Chi 192
Avila-Cle 179
Robinson-Chi 176
Fain-Phi 176

Doubles
Fain-Phi 43
Mantle-NY 37
Vernon-Was 33
Robinson-Chi 33

Triples
Avila-Cle 11
Simpson-Cle 10
Rizzuto-NY 10
Fox-Chi 10

Home Runs
Doby-Cle 32
Easter-Cle 31
Berra-NY 30
Dropo-Bos-Det 29
Zernial-Phi 29

Total Bases
Rosen-Cle 297
Mantle-NY 291
Dropo-Bos-Det ... 282
Doby-Cle 281
Robinson-Chi 277

Runs Batted In
Rosen-Cle 105
Robinson-Chi 104
Doby-Cle 104
Zernial-Phi 100
Berra-NY 98

Runs Produced
Rosen-Cle 178
Doby-Cle 176
Berra-NY 165
Robinson-Chi 161
Mantle-NY 158

Bases On Balls
Yost-Was 129
Joost-Phi 122
Fain-Phi 105
Valo-Phi 101
Doby-Cle 90

Batting Average
Fain-Phi 327
Mitchell-Cle 323
Mantle-NY 311
Kell-Det-Bos 311
Woodling-NY 309

On Base Percentage
Fain-Phi 438
Valo-Phi 432
Mantle-NY 394
Joost-Phi 388
Rosen-Cle 387

Slugging Average
Doby-Cle 541
Mantle-NY 530
Rosen-Cle 524
Easter-Cle 513
Wertz-Det-StL 506

Production
Mantle-NY 924
Doby-Cle 924
Rosen-Cle 911
Wertz-Det-StL 887
Fain-Phi 867

Adjusted Production
Doby-Cle 166
Mantle-NY 166
Rosen-Cle 162
Easter-Cle 144
Wertz-Det-StL 143

Batter Runs
Mantle-NY 40.3
Rosen-Cle 38.6
Doby-Cle 37.9
Fain-Phi 36.3
Robinson-Chi 28.3

Adjusted Batter Runs
Mantle-NY 46.9
Rosen-Cle 45.8
Doby-Cle 44.8
Fain-Phi 29.8
Woodling-NY 28.2

Clutch Hitting Index
Runnels-Was 120
Philley-Phi 116
McDougald-NY 115
Easter-Cle 110
Joost-Phi 107

Runs Created
Mantle-NY 123
Doby-Cle 116
Rosen-Cle 115
Robinson-Chi 113
Fain-Phi 107

Total Average
Doby-Cle 974
Mantle-NY 961
Wertz-Det-StL 912
Rosen-Cle 900
Valo-Phi 873

Stolen Bases
Minoso-Chi 22
Rivera-StL-Chi 21
Jensen-NY-Was 18
Rizzuto-NY 17
Throneberry-Bos 16

Stolen Base Average
Jensen-NY-Was ... 75.0
Rizzuto-NY 73.9
Rivera-StL-Chi 70.0
Throneberry-Bos ... 69.6
Minoso-Chi 57.9

Stolen Base Runs
Jensen-NY-Was 1.8
Rizzuto-NY 1.5
Michaels-Ws-SL-Phi ...1.2
Porter-StL 1.2
Goodman-Bos 1.2

Fielding Runs
Goodman-Bos 20.1
Rizzuto-NY 18.9
Martin-NY 18.3
Hatfield-Bos-Det ... 17.8
Fain-Phi 16.0

Total Player Rating
Doby-Cle 5.1
Mantle-NY 4.6
Fain-Phi 3.9
Berra-NY 3.5
Goodman-Bos 3.0

Wins
Shantz-Phi 24
Wynn-Cle 23
Lemon-Cle 22
Garcia-Cle 22
Reynolds-NY 20

Win Percentage
Shantz-Phi 774
Raschi-NY 727
Reynolds-NY 714
Lemon-Cle 667
Garcia-Cle 667

Games
Kennedy-Chi 47
Paige-StL 46
Garcia-Cle 46
Hooper-Phi 43

Complete Games
Lemon-Cle 28
Shantz-Phi 27
Reynolds-NY 24
Wynn-Cle 19
Garcia-Cle 19

Shutouts
Reynolds-NY 6
Garcia-Cle 6
Shantz-Phi 5
Lemon-Cle 5

Saves
Dorish-Chi 11
Paige-StL 10
Sain-NY 7

Innings Pitched
Lemon-Cle 309.2
Garcia-Cle 292.1
Wynn-Cle 285.2
Shantz-Phi 279.2
Pierce-Chi 255.1

Fewest Hits/Game
Lemon-Cle 6.86
Raschi-NY 7.02
Reynolds-NY 7.15
Dobson-Chi 7.36
Shantz-Phi 7.40

Fewest BB/Game
Shantz-Phi 2.03
Pillette-StL 2.41
Marrero-Was 2.59
Houtteman-Det 2.65
Garcia-Cle 2.68

Strikeouts
Reynolds-NY 160
Wynn-Cle 153
Shantz-Phi 152
Pierce-Chi 144
Garcia-Cle 143

Strikeouts/Game
McDermott-Bos ... 6.50
Reynolds-NY 5.89
Trucks-Det 5.89
Gray-Det 5.54
Grissom-Chi 5.26

Ratio
Shantz-Phi 9.56
Dobson-Chi 10.05
Lemon-Cle 10.09
Pierce-Chi 10.43
Raschi-NY 10.94

Earned Run Average
Reynolds-NY 2.06
Garcia-Cle 2.37
Shantz-Phi 2.48
Lemon-Cle 2.50
Dobson-Chi 2.51

Adjusted ERA
Reynolds-NY 161
Shantz-Phi 160
Dobson-Chi 145
Pierce-Chi 142
Garcia-Cle 141

Opponents' Batting Avg.
Lemon-Cle .... .208
Raschi-NY .... .216
Reynolds-NY .... .218
Dobson-Chi .... .222
Shantz-Phi .... .225

Opponents' On Base Pct.
Shantz-Phi 272
Lemon-Cle 279
Dobson-Chi 280
Pierce-Chi 289
Reynolds-NY 300

Starter Runs
Reynolds-NY 43.8
Garcia-Cle 42.4
Lemon-Cle 40.4
Shantz-Phi 37.2
Pierce-Chi 31.3

Adjusted Starter Runs
Shantz-Phi 46.0
Reynolds-NY 34.2
Garcia-Cle 31.6
Pierce-Chi 30.5
Lemon-Cle 29.1

Clutch Pitching Index
Garcia-Cle 127
Byrd-Phi 126
Reynolds-NY 125
Porterfield-Was ... 120
Hudson-Was-Bos 117

Relief Runs
Dorish-Chi 12.2
Kennedy-Chi 6.9
Consuegra-Was 5.1
Brissie-Cle 1.8
Littlefield-Det-SL ... 1.4

Adjusted Relief Runs
Dorish-Chi 11.9
Kennedy-Chi 6.7
Consuegra-Was 4.1
Littlefield-Det-SL ... 3.3
White-Det 8

Relief Ranking
Dorish-Chi 17.4
Kennedy-Chi 4.4
Consuegra-Was 3.6
Littlefield-Det-SL ... 2.6
White-Det 1.1

Total Pitcher Index
Shantz-Phi 5.5
Lemon-Cle 4.6
Reynolds-NY 3.9
Garcia-Cle 3.6
Pierce-Chi 3.2

Total Baseball Ranking
Shantz-Phi 5.5
Doby-Cle 5.1
Mantle-NY 4.6
Lemon-Cle 4.6
Fain-Phi 3.9

TEAM	G	W	L	PCT	GB	R	OR	AB	H	2B	3B	HR	BB	SO	AVG	OBP	SLG	PRO	PRO+	BR	/A	PF	CHI	RC	SB	CS	SBA	SBR
BRO	155	105	49	.682		955	689	5373	1529	274	59	208	655	686	.285	.366	.474	.840	121	188	167	102	101	963	90	47	66	-1
MIL	157	92	62	.597	13	738	589	5349	1422	227	52	156	439	637	.266	.325	.415	.740	104	-22	22	94	104	727	46	27	63	-2
STL	157	83	71	.539	22	768	713	5397	1474	281	56	140	574	617	.273	.347	.424	.771	107	53	54	100	95	806	18	22	45	-8
PHI	156	83	71	.539	22	716	666	5290	1400	228	62	115	530	597	.265	.335	.396	.731	97	-25	-21	99	101	727	42	21	67	0
NY	155	70	84	.455	35	768	747	5362	1452	195	45	176	499	608	.271	.336	.422	.758	101	20	6	102	101	771	31	21	60	-3
CIN	155	68	86	.442	37	714	788	5343	1396	190	34	166	485	701	.261	.325	.403	.728	94	-42	-47	101	103	711	25	20	56	-5
CHI	155	65	89	.422	40	633	835	5272	1372	204	57	137	514	746	.260	.328	.399	.727	93	-41	-56	102	92	697	49	21	70	2
PIT	154	50	104	.325	55	622	887	5253	1297	178	49	99	524	715	.247	.319	.356	.675	82	-130	-126	99	103	614	41	39	51	-11
TOT	622					5914		42639	11342	1777	414	1197	4220	5307	.266	.335	.411	.747							342	218	61	-28

TEAM	CG	SH	SV	IP	H	H/G	HR	BB	SO	RAT	ERA	ERA+	OAV	OOB	PR	/A	PF	CPI	FA	E	DP	FW	PW	BW	SBW	DIF
BRO	51	11	29	1380²	1337	8.7	169	509	817	12.1	4.10	104	.253	.320	29	25	99	97	.980	118	161	1.7	2.4	16.1	.2	7.6
MIL	72	14	15	1387	1282	8.3	107	539	738	12.0	3.30	119	.245	.318	153	96	92	106	.976	143	169	.4	9.2	2.1	.1	3.1
STL	51	11	36	1386²	1406	9.1	139	533	732	12.9	4.23	101	.262	.333	9	5	99	98	.977	138	161	.7	.5	5.2	-.4	.0
PHI	76	13	15	1369²	1410	9.3	138	410	637	12.1	3.80	111	.265	.320	74	62	98	104	.975	147	161	.0	6.0	-2.0	.3	1.6
NY	46	10	20	1365²	1403	9.2	146	610	647	13.4	4.25	101	.264	.343	5	6	100	103	.975	151	151	-.2	.6	.6	.0	-8.0
CIN	47	7	15	1365	1484	9.8	179	488	506	13.2	4.64	94	.279	.343	-53	-43	102	102	.978	129	176	1.1	-4.1	-4.5	-.1	-1.2
CHI	38	3	22	1359	1491	9.9	151	554	623	13.8	4.79	93	.276	.347	-76	-51	104	97	.967	193	141	-2.5	-4.9	-5.4	.5	.3
PIT	49	4	10	1358	1529	10.1	168	577	607	14.1	5.22	86	.285	.356	-141	-113	104	96	.973	163	139	-.9	-10.9	-12.1	-.7	-2.4
TOT	430	73	162	10971²		9.3				12.9	4.29		.266	.335					.975	1182	1259					

Runs
Snider-Bro 132
Musial-StL 127
Dark-NY 126
Gilliam-Bro 125

Hits
Ashburn-Phi 205
Musial-StL 200
Snider-Bro 198
Dark-NY 194
Schoendienst-StL ... 193

Doubles
Musial-StL 53
Dark-NY 41
Snider-Bro 38
Furillo-Bro 38
Bell-Cin 37

Triples
Gilliam-Bro 17
Bruton-Mil 14
Hemus-StL 11
Fondy-Chi 11

Home Runs
Mathews-Mil 47
Snider-Bro 42
Campanella-Bro 41
Kluszewski-Cin 40
Kiner-Pit-Chi 35

Total Bases
Snider-Bro 370
Mathews-Mil 363
Musial-StL 361
Kluszewski-Cin 325
Bell-Cin 320

Runs Batted In
Campanella-Bro 142
Mathews-Mil 135
Snider-Bro 126
Ennis-Phi 125
Hodges-Bro 122

Runs Produced
Snider-Bro 216
Musial-StL 210
Campanella-Bro ... 204
Mathews-Mil 198

Bases On Balls
Musial-StL 105
Kiner-Pit-Chi 100
Gilliam-Bro 100
Mathews-Mil 99
Hemus-StL 86

Batting Average
Furillo-Bro .... .344
Schoendienst-StL .... .342
Musial-StL .... .337
Snider-Bro .... .336
Mueller-NY .... .333

On Base Percentage
Musial-StL .... .437
Robinson-Bro .... .425
Snider-Bro .... .419
Irvin-NY .... .406
Mathews-Mil .... .406

Slugging Average
Snider-Bro .... .627
Mathews-Mil .... .627
Campanella-Bro ... .611
Musial-StL .... .609
Furillo-Bro .... .580

Production
Snider-Bro 1.046
Musial-StL 1.046
Mathews-Mil 1.033
Campanella-Bro .. 1.006
Furillo-Bro .... .973

Adjusted Production
Mathews-Mil 175
Musial-StL 169
Snider-Bro 165
Campanella-Bro ... 154
Furillo-Bro 146

Batter Runs
Musial-StL 62.7
Snider-Bro 59.3
Mathews-Mil 54.9
Campanella-Bro ... 42.9
Kluszewski-Cin ... 35.0

Adjusted Batter Runs
Mathews-Mil 63.8
Musial-StL 62.9
Snider-Bro 56.2
Campanella-Bro ... 40.4
Kluszewski-Cin ... 34.2

Clutch Hitting Index
Slaughter-StL 142
Jablonski-StL 128
Robinson-Bro 125
Ennis-Phi 121
Campanella-Bro ... 119

Runs Created
Musial-StL 166
Snider-Bro 161
Mathews-Mil 157
Campanella-Bro ... 128
Kluszewski-Cin ... 126

Total Average
Musial-StL 1.143
Snider-Bro 1.134
Mathews-Mil 1.119
Campanella-Bro .. 1.048
Robinson-Bro .... .988

Stolen Bases
Bruton-Mil 26
Reese-Bro 22
Gilliam-Bro 21
Robinson-Bro 17
Snider-Bro 16

Stolen Base Average
Robinson-Bro 81.0
Reese-Bro 78.6
Bruton-Mil 70.3
Snider-Bro 69.6
Gilliam-Bro 60.0

Stolen Base Runs
Reese-Bro 3.0
Robinson-Bro 2.7
Torgeson-Phi 1.5
Miksis-Chi 1.5
Jeffcoat-Chi 1.5

Fielding Runs
Ashburn-Phi 25.7
Schoendienst-StL .. 25.3
Logan-Mil 20.6
Crandall-Mil 14.8
Bell-Cin 13.7

Total Player Rating
Schoendienst-StL .. 5.8
Mathews-Mil 5.8
Campanella-Bro ... 4.7
Snider-Bro 4.6
Musial-StL 4.4

Wins
Spahn-Mil 23
Roberts-Phi 23
Haddix-StL 20
Erskine-Bro 20
Staley-StL 18

Win Percentage
Erskine-Bro .... .769
Spahn-Mil .... .767
Meyer-Bro .... .750
Burdette-Mil .... .750
Haddix-StL .... .690

Games
Wilhelm-NY 68
Spahn-Mil 60
Hetki-Pit 54
Smith-Cin 50

Complete Games
Roberts-Phi 33
Spahn-Mil 24
Simmons-Phi 19
Haddix-StL 19
Erskine-Bro 16

Shutouts
Haddix-StL 6
Spahn-Mil 5
Roberts-Phi 5
Simmons-Phi 4
Erskine-Bro 4

Saves
Brazle-StL 18
Wilhelm-NY 15
Hughes-Bro 9
Leonard-Chi 8
Burdette-Mil 8

Innings Pitched
Roberts-Phi 346.2
Spahn-Mil 265.2
Haddix-StL 253.0
Erskine-Bro 246.2
Simmons-Phi 238.0

Fewest Hits/Game
Spahn-Mil 7.15
Gomez-NY 7.32
Mizell-StL 7.74
Erskine-Bro 7.77
Haddix-StL 7.83

Fewest BB/Game
Roberts-Phi 1.58
Raffensberger-Cin . 1.71
Minner-Chi 1.79
Staley-StL 2.11
Hacker-Chi 2.19

Strikeouts
Roberts-Phi 198
Erskine-Bro 187
Mizell-StL 173
Haddix-StL 163
Spahn-Mil 148

Strikeouts/Game
Mizell-StL 6.94
Erskine-Bro 6.82
Antonelli-Mil 6.72
Klippstein-Chi 6.07
Haddix-StL 5.80

Ratio
Spahn-Mil 9.55
Roberts-Phi 10.05
Haddix-StL 10.42
Simmons-Phi 11.19
Erskine-Bro 11.35

Earned Run Average
Spahn-Mil 2.10
Roberts-Phi 2.75
Haddix-StL 3.06
Antonelli-Mil 3.18
Simmons-Phi 3.21

Adjusted ERA
Spahn-Mil 187
Roberts-Phi 153
Haddix-StL 139
Simmons-Phi 131
Gomez-NY 126

Opponents' Batting Avg.
Spahn-Mil .... .217
Gomez-NY .... .218
Mizell-StL .... .227
Erskine-Bro .... .230
Haddix-StL .... .232

Opponents' On Base Pct.
Spahn-Mil .... .270
Roberts-Phi .... .276
Haddix-StL .... .287
Hacker-Chi .... .299
Simmons-Phi .... .302

Starter Runs
Spahn-Mil 64.5
Roberts-Phi 59.1
Haddix-StL 34.5
Simmons-Phi 28.3
Buhl-Mil 22.5

Adjusted Starter Runs
Roberts-Phi 56.1
Spahn-Mil 53.8
Haddix-StL 33.6
Simmons-Phi 26.3
Gomez-NY 20.2

Clutch Pitching Index
Raffensberger-Cin . 115
Dickson-Pit 112
Drews-Phi 112
Burdette-Mil 110
Roe-Bro 108

Relief Runs
Wilhelm-NY 20.1
Labine-Bro 18.5
Johnson-Mil 14.6
White-StL 12.3
Hughes-Bro 7.8

Adjusted Relief Runs
Wilhelm-NY 20.1
Labine-Bro 18.2
White-StL 12.0
Johnson-Mil 11.3
Hughes-Bro 7.6

Relief Ranking
Labine-Bro 27.9
Wilhelm-NY 23.4
White-StL 16.3
Johnson-Mil 8.8
Hughes-Bro 7.3

Total Pitcher Index
Spahn-Mil 6.6
Roberts-Phi 6.1
Haddix-StL 4.7
Labine-Bro 2.7
Simmons-Phi 2.4

Total Baseball Ranking
Spahn-Mil 6.6
Roberts-Phi 6.1
Schoendienst-StL .. 5.8
Mathews-Mil 5.8
Haddix-StL 4.7

TEAM	G	W	L	PCT	GB	R	OR	AB	H	2B	3B	HR	BB	SO	AVG	OBP	SLG	PRO	PRO+	BR	/A	PF	CHI	RC	SB	CS	SBA	SBR
NY	151	99	52	.656		801	547	5194	1420	226	52	139	656	644	.273	.359	.417	.776	120	113	141	97	100	809	34	44	44	-16
CLE	155	92	62	.597	8.5	770	627	5285	1426	201	29	160	609	683	.270	.349	.410	.759	114	77	98	97	100	780	33	29	53	-8
CHI	156	89	65	.578	11.5	716	592	5212	1345	226	53	74	601	530	.258	.341	.364	.705	93	-17	-37	103	106	666	73	55	57	-11
BOS	153	84	69	.549	16	656	632	5246	1385	255	37	101	496	601	.264	.332	.384	.716	94	-10	-45	105	98	683	33	45	42	-17
WAS	152	76	76	.500	23.5	687	614	5149	1354	230	53	69	596	604	.263	.343	.368	.711	100	-6	10	98	103	675	65	36	64	-2
DET	158	60	94	.390	40.5	695	923	5553	1479	259	44	108	506	603	.266	.331	.387	.718	100	-10	-2	99	99	716	30	35	46	-12
PHI	157	59	95	.383	41.5	632	799	5455	1398	205	38	116	498	602	.256	.321	.372	.693	89	-61	-85	104	100	658	41	24	63	-2
STL	154	54	100	.351	46.5	555	778	5264	1310	214	25	112	507	644	.249	.317	.363	.680	87	-83	-94	102	93	606	17	34	33	-15
TOT	618					5512		42358	11117	1816	331	879	4469	4911	.262	.336	.383	.720							326	302	52	-83

TEAM	CG	SH	SV	IP	H	H/G	HR	BB	SO	RAT	ERA	ERA+	OAV	OOB	PR	/A	PF	CPI	FA	E	DP	FW	PW	BW	SBW	DIF
NY	50	18	39	1358¹	1286	8.5	94	500	604	12.1	3.20	115	.251	.321	120	74	92	110	.979	126	182	.3	7.4	14.1	-.6	2.2
CLE	81	11	15	1373	1311	8.6	92	519	586	12.2	3.64	103	.253	.325	53	.16	94	99	.979	127	197	.4	1.6	9.8	.2	2.9
CHI	57	17	33	1403²	1299	8.3	113	583	714	12.2	3.41	118	.246	.324	91	95	101	105	.980	125	144	.6	9.5	-3.7	-.0	5.7
BOS	41	15	37	1373	1333	8.7	92	584	642	12.7	3.58	118	.254	.331	63	96	105	104	.975	148	173	-.9	9.6	-4.5	-.7	3.9
WAS	76	16	10	1344²	1313	8.8	112	478	515	12.2	3.66	106	.258	.324	50	35	98	103	.979	120	173	.7	3.5	1.0	.8	-6.0
DET	50	2	16	1415	1633	10.4	154	585	645	14.4	5.25	77	.291	.363	-198	-187	102	96	.978	135	149	.1	-18.7	-.2	-.2	2.0
PHI	51	7	11	1409	1475	9.4	121	594	566	13.6	4.67	92	.271	.349	-106	-60	107	93	.977	137	161	-.0	-6.0	-8.5	.8	-4.3
STL	28	10	24	1383²	1467	9.5	101	626	639	13.8	4.48	94	.273	.351	-74	-43	105	97	.974	152	165	-1.0	-4.3	-9.4	-.5	-7.8
TOT	434	96	185	11060¹		9.0				12.9	3.99		.262	.336					.978	1070	1344					

Runs		Hits		Doubles		Triples		Home Runs		Total Bases	
Rosen-Cle	115	Kuenn-Det	209	Vernon-Was	43	Rivera-Chi	16	Rosen-Cle	43	Rosen-Cle	367
Yost-Was	107	Vernon-Was	205	Kell-Bos	41	Vernon-Was	11	Zernial-Phi	42	Vernon-Was	315
Mantle-NY	105	Rosen-Cle	201	White-Bos	34	Piersall-Bos	9	Doby-Cle	29	Zernial-Phi	311
Minoso-Chi	104	Philley-Phi	188	Kuenn-Det	33	Philley-Phi	9	Berra-NY	27	Philley-Phi	263
Vernon-Was	101	Busby-Was	183	Goodman-Bos	33			Boone-Cle-Det	26	Berra-NY	263

Runs Batted In		Runs Produced		Bases On Balls		Batting Average		On Base Percentage		Slugging Average	
Rosen-Cle	145	Rosen-Cle	217	Yost-Was	123	Vernon-Was	.337	Woodling-NY	.429	Rosen-Cle	.613
Vernon-Was	115	Vernon-Was	201	Fain-Chi	108	Rosen-Cle	.336	Rosen-Cle	.422	Zernial-Phi	.559
Boone-Cle-Det	114	Minoso-Chi	193	Doby-Cle	96	Goodman-Bos	.313	Minoso-Chi	.410	Berra-NY	.523
Zernial-Phi	108	Boone-Cle-Det	182	Gernert-Bos	88	Minoso-Chi	.313	Fain-Chi	.405	Boone-Cle-Det	.519
Berra-NY	108	Mantle-NY	176	Rosen-Cle	85	Busby-Was	.312	Yost-Was	.403	Vernon-Was	.518

Production		Adjusted Production		Batter Runs		Adjusted Batter Runs		Clutch Hitting Index		Runs Created	
Rosen-Cle	1.034	Rosen-Cle	181	Rosen-Cle	63.3	Rosen-Cle	67.2	Rizzuto-NY	128	Rosen-Cle	155
Vernon-Was	.921	Vernon-Was	151	Vernon-Was	39.7	Vernon-Was	42.5	Dropo-Det	122	Vernon-Was	127
Zernial-Phi	.914	Boone-Cle-Det	146	Minoso-Chi	30.6	Boone-Cle-Det	32.0	Fox-Chi	120	Zernial-Phi	113
Boone-Cle-Det	.909	Mantle-NY	145	Boone-Cle-Det	30.5	Mantle-NY	30.4	Vernon-Was	119	Boone-Cle-Det	106
Mantle-NY	.895	Berra-NY	142	Zernial-Phi	30.4	Woodling-NY	30.1	Robinson-Phi	118	Minoso-Chi	106

Total Average		Stolen Bases		Stolen Base Average		Stolen Base Runs		Fielding Runs		Total Player Rating	
Rosen-Cle	1.078	Minoso-Chi	25	Jensen-Was	69.2	Michaels-Phi	2.1	Busby-Was	18.9	Rosen-Cle	6.2
Mantle-NY	.943	Rivera-Chi	22	Minoso-Chi	61.0	Coan-Was	2.1	Groth-StL	17.1	Zernial-Phi	3.5
Boone-Cle-Det	.925	Jensen-Was	18	Rivera-Chi	59.5	Zernial-Phi	1.2	Piersall-Bos	16.1	Berra-NY	3.4
Zernial-Phi	.917	Philley-Phi	13			Souchock-Det	.9	Strickland-Cle	15.6	Boone-Cle-Det	3.2
Doby-Cle	.912	Busby-Was	13			Philley-Phi	.9	Hunter-StL	14.6	Vernon-Was	3.1

Wins		Win Percentage		Games		Complete Games		Shutouts		Saves	
Porterfield-Was	22	Lopat-NY	.800	Kinder-Bos	69	Porterfield-Was	24	Porterfield-Was	9	Kinder-Bos	27
Parnell-Bos	21	Ford-NY	.750	Stuart-StL	60	B.Lemon-Cle	23	Pierce-Chi	7	Dorish-Chi	18
B.Lemon-Cle	21	Parnell-Bos	.724	Martin-Phi	58	Garcia-Cle	21	Trucks-StL-Chi	5	Reynolds-NY	13
Trucks-StL-Chi	20	Porterfield-Was	.688	Paige-StL	57	Pierce-Chi	19	Parnell-Bos	5	Paige-StL	11
				Dorish-Chi	55	Trucks-StL-Chi	17	B.Lemon-Cle	5	Sain-NY	9

Innings Pitched		Fewest Hits/Game		Fewest BB/Game		Strikeouts		Strikeouts/Game		Ratio	
B.Lemon-Cle	286.2	Pierce-Chi	7.16	Lopat-NY	1.61	Pierce-Chi	186	Pierce-Chi	6.17	Raschi-NY	10.24
Garcia-Cle	271.2	McDermott-Bos	7.37	Sain-NY	2.14	Trucks-StL-Chi	149	Gray-Det	5.88	Lopat-NY	10.35
Pierce-Chi	271.1	Raschi-NY	7.46	A.Kellner-Phi	2.28	Wynn-Cle	138	Masterson-Was	5.14	Pierce-Chi	10.65
Trucks-StL-Chi	264.1	Masterson-Was	7.85	Porterfield-Was	2.58	Parnell-Bos	136	Parnell-Bos	5.08	Porterfield-Was	11.19
Porterfield-Was	255.0	Trucks-StL-Chi	7.97	Hoeft-Det	2.64	Garcia-Cle	134	Trucks-StL-Chi	5.07	Sain-NY	11.29

Earned Run Average		Adjusted ERA		Opponents' Batting Avg.		Opponents' On Base Pct.		Starter Runs		Adjusted Starter Runs	
Lopat-NY	2.42	Lopat-NY	152	Pierce-Chi	.218	Raschi-NY	.283	Pierce-Chi	38.4	Pierce-Chi	39.3
Pierce-Chi	2.72	Pierce-Chi	148	McDermott-Bos	.224	Lopat-NY	.288	Trucks-StL-Chi	31.3	Trucks-StL-Chi	33.9
Trucks-StL-Chi	2.93	McDermott-Bos	140	Raschi-NY	.224	Pierce-Chi	.292	Lopat-NY	31.2	Parnell-Bos	30.6
Sain-NY	3.00	Trucks-StL-Chi	139	Masterson-Was	.232	Masterson-Was	.304	Parnell-Bos	25.0	McDermott-Bos	27.4
Ford-NY	3.00	Parnell-Bos	137	Trucks-StL-Chi	.238	Garcia-Cle	.307	Ford-NY	22.9	Lopat-NY	25.1

Clutch Pitching Index		Relief Runs		Adjusted Relief Runs		Relief Ranking		Total Pitcher Index		Total Baseball Ranking	
Ford-NY	127	Kinder-Bos	25.5	Kinder-Bos	28.0	Kinder-Bos	53.6	Kinder-Bos	5.9	Rosen-Cle	6.2
Lopat-NY	123	Dorish-Chi	9.7	Dorish-Chi	10.1	Dorish-Chi	12.8	McDermott-Bos	4.4	Kinder-Bos	4.4
Sain-NY	118	Kuzava-NY	7.0	Paige-StL	8.7	Paige-StL	9.9	Trucks-StL-Chi	3.8	McDermott-Bos	4.4
B.Lemon-Cle	113	Bearden-Chi	6.9	Bearden-Chi	7.1	Bearden-Chi	6.5	Pierce-Chi	3.5	Trucks-StL-Chi	3.8
Parnell-Bos	112	Paige-StL	6.1	Kuzava-NY	3.9	Kuzava-NY	4.5	Parnell-Bos	3.4	Zernial-Phi	3.5

TEAM	G	W	L	PCT	GB	R	OR	AB	H	2B	3B	HR	BB	SO	AVG	OBP	SLG	PRO	PRO+	BR	/A	PF	CHI	RC	SB	CS	SBA	SBR
NY	154	97	57	.630		732	550	5245	1386	194	42	186	522	561	.264	.335	.424	.759	102	17	13	101	102	747	30	23	57	-5
BRO	154	92	62	.597	5	778	740	5251	1418	246	56	186	634	625	.270	.353	.444	.797	110	100	75	103	96	821	46	39	54	-10
MIL	154	89	65	.578	8	670	556	5261	1395	217	41	139	471	619	.265	.330	.401	.731	103	-33	10	94	101	697	54	31	64	-2
PHI	154	75	79	.487	22	659	614	5184	1384	243	58	102	604	620	.267	.345	.395	.740	99	-2	-1	100	95	707	30	25	53	-7
CIN	154	74	80	.481	23	729	763	5234	1369	221	46	147	557	645	.262	.336	.406	.742	96	-8	-27	103	105	726	47	30	61	-4
STL	154	72	82	.468	25	799	790	5405	1518	285	58	119	582	586	.281	.354	.421	.775	107	65	59	101	102	807	63	46	58	-9
CHI	154	64	90	.416	33	700	766	5359	1412	229	45	159	478	693	.263	.327	.412	.739	97	-21	-28	101	103	717	46	31	60	-5
PIT	154	53	101	.344	44	557	845	5088	1260	181	57	76	566	737	.248	.326	.350	.676	83	-119	-111	99	98	596	21	13	62	-2
TOT	616					5624		42027	11142	1816	403	1114	4414	5086	.265	.338	.407	.745							337	240	58	-43

TEAM	CG	SH	SV	IP	H	H/G	HR	BB	SO	RAT	ERA	ERA+	OAV	OOB	PR	/A	PF	CPI	FA	E	DP	FW	PW	BW	SBW	DIF
NY	45	19	33	1390	1258	8.1	113	613	692	12.3	3.09	130	.243	.328	151	145	99	113	.975	154	172	-.5	14.4	1.3	.0	4.9
BRO	39	8	36	1393²	1399	9.0	164	533	762	12.6	4.31	95	.261	.330	-36	-35	100	93	.978	129	138	.8	-3.5	7.4	-.5	10.7
MIL	63	13	21	1394²	1296	8.4	106	553	698	12.1	3.19	117	.250	.326	137	83	92	110	.981	116	171	1.5	8.2	1.0	.3	.9
PHI	78	14	12	1365¹	1329	8.8	133	450	570	11.8	3.59	112	.256	.318	73	68	99	100	.975	145	133	-.0	6.7	-.0	-.2	-8.4
CIN	34	8	27	1367¹	1491	9.8	169	547	537	13.6	4.50	93	.282	.354	-65	-47	103	105	.977	137	194	.4	-4.7	-2.7	.1	3.8
STL	40	11	18	1390¹	1484	9.6	170	535	680	13.4	4.50	91	.275	.346	-66	-60	101	100	.976	146	178	-.0	-5.9	5.8	-.4	-4.4
CHI	41	6	19	1374¹	1375	9.0	131	619	622	13.2	4.51	93	.264	.345	-66	-46	103	92	.974	154	164	-.5	-4.6	-2.8	.0	-5.2
PIT	37	4	15	1346	1510	10.1	128	564	525	14.0	4.92	85	.287	.359	-127	-109	103	95	.971	173	136	-1.6	-10.8	-11.0	.3	-1.0
TOT	377	83	181	11021²		9.1				12.9	4.07		.265	.338					.976	1154	1286					

Runs
Snider-Bro	120
Musial-StL	120
Mays-NY	119
Ashburn-Phi	111
Gilliam-Bro	107

Hits
Mueller-NY	212
Snider-Bro	199
Musial-StL	195
Mays-NY	195
Moon-StL	193

Doubles
Musial-StL	41
Snider-Bro	39
Repulski-StL	39
Hamner-Phi	39

Triples
Mays-NY	13
Hamner-Phi	11
Snider-Bro	10

Home Runs
Kluszewski-Cin	49
Hodges-Bro	42
Sauer-Chi	41
Mays-NY	41

Total Bases
Snider-Bro	378
Mays-NY	377
Kluszewski-Cin	368
Musial-StL	359
Hodges-Bro	335

Runs Batted In
Kluszewski-Cin	141
Snider-Bro	130
Hodges-Bro	130
Musial-StL	126
Ennis-Phi	119

Runs Produced
Musial-StL	211
Snider-Bro	210
Kluszewski-Cin	196
Hodges-Bro	194

Bases On Balls
Ashburn-Phi	125
Mathews-Mil	113
Musial-StL	103
Thompson-NY	90
Reese-Bro	90

Batting Average
Mays-NY	.345
Mueller-NY	.342
Snider-Bro	.341
Musial-StL	.330
Kluszewski-Cin	.326

On Base Percentage
Ashburn-Phi	.442
Musial-StL	.433
Mathews-Mil	.428
Snider-Bro	.427
Mays-NY	.415

Slugging Average
Mays-NY	.667
Snider-Bro	.647
Kluszewski-Cin	.642
Musial-StL	.607
Mathews-Mil	.603

Production
Mays-NY	1.083
Snider-Bro	1.074
Kluszewski-Cin	1.052
Musial-StL	1.040
Mathews-Mil	1.031

Adjusted Production
Mathews-Mil	177
Mays-NY	176
Snider-Bro	170
Musial-StL	166
Kluszewski-Cin	165

Batter Runs
Snider-Bro	64.6
Mays-NY	61.8
Musial-StL	60.7
Kluszewski-Cin	57.1
Mathews-Mil	48.6

Adjusted Batter Runs
Mays-NY	61.1
Snider-Bro	60.2
Musial-StL	59.6
Mathews-Mil	56.6
Kluszewski-Cin	53.4

Clutch Hitting Index
Ennis-Phi	132
Jablonski-StL	127
Post-Cin	126
Furillo-Bro	119
Bell-Cin	117

Runs Created
Snider-Bro	161
Mays-NY	155
Musial-StL	153
Kluszewski-Cin	151
Mathews-Mil	131

Total Average
Mathews-Mil	1.169
Mays-NY	1.158
Snider-Bro	1.156
Kluszewski-Cin	1.117
Musial-StL	1.087

Stolen Bases
Bruton-Mil	34
Temple-Cin	21
Fondy-Chi	20
Moon-StL	18
Ashburn-Phi	11

Stolen Base Average
Fondy-Chi	80.0
Temple-Cin	75.0
Bruton-Mil	72.3
Moon-StL	64.3

Stolen Base Runs
Fondy-Chi	3.0
Bruton-Mil	2.4
Temple-Cin	2.1
Torgeson-Phi	1.5

Fielding Runs
Schoendienst-StL	32.9
Grammas-StL	29.8
Ashburn-Phi	17.2
Mays-NY	15.5
Logan-Mil	14.4

Total Player Rating
Mays-NY	6.7
Mathews-Mil	5.2
Schoendienst-StL	4.8
Snider-Bro	4.6
Musial-StL	4.6

Wins
Roberts-Phi	23
Spahn-Mil	21
Antonelli-NY	21
Haddix-StL	18
Erskine-Bro	18

Win Percentage
Antonelli-NY	.750
Lawrence-StL	.714
Gomez-NY	.654
Spahn-Mil	.636
Roberts-Phi	.605

Games
Hughes-Bro	60
Hetki-Pit	58
Brazle-StL	58
Wilhelm-NY	57
Grissom-NY	56

Complete Games
Roberts-Phi	29
Spahn-Mil	23
Simmons-Phi	21
Antonelli-NY	18

Shutouts
Antonelli-NY	6

Saves
Hughes-Bro	24
Smith-Cin	20
Grissom-NY	19
Jolly-Mil	10
Hetki-Pit	9

Innings Pitched
Roberts-Phi	336.2
Spahn-Mil	283.1
Erskine-Bro	260.1
Haddix-StL	259.2
Antonelli-NY	258.2

Fewest Hits/Game
Antonelli-NY	7.27
Roberts-Phi	7.73
Conley-Mil	7.92
Lawrence-StL	8.00
Wehmeier-Cin-Phi	8.02

Fewest BB/Game
Roberts-Phi	1.50
Minner-Chi	2.06
Hacker-Chi	2.10
Burdette-Mil	2.34
Meyer-Bro	2.45

Strikeouts
Roberts-Phi	185
Haddix-StL	184
Erskine-Bro	166
Antonelli-NY	152
Spahn-Mil	136

Strikeouts/Game
Haddix-StL	6.38
Erskine-Bro	5.74
Littlefield-Pit	5.34
Antonelli-NY	5.29
Conley-Mil	5.23

Ratio
Roberts-Phi	9.36
Antonelli-NY	10.72
Burdette-Mil	10.97
Spahn-Mil	11.09
Hacker-Chi	11.23

Earned Run Average
Antonelli-NY	2.30
Burdette-Mil	2.76
Simmons-Phi	2.81
Gomez-NY	2.88
Conley-Mil	2.96

Adjusted ERA
Antonelli-NY	176
Simmons-Phi	144
Gomez-NY	140
Roberts-Phi	136
Burdette-Mil	135

Opponents' Batting Avg.
Antonelli-NY	.219
Roberts-Phi	.231
Simmons-Phi	.239
Littlefield-Pit	.239
Wehmeier-Cin-Phi	.239

Opponents' On Base Pct.
Roberts-Phi	.267
Antonelli-NY	.293
Spahn-Mil	.302
Burdette-Mil	.302
Hacker-Chi	.304

Starter Runs
Antonelli-NY	51.0
Roberts-Phi	41.3
Simmons-Phi	35.5
Burdette-Mil	34.7
Gomez-NY	29.3

Adjusted Starter Runs
Antonelli-NY	50.0
Roberts-Phi	40.1
Simmons-Phi	34.6
Gomez-NY	28.4
Burdette-Mil	25.5

Clutch Pitching Index
Gomez-NY	130
Dickson-Phi	123
Fowler-Cin	116
Conley-Mil	116
Antonelli-NY	115

Relief Runs
Wilhelm-NY	24.4
Grissom-NY	23.4
Jolly-Mil	20.4
Johnson-Mil	13.9
Smith-Cin	12.7

Adjusted Relief Runs
Wilhelm-NY	23.9
Grissom-NY	22.9
Jolly-Mil	16.1
Smith-Cin	13.7
Johnson-Mil	10.1

Relief Ranking
Grissom-NY	36.6
Wilhelm-NY	34.3
Smith-Cin	27.5
Jolly-Mil	25.4
Hughes-Bro	15.6

Total Pitcher Index
Antonelli-NY	5.5
Grissom-NY	3.6
Roberts-Phi	3.6
Wilhelm-NY	3.4
Simmons-Phi	3.3

Total Baseball Ranking
Mays-NY	6.7
Antonelli-NY	5.5
Mathews-Mil	5.2
Schoendienst-StL	4.8
Snider-Bro	4.6

TEAM	G	W	L	PCT	GB	R	OR	AB	H	2B	3B	HR	BB	SO	AVG	OBP	SLG	PRO	PRO+	BR	/A	PF	CHI	RC	SB	CS	SBA	SBR
CLE	156	111	43	.721		746	504	5222	1368	188	39	156	637	668	.262	.345	.403	.748	109	76	64	102	102	739	30	33	48	-11
NY	155	103	51	.669	8	805	563	5226	1400	215	59	133	650	632	.268	.351	.408	.759	118	101	128	97	106	768	34	41	45	-14
CHI	155	94	60	.610	17	711	521	5168	1382	203	47	94	604	536	.267	.350	.379	.729	103	51	27	103	101	700	98	58	63	-5
BOS	156	69	85	.448	42	700	728	5399	1436	244	41	123	654	660	.266	.348	.395	.743	99	73	-9	111	93	749	51	30	63	-3
DET	155	68	86	.442	43	584	664	5233	1351	215	41	90	492	603	.258	.324	.367	.691	97	-37	-26	98	97	609	48	44	52	-12
WAS	155	66	88	.429	45	632	680	5249	1292	188	69	81	610	719	.246	.328	.355	.683	98	-44	-11	95	104	631	37	21	64	-2
BAL	154	54	100	.351	57	483	668	5206	1309	195	49	52	468	634	.251	.316	.338	.654	92	-104	-65	93	91	553	30	31	49	-10
PHI	156	51	103	.331	60	542	875	5206	1228	191	41	94	504	677	.236	.307	.342	.649	84	-117	-119	100	105	553	30	29	51	-8
TOT	621					5203		41909	10766	1639	386	823	4619	5129	.257	.334	.373	.707							358	287	56	-65

TEAM	CG	SH	SV	IP	H	H/G	HR	BB	SO	RAT	ERA	ERA+	OAV	OOB	PR	/A	PF	CPI	FA	E	DP	FW	PW	BW	SBW	DIF
CLE	77	12	36	1419¹	1220	7.7	89	486	678	10.9	2.78	132	.232	.299	148	141	99	100	.979	128	148	.7	14.6	6.6	-.3	12.4
NY	51	16	37	1379¹	1284	8.4	86	552	655	12.9	3.26	105	.251	.328	71	27	92	107	.979	126	198	.8	2.8	13.2	-.6	9.8
CHI	60	23	33	1383	1255	8.2	94	517	701	11.6	3.05	122	.244	.314	103	105	100	105	.982	108	149	1.8	10.8	2.8	.3	1.2
BOS	41	10	22	1412¹	1434	9.1	118	612	707	13.3	4.01	102	.265	.344	-46	15	110	101	.972	176	163	-2.0	1.5	-.9	.5	-7.2
DET	58	13	13	1383	1375	8.9	138	506	603	12.5	3.81	97	.261	.330	-13	-17	99	103	.978	129	131	.6	-1.8	-2.7	-.4	-4.8
WAS	69	10	7	1383¹	1396	9.1	79	573	562	13.0	3.84	93	.265	.340	-18	-43	96	99	.977	137	172	.2	-4.4	-1.1	.6	-6.2
BAL	58	6	8	1373¹	1279	8.4	78	688	668	13.0	3.88	92	.250	.341	-24	-45	96	94	.975	147	152	-.4	-4.6	-6.7	-.2	-11.0
PHI	49	3	13	1371¹	1523	10.0	141	685	555	14.7	5.18	75	.285	.370	-222	-194	105	95	.972	169	163	-1.6	-20.0	-12.3	.0	7.9
TOT	463	93	169	11105		8.7				12.6	3.72		.257	.334					.977	1120	1276					

Runs		Hits		Doubles		Triples		Home Runs		Total Bases	
Mantle-NY	129	Kuenn-Det	201	Vernon-Was	33	Minoso-Chi	18	Doby-Cle	32	Minoso-Chi	304
Minoso-Chi	119	Fox-Chi	201	Smith-Cle	29	Runnels-Was	15	Williams-Bos	29	Vernon-Was	294
Avila-Cle	112	Avila-Cle	189	Minoso-Chi	29	Vernon-Was	14	Mantle-NY	27	Mantle-NY	285
Fox-Chi	111	Busby-Was	187			Mantle-NY	12	Jensen-Bos	25	Berra-NY	285
Carrasquel-Chi	106	Minoso-Chi	182			Tuttle-Det	11			Doby-Cle	279

Runs Batted In		Runs Produced		Bases On Balls		Batting Average		On Base Percentage		Slugging Average	
Doby-Cle	126	Minoso-Chi	216	Williams-Bos	136	Avila-Cle	.341	Williams-Bos	.516	Minoso-Chi	.535
Berra-NY	125	Mantle-NY	204	Yost-Was	131	Minoso-Chi	.320	Minoso-Chi	.416	Mantle-NY	.525
Jensen-Bos	117	Berra-NY	191	Mantle-NY	102	Noren-NY	.319	Rosen-Cle	.412	Rosen-Cle	.506
Minoso-Chi	116	Doby-Cle	188	Smith-Cle	88	Fox-Chi	.319	Mantle-NY	.411	Vernon-Was	.492
		Jensen-Bos	184			Berra-NY	.307	Yost-Was	.406	Berra-NY	.488

Production		Adjusted Production		Batter Runs		Adjusted Batter Runs		Clutch Hitting Index		Runs Created	
Minoso-Chi	.951	Mantle-NY	160	Williams-Bos	70.9	Williams-Bos	57.6	Berra-NY	123	Williams-Bos	139
Mantle-NY	.936	Minoso-Chi	154	Minoso-Chi	47.3	Mantle-NY	46.8	Minoso-Chi	122	Mantle-NY	127
Rosen-Cle	.918	Rosen-Cle	148	Mantle-NY	42.8	Minoso-Chi	43.2	Rosen-Cle	118	Minoso-Chi	125
Avila-Cle	.882	Noren-NY	140	Rosen-Cle	34.2	Rosen-Cle	32.6	Sievers-Was	117	Avila-Cle	109
Noren-NY	.864	Vernon-Was	140	Avila-Cle	31.5	Avila-Cle	29.8	Doby-Cle	116	Doby-Cle	108

Total Average		Stolen Bases		Stolen Base Average		Stolen Base Runs		Fielding Runs		Total Player Rating	
Williams-Bos	1.452	Jensen-Bos	22	Busby-Was	89.5	Busby-Was	3.9	Coleman-NY	17.9	Williams-Bos	5.0
Mantle-NY	1.013	Rivera-Chi	18	Jacobs-Phi	85.0	Jacobs-Phi	3.3	Carey-NY	16.7	Minoso-Chi	5.0
Minoso-Chi	.969	Minoso-Chi	18	Jensen-Bos	75.9	Jensen-Bos	2.4	Lepcio-Bos	16.1	Avila-Cle	4.7
Rosen-Cle	.959	Jacobs-Phi	17	Rivera-Chi	64.3	Cavarretta-Chi	1.2	Bolling-Bos	15.3	Mantle-NY	4.1
Doby-Cle	.862	Busby-Was	17	Fox-Chi	64.0			Minoso-Chi	13.4	Berra-NY	3.6

Wins		Win Percentage		Games		Complete Games		Shutouts		Saves	
Wynn-Cle	23	Consuegra-Chi	.842	Dixon-Was-Phi	54	Porterfield-Was	21	Trucks-Chi	5	Sain-NY	22
Lemon-Cle	23	Grim-NY	.769	Martin-Phi-Chi	48	Lemon-Cle	21	Garcia-Cle	5	Kinder-Bos	15
Grim-NY	20	Lemon-Cle	.767	Pascual-Was	48	Wynn-Cle	20			Narleski-Cle	13
Trucks-Chi	19	Garcia-Cle	.704	Kinder-Bos	48	Gromek-Det	17				
Garcia-Cle	19	Houtteman-Cle	.682								

Innings Pitched		Fewest Hits/Game		Fewest BB/Game		Strikeouts		Strikeouts/Game		Ratio	
Wynn-Cle	270.2	Turley-Bal	6.48	Lopat-NY	1.75	Turley-Bal	185	Pierce-Chi	7.06	Garcia-Cle	10.19
Trucks-Chi	264.2	Ford-NY	7.26	Gromek-Det	2.03	Wynn-Cle	155	Harshman-Chi	6.81	Wynn-Cle	10.24
Garcia-Cle	258.2	Wynn-Cle	7.48	Garver-Det	2.27	Trucks-Chi	152	Turley-Bal	6.73	Garver-Det	10.30
Lemon-Cle	258.1	Coleman-Bal	7.48	Garcia-Cle	2.47	Pierce-Chi	148	Hoeft-Det	5.86	Gromek-Det	10.86
Gromek-Det	252.2	Reynolds-NY	7.61	Zuverink-Det	2.75	Harshman-Chi	134	Reynolds-NY	5.72	Trucks-Chi	10.88

Earned Run Average		Adjusted ERA		Opponents' Batting Avg.		Opponents' On Base Pct.		Starter Runs		Adjusted Starter Runs	
Garcia-Cle	2.64	Garcia-Cle	139	Turley-Bal	.203	Garcia-Cle	.284	Garcia-Cle	31.0	Garcia-Cle	29.6
Lemon-Cle	2.72	Lemon-Cle	135	Wynn-Cle	.225	Wynn-Cle	.284	Wynn-Cle	30.0	Wynn-Cle	28.5
Wynn-Cle	2.73	Wynn-Cle	135	Ford-NY	.227	Garver-Det	.287	Lemon-Cle	28.9	Trucks-Chi	27.8
Gromek-Det	2.74	Gromek-Det	135	Trucks-Chi	.228	Gromek-Det	.297	Gromek-Det	27.5	Lemon-Cle	27.5
Trucks-Chi	2.79	Trucks-Chi	134	Garcia-Cle	.229	Trucks-Chi	.297	Trucks-Chi	27.5	Gromek-Det	26.7

Clutch Pitching Index		Relief Runs		Adjusted Relief Runs		Relief Ranking		Total Pitcher Index		Total Baseball Ranking	
Keegan-Chi	126	Mossi-Cle	18.5	Mossi-Cle	18.0	Mossi-Cle	15.2	Lemon-Cle	4.1	Williams-Bos	5.0
Gromek-Det	116	Narleski-Cle	14.8	Narleski-Cle	14.3	Narleski-Cle	13.4	Gromek-Det	3.4	Minoso-Chi	5.0
Houtteman-Cle	114	Dorish-Chi	12.1	Dorish-Chi	12.2	Dorish-Chi	11.6	Wynn-Cle	3.3	Avila-Cle	4.7
Lopat-NY	114	Miller-Det	9.8	Miller-Det	9.6	Kinder-Bos	9.7	Trucks-Chi	3.2	Lemon-Cle	4.1
Harshman-Chi	114	Sain-NY	4.9	Kinder-Bos	5.9	Sain-NY	4.9	Garcia-Cle	2.9	Mantle-NY	4.1

TEAM	G	W	L	PCT	GB	R	OR	AB	H	2B	3B	HR	BB	SO	AVG	OBP	SLG	PRO	PRO+	BR	/A	PF	CHI	RC	SB	CS	SBA	SBR
BRO	154	98	55	.641		857	650	5193	1406	230	44	201	674	718	.271	.359	.448	.807	116	142	118	103	100	834	79	56	59	-10
MIL	154	85	69	.552	13.5	743	668	5277	1377	219	55	182	504	735	.261	.329	.427	.756	109	27	63	95	102	733	42	27	61	-4
NY	154	80	74	.519	18.5	702	673	5288	1377	173	34	169	497	581	.255	.343	.395	.738	103	-15	-16	100	102	699	38	22	63	-2
PHI	154	77	77	.500	21.5	675	666	5092	1300	214	50	132	652	673	.260	.344	.425	.769	103	14	27	98	95	692	44	32	58	-6
CIN	154	75	79	.487	23.5	761	684	5270	1424	216	28	181	556	657	.270	.344	.425	.769	103	63	19	106	99	773	51	36	59	-6
CHI	154	72	81	.471	26	626	713	5214	1287	187	55	164	428	806	.247	.307	.398	.705	91	-75	-73	100	103	623	37	35	51	-10
STL	154	68	86	.442	30.5	654	757	5266	1375	228	36	143	458	597	.261	.324	.400	.724	96	-30	-29	100	99	662	64	59	52	-16
PIT	154	60	94	.390	38.5	560	767	5173	1262	210	60	91	471	652	.244	.310	.361	.671	84	-127	-119	99	100	567	22	22	50	-7
TOT	616					5578		41773	10808	1677	362	1263	4240	5419	.259	.330	.407	.737							377	289	57	-60

TEAM	CG	SH	SV	IP	H	H/G	HR	BB	SO	RAT	ERA	ERA+	OAV	OOB	PR	/A	PF	CPI	FA	E	DP	FW	PW	BW	SBW	DIF
BRO	46	11	37	1378	1296	8.5	168	483	773	11.7	3.68	110	.248	.314	54	58	101	100	.978	133	156	.5	5.8	11.7	-.2	3.8
MIL	61	5	12	1383	1339	8.7	138	591	654	12.7	3.85	98	.256	.333	29	-14	93	102	.975	152	155	-.6	-1.4	6.3	.4	3.4
NY	52	6	14	1386²	1347	8.7	155	560	721	12.7	3.77	107	.257	.334	41	39	100	107	.976	142	165	.0	3.9	-1.6	.5	.2
PHI	58	11	21	1356²	1291	8.6	161	477	657	11.9	3.93	101	.251	.318	17	6	98	96	.981	110	117	1.8	.6	2.7	.2	-5.2
CIN	38	12	22	1363	1373	9.1	161	443	576	12.1	3.95	107	.264	.324	13	43	105	102	.977	139	169	.2	4.3	1.9	.2	-8.5
CHI	47	10	23	1378¹	1306	8.5	153	601	686	12.6	4.17	98	.251	.332	-21	-13	101	95	.975	147	147	-.3	-1.3	-7.2	-.2	4.6
STL	42	10	15	1376²	1376	9.0	185	549	730	12.9	4.56	89	.262	.337	-80	-77	101	95	.975	146	152	-.2	-7.6	-2.9	-.8	2.6
PIT	41	5	16	1362	1480	9.8	142	536	622	13.5	4.39	94	.281	.350	-54	-42	102	104	.972	166	175	-1.4	-4.2	-11.8	.0	.3
TOT	385	70	160	10984¹		8.9				12.5	4.04		.259	.330					.976	1135	1236					

Runs		Hits		Doubles		Triples		Home Runs		Total Bases	
Snider-Bro	126	Kluszewski-Cin	192	Logan-Mil	37	Mays-NY	13	Mays-NY	51	Mays-NY	382
Mays-NY	123	Aaron-Mil	189	Aaron-Mil	37	Long-Pit	13	Kluszewski-Cin	47	Kluszewski-Cin	358
Post-Cin	116	Bell-Cin	188	Snider-Bro	34	Bruton-Mil	12	Banks-Chi	44	Banks-Chi	355
Kluszewski-Cin	116	Post-Cin	186	Post-Cin	33	Clemente-Pit	11	Snider-Bro	42	Post-Cin	345
Gilliam-Bro	110			Ashburn-Phi	32			Mathews-Mil	41	Snider-Bro	338

Runs Batted In		Runs Produced		Bases On Balls		Batting Average		On Base Percentage		Slugging Average	
Snider-Bro	136	Snider-Bro	220	Mathews-Mil	109	Ashburn-Phi	.338	Ashburn-Phi	.449	Mays-NY	.659
Mays-NY	127	Mays-NY	199	Ashburn-Phi	105	Mays-NY	.319	Snider-Bro	.421	Snider-Bro	.628
Ennis-Phi	120	Post-Cin	185	Snider-Bro	104	Musial-StL	.319	Mathews-Mil	.417	Mathews-Mil	.601
Banks-Chi	117	Aaron-Mil	184	Thompson-NY	84	Campanella-Bro	.318	Musial-StL	.411	Banks-Chi	.596
Kluszewski-Cin	113	Kluszewski-Cin	182			Aaron-Mil	.314	Mays-NY	.404	Kluszewski-Cin	.585

Production		Adjusted Production		Batter Runs		Adjusted Batter Runs		Clutch Hitting Index		Runs Created	
Mays-NY	1.063	Mays-NY	176	Mays-NY	62.3	Mays-NY	62.0	Long-Pit	117	Mays-NY	157
Snider-Bro	1.050	Mathews-Mil	175	Snider-Bro	58.9	Mathews-Mil	56.3	Jones-Phi	117	Snider-Bro	145
Mathews-Mil	1.018	Snider-Bro	169	Mathews-Mil	50.0	Snider-Bro	55.2	Mueller-NY	116	Kluszewski-Cin	136
Campanella-Bro	.985	Musial-StL	156	Musial-StL	46.5	Musial-StL	46.6	Ennis-Phi	116	Musial-StL	131
Musial-StL	.977	Campanella-Bro	153	Kluszewski-Cin	44.9	Ashburn-Phi	38.8	Temple-Cin	115	Mathews-Mil	131

Total Average		Stolen Bases		Stolen Base Average		Stolen Base Runs		Fielding Runs		Total Player Rating	
Mays-NY	1.180	Bruton-Mil	25	Mays-NY	85.7	Mays-NY	4.8	Mays-NY	19.8	Mays-NY	7.7
Snider-Bro	1.147	Mays-NY	24	Temple-Cin	82.6	Temple-Cin	3.3	McMillan-Cin	16.6	Banks-Chi	5.3
Mathews-Mil	1.124	Boyer-StL	22	Bruton-Mil	69.4	Robinson-Bro	1.8	O'Connell-Mil	15.8	Mathews-Mil	4.9
Musial-StL	1.020	Temple-Cin	19	Boyer-StL	56.4	Blaylock-Phi	1.2	Groat-Pit	15.4	Snider-Bro	4.7
Campanella-Bro	1.000	Gilliam-Bro	15					Bruton-Mil	14.7	Ashburn-Phi	4.0

Wins		Win Percentage		Games		Complete Games		Shutouts		Saves	
Roberts-Phi	23	Newcombe-Bro	.800	Labine-Bro	60	Roberts-Phi	26	Nuxhall-Cin	5	Meyer-Phi	16
Newcombe-Bro	20	Roberts-Phi	.622	Wilhelm-NY	59	Newcombe-Bro	17	Jones-Chi	4	Roebuck-Bro	12
Spahn-Mil	17	Nuxhall-Cin	.586	LaPalme-StL	56	Spahn-Mil	16	Dickson-Phi	4	Labine-Bro	11
Nuxhall-Cin	17	Spahn-Mil	.548	Grissom-NY	55					Freeman-Cin	11
				Freeman-Cin	52					Grissom-NY	8

Innings Pitched		Fewest Hits/Game		Fewest BB/Game		Strikeouts		Strikeouts/Game		Ratio	
Roberts-Phi	305.0	Jones-Chi	6.52	Newcombe-Bro	1.46	Jones-Chi	198	Jones-Chi	7.37	Newcombe-Bro	10.05
Nuxhall-Cin	257.0	Buhl-Mil	7.50	Roberts-Phi	1.56	Roberts-Phi	160	Haddix-StL	6.49	Roberts-Phi	10.24
Spahn-Mil	245.2	Rush-Chi	7.85	Hacker-Chi	1.82	Haddix-StL	150	Podres-Bro	6.44	Friend-Pit	10.42
Jones-Chi	241.2	Antonelli-NY	7.88	Friend-Pit	2.34	Newcombe-Bro	143	Conley-Mil	6.09	Hacker-Chi	10.44
Antonelli-NY	235.1	Dickson-Phi	7.92	Spahn-Mil	2.38	Antonelli-NY	143	Newcombe-Bro	5.51	Rush-Chi	10.73

Earned Run Average		Adjusted ERA		Opponents' Batting Avg.		Opponents' On Base Pct.		Starter Runs		Adjusted Starter Runs	
Friend-Pit	2.83	Friend-Pit	145	Jones-Chi	.206	Roberts-Phi	.280	Friend-Pit	26.9	Friend-Pit	28.6
Newcombe-Bro	3.20	Newcombe-Bro	127	Buhl-Mil	.227	Newcombe-Bro	.280	Roberts-Phi	25.8	Roberts-Phi	23.5
Buhl-Mil	3.21	Nuxhall-Cin	122	Rush-Chi	.234	Hacker-Chi	.285	Newcombe-Bro	21.8	Newcombe-Bro	22.5
Spahn-Mil	3.26	Roberts-Phi	121	Antonelli-NY	.234	Friend-Pit	.294	Spahn-Mil	21.2	Nuxhall-Cin	21.9
Roberts-Phi	3.28	Antonelli-NY	121	Dickson-Phi	.238	Rush-Chi	.295	Antonelli-NY	18.6	Schmidt-StL	18.5

Clutch Pitching Index		Relief Runs		Adjusted Relief Runs		Relief Ranking		Total Pitcher Index		Total Baseball Ranking	
Minner-Chi	122	Freeman-Cin	19.1	Freeman-Cin	21.1	Freeman-Cin	28.5	Newcombe-Bro	4.2	Mays-NY	7.7
Spahn-Mil	114	Miller-Phi	16.2	Miller-Phi	15.5	Miller-Phi	19.1	Roberts-Phi	3.7	Banks-Chi	5.3
Jackson-StL	113	LaPalme-StL	13.1	LaPalme-StL	13.4	Jeffcoat-Chi	17.6	Friend-Pit	3.3	Mathews-Mil	4.9
Law-Pit	109	Labine-Bro	12.8	Labine-Bro	13.1	Labine-Bro	17.0	Freeman-Cin	3.1	Snider-Bro	4.7
Friend-Pit	109	Jeffcoat-Chi	12.2	Jeffcoat-Chi	12.7	Bessent-Bro	13.3	Antonelli-NY	2.6	Newcombe-Bro	4.2

TEAM	G	W	L	PCT	GB	R	OR	AB	H	2B	3B	HR	BB	SO	AVG	OBP	SLG	PRO	PRO+	BR	/A	PF	CHI	RC	SB	CS	SBA	SBR
NY	154	96	58	.623		762	569	5161	1342	179	55	175	609	658	.260	.343	.418	.761	113	71	83	98	101	759	55	25	69	2
CLE	154	93	61	.604	3	698	601	5146	1325	195	31	148	723	715	.257	.353	.394	.747	104	60	32	104	93	741	28	24	54	-6
CHI	155	91	63	.591	5	725	557	5220	1401	204	36	116	567	595	.268	.347	.388	.735	101	31	11	103	101	712	69	45	61	-6
BOS	154	84	70	.545	12	755	652	5273	1392	241	39	137	707	733	.264	.354	.402	.756	101	77	7	109	97	773	43	17	72	3
DET	154	79	75	.513	17	775	658	5283	1407	211	38	130	641	583	.266	.348	.394	.742	108	46	63	98	104	736	41	22	65	-1
KC	155	63	91	.409	33	638	911	5335	1395	189	46	121	463	725	.261	.323	.382	.705	95	-40	-47	101	100	637	22	36	38	-15
BAL	156	57	97	.370	39	540	754	5257	1263	177	39	54	560	742	.240	.316	.320	.636	83	-159	-123	93	104	532	34	46	43	-17
WAS	154	53	101	.344	43	598	789	5142	1277	178	54	80	538	654	.248	.324	.351	.675	93	-86	-55	95	103	586	25	32	44	-12
TOT	618					5491		41817	10802	1574	338	961	4808	5405	.258	.339	.381	.720							317	247	56	-53

TEAM	CG	SH	SV	IP	H	H/G	HR	BB	SO	RAT	ERA	ERA+	OAV	OOB	PR	/A	PF	CPI	FA	E	DP	FW	PW	BW	SBW	DIF
NY	52	19	33	1372¹	1163	7.6	108	688	731	12.3	3.23	116	.232	.328	111	78	95	107	.978	128	180	.5	7.8	8.3	.9	1.5
CLE	45	15	36	1386¹	1285	8.3	111	558	877	12.1	3.39	118	.245	.320	88	92	101	101	.981	108	152	1.7	9.2	3.2	.0	1.9
CHI	55	20	23	1378	1301	8.5	111	497	720	11.9	3.37	117	.251	.319	90	89	100	103	.981	111	147	1.5	8.9	1.1	.0	2.4
BOS	44	9	34	1384¹	1333	8.7	128	582	674	12.7	3.72	115	.253	.331	37	88	108	102	.977	136	140	.0	8.8	.7	1.0	-3.5
DET	66	16	12	1380¹	1381	9.0	126	517	629	12.6	3.79	101	.261	.331	26	7	97	102	.976	139	159	-.2	.7	6.3	.6	-5.4
KC	29	9	22	1382	1486	9.7	175	707	572	14.6	5.35	78	.274	.367	-214	-181	105	94	.976	146	174	-.5	-18.1	-4.7	-.8	10.2
BAL	35	10	20	1388²	1403	9.1	103	625	595	13.4	4.21	91	.266	.348	-39	-61	96	98	.972	167	159	-1.7	-6.1	-12.3	-1.0	1.2
WAS	37	10	16	1354²	1450	9.6	99	634	607	14.2	4.62	83	.279	.362	-100	-119	97	98	.974	154	170	-1.0	-11.9	-5.5	-.5	-5.0
TOT	363	108	196	11026²		8.8				13.0	3.96		.258	.339					.977	1089	1281					

Runs
Smith-Cle ... 123
Mantle-NY ... 121
Kaline-Det ... 121
Tuttle-Det ... 102
Kuenn-Det ... 101

Hits
Kaline-Det ... 200
Fox-Chi ... 198
Power-KC ... 190
Kuenn-Det ... 190
Smith-Cle ... 186

Doubles
Kuenn-Det ... 38
Power-KC ... 34
Goodman-Bos ... 31
White-Bos ... 30
Finigan-KC ... 30

Triples
Mantle-NY ... 11
Carey-NY ... 11
Power-KC ... 10

Home Runs
Mantle-NY ... 37
Zernial-KC ... 30
Williams-Bos ... 28

Total Bases
Kaline-Det ... 321
Mantle-NY ... 316
Power-KC ... 301
Smith-Cle ... 287
Jensen-Bos ... 275

Runs Batted In
Jensen-Bos ... 116
Boone-Det ... 116
Berra-NY ... 108
Sievers-Was ... 106
Kaline-Det ... 102

Runs Produced
Kaline-Det ... 196
Jensen-Bos ... 185
Mantle-NY ... 183
Smith-Cle ... 178
Tuttle-Det ... 166

Bases On Balls
Mantle-NY ... 113
Goodman-Bos ... 99
Yost-Was ... 95
Fain-Det-Cle ... 94
Smith-Cle ... 93

Batting Average
Kaline-Det ... .340
Power-KC ... .319
Kell-Chi ... .312
Fox-Chi ... .311
Kuenn-Det ... .306

On Base Percentage
Mantle-NY ... .433
Kaline-Det ... .425
Smith-Cle ... .411
Yost-Was ... .410
Goodman-Bos ... .397

Slugging Average
Mantle-NY ... .611
Kaline-Det ... .546
Zernial-KC ... .508
Doby-Cle ... .505
Power-KC ... .505

Production
Mantle-NY ... 1.044
Kaline-Det ... .971
Smith-Cle ... .884
Doby-Cle ... .877
Power-KC ... .862

Adjusted Production
Mantle-NY ... 181
Kaline-Det ... 163
Sievers-Was ... 136
Vernon-Was ... 133
Smith-Cle ... 132

Batter Runs
Williams-Bos ... 59.3
Mantle-NY ... 59.0
Kaline-Det ... 50.2
Smith-Cle ... 34.7
Valo-KC ... 24.8

Adjusted Batter Runs
Mantle-NY ... 61.2
Kaline-Det ... 53.2
Williams-Bos ... 50.1
Smith-Cle ... 30.4
Vernon-Was ... 25.2

Clutch Hitting Index
Kell-Chi ... 137
Boone-Det ... 137
Zauchin-Bos ... 114
Jensen-Bos ... 111
Sievers-Was ... 111

Runs Created
Mantle-NY ... 148
Kaline-Det ... 135
Smith-Cle ... 128
Williams-Bos ... 118
Power-KC ... 103

Total Average
Mantle-NY ... 1.206
Kaline-Det ... .993
Smith-Cle ... .928
Doby-Cle ... .884
Jensen-Bos ... .849

Stolen Bases
Rivera-Chi ... 25
Minoso-Chi ... 19
Jensen-Bos ... 16
Busby-Was-Chi ... 12
Smith-Cle ... 11

Stolen Base Average
Minoso-Chi ... 70.4
Jensen-Bos ... 69.6
Rivera-Chi ... 61.0

Stolen Base Runs
Torgeson-Det ... 2.7
Busby-Was-Chi ... 1.8
Mantle-NY ... 1.8
Klaus-Bos ... 1.8

Fielding Runs
Fox-Chi ... 26.9
McDougald-NY ... 19.4
Miranda-Bal ... 19.0
Lopez-KC ... 15.1
Tuttle-Det ... 14.9

Total Player Rating
Mantle-NY ... 6.3
Kaline-Det ... 5.0
Williams-Bos ... 4.4
Fox-Chi ... 3.9
McDougald-NY ... 3.5

Wins
F.Sullivan-Bos ... 18
Lemon-Cle ... 18
Ford-NY ... 18
Wynn-Cle ... 17
Turley-NY ... 17

Win Percentage
Byrne-NY ... .762
Ford-NY ... .720
Hoeft-Det ... .696
Lemon-Cle ... .643
Donovan-Chi ... .625

Games
Narleski-Cle ... 60
Mossi-Cle ... 57
Gorman-KC ... 57
Dorish-Chi-Bal ... 48
Moore-Bal ... 46

Complete Games
Ford-NY ... 18
Hoeft-Det ... 17

Shutouts
Hoeft-Det ... 7
Wynn-Cle ... 6
Turley-NY ... 6
Pierce-Chi ... 6

Saves
Narleski-Cle ... 19
Kinder-Bos ... 18
Gorman-KC ... 18
Konstanty-NY ... 11
Morgan-NY ... 10

Innings Pitched
F.Sullivan-Bos ... 260.0
Ford-NY ... 253.2
Turley-NY ... 246.2
Wilson-Bal ... 235.1
Lary-Det ... 235.0

Fewest Hits/Game
Turley-NY ... 6.13
Score-Cle ... 6.26
Ford-NY ... 6.67
Pierce-Chi ... 7.09
Harshman-Chi ... 7.23

Fewest BB/Game
Gromek-Det ... 1.84
Donovan-Chi ... 2.31
Garcia-Cle ... 2.39
Garver-Det ... 2.61
Porterfield-Was ... 2.73

Strikeouts
Score-Cle ... 245
Turley-NY ... 210
Pierce-Chi ... 157
Ford-NY ... 137
Hoeft-Det ... 133

Strikeouts/Game
Score-Cle ... 9.70
Turley-NY ... 7.66
Pierce-Chi ... 6.87
Harshman-Chi ... 5.82
Hoeft-Det ... 5.44

Ratio
Pierce-Chi ... 10.02
Ford-NY ... 10.71
Hoeft-Det ... 10.96
Wilson-Bal ... 11.13
Wynn-Cle ... 11.35

Earned Run Average
Pierce-Chi ... 1.97
Ford-NY ... 2.63
Wynn-Cle ... 2.82
Score-Cle ... 2.85
F.Sullivan-Bos ... 2.91

Adjusted ERA
Pierce-Chi ... 201
F.Sullivan-Bos ... 148
Ford-NY ... 143
Wynn-Cle ... 142
Score-Cle ... 140

Opponents' Batting Avg.
Turley-NY ... .193
Score-Cle ... .194
Ford-NY ... .208
Pierce-Chi ... .213
Harshman-Chi ... .224

Opponents' On Base Pct.
Pierce-Chi ... .277
Ford-NY ... .297
Hoeft-Det ... .298
Wilson-Bal ... .300
Wynn-Cle ... .307

Starter Runs
Pierce-Chi ... 45.5
Ford-NY ... 37.6
F.Sullivan-Bos ... 30.4
Wynn-Cle ... 29.2
Score-Cle ... 28.1

Adjusted Starter Runs
Pierce-Chi ... 45.2
F.Sullivan-Bos ... 39.9
Ford-NY ... 31.5
Wynn-Cle ... 29.9
Score-Cle ... 28.8

Clutch Pitching Index
Pierce-Chi ... 119
Byrne-NY ... 119
F.Sullivan-Bos ... 116
Lary-Det ... 115
Schmitz-Was ... 115

Relief Runs
Consuegra-Chi ... 18.6
Mossi-Cle ... 13.9
Konstanty-NY ... 13.4
Kiely-Bos ... 11.6
Dorish-Chi-Bal ... 10.4

Adjusted Relief Runs
Consuegra-Chi ... 18.4
Kiely-Bos ... 14.9
Mossi-Cle ... 14.2
Konstanty-NY ... 11.6
Hurd-Bos ... 11.4

Relief Ranking
Kinder-Bos ... 21.1
Hurd-Bos ... 19.5
Consuegra-Chi ... 16.7
Konstanty-NY ... 16.7
Mossi-Cle ... 14.5

Total Pitcher Index
Pierce-Chi ... 5.3
F.Sullivan-Bos ... 4.2
Wynn-Cle ... 3.3
Ford-NY ... 3.1
Lary-Det ... 2.5

Total Baseball Ranking
Mantle-NY ... 6.3
Pierce-Chi ... 5.3
Kaline-Det ... 5.0
Williams-Bos ... 4.4
F.Sullivan-Bos ... 4.2

TEAM	G	W	L	PCT	GB	R	OR	AB	H	2B	3B	HR	BB	SO	AVG	OBP	SLG	PRO	PRO+	BR	/A	PF	CHI	RC	SB	CS	SBA	SBR
BRO	154	93	61	.604		720	601	5098	1315	212	36	179	649	738	.258	.344	.419	.763	103	81	24	108	97	728	65	37	64	-3
MIL	155	92	62	.597	1	709	569	5207	1350	212	54	177	486	714	.259	.325	.423	.748	113	38	80	94	101	714	29	20	59	-3
CIN	155	91	63	.591	2	775	658	5291	1406	201	32	221	528	760	.266	.338	.441	.779	107	103	54	106	100	789	45	22	67	0
STL	156	76	78	.494	17	678	698	5378	1443	234	49	124	503	622	.268	.335	.399	.734	103	25	25	100	97	707	41	35	54	-9
PHI	154	71	83	.461	22	668	738	5204	1313	207	49	121	585	673	.252	.331	.381	.712	99	-12	0	98	103	658	45	23	66	0
NY	154	67	87	.435	26	540	650	5190	1268	192	45	145	402	659	.244	.301	.382	.683	89	-85	-81	99	97	586	67	34	66	0
PIT	157	66	88	.429	27	588	653	5221	1340	199	57	110	383	752	.257	.310	.380	.690	93	-70	-57	98	102	594	24	33	42	-13
CHI	157	60	94	.390	33	597	708	5260	1281	202	50	142	446	776	.244	.304	.382	.686	91	-79	-69	98	103	606	55	38	59	-6
TOT	621					5275		41849	10716	1659	372	1219	3982	5694	.256	.324	.401	.725							371	242	61	-34

TEAM	CG	SH	SV	IP	H	H/G	HR	BB	SO	RAT	ERA	ERA+	OAV	OOB	PR	/A	PF	CPI	FA	E	DP	FW	PW	BW	SBW	DIF
BRO	46	12	30	1368²	1251	8.2	171	441	772	11.3	3.57	111	.244	.307	31	60	105	97	.981	111	149	1.4	6.1	2.5	.1	5.9
MIL	64	12	27	1393¹	1295	8.4	133	467	639	11.5	3.11	111	.247	.311	102	54	106	101	.979	130	159	.3	5.5	8.2	.1	.8
CIN	47	4	29	1389	1406	9.1	141	458	653	12.3	3.85	103	.265	.327	-12	20	106	101	.981	113	147	1.3	2.0	5.5	.4	4.6
STL	41	12	30	1388²	1339	8.7	155	546	709	12.3	3.97	95	.257	.329	-30	-28	100	98	.978	134	172	.1	-2.9	2.6	-.5	-.3
PHI	57	4	15	1377¹	1407	9.2	172	437	750	12.2	4.20	89	.266	.325	-66	-73	99	95	.975	144	143	-.6	-7.5	.0	.4	1.6
NY	31	9	28	1378	1287	8.4	144	551	765	12.2	3.78	100	.250	.326	-1	1	100	98	.976	144	143	-.6	.1	-8.3	.4	-1.7
PIT	37	8	24	1376¹	1406	9.2	144	469	662	12.4	3.74	101	.267	.329	5	5	100	105	.973	162	140	-1.5	.5	-5.8	-.9	-3.3
CHI	37	6	17	1392	1325	8.6	161	613	744	12.7	3.96	95	.252	.334	-29	-29	100	100	.976	144	141	-.4	-3.0	-7.1	-.2	-6.4
TOT	360	67	200	11063¹		8.7				12.1	3.77		.256	.324					.977	1082	1191					

Runs
Robinson-Cin 122
Snider-Bro 112
Aaron-Mil 106
Mathews-Mil 103
Gilliam-Bro 102

Hits
Aaron-Mil 200
Ashburn-Phi 190
Virdon-StL-Pit 185
Musial-StL 184
Boyer-StL 182

Doubles
Aaron-Mil 34
Snider-Bro 33
Musial-StL 33
Lopata-Phi 33
Bell-Cin 31

Triples
Bruton-Mil 15
Aaron-Mil 14
Walls-Pit 11
Moon-StL 11
Virdon-StL-Pit 10

Home Runs
Snider-Bro 43
Robinson-Cin 38
Adcock-Mil 38
Mathews-Mil 37

Total Bases
Aaron-Mil 340
Snider-Bro 324
Mays-NY 322
Robinson-Cin 319
Musial-StL 310

Runs Batted In
Musial-StL 109
Adcock-Mil 103
Kluszewski-Cin 102
Snider-Bro 101
Boyer-StL 98

Runs Produced
Aaron-Mil 172
Snider-Bro 170
Musial-StL 169
Robinson-Cin 167
Boyer-StL 163

Bases On Balls
Snider-Bro 99
Gilliam-Bro 95
Jones-Phi 92
Mathews-Mil 91
Moon-StL 80

Batting Average
Aaron-Mil 328
Virdon-StL-Pit 319
Clemente-Pit 311
Musial-StL 310
Boyer-StL 306

On Base Percentage
Snider-Bro 402
Gilliam-Bro 400
Musial-StL 390
Moon-StL 390
Jones-Phi 387

Slugging Average
Snider-Bro 598
Adcock-Mil 597
Aaron-Mil 558
Robinson-Cin 558
Mays-NY 557

Production
Snider-Bro 1.000
Robinson-Cin 939
Adcock-Mil 936
Mays-NY 928
Aaron-Mil 927

Adjusted Production
Adcock-Mil 154
Aaron-Mil 154
Snider-Bro 152
Mays-NY 146
Mathews-Mil 146

Batter Runs
Snider-Bro 50.5
Robinson-Cin 39.1
Aaron-Mil 36.3
Musial-StL 36.3
Mays-NY 35.9

Adjusted Batter Runs
Aaron-Mil 43.1
Snider-Bro 41.1
Mays-NY 36.7
Musial-StL 36.3
Mathews-Mil 36.2

Clutch Hitting Index
McMillan-Cin 145
Thomson-Mil 123
Ennis-Phi 115
Jones-Phi 109
Long-Pit 109

Runs Created
Snider-Bro 128
Robinson-Cin 121
Musial-StL 119
Mays-NY 118
Aaron-Mil 115

Total Average
Snider-Bro 1.052
Mays-NY 972
Robinson-Cin 960
Mathews-Mil 946
Adcock-Mil 916

Stolen Bases
Mays-NY 40
Gilliam-Bro 21
White-NY 15
Temple-Cin 14
Reese-Bro 13

Stolen Base Average
Mays-NY 80.0
Gilliam-Bro 70.0

Stolen Base Runs
Mays-NY 6.0
Ashburn-Phi 2.4
Temple-Cin 1.8
Post-Cin 1.8
Mathews-Mil 1.8

Fielding Runs
McMillan-Cin 29.9
Ashburn-Phi 25.3
Blasingame-StL . . . 21.9
Gilliam-Bro 17.7
Baker-Chi 17.2

Total Player Rating
Mays-NY 4.7
Aaron-Mil 4.4
McMillan-Cin 3.7
Gilliam-Bro 3.4
Musial-StL 3.3

Wins
Newcombe-Bro 27
Spahn-Mil 20
Antonelli-NY 20

Win Percentage
Newcombe-Bro . . .794
Buhl-Mil 692
Lawrence-Cin 655
Burdette-Mil 655
Spahn-Mil 645

Games
Face-Pit 68
Wilhelm-NY 64
Freeman-Cin 64
Labine-Bro 62
Lown-Chi 61

Complete Games
Roberts-Phi 22
Spahn-Mil 20
Friend-Pit 19
Newcombe-Bro 18
Burdette-Mil 16

Shutouts
Burdette-Mil 6
Newcombe-Bro 5
Antonelli-NY 5
Friend-Pit 4

Saves
Labine-Bro 19
Freeman-Cin 18
Lown-Chi 13
Jackson-StL 9
Bessent-Bro 9

Innings Pitched
Friend-Pit 314.1
Roberts-Phi 297.1
Spahn-Mil 281.1
Newcombe-Bro . . . 268.0
Kline-Pit 264.0

Fewest Hits/Game
Maglie-Bro 7.26
Newcombe-Bro 7.35
Jones-Chi 7.39
Mizell-StL 7.42
Craig-Bro 7.64

Fewest BB/Game
Roberts-Phi 1.21
Newcombe-Bro 1.54
Spahn-Mil 1.66
Fowler-Cin 1.77
Burdette-Mil 1.83

Strikeouts
Jones-Chi 176
Haddix-StL-Phi 170
Friend-Pit 166
Roberts-Phi 157
Mizell-StL 153

Strikeouts/Game
Jones-Chi 8.40
Haddix-StL-Phi 6.64
Mizell-StL 6.60
Nuxhall-Cin 5.38
Worthington-NY . . . 5.16

Ratio
Newcombe-Bro . . . 9.00
Spahn-Mil 9.73
Maglie-Bro 9.94
Burdette-Mil 10.15
Rush-Chi 10.18

Earned Run Average
Burdette-Mil 2.70
Spahn-Mil 2.78
Antonelli-NY 2.86
Maglie-Bro 2.87
Newcombe-Bro . . . 3.06

Adjusted ERA
Maglie-Bro 138
Antonelli-NY 132
Newcombe-Bro 130
Burdette-Mil 128
Spahn-Mil 124

Opponents' Batting Avg.
Newcombe-Bro 221
Jones-Chi 221
Mizell-StL 222
Maglie-Bro 222
Craig-Bro 231

Opponents' On Base Pct.
Newcombe-Bro 257
Spahn-Mil 276
Maglie-Bro 281
Burdette-Mil 282
Rush-Chi 282

Starter Runs
Spahn-Mil 30.9
Burdette-Mil 30.4
Antonelli-NY 26.3
Newcombe-Bro 21.3
Maglie-Bro 19.0

Adjusted Starter Runs
Newcombe-Bro . . . 27.1
Antonelli-NY 26.6
Maglie-Bro 23.2
Burdette-Mil 21.6
Spahn-Mil 21.2

Clutch Pitching Index
Conley-Mil 127
Klippstein-Cin 111
Kline-Pit 110
Poholsky-StL 108
Jeffcoat-Cin 105

Relief Runs
Grissom-NY 19.8
Acker-Cin 13.1
Bessent-Bro 11.2
B.Miller-Phi 7.3
Labine-Bro 5.5

Adjusted Relief Runs
Grissom-NY 19.9
Acker-Cin 15.0
Bessent-Bro 13.0
Labine-Bro 8.0
Freeman-Cin 7.0

Relief Ranking
Freeman-Cin 13.7
Bessent-Bro 13.6
Labine-Bro 12.9
Acker-Cin 11.7
Grissom-NY 8.3

Total Pitcher Index
Newcombe-Bro 4.3
Antonelli-NY 3.6
Spahn-Mil 2.9
Burdette-Mil 2.6
Dickson-Phi-StL . . . 2.2

Total Baseball Ranking
Mays-NY 4.7
Aaron-Mil 4.4
Newcombe-Bro 4.3
McMillan-Cin 3.7
Antonelli-NY 3.6

TEAM	G	W	L	PCT	GB	R	OR	AB	H	2B	3B	HR	BB	SO	AVG	OBP	SLG	PRO	PRO+	BR	/A	PF	CHI	RC	SB	CS	SBA	SBR
NY	154	97	57	.630		857	631	5312	1433	193	55	190	615	755	.270	.349	.434	.783	116	80	107	97	106	814	51	37	58	-7
CLE	155	88	66	.571	9	712	581	5148	1256	199	23	153	681	764	.244	.337	.381	.718	93	-35	-50	102	105	681	40	32	56	-7
CHI	154	85	69	.552	12	776	634	5286	1412	218	43	128	619	660	.267	.352	.397	.749	102	30	19	101	102	756	70	33	68	1
BOS	155	84	70	.545	13	780	751	5349	1473	261	45	139	727	687	.275	.365	.419	.784	101	0	-1	101	102	826	28	19	60	-3
DET	155	82	72	.532	15	789	699	5364	1494	209	50	150	644	618	.279	.359	.420	.779	111	84	82	100	97	816	43	26	62	-3
BAL	154	69	85	.448	28	571	705	5090	1242	198	34	91	563	725	.244	.322	.350	.672	90	-123	-80	92	101	572	39	42	48	-14
WAS	155	59	95	.383	38	652	924	5202	1302	198	62	112	690	877	.250	.343	.377	.720	96	-27	-26	100	94	681	37	34	52	-9
KC	154	52	102	.338	45	619	831	5256	1325	204	41	112	480	727	.252	.317	.370	.687	86	-108	-110	100	105	610	40	30	57	-6
TOT	618					5756		42007	10937	1680	353	1075	5019	5813	.260	.343	.394	.737							348	253	58	-47

TEAM	CG	SH	SV	IP	H	H/G	HR	BB	SO	RAT	ERA	ERA+	OAV	OOB	PR	/A	PF	CPI	FA	E	DP	FW	PW	BW	SBW	DIF
NY	50	10	35	1382	1285	8.4	114	652	732	12.9	3.63	107	.249	.337	82	37	93	105	.977	136	214	.6	3.6	10.5	-.1	5.4
CLE	67	17	24	1384	1233	8.0	116	564	845	11.9	3.32	127	.238	.316	129	136	101	100	.978	129	130	1.0	13.3	-4.9	-.1	1.7
CHI	65	11	13	1389	1351	8.8	118	524	722	12.3	3.73	110	.255	.325	67	58	99	99	.979	122	160	1.3	5.7	1.9	.7	-1.6
BOS	50	8	20	1398	1354	8.7	130	668	712	13.3	4.17	111	.254	.342	-1	71	111	96	.972	169	168	-1.2	7.0	-.0	.3	1.1
DET	62	10	15	1379	1389	9.1	140	655	788	13.6	4.06	101	.264	.351	15	9	99	108	.976	140	151	.4	.9	8.0	.3	-4.6
BAL	38	10	24	1360²	1362	9.0	99	547	715	12.8	4.20	93	.263	.337	-6	-42	94	93	.977	137	142	.5	-4.1	-7.8	-.8	4.2
WAS	36	1	18	1368²	1539	10.1	171	730	663	15.1	5.33	81	.287	.376	-179	-153	104	99	.972	171	173	-1.3	-15.0	-2.5	-.3	1.1
KC	30	3	18	1370¹	1424	9.4	187	679	636	14.1	4.86	89	.271	.359	-107	-81	104	101	.973	166	187	-1.1	-7.9	-10.8	.0	-5.2
TOT	398	70	167	11031²		8.9				13.2	4.16		.260	.343					.975	1170	1325					

Runs
Mantle-NY 132
Fox-Chi 109
Minoso-Chi 106

Hits
Kuenn-Det 196
Kaline-Det 194
Fox-Chi 192
Mantle-NY 188
Jensen-Bos 182

Doubles
Piersall-Bos 40
Kuenn-Det 32
Kaline-Det 32

Triples
Simpson-KC 11
Minoso-Chi 11
Lemon-Was 11
Jensen-Bos 11

Home Runs
Mantle-NY 52
Wertz-Cle 32
Berra-NY 30
Sievers-Was 29
Maxwell-Det 28

Total Bases
Mantle-NY 376
Kaline-Det 327
Jensen-Bos 287
Minoso-Chi 286

Runs Batted In
Mantle-NY 130
Kaline-Det 128
Wertz-Cle 106
Simpson-KC 105
Berra-NY 105

Runs Produced
Mantle-NY 210
Kaline-Det 197
Minoso-Chi 173
Kuenn-Det 172
Berra-NY 168

Bases On Balls
Yost-Was 151
Mantle-NY 112
Williams-Bos 102
Doby-Chi 102
Sievers-Was 100

Batting Average
Mantle-NY 353
Williams-Bos 345
Kuenn-Det 332
Maxwell-Det 326
Nieman-Chi-Bal . . .320

On Base Percentage
Williams-Bos 479
Mantle-NY 467
Nieman-Chi-Bal . . .438
Minoso-Chi 430
Maxwell-Det 420

Slugging Average
Mantle-NY 705
Williams-Bos 605
Maxwell-Det 534
Berra-NY 534
Kaline-Det 530

Production
Mantle-NY 1.172
Williams-Bos . . . 1.084
Minoso-Chi 954
Maxwell-Det 954
Nieman-Chi-Bal . . .934

Adjusted Production
Mantle-NY 213
Williams-Bos 164
Nieman-Chi-Bal . . 156
Maxwell-Det 150
Minoso-Chi 149

Batter Runs
Mantle-NY 83.3
Williams-Bos 54.1
Minoso-Chi 43.2
Maxwell-Det 37.5
Kaline-Det 33.4

Adjusted Batter Runs
Mantle-NY 88.7
Minoso-Chi 41.5
Williams-Bos 40.9
Nieman-Chi-Bal . . 38.8
Maxwell-Det 37.3

Clutch Hitting Index
Kaline-Det 117
Lollar-Chi 117
Triandos-Bal 114
Doby-Chi 113
Carey-NY 109

Runs Created
Mantle-NY 188
Minoso-Chi 130
Kaline-Det 129
Williams-Bos 121
Maxwell-Det 118

Total Average
Mantle-NY 1.426
Williams-Bos . . . 1.255
Minoso-Chi 1.031
Maxwell-Det . . . 1.015
Nieman-Chi-Bal . . .955

Stolen Bases
Aparicio-Chi 21
Rivera-Chi 20
Avila-Cle 17
Minoso-Chi 12

Stolen Base Average
Aparicio-Chi 84.0
Avila-Cle 81.0
Rivera-Chi 69.0

Stolen Base Runs
Aparicio-Chi 3.9
Avila-Cle 2.7
Mantle-NY 2.4

Fielding Runs
Piersall-Bos 17.6
Kaline-Det 17.3
Hegan-Cle 15.6
Buddin-Bos 13.9
Maxwell-Det 13.1

Total Player Rating
Mantle-NY 8.7
Kaline-Det 4.2
Berra-NY 4.2
Maxwell-Det 4.2
Minoso-Chi 3.6

Wins
Lary-Det 21

Win Percentage
Ford-NY 760
Wynn-Cle 690
Score-Cle 690
Pierce-Chi 690
Brewer-Bos 679

Games
Zuverink-Bal 62
Crimian-KC 54
Gorman-KC 52
Mossi-Cle 48
Delock-Bos 48

Complete Games
Pierce-Chi 21
Lemon-Cle 21
Lary-Det 20

Shutouts
Score-Cle 5

Saves
Zuverink-Bal 16
Mossi-Cle 11
Morgan-NY 11
Shantz-KC 9
Delock-Bos 9

Innings Pitched
Lary-Det 294.0
Wynn-Cle 277.2
Pierce-Chi 276.1
Foytack-Det 256.0
Lemon-Cle 255.1

Fewest Hits/Game
Score-Cle 5.85
Larsen-NY 6.66
Harshman-Chi . . . 7.27
Brewer-Bos 7.37
Foytack-Det 7.42

Fewest BB/Game
Stobbs-Was 2.03
Donovan-Chi 2.26
Kucks-NY 2.89
Wynn-Cle 2.95
Sturdivant-NY . . . 2.96

Strikeouts
Score-Cle 263
Pierce-Chi 192
Foytack-Det 184
Hoeft-Det 172
Lary-Det 165

Strikeouts/Game
Score-Cle 9.49
Pascual-Was 7.73
Foytack-Det 6.47
Pierce-Chi 6.25
Sturdivant-NY . . . 6.25

Ratio
Score-Cle 10.58
Donovan-Chi 10.62
Wynn-Cle 10.66
Sturdivant-NY . . . 10.80
Ford-NY 10.97

Earned Run Average
Ford-NY 2.47
Score-Cle 2.53
Wynn-Cle 2.72
Lemon-Cle 3.03
Harshman-Chi . . . 3.10

Adjusted ERA
Score-Cle 166
Ford-NY 156
Wynn-Cle 154
Lemon-Cle 139
Sullivan-Bos 135

Opponents' Batting Avg.
Score-Cle 186
Larsen-NY 204
Brewer-Bos 220
Harshman-Chi 221
Sturdivant-NY 224

Opponents' On Base Pct.
Sturdivant-NY 291
Donovan-Chi 292
Score-Cle 292
Wynn-Cle 294
Ford-NY 303

Starter Runs
Score-Cle 45.2
Wynn-Cle 44.3
Ford-NY 42.3
Lary-Det 32.9
Lemon-Cle 32.0

Adjusted Starter Runs
Score-Cle 46.5
Wynn-Cle 45.7
Ford-NY 35.0
Lemon-Cle 33.3
Sullivan-Bos 32.2

Clutch Pitching Index
Lary-Det 117
Sullivan-Bos 116
Hoeft-Det 116
Ford-NY 114
Stobbs-Was 114

Relief Runs
Narleski-Cle 17.4
Grim-NY 11.5
Byrne-NY 9.7
Byerly-Was 6.9
Mossi-Cle 5.5

Adjusted Relief Runs
Narleski-Cle 17.7
Grim-NY 9.1
Byerly-Was 7.9
Byrne-NY 6.1
Mossi-Cle 6.0

Relief Ranking
Narleski-Cle 16.1
Byerly-Was 9.6
Delock-Bos 9.2
Grim-NY 9.0
Mossi-Cle 8.4

Total Pitcher Index
Lemon-Cle 5.2
Wynn-Cle 5.1
Score-Cle 4.8
Ford-NY 4.5
Brewer-Bos 4.1

Total Baseball Ranking
Mantle-NY 8.7
Lemon-Cle 5.2
Wynn-Cle 5.1
Score-Cle 4.8
Ford-NY 4.5

TEAM	G	W	L	PCT	GB	R	OR	AB	H	2B	3B	HR	BB	SO	AVG	OBP	SLG	PRO	PRO+	BR	/A	PF	CHI	RC	SB	CS	SBA	SBR
MIL	155	95	59	.617		772	613	5458	1469	221	62	199	461	729	.269	.329	.442	.771	121	82	138	93	101	787	35	16	69	1
STL	154	87	67	.565	8	737	666	5472	1497	235	43	132	493	672	.274	.336	.405	.741	103	36	22	102	102	731	58	44	57	-9
BRO	154	84	70	.545	11	690	591	5242	1325	188	38	147	550	848	.253	.328	.387	.715	89	-11	-75	110	104	664	60	34	64	-2
CIN	154	80	74	.519	15	747	781	5389	1452	251	33	187	546	752	.269	.325	.375	.773	106	97	42	97	95	794	51	36	59	-6
PHI	156	77	77	.500	18	623	656	5241	1311	213	44	117	534	758	.250	.325	.375	.700	97	-39	-19	97	99	635	57	26	69	2
NY	154	69	85	.448	26	643	701	5346	1349	171	54	157	447	669	.252	.313	.393	.706	95	-42	-40	100	103	646	64	38	63	-4
PIT	155	62	92	.403	33	586	696	5402	1447	231	60	92	374	733	.268	.318	.384	.702	97	-46	-27	97	93	649	46	35	57	-7
CHI	156	62	92	.403	33	628	722	5369	1312	223	31	147	461	989	.244	.307	.380	.687	91	-78	-68	98	105	623	28	25	53	-7
TOT	619					5426		42919	11162	1733	365	1178	3866	6150	.260	.325	.400	.724							399	254	61	-33

TEAM	CG	SH	SV	IP	H	H/G	HR	BB	SO	RAT	ERA	ERA+	OAV	OOB	PR	/A	PF	CPI	FA	E	DP	FW	PW	BW	SBW	DIF
MIL	60	9	24	1411	1347	8.6	124	570	693	12.3	3.47	101	.253	.327	64	4	90	107	.981	120	173	1.0	.4	14.0	.5	2.0
STL	46	11	29	1413¹	1385	8.8	140	506	778	12.2	3.78	105	.257	.324	16	29	102	100	.979	131	168	.4	2.9	2.2	-.5	5.0
BRO	44	18	29	1399	1285	8.3	144	456	891	11.4	3.35	124	.244	.307	82	127	107	101	.982	107	139	.6	12.9	-7.6	.2	.9
CIN	40	5	29	1395²	1486	9.6	179	429	707	12.7	4.62	89	.275	.334	-116	-79	106	95	.976	136	117	1.7	-8.0	4.3	-.2	5.3
PHI	54	9	23	1401²	1363	8.8	139	412	858	11.5	3.79	100	.254	.310	13	1	98	92	.974	161	180	.2	.1	-1.9	.6	1.0
NY	35	9	20	1398²	1436	9.2	150	471	701	12.5	4.01	98	.267	.330	-20	-12	101	101	.972	170	143	-1.3	-1.2	-4.1	.0	-1.4
PIT	47	9	15	1395	1463	9.4	158	421	663	12.3	3.88	98	.270	.325	0	-14	98	105	.975	149	140	-1.7	-1.4	-2.7	-.3	-8.8
CHI	30	5	26	1403¹	1397	9.0	144	601	859	13.0	4.13	94	.261	.339	-39	-40	100	100	.975	127	140	-.5	-4.1	-6.9	-.3	-3.2
TOT	356	75	195	11217²		9.0				12.2	3.88		.260	.325					.977	1101	1196					

Runs
Aaron-Mil 118
Banks-Chi 113
Mays-NY 112
Mathews-Mil 109
Blasingame-StL 108

Hits
Schoendienst-NY-Mil .. 200
Aaron-Mil 198
Robinson-Cin 197
Mays-NY 195
Ashburn-Phi 186

Doubles
Hoak-Cin 39
Musial-StL 38
Bouchee-Phi 35
Banks-Chi 34
Moryn-Chi 33

Triples
Mays-NY 20
Virdon-Pit 11
Mathews-Mil 9
Bruton-Mil 9

Home Runs
Aaron-Mil 44
Banks-Chi 43
Snider-Bro 40
Mays-NY 35
Mathews-Mil 32

Total Bases
Aaron-Mil 369
Mays-NY 366
Banks-Chi 344
Robinson-Cin 323
Mathews-Mil 309

Runs Batted In
Aaron-Mil 132
Ennis-StL 105
Musial-StL 102
Banks-Chi 102
Hodges-Bro 98

Runs Produced
Aaron-Mil 206
Mays-NY 174
Banks-Chi 172
Mathews-Mil 171
Hodges-Bro 165

Bases On Balls
Temple-Cin 94
Ashburn-Phi 94
Mathews-Mil 90
Bouchee-Phi 84
Snider-Bro 77

Batting Average
Musial-StL 351
Mays-NY 333
Robinson-Cin 322
Aaron-Mil 322
Groat-Pit 315

On Base Percentage
Musial-StL 428
Mays-NY 411
Bouchee-Phi 396
Ashburn-Phi 392
Temple-Cin 391

Slugging Average
Mays-NY 626
Musial-StL 612
Aaron-Mil 600
Snider-Bro 587
Banks-Chi 579

Production
Musial-StL 1.040
Mays-NY 1.037
Aaron-Mil 979
Snider-Bro 957
Banks-Chi 942

Adjusted Production
Mays-NY 174
Musial-StL 172
Aaron-Mil 170
Mathews-Mil 157
Banks-Chi 150

Batter Runs
Mays-NY 60.5
Musial-StL 54.1
Aaron-Mil 48.3
Banks-Chi 38.6
Mathews-Mil 38.3

Adjusted Batter Runs
Mays-NY 61.0
Aaron-Mil 57.5
Musial-StL 51.8
Mathews-Mil 46.7
Banks-Chi 40.5

Clutch Hitting Index
McMillan-Cin 134
Ennis-StL 131
Hamner-Phi 115
Post-Cin 112
Hoak-Cin 112

Runs Created
Mays-NY 145
Aaron-Mil 136
Musial-StL 129
Mathews-Mil 126
Banks-Chi 123

Total Average
Musial-StL 1.103
Mays-NY 1.092
Aaron-Mil 988
Mathews-Mil 973
Snider-Bro 962

Stolen Bases
Mays-NY 38
Gilliam-Bro 26
Blasingame-StL ... 21
Temple-Cin 19
Fernandez-Phi ... 18

Stolen Base Average
Temple-Cin 79.2
Fernandez-Phi ... 78.3
Gilliam-Bro 72.2
Blasingame-StL .. 70.0
Mays-NY 66.7

Stolen Base Runs
Temple-Cin 2.7
Fernandez-Phi 2.4
Robinson-Cin 1.8
Gilliam-Bro 1.8

Fielding Runs
Ashburn-Phi 32.4
Blasingame-StL .. 25.8
Logan-Mil 23.9
Robinson-Cin 18.7
Campanella-Bro .. 16.0

Total Player Rating
Mays-NY 6.3
Aaron-Mil 5.0
Mathews-Mil 4.8
Musial-StL 4.5
Robinson-Cin 3.8

Wins
Spahn-Mil 21
Sanford-Phi 19
Buhl-Mil 18
Drysdale-Bro 17
Burdette-Mil 17

Win Percentage
Buhl-Mil 720
Sanford-Phi 704
Spahn-Mil 656
Drysdale-Bro 654
Burdette-Mil 654

Games
Lown-Chi 67
Face-Pit 59
Labine-Bro 58
Worthington-NY ... 55
Grissom-NY 55

Complete Games
Spahn-Mil 18
Friend-Pit 17
Gomez-NY 16
Sanford-Phi 15

Shutouts
Podres-Bro 6
Spahn-Mil 4
Newcombe-Bro 4
Drysdale-Bro 4

Saves
Labine-Bro 17
Grissom-NY 14
Lown-Chi 12
Wilhelm-StL 11

Innings Pitched
Friend-Pit 277.0
Spahn-Mil 271.0
Burdette-Mil 256.2
Lawrence-Cin 250.1
Roberts-Phi 249.2

Fewest Hits/Game
Sanford-Phi 7.38
Podres-Bro 7.71
Drott-Chi 7.86
Buhl-Mil 7.93
Worthington-NY ... 7.99

Fewest BB/Game
Newcombe-Bro 1.49
Roberts-Phi 1.55
Law-Pit 1.67
Purkey-Pit 1.90
Jeffcoat-Cin 2.00

Strikeouts
Sanford-Phi 188
Drott-Chi 170
Drabowsky-Chi 170
Jones-StL 154
Drysdale-Bro 148

Strikeouts/Game
Jones-StL 7.59
Haddix-Phi 7.17
Sanford-Phi 7.15
Drott-Chi 6.68
Drabowsky-Chi ... 6.38

Ratio
Podres-Bro 9.78
Roberts-Phi 10.45
Newcombe-Bro 10.56
Spahn-Mil 10.66
Law-Pit 10.74

Earned Run Average
Podres-Bro 2.66
Drysdale-Bro 2.69
Spahn-Mil 2.69
Buhl-Mil 2.74
Law-Pit 2.87

Adjusted ERA
Podres-Bro 156
Drysdale-Bro 155
Law-Pit 132
Spahn-Mil 130
Buhl-Mil 128

Opponents' Batting Avg.
Sanford-Phi 221
Podres-Bro 230
Drott-Chi 234
Drysdale-Bro 236
Spahn-Mil 237

Opponents' On Base Pct.
Podres-Bro 274
Roberts-Phi 284
Newcombe-Bro 290
Law-Pit 291
Spahn-Mil 293

Starter Runs
Spahn-Mil 35.8
Drysdale-Bro 29.2
Buhl-Mil 27.4
Podres-Bro 26.5
Sanford-Phi 21.0

Adjusted Starter Runs
Drysdale-Bro 36.3
Podres-Bro 32.7
Spahn-Mil 24.3
Sanford-Phi 19.0
Buhl-Mil 18.2

Clutch Pitching Index
Buhl-Mil 135
Barclay-NY 117
Law-Pit 113
Spahn-Mil 109
Antonelli-NY 108

Relief Runs
Farrell-Phi 13.9
Roebuck-Bro 12.5
Grissom-NY 11.6
Face-Pit 8.4
Miller-Phi 8.0

Adjusted Relief Runs
Roebuck-Bro 15.6
Farrell-Phi 13.2
Grissom-NY 12.1
Labine-Bro 8.4
Miller-Phi 7.5

Relief Ranking
Farrell-Phi 20.7
Roebuck-Bro 17.5
Grissom-NY 15.2
Labine-Bro 11.8
Miller-Phi 9.5

Total Pitcher Index
Drysdale-Bro 4.7
Podres-Bro 3.5
Spahn-Mil 3.0
Roebuck-Bro 2.3
Farrell-Phi 2.2

Total Baseball Ranking
Mays-NY 6.3
Aaron-Mil 5.0
Mathews-Mil 4.8
Drysdale-Bro 4.7
Musial-StL 4.5

TEAM	G	W	L	PCT	GB	R	OR	AB	H	2B	3B	HR	BB	SO	AVG	OBP	SLG	PRO	PRO+	BR	/A	PF	CHI	RC	SB	CS	SBA	SBR
NY	154	98	56	.636		723	534	5271	1412	200	54	145	562	709	.268	.341	.409	.750	113	76	88	98	99	729	49	38	56	-8
CHI	155	90	64	.584	8	707	566	5265	1369	208	41	106	633	745	.260	.347	.375	.722	103	40	36	101	100	708	109	51	68	2
BOS	154	82	72	.532	16	721	668	5267	1380	231	32	153	624	739	.262	.343	.405	.748	104	76	34	106	98	725	29	21	58	-4
DET	154	78	76	.506	20	614	614	5348	1376	224	37	116	504	504	.257	.324	.378	.702	96	-18	-35	103	96	644	36	47	43	-17
BAL	154	76	76	.500	21	597	588	5264	1326	191	39	87	504	699	.252	.321	.353	.674	96	-66	-30	94	101	600	57	35	62	-4
CLE	153	76	77	.497	21.5	682	722	5171	1304	199	26	140	591	786	.252	.332	.382	.714	102	10	17	99	103	661	40	47	46	-16
KC	154	59	94	.386	38.5	563	710	5170	1262	195	40	166	364	760	.244	.297	.394	.691	92	-60	-70	102	100	578	35	27	56	-6
WAS	154	55	99	.357	43	603	808	5231	1274	215	38	111	527	733	.244	.318	.363	.681	93	-56	-49	99	102	592	13	38	25	-19
TOT	616					5210		41987	10703	1663	307	1024	4309	5814	.255	.328	.382	.710							368	304	55	-72

TEAM	CG	SH	SV	IP	H	H/G	HR	BB	SO	RAT	ERA	ERA+	OAV	OOB	PR	/A	PF	CPI	FA	E	DP	FW	PW	BW	SBW	DIF
NY	41	13	42	1395¹	1198	7.7	110	580	810	11.7	3.00	120	.234	.317	122	91	95	109	.980	123	183	.2	9.4	9.1	.1	2.2
CHI	59	16	27	1401²	1305	8.4	124	470	665	11.6	3.35	112	.248	.313	69	61	99	102	.982	107	169	1.1	6.3	3.7	1.1	.7
BOS	55	9	23	1376²	1391	9.1	116	498	692	12.6	3.88	103	.264	.331	-14	17	105	100	.976	149	179	-1.2	1.8	3.5	.5	.4
DET	52	9	21	1417²	1330	8.4	147	505	756	11.9	3.56	108	.250	.320	37	47	102	104	.980	121	151	.3	4.9	-3.6	-.8	.3
BAL	44	13	25	1408	1272	8.1	95	493	767	11.5	3.46	104	.243	.312	51	20	95	92	.981	112	159	.8	2.1	-3.1	.5	-.3
CLE	46	7	23	1380²	1381	9.0	130	618	807	13.3	4.06	92	.261	.343	-42	-53	98	101	.974	153	154	-1.4	-5.5	1.8	-.7	5.4
KC	26	6	19	1369²	1344	8.8	153	565	626	12.7	4.19	94	.260	.336	-61	-35	104	99	.979	125	162	.1	-3.6	-7.2	.3	-7.1
WAS	31	5	16	1377	1482	9.7	149	580	691	13.7	4.85	80	.278	.353	-162	-146	103	95	.979	128	159	-.0	-15.1	-5.1	-1.0	-.8
TOT	354	78	196	11126²		8.7				12.4	3.79		.255	.328					.979	1018	1316					

Runs
Mantle-NY 121
Fox-Chi 110
Piersall-Bos 103
Sievers-Was 99

Hits
Fox-Chi 196
Malzone-Bos 185
Minoso-Chi 176
Mantle-NY 173
Kuenn-Det 173

Doubles
Minoso-Chi 36
Gardner-Bal 36
Malzone-Bos 31
Kuenn-Det 30

Triples
Simpson-KC-NY 9
McDougald-NY 9
Bauer-NY 9
Fox-Chi 8
Boyd-Bal 8

Home Runs
Sievers-Was 42
Williams-Bos 38
Mantle-NY 34
Wertz-Cle 28
Zernial-KC 27

Total Bases
Sievers-Was 331
Mantle-NY 315
Williams-Bos 307
Kaline-Det 276
Malzone-Bos 271

Runs Batted In
Sievers-Was 114
Wertz-Cle 105
Minoso-Chi 103
Malzone-Bos 103
Jensen-Bos 103

Runs Produced
Minoso-Chi 187
Mantle-NY 181
Sievers-Was 171
Malzone-Bos 170
Fox-Chi 165

Bases On Balls
Mantle-NY 146
Williams-Bos 119
Smith-Cle 79
Minoso-Chi 79
Wertz-Cle 78

Batting Average
Williams-Bos 388
Mantle-NY 365
Woodling-Cle 321
Boyd-Bal 318
Fox-Chi 317

On Base Percentage
Williams-Bos 528
Mantle-NY 515
Minoso-Chi 413
Woodling-Cle 412
Fox-Chi 404

Slugging Average
Williams-Bos 731
Mantle-NY 665
Sievers-Was 579
Woodling-Cle 521
Wertz-Cle 485

Production
Williams-Bos 1.259
Mantle-NY 1.179
Sievers-Was 968
Woodling-Cle 933
Minoso-Chi 867

Adjusted Production
Williams-Bos 227
Mantle-NY 223
Sievers-Was 163
Woodling-Cle 155
Minoso-Chi 136

Batter Runs
Williams-Bos 89.9
Mantle-NY 88.9
Sievers-Was 47.3
Woodling-Cle 33.0
Minoso-Chi 32.7

Adjusted Batter Runs
Mantle-NY 91.4
Williams-Bos 81.5
Sievers-Was 48.7
Woodling-Cle 33.9
Minoso-Chi 32.2

Clutch Hitting Index
Minoso-Chi 126
Doby-Cle 125
Skowron-NY 123
Malzone-Bos 117
Jensen-Bos 114

Runs Created
Mantle-NY 178
Williams-Bos 167
Sievers-Was 131
Fox-Chi 109
Minoso-Chi 106

Total Average
Williams-Bos 1.599
Mantle-NY 1.534
Sievers-Was 1.010
Woodling-Cle 944
Maxwell-Det 876

Stolen Bases
Aparicio-Chi 28
Rivera-Chi 18
Minoso-Chi 18
Mantle-NY 16

Stolen Base Average
Rivera-Chi 90.0
Mantle-NY 84.2
Aparicio-Chi 77.8
Minoso-Chi 54.5

Stolen Base Runs
Rivera-Chi 4.2
Aparicio-Chi 3.6
Mantle-NY 3.0
Landis-Chi 1.8
Martin-NY-KC 1.5

Fielding Runs
Bridges-Was 29.3
Fox-Chi 20.9
Berra-NY 15.6
Phillips-Chi 15.5
McDougald-NY 15.1

Total Player Rating
Mantle-NY 8.6
Williams-Bos 7.1
Fox-Chi 5.6
Sievers-Was 4.4
McDougald-NY 4.2

Wins
Pierce-Chi 20
Bunning-Det 20
Sturdivant-NY 16
Donovan-Chi 16
Brewer-Bos 16

Win Percentage
Sturdivant-NY 727
Donovan-Chi 727
Bunning-Det 714
Wilson-Chi 652
Pierce-Chi 625

Games
Zuverink-Bal 56
Hyde-Was 52
Clevenger-Was 52
Delock-Bos 49
Trucks-KC 48

Complete Games
Pierce-Chi 16
Donovan-Chi 16
Brewer-Bos 15

Shutouts
Wilson-Chi 5
Turley-NY 4
Pierce-Chi 4

Saves
Grim-NY 19
Narleski-Cle 16
Delock-Bos 11
Zuverink-Bal 9
Clevenger-Was 8

Innings Pitched
Bunning-Det 267.1
Wynn-Cle 263.0
Pierce-Chi 257.0
Johnson-Bal 242.0
F.Sullivan-Bos 240.2

Fewest Hits/Game
Turley-NY 6.12
Bunning-Det 7.20
Foytack-Det 7.43
Sturdivant-NY 7.59
F.Sullivan-Bos 7.70

Fewest BB/Game
F.Sullivan-Bos 1.80
Donovan-Chi 1.84
Shantz-NY 2.08
Loes-Bal 2.14
Bunning-Det 2.42

Strikeouts
Wynn-Cle 184
Bunning-Det 182
Johnson-Bal 177
Pierce-Chi 171
Turley-NY 152

Strikeouts/Game
Turley-NY 7.76
Johnson-Bal 6.58
Wynn-Cle 6.30
Bunning-Det 6.13
Pierce-Chi 5.99

Ratio
F.Sullivan-Bos 9.76
Bunning-Det 10.00
Donovan-Chi 10.44
Johnson-Bal 10.45
Pierce-Chi 10.51

Earned Run Average
Shantz-NY 2.45
Sturdivant-NY 2.54
Bunning-Det 2.69
Turley-NY 2.71
F.Sullivan-Bos 2.73

Adjusted ERA
Shantz-NY 147
F.Sullivan-Bos 146
Bunning-Det 143
Sturdivant-NY 141
Donovan-Chi 135

Opponents' Batting Avg.
Turley-NY 194
Bunning-Det 218
Foytack-Det 226
F.Sullivan-Bos 230
Sturdivant-NY 232

Opponents' On Base Pct.
F.Sullivan-Bos 275
Bunning-Det 279
Pierce-Chi 287
Johnson-Bal 289
Donovan-Chi 293

Starter Runs
Bunning-Det 32.5
F.Sullivan-Bos . . . 28.3
Sturdivant-NY 27.9
Shantz-NY 25.8
Donovan-Chi 24.9

Adjusted Starter Runs
Bunning-Det 34.5
F.Sullivan-Bos . . . 33.6
Donovan-Chi 23.6
Sturdivant-NY 23.4
Shantz-NY 22.0

Clutch Pitching Index
Shantz-NY 131
Sturdivant-NY 121
Narleski-Cle 112
Kemmerer-Bos-Was . . 110
Donovan-Chi 108

Relief Runs
Staley-Chi 20.2
Zuverink-Bal 16.4
Trucks-KC 9.8
Grim-NY 9.3
Lehman-Bal 7.6

Adjusted Relief Runs
Staley-Chi 19.6
Zuverink-Bal 14.0
Trucks-KC 12.0
Byerly-Was 8.1
Grim-NY 7.7

Relief Ranking
Grim-NY 23.8
Zuverink-Bal 20.3
Trucks-KC 16.5
Staley-Chi 13.0
Byerly-Was 10.4

Total Pitcher Index
F.Sullivan-Bos 3.5
Bunning-Det 3.3
Shantz-NY 3.1
Grim-NY 2.6
Donovan-Chi 2.5

Total Baseball Ranking
Mantle-NY 8.6
Williams-Bos 7.1
Fox-Chi 5.6
Sievers-Was 4.4
McDougald-NY 4.2

TEAM	G	W	L	PCT	GB	R	OR	AB	H	2B	3B	HR	BB	SO	AVG	OBP	SLG	PRO	PRO+	BR	/A	PF	CHI	RC	SB	CS	SBA	SBR
MIL	154	92	62	.597		675	541	5225	1388	221	21	167	478	646	.266	.331	.412	.743	111	14	72	92	98	705	26	8	76	3
PIT	154	84	70	.545	8	662	607	5247	1386	229	68	134	396	753	.264	.319	.410	.729	101	-21	-4	97	103	669	30	15	67	0
SF	154	80	74	.519	12	727	698	5318	1399	250	42	170	531	817	.263	.334	.422	.756	107	37	54	98	100	747	64	29	69	2
CIN	154	76	78	.494	16	695	621	5273	1359	242	40	123	572	765	.258	.333	.389	.722	92	-19	-54	105	104	690	61	38	62	-5
STL	154	72	82	.468	20	619	704	5255	1371	216	39	111	533	637	.261	.331	.380	.711	90	-38	-63	104	97	638	44	43	51	-13
CHI	154	72	82	.468	20	709	725	5289	1402	207	49	182	487	853	.251	.319	.426	.758	108	39	50	98	99	737	39	23	63	-2
LA	154	71	83	.461	21	668	761	5173	1297	166	50	172	495	850	.251	.319	.402	.721	93	-32	-52	103	106	650	73	47	61	-6
PHI	154	69	85	.448	23	664	762	5363	1424	238	56	124	573	871	.266	.341	.400	.741	103	20	30	99	93	729	51	33	61	-5
TOT	616							5419		42143	11026	1769	365	1183	4065	6192	.262	.330	.405	.735						388	236	62	-25

TEAM	CG	SH	SV	IP	H	H/G	HR	BB	SO	RAT	ERA	ERA+	OAV	OOB	PR	/A	PF	CPI	FA	E	DP	FW	PW	BW	SBW	DIF
MIL	72	16	17	1376	1261	8.2	125	426	773	11.2	3.21	110	.244	.305	113	47	89	99	.980	120	152	.8	4.7	7.3	.6	1.5
PIT	43	10	41	1367	1344	8.8	123	470	679	12.1	3.56	109	.261	.325	59	46	98	105	.978	133	173	.1	4.6	-.4	.3	2.3
SF	38	7	25	1389¹	1400	9.1	166	512	775	12.6	3.98	96	.263	.332	-4	-25	97	103	.975	152	156	-.9	-2.5	5.4	.5	.5
CIN	50	7	20	1385¹	1422	9.2	148	419	705	12.1	3.73	111	.267	.324	34	64	105	105	.983	100	148	1.9	6.5	-5.4	-.2	-3.7
STL	45	6	25	1381²	1398	9.1	158	567	822	13.1	4.12	100	.264	.340	-25	2	105	102	.974	153	163	-.9	.2	-6.4	-1.0	3.1
CHI	27	5	24	1361	1322	8.7	142	619	855	13.4	4.22	93	.254	.338	-40	-46	99	94	.975	150	161	-.8	-4.6	5.0	.1	-4.7
LA	30	7	31	1368¹	1399	9.2	173	606	855	13.4	4.47	92	.267	.347	-79	-57	104	100	.975	146	198	-.6	-5.7	-5.2	.3	5.9
PHI	51	6	15	1397	1480	9.5	148	446	778	12.5	4.32	92	.272	.329	-58	-56	100	93	.978	129	136	.3	-5.6	3.0	-.2	-5.5
TOT	356	64	198	11025²		9.0				12.5	3.95		.262	.330					.977	1083	1287					

Runs
Mays-SF 121
Banks-Chi 119
Aaron-Mil 109
Boyer-StL 101
Ashburn-Phi 98

Hits
Ashburn-Phi 215
Mays-SF 208
Aaron-Mil 196
Banks-Chi 193
Cepeda-SF 188

Doubles
Cepeda-SF 38
Groat-Pit 36
Musial-StL 35
H.Anderson-Phi ... 34
Aaron-Mil 34

Triples
Ashburn-Phi 13
Virdon-Pit 11
Mays-SF 11
Banks-Chi 11

Home Runs
Banks-Chi 47
Thomas-Pit 35
Robinson-Cin 31
Mathews-Mil 31
Aaron-Mil 30

Total Bases
Banks-Chi 379
Mays-SF 350
Aaron-Mil 328
Cepeda-SF 309
Thomas-Pit 297

Runs Batted In
Banks-Chi 129
Thomas-Pit 109
H.Anderson-Phi ... 97
Mays-SF 96
Cepeda-SF 96

Runs Produced
Banks-Chi 201
Mays-SF 188
Aaron-Mil 174
Boyer-StL 168
Thomas-Pit 163

Bases On Balls
Ashburn-Phi 97
Temple-Cin 91
Mathews-Mil 85
Cunningham-StL ... 82

Batting Average
Ashburn-Phi 350
Mays-SF 347
Musial-StL 337
Aaron-Mil 326
Skinner-Pit 321

On Base Percentage
Ashburn-Phi 441
Musial-StL 426
Mays-SF 423
Temple-Cin 406
Skinner-Pit.......390

Slugging Average
Banks-Chi 614
Mays-SF 583
Aaron-Mil 546
Thomas-Pit 528
Musial-StL 528

Production
Mays-SF 1.006
Banks-Chi 984
Musial-StL 953
Aaron-Mil 933
H.Anderson-Phi 900

Adjusted Production
Mays-SF 167
Banks-Chi 157
Aaron-Mil 157
Musial-StL 145
H.Anderson-Phi ... 137

Batter Runs
Mays-SF 55.3
Banks-Chi 45.7
Aaron-Mil 37.0
Musial-StL 36.7
Ashburn-Phi 36.5

Adjusted Batter Runs
Mays-SF 58.4
Banks-Chi 47.7
Aaron-Mil 46.9
Ashburn-Phi 38.2
Musial-StL 32.8

Clutch Hitting Index
H.Anderson-Phi ... 111
Fernandez-Phi 110
Long-Chi 103
Spencer-SF 103
Banks-Chi 103

Runs Created
Mays-SF 152
Banks-Chi 135
Ashburn-Phi 129
Aaron-Mil 121
Skinner-Pit 102

Total Average
Mays-SF 1.110
Banks-Chi 984
Musial-StL 970
Ashburn-Phi 929
Aaron-Mil 916

Stolen Bases
Mays-SF 31
Ashburn-Phi 21
T.Taylor-Chi 21
Blasingame-StL ... 20
Gilliam-LA 18

Stolen Base Average
Mays-SF 83.8
Blasingame-StL ... 80.0
T.Taylor-Chi 77.8
Ashburn-Phi 71.4
Gilliam-LA 62.1

Stolen Base Runs
Mays-SF 5.7
Zimmer-LA 3.0
Blasingame-StL ... 3.0
T.Taylor-Chi 2.7
Robinson-Cin 2.4

Fielding Runs
Zimmer-LA 32.6
Clemente-Pit 25.2
Boyer-StL 23.4
Ashburn-Phi 22.1
Flood-StL 19.3

Total Player Rating
Mays-SF 7.2
Banks-Chi 5.7
Ashburn-Phi 5.3
Aaron-Mil 4.1
Boyer-StL 4.0

Wins
Spahn-Mil 22
Friend-Pit 22
Burdette-Mil 20
Roberts-Phi 17
Purkey-Cin 17

Win Percentage
Spahn-Mil .... .667
Burdette-Mil .... .667
Friend-Pit ...... .611
Purkey-Cin ...... .607
Antonelli-SF .... .552

Games
Elston-Chi 69
Klippstein-Cin-LA . 57
Face-Pit 57
Hobbie-Chi........ 55

Complete Games
Spahn-Mil 23
Roberts-Phi 21
Burdette-Mil 19
Purkey-Cin 17
Friend-Pit 16

Shutouts
Willey-Mil 4
Witt-Pit 3
Purkey-Cin 3
Jay-Mil 3
Burdette-Mil 3

Saves
Face-Pit 20
Labine-LA 14
Farrell-Phi 11

Innings Pitched
Spahn-Mil 290.0
Burdette-Mil 275.1
Friend-Pit 274.0
Roberts-Phi 269.2

Fewest Hits/Game
Jones-StL 7.34
Koufax-LA 7.49
Miller-SF 7.91
Spahn-Mil 7.98
Brosnan-Chi-StL .. 7.99

Fewest BB/Game
Burdette-Mil 1.63
Roberts-Phi 1.70
Law-Pit 1.73
Purkey-Cin 1.76
Newcombe-LA-Cin .. 1.93

Strikeouts
Jones-StL 225
Spahn-Mil 150
Podres-LA 143
Antonelli-SF 143
Friend-Pit 135

Strikeouts/Game
Jones-StL 8.10
Koufax-LA 7.43
Drott-Chi 6.83
Podres-LA 6.12
Miller-SF 5.88

Ratio
Spahn-Mil 10.40
Miller-SF 10.43
Roberts-Phi 10.78
Burdette-Mil 10.92
Purkey-Cin 11.23

Earned Run Average
Miller-SF 2.47
Jones-StL 2.88
Burdette-Mil 2.91
Spahn-Mil 3.07
Roberts-Phi 3.24

Adjusted ERA
Miller-SF 154
Jones-StL 143
Roberts-Phi 122
Brosnan-Chi-StL .. 121
Burdette-Mil 121

Opponents' Batting Avg.
Koufax-LA .... .220
Jones-StL .... .223
Miller-SF .... .233
Spahn-Mil .... .237
Antonelli-SF .... .239

Opponents' On Base Pct.
Miller-SF .... .286
Spahn-Mil .... .288
Roberts-Phi ..... .294
Burdette-Mil .... .301
Purkey-Cin ...... .306

Starter Runs
Burdette-Mil 31.9
Miller-SF 29.9
Jones-StL 29.8
Spahn-Mil 28.3
Witt-Pit 27.5

Adjusted Starter Runs
Jones-StL 34.7
Miller-SF 27.1
Witt-Pit 26.5
Roberts-Phi 21.6
Burdette-Mil 18.7

Clutch Pitching Index
Haddix-Cin 116
Newcombe-LA-Cin . 115
Mizell-StL 114
Miller-SF 110
Podres-LA 109

Relief Runs
Elston-Chi 11.6
Face-Pit 9.9
Henry-Chi 9.7
Schmidt-Cin 8.4
Porterfield-Pit . 6.5

Adjusted Relief Runs
Elston-Chi 11.2
Schmidt-Cin 9.9
Henry-Chi 9.4
Face-Pit 9.1
Farrell-Phi 6.4

Relief Ranking
Elston-Chi 20.3
Farrell-Phi 12.0
Face-Pit 11.7
Henry-Chi 10.9
Schmidt-Cin 10.3

Total Pitcher Index
Spahn-Mil 3.9
Burdette-Mil 3.1
Jones-StL 2.9
Roberts-Phi 2.5
Witt-Pit 2.5

Total Baseball Ranking
Mays-SF 7.2
Banks-Chi 5.7
Ashburn-Phi 5.3
Aaron-Mil 4.1
Boyer-StL 4.0

TEAM	G	W	L	PCT	GB	R	OR	AB	H	2B	3B	HR	BB	SO	AVG	OBP	SLG	PRO	PRO+	BR	/A	PF	CHI	RC	SB	CS	SBA	SBR
NY	155	92	62	.597		759	577	5294	1418	212	39	164	537	822	.268	.338	.416	.754	117	88	115	96	102	746	48	32	60	-5
CHI	155	82	72	.532	10	634	615	5249	1348	191	42	101	518	669	.257	.329	.367	.696	99	-13	0	98	99	647	101	33	75	11
BOS	155	79	75	.513	13	697	691	5218	1335	229	30	155	638	820	.256	.340	.400	.740	102	70	21	107	96	708	29	22	57	-5
CLE	153	77	76	.503	14.5	694	635	5201	1340	210	31	161	494	819	.258	.327	.403	.730	109	38	55	98	102	677	50	49	51	-14
DET	154	77	77	.500	15	659	606	5194	1384	229	41	109	463	678	.266	.329	.389	.718	96	20	-28	107	100	657	48	32	60	-5
BAL	154	74	79	.484	17.5	521	575	5111	1233	195	19	108	483	731	.241	.310	.350	.660	92	-85	-56	95	96	546	33	35	49	-11
KC	156	73	81	.474	19	642	713	5261	1297	196	50	138	452	747	.247	.309	.381	.690	93	-40	-51	102	106	601	22	36	38	-15
WAS	156	61	93	.396	31	553	747	5156	1240	161	38	121	477	751	.240	.309	.357	.666	91	-78	-67	98	99	555	22	41	35	-18
TOT	619					5159		41684	10595	1623	290	1057	4062	6037	.254	.324	.383	.707							353	280	56	-62

TEAM	CG	SH	SV	IP	H	H/G	HR	BB	SO	RAT	ERA	ERA+	OAV	OOB	PR	/A	PF	CPI	FA	E	DP	FW	PW	BW	SBW	DIF
NY	53	21	33	1379	1201	7.8	116	557	796	11.8	3.22	110	.235	.315	85	48	94	103	.978	128	182	-.1	5.0	11.9	.3	-2.0
CHI	55	15	25	1389²	1296	8.4	152	515	751	11.8	3.61	101	.250	.320	25	5	97	104	.981	114	160	.7	.5	.0	1.9	1.9
BOS	44	5	28	1380	1396	9.1	121	521	695	12.7	3.92	102	.264	.334	-23	13	106	102	.976	145	172	-1.1	1.3	2.2	.3	-.7
CLE	51	2	20	1373¹	1283	8.4	123	604	766	12.5	3.73	98	.249	.331	6	-12	97	101	.974	152	171	-1.5	-1.2	5.7	-.6	-1.8
DET	59	8	19	1357¹	1294	8.6	133	437	797	11.8	3.59	112	.252	.316	26	67	107	101	.982	106	140	1.1	6.9	-2.9	.3	-5.4
BAL	55	15	28	1369²	1277	8.4	106	403	749	11.3	3.40	106	.249	.308	57	30	95	97	.980	114	159	.6	3.1	-5.8	-.3	-.1
KC	42	9	25	1398¹	1405	9.0	150	467	721	12.2	4.15	94	.262	.324	-59	-38	104	95	.979	125	166	.1	-3.9	-5.3	-.7	5.8
WAS	28	6	28	1376²	1443	9.4	156	558	762	13.3	4.53	84	.272	.344	-116	-110	101	98	.980	118	163	.5	-11.4	-6.9	-1.1	2.9
TOT	387	81	206	11024		8.6				12.2	3.77		.254	.324					.979	1002	1313					

Runs
Mantle-NY 127
Runnels-Bos 103
Power-KC-Cle 98
Minoso-Cle 94
Cerv-KC 93

Hits
Fox-Chi 187
Malzone-Bos 185
Power-KC-Cle 184
Runnels-Bos 183
Kuenn-Det 179

Doubles
Kuenn-Det 39
Power-KC-Cle 37
Kaline-Det 34
Runnels-Bos 32
Jensen-Bos 31

Triples
Power-KC-Cle 10
Tuttle-KC 9
Lemon-Was 9
Aparicio-Chi 9
Harris-Det 8

Home Runs
Mantle-NY 42
Colavito-Cle 41
Sievers-Was 39
Cerv-KC 38
Jensen-Bos 35

Total Bases
Mantle-NY 307
Cerv-KC 305
Colavito-Cle 303
Sievers-Was 299
Jensen-Bos 293

Runs Batted In
Jensen-Bos 122
Colavito-Cle 113
Sievers-Was 108
Cerv-KC 104
Mantle-NY 97

Runs Produced
Mantle-NY 182
Jensen-Bos 170
Power-KC-Cle 162
Cerv-KC 159

Bases On Balls
Mantle-NY 129
Jensen-Bos 99
Williams-Bos 98
Runnels-Bos 87
Colavito-Cle 84

Batting Average
Williams-Bos .... .328
Runnels-Bos ..... .322
Kuenn-Det .... .319
Kaline-Det ...... .313
Power-KC-Cle .... .312

On Base Percentage
Williams-Bos .... .462
Mantle-NY .... .445
Runnels-Bos ..... .418
Colavito-Cle .... .407
Jensen-Bos ...... .398

Slugging Average
Colavito-Cle .... .620
Cerv-KC .... .592
Mantle-NY .... .592
Williams-Bos .... .584
Sievers-Was ..... .544

Production
Williams-Bos 1.046
Mantle-NY 1.036
Colavito-Cle 1.027
Cerv-KC .... .964
Jensen-Bos ...... .933

Adjusted Production
Mantle-NY 189
Colavito-Cle 183
Williams-Bos 174
Cerv-KC 158
Sievers-Was 148

Batter Runs
Mantle-NY 64.2
Williams-Bos 53.6
Colavito-Cle 52.8
Jensen-Bos 42.7
Cerv-KC 40.7

Adjusted Batter Runs
Mantle-NY 69.2
Colavito-Cle 55.7
Williams-Bos 46.3
Cerv-KC 38.8
Jensen-Bos 35.0

Clutch Hitting Index
Courtney-Was 131
Lollar-Chi 127
F.Bolling-Det 117
Harris-Det 116
Skowron-NY 116

Runs Created
Mantle-NY 147
Colavito-Cle 122
Jensen-Bos 120
Williams-Bos 112
Runnels-Bos 107

Total Average
Mantle-NY 1.208
Williams-Bos 1.163
Colavito-Cle 1.078
Jensen-Bos ...... .980
Cerv-KC .... .947

Stolen Bases
Aparicio-Chi 29
Rivera-Chi 21
Landis-Chi 19
Mantle-NY 18
Minoso-Cle 14

Stolen Base Average
Rivera-Chi 87.5
Mantle-NY 85.7
Aparicio-Chi 82.9
Landis-Chi 73.1

Stolen Base Runs
Aparicio-Chi 5.1
Rivera-Chi 4.5
Mantle-NY 3.6
Wilson-Det 3.0

Fielding Runs
Kaline-Det 23.0
Kubek-NY 20.0
Cerv-KC 20.0
Malzone-Bos 16.6
Kuenn-Det 15.1

Total Player Rating
Mantle-NY 6.5
Cerv-KC 5.1
Colavito-Cle 5.0
Runnels-Bos 3.8
Kaline-Det 3.6

Wins
Turley-NY 21
Pierce-Chi 17
McLish-Cle 16
Lary-Det 16

Win Percentage
Turley-NY .... .750
McLish-Cle .... .667
Pierce-Chi .... .607
Portocarrero-Bal . .577
Foytack-Det ...... .536

Games
Clevenger-Was 55
Tomanek-Cle-KC ... 54
Hyde-Was 53
Wall-Bos 52

Complete Games
Turley-NY 19
Pierce-Chi 19
Lary-Det 19
Harshman-Bal 17

Shutouts
Ford-NY 7
Turley-NY 6
Wynn-Chi 4
Ramos-Was 4
Donovan-Chi 4

Saves
Duren-NY 20
Hyde-Was 18
Kiely-Bos 12
Wall-Bos 10

Innings Pitched
Lary-Det 260.1
Ramos-Was 259.1
Donovan-Chi 248.0
Turley-NY 245.1
Pierce-Chi 245.0

Fewest Hits/Game
Turley-NY 6.53
Bell-Cle 6.97
Ford-NY 7.14
Pierce-Chi 7.49
Portocarrero-Bal . 7.61

Fewest BB/Game
Donovan-Chi 1.92
O'Dell-Bal 2.07
Sullivan-Bos 2.21
Lary-Det 2.35
Pierce-Chi 2.42

Strikeouts
Wynn-Chi 179
Bunning-Det 177
Turley-NY 168
Harshman-Bal 161
Pascual-Was 146

Strikeouts/Game
Pascual-Was 7.41
Bunning-Det 7.25
Wynn-Chi 6.72
Turley-NY 6.16
Harshman-Bal 6.13

Ratio
Ford-NY 9.81
Pierce-Chi 9.96
Portocarrero-Bal . 10.25
O'Dell-Bal 10.41
Harshman-Bal 10.74

Earned Run Average
Ford-NY 2.01
Pierce-Chi 2.68
Harshman-Bal 2.89
Lary-Det 2.90
O'Dell-Bal 2.97

Adjusted ERA
Ford-NY 176
Lary-Det 139
Pierce-Chi 136
Harshman-Bal 124
McLish-Cle 122

Opponents' Batting Avg.
Turley-NY .... .206
Bell-Cle .... .213
Ford-NY .... .217
Pierce-Chi .... .227
Grant-Cle .... .228

Opponents' On Base Pct.
Ford-NY .... .276
Pierce-Chi .... .280
Portocarrero-Bal . .286
O'Dell-Bal .... .288
Harshman-Bal ..... .294

Starter Runs
Ford-NY 42.9
Pierce-Chi 29.6
Lary-Det 25.0
Harshman-Bal 23.0
Turley-NY 21.7

Adjusted Starter Runs
Ford-NY 37.1
Lary-Det 32.8
Pierce-Chi 26.0
Wilhelm-Cle-Bal .. 18.9
Harshman-Bal 18.4

Clutch Pitching Index
McLish-Cle 120
Ford-NY 117
Pierce-Chi 114
Lary-Det 113
Wilson-Chi 110

Relief Runs
Hyde-Was 23.1
Duren-NY 14.7
Kiely-Bos 6.9
Staley-Chi 5.7
Morgan-Det 4.2

Adjusted Relief Runs
Hyde-Was 23.7
Duren-NY 12.7
Kiely-Bos 9.1
Morgan-Det 6.1
Wall-Bos 4.9

Relief Ranking
Hyde-Was 36.2
Duren-NY 22.6
Kiely-Bos 10.1
Wall-Bos 7.5
Morgan-Det 6.4

Total Pitcher Index
Ford-NY 3.9
Hyde-Was 3.9
Lary-Det 3.6
Harshman-Bal 3.4
Pierce-Chi 2.8

Total Baseball Ranking
Mantle-NY 6.5
Cerv-KC 5.1
Colavito-Cle 5.0
Ford-NY 3.9
Hyde-Was 3.9

TEAM	G	W	L	PCT	GB	R	OR	AB	H	2B	3B	HR	BB	SO	AVG	OBP	SLG	PRO	PRO+	BR	/A	PF	CHI	RC	SB	CS	SBA	SBR
LA	156	88	68	.564		705	670	5282	1360	196	46	148	591	891	.257	.335	.396	.731	94	17	-34	107	99	706	84	51	62	-5
MIL	157	86	70	.551	2	724	623	5388	1426	216	36	177	488	765	.265	.329	.417	.746	115	32	93	92	100	729	41	14	75	4
SF	154	83	71	.539	4	705	680	5281	1377	239	35	167	473	875	.261	.324	.414	.738	105	16	32	98	101	711	81	34	70	4
PIT	155	78	76	.506	9	651	680	5369	1414	230	42	112	442	715	.263	.322	.384	.706	95	-39	-33	99	101	653	32	26	55	-6
CIN	154	74	80	.481	13	764	738	5288	1448	258	34	161	499	763	.274	.340	.427	.767	108	76	54	103	101	764	65	28	70	3
CHI	155	74	80	.481	13	673	688	5296	1321	209	44	163	498	911	.269	.319	.398	.717	98	-23	-16	99	102	673	32	19	63	-2
STL	154	71	83	.461	16	641	725	5317	1432	244	49	118	485	747	.269	.333	.400	.733	96	14	-30	106	92	699	65	53	55	-12
PHI	155	64	90	.416	23	599	725	5109	1237	196	38	113	498	858	.242	.314	.362	.676	86	-92	-101	102	105	574	39	46	46	-16
TOT	620					5462		42330	11015	1788	324	1159	3974	6525	.260	.327	.400	.727							439	271	62	-31

TEAM	CG	SH	SV	IP	H	H/G	HR	BB	SO	RAT	ERA	ERA+	OAV	OOB	PR	/A	PF	CPI	FA	E	DP	FW	PW	BW	SBW	DIF
LA	43	14	26	1411²	1317	8.4	157	614	1077	12.6	3.79	111	.247	.331	24	68	107	103	.981	114	154	1.5	6.8	-3.4	-.1	5.2
MIL	69	18	18	1400²	1406	9.0	128	429	775	11.9	3.51	101	.260	.317	68	5	90	104	.979	127	138	.8	.5	9.4	.8	-3.4
SF	52	12	23	1376¹	1279	8.4	139	500	873	11.8	3.47	110	.246	.316	74	52	97	103	.974	152	118	-.8	5.2	3.2	.8	-2.5
PIT	48	7	17	1393¹	1432	9.2	134	418	730	12.1	3.90	99	.267	.323	7	-5	98	100	.975	154	165	-.8	-.5	-3.3	-.2	5.9
CIN	44	7	26	1357¹	1460	9.7	162	456	690	12.9	4.31	94	.275	.337	-55	-39	100	102	.978	126	157	.7	-3.9	5.4	.7	-5.9
CHI	30	11	25	1391	1337	8.7	152	519	765	12.2	4.01	95	.254	.323	-10	-10	100	96	.977	140	142	-.0	-1.0	-1.6	.2	-.5
STL	36	8	21	1363	1427	9.4	137	564	846	13.3	4.34	98	.271	.344	-59	-15	107	100	.975	146	158	-.4	-1.5	-3.0	-.8	-.2
PHI	54	8	15	1354	1357	9.0	150	474	769	12.4	4.27	96	.261	.326	-49	-25	104	93	.973	154	132	-.8	-2.5	-10.2	-1.2	1.7
TOT	376	85	171	11047¹		9.0				12.4	3.95		.260	.327					.977	1113	1164					

Runs		Hits		Doubles		Triples		Home Runs		Total Bases	
Pinson-Cin	131	Aaron-Mil	223	Pinson-Cin	47	Neal-LA	11	Mathews-Mil	46	Aaron-Mil	400
Mays-SF	125	Pinson-Cin	205	Aaron-Mil	46	Moon-LA	11	Banks-Chi	45	Mathews-Mil	352
Mathews-Mil	118	Cepeda-SF	192	Mays-SF	43	White-StL	9	Aaron-Mil	39	Banks-Chi	351
Aaron-Mil	116	Temple-Cin	186	Cimoli-StL	40	Pinson-Cin	9	Robinson-Cin	36	Mays-SF	335
Robinson-Cin	106	Mathews-Mil	182			Dark-Chi	9	Mays-SF	34	Pinson-Cin	330

Runs Batted In		Runs Produced		Bases On Balls		Batting Average		On Base Percentage		Slugging Average	
Banks-Chi	143	Aaron-Mil	200	Gilliam-LA	96	Aaron-Mil	.355	Cunningham-StL	.456	Aaron-Mil	.636
Robinson-Cin	125	Robinson-Cin	195	Cunningham-StL	88	Cunningham-StL	.345	Aaron-Mil	.406	Banks-Chi	.596
Aaron-Mil	123	Pinson-Cin	195	Moon-LA	81	Cepeda-SF	.317	Robinson-Cin	.397	Mathews-Mil	.593
Bell-Cin	115	Mays-SF	195	Mathews-Mil	80	Pinson-Cin	.316	Moon-LA	.396	Robinson-Cin	.583
Mathews-Mil	114	Banks-Chi	195	Ashburn-Phi	79	Mays-SF	.313	Mathews-Mil	.391	Mays-SF	.583

Production		Adjusted Production		Batter Runs		Adjusted Batter Runs		Clutch Hitting Index		Runs Created	
Aaron-Mil	1.042	Aaron-Mil	188	Aaron-Mil	62.8	Aaron-Mil	75.3	Bell-Cin	134	Aaron-Mil	156
Mathews-Mil	.984	Mathews-Mil	172	Mathews-Mil	48.4	Mathews-Mil	59.4	Post-Phi	128	Mathews-Mil	143
Robinson-Cin	.980	Mays-SF	157	Banks-Chi	44.4	Banks-Chi	45.8	Mazeroski-Pit	120	Mays-SF	131
Banks-Chi	.975	Banks-Chi	156	Robinson-Cin	44.0	Mays-SF	45.3	Bouchee-Phi	111	Banks-Chi	126
Mays-SF	.967	Robinson-Cin	152	Mays-SF	42.6	Robinson-Cin	40.7	Cimoli-StL	111	Pinson-Cin	124

Total Average		Stolen Bases		Stolen Base Average		Stolen Base Runs		Fielding Runs		Total Player Rating	
Aaron-Mil	1.089	Mays-SF	27	Mays-SF	87.1	Mays-SF	5.7	Virdon-Pit	23.5	Aaron-Mil	6.6
Mathews-Mil	1.041	T.Taylor-Chi	23	Pinson-Cin	77.8	Pinson-Cin	2.7	Blasingame-StL	20.5	Banks-Chi	6.2
Mays-SF	1.037	Gilliam-LA	23	Neal-LA	73.9	Temple-Cin	2.4	Neal-LA	20.0	Mathews-Mil	6.2
Robinson-Cin	1.015	Cepeda-SF	23	T.Taylor-Chi	71.9	Aaron-Mil	2.4	Pinson-Cin	19.7	Mays-SF	5.0
Cunningham-StL	.978	Pinson-Cin	21	Cepeda-SF	71.9	Cimoli-StL	2.1	H.Anderson-Phi	18.3	Pinson-Cin	3.9

Wins		Win Percentage		Games		Complete Games		Shutouts		Saves	
Spahn-Mil	21	Face-Pit	.947	Henry-Chi	65	Spahn-Mil	21	Spahn-Mil	4	McMahon-Mil	15
S.Jones-SF	21	Law-Pit	.667	Elston-Chi	65	Law-Pit	20	S.Jones-SF	4	McDaniel-StL	15
Burdette-Mil	21	Antonelli-SF	.655	McDaniel-StL	62	Burdette-Mil	20	Drysdale-LA	4	Elston-Chi	13
Antonelli-SF	19	Buhl-Mil	.625	McMahon-Mil	60	Roberts-Phi	19	Craig-LA	4	Henry-Chi	12
				Miller-SF	59			Burdette-Mil	4		
								Buhl-Mil	4		
								Antonelli-SF	4		

Innings Pitched		Fewest Hits/Game		Fewest BB/Game		Strikeouts		Strikeouts/Game		Ratio	
Spahn-Mil	292.0	Haddix-Pit	7.58	Newcombe-Cin	1.09	Drysdale-LA	242	Drysdale-LA	8.05	Haddix-Pit	9.63
Burdette-Mil	289.2	S.Jones-SF	7.71	Burdette-Mil	1.18	S.Jones-SF	209	S.Jones-SF	6.95	Newcombe-Cin	10.05
Antonelli-SF	282.0	Hobbie-Chi	7.85	Roberts-Phi	1.22	Koufax-LA	173	Podres-LA	6.69	Conley-Phi	10.15
S.Jones-SF	270.2	Drysdale-LA	7.88	Purkey-Cin	1.78	Antonelli-SF	165	Broglio-StL	6.60	Law-Pit	10.15
Drysdale-LA	270.2	Antonelli-SF	7.88	Law-Pit	1.79	McCormick-SF	151	McCormick-SF	6.02	Antonelli-SF	10.40

Earned Run Average		Adjusted ERA		Opponents' Batting Avg.		Opponents' On Base Pct.		Starter Runs		Adjusted Starter Runs	
S.Jones-SF	2.83	Conley-Phi	137	S.Jones-SF	.228	Haddix-Pit	.273	S.Jones-SF	33.7	Craig-LA	36.7
Miller-SF	2.84	S.Jones-SF	135	Haddix-Pit	.228	Newcombe-Cin	.280	Spahn-Mil	32.1	S.Jones-SF	29.6
Buhl-Mil	2.86	Miller-SF	134	Antonelli-SF	.233	Conley-Phi	.281	Craig-LA	32.0	Jackson-StL	26.6
Spahn-Mil	2.96	Law-Pit	130	Drysdale-LA	.233	Law-Pit	.282	Law-Pit	28.7	Law-Pit	26.3
Law-Pit	2.98	Jackson-StL	128	Conley-Phi	.235	Antonelli-SF	.286	Antonelli-SF	26.7	Drysdale-LA	23.1

Clutch Pitching Index		Relief Runs		Adjusted Relief Runs		Relief Ranking		Total Pitcher Index		Total Baseball Ranking	
Miller-SF	134	Miller-SF	20.5	Henry-Chi	18.9	Henry-Chi	25.3	Newcombe-Cin	3.5	Aaron-Mil	6.6
Buhl-Mil	120	Henry-Chi	18.9	Miller-SF	18.0	Face-Pit	25.1	S.Jones-SF	3.4	Banks-Chi	6.2
Spahn-Mil	105	Face-Pit	12.9	Face-Pit	12.1	Miller-SF	16.4	Craig-LA	3.2	Mathews-Mil	6.2
Jackson-StL	104	McMahon-Mil	12.4	McMahon-Mil	8.7	Elston-Chi	13.4	Drysdale-LA	3.0	Mays-SF	5.0
S.Jones-SF	104	Elston-Chi	6.8	Meyer-Phi	7.7	McDaniel-StL	12.5	Spahn-Mil	2.8	Pinson-Cin	3.9

TEAM	G	W	L	PCT	GB	R	OR	AB	H	2B	3B	HR	BB	SO	AVG	OBP	SLG	PRO	PRO+	BR	/A	PF	CHI	RC	SB	CS	SBA	SBR
CHI	156	94	60	.610		669	588	5297	1325	220	46	97	580	634	.250	.330	.364	.694	97	-20	-11	99	100	653	113	53	68	2
CLE	154	89	65	.578	5	745	646	5288	1390	216	25	167	433	721	.263	.323	.408	.731	110	32	59	96	107	682	33	36	48	-12
NY	155	79	75	.513	15	687	647	5379	1397	224	40	153	457	828	.260	.321	.402	.723	107	17	41	97	98	695	45	22	67	0
DET	154	76	78	.494	18	713	732	5211	1346	196	30	160	580	737	.258	.338	.400	.738	102	57		105	97	720	34	17	67	0
BOS	154	75	79	.487	19	726	696	5225	1335	248	28	125	626	810	.256	.338	.385	.723	99	36	3	105	101	697	68	25	73	5
BAL	155	74	80	.481	20	551	621	5208	1240	182	23	109	536	690	.238	.312	.345	.657	88	-96	-83	98	96	563	36	24	60	-4
KC	154	66	88	.429	28	681	760	5264	1383	231	43	117	481	780	.263	.328	.390	.718	100	16	4	102	99	669	34	24	59	-4
WAS	154	63	91	.409	31	619	701	5092	1205	173	32	163	517	881	.237	.310	.379	.689	94	-43	-40	100	101	594	51	34	60	-5
TOT	618					5391		41964	10621	1690	267	1091	4210	6081	.253	.325	.384	.709							414	235	64	-17

TEAM	CG	SH	SV	IP	H	H/G	HR	BB	SO	RAT	ERA	ERA+	OAV	OOB	PR	/A	PF	CPI	FA	E	DP	FW	PW	BW	SBW	DIF
CHI	44	13	36	1425.1	1297	8.2	129	525	761	11.7	3.29	114	.242	.313	91	74	97	106	.979	130	141	.6	7.5	-1.1	.4	9.6
CLE	58	7	23	1383.2	1230	8.0	148	635	799	12.3	3.75	98	.239	.325	18	-10	95	101	.978	127	138	.7	-1.0	6.0	-1.0	7.3
NY	38	15	28	1399	1281	8.2	120	594	836	12.2	3.60	101	.244	.324	40	7	94	102	.978	131	160	.5	.7	4.2	.2	-3.6
DET	53	9	24	1360	1327	8.8	177	432	829	11.9	4.20	97	.254	.316	-52	-21	105	94	.978	124	131	.9	-2.1	1.7	-.1	-1.7
BOS	38	9	25	1364	1386	9.1	135	589	724	13.2	4.17	97	.266	.343	-47	-17	105	104	.978	131	167	.5	-1.7	.3	.7	-1.8
BAL	45	15	30	1400.1	1290	8.3	111	476	735	11.5	3.56	106	.246	.313	47	35	98	96	.976	146	163	-.4	3.5	-8.4	-.2	2.4
KC	44	8	21	1360.2	1452	9.6	148	492	703	13.2	4.35	92	.274	.341	-74	-52	104	102	.973	160	156	-1.2	-5.3	.4	-.2	-4.7
WAS	46	10	21	1360	1358	9.0	123	467	694	12.3	4.01	98	.259	.324	-23	-14	101	96	.973	162	140	-1.4	-1.4	-4.0	-.3	-6.9
TOT	366	86	208	11053		8.6				12.3	3.86		.253	.325					.977	1111	1196					

Runs
Yost-Det 115
Mantle-NY 104
Power-Cle 102
Jensen-Bos 101
Kuenn-Det 99

Hits
Kuenn-Det 198
Fox-Chi 191
Runnels-Bos 176
Power-Cle 172
Minoso-Cle 172

Doubles
Kuenn-Det 42
Malzone-Bos 34
Fox-Chi 34
Williams-KC 33
Runnels-Bos 33

Triples
Allison-Was 9
McDougald-NY 8

Home Runs
Killebrew-Was 42
Colavito-Cle 42
Lemon-Was 33
Maxwell-Det 31
Mantle-NY 31

Total Bases
Colavito-Cle 301
Killebrew-Was 282
Kuenn-Det 281
Mantle-NY 278
Allison-Was 275

Runs Batted In
Jensen-Bos 112
Colavito-Cle 111
Killebrew-Was 105
Lemon-Was 100
Maxwell-Det 95

Runs Produced
Jensen-Bos 185
Minoso-Cle 163
Malzone-Bos 163
Kuenn-Det 161
Killebrew-Was 161

Bases On Balls
Yost-Det 135
Runnels-Bos 95
Mantle-NY 93
Buddin-Bos 92
Killebrew-Was 90

Batting Average
Kuenn-Det .... .353
Kaline-Det .... .327
Runnels-Bos .... .314
Fox-Chi .... .306
Minoso-Cle .... .302

On Base Percentage
Yost-Det .... .437
Runnels-Bos .... .415
Kaline-Det .... .414
Woodling-Bal ...... .405
Kuenn-Det .... .405

Slugging Average
Kaline-Det .... .530
Killebrew-Was ..... .516
Mantle-NY .... .514
Colavito-Cle ...... .512
Lemon-Was .... .510

Production
Kaline-Det .... .944
Kuenn-Det .... .906
Mantle-NY .... .905
Yost-Det .... .873
Killebrew-Was ..... .873

Adjusted Production
Mantle-NY 152
Kaline-Det 149
Kuenn-Det 140
Woodling-Bal 139
Killebrew-Was 137

Batter Runs
Kaline-Det 41.6
Yost-Det 37.9
Francona-Cle 36.6
Kuenn-Det 36.2
Mantle-NY 36.0

Adjusted Batter Runs
Francona-Cle 40.0
Mantle-NY 39.8
Kaline-Det 35.8
Yost-Det 31.8
Kuenn-Det 30.6

Clutch Hitting Index
Strickland-Cle 125
Fox-Chi 121
Woodling-Bal 120
Jensen-Bos 115
Cerv-KC 115

Runs Created
Mantle-NY 117
Kuenn-Det 117
Yost-Det 115
Kaline-Det 114
Killebrew-Was 103

Total Average
Yost-Det .... .992
Mantle-NY .... .985
Kaline-Det .... .983
Kuenn-Det .... .903
Jensen-Bos .... .888

Stolen Bases
Aparicio-Chi 56
Mantle-NY 21
Landis-Chi 20
Jensen-Bos 20
Allison-Was 13

Stolen Base Average
Mantle-NY 87.5
Aparicio-Chi 81.2
Jensen-Bos 80.0
Landis-Chi 69.0

Stolen Base Runs
Aparicio-Chi 9.0
Mantle-NY 4.5
Jensen-Bos 3.0
Malzone-Bos 1.8
Yost-Det 1.5

Fielding Runs
Gardner-Bal 30.5
Minoso-Cle 16.2
Landis-Chi 15.8
Jensen-Bos 15.1
Colavito-Cle 11.6

Total Player Rating
Mantle-NY 4.5
Kaline-Det 4.0
Jensen-Bos 3.4
Minoso-Cle 3.4
Runnels-Bos 3.3

Wins
Wynn-Chi 22
McLish-Cle 19
Shaw-Chi 18

Win Percentage
Shaw-Chi .... .750
McLish-Cle .... .704
Wynn-Chi .... .688
Mossi-Det .... .654

Games
Staley-Chi 67
Lown-Chi 60
Clevenger-Was 50
Shaw-Chi 47

Complete Games
Pascual-Was 17
Pappas-Bal 15
Mossi-Det 15
Wynn-Chi 14
Bunning-Det 14

Shutouts
Pascual-Was 6
Wynn-Chi 5
Pappas-Bal 4

Saves
Lown-Chi 15
Staley-Chi 14
Loes-Bal 14
Duren-NY 14
Fornieles-Bos 11

Innings Pitched
Wynn-Chi 255.2
Bunning-Det 249.2
Foytack-Det 240.1
Pascual-Was 238.2
McLish-Cle 235.1

Fewest Hits/Game
Score-Cle 6.89
Ditmar-NY 6.95
Wilhelm-Bal 7.09
Wynn-Chi 7.11
O'Dell-Bal 7.36

Fewest BB/Game
Brown-Bal 1.76
Lary-Det 1.86
Garver-KC 1.88
Mossi-Det 1.93
Ramos-Was 2.00

Strikeouts
Bunning-Det 201
Pascual-Was 185
Wynn-Chi 179
Score-Cle 147
Wilhelm-Bal 139

Strikeouts/Game
Score-Cle 8.23
Bunning-Det 7.25
Pascual-Was 6.98
Turley-NY 6.47
Wynn-Chi 6.30

Ratio
Ditmar-NY 9.62
Pascual-Was 10.33
Mossi-Det 10.34
O'Dell-Bal 10.43
Brown-Bal 10.48

Earned Run Average
Wilhelm-Bal 2.19
Pascual-Was 2.64
Shaw-Chi 2.69
Ditmar-NY 2.90
Walker-Bal 2.92

Adjusted ERA
Wilhelm-Bal 173
Pascual-Was 148
Shaw-Chi 140
Walker-Bal 130
O'Dell-Bal 129

Opponents' Batting Avg.
Score-Cle .... .210
Ditmar-NY .... .211
Wynn-Chi .... .216
O'Dell-Bal .... .220
Wilhelm-Bal .... .224

Opponents' On Base Pct.
Ditmar-NY .... .270
Pascual-Was .... .284
O'Dell-Bal .... .286
Mossi-Det .... .286
Brown-Bal .... .290

Starter Runs
Wilhelm-Bal 42.0
Pascual-Was 32.4
Shaw-Chi 30.0
Ditmar-NY 21.7
Perry-Cle 20.6

Adjusted Starter Runs
Wilhelm-Bal 40.0
Pascual-Was 33.8
Shaw-Chi 27.3
Daley-KC 20.2
O'Dell-Bal 18.8

Clutch Pitching Index
Wilhelm-Bal 132
Daley-KC 122
Ford-NY 119
Shaw-Chi 114
McLish-Cle 114

Relief Runs
Staley-Chi 20.9
Duren-NY 16.9
Shantz-NY 15.6
Coates-NY 11.0
Lown-Chi 10.0

Adjusted Relief Runs
Staley-Chi 19.6
Duren-NY 15.0
Shantz-NY 13.3
Stobbs-Was 9.4
Fornieles-Bos 9.0

Relief Ranking
Staley-Chi 25.0
Duren-NY 22.1
Shantz-NY 13.6
Lown-Chi 12.7
Fornieles-Bos 10.6

Total Pitcher Index
Pascual-Was 5.0
Wilhelm-Bal 3.7
Daley-KC 3.1
Perry-Cle 2.8
Ford-NY 2.8

Total Baseball Ranking
Pascual-Was 5.0
Mantle-NY 4.5
Kaline-Det 4.0
Wilhelm-Bal 3.7
Jensen-Bos 3.4

TEAM	G	W	L	PCT	GB	R	OR	AB	H	2B	3B	HR	BB	SO	AVG	OBP	SLG	PRO	PRO+	BR	/A	PF	CHI	RC	SB	CS	SBA	SBR
PIT	155	95	59	.617		734	593	5406	1493	236	56	120	486	747	.276	.338	.407	.745	109	72	68	101	99	737	34	24	59	-4
MIL	154	88	66	.571	7	724	658	5263	1393	198	48	170	463	793	.265	.327	.393	.744	118	60	114	93	102	714	69	37	65	-2
STL	155	86	68	.558	9	639	616	5187	1317	213	48	138	501	792	.254	.323	.393	.716	94	13	-44	109	97	652	48	35	58	-7
LA	154	82	72	.532	13	662	593	5227	1333	216	38	126	529	837	.255	.327	.383	.710	94	6	-37	106	99	659	95	53	64	-3
SF	156	79	75	.513	16	671	631	5324	1357	220	62	130	467	846	.255	.319	.393	.712	106	1	41	94	102	663	86	45	66	-1
CIN	154	67	87	.435	28	640	692	5289	1324	230	40	140	512	858	.250	.320	.388	.708	98	-1	-12	102	97	661	73	37	66	0
CHI	156	60	94	.390	35	634	776	5311	1293	213	48	119	531	897	.243	.314	.369	.683	94	-48	-41	99	103	617	51	34	60	-5
PHI	154	59	95	.383	36	546	691	5169	1235	196	44	99	448	1054	.239	.304	.351	.655	85	-102	-103	100	102	546	45	48	48	-15
TOT	619					5250		42176	10745	1722	384	1042	3937	6824	.255	.322	.388	.710							501	313	62	-38

TEAM	CG	SH	SV	IP	H	H/G	HR	BB	SO	RAT	ERA	ERA+	OAV	OOB	PR	/A	PF	CPI	FA	E	DP	FW	PW	BW	SBW	DIF
PIT	47	11	33	1399²	1363	8.8	105	386	811	11.3	3.49	107	.257	.309	42	40	100	99	.979	128	163	.7	4.1	7.0	.0	6.1
MIL	55	13	28	1387¹	1327	8.6	130	518	807	12.2	3.76	91	.251	.322	0	-52	91	99	.976	141	137	-.0	-5.4	11.7	.3	4.4
STL	37	11	30	1371	1316	8.6	127	511	906	12.1	3.64	112	.253	.322	18	69	109	103	.976	141	152	.0	7.1	-4.5	-.2	6.6
LA	46	13	20	1398	1218	7.8	154	564	1122	11.7	3.40	117	.234	.312	56	89	106	103	.979	125	142	.9	9.2	-3.8	.2	-1.4
SF	55	16	26	1396	1288	8.3	107	512	897	11.8	3.44	101	.245	.315	50	6	93	99	.972	166	117	-1.3	.6	4.2	.4	-1.9
CIN	33	8	35	1390¹	1417	9.2	134	442	740	12.3	4.00	96	.267	.328	-37	-27	102	101	.979	125	155	.9	-2.8	-1.2	.5	-7.3
CHI	36	6	25	1402²	1393	8.9	152	565	805	12.8	4.35	87	.260	.335	-92	-89	100	96	.977	143	133	-.0	-9.2	-4.2	-.0	-3.6
PHI	45	6	16	1375¹	1423	9.3	133	439	736	12.3	4.01	97	.270	.328	-38	-20	103	101	.974	155	129	-.8	-2.1	-10.6	-1.1	-3.5
TOT	354	84	213	11120¹		8.7				12.1	3.76		.255	.322					.977	1124	1128					

Runs
Bruton-Mil 112
Mathews-Mil 108
Pinson-Cin 107
Mays-SF 107
Aaron-Mil 102

Hits
Mays-SF 190
Pinson-Cin 187
Groat-Pit 186
Bruton-Mil 180
Clemente-Pit 179

Doubles
Pinson-Cin 37
Cepeda-SF 36
Skinner-Pit 33
Robinson-Cin 33
Banks-Chi 32

Triples
Bruton-Mil 13
Pinson-Cin 12
Mays-SF 12
Aaron-Mil 11

Home Runs
Banks-Chi 41
Aaron-Mil 40
Mathews-Mil 39
Boyer-StL 32
Robinson-Cin 31

Total Bases
Aaron-Mil 334
Banks-Chi 331
Mays-SF 330
Boyer-StL 310
Pinson-Cin 308

Runs Batted In
Aaron-Mil 126
Mathews-Mil 124
Banks-Chi 117
Mays-SF 103
Boyer-StL 97

Runs Produced
Mathews-Mil 193
Aaron-Mil 188
Mays-SF 181
Banks-Chi 170
Clemente-Pit 167

Bases On Balls
Ashburn-Chi 116
Mathews-Mil 111
Gilliam-LA 96
Robinson-Cin 82
Spencer-StL 81

Batting Average
Groat-Pit .325
Larker-LA .323
Mays-SF .319
Clemente-Pit .314
Boyer-StL .304

On Base Percentage
Ashburn-Chi .416
Robinson-Cin .413
Mathews-Mil .401
Moon-LA .387
Mays-SF .386

Slugging Average
Robinson-Cin .595
Aaron-Mil .566
Boyer-StL .562
Mays-SF .555
Banks-Chi .554

Production
Robinson-Cin 1.007
Mathews-Mil .952
Mays-SF .941
Boyer-StL .934
Aaron-Mil .925

Adjusted Production
Mathews-Mil 170
Robinson-Cin 169
Mays-SF 164
Aaron-Mil 161
Banks-Chi 145

Batter Runs
Robinson-Cin 47.8
Mathews-Mil 46.0
Mays-SF 43.5
Boyer-StL 37.9
Aaron-Mil 37.4

Adjusted Batter Runs
Mathews-Mil 55.4
Mays-SF 50.7
Aaron-Mil 46.0
Robinson-Cin 46.0
Banks-Chi 35.6

Clutch Hitting Index
Larker-LA 149
Mathews-Mil 120
Bailey-Cin 120
Stuart-Pit 114
Clemente-Pit 112

Runs Created
Mathews-Mil 128
Mays-SF 124
Aaron-Mil 119
Banks-Chi 113
Robinson-Cin 113

Total Average
Robinson-Cin 1.069
Mathews-Mil 1.029
Mays-SF .953
Aaron-Mil .935
Boyer-StL .918

Stolen Bases
Wills-LA 50
Pinson-Cin 32
T.Taylor-Chi-Phi 26
Mays-SF 25
Bruton-Mil 22

Stolen Base Average
Javier-StL 82.6
Wills-LA 80.6
Ashburn-Chi 80.0
Pinson-Cin 72.7
Mays-SF 71.4

Stolen Base Runs
Wills-LA 7.8
Javier-StL 3.3
Blasingame-SF 3.0
Pinson-Cin 2.4
Ashburn-Chi 2.4

Fielding Runs
Mazeroski-Pit 25.4
Wills-LA 20.5
Grammas-StL 19.8
Smith-StL 18.0
Mays-SF 13.7

Total Player Rating
Mays-SF 5.9
Banks-Chi 5.8
Aaron-Mil 4.8
Robinson-Cin 4.5
Mathews-Mil 4.2

Wins
Spahn-Mil 21
Broglio-StL 21
Law-Pit 20
Burdette-Mil 19

Win Percentage
Broglio-StL .700
Law-Pit .690
Spahn-Mil .677
Buhl-Mil .640
Purkey-Cin .607

Games
Face-Pit 68
McDaniel-StL 65
Elston-Chi 60
Farrell-Phi 59
Roebuck-LA 58

Complete Games
Spahn-Mil 18
Law-Pit 18
Burdette-Mil 18
Hobbie-Chi 16
Friend-Pit 16

Shutouts
Sanford-SF 6
Drysdale-LA 5

Saves
McDaniel-StL 26
Face-Pit 24
Henry-Cin 17
Brosnan-Cin 12

Innings Pitched
Jackson-StL 282.0
Friend-Pit 275.2
Burdette-Mil 275.2
Law-Pit 271.2
Drysdale-LA 269.0

Fewest Hits/Game
Broglio-StL 6.84
Koufax-LA 6.84
Williams-LA 7.03
Drysdale-LA 7.16
Buhl-Mil 7.62

Fewest BB/Game
Burdette-Mil 1.14
Roberts-Phi 1.29
Law-Pit 1.33
Friend-Pit 1.47
Haddix-Pit 1.98

Strikeouts
Drysdale-LA 246
Koufax-LA 197
S.Jones-SF 190
Broglio-StL 188
Friend-Pit 183

Strikeouts/Game
Koufax-LA 10.13
Drysdale-LA 8.23
Williams-LA 7.60
Broglio-StL 7.48
S.Jones-SF 7.31

Ratio
Drysdale-LA 9.90
Friend-Pit 10.15
Law-Pit 10.27
Burdette-Mil 10.35
Williams-LA 10.37

Earned Run Average
McCormick-SF 2.70
Broglio-StL 2.74
Drysdale-LA 2.84
Williams-LA 3.00
Friend-Pit 3.00

Adjusted ERA
Broglio-StL 149
Drysdale-LA 140
Simmons-Phi-StL 134
Williams-LA 133
Podres-LA 129

Opponents' Batting Avg.
Koufax-LA .207
Williams-LA .210
Broglio-StL .213
Drysdale-LA .215
Buhl-Mil .229

Opponents' On Base Pct.
Drysdale-LA .275
Friend-Pit .281
Williams-LA .282
Law-Pit .287
Burdette-Mil .287

Starter Runs
McCormick-SF 29.8
Drysdale-LA 27.5
Broglio-StL 25.6
Friend-Pit 23.2
Law-Pit 20.6

Adjusted Starter Runs
Broglio-StL 34.0
Drysdale-LA 33.6
Friend-Pit 22.9
Williams-LA 22.4
Podres-LA 22.4

Clutch Pitching Index
Simmons-Phi-StL 121
Podres-LA 117
O'Dell-SF 110
Sadecki-StL 109
Buhl-Mil 108

Relief Runs
McDaniel-StL 21.6
Brosnan-Cin 15.4
Roebuck-LA 12.8
Farrell-Phi 12.2
Face-Pit 10.9

Adjusted Relief Runs
McDaniel-StL 26.0
Brosnan-Cin 16.1
Roebuck-LA 15.5
Farrell-Phi 13.6
Face-Pit 10.8

Relief Ranking
McDaniel-StL 45.2
Farrell-Phi 22.2
Face-Pit 20.3
Brosnan-Cin 17.5
Roebuck-LA 15.5

Total Pitcher Index
McDaniel-StL 5.0
Broglio-StL 4.8
Drysdale-LA 4.3
McCormick-SF 2.7
Williams-LA 2.6

Total Baseball Ranking
Mays-SF 5.9
Banks-Chi 5.8
McDaniel-StL 5.0
Aaron-Mil 4.8
Broglio-StL 4.8

TEAM	G	W	L	PCT	GB	R	OR	AB	H	2B	3B	HR	BB	SO	AVG	OBP	SLG	PRO	PRO+	BR	/A	PF	CHI	RC	SB	CS	SBA	SBR
NY	155	97	57	.630		746	627	5290	1377	215	40	193	537	818	.260	.332	.426	.758	117	63	105	94	100	747	37	23	62	-3
BAL	154	89	65	.578	8	682	606	5170	1307	206	33	123	596	801	.253	.334	.377	.711	99	-8	1	99	103	659	37	24	61	-3
CHI	154	87	67	.565	10	741	617	5191	1402	242	38	112	567	648	.270	.348	.396	.744	108	57	64	99	101	726	122	48	72	8
CLE	154	76	78	.494	21	667	693	5296	1415	218	20	127	444	573	.267	.328	.388	.716	102	-11	10	97	101	673	58	25	70	2
WAS	154	73	81	.474	24	672	696	5248	1283	205	43	147	584	883	.244	.326	.384	.710	99	-18	-11	99	101	656	52	43	55	-10
DET	154	71	83	.461	26	633	644	5202	1243	188	34	150	636	728	.239	.326	.375	.701	93	-32	-50	103	97	651	66	32	67	1
BOS	154	65	89	.422	32	658	775	5215	1359	234	32	124	570	798	.261	.336	.389	.725	99	16	-8	104	95	674	34	28	55	-7
KC	155	58	96	.377	39	615	756	5226	1303	212	34	110	513	744	.249	.318	.366	.684	90	-68	-72	101	103	598	16	11	59	-2
TOT	617					5414		41838	10689	1720	274	1086	4447	5993	.255	.331	.388	.718							422	234	64	-14

TEAM	CG	SH	SV	IP	H	H/G	HR	BB	SO	RAT	ERA	ERA+	OAV	OOB	PR	/A	PF	CPI	FA	E	DP	FW	PW	BW	SBW	DIF
NY	38	16	42	1398	1225	7.9	123	609	712	12.0	3.52	102	.238	.322	55	10	93	98	.979	129	162	.2	1.0	10.6	-.1	8.3
BAL	48	11	22	1375²	1222	8.0	117	552	785	11.8	3.52	108	.241	.320	54	44	98	98	.982	108	172	1.4	4.5	.1	-.1	6.2
CHI	42	11	26	1381	1338	8.7	127	533	695	12.3	3.60	105	.258	.329	41	27	98	106	.982	109	175	1.4	2.7	6.5	1.0	-1.5
CLE	32	10	30	1382¹	1308	8.5	161	636	771	12.8	3.95	95	.252	.336	-12	-33	97	103	.978	128	165	.2	-3.3	1.0	.4	.8
WAS	34	10	35	1405¹	1392	8.9	130	538	775	12.6	3.77	103	.260	.331	16	18	100	103	.973	165	159	-2.1	1.8	-1.1	-.8	-1.7
DET	40	7	25	1405²	1336	8.6	141	474	824	11.9	3.64	109	.251	.317	37	50	102	99	.977	138	138	-.5	5.1	-5.1	-.3	-5.8
BOS	34	6	23	1361	1440	9.5	127	580	767	13.6	4.62	87	.273	.349	-113	-88	104	94	.976	141	156	-.6	-8.9	-.8	-.5	-1.1
KC	44	4	14	1374	1428	9.4	160	525	664	13.1	4.38	91	.271	.342	-77	-60	103	100	.979	127	149	.3	-6.1	-7.3	-.0	-5.9
TOT	312	75	217	11083		8.7				12.5	3.87		.255	.331					.978	1045	1276					

Runs
Mantle-NY 119
Maris-NY 98
Minoso-Chi 89
Landis-Chi 89
Sievers-Chi 87

Hits
Minoso-Chi 184
Robinson-Bal 175
Fox-Chi 175
Smith-Chi 169
Runnels-Bos 169

Doubles
Francona-Cle 36
Skowron-NY 34
Minoso-Chi 32
Freese-Chi 32

Triples
Fox-Chi 10
Robinson-Bal 9

Home Runs
Mantle-NY 40
Maris-NY 39
Lemon-Was 38
Colavito-Det 35
Killebrew-Was ... 31

Total Bases
Mantle-NY 294
Maris-NY 290
Skowron-NY 284
Minoso-Chi 284
Lemon-Was 268

Runs Batted In
Maris-NY 112
Minoso-Chi 105
Wertz-Bos 103
Lemon-Was 100
Gentile-Bal 98

Runs Produced
Minoso-Chi 174
Mantle-NY 173
Maris-NY 171
Sievers-Chi 152
Robinson-Bal 148

Bases On Balls
Yost-Det 125
Mantle-NY 111
Allison-Was 92
Woodling-Bal 84
Landis-Chi 80

Batting Average
Runnels-Bos ...... .320
Smith-Chi .... .315
Minoso-Chi .... .311
Skowron-NY .... .309
Kuenn-Cle .... .308

On Base Percentage
Yost-Det .... .416
Woodling-Bal ..... .403
Runnels-Bos ...... .403
Mantle-NY .... .402
Sievers-Chi ...... .399

Slugging Average
Maris-NY .... .581
Mantle-NY .... .558
Killebrew-Was .... .534
Sievers-Chi ...... .534
Skowron-NY .... .528

Production
Mantle-NY .... .960
Maris-NY .... .955
Sievers-Chi ...... .933
Killebrew-Was .... .911
Skowron-NY .... .884

Adjusted Production
Mantle-NY 166
Maris-NY 164
Sievers-Chi 152
Killebrew-Was ... 145
Skowron-NY 144

Batter Runs
Mantle-NY 43.9
Williams-Bos 43.5
Maris-NY 36.5
Sievers-Chi 32.1
Killebrew-Was ... 26.9

Adjusted Batter Runs
Mantle-NY 50.6
Maris-NY 42.3
Williams-Bos 40.4
Sievers-Chi 33.0
Skowron-NY 29.7

Clutch Hitting Index
Wertz-Bos 149
Power-Cle 115
Woodling-Bal 110
Fox-Chi 109
Minoso-Chi 109

Runs Created
Mantle-NY 125
Maris-NY 111
Minoso-Chi 104
Lemon-Was 99
Francona-Cle 96

Total Average
Mantle-NY 1.053
Maris-NY .... .992
Sievers-Chi ..... .960
Killebrew-Was ... .936
Lemon-Was .... .871

Stolen Bases
Aparicio-Chi 51
Landis-Chi 23
Green-Was 21
Kaline-Det 19
Piersall-Cle 18

Stolen Base Average
Aparicio-Chi 86.4
Kaline-Det 82.6
Landis-Chi 79.3
Piersall-Cle 78.3
Green-Was 72.4

Stolen Base Runs
Aparicio-Chi 10.5
Landis-Chi 3.3
Kaline-Det 3.3
Piersall-Cle 2.4
Mantle-NY 2.4

Fielding Runs
Aparicio-Chi 30.4
Boyer-NY 27.6
Power-Cle 21.0
Tuttle-KC 17.1
Landis-Chi 12.9

Total Player Rating
Mantle-NY 4.4
Maris-NY 3.8
Aparicio-Chi 3.8
Williams-Bos 3.3
Runnels-Bos 3.2

Wins
Perry-Cle 18
Estrada-Bal 18
B.Daley-KC 16

Win Percentage
Perry-Cle .... .643
Ditmar-NY .... .625
Estrada-Bal ...... .621
Pappas-Bal .... .577

Games
Fornieles-Bos 70
Staley-Chi 64
Clevenger-Was 53
Moore-Chi-Was 51
Kutyna-KC 51

Complete Games
Lary-Det 15
Ramos-Was 14
Herbert-KC 14
Wynn-Chi 13
B.Daley-KC 13

Shutouts
Wynn-Chi 4
Perry-Cle 4
Ford-NY 4

Saves
Klippstein-Cle ... 14
Fornieles-Bos 14
Moore-Chi-Was 13
B.Shantz-NY 11

Innings Pitched
Lary-Det 274.1
Ramos-Was 274.0
Perry-Cle 261.1
Herbert-KC 252.2
Bunning-Det 252.0

Fewest Hits/Game
Estrada-Bal 6.99
Turley-NY 7.17
Barber-Bal 7.33
Bunning-Det 7.75
Ford-NY 7.85

Fewest BB/Game
Brown-Bal 1.25
Mossi-Det 1.82
Hall-KC 1.88
Lary-Det 2.03
Pierce-Chi 2.11

Strikeouts
Bunning-Det 201
Ramos-Was 160
Wynn-Chi 158
Lary-Det 149
Estrada-Bal 144

Strikeouts/Game
Bunning-Det 7.18
Bell-Cle 6.34
Estrada-Bal 6.21
Wynn-Chi 5.99
Monbouquette-Bos . 5.61

Ratio
Brown-Bal 10.08
Bunning-Det 10.43
Baumann-Chi 10.83
Mossi-Det 10.86
Ford-NY 10.93

Earned Run Average
Baumann-Chi 2.67
Bunning-Det 2.79
Brown-Bal 3.06
Ditmar-NY 3.06
Ford-NY 3.08

Adjusted ERA
Bunning-Det 142
Baumann-Chi 141
Brown-Bal 125
Herbert-KC 121
Barber-Bal 118

Opponents' Batting Avg.
Estrada-Bal ...... .218
Turley-NY .... .222
Barber-Bal .... .226
Ford-NY .... .235
Bunning-Det ...... .236

Opponents' On Base Pct.
Brown-Bal .... .286
Bunning-Det ...... .293
Mossi-Det .... .296
Ford-NY .... .299
Terry-NY .... .300

Starter Runs
Bunning-Det 30.4
Baumann-Chi 24.7
Ditmar-NY 18.0
Ford-NY 16.9
Herbert-KC 16.7

Adjusted Starter Runs
Bunning-Det 32.8
Baumann-Chi 22.8
Herbert-KC 19.7
Pascual-Was 14.5
Kralick-Was 14.2

Clutch Pitching Index
Ditmar-NY 121
Perry-Cle 113
Lee-Was 113
Baumann-Chi 113
Herbert-KC 111

Relief Runs
Staley-Chi 18.6
Fornieles-Bos ... 14.9
Sisler-Det 12.4
Aguirre-Det 10.7
B.Shantz-NY 8.1

Adjusted Relief Runs
Staley-Chi 17.4
Fornieles-Bos ... 17.0
Sisler-Det 13.2
Aguirre-Det 11.6
Stobbs-Was 7.5

Relief Ranking
Staley-Chi 32.0
Fornieles-Bos ... 25.9
Sisler-Det 20.0
Aguirre-Det 11.6
Klippstein-Cle .. 11.2

Total Pitcher Index
Staley-Chi 3.7
Fornieles-Bos ... 2.9
Bunning-Det 2.6
Herbert-KC 2.5
Pascual-Was 2.2

Total Baseball Ranking
Mantle-NY 4.4
Maris-NY 3.8
Aparicio-Chi 3.8
Staley-Chi 3.7
Williams-Bos 3.3

TEAM	G	W	L	PCT	GB	R	OR	AB	H	2B	3B	HR	BB	SO	AVG	OBP	SLG	PRO	PRO+	BR	/A	PF	CHI	RC	SB	CS	SBA	SBR
CIN	154	93	61	.604		710	653	5243	1414	247	35	158	423	761	.270	.328	.421	.749	102	19	10	101	101	713	70	33	68	1
LA	154	89	65	.578	4	735	697	5189	1358	193	40	157	596	796	.262	.340	.405	.745	95	29	-35	109	100	722	86	45	66	-1
SF	155	85	69	.552	8	773	655	5233	1379	219	32	183	506	764	.264	.332	.423	.755	109	35	62	96	106	719	79	54	59	-9
MIL	155	83	71	.539	10	712	656	5288	1365	199	34	188	534	880	.258	.330	.415	.745	110	19	63	94	98	714	70	43	62	-5
STL	155	80	74	.519	13	703	668	5307	1436	236	51	103	494	745	.271	.336	.393	.729	90	-3	-72	110	100	702	46	28	62	-3
PIT	154	75	79	.487	18	694	675	5311	1448	232	57	128	428	721	.273	.330	.410	.740	101	8	6	100	99	694	26	30	46	-10
CHI	156	64	90	.416	29	689	800	5344	1364	238	51	176	539	1027	.255	.327	.418	.745	101	16	7	101	95	726	35	25	58	-5
PHI	155	47	107	.305	46	584	796	5213	1265	185	50	103	475	928	.243	.311	.357	.668	84	-123	-115	99	102	577	56	30	65	-1
TOT	619					5600		42128	11029	1749	350	1196	3995	6622	.262	.329	.405	.735							468	288	62	-32

TEAM	CG	SH	SV	IP	H	H/G	HR	BB	SO	RAT	ERA	ERA+	OAV	OOB	PR	/A	PF	CPI	FA	E	DP	FW	PW	BW	SBW	DIF
CIN	46	12	40	1370	1300	8.5	147	500	829	12.0	3.78	107	.250	.320	38	43	101	98	.977	134	124	.7	4.3	1.0	.5	9.6
LA	40	10	35	1378[1]	1346	8.8	167	544	1105	12.7	4.04	107	.256	.331	-2	46	108	101	.975	144	162	.1	4.6	-3.5	.3	10.5
SF	39	9	30	1388	1306	8.5	152	502	924	11.9	3.77	101	.249	.318	40	6	95	98	.977	133	126	.8	.6	6.2	-.5	1.0
MIL	57	8	16	1391[1]	1357	8.8	153	493	652	12.1	3.89	96	.258	.324	21	-24	93	101	.982	111	152	2.0	-2.4	6.3	-.0	.2
STL	49	10	24	1368[2]	1334	8.8	136	570	823	12.7	3.74	118	.256	.333	44	100	109	106	.972	166	165	-1.1	9.9	-7.1	.1	1.2
PIT	34	9	29	1362	1442	9.5	121	400	759	12.3	3.92	102	.274	.328	17	10	99	102	.975	150	187	-.2	1.0	.6	-.6	-2.8
CHI	34	6	25	1385	1492	9.7	165	465	755	12.9	4.48	93	.277	.338	-70	-47	104	99	.970	183	175	-2.0	-4.7	.7	-.0	-7.0
PHI	29	9	13	1383[1]	1452	9.4	155	521	775	13.1	4.61	88	.273	.342	-88	-82	101	96	.976	146	179	.0	-8.1	-11.4	.3	-10.8
TOT	328	73	212	11026[2]		9.0				12.5	4.03		.262	.329					.976	1167	1270					

Runs
Mays-SF 129
Robinson-Cin 117
Aaron-Mil 115
Boyer-StL 109

Hits
Pinson-Cin 208
Clemente-Pit 201
Aaron-Mil 197
Boyer-StL 194
Cepeda-SF 182

Doubles
Aaron-Mil 39
Pinson-Cin 34
Santo-Chi 32
Robinson-Cin 32
Mays-SF 32

Triples
Altman-Chi 12
White-StL 11
Callison-Phi 11
Boyer-StL 11

Home Runs
Cepeda-SF 46
Mays-SF 40
Robinson-Cin 37
Stuart-Pit 35
Adcock-Mil 35

Total Bases
Aaron-Mil 358
Cepeda-SF 356
Mays-SF 334
Robinson-Cin 333
Clemente-Pit 320

Runs Batted In
Cepeda-SF 142
Robinson-Cin 124
Mays-SF 123
Aaron-Mil 120
Stuart-Pit 117

Runs Produced
Mays-SF 212
Robinson-Cin 204
Cepeda-SF 201
Aaron-Mil 201
Boyer-StL 180

Bases On Balls
Mathews-Mil 93
Moon-LA 89
Mays-SF 81
Gilliam-LA 79

Batting Average
Clemente-Pit 351
Pinson-Cin 343
Boyer-StL 329
Moon-LA 328
Aaron-Mil 327

On Base Percentage
Moon-LA 438
Robinson-Cin 411
Mathews-Mil 405
Boyer-StL 400
Mays-SF 395

Slugging Average
Robinson-Cin 611
Cepeda-SF 609
Aaron-Mil 594
Mays-SF 584
Stuart-Pit 581

Production
Robinson-Cin 1.022
Aaron-Mil 979
Mays-SF 979
Cepeda-SF 972
Clemente-Pit 951

Adjusted Production
Aaron-Mil 165
Robinson-Cin 164
Mays-SF 162
Cepeda-SF 158
Mathews-Mil 156

Batter Runs
Robinson-Cin 52.4
Aaron-Mil 46.0
Mays-SF 45.8
Cepeda-SF 40.7
Mathews-Mil 40.4

Adjusted Batter Runs
Aaron-Mil 53.8
Robinson-Cin 50.8
Mays-SF 50.4
Mathews-Mil 47.8
Cepeda-SF 45.1

Clutch Hitting Index
Moon-LA 113
McMillan-Mil 110
Davenport-SF 110
Adcock-Mil 105
Cepeda-SF 105

Runs Created
Robinson-Cin 137
Aaron-Mil 132
Mays-SF 130
Mathews-Mil 128
Boyer-StL 126

Total Average
Robinson-Cin 1.119
Mays-SF 1.017
Moon-LA 1.003
Aaron-Mil 993
Mathews-Mil 981

Stolen Bases
Wills-LA 35
Pinson-Cin 23
Robinson-Cin 22
Aaron-Mil 21
Mays-SF 18

Stolen Base Average
Robinson-Cin 88.0
Wills-LA 70.0
Aaron-Mil 70.0
Pinson-Cin 69.7
Mays-SF 66.7

Stolen Base Runs
Robinson-Cin 4.8
Maye-Mil 2.4
Williams-Chi 1.8
Wills-LA 1.5
Gonzalez-Phi 1.5

Fielding Runs
Mazeroski-Pit 30.5
Pinson-Cin 19.2
Malkmus-Phi 16.3
Clemente-Pit 14.4
Amaro-Phi 14.1

Total Player Rating
Aaron-Mil 5.6
Robinson-Cin 5.5
Mays-SF 5.0
Clemente-Pit 4.4
Mathews-Mil 4.2

Wins
Spahn-Mil 21
Jay-Cin 21
O'Toole-Cin 19

Win Percentage
Podres-LA 783
O'Toole-Cin 679
Jay-Cin 677
Burdette-Mil 621
Spahn-Mil 618

Games
Baldschun-Phi 65
Miller-SF 63
Face-Pit 62
Elston-Chi 58
Anderson-Chi 57

Complete Games
Spahn-Mil 21
Koufax-LA 15
Jay-Cin 14
Burdette-Mil 14

Shutouts
Spahn-Mil 4
Jay-Cin 4

Saves
Miller-SF 17
Face-Pit 17
Henry-Cin 16
Brosnan-Cin 16
L.Sherry-LA 15

Innings Pitched
Burdette-Mil 272.1
Spahn-Mil 262.2
Cardwell-Chi 259.1
Koufax-LA 255.2
O'Toole-Cin 252.2

Fewest Hits/Game
Koufax-LA 7.46
Jay-Cin 7.90
Gibson-StL 7.92
Sadecki-StL 7.92
Spahn-Mil 8.09

Fewest BB/Game
Burdette-Mil 1.09
Friend-Pit 1.72
Purkey-Cin 1.86
Spahn-Mil 2.19
Ellsworth-Chi 2.31

Strikeouts
Koufax-LA 269
Williams-LA 205
Drysdale-LA 182
O'Toole-Cin 178
Gibson-StL 166

Strikeouts/Game
Koufax-LA 9.47
Williams-LA 7.84
Gibson-StL 7.07
Drysdale-LA 6.71
Gibbon-Pit 6.68

Ratio
Spahn-Mil 10.42
Burdette-Mil 10.94
Koufax-LA 10.95
Purkey-Cin 11.03
Jackson-StL 11.22

Earned Run Average
Spahn-Mil 3.02
O'Toole-Cin 3.10
Simmons-StL 3.13
McCormick-SF 3.20
Gibson-StL 3.24

Adjusted ERA
Simmons-StL 141
Gibson-StL 136
O'Toole-Cin 131
Spahn-Mil 124
Koufax-LA 123

Opponents' Batting Avg.
Koufax-LA 222
Jay-Cin 236
Sadecki-StL 238
Gibson-StL 239
O'Toole-Cin 240

Opponents' On Base Pct.
Spahn-Mil 293
Koufax-LA 295
Burdette-Mil 296
Purkey-Cin 297
Jackson-StL 303

Starter Runs
Spahn-Mil 29.7
O'Toole-Cin 26.2
McCormick-SF 23.0
Simmons-StL 19.6
Gibson-StL 18.7

Adjusted Starter Runs
Simmons-StL 27.6
Gibson-StL 27.3
O'Toole-Cin 27.1
Koufax-LA 23.3
Spahn-Mil 21.2

Clutch Pitching Index
Simmons-StL 122
Ellsworth-Chi 121
Podres-LA 116
McCormick-SF 115
Gibson-StL 114

Relief Runs
Miller-SF 18.6
Perranoski-LA 14.1
McMahon-Mil 12.2
Henry-Cin 10.9
Schultz-Chi 9.9

Adjusted Relief Runs
Perranoski-LA 17.2
Miller-SF 15.6
Henry-Cin 11.1
Schultz-Chi 11.0
McMahon-Mil 9.2

Relief Ranking
Miller-SF 26.8
Perranoski-LA 22.8
Schultz-Chi 21.8
Brosnan-Cin 18.5
Henry-Cin 13.1

Total Pitcher Index
Spahn-Mil 3.9
Gibson-StL 3.3
Miller-SF 3.1
Simmons-StL 3.0
O'Toole-Cin 2.7

Total Baseball Ranking
Aaron-Mil 5.6
Robinson-Cin 5.5
Mays-SF 5.0
Clemente-Pit 4.4
Mathews-Mil 4.2

TEAM	G	W	L	PCT	GB	R	OR	AB	H	2B	3B	HR	BB	SO	AVG	OBP	SLG	PRO	PRO+	BR	/A	PF	CHI	RC	SB	CS	SBA	SBR
NY	163	109	53	.673		827	612	5559	1461	194	40	240	543	785	.263	.332	.442	.774	118	82	125	95	101	811	28	18	61	-2
DET	163	101	61	.623	8	841	671	5561	1481	215	53	180	673	867	.266	.349	.421	.770	109	96	72	103	99	835	98	36	73	8
BAL	163	95	67	.586	14	691	588	5481	1393	227	36	149	581	902	.254	.328	.390	.718	102	-16	9	97	97	699	39	30	57	-6
CHI	163	86	76	.531	23	765	726	5556	1475	216	46	138	550	612	.265	.338	.395	.733	104	17	29	98	101	754	100	40	71	6
CLE	161	78	83	.484	30.5	737	752	5609	1493	257	39	150	492	720	.266	.328	.406	.734	105	9	29	97	99	743	34	11	76	4
BOS	163	76	86	.469	33	729	792	5508	1401	251	37	112	647	847	.254	.336	.374	.710	94	-22	-39	102	101	704	56	36	61	-5
MIN	161	70	90	.438	38	707	778	5417	1353	215	40	167	597	840	.250	.328	.397	.725	95	-5	-45	106	98	698	47	43	52	-12
LA	162	70	91	.435	38.5	744	784	5424	1331	218	22	189	681	1068	.245	.333	.398	.731	91	12	-72	111	99	734	37	28	57	-6
WAS	161	61	100	.379	47.5	618	776	5366	1307	217	44	119	558	917	.244	.317	.367	.684	90	-83	-74	99	98	625	81	47	63	-4
KC	162	61	100	.379	47.5	683	863	5423	1342	216	47	90	580	772	.247	.323	.354	.677	85	-90	-101	102	107	642	58	22	73	4
TOT	811					7342		54904	14037	2226	404	1534	5902	8330	.256	.331	.395	.726							578	311	65	-13

TEAM	CG	SH	SV	IP	H	H/G	HR	BB	SO	RAT	ERA	ERA+	OAV	OOB	PR	/A	PF	CPI	FA	E	DP	FW	PW	BW	SBW	DIF
NY	47	14	39	1451	1288	8.0	137	542	866	11.5	3.46	107	.239	.312	91	42	92	99	.980	124	180	1.6	4.2	12.4	-.0	9.9
DET	62	12	30	1459¹	1404	8.7	170	469	836	11.7	3.55	116	.252	.313	78	90	102	106	.976	146	147	.3	8.9	7.1	.9	2.7
BAL	54	21	33	1471¹	1226	7.5	109	617	926	11.5	3.22	120	.227	.310	132	103	96	97	.980	128	173	1.4	10.2	.9	-.5	2.0
CHI	39	3	33	1448²	1491	9.3	158	498	814	12.4	4.06	97	.268	.329	-5	-23	97	102	.980	128	138	1.4	-2.3	2.9	-.7	2.3
CLE	35	12	23	1443¹	1426	8.9	178	599	801	12.8	4.15	95	.258	.334	-20	-34	98	102	.977	139	142	.6	-3.4	2.9	.5	-3.2
BOS	35	6	30	1442²	1472	9.2	167	679	831	13.5	4.29	97	.266	.348	-43	-20	104	105	.977	144	170	.4	-2.0	-3.9	-.4	.8
MIN	49	14	23	1432¹	1415	8.9	163	570	914	12.8	4.28	99	.256	.331	-41	-6	105	95	.972	174	150	-1.4	-6	-4.5	-1.1	-2.5
LA	25	5	34	1438	1391	8.7	180	713	973	13.4	4.31	105	.254	.343	-46	32	112	101	.969	192	154	-2.4	3.2	-7.1	-.5	-3.6
WAS	39	8	21	1425	1405	8.9	131	586	666	12.8	4.23	95	.260	.336	-33	-34	100	96	.975	156	171	-.4	-3.4	-7.3	-.3	-8.2
KC	32	5	23	1415	1519	9.7	141	629	703	14.0	4.74	88	.275	.355	-113	-89	104	97	.972	175	160	-1.4	-8.8	-10.0	.5	.2
TOT	417	100	289	14426²		8.8				12.6	4.02		.256	.331					.976	1506	1585					

Runs
Maris-NY 132
Mantle-NY 132
Colavito-Det 129
Cash-Det 119
Kaline-Det 116

Hits
Cash-Det 193
B.Robinson-Bal 192
Kaline-Det 190
Francona-Cle 178
Richardson-NY 173

Doubles
Kaline-Det 41
B.Robinson-Bal 38
Kubek-NY 38
Siebern-KC 36
Power-Cle 34

Triples
Wood-Det 14
Lumpe-KC 9
Keough-Was 9

Home Runs
Maris-NY 61
Mantle-NY 54
Killebrew-Min 46
Gentile-Bal 46
Colavito-Det 45

Total Bases
Maris-NY 366
Cash-Det 354
Mantle-NY 353
Colavito-Det 338
Killebrew-Min 328

Runs Batted In
Maris-NY 142
Gentile-Bal 141
Colavito-Det 140
Cash-Det 132
Mantle-NY 128

Runs Produced
Colavito-Det 224
Maris-NY 213
Cash-Det 210
Mantle-NY 206
Gentile-Bal 191

Bases On Balls
Mantle-NY 126
Cash-Det 124
Colavito-Det 113
Killebrew-Min 107
Allison-Min 103

Batting Average
Cash-Det .361
Kaline-Det .324
Piersall-Cle .322
Mantle-NY .317
Gentile-Bal .302

On Base Percentage
Cash-Det .488
Mantle-NY .452
Gentile-Bal .428
Pearson-LA .422
Killebrew-Min .409

Slugging Average
Mantle-NY .687
Cash-Det .662
Gentile-Bal .646
Maris-NY .620
Killebrew-Min .606

Production
Cash-Det 1.150
Mantle-NY 1.138
Gentile-Bal 1.074
Killebrew-Min 1.015
Maris-NY .997

Adjusted Production
Mantle-NY 210
Cash-Det 198
Gentile-Bal 189
Maris-NY 170
Killebrew-Min 159

Batter Runs
Cash-Det 86.1
Mantle-NY 76.3
Gentile-Bal 59.1
Killebrew-Min 52.9
Colavito-Det 51.5

Adjusted Batter Runs
Mantle-NY 84.4
Cash-Det 81.5
Gentile-Bal 63.7
Maris-NY 56.5
Colavito-Det 47.8

Clutch Hitting Index
Schilling-Bos 120
Gentile-Bal 115
Malzone-Bos 115
Allison-Min 111
Siebern-KC 109

Runs Created
Cash-Det 178
Mantle-NY 174
Colavito-Det 141
Gentile-Bal 138
Maris-NY 138

Total Average
Mantle-NY 1.384
Cash-Det 1.358
Gentile-Bal 1.196
Killebrew-Min 1.098
Colavito-Det 1.051

Stolen Bases
Aparicio-Chi 53
Howser-KC 37
Wood-Det 30
Hinton-Was 22
Bruton-Det 22

Stolen Base Average
Hinton-Was 81.5
Howser-KC 80.4
Aparicio-Chi 80.3
Geiger-Bos 80.0
Landis-Chi 79.2

Stolen Base Runs
Aparicio-Chi 8.1
Howser-KC 5.7
Wood-Det 3.6
Kaline-Det 3.6
Hinton-Was 3.6

Fielding Runs
Boyer-NY 30.3
Landis-Chi 19.3
Power-Cle 18.1
Cottier-Det-Was 16.9
Lumpe-KC 16.0

Total Player Rating
Mantle-NY 8.0
Cash-Det 7.1
Gentile-Bal 5.3
Colavito-Det 4.7
Howard-NY 4.2

Wins
Ford-NY 25
Lary-Det 23
Barber-Bal 18
Bunning-Det 17
Terry-NY 16

Win Percentage
Ford-NY .862
Terry-NY .842
Arroyo-NY .750
Lary-Det .719

Games
Arroyo-NY 65
Morgan-LA 59
Lown-Chi 59
Kunkel-KC 58
Fornieles-Bos 57

Complete Games
Lary-Det 22
Pascual-Min 15
Barber-Bal 14

Shutouts
Pascual-Min 8
Barber-Bal 8
Pappas-Bal 4
Lary-Det 4
Bunning-Det 4

Saves
Arroyo-NY 29
Wilhelm-Bal 18
Fornieles-Bos 15
Moore-Min 14
Fox-Det 12

Innings Pitched
Ford-NY 283.0
Lary-Det 275.1
Bunning-Det 268.0
Ramos-Min 264.1
Pascual-Min 252.1

Fewest Hits/Game
Estrada-Bal 6.75
Pappas-Bal 6.79
Barber-Bal 7.03
Pascual-Min 7.31
Donovan-Was 7.36

Fewest BB/Game
Mossi-Det 1.76
Brown-Bal 1.78
Donovan-Was 1.87
Terry-NY 2.01
McClain-Was 2.04

Strikeouts
Pascual-Min 221
Ford-NY 209
Bunning-Det 194
Pizarro-Chi 188
McBride-LA 180

Strikeouts/Game
Pizarro-Chi 8.69
Pascual-Min 7.88
Estrada-Bal 6.79
McBride-LA 6.70
Ford-NY 6.65

Ratio
Donovan-Was 9.39
Terry-NY 9.80
Brown-Bal 10.10
Bunning-Det 10.48
Lary-Det 10.59

Earned Run Average
Donovan-Was 2.40
Stafford-NY 2.68
Mossi-Det 2.96
Pappas-Bal 3.04
Pizarro-Chi 3.05

Adjusted ERA
Donovan-Was 167
Stafford-NY 139
Mossi-Det 139
Archer-KC 131
Schwall-Bos 129

Opponents' Batting Avg.
Estrada-Bal .207
Pappas-Bal .208
Pascual-Min .217
Barber-Bal .218
Donovan-Was .224

Opponents' On Base Pct.
Donovan-Was .269
Terry-NY .277
Bunning-Det .285
Brown-Bal .286
Ford-NY .292

Starter Runs
Hoeft-Bal 30.7
Donovan-Was 30.4
Stafford-NY 29.2
Mossi-Det 28.5
Ford-NY 25.5

Adjusted Starter Runs
Mossi-Det 30.5
Donovan-Was 30.3
Hoeft-Bal 28.0
Bunning-Det 27.1
Lary-Det 26.5

Clutch Pitching Index
Schwall-Bos 131
Mossi-Det 119
Shaw-Chi-KC 115
Monbouquette-Bos 115
McBride-LA 112

Relief Runs
Arroyo-NY 24.2
Wilhelm-Bal 21.0
Morgan-LA 17.0
Fox-Det 16.6
Lown-Chi 14.2

Adjusted Relief Runs
Morgan-LA 21.9
Arroyo-NY 20.2
Wilhelm-Bal 18.9
Fox-Det 17.1
Lown-Chi 12.9

Relief Ranking
Arroyo-NY 41.6
Wilhelm-Bal 31.8
Morgan-LA 26.9
Fox-Det 26.9
Lown-Chi 17.0

Total Pitcher Index
Arroyo-NY 4.3
Lary-Det 3.7
Donovan-Was 3.7
Wilhelm-Bal 3.2
Fox-Det 2.8

Total Baseball Ranking
Mantle-NY 8.0
Cash-Det 7.1
Gentile-Bal 5.3
Colavito-Det 4.7
Arroyo-NY 4.3

TEAM	G	W	L	PCT	GB	R	OR	AB	H	2B	3B	HR	BB	SO	AVG	OBP	SLG	PRO	PRO+	BR	/A	PF	CHI	RC	SB	CS	SBA	SBR
SF	165	103	62	.624		878	690	5588	1552	235	32	204	523	822	.278	.344	.441	.785	119	123	138	98	102	838	73	50	59	-8
LA	165	102	63	.618	1	842	697	5628	1510	192	65	140	572	886	.268	.339	.400	.739	112	41	89	94	107	783	198	43	82	34
CIN	162	98	64	.605	3.5	802	685	5645	1523	252	40	167	498	903	.270	.333	.417	.750	104	54	29	103	102	779	66	39	63	-4
PIT	161	93	68	.578	8	706	626	5483	1468	240	65	108	432	836	.268	.323	.394	.717	99	-15	-16	100	102	682	50	39	56	-8
MIL	162	86	76	.531	15.5	730	665	5458	1376	204	38	181	581	975	.252	.328	.403	.731	105	16	36	97	99	720	57	27	68	1
STL	163	84	78	.519	17.5	774	664	5643	1528	221	31	137	515	846	.271	.337	.394	.731	94	22	-51	110	102	747	86	41	68	1
PHI	161	81	80	.503	20	705	759	5420	1410	199	39	142	531	923	.260	.332	.390	.722	103	4	26	97	98	705	79	42	65	-2
HOU	162	64	96	.400	36.5	592	717	5558	1370	170	47	105	493	806	.246	.312	.351	.663	91	-117	-72	93	97	605	42	30	58	-5
CHI	162	59	103	.364	42.5	632	827	5534	1398	196	56	126	504	1044	.253	.319	.377	.696	90	-53	-77	104	94	657	78	50	61	-7
NY	161	40	120	.250	60.5	617	948	5492	1318	166	40	139	616	991	.240	.320	.361	.681	88	-75	-86	102	94	640	59	48	55	-11
TOT	812					7278		55449	14453	2075	453	1449	5265	9032	.261	.329	.393	.722							788	409	66	-9

TEAM	CG	SH	SV	IP	H	H/G	HR	BB	SO	RAT	ERA	ERA+	OAV	OOB	PR	/A	PF	CPI	FA	E	DP	FW	PW	BW	SBW	DIF
SF	62	10	39	1461²	1399	8.6	148	503	886	11.9	3.79	100	.251	.316	24	0	96	95	.977	142	153	1.0	.0	13.8	-.7	6.5
LA	44	8	46	1488²	1386	8.4	115	588	1104	12.1	3.62	100	.245	.319	54	2	92	94	.970	193	144	-2.1	.2	8.9	3.5	9.0
CIN	51	13	35	1460²	1397	8.6	149	567	964	12.4	3.75	107	.254	.329	31	44	102	104	.977	145	144	.6	4.4	2.9	-.3	9.4
PIT	40	13	41	1432¹	1433	9.0	118	466	897	12.1	3.37	117	.262	.322	90	89	100	110	.976	152	177	.2	8.9	-1.6	-.7	5.8
MIL	59	10	24	1434²	1443	9.1	151	407	802	11.8	3.68	103	.262	.317	42	19	96	103	.980	124	154	1.9	1.9	3.6	.2	-2.6
STL	53	17	25	1463¹	1394	8.6	149	517	914	11.9	3.55	120	.252	.319	64	117	108	104	.979	132	170	1.5	11.7	-5.1	.2	-5.2
PHI	43	7	24	1426²	1469	9.3	155	574	863	13.2	4.28	98	.268	.343	-53	-65	98	102	.977	138	167	1.0	-6.5	2.6	-.1	3.5
HOU	34	9	19	1453²	1446	9.0	113	471	1047	12.1	3.83	98	.259	.321	19	-15	95	95	.973	173	149	-1.0	-1.5	-7.2	-.4	-5.9
CHI	29	4	26	1438¹	1509	9.4	159	601	783	13.5	4.54	91	.272	.348	-95	-62	105	99	.977	146	171	.6	-6.2	-7.7	-.6	-8.1
NY	43	4	10	1430	1577	9.9	192	571	772	13.8	5.04	83	.281	.352	-175	-137	106	96	.967	210	167	-3.3	-13.7	-8.6	-1.0	-13.4
TOT	458	95	289	14490		9.0				12.5	3.94		.261	.329					.975	1555	1596					

Runs
Robinson-Cin 134
Wills-LA 130
Mays-SF 130
H.Aaron-Mil 127
T.Davis-LA 120

Hits
T.Davis-LA 230
Wills-LA 208
Robinson-Cin 208
White-StL 199
Groat-Pit 199

Doubles
Robinson-Cin 51
Mays-SF 36
Groat-Pit 34

Triples
Wills-LA 10
Virdon-Pit 10
W.Davis-LA 10
Callison-Phi 10

Home Runs
Mays-SF 49
H.Aaron-Mil 45
Robinson-Cin 39
Banks-Chi 37
Cepeda-SF 35

Total Bases
Mays-SF 382
Robinson-Cin 380
H.Aaron-Mil 366
T.Davis-LA 356
Cepeda-SF 324

Runs Batted In
T.Davis-LA 153
Mays-SF 141
Robinson-Cin 136
H.Aaron-Mil 128
Howard-LA 119

Runs Produced
T.Davis-LA 246
Robinson-Cin 231
Mays-SF 222
H.Aaron-Mil 210

Bases On Balls
Mathews-Mil 101
Gilliam-LA 93
Ashburn-NY 81
Mays-SF 78

Batting Average
T.Davis-LA 346
Robinson-Cin 342
Musial-StL 330
White-StL 324
H.Aaron-Mil 323

On Base Percentage
Robinson-Cin 424
Musial-StL 420
Skinner-Pit 397
Altman-Chi 394
H.Aaron-Mil 393

Slugging Average
Robinson-Cin 624
H.Aaron-Mil 618
Mays-SF 615
Howard-LA 560
T.Davis-LA 535

Production
Robinson-Cin 1.048
H.Aaron-Mil 1.012
Mays-SF 1.001
Musial-StL 928
T.Davis-LA 914

Adjusted Production
Robinson-Cin 172
H.Aaron-Mil 171
Mays-SF 167
T.Davis-LA 151
Howard-LA 149

Batter Runs
Robinson-Cin 66.6
Mays-SF 54.1
H.Aaron-Mil 54.0
T.Davis-LA 37.2
Altman-Chi 31.5

Adjusted Batter Runs
Robinson-Cin 62.0
H.Aaron-Mil 57.6
Mays-SF 56.4
T.Davis-LA 44.7
Mathews-Mil 30.5

Clutch Hitting Index
T.Davis-LA 125
Howard-LA 122
Musial-StL 112
Fairly-LA 112
Santo-Chi 111

Runs Created
Robinson-Cin 160
Mays-SF 146
H.Aaron-Mil 140
T.Davis-LA 129
White-StL 114

Total Average
Robinson-Cin 1.125
Mays-SF 1.060
H.Aaron-Mil 1.050
Musial-StL 957
Skinner-Pit 930

Stolen Bases
Wills-LA 104
W.Davis-LA 32
Pinson-Cin 26
Javier-StL 26
Taylor-Phi 20

Stolen Base Average
Mays-SF 90.0
Wills-LA 88.9
W.Davis-LA 82.1
Clendenon-Pit 80.0
Pinson-Cin 76.5

Stolen Base Runs
Wills-LA 23.4
W.Davis-LA 5.4
Mays-SF 4.2
Pinson-Cin 3.0

Fielding Runs
Mazeroski-Pit 41.1
Callison-Phi 22.9
Flood-StL 15.7
Williams-Chi 15.5
Kanehl-NY 14.5

Total Player Rating
Mays-SF 6.4
Robinson-Cin 6.0
H.Aaron-Mil 5.5
Mazeroski-Pit 5.0
Callison-Phi 3.9

Wins
Drysdale-LA 25
Sanford-SF 24
Purkey-Cin 23
Jay-Cin 21

Win Percentage
Purkey-Cin 821
Sanford-SF 774
Drysdale-LA 735
Pierce-SF 727
Shaw-Mil 625

Games
Perranoski-Phi 70
Baldschun-Phi 67
Roebuck-LA 64
Face-Pit 63
Olivo-Pit 62

Complete Games
Spahn-Mil 22
O'Dell-SF 20
Mahaffey-Phi 20
Drysdale-LA 19

Shutouts
Gibson-StL 5
Friend-Pit 5

Saves
Face-Pit 28
Perranoski-LA 20
Miller-SF 19
McDaniel-StL 14

Innings Pitched
Drysdale-LA 314.1
Purkey-Cin 288.1
O'Dell-SF 280.2
Mahaffey-Phi 274.0
Jay-Cin 273.0

Fewest Hits/Game
Koufax-LA 6.54
Gibson-StL 6.70
Bennett-Phi 7.42
Drysdale-LA 7.79
Broglio-StL 7.81

Fewest BB/Game
Shaw-Mil 1.76
Friend-Pit 1.82
Spahn-Mil 1.84
Pierce-SF 1.94
Purkey-Cin 2.00

Strikeouts
Drysdale-LA 232
Koufax-LA 216
Gibson-StL 208
Farrell-Hou 203
O'Dell-SF 195

Strikeouts/Game
Koufax-LA 10.55
Johnson-Hou 8.13
Gibson-StL 8.01
Bennett-Phi 7.68
Farrell-Hou 7.56

Ratio
Koufax-LA 9.42
Farrell-Hou 10.06
Spahn-Mil 10.23
Pierce-SF 10.26
Drysdale-LA 10.34

Earned Run Average
Koufax-LA 2.54
Shaw-Mil 2.80
Purkey-Cin 2.81
Drysdale-LA 2.83
Gibson-StL 2.85

Adjusted ERA
Gibson-StL 150
Purkey-Cin 143
Koufax-LA 143
Broglio-StL 142
Shaw-Mil 136

Opponents' Batting Avg.
Koufax-LA 197
Gibson-StL 204
Bennett-Phi 224
Drysdale-LA 230
Farrell-Hou 233

Opponents' On Base Pct.
Koufax-LA 261
Farrell-Hou 280
Drysdale-LA 283
Pierce-SF 284
Spahn-Mil 287

Starter Runs
Drysdale-LA 38.6
Purkey-Cin 36.3
Koufax-LA 28.7
Shaw-Mil 28.5
Gibson-StL 28.3

Adjusted Starter Runs
Purkey-Cin 38.9
Gibson-StL 36.8
Broglio-StL 31.4
Drysdale-LA 27.8
Friend-Pit 25.4

Clutch Pitching Index
Shaw-Mil 123
Friend-Pit 119
Broglio-StL 116
McBean-Pit 114
Koonce-Chi 111

Relief Runs
Face-Pit 20.8
McMahon-Mil-Hou 19.9
Shantz-Hou-StL . . 17.3
Umbricht-Hou 14.3
Perranoski-LA 13.0

Adjusted Relief Runs
Face-Pit 20.8
Shantz-Hou-StL . . 18.9
McMahon-Mil-Hou 18.1
Umbricht-Hou 12.8
Elston-Chi 12.6

Relief Ranking
Face-Pit 45.2
McMahon-Mil-Hou 26.6
Shantz-Hou-StL . . 23.9
Elston-Chi 23.9
Baldschun-Phi 20.3

Total Pitcher Index
Gibson-StL 5.0
Face-Pit 4.5
Purkey-Cin 3.6
Drysdale-LA 3.4
Spahn-Mil 3.1

Total Baseball Ranking
Mays-SF 6.4
Robinson-Cin 6.0
H.Aaron-Mil 5.5
Gibson-StL 5.0
Mazeroski-Pit 5.0

TEAM	G	W	L	PCT	GB	R	OR	AB	H	2B	3B	HR	BB	SO	AVG	OBP	SLG	PRO	PRO+	BR	/A	PF	CHI	RC	SB	CS	SBA	SBR
NY	162	96	66	.593		817	680	5644	1509	240	29	199	584	842	.267	.339	.426	.765	116	87	113	97	99	816	42	29	59	-5
MIN	163	91	71	.562	5	798	713	5561	1445	215	39	185	649	823	.260	.340	.412	.752	104	67	38	104	100	789	33	20	62	-2
LA	162	86	76	.531	10	718	706	5499	1377	232	35	137	602	917	.250	.328	.380	.708	100	-23	-1	97	103	698	46	27	63	-2
DET	161	85	76	.528	10.5	758	692	5456	1352	191	36	209	651	894	.248	.332	.411	.743	102	41	14	104	100	757	69	21	77	8
CHI	162	85	77	.525	11	707	658	5514	1415	250	56	92	620	674	.257	.336	.372	.708	97	-13	-9	100	99	701	76	40	66	-1
CLE	162	80	82	.494	16	682	745	5484	1341	202	22	180	502	939	.245	.314	.388	.702	97	-46	-26	97	103	671	35	16	69	1
BAL	162	77	85	.475	19	652	680	5491	1363	225	34	156	516	931	.248	.316	.387	.703	101	-42	0	94	98	665	45	32	58	-6
BOS	160	76	84	.475	19	707	756	5530	1429	257	53	146	525	923	.258	.326	.403	.729	99	9	-14	103	98	716	39	33	54	-8
KC	162	72	90	.444	24	745	837	5576	1467	220	58	116	556	803	.263	.334	.386	.720	96	3	-31	105	102	738	76	21	78	10
WAS	162	60	101	.373	35.5	599	716	5484	1370	206	38	132	466	789	.250	.310	.373	.683	90	-82	-77	99	97	623	99	53	65	-2
TOT	809					7183		55239	14068	2238	400	1552	5671	8535	.255	.328	.394	.722							560	292	66	-7

TEAM	CG	SH	SV	IP	H	H/G	HR	BB	SO	RAT	ERA	ERA+	OAV	OOB	PR	/A	PF	CPI	FA	E	DP	FW	PW	BW	SBW	DIF
NY	33	10	42	1470¹	1375	8.4	146	499	838	11.6	3.70	101	.247	.312	44	7	94	96	.979	131	151	.4	.7	11.4	-.4	3.0
MIN	53	11	27	1463¹	1400	8.6	166	493	948	11.9	3.89	105	.253	.319	13	31	103	99	.980	129	173	.5	3.1	3.8	-.1	2.7
LA	23	15	47	1466	1412	8.7	118	616	858	12.8	3.70	104	.253	.332	45	27	97	104	.973	175	153	-2.2	2.7	-.1	-.1	4.7
DET	46	8	35	1443²	1452	9.1	169	503	873	12.4	3.81	107	.259	.323	26	42	103	105	.974	156	114	-1.1	4.2	1.4	.9	-.9
CHI	50	13	28	1451²	1380	8.6	123	537	821	12.0	3.73	105	.251	.320	38	28	98	97	.982	110	153	1.6	2.8	-.9	-.0	.6
CLE	45	12	31	1441	1410	8.8	174	594	780	12.7	4.14	94	.258	.334	-27	-43	98	102	.978	139	168	-.1	-4.3	-2.6	.2	5.9
BAL	32	8	33	1462¹	1373	8.5	147	549	898	12.0	3.69	100	.249	.320	45	1	93	101	.980	122	152	.9	.1	.0	-.5	-4.4
BOS	34	12	40	1437²	1416	8.9	159	632	923	13.1	4.22	98	.258	.339	-40	-14	104	101	.979	131	152	.3	-1.4	-1.4	-.7	-.7
KC	32	4	33	1434	1450	9.1	199	655	825	13.5	4.79	88	.263	.346	-131	-91	106	97	.979	132	131	.3	-9.1	-3.1	1.1	1.9
WAS	38	11	13	1445	1400	8.7	151	593	771	12.5	4.04	100	.256	.331	-12	-1	102	100	.978	139	160	-.1	-.1	-7.7	-.1	-12.4
TOT	386	104	329	14515		8.7				12.4	3.97		.255	.328					.978	1364	1507					

Runs
Pearson-LA ... 115
Siebern-KC ... 114
Allison-Min ... 102
Yastrzemski-Bos ... 99
Richardson-NY ... 99

Hits
Richardson-NY ... 209
Lumpe-KC ... 193
B.Robinson-Bal ... 192
Yastrzemski-Bos ... 191
Robinson-Chi ... 187

Doubles
Robinson-Chi ... 45
Yastrzemski-Bos ... 43
Bressoud-Bos ... 40
Richardson-NY ... 38

Triples
Cimoli-KC ... 15
Robinson-Chi ... 10
Lumpe-KC ... 10
Clinton-Bos ... 10

Home Runs
Killebrew-Min ... 48
Cash-Det ... 39
Wagner-LA ... 37
Colavito-Det ... 37

Total Bases
Colavito-Det ... 309
B.Robinson-Bal ... 308
Wagner-LA ... 306
Yastrzemski-Bos ... 303
Killebrew-Min ... 301

Runs Batted In
Killebrew-Min ... 126
Siebern-KC ... 117
Colavito-Det ... 112
Robinson-Chi ... 109
Wagner-LA ... 107

Runs Produced
Siebern-KC ... 206
Robinson-Chi ... 187
Rollins-Min ... 176
Allison-Min ... 175
Yastrzemski-Bos ... 174

Bases On Balls
Mantle-NY ... 122
Siebern-KC ... 110
Killebrew-Min ... 106
Cash-Det ... 104
Cunningham-Chi ... 101

Batting Average
Runnels-Bos ... .326
Mantle-NY ... .321
Robinson-Chi ... .312
Hinton-Was ... .310
Siebern-KC ... .308

On Base Percentage
Mantle-NY ... .488
Siebern-KC ... .416
Cunningham-Chi ... .415
Runnels-Bos ... .411
Robinson-Chi ... .387

Slugging Average
Mantle-NY ... .605
Killebrew-Min ... .545
Colavito-Det ... .514
Cash-Det ... .513
Allison-Min ... .511

Production
Mantle-NY ... 1.093
Killebrew-Min ... .914
Siebern-KC ... .911
Cash-Det ... .897
Colavito-Det ... .889

Adjusted Production
Mantle-NY ... 198
Siebern-KC ... 138
Killebrew-Min ... 137
Cash-Det ... 134
Colavito-Det ... 132

Batter Runs
Mantle-NY ... 57.3
Siebern-KC ... 41.1
Killebrew-Min ... 33.1
Colavito-Det ... 31.4
Kaline-Det ... 30.7

Adjusted Batter Runs
Mantle-NY ... 61.0
Siebern-KC ... 35.4
Killebrew-Min ... 29.1
Kaline-Det ... 27.8
Colavito-Det ... 27.5

Clutch Hitting Index
Siebern-KC ... 125
Robinson-Chi ... 124
Rollins-Min ... 121
Howard-NY ... 115
L.Thomas-LA ... 111

Runs Created
Siebern-KC ... 129
Mantle-NY ... 126
Colavito-Det ... 117
Killebrew-Min ... 113
Robinson-Chi ... 113

Total Average
Mantle-NY ... 1.385
Siebern-KC ... .956
Cash-Det ... .950
Killebrew-Min ... .945
Allison-Min ... .901

Stolen Bases
Aparicio-Chi ... 31
Hinton-Was ... 28
Wood-Det ... 24
Charles-KC ... 20

Stolen Base Average
Howser-KC ... 90.5
Wood-Det ... 88.9
Charles-KC ... 83.3
Tartabull-KC ... 79.2
Hinton-Was ... 73.7

Stolen Base Runs
Wood-Det ... 5.4
Howser-KC ... 4.5
Charles-KC ... 3.6
Tartabull-KC ... 2.7
Mantle-NY ... 2.7

Fielding Runs
Boyer-NY ... 36.2
Versalles-Min ... 31.6
Bressoud-Bos ... 24.5
Kindall-Cle ... 20.7
Cottier-Was ... 20.5

Total Player Rating
Mantle-NY ... 5.0
Boyer-NY ... 4.0
Bressoud-Bos ... 3.8
Colavito-Det ... 3.6
Kaline-Det ... 3.4

Wins
Terry-NY ... 23
Pascual-Min ... 20
Herbert-Chi ... 20
Donovan-Cle ... 20
Bunning-Det ... 19

Win Percentage
Herbert-Chi ... .690
Ford-NY ... .680
Donovan-Cle ... .667
Aguirre-Det ... .667
Terry-NY ... .657

Games
Radatz-Bos ... 62
Wyatt-KC ... 59

Complete Games
Pascual-Min ... 18
Kaat-Min ... 16
Donovan-Cle ... 16
Terry-NY ... 14

Shutouts
Pascual-Min ... 5
Kaat-Min ... 5
Donovan-Cle ... 5
Monbouquette-Bos ... 4
McBride-LA ... 4

Saves
Radatz-Bos ... 24
Bridges-NY ... 18
Fox-Det ... 16
Wilhelm-Bal ... 15
Bell-Cle ... 12

Innings Pitched
Terry-NY ... 298.2
Kaat-Min ... 269.0
Bunning-Det ... 258.0
Pascual-Min ... 257.2
Ford-NY ... 257.2

Fewest Hits/Game
Aguirre-Det ... 6.75
Cheney-Was ... 6.96
Belinsky-LA ... 7.16
Wilson-Bos ... 7.67
Stenhouse-Was ... 7.72

Fewest BB/Game
Donovan-Cle ... 1.69
Terry-NY ... 1.72
Mossi-Det ... 1.80
Roberts-Bal ... 1.93
Pascual-Min ... 2.06

Strikeouts
Pascual-Min ... 206
Bunning-Det ... 184
Terry-NY ... 176
Pizarro-Chi ... 173
Kaat-Min ... 173

Strikeouts/Game
Pizarro-Chi ... 7.66
Cheney-Was ... 7.63
Pascual-Min ... 7.20
Belinsky-LA ... 6.97
Estrada-Bal ... 6.65

Ratio
Terry-NY ... 9.55
Aguirre-Det ... 9.67
Pascual-Min ... 10.37
Roberts-Bal ... 10.40
Fisher-Chi ... 10.59

Earned Run Average
Aguirre-Det ... 2.21
Roberts-Bal ... 2.78
Ford-NY ... 2.90
Chance-LA ... 2.96
Fisher-Chi ... 3.10

Adjusted ERA
Aguirre-Det ... 184
Roberts-Bal ... 133
Chance-LA ... 130
Kaat-Min ... 130
Ford-NY ... 129

Opponents' Batting Avg.
Aguirre-Det ... .205
Cheney-Was ... .213
Belinsky-LA ... .216
Terry-NY ... .231
Wilson-Bos ... .231

Opponents' On Base Pct.
Aguirre-Det ... .269
Terry-NY ... .270
Pascual-Min ... .286
Roberts-Bal ... .289
Fisher-Chi ... .293

Starter Runs
Aguirre-Det ... 42.3
Ford-NY ... 30.7
Terry-NY ... 25.8
Roberts-Bal ... 25.4
Kaat-Min ... 24.7

Adjusted Starter Runs
Aguirre-Det ... 44.7
Kaat-Min ... 28.1
Ford-NY ... 24.3
Pascual-Min ... 22.0
Monbouquette-Bos ... 21.0

Clutch Pitching Index
Chance-LA ... 114
Roberts-Bal ... 111
Ramos-Cle ... 110
Ford-NY ... 110
Perry-Cle ... 109

Relief Runs
Radatz-Bos ... 24.0
Hall-Bal ... 22.2
Wilhelm-Bal ... 21.0
Fox-Det ... 14.6
Fowler-LA ... 10.0

Adjusted Relief Runs
Radatz-Bos ... 26.2
Hall-Bal ... 18.7
Wilhelm-Bal ... 18.2
Fox-Det ... 15.2
Fowler-LA ... 9.0

Relief Ranking
Radatz-Bos ... 39.7
Wilhelm-Bal ... 36.6
Hall-Bal ... 19.1
Fox-Det ... 18.9
Bridges-NY ... 10.0

Total Pitcher Index
Kaat-Min ... 4.2
Wilhelm-Bal ... 3.8
Radatz-Bos ... 3.8
Aguirre-Det ... 3.7
Pascual-Min ... 3.4

Total Baseball Ranking
Mantle-NY ... 5.0
Kaat-Min ... 4.2
Boyer-NY ... 4.0
Wilhelm-Bal ... 3.8
Bressoud-Bos ... 3.8

TEAM	G	W	L	PCT	GB	R	OR	AB	H	2B	3B	HR	BB	SO	AVG	OBP	SLG	PRO	PRO+	BR	/A	PF	CHI	RC	SB	CS	SBA	SBR
LA	163	99	63	.611		640	550	5428	1361	178	34	110	453	867	.251	.311	.357	.668	106	-3	39	93	105	596	124	70	64	-5
STL	162	93	69	.574	6	747	628	5678	1540	231	66	128	458	915	.271	.328	.403	.731	107	119	50	109	99	751	77	42	65	-2
SF	162	88	74	.543	11	725	641	5579	1442	206	35	197	441	889	.258	.318	.414	.732	118	111	49	99	98	712	55	49	53	-13
PHI	162	87	75	.537	12	642	578	5524	1390	228	54	126	403	955	.252	.308	.381	.689	106	28	36	99	99	640	56	39	59	-7
CIN	162	86	76	.531	13	648	594	5416	1333	225	44	122	474	960	.246	.312	.371	.683	100	25	6	103	101	630	92	58	61	-7
MIL	163	84	78	.519	15	677	603	5518	1345	204	39	139	525	954	.244	.314	.370	.684	105	30	37	99	102	643	75	52	59	-9
CHI	162	82	80	.506	17	570	578	5404	1286	205	44	127	439	1049	.238	.300	.363	.663	92	-21	-53	105	97	573	68	60	53	-16
PIT	162	74	88	.457	25	567	595	5536	1385	181	49	108	454	940	.250	.310	.359	.669	98	-2	-6	101	92	603	57	41	58	-8
HOU	162	66	96	.407	33	464	640	5384	1184	170	39	62	456	938	.220	.284	.301	.585	80	-159	-132	94	103	461	39	30	57	-6
NY	162	51	111	.315	48	501	774	5336	1168	156	35	96	457	1078	.219	.286	.315	.601	79	-129	-137	102	106	477	41	52	44	-19
TOT	811					6181		54803	13434	1984	439	1215	4560	9545	.245	.307	.364	.671							684	493	58	-91

TEAM	CG	SH	SV	IP	H	H/G	HR	BB	SO	RAT	ERA	ERA+	OAV	OOB	PR	/A	PF	CPI	FA	E	DP	FW	PW	BW	SBW	DIF
LA	51	24	29	1469²	1329	8.1	111	402	1095	10.8	2.85	106	.239	.294	71	27	92	103	.975	159	129	-.0	2.9	4.2	.4	10.4
STL	49	17	32	1463	1329	8.2	124	463	978	11.3	3.32	107	.241	.305	-5	37	108	97	.976	147	136	.6	4.0	5.4	.8	1.2
SF	46	9	30	1469	1380	8.5	126	464	954	11.5	3.35	96	.246	.307	-9	-24	97	99	.975	156	113	.1	-2.6	12.9	-.4	-3.0
PHI	45	12	31	1457¹	1262	7.8	113	553	1052	11.4	3.09	105	.235	.311	32	23	98	104	.978	142	147	.9	2.5	3.9	.2	-1.6
CIN	55	22	36	1439²	1307	8.2	117	425	1048	11.1	3.29	102	.242	.302	-1	8	102	96	.978	135	127	1.3	.9	.7	.2	1.9
MIL	56	18	25	1471²	1327	8.1	149	489	924	11.3	3.27	99	.241	.306	4	-8	98	103	.980	129	161	1.8	-.9	4.0	.0	-1.9
CHI	45	15	28	1467	1357	8.4	119	440	851	11.0	3.08	114	.249	.303	34	70	101	105	.976	155	172	.2	7.6	-5.8	-.8	-.3
PIT	34	16	33	1448	1350	8.4	99	457	900	11.5	3.10	107	.249	.313	31	33	100	107	.972	182	195	-1.4	3.6	-.7	.1	-8.6
HOU	36	16	20	1450¹	1341	8.3	95	378	937	10.9	3.44	92	.245	.298	-24	-46	96	87	.974	162	100	-.3	-5.0	-14.3	.3	4.2
NY	42	5	12	1427²	1452	9.2	162	529	806	12.8	4.12	85	.263	.332	-132	-101	106	100	.967	210	151	-3.1	-11.0	-14.9	-1.1	.0
TOT	459	154	276	14553¹		8.3				11.4	3.29		.245	.307					.975	1577	1431					

Runs		Hits		Doubles		Triples		Home Runs		Total Bases	
H.Aaron-Mil	121	Pinson-Cin	204	Groat-StL	43	Pinson-Cin	14	McCovey-SF	44	H.Aaron-Mil	370
Mays-SF	115	Groat-StL	201	Pinson-Cin	37	Gonzalez-Phi	12	H.Aaron-Mil	44	Mays-SF	347
Flood-StL	112	H.Aaron-Mil	201	Williams-Chi	36	Groat-StL	11	Mays-SF	38	Pinson-Cin	335
White-StL	106	White-StL	200	Gonzalez-Phi	36	Callison-Phi	11	Cepeda-SF	34	Cepeda-SF	326
McCovey-SF	103	Flood-StL	200	Callison-Phi	36	Brock-Chi	11	Howard-LA	28	White-StL	323

Runs Batted In		Runs Produced		Bases On Balls		Batting Average		On Base Percentage		Slugging Average	
H.Aaron-Mil	130	H.Aaron-Mil	207	Mathews-Mil	124	T.Davis-LA	.326	Mathews-Mil	.400	H.Aaron-Mil	.586
Boyer-StL	111	White-StL	188	Robinson-Cin	81	Clemente-Pit	.320	H.Aaron-Mil	.394	Mays-SF	.582
White-StL	109	Pinson-Cin	180	H.Aaron-Mil	78	Groat-StL	.319	Mays-SF	.384	McCovey-SF	.566
Pinson-Cin	106	Mays-SF	180	Boyer-StL	70	H.Aaron-Mil	.319	Robinson-Cin	.381	Cepeda-SF	.563
Mays-SF	103	Boyer-StL	173	Schofield-Pit	69	Cepeda-SF	.316	Groat-StL	.380	Pinson-Cin	.514

Production		Adjusted Production		Batter Runs		Adjusted Batter Runs		Clutch Hitting Index		Runs Created	
H.Aaron-Mil	.980	H.Aaron-Mil	180	H.Aaron-Mil	63.0	H.Aaron-Mil	64.5	Sievers-Phi	135	H.Aaron-Mil	149
Mays-SF	.966	Mays-SF	176	Mays-SF	55.8	Mays-SF	57.2	Fairly-LA	135	Mays-SF	131
Cepeda-SF	.930	Cepeda-SF	166	Cepeda-SF	45.4	Cepeda-SF	46.6	Robinson-Cin	126	White-StL	117
McCovey-SF	.916	McCovey-SF	161	McCovey-SF	41.1	McCovey-SF	42.2	Boyer-StL	120	Cepeda-SF	113
Pinson-Cin	.864	Mathews-Mil	147	Mathews-Mil	37.4	Mathews-Mil	38.6	Edwards-Cin	120	Pinson-Cin	113

Total Average		Stolen Bases		Stolen Base Average		Stolen Base Runs		Fielding Runs		Total Player Rating	
H.Aaron-Mil	1.063	Wills-LA	40	H.Aaron-Mil	86.1	H.Aaron-Mil	6.3	Mazeroski-Pit	56.7	Mays-SF	6.6
Mays-SF	.984	H.Aaron-Mil	31	Gilliam-LA	79.2	Pinson-Cin	3.3	Callison-Phi	22.7	H.Aaron-Mil	6.5
McCovey-SF	.911	Pinson-Cin	27	Pinson-Cin	77.1	Maye-Cin	3.0	Hubbs-Chi	20.1	Mazeroski-Pit	6.0
Cepeda-SF	.906	Robinson-Cin	26	Robinson-Cin	72.2	Harper-Cin	3.0	Flood-StL	19.5	Mathews-Mil	5.3
Mathews-Mil	.894	W.Davis-LA	25	Taylor-Phi	71.9	Gilliam-LA	2.7	Harkness-NY	16.4	Callison-Phi	4.8

Wins		Win Percentage		Games		Complete Games		Shutouts		Saves	
Marichal-SF	25	Perranoski-LA	.842	Perranoski-LA	69	Spahn-Mil	22	Koufax-LA	11	McDaniel-Chi	22
Koufax-LA	25	Koufax-LA	.833	Baldschun-Phi	65	Koufax-LA	20	Spahn-Mil	7	Perranoski-LA	21
Spahn-Mil	23	Spahn-Mil	.767	Bearnarth-NY	58	Ellsworth-Chi	19	Simmons-StL	6	Face-Pit	16
Maloney-Cin	23	Maloney-Cin	.767	Sisk-Pit	57	Marichal-SF	18	Maloney-Cin	6	Baldschun-Phi	16
Ellsworth-Chi	22	Marichal-SF	.758	McDaniel-Chi	57	Drysdale-LA	17			Henry-Cin	14

Innings Pitched		Fewest Hits/Game		Fewest BB/Game		Strikeouts		Strikeouts/Game		Ratio	
Marichal-SF	321.1	Koufax-LA	6.19	Friend-Pit	1.47	Koufax-LA	306	Maloney-Cin	9.53	Koufax-LA	7.96
Drysdale-LA	315.1	Culp-Phi	6.55	Farrell-Hou	1.56	Maloney-Cin	265	Koufax-LA	8.86	Farrell-Hou	8.81
Koufax-LA	311.0	Maloney-Cin	6.58	Nuxhall-Cin	1.62	Drysdale-LA	251	Culp-Phi	7.79	Marichal-SF	9.02
Ellsworth-Chi	290.2	Ellsworth-Chi	6.90	Drysdale-LA	1.63	Marichal-SF	248	Short-Phi	7.27	Ellsworth-Chi	9.29
Sanford-SF	284.1	Farrell-Hou	7.16	Koufax-LA	1.68	Gibson-StL	204	Lemaster-Mil	7.22	Friend-Pit	9.55

Earned Run Average		Adjusted ERA		Opponents' Batting Avg.		Opponents' On Base Pct.		Starter Runs		Adjusted Starter Runs	
Koufax-LA	1.88	Ellsworth-Chi	167	Koufax-LA	.189	Koufax-LA	.230	Koufax-LA	48.6	Ellsworth-Chi	45.3
Ellsworth-Chi	2.11	Koufax-LA	161	Maloney-Cin	.202	Marichal-SF	.256	Ellsworth-Chi	38.2	Koufax-LA	39.4
Friend-Pit	2.34	Simmons-StL	143	Culp-Phi	.206	Farrell-Hou	.256	Marichal-SF	31.4	Jackson-Chi	29.2
Marichal-SF	2.41	Friend-Pit	141	Ellsworth-Chi	.210	Ellsworth-Chi	.263	Friend-Pit	28.2	Friend-Pit	28.5
Simmons-StL	2.48	Jackson-Chi	137	Broglio-StL	.216	Friend-Pit	.269	Drysdale-LA	23.2	Marichal-SF	28.2

Clutch Pitching Index		Relief Runs		Adjusted Relief Runs		Relief Ranking		Total Pitcher Index		Total Baseball Ranking	
Schwall-Pit	118	Perranoski-LA	23.1	Veale-Pit	19.5	Perranoski-LA	32.7	Ellsworth-Chi	5.2	Mays-SF	6.6
Spahn-Mil	115	Veale-Pit	19.4	Perranoski-LA	19.3	Woodeshick-Hou	26.5	Jackson-Chi	4.1	H.Aaron-Mil	6.5
Short-Phi	111	Klippstein-Phi	16.9	Klippstein-Phi	16.2	Baldschun-Phi	20.6	Perranoski-LA	3.7	Mazeroski-Pit	6.0
Cardwell-Pit	110	Woodeshick-Hou	16.6	Woodeshick-Hou	14.9	Veale-Pit	17.5	Woodeshick-Hou	3.3	Mathews-Mil	5.3
Buhl-Chi	109	Baldschun-Phi	12.5	Baldschun-Phi	11.8	Klippstein-Phi	16.9	Spahn-Mil	3.2	Ellsworth-Chi	5.2

TEAM	G	W	L	PCT	GB	R	OR	AB	H	2B	3B	HR	BB	SO	AVG	OBP	SLG	PRO	PRO+	BR	/A	PF	CHI	RC	SB	CS	SBA	SBR
NY	161	104	57	.646		714	547	5506	1387	197	35	188	434	**808**	.252	.310	.403	.713	106	27	33	99	**105**	686	42	26	62	-3
CHI	162	94	68	.580	10.5	683	**544**	5508	1379	208	**40**	114	571	896	.250	.325	.365	.690	101	4	15	98	101	675	64	28	70	2
MIN	161	91	70	.565	13	**767**	602	5531	**1408**	223	35	**225**	547	912	**.255**	.326	**.430**	**.756**	115	**116**	**101**	102	98	**777**	32	14	70	1
BAL	162	86	76	.531	18.5	644	621	5448	1359	207	32	146	469	940	.249	.312	.380	.692	102	-7	17	96	100	645	**97**	34	**74**	**9**
DET	162	79	83	.488	25.5	700	703	5500	1388	195	36	148	**592**	908	.252	**.329**	.382	.711	102	43	19	103	98	699	73	32	70	3
CLE	162	79	83	.488	25.5	635	702	5496	1314	214	29	169	469	1102	.239	.304	.381	.685	98	-26	-20	99	100	634	59	36	62	-4
BOS	161	76	85	.472	28	666	704	5575	1403	**247**	34	171	475	954	.252	.313	.400	.713	102	31	9	103	96	684	27	16	63	-2
KC	162	73	89	.451	31.5	615	704	5495	1356	225	34	95	529	829	.247	.316	.353	.669	88	-41	-76	106	99	616	47	26	64	-2
LA	161	70	91	.435	34	597	660	5506	1378	208	38	95	448	916	.250	.312	.354	.666	98	-53	-18	94	99	608	43	30	59	-5
WAS	162	56	106	.346	48.5	578	812	5446	1237	190	35	138	497	963	.227	.295	.351	.646	86	-95	-93	100	104	569	68	28	71	4
TOT	808					6599		55011	13609	2114	352	1489	5031	9228	.247	.314	.380	.694							552	270	67	4

TEAM	CG	SH	SV	IP	H	H/G	HR	BB	SO	RAT	ERA	ERA+	OAV	OOB	PR	/A	PF	CPI	FA	E	DP	FW	PW	BW	SBW	DIF
NY	**59**	19	31	1449	**1239**	7.7	115	476	965	10.8	3.07	114	**.232**	.297	89	71	97	98	.982	110	162	1.4	7.5	3.5	-.4	11.5
CHI	49	**21**	39	1469	1311	8.0	100	**440**	932	10.9	**2.97**	118	.239	.299	**107**	**87**	97	102	.979	131	163	.3	**9.1**	1.6	.2	1.9
MIN	58	13	30	1446¹	1322	8.2	162	459	941	11.2	3.28	111	.242	.303	56	59	100	105	.976	144	140	-.5	6.2	**10.6**	.0	-5.8
BAL	35	8	**43**	1452	1353	8.4	137	507	913	11.7	3.45	101	.248	.316	29	3	96	104	**.984**	99	157	**2.1**	.3	1.8	**.9**	-.0
DET	42	7	28	1456¹	1407	8.7	195	477	930	11.9	3.90	96	.253	.317	-44	-25	103	102	.982	113	124	1.3	-2.6	2.0	.3	-2.9
CLE	40	14	25	1469	1390	8.5	176	478	**1018**	11.6	3.79	95	.249	.311	-27	-28	100	98	.977	143	129	-.4	-2.9	-2.1	-.5	3.9
BOS	29	7	32	1449²	1367	8.5	152	539	1009	12.0	3.97	95	.248	.318	-55	-30	104	93	.978	135	119	-.0	-3.2	.9	-.2	-2.0
KC	35	11	29	1458	1417	8.7	156	540	887	12.4	3.92	100	.256	.327	-47	-3	108	101	.980	127	131	.5	-.3	-8.0	-.2	.0
LA	30	13	31	1455¹	1317	8.1	120	578	889	12.0	3.52	97	.242	.320	17	-16	94	100	.974	163	155	-1.6	-1.7	-1.9	-.6	-4.8
WAS	29	8	25	1447	1486	9.2	176	537	744	12.8	4.42	84	.266	.334	-126	-114	102	98	.971	182	165	-2.6	-12.0	-9.8	.4	-1.0
TOT	406	121	313	14551²		8.4				11.7	3.63		.247	.314					.978	1347	1445					

Runs
Allison-Min ... 99
Pearson-LA ... 92
Yastrzemski-Bos ... 91
Tresh-NY ... 91
Colavito-Det ... 91

Hits
Yastrzemski-Bos ... 183
Ward-Chi ... 177
Pearson-LA ... 176
Kaline-Det ... 172
Fregosi-LA ... 170

Doubles
Yastrzemski-Bos ... 40
Ward-Chi ... 34
Torres-LA ... 32
Causey-KC ... 32
Alvis-Cle ... 32

Triples
Versalles-Min ... 13
Hinton-Was ... 12
Fregosi-LA ... 12
Cimoli-KC ... 11

Home Runs
Killebrew-Min ... 45
Stuart-Bos ... 42
Allison-Min ... 35
Hall-Min ... 33
Howard-NY ... 28

Total Bases
Stuart-Bos ... 319
Ward-Chi ... 289
Killebrew-Min ... 286
Kaline-Det ... 283
Allison-Min ... 281

Runs Batted In
Stuart-Bos ... 118
Kaline-Det ... 101
Killebrew-Min ... 96
Colavito-Det ... 91
Allison-Min ... 91

Runs Produced
Kaline-Det ... 163
Colavito-Det ... 160
Stuart-Bos ... 157
Allison-Min ... 155
Siebern-KC ... 147

Bases On Balls
Yastrzemski-Bos ... 95
Pearson-LA ... 92
Allison-Min ... 90
Cash-Det ... 89
Colavito-Det ... 84

Batting Average
Yastrzemski-Bos ...321
Kaline-Det ...312
Rollins-Min ...307
Pearson-LA ...304
Ward-Chi ...295

On Base Percentage
Yastrzemski-Bos ...419
Pearson-LA ...403
Cash-Det ...388
Allison-Min ...381
Kaline-Det ...378

Slugging Average
Killebrew-Min ...555
Allison-Min ...533
Howard-NY ...528
Stuart-Bos ...521
Hall-Min ...521

Production
Allison-Min ...914
Killebrew-Min ...908
Yastrzemski-Bos ...894
Kaline-Det ...891
Howard-NY ...871

Adjusted Production
Allison-Min ...150
Killebrew-Min ...147
Yastrzemski-Bos ...145
Kaline-Det ...142
Howard-NY ...141

Batter Runs
Yastrzemski-Bos ...42.0
Allison-Min ...38.6
Kaline-Det ...34.3
Killebrew-Min ...33.5
Cash-Det ...28.7

Adjusted Batter Runs
Yastrzemski-Bos ...38.4
Allison-Min ...36.6
Killebrew-Min ...31.6
Kaline-Det ...30.9
Pearson-LA ...29.8

Clutch Hitting Index
Hansen-Chi ...127
Torres-LA ...115
Siebern-KC ...114
L.Thomas-LA ...112
Phillips-Det ...112

Runs Created
Yastrzemski-Bos ... 118
Allison-Min ... 113
Kaline-Det ... 105
Ward-Chi ... 104
Pearson-LA ... 100

Total Average
Allison-Min ...967
Yastrzemski-Bos ...916
Killebrew-Min ...907
Tresh-NY ...879
Cash-Det ...876

Stolen Bases
Aparicio-Bal ...40
Hinton-Was ...25
Wood-Det ...18
Snyder-Bal ...18
Pearson-LA ...17

Stolen Base Average
Tartabull-KC ...94.1
Aparicio-Bal ...87.0
Wood-Det ...78.3
Snyder-Bal ...78.3
Hinton-Was ...73.5

Stolen Base Runs
Aparicio-Bal ...8.4
Tartabull-KC ...4.2
Weis-Chi ...3.9
Richardson-NY ...3.9
Smith-Bal ...2.7

Fielding Runs
Hansen-Chi ...27.0
Boyer-NY ...22.3
Moran-LA ...15.2
Lock-Was ...14.8
Geiger-Bos ...13.7

Total Player Rating
Yastrzemski-Bos ...4.4
Allison-Min ...4.2
Hansen-Chi ...3.6
Battey-Min ...3.1
Pearson-LA ...2.9

Wins
Ford-NY ...24
Pascual-Min ...21
Bouton-NY ...21
Monbouquette-Bos ...20
Barber-Bal ...20

Win Percentage
Ford-NY ...774
Bouton-NY ...750
Radatz-Bos ...714
Peters-Chi ...704
Pascual-Min ...700

Games
S.Miller-Bal ...71
Radatz-Bos ...66
Dailey-Min ...66
Lamabe-Bos ...65
Wyatt-KC ...63

Complete Games
Terry-NY ...18
Pascual-Min ...18
Stigman-Min ...15
Herbert-Chi ...14
Aguirre-Det ...14

Shutouts
Herbert-Chi ...7
Bouton-NY ...6

Saves
S.Miller-Bal ...27
Radatz-Bos ...25
Wyatt-KC ...21
Wilhelm-Chi ...21
Dailey-Min ...21

Innings Pitched
Ford-NY ...269.1
Terry-NY ...268.0
Monbouquette-Bos ...266.2
Barber-Bal ...258.2
Roberts-Bal ...251.1

Fewest Hits/Game
Downing-NY ...5.84
Bouton-NY ...6.89
Drabowsky-KC ...6.97
Morehead-Bos ...7.06
McBride-LA ...7.10

Fewest BB/Game
Donovan-Cle ...1.22
Terry-NY ...1.31
Herbert-Chi ...1.40
Monbouquette-Bos ...1.42
Roberts-Bal ...1.43

Strikeouts
Pascual-Min ...202
Bunning-Det ...196
Stigman-Min ...193
Peters-Chi ...189
Ford-NY ...189

Strikeouts/Game
Downing-NY ...8.76
Ramos-Cle ...8.24
Pascual-Min ...7.32
Stigman-Min ...7.21
Bunning-Det ...7.10

Ratio
Terry-NY ...9.71
Roberts-Bal ...9.78
Ramos-Cle ...9.80
Peters-Chi ...9.93
Downing-NY ...9.94

Earned Run Average
Peters-Chi ...2.33
Pizarro-Chi ...2.39
Pascual-Min ...2.46
Bouton-NY ...2.53
Downing-NY ...2.56

Adjusted ERA
Peters-Chi ...150
Pascual-Min ...148
Pizarro-Chi ...147
Bouton-NY ...139
Stange-Min ...139

Opponents' Batting Avg.
Downing-NY ...184
Morehead-Bos ...211
Bouton-NY ...212
Drabowsky-KC ...214
Peters-Chi ...216

Opponents' On Base Pct.
Roberts-Bal ...272
Terry-NY ...273
Ramos-Cle ...273
Downing-NY ...277
Peters-Chi ...278

Starter Runs
Peters-Chi ...35.0
Pascual-Min ...32.2
Bouton-NY ...30.6
Pizarro-Chi ...29.6
Ford-NY ...26.6

Adjusted Starter Runs
Pascual-Min ...32.6
Peters-Chi ...31.7
Bouton-NY ...27.3
Pizarro-Chi ...26.6
Ford-NY ...23.2

Clutch Pitching Index
Barber-Bal ...126
Osteen-Was ...120
Stange-Min ...120
Segui-KC ...115
Pascual-Min ...115

Relief Runs
Radatz-Bos ...24.4
Dailey-Min ...19.8
S.Miller-Bal ...17.3
Wilhelm-Chi ...15.0
Fowler-LA ...12.0

Adjusted Relief Runs
Radatz-Bos ...26.7
Dailey-Min ...20.0
S.Miller-Bal ...15.4
Wilhelm-Chi ...13.1
Lamabe-Bos ...10.7

Relief Ranking
Radatz-Bos ...49.4
S.Miller-Bal ...24.3
Dailey-Min ...23.6
Wilhelm-Chi ...15.8
Kline-Was ...14.1

Total Pitcher Index
Radatz-Bos ...5.0
Pascual-Min ...4.6
Peters-Chi ...4.5
S.Miller-Bal ...3.0
Dailey-Min ...3.0

Total Baseball Ranking
Radatz-Bos ...5.0
Pascual-Min ...4.6
Peters-Chi ...4.5
Yastrzemski-Bos ...4.4
Allison-Min ...4.2

TEAM	G	W	L	PCT	GB	R	OR	AB	H	2B	3B	HR	BB	SO	AVG	OBP	SLG	PRO	PRO+	BR	/A	PF	CHI	RC	SB	CS	SBA	SBR
STL	162	93	69	.574		715	652	5625	**1531**	240	53	109	427	925	**.272**	.326	.392	.718	100	62	0	109	99	711	73	51	59	-9
PHI	162	92	70	.568	1	693	632	5493	1415	241	51	130	440	924	.258	.317	.391	.708	107	41	50	99	100	672	30	35	46	-12
CIN	163	92	70	.568	1	660	**566**	5561	1383	220	38	130	457	974	.249	.310	.372	.682	96	-10	-33	104	102	642	90	36	71	5
SF	162	90	72	.556	3	656	587	5535	1360	185	38	**165**	**505**	900	.246	.313	.382	.695	100	16	2	102	97	657	64	35	65	-2
MIL	162	88	74	.543	5	**803**	744	5591	1522	**274**	32	159	486	**825**	**.272**	**.335**	**.418**	**.753**	118	**132**	**127**	101	101	**764**	53	41	56	-9
PIT	162	80	82	.494	13	663	636	5566	1469	225	**54**	121	408	970	.264	.317	.389	.706	105	35	36	100	97	668	39	33	54	-8
LA	164	80	82	.494	13	614	572	5499	1375	180	39	79	438	893	.250	.308	.340	.648	96	-70	-28	93	105	581	**141**	60	70	**6**
CHI	162	76	86	.469	17	649	724	5545	1391	239	50	145	499	1041	.251	.316	.390	.706	101	37	9	104	94	679	70	49	59	-8
HOU	162	66	96	.407	27	495	628	5303	1214	162	41	70	381	872	.229	.287	.315	.602	81	-158	-132	94	**106**	469	40	48	45	-17
NY	163	53	109	.327	40	569	776	5566	1372	195	31	103	353	932	.246	.297	.348	.645	90	-84	-71	98	102	552	36	31	54	-8
TOT	812					6517		55284	14032	2161	427	1211	4394	9256	.254	.313	.374	.687							636	419	60	-61

TEAM	CG	SH	SV	IP	H	H/G	HR	BB	SO	RAT	ERA	ERA+	OAV	OOB	PR	/A	PF	CPI	FA	E	DP	FW	PW	BW	SBW	DIF
STL	47	10	38	1445¹	1405	8.7	133	410	877	11.5	3.43	111	.255	.310	17	60	108	104	.973	172	147	-.7	6.3	.0	-.3	6.7
PHI	37	17	**41**	1461	1402	8.6	129	440	1009	11.7	3.36	103	.252	.313	28	17	98	**106**	.975	157	150	.0	1.8	5.3	-.6	4.5
CIN	54	14	35	1467	1306	8.0	112	436	**1122**	10.9	3.07	**118**	.238	.298	75	**88**	102	100	**.979**	**130**	137	**1.6**	**9.3**	-3.5	1.2	2.4
SF	48	17	30	1476¹	1348	8.2	118	480	1023	11.4	3.19	112	.241	.306	57	61	101	102	.975	159	136	-.0	6.4	.2	.4	1.9
MIL	45	14	39	1434²	1411	8.9	160	452	906	11.8	4.12	86	.257	.316	-92	-95	100	94	.977	143	139	.8	-10.0	13.4	-.3	3.1
PIT	42	14	29	1443²	1429	8.9	92	476	951	12.1	3.52	100	.260	.322	2	-2	99	103	.972	177	**179**	-1.0	-.2	3.8	-.2	-3.4
LA	47	**19**	27	1483²	**1289**	7.8	**88**	458	1062	10.8	**2.95**	113	**.232**	**.294**	96	47	92	95	.973	170	126	-.5	5.0	-3.0	**1.3**	-3.8
CHI	**58**	11	19	1445	1510	9.4	144	423	737	12.1	4.08	91	.270	.323	-87	-59	105	98	.975	162	147	-.2	-6.2	-1.1	.0	.7
HOU	30	9	31	1428	1421	9.0	105	**353**	852	11.4	3.41	100	.260	.309	20	1	97	102	.976	149	124	.5	.1	-13.9	-1.2	-.5
NY	40	10	15	1438²	1511	9.5	130	466	717	12.7	4.25	84	.272	.334	-115	-108	101	98	.974	167	154	-.4	-11.4	-7.5	-.2	-8.5
TOT	448	135	304	14523¹		8.7				11.6	3.54		.254	.313					.975	1586	1439					

Runs		Hits		Doubles		Triples		Home Runs		Total Bases	
Allen-Phi	125	Flood-StL	211	Maye-Mil	44	Santo-Chi	13	Mays-SF	47	Allen-Phi	352
Mays-SF	121	Clemente-Pit	211	Clemente-Pit	40	Allen-Phi	13	Williams-Chi	33	Mays-SF	351
Brock-Chi-StL	111	Williams-Chi	201	Williams-Chi	39	Brock-Chi-StL	11	Hart-SF	31	Williams-Chi	343
Robinson-Cin	103	Allen-Phi	201	Robinson-Cin	38	Pinson-Cin	11	Cepeda-SF	31	Santo-Chi	334
Aaron-Mil	103	Brock-Chi-StL	200	Allen-Phi	38			Callison-Phi	31	Callison-Phi	322

Runs Batted In		Runs Produced		Bases On Balls		Batting Average		On Base Percentage		Slugging Average	
Boyer-StL	119	Boyer-StL	195	Santo-Chi	86	Clemente-Pit	.339	Santo-Chi	.401	Mays-SF	.607
Santo-Chi	114	Allen-Phi	187	Mathews-Mil	85	Carty-Mil	.330	Robinson-Cin	.399	Santo-Chi	.564
Mays-SF	111	Mays-SF	185	Mays-SF	82	Aaron-Mil	.328	Aaron-Mil	.394	Allen-Phi	.557
Torre-Mil	109	Santo-Chi	178	Robinson-Cin	79	Torre-Mil	.321	Carty-Mil	.391	Carty-Mil	.554
Callison-Phi	104	Torre-Mil	176	Boyer-StL	70	Allen-Phi	.318	Clemente-Pit	.391	Robinson-Cin	.548

Production		Adjusted Production		Batter Runs		Adjusted Batter Runs		Clutch Hitting Index		Runs Created	
Mays-SF	.992	Mays-SF	171	Mays-SF	56.5	Mays-SF	53.9	Fairly-LA	142	Mays-SF	136
Santo-Chi	.966	Allen-Phi	163	Santo-Chi	55.1	Allen-Phi	52.1	Boyer-StL	117	Santo-Chi	135
Robinson-Cin	.947	Santo-Chi	162	Allen-Phi	50.5	Santo-Chi	49.9	T.Davis-LA	116	Allen-Phi	135
Carty-Mil	.945	Carty-Mil	162	Robinson-Cin	49.5	Robinson-Cin	45.3	Torre-Mil	113	Robinson-Cin	127
Allen-Phi	.940	Robinson-Cin	158	Williams-Chi	42.5	Aaron-Mil	40.2	Javier-StL	111	Williams-Chi	125

Total Average		Stolen Bases		Stolen Base Average		Stolen Base Runs		Fielding Runs		Total Player Rating	
Mays-SF	1.059	Wills-LA	53	Harper-Cin	88.9	Wills-LA	5.7	Mazeroski-Pit	33.9	Santo-Chi	6.5
Robinson-Cin	1.012	Brock-Chi-StL	43	Aaron-Mil	84.6	Harper-Cin	5.4	W.Davis-LA	24.9	Mays-SF	6.5
Santo-Chi	.998	W.Davis-LA	42	Robinson-Cin	82.1	W.Davis-LA	4.8	Edwards-Cin	22.6	Allen-Phi	5.8
Allen-Phi	.944	Harper-Cin	24	Mays-SF	79.2	Aaron-Mil	4.2	Callison-Phi	19.4	Aaron-Mil	5.1
Carty-Mil	.920	Robinson-Cin	23	W.Davis-LA	76.4	Robinson-Cin	3.9	Rodgers-Chi	19.4	Robinson-Cin	4.6

Wins		Win Percentage		Games		Complete Games		Shutouts		Saves	
Jackson-Chi	24	Koufax-LA	.792	B.Miller-LA	74	Marichal-SF	22	Koufax-LA	7	Woodeshick-Hou	23
Marichal-SF	21	Marichal-SF	.724	Perranoski-LA	72	Drysdale-LA	21	Law-Pit	5	McBean-Pit	22
Sadecki-StL	20	O'Toole-Cin	.708	Baldschun-Phi	71	Jackson-Chi	19	Fischer-Mil	5	Baldschun-Phi	21
		Bunning-Phi	.704	Taylor-StL	63	Gibson-StL	17	Drysdale-LA	5	McDaniel-Chi	15
		Jackson-Chi	.686	McDaniel-Chi	63	Ellsworth-Chi	16	Bunning-Phi	5		

Innings Pitched		Fewest Hits/Game		Fewest BB/Game		Strikeouts		Strikeouts/Game		Ratio	
Drysdale-LA	321.1	Koufax-LA	6.22	Bunning-Phi	1.46	Veale-Pit	250	Koufax-LA	9.00	Koufax-LA	8.35
Jackson-Chi	297.2	Drysdale-LA	6.78	Bruce-Hou	1.47	Gibson-StL	245	Maloney-Cin	8.92	Drysdale-LA	8.96
Gibson-StL	287.1	Short-Phi	7.10	Law-Pit	1.50	Drysdale-LA	237	Veale-Pit	8.05	Short-Phi	9.34
Bunning-Phi	284.1	Veale-Pit	7.14	Marichal-SF	1.74	Koufax-LA	223	Gibson-StL	7.67	Bunning-Phi	9.75
Veale-Pit	279.2	Maloney-Cin	7.29	Jackson-Chi	1.75	Bunning-Phi	219	Lemaster-Mil	7.53	Jackson-Chi	9.80

Earned Run Average		Adjusted ERA		Opponents' Batting Avg.		Opponents' On Base Pct.		Starter Runs		Adjusted Starter Runs	
Koufax-LA	1.74	Koufax-LA	187	Koufax-LA	.191	Koufax-LA	.241	Drysdale-LA	48.2	Drysdale-LA	37.6
Drysdale-LA	2.18	Short-Phi	157	Drysdale-LA	.207	Drysdale-LA	.256	Koufax-LA	44.6	Koufax-LA	37.2
Short-Phi	2.20	Drysdale-LA	148	Veale-Pit	.217	Short-Phi	.268	Short-Phi	32.7	Marichal-SF	32.5
Marichal-SF	2.48	Marichal-SF	144	Short-Phi	.217	Jackson-Chi	.273	Marichal-SF	31.7	Short-Phi	31.0
Bunning-Phi	2.63	O'Toole-Cin	136	Bolin-SF	.220	Marichal-SF	.273	Bunning-Phi	28.7	Bunning-Phi	26.6

Clutch Pitching Index		Relief Runs		Adjusted Relief Runs		Relief Ranking		Total Pitcher Index		Total Baseball Ranking	
Craig-StL	122	McBean-Pit	16.2	McBean-Pit	16.0	McBean-Pit	26.5	Drysdale-LA	4.7	Santo-Chi	6.5
D.Bennett-Phi	119	B.Miller-LA	14.1	Ellis-Cin	14.1	Ellis-Cin	17.1	Koufax-LA	3.5	Mays-SF	6.5
Farrell-Hou	115	Ellis-Cin	13.1	McCool-Cin	11.9	McCool-Cin	15.2	Short-Phi	3.5	Allen-Phi	5.8
Tsitouris-Cin	115	Roebuck-Phi	11.4	Roebuck-Phi	10.8	Roebuck-Phi	13.8	Marichal-SF	3.4	Aaron-Mil	5.1
Hendley-SF	110	McCool-Cin	11.1	B.Miller-LA	9.5	Woodeshick-Hou	11.0	McBean-Pit	3.3	Drysdale-LA	4.7

TEAM	G	W	L	PCT	GB	R	OR	AB	H	2B	3B	HR	BB	SO	AVG	OBP	SLG	PRO	PRO+	BR	/A	PF	CHI	RC	SB	CS	SBA	SBR
NY	164	99	63	.611		730	577	5705	**1442**	208	35	162	520	976	.253	.319	.387	.706	100	13	2	102	**105**	705	54	18	**75**	**5**
CHI	162	98	64	.605	1	642	**501**	5491	1356	184	40	106	**562**	902	.247	.323	.353	.676	98	-32	-15	97	101	643	75	39	66	-1
BAL	163	97	65	.599	2	679	567	5463	1357	229	20	162	537	1019	.248	.319	.387	.706	102	14	17	100	101	671	78	38	67	1
DET	163	85	77	.525	14	699	678	5513	1394	199	**57**	157	517	912	.253	.321	.395	.716	103	35	25	102	100	707	60	27	69	2
LA	162	82	80	.506	17	544	551	5362	1297	186	27	102	472	920	.242	.306	.344	.650	97	-89	-36	90	99	552	49	39	56	-9
MIN	163	79	83	.488	20	**737**	678	5610	1413	227	46	**221**	553	1019	.252	**.324**	**.427**	**.751**	**113**	98	93	101	95	**775**	46	22	68	1
CLE	164	79	83	.488	20	689	693	5603	1386	208	22	164	500	1063	.247	.315	.380	.695	100	-8	-3	99	104	666	79	51	61	-7
BOS	162	72	90	.444	27	688	793	5513	1425	**253**	29	186	504	917	**.258**	**.324**	.416	.740	106	76	40	105	94	725	18	16	53	-4
WAS	162	62	100	.383	37	578	733	5396	1246	199	28	125	514	1124	.231	.301	.348	.649	86	-95	-92	100	**105**	566	47	30	61	-4
KC	163	57	105	.352	42	621	836	5524	1321	216	29	166	548	1104	.239	.313	.379	.692	95	-14	-33	103	96	645	34	20	63	-2
TOT	814					6607		55180	13637	2109	333	1551	5227	9956	.247	.316	.382	.698							540	300	64	-18

TEAM	CG	SH	SV	IP	H	H/G	HR	BB	SO	RAT	ERA	ERA+	OAV	OOB	PR	/A	PF	CPI	FA	E	DP	FW	PW	BW	SBW	DIF
NY	46	18	**45**	1506²	1312	7.8	129	504	989	11.0	3.15	115	.234	.300	79	78	100	97	.983	109	158	1.1	8.2	.2	**.7**	7.8
CHI	44	20	**45**	1467²	**1216**	**7.5**	124	**401**	955	**10.1**	**2.72**	**127**	**.226**	**.283**	**147**	**119**	95	100	.981	122	164	.2	**12.5**	-1.6	.0	5.7
BAL	44	17	41	1458²	1292	8.0	129	456	939	11.0	3.16	113	.239	.302	76	67	99	100	**.985**	**95**	159	**1.9**	7.0	1.8	.3	5.0
DET	35	11	35	1453	1343	8.3	164	536	993	12.0	3.84	99	.244	.317	-35	-29	101	95	.982	111	137	1.0	-3.0	2.6	.4	3.1
LA	30	**28**	41	1450²	1273	7.9	**100**	530	965	11.5	2.91	114	.236	.310	115	60	91	**107**	.978	138	**168**	-.7	6.3	-3.8	-.8	-.0
MIN	**47**	4	29	1477²	1361	8.3	181	545	1099	11.8	3.58	100	.243	.314	8	1	99	102	.977	145	131	-1.1	.1	**9.8**	.3	-11.1
CLE	37	16	37	1487²	1443	8.7	154	565	**1162**	12.3	3.75	96	.255	.326	-21	-25	99	103	.981	118	149	.6	-2.6	-.3	-.5	.9
BOS	21	9	38	1422	1464	9.3	178	571	1094	13.1	4.50	86	.266	.339	-138	-102	106	97	.977	138	123	-.7	-10.7	4.2	-.2	-1.5
WAS	27	5	26	1435¹	1417	8.9	172	505	794	12.2	3.98	93	.259	.324	-57	-45	102	100	.979	127	145	-.0	-4.7	-9.7	-.2	-4.3
KC	18	6	27	1455²	1516	9.4	220	614	966	13.5	4.71	81	.269	.346	-175	-144	105	101	.975	158	152	-1.9	-15.1	-3.5	-.0	-3.5
TOT	349	134	364	14615		8.4				11.8	3.63		.247	.316					.980	1261	1486					

Runs		Hits		Doubles		Triples		Home Runs		Total Bases	
Oliva-Min	109	Oliva-Min	217	Oliva-Min	43	Versalles-Min	10	Killebrew-Min	49	Oliva-Min	374
Howser-Cle	101	B.Robinson-Bal	194	Bressoud-Bos	41	Rollins-Min	10	Powell-Bal	39	B.Robinson-Bal	319
Killebrew-Min	95	Richardson-NY	181	B.Robinson-Bal	35	Yastrzemski-Bos	9	Mantle-NY	35	Killebrew-Min	316
Wagner-Cle	94	Howard-NY	172	Versalles-Min	33	Oliva-Min	9	Colavito-KC	34	Colavito-KC	298
Versalles-Min	94	Versalles-Min	171			Fregosi-LA	9	Stuart-Bos	33	Stuart-Bos	296

Runs Batted In		Runs Produced		Bases On Balls		Batting Average		On Base Percentage		Slugging Average	
B.Robinson-Bal	118	B.Robinson-Bal	172	Siebern-Bal	106	Oliva-Min	.323	Mantle-NY	.426	Powell-Bal	.606
Stuart-Bos	114	Oliva-Min	171	Mantle-NY	99	B.Robinson-Bal	.317	Allison-Min	.406	Mantle-NY	.591
Mantle-NY	111	Mantle-NY	168	Killebrew-Min	93	Howard-NY	.313	Powell-Bal	.400	Oliva-Min	.557
Killebrew-Min	111	Wagner-Cle	163	Allison-Min	92	Mantle-NY	.303	Robinson-Chi	.388	Allison-Min	.553
Colavito-KC	102			Causey-KC	88	Robinson-Chi	.301	Kaline-Det	.385	Killebrew-Min	.548

Production		Adjusted Production		Batter Runs		Adjusted Batter Runs		Clutch Hitting Index		Runs Created	
Mantle-NY	1.017	Mantle-NY	177	Mantle-NY	53.0	Mantle-NY	51.2	Rodgers-LA	125	Oliva-Min	132
Powell-Bal	1.007	Powell-Bal	176	Allison-Min	45.0	Powell-Bal	44.5	Boyer-NY	118	Killebrew-Min	122
Allison-Min	.959	Allison-Min	163	Powell-Bal	44.1	Allison-Min	44.2	Pepitone-NY	118	Mantle-NY	121
Killebrew-Min	.927	Killebrew-Min	153	Killebrew-Min	43.1	Killebrew-Min	42.3	Mantle-NY	117	Allison-Min	119
Oliva-Min	.918	Oliva-Min	150	Oliva-Min	43.0	Oliva-Min	42.2	Cash-Det	116	B.Robinson-Bal	115

Total Average		Stolen Bases		Stolen Base Average		Stolen Base Runs		Fielding Runs		Total Player Rating	
Mantle-NY	1.122	Aparicio-Bal	57	Aparicio-Bal	77.0	Aparicio-Bal	6.9	Knoop-LA	37.2	Powell-Bal	4.4
Powell-Bal	1.081	Weis-Chi	22	Weis-Chi	75.9	Tresh-NY	3.9	Yastrzemski-Bos	27.7	Fregosi-LA	4.4
Allison-Min	1.058	Davalillo-Cle	21	Howser-Cle	74.1	Wagner-Cle	3.0	Boyer-NY	19.3	Hansen-Chi	4.3
Killebrew-Min	.956	Howser-Cle	20	Hinton-Was	73.9	Weis-Chi	2.4	Green-KC	16.5	Oliva-Min	4.1
Oliva-Min	.894	Hinton-Was	17	Davalillo-Cle	65.6	Allison-Min	2.4	Brandt-Bal	16.1	Yastrzemski-Bos	3.9

Wins		Win Percentage		Games		Complete Games		Shutouts		Saves	
Peters-Chi	20	Bunker-Bal	.792	Wyatt-KC	81	Chance-LA	15	Chance-LA	11	Radatz-Bos	29
Chance-LA	20	Ford-NY	.739	Radatz-Bos	79	Pascual-Min	14	Ford-NY	8	Wilhelm-Chi	27
Wickersham-Det	19	Peters-Chi	.714	Wilhelm-Chi	73	Pappas-Bal	13	Pappas-Bal	7	Miller-Bal	23
Pizarro-Chi	19	Pappas-Bal	.696	McMahon-Cle	70	Osteen-Was	13	Lolich-Det	6	Wyatt-KC	20
Bunker-Bal	19	Chance-LA	.690	Miller-Bal	66	Kaat-Min	13	Monbouquette-Bos	5	B.Lee-LA	19

Innings Pitched		Fewest Hits/Game		Fewest BB/Game		Strikeouts		Strikeouts/Game		Ratio	
Chance-LA	278.1	Horlen-Chi	6.07	Monbouquette-Bos	1.54	Downing-NY	217	McDowell-Cle	9.19	Horlen-Chi	8.59
Peters-Chi	273.2	Chance-LA	6.27	Pappas-Bal	1.72	Pascual-Min	213	Downing-NY	8.00	Chance-LA	9.12
Bouton-NY	271.1	Bunker-Bal	6.77	Newman-LA	1.85	Chance-LA	207	Pena-KC	7.55	Pizarro-Chi	9.45
Pascual-Min	267.1	Peters-Chi	7.14	Bouton-NY	1.99	Peters-Chi	205	Stigman-Min	7.53	Bunker-Bal	9.50
Osteen-Was	257.0	Pizarro-Chi	7.27	Pizarro-Chi	2.07	Lolich-Det	192	Morehead-Bos	7.51	Bouton-NY	9.72

Earned Run Average		Adjusted ERA		Opponents' Batting Avg.		Opponents' On Base Pct.		Starter Runs		Adjusted Starter Runs	
Chance-LA	1.65	Chance-LA	199	Horlen-Chi	.190	Horlen-Chi	.250	Chance-LA	61.1	Chance-LA	50.6
Horlen-Chi	1.88	Horlen-Chi	184	Chance-LA	.195	Chance-LA	.261	Horlen-Chi	40.9	Ford-NY	40.5
Ford-NY	2.13	Ford-NY	170	Bunker-Bal	.207	Pizarro-Chi	.267	Ford-NY	40.6	Horlen-Chi	36.9
Peters-Chi	2.50	Peters-Chi	138	Peters-Chi	.219	Bunker-Bal	.269	Peters-Chi	34.2	Peters-Chi	29.1
Pizarro-Chi	2.56	Pizarro-Chi	135	Pizarro-Chi	.219	Bouton-NY	.273	Pizarro-Chi	28.3	Pizarro-Chi	23.7

Clutch Pitching Index		Relief Runs		Adjusted Relief Runs		Relief Ranking		Total Pitcher Index		Total Baseball Ranking	
McDowell-Cle	123	B.Lee-LA	32.2	Radatz-Bos	27.3	Radatz-Bos	50.4	Radatz-Bos	5.3	Radatz-Bos	5.3
Roberts-Bal	121	Wilhelm-Chi	23.9	B.Lee-LA	27.0	Wilhelm-Chi	40.7	Chance-LA	4.7	Chance-LA	4.7
Kralick-Cle	118	Radatz-Bos	23.2	Wilhelm-Chi	21.4	Worthington-Min	32.0	Wilhelm-Chi	4.3	Powell-Bal	4.4
Grant-Cle-Min	112	Worthington-Min	18.1	Stock-Bal-KC	18.6	Kline-Was	28.2	Horlen-Chi	4.2	Fregosi-LA	4.4
Peters-Chi	111	Hall-Bal	17.3	Worthington-Min	17.8	B.Lee-LA	27.9	Ford-NY	4.2	Wilhelm-Chi	4.3

TEAM	G	W	L	PCT	GB	R	OR	AB	H	2B	3B	HR	BB	SO	AVG	OBP	SLG	PRO	PRO+	BR	/A	PF	CHI	RC	SB	CS	SBA	SBR
LA	162	97	65	.599		608	521	5425	1329	193	32	78	492	891	.245	.314	.335	.649	96	-61	-22	93	103	593	172	77	69	5
SF	163	95	67	.586	2	682	593	5495	1384	169	43	159	476	844	.252	.315	.385	.700	101	24	6	103	101	649	47	27	64	-2
PIT	163	90	72	.556	7	675	580	5686	1506	217	57	111	419	1008	.265	.319	.385	.701	103	27	24	101	97	671	51	38	57	-8
CIN	162	89	73	.549	8	825	704	5658	1544	268	61	183	538	1003	.273	.341	.439	.780	118	188	129	107	95	842	82	40	67	1
MIL	162	86	76	.531	11	708	633	5542	1419	243	28	196	408	976	.256	.311	.416	.727	110	67	63	101	99	699	64	37	63	-3
PHI	162	85	76	.528	11.5	654	667	5528	1380	205	53	144	494	1091	.250	.315	.384	.699	105	24	36	98	96	665	46	32	59	-5
STL	162	80	81	.497	16.5	707	674	5579	1415	234	46	109	477	882	.254	.316	.371	.687	91	3	-59	109	107	659	100	52	66	-1
CHI	164	72	90	.444	25	635	723	5540	1316	202	33	134	532	948	.238	.309	.358	.667	92	-34	-49	102	101	613	65	47	58	-9
HOU	162	65	97	.401	32	569	711	5483	1299	188	42	97	502	877	.237	.306	.340	.646	96	-73	-33	93	98	574	90	37	71	5
NY	164	50	112	.309	47	495	752	5441	1202	203	27	107	392	1129	.221	.278	.327	.605	79	-164	-147	96	105	480	28	42	40	-17
TOT	813					6558		55377	13794	2122	422	1318	4730	9649	.249	.313	.374	.687							745	429	63	-34

TEAM	CG	SH	SV	IP	H	H/G	HR	BB	SO	RAT	ERA	ERA+	OAV	OOB	PR	/A	PF	CPI	FA	E	DP	FW	PW	BW	SBW	DIF
LA	58	23	34	1476	1223	7.5	127	425	1079	10.3	2.81	116	.224	.284	119	74	92	99	.979	134	135	.8	7.8	-2.3	.9	8.8
SF	42	17	42	1465¹	1325	8.1	137	408	1060	10.9	3.20	112	.238	.295	55	65	102	98	.976	148	124	.0	6.9	.6	.1	6.3
PIT	49	17	27	1479	1324	8.1	89	469	882	11.2	3.01	117	.241	.306	87	82	99	103	.977	152	189	-.1	8.7	2.5	-.5	-1.6
CIN	43	9	34	1457¹	1355	8.4	136	587	1113	12.3	3.88	96	.247	.325	-56	-22	106	96	.981	117	142	1.8	-2.3	13.6	.5	-5.6
MIL	43	4	38	1447²	1336	8.3	123	541	966	11.8	3.52	100	.246	.318	3	1	100	101	.978	140	145	.5	.1	6.7	.0	-2.3
PHI	50	18	21	1468²	1426	8.7	116	466	1071	12.0	3.53	98	.256	.320	2	-12	98	104	.975	157	153	-.5	-1.3	3.8	-.2	2.6
STL	40	11	35	1461¹	1414	8.7	166	467	916	11.8	3.77	102	.255	.317	-37	12	109	102	.979	130	152	1.1	1.3	-6.2	.3	3.2
CHI	33	9	35	1472	1470	9.0	154	481	855	12.1	3.78	98	.260	.321	-39	-15	104	104	.974	171	166	-1.2	-1.6	-5.2	-.6	-.5
HOU	29	7	26	1461	1459	9.0	123	388	931	11.6	3.84	87	.260	.312	-49	-79	95	94	.974	166	130	-1.0	-8.3	-3.5	.9	-4.1
NY	29	11	14	1454²	1462	9.0	147	498	776	12.4	4.06	87	.262	.328	-84	-86	100	99	.974	171	153	-1.2	-9.1	-15.5	-1.4	-3.8
TOT	416	126	306	14643		8.5				11.6	3.54		.249	.313					.977	1486	1489					

Runs		Hits		Doubles		Triples		Home Runs		Total Bases	
Harper-Cin	126	Rose-Cin	209	H.Aaron-Mil	40	Callison-Phi	16	Mays-SF	52	Mays-SF	360
Mays-SF	118	Pinson-Cin	204	Williams-Chi	39	Clendenon-Pit	14	McCovey-SF	39	Williams-Chi	356
Rose-Cin	117	Williams-Chi	203	Rose-Cin	35	Clemente-Pit	14	Williams-Chi	34	Pinson-Cin	324
Williams-Chi	115	Clemente-Pit	194	Brock-StL	35	Allen-Phi	14	Santo-Chi	33	H.Aaron-Mil	319
		Flood-StL	191	Pinson-Cin	34	Morgan-Hou	12	Robinson-Cin	33	Johnson-Cin	317

Runs Batted In		Runs Produced		Bases On Balls		Batting Average		On Base Percentage		Slugging Average	
Johnson-Cin	130	Johnson-Cin	190	Morgan-Hou	97	Clemente-Pit	.329	Mays-SF	.399	Mays-SF	.645
Robinson-Cin	113	Williams-Chi	189	Santo-Chi	88	H.Aaron-Mil	.318	Robinson-Cin	.388	H.Aaron-Mil	.560
Mays-SF	112	Robinson-Cin	189	McCovey-SF	88	Mays-SF	.317	H.Aaron-Mil	.384	Williams-Chi	.552
Williams-Chi	108	Rose-Cin	187	Wynn-Hou	84	Williams-Chi	.315	McCovey-SF	.383	Robinson-Cin	.540
Stargell-Pit	107	Mays-SF	178	Harper-Cin	78	Rose-Cin	.312	Rose-Cin	.383	McCovey-SF	.539

Production		Adjusted Production		Batter Runs		Adjusted Batter Runs		Clutch Hitting Index		Runs Created	
Mays-SF	1.044	Mays-SF	184	Mays-SF	64.7	Mays-SF	61.2	Stargell-Pit	120	Mays-SF	143
H.Aaron-Mil	.943	H.Aaron-Mil	161	Williams-Chi	49.3	Williams-Chi	46.4	Johnson-Cin	118	Williams-Chi	132
Williams-Chi	.932	Williams-Chi	155	H.Aaron-Mil	45.9	H.Aaron-Mil	45.4	Boyer-StL	118	H.Aaron-Mil	122
Robinson-Cin	.928	McCovey-SF	152	Robinson-Cin	45.9	McCovey-SF	38.9	Stuart-Phi	118	Santo-Chi	121
McCovey-SF	.922	Robinson-Cin	148	McCovey-SF	41.8	Allen-Phi	38.4	Flood-StL	118	Robinson-Cin	120

Total Average		Stolen Bases		Stolen Base Average		Stolen Base Runs		Fielding Runs		Total Player Rating	
Mays-SF	1.114	Wills-LA	94	Wynn-Hou	91.5	Wynn-Hou	10.5	Alley-Pit	29.5	Mays-SF	7.3
H.Aaron-Mil	.980	Brock-StL	63	H.Aaron-Mil	85.7	Wills-LA	9.6	Mazeroski-Pit	25.6	Wynn-Hou	6.1
McCovey-SF	.945	Wynn-Hou	43	Harper-Cin	85.4	Harper-Cin	6.9	Wine-Phi	21.7	H.Aaron-Mil	5.5
Robinson-Cin	.938	Harper-Cin	35	Wills-LA	75.2	H.Aaron-Mil	4.8	Wills-LA	21.2	Santo-Chi	5.4
Williams-Chi	.935	W.Davis-LA	25	W.Davis-LA	73.5	Allen-Phi	3.3	Wynn-Hou	20.1	Williams-Chi	4.3

Wins		Win Percentage		Games		Complete Games		Shutouts		Saves	
Koufax-LA	26	Koufax-LA	.765	Abernathy-Chi	84	Koufax-LA	27	Marichal-SF	10	Abernathy-Chi	31
Cloninger-Mil	24	Maloney-Cin	.690	Woodeshick-Hou-StL	78	Marichal-SF	24	Koufax-LA	8	McCool-Cin	21
Drysdale-LA	23	Ellis-Cin	.688	McDaniel-Chi	71	Gibson-StL	20	Veale-Pit	7	Linzy-SF	21
Marichal-SF	22	Cloninger-Mil	.686	Baldschun-Phi	65	Drysdale-LA	20	Drysdale-LA	7		
Ellis-Cin	22	Bunning-Phi	.679			Cloninger-Mil	16	Bunning-Phi	7		

Innings Pitched		Fewest Hits/Game		Fewest BB/Game		Strikeouts		Strikeouts/Game		Ratio	
Koufax-LA	335.2	Koufax-LA	5.79	Marichal-SF	1.40	Koufax-LA	382	Koufax-LA	10.24	Koufax-LA	7.83
Drysdale-LA	308.1	Maloney-Cin	6.66	Law-Pit	1.45	Veale-Pit	276	Veale-Pit	9.34	Marichal-SF	8.35
Gibson-StL	299.0	Marichal-SF	6.83	Bruce-Hou	1.49	Gibson-StL	270	Maloney-Cin	8.60	Law-Pit	9.11
Short-Phi	297.1	Bolin-SF	6.90	Farrell-Hou	1.51	Bunning-Phi	268	Bunning-Phi	8.29	Bunning-Phi	10.11
Marichal-SF	295.1	Gibson-StL	7.31	Johnson-Hou-Mil	1.87	Maloney-Cin	244	Gibson-StL	8.13	Drysdale-LA	10.16

Earned Run Average		Adjusted ERA		Opponents' Batting Avg.		Opponents' On Base Pct.		Starter Runs		Adjusted Starter Runs	
Koufax-LA	2.04	Marichal-SF	169	Koufax-LA	.179	Koufax-LA	.228	Marichal-SF	56.0	Marichal-SF	48.1
Marichal-SF	2.13	Law-Pit	163	Marichal-SF	.205	Marichal-SF	.240	Maloney-Cin	46.1	Koufax-LA	45.7
Law-Pit	2.15	Koufax-LA	160	Maloney-Cin	.206	Law-Pit	.264	Law-Pit	33.5	Maloney-Cin	34.3
Maloney-Cin	2.54	Maloney-Cin	148	Bolin-SF	.214	Drysdale-LA	.280	Bunning-Phi	30.4	Law-Pit	32.8
Bunning-Phi	2.60	Shaw-SF	136	Gibson-StL	.222	Shaw-SF	.280	Maloney-Cin	28.4	Bunning-Phi	27.8

Clutch Pitching Index		Relief Runs		Adjusted Relief Runs		Relief Ranking		Total Pitcher Index		Total Baseball Ranking	
Law-Pit	115	Linzy-SF	19.1	Linzy-SF	19.7	Linzy-SF	37.4	Marichal-SF	6.0	Mays-SF	7.3
Koonce-Chi	112	O'Dell-Mil	16.8	Abernathy-Chi	16.8	O'Dell-Mil	27.4	Koufax-LA	5.0	Wynn-Hou	6.1
Culp-Phi	108	McBean-Pit	15.8	O'Dell-Mil	16.6	Woodeshick-Hou-StL	23.5	Linzy-SF	4.9	Marichal-SF	6.0
Spahn-NY-SF	107	Perranoski-LA	15.2	McDaniel-Chi	15.7	McBean-Pit	20.2	Law-Pit	4.6	H.Aaron-Mil	5.5
Buhl-Chi	107	Abernathy-Chi	14.6	McBean-Pit	15.5	Abernathy-Chi	19.7	Maloney-Cin	4.6	Santo-Chi	5.4

TEAM	G	W	L	PCT	GB	R	OR	AB	H	2B	3B	HR	BB	SO	AVG	OBP	SLG	PRO	PRO+	BR	/A	PF	CHI	RC	SB	CS	SBA	SBR
MIN	162	102	60	.630		**774**	600	5488	**1396**	257	42	150	554	969	**.254**	.327	.399	.726	107	84	**52**	104	**106**	**730**	92	33	**74**	8
CHI	162	95	67	.586	7	647	**555**	5509	1354	200	38	125	533	916	.246	.317	.364	.681	106	1	41	94	99	636	50	33	60	-5
BAL	162	94	68	.580	8	641	578	5450	1299	227	38	125	529	907	.238	.309	.363	.672	95	-21	-33	102	103	607	67	31	68	2
DET	162	89	73	.549	13	680	602	5368	1278	190	27	162	512	952	.238	.314	.374	.688	101	10	3	101	**106**	628	57	41	58	-8
CLE	162	87	75	.537	15	663	613	5469	1367	198	21	156	506	**857**	.250	.317	.379	.696	103	26	21	i01	99	667	109	46	70	5
NY	162	77	85	.475	25	611	604	5470	1286	196	31	149	489	951	.235	.300	.364	.664	95	-42	-38	99	103	593	35	20	64	-2
CAL	162	75	87	.463	27	527	569	5354	1279	200	36	92	443	973	.239	.300	.341	.641	90	-81	-69	98	97	549	107	59	64	-3
WAS	162	70	92	.432	32	591	721	5374	1227	179	33	136	570	1125	.228	.306	.350	.656	94	-47	-38	99	101	586	30	19	61	-2
BOS	162	62	100	.383	40	669	791	5487	1378	244	40	**165**	**607**	964	.251	**.329**	**.400**	**.729**	107	**95**	51	106	90	715	47	24	66	0
KC	162	59	103	.364	43	585	755	5393	1294	186	**59**	110	521	1020	.240	.311	.358	.669	97	-25	-16	99	96	604	**110**	51	68	2
TOT	810					6388		54362	13158	2077	365	1370	5306	9634	.242	.313	.369	.682							704	357	66	-3

TEAM	CG	SH	SV	IP	H	H/G	HR	BB	SO	RAT	ERA	ERA+	OAV	OOB	PR	/A	PF	CPI	FA	E	DP	FW	PW	BW	SBW	DIF
MIN	32	12	45	1457[1]	1278	7.9	166	503	934	11.2	3.14	113	.235	.303	52	68	103	**107**	.973	172	158	-2.3	7.3	**5.5**	**.9**	9.6
CHI	21	14	**53**	1481[2]	1261	**7.7**	122	**460**	946	**10.6**	2.99	107	**.231**	**.294**	76	33	92	98	.980	127	156	.6	3.5	4.4	-.5	6.0
BAL	32	**15**	41	1477[2]	1268	**7.7**	120	510	939	11.0	**2.98**	**116**	.233	.302	**78**	**80**	100	104	.980	126	152	.6	**8.5**	-3.5	.2	7.1
DET	**45**	14	31	1455	1283	7.9	137	509	1069	11.4	3.35	104	.237	.308	17	20	101	99	.981	116	126	1.3	2.1	.3	-.8	5.1
CLE	41	13	41	1458[1]	**1254**	**7.7**	129	500	**1156**	11.0	3.30	106	.232	.300	26	30	101	94	**.981**	**114**	127	**1.4**	3.2	2.2	.6	-1.4
NY	41	11	31	1459[2]	1337	8.2	126	511	1001	11.6	3.28	104	.245	.313	29	20	98	104	.978	137	**166**	-.0	2.1	-4.1	-.2	-1.8
CAL	39	14	33	1441[2]	1259	7.9	**91**	563	847	11.5	3.17	107	.237	.313	46	37	98	100	**.981**	123	149	.8	3.9	-7.4	-.3	-3.1
WAS	21	8	40	1435[2]	1376	8.6	160	633	867	12.8	3.93	88	.254	.336	-75	-73	101	105	.977	143	148	-.4	-7.8	-4.1	-.2	1.5
BOS	33	9	25	1439[1]	1443	9.0	158	543	993	12.6	4.24	88	.260	.329	-125	-82	108	95	.974	162	129	-1.6	-8.7	5.4	.0	-14.1
KC	18	7	32	1433	1399	8.8	161	574	882	12.6	4.24	82	.256	.331	-124	-119	101	96	.977	139	142	-.2	-12.7	-1.7	.2	-7.6
TOT	323	117	372	14539[1]		8.1				11.6	3.46		.242	.313					.978	1359	1453					

Runs		Hits		Doubles		Triples		Home Runs		Total Bases	
Versalles-Min	126	Oliva-Min	185	Yastrzemski-Bos	45	Versalles-Min	12	Conigliaro-Bos	32	Versalles-Min	308
Oliva-Min	107	Versalles-Min	182	Versalles-Min	45	Campaneris-KC	12	Cash-Det	30	Tresh-NY	287
Tresh-NY	94	Colavito-Cle	170	Oliva-Min	40	Aparicio-Bal	10	Horton-Det	29	Oliva-Min	283
Buford-Chi	93	Tresh-NY	168	Tresh-NY	29	W.Smith-Cal	9	Wagner-Cle	28	Colavito-Cle	277
Colavito-Cle	92	Fregosi-Cal	167	Richardson-NY	28					Conigliaro-Bos	267

Runs Batted In		Runs Produced		Bases On Balls		Batting Average		On Base Percentage		Slugging Average	
Colavito-Cle	108	Oliva-Min	189	Colavito-Cle	93	Oliva-Min	.321	Yastrzemski-Bos	.398	Yastrzemski-Bos	.536
Horton-Det	104	Versalles-Min	184	Blefary-Bal	88	Yastrzemski-Bos	.312	Colavito-Cle	.387	Conigliaro-Bos	.512
Oliva-Min	98	Colavito-Cle	174	Mantilla-Bos	79	Davalillo-Cle	.301	Oliva-Min	.384	Cash-Det	.512
Mantilla-Bos	92	Hall-Min	147	Cash-Det	77	Robinson-Bal	.297	Blefary-Bal	.382	Wagner-Cle	.495
Whitfield-Cle	90	Horton-Det	144	Robinson-Chi	76	Wagner-Cle	.294	Mantilla-Bos	.377	Oliva-Min	.491

Production		Adjusted Production		Batter Runs		Adjusted Batter Runs		Clutch Hitting Index		Runs Created	
Yastrzemski-Bos	.935	Yastrzemski-Bos	154	Yastrzemski-Bos	41.6	Yastrzemski-Bos	35.6	Mantilla-Bos	126	Colavito-Cle	110
Cash-Det	.886	Cash-Det	147	Oliva-Min	35.3	Colavito-Cle	33.7	Horton-Det	120	Oliva-Min	109
Oliva-Min	.876	Wagner-Cle	143	Colavito-Cle	34.6	Oliva-Min	30.8	Powell-Bal	116	Yastrzemski-Bos	102
Wagner-Cle	.866	Oliva-Min	141	Cash-Det	31.0	Cash-Det	30.1	Allison-Min	116	Versalles-Min	102
Colavito-Cle	.855	Colavito-Cle	140	Wagner-Cle	29.6	Wagner-Cle	28.8	Adair-Bal	115	Tresh-NY	101

Total Average		Stolen Bases		Stolen Base Average		Stolen Base Runs		Fielding Runs		Total Player Rating	
Yastrzemski-Bos	.931	Campaneris-KC	51	Hinton-Cle	85.0	Versalles-Min	5.1	Boyer-NY	25.9	Yastrzemski-Bos	3.6
Cash-Det	.894	Cardenal-Cal	37	Versalles-Min	84.4	Campaneris-KC	3.9	Hansen-Chi	16.7	Weis-Chi	3.4
Wagner-Cle	.882	Versalles-Min	27	Howser-Cle	81.0	Davalillo-Cle	3.6	Davalillo-Cle	14.7	Buford-Chi	3.3
Blefary-Bal	.876	Davalillo-Cle	26	Davalillo-Cle	78.8	Aparicio-Bal	3.6	Conigliaro-Bos	13.5	Oliva-Min	3.3
Oliva-Min	.863	Aparicio-Bal	26	Aparicio-Bal	78.8	Hinton-Cle	3.3	Knoop-Cal	12.8	Colavito-Cle	3.1

Wins		Win Percentage		Games		Complete Games		Shutouts		Saves	
Grant-Min	21	Grant-Min	.750	Fisher-Chi	82	Stottlemyre-NY	18	Grant-Min	6	Kline-Was	29
Stottlemyre-NY	20	McLain-Det	.727	Kline-Was	74	McDowell-Cle	14	Stottlemyre-NY	4	S.Miller-Bal	24
Kaat-Min	18	Stottlemyre-NY	.690	B.Lee-Cal	69	Grant-Min	14	McLain-Det	4	Fisher-Chi	24
McDowell-Cle	17	Fisher-Chi	.682	Dickson-KC	68	McLain-Det	13	Horlen-Chi	4	B.Lee-Cal	23
		Siebert-Cle	.667	S.Miller-Bal	67			Chance-Cal	4	Radatz-Bos	22

Innings Pitched		Fewest Hits/Game		Fewest BB/Game		Strikeouts		Strikeouts/Game		Ratio	
Stottlemyre-NY	291.0	McDowell-Cle	5.87	Terry-Cle	1.25	McDowell-Cle	325	McDowell-Cle	10.71	Fisher-Chi	8.87
McDowell-Cle	273.0	Fisher-Chi	6.42	Monbouquette-Bos	1.57	Lolich-Det	226	Siebert-Cle	9.11	Siebert-Cle	9.06
Grant-Min	270.1	Siebert-Cle	6.63	Horlen-Chi	1.60	McLain-Det	192	Lolich-Det	8.35	Terry-Cle	9.67
Kaat-Min	264.1	Richert-Was	6.77	Ford-NY	1.84	Siebert-Cle	191	McLain-Det	7.84	McLain-Det	9.72
Newman-Cal	260.2	Brunet-Cal	6.81	Grant-Min	2.03	Downing-NY	179	Morehead-Bos	7.61	Newman-Cal	10.01

Earned Run Average		Adjusted ERA		Opponents' Batting Avg.		Opponents' On Base Pct.		Starter Runs		Adjusted Starter Runs	
McDowell-Cle	2.18	McDowell-Cle	160	McDowell-Cle	.185	Siebert-Cle	.262	McDowell-Cle	38.9	McDowell-Cle	39.5
Fisher-Chi	2.40	Siebert-Cle	143	Fisher-Chi	.205	Fisher-Chi	.262	Stottlemyre-NY	26.8	Stottlemyre-NY	25.0
Siebert-Cle	2.43	Perry-Min	135	Siebert-Cle	.206	Terry-Cle	.269	Siebert-Cle	21.5	Siebert-Cle	21.9
Brunet-Cal	2.56	Richert-Was	134	Brunet-Cal	.209	McLain-Det	.273	Pappas-Bal	21.1	Kaat-Min	21.4
Richert-Was	2.60	Pappas-Bal	133	Richert-Was	.210	Pappas-Bal	.281	McLain-Det	20.7	Pappas-Bal	21.3

Clutch Pitching Index		Relief Runs		Adjusted Relief Runs		Relief Ranking		Total Pitcher Index		Total Baseball Ranking	
Kaat-Min	123	Wilhelm-Chi	26.3	Wilhelm-Chi	22.1	S.Miller-Bal	42.7	S.Miller-Bal	4.8	S.Miller-Bal	4.8
Perry-Min	117	B.Lee-Cal	22.5	B.Lee-Cal	21.6	B.Lee-Cal	32.2	McDowell-Cle	4.1	McDowell-Cle	4.1
Peters-Chi	113	S.Miller-Bal	20.9	S.Miller-Bal	21.0	Worthington-Min	31.7	Worthington-Min	3.7	Worthington-Min	3.7
Richert-Was	110	Fisher-Chi	19.5	Fisher-Chi	14.6	Wilhelm-Chi	26.2	B.Lee-Cal	3.5	Yastrzemski-Bos	3.6
Pappas-Bal	110	Hamilton-NY	13.4	Hamilton-NY	13.1	Fisher-Chi	22.3	Kaat-Min	3.5	B.Lee-Cal	3.5

TEAM	G	W	L	PCT	GB	R	OR	AB	H	2B	3B	HR	BB	SO	AVG	OBP	SLG	PRO	PRO+	BR	/A	PF	CHI	RC	SB	CS	SBA	SBR
LA	162	95	67	.586		606	490	5471	1399	201	27	108	430	830	.256	.316	.362	.678	103	-37	12	92	98	615	94	64	59	-10
SF	161	93	68	.578	1.5	675	626	5539	1373	195	31	181	414	860	.248	.304	.392	.696	96	-14	-33	103	105	633	29	30	49	-9
PIT	162	92	70	.568	3	759	641	5676	1586	238	66	158	405	1011	.279	.331	.428	.759	116	117	116	100	96	779	64	60	52	-17
PHI	162	87	75	.537	8	696	640	5607	1448	224	49	117	510	969	.258	.323	.378	.701	101	12	11	100	101	683	56	42	57	-8
ATL	163	85	77	.525	10	782	683	5617	1476	220	32	207	512	913	.263	.329	.424	.753	113	106	94	102	100	775	59	47	56	-11
STL	162	83	79	.512	12	571	577	5480	1377	196	61	108	345	977	.251	.300	.368	.668	91	-66	-69	101	99	592	144	61	70	7
CIN	160	76	84	.475	18	692	702	5521	1434	232	33	149	394	877	.260	.311	.395	.706	94	7	-51	109	105	658	70	50	58	-9
HOU	163	72	90	.444	23	612	695	5511	1405	203	35	112	491	885	.255	.320	.365	.685	104	-19	25	93	94	640	90	47	66	-1
NY	161	66	95	.410	28.5	587	761	5371	1286	187	35	98	446	992	.239	.303	.342	.645	87	-99	-87	98	108	546	55	46	54	-11
CHI	162	59	103	.364	36	644	809	5592	1418	203	43	140	457	998	.254	.315	.380	.695	98	-6	-14	101	97	665	76	47	62	-5
TOT	809					6624		55385	14202	2099	412	1378	4404	9312	.256	.315	.384	.699							737	494	60	-75

TEAM	CG	SH	SV	IP	H	H/G	HR	BB	SO	RAT	ERA	ERA+	OAV	OOB	PR	/A	PF	CPI	FA	E	DP	FW	PW	BW	SBW	DIF
LA	52	20	35	1458	1287	7.9	84	356	1084	10.3	2.62	126	.237	.288	159	109	91	102	.979	133	128	.9	11.4	1.3	-.3	.7
SF	52	14	27	1476²	1370	8.3	140	359	973	10.7	3.24	113	.244	.294	61	71	102	96	.974	168	131	-1.2	7.4	-3.5	-.2	9.8
PIT	35	12	43	1463¹	1445	8.9	125	463	898	12.0	3.52	101	.261	.322	13	8	99	105	.978	141	215	.4	.8	12.2	-1.0	-1.4
PHI	52	15	23	1459²	1439	8.9	137	412	928	11.8	3.57	101	.258	.316	6	4	100	100	.982	113	147	2.0	.4	1.2	-.0	2.5
ATL	37	10	36	1469¹	1430	8.8	129	485	884	11.9	3.68	99	.257	.319	-12	-7	101	98	.976	154	139	-.3	-.7	9.9	-.4	-4.5
STL	47	19	32	1459²	1345	8.3	130	448	892	11.3	3.11	115	.246	.307	80	77	100	107	.977	145	166	.2	8.1	-7.2	1.5	-.6
CIN	28	10	35	1436	1408	8.8	153	490	1043	12.2	4.08	96	.258	.324	-76	-28	108	94	.980	122	133	1.4	-2.9	-5.3	-.2	3.0
HOU	34	13	26	1443²	1468	9.2	130	391	929	11.8	3.76	91	.262	.314	-24	-54	95	96	.972	174	126	-1.4	-5.7	2.6	.7	-5.3
NY	37	9	22	1427	1497	9.4	166	521	773	12.9	4.17	87	.272	.339	-89	-85	101	104	.975	174	171	-.6	-8.9	-9.1	-.4	4.5
CHI	28	6	24	1458	1513	9.3	184	479	908	12.5	4.33	85	.268	.328	-118	-106	102	97	.974	166	132	-1.0	-11.1	-1.5	.3	-8.7
TOT	402	128	303	14551¹		8.8				11.7	3.61		.256	.315					.977	1475	1488					

Runs		Hits		Doubles		Triples		Home Runs		Total Bases	
Alou-Atl	122	Alou-Atl	218	Callison-Phi	40	McCarver-StL	13	Aaron-Atl	44	Alou-Atl	355
Aaron-Atl	117	Rose-Cin	205	Rose-Cin	38	Brock-StL	12	Allen-Phi	40	Clemente-Pit	342
Allen-Phi	112	Clemente-Pit	202	Pinson-Cin	35	Clemente-Pit	11	Mays-SF	37	Allen-Phi	331
Clemente-Pit	105	Beckert-Chi	188	Alou-Atl	32			Torre-Atl	36	Aaron-Atl	325
Williams-Chi	100							McCovey-SF	36	Mays-SF	307

Runs Batted In		Runs Produced		Bases On Balls		Batting Average		On Base Percentage		Slugging Average	
Aaron-Atl	127	Aaron-Atl	200	Santo-Chi	95	Alou-Pit	.342	Santo-Chi	.417	Allen-Phi	.632
Clemente-Pit	119	Clemente-Pit	195	Morgan-Hou	89	Alou-Atl	.327	Morgan-Hou	.412	McCovey-SF	.586
Allen-Phi	110	Allen-Phi	182	McCovey-SF	76	Carty-Atl	.326	Allen-Phi	.398	Stargell-Pit	.581
White-Phi	103	White-Phi	166	Aaron-Atl	76	Allen-Phi	.317	Carty-Atl	.396	Torre-Atl	.560
Mays-SF	103			Menke-Atl	71	Clemente-Pit	.317	McCovey-SF	.394	Mays-SF	.556

Production		Adjusted Production		Batter Runs		Adjusted Batter Runs		Clutch Hitting Index		Runs Created	
Allen-Phi	1.030	Allen-Phi	181	Allen-Phi	56.8	Allen-Phi	56.7	White-Phi	125	Allen-Phi	131
McCovey-SF	.979	Stargell-Pit	164	Santo-Chi	51.2	Santo-Chi	49.7	Beckert-Chi	117	Santo-Chi	127
Stargell-Pit	.965	McCovey-SF	163	McCovey-SF	46.9	McCovey-SF	43.8	Clemente-Pit	117	Alou-Atl	123
Santo-Chi	.955	Santo-Chi	161	Torre-Atl	43.0	Torre-Atl	41.4	Woodward-Atl	117	McCovey-SF	119
Torre-Atl	.945	Torre-Atl	157	Stargell-Pit	41.1	Stargell-Pit	41.0	Staub-Hou	116	Clemente-Pit	119

Total Average		Stolen Bases		Stolen Base Average		Stolen Base Runs		Fielding Runs		Total Player Rating	
Allen-Phi	1.088	Brock-StL	74	Aaron-Atl	87.5	Brock-StL	11.4	Mazeroski-Pit	40.8	Santo-Chi	7.5
McCovey-SF	1.039	Jackson-Hou	49	Brock-StL	80.4	Jackson-Hou	6.3	Santo-Chi	28.8	Clemente-Pit	4.6
Santo-Chi	.988	Wills-LA	38	Jackson-Hou	77.8	Aaron-Atl	4.5	Lanier-SF	28.2	Allen-Phi	4.5
Stargell-Pit	.980	Phillips-Phi-Chi	32	Harper-Cin	74.4	Harper-Cin	2.7	Maxvill-StL	23.8	Mazeroski-Pit	4.5
Mays-SF	.941	Harper-Cin	29	White-Phi	72.7			Clemente-Pit	15.4	Aaron-Atl	4.3

Wins		Win Percentage		Games		Complete Games		Shutouts		Saves	
Koufax-LA	27	Marichal-SF	.806	Carroll-Atl	73	Koufax-LA	27	L.Jackson-Chi-Phi	5	Regan-LA	21
Marichal-SF	25	Koufax-LA	.750	Mikkelsen-Pit	71	Marichal-SF	25	Maloney-Cin	5	McCool-Cin	18
Perry-SF	21	Perry-SF	.724	Knowles-Phi	69	Gibson-StL	20	Koufax-LA	5	Face-Pit	18
Gibson-StL	21	Short-Phi	.667	Regan-LA	65	Short-Phi	19	Jaster-StL	5	Raymond-Hou	16
Short-Phi	20	Maloney-Cin	.667	McDaniel-SF	64	Bunning-Phi	16	Gibson-StL	5	Linzy-SF	16
								Bunning-Phi	5		

Innings Pitched		Fewest Hits/Game		Fewest BB/Game		Strikeouts		Strikeouts/Game		Ratio	
Koufax-LA	323.0	Marichal-SF	6.68	Marichal-SF	1.05	Koufax-LA	317	Koufax-LA	8.83	Marichal-SF	7.88
Bunning-Phi	314.0	Koufax-LA	6.72	Law-Pit	1.22	Bunning-Phi	252	Maloney-Cin	8.65	Koufax-LA	8.86
Marichal-SF	307.1	Gibson-StL	6.74	Perry-SF	1.41	Veale-Pit	229	Sutton-LA	8.34	Gibson-StL	9.41
Gibson-StL	280.1	Maloney-Cin	6.97	Drysdale-LA	1.48	Gibson-StL	225	Veale-Pit	7.68	Bunning-Phi	9.57
Drysdale-LA	273.2	Bolin-SF	6.98	Bunning-Phi	1.58	Marichal-SF	222	Jenkins-Phi-Chi	7.32	Cuellar-Hou	9.70

Earned Run Average		Adjusted ERA		Opponents' Batting Avg.		Opponents' On Base Pct.		Starter Runs		Adjusted Starter Runs	
Koufax-LA	1.73	Koufax-LA	191	Marichal-SF	.202	Marichal-SF	.230	Koufax-LA	67.4	Koufax-LA	56.3
Cuellar-Hou	2.22	Marichal-SF	165	Koufax-LA	.205	Koufax-LA	.253	Marichal-SF	47.2	Marichal-SF	49.2
Marichal-SF	2.23	Cuellar-Hou	154	Gibson-StL	.207	Gibson-StL	.267	Bunning-Phi	41.8	Bunning-Phi	41.4
Bunning-Phi	2.41	Bunning-Phi	149	Bolin-SF	.211	Bunning-Phi	.270	Gibson-StL	36.3	Gibson-StL	35.8
Gibson-StL	2.44	Gibson-StL	147	Maloney-Cin	.214	Cuellar-Hou	.274	Cuellar-Hou	35.1	Cuellar-Hou	30.5

Clutch Pitching Index		Relief Runs		Adjusted Relief Runs		Relief Ranking		Total Pitcher Index		Total Baseball Ranking	
Jackson-StL	117	Regan-LA	25.8	Regan-LA	21.7	Regan-LA	33.9	Marichal-SF	5.8	Santo-Chi	7.5
L.Jackson-Chi-Phi	110	Carroll-Atl	19.8	Carroll-Atl	20.4	McCool-Cin	29.2	Koufax-LA	5.4	Marichal-SF	5.8
Ellsworth-Chi	108	Hoerner-StL	17.5	Hoerner-StL	17.3	Carroll-Atl	22.5	Gibson-StL	4.4	Koufax-LA	5.4
Johnson-Atl	108	McCool-Cin	13.2	McCool-Cin	16.7	Hoerner-StL	19.0	Jackson-StL	4.2	Clemente-Pit	4.6
Osteen-LA	107	Woodeshick-StL	13.2	McDaniel-SF	13.6	McDaniel-SF	16.6	Bunning-Phi	4.1	Allen-Phi	4.5

TEAM	G	W	L	PCT	GB	R	OR	AB	H	2B	3B	HR	BB	SO	AVG	OBP	SLG	PRO	PRO+	BR	/A	PF	CHI	RC	SB	CS	SBA	SBR
BAL	160	97	63	.606		755	601	5529	1426	243	35	175	514	926	.258	.325	.409	.734	119	114	126	98	100	727	55	43	56	-9
MIN	162	89	73	.549	9	663	581	5390	1341	219	33	144	513	844	.249	.319	.382	.701	101	49	6	106	98	643	67	42	61	-5
DET	162	88	74	.543	10	719	698	5507	1383	224	45	179	551	987	.251	.323	.406	.729	112	102	85	102	96	714	41	34	55	-8
CHI	163	83	79	.512	15	574	517	5348	1235	193	40	87	476	872	.231	.299	.331	.630	93	-83	-47	93	106	539	153	78	66	-1
CLE	162	81	81	.500	17	574	586	5474	1300	156	25	155	460	914	.237	.299	.360	.659	95	-38	-38	100	97	579	53	41	56	-9
CAL	162	80	82	.494	18	604	643	5360	1244	179	54	122	525	1062	.232	.305	.354	.659	98	-29	-13	97	101	582	80	54	60	-8
KC	160	74	86	.463	23	564	648	5328	1259	212	56	70	421	982	.236	.295	.337	.632	90	-84	-67	97	107	535	132	50	73	10
WAS	159	71	88	.447	25.5	557	659	5318	1245	185	40	126	450	1069	.234	.296	.355	.651	94	-50	-44	99	99	548	53	37	59	-6
BOS	162	72	90	.444	26	655	731	5498	1318	228	44	145	542	1020	.240	.312	.376	.688	93	24	-44	110	98	640	35	24	59	-4
NY	160	70	89	.440	26.5	611	612	5330	1254	182	36	162	485	817	.235	.302	.374	.676	104	-5	18	96	100	598	49	29	63	-3
TOT	806					6276		54082	13005	2021	408	1365	4927	9493	.240	.308	.369	.676							718	432	62	-44

TEAM	CG	SH	SV	IP	H	H/G	HR	BB	SO	RAT	ERA	ERA+	OAV	OOB	PR	/A	PF	CPI	FA	E	DP	FW	PW	BW	SBW	DIF
BAL	23	13	51	1466[1]	1267	7.8	127	514	1070	11.1	3.32	100	.233	.303	19	2	97	97	.981	115	142	1.3	.2	13.5	-.5	2.4
MIN	52	11	28	1438[2]	1246	7.8	139	392	1015	10.4	3.13	115	.232	.287	48	74	105	97	.977	139	118	.0	8.0	.6	-.0	-.6
DET	36	11	38	1454[1]	1356	8.4	185	520	1026	11.9	3.85	90	.247	.317	-67	-60	101	102	.980	120	142	1.1	-6.4	9.1	-.4	3.6
CHI	38	22	34	1475[1]	1229	7.5	101	403	896	10.2	2.68	118	.226	.283	123	80	92	100	.976	159	149	-1.1	8.6	-5.1	.4	-.8
CLE	49	15	28	1467[1]	1260	7.7	129	489	1111	10.9	3.23	107	.232	.299	34	35	100	98	.978	138	132	.0	3.8	-4.1	-.5	.7
CAL	31	12	40	1457[1]	1364	8.4	136	511	836	11.8	3.56	94	.251	.320	-21	-33	98	105	.979	136	186	.2	-3.5	-1.4	-.4	4.1
KC	19	11	47	1435	1281	8.0	106	630	854	12.2	3.56	96	.241	.326	-19	-25	99	101	.977	139	154	-.0	-2.7	-7.2	1.5	2.4
WAS	25	6	35	1419	1282	8.1	154	448	866	11.1	3.70	93	.242	.304	-42	-39	101	95	.977	142	139	-.3	-4.2	-4.7	-.2	-9
BOS	32	10	31	1463[2]	1402	8.6	164	577	977	12.4	3.92	97	.253	.327	-78	-18	111	103	.975	155	153	-.9	-1.9	-4.7	.0	-1.5
NY	29	7	32	1415[2]	1318	8.4	124	443	842	11.3	3.41	97	.248	.308	3	-14	97	102	.977	142	142	-.3	-1.5	1.9	.1	-9.8
TOT	334	118	364	14492[2]		8.1				11.3	3.44		.240	.308					.978	1385	1457					

Runs
F.Robinson-Bal ... 122
Oliva-Min 99
Cash-Det 98
Agee-Chi 98

Hits
Oliva-Min 191
F.Robinson-Bal ... 182
Aparicio-Bal 182
Agee-Chi 172
Cash-Det 168

Doubles
Yastrzemski-Bos ... 39
B.Robinson-Bal ... 35
F.Robinson-Bal 34
Oliva-Min 32
Fregosi-Cal 32

Triples
Knoop-Cal 11
Campaneris-KC ... 10
Brinkman-Was 9

Home Runs
F.Robinson-Bal 49
Killebrew-Min 39
Powell-Bal 34
Cash-Det 32
Pepitone-NY 31

Total Bases
F.Robinson-Bal ... 367
Oliva-Min 312
Killebrew-Min 306
Cash-Det 288
Agee-Chi 281

Runs Batted In
F.Robinson-Bal ... 122
Killebrew-Min 110
Powell-Bal 109
B.Robinson-Bal ... 100
Horton-Det 100

Runs Produced
F.Robinson-Bal ... 195
B.Robinson-Bal ... 168
Agee-Chi 162
Oliva-Min 161
Killebrew-Min 160

Bases On Balls
Killebrew-Min 103
Foy-Bos 91
F.Robinson-Bal 87
Tresh-NY 86
Yastrzemski-Bos ... 84

Batting Average
F.Robinson-Bal ...316
Oliva-Min 307
Kaline-Det 288
Powell-Bal 287
Killebrew-Min 281

On Base Percentage
F.Robinson-Bal ...415
Kaline-Det 396
Killebrew-Min 393
McAuliffe-Det 375
Powell-Bal 374

Slugging Average
F.Robinson-Bal ...637
Killebrew-Min 538
Kaline-Det.........534
Powell-Bal 532
McAuliffe-Det 509

Production
F.Robinson-Bal ..1.052
Killebrew-Min 931
Kaline-Det........931
Powell-Bal 905
McAuliffe-Det.....884

Adjusted Production
F.Robinson-Bal ... 200
Kaline-Det 161
Powell-Bal 159
Killebrew-Min 155
McAuliffe-Det 148

Batter Runs
F.Robinson-Bal ... 73.6
Killebrew-Min ... 49.9
Kaline-Det 42.1
Powell-Bal 36.3
Oliva-Min 33.2

Adjusted Batter Runs
F.Robinson-Bal ...75.9
Killebrew-Min 42.4
Kaline-Det 39.8
Powell-Bal 37.8
Mantle-NY........31.4

Clutch Hitting Index
F.Robinson-Bal ... 119
Horton-Det....... 119
Green-KC......... 116
Hershberger-KC .. 115
D.Johnson-Bal 113

Runs Created
F.Robinson-Bal ... 146
Killebrew-Min 122
Oliva-Min 106
Kaline-Det 105
Cash-Det 101

Total Average
F.Robinson-Bal ..1.104
Kaline-Det........969
Killebrew-Min.....967
Powell-Bal 898
McAuliffe-Det.....877

Stolen Bases
Campaneris-KC ... 52
Buford-Chi 51
Agee-Chi 44
Aparicio-Bal 25
Cardenal-Cal 24

Stolen Base Average
Campaneris-KC ... 83.9
Tartabull-KC-Bos . 82.6
Tovar-Min 72.7
Agee-Chi 71.0
Buford-Chi 69.9

Stolen Base Runs
Campaneris-KC 9.6
Tartabull-KC-Bos ...3,3
Salmon-Cle 2.4
Agee-Chi 2.4

Fielding Runs
Weis-Chi 36.9
Tresh-NY 27.7
Boyer-NY 19.9
Yastrzemski-Bos .. 16.6
Knoop-Cal 16.5

Total Player Rating
F.Robinson-Bal ... 6.7
Tresh-NY 4.1
Fregosi-Cal 3.9
Kaline-Det 3.9
Oliva-Min 3.5

Wins
Kaat-Min 25
McLain-Det 20
Wilson-Bos-Det ... 18
Siebert-Cle 16
Palmer-Bal 15

Win Percentage
Siebert-Cle ...... .667
Kaat-Min .... .658
Wilson-Bos-Det ... .621
Palmer-Bal .... .600
McLain-Det .... .588

Games
Fisher-Chi-Bal ... 67
Cox-Was 66
Aker-KC 66
Worthington-Min .. 65
Kline-Was 63

Complete Games
Kaat-Min 19
McLain-Det 14
Wilson-Bos-Det ... 13
Bell-Cle 12

Shutouts
Tiant-Cle 5
McDowell-Cle 5
John-Chi 5

Saves
Aker-KC 32
Kline-Was 23
Sherry-Det 20
Fisher-Chi-Bal 19
S.Miller-Bal 18

Innings Pitched
Kaat-Min 304.2
McLain-Det 264.1
Wilson-Bos-Det .. 264.0
Chance-Cal 259.2
Bell-Cle 254.1

Fewest Hits/Game
McDowell-Cle 6.02
Boswell-Min 6.38
Peters-Chi 6.86
McLain-Det 6.98
Chance-Cal 7.14

Fewest BB/Game
Kaat-Min.......... 1.62
Peterson-NY 1.67
Grant-Min 1.77
Peters-Chi 1.98
Hargan-Cle 2.11

Strikeouts
McDowell-Cle 225
Kaat-Min 205
Wilson-Bos-Det ... 200
Richert-Was 195
Bell-Cle 194

Strikeouts/Game
McDowell-Cle 10.42
Boswell-Min 9.19
Lolich-Det 7.64
Richert-Was 7.14
Bell-Cle 6.87

Ratio
Peters-Chi 8.97
Kaat-Min 9.72
Richert-Was 9.74
Siebert-Cle 9.75
Ortega-Was 9.85

Earned Run Average
Peters-Chi 1.98
Horlen-Chi 2.43
Hargan-Cle 2.48
Perry-Min 2.54
John-Chi 2.62

Adjusted ERA
Peters-Chi 160
Perry-Min 142
Hargan-Cle 138
Kaat-Min 131
Horlen-Chi 130

Opponents' Batting Avg.
McDowell-Cle 188
Boswell-Min 197
Peters-Chi 212
McLain-Det 214
Richert-Was 215

Opponents' On Base Pct.
Peters-Chi.........261
Richert-Was 271
Kaat-Min 271
Ortega-Was 276
Siebert-Cle 278

Starter Runs
Peters-Chi 33.1
Horlen-Chi 23.5
Kaat-Min 23.3
Hargan-Cle 20.3
John-Chi 20.1

Adjusted Starter Runs
Kaat-Min 28.8
Peters-Chi 27.1
Perry-Min 21.7
Hargan-Cle 20.4
Nash-KC 18.9

Clutch Pitching Index
McNally-Bal 118
Horlen-Chi 114
Brunet-Cal 114
Perry-Min 113
Hargan-Cle 110

Relief Runs
Aker-KC 18.1
Wilhelm-Chi 16.0
S.Miller-Bal 12.1
Fisher-Chi-Bal 10.8
Lines-Was 10.7

Adjusted Relief Runs
Aker-KC 17.7
Wilhelm-Chi 13.7
Worthington-Min .. 11.5
S.Miller-Bal 11.1
Lines-Was 10.9

Relief Ranking
Aker-KC 28.1
McMahon-Cle-Bos .20.8
S.Miller-Bal 18.9
Kline-Was 16.8
Worthington-Min .. 14.7

Total Pitcher Index
Kaat-Min 4.1
Peters-Chi 3.9
Aker-KC 3.4
Wilson-Bos-Det ... 3.3
Perry-Min 2.4

Total Baseball Ranking
F.Robinson-Bal 6.7
Tresh-NY.......... 4.1
Kaat-Min 4.1
Fregosi-Cal 3.9
Peters-Chi 3.9

TEAM	G	W	L	PCT	GB	R	OR	AB	H	2B	3B	HR	BB	SO	AVG	OBP	SLG	PRO	PRO+	BR	/A	PF	CHI	RC	SB	CS	SBA	SBR
STL	161	101	60	.627		695	557	5566	1462	225	40	115	443	919	.263	.322	.379	.701	109	52	61	99	103	676	102	54	65	-2
SF	162	91	71	.562	10.5	652	551	5524	1354	201	39	140	520	978	.245	.315	.372	.687	104	24	33	99	100	641	22	30	42	-11
CHI	162	87	74	.540	14	702	624	5463	1373	211	49	128	509	912	.251	.319	.378	.697	101	44	13	105	105	654	63	50	56	-11
CIN	162	87	75	.537	14.5	604	563	5519	1366	251	54	109	372	969	.248	.299	.372	.671	88	-20	-88	111	102	592	92	63	59	-10
PHI	162	82	80	.506	19.5	612	581	5401	1306	221	47	103	545	1033	.242	.314	.357	.671	98	-1	-7	101	99	604	79	62	56	-14
PIT	163	81	81	.500	20.5	679	693	5724	1585	193	62	91	387	914	.277	.327	.380	.707	108	63	60	101	97	693	79	37	68	2
ATL	162	77	85	.475	24.5	631	640	5450	1307	191	39	158	512	947	.240	.309	.372	.681	102	10	19	99	100	615	55	45	55	-11
LA	162	73	89	.451	28.5	519	595	5456	1285	203	38	82	485	881	.236	.303	.332	.635	97	-74	-30	92	95	541	56	47	54	-11
HOU	162	69	93	.426	32.5	626	742	5506	1372	259	46	93	537	934	.249	.319	.364	.683	107	20	42	97	97	640	88	38	70	4
NY	162	61	101	.377	40.5	498	672	5417	1288	178	23	83	362	981	.238	.290	.325	.615	83	-118	-110	98	103	500	58	44	57	-9
TOT	810					6218		55026	13698	2133	427	1102	4672	9468	.249	.312	.363	.675							694	470	60	-74

TEAM	CG	SH	SV	IP	H	H/G	HR	BB	SO	RAT	ERA	ERA+	OAV	OOB	PR	/A	PF	CPI	FA	E	DP	FW	PW	BW	SBW	DIF
STL	44	17	45	1465	1313	8.1	97	431	956	10.9	3.05	108	.239	.299	54	39	97	98	.978	140	127	.0	4.2	6.6	.6	9.1
SF	64	17	25	1474¹	1283	7.8	113	453	990	10.8	2.92	113	.234	.296	75	61	97	101	.979	134	149	.4	6.6	3.6	-.4	-.2
CHI	47	7	28	1457	1352	8.4	142	463	888	11.4	3.48	102	.246	.308	-17	10	105	99	.981	121	143	1.1	1.1	1.4	-.4	3.3
CIN	34	18	39	1468	1328	8.1	101	498	1065	11.5	3.05	123	.241	.309	54	115	111	104	.980	121	124	1.1	12.5	-9.5	-.3	2.2
PHI	46	17	23	1453²	1372	8.5	86	403	967	11.2	3.10	110	.250	.306	44	50	101	102	.978	137	174	.2	5.4	-.8	-.7	-3.2
PIT	35	5	35	1458¹	1439	8.9	108	561	820	12.5	3.74	90	.261	.332	-59	-61	100	103	.978	141	186	.0	-6.6	6.5	1.0	-.9
ATL	35	5	32	1454	1377	8.5	118	449	862	11.6	3.47	96	.251	.313	-16	-24	98	100	.978	138	148	.2	-2.6	2.1	-.4	-3.2
LA	41	17	24	1473	1421	8.7	93	393	933	11.3	3.21	96	.254	.308	27	-19	92	102	.975	160	144	-1.1	-4.3	-3.2	-.4	-1.2
HOU	35	8	21	1445²	1444	9.0	120	485	1060	12.3	4.03	82	.260	.324	-105	-115	98	93	.974	159	120	-1.0	-12.5	4.5	1.2	-4.3
NY	36	10	19	1433²	1369	8.6	124	536	893	12.1	3.73	91	.253	.323	-56	-54	100	99	.975	157	147	-.9	-5.8	-11.9	-.2	-1.1
TOT	417	121	291	14582²		8.5				11.6	3.38		.249	.312					.978	1408	1462					

Runs
Brock-StL 113
Aaron-Atl 113
Santo-Chi 107
Clemente-Pit 103
Wynn-Hou 102

Hits
Clemente-Pit 209
Brock-StL 206
Pinson-Cin 187
Wills-Pit 186
Alou-Pit 186

Doubles
Staub-Hou 44
Cepeda-StL 37
Aaron-Atl 37

Triples
Pinson-Cin 13
Williams-Chi 12
Brock-StL 12
Morgan-Hou 11

Home Runs
Aaron-Atl 39
Wynn-Hou 37
Santo-Chi 31
McCovey-SF 31
Hart-SF 29

Total Bases
Aaron-Atl 344
Brock-StL 325
Clemente-Pit 324
Williams-Chi 305
Santo-Chi 300

Runs Batted In
Cepeda-StL 111
Clemente-Pit 110
Aaron-Atl 109
Wynn-Hou 107
Perez-Cin 102

Runs Produced
Clemente-Pit 190
Aaron-Atl 183
Cepeda-StL 177
Santo-Chi 174
Wynn-Hou 172

Bases On Balls
Santo-Chi 96
Morgan-Hou 81
Phillips-Chi 80
Hart-SF 77
Allen-Phi 75

Batting Average
Clemente-Pit 357
Gonzalez-Phi 339
Alou-Pit 338
Flood-StL 335
Staub-Hou 333

On Base Percentage
Allen-Phi 404
Cepeda-StL 403
Staub-Hou 402
Clemente-Pit 402
Santo-Chi 401

Slugging Average
Aaron-Atl 573
Allen-Phi 566
Clemente-Pit 554
McCovey-SF 535
Cepeda-StL 524

Production
Allen-Phi 970
Clemente-Pit 956
Aaron-Atl 946
Cepeda-StL 927
McCovey-SF 916

Adjusted Production
Allen-Phi 173
Clemente-Pit 170
Aaron-Atl 169
Cepeda-StL 166
McCovey-SF 162

Batter Runs
Clemente-Pit 52.1
Aaron-Atl 50.1
Santo-Chi 47.9
Cepeda-StL 47.3
Allen-Phi 46.1

Adjusted Batter Runs
Aaron-Atl 51.8
Clemente-Pit 51.6
Cepeda-StL 48.8
Allen-Phi 45.1
Santo-Chi 42.5

Clutch Hitting Index
Shannon-StL 141
Lanier-SF 125
Maxvill-StL 120
Fairly-LA 118
Boyer-Atl 117

Runs Created
Clemente-Pit 126
Aaron-Atl 126
Santo-Chi 120
Cepeda-StL 118
Hart-SF 111

Total Average
Allen-Phi 1.054
Aaron-Atl 965
Clemente-Pit 959
Cepeda-StL 950
McCovey-SF 941

Stolen Bases
Brock-StL 52
Wills-Pit 29
Morgan-Hou 29
Pinson-Cin 26
Phillips-Chi 24

Stolen Base Average
Morgan-Hou 85.3
Wynn-Hou 80.0
Allen-Phi 80.0
Davis-LA 76.9
Pinson-Cin 76.5

Stolen Base Runs
Morgan-Hou 5.7
Brock-StL 4.8
Pinson-Cin 3.0
Allen-Phi 3.0
Wills-Pit 2.7

Fielding Runs
Santo-Chi 30.6
Lanier-SF 28.9
Wine-Phi 28.9
Fuentes-SF 24.5
Mazeroski-Pit 16.7

Total Player Rating
Santo-Chi 7.3
Aaron-Atl 6.1
Clemente-Pit 5.8
Cepeda-StL 4.4
Allen-Phi 4.4

Wins
McCormick-SF 22
Jenkins-Chi 20
Osteen-LA 17
Bunning-Phi 17

Win Percentage
Hughes-StL 727
McCormick-SF 688
Veale-Pit 667
Jenkins-Chi 606
Jarvis-Atl 600

Games
Perranoski-LA 70
Abernathy-Cin 70
Willis-StL 65
Face-Pit 61

Complete Games
Jenkins-Chi 20
Seaver-NY 18
Perry-SF 18
Marichal-SF 18

Shutouts
Bunning-Phi 6
Osteen-LA 5
Nolan-Cin 5
McCormick-SF 5
L.Jackson-Phi 4

Saves
Abernathy-Cin 28
Linzy-SF 17
Face-Pit 17
Perranoski-LA 16
Hoerner-StL 15

Innings Pitched
Bunning-Phi 302.1
Perry-SF 293.0
Jenkins-Chi 289.1
Osteen-LA 288.1
Drysdale-LA 282.0

Fewest Hits/Game
Hughes-StL 6.64
Wilson-Hou 6.90
Perry-SF 7.10
Queen-Cin 7.13
Niekro-Atl 7.13

Fewest BB/Game
Pappas-Cin 1.57
Osteen-LA 1.62
Johnson-Atl 1.63
Niekro-Chi 1.70
L.Jackson-Phi 1.86

Strikeouts
Bunning-Phi 253
Jenkins-Chi 236
Perry-SF 230
Nolan-Cin 206
Cuellar-Hou 203

Strikeouts/Game
Nolan-Cin 8.18
Veale-Pit 7.94
Carlton-StL 7.83
Wilson-Hou 7.78
Gibson-StL 7.55

Ratio
Hughes-StL 8.78
Bunning-Phi 9.73
Queen-Cin 9.80
Perry-SF 9.80
Niekro-Atl 9.83

Earned Run Average
Niekro-Atl 1.87
Bunning-Phi 2.29
Short-Phi 2.39
Nolan-Cin 2.58
Perry-SF 2.61

Adjusted ERA
Niekro-Atl 178
Bunning-Phi 149
Nolan-Cin 145
Short-Phi 142
Queen-Cin 136

Opponents' Batting Avg.
Hughes-StL 203
Wilson-Hou 209
Perry-SF 214
Queen-Cin 215
Bunning-Phi 217

Opponents' On Base Pct.
Hughes-StL 252
Bunning-Phi 273
Queen-Cin 273
Perry-SF 274
Jenkins-Chi 277

Starter Runs
Bunning-Phi 36.4
Niekro-Atl 34.6
Perry-SF 24.9
Short-Phi 21.8
Nolan-Cin 20.0

Adjusted Starter Runs
Bunning-Phi 37.5
Niekro-Atl 33.4
Nolan-Cin 29.5
Jenkins-Chi 24.0
Short-Phi 22.5

Clutch Pitching Index
Ellis-Cin 123
Niekro-Atl 121
Seaver-NY 114
Marichal-SF 114
Short-Phi 114

Relief Runs
Abernathy-Cin 24.9
Linzy-SF 19.9
Nottebart-Cin 12.8
McBean-Pit 12.1
Farrell-Hou-Phi . . . 11.9

Adjusted Relief Runs
Abernathy-Cin 29.3
Linzy-SF 19.0
Nottebart-Cin 16.1
Farrell-Hou-Phi . . . 12.1
McBean-Pit 12.0

Relief Ranking
Abernathy-Cin 39.7
Linzy-SF 32.5
Hall-Phi 24.2
Farrell-Hou-Phi . . . 20.0
Face-Pit 15.3

Total Pitcher Index
Abernathy-Cin 4.5
Bunning-Phi 4.1
Linzy-SF 3.9
Niekro-Atl 3.8
Jenkins-Chi 3.1

Total Baseball Ranking
Santo-Chi 7.3
Aaron-Atl 6.1
Clemente-Pit 5.8
Abernathy-Cin 4.5
Cepeda-StL 4.4

TEAM	G	W	L	PCT	GB	R	OR	AB	H	2B	3B	HR	BB	SO	AVG	OBP	SLG	PRO	PRO+	BR	/A	PF	CHI	RC	SB	CS	SBA	SBR
BOS	162	92	70	.568		722	614	5471	1394	216	39	158	522	1020	.255	.323	.395	.718	109	118	60	108	100	694	68	59	54	-15
MIN	164	91	71	.562	1	671	590	5458	1309	216	48	131	512	976	.240	.310	.369	.679	99	44	-8	108	104	625	55	37	60	-6
DET	163	91	71	.562	1	683	587	5410	1315	192	36	152	626	994	.243	.327	.376	.703	111	100	81	103	96	681	37	21	64	-2
CHI	162	89	73	.549	3	531	491	5383	1209	181	34	89	480	849	.225	.293	.320	.613	90	-80	-61	96	104	504	124	82	60	-12
CAL	161	84	77	.522	7.5	567	587	5307	1265	170	37	114	453	1021	.238	.302	.349	.651	102	-12	10	96	99	553	40	36	53	-10
WAS	161	76	85	.472	15.5	550	637	5441	1211	168	25	115	472	1037	.223	.289	.326	.615	92	-81	-61	96	107	512	53	37	59	-6
BAL	161	76	85	.472	15.5	654	592	5456	1312	215	44	138	531	1002	.240	.313	.372	.685	110	54	59	99	99	639	54	37	59	-6
CLE	162	75	87	.463	17	559	613	5461	1282	213	35	131	413	984	.235	.295	.359	.654	98	-15	-20	101	96	563	53	65	45	-23
NY	163	72	90	.444	20	522	621	5443	1225	166	17	100	532	1043	.225	.298	.317	.615	91	-74	-54	96	98	522	63	37	63	-3
KC	161	62	99	.385	29.5	533	660	5349	1244	212	50	69	452	1019	.233	.297	.330	.627	94	-54	-37	97	100	539	132	59	69	4
TOT	810					5992		54179	12766	1949	365	1197	4993	9945	.236	.305	.351	.656							679	470	59	-78

TEAM	CG	SH	SV	IP	H	H/G	HR	BB	SO	RAT	ERA	ERA+	OAV	OOB	PR	/A	PF	CPI	FA	E	DP	FW	PW	BW	SBW	DIF
BOS	41	9	44	1459¹	1307	8.1	142	477	1010	11.3	3.36	104	.239	.306	-21	20	108	101	.977	142	142	-.6	2.2	6.6	-.8	3.6
MIN	58	18	24	1461	1336	8.2	115	396	1089	10.9	3.14	110	.243	.298	15	53	107	101	.978	132	123	.1	5.9	-.9	.2	4.7
DET	46	17	40	1443²	1230	7.7	151	472	1038	10.8	3.32	98	.230	.297	-14	-9	101	97	.978	132	126	.0	-1.0	8.9	.6	1.3
CHI	36	24	39	1490¹	1197	7.2	87	465	927	10.4	2.45	127	.219	.288	129	108	96	106	.979	138	149	-.3	11.9	-6.7	-.5	3.6
CAL	19	14	46	1430¹	1246	7.8	118	525	892	11.4	3.19	98	.237	.311	6	-8	97	105	.982	111	135	1.3	-.9	1.1	-.2	2.2
WAS	24	14	39	1473¹	1334	8.1	113	495	878	11.4	3.38	93	.242	.309	-25	-36	98	98	.978	144	167	-.8	-4.0	-6.7	.2	6.8
BAL	29	17	36	1457¹	1218	7.5	116	566	1034	11.2	3.32	95	.228	.305	-15	-27	98	95	.980	124	144	.5	-3.0	6.5	.2	-8.7
CLE	49	14	27	1477²	1258	7.7	120	559	1189	11.3	3.25	101	.231	.307	-3	3	101	99	.981	116	138	1.0	.3	-2.2	-1.7	-3.5
NY	37	16	27	1480²	1375	8.4	110	480	898	11.5	3.24	97	.249	.313	-2	-19	97	106	.976	154	144	-1.3	-2.1	-6.0	.5	-.2
KC	26	10	34	1428	1265	8.0	125	558	990	11.7	3.68	87	.238	.315	-71	-79	99	94	.978	132	120	-.0	-8.7	-4.1	1.3	-7.0
TOT	365	153	356	14601²		7.9				11.2	3.23		.236	.305					.979	1325	1388					

Runs
Yastrzemski-Bos .. 112
Killebrew-Min 105
Tovar-Min 98
Kaline-Det 94
McAuliffe-Det 92

Hits
Yastrzemski-Bos ... 189
Tovar-Min 173
Scott-Bos 171
Fregosi-Cal 171
B.Robinson-Bal 164

Doubles
Oliva-Min 34
Tovar-Min 32
Yastrzemski-Bos ... 31
D.Johnson-Bal 30
Campaneris-KC 29

Triples
Blair-Bal 12
Buford-Chi 9

Home Runs
Yastrzemski-Bos ... 44
Killebrew-Min 44
Howard-Was 36
F.Robinson-Bal 30

Total Bases
Yastrzemski-Bos ... 360
Killebrew-Min 305
F.Robinson-Bal 276
B.Robinson-Bal 265
Howard-Was 265

Runs Batted In
Yastrzemski-Bos .. 121
Killebrew-Min 113
F.Robinson-Bal 94
Howard-Was 89
Oliva-Min 83

Runs Produced
Yastrzemski-Bos ... 189
Killebrew-Min 174
F.Robinson-Bal 147
Kaline-Det 147
B.Robinson-Bal 143

Bases On Balls
Killebrew-Min 131
Mantle-NY 107
McAuliffe-Det 105
Yastrzemski-Bos ... 91
Kaline-Det 83

Batting Average
Yastrzemski-Bos ...326
F.Robinson-Bal 311
Kaline-Det 308
Scott-Bos 303
Blair-Bal 293

On Base Percentage
Yastrzemski-Bos ...421
Kaline-Det 415
Killebrew-Min 413
F.Robinson-Bal 408
Mantle-NY 394

Slugging Average
Yastrzemski-Bos ...622
F.Robinson-Bal 576
Killebrew-Min 558
Kaline-Det 541
Howard-Was 511

Production
Yastrzemski-Bos .1.043
F.Robinson-Bal ..984
Killebrew-Min 970
Kaline-Det 957
Mincher-Cal 855

Adjusted Production
Yastrzemski-Bos ... 189
F.Robinson-Bal 189
Kaline-Det 176
Killebrew-Min 170
Mincher-Cal 156

Batter Runs
Yastrzemski-Bos ... 76.4
Killebrew-Min 62.3
F.Robinson-Bal 53.3
Kaline-Det 48.4
Scott-Bos 33.8

Adjusted Batter Runs
Yastrzemski-Bos ...65.3
F.Robinson-Bal 54.2
Killebrew-Min 52.2
Kaline-Det 45.7
Mincher-Cal 34.6

Clutch Hitting Index
Hershberger-KC ...124
D.Johnson-Bal 113
Hansen-Chi 111
Northrup-Det 109
Versalles-Min 108

Runs Created
Yastrzemski-Bos .. 155
Killebrew-Min 131
F.Robinson-Bal ... 113
Kaline-Det 104
Scott-Bos 97

Total Average
Yastrzemski-Bos .1.134
Killebrew-Min 1.058
F.Robinson-Bal ..1.029
Kaline-Det 1.009
Mantle-NY 874

Stolen Bases
Campaneris-KC ... 55
Buford-Chi 34
Agee-Chi 28
McCraw-Chi 24
Clarke-NY 21

Stolen Base Average
Valentine-Was 85.0
Clarke-NY 84.0
Aparicio-Bal 78.3
Campaneris-KC 77.5
Agee-Chi 73.7

Stolen Base Runs
Campaneris-KC 6.9
Clarke-NY 3.9
Valentine-Was 3.3

Fielding Runs
B.Robinson-Bal ...30.8
Blair-Bal 20.9
Smith-Bos 16.5
Monday-KC 15.2
Clarke-NY 15.2

Total Player Rating
Yastrzemski-Bos ...7.3
Kaline-Det 5.2
B.Robinson-Bal 5.0
F.Robinson-Bal 4.8
Blair-Bal 4.1

Wins
Wilson-Det 22
Lonborg-Bos 22
Chance-Min 20
Horlen-Chi 19
McLain-Det 17

Win Percentage
Horlen-Chi 731
Lonborg-Bos 710
Wilson-Det 667
Sparma-Det 640
Peters-Chi 593

Games
Locker-Chi 77
Rojas-Cal 72
Kelso-Cal 69
Womack-NY 65
McMahon-Bos-Chi . 63

Complete Games
Chance-Min 18
Lonborg-Bos 15
Hargan-Cle 15

Shutouts
McGlothlin-Cal 6
Lolich-Det 6
John-Chi 6
Horlen-Chi 6
Hargan-Cle 6

Saves
Rojas-Cal 27
Wyatt-Bos 20
Locker-Chi 20
Womack-NY 18
Worthington-Min ... 16

Innings Pitched
Chance-Min 283.2
Lonborg-Bos ...273.1
Wilson-Det 264.0
Kaat-Min 263.1
Peters-Chi 260.0

Fewest Hits/Game
Peters-Chi 6.47
Boswell-Min 6.55
Horlen-Chi 6.56
Siebert-Cle 6.60
Downing-NY 7.05

Fewest BB/Game
Merritt-Min 1.19
Kaat-Min 1.44
Stange-Bos 1.59
Horlen-Chi 2.02
Peterson-NY 2.13

Strikeouts
Lonborg-Bos 246
McDowell-Cle 236
Chance-Min 220
Tiant-Cle 219
Peters-Chi 215

Strikeouts/Game
Tiant-Cle 9.22
McDowell-Cle 8.99
Boswell-Min 8.25
Lonborg-Bos 8.10
Phoebus-Bal 7.75

Ratio
Horlen-Chi 8.72
Merritt-Min 9.21
Siebert-Cle 9.52
John-Chi 9.84
Peters-Chi 10.00

Earned Run Average
Horlen-Chi 2.06
Peters-Chi 2.28
Siebert-Cle 2.38
John-Chi 2.47
Merritt-Min 2.53

Adjusted ERA
Horlen-Chi 151
Siebert-Cle 137
Merritt-Min 137
Peters-Chi 136
Chance-Min 127

Opponents' Batting Avg.
Peters-Chi 199
Boswell-Min 202
Siebert-Cle 202
Horlen-Chi 203
Downing-NY 217

Opponents' On Base Pct.
Horlen-Chi 253
Merritt-Min 262
Siebert-Cle 268
John-Chi 277
Peters-Chi 277

Starter Runs
Horlen-Chi 33.6
Peters-Chi 27.3
Merritt-Min 17.7
Siebert-Cle 17.5
Chance-Min 15.8

Adjusted Starter Runs
Horlen-Chi 30.0
Peters-Chi 23.7
Merritt-Min 23.5
Chance-Min 23.0
Siebert-Cle 18.3

Clutch Pitching Index
Clark-Cal 121
Stottlemyre-NY ... 117
Kaat-Min 108
Tiant-Cle 107
Stange-Bos 105

Relief Runs
Wilhelm-Chi 18.9
Drabowsky-Bal ... 17.2
Locker-Chi 15.7
McMahon-Bos-Chi .. 15.2
Baldwin-Was 11.6

Adjusted Relief Runs
Wilhelm-Chi 17.7
Drabowsky-Bal 16.4
McMahon-Bos-Chi .. 14.5
Locker-Chi 14.0
Baldwin-Was 11.1

Relief Ranking
Wilhelm-Chi 25.1
Drabowsky-Bal 23.2
Wyatt-Bos 19.4
Rojas-Cal 17.3
Locker-Chi 17.2

Total Pitcher Index
Peters-Chi 3.7
Horlen-Chi 3.5
Drabowsky-Bal 3.0
Wilhelm-Chi 2.7
Chance-Min 2.4

Total Baseball Ranking
Yastrzemski-Bos ...7.3
Kaline-Det 5.2
B.Robinson-Bal 5.0
F.Robinson-Bal 4.8
Blair-Bal 4.1

TEAM	G	W	L	PCT	GB	R	OR	AB	H	2B	3B	HR	BB	SO	AVG	OBP	SLG	PRO	PRO+	BR	/A	PF	CHI	RC	SB	CS	SBA	SBR
STL	162	97	65	.599		583	472	5561	1383	227	48	73	378	897	.249	.300	.346	.646	102	2	9	99	104	581	110	45	71	6
SF	163	88	74	.543	9	599	529	5441	1301	162	33	108	508	904	.239	.310	.341	.651	103	20	21	100	103	577	50	37	57	-7
CHI	163	84	78	.519	13	612	611	5458	1319	203	43	130	415	854	.242	.300	.366	.666	100	36	-4	107	104	593	41	30	58	-6
CIN	163	83	79	.512	14	690	673	5767	1573	281	36	106	379	938	.273	.322	.389	.711	114	130	85	106	98	688	59	55	52	-15
ATL	163	81	81	.500	16	514	549	5552	1399	179	31	80	414	782	.252	.308	.339	.647	101	9	7	100	90	564	83	44	65	-2
PIT	163	80	82	.494	17	583	532	5569	1404	180	44	80	422	953	.252	.309	.343	.652	105	19	28	99	100	580	130	59	69	4
PHI	162	76	86	.469	21	543	615	5372	1253	178	30	100	462	1003	.233	.297	.333	.630	96	-24	-24	100	104	527	58	51	53	-13
LA	162	76	86	.469	21	470	509	5354	1234	202	36	67	439	980	.230	.291	.319	.610	97	-61	-25	92	97	501	57	43	57	-9
NY	163	73	89	.451	24	473	499	5503	1252	178	30	81	379	1203	.228	.283	.315	.598	86	-91	-93	101	102	486	72	45	62	-5
HOU	162	72	90	.444	25	510	588	5336	1233	205	28	66	479	988	.231	.300	.317	.617	94	-41	-31	98	100	505	44	51	46	-17
TOT	813					5577		54913	13351	1995	359	891	4275	9502	.243	.302	.341	.643							704	460	60	-65

TEAM	CG	SH	SV	IP	H	H/G	HR	BB	SO	RAT	ERA	ERA+	OAV	OOB	PR	/A	PF	CPI	FA	E	DP	FW	PW	BW	SBW	DIF
STL	63	30	32	1479¹	1282	7.8	82	375	971	10.3	2.49	116	.234	.286	82	67	97	105	.978	140	135	-.0	7.7	1.0	1.4	5.9
SF	77	20	16	1469	1302	8.0	86	344	942	10.2	2.71	109	.236	.283	45	38	99	96	.975	162	125	-1.3	4.4	2.4	-.0	1.6
CHI	46	12	32	1453²	1399	8.7	138	392	894	11.3	3.41	93	.254	.306	-69	-40	106	100	.981	119	149	1.2	-4.6	-.5	.0	6.8
CIN	24	16	38	1490¹	1399	8.4	114	573	963	12.2	3.56	89	.250	.324	-96	-66	106	100	.978	144	144	-.2	-7.6	9.8	-1.0	1.0
ATL	44	16	29	1474²	1326	8.1	87	362	871	10.5	2.92	103	.241	.292	11	13	100	96	.980	125	139	.9	1.5	.8	.5	-3.7
PIT	42	19	30	1487	1322	8.0	73	485	897	11.2	2.74	107	.240	.306	40	31	98	107	.979	139	162	.0	3.6	3.2	1.2	-9.0
PHI	42	12	27	1448¹	1416	8.8	91	421	935	11.1	3.36	89	.257	.315	-61	-57	101	100	.980	127	163	.7	-6.5	-2.8	-.7	4.3
LA	38	23	31	1448²	1293	8.0	65	414	994	10.8	2.69	103	.241	.300	48	12	93	100	.977	144	144	-.3	1.4	-2.9	-.3	-2.9
NY	45	25	32	1483¹	1250	7.6	87	430	1014	10.5	2.72	111	.230	.292	43	49	101	98	.979	133	142	.4	5.6	-10.7	.2	-3.5
HOU	50	12	23	1446²	1362	8.5	68	479	1021	11.7	3.26	91	.249	.313	-44	-49	99	96	.975	156	129	-1.0	-5.6	-3.6	-1.2	2.4
TOT	471	185	290	14681		8.2				11.0	2.99		.243	.302					.978	1389	1432					

Runs
Beckert-Chi	98
Rose-Cin	94
Perez-Cin	93
Brock-StL	92
Williams-Chi	91

Hits
Rose-Cin	210
Alou-Atl	210
Beckert-Chi	189
A.Johnson-Cin	188
Flood-StL	186

Doubles
Brock-StL	46
Rose-Cin	42
Bench-Hou	40
Staub-Hou	37
Alou-Atl	37

Triples
Brock-StL	14
Clemente-Pit	12
Davis-LA	10
Allen-Phi	9
Williams-Chi	8

Home Runs
McCovey-SF	36
Allen-Phi	33
Banks-Chi	32
Williams-Chi	30
H.Aaron-Atl	29

Total Bases
Williams-Chi	321
H.Aaron-Atl	302
Rose-Cin	294
Alou-Atl	290
McCovey-SF	285

Runs Batted In
McCovey-SF	105
Williams-Chi	98
Santo-Chi	98
Perez-Cin	92
Allen-Phi	90

Runs Produced
Perez-Cin	167
Williams-Chi	159
Santo-Chi	158
McCovey-SF	150
Allen-Phi	144

Bases On Balls
Santo-Chi	96
Wynn-Hou	90
Hunt-SF	78
Allen-Phi	74
Staub-Hou	73

Batting Average
Rose-Cin	.335
Alou-Pit	.332
Alou-Atl	.317
A.Johnson-Cin	.312
Flood-StL	.301

On Base Percentage
Rose-Cin	.394
McCovey-SF	.383
Wynn-Hou	.378
Mays-SF	.376
Staub-Hou	.376

Slugging Average
McCovey-SF	.545
Allen-Phi	.520
Williams-Chi	.500
H.Aaron-Atl	.498
Mays-SF	.488

Production
McCovey-SF	.928
Allen-Phi	.876
Mays-SF	.864
Rose-Cin	.863
H.Aaron-Atl	.855

Adjusted Production
McCovey-SF	176
Allen-Phi	160
Mays-SF	158
Wynn-Hou	158
H.Aaron-Atl	154

Batter Runs
McCovey-SF	48.8
Rose-Cin	44.5
H.Aaron-Atl	39.0
Wynn-Hou	38.4
Allen-Phi	38.0

Adjusted Batter Runs
McCovey-SF	48.9
Wynn-Hou	40.4
H.Aaron-Atl	38.7
Allen-Phi	38.0
Rose-Cin	37.8

Clutch Hitting Index
Hundley-Chi	134
Staub-Hou	123
Clendenon-Pit	122
Santo-Chi	117
Swoboda-NY	117

Runs Created
Rose-Cin	113
McCovey-SF	110
Williams-Chi	107
H.Aaron-Atl	104
Alou-Atl	103

Total Average
McCovey-SF	.953
Allen-Phi	.869
Mays-SF	.853
H.Aaron-Atl	.852
Wynn-Hou	.826

Stolen Bases
Brock-StL	62
Wills-Pit	52
Davis-LA	36
H.Aaron-Atl	28
Jones-NY	23

Stolen Base Average
H.Aaron-Atl	84.8
Brock-StL	83.8
Taylor-Phi	81.5
Davis-LA	78.3

Stolen Base Runs
Brock-StL	11.4
H.Aaron-Atl	5.4
Davis-LA	4.8
Taylor-Phi	3.6
Wills-Pit	3.0

Fielding Runs
Mazeroski-Pit	25.7
Alley-Pit	25.6
Kessinger-Chi	17.9
Flood-StL	17.5
Santo-Chi	17.3

Total Player Rating
H.Aaron-Atl	5.5
McCovey-SF	4.6
Wynn-Hou	4.5
Santo-Chi	4.0
Clemente-Pit	3.9

Wins
Marichal-SF	26
Gibson-StL	22
Jenkins-Chi	20

Win Percentage
Blass-Pit	.750
Marichal-SF	.743
Gibson-StL	.710
Briles-StL	.633

Games
Abernathy-Cin	78
Regan-LA-Chi	73
Carroll-Atl-Cin	68
Taylor-NY	58
Linzy-SF	57

Complete Games
Marichal-SF	30
Gibson-StL	28
Jenkins-Chi	20
Perry-SF	19
Koosman-NY	17

Shutouts
Gibson-StL	13
Drysdale-LA	8
Koosman-NY	7
Blass-Pit	7

Saves
Regan-LA-Chi	25
Carroll-Atl-Cin	17
Hoerner-StL	17
Brewer-LA	14

Innings Pitched
Marichal-SF	326.0
Jenkins-Chi	308.0
Gibson-StL	304.2
Perry-SF	291.0
Seaver-NY	277.2

Fewest Hits/Game
Gibson-StL	5.85
Bolin-SF	6.52
Veale-Pit	6.86
Jarvis-Atl	7.10
Moose-Pit	7.14

Fewest BB/Game
Hands-Chi	1.25
Marichal-SF	1.27
Seaver-NY	1.56
Pappas-Cin-Atl	1.57
Niekro-Atl	1.58

Strikeouts
Gibson-StL	268
Jenkins-Chi	260
Singer-LA	227
Marichal-SF	218
Sadecki-SF	206

Strikeouts/Game
Singer-LA	7.97
Gibson-StL	7.92
Maloney-Cin	7.87
Jenkins-Chi	7.60
Wilson-Hou	7.55

Ratio
Gibson-StL	7.89
Jarvis-Atl	8.93
Bolin-SF	9.07
Seaver-NY	9.08
Hands-Chi	9.15

Earned Run Average
Gibson-StL	1.12
Bolin-SF	1.99
Veale-Pit	2.05
Koosman-NY	2.08
Blass-Pit	2.12

Adjusted ERA
Gibson-StL	258
Bolin-SF	148
Koosman-NY	145
Veale-Pit	142
Blass-Pit	138

Opponents' Batting Avg.
Gibson-StL	.184
Bolin-SF	.200
Veale-Pit	.211
Jarvis-Atl	.214
Moose-Pit	.218

Opponents' On Base Pct.
Gibson-StL	.233
Jarvis-Atl	.255
Bolin-SF	.258
Seaver-NY	.262
Hands-Chi	.264

Starter Runs
Gibson-StL	63.1
Koosman-NY	26.5
Veale-Pit	25.4
Seaver-NY	24.1
Drysdale-LA	22.3

Adjusted Starter Runs
Gibson-StL	60.0
Koosman-NY	27.5
Seaver-NY	25.2
Veale-Pit	23.8
Blass-Pit	19.6

Clutch Pitching Index
Blass-Pit	125
Briles-StL	124
Koosman-NY	123
Lemaster-Hou	122
Drysdale-LA	117

Relief Runs
Kline-Pit	16.4
Regan-LA-Chi	10.7
Linzy-SF	9.4
Grant-LA	9.4
Abernathy-Cin	7.7

Adjusted Relief Runs
Kline-Pit	15.6
Regan-LA-Chi	13.0
Abernathy-Cin	10.3
Linzy-SF	9.0
Carroll-Atl-Cin	7.2

Relief Ranking
Kline-Pit	23.4
Regan-LA-Chi	20.1
Linzy-SF	17.0
Abernathy-Cin	13.9
Upshaw-Atl	9.6

Total Pitcher Index
Gibson-StL	7.3
Seaver-NY	3.1
Koosman-NY	3.0
Marichal-SF	2.7
Kline-Pit	2.4

Total Baseball Ranking
Gibson-StL	7.3
H.Aaron-Atl	5.5
McCovey-SF	4.6
Wynn-Hou	4.5
Santo-Chi	4.0

TEAM	G	W	L	PCT	GB	R	OR	AB	H	2B	3B	HR	BB	SO	AVG	OBP	SLG	PRO	PRO+	BR	/A	PF	CHI	RC	SB	CS	SBA	SBR
DET	164	103	59	.636		671	492	5490	1292	190	39	185	521	964	.235	.309	.385	.694	114	102	82	103	100	646	26	32	45	-11
BAL	162	91	71	.562	12	579	497	5275	1187	215	28	133	570	1019	.225	.306	.352	.658	106	41	40	100	97	585	78	32	71	4
CLE	162	86	75	.534	16.5	516	504	5416	1266	210	36	75	427	858	.234	.294	.327	.621	96	-34	-26	99	100	525	115	61	65	-2
BOS	162	86	76	.531	17	614	611	5303	1253	207	17	125	582	974	.236	.306	.352	.658	102	62	21	107	99	590	76	62	55	-14
NY	164	83	79	.512	20	536	531	5310	1137	154	34	109	566	958	.214	.293	.318	.611	99	-46	-30	97	106	507	90	50	64	-3
OAK	163	82	80	.506	21	569	544	5406	1300	192	40	94	472	1022	.240	.306	.343	.649	108	19	47	95	99	580	147	61	71	8
MIN	162	79	83	.488	24	562	546	5373	1274	207	41	105	445	966	.237	.301	.350	.651	99	20	-8	105	99	564	98	54	64	-3
CAL	162	67	95	.414	36	498	615	5331	1209	170	33	83	447	1080	.227	.293	.318	.611	96	-51	-33	96	100	498	62	50	55	-11
CHI	162	67	95	.414	36	463	527	5405	1233	169	33	71	397	840	.228	.286	.312	.597	86	-82	-87	101	99	480	90	50	64	-3
WAS	161	65	96	.404	37.5	524	665	5400	1208	160	37	124	454	960	.224	.289	.336	.625	99	-31	-14	97	101	518	29	19	60	-3
TOT	812					5532		53709	12359	1874	338	1104	4881	9641	.230	.299	.339	.639							811	471	63	-39

TEAM	CG	SH	SV	IP	H	H/G	HR	BB	SO	RAT	ERA	ERA+	OAV	OOB	PR	/A	PF	CPI	FA	E	DP	FW	PW	BW	SBW	DIF
DET	59	19	29	1489²	1180	7.1	129	486	1115	10.3	2.71	111	.217	.285	44	49	101	100	.983	105	133	2.0	5.6	9.4	-.8	5.8
BAL	53	16	31	1451¹	1111	6.9	101	502	1044	10.3	2.66	110	.212	.287	51	43	98	96	.981	120	131	1.0	4.9	4.6	.9	-1.5
CLE	48	23	32	1464¹	1087	6.7	98	540	1157	10.3	2.66	111	.206	.286	53	49	99	93	.979	127	130	.6	5.6	-3.0	.2	2.0
BOS	55	17	31	1447	1303	8.1	115	523	972	11.7	3.33	95	.241	.313	-57	-28	106	100	.979	128	147	.6	-3.2	2.4	-1.2	6.4
NY	45	14	27	1467¹	1308	8.0	99	424	831	10.8	2.79	104	.240	.298	31	18	97	108	.979	139	142	.0	2.1	-3.4	.1	3.3
OAK	45	18	29	1455²	1220	7.5	124	505	997	10.9	2.94	99	.227	.297	6	-20	95	101	.977	145	136	-.4	-2.3	5.4	1.4	-3.1
MIN	46	14	29	1433¹	1224	7.7	92	414	996	10.5	2.89	107	.229	.290	13	31	104	94	.973	170	117	-2.0	3.6	-.9	.1	-2.8
CAL	29	11	31	1437	1234	7.7	131	519	869	11.2	3.43	85	.233	.306	-72	-30	98	94	.977	140	156	-.2	-9.5	-3.8	-.8	.3
CHI	20	11	40	1468	1290	7.9	97	451	834	11.1	2.75	110	.236	.303	38	46	102	110	.977	151	152	-.8	5.3	-10.0	.1	-8.6
WAS	26	11	28	1439²	1402	8.8	118	517	826	12.3	3.64	80	.258	.327	-106	-116	98	104	.976	148	144	-.7	-13.3	-1.6	.1	.0
TOT	426	154	307	14553¹		7.6				10.9	2.98		.230	.299					.978	1373	1388					

Runs
McAuliffe-Det	95
Yastrzemski-Bos	90
White-NY	89
Tovar-Min	89
Stanley-Det	88

Hits
Campaneris-Oak	177
Tovar-Min	167
F.Howard-Was	164
Aparicio-Chi	164
Yastrzemski-Bos	162

Doubles
Smith-Bos	37
B.Robinson-Bal	36
Yastrzemski-Bos	32
Tovar-Min	31

Triples
Fregosi-Cal	13
McCraw-Chi	12
Stroud-Was	10
McAuliffe-Det	10
Campaneris-Oak	9

Home Runs
F.Howard-Was	44
Horton-Det	36
Harrelson-Bos	35
Jackson-Oak	29

Total Bases
F.Howard-Was	330
Horton-Det	278
Harrelson-Bos	277
Yastrzemski-Bos	267
Northrup-Det	259

Runs Batted In
Harrelson-Bos	109
F.Howard-Was	106
Northrup-Det	90
Powell-Bal	85
Horton-Det	85

Runs Produced
Harrelson-Bos	153
Northrup-Det	145
Yastrzemski-Bos	141
F.Howard-Was	141
Stanley-Det	137

Bases On Balls
Yastrzemski-Bos	119
Mantle-NY	106
Foy-Bos	84
McAuliffe-Det	82
Andrews-Bos	81

Batting Average
Yastrzemski-Bos	.301
Cater-Oak	.290
Oliva-Min	.289
Horton-Det	.285
Uhlaender-Min	.283

On Base Percentage
Yastrzemski-Bos	.429
F.Robinson-Bal	.391
Mantle-NY	.387
Monday-Oak	.373
Andrews-Bos	.369

Slugging Average
F.Howard-Was	.552
Horton-Det	.543
Harrelson-Bos	.518
Yastrzemski-Bos	.495
Oliva-Min	.477

Production
Yastrzemski-Bos	.924
Horton-Det	.900
F.Howard-Was	.892
Harrelson-Bos	.877
Oliva-Min	.837

Adjusted Production
F.Howard-Was	172
Yastrzemski-Bos	168
Horton-Det	165
Harrelson-Bos	153
F.Robinson-Bal	153

Batter Runs
Yastrzemski-Bos	57.5
F.Howard-Was	45.1
Horton-Det	41.1
Harrelson-Bos	40.2
Freehan-Det	32.7

Adjusted Batter Runs
Yastrzemski-Bos	49.9
F.Howard-Was	48.5
Horton-Det	38.3
Harrelson-Bos	34.0
Freehan-Det	30.0

Clutch Hitting Index
Foy-Bos	118
Cater-Oak	116
Powell-Bal	113
Tresh-NY	111
Harrelson-Bos	111

Runs Created
Yastrzemski-Bos	121
F.Howard-Was	110
Horton-Det	95
Harrelson-Bos	94
Freehan-Det	94

Total Average
Yastrzemski-Bos	1.000
F.Howard-Was	.872
Horton-Det	.867
F.Robinson-Bal	.865
Harrelson-Bos	.835

Stolen Bases
Campaneris-Oak	62
Cardenal-Cle	40
Tovar-Min	35
Buford-Bal	27
Foy-Bos	26

Stolen Base Average
McCraw-Chi	80.0
Nelson-Cle	76.7
Foy-Bos	76.5
Clarke-NY	74.1
Campaneris-Oak	73.8

Stolen Base Runs
Campaneris-Oak	5.4
McCraw-Chi	3.0
Foy-Bos	3.0
Tovar-Min	2.7
Nelson-Cle	2.7

Fielding Runs
Clarke-NY	29.5
Aparicio-Chi	24.7
Unser-Was	18.8
Yastrzemski-Bos	17.3
B.Robinson-Bal	16.6

Total Player Rating
Yastrzemski-Bos	6.6
Freehan-Det	4.8
F.Howard-Was	4.6
Campaneris-Oak	3.8
Aparicio-Chi	3.7

Wins
McLain-Det	31
McNally-Bal	22
Tiant-Cle	21
Stottlemyre-NY	21
Hardin-Bal	18

Win Percentage
McLain-Det	.838
Culp-Bos	.727
Tiant-Cle	.700
Ellsworth-Bos	.696
McNally-Bal	.688

Games
Wood-Chi	88
Wilhelm-Chi	72
Locker-Chi	70
Perranoski-Min	66

Complete Games
McLain-Det	28
Tiant-Cle	19
Stottlemyre-NY	19
McNally-Bal	18
Hardin-Bal	16

Shutouts
Tiant-Cle	9

Saves
Worthington-Min	18
Wood-Chi	16
Higgins-Was	13

Innings Pitched
McLain-Det	336.0
Chance-Min	292.0
Stottlemyre-NY	278.2
McNally-Bal	273.0
McDowell-Cle	269.0

Fewest Hits/Game
Tiant-Cle	5.30
McNally-Bal	5.77
McDowell-Cle	6.06
Siebert-Cle	6.33
McLain-Det	6.46

Fewest BB/Game
Peterson-NY	1.23
McLain-Det	1.69
Ellsworth-Bos	1.70
Kaat-Min	1.73
McNally-Bal	1.81

Strikeouts
McDowell-Cle	283
McLain-Det	280
Tiant-Cle	264
Chance-Min	234
McNally-Bal	202

Strikeouts/Game
McDowell-Cle	9.47
Tiant-Cle	9.20
Lolich-Det	8.06
Culp-Bos	7.90
McLain-Det	7.50

Ratio
McNally-Bal	7.91
Tiant-Cle	7.98
McLain-Det	8.30
Chance-Min	9.15
Peterson-NY	9.32

Earned Run Average
Tiant-Cle	1.60
McDowell-Cle	1.81
McNally-Bal	1.95
McLain-Det	1.96
John-Chi	1.98

Adjusted ERA
Tiant-Cle	185
McDowell-Cle	164
McLain-Det	154
John-Chi	153
McNally-Bal	150

Opponents' Batting Avg.
Tiant-Cle	.168
McNally-Bal	.182
McDowell-Cle	.189
Siebert-Cle	.198
McLain-Det	.200

Opponents' On Base Pct.
Tiant-Cle	.233
McNally-Bal	.234
McLain-Det	.243
Chance-Min	.261
Nash-Oak	.270

Starter Runs
Tiant-Cle	39.5
McLain-Det	38.2
McDowell-Cle	35.0
McNally-Bal	31.4
Bahnsen-NY	27.5

Adjusted Starter Runs
McLain-Det	39.3
Tiant-Cle	38.9
McDowell-Cle	34.4
McNally-Bal	29.7
Bahnsen-NY	25.2

Clutch Pitching Index
Horlen-Chi	133
John-Chi	119
Fisher-Chi	116
McDowell-Cle	113
Bahnsen-NY	111

Relief Runs
Wood-Chi	19.6
Wilhelm-Chi	13.0
Romo-Cle	12.6
McMahon-Chi-Det	9.0
Drabowsky-Bal	7.3

Adjusted Relief Runs
Wood-Chi	20.5
Wilhelm-Chi	13.5
Romo-Cle	12.4
McMahon-Chi-Det	9.4
Locker-Chi	7.4

Relief Ranking
Wood-Chi	33.6
Romo-Cle	14.7
Wilhelm-Chi	14.3
Drabowsky-Bal	9.9
Locker-Chi	8.5

Total Pitcher Index
McLain-Det	4.9
Tiant-Cle	4.2
McDowell-Cle	4.0
McNally-Bal	3.9
Wood-Chi	3.9

Total Baseball Ranking
Yastrzemski-Bos	6.6
McLain-Det	4.9
Freehan-Det	4.8
F.Howard-Was	4.6
Tiant-Cle	4.2

TEAM	G	W	L	PCT	GB	R	OR	AB	H	2B	3B	HR	BB	SO	AVG	OBP	SLG	PRO	PRO+	BR	/A	PF	CHI	RC	SB	CS	SBA	SBR
EAST																												
NY	162	100	62	.617		632	541	5427	1311	184	41	109	527	1089	.242	.313	.351	.664	91	-52	-65	102	**105**	601	66	43	61	-6
CHI	163	92	70	.568	8	720	611	5530	1400	215	40	142	559	928	.253	.326	.384	.710	94	37	-53	113	102	693	30	32	48	-10
PIT	162	88	74	.543	12	725	652	5626	1557	220	**52**	119	454	944	**.277**	.336	.398	.734	**115**	84	**100**	98	97	742	74	34	**69**	**2**
STL	162	87	75	.537	13	595	**540**	5536	1403	**228**	44	90	503	876	.253	.318	.359	.677	96	-25	-27	100	94	632	87	49	64	-3
PHI	162	63	99	.389	37	645	745	5408	1304	227	35	137	549	1130	.241	.314	.372	.686	102	-12	5	97	101	629	73	49	60	-8
MON	162	52	110	.321	48	582	791	5419	1300	202	33	125	529	962	.240	.312	.359	.671	94	-40	-42	100	96	596	52	52	50	-16
WEST																												
ATL	162	93	69	.574		691	631	5460	1411	195	22	141	485	**665**	.258	.323	.380	.703	104	20	18	100	103	655	59	48	55	-11
SF	162	90	72	.556	3	713	636	5474	1325	187	28	136	**711**	1054	.242	.336	.361	.697	104	32	45	98	100	690	71	32	**69**	**2**
CIN	163	89	73	.549	4	**798**	652	5634	**1558**	224	42	**171**	474	1042	**.277**	**.338**	**.422**	**.760**	114	**133**	92	105	99	**791**	79	56	59	-10
LA	162	85	77	.525	8	645	561	5532	1405	185	**52**	97	484	823	.254	.316	.359	.675	100	-31	13	93	103	626	80	51	61	-7
HOU	162	81	81	.500	12	676	668	5348	1284	208	40	104	699	972	.240	.332	.352	.684	101	7	20	98	101	649	**101**	58	64	-5
SD	162	52	110	.321	41	468	746	5357	1203	180	42	99	423	1143	.225	.286	.329	.615	81	-153	-134	96	98	491	45	44	51	-13
TOT	973					7890		65751	16461	2455	471	1470	6397	11628	.250	.321	.369	.690							817	548	60	-84

TEAM	CG	SH	SV	IP	H	H/G	HR	BB	SO	RAT	ERA	ERA+	OAV	OOB	PR	/A	PF	CPI	FA	E	DP	FW	PW	BW	SBW	DIF
EAST																										
NY	51	**28**	35	1468¹	**1217**	**7.5**	119	517	1012	**10.8**	2.99	**122**	**.227**	**.298**	99	109	102	99	.980	122	146	1.4	11.4	-6.8	.1	12.9
CHI	58	22	27	1454¹	1366	8.5	118	475	1017	11.6	3.34	120	.248	.311	41	**110**	112	101	.979	136	149	.6	**11.5**	-5.6	-.3	4.7
PIT	39	9	33	1445²	1348	8.4	96	553	1124	12.1	3.61	97	.248	.322	-3	-20	97	95	.975	155	169	-.5	-2.1	**10.5**	**.9**	-1.9
STL	63	12	26	1460¹	1289	7.9	99	511	1004	11.3	**2.94**	121	.237	.307	106	102	99	**105**	.978	138	144	.5	10.7	-2.8	.4	-2.8
PHI	47	14	21	1434	1494	9.4	134	570	921	13.2	4.14	86	.270	.342	-88	-96	99	102	.978	137	157	.5	-10.1	.5	-.1	-8.9
MON	26	8	21	1426	1429	9.0	145	702	973	13.8	4.33	85	.263	.353	-117	-104	102	102	.971	184	**179**	-2.1	-10.9	-4.4	-.9	-10.6
WEST																										
ATL	38	7	42	1445	1334	8.3	144	438	893	11.2	3.53	102	.245	.304	11	13	100	95	**.981**	115	114	**1.8**	1.4	1.9	-.4	7.4
SF	**71**	15	17	1473²	1381	8.4	120	461	906	11.5	3.26	108	.248	.309	55	40	97	102	.974	169	155	-1.3	4.2	4.7	**.9**	.4
CIN	23	11	**44**	1465	1478	9.1	149	611	818	13.2	4.11	92	.262	.340	-84	-57	105	102	.974	167	158	-1.1	-6.0	9.7	-.3	5.8
LA	47	20	31	1457	1324	8.2	122	**420**	975	11.0	3.08	108	.242	.301	83	39	93	102	.980	126	130	1.2	4.1	1.4	.0	-2.6
HOU	52	11	34	1435²	1347	8.4	111	547	**1221**	12.1	3.60	98	.247	.319	-1	-9	99	96	.975	153	136	-.4	-.9	2.1	.2	-1.0
SD	16	9	25	1422¹	1454	9.2	113	592	764	13.2	4.24	83	.267	.343	-102	-111	98	97	.975	156	140	-.5	-11.7	-14.1	-.6	-2.1
TOT	531	166	356	17387¹		8.5				12.1	3.59		.250	.321					.977	1758	1777					

Runs		Hits		Doubles		Triples		Home Runs		Total Bases	
Rose-Cin	120	Alou-Pit	231	Alou-Pit	41	Clemente-Pit	12	McCovey-SF	45	H.Aaron-Atl	332
Bonds-SF	120	Rose-Cin	218	Kessinger-Chi	38	Rose-Cin	11	H.Aaron-Atl	44	Perez-Cin	331
Wynn-Hou	113	Brock-StL	195	Williams-Chi	33	Williams-Chi	10	May-Cin	38	McCovey-SF	322
Kessinger-Chi	109	Tolan-Cin	194	Rose-Cin	33	Tolan-Cin	10	Perez-Cin	37	Rose-Cin	321
Alou-Pit	105	Williams-Chi	188	Brock-StL	33	Brock-StL	10	Wynn-Hou	33	May-Cin	321

Runs Batted In		Runs Produced		Bases On Balls		Batting Average		On Base Percentage		Slugging Average	
McCovey-SF	126	Santo-Chi	191	Wynn-Hou	148	Rose-Cin	.348	McCovey-SF	.458	McCovey-SF	.656
Santo-Chi	123	Perez-Cin	188	McCovey-SF	121	Clemente-Pit	.345	Wynn-Hou	.440	H.Aaron-Atl	.607
Perez-Cin	122	Rose-Cin	186	Staub-Mon	110	Jones-NY	.340	Rose-Cin	.432	Allen-Phi	.573
May-Cin	110	McCovey-SF	182	Morgan-Hou	110	Alou-Pit	.331	Staub-Mon	.427	Stargell-Pit	.556
Banks-Chi	106	Bonds-SF	178	Santo-Chi	96	McCovey-SF	.320	Jones-NY	.424	Clemente-Pit	.544

Production		Adjusted Production		Batter Runs		Adjusted Batter Runs		Clutch Hitting Index		Runs Created	
McCovey-SF	1.114	McCovey-SF	212	McCovey-SF	76.1	McCovey-SF	78.7	Menke-Hou	134	McCovey-SF	151
H.Aaron-Atl	1.005	H.Aaron-Atl	177	H.Aaron-Atl	56.3	H.Aaron-Atl	55.9	Rader-Hou	132	Rose-Cin	138
Clemente-Pit	.958	Clemente-Pit	170	Rose-Cin	56.0	Wynn-Hou	53.4	Banks-Chi	132	Staub-Mon	128
Staub-Mon	.953	Wynn-Hou	168	Staub-Mon	52.6	Staub-Mon	52.2	Santo-Chi	122	H.Aaron-Atl	128
Allen-Phi	.952	Allen-Phi	168	Wynn-Hou	51.0	Rose-Cin	49.3	D.Johnson-Phi	121	Wynn-Hou	126

Total Average		Stolen Bases		Stolen Base Average		Stolen Base Runs		Fielding Runs		Total Player Rating	
McCovey-SF	1.296	Brock-StL	53	Bonds-SF	91.8	Bonds-SF	11.1	Lanier-SF	28.6	McCovey-SF	6.3
Wynn-Hou	1.118	Morgan-Hou	49	Brock-StL	79.1	Brock-StL	7.5	Kessinger-Chi	24.6	Wynn-Hou	6.0
H.Aaron-Atl	1.032	Bonds-SF	45	Morgan-Hou	77.8	Morgan-Hou	6.3	Maxvill-StL	21.1	H.Aaron-Atl	5.2
Staub-Mon	1.018	Wills-Mon-LA	40	Wynn-Hou	76.7	Wynn-Hou	2.7	Grote-NY	19.3	Staub-Mon	5.0
Allen-Phi	.988	Tolan-Cin	26	Alou-Pit	73.3	Millan-Atl	2.4	Money-Phi	17.3	Clemente-Pit	4.9

Wins		Win Percentage		Games		Complete Games		Shutouts		Saves	
Seaver-NY	25	Seaver-NY	.781	Granger-Cin	90	Gibson-StL	28	Marichal-SF	8	Gladding-Hou	29
Niekro-Atl	23	Marichal-SF	.656	McGinn-Mon	74	Marichal-SF	27	Osteen-LA	7	Upshaw-Atl	27
Marichal-SF	21	Merritt-Cin	.654	Regan-Chi	71	Perry-SF	26	Jenkins-Chi	7	Granger-Cin	27
Jenkins-Chi	21	Koosman-NY	.654	Carroll-Cin	71	Jenkins-Chi	23	Koosman-NY	6	Brewer-LA	20
		Reed-Atl	.643	Reberger-SD	67	Niekro-Atl	21	Holtzman-Chi	6	Regan-Chi	17

Innings Pitched		Fewest Hits/Game		Fewest BB/Game		Strikeouts		Strikeouts/Game		Ratio	
Perry-SF	325.1	Seaver-NY	6.65	Marichal-SF	1.62	Jenkins-Chi	273	Griffin-Hou	9.56	Marichal-SF	9.13
Osteen-LA	321.0	Maloney-Cin	6.80	Niekro-Atl	1.80	Gibson-StL	269	Wilson-Hou	9.40	Dierker-Hou	9.23
Singer-LA	315.2	Singer-LA	6.96	Jenkins-Chi	2.05	Singer-LA	247	Moose-Pit	8.74	Singer-LA	9.35
Gibson-StL	314.0	Koosman-NY	6.98	Niekro-Chi-SD	2.07	Wilson-Hou	235	Selma-SD-Chi	8.54	Niekro-Atl	9.40
Jenkins-Chi	311.1	Carlton-StL	7.05	Osteen-LA	2.07	Perry-SF	233	Veale-Pit	8.49	Seaver-NY	9.58

Earned Run Average		Adjusted ERA		Opponents' Batting Avg.		Opponents' On Base Pct.		Starter Runs		Adjusted Starter Runs	
Marichal-SF	2.10	Marichal-SF	166	Seaver-NY	.207	Dierker-Hou	.262	Marichal-SF	49.6	Hands-Chi	51.1
Carlton-StL	2.17	Seaver-NY	166	Maloney-Cin	.208	Marichal-SF	.263	Gibson-StL	49.3	Gibson-StL	48.6
Gibson-StL	2.18	Carlton-StL	165	Singer-LA	.210	Singer-LA	.263	Singer-LA	44.0	Marichal-SF	46.5
Seaver-NY	2.21	Gibson-StL	164	Dierker-Hou	.214	Niekro-Atl	.264	Dierker-Hou	42.9	Seaver-NY	44.0
Koosman-NY	2.28	Hands-Chi	162	Carlton-StL	.216	Seaver-NY	.273	Seaver-NY	42.1	Dierker-Hou	41.1

Clutch Pitching Index		Relief Runs		Adjusted Relief Runs		Relief Ranking		Total Pitcher Index		Total Baseball Ranking	
Carlton-StL	122	McGraw-NY	15.1	McGraw-NY	15.7	McGraw-NY	21.2	Gibson-StL	6.0	McCovey-SF	6.3
Perry-SF	117	Granger-Cin	12.8	Granger-Cin	15.5	Granger-Cin	20.9	Seaver-NY	5.6	Gibson-StL	6.0
Veale-Pit	114	Brewer-LA	10.3	DiLauro-NY	8.8	Taylor-NY	15.1	Hands-Chi	5.5	Wynn-Hou	6.0
Robertson-Mon	113	Gibbon-SF-Pit	9.5	Gibbon-SF-Pit	8.7	Brewer-LA	14.0	Marichal-SF	5.4	Seaver-NY	5.6
Hands-Chi	111	DiLauro-NY	8.4	Upshaw-Atl	8.2	Gibbon-SF-Pit	13.9	Carlton-StL	4.9	Hands-Chi	5.5

TEAM	G	W	L	PCT	GB	R	OR	AB	H	2B	3B	HR	BB	SO	AVG	OBP	SLG	PRO	PRO+	BR	/A	PF	CHI	RC	SB	CS	SBA	SBR
EAST																												
BAL	162	109	53	.673		779	517	5518	1465	234	29	175	634	**806**	.265	**.346**	.414	**.760**	118	135	**128**	101	96	791	82	45	65	-2
DET	162	90	72	.556	19	701	601	5441	1316	188	29	182	578	922	.242	.318	.387	.705	99	17	-12	104	104	674	35	28	56	-6
BOS	162	87	75	.537	22	743	736	5494	1381	234	37	**197**	578	923	.251	.335	**.415**	.750	110	110	69	105	95	761	41	47	47	-16
WAS	162	86	76	.531	23	694	644	5447	1365	171	40	148	630	900	.251	.332	.378	.710	111	38	75	95	99	675	52	40	57	-8
NY	162	80	81	.497	28.5	562	587	5308	1247	210	**44**	94	565	840	.235	.310	.344	.654	92	-74	-53	96	99	572	119	74	62	-9
CLE	161	62	99	.385	46.5	573	717	5365	1272	173	24	119	535	906	.237	.309	.345	.654	86	-77	-96	103	101	568	85	37	70	3
WEST																												
MIN	162	97	65	.599		**790**	618	5677	**1520**	246	32	163	599	906	**.268**	.342	.408	.750	114	118	101	102	98	**794**	115	70	62	-8
OAK	162	88	74	.543	9	740	678	5614	1400	210	28	148	617	953	.249	.330	.376	.706	109	32	63	96	103	712	100	39	72	7
CAL	163	71	91	.438	26	528	652	5316	1221	151	29	88	516	929	.230	.302	.319	.621	84	-137	-112	95	**105**	518	54	39	58	-7
KC	163	69	93	.426	28	586	688	5462	1311	179	32	98	522	901	.240	.311	.338	.649	87	-84	-87	101	102	577	129	70	65	-3
CHI	162	68	94	.420	29	625	723	5450	1346	210	27	112	552	844	.247	.322	.357	.679	92	-25	-56	105	98	638	54	22	71	3
SEA	163	64	98	.395	33	639	799	5444	1276	179	27	125	626	1015	.234	.317	.346	.663	94	-53	-43	98	104	622	**167**	59	**74**	15
TOT	973					7960		65536	16120	2385	378	1649	7032	10845	.246	.323	.369	.693							1033	570	64	-32

TEAM	CG	SH	SV	IP	H	H/G	HR	BB	SO	RAT	ERA	ERA+	OAV	OOB	PR	/A	PF	CPI	FA	E	DP	FW	PW	BW	SBW	DIF
EAST																										
BAL	50	**20**	36	1473²	**1194**	7.3	117	498	897	10.5	2.83	126	.223	.291	130	121	98	97	**.984**	101	145	2.2	12.7	13.4	.0	-.4
DET	**55**	20	28	1455¹	1250	7.7	128	586	**1032**	11.6	3.31	113	.232	.312	50	67	103	98	.979	130	130	.5	7.0	-1.3	-.3	3.0
BOS	30	7	41	1466²	1423	8.7	155	685	935	13.2	3.92	97	.256	.343	-49	-19	105	106	.975	157	**178**	-1.0	-2.0	7.2	-1.4	3.2
WAS	28	10	41	1447¹	1310	8.1	135	656	835	12.4	3.49	99	.244	.330	22	-4	96	**107**	.978	140	159	-.0	-.4	7.9	-.6	-1.8
NY	53	13	20	1440²	1258	7.9	118	522	801	11.2	3.23	108	.236	.306	63	40	96	97	.979	131	158	.5	4.2	-5.6	-.7	1.0
CLE	35	7	22	1437	1330	8.3	134	681	1000	12.9	3.94	96	.248	.338	-51	-27	104	99	.976	145	153	-.4	-2.8	-10.1	.6	-5.8
WEST																										
MIN	41	8	**43**	1497²	1388	8.3	119	524	906	11.7	3.24	113	.246	.315	64	69	101	104	.977	150	177	-.6	7.2	10.6	-.6	-.7
OAK	42	14	36	1480²	1356	8.2	163	586	887	12.0	3.71	93	.245	.322	-15	-45	95	100	.979	136	162	.2	-4.7	6.6	1.0	3.9
CAL	25	9	39	1438¹	1294	8.1	126	517	885	11.7	3.54	98	.242	.315	13	-9	96	96	.978	136	164	.2	-.9	-11.7	-.5	2.9
KC	42	10	25	1464²	1357	8.3	136	560	894	11.9	3.72	99	.246	.319	-15	-5	102	95	.975	157	114	-1.0	-.5	-9.1	-.0	-1.4
CHI	29	10	25	1437²	1470	9.2	146	564	810	12.9	4.21	92	.267	.339	-93	-56	107	99	.981	122	163	1.0	-5.9	-5.9	.6	-2.8
SEA	21	6	33	1463²	1490	9.2	172	653	963	13.5	4.35	84	.264	.345	-118	-116	100	101	.974	167	149	-1.5	-12.2	-4.5	1.9	-.6
TOT	451	134	389	17503¹		8.3				12.1	3.62		.246	.323					.978	1672	1852					

Runs
Jackson-Oak 123
F.Robinson-Bal .. 111
Howard-Was...... 111
Killebrew-Min 106
Bando-Oak 106

Hits
Oliva-Min 197
Clarke-NY 183
Blair-Bal 178
Howard-Was 175
Horton-Cle 174

Doubles
Oliva-Min 39
Jackson-Oak 36
Johnson-Bal 34
Petrocelli-Bos 32
Blair-Bal 32

Triples
Unser-Was 8
Smith-Bos 7
Clarke-NY 7

Home Runs
Killebrew-Min 49
Howard-Was 48
Jackson-Oak 47
Yastrzemski-Bos .. 40
Petrocelli-Bos 40

Total Bases
Howard-Was 340
Jackson-Oak 334
Killebrew-Min 324
Oliva-Min 316
Petrocelli-Bos..... 315

Runs Batted In
Killebrew-Min 140
Powell-Bal 121
Jackson-Oak 118
Bando-Oak 113

Runs Produced
Killebrew-Min 197
Jackson-Oak 194
Bando-Oak 188
F.Robinson-Bal ... 179

Bases On Balls
Killebrew-Min 145
Jackson-Oak 114
Bando-Oak 111
Howard-Was 102
Yastrzemski-Bos .. 101

Batting Average
Carew-Min .... .332
Smith-Bos .... .309
Oliva-Min .... .309
F.Robinson-Bal ... .308
Powell-Bal .... .304

On Base Percentage
Killebrew-Min ..... .430
F.Robinson-Bal .. .417
Jackson-Oak ...... .410
Petrocelli-Bos .... .407
Howard-Was ...... .403

Slugging Average
Jackson-Oak ...... .608
Petrocelli-Bos .... .589
Killebrew-Min .... .584
Howard-Was ...... .574
Powell-Bal .... .559

Production
Jackson-Oak 1.019
Killebrew-Min 1.014
Petrocelli-Bos.....996
Howard-Was 978
F.Robinson-Bal ..957

Adjusted Production
Jackson-Oak 190
Howard-Was 180
Killebrew-Min 177
Petrocelli-Bos 167
F.Robinson-Bal ... 164

Batter Runs
Killebrew-Min 65.6
Jackson-Oak 62.0
Howard-Was 56.8
Petrocelli-Bos 54.8
F.Robinson-Bal ... 49.9

Adjusted Batter Runs
Jackson-Oak 67.9
Howard-Was 63.8
Killebrew-Min 62.6
F.Robinson-Bal ..48.8
Petrocelli-Bos 48.4

Clutch Hitting Index
White-NY 128
Cater-Oak 120
Bando-Oak 118
Foy-KC 116
T.Conigliaro-Bos ... 113

Runs Created
Killebrew-Min 146
Jackson-Oak 144
Howard-Was 132
Petrocelli-Bos 129
F.Robinson-Bal ... 126

Total Average
Killebrew-Min 1.143
Jackson-Oak 1.139
Petrocelli-Bos....1.048
F.Robinson-Bal ..1.026
Howard-Was......1.004

Stolen Bases
Harper-Sea 73
Campaneris-Oak ... 62
Tovar-Min 45
Kelly-KC 40
Foy-KC 37

Stolen Base Average
Campaneris-Oak ... 88.6
Alomar-Chi-Cal ... 87.0
Cardenal-Cle 85.7
Aparicio-Chi 85.7
Davis-Sea 82.6

Stolen Base Runs
Campaneris-Oak ...13.8
Harper-Sea 11.1
Cardenal-Cle 7.2
Tovar-Min 6.3
Aparicio-Chi 4.8

Fielding Runs
Cardenas-Min 33.5
Aparicio-Chi 29.3
Blair-Bal 24.8
Knoop-Cal-Chi 24.5
Quilici-Min 24.2

Total Player Rating
Petrocelli-Bos 6.9
Jackson-Oak 6.6
Cardenas-Min 5.6
Aparicio-Chi 5.1
F.Robinson-Bal ... 4.2

Wins
McLain-Det........ 24
Cuellar-Bal 23

Win Percentage
Palmer-Bal .... .800
Perry-Min .... .769
McNally-Bal....... .741
McLain-Det .... .727
Odom-Oak .... .714

Games
Wood-Chi 76
Perranoski-Min 75
Lyle-Bos 71
Locker-Chi-Sea ... 68
Segui-Sea 66

Complete Games
Stottlemyre-NY 24
McLain-Det 23
McDowell-Cle 18
Cuellar-Bal 18
Peterson-NY 16

Shutouts
McLain-Det 9
Palmer-Bal 6
Cuellar-Bal 5

Saves
Perranoski-Min 31
K.Tatum-Cal 22
Lyle-Bos 17
Watt-Bal 16
Higgins-Was 16

Innings Pitched
McLain-Det 325.0
Stottlemyre-NY ..303.0
Cuellar-Bal 290.2
McDowell-Cle 285.0
Lolich-Det 280.2

Fewest Hits/Game
Messersmith-Cal .. 6.08
Palmer-Bal 6.51
Cuellar-Bal 6.60
Lolich-Det 6.86
Odom-Oak 6.96

Fewest BB/Game
Peterson-NY 1.42
Bosman-Was 1.82
McLain-Det 1.86
Perry-Min 2.27
Cuellar-Bal 2.45

Strikeouts
McDowell-Cle 279
Lolich-Det 271
Messersmith-Cal .. 211
Boswell-Min 190

Strikeouts/Game
McDowell-Cle 8.81
Lolich-Det 8.69
Messersmith-Cal .. 7.60
Butler-KC 7.25
Williams-Cle 7.01

Ratio
Peterson-NY 9.07
Cuellar-Bal 9.07
Bosman-Was 9.19
Palmer-Bal 9.75
Messersmith-Cal .. 9.86

Earned Run Average
Bosman-Was 2.19
Palmer-Bal 2.34
Cuellar-Bal 2.38
Messersmith-Cal .. 2.52
Peterson-NY 2.55

Adjusted ERA
Bosman-Was 158
Palmer-Bal 153
Cuellar-Bal 150
Messersmith-Cal .. 138
Peterson-NY 136

Opponents' Batting Avg.
Messersmith-Cal ..190
Palmer-Bal .... .200
Cuellar-Bal .... .204
Lolich-Det .... .210
McDowell-Cle .... .213

Opponents' On Base Pct.
Cuellar-Bal .... .261
Bosman-Was ...... .262
Peterson-NY ...... .263
Palmer-Bal .... .272
Messersmith-Cal ..276

Starter Runs
Cuellar-Bal 40.0
Peterson-NY 32.5
Bosman-Was 30.7
Messersmith-Cal .. 30.6
McLain-Det 29.8

Adjusted Starter Runs
Cuellar-Bal 38.1
McLain-Det 33.7
Peterson-NY 28.1
Bosman-Was 27.3
Messersmith-Cal .. 26.8

Clutch Pitching Index
Cox-Was 128
Nagy-Bos 119
Tiant-Cle 118
John-Chi 114
Wilson-Det 112

Relief Runs
K.Tatum-Cal 21.7
Perranoski-Min ... 20.2
Watt-Bal 15.6
Roland-Oak 13.7
Knowles-Was 12.9

Adjusted Relief Runs
Perranoski-Min ... 20.6
K.Tatum-Cal 20.4
Watt-Bal 15.1
Lyle-Bos 14.4
Hall-Bal 12.0

Relief Ranking
Perranoski-Min ...41.3
K.Tatum-Cal 30.9
Watt-Bal 21.1
Wood-Chi 21.0
Lyle-Bos 19.2

Total Pitcher Index
Perranoski-Min 4.4
Cuellar-Bal 4.1
Stottlemyre-NY 3.8
K.Tatum-Cal 3.8
Peterson-NY 3.7

Total Baseball Ranking
Petrocelli-Bos 6.9
Jackson-Oak 6.6
Cardenas-Min 5.6
Aparicio-Chi 5.1
Perranoski-Min ... 4.4

TEAM	G	W	L	PCT	GB	R	OR	AB	H	2B	3B	HR	BB	SO	AVG	OBP	SLG	PRO	PRO+	BR	/A	PF	CHI	RC	SB	CS	SBA	SBR
EAST																												
PIT	162	89	73	.549		729	664	5637	**1522**	235	**70**	130	444	871	**.270**	.328	.406	.734	105	12	28	98	99	740	66	34	66	-1
CHI	162	84	78	.519	5	806	679	5491	1424	228	44	179	607	844	.259	.335	.415	.750	95	49	-44	112	**104**	773	39	16	71	2
NY	162	83	79	.512	6	695	**630**	5443	1358	211	42	120	684	1062	.249	.336	.370	.706	96	-23	-24	100	98	689	118	54	69	3
STL	162	76	86	.469	13	744	747	5689	1497	218	51	113	569	961	.263	.333	.379	.712	95	-20	-35	102	103	719	117	47	71	7
PHI	161	73	88	.453	15.5	594	730	5456	1299	224	58	101	519	1066	.238	.307	.356	.663	85	-125	-109	97	101	582	72	64	53	-17
MON	162	73	89	.451	16	687	807	5411	1284	211	35	136	659	972	.237	.324	.365	.689	91	-62	-61	100	103	658	65	45	59	-8
WEST																												
CIN	162	102	60	.630		775	681	5540	1498	253	45	**191**	547	984	**.270**	.339	**.436**	.775	**113**	94	92	100	94	814	115	52	69	3
LA	161	87	74	.540	14.5	749	684	5606	1515	233	67	87	541	841	**.270**	.337	.382	.719	104	-4	28	96	102	730	**138**	57	71	7
SF	162	86	76	.531	16	**831**	826	5578	1460	257	35	165	**729**	1005	.262	**.353**	.409	.762	112	92	**102**	99	98	**821**	83	27	**75**	9
HOU	162	79	83	.488	23	744	763	5574	1446	250	47	129	598	911	.259	.334	.391	.725	104	5	36	96	100	728	114	41	74	**10**
ATL	162	76	86	.469	26	736	772	5546	1495	215	24	160	522	**736**	**.270**	.337	.404	.741	99	32	-13	106	97	742	58	34	63	-3
SD	162	63	99	.389	39	681	788	5494	1353	208	36	172	500	1164	.246	.314	.391	.705	98	-49	-22	96	102	669	60	45	57	-9
TOT	971					8771		66465	17151	2743	554	1683	6919	11417	.258	.332	.392	.724						1045	516	67	4	

TEAM	CG	SH	SV	IP	H	H/G	HR	BB	SO	RAT	ERA	ERA+	OAV	OOB	PR	/A	PF	CPI	FA	E	DP	FW	PW	BW	SBW	DIF
EAST																										
PIT	36	13	43	1453²	1386	8.6	106	625	990	12.7	3.70	106	.255	.336	56	33	96	**106**	.979	137	**195**	.3	3.3	2.8	-.1	1.8
CHI	**59**	9	25	1435	1402	8.6	143	**475**	1000	11.9	3.76	**120**	.256	.318	46	**118**	111	101	.978	137	146	.3	**11.8**	-4.4	.2	-4.8
NY	47	10	32	1459²	**1260**	**7.8**	135	575	**1064**	**11.5**	**3.45**	117	**.233**	**.310**	**97**	93	99	98	.979	124	136	1.0	9.3	-2.4	.3	-6.2
STL	51	11	20	1475²	1483	9.0	**102**	632	960	13.0	4.06	101	.263	.340	-2	10	102	100	.977	150	159	-.4	1.0	-3.5	.7	-2.8
PHI	24	8	36	1461	1483	9.1	132	538	1047	12.7	4.17	96	.265	.333	-20	-29	99	98	**.981**	114	134	**1.5**	-2.9	-10.9	-1.7	6.5
MON	29	10	32	1438²	1434	9.0	162	716	914	13.8	4.50	91	.261	.351	-73	-63	102	101	.977	141	193	.0	-6.3	-6.1	-.8	5.1
WEST																										
CIN	32	15	**60**	1444²	1370	8.5	118	592	843	12.4	3.69	109	.251	.327	57	55	100	102	.976	151	173	-.5	5.5	9.2	.3	6.6
LA	37	**17**	42	1458²	1394	8.6	164	496	880	11.9	3.82	100	.250	.316	37	2	95	99	.978	135	135	.4	.2	2.8	.7	2.5
SF	50	7	30	1457²	1514	9.3	156	604	931	13.3	4.50	88	.267	.341	-74	-86	98	98	.973	170	153	-1.5	-8.6	**10.2**	.9	4.1
HOU	36	6	35	1456	1491	9.2	131	577	942	13.0	4.23	92	.265	.338	-30	-58	96	99	.978	140	144	.1	-5.8	3.6	**1.0**	-.9
ATL	45	9	24	1430²	1451	9.1	185	478	960	12.3	4.33	99	.261	.322	-45	-6	106	96	.977	141	118	.0	-.6	-1.3	-.3	-2.9
SD	24	9	32	1440¹	1483	9.3	149	611	886	13.3	4.36	91	.267	.344	-50	-61	98	102	.975	158	159	-.9	-6.1	-2.2	-.9	-7.9
TOT	470	124	411	17411²		8.9				12.6	4.05		.258	.332					.977	1698	1845					

Runs
Williams-Chi 137
Bonds-SF 134
Rose-Cin 120
Brock-StL 114
Tolan-Cin 112

Hits
Williams-Chi 205
Rose-Cin 205
Torre-StL 203
Brock-StL 202
Alou-Pit 201

Doubles
Parker-LA 47
McCovey-SF 39
Rose-Cin 37
Dietz-SF 36
Bonds-SF 36

Triples
Davis-LA 16
Kessinger-Chi 14
Clemente-Pit 10
Bonds-SF 10

Home Runs
Bench-Cin 45
Williams-Chi 42
Perez-Cin 40
McCovey-SF 39

Total Bases
Williams-Chi 373
Bench-Cin 355
Perez-Cin 346
Bonds-SF 334
Gaston-SD 317

Runs Batted In
Bench-Cin 148
Williams-Chi 129
Perez-Cin 129
McCovey-SF 126
H.Aaron-Atl 118

Runs Produced
Williams-Chi 224
Bench-Cin 200
Perez-Cin 196
Bonds-SF 186

Bases On Balls
McCovey-SF 137
Staub-Mon 112
Dietz-SF 109
Wynn-Hou 106
Morgan-Hou 102

Batting Average
Carty-Atl 366
Torre-StL 325
Sanguillen-Pit 325
Williams-Chi 322
Parker-LA 319

On Base Percentage
Carty-Atl 456
McCovey-SF 446
Dietz-SF 430
Hickman-Chi 421
Perez-Cin 405

Slugging Average
McCovey-SF 612
Perez-Cin 589
Bench-Cin 587
Williams-Chi 586
Carty-Atl 584

Production
McCovey-SF 1.058
Carty-Atl 1.040
Hickman-Chi 1.003
Perez-Cin 994
Williams-Chi 979

Adjusted Production
McCovey-SF 183
Carty-Atl 167
Perez-Cin 162
Dietz-SF 154
Hickman-Chi 148

Batter Runs
McCovey-SF 62.0
Carty-Atl 54.4
Perez-Cin 52.1
Williams-Chi 51.1
Hickman-Chi 49.5

Adjusted Batter Runs
McCovey-SF 63.6
Perez-Cin 51.7
Carty-Atl 47.5
Dietz-SF 42.2
Carbo-Cin 40.2

Clutch Hitting Index
Parker-LA 126
Dietz-SF 122
Wine-Mon 118
Santo-Chi 117
Davis-LA 115

Runs Created
Williams-Chi 147
McCovey-SF 140
Perez-Cin 140
Bonds-SF 134
Hickman-Chi 129

Total Average
McCovey-SF 1.214
Carty-Atl 1.102
Hickman-Chi 1.080
Perez-Cin 1.045
Williams-Chi 1.018

Stolen Bases
Tolan-Cin 57
Brock-StL 51
Bonds-SF 48
Morgan-Hou 42
Davis-LA 38

Stolen Base Average
Henderson-SF 87.0
Harrelson-NY 85.2
Wynn-Hou 82.8
Bonds-SF 82.8
Cedeno-Hou 81.0

Stolen Base Runs
Bonds-SF 8.4
Brock-StL 6.3
Tolan-Cin 5.1
Morgan-Hou 4.8
Harrelson-NY 4.5

Fielding Runs
Maxvill-StL 37.5
Alley-Pit 33.7
Mazeroski-Pit 23.9
Rader-Hou 23.8
Wine-Mon 19.7

Total Player Rating
McCovey-SF 6.2
Bench-Cin 4.5
Perez-Cin 4.3
Wynn-Hou 4.2
Carty-Atl 4.2

Wins
Perry-SF 23
Gibson-StL 23
Jenkins-Chi 22
Merritt-Cin 20

Win Percentage
Gibson-StL 767
Nolan-Cin 720
Walker-Pit 714
Perry-SF 639
Merritt-Cin 625

Games
Herbel-SD-NY 76
Selma-Phi 73
Linzy-SF-StL 67
Granger-Cin 67
Giusti-Pit 66

Complete Games
Jenkins-Chi 24
Perry-SF 23
Gibson-StL 23
Seaver-NY 19
Dierker-Hou 17

Shutouts
Perry-SF 5
Sutton-LA 4
Osteen-LA 4
Morton-Mon 4
Ellis-Pit 4

Saves
Granger-Cin 35
Giusti-Pit 26
Brewer-LA 24
Raymond-Mon 23
Selma-Phi 22

Innings Pitched
Perry-SF 328.2
Jenkins-Chi 313.0
Gibson-StL 294.0
Seaver-NY 290.2
Holtzman-Chi 287.2

Fewest Hits/Game
Simpson-Cin 6.39
Seaver-NY 7.12
Walker-Pit 7.12
Gentry-NY 7.41
Jenkins-Chi 7.62

Fewest BB/Game
Jenkins-Chi 1.73
Marichal-SF 1.78
Osteen-LA 1.81
McAndrew-NY 1.86
Merritt-Cin 2.04

Strikeouts
Seaver-NY 283
Jenkins-Chi 274
Gibson-StL 274
Perry-SF 214
Holtzman-Chi 202

Strikeouts/Game
Seaver-NY 8.76
Gibson-StL 8.39
Veale-Pit 7.93
Jenkins-Chi 7.88
Stoneman-Mon 7.63

Ratio
Jenkins-Chi 9.55
Seaver-NY 9.82
McAndrew-NY 10.06
Perry-SF 10.52
Gibson-StL 10.84

Earned Run Average
Seaver-NY 2.82
Simpson-Cin 3.02
Walker-Pit 3.04
Gibson-StL 3.12
Koosman-NY 3.14

Adjusted ERA
Seaver-NY 143
Simpson-Cin 134
Pappas-Atl-Chi 133
Holtzman-Chi 133
Jenkins-Chi 133

Opponents' Batting Avg.
Simpson-Cin 198
Seaver-NY 214
Walker-Pit 219
Jenkins-Chi 224
Gentry-NY 224

Opponents' On Base Pct.
Jenkins-Chi 265
Seaver-NY 273
McAndrew-NY 281
Perry-SF 290
Gibson-StL 296

Starter Runs
Seaver-NY 39.7
Perry-SF 30.7
Gibson-StL 30.2
Jenkins-Chi 22.7
Nolan-Cin 21.7

Adjusted Starter Runs
Seaver-NY 38.9
Jenkins-Chi 38.5
Holtzman-Chi 35.8
Gibson-StL 32.4
Perry-SF 28.1

Clutch Pitching Index
Ellis-Pit 119
Morton-Mon 118
Coombs-SD 113
Pappas-Atl-Chi . . . 109
Dobson-SD 108

Relief Runs
Selma-Phi 19.4
Carroll-Cin 16.9
Gullett-Cin 13.9
Granger-Cin 13.1
C.Taylor-StL 12.9

Adjusted Relief Runs
Selma-Phi 18.5
Carroll-Cin 16.8
C.Taylor-StL 13.8
Gullett-Cin 13.8
Granger-Cin 12.9

Relief Ranking
Selma-Phi 27.9
Granger-Cin 27.2
Carroll-Cin 24.6
Hoerner-Phi 21.7
McMahon-SF 19.0

Total Pitcher Index
Seaver-NY 4.5
Gibson-StL 4.2
Jenkins-Chi 4.0
Holtzman-Chi 3.4
Selma-Phi 3.1

Total Baseball Ranking
McCovey-SF 6.2
Seaver-NY 4.5
Bench-Cin 4.5
Perez-Cin 4.3
Gibson-StL 4.2

TEAM	G	W	L	PCT	GB	R	OR	AB	H	2B	3B	HR	BB	SO	AVG	OBP	SLG	PRO	PRO+	BR	/A	PF	CHI	RC	SB	CS	SBA	SBR
EAST																												
BAL	162	108	54	.667		**792**	**574**	5545	1424	213	25	179	717	952	.257	**.346**	.401	.747	112	101	**92**	101	99	795	84	39	68	2
NY	163	93	69	.574	15	680	612	5492	1381	208	**41**	111	588	**808**	.251	.327	.365	.692	102	-18	16	95	103	662	105	61	63	-5
BOS	162	87	75	.537	21	786	722	5535	**1450**	**252**	28	**203**	594	855	**.262**	.338	**.428**	**.766**	109	**119**	63	107	98	786	50	48	51	-14
DET	162	79	83	.488	29	666	731	5377	1282	207	38	148	592	825	.238	.325	.374	.699	98	-4	-9	101	99	658	29	30	49	-9
CLE	162	76	86	.469	32	649	675	5463	1358	197	23	183	503	909	.249	.316	.394	.710	96	3	-30	105	97	670	25	36	41	-14
WAS	162	70	92	.432	38	626	689	5460	1302	184	28	138	635	989	.238	.323	.358	.681	99	-36	-5	95	97	638	72	42	63	-4
WEST																												
MIN	162	98	64	.605		744	605	5483	1438	230	**41**	153	501	905	**.262**	.329	.403	.732	107	50	40	101	103	709	57	52	52	-14
OAK	162	89	73	.549	9	678	593	5376	1338	208	24	171	584	977	.249	.327	.392	.719	108	28	53	96	98	689	**131**	68	66	-2
CAL	162	86	76	.531	12	631	630	5532	1391	197	40	114	447	922	.251	.311	.363	.674	95	-64	-43	97	104	622	69	27	**72**	5
MIL	162	65	97	.401	33	613	751	5395	1305	202	24	126	592	985	.242	.321	.358	.679	92	-42	-46	101	97	618	91	73	55	-17
KC	162	65	97	.401	33	611	705	5503	1341	202	**41**	97	514	958	.244	.311	.348	.659	88	-88	-87	100	105	593	97	53	65	-3
CHI	162	56	106	.346	42	633	822	5514	1394	192	20	123	477	872	.253	.317	.362	.679	90	-50	-74	104	102	627	53	33	62	-4
TOT	973					8109		65675	16404	2492	373	1746	6808	10957	.250	.324	.379	.703							863	562	61	-78

TEAM	CG	SH	SV	IP	H	H/G	HR	BB	SO	RAT	ERA	ERA+	OAV	OOB	PR	/A	PF	CPI	FA	E	DP	FW	PW	BW	SBW	DIF
EAST																										
BAL	60	12	31	1478²	1317	8.0	139	469	941	11.0	3.15	116	.240	**.302**	93	82	98	102	.981	117	148	1.1	8.5	9.5	.9	7.0
NY	36	6	49	1471²	1386	8.5	**130**	**451**	777	11.4	3.24	108	.249	.308	77	45	95	103	.980	130	146	.4	4.7	1.7	.2	5.1
BOS	38	8	44	1446¹	1391	8.7	156	594	1003	12.6	3.87	102	.251	.329	-25	14	107	100	.974	156	131	-1.2	1.5	6.5	-.8	-.0
DET	33	9	39	1447¹	1443	9.0	153	623	1045	13.1	4.09	91	.260	.338	-61	-59	100	100	.978	133	142	.2	-6.1	-.9	-.3	5.2
CLE	34	8	35	1451¹	1333	8.3	163	689	**1076**	12.8	3.91	101	.247	.337	-31	8	107	103	.979	133	168	.2	.8	-3.1	-.8	-2.1
WAS	20	11	40	1457²	1375	8.5	139	611	823	12.4	3.80	94	.252	.330	-13	-39	96	100	**.982**	116	173	1.1	-4.0	-.5	.3	-7.8
WEST																										
MIN	26	12	**58**	1448¹	1329	8.3	**130**	486	940	11.5	3.23	115	.244	.310	78	79	100	103	.980	123	130	.7	8.2	4.1	-.8	4.7
OAK	33	**15**	40	1442²	**1253**	**7.8**	134	542	858	11.4	3.30	107	**.234**	.308	66	38	95	98	.977	141	152	-.3	3.9	5.5	.5	-1.6
CAL	21	10	49	1462¹	1280	7.9	154	559	922	11.6	3.48	104	.237	.313	37	21	97	99	.980	127	169	.5	2.2	-4.5	**1.2**	5.6
MIL	31	2	27	1446²	1397	8.7	146	587	895	12.6	4.21	90	.255	.332	-79	-67	102	93	.978	136	142	.0	-6.9	-4.8	-1.1	-3.2
KC	30	11	25	1463²	1346	8.3	138	641	915	12.4	3.78	99	.247	.331	-11	-7	101	99	.976	152	162	-.9	-.7	-9.0	.4	-5.7
CHI	20	6	30	1430¹	1554	9.8	164	556	762	13.6	4.54	86	.280	.350	-132	-103	105	101	.975	165	**187**	-1.7	-10.7	-7.7	.3	-5.2
TOT	382	110	467	17447		8.5				12.2	3.71		.250	.324					.978	1629	1850					

Runs	Hits	Doubles	Triples	Home Runs	Total Bases
Yastrzemski-Bos .. 125	Oliva-Min 204	Tovar-Min 36	Tovar-Min 13	Howard-Was 44	Yastrzemski-Bos ... 335
Tovar-Min 120	Johnson-Cal 202	Otis-KC 36	Stanley-Det 11	Killebrew-Min 41	Oliva-Min 323
White-NY 109	Tovar-Min 195	Oliva-Min 36	Otis-KC 9	Yastrzemski-Bos ... 40	Harper-Mil 315
Smith-Bos 109	Yastrzemski-Bos ... 186	Harper-Mil 35		T.Conigliaro-Bos ... 36	Howard-Was 309
Harper-Mil 104	White-NY 180	Cardenas-Min 34		Powell-Bal 35	Powell-Bal 289

Runs Batted In	Runs Produced	Bases On Balls	Batting Average	On Base Percentage	Slugging Average
Howard-Was 126	Yastrzemski-Bos ... 187	Howard-Was 132	Johnson-Cal 329	Yastrzemski-Bos ...453	Yastrzemski-Bos ...592
T.Conigliaro-Bos ... 116	White-NY 181	Yastrzemski-Bos .. 128	Yastrzemski-Bos ..329	Howard-Was 420	Powell-Bal 549
Powell-Bal 114	Oliva-Min 180	Killebrew-Min 128	Oliva-Min.........325	Powell-Bal 417	Killebrew-Min 546
Killebrew-Min 113	Howard-Was 172	Bando-Oak 118	Aparicio-Chi 313	Killebrew-Min 416	Howard-Was 546
Oliva-Min 107	T.Conigliaro-Bos ... 169	Buford-Bal 109	F.Robinson-Bal 306	Buford-Bal 409	Harper-Mil 522

Production	Adjusted Production	Batter Runs	Adjusted Batter Runs	Clutch Hitting Index	Runs Created
Yastrzemski-Bos .1.045	Yastrzemski-Bos ...174	Yastrzemski-Bos ..71.7	Yastrzemski-Bos ..61.7	Piniella-KC 128	Yastrzemski-Bos ...157
Powell-Bal 967	Howard-Was 173	Howard-Was 54.1	Howard-Was......60.5	Cater-NY 117	Howard-Was 130
Howard-Was.......966	Powell-Bal.......163	Killebrew-Min 49.5	Powell-Bal.......47.9	McMullen-Was-Cal 116	Powell-Bal 123
Killebrew-Min 962	Killebrew-Min 161	Powell-Bal 49.2	Killebrew-Min 47.8	Howard-Was 116	Harper-Mil 122
F.Robinson-Bal ...922	F.Robinson-Bal 151	Harper-Mil 37.5	White-NY 38.2	Belanger-Bal 115	Killebrew-Min 116

Total Average	Stolen Bases	Stolen Base Average	Stolen Base Runs	Fielding Runs	Total Player Rating
Yastrzemski-Bos .1.170	Campaneris-Oak ... 42	Otis-KC 94.3	Otis-KC 8.7	Knoop-Chi 35.1	Yastrzemski-Bos .. 5.2
Powell-Bal 1.034	Harper-Mil 38	Johnson-Cal 89.5	Campaneris-Oak ...6.6	Brinkman-Was 31.1	Aparicio-Chi 4.6
Howard-Was.....1.026	Alomar-Cal 35	Campaneris-Oak ... 80.8	Stroud-Was........3.9	Nettles-Cle....... 27.8	Oliva-Min 4.3
Killebrew-Min ...1.000	Kelly-KC 34	Stroud-Was 78.4	Johnson-Cal 3.9	Cullen-Was 26.5	Fregosi-Cal 4.2
F.Robinson-Bal ...944	Otis-KC 33	Kenney-NY 76.9	Alomar-Cal 3.3	Mitterwald-Min ... 24.3	Howard-Was 4.2

Wins	Win Percentage	Games	Complete Games	Shutouts	Saves
Perry-Min 24	Cuellar-Bal 750	Wood-Chi......... 77	Cuellar-Bal 21	Palmer-Bal 5	Perranoski-Min ... 34
McNally-Bal 24	McNally-Bal 727	Grant-Oak 72	McDowell-Cle 19	Dobson-Oak 5	McDaniel-NY 29
Cuellar-Bal 24	Perry-Min........667	Knowles-Was 71	Palmer-Bal 17	Peters-Bos 4	Timmermann-Det ... 27
Wright-Cal 22	Palmer-Bal 667	Williams-Min 68	McNally-Bal 16	Perry-Min 4	Knowles-Was 27
	Siebert-Bos 652		Culp-Bos 15	Cuellar-Bal 4	Grant-Oak 24

Innings Pitched	Fewest Hits/Game	Fewest BB/Game	Strikeouts	Strikeouts/Game	Ratio
Palmer-Bal 305.0	Messersmith-Cal . 6.66	Peterson-NY 1.38	McDowell-Cle ... 304	McDowell-Cle ... 8.97	Peterson-NY 10.03
McDowell-Cle ...305.0	McDowell-Cle ... 6.96	Perry-Min 1.84	Lolich-Det 230	Johnson-KC 8.66	Cuellar-Bal 10.37
Cuellar-Bal 297.2	Segui-Oak 7.22	Cox-Was 2.06	Johnson-KC 206	Cain-Det 7.77	Perry-Min 10.46
McNally-Bal 296.0	Johnson-KC 7.49	Cuellar-Bal 2.09	Palmer-Bal 199	Lolich-Det 7.59	Blyleven-Min 10.54
Perry-Min 278.2	Culp-Bos 7.56	Horlen-Chi 2.14	Culp-Bos 197	Messersmith-Cal .. 7.49	Messersmith-Cal . 10.54

Earned Run Average	Adjusted ERA	Opponents' Batting Avg.	Opponents' On Base Pct.	Starter Runs	Adjusted Starter Runs
Segui-Oak........2.56	Segui-Oak 139	Messersmith-Cal ..205	Peterson-NY 280	Palmer-Bal 33.9	McDowell-Cle 35.2
Palmer-Bal.......2.71	McDowell-Cle 136	McDowell-Cle 213	Cuellar-Bal 286	McDowell-Cle ... 26.9	Palmer-Bal 31.6
Wright-Cal 2.83	Palmer-Bal 134	Segui-Oak 222	Perry-Min........287	Wright-Cal 25.6	Culp-Bos 25.6
Peterson-NY 2.90	Culp-Bos 130	Culp-Bos 224	Blyleven-Min......289	Peterson-NY 23.4	Wright-Cal 22.7
McDowell-Cle ... 2.92	Wright-Cal 128	Johnson-KC 228	Messersmith-Cal ..290	Perry-Min 21.0	Perry-Min 21.2

Clutch Pitching Index	Relief Runs	Adjusted Relief Runs	Relief Ranking	Total Pitcher Index	Total Baseball Ranking
Stottlemyre-NY ... 113	Grant-Oak 25.9	Grant-Oak 23.5	Knowles-Was 34.5	Knowles-Was 3.7	Yastrzemski-Bos .. 5.2
Kaat-Min 112	Knowles-Was 22.2	Williams-Min 21.9	McDaniel-NY 31.8	McDaniel-NY 3.5	Aparicio-Chi 4.6
Bahnsen-NY 109	Williams-Min 21.8	Sanders-Mil 20.9	Perranoski-Min ... 30.3	Wood-Chi 3.3	Oliva-Min 4.3
Segui-Oak....... 108	McDaniel-NY 21.1	Hall-Min 20.2	Wood-Chi 29.6	Perry-Min 3.3	Fregosi-Cal 4.2
Wright-Cal 107	Sanders-Mil 20.1	Knowles-Was 20.1	Williams-Min 25.6	McDowell-Cle 3.0	Howard-Was 4.2

TEAM	G	W	L	PCT	GB	R	OR	AB	H	2B	3B	HR	BB	SO	AVG	OBP	SLG	PRO	PRO+	BR	/A	PF	CHI	RC	SB	CS	SBA	SBR
EAST																												
PIT	162	97	65	.599		**788**	599	5674	**1555**	223	**61**	154	469	919	.274	.333	**.416**	**.749**	119	121	**125**	100	103	**776**	65	31	68	1
STL	163	90	72	.556	7	739	699	5610	1542	225	54	95	543	757	**.275**	**.342**	.385	.727	108	91	62	104	100	736	**124**	53	70	5
NY	162	83	79	.512	14	588	**550**	5477	1365	203	29	98	547	958	.249	.321	.351	.672	98	-20	-11	99	95	614	89	43	67	1
CHI	162	83	79	.512	14	637	648	5438	1401	202	34	128	527	772	.258	.327	.378	.705	93	41	-56	115	95	663	44	32	58	-6
MON	162	71	90	.441	25.5	622	729	5335	1312	197	29	88	543	800	.246	.325	.343	.668	96	-20	-22	100	102	598	51	43	54	-11
PHI	162	67	95	.414	30	558	688	5538	1289	209	35	123	499	1031	.233	.300	.350	.650	90	-74	-73	100	99	586	63	39	62	-5
WEST																												
SF	162	90	72	.556		706	644	5461	1348	224	36	140	**654**	1042	.247	.331	.378	.709	109	57	68	98	101	699	101	36	**74**	9
LA	162	89	73	.549	1	663	587	5523	1469	213	38	95	489	755	.266	.328	.370	.698	111	28	68	94	100	661	76	40	66	-1
ATL	162	82	80	.506	8	643	699	5575	1434	192	30	153	434	**747**	.257	.314	.385	.699	98	18	-23	106	98	658	57	46	55	-11
HOU	162	79	83	.488	11	585	567	5492	1319	**230**	52	71	478	888	.240	.304	.340	.644	96	-81	-67	97	**107**	573	101	51	66	0
CIN	162	79	83	.488	11	586	581	5414	1306	203	28	138	438	907	.241	.301	.366	.667	96	-45	-33	98	103	580	59	33	64	-2
SD	161	61	100	.379	28.5	486	610	5366	1250	184	31	96	438	966	.233	.294	.332	.626	89	-117	-84	93	98	513	70	45	61	-6
TOT	972					7601		65903	16590	2505	457	1379	6059	10542	.252	.318	.366	.685		900	492				65			-25

TEAM	CG	SH	SV	IP	H	H/G	HR	BB	SO	RAT	ERA	ERA+	OAV	OOB	PR	/A	PF	CPI	FA	E	DP	FW	PW	BW	SBW	DIF
EAST																									
PIT	43	15	**48**	1461	1426	8.8	108	470	813	11.9	3.31	102	.257	.318	26	12	98	105	.979	133	164	.0	1.3	**13.4**	.3	.9
STL	56	14	22	1467	1482	9.1	104	576	911	12.9	3.85	93	.263	.336	-63	-41	104	99	.978	142	155	-.4	-4.4	6.6	.8	6.4
NY	42	13	22	1466¹	**1227**	7.5	100	529	**1157**	11.0	**2.99**	114	**.227**	**.300**	78	68	98	94	.981	114	135	**1.2**	**7.3**	-1.2	-.3	-5.6
CHI	**75**	17	13	1444	1458	9.1	132	411	900	11.3	3.61	109	.262	.316	-23	52	114	101	.980	126	150	.5	5.6	-6.0	-.4	2.4
MON	49	8	25	1434¹	1418	8.9	133	658	829	13.2	4.12	86	.260	.344	-104	-94	102	100	.976	150	164	-.9	-10.1	-2.4	-1.0	4.8
PHI	31	10	25	1470²	1396	8.5	132	525	838	12.0	3.71	95	.254	.323	-41	-31	102	98	.981	122	158	.7	-3.3	-7.8	-.3	-3.3
WEST																									
SF	45	14	30	1454²	1324	8.2	128	471	831	11.3	3.32	102	.242	.306	24	13	98	97	.972	179	153	-2.6	1.4	7.3	**1.2**	1.7
LA	48	**18**	33	1449²	1363	8.5	110	**399**	853	11.1	3.23	100	.250	.304	37	-1	93	98	.979	131	159	.2	-.1	7.3	.1	.5
ATL	40	11	31	1474²	1529	9.3	152	485	823	12.5	3.75	99	.269	.330	-46	-6	107	**108**	.983	146	**180**	-.7	-.6	-2.5	-1.0	5.7
HOU	43	10	25	1471¹	1318	8.1	**75**	475	914	11.3	3.13	107	.241	.309	55	38	97	95	.983	106	152	1.6	4.1	-7.2	.2	-.8
CIN	27	11	38	1444	1298	8.1	112	501	750	11.4	3.35	100	.243	.311	18	0	97	97	**.984**	**103**	174	**1.8**	.0	-3.5	.0	-.3
SD	47	10	17	1438	1351	8.5	93	559	923	12.1	3.22	102	.249	.323	39	12	95	106	.974	161	144	-1.6	1.3	-9.0	-.4	-9.8
TOT	546	151	329	17475²		8.5				11.9	3.47		.252	.318					.979	1613	1888					

Runs
Brock-StL 126
Bonds-SF 110
Stargell-Pit 104
Garr-Atl 101
Torre-StL 97

Hits
Torre-StL 230
Garr-Atl 219
Brock-StL 200
Davis-LA 198

Doubles
Cedeno-Hou 40
Brock-StL 37
Torre-StL 34
Staub-Mon 34
Davis-LA 33

Triples
Morgan-Hou 11
Metzger-Hou 11
Davis-LA 10
Gaston-SD 9

Home Runs
Stargell-Pit 48
H.Aaron-Atl 47
May-Cin 39
Johnson-Phi 34

Total Bases
Torre-StL 352
H.Aaron-Atl 331
Stargell-Pit 321
Bonds-SF 317
Williams-Chi 300

Runs Batted In
Torre-StL 137
Stargell-Pit 125
H.Aaron-Atl 118
Bonds-SF 102
Montanez-Phi 99

Runs Produced
Torre-StL 210
Stargell-Pit 181
Brock-StL 180
Bonds-SF 179
Staub-Mon 172

Bases On Balls
Mays-SF 112
Dietz-SF 97
Bailey-Mon 97
Allen-LA 93
Morgan-Hou 88

Batting Average
Torre-StL .... .363
Garr-Atl .... .343
Beckert-Chi ...... .342
Clemente-Pit ..... .341
H.Aaron-Atl ...... .327

On Base Percentage
Mays-SF .... .429
Torre-StL .... .424
H.Aaron-Atl ...... .414
Hunt-Mon .... .403
Stargell-Pit .... .401

Slugging Average
H.Aaron-Atl ...... .669
Stargell-Pit .... .628
Torre-StL .... .555
May-Cin .... .532
Bonds-SF .... .512

Production
H.Aaron-Atl 1.082
Stargell-Pit 1.029
Torre-StL .... .979
Mays-SF .... .911
Williams-Chi ..... .889

Adjusted Production
H.Aaron-Atl 190
Stargell-Pit 188
Torre-StL 169
Mays-SF 160
Allen-LA 154

Batter Runs
H.Aaron-Atl 65.2
Torre-StL 62.5
Stargell-Pit 58.7
Williams-Chi 39.4
Staub-Mon 38.5

Adjusted Batter Runs
Stargell-Pit 59.3
H.Aaron-Atl 57.7
Torre-StL 57.3
Allen-LA 41.1
Mays-SF 39.1

Clutch Hitting Index
Fairly-Mon 129
Sanguillen-Pit 125
Bailey-Mon 123
Watson-Hou 121
Simmons-StL 120

Runs Created
Torre-StL 145
H.Aaron-Atl 137
Stargell-Pit 131
Bonds-SF 115
Brock-StL 114

Total Average
H.Aaron-Atl 1.178
Stargell-Pit 1.117
Mays-SF 1.067
Torre-StL .... .998
Bonds-SF .... .876

Stolen Bases
Brock-StL 64
Morgan-Hou 40
Garr-Atl 30

Stolen Base Average
Mays-SF 88.5
Henderson-SF 85.7
Morgan-Hou 83.3
Agee-NY 82.4
Hernandez-SD 80.8

Stolen Base Runs
Brock-StL 7.8
Morgan-Hou 7.2
Mays-SF 5.1
Agee-NY 4.8
Harrelson-NY 4.2

Fielding Runs
Maxvill-StL 29.2
Garr-Atl 16.2
Robertson-Pit 15.2
Helms-Cin 14.4
Barton-SD 14.0

Total Player Rating
Stargell-Pit 5.8
H.Aaron-Atl 4.2
Torre-StL 4.1
Staub-Mon 3.6
Mays-SF 3.6

Wins
Jenkins-Chi 24
Seaver-NY 20
Downing-LA 20
Carlton-StL 20
Ellis-Pit 19

Win Percentage
Gullett-Cin .... .727
Downing-LA ...... .690
Carlton-StL ...... .690
Ellis-Pit .... .679
Seaver-NY .... .667

Games
Granger-Cin 70
J.Johnson-SF 67
Marshall-Mon 66
McMahon-SF 61
Carroll-Cin 61

Complete Games
Jenkins-Chi 30
Seaver-NY 21
Stoneman-Mon ... 20
Gibson-StL 20

Shutouts
Pappas-Chi 5
Gibson-StL 5
Downing-LA 5
Blass-Pit 5

Saves
Giusti-Pit 30
Marshall-Mon 23
Brewer-LA 22
J.Johnson-SF 18
Upshaw-Atl 17

Innings Pitched
Jenkins-Chi 325.0
Stoneman-Mon ... 294.2
Seaver-NY 286.1
Perry-SF 280.0
Marichal-SF 279.0

Fewest Hits/Game
Wilson-Hou 6.55
Seaver-NY 6.60
Kirby-SD 7.17
Gentry-NY 7.39
Stoneman-Mon ... 7.42

Fewest BB/Game
Jenkins-Chi 1.02
Marichal-SF 1.81
Stone-Atl 1.82
Hands-Chi 1.86
Sutton-LA 1.87

Strikeouts
Seaver-NY 289
Jenkins-Chi 263
Stoneman-Mon ... 251
Kirby-SD 231
Sutton-LA 194

Strikeouts/Game
Seaver-NY 9.08
Kirby-SD 7.78
Stoneman-Mon ... 7.67
Jenkins-Chi 7.28
Gentry-NY 6.86

Ratio
Seaver-NY 8.64
Wilson-Hou 9.44
Jenkins-Chi 9.58
Marichal-SF 9.77
Sutton-LA 9.87

Earned Run Average
Seaver-NY 1.76
Roberts-SD 2.10
Wilson-Hou 2.45
Forsch-Hou 2.53
Sutton-LA 2.54

Adjusted ERA
Seaver-NY 194
Roberts-SD 157
Jenkins-Chi 142
Wilson-Hou 137
Forsch-Hou 133

Opponents' Batting Avg.
Wilson-Hou ...... .202
Seaver-NY .... .206
Kirby-SD .... .216
Cumberland-SF ... .223
Gentry-NY .... .224

Opponents' On Base Pct.
Seaver-NY .... .253
Wilson-Hou ...... .268
Jenkins-Chi ...... .271
Marichal-SF ..... .274
Nolan-Cin .... .275

Starter Runs
Seaver-NY 54.3
Roberts-SD 40.9
Wilson-Hou 30.2
Sutton-LA 27.2
Jenkins-Chi 25.2

Adjusted Starter Runs
Seaver-NY 52.4
Jenkins-Chi 42.1
Roberts-SD 35.8
Wilson-Hou 27.2
Niekro-Atl 21.8

Clutch Pitching Index
Roberts-SD 120
Downing-LA 115
Short-Phi 115
Johnson-Pit 112
Wise-Phi 112

Relief Runs
McGraw-NY 21.7
Miller-Chi-SD-Pit .. 20.0
Frisella-NY 14.9
Ray-Hou 14.6
Brewer-LA 14.3

Adjusted Relief Runs
McGraw-NY 21.0
Miller-Chi-SD-Pit .. 18.9
Frisella-NY 14.3
Ray-Hou 13.5
Hoerner-Phi 12.6

Relief Ranking
McGraw-NY 29.0
Miller-Chi-SD-Pit .. 26.7
Frisella-NY 22.7
Brewer-LA 22.3
Ray-Hou 18.4

Total Pitcher Index
Seaver-NY 6.5
Jenkins-Chi 6.4
Roberts-SD 4.6
Wise-Phi 3.4
McGraw-NY 3.4

Total Baseball Ranking
Seaver-NY 6.5
Jenkins-Chi 6.4
Stargell-Pit 5.8
Roberts-SD 4.6
H.Aaron-Atl 4.2

TEAM	G	W	L	PCT	GB	R	OR	AB	H	2B	3B	HR	BB	SO	AVG	OBP	SLG	PRO	PRO+	BR	/A	PF	CHI	RC	SB	CS	SBA	SBR
EAST																												
BAL	158	101	57	.639		**742**	**530**	5303	1382	207	25	158	**672**	844	**.261**	**.349**	.398	**.747**	120	**133**	**140**	99	97	750	66	38	63	-3
DET	162	91	71	.562	12	701	645	5502	1399	214	38	**179**	540	854	.254	.327	**.405**	.732	110	88	60	104	97	715	35	43	45	-15
BOS	162	85	77	.525	18	691	667	5401	1360	**246**	28	161	552	871	.252	.325	.397	.722	104	68	19	107	100	686	51	34	60	-5
NY	162	82	80	.506	21	648	641	5413	1377	195	**43**	97	581	717	.254	.331	.360	.691	109	22	62	94	99	643	75	55	58	-11
WAS	159	63	96	.396	38.5	537	660	5290	1219	189	30	86	575	956	.230	.309	.326	.635	91	-86	-56	94	102	538	68	45	60	-7
CLE	162	60	102	.370	43	543	747	5467	1303	200	20	109	467	868	.238	.302	.342	.644	81	-83	-133	109	101	558	57	37	61	-5
WEST																												
OAK	161	101	60	.627		691	564	5494	1383	195	25	160	542	1018	.252	.323	.384	.707	109	42	56	98	102	681	80	53	60	-8
KC	161	85	76	.528	16	603	566	5295	1323	225	40	80	490	819	.250	.316	.353	.669	97	-28	-23	99	104	594	130	46	74	11
CHI	162	79	83	.488	22.5	617	597	5382	1346	185	30	138	562	870	.250	.327	.373	.700	102	33	13	103	94	661	83	65	56	-14
CAL	162	76	86	.469	25.5	511	576	5495	1271	213	18	96	441	827	.231	.292	.329	.621	88	-131	-96	93	104	518	72	34	68	1
MIN	160	74	86	.463	26.5	654	670	5414	**1406**	197	31	116	512	846	.260	.326	.372	.698	101	28	8	103	101	641	66	44	60	-7
MIL	161	69	92	.429	32	534	609	5185	1188	160	23	104	543	924	.229	.306	.329	.635	87	-88	-82	99	103	534	82	53	61	-7
TOT	966					7472		64641	15957	2426	351	1484	6477	10414	.247	.320	.364	.684							865	547	61	-69

TEAM	CG	SH	SV	IP	H	H/G	HR	BB	SO	RAT	ERA	ERA+	OAV	OOB	PR	/A	PF	CPI	FA	E	DP	FW	PW	BW	SBW	DIF
EAST																										
BAL	**71**	15	22	1415¹	1257	8.0	125	**416**	793	10.8	**2.99**	112	.239	**.297**	74	57	97	101	.981	112	148	.7	6.1	**15.1**	.3	-.2
DET	53	11	32	1468¹	1355	8.3	126	609	**1000**	12.3	3.63	99	.247	.327	-28	-7	104	99	**.983**	106	156	**1.2**	-.8	6.5	-1.0	4.1
BOS	44	11	35	1443	1424	8.9	136	535	871	12.5	3.80	97	.259	.329	-55	-18	107	100	.981	116	149	.6	-1.9	2.0	.0	3.2
NY	67	15	12	1452	1382	8.6	126	423	707	11.3	3.43	94	.252	.308	4	-33	93	97	.981	125	159	.1	-3.5	6.7	-.6	-1.7
WAS	30	10	26	1418²	1376	8.7	132	554	762	12.5	3.70	89	.258	.333	-37	-62	96	105	.977	141	170	-1.0	-6.7	-6.0	-.1	-2.7
CLE	21	7	32	1440	1352	8.4	154	770	937	13.6	4.28	89	.252	.351	-130	-72	111	99	.981	116	159	.6	-7.7	-14.3	.0	.3
WEST																										
OAK	57	18	36	1469¹	**1229**	**7.5**	131	501	999	10.8	3.05	109	**.228**	.298	67	46	96	97	.981	117	157	.5	4.9	6.0	-.2	9.2
KC	34	15	**44**	1420¹	1301	8.2	**84**	496	775	11.6	3.25	106	.247	.316	33	28	99	98	.979	132	**178**	-.4	3.0	-2.5	**1.8**	2.5
CHI	46	19	32	1450¹	1348	8.4	100	468	976	11.4	3.12	**115**	.247	.309	55	**75**	104	101	.975	160	128	-1.9	**8.1**	1.4	-.9	-8.6
CAL	39	11	32	1481	1246	7.6	101	607	904	11.5	3.10	104	.230	.312	60	23	94	98	.980	131	159	-.2	2.5	-10.3	.7	2.4
MIN	43	9	25	1416²	1384	8.8	139	529	895	12.4	3.81	93	.257	.328	-55	-41	103	100	.980	118	134	.4	-4.4	.9	-.1	-2.7
MIL	32	**23**	32	1416¹	1303	8.3	130	569	795	12.1	3.38	103	.247	.324	13	14	100	**106**	.977	138	152	-.7	1.5	-8.8	-.1	-3.3
TOT	537	164	360	17291¹		8.3				11.9	3.46		.247	.320					.980	1512	1849					

Runs
Buford-Bal 99
Tovar-Min 94
Murcer-NY 94
Carew-Min 88
Jackson-Oak 87

Hits
Tovar-Min 204
Alomar-Cal 179
Carew-Min 177
Smith-Bos 175
Murcer-NY 175

Doubles
Smith-Bos 33
Schaal-KC 31
Rodriguez-Det 30
Oliva-Min 30

Triples
Patek-KC 11
Carew-Min 10
Blair-Bal 8

Home Runs
Melton-Chi 33
Jackson-Oak 32
Cash-Det 32
Smith-Bos 30

Total Bases
Smith-Bos 302
Jackson-Oak 288
Murcer-NY 287
Melton-Chi 267
Oliva-Min 266

Runs Batted In
Killebrew-Min 119
F.Robinson-Bal 99
Smith-Bos 96
Murcer-NY 94
Bando-Oak 94

Runs Produced
Murcer-NY 163
F.Robinson-Bal 153
Killebrew-Min 152
White-NY 151
Smith-Bos 151

Bases On Balls
Killebrew-Min 114
Yastrzemski-Bos ... 106
Schaal-KC 103
Petrocelli-Bos 91
Murcer-NY 91

Batting Average
Oliva-Min .... .337
Murcer-NY .... .331
Rettenmund-Bal .... .318
Tovar-Min .... .311
Carew-Min .... .307

On Base Percentage
Murcer-NY .... .429
Rettenmund-Bal .... .424
Kaline-Det .... .421
Buford-Bal .... .415
White-NY .... .399

Slugging Average
Oliva-Min .... .546
Murcer-NY .... .543
Cash-Det .... .531
F.Robinson-Bal .... .510
Jackson-Oak .... .508

Production
Murcer-NY .... .972
Oliva-Min .... .918
Cash-Det .... .905
F.Robinson-Bal .... .900
Buford-Bal .... .891

Adjusted Production
Murcer-NY 185
White-NY 155
F.Robinson-Bal 154
Buford-Bal 153
Oliva-Min 152

Batter Runs
Murcer-NY 53.7
Rettenmund-Bal 34.8
Buford-Bal 34.5
White-NY 33.7
Oliva-Min 33.6

Adjusted Batter Runs
White-NY 61.1
Murcer-NY 39.8
Rettenmund-Bal 35.7
Buford-Bal 35.3
F.Robinson-Bal 33.8

Clutch Hitting Index
Killebrew-Min 140
Powell-Bal 137
Alou-Oak-NY 123
F.Robinson-Bal 121
May-Chi 120

Runs Created
Murcer-NY 126
Smith-Bos 106
Jackson-Oak 103
White-NY 103
Rettenmund-Bal 99

Total Average
Murcer-NY 1.035
Buford-Bal .... .970
Cash-Det .... .933
F.Robinson-Bal .... .905
Rettenmund-Bal .... .904

Stolen Bases
Otis-KC 52
Patek-KC 49
Alomar-Cal 39
Campaneris-Oak 34

Stolen Base Average
Harper-Mil 89.3
Otis-KC 86.7
Campaneris-Oak 82.9
Pinson-Cle 80.6
Alomar-Cal 79.6

Stolen Base Runs
Otis-KC 10.8
Patek-KC 6.3
Campaneris-Oak 6.0
Harper-Mil 5.7
Alomar-Cal 5.7

Fielding Runs
Nettles-Cle 42.3
Melton-Chi 27.0
Alomar-Cal 21.4
Cullen-Was 20.5
Otis-KC 19.8

Total Player Rating
Murcer-NY 5.5
Nettles-Cle 5.3
Melton-Chi 5.1
White-NY 4.5
Otis-KC 4.2

Wins
Lolich-Det 25
Blue-Oak 24
Wood-Chi 22
McNally-Bal 21
Hunter-Oak 21

Win Percentage
McNally-Bal .... .808
Dobson-Oak .... .750
Blue-Oak .... .750
Dobson-Bal .... .714

Games
Sanders-Mil 83
Scherman-Det 69
Burgmeier-KC 67
Abernathy-KC 63

Complete Games
Lolich-Det 29
Blue-Oak 24
Wood-Chi 22
Cuellar-Bal 21
Palmer-Bal 20

Shutouts
Blue-Oak 8
Wood-Chi 7
Stottlemyre-NY 7
Bradley-Chi 6

Saves
Sanders-Mil 31
Abernathy-KC 23
Scherman-Det 20
Fingers-Oak 17
Burgmeier-KC 17

Innings Pitched
Lolich-Det 376.0
Wood-Chi 334.0
Blue-Oak 312.0
Cuellar-Bal 292.1
Coleman-Det 286.0

Fewest Hits/Game
Blue-Oak 6.03
McDowell-Cle 6.71
May-Cal 6.91
Messersmith-Cal ... 7.29
Wright-Cal 7.32

Fewest BB/Game
Peterson-NY 1.38
Kline-NY 1.50
Kaat-Min 1.62
Wood-Chi 1.67
Drago-KC 1.72

Strikeouts
Lolich-Det 308
Blue-Oak 301
Coleman-Det 236
Blyleven-Min 224
Wood-Chi 210

Strikeouts/Game
Blue-Oak 8.68
McDowell-Cle 8.05
Johnson-Chi 7.74
Coleman-Det 7.43
Lolich-Det 7.37

Ratio
Blue-Oak 8.68
Wood-Chi 9.19
Kline-NY 9.84
Dobson-Bal 9.98
McNally-Bal 10.07

Earned Run Average
Blue-Oak 1.82
Wood-Chi 1.91
Palmer-Bal 2.68
Hedlund-KC 2.71
Blyleven-Min 2.81

Adjusted ERA
Wood-Chi 188
Blue-Oak 183
Siebert-Bos 127
Hedlund-KC 126
Blyleven-Min 126

Opponents' Batting Avg.
Blue-Oak .... .189
McDowell-Cle ...... .207
May-Cal .... .213
Messersmith-Cal ... .218
Palmer-Bal .... .221

Opponents' On Base Pct.
Blue-Oak .... .252
Wood-Chi .... .264
Kline-NY .... .276
Dobson-Bal .... .279
Hunter-Oak .... .282

Starter Runs
Wood-Chi 57.5
Blue-Oak 57.0
Palmer-Bal 24.5
Lolich-Det 22.6
Blyleven-Min 20.0

Adjusted Starter Runs
Wood-Chi 62.2
Blue-Oak 52.6
Lolich-Det 28.0
Blyleven-Min 22.8
Palmer-Bal 21.0

Clutch Pitching Index
Drago-KC 119
Krausse-Mil 118
Johnson-Chi 117
Bosman-Was 112
Wood-Chi 112

Relief Runs
Sanders-Mil 23.4
Burgmeier-KC 17.0
Mingori-Cle 12.8
Queen-Cal 12.3
Grzenda-Was 12.0

Adjusted Relief Runs
Sanders-Mil 23.5
Burgmeier-KC 16.7
Mingori-Cle 15.1
Scherman-Det 11.1
Lee-Bos 10.9

Relief Ranking
Sanders-Mil 41.6
Burgmeier-KC 34.4
Scherman-Det 19.4
Abernathy-KC 13.8
Grzenda-Was 11.4

Total Pitcher Index
Wood-Chi 6.6
Blue-Oak 4.9
Sanders-Mil 4.7
Burgmeier-KC 4.4
Siebert-Bos 3.5

Total Baseball Ranking
Wood-Chi 6.6
Murcer-NY 5.5
Nettles-Cle 5.3
Melton-Chi 5.1
Blue-Oak 4.9

TEAM	G	W	L	PCT	GB	R	OR	AB	H	2B	3B	HR	BB	SO	AVG	OBP	SLG	PRO	PRO+	BR	/A	PF	CHI	RC	SB	CS	SBA	SBR
EAST																												
PIT	155	96	59	.619		691	512	5490	**1505**	251	**47**	110	404	871	**.274**	.327	**.397**	**.724**	114	74	89	98	100	**701**	49	30	62	-3
CHI	156	85	70	.548	11	685	567	5247	1346	206	40	133	565	815	.257	.332	.387	.719	100	74	2	111	100	670	69	47	59	-8
NY	156	83	73	.532	13.5	528	535	5135	1154	175	31	105	589	990	.225	.309	.332	.641	91	-68	-54	97	99	530	41	41	50	-12
STL	156	75	81	.481	21.5	568	600	5326	1383	214	42	70	437	793	.260	.319	.355	.674	99	-14	-6	99	96	591	104	48	68	2
MON	156	70	86	.449	26.5	513	609	5156	1205	156	22	91	474	828	.234	.304	.325	.629	84	-92	-101	102	102	513	68	66	51	-19
PHI	156	59	97	.378	37.5	503	635	5248	1240	200	36	98	487	930	.236	.304	.344	.648	88	-65	-78	103	94	545	42	50	46	-17
WEST																												
CIN	154	95	59	.617		707	557	5241	1317	214	44	124	**606**	914	.251	**.333**	.380	.713	**116**	67	**107**	94	104	676	**140**	63	69	4
HOU	153	84	69	.549	10.5	**708**	636	5267	1359	233	38	134	524	907	.258	.329	.393	.722	114	**75**	89	98	103	686	111	56	66	0
LA	155	85	70	.548	10.5	584	547	5270	1349	178	39	98	480	786	.256	.321	.360	.681	102	1	16	98	96	610	82	39	68	1
ATL	155	70	84	.455	25	628	730	5278	1363	186	17	144	532	770	.258	.330	.382	.712	100	60	-1	109	94	661	47	35	57	-7
SF	155	69	86	.445	26.5	662	649	5245	1281	211	36	**150**	480	964	.244	.311	.384	.695	102	17	8	101	**107**	630	123	45	**73**	**10**
SD	153	58	95	.379	36.5	488	665	5213	1181	168	38	102	407	976	.227	.284	.332	.616	87	-130	-98	93	106	489	78	46	63	-4
TOT	930					7265		63116	15683	2392	430	1359	5985	10544	.248	.317	.365	.682							954	566	63	-53

TEAM	CG	SH	SV	IP	H	H/G	HR	BB	SO	RAT	ERA	ERA+	OAV	OOB	PR	/A	PF	CPI	FA	E	DP	FW	PW	BW	SBW	DIF
EAST																										
PIT	39	15	48	1414¹	1282	8.2	90	433	838	11.1	2.81	118	.243	.304	102	81	96	**108**	.978	136	171	-.0	8.7	9.6	.2	.1
CHI	54	19	32	1398²	1329	8.6	112	**421**	824	11.5	3.22	118	.251	.311	37	**92**	110	105	.979	132	148	.2	**9.9**	.2	-.4	-2.4
NY	32	12	41	1414²	1263	8.0	118	486	**1059**	11.9	3.26	103	.240	.308	30	15	97	99	.980	116	122	1.1	1.6	-5.8	-.8	8.9
STL	**64**	13	13	1399²	1290	8.3	87	531	912	11.8	3.42	99	.247	.319	5	-3	99	97	.977	141	146	-.3	-.3	-.6	.7	-2.4
MON	39	11	23	1401¹	1281	8.2	103	579	888	12.1	3.59	99	.245	.323	-21	-6	103	97	.978	134	141	.0	-.6	-10.9	-1.6	5.0
PHI	43	13	15	1400	1318	8.5	117	536	927	12.1	3.66	98	.251	.324	-33	-11	104	99	.981	116	142	1.1	-1.2	-8.4	-1.3	-9.2
WEST																										
CIN	25	15	**60**	1412²	1313	8.4	129	435	806	11.3	3.21	100	.247	.307	38	0	93	104	**.982**	110	143	**1.3**	.0	**11.5**	.9	4.3
HOU	38	14	31	1385¹	1340	8.7	114	498	971	12.2	3.77	89	.256	.325	-48	-62	97	98	.980	116	151	.9	-6.7	9.6	.5	3.2
LA	50	**23**	29	1403	**1196**	7.7	**83**	429	856	**10.6**	**2.78**	**120**	**.230**	**.292**	104	85	97	96	.974	162	145	-1.5	9.1	1.7	.6	-2.5
ATL	40	4	27	1377	1412	9.2	155	512	732	12.7	4.27	89	.266	.333	-126	-74	110	97	.974	156	130	-1.1	-8.0	-.1	-.3	2.5
SF	44	8	23	1386¹	1309	8.5	130	507	771	12.0	3.69	94	.250	.320	-37	-32	101	98	.974	156	121	-1.1	-3.4	.9	**1.6**	-6.3
SD	39	17	19	1403²	1350	8.7	121	618	960	12.9	3.78	87	.255	.337	-50	-76	95	103	.976	144	146	-.6	-8.2	-10.5	.0	.7
TOT	507	164	361	16796²		8.4				11.8	3.45		.248	.317					.978	1619	1706					

Runs
Morgan-Cin 122
Bonds-SF 118
Wynn-Hou 117
Rose-Cin 107
Cedeno-Hou 103

Hits
Rose-Cin 198
Brock-StL 193
Williams-Chi 191
Simmons-StL 180
Garr-Atl 180

Doubles
Montanez-Phi 39
Cedeno-Hou 39
Simmons-StL 36
Williams-Chi 34

Triples
Bowa-Phi 13
Rose-Cin 11
Sanguillen-Pit 8
Cedeno-Hou 8
Brock-StL 8

Home Runs
Bench-Cin 40
Colbert-SD 38
Williams-Chi 37
Aaron-Atl 34
Stargell-Pit 33

Total Bases
Williams-Chi 348
Cedeno-Hou 300
Bench-Cin 291
May-Hou 290
Colbert-SD 286

Runs Batted In
Bench-Cin 125
Williams-Chi 122
Stargell-Pit 112
Colbert-SD 111
May-Hou 98

Runs Produced
Wynn-Hou 183
Williams-Chi 180
Morgan-Cin 179
Bonds-SF 172
Bench-Cin 172

Bases On Balls
Morgan-Cin 115
Wynn-Hou 103
Bench-Cin 100
Aaron-Atl 92
Evans-Atl 90

Batting Average
Williams-Chi 333
Garr-Atl 325
Baker-Atl 321
Cedeno-Hou 320
Watson-Hou 312

On Base Percentage
Morgan-Cin 419
Williams-Chi 403
Santo-Chi 397
Aaron-Atl 391
Wynn-Hou 391

Slugging Average
Williams-Chi 606
Stargell-Pit 558
Bench-Cin 541
Cedeno-Hou 537
Aaron-Atl 514

Production
Williams-Chi 1.010
Stargell-Pit 935
Bench-Cin 927
Cedeno-Hou 924
Aaron-Atl 906

Adjusted Production
Bench-Cin 171
Stargell-Pit 166
Williams-Chi 166
Cedeno-Hou 163
Hebner-Pit 155

Batter Runs
Williams-Chi 61.1
Bench-Cin 44.0
Cedeno-Hou 42.9
Stargell-Pit 39.6
Morgan-Cin 37.2

Adjusted Batter Runs
Bench-Cin 50.6
Williams-Chi 48.2
Cedeno-Hou 45.2
Morgan-Cin 43.5
Stargell-Pit 41.7

Clutch Hitting Index
Parker-LA 140
Tolan-Cin 131
Helms-Hou 120
Sanguillen-Pit 119
Oliver-Pit 117

Runs Created
Williams-Chi 137
Morgan-Cin 117
Cedeno-Hou 115
Bench-Cin 110
Rose-Cin 109

Total Average
Williams-Chi 1.050
Morgan-Cin 973
Cedeno-Hou 959
Stargell-Pit 958
Aaron-Atl 945

Stolen Bases
Brock-StL 63
Morgan-Cin 58
Cedeno-Hou 55
Bonds-SF 44
Tolan-Cin 42

Stolen Base Average
Hernandez-SD 88.9
Bonds-SF 88.0
Davis-LA 87.0
Brock-StL 77.8
Morgan-Cin 77.3

Stolen Base Runs
Bonds-SF 9.6
Brock-StL 8.1
Morgan-Cin 7.2
Hernandez-SD 5.4
Davis-LA 4.2

Fielding Runs
Helms-Hou 26.5
Money-Phi 20.3
Rader-Hou 18.0
Rose-Cin 16.1
Russell-LA 15.0

Total Player Rating
Cedeno-Hou 5.6
Morgan-Cin 5.5
Bench-Cin 5.1
Rose-Cin 4.3
Williams-Chi 4.1

Wins
Carlton-Phi 27
Seaver-NY 21
Osteen-LA 20
Jenkins-Chi 20

Win Percentage
Nolan-Cin 750
Carlton-Phi 730
Pappas-Chi 708
Blass-Pit 704
Ellis-Pit 682

Games
Marshall-Mon 65
Carroll-Cin 65
Borbon-Cin 62
Ross-SD 60

Complete Games
Carlton-Phi 30
Jenkins-Chi 23
Gibson-StL 23
Wise-StL 20
Sutton-LA 18

Shutouts
Sutton-LA 9
Carlton-Phi 8
Norman-SD 6
Jenkins-Chi 5
Dierker-Hou 5

Saves
Carroll-Cin 37
McGraw-NY 27
Giusti-Pit 22
Marshall-Mon 18

Innings Pitched
Carlton-Phi 346.1
Jenkins-Chi 289.1
Niekro-Atl 282.1
Gibson-StL 278.0
Sutton-LA 272.2

Fewest Hits/Game
Sutton-LA 6.14
Carlton-Phi 6.68
Gibson-StL 7.32
Seaver-NY 7.39
Bryant-SF 7.40

Fewest BB/Game
Pappas-Chi 1.34
Nolan-Cin 1.53
Niekro-Atl 1.69
Ellis-Pit 1.82
Moose-Pit 1.87

Strikeouts
Carlton-Phi 310
Seaver-NY 249
Gibson-StL 208
Sutton-LA 207
Jenkins-Chi 184

Strikeouts/Game
Seaver-NY 8.55
Reuss-Hou 8.16
Koosman-NY 8.12
Carlton-Phi 8.06
Norman-SD 7.10

Ratio
Sutton-LA 8.35
Carlton-Phi 8.97
Nolan-Cin 9.10
McAndrew-NY . . . 9.86
Niekro-Atl 9.95

Earned Run Average
Carlton-Phi 1.97
Nolan-Cin 1.99
Sutton-LA 2.08
Matlack-NY 2.32
Gibson-StL 2.46

Adjusted ERA
Carlton-Phi 182
Nolan-Cin 161
Sutton-LA 160
Matlack-NY 145
Gibson-StL 138

Opponents' Batting Avg.
Sutton-LA 189
Carlton-Phi 206
Gibson-StL 224
Seaver-NY 224
Bryant-SF 224

Opponents' On Base Pct.
Sutton-LA 240
Carlton-Phi 259
Nolan-Cin 262
Niekro-Atl 275
McAndrew-NY 278

Starter Runs
Carlton-Phi 56.9
Sutton-LA 41.6
Gibson-StL 30.7
Matlack-NY 30.6
Nolan-Cin 28.5

Adjusted Starter Runs
Carlton-Phi 62.2
Sutton-LA 38.0
Gibson-StL 29.1
Matlack-NY 28.1
Hooton-Chi 24.4

Clutch Pitching Index
Blass-Pit 131
Nolan-Cin 115
Hooton-Chi 115
Matlack-NY 115
Downing-LA 115

Relief Runs
Marshall-Mon 21.5
McGraw-NY 20.7
Brewer-LA 19.1
R.Hernandez-Pit . . 13.9
Carroll-Cin 12.8

Adjusted Relief Runs
Marshall-Mon 22.8
McGraw-NY 19.6
Brewer-LA 18.0
R.Hernandez-Pit . . 12.8
Giusti-Pit 11.6

Relief Ranking
Marshall-Mon 46.8
Brewer-LA 39.8
McGraw-NY 34.5
Giusti-Pit 23.0
Carroll-Cin 18.5

Total Pitcher Index
Carlton-Phi 7.4
Marshall-Mon 5.3
Brewer-LA 4.5
Gibson-StL 4.2
Sutton-LA 3.9

Total Baseball Ranking
Carlton-Phi 7.4
Cedeno-Hou 5.6
Morgan-Cin 5.5
Marshall-Mon 5.3
Bench-Cin 5.1

TEAM	G	W	L	PCT	GB	R	OR	AB	H	2B	3B	HR	BB	SO	AVG	OBP	SLG	PRO	PRO+	BR	/A	PF	CHI	RC	SB	CS	SBA	SBR
EAST																												
DET	156	86	70	.551		558	514	5099	1206	179	32	122	483	793	.237	.306	.356	.662	100	18	0	103	101	549	17	21	45	-8
BOS	155	85	70	.548	0.5	640	620	5208	1289	229	34	124	522	858	.248	.320	.376	.696	108	83	49	106	102	634	66	30	69	2
BAL	154	80	74	.519	5	519	430	5028	1153	193	29	100	507	935	.229	.304	.339	.643	96	-12	-25	103	100	523	78	41	66	-1
NY	155	79	76	.510	6.5	557	527	5168	1288	201	24	103	491	689	.249	.318	.357	.675	111	45	65	97	95	588	71	42	63	-4
CLE	156	72	84	.462	14	472	519	5207	1220	187	18	91	420	762	.234	.295	.330	.625	89	-54	-70	103	98	495	49	53	48	-17
MIL	156	65	91	.417	21	493	595	5124	1204	167	22	88	472	868	.235	.303	.328	.631	96	-35	-26	98	99	495	64	57	53	-15
WEST																												
OAK	155	93	62	.600		604	457	5200	1248	195	29	134	463	886	.240	.308	.366	.674	113	37	67	95	104	584	87	48	64	-3
CHI	154	87	67	.565	5.5	566	538	5083	1208	170	28	108	511	991	.238	.311	.346	.657	100	14	3	102	103	550	100	52	66	-1
MIN	154	77	77	.500	15.5	537	535	5234	1277	182	31	93	478	905	.244	.311	.344	.655	96	9	-18	105	97	554	53	41	56	-9
KC	154	76	78	.494	16.5	580	545	5167	1317	220	26	78	534	711	.255	.329	.353	.682	111	65	68	100	95	601	85	44	66	-1
CAL	155	75	80	.484	18	454	533	5165	1249	171	26	78	358	850	.242	.294	.330	.624	98	-55	-28	94	97	487	57	37	61	-5
TEX	154	54	100	.351	38.5	461	628	5029	1092	166	17	56	503	926	.217	.292	.290	.582	83	-115	-97	96	111	438	126	73	63	-6
TOT	929					6441		61712	14751	2260	316	1175	5742	10174	.239	.308	.343	.651							853	539	61	-68

TEAM	CG	SH	SV	IP	H	H/G	HR	BB	SO	RAT	ERA	ERA+	OAV	OOB	PR	/A	PF	CPI	FA	E	DP	FW	PW	BW	SBW	DIF
EAST																										
DET	46	11	33	1388[1]	1212	7.9	101	465	952	11.2	2.96	106	.236	.306	15	28	103	102	.984	96	137	1.9	3.2	.0	-.3	3.2
BOS	48	20	25	1382[2]	1309	8.5	101	512	918	12.1	3.47	93	.251	.323	-63	-39	105	100	.978	130	141	-.0	-4.4	5.6	.9	5.6
BAL	62	20	21	1371[2]	1116	7.3	85	395	788	10.0	2.53	121	.224	.283	81	82	100	97	.983	100	150	1.6	9.3	-2.8	.5	-5.6
NY	35	19	39	1373[1]	1306	8.6	87	419	625	11.5	3.05	97	.252	.312	2	-15	96	105	.978	134	179	-.3	-1.7	7.4	.2	-4.1
CLE	47	13	24	1410	1232	7.9	123	534	846	11.5	2.92	110	.237	.313	23	47	105	112	.981	116	157	.8	5.3	-8.0	-1.3	-2.9
MIL	37	14	32	1391[2]	1289	8.3	116	486	740	11.7	3.45	88	.247	.315	-61	-65	99	97	.977	139	145	-.5	-7.4	-3.0	-1.1	-1.0
WEST																										
OAK	42	23	43	1417[2]	1170	7.4	96	418	862	10.2	2.58	110	.226	.286	76	42	93	99	.979	130	146	-.0	4.8	7.6	.3	2.9
CHI	36	14	42	1385[1]	1269	8.2	94	431	936	11.2	3.12	100	.245	.307	-9	1	102	99	.977	135	136	-.4	.1	.3	.5	9.4
MIN	37	17	34	1399[1]	1188	7.6	105	444	838	10.7	2.84	113	.230	.296	35	58	105	99	.974	159	133	-1.8	6.6	-2.0	-.4	-2.4
KC	44	16	29	1381[1]	1293	8.4	85	405	801	11.3	3.24	94	.251	.309	-27	-32	97	97	.981	116	164	.7	-3.6	7.7	.5	-6.3
CAL	57	18	16	1377[2]	1109	7.2	90	620	1000	11.5	3.06	95	.222	.312	0	-23	95	96	.981	114	135	.8	-2.6	-3.2	.0	2.4
TEX	11	8	34	1374[2]	1258	8.2	92	613	868	12.6	3.53	85	.246	.332	-71	-79	98	99	.972	166	147	-2.2	-9.0	-11.0	-.0	-.8
TOT	502	193	372	16653[2]		8.0				11.3	3.06		.239	.308					.979	1535	1770					

Runs
Murcer-NY 102
Rudi-Oak 94
Harper-Bos 92
D.Allen-Chi 90
Tovar-Min 86

Hits
Rudi-Oak 181
Piniella-KC 179
Murcer-NY 171
Carew-Min 170
May-Chi 161

Doubles
Piniella-KC 33
Rudi-Oak 32
White-NY 30
Murcer-NY 30
Harper-Bos 29

Triples
Rudi-Oak 9
Fisk-Bos 9
Blair-Bal 8
Murcer-NY 7
Kelly-Chi 7

Home Runs
D.Allen-Chi 37
Murcer-NY 33
Killebrew-Min . . . 26
Epstein-Oak 26

Total Bases
Murcer-NY 314
D.Allen-Chi 305
Rudi-Oak 288
Mayberry-KC 255
Piniella-KC 253

Runs Batted In
D.Allen-Chi 113
Mayberry-KC 100
Murcer-NY 96
Scott-Mil 88
Powell-Bal 81

Runs Produced
D.Allen-Chi 166
Murcer-NY 165
Rudi-Oak 150
Mayberry-KC 140

Bases On Balls
White-NY 99
D.Allen-Chi 99
Killebrew-Min . . . 94
May-Chi 79

Batting Average
Carew-Min 318
Piniella-KC 312
D.Allen-Chi 308
May-Chi 308
Rudi-Oak 305

On Base Percentage
D.Allen-Chi 422
May-Chi 408
Mayberry-KC 396
White-NY 385
Scheinblum-KC 385

Slugging Average
D.Allen-Chi 603
Fisk-Bos 538
Murcer-NY 537
Mayberry-KC 507
Epstein-Oak 490

Production
D.Allen-Chi 1.025
Fisk-Bos 909
Mayberry-KC 903
Murcer-NY 900
Epstein-Oak 868

Adjusted Production
D.Allen-Chi 199
Murcer-NY 171
Mayberry-KC 168
Epstein-Oak 166
Fisk-Bos 159

Batter Runs
D.Allen-Chi 66.1
Murcer-NY 44.9
Mayberry-KC 43.0
Fisk-Bos 37.1
May-Chi 36.7

Adjusted Batter Runs
D.Allen-Chi 63.6
Murcer-NY 48.6
Mayberry-KC 43.5
Epstein-Oak 37.6
Rudi-Oak 35.8

Clutch Hitting Index
Billings-Tex 138
Rojas-KC 123
Scheinblum-KC . . . 123
Petrocelli-Bos 122
Bando-Oak 121

Runs Created
D.Allen-Chi 131
Murcer-NY 114
Mayberry-KC 101
May-Chi 96
Rudi-Oak 95

Total Average
D.Allen-Chi 1.121
Mayberry-KC 910
Fisk-Bos 908
Murcer-NY 888
Epstein-Oak 885

Stolen Bases
Campaneris-Oak . . . 52
Nelson-Tex 51
Patek-KC 33
Kelly-Chi 32
Otis-KC 28

Stolen Base Average
Baylor-Bal 92.3
Patek-KC 82.5
Scott-Mil 80.0
Campaneris-Oak . . 78.8
Harper-Bos 78.1

Stolen Base Runs
Campaneris-Oak . . .7.2
Baylor-Bal 6.0
Patek-KC 5.7
Nelson-Tex 5.1
Kelly-Chi 4.2

Fielding Runs
Patek-KC 29.5
Rodriguez-Det 24.0
Michael-NY 23.7
Belanger-Bal 20.8
May-Mil 14.9

Total Player Rating
Murcer-NY 5.5
D.Allen-Chi 5.4
Fisk-Bos 4.4
Patek-KC 3.8
White-NY 3.4

Wins
Wood-Chi 24
Perry-Cle 24
Lolich-Det 22

Win Percentage
Hunter-Oak 750
Tiant-Bos 714
Odom-Oak 714
Palmer-Bal 677
Kline-NY 640

Games
Lindblad-Tex 66
Fingers-Oak 65
Granger-Min 63

Complete Games
Perry-Cle 29
Lolich-Det 23
Wood-Chi 20
Ryan-Cal 20
Palmer-Bal 18

Shutouts
Ryan-Cal 9
Wood-Chi 8
Stottlemyre-NY 7

Saves
Lyle-NY 35
Forster-Chi 29
Fingers-Oak 21
Granger-Min 19
Sanders-Mil 17

Innings Pitched
Wood-Chi 376.2
Perry-Cle 342.2
Lolich-Det 327.1
Hunter-Oak 295.1
Blyleven-Min 287.1

Fewest Hits/Game
Ryan-Cal 5.26
Hunter-Oak 6.09
Nelson-KC 6.23
Tiant-Bos 6.44
Messersmith-Cal . . 6.63

Fewest BB/Game
Peterson-NY 1.58
Nelson-KC 1.61
Kline-NY 1.68
Holtzman-Oak 1.76
Wood-Chi 1.77

Strikeouts
Ryan-Cal 329
Lolich-Det 250
Perry-Cle 234
Blyleven-Min 228
Coleman-Det 222

Strikeouts/Game
Ryan-Cal 10.43
Messersmith-Cal . . 7.53
May-Cal 7.41
Bradley-Chi 7.23
Blyleven-Min 7.14

Ratio
Nelson-KC 7.89
Hunter-Oak 8.32
Perry-Cle 9.11
Palmer-Bal 9.51
Wood-Chi 9.70

Earned Run Average
Tiant-Bos 1.91
Perry-Cle 1.92
Hunter-Oak 2.04
Palmer-Bal 2.07
Nelson-KC 2.08

Adjusted ERA
Tiant-Bos 168
Perry-Cle 168
Palmer-Bal 149
Nelson-KC 146
Hunter-Oak 139

Opponents' Batting Avg.
Ryan-Cal 171
Hunter-Oak 189
Nelson-KC 196
Tiant-Bos 202
Perry-Cle 205

Opponents' On Base Pct.
Nelson-KC 236
Hunter-Oak 242
Perry-Cle 261
Palmer-Bal 269
Tiant-Bos 277

Starter Runs
Perry-Cle 43.5
Hunter-Oak 33.4
Palmer-Bal 30.3
Ryan-Cal 24.6
Wood-Chi 23.1

Adjusted Starter Runs
Perry-Cle 49.5
Palmer-Bal 30.7
Hunter-Oak 26.3
Tiant-Bos 25.9
Wood-Chi 25.8

Clutch Pitching Index
Paul-Tex 128
Odom-Oak 124
Wilcox-Cle 119
Lonborg-Mil 112
Lolich-Det 111

Relief Runs
Lyle-NY 13.6
Knowles-Oak 12.3
Bell-Mil 11.0
Forster-Chi 9.0
Abernathy-KC . . . 8.8

Adjusted Relief Runs
Lyle-NY 12.3
Bell-Mil 10.8
Knowles-Oak 10.7
Forster-Chi 9.7
Abernathy-KC . . . 8.6

Relief Ranking
Lyle-NY 23.3
Forster-Chi 16.0
Knowles-Oak 12.9
Abernathy-KC . . . 11.0
Fingers-Oak 8.5

Total Pitcher Index
Perry-Cle 7.0
Palmer-Bal 4.2
Wood-Chi 3.1
Tiant-Bos 3.0
Lyle-NY 2.7

Total Baseball Ranking
Perry-Cle 7.0
Murcer-NY 5.5
D.Allen-Chi 5.4
Fisk-Bos 4.4
Palmer-Bal 4.2

TEAM	G	W	L	PCT	GB	R	OR	AB	H	2B	3B	HR	BB	SO	AVG	OBP	SLG	PRO	PRO+	BR	/A	PF	CHI	RC	SB	CS	SBA	SBR
EAST																												
NY	161	82	79	.509		608	588	5457	1345	198	24	85	540	805	.246	.317	.338	.655	89	-81	-72	98	104	583	27	22	55	-5
STL	162	81	81	.500	1.5	643	603	5478	1418	240	35	75	531	796	.259	.328	.357	.685	96	-24	-22	100	100	635	**100**	46	68	2
PIT	162	80	82	.494	2.5	704	693	5608	1465	**257**	44	154	432	842	.261	.317	.405	.722	109	30	48	97	101	697	23	30	43	-11
MON	162	79	83	.488	3.5	668	702	5369	1345	190	23	125	**695**	**777**	.251	**.341**	.364	.705	98	30	5	104	94	672	77	68	53	-18
CHI	161	77	84	.478	5	614	655	5363	1322	201	21	117	575	855	.247	.322	.357	.679	88	-35	-81	107	99	605	65	58	53	-15
PHI	162	71	91	.438	11.5	642	717	5546	1381	218	29	134	476	979	.249	.312	.371	.683	93	-40	-56	103	102	641	51	47	52	-13
WEST																												
CIN	162	99	63	.611		741	621	5505	1398	232	34	137	639	947	.254	.335	.383	.718	111	43	81	95	102	724	**148**	55	**73**	11
LA	162	95	66	.590	3.5	675	**565**	5604	1473	219	29	110	497	795	.263	.326	.371	.697	104	-5	25	96	100	676	109	50	69	3
SF	162	88	74	.543	11	739	702	5537	1452	212	**52**	161	550	913	.262	.337	.407	.744	108	87	56	104	96	765	112	52	68	2
HOU	162	82	80	.506	17	681	672	5532	1391	216	35	134	469	962	.251	.314	.376	.690	97	-28	-26	100	107	639	92	48	66	-1
ATL	162	76	85	.472	22.5	**799**	774	5631	**1497**	219	34	**206**	608	870	**.266**	**.341**	**.427**	**.768**	111	**134**	73	108	97	**826**	84	40	68	1
SD	162	60	102	.370	39	548	770	5457	1330	198	26	112	401	966	.244	.298	.351	.649	92	-110	-67	92	102	566	88	36	71	5
TOT	971					8062		66087	16817	2600	386	1550	6453	10507	.254	.324	.376	.700							976	552	64	-38

TEAM	CG	SH	SV	IP	H	H/G	HR	BB	SO	RAT	ERA	ERA+	OAV	OOB	PR	/A	PF	CPI	FA	E	DP	FW	PW	BW	SBW	DIF
EAST																										
NY	47	15	40	1465	1345	8.3	127	490	**1027**	11.4	3.26	111	.245	.309	65	58	99	101	.980	126	140	1.1	6.0	-7.5	-.2	2.0
STL	42	14	36	1460²	1366	8.4	105	486	867	11.6	3.25	112	.248	.312	66	63	100	100	.975	159	149	-.7	6.6	-2.3	.5	-4.1
PIT	26	11	**44**	1450²	1426	8.8	110	564	839	12.6	3.73	94	.258	.331	-12	-35	96	100	.976	151	156	-.3	-3.6	5.0	-.8	-1.3
MON	26	6	38	1451²	1356	8.4	128	681	866	12.8	3.71	103	.250	.337	-9	16	104	103	.974	163	156	-.9	1.7	.5	-1.5	-1.7
CHI	27	13	40	1437²	1471	9.2	128	**438**	885	12.1	3.66	108	.267	.325	1	46	108	104	.975	157	155	-.7	4.8	-8.4	-1.2	2.0
PHI	**49**	11	22	1447¹	1435	8.9	131	632	919	13.1	3.99	95	.263	.343	-53	-31	104	103	.979	134	179	.7	-3.2	-5.8	-1.0	-.6
WEST																										
CIN	39	**17**	43	1473	1389	8.5	135	518	801	11.8	3.40	100	.252	.319	42	0	93	105	**.982**	115	162	**1.8**	.0	8.4	1.5	6.3
LA	45	15	38	1491	**1270**	**7.7**	129	461	961	10.6	**3.00**	**115**	**.231**	**.294**	**109**	72	94	97	.981	125	166	1.2	**7.5**	2.6	.6	2.5
SF	33	8	**44**	1452¹	1442	8.9	145	485	787	12.1	3.79	101	.257	.320	-21	4	104	97	.974	163	138	-.9	.4	5.8	.5	1.2
HOU	45	14	26	1460²	1389	8.6	111	575	907	12.3	3.75	97	.252	.325	-14	-19	99	95	.981	116	140	1.7	-2.0	-2.7	.2	3.7
ATL	34	9	35	1462	1467	9.0	144	575	803	12.7	4.25	93	.263	.335	-95	-51	107	95	.974	166	142	-1.1	-5.3	7.6	.4	-6.1
SD	34	10	23	1430	1461	9.2	157	548	845	12.8	4.16	83	.267	.336	-79	-110	95	100	.973	170	152	-1.3	-11.5	-7.0	.9	-2.1
TOT	447	143	429	17482		8.7				12.2	3.66		.254	.324					.977	1745	1835					

Runs		Hits		Doubles		Triples		Home Runs		Total Bases	
Bonds-SF	131	Rose-Cin	230	Stargell-Pit	43	Metzger-Hou	14	Stargell-Pit	44	Bonds-SF	341
Morgan-Cin	116	Garr-Atl	200	Oliver-Pit	38	Matthews-SF	10	Johnson-Atl	43	Stargell-Pit	337
Rose-Cin	115	Brock-StL	193	Staub-NY	36	Maddox-SF	10	Evans-Atl	41	Evans-Atl	331
Evans-Atl	114	Simmons-StL	192	Simmons-StL	36	Davis-LA	9	Aaron-Atl	40	Johnson-Atl	305
Brock-StL	110	Oliver-Pit	191	Rose-Cin	36			Bonds-SF	39	Oliver-Pit	303

Runs Batted In		Runs Produced		Bases On Balls		Batting Average		On Base Percentage		Slugging Average	
Stargell-Pit	119	Bonds-SF	188	Evans-Atl	124	Rose-Cin	.338	Singleton-Mon	.429	Stargell-Pit	.646
May-Hou	105	Stargell-Pit	181	Singleton-Mon	123	Cedeno-Hou	.320	Fairly-Mon	.422	Evans-Atl	.556
Evans-Atl	104	Singleton-Mon	180	Morgan-Cin	111	Maddox-SF	.319	Morgan-Cin	.408	Johnson-Atl	.546
Bench-Cin	104	Baker-Atl	179	McCovey-SF	105	Perez-Cin	.314	Evans-Atl	.407	Cedeno-Hou	.537
Singleton-Mon	103	Evans-Atl	177	Monday-Chi	92	Watson-Hou	.312	Watson-Hou	.405	Bonds-SF	.530

Production		Adjusted Production		Batter Runs		Adjusted Batter Runs		Clutch Hitting Index		Runs Created	
Stargell-Pit	1.041	Stargell-Pit	189	Stargell-Pit	57.8	Stargell-Pit	61.0	Cey-LA	126	Evans-Atl	143
Evans-Atl	.964	Perez-Cin	162	Evans-Atl	54.8	Morgan-Cin	47.8	Sizemore-StL	123	Stargell-Pit	136
Perez-Cin	.923	Morgan-Cin	157	Aaron-Atl	45.5	Perez-Cin	47.2	Bench-Cin	121	Bonds-SF	130
Johnson-Atl	.917	Evans-Atl	153	Singleton-Mon	44.8	Evans-Atl	45.0	Speier-SF	119	Morgan-Cin	128
Cedeno-Hou	.914	Cedeno-Hou	151	Morgan-Cin	41.6	Singleton-Mon	40.6	Tolan-Cin	116	Rose-Cin	119

Total Average		Stolen Bases		Stolen Base Average		Stolen Base Runs		Fielding Runs		Total Player Rating	
Stargell-Pit	1.129	Brock-StL	70	Baker-Atl	88.9	Morgan-Cin	11.1	Schmidt-Phi	21.2	Stargell-Pit	6.3
Evans-Atl	1.048	Morgan-Cin	67	Morgan-Cin	81.7	Brock-StL	9.0	Kessinger-Chi	17.0	Morgan-Cin	6.1
Morgan-Cin	1.034	Cedeno-Hou	56	Concepcion-Cin	81.5	Cedeno-Hou	7.8	Unser-Phi	16.7	Cedeno-Hou	5.3
Cedeno-Hou	.949	Bonds-SF	43	Cedeno-Hou	78.9	Baker-Atl	5.4	Rose-Cin	16.7	Evans-Atl	5.2
Johnson-Atl	.947	Lopes-LA	36	Brock-StL	77.8	Garr-Atl	3.9	Cey-LA	16.2	Rose-Cin	4.6

Wins		Win Percentage		Games		Complete Games		Shutouts		Saves	
Bryant-SF	24	John-LA	.696	Marshall-Mon	92	Seaver-NY	18	Billingham-Cin	7	Marshall-Mon	31
Seaver-NY	19	Gullett-Cin	.692	Borbon-Cin	80	Carlton-Phi	18	Roberts-Hou	6	McGraw-NY	25
Billingham-Cin	19	Bryant-SF	.667	Sosa-SF	71	Billingham-Cin	16	Wise-StL	5	Giusti-Pit	20
Sutton-LA	18	Seaver-NY	.655	Giusti-Pit	67			Twitchell-Phi	5	Brewer-LA	20
Gullett-Cin	18	Billingham-Cin	.655	Segui-StL	65						

Innings Pitched		Fewest Hits/Game		Fewest BB/Game		Strikeouts		Strikeouts/Game		Ratio	
Carlton-Phi	293.1	Seaver-NY	6.80	Marichal-SF	1.61	Seaver-NY	251	Seaver-NY	7.79	Seaver-NY	8.91
Billingham-Cin	293.1	Sutton-LA	6.88	Jenkins-Chi	1.89	Carlton-Phi	223	Moore-Mon	7.71	Sutton-LA	9.02
Seaver-NY	290.0	Twitchell-Phi	6.93	Barr-SF	1.91	Matlack-NY	205	Matlack-NY	7.62	Messersmith-LA	10.06
Reuss-Hou	279.1	Wilson-Hou	7.03	Sutton-LA	1.97	Sutton-LA	200	Sutton-LA	7.02	Gibson-StL	10.11
Jenkins-Chi	271.0	Messersmith-LA	7.07	Seaver-NY	1.99			Carlton-Phi	6.84	Rooker-Pit	10.41

Earned Run Average		Adjusted ERA		Opponents' Batting Avg.		Opponents' On Base Pct.		Starter Runs		Adjusted Starter Runs	
Seaver-NY	2.08	Seaver-NY	174	Seaver-NY	.206	Seaver-NY	.254	Seaver-NY	51.0	Seaver-NY	49.5
Sutton-LA	2.42	Twitchell-Phi	152	Sutton-LA	.209	Sutton-LA	.258	Sutton-LA	35.3	Rogers-Mon	33.8
Twitchell-Phi	2.50	Marshall-Mon	143	Wilson-Hou	.213	Messersmith-LA	.279	Rogers-Mon	31.5	Twitchell-Phi	32.2
Marshall-Mon	2.66	Sutton-LA	142	Messersmith-LA	.214	Gibson-StL	.284	Twitchell-Phi	28.8	Sutton-LA	28.9
Messersmith-LA	2.70	Renko-Mon	136	Renko-Mon	.218	Briles-Pit	.288	Messersmith-LA	26.6	Renko-Mon	27.8

Clutch Pitching Index		Relief Runs		Adjusted Relief Runs		Relief Ranking		Total Pitcher Index		Total Baseball Ranking	
Marshall-Mon	134	Borbon-Cin	20.2	Marshall-Mon	22.9	Marshall-Mon	37.7	Seaver-NY	5.4	Stargell-Pit	6.3
Roberts-Hou	122	Marshall-Mon	19.8	Borbon-Cin	16.8	Locker-Chi	28.8	Marshall-Mon	4.5	Morgan-Cin	6.1
Twitchell-Phi	121	Giusti-Pit	14.1	Locker-Chi	16.6	Borbon-Cin	23.1	Rogers-Mon	4.1	Seaver-NY	5.4
Grimsley-Cin	116	Moffitt-SF	13.8	Moffitt-SF	15.6	Giusti-Pit	18.3	Renko-Mon	3.6	Cedeno-Hou	5.3
Moose-Pit	113	Locker-Chi	13.3	Giusti-Pit	12.6	Scarce-Phi	16.5	Locker-Chi	3.2	Evans-Atl	5.2

TEAM	G	W	L	PCT	GB	R	OR	AB	H	2B	3B	HR	BB	SO	AVG	OBP	SLG	PRO	PRO+	BR	/A	PF	CHI	RC	SB	CS	SBA	SBR
EAST																												
BAL	162	97	65	.599		754	**561**	5537	1474	229	**48**	119	**648**	752	.266	**.348**	.389	.737	108	61	67	99	98	765	**146**	64	70	5
BOS	162	89	73	.549	8	738	647	5513	1472	235	30	147	581	799	.267	.340	**.401**	**.741**	102	58	14	106	98	751	114	45	**72**	**7**
DET	162	85	77	.525	12	642	674	5508	1400	213	32	157	509	722	.254	.322	.390	.712	94	-9	-54	107	95	674	28	30	48	-10
NY	162	80	82	.494	17	641	610	5492	1435	212	17	131	489	**680**	.261	.324	.378	.702	101	-25	-2	97	98	655	47	43	52	-12
MIL	162	74	88	.457	23	708	731	5526	1399	229	40	145	563	977	.253	.327	.388	.715	103	2	17	98	101	702	110	66	63	-7
CLE	162	71	91	.438	26	680	826	5592	1429	205	29	**158**	471	793	.256	.317	.387	.704	95	-27	-38	102	103	666	60	68	47	-23
WEST																												
OAK	162	94	68	.580		**758**	615	5507	1431	216	28	147	595	919	.260	.336	.389	.725	**110**	28	66	95	**104**	730	128	57	69	4
KC	162	88	74	.543	6	755	752	5508	1440	239	40	114	644	696	.261	.342	.381	.723	96	31	-25	108	103	720	105	69	60	-10
MIN	162	81	81	.500	13	738	692	5625	**1521**	**240**	44	120	598	954	**.270**	.344	.393	.737	103	56	26	104	97	756	87	46	65	-2
CAL	162	79	83	.488	15	629	657	5505	1395	183	29	93	509	816	.253	.320	.348	.668	95	-84	-38	92	104	609	59	47	56	-11
CHI	162	77	85	.475	17	652	705	5475	1400	228	38	111	537	952	.256	.326	.372	.698	93	-28	-50	103	99	647	83	73	53	-19
TEX	162	57	105	.352	37	619	844	5488	1397	195	29	110	503	791	.255	.320	.361	.681	95	-63	-37	96	100	629	91	53	63	-5
TOT	972					8314		66276	17193	2624	404	1552	6647	9851	.259	.331	.381	.712							1058	661	62	-79

TEAM	CG	SH	SV	IP	H	H/G	HR	BB	SO	RAT	ERA	ERA+	OAV	OOB	PR	/A	PF	CPI	FA	E	DP	FW	PW	BW	SBW	DIF
EAST																										
BAL	67	14	26	1461²	**1297**	8.0	124	475	715	**11.0**	3.07	122	**.240**	.303	122	108	98	102	.981	119	184	1.3	11.0	6.9	1.2	-4.4
BOS	67	10	33	1440¹	1417	8.9	158	499	808	12.2	3.65	110	.259	.325	27	59	105	**106**	.979	127	162	.8	6.0	1.4	**1.4**	-1.7
DET	39	11	**46**	1447²	1468	9.1	154	493	911	12.4	3.90	105	.265	.325	-13	30	107	101	**.982**	112	144	**1.7**	3.1	-5.5	-.3	5.1
NY	47	16	39	1427²	1379	8.7	109	**457**	708	11.7	3.34	110	.254	.315	75	51	96	102	.976	156	172	-.8	5.2	-.2	-.6	-4.7
MIL	50	11	28	1454	1476	9.1	119	623	671	13.2	3.98	94	.265	.342	-27	-36	99	101	.977	145	167	-.2	-3.7	1.7	-.0	-4.8
CLE	55	9	21	1464²	1532	9.4	172	602	883	13.4	4.58	85	.271	.345	-125	-108	103	96	.978	139	174	.2	-11.0	-3.9	-1.7	6.5
WEST																										
OAK	46	16	41	1457¹	1311	8.1	143	494	797	11.3	3.29	108	.241	.308	86	42	93	100	.978	137	170	.3	4.3	6.8	1.1	.6
KC	40	7	41	1449¹	1521	9.4	114	617	790	13.5	4.19	98	.273	.349	-60	-13	108	100	.974	167	**192**	-1.4	-1.3	-2.6	-.3	12.7
MIN	48	**18**	34	1451²	1443	8.9	115	519	879	12.4	3.77	105	.259	.327	7	30	104	97	.978	139	147	.2	3.1	2.7	.5	-6.4
CAL	**72**	13	19	1456¹	1351	8.3	**104**	614	**1010**	12.4	3.53	100	.246	.326	46	3	93	98	.975	156	153	-.8	.3	-3.9	-.5	2.8
CHI	48	15	35	1456	1484	9.2	110	574	848	13.0	3.86	102	.266	.338	-8	15	104	101	.977	144	165	-.1	1.5	-5.1	-1.3	1.0
TEX	35	10	27	1430	1514	9.5	130	680	831	14.1	4.64	80	.273	.357	-131	-146	98	96	.974	161	164	-1.1	-14.9	-3.8	.2	-4.4
TOT	614	150	390	17396²		8.9				12.5	3.82		.259	.331					.977	1702	1994					

Runs
Jackson-Oak ... 99
Scott-Mil ... 98
North-Oak ... 98
Carew-Min ... 98
Bando-Oak ... 97

Hits
Carew-Min ... 203
May-Mil ... 189
Murcer-NY ... 187
Scott-Mil ... 185
Johnson-Tex ... 179

Doubles
Garcia-Mil ... 32
Bando-Oak ... 32
Scott-Mil ... 30
Chambliss-Cle ... 30
Carew-Min ... 30

Triples
Carew-Min ... 11
Bumbry-Bal ... 11
Orta-Chi ... 10
Coggins-Bal ... 9
Coluccio-Mil ... 8

Home Runs
Jackson-Oak ... 32
Robinson-Cal ... 30
Burroughs-Tex ... 30
Bando-Oak ... 29

Total Bases
Scott-Mil ... 295
May-Mil ... 295
Bando-Oak ... 295
Murcer-NY ... 286
Jackson-Oak ... 286

Runs Batted In
Jackson-Oak ... 117
Scott-Mil ... 107
Mayberry-KC ... 100
Bando-Oak ... 98
Robinson-Cal ... 97

Runs Produced
Jackson-Oak ... 184
Scott-Mil ... 181
Bando-Oak ... 166
May-Mil ... 164
Mayberry-KC ... 161

Bases On Balls
Mayberry-KC ... 122
Grich-Bal ... 107
Yastrzemski-Bos ... 105
Tenace-Oak ... 101
Briggs-Mil ... 87

Batting Average
Carew-Min ... .350
Scott-Mil ... .306
Davis-Bal ... .306
Murcer-NY ... .304
May-Mil ... .303

On Base Percentage
Mayberry-KC ... .420
Carew-Min ... .415
Yastrzemski-Bos ... .411
Tenace-Oak ... .391
Jackson-Oak ... .387

Slugging Average
Jackson-Oak ... .531
Bando-Oak ... .498
Robinson-Cal ... .489
Scott-Mil ... .488
Munson-NY ... .487

Production
Jackson-Oak ... .918
Mayberry-KC ... .898
Carew-Min ... .885
Bando-Oak ... .876
Yastrzemski-Bos ... .874

Adjusted Production
Jackson-Oak ... 165
Robinson-Cal ... 153
Bando-Oak ... 153
Scott-Mil ... 144
Carew-Min ... 143

Batter Runs
Mayberry-KC ... 41.0
Jackson-Oak ... 40.5
Carew-Min ... 38.9
Yastrzemski-Bos ... 36.8
Bando-Oak ... 35.5

Adjusted Batter Runs
Jackson-Oak ... 46.4
Bando-Oak ... 41.5
Robinson-Cal ... 38.1
Carew-Min ... 34.5
Scott-Mil ... 33.9

Clutch Hitting Index
Davis-Bal ... 134
Robinson-Bal ... 124
Piniella-KC ... 123
Johnson-Oak ... 122
May-Chi ... 119

Runs Created
Bando-Oak ... 113
Carew-Min ... 113
Mayberry-KC ... 113
Jackson-Oak ... 112
Scott-Mil ... 106

Total Average
Mayberry-KC ... .995
Jackson-Oak ... .953
Carew-Min ... .885
Yastrzemski-Bos ... .879
Bando-Oak ... .876

Stolen Bases
Harper-Bos ... 54
North-Oak ... 53
Nelson-Tex ... 43
Carew-Min ... 41
Patek-KC ... 36

Stolen Base Average
Rojas-KC ... 81.8
Money-Mil ... 81.5
Harper-Bos ... 79.4
Baylor-Bal ... 78.0
Campaneris-Oak ... 77.3

Stolen Base Runs
Harper-Bos ... 7.8
Campaneris-Oak ... 4.2
Baylor-Bal ... 4.2
North-Oak ... 3.9
Money-Mil ... 3.6

Fielding Runs
Patek-KC ... 35.3
Nettles-NY ... 26.0
Bell-Cle ... 24.3
North-Oak ... 23.6
Grich-Bal ... 21.0

Total Player Rating
Carew-Min ... 5.3
Grich-Bal ... 4.7
Jackson-Oak ... 4.6
Munson-NY ... 3.8
Robinson-Cal ... 3.8

Wins
Wood-Chi ... 24
Coleman-Det ... 23
Palmer-Bal ... 22

Win Percentage
Hunter-Oak ... .808
Palmer-Bal ... .710
Blue-Oak ... .690
Splittorff-KC ... .645
Colborn-Mil ... .625

Games
Hiller-Det ... 65
Fingers-Oak ... 62
Bird-KC ... 54
Knowles-Oak ... 52

Complete Games
Perry-Cle ... 29
Ryan-Cal ... 26
Blyleven-Min ... 25
Tiant-Bos ... 23
Colborn-Mil ... 22

Shutouts
Blyleven-Min ... 9
Perry-Cle ... 7
Palmer-Bal ... 6

Saves
Hiller-Det ... 38
Lyle-NY ... 27
Fingers-Oak ... 22
Bird-KC ... 20
Acosta-Chi ... 18

Innings Pitched
Wood-Chi ... 359.1
Perry-Cle ... 344.0
Ryan-Cal ... 326.0
Blyleven-Min ... 325.0
Singer-Cal ... 315.2

Fewest Hits/Game
Bibby-Tex ... 6.04
Ryan-Cal ... 6.57
Palmer-Bal ... 6.83
Tiant-Bos ... 7.18
Blue-Oak ... 7.30

Fewest BB/Game
Kaat-Min-Chi ... 1.73
Blyleven-Min ... 1.86
Holtzman-Oak ... 2.00
Wood-Chi ... 2.28
Lolich-Det ... 2.30

Strikeouts
Ryan-Cal ... 383
Blyleven-Min ... 258
Singer-Cal ... 241
Perry-Cle ... 238
Lolich-Det ... 214

Strikeouts/Game
Ryan-Cal ... 10.57
Bibby-Tex ... 7.74
Blyleven-Min ... 7.14
Stone-Chi ... 7.04
Singer-Cal ... 6.87

Ratio
Tiant-Bos ... 9.99
Hunter-Oak ... 10.25
Blyleven-Min ... 10.30
Palmer-Bal ... 10.36
Holtzman-Oak ... 10.44

Earned Run Average
Palmer-Bal ... 2.40
Blyleven-Min ... 2.52
Lee-Bos ... 2.75
Ryan-Cal ... 2.87
Medich-NY ... 2.95

Adjusted ERA
Blyleven-Min ... 157
Palmer-Bal ... 156
Lee-Bos ... 146
Medich-NY ... 124
Ryan-Cal ... 123

Opponents' Batting Avg.
Bibby-Tex ... .192
Ryan-Cal ... .203
Palmer-Bal ... .211
Tiant-Bos ... .219
Blue-Oak ... .224

Opponents' On Base Pct.
Tiant-Bos ... .281
Hunter-Oak ... .284
Blyleven-Min ... .287
Holtzman-Oak ... .287
Palmer-Bal ... .289

Starter Runs
Blyleven-Min ... 46.8
Palmer-Bal ... 46.6
Ryan-Cal ... 34.2
Lee-Bos ... 33.7
Holtzman-Oak ... 28.1

Adjusted Starter Runs
Blyleven-Min ... 51.9
Palmer-Bal ... 43.9
Lee-Bos ... 40.1
Ryan-Cal ... 24.4
Perry-Cle ... 20.8

Clutch Pitching Index
Lee-Bos ... 119
Forster-Chi ... 116
Curtis-Bos ... 113
Drago-KC ... 112
Bahnsen-Chi ... 112

Relief Runs
Hiller-Det ... 33.1
Fingers-Oak ... 26.7
Reynolds-Bal ... 23.1
Acosta-Chi ... 17.1
Jackson-Bal ... 17.1

Adjusted Relief Runs
Hiller-Det ... 36.9
Fingers-Oak ... 22.9
Reynolds-Bal ... 22.0
Acosta-Chi ... 18.6
Jackson-Bal ... 16.3

Relief Ranking
Hiller-Det ... 64.9
Acosta-Chi ... 35.5
Fingers-Oak ... 33.3
Reynolds-Bal ... 25.5
Lyle-NY ... 23.8

Total Pitcher Index
Hiller-Det ... 6.7
Blyleven-Min ... 5.7
Palmer-Bal ... 4.5
Lee-Bos ... 4.0
Acosta-Chi ... 3.7

Total Baseball Ranking
Hiller-Det ... 6.7
Blyleven-Min ... 5.7
Carew-Min ... 5.3
Grich-Bal ... 4.7
Jackson-Oak ... 4.6

TEAM	G	W	L	PCT	GB	R	OR	AB	H	2B	3B	HR	BB	SO	AVG	OBP	SLG	PRO	PRO+	BR	/A	PF	CHI	RC	SB	CS	SBA	SBR
EAST																												
PIT	162	88	74	.543		751	657	5702	**1560**	238	46	114	514	828	**.274**	.338	.391	.729	114	66	94	96	100	745	55	31	64	-2
STL	161	86	75	.534	1.5	677	643	5620	1492	216	46	83	531	752	.265	.334	.365	.699	102	9	15	99	98	687	**172**	62	74	**14**
PHI	162	80	82	.494	8	676	701	5494	1434	233	**50**	95	469	822	.261	.322	.373	.695	96	-7	-34	104	**104**	658	115	58	66	0
MON	161	79	82	.491	8.5	662	657	5343	1355	201	29	86	652	812	.254	.338	.350	.688	93	2	-35	106	99	657	124	49	72	8
NY	162	71	91	.438	17	572	646	5468	1286	183	22	96	597	**735**	.235	.314	.329	.643	86	-99	-89	98	100	571	43	23	65	-1
CHI	162	66	96	.407	22	669	826	5574	1397	221	42	110	621	857	.251	.329	.365	.694	96	-1	-29	104	98	668	78	73	52	-20
WEST																												
LA	162	102	60	.630		**798**	**561**	5557	1511	231	34	**139**	597	820	.272	**.346**	**.401**	**.747**	120	**103**	**135**	96	102	774	149	75	67	0
CIN	163	98	64	.605	4	776	631	5535	1437	**271**	35	135	**693**	940	.260	.345	.394	.739	115	95	107	99	99	**776**	146	49	**75**	14
ATL	163	88	74	.543	14	661	563	5533	1375	202	37	120	571	772	.249	.321	.363	.684	93	-23	-51	104	101	649	72	44	62	-5
HOU	162	81	81	.500	21	653	632	5489	1441	222	41	110	471	864	.263	.324	.378	.702	107	6	35	98	98	663	108	65	62	-7
SF	162	72	90	.444	30	634	723	5482	1380	228	38	93	548	869	.252	.323	.358	.681	92	-28	-58	105	100	642	107	51	68	2
SD	162	60	102	.370	42	541	830	5415	1239	196	27	99	564	900	.229	.304	.330	.634	87	-122	-99	96	101	555	85	45	65	-2
TOT	972					8070		66212	16907	2642	447	1280	6828	9971	.255	.328	.367	.695							1254	625	67	1

TEAM	CG	SH	SV	IP	H	H/G	HR	BB	SO	RAT	ERA	ERA+	OAV	OOB	PR	/A	PF	CPI	FA	E	DP	FW	PW	BW	SBW	DIF
EAST																										
PIT	**51**	9	17	1466	1428	8.8	93	543	721	12.3	3.49	99	.256	.326	21	-7	95	100	.975	162	154	-.5	-.7	9.8	-.2	-1.4
STL	37	13	20	1473[1]	1399	8.5	97	616	794	12.5	3.48	103	.254	.331	22	15	99	**104**	.977	147	**192**	.4	1.6	1.6	**1.4**	.6
PHI	46	4	19	1447[1]	1394	8.7	111	682	892	13.1	3.91	97	.257	.343	-47	-22	104	101	.976	148	168	.4	-2.3	-3.5	-.0	4.5
MON	35	8	**27**	1429	1340	8.4	99	544	822	12.0	3.60	107	.249	.321	3	-38	106	94	.976	153	157	.0	4.0	-3.6	.8	-2.6
NY	46	15	14	1470[1]	1433	8.8	99	504	908	12.0	3.42	104	.257	.322	33	24	99	102	.975	158	150	-.2	2.5	-9.3	-.1	-2.9
CHI	23	6	26	1466[1]	1593	9.8	122	576	895	13.6	4.28	89	.277	.347	-108	-76	105	100	.969	199	141	-2.6	-7.9	-3.0	-2.1	.7
WEST																										
LA	33	19	23	1465[1]	**1272**	**7.8**	112	**464**	943	10.8	**2.97**	114	**.233**	**.296**	105	70	94	96	.975	157	122	-.2	7.3	**14.1**	-.0	-.2
CIN	34	11	**27**	1466[1]	1364	8.4	126	536	875	11.8	3.41	102	.247	.316	33	12	96	100	.979	134	151	1.2	1.2	11.1	**1.4**	1.9
ATL	46	**21**	22	1474[1]	1343	8.2	97	488	772	11.3	3.05	**124**	.244	.309	93	**119**	104	102	.979	132	161	1.3	**12.4**	-5.3	-.5	-.9
HOU	36	18	18	1450[2]	1396	8.7	**84**	601	738	12.6	3.46	100	.255	.333	25	0	96	**104**	**.982**	113	161	**2.4**	.0	3.6	-.7	-5.3
SF	27	11	25	1439	1409	8.8	116	559	756	12.5	3.78	101	.257	.328	-26	-3	105	100	.972	175	153	-1.2	.3	-6.0	-.2	-2.2
SD	25	7	19	1445[2]	1536	9.6	124	715	855	14.3	4.58	78	.275	.362	-155	-165	98	99	.973	170	126	-.9	-17.2	-10.3	-.2	7.6
TOT	439	142	257	17493[2]		8.7				12.4	3.62		.255	.328					.976	1848	1836					

Runs
Rose-Cin	110
Schmidt-Phi	108
Bench-Cin	108
Morgan-Cin	107
Brock-StL	105

Hits
Garr-Atl	214
Cash-Phi	206
Garvey-LA	200
Oliver-Pit	198
Stennett-Pit	196

Doubles
Rose-Cin	45
Oliver-Pit	38
Bench-Cin	38
Stargell-Pit	37

Triples
Garr-Atl	17
Oliver-Pit	12
Cash-Phi	11
Metzger-Hou	10
Bowa-Phi	10

Home Runs
Schmidt-Phi	36
Bench-Cin	33
Wynn-LA	32
Perez-Cin	28
Cedeno-Hou	26

Total Bases
Bench-Cin	315
Schmidt-Phi	310
Garr-Atl	305
Garvey-LA	301
Oliver-Pit	293

Runs Batted In
Bench-Cin	129
Schmidt-Phi	116
Garvey-LA	111
Wynn-LA	108
Simmons-StL	103

Runs Produced
Bench-Cin	204
Schmidt-Phi	188
Garvey-LA	185
Wynn-LA	180
Cedeno-Hou	171

Bases On Balls
Evans-Atl	126
Morgan-Cin	120
Wynn-LA	108
Schmidt-Phi	106
Rose-Cin	106

Batting Average
Garr-Atl	.353
Oliver-Pit	.321
Gross-Hou	.314
Buckner-LA	.314
Madlock-Chi	.313

On Base Percentage
Morgan-Cin	.430
Stargell-Pit	.409
Bailey-Mon	.400
Schmidt-Phi	.398
Smith-StL	.394

Slugging Average
Schmidt-Phi	.546
Stargell-Pit	.537
Smith-StL	.528
Bench-Cin	.507
Garr-Atl	.503

Production
Stargell-Pit	.947
Schmidt-Phi	.944
Morgan-Cin	.924
Smith-StL	.922
Wynn-LA	.891

Adjusted Production
Stargell-Pit	169
Morgan-Cin	160
Smith-StL	158
Schmidt-Phi	156
Wynn-LA	154

Batter Runs
Schmidt-Phi	48.3
Morgan-Cin	45.2
Stargell-Pit	44.4
Smith-StL	38.5
Wynn-LA	36.4

Adjusted Batter Runs
Stargell-Pit	48.5
Morgan-Cin	46.9
Schmidt-Phi	43.4
Wynn-LA	40.8
Smith-StL	39.4

Clutch Hitting Index
Sizemore-StL	128
Singleton-Mon	123
Montanez-Phi	121
Cey-LA	120
Zisk-Pit	119

Runs Created
Schmidt-Phi	130
Morgan-Cin	125
Stargell-Pit	115
Bench-Cin	114
Garr-Atl	113

Total Average
Morgan-Cin	1.108
Schmidt-Phi	1.017
Stargell-Pit	.997
Smith-StL	.920
Wynn-LA	.915

Stolen Bases
Brock-StL	118
Lopes-LA	59
Morgan-Cin	58
Cedeno-Hou	57
Lintz-Mon	50

Stolen Base Average
Lintz-Mon	87.7
Concepcion-Cin	87.2
Morgan-Cin	82.9
Bonds-SF	78.8
Hernandez-SD	78.7

Stolen Base Runs
Brock-StL	15.6
Lintz-Mon	10.8
Morgan-Cin	10.2
Concepcion-Cin	8.7

Fielding Runs
Cash-Phi	29.1
Schmidt-Phi	26.3
Cedeno-Hou	20.9
Foli-Mon	19.4
Rose-Cin	17.6

Total Player Rating
Schmidt-Phi	6.9
Morgan-Cin	5.2
Stargell-Pit	4.5
Wynn-LA	4.3
Concepcion-Cin	4.3

Wins
P.Niekro-Atl	20
Messersmith-LA	20
Sutton-LA	19
Billingham-Cin	19

Win Percentage
Messersmith-LA	.769
Sutton-LA	.679
Capra-Atl	.667
Torrez-Mon	.652
Billingham-Cin	.633

Games
Marshall-LA	106
Hardy-SD	76
Borbon-Cin	73
Forsch-Hou	70
Sosa-SF	68

Complete Games
P.Niekro-Atl	18
Carlton-Phi	17
Lonborg-Phi	16
Rooker-Pit	15

Shutouts
Matlack-NY	7
P.Niekro-Atl	6

Saves
Marshall-LA	21
Moffitt-SF	15
Borbon-Cin	14
Giusti-Pit	12

Innings Pitched
P.Niekro-Atl	302.1
Messersmith-LA	292.1
Carlton-Phi	291.0
Lonborg-Phi	283.0
Sutton-LA	276.0

Fewest Hits/Game
Capra-Atl	6.76
Messersmith-LA	6.99
P.Niekro-Atl	7.41
Gullett-Cin	7.44
Wilson-Hou	7.48

Fewest BB/Game
Barr-SF	1.76
Reed-Atl	1.98
Ellis-Pit	2.09
Lonborg-Phi	2.23
Marshall-LA	2.42

Strikeouts
Carlton-Phi	240
Messersmith-LA	221
Seaver-NY	201
P.Niekro-Atl	195
Matlack-NY	195

Strikeouts/Game
Seaver-NY	7.67
Carlton-Phi	7.42
Bonham-Chi	7.08
D'Acquisto-SF	6.99
Norman-Cin	6.81

Ratio
Messersmith-LA	9.97
P.Niekro-Atl	10.21
Barr-SF	10.21
Matlack-NY	10.24
Reed-Atl	10.35

Earned Run Average
Capra-Atl	2.28
P.Niekro-Atl	2.38
Matlack-NY	2.41
Marshall-LA	2.42
Messersmith-LA	2.59

Adjusted ERA
Capra-Atl	166
P.Niekro-Atl	159
Matlack-NY	148
Marshall-LA	141
Barr-SF	139

Opponents' Batting Avg.
Capra-Atl	.208
Messersmith-LA	.212
Gullett-Cin	.222
P.Niekro-Atl	.225
Matlack-NY	.226

Opponents' On Base Pct.
Messersmith-LA	.278
Matlack-NY	.285
P.Niekro-Atl	.286
Reed-Atl	.286
Capra-Atl	.287

Starter Runs
P.Niekro-Atl	41.5
Matlack-NY	35.6
Messersmith-LA	33.5
Capra-Atl	32.2
Rooker-Pit	24.6

Adjusted Starter Runs
P.Niekro-Atl	46.9
Capra-Atl	36.1
Matlack-NY	34.0
Barr-SF	28.1
Messersmith-LA	26.4

Clutch Pitching Index
Caldwell-SF	117
Morton-Atl	117
Marshall-LA	116
Schueler-Phi	113
McGlothen-StL	112

Relief Runs
Marshall-LA	27.7
Murray-Mon	20.0
House-Atl	19.3
Taylor-Mon	17.3
C.Carroll-Cin	16.5

Adjusted Relief Runs
Marshall-LA	22.7
Murray-Mon	21.7
House-Atl	21.1
Taylor-Mon	19.9
C.Carroll-Cin	15.0

Relief Ranking
Marshall-LA	31.6
C.Carroll-Cin	24.8
House-Atl	19.9
Taylor-Mon	17.9
Leon-Atl	13.4

Total Pitcher Index
P.Niekro-Atl	5.2
Capra-Atl	3.7
Marshall-LA	3.5
Messersmith-LA	3.4
Rooker-Pit	3.2

Total Baseball Ranking
Schmidt-Phi	6.9
P.Niekro-Atl	5.2
Morgan-Cin	5.2
Stargell-Pit	4.5
Wynn-LA	4.3

TEAM	G	W	L	PCT	GB	R	OR	AB	H	2B	3B	HR	BB	SO	AVG	OBP	SLG	PRO	PRO+	BR	/A	PF	CHI	RC	SB	CS	SBA	SBR
EAST																												
BAL	162	91	71	.562		659	612	5535	1418	226	27	116	509	770	.256	.325	.370	.695	103	-2	19	97	98	671	145	58	**71**	9
NY	162	89	73	.549	2	671	623	5524	1451	220	30	101	515	690	.263	.328	.368	.696	103	1	20	97	100	666	53	35	60	-5
BOS	162	84	78	.519	7	**696**	661	5499	1449	**236**	31	109	569	811	.264	.336	.377	.713	98	39	-11	107	98	699	104	58	64	-4
CLE	162	77	85	.475	14	662	694	5474	1395	201	19	131	432	756	.255	.312	.370	.682	97	-36	-30	99	**108**	610	79	68	54	-17
MIL	162	76	86	.469	15	647	660	5472	1335	228	**49**	120	500	909	.244	.310	.369	.679	96	-41	-37	99	105	622	106	75	59	-13
DET	162	72	90	.444	19	620	768	5568	1375	200	35	131	436	784	.247	.304	.366	.670	89	-64	-85	104	104	607	67	38	64	-3
WEST																												
OAK	162	90	72	.556		689	551	5331	1315	205	37	132	568	876	.247	.324	.373	.697	107	1	44	94	105	648	**164**	93	64	-7
TEX	161	84	76	.525	5	690	698	5449	1482	198	39	99	508	710	**.272**	.338	.377	.715	**108**	42	**60**	98	98	677	113	80	59	-14
MIN	163	82	80	.506	8	673	669	5632	**1530**	190	37	111	520	791	**.272**	.338	.338	.716	102	44	16	104	93	**707**	74	45	62	-5
CHI	163	80	80	.500	9	684	721	5577	1492	225	23	**135**	519	858	.268	.333	**.389**	**.722**	104	49	32	102	95	701	64	53	55	-13
KC	162	77	85	.475	13	667	662	5582	1448	232	42	93	550	768	.259	.329	.364	.693	94	-2	-40	106	99	668	146	76	66	-2
CAL	163	68	94	.420	22	618	657	5401	1372	203	31	95	509	801	.254	.323	.356	.679	101	-30	6	94	99	615	119	79	60	-12
TOT	973					7976		66044	17062	2564	400	1369	6135	9524	.258	.325	.371	.697							1234	758	62	-85

TEAM	CG	SH	SV	IP	H	H/G	HR	BB	SO	RAT	ERA	ERA+	OAV	OOB	PR	/A	PF	CPI	FA	E	DP	FW	PW	BW	SBW	DIF
EAST																										
BAL	57	**16**	25	1474	1393	8.5	101	480	701	11.6	3.27	105	.253	.316	56	29	95	102	**.980**	128	174	1.0	3.0	2.0	**1.7**	2.3
NY	53	13	24	1455¹	1402	8.7	104	528	829	12.1	3.31	105	.256	.325	50	29	96	**107**	.977	142	158	.2	3.0	2.1	.2	2.5
BOS	**71**	12	18	1455¹	1462	9.0	126	463	751	12.1	3.72	103	.262	.322	-16	20	106	99	.977	145	156	.0	2.1	-1.2	.3	1.7
CLE	45	9	27	1445²	1419	8.8	138	479	650	12.0	3.80	95	.260	.323	-30	-31	100	98	.977	146	157	-.0	-3.2	-3.1	-1.0	3.4
MIL	43	11	24	1457²	1476	9.1	126	493	621	12.3	3.76	96	.266	.329	-23	-23	100	102	**.980**	127	168	1.1	-2.4	-3.9	-.6	.8
DET	54	7	15	1455²	1443	8.9	148	621	869	13.0	4.16	91	.262	.341	-88	-58	105	99	.975	158	155	-.7	-6.1	-8.9	.4	6.2
WEST																										
OAK	49	12	28	1439²	**1322**	8.3	90	430	755	11.1	**2.95**	**112**	.246	**.305**	107	59	92	103	.977	141	154	.3	**6.2**	4.6	.0	-2.0
TEX	62	**16**	12	1433²	1423	8.9	126	449	871	12.0	3.82	93	.260	.321	-33	-41	99	95	.974	163	164	-1.1	-4.3	**6.3**	-.7	3.8
MIN	43	11	**29**	1455¹	1436	8.9	115	513	934	12.3	3.64	103	.260	.327	-4	18	104	101	.976	151	164	-.3	1.9	1.7	.2	-2.5
CHI	55	11	**29**	1465²	1470	9.0	103	548	826	12.7	3.94	95	.263	.334	-52	-34	103	96	.977	147	**188**	-.0	-3.6	3.3	-.6	.9
KC	54	13	17	1471²	1477	9.0	91	482	731	12.2	3.51	109	.263	.325	17	50	106	101	.976	152	166	-.4	5.2	-4.2	.5	-5.2
CAL	64	13	12	1439	1339	8.4	101	649	**986**	12.7	3.52	98	.248	.334	15	-14	95	102	.976	147	150	-.0	-1.5	.6	-.5	-11.6
TOT	650	144	260	17448²		8.8				12.2	3.62		.258	.325					.977	1747	1954					

Runs
Yastrzemski-Bos ... 93
Grich-Bal ... 92
Jackson-Oak ... 90
Otis-KC ... 87
Carew-Min ... 86

Hits
Carew-Min ... 218
Davis-Bal ... 181
Money-Mil ... 178
K.Henderson-Chi ... 176
Rudi-Oak ... 174

Doubles
Rudi-Oak ... 39
Scott-Mil ... 36
McRae-KC ... 36
K.Henderson-Chi ... 35
Burroughs-Tex ... 33

Triples
Rivers-Cal ... 11
Otis-KC ... 9

Home Runs
D.Allen-Chi ... 32
Jackson-Oak ... 29
Tenace-Oak ... 26
Darwin-Min ... 25
Burroughs-Tex ... 25

Total Bases
Rudi-Oak ... 287
K.Henderson-Chi ... 281
Burroughs-Tex ... 279
Carew-Min ... 267

Runs Batted In
Burroughs-Tex ... 118
Bando-Oak ... 103
Rudi-Oak ... 99
K.Henderson-Chi ... 95
Darwin-Min ... 94

Runs Produced
Burroughs-Tex ... 177
Bando-Oak ... 165
Yastrzemski-Bos ... 157
Grich-Bal ... 155
Jackson-Oak ... 154

Bases On Balls
Tenace-Oak ... 110
Yastrzemski-Bos ... 104
Burroughs-Tex ... 91
Grich-Bal ... 90

Batting Average
Carew-Min ... .364
Orta-Chi ... .316
McRae-KC ... .310
Piniella-NY ... .305
Maddox-NY ... .303

On Base Percentage
Carew-Min ... .435
Yastrzemski-Bos ... .421
Burroughs-Tex ... .405
Maddox-NY ... .397
Jackson-Oak ... .396

Slugging Average
D.Allen-Chi ... .563
Jackson-Oak ... .514
Burroughs-Tex ... .504
Rudi-Oak ... .484
Freehan-Det ... .479

Production
D.Allen-Chi ... .942
Jackson-Oak ... .910
Burroughs-Tex ... .908
Carew-Min ... .880
Yastrzemski-Bos ... .866

Adjusted Production
Jackson-Oak ... 171
Burroughs-Tex ... 164
D.Allen-Chi ... 164
Carew-Min ... 148
Robinson-Cal-Cle ... 143

Batter Runs
Burroughs-Tex ... 45.3
Carew-Min ... 44.7
Jackson-Oak ... 41.0
D.Allen-Chi ... 39.3
Yastrzemski-Bos ... 38.1

Adjusted Batter Runs
Burroughs-Tex ... 48.2
Jackson-Oak ... 48.1
Carew-Min ... 40.1
D.Allen-Chi ... 37.0
Grich-Bal ... 31.3

Clutch Hitting Index
Murcer-NY ... 134
Bando-Oak ... 132
Burroughs-Tex ... 131
Petrocelli-Bos ... 119
Evans-Bos ... 115

Runs Created
Carew-Min ... 118
Burroughs-Tex ... 113
Jackson-Oak ... 109
Yastrzemski-Bos ... 102
K.Henderson-Chi ... 100

Total Average
Jackson-Oak ... .992
D.Allen-Chi ... .953
Burroughs-Tex ... .919
Yastrzemski-Bos ... .900
Carew-Min ... .879

Stolen Bases
North-Oak ... 54
Carew-Min ... 38
Lowenstein-Cle ... 36
Campaneris-Oak ... 34
Patek-KC ... 33

Stolen Base Average
Jackson-Oak ... 83.3
Coggins-Bal ... 81.3
Pinson-KC ... 80.8
Otis-KC ... 78.3
Money-Mil ... 76.0

Stolen Base Runs
Jackson-Oak ... 4.5
Coggins-Bal ... 4.2
Pinson-KC ... 3.3
Miller-Bos ... 2.7
Blair-Bal ... 2.7

Fielding Runs
Terrell-Min ... 23.3
Rodriguez-Det ... 21.6
Robinson-Bal ... 20.5
North-Oak ... 18.4
Doyle-Cal ... 16.4

Total Player Rating
Carew-Min ... 5.9
Jackson-Oak ... 5.6
Grich-Bal ... 4.8
Burroughs-Tex ... 3.3
Robinson-Bal ... 3.2

Wins
Jenkins-Tex ... 25
Hunter-Oak ... 25

Win Percentage
Cuellar-Bal ... .688
Jenkins-Tex ... .676
Hunter-Oak ... .676
Tiant-Bos ... .629

Games
Fingers-Oak ... 76
Murphy-Mil ... 70
Foucault-Tex ... 69
Lyle-NY ... 66
Campbell-Min ... 63

Complete Games
Jenkins-Tex ... 29
G.Perry-Cle ... 28
Lolich-Det ... 27
Ryan-Cal ... 26
Tiant-Bos ... 25

Shutouts
Tiant-Bos ... 7
Jenkins-Tex ... 6
Hunter-Oak ... 6
Cuellar-Bal ... 5
Bibby-Tex ... 5

Saves
Forster-Chi ... 24
Murphy-Mil ... 20
Campbell-Min ... 19
Buskey-NY-Cle ... 18
Fingers-Oak ... 18

Innings Pitched
Ryan-Cal ... 332.2
Jenkins-Tex ... 328.1
G.Perry-Cle ... 322.1
Wood-Chi ... 320.1
Hunter-Oak ... 318.1

Fewest Hits/Game
Ryan-Cal ... 5.98
G.Perry-Cle ... 6.42
DalCanton-KC ... 6.93
Hassler-Cal ... 7.33
Hunter-Oak ... 7.58

Fewest BB/Game
Jenkins-Tex ... 1.23
Hunter-Oak ... 1.30
Holtzman-Oak ... 1.80
Kaat-Chi ... 2.04
Wright-Mil ... 2.09

Strikeouts
Ryan-Cal ... 367
Blyleven-Min ... 249
Jenkins-Tex ... 225
G.Perry-Cle ... 216
Lolich-Det ... 202

Strikeouts/Game
Ryan-Cal ... 9.93
Blyleven-Min ... 7.98
Jenkins-Tex ... 6.17
Busby-KC ... 6.10
G.Perry-Cle ... 6.03

Ratio
Hunter-Oak ... 8.99
Jenkins-Tex ... 9.29
G.Perry-Cle ... 9.35
Grimsley-Bal ... 10.53
Blyleven-Min ... 10.57

Earned Run Average
Hunter-Oak ... 2.49
G.Perry-Cle ... 2.51
Hassler-Cal ... 2.61
Blyleven-Min ... 2.66
Fitzmorris-KC ... 2.79

Adjusted ERA
G.Perry-Cle ... 144
Blyleven-Min ... 141
Fitzmorris-KC ... 137
Hunter-Oak ... 133
Hassler-Cal ... 132

Opponents' Batting Avg.
Ryan-Cal ... .190
G.Perry-Cle ... .204
DalCanton-KC ... .211
Hassler-Cal ... .225
Hunter-Oak ... .229

Opponents' On Base Pct.
Hunter-Oak ... .260
Jenkins-Tex ... .264
G.Perry-Cle ... .272
Blyleven-Min ... .292
Tiant-Bos ... .293

Starter Runs
Hunter-Oak ... 39.9
G.Perry-Cle ... 39.6
Blyleven-Min ... 29.9
Jenkins-Tex ... 29.9
Ryan-Cal ... 26.7

Adjusted Starter Runs
G.Perry-Cle ... 39.4
Blyleven-Min ... 34.1
Tiant-Bos ... 31.9
Hunter-Oak ... 29.3
Jenkins-Tex ... 27.0

Clutch Pitching Index
Goltz-Min ... 124
Hassler-Cal ... 121
Lee-Bos ... 119
Fitzmorris-KC ... 116
Tanana-Cal ... 113

Relief Runs
Lyle-NY ... 24.8
Murphy-Mil ... 23.4
Foucault-Tex ... 22.0
Lindblad-Oak ... 17.5
Hiller-Det ... 16.3

Adjusted Relief Runs
Murphy-Mil ... 23.4
Lyle-NY ... 23.2
Foucault-Tex ... 21.1
Hiller-Det ... 19.4
Campbell-Min ... 15.2

Relief Ranking
Murphy-Mil ... 42.9
Hiller-Det ... 39.8
Lyle-NY ... 28.8
Foucault-Tex ... 26.4
Campbell-Min ... 22.4

Total Pitcher Index
Murphy-Mil ... 4.9
G.Perry-Cle ... 4.4
Blyleven-Min ... 4.0
Hiller-Det ... 3.9
Hunter-Oak ... 3.0

Total Baseball Ranking
Carew-Min ... 5.9
Jackson-Oak ... 5.6
Murphy-Mil ... 4.9
Grich-Bal ... 4.8
G.Perry-Cle ... 4.4

TEAM	G	W	L	PCT	GB	R	OR	AB	H	2B	3B	HR	BB	SO	AVG	OBP	SLG	PRO	PRO+	BR	/A	PF	CHI	RC	SB	CS	SBA	SBR
EAST																												
PIT	161	92	69	.571		712	565	5489	1444	255	47	**138**	468	832	.263	.325	**.402**	.727	109	44	50	99	102	709	49	28	64	-2
PHI	162	86	76	.531	6.5	735	694	5592	1506	**283**	42	125	610	960	.269	.344	**.402**	.746	109	98	67	104	94	785	126	57	69	4
NY	162	82	80	.506	10.5	646	625	5587	1430	217	34	101	501	805	.256	.321	.361	.682	100	-36	-7	95	102	639	32	26	55	-6
STL	163	82	80	.506	10.5	662	689	5597	**1527**	239	46	81	444	**649**	**.273**	.329	.375	.704	99	7	-17	104	99	683	116	49	70	5
MON	162	75	87	.463	17.5	601	690	5518	1346	216	31	98	579	954	.244	.319	.348	.667	87	-63	-89	104	99	623	108	58	65	-2
CHI	162	75	87	.463	17.5	712	827	5470	1419	229	41	95	650	802	.259	.341	.368	.709	99	33	2	104	100	702	67	55	55	-13
WEST																												
CIN	162	108	54	.667		**840**	586	5581	1515	278	37	124	**691**	916	.271	**.355**	.401	**.756**	**114**	128	113	102	103	**829**	168	36	82	29
LA	162	88	74	.543	20	648	**534**	5453	1355	217	31	118	611	825	.248	.328	.365	.693	103	-10	18	96	98	667	138	52	73	10
SF	161	80	81	.497	27.5	659	671	5447	1412	235	45	84	604	775	.259	.336	.365	.701	97	11	-17	104	98	673	99	47	68	2
SD	162	71	91	.438	37	552	683	5429	1324	215	22	78	506	754	.244	.313	.335	.648	92	-100	-66	94	99	571	85	50	63	-5
ATL	161	67	94	.416	40.5	583	739	5424	1323	179	28	107	543	759	.244	.315	.346	.661	86	-75	-96	104	101	587	55	58	59	-6
HOU	162	64	97	.398	43.5	664	711	5515	1401	218	**54**	84	523	762	.254	.322	.359	.681	102	-36	9	93	**106**	643	133	62	68	3
TOT	971					8014		66102	17002	2781	458	1233	6730	9793	.257	.329	.369	.698							1176	558	68	18

TEAM	CG	SH	SV	IP	H	H/G	HR	BB	SO	RAT	ERA	ERA+	OAV	OOB	PR	/A	PF	CPI	FA	E	DP	FW	PW	BW	SBW	DIF
EAST																										
PIT	43	14	31	1437¹	1302	8.2	**79**	551	768	11.7	3.01	**118**	.243	.315	98	85	98	103	.976	151	147	.2	**8.9**	5.2	-.4	-2.4
PHI	33	11	30	1455	1353	8.4	111	546	897	11.9	3.82	98	.246	.320	-33	-15	103	89	.976	152	156	.2	-1.6	7.0	.3	-.9
NY	40	14	31	1466	1344	8.3	99	580	**989**	12.0	3.39	102	.246	.321	38	10	95	98	.976	151	144	.3	1.0	-.7	-.8	1.2
STL	33	13	36	1454²	1452	9.0	98	571	824	12.7	3.57	105	.260	.331	8	30	104	102	.973	171	140	-.8	3.1	-1.8	.4	.0
MON	30	12	25	1480	1448	8.8	102	665	831	13.1	3.72	103	.259	.341	-17	17	106	103	.973	180	**179**	-1.3	1.8	-9.3	-.4	3.2
CHI	27	8	33	1444¹	1587	9.9	130	551	850	13.6	4.49	86	.281	.349	-140	-105	106	98	.972	179	152	-1.3	-11.0	.2	-1.5	7.6
WEST																										
CIN	22	8	**50**	1459	1422	8.8	112	487	663	12.0	3.37	107	.257	.321	41	36	99	105	**.984**	102	173	3.0	3.8	11.8	2.9	5.6
LA	51	18	21	1469²	**1215**	7.4	104	**448**	894	10.4	**2.92**	114	**.225**	.287	114	78	94	88	.979	127	106	1.6	8.1	1.9	.9	-5.5
SF	37	9	24	1432²	1406	8.8	92	612	856	12.9	3.74	102	.259	.339	-19	10	105	101	.976	146	164	.5	1.0	-1.8	.0	-.3
SD	40	12	20	1463¹	1494	9.2	99	521	713	12.5	3.48	100	.266	.331	23	-1	96	**107**	.971	188	163	-1.8	-.1	-6.9	-.7	-.5
ATL	32	4	24	1430	1543	9.7	101	519	669	13.3	3.91	96	.278	.344	-47	-23	104	105	.972	175	147	-1.1	-2.4	-10.0	-.8	.8
HOU	39	6	25	1458¹	1436	9.0	106	679	839	13.3	4.04	83	.262	.347	-67	-108	93	99	.979	137	166	1.1	-11.3	.9	.2	-7.4
TOT	427	129	350	17450¹		8.8				12.4	3.62		.257	.329					.976	1859	1837					

Runs
Rose-Cin 112
Cash-Phi 111
Lopes-LA 108
Morgan-Cin 107
Thomas-SF 99

Hits
Cash-Phi 213
Rose-Cin 210
Garvey-LA 210
Simmons-StL 193
Millan-NY 191

Doubles
Rose-Cin 47
Cash-Phi 40
Oliver-Pit 39
Bench-Cin 39
Garvey-LA 38

Triples
Garr-Atl 11
Parker-Pit 10
Kessinger-Chi 10
Joshua-SF 10
Gross-Hou 10

Home Runs
Schmidt-Phi 38
Kingman-NY 36
Luzinski-Phi 34
Bench-Cin 28

Total Bases
Luzinski-Phi 322
Garvey-LA 314
Parker-Pit 302
Schmidt-Phi 294
Rose-Cin 286

Runs Batted In
Luzinski-Phi 120
Bench-Cin 110
Perez-Cin 109
Staub-NY 105

Runs Produced
Morgan-Cin 184
Staub-NY 179
Perez-Cin 179
Luzinski-Phi 171
Bench-Cin 165

Bases On Balls
Morgan-Cin 132
Wynn-LA 110
Evans-Atl 105
Schmidt-Phi 101

Batting Average
Madlock-Chi ...... .354
Simmons-StL ...... .332
Sanguillen-Pit .... .328
Morgan-Cin .... .327
Watson-Hou .... .324

On Base Percentage
Morgan-Cin .... .471
Wynn-LA .... .407
Rose-Cin .... .407
Madlock-Chi ...... .406
Murcer-SF .... .404

Slugging Average
Parker-Pit .... .541
Luzinski-Phi ...... .540
Schmidt-Phi .... .523
Bench-Cin .... .519
Foster-Cin .... .518

Production
Morgan-Cin ...... .979
Luzinski-Phi ..... .939
Parker-Pit .... .899
Stargell-Pit ..... .894
Schmidt-Phi ...... .890

Adjusted Production
Morgan-Cin 168
Luzinski-Phi 152
Watson-Hou 152
Parker-Pit 148
Stargell-Pit 147

Batter Runs
Morgan-Cin 57.1
Luzinski-Phi 47.5
Simmons-StL 35.7
Thornton-Chi 35.4
Schmidt-Phi 33.7

Adjusted Batter Runs
Morgan-Cin 54.9
Luzinski-Phi 42.6
Parker-Pit 32.5
Simmons-StL 32.1
Thornton-Chi 31.7

Clutch Hitting Index
Perez-Cin 133
Morales-Chi 133
Trillo-Chi 132
Montanez-Phi-SF ... 127
Murcer-SF 123

Runs Created
Morgan-Cin 145
Luzinski-Phi 128
Rose-Cin 120
Schmidt-Phi 113
Simmons-StL 108

Total Average
Morgan-Cin 1.279
Luzinski-Phi .... .956
Schmidt-Phi ..... .943
Bench-Cin .... .901
Stargell-Pit .... .895

Stolen Bases
Lopes-LA 77
Morgan-Cin 67
Brock-StL 56
Cedeno-Hou 50
Cardenal-Chi 34

Stolen Base Average
Morgan-Cin 87.0
Lopes-LA 86.5
Maddox-SF-Phi 86.2
Winfield-SD 85.2
Concepcion-Cin ... 84.6

Stolen Base Runs
Lopes-LA 15.9
Morgan-Cin 14.1
Brock-StL 7.2
Concepcion-Cin 6.3
Maddox-SF-Phi 5.1

Fielding Runs
Schmidt-Phi 24.0
Evans-Atl 23.4
Maddox-SF-Phi 21.0
Mackanin-Mon 18.2
Trillo-Chi 16.0

Total Player Rating
Morgan-Cin 7.1
Schmidt-Phi 5.7
Bench-Cin 3.9
Parker-Pit 3.7
Evans-Atl 3.5

Wins
Seaver-NY 22
Jones-SD 20
Messersmith-LA 19
Hooton-Chi-LA 18
Reuss-Pit 18

Win Percentage
Gullett-Cin ...... .789
Seaver-NY .... .710
Hooton-Chi-LA .... .667
Murray-Mon .... .652

Games
Garber-Phi 71
McEnaney-Cin 70
Tomlin-SD 67
Borbon-Cin 67
Garman-StL 66

Complete Games
Messersmith-LA 19
Jones-SD 18
Seaver-NY 15
Reuss-Pit 15

Shutouts
Messersmith-LA 7
Reuss-Pit 6
Jones-SD 6
Seaver-NY 5

Saves
Hrabosky-StL 22
Eastwick-Cin 22
Giusti-Pit 17
McEnaney-Cin 15
Knowles-Chi 15

Innings Pitched
Messersmith-LA .. 321.2
Jones-SD 285.0
Seaver-NY 280.1
Morton-Atl 277.2
Niekro-Atl 275.2

Fewest Hits/Game
Messersmith-LA ... 6.83
Seaver-NY 6.97
Warthen-Mon 6.98
Sutton-LA 7.15
Hooton-Chi-LA 7.29

Fewest BB/Game
Nolan-Cin 1.24
Jones-SD 1.77
Reed-Atl-StL 1.91
Rau-LA 2.13
Barr-SF 2.14

Strikeouts
Seaver-NY 243
Montefusco-SF 215
Messersmith-LA ... 213
Carlton-Phi 192
Richard-Hou 176

Strikeouts/Game
Montefusco-SF 7.94
Richard-Hou 7.80
Seaver-NY 7.80
Warthen-Mon 6.87
Carlton-Phi 6.77

Ratio
Jones-SD 9.41
Sutton-LA 9.45
Messersmith-LA ... 9.65
Hooton-Chi-LA 9.89
Nolan-Cin 9.91

Earned Run Average
Jones-SD 2.24
Messersmith-LA ... 2.29
Seaver-NY 2.38
Reuss-Pit 2.54
Forsch-StL 2.86

Adjusted ERA
Jones-SD 155
Messersmith-LA ... 148
Seaver-NY 145
Reuss-Pit 139
Montefusco-SF 132

Opponents' Batting Avg.
Messersmith-LA ... .213
Sutton-LA .... .213
Seaver-NY .... .214
Warthen-Mon ...... .217
Hooton-Chi-LA .... .219

Opponents' On Base Pct.
Sutton-LA .... .264
Jones-SD .... .271
Hooton-Chi-LA .... .276
Messersmith-LA ... .276
Nolan-Cin .... .278

Starter Runs
Messersmith-LA ... 47.4
Jones-SD 43.7
Seaver-NY 38.8
Reuss-Pit 28.5
Sutton-LA 21.3

Adjusted Starter Runs
Messersmith-LA ... 39.5
Jones-SD 39.0
Seaver-NY 33.5
Reuss-Pit 26.4
Montefusco-SF 24.8

Clutch Pitching Index
Reuss-Pit 122
Niekro-Atl 122
Blair-Mon 114
Koosman-NY 113
Barr-SF 110

Relief Runs
Hrabosky-StL 21.2
Apodaca-NY 20.1
Hilgendorf-Phi ... 15.9
McEnaney-Cin 11.6
Garman-StL 10.8

Adjusted Relief Runs
Hrabosky-StL 22.6
Apodaca-NY 18.5
Hilgendorf-Phi ... 17.1
Garman-StL 12.0
McEnaney-Cin 11.3

Relief Ranking
Hrabosky-StL 44.9
Apodaca-NY 20.1
Garman-StL 18.4
Hilgendorf-Phi ... 15.9
McGraw-Phi 15.0

Total Pitcher Index
Jones-SD 4.9
Hrabosky-StL 4.8
Seaver-NY 4.3
Messersmith-LA 4.1
Reuss-Pit 3.7

Total Baseball Ranking
Morgan-Cin 7.1
Schmidt-Phi 5.7
Jones-SD 4.9
Hrabosky-StL 4.8
Seaver-NY 4.3

TEAM	G	W	L	PCT	GB	R	OR	AB	H	2B	3B	HR	BB	SO	AVG	OBP	SLG	PRO	PRO+	BR	/A	PF	CHI	RC	SB	CS	SBA	SBR
EAST																												
BOS	160	95	65	.594		796	709	5448	1500	284	44	134	565	741	.275	.347	.417	.764	106	108	41	109	99	776	66	58	53	-15
BAL	159	90	69	.566	4.5	682	553	5474	1382	224	33	124	580	834	.252	.328	.373	.701	105	-14	30	94	100	680	104	55	65	-2
NY	160	83	77	.519	12	681	588	5415	1430	230	39	110	486	710	.264	.328	.382	.710	103	-3	16	97	101	665	102	59	63	-5
CLE	159	79	80	.497	15.5	688	703	5404	1409	201	25	153	525	667	.261	.329	.392	.721	103	17	18	100	99	672	106	89	54	-22
MIL	162	68	94	.420	28	675	792	5378	1343	242	34	146	553	922	.250	.323	.389	.712	100	-2	-5	101	99	663	65	64	50	-19
DET	159	57	102	.358	37.5	570	786	5366	1338	171	39	125	383	872	.249	.303	.366	.669	84	-94	-119	104	101	573	63	57	53	-15
WEST																												
OAK	162	98	64	.605		758	606	5415	1376	220	33	151	609	846	.254	.335	.391	.726	107	34	51	98	104	725	183	82	69	6
KC	162	91	71	.562	7	710	649	5491	1431	263	58	118	591	675	.261	.336	.394	.730	103	40	21	103	96	736	155	75	67	2
TEX	162	79	83	.488	19	714	733	5599	1431	208	17	134	613	863	.256	.332	.371	.703	99	-10	-4	99	102	693	102	62	62	-7
MIN	159	76	83	.478	20.5	724	736	5514	1497	215	28	121	563	746	.271	.343	.386	.729	104	46	30	102	97	732	81	48	63	-5
CHI	161	75	86	.466	22.5	655	703	5490	1400	209	38	94	611	800	.255	.334	.358	.692	95	-24	-33	101	97	659	101	54	65	-2
CAL	161	72	89	.447	25.5	628	723	5377	1324	195	41	55	593	811	.246	.324	.328	.652	91	-99	-58	93	106	596	220	108	67	1
TOT	963					8281		65371	16861	2662	429	1465	6672	9487	.258	.330	.379	.709							1348	811	62	-82

TEAM	CG	SH	SV	IP	H	H/G	HR	BB	SO	RAT	ERA	ERA+	OAV	OOB	PR	/A	PF	CPI	FA	E	DP	FW	PW	BW	SBW	DIF
EAST																										
BOS	62	11	31	1436²	1463	9.2	145	490	720	12.4	3.98	102	.265	.327	-33	14	108	99	.977	139	142	.9	1.4	4.2	-.8	9.3
BAL	70	19	21	1451	1285	8.0	110	500	717	11.1	3.17	111	.242	.308	98	55	93	100	.983	107	175	2.6	5.6	3.1	.5	-1.3
NY	70	11	20	1424	1325	8.4	104	502	809	11.7	3.29	111	.249	.317	78	56	96	103	.978	135	148	1.1	5.7	1.6	.2	-5.6
CLE	37	6	33	1435¹	1395	8.7	136	599	800	12.7	3.84	98	.258	.335	-10	-10	100	103	.978	134	156	1.1	-1.0	1.8	-1.5	-.9
MIL	36	10	34	1431²	1496	9.4	133	624	643	13.7	4.34	88	.271	.351	-89	-81	101	100	.971	180	162	-1.4	-8.3	-.5	-1.2	-1.6
DET	52	10	17	1396	1496	9.6	137	533	787	13.3	4.27	94	.275	.343	-77	-40	106	100	.972	173	141	-1.1	-4.1	-12.2	-.8	-4.3
WEST																										
OAK	36	10	44	1448	1267	7.9	102	523	784	11.4	3.27	111	.236	.308	82	58	96	94	.977	143	140	.7	5.9	5.2	1.3	3.8
KC	52	11	25	1456²	1422	8.8	108	498	815	12.0	3.47	111	.258	.322	50	62	102	102	.976	155	151	.0	6.3	2.1	.9	.6
TEX	60	16	17	1465²	1456	8.9	123	518	792	12.4	3.86	97	.261	.329	-14	-17	99	98	.971	191	173	-2.0	-1.7	-.4	-.0	2.1
MIN	57	7	22	1423	1381	8.7	137	617	846	12.9	4.05	95	.257	.337	-43	-31	102	98	.973	170	147	-.9	-3.2	3.1	.2	-2.6
CHI	34	7	39	1452¹	1489	9.2	107	655	799	13.5	3.93	99	.268	.349	-24	-9	103	105	.978	140	155	.9	-.9	-3.4	.5	-2.6
CAL	59	19	16	1453¹	1386	8.6	123	613	975	12.6	3.89	91	.253	.333	-18	-55	94	97	.971	184	164	-1.6	-5.6	-5.9	.8	3.9
TOT	625	137	319	17273²		8.8				12.5	3.78		.258	.330					.975	1851	1854					

Runs
Lynn-Bos	103
Mayberry-KC	95
Bonds-NY	93
Rice-Bos	92

Hits
Brett-KC	195
Carew-Min	192
Munson-NY	190
C.Washington-Oak	182

Doubles
Lynn-Bos	47
Jackson-Oak	39
McRae-KC	38
Mayberry-KC	38
Chambliss-NY	38

Triples
Rivers-Cal	13
Brett-KC	13
Orta-Chi	10
Cowens-KC	8

Home Runs
Scott-Mil	36
Jackson-Oak	36
Mayberry-KC	34
Bonds-NY	32

Total Bases
Scott-Mil	318
Mayberry-KC	303
Jackson-Oak	303
Lynn-Bos	299
Brett-KC	289

Runs Batted In
Scott-Mil	109
Mayberry-KC	106
Lynn-Bos	105
Jackson-Oak	104

Runs Produced
Lynn-Bos	187
Munson-NY	173
Rice-Bos	172
Mayberry-KC	167
Brett-KC	162

Bases On Balls
Mayberry-KC	119
Singleton-Bal	118
Grich-Bal	107
Tenace-Oak	106
Harrah-Tex	98

Batting Average
Carew-Min	.359
Lynn-Bos	.331
Munson-NY	.318
Rice-Bos	.309
C.Washington-Oak	.308

On Base Percentage
Carew-Min	.428
Mayberry-KC	.419
Singleton-Bal	.418
Harrah-Tex	.406
Lynn-Bos	.405

Slugging Average
Lynn-Bos	.566
Mayberry-KC	.547
Powell-Cle	.524
Scott-Mil	.515
Bonds-NY	.512

Production
Lynn-Bos	.971
Mayberry-KC	.966
Carew-Min	.926
Powell-Cle	.906
Bonds-NY	.891

Adjusted Production
Mayberry-KC	167
Lynn-Bos	158
Carew-Min	158
Singleton-Bal	156
Bonds-NY	154

Batter Runs
Mayberry-KC	56.0
Lynn-Bos	49.4
Carew-Min	44.4
Singleton-Bal	41.3
Bonds-NY	35.4

Adjusted Batter Runs
Mayberry-KC	52.6
Singleton-Bal	49.2
Carew-Min	42.1
Lynn-Bos	39.7
Bonds-NY	38.4

Clutch Hitting Index
Stanton-Cal	135
Robinson-Bal	130
Munson-NY	122
Duffy-Cle	116
Bando-Oak	115

Runs Created
Mayberry-KC	135
Lynn-Bos	120
Singleton-Bal	118
Carew-Min	118
Harrah-Tex	105

Total Average
Mayberry-KC	1.059
Lynn-Bos	1.000
Carew-Min	.986
Tenace-Oak	.919
Harrah-Tex	.914

Stolen Bases
Rivers-Cal	70
C.Washington-Oak	40
Otis-KC	39
Carew-Min	35
Remy-Cal	34

Stolen Base Average
Hisle-Min	85.0
Bumbry-Bal	84.2
Rivers-Cal	83.3
Alomar-NY	82.4
Patek-KC	82.1

Stolen Base Runs
Rivers-Cal	12.6
Patek-KC	5.4
Otis-KC	5.1
Carew-Min	5.1
Alomar-NY	4.8

Fielding Runs
Belanger-Bal	28.0
Dent-Chi	27.2
Grich-Bal	24.0
Rodriguez-Det	20.7
North-Oak	19.6

Total Player Rating
Harrah-Tex	6.2
Grich-Bal	5.8
Carew-Min	5.6
Lynn-Bos	4.7
Mayberry-KC	4.6

Wins
Palmer-Bal	23
Hunter-NY	23
Blue-Oak	22
Torrez-Bal	20
Kaat-Chi	20

Win Percentage
Torrez-Bal	.690
Leonard-KC	.682
Palmer-Bal	.676
Blue-Oak	.667
Lee-Bos	.654

Games
Fingers-Oak	75
Lindblad-Oak	68
Gossage-Chi	62
LaRoche-Cle	61
Foucault-Tex	59

Complete Games
Hunter-NY	30
G.Perry-Cle-Tex	25
Palmer-Bal	25
Jenkins-Tex	22
Blyleven-Min	20

Shutouts
Palmer-Bal	10
Hunter-NY	7

Saves
Gossage-Chi	26
Fingers-Oak	24
Murphy-Mil	20
LaRoche-Cle	17
Drago-Bos	15

Innings Pitched
Hunter-NY	328.0
Palmer-Bal	323.0
G.Perry-Cle-Tex	305.2
Kaat-Chi	303.2
Wood-Chi	291.1

Fewest Hits/Game
Hunter-NY	6.80
Ryan-Cal	6.91
Palmer-Bal	7.05
Eckersley-Cle	7.09
Blyleven-Min	7.15

Fewest BB/Game
Jenkins-Tex	1.87
G.Perry-Cle-Tex	2.06
Grimsley-Bal	2.15
Palmer-Bal	2.23
Hunter-NY	2.28

Strikeouts
Tanana-Cal	269
G.Perry-Cle-Tex	233
Blyleven-Min	233
Palmer-Bal	193
Blue-Oak	189

Strikeouts/Game
Tanana-Cal	9.41
Ryan-Cal	8.45
Blyleven-Min	7.61
Eckersley-Cle	7.33
G.Perry-Cle-Tex	6.86

Ratio
Hunter-NY	9.22
Palmer-Bal	9.33
Blyleven-Min	10.02
Tanana-Cal	10.18
G.Perry-Cle-Tex	10.33

Earned Run Average
Palmer-Bal	2.09
Hunter-NY	2.58
Eckersley-Cle	2.60
Tanana-Cal	2.62
Figueroa-Cal	2.91

Adjusted ERA
Palmer-Bal	168
Eckersley-Cle	145
Hunter-NY	141
Tanana-Cal	135
Blyleven-Min	128

Opponents' Batting Avg.
Hunter-NY	.208
Ryan-Cal	.213
Eckersley-Cle	.215
Palmer-Bal	.216
Blyleven-Min	.219

Opponents' On Base Pct.
Hunter-NY	.263
Palmer-Bal	.267
Blyleven-Min	.283
G.Perry-Cle-Tex	.284
Tanana-Cal	.288

Starter Runs
Palmer-Bal	60.6
Hunter-NY	43.7
Tanana-Cal	33.0
Eckersley-Cle	24.4
Blyleven-Min	23.7

Adjusted Starter Runs
Palmer-Bal	51.0
Hunter-NY	38.7
Tanana-Cal	26.4
Blyleven-Min	26.0
Kaat-Chi	25.7

Clutch Pitching Index
Kaat-Chi	119
Eckersley-Cle	116
Torrez-Bal	111
Osteen-Chi	110
Hargan-Tex	108

Relief Runs
Gossage-Chi	30.5
Todd-Oak	20.2
LaRoche-Cle	14.6
Lindblad-Oak	14.4
Hiller-Det	12.7

Adjusted Relief Runs
Gossage-Chi	32.0
Todd-Oak	18.2
LaRoche-Cle	14.6
Hiller-Det	14.5
Lindblad-Oak	12.3

Relief Ranking
Gossage-Chi	47.7
LaRoche-Cle	19.5
Todd-Oak	18.8
Hiller-Det	15.7
Fingers-Oak	14.1

Total Pitcher Index
Palmer-Bal	6.1
Gossage-Chi	5.2
Hunter-NY	3.8
Tanana-Cal	3.3
Busby-KC	2.6

Total Baseball Ranking
Harrah-Tex	6.2
Palmer-Bal	6.1
Grich-Bal	5.8
Carew-Min	5.6
Gossage-Chi	5.2

TEAM	G	W	L	PCT	GB	R	OR	AB	H	2B	3B	HR	BB	SO	AVG	OBP	SLG	PRO	PRO+	BR	/A	PF	CHI	RC	SB	CS	SBA	SBR
EAST																												
PHI	162	101	61	.623		770	557	5528	1505	259	45	110	542	793	.272	.342	.395	.737	112	106	83	103	101	746	127	70	64	-4
PIT	162	92	70	.568	9	708	630	5604	1499	249	56	110	433	807	.267	.323	.391	.714	107	50	44	101	102	700	130	45	74	12
NY	162	86	76	.531	15	615	**538**	5415	1334	198	34	102	561	797	.246	.320	.352	.672	103	-19	17	94	99	608	66	58	53	-15
CHI	162	75	87	.463	26	611	728	5519	1386	216	24	105	490	834	.251	.316	.356	.672	89	-27	-83	109	99	605	74	74	50	-22
STL	162	72	90	.444	29	629	671	5516	1432	243	57	63	512	860	.260	.325	.359	.684	99	1	-5	101	97	644	123	55	69	4
MON	162	55	107	.340	46	531	734	5428	1275	224	32	94	433	841	.235	.293	.340	.633	82	-109	-131	104	102	539	86	44	66	-1
WEST																												
CIN	162	102	60	.630		**857**	633	5702	**1599**	271	63	141	681	902	.280	.360	.424	**.784**	126	214	193	102	95	907	210	57	79	29
LA	162	92	70	.568	10	608	543	5472	1371	200	34	91	486	744	.251	.315	.349	.664	96	-39	-28	98	101	604	144	55	72	10
HOU	162	80	82	.494	22	625	657	5464	1401	195	50	66	530	719	.256	.325	.347	.672	107	-20	36	91	101	622	150	57	72	11
SF	162	74	88	.457	28	595	686	5452	1340	211	37	85	518	778	.246	.314	.345	.659	90	-48	-66	103	100	591	88	55	62	-7
SD	162	73	89	.451	29	570	662	5369	1327	216	37	64	488	**716**	.247	.313	.337	.650	98	-65	-19	92	100	570	92	46	67	0
ATL	162	70	92	.432	32	620	700	5345	1309	170	30	82	589	811	.245	.322	.334	.656	87	-44	-82	106	**104**	579	74	61	55	-14
TOT	972					7739		65814	16778	2652	499	1113	6263	9602	.255	.323	.361	.684							1364	677	67	3

TEAM	CG	SH	SV	IP	H	H/G	HR	BB	SO	RAT	ERA	ERA+	OAV	OOB	PR	/A	PF	CPI	FA	E	DP	FW	PW	BW	SBW	DIF
EAST																										
PHI	34	9	44	1459	1377	8.5	98	**397**	918	11.1	3.08	**115**	.250	.303	69	**76**	101	102	.981	115	148	1.7	**8.1**	8.8	-.5	1.8
PIT	45	12	35	1466	1402	8.6	95	460	762	11.5	3.36	104	.253	.313	22	20	100	99	.975	163	142	-1.0	2.1	4.7	1.2	4.0
NY	**53**	**18**	25	1449	**1248**	**7.8**	97	419	**1025**	10.5	**2.94**	112	**.233**	**.292**	91	57	94	95	.979	131	116	.8	6.1	1.8	-1.6	-2.1
CHI	27	12	33	1471¹	1511	9.2	123	490	850	12.4	3.93	98	.268	.330	-71	-12	110	100	.978	140	145	.3	-1.3	-8.8	-2.4	6.2
STL	35	15	26	1453²	1416	8.8	91	581	731	12.5	3.60	98	.258	.332	-16	-11	101	103	.973	174	163	-1.7	-1.2	-.5	.4	-6.0
MON	26	10	21	1440	1442	9.0	89	659	783	13.4	3.99	93	.266	.350	-79	-44	106	102	.976	155	**179**	-.6	-4.7	-13.9	-.1	-6.7
WEST																										
CIN	33	12	**45**	1471	1436	8.8	100	491	790	11.9	3.51	100	.258	.321	-1	0	100	101	**.984**	102	157	2.5	.0	20.5	3.1	-5.0
LA	47	17	28	1470²	1330	8.1	97	479	747	11.2	3.02	112	.243	.307	79	60	97	**104**	.980	128	154	1.0	6.4	-3.0	1.0	5.6
HOU	42	17	29	1444¹	1349	8.4	82	662	780	12.7	3.56	97	.250	.335	-9	-59	91	101	.978	140	155	.3	-6.3	3.8	1.1	.0
SF	27	**18**	31	1461²	1464	9.0	**68**	518	746	12.3	3.53	103	.263	.328	-4	16	104	100	.971	186	153	-2.4	1.7	-7.0	-.8	1.4
SD	47	11	18	1432¹	1368	8.6	87	543	652	12.1	3.65	90	.253	.323	-24	-61	93	95	.978	141	148	.2	-6.5	-2.0	-.0	.3
ATL	33	13	27	1438	1435	9.0	86	564	818	12.8	3.86	98	.261	.335	-58	-12	108	97	.973	167	151	-1.3	-1.3	-8.7	-1.5	1.8
TOT	449	164	362	17457¹		8.6				12.0	3.50		.255	.323					.977	1742	1811					

Runs
Rose-Cin 130
Morgan-Cin 113
Schmidt-Phi 112
Griffey-Cin 111
Monday-Chi 107

Hits
Rose-Cin 215
Montanez-SF-Atl ... 206
Garvey-LA 200
Buckner-LA 193

Doubles
Rose-Cin 42
Johnstone-Phi 38
Maddox-Phi 37
Garvey-LA 37

Triples
Cash-Phi 12
Geronimo-Cin 11
Parker-Pit 10
W.Davis-SD 10

Home Runs
Schmidt-Phi 38
Kingman-NY 37
Monday-Chi 32
Foster-Cin 29
Morgan-Cin 27

Total Bases
Schmidt-Phi 306
Rose-Cin 299
Foster-Cin 298
Garvey-LA 284

Runs Batted In
Foster-Cin 121
Morgan-Cin 111
Schmidt-Phi 107
Watson-Hou 102
Luzinski-Phi 95

Runs Produced
Morgan-Cin 197
Rose-Cin 183
Schmidt-Phi 181
Griffey-Cin 179
Foster-Cin 178

Bases On Balls
Wynn-Atl 127
Morgan-Cin 114
Schmidt-Phi 100
Cey-LA 89
Rose-Cin 86

Batting Average
Madlock-Chi .... .339
Griffey-Cin .... .336
Maddox-Phi .... .330
Rose-Cin .... .323
Morgan-Cin .... .320

On Base Percentage
Morgan-Cin .... .453
Madlock-Chi .... .415
Rose-Cin .... .406
Griffey-Cin .... .403
Cey-LA .... .389

Slugging Average
Morgan-Cin .... .576
Foster-Cin .... .530
Schmidt-Phi ...... .524
Monday-Chi .... .507
Kingman-NY .... .506

Production
Morgan-Cin 1.029
Madlock-Chi .... .915
Schmidt-Phi ...... .904
Foster-Cin .... .899
Rose-Cin .... .855

Adjusted Production
Morgan-Cin 186
Watson-Hou 151
Schmidt-Phi 150
Foster-Cin 149
Madlock-Chi 146

Batter Runs
Morgan-Cin 61.4
Schmidt-Phi 42.7
Madlock-Chi 40.6
Rose-Cin 39.6
Foster-Cin 36.7

Adjusted Batter Runs
Morgan-Cin 58.4
Schmidt-Phi 39.2
Watson-Hou 38.3
Rose-Cin 36.8
Foster-Cin 34.3

Clutch Hitting Index
Cruz-StL 119
Brock-StL 117
Milner-NY 117
Bench-Cin 116
Reitz-SF 116

Runs Created
Morgan-Cin 144
Rose-Cin 123
Schmidt-Phi 121
Foster-Cin 111
Griffey-Cin 109

Total Average
Morgan-Cin 1.319
Schmidt-Phi ...... .944
Foster-Cin .... .911
Madlock-Chi .... .882
Griffey-Cin .... .876

Stolen Bases
Lopes-LA 63
Morgan-Cin 60
Taveras-Pit 58
Cedeno-Hou 58
Brock-StL 56

Stolen Base Average
Morgan-Cin 87.0
Lopes-LA 86.3
Foster-Cin 85.0
Taveras-Pit 84.1
Geronimo-Cin 81.5

Stolen Base Runs
Lopes-LA 12.9
Morgan-Cin 12.6
Taveras-Pit 10.8
Cedeno-Hou 8.4
Cabell-Hou 5.7

Fielding Runs
Schmidt-Phi 24.7
Maddox-Phi 24.3
Trillo-Chi 18.3
Stennett-Pit 17.4
Royster-Atl 16.6

Total Player Rating
Schmidt-Phi 6.4
Morgan-Cin 5.8
Maddox-Phi 4.5
Cedeno-Hou 4.4
Concepcion-Cin 4.1

Wins
Jones-SD 22
Sutton-LA 21
Koosman-NY 21
Richard-Hou 20
Carlton-Phi 20

Win Percentage
Carlton-Phi .... .741
Candelaria-Pit ..... .696
Sutton-LA .... .677
Koosman-NY ...... .677
Rooker-Pit .... .652

Games
Murray-Mon 81
Metzger-SD 77
Hough-LA 77
Eastwick-Cin 71
Borbon-Cin 69

Complete Games
Jones-SD 25
Koosman-NY 17
Matlack-NY 16
Sutton-LA 15
Richard-Hou 14

Shutouts
Montefusco-SF 6
Matlack-NY 6
Seaver-NY 5
Jones-SD 5

Saves
Eastwick-Cin 26
Lockwood-NY 19
Forsch-Hou 19
Hough-LA 18
Metzger-SD 16

Innings Pitched
Jones-SD 315.1
Richard-Hou 291.0
Seaver-NY 271.0
Niekro-Atl 270.2
Sutton-LA 267.2

Fewest Hits/Game
Richard-Hou 6.84
Seaver-NY 7.01
Candelaria-Pit 7.08
Messersmith-Atl .. 7.21
Falcone-StL 7.34

Fewest BB/Game
Nolan-Cin 1.02
Kaat-Phi 1.27
Jones-SD 1.43
Matlack-NY 1.96
Lonborg-Phi 2.03

Strikeouts
Seaver-NY 235
Richard-Hou 214
Koosman-NY 200
Carlton-Phi 195
Niekro-Atl 173

Strikeouts/Game
Seaver-NY 7.80
Koosman-NY 7.28
Carlton-Phi 6.95
Richard-Hou 6.62
Zachry-Cin 6.31

Ratio
Jones-SD 9.36
Candelaria-Pit 9.61
Seaver-NY 9.70
Nolan-Cin 9.78
Koosman-NY 9.90

Earned Run Average
Denny-StL 2.52
Rau-LA 2.57
Seaver-NY 2.59
Koosman-NY 2.69
Zachry-Cin 2.74

Adjusted ERA
Denny-StL 140
Rau-LA 132
Zachry-Cin 128
Montefusco-SF ... 128
Seaver-NY 127

Opponents' Batting Avg.
Richard-Hou ...... .212
Seaver-NY .... .213
Candelaria-Pit .... .216
Messersmith-Atl ... .219
Falcone-StL .... .222

Opponents' On Base Pct.
Jones-SD .... .267
Candelaria-Pit .... .273
Seaver-NY .... .273
Nolan-Cin .... .276
Koosman-NY ...... .279

Starter Runs
Seaver-NY 27.4
Jones-SD 26.7
Richard-Hou 24.2
Rau-LA 23.9
Denny-StL 22.5

Adjusted Starter Runs
Denny-StL 23.3
Montefusco-SF ... 22.1
Seaver-NY 21.2
Rau-LA 20.8
Burris-Chi 20.8

Clutch Pitching Index
Rau-LA 139
Denny-StL 129
Burris-Chi 118
Christenson-Phi ... 112
Fryman-Mon 112

Relief Runs
Hough-LA 20.5
Eastwick-Cin 16.9
Reed-Phi 14.8
Moffitt-SF 14.1
Forsch-Hou 13.8

Adjusted Relief Runs
Hough-LA 18.6
Eastwick-Cin 16.9
Moffitt-SF 15.5
Reed-Phi 15.4
Twitchell-Phi 12.3

Relief Ranking
Eastwick-Cin 31.8
Hough-LA 28.8
Moffitt-SF 21.0
Reed-Phi 20.1
Lavelle-SF 17.8

Total Pitcher Index
Hough-LA 3.3
Eastwick-Cin 3.1
Barr-SF 2.8
Denny-StL 2.7
Rau-LA 2.6

Total Baseball Ranking
Schmidt-Phi 6.4
Morgan-Cin 5.8
Maddox-Phi 4.5
Cedeno-Hou 4.4
Concepcion-Cin 4.1

TEAM	G	W	L	PCT	GB	R	OR	AB	H	2B	3B	HR	BB	SO	AVG	OBP	SLG	PRO	PRO+	BR	/A	PF	CHI	RC	SB	CS	SBA	SBR
EAST																												
NY	159	97	62	.610		730	**575**	5555	1496	231	36	120	470	**616**	.269	.330	.389	.719	111	64	**71**	99	103	723	163	65	71	10
BAL	162	88	74	.543	10.5	619	598	5457	1326	213	28	119	519	883	.243	.311	.358	.669	102	-33	5	94	102	612	150	61	71	8
BOS	162	83	79	.512	15.5	716	660	5511	1448	257	53	**134**	500	832	.263	.327	**.402**	**.729**	101	80	-8	112	98	709	95	70	58	-14
CLE	159	81	78	.509	16	615	615	5412	1423	189	38	85	479	631	.263	.324	.359	.683	101	-2	5	99	97	611	75	69	52	-19
DET	161	74	87	.460	24	609	709	5441	1401	207	38	101	450	730	.257	.318	.365	.683	96	-7	-31	104	97	611	107	59	64	-3
MIL	161	66	95	.410	32	570	655	5396	1326	170	38	88	511	909	.246	.314	.340	.654	93	-57	-46	98	98	575	62	61	50	-18
WEST																												
KC	162	90	72	.556		713	611	5540	1490	**259**	**57**	65	484	650	.269	.331	.371	.702	104	37	32	101	103	687	218	106	67	2
OAK	161	87	74	.540	2.5	686	598	5353	1319	208	33	113	**592**	818	.246	.327	.361	.688	105	13	40	96	**105**	663	**341**	123	**73**	**29**
MIN	162	85	77	.525	5	**743**	704	5574	**1526**	222	51	81	550	714	**.274**	.343	.375	.718	107	78	57	103	100	**727**	146	75	66	-1
TEX	162	76	86	.469	14	616	652	5555	1390	213	26	80	568	809	.250	.323	.341	.664	93	-32	-45	102	98	616	87	45	66	-1
CAL	162	76	86	.469	14	550	631	5385	1265	210	23	63	634	812	.235	.309	.318	.627	90	-105	-72	94	102	531	126	80	61	-10
CHI	161	64	97	.398	25.5	586	745	5532	1410	209	46	73	471	739	.255	.317	.349	.666	94	-36	-40	101	96	622	120	53	69	4
TOT	967					7753		65711	16820	2588	467	1122	6128	9143	.256	.323	.361	.684							1690	867	66	-13

TEAM	CG	SH	SV	IP	H	H/G	HR	BB	SO	RAT	ERA	ERA+	OAV	OOB	PR	/A	PF	CPI	FA	E	DP	FW	PW	BW	SBW	DIF
EAST																										
NY	62	15	37	1455	**1300**	8.0	97	448	674	10.9	3.19	107	.241	.301	53	36	97	95	.980	126	141	.9	3.8	**7.5**	1.2	4.1
BAL	59	16	23	1468²	1396	8.6	**80**	489	678	11.7	3.32	99	.255	.318	33	-7	93	101	**.982**	118	157	**1.5**	-.7	.5	1.0	4.8
BOS	49	13	27	1458	1495	9.2	109	**409**	673	12.0	3.52	111	.267	.320	-1	62	111	104	.978	141	148	.2	6.6	-.8	-1.4	-2.5
CLE	30	**17**	**46**	1432	1361	8.6	**80**	533	928	12.1	3.47	101	.255	.326	8	3	99	101	.980	121	159	1.2	.3	.5	-1.9	1.4
DET	55	12	20	1431¹	1406	9.0	101	550	738	12.6	3.87	96	.263	.334	-56	-25	105	99	.974	168	161	-1.4	-2.7	-3.3	-.2	1.1
MIL	45	10	27	1435¹	1406	8.8	99	567	677	12.6	3.64	96	.260	.334	-20	-24	99	104	.975	152	160	-.5	-2.5	-4.9	-1.8	-4.8
WEST																										
KC	41	12	35	1472	1356	8.3	83	493	735	11.5	3.21	109	.247	.312	51	48	100	99	.978	139	147	.3	5.1	3.4	.3	-.1
OAK	39	15	29	1459¹	1412	8.7	96	415	711	11.5	3.26	103	.255	.310	42	16	95	101	.977	144	130	-.0	1.7	4.2	**3.2**	-2.6
MIN	29	11	23	1459	1421	8.8	89	610	762	12.8	3.69	97	.259	.337	-29	-16	102	102	.973	172	**182**	-1.6	-1.7	6.0	-.4	-1.8
TEX	63	15	15	1472	1464	9.0	106	461	773	12.0	3.45	104	.262	.322	10	21	102	**105**	.976	156	142	-.7	2.2	-4.8	.0	-1.8
CAL	**64**	15	17	1477¹	1323	8.1	95	553	**992**	11.7	3.36	99	**.241**	.315	26	-5	95	96	.977	150	139	-.3	-.5	-7.6	-.9	4.5
CHI	54	10	22	1448	1460	9.1	87	600	802	13.0	4.25	84	.266	.342	-118	-111	101	92	.979	130	155	.7	-11.8	-4.2	.5	-1.8
TOT	590	161	321	17468¹		8.7				12.0	3.52		.256	.323					.977	1717	1821					

Runs		Hits		Doubles		Triples		Home Runs		Total Bases	
White-NY	104	Brett-KC	215	Otis-KC	40	Brett-KC	14	Nettles-NY	32	Brett-KC	298
Carew-Min	97	Carew-Min	200	McRae-KC	34	Garner-Oak	12	R.Jackson-Bal	27	Chambliss-NY	283
Rivers-NY	95	Chambliss-NY	188	Evans-Bos	34	Carew-Min	12	Bando-Oak	27	Rice-Bos	280
Brett-KC	94	Munson-NY	186	Carty-Cle	34	Poquette-KC	10			Carew-Min	280
		Rivers-NY	184	Brett-KC	34	Bostock-Min	9			Nettles-NY	277

Runs Batted In		Runs Produced		Bases On Balls		Batting Average		On Base Percentage		Slugging Average	
L.May-Bal	109	Carew-Min	178	Hargrove-Tex	97	Brett-KC	.333	McRae-KC	.412	R.Jackson-Bal	.502
Munson-NY	105	Munson-NY	167	Harrah-Tex	91	McRae-KC	.332	Hargrove-Tex	.401	Rice-Bos	.482
Yastrzemski-Bos	102	Hisle-Min	163	Grich-Bal	86	Carew-Min	.331	Carew-Min	.398	Nettles-NY	.475
		Otis-KC	161	White-NY	83	Bostock-Min	.323	Staub-Det	.392	Lynn-Bos	.467
				Staub-Det	83	LeFlore-Det	.316	Carty-Cle	.384	Carew-Min	.463

Production		Adjusted Production		Batter Runs		Adjusted Batter Runs		Clutch Hitting Index		Runs Created	
McRae-KC	.873	R.Jackson-Bal	158	Carew-Min	40.0	McRae-KC	38.1	Mayberry-KC	137	Brett-KC	114
Carew-Min	.861	McRae-KC	154	McRae-KC	38.8	Carew-Min	36.9	Rudi-Oak	131	Carew-Min	111
R.Jackson-Bal	.855	Tenace-Oak	150	Brett-KC	36.2	Brett-KC	35.4	L.May-Bal	127	McRae-KC	101
Brett-KC	.843	Carew-Min	147	Staub-Det	33.2	R.Jackson-Bal	34.3	Yastrzemski-Bos	124	Staub-Det	99
Lynn-Bos	.842	Brett-KC	145	Carty-Cle	29.8	Carty-Cle	30.8	Hisle-Min	124	White-NY	98

Total Average		Stolen Bases		Stolen Base Average		Stolen Base Runs		Fielding Runs		Total Player Rating	
McRae-KC	.862	North-Oak	75	Rivers-NY	86.0	Campaneris-Oak	9.0	White-KC	21.1	Nettles-NY	4.1
R.Jackson-Bal	.857	LeFlore-Det	58	Campaneris-Oak	81.8	Rivers-NY	8.7	Kuiper-Cle	20.0	Brett-KC	4.0
Tenace-Oak	.855	Campaneris-Oak	54	Baylor-Oak	81.3	Baylor-Oak	8.4	Beniquez-Tex	19.5	Grich-Bal	3.9
Carew-Min	.854	Baylor-Oak	52	Bumbry-Bal	80.8	Bumbry-Bal	6.6	Brohamer-Chi	18.0	R.Jackson-Bal	3.7
Brett-KC	.797	Patek-KC	51	R.Jackson-Bal	80.0	Patek-KC	6.3	Nettles-NY	17.2	Belanger-Bal	3.6

Wins		Win Percentage		Games		Complete Games		Shutouts		Saves	
Palmer-Bal	22	Campbell-Min	.773	Campbell-Min	78	Fidrych-Det	24	Ryan-Cal	7	Lyle-NY	23
Tiant-Bos	21	Garland-Bal	.741	Fingers-Oak	70	Tanana-Cal	23	Blyleven-Min-Tex	6	LaRoche-Cle	21
Garland-Bal	20	Ellis-NY	.680	Lindblad-Oak	65	Palmer-Bal	23	Palmer-Bal	6	Fingers-Oak	20
		Fidrych-Det	.679	Lyle-NY	64			Blue-Oak	6	Campbell-Min	20
				LaRoche-Cle	61					Littell-KC	16

Innings Pitched		Fewest Hits/Game		Fewest BB/Game		Strikeouts		Strikeouts/Game		Ratio	
Palmer-Bal	315.0	Ryan-Cal	6.11	Bird-KC	1.41	Ryan-Cal	327	Ryan-Cal	10.35	Tanana-Cal	9.18
Hunter-NY	298.2	Tanana-Cal	6.62	Jenkins-Bos	1.85	Tanana-Cal	261	Eckersley-Cle	9.03	Fidrych-Det	9.81
Blue-Oak	298.1	Eckersley-Cle	7.00	Perry-Tex	1.87	Blyleven-Min-Tex	219	Tanana-Cal	8.15	Palmer-Bal	9.91
Blyleven-Min-Tex	297.2	Palmer-Bal	7.29	Blue-Oak	1.90	Eckersley-Cle	200	Blyleven-Min-Tex	6.62	Blue-Oak	10.02
Slaton-Mil	292.2	Brett-NY-Chi	7.67	Fidrych-Det	1.91	Hunter-NY	173	Campbell-Min	6.17	Perry-Tex	10.21

Earned Run Average		Adjusted ERA		Opponents' Batting Avg.		Opponents' On Base Pct.		Starter Runs		Adjusted Starter Runs	
Fidrych-Det	2.34	Fidrych-Det	159	Ryan-Cal	.195	Tanana-Cal	.261	Blue-Oak	38.6	Fidrych-Det	38.1
Blue-Oak	2.35	Blue-Oak	142	Tanana-Cal	.203	Fidrych-Det	.279	Palmer-Bal	35.1	Blue-Oak	33.1
Tanana-Cal	2.43	Tanana-Cal	137	Eckersley-Cle	.214	Blue-Oak	.280	Tanana-Cal	34.7	Tanana-Cal	28.5
Torrez-Oak	2.50	Torrez-Oak	134	Palmer-Bal	.224	Palmer-Bal	.282	Fidrych-Det	32.8	Palmer-Bal	26.5
Palmer-Bal	2.51	Palmer-Bal	130	Brett-NY-Chi	.233	Bird-KC	.283	Torrez-Oak	30.1	Tiant-Bos	26.2

Clutch Pitching Index		Relief Runs		Adjusted Relief Runs		Relief Ranking		Total Pitcher Index		Total Baseball Ranking	
Hartzell-Cal	124	Littell-KC	16.7	Hiller-Det	17.9	Hiller-Det	30.9	Fidrych-Det	5.0	Fidrych-Det	5.0
Travers-Mil	120	Fingers-Oak	15.6	Littell-KC	16.4	Fingers-Oak	25.5	Palmer-Bal	3.6	Nettles-NY	4.1
Umbarger-Tex	118	Hiller-Det	15.3	Kern-Cle	15.3	Lyle-NY	24.0	Hiller-Det	3.3	Brett-KC	4.0
Garland-Bal	116	Kern-Cle	15.0	Burgmeier-Min	14.1	Kern-Cle	23.2	Tanana-Cal	3.2	Grich-Bal	3.9
Torrez-Oak	115	Lyle-NY	14.5	Thomas-Cle	14.0	Littell-KC	22.8	Blue-Oak	3.1	R.Jackson-Bal	3.7

TEAM	G	W	L	PCT	GB	R	OR	AB	H	2B	3B	HR	BB	SO	AVG	OBP	SLG	PRO	PRO+	BR	/A	PF	CHI	RC	SB	CS	SBA	SBR
EAST																												
PHI	162	101	61	.623		847	668	5546	1548	266	56	186	573	806	.279	.351	.448	.799	114	143	105	104	98	865	135	68	67	0
PIT	162	96	66	.593	5	734	665	5662	1550	278	57	133	474	878	.274	.334	.413	.747	102	37	17	103	98	776	260	120	68	6
STL	162	83	79	.512	18	737	688	5527	1490	252	56	96	489	823	.270	.332	.388	.720	100	-13	-1	98	107	690	134	112	54	-27
CHI	162	81	81	.500	20	692	739	5604	1489	271	37	111	534	796	.266	.333	.387	.720	88	-11	-90	111	98	709	64	45	59	-8
MON	162	75	87	.463	26	665	736	5675	1474	294	50	133	478	877	.260	.320	.402	.722	101	-20	0	97	95	715	88	50	64	-4
NY	162	64	98	.395	37	587	663	5410	1319	227	30	88	529	887	.244	.315	.346	.661	87	-125	-99	95	103	577	98	81	55	-19
WEST																												
LA	162	98	64	.605		769	582	5589	1484	223	28	191	588	896	.266	.338	.418	.756	109	58	62	100	98	794	114	62	65	-3
CIN	162	88	74	.543	10	802	725	5524	1513	269	42	181	600	911	.274	.348	.436	.784	113	115	100	102	97	847	170	64	73	13
HOU	162	81	81	.500	17	680	650	5530	1405	263	60	114	515	839	.254	.322	.385	.707	104	-41	18	91	102	697	187	72	72	13
SF	162	75	87	.463	23	673	711	5497	1392	227	41	134	568	842	.253	.326	.383	.709	95	-35	-32	100	100	683	90	59	60	-8
SD	162	69	93	.426	29	692	834	5602	1397	245	49	120	602	1057	.249	.325	.375	.700	104	-49	21	90	102	700	133	57	70	6
ATL	162	61	101	.377	37	678	895	5534	1404	218	20	139	537	876	.254	.322	.376	.698	82	-58	-136	112	104	660	82	53	61	-7
TOT	972					8556		66700	17465	3033	526	1631	6487	10488	.262	.330	.396	.727							1555	843	65	-39

TEAM	CG	SH	SV	IP	H	H/G	HR	BB	SO	RAT	ERA	ERA+	OAV	OOB	PR	/A	PF	CPI	FA	E	DP	FW	PW	BW	SBW	DIF
EAST																										
PHI	31	7	47	1455²	1451	9.0	134	482	856	12.1	3.71	108	.263	.325	32	47	102	103	.981	120	168	1.3	4.8	10.6	.3	3.0
PIT	25	15	39	1481²	1406	8.5	149	485	890	11.6	3.61	110	.252	.314	50	62	102	99	.977	145	137	-.0	6.3	1.7	.9	6.1
STL	26	10	31	1446	1420	8.8	139	532	768	12.3	3.81	101	.260	.329	16	6	98	102	.978	139	174	.3	.6	-.1	-2.4	3.6
CHI	16	10	44	1468	1500	9.2	128	489	942	12.3	4.01	109	.266	.327	-16	61	112	96	.977	153	147	-.5	6.2	-9.1	-.5	3.9
MON	31	11	33	1481	1426	8.7	135	579	856	12.3	4.01	95	.255	.327	-17	-34	97	94	.980	129	128	.8	-3.4	.0	-.0	-3.3
NY	27	12	28	1433²	1378	8.7	118	490	911	11.9	3.77	99	.254	.319	22	-6	96	94	.978	134	132	.5	-.6	-10.0	-1.6	-5.3
WEST																										
LA	34	13	39	1475¹	1393	8.5	119	438	930	11.3	3.22	119	.251	.309	113	99	98	104	.981	124	160	1.1	10.0	6.3	-.0	-.4
CIN	33	12	32	1437¹	1469	9.2	156	544	868	12.8	4.21	93	.267	.337	-49	-46	101	100	.984	95	154	2.7	-4.7	10.1	1.6	-2.8
HOU	37	11	28	1465²	1384	8.5	110	545	871	12.0	3.54	101	.251	.321	61	5	91	99	.978	142	136	.0	.5	1.8	1.6	-4.1
SF	27	10	33	1459	1501	9.3	114	529	854	12.7	3.75	104	.267	.333	26	26	100	104	.972	179	136	-2.0	2.6	-3.2	-.5	-2.9
SD	6	5	44	1466¹	1556	9.6	160	673	827	13.8	4.43	80	.276	.355	-85	-146	91	105	.971	189	142	-2.5	-14.8	2.1	.9	2.2
ATL	28	5	31	1445¹	1581	9.8	169	701	915	14.5	4.85	92	.279	.363	-151	-65	114	101	.972	175	127	-1.7	-6.6	-13.8	-.4	2.5
TOT	321	121	429	17515		9.0				12.5	3.91		.262	.330					.977	1724	1741					

Runs
Foster-Cin	124
Griffey-Cin	117
Schmidt-Phi	114
Morgan-Cin	113
Parker-Pit	107

Hits
Parker-Pit	215
Rose-Phi	204
Templeton-StL	200
Foster-Cin	197
Garvey-LA	192

Doubles
Parker-Pit	44
Cash-Mon	42
Hernandez-StL	41
Cromartie-Mon	41

Triples
Templeton-StL	18
Schmidt-Phi	11
Richards-SD	11
Almon-SD	11

Home Runs
Foster-Cin	52
Burroughs-Atl	41
Luzinski-Phi	39
Schmidt-Phi	38
Garvey-LA	33

Total Bases
Foster-Cin	388
Parker-Pit	338
Luzinski-Phi	329
Garvey-LA	322
Schmidt-Phi	312

Runs Batted In
Foster-Cin	149
Luzinski-Phi	130
Garvey-LA	115
Burroughs-Atl	114

Runs Produced
Foster-Cin	221
Luzinski-Phi	190
Schmidt-Phi	177
Parker-Pit	174
Garvey-LA	173

Bases On Balls
Tenace-SD	125
Morgan-Cin	117
Smith-LA	104
Schmidt-Phi	104
Cey-LA	93

Batting Average
Parker-Pit	.338
Templeton-StL	.322
Foster-Cin	.320
Griffey-Cin	.318
Simmons-StL	.318

On Base Percentage
Smith-LA	.432
Morgan-Cin	.420
Tenace-SD	.417
Simmons-StL	.410
Parker-Pit	.399

Slugging Average
Foster-Cin	.631
Luzinski-Phi	.594
Smith-LA	.576
Schmidt-Phi	.574
Bench-Cin	.540

Production
Foster-Cin	1.017
Smith-LA	1.008
Luzinski-Phi	.993
Schmidt-Phi	.972
Parker-Pit	.929

Adjusted Production
Smith-LA	168
Foster-Cin	165
Luzinski-Phi	155
Schmidt-Phi	151
Hendrick-SD	148

Batter Runs
Foster-Cin	56.0
Smith-LA	50.3
Luzinski-Phi	48.6
Schmidt-Phi	45.8
Parker-Pit	42.0

Adjusted Batter Runs
Foster-Cin	53.6
Smith-LA	50.9
Luzinski-Phi	43.3
Schmidt-Phi	40.5
Parker-Pit	38.7

Clutch Hitting Index
Watson-Hou	121
Cey-LA	116
Bench-Cin	114
Robinson-Pit	114
Evans-SF	114

Runs Created
Foster-Cin	144
Luzinski-Phi	132
Parker-Pit	130
Schmidt-Phi	129
Smith-LA	129

Total Average
Smith-LA	1.121
Morgan-Cin	1.054
Schmidt-Phi	1.046
Luzinski-Phi	1.043
Foster-Cin	1.039

Stolen Bases
Taveras-Pit	70
Cedeno-Hou	61
Richards-SD	56
Moreno-Pit	53
Morgan-Cin	49

Stolen Base Average
Bowa-Phi	91.4
McBride-StL-Phi	83.7
Morgan-Cin	83.1
Richards-SD	82.4
Cedeno-Hou	81.3

Stolen Base Runs
Taveras-Pit	10.2
Cedeno-Hou	9.9
Richards-SD	9.6
Morgan-Cin	8.7
Bowa-Phi	7.8

Fielding Runs
DeJesus-Chi	35.8
Parker-Pit	32.5
Trillo-Chi	30.1
Schmidt-Phi	28.8
Tyson-StL	22.0

Total Player Rating
Schmidt-Phi	6.7
Foster-Cin	6.1
Parker-Pit	5.8
Hendrick-SD	3.8
Smith-LA	3.7

Wins
Carlton-Phi	23
Seaver-NY-Cin	21

Win Percentage
Candelaria-Pit	.800
Seaver-NY-Cin	.778
Christenson-Phi	.760
John-LA	.741
Forsch-StL	.741

Games
Fingers-SD	78
Tomlin-SD	76
Spillner-SD	76
Metzger-SD-StL	75

Complete Games
Niekro-Atl	20
Seaver-NY-Cin	19
Rogers-Mon	17
Carlton-Phi	17
Richard-Hou	13

Shutouts
Seaver-NY-Cin	7
Rogers-Mon	4
R.Reuschel-Chi	4

Saves
Fingers-SD	35
Sutter-Chi	31
Gossage-Pit	26
Hough-LA	22

Innings Pitched
Niekro-Atl	330.1
Rogers-Mon	301.2
Carlton-Phi	283.0
Richard-Hou	267.0
Seaver-NY-Cin	261.1

Fewest Hits/Game
Seaver-NY-Cin	6.85
Richard-Hou	7.15
Carlton-Phi	7.28
Hooton-LA	7.41
Candelaria-Pit	7.69

Fewest BB/Game
Candelaria-Pit	1.95
John-LA	2.04
Rau-LA	2.08
Barr-SF	2.15
Lemongello-Hou	2.18

Strikeouts
Niekro-Atl	262
Richard-Hou	214
Rogers-Mon	206
Carlton-Phi	198
Seaver-NY-Cin	196

Strikeouts/Game
Koosman-NY	7.62
Richard-Hou	7.21
Niekro-Atl	7.14
Seaver-NY-Cin	6.75
Matlack-NY	6.55

Ratio
Seaver-NY-Cin	9.13
Candelaria-Pit	9.72
Hooton-LA	9.95
Carlton-Phi	10.24
Sutton-LA	10.45

Earned Run Average
Candelaria-Pit	2.34
Seaver-NY-Cin	2.58
Hooton-LA	2.62
Carlton-Phi	2.64
John-LA	2.78

Adjusted ERA
Candelaria-Pit	170
R.Reuschel-Chi	157
Carlton-Phi	151
Seaver-NY-Cin	149
Hooton-LA	146

Opponents' Batting Avg.
Seaver-NY-Cin	.209
Richard-Hou	.218
Carlton-Phi	.223
Hooton-LA	.225
Koosman-NY	.232

Opponents' On Base Pct.
Seaver-NY-Cin	.260
Candelaria-Pit	.276
Hooton-LA	.281
Carlton-Phi	.287
Sutton-LA	.291

Starter Runs
Candelaria-Pit	40.2
Carlton-Phi	39.9
Seaver-NY-Cin	38.5
Hooton-LA	32.0
R.Reuschel-Chi	31.4

Adjusted Starter Runs
R.Reuschel-Chi	44.8
Carlton-Phi	42.7
Candelaria-Pit	42.1
Seaver-NY-Cin	37.0
Hooton-LA	29.9

Clutch Pitching Index
Candelaria-Pit	126
John-LA	120
Rooker-Pit	118
Lemongello-Hou	116
Rau-LA	114

Relief Runs
Gossage-Pit	33.8
Sutter-Chi	30.6
Lavelle-SF	24.4
Garber-Phi	17.9
Reed-Phi	16.0

Adjusted Relief Runs
Sutter-Chi	36.3
Gossage-Pit	34.9
Lavelle-SF	24.4
Garber-Phi	18.9
Reed-Phi	17.2

Relief Ranking
Gossage-Pit	62.5
Sutter-Chi	54.0
Lavelle-SF	35.3
Garber-Phi	30.9
W.Hernandez-Chi	21.7

Total Pitcher Index
Gossage-Pit	6.6
Carlton-Phi	6.0
R.Reuschel-Chi	5.8
Sutter-Chi	5.8
Candelaria-Pit	4.7

Total Baseball Ranking
Schmidt-Phi	6.7
Gossage-Pit	6.6
Foster-Cin	6.1
Carlton-Phi	6.0
R.Reuschel-Chi	5.8

TEAM	G	W	L	PCT	GB	R	OR	AB	H	2B	3B	HR	BB	SO	AVG	OBP	SLG	PRO	PRO+	BR	/A	PF	CHI	RC	SB	CS	SBA	SBR
EAST																												
NY	162	100	62	.617		831	651	5605	1576	267	47	184	533	681	.281	.347	.444	.791	115	104	113	99	98	853	93	57	62	-6
BAL	161	97	64	.602	2.5	719	653	5494	1433	231	25	148	560	945	.261	.332	.393	.725	103	-23	21	94	102	711	90	51	64	-4
BOS	161	97	64	.602	2.5	859	712	5510	1551	258	56	**213**	528	905	.281	.349	**.465**	**.814**	107	**144**	43	112	98	**875**	66	47	58	-8
DET	162	74	88	.457	26	714	751	5604	1480	228	45	166	452	764	.264	.321	.410	.731	93	-25	-62	105	101	717	60	46	57	-10
CLE	161	71	90	.441	28.5	676	739	5491	1476	221	46	100	531	688	.269	.337	.380	.717	90	-31	-9	97	96	682	87	87	50	-26
MIL	162	67	95	.414	33	639	765	5517	1425	255	46	125	443	862	.258	.316	.389	.705	91	-73	-72	100	99	660	85	67	56	-15
TOR	161	54	107	.335	45.5	605	822	5418	1367	230	41	100	499	819	.252	.318	.365	.683	85	-106	-115	101	99	610	65	55	54	-14
WEST																												
KC	162	102	60	.630		822	**651**	5594	1549	**299**	**77**	146	522	687	.277	.343	.436	.779	110	82	75	101	100	835	170	87	**66**	**-1**
TEX	162	94	68	.580	8	767	657	5541	1497	265	39	135	**596**	904	.270	.345	.405	.750	103	34	26	101	98	780	154	85	64	-5
CHI	162	90	72	.556	12	844	771	5633	1568	254	52	192	509	**666**	.278	.347	.444	.791	114	107	109	100	99	858	42	44	49	-14
MIN	161	84	77	.522	17.5	**867**	776	5639	**1588**	273	60	123	563	754	**.282**	**.351**	.417	.768	110	71	83	99	105	827	105	65	62	-8
CAL	162	74	88	.457	28	675	695	5410	1380	233	40	131	542	880	.255	.327	.386	.713	97	-47	-20	96	100	681	159	89	64	-6
SEA	162	64	98	.395	38	624	855	5460	1398	218	33	133	426	769	.256	.314	.381	.695	89	-91	-85	99	100	643	110	67	62	-7
OAK	161	63	98	.391	38.5	605	749	5358	1284	176	37	117	516	910	.240	.311	.352	.663	81	-145	-137	99	**107**	589	176	89	**66**	**-1**
TOT	1131					10247		77274	20572	3408	644	2013	7270	11234	.266	.333	.405	.738		1462	936	61	-123					

TEAM	CG	SH	SV	IP	H	H/G	HR	BB	SO	RAT	ERA	ERA+	OAV	OOB	PR	/A	PF	CPI	FA	E	DP	FW	PW	BW	SBW	DIF
EAST																										
NY	52	16	34	1449^1	1395	8.7	139	486	758	11.8	3.61	109	.254	.318	73	54	97	101	.979	132	151	.6	5.4	**11.2**	.3	1.5
BAL	**65**	11	23	1451	1414	8.8	124	494	737	12.0	3.74	101	.260	.325	51	8	93	101	**.983**	106	189	**2.0**	.8	2.1	.5	11.1
BOS	40	13	40	1428	1555	9.8	158	**378**	758	12.3	4.11	109	.278	.327	-8	60	111	102	.978	133	162	.5	6.0	4.3	.0	5.7
DET	44	3	23	1457	1526	9.4	162	470	784	12.5	4.13	104	.271	.329	-11	26	106	100	.978	142	153	.0	2.6	-6.2	-.1	-3.3
CLE	45	8	30	1452^1	1441	8.9	136	500	876	12.5	4.10	96	.261	.331	-6	-25	97	96	.979	130	145	.7	-2.5	-.9	-1.7	-5.1
MIL	38	6	25	1431	1461	9.2	136	566	719	13.0	4.32	94	.268	.341	-42	-40	100	97	.978	139	165	.2	-4.0	-7.2	-.6	-5.2
TOR	40	3	20	1428^1	1538	9.7	152	623	771	13.7	4.57	92	.278	.354	-81	-59	103	101	.974	164	133	-1.2	-5.9	-11.4	-.5	-7.4
WEST																										
KC	41	15	**42**	1460^2	1377	8.5	110	499	850	11.8	**3.52**	115	**.251**	.318	88	84	99	98	.978	137	145	.3	**8.3**	7.5	.8	4.1
TEX	49	**17**	31	1472^2	1412	8.6	134	471	864	**11.7**	3.56	114	.255	**.317**	81	**84**	101	101	.982	117	156	1.5	**8.3**	2.6	.4	.2
CHI	34	3	40	1444^2	1557	9.7	136	516	842	13.2	4.25	96	.277	.342	-31	-27	101	101	.974	159	125	-.9	-2.7	10.8	-.5	2.3
MIN	35	4	25	1442	1546	9.6	151	507	737	13.0	4.36	91	.278	.342	-48	-60	98	101	.978	143	184	-.0	-6.0	8.2	.0	1.2
CAL	53	13	26	1437^2	1383	8.7	136	572	**965**	12.5	3.72	105	.256	.333	54	31	96	**105**	.976	147	137	-.2	3.1	-2.0	.0	-8.1
SEA	18	1	31	1433	1508	9.5	194	578	785	13.5	4.83	85	.272	.347	-123	-114	101	96	.976	147	162	-.2	-11.3	-8.4	.2	2.8
OAK	32	4	26	1436^2	1459	9.1	145	560	788	12.8	4.04	100	.265	.336	3	-3	99	102	.970	190	136	-2.7	-.3	-13.6	.8	-1.6
TOT	586	117	416	20224		9.2				12.6	4.06		.266	.333					.977	1986	2143					

Runs		Hits		Doubles		Triples		Home Runs		Total Bases	
Carew-Min	128	Carew-Min	239	McRae-KC	54	Carew-Min	16	Rice-Bos	39	Rice-Bos	382
Fisk-Bos	106	LeFlore-Det	212	Jackson-NY	39	Rice-Bos	15	Nettles-NY	37	Carew-Min	351
Brett-KC	105	Rice-Bos	206	Lemon-Chi	38	Cowens-KC	14	Bonds-Cal	37	McRae-KC	330
		Bostock-Min	199	Carew-Min	38	Brett-KC	13	Scott-Bos	33	Cowens-KC	318
		Burleson-Bos	194			Bostock-Min	12	Jackson-NY	32	LeFlore-Det	310

Runs Batted In		Runs Produced		Bases On Balls		Batting Average		On Base Percentage		Slugging Average	
Hisle-Min	119	Carew-Min	214	Harrah-Tex	109	Carew-Min	.388	Carew-Min	.452	Rice-Bos	.593
Bonds-Cal	115	Cowens-KC	187	Singleton-Bal	107	Bostock-Min	.336	Singleton-Bal	.442	Carew-Min	.570
Rice-Bos	114	Hisle-Min	186	Hargrove-Tex	103	Singleton-Bal	.328	Hargrove-Tex	.424	Jackson-NY	.550
Hobson-Bos	112	Fisk-Bos	182	Gross-Oak	86	Rivers-NY	.326	Fisk-Bos	.408	Hisle-Min	.533
Cowens-KC	112	Bonds-Cal	181	Mayberry-KC	83	LeFlore-Det	.325	Page-Oak	.407	Brett-KC	.532

Production		Adjusted Production		Batter Runs		Adjusted Batter Runs		Clutch Hitting Index		Runs Created	
Carew-Min	1.022	Carew-Min	179	Carew-Min	67.0	Carew-Min	69.3	Wynegar-Min	130	Carew-Min	160
Rice-Bos	.972	Singleton-Bal	168	Rice-Bos	51.4	Singleton-Bal	56.5	Doyle-Bos	128	Rice-Bos	136
Singleton-Bal	.949	Page-Oak	153	Singleton-Bal	48.5	Page-Oak	39.0	Sundberg-Tex	128	Singleton-Bal	124
Fisk-Bos	.929	Jackson-NY	151	Fisk-Bos	39.9	Bostock-Min	37.6	Carty-Cle	123	McRae-KC	119
Page-Oak	.928	Thornton-Cle	149	Hargrove-Tex	37.8	Jackson-NY	36.8	Staub-Det	116	Page-Oak	117

Total Average		Stolen Bases		Stolen Base Average		Stolen Base Runs		Fielding Runs		Total Player Rating	
Carew-Min	1.093	Patek-KC	53	Page-Oak	89.4	Page-Oak	9.6	Lemon-Chi	34.9	Carew-Min	6.3
Page-Oak	1.064	Page-Oak	42	Jackson-NY	85.0	Patek-KC	8.1	Sundberg-Tex	22.9	Singleton-Bal	4.9
Singleton-Bal	1.011	Remy-Cal	41	Harrah-Tex	84.4	Harrah-Tex	5.1	R.Jones-Sea	22.0	Page-Oak	4.9
Jackson-NY	.997	Bonds-Cal	41	White-KC	82.1	White-KC	3.9	Belanger-Bal	20.7	Brett-KC	4.4
Harrah-Tex	.964	LeFlore-Det	39	Patek-KC	80.3			Smalley-Min	18.7	Lemon-Chi	4.0

Wins		Win Percentage		Games		Complete Games		Shutouts		Saves	
Palmer-Bal	20	Splittorff-KC	.727	Lyle-NY	72	Ryan-Cal	22	Tanana-Cal	7	Campbell-Bos	31
Leonard-KC	20	T.Johnson-Min	.696	T.Johnson-Min	71	Palmer-Bal	22	Leonard-KC	5	Lyle-NY	26
Goltz-Min	20	Guidry-NY	.696	Campbell-Bos	69	Leonard-KC	21	Guidry-NY	5	LaGrow-Chi	25
Ryan-Cal	19	Rozema-Det	.682	McClure-Mil	68	Garland-Cle	21	Blyleven-Tex	5	Kern-Cle	18
				LaGrow-Chi	66	Tanana-Cal	20			LaRoche-Cle-Cal	17

Innings Pitched		Fewest Hits/Game		Fewest BB/Game		Strikeouts		Strikeouts/Game		Ratio	
Palmer-Bal	319.0	Ryan-Cal	5.96	Rozema-Det	1.40	Ryan-Cal	341	Ryan-Cal	10.26	Blyleven-Tex	9.86
Goltz-Min	303.0	Blyleven-Tex	6.94	Jenkins-Bos	1.68	Leonard-KC	244	Tanana-Cal	7.65	Eckersley-Cle	10.01
Ryan-Cal	299.0	Palmer-Bal	7.42	Hartzell-Cal	1.81	Tanana-Cal	205	Guidry-NY	7.52	Guidry-NY	10.21
Leonard-KC	292.2	Guidry-NY	7.43	Eckersley-Cle	1.96	Palmer-Bal	193	Leonard-KC	7.50	Tanana-Cal	10.22
Garland-Cle	282.2	Tanana-Cal	7.50	Cleveland-Bos	2.03	Eckersley-Cle	191	Blyleven-Tex	6.98	Leonard-KC	10.24

Earned Run Average		Adjusted ERA		Opponents' Batting Avg.		Opponents' On Base Pct.		Starter Runs		Adjusted Starter Runs	
Tanana-Cal	2.54	Tanana-Cal	154	Ryan-Cal	.193	Eckersley-Cle	.278	Ryan-Cal	42.8	Ryan-Cal	38.0
Blyleven-Tex	2.72	Blyleven-Tex	150	Blyleven-Tex	.214	Blyleven-Tex	.279	Palmer-Bal	40.8	Tanana-Cal	36.9
Ryan-Cal	2.77	Ryan-Cal	141	Guidry-NY	.224	Guidry-NY	.284	Tanana-Cal	40.8	Blyleven-Tex	35.3
Guidry-NY	2.82	Guidry-NY	140	Tanana-Cal	.227	Leonard-KC	.285	Blyleven-Tex	34.8	Leonard-KC	32.2
Palmer-Bal	2.91	Rozema-Det	139	Leonard-KC	.227	Tanana-Cal	.286	Leonard-KC	33.0	Palmer-Bal	31.3

Clutch Pitching Index		Relief Runs		Adjusted Relief Runs		Relief Ranking		Total Pitcher Index		Total Baseball Ranking	
Slaton-Mil	118	Lyle-NY	28.8	Lyle-NY	27.0	Campbell-Bos	45.6	Lyle-NY	4.4	Carew-Min	6.3
Rozema-Det	116	Torrealba-Oak	18.6	Campbell-Bos	23.8	Lyle-NY	43.4	Ryan-Cal	4.2	Singleton-Bal	4.9
Grimsley-Bal	110	LaGrow-Chi	17.5	Torrealba-Oak	18.1	Romo-Sea	26.3	Campbell-Bos	3.9	Page-Oak	4.9
Splittorff-KC	108	Campbell-Bos	17.1	LaGrow-Chi	17.8	LaGrow-Chi	26.3	Blyleven-Tex	3.8	Brett-KC	4.4
Tanana-Cal	106	Coleman-Oak	15.6	Romo-Sea	16.2	T.Johnson-Min	22.8	Tanana-Cal	3.7	Lyle-NY	4.4

TEAM	G	W	L	PCT	GB	R	OR	AB	H	2B	3B	HR	BB	SO	AVG	OBP	SLG	PRO	PRO+	BR	/A	PF	CHI	RC	SB	CS	SBA	SBR
EAST																												
PHI	162	90	72	.556		708	586	5448	1404	248	32	133	552	866	.258	.331	.388	.719	106	49	43	101	101	715	152	58	72	11
PIT	161	88	73	.547	1.5	684	637	5406	1390	239	54	115	480	874	.257	.323	.385	.708	100	21	-9	105	104	676	213	90	70	10
CHI	162	79	83	.488	11	664	724	5532	1461	224	48	72	562	746	.264	.334	.361	.695	90	11	-70	112	99	673	110	58	65	-2
MON	162	76	86	.469	14	633	611	5530	1404	269	31	121	396	881	.254	.308	.379	.687	98	-27	-20	99	103	629	80	42	66	-1
STL	162	69	93	.426	21	600	657	5415	1351	263	44	79	420	713	.249	.306	.358	.664	92	-66	-58	99	98	583	97	42	70	4
NY	162	66	96	.407	24	607	690	5433	1332	227	47	86	549	829	.245	.317	.352	.669	96	-47	-25	96	101	600	100	77	56	-16
WEST																												
LA	162	95	67	.586		727	573	5437	1435	251	27	149	610	818	.264	.340	.402	.742	114	98	101	100	96	763	137	52	72	10
CIN	161	92	69	.571	2.5	710	688	5392	1378	270	32	136	636	899	.256	.337	.393	.730	110	75	75	100	97	730	137	58	70	6
SF	162	89	73	.549	6	613	594	5364	1331	240	41	117	554	814	.248	.320	.374	.694	104	-1	24	96	95	647	87	54	62	-6
SD	162	84	78	.519	11	591	598	5360	1349	208	42	75	536	848	.252	.323	.348	.671	102	-37	10	92	98	624	152	70	68	4
HOU	162	74	88	.457	21	605	634	5458	1408	231	45	70	434	743	.258	.315	.355	.670	101	-49	-5	93	103	608	178	59	75	18
ATL	162	69	93	.426	26	600	750	5381	1313	191	39	123	550	874	.244	.317	.363	.680	86	-28	-97	111	98	608	90	65	58	-12
TOT	971					7742		65156	16556	2861	482	1276	6279	9905	.254	.323	.372	.694							1533	725	68	25

TEAM	CG	SH	SV	IP	H	H/G	HR	BB	SO	RAT	ERA	ERA+	OAV	OOB	PR	/A	PF	CPI	FA	E	DP	FW	PW	BW	SBW	DIF
EAST																										
PHI	38	9	29	1436[1]	1343	8.4	118	393	813	11.0	3.33	107	.251	.305	39	37	100	99	.983	104	156	2.0	3.9	4.5	.9	-2.4
PIT	30	13	44	1444[2]	1366	8.5	103	499	880	11.8	3.41	108	.249	.315	26	46	104	98	.973	167	133	-1.4	4.9	-1.0	.8	4.2
CHI	24	7	38	1455[1]	1475	9.1	125	539	768	12.7	4.05	99	.265	.333	-77	-4	113	98	.978	144	154	-.2	-.4	-7.4	-.4	6.4
MON	42	13	32	1446	1332	8.3	117	572	740	12.0	3.42	103	.249	.325	24	16	99	106	.979	134	150	.4	1.7	-2.1	.3	-4.6
STL	42	13	22	1437[2]	1300	8.1	94	600	859	12.1	3.58	98	.245	.326	-1	-11	98	97	.978	136	155	.3	-1.2	-6.1	.2	-5.2
NY	21	7	26	1455[1]	1447	8.9	114	531	775	12.4	3.87	90	.265	.334	-48	-62	98	101	.979	132	160	.5	-6.6	-2.6	-1.9	-4.4
WEST																										
LA	46	16	38	1440[1]	1362	8.5	107	440	800	11.4	3.12	112	.250	.309	73	62	98	106	.978	140	138	.0	6.6	10.7	.8	-4.1
CIN	16	10	46	1448[1]	1437	8.9	122	567	908	12.6	3.81	93	.261	.332	-38	-42	99	102	.978	134	120	.3	-4.4	7.9	.4	7.3
SF	42	17	29	1455	1377	8.5	84	453	840	11.5	3.30	104	.252	.311	44	23	96	98	.977	146	118	-.3	2.4	2.5	-.9	4.1
SD	21	10	55	1433[2]	1385	8.7	74	483	744	11.8	3.28	101	.257	.320	47	8	93	104	.975	160	171	-1.0	.8	1.1	.2	1.9
HOU	48	17	23	1440[1]	1328	8.3	86	578	930	12.1	3.63	91	.247	.323	-9	-52	93	94	.978	133	109	.4	-5.5	-.5	1.7	-3.1
ATL	29	12	32	1440[1]	1404	8.8	132	624	848	12.9	4.08	99	.257	.337	-81	-5	113	98	.975	153	126	-.6	-.5	-10.3	-1.5	.9
TOT	389	144	414	17333[1]		8.6				12.0	3.57		.254	.323					.978	1683	1690					

Runs		Hits		Doubles		Triples		Home Runs		Total Bases	
DeJesus-Chi	104	Garvey-LA	202	Rose-Cin	51	Templeton-StL	13	Foster-Cin	40	Parker-Pit	340
Rose-Cin	103	Rose-Cin	198	Clark-SF	46	Richards-SD	12	Luzinski-Phi	35	Foster-Cin	330
Parker-Pit	102	Cabell-Hou	195	Simmons-StL	40	Parker-Pit	12	Parker-Pit	30	Garvey-LA	319
Foster-Cin	97	Parker-Pit	194	Parrish-Mon	39			Smith-LA	29	Clark-SF	318
Moreno-Pit	95	Bowa-Phi	192	Perez-Mon	38					Winfield-SD	293

Runs Batted In		Runs Produced		Bases On Balls		Batting Average		On Base Percentage		Slugging Average	
Foster-Cin	120	Parker-Pit	189	Burroughs-Atl	117	Parker-Pit	.334	Burroughs-Atl	.436	Parker-Pit	.585
Parker-Pit	117	Garvey-LA	181	Evans-SF	105	Garvey-LA	.316	Parker-Pit	.395	Smith-LA	.559
Garvey-LA	113	Foster-Cin	177	Tenace-SD	101	Cruz-Hou	.315	Tenace-SD	.394	Foster-Cin	.546
Luzinski-Phi	101	Clark-SF	163	Luzinski-Phi	100	Madlock-SF	.309	Smith-LA	.392	Clark-SF	.537
Clark-SF	98	Winfield-SD	161	Cey-LA	96	Winfield-SD	.308	Luzinski-Phi	.390	Burroughs-Atl	.529

Production		Adjusted Production		Batter Runs		Adjusted Batter Runs		Clutch Hitting Index		Runs Created	
Parker-Pit	.981	Smith-LA	164	Parker-Pit	52.9	Parker-Pit	47.6	Morgan-Cin	134	Parker-Pit	134
Burroughs-Atl	.965	Parker-Pit	163	Burroughs-Atl	50.1	Clark-SF	40.0	Reitz-StL	126	Burroughs-Atl	116
Smith-LA	.951	Clark-SF	155	Luzinski-Phi	40.9	Luzinski-Phi	39.9	Montanez-NY	119	Foster-Cin	115
Luzinski-Phi	.916	Winfield-SD	153	Foster-Cin	39.2	Foster-Cin	39.2	Watson-Hou	118	Luzinski-Phi	114
Foster-Cin	.909	Luzinski-Phi	152	Smith-LA	37.8	Winfield-SD	38.6	B.Robinson-Pit	117	Clark-SF	109

Total Average		Stolen Bases		Stolen Base Average		Stolen Base Runs		Fielding Runs		Total Player Rating	
Burroughs-Atl	1.042	Moreno-Pit	71	Cedeno-Hou	92.0	Lopes-LA	11.1	Trillo-Chi	28.9	Parker-Pit	5.3
Parker-Pit	1.025	Taveras-Pit	46	Lopes-LA	91.8	Moreno-Pit	8.1	Smith-SD	25.6	Clark-SF	4.7
Smith-LA	1.009	Lopes-LA	45	McBride-Phi	90.3	McBride-Phi	6.6	Cromartie-Mon	24.7	Foster-Cin	4.0
Luzinski-Phi	.957	DeJesus-Chi	41	Sexton-Hou	88.9			Templeton-StL	22.9	Lopes-LA	4.0
Foster-Cin	.893	Smith-SD	40	Bowa-Phi	84.4			Dawson-Mon	21.1	Templeton-StL	3.8

Wins		Win Percentage		Games		Complete Games		Shutouts		Saves	
Perry-SD	21	Perry-SD	.778	Tekulve-Pit	91	Niekro-Atl	22	Knepper-SF	6	Fingers-SD	37
Grimsley-Mon	20	Hooton-LA	.655	Littell-StL	72	Grimsley-Mon	19	Niekro-Atl	4	Tekulve-Pit	31
Niekro-Atl	19	Grimsley-Mon	.645	Moore-Chi	71	Richard-Hou	16	Halicki-SF	4	Bair-Cin	28
Hooton-LA	19	Blue-SF	.643	Moffitt-SF	70	Knepper-SF	16	Blyleven-Pit	4	Sutter-Chi	27
		John-LA	.630	Bair-Cin	70			Blue-SF	4	Garber-Phi-Atl	25

Innings Pitched		Fewest Hits/Game		Fewest BB/Game		Strikeouts		Strikeouts/Game		Ratio	
Niekro-Atl	334.1	Richard-Hou	6.28	Christenson-Phi	1.86	Richard-Hou	303	Richard-Hou	9.90	Swan-NY	9.72
Richard-Hou	275.1	Swan-NY	7.12	Barr-SF	1.93	Niekro-Atl	248	Seaver-Cin	7.83	Hooton-LA	9.80
Grimsley-Mon	263.0	Hooton-LA	7.47	R.Reuschel-Chi	2.00	Seaver-Cin	226	Vuckovich-StL	6.76	Halicki-SF	9.86
Perry-SD	260.2	Halicki-SF	7.51	Halicki-SF	2.04	Blyleven-Pit	182	Blyleven-Pit	6.72	Christenson-Phi	10.14
Knepper-SF	260.0	Knepper-SF	7.55	Sutton-LA	2.04	Montefusco-SF	177	Niekro-Atl	6.68	Rogers-Mon	10.36

Earned Run Average		Adjusted ERA		Opponents' Batting Avg.		Opponents' On Base Pct.		Starter Runs		Adjusted Starter Runs	
Swan-NY	2.43	Swan-NY	143	Richard-Hou	.196	Halicki-SF	.271	Knepper-SF	27.3	Niekro-Atl	43.3
Rogers-Mon	2.47	Rogers-Mon	143	Swan-NY	.219	Swan-NY	.277	Rogers-Mon	27.0	Rogers-Mon	25.7
Vuckovich-StL	2.54	Niekro-Atl	140	Halicki-SF	.221	Hooton-LA	.277	Swan-NY	26.4	Swan-NY	24.3
Knepper-SF	2.63	Vuckovich-StL	138	Hooton-LA	.226	Christenson-Phi	.284	Niekro-Atl	25.8	Knepper-SF	23.6
Hooton-LA	2.71	Knepper-SF	131	Seaver-Cin	.227	D.Robinson-Pit	.286	Perry-SD	24.5	Vuckovich-StL	21.4

Clutch Pitching Index		Relief Runs		Adjusted Relief Runs		Relief Ranking		Total Pitcher Index		Total Baseball Ranking	
Rau-LA	134	Tekulve-Pit	18.6	Garber-Phi-Atl	22.5	Bair-Cin	31.5	Niekro-Atl	5.7	Niekro-Atl	5.7
Vuckovich-StL	124	Garber-Phi-Atl	18.5	Tekulve-Pit	20.5	Tekulve-Pit	31.1	Tekulve-Pit	3.6	Parker-Pit	5.3
Carlton-Phi	121	Bair-Cin	17.9	Bair-Cin	17.5	Garber-Phi-Atl	29.9	Bair-Cin	3.3	Clark-SF	4.7
Jones-SD	114	Reed-Phi	16.2	Reed-Phi	16.1	Forster-LA	22.9	Carlton-Phi	3.3	Foster-Cin	4.0
Rogers-Mon	113	D'Acquisto-SD	14.9	D'Acquisto-SD	12.4	Fingers-SD	22.9	Garber-Phi-Atl	3.2	Lopes-LA	4.0

TEAM	G	W	L	PCT	GB	R	OR	AB	H	2B	3B	HR	BB	SO	AVG	OBP	SLG	PRO	PRO+	BR	/A	PF	CHI	RC	SB	CS	SBA	SBR
EAST																												
NY	163	100	63	.613		735	**582**	5583	1489	228	38	125	505	695	.267	.332	.388	.720	105	14	31	98	**105**	720	98	42	70	4
BOS	163	99	64	.607	1	796	657	5587	1493	270	46	172	582	582	.267	.339	.424	.763	102	96	12	111	100	793	74	51	59	-8
MIL	162	93	69	.574	6.5	**804**	650	5536	**1530**	265	38	**173**	520	805	**.276**	**.342**	**.432**	**.774**	116	**114**	**112**	100	100	**822**	95	53	64	-3
BAL	161	90	71	.559	9	659	633	5422	1397	248	19	154	552	864	.258	.329	.396	.725	110	18	61	94	95	691	75	61	55	-14
DET	162	86	76	.531	13.5	714	653	5601	1520	218	34	129	563	695	.271	.341	.392	.733	103	45	24	103	96	748	90	38	70	4
CLE	159	69	90	.434	29	639	694	5365	1400	223	45	106	488	698	.261	.326	.379	.705	99	-19	-11	99	99	649	64	63	50	-19
TOR	161	59	102	.366	40	590	775	5430	1358	217	39	98	448	645	.250	.310	.359	.669	86	-93	-105	102	103	587	28	52	35	-23
WEST																												
KC	162	92	70	.568		743	634	5474	1469	**305**	**59**	98	498	644	.268	.333	.399	.732	102	34	15	103	104	739	**216**	84	**72**	**14**
TEX	162	87	75	.537	5	692	632	5347	1353	216	36	132	**624**	779	.253	.335	.381	.716	101	11	10	100	100	696	196	91	68	4
CAL	162	87	75	.537	5	691	666	5472	1417	226	28	108	539	682	.259	.333	.370	.703	101	-14	-12	96	103	669	86	69	55	-16
MIN	162	73	89	.451	19	666	678	5522	1472	259	47	82	604	684	.267	**.342**	.375	.717	99	21	7	102	92	715	99	56	64	-4
CHI	161	71	90	.441	20.5	634	731	5393	1423	221	41	106	409	**625**	.264	.320	.379	.699	95	-35	-41	101	102	635	83	68	55	-16
OAK	162	69	93	.426	23	532	690	5321	1304	200	31	100	433	800	.245	.305	.351	.656	89	-117	-89	95	99	552	144	117	55	-27
SEA	160	56	104	.350	35	614	834	5358	1327	229	37	97	522	702	.248	.317	.359	.676	91	-73	-69	99	103	620	123	47	**72**	9
TOT	1131					9509		76411	19952	3325	538	1680	7287	10153	.261	.329	.385	.714							1471	892	62	-94

TEAM	CG	SH	SV	IP	H	H/G	HR	BB	SO	RAT	ERA	ERA+	OAV	OOB	PR	/A	PF	CPI	FA	E	DP	FW	PW	BW	SBW	DIF
EAST																										
NY	39	16	**36**	1460²	**1321**	8.1	111	478	817	11.3	3.18	114	.243	.308	95	72	96	99	**.982**	113	134	1.5	7.4	3.2	1.1	5.2
BOS	57	15	26	1472²	1530	9.4	137	464	706	12.4	3.54	116	.270	.329	37	94	109	111	.977	146	171	-.3	9.7	1.2	-.1	7.1
MIL	62	**19**	24	1436	1442	9.0	109	**398**	577	11.8	3.65	103	.262	.316	17	17	100	95	.977	150	144	-.6	1.8	11.5	.4	-1.0
BAL	**65**	16	33	1429	1441	8.9	107	509	754	11.7	3.56	98	.251	.318	32	-11	93	95	**.982**	110	166	**1.6**	-1.1	6.3	-.8	3.5
DET	60	12	21	1455²	1441	8.9	135	503	684	12.2	3.64	106	.263	.329	20	36	103	106	.981	118	**177**	1.2	3.7	2.5	1.1	-3.5
CLE	36	6	28	1407¹	1397	8.9	100	568	739	12.7	3.97	94	.261	.335	-33	-37	99	95	.980	123	142	.8	-3.8	-1.1	-1.3	-5.1
TOR	35	5	23	1429¹	1529	9.6	149	614	758	13.6	4.54	86	.279	.353	-123	-98	104	100	.979	131	163	.4	-10.1	-10.8	-1.7	.7
WEST																										
KC	53	14	33	1439	1350	8.4	108	478	657	11.6	3.44	111	.251	.316	52	61	102	98	.976	150	153	-.6	6.3	1.5	**2.1**	1.7
TEX	54	12	25	1456²	1431	8.8	108	421	776	11.6	3.36	112	.259	.315	66	63	100	102	.976	153	140	-.8	6.5	1.0	1.1	-1.8
CAL	44	13	33	1455²	1382	8.5	125	599	**892**	12.4	3.65	99	.259	.330	19	-6	96	102	.978	136	136	.2	-.6	1.2	-1.0	6.2
MIN	48	9	26	1459²	1468	9.1	102	520	703	12.5	3.69	103	.266	.333	11	20	102	102	.977	146	171	-.4	2.1	.7	-.3	-10.7
CHI	38	9	33	1409¹	1380	8.8	128	586	710	12.8	4.21	90	.259	.337	-71	-65	101	94	.977	139	130	-.0	-6.7	-4.2	-1.0	2.4
OAK	26	11	29	1433¹	1401	8.8	106	582	750	12.6	3.62	100	.259	.333	22	3	97	103	.971	179	145	-2.3	.3	-9.2	-2.1	1.2
SEA	28	4	20	1419¹	1540	9.8	155	567	630	13.6	4.67	81	.280	.352	-144	-136	101	98	.978	141	174	-.2	-14.0	-7.1	1.6	-4.3
TOT	645	161	390	20163¹		8.9				12.4	3.76		.261	.329					.978	1935	2146					

Runs
LeFlore-Det	126
Rice-Bos	121
Baylor-Cal	103
Thornton-Cle	97
Hisle-Mil	96

Hits
Rice-Bos	213
LeFlore-Det	198
Carew-Min	188
Munson-NY	183
Staub-Det	175

Doubles
Brett-KC	45
McRae-KC	39
Fisk-Bos	39
DeCinces-Bal	37
Ford-Min	36

Triples
Rice-Bos	15
Ford-Min	10
Carew-Min	10
Yount-Mil	9
Garr-Chi	9

Home Runs
Rice-Bos	46
Hisle-Mil	34
Baylor-Cal	34
Thornton-Cle	33
Thomas-Mil	32

Total Bases
Rice-Bos	406
Murray-Bal	293
Staub-Det	279
Baylor-Cal	279
Thompson-Det	278

Runs Batted In
Rice-Bos	139
Staub-Det	121
Hisle-Mil	115
Thornton-Cle	105

Runs Produced
Rice-Bos	214
Hisle-Mil	177
LeFlore-Det	176
Staub-Det	172
Thornton-Cle	169

Bases On Balls
Hargrove-Tex	107
Singleton-Bal	98
Kemp-Det	97
Thornton-Cle	93
Smalley-Min	85

Batting Average
Carew-Min	.333
Oliver-Tex	.324
Rice-Bos	.315
Piniella-NY	.314
Oglivie-Mil	.303

On Base Percentage
Carew-Min	.415
Singleton-Bal	.410
Hargrove-Tex	.391
Otis-KC	.387
Randolph-NY	.385

Slugging Average
Rice-Bos	.600
Hisle-Mil	.533
DeCinces-Bal	.526
Otis-KC	.525
Thornton-Cle	.516

Production
Rice-Bos	.973
Otis-KC	.911
Hisle-Mil	.909
Thornton-Cle	.898
Roberts-Sea	.881

Adjusted Production
Singleton-Bal	154
Rice-Bos	153
Hisle-Mil	153
Thornton-Cle	152
DeCinces-Bal	152

Batter Runs
Rice-Bos	58.7
Hisle-Mil	36.3
Thornton-Cle	35.6
Otis-KC	35.2
Singleton-Bal	34.0

Adjusted Batter Runs
Rice-Bos	44.1
Singleton-Bal	40.4
Thornton-Cle	36.8
Hisle-Mil	36.0
Murray-Bal	33.7

Clutch Hitting Index
Staub-Det	136
L.Johnson-Chi	127
Whitaker-Det	119
Chambliss-NY	117
Cowens-KC	116

Runs Created
Rice-Bos	147
LeFlore-Det	105
Carew-Min	105
Thompson-Det	104
Murray-Bal	104

Total Average
Rice-Bos	.973
Otis-KC	.972
Hisle-Mil	.907
Singleton-Bal	.900
Thornton-Cle	.897

Stolen Bases
LeFlore-Det	68
Cruz-Sea	59
Wills-Tex	52
Dilone-Oak	50
Wilson-KC	46

Stolen Base Average
Cruz-Sea	85.5
Campaneris-Tex	84.6
Lowenstein-Tex	84.2
Randolph-NY	83.7
Rivers-NY	83.3

Stolen Base Runs
Cruz-Sea	11.7
LeFlore-Det	10.8
Wills-Tex	7.2
Wilson-KC	6.6
Randolph-NY	6.6

Fielding Runs
Belanger-Bal	33.8
Bell-Cle	28.3
Bosetti-Tor	25.1
Yount-Mil	21.9
Wills-Tex	21.3

Total Player Rating
Smalley-Min	5.3
Rice-Bos	4.8
Yount-Mil	4.5
Otis-KC	4.2
DeCinces-Bal	4.0

Wins
Guidry-NY	25
Caldwell-Mil	22
Palmer-Bal	21
Leonard-KC	21

Win Percentage
Guidry-NY	.893
Stanley-Bos	.882
Gura-KC	.800
Eckersley-Bos	.714
Caldwell-Mil	.710

Games
Lacey-Oak	74
Heaverlo-Oak	69
Sosa-Oak	68
Gossage-NY	63

Complete Games
Caldwell-Mil	23
Leonard-KC	20
Palmer-Bal	19
Matlack-Tex	18

Shutouts
Guidry-NY	9
Palmer-Bal	6
Caldwell-Mil	6
Tiant-Bos	5

Saves
Gossage-NY	27
LaRoche-Cal	25
Stanhouse-Bal	24
Marshall-Min	21
Hrabosky-KC	20

Innings Pitched
Palmer-Bal	296.0
Leonard-KC	294.2
Caldwell-Mil	293.1
Flanagan-Bal	281.1
Sorensen-Mil	280.2

Fewest Hits/Game
Guidry-NY	6.15
Ryan-Cal	7.02
Gura-KC	7.43
Palmer-Bal	7.48
Tiant-Bos	7.84

Fewest BB/Game
Jenkins-Tex	1.48
Sorensen-Mil	1.60
Caldwell-Mil	1.66
Matlack-Tex	1.70
Rozema-Det	1.76

Strikeouts
Ryan-Cal	260
Guidry-NY	248
Leonard-KC	183
Flanagan-Bal	167
Eckersley-Bos	162

Strikeouts/Game
Ryan-Cal	9.97
Guidry-NY	8.16
Kravec-Chi	6.83
Underwood-Tor	6.33
Knapp-KC	6.02

Ratio
Guidry-NY	8.55
Caldwell-Mil	9.79
Jenkins-Tex	9.83
Gura-KC	10.03
Matlack-Tex	10.23

Earned Run Average
Guidry-NY	1.74
Matlack-Tex	2.27
Caldwell-Mil	2.36
Palmer-Bal	2.46
Goltz-Min	2.49

Adjusted ERA
Guidry-NY	208
Matlack-Tex	165
Caldwell-Mil	159
Goltz-Min	153
Palmer-Bal	142

Opponents' Batting Avg.
Guidry-NY	.193
Ryan-Cal	.220
Palmer-Bal	.227
Gura-KC	.229
Tiant-Bos	.234

Opponents' On Base Pct.
Guidry-NY	.250
Caldwell-Mil	.274
Jenkins-Tex	.279
Matlack-Tex	.284
Gura-KC	.286

Starter Runs
Guidry-NY	61.4
Caldwell-Mil	45.7
Matlack-Tex	44.9
Palmer-Bal	42.8
Goltz-Min	31.1

Adjusted Starter Runs
Guidry-NY	57.1
Caldwell-Mil	45.5
Matlack-Tex	44.3
Palmer-Bal	34.0
Eckersley-Bos	33.6

Clutch Pitching Index
Lee-Bos	130
Zahn-Min	129
Goltz-Min	125
Gale-KC	115
Eckersley-Bos	115

Relief Runs
Gossage-NY	26.2
Stanley-Bos	18.2
Hiller-Det	14.6
Marshall-Min	14.4
Sosa-Oak	13.6

Adjusted Relief Runs
Gossage-NY	24.0
Stanley-Bos	23.7
Hiller-Det	15.7
Marshall-Min	15.0
Sosa-Oak	12.1

Relief Ranking
Gossage-NY	44.7
Marshall-Min	37.2
Stanley-Bos	29.4
Hiller-Det	25.6
LaRoche-Cal	19.9

Total Pitcher Index
Guidry-NY	6.2
Caldwell-Mil	5.0
Matlack-Tex	4.7
Gossage-NY	4.7
Palmer-Bal	4.3

Total Baseball Ranking
Guidry-NY	6.2
Smalley-Min	5.3
Caldwell-Mil	5.0
Rice-Bos	4.8
Matlack-Tex	4.7

TEAM	G	W	L	PCT	GB	R	OR	AB	H	2B	3B	HR	BB	SO	AVG	OBP	SLG	PRO	PRO+	BR	/A	PF	CHI	RC	SB	CS	SBA	SBR
EAST																												
PIT	163	98	64	.605		775	643	5661	1541	264	52	148	483	855	.272	.333	.416	.749	105	68	32	105	101	781	180	66	73	14
MON	160	95	65	.594	2	701	581	5465	1445	273	42	143	432	890	.264	.321	.408	.729	105	23	29	99	102	701	121	56	68	3
STL	163	86	76	.531	12	731	693	5734	1594	279	63	100	460	838	.278	.335	.401	.736	106	46	40	101	98	757	116	69	63	-7
PHI	163	84	78	.519	14	683	718	5463	1453	250	53	119	602	764	.266	.343	.396	.739	105	63	39	103	91	743	128	76	63	-7
CHI	162	80	82	.494	18	706	707	5550	1494	250	43	135	478	762	.269	.331	.403	.734	97	40	-28	110	98	726	73	52	58	-9
NY	163	63	99	.389	35	593	706	5591	1399	255	41	74	498	817	.250	.315	.350	.665	90	-90	-68	96	99	615	135	79	63	-7
WEST																												
CIN	161	90	71	.559		731	644	5477	1445	266	31	132	614	902	.264	.340	.396	.736	106	55	51	101	99	741	99	47	68	2
HOU	162	89	73	.549	1.5	583	582	5394	1382	224	52	49	461	745	.256	.317	.344	.661	91	-93	-60	94	102	591	190	95	67	0
LA	162	79	83	.488	11.5	739	717	5490	1443	220	24	183	556	834	.263	.333	.412	.745	111	62	73	99	99	743	106	46	70	4
SF	162	71	91	.438	19.5	672	751	5395	1328	192	36	125	580	925	.246	.322	.365	.687	100	-46	-3	93	106	644	140	73	66	-2
SD	161	68	93	.422	22	603	681	5446	1316	193	53	93	534	770	.242	.313	.348	.661	91	-97	-62	94	103	600	100	58	63	-5
ATL	160	66	94	.413	23.5	669	763	5422	1389	220	28	126	490	818	.256	.320	.377	.697	89	-31	-78	107	105	654	98	50	66	-1
TOT	971					8186		66088	17229	2886	518	1427	6188	9920	.261	.327	.385	.712							1486	767	66	-14

TEAM	CG	SH	SV	IP	H	H/G	HR	BB	SO	RAT	ERA	ERA+	OAV	OOB	PR	/A	PF	CPI	FA	E	DP	FW	PW	BW	SBW	DIF
EAST																										
PIT	24	7	52	1493¹	1424	8.6	125	504	904	11.8	3.41	114	.254	.318	53	77	104	103	.979	134	163	.4	7.9	3.3	1.6	3.8
MON	33	18	39	1447¹	1379	8.6	116	450	813	11.5	3.14	117	.253	.312	95	84	98	107	.979	131	123	.4	8.7	3.0	.4	2.5
STL	38	10	25	1486²	1449	8.8	127	501	788	11.9	3.72	101	.258	.321	1	6	101	97	.980	132	166	.5	.6	4.1	-.6	.3
PHI	33	14	29	1441¹	1455	9.1	135	477	787	12.2	4.16	92	.266	.328	-69	-54	103	94	.983	106	148	2.1	-5.6	4.0	-.6	3.1
CHI	20	11	44	1446²	1500	9.3	127	521	933	12.8	3.88	106	.270	.338	-24	37	110	105	.975	159	163	-1.1	3.8	-2.9	-.8	.0
NY	16	10	36	1482²	1486	9.0	120	607	819	12.9	3.84	95	.266	.341	-18	-34	98	105	.978	140	168	.0	-3.5	-7.6	-.6	-6.9
WEST																										
CIN	27	10	40	1440¹	1415	8.8	103	485	773	10.9	3.58	104	.260	.322	24	24	100	99	.980	124	152	.9	2.5	5.3	.3	.5
HOU	55	19	31	1447²	1278	7.9	90	504	854	11.2	3.20	110	.237	.306	86	51	94	93	.978	138	146	.1	5.3	-6.2	.1	8.7
LA	30	6	34	1444	1425	8.9	101	555	811	12.5	3.83	95	.260	.331	-15	-31	97	97	.981	118	123	1.3	-3.2	7.5	.5	-8.2
SF	25	6	34	1436	1484	9.3	143	577	880	13.1	4.16	84	.269	.341	-69	-107	94	101	.974	163	138	-1.4	-11.0	-.3	-.0	2.8
SD	29	7	25	1453	1438	8.9	108	513	779	12.2	3.69	96	.263	.328	6	-27	95	101	.978	141	154	-.1	-2.8	-6.4	-.4	-2.8
ATL	32	3	34	1407²	1496	9.6	132	494	779	13.0	4.18	91	.272	.337	-70	-21	109	99	.970	183	139	-2.7	-2.2	-8.0	-.0	-1.1
TOT	362	121	423	17426²		8.9				12.3	3.73		.261	.327					.978	1669	1783					

<table>
<tr><td>

Runs
Hernandez-StL 116
Moreno-Pit 110
Schmidt-Phi 109
Parker-Pit 109
Lopes-LA 109

</td><td>

Hits
Templeton-StL ... 211
Hernandez-StL ... 210
Rose-Phi 208
Garvey-LA 204
Moreno-Pit 196

</td><td>

Doubles
Hernandez-StL 48
Cromartie-Mon 46
Parker-Pit 45
Reitz-StL 41
Rose-Phi 40

</td><td>

Triples
Templeton-StL 19
Moreno-Pit 12
McBride-Phi 12
Winfield-SD 12
Dawson-Mon 12

</td><td>

Home Runs
Kingman-Chi 48
Schmidt-Phi 45
Winfield-SD 34
Horner-Atl 33
Stargell-Pit 32

</td><td>

Total Bases
Winfield-SD 333
Parker-Pit 327
Kingman-Chi 326
Garvey-LA 322
Matthews-Atl 317

</td></tr>
<tr><td>

Runs Batted In
Winfield-SD 118
Kingman-Chi 115
Schmidt-Phi 114
Garvey-LA 110
Hernandez-StL 105

</td><td>

Runs Produced
Hernandez-StL 210
Winfield-SD 181
Schmidt-Phi 178
Parker-Pit 178
Garvey-LA 174

</td><td>

Bases On Balls
Schmidt-Phi 120
Tenace-SD 105
Lopes-LA 97
North-SF 96
Rose-Phi 95

</td><td>

Batting Average
Hernandez-StL 344
Rose-Phi 331
Knight-Cin 318
Garvey-LA 315
Horner-Atl 314

</td><td>

On Base Percentage
Hernandez-StL ... .421
Rose-Phi ...... .421
Tenace-SD ..... .407
Mazzilli-NY ..... .397
Winfield-SD ..... .396

</td><td>

Slugging Average
Kingman-Chi 613
Schmidt-Phi 564
Foster-Cin 561
Winfield-SD 558
Horner-Atl 552

</td></tr>
<tr><td>

Production
Kingman-Chi 960
Schmidt-Phi 955
Winfield-SD 954
Foster-Cin 950
Hernandez-StL 934

</td><td>

Adjusted Production
Winfield-SD 167
Foster-Cin 155
Schmidt-Phi 153
Hernandez-StL 152
Parrish-Mon 146

</td><td>

Batter Runs
Winfield-SD 47.4
Hernandez-StL 47.1
Schmidt-Phi 44.9
Parker-Pit 39.3
Kingman-Chi 37.8

</td><td>

Adjusted Batter Runs
Winfield-SD 55.0
Hernandez-StL 46.1
Schmidt-Phi 41.1
Parker-Pit 33.8
Foster-Cin 33.1

</td><td>

Clutch Hitting Index
Foli-NY-Pit 140
Hebner-NY 137
Flynn-NY 124
Luzinski-Phi 122
Concepcion-Cin ... 114

</td><td>

Runs Created
Hernandez-StL 135
Winfield-SD 132
Parker-Pit 131
Schmidt-Phi 123
Matthews-Atl 118

</td></tr>
<tr><td>

Total Average
Schmidt-Phi 1.024
Winfield-SD 988
Kingman-Chi 972
Hernandez-StL 961
Foster-Cin........959

</td><td>

Stolen Bases
Moreno-Pit 77
North-SF 58
Taveras-Pit-NY ... 44
Lopes-LA 44
Scott-Mon 39

</td><td>

Stolen Base Average
Lopes-LA 91.7
Parker-Pit 83.3
Morgan-Cin 82.4
Royster-Atl 81.4
Smith-SD 80.0

</td><td>

Stolen Base Runs
Lopes-LA 10.8
Moreno-Pit 10.5
Royster-Atl 5.7
Morgan-Cin 4.8

</td><td>

Fielding Runs
Maddox-Phi 26.9
Moreno-Pit 22.8
Evans-SF 22.4
Smith-SD 21.0
Cromartie-Mon ... 20.4

</td><td>

Total Player Rating
Winfield-SD 5.9
Schmidt-Phi 5.8
Hernandez-StL 5.6
Templeton-StL 4.7
Parker-Pit 4.0

</td></tr>
<tr><td>

Wins
Niekro-Atl 21
Niekro-Hou 21
Richard-Hou 18
Reuschel-Chi 18
Carlton-Phi 18

</td><td>

Win Percentage
Seaver-Cin ...... .727
Niekro-Hou ..... .656
Martinez-StL .... .652
Sutcliffe-LA ..... .630
Carlton-Phi ...... .621

</td><td>

Games
Tekulve-Pit 94
Romo-Pit 84
Jackson-Pit 72
Lavelle-SF 70
Garber-Atl 68

</td><td>

Complete Games
Niekro-Atl 23
Richard-Hou 19
Rogers-Mon 13
Carlton-Phi 13
Hooton-LA 12

</td><td>

Shutouts
Seaver-Cin 5
Rogers-Mon 5
Niekro-Hou 5
Richard-Hou 4
Carlton-Phi 4

</td><td>

Saves
Sutter-Chi 37
Tekulve-Pit 31
Garber-Atl 25
Sambito-Hou 22
Lavelle-SF 20

</td></tr>
<tr><td>

Innings Pitched
Niekro-Atl 342.0
Richard-Hou 292.1
Niekro-Hou 263.2
Jones-SD 263.0
Swan-NY 251.1

</td><td>

Fewest Hits/Game
Richard-Hou 6.77
Carlton-Phi 7.24
Niekro-Hou 7.54
Schatzeder-Mon .. 7.56
Andujar-Hou 7.79

</td><td>

Fewest BB/Game
Forsch-Hou 1.77
Candelaria-Pit 1.78
Hume-Cin 1.82
Lee-Mon 1.86
Swan-NY 2.04

</td><td>

Strikeouts
Richard-Hou 313
Carlton-Phi 213
Niekro-Atl 208
Blyleven-Pit 172
McGlothen-Chi 147

</td><td>

Strikeouts/Game
Richard-Hou 9.64
Carlton-Phi 7.64
Sanderson-Mon ... 7.39
Blyleven-Pit 6.52
Krukow-Chi 6.50

</td><td>

Ratio
Forsch-Hou 9.62
Richard-Hou 9.88
Seaver-Cin 10.38
Sutton-LA 10.47
Carlton-Phi 10.61

</td></tr>
<tr><td>

Earned Run Average
Richard-Hou 2.71
Hume-Cin 2.76
Schatzeder-Mon ...2.83
Hooton-LA 2.97
Niekro-Hou 3.00

</td><td>

Adjusted ERA
Hume-Cin 135
Richard-Hou 130
Schatzeder-Mon ... 129
Hooton-LA 122
Rogers-Mon 122

</td><td>

Opponents' Batting Avg.
Richard-Hou ..... .209
Carlton-Phi ...... .219
Schatzeder-Mon ... .225
Niekro-Hou ..... .228
Andujar-Hou ..... .233

</td><td>

Opponents' On Base Pct.
Forsch-Hou ..... .275
Richard-Hou ...... .278
Seaver-Cin ..... .291
Sutton-LA ...... .291
Carlton-Phi ...... .292

</td><td>

Starter Runs
Richard-Hou 33.2
Niekro-Hou 21.3
Rogers-Mon 20.1
Fulgham-StL 19.5
Hooton-LA 17.9

</td><td>

Adjusted Starter Runs
Richard-Hou 26.0
Niekro-Atl 24.8
Fulgham-StL 20.0
Rogers-Mon 18.2
Bibby-Pit......... 16.3

</td></tr>
<tr><td>

Clutch Pitching Index
Hume-Cin 117
Lamp-Chi 114
Lee-Mon 113
Kobel-NY 112
Blyleven-Pit 112

</td><td>

Relief Runs
Sambito-Hou 19.9
Sosa-Mon 19.1
Hume-Cin 17.6
Minton-SF 17.0
Sutter-Chi 17.0

</td><td>

Adjusted Relief Runs
Sutter-Chi 21.3
Sosa-Mon 18.4
Sambito-Hou 17.6
Hume-Cin 17.6
Tekulve-Pit 16.9

</td><td>

Relief Ranking
Sutter-Chi 40.3
Sambito-Hou 35.6
Sosa-Mon 33.3
Tekulve-Pit 29.1
Littell-StL 25.6

</td><td>

Total Pitcher Index
Sutter-Chi 4.5
Sambito-Hou 4.1
Niekro-Atl 3.4
Sosa-Mon 3.3
Tekulve-Pit 3.2

</td><td>

Total Baseball Ranking
Winfield-SD 5.9
Schmidt-Phi 5.8
Hernandez-StL 5.6
Templeton-StL 4.7
Sutter-Chi 4.5

</td></tr>
</table>

TEAM	G	W	L	PCT	GB	R	OR	AB	H	2B	3B	HR	BB	SO	AVG	OBP	SLG	PRO	PRO+	BR	/A	PF	CHI	RC	SB	CS	SBA	SBR
EAST																												
BAL	159	102	57	.642		757	582	5371	1401	258	24	181	608	847	.261	.339	.419	.758	107	25	54	96	98	758	99	49	67	0
MIL	161	95	66	.590	8	807	722	5536	1552	291	41	185	549	745	.280	.347	.448	.795	113	95	95	100	94	850	100	53	65	-2
BOS	160	91	69	.569	11.5	841	711	5538	1567	310	34	194	512	708	.283	.347	.456	.803	109	108	61	106	97	848	60	43	58	-8
NY	160	89	71	.556	13.5	734	672	5421	1443	226	40	150	509	590	.266	.331	.406	.737	100	-21	-5	98	102	708	65	46	59	-8
DET	161	85	76	.528	18	770	738	5375	1446	221	35	164	575	814	.269	.342	.415	.757	100	24	0	103	100	754	176	86	67	1
CLE	161	81	80	.503	22	760	805	5376	1388	206	29	138	657	786	.258	.344	.384	.728	96	-21	-24	100	103	720	143	90	61	-11
TOR	162	53	109	.327	50.5	613	862	5423	1362	253	34	95	448	663	.251	.313	.363	.676	81	-142	-149	101	104	602	75	56	57	-11
WEST																												
CAL	162	88	74	.543		866	768	5550	1563	242	43	164	589	843	.282	.354	.429	.783	114	83	112	97	101	842	100	53	65	-2
KC	162	85	77	.525	3	851	816	5653	1596	286	79	116	528	675	.282	.347	.422	.769	104	51	35	102	103	836	207	76	73	17
TEX	162	83	79	.512	5	750	698	5562	1549	252	26	140	461	607	.278	.337	.409	.746	101	-1	8	99	99	750	79	51	61	-7
MIN	162	82	80	.506	6	764	725	5544	1544	256	46	112	526	693	.278	.344	.402	.746	96	7	-22	104	99	770	66	45	59	-7
CHI	160	73	87	.456	14	730	748	5463	1505	290	33	127	454	668	.275	.335	.410	.745	100	-4	-4	100	99	726	97	62	61	-8
SEA	162	67	95	.414	21	711	820	5544	1490	250	52	132	515	725	.269	.334	.404	.738	96	-17	-30	102	96	733	126	54	71	7
OAK	162	54	108	.333	34	573	860	5348	1276	188	32	108	482	751	.239	.304	.346	.650	79	-189	-160	95	106	552	104	69	60	-10
TOT	1128					10527		76704	20682	3529	548	2006	7413	10115	.270	.337	.408	.746							1497	831	64	-50

TEAM	CG	SH	SV	IP	H	H/G	HR	BB	SO	RAT	ERA	ERA+	OAV	OOB	PR	/A	PF	CPI	FA	E	DP	FW	PW	BW	SBW	DIF
EAST																										
BAL	52	12	30	1434¹	1279	8.0	133	467	786	11.0	3.26	123	.241	.304	152	119	95	100	.980	125	161	.8	11.6	5.3	.3	4.5
MIL	61	12	23	1439²	1563	9.8	162	381	580	12.3	4.03	103	.279	.327	29	21	99	105	.980	127	153	.7	2.0	9.3	.1	2.3
BOS	47	11	29	1431¹	1487	9.4	133	463	731	12.5	4.03	110	.270	.330	29	61	105	100	.977	142	166	-.2	6.0	6.0	-.4	-.3
NY	43	10	37	1432¹	1446	9.1	123	455	731	12.0	3.83	106	.268	.326	61	38	97	102	.981	122	183	1.0	3.7	-.5	-.4	5.2
DET	25	5	37	1423¹	1429	9.0	167	547	802	12.8	4.27	101	.265	.338	-9	8	103	101	.981	120	184	1.1	.8	.0	.4	2.1
CLE	28	7	32	1431²	1502	9.4	138	570	781	13.2	4.57	93	.272	.343	-56	-50	101	94	.978	134	149	.3	-4.9	-2.3	-.7	8.1
TOR	44	7	11	1417	1537	9.8	165	594	613	13.8	4.82	90	.281	.356	-95	-75	103	100	.975	159	187	-1.0	-7.3	-14.5	-.7	-4.4
WEST																										
CAL	46	9	33	1436	1463	9.2	131	573	820	13.0	4.34	94	.267	.340	-19	-42	97	96	.978	135	172	.3	-4.1	10.9	.1	-.3
KC	42	7	27	1448¹	1477	9.2	165	536	640	12.7	4.45	96	.267	.335	-38	-30	101	95	.977	146	160	-.3	-2.9	3.4	2.0	1.8
TEX	26	10	42	1444¹	1371	8.6	135	532	773	12.1	3.86	107	.253	.323	56	45	98	97	.979	130	151	.6	4.4	.8	-.3	-3.5
MIN	31	6	33	1444¹	1590	9.9	128	452	721	12.8	4.13	106	.285	.340	14	40	104	106	.979	134	203	.4	3.9	-2.1	-.3	4.3
CHI	28	9	37	1409	1365	8.7	114	618	675	12.9	4.10	104	.256	.338	18	23	101	96	.972	173	142	-1.9	2.2	-.4	-.4	-6.5
SEA	37	7	26	1438	1567	9.8	165	571	736	13.6	4.58	95	.281	.351	-57	-34	103	103	.978	141	170	.0	-3.3	-2.9	1.0	-8.8
OAK	41	4	20	1429¹	1606	10.1	147	654	726	14.5	4.75	85	.288	.367	-84	-112	96	105	.972	174	137	-1.9	-10.9	-15.6	-.6	2.0
TOT	551	116	417	20051²		9.3				12.8	4.22		.270	.337					.978	1962	2318					

Runs
Baylor-Cal 120
Brett-KC 119
Rice-Bos 117
Lynn-Bos 116
Lansford-Cal 114

Hits
Brett-KC 212
Rice-Bos 201
Bell-Tex 200
Molitor-Mil 188
Lansford-Cal 188

Doubles
Lemon-Chi 44
Cooper-Mil 44
Lynn-Bos 42
Brett-KC 42
Bell-Tex 42

Triples
Brett-KC 20
Molitor-Mil 16
Wilson-KC 13
Randolph-NY 13

Home Runs
Thomas-Mil 45
Rice-Bos 39
Lynn-Bos 39
Baylor-Cal 36
Singleton-Bal 35

Total Bases
Rice-Bos 369
Brett-KC 363
Lynn-Bos 338
Baylor-Cal 333
Singleton-Bal 304

Runs Batted In
Baylor-Cal 139
Rice-Bos 130
Thomas-Mil 123
Lynn-Bos 122
Porter-KC 112

Runs Produced
Baylor-Cal 223
Rice-Bos 208
Brett-KC 203
Lynn-Bos 199
Porter-KC 193

Bases On Balls
Porter-KC 121
Singleton-Bal 109
Thomas-Mil 98
Randolph-NY 95
Thornton-Cle 90

Batting Average
Lynn-Bos .... .333
Brett-KC .... .329
Downing-Cal ...... .326
Rice-Bos .... .325
Oliver-Tex .... .323

On Base Percentage
Porter-KC .... .429
Lynn-Bos .... .426
Downing-Cal ...... .420
Lezcano-Mil ...... .420
Singleton-Bal ..... .409

Slugging Average
Lynn-Bos .... .637
Rice-Bos .... .596
Lezcano-Mil ...... .573
Brett-KC .... .563
Jackson-NY ...... .544

Production
Lynn-Bos 1.063
Lezcano-Mil ...... .992
Rice-Bos .... .981
Kemp-Det .... .946
Singleton-Bal ..... .942

Adjusted Production
Lynn-Bos 173
Lezcano-Mil 165
Singleton-Bal 158
Rice-Bos 152
Jackson-NY 151

Batter Runs
Lynn-Bos 62.1
Rice-Bos 50.2
Lezcano-Mil 44.6
Singleton-Bal 44.4
Brett-KC 42.8

Adjusted Batter Runs
Lynn-Bos 54.7
Singleton-Bal 49.2
Lezcano-Mil 44.6
Rice-Bos 42.9
Baylor-Cal 40.8

Clutch Hitting Index
Porter-KC 123
Baylor-Cal 121
Sundberg-Tex 120
Cerone-Tor 117
Dauer-Bal 114

Runs Created
Lynn-Bos 147
Rice-Bos 138
Brett-KC 134
Singleton-Bal 127
Baylor-Cal 126

Total Average
Lynn-Bos 1.162
Lezcano-Mil 1.051
Rice-Bos .... .993
Singleton-Bal ..... .993
Porter-KC .... .982

Stolen Bases
Wilson-KC 83
LeFlore-Det 78
Cruz-Sea 49
Bumbry-Bal 37
Wills-Tex 35

Stolen Base Average
Wilson-KC 87.4
Otis-KC 85.7
LeFlore-Det 84.8
Cruz-Sea 84.5
Lowenstein-Bal ... 80.0

Stolen Base Runs
Wilson-KC 17.7
LeFlore-Det 15.0
Cruz-Sea 9.3
Otis-KC 6.0
Manning-Cle 4.2

Fielding Runs
Smalley-Min 33.1
Dent-NY 32.0
Mendoza-Sea 28.0
Burleson-Bos 22.1
Wilfong-Min 20.7

Total Player Rating
Smalley-Min 5.6
Lynn-Bos 5.2
Brett-KC 4.9
Grich-Cal 4.3
Lezcano-Mil 4.0

Wins
Flanagan-Bal 23
John-NY 21
Koosman-Min 20
Guidry-NY 18

Win Percentage
Caldwell-Mil ...... .727
Flanagan-Bal ..... .719
Morris-Det .... .708
John-NY .... .700
Guidry-NY .... .692

Games
Marshall-Min 90
Monge-Cle 76
Kern-Tex 71
Lyle-Tex 67
Heaverlo-Oak 62

Complete Games
D.Martinez-Bal 18
Ryan-Cal 17
John-NY 17
Eckersley-Bos 17

Shutouts
Ryan-Cal 5
Leonard-KC 5
Flanagan-Bal 5
Stanley-Bos 4
Caldwell-Mil 4

Saves
Marshall-Min 32
Kern-Tex 29
Stanhouse-Bal 21
Lopez-Det 21
Monge-Cle 19

Innings Pitched
D.Martinez-Bal ... 292.1
John-NY 276.1
Flanagan-Bal ... 265.2
Koosman-Min ... 263.2
Jenkins-Tex 259.0

Fewest Hits/Game
Ryan-Cal 6.83
Kravec-Chi 7.49
Guidry-NY 7.73
Morris-Det 8.15
Baumgarten-Chi ... 8.26

Fewest BB/Game
McGregor-Bal 1.19
Caldwell-Mil 1.49
Sorensen-Mil 1.61
Stanley-Bos 1.83
John-NY 2.12

Strikeouts
Ryan-Cal 223
Guidry-NY 201
Flanagan-Bal 190
Jenkins-Tex 164
Koosman-Min 157

Strikeouts/Game
Ryan-Cal 9.01
Guidry-NY 7.65
Flanagan-Bal 6.44
Jenkins-Tex 5.70
Bannister-Sea 5.68

Ratio
McGregor-Bal 9.79
Guidry-NY 10.43
Flanagan-Bal ... 10.77
Leonard-KC 10.83
Eckersley-Bos ... 10.91

Earned Run Average
Guidry-NY 2.78
John-NY 2.96
Eckersley-Bos 2.99
Flanagan-Bal 3.08
Morris-Det 3.28

Adjusted ERA
Eckersley-Bos 148
Guidry-NY 146
John-NY 137
Morris-Det 132
Flanagan-Bal 130

Opponents' Batting Avg.
Ryan-Cal .... .212
Kravec-Chi .... .233
Guidry-NY .... .236
Baumgarten-Chi ... .243
Morris-Det .... .244

Opponents' On Base Pct.
McGregor-Bal ..... .275
Guidry-NY .... .294
Flanagan-Bal ..... .297
Eckersley-Bos ..... .298
Leonard-KC .... .299

Starter Runs
John-NY 38.4
Guidry-NY 37.7
Eckersley-Bos 33.5
Flanagan-Bal 33.4
Koosman-Min 24.5

Adjusted Starter Runs
Eckersley-Bos 39.0
John-NY 34.0
Guidry-NY 33.9
Koosman-Min 29.3
Flanagan-Bal 27.4

Clutch Pitching Index
Eckersley-Bos 115
Keough-Oak 114
McCatty-Oak 114
Travers-Mil 113
Koosman-Min 112

Relief Runs
Kern-Tex 42.0
Monge-Cle 26.4
Lopez-Det 25.5
Marshall-Min 24.8
Stoddard-Bal 16.2

Adjusted Relief Runs
Kern-Tex 40.9
Marshall-Min 27.4
Lopez-Det 26.9
Monge-Cle 26.9
Burgmeier-Bos 16.5

Relief Ranking
Kern-Tex 65.0
Marshall-Min 57.1
Monge-Cle 49.5
Lopez-Det 38.8
Drago-Bos 26.6

Total Pitcher Index
Kern-Tex 6.7
Marshall-Min 5.7
Monge-Cle 5.0
Eckersley-Bos 4.0
John-NY 3.8

Total Baseball Ranking
Kern-Tex 6.7
Marshall-Min 5.7
Smalley-Min 5.6
Lynn-Bos 5.2
Monge-Cle 5.0

TEAM	G	W	L	PCT	GB	R	OR	AB	H	2B	3B	HR	BB	SO	AVG	OBP	SLG	PRO	PRO+	BR	/A	PF	CHI	RC	SB	CS	SBA	SBR
EAST																												
PHI	162	91	71	.562		728	639	5625	1517	272	54	117	472	**708**	.270	.330	**.400**	.730	103	61	21	106	100	**736**	140	62	69	5
MON	162	90	72	.556	1	694	629	5465	1407	250	61	114	542	865	.257	.327	.388	.715	105	36	35	100	101	709	237	82	74	22
PIT	162	83	79	.512	8	666	646	5517	1469	249	38	116	452	760	.266	.325	.388	.713	102	27	17	102	98	686	209	102	67	2
STL	162	74	88	.457	17	**738**	710	5608	**1541**	300	49	101	451	781	**.275**	**.331**	**.400**	**.731**	106	**63**	41	103	102	724	117	54	68	3
NY	162	67	95	.414	24	611	702	5478	1407	218	41	61	501	840	.257	.322	.345	.667	95	-52	-35	97	102	601	158	99	61	-12
CHI	162	64	98	.395	27	614	728	5619	1411	251	35	107	471	912	.251	.311	.365	.676	88	-47	-93	107	100	627	93	64	59	-11
WEST																												
HOU	163	93	70	.571		637	**589**	5566	1455	231	**67**	75	540	755	.261	.328	.367	.695	**109**	2	**55**	92	96	688	194	74	72	14
LA	163	92	71	.564	1	663	663	5568	1462	209	24	**148**	492	846	.263	.325	.386	.713	106	29	42	98	96	699	123	72	63	-6
CIN	163	89	73	.549	3.5	707	670	5516	1445	256	45	113	537	852	.262	.330	.386	.716	105	39	39	100	101	716	156	43	**78**	21
ATL	161	81	80	.503	11	630	660	5402	1352	226	22	144	434	899	.250	.308	.380	.688	94	-27	-47	103	**104**	616	73	52	58	-9
SF	161	75	86	.466	17	573	634	5368	1310	199	44	80	509	840	.244	.311	.342	.653	90	-82	-69	98	102	571	100	58	63	-5
SD	163	73	89	.451	19.5	591	654	5540	1410	195	43	67	**563**	791	.255	.326	.342	.668	98	-48	-12	94	96	641	**239**	73	77	**28**
TOT	973					7852		66272	17186	2856	523	1243	5969	9849	.259	.323	.374	.697							1839	835	69	51

TEAM	CG	SH	SV	IP	H	H/G	HR	BB	SO	RAT	ERA	ERA+	OAV	OOB	PR	/A	PF	CPI	FA	E	DP	FW	PW	BW	SBW	DIF
EAST																										
PHI	25	8	40	1480	1419	8.6	87	530	889	12.0	3.43	110	.255	.322	28	**59**	105	100	.979	136	136	.2	**6.2**	2.2	.0	1.2
MON	33	15	36	1456²	1447	8.9	100	460	823	11.9	3.48	102	.261	.320	20	14	99	102	.977	144	126	-.2	1.5	3.7	1.9	2.1
PIT	25	8	**43**	1458¹	1422	8.8	110	**451**	832	11.7	3.58	102	.259	.318	4	10	101	99	.978	137	154	.2	1.1	1.8	-.2	-.8
STL	**34**	9	27	1447	1454	9.0	90	495	664	12.3	3.93	94	.265	.329	-53	-39	103	94	.981	122	**174**	1.0	-4.1	4.3	-.1	-8.1
NY	17	9	33	1451¹	1473	9.1	140	510	886	12.4	3.85	92	.267	.331	-40	-48	99	104	.975	154	132	-.7	-5.1	-3.7	-1.7	-2.8
CHI	13	6	35	1479	1525	9.3	109	589	923	13.0	3.89	101	.272	.344	-47	4	109	**106**	.974	174	149	-1.7	.4	-9.8	-1.6	-4.2
WEST																										
HOU	31	18	41	1482²	1367	**8.3**	**69**	466	**929**	11.3	**3.10**	106	**.246**	**.307**	82	31	91	96	.978	140	145	.0	3.3	**5.8**	1.0	1.3
LA	24	**19**	42	1472²	1358	8.3	105	480	835	11.3	3.25	108	.248	.309	58	41	97	100	.981	123	149	1.0	4.3	4.4	-1.1	1.8
CIN	30	12	37	1459¹	1404	8.7	113	506	833	11.9	3.85	93	.255	.319	-40	-44	99	92	**.983**	**106**	144	**1.9**	-4.6	4.1	1.8	4.9
ATL	29	9	37	1428	1397	8.8	131	454	696	11.8	3.77	99	.258	.318	-27	-4	104	97	.975	162	156	-1.2	-.4	-5.0	-1.4	8.4
SF	27	10	35	1448¹	1446	9.0	92	492	811	12.2	3.46	102	.261	.325	24	13	98	104	.975	159	124	-1.0	1.4	-7.3	-1.0	2.4
SD	19	9	39	1466¹	1474	9.0	97	536	728	12.4	3.65	94	.267	.333	-8	-36	95	105	.980	132	157	.5	-3.8	-1.3	**2.5**	-5.9
TOT	307	132	445	17529²		8.8				12.0	3.60		.259	.323					.978	1689	1746					

Runs		Hits		Doubles		Triples		Home Runs		Total Bases	
Hernandez-StL	111	Garvey-LA	200	Rose-Phi	42	Scott-Mon	13	Schmidt-Phi	48	Schmidt-Phi	342
Schmidt-Phi	104	Richards-SD	193	Dawson-Mon	41	Moreno-Pit	13	Horner-Atl	35	Garvey-LA	307
Murphy-Atl	98	Hernandez-StL	191	Buckner-Chi	41	LeFlore-Mon	11	Murphy-Atl	33	Hernandez-StL	294
Dawson-Mon	96	Buckner-Chi	187	Knight-Cin	39	Herndon-SF	11	Carter-Mon	29	Baker-LA	291
				Hernandez-StL	39			Baker-LA	29	Murphy-Atl	290

Runs Batted In		Runs Produced		Bases On Balls		Batting Average		On Base Percentage		Slugging Average	
Schmidt-Phi	121	Hernandez-StL	194	Morgan-Hou	93	Buckner-Chi	.324	Hernandez-StL	.410	Schmidt-Phi	.624
Hendrick-StL	109	Schmidt-Phi	177	Driessen-Cin	93	Hernandez-StL	.321	Cedeno-Hou	.390	Clark-SF	.517
Garvey-LA	106	Dawson-Mon	166	Tenace-SD	92	Templeton-StL	.319	Clark-SF	.390	Murphy-Atl	.510
Carter-Mon	101	Simmons-StL	161	Schmidt-Phi	89	McBride-Phi	.309	Schmidt-Phi	.388	Simmons-StL	.505
Hernandez-StL	99	Griffey-Cin	161	Hernandez-StL	86	Cedeno-Hou	.309	Driessen-Cin	.382	Baker-LA	.503

Production		Adjusted Production		Batter Runs		Adjusted Batter Runs		Clutch Hitting Index		Runs Created	
Schmidt-Phi	1.012	Schmidt-Phi	169	Schmidt-Phi	56.5	Schmidt-Phi	49.7	Montanez-SD-Mon	.124	Schmidt-Phi	137
Clark-SF	.907	Clark-SF	155	Hernandez-StL	43.3	Hernandez-StL	39.7	Rose-Phi	117	Hernandez-StL	122
Hernandez-StL	.904	Cedeno-Hou	150	Easler-Pit	37.2	Easler-Pit	35.9	Youngblood-NY	117	Dawson-Mon	105
Simmons-StL	.885	Hernandez-StL	147	Clark-SF	31.1	Cedeno-Hou	33.6	Simmons-StL	117	Murphy-Atl	101
Murphy-Atl	.859	Simmons-StL	140	Simmons-StL	29.6	Clark-SF	33.1	Concepcion-Cin	116	Griffey-Cin	99

Total Average		Stolen Bases		Stolen Base Average		Stolen Base Runs		Fielding Runs		Total Player Rating	
Schmidt-Phi	1.095	LeFlore-Mon	97	Griffey-Cin	95.8	LeFlore-Mon	17.7	Smith-SD	40.8	Schmidt-Phi	7.3
Hernandez-StL	.915	Moreno-Pit	96	Mumphrey-SD	91.2	Mumphrey-SD	12.6	Templeton-StL	27.6	Dawson-Mon	4.8
Clark-SF	.906	Collins-Cin	79	LeFlore-Mon	83.6	Scott-Mon	11.1	Moreno-Pit	27.4	Templeton-StL	4.7
Cedeno-Hou	.890	Scott-Mon	63	Maddox-Phi	83.3	Collins-Cin	11.1	Schmidt-Phi	23.2	Smith-SD	4.7
Simmons-StL	.872	Richards-SD	61	Scott-Mon	82.9	Moreno-Pit	9.0	Dawson-Mon	20.1	Cedeno-Hou	4.3

Wins		Win Percentage		Games		Complete Games		Shutouts		Saves	
Carlton-Phi	24	Bibby-Pit	.760	Tidrow-Chi	84	Rogers-Mon	14	Reuss-LA	6	Sutter-Chi	28
Niekro-Hou	20	Reuss-LA	.750	Tekulve-Pit	78	Carlton-Phi	13	Rogers-Mon	4	Hume-Cin	25
Bibby-Pit	19	Carlton-Phi	.727	Hume-Cin	78	Niekro-Atl	11	Richard-Hou	4	Fingers-SD	23
Reuss-LA	18	Ruthven-Phi	.630	Camp-Atl	77	Niekro-Hou	11			Camp-Atl	22
Ruthven-Phi	17	Niekro-Hou	.625	Romo-Pit	74					Allen-NY	22

Innings Pitched		Fewest Hits/Game		Fewest BB/Game		Strikeouts		Strikeouts/Game		Ratio	
Carlton-Phi	304.0	Soto-Cin	5.96	Forsch-StL	1.38	Carlton-Phi	286	Soto-Cin	8.61	Sutton-LA	8.99
Rogers-Mon	281.0	Sutton-LA	6.91	Reuss-LA	1.57	Ryan-Hou	200	Carlton-Phi	8.47	Reuss-LA	9.14
Niekro-Atl	275.0	Carlton-Phi	7.19	Forsch-Hou	1.66	Soto-Cin	182	Ryan-Hou	7.70	Pastore-Cin	9.89
Reuschel-Chi	257.0	Seaver-Cin	7.50	Candelaria-Pit	1.93	Niekro-Atl	176	Blyleven-Pit	6.98	Carlton-Phi	9.92
Niekro-Hou	256.0	Reuss-LA	7.57	Sutton-LA	1.99	Blyleven-Pit	168	Welch-LA	5.94	Soto-Cin	10.02

Earned Run Average		Adjusted ERA		Opponents' Batting Avg.		Opponents' On Base Pct.		Starter Runs		Adjusted Starter Runs	
Sutton-LA	2.20	Carlton-Phi	162	Soto-Cin	.187	Sutton-LA	.258	Carlton-Phi	42.6	Carlton-Phi	49.0
Carlton-Phi	2.34	Sutton-LA	159	Sutton-LA	.211	Reuss-LA	.261	Sutton-LA	33.0	Sutton-LA	30.5
Reuss-LA	2.51	Reuss-LA	139	Carlton-Phi	.218	Pastore-Cin	.277	Reuss-LA	27.8	Reuss-LA	25.1
Blue-SF	2.97	Rogers-Mon	120	Seaver-Cin	.225	Carlton-Phi	.278	Ruhle-Hou	21.8	Rogers-Mon	18.3
Rogers-Mon	2.98	Blue-SF	119	Reuss-LA	.227	Soto-Cin	.279	Richard-Hou	21.5	Richard-Hou	17.5

Clutch Pitching Index		Relief Runs		Adjusted Relief Runs		Relief Ranking		Total Pitcher Index		Total Baseball Ranking	
Reuschel-Chi	119	McGraw-Phi	21.9	Caudill-Chi	24.5	McGraw-Phi	32.6	Carlton-Phi	5.3	Schmidt-Phi	7.3
Bomback-NY	116	Camp-Atl	20.3	McGraw-Phi	23.9	Camp-Atl	28.4	McGraw-Phi	3.6	Carlton-Phi	5.3
Zachry-NY	114	Caudill-Chi	20.1	Camp-Atl	22.0	Hume-Cin	25.6	Camp-Atl	3.4	Dawson-Mon	4.8
Ruthven-Phi	112	Smith-Hou	19.1	Holland-SF	16.4	Sutter-Chi	25.5	Hume-Cin	3.1	Templeton-StL	4.7
Sanderson-Mon	111	Holland-SF	16.9	Smith-Hou	15.5	Fryman-Mon	20.1	Sutter-Chi	2.7	Smith-SD	4.7

TEAM	G	W	L	PCT	GB	R	OR	AB	H	2B	3B	HR	BB	SO	AVG	OBP	SLG	PRO	PRO+	BR	/A	PF	CHI	RC	SB	CS	SBA	SBR
EAST																												
NY	162	103	59	.636		820	662	5553	1484	239	34	189	643	739	.267	.346	.425	.771	112	79	93	98	100	820	86	36	70	4
BAL	162	100	62	.617	3	805	640	5585	1523	258	29	156	587	766	.273	.344	.413	.757	107	52	60	99	102	788	111	38	74	11
MIL	162	86	76	.531	17	811	682	5653	1555	298	36	203	455	745	.275	.332	.448	.780	116	78	104	97	100	834	131	56	70	6
BOS	160	83	77	.519	19	757	767	5603	1588	297	36	162	475	720	.283	.343	.436	.779	107	86	45	105	93	810	79	48	62	-5
DET	163	84	78	.519	19	830	757	5648	1543	232	53	143	645	844	.273	.351	.409	.760	106	66	47	102	101	804	75	68	52	-18
CLE	160	79	81	.494	23	738	667	5470	1517	221	40	89	617	625	.277	.335	.381	.736	102	26	23	100	97	739	118	58	67	1
TOR	162	67	95	.414	36	624	762	5571	1398	249	53	126	448	813	.251	.310	.383	.693	85	-92	-121	105	99	640	67	72	48	-23
WEST																												
KC	162	97	65	.599		809	694	5714	1633	266	59	115	508	709	.286	.348	.413	.761	107	62	56	101	100	826	185	43	81	30
OAK	162	83	79	.512	14	686	642	5495	1424	212	35	137	506	824	.259	.324	.385	.709	100	-51	-4	93	102	680	175	82	68	3
MIN	161	77	84	.478	19.5	670	724	5530	1468	252	46	99	436	703	.265	.322	.381	.703	86	-65	-113	107	103	655	62	46	57	-9
TEX	163	76	85	.472	20.5	756	752	5690	1616	263	27	124	480	589	.284	.342	.405	.747	107	30	53	97	98	768	91	49	65	-2
CHI	162	70	90	.438	26	587	722	5444	1408	255	38	91	399	670	.259	.314	.370	.684	87	-104	-101	100	98	608	68	54	56	-12
CAL	160	65	95	.406	31	698	797	5443	1442	236	32	106	539	889	.265	.335	.378	.713	97	-33	-16	98	102	681	91	63	59	-11
SEA	163	59	103	.364	38	610	793	5489	1359	211	35	104	483	727	.248	.311	.356	.667	81	-136	-141	101	105	598	116	62	65	-2
TOT	1132					10201		77888	20958	3489	553	1844	7221	10363	.269	.334	.399	.733							1455	775	65	-29

TEAM	CG	SH	SV	IP	H	H/G	HR	BB	SO	RAT	ERA	ERA+	OAV	OOB	PR	/A	PF	CPI	FA	E	DP	FW	PW	BW	SBW	DIF
EAST																										
NY	29	15	50	1464¹	1433	8.8	102	463	845	11.8	3.58	109	.259	.319	73	55	97	98	.978	138	160	.0	5.5	9.3	.6	6.6
BAL	42	10	41	1460	1438	8.9	134	507	789	12.1	3.64	109	.265	.325	63	50	98	104	.985	95	178	2.4	5.0	6.0	1.3	4.3
MIL	48	14	30	1450	1530	9.5	137	420	575	12.3	3.71	104	.273	.326	53	26	96	107	.977	147	189	-.5	2.6	10.4	.8	-8.3
BOS	30	8	43	1441¹	1557	9.7	129	481	696	12.9	4.38	96	.279	.340	-55	-26	105	97	.977	149	206	-.7	-2.6	4.5	-.3	2.1
DET	40	9	30	1467¹	1505	9.2	152	558	741	12.8	4.25	97	.267	.336	-35	-23	102	98	.979	133	165	.3	-2.3	4.7	-1.6	1.9
CLE	35	8	32	1428	1519	9.6	137	552	843	13.3	4.68	87	.275	.344	-103	-107	101	92	.983	105	143	1.8	-9.7	2.3	.3	4.3
TOR	39	9	23	1466	1523	9.3	135	635	705	13.4	4.19	103	.274	.351	-26	17	107	105	.979	133	206	.3	1.7	-12.1	-2.1	-1.8
WEST																										
KC	37	10	42	1459¹	1496	9.2	129	465	614	12.2	3.83	106	.267	.325	33	36	100	100	.978	141	150	-.2	3.6	5.6	3.2	3.8
OAK	94	9	13	1471²	1347	8.2	142	521	769	11.6	3.46	109	.244	.312	94	50	93	99	.979	130	115	.5	5.0	-.4	.5	-3.5
MIN	35	9	30	1451	1502	9.3	120	468	744	12.4	3.93	111	.272	.331	16	68	108	100	.977	148	192	-.6	6.8	-11.3	-.7	2.3
TEX	35	6	25	1451²	1561	9.7	119	519	890	13.1	4.02	97	.277	.342	2	-21	97	104	.977	147	169	-.5	-2.1	5.3	.0	-7.2
CHI	32	12	42	1435¹	1434	9.0	108	563	724	12.8	3.92	103	.263	.337	18	17	100	99	.973	171	162	-1.9	1.7	-10.1	-1.0	1.2
CAL	22	6	30	1428¹	1548	9.8	141	529	725	13.3	4.52	87	.278	.345	-77	-94	97	97	.978	134	144	.1	-9.4	-1.6	-.9	-3.3
SEA	31	7	26	1457¹	1565	9.7	159	540	703	13.2	4.38	94	.278	.344	-56	-40	102	101	.977	149	189	-.6	-4.0	-14.1	.0	-3.4
TOT	549	132	457	20331²		9.3				12.7	4.03		.269	.334					.978	1920	2368					

Runs
Wilson-KC 133
Yount-Mil 121
Bumbry-Bal 118
Henderson-Oak 111
Trammell-Det 107

Hits
Wilson-KC 230
Cooper-Mil 219
Rivers-Tex 210
Oliver-Tex 209
Bumbry-Bal 205

Doubles
Yount-Mil 49
Oliver-Tex 43
Morrison-Chi 40
McRae-KC 39
Evans-Bos 37

Triples
Wilson-KC 15
Griffin-Tor 15
Washington-KC 11
Landreaux-Min 11
Yount-Mil 10

Home Runs
Oglivie-Mil 41
Jackson-NY 41
Thomas-Mil 38
Armas-Oak 35
Murray-Bal 32

Total Bases
Cooper-Mil 335
Oglivie-Mil 333
Murray-Bal 322
Yount-Mil 317
Oliver-Tex 315

Runs Batted In
Cooper-Mil 122
Oglivie-Mil 118
G.Brett-KC 118
Oliver-Tex 117
Murray-Bal 116

Runs Produced
Oliver-Tex 194
Cooper-Mil 193
Yount-Mil 185
Murray-Bal 184
G.Brett-KC 181

Bases On Balls
Randolph-NY 119
Henderson-Oak ... 117
Hargrove-Cle 111
Murphy-Oak 102
Harrah-Cle 98

Batting Average
G.Brett-KC .... .390
Cooper-Mil .... .352
Dilone-Cle .... .341
Rivers-Tex .... .333
Carew-Cal .... .331

On Base Percentage
G.Brett-KC .... .461
Randolph-NY ..... .429
Henderson-Oak ... .422
Hargrove-Cle ..... .421
Thompson-Det-Cal ... .402

Slugging Average
G.Brett-KC .... .664
Jackson-NY .... .597
Oglivie-Mil .... .563
Cooper-Mil .... .539
Yount-Mil .... .519

Production
G.Brett-KC 1.124
Jackson-NY .... .996
Cooper-Mil .... .931
Oglivie-Mil .... .930
Singleton-Bal ..... .885

Adjusted Production
G.Brett-KC 202
Jackson-NY 172
Cooper-Mil 157
Oglivie-Mil 156
Singleton-Bal 143

Batter Runs
G.Brett-KC 64.8
Jackson-NY 49.1
Cooper-Mil 42.9
Oglivie-Mil 39.2
Singleton-Bal 35.4

Adjusted Batter Runs
G.Brett-KC 63.8
Jackson-NY 51.1
Cooper-Mil 46.9
Oglivie-Mil 43.0
Henderson-Oak ... 36.6

Clutch Hitting Index
Manning-Cle 125
Thompson-Det-Cal ... 125
Hargrove-Cle 122
Whitaker-Det 122
Aikens-KC 122

Runs Created
G.Brett-KC 135
Cooper-Mil 126
Jackson-NY 125
Oglivie-Mil 121
Henderson-Oak ... 120

Total Average
G.Brett-KC 1.258
Jackson-NY 1.060
Henderson-Oak ... .973
Randolph-NY ..... .952
Oglivie-Mil .... .925

Stolen Bases
Henderson-Oak ... 100
Wilson-KC 79
Dilone-Cle 61
Cruz-Sea 45
Bumbry-Bal 44

Stolen Base Average
Otis-KC 94.1
Harrah-Cle 89.5
Kelly-Bal 88.9
Wilson-KC 88.8
Cruz-Sea 86.5

Stolen Base Runs
Wilson-KC 17.7
Henderson-Oak ... 14.4
Cruz-Sea 9.3
Dilone-Cle 7.5
Bumbry-Bal 6.6

Fielding Runs
Castino-Min 27.8
Burleson-Bos 25.5
DeCinces-Bal 24.5
Murphy-Oak 23.9
Henderson-Oak ... 23.3

Total Player Rating
Henderson-Oak 6.6
G.Brett-KC 6.4
Oglivie-Mil 5.4
Bell-Tex 4.7
Cooper-Mil 4.3

Wins
Stone-Bal 25
Norris-Oak 22
John-NY 22
McGregor-Bal 20
Leonard-KC 20

Win Percentage
Stone-Bal .... .781
May-NY .... .750
McGregor-Bal ..... .714
Norris-Oak .... .710
John-NY .... .710

Games
Quisenberry-KC 75
Corbett-Min 73
Monge-Cle 67
Lopez-Det 67

Complete Games
Langford-Oak 28
Norris-Oak 24
Keough-Oak 20
John-NY 16
Gura-KC 16

Shutouts
John-NY 6
Zahn-Min 5
Stieb-Tor 4
McGregor-Bal 4
Gura-KC 4

Saves
Quisenberry-KC 33
Gossage-NY 33
Farmer-Chi 30
Stoddard-Bal 26
Burgmeier-Bos 24

Innings Pitched
Langford-Oak 290.0
Norris-Oak 284.1
Gura-KC 283.1
Leonard-KC 280.1
John-NY 265.1

Fewest Hits/Game
Norris-Oak 6.81
May-NY 7.39
Clancy-Tor 7.79
Underwood-NY ... 7.84
Keough-Oak 7.85

Fewest BB/Game
Matlack-Tex 1.84
Splittorff-KC 1.90
John-NY 1.90
Tanana-Cal 1.99
Langford-Oak 1.99

Strikeouts
Barker-Cle 187
Norris-Oak 180
Guidry-NY 166
Leonard-KC 155
Bannister-Sea 155

Strikeouts/Game
Barker-Cle 6.83
May-NY 6.83
Guidry-NY 6.80
Bannister-Sea 6.41
Perry-Tex-NY 5.91

Ratio
May-NY 9.39
Norris-Oak 9.62
Langford-Oak 10.58
Burns-Chi 10.59
Eckersley-Bos ... 10.65

Earned Run Average
May-NY 2.46
Norris-Oak 2.53
Burns-Chi 2.84
Keough-Oak 2.92
Gura-KC 2.95

Adjusted ERA
May-NY 159
Norris-Oak 149
Burns-Chi 142
Gura-KC 137
Erickson-Min 134

Opponents' Batting Avg.
Norris-Oak .... .209
May-NY .... .224
Clancy-Tor .... .233
Keough-Oak .... .236
Underwood-NY ... .237

Opponents' On Base Pct.
May-NY .... .268
Norris-Oak .... .272
Eckersley-Bos .... .291
Burns-Chi .... .295
Bannister-Sea ..... .296

Starter Runs
Norris-Oak 47.4
Gura-KC 34.0
Burns-Chi 31.7
Keough-Oak 31.0
May-NY 30.6

Adjusted Starter Runs
Norris-Oak 39.0
Gura-KC 34.5
Burns-Chi 31.5
May-NY 28.4
Clancy-Tor 27.8

Clutch Pitching Index
Sorensen-Mil 126
Stanley-Bos 117
Keough-Oak 113
Trout-Chi 113
Perry-Tex-NY 112

Relief Runs
Corbett-Min 31.1
Burgmeier-Bos 22.4
Gossage-NY 19.4
Darwin-Tex 17.1
Garvin-Tor 16.0

Adjusted Relief Runs
Corbett-Min 36.0
Burgmeier-Bos 24.4
Garvin-Tor 18.5
Gossage-NY 18.1
Proly-Chi 15.6

Relief Ranking
Corbett-Min 46.9
Burgmeier-Bos 33.2
Gossage-NY 26.8
Quisenberry-KC ... 26.3
Garvin-Tor 26.2

Total Pitcher Index
Norris-Oak 4.7
Corbett-Min 4.6
Burgmeier-Bos 3.8
Burns-Chi 3.5
Gura-KC 3.3

Total Baseball Ranking
Henderson-Oak 6.6
G.Brett-KC 6.4
Oglivie-Mil 5.4
Norris-Oak 4.7
Bell-Tex 4.7

TEAM	G	W	L	PCT	GB	R	OR	AB	H	2B	3B	HR	BB	SO	AVG	OBP	SLG	PRO	PRO+	BR	/A	PF	CHI	RC	SB	CS	SBA	SBR
EAST																												
Split Season: First-half Winner PHI (34-21); Second-half Winner MON (30-23)																												
STL	103	59	43	.578		464	417	3537	936	158	45	50	379	495	.265	.339	.377	.716	106	43	31	103	102	454	88	45	66	-1
MON	108	60	48	.556	2	443	394	3591	883	146	28	81	368	498	.246	.319	.370	.689	100	3	-2	101	105	435	138	40	78	17
PHI	107	59	48	.551	2.5	491	472	3665	1002	165	25	69	372	432	.273	.344	.389	.733	109	66	45	104	100	495	103	46	69	3
PIT	103	46	56	.451	13	407	425	3576	920	176	30	55	278	494	.257	.314	.369	.683	96	-9	-21	103	102	417	122	52	70	5
NY	105	41	62	.398	18.5	348	432	3493	868	136	35	57	304	603	.248	.311	.356	.667	96	-26	-20	98	93	387	103	42	71	6
CHI	106	38	65	.369	21.5	370	483	3546	838	138	29	57	342	611	.236	.306	.340	.646	84	-52	-68	104	104	368	72	41	64	-3
WEST																												
Split Season: First-half Winner LA (36-21); Second-half Winner HOU (33-20)																												
CIN	108	66	42	.611		464	440	3637	972	190	24	64	375	553	.267	.339	.385	.724	109	53	45	102	97	469	58	37	61	-5
LA	110	63	47	.573	4	450	356	3751	984	133	20	82	331	550	.262	.325	.374	.699	108	16	32	96	101	450	73	46	61	-6
HOU	110	61	49	.555	6	394	331	3693	948	160	35	45	340	488	.257	.321	.356	.677	103	-12	9	95	95	425	81	43	65	-2
SF	111	56	55	.505	11.5	427	414	3766	941	161	26	63	386	543	.250	.322	.357	.679	100	-8	0	98	99	431	89	50	64	-3
ATL	107	50	56	.472	15	395	416	3642	886	148	22	64	321	540	.243	.308	.349	.657	90	-41	-51	103	105	391	98	39	72	6
SD	110	41	69	.373	26	382	455	3757	963	170	35	32	311	525	.256	.316	.346	.662	100	-33	-4	93	96	400	83	62	57	-12
TOT	644					5035		43654	11141	1881	354	719	4107	6332	.255	.322	.364	.686							1108	543	67	7

TEAM	CG	SH	SV	IP	H	H/G	HR	BB	SO	RAT	ERA	ERA+	OAV	OOB	PR	/A	PF	CPI	FA	E	DP	FW	PW	BW	SBW	DIF
EAST																										
STL	11	5	33	943	902	8.6	52	290	388	11.5	3.63	98	.255	.314	-14	-7	102	91	.981	82	108	.6	-.8	3.3	-.2	5.0
MON	20	12	23	975	902	8.3	58	268	520	11.0	3.30	108	.247	.302	21	21	100	92	.980	81	88	.9	2.3	-.2	1.8	1.3
PHI	19	5	23	960¹	967	9.1	72	347	580	12.4	4.05	90	.267	.333	-60	-45	104	97	.980	86	90	.6	-4.8	4.8	.3	4.6
PIT	11	5	29	942	953	9.1	60	346	492	12.6	3.56	101	.266	.333	-8	3	103	107	.979	86	106	.4	.3	-2.3	.5	-4.0
NY	7	3	24	926¹	906	8.8	74	336	490	12.2	3.55	98	.259	.326	-6	-7	100	105	.968	130	89	-1.6	-.8	-2.1	.6	-6.5
CHI	6	2	20	956²	983	9.2	59	388	532	13.1	4.01	92	.270	.344	-55	-33	106	101	.974	113	103	-.8	-3.5	-7.3	-.4	-1.5
WEST																										
CIN	25	14	20	965²	863	8.0	67	393	593	11.8	3.73	95	.241	.318	-26	-19	102	90	.981	80	99	1.0	-2.0	4.8	-.6	8.8
LA	26	19	24	997	904	8.2	54	302	603	11.0	3.01	110	.245	.304	54	35	95	100	.980	87	101	.7	3.8	3.4	-.7	.8
HOU	23	19	25	990	842	7.7	40	300	610	10.5	2.66	124	.231	.291	91	69	94	96	.980	87	81	.7	7.4	1.0	-.3	-2.8
SF	8	9	33	1009¹	970	8.6	57	393	561	12.4	3.28	105	.256	.330	23	17	98	109	.977	102	102	.0	1.8	.0	-.4	-1.0
ATL	11	4	24	968	936	8.7	62	330	471	11.9	3.45	104	.257	.321	4	14	103	102	.976	102	93	-.2	1.5	-5.5	.6	.6
SD	9	6	23	1002	1013	9.1	64	414	492	10.5	3.72	98	.268	.343	-25	-51	93	108	.977	102	117	-.0	-5.5	-.4	-1.3	-6.7
TOT	176	103	301	11635¹		8.6				11.9	3.49		.255	.322					.978	1138	1177					

Runs		Hits		Doubles		Triples		Home Runs		Total Bases	
Schmidt-Phi	78	Rose-Phi	140	Buckner-Chi	35	Richards-SD	12	Schmidt-Phi	31	Schmidt-Phi	228
Rose-Phi	73	Buckner-Chi	131	Jones-SD	34	Reynolds-Hou	12	Dawson-Mon	24	Dawson-Mon	218
Dawson-Mon	71	Concepcion-Cin	129	Concepcion-Cin	28	Herr-StL	9	Kingman-NY	22	Foster-Cin	215
Hendrick-StL	67	Baker-LA	128	Hernandez-StL	27			Foster-Cin	22	Buckner-Chi	202
		Griffey-Cin	123	Chambliss-Atl	25			Hendrick-StL	18	Hendrick-StL	191

Runs Batted In		Runs Produced		Bases On Balls		Batting Average		On Base Percentage		Slugging Average	
Schmidt-Phi	91	Schmidt-Phi	138	Schmidt-Phi	73	Madlock-Pit	.341	Schmidt-Phi	.439	Schmidt-Phi	.644
Foster-Cin	90	Foster-Cin	132	Morgan-SF	66	Rose-Phi	.325	Madlock-Pit	.418	Dawson-Mon	.553
Buckner-Chi	75	Matthews-Phi	120	Hernandez-StL	61	Baker-LA	.320	Hernandez-StL	.405	Foster-Cin	.519
Carter-Mon	68	Concepcion-Cin	119	Thompson-Pit	59	Schmidt-Phi	.316	Matthews-Phi	.404	Madlock-Pit	.495
		Garvey-LA	117	Matthews-Phi	59	Buckner-Chi	.311	Raines-Mon	.394	Hendrick-StL	.485

Production		Adjusted Production		Batter Runs		Adjusted Batter Runs		Clutch Hitting Index		Runs Created	
Schmidt-Phi	1.083	Schmidt-Phi	195	Schmidt-Phi	50.1	Schmidt-Phi	46.0	Concepcion-Cin	141	Schmidt-Phi	102
Dawson-Mon	.923	Dawson-Mon	157	Dawson-Mon	28.8	Dawson-Mon	28.0	Herr-StL	127	Dawson-Mon	83
Madlock-Pit	.912	Madlock-Pit	153	Foster-Cin	27.7	Foster-Cin	26.5	Matthews-Phi	126	Foster-Cin	81
Foster-Cin	.895	Foster-Cin	150	Hernandez-StL	24.6	Hernandez-StL	22.8	Foster-Cin	126	Hernandez-StL	73
Hernandez-StL	.868	Cey-LA	145	Matthews-Phi	22.0	Madlock-Pit	20.4	Maddox-Phi	122	Matthews-Phi	71

Total Average		Stolen Bases		Stolen Base Average		Stolen Base Runs		Fielding Runs		Total Player Rating	
Schmidt-Phi	1.227	Raines-Mon	71	Lopes-LA	90.9	Raines-Mon	14.7	Smith-SD	25.9	Schmidt-Phi	7.0
Raines-Mon	1.034	Moreno-Pit	39	Lacy-Pit	88.9	Lacy-Pit	5.4	Schmidt-Phi	22.5	Dawson-Mon	5.0
Dawson-Mon	.989	Scott-Mon	30	Dawson-Mon	86.7	Dawson-Mon	5.4	Dawson-Mon	17.8	Foster-Cin	3.4
Madlock-Pit	.959			Raines-Mon	86.6	Scott-Mon	4.8	Flynn-NY	12.2	Raines-Mon	3.1
Matthews-Phi	.908			Puhl-Hou	84.6	Lopes-LA	4.8	Clark-SF	11.9	Hernandez-StL	2.5

Wins		Win Percentage		Games		Complete Games		Shutouts		Saves	
Seaver-Cin	14	Seaver-Cin	.875	Lucas-SD	57	Valenzuela-LA	11	Valenzuela-LA	8	Sutter-StL	25
Valenzuela-LA	13	Carlton-Phi	.765	Minton-SF	55	Soto-Cin	10	Knepper-Hou	5	Minton-SF	21
Carlton-Phi	13	Ryan-Hou	.688	Tidrow-Chi	51	Carlton-Phi	10	Hooton-LA	4	Allen-NY	18
		Valenzuela-LA	.650	Hume-Cin	51	Reuss-LA	8			Camp-Atl	17
		Hooton-LA	.647	Sambito-Hou	49	Rogers-Mon	7				

Innings Pitched		Fewest Hits/Game		Fewest BB/Game		Strikeouts		Strikeouts/Game		Ratio	
Valenzuela-LA	192.1	Ryan-Hou	5.98	Perry-Atl	1.43	Valenzuela-LA	180	Carlton-Phi	8.48	Sutton-Hou	9.19
Carlton-Phi	190.0	Seaver-Cin	6.49	Reuss-LA	1.59	Carlton-Phi	179	Ryan-Hou	8.46	Valenzuela-LA	9.45
Soto-Cin	175.0	Valenzuela-LA	6.55	Sutton-Hou	1.64	Soto-Cin	151	Valenzuela-LA	8.42	Knepper-Hou	9.77
Seaver-Cin	166.1	Berenyi-Cin	6.93	Sorensen-StL	1.67	Ryan-Hou	140	Soto-Cin	7.77	Reuss-LA	9.96
Niekro-Hou	166.0	Blue-SF	7.00	Solomon-Pit	1.91	Gullickson-Mon	115	Berenyi-Cin	7.57	Hooton-LA	10.05

Earned Run Average		Adjusted ERA		Opponents' Batting Avg.		Opponents' On Base Pct.		Starter Runs		Adjusted Starter Runs	
Ryan-Hou	1.69	Ryan-Hou	195	Ryan-Hou	.188	Sutton-Hou	.268	Ryan-Hou	29.8	Ryan-Hou	26.5
Knepper-Hou	2.18	Knepper-Hou	151	Valenzuela-LA	.205	Valenzuela-LA	.271	Knepper-Hou	22.8	Carlton-Phi	25.6
Hooton-LA	2.28	Carlton-Phi	150	Seaver-Cin	.205	Knepper-Hou	.280	Carlton-Phi	22.7	Knepper-Hou	19.4
Reuss-LA	2.30	Hooton-LA	146	Berenyi-Cin	.211	Sanderson-Mon	.281	Valenzuela-LA	21.6	Seaver-Cin	18.7
Carlton-Phi	2.42	Reuss-LA	144	Blue-SF	.217	Ryan-Hou	.281	Reuss-LA	20.2	Valenzuela-LA	17.9

Clutch Pitching Index		Relief Runs		Adjusted Relief Runs		Relief Ranking		Total Pitcher Index		Total Baseball Ranking	
Mahler-Atl	124	Lucas-SD	14.9	Camp-Atl	15.2	Camp-Atl	29.3	Ryan-Hou	3.3	Schmidt-Phi	7.0
Solomon-Pit	124	Camp-Atl	14.5	Lucas-SD	12.6	Lucas-SD	21.7	Camp-Atl	3.1	Dawson-Mon	5.0
Alexander-SF	122	Holland-SF	12.0	Holland-SF	11.4	Sambito-Hou	18.2	Valenzuela-LA	2.5	Foster-Cin	3.4
Blue-SF	112	Sambito-Hou	11.7	Sambito-Hou	10.3	Fryman-Mon	15.7	Lucas-SD	2.3	Ryan-Hou	3.3
Zachry-NY	111	Reardon-NY-Mon	10.3	Reardon-NY-Mon	10.3	Holland-SF	14.0	Carlton-Phi	2.2	Camp-Atl	3.1

TEAM	G	W	L	PCT	GB	R	OR	AB	H	2B	3B	HR	BB	SO	AVG	OBP	SLG	PRO	PRO+	BR	/A	PF	CHI	RC	SB	CS	SBA	SBR
EAST																												
Split Season: First-half Winner NY (34-22); Second-half Winner MIL (31-22)																												
MIL	109	62	47	.569		493	459	3743	961	173	20	96	300	461	.257	.317	.391	.708	109	9	33	95	108	451	39	36	52	-10
BAL	105	59	46	.562	1	429	437	3516	883	165	11	88	404	454	.251	.331	.379	.710	104	22	23	100	95	431	41	34	55	-8
NY	107	59	48	.551	2	421	343	3529	889	148	22	100	391	434	.252	.328	.391	.719	108	29	35	99	92	445	47	30	61	-4
DET	109	60	49	.550	2	427	404	3600	922	148	29	65	404	500	.256	.334	.368	.702	98	14	-2	104	94	442	61	37	62	-9
BOS	108	59	49	.546	2.5	519	481	3820	1052	168	17	90	378	520	.275	.343	.399	.742	107	65	33	106	99	514	32	31	51	-9
CLE	103	52	51	.505	7	431	442	3507	922	150	21	39	343	379	.263	.331	.351	.682	98	-11	-5	99	104	414	119	37	76	14
TOR	106	37	69	.349	23.5	329	466	3521	797	137	23	61	284	556	.226	.288	.330	.618	73	-103	-124	106	105	326	66	57	54	-14
WEST																												
Split Season: First-half Winner OAK (37-23); Second-half Winner KC (30-23)																												
OAK	109	64	45	.587		458	403	3677	910	119	26	104	342	647	.247	.314	.379	.693	104	-8	13	95	106	438	98	47	68	1
TEX	105	57	48	.543	5	452	389	3581	968	178	15	49	295	396	.270	.329	.369	.698	107	5	28	95	105	425	46	41	53	-11
CHI	106	54	52	.509	8.5	476	423	3615	982	135	27	76	322	518	.272	.338	.387	.725	110	41	51	98	100	471	86	44	66	-1
KC	103	50	53	.485	11	397	405	3560	952	169	29	61	301	419	.267	.327	.383	.710	105	17	21	99	90	437	100	53	65	-2
CAL	110	51	59	.464	13.5	476	453	3688	944	134	16	97	393	571	.256	.332	.380	.712	105	26	26	100	100	463	44	33	57	-7
SEA	110	44	65	.404	20	426	521	3780	950	148	13	89	329	553	.251	.316	.368	.684	93	-19	-36	104	98	441	100	50	67	0
MIN	110	41	68	.376	23	378	486	3676	884	147	36	47	275	497	.240	.295	.338	.633	77	-87	-111	107	109	355	34	27	56	-6
TOT	750					6112		50813	13016	2119	305	1062	4761	6905	.256	.323	.373	.696							913	557	62	-60

TEAM	CG	SH	SV	IP	H	H/G	HR	BB	SO	RAT	ERA	ERA+	OAV	OOB	PR	/A	PF	CPI	FA	E	DP	FW	PW	BW	SBW	DIF
EAST																										
MIL	11	4	35	986	994	9.1	72	352	448	12.4	3.91	88	.266	.331	-27	-53	94	99	.982	79	135	.5	-5.6	3.5	-.6	9.7
BAL	25	10	23	940	923	8.8	83	347	489	12.3	3.70	98	.260	.328	-4	-7	99	104	.983	68	114	1.0	-.7	2.4	-.4	4.2
NY	16	13	30	948	827	7.9	64	287	606	10.7	2.90	123	.235	.295	80	71	98	99	.982	72	100	.8	7.5	3.7	-.6	-6.5
DET	33	13	22	969¹	840	7.8	83	373	476	11.5	3.53	107	.236	.313	14	26	103	94	.984	67	109	1.2	2.7	-.2	.0	1.7
BOS	19	4	24	987¹	983	9.0	90	354	536	12.4	3.81	102	.262	.330	-17	7	106	103	.979	91	108	-.2	.7	3.5	-.5	1.5
CLE	33	10	13	931	989	9.6	67	311	569	12.7	3.88	94	.274	.333	-23	-26	99	102	.978	87	91	-.2	-2.7	-.5	1.9	2.0
TOR	20	4	18	953¹	908	8.6	72	377	451	12.5	3.81	103	.252	.329	-17	13	108	97	.975	105	102	-1.1	1.4	-13.0	-1.0	-2.2
WEST																										
OAK	60	11	10	993	883	8.0	80	370	505	11.6	3.30	105	.240	.314	40	20	95	101	.980	81	74	.4	2.1	1.4	.6	5.1
TEX	23	13	18	940¹	851	8.1	67	322	488	11.4	3.40	102	.243	.310	27	7	95	95	.984	69	102	.9	.7	2.9	-.7	.6
CHI	20	8	23	940²	891	8.5	73	336	529	12.0	3.47	103	.252	.321	19	11	98	102	.979	83	113	-.0	1.2	5.4	.3	-5.8
KC	24	8	24	922¹	909	8.9	75	273	404	11.7	3.46	100	.260	.317	10	5	99	101	.982	72	94	.7	.5	2.2	.2	-5.1
CAL	27	8	19	971¹	958	8.9	81	323	426	12.1	3.70	99	.261	.324	-4	-5	100	102	.977	101	120	-.7	-.5	2.7	-.3	-5.2
SEA	10	5	23	997¹	1039	9.4	76	360	478	12.8	4.23	91	.271	.336	-64	-42	105	95	.979	91	122	-.1	-4.4	-3.8	.5	-2.6
MIN	13	6	22	979²	1021	9.4	79	376	500	13.0	3.98	99	.272	.341	-35	-3	108	104	.978	96	103	-.4	-.3	-11.6	-.2	-1.0
TOT	334	117	304	13459²		8.7				12.1	3.66		.256	.323					.980	1166	1487					

Runs
Henderson-Oak 89
Evans-Bos 84
Cooper-Mil 70
Harrah-Cle 64
Rivers-Tex 62

Hits
Henderson-Oak 135
Lansford-Bos 134
Wilson-KC 133
Cooper-Mil 133
Paciorek-Sea 132

Doubles
Cooper-Mil 35
Oliver-Tex 29
Paciorek-Sea 28
Dauer-Bal 27
G.Brett-KC 27

Triples
Castino-Min 9
Wilson-KC 7
Henderson-Oak 7
G.Brett-KC 7
Baines-Chi 7

Home Runs
Murray-Bal 22
Grich-Cal 22
Evans-Bos 22
Armas-Oak 22

Total Bases
Evans-Bos 215
Armas-Oak 211
Paciorek-Sea 206
Cooper-Mil 206
Murray-Bal 202

Runs Batted In
Murray-Bal 78
Armas-Oak 76
Oglivie-Mil....... 72
Evans-Bos 71
Winfield-NY 68

Runs Produced
Evans-Bos 133
Henderson-Oak 118
Cooper-Mil 118
Murray-Bal 113
Oglivie-Mil 111

Bases On Balls
Evans-Bos 85
Murphy-Oak 73
Kemp-Det 70
Henderson-Oak 64
Aikens-KC 62

Batting Average
Lansford-Bos 336
Paciorek-Sea 326
Cooper-Mil 320
Henderson-Oak 319
Hargrove-Cle 317

On Base Percentage
Hargrove-Cle 432
Evans-Bos 418
Henderson-Oak 411
Kemp-Det 393
Lansford-Bos......391

Slugging Average
Grich-Cal 543
Murray-Bal 534
Evans-Bos 522
Paciorek-Sea 509
Cooper-Mil 495

Production
Evans-Bos 940
Grich-Cal 924
Murray-Bal 897
Paciorek-Sea 894
Lemon-Chi 879

Adjusted Production
Grich-Cal 164
Evans-Bos 160
Murray-Bal 156
Lemon-Chi 155
Cooper-Mil 154

Batter Runs
Evans-Bos 39.8
Paciorek-Sea 28.4
Grich-Cal 28.3
Henderson-Oak 26.9
Murray-Bal 25.9

Adjusted Batter Runs
Evans-Bos 34.2
Henderson-Oak 30.8
Grich-Cal.......28.3
Cooper-Mil 27.3
Murray-Bal 26.0

Clutch Hitting Index
Yastrzemski-Bos ...139
Wills-Tex 132
Hargrove-Cle 129
Oglivie-Mil 128
Murphy-Oak 125

Runs Created
Evans-Bos 95
Henderson-Oak 81
Paciorek-Sea 76
Grich-Cal 73
Murray-Bal 70

Total Average
Evans-Bos 1.007
Grich-Cal 917
Henderson-Oak ...899
Murray-Bal 864
Paciorek-Sea 846

Stolen Bases
Henderson-Oak 56
Cruz-Sea 43
LeFlore-Chi 36
Wilson-KC 34
Dilone-Cle 29

Stolen Base Average
Manning-Cle 89.3
Bannister-Cle 88.9
Cruz-Sea 84.3
Wilson-KC 81.0
Gibson-Det 77.3

Stolen Base Runs
Cruz-Sea 8.1
Manning-Cle 5.7
Wilson-KC 5.4
LeFlore-Chi 4.2

Fielding Runs
Bell-Tex 30.0
Yount-Mil 27.5
Wilson-KC 22.1
Burleson-Cal 21.0
Henderson-Oak 20.1

Total Player Rating
Henderson-Oak 5.2
Bell-Tex 4.6
Yount-Mil 4.5
Grich-Cal 4.5
Evans-Bos 4.5

Wins
Vuckovich-Mil...... 14
Morris-Det 14
McCatty-Oak 14
D.Martinez-Bal 14

Win Percentage
Vuckovich-Mil .... .778
D.Martinez-Bal ... .737
McGregor-Bal ..... .722
Guidry-NY 688

Games
Corbett-Min 54
Fingers-Mil 47
Rawley-Sea 46
Easterly-Mil 44

Complete Games
Langford-Oak 18
McCatty-Oak 16
Morris-Det 15
Norris-Oak 12
Gura-KC 12

Shutouts
Medich-Tex 4
McCatty-Oak 4
Forsch-Cal 4
Dotson-Chi 4

Saves
Fingers-Mil 28
Gossage-NY 20
Quisenberry-KC ... 18
Corbett-Min 17
Saucier-Det 13

Innings Pitched
Leonard-KC 201.2
Morris-Det 198.0
Langford-Oak 195.1
McCatty-Oak 185.2
Stieb-Tor 183.2

Fewest Hits/Game
Righetti-NY 6.41
McCatty-Oak 6.79
Morris-Det 6.95
Guidry-NY 7.09
Darwin-Tex 7.09

Fewest BB/Game
Honeycutt-Tex 1.20
Forsch-Cal 1.59
Gura-KC 1.83
Leonard-KC 1.83
Guidry-NY 1.84

Strikeouts
Barker-Cle 127
Burns-Chi 108
Leonard-KC 107
Blyleven-Cle 107
Guidry-NY 104

Strikeouts/Game
Righetti-NY 7.60
Barker-Cle 7.41
Guidry-NY 7.37
Bannister-Sea 6.30
Burns-Chi 6.20

Ratio
Guidry-NY 9.00
Gura-KC 9.30
Righetti-NY 9.66
Honeycutt-Tex 9.66
McCatty-Oak 9.84

Earned Run Average
Righetti-NY 2.05
Stewart-Bal 2.32
McCatty-Oak 2.33
Lamp-Chi 2.41
John-NY 2.63

Adjusted ERA
Righetti-NY 174
Stewart-Bal 156
McCatty-Oak 149
Lamp-Chi 148
John-NY 136

Opponents' Batting Avg.
Righetti-NY 196
McCatty-Oak 211
Guidry-NY 214
Darwin-Tex 218
Morris-Det 218

Opponents' On Base Pct.
Guidry-NY 257
Gura-KC 269
Righetti-NY 269
Honeycutt-Tex 272
McCatty-Oak 279

Starter Runs
McCatty-Oak 27.5
Righetti-NY 18.8
Gura-KC 18.0
Burns-Chi 17.7
Lamp-Chi 17.6

Adjusted Starter Runs
McCatty-Oak 23.8
Righetti-NY 17.8
Gura-KC 17.1
Lamp-Chi 16.5
Burns-Chi 16.3

Clutch Pitching Index
Stewart-Bal 145
John-NY 129
Burns-Chi 121
Denny-Cle 119
McGregor-Bal 116

Relief Runs
Fingers-Mil 22.7
Gossage-NY 15.0
Quisenberry-KC ... 13.3
Saucier-Det 10.9
Corbett-Min 10.6

Adjusted Relief Runs
Fingers-Mil 20.7
Gossage-NY 14.5
Corbett-Min 13.4
Quisenberry-KC ... 13.0
Saucier-Det 11.5

Relief Ranking
Fingers-Mil 38.2
Gossage-NY 28.0
Saucier-Det 19.6
Quisenberry-KC ...17.8
Corbett-Min 16.9

Total Pitcher Index
Fingers-Mil 4.3
Gossage-NY 3.2
McCatty-Oak 2.8
Quisenberry-KC ... 2.3
Saucier-Det 2.0

Total Baseball Ranking
Henderson-Oak 5.2
Bell-Tex 4.6
Yount-Mil 4.5
Grich-Cal 4.5
Evans-Bos 4.5

TEAM	G	W	L	PCT	GB	R	OR	AB	H	2B	3B	HR	BB	SO	AVG	OBP	SLG	PRO	PRO+	BR	/A	PF	CHI	RC	SB	CS	SBA	SBR
EAST																												
STL	162	92	70	.568		685	**609**	5455	1439	239	**52**	67	569	805	.264	**.337**	.364	.701	101	24	17	101	99	682	**200**	91	69	5
PHI	162	89	73	.549	3	664	654	5454	1417	245	25	112	506	831	.260	.325	.376	.701	100	14	-1	102	99	654	128	76	63	-7
MON	162	86	76	.531	6	697	616	5557	1454	270	38	133	503	816	.262	.327	.396	.723	106	52	38	102	97	725	156	56	**74**	13
PIT	162	84	78	.519	8	724	696	5614	**1535**	**272**	40	134	447	862	**.273**	.330	**.408**	**.738**	109	**80**	58	103	97	**745**	161	75	68	3
CHI	162	73	89	.451	19	676	709	5531	1436	239	46	102	460	869	.260	.319	.375	.694	97	-4	-22	103	103	662	132	70	65	-2
NY	162	65	97	.401	27	609	723	5510	1361	227	26	97	456	1005	.247	.307	.350	.657	90	-75	-71	99	105	595	137	58	70	6
WEST																												
ATL	162	89	73	.549		**739**	702	5507	1411	215	22	**146**	554	869	.256	.327	.383	.710	100	33	4	104	105	697	151	77	66	-1
LA	162	88	74	.543	1	691	612	5642	1487	222	32	138	528	**804**	.264	.330	.388	.718	110	47	**65**	98	95	735	151	56	73	12
SF	162	87	75	.537	2	673	687	5499	1393	213	30	133	**607**	915	.253	.329	.384	.705	103	27	28	100	97	685	130	56	70	5
SD	162	81	81	.500	8	675	658	5575	1435	217	**52**	81	429	877	.257	.313	.359	.672	99	-49	-17	95	**110**	626	165	77	68	3
HOU	162	77	85	.475	12	569	620	5440	1342	236	48	74	435	830	.247	.305	.349	.654	95	-84	-42	92	102	578	140	61	70	5
CIN	162	61	101	.377	28	545	661	5479	1375	228	34	82	470	817	.251	.313	.350	.663	89	-63	-75	102	92	588	131	69	66	-2
TOT	972					7947		66263	17085	2823	445	1299	5964	10300	.258	.322	.373	.695							1782	822	68	41

TEAM	CG	SH	SV	IP	H	H/G	HR	BB	SO	RAT	ERA	ERA+	OAV	OOB	PR	/A	PF	CPI	FA	E	DP	FW	PW	BW	SBW	DIF
EAST																										
STL	25	10	47	1465¹	1420	8.7	94	502	689	11.9	3.37	107	.258	.322	37	40	101	105	**.981**	124	169	.9	4.2	1.8	.2	3.9
PHI	**38**	13	33	1456¹	1395	8.6	86	472	**1002**	11.7	3.61	102	.255	.317	-1	9	102	93	**.981**	121	138	**1.1**	.9	-.1	-1.1	7.1
MON	34	10	43	1460²	1371	8.4	110	**448**	936	11.3	3.31	**110**	.250	.309	46	**53**	101	99	.980	122	117	**1.1**	**5.6**	4.0	**1.0**	-6.6
PIT	19	7	39	1466²	1434	8.8	118	521	933	12.2	3.81	97	.257	.324	-34	-17	103	96	.977	145	133	-.3	-1.8	6.1	-.0	-1.0
CHI	9	7	43	1447¹	1510	9.4	125	452	764	12.4	3.92	95	.272	.330	-51	-30	104	102	.979	132	110	.5	-3.2	-2.3	-.6	-2.4
NY	15	5	37	1447¹	1508	9.4	119	582	759	13.1	3.88	94	.273	.344	-45	-40	101	**109**	.972	175	134	-2.0	-4.2	-7.5	.3	-2.6
WEST																										
ATL	15	11	**51**	1463	1484	9.1	126	502	813	12.4	3.82	98	.267	.331	-36	-15	104	103	.979	137	**186**	.2	-1.6	.4	-.5	9.4
LA	37	**16**	28	1488¹	1356	**8.2**	81	468	932	**11.2**	**3.26**	106	.244	**.305**	56	34	96	92	.979	139	131	.1	3.6	**6.8**	.9	-4.4
SF	18	4	45	1465¹	1507	9.3	109	466	810	12.3	3.64	99	.270	.329	-6	-7	100	106	.973	173	125	-1.9	-.7	2.9	.2	5.5
SD	20	11	41	1476	1348	**8.2**	139	502	765	11.4	3.52	97	**.244**	.310	13	-16	95	96	.976	152	142	-.7	-1.7	-1.8	-.0	4.2
HOU	37	**16**	31	1446²	**1338**	8.3	87	479	899	11.5	3.42	97	.247	.312	30	-16	92	94	.978	136	154	.3	-1.7	-4.4	.2	1.7
CIN	22	7	31	1460¹	1414	8.7	105	570	998	12.4	3.66	101	.258	.330	-10	6	103	102	.980	128	158	.7	.6	-7.9	-.6	-12.9
TOT	289	117	469	17543¹		8.8				12.0	3.60		.258	.322					.978	1684	1697					

Runs	**Hits**	**Doubles**	**Triples**	**Home Runs**	**Total Bases**
L.Smith-StL 120	Oliver-Mon 204	Oliver-Mon 43	Thon-Hou 10	Kingman-NY 37	Oliver-Mon 317
Murphy-Atl 113	Buckner-Chi 201	Kennedy-SD 42	Wilson-NY 9	Murphy-Atl......... 36	Guerrero-LA 308
Schmidt-Phi 108	Dawson-Mon 183	Dawson-Mon 37	Puhl-Hou 9	Schmidt-Phi....... 35	Murphy-Atl 303
Dawson-Mon 107	L.Smith-StL 182	Knight-Hou 36	Moreno-Pit 9	Horner-Atl 32	Dawson-Mon 303
Sandberg-Chi 103	Ray-Pit............. 182			Guerrero-LA 32	Buckner-Chi 290

Runs Batted In	**Runs Produced**	**Bases On Balls**	**Batting Average**	**On Base Percentage**	**Slugging Average**
Oliver-Mon 109	Murphy-Atl 186	Schmidt-Phi 107	Oliver-Mon .... .331	Schmidt-Phi .... .407	Schmidt-Phi........ .547
Murphy-Atl 109	Buckner-Chi 183	Thompson-Pit 101	Madlock-Pit .... .319	Hernandez-StL .... .404	Guerrero-LA .... .536
Buckner-Chi 105	L.Smith-StL 181	Hernandez-StL 100	Durham-Chi .... .312	Morgan-SF .... .402	Durham-Chi .... .521
Hendrick-StL 104	Oliver-Mon 177	Murphy-Atl 93	L.Smith-StL .... .307	Thompson-Pit ..... .397	Oliver-Mon .... .514
Clark-SF 103	Madlock-Pit....... 168	Clark-SF 90	Buckner-Chi .... .306	Oliver-Mon .... .394	Thompson-Pit ..... .511

Production	**Adjusted Production**	**Batter Runs**	**Adjusted Batter Runs**	**Clutch Hitting Index**	**Runs Created**
Schmidt-Phi 954	Schmidt-Phi 161	Schmidt-Phi 47.2	Schmidt-Phi 44.7	Hernandez-StL 129	Oliver-Mon 125
Guerrero-LA 915	Guerrero-LA 157	Oliver-Mon 42.7	Guerrero-LA 43.1	Hendrick-StL 128	Guerrero-LA 120
Durham-Chi 910	Oliver-Mon 149	Thompson-Pit 40.7	Oliver-Mon 40.5	DeJesus-Phi 123	Murphy-Atl 118
Oliver-Mon 908	Lezcano-SD 149	Guerrero-LA 40.3	Thompson-Pit 37.4	Buckner-Chi 123	Schmidt-Phi 118
Thompson-Pit 908	Durham-Chi....... 148	Murphy-Atl 37.8	Durham-Chi 35.0	Lezcano-SD........ 115	Thompson-Pit 117

Total Average	**Stolen Bases**	**Stolen Base Average**	**Stolen Base Runs**	**Fielding Runs**	**Total Player Rating**
Schmidt-Phi 1.026	Raines-Mon 78	Bailor-NY 87.0	Raines-Mon 13.8	O.Smith-StL 33.1	Schmidt-Phi 6.1
Guerrero-LA 959	L.Smith-StL 68	Morgan-SF 85.7	Wilson-NY 7.8	Dawson-Mon 20.8	Carter-Mon 5.4
Thompson-Pit 951	Moreno-Pit 60	Wiggins-SD 84.6	Wiggins-SD........6.3	Hubbard-Atl 19.9	Dawson-Mon 4.7
Morgan-SF 923	Wilson-NY 58	Matthews-Phi..... 84.0	Thon-Hou 6.3	Schmidt-Phi 18.8	Guerrero-LA 4.6
Durham-Chi 917	S.Sax-LA 49	O.Smith-StL 83.3	Dawson-Mon 5.7	Davis-SF 17.9	Lezcano-SD 4.6

Wins	**Win Percentage**	**Games**	**Complete Games**	**Shutouts**	**Saves**
Carlton-Phi 23	Niekro-Atl .... .810	Tekulve-Pit 85	Carlton-Phi 19	Carlton-Phi 6	Sutter-StL 36
Valenzuela-LA...... 19	Rogers-Mon ...... .704	Minton-SF 78	Valenzuela-LA...... 18	Niekro-Hou 5	Minton-SF 30
Rogers-Mon 19	Carlton-Phi ...... .676	Scurry-Pit 76	Niekro-Hou 16	Andujar-StL 5	Garber-Atl......... 30
Reuss-LA 18	Lollar-SD .... .640	Reardon-Mon 75	Rogers-Mon 14		Reardon-Mon 26
	Forsch-StL .... .625	Hernandez-Chi 75	Soto-Cin 13		Tekulve-Pit 20

Innings Pitched	**Fewest Hits/Game**	**Fewest BB/Game**	**Strikeouts**	**Strikeouts/Game**	**Ratio**
Carlton-Phi 295.2	Ryan-Hou 7.05	Bird-Chi 1.41	Carlton-Phi 286	Soto-Cin 9.57	Soto-Cin 9.68
Valenzuela-LA....285.0	Soto-Cin 7.06	Hammaker-SF 1.44	Soto-Cin 274	Ryan-Hou 8.81	Niekro-Hou 9.77
Rogers-Mon 277.0	Lea-Mon 7.35	Andujar-StL 1.69	Ryan-Hou 245	Carlton-Phi 8.71	Andujar-StL 9.96
Niekro-Hou 270.0	Lollar-SD 7.43	Reuss-LA 1.77	Valenzuela-LA..... 199	Candelaria-Pit ... 6.85	Sutton-Hou 9.97
Andujar-StL 265.2	Niekro-Hou 7.47	Candelaria-Pit 1.91	Rogers-Mon 179	Welch-LA 6.72	Reuss-LA 10.04

Earned Run Average	**Adjusted ERA**	**Opponents' Batting Avg.**	**Opponents' On Base Pct.**	**Starter Runs**	**Adjusted Starter Runs**
Rogers-Mon 2.40	Rogers-Mon 151	Ryan-Hou .... .213	Soto-Cin .... .273	Rogers-Mon 36.8	Rogers-Mon 38.0
Niekro-Hou 2.47	Andujar-StL 146	Soto-Cin .... .215	Reuss-LA .... .278	Niekro-Hou 34.0	Andujar-StL 33.8
Andujar-StL 2.47	Niekro-Hou 134	Lea-Mon .... .222	Sutton-Hou .... .279	Andujar-StL 33.3	Soto-Cin 25.9
Soto-Cin 2.79	Soto-Cin 132	Lollar-SD .... .224	Niekro-Hou .... .279	Soto-Cin 23.1	Niekro-Hou 25.5
Valenzuela-LA....2.87	Candelaria-Pit 126	Niekro-Hou .... .229	Andujar-StL....... .282	Valenzuela-LA 23.0	Valenzuela-LA 18.8

Clutch Pitching Index	**Relief Runs**	**Adjusted Relief Runs**	**Relief Ranking**	**Total Pitcher Index**	**Total Baseball Ranking**
Camp-Atl 124	Minton-SF 24.2	Minton-SF 24.1	Minton-SF 37.9	Minton-SF 4.2	Schmidt-Phi 6.1
Jenkins-Chi 121	Scurry-Pit 21.5	Scurry-Pit 22.7	Garber-Atl 35.5	Garber-Atl 4.1	Carter-Mon 5.4
Krukow-Phi....... 120	Reardon-Mon 18.6	Bedrosian-Atl 20.1	Reardon-Mon 27.6	Rogers-Mon 3.7	Dawson-Mon 4.7
Gale-SF 114	Bedrosian-Atl 18.1	Reardon-Mon 19.1	DeLeon-SD 24.8	Andujar-StL 3.2	Guerrero-LA 4.6
Mura-StL........ 110	DeLeon-SD 17.8	Garber-Atl 18.5	Scurry-Pit 24.6	Reardon-Mon ... 2.8	Lezcano-SD 4.6

TEAM	G	W	L	PCT	GB	R	OR	AB	H	2B	3B	HR	BB	SO	AVG	OBP	SLG	PRO	PRO+	BR	/A	PF	CHI	RC	SB	CS	SBA	SBR
EAST																												
MIL	163	95	67	.586		**891**	717	5733	1599	277	41	**216**	484	714	.279	.337	**.455**	.792	123	109	162	94	105	**865**	84	52	62	-6
BAL	163	94	68	.580	1	774	687	5557	1478	259	27	179	634	796	.266	.344	.419	.763	108	67	70	100	96	795	49	38	56	-8
BOS	162	89	73	.549	6	753	713	5596	1536	271	31	136	547	736	.274	.342	.407	.749	99	39	-6	106	98	755	42	39	52	-11
DET	162	83	79	.512	12	729	685	5590	1489	237	40	177	470	807	.266	.326	.418	.744	103	15	12	100	99	752	93	66	58	-12
NY	162	79	83	.488	16	709	716	5526	1417	225	37	161	590	719	.256	.331	.398	.729	101	-5	7	98	98	716	69	45	61	-6
TOR	162	78	84	.481	17	651	701	5526	1447	262	45	106	415	749	.262	.317	.383	.700	83	-70	-129	109	102	655	118	81	59	-13
CLE	162	78	84	.481	17	683	748	5559	1458	225	32	109	**651**	625	.262	.343	.373	.716	97	-13	-9	100	94	723	151	66	69	5
WEST																												
CAL	162	93	69	.574		814	**670**	5532	1518	268	26	186	613	760	.274	**.350**	.433	.783	114	108	108	100	96	834	55	53	51	-15
KC	162	90	72	.556	3	784	717	5629	**1603**	295	58	132	442	758	**.285**	.340	.428	.768	109	67	66	100	99	802	133	48	**73**	11
CHI	162	87	75	.537	6	786	710	5575	1523	266	52	136	533	866	.273	.340	.413	.753	106	43	43	100	102	784	136	58	70	6
SEA	162	76	86	.469	17	651	712	5626	1431	259	33	130	456	806	.254	.313	.381	.694	87	-84	-102	103	102	657	131	82	62	-10
OAK	162	68	94	.420	25	691	819	5448	1286	211	27	149	582	948	.236	.312	.367	.679	90	-106	-79	96	**113**	644	**232**	87	73	**17**
TEX	162	64	98	.395	29	590	749	5445	1354	204	26	115	447	750	.249	.309	.359	.668	87	-128	-100	95	103	593	63	45	58	-8
MIN	162	60	102	.370	33	657	819	5544	1427	234	44	148	474	887	.257	.319	.396	.715	93	-43	-61	103	98	676	38	33	54	-8
TOT	1135					10163		77886	20566	3493	519	2080	7338	10921	.264	.330	.402	.733							1394	795	64	-59

TEAM	CG	SH	SV	IP	H	H/G	HR	BB	SO	RAT	ERA	ERA+	OAV	OOB	PR	/A	PF	CPI	FA	E	DP	FW	PW	BW	SBW	DIF
EAST																										
MIL	34	6	**47**	1467¹	1514	9.3	152	511	717	12.5	3.98	95	.270	.333	15	-32	93	106	.980	125	**185**	.1	-3.2	**16.2**	-.2	1.1
BAL	38	8	34	1462¹	1436	8.8	147	488	719	**12.0**	3.99	101	.257	**.320**	14	7	99	95	**.984**	**101**	140	**1.4**	.7	7.0	-.4	4.3
BOS	23	11	33	1453	1557	9.6	155	478	816	12.8	4.03	107	.276	.336	7	44	106	**108**	.981	121	172	.3	4.4	-.6	-.7	4.6
DET	**45**	5	27	1451	**1371**	**8.5**	172	554	740	12.1	**3.80**	107	**.251**	.323	44	42	100	104	.981	117	165	.5	4.2	1.2	-.8	-3.1
NY	24	8	39	1459	1471	9.1	113	491	939	12.2	3.99	100	.264	.326	13	-1	98	95	.979	128	158	-.0	-.1	.7	-.2	-2.3
TOR	41	**13**	25	1443²	1428	8.9	147	493	776	12.1	3.95	113	.257	.321	20	**85**	110	97	.978	136	146	-.5	**8.5**	-12.9	-.9	2.8
CLE	31	9	30	1468¹	1433	8.8	122	589	882	12.5	4.11	99	.257	.330	-5	-5	100	94	.980	123	129	.2	-.5	-.9	.9	-2.7
WEST																										
CAL	40	10	27	1464	1436	8.8	124	482	728	**12.0**	3.82	106	.259	.322	42	38	100	98	.983	108	171	1.0	3.8	10.8	-1.1	-2.5
KC	16	12	45	1431	1443	9.1	163	471	650	12.2	4.08	100	.262	.323	-1	0	100	98	.979	127	140	-.0	.0	6.6	1.5	.9
CHI	30	10	41	1439	1502	9.4	**99**	**460**	753	12.4	3.87	104	.270	.329	33	27	99	100	.976	154	173	-1.5	2.7	4.3	1.0	-.5
SEA	23	11	39	1476¹	1431	8.7	173	547	**1002**	12.3	3.88	109	.256	.325	32	60	104	104	.978	139	158	-.7	6.0	-10.2	-.6	-.5
OAK	42	6	22	1456	1506	9.3	177	648	697	13.5	4.54	86	.268	.346	-76	-103	96	100	.974	160	140	-1.8	-10.3	-7.9	2.1	4.9
TEX	32	5	24	1431	1554	9.8	128	483	690	13.1	4.28	90	.280	.342	-33	-66	95	102	.981	121	169	.3	-6.6	-10.0	-.4	-.3
MIN	26	7	30	1433	1484	9.3	208	643	812	13.4	4.72	90	.269	.347	-103	-77	104	101	.982	108	162	1.0	-7.7	-6.1	-.4	-7.8
TOT	445	121	463	20335		9.1				12.5	4.07		.264	.330					.980	1768	2208					

Runs		Hits		Doubles		Triples		Home Runs		Total Bases	
Molitor-Mil	136	Yount-Mil	210	Yount-Mil	46	Wilson-KC	15	Thomas-Mil	39	Yount-Mil	367
Yount-Mil	129	Cooper-Mil	205	McRae-KC	46	Herndon-Det	13	R.Jackson-Cal	39	Cooper-Mil	345
Evans-Bos	122	Molitor-Mil	201	White-KC	45	Yount-Mil	12	Winfield-NY	37	McRae-KC	332
Henderson-Oak	119	Wilson-KC	194	DeCinces-Cal	42	Mumphrey-NY	10	Oglivie-Mil	34	Evans-Bos	325
Downing-Cal	109	McRae-KC	189	Cowens-Sea	39					DeCinces-Cal	315

Runs Batted In		Runs Produced		Bases On Balls		Batting Average		On Base Percentage		Slugging Average	
McRae-KC	133	Yount-Mil	214	Henderson-Oak	116	Wilson-KC	.332	Evans-Bos	.403	Yount-Mil	.578
Cooper-Mil	121	McRae-KC	197	Evans-Bos	112	Yount-Mil	.331	Harrah-Cle	.400	Winfield-NY	.560
Thornton-Cle	116	Cooper-Mil	193	Thornton-Cle	109	Carew-Cal	.319	Henderson-Oak	.399	Murray-Bal	.549
Yount-Mil	114	Molitor-Mil	188	Hargrove-Cle	101	Murray-Bal	.316	Carew-Cal	.399	DeCinces-Cal	.548
Thomas-Mil	112	Evans-Bos	188	Murphy-Oak	94	Cooper-Mil	.313	Murray-Bal	.395	McRae-KC	.542

Production		Adjusted Production		Batter Runs		Adjusted Batter Runs		Clutch Hitting Index		Runs Created	
Yount-Mil	.962	Yount-Mil	170	Yount-Mil	50.3	Yount-Mil	58.7	Otis-KC	137	Yount-Mil	136
Murray-Bal	.944	Murray-Bal	157	Evans-Bos	48.5	Murray-Bal	42.9	Foli-Cal	137	Evans-Bos	134
Evans-Bos	.937	DeCinces-Cal	149	Murray-Bal	42.5	Evans-Bos	40.9	Hayes-Cle	128	Harrah-Cle	123
DeCinces-Cal	.922	R.Jackson-Cal	147	DeCinces-Cal	38.1	Harrah-Cle	38.6	Boone-Cal	124	McRae-KC	123
McRae-KC	.912	McRae-KC	146	Harrah-Cle	38.0	DeCinces-Cal	38.1	Murphy-Oak	122	Cooper-Mil	118

Total Average		Stolen Bases		Stolen Base Average		Stolen Base Runs		Fielding Runs		Total Player Rating	
Evans-Bos	.976	Henderson-Oak	130	Sexton-Oak	100.0	Henderson-Oak	13.8	Bell-Tex	34.4	Yount-Mil	7.0
Yount-Mil	.969	Garcia-Tor	54	Fisk-Chi	89.5	Molitor-Mil	6.9	Bernazard-Chi	24.6	DeCinces-Cal	5.3
Murray-Bal	.957	J.Cruz-Sea	46	Dilone-Cle	86.8	Dilone-Cle	6.9	Murphy-Oak	21.8	Bell-Tex	5.1
Henderson-Oak	.934	Molitor-Mil	41	Harrah-Cle	85.0	J.Cruz-Sea	6.0	DeCinces-Cal	20.6	Evans-Bos	4.2
Harrah-Cle	.931	Wilson-KC	37	Brown-Sea	82.4	Wathan-KC	5.4	Almon-Chi	20.0	Henderson-Oak	4.0

Wins		Win Percentage		Games		Complete Games		Shutouts		Saves	
Hoyt-Chi	19	Vuckovich-Mil	.750	VandeBerg-Sea	78	Stieb-Tor	19	Stieb-Tor	5	Quisenberry-KC	35
Zahn-Cal	18	Palmer-Bal	.750	T.Martinez-Bal	76	Morris-Det	17	Zahn-Cal	4	Gossage-NY	30
Vuckovich-Mil	18	Zahn-Cal	.692	Quisenberry-KC	72	Langford-Oak	15	Forsch-Cal	4	Fingers-Mil	29
Gura-KC	18	Petry-Det	.625	Caudill-Sea	70	Hoyt-Chi	14			Caudill-Sea	26
		Gura-KC	.600	Spillner-Cle	65					Davis-Min	22

Innings Pitched		Fewest Hits/Game		Fewest BB/Game		Strikeouts		Strikeouts/Game		Ratio	
Stieb-Tor	288.1	Sutcliffe-Cle	7.25	John-NY-Cal	1.58	Bannister-Sea	209	Righetti-NY	8.02	Palmer-Bal	10.39
Clancy-Tor	266.2	Ujdur-Det	7.58	Eckersley-Bos	1.73	Barker-Cle	187	Bannister-Sea	7.62	Eckersley-Bos	10.95
Morris-Det	266.1	Righetti-NY	7.62	Hoyt-Chi	1.80	Righetti-NY	163	Beattie-Sea	7.31	Stieb-Tor	10.96
Caldwell-Mil	258.0	Palmer-Bal	7.73	Haas-Mil	1.82	Guidry-NY	162	Barker-Cle	6.88	Barker-Cle	11.11
D.Martinez-Bal	252.0	Barker-Cle	7.76	Langford-Oak	1.86	Tudor-Bos	146	Tudor-Bos	6.72	Bannister-Sea	11.11

Earned Run Average		Adjusted ERA		Opponents' Batting Avg.		Opponents' On Base Pct.		Starter Runs		Adjusted Starter Runs	
Sutcliffe-Cle	2.96	Stanley-Bos	139	Sutcliffe-Cle	.226	Palmer-Bal	.287	Sutcliffe-Cle	26.8	Stieb-Tor	39.4
Stanley-Bos	3.10	Stieb-Tor	138	Righetti-NY	.229	Eckersley-Bos	.297	Stieb-Tor	26.5	Sutcliffe-Cle	26.9
Palmer-Bal	3.13	Sutcliffe-Cle	138	Ujdur-Det	.230	Stieb-Tor	.299	Palmer-Bal	23.7	Petry-Det	23.0
Petry-Det	3.22	Palmer-Bal	129	Palmer-Bal	.231	Barker-Cle	.301	Petry-Det	23.3	Palmer-Bal	22.7
Stieb-Tor	3.25	Beattie-Sea	127	Barker-Cle	.232	Clancy-Tor	.302	Vuckovich-Mil	18.2	Clancy-Tor	22.6

Clutch Pitching Index		Relief Runs		Adjusted Relief Runs		Relief Ranking		Total Pitcher Index		Total Baseball Ranking	
Vuckovich-Mil	131	Spillner-Cle	23.5	Spillner-Cle	23.6	Caudill-Sea	51.9	Caudill-Sea	5.1	Yount-Mil	7.0
Tudor-Bos	121	Quisenberry-KC	22.9	Quisenberry-KC	23.0	Spillner-Cle	43.2	Quisenberry-KC	4.5	DeCinces-Cal	5.3
Dotson-Chi	118	Burgmeier-Bos	20.3	Burgmeier-Bos	23.0	Quisenberry-KC	37.4	Spillner-Cle	4.2	Caudill-Sea	5.1
Wilcox-Det	113	Gossage-NY	19.1	Stanley-Bos	22.5	Clear-Bos	34.6	Stieb-Tor	4.2	Bell-Tex	5.1
Stanley-Bos	110	Caudill-Sea	18.3	Caudill-Sea	20.1	Gossage-NY	29.0	Clear-Bos	3.5	Quisenberry-KC	4.5

TEAM	G	W	L	PCT	GB	R	OR	AB	H	2B	3B	HR	BB	SO	AVG	OBP	SLG	PRO	PRO+	BR	/A	PF	CHI	RC	SB	CS	SBA	SBR
EAST																												
PHI	163	90	72	.556		696	635	5426	1352	209	45	125	**640**	906	.249	.331	.373	.704	102	17	25	99	101	676	143	75	66	-2
PIT	162	84	78	.519	6	659	648	5531	1460	238	29	121	497	873	.264	.327	.383	.710	100	17	0	103	96	682	124	77	62	-9
MON	163	82	80	.506	8	677	646	5611	1482	**297**	41	102	509	733	.264	.329	.386	.715	105	30	34	99	95	716	138	44	**76**	15
STL	162	79	83	.488	11	679	710	5550	**1496**	262	**63**	83	543	879	.270	.337	.384	.721	**106**	47	**47**	100	94	725	**207**	89	70	9
CHI	162	71	91	.438	19	701	719	5512	1436	272	42	140	470	868	.261	.322	**.401**	.723	101	35	2	105	100	707	84	40	68	1
NY	162	68	94	.420	22	575	680	5444	1314	172	26	112	436	1031	.241	.301	.344	.645	85	-112	-107	99	107	562	141	64	69	4
WEST																												
LA	163	91	71	.562		654	**609**	5440	1358	197	34	**146**	541	925	.250	.320	.379	.699	100	-6	-2	99	100	663	166	76	69	4
ATL	162	88	74	.543	3	**746**	640	5472	1489	218	45	130	582	847	**.272**	**.344**	**.400**	**.744**	104	**91**	35	107	98	**744**	146	88	62	-9
HOU	162	85	77	.525	6	643	646	5502	1412	239	60	97	517	882	.257	.323	.375	.698	106	-7	34	94	97	673	164	95	63	-8
SD	163	81	81	.500	10	653	653	5527	1384	207	34	93	482	822	.250	.313	.351	.664	93	-74	-53	97	**110**	609	179	67	73	14
SF	162	79	83	.488	12	687	697	5369	1324	206	30	142	619	990	.247	.328	.375	.703	104	11	33	97	102	662	140	78	64	-5
CIN	162	74	88	.457	17	623	710	5333	1274	236	35	107	588	1006	.239	.317	.356	.673	89	-49	-70	104	103	606	154	77	67	0
TOT	974					7993		65717	16781	2753	484	1398	6424	10749	.255	.324	.376	.700							1786	870	67	14

TEAM	CG	SH	SV	IP	H	H/G	HR	BB	SO	RAT	ERA	ERA+	OAV	OOB	PR	/A	PF	CPI	FA	E	DP	FW	PW	BW	SBW	DIF
EAST																										
PHI	20	10	41	1461²	1429	8.8	111	**464**	**1092**	11.8	3.34	107	.256	.316	47	37	98	103	.976	152	117	-.7	3.9	2.6	-.3	3.6
PIT	25	14	41	1462¹	1378	8.5	109	563	1061	12.1	3.55	104	.252	.323	12	25	102	99	**.982**	165	145	1.4	2.6	.0	-1.1	.0
MON	**38**	**15**	34	1471	1406	8.6	120	479	899	11.7	3.58	100	.254	.317	8	1	99	99	.981	116	130	1.4	.1	3.6	**1.4**	-5.5
STL	22	10	27	1460²	1479	9.1	115	525	709	12.5	3.79	96	.266	.332	-26	-28	100	102	.976	152	173	-.8	-2.9	**4.9**	.8	-4.0
CHI	9	10	42	1428²	1496	9.4	117	498	807	12.7	4.08	93	.274	.337	-71	-45	105	100	**.982**	115	164	1.4	-4.7	.2	-.0	-6.9
NY	18	7	33	1451	1384	8.6	97	615	717	12.5	3.68	99	.256	.334	-8	-8	100	100	.976	151	171	-.7	-.8	-11.2	.3	-.6
WEST																										
LA	27	12	40	1464	1336	8.2	97	495	1000	**11.4**	**3.10**	116	.244	**.309**	85	79	99	101	.974	168	132	-1.7	**8.3**	-.2	.3	3.3
ATL	18	4	**48**	1440²	1412	8.8	132	540	895	12.3	3.67	106	.260	.329	-7	33	107	**105**	.978	137	**176**	.1	3.4	3.7	-1.1	.8
HOU	22	14	**48**	1466¹	**1276**	**7.8**	**94**	570	904	11.5	3.45	99	**.236**	.312	29	-8	94	90	.977	147	165	-.5	-.8	3.6	-1.0	2.7
SD	23	5	44	1467²	1389	8.5	144	528	850	11.9	3.62	96	.253	.322	1	-22	96	102	.979	129	135	.6	-2.3	-5.5	1.3	5.8
SF	20	9	47	1445²	1431	8.9	127	520	881	12.3	3.70	96	.259	.326	-11	-27	97	101	.973	171	109	-1.9	-2.8	3.4	-.6	-.0
CIN	34	5	29	1441¹	1365	8.5	135	627	934	12.6	3.98	95	.253	.333	-57	-29	105	97	.981	114	121	1.5	-3.0	-7.3	-.1	2.0
TOT	276	115	474	17461		8.6				12.1	3.63		.255	.324					.978	1667	1758					

Runs		Hits		Doubles		Triples		Home Runs		Total Bases	
Raines-Mon	133	Dawson-Mon	189	Ray-Pit	38	Butler-Atl	13	Schmidt-Phi	40	Dawson-Mon	341
Murphy-Atl	131	Cruz-Hou	189	Oliver-Mon	38	Moreno-Hou	11	Murphy-Atl	36	Murphy-Atl	318
Schmidt-Phi	104	Ramirez-Atl	185	Buckner-Chi	38	Green-StL	10	Guerrero-LA	32	Guerrero-LA	310
Dawson-Mon	104	Oliver-Mon	184	Carter-Mon	37	Dawson-Mon	10	Dawson-Mon	32	Thon-Hou	283
		Raines-Mon	183					Evans-SF	30	Schmidt-Phi	280

Runs Batted In		Runs Produced		Bases On Balls		Batting Average		On Base Percentage		Slugging Average	
Murphy-Atl	121	Murphy-Atl	216	Schmidt-Phi	128	Madlock-Pit	.323	Schmidt-Phi	.402	Murphy-Atl	.540
Dawson-Mon	113	Raines-Mon	193	Thompson-Pit	99	L.Smith-StL	.321	Hernandez-StL-NY	.398	Dawson-Mon	.539
Schmidt-Phi	109	Dawson-Mon	185	Raines-Mon	97	Cruz-Hou	.318	Murphy-Atl	.396	Guerrero-LA	.531
Guerrero-LA	103	Schmidt-Phi	173	Murphy-Atl	90	Hendrick-StL	.318	Raines-Mon	.395	Schmidt-Phi	.524
Kennedy-SD	98	Cruz-Hou	163	Morgan-Phi	89	Knight-Hou	.304	Madlock-Pit	.389	Evans-SF	.516

Production		Adjusted Production		Batter Runs		Adjusted Batter Runs		Clutch Hitting Index		Runs Created	
Murphy-Atl	.936	Schmidt-Phi	156	Murphy-Atl	46.2	Schmidt-Phi	44.6	Kennedy-SD	122	Murphy-Atl	131
Schmidt-Phi	.926	Evans-SF	151	Schmidt-Phi	43.2	Guerrero-LA	38.4	Rose-Phi	121	Raines-Mon	120
Guerrero-LA	.908	Guerrero-LA	150	Guerrero-LA	37.8	Murphy-Atl	37.5	Garner-Hou	115	Guerrero-LA	118
Evans-SF	.896	Murphy-Atl	146	Evans-SF	33.0	Evans-SF	36.2	Hendrick-StL	115	Schmidt-Phi	117
Dawson-Mon	.886	Cruz-Hou	143	Dawson-Mon	32.4	Cruz-Hou	34.5	McGee-StL	112	Dawson-Mon	113

Total Average		Stolen Bases		Stolen Base Average		Stolen Base Runs		Fielding Runs		Total Player Rating	
Murphy-Atl	1.014	Raines-Mon	90	Morgan-Phi	90.0	Raines-Mon	18.6	Sandberg-Chi	41.1	Schmidt-Phi	6.4
Schmidt-Phi	.986	Wiggins-SD	66	Murphy-Atl	88.2	Wiggins-SD	12.0	Schmidt-Phi	23.3	Thon-Hou	5.9
Raines-Mon	.959	S.Sax-LA	56	Raines-Mon	86.5	McGee-StL	6.9	Hubbard-Atl	21.6	Raines-Mon	5.8
Guerrero-LA	.935	Wilson-NY	54	Bailor-NY	85.7	Wilson-NY	6.6	Buckner-Chi	21.0	Guerrero-LA	4.6
Evans-SF	.908	L.Smith-StL	43	Wiggins-SD	83.5	Murphy-Atl	6.6	Thon-Hou	20.8	Murphy-Atl	4.6

Wins		Win Percentage		Games		Complete Games		Shutouts		Saves	
Denny-Phi	19	Denny-Phi	.760	Campbell-Chi	82	Soto-Cin	18	Rogers-Mon	5	Smith-Chi	29
Soto-Cin	17	Perez-Atl	.652	Tekulve-Pit	76	Rogers-Mon	13	Valenzuela-LA	4	Holland-Phi	25
Rogers-Mon	17	McWilliams-Pit	.652	Hernandez-Chi-Phi	74	Gullickson-Mon	10	McWilliams-Pit	4	Minton-SF	22
Gullickson-Mon	17	Candelaria-Pit	.652	Scherrer-Cin	73			Lea-Mon	4	Sutter-StL	21
Lea-Mon	16	McMurtry-Atl	.625	Minton-SF	73					Reardon-Mon	21

Innings Pitched		Fewest Hits/Game		Fewest BB/Game		Strikeouts		Strikeouts/Game		Ratio	
Carlton-Phi	283.2	Ryan-Hou	6.14	Hammaker-SF	1.67	Carlton-Phi	275	Carlton-Phi	8.73	Hammaker-SF	9.50
Soto-Cin	273.2	Soto-Cin	6.81	Ruthven-Phi-Chi	1.87	Soto-Cin	242	Ryan-Hou	8.39	Soto-Cin	10.10
Rogers-Mon	273.0	Welch-LA	7.24	Denny-Phi	1.97	McWilliams-Pit	199	Soto-Cin	7.96	Pena-LA	10.37
Niekro-Hou	263.2	Hammaker-SF	7.68	Reuss-LA	2.01	Valenzuela-LA	189	McWilliams-Pit	7.53	Welch-LA	10.54
Valenzuela-LA	257.0	Pena-LA	7.73	Candelaria-Pit	2.05	Ryan-Hou	183	Berenyi-Cin	7.29	Denny-Phi	10.61

Earned Run Average		Adjusted ERA		Opponents' Batting Avg.		Opponents' On Base Pct.		Starter Runs		Adjusted Starter Runs	
Hammaker-SF	2.25	Hammaker-SF	157	Ryan-Hou	.195	Hammaker-SF	.267	Denny-Phi	33.8	Soto-Cin	33.7
Denny-Phi	2.37	Denny-Phi	150	Soto-Cin	.208	Soto-Cin	.280	Soto-Cin	28.3	Denny-Phi	32.1
Welch-LA	2.65	Soto-Cin	141	Welch-LA	.222	Pena-LA	.285	Hammaker-SF	26.4	Hammaker-SF	24.6
Soto-Cin	2.70	Welch-LA	136	Hammaker-SF	.228	Welch-LA	.294	Welch-LA	22.2	Welch-LA	21.4
Pena-LA	2.75	Pena-LA	131	Pena-LA	.229	Denny-Phi	.294	Smith-Mon	19.6	McMurtry-Atl	19.8

Clutch Pitching Index		Relief Runs		Adjusted Relief Runs		Relief Ranking		Total Pitcher Index		Total Baseball Ranking	
Rhoden-Pit	119	Orosco-NY	26.3	Orosco-NY	26.3	Orosco-NY	52.2	Orosco-NY	6.0	Schmidt-Phi	6.4
Niekro-Atl	117	Smith-Chi	22.6	Smith-Chi	24.5	Smith-Chi	45.4	Smith-Chi	4.9	Orosco-NY	6.0
Reuss-LA	116	Tekulve-Pit	21.9	Tekulve-Pit	22.7	Tekulve-Pit	34.1	Howe-LA	3.8	Thon-Hou	5.9
Denny-Phi	115	Niedenfuer-LA	18.1	Niedenfuer-LA	17.8	Howe-LA	33.3	Tekulve-Pit	3.7	Raines-Mon	5.8
Knepper-Hou	111	Howe-LA	16.7	Howe-LA	16.4	Holland-Phi	23.8	Denny-Phi	3.5	Smith-Chi	4.9

TEAM	G	W	L	PCT	GB	R	OR	AB	H	2B	3B	HR	BB	SO	AVG	OBP	SLG	PRO	PRO+	BR	/A	PF	CHI	RC	SB	CS	SBA	SBR
EAST																												
BAL	162	98	64	.605		799	652	5546	1492	283	27	**168**	601	800	.269	**.343**	.421	.764	111	70	85	98	99	794	61	33	65	-2
DET	162	92	70	.568	6	789	679	5592	1530	283	53	156	508	831	.274	.338	.427	.765	112	67	88	97	99	799	93	53	64	-4
NY	162	91	71	.562	7	770	703	5631	1535	269	40	153	533	686	.273	.339	.416	.755	110	52	81	96	98	783	84	42	67	0
TOR	162	89	73	.549	9	795	726	5581	1546	268	**58**	167	510	810	**.277**	.341	**.436**	**.777**	106	**89**	39	106	97	**818**	131	72	65	-4
MIL	162	87	75	.537	11	764	708	5620	**1556**	281	57	132	475	665	**.277**	.336	.418	.754	**115**	44	**103**	92	98	774	101	49	67	1
BOS	162	78	84	.481	20	724	775	5590	1512	**287**	32	142	536	758	.270	.337	.409	.746	97	35	-20	107	94	749	30	26	54	-7
CLE	162	70	92	.432	28	704	785	5476	1451	249	31	86	**605**	691	.265	.341	.369	.710	92	-23	-50	104	100	687	109	71	61	-10
WEST																												
CHI	162	99	63	.611		**800**	650	5484	1439	270	42	157	527	888	.262	.332	.413	.745	100	26	-2	104	**107**	762	165	50	77	20
KC	163	79	83	.488	20	696	767	5598	1515	273	54	109	397	722	.271	.322	.397	.719	97	-31	-32	100	102	711	182	47	**79**	**26**
TEX	163	77	85	.475	22	639	**609**	5610	1429	242	33	106	442	767	.255	.312	.366	.678	88	-108	-96	98	104	633	119	60	66	0
OAK	162	74	88	.457	25	708	782	5516	1447	237	28	121	524	872	.262	.330	.381	.711	101	-34	7	94	102	694	**235**	98	71	12
CAL	162	70	92	.432	29	722	779	5640	1467	241	22	154	509	835	.260	.325	.393	.718	98	-29	-23	99	102	702	41	39	51	-11
MIN	162	70	92	.432	29	709	822	5601	1463	280	41	141	467	802	.261	.321	.401	.722	94	-23	-48	104	101	701	44	29	60	-4
SEA	162	60	102	.370	39	558	740	5336	1280	247	31	111	460	840	.240	.303	.360	.663	79	-135	-156	104	100	574	144	80	64	-5
TOT	1135					10177		77821	20662	3710	549	1903	7094	10967	.266	.330	.401	.731							1539	749	67	12

TEAM	CG	SH	SV	IP	H	H/G	HR	BB	SO	RAT	ERA	ERA+	OAV	OOB	PR	/A	PF	CPI	FA	E	DP	FW	PW	BW	SBW	DIF
EAST																										
BAL	36	**15**	38	1452¹	1451	9.0	130	452	774	11.9	3.63	109	.261	.318	70	53	97	104	.981	121	159	.5	5.3	8.5	-.3	3.0
DET	42	9	28	1451	1318	8.2	146	522	875	11.6	3.80	103	**.242**	.312	42	17	96	96	.980	125	142	.3	1.7	8.8	-.5	.7
NY	**47**	12	32	1456²	1449	9.0	116	455	892	11.9	3.86	101	.260	.318	33	6	96	95	.978	139	157	-.5	.6	8.1	-.0	1.9
TOR	43	8	32	1445¹	1434	8.9	145	517	835	12.4	4.12	104	.259	.327	-10	29	106	97	.981	115	148	.9	2.9	3.9	-.5	.8
MIL	35	10	43	1454	1513	9.4	133	491	689	12.6	4.02	93	.270	.332	6	-46	92	103	**.982**	113	162	**1.0**	-4.6	**10.3**	.0	-.7
BOS	29	7	42	1446¹	1572	9.8	158	493	767	13.0	4.34	100	.279	.340	-44	2	107	104	.979	130	168	.0	.2	-2.0	-.8	-.5
CLE	34	8	25	1441²	1531	9.6	120	529	794	13.1	4.43	96	.275	.342	-60	-32	104	97	.980	122	174	.5	-3.2	-5.0	-1.1	-2.2
WEST																										
CHI	35	12	48	1445¹	1355	8.4	128	**447**	877	**11.4**	3.67	114	.248	**.309**	63	83	103	94	.981	120	158	.6	8.3	-.2	1.9	7.4
KC	19	8	**49**	1437²	1535	9.6	133	471	593	12.7	4.25	96	.274	.333	-30	-28	100	99	.974	165	178	-1.9	-2.8	-3.2	**2.5**	3.4
TEX	43	11	32	1466²	1392	8.5	**97**	471	826	11.7	**3.31**	121	.252	.315	122	113	99	104	**.982**	113	151	**1.0**	11.3	-9.6	-.0	-6.6
OAK	22	12	33	1454¹	1462	9.0	135	626	719	13.1	4.34	89	.263	.340	-46	-79	95	97	.974	157	157	-1.5	-7.9	.7	1.1	.5
CAL	39	7	23	1474	1636	10.0	130	496	668	13.2	4.31	93	.284	.344	-41	-49	99	104	.977	154	**190**	-1.3	-4.9	-2.3	-1.2	-1.3
MIN	20	5	39	1437¹	1559	9.8	163	580	748	13.6	4.66	91	.280	.351	-96	-67	105	102	.980	121	170	.5	-6.7	-4.8	-.5	.4
SEA	25	9	39	1418¹	1455	9.2	145	544	**910**	12.9	4.12	103	.268	.339	-9	22	105	**105**	.978	136	159	-.3	2.2	-15.6	-.6	-6.7
TOT	469	133	503	20281		9.2				12.5	4.06		.266	.330					.979	1831	2273					

Runs		Hits		Doubles		Triples		Home Runs		Total Bases	
Ripken-Bal	121	Ripken-Bal	211	Ripken-Bal	47	Yount-Mil	10	Rice-Bos	39	Rice-Bos	344
Murray-Bal	115	Boggs-Bos	210	Boggs-Bos	44	Herndon-Det	9	Armas-Bos	36	Ripken-Bal	343
Cooper-Mil	106	Whitaker-Det	206	Yount-Mil	42	Griffin-Tor	9	Kittle-Chi	35	Cooper-Mil	336
Henderson-Oak	105	Cooper-Mil	203	Parrish-Det	42	Gibson-Det	9	Murray-Bal	33	Murray-Bal	313
Moseby-Tor	104	Rice-Bos	191							Winfield-NY	307

Runs Batted In		Runs Produced		Bases On Balls		Batting Average		On Base Percentage		Slugging Average	
Rice-Bos	126	Cooper-Mil	202	Henderson-Oak	103	Boggs-Bos	.361	Boggs-Bos	.449	Brett-KC	.563
Cooper-Mil	126	Ripken-Bal	196	Singleton-Bal	99	Carew-Cal	.339	Henderson-Oak	.415	Rice-Bos	.550
Winfield-NY	116	Murray-Bal	193	Boggs-Bos	92	Whitaker-Det	.320	Carew-Cal	.411	Murray-Bal	.538
Parrish-Det	114	Winfield-NY	183	Thornton-Cle	87	Trammell-Det	.319	Murray-Bal	.398	Fisk-Chi	.518
Murray-Bal	111	Rice-Bos	177	Murray-Bal	86	Ripken-Bal	.318	Singleton-Bal	.395	Ripken-Bal	.517

Production		Adjusted Production		Batter Runs		Adjusted Batter Runs		Clutch Hitting Index		Runs Created	
Brett-KC	.949	Murray-Bal	158	Boggs-Bos	50.6	Murray-Bal	47.3	Simmons-Mil	124	Boggs-Bos	130
Murray-Bal	.936	Brett-KC	157	Murray-Bal	44.9	Yount-Mil	43.6	Franco-Cle	122	Murray-Bal	127
Boggs-Bos	.935	Yount-Mil	155	Rice-Bos	38.7	Boggs-Bos	41.4	Murphy-Oak	116	Ripken-Bal	120
Rice-Bos	.914	Boggs-Bos	147	Ripken-Bal	37.1	Ripken-Bal	39.4	Cooper-Mil	116	Yount-Mil	115
Upshaw-Tor	.891	Ripken-Bal	145	Brett-KC	36.3	Brett-KC	36.1	Singleton-Bal	113	Whitaker-Det	114

Total Average		Stolen Bases		Stolen Base Average		Stolen Base Runs		Fielding Runs		Total Player Rating	
Henderson-Oak	1.048	Henderson-Oak	108	Wilson-KC	88.1	Henderson-Oak	21.0	Ward-Min	25.9	Ripken-Bal	6.7
Murray-Bal	.971	R.Law-Chi	77	R.Law-Chi	86.5	R.Law-Chi	15.9	T.Cruz-Sea-Bal	25.4	Henderson-Oak	5.7
Boggs-Bos	.964	Wilson-KC	59	Washington-KC	85.1	Wilson-KC	12.9	Dempsey-Bal	20.6	Yount-Mil	5.2
Brett-KC	.964	J.Cruz-Sea-Chi	57	Henderson-Oak	85.0	J.Cruz-Sea-Chi	9.9	Fletcher-Chi	18.2	Boggs-Bos	4.5
Yount-Mil	.897	Sample-Tex	44			Sample-Tex	8.4	Brunansky-Min	17.8	Grich-Cal	4.5

Wins		Win Percentage		Games		Complete Games		Shutouts		Saves	
Hoyt-Chi	24	Dotson-Chi	.759	Quisenberry-KC	69	Guidry-NY	21	Boddicker-Bal	5	Quisenberry-KC	45
Dotson-Chi	22	McGregor-Bal	.720	VandeBerg-Sea	68	Morris-Det	20	Stieb-Tor	4	Stanley-Bos	33
Guidry-NY	21	Hoyt-Chi	.706	Davis-Min	66	Stieb-Tor	14	Burns-Chi	4	Davis-Min	30
Morris-Det	20	Guidry-NY	.700	T.Martinez-Bal	65	Rawley-NY	13			Caudill-Sea	26
Petry-Det	19	Boddicker-Bal	.667	Stanley-Bos	64	McGregor-Bal	12			Ladd-Mil	25

Innings Pitched		Fewest Hits/Game		Fewest BB/Game		Strikeouts		Strikeouts/Game		Ratio	
Morris-Det	293.2	Boddicker-Bal	7.09	Hoyt-Chi	1.07	Morris-Det	232	Bannister-Chi	7.99	Hoyt-Chi	9.25
Stieb-Tor	278.0	Stieb-Tor	7.22	McGregor-Bal	1.56	Bannister-Chi	193	Morris-Det	7.11	Boddicker-Bal	9.70
Petry-Det	266.1	Conroy-Oak	7.82	John-Cal	1.88	Stieb-Tor	187	Righetti-NY	7.01	Morris-Det	10.51
Hoyt-Chi	260.2	Hough-Tex	7.82	Honeycutt-Tex	1.91	Righetti-NY	169	Conroy-Oak	6.21	Guidry-NY	10.57
McGregor-Bal	260.0	Dotson-Chi	7.84	Eckersley-Bos	1.99	Sutcliffe-Cle	160	Gott-Tor	6.16	Stieb-Tor	10.68

Earned Run Average		Adjusted ERA		Opponents' Batting Avg.		Opponents' On Base Pct.		Starter Runs		Adjusted Starter Runs	
Honeycutt-Tex	2.42	Honeycutt-Tex	165	Boddicker-Bal	.216	Hoyt-Chi	.262	Honeycutt-Tex	31.8	Stieb-Tor	38.8
Boddicker-Bal	2.77	Boddicker-Bal	143	Stieb-Tor	.219	Boddicker-Bal	.274	Stieb-Tor	31.4	Honeycutt-Tex	30.7
Stieb-Tor	3.04	Stieb-Tor	141	Conroy-Oak	.232	Morris-Det	.289	Boddicker-Bal	25.8	Dotson-Chi	25.6
Hough-Tex	3.18	Young-Sea	130	Bannister-Chi	.233	Guidry-NY	.291	McGregor-Bal	25.3	Boddicker-Bal	23.6
McGregor-Bal	3.18	Dotson-Chi	130	Morris-Det	.233	Stieb-Tor	.293	Hough-Tex	24.7	Hough-Tex	23.1

Clutch Pitching Index		Relief Runs		Adjusted Relief Runs		Relief Ranking		Total Pitcher Index		Total Baseball Ranking	
Honeycutt-Tex	139	Quisenberry-KC	32.7	Quisenberry-KC	32.9	Quisenberry-KC	41.0	Quisenberry-KC	4.4	Ripken-Bal	6.7
Zahn-Cal	118	T.Martinez-Bal	19.6	Stanley-Bos	24.2	Stanley-Bos	39.4	Honeycutt-Tex	4.3	Henderson-Oak	5.7
Hurst-Bos	113	Stanley-Bos	19.6	T.Martinez-Bal	18.4	Gossage-NY	38.1	Stieb-Tor	3.9	Yount-Mil	5.2
Dotson-Chi	113	Gossage-NY	17.4	Barojas-Chi	16.6	T.Martinez-Bal	27.6	Stanley-Bos	3.9	Boggs-Bos	4.5
McGregor-Bal	113	Lopez-Det	16.0	Gossage-NY	15.8	Lopez-Det	23.6	Gossage-NY	3.8	Grich-Cal	4.5

1984 National League

TEAM	G	W	L	PCT	GB	R	OR	AB	H	2B	3B	HR	BB	SO	AVG	OBP	SLG	PRO	PRO+	BR	/A	PF	CHI	RC	SB	CS	SBA	SBR
EAST																												
CHI	161	96	65	.596		**762**	658	5437	1415	240	47	136	**567**	967	.260	.333	.397	.730	102	78	12	109	104	729	154	66	70	7
NY	162	90	72	.556	6.5	652	676	5438	1400	235	25	107	500	1001	.257	.322	.369	.691	102	1	11	99	100	645	149	54	73	12
STL	162	84	78	.519	12.5	652	645	5433	1369	225	44	75	516	924	.252	.319	.351	.670	97	-35	-19	99	106	623	220	71	76	23
PHI	162	81	81	.500	15.5	720	690	5614	1494	**248**	51	**147**	555	1084	**.266**	**.335**	**.407**	**.742**	112	102	90	102	93	**766**	186	60	76	20
MON	161	78	83	.484	18	593	585	5439	1367	242	36	96	470	**782**	.251	.314	.362	.676	101	-32	-4	96	96	630	131	38	**78**	17
PIT	162	75	87	.463	21.5	615	**567**	5537	1412	237	33	98	438	841	.255	.312	.363	.675	95	-37	-37	100	99	611	96	62	61	-8
WEST																												
SD	162	92	70	.568		686	634	5504	1425	207	42	109	472	810	.259	.320	.371	.691	100	-1	0	100	105	645	152	68	69	5
HOU	162	80	82	.494	12	693	630	5548	1465	222	**67**	79	494	837	.264	.326	.371	.697	110	14	63	93	102	679	105	61	63	-5
ATL	162	80	82	.494	12	632	655	5422	1338	234	27	111	555	896	.247	.319	.361	.680	90	-18	-64	107	99	623	140	85	62	-9
LA	162	79	83	.488	13	580	600	5399	1316	213	23	102	488	829	.244	.308	.348	.656	91	-68	-62	99	100	573	109	69	61	-9
CIN	162	70	92	.432	22	627	747	5498	1342	238	30	106	566	978	.244	.316	.356	.672	91	-34	-62	105	100	635	160	63	72	10
SF	162	66	96	.407	26	682	807	5650	**1499**	229	26	112	528	980	.265	.330	.375	.705	108	31	54	97	97	686	126	76	62	-8
TOT	971					7894		65919	16842	2770	451	1278	6149	10929	.255	.321	.369	.691							1728	773	69	55

TEAM	CG	SH	SV	IP	H	H/G	HR	BB	SO	RAT	ERA	ERA+	OAV	OOB	PR	/A	PF	CPI	FA	E	DP	FW	PW	BW	SBW	DIF
EAST																										
CHI	19	8	50	1434	1458	9.2	99	**442**	879	12.1	3.75	104	.267	.324	-26	25	109	99	.981	121	137	1.1	2.6	1.3	.3	10.3
NY	12	15	50	1442²	1371	8.6	104	573	1028	12.3	3.60	98	.251	.326	-2	-10	99	101	.979	129	154	.7	-1.1	1.2	.8	7.4
STL	19	12	**51**	1449	1427	8.9	94	494	808	12.1	3.58	97	.262	.326	1	-18	97	103	**.982**	118	**184**	**1.3**	-1.9	-2.0	**1.9**	3.6
PHI	11	6	35	1458¹	1416	8.7	101	448	904	11.6	3.62	100	.253	**.310**	-5	2	101	92	.975	161	112	-1.2	.2	**9.5**	1.6	-10.1
MON	19	10	48	1431	1333	8.4	114	474	861	11.5	3.31	103	.249	.312	45	18	95	103	.978	132	147	.4	1.9	-.4	1.3	-5.7
PIT	27	13	34	1470	1344	**8.2**	102	502	995	**11.4**	**3.11**	**116**	.246	.310	78	80	100	**105**	.980	128	142	.7	**8.4**	-3.9	-1.3	-9.9
WEST																										
SD	13	**17**	44	1460¹	**1327**	**8.2**	122	563	812	11.8	3.48	102	**.244**	.317	17	14	99	99	.978	138	144	.1	1.5	.0	.0	9.3
HOU	24	13	29	1449¹	1350	8.4	91	502	950	11.3	3.32	100	.248	.314	44	0	93	99	.979	133	160	.4	.0	6.6	-1.0	-7.1
ATL	17	7	49	1447	1401	8.7	122	525	859	12.1	3.57	108	.257	.324	3	46	107	**105**	.978	139	153	.0	4.8	-6.7	-1.4	2.2
LA	**39**	16	27	1460²	1381	8.5	76	499	**1033**	11.7	3.17	111	.250	.314	68	59	98	102	.975	163	146	-1.3	6.2	-6.5	-1.4	1.1
CIN	25	6	25	1461¹	1445	8.9	128	578	946	12.6	4.16	91	.259	.330	-92	-62	105	94	.977	139	116	.0	-6.5	-6.5	.6	1.4
SF	9	7	38	1461	**1589**	9.8	125	549	854	13.4	4.39	80	.278	.345	-131	-143	98	99	.973	173	134	-1.9	-15.0	5.7	-1.3	-2.4
TOT	234	130	480	17424²		8.7				12.0	3.59		.255	.321					.978	1674	1729					

Runs		Hits		Doubles		Triples		Home Runs		Total Bases	
Sandberg-Chi	114	Gwynn-SD	213	Ray-Pit	38	Sandberg-Chi	19	Schmidt-Phi	36	Murphy-Atl	332
Wiggins-SD	106	Sandberg-Chi	200	Raines-Mon	38	Samuel-Phi	19	Murphy-Atl	36	Sandberg-Chi	331
Raines-Mon	106	Raines-Mon	192	Sandberg-Chi	36	Cruz-Hou	13	Carter-Mon	27	Samuel-Phi	310
Samuel-Phi	105	Samuel-Phi	191	Samuel-Phi	36			Strawberry-NY	26	Carter-Mon	290
Matthews-Chi	101	Cruz-Hou	187					Cey-Chi	25	Schmidt-Phi	283

Runs Batted In		Runs Produced		Bases On Balls		Batting Average		On Base Percentage		Slugging Average	
Schmidt-Phi	106	Sandberg-Chi	179	Matthews-Chi	103	Gwynn-SD	.351	Matthews-Chi	.417	Murphy-Atl	.547
Carter-Mon	106	Cruz-Hou	179	Hernandez-NY	97	Lacy-Pit	.321	Hernandez-NY	.415	Schmidt-Phi	.536
Murphy-Atl	100	Matthews-Chi	169	Schmidt-Phi	92	C.Davis-SF	.315	Gwynn-SD	.411	Sandberg-Chi	.520
Strawberry-NY	97	Schmidt-Phi	163	Thompson-Pit	87	Sandberg-Chi	.314	Raines-Mon	.395	C.Davis-SF	.507
Cey-Chi	97	Hernandez-NY	162	Raines-Mon	87	Ray-Pit	.312	Schmidt-Phi	.388	Durham-Chi	.505

Production		Adjusted Production		Batter Runs		Adjusted Batter Runs		Clutch Hitting Index		Runs Created	
Schmidt-Phi	.924	Schmidt-Phi	155	Murphy-Atl	43.8	Schmidt-Phi	39.5	Mumphrey-Hou	132	Sandberg-Chi	126
Murphy-Atl	.920	C.Davis-SF	149	Schmidt-Phi	41.2	Cruz-Hou	38.4	Davis-Chi	125	Raines-Mon	124
Sandberg-Chi	.889	Cruz-Hou	148	Sandberg-Chi	37.5	Hernandez-NY	37.0	Garvey-SD	125	Murphy-Atl	123
Durham-Chi	.877	Murphy-Atl	145	Hernandez-NY	35.5	Murphy-Atl	35.5	Cey-Chi	120	Cruz-Hou	111
C.Davis-SF	.876	Hernandez-NY	145	Gwynn-SD	33.9	Raines-Mon	35.4	Concepcion-Cin	118	Carter-Mon	108

Total Average		Stolen Bases		Stolen Base Average		Stolen Base Runs		Fielding Runs		Total Player Rating	
Raines-Mon	.953	Raines-Mon	75	Dilone-Mon	93.1	Raines-Mon	16.5	O.Smith-StL	26.2	Sandberg-Chi	6.4
Murphy-Atl	.942	Samuel-Phi	72	Raines-Mon	88.2	Samuel-Phi	12.6	Sandberg-Chi	23.3	Raines-Mon	5.8
Schmidt-Phi	.933	Wiggins-SD	70	Cedeno-Cin	86.4	Wilson-NY	8.4	Garner-Hou	23.1	Cruz-Hou	4.9
Sandberg-Chi	.913	L.Smith-StL	50	VanSlyke-StL	84.8	Wiggins-SD	8.4	Martinez-SD	20.6	Schmidt-Phi	4.8
Matthews-Chi	.888			Stone-Phi	84.4	Redus-Cin	7.8	Hubbard-Atl	19.6	Hernandez-NY	4.6

Wins		Win Percentage		Games		Complete Games		Shutouts		Saves	
Andujar-StL	20	Sutcliffe-Chi	.941	Power-Cin	78	Soto-Cin	13	Pena-LA	4	Sutter-StL	45
Soto-Cin	18	Soto-Cin	.720	Lavelle-SF	77	Valenzuela-LA	12	Hershiser-LA	4	Smith-Chi	33
Gooden-NY	17	Gooden-NY	.654	Minton-SF	74	Andujar-StL	12	Andujar-StL	4	Orosco-NY	31
Sutcliffe-Chi	16	Show-SD	.625	Tekulve-Pit	72	Knepper-Hou	11			Holland-Phi	29
Niekro-Hou	16			Sutter-StL	71	Mahler-Atl	9			Gossage-SD	25

Innings Pitched		Fewest Hits/Game		Fewest BB/Game		Strikeouts		Strikeouts/Game		Ratio	
Andujar-StL	261.1	Gooden-NY	6.65	Gullickson-Mon	1.47	Gooden-NY	276	Gooden-NY	11.39	Gooden-NY	9.74
Valenzuela-LA	261.0	Soto-Cin	6.86	Candelaria-Pit	1.65	Valenzuela-LA	240	Ryan-Hou	9.65	Hershiser-LA	10.15
Niekro-Hou	248.1	DeLeon-Pit	6.88	Whitson-SD	2.00	Ryan-Hou	197	Valenzuela-LA	8.28	Andujar-StL	10.16
Rhoden-Pit	238.1	Ryan-Hou	7.01	Pena-LA	2.08	Soto-Cin	185	Berenyi-Cin-NY	7.27	Soto-Cin	10.35
Soto-Cin	237.1	Andujar-StL	7.51	Knepper-Hou	2.12	Carlton-Phi	163	DeLeon-Pit	7.16	Candelaria-Pit	10.39

Earned Run Average		Adjusted ERA		Opponents' Batting Avg.		Opponents' On Base Pct.		Starter Runs		Adjusted Starter Runs	
Pena-LA	2.48	Pena-LA	142	Gooden-NY	.202	Gooden-NY	.270	Pena-LA	24.5	Rhoden-Pit	23.3
Gooden-NY	2.60	Gooden-NY	136	Soto-Cin	.209	Hershiser-LA	.279	Gooden-NY	23.9	Pena-LA	23.2
Hershiser-LA	2.66	Hershiser-LA	133	Ryan-Hou	.211	Soto-Cin	.286	Rhoden-Pit	23.0	Gooden-NY	22.6
Rhoden-Pit	2.72	Rhoden-Pit	132	DeLeon-Pit	.214	Andujar-StL	.286	Hershiser-LA	19.6	Sutcliffe-Chi	20.3
Candelaria-Pit	2.72	Candelaria-Pit	132	Hershiser-LA	.225	Ryan-Hou	.288	Denny-Phi	19.5	Denny-Phi	20.3

Clutch Pitching Index		Relief Runs		Adjusted Relief Runs		Relief Ranking		Total Pitcher Index		Total Baseball Ranking	
McWilliams-Pit	130	Sutter-StL	27.9	Sutter-StL	26.3	Sutter-StL	44.8	Sutter-StL	4.9	Sandberg-Chi	6.4
Terrell-NY	124	Dawley-Hou	18.1	Lefferts-SD	16.9	Bedrosian-Atl	26.4	Rhoden-Pit	3.5	Raines-Mon	5.8
Candelaria-Pit	122	Lefferts-SD	17.1	Dawley-Hou	15.1	Dawley-Hou	22.6	Gooden-NY	2.9	Cruz-Hou	4.9
Honeycutt-LA	117	Sisk-NY	13.0	Bedrosian-Atl	13.8	Orosco-NY	22.5	Sutcliffe-Chi	2.8	Sutter-StL	4.9
Trout-Chi	117	Andersen-Phi	12.1	Andersen-Phi	12.6	Power-Cin	18.0	Bedrosian-Atl	2.7	Schmidt-Phi	4.8

TEAM	G	W	L	PCT	GB	R	OR	AB	H	2B	3B	HR	BB	SO	AVG	OBP	SLG	PRO	PRO+	BR	/A	PF	CHI	RC	SB	CS	SBA	SBR
EAST																												
DET	162	104	58	.642		829	643	5644	1529	254	46	187	602	941	.271	.345	.432	.777	114	103	109	99	99	843	106	68	61	-9
TOR	163	89	73	.549	15	750	696	5687	1555	275	68	143	460	816	.273	.333	.421	.754	103	52	24	104	96	808	193	67	74	18
NY	162	87	75	.537	17	758	679	5661	1560	275	32	130	534	673	.276	.342	.404	.746	110	47	78	96	97	773	62	38	62	-4
BOS	162	86	76	.531	18	810	764	5648	1598	259	45	181	500	842	.283	.343	.441	.784	110	113	75	105	97	832	38	25	60	-4
BAL	162	85	77	.525	19	681	667	5456	1374	234	23	160	620	884	.252	.331	.391	.722	101	-4	12	98	96	705	51	36	59	-6
CLE	163	75	87	.463	29	761	764	5643	1498	222	39	123	600	815	.265	.339	.384	.723	98	4	-9	102	103	732	126	77	62	-8
MIL	161	67	94	.416	36.5	641	734	5511	1446	232	36	96	432	673	.262	.319	.370	.689	94	-75	-50	96	103	621	52	57	48	-19
WEST																												
KC	162	84	78	.519		673	686	5543	1487	269	52	117	400	832	.268	.320	.399	.719	97	-23	-28	101	99	685	106	64	62	-7
CAL	162	81	81	.500	3	696	697	5470	1363	211	30	150	556	928	.249	.322	.381	.703	95	-46	-41	99	105	663	80	51	61	-7
MIN	162	81	81	.500	3	673	675	5562	1473	259	33	114	437	735	.265	.321	.385	.706	90	-45	-75	105	102	669	39	30	57	-6
OAK	162	77	85	.475	7	738	794	5457	1415	257	29	158	568	871	.259	.332	.404	.736	109	18	67	93	101	732	145	64	69	5
SEA	162	74	88	.457	10	682	774	5546	1429	244	34	129	519	871	.258	.326	.384	.710	97	-32	-23	99	100	700	116	62	65	-2
CHI	162	74	88	.457	10	679	736	5513	1360	225	38	172	523	883	.247	.316	.395	.711	91	-37	-67	105	101	690	109	49	69	3
TEX	161	69	92	.429	14.5	656	714	5569	1452	227	29	120	420	807	.261	.315	.377	.692	88	-75	-95	103	104	643	81	50	62	-6
TOT	1134					10027		77910	20593	3443	534	1980	7171	11571	.264	.329	.398	.727							1304	738	64	-52

TEAM	CG	SH	SV	IP	H	H/G	HR	BB	SO	RAT	ERA	ERA+	OAV	OOB	PR	/A	PF	CPI	FA	E	DP	FW	PW	BW	SBW	DIF
EAST																										
DET	19	8	51	1464	1358	8.3	130	489	914	11.5	3.49	112	.246	.311	81	70	98	98	.979	127	162	.3	7.0	11.0	-.5	5.2
TOR	34	10	33	1464	1433	8.8	140	528	875	12.3	3.86	106	.257	.325	21	38	103	99	.980	123	166	.6	3.8	2.4	2.2	-1.0
NY	15	12	43	1465¹	1485	9.1	120	518	992	12.4	3.78	100	.264	.328	35	2	95	102	.977	142	177	-.5	.2	7.8	-.0	-1.5
BOS	40	12	32	1442	1524	9.5	141	517	927	12.9	4.18	100	.270	.334	-29	-2	104	99	.977	143	128	-.6	-.2	7.5	-.0	-1.7
BAL	48	13	32	1439¹	1393	8.7	137	512	714	12.1	3.71	104	.256	.323	44	25	97	102	.981	123	166	.5	2.5	1.2	-.2	-.0
CLE	21	7	35	1467²	1523	9.3	141	545	803	12.8	4.26	96	.269	.336	-43	-27	102	98	.977	146	163	-.7	-2.7	-.9	-.4	-1.2
MIL	13	7	41	1433	1532	9.6	137	480	785	12.8	4.06	91	.274	.334	-10	-33	96	103	.978	136	156	-.3	-3.3	-5.0	-1.5	-3.4
WEST																										
KC	18	9	50	1444	1426	8.9	136	433	724	11.8	3.92	103	.258	.315	11	17	101	93	.979	131	157	.0	1.7	-2.8	-.3	4.4
CAL	36	12	26	1458	1526	9.4	143	474	754	12.5	3.96	100	.271	.331	6	2	99	104	.980	128	170	.2	.2	-4.1	-.3	4.0
MIN	32	9	38	1437²	1429	8.9	159	463	713	12.1	3.85	109	.260	.321	23	56	105	101	.980	120	134	.7	5.6	-7.5	-.2	1.5
OAK	15	6	44	1444	1554	9.8	155	592	695	13.7	4.48	84	.278	.351	-78	-117	94	103	.975	146	159	-.8	-11.8	6.7	.9	.9
SEA	26	4	35	1442	1497	9.3	138	619	972	13.5	4.31	93	.270	.348	-50	-51	100	102	.979	128	143	.2	-5.1	-2.3	-.2	.0
CHI	43	9	32	1454¹	1416	8.8	155	483	840	12.0	4.13	101	.256	.320	-23	4	104	93	.981	122	160	.6	.4	-6.7	.7	-1.9
TEX	38	6	21	1438²	1443	9.0	148	518	863	12.5	3.91	106	.260	.327	13	38	104	101	.977	138	138	-.4	3.8	-9.6	-.2	-5.2
TOT	398	124	513	20280		9.1				12.5	3.99		.264	.329					.979	1853	2179					

Runs
Evans-Bos ... 121
Henderson-Oak ... 113
Boggs-Bos ... 109
Butler-Cle ... 108
Armas-Bos ... 107

Hits
Mattingly-NY ... 207
Boggs-Bos ... 203
Ripken-Bal ... 195
Winfield-NY ... 193

Doubles
Mattingly-NY ... 44
Parrish-Tex ... 42
Bell-Tor ... 39
Ripken-Bal ... 37
Evans-Bos ... 37

Triples
Moseby-Tor ... 15
Collins-Tor ... 15
Gibson-Det ... 10
Baines-Chi ... 10

Home Runs
Armas-Bos ... 43
Kingman-Oak ... 35
Thornton-Cle ... 33
Parrish-Det ... 33
Murphy-Oak ... 33

Total Bases
Armas-Bos ... 339
Evans-Bos ... 335
Ripken-Bal ... 327
Mattingly-NY ... 324
Easler-Bos ... 310

Runs Batted In
Armas-Bos ... 123
Rice-Bos ... 122
Kingman-Oak ... 118
Davis-Sea ... 116

Runs Produced
Evans-Bos ... 193
Rice-Bos ... 192
Winfield-NY ... 187
Armas-Bos ... 187

Bases On Balls
Murray-Bal ... 107
Davis-Sea ... 97
Evans-Bos ... 96
Thornton-Cle ... 91
Boggs-Bos ... 89

Batting Average
Mattingly-NY ... .343
Winfield-NY ... .340
Boggs-Bos ... .325
Bell-Tex ... .315
Trammell-Det ... .314

On Base Percentage
Murray-Bal ... .415
Boggs-Bos ... .409
Henderson-Oak ... .401
Winfield-NY ... .397
Davis-Sea ... .395

Slugging Average
Baines-Chi ... .541
Mattingly-NY ... .537
Evans-Bos ... .532
Armas-Bos ... .531
Hrbek-Min ... .522

Production
Evans-Bos ... .924
Mattingly-NY ... .923
Murray-Bal ... .923
Winfield-NY ... .912
Hrbek-Min ... .909

Adjusted Production
Mattingly-NY ... 159
Murray-Bal ... 157
Winfield-NY ... 156
Henderson-Oak ... 147
Davis-Sea ... 147

Batter Runs
Murray-Bal ... 46.8
Evans-Bos ... 46.6
Mattingly-NY ... 41.3
Winfield-NY ... 38.4
Davis-Sea ... 37.5

Adjusted Batter Runs
Murray-Bal ... 49.7
Mattingly-NY ... 46.0
Winfield-NY ... 42.8
Evans-Bos ... 40.6
Ripken-Bal ... 39.3

Clutch Hitting Index
Franco-Cle ... 132
Davis-Sea ... 127
Rice-Bos ... 124
Simmons-Mil ... 121
Tabler-Cle ... 116

Runs Created
Evans-Bos ... 132
Murray-Bal ... 130
Ripken-Bal ... 122
Mattingly-NY ... 120
Easler-Bos ... 118

Total Average
Murray-Bal ... .993
Henderson-Oak ... .971
Evans-Bos ... .942
Davis-Sea ... .928
Gibson-Det ... .926

Stolen Bases
Henderson-Oak ... 66
Collins-Tor ... 60
Butler-Cle ... 52
Pettis-Cal ... 48
Wilson-KC ... 47

Stolen Base Average
Wilson-KC ... 90.4
Tolleson-Tex ... 84.6
Perconte-Sea ... 82.9
Moseby-Tor ... 81.3
Collins-Tor ... 81.1

Stolen Base Runs
Wilson-KC ... 11.1
Collins-Tor ... 9.6
Henderson-Oak ... 9.0
Garcia-Tor ... 6.6
Moseby-Tor ... 6.3

Fielding Runs
Ripken-Bal ... 38.8
Puckett-Min ... 30.1
Cruz-Chi ... 22.1
Boggs-Bos ... 21.0
Murphy-Oak ... 21.0

Total Player Rating
Ripken-Bal ... 9.1
Yount-Mil ... 5.0
Murray-Bal ... 4.9
Mattingly-NY ... 4.9
Henderson-Oak ... 4.7

Wins
Boddicker-Bal ... 20
Morris-Det ... 19
Blyleven-Cle ... 19
Viola-Min ... 18
Petry-Det ... 18

Win Percentage
Alexander-Tor ... .739
Blyleven-Cle ... .731
Petry-Det ... .692
Wilcox-Det ... .680

Games
Hernandez-Det ... 80
Quisenberry-KC ... 72
Lopez-Det ... 71
Camacho-Cle ... 69
Caudill-Oak ... 68

Complete Games
Hough-Tex ... 17
Boddicker-Bal ... 16
Dotson-Chi ... 14
Blyleven-Cle ... 12
Beattie-Sea ... 12

Shutouts
Zahn-Cal ... 5
Ojeda-Bos ... 5

Saves
Quisenberry-KC ... 44
Caudill-Oak ... 36
Hernandez-Det ... 32
Righetti-NY ... 31
Davis-Min ... 29

Innings Pitched
Stieb-Tor ... 267.0
Hough-Tex ... 266.0
Alexander-Tor ... 261.2
Boddicker-Bal ... 261.1
Viola-Min ... 257.2

Fewest Hits/Game
Stieb-Tor ... 7.25
Blyleven-Cle ... 7.49
Boddicker-Bal ... 7.51
Langston-Sea ... 7.52
Mason-Tex ... 7.76

Fewest BB/Game
Hoyt-Chi ... 1.64
Smithson-Min ... 1.93
Guidry-NY ... 2.02
Alexander-Tor ... 2.03
Haas-Mil ... 2.04

Strikeouts
Langston-Sea ... 204
Stieb-Tor ... 198
Witt-Cal ... 196
Blyleven-Cle ... 170
Hough-Tex ... 164

Strikeouts/Game
Langston-Sea ... 8.16
Witt-Cal ... 7.15
Moore-Sea ... 6.71
Stieb-Tor ... 6.67
Berenguer-Det ... 6.31

Ratio
Black-KC ... 10.30
Alexander-Tor ... 10.32
Mason-Tex ... 10.35
Blyleven-Cle ... 10.43
Boddicker-Bal ... 10.47

Earned Run Average
Boddicker-Bal ... 2.79
Stieb-Tor ... 2.83
Blyleven-Cle ... 2.87
Niekro-NY ... 3.09
Zahn-Cal ... 3.12

Adjusted ERA
Stieb-Tor ... 145
Blyleven-Cle ... 143
Boddicker-Bal ... 139
Alexander-Tor ... 131
Viola-Min ... 131

Opponents' Batting Avg.
Stieb-Tor ... .221
Blyleven-Cle ... .224
Boddicker-Bal ... .228
Langston-Sea ... .230
Berenguer-Det ... .232

Opponents' On Base Pct.
Black-KC ... .283
Blyleven-Cle ... .287
Alexander-Tor ... .287
Mason-Tex ... .288
Seaver-Chi ... .290

Starter Runs
Boddicker-Bal ... 34.9
Stieb-Tor ... 34.4
Blyleven-Cle ... 30.7
Alexander-Tor ... 25.0
Black-KC ... 25.0

Adjusted Starter Runs
Stieb-Tor ... 37.5
Blyleven-Cle ... 33.3
Boddicker-Bal ... 31.4
Viola-Min ... 28.3
Alexander-Tor ... 28.1

Clutch Pitching Index
Niekro-NY ... 125
Fontenot-NY ... 119
Cocanower-Mil ... 114
Hurst-Bos ... 113
Burris-Oak ... 112

Relief Runs
Hernandez-Det ... 32.2
Quisenberry-KC ... 19.4
Righetti-NY ... 17.7
Corbett-Cal ... 17.7
Camacho-Cle ... 17.3

Adjusted Relief Runs
Hernandez-Det ... 31.1
Quisenberry-KC ... 19.9
Camacho-Cle ... 18.4
Corbett-Cal ... 17.5
Righetti-NY ... 15.6

Relief Ranking
Hernandez-Det ... 39.9
Camacho-Cle ... 32.7
Quisenberry-KC ... 27.7
Righetti-NY ... 27.3
Caudill-Oak ... 25.9

Total Pitcher Index
Boddicker-Bal ... 4.2
Hernandez-Det ... 4.1
Blyleven-Cle ... 3.4
Camacho-Cle ... 3.3
Stieb-Tor ... 3.3

Total Baseball Ranking
Ripken-Bal ... 9.1
Yount-Mil ... 5.0
Murray-Bal ... 4.9
Mattingly-NY ... 4.9
Henderson-Oak ... 4.7

1985 National League

TEAM	G	W	L	PCT	GB	R	OR	AB	H	2B	3B	HR	BB	SO	AVG	OBP	SLG	PRO	PRO+	BR	/A	PF	CHI	RC	SB	CS	SBA	SBR
EAST																												
STL	162	101	61	.623		**747**	572	5467	1446	245	**59**	87	**586**	853	**.264**	.338	.379	**.717**	108	52	58	99	**105**	733	314	96	77	**37**
NY	162	98	64	.605	3	695	**568**	5549	1425	239	35	134	546	872	.257	.326	.385	.711	108	31	49	98	99	691	117	53	69	3
MON	161	84	77	.522	16.5	633	636	5429	1342	242	49	118	490	880	.247	.313	.375	.688	104	-19	17	94	101	633	169	77	69	5
CHI	162	77	84	.478	23.5	686	729	5492	1397	239	28	**150**	562	937	.254	.326	**.390**	.716	95	40	-37	111	98	710	182	49	**79**	25
PHI	162	75	87	.463	26	667	673	5477	1343	238	47	141	527	1095	.245	.314	.383	.697	97	0	-18	103	102	657	122	51	71	6
PIT	161	57	104	.354	43.5	568	708	5436	1340	251	28	80	514	842	.247	.313	.347	.660	91	-64	-58	99	97	587	110	60	65	-3
WEST																												
LA	162	95	67	.586		682	579	5502	1434	226	28	129	539	846	.261	.330	.382	.712	108	38	**59**	97	97	704	136	58	70	6
CIN	162	89	72	.553	5.5	677	666	5431	1385	249	34	114	576	856	.255	.329	.376	.705	98	26	-8	105	99	672	159	70	69	6
SD	162	83	79	.512	12	650	622	5507	1405	241	28	109	513	**809**	.255	.321	.368	.689	101	-9	1	99	100	645	60	39	61	-5
HOU	162	83	79	.512	12	706	691	5582	**1457**	**261**	42	121	477	873	.261	.322	.368	.710	107	25	45	97	103	684	95	56	63	-5
ATL	162	66	96	.407	29	632	781	5526	1359	213	28	126	553	849	.246	.317	.363	.680	91	-28	-66	106	99	622	72	52	58	-10
SF	162	62	100	.383	33	556	674	5420	1263	217	31	115	488	962	.233	.301	.348	.649	91	-93	-66	95	100	564	99	55	64	-3
TOT	971					7899		65818	16596	2861	437	1424	6373	10674	.252	.321	.374	.695							1636	716	70	61

TEAM	CG	SH	SV	IP	H	H/G	HR	BB	SO	RAT	ERA	ERA+	OAV	OOB	PR	/A	PF	CPI	FA	E	DP	FW	PW	BW	SBW	DIF
EAST																										
STL	**37**	20	44	1464	1343	8.3	**98**	453	798	11.2	3.10	114	.246	.307	79	70	98	102	**.983**	**108**	166	**1.7**	7.4	6.1	**3.4**	1.5
NY	32	19	37	1488	1306	**7.9**	111	515	**1039**	11.1	3.11	111	.237	.304	80	57	96	99	.982	115	138	1.3	6.0	5.2	-.2	4.8
MON	13	13	**53**	1457	1346	8.3	99	509	870	11.6	3.55	96	.247	.313	7	-25	94	93	.981	121	152	.8	-2.6	1.8	-.0	3.5
CHI	20	8	42	1442¹	1492	9.3	156	519	820	12.7	4.16	96	.271	.336	-91	-27	111	100	.979	134	150	.1	-2.8	-3.9	2.1	1.0
PHI	24	9	30	1447	1424	8.9	115	596	899	12.7	3.68	100	.259	.334	-15	0	103	105	.978	139	142	-.2	.0	-1.9	.0	-4.0
PIT	15	6	29	1445¹	1406	8.8	107	584	962	12.6	3.97	90	.255	.330	-61	-64	100	94	.979	133	127	.1	-6.7	-6.1	-.9	-9.9
WEST																										
LA	37	21	36	1465	**1280**	**7.9**	102	462	979	**10.8**	**2.96**	117	**.234**	**.296**	102	84	97	98	.974	166	131	-1.8	**8.8**	6.2	.0	.7
CIN	24	11	45	1451¹	1347	8.4	131	535	910	11.8	3.71	102	.248	.317	-19	12	105	96	.980	122	142	.8	1.3	-.8	.0	7.1
SD	26	19	44	1451¹	1399	8.7	127	**443**	727	11.6	3.40	104	.257	.316	30	21	98	**106**	.980	124	158	.7	2.2	-1.1		.0
HOU	17	9	42	1458	1393	8.6	119	543	909	12.1	3.66	95	.254	.324	-11	-32	96	100	.976	152	159	-1.0	-3.4	4.7	-1.1	2.7
ATL	9	9	29	1457¹	1512	9.3	134	642	776	13.5	4.19	92	.271	.349	-98	-56	107	104	.976	159	**197**	-1.4	-5.9	-6.9	-1.6	.8
SF	13	5	24	1448	1348	8.4	125	572	985	12.1	3.61	95	.247	.321	-3	-28	96	99	.976	148	134	-.7	-2.9	-6.9	-.9	-7.5
TOT	267	149	455	17474²		8.5				12.0	3.59		.252	.321					.979	1621	1796					

Runs
Murphy-Atl 118
Raines-Mon 115
McGee-StL 114
Sandberg-Chi 113
Coleman-StL 107

Hits
McGee-StL 216
Parker-Cin 198
Gwynn-SD 197
Sandberg-Chi 186
Murphy-Atl 185

Doubles
Parker-Cin 42
Wilson-Phi 39
Herr-StL 38
Wallach-Mon 36

Triples
McGee-StL 18
Samuel-Phi 13
Raines-Mon 13
Garner-Hou 10
Coleman-StL 10

Home Runs
Murphy-Atl 37
Parker-Cin 34
Schmidt-Phi 33
Guerrero-LA 33
Carter-NY 32

Total Bases
Parker-Cin 350
Murphy-Atl 332
McGee-StL 308
Sandberg-Chi 307
Schmidt-Phi 292

Runs Batted In
Parker-Cin 125
Murphy-Atl 111
Herr-StL 110
Moreland-Chi 106
Wilson-Phi 102

Runs Produced
Herr-StL 199
Murphy-Atl 192
McGee-StL 186
Parker-Cin 179
Sandberg-Chi 170

Bases On Balls
Murphy-Atl 90
Schmidt-Phi 87
Martinez-SD 87
Rose-Cin 86
Law-Mon 86

Batting Average
McGee-StL .... .353
Guerrero-LA ...... .320
Raines-Mon .... .320
Gwynn-SD .... .317
Parker-Cin .... .312

On Base Percentage
Guerrero-LA ...... .425
Scioscia-LA ...... .409
Raines-Mon .... .407
Rose-Cin .... .398
Clark-StL .... .397

Slugging Average
Guerrero-LA ...... .577
Parker-Cin .... .551
Murphy-Atl .... .539
Schmidt-Phi ...... .532
Marshall-LA ...... .515

Production
Guerrero-LA 1.002
Murphy-Atl .... .929
Parker-Cin .... .918
Schmidt-Phi ...... .911
Clark-StL .... .899

Adjusted Production
Guerrero-LA 183
Raines-Mon 155
Clark-StL 151
McGee-StL 148
Murphy-Atl 148

Batter Runs
Guerrero-LA 52.8
Murphy-Atl 47.6
Parker-Cin 42.5
Schmidt-Phi 38.5
Raines-Mon 37.5

Adjusted Batter Runs
Guerrero-LA 56.3
Raines-Mon 43.9
Murphy-Atl 40.4
McGee-StL 37.6
Parker-Cin 36.8

Clutch Hitting Index
Herr-StL 161
Pendleton-StL 139
Moreland-Chi 128
Wilson-Phi 128
Brooks-Mon 125

Runs Created
Murphy-Atl 131
Raines-Mon 124
McGee-StL 123
Guerrero-LA 121
Sandberg-Chi 117

Total Average
Guerrero-LA 1.086
Raines-Mon 1.022
Murphy-Atl .... .960
Schmidt-Phi ...... .927
McGee-StL .... .920

Stolen Bases
Coleman-StL 110
Raines-Mon 70
McGee-StL 56
Sandberg-Chi 54
Samuel-Phi 53

Stolen Base Average
Lopes-Chi 92.2
Herr-StL 91.2
Raines-Mon 88.6
VanSlyke-StL 85.0
Davis-Cin 84.2

Stolen Base Runs
Coleman-StL 18.0
Raines-Mon 15.6
Lopes-Chi 11.7
Sandberg-Chi 9.6
Herr-StL 7.5

Fielding Runs
Hubbard-Atl 61.8
Wallach-Mon 36.7
McReynolds-SD 23.1
Pendleton-StL 22.7
Wilson-Phi 20.4

Total Player Rating
Raines-Mon 6.6
Guerrero-LA 6.3
McGee-StL 5.4
Hubbard-Atl 5.4
Sandberg-Chi 4.6

Wins
Gooden-NY 24
Tudor-StL 21
Andujar-StL 21
Browning-Cin 20
Hershiser-LA 19

Win Percentage
Hershiser-LA ..... .864
Gooden-NY .... .857
Smith-Mon .... .783
Darling-NY .... .727
Tudor-StL .... .724

Games
Burke-Mon 78
M.Davis-SF 77
Garrelts-SF 74
Carman-Phi 71
Minton-SF 68

Complete Games
Gooden-NY 16
Valenzuela-LA 14
Tudor-StL 14
Cox-StL 10
Andujar-StL 10

Shutouts
Tudor-StL 10
Gooden-NY 8
Valenzuela-LA 5
Hershiser-LA 5

Saves
Reardon-Mon 41
Smith-Chi 33
Smith-Hou 27
Power-Cin 27
Gossage-SD 26

Innings Pitched
Gooden-NY 276.2
Tudor-StL 275.0
Valenzuela-LA .. 272.1
Andujar-StL ... 269.2
Mahler-Atl 266.2

Fewest Hits/Game
Fernandez-NY 5.71
Gooden-NY 6.44
Hershiser-LA 6.72
Tudor-StL 6.84
Soto-Cin 6.87

Fewest BB/Game
Hoyt-SD .... .86
Eckersley-Chi 1.01
Lynch-NY 1.27
Tudor-StL 1.60
Smith-Mon 1.66

Strikeouts
Gooden-NY 268
Soto-Cin 214
Ryan-Hou 209
Valenzuela-LA ... 208
Fernandez-NY 180

Strikeouts/Game
Fernandez-NY 9.51
Gooden-NY 8.72
DeLeon-Pit 8.24
Ryan-Hou 8.11
Soto-Cin 7.50

Ratio
Tudor-StL 8.61
Gooden-NY 8.75
Eckersley-Chi ... 8.88
Hershiser-LA 9.50
Smith-Mon 9.51

Earned Run Average
Gooden-NY 1.53
Tudor-StL 1.93
Hershiser-LA 2.03
Reuschel-Pit 2.27
Welch-LA 2.31

Adjusted ERA
Gooden-NY 226
Tudor-StL 183
Hershiser-LA 171
Reuschel-Pit 157
Welch-LA 150

Opponents' Batting Avg.
Fernandez-NY .... .181
Gooden-NY .... .201
Hershiser-LA .... .206
Tudor-StL .... .209
Soto-Cin .... .211

Opponents' On Base Pct.
Tudor-StL .... .249
Gooden-NY .... .254
Eckersley-Chi ... .255
Hershiser-LA .... .268
Smith-Mon .... .269

Starter Runs
Gooden-NY 63.4
Tudor-StL 50.7
Hershiser-LA 41.6
Valenzuela-LA ... 34.6
Reuschel-Pit 28.4

Adjusted Starter Runs
Gooden-NY 59.2
Tudor-StL 48.9
Hershiser-LA 38.5
Valenzuela-LA ... 31.2
Reuschel-Pit 28.1

Clutch Pitching Index
Darling-NY 120
Hawkins-SD 119
Show-SD 119
Reuss-LA 115
Gooden-NY 115

Relief Runs
Burke-Mon 16.0
Gossage-SD 15.5
Franco-Cin 15.5
Garrelts-SF 15.2
Carman-Phi 14.4

Adjusted Relief Runs
Franco-Cin 17.6
Carman-Phi 15.3
Gossage-SD 15.0
Garrelts-SF 13.3
Burke-Mon 13.3

Relief Ranking
Franco-Cin 28.8
Gossage-SD 24.8
Smith-Hou 24.7
Carman-Phi 23.5
Power-Cin 22.5

Total Pitcher Index
Gooden-NY 7.3
Tudor-StL 5.5
Hershiser-LA 4.2
Reuschel-Pit 4.0
Valenzuela-LA 3.6

Total Baseball Ranking
Gooden-NY 7.3
Raines-Mon 6.6
Guerrero-LA 6.3
Tudor-StL 5.5
McGee-StL 5.4

TEAM	G	W	L	PCT	GB	R	OR	AB	H	2B	3B	HR	BB	SO	AVG	OBP	SLG	PRO	PRO+	BR	/A	PF	CHI	RC	SB	CS	SBA	SBR
EAST
TOR	161	99	62	.615		759	**588**	5508	1482	281	**53**	158	503	807	.269	.334	.425	.759	103	43	24	103	98	767	144	77	65	-3
NY	161	97	64	.602	2	**839**	660	5458	1458	272	31	176	620	771	.267	.347	.425	.772	113	82	**102**	98	102	821	**155**	53	**75**	**15**
DET	161	84	77	.522	15	729	688	5575	1413	254	45	202	526	926	.253	.321	.424	.745	103	8	13	99	97	765	75	41	65	-2
BAL	161	83	78	.516	16	818	764	5517	1451	234	22	**214**	604	908	.263	.338	**.430**	.768	112	64	86	97	102	794	69	43	62	-5
BOS	163	81	81	.500	18.5	800	720	5720	**1615**	292	31	162	562	816	**.282**	**.350**	.429	**.779**	108	**96**	61	104	93	**844**	66	27	71	4
MIL	161	71	90	.441	28	690	802	5568	1467	250	44	101	462	**746**	.263	.322	.379	.701	95	-68	-65	100	103	666	69	34	67	0
CLE	162	60	102	.370	39.5	729	861	5527	1465	254	31	116	492	817	.265	.327	.385	.712	95	-44	-39	99	106	681	132	72	65	-4
WEST
KC	162	91	71	.562		687	639	5500	1384	261	49	154	473	840	.252	.315	.401	.716	94	-47	-49	100	101	687	128	48	73	10
CAL	162	90	72	.556	1	732	703	5442	1364	215	31	153	**648**	902	.251	.335	.386	.721	97	-17	-13	100	100	711	106	51	68	1
CHI	163	85	77	.525	6	736	720	5470	1386	247	37	146	471	843	.253	.318	.392	.710	90	-55	-81	104	**110**	674	108	56	66	-1
MIN	162	77	85	.475	14	705	782	5509	1453	282	41	141	502	779	.264	.329	.407	.736	95	-1	-43	106	97	729	68	44	61	-6
OAK	162	77	85	.475	14	757	787	5581	1475	230	34	155	508	861	.264	.327	.401	.728	106	-15	39	93	104	725	117	58	67	0
SEA	162	74	88	.457	17	719	818	5521	1410	277	38	171	564	942	.255	.328	.412	.740	100	7	3	101	96	739	94	35	73	7
TEX	161	62	99	.385	28.5	617	785	5361	1359	213	41	129	530	819	.253	.324	.381	.705	91	-54	-63	101	93	652	130	76	63	-7
TOT	1132					10317		77257	20182	3562	528	2178	7465	11777	.261	.330	.406	.735							1461	715	67	9

TEAM	CG	SH	SV	IP	H	H/G	HR	BB	SO	RAT	ERA	ERA+	OAV	OOB	PR	/A	PF	CPI	FA	E	DP	FW	PW	BW	SBW	DIF
EAST
TOR	18	9	47	1448	**1312**	8.2	147	484	823	**11.3**	**3.31**	127	.243	**.308**	135	**145**	102	107	.980	125	164	.2	**14.3**	2.4	-.4	1.9
NY	25	9	**49**	1440¹	1373	8.6	157	518	907	11.9	3.69	109	.251	.318	74	50	97	104	.979	126	172	.2	4.9	**10.1**	**1.4**	-.1
DET	31	**11**	40	1456	1313	**8.1**	141	556	943	11.7	3.78	108	**.240**	.313	59	47	98	94	.977	143	152	-.8	4.6	1.3	-.3	-1.4
BAL	32	6	33	1427¹	1480	9.3	160	568	793	13.1	4.38	92	.270	.341	-36	-55	97	102	.979	129	168	-.0	-5.4	8.5	-.6	.0
BOS	35	8	29	1461¹	1487	9.2	130	540	913	12.7	4.06	106	.265	.333	14	37	103	101	.977	145	161	-.8	3.7	6.0	.3	-9.2
MIL	34	5	37	1437	1510	9.5	175	499	777	12.8	4.39	95	.271	.334	-39	-36	100	97	.977	142	153	-.7	-3.6	-6.4	-.0	1.3
CLE	24	7	28	1421	1556	9.9	170	547	702	13.6	4.91	84	.281	.350	-121	-123	100	98	.977	141	161	-.6	-12.2	-3.9	-.5	-3.9
WEST
KC	27	**11**	41	1461	1433	8.8	**103**	463	846	11.9	3.49	119	.257	.317	107	109	100	103	.980	127	160	.1	10.8	-4.8	.9	3.0
CAL	22	8	41	1457¹	1453	9.0	171	514	767	12.3	3.91	105	.263	.328	38	32	99	**108**	**.982**	112	**202**	1.0	3.2	-1.3	.0	6.1
CHI	20	8	39	1451²	1411	8.7	161	569	**1023**	12.5	4.07	106	.256	.330	13	40	104	101	**.982**	111	152	**1.1**	4.0	-8.0	-.2	7.1
MIN	**41**	7	34	1426¹	1468	9.3	164	**462**	767	12.4	4.48	98	.268	.329	-53	-11	106	95	.980	120	139	.5	-1.1	-4.3	-.1	1.5
OAK	10	6	41	1453	1451	9.0	172	607	785	12.9	4.41	98	.259	.334	-43	-89	93	97	.977	140	137	-.6	-8.8	3.9	-.0	1.6
SEA	23	8	30	1432	1456	9.2	154	637	868	13.4	4.68	90	.265	.346	-84	-74	102	96	.980	122	156	.4	-7.3	.3	.6	-1.0
TEX	18	5	33	1411²	1479	9.4	173	501	863	12.9	4.56	93	.269	.334	-65	-52	102	97	.980	120	145	.5	-5.1	-6.2	-.8	-6.9
TOT	360	108	522	20184		9.0				12.5	4.15		.261	.330					.979	1803	2222					

Runs		Hits		Doubles		Triples		Home Runs		Total Bases	
Henderson-NY	146	Boggs-Bos	240	Mattingly-NY	48	Wilson-KC	21	Evans-Det	40	Mattingly-NY	370
Ripken-Bal	116	Mattingly-NY	211	Buckner-Bos	46	Butler-Cle	14	Fisk-Chi	37	Brett-KC	322
Murray-Bal	111	Buckner-Bos	201	Boggs-Bos	42	Puckett-Min	13	Balboni-KC	36	Bradley-Sea	319
Evans-Bos	110	Puckett-Min	199	Cooper-Mil	39	Fernandez-Tor	10	Mattingly-NY	35	Boggs-Bos	312
Brett-KC	108	Baines-Chi	198					G.Thomas-Sea	32	Murray-Bal	305

Runs Batted In		Runs Produced		Bases On Balls		Batting Average		On Base Percentage		Slugging Average	
Mattingly-NY	145	Mattingly-NY	217	Evans-Bos	114	Boggs-Bos	.368	Boggs-Bos	.452	Brett-KC	.585
Murray-Bal	124	Murray-Bal	204	Harrah-Tex	113	Brett-KC	.335	Brett-KC	.442	Mattingly-NY	.567
Winfield-NY	114	Ripken-Bal	200	Brett-KC	103	Mattingly-NY	.324	Harrah-Tex	.437	Barfield-Tor	.536
Baines-Chi	113	Henderson-NY	194	Henderson-NY	99	Henderson-NY	.314	Henderson-NY	.422	Murray-Bal	.523
Brett-KC	112	Winfield-NY	193	Boggs-Bos	96	Butler-Cle	.311	Murray-Bal	.387	Evans-Det	.519

Production		Adjusted Production		Batter Runs		Adjusted Batter Runs		Clutch Hitting Index		Runs Created	
Brett-KC	1.028	Brett-KC	178	Brett-KC	63.4	Brett-KC	63.0	Franco-Cle	137	Brett-KC	146
Mattingly-NY	.946	Henderson-NY	159	Boggs-Bos	54.8	Mattingly-NY	50.8	Meacham-NY	137	Boggs-Bos	143
Henderson-NY	.938	Mattingly-NY	159	Mattingly-NY	47.5	Boggs-Bos	48.9	Mattingly-NY	132	Henderson-NY	138
Boggs-Bos	.929	Murray-Bal	150	Henderson-NY	45.5	Henderson-NY	48.5	Boone-Cal	130	Mattingly-NY	136
Murray-Bal	.910	Boggs-Bos	149	Murray-Bal	38.4	Murray-Bal	41.6	Thornton-Cle	125	Murray-Bal	122

Total Average		Stolen Bases		Stolen Base Average		Stolen Base Runs		Fielding Runs		Total Player Rating	
Henderson-NY	1.155	Henderson-NY	80	Perconte-Sea	93.9	Henderson-NY	18.0	Owen-Sea	30.3	Henderson-NY	7.4
Brett-KC	1.150	Pettis-Cal	56	Pettis-Cal	88.9	Pettis-Cal	11.4	Buckner-Bos	25.4	Brett-KC	7.2
Gibson-Det	.953	Butler-Cle	47	Gibson-Det	88.2	Perconte-Sea	8.1	Barfield-Tor	21.9	Boggs-Bos	5.3
Boggs-Bos	.952	Wilson-KC	43	Pettis-Cal	86.2	Smith-KC	7.8	Butler-Cle	21.8	Barfield-Tor	4.8
Murray-Bal	.938	Smith-KC	40	Smith-KC	85.1	Gibson-Det	6.6	Puckett-Min	21.2	Murray-Bal	4.4

Wins		Win Percentage		Games		Complete Games		Shutouts		Saves	
Guidry-NY	22	Guidry-NY	.786	Quisenberry-KC	84	Blyleven-Cle-Min	24	Blyleven-Cle-Min	5	Quisenberry-KC	37
Saberhagen-KC	20	Saberhagen-KC	.769	VandeBerg-Sea	76	Moore-Sea	14	Morris-Det	4	James-Cal	32
Viola-Min	18	Leibrandt-KC	.654	Righetti-NY	74	Hough-Tex	14	Burns-Chi	4	Moore-Cal	31
Burns-Chi	18	Higuera-Mil	.652	Hernandez-Det	74	Morris-Det	13			Hernandez-Det	31
				Nunez-Sea	70	Boyd-Bos	13				

Innings Pitched		Fewest Hits/Game		Fewest BB/Game		Strikeouts		Strikeouts/Game		Ratio	
Blyleven-Cle-Min	293.2	Stieb-Tor	7.00	Haas-Mil	1.39	Blyleven-Cle-Min	206	Bannister-Chi	8.46	Saberhagen-KC	9.56
Boyd-Bos	272.1	Hough-Tex	7.12	Saberhagen-KC	1.45	Bannister-Chi	198	Hurst-Bos	7.42	Guidry-NY	9.90
Stieb-Tor	265.0	Petry-Det	7.16	Guidry-NY	1.46	Morris-Det	191	Burns-Chi	6.82	Key-Tor	10.16
Alexander-Tor	260.2	Morris-Det	7.42	Butcher-Min	1.86	Hurst-Bos	189	Morris-Det	6.69	Petry-Det	10.33
Guidry-NY	259.0	Higuera-Mil	7.88	Key-Tor	2.12	Witt-Cal	180	Tanana-Tex-Det	6.66	Hough-Tex	10.35

Earned Run Average		Adjusted ERA		Opponents' Batting Avg.		Opponents' On Base Pct.		Starter Runs		Adjusted Starter Runs	
Stieb-Tor	2.48	Stieb-Tor	170	Stieb-Tor	.213	Saberhagen-KC	.273	Stieb-Tor	49.1	Stieb-Tor	50.9
Leibrandt-KC	2.69	Leibrandt-KC	155	Hough-Tex	.215	Guidry-NY	.279	Leibrandt-KC	38.5	Leibrandt-KC	38.8
Saberhagen-KC	2.87	Saberhagen-KC	145	Petry-Det	.217	Key-Tor	.284	Saberhagen-KC	33.4	Blyleven-Cle-Min	35.4
Key-Tor	3.00	Key-Tor	140	Morris-Det	.225	Hough-Tex	.285	Blyleven-Cle-Min	32.3	Saberhagen-KC	33.8
Blyleven-Cle-Min	3.16	Seaver-Chi	136	Higuera-Mil	.235	Petry-Det	.285	Key-Tor	27.0	Seaver-Chi	30.5

Clutch Pitching Index		Relief Runs		Adjusted Relief Runs		Relief Ranking		Total Pitcher Index		Total Baseball Ranking	
Leibrandt-KC	121	Moore-Cal	25.5	James-Chi	26.8	Moore-Cal	51.9	Stieb-Tor	5.5	Henderson-NY	7.4
Romanick-Cal	117	Quisenberry-KC	25.4	Quisenberry-KC	25.6	James-Chi	50.4	Moore-Cal	5.3	Brett-KC	7.2
Boddicker-Bal	115	James-Chi	24.7	Moore-Cal	25.0	Quisenberry-KC	46.9	James-Chi	5.1	Stieb-Tor	5.5
Alexander-Tor	114	Cliburn-Cal	22.6	Cliburn-Cal	22.2	Hernandez-Det	35.3	Quisenberry-KC	4.9	Moore-Cal	5.3
Stieb-Tor	112	Harris-Tex	21.1	Harris-Tex	22.1	Righetti-NY	32.2	Leibrandt-KC	4.5	Boggs-Bos	5.3

TEAM	G	W	L	PCT	GB	R	OR	AB	H	2B	3B	HR	BB	SO	AVG	OBP	SLG	PRO	PRO+	BR	/A	PF	CHI	RC	SB	CS	SBA	SBR
EAST																												
NY	162	108	54	.667		**783**	578	5558	**1462**	261	31	148	**631**	968	**.263**	.341	.401	.742	114	**84**	107	97	101	**773**	118	48	71	7
PHI	161	86	75	.534	21.5	739	713	5483	1386	266	39	154	589	1154	.253	.330	.400	.730	103	50	24	104	101	739	153	59	72	11
STL	161	79	82	.491	28.5	601	611	5378	1270	216	48	58	568	905	.236	.311	.327	.638	83	-119	-114	99	**109**	584	**262**	78	**77**	**32**
MON	161	78	83	.484	29.5	637	688	5508	1401	255	**50**	110	537	1016	.254	.324	.379	.703	101	-1	5	99	94	676	193	95	67	1
CHI	160	70	90	.438	37	680	781	5499	1409	258	27	**155**	508	966	.256	.321	.398	.719	96	21	-33	108	98	697	132	62	68	2
PIT	162	64	98	.395	44	663	700	5456	1366	**273**	33	111	569	929	.250	.323	.374	.697	96	-12	-27	102	100	654	152	84	64	-5
WEST																												
HOU	162	96	66	.593		654	**569**	5441	1388	244	32	125	536	916	.255	.325	.381	.706	104	3	22	97	98	668	163	75	68	4
CIN	162	86	76	.531	10	732	717	5536	1404	237	35	144	586	942	.254	.327	.387	.714	99	21	-9	104	104	712	177	53	**77**	21
SF	162	83	79	.512	13	698	618	5501	1394	269	29	114	536	1087	.253	.324	.375	.699	104	-9	24	95	104	674	148	93	61	-11
SD	162	74	88	.457	22	656	723	5515	1442	239	25	136	484	917	.261	.323	.388	.711	104	9	23	98	97	671	96	68	59	-12
LA	162	73	89	.451	23	638	679	5471	1373	232	14	130	478	966	.251	.315	.370	.685	102	-42	2	93	102	639	155	67	70	6
ATL	161	72	89	.447	23.5	615	719	5384	1348	241	24	138	538	**904**	.250	.321	.381	.702	94	-5	-42	106	93	646	93	76	55	-18
TOT	969					8096		65730	16643	2991	387	1523	6560	11648	.253	.324	.380	.704							1842	858	68	38

TEAM	CG	SH	SV	IP	H	H/G	HR	BB	SO	RAT	ERA	ERA+	OAV	OOB	PR	/A	PF	CPI	FA	E	DP	FW	PW	BW	SBW	DIF
EAST																										
NY	27	11	46	1484	1304	7.9	**103**	509	1083	11.2	**3.11**	114	.236	.304	**100**	70	95	98	.978	138	145	.1	7.3	**11.1**	.4	8.1
PHI	22	11	39	1451[2]	1473	9.1	130	553	874	12.7	3.85	100	.265	.334	-22	0	104	105	.978	137	157	.1	.0	2.5	.8	2.1
STL	17	4	46	1466[1]	1364	8.4	135	**485**	761	11.5	3.37	108	.250	.314	56	44	98	**106**	**.981**	**123**	178	**.9**	4.6	-11.8	3.0	1.9
MON	15	9	50	1466[1]	1350	8.3	119	566	1051	12.0	3.78	98	.246	.320	-11	-15	99	99	.979	133	132	.3	-1.6	.5	-.2	-1.6
CHI	11	6	42	1445	1546	9.6	143	557	962	13.2	4.49	90	.279	.346	-124	-72	109	100	.980	124	147	.8	-7.5	-3.4	-.1	.2
PIT	17	9	30	1450[2]	1397	8.7	138	570	924	12.4	3.90	98	.255	.329	-30	-11	103	100	.978	143	134	-.2	-1.1	-2.8	-.8	-12.0
WEST																										
HOU	18	**19**	51	1456[1]	**1203**	**7.4**	116	523	**1160**	**10.8**	3.15	114	**.225**	**.297**	92	**73**	97	93	.979	130	108	.6	**7.6**	2.3	.0	4.5
CIN	14	8	45	1468	1465	9.0	136	524	924	12.3	3.91	99	.264	.329	-32	-7	104	101	.978	140	160	.0	-.7	-.9	1.9	4.8
SF	18	10	35	1460[1]	1264	7.8	121	591	992	11.6	3.33	106	.236	.316	62	30	95	101	.977	143	149	-.2	3.1	2.5	-1.5	-2.0
SD	13	7	32	1443[1]	1406	8.8	150	607	934	12.7	3.99	92	.258	.335	-44	-54	98	102	.978	137	135	.2	-5.6	2.4	-1.6	-2.4
LA	**35**	14	25	1454[1]	1428	8.8	115	499	1051	12.1	3.76	92	.256	.320	-7	-51	93	96	.971	181	118	-2.2	-5.3	.2	.3	-1.0
ATL	17	5	39	1424[2]	1443	9.1	117	576	932	12.9	3.97	100	.266	.340	-41	0	107	103	.978	141	**181**	-.1	.0	-4.4	-2.2	-1.8
TOT	224	113	480	17471		8.6				12.1	3.72		.253	.324					.978	1670	1744					

Runs		Hits		Doubles		Triples		Home Runs		Total Bases	
Hayes-Phi	107	Gwynn-SD	211	Hayes-Phi	46	Webster-Mon	13	Schmidt-Phi	37	Parker-Cin	304
Gwynn-SD	107	Sax-LA	210	Sax-LA	43	Samuel-Phi	12	Parker-Cin	31	Schmidt-Phi	302
Schmidt-Phi	97	Raines-Mon	194	Dunston-Chi	37	Raines-Mon	10	Davis-Hou	31	Gwynn-SD	300
Davis-Cin	97	Hayes-Phi	186	Bream-Pit	37	Coleman-StL	8	Murphy-Atl	29	Murphy-Atl	293
		Bass-Hou	184	Samuel-Phi	36					Hayes-Phi	293

Runs Batted In		Runs Produced		Bases On Balls		Batting Average		On Base Percentage		Slugging Average	
Schmidt-Phi	119	Hayes-Phi	186	Hernandez-NY	94	Raines-Mon	.334	Raines-Mon	.415	Schmidt-Phi	.547
Parker-Cin	116	Schmidt-Phi	179	Schmidt-Phi	89	Sax-LA	.332	Hernandez-NY	.414	Strawberry-NY	.507
Carter-NY	105	Parker-Cin	174	C.Davis-SF	84	Gwynn-SD	.329	Schmidt-Phi	.395	McReynolds-SD	.504
Davis-Hou	101	Hernandez-NY	164	Oberkfell-Atl	83	Bass-Hou	.311	Sax-LA	.391	Davis-Hou	.493
Hayes-Phi	98	Carter-NY	162	Doran-Hou	81	Hernandez-NY	.310	Gwynn-SD	.382	Bass-Hou	.486

Production		Adjusted Production		Batter Runs		Adjusted Batter Runs		Clutch Hitting Index		Runs Created	
Schmidt-Phi	.942	Schmidt-Phi	152	Schmidt-Phi	44.0	Schmidt-Phi	40.0	Carter-NY	132	Raines-Mon	130
Raines-Mon	.891	Raines-Mon	146	Raines-Mon	38.0	Raines-Mon	39.0	Pendleton-StL	123	Schmidt-Phi	122
Strawberry-NY	.871	Strawberry-NY	142	Hernandez-NY	32.2	Hernandez-NY	35.3	Cruz-Hou	121	Gwynn-SD	113
McReynolds-SD	.867	Hernandez-NY	141	Hayes-Phi	30.3	Sax-LA	33.4	Uribe-SF	121	Hayes-Phi	111
Hayes-Phi	.861	McReynolds-SD	140	Gwynn-SD	28.4	Gwynn-SD	30.6	Jeltz-Phi	120	Sax-LA	110

Total Average		Stolen Bases		Stolen Base Average		Stolen Base Runs		Fielding Runs		Total Player Rating	
Raines-Mon	1.040	Coleman-StL	107	Dernier-Chi	93.1	Coleman-StL	23.7	Hubbard-Atl	41.0	Raines-Mon	6.2
Schmidt-Phi	.988	Davis-Cin	80	Raines-Mon	88.6	Davis-Cin	17.4	Pendleton-StL	24.2	Gwynn-SD	5.2
Strawberry-NY	.910	Raines-Mon	70	Coleman-StL	88.4	Raines-Mon	15.6	Bream-Pit	22.8	Hernandez-NY	4.4
Hernandez-NY	.873	Duncan-LA	48	Davis-Cin	87.9	Dernier-Chi	6.9	Wilson-Phi	20.6	Sax-LA	3.7
McReynolds-SD	.848			Leonard-SF	84.2			Dunston-Chi	20.3	Hubbard-Atl	3.5

Wins		Win Percentage		Games		Complete Games		Shutouts		Saves	
Valenzuela-LA	21	Ojeda-NY	.783	Lefferts-SD	83	Valenzuela-LA	20	Scott-Hou	5	Worrell-StL	36
Krukow-SF	20	Gooden-NY	.739	McDowell-NY	75	Rhoden-Pit	12	Knepper-Hou	5	Reardon-Mon	35
Scott-Hou	18	Fernandez-NY	.727	Worrell-StL	74	Gooden-NY	12	Welch-LA	3	Smith-Hou	33
Ojeda-NY	18	Darling-NY	.714	Franco-Cin	74	Krukow-SF	10	Valenzuela-LA	3	Smith-Chi	31
		Krukow-SF	.690	Tekulve-Phi	73						

Innings Pitched		Fewest Hits/Game		Fewest BB/Game		Strikeouts		Strikeouts/Game		Ratio	
Scott-Hou	275.1	Scott-Hou	5.95	Eckersley-Chi	1.93	Scott-Hou	306	Scott-Hou	10.00	Scott-Hou	8.37
Valenzuela-LA	269.1	Youmans-Mon	5.96	Sanderson-Chi	1.96	Valenzuela-LA	242	Ryan-Hou	9.81	Krukow-SF	9.66
Knepper-Hou	258.0	Ryan-Hou	6.02	Krukow-SF	2.02	Youmans-Mon	202	Fernandez-NY	8.81	Ojeda-NY	9.90
Rhoden-Pit	253.2	Fernandez-NY	7.09	Welch-LA	2.10	Gooden-NY	200	Youmans-Mon	8.30	Gooden-NY	10.12
Gooden-NY	250.0	Gooden-NY	7.09	Ojeda-NY	2.15	Fernandez-NY	200	Valenzuela-LA	8.09	Rhoden-Pit	10.25

Earned Run Average		Adjusted ERA		Opponents' Batting Avg.		Opponents' On Base Pct.		Starter Runs		Adjusted Starter Runs	
Scott-Hou	2.22	Scott-Hou	162	Scott-Hou	.186	Scott-Hou	.244	Scott-Hou	45.7	Scott-Hou	42.1
Ojeda-NY	2.57	Ojeda-NY	138	Ryan-Hou	.188	Krukow-SF	.271	Ojeda-NY	27.7	Rhoden-Pit	28.0
Darling-NY	2.81	Rhoden-Pit	135	Youmans-Mon	.188	Ojeda-NY	.279	Rhoden-Pit	24.7	Ojeda-NY	23.3
Rhoden-Pit	2.84	Darling-NY	126	Gooden-NY	.215	Gooden-NY	.280	Gooden-NY	24.2	Ruffin-Phi	22.6
Gooden-NY	2.84	Cox-StL	125	Fernandez-NY	.216	Ryan-Hou	.285	Darling-NY	23.9	Gooden-NY	19.2

Clutch Pitching Index		Relief Runs		Adjusted Relief Runs		Relief Ranking		Total Pitcher Index		Total Baseball Ranking	
Dravecky-SD	115	Worrell-StL	18.8	Worrell-StL	17.9	Worrell-StL	43.5	Worrell-StL	4.5	Raines-Mon	6.2
Darling-NY	113	McGaffigan-Mon	16.9	McGaffigan-Mon	16.5	Smith-Chi	24.5	Scott-Hou	4.3	Gwynn-SD	5.2
Garrelts-SF	110	Horton-StL	16.4	Tekulve-Phi	16.1	Orosco-NY	23.1	Rhoden-Pit	4.0	Worrell-StL	4.4
Tudor-StL	109	Tekulve-Phi	14.4	Horton-StL	15.6	Garber-Atl	22.9	Garber-Atl	2.6	Hernandez-NY	4.4
Gullickson-Cin	109	McCullers-SD	14.2	McCullers-SD	13.2	Tekulve-Phi	22.3	Smith-Chi	2.5	Scott-Hou	4.3

TEAM	G	W	L	PCT	GB	R	OR	AB	H	2B	3B	HR	BB	SO	AVG	OBP	SLG	PRO	PRO+	BR	/A	PF	CHI	RC	SB	CS	SBA	SBR
EAST																												
BOS	161	95	66	.590		794	696	5498	1488	**320**	21	144	595	**707**	.271	.349	.415	.764	107	59	57	100	98	792	41	34	55	-8
NY	162	90	72	.556	5.5	797	738	5570	1512	275	23	188	645	911	.271	**.350**	**.430**	**.780**	**112**	**89**	**99**	99	94	**843**	139	48	**74**	**13**
DET	162	87	75	.537	8.5	798	714	5512	1447	234	30	**198**	613	885	.263	.341	.424	.765	107	52	55	100	99	814	138	58	70	7
TOR	163	86	76	.531	9.5	809	733	5716	1540	285	35	181	496	848	.269	.331	.427	.758	102	29	10	102	103	796	110	59	65	-2
CLE	163	84	78	.519	11.5	**831**	841	5702	**1620**	270	**45**	157	456	944	**.284**	.340	**.430**	.770	110	57	72	98	102	822	**141**	54	72	10
MIL	161	77	84	.478	18	667	734	5461	1393	255	38	127	530	986	.255	.324	.385	.709	89	-59	-80	103	98	682	100	50	67	0
BAL	162	73	89	.451	22.5	708	760	5524	1425	223	13	169	563	862	.258	.330	.395	.725	97	-28	-17	99	99	708	64	34	65	-1
WEST																												
CAL	162	92	70	.568		786	684	5433	1387	236	36	167	**671**	860	.255	.341	.404	.745	103	22	31	99	101	765	109	42	72	8
TEX	162	87	75	.537	5	771	743	5529	1479	248	43	184	511	1088	.267	.333	.428	.761	103	37	18	102	99	761	103	85	55	-20
KC	162	76	86	.469	16	654	**673**	5561	1403	264	**45**	137	474	919	.252	.315	.390	.705	88	-77	-90	102	99	683	97	46	68	2
OAK	162	76	86	.469	16	731	760	5435	1370	213	25	163	553	983	.252	.325	.390	.715	101	-48	3	93	106	700	139	61	70	5
CHI	162	72	90	.444	20	644	699	5406	1335	197	34	121	487	940	.247	.313	.363	.676	81	-125	-144	103	**107**	614	115	54	68	2
MIN	162	71	91	.438	21	741	839	5531	1446	257	39	196	501	977	.261	.327	.428	.755	100	21	2	103	97	756	81	61	57	-12
SEA	162	67	95	.414	25	718	835	5498	1392	243	41	158	572	1148	.253	.327	.399	.726	95	-28	-33	101	100	706	93	76	55	-18
TOT	1134					10449		77376	20237	3520	468	2290	7667	13058	.262	.332	.408	.740							1470	762	66	-16

TEAM	CG	SH	SV	IP	H	H/G	HR	BB	SO	RAT	ERA	ERA+	OAV	OOB	PR	/A	PF	CPI	FA	E	DP	FW	PW	BW	SBW	DIF
EAST																										
BOS	36	6	41	1429²	1469	9.2	167	**474**	1033	12.4	3.93	106	.266	.327	38	36	100	**106**	.979	129	146	-.2	3.5	5.6	-.7	6.2
NY	13	8	**58**	1443¹	1461	9.1	175	492	878	12.3	4.11	99	.263	.325	11	-3	98	100	.979	127	153	.0	-.3	**9.7**	**1.4**	-1.8
DET	33	12	38	1443²	1374	8.6	183	571	880	12.3	4.02	102	.251	.325	25	16	99	100	.982	108	163	1.1	1.6	5.4	.8	-2.9
TOR	16	12	44	1476	1467	8.9	164	487	1002	12.2	4.08	103	.261	.325	16	23	101	99	**.984**	**100**	150	**1.7**	2.3	1.0	-.0	.2
CLE	31	7	34	1447²	1548	9.6	167	605	744	13.7	4.58	91	.273	.349	-64	-70	99	101	.975	157	148	-1.7	-6.9	7.1	1.1	3.4
MIL	29	12	32	1431²	1478	9.3	158	494	952	12.6	4.01	108	.267	.330	26	50	104	104	.976	146	146	-1.2	4.9	-7.9	.1	.5
BAL	17	6	39	1436²	1451	9.1	177	535	954	12.6	4.30	96	.263	.330	-20	-27	99	98	.978	135	163	-.5	-2.7	-1.7	.0	-3.2
WEST																										
CAL	29	12	40	1456	1356	**8.4**	153	478	955	**11.5**	3.84	107	.248	**.311**	54	44	98	94	.983	107	156	1.2	4.3	.3	.9	1.5
TEX	15	8	41	1450¹	1356	**8.4**	145	736	**1059**	13.2	4.11	105	.249	.342	11	31	103	100	.980	122	160	.3	3.0	1.8	-1.9	2.7
KC	24	**13**	31	1440²	1413	8.8	**121**	479	888	12.1	**3.82**	**111**	.258	.322	**56**	**68**	102	98	.980	123	153	.2	**6.7**	-8.8	.3	-3.4
OAK	22	8	37	1433	**1334**	**8.4**	166	667	937	12.8	4.31	90	**.247**	.333	-21	-70	93	94	.978	135	120	-.5	-6.9	.3	.6	1.4
CHI	18	8	38	1442¹	1361	8.5	143	561	895	12.2	3.93	110	.251	.325	39	61	103	97	.981	117	142	.6	6.0	-14.2	-.3	-1.8
MIN	**39**	6	24	1432²	1579	9.9	200	503	937	13.4	4.77	90	.281	.345	-94	-74	103	101	.980	118	168	.5	-7.3	.2	-1.1	-2.4
SEA	33	5	27	1439²	1590	9.9	171	585	944	13.9	4.65	91	.283	.355	-76	-65	102	105	.975	156	**191**	-1.7	-6.4	-3.2	-1.7	-1.0
TOT	355	123	524	20203¹		9.0				12.7	4.18		.262	.332					.979	1780	2159					

Runs		Hits		Doubles		Triples		Home Runs		Total Bases	
Henderson-NY	130	Mattingly-NY	238	Mattingly-NY	53	Butler-Cle	14	Barfield-Tor	40	Mattingly-NY	388
Puckett-Min	119	Puckett-Min	223	Boggs-Bos	47	Sierra-Tex	10	Kingman-Oak	35	Puckett-Min	365
Mattingly-NY	117	Fernandez-Tor	213	Rice-Bos	39	Fernandez-Tor	9	Gaetti-Min	34	Carter-Cle	341
Carter-Cle	108	Boggs-Bos	207	Buckner-Bos	39	Carter-Cle	9	Deer-Mil	33	Bell-Tor	341
				Barrett-Bos	39			Canseco-Oak	33	Barfield-Tor	329

Runs Batted In		Runs Produced		Bases On Balls		Batting Average		On Base Percentage		Slugging Average	
Carter-Cle	121	Carter-Cle	200	Boggs-Bos	105	Boggs-Bos	.357	Boggs-Bos	.455	Mattingly-NY	.573
Canseco-Oak	117	Mattingly-NY	199	Evans-Bos	97	Mattingly-NY	.352	P.Bradley-Sea	.406	Barfield-Tor	.559
Mattingly-NY	113	Rice-Bos	188	Randolph-NY	94	Puckett-Min	.328	Brett-KC	.404	Puckett-Min	.537
Rice-Bos	110	Puckett-Min	184	Jackson-Cal	92	Tabler-Cle	.326	Murray-Bal	.400	Bell-Tor	.532
		Bell-Tor	178	Evans-Det	91	Rice-Bos	.324	Mattingly-NY	.399	Gaetti-Min	.518

Production		Adjusted Production		Batter Runs		Adjusted Batter Runs		Clutch Hitting Index		Runs Created	
Mattingly-NY	.973	Mattingly-NY	163	Mattingly-NY	55.6	Mattingly-NY	57.3	Phillips-Oak	135	Mattingly-NY	150
Boggs-Bos	.942	Boggs-Bos	156	Boggs-Bos	51.6	Boggs-Bos	51.1	Buckner-Bos	127	Boggs-Bos	133
Barfield-Tor	.929	Barfield-Tor	145	Barfield-Tor	39.0	Barfield-Tor	36.1	Cooper-Mil	126	Puckett-Min	127
Puckett-Min	.903	Puckett-Min	138	Puckett-Min	37.1	Puckett-Min	34.1	Canseco-Oak	125	Barfield-Tor	122
Brett-KC	.885	Rice-Bos	137	Rice-Bos	32.6	Rice-Bos	32.3	Downing-Cal	122	Carter-Cle	116

Total Average		Stolen Bases		Stolen Base Average		Stolen Base Runs		Fielding Runs		Total Player Rating	
Boggs-Bos	.987	Henderson-NY	87	Felder-Mil	88.9	Henderson-NY	15.3	Owen-Sea-Bos	31.9	Barfield-Tor	4.8
Mattingly-NY	.969	Pettis-Cal	50	Davis-Oak	87.1	Pettis-Cal	7.2	Reynolds-Sea	29.0	Ripken-Bal	4.4
Gibson-Det	.950	Cangelosi-Chi	50	Gibson-Det	85.0	Gibson-Det	6.6	Barfield-Tor	20.9	Boggs-Bos	4.3
Barfield-Tor	.931	Wilson-KC	34	Henderson-NY	82.9	Davis-Oak	5.7	Pettis-Cal	20.7	Rice-Bos	4.2
Henderson-NY	.931	Gibson-Det	34			Wilson-KC	5.4	Buckner-Bos	20.1	Henderson-NY	4.2

Wins		Win Percentage		Games		Complete Games		Shutouts		Saves	
Clemens-Bos	24	Clemens-Bos	.857	Williams-Tex	80	Candiotti-Cle	17	Morris-Det	6	Righetti-NY	46
Morris-Det	21	Rasmussen-NY	.750	Righetti-NY	74	Blyleven-Min	16	Hurst-Bos	4	Aase-Bal	34
Higuera-Mil	20	Morris-Det	.724	Harris-Tex	73	Morris-Det	15	Higuera-Mil	4	Henke-Tor	27
Witt-Cal	18	Higuera-Mil	.645	Eichhorn-Tor	69	Higuera-Mil	15			Hernandez-Det	24
Rasmussen-NY	18	Witt-Cal	.643			Witt-Cal	14			Moore-Cal	21

Innings Pitched		Fewest Hits/Game		Fewest BB/Game		Strikeouts		Strikeouts/Game		Ratio	
Blyleven-Min	271.2	Clemens-Bos	6.34	Guidry-NY	1.78	Langston-Sea	245	Langston-Sea	9.21	Clemens-Bos	8.86
Witt-Cal	269.0	Rasmussen-NY	7.13	Boyd-Bos	1.89	Clemens-Bos	238	Hurst-Bos	8.62	Witt-Cal	9.84
Morris-Det	267.0	Witt-Cal	7.29	Blyleven-Min	1.92	Morris-Det	223	Clemens-Bos	8.43	Morris-Det	10.48
Moore-Sea	266.0	Hough-Tex	7.35	Wegman-Mil	1.95	Blyleven-Min	215	Correa-Tex	8.41	Rasmussen-NY	10.51
Clemens-Bos	254.0	Cowley-Chi	7.37	Sutton-Cal	2.13	Witt-Cal	208	Rijo-Oak	8.18	Sutton-Cal	10.61

Earned Run Average		Adjusted ERA		Opponents' Batting Avg.		Opponents' On Base Pct.		Starter Runs		Adjusted Starter Runs	
Clemens-Bos	2.48	Clemens-Bos	168	Clemens-Bos	.195	Clemens-Bos	.253	Clemens-Bos	47.8	Clemens-Bos	47.5
Higuera-Mil	2.79	Higuera-Mil	155	Rasmussen-NY	.217	Witt-Cal	.277	Witt-Cal	39.8	Higuera-Mil	42.4
Witt-Cal	2.84	Witt-Cal	144	Witt-Cal	.221	Morris-Det	.287	Higuera-Mil	38.2	Witt-Cal	37.8
Hurst-Bos	2.99	Hurst-Bos	139	Hough-Tex	.221	Sutton-Cal	.288	Morris-Det	26.9	Morris-Det	25.3
D.Jackson-KC	3.20	D.Jackson-KC	133	Correa-Tex	.223	Rasmussen-NY	.290	Hurst-Bos	22.9	Hurst-Bos	22.6

Clutch Pitching Index		Relief Runs		Adjusted Relief Runs		Relief Ranking		Total Pitcher Index		Total Baseball Ranking	
Hurst-Bos	123	Eichhorn-Tor	42.8	Eichhorn-Tor	43.6	Eichhorn-Tor	56.2	Eichhorn-Tor	5.8	Eichhorn-Tor	5.8
D.Jackson-KC	121	Righetti-NY	20.5	Righetti-NY	19.4	Righetti-NY	45.1	Clemens-Bos	4.9	Clemens-Bos	4.9
Higuera-Mil	119	Harris-Tex	16.7	Harris-Tex	18.2	Harris-Tex	33.8	Higuera-Mil	4.8	Higuera-Mil	4.8
Stieb-Tor	119	Clear-Mil	16.2	Clear-Mil	17.4	Clear-Mil	29.8	Righetti-NY	4.6	Barfield-Tor	4.8
Niekro-Cle	117	Mohorcic-Tex	14.7	Mohorcic-Tex	15.8	Plesac-Mil	27.9	Witt-Cal	4.0	Righetti-NY	4.6

TEAM	G	W	L	PCT	GB	R	OR	AB	H	2B	3B	HR	BB	SO	AVG	OBP	SLG	PRO	PRO+	BR	/A	PF	CHI	RC	SB	CS	SBA	SBR
EAST
STL	162	95	67	.586		798	693	5500	1449	252	49	94	644	933	.263	.343	.378	.721	95	-9	-23	102	109	740	248	72	78	31
NY	162	92	70	.568	3	823	698	5601	1499	287	34	192	592	1012	.268	.341	.434	.775	117	81	124	95	100	848	159	49	76	18
MON	162	91	71	.562	4	741	720	5527	1467	310	39	120	501	918	.265	.330	.401	.731	99	-6	-28	103	103	734	166	74	69	5
PIT	162	80	82	.494	15	723	744	5536	1464	282	45	131	535	914	.264	.332	.403	.735	99	3	-1	101	98	741	140	58	71	7
PHI	162	80	82	.494	15	702	749	5475	1390	248	51	169	587	1109	.254	.329	.410	.739	98	8	-16	103	95	736	111	49	69	4
CHI	161	76	85	.472	18.5	720	801	5583	1475	244	33	209	504	1064	.264	.327	.432	.759	102	40	10	104	94	785	109	48	69	4
WEST
SF	162	90	72	.556		783	669	5608	1458	274	32	205	511	1094	.260	.326	.430	.756	110	33	70	95	102	768	126	97	57	-20
CIN	162	84	78	.519	6	783	752	5560	1478	262	29	192	514	928	.266	.331	.427	.758	102	42	8	104	102	786	169	46	79	23
HOU	162	76	86	.469	14	648	678	5485	1386	238	28	122	480	936	.253	.321	.373	.694	94	-78	-54	96	100	669	162	46	78	21
LA	162	73	89	.451	17	635	675	5517	1389	236	23	125	445	923	.252	.311	.371	.682	88	-108	-92	97	104	627	128	59	68	3
ATL	161	69	92	.429	20.5	747	829	5428	1401	284	24	152	641	834	.258	.341	.403	.744	98	28	-9	105	98	747	135	68	67	0
SD	162	65	97	.401	25	668	763	5456	1419	209	48	113	577	992	.260	.334	.378	.712	99	-34	-9	96	96	693	198	91	69	5
TOT	971					8771		66276	17275	3126	435	1824	6577	11657	.261	.331	.404	.734							1851	757	71	101

TEAM	CG	SH	SV	IP	H	H/G	HR	BB	SO	RAT	ERA	ERA+	OAV	OOB	PR	/A	PF	CPI	FA	E	DP	FW	PW	BW	SBW	DIF
EAST
STL	10	7	48	1466	1484	9.1	129	533	873	12.5	3.91	106	.265	.332	28	40	102	103	.982	116	172	.9	4.0	-2.3	2.2	9.2
NY	16	7	51	1454	1407	8.7	135	510	1032	12.1	3.84	98	.254	.321	38	-11	93	97	.978	137	137	-.3	-1.1	12.3	1.0	-.9
MON	16	8	50	1450¹	1428	8.9	145	446	1012	11.8	3.92	107	.257	.315	26	46	103	95	.976	147	122	-.9	4.6	-2.8	-.3	9.4
PIT	25	13	39	1445	1377	8.6	164	562	914	12.0	4.20	98	.253	.326	-19	-14	101	95	.980	123	147	.5	-1.4	-.0	-.1	.2
PHI	13	7	48	1448¹	1453	9.0	167	587	877	12.9	4.18	101	.263	.338	-16	9	104	103	.980	121	137	.6	.9	-1.6	-.4	-.5
CHI	11	5	48	1434²	1524	9.6	159	628	1024	13.7	4.55	94	.275	.352	-76	-44	105	103	.979	130	154	.0	-4.4	1.0	-.4	-.7
WEST
SF	19	10	38	1471	1407	8.6	146	547	1038	12.1	3.68	105	.255	.325	66	27	94	106	.980	129	183	.1	2.7	7.0	-2.8	2.0
CIN	7	6	44	1452¹	1486	9.2	170	485	919	12.4	4.24	100	.267	.328	-27	0	104	99	.979	130	137	.0	.0	.8	1.5	.7
HOU	13	13	33	1441¹	1363	8.5	141	525	1137	12.0	3.84	102	.250	.319	38	12	96	96	.981	116	113	.9	1.2	-5.4	1.3	-2.9
LA	29	8	32	1455	1415	8.8	130	565	1097	12.4	3.72	107	.255	.327	59	40	97	103	.975	155	144	-1.3	4.0	-9.2	-.5	-.9
ATL	16	4	32	1427²	1529	9.6	163	587	837	13.6	4.63	94	.276	.350	-87	-45	107	101	.982	116	170	.8	-4.5	-.9	-.8	-6.1
SD	14	10	33	1433¹	1402	8.8	175	602	897	12.8	4.27	93	.256	.334	-30	-50	97	98	.976	147	135	-.9	-5.0	-.9	-.3	-8.9
TOT	189	98	496	17379		8.9				12.5	4.08		.261	.331					.979	1567	1751

Runs		Hits		Doubles		Triples		Home Runs		Total Bases	
Raines-Mon	123	Gwynn-SD	218	Wallach-Mon	42	Samuel-Phi	15	Dawson-Chi	49	Dawson-Chi	353
Coleman-StL	121	Guerrero-LA	184	Smith-StL	40	Gwynn-SD	13	Murphy-Atl	44	Samuel-Phi	329
Davis-Cin	120	Smith-StL	182	Galarraga-Mon	40	VanSlyke-Pit	11	Strawberry-NY	39	Murphy-Atl	328
Gwynn-SD	119	Coleman-StL	180			McGee-StL	11	Davis-Cin	37	Strawberry-NY	310
Murphy-Atl	115					Coleman-StL	10	Johnson-NY	36	Clark-SF	307

Runs Batted In		Runs Produced		Bases On Balls		Batting Average		On Base Percentage		Slugging Average	
Dawson-Chi	137	Wallach-Mon	186	Clark-StL	136	Gwynn-SD	.370	Clark-StL	.461	Clark-StL	.597
Wallach-Mon	123	Samuel-Phi	185	Hayes-Phi	121	Guerrero-LA	.338	Gwynn-SD	.450	Davis-Cin	.593
Schmidt-Phi	113	Davis-Cin	183	Murphy-Atl	115	Raines-Mon	.330	Raines-Mon	.431	Strawberry-NY	.583
Clark-StL	106	Smith-StL	179	Strawberry-NY	97	Kruk-SD	.313	Guerrero-LA	.421	Clark-SF	.580
		Dawson-Chi	178	Raines-Mon	90	James-Atl	.312	Murphy-Atl	.420	Murphy-Atl	.580

Production		Adjusted Production		Batter Runs		Adjusted Batter Runs		Clutch Hitting Index		Runs Created	
Clark-StL	1.058	Clark-StL	174	Clark-StL	54.3	Gwynn-SD	54.3	Herr-StL	172	Murphy-Atl	143
Murphy-Atl	1.000	Strawberry-NY	165	Murphy-Atl	53.3	Clark-StL	52.0	Pendleton-StL	131	Gwynn-SD	143
Davis-Cin	.994	Gwynn-SD	160	Gwynn-SD	49.6	Strawberry-NY	51.1	Smith-StL	130	Strawberry-NY	132
Strawberry-NY	.984	Guerrero-LA	156	Strawberry-NY	44.7	Murphy-Atl	46.8	McGee-StL	126	Raines-Mon	132
Gwynn-SD	.961	Clark-SF	155	Raines-Mon	43.2	Guerrero-LA	45.7	Diaz-Cin	124	Clark-StL	127

Total Average		Stolen Bases		Stolen Base Average		Stolen Base Runs		Fielding Runs		Total Player Rating	
Clark-StL	1.258	Coleman-StL	109	Sandberg-Chi	91.3	Coleman-StL	19.5	Hubbard-Atl	28.2	Davis-Cin	6.9
Davis-Cin	1.182	Gwynn-SD	56	Raines-Mon	90.9	Raines-Mon	12.0	Davis-Cin	28.1	Gwynn-SD	6.6
Raines-Mon	1.133	Hatcher-Hou	53	Davis-Cin	89.3	Davis-Cin	11.4	Bonds-Pit	19.7	Raines-Mon	6.1
Murphy-Atl	1.106	Raines-Mon	50	Hatcher-Hou	85.5	Hatcher-Hou	10.5	Smith-StL	19.3	Murphy-Atl	5.4
Strawberry-NY	1.103	Davis-Cin	50	Coleman-StL	83.2	Gwynn-SD	9.6	Hernandez-NY	17.7	Strawberry-NY	5.0

Wins		Win Percentage		Games		Complete Games		Shutouts		Saves	
Sutcliffe-Chi	18	Gooden-NY	.682	Tekulve-Phi	90	Reuschel-Pit-SF	12	Reuschel-Pit-SF	4	Bedrosian-Phi	40
Rawley-Phi	17	Sutcliffe-Chi	.643	Murphy-Cin	87	Valenzuela-LA	12	Welch-LA	4	Smith-Chi	36
Scott-Hou	16	Welch-LA	.625	Williams-Cin	85	Hershiser-LA	10			Worrell-StL	33
Hershiser-LA	16	Rawley-Phi	.607	J.Robinson-SF-Pit	81	Z.Smith-Atl	9			Franco-Cin	32
		Z.Smith-Atl	.600	McCullers-SD	78	Scott-Hou	8			McDowell-NY	25

Innings Pitched		Fewest Hits/Game		Fewest BB/Game		Strikeouts		Strikeouts/Game		Ratio	
Hershiser-LA	264.2	Ryan-Hou	6.55	Reuschel-Pit-SF	1.67	Ryan-Hou	270	Ryan-Hou	11.48	Reuschel-Pit-SF	10.19
Welch-LA	251.2	Scott-Hou	7.23	Heaton-Mon	1.72	Scott-Hou	233	Scott-Hou	8.47	Scott-Hou	10.25
Valenzuela-LA	251.0	Welch-LA	7.30	Gullickson-Cin	2.13	Welch-LA	196	Sebra-Mon	7.92	Ryan-Hou	10.42
Scott-Hou	247.2	Dunne-Pit	7.88	Forsch-StL	2.26	Valenzuela-LA	190	Gooden-NY	7.41	Welch-LA	10.51
Z.Smith-Atl	242.0	Darling-NY	7.93	Drabek-Pit	2.35	Hershiser-LA	190	Darling-NY	7.24	Drabek-Pit	10.77

Earned Run Average		Adjusted ERA		Opponents' Batting Avg.		Opponents' On Base Pct.		Starter Runs		Adjusted Starter Runs	
Ryan-Hou	2.76	Ryan-Hou	142	Ryan-Hou	.199	Scott-Hou	.282	Ryan-Hou	30.9	Ryan-Hou	27.1
Dunne-Pit	3.03	Dunne-Pit	136	Scott-Hou	.217	Ryan-Hou	.284	Hershiser-LA	30.0	Hershiser-LA	26.6
Hershiser-LA	3.06	Reuschel-Pit-SF	131	Welch-LA	.221	Reuschel-Pit-SF	.284	Reuschel-Pit-SF	24.9	Reuschel-Pit-SF	24.1
Reuschel-Pit-SF	3.09	Hershiser-LA	130	Darling-NY	.233	Welch-LA	.291	Welch-LA	24.1	Welch-LA	20.9
Gooden-NY	3.21	Welch-LA	123	Dunne-Pit	.240	Drabek-Pit	.296	Scott-Hou	23.3	Dunne-Pit	19.6

Clutch Pitching Index		Relief Runs		Adjusted Relief Runs		Relief Ranking		Total Pitcher Index		Total Baseball Ranking	
LaCoss-SF	124	Burke-Mon	29.3	Burke-Mon	30.5	Franco-Cin	36.1	Hershiser-LA	3.6	Davis-Cin	6.9
Cox-StL	120	McGaffigan-Mon	22.5	McGaffigan-Mon	24.2	Burke-Mon	34.7	Franco-Cin	3.6	Gwynn-SD	6.6
Dravecky-SD-SF	113	Williams-Cin	20.9	Williams-Cin	22.8	Worrell-StL	33.2	Burke-Mon	3.5	Raines-Mon	6.1
Ruffin-Phi	112	J.Robinson-SF-Pit	16.9	Worrell-StL	15.7	Smith-Chi	26.6	Worrell-StL	3.4	Murphy-Atl	5.4
Grant-SF-SD	111	Smith-Hou	16.2	Franco-Cin	15.7	Bedrosian-Phi	25.3	Smith-Chi	2.6	Strawberry-NY	5.0

TEAM	G	W	L	PCT	GB	R	OR	AB	H	2B	3B	HR	BB	SO	AVG	OBP	SLG	PRO	PRO+	BR	/A	PF	CHI	RC	SB	CS	SBA	SBR
EAST																												
DET	162	98	64	.605		**896**	735	5649	1535	274	32	**225**	653	913	.272	.352	**.451**	**.803**	116	91	131	96	98	**910**	106	50	68	2
TOR	162	96	66	.593	2	845	**655**	5635	1514	277	38	215	555	970	.269	.338	.446	.784	103	42	26	102	100	841	126	50	72	8
MIL	162	91	71	.562	7	862	817	5625	1552	272	46	163	598	1040	.276	.349	.428	.777	102	40	17	103	101	852	**176**	74	70	8
NY	162	89	73	.549	9	788	758	5511	1445	239	16	196	604	949	.262	.338	.418	.756	100	-6	3	99	100	773	105	43	71	6
BOS	162	78	84	.481	20	842	825	5586	**1554**	273	26	174	606	**825**	**.278**	**.355**	.430	.785	104	61	38	103	97	855	77	45	63	-4
BAL	162	67	95	.414	31	729	880	5576	1437	219	20	211	524	939	.258	.324	.418	.742	98	-47	-27	97	99	736	69	45	61	-6
CLE	162	61	101	.377	37	742	957	5606	1476	267	30	187	489	977	.263	.326	.422	.748	95	-35	-40	101	98	772	140	54	72	10
WEST																												
MIN	162	85	77	.525		786	806	5441	1422	258	35	196	523	898	.261	.330	.430	.760	96	-8	-35	104	103	757	113	65	63	-5
KC	162	83	79	.512	2	715	691	5499	1443	239	40	168	523	1034	.262	.330	.412	.742	93	-40	-58	102	97	747	125	43	**74**	**12**
OAK	162	81	81	.500	4	806	789	5511	1432	263	33	199	593	1056	.260	.336	.428	.764	108	4	58	93	101	796	140	63	69	4
SEA	162	78	84	.481	7	760	801	5508	1499	282	48	161	500	863	.272	.337	.428	.765	96	9	-31	105	96	788	174	73	70	8
CHI	162	77	85	.475	8	748	746	5538	1427	**283**	36	173	621	971	.258	.321	.415	.736	91	-57	-74	102	103	737	138	52	73	10
TEX	162	75	87	.463	10	823	849	5564	1478	264	35	194	567	1081	.266	.336	.430	.766	101	9	8	100	102	798	120	71	63	-7
CAL	162	75	87	.463	10	770	803	5570	1406	257	26	172	590	926	.252	.328	.401	.729	95	-65	-39	97	**105**	744	125	44	**74**	11
TOT	1134					11112		77819	20620	3667	461	2634	7812	13442	.265	.336	.425	.761							1734	772	69	57

TEAM	CG	SH	SV	IP	H	H/G	HR	BB	SO	RAT	ERA	ERA+	OAV	OOB	PR	/A	PF	CPI	FA	E	DP	FW	PW	BW	SBW	DIF
EAST																										
DET	33	10	31	1456	1430	8.8	180	563	976	12.5	4.02	105	.256	.328	70	32	95	103	.980	122	147	.1	3.1	**12.5**	-.2	1.6
TOR	18	8	43	1454	1323	8.2	158	567	1064	11.8	3.74	120	.244	.318	115	121	101	100	.982	111	148	.8	**11.5**	2.5	.4	-.2
MIL	28	6	45	1464	1548	9.5	169	529	1039	12.9	4.62	99	.271	.336	-27	-8	103	96	.976	145	155	-1.3	-.8	1.6	.4	10.1
NY	19	10	**47**	1446¹	1475	9.2	179	542	900	12.8	4.36	101	.266	.334	16	5	98	101	.983	102	155	1.3	.5	.3	.2	5.7
BOS	47	**13**	16	1436	1584	9.9	190	517	1034	13.4	4.77	95	.282	.346	-50	-37	102	102	.982	110	158	.8	-3.5	3.6	-.8	-3.2
BAL	17	6	30	1439²	1555	9.7	226	547	870	13.3	5.01	88	.276	.343	-88	-97	99	98	.982	111	174	.8	-9.2	-2.6	-1.0	-2.0
CLE	24	8	25	1422²	1566	9.9	219	606	849	14.1	5.28	86	.278	.354	-131	-120	102	97	.975	153	128	-1.8	-11.4	-3.8	.6	-3.5
WEST																										
MIN	16	4	39	1427¹	1465	9.2	210	564	990	13.1	4.63	100	.266	.339	-27	-2	104	100	**.984**	98	147	**1.6**	-.2	-3.3	-.9	6.8
KC	44	11	26	1424	1424	9.0	**128**	548	923	12.7	3.86	118	.261	.333	95	111	102	**105**	.979	131	151	-.5	10.6	-5.5	**.8**	-3.4
OAK	18	6	40	1445²	1442	9.0	176	531	1042	12.5	4.32	96	.258	.327	22	-31	93	96	.977	142	122	-1.1	-3.0	5.5	.0	-1.4
SEA	39	10	33	1430²	1503	9.5	199	**497**	919	12.8	4.49	105	.272	.335	-5	-37	106	102	.980	122	150	.1	3.5	-3.0	.4	-4.0
CHI	29	12	37	1447²	1436	8.9	189	537	792	12.5	4.30	107	.259	.349	26	46	103	99	.981	116	174	.5	4.4	-7.1	.6	-2.4
TEX	20	3	27	1444¹	1388	8.6	199	760	**1103**	13.7	4.63	97	.253	.350	-28	-25	100	100	.976	151	148	-1.7	-2.4	.8	-1.1	-1.6
CAL	20	7	36	1457¹	1481	9.1	212	504	941	12.5	4.38	98	.264	.329	13	-13	97	101	.981	117	162	.4	-1.2	-3.7	.7	-2.1
TOT	372	114	475	20195²		9.2				12.9	4.46		.265	.336					.980	1731	2119					

Runs
Molitor-Mil 114
Bell-Tor 111
Whitaker-Det 110
Downing-Cal 110

Hits
Seitzer-KC 207
Puckett-Min 207
Trammell-Det 205
Boggs-Bos 200
Yount-Mil 198

Doubles
Molitor-Mil 41
Boggs-Bos 40

Triples
Wilson-KC 15
Polonia-Oak 10
P.Bradley-Sea 10
Yount-Mil 9

Home Runs
McGwire-Oak 49
Bell-Tor 47

Total Bases
Bell-Tor 369
McGwire-Oak 344
Puckett-Min 333
Trammell-Det 329
Boggs-Bos 324

Runs Batted In
Bell-Tor 134
Evans-Bos 123
McGwire-Oak 118
Joyner-Cal 117
Mattingly-NY 115

Runs Produced
Evans-Bos 198
Bell-Tor 198
Trammell-Det 186
Joyner-Cal 183
Yount-Mil 181

Bases On Balls
Evans-Bos 106
Downing-Cal 106
Boggs-Bos 105
Evans-Det 100
Butler-Cle 91

Batting Average
Boggs-Bos .... .363
Molitor-Mil .... .353
Trammell-Det ...... .343
Puckett-Min .... .332
Mattingly-NY ...... .327

On Base Percentage
Boggs-Bos .... .467
Molitor-Mil .... .438
Evans-Bos .... .422
Randolph-NY .... .415
Trammell-Det ...... .406

Slugging Average
McGwire-Oak .... .618
Bell-Tor .... .605
Boggs-Bos .... .588
Evans-Bos .... .569
Molitor-Mil .... .566

Production
Boggs-Bos 1.055
Molitor-Mil 1.004
McGwire-Oak .... .992
Evans-Bos .... .991
Bell-Tor .... .962

Adjusted Production
Boggs-Bos 173
McGwire-Oak 168
Molitor-Mil 159
Trammell-Det 157
Evans-Bos 155

Batter Runs
Boggs-Bos 66.6
Evans-Bos 49.6
Molitor-Mil 44.8
McGwire-Oak 44.2
Trammell-Det 43.7

Adjusted Batter Runs
Boggs-Bos 62.7
McGwire-Oak 53.0
Trammell-Det 49.5
Evans-Bos 46.1
Molitor-Mil 41.8

Clutch Hitting Index
Randolph-NY 141
Griffin-Oak 127
Owen-Bos 118
Tabler-Cle 117
Ward-NY 117

Runs Created
Boggs-Bos 154
Trammell-Det 137
Evans-Bos 134
McGwire-Oak 131
Molitor-Mil 125

Total Average
Molitor-Mil 1.171
Boggs-Bos 1.169
Evans-Bos 1.059
McGwire-Oak 1.042
Trammell-Det 1.015

Stolen Bases
Reynolds-Sea 60
Wilson-KC 59
Redus-Chi 52
Molitor-Mil 45
Henderson-NY 41

Stolen Base Average
McDowell-Tex 92.3
Trammell-Det 91.3
Schofield-Cal 86.4
Moseby-Tor 84.8
Wilson-KC 84.3

Stolen Base Runs
Wilson-KC 11.1
Redus-Chi 9.0
Moseby-Tor 7.5
Molitor-Mil 7.5
Henderson-NY 7.5

Fielding Runs
Barrett-Bos 32.3
Salazar-KC 21.8
Manrique-Chi 18.9
Reynolds-Sea 18.8
Gagne-Min 16.9

Total Player Rating
Boggs-Bos 5.8
Trammell-Det 5.4
Molitor-Mil 3.5
Henderson-NY 3.5
McGwire-Oak 3.3

Wins
Stewart-Oak 20
Clemens-Bos 20
Langston-Sea 19

Win Percentage
Clemens-Bos .... .690
Key-Tor .... .680
Saberhagen-KC ..... .643
Higuera-Mil .... .643

Games
Eichhorn-Tor 89
Williams-Tex 85
Mohorcic-Tex 74
Henke-Tor 72
Musselman-Tor 68

Complete Games
Clemens-Bos 18
Saberhagen-KC 15
Hurst-Bos 15
Langston-Sea 14
Higuera-Mil 14

Shutouts
Clemens-Bos 7
Saberhagen-KC 4

Saves
Henke-Tor 34
Righetti-NY 31
Reardon-Min 31
Plesac-Mil 23
Buice-Cal 17

Innings Pitched
Hough-Tex 285.1
Clemens-Bos 281.2
Langston-Sea 272.0
Blyleven-Min 267.0
Morris-Det 266.0

Fewest Hits/Game
Key-Tor 7.24
Hough-Tex 7.51
Morris-Det 7.68
Stewart-Oak 7.71
DeLeon-Chi 7.73

Fewest BB/Game
Long-Chi 1.49
Saberhagen-KC 1.86
Sutton-Cal 1.93
Bannister-Chi 1.93
Young-Oak 1.95

Strikeouts
Langston-Sea 262
Clemens-Bos 256
Higuera-Mil 240
Hough-Tex 223
Morris-Det 208

Strikeouts/Game
Langston-Sea 8.67
Higuera-Mil 8.25
Clemens-Bos 8.18
Bosio-Mil 7.94
Nieves-Mil 7.50

Ratio
Key-Tor 9.59
Bannister-Chi 10.43
Saberhagen-KC 10.68
Young-Oak 10.68
Viola-Min 10.80

Earned Run Average
Key-Tor 2.76
Viola-Min 2.90
Clemens-Bos 2.97
Saberhagen-KC 3.36
Morris-Det 3.38

Adjusted ERA
Key-Tor 163
Viola-Min 159
Clemens-Bos 153
Saberhagen-KC 135
Leibrandt-KC 134

Opponents' Batting Avg.
Key-Tor .... .221
Hough-Tex .... .223
Morris-Det .... .228
Stewart-Oak .... .229
DeLeon-Chi .... .230

Opponents' On Base Pct.
Key-Tor .... .273
Bannister-Chi ..... .286
Viola-Min .... .294
Morris-Det .... .294
Young-Oak .... .295

Starter Runs
Key-Tor 49.2
Clemens-Bos 46.5
Viola-Min 43.6
Morris-Det 31.7
Saberhagen-KC 31.2

Adjusted Starter Runs
Key-Tor 50.3
Clemens-Bos 49.0
Viola-Min 48.1
Saberhagen-KC 34.0
Leibrandt-KC 30.6

Clutch Pitching Index
Viola-Min 115
Rhoden-NY 112
Terrell-Det 110
Blyleven-Min 109
Gubicza-KC 107

Relief Runs
Henke-Tor 20.5
Eckersley-Oak 18.3
Eichhorn-Tor 18.2
Thigpen-Chi 17.1
Plesac-Mil 16.3

Adjusted Relief Runs
Henke-Tor 20.9
Eichhorn-Tor 18.7
Thigpen-Chi 18.3
Plesac-Mil 17.3
Mohorcic-Tex 16.4

Relief Ranking
Plesac-Mil 32.9
Thigpen-Chi 29.6
Henke-Tor 29.0
Mohorcic-Tex 25.2
Eichhorn-Tor 22.4

Total Pitcher Index
Viola-Min 4.6
Key-Tor 4.4
Clemens-Bos 4.4
Leibrandt-KC 3.5
Saberhagen-KC 3.4

Total Baseball Ranking
Boggs-Bos 5.8
Trammell-Det 5.4
Viola-Min 4.6
Key-Tor 4.4
Clemens-Bos 4.4

TEAM	G	W	L	PCT	GB	R	OR	AB	H	2B	3B	HR	BB	SO	AVG	OBP	SLG	PRO	PRO+	BR	/A	PF	CHI	RC	SB	CS	SBA	SBR
EAST																												
NY	160	100	60	.625		**703**	532	5408	1387	251	24	**152**	544	842	.256	**.328**	**.396**	**.724**	120	**95**	**131**	95	97	**717**	140	51	73	11
PIT	160	85	75	.531	15	651	616	5379	1327	240	45	110	**553**	947	.247	.321	.369	.690	105	33	42	99	99	648	119	60	66	0
MON	163	81	81	.500	20	628	592	5573	1400	260	**48**	107	454	1053	.251	.311	.373	.684	98	12	-18	105	97	636	189	89	68	3
CHI	163	77	85	.475	24	660	694	5675	**1481**	**262**	46	113	403	910	**.261**	.312	.383	.695	100	31	1	105	99	673	120	46	72	8
STL	162	76	86	.469	25	578	633	5518	1373	207	33	71	484	**827**	.249	.312	.337	.649	92	-47	-53	101	98	601	**234**	64	**79**	**32**
PHI	162	65	96	.404	35.5	597	734	5403	1294	246	31	106	489	981	.239	.308	.355	.663	94	-22	-35	102	100	599	112	49	70	4
WEST																												
LA	162	94	67	.584		628	544	5431	1346	217	25	99	437	947	.248	.308	.352	.660	99	-32	-14	97	**107**	590	131	46	74	12
CIN	161	87	74	.540	7	641	596	5426	1334	246	25	122	479	922	.246	.311	.368	.679	97	6	-19	104	102	639	207	56	**79**	29
SD	161	83	78	.516	11	594	583	5325	1325	205	35	94	494	892	.247	.313	.351	.664	99	-19	-8	98	99	594	123	50	71	7
SF	162	83	79	.512	11.5	670	626	5450	1353	227	44	113	550	1023	.248	.321	.368	.689	109	32	61	96	101	650	121	78	61	-11
HOU	162	82	80	.506	12.5	617	631	5494	1338	239	31	96	474	840	.244	.308	.351	.659	99	-32	-9	96	103	604	198	71	74	17
ATL	160	54	106	.338	39.5	555	741	5440	1319	228	28	96	432	848	.242	.301	.348	.649	88	-56	-84	105	99	549	95	69	58	-13
TOT	969					7522		65563	16277	2828	415	1279	5793	11032	.248	.313	.363	.675							1789	729	71	99

TEAM	CG	SH	SV	IP	H	H/G	HR	BB	SO	RAT	ERA	ERA+	OAV	OOB	PR	/A	PF	CPI	FA	E	DP	FW	PW	BW	SBW	DIF
EAST																										
NY	31	22	46	1439	**1253**	7.8	78	404	**1100**	10.6	2.91	111	.235	.293	86	50	93	97	**.981**	115	127	.9	5.4	**14.1**	.3	-.7
PIT	12	11	46	1440²	1349	8.4	108	469	790	11.6	3.47	98	.250	.314	-3	-10	99	101	.980	125	128	.3	-1.1	4.5	-.9	2.1
MON	18	12	43	1482²	1310	8.0	122	476	923	11.1	3.08	**117**	.238	.303	60	**84**	104	**105**	.978	142	145	-.5	**9.1**	-1.9	-.6	-6.0
CHI	30	10	29	1464¹	1494	9.2	115	490	897	12.4	3.84	94	.265	.327	-64	-38	105	102	.980	125	128	.5	-4.1	.1	-.0	-.4
STL	17	14	42	1470²	1387	8.5	91	486	881	11.6	3.47	100	.252	.314	-4	1	101	99	**.981**	121	131	.6	.1	-5.7	**2.6**	-2.6
PHI	16	6	36	1433	1447	9.1	118	628	859	13.3	4.14	86	.265	.344	-110	-92	103	102	.976	145	139	-.7	-9.9	-3.8	-.5	-.6
WEST																										
LA	**32**	**24**	49	1463¹	1291	7.9	84	473	1029	11.0	2.96	112	.237	.301	78	59	97	102	.977	142	126	-.5	6.4	-1.5	.4	8.8
CIN	24	13	43	1455	1271	7.9	121	504	934	11.1	3.35	107	.237	.306	16	38	104	98	.980	125	131	.4	4.1	-2.0	2.2	1.9
SD	30	9	39	1449	1332	8.3	112	439	885	11.1	3.28	104	.247	.306	27	19	99	102	**.981**	120	**147**	.6	2.0	-.9	-.1	.8
SF	25	13	42	1462¹	1323	8.1	99	422	875	10.9	3.39	96	.242	.300	10	-20	95	93	.980	129	145	-.2	-2.2	6.6	-2.1	-.5
HOU	21	15	40	1474²	1339	8.2	123	478	1049	11.3	3.41	97	.242	.307	7	-14	96	99	.978	138	124	-.3	-1.5	-1.0	.9	2.9
ATL	14	4	25	1446	1481	9.2	108	524	810	12.7	4.09	90	.268	.336	-103	-67	107	100	.976	151	138	-1.1	-7.2	-9.1	-2.0	-6.3
TOT	270	153	480	17480²		8.4				11.6	3.45		.248	.313					.979	1578	1609					

Runs
Butler-SF 109
Gibson-LA 106
Clark-SF 102
VanSlyke-Pit 101
Strawberry-NY 101

Hits
Galarraga-Mon 184
Dawson-Chi 179
Palmeiro-Chi 178
Sax-LA 175
Larkin-Cin 174

Doubles
Galarraga-Mon 42
Palmeiro-Chi 41
Sabo-Cin 40
Bream-Pit 37

Triples
VanSlyke-Pit 15
Coleman-StL 10
Young-Hou 9
Samuel-Phi 9
Butler-SF 9

Home Runs
Strawberry-NY 39
Davis-Hou 30
Galarraga-Mon 29
Clark-SF 29
McReynolds-NY ... 27

Total Bases
Galarraga-Mon.... 329
Dawson-Chi 298
VanSlyke-Pit 297
Strawberry-NY ... 296
Clark-SF 292

Runs Batted In
Clark-SF 109
Strawberry-NY 101
VanSlyke-Pit 100
Bonilla-Pit 100

Runs Produced
Clark-SF 182
VanSlyke-Pit 176
Strawberry-NY ... 163
Bonilla-Pit 163
Galarraga-Mon ... 162

Bases On Balls
Clark-SF 100
Butler-SF 97
Daniels-Cin 87
Johnson-NY 86

Batting Average
Gwynn-SD 313
Palmeiro-Chi 307
Dawson-Chi 303
Galarraga-Mon ..302
Perry-Atl 300

On Base Percentage
Daniels-Cin 400
Butler-SF 395
Clark-SF 392
Gibson-LA 381
Gwynn-SD 374

Slugging Average
Strawberry-NY 545
Galarraga-Mon ...540
Clark-SF 508
VanSlyke-Pit 506
Dawson-Chi 504

Production
Strawberry-NY 916
Clark-SF 900
Galarraga-Mon ...894
Gibson-LA 864
Daniels-Cin 863

Adjusted Production
Strawberry-NY ... 168
Clark-SF 163
Gibson-LA 151
Bonds-Pit 147
Galarraga-Mon ... 147

Batter Runs
Clark-SF 44.3
Strawberry-NY ... 42.0
Galarraga-Mon ... 39.2
Gibson-LA 33.8
Daniels-Cin 33.2

Adjusted Batter Runs
Clark-SF 49.3
Strawberry-NY ...47.4
Gibson-LA........36.9
Galarraga-Mon ..34.3
Bonilla-Pit 33.6

Clutch Hitting Index
Moreland-SD 131
Gwynn-SD 118
Maldonado-SF ... 114
Bream-Pit 114
Davis-Cin 113

Runs Created
Clark-SF 120
Galarraga-Mon .. 114
Strawberry-NY .. 111
Gibson-LA 107
VanSlyke-Pit ... 107

Total Average
Strawberry-NY 957
Clark-SF 955
Gibson-LA 929
Davis-Cin 927
Daniels-Cin 924

Stolen Bases
Coleman-StL 81
Young-Hou 65
Smith-StL 57
Sabo-Cin 46
Nixon-Mon 46

Stolen Base Average
McReynolds-NY . 100.0
Davis-Cin 92.1
Gibson-LA 88.6
McGee-StL 87.2
Smith-StL 86.4

Stolen Base Runs
Smith-StL 11.7
McGee-StL 8.7
Davis-Cin 8.7
Coleman-StL 8.1
Larkin-Cin 7.8

Fielding Runs
Smith-StL 22.9
Bream-Pit 20.9
Sabo-Cin 18.8
Murphy-Atl 17.5
VanSlyke-Pit ... 16.7

Total Player Rating
Strawberry-NY ... 5.2
VanSlyke-Pit 5.1
Smith-StL 5.1
Gibson-LA 5.0
Larkin-Cin 4.5

Wins
Jackson-Cin 23
Hershiser-LA 23
Cone-NY 20
Reuschel-SF 19

Win Percentage
Cone-NY 870
Browning-Cin 783
Jackson-Cin ..... .742
Hershiser-LA .... .742
Maddux-Chi ..... .692

Games
Murphy-NY 76
Robinson-Pit 75
Agosto-Hou 75
Tekulve-Phi 70
Franco-Cin 70

Complete Games
Jackson-Cin 15
Hershiser-LA 15
Show-SD 13
Sutcliffe-Chi 12
Gooden-NY 10

Shutouts
Hershiser-LA 8
Leary-LA 6
Jackson-Cin 6
Scott-Hou 5
Ojeda-NY 5

Saves
Franco-Cin 39
Gott-Pit 34
Worrell-StL 32
Davis-SD 28
Bedrosian-Phi 28

Innings Pitched
Hershiser-LA 267.0
Jackson-Cin 260.2
Browning-Cin ...250.2
Mahler-Atl 249.0
Maddux-Chi 249.0

Fewest Hits/Game
Fernandez-NY ... 6.11
Perez-Mon 6.37
Rijo-Cin 6.67
Scott-Hou 6.67
Cone-NY 6.93

Fewest BB/Game
B.Smith-Mon 1.45
Mahler-Atl 1.52
Reuschel-SF 1.54
Ojeda-NY 1.56
Tudor-StL-LA 1.87

Strikeouts
Ryan-Hou 228
Cone-NY 213
DeLeon-StL 208
Scott-Hou 190
Fernandez-NY ... 189

Strikeouts/Game
Ryan-Hou 9.33
Fernandez-NY ... 9.10
Rijo-Cin 8.89
DeLeon-StL 8.31
Cone-NY 8.29

Ratio
Perez-Mon 8.81
Scott-Hou 9.18
Ojeda-NY 9.22
Hershiser-LA 9.61
Jackson-Cin 9.63

Earned Run Average
Magrane-StL 2.18
Cone-NY 2.22
Hershiser-LA 2.26
Tudor-StL-LA 2.32
Rijo-Cin 2.39

Adjusted ERA
Magrane-StL 160
Rijo-Cin 150
Tudor-StL-LA ... 148
Hershiser-LA ... 147
Perez-Mon 147

Opponents' Batting Avg.
Fernandez-NY 191
Perez-Mon 196
Scott-Hou 204
Rijo-Cin 209
Cone-NY 213

Opponents' On Base Pct.
Perez-Mon 253
Scott-Hou 261
Ojeda-NY 264
Hershiser-LA 271
Fernandez-NY ...274

Starter Runs
Hershiser-LA 35.3
Cone-NY 31.6
Tudor-StL-LA ... 24.7
Magrane-StL ... 23.3
Perez-Mon 21.0

Adjusted Starter Runs
Hershiser-LA ... 31.8
Cone-NY 25.8
Jackson-Cin 24.7
Tudor-StL-LA ... 24.5
Perez-Mon 24.1

Clutch Pitching Index
Tudor-StL-LA 135
Rawley-Phi 122
Moyer-Chi 118
Robinson-SF 113
D.Martinez-Mon ... 112

Relief Runs
Franco-Cin 17.9
Holton-LA 16.4
Pena-LA 16.1
Davis-SD 15.7
Myers-NY 13.0

Adjusted Relief Runs
Franco-Cin 19.2
Holton-LA 16.1
Davis-SD 15.1
Pena-LA 14.9
Harris-Phi 14.3

Relief Ranking
Franco-Cin 43.8
Davis-SD 30.4
Myers-NY 24.7
Pena-LA 22.7
Holton-LA 16.7

Total Pitcher Index
Franco-Cin 5.0
Hershiser-LA 4.5
Davis-SD 3.8
Jackson-Cin 3.2
D.Martinez-Mon ... 3.0

Total Baseball Ranking
Strawberry-NY ... 5.2
VanSlyke-Pit 5.1
Smith-StL 5.1
Franco-Cin 5.0
Gibson-LA 5.0

TEAM	G	W	L	PCT	GB	R	OR	AB	H	2B	3B	HR	BB	SO	AVG	OBP	SLG	PRO	PRO+	BR	/A	PF	CHI	RC	SB	CS	SBA	SBR
EAST																												
BOS	162	89	73	.549		**813**	689	5545	**1569**	310	39	124	**623**	728	**.283**	.360	.420	**.780**	113	**140**	**104**	104	94	**842**	65	36	64	-2
DET	162	88	74	.543	1	703	658	5433	1358	213	28	143	588	841	.250	.326	.378	.704	100	-20	6	96	103	673	87	42	67	1
TOR	162	87	75	.537	2	763	680	5557	1491	271	47	158	521	935	.268	.334	.419	.753	109	68	65	100	98	771	107	36	75	11
MIL	162	87	75	.537	2	682	**616**	5488	1409	258	26	113	439	911	.257	.316	.375	.691	92	-56	-61	101	**107**	648	**159**	55	74	15
NY	161	85	76	.528	3.5	772	748	5592	1469	272	12	148	588	935	.263	.336	.395	.731	105	33	39	99	102	754	146	39	**79**	**20**
CLE	162	78	84	.481	11	666	731	5505	1435	235	28	134	416	866	.261	.317	.387	.704	94	-35	-52	103	101	667	97	50	66	-1
BAL	161	54	107	.335	34.5	550	789	5358	1275	199	20	137	504	869	.238	.307	.359	.666	88	-101	-85	97	94	581	69	44	61	-6
WEST																												
OAK	162	104	58	.642		800	620	5602	1474	251	22	156	580	926	.263	.339	.399	.738	110	50	77	97	103	763	129	54	70	6
MIN	162	91	71	.562	13	759	672	5510	1508	294	31	151	528	832	.274	.343	**.421**	.764	110	94	71	103	95	785	107	63	63	-6
KC	162	84	77	.522	19.5	704	648	5469	1419	275	40	121	486	944	.259	.324	.391	.715	98	-9	-15	101	102	696	137	54	72	9
CAL	162	75	87	.463	29	714	771	5582	1458	258	31	124	469	819	.261	.324	.385	.709	101	-18	1	97	103	690	86	52	62	-5
CHI	161	71	90	.441	32.5	631	757	5449	1327	224	35	132	446	908	.244	.305	.370	.675	88	-92	-90	100	105	609	98	46	68	2
TEX	161	70	91	.435	33.5	637	735	5479	1378	227	39	112	542	1022	.252	.323	.368	.691	91	-47	-63	102	97	661	130	57	70	5
SEA	161	68	93	.422	35.5	664	744	5436	1397	271	27	148	461	787	.257	.319	.398	.717	95	-7	-37	104	97	673	95	61	70	-8
TOT	1131					9858		77005	19967	3558	425	1901	7191	12323	.259	.327	.391	.718							1512	689	69	40

TEAM	CG	SH	SV	IP	H	H/G	HR	BB	SO	RAT	ERA	ERA+	OAV	OOB	PR	/A	PF	CPI	FA	E	DP	FW	PW	BW	SBW	DIF
EAST																										
BOS	26	14	37	1426¹	1415	8.9	143	493	**1085**	12.3	3.97	104	.259	.324	-1	23	104	99	.984	93	123	1.6	2.3	**10.5**	-.5	-5.9
DET	34	8	36	1445²	1361	8.5	150	497	890	11.8	3.71	103	.248	.314	41	17	96	99	.982	109	129	.6	1.7	.6	-.2	4.2
TOR	16	**17**	47	1449	1404	8.7	143	528	904	12.4	3.80	104	.256	.328	27	22	99	**105**	.982	110	170	.6	2.2	6.6	.8	-4.2
MIL	30	8	51	1449¹	1355	8.4	125	**437**	832	**11.2**	3.45	**115**	.248	**.306**	84	**85**	100	99	.981	120	146	-.0	**8.6**	-6.2	1.2	2.4
NY	16	5	43	1456	1512	9.3	157	487	861	12.7	4.26	92	.267	.331	-48	-52	99	104	.978	134	161	-.9	-5.3	3.9	**1.7**	5.0
CLE	35	10	46	1434	1501	9.4	120	442	812	12.4	4.16	99	.270	.328	-31	-8	104	97	.980	124	131	-.3	-.8	-5.3	-.4	3.7
BAL	20	7	26	1416	1506	9.6	153	523	709	13.2	4.54	86	.274	.342	-90	-100	98	99	.980	119	172	.0	-10.1	-8.6	-.9	-6.9
WEST																										
OAK	22	9	**64**	1489¹	1376	8.3	116	553	983	11.8	**3.44**	110	.247	.318	**87**	56	95	104	.983	105	151	.9	5.7	7.8	.3	8.4
MIN	18	9	52	1431²	1457	9.2	146	453	897	12.3	3.93	104	.266	.327	6	22	103	104	**.986**	**84**	155	**2.1**	2.2	7.2	-.9	-.6
KC	29	12	32	1428¹	1415	8.9	102	465	886	12.1	3.65	109	.258	.320	49	52	101	100	.980	124	147	-.3	5.3	-1.5	.6	-.6
CAL	26	9	33	1455²	1503	9.3	135	568	817	13.1	4.32	89	.270	.342	-57	-74	97	101	.979	135	175	-.9	-7.5	-.1	-.8	3.1
CHI	11	9	43	1439	1467	9.2	138	533	754	12.7	4.12	96	.266	.334	-25	-24	100	101	.976	154	**177**	-2.1	-2.4	-9.1	-.0	4.2
TEX	**41**	11	31	1438²	**1310**	**8.2**	129	654	912	12.6	4.05	101	**.244**	.332	-13	5	103	95	.979	131	145	-.7	.5	-6.4	.2	-4.1
SEA	28	11	28	1428	1385	8.7	144	558	981	12.5	4.15	100	.256	.330	-30	1	105	97	.980	123	168	-.2	.1	-3.7	-1.1	-7.5
TOT	352	139	569	20187		8.9				12.4	3.97		.259	.327					.981	1665	2150					

Runs		Hits		Doubles		Triples		Home Runs		Total Bases	
Boggs-Bos	128	Puckett-Min	234	Boggs-Bos	45	Yount-Mil	11	Canseco-Oak	42	Puckett-Min	358
Canseco-Oak	120	Boggs-Bos	214	Ray-Cal	42	Wilson-KC	11	McGriff-Tor	34	Canseco-Oak	347
Henderson-NY	118	Greenwell-Bos	192	Puckett-Min	42	Reynolds-Sea	11	McGwire-Oak	32	Greenwell-Bos	313
Molitor-Mil	115	Yount-Mil	190	Brett-KC	42	Greenwell-Bos	8	Murray-Bal	28	Brett-KC	300
Puckett-Min	109	Molitor-Mil	190	Fernandez-Tor	41			Gaetti-Min	28	Carter-Cle	297

Runs Batted In		Runs Produced		Bases On Balls		Batting Average		On Base Percentage		Slugging Average	
Canseco-Oak	124	Puckett-Min	206	Boggs-Bos	125	Boggs-Bos	.366	Boggs-Bos	.480	Canseco-Oak	.569
Puckett-Min	121	Canseco-Oak	202	Clark-NY	113	Puckett-Min	.356	Greenwell-Bos	.420	McGriff-Tor	.552
Greenwell-Bos	119	Evans-Bos	186	C.Ripken-Bal	102	Greenwell-Bos	.325	Davis-Sea	.416	Gaetti-Min	.551
Evans-Bos	111	Greenwell-Bos	183	Davis-Sea	95	Winfield-NY	.322	Winfield-NY	.398	Puckett-Min	.545
Winfield-NY	107	Boggs-Bos	181	Greenwell-Bos	87	Molitor-Mil	.312	Henderson-NY	.397	Greenwell-Bos	.531

Production		Adjusted Production		Batter Runs		Adjusted Batter Runs		Clutch Hitting Index		Runs Created	
Boggs-Bos	.970	Canseco-Oak	172	Boggs-Bos	65.8	Boggs-Bos	59.7	Barrett-Bos	135	Boggs-Bos	140
Canseco-Oak	.963	Boggs-Bos	165	Canseco-Oak	54.1	Canseco-Oak	58.9	Hall-Cle	123	Canseco-Oak	136
Greenwell-Bos	.950	Winfield-NY	159	Greenwell-Bos	53.4	Greenwell-Bos	47.9	Larkin-Min	121	Greenwell-Bos	134
McGriff-Tor	.930	Greenwell-Bos	158	Puckett-Min	45.5	Winfield-NY	44.4	Evans-Bos	120	Puckett-Min	126
Winfield-NY	.928	McGriff-Tor	156	Winfield-NY	43.4	Puckett-Min	42.0	Clark-NY	118	Brett-KC	119

Total Average		Stolen Bases		Stolen Base Average		Stolen Base Runs		Fielding Runs		Total Player Rating	
Boggs-Bos	1.043	Henderson-NY	93	Javier-Oak	95.2	Henderson-NY	20.1	Guillen-Chi	42.6	Canseco-Oak	6.4
Canseco-Oak	1.011	Pettis-Det	44	Redus-Chi	92.9	Pettis-Det	7.2	Gruber-Tor	25.1	Puckett-Min	5.4
Greenwell-Bos	1.000	Molitor-Mil	41	Cotto-Sea	90.0	Redus-Chi	6.6	Schofield-Cal	23.2	Boggs-Bos	5.3
McGriff-Tor	.958	Canseco-Oak	40	Henderson-NY	87.7			Puckett-Min	19.5	Greenwell-Bos	4.9
Henderson-NY	.955			Yount-Mil	84.6			Gladden-Min	16.3	Henderson-NY	4.7

Wins		Win Percentage		Games		Complete Games		Shutouts		Saves	
Viola-Min	24	Viola-Min	.774	Crim-Mil	70	Stewart-Oak	14	Clemens-Bos	8	Eckersley-Oak	45
Stewart-Oak	21	Hurst-Bos	.750	Thigpen-Chi	68	Clemens-Bos	14	Swindell-Cle	4	Reardon-Min	42
Gubicza-KC	20	Gubicza-KC	.714	Williams-Tex	67	Witt-Tex	13	Stieb-Tor	4	Jones-Cle	37
		Davis-Oak	.696	Henneman-Det	65	Witt-Cal	12	Gubicza-KC	4	Thigpen-Chi	34
		Stieb-Tor	.667			Swindell-Cle	12			Plesac-Mil	30

Innings Pitched		Fewest Hits/Game		Fewest BB/Game		Strikeouts		Strikeouts/Game		Ratio	
Stewart-Oak	275.2	Robinson-Det	6.33	Anderson-Min	1.65	Clemens-Bos	291	Clemens-Bos	9.92	Higuera-Mil	9.22
Gubicza-KC	269.2	Higuera-Mil	6.65	Swindell-Cle	1.67	Langston-Sea	235	Langston-Sea	8.09	Clemens-Bos	9.72
Clemens-Bos	264.0	Stieb-Tor	6.82	Alexander-Det	1.81	Viola-Min	193	Witt-Tex	7.64	Robinson-Det	10.26
Langston-Sea	261.1	Witt-Tex	6.92	Bosio-Mil	1.88	Stewart-Oak	192	Higuera-Mil	7.60	Moore-Sea	10.31
Saberhagen-KC	260.2	Hough-Tex	7.21	Viola-Min	1.90	Higuera-Mil	192	Moore-Sea	7.16	Viola-Min	10.33

Earned Run Average		Adjusted ERA		Opponents' Batting Avg.		Opponents' On Base Pct.		Starter Runs		Adjusted Starter Runs	
Anderson-Min	2.45	Anderson-Min	166	Robinson-Det	.197	Higuera-Mil	.265	Higuera-Mil	38.2	Viola-Min	40.4
Higuera-Mil	2.45	Higuera-Mil	162	Higuera-Mil	.207	Clemens-Bos	.270	Gubicza-KC	37.8	Higuera-Mil	38.5
Viola-Min	2.64	Viola-Min	154	Stieb-Tor	.210	Robinson-Det	.284	Viola-Min	37.5	Gubicza-KC	38.4
Gubicza-KC	2.70	Gubicza-KC	147	Witt-Tex	.216	Moore-Sea	.287	Anderson-Min	34.1	Anderson-Min	36.5
Clemens-Bos	2.93	Clemens-Bos	140	Clemens-Bos	.220	Swindell-Cle	.287	Clemens-Bos	30.3	Clemens-Bos	34.6

Clutch Pitching Index		Relief Runs		Adjusted Relief Runs		Relief Ranking		Total Pitcher Index		Total Baseball Ranking	
Anderson-Min	138	Henneman-Det	21.2	Henneman-Det	19.7	Henneman-Det	39.8	Viola-Min	4.6	Canseco-Oak	6.4
Davis-Oak	121	Jones-Cle	15.7	Jones-Cle	17.1	Jones-Cle	30.0	Anderson-Min	4.5	Puckett-Min	5.4
Candiotti-Cle	116	Harvey-Cal	15.5	Jackson-Sea	16.9	Harvey-Cal	28.1	Higuera-Mil	4.3	Boggs-Bos	5.3
Leibrandt-KC	116	Mirabella-Mil	15.4	Mirabella-Mil	15.5	Reardon-Min	26.4	Gubicza-KC	4.2	Greenwell-Bos	4.9
Viola-Min	115	Jackson-Sea	14.8	Harvey-Cal	14.6	Eckersley-Oak	24.6	Henneman-Det	4.1	Henderson-NY	4.7

TEAM	G	W	L	PCT	GB	R	OR	AB	H	2B	3B	HR	BB	SO	AVG	OBP	SLG	PRO	PRO+	BR	/A	PF	CHI	RC	SB	CS	SBA	SBR
EAST																												
CHI	162	93	69	.574		**702**	623	5513	**1438**	235	45	124	472	921	**.261**	.322	.387	**.709**	101	54	3	107	101	**685**	136	57	70	7
NY	162	87	75	.537	6	683	595	5489	1351	**280**	21	**147**	504	934	.246	.313	.385	.698	110	30	62	95	102	676	158	53	**75**	**16**
STL	164	86	76	.531	7	632	608	5492	1418	263	47	73	507	848	.258	**.323**	.363	.686	99	16	-5	103	97	652	155	54	74	14
MON	162	81	81	.500	12	632	630	5482	1353	267	30	100	**572**	958	.247	.322	.361	.683	100	13	4	101	96	645	**160**	70	70	6
PIT	164	74	88	.457	19	637	680	5539	1334	263	**53**	95	563	914	.241	.314	.359	.673	102	-13	9	97	100	629	155	69	69	5
PHI	163	67	95	.414	26	629	735	5447	1324	215	36	123	558	926	.243	.316	.364	.680	100	1	1	100	99	634	106	50	68	2
WEST																												
SF	162	92	70	.568		699	600	5469	1365	241	52	141	508	1071	.250	.318	**.390**	.708	**111**	50	**69**	97	102	683	87	54	62	-6
SD	162	89	73	.549	3	642	626	5422	1360	215	32	120	552	1013	.251	.321	.369	.690	103	22	21	100	98	644	136	67	67	1
HOU	162	86	76	.531	6	647	669	5516	1316	239	28	97	530	860	.239	.308	.345	.653	95	-50	-29	97	109	606	144	62	70	6
LA	160	77	83	.481	14	554	**536**	5465	1313	241	17	89	507	885	.240	.308	.339	.647	93	-61	-51	98	96	576	81	54	60	-8
CIN	162	75	87	.463	17	632	691	5520	1362	243	28	128	493	1028	.247	.312	.370	.682	97	1	-21	103	99	639	128	71	64	-4
ATL	161	63	97	.394	28	584	680	5463	1281	201	22	128	485	996	.234	.300	.350	.650	89	-64	-79	103	103	575	83	54	61	-8
TOT	973					7673		65817	16215	2903	411	1365	6251	11354	.246	.315	.365	.680							1529	715	68	30

TEAM	CG	SH	SV	IP	H	H/G	HR	BB	SO	RAT	ERA	ERA+	OAV	OOB	PR	/A	PF	CPI	FA	E	DP	FW	PW	BW	SBW	DIF
EAST																										
CHI	18	10	55	1460¹	1369	8.4	106	532	918	11.9	3.43	110	.250	.319	11	54	108	104	.980	124	130	.6	5.8	.3	.5	4.8
NY	24	12	38	1454¹	**1260**	7.8	115	532	**1108**	11.3	3.29	99	**.231**	**.303**	33	-5	93	95	.976	144	110	-.6	-.5	6.6	**1.4**	-1.0
STL	18	18	43	1461	1330	8.2	**84**	482	844	11.3	3.36	108	.243	.308	21	43	104	95	**.982**	112	134	**1.4**	4.6	-.5	1.2	-1.7
MON	20	13	35	1468¹	1344	8.2	120	519	1059	11.6	3.48	102	.245	.314	3	9	101	101	.979	136	126	-.1	1.0	.4	.4	-1.7
PIT	20	9	40	1487²	1394	8.4	121	539	827	11.9	3.64	92	.248	.317	-24	-47	96	98	.975	160	130	-1.4	-5.0	1.0	.3	-1.8
PHI	10	10	33	1433¹	1408	8.8	127	613	899	12.9	4.04	88	.259	.337	-87	-80	101	101	.979	133	136	.1	-8.6	.1	-.0	-5.6
WEST																										
SF	12	16	47	1457	1320	8.2	120	471	802	11.2	3.30	102	.243	.307	31	11	97	102	**.982**	114	135	1.2	1.2	**7.4**	-.9	2.2
SD	21	11	52	1457¹	1359	8.4	133	481	933	11.5	3.38	103	.249	.312	19	19	100	106	.976	154	147	-1.1	2.0	2.2	-.2	5.0
HOU	19	12	38	1479¹	1379	8.4	105	551	965	11.9	3.64	93	.247	.318	-25	-42	97	96	.977	142	121	-.4	-4.5	-3.1	.4	12.7
LA	**25**	**19**	36	1463¹	1278	7.9	95	504	1052	**11.1**	**2.95**	**116**	.237	.306	89	76	101	107	.981	118	**153**	.8	**8.1**	-5.5	-1.1	-5.4
CIN	16	9	37	1464¹	1404	8.6	125	559	981	12.3	3.73	96	.253	.326	-38	-21	103	102	.980	121	108	.8	-2.2	-2.2	-.7	-1.6
ATL	15	8	33	1447²	1370	8.5	114	**468**	966	11.5	3.70	99	.250	.311	-33	-8	104	94	.976	152	124	-1.1	-.9	-8.4	-1.1	-5.5
TOT	218	147	487	17534		8.3				11.7	3.49		.246	.315					.978	1610	1554					

Runs		Hits		Doubles		Triples		Home Runs		Total Bases	
Sandberg-Chi	104	Gwynn-SD	203	Wallach-Mon	42	Thompson-SF	11	Mitchell-SF	47	Mitchell-SF	345
Johnson-NY	104	Clark-SF	196	Guerrero-StL	42	Bonilla-Pit	10	Johnson-NY	36	Clark-SF	321
Clark-SF	104	R.Alomar-SD	184	Johnson-NY	41	VanSlyke-Pit	9	Davis-Hou	34	Johnson-NY	319
Mitchell-SF	100	Guerrero-StL	177	Clark-SF	38	Coleman-StL	9	Davis-Cin	34	Bonilla-Pit	302
Butler-SF	100	Sandberg-Chi	176	Bonilla-Pit	37	Clark-SF	9	Sandberg-Chi	30	Sandberg-Chi	301

Runs Batted In		Runs Produced		Bases On Balls		Batting Average		On Base Percentage		Slugging Average	
Mitchell-SF	125	Clark-SF	192	J.Clark-SD	132	Gwynn-SD	.336	L.Smith-Atl	.420	Mitchell-SF	.635
Guerrero-StL	117	Mitchell-SF	178	V.Hayes-Phi	101	Clark-SF	.333	J.Clark-SD	.413	Johnson-NY	.559
Clark-SF	111	Johnson-NY	169	Raines-Mon	93	L.Smith-Atl	.315	Clark-SF	.412	Clark-SF	.546
Johnson-NY	101	Guerrero-StL	160	Bonds-Pit	93	Grace-Chi	.314	Grace-Chi	.407	Davis-Cin	.541
Davis-Cin	101	Bonilla-Pit	158			Guerrero-StL	.311	Guerrero-StL	.398	L.Smith-Atl	.533

Production		Adjusted Production		Batter Runs		Adjusted Batter Runs		Clutch Hitting Index		Runs Created	
Mitchell-SF	1.027	Mitchell-SF	194	Mitchell-SF	62.1	Mitchell-SF	65.8	Guerrero-StL	132	Mitchell-SF	136
Clark-SF	.958	Clark-SF	177	Clark-SF	55.6	Clark-SF	59.2	Hatcher-Hou-Pit	121	Johnson-NY	127
L.Smith-Atl	.953	Johnson-NY	171	L.Smith-Atl	47.0	Johnson-NY	51.3	J.Clark-SD	120	L.Smith-Atl	113
Johnson-NY	.932	L.Smith-Atl	166	Johnson-NY	45.7	L.Smith-Atl	44.2	Doran-Hou	117	Guerrero-StL	109
Davis-Cin	.916	Davis-Cin	154	Guerrero-StL	38.3	Bonilla-Pit	36.1	Murphy-Atl	115		

Total Average		Stolen Bases		Stolen Base Average		Stolen Base Runs		Fielding Runs		Total Player Rating	
Mitchell-SF	1.099	Coleman-StL	65	Doran-Hou	88.0	Coleman-StL	13.5	Pendleton-StL	30.2	Mitchell-SF	7.0
Johnson-NY	1.026	Samuel-Phi-NY	42	Biggio-Hou	87.5	Johnson-NY	7.5	Young-Hou	26.3	L.Smith-Atl	5.2
L.Smith-Atl	1.023	R.Alomar-SD	42	Coleman-StL	86.7	Raines-Mon	6.9	Oquendo-StL	20.4	Clark-SF	5.0
Clark-SF	1.010	Raines-Mon	41	D.Martinez-Mon	85.2	Samuel-Phi-NY	5.4	Foley-Mon	19.8	Bonds-Pit	4.2
J.Clark-SD	.969	Johnson-NY	41	Johnson-NY	83.7	Doran-Hou	4.8	Bonds-Pit	19.7	Bonilla-Pit	4.2

Wins		Win Percentage		Games		Complete Games		Shutouts		Saves	
Scott-Hou	20	Bielecki-Chi	.720	Williams-Chi	76	Hurst-SD	10	Belcher-LA	8	Davis-SD	44
Maddux-Chi	19	D.Martinez-Mon	.696	Dibble-Cin	74	Belcher-LA	10	Drabek-Pit	5	Williams-Chi	36
Magrane-StL	18	Reuschel-SF	.680	Parrett-Phi	72	Scott-Hou	9	Langston-Mon	4	Franco-Cin	32
Bielecki-Chi	18	Scott-Hou	.667	Dayley-StL	71	Magrane-StL	9	Hershiser-LA	4	Howell-LA	28
Reuschel-SF	17	Magrane-StL	.667	Agosto-Hou	71	Browning-Cin	9	Glavine-Atl	4	Burke-Mon	28

Innings Pitched		Fewest Hits/Game		Fewest BB/Game		Strikeouts		Strikeouts/Game		Ratio	
Hershiser-LA	256.2	DeLeon-StL	6.36	Robinson-SF	1.69	DeLeon-StL	201	Langston-Mon	8.92	Garrelts-SF	9.08
Browning-Cin	249.2	Fernandez-NY	6.44	Lilliquist-Atl	1.85	Belcher-LA	200	Fernandez-NY	8.12	DeLeon-StL	9.53
Hurst-SD	244.2	Howell-Phi	6.84	D.Martinez-Mon	1.90	Fernandez-NY	198	Belcher-LA	7.83	Scott-Hou	9.63
DeLeon-StL	244.2	Smoltz-Atl	6.92	Whitson-SD	1.90	Cone-NY	190	Cone-NY	7.78	Fernandez-NY	9.77
Drabek-Pit	244.1	Garrelts-SF	6.94	Glavine-Atl	1.94	Hurst-SD	179	DeLeon-StL	7.39	B.Smith-Mon	9.81

Earned Run Average		Adjusted ERA		Opponents' Batting Avg.		Opponents' On Base Pct.		Starter Runs		Adjusted Starter Runs	
Garrelts-SF	2.28	Garrelts-SF	148	DeLeon-StL	.197	Garrelts-SF	.260	Hershiser-LA	33.7	Hershiser-LA	31.4
Hershiser-LA	2.31	Hershiser-LA	148	Fernandez-NY	.198	Scott-Hou	.268	Garrelts-SF	26.1	Garrelts-SF	23.4
Langston-Mon	2.39	Langston-Mon	147	Smoltz-Atl	.212	DeLeon-StL	.269	Hurst-SD	22.0	Langston-Mon	22.3
Whitson-SD	2.66	Whitson-SD	132	Garrelts-SF	.212	Fernandez-NY	.272	Langston-Mon	21.6	Hurst-SD	22.0
Hurst-SD	2.69	Hurst-SD	130	Scott-Hou	.212	Smiley-Pit	.276	Whitson-SD	21.2	Maddux-Chi	21.5

Clutch Pitching Index		Relief Runs		Adjusted Relief Runs		Relief Ranking		Total Pitcher Index		Total Baseball Ranking	
Langston-Mon	135	Andersen-Hou	19.0	Lancaster-Chi	19.3	Davis-SD	29.7	Hershiser-LA	4.6	Mitchell-SF	7.0
Hershiser-LA	124	Lancaster-Chi	17.2	Andersen-Hou	18.0	Howell-LA	27.5	Maddux-Chi	3.4	L.Smith-Atl	5.2
Lilliquist-Atl	117	Davis-SD	17.0	Davis-SD	17.0	McDowell-NY-Phi	26.3	McDowell-NY-Phi	3.3	Clark-SF	5.0
Maddux-Chi	115	Howell-LA	16.9	Dibble-Cin	16.6	Dibble-Cin	23.4	Davis-SD	3.0	Hershiser-LA	4.6
Drabek-Pit	113	Landrum-Pit	16.5	Howell-LA	16.2	Landrum-Pit	19.4	Howell-LA	3.0	Bonds-Pit	4.2

TEAM	G	W	L	PCT	GB	R	OR	AB	H	2B	3B	HR	BB	SO	AVG	OBP	SLG	PRO	PRO+	BR	/A	PF	CHI	RC	SB	CS	SBA	SBR
EAST																												
TOR	162	89	73	.549		731	651	5581	1449	265	40	142	521	923	.260	.326	.398	.724	105	18	32	98	102	724	144	58	71	8
BAL	162	87	75	.537	2	708	686	5440	1369	238	33	129	593	957	.252	.329	.379	.708	102	-6	15	97	102	678	118	55	68	2
BOS	162	83	79	.512	6	774	735	5666	1571	326	30	108	643	755	.277	.355	.403	.758	106	106	55	106	93	802	56	35	62	-4
MIL	162	81	81	.500	8	707	679	5473	1415	235	32	126	455	791	.259	.321	.382	.703	98	-22	-15	99	106	677	165	62	73	12
NY	161	74	87	.460	14.5	698	792	5458	1470	229	23	130	502	831	.269	.334	.391	.725	105	26	35	99	99	709	137	60	70	5
CLE	162	73	89	.451	16	604	654	5463	1340	221	26	127	499	934	.245	.312	.365	.677	89	-72	-82	102	98	622	74	51	59	-8
DET	162	59	103	.364	30	617	816	5432	1315	198	24	116	585	899	.242	.320	.351	.671	91	-74	-60	98	100	616	103	50	67	1
WEST																												
OAK	162	99	63	.611		712	576	5416	1414	220	25	127	562	855	.261	.334	.381	.715	105	12	37	96	101	687	157	55	74	14
KC	162	92	70	.568	7	690	635	5475	1428	227	41	101	554	897	.261	.332	.373	.705	98	-9	-6	100	101	682	154	51	75	16
CAL	162	91	71	.562	8	669	578	5545	1422	208	37	145	429	1011	.256	.313	.386	.699	98	-38	-26	98	103	663	89	40	69	3
TEX	162	83	79	.512	16	695	714	5458	1433	260	46	122	503	989	.263	.329	.394	.723	101	18	7	102	98	694	101	49	67	1
MIN	162	80	82	.494	19	740	738	5581	1442	278	35	117	478	743	.276	.338	.402	.740	101	53	3	107	98	751	111	53	68	2
SEA	162	73	89	.451	26	694	728	5512	1417	237	29	134	489	838	.257	.323	.384	.707	95	-16	-38	103	103	679	81	55	60	-9
CHI	161	69	92	.429	29.5	693	750	5504	1493	262	36	94	464	873	.271	.331	.383	.714	103	4	21	98	100	696	97	52	65	-2
TOT	1133					9732		77004	20078	3404	457	1718	7277	12296	.261	.328	.384	.712							1587	726	69	41

TEAM	CG	SH	SV	IP	H	H/G	HR	BB	SO	RAT	ERA	ERA+	OAV	OOB	PR	/A	PF	CPI	FA	E	DP	FW	PW	BW	SBW	DIF
EAST																										
TOR	12	12	38	1467	1408	8.6	99	478	849	11.8	3.58	105	.255	.320	49	31	97	99	.980	127	164	-.1	3.2	3.3	.5	1.2
BAL	16	7	44	1448[1]	1518	9.4	134	486	676	12.6	4.00	95	.272	.333	-19	-33	98	104	.986	87	163	2.3	-3.4	1.5	-.0	5.6
BOS	14	9	42	1460[1]	1448	8.9	131	548	1054	12.5	4.01	102	.261	.331	-20	15	106	99	.980	127	162	-.1	1.5	5.6	-.7	-4.3
MIL	16	8	45	1432[1]	1463	9.2	129	457	812	12.2	3.80	101	.264	.324	14	7	99	102	.975	155	164	-1.8	.7	-1.5	.9	1.7
NY	15	9	44	1414[2]	1550	9.9	150	521	787	13.4	4.50	86	.281	.347	-98	-100	100	102	.980	122	183	.1	-10.2	3.6	.2	-.2
CLE	23	13	38	1453	1423	8.8	107	452	844	11.8	3.65	109	.257	.315	38	50	102	96	.981	118	126	.4	5.1	-8.3	-1.1	-4.1
DET	24	4	26	1427[1]	1514	9.5	150	652	831	13.9	4.53	84	.274	.355	-103	-114	98	103	.979	130	153	-.3	-11.6	-6.1	-.2	-3.8
WEST																										
OAK	17	20	57	1448[1]	1287	8.0	103	510	930	11.3	3.09	119	.238	.307	128	95	95	103	.979	129	159	-.2	9.7	3.8	1.1	3.7
KC	27	13	38	1451[2]	1415	8.8	86	455	978	11.7	3.55	109	.257	.316	54	49	99	97	.982	114	139	.7	5.0	-.6	1.3	4.6
CAL	32	20	38	1454[1]	1384	8.6	113	465	897	11.6	3.28	116	.253	.315	97	86	98	107	.985	96	173	1.7	8.8	-2.6	-.0	2.1
TEX	26	7	44	1434[1]	1279	8.0	119	654	1112	12.4	3.91	101	.239	.327	-4	9	102	92	.978	136	137	-.6	.9	.7	-.2	1.2
MIN	19	8	38	1429[1]	1495	9.4	139	500	851	12.8	4.28	97	.269	.334	-63	-23	107	97	.982	107	141	1.1	-2.3	.3	-.0	-.0
SEA	15	10	44	1438	1422	8.9	114	560	897	12.7	4.00	101	.259	.333	-19	4	104	98	.977	143	168	-1.1	.4	-3.9	-1.2	-2.3
CHI	9	5	46	1422	1472	9.3	144	539	778	12.9	4.23	90	.269	.338	-54	-67	98	101	.975	151	176	-1.6	-6.8	2.1	-.5	-4.7
TOT	265	145	582	20181		9.0				12.4	3.88		.261	.328					.980	1742	2208					

Runs
R.Henderson-NY-Oak .. 113
Boggs-Bos 113
Yount-Mil 101
Sierra-Tex 101
McGriff-Tor 98

Hits
Puckett-Min 215
Sax-NY 205
Boggs-Bos 205
Reed-Bos 195

Doubles
Boggs-Bos 51
Puckett-Min 45
Reed-Bos 42
Bell-Tor 41
Yount-Mil 38

Triples
Sierra-Tex 14
White-Cal 13
Bradley-Bal 10

Home Runs
McGriff-Tor 36
Carter-Cle 35
McGwire-Oak 33
Jackson-KC 32
Esasky-Bos 30

Total Bases
Sierra-Tex 344
Yount-Mil 314
Carter-Cle 303
Mattingly-NY 301
Puckett-Min 295

Runs Batted In
Sierra-Tex 119
Mattingly-NY 113
Esasky-Bos 108
Jackson-KC 105
Carter-Cle 105

Runs Produced
Sierra-Tex 191
Yount-Mil 183
Bell-Tor 174
Mattingly-NY 169
Greenwell-Bos 168

Bases On Balls
R.Henderson-NY-Oak . 126
McGriff-Tor 119
Boggs-Bos 107
Seitzer-KC 102
Davis-Sea 101

Batting Average
Puckett-Min 339
Lansford-Oak 336
Boggs-Bos 330
Yount-Mil 318
Franco-Tex 316

On Base Percentage
Boggs-Bos 434
Davis-Sea 428
R.Henderson-NY-Oak .413
McGriff-Tor 402
Evans-Bos 402

Slugging Average
Sierra-Tex 543
McGriff-Tor 525
Yount-Mil 511
Esasky-Bos 500
Davis-Sea 496

Production
McGriff-Tor 927
Davis-Sea 924
Yount-Mil 898
Sierra-Tex 895
Boggs-Bos 883

Adjusted Production
McGriff-Tor 162
Davis-Sea 155
Yount-Mil 152
Sierra-Tex 146
Baines-Chi-Tex 144

Batter Runs
McGriff-Tor 46.8
Boggs-Bos 46.6
Davis-Sea 44.2
Yount-Mil 41.2
Sierra-Tex 37.4

Adjusted Batter Runs
McGriff-Tor 49.1
Yount-Mil 42.3
Davis-Sea 40.7
Boggs-Bos 38.7
Sierra-Tex 35.6

Clutch Hitting Index
Evans-Bos 122
Brett-KC 121
Mattingly-NY 119
Ray-Cal 118
Greenwell-Bos 113

Runs Created
Yount-Mil 125
Boggs-Bos 122
Sierra-Tex 122
McGriff-Tor 121
R.Henderson-NY-Oak . 110

Total Average
McGriff-Tor 986
R.Henderson-NY-Oak ..983
Davis-Sea 975
Yount-Mil 926
Boggs-Bos 882

Stolen Bases
R.Henderson-NY-Oak .. 77
Espy-Tex 45
White-Cal 44
Sax-NY 43
Pettis-Det 43

Stolen Base Average
Thurman-KC 100.0
Franco-Tex 87.5
Yount-Mil 86.4
Finley-Bal 85.0
R.Henderson-NY-Oak . 84.6

Stolen Base Runs
R.Henderson-NY-Oak .14.7
Thurman-KC 4.8
Felder-Mil 4.8
Franco-Tex 4.5

Fielding Runs
Reynolds-Sea 27.0
Howell-Cal 22.5
Gruber-Tor 19.2
Snyder-Cle 18.6
Puckett-Min 18.4

Total Player Rating
R.Henderson-NY-Oak .. 5.2
Yount-Mil 4.6
Sierra-Tex 3.9
Puckett-Min 3.9
McGriff-Tor 3.5

Wins
Saberhagen-KC 23
Stewart-Oak 21
Moore-Oak 19
Davis-Oak 19
Ballard-Bal 18

Win Percentage
Saberhagen-KC .... .793
Blyleven-Cal 773
Davis-Oak 731
Stewart-Oak 700
Ballard-Bal 692

Games
Crim-Mil 76
Murphy-Bos 74
Rogers-Tex 73
Russell-Tex 71
Guetterman-NY 70

Complete Games
Saberhagen-KC 12
Morris-Det 10
Finley-Cal 9

Shutouts
Blyleven-Cal 5
Saberhagen-KC 4
McCaskill-Cal 4

Saves
Russell-Tex 38
Thigpen-Chi 34
Schooler-Sea ... 33
Plesac-Mil 33
Eckersley-Oak 33

Innings Pitched
Saberhagen-KC ... 262.1
Stewart-Oak 257.2
Gubicza-KC 255.0
Clemens-Bos ... 253.1
Milacki-Bal 243.0

Fewest Hits/Game
Ryan-Tex 6.09
Gordon-KC 6.74
Stieb-Tor 7.14
Saberhagen-KC ... 7.17
Moore-Oak 7.19

Fewest BB/Game
Key-Tor 1.13
Saberhagen-KC ... 1.48
Blyleven-Cal 1.64
Bosio-Mil 1.84
Witt-Cal 1.96

Strikeouts
Ryan-Tex 301
Clemens-Bos 230
Saberhagen-KC ... 193
Gubicza-KC 173
Bosio-Mil 173

Strikeouts/Game
Ryan-Tex 11.32
Gordon-KC 8.45
Clemens-Bos 8.17
Witt-Tex 7.69
Viola-Min 7.07

Ratio
Saberhagen-KC ... 8.71
Ryan-Tex 10.12
Blyleven-Cal ... 10.34
Moore-Oak 10.35
Key-Tor 10.67

Earned Run Average
Saberhagen-KC ... 2.16
Finley-Cal 2.57
Moore-Oak 2.61
Blyleven-Cal 2.73
McCaskill-Cal 2.93

Adjusted ERA
Saberhagen-KC ... 178
Finley-Cal 148
Moore-Oak 141
Blyleven-Cal 140
Clemens-Bos 131

Opponents' Batting Avg.
Ryan-Tex 187
Gordon-KC 210
Saberhagen-KC ...217
Stieb-Tor 219
Moore-Oak 219

Opponents' On Base Pct.
Saberhagen-KC ...252
Ryan-Tex 276
Moore-Oak 288
Blyleven-Cal 289
Bosio-Mil 291

Starter Runs
Saberhagen-KC .. 50.2
Moore-Oak 34.3
Blyleven-Cal ... 31.0
Finley-Cal 29.1
Bosio-Mil 24.2

Adjusted Starter Runs
Saberhagen-KC ... 49.2
Blyleven-Cal 29.1
Moore-Oak 28.8
Finley-Cal 27.6
Clemens-Bos 27.4

Clutch Pitching Index
Cerutti-Tor 130
Ballard-Bal 123
Finley-Cal 123
McCaskill-Cal 116
Davis-Oak 113

Relief Runs
Montgomery-KC .. 25.7
Olson-Bal 20.7
Lamp-Bos 19.5
Henke-Tor 19.4
Burns-Oak 17.6

Adjusted Relief Runs
Montgomery-KC .. 25.3
Lamp-Bos 22.2
Olson-Bal 19.8
Henke-Tor 18.3
Orosco-Cle 16.3

Relief Ranking
Jones-Cle 40.4
Russell-Tex 38.7
Montgomery-KC .. 35.9
Henke-Tor 29.6
Olson-Bal 28.9

Total Pitcher Index
Saberhagen-KC ... 5.5
Jones-Cle 4.3
Russell-Tex 4.2
Moore-Oak 4.0
Montgomery-KC .. 3.8

Total Baseball Ranking
Saberhagen-KC 5.5
R.Henderson-NY-Oak .. 5.2
Yount-Mil 4.6
Jones-Cle 4.3
Russell-Tex 4.2

TEAM	G	W	L	PCT	GB	R	OR	AB	H	2B	3B	HR	BB	SO	AVG	OBP	SLG	PRO	PRO+	BR	/A	PF	CHI	RC	SB	CS	SBA	SBR
EAST																												
PIT	162	95	67	.586		733	619	5388	1395	**288**	42	138	**582**	914	.259	**.334**	.405	**.739**	113	64	**92**	96	99	738	137	52	72	10
NY	162	91	71	.562	4	**775**	613	5504	1410	278	21	**172**	536	851	.256	.326	**.408**	.734	107	48	50	100	**106**	**748**	110	33	**77**	13
MON	162	85	77	.525	10	662	598	5453	1363	227	**43**	114	576	1024	.250	.325	.370	.695	101	-18	7	96	99	672	**235**	99	70	11
PHI	162	77	85	.475	18	646	729	5535	1410	237	27	103	**582**	915	.255	.329	.363	.692	96	-19	-17	100	96	675	108	35	76	11
CHI	162	77	85	.475	18	690	774	5600	**1474**	240	36	136	406	869	.263	.316	.392	.708	93	-7	-56	107	103	695	151	50	75	15
STL	162	70	92	.432	25	599	698	5462	1398	255	41	73	517	**844**	.256	.323	.358	.681	93	-46	-49	100	95	650	221	74	75	**22**
WEST																												
CIN	162	91	71	.562		693	**597**	5525	1466	284	40	125	466	913	**.265**	.327	.399	.726	101	35	5	104	97	726	166	66	72	10
LA	162	86	76	.531	5	728	685	5491	1436	222	27	129	538	952	.262	.331	.382	.713	105	17	37	97	104	699	141	65	68	3
SF	162	85	77	.525	6	719	710	5573	1459	221	35	152	488	973	.262	.325	.396	.721	108	24	50	96	101	724	109	56	66	-1
SD	162	75	87	.463	16	673	673	5554	1429	243	35	123	509	902	.257	.323	.380	.703	98	-8	-13	101	99	682	138	59	70	6
HOU	162	75	87	.463	16	573	656	5379	1301	209	32	94	548	997	.242	.315	.345	.660	90	-83	-66	97	97	596	179	83	68	4
ATL	162	65	97	.401	26	682	821	5504	1376	263	26	162	473	1010	.250	.312	.396	.708	95	-8	-47	106	103	675	92	55	63	-5
TOT	972						8173	65968	16917	2967	405	1521	6221	11164	.256	.324	.383	.707							1787	727	71	100

TEAM	CG	SH	SV	IP	H	H/G	HR	BB	SO	RAT	ERA	ERA+	OAV	OOB	PR	/A	PF	CPI	FA	E	DP	FW	PW	BW	SBW	DIF
EAST																										
PIT	18	8	43	1447	1367	8.5	135	413	848	11.3	3.40	106	.251	.307	63	35	95	103	.979	134	125	-.4	3.6	**9.5**	.2	1.2
NY	18	**14**	41	1440	1339	8.4	119	444	**1217**	11.3	3.42	109	.246	**.306**	59	51	99	97	.978	132	107	-.3	5.3	5.2	.5	-.6
MON	18	11	**50**	1473¹	1349	**8.2**	127	510	991	11.6	3.37	108	**.245**	.313	**70**	46	96	103	.982	110	134	.9	4.7	.7	.3	-2.7
PHI	18	7	35	1449	1381	8.6	124	651	840	12.8	4.07	94	.253	.336	-45	-40	101	97	.981	117	**150**	.5	-4.1	-1.8	.3	1.1
CHI	13	7	42	1442²	1510	9.4	121	572	877	13.2	4.34	94	.271	.342	-87	-42	108	98	.980	124	136	.1	-4.3	-5.8	.7	5.3
STL	8	13	39	1443¹	1432	8.9	**98**	475	833	12.1	3.87	98	.261	.324	-13	-9	101	95	.979	130	114	-.2	-.9	-5.1	**1.4**	-6.2
WEST																										
CIN	14	12	**50**	1456¹	**1338**	8.3	124	543	1029	11.8	3.39	**116**	.246	.318	64	**89**	104	105	**.983**	102	126	1.4	**9.2**	.5	.2	-1.3
LA	**29**	12	29	1442	1364	8.5	137	478	1021	11.7	3.72	98	.249	.313	11	-10	97	96	.979	130	123	-.2	-1.0	3.8	-.5	3.0
SF	14	6	45	1446¹	1477	9.2	131	553	788	12.8	4.08	89	.267	.335	-46	-70	96	101	**.983**	107	148	-.1	-7.2	5.2	-1.0	5.9
SD	21	12	35	1461²	1437	8.8	147	507	928	12.1	3.68	104	.258	.322	19	24	101	106	.977	141	141	-.8	2.5	-1.3	-.2	-6.0
HOU	12	6	37	1450	1396	8.7	130	496	854	12.0	3.61	103	.255	.321	30	17	98	104	.978	131	124	-.3	1.8	-6.8	-.4	-.2
ATL	17	8	30	1429²	1527	9.6	128	579	938	13.4	4.58	88	.275	.346	-125	-86	106	97	.974	158	133	-1.8	-8.9	-4.8	-1.4	.9
TOT	200	116	476	17381¹		8.8				12.2	3.79		.256	.324					.980	1516	1561					

Runs		Hits		Doubles		Triples		Home Runs		Total Bases	
Sandberg-Chi	116	Dykstra-Phi	192	Jefferies-NY	40	Duncan-Cin	11	Sandberg-Chi	40	Sandberg-Chi	344
Bonilla-Pit	112	Butler-SF	192	Bonilla-Pit	39	Gwynn-SD	10	Strawberry-NY	37	Bonilla-Pit	324
Butler-SF	108	Sandberg-Chi	188	Sabo-Cin	38	L.Smith-Atl	9	Mitchell-SF	35	Gant-Atl	310
Gant-Atl	107	Wallach-Mon	185	Wallach-Mon	37	Coleman-StL	9	Williams-SF	33	Williams-SF	301
Dykstra-Phi	106	Larkin-Cin	185	Johnson-NY	37	Butler-SF	9	Bonds-Pit	33	Wallach-Mon	295

Runs Batted In		Runs Produced		Bases On Balls		Batting Average		On Base Percentage		Slugging Average	
Williams-SF	122	Bonilla-Pit	200	J.Clark-SD	104	McGee-StL	.335	Magadan-NY	.425	Bonds-Pit	.565
Bonilla-Pit	120	Bonds-Pit	185	Bonds-Pit	93	Murray-LA	.330	Dykstra-Phi	.420	Sandberg-Chi	.559
Carter-SD	115	Williams-SF	176	Butler-SF	90	Magadan-NY	.328	Murray-LA	.417	Mitchell-SF	.544
Bonds-Pit	114	Sandberg-Chi	176	Dykstra-Phi	89	Dykstra-Phi	.325	Bonds-Pit	.410	Gant-Atl	.539
Strawberry-NY	108	Carter-SD	170	V.Hayes-Phi	87	Dawson-Chi	.310	Butler-SF	.401	Justice-Atl	.535

Production		Adjusted Production		Batter Runs		Adjusted Batter Runs		Clutch Hitting Index		Runs Created	
Bonds-Pit	.974	Bonds-Pit	172	Bonds-Pit	48.1	Bonds-Pit	52.6	Carter-SD	130	Bonds-Pit	128
Murray-LA	.936	Murray-LA	160	Murray-LA	44.7	Murray-LA	48.0	Magadan-NY	123	Sandberg-Chi	124
Daniels-LA	.923	Daniels-LA	156	Sandberg-Chi	37.9	J.Clark-SD	35.9	Kruk-Phi	121	Dykstra-Phi	121
Sandberg-Chi	.918	Mitchell-SF	151	J.Clark-SD	36.5	Mitchell-SF	35.0	Guerrero-StL	119	Murray-LA	118
Justice-Atl	.909	Magadan-NY	143	Dykstra-Phi	34.3	Daniels-LA	34.9	V.Hayes-Phi	119	Gant-Atl	109

Total Average		Stolen Bases		Stolen Base Average		Stolen Base Runs		Fielding Runs		Total Player Rating	
Bonds-Pit	1.115	Coleman-StL	77	Gibson-LA	92.9	Coleman-StL	12.9	Thompson-SF	27.7	Bonds-Pit	7.2
Daniels-LA	.945	Yelding-Hou	64	Grissom-Mon	91.7	Bonds-Pit	7.8	Grace-Chi	26.7	Dykstra-Phi	5.8
Murray-LA	.945	Bonds-Pit	52	Dawson-Chi	88.9	Nixon-Mon	7.2	C.Hayes-Phi	23.6	Sandberg-Chi	4.3
Justice-Atl	.941	Butler-SF	51	Davis-Cin	87.5	Dykstra-Phi	6.9	Dykstra-Phi	20.1	Larkin-Cin	4.3
Dykstra-Phi	.941	Nixon-Mon	50	Dykstra-Phi	86.8			Larkin-Cin	19.9	Murray-LA	4.1

Wins		Win Percentage		Games		Complete Games		Shutouts		Saves	
Drabek-Pit	22	Drabek-Pit	.786	Agosto-Hou	82	Martinez-LA	12	Morgan-LA	4	Franco-NY	33
Viola-NY	20	Martinez-LA	.769	Assenmacher-Chi	74	Hurst-SD	9	Hurst-SD	4	Myers-Cin	31
Martinez-LA	20	Gooden-NY	.731	Harris-SD	73	Drabek-Pit	9			L.Smith-StL	27
Gooden-NY	19	Viola-NY	.625	McDowell-Phi	72	Maddux-Chi	8			Smith-Hou	23
		Browning-Cin	.625	Akerfelds-Phi	71					Lefferts-SD	23

Innings Pitched		Fewest Hits/Game		Fewest BB/Game		Strikeouts		Strikeouts/Game		Ratio	
Viola-NY	249.2	Fernandez-NY	6.52	Darwin-Hou	1.72	Cone-NY	233	Cone-NY	9.91	Darwin-Hou	9.46
Maddux-Chi	237.0	Rijo-Cin	6.90	Whitson-SD	1.85	Martinez-LA	223	Fernandez-NY	9.08	Drabek-Pit	9.69
Martinez-LA	234.1	Martinez-LA	7.34	Leibrandt-Atl	1.94	Gooden-NY	223	Gooden-NY	8.63	D.Martinez-Mon	9.80
Gooden-NY	232.2	Drabek-Pit	7.39	D.Martinez-Mon	1.95	Viola-NY	182	Martinez-LA	8.56	Martinez-LA	10.06
		Darwin-Hou	7.52	Browning-Cin	2.06	Fernandez-NY	181	DeLeon-StL	8.08	Fernandez-NY	10.14

Earned Run Average		Adjusted ERA		Opponents' Batting Avg.		Opponents' On Base Pct.		Starter Runs		Adjusted Starter Runs	
Darwin-Hou	2.21	Darwin-Hou	168	Fernandez-NY	.200	Darwin-Hou	.267	Viola-NY	31.2	Whitson-SD	31.1
Smith-Mon-Pit	2.55	Whitson-SD	147	Rijo-Cin	.212	Drabek-Pit	.275	Whitson-SD	30.3	Viola-NY	29.8
Whitson-SD	2.60	Rijo-Cin	146	Martinez-LA	.220	D.Martinez-Mon	.275	Smith-Mon-Pit	29.7	Rijo-Cin	27.3
Viola-NY	2.67	Smith-Mon-Pit	143	Drabek-Pit	.225	Martinez-LA	.279	Darwin-Hou	28.5	Darwin-Hou	27.1
Rijo-Cin	2.70	Viola-NY	140	Darwin-Hou	.225	Fernandez-NY	.280	Drabek-Pit	26.4	Smith-Mon-Pit	26.0

Clutch Pitching Index		Relief Runs		Adjusted Relief Runs		Relief Ranking		Total Pitcher Index		Total Baseball Ranking	
Gullickson-Hou	121	Dibble-Cin	22.3	Dibble-Cin	23.9	Myers-Cin	33.1	Viola-NY	3.6	Bonds-Pit	7.2
Smith-Mon-Pit	118	Brantley-SF	21.5	Charlton-Cin	20.6	Dibble-Cin	30.2	Myers-Cin	3.6	Dykstra-Phi	5.8
Whitson-SD	115	Harris-SD	19.4	Brantley-SF	20.1	Harris-SD	27.7	Whitson-SD	3.4	Sandberg-Chi	4.3
Rasmussen-SD	114	Charlton-Cin	18.0	Harris-SD	19.8	Brantley-SF	26.6	Drabek-Pit	3.4	Larkin-Cin	4.3
Darwin-Hou	107	Myers-Cin	16.5	Myers-Cin	18.0	Charlton-Cin	25.8	Rijo-Cin	3.1	Murray-LA	4.1

TEAM	G	W	L	PCT	GB	R	OR	AB	H	2B	3B	HR	BB	SO	AVG	OBP	SLG	PRO	PRO+	BR	/A	PF	CHI	RC	SB	CS	SBA	SBR
EAST																												
BOS	162	88	74	.543		699	664	5516	**1502**	298	31	106	598	795	**.272**	**.346**	.395	.741	102	57	22	105	92	733	53	52	50	-15
TOR	162	86	76	.531	2	**767**	661	5589	1479	263	**50**	167	526	970	.265	.331	**.419**	**.750**	106	56	42	102	101	**769**	111	52	68	2
DET	162	79	83	.488	9	750	754	5479	1418	241	32	**172**	634	952	.259	.339	.409	.748	107	62	57	101	98	754	82	57	59	-10
CLE	162	77	85	.475	11	732	737	5485	1465	266	41	110	458	836	.267	.327	.391	.718	101	-5	-2	100	107	694	107	52	67	1
BAL	161	76	85	.472	11.5	669	698	5410	1328	234	22	132	**660**	962	.245	.332	.370	.702	99	-21	1	97	98	676	94	52	64	-3
MIL	162	74	88	.457	14	732	760	5503	1408	247	36	128	519	821	.256	.324	.384	.708	98	-24	-19	99	**109**	692	**164**	72	69	6
NY	162	67	95	.414	21	603	749	5483	1322	208	19	147	427	1027	.241	.302	.366	.668	86	-109	-111	100	105	605	119	45	**73**	9
WEST																												
OAK	162	103	59	.636		733	**570**	5433	1379	209	22	164	651	992	.254	.339	.391	.730	**108**	31	**61**	96	100	739	141	54	72	**10**
CHI	162	94	68	.580	9	682	633	5402	1393	251	44	106	478	903	.258	.322	.379	.701	97	-35	-21	98	105	651	140	90	61	-12
TEX	162	83	79	.512	20	676	696	5469	1416	257	27	110	575	1054	.259	.333	.376	.709	98	-11	-12	100	98	688	115	48	71	6
CAL	162	80	82	.494	23	690	706	5570	1448	237	27	147	566	1000	.260	.331	.391	.722	103	10	24	98	96	715	69	43	62	-5
SEA	162	77	85	.475	26	640	680	5474	1419	251	26	107	596	**749**	.259	.336	.373	.709	97	-7	-15	101	92	691	105	51	67	1
KC	161	75	86	.466	27.5	707	709	5488	1465	**316**	44	100	498	879	.267	.331	.395	.726	104	14	25	98	101	706	107	62	63	-5
MIN	162	74	88	.457	29	666	729	5499	1458	281	39	100	445	**749**	.265	.326	.385	.711	92	-17	-61	107	99	673	96	53	64	-3
TOT	1133					9746		76800	19900	3559	460	1796	7631	12689	.259	.330	.388	.718						1503	783	66		-19

TEAM	CG	SH	SV	IP	H	H/G	HR	BB	SO	RAT	ERA	ERA+	OAV	OOB	PR	/A	PF	CPI	FA	E	DP	FW	PW	BW	SBW	DIF
EAST																										
BOS	15	13	44	1442	1439	9.0	**92**	519	997	12.5	3.72	110	.261	.329	30	57	104	100	.980	123	154	-.2	5.8	2.2	-1.4	.6
TOR	9	6	48	1454	1434	8.9	143	**445**	892	11.9	3.84	103	.260	.319	11	17	101	99	**.986**	86	144	**2.0**	1.7	4.3	.3	-3.4
DET	15	12	45	1430[1]	1401	8.8	154	661	856	13.3	4.39	90	.259	.345	-76	-68	101	98	.979	131	178	-.7	-6.9	5.8	-.9	.7
CLE	12	10	47	1427[1]	1491	9.4	163	518	860	12.9	4.26	92	.270	.337	-57	-55	100	102	.981	117	146	.2	-5.6	-.2	.2	1.4
BAL	10	5	43	1435[1]	1445	9.1	161	537	776	12.5	4.04	94	.264	.331	-21	-39	97	103	.985	93	151	1.6	-4.0	.1	-.2	-2.0
MIL	23	13	42	1445	1558	9.7	121	469	771	12.9	4.08	95	.275	.335	-28	-34	99	101	.976	149	152	-1.8	-3.5	-1.9	.7	-.6
NY	15	6	41	1444[2]	1430	8.9	144	618	909	12.9	4.21	94	.261	.339	-49	-39	102	99	.980	126	164	-.4	-4.0	-11.3	1.1	.6
WEST																										
OAK	18	**16**	64	1456	**1287**	**8.0**	123	494	831	**11.2**	**3.18**	**117**	**.238**	**.305**	118	87	95	101	**.986**	87	152	**2.0**	**8.9**	**6.2**	**1.2**	3.8
CHI	17	10	**68**	1449[1]	1313	8.2	106	548	914	11.8	3.61	106	.244	.318	48	34	98	95	.980	124	169	-.3	3.5	-2.1	-1.1	13.0
TEX	**25**	9	36	1444[2]	1343	8.4	113	623	997	12.5	3.83	102	.248	.330	12	14	100	97	.979	133	161	-.8	1.4	-1.2	.7	1.9
CAL	21	13	42	1454	1482	9.2	106	544	944	12.5	3.79	101	.267	.337	18	3	98	**105**	.978	142	186	-1.4	.3	2.4	-.4	-2.0
SEA	21	7	41	1443[1]	1319	8.2	120	606	**1064**	12.3	3.69	107	.243	.335	34	42	101	99	.979	130	152	-.6	4.3	-1.5	.2	-6.4
KC	18	8	33	1420[2]	1449	9.2	116	560	1006	13.0	3.93	97	.264	.337	-5	-16	98	102	.980	122	161	-.2	-1.6	2.5	-.4	-5.9
MIN	13	13	43	1435[2]	1509	9.5	134	489	872	12.7	4.12	101	.273	.335	-35	4	106	101	.983	101	161	1.1	.4	-6.2	-.2	-2.2
TOT	229	144	637	20182[1]		8.9				12.5	3.91		.259	.330					.981	1664	2231					

Runs
R.Henderson-Oak 119
Fielder-Det 104
Reynolds-Sea 100
Yount-Mil 98
Phillips-Det 97

Hits
Palmeiro-Tex 191
Boggs-Bos 187
Kelly-NY 183
Greenwell-Bos 181

Doubles
J.Reed-Bos 45
Brett-KC 45
Calderon-Chi 44
Boggs-Bos 44
Harper-Min 42

Triples
Fernandez-Tor 17
Sosa-Chi 10
Polonia-NY-Cal 9
Liriano-Tor-Min ... 9
Johnson-Chi 9

Home Runs
Fielder-Det 51
McGwire-Oak 39
J.Canseco-Oak 37
McGriff-Tor 35
Gruber-Tor 31

Total Bases
Fielder-Det 339
Gruber-Tor 303
McGriff-Tor 295
K.Griffey-Sea 287
Burks-Bos 286

Runs Batted In
Fielder-Det 132
Gruber-Tor 118
McGwire-Oak 108
J.Canseco-Oak 101
Sierra-Tex 96

Runs Produced
Fielder-Det 185
Gruber-Tor 179
Yount-Mil 158
Burks-Bos 157
McGwire-Oak 156

Bases On Balls
McGwire-Oak 110
Tettleton-Bal 106
Phillips-Det 99
R.Henderson-Oak ... 97
McGriff-Tor 94

Batting Average
Brett-KC 329
R.Henderson-Oak ..325
Palmeiro-Tex 319
Trammell-Det 304
Boggs-Bos 302

On Base Percentage
R.Henderson-Oak ...441
McGriff-Tor 403
E.Martinez-Sea ...399
Davis-Sea 393
Brett-KC 392

Slugging Average
Fielder-Det 592
R.Henderson-Oak ..577
J.Canseco-Oak ...543
McGriff-Tor 530
Brett-KC 515

Production
R.Henderson-Oak ..1.017
Fielder-Det 972
McGriff-Tor 932
J.Canseco-Oak ...917
Brett-KC 906

Adjusted Production
R.Henderson-Oak 190
Fielder-Det 167
J.Canseco-Oak 160
McGriff-Tor 156
Brett-KC 154

Batter Runs
R.Henderson-Oak ... 57.5
Fielder-Det 51.3
McGriff-Tor 45.5
Brett-KC 37.0
J.Canseco-Oak ... 34.3

Adjusted Batter Runs
R.Henderson-Oak ... 62.7
Fielder-Det 50.4
McGriff-Tor 43.4
Brett-KC 38.7
J.Canseco-Oak ... 38.4

Clutch Hitting Index
Leonard-Sea 138
Guillen-Chi 122
Fletcher-Chi 121
Gaetti-Min 118
Gruber-Tor 117

Runs Created
R.Henderson-Oak ... 137
Fielder-Det 129
McGriff-Tor 124
Brett-KC 106
K.Griffey-Sea 103

Total Average
R.Henderson-Oak ..1.241
Fielder-Det 1.007
McGriff-Tor 983
J.Canseco-Oak ...943
McGwire-Oak 903

Stolen Bases
R.Henderson-Oak 65
Sax-NY 43
Kelly-NY 42
Cole-Cle 40
Pettis-Tex 38

Stolen Base Average
Cotto-Sea 87.5
R.Henderson-Oak .. 86.7
Molitor-Mil 85.7
Gantner-Mil 85.7
Wilson-Tor 85.2

Stolen Base Runs
R.Henderson-Oak ...13.5
Sax-NY 7.5
Cole-Cle 6.6
Wilson-Tor 4.5
Cotto-Sea 4.5

Fielding Runs
Espinoza-NY 21.1
Reynolds-Sea 15.1
Quintana-Bos 14.5
Gaetti-Min 13.8
Gallego-Oak 13.7

Total Player Rating
R.Henderson-Oak ... 8.2
Fielder-Det 4.2
McGriff-Tor 4.1
J.Canseco-Oak ... 4.0
Fisk-Chi 3.5

Wins
Welch-Oak 27
Stewart-Oak 22
Clemens-Bos 21

Win Percentage
Welch-Oak 818
Clemens-Bos 778
Stieb-Tor 750
Boddicker-Bos ...680

Games
Thigpen-Chi 77
Ward-Tor 73
Montgomery-KC ... 73
Rogers-Tex 69
Henneman-Det 69

Complete Games
Stewart-Oak 11
Morris-Det 11

Shutouts
Stewart-Oak 4
Clemens-Bos 4
Perez-Chi 3
Morris-Det 3
Appier-KC 3

Saves
Thigpen-Chi 57
Eckersley-Oak 48
Jones-Cle 43
Olson-Bal 37
Righetti-NY 36

Innings Pitched
Stewart-Oak 267.0
Morris-Det 249.2
Welch-Oak 238.0
Hanson-Sea 236.0
Finley-Cal 236.0

Fewest Hits/Game
Ryan-Tex 6.04
Johnson-Sea 7.13
Clemens-Bos 7.61
Stewart-Oak 7.62
Stieb-Tor 7.72

Fewest BB/Game
Anderson-Min 1.86
Swindell-Cle 1.97
Clemens-Bos 2.13
Knudson-Mil 2.14
Wells-Tor 2.14

Strikeouts
Ryan-Tex 232
Witt-Tex 221
Hanson-Sea 211
Clemens-Bos 209
Langston-Cal 195

Strikeouts/Game
Ryan-Tex 10.24
Witt-Tex 8.96
Clemens-Bos 8.24
Gordon-KC 8.06
Hanson-Sea 8.05

Ratio
Ryan-Tex 9.62
Clemens-Bos 10.01
Wells-Tor 10.10
Hanson-Sea 10.49
Stewart-Oak 10.58

Earned Run Average
Clemens-Bos .. 1.93
Finley-Cal 2.40
Stewart-Oak 2.56
Appier-KC 2.76
Stieb-Tor 2.93

Adjusted ERA
Clemens-Bos 211
Finley-Cal 159
Stewart-Oak 145
Appier-KC 139
Stieb-Tor 134

Opponents' Batting Avg.
Ryan-Tex 188
Johnson-Sea 216
Clemens-Bos 228
Stieb-Tor 230
Stewart-Oak 231

Opponents' On Base Pct.
Ryan-Tex 269
Clemens-Bos 280
Wells-Tor 283
Hanson-Sea 289
Black-Cle-Tor 293

Starter Runs
Clemens-Bos..... 50.1
Stewart-Oak 39.9
Finley-Cal 39.4
Welch-Oak 25.3
Appier-KC 23.6

Adjusted Starter Runs
Clemens-Bos 54.3
Finley-Cal 37.1
Stewart-Oak 34.2
Stieb-Tor 23.4
Appier-KC 22.0

Clutch Pitching Index
Finley-Cal 136
Appier-KC 121
Clemens-Bos 118
Welch-Oak 117
Johnson-Bal 113

Relief Runs
Farr-KC 27.1
Eckersley-Oak ... 26.8
Swift-Sea 21.5
Thigpen-Chi 20.5
Nelson-Oak 19.4

Adjusted Relief Runs
Farr-KC 26.1
Eckersley-Oak ... 25.3
Swift-Sea 22.3
Thigpen-Chi 19.6
Nelson-Oak 17.8

Relief Ranking
Eckersley-Oak ... 55.8
Thigpen-Chi 48.3
Farr-KC 37.4
Jones-Cle 28.1
Olson-Bal 27.8

Total Pitcher Index
Clemens-Bos..... 6.7
Eckersley-Oak ... 5.9
Thigpen-Chi 5.3
Finley-Cal 4.1
Stewart-Oak 4.1

Total Baseball Ranking
R.Henderson-Oak ... 8.2
Clemens-Bos 6.7
Eckersley-Oak ... 5.9
Thigpen-Chi 5.3
Fielder-Det 4.2

TEAM	G	W	L	PCT	GB	R	OR	AB	H	2B	3B	HR	BB	SO	AVG	OBP	SLG	PRO	PRO+	BR	/A	PF	CHI	RC	SB	CS	SBA	SBR
EAST																												
PIT	162	98	64	.605		**768**	632	5449	**1433**	**259**	50	126	**620**	901	**.263**	**.342**	.398	**.740**	116	**104**	117	98	98	762	124	46	73	10
STL	162	84	78	.519	14	651	648	5362	1366	239	**53**	68	532	857	.255	.324	.357	.681	96	-13	-17	101	102	628	202	110	65	-5
PHI	162	78	84	.481	20	629	680	5521	1332	248	33	111	490	1026	.241	.306	.358	.664	93	-60	-53	99	**104**	609	92	30	**75**	10
CHI	160	77	83	.481	20	695	734	5522	1395	232	26	159	442	879	.253	.312	.390	.702	97	11	-21	105	103	675	123	64	66	-2
NY	161	77	84	.478	20.5	640	646	5359	1305	250	24	117	578	**789**	.244	.320	.365	.685	99	-9	-4	99	99	641	153	70	69	4
MON	161	71	90	.441	26.5	579	655	5412	1329	236	42	95	484	1056	.246	.311	.357	.668	94	-47	-38	99	95	607	**221**	100	69	6
WEST																												
ATL	162	94	68	.580		749	644	5456	1407	255	30	141	563	906	.258	.331	.393	.724	103	65	22	106	102	719	165	76	68	4
LA	162	93	69	.574	1	665	**565**	5408	1366	191	29	108	583	957	.253	.328	.359	.687	101	1	16	98	100	650	126	68	65	-3
SD	162	84	78	.519	10	636	646	5408	1321	204	36	121	501	1069	.244	.312	.362	.674	92	-35	-54	103	102	605	101	64	61	-8
SF	162	75	87	.463	19	649	697	5463	1345	215	48	141	471	973	.246	.311	.381	.692	103	-9	12	97	100	647	95	57	63	-6
CIN	162	74	88	.457	20	689	691	5501	1419	250	27	**164**	488	1006	.258	.322	**.403**	.725	105	57	30	104	96	721	124	56	69	4
HOU	162	65	97	.401	29	605	717	5504	1345	240	43	79	502	1027	.244	.312	.347	.659	97	-64	-29	94	101	606	125	68	65	-3
TOT	970					7955		65365	16363	2819	441	1430	6254	11446	.250	.319	.373	.692							1651	809	67	10

TEAM	CG	SH	SV	IP	H	H/G	HR	BB	SO	RAT	ERA	ERA+	OAV	OOB	PR	/A	PF	CPI	FA	E	DP	FW	PW	BW	SBW	DIF
EAST																										
PIT	**18**	11	**51**	1456¹	1411	8.7	117	**401**	919	11.4	3.44	104	.256	.309	39	21	97	103	.981	120	134	.4	2.2	**12.2**	**1.0**	1.3
STL	9	5	**51**	1435¹	1367	8.6	114	454	822	11.7	3.69	101	.255	.318	0	5	101	100	**.982**	**107**	133	**1.1**	.5	-1.8	-.6	3.8
PHI	16	11	35	1463	1346	8.3	111	670	988	12.7	3.86	95	.246	.332	-29	-32	100	99	.981	119	111	.4	-3.3	-5.5	**1.0**	4.5
CHI	12	4	40	1456²	1415	8.7	117	542	927	12.3	4.03	96	.257	.327	-57	-24	105	96	**.982**	113	120	.7	-2.5	-2.2	-.3	1.3
NY	12	11	39	1437¹	1403	8.8	108	410	1028	11.5	3.56	102	.257	.311	20	13	99	100	.977	143	112	-1.0	1.4	-.4	.3	-3.7
MON	12	**14**	39	1440¹	**1304**	**8.1**	111	584	909	12.0	3.64	99	.244	.322	7	-4	98	100	.979	133	128	-.4	-.4	-4.0	.5	-5.2
WEST																										
ATL	**18**	7	48	1452²	**1304**	**8.1**	118	481	969	**11.2**	3.49	111	**.240**	**.305**	32	64	106	95	.978	138	122	-.7	6.7	2.3	.3	4.4
LA	15	**14**	40	1458	1312	**8.1**	**96**	500	1028	11.4	**3.06**	117	.241	.308	**101**	**86**	98	**107**	.980	123	126	.2	**9.0**	1.7	-.4	1.6
SD	14	11	47	1452²	1385	8.6	139	457	921	11.5	3.57	106	.252	.311	18	36	103	102	**.982**	113	130	.8	3.8	-5.6	-.9	5.0
SF	10	10	45	1442	1397	8.7	143	544	905	12.3	4.03	96	.257	.329	-56	-72	97	100	**.982**	109	151	1.0	-7.5	1.3	-.7	.0
CIN	7	11	43	1440	1372	8.6	127	560	997	12.3	3.83	99	.253	.326	-24	-5	103	101	.979	125	131	.0	-.5	3.1	.3	-10.0
HOU	7	13	36	1453	1347	8.3	129	651	**1033**	12.6	4.00	88	.247	.330	-51	-80	95	97	.974	161	129	-2.0	-8.4	-3.0	-.4	-2.2
TOT	150	122	514	17387²		8.5				11.9	3.68		.250	.319					.980	1504	1527					

Runs		Hits		Doubles		Triples		Home Runs		Total Bases	
Butler-LA	112	Pendleton-Atl	187	Bonilla-Pit	44	Lankford-StL	15	Johnson-NY	38	Pendleton-Atl	303
Johnson-NY	108	Butler-LA	182	Jose-StL	40	Gwynn-SD	11	Williams-SF	34	Clark-SF	303
Sandberg-Chi	104	Sabo-Cin	175	Zeile-StL	36	Finley-Hou	10	Gant-Atl	32	Johnson-NY	302
Bonilla-Pit	102	Bonilla-Pit	174	O'Neill-Cin	36	Grissom-Mon	9	McGriff-SD	31	Williams-SF	294
Gant-Atl	101	Jose-StL	173			Gonzalez-Hou	9	Dawson-Chi	31	Sabo-Cin	294

Runs Batted In		Runs Produced		Bases On Balls		Batting Average		On Base Percentage		Slugging Average	
Johnson-NY	117	Johnson-NY	187	Butler-LA	108	Pendleton-Atl	.319	Bonds-Pit	.419	Clark-SF	.536
Clark-SF	116	Bonds-Pit	186	Bonds-Pit	107	Morris-Cin	.318	Butler-LA	.402	Johnson-NY	.535
Bonds-Pit	116	Bonilla-Pit	184	McGriff-SD	105	Gwynn-SD	.317	McGriff-SD	.400	Pendleton-Atl	.517
McGriff-SD	106	Sandberg-Chi	178	DeShields-Mon	95	McGee-SF	.312	Bonilla-Pit	.398	Bonds-Pit	.514
Gant-Atl	105	Gant-Atl	174	Bonilla-Pit	90	Jose-StL	.305	Bagwell-Hou	.391	Larkin-Cin	.506

Production		Adjusted Production		Batter Runs		Adjusted Batter Runs		Clutch Hitting Index		Runs Created	
Bonds-Pit	.932	Bonds-Pit	163	Bonds-Pit	45.5	Bonds-Pit	47.3	Pagnozzi-StL	129	Bonds-Pit	118
Clark-SF	.897	Clark-SF	154	Bonilla-Pit	39.5	Bonilla-Pit	41.3	Bonds-Pit	127	Sandberg-Chi	114
McGriff-SD	.894	Bonilla-Pit	151	McGriff-SD	38.4	Clark-SF	38.1	Murray-LA	118	Bonilla-Pit	114
Bonilla-Pit	.890	Johnson-NY	147	Sandberg-Chi	34.8	McGriff-SD	35.2	Magadan-NY	117	Clark-SF	110
Larkin-Cin	.886	McGriff-SD	146	Clark-SF	34.7	Johnson-NY	33.5	Daniels-LA	116	Pendleton-Atl	107

Total Average		Stolen Bases		Stolen Base Average		Stolen Base Runs		Fielding Runs		Total Player Rating	
Bonds-Pit	1.055	Grissom-Mon	76	Dykstra-Phi	85.7	Grissom-Mon	12.6	Pendleton-Atl	27.9	Bonds-Pit	6.4
McGriff-SD	.937	Nixon-Atl	72	Redus-Pit	85.0	Nixon-Atl	9.0	Belliard-Atl	26.1	Pendleton-Atl	5.9
Larkin-Cin	.923	DeShields-Mon	56	Landrum-Chi	84.4	O.Smith-StL	5.1	Lind-Pit	22.6	Larkin-Cin	5.8
Johnson-NY	.902	Lankford-StL	44	Jefferies-NY	83.9	Landrum-Chi	5.1	Grissom-Mon	20.4	Sandberg-Chi	4.7
Sandberg-Chi	.896	Bonds-Pit	43	Grissom-Mon	81.7	Bonds-Pit	5.1	Grace-Chi	20.0	Bonilla-Pit	4.1

Wins		Win Percentage		Games		Complete Games		Shutouts		Saves	
Smiley-Pit	20	Smiley-Pit	.714	Jones-NY	77	D.Martinez-Mon	9	D.Martinez-Mon	5	L.Smith-StL	47
Glavine-Atl	20	Rijo-Cin	.714	Assenmacher-Chi	75	Glavine-Atl	9	Martinez-LA	4	Dibble-Cin	31
Avery-Atl	18	Avery-Atl	.692	Stanton-Atl	74	Mulholland-Phi	8	Smith-Pit	3	Williams-Phi	30
Martinez-LA	17	Hurst-SD	.652	Burke-Mon-NY	72	Maddux-Chi	7	Mulholland-Phi	3	Franco-NY	30
		Glavine-Atl	.645	Agosto-StL	72			Black-SF	3	Righetti-SF	24

Innings Pitched		Fewest Hits/Game		Fewest BB/Game		Strikeouts		Strikeouts/Game		Ratio	
Maddux-Chi	263.0	Harnisch-Hou	7.02	Smith-Pit	1.14	Cone-NY	241	Cone-NY	9.32	Rijo-Cin	9.82
Glavine-Atl	246.2	Rijo-Cin	7.27	Tewksbury-StL	1.79	Maddux-Chi	198	Rijo-Cin	7.58	Glavine-Atl	9.92
Morgan-LA	236.1	DeJesus-Phi	7.28	Mulholland-Phi	1.90	Glavine-Atl	192	Harnisch-Hou	7.14	Morgan-LA	9.94
Drabek-Pit	234.2	Hill-StL	7.30	Smiley-Pit	1.91	Rijo-Cin	172	Gooden-NY	7.11	D.Martinez-Mon	10.26
Cone-NY	232.2	Glavine-Atl	7.33	B.Smith-StL	2.04	Harnisch-Hou	172	Glavine-Atl	7.01	Benes-SD	10.37

Earned Run Average		Adjusted ERA		Opponents' Batting Avg.		Opponents' On Base Pct.		Starter Runs		Adjusted Starter Runs	
D.Martinez-Mon	2.39	Glavine-Atl	152	Harnisch-Hou	.212	Rijo-Cin	.274	D.Martinez-Mon	31.9	Glavine-Atl	36.5
Rijo-Cin	2.51	Rijo-Cin	151	Rijo-Cin	.219	Glavine-Atl	.279	Glavine-Atl	31.0	D.Martinez-Mon	30.2
Glavine-Atl	2.55	D.Martinez-Mon	151	Glavine-Atl	.222	Morgan-LA	.279	Rijo-Cin	26.6	Rijo-Cin	29.3
Belcher-LA	2.62	DeLeon-StL	137	Hill-StL	.224	D.Martinez-Mon	.283	Belcher-LA	24.7	Harris-SD	23.1
Harnisch-Hou	2.70	Belcher-LA	137	DeJesus-Phi	.224	Benes-SD	.286	Morgan-LA	23.7	Belcher-LA	22.6

Clutch Pitching Index		Relief Runs		Adjusted Relief Runs		Relief Ranking		Total Pitcher Index		Total Baseball Ranking	
DeLeon-StL	131	McElroy-Chi	19.5	McElroy-Chi	21.7	Williams-Phi	32.4	Glavine-Atl	5.5	Bonds-Pit	6.4
Drabek-Pit	127	Maddux-SD	13.4	Maddux-SD	14.6	L.Smith-StL	28.5	D.Martinez-Mon	3.9	Pendleton-Atl	5.9
Tewksbury-StL	121	Williams-Phi	13.2	Williams-Phi	13.0	McElroy-Chi	16.9	Williams-Phi	3.4	Larkin-Cin	5.8
Ojeda-LA	121	Brantley-SF	13.0	Brantley-SF	11.9	Pena-NY-Atl	16.5	Rijo-Cin	3.0	Glavine-Atl	5.5
Belcher-LA	118	Pena-NY-Atl	11.7	Pena-NY-Atl	11.8	Franco-NY	15.3	L.Smith-StL	3.0	Sandberg-Chi	4.7

TEAM	G	W	L	PCT	GB	R	OR	AB	H	2B	3B	HR	BB	SO	AVG	OBP	SLG	PRO	PRO+	BR	/A	PF	CHI	RC	SB	CS	SBA	SBR
EAST																												
TOR	162	91	71	.562		684	**622**	5489	1412	295	45	133	499	1043	.257	.326	.400	.726	96	-7	-33	104	96	724	148	53	74	**13**
DET	162	84	78	.519	7	817	794	5547	1372	259	26	**209**	**699**	1185	.247	.335	.416	.751	105	50	39	101	103	800	109	47	70	5
BOS	162	84	78	.519	7	731	712	5530	1486	**305**	25	126	593	820	.269	.343	.401	.744	100	42	4	105	95	756	59	39	60	-6
MIL	162	83	79	.512	8	799	744	5611	1523	247	**53**	116	556	802	.271	.340	.396	.736	106	24	43	98	105	745	106	68	61	-9
NY	162	71	91	.438	20	674	777	5541	1418	249	19	147	473	861	.256	.319	.387	.706	94	-47	-48	100	101	683	109	36	**75**	11
BAL	162	67	95	.414	24	686	796	5604	1421	256	29	170	528	974	.254	.321	.401	.722	102	-17	12	96	96	707	50	33	60	-5
CLE	162	57	105	.352	34	576	759	5470	1390	236	26	79	449	888	.254	.316	.350	.666	83	-118	-122	101	98	591	84	58	59	-10
WEST																												
MIN	162	95	67	.586		776	652	5556	**1557**	270	42	140	526	**747**	**.280**	**.347**	.420	**.767**	106	82	45	105	96	786	107	68	61	-9
CHI	162	87	75	.537	8	758	681	5594	1464	226	39	139	610	896	.262	.338	.391	.729	103	12	30	98	101	741	134	74	64	-4
TEX	162	85	77	.525	10	**829**	814	5703	1539	288	31	177	596	1039	.270	.343	**.424**	**.767**	113	85	100	98	99	**831**	102	50	67	1
OAK	162	84	78	.519	11	760	776	5410	1342	246	19	159	642	981	.248	.333	.389	.722	105	-2	39	94	**106**	711	**151**	64	70	7
SEA	162	83	79	.512	12	702	674	5494	1400	268	29	126	588	811	.255	.331	.383	.714	97	-21	-22	100	99	698	97	44	69	3
KC	162	82	80	.506	13	727	722	5584	1475	290	41	117	523	969	.264	.331	.394	.725	100	-4	-7	100	101	720	119	68	64	-5
CAL	162	81	81	.500	14	653	649	5470	1396	245	29	115	448	928	.255	.316	.374	.690	90	-78	-77	100	104	640	94	56	63	-5
TOT	1134					10172		77603	20195	3680	453	1953	7730	12944	.260	.331	.395	.726							1469	758	66	-14

TEAM	CG	SH	SV	IP	H	H/G	HR	BB	SO	RAT	ERA	ERA+	OAV	OOB	PR	/A	PF	CPI	FA	E	DP	FW	PW	BW	SBW	DIF
EAST																										
TOR	10	**16**	60	1462²	1301	8.0	121	523	971	**11.5**	**3.50**	120	**.238**	**.309**	96	**114**	103	96	.980	127	115	-.6	**11.4**	-3.3	**1.4**	1.1
DET	18	8	38	1450¹	1570	9.7	148	593	739	13.6	4.51	92	.280	.352	-66	-57	101	105	.983	104	171	.7	-5.7	3.9	.6	3.5
BOS	15	13	45	1439²	1405	8.8	147	530	999	12.3	4.01	107	.257	.326	13	46	105	100	.981	116	165	.0	4.6	.4	-.5	-1.5
MIL	23	11	41	1463²	1498	9.2	147	527	859	12.7	4.14	96	.266	.334	-8	-28	97	102	.981	118	176	-.0	-2.8	4.3	-.8	1.4
NY	3	11	37	1444	1510	9.4	152	506	936	12.8	4.42	94	.271	.336	-52	-45	101	99	.979	133	181	-.9	-4.5	-4.8	1.2	-1.0
BAL	8	8	44	1457²	1534	9.5	147	504	868	12.8	4.59	86	.273	.335	-80	-103	97	95	**.985**	**91**	172	**1.4**	-10.3	1.2	-.4	-5.9
CLE	22	8	33	1441¹	1551	9.7	110	**441**	862	12.7	4.23	98	.276	.333	-22	-13	101	98	.976	149	150	-1.8	-1.3	-12.2	-.9	-7.8
WEST																										
MIN	21	12	53	1449¹	1402	8.7	139	488	876	11.9	3.69	115	.255	.319	64	92	104	104	**.985**	95	161	1.2	9.2	4.5	-.8	-.0
CHI	**28**	8	40	1478	1302	**7.9**	154	601	923	11.8	3.79	105	.239	.318	50	30	97	98	.982	116	151	.0	3.0	3.0	-.3	.3
TEX	9	10	41	1479	1486	9.0	151	662	**1022**	13.3	4.47	90	.262	.344	-61	-72	98	98	.979	134	138	-1.0	-7.2	**10.0**	.2	2.0
OAK	14	10	49	1444¹	1425	8.9	155	655	892	13.3	4.57	84	.267	.341	-77	-119	94	97	.982	107	150	.5	-11.9	3.9	.8	9.7
SEA	10	13	48	1464¹	1387	8.5	136	628	1003	12.7	3.79	109	.253	.335	50	54	101	**107**	.983	110	**187**	.3	5.4	-2.2	.4	-1.9
KC	17	12	41	1466	1473	9.0	**105**	529	1004	12.6	3.92	105	.261	.329	28	32	101	101	.980	125	141	-.5	3.2	-.7	-.4	-.6
CAL	18	10	50	1441²	1351	8.4	141	543	990	12.1	3.69	111	.250	.323	65	66	100	105	.984	102	156	.8	6.6	-7.7	-.4	.7
TOT	216	150	618	20382²		8.9				12.6	4.09		.260	.331					.981	1627	2214					

Runs
Molitor-Mil 133
Palmeiro-Tex 115
Canseco-Oak 115
White-Tor 110
Sierra-Tex 110

Hits
Molitor-Mil 216
C.Ripken-Bal 210
Sierra-Tex 203
Palmeiro-Tex 203
Franco-Tex 201

Doubles
Palmeiro-Tex 49
C.Ripken-Bal 46
Sierra-Tex 44

Triples
Molitor-Mil 13
Johnson-Chi 13
Alomar-Tor 11
White-Tor 10
Devereaux-Bal 10

Home Runs
Fielder-Det 44
Canseco-Oak 44
C.Ripken-Bal 34
Carter-Tor 33
Thomas-Chi 32

Total Bases
C.Ripken-Bal 368
Palmeiro-Tex 336
Sierra-Tex 332
Molitor-Mil 325
Carter-Tor 321

Runs Batted In
Fielder-Det 133
Canseco-Oak 122
Sierra-Tex 116
C.Ripken-Bal 114
Thomas-Chi 109

Runs Produced
Sierra-Tex 201
Canseco-Oak 193
Molitor-Mil 191
Fielder-Det 191
Thomas-Chi 181

Bases On Balls
Thomas-Chi 138
Tettleton-Det 101
R.Henderson-Oak . . . 98
Clark-Bos 96
Davis-Min 95

Batting Average
Franco-Tex 341
Boggs-Bos 332
Randolph-Mil 327
K.Griffey-Sea 327
Molitor-Mil 325

On Base Percentage
Thomas-Chi 454
Randolph-Mil 427
Boggs-Bos 425
Franco-Tex 409
E.Martinez-Sea 407

Slugging Average
Tartabull-KC 593
C.Ripken-Bal 566
Canseco-Oak 556
Thomas-Chi 553
Palmeiro-Tex 532

Production
Thomas-Chi 1.007
Tartabull-KC 993
C.Ripken-Bal 945
K.Griffey-Sea 932
Palmeiro-Tex 925

Adjusted Production
Thomas-Chi 181
Tartabull-KC 170
C.Ripken-Bal 164
Canseco-Oak 159
Palmeiro-Tex 156

Batter Runs
Thomas-Chi 65.9
C.Ripken-Bal 48.5
Tartabull-KC 46.4
Palmeiro-Tex 45.6
K.Griffey-Sea 42.3

Adjusted Batter Runs
Thomas-Chi 69.4
C.Ripken-Bal 53.9
Palmeiro-Tex 47.9
Tartabull-KC 45.9
Canseco-Oak 44.7

Clutch Hitting Index
Davis-Sea 135
Surhoff-Mil 125
Yount-Mil 124
Randolph-Mil 122
Hrbek-Min 119

Runs Created
Thomas-Chi 145
C.Ripken-Bal 134
Molitor-Mil 132
Palmeiro-Tex 129
K.Griffey-Sea 118

Total Average
Thomas-Chi 1.109
Tartabull-KC 1.044
K.Griffey-Sea 969
Canseco-Oak 962
Whitaker-Det 942

Stolen Bases
R.Henderson-Oak . . . 58
Alomar-Tor 53
Raines-Chi 51
Polonia-Cal 48
Cuyler-Det 41

Stolen Base Average
Cotto-Sea 84.2
Knoblauch-Min 83.3
Alomar-Tor 82.8
Gibson-KC 81.8
Canseco-Oak 81.3

Stolen Base Runs
Alomar-Tor 9.3
R.Henderson-Oak . . . 6.6
Raines-Chi 6.3
Cuyler-Det 6.3
Franco-Tex 5.4

Fielding Runs
Gaetti-Cal 24.6
Vizquel-Sea 23.5
Espinoza-NY 20.3
Buechele-Tex 19.9
Sojo-Cal 19.5

Total Player Rating
C.Ripken-Bal 8.3
Thomas-Chi 5.5
K.Griffey-Sea 4.9
Canseco-Oak 4.2
R.Henderson-Oak . . . 4.1

Wins
Gullickson-Det 20
Erickson-Min 20
Langston-Cal 19

Win Percentage
Erickson-Min 714
Langston-Cal 704
Gullickson-Det 690
Wegman-Mil 682
Moore-Oak 680

Games
D.Ward-Tor 81
Olson-Bal 72
Jackson-Sea 72
Swift-Sea 71

Complete Games
McDowell-Chi 15
Clemens-Bos 13
Navarro-Mil 10
Morris-Min 10
Terrell-Det 8

Shutouts
Clemens-Bos 4
McDowell-Chi 3
Holman-Sea 3
Erickson-Min 3
Appier-KC 3

Saves
Harvey-Cal 46
Eckersley-Oak 43
Aguilera-Min 42
Reardon-Bos 40
Montgomery-KC . . . 33

Innings Pitched
Clemens-Bos 271.1
McDowell-Chi . . . 253.2
Morris-Min 246.2
Langston-Cal 246.1
Tapani-Min 244.0

Fewest Hits/Game
Ryan-Tex 5.31
Johnson-Sea 6.75
Langston-Cal 6.94
Clemens-Bos 7.26
McDowell-Chi 7.52

Fewest BB/Game
Swindell-Cle 1.17
Sanderson-NY 1.25
Tapani-Min 1.48
Gullickson-Det 1.75
Wegman-Mil 1.86

Strikeouts
Clemens-Bos 241
Johnson-Sea 228
Ryan-Tex 203
McDowell-Chi 191
Langston-Cal 183

Strikeouts/Game
Ryan-Tex 10.56
Johnson-Sea 10.19
Clemens-Bos 7.99
Hanson-Sea 7.37
Appier-KC 6.85

Ratio
Ryan-Tex 9.31
Clemens-Bos 9.59
Tapani-Min 9.85
Sanderson-NY . . . 10.04
Saberhagen-KC . . 10.04

Earned Run Average
Clemens-Bos 2.62
Candiotti-Cle-Tor . . 2.65
Wegman-Mil 2.84
J.Abbott-Cal 2.89
Ryan-Tex 2.91

Adjusted ERA
Clemens-Bos 164
Candiotti-Cle-Tor . . 158
Tapani-Min 143
J.Abbott-Cal 142
Wegman-Mil 140

Opponents' Batting Avg.
Ryan-Tex 172
Johnson-Sea 213
Langston-Cal 215
Clemens-Bos 221
Candiotti-Cle-Tor . . .228

Opponents' On Base Pct.
Ryan-Tex 267
Clemens-Bos 272
Tapani-Min 278
Sanderson-NY 281
Saberhagen-KC 281

Starter Runs
Clemens-Bos 44.4
Candiotti-Cle-Tor . . 38.3
J.Abbott-Cal 32.5
Langston-Cal 30.1
Tapani-Min 30.0

Adjusted Starter Runs
Clemens-Bos 50.6
Candiotti-Cle-Tor . . 40.6
Tapani-Min 34.7
J.Abbott-Cal 32.8
Langston-Cal 30.3

Clutch Pitching Index
Krueger-Sea 130
Holman-Sea 117
Terrell-Det 117
Guzman-Tex 116
Tanana-Det 115

Relief Runs
Frohwirth-Bal 23.8
Harvey-Cal 21.8
Swift-Sea 21.1
Eichhorn-Cal 19.2
Flanagan-Bal 18.7

Adjusted Relief Runs
Frohwirth-Bal 22.3
Harvey-Cal 21.9
Swift-Sea 21.3
Eichhorn-Cal 19.2
Habyan-NY 18.4

Relief Ranking
Harvey-Cal 43.8
Aguilera-Min 37.4
Farr-NY 30.8
D.Ward-Tor 27.0
Radinsky-Chi 23.4

Total Pitcher Index
Clemens-Bos 4.8
Harvey-Cal 4.5
Candiotti-Cle-Tor . . 4.5
J.Abbott-Cal 4.1
Aguilera-Min 3.8

Total Baseball Ranking
C.Ripken-Bal 8.3
Thomas-Chi 5.5
K.Griffey-Sea 4.9
Clemens-Bos 4.8
Harvey-Cal 4.5

TEAM	G	W	L	PCT	GB	R	OR	AB	H	2B	3B	HR	BB	SO	AVG	OBP	SLG	PRO	PRO+	BR	/A	PF	CHI	RC	SB	CS	SBA	SBR
EAST																												
PIT	162	96	66	.593		**693**	595	5527	1409	272	**54**	106	569	872	.255	.327	.381	.708	**107**	48	**56**	99	101	**699**	110	53	67	1
MON	162	87	75	.537	9	648	581	5477	1381	263	37	102	463	976	.252	.315	.370	.685	101	-4	2	99	104	651	196	63	76	**21**
STL	162	83	79	.512	13	631	604	5594	**1464**	262	44	94	495	996	**.262**	.325	.375	.700	**107**	30	51	97	94	680	**208**	118	64	-8
CHI	162	78	84	.481	18	593	624	5590	1420	221	41	104	417	**816**	.254	.309	.364	.673	94	-31	-46	103	99	617	77	51	60	-8
NY	162	72	90	.444	24	599	653	5340	1254	259	17	93	**572**	956	.235	.312	.342	.654	92	-54	-46	99	**106**	583	129	52	71	8
PHI	162	70	92	.432	26	686	717	5500	1392	255	36	118	509	1059	.253	.322	.377	.699	104	27	29	100	104	684	127	31	**80**	20
WEST																												
ATL	162	98	64	.605		682	**569**	5480	1391	223	48	**138**	493	924	.254	.318	**.388**	.706	99	34	-6	106	103	686	126	60	68	2
CIN	162	90	72	.556	8	660	609	5460	1418	**281**	44	99	563	888	.260	**.331**	.382	**.713**	105	**58**	39	103	96	689	125	65	66	-2
SD	162	82	80	.506	16	617	636	5476	1396	255	30	135	453	864	.255	.315	.386	.701	102	22	11	102	96	648	69	52	57	-11
HOU	162	81	81	.500	17	608	668	5480	1350	255	38	96	435	1025	.246	.316	.359	.675	102	-20	7	96	100	636	139	54	72	9
SF	162	72	90	.444	26	574	647	5456	1330	220	36	105	435	1067	.244	.304	.355	.659	97	-57	-26	94	102	584	112	64	64	-5
LA	162	63	99	.389	35	548	636	5368	1333	201	34	72	503	899	.248	.316	.339	.655	93	-54	-45	98	97	579	142	78	65	-4
TOT	972					7539		65748	16538	2967	459	1262	5978	11342	.252	.318	.368	.686							1560	741	68	23

TEAM	CG	SH	SV	IP	H	H/G	HR	BB	SO	RAT	ERA	ERA+	OAV	OOB	PR	/A	PF	CPI	FA	E	DP	FW	PW	BW	SBW	DIF
EAST																										
PIT	20	20	43	1479²	1410	8.6	101	455	844	11.5	3.35	103	.254	.314	25	14	98	103	.984	101	144	.9	1.5	**6.0**	-.1	6.7
MON	11	14	49	1468	**1296**	**7.9**	92	525	1014	11.5	3.25	107	**.238**	.310	41	35	99	97	.980	124	113	-.4	3.8	.2	**2.1**	.4
STL	10	9	47	1480	1405	8.5	118	**400**	842	**11.2**	3.38	100	.305		20	1	97	99	**.985**	94	146	**1.3**	.1	5.5	-1.1	-3.8
CHI	16	11	37	1469	1337	8.2	107	575	901	12.0	3.39	106	.246	.323	18	34	103	104	.982	114	142	.2	3.7	-5.0	-1.1	-.8
NY	17	13	34	1446²	1404	8.7	98	482	1025	12.0	3.66	95	.256	.321	-25	-30	99	98	.981	116	134	.0	-3.2	-5.0	.7	-1.5
PHI	**27**	7	34	1428	1387	8.7	113	549	851	12.4	4.11	85	.257	.328	-96	-98	100	92	.978	131	128	-.8	-10.6	3.1	1.9	-4.7
WEST																										
ATL	26	**24**	41	1460	1321	8.1	89	489	948	11.3	**3.14**	116	.242	.307	58	83	104	99	.982	109	121	.4	**8.9**	-.6	.0	8.3
CIN	9	11	**55**	1449²	1362	8.5	109	470	**1060**	11.5	3.46	104	.251	.314	6	21	103	100	.984	96	128	1.2	2.3	4.2	-.4	1.8
SD	9	11	46	1461¹	1444	8.9	111	480	971	11.7	3.56	100	.251	.318	-9	3	102	102	.982	115	127	.0	.3	1.2	-1.4	.8
HOU	5	12	45	1459¹	1386	8.5	114	539	978	12.1	3.72	90	.252	.323	-35	-58	96	98	.981	114	125	.2	-6.2	.8	.8	4.6
SF	9	12	30	1461	1385	8.5	128	502	927	11.8	3.61	91	.253	.320	-17	-50	94	102	.982	113	**174**	.2	-5.4	-2.8	-.7	-.3
LA	18	13	29	1438	1401	8.8	**82**	553	981	12.4	3.41	101	.257	.328	15	5	98	**106**	.972	174	136	-3.2	.5	-4.8	-.6	-9.8
TOT	177	157	490	17500²		8.5				11.8	3.50		.252	.318					.981	1401	1618					

Runs
- Bonds-Pit 109
- Hollins-Phi 104
- VanSlyke-Pit 103
- Sandberg-Chi 100
- Grissom-Mon 99

Hits
- VanSlyke-Pit 199
- Pendleton-Atl 199
- Sandberg-Chi 186
- Grace-Chi 185
- Sheffield-SD 184

Doubles
- VanSlyke-Pit 45
- Lankford-StL 40
- Duncan-Phi 40
- Clark-SF 40

Triples
- Sanders-Atl 14
- Finley-Hou 13
- VanSlyke-Pit 12
- Butler-LA 11
- Alicea-StL 11

Home Runs
- McGriff-SD 35
- Bonds-Pit 34
- Sheffield-SD 33
- Hollins-Phi 27
- Daulton-Phi 27

Total Bases
- Sheffield-SD 323
- Sandberg-Chi 312
- VanSlyke-Pit 310
- Pendleton-Atl 303

Runs Batted In
- Daulton-Phi 109
- Pendleton-Atl 105
- McGriff-SD 104
- Bonds-Pit 103
- Sheffield-SD 100

Runs Produced
- Pendleton-Atl 182
- VanSlyke-Pit 178
- Bonds-Pit 178
- Hollins-Phi 170
- Bagwell-Hou 165

Bases On Balls
- Bonds-Pit 127
- McGriff-SD 96
- Butler-LA 95
- Biggio-Hou 94
- Kruk-Phi 92

Batting Average
- Sheffield-SD ...... .330
- VanSlyke-Pit ...... .324
- Kruk-Phi .... .323
- Roberts-Cin .... .323
- Gwynn-SD .... .317

On Base Percentage
- Bonds-Pit .... .461
- Kruk-Phi .... .428
- Butler-LA .... .413
- McGriff-SD .... .396
- Roberts-Cin .... .396

Slugging Average
- Bonds-Pit .... .624
- Sheffield-SD ...... .580
- McGriff-SD .... .556
- Daulton-Phi .... .524
- Sandberg-Chi ...... .510

Production
- Bonds-Pit 1.085
- Sheffield-SD ...... .969
- McGriff-SD .... .952
- Daulton-Phi .... .912
- VanSlyke-Pit ...... .891

Adjusted Production
- Bonds-Pit 207
- Sheffield-SD 168
- McGriff-SD 164
- Daulton-Phi 157
- Clark-SF 153

Batter Runs
- Bonds-Pit 71.8
- Sheffield-SD 50.1
- McGriff-SD 48.1
- VanSlyke-Pit 40.2
- Kruk-Phi 38.6

Adjusted Batter Runs
- Bonds-Pit 73.3
- Sheffield-SD 48.2
- McGriff-SD 46.2
- VanSlyke-Pit 41.4
- Kruk-Phi 38.9

Clutch Hitting Index
- Murray-NY 126
- Daulton-Phi 124
- Lind-Pit 120
- Karros-LA 115
- Larkin-Cin 114

Runs Created
- Bonds-Pit 148
- VanSlyke-Pit 122
- Sheffield-SD 118
- Sandberg-Chi 117
- McGriff-SD 116

Total Average
- Bonds-Pit 1.335
- Daulton-Phi .... .994
- McGriff-SD .... .987
- Sheffield-SD ...... .945
- Kruk-Phi .... .900

Stolen Bases
- Grissom-Mon 78
- DeShields-Mon 46
- Roberts-Cin 44
- Finley-Hou 44
- O.Smith-StL 43

Stolen Base Average
- Davis-LA 95.0
- Alou-Mon 88.9
- Duncan-Phi 88.5

Stolen Base Runs
- Grissom-Mon 15.6
- Finley-Hou 7.8
- O.Smith-StL 7.5
- Bonds-Pit 6.9
- Dykstra-Phi 6.0

Fielding Runs
- Belliard-Atl 26.6
- Jackson-SD 24.2
- Thompson-SF 20.3
- Wallach-Mon 18.2
- Harris-LA 16.6

Total Player Rating
- Bonds-Pit 9.2
- Sheffield-SD 5.8
- Sandberg-Chi 5.7
- VanSlyke-Pit 5.4
- Larkin-Cin 4.7

Wins
- Maddux-Chi 20
- Glavine-Atl 20

Win Percentage
- Tewksbury-StL ..... .762
- Glavine-Atl .... .714
- Leibrandt-Atl ..... .682
- Morgan-Chi .... .667
- Maddux-Chi .... .645

Games
- Boever-Phi 81
- D.Jones-Hou 80
- Perez-StL 77
- Hernandez-Hou 77
- Innis-NY 76

Complete Games
- Mulholland-Phi 12
- Schilling-Phi 10
- Drabek-Pit 10
- Smoltz-Atl 9
- Maddux-Chi 9

Shutouts
- Glavine-Atl 5
- Cone-NY 5

Saves
- L.Smith-StL 43
- Myers-SD 38
- Wetteland-Mon 37
- D.Jones-Hou 36
- M.Williams-Phi 29

Innings Pitched
- Maddux-Chi 268.0
- Drabek-Pit 256.2
- Smoltz-Atl 246.2
- Morgan-Chi 240.0
- Avery-Atl 233.2

Fewest Hits/Game
- Schilling-Phi 6.56
- Maddux-Chi 6.75
- Fernandez-NY 6.79
- Martinez-Mon 6.84
- Cone-NY 7.41

Fewest BB/Game
- Tewksbury-StL ..... .77
- Cormier-StL 1.60
- Swindell-Cin 1.73
- Mulholland-Phi 1.81
- Tomlin-Pit 1.81

Strikeouts
- Smoltz-Atl 215
- Cone-NY 214
- Maddux-Chi 199
- Fernandez-NY 193
- Drabek-Pit 177

Strikeouts/Game
- Cone-NY 9.79
- Fernandez-NY 8.09
- Smoltz-Atl 7.84
- Rijo-Cin 7.29
- Harnisch-Hou 7.14

Ratio
- Schilling-Phi 8.95
- Tewksbury-StL 9.27
- Maddux-Chi 9.57
- Martinez-Mon 9.58
- Drabek-Pit 9.75

Earned Run Average
- Swift-SF 2.08
- Tewksbury-StL 2.16
- Maddux-Chi 2.18
- Schilling-Phi 2.35
- Martinez-Mon 2.47

Adjusted ERA
- Maddux-Chi 165
- Swift-SF 159
- Tewksbury-StL 157
- Schilling-Phi 149
- Morgan-Chi 141

Opponents' Batting Avg.
- Schilling-Phi ..... .201
- Maddux-Chi .... .210
- Fernandez-NY ...... .210
- Martinez-Mon ...... .211
- Cone-NY .... .223

Opponents' On Base Pct.
- Schilling-Phi ..... .256
- Tewksbury-StL ..... .267
- Martinez-Mon ...... .273
- Maddux-Chi .... .273
- Drabek-Pit .... .277

Starter Runs
- Maddux-Chi 39.3
- Tewksbury-StL 34.7
- Schilling-Phi 29.1
- Swift-SF 26.1
- Martinez-Mon 26.1

Adjusted Starter Runs
- Maddux-Chi 42.2
- Tewksbury-StL 31.7
- Schilling-Phi 28.7
- Morgan-Chi 28.0
- Martinez-Mon 25.1

Clutch Pitching Index
- Swift-SF 131
- Tewksbury-StL 120
- Swindell-Cin 119
- Morgan-Chi 115
- Ojeda-LA 113

Relief Runs
- Rojas-Mon 23.2
- D.Jones-Hou 20.5
- Beck-SF 17.8
- Hernandez-Hou 17.2
- Perez-StL 17.2

Adjusted Relief Runs
- Rojas-Mon 22.7
- D.Jones-Hou 18.7
- Perez-StL 16.0
- Beck-SF 15.8
- Hernandez-Hou 15.4

Relief Ranking
- D.Jones-Hou 42.1
- Rojas-Mon 21.4
- Perez-StL 18.6
- Beck-SF 15.8
- Hernandez-Hou 14.7

Total Pitcher Index
- Maddux-Chi 6.2
- D.Jones-Hou 4.5
- Martinez-Mon 3.5
- Glavine-Atl 3.3
- Rijo-Cin 3.2

Total Baseball Ranking
- Bonds-Pit 9.2
- Maddux-Chi 6.2
- Sheffield-SD 5.8
- Sandberg-Chi 5.7
- VanSlyke-Pit 5.4

TEAM	G	W	L	PCT	GB	R	OR	AB	H	2B	3B	HR	BB	SO	AVG	OBP	SLG	PRO	PRO+	BR	/A	PF	CHI	RC	SB	CS	SBA	SBR
EAST																												
TOR	162	96	66	.593		780	682	5536	1458	265	40	163	561	933	.263	.336	**.414**	**.750**	104	63	29	105	102	**779**	129	39	77	**15**
MIL	162	92	70	.568	4	740	**604**	5504	1477	272	35	82	511	779	.268	.334	.375	.709	100	-10	4	98	108	700	89	115	69	8
BAL	162	89	73	.549	7	705	656	5485	1423	243	36	148	647	827	.259	.343	.398	.741	104	56	37	103	92	754	89	48	65	-2
NY	162	76	86	.469	20	733	746	5593	1462	281	18	163	536	903	.261	.331	.406	.737	106	33	39	99	99	742	78	37	68	1
CLE	162	76	86	.469	20	674	746	5620	1495	227	24	127	448	885	.266	.325	.383	.708	100	-22	-10	98	99	686	144	67	68	3
DET	162	75	87	.463	21	791	794	5515	1411	256	16	**182**	675	1055	.256	.340	.407	.747	107	63	59	101	102	769	66	45	59	-7
BOS	162	73	89	.451	23	599	669	5461	1343	259	21	84	591	865	.246	.323	.347	.670	83	-84	-125	107	98	617	44	48	48	-16
WEST																												
OAK	162	96	66	.593		745	672	5387	1389	219	24	142	**707**	831	.258	**.349**	.386	.735	**112**	54	**95**	95	98	748	143	59	71	8
MIN	162	90	72	.556	6	747	653	5582	**1544**	275	27	104	527	834	**.277**	.345	.391	.736	103	46	22	103	99	748	123	74	62	-8
CHI	162	86	76	.531	10	738	690	5498	1434	269	36	110	622	784	.261	.339	.383	.722	103	19	28	99	102	728	160	57	74	14
TEX	162	77	85	.475	19	682	753	5537	1387	266	23	159	510	1036	.250	.324	.393	.717	104	-5	20	96	98	708	81	44	65	-2
KC	162	72	90	.444	24	610	667	5501	1411	**284**	**42**	75	439	741	.256	.317	.364	.681	88	-73	-90	103	99	629	131	71	65	-3
CAL	162	72	90	.444	24	579	671	5364	1306	202	20	88	416	882	.243	.303	.338	.641	79	-152	-155	101	**112**	529	160	101	61	-13
SEA	162	64	98	.395	32	679	799	5564	1466	278	24	149	474	841	.263	.326	.402	.728	102	13	9	101	96	708	100	55	65	-3
TOT	1134					9802		77147	20006	3596	386	1776	7704	12196	.259	.331	.385	.716							1704	860	66	-5

TEAM	CG	SH	SV	IP	H	H/G	HR	BB	SO	RAT	ERA	ERA+	OAV	OOB	PR	/A	PF	CPI	FA	E	DP	FW	PW	BW	SBW	DIF
EAST																										
TOR	18	14	49	1440²	1346	8.4	124	541	954	12.1	3.91	104	.248	.321	5	27	104	93	.985	93	109	1.4	2.7	3.0	**1.6**	6.3
MIL	19	14	39	1457	**1344**	**8.3**	127	**435**	793	**11.3**	**3.43**	112	**.246**	**.307**	82	65	97	98	**.986**	**89**	146	**1.6**	6.6	.4	.8	1.5
BAL	20	**16**	48	1464	1419	8.7	124	518	846	12.1	3.79	106	.256	.324	25	38	102	99	.985	93	168	1.4	3.9	3.8	-.2	-.9
NY	20	9	44	1452²	1453	9.0	129	612	851	13.0	4.21	93	.263	.341	-43	-47	99	99	.982	114	165	.2	-4.8	4.0	.1	-4.6
CLE	13	7	46	1470	1507	9.2	159	566	890	12.9	4.11	95	.268	.339	-28	-33	99	106	.978	141	176	-1.3	-3.4	-1.0	.3	.3
DET	10	4	36	1435²	1534	9.6	155	564	693	13.3	4.60	86	.277	.346	-105	-103	100	99	.981	116	164	.1	-10.5	6.0	-.7	-1.0
BOS	22	13	39	1448²	1403	8.7	107	535	943	12.3	3.58	**117**	.255	.326	57	**101**	107	103	.978	139	170	-1.2	**10.3**	-12.7	-1.6	-2.8
WEST																										
OAK	8	9	**58**	1447	1396	8.7	129	601	843	12.7	3.73	100	.256	.335	34	3	95	**107**	.979	125	158	-.4	.3	**9.7**	.8	4.5
MIN	16	13	50	1453	1391	8.6	121	479	923	11.8	3.70	109	.254	.318	38	56	103	98	.985	95	155	1.3	5.7	2.2	-.8	.5
CHI	21	5	52	1461²	1400	8.6	123	550	810	12.3	3.82	101	.252	.326	19	6	98	98	.979	129	134	-.6	.6	2.9	1.5	.7
TEX	19	3	42	1460¹	1471	9.1	113	598	**1034**	13.0	4.09	93	.264	.341	-24	-47	96	100	.975	154	153	-2.0	-4.8	2.0	-.2	.9
KC	9	12	44	1447¹	1426	8.9	**106**	512	834	12.3	3.81	106	.259	.327	21	39	103	98	.980	122	164	-.2	4.0	-9.2	-.3	-3.3
CAL	**26**	13	42	1446	1449	9.0	130	532	888	12.6	3.84	104	.264	.333	16	23	101	96	.979	134	172	-.9	2.3	-15.8	-1.3	6.6
SEA	21	9	30	1445	1467	9.1	129	661	894	13.6	4.55	87	.266	.351	-97	-92	101	96	.982	112	170	.3	-9.4	.9	-.3	-8.6
TOT	242	141	619	20329		8.9				12.5	3.94		.259	.331					.981	1656	2204					

Runs		Hits		Doubles		Triples		Home Runs		Total Bases	
Phillips-Det	114	Puckett-Min	210	Thomas-Chi	46	Johnson-Chi	12	Gonzalez-Tex	43	Puckett-Min	313
Thomas-Chi	108	Baerga-Cle	205	E.Martinez-Sea	46	Devereaux-Bal	11	McGwire-Oak	42	Carter-Tor	310
Alomar-Tor	105	Molitor-Mil	195	Yount-Mil	40	Anderson-Bal	10	Fielder-Det	35	Gonzalez-Tex	309
Puckett-Min	104	Mack-Min	189	Mattingly-NY	40	Raines-Chi	9	Carter-Tor	34	Thomas-Chi	307
Knoblauch-Min	104	Thomas-Chi	185	Griffey-Sea	39			Belle-Cle	34	Devereaux-Bal	303

Runs Batted In		Runs Produced		Bases On Balls		Batting Average		On Base Percentage		Slugging Average	
Fielder-Det	124	Thomas-Chi	199	Thomas-Chi	122	E.Martinez-Sea	.343	Thomas-Chi	.446	McGwire-Oak	.585
Carter-Tor	119	Puckett-Min	195	Tettleton-Det	122	Puckett-Min	.329	Tartabull-NY	.410	E.Martinez-Sea	.544
Thomas-Chi	115	Carter-Tor	182	Phillips-Det	114	Thomas-Chi	.323	E.Martinez-Sea	.408	Thomas-Chi	.536
Belle-Cle	112	Baerga-Cle	177	Milligan-Bal	106	Molitor-Mil	.320	Alomar-Tor	.406	Griffey-Sea	.535
Bell-Chi	112	Winfield-Tor	174	Tartabull-NY	103	Mack-Min	.315	Molitor-Mil	.396	Gonzalez-Tex	.529

Production		Adjusted Production		Batter Runs		Adjusted Batter Runs		Clutch Hitting Index		Runs Created	
Thomas-Chi	.981	McGwire-Oak	180	Thomas-Chi	62.4	Thomas-Chi	64.3	Surhoff-Mil	136	Thomas-Chi	142
McGwire-Oak	.976	Thomas-Chi	176	E.Martinez-Sea	44.9	McGwire-Oak	50.3	Lansford-Oak	134	Anderson-Bal	118
E.Martinez-Sea	.951	E.Martinez-Sea	164	McGwire-Oak	44.4	E.Martinez-Sea	44.4	Devereaux-Bal	120	E.Martinez-Sea	116
Tartabull-NY	.900	Tartabull-NY	152	Griffey-Sea	34.2	Molitor-Mil	35.7	Felix-Cal	120	Molitor-Mil	116
Griffey-Sea	.898	Griffey-Sea	148	Mack-Min	33.8	R.Henderson-Oak	35.6	Ventura-Chi	119	Mack-Min	114

Total Average		Stolen Bases		Stolen Base Average		Stolen Base Runs		Fielding Runs		Total Player Rating	
Thomas-Chi	1.066	Lofton-Cle	66	Cotto-Sea	92.0	Lofton-Cle	12.6	Reed-Bos	23.8	R.Henderson-Oak	4.7
McGwire-Oak	1.040	Listach-Mil	54	White-Tor	90.2	Raines-Chi	9.9	Ventura-Chi	23.7	Ventura-Chi	4.6
Tartabull-NY	.972	Anderson-Bal	53	Raines-Chi	88.2	Alomar-Tor	9.3	Gagne-Min	20.9	E.Martinez-Sea	4.6
E.Martinez-Sea	.970	Polonia-Cal	51	B.Kelly-NY	84.8	White-Tor	8.7	Lofton-Cle	16.7	Thomas-Chi	4.3
Alomar-Tor	.915	Alomar-Tor	49	Lofton-Cle	84.6	R.Henderson-Oak	7.8	White-Tor	15.1	Anderson-Bal	4.2

Wins		Win Percentage		Games		Complete Games		Shutouts		Saves	
Morris-Tor	21	Mussina-Bal	.783	Rogers-Tex	81	McDowell-Chi	13	Clemens-Bos	5	Eckersley-Oak	51
Brown-Tex	21	Morris-Tor	.778	D.Ward-Tor	79	Clemens-Bos	11	Mussina-Bal	4	Aguilera-Min	41
McDowell-Chi	20	Guzman-Tor	.762	Olin-Cle	72	Brown-Tex	11	Fleming-Sea	4	Montgomery-KC	39
Mussina-Bal	18	Bosio-Mil	.727	Lilliquist-Cle	71	Perez-NY	10			Olson-Bal	36
Clemens-Bos	18	McDowell-Chi	.667	Harris-Bos	70	Nagy-Cle	10			Henke-Tor	34

Innings Pitched		Fewest Hits/Game		Fewest BB/Game		Strikeouts		Strikeouts/Game		Ratio	
Brown-Tex	265.2	Johnson-Sea	6.59	Bosio-Mil	1.71	Johnson-Sea	241	Johnson-Sea	10.31	Mussina-Bal	9.78
Wegman-Mil	261.2	Guzman-Tor	6.73	Mussina-Bal	1.79	Perez-NY	218	Guzman-Tor	8.22	Clemens-Bos	10.00
McDowell-Chi	260.2	Appier-KC	7.21	Wegman-Mil	1.89	Clemens-Bos	208	Perez-NY	7.92	Appier-KC	10.24
Nagy-Cle	252.0	Clemens-Bos	7.41	Tapani-Min	1.96	Guzman-Tor	179	Clemens-Bos	7.59	Smiley-Min	10.31
Perez-NY	247.2	Smiley-Min	7.66	Gullickson-Det	2.03	McDowell-Chi	178	Guzman-Tex	7.19	Guzman-Tor	10.36

Earned Run Average		Adjusted ERA		Opponents' Batting Avg.		Opponents' On Base Pct.		Starter Runs		Adjusted Starter Runs	
Clemens-Bos	2.41	Clemens-Bos	175	Johnson-Sea	.206	Mussina-Bal	.279	Clemens-Bos	42.0	Clemens-Bos	49.4
Appier-KC	2.46	Appier-KC	165	Guzman-Tor	.207	Clemens-Bos	.280	Mussina-Bal	37.5	Mussina-Bal	39.7
Mussina-Bal	2.54	Mussina-Bal	158	Appier-KC	.217	Appier-KC	.282	Appier-KC	34.2	Appier-KC	36.8
Guzman-Tor	2.64	Guzman-Tor	155	Clemens-Bos	.224	Guzman-Tor	.287	Perez-NY	29.4	Guzman-Tor	28.9
Abbott-Cal	2.77	Abbott-Cal	144	Smiley-Min	.231	Smiley-Min	.288	Abbott-Cal	27.4	Perez-NY	28.8

Clutch Pitching Index		Relief Runs		Adjusted Relief Runs		Relief Ranking		Total Pitcher Index		Total Baseball Ranking	
Abbott-Cal	132	D.Ward-Tor	22.4	D.Ward-Tor	24.0	Eckersley-Oak	38.0	Clemens-Bos	5.8	Clemens-Bos	5.8
Finley-Cal	124	Hernandez-Chi	18.1	Harris-Bos	20.4	Olin-Cle	31.6	Eckersley-Oak	4.2	R.Henderson-Oak	4.7
Erickson-Min	113	Eckersley-Oak	18.0	Frohwirth-Bal	18.4	Montgomery-KC	31.4	Appier-KC	3.8	Ventura-Chi	4.6
Perez-NY	110	Frohwirth-Bal	17.4	Hernandez-Chi	17.5	J.Russell-Tex-Oak	31.3	Olin-Cle	3.5	E.Martinez-Sea	4.6
Moore-Oak	108	Harris-Bos	17.1	Montgomery-KC	17.2	D.Ward-Tor	29.8	Mussina-Bal	3.5	Thomas-Chi	4.3

TEAM	G	W	L	PCT	GB	R	OR	AB	H	2B	3B	HR	BB	SO	AVG	OBP	SLG	PRO	PRO+	BR	/A	PF	CHI	RC	SB	CS	SBA	SBR
EAST																												
PHI	162	97	65	.599		877	740	5685	1555	297	51	156	665	1049	.274	.354	.426	.780	116	117	130	99	99	880	91	32	74	8
MON	163	94	68	.580	3	732	682	5493	1410	270	36	122	542	860	.257	.329	.386	.715	92	-25	-55	104	104	727	228	56	80	35
STL	162	87	75	.537	10	758	744	5551	1508	262	34	118	588	882	.272	.344	.395	.739	105	32	48	98	99	759	153	72	68	3
CHI	163	84	78	.519	13	738	739	5627	1521	259	32	161	446	923	.270	.328	.414	.742	105	18	31	98	99	748	100	43	70	4
PIT	162	75	87	.463	22	707	806	5549	1482	267	50	110	536	972	.267	.338	.393	.731	101	10	12	100	95	734	92	55	63	-5
FLA	162	64	98	.395	33	581	724	5475	1356	197	31	94	498	1054	.248	.316	.346	.662	79	-124	-157	106	98	604	117	56	68	2
NY	162	59	103	.364	38	672	744	5448	1350	228	37	158	448	879	.248	.308	.390	.698	92	-72	-64	99	105	646	79	50	61	-6
WEST																												
ATL	162	104	58	.642		767	559	5515	1444	239	29	169	560	946	.262	.334	.408	.742	103	26	19	101	101	754	125	48	72	9
SF	162	103	59	.636	1	808	636	5557	1534	269	33	168	516	930	.276	.343	.427	.770	115	82	107	97	99	803	120	65	65	-3
HOU	162	85	77	.525	19	716	630	5464	1459	288	37	138	497	911	.267	.333	.409	.742	107	24	51	96	96	733	103	60	63	-5
LA	162	81	81	.500	23	675	660	5588	1458	234	28	130	492	937	.261	.324	.383	.707	100	-45	-5	94	98	696	126	61	67	1
CIN	162	73	89	.451	31	722	785	5517	1457	261	24	137	485	1025	.264	.327	.396	.723	98	-13	-14	100	102	720	142	59	71	7
COL	162	67	95	.414	37	758	967	5517	1507	278	59	142	388	944	.273	.326	.422	.748	90	28	-93	116	102	731	146	90	62	-10
SD	162	61	101	.377	43	679	772	5503	1386	239	28	153	443	1046	.252	.314	.389	.703	91	-58	-69	102	103	672	92	41	69	3
TOT	1135					10190		77489	20427	3588	513	1956	7104	13358	.264	.330	.399	.729							1714	788	69	41

TEAM	CG	SH	SV	IP	H	H/G	HR	BB	SO	RAT	ERA	ERA+	OAV	OOB	PR	/A	PF	CPI	FA	E	DP	FW	PW	BW	SBW	DIF
EAST																										
PHI	24	11	46	1472²	1419	8.7	129	573	1117	12.4	3.95	100	.251	.324	14	1	98	94	.977	141	123	-.4	.0	13.0	.5	2.8
MON	8	7	61	1456²	1369	8.5	119	521	934	12.0	3.55	118	.249	.319	80	101	103	101	.975	159	144	-1.4	10.1	-5.5	3.2	6.6
STL	5	7	54	1453	1553	9.6	152	383	775	12.3	4.09	97	.276	.327	-8	-20	98	102	.975	159	157	-1.4	-2.0	4.8	.0	4.6
CHI	8	5	56	1449²	1514	9.4	153	470	905	12.6	4.18	95	.273	.335	-22	-31	99	103	.982	115	162	1.1	-3.1	3.1	.1	1.8
PIT	12	5	34	1445²	1557	9.7	153	485	832	13.0	4.77	85	.280	.342	-117	-116	100	95	.983	105	161	1.7	-11.6	1.2	-.8	3.5
FLA	4	5	48	1440¹	1437	9.0	135	598	945	12.9	4.13	105	.261	.337	-14	30	107	100	.980	125	130	.5	3.0	-15.7	-.0	-4.8
NY	16	8	22	1438	1483	9.3	139	434	867	12.3	4.05	99	.269	.328	-2	-6	99	100	.975	156	143	-1.3	-.6	-6.4	-.9	-12.9
WEST																										
ATL	18	16	46	1455	1297	8.0	101	480	1036	11.1	3.14	128	.240	.305	146	142	99	101	.983	108	146	1.5	14.2	1.9	.6	4.8
SF	4	9	50	1456²	1385	8.6	168	442	982	11.6	3.61	108	.253	.315	69	47	97	105	.984	101	169	1.9	4.7	10.7	-.6	5.3
HOU	18	14	42	1441¹	1363	8.5	117	476	1056	11.7	3.49	111	.251	.316	88	61	96	101	.979	126	141	.5	6.1	5.1	-.8	-6.8
LA	17	9	36	1472²	1406	8.6	103	567	1043	12.3	3.50	109	.254	.327	88	51	94	105	.979	133	141	.0	5.1	-.5	-.2	-4.5
CIN	11	8	37	1434	1510	9.5	158	508	996	12.9	4.51	89	.272	.338	-74	-77	100	97	.980	121	133	.8	-7.7	-1.4	.4	-.0
COL	9	0	35	1431¹	1664	10.5	181	609	913	14.6	5.41	88	.294	.367	-218	-102	118	98	.973	167	149	-1.9	-10.2	-9.3	-1.3	8.7
SD	8	6	32	1437²	1470	9.2	148	558	957	12.9	4.23	98	.266	.337	-30	-15	102	100	.974	160	129	-1.5	-1.5	-6.9	.0	-10.1
TOT	162	110	599	20284²		9.1				12.5	4.04		.264	.330					.978	1876	2028					

Runs		Hits		Doubles		Triples		Home Runs		Total Bases	
Dykstra-Phi	143	Dykstra-Phi	194	Hayes-Col	45	Finley-Hou	13	Bonds-SF	46	Bonds-SF	365
Bonds-SF	129	Grace-Chi	193	Dykstra-Phi	44	Butler-LA	10	Justice-Atl	40	Williams-SF	325
Gant-Atl	113	Grissom-Mon	188	Bichette-Col	43	Morandini-Phi	9	Williams-SF	38	Gant-Atl	309
McGriff-SD-Atl	111	Bell-Pit	187	Gwynn-SD	41	Bell-Pit	9	McGriff-SD-Atl	37	Piazza-LA	307
Blauser-Atl	110	Jefferies-StL	186	Biggio-Hou	41			Gant-Atl	36	Dykstra-Phi	307

Runs Batted In		Runs Produced		Bases On Balls		Batting Average		On Base Percentage		Slugging Average	
Bonds-SF	123	Bonds-SF	206	Dykstra-Phi	129	Galarraga-Col	.370	Bonds-SF	.463	Bonds-SF	.677
Justice-Atl	120	Gant-Atl	194	Bonds-SF	126	Gwynn-SD	.358	Kruk-Phi	.433	Galarraga-Col	.602
Gant-Atl	117	Dykstra-Phi	190	Daulton-Phi	117	Jefferies-StL	.342	Dykstra-Phi	.423	Williams-SF	.561
Piazza-LA	112	Grissom-Mon	180	Kruk-Phi	111	Bonds-SF	.336	Merced-Pit	.415	Piazza-LA	.561
Williams-SF	110	Hollins-Phi	179	Butler-LA	86	Grace-Chi	.325	Jefferies-StL	.411	McGriff-SD-Atl	.549

Production		Adjusted Production		Batter Runs		Adjusted Batter Runs		Clutch Hitting Index		Runs Created	
Bonds-SF	1.140	Bonds-SF	207	Bonds-SF	82.0	Bonds-SF	87.0	Zeile-StL	128	Bonds-SF	172
Galarraga-Col	1.010	Piazza-LA	155	Dykstra-Phi	43.3	Dykstra-Phi	45.3	King-Pit	127	Dykstra-Phi	142
Piazza-LA	.935	Bagwell-Hou	146	Galarraga-Col	42.3	Piazza-LA	40.5	May-Chi	126	Kruk-Phi	117
McGriff-SD-Atl	.927	Kruk-Phi	145	Kruk-Phi	38.1	Kruk-Phi	39.9	Oliver-Cin	125	McGriff-SD-Atl	115
Bagwell-Hou	.909	Dykstra-Phi	144	McGriff-SD-Atl	34.8	Bagwell-Hou	35.4	Daulton-Phi	122	Jefferies-StL	113

Total Average		Stolen Bases		Stolen Base Average		Stolen Base Runs		Fielding Runs		Total Player Rating	
Bonds-SF	1.339	Carr-Fla	58	Frazier-Mon	89.5	Grissom-Mon	9.9	Bell-Pit	25.5	Bonds-SF	8.8
Galarraga-Col	1.006	Grissom-Mon	53	Davis-LA	86.8	Jefferies-StL	8.4	King-Pit	20.6	Dykstra-Phi	6.1
Dykstra-Phi	1.000	Nixon-Atl	47	Grissom-Mon	84.1	DeShields-Mon	6.9	Gonzalez-Hou	19.8	Bell-Pit	5.7
Kruk-Phi	.974	Lewis-SF	46	Bell-SD	83.9	Davis-LA	6.9	Reed-LA	19.4	Piazza-LA	5.2
Daulton-Phi	.971	Jefferies-StL	46	Jefferies-StL	83.6	Nixon-Atl	6.3	O.Smith-StL	18.4	Wilkins-Chi	4.3

Wins		Win Percentage		Games		Complete Games		Shutouts		Saves	
Glavine-Atl	22	Portugal-Hou	.818	Jackson-SF	81	Maddux-Atl	8	Harnisch-Hou	4	Myers-Chi	53
Burkett-SF	22	Greene-Phi	.800	West-Phi	76			R.Martinez-LA	3	Beck-SF	48
Swift-SF	21	Glavine-Atl	.786	Beck-SF	76					Harvey-Fla	45
Maddux-Atl	20	Burkett-SF	.759	McMichael-Atl	74						
		Avery-Atl	.750								

Innings Pitched		Fewest Hits/Game		Fewest BB/Game		Strikeouts		Strikeouts/Game		Ratio	
Maddux-Atl	267.0	Harnisch-Hou	7.07	Tewksbury-StL	.84	Rijo-Cin	227	Rijo-Cin	7.94	Maddux-Atl	9.64
Rijo-Cin	257.1	Swift-SF	7.54	Arocha-StL	1.48	Smoltz-Atl	208	Smoltz-Atl	7.68	Rijo-Cin	9.86
Smoltz-Atl	243.2	Rijo-Cin	7.62	Burkett-SF	1.55	Maddux-Atl	197	Guzman-Chi	7.68	Swift-SF	9.90
Glavine-Atl	239.1	Smoltz-Atl	7.68	Avery-Atl	1.73	Schilling-Phi	186	Harnisch-Hou	7.65	Mulholland-Phi	10.37
Drabek-Hou	237.2	Maddux-Atl	7.69	Maddux-Atl	1.75	Harnisch-Hou	185	Greene-Phi	7.52	Avery-Atl	10.44

Earned Run Average		Adjusted ERA		Opponents' Batting Avg.		Opponents' On Base Pct.		Starter Runs		Adjusted Starter Runs	
Maddux-Atl	2.36	Maddux-Atl	170	Harnisch-Hou	.214	Maddux-Atl	.274	Maddux-Atl	49.8	Maddux-Atl	49.0
Rijo-Cin	2.48	Rijo-Cin	162	Swift-SF	.226	Swift-SF	.278	Rijo-Cin	44.5	Rijo-Cin	44.0
Portugal-Hou	2.77	Portugal-Hou	140	Rijo-Cin	.230	Rijo-Cin	.278	Swift-SF	31.4	Swift-SF	28.0
Swift-SF	2.82	Swift-SF	138	Smoltz-Atl	.230	Mulholland-Phi	.283	Portugal-Hou	29.4	Avery-Atl	26.5
Avery-Atl	2.94	Avery-Atl	136	Maddux-Atl	.232	Harnisch-Hou	.290	Avery-Atl	27.2	Portugal-Hou	25.4

Clutch Pitching Index		Relief Runs		Adjusted Relief Runs		Relief Ranking		Total Pitcher Index		Total Baseball Ranking	
Portugal-Hou	120	Fassero-Mon	29.2	Fassero-Mon	31.3	Wetteland-Mon	63.7	Wetteland-Mon	6.5	Bonds-SF	8.8
Glavine-Atl	116	Wetteland-Mon	25.3	Wetteland-Mon	26.5	Harvey-Fla	45.2	Maddux-Atl	6.1	Wetteland-Mon	6.5
R.Martinez-LA	116	McMichael-Atl	20.1	Harvey-Fla	20.1	Fassero-Mon	32.5	Rijo-Cin	4.8	Dykstra-Phi	6.1
Reynoso-Col	113	Harvey-Fla	18.0	McMichael-Atl	19.9	Beck-SF	28.0	Harvey-Fla	4.6	Maddux-Atl	6.1
Avery-Atl	110	P.Martinez-LA	17.0	Beck-SF	15.4	Gott-LA	27.3	Swift-SF	4.2	Bell-Pit	5.7

TEAM	G	W	L	PCT	GB	R	OR	AB	H	2B	3B	HR	BB	SO	AVG	OBP	SLG	PRO	PRO+	BR	/A	PF	CHI	RC	SB	CS	SBA	SBR
EAST																												
TOR	162	95	67	.586		847	742	5579	1556	317	42	159	588	861	**.279**	.353	**.436**	.789	110	85	81	101	99	867	**170**	49	**78**	**22**
NY	162	88	74	.543	7	821	761	5615	**1568**	294	24	178	629	910	**.279**	.356	.435	.791	**115**	93	122	97	95	861	39	35	53	-9
BAL	162	85	77	.525	10	786	745	5508	1470	287	24	157	655	930	.267	.349	.413	.762	100	36	3	104	98	796	73	54	57	-11
DET	162	85	77	.525	10	**899**	837	5620	1546	282	38	178	**765**	1122	.275	**.365**	.434	**.799**	**115**	120	126	99	98	**916**	104	63	62	-7
BOS	162	80	82	.494	15	686	698	5496	1451	**319**	29	114	508	871	.264	.333	.395	.728	89	-41	-85	106	96	713	73	38	66	-1
CLE	162	76	86	.469	19	790	813	5619	1547	264	31	141	488	843	.275	.339	.409	.748	100	-5	-2	100	104	776	159	55	74	15
MIL	162	69	93	.426	26	733	792	5525	1426	240	25	125	555	932	.258	.330	.378	.708	91	-77	-67	99	108	686	138	93	60	-14
WEST																												
CHI	162	94	68	.580		776	**664**	5483	1454	228	**44**	162	604	834	.265	.342	.411	.753	103	11	28	98	100	773	106	57	65	-2
TEX	162	86	76	.531	8	835	751	5510	1472	284	39	**181**	483	984	.267	.332	.431	.763	107	16	46	96	**109**	777	113	67	63	-6
KC	162	84	78	.519	10	675	694	5522	1455	294	35	125	428	936	.263	.322	.397	.719	87	-67	-107	106	100	692	100	75	57	-15
SEA	162	82	80	.506	12	734	731	5494	1429	272	24	161	624	901	.260	.342	.406	.748	99	3	-8	101	95	758	91	68	57	-14
CAL	162	71	91	.438	23	684	770	5391	1399	259	24	114	564	930	.260	.334	.380	.714	88	-63	-85	103	101	679	169	104	63	-9
MIN	162	71	91	.438	23	693	830	5601	1480	261	27	121	493	850	.264	.329	.385	.714	91	-70	-72	100	101	692	83	59	58	-11
OAK	162	68	94	.420	26	715	846	5543	1408	260	21	158	622	1048	.254	.333	.394	.727	101	-42	1	94	99	735	131	59	69	4
TOT	1134					10674		77506	20661	3861	427	2074	8006	12952	.267	.340	.408	.748							1549	872	64	-59

TEAM	CG	SH	SV	IP	H	H/G	HR	BB	SO	RAT	ERA	ERA+	OAV	OOB	PR	/A	PF	CPI	FA	E	DP	FW	PW	BW	SBW	DIF
EAST																										
TOR	11	11	**50**	1441¹	1441	9.0	134	620	1023	13.1	4.21	103	.261	.339	18	17	100	99	.982	107	144	.5	1.7	7.9	**2.5**	1.5
NY	11	**13**	38	1438¹	1467	9.2	170	552	899	12.8	4.35	95	.266	.336	-4	-31	96	100	.983	105	166	.6	-3.0	11.9	-.5	-2.0
BAL	21	10	42	1442²	1427	8.9	153	579	900	12.8	4.31	104	.261	.336	2	26	104	98	.984	100	171	.9	2.5	.3	-.7	1.0
DET	11	7	36	1436²	1547	9.7	188	542	828	13.4	4.65	92	.276	.345	-52	-58	99	102	.979	132	148	-1.0	-5.6	12.3	-.3	-1.3
BOS	9	11	44	1452¹	**1379**	8.5	127	552	997	12.3	**3.77**	122	.252	.325	88	136	107	100	.980	122	155	-.4	13.2	-8.3	.3	-5.9
CLE	7	8	45	1445²	1591	9.9	182	591	888	13.8	4.58	94	.281	.353	-42	-41	100	**107**	.976	148	174	-1.9	-4.0	-.2	1.9	-.7
MIL	**26**	6	29	1447	1511	9.4	153	522	810	13.0	4.45	95	.271	.340	-21	-33	99	99	.979	131	148	-.9	-3.2	-6.5	-1.0	-.4
WEST																										
CHI	16	11	48	1454	1398	8.7	125	566	974	12.4	**3.70**	113	.255	.330	**100**	77	97	105	.982	112	153	.2	7.5	2.7	.2	2.4
TEX	20	6	45	1438¹	1476	9.2	144	562	957	13.0	4.28	97	.267	.339	7	-21	96	100	.979	132	145	-1.0	-2.0	4.5	-.2	3.8
KC	16	6	48	1445¹	1379	8.6	**105**	571	985	12.4	4.04	113	.254	.329	45	87	106	93	.984	97	150	1.0	8.5	-10.4	-1.1	5.0
SEA	22	10	41	1453²	1421	8.8	135	605	**1083**	13.0	4.20	105	.259	.340	20	33	102	99	**.985**	**90**	173	**1.4**	3.2	-.8	-1.0	-1.9
CAL	**26**	6	41	1430¹	1482	9.3	153	550	843	13.1	4.34	104	.270	.342	-3	26	104	102	.980	120	161	-.3	2.5	-8.3	-.5	-3.5
MIN	5	3	44	1444¹	1591	9.9	148	**514**	901	13.4	4.71	92	.283	.348	-63	-57	101	99	.984	100	160	.9	-5.5	-7.0	-.7	2.4
OAK	8	2	42	1452¹	1551	9.6	157	680	864	14.1	4.90	83	.276	.359	-94	-133	94	98	.982	111	161	.2	-12.9	.0	.8	-1.2
TOT	209	110	593	20222¹		9.2				13.0	4.32		.267	.340					.981	1607	2209					

Runs
Palmeiro-Tex 124
Molitor-Tor 121
White-Tor 116
Lofton-Cle 116
R.Henderson-Oak-Tor . 114

Hits
Molitor-Tor 211
Olerud-Tor 200
Baerga-Cle 200
Alomar-Tor 192
Lofton-Cle 185

Doubles
Olerud-Tor 54
White-Tor 42
Valentin-Bos 40
Palmeiro-Tex 40
Puckett-Min 39

Triples
Johnson-Chi 14
Cora-Chi 13
Hulse-Tex 10
McRae-KC 9
Fernandez-Tor 9

Home Runs
Gonzalez-Tex 46
Griffey-Sea 45
Thomas-Chi 41
Belle-Cle 38
Palmeiro-Tex 37

Total Bases
Griffey-Sea 359
Gonzalez-Tex 339
Thomas-Chi 333
Palmeiro-Tex 331
Olerud-Tor 330

Runs Batted In
Belle-Cle 129
Thomas-Chi 128
Carter-Tor 121
Gonzalez-Tex 118
Fielder-Det 117

Runs Produced
Molitor-Tor 210
Baerga-Cle 198
Thomas-Chi 193
Palmeiro-Tex 192
Olerud-Tor 192

Bases On Balls
Phillips-Det 132
R.Henderson-Oak-Tor 120
Olerud-Tor 114
Thomas-Chi 112
Tettleton-Det 109

Batting Average
Olerud-Tor ..... .363
Molitor-Tor ..... .332
Alomar-Tor ..... .326
Lofton-Cle ..... .325
Baerga-Cle ..... .321

On Base Percentage
Olerud-Tor ..... .478
Phillips-Det ..... .446
R.Henderson-Oak-Tor ..... .435
Thomas-Chi ..... .434
Hoiles-Bal ..... .419

Slugging Average
Gonzalez-Tex ..... .632
Griffey-Sea ..... .617
Thomas-Chi ..... .607
Olerud-Tor ..... .599
Hoiles-Bal ..... .585

Production
Olerud-Tor 1.077
Thomas-Chi 1.041
Griffey-Sea 1.029
Hoiles-Bal 1.003
Gonzalez-Tex 1.001

Adjusted Production
Olerud-Tor 186
Thomas-Chi 180
Gonzalez-Tex 170
Griffey-Sea 170
Hoiles-Bal 160

Batter Runs
Olerud-Tor 74.4
Thomas-Chi 62.3
Griffey-Sea 60.1
Gonzalez-Tex 44.4
Molitor-Tor 41.0

Adjusted Batter Runs
Olerud-Tor 73.6
Thomas-Chi 65.5
Griffey-Sea 58.1
Gonzalez-Tex 49.0
Palmeiro-Tex 42.9

Clutch Hitting Index
McLemore-Bal 122
Surhoff-Mil 120
Baerga-Cle 119
Davis-Cal 117
Kirby-Cle 115

Runs Created
Olerud-Tor 161
Thomas-Chi 149
Griffey-Sea 147
Molitor-Tor 136
Palmeiro-Tex 128

Total Average
Olerud-Tor 1.230
Thomas-Chi 1.160
R.Henderson-Oak-Tor 1.106
Griffey-Sea 1.104
Hoiles-Bal 1.077

Stolen Bases
Lofton-Cle 70
Polonia-Cal 55
Alomar-Tor 55
R.Henderson-Oak-Tor 53
Curtis-Cal 48

Stolen Base Average
White-Tor 89.5
Palmeiro-Tex 88.0
R.Henderson-Oak-Tor 86.9
Molitor-Tor 84.6
Fletcher-Bos 84.2

Stolen Base Runs
Lofton-Cle 12.6
R.Henderson-Oak-Tor 11.1
White-Tor 7.8
Alomar-Tor 7.5
Johnson-Chi 6.3

Fielding Runs
Vizquel-Sea 22.9
Pena-Bos 22.2
Joyner-KC 20.5
Boggs-NY 19.6
Belle-Cle 19.1

Total Player Rating
Olerud-Tor 5.9
R.Henderson-Oak-Tor 5.3
Griffey-Sea 5.3
Belle-Cle 5.2
Gonzalez-Tex 4.9

Wins
McDowell-Chi 22
Johnson-Sea 19
Hentgen-Tor 19

Win Percentage
Key-NY ..... .750
Johnson-Sea ..... .704
Appier-KC ..... .692
McDowell-Chi ..... .688
Hentgen-Tor ..... .679

Games
Harris-Cal 80
Radinsky-Chi 73
D.Ward-Tor 71
Nelson-Sea 71
Fossas-Bos 71

Complete Games
Finley-Cal 13
Brown-Tex 12
McDowell-Chi 10
Johnson-Sea 10
Eldred-Mil 8

Shutouts
McDowell-Chi 4
Moore-Det 3
Johnson-Sea 3
Brown-Tex 3

Saves
D.Ward-Tor 45
Montgomery-KC 45
Henke-Tex 40
Hernandez-Chi 38
Eckersley-Oak 36

Innings Pitched
Eldred-Mil 258.0
McDowell-Chi 256.2
Langston-Cal 256.1
Johnson-Sea 255.1
Cone-KC 254.0

Fewest Hits/Game
Johnson-Sea 6.52
Appier-KC 6.90
Cone-KC 7.26
Alvarez-Chi 7.28
McDonald-Bal 7.56

Fewest BB/Game
Key-NY 1.64
Darwin-Bos 1.92
Wells-Det 2.02
Tapani-Min 2.27
Doherty-Det 2.34

Strikeouts
Johnson-Sea 308
Langston-Cal 196
Guzman-Tor 194
Cone-KC 191
Finley-Cal 187

Strikeouts/Game
Johnson-Sea 10.86
Perez-NY 8.17
Guzman-Tor 7.90
Clemens-Bos 7.51
Banks-Min 7.25

Ratio
Darwin-Bos 9.73
Appier-KC 9.99
Key-NY 10.00
Johnson-Sea 10.57
Fernandez-Chi 10.70

Earned Run Average
Appier-KC 2.56
Alvarez-Chi 2.95
Key-NY 3.00
Fernandez-Chi 3.13
Viola-Bos 3.14

Adjusted ERA
Appier-KC 179
Viola-Bos 147
Finley-Cal 143
Alvarez-Chi 142
Darwin-Bos 142

Opponents' Batting Avg.
Johnson-Sea ..... .203
Appier-KC ..... .212
Cone-KC ..... .223
McDonald-Bal ..... .228
Bosio-Sea ..... .228

Opponents' On Base Pct.
Darwin-Bos ..... .274
Appier-KC ..... .280
Key-NY ..... .282
Johnson-Sea ..... .292
Fernandez-Chi ..... .296

Starter Runs
Appier-KC 46.6
Key-NY 34.6
Fernandez-Chi 32.7
Finley-Cal 32.7
Langston-Cal 32.1

Adjusted Starter Runs
Appier-KC 53.5
Finley-Cal 37.9
Langston-Cal 37.4
Cone-KC 35.3
Darwin-Bos 34.6

Clutch Pitching Index
Alvarez-Chi 129
Viola-Bos 123
Pavlik-Tex 119
Banks-Min 118
Finley-Cal 115

Relief Runs
Montgomery-KC 19.9
Hernandez-Chi 17.8
D.Ward-Tor 17.4
Lilliquist-Cle 14.7
Henneman-Det 13.4

Adjusted Relief Runs
Montgomery-KC 22.4
D.Ward-Tor 17.4
Hernandez-Chi 16.5
Lilliquist-Cle 14.8
Mills-Bal 13.9

Relief Ranking
Montgomery-KC 53.8
D.Ward-Tor 35.5
Hernandez-Chi 31.2
Henke-Tex 24.8
Fernandez-Chi 23.1

Total Pitcher Index
Montgomery-KC 5.0
Appier-KC 4.8
Langston-Cal 3.9
Finley-Cal 3.7
D.Ward-Tor 3.5

Total Baseball Ranking
Olerud-Tor 5.9
R.Henderson-Oak-Tor 5.3
Griffey-Sea 5.3
Belle-Cle 5.2
Montgomery-KC 5.0

TEAM	G	W	L	PCT	GB	R	OR	AB	H	2B	3B	HR	BB	SO	AVG	OBP	SLG	PRO	PRO+	BR	/A	PF	CHI	RC	SB	CS	SBA	SBR
EAST																												
MON	114	74	40	.649		585	454	4000	1111	246	30	108	379	669	.278	.346	.435	.781	106	47	36	102	99	615	**137**	36	**79**	**20**
ATL	114	68	46	.596	6	542	**448**	3861	1031	198	18	**137**	377	**668**	.267	.336	.434	.770	105	25	24	100	99	548	48	31	61	-4
NY	113	55	58	.487	18.5	506	526	3869	966	164	21	117	336	807	.250	.318	.394	.712	89	-57	-60	101	**109**	484	25	26	49	-8
PHI	115	54	61	.470	20.5	521	497	3927	1028	208	28	80	396	711	.262	.334	.390	.724	95	-31	-25	99	104	515	67	24	74	6
FLA	115	51	64	.443	23.5	468	576	3926	1043	180	24	94	349	746	.266	.332	.396	.728	90	-29	-56	106	94	519	65	26	71	4
CENTRAL																												
CIN	115	66	48	.579		**609**	490	3999	**1142**	211	36	124	388	738	**.286**	**.353**	**.449**	**.802**	115	78	83	99	98	**633**	119	51	70	5
HOU	115	66	49	.574		602	503	3955	1099	**252**	25	120	394	718	.278	.350	.445	.795	115	66	80	98	99	624	124	44	74	11
STL	115	53	61	.465	13	535	621	3902	1026	213	27	108	**434**	686	.263	.342	.414	.756	106	14	35	96	98	555	76	46	62	-5
PIT	114	53	61	.465	13	466	580	3864	1001	198	23	80	349	725	.259	.324	.384	.708	89	-57	-55	100	102	478	53	25	68	1
CHI	113	49	64	.434	16.5	500	549	3918	1015	189	26	80	364	750	.259	.326	.404	.730	98	-29	-16	97	101	507	69	53	57	-11
WEST																												
LA	114	58	56	.509		532	509	3904	1055	160	29	115	366	687	.270	.336	.414	.750	106	1	32	94	101	538	74	37	67	0
SF	115	55	60	.478	3.5	504	500	3869	963	159	32	123	364	719	.249	.320	.402	.722	96	-44	-26	96	105	504	114	40	74	10
COL	117	53	64	.453	6.5	573	638	4006	1098	206	**39**	125	378	761	.274	.340	.439	.779	92	40	-54	116	99	584	91	53	63	-5
SD	117	47	70	.402	12.5	479	531	4068	1117	200	19	92	319	762	.275	.332	.401	.733	97	-24	-19	99	93	526	79	37	68	2
TOT	803					7422		55068	14695	2784	377	1532	5193	10147	.267	.335	.415	.750							1141	529	68	25

TEAM	CG	SH	SV	IP	H	H/G	HR	BB	SO	RAT	ERA	ERA+	OAV	OOB	PR	/A	PF	CPI	FA	E	DP	FW	PW	BW	SBW	DIF
EAST																										
MON	4	8	46	1036²	970	8.4	100	288	805	11.3	3.56	119	.247	**.305**	75	78	101	95	.979	94	90	-.5	**7.7**	3.5	**1.8**	4.5
ATL	16	8	26	1026¹	**929**	8.1	76	378	865	11.7	3.57	116	**.242**	.314	73	66	99	93	.982	81	85	.3	6.5	2.4	-.6	2.4
NY	7	3	35	1023	1069	9.4	117	332	640	12.5	4.13	103	.271	.331	9	14	101	103	.980	89	112	-.2	1.4	-5.9	-1.0	4.2
PHI	7	6	30	1024¹	1028	9.0	98	377	699	12.6	3.85	107	.261	.330	41	31	98	103	.978	94	96	-.4	3.0	-2.5	.4	-4.1
FLA	5	7	30	1015	1069	9.5	120	428	649	13.6	4.50	100	.274	.352	-32	1	107	104	.978	95	111	-.5	.0	-5.5	.2	-.8
CENTRAL																										
CIN	6	6	27	1038¹	1037	9.0	117	339	799	12.2	3.78	110	.262	.324	50	43	99	**106**	.983	73	91	.8	4.2	**8.2**	.3	-4.5
HOU	9	6	29	1029²	1043	9.1	102	367	739	12.6	3.97	103	.265	.333	28	11	97	104	.983	76	110	.6	1.1	7.9	.9	-2.0
STL	7	7	29	1018	1154	10.2	134	355	632	13.7	5.14	79	.289	.353	-105	-121	97	97	.982	80	119	.4	-11.9	3.4	-.7	4.7
PIT	8	2	24	1005²	1094	9.8	117	370	650	13.5	4.64	92	.281	.350	-47	-44	101	102	.980	91	**131**	-.3	-4.3	-5.4	-.0	6.1
CHI	5	5	27	1023²	1054	9.3	120	392	717	12.9	4.47	92	.268	.338	-29	-41	98	97	.982	81	110	.2	-4.0	-1.6	-1.3	-.9
WEST																										
LA	14	5	20	1014	1041	9.2	90	354	732	12.7	4.17	95	.267	.333	4	-25	94	97	.980	88	104	-.1	-2.5	3.1	-.2	.6
SF	2	4	33	1025¹	1014	8.9	122	372	655	12.5	3.99	101	.262	.333	26	4	96	106	**.985**	**68**	113	**1.1**	.4	-2.6	.8	-2.2
COL	4	5	28	1031	1185	10.3	120	448	703	14.7	5.15	96	.292	.369	-108	-21	118	101	.981	84	117	.2	-2.1	-5.3	-.7	2.3
SD	8	6	27	1045²	1008	8.7	99	393	862	12.3	4.08	103	.283	.323	15	14	100	91	.975	111	82	-1.3	1.4	-1.9	.0	-9.7
TOT	102	78	411	14356²		9.2				12.8	4.21		.267	.335					.980	1205	1471					

Runs		Hits		Doubles		Triples		Home Runs		Total Bases	
Bagwell-Hou	104	Gwynn-SD	165	Walker-Mon	44	Lewis-SF	9	Williams-SF	43	Bagwell-Hou	300
Grissom-Mon	96	Bichette-Col	147	Biggio-Hou	44	Butler-LA	9	Bagwell-Hou	39	Williams-SF	270
Lankford-StL	89	Bagwell-Hou	147	Gwynn-SD	35	R.Sanders-Cin	8	Bonds-SF	37	Bichette-Col	265
Bonds-SF	89	Morris-Cin	146	Bell-Pit	35	Mondesi-LA	8	McGriff-Atl	34	McGriff-Atl	264
Biggio-Hou	88	Conine-Fla	144	Bichette-Col	33	Kingery-Col	8	Galarraga-Col	31	Bonds-SF	253

Runs Batted In		Runs Produced		Bases On Balls		Batting Average		On Base Percentage		Slugging Average	
Bagwell-Hou	116	Bagwell-Hou	181	Bonds-SF	74	Gwynn-SD	.394	Bagwell-Hou	.461	Bagwell-Hou	.750
Williams-SF	96	Walker-Mon	143	Justice-Atl	69	Bagwell-Hou	.368	Gwynn-SD	.458	Mitchell-Cin	.681
Bichette-Col	95	Bichette-Col	142	Dykstra-Phi	68	Alou-Mon	.339	Mitchell-Cin	.438	Bonds-SF	.647
McGriff-Atl	94	McGriff-Atl	141	Butler-LA	68	Morris-Cin	.335	Bonds-SF	.429	McGriff-Atl	.623
Piazza-LA	92	Biggio-Hou	138	Bagwell-Hou	65	Mitchell-Cin	.326	Justice-Atl	.428	Williams-SF	.607

Production		Adjusted Production		Batter Runs		Adjusted Batter Runs		Clutch Hitting Index		Runs Created	
Bagwell-Hou	1.211	Bagwell-Hou	213	Bagwell-Hou	64.7	Bagwell-Hou	67.5	Gonzalez-Hou	132	Bagwell-Hou	137
Mitchell-Cin	1.119	Mitchell-Cin	187	Bonds-SF	44.9	Bonds-SF	48.7	Blauser-Atl	121	Bonds-SF	115
Bonds-SF	1.076	Bonds-SF	182	Gwynn-SD	42.2	Gwynn-SD	43.2	Piazza-LA	120	Gwynn-SD	104
Gwynn-SD	1.026	Gwynn-SD	167	Mitchell-Cin	40.3	Mitchell-Cin	41.0	Morris-Cin	116	McGriff-Atl	103
McGriff-Atl	1.014	McGriff-Atl	159	McGriff-Atl	35.6	McGriff-Atl	35.5	Sheffield-Fla	116	Biggio-Hou	98

Total Average		Stolen Bases		Stolen Base Average		Stolen Base Runs		Fielding Runs		Total Player Rating	
Bagwell-Hou	1.413	Biggio-Hou	39	Larkin-Cin	92.9	Biggio-Hou	9.3	Sanchez-Chi	28.5	Bagwell-Hou	7.4
Bonds-SF	1.256	D.Sanders-Atl-Cin	38	Biggio-Hou	90.7	Grissom-Mon	7.2	Bell-Pit	19.3	Bonds-SF	5.5
Mitchell-Cin	1.244	Grissom-Mon	36	Clayton-SF	88.5	Larkin-Cin	6.6	Bagwell-Hou	17.1	Gwynn-SD	4.3
Gwynn-SD	1.069	Carr-Fla	32	Grissom-Mon	85.7	Clayton-SF	5.1	Grissom-Mon	16.3	Mitchell-Cin	4.2
McGriff-Atl	1.063	Lewis-SF	30	Cordero-Mon	84.2	Carr-Fla	4.8	Karros-LA	16.0	Biggio-Hou	3.2

Wins		Win Percentage		Games		Complete Games		Shutouts		Saves	
Maddux-Atl	16	Saberhagen-NY	.778	Reed-Col	61	Maddux-Atl	10	Martinez-LA	3	Franco-NY	30
Hill-Mon	16	Hill-Mon	.762	Rojas-Phi	58	Drabek-Hou	6	Maddux-Atl	3	Beck-SF	28
Saberhagen-NY	14	Maddux-Atl	.727	Bautista-Chi	58	Candiotti-LA	5	Drabek-Hou	2	Jones-Phi	27
Jackson-Phi	14	Jackson-Phi	.700	Munoz-Col	57			Benes-SD	2	Wetteland-Mon	25
Glavine-Atl	13	Martinez-Mon	.688	Burba-SF	57						

Innings Pitched		Fewest Hits/Game		Fewest BB/Game		Strikeouts		Strikeouts/Game		Ratio	
Maddux-Atl	202.0	Maddux-Atl	6.68	Saberhagen-NY	.66	Benes-SD	189	Benes-SD	9.87	Maddux-Atl	8.33
Jackson-Phi	179.1	Martinez-Mon	7.15	Tewksbury-StL	1.27	Rijo-Cin	171	Rijo-Cin	8.93	Saberhagen-NY	9.44
Saberhagen-NY	177.1	Drabek-Hou	7.21	Maddux-Atl	1.38	Maddux-Atl	156	Martinez-Mon	8.83	Drabek-Hou	9.78
Rijo-Cin	172.1	Avery-Atl	7.54	Reynolds-Hou	1.52	Saberhagen-NY	143	Neagle-Pit	8.01	Fassero-Mon	10.38
Benes-SD	172.1	Fassero-Mon	7.72	Swindell-Hou	1.58	Martinez-Mon	142	Reynolds-Hou	7.98	Ashby-SD	10.46

Earned Run Average		Adjusted ERA		Opponents' Batting Avg.		Opponents' On Base Pct.		Starter Runs		Adjusted Starter Runs	
Maddux-Atl	1.56	Maddux-Atl	266	Maddux-Atl	.207	Maddux-Atl	.245	Maddux-Atl	59.5	Maddux-Atl	58.1
Saberhagen-NY	2.74	Saberhagen-NY	155	Martinez-Mon	.220	Saberhagen-NY	.273	Saberhagen-NY	29.0	Saberhagen-NY	30.0
Drabek-Hou	2.84	Drabek-Hou	143	Drabek-Hou	.220	Drabek-Hou	.277	Drabek-Hou	25.0	Freeman-Col	27.2
Fassero-Mon	2.99	Fassero-Mon	142	Avery-Atl	.227	Fassero-Mon	.286	Rijo-Cin	21.6	Drabek-Hou	22.4
Reynolds-Hou	3.05	Jones-NY	135	Fassero-Mon	.229	Ashby-SD	.286	Henry-Mon	21.2	Henry-Mon	21.6

Clutch Pitching Index		Relief Runs		Adjusted Relief Runs		Relief Ranking		Total Pitcher Index		Total Baseball Ranking	
Rijo-Cin	125	Jackson-SF	12.8	Brantley-Cin	12.2	Brantley-Cin	26.4	Maddux-Atl	7.1	Bagwell-Hou	7.4
Rapp-Fla	121	Brantley-Cin	12.6	Carrasco-Cin	12.0	Jones-Phi	24.9	Saberhagen-NY	3.2	Maddux-Atl	7.1
Smith-Pit	118	Carrasco-Cin	12.4	Jackson-SF	11.9	Carrasco-Cin	24.0	Drabek-Hou	2.9	Bonds-SF	5.5
Burkett-SF	118	Jones-Phi	12.3	Jones-Phi	11.7	Wetteland-Mon	23.0	Freeman-Col	2.8	Gwynn-SD	4.3
Trachsel-Chi	116	Jones-Hou	12.0	McElroy-Cin	11.6	Nen-Fla	21.4	Brantley-Cin	2.7	Mitchell-Cin	4.2

TEAM	G	W	L	PCT	GB	R	OR	AB	H	2B	3B	HR	BB	SO	AVG	OBP	SLG	PRO	PRO+	BR	/A	PF	CHI	RC	SB	CS	SBA	SBR
EAST																												
NY	113	70	43	.619		670	534	3986	1155	238	16	139	**530**	660	.290	.377	.462	.839	123	97	145	93	94	**692**	55	40	58	-8
BAL	112	63	49	.563	6.5	589	**497**	3856	1047	185	20	139	448	655	.272	.352	.438	.790	96	13	-25	106	99	606	69	13	**84**	**13**
TOR	115	55	60	.478	16	566	579	3962	1064	210	30	115	387	691	.269	.339	.424	.763	94	-30	-35	101	100	570	79	26	75	8
BOS	115	54	61	.470	17	552	621	3940	1038	222	19	120	404	723	.263	.337	.421	.758	88	-39	-75	107	100	558	81	38	68	2
DET	115	53	62	.461	18	652	671	3955	1048	216	25	161	520	897	.265	.355	.454	.809	108	42	46	99	100	646	46	33	58	-6
CENTRAL																												
CHI	113	67	46	.593		633	498	3942	1133	175	**39**	121	497	568	.287	.370	.444	.814	110	58	64	99	95	660	77	27	74	7
CLE	113	66	47	.584	1	**679**	562	4022	**1165**	**240**	20	**167**	382	629	.290	.354	**.484**	.838	108	73	44	104	101	686	131	48	73	11
KC	115	64	51	.557	4	574	532	3911	1051	211	38	100	376	698	.269	.338	.419	.757	87	-38	-82	105	105	558	**140**	62	69	5
MIN	113	53	60	.469	14	594	688	3952	1092	239	23	103	359	635	.276	.343	.427	.770	97	-20	-20	100	105	578	94	30	76	10
MIL	115	53	62	.461	15	547	586	3978	1045	238	21	99	417	680	.263	.338	.408	.746	89	-53	-64	102	100	549	59	37	61	-5
WEST																												
TEX	114	52	62	.456		613	697	3983	1114	198	27	124	437	730	.280	.356	.436	.792	110	20	62	93	98	622	82	35	70	4
OAK	114	51	63	.447	1	549	589	3885	1009	178	13	113	417	686	.260	.334	.399	.733	96	-68	-26	92	**106**	527	91	39	70	4
SEA	112	49	63	.438	2	569	616	3883	1045	211	18	153	372	652	.269	.337	.451	.788	99	-1	-13	102	99	585	48	21	70	2
CAL	115	47	68	.409	5.5	543	660	3943	1042	178	16	120	402	715	.264	.336	.409	.745	88	-54	-70	103	101	536	65	54	55	-13
TOT	797					8330		55198	15048	2939	325	1774	5938	9619	.273	.348	.434	.782							1117	503	69	33

TEAM	CG	SH	SV	IP	H	H/G	HR	BB	SO	RAT	ERA	ERA+	OAV	OOB	PR	/A	PF	CPI	FA	E	DP	FW	PW	BW	SBW	DIF
EAST																										
NY	8	2	31	1019²	1045	9.2	120	398	656	12.9	4.34	102	.267	.337	52	10	92	103	.982	80	122	.1	.9	**13.4**	-1.0	-.0
BAL	13	4	37	997²	1005	9.1	131	351	666	12.5	4.31	118	.263	.330	54	84	106	102	**.986**	57	103	**1.5**	7.8	-2.3	**1.0**	-.9
TOR	13	4	26	1025	1053	9.2	127	482	**832**	13.8	4.70	103	.266	.351	12	14	101	102	.981	81	105	.2	1.3	-3.2	.5	-1.3
BOS	6	3	30	1029¹	1104	9.7	120	450	729	13.9	4.93	104	.276	.354	-15	24	107	99	.981	81	124	.2	2.2	-6.9	-.0	1.1
DET	15	1	20	1018	1139	10.1	148	449	560	14.3	5.38	88	.282	.358	-66	-71	99	98	.981	82	90	.1	-6.6	4.3	-.8	-1.5
CENTRAL																										
CHI	13	**9**	20	1011¹	**964**	**8.6**	115	377	754	**12.1**	**3.96**	119	**.250**	**.320**	**94**	82	98	100	.981	79	91	.2	7.6	5.9	.4	-3.6
CLE	**17**	5	21	1018²	1097	9.7	**94**	404	666	13.6	4.36	113	.275	.348	49	65	103	**105**	.980	90	119	-.4	6.0	4.1	.8	-.9
KC	5	6	**38**	1031²	1018	8.9	95	392	717	12.6	4.23	**122**	.260	.332	65	**108**	108	97	.982	80	102	.2	**10.0**	-7.6	.2	3.6
MIN	6	4	29	1005	1197	10.7	153	388	602	14.5	5.68	86	.299	.365	-98	-92	101	100	.982	75	99	.4	-8.5	-1.8	.7	5.7
MIL	11	3	23	1036	1071	9.3	127	421	577	13.2	4.62	106	.269	.343	20	34	103	101	.981	85	**130**	-.0	3.1	-5.9	-.7	-1.0
WEST																										
TEX	10	4	26	1023	1176	10.3	157	394	683	14.1	5.45	83	.288	.355	-75	-105	94	98	.976	106	106	-1.4	-9.7	5.7	.1	.2
OAK	12	**9**	23	1003¹	979	8.8	128	510	732	13.7	4.80	93	.257	.350	0	-40	93	105	.979	88	105	-.3	-3.7	-2.4	.1	.2
SEA	13	7	21	984	1051	9.6	109	486	763	14.3	4.99	98	.274	.360	-21	-10	102	99	.977	95	102	-.8	-.9	-1.2	-.0	-4.1
CAL	11	4	21	1027	1149	10.1	150	436	682	14.3	5.42	92	.287	.363	-70	-49	104	100	.983	76	110	.5	-4.5	-6.5	-1.4	1.4
TOT	153	65	366	14229²		9.5				13.5	4.80		.273	.348					.981	1155	1508					

Runs
Thomas-Chi 106
Lofton-Cle 105
Griffey-Sea 94
Phillips-Det 91
Belle-Cle 90

Hits
Lofton-Cle 160
Molitor-Tor 155
Belle-Cle 147
Thomas-Chi 141

Doubles
Knoblauch-Min . . . 45
Belle-Cle 35
Thomas-Chi 34
Fryman-Det 34

Triples
L.Johnson-Chi 14
Coleman-KC 12
Lofton-Cle 9
Diaz-Mil 7

Home Runs
Griffey-Sea 40
Thomas-Chi 38
Belle-Cle 36
Canseco-Tex 31
Fielder-Det 28

Total Bases
Belle-Cle 294
Griffey-Sea 292
Thomas-Chi 291
Lofton-Cle 246
Palmeiro-Bal 240

Runs Batted In
Puckett-Min 112
Carter-Tor 103
Thomas-Chi 101
Belle-Cle 101
Franco-Chi 98

Runs Produced
Puckett-Min 171
Thomas-Chi 169
Belle-Cle 155
Lofton-Cle 150
Franco-Chi 150

Bases On Balls
Thomas-Chi 109
Tettleton-Det 97
Phillips-Det 95
O'Neill-NY 72
Henderson-Oak . . 72

Batting Average
O'Neill-NY 359
Belle-Cle 357
Thomas-Chi 353
Lofton-Cle 349
Boggs-NY 342

On Base Percentage
Thomas-Chi 494
O'Neill-NY 464
Belle-Cle 442
Boggs-NY 437
Clark-Tex 436

Slugging Average
Thomas-Chi 729
Belle-Cle 714
Griffey-Sea 674
O'Neill-NY 603
Hamelin-KC 599

Production
Thomas-Chi 1.223
Belle-Cle 1.156
Griffey-Sea 1.078
O'Neill-NY 1.067
Hamelin-KC 992

Adjusted Production
Thomas-Chi 212
O'Neill-NY 185
Belle-Cle 183
Griffey-Sea 168
Clark-Tex 151

Batter Runs
Thomas-Chi 71.3
Belle-Cle 56.3
Griffey-Sea 44.7
O'Neill-NY 42.8
Vaughn-Bos 30.7

Adjusted Batter Runs
Thomas-Chi 72.6
Belle-Cle 51.1
O'Neill-NY 49.9
Griffey-Sea 42.5
Clark-Tex 33.2

Clutch Hitting Index
Puckett-Min 143
Clark-Tex 122
Sorrento-Cle 120
Franco-Chi 120
Fryman-Det 118

Runs Created
Thomas-Chi 145
Belle-Cle 131
Griffey-Sea 117
Lofton-Cle 111
Molitor-Tor 101

Total Average
Thomas-Chi 1.453
Belle-Cle 1.304
Griffey-Sea 1.174
O'Neill-NY 1.152
Lofton-Cle 1.101

Stolen Bases
Lofton-Cle 60
Coleman-KC 50
Nixon-Bos 42
Knoblauch-Min . . . 35
Anderson-Bal 31

Stolen Base Average
Molitor-Tor 100.0
Anderson-Bal 96.9
Hulse-Tex 90.0
Coleman-KC 86.2
Shumpert-KC 85.7

Stolen Base Runs
Lofton-Cle 10.8
Coleman-KC 10.2
Anderson-Bal 8.7
Knoblauch-Min . . . 6.9
Nixon-Bos 6.6

Fielding Runs
Valentin-Mil 28.1
Espinoza-Cle 24.4
Gallego-NY 19.6
Fielder-Det 15.7
Curtis-Cal 14.6

Total Player Rating
Thomas-Chi 5.0
Belle-Cle 4.6
O'Neill-NY 4.4
Griffey-Sea 4.2
Lofton-Cle 3.8

Wins
Key-NY 17
Mussina-Bal 16
Cone-KC 16
McDonald-Bal 14

Win Percentage
Bere-Chi 857
Key-NY 810
Clark-Cle 786
Mussina-Bal 762
Cone-KC 762

Games
Wickman-NY 53
Mesa-Cle 51
Guthrie-Min 50
Brewer-KC 50
Willis-Min 49

Complete Games
Johnson-Sea 9
Martinez-Cle 7
Finley-Cal 7

Shutouts
Johnson-Sea 4

Saves
L.Smith-Bal 33
Montgomery-KC . . 27
Aguilera-Min 23
Eckersley-Oak . . . 19
Ayala-Sea 18

Innings Pitched
Finley-Cal 183.1
McDowell-Chi . . 181.0
Eldred-Mil 179.0
Martinez-Cle . . . 176.2
Mussina-Bal . . . 176.1

Fewest Hits/Game
Clemens-Bos . . . 6.54
Cone-KC 6.82
Johnson-Sea . . . 6.91
Ontiveros-Oak . . 7.26
Bere-Chi 7.56

Fewest BB/Game
Gubicza-KC 1.80
Gullickson-Det . . . 1.95
Wegman-Mil 2.02
Ontiveros-Oak . . . 2.03
McDowell-Chi . . . 2.09

Strikeouts
Johnson-Sea 204
Clemens-Bos 168
Finley-Cal 148
Hentgen-Tor 147
Appier-KC 145

Strikeouts/Game
Johnson-Sea 10.67
Clemens-Bos 8.86
Appier-KC 8.42
Langston-Cal 8.22
Bere-Chi 8.07

Ratio
Ontiveros-Oak . . . 9.75
Cone-KC 10.01
Clemens-Bos 10.49
Mussina-Bal 10.51
Johnson-Sea 10.99

Earned Run Average
Ontiveros-Oak . . . 2.65
Clemens-Bos 2.85
Cone-KC 2.94
Mussina-Bal 3.06
Johnson-Sea 3.19

Adjusted ERA
Clemens-Bos . . . 180
Cone-KC 176
Ontiveros-Oak . . 167
Mussina-Bal . . . 166
Johnson-Sea . . . 154

Opponents' Batting Avg.
Clemens-Bos 203
Cone-KC 209
Johnson-Sea 216
Ontiveros-Oak 217
Bere-Chi 229

Opponents' On Base Pct.
Ontiveros-Oak 272
Cone-KC 279
Clemens-Bos 291
Mussina-Bal 294
Martinez-Cle 301

Starter Runs
Clemens-Bos 37.0
Cone-KC 35.5
Mussina-Bal 34.0
Johnson-Sea 30.7
Key-NY 28.6

Adjusted Starter Runs
Clemens-Bos 43.5
Cone-KC 42.7
Mussina-Bal 39.4
Johnson-Sea 32.7
Bones-Mil 28.3

Clutch Pitching Index
Kamieniecki-NY . . 124
Key-NY 122
Clark-Cle 117
Mahomes-Min . . . 115
Stottlemyre-Tor . . 114

Relief Runs
Eichhorn-Bal . . . 20.9
Plunk-Cle 17.9
Castillo-Tor 17.3
Howe-NY 13.3
Wickman-NY . . . 13.3

Adjusted Relief Runs
Eichhorn-Bal . . . 23.0
Plunk-Cle 17.9
Castillo-Tor 17.4
Ryan-Bos 14.4
Ayala-Sea 12.9

Relief Ranking
Eichhorn-Bal . . . 32.8
L.Smith-Bal 23.7
Ayala-Sea 23.5
Plunk-Cle 23.4
Ryan-Bos 22.3

Total Pitcher Index
Cone-KC 4.6
Mussina-Bal 3.8
Clemens-Bos 3.2
Eichhorn-Bal 3.1
Johnson-Sea 3.1

Total Baseball Ranking
Thomas-Chi 5.0
Cone-KC 4.6
Belle-Cle 4.6
O'Neill-NY 4.4
Griffey-Sea 4.2

Home–Road Statistics

This section consists of two parts, each illustrating the powerful effects a ballpark can have on batting and pitching performance. (Parks affect fielding and baserunning as well, but to a far lesser degree.) The first component is a summary of the won-lost records and run-scoring characteristics of every park for all years of the four most significant major leagues—the American and National leagues and the American and National associations. The second is a breakdown of the home-road records for all teams in all leagues since 1871; detailed here are the won-lost records, runs scored and allowed; home runs hit and allowed; and a variety of hitting and pitching factors that are helpful for evaluation of a team and, by extension, its players.

What is the definition of success at home and on the road? Every team is expected to win more games at home than it does on the road, to the extent that if it only breaks even on the road it is thought to have a shot at the pennant. No matter whether its home park favors hitters or pitchers, a home team should be able to take advantage of the park's peculiarities better than the visiting team can. The Houston Astros may score fewer (and the Colorado Rockies more) runs at home than they do on the road, but their *differential* between runs scored and runs allowed will be greater than their run differential on the road. Greater run differential means more wins.

Almost anybody, it seems, can play .500 ball at home (in the NL of 1983, for example, only one team had a losing record on its own turf). This is somewhat deceptive, for while .500 is the average of all games played, and a team that goes 81–81 is thus defined as average, .500 is not the average at home nor, for that matter, away. The table below, which gives the home park won-lost records of all major leagues since 1900, shows the home average to be .543. The inverse, .457, is the average road record in this century.

If the average home winning percentage is .543, then an average team (81–81) should be expected to go 44–37 at home and 37–44 on the road. Until 1987, only four teams with road records that were below average—that is, 37–44—ever won the pennant, and none went on to win the World Series. Then the Minnesota Twins took the American League flag with a regular-season road mark of 29–52, by far the worst ever for a pennant or division winner, and then proceeded to lose all three World Series road games while winning all four at home. We are not likely to see such a performance again.

Just as runs scored and runs allowed may predict won-lost records, as discussed in the Introduction to the Annual Record, so may we move backward from won-lost

records (the actual home-park norm of 44–37, which is between 5 and 10 percent better than the theoretical norm of 41–40) to examine runs scored and runs allowed. Runs (and home runs) per inning at home are indeed accumulated at a rate per inning about 10 percent higher than on the road, but the totals presented in this section fall short of that mark. The reason: since the number of innings played at home is about 5 percent lower than on the road (leading home teams do not bat in the bottom half of final innings), total runs and homers are in actuality only about 5 percent higher.

Home Park Won-Lost Records

National League

Years	W	L	Pct.
1900–10 ('01 AL)	3489	2995	.538
1911–20	3189	2775	.537
1921–30	3359	2771	.548
1931–40	3353	2760	.549
1941–50	3319	2823	.540
1951–61	3681	3098	.543
1962–68	3075	2591	.543
1969–76	4088	3638	.529
1977–94	9285	7851	.542
	36,838	31,282	.541

American League

Years	W	L	Pct.
1901–10	3347	2528	.570
1911–20	3204	2751	.538
1921–30	3344	2787	.545
1931–40	3349	2753	.549
1941–50	3383	2754	.551
1951–60	3291	2863	.535
1961–68	3462	3003	.535
1969–76	4142	3568	.537
1977–94	10,660	9033	.542
	38,182	32,010	.544

Federal League

Years	W	L	Pct.
1914–15	660	560	.541

Major League

Years	W	L	Pct.
1900–94	75,680	63,852	.542

Detailed technical information about the formulas and calculations behind Park Factor, as applied to teams as well as individuals, will be found in the Glossary. For the general reader, suffice it to say that all factors and ratings related to home-park effects are calculated by comparing runs scored and allowed per inning at home to runs scored and allowed per inning on the road. The same holds true for home runs.

Adjustments such as the Run Rating for Batters (RB) and the Home Run rating for Batters (HRB) are made to team measures of batting strength to take into account the fact that a team's batters do not have to face its own pitchers. Innings are estimated from the number of games and games won (leading home teams not batting in the final inning).

For additional useful information about home-road differences, we refer the reader to the Annual Record and the Glossary. For a key to the team and league abbreviations used throughout this section, flip to the last pages of this volume.

Other abbreviations follow.

TM	Team
LG	League
W	Wins
L	Losses
T	Ties
R	Runs
OR	Opponents' Runs
HR	Home Runs
OHR	Opponents' Home Runs

HRF   Home Run Factor (A measure of the home runs hit in a given ballpark, with 100 representing the average home park and the highest figure above that representing the best home-run park.)

HRB   Home Run Batter Rating (A measure of a team's home-run ability, taking into account the HRF and the fact that its batters do not face its own pitchers, with 100 representing the average and the highest figure above that representing the best.)

HRP   Home Run Pitcher Rating (A measure of a team's ability to prevent home runs, taking into account the HRF and the fact that its pitchers do not face its own batters, with 100 representing the average and the lowest figure beneath that representing the best.)

RF   Run Factor (A measure of the runs scored in a given ballpark compared to other ballparks, with 100 representing the average home park and the highest figure above that representing the best hitters' park.)

RB   Run Rating for Batters (A measure of a team's run-scoring ability, taking into account the HRF and the fact that its batters do not face its own pitchers, with 100 representing the average and the highest figure above that representing the best.)

RP   Run Rating for Pitchers (A measure of a team's run-prevention ability, taking into account the HRF and the fact that its pitchers do not face its own batters, with 100 representing the average and the lowest figure beneath that representing the best.)

BPF   Batting Park Factor (Equivalent to the Park Factor shown in the batters' section of the team statistics in the Annual Record; above 100 means batters benefited from playing half their games in a good hitting park.)

PPF   Pitching Park Factor (Equivalent to the Park Factor shown in the pitchers' section of the team statistics in the Annual Record; above 100 means a pitcher was hurt by playing half his games in a good hitting park.)

PARK	TM	LG	YEARS	RF	HRF	HOME							ROAD						
						W	L	T	R	OR	HR	OHR	W	L	T	R	OR	HR	OHR
AMERICAN LEAGUE																			
Oriole Park	BAL	A	1901–1902	115	120	72	56	2	821	736	27	29	46	97	3	654	862	30	22
Memorial Stadium	BAL	A	1954–1991	92	91	1687	1310	9	12247	11263	2490	2262	1515	1502	0	13030	12657	2804	2475
Oriole Park at Camden Yards	BAL	A	1992–1994	107	117	119	98	0	1067	976	237	220	118	101	0	1013	922	207	188
Huntington Avenue Grounds	BOS	A	1901–1911	102	172	464	357	10	3494	3075	219	173	386	424	14	3230	3201	106	120
Fenway Park (I)	BOS	A	1912–1933	96	52	834	821	15	6819	7273	180	359	679	983	16	6743	8007	476	557
Fenway Park (II)	BOS	A	1934–1994	114	111	2801	1969	16	24917	22089	4267	3807	2211	2550	12	20520	20882	3700	3550
Chavez Ravine	CAL	A	1965–1965	92	65	46	34	0	265	254	36	35	29	53	0	262	315	56	56
Anaheim Stadium	CAL	A	1966–1994	94	100	1176	1128	1	9163	9358	1722	1902	1041	1243	2	9513	10066	1720	1852
South Side Park (II)	CHI	A	1901–1909	89	32	433	235	21	2811	1987	31	31	311	340	13	2598	2659	73	116
Comiskey/White Sox Park	CHI	A	1910–1990	97	86	3346	2917	32	26769	26375	2811	3463	2871	3416	34	26920	27825	3351	3992
Comiskey Park (II)	CHI	A	1991–1994	95	103	175	122	0	1426	1190	272	254	159	143	0	1479	1343	260	263
League Park (I)	CLE	A	1901–1909	96	64	385	280	14	2842	2379	65	60	312	352	8	2614	2763	107	86
League Park (II)	CLE	A	1910–1931	107	67	907	762	15	8165	7767	287	295	780	883	19	7362	7567	415	450
League/Municipal shared	CLE	A	1932–1946	95	73	667	495	7	5485	4939	558	418	532	598	12	5300	5495	710	592
League Park (II)				110	96	408	280	2	3706	3224	443	312							
Municipal Stadium				77	40	259	215	5	1779	1715	115	106							
Municipal/Cleveland Stadium	CLE	A	1947–1993	98	110	1975	1736	7	15906	15850	3254	3217	1711	1998	9	15948	16332	2966	2927
Jacobs Field	CLE	A	1994–1994	109	124	35	16	0	335	248	87	44	31	31	0	344	314	80	50
Bennett Park	DET	A	1901–1911	107	97	483	327	15	3727	3284	105	93	375	438	13	3199	3364	99	107
Navin Field	DET	A	1912–1937	102	93	1089	891	9	10250	9715	631	727	939	1031	22	9832	9783	751	709
Briggs/Tiger Stadium	DET	A	1938–1994	105	127	2501	1977	16	21036	19652	4441	4267	2122	2336	18	19443	19302	3526	3323
Municipal Stadium (I)	KC	A	1955–1967	107	108	452	575	2	4285	5087	767	1086	377	649	5	3819	4897	713	995
Municipal Stadium (II)	KC	A	1969–1972	100	65	159	159	1	1211	1227	137	175	136	185	0	1169	1277	216	268
Royals Stadium	KC	A	1973–1994	104	74	1005	721	1	8033	7201	1047	1058	823	907	0	7330	7453	1431	1424
Wrigley Field	LA	A	1961–1961	127	199	46	36	0	447	421	122	126	24	55	1	297	363	67	54
Chavez Ravine	LA	A	1962–1964	86	52	124	119	0	851	900	106	125	114	128	0	1008	1017	228	213
Lloyd Street Grounds	MIL	A	1901–1901	92	97	32	37	1	342	373	15	14	16	52	1	299	455	11	18
County Stadium	MIL	A	1970–1994	97	88	1028	937	1	8548	8470	1522	1550	885	1088	1	8701	8894	1701	1788
Metropolitan Stadium	MIN	A	1961–1981	108	110	910	759	5	7691	7018	1424	1443	809	853	2	6936	6688	1325	1270
Humphrey Metrodome	MIN	A	1982–1994	108	102	569	465	0	4976	4923	896	1066	429	594	0	4270	4782	876	1018
Hilltop Park	NY	A	1903–1912	116	166	400	344	8	3299	3270	134	124	334	415	19	2702	3082	58	101
Polo Grounds (IV)	NY	A	1913–1922	101	197	416	335	10	3312	2916	332	292	358	378	6	3054	2945	190	119
Yankee Stadium (I)	NY	A	1923–1973	91	103	2553	1410	16	19607	14741	3654	2408	2168	1790	26	20696	17497	3532	2427
Shea Stadium	NY	A	1974–1975	94	92	90	69	0	646	578	92	106	82	81	0	706	633	119	102
Yankee Stadium (II)	NY	A	1976–1994	95	99	872	609	0	6871	6128	1445	1255	740	746	0	7032	6718	1479	1263
Oakland Coliseum	OAK	A	1968–1994	88	89	1198	935	1	8823	8229	1806	1661	1015	1115	0	9649	9723	1974	1922
Columbia Park	PHI	A	1901–1908	108	109	384	188	11	2758	2121	128	65	255	322	14	2228	2402	107	74
Shibe Park/Connie Mack Stadium	PHI	A	1909–1954	102	125	1762	1704	31	16078	16880	1809	1900	1485	2034	23	15449	17217	1458	1533
Sportsman's Park (III)	STL	A	1902–1908	93	104	275	243	12	1906	1793	61	73	215	300	10	1849	2087	56	71
Sportsman's Park (IV)	STL	A	1909–1953	108	137	1615	1726	40	15888	17694	1680	2004	1309	2126	34	13902	17170	1217	1459
Sicks Stadium	SEA	A	1969–1969	100	125	34	47	1	329	399	74	93	30	51	0	310	400	51	79
Kingdome	SEA	A	1977–1994	104	127	656	744	0	6132	6716	1347	1450	559	851	2	5623	6759	1046	1166
Arlington Stadium	TEX	A	1972–1993	98	95	906	844	0	7528	7641	1323	1391	759	984	4	7439	7954	1445	1408
The Ballpark in Arlington	TEX	A	1994–1994	89	69	31	32	0	334	353	63	67	21	30	0	279	344	61	90
Exhibition Stadium	TOR	A	1977–1988	107	106	480	462	0	4243	4319	798	914	414	529	2	3890	4147	810	803
SkyDome	TOR	A	1989–1994	101	116	270	194	0	2194	1992	464	409	242	219	0	2181	1945	415	339
American League Park (I)	WAS	A	1901–1903	104	214	100	103	4	1015	1065	67	98	65	138	6	811	1187	30	47
American League Park (II)	WAS	A	1904–1910	92	46	224	297	16	1709	2048	31	32	157	380	10	1671	2418	65	71
Griffith Stadium (I)	WAS	A	1911–1955	93	39	1841	1602	38	15218	14998	529	784	1525	1885	24	15537	16599	1410	1870
Griffith Stadium (II)	WAS	A	1956–1961	101	99	192	272	1	1858	2361	364	449	180	287	2	1859	2291	409	411
R.F.K. Stadium	WAS	A	1962–1971	96	96	363	441	0	2906	3356	616	715	316	491	1	2928	3580	652	735
NATIONAL LEAGUE																			
Atlanta/Fulton County Stadium	ATL	N	1966–1994	112	135	1165	1113	4	10046	10333	2185	2100	1037	1260	3	8886	9419	1743	1452
Union Park	BAL	N	1892–1899	103	46	380	167	15	4107	2772	72	54	264	280	11	3391	3256	114	158
South End Grounds (I)	BOS	N	1876–1893	103	101	624	327	16	6241	4295	296	200	478	467	16	5090	5188	229	265
South End Grounds (II)	BOS	N	1894–1914	110	200	807	718	28	7845	7453	517	536	610	917	27	6382	7479	209	315
Braves Field	BOS	N	1915–1952	89	67	1411	1430	23	10995	11822	893	1002	1188	1739	27	12211	14098	1281	1632
Washington Park (II)	BRO	N	1890–1890	98	80	58	16	0	547	303	27	9	28	27	0	337	318	16	18
Eastern Park	BRO	N	1891–1897	89	88	293	182	11	3026	2567	117	117	188	281	6	2831	3282	114	145
Washington Park (III)	BRO	N	1898–1912	96	81	554	556	17	4460	4647	168	155	436	662	20	4314	5092	184	207
Ebbets Field	BRO	N	1913–1957	102	110	1974	1453	34	16259	14848	1957	1933	1683	1749	24	15470	15108	1753	1783
Riverside Park	BUF	N	1879–1883	104	35	123	87	3	1278	1068	12	12	89	125	2	997	1285	31	38
Olympic Park (I)	BUF	N	1884–1885	113	96	56	56	3	674	717	36	33	46	65	1	521	668	26	44
23rd Street Grounds	CHI	N	1876–1877	125	69	42	18	0	558	299	3	5	36	29	1	432	333	5	8
Lake Front Park (I)	CHI	N	1878–1882	109	78	150	56	2	1443	875	21	16	104	81	5	1056	916	16	28
Lake Front Park (II)	CHI	N	1882–1884	120	475	75	30	1	908	566	142	72	46	59	0	605	621	13	32
West Side Park (I)	CHI	N	1885–1890	121	300	267	123	6	2934	1994	318	230	209	162	10	2069	1916	92	86
South Side Park (I)	CHI	N	1891–1893	105	110	117	87	3	1297	1092	68	54	91	113	1	1000	1247	50	60
West Side Park (II)	CHI	N	1894–1915	101	90	1008	635	28	8152	6881	333	246	816	750	35	7404	6967	361	263
Wrigley Field	CHI	N	1916–1994	106	116	3294	2863	31	27908	27363	4579	4437	2730	3365	32	25177	26511	3895	3785
Avenue Grounds	CIN	N	1876–1879	86	147	64	65	2	681	766	18	11	40	93	1	666	1043	5	15
Bank Street Grounds	CIN	N	1880–1880	103	341	14	25	1	163	216	5	8	7	34	2	131	256	2	2
League Park (I)	CIN	N	1890–1893	99	126	158	123	5	1630	1378	86	84	122	144	6	1294	1590	54	74
League Park (II)	CIN	N	1894–1901	105	61	349	217	12	3532	3113	100	108	214	319	14	2778	3224	142	182
Palace of the Fans	CIN	N	1902–1911	108	58	410	355	14	3436	3108	84	61	326	412	14	2848	2993	121	120
Redland/Crosley Field	CIN	N	1912–1969	99	86	2441	2043	26	19346	18722	2315	2156	1961	2484	26	18426	19751	2475	2653
Riverfront Stadium	CIN	N	1970–1994	103	109	1118	850	3	8835	8130	1683	1620	1010	958	1	8494	8039	1577	1459
Kennard Street Park	CLE	N	1879–1884	94	39	132	139	3	1226	1310	17	23	110	160	5	1209	1471	45	58
National League Park	CLE	N	1889–1890	95	53	63	72	3	710	696	21	20	42	88	4	570	855	25	49
League Park (I)	CLE	N	1891–1899	107	38	360	198	7	3818	2956	56	68	273	406	17	3570	4265	164	234
Mile High Stadium	COL	N	1993–1994	124	117	64	74	0	806	907	136	168	56	85	0	525	698	131	133
Recreation Park	DET	N	1881–1888	100	108	248	179	8	2602	2146	153	95	178	258	9	2245	2621	111	124
Joe Robbie Stadium	FLA	N	1993–1994	111	107	60	80	0	544	710	90	142	55	82	0	505	590	98	113

PARK	TM	LG	YEARS	RF	HRF	HOME							ROAD						
						W	L	T	R	OR	HR	OHR	W	L	T	R	OR	HR	OHR
Hartford Ball Club Grounds	HAR	N	1876–1876	106	0	23	9	0	220	107	0	0	24	12	1	209	154	2	2
Union Grounds (Brooklyn)	HAR	N	1877–1877	71	107	19	8	2	167	92	2	1	12	19	0	174	219	2	1
Colt Stadium	HOU	N	1962–1964	86	64	117	125	2	750	898	98	119	79	163	0	801	1087	139	194
Astrodome	HOU	N	1965–1994	89	63	1329	1048	0	9255	8658	1140	1190	1014	1361	2	9578	10478	1751	1928
South Street Park	IND	N	1878–1878	68	62	10	17	1	106	115	1	1	14	19	2	187	213	2	2
Athletic Park (I)	IND	N	1887–1887	99	98	24	39	1	349	456	19	28	13	50	0	278	507	14	32
Athletic Park (II)	IND	N	1888–1889	111	275	63	71	1	823	780	77	94	46	89	1	595	842	19	43
Association Park	KC	N	1886–1886	124	40	19	42	1	301	456	9	4	11	49	4	193	420	10	23
Memorial Coliseum	LA	N	1958–1961	113	146	172	137	0	1474	1430	346	397	158	151	0	1296	1291	257	254
Chavez Ravine/Dodger Stadium	LA	N	1962–1994	89	87	1511	1107	0	10128	8802	1718	1583	1312	1308	6	11099	10404	2046	1795
Louisville Baseball Park	LOU	N	1876–1877	133	675	36	25	2	368	326	13	6	29	36	2	251	307	2	1
Eclipse Park (I)	LOU	N	1892–1892	82	35	37	31	2	309	286	7	3	26	58	0	340	518	11	23
Eclipse Park (II)	LOU	N	1893–1899	93	123	202	233	12	2422	2727	130	136	154	361	4	2604	3770	114	134
Milwaukee Baseball Grounds	MIL	N	1878–1878	126	35	7	18	0	127	177	1	0	8	27	1	129	209	1	3
County Stadium	MIL	N	1953–1965	87	82	602	414	7	4408	3694	998	776	544	476	1	4977	4424	1232	951
Jarry Park	MON	N	1969–1976	106	119	285	356	0	2519	2927	461	519	269	378	1	2347	2792	382	442
Olympic Stadium	MON	N	1977–1994	98	86	774	614	0	5734	5310	902	948	694	726	3	5846	5724	1122	1082
Union Grounds (Brooklyn)	NY	N	1876–1876	78	646	13	20	1	143	207	2	7	8	15	1	117	205	0	1
Polo Grounds (I)	NY	N	1883–1888	92	71	234	112	12	2111	1418	87	46	186	161	12	1973	1905	100	89
Polo Grounds (II)	NY	N	1889–1890	98	54	84	42	3	874	583	26	17	62	69	6	769	820	51	35
Polo Grounds (III)	NY	N	1891–1910	97	134	876	564	38	7664	6329	377	279	686	736	27	7029	7160	227	254
Polo Grounds (IV)	NY	N	1911–1957	97	170	2106	1465	24	16900	14430	3146	2524	1833	1749	29	16963	15533	1763	1603
Polo Grounds (IV)	NY	N	1962–1963	110	162	56	105	0	611	891	154	213	35	126	1	507	831	81	141
Shea Stadium	NY	N	1964–1994	94	98	1235	1214	4	9315	9410	1672	1780	1101	1353	2	9652	10171	1728	1771
Jefferson Street Grounds	PHI	N	1876–1876	114	55	10	24	1	259	309	4	0	4	21	0	119	225	3	2
Recreation Park	PHI	N	1883–1886	95	32	102	117	5	1115	1286	21	21	81	134	3	1013	1435	42	84
Philadelphia Baseball Grounds	PHI	N	1887–1894	102	96	353	200	6	3889	2735	185	117	230	276	13	2871	3201	136	157
Baker Bowl	PHI	N	1895–1937	114	159	1607	1577	25	16007	16788	1617	1393	1288	1913	35	13361	15590	905	997
Shibe Park/Connie Mack Stadium	PHI	N	1938–1970	96	89	1211	1350	13	10001	11185	1552	1731	1062	1516	7	10096	11829	1702	1971
Veterans Stadium	PHI	N	1971–1994	104	107	1056	839	3	8527	7929	1586	1390	842	1041	1	7587	8092	1368	1386
Recreation Park	PIT	N	1887–1890	79	14	122	117	7	1229	1138	15	12	83	204	3	1249	2230	81	144
Exposition Park	PIT	N	1891–1908	99	65	813	503	9	7060	5718	226	103	641	603	32	6374	6192	245	245
Forbes Field	PIT	N	1909–1969	102	69	2593	2113	35	21368	20076	1849	1930	2162	2508	38	20019	20318	2533	2924
Three Rivers Stadium	PIT	N	1970–1994	100	93	1118	854	1	8674	7762	1414	1358	947	1011	3	8282	8165	1503	1460
Messer Street Grounds	PRO	N	1878–1885	91	61	244	114	4	2027	1354	44	28	194	164	5	2010	1774	54	66
Grand Avenue Park	STL	N	1876–1877	77	65	44	16	0	327	182	1	2	29	35	0	344	365	2	3
Union Park	STL	N	1885–1886	87	58	50	67	4	503	575	19	14	29	84	3	435	731	19	35
Sportsman's Park (I)	STL	N	1892–1892	92	241	37	36	2	379	380	32	32	19	58	3	324	542	13	15
Robison Field	STL	N	1893–1919	97	110	885	1063	39	8223	9497	385	424	691	1268	25	7718	10289	275	450
Sportsman's Park (IV)	STL	N	1920–1965	106	103	2133	1429	28	18069	15545	2305	2266	1810	1730	24	16384	15239	2192	2222
Busch Stadium	STL	N	1966–1994	100	80	1242	1054	5	9524	9114	1113	1350	1128	1157	2	9398	9245	1348	1700
Jack Murphy Stadium	SD	N	1969–1994	92	98	993	1061	4	7635	8244	1342	1579	837	1212	1	7866	9252	1346	1613
Seals Stadium	SF	N	1958–1959	94	97	86	68	0	702	625	165	151	77	77	0	730	686	172	154
Candlestick Park	SF	N	1960–1994	96	97	1554	1222	0	11746	10840	2358	2072	1305	1468	5	11764	11872	2406	2164
Newell Park	SYR	N	1879–1879	80	53	11	32	1	115	200	1	2	11	26	0	160	257	4	2
Putnam Grounds	TRO	N	1879–1879	94	96	12	27	2	191	263	3	6	7	29	0	130	281	1	7
Haymakers' Grounds	TRO	N	1880–1881	113	479	44	39	1	426	453	9	15	36	48	0	365	413	1	4
Troy Ball Club Grounds	TRO	N	1882–1882	93	57	22	20	0	238	217	7	2	13	28	2	192	305	5	11
Swampoodle Grounds	WAS	N	1886–1889	90	91	96	141	13	1136	1362	71	66	67	196	1	1023	1865	54	102
Boundary Field	WAS	N	1892–1899	99	126	265	269	11	3416	3346	222	139	145	428	7	2802	4360	116	184
Worcester Driving Park Grounds	WOR	N	1880–1882	118	151	55	69	2	703	777	21	25	35	90	1	498	737	10	20

AMERICAN ASSOCIATION

PARK	TM	LG	YEARS	RF	HRF	HOME							ROAD						
Newington Park	BAL	AA	1882–1882	94	98	9	25	1	138	225	2	7	10	29	0	134	287	2	8
Oriole Park	BAL	AA	1883–1890	98	75	240	181	18	2689	2263	72	39	159	303	7	2168	3179	62	95
Union Park	BAL	AA	1891–1891	102	49	44	24	2	481	354	13	8	27	40	2	367	442	17	25
Congress Street Grounds	BOS	AA	1891–1891	93	170	51	17	2	520	295	37	22	42	25	2	507	379	15	20
Washington Park (I)	BRO	AA	1884–1889	99	132	241	149	10	2555	1971	91	72	169	205	9	2045	2360	52	67
Ridgewood Park	BRO	AA	1890–1890	100	41	15	22	1	220	252	4	3	11	51	0	272	481	9	18
Bank Street Grounds	CIN	AA	1882–1883	100	273	69	24	0	651	294	29	18	47	38	0	495	387	10	6
League Park (I)	CIN	AA	1884–1889	105	180	264	146	3	2838	1973	165	93	169	188	9	1970	2122	63	65
Pendleton Park	CIN	AA	1891–1891	122	210	24	29	1	297	289	21	9	19	37	1	250	354	7	11
National League Park (II)	CLE	AA	1887–1888	100	50	55	64	2	734	777	10	19	34	110	3	647	1162	16	53
Recreation Park (I)	COL	AA	1883–1884	83	120	56	45	2	480	490	28	22	45	59	1	579	628	27	16
Recreation Park (II)	COL	AA	1889–1891	83	56	117	84	2	1169	859	26	27	83	125	7	1144	1456	46	55
Seventh Street Park	IND	AA	1884–1884	99	115	17	39	1	257	380	13	15	12	39	2	206	375	7	15
Association Park (I)	KC	AA	1888–1888	124	124	23	34	2	330	392	15	10	20	55	0	249	502	4	22
Exposition Park	KC	AA	1889–1889	121	55	35	35	0	523	518	8	17	20	47	2	329	512	10	34
Eclipse Park (I)	LOU	AA	1882–1891	96	67	357	238	12	3704	2949	83	66	218	400	8	3074	4083	91	138
Athletic Field	MIL	AA	1891–1891	140	383	16	5	0	172	82	11	5	5	10	0	56	74	2	1
Polo Grounds (I) West Diamond	NY	AA	1883–1885	88	53	99	50	2	902	578	24	13	74	88	1	857	938	25	50
St. George Cricket Grounds	NY	AA	1886–1887	89	72	55	67	5	658	750	20	19	42	104	2	715	1108	19	43
Oakdale Park	PHI	AA	1882–1882	127	325	21	18	0	236	220	3	11	20	16	0	166	166	2	2
Jefferson Street Grounds	PHI	AA	1883–1890	104	84	322	190	10	3701	2783	122	70	197	274	8	2557	3161	102	109
Athletic Park	PHI	AA	1891–1891	105	72	43	26	3	465	366	29	9	30	40	1	354	427	26	26
Expositon Park (I)	PIT	AA	1882–1883	95	110	35	49	2	477	493	22	6	35	57	1	470	646	9	19
Recreation Park	PIT	AA	1884–1886	92	26	101	86	2	990	864	6	10	65	104	3	774	1043	17	39
Allen Pasture	RIC	AA	1884–1884	101	117	5	15	2	96	142	3	8	7	15	2	98	153	4	6
Culver Field (I)	ROC	AA	1890–1890	82	57	40	22	1	348	252	13	4	23	41	6	361	458	18	15
Sportsman's Park (I)	STL	AA	1882–1891	116	202	460	177	6	4749	2924	214	145	322	256	14	3196	2999	91	75
Star Park (II)	SYR	AA	1890–1890	81	19	30	30	4	321	320	2	4	25	42	1	378	511	12	24
League Park	TOL	AA	1884–1884	107	33	28	25	2	270	267	3	2	18	33	4	193	305	5	10
Speranza Park	TOL	AA	1890–1890	104	143	40	27	1	422	316	11	11	28	37	1	316	374	7	12
Athletic Park	WAS	AA	1884–1884	82	37	10	20	1	137	181	3	4	2	31	0	111	300	3	17
Boundary Field	WAS	AA	1891–1891	98	88	28	40	4	389	519	13	18	16	51	0	300	547	6	26

NATIONAL ASSOCIATION

PARK	TM	LG	YEARS	RF	HRF	HOME							ROAD						
						W	L	T	R	OR	HR	OHR	W	L	T	R	OR	HR	OHR
Jefferson Street Grounds	ATH	NA	1871–1875	109	102	104	28	5	1516	834	23	4	61	58	3	1013	930	10	14
Capitoline Grounds	ATL	NA	1872–1872	147	205	6	12	0	153	265	0	4	3	16	0	84	208	0	2
Union Grounds	ATL	NA	1873–1875	78	93	30	53	2	464	641	8	14	11	59	0	335	795	1	18
Newington Park	BAL	NA	1872–1874	102	285	46	26	3	799	544	22	5	32	53	2	689	846	5	6
South End Grounds (I)	BOS	NA	1871–1875	109	170	120	23	1	1714	806	36	4	105	37	6	1513	951	19	6
Centennial Grounds	CEN	NA	1875–1875	93	0	0	7	0	25	77	0	0	2	5	0	45	61	0	0
Union Base-Ball Grounds	CHI	NA	1871–1871	119	98	13	3	0	196	135	6	3	6	6	0	106	106	4	3
23rd Street Grounds	CHI	NA	1874–1875	101	27	34	26	1	439	373	1	1	24	42	1	358	523	2	6
National Association Grounds	CLE	NA	1871–1872	95	286	5	15	0	165	227	4	13	11	20	0	258	368	3	6
Union Grounds	ECK	NA	1872–1872	77	21	3	11	0	75	167	0	1	0	15	0	77	246	0	5
Hartford Ball Club Grounds	HAR	NA	1874–1875	116	25	39	28	2	533	397	1	1	31	37	2	395	417	3	5
Hamilton Field	KEK	NA	1871–1871	110	0	5	4	0	78	112	0	0	2	8	0	59	131	2	5
Mansfield Club Grounds	MAN	NA	1872–1872	99	23	4	7	0	130	133	1	0	1	12	0	90	215	0	5
Newington Park	MAR	NA	1873–1873	85	0	0	1	0	3	24	0	0	0	5	0	23	128	0	4
Union Grounds (Brooklyn)	MUT	NA	1871–1875	93	161	94	53	3	1213	837	21	9	57	69	2	864	1025	5	11
Nationals Grounds	NAT	NA	1872–1872	154	0	0	7	0	65	135	0	0	0	4	0	15	55	0	2
Hamilton Park	NH	NA	1875–1875	79	95	3	24	0	87	211	1	3	4	16	0	83	186	1	2
Olympics Grounds	OLY	NA	1871–1872	111	244	9	11	0	197	218	5	2	8	11	2	167	225	1	2
Jefferson Street Grounds	PHI	NA	1873–1875	106	48	54	30	1	760	527	8	0	48	47	1	712	673	6	13
Waverly Fairgrounds	RES	NA	1873–1873	92	0	0	8	0	34	101	0	0	2	13	0	64	198	0	8
Agricultural Society Fair Gnds	ROK	NA	1871–1871	91	0	3	4	0	72	66	0	0	1	17	0	159	221	3	3
Red Stocking Base Ball Park	RS	NA	1875–1875	87	0	3	11	0	50	108	0	0	1	4	0	10	53	0	0
Grand Avenue Park	STL	NA	1875–1875	78	53	21	12	1	183	135	0	1	18	17	1	203	234	0	2
Haymakers' Grounds	TRO	NA	1871–1872	108	123	13	15	1	326	327	7	3	15	10	0	298	226	4	3
Olympics Grounds	WAS	NA	1873–1873	102	45	6	12	0	157	208	3	1	2	19	0	126	277	0	10
Olympics Grounds	WAS	NA	1875–1875	108	0	2	10	0	45	158	0	0	3	13	0	62	180	0	6
Perry Park	WES	NA	1875–1875	113	0	1	7	0	30	57	0	0	0	5	0	15	31	0	0

TM	HOME								ROAD								ALL															
	G	W	L	T	R	OR	HR	OHR	G	W	L	T	R	OR	HR	OHR	G	W	L	T	R	OR	HR	OHR	HRF	HRB	HRP	RF	RB	RP	BPF	PPF
1871 NATIONAL ASSOCIATION																																
ATH	15	12	3	0	184	125	3	0	13	9	4	0	192	141	6	3	28	21	7	0	376	266	9	3	32	273	70	84	139	103	93	89
BOS	18	12	5	1	230	168	2	1	13	8	5	0	171	135	1	1	31	20	10	1	401	303	3	2	109	44	32	96	126	99	98	95
CHI	16	13	3	0	196	135	6	3	12	6	6	0	106	106	4	3	28	19	9	0	302	241	10	6	98	201	134	117	90	77	111	109
CLE	13	3	10	0	119	162	4	10	16	7	9	0	130	179	3	3	29	10	19	0	249	341	7	13	235	99	147	109	80	106	103	107
KEK	9	5	4	0	78	112	0	0	10	2	8	0	59	131	2	5	19	7	12	0	137	243	2	5	0	100	100	108	68	113	102	108
MUT	19	12	7	0	178	127	0	4	14	4	10	0	124	186	1	3	33	16	17	0	302	313	1	7	76	19	118	74	102	105	88	88
OLY	13	8	5	0	163	113	5	2	19	7	10	2	147	190	1	2	32	15	15	2	310	303	6	4	270	52	46	118	87	83	110	110
ROK	7	3	4	0	72	66	0	0	18	1	17	0	159	221	3	3	25	4	21	0	231	287	3	3	0	100	100	92	96	107	95	97
TRO	17	7	9	1	200	231	4	3	12	6	6	0	151	131	2	1	29	13	15	1	351	362	6	4	153	84	54	106	116	116	101	101
1872 NATIONAL ASSOCIATION																																
ATH	28	22	4	2	371	171	3	1	19	8	10	1	168	178	1	2	47	30	14	3	539	349	4	3	92	86	74	107	113	83	105	102
ATL	18	6	12	0	153	265	0	4	19	3	16	0	84	208	0	2	37	9	28	0	237	473	0	6	187	0	109	141	58	113	117	124
BAL	29	20	7	2	321	189	12	3	29	15	12	2	296	245	2	0	58	35	19	4	617	434	14	3	476	86	11	96	115	83	100	97
BOS	21	20	1	0	249	87	2	0	27	19	7	1	272	149	5	0	48	39	8	1	521	236	7	0	56	164	0	106	109	52	108	102
CLE	7	2	5	0	46	65	0	3	15	4	11	0	128	189	0	3	22	6	16	0	174	254	0	6	190	0	208	75	95	133	86	89
ECK	14	3	11	0	75	167	0	1	15	0	15	0	77	246	0	3	29	3	26	0	152	413	0	6	22	0	298	78	68	163	85	93
MAN	11	4	7	0	130	133	1	0	13	1	12	0	90	215	0	4	24	5	19	0	220	348	1	5	25	214	209	99	108	156	94	99
MUT	29	20	8	1	263	144	2	0	27	14	12	1	260	218	2	2	56	34	20	2	523	362	4	2	50	103	37	82	108	76	94	91
NAT	7	0	7	0	65	135	0	2	4	0	4	0	15	55	0	0	11	0	11	0	80	190	0	2	0	100	100	147	57	142	117	127
OLY	7	1	6	0	34	105	0	0	2	1	1	0	20	35	0	0	9	2	7	0	54	140	0	0	0	100	100	73	98	203	79	88
TRO	12	6	6	0	126	96	3	0	13	9	4	0	147	95	2	2	25	15	10	0	273	191	5	2	83	233	90	100	116	84	102	99
1873 NATIONAL ASSOCIATION																																
ATH	27	21	6	0	298	165	3	0	25	7	17	1	176	238	1	3	52	28	23	1	474	403	4	3	72	71	45	104	97	86	103	102
ATL	29	14	14	1	215	228	6	4	26	3	23	0	151	321	0	3	55	17	37	1	366	549	6	7	241	33	70	84	83	117	91	95
BAL	26	19	6	1	363	178	9	1	31	15	16	0	281	273	3	3	57	34	22	1	644	451	12	4	181	111	51	116	116	84	109	105
BOS	32	24	8	0	444	238	11	2	28	19	8	1	295	222	2	3	60	43	16	1	739	460	13	5	203	94	59	116	123	83	110	104
MAR	1	0	1	0	3	24	0	0	5	0	5	0	23	128	0	4	6	0	6	0	26	152	0	4	0	100	100	86	54	278	77	99
MUT	31	22	9	0	286	170	6	1	22	7	15	0	138	215	0	4	53	29	24	0	424	385	6	5	121	62	81	93	88	86	99	98
PHI	27	22	5	0	283	185	3	0	26	14	12	0	243	211	3	3	53	36	17	0	526	396	6	3	52	120	45	101	107	84	103	100
RES	8	0	8	0	34	101	0	0	15	2	13	0	64	198	0	8	23	2	21	0	98	299	0	8	0	100	100	93	51	139	92	103
WAS	18	6	12	0	157	208	3	1	21	2	19	0	126	277	0	10	39	8	31	0	283	485	3	11	48	162	242	102	84	134	97	103
1874 NATIONAL ASSOCIATION																																
ATH	29	21	8	0	275	183	6	3	26	12	14	0	166	161	0	2	55	33	22	0	441	344	6	5	294	37	66	123	92	76	114	111
ATL	29	15	13	1	170	164	0	5	27	7	20	0	131	285	1	11	56	22	33	1	301	449	1	16	42	27	392	76	85	115	88	92
BAL	20	7	13	0	115	177	1	1	27	2	25	0	112	328	0	3	47	9	38	0	227	505	1	4	89	30	83	88	75	142	89	98
BOS	36	27	9	0	411	194	11	1	35	25	9	1	324	221	7	0	71	52	18	1	735	415	18	1	157	197	11	109	128	79	107	100
CHI	28	18	10	0	228	174	1	1	31	10	21	0	190	306	2	6	59	28	31	0	418	480	3	7	30	106	164	91	102	111	94	96
HAR	30	13	17	0	244	242	1	1	23	3	20	0	127	229	1	1	53	16	37	0	371	471	2	2	77	43	43	102	93	118	98	102
MUT	35	27	8	0	307	173	6	3	30	15	15	0	193	204	2	0	65	42	23	0	500	377	8	3	287	69	16	105	96	77	105	103
PHI	25	16	9	0	246	166	1	0	33	13	20	0	230	262	2	4	58	29	29	0	476	428	3	4	24	114	62	109	107	95	105	103
1875 NATIONAL ASSOCIATION																																
ATH	38	28	7	3	388	190	8	0	39	25	13	1	311	212	2	4	77	53	20	4	699	402	10	4	136	169	92	115	136	83	108	104
ATL	27	1	26	0	79	249	2	5	17	1	16	0	53	189	0	4	44	2	42	0	132	438	2	9	104	69	331	82	57	174	87	95
BOS	37	37	0	0	380	119	10	0	45	34	8	3	451	224	4	2	82	71	8	3	831	343	14	2	195	183	42	95	166	72	100	92
CEN	7	0	7	0	25	77	0	0	7	2	5	0	45	61	0	0	14	2	12	0	70	138	0	0	0	100	100	93	88	165	92	98
CHI	33	16	16	1	211	199	0	0	36	14	21	1	168	217	0	0	69	30	37	2	379	416	0	0	0	100	100	114	83	91	107	108
HAR	39	26	11	2	289	155	0	0	47	28	17	2	268	188	2	4	86	54	28	4	557	343	2	4	0	100	100	118	95	60	112	109
MUT	36	13	21	2	179	223	7	1	35	17	17	1	149	202	0	2	71	30	38	3	328	425	7	3	317	49	59	110	71	91	105	107
NH	27	3	24	0	87	211	1	3	20	4	16	0	83	186	1	2	47	7	40	0	170	397	2	5	95	77	174	80	69	150	87	93
PHI	33	16	16	1	231	176	4	0	37	21	15	1	239	200	1	6	70	37	31	2	470	376	5	6	66	178	138	104	106	86	103	101
RS	14	3	11	0	50	108	0	0	5	1	4	0	10	53	0	0	19	4	15	0	60	161	0	0	0	100	100	88	51	151	90	98
STL	34	21	12	1	183	135	0	1	36	18	17	1	203	234	0	2	70	39	29	2	386	369	0	3	55	0	80	79	100	93	91	90
WES	8	1	7	0	30	57	0	0	5	0	5	0	15	31	0	0	13	1	12	0	45	88	0	0	0	100	100	111	52	99	105	110
WAS	12	2	10	0	45	158	0	0	16	3	13	0	62	180	0	6	28	5	23	0	107	338	0	6	0	100	100	107	65	187	96	106
1882 AMERICAN ASSOCIATION																																
BAL	35	9	25	1	138	225	2	7	39	10	29	0	134	287	2	8	74	19	54	1	272	512	4	15	98	56	168	95	77	129	92	102
CIN	42	31	11	0	270	130	0	5	38	24	14	0	219	138	5	2	80	55	25	0	489	268	5	7	70	55	90	103	108	65	109	100
LOU	39	26	13	0	215	129	0	0	41	16	25	0	230	229	9	6	80	42	38	0	445	358	9	6	0	100	100	82	115	94	94	90
PHI	39	21	18	0	236	220	3	11	36	20	16	0	166	166	2	2	75	41	34	0	402	386	5	13	236	43	75	122	92	89	112	111
PIT	35	17	18	0	185	172	12	3	44	22	21	1	239	241	6	1	79	39	39	1	424	413	18	4	210	126	32	95	106	103	97	97
STL	44	24	20	0	253	262	7	2	36	13	23	0	150	236	4	5	80	37	43	0	403	498	11	7	84	131	91	107	95	116	100	104
1883 AMERICAN ASSOCIATION																																
BAL	49	18	31	0	300	395	4	6	47	10	37	0	173	342	1	6	96	28	68	0	473	737	5	12	128	28	70	122	79	119	107	113
CIN	51	38	13	0	381	164	29	13	47	23	24	0	276	249	5	4	98	61	37	0	657	413	34	17	307	104	65	97	114	77	102	97
COL	47	18	29	0	198	283	5	8	50	14	36	0	276	376	0	8	97	32	65	0	474	659	15	16	78	118	131	79	98	130	87	91
LOU	47	29	18	0	281	226	4	0	51	23	27	1	283	337	10	7	98	52	45	1	564	563	14	7	28	151	46	90	107	105	95	95
NY	47	29	17	1	270	187	3	4	50	25	25	0	228	218	3	8	97	54	42	1	498	405	6	12	71	50	87	108	83	69	108	106
PHI	51	37	14	0	404	261	9	8	47	29	18	0	316	286	11	14	98	66	32	0	720	547	20	22	67	191	201	103	126	100	101	98
PIT	49	18	31	0	292	321	10	3	49	13	36	0	231	405	3	18	98	31	67	0	523	726	13	21	64	141	162	95	100	132	94	98
STL	49	35	14	0	298	197	5	3	49	30	19	0	251	211	2	4	98	65	33	0	549	408	7	7	130	38	41	108	90	70	108	105
1884 AMERICAN ASSOCIATION																																
BAL	57	42	13	2	371	224	21	8	51	21	30	0	264	292	11	8	108	63	43	2	635	516	32	16	134	132	74	97	113	94	99	97
BRO	52	23	26	3	263	265	9	8	57	17	38	2	213	379	7	12	109	40	64	5	476	644	16	20	97	81	98	97	87	113	98	100
CIN	57	40	16	1	439	233	31	20	55	28	25	2	315	279	5	7	112	68	41	3	754	512	36	27	335	71	68	110	121	86	106	103
COL	55	38	16	1	282	207	23	14	55	31	23	1	303	252	17	8	110	69	39	2	585	459	40	22	145	164	93	90	105	84	97	95
IND	57	17	39	1	257	380	13	15	53	12	39	2	206	375	7	15	110	29	78	3	463	755	20	30	114	93	139	100	82	130	97	101
LOU	57	41	14	1	278	145	4	2	54	27	26	1	295	280	13	7	110	68	40	2	573	425	17	9	31	121	66	74	114	83	89	87
NY	55	42	9	4	370	179	11	4	57	33	23	1	364	244	11	11	112	75	32	5	734	423	22	15	74	123	80	96	125	75	100	96
PHI	54	38	16	0	438	268	12	4	54	23	30	1	262	278	14	12	108	61	46	1	700	546	26	16	64	162	95	129	107	88	114	113
PIT	56	18	37	1	225	350	1	4	54	12	41	1	182	375	1	21	110	30	78	2	407	725	2	25	23	28	173	97	73	125	97	101
RIC	22	5	15	2	96	142	3	8	24	7	15	2	98	153	4	6	46	12	30	4	194	295	7	14	116	81	151	101	82	120	99	102
STL	53	38	14	1	380	243	6	10	57	29	26	2	278	294	5	6	110	67	40	3	658	537	11	16	152	43	60	117	105	88	109	108
TOL	55	28	25	2	270	267	3	2	55	18	33	4	193	305	5	10	110	46	58	6	463	572	8	12	35	64	73	107	77	95	104	105
WAS	30	10	20	0	137	181	3	4	33	2	31	0	111	300	3	17	63	12	51	0	248	481	6	21	39	103	226	83	88	153	88	93
1885 AMERICAN ASSOCIATION																																
BAL	54	29	25	0	360	296	11	2	56	12	43	1	182	388	6	10	110	41	68	1	542	684	17	12	85	98	65	115	83	105	106	109
BRO	58	36	22	0	386	308	9	14	54	17	37	0	238	342	5	13	112	53	59	0	624	650	14	27	116	71	130	109	96	102	104	105
CIN	56	35	21	0	358	269	17	17	56	28	28	0	284	307	9	7	112	63	49	0	642	576	26	24	187	100	90	106	100	92	104	103
LOU	56	37	19	0	334	259	16	4	56	16	40	0	228	339	3	9	112	53	59	0	562	598	19	13	153	69	62	104	89	94	102	103

TM	HOME G	W	L	T	R	OR	HR	OHR	ROAD G	W	L	T	R	OR	HR	OHR	ALL G	W	L	T	R	OR	HR	OHR	HRF	HRB	HRP	RF	RB	RP	BPF	PPF
NY	52	28	24	0	262	212	10	5	56	16	40	0	265	476	11	31	108	44	64	0	527	688	21	36	41	240	267	71	111	129	84	86
PHI	57	33	23	1	449	330	18	9	56	22	34	0	315	362	12	2	113	55	57	1	764	692	30	11	170	114	40	111	118	110	103	102
PIT	57	37	20	0	342	242	3	3	54	19	35	0	206	295	2	11	111	56	55	0	548	537	5	14	47	43	83	109	83	84	106	106
STL	55	44	11	0	319	160	6	5	57	35	22	0	358	301	11	7	112	79	33	0	677	461	17	12	68	100	75	79	119	82	93	89

1886 AMERICAN ASSOCIATION

TM	HOME G	W	L	T	R	OR	HR	OHR	ROAD G	W	L	T	R	OR	HR	OHR	ALL G	W	L	T	R	OR	HR	OHR	HRF	HRB	HRP	RF	RB	RP	BPF	PPF
BAL	66	30	31	5	320	315	2	2	73	18	52	3	298	560	6	23	139	48	83	8	618	875	8	25	17	93	155	83	89	115	90	94
BRO	69	43	25	1	453	364	9	7	72	33	36	3	379	462	7	10	141	76	61	4	832	826	16	17	99	75	79	102	104	103	100	100
CIN	71	40	31	0	472	380	32	16	70	25	42	3	406	484	13	9	141	65	73	3	878	864	45	25	188	151	96	95	115	113	96	96
LOU	69	37	30	2	484	402	19	9	69	29	40	0	345	395	1	7	138	66	70	2	829	797	20	16	266	38	53	117	98	95	108	108
NY	65	30	33	2	336	352	10	9	72	23	49	0	290	415	8	14	137	53	82	2	626	767	18	23	95	94	114	106	78	93	104	106
PHI	71	37	32	2	434	468	13	11	68	26	40	2	337	472	8	24	139	63	72	4	771	940	21	35	74	140	197	106	97	116	100	103
PIT	76	46	29	1	423	272	2	3	64	34	28	2	386	373	14	7	140	80	57	3	809	645	16	10	22	106	94	80	112	91	92	90
STL	70	52	18	0	546	286	13	7	69	41	28	0	398	307	7	6	139	93	46	0	944	593	20	13	145	75	53	116	107	72	111	106

1887 AMERICAN ASSOCIATION

TM	HOME G	W	L	T	R	OR	HR	OHR	ROAD G	W	L	T	R	OR	HR	OHR	ALL G	W	L	T	R	OR	HR	OHR	HRF	HRB	HRP	RF	RB	RP	BPF	PPF
BAL	68	42	21	5	500	328	16	6	73	35	37	1	470	536	15	10	141	77	58	6	970	864	31	16	96	104	57	90	110	97	96	94
BRO	75	36	38	1	514	470	18	14	63	24	36	3	398	448	7	13	138	60	74	4	912	918	25	27	128	73	85	98	102	103	98	99
CIN	73	46	27	0	542	396	24	16	63	35	27	1	351	350	13	12	136	81	54	1	893	746	37	28	133	113	91	114	90	78	110	108
CLE	60	22	36	2	373	463	2	7	73	17	56	0	356	637	12	27	133	39	92	2	729	1100	14	34	30	71	171	100	87	123	97	102
LOU	69	45	23	1	553	402	14	15	70	31	37	2	402	457	13	16	139	76	60	3	955	859	27	31	102	96	109	112	98	90	107	105
NY	62	25	34	3	322	398	10	10	76	19	55	2	425	693	11	29	138	44	89	5	747	1091	21	39	63	104	154	80	95	128	88	92
PHI	70	41	27	2	502	404	18	11	67	23	42	2	387	492	11	18	137	64	69	4	889	896	29	29	96	107	107	99	99	100	99	100
STL	73	58	15	0	679	381	26	16	65	37	25	3	453	372	13	3	138	95	40	3	1132	753	39	19	204	90	39	115	113	80	109	105

1888 AMERICAN ASSOCIATION

TM	HOME G	W	L	T	R	OR	HR	OHR	ROAD G	W	L	T	R	OR	HR	OHR	ALL G	W	L	T	R	OR	HR	OHR	HRF	HRB	HRP	RF	RB	RP	BPF	PPF
BAL	56	30	26	0	285	276	7	11	81	27	54	0	361	503	12	12	137	57	80	0	646	779	19	23	107	77	94	94	96	109	96	98
BRO	76	53	20	3	451	267	18	10	67	35	32	0	307	312	7	5	143	88	52	3	758	579	25	15	183	65	43	103	97	78	105	102
CIN	82	56	25	1	484	333	24	5	55	24	29	2	260	295	8	14	137	80	54	3	744	628	32	19	90	136	98	100	101	91	101	100
CLE	61	33	28	0	361	314	8	12	74	17	54	3	291	525	4	26	135	50	82	3	652	839	12	38	82	67	162	99	98	118	97	100
KC	57	23	34	0	330	392	15	10	75	20	55	0	249	502	4	22	132	43	89	0	579	894	19	32	121	83	127	121	81	118	106	112
LOU	60	27	29	4	321	298	1	4	79	21	58	0	365	572	13	24	139	48	87	4	686	870	14	28	20	75	173	87	107	125	91	94
PHI	74	54	20	0	505	253	20	8	62	27	32	3	320	338	11	6	136	81	52	3	825	591	31	14	133	106	53	98	115	88	101	97
STL	82	60	21	1	525	284	22	13	55	32	22	1	264	215	14	3	137	92	43	2	789	499	36	19	117	138	76	113	97	68	111	106

1889 AMERICAN ASSOCIATION

TM	HOME G	W	L	T	R	OR	HR	OHR	ROAD G	W	L	T	R	OR	HR	OHR	ALL G	W	L	T	R	OR	HR	OHR	HRF	HRB	HRP	RF	RB	RP	BPF	PPF
BAL	67	41	23	3	436	314	10	4	72	29	42	1	355	481	10	23	139	70	65	4	791	795	20	27	49	79	77	97	95	94	100	99
BRO	70	50	18	2	488	297	28	19	70	43	26	1	510	417	19	14	140	93	44	3	998	714	47	33	137	105	77	88	123	91	96	92
CIN	74	47	26	1	543	362	37	19	67	29	37	1	354	407	15	13	141	76	63	2	897	769	52	35	152	104	80	107	99	88	105	103
COL	69	36	33	0	407	350	13	11	71	24	45	2	376	573	23	22	140	60	78	2	783	923	36	33	58	121	111	83	103	116	91	92
KC	70	35	35	0	523	518	8	17	69	20	47	2	329	512	10	34	139	55	82	2	852	1030	18	51	59	68	159	118	94	113	106	109
LOU	65	18	47	0	330	473	10	18	75	9	64	2	302	617	12	29	140	27	111	2	632	1090	22	43	86	65	116	98	78	125	96	102
PHI	73	46	22	5	506	347	16	13	65	29	36	0	380	440	27	22	138	75	58	5	886	787	43	35	56	154	130	94	108	98	98	96
STL	71	51	18	2	581	317	45	28	70	39	27	4	372	367	13	11	141	90	45	6	953	684	58	39	243	86	64	119	98	75	112	109

1890 AMERICAN ASSOCIATION

TM	HOME G	W	L	T	R	OR	HR	OHR	ROAD G	W	L	T	R	OR	HR	OHR	ALL G	W	L	T	R	OR	HR	OHR	HRF	HRB	HRP	RF	RB	RP	BPF	PPF
BAL	22	8	11	3	117	115	1	0	16	7	8	1	65	77	1	3	38	15	19	4	182	192	2	3	20	77	48	116	76	82	109	110
BRO	38	15	22	1	220	252	4	3	62	11	51	0	272	481	9	18	100	26	73	1	492	733	13	21	44	112	132	100	94	128	97	101
COL	71	47	22	2	453	246	9	8	69	32	33	4	377	369	7	12	140	79	55	6	830	615	16	20	89	69	83	93	107	82	99	96
LOU	74	57	13	4	513	280	8	8	62	31	31	0	307	304	7	10	136	88	44	4	820	584	15	18	82	68	80	109	98	75	107	104
PHI	72	36	36	0	463	452	16	6	60	18	42	0	240	493	8	11	132	54	78	0	703	945	24	17	96	102	78	103	95	108	98	102
ROC	63	40	22	1	348	252	13	4	70	23	41	6	361	458	18	15	133	63	63	7	709	710	31	19	60	169	97	83	105	101	92	92
STL	72	45	25	2	551	396	42	31	67	33	33	1	313	341	6	7	139	78	58	3	864	737	48	38	357	78	72	131	94	84	116	115
SYR	60	30	30	0	321	320	2	4	68	25	42	1	378	511	12	24	128	55	72	1	699	831	14	28	21	103	187	83	110	125	90	91
TOL	68	40	27	1	422	316	17	11	66	28	37	1	316	374	7	12	134	68	64	2	738	690	24	23	137	83	87	104	95	91	103	102

1891 AMERICAN ASSOCIATION

TM	HOME G	W	L	T	R	OR	HR	OHR	ROAD G	W	L	T	R	OR	HR	OHR	ALL G	W	L	T	R	OR	HR	OHR	HRF	HRB	HRP	RF	RB	RP	BPF	PPF
BAL	70	44	24	2	481	354	13	8	69	27	40	2	367	442	17	25	139	71	64	4	848	796	30	33	52	114	109	102	103	98	101	100
BOS	70	51	17	2	520	295	37	22	69	42	25	2	507	379	15	20	139	93	42	4	1027	674	52	42	157	108	98	93	128	88	98	94
CIN	45	24	20	1	297	289	21	9	57	19	37	1	250	354	7	11	102	43	57	2	547	643	28	20	187	70	59	119	85	98	109	111
COL	63	34	29	0	309	263	4	8	75	27	47	1	391	514	16	21	138	61	76	1	700	777	20	29	41	68	105	77	98	103	89	90
LOU	72	40	32	0	395	335	7	6	69	15	52	2	317	553	10	27	141	55	84	2	712	888	17	33	36	79	111	81	98	116	90	92
MIL	21	16	5	0	172	82	11	5	15	5	10	0	56	74	2	1	36	21	15	0	228	156	13	6	291	60	30	134	82	67	120	118
PHI	72	43	26	3	465	366	29	9	71	30	40	1	354	427	26	26	143	73	66	4	819	793	55	35	74	174	109	105	95	93	103	103
STL	74	53	21	0	617	398	42	30	67	33	31	3	359	355	16	20	141	86	52	3	976	753	58	50	168	115	110	126	101	83	114	112
WAS	72	28	40	4	389	519	13	18	67	16	51	0	300	547	6	26	139	44	91	4	689	1066	19	44	89	57	120	98	88	130	95	101

1884 UNION ASSOCIATION

TM	HOME G	W	L	T	R	OR	HR	OHR	ROAD G	W	L	T	R	OR	HR	OHR	ALL G	W	L	T	R	OR	HR	OHR	HRF	HRB	HRP	RF	RB	RP	BPF	PPF
ALT	18	6	12	0	73	156	0	2	7	0	7	0	17	60	2	1	25	6	19	0	90	216	2	3	27	99	190	110	56	140	101	109
BAL	50	29	21	0	372	312	12	16	56	29	26	1	304	318	5	8	106	58	47	1	676	630	17	24	219	71	101	122	102	97	110	110
BOS	58	34	23	1	346	260	7	5	53	24	28	1	290	297	12	12	111	58	51	2	636	557	19	17	48	167	144	95	103	91	98	97
CHI	35	20	14	1	177	159	2	2	39	14	25	0	183	252	8	9	74	34	39	1	360	411	10	11	28	143	150	87	93	102	94	94
CIN	52	35	17	0	382	239	18	12	53	34	19	0	325	241	8	5	105	69	36	0	707	480	26	17	216	109	72	113	110	77	108	105
KC	36	11	23	2	150	205	3	6	46	5	40	1	159	414	3	8	82	16	63	3	309	619	6	14	101	51	111	78	80	140	87	91
MIL	12	8	4	0	53	35	0	1	0	0	0	0	0	0	0	0	12	8	4	0	53	35	0	1	0	100	0	100	0	100	54	54
PHI	34	13	21	0	223	249	4	1	33	8	25	0	192	296	3	6	67	21	46	0	415	545	7	7	55	102	79	93	119	151	93	95
PIT	5	1	4	0	22	29	0	1	14	6	7	1	56	42	0	0	19	7	11	1	78	71	0	1			0	100	139	62	122	122
STL	56	50	6	0	461	179	10	4	58	44	13	1	426	250	22	5	114	94	19	1	887	429	32	9	58	227	78	102	133	68	104	98
STP	0	0	0	0	0	0	0	0	9	2	6	1	24	57	0	1	9	2	6	1	24	57	0	1	0	100	100	0	100	100	54	54
WAS	65	36	27	2	382	318	4	10	49	11	38	0	192	362	0	6	114	47	65	2	574	680	4	16	164	13	71	95	90	110	97	98
WIL	7	1	6	0	16	46	1	4	11	1	10	0	19	68	1	0	18	2	16	0	35	114	2	4	501	48	37	104	34	103	103	109

1890 PLAYERS LEAGUE

TM	HOME G	W	L	T	R	OR	HR	OHR	ROAD G	W	L	T	R	OR	HR	OHR	ALL G	W	L	T	R	OR	HR	OHR	HRF	HRB	HRP	RF	RB	RP	BPF	PPF
BOS	70	48	21	1	602	383	42	38	60	33	27	0	386	384	12	11	130	81	48	1	988	767	54	49	241	78	71	110	102	84	107	104
BRO	66	46	19	1	564	410	20	7	67	30	37	0	398	480	14	19	133	76	56	1	962	890	34	26	85	89	66	112	99	93	106	105
BUF	65	23	42	0	425	498	7	20	63	13	54	2	367	698	13	47	128	36	96	2	792	1196	20	67	50	75	203	91	95	133	92	97
CHI	70	46	23	1	504	345	18	12	68	29	39	0	381	425	13	15	138	75	62	1	885	770	31	27	104	70	62	102	89	79	104	103
CLE	62	31	30	1	416	403	10	15	69	24	45	0	433	623	17	30	131	55	75	1	849	1026	27	45	62	87	132	87	104	119	92	94
NY	66	47	19	0	628	404	35	21	66	27	38	1	389	477	31	16	132	74	57	1	1017	881	66	37	117	155	94	117	102	92	109	107
PHI	65	35	30	0	482	418	20	15	67	33	33	1	465	434	29	33	132	68	63	1	947	852	49	33	79	135	97	103	102	93	102	101
PIT	65	37	28	0	435	356	21	15	63	23	40	0	398	535	14	17	128	60	68	0	833	891	35	32	110	84	79	84	104	109	92	92

1914 FEDERAL LEAGUE

TM	HOME G	W	L	T	R	OR	HR	OHR	ROAD G	W	L	T	R	OR	HR	OHR	ALL G	W	L	T	R	OR	HR	OHR	HRF	HRB	HRP	RF	RB	RP	BPF	PPF
BAL	83	53	26	4	350	298	25	15	77	31	44	2	295	330	7	19	160	84	70	6	645	628	32	34	136	65	79	97	99	97	99	99
BRO	80	47	32	1	358	335	27	13	77	30	45	2	304	342	15	18	157	77	77	3	662	677	42	31	114	102	81	103	102	104	101	101
BUF	79	47	29	3	345	300	20	18	76	33	42	1	275	302	17	27	155	80	71	4	620	602	37	45	85	115	133	107	93	91	104	104
CHI	75	41	34	0	248	208	30	19	82	46	33	3	373	309	22	24	157	87	67	3	621	517	52	43	115	134	115	76	105	89	91	89
IND	80	53	23	4	439	339	14	8	77	35	42	0	323	283	19	21	157	88	65	4	762	622	33	29	57	114	94	121	106	89	111	108

	HOME								ROAD								ALL															
TM	G	W	L	T	R	OR	HR	OHR	G	W	L	T	R	OR	HR	OHR	G	W	L	T	R	OR	HR	OHR	HRF	HRB	HRP	RF	RB	RP	BPF	PPF
KC	76	38	37	1	322	306	28	21	78	29	47	2	322	377	11	16	154	67	84	3	644	683	39	37	167	77	79	93	107	112	95	96
PIT	75	37	37	1	297	307	11	10	79	27	49	3	308	391	23	28	154	64	86	4	605	698	34	38	46	131	137	91	102	114	94	96
STL	76	31	44	1	304	368	13	23	78	31	45	2	261	329	13	15	154	62	89	3	565	697	26	38	126	64	88	114	85	102	106	108

1915 FEDERAL LEAGUE

	HOME								ROAD								ALL															
TM	G	W	L	T	R	OR	HR	OHR	G	W	L	T	R	OR	HR	OHR	G	W	L	T	R	OR	HR	OHR	HRF	HRB	HRP	RF	RB	RP	BPF	PPF
BAL	75	24	51	0	299	419	29	36	79	23	56	0	251	341	7	16	154	47	107	0	550	760	36	52	235	67	104	121	87	115	107	111
BRO	74	34	40	0	315	324	20	11	79	36	42	1	332	349	16	16	153	70	82	1	647	673	36	27	103	114	88	100	112	116	98	98
BUF	77	37	40	0	290	324	21	21	76	37	38	1	284	310	19	14	153	74	78	1	574	634	40	35	122	120	105	102	98	106	100	101
CHI	78	44	32	2	310	252	21	10	77	42	34	1	330	286	29	23	155	86	66	3	640	538	50	33	62	207	140	92	110	95	97	95
KC	77	46	31	0	274	249	15	19	76	35	41	0	273	302	13	10	153	81	72	0	547	551	28	29	138	76	76	91	96	97	97	97
NEW	79	40	39	0	267	271	4	2	76	40	33	3	318	291	13	13	155	80	72	3	585	562	17	15	25	84	62	87	104	101	94	94
PIT	77	45	31	1	292	269	4	10	79	41	36	2	300	255	16	27	156	86	67	3	592	524	20	37	37	89	163	104	95	85	104	102
STL	82	43	34	5	334	280	12	15	77	44	33	0	300	247	11	7	159	87	67	5	634	527	23	22	135	60	54	105	99	84	105	102

1876 NATIONAL LEAGUE

	HOME								ROAD								ALL															
TM	G	W	L	T	R	OR	HR	OHR	G	W	L	T	R	OR	HR	OHR	G	W	L	T	R	OR	HR	OHR	HRF	HRB	HRP	RF	RB	RP	BPF	PPF
BOS	36	19	17	0	253	200	5	3	34	20	14	0	218	250	4	4	70	39	31	0	471	450	9	7	96	182	148	93	121	116	95	94
CHI	31	25	6	0	352	143	3	1	35	27	8	0	272	114	5	5	66	52	14	0	624	257	8	6	50	229	153	141	130	59	125	113
CIN	30	6	24	0	119	243	2	2	35	3	32	0	119	336	2	2	65	9	56	0	238	579	4	9	53	135	214	90	70	150	89	100
HAR	32	23	9	0	220	107	0	0	37	24	12	1	209	154	2	2	69	47	21	1	429	261	2	2	0	100	106	98	62	108	103	
LOU	33	15	16	2	149	154	6	3	36	15	20	1	131	190	0	0	69	30	36	3	280	344	6	3	0	100	102	66	80	104	106	
NY	33	13	20	0	143	207	2	7	24	8	15	1	117	205	0	1	57	21	35	1	260	412	2	8	384	10	63	80	90	135	87	93
PHI	35	10	24	1	259	309	4	0	25	4	21	0	119	225	3	2	60	14	45	1	378	534	7	2	59	188	56	112	103	145	99	105
STL	30	24	6	0	150	58	1	1	34	21	13	0	236	171	1	2	64	45	19	0	386	229	2	3	80	43	59	62	118	69	88	82

1877 NATIONAL LEAGUE

	HOME								ROAD								ALL															
TM	G	W	L	T	R	OR	HR	OHR	G	W	L	T	R	OR	HR	OHR	G	W	L	T	R	OR	HR	OHR	HRF	HRB	HRP	RF	RB	RP	BPF	PPF
BOS	32	27	5	0	260	110	0	1	29	15	13	1	159	153	4	4	61	42	18	1	419	263	4	5	14	119	271	108	110	77	108	101
CHI	29	17	12	0	206	156	0	4	31	9	21	1	160	219	0	3	60	26	33	1	366	375	0	7	133	0	124	101	110	111	98	99
CIN	30	12	17	1	157	201	4	1	28	3	25	1	134	284	2	3	58	15	42	1	291	485	6	4	92	168	121	81	110	163	82	90
HAR	29	19	8	2	167	92	2	1	31	12	19	0	174	219	2	1	60	31	27	2	341	311	4	2	106	87	48	74	116	100	89	87
LOU	30	21	9	0	219	172	7	3	31	14	16	1	120	117	2	1	61	35	25	1	339	289	9	4	246	122	63	154	74	66	132	130
STL	30	20	10	0	177	124	0	1	30	8	22	0	108	194	1	1	60	28	32	0	285	318	1	2	54	21	58	99	82	90	102	103

1878 NATIONAL LEAGUE

	HOME								ROAD								ALL															
TM	G	W	L	T	R	OR	HR	OHR	G	W	L	T	R	OR	HR	OHR	G	W	L	T	R	OR	HR	OHR	HRF	HRB	HRP	RF	RB	RP	BPF	PPF
BOS	30	23	7	0	171	104	1	3	30	18	12	0	127	137	1	3	60	41	19	0	298	241	2	6	102	58	145	105	89	75	108	105
CHI	35	17	18	0	226	210	2	2	26	13	12	1	145	121	1	2	61	30	30	1	371	331	3	4	99	77	103	118	108	97	108	106
CIN	34	25	8	1	190	126	4	2	27	12	15	0	143	155	1	0	61	37	23	1	333	281	5	2	294	59	15	87	111	98	95	93
IND	28	10	17	1	106	115	1	1	35	14	19	2	187	213	2	2	63	24	36	3	293	328	3	3	66	84	84	72	102	112	87	88
MIL	25	7	18	0	127	177	1	0	36	8	27	1	129	209	1	3	61	15	45	1	256	386	2	3	39	93	59	121	78	110	107	114
PRO	32	17	13	2	182	170	4	2	30	16	14	0	171	167	4	3	62	33	27	2	353	337	8	5	83	260	182	98	113	109	98	97

1879 NATIONAL LEAGUE

	HOME								ROAD								ALL															
TM	G	W	L	T	R	OR	HR	OHR	G	W	L	T	R	OR	HR	OHR	G	W	L	T	R	OR	HR	OHR	HRF	HRB	HRP	RF	RB	RP	BPF	PPF
BOS	42	29	13	0	308	165	11	2	42	25	17	0	254	183	9	7	84	54	30	0	562	348	20	9	84	312	159	109	117	78	107	101
BUF	40	23	16	1	223	204	1	0	39	23	16	0	167	161	1	3	79	46	32	1	390	365	2	3	27	58	36	124	81	77	114	113
CHI	43	29	13	1	264	191	2	0	40	17	20	3	173	219	1	5	83	46	33	4	437	410	3	5	34	83	62	108	94	90	105	104
CIN	37	21	16	0	215	196	8	0	44	22	21	1	270	268	0	5	81	43	37	1	485	464	8	11	259	46	102	92	119	114	95	94
CLE	42	15	27	0	167	236	2	1	40	12	28	0	155	225	2	3	82	27	55	0	322	461	4	4	59	67	59	99	75	103	99	103
PRO	42	34	8	0	323	143	9	4	43	25	17	1	289	212	3	5	85	59	25	1	612	355	12	9	157	118	105	98	134	83	101	94
SYR	34	11	22	1	115	200	1	2	37	11	26	0	160	257	4	2	71	22	48	1	275	457	5	4	57	83	84	83	82	128	89	95
TRO	41	12	27	2	191	263	3	6	36	7	29	0	130	281	1	7	77	19	56	2	321	544	4	13	96	64	181	95	84	134	93	100

1880 NATIONAL LEAGUE

	HOME								ROAD								ALL															
TM	G	W	L	T	R	OR	HR	OHR	G	W	L	T	R	OR	HR	OHR	G	W	L	T	R	OR	HR	OHR	HRF	HRB	HRP	RF	RB	RP	BPF	PPF
BOS	43	25	17	1	213	190	14	1	43	15	27	1	203	265	6	1	86	40	44	2	416	455	20	2	187	160	23	87	113	121	92	93
BUF	44	13	29	2	173	233	1	1	41	11	29	1	159	269	2	9	85	24	58	3	332	502	3	10	18	101	176	88	92	132	91	96
CHI	43	37	5	1	284	148	1	0	43	30	12	1	254	169	2	8	86	67	17	2	538	317	4	8	11	154	98	105	127	80	105	98
CIN	40	14	25	1	163	216	5	8	43	7	34	2	131	256	2	2	83	21	59	3	294	472	7	10	262	54	68	102	77	116	99	105
CLE	43	23	19	1	182	168	2	1	42	24	18	0	205	169	5	1	85	47	37	1	387	337	7	4	40	119	70	93	87	99	97	
PRO	44	31	12	1	210	116	4	2	43	21	20	2	209	183	4	5	87	52	32	3	419	299	8	7	69	121	100	84	108	79	96	92
TRO	41	20	21	0	204	257	5	6	42	21	21	0	188	181	0	2	83	41	42	0	392	438	5	8	357	17	50	124	92	100	110	112
WOR	42	24	17	1	247	186	5	6	43	16	26	1	165	184	3	7	85	40	43	2	412	370	8	13	111	107	163	123	91	84	112	111

1881 NATIONAL LEAGUE

	HOME								ROAD								ALL															
TM	G	W	L	T	R	OR	HR	OHR	G	W	L	T	R	OR	HR	OHR	G	W	L	T	R	OR	HR	OHR	HRF	HRB	HRP	RF	RB	RP	BPF	PPF
BOS	41	19	22	0	151	180	2	4	42	19	23	0	197	230	3	5	83	38	45	0	348	410	5	9	79	58	100	81	90	104	91	93
BUF	41	25	16	0	241	206	2	0	42	20	22	0	199	242	10	9	83	45	38	0	440	448	12	9	12	273	105	104	103	105	101	101
CHI	42	32	10	0	309	186	7	6	42	24	18	0	241	194	5	8	84	56	28	0	550	380	12	14	102	135	154	114	118	86	108	103
CLE	42	20	22	0	190	185	3	4	43	16	26	1	201	229	4	5	85	36	48	1	391	414	7	9	81	79	99	90	94	99	96	96
DET	42	23	19	0	252	213	14	4	42	18	24	0	188	216	3	4	84	41	43	0	440	429	17	8	215	100	68	113	96	95	106	106
PRO	43	23	20	0	209	194	4	2	42	24	17	1	240	232	7	3	85	47	37	1	449	426	11	5	62	130	66	86	112	107	93	92
TRO	43	24	18	1	222	196	4	9	42	15	27	0	177	232	1	2	85	39	45	1	399	428	5	11	301	25	51	99	92	98	100	101
WOR	42	19	22	1	240	253	7	4	41	13	28	0	170	239	0	7	83	32	50	1	410	492	7	11	142	52	102	114	92	109	105	107

1882 NATIONAL LEAGUE

	HOME								ROAD								ALL															
TM	G	W	L	T	R	OR	HR	OHR	G	W	L	T	R	OR	HR	OHR	G	W	L	T	R	OR	HR	OHR	HRF	HRB	HRP	RF	RB	RP	BPF	PPF
BOS	43	27	15	1	263	191	8	7	42	18	24	0	209	220	7	3	85	45	39	1	472	411	15	10	139	77	50	103	99	88	103	102
BUF	39	26	13	0	286	184	5	7	45	19	26	0	214	278	13	9	84	45	39	0	500	462	18	16	66	131	130	109	106	99	104	103
CHI	45	35	10	0	360	140	9	8	39	20	19	0	243	213	6	5	84	55	29	0	603	353	15	13	130	80	70	97	130	83	101	95
CLE	42	21	19	2	175	170	6	7	42	21	21	0	227	240	14	15	84	42	40	2	402	410	20	22	48	188	205	76	99	100	90	90
DET	43	24	18	1	221	238	4	10	43	18	23	2	186	252	5	9	86	42	41	3	407	490	19	19	158	89	98	104	86	101	102	104
PRO	42	30	12	0	247	172	6	6	42	22	20	0	216	184	5	6	84	52	32	0	463	356	11	12	109	65	70	105	96	76	106	103
TRO	42	22	20	0	238	217	7	2	43	13	28	0	192	305	5	11	85	35	48	2	430	522	12	13	60	102	87	94	99	116	95	97
WOR	42	12	30	0	216	338	9	15	42	6	36	0	163	314	7	6	84	18	66	0	379	652	16	21	163	83	98	111	83	134	100	107

1883 NATIONAL LEAGUE

	HOME								ROAD								ALL															
TM	G	W	L	T	R	OR	HR	OHR	G	W	L	T	R	OR	HR	OHR	G	W	L	T	R	OR	HR	OHR	HRF	HRB	HRP	RF	RB	RP	BPF	PPF
BOS	49	41	8	0	391	190	21	3	49	22	27	0	277	267	13	8	98	63	35	0	668	457	34	11	114	200	80	107	110	80	106	102
BUF	49	36	13	0	355	241	3	4	49	16	32	1	258	335	5	8	98	52	45	1	613	576	8	12	57	64	90	101	108	102	100	99
CHI	49	36	13	0	410	254	11	6	49	23	26	0	269	287	2	15	98	59	39	0	679	541	13	21	101	88	134	118	109	91	109	106
CLE	49	31	18	0	248	203	0	4	51	24	24	3	227	240	8	3	100	55	42	3	475	443	8	7	41	45	74	101	79	74	104	104
DET	51	23	26	2	264	207	12	9	50	17	32	1	260	371	1	13	101	40	58	3	524	661	13	22	138	63	121	85	99	118	91	94
NY	49	28	19	2	292	262	20	15	49	18	31	0	238	315	4	4	98	46	50	2	530	577	24	19	307	71	62	100	94	110	100	101
PHI	50	9	40	1	224	439	0	1	49	8	41	0	222	449	3	19	99	17	81	1	446	888	3	20	5	20	212	94	86	156	90	99
PRO	49	34	15	0	330	186	10	5	49	24	25	0	304	250	11	7	98	58	40	0	634	436	21	12	86	143	88	95	111	80	101	96

1884 NATIONAL LEAGUE

	HOME								ROAD								ALL															
TM	G	W	L	T	R	OR	HR	OHR	G	W	L	T	R	OR	HR	OHR	G	W	L	T	R	OR	HR	OHR	HRF	HRB	HRP	RF	RB	RP	BPF	PPF
BOS	58	40	16	0	328	181	14	4	60	33	22	5	356	288	22	26	118	73	38	5	684	469	36	30	44	126	83	88	110	78	98	93
BUF	58	37	18	3	409	311	23	20	57	27	29	1	292	314	16	26	115	64	47	4	701	625	39	46	101	97	113	115	102	94	108	106
CHI	57	39	17	1	498	312	131	66	56	23	33	0	336	334	11	17	113	62	50	1	834	646	142	83	399	121	103	117	124	101	107	104
CLE	51	22	34	0	264	348	4	6	57	13	43	1	194	360	5	23	108	35	77	1	458	716	16	35	27	66	116	100	72	107	102	108
DET	58	18	38	2	228	347	14	16	56	10	46	0	215	389	17	20	114	28	84	2	443	736	31	36	78	85	97	91	76	118	93	99
NY	58	34	22	2	378	261	8	4	58	28	28	2	315	362	15	24	116	62	50	4	693	623	23	28	34	89	81	96	111	101	98	96
PHI	57	19	37	1	281	388	1	1	56	20	36	0	268	436	13	37	113	39	73	1	549	824	14	38	4	90	137	93	96	136	92	97

TM	HOME								ROAD								ALL															
	G	W	L	T	R	OR	HR	OHR	G	W	L	T	R	OR	HR	OHR	G	W	L	T	R	OR	HR	OHR	HRF	HRB	HRP	RF	RB	RP	BPF	PPF
PRO	57	45	11	1	329	164	4	6	57	39	17	1	336	224	17	20	114	84	28	2	665	388	21	26	31	70	90	92	105	64	101	96

1885 NATIONAL LEAGUE

TM	G	W	L	T	R	OR	HR	OHR	G	W	L	T	R	OR	HR	OHR	G	W	L	T	R	OR	HR	OHR	HRF	HRB	HRP	RF	RB	RP	BPF	PPF
BOS	58	22	35	1	254	289	7	5	55	24	31	0	274	300	15	21	113	46	66	1	528	589	22	26	34	169	169	90	100	110	94	96
BUF	57	19	38	0	265	406	13	13	55	19	36	0	229	354	10	18	112	38	74	0	494	760	23	31	89	119	152	108	90	130	99	105
CHI	57	43	14	0	458	269	47	27	56	44	11	1	377	200	7	10	113	87	25	1	835	469	54	37	309	108	98	123	132	79	114	106
DET	52	29	23	0	294	228	13	8	56	12	44	0	220	355	12	10	108	41	67	0	514	583	25	18	101	116	86	97	100	109	97	99
NY	55	45	10	0	362	178	7	6	57	40	17	0	329	192	9	5	112	85	27	0	691	370	16	11	99	68	48	109	114	66	109	102
PHI	55	29	26	0	277	244	7	7	56	27	28	1	236	267	13	11	111	56	54	1	513	511	20	18	63	109	101	105	90	90	104	104
PRO	53	30	23	0	197	209	3	1	57	23	34	0	245	322	3	17	110	53	57	0	442	531	6	18	24	71	86	79	90	104	90	92
STL	58	23	33	2	215	262	6	4	53	13	39	1	175	332	2	11	111	36	72	3	390	594	8	15	72	44	70	86	78	111	92	97

1886 NATIONAL LEAGUE

TM	G	W	L	T	R	OR	HR	OHR	G	W	L	T	R	OR	HR	OHR	G	W	L	T	R	OR	HR	OHR	HRF	HRB	HRP	RF	RB	RP	BPF	PPF
BOS	58	32	25	1	354	280	15	8	60	24	36	0	303	379	9	25	118	56	61	1	657	659	24	33	73	102	118	96	110	109	97	97
CHI	62	52	10	0	539	275	45	34	64	38	24	2	364	281	8	15	126	90	34	2	903	556	53	49	274	82	94	128	117	78	116	110
DET	60	48	12	0	441	255	37	10	66	39	24	3	388	283	16	10	126	87	36	3	829	538	53	20	180	113	52	114	115	79	110	104
KC	62	19	42	1	301	456	9	4	64	11	49	4	193	420	10	23	126	30	91	5	494	876	19	27	43	96	96	121	70	117	106	114
NY	63	47	12	4	327	195	10	4	61	28	32	1	366	363	11	19	124	75	44	5	693	558	21	23	49	96	83	73	123	98	88	85
PHI	62	45	14	3	333	215	13	12	57	26	29	2	287	283	13	17	119	71	43	5	620	498	26	29	80	97	106	91	102	83	98	96
STL	63	27	34	2	288	313	13	10	63	16	45	2	260	399	17	24	126	43	79	4	548	712	30	34	58	126	130	91	88	110	95	98
WAS	65	19	42	4	245	372	13	12	60	9	50	1	200	420	10	22	125	28	92	5	445	792	23	34	73	89	119	90	73	122	93	100

1887 NATIONAL LEAGUE

TM	G	W	L	T	R	OR	HR	OHR	G	W	L	T	R	OR	HR	OHR	G	W	L	T	R	OR	HR	OHR	HRF	HRB	HRP	RF	RB	RP	BPF	PPF
BOS	63	39	21	3	466	322	29	17	64	22	39	3	367	471	24	38	127	61	60	6	833	793	53	55	78	132	128	96	111	106	98	97
CHI	64	44	18	2	540	347	67	44	63	27	32	4	278	372	13	11	127	71	50	6	818	719	80	55	317	74	56	130	89	83	116	115
DET	61	43	17	1	502	306	25	20	66	36	28	2	467	405	30	32	127	79	45	3	969	711	55	52	82	129	121	102	124	94	102	97
IND	64	24	39	1	349	456	19	28	63	13	50	0	278	507	14	32	127	37	89	1	627	963	33	60	98	71	121	99	84	123	96	102
NY	63	36	26	1	439	340	21	8	66	32	29	5	378	377	27	19	129	68	55	6	817	717	48	27	69	110	62	108	99	89	105	103
PHI	64	38	23	3	438	321	25	22	64	37	25	2	453	380	22	26	128	75	48	5	891	701	47	48	99	98	99	93	117	95	98	95
PIT	66	31	34	1	336	336	6	4	59	24	35	0	285	421	14	35	125	55	69	1	621	757	20	39	20	89	109	86	88	104	93	96
WAS	63	27	32	4	329	349	29	19	63	19	44	0	271	466	18	28	126	46	76	4	600	815	47	47	102	97	98	92	83	107	95	99

1888 NATIONAL LEAGUE

TM	G	W	L	T	R	OR	HR	OHR	G	W	L	T	R	OR	HR	OHR	G	W	L	T	R	OR	HR	OHR	HRF	HRB	HRP	RF	RB	RP	BPF	PPF
BOS	68	36	30	2	365	315	23	16	69	34	34	1	304	305	33	20	137	70	64	3	669	620	56	36	77	148	102	112	102	95	106	105
CHI	70	43	27	0	438	336	50	44	66	34	31	1	294	323	27	19	136	77	58	1	732	659	77	63	174	144	117	116	110	102	107	106
DET	68	40	26	2	400	279	24	18	66	28	37	1	321	350	27	26	134	68	63	3	721	629	51	44	79	143	124	99	121	107	98	97
IND	66	31	35	0	328	302	27	40	70	19	50	1	270	426	7	24	136	50	85	1	598	728	34	64	195	53	106	95	103	120	95	98
NY	70	44	23	3	313	182	21	9	68	40	24	4	347	296	34	18	138	84	47	7	660	478	55	27	60	155	82	78	115	85	92	89
PHI	66	37	29	0	313	268	6	12	66	32	32	2	222	241	10	14	132	69	61	2	535	509	16	26	78	41	66	122	78	76	114	113
PIT	70	37	30	3	280	234	0	1	69	29	38	2	254	346	14	22	139	66	68	5	534	580	14	23	3	29	109	86	91	96	94	95
WAS	66	26	38	2	260	318	17	25	70	22	48	0	222	410	13	25	136	48	86	2	482	728	30	50	113	69	109	96	82	117	96	101

1889 NATIONAL LEAGUE

TM	G	W	L	T	R	OR	HR	OHR	G	W	L	T	R	OR	HR	OHR	G	W	L	T	R	OR	HR	OHR	HRF	HRB	HRP	RF	RB	RP	BPF	PPF
BOS	68	48	17	3	455	272	24	14	65	35	28	2	371	352	18	27	133	83	45	5	826	624	42	41	84	98	93	98	104	82	102	98
CHI	69	37	30	2	450	398	54	52	67	30	35	2	416	417	25	19	136	67	65	4	866	815	79	71	200	116	102	99	110	105	99	98
CLE	68	33	35	0	353	341	8	13	68	28	37	3	302	379	17	23	136	61	72	3	655	720	25	36	56	63	90	101	81	88	102	103
IND	69	32	36	1	495	478	50	54	66	27	39	0	325	416	12	19	135	59	75	1	820	894	62	73	250	71	90	121	95	104	109	110
NY	63	47	15	1	513	311	18	15	68	36	28	4	422	396	34	23	131	83	43	5	935	707	52	38	67	130	102	109	116	91	105	102
PHI	68	43	24	1	467	347	27	12	62	20	40	2	274	402	17	21	130	63	64	3	741	749	44	33	94	96	74	108	92	95	104	105
PIT	70	40	28	2	388	307	6	2	64	21	43	0	337	492	36	40	134	61	71	2	725	799	42	42	11	194	133	79	106	113	89	90
WAS	56	24	29	3	302	323	12	10	71	17	54	0	330	569	13	27	127	41	83	3	632	892	25	37	71	67	84	88	95	123	92	95

1890 NATIONAL LEAGUE

TM	G	W	L	T	R	OR	HR	OHR	G	W	L	T	R	OR	HR	OHR	G	W	L	T	R	OR	HR	OHR	HRF	HRB	HRP	RF	RB	RP	BPF	PPF
BOS	66	43	23	0	435	284	20	11	68	33	34	1	328	308	11	16	134	76	57	1	763	592	31	27	116	86	79	115	92	74	111	108
BRO	74	58	16	0	547	303	27	9	55	28	27	0	337	318	16	18	129	86	43	0	884	621	43	27	82	154	106	98	121	92	100	96
CHI	74	48	24	2	509	369	55	29	65	36	29	0	340	323	12	12	139	84	53	2	849	692	67	41	246	106	80	115	99	84	109	107
CIN	73	50	23	0	470	323	19	25	61	27	32	2	283	309	8	16	134	77	55	2	753	632	27	41	145	67	103	111	92	81	108	106
CLE	70	30	37	3	357	355	13	7	66	14	51	1	268	476	8	26	136	44	88	4	625	831	21	33	58	93	114	90	89	113	94	97
NY	66	37	27	2	361	272	8	2	69	26	41	2	347	424	17	12	135	63	68	4	708	696	25	14	39	105	50	87	100	97	95	94
PHI	76	54	22	0	554	378	14	10	57	24	32	1	269	329	9	12	133	78	54	1	823	707	23	22	88	73	72	115	99	91	108	107
PIT	40	14	25	1	225	261	3	5	98	9	88	1	373	971	17	47	138	23	113	2	598	1232	20	52	33	90	170	87	98	154	88	95

1891 NATIONAL LEAGUE

TM	G	W	L	T	R	OR	HR	OHR	G	W	L	T	R	OR	HR	OHR	G	W	L	T	R	OR	HR	OHR	HRF	HRB	HRP	RF	RB	RP	BPF	PPF
BOS	73	51	20	2	527	328	34	33	67	36	31	0	320	330	19	18	140	87	51	2	847	658	53	51	155	115	111	119	96	79	112	109
BRO	72	41	31	0	438	383	11	19	65	20	45	0	327	438	12	21	137	61	76	0	765	821	23	40	83	70	114	97	104	111	97	98
CHI	67	43	22	2	467	343	39	30	70	39	31	0	366	387	21	23	137	82	53	2	833	730	60	53	153	137	127	112	103	92	106	105
CIN	67	26	41	0	296	328	19	17	71	30	40	1	350	463	21	23	138	56	81	1	646	791	40	40	87	118	117	83	93	110	91	93
CLE	69	40	28	1	484	426	4	6	72	25	46	1	352	462	18	18	141	65	74	2	836	888	22	24	32	76	91	114	102	108	105	106
NY	69	39	28	2	377	361	28	14	67	32	33	2	377	409	18	12	136	71	61	4	754	711	46	26	131	105	65	86	107	101	94	93
PHI	69	35	34	0	372	350	8	9	69	33	35	1	384	423	13	20	138	68	69	1	756	773	21	29	55	72	92	91	104	106	95	95
PIT	66	32	34	0	379	316	14	9	71	23	46	2	300	428	15	22	137	55	80	2	679	744	29	31	69	95	92	102	89	95	101	102

1892 NATIONAL LEAGUE

TM	G	W	L	T	R	OR	HR	OHR	G	W	L	T	R	OR	HR	OHR	G	W	L	T	R	OR	HR	OHR	HRF	HRB	HRP	RF	RB	RP	BPF	PPF
BAL	79	29	46	4	472	486	13	14	73	17	55	1	307	534	17	37	152	46	101	5	779	1020	30	51	47	137	196	103	101	131	99	101
BOS	76	54	21	1	490	344	20	27	76	48	27	1	372	305	14	14	152	102	48	2	862	649	34	41	162	78	89	123	98	76	113	111
BRO	78	51	24	3	485	340	14	8	80	44	35	1	450	393	16	18	158	95	59	4	935	733	30	26	69	99	81	101	114	92	101	99
CHI	67	36	31	0	292	278	9	9	80	34	45	1	343	457	17	26	147	70	76	1	635	735	26	35	52	104	126	86	91	102	93	94
CIN	80	45	32	3	414	352	29	21	75	37	36	2	326	379	15	18	155	82	68	5	766	731	44	39	138	103	97	105	93	90	103	103
CLE	79	54	24	1	483	281	4	4	74	39	32	3	372	332	22	24	153	93	56	4	855	613	26	28	18	128	133	103	106	78	103	101
LOU	70	37	31	2	309	286	7	3	84	26	58	0	340	518	11	23	154	63	89	2	649	804	18	26	37	86	82	84	91	107	92	93
NY	79	42	36	1	452	382	26	12	74	29	44	1	359	444	13	20	153	71	80	2	811	826	39	32	107	106	92	97	106	108	98	98
PHI	81	55	26	0	512	322	34	8	74	32	40	2	348	368	16	16	155	87	66	2	860	690	50	24	119	123	68	107	103	86	104	103
PIT	87	52	34	1	477	363	32	14	68	28	39	1	325	433	6	14	155	80	73	2	802	796	38	28	169	67	88	109	109	94	94	
STL	75	37	36	2	379	380	32	32	80	19	58	3	324	542	13	15	155	56	94	5	703	922	45	47	215	82	88	93	94	119	95	97
WAS	70	34	36	0	404	379	23	22	83	24	57	2	327	490	14	18	153	58	93	2	731	869	37	40	156	85	93	111	90	105	105	106

1893 NATIONAL LEAGUE

TM	G	W	L	T	R	OR	HR	OHR	G	W	L	T	R	OR	HR	OHR	G	W	L	T	R	OR	HR	OHR	HRF	HRB	HRP	RF	RB	RP	BPF	PPF
BAL	60	36	24	0	451	404	16	9	70	24	46	0	369	489	11	20	130	60	70	0	820	893	27	29	94	73	74	114	90	98	107	108
BOS	65	49	15	1	557	350	48	41	66	37	28	1	451	445	17	25	131	86	43	2	1008	795	65	66	199	113	125	104	114	92	103	101
BRO	67	43	24	0	393	348	24	17	63	22	39	2	382	497	21	24	130	65	63	2	775	845	45	41	87	129	117	81	101	108	91	91
CHI	73	38	34	1	538	471	20	15	55	18	37	0	291	403	12	11	128	56	71	1	829	874	32	26	112	77	64	108	93	101	104	104
CIN	66	37	27	2	424	375	19	21	65	28	36	1	335	439	10	17	131	65	63	3	759	814	29	38	141	61	82	102	87	93	101	102
CLE	72	49	23	0	579	440	10	9	59	26	33	0	397	399	22	26	131	75	56	1	976	839	32	35	36	133	137	108	110	97	104	103
LOU	53	24	28	1	329	367	3	14	73	26	47	0	430	575	16	24	126	50	75	1	759	942	19	38	60	53	124	95	96	115	96	98
NY	71	49	20	2	571	390	48	19	65	19	44	2	370	455	13	17	136	68	64	4	941	845	61	36	188	95	72	106	101	93	103	103
PHI	66	43	22	1	569	451	35	13	67	29	35	3	452	490	15	11	133	72	57	4	1011	841	80	30	113	90	80	116	99	88	100	98
PIT	73	54	19	0	593	417	25	8	58	27	29	2	377	349	12	21	131	81	48	2	970	766	37	29	82	105	84	111	104	86	106	105
STL	72	40	30	2	424	405	7	14	63	17	45	1	321	424	3	24	135	57	75	3	745	829	10	38	69	32	104	97	85	94	99	100

	HOME								ROAD								ALL															
TM	G	W	L	T	R	OR	HR	OHR	G	W	L	T	R	OR	HR	OHR	G	W	L	T	R	OR	HR	OHR	HRF	HRB	HRP	RF	RB	RP	BPF	PPF
WAS	49	21	27	1	281	298	8	7	81	19	62	0	441	734	15	47	130	40	89	1	722	1032	23	54	41	102	153	81	97	124	89	92

1894 NATIONAL LEAGUE

TM	G	W	L	T	R	OR	HR	OHR	G	W	L	T	R	OR	HR	OHR	G	W	L	T	R	OR	HR	OHR	HRF	HRB	HRP	RF	RB	RP	BPF	PPF
BAL	67	52	15	0	626	378	13	9	62	37	24	1	545	441	20	22	129	89	39	1	1171	819	33	31	52	85	75	97	124	90	99	96
BOS	63	44	19	0	670	519	77	70	70	39	30	1	550	483	26	19	133	83	49	1	1220	1002	103	89	301	105	87	127	111	93	113	111
BRO	68	42	24	2	512	452	22	15	66	28	37	1	509	555	20	26	134	70	61	3	1021	1007	42	41	80	88	83	89	110	108	94	94
CHI	67	35	30	2	625	513	26	13	68	22	45	1	416	553	39	30	135	57	75	3	1041	1066	65	43	59	153	100	116	97	100	108	108
CIN	67	38	28	1	512	515	43	45	65	17	47	1	398	570	18	40	132	55	75	2	910	1085	61	85	141	97	141	102	93	110	100	101
CLE	59	35	24	0	511	411	8	18	71	33	37	1	421	485	29	36	130	68	61	1	932	896	37	54	51	86	136	121	89	85	111	111
LOU	61	24	37	0	317	366	16	7	69	12	57	0	375	635	26	32	130	36	94	0	692	1001	42	39	46	117	89	76	83	113	88	91
NY	69	49	17	3	477	362	29	21	68	39	27	2	463	427	14	16	137	88	44	5	940	789	43	37	158	58	53	95	94	80	100	98
PHI	69	48	20	1	674	398	26	31	60	23	37	0	469	568	14	31	129	71	57	1	1143	966	40	62	110	74	115	91	127	109	95	94
PIT	75	46	28	1	559	475	26	11	57	19	37	1	396	497	22	28	132	65	65	2	955	972	48	39	58	122	94	89	104	108	94	94
STL	66	34	32	0	429	438	30	16	67	22	44	1	342	515	24	32	133	56	76	1	771	953	54	48	84	113	97	102	78	95	101	103
WAS	62	32	30	0	476	463	35	20	70	13	57	0	406	659	24	39	132	45	87	0	882	1122	59	59	97	118	114	98	94	115	98	100

1895 NATIONAL LEAGUE

TM	G	W	L	T	R	OR	HR	OHR	G	W	L	T	R	OR	HR	OHR	G	W	L	T	R	OR	HR	OHR	HRF	HRB	HRP	RF	RB	RP	BPF	PPF
BAL	67	54	12	1	581	293	10	8	65	33	31	1	428	353	15	23	132	87	43	2	1009	646	25	31	49	86	95	110	108	72	107	104
BOS	67	48	19	0	537	363	50	38	65	23	41	1	370	463	4	18	132	71	60	1	907	826	54	56	314	50	80	105	101	94	103	102
BRO	66	43	22	1	444	334	22	20	67	28	38	1	423	500	17	21	133	71	60	2	867	834	39	41	112	91	96	87	106	101	94	94
CHI	69	43	26	0	477	439	32	23	64	29	32	3	389	415	23	15	133	72	58	3	866	854	55	38	131	117	83	106	96	95	103	103
CIN	65	42	22	1	528	404	8	7	67	24	42	1	375	450	28	32	132	66	64	2	903	854	36	39	27	144	144	115	96	92	108	107
CLE	60	47	13	0	423	274	5	10	71	37	33	1	494	446	24	23	131	84	46	1	917	720	29	33	41	88	117	90	110	87	97	95
LOU	59	19	38	2	328	447	14	12	74	16	58	0	370	643	20	28	133	35	96	2	698	1090	34	40	68	101	110	94	85	125	95	99
NY	67	40	27	0	424	376	14	8	65	26	38	1	428	458	18	26	132	66	65	1	852	834	32	34	51	112	103	89	104	101	95	94
PHI	73	51	21	1	653	455	42	16	60	27	32	1	415	502	19	20	133	78	53	2	1068	957	61	36	121	130	88	100	122	113	99	98
PIT	67	44	21	2	422	334	9	3	67	27	40	0	389	453	17	14	134	71	61	2	811	787	26	17	41	89	50	91	96	92	96	96
STL	67	25	41	1	411	491	26	35	68	14	51	3	336	541	12	29	135	39	92	4	747	1032	38	64	142	77	130	102	84	113	100	102
WAS	69	31	34	4	523	521	39	33	63	12	51	0	314	527	16	22	132	43	85	4	837	1048	55	55	160	103	110	110	92	115	103	105

1896 NATIONAL LEAGUE

TM	G	W	L	T	R	OR	HR	OHR	G	W	L	T	R	OR	HR	OHR	G	W	L	T	R	OR	HR	OHR	HRF	HRB	HRP	RF	RB	RP	BPF	PPF
BAL	67	49	16	2	528	310	8	4	65	41	23	1	467	352	15	18	132	90	39	3	995	662	23	22	38	103	82	101	122	84	102	99
BOS	67	42	24	1	510	371	23	39	65	32	33	0	350	390	13	18	132	74	57	1	860	761	36	57	181	80	119	115	99	90	108	107
BRO	65	35	28	2	298	298	13	19	68	23	45	0	394	466	15	20	133	58	73	2	692	764	28	39	95	85	116	74	99	107	87	88
CHI	68	42	24	2	470	427	19	16	64	29	33	2	345	372	15	14	132	71	57	4	815	799	34	30	113	94	84	117	94	93	108	108
CIN	66	51	15	0	450	292	6	1	62	26	35	1	333	328	14	26	128	77	50	1	783	620	20	27	18	141	97	106	96	78	105	103
CLE	64	43	19	2	445	315	9	4	71	37	29	5	395	335	19	23	135	80	48	7	840	650	28	27	37	124	95	116	94	75	110	108
LOU	64	25	37	2	326	471	24	38	70	13	56	1	327	526	13	10	134	38	93	3	653	997	37	48	249	69	76	100	83	121	98	102
NY	66	39	26	1	438	371	21	14	67	25	41	1	391	450	19	19	133	64	67	2	829	821	40	33	94	122	102	98	105	104	99	99
PHI	69	42	27	0	530	448	30	24	61	20	41	0	360	443	19	15	130	62	68	0	890	891	49	39	135	126	102	107	110	112	102	102
PIT	66	35	31	0	369	335	5	2	65	31	32	2	418	406	22	16	131	66	63	2	787	741	27	18	20	135	78	85	107	101	93	93
STL	62	27	34	1	322	374	25	18	69	13	56	0	271	555	12	22	131	40	90	1	593	929	37	40	134	95	106	92	80	118	95	98
WAS	68	38	29	1	462	395	30	12	65	20	44	1	356	525	15	12	133	58	73	2	818	920	45	24	142	104	62	93	108	119	95	96

1897 NATIONAL LEAGUE

TM	G	W	L	T	R	OR	HR	OHR	G	W	L	T	R	OR	HR	OHR	G	W	L	T	R	OR	HR	OHR	HRF	HRB	HRP	RF	RB	RP	BPF	PPF
BAL	69	51	15	3	470	293	4	7	67	39	25	3	494	381	15	11	136	90	40	6	964	674	19	18	44	75	83	87	127	91	95	92
BOS	67	54	12	1	573	307	26	26	68	39	27	2	452	358	19	13	135	93	39	3	1025	665	45	39	160	118	99	112	120	82	107	103
BRO	70	38	29	3	456	412	11	19	66	23	42	1	346	433	13	15	136	61	71	4	802	845	24	34	100	78	108	104	98	104	102	102
CHI	67	36	30	1	444	405	16	15	71	23	43	5	388	489	22	15	138	59	73	6	832	894	38	30	89	127	104	102	103	109	100	101
CIN	68	49	18	1	444	345	4	3	66	27	38	1	319	360	18	15	134	76	56	2	763	705	22	18	22	114	92	112	90	84	107	107
CLE	65	49	16	0	477	306	8	11	67	20	46	1	296	374	8	21	132	69	62	1	773	680	16	32	70	66	117	119	89	81	111	110
LOU	68	34	31	3	343	402	26	23	66	18	47	1	326	457	14	16	134	52	78	4	669	859	40	39	150	106	106	92	89	112	95	97
NY	75	51	19	5	495	347	16	12	62	32	29	1	400	348	15	14	137	83	48	6	895	695	31	26	82	109	93	95	113	90	98	96
PHI	67	32	34	1	381	357	17	6	67	23	43	1	371	435	23	22	134	55	77	2	752	792	40	28	53	181	115	91	100	104	96	96
PIT	65	38	27	0	354	363	10	5	70	22	44	4	322	472	15	17	135	60	71	4	676	835	25	22	53	108	84	97	87	105	98	100
STL	60	18	41	1	273	467	20	41	72	11	61	0	315	616	11	13	132	29	102	1	588	1083	31	54	254	67	101	93	81	141	93	99
WAS	68	40	26	2	434	372	28	13	67	21	45	1	347	421	8	14	135	61	71	3	781	793	36	27	171	79	72	103	99	101	102	

1898 NATIONAL LEAGUE

TM	G	W	L	T	R	OR	HR	OHR	G	W	L	T	R	OR	HR	OHR	G	W	L	T	R	OR	HR	OHR	HRF	HRB	HRP	RF	RB	RP	BPF	PPF
BAL	76	58	15	3	505	268	4	1	78	38	38	2	428	355	8	16	154	96	53	5	933	623	12	17	23	97	76	103	119	82	103	100
BOS	79	62	15	2	510	272	45	22	73	40	32	1	362	342	8	15	152	102	47	3	872	614	53	37	240	112	108	104	111	82	104	101
BRO	74	30	41	3	319	367	10	15	75	24	50	1	319	440	4	19	149	54	91	4	638	811	17	34	96	74	139	91	92	114	95	96
CHI	89	58	31	0	520	378	10	4	63	27	34	2	308	301	8	13	152	85	65	2	828	679	18	17	50	106	89	105	105	90	103	102
CIN	89	58	28	3	521	423	2	3	68	34	32	2	310	317	17	13	157	92	60	5	831	740	19	16	14	125	132	115	97	89	108	107
CLE	57	36	19	2	264	210	5	1	99	45	49	5	466	473	13	25	156	81	68	7	730	683	18	26	29	129	94	89	98	96	96	95
LOU	79	43	34	2	410	368	24	25	75	27	47	1	318	465	8	8	154	70	81	3	728	833	32	33	250	73	74	94	99	112	96	98
NY	76	45	28	3	423	322	18	10	81	32	45	4	414	478	16	11	157	77	73	7	837	800	34	21	110	126	81	90	114	108	95	94
PHI	81	49	31	1	452	371	13	9	69	29	40	0	371	413	20	14	150	78	71	1	823	784	33	23	57	177	128	90	117	113	94	94
PIT	75	39	35	1	316	312	6	3	77	33	41	3	318	382	8	11	152	72	76	4	634	694	14	14	51	77	65	93	87	94	97	98
STL	66	20	44	2	285	424	8	15	88	19	67	2	286	505	5	17	154	39	111	4	571	929	13	32	132	47	109	115	72	112	106	110
WAS	80	34	44	2	418	471	29	17	75	17	57	1	286	468	7	12	155	51	101	3	704	939	36	29	202	85	85	108	89	117	102	105

1899 NATIONAL LEAGUE

TM	G	W	L	T	R	OR	HR	OHR	G	W	L	T	R	OR	HR	OHR	G	W	L	T	R	OR	HR	OHR	HRF	HRB	HRP	RF	RB	RP	BPF	PPF
BAL	77	51	24	2	474	340	4	2	75	35	38	2	353	351	13	11	152	86	62	4	827	691	17	13	26	92	62	112	96	82	107	106
BOS	80	53	26	1	460	346	32	33	73	42	31	0	398	299	7	11	153	95	57	1	858	645	39	44	279	66	82	106	102	78	105	103
BRO	78	61	16	1	510	315	13	18	72	40	31	1	382	343	14	14	150	101	47	2	892	658	27	32	104	94	109	106	108	83	105	102
CHI	85	44	39	2	429	415	14	14	67	31	34	2	383	348	13	6	152	75	73	4	812	763	27	20	115	86	61	92	107	101	96	96
CIN	88	57	29	2	543	416	2	7	68	26	38	4	313	354	11	19	156	83	67	6	856	770	13	26	25	67	148	111	97	91	106	105
CLE	42	9	33	0	152	293	3	5	112	11	101	0	377	959	9	38	154	20	134	0	529	1252	12	43	46	64	149	87	75	154	89	96
LOU	63	33	28	2	369	306	23	17	92	42	49	1	458	469	17	16	155	75	77	3	827	775	40	33	166	108	92	106	100	93	103	103
NY	75	35	38	2	382	394	7	6	77	25	52	0	352	469	16	13	152	60	90	2	734	863	23	19	48	103	87	96	95	110	97	99
PHI	83	58	25	0	503	353	11	3	71	36	33	2	413	390	20	14	154	94	58	2	916	743	31	17	38	160	78	93	117	97	97	95
PIT	81	49	34	1	475	381	12	8	70	27	39	4	359	384	15	19	154	76	73	5	834	765	27	27	51	130	121	96	105	98	99	98
STL	87	50	33	4	480	446	38	33	68	34	34	0	339	293	9	8	155	84	67	4	819	739	47	41	275	79	70	114	93	84	108	107
WAS	79	35	43	1	418	447	30	15	76	19	55	2	325	536	17	20	155	54	98	3	743	983	47	35	114	150	119	96	96	123	96	98

1900 NATIONAL LEAGUE

TM	G	W	L	T	R	OR	HR	OHR	G	W	L	T	R	OR	HR	OHR	G	W	L	T	R	OR	HR	OHR	HRF	HRB	HRP	RF	RB	RP	BPF	PPF
BOS	73	42	29	2	507	420	40	43	69	24	43	2	271	319	8	16	142	66	72	4	778	739	48	59	254	80	111	140	85	84	120	120
BRO	73	43	26	4	452	394	15	15	69	39	28	2	364	328	11	15	142	82	54	6	816	722	26	30	109	77	89	114	102	92	108	106
CHI	77	45	30	2	337	329	12	5	69	20	45	4	298	422	21	18	146	65	75	6	635	751	33	21	44	139	86	84	91	105	93	94
CIN	63	27	34	2	255	309	12	9	81	35	43	3	448	436	21	19	144	62	77	5	703	745	33	28	70	117	99	83	99	107	92	93
NY	71	38	31	2	393	375	13	7	70	42	30	1	320	448	10	18	141	60	78	3	713	823	23	26	76	83	87	98	100	113	97	99
PHI	70	45	23	2	434	353	13	6	71	30	40	1	376	439	16	22	141	75	63	3	810	792	29	29	57	122	108	99	113	110	98	98
PIT	70	42	28	0	359	315	14	7	70	37	32	1	374	297	12	17	140	79	60	1	733	612	26	24	76	94	82	101	98	83	103	101
STL	72	40	31	1	383	317	23	18	70	25	44	1	361	431	13	19	142	65	75	2	744	748	36	37	120	103	109	87	108	108	93	98

1901 NATIONAL LEAGUE

TM	G	W	L	T	R	OR	HR	OHR	G	W	L	T	R	OR	HR	OHR	G	W	L	T	R	OR	HR	OHR	HRF	HRB	HRP	RF	RB	RP	BPF	PPF
BOS	70	41	29	0	297	298	18	17	70	28	40	2	234	258	10	12	140	69	69	2	531	556	28	29	148	78	83	118	73	77	112	112

TM	HOME								ROAD								ALL															
	G	W	L	T	R	OR	HR	OHR	G	W	L	T	R	OR	HR	OHR	G	W	L	T	R	OR	HR	OHR	HRF	HRB	HRP	RF	RB	RP	BPF	PPF
BRO	68	43	25	0	400	303	13	6	69	36	32	1	344	297	19	12	137	79	57	1	744	600	32	18	66	133	78	111	111	92	106	103
CHI	70	30	39	1	293	357	6	10	70	23	47	0	285	342	12	17	140	53	86	1	578	699	18	27	58	78	114	102	89	105	100	102
CIN	72	27	43	2	279	409	23	33	70	25	44	1	282	409	15	18	142	52	87	3	561	818	38	51	151	116	146	96	90	125	95	100
NY	71	30	38	3	255	350	8	11	70	22	47	1	289	405	11	13	141	52	85	4	544	755	19	24	79	72	89	86	91	122	91	95
PHI	69	46	23	0	349	247	11	6	71	37	34	0	319	296	13	13	140	83	57	0	668	543	24	19	71	95	73	101	100	84	103	100
PIT	69	45	24	0	372	255	15	8	71	45	25	1	404	279	14	12	140	90	49	1	776	534	29	20	93	102	72	97	119	86	101	96
STL	72	40	31	1	392	338	21	21	70	36	33	1	400	351	18	18	142	76	64	2	792	689	39	39	112	135	135	96	125	111	97	95

1902 NATIONAL LEAGUE

TM	HOME								ROAD								ALL															
	G	W	L	T	R	OR	HR	OHR	G	W	L	T	R	OR	HR	OHR	G	W	L	T	R	OR	HR	OHR	HRF	HRB	HRP	RF	RB	RP	BPF	PPF
BOS	72	42	27	3	283	230	13	11	70	31	37	2	289	286	1	5	142	73	64	5	572	516	14	16	286	45	75	88	106	97	95	94
BRO	69	45	23	1	277	210	8	2	72	30	40	2	287	309	11	8	141	75	63	3	564	519	19	10	58	197	101	87	107	98	95	94
CHI	70	31	38	1	228	249	1	3	71	37	31	3	302	252	5	6	141	68	69	4	530	501	6	9	40	58	100	89	98	94	96	95
CIN	70	35	35	0	353	305	11	8	71	35	35	1	280	261	7	7	141	70	70	1	633	566	18	15	132	130	113	120	103	93	110	108
NY	71	24	44	3	214	297	7	7	68	24	44	0	187	293	1	9	139	48	88	3	401	590	8	16	127	54	115	100	73	102	100	104
PHI	69	29	39	1	264	351	6	6	69	27	42	0	220	298	4	6	138	56	81	1	484	649	5	12	72	44	108	115	84	108	105	109
PIT	71	56	15	0	410	207	9	2	71	47	21	3	365	233	9	2	142	103	36	3	775	440	18	4	102	130	33	105	130	80	105	98
STL	70	28	38	4	262	336	3	6	70	28	40	2	255	359	7	10	140	56	78	6	517	695	10	16	56	108	167	97	98	126	95	99

1903 NATIONAL LEAGUE

TM	HOME								ROAD								ALL															
	G	W	L	T	R	OR	HR	OHR	G	W	L	T	R	OR	HR	OHR	G	W	L	T	R	OR	HR	OHR	HRF	HRB	HRP	RF	RB	RP	BPF	PPF
BOS	68	31	35	2	283	314	11	19	72	27	45	0	295	385	14	11	140	58	80	2	578	699	25	30	122	132	150	93	90	106	96	98
BRO	73	40	33	0	359	361	8	9	66	30	33	3	308	321	7	9	139	70	66	3	667	682	15	18	97	81	95	103	99	101	101	102
CHI	73	45	28	0	345	285	2	7	66	37	28	1	350	314	7	7	139	82	56	1	695	599	9	14	62	53	89	88	110	97	95	93
CIN	76	41	35	0	440	389	12	7	65	33	30	2	325	267	16	7	141	74	65	2	765	656	28	14	74	96	93	117	104	90	109	107
NY	70	41	27	2	368	296	9	10	72	43	28	1	361	271	11	10	142	84	55	3	729	567	20	20	95	108	108	108	101	81	106	103
PHI	61	25	33	3	250	298	9	6	78	24	53	1	367	440	3	15	139	49	86	4	617	738	12	21	104	67	102	87	100	117	92	94
PIT	70	46	24	0	393	327	17	5	71	45	25	1	400	286	17	4	141	91	49	1	793	613	34	9	107	161	50	107	113	90	105	101
STL	69	22	45	2	248	393	7	13	70	21	49	0	257	402	1	12	139	43	94	2	505	795	8	25	143	32	105	97	79	118	96	102

1904 NATIONAL LEAGUE

TM	HOME								ROAD								ALL															
	G	W	L	T	R	OR	HR	OHR	G	W	L	T	R	OR	HR	OHR	G	W	L	T	R	OR	HR	OHR	HRF	HRB	HRP	RF	RB	RP	BPF	PPF
BOS	79	34	45	0	269	363	13	11	76	21	53	2	222	386	11	14	155	55	98	2	491	749	24	25	92	118	122	99	84	121	96	102
BRO	76	31	44	1	234	287	3	11	78	25	53	0	263	327	12	16	154	56	97	1	497	614	15	27	54	84	161	90	87	104	95	98
CHI	78	49	27	2	303	240	6	10	78	44	33	1	296	277	16	6	156	93	60	3	599	517	22	16	76	105	87	96	98	86	100	99
CIN	79	49	27	3	409	295	12	6	78	39	38	1	286	252	9	7	157	88	65	4	695	547	21	13	110	85	56	125	98	80	114	111
NY	84	56	26	2	397	258	23	30	74	50	21	3	347	218	8	6	158	106	47	5	744	476	31	36	262	81	81	104	115	77	105	100
PHI	73	28	43	2	269	348	7	7	82	24	57	1	302	436	16	15	155	52	100	3	571	784	23	22	53	135	132	93	102	133	93	97
PIT	78	48	30	0	338	286	5	2	78	39	36	3	337	306	10	11	156	87	66	3	675	592	15	13	37	100	71	98	111	99	99	98
STL	76	39	36	1	298	280	14	15	79	36	43	0	304	315	10	8	155	75	79	1	602	595	24	23	154	88	83	97	100	99	99	99

1905 NATIONAL LEAGUE

TM	HOME								ROAD								ALL															
	G	W	L	T	R	OR	HR	OHR	G	W	L	T	R	OR	HR	OHR	G	W	L	T	R	OR	HR	OHR	HRF	HRB	HRP	RF	RB	RP	BPF	PPF
BOS	76	29	46	1	234	344	14	14	80	22	57	1	234	389	3	22	156	51	103	2	468	733	17	36	114	73	145	96	76	112	97	102
BRO	77	29	47	1	273	379	16	16	78	19	57	2	233	428	13	8	155	48	104	3	506	807	29	24	142	108	87	98	83	125	96	102
CHI	81	54	25	2	365	212	9	4	74	38	36	0	302	230	5	10	155	92	61	2	667	442	14	14	71	61	64	100	100	70	105	100
CIN	79	50	28	1	438	330	12	2	76	29	46	1	297	368	15	20	155	79	74	2	735	698	27	22	42	191	117	110	111	108	103	103
NY	76	54	21	1	379	234	33	19	79	51	27	1	401	271	6	6	155	105	48	2	780	505	39	25	317	75	58	97	121	83	101	96
PHI	76	39	36	1	353	314	8	9	79	44	33	2	355	288	8	12	155	83	69	3	708	602	16	21	90	73	92	107	107	93	104	102
PIT	78	49	28	1	362	287	4	1	77	47	29	1	330	283	18	11	155	96	57	2	692	570	22	12	19	156	72	105	104	88	104	102
STL	77	32	45	0	245	342	13	10	77	26	51	0	290	392	7	18	154	58	96	0	535	734	20	28	92	97	126	87	93	122	91	95

1906 NATIONAL LEAGUE

TM	HOME								ROAD								ALL															
	G	W	L	T	R	OR	HR	OHR	G	W	L	T	R	OR	HR	OHR	G	W	L	T	R	OR	HR	OHR	HRF	HRB	HRP	RF	RB	RP	BPF	PPF
BOS	76	28	47	1	218	329	11	16	76	21	55	0	190	320	5	8	152	49	102	1	408	649	16	24	180	76	110	104	75	113	100	106
BRO	76	31	44	1	191	287	9	5	77	35	42	0	305	338	16	10	153	66	86	1	496	625	25	15	57	206	133	77	104	129	86	90
CHI	79	56	21	2	345	214	7	6	76	60	15	1	360	167	13	6	155	116	36	3	705	381	20	12	71	141	95	104	120	69	107	99
CIN	78	36	40	2	316	333	10	10	77	28	47	2	217	249	6	4	155	64	87	4	533	582	16	14	175	73	61	130	83	91	115	116
NY	75	51	24	0	309	239	9	8	78	45	32	1	316	271	6	5	153	96	56	1	625	510	15	13	151	73	65	99	114	96	100	97
PHI	77	37	40	0	226	270	2	5	77	34	42	1	302	294	10	13	154	71	82	1	528	564	12	18	33	106	172	85	104	111	92	93
PIT	77	49	27	1	325	232	4	8	77	44	33	0	298	238	8	5	154	93	60	1	623	470	12	13	94	75	82	104	109	85	104	101
STL	77	28	48	1	241	313	6	10	77	24	50	3	229	294	4	7	154	52	98	4	470	607	10	17	136	53	87	104	85	106	101	104

1907 NATIONAL LEAGUE

TM	HOME								ROAD								ALL															
	G	W	L	T	R	OR	HR	OHR	G	W	L	T	R	OR	HR	OHR	G	W	L	T	R	OR	HR	OHR	HRF	HRB	HRP	RF	RB	RP	BPF	PPF
BOS	74	31	42	1	253	304	14	20	78	27	48	1	249	348	8	8	152	58	90	4	502	652	22	28	192	94	110	98	102	128	95	99
BRO	77	37	38	2	223	232	9	10	76	28	45	3	223	290	9	6	153	65	83	5	446	522	18	16	121	93	82	88	91	104	94	96
CHI	76	54	19	3	282	198	2	5	79	53	26	0	292	192	11	6	155	107	45	3	574	390	13	11	47	80	89	105	103	73	106	102
CIN	81	43	36	2	287	227	3	5	75	23	51	1	239	292	12	11	156	66	87	3	526	519	15	16	35	117	139	90	105	103	95	95
NY	77	45	30	2	317	250	19	19	78	37	41	0	257	260	4	6	155	82	71	2	574	510	23	25	284	63	75	110	103	94	105	104
PHI	75	45	30	0	265	247	2	4	74	38	34	2	247	229	10	9	149	83	64	2	512	476	12	13	34	90	115	106	97	91	104	103
PIT	77	47	29	1	330	258	7	3	80	44	34	2	304	252	12	9	157	91	63	3	634	510	19	12	53	133	82	110	113	94	105	102
STL	79	31	47	1	223	291	9	10	76	21	54	1	196	317	10	10	155	52	101	2	419	608	19	20	91	115	120	95	83	115	96	100

1908 NATIONAL LEAGUE

TM	HOME								ROAD								ALL															
	G	W	L	T	R	OR	HR	OHR	G	W	L	T	R	OR	HR	OHR	G	W	L	T	R	OR	HR	OHR	HRF	HRB	HRP	RF	RB	RP	BPF	PPF
BOS	78	35	42	1	295	328	13	20	78	28	49	1	242	294	4	9	156	63	91	2	537	622	17	29	211	56	98	113	100	113	104	106
BRO	77	27	50	0	179	243	16	3	77	26	51	0	198	273	12	14	154	53	101	0	377	516	28	17	74	178	105	89	77	102	95	99
CHI	78	47	30	1	294	264	9	15	80	52	25	3	330	197	10	6	158	99	55	4	624	461	19	20	154	83	77	109	112	86	106	102
CIN	77	40	37	0	260	272	8	7	78	33	44	1	229	272	6	12	155	73	81	1	489	544	14	19	86	81	103	106	92	102	103	104
NY	80	52	25	3	343	235	10	11	77	46	31	0	309	221	10	15	157	98	56	3	652	456	20	26	84	122	151	106	120	88	104	100
PHI	78	43	34	1	251	213	0	3	77	40	37	0	253	232	11	5	155	83	71	1	504	445	11	8	21	53	94	95	98	88	100	98
PIT	77	42	35	0	227	255	12	4	78	56	21	1	358	214	13	12	155	98	56	1	585	469	25	16	69	159	100	88	118	100	95	92
STL	77	28	49	0	185	295	9	11	77	21	56	0	186	331	8	5	154	49	105	0	371	626	17	16	142	75	67	92	78	122	94	100

1909 NATIONAL LEAGUE

TM	HOME								ROAD								ALL															
	G	W	L	T	R	OR	HR	OHR	G	W	L	T	R	OR	HR	OHR	G	W	L	T	R	OR	HR	OHR	HRF	HRB	HRP	RF	RB	RP	BPF	PPF
BOS	76	27	47	2	219	326	11	9	79	18	61	0	216	357	4	14	155	45	108	2	435	683	15	23	119	76	114	97	80	118	96	102
BRO	79	34	45	0	238	311	12	9	76	21	53	2	206	316	4	23	155	55	98	2	444	627	16	32	76	115	186	100	79	107	99	103
CHI	77	47	29	1	281	199	8	0	78	57	20	1	354	191	12	6	155	104	49	2	635	390	20	6	49	131	31	92	111	73	100	95
CIN	80	39	38	3	282	299	5	2	76	38	38	0	324	300	17	3	156	77	76	3	606	599	22	5	36	143	46	90	113	112	94	94
NY	77	44	33	0	298	294	19	23	81	48	28	5	325	252	7	5	158	92	61	5	623	546	26	28	278	77	73	108	103	92	105	103
PHI	77	40	37	0	266	279	6	10	77	34	42	1	250	239	6	13	154	74	79	1	516	518	12	23	86	71	125	110	86	86	106	106
PIT	78	56	21	1	354	237	10	6	75	54	21	0	345	210	15	6	153	110	42	1	699	447	25	12	77	143	77	104	119	80	105	99
STL	76	26	48	2	271	387	9	12	78	28	50	0	312	344	6	10	154	54	98	2	583	731	15	22	127	71	101	101	107	130	96	99

1910 NATIONAL LEAGUE

TM	HOME								ROAD								ALL															
	G	W	L	T	R	OR	HR	OHR	G	W	L	T	R	OR	HR	OHR	G	W	L	T	R	OR	HR	OHR	HRF	HRB	HRP	RF	RB	RP	BPF	PPF
BOS	78	29	48	1	292	396	25	25	79	24	52	3	203	305	6	11	157	53	100	4	495	701	31	36	236	64	82	129	68	94	114	118
BRO	80	39	39	2	255	287	9	5	76	25	51	0	242	336	16	12	156	64	90	2	497	623	25	17	50	119	81	89	83	101	95	98
CHI	77	58	19	0	354	231	18	9	78	54	23	1	358	268	16	9	155	104	50	0	712	499	34	18	109	118	67	96	114	83	101	96
CIN	77	39	37	1	320	341	6	8	79	36	42	1	300	343	17	19	156	75	79	2	620	684	23	27	43	116	138	105	98	106	101	102
NY	79	52	26	1	352	255	20	17	76	39	37	0	363	312	11	13	155	91	63	1	715	567	31	30	141	96	96	89	120	98	95	92
PHI	78	40	36	2	333	290	12	10	79	41	35	2	341	349	10	11	157	78	73	4	674	639	22	36	107	81	126	93	111	106	96	95
PIT	76	46	30	0	365	308	17	8	78	40	37	1	290	268	16	12	154	86	67	1	655	576	33	20	93	125	80	121	94	85	112	110
STL	76	35	41	0	312	316	3	14	77	28	49	0	327	402	12	16	153	63	90	0	639	718	15	30	64	64	134	88	114	125	91	93

1911 NATIONAL LEAGUE

TM	HOME G	W	L	T	R	OR	HR	OHR	ROAD G	W	L	T	R	OR	HR	OHR	ALL G	W	L	T	R	OR	HR	OHR	HRF	HRB	HRP	RF	RB	RP	BPF	PPF
BOS	75	19	54	2	391	536	28	47	81	25	53	3	308	485	9	29	156	44	107	5	699	1021	37	76	184	68	139	120	98	136	103	109
BRO	74	31	42	1	247	303	10	11	80	33	44	3	292	356	18	16	154	64	86	4	539	659	28	27	69	79	78	92	82	98	97	99
CHI	84	49	32	3	380	306	26	13	73	43	30	0	377	301	28	13	157	92	62	3	757	607	54	26	85	140	74	90	114	94	97	94
CIN	82	38	42	2	331	317	5	6	77	32	41	4	351	389	16	30	159	70	83	6	682	706	21	36	25	89	126	84	106	109	92	92
NY	75	49	25	1	357	267	25	13	79	50	29	0	399	275	16	20	154	99	54	1	756	542	41	33	111	97	81	99	108	81	102	98
PHI	76	42	34	0	352	357	48	26	77	37	39	1	306	312	12	17	153	79	73	1	658	669	60	43	216	90	80	114	91	92	107	108
PIT	78	48	29	1	393	246	29	6	77	37	40	0	351	311	20	30	155	85	69	1	744	557	49	36	72	151	102	96	108	83	101	97
STL	79	36	38	5	343	380	11	12	79	39	36	4	328	365	15	27	158	75	74	9	671	745	26	39	58	84	113	104	95	104	101	102

1912 NATIONAL LEAGUE

TM	HOME G	W	L	T	R	OR	HR	OHR	ROAD G	W	L	T	R	OR	HR	OHR	ALL G	W	L	T	R	OR	HR	OHR	HRF	HRB	HRP	RF	RB	RP	BPF	PPF
BOS	79	31	47	1	407	471	22	28	76	21	54	1	286	390	13	15	155	52	101	2	693	861	35	43	155	76	91	119	90	109	107	110
BRO	76	33	43	0	303	368	17	20	77	25	52	0	348	386	15	25	153	58	95	0	651	754	32	45	93	96	128	92	97	110	95	97
CHI	77	46	29	2	394	347	22	18	75	45	30	0	362	321	21	15	152	91	59	2	756	668	43	33	108	115	91	106	104	93	104	102
CIN	77	45	32	0	309	311	7	2	78	30	46	2	347	411	14	26	155	75	78	2	656	722	21	28	25	110	88	85	100	108	92	93
NY	76	49	25	2	387	302	31	21	78	54	23	1	436	269	16	15	154	103	48	3	823	571	47	36	160	99	81	102	112	81	104	99
PHI	75	34	41	0	318	352	25	26	77	39	38	0	352	336	18	17	152	73	79	0	670	688	43	43	141	103	103	100	95	98	100	101
PIT	76	45	31	0	347	275	15	10	76	48	27	1	404	290	24	18	152	93	58	1	751	565	39	28	63	130	97	92	108	85	99	95
STL	77	37	40	0	354	414	14	9	76	26	50	0	305	416	13	22	153	63	90	0	659	830	27	31	67	92	95	104	94	115	99	102

1913 NATIONAL LEAGUE

TM	HOME G	W	L	T	R	OR	HR	OHR	ROAD G	W	L	T	R	OR	HR	OHR	ALL G	W	L	T	R	OR	HR	OHR	HRF	HRB	HRP	RF	RB	RP	BPF	PPF
BOS	77	34	40	3	298	337	14	12	77	35	42	0	343	353	18	25	154	69	82	3	641	690	32	37	63	104	112	92	106	113	95	96
BRO	77	29	47	1	296	343	20	14	75	36	37	2	299	270	19	19	152	65	84	3	595	613	39	33	88	108	92	108	91	93	104	105
CHI	76	51	25	0	372	278	37	20	79	37	40	2	348	352	22	19	155	88	65	2	720	630	59	39	138	127	92	98	113	101	99	97
CIN	78	32	44	2	307	380	15	13	78	32	45	1	300	337	12	27	156	64	89	3	607	717	27	40	74	83	109	106	92	107	102	104
NY	81	54	23	4	367	250	22	22	75	47	28	0	317	265	8	16	156	101	51	4	684	515	30	38	158	55	75	100	103	80	103	100
PHI	78	43	33	2	361	366	51	23	81	45	30	6	332	270	22	17	159	88	63	8	693	636	73	40	177	130	83	123	95	87	112	111
PIT	79	41	35	3	324	277	13	6	76	37	36	3	349	308	22	20	155	78	71	6	673	585	35	26	47	121	84	90	109	97	96	94
STL	74	25	48	1	239	346	8	20	79	26	51	2	289	409	7	37	153	51	99	3	528	755	15	57	70	52	156	89	90	123	92	97

1914 NATIONAL LEAGUE

TM	HOME G	W	L	T	R	OR	HR	OHR	ROAD G	W	L	T	R	OR	HR	OHR	ALL G	W	L	T	R	OR	HR	OHR	HRF	HRB	HRP	RF	RB	RP	BPF	PPF
BOS	79	51	25	3	339	279	17	16	79	43	34	2	318	269	18	22	158	94	59	5	657	548	35	38	85	115	122	106	104	89	104	102
BRO	79	45	34	0	342	306	17	17	75	30	45	0	280	312	14	19	154	75	79	0	622	618	31	36	98	96	110	103	104	104	101	101
CHI	76	46	30	0	318	281	22	20	80	32	46	2	287	357	20	17	156	78	76	2	605	638	42	37	117	119	106	98	103	107	98	99
CIN	77	34	42	1	290	328	4	5	79	26	52	2	240	323	12	25	157	60	94	3	530	651	16	30	28	78	118	111	84	101	105	107
NY	80	43	36	1	316	288	16	24	76	41	34	1	356	288	14	23	156	84	70	2	672	576	30	47	103	94	138	91	118	103	96	94
PHI	78	48	30	0	377	321	50	16	76	26	50	0	274	366	12	10	154	74	80	0	651	687	62	26	235	100	56	105	109	116	100	101
PIT	77	39	36	2	234	214	3	6	81	30	49	2	269	326	15	21	158	69	85	4	503	540	18	27	29	73	114	81	90	95	92	93
STL	79	42	34	3	285	280	20	14	79	39	38	1	273	260	13	12	157	81	72	4	558	540	33	26	129	82	68	104	89	87	104	103

1915 NATIONAL LEAGUE

TM	HOME G	W	L	T	R	OR	HR	OHR	ROAD G	W	L	T	R	OR	HR	OHR	ALL G	W	L	T	R	OR	HR	OHR	HRF	HRB	HRP	RF	RB	RP	BPF	PPF
BOS	78	49	27	2	280	263	3	5	79	34	42	3	302	282	14	18	157	83	69	5	582	545	17	23	28	85	118	95	104	98	98	97
BRO	78	51	26	1	299	263	9	14	76	29	46	1	237	297	5	15	154	80	72	2	536	560	14	29	111	47	93	102	95	99	101	102
CHI	77	42	34	1	296	314	31	16	79	31	46	2	274	306	22	12	156	73	80	3	570	620	53	28	135	162	94	107	99	106	102	103
CIN	79	39	37	3	265	295	6	7	81	32	46	3	251	290	9	21	160	71	83	6	516	585	15	28	48	75	115	105	87	97	103	104
NY	76	37	38	1	275	270	15	20	79	32	45	2	307	358	9	20	155	69	83	3	582	628	24	40	121	81	129	86	114	121	91	92
PHI	77	49	27	0	313	235	46	18	77	41	35	1	276	228	12	8	153	90	62	1	589	463	58	26	255	111	61	110	99	80	107	104
PIT	79	40	37	2	290	241	8	6	77	33	44	0	267	279	16	15	156	73	81	2	557	520	24	21	47	113	97	95	100	94	99	98
STL	81	42	36	3	320	303	11	10	76	30	45	1	270	298	9	20	157	72	81	4	590	601	20	30	71	87	117	102	103	105	100	100

1916 NATIONAL LEAGUE

TM	HOME G	W	L	T	R	OR	HR	OHR	ROAD G	W	L	T	R	OR	HR	OHR	ALL G	W	L	T	R	OR	HR	OHR	HRF	HRB	HRP	RF	RB	RP	BPF	PPF
BOS	78	41	31	6	224	207	6	4	80	48	32	0	318	246	16	20	158	89	63	6	542	453	22	24	31	112	104	81	106	92	93	91
BRO	78	50	27	1	300	233	19	9	78	44	33	1	285	238	9	15	156	94	60	2	585	471	28	24	115	82	75	103	105	87	103	100
CHI	79	37	41	1	309	317	34	22	77	30	45	2	211	224	12	10	156	67	86	3	520	541	46	32	208	96	73	133	82	85	117	117
CIN	76	32	44	0	242	312	4	10	79	28	49	2	263	305	10	25	155	60	93	2	505	617	14	35	44	66	146	100	96	115	98	101
NY	78	47	30	1	291	229	21	23	77	39	36	2	306	275	21	18	155	86	66	3	597	504	42	41	111	143	139	90	117	101	96	93
PHI	79	50	29	0	281	233	29	17	75	41	33	1	300	256	13	11	154	91	62	1	581	489	42	28	166	102	75	90	114	98	96	94
PIT	78	37	40	1	268	298	9	5	79	28	49	2	216	288	11	19	157	65	89	3	484	586	20	24	50	93	91	111	85	101	105	107
STL	76	36	40	0	251	295	12	15	77	24	53	0	225	334	13	16	153	60	93	0	476	629	25	31	94	88	106	98	94	119	97	100

1917 NATIONAL LEAGUE

TM	HOME G	W	L	T	R	OR	HR	OHR	ROAD G	W	L	T	R	OR	HR	OHR	ALL G	W	L	T	R	OR	HR	OHR	HRF	HRB	HRP	RF	RB	RP	BPF	PPF
BOS	77	35	42	0	240	269	13	3	80	37	39	4	296	283	9	16	157	72	81	4	536	552	22	19	69	105	77	92	100	103	96	97
BRO	78	36	38	4	270	288	14	14	78	34	43	1	241	271	11	16	156	70	81	5	511	559	25	32	97	105	130	107	90	97	104	105
CHI	77	35	42	0	273	305	11	14	80	39	38	3	279	262	6	20	157	74	80	3	552	567	17	34	100	70	128	109	96	98	104	105
CIN	80	39	38	3	279	296	10	3	77	39	38	0	322	315	16	17	157	78	76	3	601	611	26	20	41	153	98	88	118	119	92	93
NY	80	50	28	2	294	220	21	17	78	48	28	2	341	237	18	12	158	98	56	4	635	457	39	29	121	142	109	89	117	88	97	93
PHI	76	46	29	1	297	270	26	20	78	41	36	1	281	230	12	5	154	87	65	2	578	500	38	25	229	96	58	113	99	87	108	106
PIT	79	25	53	1	232	307	2	4	78	26	50	2	232	288	7	10	157	51	103	3	464	595	9	14	37	45	72	100	84	105	100	103
STL	78	38	38	2	266	302	15	15	76	44	32	0	265	265	11	14	154	82	70	2	531	567	26	29	115	99	110	104	96	102	102	102

1918 NATIONAL LEAGUE

TM	HOME G	W	L	T	R	OR	HR	OHR	ROAD G	W	L	T	R	OR	HR	OHR	ALL G	W	L	T	R	OR	HR	OHR	HRF	HRB	HRP	RF	RB	RP	BPF	PPF
BOS	52	23	29	0	163	183	5	2	72	30	42	0	261	286	8	12	124	53	71	0	424	469	13	14	51	104	85	88	99	109	94	95
BRO	54	33	21	0	173	185	4	12	72	24	48	0	187	278	6	10	126	57	69	0	360	463	10	22	128	53	108	102	79	97	101	104
CHI	76	50	26	0	300	235	9	5	55	34	19	2	238	158	12	8	131	84	45	2	538	393	21	13	55	154	101	100	112	84	102	98
CIN	71	46	24	1	298	256	9	8	58	22	36	0	232	240	6	14	129	68	60	1	530	496	15	19	61	117	130	97	117	111	97	96
NY	56	35	21	0	204	181	9	13	68	36	32	0	276	234	4	7	124	71	53	0	480	415	13	20	207	51	78	93	109	96	98	96
PHI	57	27	29	1	220	261	19	13	68	28	39	1	210	246	6	9	125	55	68	2	430	507	25	22	212	93	93	121	88	102	109	111
PIT	69	41	27	1	270	232	9	4	57	24	33	0	196	180	6	9	126	65	60	1	466	412	15	13	74	99	84	109	96	86	106	105
STL	73	32	40	1	241	280	14	7	58	19	38	1	213	247	13	9	131	51	78	2	454	527	27	16	77	173	111	90	103	117	93	95

1919 NATIONAL LEAGUE

TM	HOME G	W	L	T	R	OR	HR	OHR	ROAD G	W	L	T	R	OR	HR	OHR	ALL G	W	L	T	R	OR	HR	OHR	HRF	HRB	HRP	RF	RB	RP	BPF	PPF
BOS	68	29	38	1	231	265	11	9	72	28	44	0	234	298	13	20	140	57	82	1	465	563	24	29	67	117	128	98	93	110	98	100
BRO	69	36	33	0	243	227	12	10	72	33	38	1	282	286	13	11	141	69	71	1	525	513	25	21	96	95	81	88	109	106	94	94
CHI	71	40	31	0	232	190	11	7	69	35	34	0	222	217	10	7	140	75	65	0	454	407	21	14	103	74	51	95	89	80	100	99
CIN	71	52	19	0	315	189	10	5	69	44	25	0	262	212	10	16	140	96	44	0	577	401	20	21	60	99	91	105	107	78	105	101
NY	69	46	23	0	310	209	28	17	71	41	30	0	295	261	12	17	140	87	53	0	605	470	40	34	150	124	117	98	119	95	100	96
PHI	71	26	44	0	307	378	29	24	67	21	46	0	203	321	3	16	138	47	90	1	510	699	42	40	156	133	133	118	96	128	104	108
PIT	70	40	30	0	273	218	8	7	69	31	38	0	199	248	9	16	139	71	68	0	472	466	17	23	62	83	100	107	88	88	105	105
STL	69	34	35	0	240	244	9	10	69	20	48	1	223	308	9	15	138	54	83	1	463	552	18	25	80	78	102	91	98	113	94	96

1920 NATIONAL LEAGUE

TM	HOME G	W	L	T	R	OR	HR	OHR	ROAD G	W	L	T	R	OR	HR	OHR	ALL G	W	L	T	R	OR	HR	OHR	HRF	HRB	HRP	RF	RB	RP	BPF	PPF
BOS	74	36	37	1	271	292	5	11	79	26	53	0	252	378	18	28	153	62	90	1	523	670	23	39	40	98	165	95	90	111	96	99
BRO	78	49	29	0	360	291	17	14	77	44	32	1	300	237	11	11	155	93	61	0	660	528	28	25	134	70	64	118	97	79	111	108
CHI	77	43	34	0	322	302	19	15	77	32	45	0	297	333	15	22	154	75	79	0	619	635	34	37	93	111	118	99	103	105	99	99
CIN	77	42	34	1	281	238	5	1	77	32	45	0	358	331	13	25	154	74	79	1	639	569	18	26	18	121	89	78	117	105	90	88
NY	80	45	35	0	334	282	31	33	75	41	33	1	348	261	15	11	155	86	68	1	682	543	46	44	199	97	88	96	112	91	99	97
PHI	77	32	45	0	339	380	50	30	76	30	46	0	226	334	14	5	153	62	91	0	565	714	64	35	296	99	50	122	85	106	109	112
PIT	78	42	35	1	276	263	6	4	77	37	40	0	254	289	10	21	155	79	75	1	530	552	16	25	35	79	91	98	85	89	101	101

| | HOME | | | | | | | | ROAD | | | | | | | | ALL | | | | | | | | | | | | | | | |
TM	G	W	L	T	R	OR	HR	OHR	G	W	L	T	R	OR	HR	OHR	G	W	L	T	R	OR	HR	OHR	HRF	HRB	HRP	RF	RB	RP	BPF	PPF
STL	76	38	38	0	330	332	10	10	79	37	41	1	345	350	22	20	155	75	79	1	675	682	32	30	53	124	119	99	112	113	98	98

1921 NATIONAL LEAGUE

| | HOME | | | | | | | | ROAD | | | | | | | | ALL | | | | | | | | | | | | | | | |
TM	G	W	L	T	R	OR	HR	OHR	G	W	L	T	R	OR	HR	OHR	G	W	L	T	R	OR	HR	OHR	HRF	HRB	HRP	RF	RB	RP	BPF	PPF
BOS	74	42	32	0	332	292	20	18	79	37	42	0	389	405	41	36	153	79	74	0	721	697	61	54	56	133	121	86	111	106	93	92
BRO	78	41	37	0	360	361	32	23	74	36	38	0	307	320	27	23	152	77	75	0	667	681	59	46	104	98	79	108	91	93	105	105
CHI	76	32	44	0	345	434	23	37	77	32	45	0	323	339	14	30	153	64	89	0	668	773	37	67	131	56	97	116	89	101	107	108
CIN	76	40	36	0	321	306	5	2	77	30	47	0	297	343	15	35	153	70	83	0	618	649	20	37	16	76	74	99	87	91	101	101
NY	79	53	26	0	407	321	47	46	74	41	33	0	433	316	28	33	153	94	59	0	840	637	75	79	137	114	121	93	123	97	97	94
PHI	76	29	47	0	326	485	67	49	78	22	56	0	291	434	21	30	154	51	103	0	617	919	88	79	197	100	101	111	86	121	102	107
PIT	76	45	31	0	343	295	13	10	78	45	32	1	349	300	24	27	154	90	63	1	692	595	37	37	50	81	76	102	95	83	103	101
STL	78	48	29	1	397	307	43	25	76	39	37	0	412	374	40	36	154	87	66	1	809	681	83	61	89	156	119	89	121	104	95	93

1922 NATIONAL LEAGUE

| | HOME | | | | | | | | ROAD | | | | | | | | ALL | | | | | | | | | | | | | | | |
TM	G	W	L	T	R	OR	HR	OHR	G	W	L	T	R	OR	HR	OHR	G	W	L	T	R	OR	HR	OHR	HRF	HRB	HRP	RF	RB	RP	BPF	PPF
BOS	76	32	43	1	287	373	6	15	78	21	57	0	309	449	26	42	154	53	100	1	596	822	32	57	34	65	119	89	83	109	94	98
BRO	78	44	34	0	380	326	25	35	77	32	44	1	363	428	31	35	155	76	78	1	743	754	56	74	86	92	118	89	101	102	95	95
CHI	76	39	37	0	344	382	22	37	80	41	37	2	427	426	20	40	156	80	74	2	771	808	42	77	103	63	108	91	104	109	95	96
CIN	79	48	29	2	378	297	8	13	77	38	39	0	388	380	37	36	156	86	68	2	766	677	45	49	31	91	111	88	103	92	96	94
NY	79	51	27	1	439	333	48	38	77	42	34	1	413	325	32	33	156	93	61	2	852	658	80	71	126	106	97	103	106	84	104	100
PHI	77	35	41	1	449	517	95	60	77	22	55	0	289	403	21	29	154	57	96	1	738	920	116	89	243	95	89	131	84	103	113	117
PIT	78	45	33	0	439	390	22	16	77	40	36	1	426	346	30	36	155	85	69	1	865	736	52	52	60	97	91	106	108	94	103	101
STL	77	42	35	0	446	414	59	31	77	43	34	0	417	405	48	30	154	85	69	0	863	819	107	61	114	152	98	105	111	106	101	100

1923 NATIONAL LEAGUE

| | HOME | | | | | | | | ROAD | | | | | | | | ALL | | | | | | | | | | | | | | | |
TM	G	W	L	T	R	OR	HR	OHR	G	W	L	T	R	OR	HR	OHR	G	W	L	T	R	OR	HR	OHR	HRF	HRB	HRP	RF	RB	RP	BPF	PPF
BOS	77	22	55	0	291	429	7	27	78	32	45	1	345	369	25	37	155	54	100	1	636	798	32	64	58	54	113	100	85	104	100	102
BRO	78	37	40	1	348	383	26	27	77	39	38	0	405	358	36	28	155	76	78	1	753	741	62	55	84	97	88	95	102	101	98	98
CHI	77	46	31	0	402	354	63	57	77	37	40	0	354	350	27	29	154	83	71	0	756	704	90	86	188	93	92	107	97	91	104	103
CIN	78	46	32	0	337	300	6	4	76	45	31	0	371	329	39	24	154	91	63	0	708	629	45	28	17	98	66	91	97	87	98	96
NY	77	47	30	0	408	362	41	53	76	48	28	0	446	317	44	39	153	95	58	0	854	679	85	82	124	119	112	101	114	93	101	98
PHI	75	20	55	0	418	597	76	77	80	30	49	1	330	411	36	23	155	50	104	1	748	1008	112	100	223	110	92	136	88	114	114	118
PIT	77	47	30	0	381	322	16	9	77	40	37	0	405	374	33	44	154	87	67	0	786	696	49	53	36	112	99	92	109	98	97	95
STL	78	42	35	1	335	320	22	27	76	37	39	0	411	412	41	43	154	79	74	1	746	732	63	70	60	118	131	80	111	109	90	90

1924 NATIONAL LEAGUE

| | HOME | | | | | | | | ROAD | | | | | | | | ALL | | | | | | | | | | | | | | | |
TM	G	W	L	T	R	OR	HR	OHR	G	W	L	T	R	OR	HR	OHR	G	W	L	T	R	OR	HR	OHR	HRF	HRB	HRP	RF	RB	RP	BPF	PPF
BOS	76	28	48	0	254	366	9	8	78	25	52	1	266	434	16	41	154	53	100	1	520	800	25	49	33	67	94	91	79	115	94	99
BRO	77	46	31	0	342	338	26	30	77	46	31	0	375	337	46	28	154	92	62	0	717	675	72	58	79	126	108	97	104	98	99	98
CHI	78	46	31	1	373	341	33	68	76	35	41	0	325	358	33	21	154	81	72	1	698	699	66	89	166	89	100	102	99	99	101	101
CIN	76	43	33	0	311	283	3	3	77	40	37	0	338	296	33	27	153	83	70	0	649	579	36	30	11	87	79	96	93	84	101	99
NY	77	51	26	0	385	272	51	40	77	42	34	1	472	369	44	37	154	93	60	1	857	641	95	77	112	149	125	81	134	104	91	88
PHI	76	26	49	1	369	483	58	64	76	29	47	0	307	366	36	20	152	55	96	1	676	849	94	84	188	114	93	121	91	111	108	111
PIT	77	49	28	0	393	293	20	17	76	41	35	0	331	295	24	25	153	90	63	0	724	588	44	42	78	76	72	108	98	82	106	104
STL	77	40	37	0	419	359	32	37	77	25	52	0	321	391	35	33	154	65	89	0	740	750	67	70	101	109	113	107	103	105	102	103

1925 NATIONAL LEAGUE

| | HOME | | | | | | | | ROAD | | | | | | | | ALL | | | | | | | | | | | | | | | |
TM	G	W	L	T	R	OR	HR	OHR	G	W	L	T	R	OR	HR	OHR	G	W	L	T	R	OR	HR	OHR	HRF	HRB	HRP	RF	RB	RP	BPF	PPF
BOS	76	37	39	0	315	383	15	14	77	33	44	0	393	419	26	53	153	70	83	0	708	802	41	67	40	78	102	88	97	109	94	95
BRO	77	40	37	0	383	407	25	41	76	28	48	0	403	459	39	34	153	68	85	0	786	866	64	75	90	83	97	91	108	118	94	95
CHI	77	37	40	0	367	359	57	63	77	31	46	0	356	414	29	39	154	68	86	0	723	773	86	102	160	83	99	94	95	101	97	98
CIN	76	44	32	0	334	285	10	5	77	36	41	0	356	358	34	30	153	80	73	0	690	643	44	35	26	81	57	89	92	86	97	97
NY	76	47	29	0	362	334	55	39	76	39	37	0	374	368	59	34	152	86	66	0	736	702	114	73	102	143	97	95	97	93	99	98
PHI	77	38	39	0	488	547	73	74	76	30	46	0	324	383	27	43	153	68	85	0	812	930	100	117	182	89	109	136	90	102	116	118
PIT	77	52	25	0	481	342	27	31	76	43	33	0	431	373	51	50	153	95	58	0	912	715	78	81	61	122	128	102	116	94	102	99
STL	76	48	28	0	449	359	66	41	77	29	48	0	379	405	43	45	153	77	76	0	828	764	109	86	120	126	105	104	105	98	102	101

1926 NATIONAL LEAGUE

| | HOME | | | | | | | | ROAD | | | | | | | | ALL | | | | | | | | | | | | | | | |
TM	G	W	L	T	R	OR	HR	OHR	G	W	L	T	R	OR	HR	OHR	G	W	L	T	R	OR	HR	OHR	HRF	HRB	HRP	RF	RB	RP	BPF	PPF
BOS	77	43	34	0	296	266	4	5	76	23	52	1	328	453	12	41	153	66	86	1	624	719	16	46	19	60	111	73	106	116	86	88
BRO	76	38	38	0	314	331	23	26	79	33	44	2	309	374	17	24	155	71	82	2	623	705	40	50	120	65	80	98	89	99	99	101
CHI	78	49	28	1	377	295	35	16	77	33	44	0	305	307	31	23	155	82	72	1	682	602	66	39	94	119	74	108	91	82	106	105
CIN	77	53	23	1	372	259	8	8	80	34	44	2	375	392	27	32	157	87	67	3	747	651	35	40	31	90	97	88	111	97	95	93
NY	76	43	33	0	333	317	45	43	75	31	44	0	330	351	28	27	151	74	77	0	663	668	73	70	147	114	110	95	99	100	98	98
PHI	76	33	42	1	392	470	51	42	76	25	51	0	295	430	24	26	152	58	93	1	687	900	75	68	166	105	100	115	96	122	103	107
PIT	79	49	28	2	446	374	18	19	78	35	41	2	323	315	26	31	157	84	69	4	769	689	44	50	67	93	103	123	96	87	112	111
STL	79	47	30	2	411	359	54	42	77	42	35	0	406	319	36	34	156	89	65	2	817	678	90	76	129	149	131	96	104	113	96	100

1927 NATIONAL LEAGUE

| | HOME | | | | | | | | ROAD | | | | | | | | ALL | | | | | | | | | | | | | | | |
TM	G	W	L	T	R	OR	HR	OHR	G	W	L	T	R	OR	HR	OHR	G	W	L	T	R	OR	HR	OHR	HRF	HRB	HRP	RF	RB	RP	BPF	PPF
BOS	74	32	41	1	296	339	5	10	81	28	53	0	355	432	32	33	155	60	94	1	651	771	37	43	28	78	107	89	98	114	93	95
BRO	74	34	39	1	266	296	20	35	80	31	49	0	275	323	19	28	154	65	88	1	541	619	39	63	122	59	90	101	75	84	103	104
CHI	78	50	28	0	398	315	37	19	75	35	40	0	352	346	37	31	153	85	68	0	750	661	74	50	82	135	94	99	107	96	100	99
CIN	80	45	35	0	348	320	3	11	73	30	43	0	295	333	26	25	153	75	78	0	643	653	29	36	28	59	97	97	92	93	100	100
NY	74	49	25	0	389	342	62	49	81	43	37	1	428	378	47	28	155	92	62	1	817	720	109	77	152	152	110	100	115	103	100	98
PHI	78	34	43	1	375	429	32	46	77	17	60	0	303	474	25	35	155	51	103	1	678	903	57	84	117	91	127	100	99	127	96	100
PIT	79	48	31	0	406	345	25	23	77	46	29	2	411	314	29	35	156	94	60	2	817	659	54	58	77	100	105	102	112	93	102	99
STL	80	55	25	0	433	354	55	51	73	37	36	0	321	311	29	21	153	92	61	0	754	665	84	72	175	104	87	113	100	90	107	106

1928 NATIONAL LEAGUE

| | HOME | | | | | | | | ROAD | | | | | | | | ALL | | | | | | | | | | | | | | | |
TM	G	W	L	T	R	OR	HR	OHR	G	W	L	T	R	OR	HR	OHR	G	W	L	T	R	OR	HR	OHR	HRF	HRB	HRP	RF	RB	RP	BPF	PPF
BOS	76	25	51	0	309	448	24	62	77	25	52	0	322	430	28	38	153	50	103	0	631	878	52	100	125	64	111	100	90	120	97	101
BRO	77	41	35	1	330	296	30	25	78	36	41	1	335	344	36	34	155	77	76	2	665	640	66	59	82	91	82	94	92	89	99	99
CHI	77	52	25	0	335	264	40	18	77	39	38	0	379	351	52	38	154	91	63	0	714	615	92	56	68	139	87	85	105	91	95	93
CIN	78	44	33	1	324	318	3	17	75	34	41	0	324	368	29	41	153	78	74	1	648	686	32	58	30	49	114	91	94	99	96	97
NY	77	51	26	0	411	315	80	46	78	42	35	1	396	338	38	31	155	93	61	1	807	653	118	77	169	112	80	101	109	90	102	99
PHI	75	26	49	0	360	521	54	67	77	17	60	0	300	436	31	41	152	43	109	0	660	957	85	108	155	92	114	117	89	123	104	109
PIT	77	47	30	0	479	356	16	15	75	38	37	0	358	348	36	51	152	85	67	0	837	704	52	66	38	102	115	114	109	95	107	105
STL	77	42	35	0	367	336	62	51	77	53	24	0	440	300	51	35	154	95	59	0	807	636	113	86	128	133	104	97	112	91	100	97

1929 NATIONAL LEAGUE

| | HOME | | | | | | | | ROAD | | | | | | | | ALL | | | | | | | | | | | | | | | |
TM	G	W	L	T	R	OR	HR	OHR	G	W	L	T	R	OR	HR	OHR	G	W	L	T	R	OR	HR	OHR	HRF	HRB	HRP	RF	RB	RP	BPF	PPF
BOS	77	34	43	0	318	403	11	39	77	22	55	0	339	473	22	64	154	56	98	0	657	876	33	103	60	43	122	89	85	109	94	97
BRO	77	42	35	0	371	413	53	48	76	28	48	0	384	475	46	44	153	70	83	0	755	888	99	92	109	101	95	91	98	112	94	96
CHI	78	52	25	1	490	374	76	41	78	46	29	3	492	384	63	36	156	98	54	4	982	758	139	77	117	131	79	100	116	93	101	98
CIN	78	38	39	1	356	356	7	18	77	30	47	0	330	404	27	43	155	68	86	1	686	760	34	61	38	45	84	96	83	91	99	100
NY	77	39	37	1	418	374	79	59	75	45	30	0	479	335	57	43	152	84	67	1	897	709	136	102	130	129	101	96	110	90	100	97
PHI	76	39	37	0	503	580	86	74	78	32	45	1	394	452	67	48	154	71	82	1	897	1032	153	122	135	145	119	126	99	112	110	112
PIT	76	45	31	0	471	382	27	37	78	43	42	0	433	398	33	59	154	88	65	1	904	780	60	96	75	73	109	105	106	93	103	102
STL	77	43	32	2	414	386	48	51	77	35	42	0	417	420	52	50	154	78	74	2	831	806	100	101	97	109	110	96	102	100	98	98

1930 NATIONAL LEAGUE

| | HOME | | | | | | | | ROAD | | | | | | | | ALL | | | | | | | | | | | | | | | |
TM	G	W	L	T	R	OR	HR	OHR	G	W	L	T	R	OR	HR	OHR	G	W	L	T	R	OR	HR	OHR	HRF	HRB	HRP	RF	RB	RP	BPF	PPF
BOS	77	39	38	0	329	401	29	51	77	31	46	0	364	434	37	66	154	70	84	0	693	835	66	117	80	66	110	92	82	96	97	99
BRO	77	49	28	0	442	346	73	66	77	37	40	0	429	392	49	49	154	86	68	0	871	738	122	115	136	93	89	97	99	85	101	99
CHI	79	51	26	2	538	454	96	62	77	39	40	0	460	416	75	49	156	90	64	2	998	870	171	111	121	138	95	110	107	95	105	103
CIN	77	37	40	0	300	368	20	21	77	22	55	0	365	489	54	54	154	59	95	0	665	857	74	75	41	88	90	79	84	105	90	93
NY	77	46	31	0	458	391	91	63	77	41	36	0	501	423	52	54	154	87	67	0	959	814	143	117	138	107	93	93	112	97	97	95

	HOME								ROAD								ALL														
TM	G	W	L	T	R	OR	HR	OHR	G	W	L	T	R	OR	HR	OHR	G	W	L	T	R	OR	HR	OHR	HRF	HRB	HRP	RF	RB	RP	BPF	PPF
PHI	77	35	42	0	543	644	72	72	79	17	60	2	401	555	54	70	156	52	102	2	944	1199	126	142	115	108	120	121	100	124	106	109
PIT	77	42	35	0	433	454	27	48	77	38	39	0	458	474	59	80	154	80	74	0	891	928	86	128	57	98	143	96	105	109	97	98
STL	77	53	24	0	541	383	52	49	77	39	38	0	463	401	52	38	154	92	62	0	1004	784	104	87	112	86	73	107	109	88	105	102

1931 NATIONAL LEAGUE

TM	G	W	L	T	R	OR	HR	OHR	G	W	L	T	R	OR	HR	OHR	G	W	L	T	R	OR	HR	OHR	HRF	HRB	HRP	RF	RB	RP	BPF	PPF
BOS	78	36	41	1	278	318	16	24	78	28	49	1	255	362	18	42	156	64	90	2	533	680	34	66	69	66	115	96	77	96	99	102
BRO	76	46	29	1	363	317	44	24	77	33	44	0	318	356	27	32	153	79	73	1	681	673	71	56	115	106	88	102	98	97	101	101
CHI	77	50	27	0	414	311	40	22	79	34	43	2	414	399	44	32	156	84	70	2	828	710	84	54	86	144	97	93	124	108	96	94
CIN	77	38	39	0	312	328	6	4	77	20	57	0	280	414	15	47	154	58	96	0	592	742	21	51	18	77	102	92	91	110	95	98
NY	78	50	27	1	379	274	80	47	75	37	38	0	389	325	21	24	153	87	65	1	768	599	101	71	225	95	79	90	116	94	96	93
PHI	76	40	36	0	391	423	51	35	79	26	52	1	293	405	30	40	155	66	88	1	684	828	81	75	123	120	116	117	93	110	106	109
PIT	78	44	33	1	343	327	25	16	77	31	46	0	293	364	16	39	155	75	79	1	636	691	41	55	76	77	92	100	91	98	100	101
STL	78	54	24	0	439	320	30	29	76	47	29	0	376	294	30	36	154	101	53	0	815	614	60	65	90	104	111	111	111	86	107	103

1932 NATIONAL LEAGUE

TM	G	W	L	T	R	OR	HR	OHR	G	W	L	T	R	OR	HR	OHR	G	W	L	T	R	OR	HR	OHR	HRF	HRB	HRP	RF	RB	RP	BPF	PPF
BOS	77	44	33	0	299	285	27	20	78	33	44	1	350	370	36	41	155	77	77	1	649	655	63	61	65	91	85	84	98	98	93	93
BRO	78	44	34	0	378	353	59	31	76	37	39	0	374	394	51	41	154	81	73	0	752	747	110	72	96	137	95	94	111	110	96	96
CHI	77	53	24	0	390	303	32	33	77	37	40	0	330	330	37	35	154	90	64	0	720	633	69	68	92	86	85	105	98	87	104	103
CIN	77	33	44	0	270	344	11	11	78	27	50	1	305	371	36	58	155	60	94	1	575	715	47	69	26	94	115	92	84	102	96	99
NY	77	37	40	0	362	359	78	71	77	35	42	0	393	347	38	41	154	72	82	0	755	706	116	112	169	109	108	97	108	102	99	98
PHI	77	45	32	0	507	429	86	71	77	33	44	0	337	367	36	36	154	78	76	0	844	796	122	107	190	105	96	128	106	102	112	111
PIT	76	45	31	0	352	338	22	25	78	41	37	0	349	373	26	61	154	86	68	0	701	711	48	86	59	79	120	99	100	101	99	100
STL	79	42	35	2	354	357	36	38	77	30	47	0	330	360	40	38	156	72	82	2	684	717	76	76	93	95	95	100	95	99	100	101

1933 NATIONAL LEAGUE

TM	G	W	L	T	R	OR	HR	OHR	G	W	L	T	R	OR	HR	OHR	G	W	L	T	R	OR	HR	OHR	HRF	HRB	HRP	RF	RB	RP	BPF	PPF
BOS	77	45	31	1	265	230	27	26	79	38	40	1	287	301	27	28	156	83	71	2	552	531	54	54	99	92	92	88	93	89	96	96
BRO	80	36	41	3	306	352	33	29	77	29	47	1	311	343	29	22	157	65	88	4	617	695	62	51	114	98	82	96	103	114	97	98
CHI	79	55	24	0	334	239	40	32	75	31	44	0	312	297	32	19	154	86	68	0	646	536	72	51	129	109	78	91	109	92	97	95
CIN	79	37	42	0	264	321	5	10	74	21	52	1	232	322	29	37	153	58	94	1	496	643	34	47	23	88	131	98	83	104	98	102
NY	77	48	27	2	298	241	55	44	79	43	34	2	338	274	27	17	156	91	61	4	636	515	82	61	200	95	70	92	104	86	99	96
PHI	72	32	40	0	355	437	45	46	80	28	52	0	252	323	15	41	152	60	92	0	607	760	60	87	163	81	124	142	86	105	118	121
PIT	77	50	27	0	332	272	12	13	77	37	40	0	335	347	27	41	154	87	67	0	667	619	39	54	40	99	122	90	115	108	95	94
STL	77	46	31	0	347	315	18	25	77	36	40	1	340	294	39	30	154	82	71	1	687	609	57	55	66	116	119	104	110	99	102	100

1934 NATIONAL LEAGUE

TM	G	W	L	T	R	OR	HR	OHR	G	W	L	T	R	OR	HR	OHR	G	W	L	T	R	OR	HR	OHR	HRF	HRB	HRP	RF	RB	RP	BPF	PPF
BOS	75	40	35	0	280	280	36	28	77	38	38	1	403	434	47	50	152	78	73	1	683	714	83	78	71	119	110	72	112	116	86	86
BRO	77	43	33	1	390	355	40	38	76	28	48	0	358	440	39	43	153	71	81	1	748	795	79	81	94	98	100	93	111	116	95	95
CHI	77	47	30	0	347	301	53	44	75	39	35	1	358	338	48	36	152	86	65	1	705	639	101	80	112	117	95	92	102	93	98	96
CIN	78	30	47	1	331	406	17	24	74	22	52	0	259	395	38	37	152	52	99	1	590	801	55	61	54	81	94	104	82	108	101	105
NY	75	49	26	0	363	254	75	43	78	44	34	0	397	329	51	32	153	93	60	0	760	583	126	75	141	126	81	91	108	85	98	95
PHI	71	35	36	0	384	400	28	71	78	21	57	0	291	394	28	55	149	56	93	0	675	794	56	126	125	67	135	120	89	104	108	111
PIT	78	45	32	1	421	369	22	38	73	29	44	0	314	344	30	40	151	74	76	1	735	713	52	78	82	69	100	111	98	96	105	105
STL	77	48	29	0	451	363	56	43	77	47	29	1	348	293	48	34	154	95	58	1	799	656	104	77	119	114	87	124	97	82	114	111

1935 NATIONAL LEAGUE

TM	G	W	L	T	R	OR	HR	OHR	G	W	L	T	R	OR	HR	OHR	G	W	L	T	R	OR	HR	OHR	HRF	HRB	HRP	RF	RB	RP	BPF	PPF
BOS	75	25	50	0	309	381	34	41	78	13	65	0	266	471	41	40	153	38	115	0	575	852	75	81	94	93	100	95	84	118	96	100
BRO	77	38	38	1	349	346	32	43	77	32	45	0	362	421	27	45	154	70	83	1	711	767	59	88	103	70	101	90	105	111	94	95
CHI	77	56	21	0	426	264	43	40	77	44	33	0	421	333	45	45	154	100	54	0	847	597	88	85	95	110	107	94	118	87	99	95
CIN	76	41	35	0	331	320	18	18	78	27	50	1	315	452	55	47	154	68	85	1	646	772	73	65	39	119	111	88	96	111	93	95
NY	79	50	27	2	386	302	84	66	77	41	35	1	384	373	39	40	156	91	62	3	770	675	123	106	169	110	100	91	109	97	96	95
PHI	79	35	43	1	416	499	52	68	77	29	46	2	269	372	40	38	156	64	89	3	685	871	92	106	140	95	105	132	81	102	114	117
PIT	77	46	31	0	398	340	32	25	76	40	36	0	345	307	34	38	153	86	67	0	743	647	66	63	81	86	81	111	96	85	107	105
STL	77	53	24	0	441	298	39	27	77	43	34	0	388	327	47	41	154	96	58	0	829	625	86	68	78	114	92	104	110	86	104	100

1936 NATIONAL LEAGUE

TM	G	W	L	T	R	OR	HR	OHR	G	W	L	T	R	OR	HR	OHR	G	W	L	T	R	OR	HR	OHR	HRF	HRB	HRP	RF	RB	RP	BPF	PPF
BOS	79	35	43	1	292	339	26	23	78	36	40	2	339	376	41	46	157	71	83	3	631	715	67	69	59	110	110	88	90	101	95	96
BRO	79	37	40	2	360	397	15	46	77	30	47	0	302	355	18	38	156	67	87	2	662	752	33	84	105	43	99	110	86	96	105	106
CHI	77	50	27	0	404	290	34	41	77	37	40	0	351	313	42	36	154	87	67	0	755	603	76	77	97	103	104	105	99	82	105	102
CIN	76	42	34	0	358	350	24	21	78	32	46	0	364	410	58	30	154	74	80	0	722	760	82	51	56	128	91	94	103	108	96	97
NY	78	52	26	0	378	296	68	54	76	40	36	0	364	325	29	21	154	92	62	0	742	621	97	75	204	83	65	97	102	87	100	98
PHI	78	30	48	0	408	499	69	56	76	24	52	0	318	375	34	31	154	54	100	0	726	874	103	87	167	102	90	122	92	109	108	111
PIT	76	46	30	0	375	342	23	25	80	38	40	2	429	376	37	49	156	84	70	2	804	718	60	74	62	97	113	95	112	102	98	96
STL	77	43	33	1	363	386	38	43	78	44	34	0	432	408	50	46	155	87	67	1	795	794	88	89	88	127	130	92	115	115	94	94

1937 NATIONAL LEAGUE

TM	G	W	L	T	R	OR	HR	OHR	G	W	L	T	R	OR	HR	OHR	G	W	L	T	R	OR	HR	OHR	HRF	HRB	HRP	RF	RB	RP	BPF	PPF
BOS	76	43	33	0	252	224	26	15	76	36	40	0	327	332	37	45	152	79	73	0	579	556	63	60	53	107	93	75	94	90	90	90
BRO	76	36	39	1	336	389	20	30	79	26	52	1	280	383	17	38	155	62	91	2	616	772	37	68	94	47	82	111	84	103	104	107
CHI	78	46	32	0	412	361	47	48	76	47	29	0	399	321	49	43	154	93	61	0	811	682	96	91	102	126	120	105	114	98	103	100
CIN	80	28	51	1	268	347	13	14	75	28	47	0	344	360	42	10	155	56	98	1	612	707	73	38	33	119	84	83	96	110	91	93
NY	75	50	25	0	353	288	76	57	77	45	32	0	379	314	35	28	152	95	57	0	732	602	111	85	191	99	79	97	107	90	100	98
PHI	74	29	45	0	379	481	65	69	81	32	47	2	345	388	38	47	155	61	92	2	724	869	103	116	157	108	122	123	96	113	108	111
PIT	78	46	32	0	360	332	13	28	76	40	36	0	344	314	43	43	154	86	68	0	704	646	47	71	56	73	112	103	99	92	102	101
STL	80	45	33	2	406	379	52	51	77	36	40	1	383	354	42	44	157	81	73	3	789	733	94	95	113	114	115	102	111	104	100	100

1938 NATIONAL LEAGUE

TM	G	W	L	T	R	OR	HR	OHR	G	W	L	T	R	OR	HR	OHR	G	W	L	T	R	OR	HR	OHR	HRF	HRB	HRP	RF	RB	RP	BPF	PPF
BOS	75	45	30	0	233	241	12	19	78	32	45	1	328	377	42	47	153	77	75	1	561	618	54	66	39	93	119	73	95	102	88	89
BRO	74	31	41	2	319	349	38	44	77	38	39	0	385	361	23	44	151	69	80	2	704	710	61	88	123	73	103	94	110	111	96	96
CHI	77	44	33	0	349	326	24	41	77	45	30	2	364	272	41	30	154	89	63	2	713	598	65	71	93	85	94	106	100	85	105	103
CIN	77	43	34	0	344	323	50	31	74	39	34	1	379	311	60	44	151	82	68	1	723	634	110	75	78	167	120	94	111	99	98	96
NY	73	43	30	0	365	297	89	58	79	40	37	2	340	401	36	29	152	83	67	2	705	698	125	87	208	107	80	105	102	93	103	102
PHI	75	26	48	1	286	439	18	40	76	19	57	0	264	401	22	36	151	45	105	1	550	840	40	76	99	53	94	107	82	119	100	106
PIT	78	44	33	1	348	330	22	22	74	42	31	1	359	300	43	49	152	86	64	2	707	630	65	71	49	115	122	99	105	95	100	99
STL	81	36	41	4	414	425	58	45	75	35	39	1	311	296	33	32	156	71	80	5	725	721	91	77	138	96	84	123	94	93	111	111

1939 NATIONAL LEAGUE

TM	G	W	L	T	R	OR	HR	OHR	G	W	L	T	R	OR	HR	OHR	G	W	L	T	R	OR	HR	OHR	HRF	HRB	HRP	RF	RB	RP	BPF	PPF
BOS	73	37	35	1	254	272	13	14	79	26	53	0	318	387	43	49	152	63	88	1	572	659	56	63	34	97	107	82	93	104	92	93
BRO	78	51	27	0	385	329	41	49	79	33	42	4	323	316	37	44	157	84	69	4	708	645	78	93	111	91	106	112	95	87	107	106
CHI	80	44	34	2	379	343	46	35	76	40	36	0	345	335	47	39	156	84	70	2	724	678	91	74	89	116	97	101	104	98	101	100
CIN	81	55	25	1	404	307	48	39	75	42	32	1	363	288	50	42	156	97	57	2	767	595	98	81	90	126	107	102	107	86	103	100
NY	74	41	33	0	360	315	84	58	77	36	41	0	343	382	32	28	151	77	74	0	703	685	116	86	208	93	74	99	106	103	99	99
PHI	74	29	44	1	288	384	19	49	78	16	62	0	265	472	30	57	152	45	106	1	553	856	49	106	83	69	138	95	88	127	94	99
PIT	77	35	42	0	339	365	22	29	76	33	43	0	327	356	41	41	153	68	85	0	666	721	63	70	64	92	103	101	98	105	100	101
STL	79	51	27	1	431	317	63	42	76	41	34	1	348	316	35	40	155	92	61	2	779	633	98	76	140	97	80	108	107	90	105	103

1940 NATIONAL LEAGUE

TM	G	W	L	T	R	OR	HR	OHR	G	W	L	T	R	OR	HR	OHR	G	W	L	T	R	OR	HR	OHR	HRF	HRB	HRP	RF	RB	RP	BPF	PPF
BOS	75	35	40	0	328	352	25	30	77	30	47	0	295	393	34	53	152	65	87	0	623	745	59	83	67	83	110	101	95	110	99	101
BRO	81	41	37	3	369	358	40	55	75	47	28	0	328	263	53	46	156	88	65	3	697	621	93	101	91	115	124	113	94	85	108	106
CHI	77	40	37	0	333	316	40	32	77	35	42	0	348	320	46	42	154	75	79	0	681	636	86	74	84	107	93	97	101	95	100	99

TM	HOME								ROAD								ALL															
	G	W	L	T	R	OR	HR	OHR	G	W	L	T	R	OR	HR	OHR	G	W	L	T	R	OR	HR	OHR	HRF	HRB	HRP	RF	RB	RP	BPF	PPF
CIN	77	55	21	1	352	240	47	36	78	45	32	1	355	288	42	37	155	100	53	2	707	528	89	73	107	97	82	95	103	79	101	98
NY	76	33	43	0	323	339	61	75	76	39	37	0	340	320	30	35	152	72	80	0	663	659	91	110	184	77	91	100	99	99	100	100
PHI	79	24	55	0	232	403	33	50	74	26	48	0	262	347	42	42	153	50	103	0	494	750	75	92	92	93	111	96	76	109	97	102
PIT	75	40	34	1	390	354	26	22	81	38	42	1	419	429	50	50	156	78	76	2	809	783	76	72	55	109	101	95	124	120	95	95
STL	77	41	36	0	368	364	69	47	79	43	33	3	379	335	50	36	156	84	69	3	747	699	119	83	133	117	86	105	107	101	102	101

1941 NATIONAL LEAGUE

TM	HOME								ROAD								ALL															
	G	W	L	T	R	OR	HR	OHR	G	W	L	T	R	OR	HR	OHR	G	W	L	T	R	OR	HR	OHR	HRF	HRB	HRP	RF	RB	RP	BPF	PPF
BOS	76	32	44	0	276	321	17	28	80	30	48	2	316	399	31	47	156	62	92	2	592	720	48	75	63	77	115	88	96	114	93	95
BRO	79	52	25	2	421	282	55	40	78	48	29	1	379	299	46	41	157	100	54	3	800	581	101	81	108	131	109	103	116	88	103	99
CHI	77	38	39	0	311	306	37	20	78	32	45	1	355	364	62	40	155	70	84	1	666	670	99	60	60	164	105	88	109	109	94	94
CIN	79	45	34	0	308	273	27	27	75	43	32	0	308	291	37	34	154	88	66	0	616	564	64	61	75	96	93	94	96	88	99	98
NY	78	38	39	1	360	358	68	69	78	36	40	2	307	348	27	21	156	74	79	3	667	706	95	90	231	78	70	108	98	103	103	104
PHI	76	23	52	1	255	384	34	37	79	20	59	0	246	409	30	42	155	43	111	1	501	793	64	79	100	87	104	99	79	118	97	103
PIT	78	45	32	1	346	336	20	28	78	36	41	1	344	307	36	38	156	81	73	2	690	643	56	66	68	86	102	104	102	96	103	102
STL	79	53	24	2	405	324	37	53	76	44	32	0	329	265	33	32	155	97	56	2	734	589	70	85	129	84	97	117	102	84	110	107

1942 NATIONAL LEAGUE

TM	HOME								ROAD								ALL															
	G	W	L	T	R	OR	HR	OHR	G	W	L	T	R	OR	HR	OHR	G	W	L	T	R	OR	HR	OHR	HRF	HRB	HRP	RF	RB	RP	BPF	PPF
BOS	70	33	36	1	250	271	36	34	80	26	53	1	265	374	32	48	150	59	89	2	515	645	68	82	99	109	126	93	93	111	95	98
BRO	79	57	22	0	381	250	30	35	76	47	28	1	361	260	32	38	155	104	50	1	742	510	62	73	92	96	111	100	121	87	102	97
CHI	78	36	41	1	298	318	36	27	77	32	45	0	293	347	39	43	155	68	86	1	591	665	75	70	78	127	117	95	102	113	96	98
CIN	78	38	39	1	264	276	30	23	76	38	37	1	263	269	36	24	154	76	76	2	527	545	66	47	88	99	74	99	87	89	101	102
NY	79	47	31	1	376	296	80	67	75	38	36	1	299	304	29	27	154	85	67	2	675	600	109	94	211	104	93	106	109	99	103	101
PHI	74	23	51	0	182	340	18	31	77	19	58	0	212	366	26	30	151	42	109	0	394	706	44	61	90	68	92	93	71	119	94	101
PIT	77	41	34	2	333	301	15	21	74	25	47	2	252	330	39	41	151	66	81	4	585	631	54	62	46	108	127	104	98	105	101	102
STL	78	60	17	1	419	229	31	24	78	46	31	1	336	253	29	25	156	106	48	2	755	482	60	49	103	82	69	111	114	78	108	103

1943 NATIONAL LEAGUE

TM	HOME								ROAD								ALL															
	G	W	L	T	R	OR	HR	OHR	G	W	L	T	R	OR	HR	OHR	G	W	L	T	R	OR	HR	OHR	HRF	HRB	HRP	RF	RB	RP	BPF	PPF
BOS	77	38	39	0	247	327	25	34	76	30	46	0	218	285	14	32	153	68	85	0	465	612	39	66	122	66	109	110	73	93	106	109
BRO	77	46	31	0	389	323	21	30	76	35	41	0	327	351	18	29	153	81	72	0	716	674	39	59	106	72	104	103	119	113	100	99
CHI	75	36	38	1	292	300	24	19	79	38	41	0	340	300	28	34	154	74	79	1	632	600	52	53	75	112	110	98	105	101	99	98
CIN	78	48	29	1	282	280	17	15	77	39	38	0	326	263	26	23	155	87	67	1	608	543	43	38	68	90	81	95	100	91	99	98
NY	77	34	43	0	291	326	63	52	79	21	55	3	267	387	18	28	156	55	98	3	558	713	81	80	212	93	103	96	95	117	96	99
PHI	78	33	43	2	269	314	29	18	79	31	47	1	302	362	37	41	157	64	90	3	571	676	66	59	64	155	133	89	99	114	93	96
PIT	78	47	30	1	364	296	20	15	79	33	44	2	305	309	22	29	157	80	74	3	669	605	42	44	72	88	88	108	104	95	104	103
STL	81	58	21	2	355	243	33	17	76	47	28	1	324	232	37	16	157	105	49	3	679	475	70	33	91	127	65	103	105	76	105	100

1944 NATIONAL LEAGUE

TM	HOME								ROAD								ALL															
	G	W	L	T	R	OR	HR	OHR	G	W	L	T	R	OR	HR	OHR	G	W	L	T	R	OR	HR	OHR	HRF	HRB	HRP	RF	RB	RP	BPF	PPF
BOS	78	38	40	0	293	307	51	44	77	27	49	1	300	367	28	36	155	65	89	1	593	674	79	80	138	92	96	89	96	106	95	96
BRO	77	37	39	1	372	413	27	34	78	26	52	0	318	419	29	41	155	63	91	1	690	832	56	75	89	83	107	106	106	124	99	102
CHI	78	35	42	1	346	342	33	40	79	40	37	2	356	327	38	35	157	75	79	3	702	669	71	75	101	98	103	102	104	100	101	100
CIN	78	45	33	0	252	252	14	23	77	44	32	1	320	285	37	37	155	89	65	1	573	537	51	60	53	86	107	85	91	86	95	95
NY	75	39	36	0	372	382	75	86	80	28	51	1	310	391	18	30	155	67	87	1	682	773	93	116	269	69	91	112	100	112	104	105
PHI	79	29	49	1	271	346	20	21	75	32	43	0	268	312	35	28	154	61	92	1	539	658	55	49	64	89	82	100	82	98	100	103
PIT	81	49	28	4	399	357	23	31	77	41	35	1	345	305	47	34	158	90	63	5	744	662	70	65	67	111	109	110	105	95	105	104
STL	77	54	22	1	360	230	39	14	80	51	27	2	412	260	61	41	157	105	49	3	772	490	100	55	58	171	95	94	115	77	101	95

1945 NATIONAL LEAGUE

TM	HOME								ROAD								ALL															
	G	W	L	T	R	OR	HR	OHR	G	W	L	T	R	OR	HR	OHR	G	W	L	T	R	OR	HR	OHR	HRF	HRB	HRP	RF	RB	RP	BPF	PPF
BOS	75	36	38	1	411	395	68	63	79	31	47	1	310	333	33	36	154	67	85	2	721	728	101	99	177	105	105	126	93	95	112	113
BRO	78	48	30	0	387	347	29	34	77	39	37	1	408	377	28	40	155	87	67	1	795	724	57	74	93	82	103	94	120	111	96	95
CHI	76	49	26	1	330	253	24	17	79	49	30	0	405	279	33	40	155	98	56	1	735	532	57	57	62	95	89	91	107	81	99	95
CIN	77	36	41	0	267	307	25	23	77	25	52	0	269	387	31	47	154	61	93	0	536	694	56	70	64	97	112	88	83	104	94	97
NY	78	47	30	1	366	325	83	47	76	31	44	1	302	375	31	38	154	78	74	2	668	700	114	85	166	116	99	100	98	102	100	100
PHI	77	22	55	0	261	450	23	28	77	24	53	0	287	415	33	33	154	46	108	0	548	865	56	61	78	85	93	99	83	123	96	102
PIT	79	45	34	0	407	352	31	25	76	37	38	1	346	334	41	36	155	82	72	1	753	686	72	61	73	113	97	107	105	97	103	102
STL	78	48	29	1	368	286	28	29	77	47	30	0	388	297	36	41	155	95	59	1	756	583	64	70	76	100	107	96	109	87	100	97

1946 NATIONAL LEAGUE

TM	HOME								ROAD								ALL															
	G	W	L	T	R	OR	HR	OHR	G	W	L	T	R	OR	HR	OHR	G	W	L	T	R	OR	HR	OHR	HRF	HRB	HRP	RF	RB	RP	BPF	PPF
BOS	77	45	31	1	300	268	14	31	77	36	41	0	330	324	30	45	154	81	72	1	630	592	44	76	63	76	127	89	109	103	95	94
BRO	79	56	22	1	379	273	20	22	78	40	38	0	327	297	35	36	157	96	60	1	701	570	55	58	62	92	97	103	110	92	103	100
CHI	77	44	33	0	291	260	24	30	78	38	38	2	335	321	32	26	155	82	71	2	626	581	56	58	93	80	83	87	108	101	94	93
CIN	77	35	42	0	267	289	37	39	79	32	45	2	256	281	28	31	156	67	87	2	523	570	65	70	126	81	87	105	82	88	104	105
NY	77	38	39	0	340	336	76	75	77	23	54	0	272	349	45	39	154	61	93	0	612	685	121	114	162	144	135	107	99	109	102	103
PHI	78	41	36	1	280	335	38	34	77	28	49	0	280	370	42	39	155	69	85	1	560	705	80	73	89	122	113	94	96	118	95	98
PIT	78	37	40	1	303	342	24	23	77	26	51	0	249	326	36	27	155	63	91	1	552	668	60	50	75	92	80	108	87	103	103	106
STL	78	49	29	0	370	288	39	36	78	49	29	0	342	257	42	27	156	98	58	0	712	545	81	63	109	109	87	110	108	86	107	103

1947 NATIONAL LEAGUE

TM	HOME								ROAD								ALL															
	G	W	L	T	R	OR	HR	OHR	G	W	L	T	R	OR	HR	OHR	G	W	L	T	R	OR	HR	OHR	HRF	HRB	HRP	RF	RB	RP	BPF	PPF
BOS	77	50	27	0	332	289	29	39	77	36	41	0	369	333	56	54	154	86	68	0	701	622	85	93	65	90	103	93			97	95
BRO	78	52	25	1	409	343	37	57	77	42	35	0	365	325	46	47	155	94	60	1	774	668	83	104	101	74	90	108	104	92	105	103
CHI	79	36	43	0	280	384	29	51	76	33	42	1	287	338	42	55	155	69	85	1	567	722	71	106	81	70	101	101	79	98	101	104
CIN	77	42	35	0	318	330	48	47	77	31	46	0	363	425	47	55	154	73	81	0	681	755	95	102	94	88	94	84	107	116	91	92
NY	76	45	31	0	417	380	131	45	79	36	42	1	413	381	90	47	155	81	73	1	830	761	221	122	146	167	100	104	117	108	101	99
PHI	77	38	38	1	309	323	24	43	78	24	54	0	280	364	36	55	155	62	92	1	589	687	60	98	76	59	93	99	83	95	100	102
PIT	79	32	45	2	384	437	95	87	77	30	47	0	360	380	61	68	156	62	92	2	744	817	156	155	130	127	128	106	109	112	101	102
STL	77	46	31	0	400	331	45	49	79	43	34	2	380	303	70	57	156	89	65	2	780	634	115	106	79	113	108	109	103	86	106	104

1948 NATIONAL LEAGUE

TM	HOME								ROAD								ALL															
	G	W	L	T	R	OR	HR	OHR	G	W	L	T	R	OR	HR	OHR	G	W	L	T	R	OR	HR	OHR	HRF	HRB	HRP	RF	RB	RP	BPF	PPF
BOS	76	45	31	0	349	297	32	40	78	46	31	1	390	287	63	53	154	91	62	1	739	584	95	93	67	103	105	99	107	87	102	99
BRO	78	36	41	1	352	386	43	68	77	48	29	0	392	281	48	51	155	84	70	1	744	667	91	119	110	84	105	108	104	94	104	103
CHI	78	35	42	1	282	323	38	34	77	29	48	0	315	383	49	55	155	64	90	1	597	706	87	89	71	95	95	86	94	108	93	95
CIN	77	32	45	0	312	398	68	52	76	32	44	0	276	354	36	52	153	64	89	0	588	752	104	104	128	85	89	109	84	104	103	106
NY	77	37	40	0	366	374	89	82	78	41	36	1	414	330	75	40	155	78	76	1	780	704	164	122	142	134	99	101	114	104	100	98
PHI	76	32	44	0	276	332	32	44	79	34	44	1	315	397	59	51	155	66	88	1	591	729	91	95	74	95	102	89	91	110	94	97
PIT	80	47	31	2	384	370	69	64	76	36	40	0	322	329	39	56	156	83	71	2	706	699	108	120	128	88	100	109	98	97	104	104
STL	77	44	33	0	359	327	47	43	78	41	36	1	383	319	58	60	155	85	69	1	742	646	105	103	80	110	108	100	107	95	104	99

1949 NATIONAL LEAGUE

TM	HOME								ROAD								ALL															
	G	W	L	T	R	OR	HR	OHR	G	W	L	T	R	OR	HR	OHR	G	W	L	T	R	OR	HR	OHR	HRF	HRB	HRP	RF	RB	RP	BPF	PPF
BOS	77	43	34	0	344	328	40	40	80	32	45	3	362	391	63	70	157	75	79	3	706	719	103	110	66	104	109	94	103	104	97	97
BRO	78	48	29	1	431	335	86	73	78	49	28	1	448	316	66	59	156	97	57	2	879	651	152	132	125	118	104	101	122	94	101	98
CHI	77	33	44	0	285	365	53	38	77	28	49	0	308	408	44	66	154	61	93	0	593	773	97	104	84	91	94	91	90	113	94	97
CIN	78	35	42	1	326	349	50	54	78	27	50	1	301	421	36	70	156	62	92	2	627	770	86	124	97	75	103	93	93	111	96	98
NY	79	43	34	2	404	331	94	78	77	30	49	0	332	362	53	54	156	73	81	2	736	693	147	132	146	102	95	102	103	97	101	101
PHI	77	40	37	0	336	326	61	35	77	41	36	0	326	342	61	69	154	81	73	0	662	668	122	104	77	120	100	99	94	95	100	101
PIT	77	36	41	0	341	397	77	75	77	35	42	0	340	363	49	67	154	71	83	0	681	760	126	142	126	98	111	104	97	106	100	102
STL	79	51	26	2	427	325	48	33	78	45	32	1	339	291	54	54	157	96	58	3	766	616	102	87	77	94	80	117	97	80	110	108

1950 NATIONAL LEAGUE

TM	HOME								ROAD								ALL															
	G	W	L	T	R	OR	HR	OHR	G	W	L	T	R	OR	HR	OHR	G	W	L	T	R	OR	HR	OHR	HRF	HRB	HRP	RF	RB	RP	BPF	PPF
BOS	79	46	31	2	343	294	59	45	77	37	40	0	442	442	89	84	156	83	71	2	785	736	148	129	62	132	115	73	126	118	86	85

TM	HOME G	W	L	T	R	OR	HR	OHR	ROAD G	W	L	T	R	OR	HR	OHR	ALL G	W	L	T	R	OR	HR	OHR	HRF	HRB	HRP	RF	RB	RP	BPF	PPF
BRO	78	48	30	0	458	386	110	96	77	41	35	1	389	338	84	67	155	89	65	1	847	724	194	163	130	126	108	113	110	96	106	104
CHI	78	35	42	1	352	411	79	63	76	29	47	0	291	361	82	67	154	64	89	1	643	772	161	130	93	121	101	111	85	100	105	107
CIN	76	38	38	0	355	373	52	81	77	28	49	0	299	361	47	64	153	66	87	0	654	734	99	145	117	67	94	109	88	97	105	106
NY	76	44	32	0	362	290	84	67	78	42	36	0	373	353	49	73	154	86	68	0	735	643	133	140	124	86	92	94	104	92	98	97
PHI	78	47	30	1	348	279	58	53	79	44	33	2	374	345	67	69	157	91	63	3	722	624	125	122	85	95	92	90	101	89	97	96
PIT	77	33	44	0	370	447	81	79	77	24	52	1	311	410	57	73	154	57	96	1	681	857	138	152	118	93	102	110	92	113	103	106
STL	76	47	29	0	389	303	50	43	77	31	46	0	304	367	52	76	153	78	75	0	693	670	102	119	76	85	93	104	94	92	103	103
1951 NATIONAL LEAGUE																																
BOS	78	42	35	1	367	310	59	37	77	34	43	0	356	352	71	59	155	76	78	1	723	662	130	96	75	113	85	95	107	99	98	97
BRO	78	49	29	0	412	316	100	81	80	48	31	1	443	356	84	69	158	97	60	1	855	672	184	150	120	133	111	95	124	100	98	95
CHI	77	32	45	0	304	364	45	59	78	30	47	1	310	386	58	66	155	62	92	1	614	750	103	125	86	86	103	97	91	109	97	100
CIN	77	35	42	0	289	320	44	46	78	33	44	1	270	347	44	73	155	68	86	1	559	667	88	119	80	77	99	99	80	94	101	103
NY	78	50	28	0	399	308	115	89	79	48	31	0	382	333	64	59	157	98	59	0	781	641	179	148	157	109	94	101	110	92	102	99
PHI	77	38	39	0	312	305	43	50	77	35	42	0	336	339	65	60	154	73	81	0	648	644	108	110	77	94	97	92	97	97	97	97
PIT	78	32	45	1	388	465	72	84	77	32	45	0	301	380	65	73	155	64	90	1	689	845	137	157	109	106	119	119	93	112	107	109
STL	79	44	34	1	370	323	44	56	76	37	39	0	313	348	51	63	155	81	73	1	683	671	95	119	86	79	96	101	98	96	101	101
1952 NATIONAL LEAGUE																																
BOS	77	31	45	1	257	314	48	44	78	33	44	1	312	337	62	62	155	64	89	2	569	651	110	106	77	108	104	90	93	104	95	97
BRO	80	45	33	2	389	324	76	78	75	51	24	0	386	279	77	43	155	96	57	2	775	603	153	121	119	126	100	102	118	95	101	98
CHI	77	42	35	0	329	316	51	40	78	35	42	1	299	315	56	61	155	77	77	1	628	631	107	101	81	103	96	106	94	94	103	103
CIN	77	38	39	0	318	319	43	43	77	31	46	0	297	340	61	68	154	69	85	0	615	659	104	111	69	109	114	99	96	102	99	100
NY	77	50	27	0	369	327	103	74	77	42	35	0	353	312	48	47	154	92	62	0	722	639	151	121	170	98	84	105	110	99	102	101
PHI	76	47	29	0	318	269	42	43	78	40	38	0	339	283	51	52	154	87	67	0	657	552	93	95	87	86	87	98	101	87	101	99
PIT	77	23	54	0	261	414	45	72	78	19	58	1	254	379	47	61	155	42	112	1	515	793	92	133	106	80	110	105	80	117	100	105
STL	77	48	29	0	343	291	46	59	77	40	37	0	334	339	51	60	154	88	66	0	677	630	97	119	96	88	105	96	108	101	98	97
1953 NATIONAL LEAGUE																																
BRO	78	60	17	1	517	333	110	82	77	45	32	0	438	356	98	87	155	105	49	1	955	689	208	169	104	141	118	107	125	94	104	99
CHI	77	43	34	0	351	417	74	69	78	22	55	1	282	418	63	82	155	65	89	1	633	835	137	151	99	92	100	109	83	107	103	106
CIN	78	38	39	1	367	391	89	96	77	30	47	0	347	397	77	83	155	68	86	1	714	788	166	179	111	108	116	100	98	107	99	100
MIL	79	45	31	3	332	260	51	44	78	47	31	0	406	329	105	63	157	92	62	3	738	589	156	107	60	121	91	82	105	86	94	92
NY	77	38	39	0	395	345	109	81	78	32	45	1	373	402	67	65	155	70	84	1	768	747	176	146	137	98	85	97	106	104	98	98
PHI	78	48	29	1	363	304	63	65	78	35	42	1	353	362	52	73	156	83	71	2	716	666	115	138	102	74	88	94	98	92	99	98
PIT	77	26	51	0	338	460	53	88	77	24	53	0	284	427	46	80	154	50	104	0	622	887	99	168	108	65	104	109	83	114	102	106
STL	78	48	30	0	420	321	65	58	79	35	41	3	348	392	75	81	157	83	71	3	768	713	140	139	82	101	99	102	101	95	101	101
1954 NATIONAL LEAGUE																																
BRO	77	45	32	0	380	393	101	92	77	47	30	0	398	347	85	72	154	92	62	0	778	740	186	164	121	125	112	104	109	105	101	100
CHI	77	40	37	0	366	385	86	59	77	24	53	0	334	381	73	72	154	64	90	0	700	766	159	131	99	114	96	104	99	107	101	102
CIN	77	41	36	0	380	380	47	59	77	33	44	0	349	356	53	64	154	74	80	0	729	763	147	169	156	83	95	110	100	104	104	104
MIL	77	43	34	0	285	251	43	29	77	46	31	0	385	305	96	77	154	89	65	0	670	556	139	106	44	133	102	81	102	87	93	91
NY	76	53	23	0	387	254	120	67	78	44	34	0	345	296	66	46	154	97	57	0	732	550	186	113	159	100	66	104	99	77	105	102
PHI	78	39	39	0	315	305	47	60	76	36	40	0	344	309	55	73	154	75	79	0	659	614	102	133	83	79	100	93	95	89	99	98
PIT	77	31	46	0	277	422	22	42	77	22	55	0	280	423	54	86	154	53	101	0	557	845	76	128	98	71	115	98	82	118	97	102
STL	77	33	44	0	386	431	57	90	77	39	38	0	413	359	62	80	154	72	82	0	799	790	119	170	103	87	118	105	113	112	100	100
1955 NATIONAL LEAGUE																																
BRO	77	56	21	0	461	318	119	85	77	42	34	1	396	332	82	83	154	98	55	1	857	650	201	168	122	115	100	108	118	93	104	101
CHI	77	43	33	1	348	322	80	62	77	29	48	0	278	391	84	91	154	72	81	1	626	713	164	153	83	114	106	100	90	101	100	101
CIN	77	46	31	0	425	341	102	91	77	29	48	0	336	343	79	70	154	75	79	0	761	684	181	161	125	102	92	111	103	94	106	104
MIL	77	46	31	0	342	297	75	51	77	39	38	0	401	371	107	87	154	85	69	0	743	668	182	138	68	136	105	85	115	104	93	92
NY	79	44	35	0	362	327	95	91	75	36	39	0	340	346	74	64	154	80	74	0	702	673	169	155	124	95	88	96	102	99	98	98
PHI	77	46	31	0	371	309	76	78	77	31	46	0	304	357	56	83	154	77	77	0	675	666	132	161	109	79	95	103	95	94	102	102
PIT	75	36	39	0	298	337	34	48	79	24	55	0	262	430	57	94	154	60	94	0	560	767	91	142	60	71	103	96	83	109	97	101
STL	77	41	36	0	358	362	84	92	77	27	50	0	296	395	59	93	154	68	86	0	654	757	143	185	113	86	109	103	93	106	100	102
1956 NATIONAL LEAGUE																																
BRO	77	52	25	0	369	300	102	89	77	41	36	0	351	301	77	82	154	93	61	0	720	601	179	171	118	110	107	103	107	92	103	100
CHI	80	39	38	3	335	328	78	77	77	21	56	0	262	380	64	84	157	60	94	3	597	708	142	161	100	93	104	98	91	106	98	101
CIN	77	51	26	0	426	346	128	75	78	40	37	1	349	312	93	66	155	91	63	1	775	658	221	141	126	128	87	117	109	95	108	106
MIL	77	47	29	1	344	265	77	53	78	45	33	0	365	304	100	80	155	92	62	1	709	569	177	133	76	130	101	94	109	90	99	96
NY	77	37	40	0	269	306	94	86	77	30	47	0	271	344	51	58	154	67	87	0	540	650	145	144	152	74	75	94	85	100	97	99
PHI	77	40	37	0	337	335	61	74	77	31	46	0	331	403	60	98	154	71	83	0	668	738	121	172	87	88	118	92	109	118	94	95
PIT	77	35	43	0	301	328	49	45	79	31	45	3	287	325	61	97	157	66	88	3	588	653	110	142	63	89	105	103	86	95	102	103
STL	78	43	34	1	358	328	58	73	78	33	44	1	320	370	66	82	156	76	78	2	678	698	124	155	90	85	104	99	104	106	99	99
1957 NATIONAL LEAGUE																																
BRO	77	43	34	0	383	348	84	88	77	41	36	0	307	243	63	56	154	84	70	0	690	591	147	144	137	84	82	128	88	76	116	114
CHI	78	31	46	1	301	353	81	68	78	31	46	1	327	369	66	76	156	62	92	2	628	722	147	144	103	97	95	94	95	108	96	98
CIN	77	45	32	0	417	410	118	101	77	35	42	0	330	371	69	78	154	80	74	0	747	781	187	179	141	108	106	116	105	109	105	106
MIL	78	45	32	1	312	289	75	51	77	50	27	0	460	324	124	73	155	95	59	1	772	613	199	124	67	158	107	79	125	104	90	88
NY	77	37	40	0	353	341	99	86	77	32	45	0	290	360	58	64	154	69	85	0	643	701	157	150	142	87	86	105	93	101	102	103
PHI	78	38	39	1	299	322	60	60	77	34	43	0	324	334	57	79	155	72	77	2	623	656	117	139	90	82	95	95	93	97	98	99
PIT	77	36	41	0	273	321	20	53	78	26	51	0	313	375	72	105	155	62	92	1	586	696	92	158	45	80	143	88	92	107	94	96
STL	77	42	35	0	356	348	64	70	77	45	32	0	381	318	68	70	154	87	67	0	737	666	132	140	98	90	95	101	109	99	101	99
1958 NATIONAL LEAGUE																																
CHI	77	35	42	0	350	381	101	72	77	37	40	0	359	344	81	70	154	72	82	0	709	725	182	142	112	115	93	103	104	106	100	101
CIN	77	40	37	0	364	337	71	86	77	36	41	0	331	284	52	62	154	76	78	0	695	621	123	148	131	71	84	112	96	86	107	106
LA	77	39	38	0	359	405	92	101	77	32	45	0	309	356	80	72	154	71	83	0	668	761	172	173	122	108	107	112	94	106	105	106
MIL	77	48	29	0	291	207	72	48	77	44	33	0	384	334	95	77	154	92	62	0	675	541	167	125	73	128	98	73	112	91	89	87
PHI	77	35	42	0	318	297	59	77	77	34	43	0	346	365	65	71	154	69	85	0	664	762	124	148	99	84	98	100	100	112	98	100
PIT	77	49	28	0	323	260	41	40	77	35	42	0	339	347	93	83	154	84	70	0	662	607	134	123	50	116	110	87	103	95	95	94
STL	77	39	38	0	329	381	62	88	77	33	44	0	290	323	49	70	154	72	82	0	619	704	111	158	122	68	93	113	86	96	106	100
SF	77	44	33	0	363	354	85	88	77	36	41	0	364	344	85	78	154	80	74	0	727	698	170	166	106	114	112	101	107	104	100	100
1959 NATIONAL LEAGUE																																
CHI	77	38	39	0	336	329	87	76	78	36	41	1	337	359	76	76	155	74	80	1	673	688	163	152	107	109	103	97	100	99	98	99
CIN	77	43	34	0	423	367	101	84	77	31	46	0	341	371	60	78	154	74	80	0	764	738	161	162	128	98	101	109	109	106	103	103
LA	78	46	32	0	363	333	82	90	78	42	36	0	342	337	66	67	156	88	68	0	705	670	148	157	126	91	95	103	101	96	102	101
MIL	79	49	29	1	350	274	83	64	78	37	41	0	374	349	94	61	157	86	70	1	724	623	177	128	93	123	93	87	111	97	95	93
PHI	78	37	40	1	316	354	55	66	77	27	50	0	283	371	58	84	155	64	90	1	599	725	113	150	85	85	108	100	88	104	99	102
PIT	77	47	30	0	348	334	47	53	78	31	46	1	303	346	51	60	155	78	76	1	651	680	112	134	72	89	103	106	92	96	103	104
STL	77	42	35	0	366	359	64	63	77	29	48	0	275	366	54	73	154	71	83	0	641	725	118	137	100	81	92	111	90	101	105	106
SF	77	46	31	0	339	271	80	63	77	41	36	0	366	342	87	76	154	83	71	0	705	613	167	139	89	123	104	88	109	96	95	94

	HOME								ROAD								ALL															
TM	G	W	L	T	R	OR	HR	OHR	G	W	L	T	R	OR	HR	OHR	G	W	L	T	R	OR	HR	OHR	HRF	HRB	HRP	RF	RB	RP	BPF	PPF
1960 NATIONAL LEAGUE																																
CHI	79	33	44	2	331	390	52	78	77	27	50	0	303	386	67	74	156	60	94	2	634	776	119	152	90	97	121	101	98	117	98	101
CIN	77	37	40	0	314	347	75	68	77	30	47	0	326	345	65	66	154	67	87	0	640	692	140	134	107	105	101	98	100	107	98	99
LA	77	42	35	0	379	334	89	97	77	40	37	0	283	259	37	57	154	82	72	0	662	593	126	154	177	69	86	127	88	80	115	114
MIL	77	51	26	0	342	270	90	56	77	37	40	0	382	388	80	74	154	88	66	0	724	658	170	130	96	135	107	82	123	112	91	89
PHI	77	31	46	0	300	373	54	74	77	28	49	0	246	318	45	59	154	59	95	0	546	691	99	133	118	70	91	115	78	96	107	110
PIT	78	52	25	1	362	287	51	36	77	43	34	0	372	306	69	69	155	95	59	1	734	593	120	105	66	109	94	96	112	93	99	97
STL	77	51	26	0	361	308	78	64	78	35	42	1	278	308	60	63	155	86	68	1	639	616	138	127	115	98	91	114	90	87	108	108
SF	77	45	32	0	296	256	46	34	79	34	43	2	375	375	84	73	156	79	75	2	671	631	130	107	56	124	102	78	114	107	90	89
1961 NATIONAL LEAGUE																																
CHI	78	40	37	1	372	391	102	81	78	24	53	1	317	409	74	84	156	64	90	2	689	800	176	165	113	111	106	104	98	111	100	102
CIN	77	47	30	0	345	355	70	75	77	46	31	0	365	298	88	72	154	93	61	0	710	653	158	147	93	110	104	106	98	91	104	103
LA	77	45	32	0	373	358	83	109	77	44	33	0	362	339	74	58	154	89	65	0	735	697	157	167	139	91	93	105	103	99	102	101
MIL	77	45	32	0	324	280	84	72	78	38	39	1	388	376	104	81	155	83	71	1	712	656	188	153	87	135	114	82	111	102	92	91
PHI	78	22	55	1	256	408	43	77	77	25	52	0	328	388	60	78	155	47	107	1	584	796	103	155	86	74	107	91	89	117	94	98
PIT	77	38	39	0	338	338	49	54	77	37	40	0	356	337	79	67	154	75	79	0	694	675	128	121	73	95	93	98	100	98	99	99
STL	78	48	29	1	413	362	54	69	77	32	45	0	290	306	49	67	155	80	74	1	703	668	103	136	104	66	85	124	88	85	113	113
SF	77	45	32	0	371	316	97	77	78	40	37	1	402	339	86	75	155	85	69	1	773	655	183	152	109	118	100	95	112	97	98	96
1962 NATIONAL LEAGUE																																
CHI	81	32	49	0	333	456	71	94	81	27	54	0	299	371	55	65	162	59	103	0	632	827	126	159	131	76	94	114	82	105	106	109
CIN	81	58	23	0	456	294	95	68	81	40	41	0	346	391	72	81	162	98	64	0	802	685	167	149	107	112	102	103	108	94	102	100
HOU	82	32	48	2	268	340	44	41	80	32	48	0	324	377	61	72	162	64	96	2	592	717	105	113	64	87	91	85	88	105	93	95
LA	83	54	29	0	409	289	47	39	82	48	34	0	433	408	93	76	165	102	63	0	842	697	140	115	54	120	101	85	124	103	93	91
MIL	81	49	32	0	374	307	93	74	81	37	44	0	356	358	88	77	162	86	76	0	730	665	181	151	101	125	107	96	102	93	99	98
NY	80	22	58	0	335	510	93	120	81	18	62	1	282	438	46	72	161	40	120	1	617	948	139	192	165	73	101	114	82	121	104	108
PHI	80	46	34	0	341	346	70	66	81	35	46	0	364	413	72	89	161	81	80	0	705	759	142	155	87	107	115	91	103	110	95	95
PIT	81	51	30	0	358	315	48	56	80	42	38	0	348	311	60	62	161	93	68	0	706	626	108	118	86	79	86	102	96	86	102	101
STL	81	44	37	0	407	362	64	83	82	40	41	1	367	302	73	66	163	84	78	1	774	664	137	149	107	92	98	115	98	85	108	107
SF	82	61	21	0	479	299	109	74	83	42	41	0	399	391	95	74	165	103	62	0	878	690	204	148	110	133	100	101	118	95	101	99
1963 NATIONAL LEAGUE																																
CHI	81	43	38	0	298	302	63	70	81	39	42	0	272	276	64	49	162	82	80	0	570	578	127	119	116	97	91	109	88	89	105	105
CIN	81	46	35	0	344	300	65	46	81	40	41	0	304	294	57	71	162	86	76	0	648	594	122	117	88	107	102	107	101	93	104	103
HOU	81	44	37	0	236	268	25	34	81	22	59	0	228	372	37	61	162	66	96	0	464	640	62	95	62	62	90	85	82	108	92	95
LA	81	53	28	0	296	248	42	43	82	46	35	1	344	302	68	68	163	99	63	1	640	550	110	111	66	106	108	88	108	94	95	94
MIL	82	45	36	1	341	307	68	81	81	39	42	0	336	296	71	68	163	84	78	1	677	603	139	149	105	114	121	101	108	97	101	100
NY	81	34	47	0	276	381	61	93	81	17	64	0	225	393	35	69	162	51	111	0	501	774	96	162	139	67	110	104	82	121	99	104
PHI	81	45	36	0	340	282	61	60	81	42	39	0	302	296	65	53	162	87	75	0	642	578	126	113	103	102	92	104	101	92	103	102
PIT	81	42	39	0	275	295	47	42	81	32	49	0	292	300	61	57	162	74	88	0	567	595	108	99	77	98	91	96	93	97	99	99
STL	81	53	28	0	429	311	79	70	81	40	41	0	318	317	49	54	162	93	69	0	747	628	128	124	139	87	86	115	112	97	107	106
SF	81	50	31	0	363	289	101	64	81	38	43	0	362	352	96	62	162	88	74	0	725	641	197	126	104	161	109	93	123	110	96	94
1964 NATIONAL LEAGUE																																
CHI	81	40	41	0	337	397	84	88	81	36	45	0	312	327	61	56	162	76	86	0	649	724	145	144	140	102	100	113	95	104	105	106
CIN	82	47	34	1	331	294	62	59	81	45	36	0	329	272	68	53	163	92	70	1	660	566	130	112	100	106	93	103	98	85	103	102
HOU	81	41	40	0	246	290	29	44	81	25	56	0	249	338	41	61	162	66	96	0	495	628	70	105	73	66	95	91	79	98	96	98
LA	81	41	40	0	259	259	26	38	83	39	42	2	355	313	53	50	164	80	82	2	614	572	79	88	66	73	84	81	101	95	92	91
MIL	81	45	36	0	405	356	89	78	81	43	38	0	398	388	70	82	162	88	74	0	803	744	159	160	109	130	132	98	128	119	97	96
NY	82	33	48	1	298	363	58	61	81	20	61	0	271	413	45	69	163	53	109	1	569	776	103	130	101	85	105	94	92	121	95	98
PHI	81	46	35	0	352	298	59	61	81	46	35	0	341	334	71	68	162	92	70	0	693	632	130	129	88	115	115	97	108	99	99	98
PIT	81	42	39	0	340	315	55	31	81	38	43	0	323	321	66	61	162	80	82	0	663	636	121	92	70	116	87	101	101	97	101	101
STL	81	48	33	0	386	378	59	81	81	45	36	0	329	274	50	52	162	93	69	0	715	652	109	133	133	79	93	124	98	90	112	111
SF	81	44	37	0	314	299	86	63	81	46	35	0	342	288	79	55	162	90	72	0	656	587	165	118	111	130	96	98	101	91	100	99
1965 NATIONAL LEAGUE																																
CHI	83	40	41	2	330	380	79	94	81	32	49	0	305	343	55	60	164	72	90	2	635	723	134	154	139	85	96	106	94	106	102	103
CIN	81	49	32	0	450	352	108	69	81	40	41	0	375	352	75	67	162	89	73	0	825	704	183	136	122	125	98	110	122	106	104	102
HOU	81	36	45	0	250	313	25	32	81	29	52	0	319	398	72	91	162	65	97	0	569	711	97	123	37	106	132	79	98	120	89	91
LA	81	50	31	0	268	218	26	41	81	47	34	0	340	303	52	86	162	97	65	0	608	521	78	127	52	78	120	78	102	88	91	90
MIL	82	29	52	1	258	380	50	81	82	21	60	1	237	372	57	66	164	50	112	2	495	752	107	147	104	80	106	102	75	109	100	104
PHI	80	45	35	0	312	300	77	55	82	40	41	1	342	367	67	61	162	85	76	1	654	667	144	116	105	105	87	90	106	107	95	95
PIT	82	49	32	1	334	284	37	38	81	41	40	0	341	296	74	51	163	90	72	1	675	580	111	89	62	97	83	97	103	90	100	98
STL	81	42	39	0	379	361	68	103	81	38	42	1	328	313	41	63	162	80	81	1	707	674	109	166	154	66	98	114	102	97	106	106
SF	81	51	30	0	365	327	81	81	82	44	37	1	317	266	78	56	163	95	67	1	682	593	159	137	121	110	95	119	94	83	111	109
1966 NATIONAL LEAGUE																																
ATL	82	43	38	1	394	335	119	82	81	42	39	0	388	348	88	47	163	85	77	1	782	683	207	129	141	124	79	98	119	105	99	97
CHI	81	32	49	0	342	410	80	100	81	27	54	0	302	399	60	84	162	59	103	0	644	809	140	184	120	95	122	105	97	119	100	103
CIN	79	46	33	0	417	372	91	63	81	30	51	0	275	330	58	60	160	76	84	0	692	702	149	153	151	88	90	129	92	95	114	114
HOU	81	45	36	0	318	317	48	48	82	27	54	1	294	378	64	82	163	72	90	1	612	695	112	130	68	96	107	96	94	105	97	99
LA	81	53	28	0	286	220	43	36	81	42	39	0	320	270	65	48	162	95	67	0	606	490	108	84	73	86	69	88	94	78	97	95
NY	81	32	49	0	276	372	51	94	80	34	46	0	311	389	47	72	161	66	95	0	587	761	98	166	117	67	108	91	95	120	94	97
PHI	81	48	33	0	354	319	52	65	81	39	42	0	342	321	65	72	162	87	75	0	696	640	117	137	87	90	105	102	104	96	101	100
PIT	81	46	35	0	384	317	48	48	81	46	35	0	375	324	110	77	162	92	70	0	759	641	158	125	54	144	123	101	114	98	101	99
STL	81	43	38	0	274	288	48	64	81	40	41	0	297	289	60	66	162	83	79	0	571	577	108	130	90	81	97	96	86	87	100	100
SF	81	47	34	0	317	312	91	77	80	46	34	0	358	314	90	63	161	93	68	0	675	626	181	140	108	128	101	94	105	98	97	97
1967 NATIONAL LEAGUE																																
ATL	81	48	33	0	352	316	91	74	81	29	52	0	279	324	67	44	162	77	85	0	631	640	158	118	141	121	91	109	97	99	104	105
CHI	84	49	34	1	366	332	70	90	78	38	40	0	336	292	58	52	162	87	74	1	702	624	128	142	131	104	111	103	111	100	101	100
CIN	81	49	32	0	343	287	57	66	81	38	43	0	261	275	52	35	162	87	75	0	604	563	109	101	136	85	76	116	89	84	109	108
HOU	81	46	35	0	337	315	31	32	81	23	58	0	289	427	62	88	162	69	93	0	626	742	93	120	44	122	145	91	108	125	93	95
LA	81	42	39	0	241	230	36	35	81	31	50	0	278	365	46	58	162	73	89	0	519	595	82	93	70	87	95	75	96	106	88	89
NY	78	36	42	0	258	307	44	61	84	25	59	0	240	365	39	63	162	61	101	0	498	672	83	124	108	73	105	99	81	106	99	102
PHI	80	45	35	0	320	292	48	44	82	37	45	0	292	289	55	42	162	82	80	0	612	581	103	86	98	92	78	107	94	90	104	104
PIT	81	49	32	0	370	321	43	49	82	32	49	1	309	372	48	59	163	81	81	1	679	693	91	108	88	87	101	102	109	111	100	100
STL	81	49	32	0	326	301	53	54	80	52	28	0	369	256	62	43	161	101	60	0	695	557	115	97	102	103	88	100	111	91	101	99
SF	82	51	31	0	333	271	65	59	80	40	40	0	319	280	75	54	162	91	71	0	652	551	140	113	95	131	109	99	104	89	101	99
1968 NATIONAL LEAGUE																																
ATL	81	41	40	0	241	241	42	43	82	40	41	1	273	308	38	44	163	81	81	1	514	549	80	87	104	87	94	85	99	105	93	94
CHI	82	47	34	1	363	332	83	83	81	37	44	0	249	279	47	55	163	84	78	1	612	611	130	138	152	120	129	126	97	98	112	112
CIN	82	40	41	1	377	400	55	88	81	43	38	0	313	273	51	48	163	83	79	1	690	673	106	114	118	112	108	111	127	111	108	111
HOU	81	42	39	0	279	269	22	30	81	30	51	0	231	319	44	38	162	72	90	0	510	588	66	68	65	85	91	99	93	105	99	100
LA	81	41	40	0	212	215	25	24	81	35	46	0	258	294	42	41	162	76	86	0	470	509	67	65	61	90	87	79	94	100	91	91

TM	HOME G	W	L	T	R	OR	HR	OHR	ROAD G	W	L	T	R	OR	HR	OHR	ALL G	W	L	T	R	OR	HR	OHR	HRF	HRB	HRP	RF	RB	RP	BPF	PPF
NY	82	32	49	1	224	270	49	50	81	41	40	0	249	229	32	37	163	73	89	1	473	499	81	87	135	76	82	101	83	87	102	103
PHI	81	38	43	0	274	297	52	46	81	38	43	0	269	318	48	45	162	76	86	0	543	615	100	91	104	111	102	97	100	112	97	99
PIT	81	40	41	0	289	268	33	30	82	40	41	1	294	264	47	43	163	80	82	1	583	532	80	73	73	101	93	101	103	95	101	100
STL	81	47	34	0	267	218	31	35	81	50	31	0	316	254	42	47	162	97	65	0	583	472	73	82	77	92	102	87	110	91	95	93
SF	81	42	39	0	299	242	60	32	82	46	35	1	300	287	48	54	163	88	74	1	599	529	108	86	93	126	101	94	110	98	98	96

1969 NATIONAL LEAGUE

TM	HOME G	W	L	T	R	OR	HR	OHR	ROAD G	W	L	T	R	OR	HR	OHR	ALL G	W	L	T	R	OR	HR	OHR	HRF	HRB	HRP	RF	RB	RP	BPF	PPF
ATL	81	50	31	0	360	321	77	84	81	43	38	0	331	310	64	60	162	93	69	0	691	631	141	144	128	103	104	106	102	93	104	103
CHI	82	49	32	1	387	321	84	64	81	43	38	0	333	290	58	54	163	92	70	1	720	611	142	118	128	100	85	112	102	88	107	105
CIN	81	50	31	0	407	373	97	74	82	39	42	1	391	395	74	75	163	89	73	1	798	768	171	149	115	131	117	101	122	118	99	98
HOU	81	52	29	0	371	313	47	43	81	29	52	0	305	355	57	68	162	81	81	0	676	668	104	111	74	98	102	103	101	100	101	101
LA	81	50	31	0	325	258	41	55	81	35	46	0	320	303	56	67	162	85	77	0	645	561	97	122	80	88	109	94	100	88	99	97
MON	81	24	57	0	288	421	73	87	81	28	53	0	294	370	52	58	162	52	110	0	582	791	125	145	138	87	99	104	88	117	100	103
NY	82	52	30	0	312	270	56	59	80	48	32	0	320	271	53	60	162	100	62	0	632	541	109	119	101	89	96	98	96	83	100	99
PHI	81	30	51	0	317	378	75	64	81	33	48	0	328	367	62	70	162	63	99	0	645	745	137	134	104	111	109	99	100	114	98	99
PIT	81	47	34	0	324	322	41	33	81	41	40	0	401	330	78	63	162	88	74	0	725	652	119	96	55	122	101	90	116	106	95	94
STL	80	42	38	0	273	273	41	43	82	45	37	0	322	267	49	56	162	87	75	0	595	540	90	99	84	79	85	96	91	83	100	99
SD	81	28	53	0	239	358	47	47	81	24	57	0	229	388	52	66	162	52	110	0	468	746	99	113	80	90	100	95	74	113	97	100
SF	81	52	29	0	362	317	77	61	81	38	43	0	351	319	59	59	162	90	72	0	713	636	136	120	116	102	92	102	107	97	101	100

1970 NATIONAL LEAGUE

TM	HOME G	W	L	T	R	OR	HR	OHR	ROAD G	W	L	T	R	OR	HR	OHR	ALL G	W	L	T	R	OR	HR	OHR	HRF	HRB	HRP	RF	RB	RP	BPF	PPF
ATL	81	42	39	0	395	398	92	119	81	34	47	0	341	374	68	66	162	76	86	0	736	772	160	185	150	95	105	110	96	101	104	105
CHI	80	46	34	0	471	394	109	92	82	38	44	0	335	285	70	51	162	84	78	0	806	679	179	143	161	99	79	138	92	79	120	118
CIN	81	57	24	0	416	334	100	58	81	45	36	0	359	347	91	60	162	102	60	0	775	681	191	118	106	131	84	107	102	90	104	103
HOU	81	44	37	0	350	351	51	64	81	35	46	0	394	412	78	67	162	79	83	0	744	763	129	131	81	100	104	88	109	111	93	94
LA	81	39	42	0	310	316	35	82	80	48	32	0	439	368	52	82	161	87	74	0	749	684	87	164	88	67	121	78	114	106	90	89
MON	81	39	41	0	363	385	77	91	82	34	48	0	324	422	59	71	162	73	89	0	687	807	136	162	128	86	101	102	94	109	100	102
NY	82	44	38	0	374	314	63	75	80	39	41	0	321	316	57	60	162	83	79	0	695	630	120	135	114	80	88	105	91	84	104	103
PHI	80	40	40	0	293	337	48	63	81	33	48	0	301	393	53	69	161	73	88	0	594	730	101	132	92	75	96	92	85	103	96	98
PIT	82	50	32	0	356	315	43	41	80	39	41	0	373	349	87	65	162	89	73	0	729	664	130	106	56	114	98	92	103	95	97	96
STL	81	34	47	0	377	418	51	44	81	42	39	0	367	329	62	58	162	76	86	0	744	747	113	102	80	87	79	113	96	95	106	106
SD	81	31	50	0	312	393	68	56	81	32	49	0	369	395	104	93	162	63	99	0	681	788	172	149	64	152	132	92	98	112	95	96
SF	81	48	33	0	413	386	84	77	81	38	43	0	418	440	81	79	162	86	76	0	831	826	165	156	101	118	113	94	119	118	96	96

1971 NATIONAL LEAGUE

TM	HOME G	W	L	T	R	OR	HR	OHR	ROAD G	W	L	T	R	OR	HR	OHR	ALL G	W	L	T	R	OR	HR	OHR	HRF	HRB	HRP	RF	RB	RP	BPF	PPF
ATL	82	43	39	0	366	384	96	90	80	39	41	0	277	315	57	62	162	82	80	0	643	699	153	152	146	110	111	121	92	100	110	111
CHI	81	44	37	0	363	342	74	70	81	39	42	0	274	306	54	62	162	83	79	0	637	648	128	132	122	101	105	120	91	94	110	110
CIN	81	46	35	0	303	251	69	51	81	33	48	0	283	330	69	61	162	79	83	0	586	581	138	112	93	125	103	91	96	95	96	96
HOU	81	39	42	0	256	263	18	27	81	40	41	0	329	304	53	48	162	79	83	0	585	567	71	75	47	77	88	83	100	97	93	92
LA	81	42	39	0	324	286	43	56	81	47	34	0	339	301	52	54	162	89	73	0	663	587	95	110	94	84	97	96	106	95	99	98
MON	80	36	44	0	304	366	50	68	82	35	46	1	318	363	38	65	162	71	90	1	622	729	88	133	115	72	106	100	99	115	99	100
NY	81	44	37	0	281	256	48	50	81	39	42	0	307	294	50	50	162	83	79	0	588	550	98	100	98	85	87	90	96	91	96	96
PHI	81	34	47	0	296	353	73	80	81	33	48	0	262	335	50	52	162	67	95	0	558	688	123	132	143	89	95	107	86	104	103	105
PIT	80	52	28	0	393	279	66	49	82	45	37	0	395	320	88	59	162	97	65	0	788	599	154	108	82	146	107	98	126	98	99	97
STL	82	45	36	1	376	358	38	49	81	45	36	0	363	341	57	51	163	90	72	1	739	699	95	100	79	90	100	103	115	110	101	100
SD	81	33	48	0	233	296	42	43	80	28	52	0	253	314	54	50	161	61	100	0	486	610	96	93	81	91	89	92	80	99	96	98
SF	81	51	30	0	372	300	71	58	81	39	42	0	334	344	69	70	162	90	72	0	706	644	140	128	94	127	117	100	112	103	100	99

1972 NATIONAL LEAGUE

TM	HOME G	W	L	T	R	OR	HR	OHR	ROAD G	W	L	T	R	OR	HR	OHR	ALL G	W	L	T	R	OR	HR	OHR	HRF	HRB	HRP	RF	RB	RP	BPF	PPF
ATL	78	36	41	1	339	392	86	88	77	34	43	0	289	338	58	67	155	70	84	1	628	730	144	155	133	112	121	113	99	114	105	106
CHI	77	46	31	0	392	305	83	63	79	39	39	1	293	262	50	49	156	85	70	1	685	567	133	112	146	94	82	126	99	83	114	112
CIN	76	42	34	0	300	266	58	59	78	53	25	0	407	291	66	70	154	95	59	0	707	557	124	129	90	118	122	85	125	102	93	91
HOU	77	41	36	0	367	355	58	56	76	43	33	0	341	281	76	58	153	84	69	0	708	636	134	114	86	129	113	114	112	101	106	105
LA	75	41	34	0	267	221	46	37	80	44	36	0	317	306	52	46	155	85	70	0	584	527	98	83	92	88	75	85	103	93	94	93
MON	78	35	43	0	252	324	50	56	78	35	43	0	261	285	41	47	156	70	86	0	513	609	91	103	118	72	81	104	82	96	102	104
NY	78	41	37	0	254	264	45	56	78	42	36	0	274	314	60	62	156	83	73	0	528	578	105	118	84	100	112	89	91	99	95	96
PHI	79	28	51	0	246	316	49	57	77	31	46	0	257	319	49	60	156	59	97	0	503	635	98	117	94	89	105	94	85	106	97	99
PIT	78	49	29	0	351	259	53	34	77	47	30	0	340	253	57	56	155	96	59	0	691	512	110	90	79	108	87	103	111	84	103	100
STL	77	40	37	0	298	308	31	38	79	35	44	0	270	292	39	49	156	75	81	0	568	600	70	87	82	66	81	109	89	94	105	105
SD	80	26	54	0	217	315	41	64	73	32	41	0	271	350	61	57	153	58	95	0	488	665	102	121	81	101	120	79	93	124	88	91
SF	77	34	43	0	336	321	86	65	78	35	43	0	326	328	64	65	155	69	86	0	662	649	150	130	116	124	110	101	110	108	100	100

1973 NATIONAL LEAGUE

TM	HOME G	W	L	T	R	OR	HR	OHR	ROAD G	W	L	T	R	OR	HR	OHR	ALL G	W	L	T	R	OR	HR	OHR	HRF	HRB	HRP	RF	RB	RP	BPF	PPF
ATL	81	40	40	1	460	437	118	87	81	36	45	0	339	337	88	57	162	76	85	1	799	774	206	144	136	137	98	129	105	102	113	113
CHI	80	41	39	0	327	356	66	72	81	36	45	0	287	299	51	56	161	77	84	0	614	655	117	128	127	80	87	116	85	90	108	109
CIN	81	50	31	0	330	287	47	67	81	49	32	0	411	334	90	68	162	99	63	0	741	621	137	135	75	119	123	85	118	101	93	92
HOU	81	41	40	0	315	322	58	53	81	41	40	0	366	350	76	58	162	82	80	0	681	672	134	111	84	111	94	90	107	106	95	95
LA	81	50	31	0	338	271	63	62	81	45	35	1	337	294	47	67	162	95	66	1	675	565	110	129	110	81	94	98	100	85	100	99
MON	81	43	38	0	364	353	63	70	81	36	45	0	304	349	62	58	162	79	83	0	668	702	125	128	110	92	94	109	95	100	104	104
NY	81	43	38	0	314	283	39	61	80	39	41	0	294	305	46	66	161	82	79	0	608	588	85	127	89	70	101	99	91	88	101	100
PHI	81	38	43	0	358	381	78	80	81	33	48	0	284	336	56	51	162	71	91	0	642	717	134	131	141	86	84	117	88	98	108	109
PIT	81	41	40	0	334	301	72	42	81	39	42	0	370	392	82	68	162	80	82	0	704	693	154	110	78	134	96	84	114	112	92	92
STL	81	43	38	0	290	255	27	30	81	38	43	0	353	348	48	75	162	81	81	0	643	603	75	105	49	79	101	79	106	99	91	90
SD	81	31	50	0	273	355	51	80	81	29	52	0	275	415	61	77	162	60	102	0	548	770	112	157	94	91	124	90	87	118	94	97
SF	81	47	34	0	395	363	85	79	81	41	40	0	344	339	76	66	162	88	74	0	739	702	161	145	115	118	107	110	105	100	105	104

1974 NATIONAL LEAGUE

TM	HOME G	W	L	T	R	OR	HR	OHR	ROAD G	W	L	T	R	OR	HR	OHR	ALL G	W	L	T	R	OR	HR	OHR	HRF	HRB	HRP	RF	RB	RP	BPF	PPF
ATL	81	46	35	0	337	290	65	44	82	42	39	1	324	273	55	53	163	88	74	1	661	563	120	97	102	110	90	106	93	80	105	104
CHI	81	32	49	0	344	424	67	72	81	34	47	0	325	402	43	50	162	66	96	0	669	826	110	122	142	85	95	104	99	120	100	102
CIN	82	50	31	1	389	295	74	62	81	48	33	0	387	336	61	64	163	98	64	1	776	631	135	126	108	123	116	95	117	97	98	96
HOU	81	46	35	0	330	293	58	35	81	35	46	0	323	339	52	49	162	81	81	0	653	632	110	84	93	85	95	99	96	98	98	98
LA	81	52	29	0	355	250	68	51	81	50	31	0	443	311	71	61	162	102	60	0	798	561	139	112	92	137	112	83	128	93	93	90
MON	80	42	38	0	356	329	50	49	81	37	44	0	306	328	36	50	161	79	82	0	662	657	86	99	115	75	86	108	95	94	104	104
NY	81	36	45	0	279	325	43	49	81	35	46	0	293	321	53	50	162	71	91	0	572	646	96	99	90	94	97	98	96	99	100	100
PHI	81	46	35	0	378	337	55	56	81	34	47	0	298	364	40	55	162	80	82	0	676	701	95	111	115	82	94	107	97	101	103	104
PIT	81	52	29	0	380	303	47	32	81	36	45	0	371	354	67	61	162	88	74	0	751	657	114	93	64	130	105	95	114	101	98	96
STL	81	44	37	0	356	329	45	46	80	42	38	0	321	314	38	51	162	86	75	0	677	643	83	97	77	89	106	98	93	104	103	103
SD	81	36	45	0	272	381	47	54	81	24	57	0	269	449	52	70	162	60	102	0	541	830	99	124	83	104	126	90	87	127	93	97
SF	81	37	44	0	340	398	50	61	81	35	46	0	294	325	43	55	162	72	90	0	634	723	93	116	111	83	102	117	88	99	108	109

1975 NATIONAL LEAGUE

TM	HOME G	W	L	T	R	OR	HR	OHR	ROAD G	W	L	T	R	OR	HR	OHR	ALL G	W	L	T	R	OR	HR	OHR	HRF	HRB	HRP	RF	RB	RP	BPF	PPF
ATL	80	37	43	0	280	350	58	63	81	30	51	0	303	389	49	38	161	67	94	0	583	739	107	101	135	90	83	92	92	115	95	97
CHI	81	42	39	0	392	427	54	71	81	33	48	0	320	400	41	59	162	75	87	0	712	827	95	130	122	85	113	112	102	118	104	105
CIN	81	64	17	0	457	275	70	52	81	44	37	0	383	311	54	60	162	108	54	0	840	586	124	112	108	116	107	107	120	87	104	101
HOU	81	37	44	0	313	338	40	43	81	27	53	1	351	373	44	63	162	64	97	1	664	711	84	106	78	93	113	90	105	112	94	95
LA	81	49	32	0	319	221	64	52	81	39	42	0	329	313	54	52	162	88	74	0	648	534	118	104	109	110	98	86	103	85	95	93
MON	81	39	42	0	326	375	53	57	81	36	45	0	275	315	45	45	162	75	87	0	601	690	98	102	120	87	90	117	83	94	108	109
NY	81	42	39	0	294	301	52	48	81	40	41	0	352	324	49	51	162	82	80	0	646	625	101	99	100	98	96	89	101	99	95	95

TM	HOME								ROAD								ALL																
	G	W	L	T	R	OR	HR	OHR	G	W	L	T	R	OR	HR	OHR	G	W	L	T	R	OR	HR	OHR	HRF	HRB	HRP	RF	RB	RP	BPF	PPF
PHI	81	51	30	0	401	326	72	47	81	35	46	0	334	368	53	64	162	86	76	0	735	694	125	111	102	121	109	104	108	103	101	101
PIT	80	52	28	0	348	270	67	41	81	40	41	0	364	295	71	38	161	92	69	0	712	565	138	79	101	132	79	96	108	87	99	97
STL	82	45	36	1	351	352	46	39	81	37	44	0	311	337	35	59	163	82	80	1	662	689	81	98	90	83	97	107	95	99	103	103
SD	81	38	43	0	279	338	33	38	81	33	48	0	273	345	45	61	162	71	91	0	552	683	78	99	68	90	111	99	83	101	100	100
SF	81	46	35	0	346	335	36	37	80	34	46	0	313	336	48	55	161	80	81	0	659	671	84	92	72	95	103	103	98	99	102	102

1976 NATIONAL LEAGUE

TM	G	W	L	T	R	OR	HR	OHR	G	W	L	T	R	OR	HR	OHR	G	W	L	T	R	OR	HR	OHR	HRF	HRB	HRP	RF	RB	RP	BPF	PPF
ATL	81	34	47	0	338	401	43	56	81	36	45	0	282	299	39	30	162	70	92	0	620	700	82	86	138	75	76	124	87	96	111	112
CHI	81	42	39	0	355	385	71	84	81	33	48	0	256	343	34	39	162	75	87	0	611	728	105	123	193	78	90	121	86	102	109	111
CIN	81	49	32	0	426	337	73	46	81	53	28	0	431	296	68	54	162	102	60	0	857	633	141	100	99	155	114	106	129	98	103	100
HOU	82	46	36	0	277	264	30	27	80	34	46	0	348	393	36	55	162	80	82	0	625	657	66	82	63	89	103	73	113	117	86	87
LA	81	49	32	0	296	265	42	48	81	43	38	0	312	278	49	49	162	92	70	0	608	543	91	97	93	102	108	96	95	85	100	99
MON	80	27	53	0	266	374	45	41	82	28	54	0	265	360	49	46	162	55	107	0	531	734	94	89	90	106	101	103	82	111	100	103
NY	82	45	37	0	269	245	43	43	80	41	39	0	346	293	59	54	162	86	76	0	615	538	102	97	76	126	121	80	104	92	92	91
PHI	81	53	28	0	424	277	63	49	81	48	33	0	346	280	47	49	162	101	61	0	770	557	110	98	117	110	100	112	111	83	107	105
PIT	81	47	34	0	366	302	54	44	81	45	36	0	342	328	56	51	162	92	70	0	708	630	110	95	93	124	108	100	109	100	100	100
STL	81	37	44	0	335	346	27	40	81	35	46	0	294	325	36	51	162	72	90	0	629	671	63	91	78	76	107	108	94	100	104	104
SD	80	42	38	0	254	271	30	38	82	31	51	0	316	391	34	49	162	73	89	0	570	662	64	87	85	74	98	77	100	114	88	90
SF	81	40	41	0	314	352	44	32	81	34	47	0	281	334	41	36	162	74	88	0	595	686	85	68	98	90	73	107	89	102	103	104

1977 NATIONAL LEAGUE

TM	G	W	L	T	R	OR	HR	OHR	G	W	L	T	R	OR	HR	OHR	G	W	L	T	R	OR	HR	OHR	HRF	HRB	HRP	RF	RB	RP	BPF	PPF
ATL	81	40	41	0	416	488	97	111	81	21	60	0	262	407	42	58	162	61	101	0	678	895	139	169	189	70	87	130	83	110	113	115
CHI	81	46	35	0	411	402	69	82	81	35	46	0	281	337	42	46	162	81	81	0	692	739	111	128	162	62	70	128	85	91	114	115
CIN	81	48	33	0	408	355	83	83	81	40	41	0	394	370	98	73	162	88	74	0	802	725	181	156	98	137	120	100	113	103	100	99
HOU	81	46	35	0	309	291	40	33	81	35	46	0	371	359	74	77	162	81	81	0	680	650	114	110	51	111	103	83	103	93	92	
LA	81	51	30	0	386	273	96	65	81	47	34	0	383	309	95	54	162	98	64	0	769	582	191	119	108	134	87	97	108	83	100	98
MON	81	38	43	0	329	362	66	65	81	37	47	0	336	374	72	70	162	75	87	0	665	736	138	135	93	105	103	97	95	104	98	99
NY	79	35	44	0	282	297	46	56	83	29	54	0	305	366	42	62	162	64	98	0	587	663	88	118	102	63	83	90	86	96	96	97
PHI	81	60	21	0	453	299	101	63	81	41	40	0	394	369	85	71	162	101	61	0	847	668	186	134	106	133	99	100	118	95	100	98
PIT	81	58	23	0	396	315	64	76	81	38	43	0	338	350	69	73	162	96	66	0	734	665	133	149	100	99	110	104	100	92	103	102
STL	83	52	31	0	379	314	41	53	79	31	48	0	358	374	55	86	162	83	79	0	737	688	96	139	66	87	120	91	108	101	96	95
SD	81	35	46	0	299	368	53	70	81	34	47	0	393	466	67	90	162	69	93	0	692	834	120	160	79	100	130	79	111	131	88	89
SF	81	38	43	0	353	371	62	56	81	37	44	0	320	340	72	58	162	75	87	0	673	711	134	114	91	101	88	108	90	95	104	105

1978 NATIONAL LEAGUE

TM	G	W	L	T	R	OR	HR	OHR	G	W	L	T	R	OR	HR	OHR	G	W	L	T	R	OR	HR	OHR	HRF	HRB	HRP	RF	RB	RP	BPF	PPF
ATL	81	39	42	0	364	400	87	89	81	30	51	0	236	350	36	43	162	69	93	0	600	750	123	132	201	76	84	126	82	103	112	114
CHI	82	44	38	0	393	387	41	76	80	35	45	0	271	337	31	49	162	79	83	0	664	724	72	125	138	58	96	122	93	101	110	111
CIN	80	49	31	0	379	338	74	61	81	43	38	0	331	350	62	61	161	92	69	0	710	688	136	122	111	124	113	107	108	105	103	102
HOU	81	50	31	0	327	254	30	29	81	24	57	0	278	380	40	57	162	74	88	0	605	634	70	86	63	81	94	89	100	103	95	95
LA	81	54	27	0	361	272	78	59	81	41	40	0	366	301	71	48	162	95	67	0	727	573	149	107	115	131	97	96	114	91	99	97
MON	80	41	39	0	299	283	46	49	82	35	47	0	334	328	75	68	162	76	86	0	633	611	121	117	70	134	132	91	102	99	96	95
NY	80	33	47	0	295	340	37	60	82	33	49	0	312	350	49	54	162	66	96	0	607	690	86	114	96	83	108	98	96	108	98	99
PHI	82	54	28	0	405	279	80	70	80	36	44	0	303	307	53	48	162	90	72	0	708	586	133	118	140	104	94	109	103	88	105	104
PIT	81	55	26	0	389	310	57	61	80	33	47	0	295	327	58	42	161	88	73	0	684	637	115	103	115	101	90	110	101	95	105	105
STL	81	37	44	0	289	307	29	32	81	32	49	0	311	350	50	62	162	69	93	0	600	657	79	94	56	95	100	90	98	106	95	96
SD	81	50	31	0	291	245	31	23	81	34	47	0	300	353	44	51	162	84	78	0	591	598	75	74	59	88	82	83	100	99	92	92
SF	81	50	31	0	291	244	47	30	81	39	42	0	322	350	70	54	162	89	73	0	613	594	117	84	64	132	96	81	104	100	91	91

1979 NATIONAL LEAGUE

TM	G	W	L	T	R	OR	HR	OHR	G	W	L	T	R	OR	HR	OHR	G	W	L	T	R	OR	HR	OHR	HRF	HRB	HRP	RF	RB	RP	BPF	PPF
ATL	79	34	45	0	359	425	73	80	81	32	49	0	310	338	53	52	160	66	94	0	669	763	126	132	142	90	93	121	91	102	109	110
CHI	81	45	36	0	423	370	79	72	81	35	46	0	283	337	56	55	162	80	82	0	706	707	135	127	132	98	93	125	91	93	112	112
CIN	80	48	32	0	360	298	71	53	81	42	39	0	371	346	61	50	161	90	71	0	731	644	132	103	113	104	83	94	111	99	97	96
HOU	81	52	29	0	269	234	15	31	81	37	44	0	314	348	34	59	162	89	73	0	583	582	49	90	52	51	93	78	95	94	90	90
LA	81	46	35	0	389	341	106	93	81	33	48	0	350	376	77	46	162	79	83	0	739	717	183	101	127	133	78	100	109	100	100	99
MON	81	56	25	0	378	275	68	51	79	39	40	0	323	306	75	65	160	95	65	0	701	581	143	116	85	132	109	102	101	86	102	101
NY	82	28	53	1	267	354	30	58	81	35	46	0	326	352	44	62	163	63	99	1	593	706	74	120	82	67	107	90	91	107	95	96
PHI	81	43	38	0	332	342	52	72	82	41	40	1	351	376	63	67	163	84	78	1	683	718	119	135	97	102	115	95	103	107	97	97
PIT	81	48	33	0	399	339	74	77	82	50	31	1	376	304	74	48	163	98	64	1	775	643	148	125	124	112	94	110	107	90	106	104
STL	82	42	39	1	379	372	48	65	81	44	37	0	352	321	52	62	163	86	76	1	731	693	100	127	98	85	105	110	102	97	105	104
SD	81	39	42	0	287	335	36	47	80	29	51	0	316	346	57	61	161	68	93	0	603	681	93	108	71	91	106	93	92	103	96	97
SF	81	38	43	0	298	361	53	61	81	33	48	0	374	390	72	82	162	71	91	0	672	751	125	143	75	123	138	87	106	118	92	93

1980 NATIONAL LEAGUE

TM	G	W	L	T	R	OR	HR	OHR	G	W	L	T	R	OR	HR	OHR	G	W	L	T	R	OR	HR	OHR	HRF	HRB	HRP	RF	RB	RP	BPF	PPF
ATL	80	50	30	0	352	297	84	79	81	31	50	0	278	363	60	52	161	81	80	0	630	660	144	131	142	119	108	102	96	100	101	101
CHI	81	37	44	0	338	385	54	62	81	27	54	0	276	343	53	47	162	64	98	0	614	728	107	109	113	98	99	114	88	104	106	108
CIN	82	44	37	1	356	349	66	70	81	45	36	0	351	321	47	43	163	89	73	1	707	670	113	113	144	90	89	104	106	101	102	101
HOU	81	55	26	0	329	255	26	22	82	38	44	0	308	334	49	47	163	93	70	0	637	589	75	69	53	91	82	93	99	92	98	97
LA	82	55	27	0	327	272	82	58	81	37	44	0	336	319	66	47	163	92	71	0	663	591	148	105	121	129	94	92	104	94	97	96
MON	80	51	29	0	357	286	51	40	82	39	43	0	337	343	63	60	162	90	72	0	694	629	114	100	78	124	109	98	107	98	99	98
NY	82	38	44	0	306	336	35	40	80	29	51	0	305	366	26	60	162	67	95	0	611	702	61	140	126	53	115	93	98	111	96	97
PHI	81	49	32	0	398	334	64	44	81	42	39	0	330	305	54	43	162	91	71	0	728	639	117	87	112	105	80	115	104	92	107	106
PIT	81	47	34	0	355	322	63	53	81	36	45	0	311	353	57	56	162	83	79	0	666	646	116	110	105	110	106	99	96	103	103	
STL	81	41	40	0	396	357	41	42	81	33	48	0	342	353	60	48	162	74	88	0	738	710	101	90	78	108	98	107	110	106	103	102
SD	81	45	36	0	295	274	29	33	82	28	53	1	296	380	38	64	163	73	89	1	591	654	67	97	63	80	108	86	97	105	93	94
SF	81	44	37	0	283	293	24	41	80	31	49	0	290	341	56	51	161	75	86	0	573	634	80	92	62	92	112	91	92	101	96	96

1981 NATIONAL LEAGUE

TM	G	W	L	T	R	OR	HR	OHR	G	W	L	T	R	OR	HR	OHR	G	W	L	T	R	OR	HR	OHR	HRF	HRB	HRP	RF	RB	RP	BPF	PPF
ATL	50	22	27	1	182	195	37	41	57	28	29	2	213	221	27	21	107	50	56	1	395	416	64	62	172	82	76	99	95	100	99	100
CHI	58	27	30	1	239,	254	41	38	48	11	35	2	131	229	16	21	106	38	65	3	370	483	57	59	164	68	75	111	84	111	104	106
CIN	54	32	22	0	226	230	26	41	54	34	20	0	238	210	38	26	108	66	42	0	464	440	64	67	105	105	108	103	109	104	101	100
HOU	51	31	20	0	166	106	16	9	53	30	29	0	228	225	29	31	110	61	49	0	394	331	45	40	51	96	76	72	105	85	88	87
LA	56	33	23	0	221	171	37	34	54	30	24	0	229	185	45	20	110	63	47	0	450	356	82	54	106	129	87	93	107	83	100	96
MON	56	38	18	0	255	170	39	23	52	22	30	0	188	224	42	35	108	60	48	0	443	394	81	58	77	154	112	97	106	96	101	98
NY	52	24	27	1	186	207	30	38	53	17	35	1	162	225	27	36	105	41	62	2	348	432	57	74	108	96	121	102	84	103	101	102
PHI	55	36	19	0	295	261	41	39	52	23	29	0	196	211	28	33	107	59	48	0	491	472	69	72	122	105	110	127	104	101	112	112
PIT	51	22	28	1	189	207	29	29	52	24	28	0	218	218	26	31	103	46	56	1	407	425	55	60	103	95	103	93	105	110	96	96
STL	53	32	21	0	244	218	22	26	52	27	22	1	220	199	28	26	105	59	43	1	464	417	50	52	86	93	97	105	113	103	102	101
SD	55	20	35	0	168	223	9	27	55	21	34	0	214	232	28	37	110	41	69	0	382	455	32	64	61	62	126	87	95	112	93	95
SF	53	29	24	0	218	204	28	19	58	27	31	0	209	210	35	38	111	56	55	0	427	414	63	57	72	119	103	109	94	91	105	105

1982 NATIONAL LEAGUE

TM	G	W	L	T	R	OR	HR	OHR	G	W	L	T	R	OR	HR	OHR	G	W	L	T	R	OR	HR	OHR	HRF	HRB	HRP	RF	RB	RP	BPF	PPF
ATL	81	42	39	0	388	387	95	86	81	47	34	0	351	315	51	40	162	89	73	0	739	702	146	126	185	96	82	115	104	99	107	107
CHI	81	38	43	0	352	371	53	62	81	35	46	0	324	338	49	63	162	73	89	0	676	709	102	125	102	95	114	108	99	103	103	104
CIN	81	33	48	0	296	325	37	47	81	28	53	0	249	336	45	58	162	61	101	0	545	661	82	105	82	83	104	104	80	96	102	104
HOU	81	43	38	0	290	294	31	26	81	34	47	0	279	326	43	61	162	77	85	0	569	620	74	87	57	88	96	97	87	94	99	100
LA	81	43	38	0	321	283	57	35	81	45	36	0	370	329	81	46	162	88	74	0	691	612	138	81	74	142	88	88	110	99	95	94
MON	81	40	41	0	335	352	59	65	81	46	35	0	362	264	74	45	162	86	76	0	697	616	133	110	104	121	101	109	100	89	105	104
NY	81	33	48	0	307	357	48	60	81	32	49	0	302	366	49	59	162	65	97	0	609	723	97	119	99	91	110	98	93	109	98	100

TM	HOME G	W	L	T	R	OR	HR	OHR	ROAD G	W	L	T	R	OR	HR	OHR	ALL G	W	L	T	R	OR	HR	OHR	HRF	HRB	HRP	RF	RB	RP	BPF	PPF
PHI	81	51	30	0	301	307	57	46	81	38	43	0	363	347	55	40	162	89	73	0	664	654	112	86	108	98	76	87	107	106	94	94
PIT	81	42	39	0	391	394	77	65	81	42	39	0	333	302	57	53	162	84	78	0	724	696	134	118	126	110	98	121	99	95	110	110
STL	81	46	35	0	338	325	27	48	81	46	35	0	347	284	40	46	162	92	70	0	685	609	67	94	89	64	89	105	100	90	103	102
SD	81	43	38	0	316	286	33	76	81	38	43	0	359	372	48	63	162	81	81	0	675	658	81	139	98	77	127	84	111	108	92	92
SF	81	45	36	0	319	312	55	54	81	42	39	0	354	375	78	55	162	87	75	0	673	687	133	109	84	133	113	88	109	111	94	94
1983 NATIONAL LEAGUE																																
ATL	80	46	34	0	394	327	66	71	82	42	40	0	352	313	64	61	162	88	74	0	746	640	130	132	112	107	108	111	106	92	106	104
CHI	81	43	38	0	384	341	71	69	81	28	53	0	317	378	69	48	162	71	91	0	701	719	140	117	117	112	94	103	104	107	101	101
CIN	81	36	45	0	331	360	52	64	81	38	43	0	292	355	55	71	162	74	88	0	623	710	107	135	92	97	120	106	91	103	103	104
HOU	82	46	36	0	294	278	26	28	80	39	41	0	349	368	71	66	162	85	77	0	643	646	97	94	41	115	115	79	108	108	90	90
LA	80	48	32	0	316	296	74	49	83	43	39	1	338	313	72	48	163	91	71	1	654	609	146	97	106	119	82	98	98	92	100	99
MON	81	46	35	0	341	325	40	56	82	36	45	1	336	321	62	64	163	82	80	1	677	646	102	120	79	97	114	102	100	95	102	101
NY	82	41	41	0	300	329	63	53	80	27	53	0	275	351	49	44	162	68	94	0	575	680	112	97	119	87	76	97	88	102	99	100
PHI	82	50	31	1	361	310	61	61	81	40	41	0	335	325	64	50	163	90	72	1	696	635	125	111	106	104	93	101	103	95	101	100
PIT	81	41	40	0	335	336	60	63	81	43	38	0	324	312	61	46	162	84	78	0	659	648	121	109	114	97	87	105	96	95	103	103
STL	81	44	37	0	334	350	38	58	81	35	46	0	345	360	45	57	162	79	83	0	679	710	83	115	94	73	99	97	104	109	98	98
SD	82	47	34	1	350	299	53	82	81	34	47	0	303	354	40	62	163	81	81	1	653	653	93	144	127	71	106	98	99	98	99	99
SF	81	43	38	0	346	356	73	67	81	36	45	0	341	341	46	56	162	79	83	0	687	697	142	127	108	119	107	103	103	104	101	101
1984 NATIONAL LEAGUE																																
ATL	81	38	43	0	328	376	53	72	81	42	39	0	304	279	58	50	162	80	82	0	632	655	111	122	114	99	107	119	88	90	110	110
CHI	80	51	29	0	414	360	86	70	81	45	36	0	348	298	50	29	161	96	65	0	762	658	136	99	186	91	64	120	106	93	110	109
CIN	81	39	42	0	356	381	58	73	81	31	50	0	271	366	48	55	162	70	92	0	627	747	106	128	124	91	107	113	90	106	106	107
HOU	81	43	38	0	309	292	18	29	81	37	44	0	384	338	61	62	162	80	82	0	693	630	79	91	40	98	123	84	114	104	92	92
LA	81	40	41	0	287	321	49	40	81	39	42	0	293	279	53	36	162	79	83	0	580	600	102	76	100	93	71	106	85	88	104	104
MON	81	39	42	0	266	260	45	56	80	39	41	0	327	325	51	68	161	78	83	0	593	585	96	114	92	95	111	81	99	98	91	91
NY	81	48	33	0	336	327	56	47	81	42	39	0	316	349	51	57	162	90	72	0	652	676	107	104	96	102	99	100	99	102	100	100
PHI	81	39	42	0	353	369	79	45	81	42	39	0	367	321	68	56	162	81	81	0	720	690	147	101	100	138	98	105	108	103	102	101
PIT	81	41	40	0	282	304	63	48	81	34	47	0	333	304	50	58	162	75	87	0	615	567	98	102	86	99	102	86	99	92	94	94
STL	81	44	37	0	327	310	29	42	81	40	41	0	325	335	46	52	162	84	78	0	652	645	75	94	74	79	99	97	100	99	99	99
SD	81	48	33	0	344	300	60	61	81	44	37	0	342	334	49	61	162	92	70	0	686	634	109	122	110	98	110	96	106	98	98	98
SF	81	35	46	0	340	393	55	63	81	31	50	0	342	414	57	62	162	66	96	0	682	807	112	125	98	108	119	96	108	126	96	98
1985 NATIONAL LEAGUE																																
ATL	81	32	49	0	336	431	65	80	81	34	47	0	296	350	61	54	162	66	96	0	632	781	126	134	122	97	101	116	90	109	106	108
CHI	81	41	39	1	399	423	98	104	81	36	45	0	287	306	52	52	162	77	84	1	686	729	150	156	180	92	95	134	90	95	116	117
CIN	81	47	34	0	347	359	49	65	81	42	38	1	330	307	65	66	162	89	72	1	677	666	114	131	88	102	117	110	98	96	105	105
HOU	81	44	37	0	333	338	47	42	81	39	42	0	373	353	74	72	162	83	79	0	706	691	121	119	66	122	121	93	112	109	96	96
LA	81	48	33	0	310	258	47	54	81	47	34	0	372	321	82	48	162	95	67	0	682	579	129	102	80	117	98	84	111	96	93	92
MON	81	44	37	0	300	289	45	45	80	40	40	0	333	347	73	54	161	84	77	0	633	636	118	99	72	113	99	87	103	104	94	94
NY	81	51	30	0	344	254	58	58	81	47	34	0	351	314	76	53	162	98	64	0	695	568	134	111	92	117	99	92	109	90	97	95
PHI	81	41	40	0	350	338	72	57	81	34	47	0	317	335	69	58	162	75	87	0	667	673	141	115	101	118	98	105	99	100	102	102
PIT	80	35	45	0	314	347	39	53	81	22	59	0	254	361	41	54	161	57	104	0	568	708	80	107	97	68	89	106	84	104	103	104
STL	81	54	27	0	358	255	36	39	81	47	34	0	389	317	51	59	162	101	61	0	747	572	87	98	71	84	93	89	119	93	96	93
SD	81	44	37	0	321	323	64	77	81	39	42	0	329	299	45	50	162	83	79	0	650	622	109	127	143	76	87	102	97	93	102	101
SF	81	38	43	0	265	307	58	67	81	24	57	0	291	367	57	58	162	62	100	0	556	674	115	125	107	94	101	87	91	108	93	95
1986 NATIONAL LEAGUE																																
ATL	81	41	40	0	331	360	77	71	80	31	49	0	284	359	61	46	161	72	89	0	615	719	138	117	132	94	79	105	90	104	102	103
CHI	80	42	38	0	394	399	89	79	80	28	52	0	286	382	66	54	160	70	90	0	680	781	155	143	125	110	103	116	95	109	107	108
CIN	81	43	38	0	383	377	86	73	81	43	38	0	349	340	58	63	162	86	76	0	732	717	144	136	128	99	95	110	104	102	104	104
HOU	81	52	29	0	327	289	49	56	81	44	37	0	327	280	76	60	162	96	66	0	654	569	125	116	79	107	102	102	94	83	103	102
LA	81	46	35	0	326	290	57	46	81	27	54	0	312	389	73	49	162	73	89	0	638	679	130	115	74	117	104	88	101	106	94	95
MON	80	36	44	0	296	347	42	56	81	42	39	0	341	341	68	63	161	78	83	0	637	688	110	119	77	96	106	96	97	104	98	98
NY	81	55	26	0	379	251	77	47	81	53	28	0	404	327	71	56	162	108	54	0	783	578	148	103	100	115	82	89	121	91	96	93
PHI	80	49	31	0	413	344	86	49	81	37	44	0	326	369	68	81	161	86	75	0	739	713	154	130	93	120	108	110	105	102	104	104
PIT	81	31	50	0	331	357	49	75	81	33	48	0	332	343	62	63	162	64	98	0	663	700	111	138	98	88	108	101	98	103	100	101
STL	81	42	39	0	321	303	27	63	80	37	43	0	280	308	31	72	161	79	82	0	601	611	58	135	87	49	108	104	87	88	103	103
SD	81	43	38	0	339	319	80	78	81	31	50	0	317	404	56	72	162	74	88	0	656	723	136	150	121	98	108	92	102	111	95	96
SF	81	46	35	0	345	275	50	61	81	37	44	0	353	343	64	60	162	83	79	0	698	618	114	121	90	93	99	90	108	96	96	95
1987 NATIONAL LEAGUE																																
ATL	81	42	39	0	421	450	82	88	80	27	53	0	326	379	70	75	161	69	92	0	747	829	152	163	113	95	101	119	95	104	108	109
CHI	80	40	40	0	381	389	114	90	81	36	45	0	339	412	95	69	161	76	85	0	720	801	209	159	123	125	97	103	98	108	101	102
CIN	81	42	39	0	396	401	94	97	81	42	39	0	387	351	98	81	162	84	78	0	783	752	192	170	111	122	108	107	104	100	103	103
HOU	81	47	34	0	334	268	51	46	81	29	52	0	314	410	71	95	162	76	86	0	648	678	122	141	60	102	111	84	97	99	93	93
LA	81	40	41	0	280	306	52	56	81	33	48	0	355	369	73	74	162	73	89	0	635	675	125	130	75	92	96	82	95	100	92	92
MON	81	48	33	0	401	371	62	74	81	43	38	0	340	349	58	71	162	91	71	0	741	720	120	145	106	76	91	112	95	93	106	106
NY	81	49	32	0	407	335	93	63	81	43	38	0	416	363	99	72	162	92	70	0	823	698	192	135	92	130	94	96	114	98	98	97
PHI	81	43	38	0	385	373	80	78	81	37	44	0	317	376	89	89	162	80	82	0	702	749	169	167	90	119	117	108	92	98	104	105
PIT	81	47	34	0	404	363	71	84	81	33	48	0	319	381	60	80	162	80	82	0	723	744	131	164	110	82	102	109	95	98	104	104
STL	81	49	32	0	387	339	42	60	81	46	35	0	411	354	52	69	162	95	67	0	798	693	94	129	86	65	88	96	111	97	98	97
SD	81	37	44	0	338	357	60	97	81	28	53	0	330	406	53	78	162	65	97	0	668	763	113	175	117	60	104	95	97	97	98	
SF	81	46	35	0	373	312	118	72	81	44	37	0	410	357	87	74	162	90	72	0	783	669	205	146	117	123	92	91	111	96	96	95
1988 NATIONAL LEAGUE																																
ATL	79	28	51	0	295	391	48	64	81	26	55	0	260	350	48	44	160	54	106	0	555	741	96	108	120	83	91	112	86	112	104	107
CHI	82	39	42	1	346	373	58	71	81	38	43	0	314	321	55	44	163	77	85	1	660	694	113	115	125	95	94	110	100	105	104	105
CIN	80	45	35	0	333	312	75	71	81	42	39	0	308	284	47	50	161	87	74	0	641	596	122	121	147	94	94	110	97	91	105	105
HOU	81	44	37	0	293	282	33	50	81	38	43	0	324	349	63	73	162	82	80	0	617	631	96	123	63	110	142	87	105	107	93	93
LA	81	45	36	0	316	297	49	38	81	49	31	1	312	247	50	46	162	94	67	1	628	544	99	84	92	95	81	110	94	82	106	105
MON	81	43	38	0	333	304	47	62	82	38	43	1	295	288	60	60	163	81	81	1	628	592	107	122	93	104	118	110	94	89	105	105
NY	80	56	24	0	313	218	67	34	80	44	36	0	390	314	85	44	160	100	60	0	703	532	152	78	81	156	85	78	126	97	90	88
PHI	81	38	42	1	327	361	62	64	81	27	54	0	270	373	44	54	162	65	96	1	597	734	106	118	124	89	99	105	94	113	101	103
PIT	81	43	38	0	326	298	56	50	79	42	37	0	325	318	54	58	160	85	75	0	651	616	110	108	93	108	106	95	107	102	98	97
STL	81	41	40	0	314	318	29	39	81	35	46	0	264	315	42	52	162	76	86	0	578	633	71	91	74	75	95	108	88	96	104	105
SD	81	47	34	0	303	267	56	56	80	34	44	0	291	316	38	56	161	81	78	0	594	583	94	112	116	81	97	93	98	96	97	97
SF	81	45	36	0	318	284	58	42	81	38	43	0	352	342	55	57	162	83	79	0	670	626	113	99	90	111	97	88	114	107	94	93
1989 NATIONAL LEAGUE																																
ATL	79	33	46	0	309	334	55	61	82	30	51	1	275	346	73	53	161	63	97	1	584	680	128	114	95	116	105	106	90	104	102	104
CHI	81	48	33	0	381	334	61	64	81	45	36	0	321	289	63	42	162	93	69	0	702	623	124	106	118	100	85	116	101	91	108	107
CIN	81	38	43	0	312	377	59	71	81	37	44	0	320	314	69	54	162	75	87	0	632	691	128	125	105	111	108	107	96	104	103	104
HOU	82	47	35	0	340	344	42	50	80	39	41	0	307	325	74	76	162	86	76	0	647	669	97	105	83	92	100	105	99	102	102	103
LA	81	44	37	0	253	244	59	46	79	33	46	0	301	292	52	49	160	77	83	0	554	536	89	95	81	86	92	93	93	92	93	93
MON	81	44	37	0	336	309	55	60	81	37	44	0	296	321	45	60	162	81	81	0	632	630	100	120	109	84	100	104	97	97	102	102
NY	81	51	30	0	333	275	78	56	81	36	45	0	350	320	69	59	162	87	75	0	683	595	147	115	105	127	102	92	111	98	96	95

TM	HOME G	W	L	T	R	OR	HR	OHR	ROAD G	W	L	T	R	OR	HR	OHR	ALL G	W	L	T	R	OR	HR	OHR	HRF	HRB	HRP	RF	RB	RP	BPF	PPF
PHI	81	38	42	1	321	376	61	67	82	29	53	0	308	359	62	60	163	67	95	1	629	735	123	127	105	106	109	104	97	112	101	102
PIT	81	39	42	0	296	313	45	62	83	35	46	2	341	367	50	59	164	74	88	2	637	680	95	121	100	83	103	89	105	111	94	94
STL	83	46	35	2	319	308	27	36	81	40	41	0	313	300	46	48	164	86	76	2	632	608	73	84	68	73	85	100	97	94	101	100
SD	81	46	35	0	324	312	66	82	81	43	38	0	318	314	54	51	162	89	73	0	642	626	120	133	137	91	98	101	100	98	101	101
SF	81	53	28	0	368	255	63	61	81	39	42	0	331	345	78	59	162	92	70	0	699	600	141	120	92	130	113	93	113	98	97	96

1990 NATIONAL LEAGUE

TM	HOME G	W	L	T	R	OR	HR	OHR	ROAD G	W	L	T	R	OR	HR	OHR	ALL G	W	L	T	R	OR	HR	OHR	HRF	HRB	HRP	RF	RB	RP	BPF	PPF
ATL	81	37	44	0	352	427	85	70	81	28	53	0	330	394	77	58	162	65	97	0	682	821	162	128	112	121	97	106	99	117	101	103
CHI	81	39	42	0	372	435	75	73	81	38	43	0	318	337	61	48	162	77	85	0	690	774	136	121	132	93	82	121	93	103	109	110
CIN	81	46	35	0	334	312	70	73	81	45	36	0	359	285	55	51	162	91	71	0	693	597	125	124	132	85	84	101	100	87	102	100
HOU	81	49	32	0	298	271	35	47	81	26	55	0	275	385	59	83	162	75	87	0	573	656	94	130	60	93	125	87	90	101	94	95
LA	81	47	34	0	351	323	54	73	81	39	42	0	377	362	75	64	162	86	76	0	728	685	129	137	92	106	113	92	111	105	96	95
MON	81	47	34	0	328	268	48	62	81	38	43	0	334	330	66	65	162	85	77	0	662	598	114	127	85	96	108	91	101	92	97	96
NY	81	52	29	0	397	280	86	52	81	39	42	0	378	333	86	67	162	91	71	0	775	613	172	119	92	142	101	96	115	93	99	97
PHI	81	41	40	0	311	367	47	67	81	36	45	0	335	362	56	57	162	77	85	0	646	729	103	124	101	81	96	97	97	108	98	99
PIT	81	49	32	0	351	299	59	63	81	46	35	0	382	320	79	72	162	95	67	0	733	619	138	135	83	120	118	94	110	94	98	96
STL	81	34	47	0	319	366	43	47	81	36	45	0	280	332	30	51	162	70	92	0	599	698	73	98	109	53	71	110	84	97	105	106
SD	81	37	44	0	342	348	63	78	81	38	43	0	331	325	60	69	162	75	87	0	673	673	123	147	108	95	111	104	97	97	102	102
SF	81	49	32	0	380	340	81	70	81	36	45	0	339	370	71	61	162	85	77	0	719	710	152	131	113	113	99	102	105	104	100	100

1991 NATIONAL LEAGUE

TM	HOME G	W	L	T	R	OR	HR	OHR	ROAD G	W	L	T	R	OR	HR	OHR	ALL G	W	L	T	R	OR	HR	OHR	HRF	HRB	HRP	RF	RB	RP	BPF	PPF
ATL	81	48	33	0	418	368	83	73	81	46	35	0	331	276	58	45	162	94	68	0	749	644	141	118	146	96	81	127	99	86	114	113
CHI	83	46	37	0	386	396	93	75	77	31	46	0	309	338	66	42	160	77	83	0	695	734	159	117	139	113	83	111	101	107	104	105
CIN	81	39	42	0	373	376	104	77	81	35	46	0	316	315	60	50	162	74	88	0	689	691	164	127	155	107	86	116	96	96	108	108
HOU	81	37	44	0	302	330	27	44	81	28	53	0	303	387	52	85	162	65	97	0	605	717	79	129	53	87	136	91	96	112	95	96
LA	81	54	27	0	342	280	57	46	81	39	42	0	323	285	51	50	162	93	69	0	665	565	108	96	103	88	79	103	97	84	103	102
MON	68	33	35	0	216	233	35	33	93	38	55	0	363	462	60	78	161	71	90	0	579	695	95	111	69	94	103	79	96	107	90	91
NY	82	40	42	0	332	348	57	55	79	37	42	0	308	298	60	53	161	77	84	0	640	646	117	108	96	100	93	107	93	94	104	104
PHI	83	47	36	0	341	334	61	53	79	31	48	0	288	346	50	58	162	78	84	0	629	680	111	111	100	92	92	101	94	101	100	101
PIT	84	52	32	0	382	314	61	55	78	46	32	0	386	318	65	62	162	98	64	0	768	632	126	117	87	113	106	93	119	100	97	95
STL	84	52	32	0	345	293	32	41	78	32	46	0	306	355	36	73	162	84	78	0	651	648	68	114	64	71	110	91	103	102	95	95
SD	81	42	39	0	315	320	65	72	81	42	39	0	321	326	56	67	162	84	78	0	636	646	121	139	111	98	111	98	96	98	100	100
SF	81	43	38	0	306	305	69	62	81	32	49	0	343	392	72	81	162	75	87	0	649	697	141	143	86	130	131	84	107	114	92	92

1992 NATIONAL LEAGUE

TM	HOME G	W	L	T	R	OR	HR	OHR	ROAD G	W	L	T	R	OR	HR	OHR	ALL G	W	L	T	R	OR	HR	OHR	HRF	HRB	HRP	RF	RB	RP	BPF	PPF
ATL	81	51	30	0	343	290	72	45	81	47	34	0	339	279	66	44	162	98	64	0	682	569	138	89	107	125	84	103	106	90	102	101
CHI	81	43	38	0	315	297	59	49	81	35	46	0	278	327	45	58	162	78	84	0	593	624	104	107	104	97	100	101	94	98	101	101
CIN	81	53	28	0	355	289	60	60	81	37	44	0	305	320	39	49	162	90	72	0	660	609	99	109	133	80	89	103	103	96	102	101
HOU	81	47	34	0	302	293	49	41	81	34	47	0	306	355	47	73	162	81	81	0	608	648	96	114	77	107	120	88	104	112	94	94
LA	81	37	44	0	277	281	26	33	81	26	55	0	271	355	46	49	162	63	99	0	548	636	72	82	63	81	93	89	93	106	94	96
MON	81	43	38	0	331	334	50	54	81	44	37	0	317	247	52	44	162	87	75	0	648	581	102	98	108	93	89	117	95	85	109	108
NY	81	41	40	0	288	305	42	43	81	31	50	0	311	348	51	49	162	72	90	0	599	653	93	92	86	94	93	90	101	109	95	95
PHI	81	41	40	0	369	331	67	49	81	29	52	0	317	386	51	64	162	70	92	0	686	717	118	113	100	113	109	99	111	116	98	98
PIT	81	53	28	0	363	277	51	37	81	43	38	0	330	318	55	64	162	96	66	0	693	595	106	101	76	116	107	100	110	96	100	99
STL	81	45	36	0	328	297	55	52	81	38	43	0	303	307	39	66	162	83	79	0	631	604	94	118	102	89	110	102	99	95	102	101
SD	81	45	36	0	339	334	87	64	81	37	44	0	278	302	48	47	162	82	80	0	617	636	135	111	152	101	87	115	91	94	107	108
SF	81	42	39	0	307	294	57	60	81	30	51	0	267	353	48	68	162	72	90	0	574	647	105	128	100	102	122	97	93	104	98	99

1993 NATIONAL LEAGUE

TM	HOME G	W	L	T	R	OR	HR	OHR	ROAD G	W	L	T	R	OR	HR	OHR	ALL G	W	L	T	R	OR	HR	OHR	HRF	HRB	HRP	RF	RB	RP	BPF	PPF
ATL	81	51	30	0	366	291	78	52	81	53	28	0	401	268	91	49	162	104	58	0	767	559	169	101	95	122	76	100	104	77	102	100
CHI	82	43	38	1	381	382	78	94	81	41	40	0	357	357	85	59	163	84	78	1	738	739	161	153	115	108	101	105	98	98	103	103
CIN	81	41	40	0	363	383	69	81	81	32	49	0	359	402	68	77	162	73	89	0	722	785	137	158	103	98	112	98	101	109	98	99
COL	81	39	42	0	489	551	77	107	81	28	53	0	269	416	65	74	162	67	95	0	758	967	142	181	128	91	113	145	85	110	120	122
FLA	81	35	46	0	299	369	44	72	81	29	52	0	282	355	50	63	162	64	98	0	581	724	94	135	101	67	94	103	78	96	102	103
HOU	81	44	37	0	363	285	62	56	81	41	40	0	353	345	76	61	162	85	77	0	716	630	138	117	87	104	90	94	101	89	98	97
LA	81	41	40	0	330	318	66	48	81	40	41	0	345	344	64	55	162	81	81	0	675	662	130	103	96	93	75	94	95	93	98	98
MON	81	55	26	0	367	315	62	50	82	39	42	1	365	367	60	69	163	94	68	1	732	682	122	119	89	91	88	96	102	95	98	98
NY	81	28	53	0	317	376	75	72	81	31	50	0	355	368	83	67	162	59	103	0	672	744	158	139	97	115	102	95	95	105	97	98
PHI	81	52	29	0	441	371	80	57	81	45	36	0	436	369	76	72	162	97	65	0	877	740	156	129	94	115	96	102	120	102	101	99
PIT	81	40	41	0	372	388	64	67	81	35	46	0	335	418	46	86	162	75	87	0	707	806	110	153	99	80	108	100	98	110	99	100
STL	81	49	32	0	376	321	59	59	81	38	43	0	382	423	59	93	162	87	75	0	758	744	118	152	79	96	119	88	112	109	94	93
SD	81	34	47	0	345	376	87	79	81	27	54	0	334	396	66	69	162	61	101	0	679	772	153	148	119	100	97	98	95	107	98	99
SF	81	50	31	0	362	293	82	81	81	53	28	0	446	343	86	87	162	103	59	0	808	636	168	168	96	125	125	85	119	95	93	92

1994 NATIONAL LEAGUE

TM	HOME G	W	L	T	R	OR	HR	OHR	ROAD G	W	L	T	R	OR	HR	OHR	ALL G	W	L	T	R	OR	HR	OHR	HRF	HRB	HRP	RF	RB	RP	BPF	PPF
ATL	55	31	24	0	230	231	61	37	59	37	22	0	312	217	76	39	114	68	46	0	542	448	137	76	93	127	74	95	104	88	99	97
CHI	59	20	39	0	216	287	47	71	54	29	25	0	284	262	62	49	113	49	64	0	500	549	109	120	97	104	113	85	104	114	92	93
CIN	60	37	22	1	306	263	59	65	55	29	26	0	303	227	65	52	115	66	48	1	609	490	124	117	98	115	109	99	115	93	100	99
COL	57	25	32	0	317	356	59	61	58	20	28	0	256	227	66	39	115	45	60	0	573	638	125	120	100	112	108	128	94	104	113	114
FLA	59	25	34	0	245	341	46	70	56	26	30	0	223	235	48	50	115	51	64	0	468	576	94	120	111	82	102	119	81	97	109	110
HOU	59	37	22	0	307	241	57	56	56	29	27	0	295	262	63	46	115	66	49	0	602	503	120	102	99	109	94	95	116	98	98	96
LA	55	33	22	0	230	209	47	49	59	25	34	0	302	300	68	41	114	58	56	0	532	509	115	90	95	105	86	80	112	107	90	90
MON	52	32	20	0	266	227	42	47	62	42	20	0	319	227	66	53	114	74	40	0	585	454	108	100	91	102	97	109	106	84	105	104
NY	53	23	30	0	235	271	53	60	60	32	28	0	271	255	64	57	113	55	58	0	506	526	117	117	105	107	107	108	93	97	104	104
PHI	60	34	26	0	268	243	45	40	55	20	35	0	253	254	35	58	115	54	61	0	521	497	80	98	84	79	94	93	101	97	97	96
PIT	61	32	29	0	271	291	45	61	53	21	32	0	195	289	35	56	114	53	61	0	466	580	80	117	101	73	105	100	88	109	99	101
STL	56	23	33	0	248	315	50	66	59	30	28	1	287	306	58	68	115	53	61	1	535	621	108	134	97	102	124	100	102	117	99	100
SD	57	26	31	0	240	251	51	57	60	21	39	0	239	280	41	42	117	47	70	0	479	531	92	99	132	71	75	99	89	98	100	100
SF	60	29	31	0	259	258	56	74	55	26	29	0	245	242	67	48	115	55	60	0	504	500	123	122	103	112	110	97	96	95	99	99

1901 AMERICAN LEAGUE

TM	HOME G	W	L	T	R	OR	HR	OHR	ROAD G	W	L	T	R	OR	HR	OHR	ALL G	W	L	T	R	OR	HR	OHR	HRF	HRB	HRP	RF	RB	RP	BPF	PPF
BAL	66	40	25	1	430	367	10	11	69	28	40	1	330	383	14	10	135	68	65	2	760	750	24	21	93	85	76	115	98	98	107	107
BOS	69	49	20	0	383	252	21	18	69	30	37	2	376	356	16	15	138	79	57	2	759	608	37	33	123	118	108	89	106	87	97	94
CHI	71	49	21	1	441	285	14	11	66	34	32	0	378	346	18	16	137	83	53	1	819	631	32	27	72	132	113	95	113	90	99	96
CLE	69	28	39	2	321	403	0	12	69	26	43	0	346	428	12	10	138	54	82	2	667	831	12	22	57	39	97	93	95	115	95	98
DET	70	42	27	1	438	369	15	10	66	32	34	0	303	325	14	12	136	74	61	1	741	694	29	22	92	104	81	119	92	88	110	109
MIL	70	32	37	1	342	373	15	14	69	16	52	1	299	455	11	18	139	48	89	2	641	828	26	32	97	93	111	93	91	113	91	98
PHI	66	42	24	0	410	352	15	9	71	32	38	1	395	409	20	11	137	74	62	1	805	761	35	20	85	126	78	102	110	104	100	100
WAS	68	31	35	2	333	375	17	36	70	30	37	3	349	396	16	15	138	61	72	5	682	771	33	51	160	102	135	98	94	105	98	100

1902 AMERICAN LEAGUE

TM	HOME G	W	L	T	R	OR	HR	OHR	ROAD G	W	L	T	R	OR	HR	OHR	ALL G	W	L	T	R	OR	HR	OHR	HRF	HRB	HRP	RF	RB	RP	BPF	PPF
BAL	64	32	31	1	391	369	17	18	77	18	57	2	324	479	16	12	141	50	88	3	715	848	33	30	140	85	76	111	103	118	102	104
BOS	71	43	27	1	348	284	23	15	67	34	33	0	316	316	19	12	138	77	60	1	664	600	42	27	114	119	81	96	99	91	98	98
CHI	71	48	19	4	371	238	5	2	67	26	41	0	304	364	9	28	138	74	60	4	675	602	14	30	20	103	111	88	106	95	95	94
CLE	65	40	25	0	357	257	15	7	72	29	42	1	329	410	18	19	137	69	67	1	686	667	33	26	69	122	91	93	107	102	97	96
DET	68	35	33	0	312	286	13	8	69	17	50	2	254	371	9	12	137	52	83	2	566	657	22	20	100	65	59	96	86	97	99	100
PHI	73	56	17	0	477	330	19	13	64	27	36	1	298	306	19	20	137	83	53	1	775	636	38	33	75	140	122	116	105	90	108	106
STL	73	49	21	3	350	289	16	14	67	29	37	1	269	318	13	22	140	78	58	4	619	607	29	36	81	101	119	101	88	87	102	102

TM	HOME G	W	L	T	R	OR	HR	OHR	ROAD G	W	L	T	R	OR	HR	OHR	ALL G	W	L	T	R	OR	HR	OHR	HRF	HRB	HRP	RF	RB	RP	BPF	PPF
WAS	68	40	28	0	407	341	35	38	70	21	47	2	300	449	12	18	138	61	75	2	707	790	47	56	210	97	119	102	106	117	98	100

1903 AMERICAN LEAGUE

TM	HOME G	W	L	T	R	OR	HR	OHR	ROAD G	W	L	T	R	OR	HR	OHR	ALL G	W	L	T	R	OR	HR	OHR	HRF	HRB	HRP	RF	RB	RP	BPF	PPF
BOS	70	49	20	1	395	266	35	12	71	42	27	2	313	238	13	11	141	91	47	3	708	504	48	23	179	141	85	120	109	82	112	107
CHI	70	41	28	1	284	244	5	2	68	19	49	0	232	369	9	21	138	60	77	1	516	613	14	23	25	127	123	86	100	114	92	94
CLE	74	49	25	0	364	256	11	5	66	28	38	0	275	323	20	11	140	77	63	0	639	579	31	16	50	175	97	94	115	107	96	95
DET	65	37	28	0	279	222	5	7	72	28	43	1	288	317	7	12	137	65	71	1	567	539	12	19	73	59	88	93	105	99	97	96
NY	67	41	26	0	301	269	10	6	69	31	36	2	278	304	8	13	136	72	62	2	579	573	18	19	81	88	87	101	104	103	100	100
PHI	67	44	21	2	323	238	17	8	70	31	39	0	274	281	15	12	137	75	60	2	597	519	32	20	98	141	93	105	102	91	104	102
STL	70	38	32	0	250	228	7	15	69	27	42	0	250	297	5	11	139	65	74	0	500	525	12	26	129	45	92	87	93	96	95	95
WAS	71	29	40	2	275	349	15	24	69	14	54	1	162	342	2	14	140	43	94	3	437	691	17	38	199	42	110	115	71	109	105	111

1904 AMERICAN LEAGUE

TM	HOME G	W	L	T	R	OR	HR	OHR	ROAD G	W	L	T	R	OR	HR	OHR	ALL G	W	L	T	R	OR	HR	OHR	HRF	HRB	HRP	RF	RB	RP	BPF	PPF
BOS	81	49	30	2	325	240	18	18	76	46	29	1	283	226	8	13	157	95	59	3	608	466	26	31	151	109	134	105	104	83	105	101
CHI	78	50	27	1	297	226	0	2	78	39	38	1	303	256	14	11	156	89	65	2	600	482	14	13	9	69	156	95	110	90	99	97
CLE	78	44	31	3	329	242	14	2	76	42	34	0	318	240	13	8	154	86	65	3	647	482	27	10	77	150	58	100	117	90	102	98
DET	79	34	40	5	237	295	3	4	83	28	50	5	268	332	8	12	162	62	90	10	505	627	11	16	40	74	101	93	92	111	95	98
NY	75	46	29	0	321	288	22	25	80	46	30	4	277	238	5	4	155	92	59	4	598	526	27	29	357	62	61	124	97	87	112	111
PHI	79	47	31	1	308	235	19	8	76	34	39	3	249	268	12	5	155	81	70	4	557	503	31	13	144	126	58	101	99	91	102	101
STL	78	32	43	3	231	288	2	14	78	33	44	1	250	316	8	11	156	65	87	4	481	604	10	25	85	55	131	92	92	112	95	98
WAS	78	23	52	3	221	350	3	2	79	15	61	2	216	393	7	17	157	38	113	6	437	743	10	19	23	103	124	93	85	135	93	99

1905 AMERICAN LEAGUE

TM	HOME G	W	L	T	R	OR	HR	OHR	ROAD G	W	L	T	R	OR	HR	OHR	ALL G	W	L	T	R	OR	HR	OHR	HRF	HRB	HRP	RF	RB	RP	BPF	PPF
BOS	77	44	32	1	296	281	21	21	76	34	42	0	283	283	8	12	153	78	74	1	579	564	29	33	183	109	130	101	102	100	100	100
CHI	82	50	29	3	300	207	3	2	76	42	31	3	312	244	8	9	158	92	60	6	612	451	11	11	30	82	73	87	109	83	97	93
CLE	77	41	36	0	286	284	5	13	78	35	42	1	277	303	13	10	155	76	78	1	563	587	18	23	81	100	132	100	99	103	99	100
DET	76	45	30	1	267	275	5	5	78	34	44	0	245	327	8	6	154	79	74	1	512	602	13	11	76	70	61	98	92	106	98	100
NY	75	40	35	0	316	303	15	16	77	31	43	3	270	319	8	10	152	71	78	3	586	622	23	26	161	94	107	107	103	109	102	103
PHI	74	51	22	1	337	247	12	12	78	41	34	3	286	241	12	9	152	92	56	4	623	488	24	21	119	117	103	116	101	82	110	107
STL	79	34	42	3	250	267	5	7	77	20	57	0	261	341	11	12	156	54	99	3	511	608	16	19	53	104	124	84	98	113	91	93
WAS	77	33	42	2	289	340	10	4	77	31	45	1	270	283	12	8	154	64	87	3	559	623	22	12	72	125	71	111	95	104	104	106

1906 AMERICAN LEAGUE

TM	HOME G	W	L	T	R	OR	HR	OHR	ROAD G	W	L	T	R	OR	HR	OHR	ALL G	W	L	T	R	OR	HR	OHR	HRF	HRB	HRP	RF	RB	RP	BPF	PPF
BOS	77	22	54	1	230	364	10	21	78	27	51	0	233	342	3	16	155	49	105	1	463	706	13	37	150	63	169	102	83	120	98	103
CHI	79	54	23	2	275	180	2	1	75	39	35	1	295	280	5	10	154	93	58	3	570	460	7	11	21	77	78	78	111	91	92	89
CLE	79	47	30	2	351	229	4	8	78	42	34	2	312	253	8	8	157	89	64	4	663	482	12	16	77	74	99	102	112	84	103	99
DET	78	42	34	2	315	317	4	5	73	29	44	0	203	282	6	9	151	71	78	2	518	599	10	14	59	73	97	118	85	99	108	110
NY	76	53	23	0	398	294	14	8	79	37	38	4	246	249	3	13	155	90	61	4	644	543	17	21	137	79	108	139	94	82	120	118
PHI	73	48	23	2	285	212	21	4	76	30	44	2	276	331	11	5	149	78	67	4	561	543	32	9	151	143	50	87	111	105	94	93
STL	76	40	34	2	272	225	13	10	78	36	39	3	286	273	7	4	154	76	73	5	558	498	20	14	188	80	55	92	101	91	98	97
WAS	75	33	41	1	260	288	7	5	76	22	54	0	258	376	19	10	151	55	95	1	518	664	26	15	45	209	141	88	103	127	91	94

1907 AMERICAN LEAGUE

TM	HOME G	W	L	T	R	OR	HR	OHR	ROAD G	W	L	T	R	OR	HR	OHR	ALL G	W	L	T	R	OR	HR	OHR	HRF	HRB	HRP	RF	RB	RP	BPF	PPF
BOS	78	34	41	3	249	270	12	11	77	25	49	3	215	288	6	11	155	59	90	6	464	558	18	22	127	130	160	101	81	96	101	103
CHI	79	48	29	2	316	222	0	4	78	39	35	4	272	252	5	9	157	87	64	6	588	474	5	13	31	37	144	102	99	82	104	101
CLE	82	46	31	5	267	226	6	5	76	39	36	1	263	299	5	3	158	85	67	6	530	525	11	8	124	70	51	84	99	98	93	93
DET	79	50	27	2	373	265	3	3	74	42	31	1	321	267	8	5	153	92	58	3	694	532	11	8	47	106	86	102	122	97	101	98
NY	75	33	40	2	331	372	10	7	77	37	38	2	274	293	5	6	152	70	78	4	605	665	15	13	147	93	86	123	100	109	109	110
PHI	73	50	20	3	324	235	14	7	77	38	37	2	258	276	8	6	150	88	57	5	582	511	22	13	149	140	92	110	100	90	106	104
STL	76	36	40	0	261	262	6	11	79	33	43	3	281	293	4	6	155	69	83	3	542	555	10	17	161	61	96	95	98	100	98	98
WAS	75	27	47	1	228	310	2	3	79	22	55	2	278	381	10	7	154	49	102	3	506	691	12	10	33	120	123	86	100	130	90	94

1908 AMERICAN LEAGUE

TM	HOME G	W	L	T	R	OR	HR	OHR	ROAD G	W	L	T	R	OR	HR	OHR	ALL G	W	L	T	R	OR	HR	OHR	HRF	HRB	HRP	RF	RB	RP	BPF	PPF
BOS	77	37	40	0	273	249	9	8	78	38	39	1	291	264	5	10	155	75	79	1	564	513	14	18	113	96	107	99	98	97	98	97
CHI	78	51	25	2	271	184	1	4	78	37	39	2	266	286	2	7	156	88	64	4	537	470	3	11	59	24	82	85	107	93	94	93
CLE	78	51	26	1	305	223	8	7	79	39	38	2	263	234	10	9	157	90	64	3	568	457	18	16	83	137	124	107	99	82	106	103
DET	78	44	33	1	315	300	6	6	76	46	30	0	332	247	13	6	154	90	63	1	647	547	19	12	65	154	112	104	121	104	101	99
NY	77	30	47	0	234	352	11	16	78	21	56	1	225	361	2	10	155	51	103	1	459	713	13	26	194	57	126	100	90	132	95	101
PHI	78	46	30	2	294	272	11	4	79	22	55	2	192	290	10	6	157	68	85	4	486	562	21	10	95	141	74	116	83	96	107	110
STL	78	46	31	1	292	234	12	2	77	37	38	2	252	249	8	5	155	83	69	3	544	483	20	7	106	124	50	104	99	89	103	102
WAS	78	43	32	3	249	237	2	9	77	24	53	0	230	302	6	7	155	67	85	3	479	539	8	16	85	58	114	91	95	104	95	97

1909 AMERICAN LEAGUE

TM	HOME G	W	L	T	R	OR	HR	OHR	ROAD G	W	L	T	R	OR	HR	OHR	ALL G	W	L	T	R	OR	HR	OHR	HRF	HRB	HRP	RF	RB	RP	BPF	PPF
BOS	75	47	28	0	329	295	18	13	77	41	35	1	268	255	2	5	152	88	63	1	597	550	20	18	317	60	74	120	105	98	109	108
CHI	81	42	34	5	256	201	1	3	78	36	40	2	236	262	3	5	159	78	74	7	492	463	4	8	52	33	68	90	93	88	97	96
CLE	77	39	37	1	262	259	2	1	78	32	45	1	231	273	8	8	155	71	82	2	493	532	10	9	21	121	90	104	91	97	102	103
DET	78	57	19	2	377	246	12	9	80	41	35	4	289	247	7	7	158	98	54	6	666	493	19	16	146	112	99	118	111	86	110	106
NY	77	41	35	1	338	263	11	9	76	33	42	1	252	324	5	12	153	74	77	2	590	587	16	21	114	118	154	103	113	113	99	99
PHI	76	49	27	0	293	200	9	4	77	46	31	0	312	208	12	5	153	95	58	0	605	408	21	9	81	165	80	113	80	102	97	97
STL	79	40	37	2	242	235	4	6	75	21	52	2	199	340	6	10	154	61	89	4	441	575	10	16	62	95	141	85	92	114	92	94
WAS	77	27	48	2	197	271	5	2	79	15	62	2	183	385	4	10	156	42	110	4	380	656	9	12	53	96	95	84	80	126	90	96

1910 AMERICAN LEAGUE

TM	HOME G	W	L	T	R	OR	HR	OHR	ROAD G	W	L	T	R	OR	HR	OHR	ALL G	W	L	T	R	OR	HR	OHR	HRF	HRB	HRP	RF	RB	RP	BPF	PPF
BOS	80	51	28	1	338	262	32	21	78	30	44	4	300	302	11	9	158	81	72	5	638	564	43	30	216	151	116	98	112	101	99	97
CHI	79	41	37	1	233	198	2	2	77	27	48	2	224	281	5	14	156	68	85	3	457	479	7	16	23	74	114	85	86	88	95	95
CLE	80	39	36	5	278	330	4	2	81	32	45	4	270	327	5	8	161	71	81	9	548	657	9	10	50	63	58	102	94	110	100	102
DET	78	46	31	1	346	306	18	21	77	40	37	0	333	276	10	13	155	86	68	1	679	582	28	34	155	133	158	105	118	103	102	100
NY	78	49	25	3	343	284	13	7	79	39	38	2	283	273	7	9	156	88	63	5	626	557	20	16	125	94	81	114	103	93	107	106
PHI	78	57	19	2	339	211	9	0	77	45	29	3	334	230	10	8	155	102	48	5	673	441	19	8	54	133	44	98	117	81	102	97
STL	79	26	51	2	229	359	4	3	79	21	56	2	222	384	8	11	158	47	107	4	451	743	12	14	39	95	96	96	83	129	94	100
WAS	77	38	35	4	265	252	2	7	80	28	50	2	236	298	7	12	157	66	85	6	501	550	9	19	52	59	127	100	87	94	101	102

1911 AMERICAN LEAGUE

TM	HOME G	W	L	T	R	OR	HR	OHR	ROAD G	W	L	T	R	OR	HR	OHR	ALL G	W	L	T	R	OR	HR	OHR	HRF	HRB	HRP	RF	RB	RP	BPF	PPF
BOS	78	39	37	0	328	312	20	15	77	39	38	0	352	331	15	6	153	78	75	0	680	643	35	21	156	110	66	96	97	93	99	98
CHI	78	40	37	1	341	299	8	13	76	37	37	2	378	325	12	9	154	77	74	3	719	624	20	22	98	80	87	90	105	93	97	95
CLE	77	46	30	1	368	344	7	4	79	34	43	2	323	368	13	13	156	80	73	3	691	712	20	17	47	105	83	105	93	96	103	103
DET	78	51	25	0	468	403	21	15	78	38	40	0	363	373	9	13	156	89	65	0	831	776	30	28	156	92	94	119	108	103	108	107
NY	77	36	40	1	365	422	14	14	76	40	36	0	319	302	11	12	153	76	76	1	684	724	25	26	117	94	97	121	88	92	111	111
PHI	75	54	20	1	384	253	11	5	77	47	30	0	477	348	24	12	152	101	50	1	861	601	35	17	50	181	97	83	132	96	93	88
STL	78	25	53	0	296	396	9	10	74	20	54	0	271	416	8	18	152	45	107	0	567	812	17	28	71	86	126	94	85	117	95	100
WAS	77	39	38	0	323	356	11	21	77	25	52	0	302	410	5	18	154	64	90	0	625	766	16	39	132	57	131	95	91	109	97	99

1912 AMERICAN LEAGUE

TM	HOME G	W	L	T	R	OR	HR	OHR	ROAD G	W	L	T	R	OR	HR	OHR	ALL G	W	L	T	R	OR	HR	OHR	HRF	HRB	HRP	RF	RB	RP	BPF	PPF
BOS	78	57	20	1	417	286	10	10	76	48	27	1	382	258	19	8	154	105	47	2	799	544	29	18	76	167	118	108	109	78	107	102
CHI	78	34	43	1	277	340	11	12	80	44	33	3	362	308	6	14	158	78	76	4	639	648	17	26	115	81	120	95	92	94	99	99
CLE	77	41	35	1	350	329	4	6	78	34	43	1	327	352	8	9	155	75	78	2	677	681	12	15	63	71	89	101	98	98	101	101
DET	76	37	39	0	344	370	8	6	78	32	45	1	376	407	11	10	154	69	84	1	720	777	19	16	71	112	95	94	111	119	95	96
NY	76	31	44	1	352	423	14	16	77	19	58	0	278	419	4	12	153	50	102	1	630	842	18	28	168	67	111	109	91	118	101	105

	HOME								ROAD								ALL																
TM	G	W	L	T	R	OR	HR	OHR	G	W	L	T	R	OR	HR	OHR	G	W	L	T	R	OR	HR	OHR	HRF	HRB	HRP	RF	RB	RP	BPF	PPF
PHI	77	45	31	1	379	337	11	6	76	45	31	0	400	321	11	6	153	90	62	1	779	658	22	12	100	108	63	99	115	99	100	98
STL	79	27	50	2	287	379	6	11	78	26	51	1	265	385	13	6	157	53	101	3	552	764	19	17	88	98	92	99	80	107	99	103
WAS	78	45	32	1	336	289	13	12	76	46	29	1	363	292	7	12	154	91	61	2	699	581	20	24	125	92	112	95	103	87	99	97

1913 AMERICAN LEAGUE

TM	G	W	L	T	R	OR	HR	OHR	G	W	L	T	R	OR	HR	OHR	G	W	L	T	R	OR	HR	OHR	HRF	HRB	HRP	RF	RB	RP	BPF	PPF
BOS	75	41	34	0	328	312	3	0	76	38	37	1	303	298	14	6	151	79	71	1	631	610	17	6	17	139	29	107	103	100	103	103
CHI	77	40	37	0	216	233	5	4	76	38	37	1	272	265	19	6	153	78	74	1	488	498	24	10	39	151	86	85	85	87	95	95
CLE	80	45	32	3	337	290	4	9	75	41	34	0	296	246	12	10	155	86	66	3	633	536	16	19	59	94	121	108	98	85	106	104
DET	76	34	42	0	312	368	9	5	77	32	45	0	312	348	15	8	153	66	87	0	624	716	24	13	64	139	82	103	105	118	99	101
NY	75	27	47	1	265	339	5	20	78	30	47	1	264	329	3	11	153	57	94	2	529	668	8	31	166	32	109	104	87	107	101	104
PHI	76	50	26	0	388	271	19	14	77	46	31	0	406	321	14	10	153	96	57	0	794	592	33	24	134	148	112	94	137	106	96	92
STL	77	31	46	0	247	309	13	11	78	26	50	2	281	333	5	10	155	57	96	2	528	642	18	21	149	69	86	92	91	108	95	98
WAS	78	42	35	1	291	317	9	29	77	48	29	0	305	244	10	6	155	90	64	1	596	561	19	35	202	79	102	109	93	87	106	105

1914 AMERICAN LEAGUE

TM	G	W	L	T	R	OR	HR	OHR	G	W	L	T	R	OR	HR	OHR	G	W	L	T	R	OR	HR	OHR	HRF	HRB	HRP	RF	RB	RP	BPF	PPF
BOS	79	44	31	4	270	246	3	5	80	47	31	2	318	264	15	13	159	91	62	6	588	510	18	18	32	133	155	92	104	92	98	96
CHI	81	43	37	1	271	285	7	4	76	27	47	2	216	275	12	11	157	70	84	3	487	560	19	15	48	141	108	105	82	93	103	105
CLE	79	32	47	0	289	380	4	3	78	19	55	4	249	329	6	7	157	51	102	4	538	709	10	10	56	66	62	111	92	117	102	106
DET	78	42	35	1	315	318	11	9	79	38	38	3	300	300	14	8	157	80	73	4	615	618	25	17	93	140	101	106	105	106	102	102
NY	78	36	40	2	278	259	8	24	79	34	44	1	259	291	4	6	157	70	84	3	537	550	12	30	252	42	83	99	94	96	100	100
PHI	78	51	24	3	354	247	17	13	80	48	29	3	395	282	12	5	158	99	53	6	749	529	29	18	166	120	74	93	133	99	97	93
STL	81	42	36	3	271	298	11	14	78	29	46	3	252	316	6	0	159	71	82	6	523	614	17	20	178	66	74	97	92	106	98	100
WAS	77	40	33	4	282	246	8	7	81	41	40	0	290	273	10	13	158	81	73	4	572	519	18	20	72	116	123	99	98	90	101	100

1915 AMERICAN LEAGUE

TM	G	W	L	T	R	OR	HR	OHR	G	W	L	T	R	OR	HR	OHR	G	W	L	T	R	OR	HR	OHR	HRF	HRB	HRP	RF	RB	RP	BPF	PPF
BOS	76	55	20	1	324	221	5	4	79	46	30	3	345	278	9	14	155	101	50	4	669	499	14	18	45	100	110	94	110	84	99	96
CHI	79	54	24	1	353	236	9	4	76	39	37	0	364	273	16	10	155	93	61	1	717	509	25	14	52	160	93	91	120	89	98	93
CLE	77	27	50	0	277	362	7	9	77	30	45	2	262	308	13	9	154	57	95	2	539	670	20	18	74	112	107	109	85	103	104	106
DET	77	51	26	0	416	318	11	7	79	49	28	2	362	279	12	7	156	100	54	2	778	597	23	14	99	110	71	117	116	92	109	105
NY	82	37	43	2	306	303	28	32	72	32	40	0	278	285	3	9	154	69	83	2	584	588	31	41	307	64	105	95	98	98	98	98
PHI	74	19	53	2	274	424	9	17	80	24	56	0	271	464	7	5	154	43	109	2	545	888	16	22	197	59	68	100	95	144	94	101
STL	76	35	38	3	237	315	6	7	83	28	53	2	284	365	13	14	159	63	91	5	521	680	19	21	55	117	130	93	86	109	96	99
WAS	80	50	29	1	310	246	3	2	75	35	39	1	259	245	9	10	155	85	68	2	569	491	12	12	27	93	82	104	88	78	105	103

1916 AMERICAN LEAGUE

TM	G	W	L	T	R	OR	HR	OHR	G	W	L	T	R	OR	HR	OHR	G	W	L	T	R	OR	HR	OHR	HRF	HRB	HRP	RF	RB	RP	BPF	PPF
BOS	78	49	28	1	252	205	1	1	78	42	35	1	298	275	13	9	156	91	63	2	550	480	14	10	10	118	101	83	103	90	94	92
CHI	77	49	28	0	326	254	9	5	78	40	37	1	275	243	8	9	155	89	65	1	601	497	17	14	86	100	82	112	97	83	108	106
CLE	78	44	33	1	323	293	4	9	79	33	44	2	307	309	12	7	157	77	77	3	630	602	16	16	72	95	106	101	109	105	100	99
DET	77	49	28	0	350	313	7	8	78	38	39	1	320	282	10	4	155	87	67	1	670	595	17	12	108	88	63	111	113	101	104	103
NY	79	46	31	2	306	277	22	22	77	34	43	0	271	284	13	15	156	80	74	2	577	561	35	37	144	183	194	102	99	97	101	101
PHI	76	23	53	0	231	399	15	17	78	13	64	1	216	377	4	9	154	36	117	1	447	776	19	26	208	66	99	105	80	130	98	105
STL	79	45	32	2	290	238	7	10	79	34	43	2	298	307	7	5	158	79	75	4	588	545	14	15	135	65	66	89	107	99	95	94
WAS	81	49	28	4	294	248	6	1	78	27	49	2	242	295	6	13	159	76	77	6	536	543	12	14	39	111	82	97	92	93	100	100

1917 AMERICAN LEAGUE

TM	G	W	L	T	R	OR	HR	OHR	G	W	L	T	R	OR	HR	OHR	G	W	L	T	R	OR	HR	OHR	HRF	HRB	HRP	RF	RB	RP	BPF	PPF
BOS	80	45	33	2	293	245	3	4	77	45	29	3	262	209	11	8	157	90	62	5	555	454	14	12	39	108	106	110	90	75	108	106
CHI	79	56	21	2	327	204	7	3	77	44	33	0	329	260	11	7	156	100	54	2	656	464	18	10	58	129	74	90	118	87	98	93
CLE	77	43	34	0	317	314	5	8	79	45	32	2	267	229	8	9	156	88	66	2	584	543	13	17	81	85	109	127	90	84	114	113
DET	76	34	41	1	285	303	5	5	78	44	34	0	354	274	20	7	154	78	75	1	639	577	25	12	41	193	129	97	116	107	98	96
NY	75	35	40	0	269	292	19	24	80	36	42	2	255	266	8	4	155	71	82	2	524	558	27	28	282	97	81	112	87	92	107	107
PHI	76	29	47	0	264	319	11	17	78	26	51	1	265	372	6	6	154	55	98	1	529	691	17	23	202	73	89	93	101	127	94	97
STL	78	31	46	1	252	337	7	11	77	26	51	0	258	350	8	3	155	57	97	1	510	687	15	19	108	89	108	95	95	123	95	98
WAS	81	42	36	3	264	255	1	3	76	32	43	1	279	311	3	9	157	74	79	4	543	566	4	12	34	33	92	84	103	107	92	93

1918 AMERICAN LEAGUE

TM	G	W	L	T	R	OR	HR	OHR	G	W	L	T	R	OR	HR	OHR	G	W	L	T	R	OR	HR	OHR	HRF	HRB	HRP	RF	RB	RP	BPF	PPF
BOS	70	49	21	0	272	165	2	3	56	26	30	0	202	215	13	6	126	75	51	0	474	380	15	9	24	192	167	86	109	90	95	93
CHI	56	30	26	0	216	194	4	4	68	27	41	0	241	252	4	5	124	57	67	0	457	446	8	9	107	64	71	101	101	98	100	100
CLE	62	38	22	2	274	219	1	4	67	35	32	0	230	228	8	5	129	73	54	2	504	447	9	9	45	79	109	115	99	90	108	107
DET	58	28	29	1	221	246	2	6	70	27	42	1	255	311	11	4	128	55	71	2	476	557	13	10	67	109	112	99	106	121	97	99
NY	67	37	29	1	251	237	10	22	59	23	34	2	242	238	10	3	126	60	63	3	493	475	20	25	189	148	130	91	114	110	94	94
PHI	68	35	32	1	256	273	15	8	62	17	44	1	156	265	7	5	130	52	76	2	412	538	22	13	158	136	89	111	82	106	104	108
STL	53	23	30	0	178	195	1	7	70	35	34	1	248	253	4	4	123	58	64	1	426	448	5	11	127	38	79	98	95	100	99	100
WAS	74	41	32	1	268	238	1	6	56	31	24	1	193	174	3	4	130	72	56	2	461	412	4	10	79	36	83	104	93	84	104	103

1919 AMERICAN LEAGUE

TM	G	W	L	T	R	OR	HR	OHR	G	W	L	T	R	OR	HR	OHR	G	W	L	T	R	OR	HR	OHR	HRF	HRB	HRP	RF	RB	RP	BPF	PPF
BOS	66	35	30	1	233	241	10	3	72	31	41	0	331	311	23	13	138	66	71	1	564	552	33	16	43	145	68	82	108	107	91	91
CHI	70	48	22	0	344	279	5	10	70	40	30	0	323	255	20	14	140	88	52	0	667	534	25	24	48	99	113	108	111	91	105	102
CLE	69	44	25	0	340	276	12	4	70	40	30	0	296	261	12	15	139	84	55	0	636	537	24	19	64	97	69	112	105	91	107	104
DET	70	46	24	0	307	243	10	14	70	34	36	0	311	335	13	21	140	80	60	0	618	578	23	35	74	91	129	87	116	108	93	92
NY	73	46	25	2	326	255	33	30	68	34	34	0	252	251	12	17	141	80	59	2	578	506	45	47	180	107	118	107	94	85	106	104
PHI	70	21	49	0	266	400	29	31	70	15	55	0	191	342	6	13	140	36	104	0	457	742	35	44	244	62	88	118	75	116	106	112
STL	70	40	30	0	280	249	19	23	70	27	42	1	253	318	12	12	140	67	72	1	533	567	31	35	160	81	89	93	96	101	97	98
WAS	72	32	40	0	265	282	2	5	70	24	44	2	268	288	22	15	142	56	84	2	533	570	24	20	102	125	95	94	99	98	99	99

1920 AMERICAN LEAGUE

TM	G	W	L	T	R	OR	HR	OHR	G	W	L	T	R	OR	HR	OHR	G	W	L	T	R	OR	HR	OHR	HRF	HRB	HRP	RF	RB	RP	BPF	PPF
BOS	76	41	35	0	327	300	3	14	78	31	46	1	323	398	19	25	154	72	81	1	650	698	22	39	43	54	114	90	93	98	96	97
CHI	77	52	25	0	381	298	18	10	77	44	33	0	413	367	19	35	154	96	58	0	794	665	37	45	56	111	112	90	113	97	96	94
CLE	78	51	27	0	441	330	20	10	76	47	29	0	416	312	15	21	154	98	56	0	857	642	35	31	84	79	69	104	113	88	104	100
DET	78	32	46	0	336	452	12	24	77	29	47	1	316	381	18	22	155	61	93	1	652	833	30	46	89	67	100	109	86	106	103	106
NY	77	49	28	0	424	308	71	36	77	46	31	0	414	321	44	12	154	95	59	0	838	629	115	48	173	189	83	101	112	87	102	99
PHI	77	25	50	2	254	401	35	40	79	23	56	0	304	433	9	16	156	48	106	2	558	834	44	56	241	52	71	90	80	114	94	99
STL	78	40	38	0	473	415	31	33	76	36	39	1	324	351	19	20	154	76	77	1	797	766	50	53	149	88	93	124	97	95	111	111
WAS	76	37	38	1	343	386	5	7	77	31	46	0	380	416	31	44	153	68	84	1	723	802	36	51	18	135	180	93	104	114	95	96

1921 AMERICAN LEAGUE

TM	G	W	L	T	R	OR	HR	OHR	G	W	L	T	R	OR	HR	OHR	G	W	L	T	R	OR	HR	OHR	HRF	HRB	HRP	RF	RB	RP	BPF	PPF
BOS	77	41	36	0	332	333	3	16	77	34	43	0	336	363	14	37	154	75	79	0	668	696	17	53	40	35	112	96	85	88	100	100
CHI	77	37	40	0	378	399	13	20	77	25	52	0	305	429	22	32	154	62	92	0	683	858	35	52	64	69	99	101	87	107	99	102
CLE	77	51	26	0	467	330	15	10	77	43	34	0	458	382	27	33	154	94	60	0	925	712	42	43	45	96	88	97	118	94	99	96
DET	77	37	40	0	433	412	19	28	77	34	42	1	450	440	39	43	154	71	82	1	883	852	58	71	60	123	151	95	117	113	96	96
NY	77	53	25	0	500	355	83	34	75	45	30	0	448	353	51	17	153	98	55	0	948	708	134	51	155	176	75	104	118	91	103	99
PHI	77	28	47	2	353	464	65	59	78	25	53	0	304	430	17	26	155	53	100	2	657	894	82	85	233	79	90	109	80	105	103	107
STL	77	43	34	0	423	434	42	43	77	38	39	0	412	411	25	28	154	81	73	0	835	845	67	71	149	91	97	104	105	106	101	101
WAS	76	46	30	0	358	332	14	13	78	34	43	1	346	406	28	38	154	80	73	1	704	738	42	51	45	97	107	95	91	94	99	99

1922 AMERICAN LEAGUE

TM	G	W	L	T	R	OR	HR	OHR	G	W	L	T	R	OR	HR	OHR	G	W	L	T	R	OR	HR	OHR	HRF	HRB	HRP	RF	RB	RP	BPF	PPF
BOS	73	31	42	0	280	344	6	17	81	30	51	0	318	425	39	31	154	61	93	0	598	769	45	48	39	78	108	93	85	106	99	99
CHI	77	43	34	0	351	335	10	21	78	34	43	1	340	356	35	36	155	77	77	1	691	691	45	57	48	83	115	100	93	93	101	101
CLE	80	44	35	1	423	424	12	20	75	34	41	0	345	393	20	38	155	78	76	1	768	817	32	58	55	62	104	107	102	108	102	103

	HOME								ROAD								ALL															
TM	G	W	L	T	R	OR	HR	OHR	G	W	L	T	R	OR	HR	OHR	G	W	L	T	R	OR	HR	OHR	HRF	HRB	HRP	RF	RB	RP	BPF	PPF
DET	77	43	34	0	426	370	15	32	78	36	41	1	402	421	39	30	155	79	75	1	828	791	54	62	72	90	110	98	115	111	98	97
NY	77	50	27	0	387	291	53	48	77	44	33	0	371	327	42	25	154	94	60	0	758	618	95	73	143	123	95	99	102	85	101	99
PHI	78	38	39	1	388	437	80	82	77	27	50	0	317	393	31	25	155	65	89	1	705	830	111	107	230	107	99	112	92	106	104	106
STL	77	54	23	0	471	314	70	41	77	39	38	0	396	329	28	30	154	93	61	0	867	643	98	71	173	106	87	108	112	87	106	102
WAS	79	40	39	0	329	295	15	3	75	29	46	0	321	411	30	46	154	69	85	0	650	706	45	49	25	130	87	82	98	104	92	93

1923 AMERICAN LEAGUE

TM	G	W	L	T	R	OR	HR	OHR	G	W	L	T	R	OR	HR	OHR	G	W	L	T	R	OR	HR	OHR	HRF	HRB	HRP	RF	RB	RP	BPF	PPF
BOS	78	37	40	1	327	402	11	15	76	24	51	1	257	407	23	33	154	61	91	2	584	809	34	48	48	81	109	105	78	104	102	106
CHI	75	30	45	0	327	348	13	24	81	39	40	2	365	393	29	25	156	69	85	2	692	741	42	49	76	80	97	96	94	100	98	99
CLE	78	42	36	0	455	393	22	16	75	40	35	0	433	353	37	20	153	82	71	0	888	746	59	36	67	121	80	104	120	103	101	99
DET	77	45	32	0	400	351	21	31	78	38	39	1	431	390	20	27	155	83	71	1	831	741	41	58	111	70	95	94	116	105	97	95
NY	76	46	30	0	407	329	62	50	76	52	24	0	416	293	43	18	152	98	54	0	823	622	105	68	168	152	97	105	109	85	104	101
PHI	75	34	41	0	345	360	28	32	78	35	42	1	316	401	25	36	153	69	83	1	661	761	53	68	102	99	123	102	90	102	100	102
STL	78	40	36	2	377	364	50	44	76	34	42	0	311	356	32	15	154	74	78	2	688	720	82	59	174	112	76	107	90	94	104	105
WAS	79	43	34	2	363	339	7	16	76	32	44	0	357	408	19	40	155	75	78	2	720	747	26	56	41	65	131	89	103	106	95	95

1924 AMERICAN LEAGUE

TM	G	W	L	T	R	OR	HR	OHR	G	W	L	T	R	OR	HR	OHR	G	W	L	T	R	OR	HR	OHR	HRF	HRB	HRP	RF	RB	RP	BPF	PPF
BOS	77	41	36	0	402	391	8	17	80	26	51	3	335	415	22	26	157	67	87	3	737	806	30	43	57	69	103	108	91	99	104	105
CHI	77	37	39	1	403	414	13	23	77	29	48	0	390	444	28	29	154	66	87	1	793	858	41	52	66	98	126	98	107	114	97	98
CLE	75	37	38	0	374	375	13	18	78	30	48	0	381	439	28	25	153	67	86	0	755	814	41	43	64	96	106	95	103	110	97	97
DET	78	45	33	0	427	393	17	28	78	41	35	2	422	403	18	27	156	86	68	2	849	796	35	55	101	70	105	100	110	104	99	99
NY	78	45	32	1	397	324	57	46	75	44	31	0	401	343	41	13	153	89	63	1	798	667	98	59	167	158	91	95	106	90	99	97
PHI	75	36	39	0	328	391	32	24	77	35	42	0	357	387	31	19	152	71	81	0	685	778	63	43	113	120	86	99	91	102	99	101
STL	78	41	36	1	426	445	44	49	75	33	42	0	343	364	23	19	153	74	78	1	769	809	67	68	186	99	116	94	98	107	108	
WAS	79	47	30	2	371	280	1	7	75	45	32	0	384	333	21	27	156	92	62	2	755	613	22	34	18	50	115	91	99	82	98	96

1925 AMERICAN LEAGUE

TM	G	W	L	T	R	OR	HR	OHR	G	W	L	T	R	OR	HR	OHR	G	W	L	T	R	OR	HR	OHR	HRF	HRB	HRP	RF	RB	RP	BPF	PPF
BOS	75	28	47	0	309	441	10	28	77	19	58	0	330	481	31	39	152	47	105	0	639	922	41	67	58	73	125	94	85	117	95	99
CHI	77	44	33	0	366	378	13	32	77	35	42	0	445	392	25	37	154	79	75	0	811	770	38	69	75	63	111	90	106	102	96	95
CLE	77	37	39	1	421	430	23	19	78	33	45	0	361	387	29	22	155	70	84	1	782	817	52	41	85	79	64	113	91	95	106	107
DET	77	43	34	0	451	399	18	36	79	38	39	2	452	430	32	34	156	81	73	2	903	829	50	70	86	78	108	99	112	104	99	98
NY	79	42	36	1	354	356	54	56	77	27	49	1	352	418	56	22	156	69	85	2	706	774	110	78	131	149	104	91	91	98	96	97
PHI	77	51	26	0	435	351	35	37	76	37	38	1	396	362	41	23	153	88	64	1	831	713	76	60	110	109	87	103	102	89	103	101
STL	78	45	32	1	503	501	73	73	76	37	39	0	397	405	37	26	154	82	71	1	900	906	110	99	196	119	102	119	104	105	108	108
WAS	76	53	22	1	408	298	13	13	76	43	33	0	421	372	43	36	152	96	55	1	829	670	56	49	36	116	107	91	107	89	98	95

1926 AMERICAN LEAGUE

TM	G	W	L	T	R	OR	HR	OHR	G	W	L	T	R	OR	HR	OHR	G	W	L	T	R	OR	HR	OHR	HRF	HRB	HRP	RF	RB	RP	BPF	PPF
BOS	77	25	51	1	288	438	9	16	77	21	56	0	274	397	23	29	154	46	107	1	562	835	32	45	50	75	107	105	76	108	101	106
CHI	79	47	31	1	332	294	8	19	76	34	41	1	398	371	24	28	154	81	72	2	730	665	32	47	53	72	111	81	109	100	92	90
CLE	80	49	31	0	376	301	11	19	74	39	35	0	362	311	16	30	154	88	66	0	738	612	27	49	64	62	104	95	102	86	100	97
DET	81	39	41	0	380	445	16	38	76	40	34	2	413	385	20	20	157	79	75	3	793	830	36	58	123	62	90	98	110	115	97	97
NY	75	50	25	0	417	326	58	33	80	41	38	1	430	387	63	23	155	91	63	1	847	713	121	56	112	222	117	98	116	100	99	97
PHI	71	44	27	0	365	314	34	27	79	39	40	0	312	256	27	11	150	83	67	0	677	570	61	38	163	90	55	128	92	70	118	115
STL	79	40	39	0	375	429	53	64	76	22	53	1	307	416	19	22	155	62	92	1	682	845	72	86	224	85	99	105	92	112	101	103
WAS	74	42	30	2	373	378	4	15	78	39	39	0	429	383	39	30	152	81	69	2	802	761	43	45	32	97	143	98	114	109	98	97

1927 AMERICAN LEAGUE

TM	G	W	L	T	R	OR	HR	OHR	G	W	L	T	R	OR	HR	OHR	G	W	L	T	R	OR	HR	OHR	HRF	HRB	HRP	RF	RB	RP	BPF	PPF
BOS	78	29	49	0	299	409	5	29	76	22	54	0	298	447	23	27	154	51	103	0	597	856	28	56	68	56	117	92	83	114	95	99
CHI	75	38	37	0	337	343	6	22	78	32	46	0	325	365	30	33	153	70	83	0	662	708	36	55	49	77	135	102	86	91	102	103
CLE	77	35	42	0	333	367	10	11	76	31	45	0	335	399	16	26	153	66	87	0	668	766	26	37	52	61	79	94	91	103	97	99
DET	78	44	32	2	467	433	25	28	78	38	39	1	378	372	26	24	156	82	71	3	845	805	51	52	106	89	90	117	102	98	108	107
NY	77	57	19	1	479	267	83	30	78	53	25	0	496	332	75	12	155	110	44	1	975	599	158	42	129	251	79	94	128	84	100	94
PHI	77	50	27	0	412	327	26	36	78	41	36	1	429	399	30	29	155	91	63	1	841	726	56	65	107	101	115	92	114	100	97	95
STL	78	38	38	2	440	457	42	57	77	21	56	0	284	447	13	22	155	59	94	2	724	904	55	79	226	60	87	117	89	109	106	109
WAS	79	51	28	0	416	308	10	19	78	34	41	3	366	422	19	34	157	85	69	3	782	730	29	53	58	64	111	92	105	98	97	96

1928 AMERICAN LEAGUE

TM	G	W	L	T	R	OR	HR	OHR	G	W	L	T	R	OR	HR	OHR	G	W	L	T	R	OR	HR	OHR	HRF	HRB	HRP	RF	RB	RP	BPF	PPF
BOS	74	26	47	1	283	363	10	15	80	31	49	0	306	407	28	34	154	57	96	1	589	770	38	49	46	79	103	97	82	104	98	101
CHI	78	37	40	1	316	369	11	28	77	35	42	0	340	356	13	38	155	72	82	1	656	725	24	66	78	45	111	97	90	98	99	100
CLE	77	29	48	0	366	443	10	15	78	33	44	1	308	387	24	37	155	62	92	1	674	830	34	52	44	75	108	114	86	104	106	108
DET	77	36	41	0	382	400	33	26	77	32	45	0	362	404	29	32	154	68	86	0	744	804	62	58	97	104	98	101	102	109	99	100
NY	77	52	25	0	400	301	69	36	77	49	28	0	494	384	64	23	154	101	53	0	894	685	133	59	119	205	103	83	133	105	92	89
PHI	77	52	25	0	430	295	54	33	76	46	30	0	399	320	35	33	153	98	55	0	829	615	89	66	124	134	106	101	111	85	103	99
STL	77	44	33	0	398	389	51	64	77	38	39	0	374	353	12	29	154	82	72	0	772	742	63	93	229	60	87	107	102	98	104	103
WAS	80	37	43	0	363	378	16	12	75	38	36	1	355	327	24	28	155	75	79	1	718	705	40	40	54	83	79	102	96	94	102	101

1929 AMERICAN LEAGUE

TM	G	W	L	T	R	OR	HR	OHR	G	W	L	T	R	OR	HR	OHR	G	W	L	T	R	OR	HR	OHR	HRF	HRB	HRP	RF	RB	RP	BPF	PPF
BOS	78	32	45	1	328	399	11	36	77	26	51	0	277	404	17	42	155	58	96	1	605	803	28	78	80	41	105	103	77	99	102	105
CHI	76	35	41	0	306	366	19	41	76	24	52	0	321	426	18	43	152	59	93	0	627	792	37	84	97	51	107	90	87	107	95	97
CLE	76	44	32	0	359	363	27	21	76	37	39	0	358	373	35	35	152	81	71	0	717	736	62	56	72	95	85	99	94	96	100	101
DET	77	38	39	0	476	453	57	33	78	32	45	1	450	475	53	40	155	70	84	1	926	928	110	73	98	149	105	101	123	123	97	97
NY	77	49	28	0	463	362	69	55	77	39	38	0	436	413	73	28	154	88	66	0	899	775	142	83	120	180	111	98	118	104	99	97
PHI	74	57	16	1	484	302	72	47	77	47	30	0	417	313	50	26	151	104	46	1	901	615	122	73	154	133	84	112	110	79	109	104
STL	77	41	36	0	370	341	22	58	77	38	37	2	363	372	24	42	154	79	73	2	733	713	46	100	118	59	116	97	95	100	100	100
WAS	78	37	40	1	376	390	10	17	75	34	40	0	354	386	38	31	153	71	81	1	730	776	48	48	41	80	92	99	96	101	100	100

1930 AMERICAN LEAGUE

TM	G	W	L	T	R	OR	HR	OHR	G	W	L	T	R	OR	HR	OHR	G	W	L	T	R	OR	HR	OHR	HRF	HRB	HRP	RF	RB	RP	BPF	PPF
BOS	76	30	46	0	287	354	15	31	78	22	56	0	325	460	32	44	154	52	102	0	612	814	47	75	64	64	102	84	79	101	93	96
CHI	78	34	44	0	393	457	25	42	76	28	48	0	336	427	38	32	154	62	92	0	729	884	63	74	93	76	88	106	85	101	103	105
CLE	77	44	33	0	494	469	34	46	77	37	40	0	396	446	38	39	154	81	73	0	890	915	72	85	104	84	97	113	102	105	105	105
DET	77	45	33	0	441	419	45	48	76	30	46	0	342	414	37	38	154	75	79	0	783	833	82	86	118	90	109	89	95	105	106	
NY	76	47	29	0	471	390	69	54	78	39	39	0	591	508	83	39	154	86	68	0	1062	898	152	93	104	184	122	83	142	123	90	87
PHI	76	58	18	0	485	329	76	49	78	44	34	0	466	422	49	35	154	102	52	0	951	751	125	84	145	121	87	96	115	93	99	96
STL	78	38	40	0	432	475	35	72	76	26	50	0	319	411	40	52	154	64	90	0	751	886	75	124	111	91	138	117	83	97	108	110
WAS	77	56	21	0	474	300	17	15	77	38	39	0	418	389	40	37	154	94	60	0	892	689	57	52	45	86	79	97	106	84	101	98

1931 AMERICAN LEAGUE

TM	G	W	L	T	R	OR	HR	OHR	G	W	L	T	R	OR	HR	OHR	G	W	L	T	R	OR	HR	OHR	HRF	HRB	HRP	RF	RB	RP	BPF	PPF
BOS	80	39	40	1	332	362	11	29	73	23	50	0	293	438	26	25	153	62	90	1	625	800	37	54	73	56	83	87	85	106	94	96
CHI	77	31	45	1	341	421	11	45	79	25	52	2	363	518	16	37	156	56	97	3	704	939	27	82	106	36	100	89	95	122	92	96
CLE	76	45	31	0	503	405	38	32	79	33	45	1	382	428	33	32	155	78	76	1	885	833	71	64	110	92	84	114	100	106	106	106
DET	77	36	41	0	349	432	19	43	77	25	52	0	302	404	24	36	154	61	93	0	651	836	43	79	92	60	103	108	79	99	104	107
NY	77	51	25	1	545	337	84	39	78	43	34	1	522	423	71	28	155	94	59	2	1067	760	155	67	123	194	95	96	137	102	98	93
PHI	77	60	15	0	446	289	61	37	78	47	30	1	412	337	46	31	155	107	45	1	858	626	118	73	110	160	106	104	104	79	105	101
STL	77	39	38	0	407	425	42	48	77	24	53	0	315	445	34	36	154	63	91	0	722	870	76	84	123	97	106	107	89	105	102	105
WAS	79	55	22	2	453	308	13	24	77	37	40	0	390	383	36	49	156	92	62	2	843	691	49	73	46	89	132	97	105	88	101	98

1932 AMERICAN LEAGUE

TM	G	W	L	T	R	OR	HR	OHR	G	W	L	T	R	OR	HR	OHR	G	W	L	T	R	OR	HR	OHR	HRF	HRB	HRP	RF	RB	RP	BPF	PPF
BOS	77	27	50	0	295	439	18	31	77	16	61	0	271	476	35	48	154	43	111	0	566	915	53	79	61	72	105	96	73	111	97	102

	HOME								ROAD								ALL														
TM	G	W	L	T	R	OR	HR	OHR	G	W	L	T	R	OR	HR	OHR	G	W	L	T	R	OR	HR	OHR	HRF	HRB	HRP	RF	RB	RP	BPF	PPF
CHI	77	28	49	0	300	390	10	36	75	21	53	1	367	507	26	52	152	49	102	1	667	897	36	88	60	49	116	78	97	124	87	91
CLE	77	43	33	1	460	401	36	33	76	44	32	0	385	346	42	37	153	87	65	1	845	747	78	70	88	91	83	115	97	87	108	107
DET	78	42	34	2	423	399	29	50	75	34	41	0	376	388	51	39	153	76	75	2	799	787	80	89	86	97	109	103	98	97	102	102
NY	77	62	15	0	482	300	81	44	79	45	32	2	520	424	79	49	156	107	47	2	1002	724	160	93	102	180	115	88	129	97	95	91
PHI	77	51	26	0	572	406	109	80	77	43	34	0	409	346	63	32	154	94	60	0	981	752	172	112	179	146	96	126	106	85	114	111
STL	75	33	42	0	385	428	47	56	79	30	49	0	351	470	20	47	154	63	91	0	736	898	67	103	149	59	93	103	91	109	100	103
WAS	77	51	26	0	431	325	21	26	77	42	35	0	409	391	40	47	154	93	61	0	840	716	61	73	58	84	99	96	105	91	100	98

1933 AMERICAN LEAGUE

TM	G	W	L	T	R	OR	HR	OHR	G	W	L	T	R	OR	HR	OHR	G	W	L	T	R	OR	HR	OHR	HRF	HRB	HRP	RF	RB	RP	BPF	PPF
BOS	72	32	40	0	341	377	23	35	77	31	46	0	359	381	27	40	149	63	86	0	700	758	50	75	93	69	99	103	93	100	101	102
CHI	77	35	41	1	355	426	20	42	74	32	42	0	328	388	23	43	151	67	83	1	683	814	43	85	91	60	111	104	90	104	101	103
CLE	77	45	32	0	353	341	22	24	74	30	44	0	301	328	28	36	151	75	76	0	654	669	50	60	72	75	87	105	83	85	105	105
DET	78	43	35	0	394	382	27	36	77	32	44	1	328	351	30	48	155	75	79	1	722	733	57	84	82	82	115	111	87	89	107	107
NY	75	51	23	1	421	324	79	26	77	40	36	1	506	444	65	40	152	91	59	2	927	768	144	66	103	186	96	83	134	114	91	88
PHI	76	46	29	1	414	387	82	50	76	33	43	0	461	466	57	27	152	79	72	1	875	853	139	77	147	151	88	88	126	123	92	91
STL	77	30	46	1	389	480	43	68	76	25	50	1	280	340	21	28	153	55	96	2	669	820	64	96	191	59	82	130	76	91	115	117
WAS	76	46	30	0	358	338	14	16	77	53	23	1	492	327	46	48	153	99	53	1	850	665	60	64	36	109	118	89	115	94	96	93

1934 AMERICAN LEAGUE

TM	G	W	L	T	R	OR	HR	OHR	G	W	L	T	R	OR	HR	OHR	G	W	L	T	R	OR	HR	OHR	HRF	HRB	HRP	RF	RB	RP	BPF	PPF
BOS	77	42	35	0	447	405	23	24	76	34	41	1	373	370	28	46	153	76	76	1	820	775	51	70	66	71	90	111	99	94	106	105
CHI	75	29	46	0	370	464	47	82	78	24	53	1	334	482	24	57	153	53	99	1	704	946	71	139	151	69	128	104	90	117	99	103
CLE	78	47	31	0	435	362	45	34	76	38	38	0	379	401	55	36	154	85	69	0	814	763	100	70	87	121	89	100	103	97	100	100
DET	80	54	26	0	479	345	28	32	74	47	27	0	479	363	46	54	154	101	53	0	958	708	74	86	60	109	123	93	125	96	98	94
NY	77	53	24	0	416	275	75	34	77	41	36	0	426	394	60	37	154	94	60	0	842	669	135	71	112	145	84	87	112	91	96	93
PHI	76	34	40	2	371	410	81	48	77	34	42	1	393	428	63	36	153	68	82	3	764	838	144	84	126	150	94	96	100	109	97	98
STL	76	36	39	1	356	405	35	60	78	31	46	1	318	395	27	34	154	67	85	2	674	800	62	94	148	59	84	108	82	96	104	106
WAS	76	34	40	2	368	397	14	26	79	32	46	1	361	409	37	48	155	66	86	3	729	806	51	74	52	72	106	102	91	99	101	102

1935 AMERICAN LEAGUE

TM	G	W	L	T	R	OR	HR	OHR	G	W	L	T	R	OR	HR	OHR	G	W	L	T	R	OR	HR	OHR	HRF	HRB	HRP	RF	RB	RP	BPF	PPF
BOS	79	41	37	1	393	404	26	29	75	37	38	0	325	328	43	38	154	78	75	1	718	732	69	67	68	95	94	114	85	86	108	108
CHI	77	42	34	1	418	396	50	61	76	32	44	0	320	354	24	44	153	74	78	1	738	750	74	105	149	71	101	116	87	88	109	109
CLE	77	48	29	0	391	340	53	30	79	34	42	3	385	399	40	38	156	82	71	3	776	739	93	68	108	102	78	97	98	94	99	99
DET	79	53	25	1	467	304	45	38	73	40	33	0	452	361	61	40	152	93	58	1	919	665	106	78	79	144	112	90	123	93	97	93
NY	74	41	33	0	341	294	60	51	75	48	27	0	477	338	44	40	149	89	60	0	818	632	104	91	130	114	102	82	115	93	93	90
PHI	72	30	42	0	369	414	63	39	77	28	49	0	341	455	49	34	149	58	91	0	710	869	112	73	125	122	84	103	94	112	100	102
STL	76	31	44	1	374	513	36	49	79	34	43	2	344	417	37	43	155	65	87	3	718	930	73	92	108	84	103	117	86	107	106	110
WAS	77	37	39	1	388	414	5	28	77	30	47	0	435	489	27	61	154	67	86	1	823	903	32	89	40	47	139	88	115	124	91	93

1936 AMERICAN LEAGUE

TM	G	W	L	T	R	OR	HR	OHR	G	W	L	T	R	OR	HR	OHR	G	W	L	T	R	OR	HR	OHR	HRF	HRB	HRP	RF	RB	RP	BPF	PPF
BOS	77	47	29	1	437	360	38	31	78	27	51	0	338	404	48	47	155	74	80	1	775	764	86	78	76	100	91	107	83	82	106	106
CHI	75	43	32	0	453	419	23	55	78	38	38	2	467	454	37	49	153	81	70	2	920	873	60	104	95	65	108	99	107	102	99	99
CLE	81	49	30	2	535	433	73	33	76	31	44	1	386	429	50	40	157	80	74	3	921	862	123	73	109	117	76	110	97	93	105	105
DET	77	44	33	0	448	399	51	58	77	39	38	0	473	472	43	42	154	83	71	0	921	871	94	100	124	90	94	91	111	105	95	95
NY	76	55	21	0	492	311	82	41	77	46	30	2	573	420	100	43	153	101	51	2	1065	731	182	84	90	201	106	85	128	92	95	90
PHI	77	31	46	0	383	531	43	77	77	22	54	1	331	514	29	54	154	53	100	1	714	1045	72	131	135	67	114	106	81	114	100	105
STL	77	31	43	3	443	552	47	63	78	26	52	0	361	512	32	52	155	57	95	3	804	1064	79	115	126	75	105	112	88	113	103	107
WAS	77	42	35	0	433	380	16	27	76	40	36	0	456	419	46	46	153	82	71	0	889	799	62	73	50	80	101	93	105	96	98	96

1937 AMERICAN LEAGUE

TM	G	W	L	T	R	OR	HR	OHR	G	W	L	T	R	OR	HR	OHR	G	W	L	T	R	OR	HR	OHR	HRF	HRB	HRP	RF	RB	RP	BPF	PPF
BOS	74	44	29	1	420	368	53	43	80	36	43	1	401	407	47	49	154	80	72	2	821	775	100	92	107	96	89	105	99	94	103	102
CHI	77	47	30	0	397	365	39	62	77	39	38	1	383	365	28	53	154	86	68	0	780	730	67	115	122	61	100	102	94	89	103	102
CLE	78	50	28	0	430	329	48	22	78	33	43	2	387	439	55	39	156	83	71	2	817	768	103	61	77	109	66	93	103	97	97	97
DET	77	49	28	0	521	448	91	58	78	40	37	1	414	393	59	44	155	89	65	1	935	841	150	102	140	125	90	119	106	97	109	108
NY	79	57	20	2	520	298	94	41	78	45	32	1	459	373	80	51	157	102	52	3	979	671	174	92	103	168	98	99	117	84	102	97
PHI	79	27	50	2	333	419	51	47	75	27	47	1	366	435	43	58	154	54	97	3	699	854	94	105	92	99	109	93	110	94	96	
STL	78	25	51	2	385	513	39	74	78	21	57	0	330	510	32	69	156	46	108	2	715	1023	71	143	108	71	131	104	89	121	99	103
WAS	80	43	35	2	376	381	14	30	78	30	45	3	381	460	33	66	158	73	80	5	757	841	47	96	47	61	116	89	98	106	94	96

1938 AMERICAN LEAGUE

TM	G	W	L	T	R	OR	HR	OHR	G	W	L	T	R	OR	HR	OHR	G	W	L	T	R	OR	HR	OHR	HRF	HRB	HRP	RF	RB	RP	BPF	PPF
BOS	75	52	23	0	481	356	67	52	75	36	38	1	421	395	31	50	150	88	61	1	902	751	98	102	140	74	82	103	109	93	102	100
CHI	73	33	39	1	326	364	24	41	76	32	44	0	383	388	43	60	149	65	83	1	709	752	67	101	68	74	108	93	91	96	98	98
CLE	76	46	30	0	425	363	54	35	77	40	36	1	422	419	59	65	153	86	66	1	847	782	113	100	76	120	104	96	105	97	99	98
DET	79	48	31	0	447	392	83	60	76	36	39	1	415	403	54	50	155	84	70	1	862	795	137	110	128	109	92	99	103	96	100	99
NY	79	55	22	2	524	342	112	43	78	44	31	3	442	368	62	42	157	99	53	5	966	710	174	85	141	125	70	106	109	83	105	102
PHI	76	28	47	1	378	486	55	64	78	25	52	1	348	470	43	78	154	53	99	2	726	956	98	142	99	95	130	106	87	111	101	104
STL	77	31	43	3	385	487	52	62	79	24	54	1	370	475	40	70	156	55	97	4	755	962	92	132	104	84	115	104	90	112	100	103
WAS	78	44	33	1	412	413	33	27	74	31	43	0	402	460	52	65	152	75	76	1	814	873	85	92	52	106	107	92	105	112	95	96

1939 AMERICAN LEAGUE

TM	G	W	L	T	R	OR	HR	OHR	G	W	L	T	R	OR	HR	OHR	G	W	L	T	R	OR	HR	OHR	HRF	HRB	HRP	RF	RB	RP	BPF	PPF
BOS	75	42	32	1	458	445	57	39	77	47	30	0	432	350	67	38	152	89	62	1	890	795	124	77	95	125	83	117	104	94	108	107
CHI	77	50	27	0	414	366	38	51	78	35	42	1	341	371	26	48	155	85	69	1	755	737	64	99	119	57	86	110	88	86	107	106
CLE	77	44	33	0	363	347	30	33	77	43	34	0	434	353	55	42	154	87	67	0	797	700	85	75	68	95	88	92	101	91	99	96
DET	78	42	35	1	461	434	66	65	77	39	38	0	388	328	58	39	155	81	73	1	849	762	124	104	128	110	92	120	95	86	111	110
NY	77	52	25	0	382	261	84	48	75	54	20	1	585	295	82	37	152	106	45	1	967	556	166	85	109	160	90	75	133	84	91	85
PHI	76	28	48	0	354	523	45	83	77	27	49	1	357	499	53	65	153	55	97	1	711	1022	98	148	107	103	145	102	92	126	97	102
STL	78	18	59	1	372	561	47	80	78	25	52	1	361	474	44	53	156	43	111	2	733	1035	91	133	124	84	116	108	90	121	100	105
WAS	77	37	39	1	326	337	11	19	76	28	48	0	376	460	33	56	153	65	87	1	702	797	44	75	36	61	100	80	98	109	90	91

1940 AMERICAN LEAGUE

TM	G	W	L	T	R	OR	HR	OHR	G	W	L	T	R	OR	HR	OHR	G	W	L	T	R	OR	HR	OHR	HRF	HRB	HRP	RF	RB	RP	BPF	PPF
BOS	79	45	34	0	468	421	73	64	75	37	38	0	404	404	72	60	154	82	72	0	872	825	145	124	99	136	119	104	113	108	101	100
CHI	78	41	36	1	357	363	36	65	77	41	36	0	378	309	37	46	155	82	72	1	735	672	73	111	118	61	87	103	92	85	104	103
CLE	82	51	30	1	350	281	37	27	73	38	35	0	360	356	64	59	155	89	65	1	710	637	101	86	50	121	102	81	100	90	93	92
DET	79	50	29	0	512	389	82	64	76	40	35	1	376	328	52	38	155	90	64	1	888	717	134	102	147	97	75	121	103	86	111	109
NY	76	52	24	0	414	284	83	63	79	36	42	1	403	387	72	56	155	88	66	1	817	671	155	119	117	132	105	93	108	90	99	96
PHI	71	29	42	0	336	409	44	62	83	25	58	0	367	523	61	73	154	54	100	0	703	932	105	135	92	102	128	97	97	123	95	99
STL	77	37	39	1	419	460	68	68	79	30	48	1	338	422	50	45	156	67	87	2	757	882	118	113	138	89	85	115	92	106	106	108
WAS	77	36	41	0	316	368	19	28	77	28	49	0	349	443	33	65	154	64	90	0	665	811	52	93	51	62	100	87	94	111	93	95

1941 AMERICAN LEAGUE

TM	G	W	L	T	R	OR	HR	OHR	G	W	L	T	R	OR	HR	OHR	G	W	L	T	R	OR	HR	OHR	HRF	HRB	HRP	RF	RB	RP	BPF	PPF
BOS	77	47	30	0	461	371	70	51	78	37	40	1	404	379	54	37	155	84	70	1	865	750	124	88	130	118	87	107	114	101	103	101
CHI	79	38	39	2	288	297	17	40	77	39	38	0	350	352	30	49	156	77	77	2	638	649	47	89	73	57	104	83	92	94	93	94
CLE	77	42	35	0	340	322	45	35	78	33	44	1	337	346	58	36	155	75	79	1	677	668	103	71	88	116	84	98	91	90	101	100
DET	77	43	34	0	381	377	51	43	78	32	45	1	305	366	30	37	155	75	79	1	686	743	81	80	135	73	74	112	88	94	106	107
NY	78	51	26	1	396	295	76	44	78	50	27	1	434	336	75	37	156	101	53	2	830	631	151	81	108	157	92	92	114	90	98	95
PHI	77	36	41	0	373	432	43	75	77	28	49	0	340	408	42	61	154	64	90	0	713	840	85	136	112	95	141	106	97	112	101	103
STL	79	40	37	2	407	408	49	63	78	30	47	1	358	415	42	57	157	70	84	3	765	823	91	120	110	97	124	103	103	109	100	101
WAS	78	40	37	1	367	387	13	19	78	30	47	1	361	411	39	50	156	70	84	2	728	798	52	69	39	75	100	98	101	109	98	99

TM	HOME G	W	L	T	R	OR	HR	OHR	ROAD G	W	L	T	R	OR	HR	OHR	ALL G	W	L	T	R	OR	HR	OHR	HRF	HRB	HRP	RF	RB	RP	BPF	PPF
1942 AMERICAN LEAGUE																																
BOS	77	53	24	0	403	299	54	33	75	40	35	0	358	295	49	32	152	93	59	0	761	594	103	65	105	153	103	105	113	91	104	100
CHI	70	35	35	0	256	275	6	31	78	31	47	0	282	334	19	43	148	66	82	0	538	609	25	74	69	42	123	96	86	96	99	100
CLE	80	39	39	2	266	308	20	24	76	36	40	0	324	351	30	37	156	75	79	2	590	659	50	61	65	88	104	83	97	107	91	93
DET	77	43	34	0	344	302	50	40	79	30	47	2	245	285	26	20	156	73	81	2	589	587	76	60	178	79	63	121	78	79	113	113
NY	77	58	19	0	394	226	62	39	77	45	32	0	407	281	46	32	154	103	51	0	801	507	108	71	127	144	101	93	123	82	99	94
PHI	76	25	51	0	249	415	16	42	78	30	48	0	300	386	17	47	154	55	99	0	549	801	33	89	93	53	128	98	87	121	96	101
STL	77	40	37	0	376	350	55	37	74	42	32	0	354	287	43	26	151	82	69	0	730	637	98	63	124	133	90	108	109	96	104	102
WAS	77	35	42	0	339	409	13	11	74	27	47	0	314	408	27	39	151	62	89	0	653	817	40	50	38	90	98	99	106	129	96	99
1943 AMERICAN LEAGUE																																
BOS	77	39	36	2	293	312	29	25	78	29	48	1	270	295	28	36	155	68	84	3	563	607	57	61	87	104	109	107	90	97	103	104
CHI	76	40	36	0	264	311	20	25	79	42	36	1	309	283	13	29	155	82	72	1	573	594	33	54	110	51	81	101	94	97	101	101
CLE	77	44	33	0	269	247	16	21	76	38	38	0	331	330	39	31	153	82	71	0	600	577	55	52	56	115	117	80	112	108	90	90
DET	78	45	32	1	345	284	45	26	77	33	44	0	287	276	32	25	155	78	76	1	632	560	77	51	120	115	82	109	99	90	105	104
NY	77	54	23	0	321	241	60	33	78	44	33	1	348	301	40	27	155	98	56	1	669	542	100	60	136	144	94	90	115	96	96	94
PHI	79	27	51	1	261	387	14	36	76	22	54	0	236	330	12	37	155	49	105	1	497	717	26	73	97	45	115	107	81	112	101	106
STL	77	44	33	0	319	290	49	51	76	28	47	1	277	314	29	23	153	72	80	1	596	604	78	74	170	102	94	101	100	101	100	101
WAS	76	44	32	0	345	307	9	14	77	40	37	0	321	288	38	34	153	84	69	0	666	595	47	48	36	106	122	108	108	98	104	102
1944 AMERICAN LEAGUE																																
BOS	78	47	30	1	389	311	48	34	78	30	47	1	350	365	21	32	156	77	77	2	739	676	69	66	145	95	98	98	119	110	98	97
CHI	77	41	36	0	302	304	11	24	77	30	47	0	241	358	12	44	154	71	83	0	543	662	23	68	65	52	129	101	86	103	100	102
CLE	78	39	38	1	345	328	27	16	77	33	44	0	298	349	43	24	155	72	82	1	643	677	70	40	66	140	87	102	101	106	100	101
DET	78	43	34	1	325	318	38	21	78	45	32	1	333	263	22	18	156	88	66	2	658	581	60	39	140	82	57	108	88	88	105	104
NY	78	47	31	0	388	307	58	45	76	36	40	0	286	310	38	37	154	83	71	0	674	617	96	82	129	156	139	112	100	94	106	105
PHI	76	39	37	0	277	270	18	28	79	33	45	1	248	324	18	30	155	72	82	1	525	594	36	58	99	62	96	99	82	92	101	102
STL	77	54	23	0	368	272	45	24	77	35	42	0	316	315	27	34	154	89	65	0	684	587	72	58	112	118	101	102	107	93	102	100
WAS	77	40	37	0	286	268	9	13	77	24	53	0	306	396	24	35	154	64	90	0	592	664	33	48	40	79	110	80	106	115	89	91
1945 AMERICAN LEAGUE																																
BOS	78	42	35	1	306	299	22	28	79	29	48	2	293	375	28	30	157	71	83	3	599	674	50	58	88	97	111	92	104	114	95	96
CHI	74	44	29	1	305	277	8	34	76	27	49	0	291	356	14	29	150	71	78	1	596	633	22	63	100	42	110	93	107	112	95	96
CLE	77	44	33	0	292	273	27	15	70	29	39	2	265	275	38	24	147	73	72	2	557	548	65	39	65	150	96	96	99	97	99	98
DET	78	50	26	0	333	285	43	28	79	38	39	2	300	280	34	20	155	88	65	2	633	565	77	48	132	121	80	110	99	89	106	105
NY	76	48	28	0	395	297	65	51	76	33	43	0	281	309	28	15	152	81	71	0	676	606	93	66	223	111	76	115	106	97	107	106
PHI	77	39	35	3	265	270	16	21	76	13	63	0	229	368	17	34	153	52	98	3	494	638	33	55	73	72	110	88	89	110	94	96
STL	76	47	27	2	353	291	32	33	78	34	43	1	244	257	31	26	154	81	70	3	597	548	63	59	115	110	104	127	86	81	115	114
WAS	78	46	31	1	278	255	1	6	78	41	36	1	344	307	26	36	156	87	67	2	622	562	27	42	13	59	136	84	110	101	93	92
1946 AMERICAN LEAGUE																																
BOS	78	61	16	1	469	315	65	44	78	43	34	1	323	279	44	45	156	104	50	2	792	594	109	89	121	121	104	128	109	86	114	111
CHI	79	40	38	1	272	290	17	46	76	34	42	0	290	305	20	34	155	74	80	1	562	595	37	80	110	43	86	92	92	97	97	97
CLE	78	36	41	0	231	264	25	36	79	32	45	2	306	374	54	48	156	68	86	2	537	638	79	84	64	114	127	77	96	111	88	90
DET	79	48	30	1	391	300	75	68	76	44	32	0	313	267	33	29	155	92	62	1	704	567	108	97	194	90	82	114	103	86	108	105
NY	77	47	30	0	342	262	68	34	77	40	37	0	342	285	68	32	154	87	67	0	684	547	136	66	102	163	88	97	109	90	100	98
PHI	78	31	46	1	297	351	21	38	77	18	59	0	232	329	19	45	155	49	105	1	529	680	40	83	90	51	99	110	80	101	104	107
STL	77	35	41	1	313	344	46	29	79	31	47	1	308	366	38	44	156	66	88	2	621	710	84	73	94	105	91	99	100	113	98	100
WAS	76	38	38	0	253	343	16	25	79	38	40	1	355	363	44	56	155	76	78	1	608	706	60	81	46	97	130	88	104	120	92	94
1947 AMERICAN LEAGUE																																
BOS	81	49	30	2	421	355	61	39	76	34	41	1	299	314	42	45	157	83	71	3	720	669	103	84	107	115	98	116	102	97	108	107
CHI	75	32	43	0	244	322	20	31	80	38	41	1	309	339	33	45	155	70	84	1	553	661	53	76	72	70	98	94	89	104	97	99
CLE	78	38	39	1	314	279	52	51	79	42	35	2	373	309	60	43	157	80	74	3	687	588	112	94	101	133	114	90	110	96	96	94
DET	80	46	31	3	370	345	62	47	78	39	38	1	344	297	41	32	158	85	69	4	714	642	103	79	138	99	78	108	105	95	104	103
NY	77	55	22	0	392	242	54	49	78	42	35	1	402	326	61	46	155	97	57	1	794	568	115	95	99	140	119	91	128	95	97	92
PHI	78	39	38	1	296	324	33	41	78	39	38	1	337	290	28	44	156	78	76	2	633	614	61	85	102	70	95	99	99	98	95	100
STL	77	29	48	0	286	401	52	57	77	30	47	0	278	343	38	46	154	59	95	0	564	744	90	103	124	98	111	108	87	110	102	105
WAS	77	36	41	0	244	326	10	20	77	28	49	0	252	349	32	43	154	64	90	0	496	675	42	63	43	63	98	95	80	105	97	101
1948 AMERICAN LEAGUE																																
BOS	77	55	23	0	481	336	60	43	77	41	36	0	426	384	61	40	155	96	59	0	907	720	121	83	102	134	97	101	124	101	100	97
CHI	76	27	48	1	278	378	21	36	78	24	53	1	281	436	34	53	154	51	101	2	559	814	55	89	69	73	112	93	81	112	95	100
CLE	79	48	30	1	398	272	77	41	77	49	28	0	442	296	78	41	156	97	58	1	840	568	155	82	98	175	102	91	116	82	99	94
DET	77	39	38	0	327	355	39	61	77	39	38	0	373	371	39	31	154	78	76	0	700	726	78	92	136	77	85	93	100	103	96	97
NY	77	50	27	0	413	315	70	54	77	44	33	0	444	318	69	40	154	94	60	0	857	633	139	94	113	151	107	97	118	90	100	96
PHI	77	36	41	0	347	396	33	47	77	48	29	0	382	339	35	39	154	84	70	0	729	735	68	86	107	74	90	103	99	99	101	102
STL	76	34	42	0	363	451	29	64	79	25	52	2	308	398	34	39	155	59	94	2	671	849	63	103	126	65	97	116	87	106	106	109
WAS	77	29	48	1	312	419	11	24	76	27	49	0	266	377	20	57	154	56	97	1	578	796	31	81	47	48	109	108	77	102	103	107
1949 AMERICAN LEAGUE																																
BOS	77	61	16	0	514	310	71	43	78	35	42	1	382	357	60	39	155	96	58	1	896	667	131	82	116	124	82	113	115	90	107	103
CHI	77	32	45	0	327	353	15	52	77	31	46	0	321	384	28	56	154	63	91	0	648	737	43	108	81	49	115	96	92	103	98	99
CLE	77	49	28	0	319	263	61	42	77	40	37	0	356	311	51	40	154	89	65	0	675	574	112	82	112	108	82	89	96	83	98	96
DET	78	50	27	1	402	350	57	60	77	37	40	0	349	305	31	42	155	87	67	1	751	655	88	102	148	72	85	112	96	85	108	106
NY	78	54	23	1	419	304	72	53	77	43	34	0	410	333	43	45	155	97	57	1	829	637	115	98	135	100	89	98	114	91	100	97
PHI	77	52	25	0	389	326	42	42	77	29	48	0	337	399	40	63	154	81	73	0	726	725	82	105	84	95	116	98	102	102	99	99
STL	77	36	41	0	394	426	69	56	78	17	60	1	273	487	48	57	155	53	101	1	667	913	117	113	116	115	113	106	92	122	100	104
WAS	77	26	51	0	254	426	20	14	77	24	53	0	330	442	61	65	154	50	104	0	584	868	81	79	29	133	117	88	88	126	91	96
1950 AMERICAN LEAGUE																																
BOS	77	55	22	0	625	427	100	67	77	39	38	0	402	377	61	54	154	94	60	0	1027	804	161	121	139	111	88	131	114	94	114	111
CHI	79	35	42	2	316	352	52	55	77	25	52	0	309	397	41	52	156	60	94	2	625	749	93	107	109	71	81	92	82	96	97	99
CLE	78	49	28	0	386	297	102	57	78	43	34	1	420	357	62	63	155	92	62	1	806	654	164	120	126	118	93	91	105	87	98	95
DET	81	50	30	1	405	346	60	72	76	45	29	2	432	367	54	69	157	95	59	3	837	713	114	141	102	93	113	91	110	95	97	95
NY	77	53	24	0	440	333	78	51	78	45	32	1	474	358	81	67	155	98	56	1	914	691	159	118	91	138	106	96	118	92	99	96
PHI	77	29	48	0	314	406	45	67	77	23	54	0	356	507	55	71	154	52	102	0	670	913	100	138	89	89	119	84	97	126	90	93
STL	74	27	47	0	368	484	52	69	80	31	49	0	316	432	54	60	154	58	96	0	684	916	106	129	111	84	99	118	83	107	107	111
WAS	78	35	42	1	347	407	18	28	77	32	45	0	343	406	58	71	155	67	87	1	690	813	76	99	38	84	112	99	89	103	99	101
1951 AMERICAN LEAGUE																																
BOS	75	50	25	0	460	348	80	65	79	37	42	0	344	377	47	35	154	87	67	0	804	725	127	100	169	90	72	116	104	96	108	106
CHI	78	39	38	1	334	310	28	47	77	42	35	0	380	334	58	62	155	81	73	1	714	644	86	109	65	97	124	90	103	94	97	95
CLE	77	53	24	0	324	249	76	42	78	40	37	1	372	345	64	44	155	93	61	1	696	594	140	86	110	123	81	84	103	89	94	93
DET	77	36	41	0	358	402	58	60	77	37	40	0	327	339	46	42	154	73	81	0	685	741	104	102	128	87	85	112	91	97	106	107
NY	78	56	22	0	366	258	72	43	76	42	34	0	432	363	68	49	154	98	56	0	798	621	140	92	98	134	93	80	123	98	91	88
PHI	79	38	41	0	406	407	54	59	75	32	43	0	330	338	48	50	154	70	84	0	736	745	102	109	108	94	100	113	97	98	106	106
STL	77	24	53	0	327	486	41	66	77	28	49	0	284	396	45	65	154	52	102	0	611	882	86	131	96	86	125	115	82	113	105	109

	HOME								ROAD								ALL															
TM	G	W	L	T	R	OR	HR	OHR	G	W	L	T	R	OR	HR	OHR	G	W	L	T	R	OR	HR	OHR	HRF	HRB	HRP	RF	RB	RP	BPF	PPF
WAS	76	32	44	0	319	362	13	35	78	30	48	0	353	402	41	75	154	62	92	0	672	764	54	110	45	67	134	93	99	110	95	97

1952 AMERICAN LEAGUE

TM	G	W	L	T	R	OR	HR	OHR	G	W	L	T	R	OR	HR	OHR	G	W	L	T	R	OR	HR	OHR	HRF	HRB	HRP	RF	RB	RP	BPF	PPF
BOS	77	50	27	0	406	309	68	49	77	26	51	0	262	349	45	58	154	76	78	0	668	658	113	107	112	109	106	115	96	97	107	107
CHI	79	44	33	2	305	276	42	39	77	37	40	0	305	292	38	47	156	81	73	2	610	568	80	86	94	81	86	96	94	88	100	99
CLE	77	49	28	0	333	260	72	43	78	44	33	1	430	346	76	51	155	93	61	1	763	606	148	94	94	155	105	81	130	106	91	88
DET	77	32	45	0	284	366	65	59	79	18	59	2	273	372	38	52	156	50	104	2	557	738	103	111	132	89	97	101	86	110	99	103
NY	77	49	28	0	345	264	64	48	77	46	31	0	382	293	65	46	154	95	59	0	727	557	129	94	102	130	99	92	115	91	98	95
PHI	78	45	32	1	382	403	55	60	77	34	43	0	282	320	34	53	155	79	75	1	664	723	89	113	126	80	100	124	92	100	111	112
STL	78	42	35	1	321	346	47	52	77	22	55	0	283	387	35	59	155	64	90	1	604	733	82	111	103	83	108	98	96	114	97	100
WAS	78	42	35	1	299	292	13	18	79	36	41	2	299	316	37	60	157	78	76	3	598	608	50	78	35	71	101	98	91	92	100	100

1953 AMERICAN LEAGUE

TM	G	W	L	T	R	OR	HR	OHR	G	W	L	T	R	OR	HR	OHR	G	W	L	T	R	OR	HR	OHR	HRF	HRB	HRP	RF	RB	RP	BPF	PPF
BOS	76	38	38	0	335	354	57	59	77	46	31	0	321	278	44	33	153	84	69	0	656	632	101	92	144	75	67	115	89	85	109	108
CHI	78	41	36	1	349	328	30	56	78	48	29	1	367	264	44	57	156	89	65	2	716	592	74	113	87	70	104	107	97	82	106	103
CLE	78	53	24	1	379	272	90	46	77	39	38	0	391	355	70	46	155	92	62	1	770	627	160	92	115	133	83	88	117	97	95	93
DET	79	30	47	2	369	462	55	97	79	30	47	2	326	461	53	57	158	60	94	4	695	923	108	154	131	89	117	104	101	129	98	102
NY	77	50	27	0	347	255	64	39	74	49	25	0	454	292	75	55	151	99	52	0	801	547	139	94	80	143	101	81	128	93	93	88
PHI	78	27	50	1	299	447	49	74	79	32	45	2	333	352	67	47	157	59	95	3	632	799	116	121	107	102	105	108	89	108	102	105
STL	77	23	54	0	281	447	58	64	77	31	46	0	274	331	54	37	154	54	100	0	555	778	112	101	127	90	80	116	76	107	107	111
WAS	75	39	36	0	305	283	10	31	77	37	40	0	382	331	59	81	152	76	76	0	687	614	69	112	33	84	152	86	107	97	94	93

1954 AMERICAN LEAGUE

TM	G	W	L	T	R	OR	HR	OHR	G	W	L	T	R	OR	HR	OHR	G	W	L	T	R	OR	HR	OHR	HRF	HRB	HRP	RF	RB	RP	BPF	PPF
BAL	77	32	45	0	235	313	19	23	77	22	55	0	248	355	33	55	154	54	100	0	483	668	52	78	50	66	91	91	79	105	95	99
BOS	79	38	39	2	357	384	69	70	77	31	46	0	343	344	54	48	156	69	85	2	700	728	123	118	127	107	102	104	107	111	100	101
CHI	78	45	32	1	327	294	39	51	77	49	28	0	384	227	55	43	155	94	60	1	711	521	94	94	93	93	94	101	106	80	103	100
CLE	77	59	18	0	376	252	78	57	79	52	25	2	370	252	78	32	156	111	43	2	746	504	156	89	125	134	80	105	108	76	106	101
DET	77	35	42	0	285	336	44	80	78	33	44	1	299	328	46	58	155	68	86	1	584	664	90	138	117	85	122	100	90	101	100	101
NY	78	54	23	1	388	274	68	42	77	49	28	0	417	289	65	44	155	103	51	1	805	563	133	86	101	126	86	95	125	92	99	94
PHI	77	29	47	1	260	467	44	85	79	22	56	1	282	408	50	56	156	51	103	2	542	875	94	141	119	88	122	105	84	128	98	105
WAS	78	37	41	0	320	335	27	27	77	29	47	1	312	345	54	52	155	66	88	1	632	680	81	79	53	98	97	98	99	106	98	99

1955 AMERICAN LEAGUE

TM	G	W	L	T	R	OR	HR	OHR	G	W	L	T	R	OR	HR	OHR	G	W	L	T	R	OR	HR	OHR	HRF	HRB	HRP	RF	RB	RP	BPF	PPF
BAL	79	30	47	2	249	335	15	42	77	27	50	0	291	419	39	61	156	57	97	2	540	754	54	103	58	52	100	81	87	116	90	93
BOS	78	47	31	0	470	395	84	79	76	37	39	0	285	257	53	49	154	84	70	0	755	652	137	128	146	93	88	146	88	78	124	122
CHI	77	49	28	0	357	262	54	47	78	42	35	1	368	295	62	64	155	91	63	1	725	557	116	111	94	104	99	96	104	83	101	98
CLE	77	49	28	0	343	318	84	58	77	44	33	0	355	283	64	53	154	93	61	0	698	601	148	111	119	111	87	104	98	86	104	102
DET	77	46	31	0	386	301	81	59	77	33	44	0	389	357	49	67	154	79	75	0	775	658	130	126	118	99	99	93	117	101	97	95
KC	76	33	43	0	333	477	70	110	79	30	48	1	305	434	51	65	155	63	91	1	638	911	121	175	149	86	116	111	92	125	101	106
NY	77	52	25	0	378	248	89	44	77	44	33	0	384	321	86	64	154	96	58	0	762	569	175	108	91	153	100	91	114	88	98	94
WAS	77	28	49	0	282	357	20	25	77	25	52	0	316	432	60	74	154	53	101	0	598	789	80	99	36	94	114	86	96	122	91	94

1956 AMERICAN LEAGUE

TM	G	W	L	T	R	OR	HR	OHR	G	W	L	T	R	OR	HR	OHR	G	W	L	T	R	OR	HR	OHR	HRF	HRB	HRP	RF	RB	RP	BPF	PPF
BAL	77	41	36	0	275	315	35	39	77	28	49	0	296	390	56	60	154	69	85	0	571	705	91	99	66	78	84	87	85	102	94	96
BOS	78	43	34	1	408	388	68	64	77	41	36	0	372	363	71	66	155	84	70	1	780	751	139	130	96	105	99	106	105	102	103	102
CHI	77	46	31	0	403	320	69	47	77	39	38	0	373	314	59	71	154	85	69	0	776	634	128	118	91	99	91	105	104	87	104	102
CLE	77	46	31	0	340	287	71	61	78	42	35	1	372	294	82	55	155	88	66	1	712	581	153	116	99	112	88	97	97	81	101	99
DET	78	37	40	1	359	357	75	77	77	45	32	0	430	342	75	63	155	82	72	1	789	699	150	140	108	108	101	93	113	102	97	95
KC	77	22	55	0	305	449	62	113	77	30	47	0	314	382	50	74	154	52	102	0	619	831	112	187	132	76	117	106	86	111	101	105
NY	77	49	28	0	412	303	88	48	77	48	29	0	445	328	102	66	154	97	57	0	857	631	190	114	84	152	98	95	121	93	99	95
WAS	77	32	45	0	354	481	63	95	78	27	50	1	298	443	49	76	155	59	95	1	652	924	112	171	122	77	112	111	89	120	102	107

1957 AMERICAN LEAGUE

TM	G	W	L	T	R	OR	HR	OHR	G	W	L	T	R	OR	HR	OHR	G	W	L	T	R	OR	HR	OHR	HRF	HRB	HRP	RF	RB	RP	BPF	PPF
BAL	77	42	33	2	283	248	36	30	77	34	43	0	314	340	51	65	154	76	76	2	597	588	87	95	60	83	85	83	99	97	93	93
BOS	77	44	33	0	408	360	72	67	77	38	39	0	313	308	81	49	154	82	72	0	721	668	153	116	106	115	90	120	100	94	110	109
CHI	77	45	32	0	347	263	40	59	78	45	32	1	360	303	66	65	155	90	64	1	707	566	106	124	80	90	105	95	109	89	99	97
CLE	77	40	37	0	348	384	71	74	76	36	40	0	334	338	69	56	153	76	77	0	682	722	140	130	112	104	97	106	104	109	102	102
DET	77	45	32	0	351	304	71	86	77	33	44	0	263	310	45	61	154	78	76	0	614	614	116	147	140	76	95	112	87	88	107	107
KC	77	37	40	0	294	344	91	77	77	22	54	1	269	366	75	76	154	59	94	1	563	710	166	153	109	128	120	99	88	107	99	102
NY	77	48	29	0	316	241	60	51	77	50	27	0	407	293	85	59	154	98	56	0	723	534	145	110	80	123	98	83	118	91	94	90
WAS	77	28	49	0	304	415	60	79	77	27	50	0	299	393	51	70	154	55	99	0	603	808	111	149	111	84	108	102	95	122	98	102

1958 AMERICAN LEAGUE

TM	G	W	L	T	R	OR	HR	OHR	G	W	L	T	R	OR	HR	OHR	G	W	L	T	R	OR	HR	OHR	HRF	HRB	HRP	RF	RB	RP	BPF	PPF
BAL	78	46	31	1	248	256	46	36	76	28	48	0	273	319	62	70	154	74	79	1	521	575	108	106	64	99	94	85	87	94	94	95
BOS	77	49	28	0	384	350	73	65	78	30	47	1	313	341	82	56	155	79	75	1	697	691	155	121	101	115	93	112	103	102	105	105
CHI	77	47	30	0	318	282	47	68	78	35	42	1	316	333	54	84	155	82	72	1	634	615	101	152	86	83	119	95	100	97	98	98
CLE	76	42	34	0	324	293	72	59	77	35	42	0	370	342	89	64	153	77	76	0	694	635	161	123	88	130	104	89	115	107	94	93
DET	77	43	34	0	348	306	59	79	77	34	43	0	311	300	50	54	154	77	77	0	659	606	109	133	127	73	86	106	99	92	104	103
KC	78	43	34	1	365	363	88	96	78	30	47	1	277	350	50	64	156	73	81	2	642	713	138	160	161	80	86	114	93	103	105	107
NY	78	44	33	1	362	318	78	62	77	48	29	0	397	259	86	54	155	92	62	1	759	577	164	116	100	122	91	103	114	90	103	99
WAS	78	33	44	1	269	373	49	80	78	28	49	1	284	374	72	76	156	61	93	2	553	747	121	156	88	98	124	97	88	115	97	100

1959 AMERICAN LEAGUE

TM	G	W	L	T	R	OR	HR	OHR	G	W	L	T	R	OR	HR	OHR	G	W	L	T	R	OR	HR	OHR	HRF	HRB	HRP	RF	RB	RP	BPF	PPF
BAL	78	38	39	1	260	299	53	50	77	36	41	0	291	322	56	61	155	74	80	1	551	621	109	111	88	82	83	91	84	94	97	98
BOS	77	43	34	0	404	356	62	66	77	32	45	0	322	340	63	69	154	75	79	0	726	696	125	135	97	93	100	113	102	99	106	105
CHI	78	47	30	1	313	272	44	61	78	47	30	1	356	316	53	68	156	94	60	2	669	588	97	129	89	73	95	89	102	91	97	95
CLE	77	43	34	0	346	316	84	74	77	46	31	0	399	330	83	74	154	89	65	0	745	646	167	148	101	124	112	93	115	102	97	95
DET	77	41	36	0	401	411	95	105	77	35	42	0	312	321	65	72	154	76	78	0	713	732	160	177	138	102	112	124	96	98	111	111
KC	77	37	40	0	362	386	58	80	77	29	48	0	319	374	59	68	154	66	88	0	681	760	117	148	107	84	103	106	100	110	101	103
NY	77	40	37	0	293	305	63	45	78	39	38	1	394	342	90	75	155	79	75	1	687	647	153	120	69	131	104	84	109	104	93	92
WAS	77	34	43	0	307	360	83	68	77	29	48	0	312	341	80	55	154	63	91	0	619	701	163	123	109	114	88	101	92	103	100	102

1960 AMERICAN LEAGUE

TM	G	W	L	T	R	OR	HR	OHR	G	W	L	T	R	OR	HR	OHR	G	W	L	T	R	OR	HR	OHR	HRF	HRB	HRP	RF	RB	RP	BPF	PPF
BAL	77	44	33	0	332	313	50	52	77	45	32	0	350	293	73	66	154	89	65	0	682	606	123	117	77	100	96	101	99	89	102	101
BOS	77	36	41	0	347	413	65	69	77	29	48	0	311	362	59	58	154	65	89	0	658	775	124	127	112	86	87	110	94	109	103	105
CHI	77	51	26	0	379	298	57	54	77	36	41	0	362	319	55	73	154	87	67	0	741	617	112	127	89	87	96	100	108	92	101	99
CLE	77	39	38	0	315	351	62	84	77	37	40	0	352	342	65	77	154	76	78	0	667	693	127	161	102	95	117	96	101	104	98	98
DET	77	40	37	0	322	323	78	85	77	31	46	0	311	321	72	56	154	71	83	0	633	644	150	141	123	101	94	101	92	94	102	102
KC	78	34	43	1	327	369	58	79	77	24	53	0	288	387	52	81	155	58	96	1	615	756	110	160	100	82	114	100	92	110	99	101
NY	77	55	22	0	350	273	92	52	78	42	35	1	396	354	101	71	155	97	57	1	746	627	193	123	88	150	102	87	116	100	94	92
WAS	77	32	45	0	336	366	75	74	77	41	36	0	336	330	72	56	154	73	81	0	672	696	147	130	114	101	90	104	98	101	102	102

1961 AMERICAN LEAGUE

TM	G	W	L	T	R	OR	HR	OHR	G	W	L	T	R	OR	HR	OHR	G	W	L	T	R	OR	HR	OHR	HRF	HRB	HRP	RF	RB	RP	BPF	PPF
BAL	82	48	33	1	320	283	61	46	81	47	34	0	371	305	88	63	163	95	67	1	691	588	149	109	73	108	81	90	96	83	97	96
BOS	82	50	31	1	401	386	63	91	81	26	55	0	328	406	49	76	163	76	86	1	729	792	112	167	119	67	96	105	97	105	102	103
CHI	81	53	28	0	411	320	80	55	82	33	48	1	354	406	58	103	163	86	76	1	765	726	138	158	86	98	107	98	105	100	99	99
CLE	81	40	41	0	342	380	74	98	80	38	42	0	395	372	76	80	161	78	83	0	737	752	150	178	108	97	112	93	105	107	96	97
DET	82	50	31	1	389	324	90	95	81	51	30	0	452	347	90	75	163	101	61	1	841	671	180	170	111	112	106	90	119	97	96	94

TM	G	W	L	T	R	OR	HR	OHR	G	W	L	T	R	OR	HR	OHR	G	W	L	T	R	OR	HR	OHR	HRF	HRB	HRP	RF	RB	RP	BPF	PPF
			HOME								ROAD									ALL												
KC	80	33	47	0	365	434	33	61	82	28	53	1	318	429	57	80	162	61	100	1	683	863	90	141	72	66	102	107	91	113	102	104
LA	82	46	36	0	447	421	122	126	80	24	55	1	297	363	67	54	162	70	91	1	744	784	189	180	181	90	83	124	90	96	111	112
MIN	81	36	44	1	380	423	92	89	80	34	46	0	327	355	75	74	161	70	90	1	707	778	167	163	117	102	100	114	91	99	106	107
NY	81	65	16	0	411	251	112	59	82	44	37	1	416	361	128	78	163	109	53	1	827	612	240	137	87	166	101	89	117	88	96	93
WAS	79	33	46	0	288	366	34	53	82	28	54	0	330	410	85	78	161	61	100	0	618	776	119	131	57	93	109	91	89	109	95	97

1962 AMERICAN LEAGUE

TM	G	W	L	T	R	OR	HR	OHR	G	W	L	T	R	OR	HR	OHR	G	W	L	T	R	OR	HR	OHR	HRF	HRB	HRP	RF	RB	RP	BPF	PPF
BAL	82	44	38	0	313	276	66	65	80	33	47	0	339	404	90	82	162	77	85	0	652	680	156	147	76	113	108	79	102	104	90	90
BOS	79	39	40	0	369	377	72	76	81	37	44	0	338	379	74	83	160	76	84	0	707	756	146	159	97	97	105	106	97	104	102	103
CHI	81	43	38	0	315	319	36	58	81	42	39	0	392	339	56	65	162	85	77	0	707	658	92	123	80	63	84	88	103	97	95	94
CLE	81	43	38	0	348	350	103	89	81	37	44	0	334	395	77	85	162	80	82	0	682	745	180	174	116	108	106	96	97	105	98	99
DET	82	49	33	0	448	368	117	91	79	36	43	0	310	324	92	78	161	85	76	0	758	692	209	169	116	126	105	121	95	88	111	110
KC	81	39	42	0	405	443	64	118	81	33	48	0	340	394	52	81	162	72	90	0	745	837	116	199	131	66	107	113	99	110	105	106
LA	81	40	41	0	357	368	50	50	81	46	35	0	361	338	87	68	162	86	76	0	718	706	137	118	67	101	90	104	98	96	102	102
MIN	82	45	36	1	417	378	97	97	81	46	35	0	381	335	88	69	163	91	71	1	798	713	185	166	120	109	98	109	105	95	105	104
NY	80	50	30	0	369	306	92	67	82	46	36	0	448	374	107	79	162	96	66	0	817	680	199	146	90	135	102	86	121	103	94	92
WAS	80	27	53	0	293	364	65	79	82	33	48	1	306	352	67	72	162	60	101	1	599	716	132	151	104	83	94	101	83	97	101	102

1963 AMERICAN LEAGUE

TM	G	W	L	T	R	OR	HR	OHR	G	W	L	T	R	OR	HR	OHR	G	W	L	T	R	OR	HR	OHR	HRF	HRB	HRP	RF	RB	RP	BPF	PPF
BAL	81	48	33	0	311	268	72	56	81	38	43	0	333	353	74	81	162	86	76	0	644	621	146	137	84	106	99	86	104	100	94	93
BOS	80	44	36	0	383	346	95	73	81	32	49	0	283	358	76	79	161	76	85	0	666	704	171	152	108	111	100	113	95	101	106	106
CHI	82	49	33	0	362	272	63	46	80	45	35	0	321	272	51	54	162	94	68	0	683	544	114	100	102	73	65	105	99	81	104	102
CLE	81	41	40	0	308	341	88	87	81	38	43	0	327	361	81	89	162	79	83	0	635	702	169	176	103	114	118	95	99	109	97	98
DET	81	47	34	0	395	339	94	109	81	32	49	0	305	364	54	86	162	79	83	0	700	703	148	195	139	84	111	109	102	103	104	104
KC	81	36	45	0	326	390	52	87	81	37	44	0	289	314	43	69	162	73	89	0	615	704	95	156	121	58	91	116	87	98	107	109
LA	81	39	42	0	264	306	24	44	80	31	49	0	333	354	71	76	161	70	91	0	597	660	95	120	48	80	108	83	99	109	91	92
MIN	81	48	33	0	377	306	112	99	80	43	37	0	390	296	113	63	161	91	70	0	767	602	225	162	117	143	105	99	116	94	100	98
NY	80	58	22	0	367	246	88	55	81	46	35	0	347	301	100	60	161	104	57	0	714	547	188	115	93	128	83	98	108	85	101	98
WAS	80	31	49	0	286	406	63	82	82	25	57	0	292	406	75	94	162	56	106	0	578	812	138	176	88	100	125	100	89	121	98	101

1964 AMERICAN LEAGUE

TM	G	W	L	T	R	OR	HR	OHR	G	W	L	T	R	OR	HR	OHR	G	W	L	T	R	OR	HR	OHR	HRF	HRB	HRP	RF	RB	RP	BPF	PPF
BAL	82	49	32	1	351	296	79	64	81	48	33	0	328	271	83	65	163	97	65	1	679	567	162	129	97	104	85	107	98	83	105	103
BOS	81	45	36	0	393	382	100	87	81	27	54	0	295	411	86	91	162	72	90	0	688	793	186	178	104	120	116	108	102	117	102	103
CHI	81	52	29	0	306	213	43	42	81	46	35	0	336	288	63	82	162	98	64	0	642	501	106	124	62	84	93	86	103	81	95	93
CLE	82	41	40	1	365	351	84	82	82	38	43	1	324	342	80	72	164	79	83	2	689	693	164	154	108	101	95	107	101	101	103	103
DET	82	46	35	1	340	320	85	89	81	39	42	0	359	358	72	75	163	85	77	1	699	678	157	164	115	94	98	92	111	108	96	95
KC	81	26	55	0	330	455	107	132	82	31	50	1	291	381	59	88	163	57	105	1	621	836	166	220	153	86	114	115	90	117	105	108
LA	81	45	36	0	230	226	32	31	81	37	44	0	314	325	70	69	162	82	80	0	544	551	102	100	48	85	83	74	93	94	89	89
MIN	82	40	41	1	386	336	115	88	81	39	42	0	351	342	106	93	163	79	83	1	737	678	221	181	101	145	122	102	110	103	101	100
NY	81	50	31	0	363	290	69	56	83	49	32	2	367	287	93	73	164	99	63	2	730	577	162	129	80	113	92	103	106	86	103	101
WAS	81	31	50	0	294	380	71	95	81	31	50	0	284	353	54	77	162	62	100	0	578	733	125	172	122	73	98	104	87	108	101	103

1965 AMERICAN LEAGUE

TM	G	W	L	T	R	OR	HR	OHR	G	W	L	T	R	OR	HR	OHR	G	W	L	T	R	OR	HR	OHR	HRF	HRB	HRP	RF	RB	RP	BPF	PPF
BAL	79	46	33	0	302	282	62	71	83	48	35	0	339	296	63	49	162	94	68	0	641	578	125	120	123	82	77	98	100	91	100	99
BOS	81	34	47	0	375	433	94	88	81	28	53	0	294	358	71	70	162	62	100	0	669	791	165	158	124	109	105	120	97	113	107	109
CAL	80	46	34	0	265	254	36	35	82	29	53	0	262	315	56	56	162	75	87	0	527	569	92	91	67	77	76	93	85	90	98	98
CHI	81	48	33	0	288	241	45	51	81	47	34	0	359	314	80	71	162	95	67	0	647	555	125	122	67	107	107	81	110	96	92	90
CLE	82	52	30	0	342	287	90	58	80	35	45	0	321	326	66	71	162	87	75	0	663	613	156	129	105	110	94	96	106	98	98	97
DET	81	47	34	0	362	310	96	85	81	42	39	0	318	292	66	52	162	89	73	0	680	602	162	137	146	96	82	110	101	91	105	104
KC	81	33	48	0	301	365	47	68	81	26	55	0	284	390	63	93	162	59	103	0	585	755	110	161	75	94	132	98	95	119	97	100
MIN	81	51	30	0	379	308	67	89	81	51	30	0	395	292	83	77	162	102	60	0	774	600	150	166	99	113	123	101	120	95	101	98
NY	83	40	43	0	320	306	77	63	79	37	42	0	291	298	72	63	162	77	85	0	611	604	149	126	99	109	93	101	95	94	101	101
WAS	81	36	45	0	302	366	62	86	81	34	47	0	289	355	74	74	162	70	92	0	591	721	136	160	99	101	117	103	92	111	100	102

1966 AMERICAN LEAGUE

TM	G	W	L	T	R	OR	HR	OHR	G	W	L	T	R	OR	HR	OHR	G	W	L	T	R	OR	HR	OHR	HRF	HRB	HRP	RF	RB	RP	BPF	PPF
BAL	79	48	31	0	375	296	85	65	81	49	32	0	380	305	90	62	160	97	63	0	755	601	175	127	102	127	96	101	120	98	101	98
BOS	81	40	41	0	374	397	80	97	81	32	49	0	281	334	65	67	162	72	90	0	655	731	145	164	129	94	104	122	95	105	109	110
CAL	81	42	39	0	303	315	54	67	81	38	43	0	301	328	68	69	162	80	82	0	604	643	122	136	89	94	104	98	97	102	99	100
CHI	81	45	36	0	273	217	31	36	82	38	43	1	301	300	56	65	163	83	79	1	574	517	87	101	59	76	87	84	96	87	94	93
CLE	81	41	40	0	283	300	82	65	81	40	41	0	291	286	73	64	162	81	81	0	574	586	155	129	107	109	92	101	90	91	101	102
DET	81	42	39	0	360	374	97	101	81	46	35	0	359	324	82	84	162	88	74	0	719	698	179	185	118	125	128	107	112	108	102	102
KC	81	42	39	0	284	292	18	27	79	32	47	0	280	356	52	79	160	74	86	0	564	648	70	106	36	74	107	89	97	109	94	95
MIN	81	49	32	0	375	311	94	83	81	40	41	0	288	270	50	56	162	89	73	0	663	581	144	139	157	80	80	121	94	84	111	110
NY	82	35	46	1	302	280	74	63	78	35	43	0	309	332	88	61	160	70	89	1	611	612	162	124	88	126	100	87	105	105	94	94
WAS	78	42	36	0	273	292	62	84	81	29	52	0	284	367	64	70	159	71	88	0	557	659	126	154	111	90	108	91	95	110	95	96

1967 AMERICAN LEAGUE

TM	G	W	L	T	R	OR	HR	OHR	G	W	L	T	R	OR	HR	OHR	G	W	L	T	R	OR	HR	OHR	HRF	HRB	HRP	RF	RB	RP	BPF	PPF
BAL	77	35	42	0	283	275	64	49	84	41	43	0	371	317	74	67	161	76	85	0	654	592	138	116	88	123	105	89	116	106	95	94
BOS	81	49	32	0	408	355	90	88	81	43	38	0	314	259	68	54	162	92	70	0	722	614	158	142	140	113	101	130	105	91	115	113
CAL	83	53	30	0	288	276	56	59	78	31	47	0	279	311	58	59	161	84	77	0	567	587	114	118	93	99	102	91	100	103	96	96
CHI	82	49	33	0	243	222	38	38	80	40	40	0	288	269	51	49	162	89	73	0	531	491	89	87	76	81	80	83	95	88	94	93
CLE	81	36	45	0	274	316	76	69	81	39	42	0	285	297	55	51	162	75	87	0	559	613	131	120	131	94	87	101	93	101	100	101
DET	81	52	29	1	360	272	83	79	81	39	42	0	323	315	69	72	163	91	71	1	683	587	152	151	113	122	122	99	114	99	99	98
KC	81	37	44	0	288	320	19	38	81	25	55	0	245	340	50	87	162	62	99	0	533	660	69	125	43	80	140	101	90	109	100	102
MIN	81	52	29	0	372	292	70	63	83	39	42	2	299	298	61	52	164	91	71	2	671	590	131	115	119	98	87	113	103	93	107	106
NY	82	43	38	1	268	271	60	47	81	29	52	0	254	350	40	63	163	72	90	1	522	621	100	110	102	81	89	89	92	107	94	96
WAS	82	40	40	0	277	332	57	54	81	36	45	0	273	305	58	59	161	76	85	0	550	637	115	113	96	98	96	106	90	103	102	104

1968 AMERICAN LEAGUE

TM	G	W	L	T	R	OR	HR	OHR	G	W	L	T	R	OR	HR	OHR	G	W	L	T	R	OR	HR	OHR	HRF	HRB	HRP	RF	RB	RP	BPF	PPF
BAL	80	47	33	0	288	248	57	54	82	44	38	0	291	249	76	47	162	91	71	0	579	497	133	101	94	123	97	102	103	89	102	101
BOS	81	46	35	0	325	299	58	61	81	40	41	0	289	312	67	54	162	86	76	0	614	611	125	115	99	115	107	104	111	110	101	101
CAL	81	32	49	0	229	299	49	66	81	35	46	0	269	316	34	65	162	67	95	0	498	615	83	131	113	71	109	90	96	116	94	96
CHI	81	36	45	0	225	273	29	47	81	31	50	0	238	254	42	50	162	67	95	0	463	527	71	97	83	69	93	100	83	94	101	102
CLE	81	43	37	1	246	262	36	56	81	43	38	0	270	242	39	42	162	86	75	1	516	504	75	98	112	64	80	100	93	91	101	101
DET	81	56	25	0	348	254	107	76	83	47	34	2	323	238	78	54	164	103	59	2	671	492	185	129	138	143	104	110	113	85	106	103
MIN	81	41	40	0	299	290	50	51	81	38	43	0	263	256	55	41	162	79	83	0	562	546	105	92	105	92	81	112	96	94	106	106
NY	82	39	42	1	268	268	56	50	82	44	37	1	268	263	53	49	164	83	79	2	536	531	109	99	104	95	87	101	95	94	101	101
OAK	83	44	38	1	296	258	38	58	80	38	42	0	273	286	56	66	163	82	80	1	569	544	94	124	78	96	125	96	104	100	98	98
WAS	81	34	47	0	257	300	53	53	80	31	49	0	267	365	71	65	161	65	96	0	524	665	124	118	78	129	124	87	105	129	91	94

1969 AMERICAN LEAGUE

TM	G	W	L	T	R	OR	HR	OHR	G	W	L	T	R	OR	HR	OHR	G	W	L	T	R	OR	HR	OHR	HRF	HRB	HRP	RF	RB	RP	BPF	PPF
BAL	81	60	21	0	402	251	82	51	81	49	32	0	377	266	93	66	162	109	53	0	779	517	175	117	86	135	93	103	113	78	104	100
BOS	81	46	35	0	392	391	105	78	81	41	40	0	351	345	92	77	162	87	75	0	743	736	197	155	108	140	113	112	107	106	105	105
CAL	81	43	39	0	277	305	49	65	82	28	53	1	251	347	39	61	163	71	91	1	528	652	88	126	113	59	83	98	80	97	99	101
CHI	81	41	40	0	352	387	61	80	81	27	54	0	273	336	51	56	162	68	94	0	625	723	112	146	118	75	96	118	87	100	108	110
CLE	81	33	48	0	276	341	56	60	80	29	51	0	297	376	63	74	161	62	99	0	573	717	119	134	84	95	106	90	92	113	94	96
DET	81	46	35	0	361	305	104	72	81	44	37	0	340	296	78	56	162	90	72	0	701	601	182	128	129	115	84	105	102	89	103	102
KC	82	36	45	1	301	362	39	63	81	33	48	0	285	326	59	73	163	69	93	1	586	688	98	136	77	79	109	106	86	99	103	104

	HOME								ROAD								ALL															
TM	G	W	L	T	R	OR	HR	OHR	G	W	L	T	R	OR	HR	OHR	G	W	L	T	R	OR	HR	OHR	HRF	HRB	HRP	RF	RB	RP	BPF	PPF
MIN	81	57	24	0	414	298	79	61	81	40	41	0	376	320	84	58	162	97	65	0	790	618	163	119	100	118	88	103	117	93	102	100
NY	80	48	32	0	284	245	44	51	82	32	49	1	278	342	50	67	162	80	81	1	562	587	94	118	84	73	90	88	89	92	95	96
OAK	81	49	32	0	330	315	73	70	81	39	42	0	410	363	75	93	162	88	74	0	740	678	148	163	87	118	128	85	121	112	92	91
SEA	82	34	47	1	329	399	74	93	81	30	51	0	310	400	51	79	163	64	98	1	639	799	125	172	123	82	111	100	97	120	98	100
WAS	81	47	34	0	353	290	77	62	81	39	42	0	341	354	71	73	162	86	76	0	694	644	148	135	97	109	100	93	108	101	97	96

1970 AMERICAN LEAGUE

TM	G	W	L	T	R	OR	HR	OHR	G	W	L	T	R	OR	HR	OHR	G	W	L	T	R	OR	HR	OHR	HRF	HRB	HRP	RF	RB	RP	BPF	PPF
BAL	81	59	22	0	386	256	88	58	81	49	32	0	406	318	91	81	162	108	54	0	792	574	179	139	87	132	104	91	121	90	97	94
BOS	81	52	29	0	455	382	117	75	81	35	46	0	331	340	86	81	162	87	75	0	786	722	203	156	114	131	105	123	105	98	111	110
CAL	81	43	38	0	287	274	41	59	81	43	38	0	344	356	73	95	162	86	76	0	631	630	114	154	62	97	129	82	102	102	91	91
CHI	84	31	53	0	346	469	78	97	78	25	53	0	287	333	45	67	162	56	106	0	633	822	123	164	138	70	94	115	89	112	106	108
CLE	81	43	38	0	386	370	133	103	81	33	48	0	263	305	50	60	162	76	86	0	649	675	183	163	195	82	80	129	83	87	115	115
DET	81	42	39	0	348	379	86	86	81	37	44	0	318	352	62	67	162	79	83	0	666	731	148	153	130	89	92	108	96	104	103	104
KC	79	35	44	0	305	331	46	48	83	30	53	0	306	374	51	90	162	65	97	0	611	705	97	138	71	79	105	97	92	105	98	100
MIL	81	38	42	1	313	362	68	72	82	27	55	0	300	389	58	74	163	65	97	1	613	751	126	146	106	84	96	98	92	111	98	100
MIN	81	51	30	0	366	285	66	53	81	47	34	0	378	320	87	77	162	98	64	0	744	605	153	130	75	119	102	95	112	93	98	97
NY	81	53	28	0	317	257	60	40	82	40	41	1	363	355	51	90	163	93	69	1	680	612	111	130	74	89	96	83	109	98	92	91
OAK	81	49	32	0	337	265	83	56	81	40	40	0	341	328	88	78	162	89	73	0	678	593	171	134	85	127	101	91	104	92	97	96
WAS	81	40	41	0	303	330	72	61	81	30	51	0	323	359	66	78	162	70	92	0	626	689	138	139	92	99	99	93	96	105	96	97

1971 AMERICAN LEAGUE

TM	G	W	L	T	R	OR	HR	OHR	G	W	L	T	R	OR	HR	OHR	G	W	L	T	R	OR	HR	OHR	HRF	HRB	HRP	RF	RB	RP	BPF	PPF
BAL	77	53	24	0	374	254	78	67	81	48	33	0	368	276	80	58	158	101	57	0	742	530	158	125	111	124	100	104	118	87	103	100
BOS	80	47	33	0	375	338	88	75	82	38	44	0	316	329	73	61	162	85	77	0	691	667	161	136	122	118	101	112	104	101	106	105
CAL	81	35	46	0	233	297	39	55	81	41	40	0	278	279	57	46	162	76	86	0	511	576	96	101	92	78	83	95	83	93	98	99
CHI	81	39	42	0	278	310	60	53	81	40	41	0	339	287	78	47	162	79	83	0	617	597	138	100	91	114	85	94	101	98	98	97
CLE	81	29	52	0	297	400	62	99	81	31	50	0	246	347	47	55	162	60	102	0	543	747	109	154	149	73	97	114	82	110	106	108
DET	81	54	27	0	352	289	90	70	81	37	44	0	349	356	89	56	162	91	71	0	701	645	179	126	110	138	100	92	117	108	96	95
KC	81	44	37	0	296	277	23	36	80	41	39	0	307	289	57	48	161	85	76	0	603	566	80	84	58	76	86	96	98	93	99	98
MIL	82	34	48	0	282	319	46	64	79	35	44	0	252	290	58	66	161	69	92	0	534	609	104	130	86	91	112	105	83	94	103	104
MIN	79	37	42	0	332	356	57	71	81	37	44	0	322	314	59	68	160	74	86	0	654	670	116	139	103	94	111	110	102	104	104	104
NY	81	44	37	0	327	297	39	61	81	38	43	0	321	344	58	65	162	82	80	0	648	641	97	126	83	85	109	94	107	106	97	97
OAK	81	46	35	0	325	300	84	74	80	55	25	0	366	264	76	57	161	101	60	0	691	564	160	131	117	120	100	99	110	92	100	99
WAS	81	35	46	0	268	296	34	59	78	28	50	0	269	364	52	73	159	63	96	0	537	660	86	132	73	82	123	86	95	114	92	94

1972 AMERICAN LEAGUE

TM	G	W	L	T	R	OR	HR	OHR	G	W	L	T	R	OR	HR	OHR	G	W	L	T	R	OR	HR	OHR	HRF	HRB	HRP	RF	RB	RP	BPF	PPF
BAL	77	38	39	0	240	211	44	40	77	42	35	0	279	219	56	45	154	80	74	0	519	430	100	85	85	110	95	91	100	84	98	96
BOS	78	52	26	0	373	303	71	49	77	33	44	0	267	317	53	52	155	85	70	0	640	620	124	101	112	119	100	113	112	111	105	105
CAL	80	44	36	0	221	218	30	31	75	31	44	0	233	315	48	59	155	75	80	0	454	533	78	90	55	104	115	77	97	110	88	90
CHI	78	55	23	0	341	252	65	44	76	32	44	0	225	286	43	50	154	87	67	0	566	538	108	94	114	103	92	113	99	96	106	106
CLE	77	43	34	0	263	261	59	79	79	29	50	0	209	258	32	44	156	72	84	0	472	519	91	123	173	68	91	113	81	89	107	108
DET	78	44	34	0	312	288	68	67	78	42	36	0	246	226	54	34	156	86	70	0	558	514	122	101	148	102	82	125	91	85	113	112
KC	77	44	33	0	309	257	29	28	77	32	45	0	271	288	49	57	154	76	78	0	580	545	78	85	56	102	108	101	108	102	100	100
MIL	79	37	42	0	243	286	36	45	77	28	49	0	250	309	52	71	156	65	91	0	493	595	88	116	66	111	141	92	96	114	95	97
MIN	74	42	32	0	299	255	52	54	80	35	45	0	238	280	41	51	154	77	77	0	537	535	93	105	122	87	97	114	94	94	107	107
NY	77	46	31	0	270	219	53	37	78	33	45	0	287	308	50	50	155	79	76	0	557	527	103	87	92	109	92	85	113	106	92	92
OAK	77	48	29	0	287	210	68	52	78	45	33	0	317	247	66	44	155	93	62	0	604	457	134	96	111	130	96	91	116	90	97	94
TEX	77	31	46	0	235	288	33	41	77	23	54	0	226	340	23	51	154	54	100	0	461	628	56	92	98	58	91	92	92	121	94	97

1973 AMERICAN LEAGUE

TM	G	W	L	T	R	OR	HR	OHR	G	W	L	T	R	OR	HR	OHR	G	W	L	T	R	OR	HR	OHR	HRF	HRB	HRP	RF	RB	RP	BPF	PPF
BAL	81	50	31	0	408	284	63	60	81	47	34	0	346	277	56	64	162	97	65	0	754	561	119	124	103	90	94	111	101	77	107	105
BOS	81	48	33	0	390	339	83	83	81	41	40	0	348	308	64	75	162	89	73	0	738	647	147	158	118	106	114	111	101	89	106	105
CAL	81	43	38	0	316	294	41	49	81	36	45	0	313	363	52	55	162	79	83	0	629	657	93	104	85	76	85	91	95	98	96	96
CHI	81	40	41	0	329	368	56	58	81	37	44	0	323	337	55	52	162	77	85	0	652	705	111	110	106	82	81	105	92	99	102	103
CLE	81	34	47	0	320	427	92	100	81	37	44	0	360	399	66	72	162	71	91	0	680	826	158	172	134	107	116	98	101	121	97	99
DET	81	47	34	0	329	332	86	71	81	38	43	0	313	342	71	83	162	85	77	0	642	674	157	154	102	122	120	101	92	96	101	101
KC	81	48	33	0	422	404	54	61	81	40	41	0	333	348	60	53	162	88	74	0	755	752	114	114	102	86	86	120	100	100	109	109
MIL	81	40	41	0	349	343	73	52	81	34	47	0	359	388	72	67	162	74	88	0	708	731	145	119	90	117	97	93	107	110	96	96
MIN	81	37	44	0	357	386	56	60	81	44	37	0	381	306	64	55	162	81	81	0	738	692	120	115	98	93	89	107	103	97	104	103
NY	81	50	31	0	359	263	74	42	81	30	51	0	282	347	57	67	162	80	82	0	641	610	131	109	94	103	86	99	99	88	101	100
OAK	81	50	31	0	313	253	70	70	81	44	37	0	445	362	77	73	162	94	68	0	758	615	147	143	95	118	115	73	125	104	87	85
TEX	81	35	46	0	321	408	47	51	81	22	59	0	298	436	63	79	162	57	105	0	619	844	110	130	70	101	116	98	92	122	97	100

1974 AMERICAN LEAGUE

TM	G	W	L	T	R	OR	HR	OHR	G	W	L	T	R	OR	HR	OHR	G	W	L	T	R	OR	HR	OHR	HRF	HRB	HRP	RF	RB	RP	BPF	PPF
BAL	81	46	35	0	281	293	48	46	81	45	36	0	378	319	68	55	162	91	71	0	659	612	116	101	78	112	100	84	107	100	93	92
BOS	81	46	35	0	375	348	58	66	81	38	43	0	321	313	51	60	162	84	78	0	696	661	109	126	111	91	105	113	98	94	107	106
CAL	81	36	45	0	291	287	46	47	82	32	49	1	327	370	49	54	163	68	94	1	618	657	95	101	91	86	90	84	100	106	92	93
CHI	82	46	34	2	360	365	66	43	81	34	46	1	324	356	69	60	163	80	80	3	684	721	135	103	85	127	98	105	101	106	102	102
CLE	81	40	41	0	338	349	72	92	81	37	44	0	324	345	59	46	162	77	85	0	662	694	131	138	149	96	96	102	99	103	101	101
DET	81	36	45	0	335	412	74	84	81	36	45	0	285	356	57	64	162	72	90	0	620	768	131	148	127	104	116	114	88	107	106	108
KC	81	40	41	0	355	353	38	42	81	37	44	0	312	309	51	49	162	77	85	0	667	662	89	91	81	84	86	112	95	94	106	106
MIL	81	40	41	0	342	329	58	69	81	36	45	0	305	331	62	57	162	76	86	0	647	660	120	126	106	104	108	105	95	97	102	103
MIN	82	48	33	1	365	317	60	56	81	34	47	0	308	352	51	59	163	82	80	1	673	669	111	115	104	95	98	102	100	99	101	101
NY	81	47	34	0	315	295	42	50	81	42	39	0	356	328	59	54	162	89	73	0	671	623	101	104	83	95	99	90	106	99	96	95
OAK	81	49	32	0	345	265	69	43	81	41	40	0	344	286	63	47	162	90	72	0	689	551	132	90	102	112	79	98	103	84	100	99
TEX	80	42	38	0	321	340	43	57	81	42	38	1	369	358	56	69	161	84	76	1	690	698	99	126	83	96	121	93	109	110	96	96

1975 AMERICAN LEAGUE

TM	G	W	L	T	R	OR	HR	OHR	G	W	L	T	R	OR	HR	OHR	G	W	L	T	R	OR	HR	OHR	HRF	HRB	HRP	RF	RB	RP	BPF	PPF
BAL	77	44	33	0	282	231	46	45	82	46	36	0	400	322	78	65	159	90	69	0	682	553	124	110	70	118	107	78	109	90	91	89
BOS	81	47	34	0	427	399	74	83	79	48	31	0	369	310	60	62	160	95	65	0	796	709	134	145	124	100	107	118	107	95	109	108
CAL	81	35	46	0	294	349	24	52	80	37	43	0	334	374	31	71	161	72	89	0	628	723	55	123	75	51	108	90	96	109	95	96
CHI	81	42	39	0	350	359	42	54	80	37	43	0	305	344	52	53	161	79	82	0	655	703	94	107	91	79	90	107	91	98	103	104
CLE	80	41	39	0	331	367	79	85	79	38	41	0	357	336	74	51	159	79	80	0	688	703	153	136	126	114	100	99	101	103	99	100
DET	80	31	49	0	301	421	63	83	79	26	53	0	269	365	62	54	159	57	102	0	570	786	125	137	120	96	102	110	80	108	104	106
KC	81	51	30	0	377	309	46	45	81	40	41	0	333	340	72	63	162	91	71	0	710	649	118	108	70	111	103	102	100	92	102	101
MIL	81	36	45	0	348	398	72	63	81	32	49	0	327	394	74	70	162	68	94	0	675	792	146	133	93	124	114	102	97	112	100	101
MIN	82	39	42	0	394	402	75	88	77	37	40	0	330	334	46	45	159	76	83	0	724	736	121	137	155	79	88	111	101	102	105	105
NY	78	43	35	0	331	283	50	56	82	40	42	0	350	305	60	48	160	83	77	0	681	588	110	104	103	88	83	99	98	86	101	100
OAK	81	54	27	0	366	247	75	43	81	44	37	0	392	359	76	59	162	98	64	0	758	606	151	102	89	128	89	84	118	95	93	91
TEX	80	39	41	0	349	366	52	70	82	40	42	0	365	367	82	53	162	79	83	0	714	733	134	123	93	112	105	100	103	106	99	100

1976 AMERICAN LEAGUE

TM	G	W	L	T	R	OR	HR	OHR	G	W	L	T	R	OR	HR	OHR	G	W	L	T	R	OR	HR	OHR	HRF	HRB	HRP	RF	RB	RP	BPF	PPF
BAL	81	42	39	0	280	306	58	38	81	46	35	0	339	292	61	42	162	88	74	0	619	598	119	80	94	129	90	94	97	95	98	97
BOS	81	46	35	0	408	352	71	61	81	37	44	0	308	308	63	48	162	83	79	0	716	660	134	109	117	134	110	121	99	93	110	110
CAL	81	38	43	0	249	284	24	35	81	38	43	0	301	347	39	60	162	76	86	0	550	631	63	95	61	83	121	83	92	104	92	93
CHI	81	40	41	0	300	369	31	34	81	29	52	0	286	376	42	53	161	64	97	0	586	745	73	87	70	92	106	101	92	114	99	101
CLE	79	44	35	0	311	295	40	43	80	37	43	0	304	320	45	37	159	81	78	0	615	615	85	80	102	90	85	99	99	97	100	100
DET	80	36	44	0	305	381	51	62	81	38	43	0	304	328	50	39	161	74	87	0	609	709	101	101	125	98	96	109	91	105	103	105
KC	81	49	32	0	368	287	37	35	81	41	40	0	345	324	28	48	162	90	72	0	713	611	65	83	96	70	87	99	110	96	100	98

TM	HOME								ROAD								ALL															
	G	W	L	T	R	OR	HR	OHR	G	W	L	T	R	OR	HR	OHR	G	W	L	T	R	OR	HR	OHR	HRF	HRB	HRP	RF	RB	RP	BPF	PPF
MIL	81	36	45	0	292	321	45	43	80	30	50	0	278	334	43	56	161	66	95	0	570	655	88	99	88	101	112	98	89	101	99	100
MIN	81	44	37	0	368	348	34	52	81	41	40	0	375	356	47	37	162	85	77	0	743	704	81	89	102	85	92	98	116	111	98	98
NY	80	45	35	0	349	294	67	51	79	52	27	0	381	281	53	46	159	97	62	0	730	575	120	97	117	120	100	97	115	93	99	97
OAK	81	51	30	0	353	284	56	57	80	36	44	0	333	314	57	39	161	87	74	0	686	598	113	96	115	114	96	98	107	94	100	98
TEX	81	39	42	0	319	330	40	57	81	37	44	0	297	322	40	49	162	76	86	0	616	652	80	106	108	83	107	104	93	98	102	103

1977 AMERICAN LEAGUE

TM	HOME								ROAD								ALL															
	G	W	L	T	R	OR	HR	OHR	G	W	L	T	R	OR	HR	OHR	G	W	L	T	R	OR	HR	OHR	HRF	HRB	HRP	RF	RB	RP	BPF	PPF
BAL	81	54	27	0	356	269	74	62	80	43	37	0	363	384	74	62	161	97	64	0	719	653	148	124	100	102	87	85	107	96	93	92
BOS	80	51	29	0	495	407	124	95	81	46	35	0	364	305	89	63	161	97	64	0	859	712	213	158	143	124	93	134	100	84	117	116
CAL	81	39	42	0	320	321	69	65	81	35	46	0	355	374	62	71	162	74	88	0	675	695	131	136	100	90	94	88	97	100	95	95
CHI	81	48	33	0	434	370	85	58	81	42	39	0	410	401	107	78	162	90	72	0	844	771	192	136	79	149	108	100	116	106	99	99
CLE	81	37	44	0	339	357	54	66	80	34	46	0	337	382	46	70	161	71	90	0	676	739	100	136	101	69	92	95	95	103	98	98
DET	81	39	42	0	369	401	81	100	81	35	46	0	345	350	85	62	162	74	88	0	714	751	166	162	121	107	102	109	93	97	105	105
KC	81	55	26	0	408	320	56	50	81	47	34	0	414	331	90	60	162	102	60	0	822	651	146	110	73	113	89	99	112	90	100	99
MIL	81	37	44	0	305	365	49	54	81	30	51	0	334	400	76	82	162	67	95	0	639	765	125	136	66	104	112	91	91	108	95	96
MIN	80	48	32	0	469	376	61	79	81	36	45	0	398	400	62	72	161	84	77	0	867	776	123	151	106	84	101	107	115	105	103	102
NY	81	55	26	0	412	305	84	63	81	45	36	0	419	346	100	76	162	100	62	0	831	651	184	139	86	137	106	95	115	92	98	97
OAK	81	35	46	0	302	347	58	69	80	28	52	0	303	402	59	76	161	63	98	0	605	749	117	145	92	85	104	90	87	106	95	97
SEA	81	29	52	0	303	419	75	103	81	35	46	0	321	436	58	91	162	64	98	0	624	855	133	194	117	87	124	95	88	118	96	98
TEX	81	44	37	0	369	368	62	78	81	50	31	0	398	289	73	56	162	94	68	0	767	657	135	134	109	90	88	108	100	86	105	104
TOR	80	25	55	0	297	444	45	94	81	29	52	0	308	378	55	58	161	54	107	0	605	822	100	152	120	65	93	107	81	108	103	105

1978 AMERICAN LEAGUE

TM	HOME								ROAD								ALL															
	G	W	L	T	R	OR	HR	OHR	G	W	L	T	R	OR	HR	OHR	G	W	L	T	R	OR	HR	OHR	HRF	HRB	HRP	RF	RB	RP	BPF	PPF
BAL	81	51	30	0	316	258	74	42	80	39	41	0	343	375	80	65	161	90	71	0	659	633	154	107	81	143	100	81	108	103	91	90
BOS	82	59	23	0	445	334	94	72	81	40	41	0	351	323	78	65	163	99	64	0	796	657	172	137	115	134	109	114	108	91	107	106
CAL	81	50	31	0	371	316	56	58	81	37	44	0	320	350	52	67	162	87	75	0	691	666	108	125	96	92	105	103	100	97	102	101
CHI	80	38	42	0	342	349	56	58	81	33	48	0	292	382	50	70	161	71	90	0	634	731	106	128	96	91	108	103	93	106	101	102
CLE	78	42	36	0	319	287	50	37	81	27	54	0	320	407	56	63	159	69	90	0	639	694	106	100	77	101	93	87	103	110	93	94
DET	81	47	34	0	395	338	74	78	81	39	42	0	319	315	55	57	162	86	76	0	714	653	129	135	133	93	97	115	97	90	108	107
KC	81	56	25	0	434	264	43	44	81	36	45	0	309	370	55	64	162	92	70	0	743	634	98	108	75	93	100	103	107	92	102	101
MIL	81	54	27	0	446	318	94	50	81	39	42	0	358	332	79	59	162	93	69	0	804	650	173	109	105	140	92	111	111	92	106	104
MIN	81	38	43	0	322	308	44	39	81	35	46	0	344	370	38	63	162	73	89	0	666	678	82	102	83	75	89	89	104	105	94	94
NY	81	55	26	0	358	275	68	59	82	45	37	0	377	307	57	52	163	100	63	0	735	582	125	111	118	94	84	95	109	87	99	97
OAK	80	38	42	0	281	330	52	51	82	31	51	0	251	360	48	55	162	69	93	0	532	690	100	106	102	82	86	102	78	99	101	102
SEA	81	32	49	0	343	423	58	93	79	24	55	0	271	411	39	62	160	56	104	0	614	834	97	155	139	69	107	107	89	119	102	104
TEX	82	52	30	0	348	289	62	49	80	35	45	0	344	343	70	59	162	87	75	0	692	632	132	108	85	118	98	91	106	97	96	96
TOR	81	37	44	0	334	366	50	75	80	22	58	0	256	409	48	74	161	59	102	0	590	775	98	149	100	84	123	102	87	112	100	102

1979 AMERICAN LEAGUE

TM	HOME								ROAD								ALL															
	G	W	L	T	R	OR	HR	OHR	G	W	L	T	R	OR	HR	OHR	G	W	L	T	R	OR	HR	OHR	HRF	HRB	HRP	RF	RB	RP	BPF	PPF
BAL	79	55	24	0	369	259	74	57	80	47	33	0	388	323	107	76	159	102	57	0	757	582	181	133	75	145	110	91	105	82	97	96
BOS	80	51	29	0	470	357	121	59	80	40	40	0	371	354	73	74	160	91	69	0	841	711	194	133	121	121	88	114	105	90	107	106
CAL	81	49	32	0	408	339	71	55	81	39	42	0	458	429	93	76	162	88	74	0	866	768	164	131	76	128	104	86	124	111	93	92
CHI	79	33	46	0	349	401	56	60	81	40	41	0	381	347	71	54	160	73	87	0	730	748	127	114	95	90	82	105	96	98	102	103
CLE	81	47	34	0	428	409	87	72	80	34	46	0	332	396	51	66	161	81	80	0	760	805	138	138	131	82	84	112	95	101	106	106
DET	80	46	34	0	394	323	101	74	81	39	42	0	376	415	63	93	161	85	76	0	770	738	164	167	113	108	112	93	107	102	96	96
KC	81	46	35	0	462	421	53	81	81	39	42	0	389	395	63	84	162	85	77	0	851	816	116	165	92	85	118	112	107	103	105	105
MIL	81	52	29	0	401	362	91	81	80	43	37	0	406	360	94	81	161	95	66	0	807	722	185	162	98	132	117	99	107	97	100	99
MIN	81	39	42	0	415	390	67	61	81	43	38	0	349	335	45	67	162	82	80	0	764	725	112	128	113	72	83	116	93	89	109	108
NY	81	51	30	0	360	308	77	59	79	38	41	0	374	364	73	64	160	89	71	0	734	672	150	123	98	106	88	90	103	95	96	95
OAK	81	31	50	0	262	371	46	65	81	23	58	0	311	489	62	82	162	54	108	0	573	860	108	147	77	85	113	79	86	125	89	91
SEA	81	36	45	0	371	404	88	94	81	31	50	0	340	416	44	71	162	67	95	0	711	820	132	165	151	72	92	101	94	107	100	101
TEX	81	44	37	0	382	335	69	63	81	39	42	0	368	363	71	72	162	83	79	0	750	698	140	135	93	100	97	98	99	93	100	99
TOR	81	32	49	0	345	432	50	74	81	21	60	0	268	430	45	91	162	53	109	0	613	862	95	165	90	70	117	108	78	108	103	106

1980 AMERICAN LEAGUE

TM	HOME								ROAD								ALL															
	G	W	L	T	R	OR	HR	OHR	G	W	L	T	R	OR	HR	OHR	G	W	L	T	R	OR	HR	OHR	HRF	HRB	HRP	RF	RB	RP	BPF	PPF
BAL	81	50	31	0	397	319	75	81	81	50	31	0	408	321	81	53	162	100	62	0	805	640	156	134	116	110	94	100	110	89	101	99
BOS	81	36	45	0	370	420	79	74	79	47	32	0	387	347	83	55	160	83	77	0	757	767	162	129	108	120	97	105	103	104	102	102
CAL	81	30	51	0	330	403	49	76	79	35	44	0	368	394	57	65	160	65	95	0	698	797	106	141	99	82	107	93	101	114	96	97
CHI	81	37	42	2	281	350	41	37	81	33	48	0	306	372	50	71	162	70	90	2	587	722	91	108	66	84	94	93	83	101	97	98
CLE	79	44	35	0	400	389	55	66	81	35	46	0	338	418	34	71	160	79	81	0	738	807	89	137	117	63	96	106	100	109	102	103
DET	82	43	38	1	440	404	77	95	81	41	40	0	390	353	66	57	163	84	78	1	830	757	143	152	135	94	97	111	107	98	105	105
KC	81	49	32	0	397	335	47	51	81	48	33	0	412	359	68	78	162	97	65	0	809	694	115	129	69	103	114	96	113	98	98	97
MIL	82	40	42	0	368	336	90	65	80	46	34	0	443	346	113	72	162	86	76	0	811	682	203	137	83	169	119	88	117	101	94	93
MIN	80	44	36	0	392	361	51	63	81	33	48	0	278	363	48	57	161	77	84	0	670	724	99	120	109	72	86	117	84	92	109	109
NY	81	53	28	0	409	315	91	47	81	50	31	0	411	347	98	55	162	103	59	0	820	662	189	102	92	147	83	97	113	93	99	98
OAK	81	46	35	0	337	277	58	57	81	37	44	0	349	365	79	85	162	83	79	0	686	642	137	142	72	122	125	87	100	93	94	94
SEA	81	36	45	0	340	389	74	99	82	23	58	1	270	404	30	60	163	59	103	1	610	793	104	159	180	54	86	107	80	103	103	105
TEX	80	39	41	0	380	365	58	57	83	37	44	2	376	387	66	62	163	76	85	2	756	752	124	119	93	96	92	101	103	102	100	100
TOR	81	35	46	0	311	386	56	75	81	32	49	0	313	376	70	60	162	67	95	0	624	762	126	135	100	96	102	100	86	103	100	101

1981 AMERICAN LEAGUE

TM	HOME								ROAD								ALL															
	G	W	L	T	R	OR	HR	OHR	G	W	L	T	R	OR	HR	OHR	G	W	L	T	R	OR	HR	OHR	HRF	HRB	HRP	RF	RB	RP	BPF	PPF
BAL	55	33	22	0	231	217	49	47	50	26	24	0	198	220	39	36	105	59	46	0	429	437	88	83	116	110	104	98	101	103	99	99
BOS	53	30	23	0	278	247	52	47	55	29	26	0	241	234	38	43	108	59	49	0	519	481	90	90	125	106	107	114	111	104	106	106
CAL	54	26	28	0	244	233	48	39	56	25	31	0	232	220	49	42	110	51	59	0	476	453	97	81	99	126	107	108	102	98	104	104
CHI	49	25	24	0	215	198	31	33	57	29	28	0	261	225	45	40	106	54	52	0	476	423	76	73	88	106	103	99	110	99	100	99
CLE	54	25	29	0	210	216	19	33	49	27	22	0	221	226	20	34	103	52	51	0	431	442	39	67	88	56	94	87	111	113	93	93
DET	55	32	23	0	241	194	43	44	54	28	26	0	186	208	22	39	109	60	49	0	427	404	65	83	137	69	91	109	91	87	105	105
KC	47	19	28	0	163	197	17	27	56	31	25	0	234	208	44	48	103	50	53	0	397	405	61	75	59	99	128	97	95	98	99	99
MIL	49	28	21	0	203	203	33	29	60	34	26	0	290	256	63	43	109	62	47	0	493	459	96	72	74	138	110	92	115	108	96	95
MIN	61	24	36	1	213	292	25	47	49	17	32	0	165	194	22	31	110	41	68	1	378	486	47	79	105	59	95	110	80	101	105	106
NY	51	32	19	0	203	154	47	24	56	27	29	0	218	189	53	40	107	59	48	0	421	343	100	64	85	142	92	97	96	79	100	99
OAK	56	35	21	0	234	183	57	46	53	29	24	0	224	220	47	34	109	64	45	0	458	403	104	80	120	123	96	90	108	96	96	96
SEA	57	20	37	0	226	271	52	53	53	24	28	1	200	250	37	23	110	44	65	1	426	521	89	76	154	91	74	102	95	115	100	101
TEX	56	32	24	0	232	168	21	24	49	25	24	0	220	221	28	43	105	57	48	0	452	389	49	67	58	86	111	81	117	101	91	90
TOR	53	17	36	0	172	272	34	41	53	20	33	0	157	194	27	31	106	37	69	0	329	466	61	72	125	72	84	122	69	95	111	113

1982 AMERICAN LEAGUE

TM	HOME								ROAD								ALL															
	G	W	L	T	R	OR	HR	OHR	G	W	L	T	R	OR	HR	OHR	G	W	L	T	R	OR	HR	OHR	HRF	HRB	HRP	RF	RB	RP	BPF	PPF
BAL	82	53	28	1	397	330	87	87	81	41	40	0	377	357	92	60	163	94	68	1	774	687	179	147	113	113	93	99	106	95	100	99
BOS	81	49	32	0	434	370	67	82	81	40	41	0	319	343	69	73	162	89	73	0	753	713	136	155	105	90	101	120	94	90	110	110
CAL	81	52	29	0	414	322	99	69	81	41	40	0	400	348	87	55	162	93	69	0	814	670	186	124	118	114	78	99	112	94	100	99
CHI	80	49	31	0	383	332	51	43	82	38	44	0	403	378	85	56	162	87	75	0	786	710	136	99	70	103	78	95	111	101	97	97
CLE	81	41	40	0	342	377	49	64	81	36	45	0	341	357	60	58	162	77	84	0	683	748	109	122	96	74	82	101	94	102	100	101
DET	81	47	34	0	378	328	108	100	81	36	45	0	351	357	69	72	162	83	79	0	729	685	177	172	143	99	97	100	95	100	100	100
KC	81	56	25	0	431	318	61	64	81	34	47	0	353	399	71	99	162	90	72	0	784	717	132	163	75	103	123	100	108	99	100	99
MIL	82	48	34	0	431	319	89	64	81	47	33	1	460	398	127	88	163	95	67	1	891	717	216	152	72	169	123	88	130	96	94	92
MIN	81	37	44	0	351	401	81	110	81	23	58	0	306	418	67	98	162	60	102	0	657	819	148	208	113	96	132	102	90	111	100	102
NY	81	42	39	0	346	338	73	55	81	37	44	0	363	378	88	58	162	79	83	0	709	716	161	113	88	113	81	93	101	102	96	97
OAK	81	36	45	0	328	398	71	83	81	32	49	0	363	421	78	94	162	68	94	0	691	819	149	177	89	108	126	92	100	117	95	96

TM	HOME								ROAD								ALL															
	G	W	L	T	R	OR	HR	OHR	G	W	L	T	R	OR	HR	OHR	G	W	L	T	R	OR	HR	OHR	HRF	HRB	HRP	RF	RB	RP	BPF	PPF
SEA	81	42	39	0	356	388	78	104	81	34	47	0	295	324	52	69	162	76	86	0	651	712	130	173	145	72	94	118	82	89	109	110
TEX	81	38	43	0	286	333	43	66	81	26	55	0	304	416	72	62	162	64	98	0	590	749	115	128	82	83	94	86	88	109	93	94
TOR	81	44	37	0	353	379	62	70	81	34	47	0	298	322	44	77	162	78	84	0	651	701	106	147	108	68	93	116	83	89	109	109

1983 AMERICAN LEAGUE

TM	HOME								ROAD								ALL															
	G	W	L	T	R	OR	HR	OHR	G	W	L	T	R	OR	HR	OHR	G	W	L	T	R	OR	HR	OHR	HRF	HRB	HRP	RF	RB	RP	BPF	PPF
BAL	81	50	31	0	389	328	79	66	81	48	33	0	410	324	89	64	162	98	64	0	799	652	168	130	96	126	99	99	110	91	100	99
BOS	81	38	43	0	373	390	65	76	81	40	41	0	351	385	77	82	162	78	84	0	724	775	142	158	89	112	124	103	99	105	101	102
CAL	81	35	46	0	368	354	86	67	81	35	46	0	354	425	68	63	162	70	92	0	722	779	154	130	115	105	90	93	104	111	96	96
CHI	81	55	26	0	432	306	84	64	81	44	37	0	368	344	73	64	162	99	63	0	800	650	157	128	109	110	92	105	107	88	103	102
CLE	81	36	45	0	367	424	48	71	81	34	47	0	337	361	38	49	162	70	92	0	704	785	86	120	132	54	74	111	92	102	105	106
DET	81	48	33	0	377	314	83	87	81	44	37	0	412	365	73	83	162	92	70	0	789	679	156	170	109	112	121	90	114	99	96	94
KC	82	45	36	1	381	369	50	66	81	34	47	0	315	398	59	67	163	79	83	1	696	767	109	133	91	83	100	103	94	103	101	102
MIL	81	52	29	0	356	305	64	57	81	35	46	0	408	403	68	76	162	87	75	0	764	708	132	133	85	105	105	83	115	107	92	91
MIN	81	37	44	0	389	427	56	91	81	33	48	0	320	395	85	72	162	70	92	0	709	822	141	163	93	109	125	112	93	107	105	106
NY	81	51	30	0	398	323	67	55	81	40	41	0	372	380	86	61	162	91	71	0	770	703	153	116	85	120	94	97	108	99	99	98
OAK	81	42	39	0	348	367	60	54	81	32	49	0	360	415	61	81	162	74	88	0	708	782	121	135	81	99	108	92	102	112	96	96
SEA	81	30	51	0	281	369	64	80	81	30	51	0	277	371	47	65	162	60	102	0	558	740	111	145	124	73	94	99	77	101	99	101
TEX	81	44	37	0	326	294	45	33	82	33	48	1	313	315	61	64	163	77	85	1	639	609	106	97	65	93	82	100	86	83	101	101
TOR	81	48	33	0	437	385	101	84	81	41	40	0	358	341	66	61	162	89	73	0	795	726	167	145	142	102	90	117	101	93	108	108

1984 AMERICAN LEAGUE

TM	HOME								ROAD								ALL															
	G	W	L	T	R	OR	HR	OHR	G	W	L	T	R	OR	HR	OHR	G	W	L	T	R	OR	HR	OHR	HRF	HRB	HRP	RF	RB	RP	BPF	PPF
BAL	81	44	37	0	319	306	82	59	81	41	40	0	362	361	78	78	162	85	77	0	681	667	160	137	91	119	102	88	101	99	94	94
BOS	81	41	40	0	456	433	100	76	81	45	36	0	354	351	81	65	162	86	76	0	810	764	181	141	119	117	93	122	102	97	110	110
CAL	81	37	44	0	341	364	79	83	81	44	37	0	355	333	71	60	162	81	81	0	696	697	150	143	122	96	91	102	96	96	101	101
CHI	81	43	38	0	394	389	103	77	81	31	50	0	285	347	69	78	162	74	88	0	679	736	172	155	120	110	102	121	85	93	110	111
CLE	81	41	39	1	411	399	65	73	82	34	48	0	350	367	58	68	163	75	87	1	761	766	123	141	110	82	94	113	100	100	106	106
DET	82	53	29	0	406	295	85	69	80	51	29	0	423	348	102	61	162	104	58	0	829	643	187	130	94	136	97	91	121	95	96	94
KC	81	44	37	0	344	326	48	59	81	40	41	0	329	360	69	77	162	84	78	0	673	686	117	136	75	94	109	98	95	96	99	99
MIL	81	38	43	0	286	344	42	68	80	29	51	0	355	390	54	69	161	67	94	0	641	734	96	137	88	72	101	84	98	112	92	93
MIN	81	47	34	0	372	337	63	77	81	34	47	0	301	338	51	82	162	81	81	0	673	675	114	159	105	79	108	110	89	89	106	106
NY	81	51	30	0	372	292	62	49	81	36	45	0	386	387	68	71	162	87	75	0	758	679	130	120	81	101	92	87	113	101	94	93
OAK	81	44	37	0	356	344	77	72	81	33	48	0	382	452	81	83	162	77	85	0	738	796	158	155	91	118	116	85	113	120	91	92
SEA	81	42	39	0	357	394	68	82	81	32	49	0	325	380	61	56	162	74	88	0	682	774	129	138	125	81	85	106	93	105	102	103
TEX	80	34	46	0	327	357	55	70	81	35	46	0	329	357	65	78	161	69	92	0	656	714	120	148	89	91	110	100	92	100	100	101
TOR	81	49	32	0	387	339	59	78	82	40	41	1	363	357	84	62	163	89	73	1	750	696	143	140	96	102	101	102	103	96	101	101

1985 AMERICAN LEAGUE

TM	HOME								ROAD								ALL															
	G	W	L	T	R	OR	HR	OHR	G	W	L	T	R	OR	HR	OHR	G	W	L	T	R	OR	HR	OHR	HRF	HRB	HRP	RF	RB	RP	BPF	PPF
BAL	81	45	36	0	414	374	103	87	80	38	42	0	404	390	111	73	161	83	78	0	818	764	214	160	102	138	105	98	113	106	99	98
BOS	81	43	37	1	415	357	73	64	82	38	44	0	385	363	89	66	163	81	81	1	800	720	162	130	90	107	88	104	105	96	102	101
CAL	79	49	30	0	370	331	75	93	83	41	42	0	362	372	78	78	162	90	72	0	732	703	153	171	113	93	103	101	98	95	101	101
CHI	81	45	36	0	359	361	74	83	82	40	41	1	377	359	72	78	163	85	77	1	736	720	146	161	100	91	99	99	99	97	100	100
CLE	81	38	43	0	380	379	52	76	81	22	59	0	349	482	64	94	162	60	102	0	729	861	116	170	81	83	118	91	105	122	94	95
DET	81	44	37	0	386	368	108	93	80	40	40	0	343	320	94	48	161	84	77	0	729	688	202	141	136	111	76	112	93	88	106	106
KC	82	50	32	0	357	317	67	43	80	41	39	0	330	322	87	60	162	91	71	0	687	639	154	103	75	110	75	101	91	85	102	101
MIL	80	40	40	0	368	416	50	86	81	31	50	0	322	386	51	89	161	71	90	0	690	802	101	175	98	66	111	110	90	104	105	106
MIN	84	49	35	0	407	393	71	83	78	28	50	0	298	389	70	81	162	77	85	0	705	782	141	164	95	93	107	107	92	102	103	104
NY	80	58	22	0	411	288	92	67	81	39	42	0	428	372	84	90	161	97	64	0	839	660	176	157	94	118	105	90	120	95	96	94
OAK	79	43	36	0	348	347	66	71	83	34	49	0	409	440	89	101	162	77	85	0	757	787	155	172	77	113	124	87	111	114	93	93
SEA	83	42	41	0	360	389	92	78	79	32	47	0	359	429	79	76	162	74	88	0	719	818	171	154	104	108	98	91	103	116	94	95
TEX	77	37	43	0	356	406	76	102	81	25	56	0	261	379	53	71	161	62	99	0	617	785	129	173	139	77	92	117	77	98	104	110
TOR	80	54	26	0	396	264	75	78	81	45	36	0	363	324	83	69	161	99	62	0	759	588	158	147	103	100	94	99	103	81	101	99

1986 AMERICAN LEAGUE

TM	HOME								ROAD								ALL															
	G	W	L	T	R	OR	HR	OHR	G	W	L	T	R	OR	HR	OHR	G	W	L	T	R	OR	HR	OHR	HRF	HRB	HRP	RF	RB	RP	BPF	PPF
BAL	79	37	42	0	348	362	91	98	83	36	47	0	360	398	78	79	162	73	89	0	708	760	169	177	124	93	97	98	96	102	99	99
BOS	81	51	30	0	389	350	55	85	80	44	36	0	405	346	89	82	161	95	66	0	794	696	144	167	83	96	113	98	107	95	100	99
CAL	82	50	32	0	371	335	88	84	80	42	38	0	415	349	79	69	162	92	70	0	786	684	167	153	113	95	88	91	109	96	96	95
CHI	81	41	40	0	341	335	51	63	81	31	50	0	303	364	70	80	162	72	90	0	644	699	121	143	77	82	97	101	85	92	101	101
CLE	81	45	35	1	403	415	80	80	82	39	43	0	428	426	77	87	163	84	78	1	831	841	157	167	99	96	102	97	113	115	98	98
DET	81	49	32	0	403	310	96	83	81	38	43	0	395	404	102	100	162	87	75	0	798	714	198	183	90	129	120	90	112	101	95	95
KC	81	45	36	0	342	317	60	46	81	31	50	0	312	356	77	75	162	76	86	0	654	673	137	121	71	97	84	98	88	90	100	100
MIL	80	41	39	0	338	375	63	79	81	36	45	0	329	359	64	79	161	77	84	0	667	734	127	158	100	78	95	104	88	96	102	103
MIN	81	43	38	0	426	439	116	107	81	28	53	0	315	400	80	93	162	71	91	0	741	839	196	200	126	107	111	118	91	103	108	109
NY	80	41	39	0	384	396	93	96	82	49	33	0	413	342	95	79	162	90	72	0	797	738	188	175	111	110	102	106	104	96	103	103
OAK	83	47	36	0	363	349	75	81	79	29	50	0	368	411	88	85	162	76	86	0	731	760	163	166	86	107	109	88	105	109	94	94
SEA	82	41	41	0	410	427	97	98	80	26	54	0	308	408	61	72	162	67	95	0	718	835	158	171	138	80	88	112	91	106	105	106
TEX	81	51	30	0	374	343	87	61	81	36	45	0	397	400	97	84	162	87	75	0	771	743	184	145	83	122	97	91	108	104	95	95
TOR	81	42	39	0	415	389	87	89	82	44	37	1	394	344	94	75	163	86	76	1	809	733	181	164	105	107	98	110	103	93	105	104

1987 AMERICAN LEAGUE

TM	HOME								ROAD								ALL															
	G	W	L	T	R	OR	HR	OHR	G	W	L	T	R	OR	HR	OHR	G	W	L	T	R	OR	HR	OHR	HRF	HRB	HRP	RF	RB	RP	BPF	PPF
BAL	82	31	51	0	351	456	110	125	80	36	44	0	378	424	101	101	162	67	95	0	729	880	211	226	111	108	114	97	94	112	99	99
BOS	80	50	30	0	436	383	86	75	82	28	54	0	406	442	88	115	162	78	84	0	842	825	174	190	82	103	109	99	107	105	99	99
CAL	81	38	43	0	377	405	88	116	81	37	44	0	393	398	84	96	162	75	87	0	770	803	172	212	112	87	106	99	98	102	99	100
CHI	81	38	43	0	394	414	72	90	81	39	42	0	354	332	101	99	162	77	85	0	748	746	173	189	82	101	110	116	87	86	109	109
CLE	81	35	46	0	373	519	94	118	81	26	55	0	369	438	93	101	162	61	101	0	742	957	187	219	107	97	112	108	91	115	103	105
DET	81	54	27	0	442	338	125	101	81	44	37	0	454	397	100	79	162	98	64	0	896	735	225	180	125	106	86	93	116	97	97	96
KC	81	46	35	0	375	349	73	57	81	37	44	0	340	342	95	71	162	83	79	0	715	691	168	128	80	97	75	106	87	84	104	104
MIL	81	48	33	0	440	420	72	79	81	43	38	0	422	397	91	90	162	91	71	0	862	817	163	169	85	93	96	105	106	101	102	102
MIN	81	56	25	0	411	348	106	92	81	29	52	0	375	458	90	118	162	85	77	0	786	806	196	210	96	108	114	92	104	105	96	96
NY	81	51	30	0	401	346	98	88	81	38	43	0	387	412	98	91	162	89	73	0	788	758	196	179	99	104	96	94	102	98	98	97
OAK	81	42	39	0	363	351	88	75	81	39	42	0	443	438	111	101	162	81	81	0	806	789	199	176	118	105	82	112	109	91	91	91
SEA	81	40	41	0	403	400	103	115	81	38	43	0	357	401	58	84	162	78	84	0	760	801	161	199	148	68	85	105	93	98	103	103
TEX	81	43	38	0	426	447	93	111	81	32	49	0	397	402	101	88	162	75	87	0	823	849	194	199	107	100	102	108	100	103	104	104
TOR	81	52	29	0	425	319	101	83	81	44	37	0	420	336	114	75	162	96	66	0	845	655	215	158	99	114	86	99	105	83	101	99

1988 AMERICAN LEAGUE

TM	HOME								ROAD								ALL															
	G	W	L	T	R	OR	HR	OHR	G	W	L	T	R	OR	HR	OHR	G	W	L	T	R	OR	HR	OHR	HRF	HRB	HRP	RF	RB	RP	BPF	PPF
BAL	80	34	46	0	286	354	70	77	81	20	61	0	264	435	67	76	161	54	107	0	550	789	137	153	102	101	112	92	83	115	95	97
BOS	81	53	28	0	456	360	68	73	81	36	45	0	357	329	56	70	162	89	73	0	813	689	124	143	112	86	99	118	105	91	109	108
CAL	81	35	46	0	333	368	58	71	81	40	41	0	381	403	66	64	162	75	87	0	714	771	124	135	99	91	99	90	107	115	94	95
CHI	81	40	41	0	311	373	55	64	80	31	49	0	320	384	77	74	161	71	90	0	631	757	132	138	75	109	115	96	92	109	98	99
CLE	81	44	37	0	353	359	62	52	81	34	47	0	313	372	72	68	162	78	84	0	666	731	134	120	82	107	96	103	93	101	101	102
DET	81	50	31	0	328	303	83	76	81	38	43	0	375	355	60	74	162	88	74	0	703	658	143	150	118	97	102	88	106	99	94	94
KC	80	44	36	0	359	330	55	37	81	40	41	0	345	318	66	65	162	87	77	0	704	648	121	102	73	103	85	105	97	90	103	103
MIL	81	47	34	0	354	310	60	65	81	40	41	0	328	306	53	60	162	87	75	0	682	616	113	125	110	78	86	105	93	85	103	103
MIN	81	47	34	0	402	354	76	79	81	44	37	0	357	318	75	67	162	91	71	0	759	672	151	146	109	107	103	112	101	90	106	105
NY	80	46	34	0	378	345	77	75	81	39	42	0	394	403	71	82	161	85	76	0	772	748	148	157	101	110	116	93	115	110	96	95
OAK	81	54	27	0	362	294	67	47	81	50	31	0	438	326	89	69	162	104	58	0	800	620	156	116	75	130	98	88	119	94	95	93
SEA	81	37	44	0	362	405	97	81	80	31	49	0	302	339	51	63	161	68	93	0	664	744	148	144	147	87	88	116	88	98	107	108
TEX	81	38	43	0	336	368	58	67	80	32	48	0	301	367	54	62	161	70	91	0	637	735	112	129	105	80	92	103	90	102	101	102

TM	HOME								ROAD								ALL														
	G	W	L	T	R	OR	HR	OHR	G	W	L	T	R	OR	HR	OHR	G	W	L	T	R	OR	HR	OHR	HRF	HRB	HRP	RF	RB	RP	BPF	PPF
TOR	81	45	36	0	371	344	78	73	81	42	39	0	392	336	80	70	162	87	75	0	763	680	158	143	101	116	106	99	108	98	100	99

1989 AMERICAN LEAGUE

TM	G	W	L	T	R	OR	HR	OHR	G	W	L	T	R	OR	HR	OHR	G	W	L	T	R	OR	HR	OHR	HRF	HRB	HRP	RF	RB	RP	BPF	PPF
BAL	81	47	34	0	347	338	61	65	81	40	41	0	361	348	68	69	162	87	75	0	708	686	129	134	93	110	114	97	103	100	99	98
BOS	81	46	35	0	419	374	52	70	81	37	44	0	355	361	56	61	162	83	79	0	774	735	108	131	104	87	103	110	106	102	105	104
CAL	81	52	29	0	317	285	73	75	81	39	42	0	352	293	72	38	162	91	71	0	669	578	145	113	132	103	78	94	98	85	99	98
CHI	80	35	45	0	301	365	36	58	81	34	47	0	392	385	58	86	161	69	92	0	693	750	94	144	67	93	139	87	108	117	93	93
CLE	81	41	40	0	319	332	56	51	81	32	49	0	285	322	71	56	162	73	89	0	604	654	127	107	85	111	95	106	84	90	104	104
DET	81	38	43	0	321	389	74	77	81	21	60	0	296	427	42	73	162	59	103	0	617	816	116	150	127	83	109	97	91	118	97	99
KC	81	55	26	0	335	288	38	26	81	37	44	0	355	347	63	60	162	92	70	0	690	635	101	86	54	106	87	90	104	96	96	95
MIL	81	45	36	0	344	321	69	54	81	36	45	0	363	358	57	75	162	81	81	0	707	679	126	129	94	107	108	93	105	101	97	96
MIN	81	45	36	0	387	404	59	69	81	35	46	0	353	334	58	70	162	80	82	0	740	738	117	139	100	96	113	114	100	99	106	106
NY	81	41	40	0	373	419	64	88	80	33	47	0	325	373	66	62	161	74	87	0	698	792	130	150	115	101	114	111	97	109	104	105
OAK	81	54	27	0	370	284	65	51	81	45	36	0	342	292	62	52	162	99	63	0	712	576	127	103	103	101	83	104	99	81	103	102
SEA	81	40	41	0	353	386	68	67	81	33	48	0	341	342	66	47	162	73	89	0	694	728	134	114	117	100	85	107	97	101	103	103
TEX	81	45	36	0	352	371	75	63	81	38	43	0	343	343	47	56	162	83	79	0	695	714	122	119	131	85	85	105	98	100	102	103
TOR	81	46	35	0	330	308	64	50	81	43	38	0	401	343	78	49	162	89	73	0	731	651	142	99	91	119	86	87	112	101	94	93

1990 AMERICAN LEAGUE

TM	G	W	L	T	R	OR	HR	OHR	G	W	L	T	R	OR	HR	OHR	G	W	L	T	R	OR	HR	OHR	HRF	HRB	HRP	RF	RB	RP	BPF	PPF
BAL	80	40	40	0	320	337	74	82	81	36	45	0	349	361	58	79	161	76	85	0	669	698	132	161	114	98	119	94	100	104	97	97
BOS	81	51	30	0	394	318	61	44	81	37	44	0	305	346	45	48	162	88	74	0	699	664	106	92	112	76	67	109	95	91	105	105
CAL	81	42	39	0	360	354	89	55	81	38	43	0	330	352	58	51	162	80	82	0	690	706	147	106	129	98	74	104	97	99	102	102
CHI	80	49	31	0	345	315	41	53	82	45	37	0	337	318	65	53	162	94	68	0	682	633	106	106	83	87	90	104	95	89	103	102
CLE	81	41	40	0	363	373	52	86	81	36	45	0	369	364	58	77	162	77	85	0	732	737	110	163	102	87	125	100	105	106	100	100
DET	81	39	42	0	372	399	92	75	81	40	41	0	378	355	80	79	162	79	83	0	750	754	172	154	105	133	121	105	106	106	102	102
KC	81	45	36	0	370	342	42	46	80	30	50	0	337	367	58	70	161	75	86	0	707	709	100	116	69	92	105	100	103	103	100	100
MIL	81	39	42	0	356	374	60	59	81	35	46	0	376	386	68	62	162	74	88	0	732	760	128	121	92	103	98	96	108	112	97	97
MIN	81	41	40	0	373	380	46	69	81	33	48	0	293	349	54	65	162	74	88	0	666	729	100	134	96	79	105	115	89	97	107	108
NY	81	37	44	0	296	361	64	78	81	30	51	0	307	388	83	66	162	67	95	0	603	749	147	144	95	119	117	94	90	110	97	98
OAK	81	51	30	0	321	244	69	52	81	52	29	0	412	326	95	71	162	103	59	0	733	570	164	123	75	145	112	79	116	92	91	89
SEA	81	38	43	0	310	341	49	60	81	39	42	0	330	339	58	60	162	77	85	0	640	680	107	120	93	86	96	97	93	98	99	99
TEX	82	47	35	0	354	348	64	59	80	36	44	0	322	348	46	54	162	83	79	0	676	696	110	113	118	77	80	102	96	99	101	101
TOR	81	44	37	0	385	341	93	82	81	42	39	0	382	320	74	61	162	86	76	0	767	661	167	143	127	116	100	103	108	94	102	101

1991 AMERICAN LEAGUE

TM	G	W	L	T	R	OR	HR	OHR	G	W	L	T	R	OR	HR	OHR	G	W	L	T	R	OR	HR	OHR	HRF	HRB	HRP	RF	RB	RP	BPF	PPF
BAL	81	33	48	0	329	367	80	80	81	34	47	0	357	409	90	75	162	67	95	0	686	776	170	155	96	125	115	91	100	112	95	96
BOS	81	43	38	0	378	374	69	76	81	41	40	0	353	338	57	71	162	84	78	0	731	712	126	147	112	85	99	108	96	94	104	104
CAL	81	40	41	0	291	303	59	74	81	41	40	0	362	346	56	67	162	81	81	0	653	649	115	141	108	79	96	85	96	93	93	93
CHI	81	46	35	0	378	337	74	79	81	41	40	0	380	344	65	75	162	87	75	0	758	681	139	154	109	96	106	99	104	94	100	100
CLE	82	30	52	0	271	377	22	41	80	27	53	0	305	382	57	69	162	57	105	0	576	759	79	110	50	71	104	91	83	108	95	97
DET	81	54	27	0	437	402	109	89	81	35	46	0	380	392	100	59	162	84	78	0	817	794	209	148	123	136	98	108	109	106	103	103
KC	81	40	41	0	344	378	47	40	81	42	39	0	383	344	70	65	162	82	80	0	727	722	117	105	66	99	89	99	100	100	100	100
MIL	80	43	37	0	398	398	62	73	82	40	42	0	401	346	54	74	162	83	79	0	799	744	116	147	108	80	100	109	106	99	104	104
MIN	81	51	30	0	404	342	62	75	81	44	37	0	372	310	78	64	162	95	67	0	776	652	140	139	98	101	101	100	101	86	106	104
NY	81	39	42	0	356	380	82	84	81	32	49	0	318	397	65	68	162	71	91	0	674	777	147	152	122	95	99	102	92	105	101	102
OAK	81	47	34	0	357	371	76	59	81	37	44	0	403	425	83	88	162	84	78	0	760	796	159	147	80	128	117	89	112	117	94	94
SEA	81	45	36	0	374	319	69	69	81	38	43	0	328	355	57	67	162	83	79	0	702	674	126	136	111	85	92	101	95	92	101	101
TEX	81	46	35	0	404	400	79	77	81	39	42	0	425	414	98	74	162	85	77	0	829	814	177	151	92	133	116	96	117	115	97	97
TOR	81	46	35	0	359	344	75	72	81	45	36	0	325	278	58	49	162	91	71	0	684	622	133	121	135	81	73	116	86	79	109	109

1992 AMERICAN LEAGUE

TM	G	W	L	T	R	OR	HR	OHR	G	W	L	T	R	OR	HR	OHR	G	W	L	T	R	OR	HR	OHR	HRF	HRB	HRP	RF	RB	RP	BPF	PPF
BAL	81	43	38	0	339	333	75	69	81	46	35	0	366	323	73	55	162	89	73	0	705	656	148	124	112	110	93	98	101	95	100	99
BOS	81	44	37	0	328	341	45	46	81	29	52	0	271	328	39	61	162	73	89	0	599	669	84	107	91	69	85	110	81	90	106	106
CAL	81	41	40	0	311	340	44	60	81	31	50	0	268	331	44	70	162	72	90	0	579	671	88	130	91	73	104	107	79	91	104	105
CHI	82	50	32	0	368	314	54	62	80	36	44	0	370	376	56	61	162	86	76	0	738	690	110	123	97	88	97	90	111	104	95	95
CLE	81	41	40	0	366	397	62	94	81	35	46	0	308	349	65	65	162	76	86	0	674	746	127	159	118	94	114	114	90	99	107	108
DET	80	38	42	0	389	399	91	90	82	37	45	0	402	395	91	65	162	75	87	0	791	794	182	155	117	135	116	101	114	114	99	99
KC	81	44	37	0	314	336	24	41	81	28	53	0	296	331	51	65	162	72	90	0	610	667	75	106	58	72	104	103	86	93	102	102
MIL	81	53	28	0	339	254	35	51	81	39	42	0	401	350	47	76	162	92	70	0	740	604	82	127	72	75	112	81	116	95	91	90
MIN	81	48	33	0	375	326	56	56	81	42	39	0	372	327	48	65	162	90	72	0	747	653	104	121	100	82	94	101	106	93	101	100
NY	81	41	40	0	385	387	88	70	81	35	46	0	348	359	75	59	162	76	86	0	733	746	163	129	116	119	96	108	101	103	104	104
OAK	81	51	30	0	365	326	76	73	81	45	36	0	380	346	66	56	162	96	66	0	745	672	142	129	121	102	92	96	108	98	98	98
SEA	81	38	43	0	355	398	78	63	81	26	55	0	324	401	71	66	162	64	98	0	679	799	149	129	102	117	102	102	97	113	100	101
TEX	81	36	45	0	317	376	71	63	81	41	40	0	365	377	88	50	162	77	85	0	682	753	159	113	97	126	92	94	101	111	96	97
TOR	81	53	28	0	390	334	79	60	81	43	38	0	390	348	84	64	162	96	66	0	780	682	163	124	95	132	102	99	112	99	100	99

1993 AMERICAN LEAGUE

TM	G	W	L	T	R	OR	HR	OHR	G	W	L	T	R	OR	HR	OHR	G	W	L	T	R	OR	HR	OHR	HRF	HRB	HRP	RF	RB	RP	BPF	PPF
BAL	81	48	33	0	434	371	87	81	81	37	44	0	352	374	70	72	162	85	77	0	786	745	157	153	117	98	96	110	98	93	105	105
BOS	81	43	38	0	393	363	54	53	81	37	44	0	293	335	60	74	162	80	82	0	686	698	114	127	81	84	92	119	81	83	110	110
CAL	81	44	37	0	363	398	64	84	81	27	54	0	321	372	50	69	162	71	91	0	684	770	114	153	121	69	92	108	86	96	104	105
CHI	81	45	36	0	384	333	82	70	81	49	32	0	392	331	80	55	162	94	68	0	776	664	162	125	113	102	91	100	87	101	100	100
CLE	81	46	35	0	387	351	69	83	81	30	51	0	403	462	72	99	162	76	86	0	790	813	141	182	89	103	129	86	113	115	92	93
DET	81	44	37	0	457	408	103	99	81	41	40	0	442	429	75	89	162	85	77	0	899	837	178	188	121	110	117	100	119	112	99	98
KC	81	43	38	0	370	354	50	49	81	41	40	0	305	340	75	56	162	84	78	0	675	694	125	105	77	92	80	111	83	85	107	107
MIL	81	38	43	0	371	381	53	65	81	31	50	0	362	411	72	88	162	69	93	0	733	792	125	153	75	97	117	97	98	105	98	99
MIN	81	36	45	0	360	433	56	70	81	35	46	0	333	397	65	78	162	71	91	0	693	830	121	148	88	87	105	107	88	104	103	104
NY	81	50	31	0	389	342	88	85	81	38	43	0	432	419	90	85	162	88	74	0	821	761	178	170	99	122	117	87	115	107	94	93
OAK	81	38	43	0	333	387	78	78	81	30	51	0	382	459	80	79	162	68	94	0	715	846	158	157	97	109	108	86	102	119	92	93
SEA	81	46	35	0	380	350	74	66	81	36	45	0	354	381	87	69	162	82	80	0	734	731	161	135	90	113	96	99	96	96	100	100
TEX	81	50	31	0	414	341	90	72	81	36	45	0	421	410	91	72	162	86	76	0	835	751	181	144	100	122	99	92	114	103	96	95
TOR	81	48	33	0	437	390	90	81	81	47	34	0	410	352	69	53	162	95	67	0	847	742	159	134	137	90	76	109	106	94	105	104

1994 AMERICAN LEAGUE

TM	G	W	L	T	R	OR	HR	OHR	G	W	L	T	R	OR	HR	OHR	G	W	L	T	R	OR	HR	OHR	HRF	HRB	HRP	RF	RB	RP	BPF	PPF
BAL	55	28	27	0	294	272	75	70	57	35	22	0	295	225	64	61	112	63	49	0	589	497	139	131	119	102	97	112	94	80	107	106
BOS	64	31	33	0	320	353	68	67	51	23	28	0	232	268	52	53	115	54	61	0	552	621	120	120	102	92	92	106	89	99	103	104
CAL	63	23	40	0	286	389	74	93	52	24	28	0	257	271	46	57	115	47	68	0	543	660	120	150	130	81	100	104	90	106	101	103
CHI	53	34	19	0	296	206	62	43	60	33	27	0	337	292	59	72	113	67	46	0	633	498	121	115	92	100	93	92	111	87	97	95
CLE	51	35	16	0	335	248	87	44	62	31	31	0	344	314	80	50	113	66	47	0	679	562	167	94	122	119	70	108	111	93	104	103
DET	58	34	24	0	350	324	85	76	57	19	38	0	302	347	76	72	115	53	62	0	652	671	161	148	106	124	115	101	109	112	100	100
KC	59	35	24	0	325	287	41	48	56	29	27	0	249	245	59	47	115	64	51	0	574	532	100	95	81	84	81	117	87	81	109	109
MIL	56	24	32	0	275	311	48	63	59	29	30	0	272	275	51	64	115	53	62	0	547	586	99	127	101	77	97	111	86	92	106	106
MIN	59	32	27	0	319	339	48	88	54	21	33	0	275	349	55	65	113	53	60	0	594	688	103	153	103	82	118	96	104	119	97	98
NY	57	33	24	0	291	260	63	62	56	37	19	0	379	274	76	58	113	70	43	0	670	534	139	120	93	114	100	85	121	99	93	92
OAK	56	24	32	0	241	262	51	54	58	27	31	0	308	327	62	74	114	51	63	0	549	589	113	128	81	99	110	83	101	107	91	92
SEA	44	22	22	0	248	244	63	44	68	27	41	0	321	372	90	59	112	49	63	0	569	616	153	109	106	119	87	108	95	101	104	104
TEX	63	31	32	0	334	353	63	67	51	21	30	0	279	344	61	90	114	52	62	0	613	697	124	157	71	120	147	90	111	125	93	94
TOR	59	33	26	0	293	275	63	64	56	22	34	0	273	304	52	63	115	55	60	0	566	579	115	127	104	88	97	94	97	99	97	97

The All-Time Leaders

This section is divided into two parts: lifetime leaders and single-season leaders. Both groups command our attention and convey the pleasures of the game, which lie as much in contemplation of the past as in experiencing the present: Henry Aaron, 755; Babe Ruth, 714; Willie Mays, 660—this is no mere aggregation of names and numbers, as in a telephone directory . . . it comprises the romance and lore of the home run, and of baseball itself. Jack Chesbro, 41, 1904; Bob Gibson, 1.12, 1968; Nolan Ryan, 383, 1973 . . . you can fill in the blanks that tell the story of pitching's most glorious seasons.

What follows are the all-time great achievements in 219 categories, both the traditional statistics and the new. For most of these we will give not the top 10 or 20 but the top 100, because some categories would otherwise be dominated by players of a certain era (for example, slugging average by batters of the 1920s and 1930s, earned run average by pitchers of 1900–1919). And for many stats we will offer a second kind of ranking, broken down into six distinct eras of baseball, with the top 10 or 15 leaders in each. For example, breaking down single-season home runs this way would produce lists topped by these men:

> 1876–1892: Ned Williamson, 27, 1884
> 1893–1919: Babe Ruth, 29, 1919
> 1920–1941: Babe Ruth, 60, 1927
> 1942–1960: Ralph Kiner, 54, 1949
> 1961–1976: Roger Maris, 61, 1961
> 1977–1994: George Foster, 52, 1977

And for single-season Adjusted ERA (normalized to league average and adjusted for home-park factor), we get:

> 1876–1892: Tim Keefe, 294
> (adjusted from actual 0.80), 1880
> 1893–1919: Dutch Leonard, 280
> (adjusted from actual 0.96), 1914
> 1920–1941: Lefty Grove, 218
> (adjusted from actual 2.06), 1931
> 1942–1960: Billy Pierce, 201
> (adjusted from actual 1.97), 1955
> 1961–1976: Bob Gibson, 258
> (adjusted from actual 1.12), 1968
> 1977–1994: Greg Maddux, 266
> (adjusted from actual 1.56), 1994

This is quite a different lineup from the traditional list of ERA leaders (which relegates pre-1900 pitching to the shadows), where of the 15 top spots, 14 are accorded to pitchers active from 1905 to 1918. Is there a baseball fan alive who thinks that all the great pitchers were created in that 14-year span and that the mold was then broken?

But enough expostulation and fulmination. Let's set some ground rules, define some terms that may still be unfamiliar after you've browsed through the Player and Pitcher registers, and get on with the show.

To be eligible for a lifetime pitching category that is stated as an average, a man must have pitched 1,500 or more innings, or 750 or more innings if he is a relief pitcher, in the major leagues; for a counting statistic, he must simply have attained the necessary quantity to crack the list. For a single-season category expressed as an average, he must have pitched one inning per league scheduled game or have attained the necessary quantity (wins, strikeouts, saves) to head a counted list.

To be eligible for a lifetime batting category that is stated as an average, a man must have played in 1,000 or more games; for counting stats such as strikeouts, a Rob Deer earned his place on the list before he played his 1,000th game. For Pitcher Batting Average, the criterion is 1,500 innings pitched or 100 hits. And to reach the single-season batting lists, a man must have 3.1 plate appearances per scheduled game.

We provide tables of the top fielding performances, too, sorted by position as you would expect (and, in this edition, including only games played at the position, rather than combining data from secondary positions under the dominant postion). But we go one step further and rank several *batting* categories by position, thus recognizing and illustrating the greater demands for fielding skill at such positions as shortstop, catcher, and second base, and the comparatively plentiful supply of batting talent in the outfield and at first base. As we establish a 1,000-game minimum for inclusion in all but a few batting and baserunning categories, we likewise establish for these positional rankings a minimum of 1,000 games played at the position.

For the three principal categories—Total Player Rating, Total Pitcher Index, and Total Baseball Ranking—we have introduced several variations. For example, TPR and TBR are shown 500 deep for lifetime leaders—sorted first by highest value; then alphabetically so that the reader may find a particular player without scanning 500 names; and last by the above-named eras, the top 25 in each. Total Pitcher Index is also sorted this way, but because far fewer pitchers than position players meet the longevity criteria, the lifetime groupings go 300 and 200 deep rather than 500 and 300. Ties are calculated to as many decimal places as needed to break them, but averages are shown to only three places. When two or more players are tied in an averaged category with a narrow base of data, such as a season's won-lost percentage, the reader can presume a numerical dead heat (and obviously this goes for counting stats, too—one man's 39 doubles are as good as another's). But where there is a tie for batting average, earned run average, or any of the sabermetric measures, the reader may assume that the man listed above the other(s) has the minutely higher average.

Here are the few stats carried in this section that are not carried in the Annual Record or Registers, with definitions where the terms are not self-explanatory (see Glossary for formulas):

Batting, Baserunning, Fielding

Runs (Scored) Per Game   Broken down by era
Home Run Percentage   Home runs per 100 at bats
Bases on Balls Percentage   Walks (most) per 100 appearances (at bats plus walks)
At-Bats Per Strikeout   Broken down by era
Relative Batting Average   Normalized to league average
Isolated Power   Slugging average minus batting average
Extra Base Hits
Pinch Hits
Pinch Hit Batting Average
Pinch Hit Home Runs
Strikeout Percentage
Total Player Rating Per 150 Games   Highlighting the achievements of modern players and those with comparatively short careers (though at least 1,000 games)
Total Chances Per Game   Broken down by position
Chances Accepted Per Game   Broken down by position

Putouts   Broken down by position
Putouts Per Game   Broken down by position
Assists   Broken down by position
Assists Per Game   Broken down by position
Double Plays   Broken down by position

Pitching

Wins Above Team   How many wins a pitcher garnered beyond those expected of an average pitcher for that team; the formula is weighted so that a pitcher on a good team has a chance to compete with pitchers on poor teams who otherwise would benefit from the larger potential spread between their team's won-lost percentage and their own; see Glossary for more information.
Wins Above League   A pitcher's won-lost record restated by adding his Pitching Wins above the league average to the record that a league-average pitcher would have had with the same number of decisions (for example, Tom Seaver goes 20–10 with 7 Pitching Wins; applying the 7 wins to a 15–15 mark in the same 30 decisions results in a WAL of 22–8).
Percentage of Team Wins
Relief Games
Pitchers' Batting Runs
Pitchers' Fielding Runs
Relief Wins   This statistic, like the relief stats below, includes only games in relief.
Relief Losses
Relief Innings Pitched
Relief Points   Relief wins plus saves minus losses

Games

1	Pete Rose	3562
2	Carl Yastrzemski	3308
3	Hank Aaron	3298
4	Ty Cobb	3035
5	Stan Musial	3026
6	Willie Mays	2992
7	Rusty Staub	2951
8	Dave Winfield	2927
9	Brooks Robinson	2896
10	Robin Yount	2856
11	Al Kaline	2834
12	Eddie Collins	2826
13	Reggie Jackson	2820
14	Frank Robinson	2808
15	Honus Wagner	2792
16	Tris Speaker	2789
17	Tony Perez	2777
18	Mel Ott	2730
19	George Brett	2707
20	Eddie Murray	2706
21	Graig Nettles	2700
22	Darrell Evans	2687
23	Rabbit Maranville	2670
24	Joe Morgan	2649
25	Lou Brock	2616
26	Dwight Evans	2606
27	Luis Aparicio	2599
28	Willie McCovey	2588
29	Paul Waner	2549
30	Ernie Banks	2528
31	Bill Buckner	2517
	Sam Crawford	2517
33	Andre Dawson	2506
34	Babe Ruth	2503
35	Carlton Fisk	2499
36	Dave Concepcion	2488
	Billy Williams	2488
38	Nap Lajoie	2480
39	Max Carey	2476
40	Rod Carew	2469
	Vada Pinson	2469
42	Dave Parker	2466
43	Ted Simmons	2456
44	Ozzie Smith	2447
45	Bill Dahlen	2443
46	Ron Fairly	2442
47	Harmon Killebrew	2435
48	Roberto Clemente	2433
49	Willie Davis	2429
50	Luke Appling	2422
51	Zack Wheat	2410
52	Mickey Vernon	2409
53	Buddy Bell	2405
54	Sam Rice	2404
	Mike Schmidt	2404
56	Mickey Mantle	2401
57	Eddie Mathews	2391
58	Jake Beckley	2386
59	Bobby Wallace	2383
60	Enos Slaughter	2380
61	George Davis	2368
	Al Oliver	2368
63	Nellie Fox	2367
64	Willie Stargell	2360
65	Jose Cruz	2353
66	Brian Downing	2344
67	Steve Garvey	2332
68	Bert Campaneris	2328
69	Frank White	2324
70	Charlie Gehringer	2323
71	Jimmie Foxx	2317
72	Frankie Frisch	2311
73	Harry Hooper	2309
74	Lou Whitaker	2306
75	Gary Carter	2296
76	Don Baylor	2292
	Ted Williams	2292
78	Goose Goslin	2287
79	Jimmy Dykes	2282
80	Cap Anson	2276
81	Lave Cross	2275
82	Bob Boone	2264
83	Chris Speier	2260
84	Rogers Hornsby	2259
85	Larry Bowa	2247
86	Ron Santo	2243
87	Fred Clarke	2242
88	Doc Cramer	2239
89	Red Schoendienst	2216
90	Al Simmons	2215
91	Joe Torre	2209
92	Willie Randolph	2202
93	Tommy Corcoran	2200
94	Tony Taylor	2195
95	Richie Ashburn	2189
96	Bill Russell	2181
97	Dale Murphy	2180
98	Chris Chambliss	2175
99	Joe Judge	2171
100	2 players tied	2166

At Bats

1	Pete Rose	14053
2	Hank Aaron	12364
3	Carl Yastrzemski	11988
4	Ty Cobb	11434
5	Robin Yount	11008
6	Stan Musial	10972
7	Dave Winfield	10888
8	Willie Mays	10881
9	Brooks Robinson	10654
10	Honus Wagner	10430
11	George Brett	10349
12	Lou Brock	10332
13	Luis Aparicio	10230
14	Tris Speaker	10195
15	Eddie Murray	10167
16	Al Kaline	10116
17	Rabbit Maranville	10078
18	Frank Robinson	10006
19	Eddie Collins	9949
20	Reggie Jackson	9864
21	Tony Perez	9778
22	Rusty Staub	9720
23	Vada Pinson	9645
24	Andre Dawson	9643
25	Nap Lajoie	9589
26	Sam Crawford	9570
27	Jake Beckley	9526
28	Paul Waner	9459
29	Mel Ott	9456
30	Roberto Clemente	9454
31	Ernie Banks	9421
32	Bill Buckner	9397
33	Max Carey	9363
34	Dave Parker	9358
35	Billy Williams	9350
36	Rod Carew	9315
37	Joe Morgan	9277
38	Sam Rice	9269
39	Nellie Fox	9232
40	Willie Davis	9174
41	Doc Cramer	9140
42	Frankie Frisch	9112
43	Zack Wheat	9106
44	Cap Anson	9101
45	Lave Cross	9072
46	Al Oliver	9049
47	Bill Dahlen	9031
	George Davis	9031
49	Ozzie Smith	9013
50	Dwight Evans	8996
51	Buddy Bell	8995
52	Graig Nettles	8986
53	Darrell Evans	8973
54	Charlie Gehringer	8860
55	Luke Appling	8856
56	Steve Garvey	8835
57	Tommy Corcoran	8804
58	Harry Hooper	8785
59	Al Simmons	8759
60	Carlton Fisk	8756
61	Mickey Vernon	8731
62	Dave Concepcion	8723
63	Bert Campaneris	8684
64	Ted Simmons	8680
65	Goose Goslin	8656
66	Bobby Wallace	8618
67	Paul Molitor	8610
68	Willie Keeler	8591
69	Fred Clarke	8568
70	Eddie Mathews	8537
71	Red Schoendienst	8479
72	Jesse Burkett	8421
73	Larry Bowa	8418
74	Babe Ruth	8399
75	Richie Ashburn	8365
76	Mike Schmidt	8352
77	Lou Whitaker	8321
78	Bid McPhee	8291
79	George Sisler	8267
80	Jim Rice	8225
81	Don Baylor	8198
82	Willie McCovey	8197
83	Rogers Hornsby	8173
84	Jimmy Ryan	8164
85	Harmon Killebrew	8147
86	Ron Santo	8143
87	Jimmie Foxx	8134
88	Mickey Mantle	8102
89	Pee Wee Reese	8058
90	Jimmy Dykes	8046
91	Cal Ripken	8027
92	George Van Haltren	8021
93	Willie Randolph	8018
94	Lou Gehrig	8001
95	Joe Kuhel	7984
96	Gary Carter	7971
97	Dale Murphy	7960
98	Tommy Leach	7959
99	Enos Slaughter	7946
100	2 players tied	7927

Runs

1	Ty Cobb	2246
2	Hank Aaron	2174
	Babe Ruth	2174
4	Pete Rose	2165
5	Willie Mays	2062
6	Stan Musial	1949
7	Lou Gehrig	1888
8	Tris Speaker	1882
9	Mel Ott	1859
10	Frank Robinson	1829
11	Eddie Collins	1821
12	Carl Yastrzemski	1816
13	Ted Williams	1798
14	Charlie Gehringer	1774
15	Jimmie Foxx	1751
16	Honus Wagner	1736
17	Jesse Burkett	1720
18	Cap Anson	1719
	Willie Keeler	1719
20	Billy Hamilton	1690
21	Bid McPhee	1678
22	Mickey Mantle	1677
23	Dave Winfield	1658
24	Rickey Henderson	1652
25	Joe Morgan	1650
26	Jimmy Ryan	1642
27	George Van Haltren	1639
28	Robin Yount	1632
29	Paul Waner	1627
30	Al Kaline	1622
31	Roger Connor	1620
32	Fred Clarke	1619
33	Lou Brock	1610
34	Jake Beckley	1600
35	Ed Delahanty	1599
36	Bill Dahlen	1589
37	George Brett	1583
38	Rogers Hornsby	1579
39	Hugh Duffy	1552
40	Reggie Jackson	1551
41	Max Carey	1545
42	George Davis	1539
43	Frankie Frisch	1532
44	Dan Brouthers	1523
45	Tom Brown	1521
46	Sam Rice	1514
47	Eddie Mathews	1509
48	Al Simmons	1507
49	Mike Schmidt	1506
50	Nap Lajoie	1504
51	Harry Stovey	1492
52	Goose Goslin	1483
53	Paul Molitor	1482
54	Arlie Latham	1478
55	Eddie Murray	1477
56	Dwight Evans	1470
57	Herman Long	1455
58	Jim O'Rourke	1446
59	Harry Hooper	1429
60	Dummy Hoy	1426
61	Rod Carew	1424
62	Joe Kelley	1421
63	Roberto Clemente	1416
64	Billy Williams	1410
65	John Ward	1408
66	Mike Griffin	1405
67	Sam Crawford	1391
68	Joe DiMaggio	1390
69	Vada Pinson	1366
70	Doc Cramer	1357
	King Kelly	1357
72	Tommy Leach	1355
73	Lou Whitaker	1350
74	Darrell Evans	1344
75	Pee Wee Reese	1338
76	Andre Dawson	1337
77	Luis Aparicio	1335
78	Lave Cross	1333
79	George Gore	1327
80	Richie Ashburn	1322
81	Luke Appling	1319
82	Patsy Donovan	1318
83	Mike Tiernan	1313
84	Ernie Banks	1305
85	Jimmy Sheckard	1296
86	Kiki Cuyler	1295
87	Tim Raines	1293
88	Harry Heilmann	1291
89	Zack Wheat	1289
90	Heinie Manush	1287
91	George Sisler	1284
92	Harmon Killebrew	1283
93	Donie Bush	1280
94	Nellie Fox	1279
95	Fred Tenney	1278
96	Carlton Fisk	1276
97	Dave Parker	1272
	Tony Perez	1272
99	Duke Snider	1259
100	Bobby Bonds	1258

Runs per Game

1876-1892

1	George Gore	1.01
2	Harry Stovey	1.00
3	King Kelly	.93
4	Dan Brouthers	.91
5	Arlie Latham	.91
6	Sam Thompson	.89
7	Buck Ewing	.86
8	Tom Brown	.85
9	Hardy Richardson	.84
10	Tommy McCarthy	.84
11	Tip O'Neill	.83
12	Denny Lyons	.83
13	Curt Welch	.83
14	Jim O'Rourke	.82
15	Roger Connor	.81

1893-1919

1	Billy Hamilton	1.06
2	John McGraw	.93
3	Mike Griffin	.93
4	Hugh Duffy	.89
5	Mike Tiernan	.89
6	Ed Delahanty	.87
7	Cupid Childs	.83
8	Jesse Burkett	.83
9	George Van Haltren	.83
10	Jimmy Ryan	.82
11	Willie Keeler	.81
12	Dummy Hoy	.79
13	Herman Long	.78
14	Hughie Jennings	.77
15	Joe Kelley	.77

1920-1941

1	Lou Gehrig	.87
2	Babe Ruth	.87
3	Earle Combs	.82
4	Red Rolfe	.80
5	Charlie Gehringer	.76
6	Jimmie Foxx	.76
7	Hank Greenberg	.75
8	Earl Averill	.73
9	Max Bishop	.72
10	Lu Blue	.71
11	Mickey Cochrane	.70
12	Rogers Hornsby	.70
13	Kiki Cuyler	.69
14	Mel Ott	.68
15	Al Simmons	.68

1942-1960

1	Joe DiMaggio	.80
2	Ted Williams	.78
3	Dom DiMaggio	.75
4	Tommy Henrich	.70
5	Mickey Mantle	.70
6	Jackie Robinson	.69
7	Johnny Pesky	.68
8	Ralph Kiner	.66
9	Eddie Stanky	.64
10	Stan Musial	.64
11	George Case	.64
12	Eddie Mathews	.63
13	Larry Doby	.63
14	Charlie Keller	.62
15	Minnie Minoso	.62

1961-1976

1	Willie Mays	.69
2	Bobby Bonds	.68
3	Hank Aaron	.66
4	Frank Robinson	.65
5	Dick Allen	.63
6	Joe Morgan	.62
7	Lou Brock	.62
8	Pete Rose	.61
9	Roberto Clemente	.58
10	Rod Carew	.58
11	Jim Wynn	.58
12	Al Kaline	.57
13	Billy Williams	.57
14	Reggie Smith	.57
15	Roger Maris	.56

1977-1994

1	Rickey Henderson	.79
2	Paul Molitor	.70
3	Barry Bonds	.69
4	Tim Raines	.67
5	Ron LeFlore	.67
6	Wade Boggs	.65
7	Jose Canseco	.64
8	Vince Coleman	.64
9	Lenny Dykstra	.63
10	Ryne Sandberg	.63
11	Mike Schmidt	.63
12	Devon White	.62
13	Brett Butler	.62
14	Roberto Alomar	.61
15	Fred McGriff	.61

Hits

1	Pete Rose	4256
2	Ty Cobb	4189
3	Hank Aaron	3771
4	Stan Musial	3630
5	Tris Speaker	3514
6	Carl Yastrzemski	3419
7	Honus Wagner	3415
8	Eddie Collins	3312
9	Willie Mays	3283
10	Nap Lajoie	3242
11	George Brett	3154
12	Paul Waner	3152
13	Robin Yount	3142
14	Dave Winfield	3088
15	Rod Carew	3053
16	Lou Brock	3023
17	Al Kaline	3007
18	Roberto Clemente	3000
19	Cap Anson	2995
20	Sam Rice	2987
21	Sam Crawford	2961
22	Frank Robinson	2943
23	Willie Keeler	2932
24	Jake Beckley	2930
	Rogers Hornsby	2930
	Eddie Murray	2930
27	Al Simmons	2927
28	Zack Wheat	2884
29	Frankie Frisch	2880
30	Mel Ott	2876
31	Babe Ruth	2873
32	Jesse Burkett	2850
33	Brooks Robinson	2848
34	Charlie Gehringer	2839
35	George Sisler	2812
36	Vada Pinson	2757
37	Luke Appling	2749
38	Al Oliver	2743
39	Goose Goslin	2735
40	Tony Perez	2732
41	Lou Gehrig	2721
42	Rusty Staub	2716
43	Bill Buckner	2715
44	Dave Parker	2712
45	Billy Williams	2711
46	Doc Cramer	2705
47	Andre Dawson	2700
48	Luis Aparicio	2677
49	Fred Clarke	2672
50	Max Carey	2665
51	Nellie Fox	2663
52	George Davis	2660
	Harry Heilmann	2660
54	Ted Williams	2654
55	Paul Molitor	2647
56	Jimmie Foxx	2646
57	Lave Cross	2645
58	Rabbit Maranville	2605
59	Steve Garvey	2599
60	Ed Delahanty	2597
61	Reggie Jackson	2584
62	Ernie Banks	2583
63	Richie Ashburn	2574
64	Willie Davis	2561
65	George Van Haltren	2532
66	Heinie Manush	2524
67	Joe Morgan	2517
68	Buddy Bell	2514
69	Jimmy Ryan	2502
70	Mickey Vernon	2495
71	Ted Simmons	2472
72	Joe Medwick	2471
73	Roger Connor	2467
74	Harry Hooper	2466
75	Lloyd Waner	2459
76	Bill Dahlen	2457
77	Jim Rice	2452
78	Red Schoendienst	2449
79	Dwight Evans	2446
80	Pie Traynor	2416
81	Mickey Mantle	2415
82	Stuffy McInnis	2405
83	Wade Boggs	2392
84	Enos Slaughter	2383
85	Edd Roush	2376
86	Ozzie Smith	2365
87	Carlton Fisk	2356
88	Joe Judge	2352
89	Orlando Cepeda	2351
90	Billy Herman	2345
91	Joe Torre	2342
92	Dave Concepcion	2326
	Jake Daubert	2326
94	Eddie Mathews	2315
95	Jim Bottomley	2313
96	Bobby Wallace	2309
97	Jim O'Rourke	2304
98	Kiki Cuyler	2299
	Charlie Grimm	2299
100	2 players tied	2296

Doubles

1	Tris Speaker	792
2	Pete Rose	746
3	Stan Musial	725
4	Ty Cobb	724
5	George Brett	665
6	Nap Lajoie	657
7	Carl Yastrzemski	646
8	Honus Wagner	640
9	Hank Aaron	624
10	Paul Waner	605
11	Robin Yount	583
12	Charlie Gehringer	574
13	Harry Heilmann	542
14	Rogers Hornsby	541
15	Joe Medwick	540
16	Al Simmons	539
17	Dave Winfield	535
18	Lou Gehrig	534
19	Al Oliver	529
20	Cap Anson	528
	Frank Robinson	528
22	Dave Parker	526
23	Ted Williams	525
24	Willie Mays	523
25	Ed Delahanty	522
26	Joe Cronin	515
27	Eddie Murray	511
28	Babe Ruth	506
29	Tony Perez	505
30	Goose Goslin	500
31	Rusty Staub	499
32	Bill Buckner	498
	Al Kaline	498
	Sam Rice	498
35	Andre Dawson	491
	Heinie Manush	491
37	Mickey Vernon	490
38	Mel Ott	488
39	Lou Brock	486
	Billy Herman	486
41	Vada Pinson	485
42	Hal McRae	484
43	Dwight Evans	483
	Ted Simmons	483
45	Brooks Robinson	482
46	Zack Wheat	476
47	Jake Beckley	473
48	Paul Molitor	472
49	Wade Boggs	467
50	Frankie Frisch	466
51	Jim Bottomley	465
52	Reggie Jackson	463
53	Dan Brouthers	460
54	Sam Crawford	458
	Jimmie Foxx	458
56	Jimmy Dykes	453
57	George Davis	451
	Jimmy Ryan	451
59	Joe Morgan	449
60	Rod Carew	445
61	George Burns	444
62	Dick Bartell	442
63	Roger Connor	441
64	Luke Appling	440
	Roberto Clemente	440
	Steve Garvey	440
67	Eddie Collins	438
68	Cesar Cedeno	436
	Joe Sewell	436
70	Wally Moses	435
71	Billy Williams	434
72	Joe Judge	433
73	Red Schoendienst	427
74	Keith Hernandez	426
75	Buddy Bell	425
	Sherry Magee	425
	George Sisler	425
78	Willie Stargell	423
79	Carlton Fisk	421
80	Max Carey	419
81	Orlando Cepeda	417
82	Cecil Cooper	415
83	Jim O'Rourke	414
	Cal Ripken	414
85	Bill Dahlen	413
	Enos Slaughter	413
87	Joe Kuhel	412
88	Lave Cross	411
89	Don Mattingly	410
90	Mike Schmidt	408
91	Ernie Banks	407
	Ben Chapman	407
	Frank White	407
94	Lou Whitaker	406
95	Earl Averill	401
	Marty McManus	401
97	Tim Wallach	400
98	Babe Herman	399
	Gee Walker	399
100	2 players tied	398

Triples

1	Sam Crawford	309
2	Ty Cobb	295
3	Honus Wagner	252
4	Jake Beckley	243
5	Roger Connor	233
6	Tris Speaker	222
7	Fred Clarke	220
8	Dan Brouthers	205
9	Joe Kelley	194
10	Paul Waner	191
11	Bid McPhee	188
12	Eddie Collins	186
13	Ed Delahanty	185
14	Sam Rice	184
15	Jesse Burkett	182
	Edd Roush	182
17	Ed Konetchy	181
18	Buck Ewing	178
19	Rabbit Maranville	177
	Stan Musial	177
21	Harry Stovey	174
22	Goose Goslin	173
23	Tommy Leach	172
	Zack Wheat	172
25	Rogers Hornsby	169
26	Joe Jackson	168
27	Roberto Clemente	166
	Sherry Magee	166
29	Jake Daubert	165
30	Elmer Flick	164
	George Sisler	164
	Pie Traynor	164
33	Bill Dahlen	163
	George Davis	163
	Lou Gehrig	163
	Nap Lajoie	163
37	Mike Tiernan	162
38	George Van Haltren	161
39	Harry Hooper	160
	Heinie Manush	160
	Sam Thompson	160
42	Max Carey	159
	Joe Judge	159
44	Ed McKean	158
45	Kiki Cuyler	157
	Jimmy Ryan	157
47	Tommy Corcoran	155
48	Earle Combs	154
49	Jim Bottomley	151
	Harry Heilmann	151
51	Kip Selbach	149
	Al Simmons	149
53	Wally Pipp	148
	Enos Slaughter	148
55	Bobby Veach	147
	Willie Wilson	147
57	Charlie Gehringer	146
58	Harry Davis	145
	Willie Keeler	145
60	Bobby Wallace	143
61	Lou Brock	141
62	Willie Mays	140
63	John Reilly	139
64	Tom Brown	138
	Willie Davis	138
	Frankie Frisch	138
	Jimmy Williams	138
68	George Brett	137
69	Babe Ruth	136
	Jimmy Sheckard	136
	Elmer Smith	136
72	Lave Cross	135
	Pete Rose	135
74	Shano Collins	133
75	Jim O'Rourke	132
	George Wood	132
77	Joe DiMaggio	131
	Buck Freeman	131
79	Buddy Myer	130
80	Oyster Burns	129
	Larry Gardner	129
82	Earl Averill	128
	Arky Vaughan	128
84	Vada Pinson	127
85	Hardy Richardson	126
	Robin Yount	126
87	Jimmie Foxx	125
88	John Anderson	124
	Cap Anson	124
	Hal Chase	124
	Frank Schulte	124
92	Larry Doyle	123
	Duke Farrell	123
94	Dummy Hoy	121
95	Mickey Vernon	120
96	Hugh Duffy	119
	Fred Pfeffer	119
98	4 players tied	118

Triples (by era)

1876-1892

1	Roger Connor	233
2	Dan Brouthers	205
3	Bid McPhee	188
4	Buck Ewing	178
5	Harry Stovey	174
6	Sam Thompson	160
7	John Reilly	139
8	Tom Brown	138
9	Jim O'Rourke	132
	George Wood	132
11	Oyster Burns	129
12	Hardy Richardson	126
13	Cap Anson	124
14	Fred Pfeffer	119
15	Bill Kuehne	115

1893-1919

1	Sam Crawford	309
2	Ty Cobb	295
3	Honus Wagner	252
4	Jake Beckley	243
5	Tris Speaker	222
6	Fred Clarke	220
7	Joe Kelley	194
8	Eddie Collins	186
9	Ed Delahanty	185
10	Jesse Burkett	182
11	Ed Konetchy	181
12	Tommy Leach	172
	Zack Wheat	172
14	Joe Jackson	168
15	Sherry Magee	166

1920-1941

1	Paul Waner	191
2	Sam Rice	184
3	Edd Roush	182
4	Rabbit Maranville	177
5	Goose Goslin	173
6	Rogers Hornsby	169
7	George Sisler	164
	Pie Traynor	164
9	Lou Gehrig	163
10	Heinie Manush	160
11	Max Carey	159
	Joe Judge	159
13	Kiki Cuyler	157
14	Earle Combs	154
15	2 players tied	151

1942-1960

1	Stan Musial	177
2	Enos Slaughter	148
3	Joe DiMaggio	131
4	Mickey Vernon	120
5	Nellie Fox	112
6	Wally Moses	110
7	Richie Ashburn	109
8	Bill Bruton	102
	Jeff Heath	102
10	Phil Cavarretta	99
11	Dixie Walker	96
12	Bob Elliott	94
13	Bobby Doerr	89
14	Duke Snider	85
15	2 players tied	83

1961-1976

1	Roberto Clemente	166
2	Lou Brock	141
3	Willie Mays	140
4	Willie Davis	138
5	Pete Rose	135
6	Vada Pinson	127
7	Rod Carew	112
8	Hank Aaron	98
9	Joe Morgan	96
10	Luis Aparicio	92
11	Ernie Banks	90
12	Johnny Callison	89
13	Billy Williams	88
14	Bert Campaneris	86
	Tony Taylor	86

1977-1994

1	Willie Wilson	147
2	George Brett	137
3	Robin Yount	126
4	Brett Butler	118
5	Garry Templeton	106
6	Tim Raines	105
7	Larry Bowa	99
8	Andre Dawson	95
	Paul Molitor	95
10	Jose Cruz	94
	Juan Samuel	94
12	Andy Van Slyke	89
13	Dave Winfield	88
14	Tony Fernandez	87
	Omar Moreno	87

Home Runs

1	Hank Aaron	755
2	Babe Ruth	714
3	Willie Mays	660
4	Frank Robinson	586
5	Harmon Killebrew	573
6	Reggie Jackson	563
7	Mike Schmidt	548
8	Mickey Mantle	536
9	Jimmie Foxx	534
10	Willie McCovey	521
	Ted Williams	521
12	Ernie Banks	512
	Eddie Mathews	512
14	Mel Ott	511
15	Lou Gehrig	493
16	Stan Musial	475
	Willie Stargell	475
18	Dave Winfield	463
19	Eddie Murray	458
20	Carl Yastrzemski	452
21	Dave Kingman	442
22	Andre Dawson	428
23	Billy Williams	426
24	Darrell Evans	414
25	Duke Snider	407
26	Al Kaline	399
27	Dale Murphy	398
28	Graig Nettles	390
29	Johnny Bench	389
30	Dwight Evans	385
31	Frank Howard	382
	Jim Rice	382
33	Orlando Cepeda	379
	Tony Perez	379
35	Norm Cash	377
36	Carlton Fisk	376
37	Rocky Colavito	374
38	Gil Hodges	370
39	Ralph Kiner	369
40	Joe DiMaggio	361
41	Johnny Mize	359
42	Yogi Berra	358
43	Lee May	354
44	Dick Allen	351
45	George Foster	348
46	Ron Santo	342
47	Jack Clark	340
48	Dave Parker	339
	Boog Powell	339
50	Don Baylor	338
51	Joe Adcock	336
52	Bobby Bonds	332
53	Hank Greenberg	331
54	Willie Horton	325
55	Gary Carter	324
56	Lance Parrish	320
57	Roy Sievers	318
58	George Brett	317
59	Ron Cey	316
60	Reggie Smith	314
61	Cal Ripken	310
62	Greg Luzinski	307
	Al Simmons	307
64	Fred Lynn	306
65	Joe Carter	302
66	Rogers Hornsby	301
67	Chuck Klein	300
68	Darryl Strawberry	294
69	Kent Hrbek	293
70	Rusty Staub	292
71	Jim Wynn	291
72	Del Ennis	288
	Bob Johnson	288
	Hank Sauer	288
75	Frank Thomas	286
76	Ken Boyer	282
77	Ted Kluszewski	279
78	Harold Baines	277
	Rudy York	277
80	Jose Canseco	276
81	Brian Downing	275
	Roger Maris	275
83	Steve Garvey	272
84	Tom Brunansky	271
	George Scott	271
86	Joe Morgan	268
	Brooks Robinson	268
	Gorman Thomas	268
89	George Hendrick	267
90	Vic Wertz	266
91	George Bell	265
92	Bobby Thomson	264
93	Fred McGriff	262
94	Barry Bonds	259
95	Gary Gaetti	257
96	Bob Allison	256
	Larry Parrish	256
	Vada Pinson	256
99	John Mayberry	255
100	3 players tied	253

Home Runs (by era)

1876-1892

1	Roger Connor	138
2	Sam Thompson	127
3	Harry Stovey	122
4	Dan Brouthers	106
5	Cap Anson	97
6	Fred Pfeffer	94
7	Jack Clements	77
8	Jerry Denny	74
9	Buck Ewing	71
10	Hardy Richardson	70
11	King Kelly	69
	John Reilly	69
13	George Wood	68
14	Oyster Burns	65
	Bug Holliday	65

1893-1919

1	Zack Wheat	132
2	Gavvy Cravath	119
3	Jimmy Ryan	118
	Tilly Walker	118
5	Ty Cobb	117
	Tris Speaker	117
7	Hugh Duffy	106
	Mike Tiernan	106
9	Ed Delahanty	101
	Honus Wagner	101
11	Sam Crawford	97
12	Frank Baker	96
13	Frank Schulte	92
14	Herman Long	91
15	Jake Beckley	86

1920-1941

1	Babe Ruth	714
2	Jimmie Foxx	534
3	Mel Ott	511
4	Lou Gehrig	493
5	Hank Greenberg	331
6	Al Simmons	307
7	Rogers Hornsby	301
8	Chuck Klein	300
9	Bob Johnson	288
10	Cy Williams	251
11	Goose Goslin	248
12	Hack Wilson	244
13	Wally Berger	242
14	Dolph Camilli	239
15	Earl Averill	238

1942-1960

1	Mickey Mantle	536
2	Ted Williams	521
3	Eddie Mathews	512
4	Stan Musial	475
5	Duke Snider	407
6	Gil Hodges	370
7	Ralph Kiner	369
8	Joe DiMaggio	361
9	Johnny Mize	359
10	Yogi Berra	358
11	Joe Adcock	336
12	Roy Sievers	318
13	Del Ennis	288
	Hank Sauer	288
15	Frank Thomas	286

1961-1976

1	Hank Aaron	755
2	Willie Mays	660
3	Frank Robinson	586
4	Harmon Killebrew	573
5	Willie McCovey	521
6	Ernie Banks	512
7	Willie Stargell	475
8	Carl Yastrzemski	452
9	Billy Williams	426
10	Al Kaline	399
11	Johnny Bench	389
12	Frank Howard	382
13	Orlando Cepeda	379
	Tony Perez	379
15	Norm Cash	377

1977-1994

1	Reggie Jackson	563
2	Mike Schmidt	548
3	Dave Winfield	463
4	Eddie Murray	458
5	Dave Kingman	442
6	Andre Dawson	428
7	Darrell Evans	414
8	Dale Murphy	398
9	Graig Nettles	390
10	Dwight Evans	385
11	Jim Rice	382
12	Carlton Fisk	376
13	George Foster	348
14	Jack Clark	340
15	Dave Parker	339

Home Run Percentage

1	Babe Ruth	8.50
2	Ralph Kiner	7.09
3	Harmon Killebrew	7.03
4	Ted Williams	6.76
5	Dave Kingman	6.62
6	Mickey Mantle	6.62
7	Fred McGriff	6.58
8	Jimmie Foxx	6.57
9	Mike Schmidt	6.56
10	Jose Canseco	6.40
11	Hank Greenberg	6.37
12	Willie McCovey	6.36
13	Darryl Strawberry	6.18
14	Lou Gehrig	6.16
15	Hank Aaron	6.11
16	Willie Mays	6.07
17	Hank Sauer	6.01
18	Eddie Mathews	6.00
19	Willie Stargell	5.99
20	Rob Deer	5.90
21	Frank Howard	5.89
22	Kevin Mitchell	5.88
23	Frank Robinson	5.86
24	Bob Horner	5.77
25	Roy Campanella	5.76
26	Rocky Colavito	5.75
27	Barry Bonds	5.74
28	Gus Zernial	5.74
29	Gorman Thomas	5.73
30	Reggie Jackson	5.71
31	Dick Stuart	5.70
32	Duke Snider	5.68
33	Norm Cash	5.62
34	Johnny Mize	5.57
35	Eric Davis	5.55
36	Dick Allen	5.54
37	Ernie Banks	5.43
38	Mel Ott	5.40
39	Roger Maris	5.39
40	Danny Tartabull	5.34
41	Joe DiMaggio	5.29
42	Gil Hodges	5.26
43	Wally Post	5.24
44	Al Rosen	5.15
45	Hack Wilson	5.13
46	Glenn Davis	5.11
47	Bob Allison	5.09
48	Joe Adcock	5.09
49	Johnny Bench	5.08
50	Boog Powell	5.07
51	Jesse Barfield	5.06
52	Nate Colbert	5.06
53	Dale Murphy	5.00
54	Charlie Keller	4.99
55	Mickey Tettleton	4.98
56	Roy Sievers	4.98
57	Cliff Johnson	4.97
58	Don Mincher	4.97
59	Jack Clark	4.97
60	George Foster	4.96
61	Pete Incaviglia	4.88
62	Tony Armas	4.86
63	Joe Carter	4.84
64	Andy Thornton	4.78
65	Orlando Cepeda	4.78
66	Leon Wagner	4.77
67	Jim Lemon	4.76
68	Yogi Berra	4.74
69	Don Demeter	4.73
70	Kent Hrbek	4.73
71	Larry Doby	4.73
72	Greg Luzinski	4.72
73	Bobby Bonds	4.71
74	Ted Kluszewski	4.71
75	Rudy York	4.70
76	Wally Berger	4.69
77	John Mayberry	4.68
78	Lee May	4.65
79	Lance Parrish	4.65
80	Jim Rice	4.64
81	Howard Johnson	4.63
82	Chuck Klein	4.63
83	Darrell Evans	4.61
84	Gene Tenace	4.58
85	Charlie Maxwell	4.56
86	Billy Williams	4.56
87	Frank Thomas	4.55
88	Eddie Murray	4.50
89	Jim Ray Hart	4.49
90	Gary Roenicke	4.47
91	Dolph Camilli	4.46
92	Reggie Smith	4.46
93	Woodie Held	4.45
94	Willie Horton	4.45
95	Oscar Gamble	4.44
96	Andre Dawson	4.44
97	Joe Gordon	4.43
98	Fred Lynn	4.42
99	Hal Trosky	4.42
100	Kirk Gibson	4.42

Home Run Pct. (by era)

1876-1892

1	Sam Thompson	2.12
2	Harry Stovey	1.99
3	Jack Clements	1.80
4	Roger Connor	1.77
5	Dan Brouthers	1.58
6	Jerry Denny	1.50
7	John Reilly	1.47
8	Denny Lyons	1.44
9	Charlie Bennett	1.44
10	Fred Pfeffer	1.43
11	Ned Williamson	1.41
12	Oyster Burns	1.40
13	Buck Ewing	1.32
14	George Wood	1.27
15	Hardy Richardson	1.24

1893-1919

1	Gavvy Cravath	3.01
2	Tilly Walker	2.33
3	Buck Freeman	1.95
4	Mike Tiernan	1.79
5	Fred Luderus	1.73
6	Frank Baker	1.60
7	Hugh Duffy	1.51
8	Charlie Hickman	1.48
9	Zack Wheat	1.45
10	Jimmy Ryan	1.45
11	Frank Schulte	1.41
12	Casey Stengel	1.40
13	Ed Delahanty	1.35
14	Mike Donlin	1.32
15	Chief Wilson	1.28

1920-1941

1	Babe Ruth	8.50
2	Jimmie Foxx	6.57
3	Hank Greenberg	6.37
4	Lou Gehrig	6.16
5	Mel Ott	5.40
6	Hack Wilson	5.13
7	Wally Berger	4.69
8	Chuck Klein	4.63
9	Dolph Camilli	4.46
10	Hal Trosky	4.42
11	Bob Johnson	4.16
12	Ken Williams	4.03
13	Earl Averill	3.75
14	Cy Williams	3.70
15	Rogers Hornsby	3.68

1942-1960

1	Ralph Kiner	7.09
2	Ted Williams	6.76
3	Mickey Mantle	6.62
4	Hank Sauer	6.01
5	Eddie Mathews	6.00
6	Roy Campanella	5.76
7	Gus Zernial	5.74
8	Duke Snider	5.68
9	Johnny Mize	5.57
10	Joe DiMaggio	5.29
11	Gil Hodges	5.26
12	Wally Post	5.24
13	Al Rosen	5.15
14	Joe Adcock	5.09
15	Charlie Keller	4.99

1961-1976

1	Harmon Killebrew	7.03
2	Willie McCovey	6.36
3	Hank Aaron	6.11
4	Willie Mays	6.07
5	Willie Stargell	5.99
6	Frank Howard	5.89
7	Frank Robinson	5.86
8	Rocky Colavito	5.75
9	Dick Stuart	5.70
10	Norm Cash	5.62
11	Dick Allen	5.54
12	Ernie Banks	5.43
13	Roger Maris	5.39
14	Bob Allison	5.09
15	Johnny Bench	5.08

1977-1994

1	Dave Kingman	6.62
2	Fred McGriff	6.58
3	Mike Schmidt	6.56
4	Jose Canseco	6.40
5	Darryl Strawberry	6.18
6	Rob Deer	5.90
7	Kevin Mitchell	5.88
8	Bob Horner	5.77
9	Barry Bonds	5.74
10	Gorman Thomas	5.73
11	Reggie Jackson	5.71
12	Eric Davis	5.55
13	Danny Tartabull	5.34
14	Glenn Davis	5.11
15	Jesse Barfield	5.06

Total Bases

1	Hank Aaron	6856
2	Stan Musial	6134
3	Willie Mays	6066
4	Ty Cobb	5854
5	Babe Ruth	5793
6	Pete Rose	5752
7	Carl Yastrzemski	5539
8	Frank Robinson	5373
9	Dave Winfield	5188
10	Tris Speaker	5101
11	Lou Gehrig	5060
12	George Brett	5044
13	Mel Ott	5041
14	Jimmie Foxx	4956
15	Ted Williams	4884
16	Eddie Murray	4883
17	Honus Wagner	4862
18	Al Kaline	4852
19	Reggie Jackson	4834
20	Robin Yount	4730
21	Rogers Hornsby	4712
22	Ernie Banks	4706
23	Al Simmons	4685
24	Andre Dawson	4665
25	Billy Williams	4599
26	Tony Perez	4532
27	Mickey Mantle	4511
28	Roberto Clemente	4492
29	Paul Waner	4478
30	Nap Lajoie	4474
31	Dave Parker	4405
32	Mike Schmidt	4404
33	Eddie Mathews	4349
34	Sam Crawford	4328
35	Goose Goslin	4325
36	Brooks Robinson	4270
37	Vada Pinson	4264
38	Eddie Collins	4263
39	Charlie Gehringer	4257
40	Lou Brock	4238
41	Dwight Evans	4230
42	Willie McCovey	4219
43	Willie Stargell	4190
44	Rusty Staub	4185
45	Jake Beckley	4147
46	Harmon Killebrew	4143
47	Jim Rice	4129
48	Zack Wheat	4100
49	Al Oliver	4083
50	Cap Anson	4062
51	Harry Heilmann	4053
52	Carlton Fisk	3999
53	Rod Carew	3998
54	Joe Morgan	3962
55	Orlando Cepeda	3959
56	Sam Rice	3955
57	Joe DiMaggio	3948
58	Steve Garvey	3941
59	Frankie Frisch	3937
60	Paul Molitor	3897
61	George Sisler	3871
62	Darrell Evans	3866
63	Duke Snider	3865
64	Joe Medwick	3852
65	Bill Buckner	3833
66	Ted Simmons	3793
67	Ed Delahanty	3792
68	Roger Connor	3788
69	Graig Nettles	3779
	Ron Santo	3779
71	Willie Davis	3778
72	Jesse Burkett	3759
73	Mickey Vernon	3741
74	Jim Bottomley	3737
75	Dale Murphy	3733
76	Fred Clarke	3674
77	Heinie Manush	3665
78	George Davis	3656
79	Buddy Bell	3654
80	Cal Ripken	3651
81	Johnny Bench	3644
82	Yogi Berra	3643
83	Johnny Mize	3621
	Jimmy Ryan	3621
85	Max Carey	3612
86	Enos Slaughter	3599
87	Don Baylor	3571
88	Willie Keeler	3562
89	Joe Torre	3560
90	Joe Cronin	3546
91	Luke Appling	3528
92	Chuck Klein	3522
	Lou Whitaker	3522
94	Luis Aparicio	3504
95	Bob Johnson	3501
96	Gary Carter	3497
97	Lee May	3495
98	Dan Brouthers	3484
99	Lave Cross	3467
100	Harold Baines	3449

Runs Batted In

1	Hank Aaron	2297
2	Babe Ruth	2213
3	Lou Gehrig	1995
4	Stan Musial	1951
5	Ty Cobb	1937
6	Jimmie Foxx	1922
7	Willie Mays	1903
8	Cap Anson	1879
9	Mel Ott	1860
10	Carl Yastrzemski	1844
11	Ted Williams	1839
12	Dave Winfield	1829
13	Al Simmons	1827
14	Frank Robinson	1812
15	Eddie Murray	1738
16	Honus Wagner	1732
17	Reggie Jackson	1702
18	Tony Perez	1652
19	Ernie Banks	1636
20	Goose Goslin	1609
21	Nap Lajoie	1599
22	George Brett	1595
	Mike Schmidt	1595
24	Rogers Hornsby	1584
	Harmon Killebrew	1584
26	Al Kaline	1583
27	Jake Beckley	1575
28	Willie McCovey	1555
29	Andre Dawson	1540
	Willie Stargell	1540
31	Harry Heilmann	1539
32	Joe DiMaggio	1537
33	Tris Speaker	1529
34	Sam Crawford	1525
35	Mickey Mantle	1509
36	Dave Parker	1493
37	Billy Williams	1475
38	Rusty Staub	1466
39	Ed Delahanty	1464
40	Eddie Mathews	1453
41	Jim Rice	1451
42	George Davis	1437
43	Yogi Berra	1430
44	Charlie Gehringer	1427
45	Joe Cronin	1424
46	Jim Bottomley	1422
47	Robin Yount	1406
48	Ted Simmons	1389
49	Dwight Evans	1384
50	Joe Medwick	1383
51	Johnny Bench	1376
52	Orlando Cepeda	1365
53	Brooks Robinson	1357
54	Darrell Evans	1354
55	Johnny Mize	1337
56	Duke Snider	1333
57	Ron Santo	1331
58	Carlton Fisk	1330
59	Al Oliver	1326
60	Roger Connor	1322
61	Graig Nettles	1314
	Pete Rose	1314
63	Mickey Vernon	1311
64	Paul Waner	1309
65	Steve Garvey	1308
66	Roberto Clemente	1305
67	Enos Slaughter	1304
68	Hugh Duffy	1302
69	Eddie Collins	1300
70	Sam Thompson	1299
71	Dan Brouthers	1296
72	Del Ennis	1284
73	Bob Johnson	1283
74	Don Baylor	1276
	Hank Greenberg	1276
76	Gil Hodges	1274
77	Pie Traynor	1273
78	Dale Murphy	1266
79	Zack Wheat	1248
80	Bobby Doerr	1247
81	Frankie Frisch	1244
	Lee May	1244
83	George Foster	1239
84	Bill Dahlen	1233
85	Gary Carter	1225
86	Dave Kingman	1210
87	Bill Dickey	1209
88	Bill Buckner	1208
89	Chuck Klein	1201
90	Harold Baines	1198
91	Bob Elliott	1195
92	Joe Kelley	1194
93	Tony Lazzeri	1191
94	Boog Powell	1187
95	Joe Torre	1185
96	Heinie Manush	1183
97	Jack Clark	1180
98	Gabby Hartnett	1179
	Cal Ripken	1179
100	Vic Wertz	1178

Runs Batted In (by era)

1876-1892

1	Cap Anson	1879
2	Roger Connor	1322
3	Sam Thompson	1299
4	Dan Brouthers	1296
5	Fred Pfeffer	1019
6	Jim O'Rourke	1010
7	King Kelly	950
8	Buck Ewing	883
9	John Ward	867
10	Hardy Richardson	822
11	Deacon White	756
12	Paul Hines	751
13	Tom Burns	683
14	Sam Wise	672
15	2 players tied	667

1893-1919

1	Ty Cobb	1937
2	Honus Wagner	1732
3	Nap Lajoie	1599
4	Jake Beckley	1575
5	Tris Speaker	1529
6	Sam Crawford	1525
7	Ed Delahanty	1464
8	George Davis	1437
9	Hugh Duffy	1302
10	Eddie Collins	1300
11	Zack Wheat	1248
12	Bill Dahlen	1233
13	Joe Kelley	1194
14	Sherry Magee	1176
15	Bobby Veach	1166

1920-1941

1	Babe Ruth	2213
2	Lou Gehrig	1995
3	Jimmie Foxx	1922
4	Mel Ott	1860
5	Al Simmons	1827
6	Goose Goslin	1609
7	Rogers Hornsby	1584
8	Harry Heilmann	1539
9	Charlie Gehringer	1427
10	Joe Cronin	1424
11	Jim Bottomley	1422
12	Joe Medwick	1383
13	Paul Waner	1309
14	Bob Johnson	1283
15	Hank Greenberg	1276

1942-1960

1	Stan Musial	1951
2	Ted Williams	1839
3	Joe DiMaggio	1537
4	Mickey Mantle	1509
5	Eddie Mathews	1453
6	Yogi Berra	1430
7	Johnny Mize	1337
8	Duke Snider	1333
9	Mickey Vernon	1311
10	Enos Slaughter	1304
11	Del Ennis	1284
12	Gil Hodges	1274
13	Bobby Doerr	1247
14	Bob Elliott	1195
15	Vic Wertz	1178

1961-1976

1	Hank Aaron	2297
2	Willie Mays	1903
3	Carl Yastrzemski	1844
4	Frank Robinson	1812
5	Tony Perez	1652
6	Ernie Banks	1636
7	Harmon Killebrew	1584
8	Al Kaline	1583
9	Willie McCovey	1555
10	Willie Stargell	1540
11	Billy Williams	1475
12	Rusty Staub	1466
13	Johnny Bench	1376
14	Orlando Cepeda	1365
15	Brooks Robinson	1357

1977-1994

1	Dave Winfield	1829
2	Eddie Murray	1738
3	Reggie Jackson	1702
4	George Brett	1595
	Mike Schmidt	1595
6	Andre Dawson	1540
7	Dave Parker	1493
8	Jim Rice	1451
9	Robin Yount	1406
10	Ted Simmons	1389
11	Dwight Evans	1384
12	Darrell Evans	1354
13	Carlton Fisk	1330
14	Al Oliver	1326
15	Graig Nettles	1314

Runs Batted In per Game

1	Sam Thompson	.92
2	Lou Gehrig	.92
3	Hank Greenberg	.92
4	Joe DiMaggio	.89
5	Babe Ruth	.88
6	Jimmie Foxx	.83
7	Cap Anson	.83
8	Al Simmons	.82
9	Ted Williams	.80
10	Ed Delahanty	.80
11	Hack Wilson	.79
12	Dan Brouthers	.77
13	Jose Canseco	.76
14	Bob Meusel	.76
15	Hal Trosky	.75
16	Hugh Duffy	.75
17	Rudy York	.72
18	Harry Heilmann	.72
19	Jim Bottomley	.71
20	Johnny Mize	.71
21	Roy Campanella	.70
22	Goose Goslin	.70
23	Rogers Hornsby	.70
24	Earl Averill	.70
25	Joe Medwick	.70
26	Hank Aaron	.70
27	Jim Rice	.69
28	Ralph Kiner	.69
29	Bob Johnson	.69
30	Al Rosen	.69
31	Chuck Klein	.69
32	Tony Lazzeri	.68
33	Vern Stephens	.68
34	Joe Carter	.68
35	Mel Ott	.68
36	Bill Dickey	.68
37	Del Ennis	.67
38	Yogi Berra	.67
39	Bob Horner	.67
40	Buck Ewing	.67
41	Joe Cronin	.67
42	Bobby Doerr	.67
43	Dick Stuart	.67
44	Wally Berger	.67
45	Danny Tartabull	.66
46	Mike Schmidt	.66
47	Roger Connor	.66
48	Jake Beckley	.66
49	Pie Traynor	.66
50	Darryl Strawberry	.66
51	Hughie Jennings	.65
52	Ken Williams	.65
53	King Kelly	.65
54	Willie Stargell	.65
55	Ruben Sierra	.65
56	Harmon Killebrew	.65
57	Charlie Keller	.65
58	Chick Hafey	.65
59	Ernie Banks	.65
60	Glenn Wright	.65
61	Jackie Jensen	.65
62	Frank Robinson	.65
63	Nap Lajoie	.64
64	Stan Musial	.64
65	Joe Kelley	.64
66	Orlando Cepeda	.64
67	Babe Herman	.64
68	Eddie Murray	.64
69	Jeff Heath	.64
70	Bobby Veach	.64
71	Dick Allen	.64
72	Ty Cobb	.64
73	Johnny Bench	.64
74	Dolph Camilli	.64
75	Willie Mays	.64
76	Irish Meusel	.64
77	Don Mattingly	.63
78	Kevin Mitchell	.63
79	Buck Freeman	.63
80	Larry Doby	.63
81	Vic Wertz	.63
82	George Bell	.63
83	Patsy Tebeau	.63
84	Rocky Colavito	.63
85	George Kelly	.63
86	Gus Zernial	.63
87	Mickey Mantle	.63
88	George Foster	.63
89	Frank Baker	.63
90	Bill Terry	.63
91	Steve Brodie	.63
92	Hank Sauer	.63
93	Dave Winfield	.62
94	Dave Kingman	.62
95	Joe Gordon	.62
96	Duke Snider	.62
97	Kent Hrbek	.62
98	Will Clark	.62
99	Honus Wagner	.62
100	Frank McCormick	.62

Walks

#	Player	Walks
1	Babe Ruth	2056
2	Ted Williams	2019
3	Joe Morgan	1865
4	Carl Yastrzemski	1845
5	Mickey Mantle	1733
6	Mel Ott	1708
7	Eddie Yost	1614
8	Darrell Evans	1605
9	Stan Musial	1599
10	Pete Rose	1566
11	Harmon Killebrew	1559
12	Lou Gehrig	1508
13	Mike Schmidt	1507
14	Eddie Collins	1499
15	Rickey Henderson	1478
16	Willie Mays	1464
17	Jimmie Foxx	1452
18	Eddie Mathews	1444
19	Frank Robinson	1420
20	Hank Aaron	1402
21	Dwight Evans	1391
22	Tris Speaker	1381
23	Reggie Jackson	1375
24	Willie McCovey	1345
25	Luke Appling	1302
26	Al Kaline	1277
27	Ken Singleton	1263
28	Jack Clark	1262
29	Rusty Staub	1255
30	Ty Cobb	1249
31	Willie Randolph	1243
32	Jim Wynn	1224
33	Eddie Murray	1218
34	Pee Wee Reese	1210
35	Dave Winfield	1202
36	Richie Ashburn	1198
37	Brian Downing	1197
38	Billy Hamilton	1187
39	Charlie Gehringer	1186
40	Lou Whitaker	1166
41	Donie Bush	1158
42	Max Bishop	1153
	Toby Harrah	1153
44	Wade Boggs	1139
45	Harry Hooper	1136
46	Jimmy Sheckard	1135
47	Ron Santo	1108
48	George Brett	1096
49	Lu Blue	1092
	Stan Hack	1092
51	Paul Waner	1091
52	Graig Nettles	1088
53	Bobby Grich	1087
54	Bob Johnson	1075
55	Harland Clift	1070
	Keith Hernandez	1070
57	Bill Dahlen	1064
	Tim Raines	1064
59	Joe Cronin	1059
60	Ron Fairly	1052
61	Billy Williams	1045
62	Norm Cash	1043
	Eddie Joost	1043
64	Roy Thomas	1042
65	Max Carey	1040
66	Rogers Hornsby	1038
67	Jim Gilliam	1036
68	Sal Bando	1031
69	Ozzie Smith	1030
70	Jesse Burkett	1029
71	Rod Carew	1018
	Enos Slaughter	1018
73	Ron Cey	1012
74	Brett Butler	1011
	Ralph Kiner	1011
76	Dummy Hoy	1004
77	Miller Huggins	1003
78	Roger Connor	1002
79	Boog Powell	1001
80	Eddie Stanky	996
81	Cupid Childs	991
82	Dale Murphy	986
83	Gene Tenace	984
84	Bid McPhee	981
85	Joe Kuhel	980
	Earl Torgeson	980
87	Augie Galan	979
88	Duke Snider	971
89	Bob Elliott	967
90	Robin Yount	966
91	Mike Hargrove	965
	Joe Judge	965
	Buddy Myer	965
94	Honus Wagner	963
95	Jimmy Dykes	958
96	Mickey Vernon	955
97	Cap Anson	952
98	Rocky Colavito	951
99	Goose Goslin	949
100	Dolph Camilli	947

Walk Percentage

#	Player	Walk %
1	Ted Williams	20.76
2	Max Bishop	20.42
3	Babe Ruth	19.67
4	Eddie Stanky	18.80
5	Ferris Fain	18.70
6	Gene Tenace	18.31
7	Roy Cullenbine	18.03
8	Eddie Yost	18.01
9	Mickey Mantle	17.62
10	John McGraw	17.56
11	Charlie Keller	17.14
12	Joe Morgan	16.74
13	Mickey Tettleton	16.61
14	Earl Torgeson	16.47
15	Bernie Carbo	16.45
16	Roy Thomas	16.44
17	Ralph Kiner	16.26
18	Rickey Henderson	16.18
19	Harmon Killebrew	16.06
20	Billy Hamilton	15.92
21	Lou Gehrig	15.86
22	Elmer Valo	15.78
23	Joe Ferguson	15.77
24	Harland Clift	15.74
25	Eddie Joost	15.69
26	Lu Blue	15.61
27	Jack Clark	15.56
28	Jim Wynn	15.54
29	Mel Ott	15.30
30	Miller Huggins	15.29
31	Mike Schmidt	15.29
32	Barry Bonds	15.23
33	Darrell Evans	15.17
34	Jimmie Foxx	15.15
35	Joe Cunningham	15.12
36	Dolph Camilli	15.03
37	Cupid Childs	14.99
38	Ken Singleton	14.94
39	Elbie Fletcher	14.85
40	Merv Rettenmund	14.83
41	Mike Hargrove	14.78
42	Topsy Hartsel	14.72
43	Dwayne Murphy	14.66
44	Wayne Garrett	14.59
45	Fred McGriff	14.56
46	Jason Thompson	14.52
47	Eddie Mathews	14.47
48	John Kruk	14.29
49	Mickey Cochrane	14.22
50	Andy Thornton	14.20
51	Augie Galan	14.16
52	Gene Woodling	14.15
53	Willie McCovey	14.10
54	Hank Greenberg	14.09
55	Darrell Porter	14.04
56	Larry Doby	14.01
57	John Mayberry	13.92
58	Alvin Davis	13.91
59	Tony Phillips	13.90
60	John Briggs	13.87
61	Billy North	13.85
62	Donie Bush	13.84
63	Wally Schang	13.79
64	Wade Boggs	13.76
65	Roger Bresnahan	13.74
66	Paul Radford	13.71
67	Steve Braun	13.69
68	Norm Siebern	13.64
69	Bob Allison	13.64
70	Bobby Grich	13.63
71	Al Rosen	13.61
72	Toby Harrah	13.48
73	Lee Mazzilli	13.47
74	Norm Cash	13.46
75	Mike Jorgensen	13.46
76	Bob Johnson	13.45
77	Willie Randolph	13.42
78	Tommy Henrich	13.40
79	Dwight Evans	13.39
80	Danny Tartabull	13.38
81	Rick Ferrell	13.38
82	Wayne Gross	13.36
83	Carl Yastrzemski	13.34
84	Grady Hatton	13.31
85	Lyn Lary	13.28
86	Brian Downing	13.23
87	Ed Bailey	13.21
88	Jackie Robinson	13.17
89	Jack Graney	13.14
90	Eddie Collins	13.09
91	Rick Monday	13.09
92	Don Mincher	13.08
93	Pee Wee Reese	13.06
94	Jeff Burroughs	13.05
95	Stan Hack	13.05
96	Gary Roenicke	13.04
97	Boog Powell	13.03
98	Jimmy Sheckard	12.99
99	Charlie Maxwell	12.98
100	Darryl Strawberry	12.97

Strikeouts

#	Player	Strikeouts
1	Reggie Jackson	2597
2	Willie Stargell	1936
3	Mike Schmidt	1883
4	Tony Perez	1867
5	Dave Kingman	1816
6	Bobby Bonds	1757
7	Dale Murphy	1748
8	Lou Brock	1730
9	Mickey Mantle	1710
10	Harmon Killebrew	1699
11	Dwight Evans	1697
12	Dave Winfield	1660
13	Lee May	1570
14	Dick Allen	1556
15	Willie McCovey	1550
16	Dave Parker	1537
17	Frank Robinson	1532
18	Willie Mays	1526
19	Rick Monday	1513
20	Greg Luzinski	1495
21	Eddie Mathews	1487
22	Lance Parrish	1475
23	Frank Howard	1460
24	Andre Dawson	1451
25	Jack Clark	1441
26	Jim Wynn	1427
27	Jim Rice	1423
28	George Foster	1419
29	George Scott	1418
30	Darrell Evans	1410
31	Carl Yastrzemski	1393
32	Carlton Fisk	1386
33	Hank Aaron	1383
34	Rob Deer	1379
35	Larry Parrish	1359
36	Robin Yount	1350
37	Ron Santo	1343
38	Gorman Thomas	1339
39	Eddie Murray	1338
40	Babe Ruth	1330
41	Deron Johnson	1318
42	Willie Horton	1313
43	Jimmie Foxx	1311
44	Chili Davis	1306
45	Juan Samuel	1287
46	Johnny Bench	1278
	Bobby Grich	1278
48	Claudell Washington	1266
49	Ken Singleton	1246
50	Duke Snider	1237
51	Ernie Banks	1236
52	Ron Cey	1235
53	Jesse Barfield	1234
54	Roberto Clemente	1230
55	Boog Powell	1226
56	Kirk Gibson	1224
57	Gary Gaetti	1210
58	Graig Nettles	1209
59	Tony Armas	1201
60	Vada Pinson	1196
61	Tom Brunansky	1187
62	Dave Concepcion	1186
63	Jose Canseco	1174
64	Orlando Cepeda	1169
65	Darryl Strawberry	1160
66	Tim Wallach	1159
67	Danny Tartabull	1148
68	Willie Wilson	1144
69	Pete Rose	1143
70	Bert Campaneris	1142
71	Donn Clendenon	1140
72	Gil Hodges	1137
73	Jeff Burroughs	1135
	Leo Cardenas	1135
	Lloyd Moseby	1135
76	Pete Incaviglia	1132
77	Brian Downing	1127
78	Bob Bailey	1126
79	Gary Matthews	1125
80	Harold Baines	1118
81	Fred Lynn	1116
82	Dave Henderson	1105
83	Jim Fregosi	1097
84	Joe Torre	1094
85	Garry Templeton	1092
86	Norm Cash	1091
87	Tony Taylor	1083
88	Tommy Harper	1080
89	Don Baylor	1069
90	Johnny Callison	1064
91	Joe Adcock	1059
92	Lou Whitaker	1058
93	Doug Rader	1055
94	Ryne Sandberg	1050
95	Mickey Tettleton	1048
96	Billy Williams	1046
97	Rickey Henderson	1035
	Frank White	1035
99	Bob Allison	1033
100	Jose Cruz	1031

At Bats per Strikeout

#	Player	AB/SO
1	Joe Sewell	62.6
2	Lloyd Waner	44.9
3	Nellie Fox	42.7
4	Tommy Holmes	40.9
5	Andy High	33.8
6	Sam Rice	33.7
7	Frankie Frisch	33.5
8	Dale Mitchell	33.5
9	Johnny Cooney	31.5
10	Frank McCormick	30.3
11	Don Mueller	29.9
12	Billy Southworth	29.5
13	Rip Radcliff	28.9
14	Edd Roush	28.3
15	Pie Traynor	27.2
16	Doc Cramer	26.5
17	Carson Bigbee	26.0
18	Hank Severeid	25.5
19	George Sisler	25.3
20	Paul Waner	25.2
21	Sparky Adams	24.9
22	Lou Finney	24.9
23	Deacon White	24.8
24	Jack Rowe	24.8
25	Irish Meusel	24.6
26	Ezra Sutton	24.6
27	Red Schoendienst	24.5
28	Vic Power	24.5
29	Arky Vaughan	24.0
30	Felix Millan	23.9
31	Mickey Cochrane	23.8
32	Charlie Gehringer	23.8
33	John Ward	23.5
34	George Kell	23.4
35	George Cutshaw	23.2
36	Jack Tobin	23.1
37	Taffy Wright	23.1
38	Hughie Critz	23.1
39	Mark Koenig	22.5
40	Ernie Lombardi	22.3
41	Heinie Manush	22.2
42	Bobby Richardson	22.2
43	Jo-Jo Moore	22.0
44	Earl Sheely	21.8
45	Bill Dickey	21.8
46	Johnny Pesky	21.8
47	Rick Ferrell	21.8
48	Glenn Beckert	21.4
49	Dick Siebert	21.2
50	Eddie Waitkus	20.9
51	Max Flack	20.8
52	Bill Buckner	20.7
53	Dixie Walker	20.7
54	Everett Scott	20.7
55	Earle Combs	20.7
56	Paul Hines	20.6
57	Freddy Lindstrom	20.3
58	Mickey Owen	20.2
59	Joe Vosmik	20.1
60	Tony Gwynn	20.1
61	Lou Boudreau	19.5
62	Milt Stock	19.5
63	Willard Marshall	19.3
64	Debs Garms	19.3
65	Charlie Grimm	19.3
66	Harry Rice	19.3
67	Skeeter Newsome	19.2
68	Curt Walker	19.1
69	Peanuts Lowrey	19.1
70	Charlie Jamieson	19.0
71	Muddy Ruel	19.0
72	Tommy Griffith	18.9
73	Tommy Thevenow	18.8
74	Joe Stripp	18.6
75	Joe DiMaggio	18.5
76	Bob Fothergill	18.5
77	Bing Miller	18.3
78	Riggs Stephenson	18.3
79	Yogi Berra	18.2
80	Billy Herman	18.0
81	Lee Magee	18.0
82	Dave Cash	18.0
83	Elmer Valo	17.7
84	Heinie Groh	17.6
85	Luke Sewell	17.5
86	Rich Dauer	17.5
87	Buddy Lewis	17.4
88	Billy Goodman	17.2
89	Jim Gilliam	17.1
90	Harvey Kuenn	17.1
91	Gus Mancuso	17.1
92	Jimmie Wilson	17.0
93	Billy Cox	17.0
94	Ken Williams	16.9
95	George Case	16.9
96	Cecil Travis	16.9
97	Luke Appling	16.8
98	Jackie Hayes	16.8
99	Jackie Robinson	16.8
100	Bibb Falk	16.7

Batting Average

1	Ty Cobb	.366
2	Rogers Hornsby	.358
3	Joe Jackson	.356
4	Ed Delahanty	.346
5	Tris Speaker	.345
6	Ted Williams	.344
7	Billy Hamilton	.344
8	Dan Brouthers	.342
9	Babe Ruth	.342
10	Harry Heilmann	.342
11	Pete Browning	.341
12	Willie Keeler	.341
13	Bill Terry	.341
14	George Sisler	.340
15	Lou Gehrig	.340
16	Jesse Burkett	.338
17	Nap Lajoie	.338
18	Riggs Stephenson	.336
19	Wade Boggs	.335
20	Al Simmons	.334
21	John McGraw	.334
22	Tony Gwynn	.333
23	Paul Waner	.333
24	Eddie Collins	.333
25	Mike Donlin	.333
26	Stan Musial	.331
27	Sam Thompson	.331
28	Heinie Manush	.330
29	Cap Anson	.329
30	Rod Carew	.328
31	Honus Wagner	.327
32	Tip O'Neill	.326
33	Bob Fothergill	.325
34	Jimmie Foxx	.325
35	Earle Combs	.325
36	Joe DiMaggio	.325
37	Babe Herman	.324
38	Hugh Duffy	.324
39	Joe Medwick	.324
40	Edd Roush	.323
41	Sam Rice	.322
42	Ross Youngs	.322
43	Kiki Cuyler	.321
44	Charlie Gehringer	.320
45	Chuck Klein	.320
46	Pie Traynor	.320
47	Mickey Cochrane	.320
48	Ken Williams	.319
49	Kirby Puckett	.318
50	Earl Averill	.318
51	Arky Vaughan	.318
52	Roberto Clemente	.317
53	Chick Hafey	.317
54	Joe Kelley	.317
55	Zack Wheat	.317
56	Roger Connor	.317
57	Lloyd Waner	.316
58	Frankie Frisch	.316
59	Goose Goslin	.316
60	George Van Haltren	.316
61	Bibb Falk	.314
62	Cecil Travis	.314
63	Hank Greenberg	.313
64	Jack Fournier	.313
65	Elmer Flick	.313
66	Bill Dickey	.313
67	Dale Mitchell	.312
68	Johnny Mize	.312
69	Joe Sewell	.312
70	Fred Clarke	.312
71	Barney McCosky	.312
72	Bing Miller	.312
73	Hughie Jennings	.311
74	Freddy Lindstrom	.311
75	Jackie Robinson	.311
76	Baby Doll Jacobson	.311
77	Taffy Wright	.311
78	Rip Radcliff	.311
79	Ginger Beaumont	.311
80	Mike Tiernan	.311
81	Denny Lyons	.310
82	Elmer Smith	.310
83	Luke Appling	.310
84	Irish Meusel	.310
85	Bobby Veach	.310
86	Jim O'Rourke	.310
87	Jim Bottomley	.310
88	John Stone	.310
89	Sam Crawford	.309
90	Bob Meusel	.309
91	Don Mattingly	.309
92	Jack Tobin	.309
93	Spud Davis	.308
94	Richie Ashburn	.308
95	King Kelly	.308
96	Jake Beckley	.308
97	Stuffy McInnis	.307
98	Paul Molitor	.307
99	Joe Vosmik	.307
100	Frank Baker	.307

Batting Average (by era)

1876-1892

1	Dan Brouthers	.342
2	Pete Browning	.341
3	Sam Thompson	.331
4	Cap Anson	.329
5	Tip O'Neill	.326
6	Roger Connor	.317
7	Denny Lyons	.310
8	Jim O'Rourke	.310
9	King Kelly	.308
10	Deacon White	.303
11	Henry Larkin	.303
12	Buck Ewing	.303
13	George Gore	.301
14	Paul Hines	.301
15	Oyster Burns	.300

1893-1919

1	Ty Cobb	.366
2	Joe Jackson	.356
3	Ed Delahanty	.346
4	Tris Speaker	.345
5	Billy Hamilton	.344
6	Willie Keeler	.341
7	Jesse Burkett	.338
8	Nap Lajoie	.338
9	John McGraw	.334
10	Eddie Collins	.333
11	Mike Donlin	.333
12	Honus Wagner	.327
13	Hugh Duffy	.324
14	Joe Kelley	.317
15	Zack Wheat	.317

1920-1941

1	Rogers Hornsby	.358
2	Babe Ruth	.342
3	Harry Heilmann	.342
4	Bill Terry	.341
5	George Sisler	.340
6	Lou Gehrig	.340
7	Riggs Stephenson	.336
8	Al Simmons	.334
9	Paul Waner	.333
10	Heinie Manush	.330
11	Bob Fothergill	.325
12	Jimmie Foxx	.325
13	Earle Combs	.325
14	Babe Herman	.324
15	Joe Medwick	.324

1942-1960

1	Ted Williams	.344
2	Stan Musial	.331
3	Joe DiMaggio	.325
4	Dale Mitchell	.312
5	Johnny Mize	.312
6	Barney McCosky	.312
7	Jackie Robinson	.311
8	Taffy Wright	.311
9	Richie Ashburn	.308
10	Johnny Pesky	.307
11	George Kell	.306
12	Dixie Walker	.306
13	Harvey Kuenn	.303
14	Tommy Holmes	.302
15	Enos Slaughter	.300

1961-1976

1	Rod Carew	.328
2	Roberto Clemente	.317
3	Matty Alou	.307
4	Ralph Garr	.306
5	Hank Aaron	.305
6	Tony Oliva	.304
7	Manny Mota	.304
8	Pete Rose	.303
9	Willie Mays	.302
10	Rico Carty	.299
11	Joe Torre	.297
12	Al Kaline	.297
13	Orlando Cepeda	.297
14	Manny Sanguillen	.296
15	Bob Watson	.295

1977-1994

1	Wade Boggs	.335
2	Tony Gwynn	.333
3	Kirby Puckett	.318
4	Don Mattingly	.309
5	Paul Molitor	.307
6	George Brett	.305
7	Bill Madlock	.305
8	Mike Greenwell	.304
9	Al Oliver	.303
10	Mark Grace	.303
11	Will Clark	.302
12	Julio Franco	.301
13	Pedro Guerrero	.300
14	John Kruk	.300
15	Bake McBride	.299

Batting Average (by position)

First Base

1	Dan Brouthers	.342
2	Bill Terry	.341
3	George Sisler	.340
4	Lou Gehrig	.340
5	Cap Anson	.329
6	Rod Carew	.328
7	Jimmie Foxx	.325
8	Roger Connor	.317
9	Hank Greenberg	.313
10	Jack Fournier	.313

Second Base

1	Rogers Hornsby	.358
2	Nap Lajoie	.338
3	Eddie Collins	.333
4	Charlie Gehringer	.320
5	Frankie Frisch	.316
6	Cupid Childs	.306
7	Billy Herman	.304
8	Buddy Myer	.303
9	Roberto Alomar	.298
10	Del Pratt	.292

Shortstop

1	Honus Wagner	.327
2	Arky Vaughan	.318
3	Joe Sewell	.312
4	Luke Appling	.310
5	Ed McKean	.302
6	Joe Cronin	.301
7	Barry Larkin	.296
8	Lou Boudreau	.295
9	George Davis	.295
10	Glenn Wright	.294

Third Base

1	Wade Boggs	.335
2	Pie Traynor	.320
3	Denny Lyons	.310
4	Frank Baker	.307
5	George Kell	.306
6	George Brett	.305
7	Bill Madlock	.305
8	Stan Hack	.301
9	Pinky Whitney	.295
10	Jimmy Collins	.294

Outfield

1	Ty Cobb	.366
2	Joe Jackson	.356
3	Ed Delahanty	.346
4	Tris Speaker	.345
5	Ted Williams	.344
6	Billy Hamilton	.344
7	Babe Ruth	.342
8	Harry Heilmann	.342
9	Willie Keeler	.341
10	Jesse Burkett	.338
11	Al Simmons	.334
12	Tony Gwynn	.333
13	Paul Waner	.333
14	Stan Musial	.331
15	Sam Thompson	.331
16	Heinie Manush	.330
17	Tip O'Neill	.326
18	Earle Combs	.325
19	Joe DiMaggio	.325
20	Babe Herman	.324

Catcher

1	Mickey Cochrane	.320
2	Bill Dickey	.313
3	Spud Davis	.308
4	Ernie Lombardi	.306
5	Gabby Hartnett	.297
6	Manny Sanguillen	.296
7	Smoky Burgess	.295
8	Thurman Munson	.292
9	Hank Severeid	.289
10	Jack Clements	.286

Relative Batting Average

1	Ty Cobb	134.7
2	Joe Jackson	133.1
3	Pete Browning	131.6
4	Ted Williams	128.1
5	Dan Brouthers	127.8
6	Wade Boggs	127.6
7	Nap Lajoie	127.3
8	Rod Carew	127.0
9	Tony Gwynn	127.0
10	Rogers Hornsby	126.2
11	Tris Speaker	125.4
12	Tip O'Neill	125.3
13	Willie Keeler	124.5
14	Stan Musial	123.9
15	Mike Donlin	123.6
16	Honus Wagner	123.1
17	Billy Hamilton	122.7
18	Ed Delahanty	122.7
19	Cap Anson	122.7
20	Jesse Burkett	121.7
21	Eddie Collins	121.6
22	Kirby Puckett	121.4
23	Sam Thompson	121.1
24	Roberto Clemente	120.7
25	Tony Oliva	120.4
26	Harry Heilmann	119.4
27	Babe Ruth	119.2
28	George Sisler	118.9
29	Sam Crawford	118.8
30	King Kelly	118.2
31	Jim O'Rourke	118.1
32	Matty Alou	117.9
33	Joe Medwick	117.8
34	Paul Waner	117.8
35	Don Mattingly	117.6
36	Elmer Flick	117.4
37	Roger Connor	117.4
38	Bill Terry	117.3
39	Lou Gehrig	117.2
40	Joe DiMaggio	117.1
41	Ginger Beaumont	117.0
42	Paul Molitor	116.8
43	Ralph Garr	116.7
44	Manny Mota	116.4
45	George Brett	116.3
46	Dale Mitchell	116.3
47	Henry Larkin	116.3
48	John McGraw	116.2
49	Deacon White	116.0
50	Hank Aaron	116.0
51	Mike Greenwell	115.9
52	Paul Hines	115.8
53	George Gore	115.7
54	Jackie Robinson	115.7
55	Mark Grace	115.7
56	Pete Rose	115.6
57	Al Simmons	115.4
58	Frank Baker	115.4
59	Al Kaline	115.4
60	Bill Madlock	115.2
61	Arky Vaughan	115.1
62	Will Clark	115.1
63	Al Oliver	115.1
64	Riggs Stephenson	115.0
65	Mickey Mantle	115.0
66	Johnny Mize	115.0
67	Zack Wheat	114.9
68	Hugh Duffy	114.8
69	George Kell	114.8
70	Barney McCosky	114.7
71	Richie Ashburn	114.6
72	Hardy Richardson	114.6
73	Julio Franco	114.6
74	Pedro Guerrero	114.5
75	Johnny Pesky	114.5
76	Harvey Kuenn	114.5
77	Rico Carty	114.4
78	Willie Mays	114.3
79	John Kruk	114.2
80	Fred Clarke	114.0
81	Heinie Manush	114.0
82	Cy Seymour	113.9
83	Roberto Alomar	113.9
84	Jimmie Foxx	113.8
85	Joe Torre	113.8
86	Edd Roush	113.8
87	Rafael Palmeiro	113.7
88	Denny Lyons	113.6
89	Cecil Cooper	113.5
90	Jim Rice	113.5
91	Frank Robinson	113.4
92	Tommy Davis	113.4
93	Taffy Wright	113.4
94	Willie McGee	113.3
95	Minnie Minoso	113.1
96	Jimmy Wolf	113.0
97	Tommy Holmes	113.0
98	Joe Kelley	112.9
99	Orlando Cepeda	112.9
100	Mickey Rivers	112.9

On Base Percentage

1	Ted Williams	.483
2	Babe Ruth	.474
3	John McGraw	.466
4	Billy Hamilton	.455
5	Lou Gehrig	.447
6	Rogers Hornsby	.434
7	Ty Cobb	.433
8	Wade Boggs	.428
	Jimmie Foxx	.428
	Tris Speaker	.428
11	Ferris Fain	.425
12	Eddie Collins	.424
13	Max Bishop	.423
	Dan Brouthers	.423
	Joe Jackson	.423
	Mickey Mantle	.423
17	Mickey Cochrane	.419
18	Stan Musial	.418
19	Cupid Childs	.416
20	Jesse Burkett	.415
21	Mel Ott	.414
22	Roy Thomas	.413
23	Ed Delahanty	.412
	Hank Greenberg	.412
25	Harry Heilmann	.410
	Charlie Keller	.410
	Jackie Robinson	.410
	Eddie Stanky	.410
29	Roy Cullenbine	.408
	Rickey Henderson	.408
31	Denny Lyons	.407
	Riggs Stephenson	.407
33	Joe Cunningham	.406
	Arky Vaughan	.406
35	Charlie Gehringer	.404
	Paul Waner	.404
37	Pete Browning	.403
38	Lu Blue	.402
	Joe Kelley	.402
40	Mike Hargrove	.400
	John Kruk	.400
42	Luke Appling	.399
	Elmer Valo	.399
	Ross Youngs	.399
45	Joe DiMaggio	.398
	Ralph Kiner	.398
	Elmer Smith	.398
48	Richie Ashburn	.397
	Barry Bonds	.397
	Earle Combs	.397
	Roger Connor	.397
	Johnny Mize	.397
53	Cap Anson	.395
	Earl Averill	.395
	Rod Carew	.395
	Joe Morgan	.395
	Hack Wilson	.395
	Eddie Yost	.395
59	Frank Chance	.394
	Stan Hack	.394
	Johnny Pesky	.394
62	Bob Johnson	.393
	Wally Schang	.393
	Bill Terry	.393
	Ken Williams	.393
66	Jack Fournier	.392
	George Grantham	.392
	Tip O'Neill	.392
	Frank Robinson	.392
	Mike Tiernan	.392
71	Fred McGriff	.391
	Minnie Minoso	.391
	Joe Sewell	.391
	Ken Singleton	.391
	Gene Tenace	.391
	Honus Wagner	.391
77	Harlond Clift	.390
	Joe Cronin	.390
	Augie Galan	.390
	Hughie Jennings	.390
81	Bernie Carbo	.389
	Elmer Flick	.389
	Tony Gwynn	.389
	Buddy Myer	.389
	Tim Raines	.389
86	Dolph Camilli	.388
	Mike Griffin	.388
	Keith Hernandez	.388
	Willie Keeler	.388
	Gene Woodling	.388
91	Larry Doby	.387
	Goose Goslin	.387
	Willie Mays	.387
	Earl Torgeson	.387
95	8 players tied	.386

Slugging Average

1	Babe Ruth	.690
2	Ted Williams	.634
3	Lou Gehrig	.632
4	Jimmie Foxx	.609
5	Hank Greenberg	.605
6	Joe DiMaggio	.579
7	Rogers Hornsby	.577
8	Johnny Mize	.562
9	Stan Musial	.559
10	Willie Mays	.557
11	Mickey Mantle	.557
12	Hank Aaron	.555
13	Ralph Kiner	.548
14	Hack Wilson	.545
15	Chuck Klein	.543
16	Fred McGriff	.541
17	Duke Snider	.540
18	Frank Robinson	.537
19	Barry Bonds	.537
20	Al Simmons	.535
21	Dick Allen	.534
22	Earl Averill	.534
23	Mel Ott	.533
24	Babe Herman	.532
25	Ken Williams	.530
26	Kevin Mitchell	.529
27	Willie Stargell	.529
28	Mike Schmidt	.527
29	Chick Hafey	.526
30	Hal Trosky	.522
31	Wally Berger	.522
32	Harry Heilmann	.520
33	Dan Brouthers	.519
34	Charlie Keller	.518
35	Joe Jackson	.517
36	Willie McCovey	.515
37	Ty Cobb	.512
38	Jose Canseco	.512
39	Eddie Mathews	.509
40	Jeff Heath	.509
41	Harmon Killebrew	.509
42	Bob Johnson	.506
43	Bill Terry	.506
44	Darryl Strawberry	.506
45	Danny Tartabull	.505
46	Ed Delahanty	.505
47	Sam Thompson	.505
48	Joe Medwick	.505
49	Jim Rice	.502
50	Tris Speaker	.500
51	Jim Bottomley	.500
52	Goose Goslin	.500
53	Roy Campanella	.500
54	Ernie Banks	.500
55	Orlando Cepeda	.499
56	Bob Horner	.499
57	Will Clark	.499
58	Frank Howard	.499
59	Ted Kluszewski	.498
60	Bob Meusel	.497
61	Hank Sauer	.496
62	Al Rosen	.495
63	Billy Williams	.492
64	Ripper Collins	.492
65	Dolph Camilli	.492
66	Tommy Henrich	.491
67	Larry Doby	.490
68	Reggie Jackson	.490
69	Dick Stuart	.489
70	Reggie Smith	.489
71	Gabby Hartnett	.489
72	Rocky Colavito	.489
73	Norm Cash	.488
74	George Brett	.487
75	Gil Hodges	.487
76	Bill Dickey	.486
77	Roger Connor	.486
78	Gus Zernial	.486
79	Joe Adcock	.485
80	Wally Post	.485
81	Fred Lynn	.484
82	Andre Dawson	.484
83	Jack Fournier	.483
84	Rudy York	.483
85	Yogi Berra	.482
86	Kent Hrbek	.481
87	Charlie Gehringer	.480
88	Eddie Murray	.480
89	Pedro Guerrero	.480
90	George Foster	.480
91	Rafael Palmeiro	.480
92	Al Kaline	.480
93	Heinie Manush	.479
94	Gavvy Cravath	.478
95	Dave Kingman	.478
96	Mickey Cochrane	.478
97	Greg Luzinski	.478
98	Eric Davis	.477
99	Dave Winfield	.476
100	Tony Oliva	.476

Production

1	Babe Ruth	1.163
2	Ted Williams	1.116
3	Lou Gehrig	1.080
4	Jimmie Foxx	1.038
5	Hank Greenberg	1.017
6	Rogers Hornsby	1.010
7	Mickey Mantle	.979
8	Joe DiMaggio	.977
	Stan Musial	.977
10	Johnny Mize	.959
11	Mel Ott	.947
12	Ralph Kiner	.946
13	Ty Cobb	.945
14	Willie Mays	.944
15	Dan Brouthers	.942
16	Joe Jackson	.940
	Hack Wilson	.940
18	Barry Bonds	.934
19	Fred McGriff	.933
20	Hank Aaron	.932
21	Harry Heilmann	.930
22	Frank Robinson	.929
23	Earl Averill	.928
	Charlie Keller	.928
	Tris Speaker	.928
26	Ken Williams	.924
27	Chuck Klein	.922
28	Duke Snider	.921
29	Ed Delahanty	.917
30	Babe Herman	.915
	Al Simmons	.915
32	Dick Allen	.914
33	Mike Schmidt	.912
34	Bob Johnson	.899
	Bill Terry	.899
36	Chick Hafey	.898
37	Mickey Cochrane	.897
38	Kevin Mitchell	.893
39	Willie McCovey	.892
	Willie Stargell	.892
	Hal Trosky	.892
42	Eddie Mathews	.888
	Sam Thompson	.888
44	Goose Goslin	.887
	Billy Hamilton	.887
	Harmon Killebrew	.887
47	Wade Boggs	.884
	Charlie Gehringer	.884
49	Roger Connor	.883
	Jackie Robinson	.883
51	Will Clark	.882
	Al Simmons	.882
	Danny Tartabull	.882
54	Wally Berger	.881
55	Dolph Camilli	.880
	Riggs Stephenson	.880
57	Jeff Heath	.879
58	Paul Waner	.878
59	Larry Doby	.877
60	John McGraw	.876
61	Jack Fournier	.875
62	Tommy Henrich	.873
63	Jim Bottomley	.869
	Pete Browning	.869
65	Bill Dickey	.868
66	Joe Medwick	.867
67	Norm Cash	.865
	Darryl Strawberry	.865
69	Jose Canseco	.864
70	Jesse Burkett	.862
71	George Brett	.861
	Roy Campanella	.861
73	Kiki Cuyler	.860
74	Earle Combs	.859
	Al Kaline	.859
	Reggie Smith	.859
	Arky Vaughan	.859
78	Jack Clark	.858
	Gavvy Cravath	.858
	Gabby Hartnett	.858
	Jim Rice	.858
82	Joe Cronin	.857
	Honus Wagner	.857
84	Heinie Manush	.856
	Billy Williams	.856
86	Mike Donlin	.854
	George Grantham	.854
	Pedro Guerrero	.854
	Mike Tiernan	.854
90	Eddie Collins	.853
	Frank Howard	.853
	Joe Kelley	.853
93	Orlando Cepeda	.852
	Ripper Collins	.852
	Ted Kluszewski	.852
	Bob Meusel	.852
97	Rocky Colavito	.851
	Kent Hrbek	.851
	Minnie Minoso	.851
100	2 players tied	.850

Adjusted Production

1	Babe Ruth	209
2	Ted Williams	186
3	Lou Gehrig	182
4	Rogers Hornsby	176
5	Mickey Mantle	173
6	Dan Brouthers	170
7	Joe Jackson	169
8	Ty Cobb	167
9	Pete Browning	164
10	Jimmie Foxx	161
11	Barry Bonds	158
12	Hank Greenberg	157
	Willie Mays	157
	Johnny Mize	157
	Stan Musial	157
16	Hank Aaron	156
	Dick Allen	156
	Joe DiMaggio	156
	Tris Speaker	156
20	Mel Ott	155
21	Roger Connor	154
	Frank Robinson	154
23	Ed Delahanty	153
	Fred McGriff	153
25	Charlie Keller	152
26	Nap Lajoie	150
	Honus Wagner	150
28	Gavvy Cravath	149
	Elmer Flick	149
30	Will Clark	148
	Harry Heilmann	148
	Ralph Kiner	148
	Willie McCovey	148
34	Kevin Mitchell	147
	Mike Schmidt	147
	Willie Stargell	147
37	Sam Thompson	146
38	Eddie Mathews	145
	Hack Wilson	145
40	Sam Crawford	143
	Jack Fournier	143
	Frank Howard	143
43	Mike Donlin	142
	Harmon Killebrew	142
	Darryl Strawberry	142
46	Eddie Collins	141
	Babe Herman	141
	Henry Larkin	141
	Harry Stovey	141
50	Wally Berger	140
	Jesse Burkett	140
	Jose Canseco	140
	Jeff Heath	140
	Reggie Jackson	140
	Tip O'Neill	140
56	Billy Hamilton	139
	Rickey Henderson	139
	Bob Johnson	139
	Denny Lyons	139
	Danny Tartabull	139
61	Cap Anson	138
	Wade Boggs	138
	Norm Cash	138
	Jack Clark	138
	Pedro Guerrero	138
	Al Rosen	138
	Duke Snider	138
	Mike Tiernan	138
69	Larry Doby	137
	Sherry Magee	137
	Gene Tenace	137
	Bill Terry	137
73	Frank Baker	136
	King Kelly	136
	Reggie Smith	136
	Arky Vaughan	136
	Ken Williams	136
78	George Brett	135
	Oyster Burns	135
	Frank Chance	135
	Chuck Klein	135
	John Kruk	135
	John McGraw	135
84	Dolph Camilli	134
	George Gore	134
	Charlie Hickman	134
	Al Kaline	134
	Boog Powell	134
89	Orlando Cepeda	133
	Chick Hafey	133
	Paul Hines	133
	Joe Medwick	133
	Joe Morgan	133
	Eddie Murray	133
	Bill Nicholson	133
	Jim O'Rourke	133
	Paul Waner	133
98	10 players tied	132

Batting Runs

1	Babe Ruth	1322
2	Ted Williams	1166
3	Ty Cobb	1031
4	Stan Musial	983
5	Lou Gehrig	917
6	Hank Aaron	878
7	Rogers Hornsby	844
8	Tris Speaker	843
9	Willie Mays	827
10	Jimmie Foxx	803
	Mickey Mantle	803
12	Frank Robinson	773
13	Mel Ott	767
14	Honus Wagner	664
15	Dan Brouthers	636
16	Carl Yastrzemski	617
17	Eddie Collins	605
18	Mike Schmidt	592
19	Nap Lajoie	556
20	Cap Anson	548
	Roger Connor	548
22	Harmon Killebrew	532
23	Ed Delahanty	526
24	Willie McCovey	524
25	Johnny Mize	520
26	Harry Heilmann	517
27	Al Kaline	513
28	George Brett	511
29	Joe DiMaggio	507
30	Jesse Burkett	504
31	Sam Crawford	493
32	Paul Waner	491
33	Willie Stargell	483
34	Eddie Mathews	480
35	Wade Boggs	473
36	Billy Hamilton	471
37	Dick Allen	470
38	Hank Greenberg	468
39	Reggie Jackson	466
40	Billy Williams	463
41	Joe Jackson	452
42	Duke Snider	441
43	Joe Morgan	438
44	Rod Carew	431
45	Eddie Murray	423
46	Dwight Evans	418
47	Pete Rose	416
48	Rickey Henderson	415
49	Al Simmons	399
50	Ralph Kiner	391
	Dave Winfield	391
52	Norm Cash	390
53	Reggie Smith	379
54	Fred Clarke	376
	Charlie Gehringer	376
	Joe Kelley	376
57	Chuck Klein	375
58	Jack Clark	367
	Jim Rice	367
60	Bob Johnson	366
61	Arky Vaughan	361
62	Sam Thompson	360
63	Pete Browning	356
64	Barry Bonds	354
	Roberto Clemente	354
	Joe Medwick	354
67	Harry Stovey	346
68	Ron Santo	345
69	Elmer Flick	342
70	Goose Goslin	341
	Willie Keeler	341
72	Orlando Cepeda	337
73	Earl Averill	334
	Zack Wheat	334
75	Ken Singleton	332
76	Sherry Magee	331
77	Frank Howard	324
78	Dolph Camilli	319
79	Rusty Staub	318
	Bill Terry	318
81	Paul Molitor	315
82	King Kelly	313
83	Keith Hernandez	310
84	Fred Lynn	309
85	Enos Slaughter	306
86	Boog Powell	305
	Hack Wilson	305
88	Babe Herman	304
	Fred McGriff	304
90	Minnie Minoso	299
91	Joe Torre	298
92	Rocky Colavito	297
93	Jim O'Rourke	293
94	Tony Perez	292
95	Greg Luzinski	291
	Jimmy Ryan	291
97	George Gore	290
	Mike Tiernan	290
99	Ernie Banks	288
100	2 players tied	287

Adjusted Batting Runs

1	Babe Ruth	1382
2	Ted Williams	1024
3	Lou Gehrig	1005
4	Ty Cobb	1004
5	Hank Aaron	914
6	Stan Musial	899
7	Rogers Hornsby	874
8	Mickey Mantle	863
9	Willie Mays	844
10	Tris Speaker	793
11	Mel Ott	776
12	Jimmie Foxx	746
13	Frank Robinson	744
14	Honus Wagner	631
15	Eddie Collins	619
16	Dan Brouthers	609
17	Eddie Mathews	559
18	Nap Lajoie	558
19	Roger Connor	549
20	Ed Delahanty	544
21	Mike Schmidt	543
22	Willie McCovey	540
23	Harry Heilmann	532
24	Joe DiMaggio	529
25	Reggie Jackson	519
26	Johnny Mize	490
27	George Brett	488
	Willie Stargell	488
29	Harmon Killebrew	482
30	Rickey Henderson	480
31	Joe Morgan	478
32	Jesse Burkett	474
	Carl Yastrzemski	474
34	Dick Allen	469
35	Al Kaline	468
36	Sam Crawford	464
	Paul Waner	464
38	Eddie Murray	463
39	Dave Winfield	448
40	Joe Jackson	433
41	Wade Boggs	425
42	Hank Greenberg	422
43	Cap Anson	417
44	Billy Hamilton	414
45	Rod Carew	408
46	Duke Snider	388
47	Bob Johnson	387
48	Pete Browning	384
49	Jack Clark	377
50	Barry Bonds	373
51	Billy Williams	371
52	Fred Clarke	366
	Pete Rose	366
54	Roberto Clemente	363
	Ralph Kiner	363
56	Al Simmons	361
57	Ken Singleton	359
58	Frank Howard	357
59	Norm Cash	355
60	Elmer Flick	353
61	Arky Vaughan	352
62	Goose Goslin	347
63	Sam Thompson	344
64	Reggie Smith	342
65	Orlando Cepeda	338
	Bill Terry	338
67	Zack Wheat	335
68	Rusty Staub	334
69	Paul Molitor	333
70	Charlie Gehringer	332
71	Dwight Evans	331
72	Sherry Magee	324
73	Babe Herman	323
74	Joe Kelley	321
75	Keith Hernandez	320
76	Mike Tiernan	314
77	Hack Wilson	311
78	Joe Medwick	310
	Boog Powell	310
80	Jack Fournier	308
81	Will Clark	303
82	Jake Beckley	299
	Tim Raines	299
	Joe Torre	299
85	Chuck Klein	298
86	Minnie Minoso	297
87	Earl Averill	296
	Fred McGriff	296
89	Frank Thomas	295
90	Charlie Keller	293
	Harry Stovey	293
92	Tony Gwynn	290
93	Jim Wynn	289
94	Rocky Colavito	287
95	Willie Keeler	286
	Jim O'Rourke	286
97	Larry Doby	285
98	Bobby Bonds	277
	Pedro Guerrero	277
100	Brian Downing	276

Batting Wins

1	Babe Ruth	127.5
2	Ted Williams	115.9
3	Ty Cobb	106.3
4	Stan Musial	99.7
5	Hank Aaron	91.1
6	Tris Speaker	86.1
7	Willie Mays	85.5
8	Lou Gehrig	85.3
9	Rogers Hornsby	84.9
10	Mickey Mantle	82.9
11	Frank Robinson	80.7
12	Mel Ott	76.2
13	Jimmie Foxx	75.3
14	Honus Wagner	68.5
15	Carl Yastrzemski	64.3
16	Eddie Collins	62.1
17	Mike Schmidt	61.8
18	Nap Lajoie	57.0
19	Harmon Killebrew	55.8
20	Dan Brouthers	55.6
21	Willie McCovey	54.9
22	Al Kaline	53.4
23	Sam Crawford	52.4
24	Johnny Mize	52.2
25	George Brett	51.4
26	Willie Stargell	51.0
27	Harry Heilmann	50.8
28	Dick Allen	50.0
29	Eddie Mathews	49.2
30	Joe DiMaggio	48.6
31	Billy Williams	48.6
32	Paul Waner	48.6
33	Cap Anson	48.5
34	Reggie Jackson	47.9
35	Roger Connor	47.9
36	Joe Jackson	47.4
37	Wade Boggs	47.0
38	Ed Delahanty	46.4
39	Jesse Burkett	46.2
40	Joe Morgan	45.9
41	Rod Carew	44.7
42	Hank Greenberg	44.5
43	Duke Snider	44.4
44	Pete Rose	43.9
45	Eddie Murray	42.6
46	Dwight Evans	42.2
47	Rickey Henderson	41.3
48	Norm Cash	41.1
49	Billy Hamilton	41.1
50	Reggie Smith	40.3
51	Dave Winfield	39.6
52	Ralph Kiner	39.1
53	Jack Clark	38.0
54	Al Simmons	37.4
55	Jim Rice	36.9
56	Roberto Clemente	36.8
57	Chuck Klein	36.7
58	Fred Clarke	36.7
59	Barry Bonds	36.6
60	Arky Vaughan	36.4
61	Ron Santo	36.3
62	Sherry Magee	35.8
63	Joe Medwick	35.8
64	Bob Johnson	35.2
65	Charlie Gehringer	35.1
66	Orlando Cepeda	35.1
67	Elmer Flick	34.8
68	Joe Kelley	34.6
69	Frank Howard	34.4
70	Zack Wheat	34.4
71	Ken Singleton	34.0
72	Rusty Staub	33.3
73	Willie Keeler	33.0
74	Boog Powell	32.4
75	Keith Hernandez	32.4
76	Dolph Camilli	32.2
77	Goose Goslin	31.9
78	Joe Torre	31.4
79	Paul Molitor	31.3
80	Sam Thompson	31.2
81	Fred Lynn	31.1
82	Pete Browning	31.0
83	Enos Slaughter	30.9
84	Fred McGriff	30.9
85	Earl Averill	30.8
86	Rocky Colavito	30.8
87	Bill Terry	30.8
88	Tony Perez	30.6
89	Harry Stovey	30.5
90	Minnie Minoso	30.3
91	Greg Luzinski	30.1
92	Ernie Banks	29.8
93	Gavvy Cravath	29.7
94	Tim Raines	29.5
95	Hack Wilson	29.5
96	Babe Herman	29.5
97	Tony Gwynn	29.3
98	Tony Oliva	28.9
99	Jack Fournier	28.8
100	Charlie Keller	28.6

Adjusted Batting Wins

1	Babe Ruth	133.3
2	Ty Cobb	103.6
3	Ted Williams	101.7
4	Hank Aaron	94.8
5	Lou Gehrig	93.5
6	Stan Musial	91.1
7	Mickey Mantle	89.1
8	Rogers Hornsby	87.9
9	Willie Mays	87.3
10	Tris Speaker	81.0
11	Frank Robinson	77.7
12	Mel Ott	77.1
13	Jimmie Foxx	69.9
14	Honus Wagner	65.1
15	Eddie Collins	63.5
16	Eddie Mathews	57.3
17	Nap Lajoie	57.2
18	Mike Schmidt	56.7
19	Willie McCovey	56.6
20	Reggie Jackson	53.4
21	Dan Brouthers	53.2
22	Harry Heilmann	52.2
23	Willie Stargell	51.5
24	Joe DiMaggio	50.8
25	Harmon Killebrew	50.6
26	Joe Morgan	50.1
27	Dick Allen	49.8
28	Carl Yastrzemski	49.4
29	Sam Crawford	49.4
30	Johnny Mize	49.2
31	George Brett	49.1
32	Al Kaline	48.7
33	Roger Connor	48.0
34	Ed Delahanty	48.0
35	Rickey Henderson	47.8
36	Eddie Murray	46.6
37	Paul Waner	45.9
38	Joe Jackson	45.4
39	Dave Winfield	45.4
40	Jesse Burkett	43.5
41	Rod Carew	42.3
42	Wade Boggs	42.2
43	Hank Greenberg	40.1
44	Duke Snider	39.1
45	Jack Clark	39.1
46	Billy Williams	39.0
47	Barry Bonds	38.6
48	Pete Rose	38.6
49	Frank Howard	37.9
50	Roberto Clemente	37.8
51	Norm Cash	37.5
52	Bob Johnson	37.2
53	Cap Anson	36.9
54	Ken Singleton	36.7
55	Reggie Smith	36.4
56	Ralph Kiner	36.3
57	Billy Hamilton	36.1
58	Elmer Flick	35.9
59	Fred Clarke	35.7
60	Arky Vaughan	35.5
61	Orlando Cepeda	35.2
62	Sherry Magee	35.1
63	Rusty Staub	35.0
64	Zack Wheat	34.5
65	Al Simmons	33.8
66	Pete Browning	33.4
67	Keith Hernandez	33.4
68	Dwight Evans	33.4
69	Paul Molitor	33.1
70	Boog Powell	32.9
71	Bill Terry	32.7
72	Goose Goslin	32.5
73	Joe Torre	31.5
74	Joe Medwick	31.4
75	Babe Herman	31.3
76	Will Clark	31.2
77	Jack Fournier	31.1
78	Charlie Gehringer	31.0
79	Tim Raines	30.8
80	Jim Wynn	30.6
81	Tony Gwynn	30.1
82	Minnie Minoso	30.1
83	Hack Wilson	30.1
84	Fred McGriff	30.1
85	Sam Thompson	29.8
86	Rocky Colavito	29.8
87	Joe Kelley	29.5
88	Chuck Klein	29.2
89	Charlie Keller	29.2
90	Frank Thomas	29.1
91	Pedro Guerrero	29.0
92	Bobby Bonds	28.7
93	Larry Doby	28.4
94	Tony Perez	28.3
95	Brian Downing	27.8
96	Ron Santo	27.7
97	Jim Rice	27.6
98	Willie Keeler	27.6
99	Darryl Strawberry	27.6
100	Johnny Bench	27.5

Runs Created

1	Babe Ruth	2847
2	Ty Cobb	2810
3	Stan Musial	2625
4	Hank Aaron	2550
5	Ted Williams	2538
6	Willie Mays	2372
7	Tris Speaker	2325
8	Lou Gehrig	2321
9	Mel Ott	2235
	Honus Wagner	2235
11	Pete Rose	2220
12	Jimmie Foxx	2191
13	Carl Yastrzemski	2147
14	Frank Robinson	2126
15	Rogers Hornsby	2074
16	Mickey Mantle	2069
17	Eddie Collins	2059
18	Nap Lajoie	1907
19	George Brett	1878
20	Paul Waner	1853
21	Al Kaline	1846
22	Ed Delahanty	1832
23	Jesse Burkett	1804
	Joe Morgan	1804
	Dave Winfield	1804
26	Charlie Gehringer	1787
27	Al Simmons	1777
28	Reggie Jackson	1772
29	Eddie Murray	1766
30	Mike Schmidt	1757
31	Cap Anson	1756
32	Eddie Mathews	1738
33	Sam Crawford	1716
34	Goose Goslin	1707
35	Billy Hamilton	1706
36	Harry Heilmann	1698
37	Willie Keeler	1688
38	Jake Beckley	1685
39	Fred Clarke	1677
40	Billy Williams	1671
41	Robin Yount	1655
42	Roger Connor	1648
43	Willie McCovey	1638
44	George Davis	1634
45	Dan Brouthers	1624
46	Dwight Evans	1611
47	Harmon Killebrew	1609
48	Joe DiMaggio	1606
49	Rickey Henderson	1602
50	Rod Carew	1595
51	George Van Haltren	1566
52	Jimmy Ryan	1562
53	Roberto Clemente	1557
54	Zack Wheat	1540
55	Joe Kelley	1535
56	Rusty Staub	1534
57	Willie Stargell	1531
58	Paul Molitor	1524
59	Tony Perez	1523
60	Ernie Banks	1513
61	Lou Brock	1512
62	Bill Dahlen	1508
	Hugh Duffy	1508
64	Johnny Mize	1502
65	Sam Rice	1501
66	Darrell Evans	1499
67	George Sisler	1498
68	Luke Appling	1493
69	Duke Snider	1487
70	Andre Dawson	1483
71	Max Carey	1472
72	Frankie Frisch	1464
73	Dave Parker	1452
74	Wade Boggs	1433
75	Enos Slaughter	1432
76	Joe Cronin	1426
77	Bob Johnson	1418
78	Vada Pinson	1394
79	Heinie Manush	1389
80	Mickey Vernon	1387
81	Richie Ashburn	1386
82	Jim Bottomley	1384
83	Jim Rice	1382
84	Ron Santo	1379
85	Chuck Klein	1378
86	Carlton Fisk	1375
87	Joe Medwick	1372
88	Tim Raines	1360
89	Earl Averill	1358
	Brooks Robinson	1358
91	Harry Hooper	1349
92	Al Oliver	1348
93	Lou Whitaker	1347
94	Bid McPhee	1345
95	Orlando Cepeda	1338
96	Kiki Cuyler	1336
97	Hank Greenberg	1331
98	Sherry Magee	1328
99	Arky Vaughan	1323
100	Jimmy Sheckard	1316

Total Average

1	Babe Ruth	1.399
2	Ted Williams	1.320
3	Lou Gehrig	1.229
4	Billy Hamilton	1.191
5	John McGraw	1.153
6	Jimmie Foxx	1.143
7	Hank Greenberg	1.105
	Rogers Hornsby	1.105
9	Mickey Mantle	1.091
10	Ty Cobb	1.066
11	Dan Brouthers	1.061
12	Mel Ott	1.036
13	Ed Delahanty	1.035
14	Barry Bonds	1.029
15	Stan Musial	1.028
16	Joe DiMaggio	1.012
17	Tris Speaker	1.011
18	Joe Jackson	1.008
19	Ralph Kiner	1.006
20	Johnny Mize	1.005
	Hack Wilson	1.005
22	Charlie Keller	1.000
23	Rickey Henderson	.992
24	Willie Mays	.982
25	Fred McGriff	.971
26	Mike Tiernan	.970
27	Harry Heilmann	.963
28	Joe Kelley	.961
	Frank Robinson	.961
30	Earl Averill	.957
31	Denny Lyons	.955
32	Mike Schmidt	.954
33	Roger Connor	.952
34	Mickey Cochrane	.947
	Honus Wagner	.947
36	Pete Browning	.946
37	Chuck Klein	.944
38	Jesse Burkett	.943
	Ken Williams	.943
40	Babe Herman	.942
41	Eddie Collins	.941
42	Hank Aaron	.940
43	Jackie Robinson	.939
	Sam Thompson	.939
45	Duke Snider	.933
46	Dick Allen	.930
	Hugh Duffy	.930
48	Dolph Camilli	.928
49	Harry Stovey	.923
50	Frank Chance	.920
	Bob Johnson	.920
52	Eddie Mathews	.916
53	Elmer Flick	.915
54	Mike Donlin	.914
55	Willie McCovey	.912
56	Elmer Smith	.911
57	Charlie Gehringer	.910
	Harmon Killebrew	.910
	Joe Morgan	.910
60	Chick Hafey	.908
61	Gavvy Cravath	.905
	Mike Griffin	.905
	Al Simmons	.905
64	Tim Raines	.903
65	Kiki Cuyler	.901
	Goose Goslin	.901
67	Cupid Childs	.900
	Eric Davis	.900
69	Riggs Stephenson	.899
	Bill Terry	.899
71	Tip O'Neill	.897
72	Arky Vaughan	.894
73	Larry Doby	.893
	Tommy Henrich	.893
75	Darryl Strawberry	.890
76	Willie Stargell	.889
	Hal Trosky	.889
78	Wade Boggs	.888
	Danny Tartabull	.888
	Paul Waner	.888
81	Jack Fournier	.884
82	Fred Clarke	.883
	Hughie Jennings	.883
84	Will Clark	.882
	George Grantham	.882
86	Roy Cullenbine	.881
	George Van Haltren	.881
88	Kevin Mitchell	.878
89	Norm Cash	.875
	Al Rosen	.875
91	Oyster Burns	.873
92	Wally Berger	.870
	Jimmy Ryan	.870
94	Jeff Heath	.869
95	Cap Anson	.867
	Jack Clark	.867
97	Dummy Hoy	.865
98	Jim Bottomley	.862
99	King Kelly	.861
	Nap Lajoie	.861

Runs Produced

1	Ty Cobb	4066
2	Hank Aaron	3716
3	Babe Ruth	3673
4	Cap Anson	3501
5	Stan Musial	3425
6	Lou Gehrig	3390
7	Honus Wagner	3367
8	Pete Rose	3319
9	Willie Mays	3305
10	Tris Speaker	3294
11	Mel Ott	3208
	Carl Yastrzemski	3208
13	Jimmie Foxx	3139
14	Ted Williams	3116
15	Jake Beckley	3089
16	Eddie Collins	3074
17	Frank Robinson	3055
18	Al Simmons	3027
19	Dave Winfield	3024
20	Nap Lajoie	3020
21	Charlie Gehringer	3017
22	Ed Delahanty	2962
23	George Davis	2903
24	Rogers Hornsby	2862
25	George Brett	2861
26	Goose Goslin	2844
27	Paul Waner	2823
28	Sam Crawford	2819
29	Al Kaline	2806
30	Roger Connor	2804
31	Robin Yount	2787
32	Eddie Murray	2757
33	Hugh Duffy	2748
34	Bill Dahlen	2738
35	Dan Brouthers	2713
36	Reggie Jackson	2690
37	Frankie Frisch	2671
38	Mickey Mantle	2650
39	Harry Heilmann	2647
40	Jimmy Ryan	2617
41	Jesse Burkett	2597
42	George Van Haltren	2584
43	Fred Clarke	2567
44	Joe DiMaggio	2566
45	Sam Rice	2558
46	Mike Schmidt	2553
47	Joe Kelley	2550
48	Tony Perez	2545
49	Joe Morgan	2515
50	Willie Keeler	2496
51	Joe Cronin	2487
52	Roberto Clemente	2481
53	Dwight Evans	2469
54	Billy Williams	2459
55	Eddie Mathews	2450
56	Andre Dawson	2449
57	Ernie Banks	2429
58	Sam Thompson	2428
59	Dave Parker	2426
60	Herman Long	2419
61	Jim O'Rourke	2406
62	Zack Wheat	2405
63	Pie Traynor	2398
64	Luke Appling	2390
65	Billy Hamilton	2386
66	Enos Slaughter	2382
67	Jim Bottomley	2380
68	Joe Medwick	2376
69	Rusty Staub	2363
70	Lou Brock	2361
71	Heinie Manush	2360
72	George Sisler	2357
73	Rod Carew	2347
74	Mickey Vernon	2335
75	Brooks Robinson	2321
76	Jim Rice	2318
77	Al Oliver	2296
78	Harmon Killebrew	2294
79	Tommy Corcoran	2285
80	Darrell Evans	2284
81	Vada Pinson	2280
82	Max Carey	2275
83	Willie McCovey	2263
84	Paul Molitor	2262
85	Willie Stargell	2260
86	John Ward	2249
87	Yogi Berra	2247
88	King Kelly	2238
89	Bob Johnson	2234
90	Kiki Cuyler	2232
91	Carlton Fisk	2230
	Rickey Henderson	2230
93	Ted Simmons	2215
94	Sherry Magee	2205
95	Duke Snider	2185
96	Steve Garvey	2179
97	Don Baylor	2174
98	Harry Hooper	2171
99	Doc Cramer	2162
100	Lou Whitaker	2160

Clutch Hitting Index

1	Cap Anson	132
2	Earl Sheely	127
3	Tommy Thevenow	126
4	Bobby Veach	124
5	Pat Tabler	120
	Pie Traynor	120
7	Sam Mertes	119
8	Hughie Jennings	118
	Duffy Lewis	118
	Jack Rowe	118
	Luke Sewell	118
12	Rube Bressler	117
	Tommy Davis	117
	Bob Fothergill	117
	Chick Gandil	117
	King Kelly	117
	Cookie Lavagetto	117
	Muddy Ruel	117
	Ray Schalk	117
	Billy Sullivan	117
21	John Anderson	116
	Frank Bowerman	116
	Sherry Magee	116
	Elmer Smith	116
	Red Smith	116
26	Kitty Bransfield	115
	Lou Criger	115
	Ron Fairly	115
	Sam Mele	115
	Pinky Whitney	115
	Possum Whitted	115
32	Roy Campanella	114
	Sam Crawford	114
	George Cutshaw	114
	Art Devlin	114
	Ferris Fain	114
	Carl Furillo	114
	Red Murray	114
	Lee Tannehill	114
	Denny Walling	114
	Deacon White	114
	Jimmie Wilson	114
	Heinie Zimmerman	114
44	Bob Elliott	113
	Larry Gardner	113
	Frank LaPorte	113
	Stuffy McInnis	113
	Enos Slaughter	113
	Frank Snyder	113
	Vic Wertz	113
	Taffy Wright	113
52	Alan Ashby	112
	Frank Baker	112
	Larry Biittner	112
	Smoky Burgess	112
	Frank Chance	112
	Johnny Edwards	112
	Kid Elberfeld	112
	Art Fletcher	112
	Sherm Lollar	112
	Frank McCormick	112
	Keith Moreland	112
	Manny Mota	112
	Mickey Owen	112
	Fred Pfeffer	112
	Boog Powell	112
	Cy Seymour	112
	Ted Simmons	112
	Sam Thompson	112
	Mike Tresh	112
71	Bob Boone	111
	Sid Bream	111
	Steve Brodie	111
	Gavvy Cravath	111
	Joe Cronin	111
	Hugh Duffy	111
	Hank Gowdy	111
	Ron Hassey	111
	Jim Kaat	111
	Willie Kamm	111
	Ed Kirkpatrick	111
	Steve O'Neill	111
	Terry Pendleton	111
	Del Pratt	111
	Rusty Staub	111
	Harry Steinfeldt	111
	Riggs Stephenson	111
	Patsy Tebeau	111
	Joe Tinker	111
	Jimmy Williams	111
	Glenn Wright	111
92	22 players tied	110

Isolated Power

1	Babe Ruth	.348
2	Lou Gehrig	.292
3	Hank Greenberg	.292
4	Ted Williams	.289
5	Jimmie Foxx	.284
6	Ralph Kiner	.269
7	Mike Schmidt	.260
8	Mickey Mantle	.259
9	Fred McGriff	.256
10	Willie Mays	.256
11	Joe DiMaggio	.254
12	Harmon Killebrew	.252
13	Barry Bonds	.251
14	Johnny Mize	.250
15	Hank Aaron	.250
16	Willie Stargell	.247
17	Darryl Strawberry	.247
18	Willie McCovey	.245
19	Jose Canseco	.244
20	Duke Snider	.244
21	Kevin Mitchell	.243
22	Frank Robinson	.243
23	Dave Kingman	.242
24	Dick Allen	.242
25	Eddie Mathews	.238
26	Hack Wilson	.238
27	Charlie Keller	.231
28	Hank Sauer	.230
29	Mel Ott	.229
30	Stan Musial	.228
31	Reggie Jackson	.228
32	Danny Tartabull	.228
33	Dick Stuart	.225
34	Ernie Banks	.225
35	Frank Howard	.225
36	Roy Campanella	.224
37	Chuck Klein	.223
38	Gorman Thomas	.223
39	Rocky Colavito	.223
40	Bob Horner	.222
41	Rob Deer	.222
42	Wally Berger	.221
43	Gus Zernial	.221
44	Wally Post	.220
45	Hal Trosky	.219
46	Rogers Hornsby	.218
47	Eric Davis	.218
48	Norm Cash	.217
49	Bob Allison	.217
50	Roger Maris	.216
51	Earl Averill	.216
52	Jeff Heath	.216
53	Dolph Camilli	.215
54	Gil Hodges	.214
55	Ken Williams	.211
56	Joe Carter	.210
57	Jesse Barfield	.210
58	Al Rosen	.210
59	Bob Johnson	.210
60	Tommy Henrich	.209
61	Chick Hafey	.209
62	Jack Clark	.209
63	Johnny Bench	.208
64	Roy Sievers	.208
65	Rudy York	.208
66	Glenn Davis	.208
67	Joe Adcock	.208
68	Nate Colbert	.207
69	Babe Herman	.207
70	Larry Doby	.207
71	George Foster	.206
72	Pete Incaviglia	.205
73	Jim Rice	.204
74	Andre Dawson	.204
75	Dale Murphy	.204
76	Bobby Bonds	.203
77	Orlando Cepeda	.203
78	Billy Williams	.202
79	Greg Luzinski	.202
80	Cliff Johnson	.202
81	Reggie Smith	.202
82	Fred Lynn	.201
83	Mickey Tettleton	.201
84	Al Simmons	.201
85	Don Mincher	.201
86	Tony Armas	.200
87	Ted Kluszewski	.200
88	Leon Durham	.199
89	Howard Johnson	.199
90	Dwight Evans	.198
91	Jim Lemon	.198
92	Kent Hrbek	.198
93	Bobby Bonilla	.198
94	Andy Thornton	.198
95	Bill Nicholson	.198
96	Dale Long	.198
97	Yogi Berra	.198
98	Joe Gordon	.197
99	Will Clark	.197
100	Boog Powell	.196

Extra Base Hits

1	Hank Aaron	1477
2	Stan Musial	1377
3	Babe Ruth	1356
4	Willie Mays	1323
5	Lou Gehrig	1190
6	Frank Robinson	1186
7	Carl Yastrzemski	1157
8	Ty Cobb	1136
9	Tris Speaker	1131
10	George Brett	1119
11	Jimmie Foxx	1117
	Ted Williams	1117
13	Dave Winfield	1086
14	Reggie Jackson	1075
15	Mel Ott	1071
16	Pete Rose	1041
17	Mike Schmidt	1015
18	Andre Dawson	1014
19	Rogers Hornsby	1011
20	Ernie Banks	1009
21	Eddie Murray	1003
22	Al Simmons	995
23	Honus Wagner	993
24	Al Kaline	972
25	Tony Perez	963
26	Robin Yount	960
27	Willie Stargell	953
28	Mickey Mantle	952
29	Billy Williams	948
30	Dwight Evans	941
31	Dave Parker	940
32	Eddie Mathews	938
33	Goose Goslin	921
34	Willie McCovey	920
35	Paul Waner	909
36	Charlie Gehringer	904
37	Nap Lajoie	903
38	Harmon Killebrew	887
39	Joe DiMaggio	881
40	Harry Heilmann	876
41	Vada Pinson	868
42	Sam Crawford	864
43	Joe Medwick	858
44	Duke Snider	850
45	Roberto Clemente	846
46	Carlton Fisk	844
47	Rusty Staub	838
48	Jim Bottomley	835
49	Jim Rice	834
50	Al Oliver	825
51	Orlando Cepeda	823
52	Brooks Robinson	818
53	Joe Morgan	813
54	Roger Connor	812
55	Johnny Mize	809
56	Ed Delahanty	808
57	Joe Cronin	803
58	Jake Beckley	802
59	Johnny Bench	794
60	Dale Murphy	787
61	Mickey Vernon	782
62	Hank Greenberg	781
63	Zack Wheat	780
64	Darrell Evans	779
	Bob Johnson	779
66	Ted Simmons	778
67	Lou Brock	776
68	Ron Santo	774
69	Chuck Klein	772
70	Dan Brouthers	771
71	Earl Averill	767
72	Cal Ripken	764
73	Paul Molitor	763
74	Heinie Manush	761
75	Steve Garvey	755
76	Dick Allen	750
77	Cap Anson	749
78	Graig Nettles	746
79	Hal McRae	741
80	Fred Lynn	737
81	Reggie Smith	734
82	Don Baylor	732
83	Enos Slaughter	730
84	Yogi Berra	728
85	Gary Carter	726
	Jimmy Ryan	726
87	Lee May	725
88	Bill Buckner	721
89	Sam Rice	716
90	Willie Davis	715
	Del Ennis	715
92	Gil Hodges	713
93	Jack Clark	711
94	Frankie Frisch	709
95	Dave Kingman	707
96	Cecil Cooper	703
97	George Foster	702
98	Lou Whitaker	701
99	Bobby Bonds	700
100	Gabby Hartnett	696

Pinch Hits

1	Manny Mota	150
2	Smoky Burgess	145
3	Greg Gross	143
4	Jose Morales	123
5	Jerry Lynch	116
6	Red Lucas	114
7	Steve Braun	113
8	Terry Crowley	108
	Denny Walling	108
10	Gates Brown	107
11	Mike Lum	103
12	Jim Dwyer	102
13	Rusty Staub	100
14	Larry Biittner	95
	Vic Davalillo	95
16	Jerry Hairston	94
17	Dave Philley	93
	Joel Youngblood	93
19	Jay Johnstone	92
20	Ed Kranepool	90
	Elmer Valo	90
22	Dave Collins	85
23	Gerald Perry	84
24	Jesus Alou	82
	Thad Bosley	82
	Kurt Bevacqua	82
	Tim McCarver	82

Pinch Hit Average
(150 at-bats minimum)

1	Tommy Davis	.320
2	Frenchy Bordagaray	.312
3	Frankie Baumholtz	.307
4	Sid Bream	.306
5	Red Schoendienst	.303
6	Bob Fothergill	.300
7	Dave Philley	.299
8	Manny Mota	.297
9	Ted Easterly	.296
10	Dwight Smith	.296
11	Harvey Hendrick	.295
12	Larry Herndon	.294
13	Rance Mulliniks	.292
14	Milt Thompson	.289
15	Terry Puhl	.289
16	Manny Sanguillen	.288
17	Ricky Jordan	.287
18	Mark Carreon	.287
19	Smoky Burgess	.286
20	Rick Miller	.286
21	Johnny Mize	.283
22	Ken Griffey Sr.	.282
23	Bubba Morton	.281
24	Steve Braun	.281
25	Don Mueller	.280

Pinch Hit Home Runs

1	Cliff Johnson	20
2	Jerry Lynch	18
3	Gates Brown	16
	Smoky Burgess	16
	Willie McCovey	16
6	George Crowe	14
7	Joe Adcock	12
	Bob Cerv	12
	Jose Morales	12
	Graig Nettles	12
11	Jeff Burroughs	11
	Jay Johnstone	11
	Candy Maldonado	11
	Fred Whitfield	11
	Cy Williams	11
16	Jim Dwyer	10
	Mike Lum	10
	Ken McMullen	10
	Don Mincher	10
	Wally Post	10
	Champ Summers	10
	Jerry Turner	10
	Gus Zernial	10

Total Player Rating / 150g

1	Babe Ruth	6.45
2	Barry Bonds	5.78
3	Nap Lajoie	5.70
4	Ted Williams	5.61
5	Rogers Hornsby	5.39
6	Rickey Henderson	5.38
7	Mike Schmidt	4.89
8	Mickey Mantle	4.75
9	Tris Speaker	4.65
10	Willie Mays	4.62
11	Lou Gehrig	4.55
12	Ty Cobb	4.50
13	Honus Wagner	4.37
14	Joe Jackson	4.22
15	Hank Aaron	4.08
16	Joe DiMaggio	4.05
17	Tim Raines	3.98
18	Barry Larkin	3.96
19	Lou Boudreau	3.76
20	Eddie Collins	3.70
21	Frank Robinson	3.69
22	Dan Brouthers	3.68
23	Pete Browning	3.65
24	Ed Delahanty	3.62
25	Wade Boggs	3.57
26	Jimmie Foxx	3.50
27	Stan Musial	3.49
28	Jackie Robinson	3.45
29	Mel Ott	3.45
30	Tony Gwynn	3.41
31	Buck Ewing	3.35
32	Bobby Grich	3.29
33	Eddie Mathews	3.24
34	George Davis	3.24
35	Arky Vaughan	3.24
36	Hank Greenberg	3.23
37	Frank Baker	3.22
38	Roger Connor	3.21
39	Joe Morgan	3.19
40	Mickey Cochrane	3.18
41	Lenny Dykstra	3.16
42	Bill Dahlen	3.16
43	Bobby Doerr	3.14
44	Jack Glasscock	3.12
45	Ryne Sandberg	3.10
46	Cupid Childs	3.09
47	Hardy Richardson	3.08
48	Hughie Jennings	3.06
49	Sam Thompson	3.03
50	Dick Allen	3.03
51	Gabby Hartnett	3.02
52	Charlie Keller	3.01
53	Darryl Strawberry	2.98
54	Bill Dickey	2.97
55	Jose Canseco	2.95
56	Ralph Kiner	2.94
57	Elmer Flick	2.90
58	Johnny Mize	2.88
59	Kevin Mitchell	2.88
60	Charlie Gehringer	2.87
61	Bob Johnson	2.87
62	Cal Ripken	2.84
63	Bid McPhee	2.82
64	Joe Cronin	2.78
65	Dave Bancroft	2.77
66	Charlie Bennett	2.71
67	Joe Sewell	2.71
68	Joe Gordon	2.70
69	Eric Davis	2.67
70	Roy Campanella	2.67
71	Denny Lyons	2.65
72	Roberto Clemente	2.64
73	Reggie Smith	2.64
74	Ron Santo	2.64
75	Ozzie Smith	2.64
76	Jim Wynn	2.59
77	Yogi Berra	2.56
78	King Kelly	2.55
79	Frankie Frisch	2.54
80	Art Fletcher	2.53
81	Luke Appling	2.52
82	Bill Mazeroski	2.52
83	Kirby Puckett	2.50
84	Billy Hamilton	2.49
85	Fred McGriff	2.48
86	Paul Molitor	2.48
87	Billy Herman	2.47
88	Keith Hernandez	2.47
89	Wally Berger	2.47
90	Will Clark	2.46
91	Heinie Groh	2.42
92	Bobby Bonds	2.40
93	Frank Chance	2.40
94	Al Kaline	2.36
95	Art Devlin	2.35
96	Jack Fournier	2.35
97	Jack Clark	2.34
98	Roy Thomas	2.33
99	Gavvy Cravath	2.32
100	Bobby Wallace	2.32

Stolen Bases

1	Rickey Henderson	1117
2	Lou Brock	938
3	Billy Hamilton	912
4	Ty Cobb	892
5	Tim Raines	764
6	Eddie Collins	744
7	Arlie Latham	739
8	Max Carey	738
9	Honus Wagner	722
10	Vince Coleman	698
11	Joe Morgan	689
12	Willie Wilson	668
13	Tom Brown	657
14	Bert Campaneris	649
15	George Davis	616
16	Dummy Hoy	594
17	Maury Wills	586
18	George Van Haltren	583
19	Hugh Duffy	574
20	Ozzie Smith	569
21	Bid McPhee	568
22	Davey Lopes	557
23	Cesar Cedeno	550
24	Bill Dahlen	547
25	John Ward	540
26	Herman Long	534
27	Patsy Donovan	518
28	Jack Doyle	516
29	Harry Stovey	509
30	Luis Aparicio	506
	Fred Clarke	506
32	Brett Butler	503
33	Willie Keeler	495
	Clyde Milan	495
35	Omar Moreno	487
36	Mike Griffin	473
37	Tommy McCarthy	468
38	Jimmy Sheckard	465
39	Bobby Bonds	461
40	Ed Delahanty	455
	Ron LeFlore	455
42	Paul Molitor	454
43	Curt Welch	453
44	Steve Sax	444
45	Joe Kelley	443
46	Sherry Magee	441
47	John McGraw	436
48	Tris Speaker	432
49	Mike Tiernan	428
50	Bob Bescher	427
51	Charlie Comiskey	419
	Frankie Frisch	419
53	Jimmy Ryan	418
54	Tommy Harper	408
55	Donie Bush	404
56	Frank Chance	401
57	Bill Lange	399
58	Willie Davis	398
59	Sam Mertes	396
60	Dave Collins	395
	Billy North	395
62	Otis Nixon	394
63	Jesse Burkett	389
64	Tommy Corcoran	387
65	Tom Daly	385
	Freddie Patek	385
67	George Burns	383
	Hugh Nicol	383
69	Fred Pfeffer	382
70	Walt Wilmot	381
71	Nap Lajoie	380
72	Harry Hooper	375
	George Sisler	375
74	Jack Glasscock	372
75	Lonnie Smith	370
76	King Kelly	368
77	Sam Crawford	366
	Tommy Dowd	366
79	Hal Chase	363
	Juan Samuel	363
81	Tommy Leach	361
82	Hughie Jennings	359
	Fielder Jones	359
84	Buck Ewing	354
	Gary Pettis	354
86	Rod Carew	353
87	Tommy Tucker	352
88	Sam Rice	351
89	George Case	349
90	Paul Radford	346
91	Julio Cruz	343
92	Amos Otis	341
93	John Anderson	338
	Willie Mays	338
95	Joe Tinker	336
96	Kip Selbach	334
97	Elmer Flick	330
98	Jose Cardenal	329
	Ned Hanlon	329
100	3 players tied	328

Stolen Base Average

1	Eric Davis	87.2
2	Tim Raines	85.1
3	Marquis Grissom	84.7
4	Barry Larkin	83.9
5	Kenny Lofton	83.5
6	Henry Cotto	83.3
7	Willie Wilson	83.3
8	Davey Lopes	83.0
9	Stan Javier	82.6
10	Julio Cruz	81.5
11	Vince Coleman	81.4
12	Rickey Henderson	81.4
13	Joe Morgan	81.0
14	Lenny Dykstra	80.5
15	Ozzie Smith	80.3
16	Andy Van Slyke	80.1
17	Mickey Mantle	80.1
18	Enzo Hernandez	79.6
19	Gary Redus	79.5
20	Paul Molitor	79.2
21	Gregg Jefferies	79.1
22	Devon White	79.1
23	R. J. Reynolds	79.0
24	Luis Aparicio	78.8
25	Amos Otis	78.6
26	Roberto Alomar	78.5
27	Kirk Gibson	78.3
28	Joe Carter	78.1
29	Tommy Harper	77.9
30	Rudy Law	77.8
31	Brady Anderson	77.8
	Mike Felder	77.8
33	Bob Dernier	77.6
34	Miguel Dilone	77.4
35	Ryne Sandberg	77.4
36	Gary Pettis	77.3
37	Mariano Duncan	77.3
38	Mookie Wilson	76.9
39	Barry Bonds	76.9
40	Milt Thompson	76.8
41	Hank Aaron	76.7
42	Willie Mays	76.6
43	Bert Campaneris	76.5
44	Ron LeFlore	76.2
45	George Case	76.2
46	Oddibe McDowell	76.1
47	Otis Nixon	75.8
48	Dick Howser	75.5
49	Cesar Cedeno	75.4
50	Lou Brock	75.3

Stolen Base Runs

1	Rickey Henderson	182
2	Tim Raines	149
3	Willie Wilson	120
4	Vince Coleman	114
5	Joe Morgan	110
6	Davey Lopes	99
7	Lou Brock	97
8	Ozzie Smith	87
9	Bert Campaneris	75
10	Luis Aparicio	70
11	Eric Davis	65
	Paul Molitor	65
13	Cesar Cedeno	58
14	Julio Cruz	56
15	Tommy Harper	53
16	Marquis Grissom	51
	Ron LeFlore	51
	Maury Wills	51
19	Amos Otis	47
	Gary Redus	47
21	Gary Pettis	44
22	Otis Nixon	43
23	Lenny Dykstra	42
24	Willie Davis	41
	Ryne Sandberg	41
26	Willie Mays	40
27	George Case	39
	Mookie Wilson	39
29	Barry Bonds	37
	Bobby Bonds	37
	Kirk Gibson	37
	Omar Moreno	37
	Freddie Patek	37
34	Roberto Alomar	36
	Kenny Lofton	36
	Andy Van Slyke	36
37	Dave Collins	35
	Barry Larkin	35
39	Devon White	34
40	Miguel Dilone	33
	Juan Samuel	33
42	Larry Bowa	32
43	Dave Concepcion	31
	Willie McGee	31
45	Andre Dawson	29
	Rudy Law	29
	Lloyd Moseby	29
48	Hank Aaron	28
	Bob Dernier	28
50	Lonnie Smith	27

Stolen Base Wins

1	Rickey Henderson	18.1
2	Tim Raines	15.3
3	Willie Wilson	12.0
4	Vince Coleman	11.7
5	Joe Morgan	11.5
6	Davey Lopes	10.2
7	Lou Brock	10.2
8	Ozzie Smith	9.1
9	Bert Campaneris	7.9
10	Luis Aparicio	7.3
11	Eric Davis	6.7
12	Paul Molitor	6.5
13	Cesar Cedeno	6.1
14	Tommy Harper	5.6
15	Julio Cruz	5.6
16	Maury Wills	5.3
17	Marquis Grissom	5.3
18	Ron LeFlore	5.2
19	Amos Otis	4.9
20	Gary Redus	4.8
21	Gary Pettis	4.4
22	Otis Nixon	4.4
23	Lenny Dykstra	4.3
24	Willie Davis	4.3
25	Ryne Sandberg	4.3
26	Willie Mays	4.1
27	Mookie Wilson	4.1
28	George Case	3.9
29	Freddie Patek	3.8
30	Omar Moreno	3.8
31	Bobby Bonds	3.8
32	Barry Bonds	3.8
33	Andy Van Slyke	3.7
34	Kirk Gibson	3.7
35	Roberto Alomar	3.7
36	Barry Larkin	3.6
37	Dave Collins	3.6
38	Kenny Lofton	3.4
39	Juan Samuel	3.4
40	Miguel Dilone	3.4
41	Devon White	3.4
42	Larry Bowa	3.3
43	Dave Concepcion	3.2
44	Willie McGee	3.2
45	Andre Dawson	3.0
46	Bob Dernier	2.9
47	Rudy Law	2.9
48	Hank Aaron	2.9
49	Lloyd Moseby	2.9
50	Lonnie Smith	2.8

Games

First Base
1 Eddie Murray 2394
2 Jake Beckley 2377
3 Mickey Vernon 2237
4 Lou Gehrig 2137
5 Charlie Grimm 2131
6 Joe Judge 2084
7 Ed Konetchy 2073
8 Steve Garvey 2059
9 Cap Anson 2058
10 Joe Kuhel 2057

Second Base
1 Eddie Collins 2650
2 Joe Morgan 2527
3 Nellie Fox 2295
4 Lou Whitaker 2245
5 Charlie Gehringer 2206
6 Willie Randolph 2152
7 Frank White 2150
8 Bid McPhee 2126
9 Bill Mazeroski 2094
10 Nap Lajoie 2035

Shortstop
1 Luis Aparicio 2581
2 Ozzie Smith 2418
3 Larry Bowa 2222
4 Luke Appling 2218
5 Dave Concepcion 2178
6 Rabbit Maranville 2153
7 Bill Dahlen 2132
8 Bert Campaneris 2097
9 Tommy Corcoran 2073
10 Alan Trammell 2036

Third Base
1 Brooks Robinson 2870
2 Graig Nettles 2412
3 Mike Schmidt 2212
4 Buddy Bell 2183
5 Eddie Mathews 2181
6 Ron Santo 2130
7 Eddie Yost 2008
8 Ron Cey 1989
9 Aurelio Rodriguez 1983
10 Sal Bando 1896

Outfield
1 Ty Cobb 2935
2 Willie Mays 2842
3 Hank Aaron 2760
4 Tris Speaker 2698
5 Lou Brock 2507
6 Al Kaline 2488
7 Dave Winfield 2469
8 Max Carey 2421
9 Vada Pinson 2403
10 Roberto Clemente 2370
11 Zack Wheat 2337
12 Willie Davis 2323
13 Mel Ott 2313
14 Sam Crawford 2299
15 Paul Waner 2288
16 Harry Hooper 2284
17 Sam Rice 2270
18 Andre Dawson 2258
19 Babe Ruth 2241
20 Goose Goslin 2188

Catcher
1 Carlton Fisk 2229
2 Bob Boone 2225
3 Gary Carter 2056
4 Jim Sundberg 1927
5 Al Lopez 1918
6 Rick Ferrell 1806
7 Gabby Hartnett 1793
8 Ted Simmons 1771
9 Tony Pena 1754
10 Lance Parrish 1751

Pitcher
1 Hoyt Wilhelm 1070
2 Kent Tekulve 1050
3 Rich Gossage 1002
4 Lindy McDaniel 987
5 Rollie Fingers 944
6 Gene Garber 931
7 Cy Young 906
8 Sparky Lyle 899
9 Jim Kaat 898
10 Lee Smith 891

Fielding Average

First Base
1 Don Mattingly .... .996
2 Steve Garvey .... .996
3 Wes Parker .... .996
4 Dan Driessen .... .995
5 Jim Spencer .... .995
6 Frank McCormick .... .995
7 Mark Grace .... .994
8 Keith Hernandez .... .994
9 Kent Hrbek .... .994
10 Vic Power .... .994

Second Base
1 Ryne Sandberg .... .990
2 Tom Herr .... .989
3 Jim Gantner .... .985
4 Frank White .... .984
5 Bobby Grich .... .984
6 Jerry Lumpe .... .984
7 Lou Whitaker .... .984
8 Cookie Rojas .... .984
9 Dave Cash .... .984
10 Nellie Fox .... .984

Shortstop
1 Tony Fernandez .... .980
2 Larry Bowa .... .980
3 Ozzie Smith .... .979
4 Cal Ripken .... .979
5 Spike Owen .... .977
6 Alan Trammell .... .977
7 Mark Belanger .... .977
8 Bucky Dent .... .976
9 Dick Schofield .... .976
10 Roger Metzger .... .976

Third Base
1 Brooks Robinson .... .971
2 Ken Reitz .... .970
3 Steve Buechele .... .969
4 George Kell .... .969
5 Don Money .... .968
6 Don Wert .... .968
7 Willie Kamm .... .967
8 Heinie Groh .... .967
9 Carney Lansford .... .966
10 Clete Boyer .... .965

Outfield
1 Terry Puhl .... .993
2 Brett Butler .... .992
3 Pete Rose .... .991
4 Amos Otis .... .991
5 Joe Rudi .... .991
6 Mickey Stanley .... .991
7 Robin Yount .... .990
8 Jim Piersall .... .990
9 Jim Landis .... .989
10 Ken Berry .... .989
11 Kirby Puckett .... .989
12 Tommy Holmes .... .989
13 Gene Woodling .... .989
14 Cesar Geronimo .... .988
15 Fred Lynn .... .988
16 Tim Raines .... .988
17 Paul Blair .... .988
18 Andy Van Slyke .... .988
19 Roy White .... .988
20 Jim Busby .... .988

Catcher
1 Bill Freehan .... .993
2 Elston Howard .... .993
3 Jim Sundberg .... .993
4 Sherm Lollar .... .992
5 Johnny Edwards .... .992
6 Tom Haller .... .992
7 Jerry Grote .... .991
8 Ernie Whitt .... .991
9 Lance Parrish .... .991
10 Gary Carter .... .991

Pitcher
1 Don Mossi .... .990
2 Gary Nolan .... .990
3 Rick Rhoden .... .989
4 Lon Warneke .... .988
5 Jim Wilson .... .988
6 Woodie Fryman .... .988
7 Larry Gura .... .986
8 Pete Alexander .... .985
9 Alvin Crowder .... .984
10 Bill Monbouquette ...... .984

Total Chances per Game

First Base
1 Tom Jones 11.38
2 George Stovall 11.30
3 George Kelly 11.09
4 Candy LaChance 11.05
5 Wally Pipp 11.05
6 Ed Konetchy 11.04
7 George Burns 10.92
8 Bill Terry 10.91
9 Cap Anson 10.86
10 Walter Holke 10.83
11 Bill Phillips 10.83
12 Fred Tenney 10.83

Second Base
1 Fred Pfeffer 6.95
2 Bid McPhee 6.70
3 Cub Stricker 6.59
4 Lou Bierbauer 6.50
5 Cupid Childs 6.32
6 Ski Melillo 6.16
7 Hughie Critz 6.07
8 Frankie Frisch 6.05
9 Bobby Lowe 6.02
10 Bucky Harris 6.00
11 Nap Lajoie 6.00

Shortstop
1 Herman Long 6.38
2 Dave Bancroft 6.33
3 Bill Dahlen 6.26
4 George Davis 6.22
5 Rabbit Maranville 6.10
6 Bobby Wallace 6.10
7 Tommy Corcoran 6.09
8 Monte Cross 6.06
9 Bones Ely 6.06
10 Honus Wagner 5.99

Third Base
1 Jerry Denny 4.21
2 Billy Shindle 4.15
3 Billy Nash 4.07
4 Arlie Latham 4.04
5 Denny Lyons 3.98
6 Jimmy Collins 3.89
7 Hick Carpenter 3.81
8 Jimmy Austin 3.74
9 Lave Cross 3.73
10 Frank Baker 3.64

Outfield
1 Taylor Douthit 3.16
2 Richie Ashburn 3.04
3 Dom DiMaggio 2.99
4 Mike Kreevich 2.95
5 Dwayne Murphy 2.92
6 Sam Chapman 2.91
7 Sam West 2.88
8 Max Carey 2.87
9 Fred Schulte 2.84
10 Devon White 2.84
11 Lloyd Waner 2.81
12 Vince DiMaggio 2.80
13 Joe DiMaggio 2.78
14 Tris Speaker 2.77
15 Billy North 2.76
16 Kirby Puckett 2.76
17 Terry Moore 2.75
18 Garry Maddox 2.74
19 Jimmy McAleer 2.73
20 Wally Berger 2.71
21 Gary Pettis 2.71

Catcher
1 Johnny Edwards 6.98
2 Johnny Roseboro 6.83
3 Bill Freehan 6.79
4 Mike Scioscia 6.59
5 Jerry Grote 6.53
6 Tony Pena 6.42
7 Tim McCarver 6.41
8 Gary Carter 6.38
9 Tom Haller 6.33
10 Bill Killefer 6.27

Pitcher
1 Nick Altrock 3.72
2 Harry Howell 3.61
3 Addie Joss 3.60
4 Ed Walsh 3.49
5 Nixey Callahan 3.47
6 Willie Sudhoff 3.31
7 George Mullin 3.20
8 Barney Pelty 3.20
9 Chick Fraser 3.12
10 Red Donahue 2.95
11 Ed Willett 2.95

Chances Accepted per Game

First Base
1 Tom Jones 11.21
2 George Stovall 11.15
3 George Kelly 11.00
4 Wally Pipp 10.96
5 Ed Konetchy 10.93
6 Candy LaChance 10.87
7 Bill Terry 10.82
8 George Burns 10.77
9 Walter Holke 10.75
10 Fred Tenney 10.65

Second Base
1 Fred Pfeffer 6.39
2 Bid McPhee 6.33
3 Lou Bierbauer 6.07
4 Ski Melillo 6.00
5 Cub Stricker 5.97
6 Hughie Critz 5.91
7 Frankie Frisch 5.89
8 Cupid Childs 5.88
9 Bucky Harris 5.79
10 Nap Lajoie 5.78

Shortstop
1 Dave Bancroft 5.98
2 George Davis 5.85
3 Rabbit Maranville 5.81
4 Bill Dahlen 5.80
5 Herman Long 5.78
6 Bobby Wallace 5.73
7 Travis Jackson 5.67
8 Dick Bartell 5.64
9 Tommy Corcoran 5.63
10 Honus Wagner 5.63

Third Base
1 Jerry Denny 3.72
2 Billy Shindle 3.70
3 Billy Nash 3.65
4 Jimmy Collins 3.61
5 Arlie Latham 3.52
6 Denny Lyons 3.51
7 Lave Cross 3.50
8 Jimmy Austin 3.49
9 Frank Baker 3.43
10 Bill Bradley 3.38

Outfield
1 Taylor Douthit 3.07
2 Richie Ashburn 2.98
3 Dom DiMaggio 2.92
4 Mike Kreevich 2.89
5 Dwayne Murphy 2.88
6 Sam Chapman 2.83
7 Sam West 2.83
8 Devon White 2.80
9 Max Carey 2.77
10 Fred Schulte 2.77
11 Lloyd Waner 2.76
12 Vince DiMaggio 2.75
13 Kirby Puckett 2.73
14 Joe DiMaggio 2.72
15 Terry Moore 2.71
16 Billy North 2.71
17 Garry Maddox 2.70
18 Tris Speaker 2.69
19 Robin Yount 2.68
20 Chet Lemon 2.66

Catcher
1 Johnny Edwards 6.92
2 Johnny Roseboro 6.76
3 Bill Freehan 6.75
4 Mike Scioscia 6.51
5 Jerry Grote 6.47
6 Tony Pena 6.36
7 Tim McCarver 6.35
8 Gary Carter 6.32
9 Tom Haller 6.28
10 Earl Battey 6.15

Pitcher
1 Nick Altrock 3.59
2 Addie Joss 3.47
3 Harry Howell 3.46
4 Ed Walsh 3.36
5 Nixey Callahan 3.25
6 Willie Sudhoff 3.11
7 George Mullin 3.03
8 Barney Pelty 3.00
9 Chick Fraser 2.90
10 Red Donahue 2.81
11 Christy Mathewson 2.81

Putouts

First Base
1	Jake Beckley	23709
2	Ed Konetchy	21361
3	Eddie Murray	21085
4	Cap Anson	20794
5	Charlie Grimm	20711
6	Stuffy McInnis	19962
7	Mickey Vernon	19808
8	Jake Daubert	19634
9	Lou Gehrig	19510
10	Joe Kuhel	19386

Second Base
1	Bid McPhee	6545
2	Eddie Collins	6526
3	Nellie Fox	6090
4	Joe Morgan	5742
5	Nap Lajoie	5496
6	Charlie Gehringer	5369
7	Bill Mazeroski	4974
8	Bobby Doerr	4928
9	Willie Randolph	4859
10	Billy Herman	4780

Shortstop
1	Rabbit Maranville	5139
2	Bill Dahlen	4850
3	Dave Bancroft	4623
4	Honus Wagner	4576
5	Tommy Corcoran	4550
6	Luis Aparicio	4548
7	Luke Appling	4398
8	Herman Long	4225
9	Bobby Wallace	4142
10	Ozzie Smith	4100

Third Base
1	Brooks Robinson	2697
2	Jimmy Collins	2372
3	Eddie Yost	2356
4	Lave Cross	2306
5	Pie Traynor	2289
6	Billy Nash	2219
7	Frank Baker	2154
8	Willie Kamm	2151
9	Eddie Mathews	2049
10	Willie Jones	2045

Outfield
1	Willie Mays	7095
2	Tris Speaker	6788
3	Max Carey	6363
4	Ty Cobb	6361
5	Richie Ashburn	6089
6	Hank Aaron	5539
7	Willie Davis	5449
8	Doc Cramer	5412
9	Vada Pinson	5097
10	Andre Dawson	5077
11	Willie Wilson	5060
12	Al Kaline	5035
13	Zack Wheat	4996
14	Chet Lemon	4993
15	Al Simmons	4988
16	Dave Winfield	4975
17	Amos Otis	4936
18	Rickey Henderson	4920
19	Paul Waner	4872
20	Lloyd Waner	4860

Catcher
1	Gary Carter	11785
2	Carlton Fisk	11369
3	Bob Boone	11260
4	Tony Pena	10177
5	Bill Freehan	9941
6	Jim Sundberg	9767
7	Lance Parrish	9301
8	Johnny Roseboro	9291
9	Johnny Bench	9249
10	Johnny Edwards	8925

Pitcher
1	Jack Morris	387
2	Phil Niekro	386
3	Fergie Jenkins	363
4	Gaylord Perry	349
5	Don Sutton	334
6	Tony Mullane	328
	Rick Reuschel	328
	Tom Seaver	328
9	Jim Galvin	324
10	Robin Roberts	316

Putouts per Game

First Base
1	Tom Jones	10.53
2	Candy LaChance	10.48
3	George Stovall	10.45
4	George Kelly	10.37
5	Wally Pipp	10.33
6	Ed Konetchy	10.31
7	Bill Phillips	10.22
8	Walter Holke	10.20
9	Charlie Comiskey	10.15
10	John Reilly	10.12
11	Bill Terry	10.12

Second Base
1	Bid McPhee	3.08
2	Fred Pfeffer	3.07
3	Cub Stricker	3.02
4	Lou Bierbauer	2.74
5	Jerry Priddy	2.74
6	Bucky Harris	2.73
7	Nap Lajoie	2.71
8	Bobby Doerr	2.67
9	Cupid Childs	2.66
10	Nellie Fox	2.66

Shortstop
1	Dave Bancroft	2.47
2	Honus Wagner	2.43
3	Rabbit Maranville	2.39
4	Monte Cross	2.38
5	George Davis	2.36
6	Herman Long	2.36
7	Dick Bartell	2.31
8	Bill Dahlen	2.28
9	Ivy Olson	2.27
10	Bobby Wallace	2.27

Third Base
1	Jerry Denny	1.61
2	Denny Lyons	1.55
3	Billy Nash	1.52
4	Jimmy Austin	1.43
5	Billy Shindle	1.43
6	Jimmy Collins	1.41
7	Frank Baker	1.40
8	Hick Carpenter	1.37
9	Lave Cross	1.34
10	Hans Lobert	1.30

Outfield
1	Taylor Douthit	3.01
2	Richie Ashburn	2.90
3	Dom DiMaggio	2.82
4	Dwayne Murphy	2.82
5	Mike Kreevich	2.81
6	Sam Chapman	2.74
7	Sam West	2.74
8	Devon White	2.73
9	Fred Schulte	2.70
10	Lloyd Waner	2.68
11	Billy North	2.65
12	Kirby Puckett	2.65
13	Garry Maddox	2.64
14	Max Carey	2.63
15	Joe DiMaggio	2.63
16	Vince DiMaggio	2.63
17	Terry Moore	2.63
18	Robin Yount	2.63
19	Gary Pettis	2.62
20	Chet Lemon	2.60

Catcher
1	Johnny Edwards	6.42
2	Johnny Roseboro	6.30
3	Bill Freehan	6.29
4	Jerry Grote	6.00
5	Mike Scioscia	5.98
6	Tim McCarver	5.92
7	Tom Haller	5.85
8	Tony Pena	5.81
9	Gary Carter	5.74
10	Earl Battey	5.69

Pitcher
1	Greg Maddux	0.91
2	Nick Altrock	0.78
3	Dave Foutz	0.78
4	Chick Fraser	0.73
5	Mike Boddicker	0.72
6	Doug Drabek	0.72
7	Carl Morton	0.72
8	Jack Morris	0.71
9	Orel Hershiser	0.69
10	Dan Petry	0.69

Assists

First Base
1	Eddie Murray	1842
2	Keith Hernandez	1682
3	George Sisler	1529
4	Mickey Vernon	1448
5	Fred Tenney	1363
6	Bill Buckner	1351
	Chris Chambliss	1351
8	Norm Cash	1317
9	Jake Beckley	1315
10	Joe Judge	1301

Second Base
1	Eddie Collins	7630
2	Charlie Gehringer	7068
3	Joe Morgan	6967
4	Bid McPhee	6905
5	Bill Mazeroski	6685
6	Lou Whitaker	6490
7	Nellie Fox	6373
8	Willie Randolph	6336
9	Nap Lajoie	6262
10	Frank White	6250

Shortstop
1	Ozzie Smith	8084
2	Luis Aparicio	8016
3	Bill Dahlen	7500
4	Rabbit Maranville	7354
5	Luke Appling	7218
6	Tommy Corcoran	7106
7	Larry Bowa	6857
8	Dave Concepcion	6594
9	Dave Bancroft	6561
10	Roger Peckinpaugh	6337

Third Base
1	Brooks Robinson	6205
2	Graig Nettles	5279
3	Mike Schmidt	5045
4	Buddy Bell	4925
5	Ron Santo	4581
6	Eddie Mathews	4322
7	Aurelio Rodriguez	4150
8	Ron Cey	4018
9	Sal Bando	3720
10	Lave Cross	3706

Outfield
1	Tris Speaker	449
2	Ty Cobb	392
3	Jimmy Ryan	375
4	Tom Brown	348
	George Van Haltren	348
6	Harry Hooper	344
7	Max Carey	339
8	Jimmy Sheckard	307
9	Clyde Milan	294
10	Orator Shaffer	289
11	King Kelly	285
12	Sam Thompson	283
13	Sam Rice	278
14	Dummy Hoy	273
15	Jesse Burkett	270
16	Sam Crawford	268
	Tommy McCarthy	268
18	Roberto Clemente	266
19	Patsy Donovan	264
20	Willie Keeler	258

Catcher
1	Deacon McGuire	1859
2	Ray Schalk	1811
3	Steve O'Neill	1698
4	Red Dooin	1590
5	Chief Zimmer	1580
6	Johnny Kling	1552
7	Ivey Wingo	1487
8	Wilbert Robinson	1454
9	Bill Bergen	1444
10	Wally Schang	1420

Pitcher
1	Cy Young	2014
2	Christy Mathewson	1503
3	Pete Alexander	1419
4	Jim Galvin	1382
5	Walter Johnson	1351
6	Burleigh Grimes	1252
7	George Mullin	1244
8	Jack Quinn	1240
9	Ed Walsh	1208
10	Eppa Rixey	1195

Assists per Game

First Base
1	Mark Grace	0.89
2	Bill Buckner	0.87
3	Ferris Fain	0.84
4	Keith Hernandez	0.84
5	Vic Power	0.83
6	Wally Joyner	0.81
7	Pete O'Brien	0.78
8	George Sisler	0.78
9	Eddie Murray	0.77
10	Rudy York	0.77

Second Base
1	Hughie Critz	3.54
2	Frankie Frisch	3.42
3	Ski Melillo	3.38
4	Lou Bierbauer	3.34
5	Glenn Hubbard	3.34
6	Fred Pfeffer	3.33
7	Rogers Hornsby	3.31
8	Ryne Sandberg	3.28
9	Bid McPhee	3.25
10	Tony Cuccinello	3.23

Shortstop
1	Germany Smith	3.70
2	Art Fletcher	3.55
3	Bill Dahlen	3.52
4	Dave Bancroft	3.51
5	Bones Ely	3.50
6	Travis Jackson	3.50
7	George Davis	3.49
8	Jack Glasscock	3.46
9	Bobby Wallace	3.46
10	Tommy Corcoran	3.43
11	Herman Long	3.43

Third Base
1	Mike Schmidt	2.29
2	Billy Shindle	2.27
3	Buddy Bell	2.26
4	Arlie Latham	2.26
5	Terry Pendleton	2.26
6	Clete Boyer	2.24
7	Jimmy Collins	2.20
8	Graig Nettles	2.19
9	George Brett	2.18
10	Darrell Evans	2.17
11	Brooks Robinson	2.17

Outfield
1	Tommy McCarthy	0.23
2	Pop Corkhill	0.22
3	Jimmy Wolf	0.22
4	Sam Thompson	0.21
5	Tom Brown	0.20
6	Jimmy Ryan	0.20
7	George Van Haltren	0.20
8	Curt Welch	0.20
9	Ed Delahanty	0.19
10	George Gore	0.19
11	Paul Hines	0.18
12	Gavvy Cravath	0.17
13	Mike Griffin	0.17
14	Ned Hanlon	0.17
15	Joe Hornung	0.17
16	Mike Mitchell	0.17
17	Tris Speaker	0.17
18	Tilly Walker	0.17
19	George Wood	0.17
20	Ross Youngs	0.17

Catcher
1	Duke Farrell	1.42
2	Red Dooin	1.34
3	Johnny Kling	1.33
4	Bill Killefer	1.32
5	Oscar Stanage	1.29
6	Chief Zimmer	1.28
7	John Warner	1.27
8	Ivey Wingo	1.21
9	Billy Sullivan	1.18
10	George Gibson	1.17

Pitcher
1	Addie Joss	2.96
2	Harry Howell	2.84
3	Nick Altrock	2.81
4	Ed Walsh	2.81
5	Willie Sudhoff	2.73
6	Nixey Callahan	2.60
7	George Mullin	2.56
8	Ed Willett	2.54
9	Barney Pelty	2.51
10	Red Donahue	2.46

Double Plays

First Base

1	Mickey Vernon	2044
2	Eddie Murray	2021
3	Joe Kuhel	1769
4	Charlie Grimm	1733
5	Chris Chambliss	1687
6	Keith Hernandez	1654
7	Gil Hodges	1614
8	Lou Gehrig	1575
9	Jim Bottomley	1562
10	Jimmie Foxx	1528

Second Base

1	Bill Mazeroski	1706
2	Nellie Fox	1619
3	Willie Randolph	1547
4	Bobby Doerr	1507
5	Joe Morgan	1505
6	Lou Whitaker	1495
7	Charlie Gehringer	1444
8	Frank White	1382
9	Red Schoendienst	1368
10	Bobby Grich	1302

Shortstop

1	Luis Aparicio	1553
2	Ozzie Smith	1526
3	Luke Appling	1424
4	Cal Ripken	1356
5	Roy McMillan	1304
6	Dave Concepcion	1290
7	Larry Bowa	1265
8	Alan Trammell	1258
9	Pee Wee Reese	1246
10	Dick Groat	1237

Third Base

1	Brooks Robinson	618
2	Graig Nettles	470
3	Mike Schmidt	450
4	Buddy Bell	430
5	Aurelio Rodriguez	408
6	Ron Santo	395
7	Gary Gaetti	374
8	Eddie Mathews	369
9	Ken Boyer	355
10	Wade Boggs	347

Outfield

1	Tris Speaker	139
2	Ty Cobb	107
3	Max Carey	86
4	Tom Brown	85
5	Harry Hooper	81
6	Jimmy Sheckard	80
7	Mike Griffin	75
8	Dummy Hoy	72
9	Jimmy Ryan	71
10	Fielder Jones	70
11	Patsy Donovan	69
12	Sam Rice	67
13	George Van Haltren	64
14	Jesse Burkett	62
15	Sam Thompson	61
16	Willie Keeler	60
	Willie Mays	60
	Tommy McCarthy	60
	Mel Ott	60
20	Sam Crawford	59

Catcher

1	Ray Schalk	226
2	Steve O'Neill	193
3	Yogi Berra	175
4	Gabby Hartnett	163
5	Bob Boone	154
6	Jimmie Wilson	153
7	Gary Carter	149
	Wally Schang	149
9	Carlton Fisk	147
10	Jim Sundberg	145

Pitcher

1	Phil Niekro	83
2	Warren Spahn	82
3	Freddie Fitzsimmons	79
4	Bob Lemon	78
5	Bucky Walters	76
6	Burleigh Grimes	74
7	Walter Johnson	72
8	Tommy John	69
9	Jim Kaat	65
10	Dizzy Trout	63

Fielding Runs

1	Nap Lajoie	367
2	Bill Mazeroski	362
3	Bill Dahlen	348
4	Bid McPhee	314
5	Fred Pfeffer	266
6	Mike Schmidt	265
7	George Davis	249
8	Tris Speaker	248
9	Jack Glasscock	240
10	Ozzie Smith	236
11	Clete Boyer	233
12	Glenn Hubbard	229
13	Richie Ashburn	227
14	Bobby Wallace	212
15	Joe Tinker	208
16	Max Carey	199
17	Dave Bancroft	198
18	Buddy Bell	191
19	Aurelio Rodriguez	184
20	Bobby Doerr	181
21	Willie Mays	180
22	Dick Bartell	178
	Mickey Doolan	178
	Terry Pendleton	178
25	Roberto Clemente	175
26	Joe Gerhardt	173
27	George McBride	170
28	Mark Belanger	167
29	Lee Tannehill	166
30	Darrell Evans	165
31	Rickey Henderson	164
32	Art Fletcher	162
33	Dal Maxvill	160
34	Rabbit Maranville	158
35	Germany Smith	157
36	Danny Richardson	156
37	Ski Melillo	151
	Brooks Robinson	151
39	Lou Bierbauer	150
	Frankie Frisch	150
	Hughie Jennings	150
	Bobby Knoop	150
43	Jim Hegan	149
	Carl Yastrzemski	149
45	Keith Hernandez	148
	Pop Snyder	148
47	Lave Cross	145
48	Garry Maddox	142
49	Billy Jurges	140
50	Jimmy Collins	139
51	Ron Santo	138
52	Willie Davis	137
	Fred Dunlap	137
	Bobby Wine	137
55	Kirby Puckett	135
56	Lou Boudreau	134
57	John Ward	133
58	Hal Lanier	132
	Graig Nettles	132
60	Lou Criger	131
	Bill Killefer	131
62	Andre Dawson	130
	Ryne Sandberg	130
64	Manny Trillo	129
65	Mick Kelleher	128
66	Bill Buckner	127
67	Gene Alley	125
	Gary Gaetti	125
69	Fred Tenney	124
70	Vic Power	123
71	Tony Gwynn	121
	Al Weis	121
73	Bill Bergen	119
74	Chet Lemon	116
	Harold Reynolds	116
76	Everett Scott	115
77	Jesse Barfield	114
	Curt Flood	114
	Tommy Leach	114
80	Barry Bonds	113
	Johnny Callison	113
	Hank DeBerry	113
	Hobe Ferris	113
	Hardy Richardson	113
85	Hughie Critz	111
	Jose Cruz	111
87	Jim Wynn	110
88	Jerry Denny	109
89	Curt Welch	107
90	Tommy Corcoran	106
	Tim Raines	106
	Joe Sewell	106
93	Brett Butler	105
	Johnny Logan	105
95	Travis Jackson	104
96	Al Kaline	103
	Omar Moreno	103
98	Eddie Miller	102
	Dwayne Murphy	102
	Chief Zimmer	102

Fielding Runs (by position)

First Base

1	Keith Hernandez	150
2	Fred Tenney	129
3	Vic Power	124
4	Bill Buckner	121
5	George Sisler	89
6	Sid Bream	76
	Darrell Evans	76
8	Mark Grace	67
	Bill Terry	67
10	Ed Konetchy	60
	Eddie Murray	60

Second Base

1	Nap Lajoie	368
2	Bill Mazeroski	363
3	Bid McPhee	314
4	Fred Pfeffer	257
5	Glenn Hubbard	229
6	Bobby Doerr	180
7	Joe Gerhardt	160
8	Lou Bierbauer	153
9	Bobby Knoop	150
10	Ski Melillo	148

Shortstop

1	Bill Dahlen	302
2	Jack Glasscock	243
3	Ozzie Smith	235
4	Joe Tinker	210
5	Dave Bancroft	200
6	George Davis	187
7	Rabbit Maranville	177
8	George McBride	173
9	Mickey Doolan	167
10	Mark Belanger	164

Third Base

1	Mike Schmidt	265
2	Clete Boyer	201
3	Buddy Bell	199
4	Aurelio Rodriguez	185
5	Terry Pendleton	180
6	Brooks Robinson	152
7	Jimmy Collins	138
8	Graig Nettles	136
9	Ron Santo	135
10	Lave Cross	132

Outfield

1	Tris Speaker	248
2	Richie Ashburn	227
3	Max Carey	202
4	Willie Mays	184
5	Roberto Clemente	173
6	Rickey Henderson	165
7	Carl Yastrzemski	143
8	Garry Maddox	142
9	Willie Davis	137
	Kirby Puckett	137
11	Andre Dawson	131
12	Tony Gwynn	120
13	Chet Lemon	119
14	Jim Wynn	118
15	Curt Flood	116
16	Johnny Callison	114
17	Barry Bonds	113
18	Jesse Barfield	112
19	Jose Cruz	111
20	Jim Fogarty	110

Catcher

1	Pop Snyder	151
2	Jim Hegan	149
3	Lou Criger	134
4	Bill Killefer	131
5	Bill Bergen	118
6	Chief Zimmer	103
7	Jim Sundberg	99
8	Ossee Schreckengost	98
9	Johnny Edwards	97
10	Tony Pena	96

Pitcher

1	Ed Walsh	84
2	Carl Mays	74
3	Christy Mathewson	69
4	Freddie Fitzsimmons	61
5	Bob Lemon	59
6	Burleigh Grimes	58
7	Tommy John	56
8	Harry Gumbert	51
9	Harry Howell	50
10	John Clarkson	45

Fielding Wins

1	Bill Mazeroski	37.7
2	Nap Lajoie	37.6
3	Bill Dahlen	33.1
4	Mike Schmidt	27.7
5	Bid McPhee	27.3
6	Tris Speaker	25.3
7	Ozzie Smith	24.6
8	Clete Boyer	24.2
9	Glenn Hubbard	23.8
10	George Davis	23.4
11	Fred Pfeffer	23.2
12	Richie Ashburn	22.7
13	Joe Tinker	21.9
14	Bobby Wallace	21.4
15	Jack Glasscock	21.3
16	Max Carey	20.4
17	Dave Bancroft	20.2
18	Buddy Bell	19.6
19	Aurelio Rodriguez	19.2
20	Mickey Doolan	19.0
21	Willie Mays	18.6
22	Terry Pendleton	18.5
23	George McBride	18.3
24	Roberto Clemente	18.2
25	Lee Tannehill	18.0
26	Bobby Doerr	17.8
27	Dick Bartell	17.5
28	Mark Belanger	17.5
29	Art Fletcher	17.3
30	Darrell Evans	17.0
31	Dal Maxvill	16.9
32	Rickey Henderson	16.3
33	Bobby Knoop	16.2
34	Rabbit Maranville	16.0
35	Brooks Robinson	15.9
36	Carl Yastrzemski	15.5
37	Joe Gerhardt	15.5
38	Keith Hernandez	15.5
39	Jim Hegan	14.9
40	Garry Maddox	14.9
41	Frankie Frisch	14.7
42	Ron Santo	14.5
43	Bobby Wine	14.4
	Willie Davis	14.4
45	Bill Killefer	14.2
46	Billy Jurges	14.2
47	Ski Melillo	14.1
48	Hal Lanier	14.1
49	Graig Nettles	13.7
50	Danny Richardson	13.6
51	Ryne Sandberg	13.6
52	Andre Dawson	13.5
53	Germany Smith	13.5
54	Lou Boudreau	13.5
55	Manny Trillo	13.5
56	Jimmy Collins	13.4
57	Kirby Puckett	13.4
58	Mick Kelleher	13.4
59	Lave Cross	13.3
60	Gene Alley	13.3
61	Lou Criger	13.2
62	Pop Snyder	13.2
63	Hughie Jennings	13.2
64	Bill Buckner	13.1
65	Al Weis	12.9
66	Lou Bierbauer	12.7
67	Bill Bergen	12.6
68	Tony Gwynn	12.6
69	Vic Power	12.6
70	Gary Gaetti	12.4
71	Fred Dunlap	12.4
72	Fred Tenney	12.3
73	Hobe Ferris	12.0
74	Curt Flood	11.9
75	Tommy Leach	11.9
76	Johnny Callison	11.9
77	John Ward	11.7
78	Barry Bonds	11.7
79	Everett Scott	11.7
80	Chet Lemon	11.6
81	Jim Wynn	11.6
82	Jose Cruz	11.6
83	Harold Reynolds	11.5
84	Jesse Barfield	11.4
85	Tim Raines	10.9
86	Hank DeBerry	10.9
87	Brett Butler	10.8
88	Hughie Critz	10.7
89	Al Kaline	10.7
90	Omar Moreno	10.7
91	Johnny Logan	10.6
92	Hank Aaron	10.5
93	Honus Wagner	10.4
94	Eddie Miller	10.4
95	Dwayne Murphy	10.2
96	Johnny Edwards	10.2
97	Dave Parker	10.1
98	Tony Pena	10.1
99	Hardy Richardson	10.1
100	Travis Jackson	10.0

Total Player Rating

1	Babe Ruth	107.6
2	Nap Lajoie	94.3
3	Willie Mays	92.2
4	Ty Cobb	91.1
5	Hank Aaron	89.8
6	Tris Speaker	86.5
7	Ted Williams	85.7
8	Honus Wagner	81.3
9	Rogers Hornsby	81.1
10	Mike Schmidt	78.4
11	Mickey Mantle	76.1
12	Rickey Henderson	74.6
13	Stan Musial	70.5
14	Eddie Collins	69.7
15	Frank Robinson	69.0
16	Lou Gehrig	65.7
17	Mel Ott	62.7
18	Joe Morgan	56.3
19	Jimmie Foxx	54.0
20	Eddie Mathews	51.6
21	Bill Dahlen	51.4
22	George Davis	51.1
23	Tim Raines	51.0
24	Barry Bonds	49.4
25	Joe DiMaggio	46.9
26	Carl Yastrzemski	45.5
27	Al Kaline	44.6
28	Wade Boggs	44.4
	Charlie Gehringer	44.4
30	Ed Delahanty	44.3
31	Bobby Grich	44.1
32	Robin Yount	43.1
33	Ozzie Smith	43.0
34	Roberto Clemente	42.9
35	Reggie Jackson	42.8
36	Roger Connor	42.7
37	Lou Boudreau	41.3
38	Dan Brouthers	41.1
39	Luke Appling	40.7
40	Gabby Hartnett	40.1
	Bid McPhee	40.1
42	Dave Winfield	39.7
43	Ron Santo	39.5
44	Joe Cronin	39.4
45	Cal Ripken	39.2
	Arky Vaughan	39.2
47	Frankie Frisch	39.1
48	George Brett	39.0
	Bobby Doerr	39.0
50	Ryne Sandberg	38.8
51	Tony Gwynn	38.5
52	Joe Jackson	37.5
53	Bobby Wallace	36.9
54	Willie McCovey	36.5
55	Bill Mazeroski	36.3
56	Yogi Berra	36.2
	Johnny Mize	36.2
58	Jack Glasscock	36.1
	Paul Waner	36.1
60	Bob Johnson	35.6
	Eddie Murray	35.6
62	Bill Dickey	35.4
63	Dick Allen	35.3
	Dave Bancroft	35.3
65	Paul Molitor	35.2
66	Reggie Smith	35.0
67	Darrell Evans	34.6
68	Keith Hernandez	34.4
	Joe Sewell	34.4
70	Frank Baker	33.8
71	Jim Wynn	33.2
72	Willie Stargell	32.8
73	Harry Heilmann	32.4
74	Jackie Robinson	31.8
75	Billy Herman	31.7
76	Rod Carew	31.4
	Mickey Cochrane	31.4
78	Jack Clark	31.1
	Andre Dawson	31.1
	Billy Williams	31.1
81	Cap Anson	30.7
82	Dwight Evans	30.4
83	Richie Ashburn	30.2
	Sam Crawford	30.2
85	Cupid Childs	30.0
	Hank Greenberg	30.0
87	Bobby Bonds	29.6
	Gary Carter	29.6
89	Buck Ewing	29.4
90	Ralph Kiner	28.9
91	Pete Browning	28.8
	Jose Cruz	28.8
93	Elmer Flick	28.7
94	Fred Clarke	28.6
95	Jesse Burkett	28.5
96	Sam Thompson	28.4
97	Cesar Cedeno	28.3
98	Joe Gordon	28.2
99	Dick Bartell	27.9
100	Barry Larkin	27.6

Total Player Rating

	Rusty Staub	27.6
102	Norm Cash	27.5
103	Fred Dunlap	27.4
	Kirby Puckett	27.4
105	Hardy Richardson	27.3
106	Stan Hack	27.2
107	Joe Medwick	27.1
108	Heinie Groh	27.0
	Jim Rice	27.0
110	Darryl Strawberry	26.9
111	Sherry Magee	26.6
112	Billy Hamilton	26.4
	Harmon Killebrew	26.4
114	Hughie Jennings	26.2
115	Goose Goslin	26.1
116	Minnie Minoso	26.0
117	Ernie Banks	25.9
	Art Fletcher	25.9
119	Al Simmons	25.6
120	Rocky Colavito	25.2
121	Bill Terry	24.9
122	Lenny Dykstra	24.8
	Tony Oliva	24.8
124	King Kelly	24.7
125	Zack Wheat	24.5
	Lou Whitaker	24.5
127	Johnny Bench	24.3
128	Travis Jackson	24.2
129	Carlton Fisk	24.0
	Jack Fournier	24.0
	Alan Trammell	24.0
132	Charlie Keller	23.5
133	Jimmy Collins	23.4
134	Willie Randolph	23.1
135	Max Carey	23.0
	Dave Parker	23.0
	Joe Tinker	23.0
138	Jake Beckley	22.9
	Buddy Bell	22.9
140	Roy Thomas	22.8
141	Harland Clift	22.7
	George Sisler	22.7
143	Jose Canseco	22.5
144	George Foster	22.3
	Ed Konetchy	22.3
	Chet Lemon	22.3
	Fred Lynn	22.3
	Duke Snider	22.3
149	Wally Berger	22.2
150	Brett Butler	22.1
151	Ron Cey	21.9
152	Fred Pfeffer	21.7
153	Roy Campanella	21.6
154	Chuck Klein	21.5
155	Graig Nettles	21.4
156	Frank Howard	21.3
	Harry Stovey	21.3
	Roy White	21.3
159	Larry Doby	21.2
160	Andy Van Slyke	21.0
161	Ken Griffey	20.9
	Kevin Mitchell	20.9
	Ken Singleton	20.9
	Fred Tenney	20.9
165	Will Clark	20.8
	Pie Traynor	20.8
167	Charley Jones	20.7
168	Frank Chance	20.6
	Art Devlin	20.6
	Jim Fregosi	20.6
171	Mike Griffin	20.5
	Frank Thomas	20.5
173	Del Pratt	20.4
174	Glenn Hubbard	20.2
	Joe Kelley	20.2
176	Pete Rose	20.0
177	Denny Lyons	19.8
	Brooks Robinson	19.8
179	Roger Bresnahan	19.7
180	Eric Davis	19.6
	Vern Stephens	19.6
	Joe Torre	19.6
183	Dale Murphy	19.3
	Amos Otis	19.3
	Jimmy Sheckard	19.3
186	Charlie Bennett	19.2
187	Bill Joyce	19.0
	Fred McGriff	19.0
	Bill Nicholson	19.0
190	Gavvy Cravath	18.9
	Bob Elliott	18.9
192	Ken Boyer	18.6
	Brian Downing	18.6
194	Eddie Stanky	18.4
195	Wally Schang	18.3
196	Miller Huggins	18.2
197	Roy Cullenbine	18.1
198	Gene Alley	18.0
199	Rico Carty	17.9
200	Ferris Fain	17.8

Total Player Rating

201	Earl Averill	17.6
202	Tommy Leach	17.4
203	Babe Herman	17.3
	Johnny Logan	17.3
	Ernie Lombardi	17.3
206	Paul Hines	17.2
	Ken Williams	17.2
208	Tony Fernandez	17.1
209	Tony Lazzeri	16.9
210	Gil McDougald	16.8
	Ted Simmons	16.8
212	Orlando Cepeda	16.7
	Pedro Guerrero	16.7
214	Jesse Barfield	16.4
	Jeff Heath	16.4
	Dwayne Murphy	16.4
217	Enos Slaughter	16.3
	Danny Tartabull	16.3
219	Kirk Gibson	16.2
	George Gore	16.2
221	John McGraw	16.1
	Jim O'Rourke	16.1
	Jimmy Williams	16.1
224	Kiki Cuyler	15.8
	Phil Rizzuto	15.8
	Chief Zimmer	15.8
227	Mike Hargrove	15.7
	Robby Thompson	15.7
229	Davey Johnson	15.6
	Jocko Milligan	15.6
	Hack Wilson	15.6
232	Ray Chapman	15.5
233	Bobby Bonilla	15.4
234	Jeff Bagwell	15.3
	Thurman Munson	15.3
	Gene Tenace	15.3
237	Sid Gordon	15.1
238	Mark Belanger	15.0
	Bobby Knoop	15.0
240	Henry Larkin	14.9
	Boog Powell	14.9
	Bobby Veach	14.9
243	Benny Kauff	14.8
	Mike Scioscia	14.8
245	Sixto Lezcano	14.7
246	Augie Galan	14.6
	Greg Luzinski	14.6
	Pee Wee Reese	14.6
249	Lave Cross	14.5
	Duke Farrell	14.5
	Tommy Henrich	14.5
252	Kevin McReynolds	14.4
253	Bob Allison	14.3
254	Ron Hansen	14.2
255	Johnny Callison	14.1
256	Ben Chapman	14.0
257	Rafael Palmeiro	13.9
258	Harold Baines	13.8
259	Gil Hodges	13.7
	Roy Smalley	13.7
261	Willie Kamm	13.6
262	Fred Carroll	13.5
	Tommy Holmes	13.5
	Kip Selbach	13.5
	Richie Zisk	13.5
266	Chief Meyers	13.4
	Al Oliver	13.4
268	Roger Peckinpaugh	13.3
	Jimmy Ryan	13.3
	George Stone	13.3
271	Bill Freehan	13.2
	Dave Orr	13.2
273	Doug DeCinces	13.1
	Johnny Evers	13.1
	Rabbit Maranville	13.1
	Edd Roush	13.1
277	Bobby Murcer	13.0
	Red Smith	13.0
	John Titus	13.0
	Larry Walker	13.0
281	Don Mattingly	12.9
	Terry Pendleton	12.9
	Mike Tiernan	12.9
284	Kal Daniels	12.8
285	Lou Brock	12.7
	Dolph Camilli	12.7
	Jack Clements	12.7
	Kid Elberfeld	12.7
	Harry Hooper	12.7
	Billy Nash	12.7
	Roy Sievers	12.7
292	Clete Boyer	12.6
	Deacon McGuire	12.6
	Riggs Stephenson	12.6
295	Chick Hafey	12.5
	Matt Williams	12.5
297	Luis Aparicio	12.4
	Jay Bell	12.4
	Ken Griffey	12.4
	Johnny Pesky	12.4

Total Player Rating

	Al Rosen	12.4
302	Darrell Porter	12.1
	Bob Watson	12.1
304	Roberto Alomar	12.0
	Gary Matthews	12.0
	Lance Parrish	12.0
307	Rick Burleson	11.9
	Lou Criger	11.9
	Jake Daubert	11.9
	Chili Davis	11.9
	Nellie Fox	11.9
	Lonny Frey	11.9
313	Albert Belle	11.8
	Ossee Schreckengost	11.8
315	Jim Gentile	11.7
	Roger Maris	11.7
	Jerry Priddy	11.7
	Andy Thornton	11.7
319	Earle Combs	11.6
	Ken Keltner	11.6
	Hal McRae	11.6
	Lefty O'Doul	11.6
	Lonnie Smith	11.6
	Stan Spence	11.6
325	Johnny Kling	11.5
326	Buck Herzog	11.4
	Dan McGann	11.4
	Orator Shaffer	11.4
329	Julio Franco	11.3
	Toby Harrah	11.3
	Andy Seminick	11.3
	Ed Swartwood	11.3
333	Tom Haller	11.1
	David Justice	11.1
	Freddy Lindstrom	11.1
	George Van Haltren	11.1
337	Harry Davis	11.0
	John Kruk	11.0
	Mark McGwire	11.0
	Danny Murphy	11.0
	Paul O'Neill	11.0
	Hank Sauer	11.0
343	Don Baylor	10.9
	Joe Harris	10.9
	Monte Irvin	10.9
	Ben Oglivie	10.9
347	Earl Battey	10.8
	Tony Cuccinello	10.8
	Willie Davis	10.8
	Dom DiMaggio	10.8
	Jackie Jensen	10.8
	Ross Youngs	10.8
353	Tom Daly	10.7
	Mike Greenwell	10.7
355	Mike Donlin	10.6
	Red Schoendienst	10.6
	Dixie Walker	10.6
	Curt Welch	10.6
	Deacon White	10.6
360	Billy Jurges	10.5
	Kenny Lofton	10.5
	Maury Wills	10.5
363	Ed McFarland	10.4
	Tip O'Neill	10.4
	Cy Seymour	10.4
366	Willie Keeler	10.3
	Whitey Kurowski	10.3
	Willie McGee	10.3
	Rico Petrocelli	10.3
370	Bill Melton	10.2
	Buddy Myer	10.2
	Cecil Travis	10.2
	Jimmy Wolf	10.2
	Rudy York	10.2
375	Jack Crooks	10.1
	Rick Ferrell	10.1
377	Mark Grace	10.0
	Ned Williamson	10.0
379	Jerry Denny	9.9
	Charlie Hickman	9.9
	Tony Perez	9.9
382	Larry Hisle	9.8
	Edgar Martinez	9.8
	Doug Rader	9.8
385	Johnny Romano	9.7
	Heinie Zimmerman	9.7
387	Carlos Baerga	9.5
	Oscar Gamble	9.5
	Elmer Smith	9.5
390	John Farrell	9.4
	Hank Gowdy	9.4
	Vic Wertz	9.4
393	Oyster Burns	9.3
	Walker Cooper	9.3
	Jimmy Dykes	9.3
	Kent Hrbek	9.3
	Bump Wills	9.3
398	Craig Biggio	9.2
	Don Buford	9.2
	Dave Concepcion	9.2

Total Player Rating

	Sherm Lollar	9.2
	Wes Westrum	9.2
403	Bill Lange	9.1
	Sam Rice	9.1
405	Bill Bradley	9.0
	Claude Ritchey	9.0
407	Del Ennis	8.9
	Pinky May	8.9
409	Garry Maddox	8.8
	Marty McManus	8.8
	Vada Pinson	8.8
	Gene Woodling	8.8
413	Dal Maxvill	8.7
414	Happy Felsch	8.6
	Fred Luderus	8.6
	Bob Nieman	8.6
417	Bernie Carbo	8.5
	Marquis Grissom	8.5
	Rick Monday	8.5
420	Sal Bando	8.4
	Bert Campaneris	8.4
	Eddie Joost	8.4
423	Steve Kemp	8.3
424	Del Crandall	8.2
	George Selkirk	8.2
	Snuffy Stirnweiss	8.2
	Pinky Whitney	8.2
428	Hank DeBerry	8.1
429	Mike Mitchell	8.0
	Jim Sundberg	8.0
431	Topsy Hartsel	7.9
	Bill Sweeney	7.9
	Al Weis	7.9
	Ernie Whitt	7.9
435	Bob Allen	7.8
	Johnny Bassler	7.8
	Frank Fennelly	7.8
	Cecil Fielder	7.8
	Wally Joyner	7.8
	John Ward	7.8
441	Jimmy Barrett	7.7
	Elbie Fletcher	7.7
	Solly Hemus	7.7
444	Cecil Cooper	7.6
	Ron Karkovice	7.6
	Johnny Mostil	7.6
	Robin Ventura	7.6
	Billy Werber	7.6
449	Dusty Baker	7.5
	Jay Buhner	7.5
	Mike Gallego	7.5
	Pop Snyder	7.5
	Mickey Tettleton	7.5
454	Donie Bush	7.4
	Phil Garner	7.4
	Cliff Johnson	7.4
	Harry Steinfeldt	7.4
458	Joe Adcock	7.3
	Phil Bradley	7.3
	Ken McMullen	7.3
	Jim McTamany	7.3
	Spike Owen	7.3
	Lee Tannehill	7.3
	Cy Williams	7.3
465	Johnny Bates	7.2
	Luis Gonzalez	7.2
	John Olerud	7.2
	Jody Reed	7.2
	Danny Richardson	7.2
	Socks Seybold	7.2
471	Julio Cruz	7.1
	Dick Dietz	7.1
	Ival Goodman	7.1
	Tony Pena	7.1
	Perry Werden	7.1
476	Dave Brain	7.0
	Spud Davis	7.0
	Joe Gerhardt	7.0
	Elston Howard	7.0
	Mick Kelleher	7.0
	Buddy Lewis	7.0
	Charlie Maxwell	7.0
	Bake McBride	7.0
	Matty McIntyre	7.0
	Johnny Ray	7.0
	Pete Reiser	7.0
	Ruben Sierra	7.0
488	Ellis Burks	6.9
	Jim Fogarty	6.9
	Tony Phillips	6.9
	George Wood	6.9
492	Sam Wise	6.8
493	Dave Cash	6.7
	Harry Danning	6.7
	Kelly Gruber	6.7
496	9 players tied	6.6

Total Player Rating (alpha.)

Hank Aaron	89.8
Joe Adcock	7.3
Dick Allen	35.3
Bob Allen	7.8
Gene Alley	18.0
Bob Allison	14.3
Roberto Alomar	12.0
Cap Anson	30.7
Luis Aparicio	12.4
Luke Appling	40.7
Richie Ashburn	30.2
Earl Averill	17.6
Carlos Baerga	9.5
Jeff Bagwell	15.3
Harold Baines	13.8
Frank Baker	33.8
Dusty Baker	7.5
Dave Bancroft	35.3
Sal Bando	8.4
Ernie Banks	25.9
Jesse Barfield	16.4
Jimmy Barrett	7.7
Dick Bartell	27.9
Johnny Bassler	7.8
Johnny Bates	7.2
Earl Battey	10.8
Don Baylor	10.9
Jake Beckley	22.9
Mark Belanger	15.0
Buddy Bell	22.9
Jay Bell	12.4
Albert Belle	11.8
Johnny Bench	24.3
Charlie Bennett	19.2
Wally Berger	22.2
Yogi Berra	36.2
Craig Biggio	9.2
Wade Boggs	44.4
Bobby Bonds	29.6
Bobby Bonilla	15.4
Lou Boudreau	41.3
Clete Boyer	12.6
Ken Boyer	18.6
Phil Bradley	7.3
Bill Bradley	9.0
Dave Brain	7.0
Roger Bresnahan	19.7
George Brett	39.0
Lou Brock	12.7
Dan Brouthers	41.1
Pete Browning	28.8
Don Buford	9.2
Jay Buhner	7.5
Jesse Burkett	28.5
Ellis Burks	6.9
Rick Burleson	11.9
Oyster Burns	9.3
Donie Bush	7.4
Brett Butler	22.1
Johnny Callison	14.1
Dolph Camilli	12.7
Roy Campanella	21.6
Bert Campaneris	8.4
Jose Canseco	22.5
Bernie Carbo	8.5
Rod Carew	31.4
Max Carey	23.0
Fred Carroll	13.5
Gary Carter	29.6
Rico Carty	17.9
Dave Cash	6.7
Norm Cash	27.5
Cesar Cedeno	28.3
Orlando Cepeda	16.7
Ron Cey	21.9
Frank Chance	20.6
Ray Chapman	15.5
Ben Chapman	14.0
Cupid Childs	30.0
Jack Clark	31.1
Will Clark	20.8
Fred Clarke	28.6
Roberto Clemente	42.9
Jack Clements	12.7
Harlond Clift	22.7
Ty Cobb	91.1
Mickey Cochrane	31.4
Rocky Colavito	25.2
Eddie Collins	69.7
Jimmy Collins	23.4
Earle Combs	11.6
Dave Concepcion	9.2
Roger Connor	42.7
Cecil Cooper	7.6
Walker Cooper	9.3
Del Crandall	8.2
Gavvy Cravath	18.9
Sam Crawford	30.2
Lou Criger	11.9

Total Player Rating (alpha.)

Joe Cronin	39.4
Jack Crooks	10.1
Lave Cross	14.5
Jose Cruz	28.8
Julio Cruz	7.1
Tony Cuccinello	10.8
Roy Cullenbine	18.1
Kiki Cuyler	15.8
Bill Dahlen	51.4
Tom Daly	10.7
Kal Daniels	12.8
Harry Danning	6.7
Jake Daubert	11.9
Chili Davis	11.9
Eric Davis	19.6
George Davis	51.1
Harry Davis	11.0
Spud Davis	7.0
Willie Davis	10.8
Andre Dawson	31.1
Hank DeBerry	8.1
Doug DeCinces	13.1
Ed Delahanty	44.3
Jerry Denny	9.9
Art Devlin	20.6
Bill Dickey	35.4
Dick Dietz	7.1
Dom DiMaggio	10.8
Joe DiMaggio	46.9
Larry Doby	21.2
Bobby Doerr	39.0
Mike Donlin	10.6
Brian Downing	18.6
Fred Dunlap	27.4
Jimmy Dykes	9.3
Lenny Dykstra	24.8
Kid Elberfeld	12.7
Bob Elliott	18.9
Del Ennis	8.9
Darrell Evans	34.6
Dwight Evans	30.4
Johnny Evers	13.1
Buck Ewing	29.4
Ferris Fain	17.8
Duke Farrell	14.5
John Farrell	9.4
Happy Felsch	8.6
Frank Fennelly	7.8
Tony Fernandez	17.1
Rick Ferrell	10.1
Cecil Fielder	7.8
Carlton Fisk	24.0
Art Fletcher	25.9
Elbie Fletcher	7.7
Elmer Flick	28.7
Jim Fogarty	6.9
George Foster	22.3
Jack Fournier	24.0
Nellie Fox	11.9
Jimmie Foxx	54.0
Julio Franco	11.3
Bill Freehan	13.2
Jim Fregosi	20.6
Lonny Frey	11.9
Frankie Frisch	39.1
Augie Galan	14.6
Mike Gallego	7.5
Oscar Gamble	9.5
Phil Garner	7.4
Lou Gehrig	65.7
Charlie Gehringer	44.4
Jim Gentile	11.7
Joe Gerhardt	7.0
Kirk Gibson	16.2
Jack Glasscock	36.1
Luis Gonzalez	7.2
Ival Goodman	7.1
Joe Gordon	28.2
Sid Gordon	15.1
George Gore	16.2
Goose Goslin	26.1
Hank Gowdy	9.4
Mark Grace	10.0
Hank Greenberg	30.0
Mike Greenwell	10.7
Bobby Grich	44.1
Ken Griffey	20.9
Ken Griffey	12.4
Mike Griffin	20.5
Marquis Grissom	8.5
Heinie Groh	27.0
Kelly Gruber	6.7
Pedro Guerrero	16.7
Tony Gwynn	38.5
Stan Hack	27.2
Chick Hafey	12.5
Tom Haller	11.1
Billy Hamilton	26.4
Ron Hansen	14.2
Mike Hargrove	15.7

Total Player Rating (alpha.)

Toby Harrah	11.3
Joe Harris	10.9
Gabby Hartnett	40.1
Topsy Hartsel	7.9
Jeff Heath	16.4
Harry Heilmann	32.4
Solly Hemus	7.7
Rickey Henderson	74.6
Tommy Henrich	14.5
Babe Herman	17.3
Billy Herman	31.7
Keith Hernandez	34.4
Buck Herzog	11.4
Charlie Hickman	9.9
Paul Hines	17.2
Larry Hisle	9.8
Gil Hodges	13.7
Tommy Holmes	13.5
Harry Hooper	12.7
Rogers Hornsby	81.1
Elston Howard	7.0
Frank Howard	21.3
Kent Hrbek	9.3
Glenn Hubbard	20.2
Miller Huggins	18.2
Monte Irvin	10.9
Joe Jackson	37.5
Reggie Jackson	42.8
Travis Jackson	24.2
Hughie Jennings	26.2
Jackie Jensen	10.8
Cliff Johnson	7.4
Davey Johnson	15.6
Bob Johnson	35.6
Charley Jones	20.7
Eddie Joost	8.4
Bill Joyce	19.0
Wally Joyner	7.8
Billy Jurges	10.5
David Justice	11.1
Al Kaline	44.6
Willie Kamm	13.6
Ron Karkovice	7.6
Benny Kauff	14.8
Willie Keeler	10.3
Mick Kelleher	7.0
Charlie Keller	23.5
Joe Kelley	20.2
King Kelly	24.7
Ken Keltner	11.6
Steve Kemp	8.3
Harmon Killebrew	26.4
Ralph Kiner	28.9
Chuck Klein	21.5
Johnny Kling	11.5
Bobby Knoop	15.0
Ed Konetchy	22.3
John Kruk	11.0
Whitey Kurowski	10.3
Nap Lajoie	94.3
Bill Lange	9.1
Barry Larkin	27.6
Henry Larkin	14.9
Tony Lazzeri	16.9
Tommy Leach	17.4
Chet Lemon	22.3
Buddy Lewis	7.0
Sixto Lezcano	14.7
Freddy Lindstrom	11.1
Kenny Lofton	10.5
Johnny Logan	17.3
Sherm Lollar	9.2
Ernie Lombardi	17.3
Fred Luderus	8.6
Greg Luzinski	14.6
Fred Lynn	22.3
Denny Lyons	19.8
Garry Maddox	8.8
Sherry Magee	26.6
Mickey Mantle	76.1
Rabbit Maranville	13.1
Roger Maris	11.7
Edgar Martinez	9.8
Eddie Mathews	51.6
Gary Matthews	12.0
Don Mattingly	12.9
Dal Maxvill	8.7
Charlie Maxwell	7.0
Pinky May	8.9
Willie Mays	92.2
Bill Mazeroski	36.3
Bake McBride	7.0
Willie McCovey	36.5
Gil McDougald	16.8
Ed McFarland	10.4
Dan McGann	11.4
Willie McGee	10.3
John McGraw	16.1
Fred McGriff	19.0
Deacon McGuire	12.6

Total Player Rating (alpha.)

Mark McGwire	11.0
Matty McIntyre	7.0
Marty McManus	8.8
Ken McMullen	7.3
Bid McPhee	40.1
Hal McRae	11.6
Kevin McReynolds	14.4
Jim McTamany	7.3
Joe Medwick	27.1
Bill Melton	10.2
Chief Meyers	13.4
Jocko Milligan	15.6
Minnie Minoso	26.0
Kevin Mitchell	20.9
Mike Mitchell	8.0
Johnny Mize	36.2
Paul Molitor	35.2
Rick Monday	8.5
Joe Morgan	56.3
Johnny Mostil	7.6
Thurman Munson	15.3
Bobby Murcer	13.0
Dale Murphy	19.3
Danny Murphy	11.0
Dwayne Murphy	16.4
Eddie Murray	35.6
Stan Musial	70.5
Buddy Myer	10.2
Billy Nash	12.7
Graig Nettles	21.4
Bill Nicholson	19.0
Bob Nieman	8.6
Lefty O'Doul	11.6
Tip O'Neill	10.4
Paul O'Neill	11.0
Jim O'Rourke	16.1
Ben Oglivie	10.9
John Olerud	7.2
Tony Oliva	24.8
Al Oliver	13.4
Dave Orr	13.2
Amos Otis	19.3
Mel Ott	62.7
Spike Owen	7.3
Rafael Palmeiro	13.9
Dave Parker	23.0
Lance Parrish	12.0
Roger Peckinpaugh	13.3
Tony Pena	7.1
Terry Pendleton	12.9
Tony Perez	9.9
Johnny Pesky	12.4
Rico Petrocelli	10.3
Fred Pfeffer	21.7
Tony Phillips	6.9
Vada Pinson	8.8
Darrell Porter	12.1
Boog Powell	14.9
Del Pratt	20.4
Jerry Priddy	11.7
Kirby Puckett	27.4
Doug Rader	9.8
Tim Raines	51.0
Willie Randolph	23.1
Johnny Ray	7.0
Jody Reed	7.2
Pee Wee Reese	14.6
Pete Reiser	7.0
Sam Rice	9.1
Jim Rice	27.0
Hardy Richardson	27.3
Danny Richardson	7.2
Cal Ripken	39.2
Claude Ritchey	9.0
Phil Rizzuto	15.8
Brooks Robinson	19.8
Frank Robinson	69.0
Jackie Robinson	31.8
Johnny Romano	9.7
Pete Rose	20.0
Al Rosen	12.4
Edd Roush	13.1
Babe Ruth	107.6
Jimmy Ryan	13.3
Ryne Sandberg	38.8
Ron Santo	39.5
Hank Sauer	11.0
Wally Schang	18.3
Mike Schmidt	78.4
Red Schoendienst	10.6
Ossee Schreckengost	11.8
Mike Scioscia	14.8
Kip Selbach	13.5
George Selkirk	8.2
Andy Seminick	11.3
Joe Sewell	34.4
Socks Seybold	7.2
Cy Seymour	10.4
Orator Shaffer	11.4
Jimmy Sheckard	19.3

Total Player Rating (alpha.)

Ruben Sierra	7.0
Roy Sievers	12.7
Al Simmons	25.6
Ted Simmons	16.8
Ken Singleton	20.9
George Sisler	22.7
Enos Slaughter	16.3
Roy Smalley	13.7
Reggie Smith	35.0
Elmer Smith	9.5
Red Smith	13.0
Lonnie Smith	11.6
Ozzie Smith	43.0
Duke Snider	22.3
Pop Snyder	7.5
Tris Speaker	86.5
Stan Spence	11.6
Eddie Stanky	18.4
Willie Stargell	32.8
Rusty Staub	27.6
Harry Steinfeldt	7.4
Vern Stephens	19.6
Riggs Stephenson	12.6
Snuffy Stirnweiss	8.2
George Stone	13.3
Harry Stovey	21.3
Darryl Strawberry	26.9
Jim Sundberg	8.0
Ed Swartwood	11.3
Bill Sweeney	7.9
Lee Tannehill	7.3
Danny Tartabull	16.3
Gene Tenace	15.3
Fred Tenney	20.9
Bill Terry	24.9
Mickey Tettleton	7.5
Frank Thomas	20.5
Roy Thomas	22.8
Robby Thompson	15.7
Sam Thompson	28.4
Andy Thornton	11.7
Mike Tiernan	12.9
Joe Tinker	23.0
John Titus	13.0
Joe Torre	19.6
Alan Trammell	24.0
Cecil Travis	10.2
Pie Traynor	20.8
George Van Haltren	11.1
Andy Van Slyke	21.0
Arky Vaughan	39.2
Bobby Veach	14.9
Robin Ventura	7.6
Honus Wagner	81.3
Dixie Walker	10.6
Larry Walker	13.0
Bobby Wallace	36.9
Paul Waner	36.1
John Ward	7.8
Bob Watson	12.1
Al Weis	7.9
Curt Welch	10.6
Billy Werber	7.6
Perry Werden	7.1
Vic Wertz	9.4
Wes Westrum	9.2
Zack Wheat	24.5
Lou Whitaker	24.5
Deacon White	10.6
Roy White	21.3
Pinky Whitney	8.2
Ernie Whitt	7.9
Billy Williams	31.1
Cy Williams	7.3
Jimmy Williams	16.1
Ken Williams	17.2
Matt Williams	12.5
Ted Williams	85.7
Ned Williamson	10.0
Bump Wills	9.3
Maury Wills	10.5
Hack Wilson	15.6
Dave Winfield	39.7
Sam Wise	6.8
Jimmy Wolf	10.2
George Wood	6.9
Gene Woodling	8.8
Jim Wynn	33.2
Carl Yastrzemski	45.5
Rudy York	10.2
Ross Youngs	10.8
Robin Yount	43.1
Chief Zimmer	15.8
Heinie Zimmerman	9.7
Richie Zisk	13.5

Total Player Rating (by era)

1876-1892

1	Roger Connor	42.7
2	Dan Brouthers	41.1
3	Bid McPhee	40.1
4	Jack Glasscock	36.1
5	Cap Anson	30.7
6	Buck Ewing	29.4
7	Pete Browning	28.8
8	Sam Thompson	28.4
9	Fred Dunlap	27.4
10	Hardy Richardson	27.3
11	King Kelly	24.7
12	Fred Pfeffer	21.7
13	Harry Stovey	21.3
14	Charley Jones	20.7
15	Denny Lyons	19.8
16	Charlie Bennett	19.2
17	Paul Hines	17.2
18	George Gore	16.2
19	Jim O'Rourke	16.1
20	Jocko Milligan	15.6
21	Henry Larkin	14.9
22	Fred Carroll	13.5
23	Dave Orr	13.2
24	Jack Clements	12.7
	Billy Nash	12.7

1893-1919

1	Nap Lajoie	94.3
2	Ty Cobb	91.1
3	Tris Speaker	86.5
4	Honus Wagner	81.3
5	Eddie Collins	69.7
6	Bill Dahlen	51.4
7	George Davis	51.1
8	Ed Delahanty	44.3
9	Joe Jackson	37.5
10	Bobby Wallace	36.9
11	Frank Baker	33.8
12	Sam Crawford	30.2
13	Cupid Childs	30.0
14	Elmer Flick	28.7
15	Fred Clarke	28.6
16	Jesse Burkett	28.5
17	Heinie Groh	27.0
18	Sherry Magee	26.6
19	Billy Hamilton	26.4
20	Hughie Jennings	26.2
21	Art Fletcher	25.9
22	Zack Wheat	24.5
23	Jimmy Collins	23.4
24	Joe Tinker	23.0
25	Jake Beckley	22.9

1920-1941

1	Babe Ruth	107.6
2	Rogers Hornsby	81.1
3	Lou Gehrig	65.7
4	Mel Ott	62.7
5	Jimmie Foxx	54.0
6	Charlie Gehringer	44.4
7	Luke Appling	40.7
8	Gabby Hartnett	40.1
9	Joe Cronin	39.4
10	Arky Vaughan	39.2
11	Frankie Frisch	39.1
12	Paul Waner	36.1
13	Bob Johnson	35.6
14	Bill Dickey	35.4
15	Dave Bancroft	35.3
16	Joe Sewell	34.4
17	Harry Heilmann	32.4
18	Billy Herman	31.7
19	Mickey Cochrane	31.4
20	Hank Greenberg	30.0
21	Dick Bartell	27.9
22	Stan Hack	27.2
23	Joe Medwick	27.1
24	Goose Goslin	26.1
25	Al Simmons	25.6

Total Player Rating (by era)

1942-1960

1	Ted Williams	85.7
2	Mickey Mantle	76.1
3	Stan Musial	70.5
4	Eddie Mathews	51.6
5	Joe DiMaggio	46.9
6	Lou Boudreau	41.3
7	Bobby Doerr	39.0
8	Yogi Berra	36.2
	Johnny Mize	36.2
10	Jackie Robinson	31.8
11	Richie Ashburn	30.2
12	Ralph Kiner	28.9
13	Joe Gordon	28.2
14	Minnie Minoso	26.0
15	Charlie Keller	23.5
16	Duke Snider	22.3
17	Roy Campanella	21.6
18	Larry Doby	21.2
19	Vern Stephens	19.6
20	Bill Nicholson	19.0
21	Bob Elliott	18.9
22	Eddie Stanky	18.4
23	Roy Cullenbine	18.1
24	Ferris Fain	17.8
25	Johnny Logan	17.3

1961-1976

1	Willie Mays	92.2
2	Hank Aaron	89.8
3	Frank Robinson	69.0
4	Joe Morgan	56.3
5	Carl Yastrzemski	45.5
6	Al Kaline	44.6
7	Roberto Clemente	42.9
8	Ron Santo	39.5
9	Willie McCovey	36.5
10	Bill Mazeroski	36.3
11	Dick Allen	35.3
12	Reggie Smith	35.0
13	Jim Wynn	33.2
14	Willie Stargell	32.8
15	Rod Carew	31.4
16	Billy Williams	31.1
17	Bobby Bonds	29.6
18	Rusty Staub	27.6
19	Norm Cash	27.5
20	Harmon Killebrew	26.4
21	Ernie Banks	25.9
22	Rocky Colavito	25.2
23	Tony Oliva	24.8
24	Johnny Bench	24.3
25	2 players tied	21.3

1977-1994

1	Mike Schmidt	78.4
2	Rickey Henderson	74.6
3	Tim Raines	51.0
4	Barry Bonds	49.4
5	Wade Boggs	44.4
6	Bobby Grich	44.1
7	Robin Yount	43.1
8	Ozzie Smith	43.0
9	Reggie Jackson	42.8
10	Dave Winfield	39.7
11	Cal Ripken	39.2
12	George Brett	39.0
13	Ryne Sandberg	38.8
14	Tony Gwynn	38.5
15	Eddie Murray	35.6
16	Paul Molitor	35.2
17	Darrell Evans	34.6
18	Keith Hernandez	34.4
19	Jack Clark	31.1
	Andre Dawson	31.1
21	Dwight Evans	30.4
22	Gary Carter	29.6
23	Jose Cruz	28.8
24	Cesar Cedeno	28.3
25	Barry Larkin	27.6

Wins

#	Player	Wins
1	Cy Young	511
2	Walter Johnson	417
3	Pete Alexander	373
	Christy Mathewson	373
5	Warren Spahn	363
6	Kid Nichols	361
7	Jim Galvin	360
8	Tim Keefe	342
9	Steve Carlton	329
10	John Clarkson	328
11	Eddie Plank	326
12	Nolan Ryan	324
	Don Sutton	324
14	Phil Niekro	318
15	Gaylord Perry	314
16	Tom Seaver	311
17	Charley Radbourn	309
18	Mickey Welch	307
19	Lefty Grove	300
	Early Wynn	300
21	Tommy John	288
22	Bert Blyleven	287
23	Robin Roberts	286
24	Fergie Jenkins	284
	Tony Mullane	284
26	Jim Kaat	283
27	Red Ruffing	273
28	Burleigh Grimes	270
29	Jim Palmer	268
30	Bob Feller	266
	Eppa Rixey	266
32	Jim McCormick	265
33	Gus Weyhing	264
34	Ted Lyons	260
35	Red Faber	254
	Jack Morris	254
37	Carl Hubbell	253
38	Bob Gibson	251
39	Vic Willis	249
40	Jack Quinn	247
41	Joe McGinnity	246
42	Jack Powell	245
	Amos Rusie	245
44	Juan Marichal	243
45	Herb Pennock	240
	Frank Tanana	240
47	Mordecai Brown	239
48	Clark Griffith	237
	Waite Hoyt	237
50	Whitey Ford	236
51	Charlie Buffinton	233
52	Sam Jones	229
	Luis Tiant	229
	Will White	229
55	George Mullin	228
56	Jim Bunning	224
	Catfish Hunter	224
58	Paul Derringer	223
	Mel Harder	223
60	Hooks Dauss	222
	Jerry Koosman	222
62	Joe Niekro	221
63	Jerry Reuss	220
64	Dennis Martinez	219
65	Bob Caruthers	218
	Earl Whitehill	218
67	Freddie Fitzsimmons	217
	Mickey Lolich	217
69	Wilbur Cooper	216
	Charlie Hough	216
71	Stan Coveleski	215
	Jim Perry	215
73	Rick Reuschel	214
74	Chief Bender	212
75	Bobo Newsom	211
	Billy Pierce	211
	Bob Welch	211
78	Jesse Haines	210
79	Vida Blue	209
	Don Drysdale	209
	Milt Pappas	209
82	Eddie Cicotte	208
83	Bob Lemon	207
	Carl Mays	207
	Hal Newhouser	207
86	Silver King	204
	Al Orth	204
88	Lew Burdette	203
	Jack Stivetts	203
90	Rube Marquard	201
	Charlie Root	201
92	George Uhle	200
93	Jack Chesbro	198
	Bucky Walters	198
95	Larry French	197
	Bob Friend	197
	Jesse Tannehill	197
	Adonis Terry	197
	Dazzy Vance	197
100	2 players tied	196

Losses

#	Player	Losses
1	Cy Young	316
2	Jim Galvin	308
3	Nolan Ryan	292
4	Walter Johnson	279
5	Phil Niekro	274
6	Gaylord Perry	265
7	Don Sutton	256
8	Jack Powell	254
9	Eppa Rixey	251
10	Bert Blyleven	250
11	Robin Roberts	245
	Warren Spahn	245
13	Steve Carlton	244
	Early Wynn	244
15	Jim Kaat	237
16	Frank Tanana	236
17	Gus Weyhing	232
18	Tommy John	231
19	Bob Friend	230
	Ted Lyons	230
21	Fergie Jenkins	226
22	Tim Keefe	225
	Red Ruffing	225
24	Bobo Newsom	222
25	Tony Mullane	220
26	Jack Quinn	218
27	Sam Jones	217
28	Charlie Hough	216
29	Jim McCormick	214
30	Red Faber	213
31	Paul Derringer	212
	Chick Fraser	212
	Burleigh Grimes	212
34	Mickey Welch	210
35	Jerry Koosman	209
36	Pete Alexander	208
	Kid Nichols	208
38	Tom Seaver	205
	Vic Willis	205
40	Joe Niekro	204
	Jim Whitney	204
42	George Mullin	196
	Adonis Terry	196
44	Claude Osteen	195
	Charley Radbourn	195
46	Eddie Plank	194
47	Mickey Lolich	191
	Rick Reuschel	191
	Jerry Reuss	191
	Tom Zachary	191
51	Al Orth	189
52	Christy Mathewson	188
53	Mel Harder	186
	Jack Morris	186
55	Earl Whitehill	185
56	Jim Bunning	184
57	Joe Bush	183
	Larry Jackson	183
	Curt Simmons	183
60	Hooks Dauss	182
	Waite Hoyt	182
62	Murry Dickson	181
	Dutch Leonard	181
	Rick Wise	181
65	Lee Meadows	180
66	Pink Hawley	179
	Dolf Luque	179
68	John Clarkson	178
	Wilbur Cooper	178
70	Bill Dinneen	177
	Rube Marquard	177
72	Red Donahue	175
	Tom Hughes	175
74	Doyle Alexander	174
	Bob Gibson	174
	Jim Perry	174
	Amos Rusie	174
78	Luis Tiant	172
79	Larry French	171
	Dennis Martinez	171
81	Ted Breitenstein	170
	Camilo Pascual	170
83	Billy Pierce	169
84	Red Ames	167
	Jim Clancy	167
	Bert Cunningham	167
	Red Ehret	167
88	Don Drysdale	166
	Howard Ehmke	166
	Catfish Hunter	166
	George Uhle	166
	Will White	166
93	Mark Baldwin	165
	Bump Hadley	165
	Si Johnson	165
96	Milt Gaston	164
	Win Mercer	164
	Milt Pappas	164
99	Bill Hutchison	163
100	2 players tied	162

Winning Percentage

#	Player	Pct.
1	Dave Foutz	.690
2	Whitey Ford	.690
3	Bob Caruthers	.688
4	Lefty Grove	.680
5	Vic Raschi	.667
6	Larry Corcoran	.665
7	Christy Mathewson	.665
8	Sam Leever	.660
9	Sal Maglie	.657
10	Sandy Koufax	.655
11	Johnny Allen	.654
12	Ron Guidry	.651
13	Lefty Gomez	.649
14	Roger Clemens	.649
15	Dwight Gooden	.649
16	John Clarkson	.648
17	Mordecai Brown	.648
18	Dizzy Dean	.644
19	Pete Alexander	.642
20	Jim Palmer	.638
21	Kid Nichols	.634
22	Deacon Phillippe	.634
23	Joe McGinnity	.634
24	Ed Reulbach	.632
25	Juan Marichal	.631
26	Mort Cooper	.631
27	Allie Reynolds	.630
28	Jesse Tannehill	.629
29	Ray Kremer	.627
30	Firpo Marberry	.627
31	Eddie Plank	.627
32	Tommy Bond	.627
33	Chief Bender	.625
34	Jimmy Key	.624
35	Don Newcombe	.623
36	Nig Cuppy	.623
37	Addie Joss	.623
38	Fred Goldsmith	.622
39	Doc Crandall	.622
40	Carl Hubbell	.622
	Carl Mays	.622
42	Bob Feller	.621
43	Mel Parnell	.621
44	John Tudor	.619
45	Clark Griffith	.619
46	Bob Lemon	.618
47	Cy Young	.618
48	John Ward	.617
49	Urban Shocker	.615
50	Jeff Tesreau	.615
51	Jim Maloney	.615
52	Lon Warneke	.613
53	David Cone	.613
54	Charley Radbourn	.613
55	Gary Nolan	.611
56	Schoolboy Rowe	.610
57	Carl Erskine	.610
58	Ed Walsh	.607
59	Charlie Ferguson	.607
60	Dave McNally	.607
61	Hooks Wiltse	.607
62	Jack Stivetts	.606
63	Art Nehf	.605
64	Charlie Buffinton	.605
65	Orval Overall	.603
66	Tim Keefe	.603
67	Tom Seaver	.603
68	Stan Coveleski	.602
69	Preacher Roe	.602
70	Wes Ferrell	.601
71	J.R. Richard	.601
72	Jack Chesbro	.600
73	Walter Johnson	.599
74	Freddie Fitzsimmons	.598
75	Ed Lopat	.597
76	Warren Spahn	.597
77	Herb Pennock	.597
78	Rip Sewell	.596
79	Mike Garcia	.594
80	Mickey Welch	.594
81	Pat Malone	.593
82	Alvin Crowder	.592
83	John Candelaria	.592
84	Harry Brecheen	.591
85	Bob Welch	.591
86	Jim Bagby	.591
87	Bob Gibson	.591
88	Dutch Ruether	.591
89	Tom Glavine	.590
90	Greg Maddux	.590
	Denny McLain	.590
92	Eddie Rommel	.590
93	Jack Coombs	.590
94	Tiny Bonham	.589
95	Bret Saberhagen	.588
96	Mike Cuellar	.587
97	Bill Bernhard	.586
98	Jeff Pfeffer	.585
99	Lew Burdette	.585
100	Amos Rusie	.585

Games

#	Player	Games
1	Hoyt Wilhelm	1070
2	Kent Tekulve	1050
3	Rich Gossage	1002
4	Lindy McDaniel	987
5	Rollie Fingers	944
6	Gene Garber	931
7	Cy Young	906
8	Sparky Lyle	899
9	Jim Kaat	898
10	Lee Smith	891
11	Jeff Reardon	880
12	Don McMahon	874
13	Phil Niekro	864
14	Charlie Hough	858
15	Dennis Eckersley	849
16	Roy Face	848
17	Tug McGraw	824
18	Nolan Ryan	807
19	Walter Johnson	802
20	Gaylord Perry	777
21	Don Sutton	774
22	Darold Knowles	765
23	Tommy John	760
24	Jack Quinn	756
25	Jesse Orosco	754
26	Ron Reed	751
27	Warren Spahn	750
28	Tom Burgmeier	745
	Gary Lavelle	745
30	Willie Hernandez	744
31	Steve Carlton	741
32	Ron Perranoski	737
33	Ron Kline	736
34	Clay Carroll	731
35	Mike Marshall	723
36	Johnny Klippstein	711
37	Greg Minton	710
38	Dave Righetti	708
39	Stu Miller	704
40	Steve Bedrosian	703
41	Joe Niekro	702
42	Bill Campbell	700
43	Larry Andersen	699
44	Bob McClure	698
45	Jim Galvin	697
46	Pete Alexander	696
	Craig Lefferts	696
48	Bob Miller	694
49	Bert Blyleven	692
	Grant Jackson	692
	Eppa Rixey	692
52	Early Wynn	691
53	Eddie Fisher	690
54	Rick Honeycutt	682
55	Ted Abernathy	681
56	Robin Roberts	676
57	Waite Hoyt	674
	Dan Quisenberry	674
59	Red Faber	669
60	Dave Giusti	668
61	Fergie Jenkins	664
62	Bruce Sutter	661
63	Greg Harris	658
64	Tom Seaver	656
65	Paul Lindblad	655
66	Wilbur Wood	651
67	Sam Jones	647
	Dave LaRoche	647
69	Dutch Leonard	640
	Gerry Staley	640
71	Dennis Lamp	639
	Diego Segui	639
73	Frank Tanana	638
74	Bob Stanley	637
75	Christy Mathewson	635
76	Charlie Root	632
77	Jim Perry	630
78	Jerry Reuss	628
79	Lew Burdette	626
80	Murry Dickson	625
	Woodie Fryman	625
82	Red Ruffing	624
83	Eddie Plank	623
84	Kid Nichols	620
	Dick Tidrow	620
86	Roger McDowell	618
87	Herb Pennock	617
88	Burleigh Grimes	616
	Lefty Grove	616
90	Terry Forster	614
91	John Franco	613
92	Jerry Koosman	612
93	Dave Smith	609
94	Mark Davis	605
95	Bob Friend	602
	Al Worthington	602
97	Elias Sosa	601
98	John Candelaria	600
	Bobo Newsom	600
100	Tim Keefe	599

Games Started

1	Cy Young	815
2	Nolan Ryan	773
3	Don Sutton	756
4	Phil Niekro	716
5	Steve Carlton	709
6	Tommy John	700
7	Gaylord Perry	690
8	Bert Blyleven	685
9	Jim Galvin	682
10	Walter Johnson	666
11	Warren Spahn	665
12	Tom Seaver	647
13	Jim Kaat	625
14	Frank Tanana	616
15	Early Wynn	612
16	Robin Roberts	609
17	Pete Alexander	599
18	Fergie Jenkins	594
19	Tim Keefe	593
20	Kid Nichols	561
21	Eppa Rixey	553
22	Christy Mathewson	551
23	Mickey Welch	549
24	Jerry Reuss	547
25	Red Ruffing	536
26	Eddie Plank	529
	Rick Reuschel	529
28	Jerry Koosman	527
	Jack Morris	527
30	Jim Palmer	521
31	Jim Bunning	519
32	John Clarkson	518
33	Jack Powell	516
34	Tony Mullane	504
35	Charley Radbourn	503
	Gus Weyhing	503
37	Dennis Martinez	500
	Joe Niekro	500
39	Bob Friend	497
	Burleigh Grimes	497
41	Mickey Lolich	496
42	Claude Osteen	488
43	Sam Jones	487
44	Jim McCormick	485
45	Bob Feller	484
	Ted Lyons	484
	Luis Tiant	484
48	Red Faber	483
	Bobo Newsom	483
50	Bob Gibson	482
51	Catfish Hunter	476
52	Vida Blue	473
	Earl Whitehill	473
54	Vic Willis	471
55	Don Drysdale	465
	Milt Pappas	465
57	Doyle Alexander	464
58	Bob Welch	462
59	Curt Simmons	461
60	Mike Torrez	458
61	Lefty Grove	457
	Juan Marichal	457
63	Rick Wise	455
64	Jim Perry	447
65	Paul Derringer	445
66	Jack Quinn	444
67	Charlie Hough	440
68	Whitey Ford	438
69	Mel Harder	433
70	Billy Pierce	432
71	Carl Hubbell	431
72	Larry Jackson	429
73	George Mullin	428
74	Amos Rusie	427
75	Freddie Fitzsimmons	426
76	Waite Hoyt	423
77	Bob Forsch	422
78	Herb Pennock	420
79	Mike Moore	415
80	Bob Knepper	413
81	Frank Viola	411
82	Ken Holtzman	410
83	Dave Stieb	409
	Tom Zachary	409
85	Wilbur Cooper	408
86	Lee Meadows	406
	Adonis Terry	406
88	Mike Flanagan	404
	Rube Marquard	404
	Camilo Pascual	404
91	Will White	401
92	Bucky Walters	398
93	Charlie Buffinton	396
	Dave McNally	396
	Scott Sanderson	396
	Jim Whitney	396
97	Al Orth	394
98	Steve Rogers	393
99	Paul Splittorff	392
	Rick Sutcliffe	392

Games Started (by era)

1876-1892

1	Jim Galvin	682
2	Tim Keefe	593
3	Mickey Welch	549
4	John Clarkson	518
5	Tony Mullane	504
6	Charley Radbourn	503
	Gus Weyhing	503
8	Jim McCormick	485
9	Adonis Terry	406
10	Will White	401
11	Charlie Buffinton	396
	Jim Whitney	396
13	Silver King	371
14	Bill Hutchison	347
15	Jack Stivetts	333

1893-1919

1	Cy Young	815
2	Walter Johnson	666
3	Pete Alexander	599
4	Kid Nichols	561
5	Christy Mathewson	551
6	Eddie Plank	529
7	Jack Powell	516
8	Vic Willis	471
9	George Mullin	428
10	Amos Rusie	427
11	Rube Marquard	404
12	Al Orth	394
13	Chick Fraser	389
14	Hooks Dauss	388
15	Joe McGinnity	381

1920-1941

1	Eppa Rixey	553
2	Red Ruffing	536
3	Burleigh Grimes	497
4	Sam Jones	487
5	Ted Lyons	484
6	Red Faber	483
	Bobo Newsom	483
8	Earl Whitehill	473
9	Lefty Grove	457
10	Paul Derringer	445
11	Jack Quinn	444
12	Mel Harder	433
13	Carl Hubbell	431
14	Freddie Fitzsimmons	426
15	Waite Hoyt	423

1942-1960

1	Warren Spahn	665
2	Early Wynn	612
3	Robin Roberts	609
4	Bob Friend	497
5	Bob Feller	484
6	Curt Simmons	461
7	Whitey Ford	438
8	Billy Pierce	432
9	Dutch Leonard	375
10	Hal Newhouser	374
11	Lew Burdette	373
12	Bob Buhl	369
13	Vern Law	364
14	Bob Lemon	350

1961-1976

1	Don Sutton	756
2	Phil Niekro	716
3	Steve Carlton	709
4	Tommy John	700
5	Gaylord Perry	690
6	Tom Seaver	647
7	Jim Kaat	625
8	Fergie Jenkins	594
9	Jerry Koosman	527
10	Jim Palmer	521
11	Jim Bunning	519
12	Mickey Lolich	496
13	Claude Osteen	488
14	Luis Tiant	484
15	Bob Gibson	482

1977-1994

1	Nolan Ryan	773
2	Bert Blyleven	685
3	Frank Tanana	616
4	Jerry Reuss	547
5	Rick Reuschel	529
6	Jack Morris	527
7	Dennis Martinez	500
	Joe Niekro	500
9	Vida Blue	473
10	Doyle Alexander	464
11	Bob Welch	462
12	Charlie Hough	440
13	Bob Forsch	422
14	Mike Moore	415
15	Bob Knepper	413

Complete Games

1	Cy Young	749
2	Jim Galvin	639
3	Tim Keefe	554
4	Walter Johnson	531
	Kid Nichols	531
6	Mickey Welch	525
7	Charley Radbourn	489
8	John Clarkson	485
9	Tony Mullane	468
10	Jim McCormick	466
11	Gus Weyhing	448
12	Pete Alexander	437
13	Christy Mathewson	434
14	Jack Powell	422
15	Eddie Plank	410
16	Will White	394
17	Amos Rusie	392
18	Vic Willis	388
19	Warren Spahn	382
20	Jim Whitney	377
21	Adonis Terry	367
22	Ted Lyons	356
23	George Mullin	353
24	Charlie Buffinton	351
25	Chick Fraser	342
26	Clark Griffith	337
27	Red Ruffing	335
28	Silver King	329
29	Al Orth	324
30	Bill Hutchison	321
31	Burleigh Grimes	314
	Joe McGinnity	314
33	Red Donahue	313
34	Guy Hecker	310
35	Bill Dinneen	306
36	Robin Roberts	305
37	Gaylord Perry	303
38	Ted Breitenstein	300
39	Bob Caruthers	298
	Lefty Grove	298
41	Pink Hawley	297
	Ed Morris	297
43	Mark Baldwin	296
44	Tommy Bond	294
45	Brickyard Kennedy	293
46	Eppa Rixey	290
	Early Wynn	290
48	Bill Donovan	289
	Bobby Mathews	289
50	Bert Cunningham	286
51	Wilbur Cooper	279
	Bob Feller	279
	Sadie McMahon	279
54	Jack Stivetts	278
	Jack Taylor	278
56	Charlie Getzien	277
57	Red Faber	273
58	Mordecai Brown	271
59	Frank Dwyer	270
	Jouett Meekin	270
61	Fergie Jenkins	267
62	Elton Chamberlain	264
	Matt Kilroy	264
64	Jesse Tannehill	263
65	Doc White	262
66	Rube Waddell	261
67	Jack Chesbro	260
	Red Ehret	260
	Carl Hubbell	260
70	Larry Corcoran	256
71	Chief Bender	255
	Bob Gibson	255
73	Steve Carlton	254
74	Frank Killen	253
75	Paul Derringer	251
	Win Mercer	251
77	Sam Jones	250
	Ed Walsh	250
79	Eddie Cicotte	249
	Stump Weidman	249
81	Herb Pennock	247
82	Bobo Newsom	246
83	George Bradley	245
	Hooks Dauss	245
	Phil Niekro	245
86	Harry Howell	244
	Juan Marichal	244
	John Ward	244
89	Jack Quinn	243
90	Bert Blyleven	242
	Deacon Phillippe	242
	Bucky Walters	242
93	Sam Leever	241
94	Kid Gleason	240
95	Addie Joss	234
96	George Uhle	232
97	Carl Mays	231
	Tom Lovett	231
	Harry Staley	231
100	Earl Moore	230

Complete Games (by era)

1876-1892

1	Jim Galvin	639
2	Tim Keefe	554
3	Mickey Welch	525
4	Charley Radbourn	489
5	John Clarkson	485
6	Tony Mullane	468
7	Jim McCormick	466
8	Gus Weyhing	448
9	Will White	394
10	Jim Whitney	377
11	Adonis Terry	367
12	Charlie Buffinton	351
13	Silver King	329
14	Bill Hutchison	321
15	Guy Hecker	310

1893-1919

1	Cy Young	749
2	Walter Johnson	531
	Kid Nichols	531
4	Pete Alexander	437
5	Christy Mathewson	434
6	Jack Powell	422
7	Eddie Plank	410
8	Amos Rusie	392
9	Vic Willis	388
10	George Mullin	353
11	Chick Fraser	342
12	Clark Griffith	337
13	Al Orth	324
14	Joe McGinnity	314
15	Red Donahue	313

1920-1941

1	Ted Lyons	356
2	Red Ruffing	335
3	Burleigh Grimes	314
4	Lefty Grove	298
5	Eppa Rixey	290
6	Wilbur Cooper	279
7	Red Faber	273
8	Carl Hubbell	260
9	Paul Derringer	251
10	Sam Jones	250
11	Herb Pennock	247
12	Bobo Newsom	246
13	Jack Quinn	243
14	Bucky Walters	242
15	George Uhle	232

1942-1960

1	Warren Spahn	382
2	Robin Roberts	305
3	Early Wynn	290
4	Bob Feller	279
5	Hal Newhouser	212
6	Billy Pierce	193
7	Dutch Leonard	192
8	Bob Lemon	188
9	Ed Lopat	164
10	Bob Friend	163
	Curt Simmons	163
12	Lew Burdette	158
	Dizzy Trout	158
14	Whitey Ford	156
	Jim Tobin	156

1961-1976

1	Gaylord Perry	303
2	Fergie Jenkins	267
3	Bob Gibson	255
4	Steve Carlton	254
5	Phil Niekro	245
6	Juan Marichal	244
7	Tom Seaver	231
8	Jim Palmer	211
9	Mickey Lolich	195
10	Luis Tiant	187
11	Catfish Hunter	181
12	Jim Kaat	180
13	Don Sutton	178
14	Mike Cuellar	172
15	Don Drysdale	167

1977-1994

1	Bert Blyleven	242
2	Nolan Ryan	222
3	Jack Morris	175
4	Vida Blue	143
	Frank Tanana	143
6	Steve Rogers	129
7	Jerry Reuss	127
8	Dennis Martinez	117
9	Fernando Valenzuela	112
10	Charlie Hough	107
	Joe Niekro	107
12	Dennis Leonard	103
	Dave Stieb	103
14	Rick Reuschel	102
15	Mike Flanagan	101

Shutouts

1	Walter Johnson	110
2	Pete Alexander	90
3	Christy Mathewson	79
4	Cy Young	76
5	Eddie Plank	69
6	Warren Spahn	63
7	Nolan Ryan	61
	Tom Seaver	61
9	Bert Blyleven	60
10	Don Sutton	58
11	Jim Galvin	57
	Ed Walsh	57
13	Bob Gibson	56
14	Mordecai Brown	55
	Steve Carlton	55
16	Jim Palmer	53
	Gaylord Perry	53
18	Juan Marichal	52
19	Rube Waddell	50
	Vic Willis	50
21	Don Drysdale	49
	Fergie Jenkins	49
	Luis Tiant	49
	Early Wynn	49
25	Kid Nichols	48
26	Tommy John	46
	Jack Powell	46
28	Whitey Ford	45
	Addie Joss	45
	Phil Niekro	45
	Robin Roberts	45
	Red Ruffing	45
	Doc White	45
34	Babe Adams	44
	Bob Feller	44
36	Milt Pappas	43
37	Catfish Hunter	42
	Bucky Walters	42
39	Mickey Lolich	41
	Hippo Vaughn	41
	Mickey Welch	41
42	Chief Bender	40
	Jim Bunning	40
	Larry French	40
	Sandy Koufax	40
	Claude Osteen	40
	Ed Reulbach	40
	Mel Stottlemyre	40
49	Tim Keefe	39
	Sam Leever	39
	Jerry Reuss	39
52	Stan Coveleski	38
	Billy Pierce	38
	Nap Rucker	38
55	Vida Blue	37
	John Clarkson	37
	Larry Jackson	37
	Eppa Rixey	37
	Steve Rogers	37
60	Roger Clemens	36
	Mike Cuellar	36
	Bob Friend	36
	Carl Hubbell	36
	Sam Jones	36
	Camilo Pascual	36
	Allie Reynolds	36
	Curt Simmons	36
	Will White	36
69	Tommy Bond	35
	Joe Bush	35
	Jack Chesbro	35
	Eddie Cicotte	35
	Jack Coombs	35
	Wilbur Cooper	35
	Bill Donovan	35
	Burleigh Grimes	35
	Lefty Grove	35
	George Mullin	35
	Herb Pennock	35
	Charley Radbourn	35
81	Bill Doak	34
	Earl Moore	34
	Frank Tanana	34
	Jesse Tannehill	34
85	Tommy Bridges	33
	Lew Burdette	33
	Dean Chance	33
	Mort Cooper	33
	Jerry Koosman	33
	Lefty Leifield	33
	Dutch Leonard	33
	Jim McCormick	33
	Dave McNally	33
	Hal Newhouser	33
	Bob Shawkey	33
	Virgil Trucks	33
97	Paul Derringer	32
	Joe McGinnity	32
	Jim Perry	32
100	7 players tied	31

Saves

1	Lee Smith	434
2	Jeff Reardon	367
3	Rollie Fingers	341
4	Rich Gossage	310
5	Bruce Sutter	300
6	Dennis Eckersley	294
7	Tom Henke	275
8	John Franco	266
9	Dave Righetti	252
10	Dan Quisenberry	244
11	Sparky Lyle	238
12	Hoyt Wilhelm	227
13	Gene Garber	218
14	Doug Jones	217
15	Dave Smith	216
16	Randy Myers	205
17	Bobby Thigpen	201
18	Roy Face	193
19	Mitch Williams	192
20	Mike Marshall	188
21	Jeff Montgomery	187
22	Steve Bedrosian	184
	Kent Tekulve	184
24	Tug McGraw	180
25	Rick Aguilera	179
	Ron Perranoski	179
27	Bryan Harvey	177
28	Lindy McDaniel	172
29	Jeff Russell	163
30	Gregg Olson	161
31	Jay Howell	155
32	Stu Miller	154
33	Don McMahon	153
34	Roger McDowell	151
35	Greg Minton	150
36	Ted Abernathy	148
37	Willie Hernandez	147
38	Dave Giusti	145
	Todd Worrell	145
40	Clay Carroll	143
	Darold Knowles	143
42	Mike Henneman	136
	Gary Lavelle	136
44	Dan Plesac	134
45	Jim Brewer	132
	Steve Farr	132
	Bob Stanley	132
48	Ron Davis	130
	Jesse Orosco	130
50	Terry Forster	127
51	Bill Campbell	126
	Dave LaRoche	126
53	John Hiller	125
54	Jack Aker	123
55	Dick Radatz	122
56	Duane Ward	121
57	Tippy Martinez	115
58	Frank Linzy	111
59	Al Worthington	110
60	Fred Gladding	109
61	Wayne Granger	108
	Ron Kline	108
63	Johnny Murphy	107
64	Bill Caudill	106
	John Wetteland	106
66	Ron Reed	103
	John Wyatt	103
68	Tom Burgmeier	102
	Tim Burke	102
	Ellis Kinder	102
71	Craig Lefferts	101
	Firpo Marberry	101
73	Joe Hoerner	99
74	Mike Schooler	98
75	Al Hrabosky	97
	Tom Niedenfuer	97
77	Mark Davis	96
	Clem Labine	96
	Randy Moffitt	96
80	Bob Locker	95
81	Rod Beck	94
82	Aurelio Lopez	93
83	Tom Hume	92
	Phil Regan	92
85	Bill Henry	90
86	Donnie Moore	89
87	Rob Dibble	88
	Jim Gott	88
	Steve Howe	88
	Jim Kern	88
91	Ken Sanders	86
	Cecil Upshaw	86
93	Joe Sambito	84
94	Mark Clear	83
	Turk Farrell	83
	Claude Raymond	83
	Elias Sosa	83
98	Don Aase	82
	Larry Sherry	82
100	2 players tied	81

Innings Pitched

1	Cy Young	7356.2
2	Jim Galvin	5941.1
3	Walter Johnson	5914.2
4	Phil Niekro	5404.1
5	Nolan Ryan	5386.0
6	Gaylord Perry	5350.1
7	Don Sutton	5282.1
8	Warren Spahn	5243.2
9	Steve Carlton	5217.1
10	Pete Alexander	5190.0
11	Kid Nichols	5056.1
12	Tim Keefe	5047.1
13	Bert Blyleven	4970.0
14	Mickey Welch	4802.0
15	Tom Seaver	4782.2
16	Christy Mathewson	4780.2
17	Tommy John	4710.1
18	Robin Roberts	4688.2
19	Early Wynn	4564.0
20	John Clarkson	4536.1
21	Charley Radbourn	4535.1
22	Tony Mullane	4531.1
23	Jim Kaat	4530.1
24	Fergie Jenkins	4500.2
25	Eddie Plank	4495.2
26	Eppa Rixey	4494.2
27	Jack Powell	4389.0
28	Red Ruffing	4344.0
29	Gus Weyhing	4324.1
30	Jim McCormick	4275.2
31	Frank Tanana	4188.1
32	Burleigh Grimes	4179.2
33	Ted Lyons	4161.0
34	Red Faber	4086.2
35	Vic Willis	3996.0
36	Jim Palmer	3948.0
37	Lefty Grove	3940.2
38	Jack Quinn	3920.1
39	Bob Gibson	3884.1
40	Sam Jones	3883.0
41	Jerry Koosman	3839.1
42	Bob Feller	3827.0
43	Jack Morris	3824.0
44	Charlie Hough	3801.1
45	Amos Rusie	3769.2
46	Waite Hoyt	3762.1
47	Jim Bunning	3760.1
48	Bobo Newsom	3759.1
49	George Mullin	3686.2
50	Jerry Reuss	3669.2
51	Paul Derringer	3645.0
52	Mickey Lolich	3638.1
53	Bob Friend	3611.0
54	Carl Hubbell	3590.1
55	Joe Niekro	3584.0
56	Herb Pennock	3571.2
57	Earl Whitehill	3564.2
58	Dennis Martinez	3560.2
59	Rick Reuschel	3548.1
60	Will White	3542.2
61	Adonis Terry	3514.0
62	Juan Marichal	3507.1
63	Jim Whitney	3496.1
64	Luis Tiant	3486.1
65	Wilbur Cooper	3480.0
66	Claude Osteen	3460.1
67	Catfish Hunter	3449.1
68	Joe McGinnity	3441.1
69	Don Drysdale	3432.0
70	Mel Harder	3426.1
71	Charlie Buffinton	3404.0
72	Hooks Dauss	3390.2
73	Clark Griffith	3385.2
74	Doyle Alexander	3367.2
75	Chick Fraser	3356.0
76	Al Orth	3354.2
77	Curt Simmons	3348.1
78	Vida Blue	3343.1
79	Rube Marquard	3306.2
	Billy Pierce	3306.2
81	Jim Perry	3285.2
82	Larry Jackson	3262.2
83	Freddie Fitzsimmons	3223.2
84	Eddie Cicotte	3223.1
85	Dolf Luque	3220.1
86	Dutch Leonard	3218.1
87	Jesse Haines	3208.2
88	Red Ames	3198.0
89	Charlie Root	3197.1
90	Silver King	3190.2
91	Milt Pappas	3186.0
92	Mordecai Brown	3172.1
93	Whitey Ford	3170.1
94	Lee Meadows	3160.2
95	Larry French	3152.0
96	Rick Wise	3127.0
97	Tom Zachary	3126.1
98	George Uhle	3119.2
99	Bucky Walters	3104.2
100	Bob Welch	3092.0

Innings Pitched (by era)

1876-1892

1	Jim Galvin	5941.1
2	Tim Keefe	5047.1
3	Mickey Welch	4802.0
4	John Clarkson	4536.1
5	Charley Radbourn	4535.1
6	Tony Mullane	4531.1
7	Gus Weyhing	4324.1
8	Jim McCormick	4275.2
9	Will White	3542.2
10	Adonis Terry	3514.0
11	Jim Whitney	3496.1
12	Charlie Buffinton	3404.0
13	Silver King	3190.2
14	Bill Hutchison	3083.0
15	Guy Hecker	2906.0

1893-1919

1	Cy Young	7356.2
2	Walter Johnson	5914.2
3	Pete Alexander	5190.0
4	Kid Nichols	5056.1
5	Christy Mathewson	4780.2
6	Eddie Plank	4495.2
7	Jack Powell	4389.0
8	Vic Willis	3996.0
9	Amos Rusie	3769.2
10	George Mullin	3686.2
11	Joe McGinnity	3441.1
12	Hooks Dauss	3390.2
13	Clark Griffith	3385.2
14	Chick Fraser	3356.0
15	Al Orth	3354.2

1920-1941

1	Eppa Rixey	4494.2
2	Red Ruffing	4344.0
3	Burleigh Grimes	4179.2
4	Ted Lyons	4161.0
5	Red Faber	4086.2
6	Lefty Grove	3940.2
7	Jack Quinn	3920.1
8	Sam Jones	3883.0
9	Waite Hoyt	3762.1
10	Bobo Newsom	3759.1
11	Paul Derringer	3645.0
12	Carl Hubbell	3590.1
13	Herb Pennock	3571.2
14	Earl Whitehill	3564.2
15	Wilbur Cooper	3480.0

1942-1960

1	Warren Spahn	5243.2
2	Robin Roberts	4688.2
3	Early Wynn	4564.0
4	Bob Feller	3827.0
5	Bob Friend	3611.0
6	Curt Simmons	3348.1
7	Billy Pierce	3306.2
8	Dutch Leonard	3218.1
9	Whitey Ford	3170.1
10	Lew Burdette	3067.1
11	Murry Dickson	3052.1
12	Hal Newhouser	2993.0
13	Bob Lemon	2850.0
14	Dizzy Trout	2725.2
15	Virgil Trucks	2682.1

1961-1976

1	Phil Niekro	5404.1
2	Gaylord Perry	5350.1
3	Don Sutton	5282.1
4	Steve Carlton	5217.1
5	Tom Seaver	4782.2
6	Tommy John	4710.1
7	Jim Kaat	4530.1
8	Fergie Jenkins	4500.2
9	Jim Palmer	3948.0
10	Bob Gibson	3884.1
11	Jerry Koosman	3839.1
12	Jim Bunning	3760.1
13	Mickey Lolich	3638.1
14	Juan Marichal	3507.1
15	Luis Tiant	3486.1

1977-1994

1	Nolan Ryan	5386.0
2	Bert Blyleven	4970.0
3	Frank Tanana	4188.1
4	Jack Morris	3824.0
5	Charlie Hough	3801.1
6	Jerry Reuss	3669.2
7	Joe Niekro	3584.0
8	Dennis Martinez	3560.2
9	Rick Reuschel	3548.1
10	Doyle Alexander	3367.2
11	Vida Blue	3343.1
12	Bob Welch	3092.0
13	Dennis Eckersley	3082.2
14	Dave Stieb	2845.0
15	Steve Rogers	2837.2

Hits per Game

1	Nolan Ryan	6.56
2	Sid Fernandez	6.77
3	Sandy Koufax	6.79
4	J.R. Richard	6.88
5	Andy Messersmith	6.94
6	Hoyt Wilhelm	7.01
7	Sam McDowell	7.03
8	Ed Walsh	7.12
9	Bob Turley	7.18
10	Orval Overall	7.22
11	Jeff Tesreau	7.24
12	Ed Reulbach	7.24
13	Mario Soto	7.26
14	Addie Joss	7.30
15	Jose DeLeon	7.36
16	Jim Maloney	7.39
17	David Cone	7.41
18	Rich Gossage	7.45
19	Tom Seaver	7.47
20	Walter Johnson	7.48
21	Rube Waddell	7.48
22	Roger Clemens	7.53
23	Bob Gibson	7.60
24	Don Wilson	7.61
25	Jim Palmer	7.63
26	Larry Cheney	7.68
27	Mordecai Brown	7.68
28	Sam Jones	7.68
29	Bob Feller	7.69
30	Johnny Vander Meer	7.69
31	Catfish Hunter	7.72
32	Al Downing	7.72
33	Jim Scott	7.73
34	Charlie Hough	7.77
35	Bobby Bolin	7.79
36	Stan Williams	7.79
37	Rollie Fingers	7.80
38	Dean Chance	7.81
39	Frank Smith	7.82
40	Tug McGraw	7.83
41	Barney Pelty	7.84
42	Whitey Ford	7.85
43	Denny McLain	7.85
44	Bob Veale	7.87
45	Dwight Gooden	7.87
46	Chief Bender	7.89
47	George McQuillan	7.89
48	Jack Coombs	7.89
49	Moe Drabowsky	7.90
50	Vida Blue	7.91
51	Nap Rucker	7.92
52	Tim Keefe	7.92
53	Allie Reynolds	7.92
54	Eddie Plank	7.92
55	Mark Langston	7.93
56	Luis Tiant	7.94
57	Christy Mathewson	7.94
58	Rudy May	7.94
59	Ray Culp	7.95
60	Dave Stieb	7.95
61	Bill Donovan	7.99
62	Howie Camnitz	7.99
63	Don Sutton	7.99
64	Juan Pizarro	7.99
65	Jose Rijo	8.00
66	Gary Bell	8.01
67	Earl Moore	8.02
68	Sonny Siebert	8.03
69	Lefty Tyler	8.03
70	Hal Newhouser	8.04
71	Claude Hendrix	8.06
72	Steve Carlton	8.06
73	Hooks Wiltse	8.06
74	Orel Hershiser	8.07
75	Willie Mitchell	8.07
76	Larry Corcoran	8.08
77	Amos Rusie	8.08
78	Bill Singer	8.08
79	Bob Lemon	8.08
80	Mike Scott	8.08
81	Stu Miller	8.09
82	Don Drysdale	8.09
83	Gary Nolan	8.09
84	Eddie Cicotte	8.09
85	Juan Marichal	8.09
86	Virgil Trucks	8.11
87	Hippo Vaughn	8.11
88	Doc White	8.12
89	Blue Moon Odom	8.12
90	Kirby Higbe	8.13
91	Jim Shaw	8.13
92	Mike Cuellar	8.13
93	Billy Pierce	8.14
94	Fernando Valenzuela	8.15
95	Mort Cooper	8.15
96	Greg Maddux	8.15
97	Red Ames	8.15
98	Vic Willis	8.16
99	Harry Brecheen	8.17
100	Earl Wilson	8.17

Home Runs Allowed

1	Robin Roberts	505
2	Fergie Jenkins	484
3	Phil Niekro	482
4	Don Sutton	472
5	Frank Tanana	448
6	Warren Spahn	434
7	Bert Blyleven	430
8	Steve Carlton	414
9	Gaylord Perry	399
10	Jim Kaat	395
11	Jack Morris	389
12	Charlie Hough	383
13	Tom Seaver	380
14	Catfish Hunter	374
15	Jim Bunning	372
16	Mickey Lolich	347
17	Luis Tiant	346
18	Early Wynn	338
19	Dennis Martinez	327
20	Doyle Alexander	324
21	Nolan Ryan	321
22	Juan Marichal	320
23	Dennis Eckersley	319
24	Pedro Ramos	315
25	Jim Perry	308
26	Jim Palmer	303
27	Murry Dickson	302
	Tommy John	302
29	Milt Pappas	298
30	Mudcat Grant	292
31	Floyd Bannister	291
32	Jerry Koosman	290
33	Lew Burdette	289
34	Bob Friend	286
	Scott Sanderson	286
36	Frank Viola	285
37	Billy Pierce	284
38	Bill Gullickson	282
39	Don Drysdale	280
40	Jim Slaton	277
41	Joe Niekro	276
42	Vern Law	268
43	Mike Moore	267
	Bob Welch	267
45	Vida Blue	263
46	Rick Wise	261
47	Larry Jackson	259
48	Bruce Hurst	258
49	Bob Gibson	257
50	Camilo Pascual	256
51	Mike McCormick	255
	Curt Simmons	255
53	Red Ruffing	254
54	Dave Stewart	253
55	Don Newcombe	252
56	Mike Flanagan	251
57	Ken Holtzman	249
	Claude Osteen	249
59	Steve Renko	248
60	John Candelaria	245
	Jerry Reuss	245
62	Jim Clancy	244
	Mark Langston	244
64	Denny McLain	242
	Johnny Podres	242
66	Harvey Haddix	240
	Ray Sadecki	240
68	Bob Buhl	238
69	Rick Sutcliffe	236
	Earl Wilson	236
71	Scott McGregor	235
72	Tom Browning	234
	Joe Coleman	234
74	Jim Lonborg	233
75	Danny Darwin	231
76	Dave McNally	230
77	Whitey Ford	228
	Bob Knepper	228
79	Carl Hubbell	227
80	Ron Guidry	226
81	Don Cardwell	225
82	Bob Feller	224
83	Stan Bahnsen	223
	Ron Darling	223
	Ted Lyons	223
	Mike Torrez	223
87	Mike Cuellar	222
88	Ray Burris	221
	Rick Reuschel	221
90	Dave Stieb	219
91	Mike Caldwell	218
	Ron Kline	218
	Dan Petry	218
94	Bob Forsch	216
	Ralph Terry	216
96	Ned Garver	213
97	Bill Monbouquette	211
	Ed Whitson	211
99	Herm Wehmeier	210
100	4 players tied	209

Home Runs Allowed (by era)

1876-1892

1	John Clarkson	161
2	Jack Stivetts	131
3	Jim Galvin	122
4	Gus Weyhing	120
5	Charley Radbourn	117
6	Mickey Welch	106
7	Bill Hutchison	104
8	Tony Mullane	98
9	Charlie Getzien	95
10	Harry Staley	92
11	Charlie Buffinton	87
12	Jim McCormick	84
13	Mark Baldwin	82
14	Jim Whitney	79
15	Adonis Terry	76

1893-1919

1	Pete Alexander	164
2	Kid Nichols	156
3	Cy Young	138
4	Jack Powell	110
5	Frank Dwyer	109
6	Rube Marquard	107
7	Walter Johnson	97
8	Brickyard Kennedy	93
9	Christy Mathewson	91
10	Hooks Dauss	87
11	Ad Gumbert	81
12	Kid Carsey	80
13	Ted Breitenstein	79
14	Bill Dinneen	78
15	Clark Griffith	76

1920-1941

1	Red Ruffing	254
2	Carl Hubbell	227
3	Ted Lyons	223
4	Bobo Newsom	206
5	Earl Whitehill	192
6	Charlie Root	187
7	Freddie Fitzsimmons	186
8	Tommy Bridges	181
9	Lon Warneke	175
10	George Blaeholder	173
	Syl Johnson	173
12	Bump Hadley	167
13	Jesse Haines	165
14	Larry French	164
15	Rube Walberg	163

1942-1960

1	Robin Roberts	505
2	Warren Spahn	434
3	Early Wynn	338
4	Pedro Ramos	315
5	Murry Dickson	302
6	Lew Burdette	289
7	Bob Friend	286
8	Billy Pierce	284
9	Vern Law	268
10	Curt Simmons	255
11	Don Newcombe	252
12	Johnny Podres	242
13	Harvey Haddix	240
14	Bob Buhl	238
15	Whitey Ford	228

1961-1976

1	Fergie Jenkins	484
2	Phil Niekro	482
3	Don Sutton	472
4	Steve Carlton	414
5	Gaylord Perry	399
6	Jim Kaat	395
7	Tom Seaver	380
8	Catfish Hunter	374
9	Jim Bunning	372
10	Mickey Lolich	347
11	Luis Tiant	346
12	Juan Marichal	320
13	Jim Perry	308
14	Jim Palmer	303
15	Tommy John	302

1977-1994

1	Frank Tanana	448
2	Bert Blyleven	430
3	Jack Morris	389
4	Charlie Hough	383
5	Dennis Martinez	327
6	Doyle Alexander	324
7	Nolan Ryan	321
8	Dennis Eckersley	319
9	Floyd Bannister	291
10	Scott Sanderson	286
11	Frank Viola	285
12	Bill Gullickson	282
13	Jim Slaton	277
14	Joe Niekro	276
15	2 players tied	267

Walks

1	Nolan Ryan	2795
2	Steve Carlton	1833
3	Phil Niekro	1809
4	Early Wynn	1775
5	Bob Feller	1764
6	Bobo Newsom	1732
7	Amos Rusie	1704
8	Charlie Hough	1665
9	Gus Weyhing	1566
10	Red Ruffing	1541
11	Bump Hadley	1442
12	Warren Spahn	1434
13	Earl Whitehill	1431
14	Tony Mullane	1408
15	Sam Jones	1396
16	Jack Morris	1390
	Tom Seaver	1390
18	Gaylord Perry	1379
19	Mike Torrez	1371
20	Walter Johnson	1363
21	Don Sutton	1343
22	Bob Gibson	1336
23	Chick Fraser	1332
24	Bert Blyleven	1322
25	Sam McDowell	1312
26	Jim Palmer	1311
27	Mark Baldwin	1307
28	Adonis Terry	1298
29	Mickey Welch	1297
30	Burleigh Grimes	1295
31	Kid Nichols	1268
32	Joe Bush	1263
33	Joe Niekro	1262
34	Allie Reynolds	1261
35	Tommy John	1259
36	Frank Tanana	1255
37	Bob Lemon	1251
38	Hal Newhouser	1249
39	George Mullin	1238
40	Tim Keefe	1234
41	Cy Young	1217
42	Red Faber	1213
43	Vic Willis	1212
44	Ted Breitenstein	1203
45	Brickyard Kennedy	1201
46	Jerry Koosman	1198
47	Tommy Bridges	1192
48	John Clarkson	1191
49	Lefty Grove	1187
50	Vida Blue	1185
51	Billy Pierce	1178
52	Jack Stivetts	1155
53	Johnny Vander Meer	1132
54	Bill Hutchison	1129
55	Jerry Reuss	1127
56	Ted Lyons	1121
	Bucky Walters	1121
58	Mel Harder	1118
59	Earl Moore	1108
60	Bob Buhl	1105
61	Luis Tiant	1104
62	Mickey Lolich	1099
63	Lefty Gomez	1095
64	Mike Moore	1088
	Virgil Trucks	1088
66	Whitey Ford	1086
67	Jim Kaat	1083
68	Eppa Rixey	1082
69	Mark Langston	1081
	Rick Sutcliffe	1081
71	Eddie Plank	1072
72	Camilo Pascual	1069
73	Bob Turley	1068
74	Hooks Dauss	1067
75	Elton Chamberlain	1065
76	Bert Cunningham	1064
77	Curt Simmons	1063
78	Bill Donovan	1059
79	Murry Dickson	1058
	Jouett Meekin	1058
81	Vern Kennedy	1049
82	Dizzy Trout	1046
83	Howard Ehmke	1042
84	Wes Ferrell	1040
85	Tommy Byrne	1037
86	Red Ames	1034
	Dennis Martinez	1034
	Bob Welch	1034
89	Rube Walberg	1031
90	Jack Powell	1021
91	Bob Shawkey	1018
92	Dave Stieb	1017
93	Steve Renko	1010
94	Jim Slaton	1004
	Fernando Valenzuela	1004
96	Joe Coleman	1003
	Waite Hoyt	1003
98	Jim Bunning	1000
99	Jim Perry	998
100	Fergie Jenkins	997

Fewest Walks per Game

1876-1892

1	Tommy Bond	0.58
2	George Bradley	0.67
3	Terry Larkin	0.71
4	John Ward	0.92
5	Fred Goldsmith	0.96
6	Jim Whitney	1.06
7	Bobby Mathews	1.11
8	Jim Galvin	1.13
9	Will White	1.26
10	Jack Lynch	1.38
11	Guy Hecker	1.51
12	Lee Richmond	1.53
13	Jim McCormick	1.58
14	Jumbo McGinnis	1.65
15	Ed Morris	1.67

1893-1919

1	Deacon Phillippe	1.25
2	Babe Adams	1.29
3	Addie Joss	1.41
4	Cy Young	1.49
5	Jesse Tannehill	1.56
6	Christy Mathewson	1.59
7	Nick Altrock	1.62
8	Pete Alexander	1.65
9	Noodles Hahn	1.69
10	Dick Rudolph	1.77
11	Al Orth	1.77
12	Slim Sallee	1.83
13	Bill Bernhard	1.83
14	Ed Siever	1.86
15	Ed Walsh	1.87

1920-1941

1	Red Lucas	1.61
2	Pete Donohue	1.80
3	Jesse Barnes	1.80
4	Carl Hubbell	1.82
5	Curt Davis	1.85
6	Paul Derringer	1.88
7	Bill Swift	1.93
8	Sherry Smith	1.93
9	Watty Clark	1.97
10	Jack Quinn	1.97
11	Syl Johnson	2.03
12	Dizzy Dean	2.07
13	Art Nehf	2.13
14	Sloppy Thurston	2.15
15	Eppa Rixey	2.17

1942-1960

1	Tiny Bonham	1.67
2	Robin Roberts	1.73
3	Lew Burdette	1.84
4	Ken Raffensberger	1.88
5	Vern Law	2.01
6	Don Newcombe	2.05
7	Dutch Leonard	2.06
8	Hal Brown	2.08
9	Larry Jansen	2.09
10	Bob Purkey	2.17
11	Dick Donovan	2.21
12	Bob Friend	2.23
13	Don Mossi	2.24
14	Preacher Roe	2.37
15	Ed Lopat	2.40

1961-1976

1	Fritz Peterson	1.73
2	Juan Marichal	1.82
3	Fergie Jenkins	1.99
4	Jim Barr	2.04
5	Bill Monbouquette	2.12
6	Ken Johnson	2.14
7	Jim Kaat	2.15
8	Ralph Terry	2.17
9	Gary Nolan	2.22
10	Don Drysdale	2.24
11	Bill Hands	2.27
12	Larry Jackson	2.27
13	Don Sutton	2.29
14	Ron Reed	2.30
15	Rick Wise	2.31

1977-1994

1	Bret Saberhagen	1.68
2	Greg Swindell	1.88
3	Dennis Eckersley	2.06
4	Lary Sorensen	2.08
5	John Candelaria	2.11
6	Jimmy Key	2.14
7	Bryn Smith	2.17
8	Scott McGregor	2.18
9	Bill Gullickson	2.19
10	Scott Sanderson	2.22
11	Mike Caldwell	2.23
12	Doug Drabek	2.33
13	Randy Jones	2.34
14	Moose Haas	2.37
15	Rick Reuschel	2.37

Strikeouts

1	Nolan Ryan	5714
2	Steve Carlton	4136
3	Bert Blyleven	3701
4	Tom Seaver	3640
5	Don Sutton	3574
6	Gaylord Perry	3534
7	Walter Johnson	3509
8	Phil Niekro	3342
9	Fergie Jenkins	3192
10	Bob Gibson	3117
11	Jim Bunning	2855
12	Mickey Lolich	2832
13	Cy Young	2803
14	Frank Tanana	2773
15	Warren Spahn	2583
16	Bob Feller	2581
17	Jerry Koosman	2556
18	Tim Keefe	2543
19	Christy Mathewson	2502
20	Don Drysdale	2486
21	Jack Morris	2478
22	Jim Kaat	2461
23	Sam McDowell	2453
24	Luis Tiant	2416
25	Sandy Koufax	2396
26	Charlie Hough	2362
27	Robin Roberts	2357
28	Early Wynn	2334
29	Rube Waddell	2316
30	Juan Marichal	2303
31	Lefty Grove	2266
32	Eddie Plank	2246
33	Dennis Eckersley	2245
	Tommy John	2245
35	Jim Palmer	2212
36	Roger Clemens	2201
37	Pete Alexander	2198
38	Vida Blue	2175
39	Camilo Pascual	2167
40	Mark Langston	2110
41	Bobo Newsom	2082
42	Dazzy Vance	2045
43	Rick Reuschel	2015
44	Catfish Hunter	2012
45	Billy Pierce	1999
46	Red Ruffing	1987
47	John Clarkson	1978
48	Bob Welch	1969
49	Whitey Ford	1956
50	Amos Rusie	1934
51	Dennis Martinez	1923
52	Jerry Reuss	1907
53	Dwight Gooden	1875
54	Kid Nichols	1868
55	Fernando Valenzuela	1861
56	Mickey Welch	1850
57	Charley Radbourn	1830
58	Frank Viola	1822
59	Tony Mullane	1803
60	Jim Galvin	1799
61	Hal Newhouser	1796
62	Ron Guidry	1778
63	Rudy May	1760
64	Joe Niekro	1747
65	Ed Walsh	1736
66	Bob Friend	1734
67	Joe Coleman	1728
	Milt Pappas	1728
69	Floyd Bannister	1723
70	Chief Bender	1711
71	Larry Jackson	1709
72	Jim McCormick	1704
73	Bob Veale	1703
74	Red Ames	1702
75	Charlie Buffinton	1700
76	Curt Simmons	1697
77	Bruce Hurst	1689
78	Dave Stewart	1683
79	Rick Sutcliffe	1679
80	Carl Hubbell	1677
81	Tommy Bridges	1674
82	John Candelaria	1673
83	Gus Weyhing	1665
84	Vic Willis	1651
85	Rick Wise	1647
86	Dave Stieb	1642
87	Al Downing	1639
88	Mike Cuellar	1632
89	Chris Short	1629
90	Andy Messersmith	1625
91	Jack Powell	1621
	Steve Rogers	1621
93	Danny Darwin	1615
94	Ray Sadecki	1614
95	Claude Osteen	1612
96	Hoyt Wilhelm	1610
97	Jim Maloney	1605
98	Mike Moore	1603
99	Ken Holtzman	1601
100	Rube Marquard	1593

Strikeouts per Game

1	Nolan Ryan	9.55
2	Sandy Koufax	9.28
3	Sam McDowell	8.86
4	J.R. Richard	8.37
5	Roger Clemens	8.28
6	David Cone	8.24
7	Sid Fernandez	8.19
8	Bob Veale	7.96
9	Jose Rijo	7.83
10	Jim Maloney	7.81
11	Dwight Gooden	7.78
12	Bobby Witt	7.76
13	Mark Langston	7.76
14	Jose DeLeon	7.56
15	Mario Soto	7.54
16	Sam Jones	7.54
17	Rich Gossage	7.47
18	Bob Gibson	7.22
19	Steve Carlton	7.13
20	Rube Waddell	7.04
21	Mickey Lolich	7.01
22	Rollie Fingers	6.87
23	Tom Seaver	6.85
24	Jim Bunning	6.83
25	Juan Pizarro	6.73
26	Bobby Bolin	6.71
27	Bert Blyleven	6.70
28	Ron Guidry	6.69
29	Ray Culp	6.69
30	Stan Williams	6.66
31	Camilo Pascual	6.65
32	Bob Turley	6.65
33	Don Wilson	6.60
34	Tug McGraw	6.59
35	Denny Lemaster	6.57
36	Andy Messersmith	6.56
37	Dennis Eckersley	6.55
38	Don Drysdale	6.52
39	Al Downing	6.50
40	Fernando Valenzuela	6.49
41	Floyd Bannister	6.49
42	Toad Ramsey	6.49
43	Chuck Finley	6.47
44	Diego Segui	6.46
45	Dean Chance	6.43
46	Hoyt Wilhelm	6.43
47	Mike Scott	6.39
48	Fergie Jenkins	6.38
49	Kevin Gross	6.38
50	Moe Drabowsky	6.37
51	Earl Wilson	6.37
52	Harvey Haddix	6.34
53	Sonny Siebert	6.32
54	Chris Short	6.31
55	Bruce Hurst	6.29
56	Bill Singer	6.27
57	Luis Tiant	6.24
58	Turk Farrell	6.21
59	Dazzy Vance	6.20
60	Stu Miller	6.18
61	Clay Kirby	6.17
62	Greg Swindell	6.16
63	Gary Bell	6.15
64	Gary Peters	6.14
65	Denny McLain	6.12
66	Bret Saberhagen	6.12
67	Don Sutton	6.09
68	Greg Maddux	6.08
69	Mike Krukow	6.07
70	Bob Feller	6.07
71	Ron Darling	6.07
72	Joe Coleman	6.05
73	Fred Norman	6.05
74	Rudy May	6.04
75	Orel Hershiser	6.02
76	Jerry Koosman	5.99
77	John Candelaria	5.96
78	Frank Tanana	5.96
79	Gaylord Perry	5.94
80	Dave Stewart	5.94
81	Danny Darwin	5.94
82	Woodie Fryman	5.92
83	Juan Marichal	5.91
84	Steve Barber	5.89
85	John Montefusco	5.89
86	Frank Viola	5.87
87	Mark Gubicza	5.87
88	Tom Candiotti	5.86
89	Mike Witt	5.86
90	Vida Blue	5.85
91	Jack Morris	5.83
92	Joey Jay	5.81
93	Ray Sadecki	5.81
94	Jim O'Toole	5.79
95	Dave Giusti	5.78
96	Jon Matlack	5.77
97	Larry Dierker	5.76
98	Don Robinson	5.75
99	Bob Welch	5.73
100	Lindy McDaniel	5.73

Ratio

1	Addie Joss	8.9
2	Ed Walsh	9.2
3	John Ward	9.4
4	Christy Mathewson	9.6
5	Tommy Bond	9.8
	Mordecai Brown	9.8
7	George Bradley	9.9
	Walter Johnson	9.9
9	Babe Adams	10.0
	Larry Corcoran	10.0
	Sandy Koufax	10.0
	Juan Marichal	10.0
13	Charlie Ferguson	10.1
	Terry Larkin	10.1
	Deacon Phillippe	10.1
16	Pete Alexander	10.2
	Jim McCormick	10.2
	Ed Morris	10.2
	Bret Saberhagen	10.2
	Tom Seaver	10.2
	Will White	10.2
22	Chief Bender	10.3
	Catfish Hunter	10.3
	Tim Keefe	10.3
	Rube Waddell	10.3
26	Nick Altrock	10.4
	Tiny Bonham	10.4
	Roger Clemens	10.4
	Sid Fernandez	10.4
	Fred Goldsmith	10.4
	Noodles Hahn	10.4
	Fergie Jenkins	10.4
	George McQuillan	10.4
	Gary Nolan	10.4
	Charley Radbourn	10.4
	Don Sutton	10.4
	Jim Whitney	10.4
	Hoyt Wilhelm	10.4
	Hooks Wiltse	10.4
	Cy Young	10.4
41	Eddie Cicotte	10.5
	Andy Messersmith	10.5
	Eddie Plank	10.5
	Dick Rudolph	10.5
	Jeff Tesreau	10.5
	Doc White	10.5
47	Dennis Eckersley	10.6
	Rollie Fingers	10.6
	Carl Hubbell	10.6
	Sam Leever	10.6
	Denny McLain	10.6
	Robin Roberts	10.6
53	Bob Caruthers	10.7
	Jack Chesbro	10.7
	Doug Drabek	10.7
	Don Drysdale	10.7
	Dwight Gooden	10.7
	Ron Guidry	10.7
	Guy Hecker	10.7
	Jumbo McGinnis	10.7
	Orval Overall	10.7
	Jim Palmer	10.7
	Ed Reulbach	10.7
	Slim Sallee	10.7
	Frank Smith	10.7
	George Winter	10.7
67	John Candelaria	10.8
	Mike Cuellar	10.8
	Bob Ewing	10.8
	Jim Galvin	10.8
	Barney Pelty	10.8
	Gaylord Perry	10.8
	Nap Rucker	10.8
	Dupee Shaw	10.8
	Mario Soto	10.8
	Warren Spahn	10.8
	Ralph Terry	10.8
78	Harry Brecheen	10.9
	Phil Douglas	10.9
	Eddie Fisher	10.9
	Dave Foutz	10.9
	Bob Gibson	10.9
	Claude Hendrix	10.9
	Jimmy Key	10.9
	Greg Maddux	10.9
	Fritz Peterson	10.9
	Jim Scott	10.9
	Jack Taylor	10.9
	Luis Tiant	10.9
	Fred Toney	10.9
	John Tudor	10.9
	Carl Weilman	10.9
93	11 players tied	11.0

Earned Run Average

1	Ed Walsh	1.82
2	Addie Joss	1.89
3	Mordecai Brown	2.06
4	John Ward	2.10
5	Christy Mathewson	2.13
6	Rube Waddell	2.16
7	Walter Johnson	2.17
8	Orval Overall	2.23
9	Tommy Bond	2.25
10	Ed Reulbach	2.28
	Will White	2.28
12	Jim Scott	2.30
13	Eddie Plank	2.35
14	Larry Corcoran	2.36
15	Eddie Cicotte	2.38
	Ed Killian	2.38
	George McQuillan	2.38
18	Doc White	2.39
19	Nap Rucker	2.42
20	Terry Larkin	2.43
	Jim McCormick	2.43
	Jeff Tesreau	2.43
23	Chief Bender	2.46
24	Sam Leever	2.47
	Lefty Leifield	2.47
	Hooks Wiltse	2.47
27	Bob Ewing	2.49
	Hippo Vaughn	2.49
29	George Bradley	2.50
30	Hoyt Wilhelm	2.52
31	Noodles Hahn	2.55
32	Pete Alexander	2.56
	Slim Sallee	2.56
34	Deacon Phillippe	2.59
	Frank Smith	2.59
36	Ed Siever	2.60
37	Bob Rhoads	2.61
38	Tim Keefe	2.62
39	Red Ames	2.63
	Barney Pelty	2.63
	Vic Willis	2.63
	Cy Young	2.63
43	Claude Hendrix	2.65
44	Joe McGinnity	2.66
	Dick Rudolph	2.66
	Jack Taylor	2.66
47	Nick Altrock	2.67
	Charlie Ferguson	2.67
	Charley Radbourn	2.67
	Carl Weilman	2.67
51	Jack Chesbro	2.68
	Cy Falkenberg	2.68
53	Bill Donovan	2.69
	Fred Toney	2.69
55	Larry Cheney	2.70
56	Mickey Welch	2.71
57	Fred Goldsmith	2.73
58	Harry Howell	2.74
59	Howie Camnitz	2.75
	Whitey Ford	2.75
	Dummy Taylor	2.75
62	Babe Adams	2.76
	Sandy Koufax	2.76
	Dutch Leonard	2.76
65	Jeff Pfeffer	2.77
66	Jack Coombs	2.78
	Earl Moore	2.78
68	Tully Sparks	2.79
	Jesse Tannehill	2.79
70	Phil Douglas	2.80
71	John Clarkson	2.81
72	Ray Fisher	2.82
	Ed Morris	2.82
	George Mullin	2.82
75	Bob Caruthers	2.83
76	Dave Foutz	2.84
77	Andy Messersmith	2.86
	Jim Palmer	2.86
	Tom Seaver	2.86
80	Jim Galvin	2.87
	George Winter	2.87
82	Willie Mitchell	2.88
83	Wilbur Cooper	2.89
	Stan Coveleski	2.89
	Juan Marichal	2.89
86	Rollie Fingers	2.90
87	Bob Gibson	2.91
88	Harry Brecheen	2.92
	Dean Chance	2.92
	Doc Crandall	2.92
	Guy Hecker	2.92
	Carl Mays	2.92
93	Roger Clemens	2.93
	Dave Davenport	2.93
95	Don Drysdale	2.95
	Jumbo McGinnis	2.95
	Kid Nichols	2.95
	Lefty Tyler	2.95
99	Charlie Buffinton	2.96
100	4 players tied	2.97

Earned Run Average (by era)

1876-1892

1	John Ward	2.10
2	Tommy Bond	2.25
3	Will White	2.28
4	Larry Corcoran	2.36
5	Terry Larkin	2.43
	Jim McCormick	2.43
7	George Bradley	2.50
8	Tim Keefe	2.62
9	Charlie Ferguson	2.67
	Charley Radbourn	2.67
11	Mickey Welch	2.71
12	Fred Goldsmith	2.73
13	John Clarkson	2.81
14	Ed Morris	2.82
15	Bob Caruthers	2.83

1893-1919

1	Ed Walsh	1.82
2	Addie Joss	1.89
3	Mordecai Brown	2.06
4	Christy Mathewson	2.13
5	Rube Waddell	2.16
6	Walter Johnson	2.17
7	Orval Overall	2.23
8	Ed Reulbach	2.28
9	Jim Scott	2.30
10	Eddie Plank	2.35
11	Eddie Cicotte	2.38
	Ed Killian	2.38
	George McQuillan	2.38
14	Doc White	2.39
15	Nap Rucker	2.42

1920-1941

1	Wilbur Cooper	2.89
	Stan Coveleski	2.89
3	Carl Mays	2.92
4	Carl Hubbell	2.98
5	Dizzy Dean	3.02
6	Lefty Grove	3.06
7	Bob Shawkey	3.09
8	Red Faber	3.15
	Eppa Rixey	3.15
10	Urban Shocker	3.17
11	Lon Warneke	3.18
12	Art Nehf	3.20
13	Jesse Barnes	3.22
14	George Mogridge	3.23
15	2 players tied	3.24

1942-1960

1	Hoyt Wilhelm	2.52
2	Whitey Ford	2.75
3	Harry Brecheen	2.92
4	Mort Cooper	2.97
5	Max Lanier	3.01
6	Tiny Bonham	3.06
	Hal Newhouser	3.06
8	Warren Spahn	3.09
9	Sal Maglie	3.15
10	Ed Lopat	3.21
11	Bob Lemon	3.23
	Dizzy Trout	3.23
13	Stu Miller	3.24
14	Bob Feller	3.25
	Dutch Leonard	3.25

1961-1976

1	Sandy Koufax	2.76
2	Andy Messersmith	2.86
	Jim Palmer	2.86
	Tom Seaver	2.86
5	Juan Marichal	2.89
6	Rollie Fingers	2.90
7	Bob Gibson	2.91
8	Dean Chance	2.92
9	Don Drysdale	2.95
10	Mel Stottlemyre	2.97
11	Bob Veale	3.07
12	Gary Nolan	3.08
13	Joe Horlen	3.11
	Gaylord Perry	3.11
15	2 players tied	3.14

1977-1994

1	Roger Clemens	2.93
2	Orel Hershiser	3.00
3	Rich Gossage	3.01
4	Greg Maddux	3.02
5	Dwight Gooden	3.10
6	David Cone	3.12
	Jose Rijo	3.12
	John Tudor	3.12
9	J.R. Richard	3.15
10	Doug Drabek	3.17
	Steve Rogers	3.17
12	Nolan Ryan	3.19
	Bret Saberhagen	3.19
14	Vida Blue	3.27
15	2 players tied	3.29

Adjusted Earned Run Average

1	Lefty Grove	148
2	Roger Clemens	147
	Walter Johnson	147
4	Hoyt Wilhelm	146
5	Ed Walsh	145
6	Addie Joss	142
7	Kid Nichols	139
8	Cy Young	138
9	Mordecai Brown	137
10	Christy Mathewson	136
11	Pete Alexander	135
	Rube Waddell	135
13	John Clarkson	134
14	Harry Brecheen	133
	Whitey Ford	133
	Noodles Hahn	133
17	Sandy Koufax	131
18	Dizzy Dean	130
	Carl Hubbell	130
	Hal Newhouser	130
	Amos Rusie	130
22	Greg Maddux	129
23	Stan Coveleski	128
	Bret Saberhagen	128
25	Nig Cuppy	127
	Bob Gibson	127
	Sal Maglie	127
	Tom Seaver	127
29	Tommy Bridges	126
30	Lefty Gomez	125
	Rich Gossage	125
	Tim Keefe	125
	Max Lanier	125
	Jim Palmer	125
	Mel Parnell	125
	Dazzy Vance	125
37	Dave Foutz	124
	Jimmy Key	124
	Jose Rijo	124
	Urban Shocker	124
	Dizzy Trout	124
42	Bob Caruthers	123
	Eddie Cicotte	123
	David Cone	123
	Mort Cooper	123
	Sam Leever	123
	Orval Overall	123
	John Tudor	123
49	Larry Corcoran	122
	Bob Feller	122
	Charlie Ferguson	122
	Silver King	122
	Juan Marichal	122
	Eddie Plank	122
	Ed Reulbach	122
	Eddie Rommel	122
	Dave Stieb	122
58	Don Drysdale	121
	Clark Griffith	121
	Andy Messersmith	121
	Jack Stivetts	121
62	Tiny Bonham	120
	Joe McGinnity	120
	Deacon Phillippe	120
	Charley Radbourn	120
	Jim Scott	120
	Hippo Vaughn	120
	Will White	120
69	Dean Chance	119
	Red Faber	119
	Rollie Fingers	119
	Ron Guidry	119
	Orel Hershiser	119
	Thornton Lee	119
	Bob Lemon	119
	Dutch Leonard	119
	Carl Mays	119
	Billy Pierce	119
	Nap Rucker	119
	Bobby Shantz	119
	Lon Warneke	119
82	Babe Adams	118
	Chuck Finley	118
	Ted Lyons	118
	Sadie McMahon	118
	Tony Mullane	118
	Warren Spahn	118
	John Ward	118
	Vic Willis	118
90	Bert Blyleven	117
	Dennis Eckersley	117
	Wes Ferrell	117
	Mike Garcia	117
	Dolf Luque	117
	Jim McCormick	117
	Gaylord Perry	117
	Toad Ramsey	117
	Bob Stanley	117
	Virgil Trucks	117
100	17 players tied	116

Adjusted ERA (by era)

1876-1892

1	John Clarkson	134
2	Tim Keefe	125
3	Dave Foutz	124
4	Bob Caruthers	123
5	Larry Corcoran	122
	Charlie Ferguson	122
	Silver King	122
8	Jack Stivetts	121
9	Charley Radbourn	120
	Will White	120
11	Sadie McMahon	118
	Tony Mullane	118
	John Ward	118
14	Jim McCormick	117
	Toad Ramsey	117

1893-1919

1	Walter Johnson	147
2	Ed Walsh	145
3	Addie Joss	142
4	Kid Nichols	139
5	Cy Young	138
6	Mordecai Brown	137
7	Christy Mathewson	136
8	Pete Alexander	135
	Rube Waddell	135
10	Noodles Hahn	133
11	Amos Rusie	130
12	Nig Cuppy	127
13	Eddie Cicotte	123
	Sam Leever	123
	Orval Overall	123

1920-1941

1	Lefty Grove	148
2	Dizzy Dean	130
	Carl Hubbell	130
4	Stan Coveleski	128
5	Tommy Bridges	126
6	Lefty Gomez	125
	Dazzy Vance	125
8	Urban Shocker	124
9	Eddie Rommel	122
10	Red Faber	119
	Thornton Lee	119
	Carl Mays	119
	Lon Warneke	119
14	Ted Lyons	118
15	2 players tied	117

1942-1960

1	Hoyt Wilhelm	146
2	Harry Brecheen	133
	Whitey Ford	133
4	Hal Newhouser	130
5	Sal Maglie	127
6	Max Lanier	125
	Mel Parnell	125
8	Dizzy Trout	124
9	Mort Cooper	123
10	Bob Feller	122
11	Tiny Bonham	120
12	Bob Lemon	119
	Dutch Leonard	119
	Billy Pierce	119
	Bobby Shantz	119

1961-1976

1	Sandy Koufax	131
2	Bob Gibson	127
	Tom Seaver	127
4	Jim Palmer	125
5	Juan Marichal	122
6	Don Drysdale	121
	Andy Messersmith	121
8	Dean Chance	119
	Rollie Fingers	119
10	Gaylord Perry	117
11	Tug McGraw	116
	Gary Nolan	116
13	4 players tied	115

1977-1994

1	Roger Clemens	147
2	Greg Maddux	129
3	Bret Saberhagen	128
4	Rich Gossage	125
5	Jimmy Key	124
	Jose Rijo	124
7	David Cone	123
	John Tudor	123
9	Dave Stieb	122
10	Ron Guidry	119
	Orel Hershiser	119
12	Chuck Finley	118
13	Bert Blyleven	117
	Dennis Eckersley	117
	Bob Stanley	117

Pitching Runs

#	Player	Runs
1	Cy Young	754
2	Walter Johnson	706
3	Lefty Grove	595
4	Kid Nichols	531
5	Pete Alexander	484
6	Warren Spahn	470
7	Christy Mathewson	420
8	Tom Seaver	419
9	Amos Rusie	416
10	Tim Keefe	404
11	Carl Hubbell	393
12	Whitey Ford	386
13	Bob Feller	385
14	Jim Palmer	374
15	John Clarkson	371
16	Lefty Gomez	322
17	Roger Clemens	321
18	Ted Lyons	313
19	Gaylord Perry	311
20	Ed Walsh	310
	Hoyt Wilhelm	310
22	Nolan Ryan	309
23	Charley Radbourn	302
24	Red Faber	294
25	Bob Gibson	290
26	Dazzy Vance	281
27	Mordecai Brown	279
28	Red Ruffing	272
29	Bert Blyleven	271
30	Dutch Leonard	267
31	Don Drysdale	266
32	Robin Roberts	264
33	Juan Marichal	262
34	Stan Coveleski	259
	Don Sutton	259
36	Eddie Plank	258
37	Hal Newhouser	257
38	Tommy Bridges	256
39	Bob Lemon	251
	Eppa Rixey	251
41	Billy Pierce	250
42	Dolf Luque	245
	Tony Mullane	245
44	Sandy Koufax	243
45	Rube Waddell	241
46	Steve Carlton	236
47	Clark Griffith	233
48	Carl Mays	217
49	Addie Joss	216
	Mickey Welch	216
51	Bob Caruthers	214
	Tommy John	214
53	Waite Hoyt	210
	Urban Shocker	210
55	Silver King	207
56	Jim McCormick	202
57	Ron Guidry	201
	Bret Saberhagen	201
59	Eddie Cicotte	200
	Nig Cuppy	200
61	Dave Stieb	199
62	Will White	198
63	Harry Brecheen	194
64	Phil Niekro	192
65	Mel Harder	190
66	Jimmy Key	189
67	Lon Warneke	188
68	Dizzy Dean	187
69	Ed Lopat	186
	Joe McGinnity	186
71	Jim Bunning	179
	Ed Morris	179
	Eddie Rommel	179
74	Larry French	178
75	Dizzy Trout	177
76	Spud Chandler	176
77	Sam Leever	175
78	Freddie Fitzsimmons	174
	Mike Garcia	174
80	Orel Hershiser	172
	Sadie McMahon	172
	Andy Messersmith	172
	Vic Willis	172
84	Early Wynn	170
85	Thornton Lee	169
86	Wilbur Cooper	168
87	Charlie Buffinton	162
88	Babe Adams	161
	Noodles Hahn	161
90	Jim Galvin	160
91	Ed Reulbach	159
92	Rich Gossage	158
93	Dennis Eckersley	157
	Fergie Jenkins	157
	Greg Maddux	157
96	Sal Maglie	156
	Firpo Marberry	156
98	Guy Hecker	154
99	Deacon Phillippe	153
100	2 players tied	152

Adjusted Pitching Runs

#	Player	Runs
1	Cy Young	820
2	Walter Johnson	668
3	Kid Nichols	653
4	Lefty Grove	643
5	Pete Alexander	522
6	John Clarkson	480
7	Tom Seaver	411
8	Christy Mathewson	403
9	Amos Rusie	381
10	Tim Keefe	375
11	Roger Clemens	368
12	Carl Hubbell	355
13	Bob Gibson	335
14	Warren Spahn	330
15	Bert Blyleven	319
16	Whitey Ford	315
	Jim Palmer	315
18	Hal Newhouser	305
	Gaylord Perry	305
20	Ted Lyons	302
21	Bob Feller	301
22	Phil Niekro	299
23	Tommy Bridges	291
24	Hoyt Wilhelm	288
25	Steve Carlton	277
26	Stan Coveleski	276
27	Red Faber	274
28	Tony Mullane	270
	Ed Walsh	270
30	Mordecai Brown	267
	Charley Radbourn	267
32	Clark Griffith	266
	Dazzy Vance	266
34	Eddie Plank	255
35	Fergie Jenkins	254
36	Silver King	253
37	Eppa Rixey	248
	Rube Waddell	248
39	Juan Marichal	247
	Jack Stivetts	247
41	Dave Stieb	240
42	Nig Cuppy	239
43	Robin Roberts	236
44	Dizzy Trout	232
45	Don Drysdale	230
46	Lefty Gomez	229
	Billy Pierce	229
48	Urban Shocker	226
49	Dutch Leonard	224
50	Sandy Koufax	221
51	Nolan Ryan	218
52	Eddie Rommel	217
53	Vic Willis	208
54	Addie Joss	207
	Joe McGinnity	207
56	Bob Caruthers	206
57	Harry Brecheen	205
	Bret Saberhagen	205
59	Dizzy Dean	201
	Jim McCormick	201
61	Dolf Luque	200
62	Dennis Eckersley	197
63	Mickey Welch	196
64	Eddie Cicotte	195
	Wes Ferrell	195
66	Bob Lemon	193
67	Jim Bunning	192
68	Carl Mays	189
69	Lon Warneke	188
70	Noodles Hahn	187
	Greg Maddux	187
72	Jimmy Key	186
73	Rick Reuschel	183
74	Mel Harder	182
	Sadie McMahon	182
	Jack Quinn	182
77	Wilbur Cooper	180
78	Tommy John	179
	Will White	179
80	Frank Dwyer	177
81	Red Ruffing	174
82	Waite Hoyt	173
	Luis Tiant	173
84	Thornton Lee	172
85	Larry French	171
86	Mel Parnell	170
87	Sam Leever	169
88	Bucky Walters	168
89	Ron Guidry	167
	Virgil Trucks	167
91	Jim Galvin	162
92	Babe Adams	161
	Charlie Buffinton	161
94	Sal Maglie	160
95	Larry Jackson	155
	Frank Viola	155
97	Rich Gossage	154
	Steve Rogers	154
99	Hippo Vaughn	152
100	2 players tied	150

Pitching Wins

#	Player	Wins
1	Walter Johnson	73.2
2	Cy Young	70.8
3	Lefty Grove	55.5
4	Pete Alexander	49.7
5	Warren Spahn	47.4
6	Kid Nichols	47.1
7	Christy Mathewson	44.2
8	Tom Seaver	43.8
9	Whitey Ford	39.3
10	Jim Palmer	38.8
11	Carl Hubbell	38.7
12	Bob Feller	37.5
13	Tim Keefe	36.3
14	Amos Rusie	35.7
15	Ed Walsh	33.4
16	John Clarkson	33.1
17	Gaylord Perry	32.6
18	Nolan Ryan	32.1
19	Hoyt Wilhelm	31.9
20	Roger Clemens	31.8
21	Bob Gibson	30.5
22	Lefty Gomez	29.9
23	Mordecai Brown	29.7
24	Ted Lyons	29.4
25	Red Faber	28.9
26	Bert Blyleven	27.8
27	Don Drysdale	27.7
28	Juan Marichal	27.6
29	Eddie Plank	27.3
30	Dazzy Vance	27.0
31	Don Sutton	26.9
32	Charley Radbourn	26.9
33	Robin Roberts	26.6
34	Dutch Leonard	26.4
35	Hal Newhouser	26.0
36	Stan Coveleski	25.9
37	Red Ruffing	25.6
38	Rube Waddell	25.3
39	Eppa Rixey	25.2
40	Sandy Koufax	25.1
41	Billy Pierce	25.1
42	Bob Lemon	25.0
43	Steve Carlton	24.7
44	Tommy Bridges	24.1
45	Dolf Luque	23.9
46	Addie Joss	23.4
47	Tommy John	22.1
48	Carl Mays	22.0
49	Tony Mullane	21.5
50	Eddie Cicotte	21.4
51	Clark Griffith	20.8
52	Urban Shocker	20.5
53	Waite Hoyt	20.2
54	Ron Guidry	20.1
55	Bret Saberhagen	20.1
56	Phil Niekro	20.0
57	Dave Stieb	19.9
58	Mickey Welch	19.7
59	Harry Brecheen	19.6
60	Lon Warneke	18.9
61	Bob Caruthers	18.8
62	Ed Lopat	18.8
63	Jimmy Key	18.7
64	Jim Bunning	18.6
65	Joe McGinnity	18.6
66	Dizzy Dean	18.6
67	Jim McCormick	18.4
68	Will White	18.2
69	Andy Messersmith	18.2
70	Mel Harder	18.1
71	Dizzy Trout	17.9
72	Orel Hershiser	17.9
73	Silver King	17.8
74	Sam Leever	17.8
75	Vic Willis	17.6
76	Spud Chandler	17.6
77	Larry French	17.6
78	Wilbur Cooper	17.5
79	Mike Garcia	17.4
80	Early Wynn	17.2
81	Ed Reulbach	17.1
82	Freddie Fitzsimmons	17.1
83	Nig Cuppy	17.0
84	Eddie Rommel	17.0
85	Babe Adams	16.7
86	Fergie Jenkins	16.4
87	Thornton Lee	16.3
88	Greg Maddux	16.3
89	Rich Gossage	16.2
90	Ed Morris	16.0
91	Dennis Eckersley	15.9
92	Vida Blue	15.9
93	Noodles Hahn	15.8
94	Joe Wood	15.7
95	Sal Maglie	15.6
96	Bucky Walters	15.4
97	Deacon Phillippe	15.4
98	Steve Rogers	15.3
99	Bob Shawkey	15.2
100	Rollie Fingers	15.1

Adjusted Pitching Wins

#	Player	Wins
1	Cy Young	77.0
2	Walter Johnson	69.2
3	Lefty Grove	59.9
4	Kid Nichols	57.9
5	Pete Alexander	53.6
6	Tom Seaver	43.0
7	John Clarkson	42.8
8	Christy Mathewson	42.4
9	Roger Clemens	36.5
10	Bob Gibson	35.2
11	Carl Hubbell	35.0
12	Tim Keefe	33.7
13	Warren Spahn	33.3
14	Bert Blyleven	32.8
15	Amos Rusie	32.7
16	Jim Palmer	32.7
17	Whitey Ford	32.1
18	Gaylord Perry	32.0
19	Phil Niekro	31.2
20	Hal Newhouser	30.9
21	Hoyt Wilhelm	29.6
22	Bob Feller	29.3
23	Ed Walsh	29.1
24	Steve Carlton	29.0
25	Mordecai Brown	28.4
26	Ted Lyons	28.4
27	Stan Coveleski	27.6
28	Tommy Bridges	27.4
29	Eddie Plank	27.0
30	Red Faber	27.0
31	Fergie Jenkins	26.5
32	Rube Waddell	26.1
33	Juan Marichal	26.0
34	Dazzy Vance	25.6
35	Eppa Rixey	24.9
36	Dave Stieb	24.0
37	Don Drysdale	24.0
38	Robin Roberts	23.8
39	Clark Griffith	23.8
40	Charley Radbourn	23.7
41	Tony Mullane	23.7
42	Dizzy Trout	23.5
43	Billy Pierce	23.0
44	Sandy Koufax	22.9
45	Nolan Ryan	22.6
46	Addie Joss	22.4
47	Dutch Leonard	22.1
48	Urban Shocker	22.1
49	Silver King	21.8
50	Vic Willis	21.3
51	Lefty Gomez	21.3
52	Jack Stivetts	20.9
53	Eddie Cicotte	20.8
54	Harry Brecheen	20.7
55	Joe McGinnity	20.7
56	Eddie Rommel	20.6
57	Bret Saberhagen	20.5
58	Nig Cuppy	20.4
59	Dennis Eckersley	20.0
60	Dizzy Dean	20.0
61	Jim Bunning	19.9
62	Dolf Luque	19.5
63	Greg Maddux	19.4
64	Bob Lemon	19.2
65	Rick Reuschel	19.1
66	Carl Mays	19.1
67	Lon Warneke	18.9
68	Wilbur Cooper	18.7
69	Tommy John	18.5
70	Jimmy Key	18.4
71	Jim McCormick	18.4
72	Noodles Hahn	18.3
73	Luis Tiant	18.2
74	Jack Quinn	18.1
75	Bob Caruthers	18.1
76	Wes Ferrell	18.0
77	Mickey Welch	17.9
78	Mel Harder	17.3
79	Sam Leever	17.2
80	Bucky Walters	17.1
81	Virgil Trucks	16.9
82	Larry French	16.9
83	Mel Parnell	16.8
84	Babe Adams	16.7
85	Ron Guidry	16.7
86	Waite Hoyt	16.6
87	Thornton Lee	16.6
88	Hippo Vaughn	16.5
89	Will White	16.5
90	Red Ruffing	16.4
91	Larry Jackson	16.1
92	Steve Rogers	16.1
93	Sal Maglie	16.0
94	Rich Gossage	15.8
95	Joe Wood	15.7
96	Ed Reulbach	15.7
97	Frank Viola	15.5
98	Sadie McMahon	15.5
99	Andy Messersmith	15.3
100	Don Sutton	15.2

Opponents' Batting Average

#	Player	Avg
1	Nolan Ryan	.204
2	Sandy Koufax	.205
3	Sid Fernandez	.208
4	Andy Messersmith	.212
	J.R. Richard	.212
6	Sam McDowell	.215
7	Hoyt Wilhelm	.216
8	Ed Walsh	.218
9	Mario Soto	.220
	Bob Turley	.220
11	Addie Joss	.223
	Orval Overall	.223
	Jeff Tesreau	.223
14	David Cone	.224
	Jose DeLeon	.224
	Jim Maloney	.224
	Ed Reulbach	.224
18	Roger Clemens	.226
	Larry Corcoran	.226
	Tom Seaver	.226
21	Walter Johnson	.227
	Tim Keefe	.227
23	Bob Gibson	.228
	Rich Gossage	.228
	Rube Waddell	.228
	Don Wilson	.228
27	Sam Jones	.230
	Jim Palmer	.230
29	Bobby Bolin	.231
	Bob Feller	.231
	Catfish Hunter	.231
32	Al Downing	.232
	Johnny Vander Meer	.232
	Stan Williams	.232
35	Mordecai Brown	.233
	Charlie Ferguson	.233
	Charlie Hough	.233
38	Dean Chance	.234
	Larry Cheney	.234
	Denny McLain	.234
	Toad Ramsey	.234
	Amos Rusie	.234
43	Ray Culp	.235
	Rollie Fingers	.235
	Whitey Ford	.235
	Dave Foutz	.235
	Dwight Gooden	.235
	Ed Morris	.235
	Tony Mullane	.235
	John Ward	.235
51	Moe Drabowsky	.236
	Christy Mathewson	.236
	Don Sutton	.236
	Luis Tiant	.236
	Bob Veale	.236
56	Vida Blue	.237
	Juan Marichal	.237
	Tug McGraw	.237
	Juan Pizarro	.237
	Frank Smith	.237
61	Rudy May	.238
	Allie Reynolds	.238
	Jim Scott	.238
	Sonny Siebert	.238
65	Gary Bell	.239
	Chief Bender	.239
	Bill Donovan	.239
	Don Drysdale	.239
	Orel Hershiser	.239
	Mark Langston	.239
	Hal Newhouser	.239
	Gary Nolan	.239
	Barney Pelty	.239
	Eddie Plank	.239
	Jose Rijo	.239
	Dupee Shaw	.239
	Dave Stieb	.239
	Will White	.239
79	Steve Carlton	.240
	Bob Caruthers	.240
	John Clarkson	.240
	Mort Cooper	.240
	Billy Pierce	.240
	Mike Scott	.240
	Bill Singer	.240
	Virgil Trucks	.240
87	Jack Coombs	.241
	Kirby Higbe	.241
	Bob Lemon	.241
	George McQuillan	.241
	Earl Moore	.241
	Charley Radbourn	.241
	Hooks Wiltse	.241
94	10 players tied	.242

Opponents' On Base Pct.

#	Player	Pct
1	John Ward	.254
2	Addie Joss	.260
3	George Bradley	.262
4	Terry Larkin	.263
5	Larry Corcoran	.264
	Ed Walsh	.264
7	Tommy Bond	.267
8	Will White	.268
9	Charlie Ferguson	.270
10	Christy Mathewson	.273
	Ed Morris	.273
12	Jim McCormick	.274
13	Fred Goldsmith	.275
	Jim Whitney	.275
15	Tim Keefe	.276
	Sandy Koufax	.276
17	Mordecai Brown	.278
	Juan Marichal	.278
	Charley Radbourn	.278
20	Walter Johnson	.279
	Dupee Shaw	.279
22	Guy Hecker	.281
	Jumbo McGinnis	.281
24	Deacon Phillippe	.283
25	Babe Adams	.284
	Jim Galvin	.284
27	Bob Caruthers	.285
	Bobby Mathews	.285
	Tom Seaver	.285
30	Dave Foutz	.286
	Bret Saberhagen	.286
	Cy Young	.286
33	Roger Clemens	.287
	Sid Fernandez	.287
	Catfish Hunter	.287
	Gary Nolan	.287
	Don Sutton	.287
38	Pete Alexander	.288
	Rube Waddell	.288
40	Tiny Bonham	.289
	Henry Boyle	.289
	Noodles Hahn	.289
	Fergie Jenkins	.289
	Jack Lynch	.289
	Andy Messersmith	.289
46	Hoyt Wilhelm	.290
	Hooks Wiltse	.290
48	Nick Altrock	.291
	Chief Bender	.291
	John Clarkson	.291
	Dennis Eckersley	.291
	Carl Hubbell	.291
53	Charlie Buffinton	.292
	Denny McLain	.292
	Mickey Welch	.292
	Doc White	.292
57	Sam Leever	.293
	Eddie Plank	.293
	Robin Roberts	.293
60	Don Drysdale	.294
	Ron Guidry	.294
	George McQuillan	.294
63	Rollie Fingers	.295
	Dwight Gooden	.295
	Toad Ramsey	.295
	Jeff Tesreau	.295
67	Jack Chesbro	.296
	Doug Drabek	.296
	Jim Palmer	.296
	Mario Soto	.296
	Ralph Terry	.296
72	Gaylord Perry	.297
	Frank Smith	.297
	Warren Spahn	.297
	George Winter	.297
76	Harry Brecheen	.298
	John Candelaria	.298
	Eddie Cicotte	.298
	Dizzy Dean	.298
	Tony Mullane	.298
	Orval Overall	.298
	Lee Richmond	.298
	Dick Rudolph	.298
	Jack Taylor	.298
	Luis Tiant	.298
86	Jim Bunning	.299
	Mike Cuellar	.299
	Eddie Fisher	.299
	Bob Gibson	.299
	Jimmy Key	.299
	Don Mossi	.299
	Don Newcombe	.299
	Ed Reulbach	.299
	Slim Sallee	.299
95	8 players tied	.300

Wins Above Team

#	Player	Value
1	Cy Young	99.7
2	Walter Johnson	90.0
3	Pete Alexander	81.6
4	Christy Mathewson	64.9
5	Lefty Grove	62.9
6	Tom Seaver	58.9
7	Jim McCormick	56.3
8	Jim Galvin	53.7
9	Charley Radbourn	50.3
10	Warren Spahn	45.8
11	Clark Griffith	45.6
12	Whitey Ford	44.4
13	Will White	43.5
14	Roger Clemens	41.6
15	Juan Marichal	38.7
16	Bob Feller	36.8
	Mickey Welch	36.8
18	Ted Lyons	36.2
	Phil Niekro	36.2
20	Amos Rusie	35.9
21	Tony Mullane	35.8
	Eddie Plank	35.8
23	Jesse Tannehill	35.6
24	Charlie Buffinton	35.0
25	Wes Ferrell	34.8
26	Carl Hubbell	34.6
27	Kid Nichols	34.4
28	Steve Carlton	33.5
29	Dwight Gooden	33.4
30	Dazzy Vance	33.2
31	Jim Devlin	32.5
32	Joe McGinnity	32.4
33	Ed Walsh	31.5
34	Bob Gibson	31.0
35	Ed Morris	30.8
	Eddie Rommel	30.8
37	Sandy Koufax	30.6
38	Bob Caruthers	30.4
39	Jim Palmer	30.2
	Urban Shocker	30.2
41	Robin Roberts	30.0
42	Guy Hecker	29.5
	Sadie McMahon	29.5
44	Fergie Jenkins	29.3
45	Ron Guidry	29.1
46	Mordecai Brown	29.0
47	Addie Joss	28.7
48	Dizzy Dean	27.6
49	Bobby Mathews	26.7
50	Schoolboy Rowe	26.5
51	Sam Leever	25.7
52	Rip Sewell	25.4
53	Frank Killen	25.1
54	Jack Chesbro	24.8
55	Nap Rucker	24.7
56	Red Lucas	24.5
57	Russ Ford	24.3
58	John Candelaria	23.9
	Herb Pennock	23.9
60	Charlie Ferguson	23.6
61	Red Faber	23.5
62	Johnny Allen	23.4
	Chief Bender	23.4
64	John Clarkson	23.2
65	Gaylord Perry	23.1
	Rick Reuschel	23.1
67	Joe Wood	23.0
68	Noodles Hahn	22.9
	Firpo Marberry	22.9
70	Sal Maglie	22.7
71	Gus Weyhing	22.6
72	Tim Keefe	22.5
73	Tommy John	22.2
74	Bob Welch	21.9
75	Carl Mays	21.6
	Bret Saberhagen	21.6
77	Orel Hershiser	21.4
78	Burleigh Grimes	21.3
	Claude Passeau	21.3
	Hippo Vaughn	21.3
81	Spud Chandler	21.2
82	Dutch Leonard	21.1
	J.R. Richard	21.1
84	John Tudor	21.0
	George Uhle	21.0
	Bucky Walters	21.0
87	Jim Maloney	20.9
88	Mark Langston	20.8
89	Slim Sallee	20.6
90	Vida Blue	20.4
	Hal Newhouser	20.4
	Frank Viola	20.4
93	Bert Blyleven	20.3
	Freddie Fitzsimmons	20.3
95	Babe Adams	20.2
	Allie Reynolds	20.2
97	Ted Breitenstein	20.1
	Stan Coveleski	20.1
99	Art Nehf	20.0
100	2 players tied	19.9

Wins Above League

#	Player	Value
1	Cy Young	413.5
2	Walter Johnson	348.0
3	Jim Galvin	334.0
4	Nolan Ryan	308.0
5	Warren Spahn	304.0
6	Phil Niekro	296.0
7	Pete Alexander	290.5
8	Don Sutton	290.0
9	Gaylord Perry	289.5
10	Steve Carlton	286.5
11	Kid Nichols	284.5
12	Tim Keefe	283.5
13	Christy Mathewson	280.5
14	Early Wynn	272.0
15	Bert Blyleven	268.5
16	Robin Roberts	265.5
17	Jim Kaat	260.0
	Eddie Plank	260.0
19	Tommy John	259.5
20	Eppa Rixey	258.5
	Mickey Welch	258.5
22	Tom Seaver	258.0
23	Fergie Jenkins	255.0
24	John Clarkson	253.0
25	Tony Mullane	252.0
	Charley Radbourn	252.0
27	Jack Powell	249.5
28	Red Ruffing	249.0
29	Gus Weyhing	248.0
30	Ted Lyons	245.0
31	Burleigh Grimes	241.0
32	Jim McCormick	239.5
33	Frank Tanana	238.0
34	Red Faber	233.5
35	Jack Quinn	232.5
36	Vic Willis	227.0
37	Sam Jones	223.0
38	Lefty Grove	220.5
39	Jack Morris	220.0
40	Paul Derringer	217.5
41	Bobo Newsom	216.5
42	Charlie Hough	216.0
43	Jerry Koosman	215.5
44	Bob Feller	214.0
45	Bob Friend	213.5
46	Bob Gibson	212.5
	Joe Niekro	212.5
48	George Mullin	212.0
49	Jim Palmer	210.0
50	Waite Hoyt	209.5
	Amos Rusie	209.5
52	Jerry Reuss	205.5
53	Mel Harder	204.5
54	Jim Bunning	204.0
	Mickey Lolich	204.0
56	Carl Hubbell	203.5
57	Rick Reuschel	202.5
58	Hooks Dauss	202.0
59	Earl Whitehill	201.5
60	Herb Pennock	201.0
61	Luis Tiant	200.5
62	Will White	197.5
	Jim Whitney	197.5
64	Wilbur Cooper	197.0
65	Al Orth	196.5
	Adonis Terry	196.5
67	Claude Osteen	195.5
68	Catfish Hunter	195.0
	Dennis Martinez	195.0
70	Jim Perry	194.5
71	Joe McGinnity	194.0
72	Chick Fraser	193.5
73	Charlie Buffinton	192.5
	Juan Marichal	192.5
75	Clark Griffith	191.5
76	Billy Pierce	190.0
77	Joe Bush	189.0
	Rube Marquard	189.0
79	Larry Jackson	188.5
	Tom Zachary	188.5
81	Curt Simmons	188.0
82	Don Drysdale	187.5
83	Dolf Luque	186.5
	Milt Pappas	186.5
85	Dutch Leonard	186.0
86	Vida Blue	185.0
87	Mordecai Brown	184.5
	Rick Wise	184.5
89	Doyle Alexander	184.0
	Larry French	184.0
	Jesse Haines	184.0
	Lee Meadows	184.0
93	George Uhle	183.0
94	Freddie Fitzsimmons	181.5
95	Charlie Root	180.5
96	Bucky Walters	179.0
97	5 players tied	178.5

Relief Games

1	Kent Tekulve	1050
2	Hoyt Wilhelm	1018
3	Rich Gossage	965
4	Gene Garber	922
5	Lindy McDaniel	913
6	Rollie Fingers	907
7	Sparky Lyle	899
8	Lee Smith	885
9	Jeff Reardon	880
10	Don McMahon	872
11	Roy Face	821
12	Tug McGraw	785
13	Darold Knowles	757
14	Jesse Orosco	750
15	Tom Burgmeier	742
	Gary Lavelle	742
17	Ron Perranoski	736
18	Willie Hernandez	733
19	Clay Carroll	703
	Greg Minton	703
21	Mike Marshall	699
22	Larry Andersen	698
23	Bill Campbell	691
24	Dan Quisenberry	674
25	Bruce Sutter	661
26	Steve Bedrosian	657
27	Craig Lefferts	651
28	Ted Abernathy	647
29	Dave LaRoche	632
30	Dave Righetti	628
31	Eddie Fisher	627
32	Bob McClure	625
33	Paul Lindblad	623
34	Roger McDowell	616
35	John Franco	613
36	Stu Miller	611
37	Grant Jackson	609
38	Dave Smith	608
39	Elias Sosa	598
40	Bob Miller	595
41	Tom Henke	590
42	Pedro Borbon	589
	Mitch Williams	589
44	Rob Murphy	583
45	Doug Bair	579
46	Bob Locker	576
47	Terry Forster	575
48	Paul Assenmacher	574
49	Greg Harris	560
50	Bob Stanley	552

Relief Wins

1	Hoyt Wilhelm	124
2	Lindy McDaniel	119
3	Rich Gossage	112
4	Rollie Fingers	107
5	Sparky Lyle	99
6	Roy Face	96
7	Gene Garber	94
	Kent Tekulve	94
9	Mike Marshall	92
10	Don McMahon	90
11	Tug McGraw	89
12	Clay Carroll	88
13	Bob Stanley	85
14	Bill Campbell	80
	Gary Lavelle	80
16	Tom Burgmeier	79
	Stu Miller	79
	Ron Perranoski	79
19	Johnny Murphy	73
20	John Hiller	72
	Jeff Reardon	72
22	Mark Clear	71
	Dick Hall	71
24	Willie Hernandez	70
25	Pedro Borbon	69
26	Bruce Sutter	68
27	Lee Smith	67
28	Jesse Orosco	66
29	Steve Bedrosian	64
	Al Hrabosky	64
31	Darold Knowles	63
	Clem Labine	63
	Dave LaRoche	63
34	Jim Brewer	62
	Turk Farrell	62
	Eddie Fisher	62
	John Franco	62
	Grant Jackson	62
	Paul Lindblad	62
	Frank Linzy	62
	Roger McDowell	62
42	Joe Heving	60
43	Johnny Klippstein	59
	Elias Sosa	59
45	Aurelio Lopez	58
	Phil Regan	58
47	Ted Abernathy	57
	Bob Locker	57
	Greg Minton	57
50	4 players tied	56

Relief Losses

1	Gene Garber	108
2	Hoyt Wilhelm	103
3	Rollie Fingers	101
4	Mike Marshall	98
5	Kent Tekulve	90
6	Lindy McDaniel	88
7	Rich Gossage	85
8	Roy Face	82
9	Jeff Reardon	77
10	Sparky Lyle	76
11	Gary Lavelle	75
12	Ron Perranoski	74
13	Lee Smith	73
14	Darold Knowles	71
	Bruce Sutter	71
16	Tug McGraw	69
17	Stu Miller	67
18	Clay Carroll	66
	Don McMahon	66
20	Bill Campbell	65
21	Greg Minton	62
22	Roger McDowell	61
	Jesse Orosco	61
	Bob Stanley	61
25	John Hiller	58
26	Steve Bedrosian	57
	Frank Linzy	57
28	Willie Hernandez	55
29	Tom Burgmeier	53
	Ron Davis	53
	Craig Lefferts	53
	Dave Smith	53
33	Jim Kern	52
	Randy Moffitt	52
35	Turk Farrell	51
	Eddie Fisher	51
	Dave LaRoche	51
	Claude Raymond	51
	Dave Righetti	51
40	Dale Murray	50
	Al Worthington	50
42	Jim Brewer	49
	Mark Davis	49
	Doug Jones	49
	Elias Sosa	49
	Mitch Williams	49
47	Ted Abernathy	48
	Mark Clear	48
49	3 players tied	47

Relief Innings Pitched

1	Hoyt Wilhelm	1871.0
2	Lindy McDaniel	1694.0
3	Rich Gossage	1510.0
4	Rollie Fingers	1501.0
5	Gene Garber	1454.1
6	Kent Tekulve	1437.0
7	Sparky Lyle	1391.0
8	Tug McGraw	1302.0
9	Don McMahon	1297.0
10	Mike Marshall	1260.0
11	Tom Burgmeier	1250.1
12	Roy Face	1213.0
13	Clay Carroll	1206.1
14	Eddie Fisher	1186.0
15	Bill Campbell	1178.0
16	Ron Perranoski	1172.1
17	Bob Stanley	1157.0
18	Jeff Reardon	1124.1
19	Stu Miller	1096.1
20	Lee Smith	1089.1
21	Greg Minton	1088.0
22	Gary Lavelle	1079.1
23	Darold Knowles	1053.0
24	Paul Lindblad	1044.0
	Dan Quisenberry	1044.0
26	Bruce Sutter	1043.0
27	Johnny Klippstein	1042.1
28	Pedro Borbon	1017.0
29	Willie Hernandez	995.0
30	Bob Miller	994.1
31	Dave LaRoche	976.0
32	Ted Abernathy	970.0
33	John Hiller	964.1
34	Larry Andersen	958.0
35	Jesse Orosco	915.0
36	Elias Sosa	905.0
37	Dale Murray	902.0
38	Doug Bair	890.0
39	Terry Forster	888.0
40	Bob Locker	879.0
41	Dennis Lamp	876.0
42	Ron Reed	875.0
43	Jim Brewer	861.0
44	Aurelio Lopez	860.0
45	Dick Tidrow	859.1
46	Steve Bedrosian	857.0
47	Dave Giusti	856.1
48	Clem Labine	854.0
	Roger McDowell	854.0
50	Grant Jackson	849.0

Relief Points

1. Lee Smith 863
2. Jeff Reardon 797
3. Rollie Fingers 795
4. Rich Gossage 757
5. Bruce Sutter 665
6. Dennis Eckersley 599
   Hoyt Wilhelm 599
8. Sparky Lyle 598
9. Tom Henke 559
10. Dan Quisenberry 554
11. John Franco 549
12. Dave Righetti 545
13. Gene Garber 516
14. Roy Face 496
15. Lindy McDaniel 494
16. Dave Smith 485
17. Tug McGraw 469
18. Kent Tekulve 466
19. Mike Marshall 462
20. Ron Perranoski 442
21. Steve Bedrosian 439
22. Bobby Thigpen 430
23. Don McMahon 420
24. Mitch Williams 409
25. Doug Jones 407
26. Stu Miller 399
27. Clay Carroll 396
28. Randy Myers 392
29. Willie Hernandez 379
30. Bob Stanley 373
31. Roger McDowell 365
32. Dave Giusti 363
33. Ted Abernathy 362
    Jeff Montgomery 362
35. Jay Howell 358
36. Gary Lavelle 357
37. Greg Minton 352
38. Bryan Harvey 351
39. Bill Campbell 347
40. Darold Knowles 341
41. Jim Brewer 339
42. Mike Henneman 338
43. John Hiller 336
44. Gregg Olson 333
45. Rick Aguilera 332
46. Jesse Orosco 331
47. Dave LaRoche 327
48. Jeff Russell 325
49. Johnny Murphy 317
50. Tom Burgmeier 309

Relief Ranking

1. Hoyt Wilhelm 334
2. Rich Gossage 285
3. Lee Smith 251
4. Bruce Sutter 215
5. Rollie Fingers 211
6. Dan Quisenberry 207
7. Kent Tekulve 204
8. Tom Henke 196
9. John Franco 194
10. Dennis Eckersley 192
11. Sparky Lyle 179
12. Mike Marshall 175
13. John Hiller 173
14. Jeff Reardon 169
15. Bob Stanley 168
16. Jeff Montgomery 160
17. Tug McGraw 159
18. Gary Lavelle 152
19. Gene Garber 148
20. Jesse Orosco 146
21. Ellis Kinder 145
22. Lindy McDaniel 143
23. Clay Carroll 138
    Bryan Harvey 138
25. Gregg Olson 132
26. Dave Smith 131
27. Ron Perranoski 128
28. Doug Jones 125
    Stu Miller 125
30. Willie Hernandez 123
31. Mike Henneman 120
32. Don McMahon 114
33. Jay Howell 112
    Dave Righetti 112
35. Steve Bedrosian 111
    Steve Farr 111
    Johnny Murphy 111
38. Rick Aguilera 109
39. Greg Harris 107
40. Lefty Grove 106
    Jeff Russell 106
42. Mark Eichhorn 102
    Roy Face 102
44. Tom Burgmeier 99
45. Terry Forster 98
    Greg Minton 98
47. Tim Burke 97
    Frank Linzy 97
49. Ron Reed 95
    Mitch Williams 95

Relievers' Runs

1. Hoyt Wilhelm 261
2. Rich Gossage 181
3. Rollie Fingers 156
4. Dan Quisenberry 144
5. Kent Tekulve 128
6. Sparky Lyle 121
7. Dennis Eckersley 111
   Tom Henke 111
9. Tug McGraw 110
10. Lee Smith 106
11. Mark Eichhorn 101
12. Clay Carroll 100
    Mike Marshall 100
    Jesse Orosco 100
    Ron Perranoski 100
16. John Hiller 99
    Gary Lavelle 99
    Don McMahon 99
19. Stu Miller 96
20. Lindy McDaniel 94
21. Bob Stanley 93
22. Jeff Montgomery 91
    Bruce Sutter 91
24. Dave Smith 89
25. Greg Minton 88
26. Greg Harris 86
27. John Franco 85
    Johnny Murphy 85
29. Jeff Reardon 84
30. Ellis Kinder 82
31. Tom Burgmeier 78
    Steve Farr 78
    Jay Howell 78
34. Willie Hernandez 74
35. Jim Brewer 73
36. Tim Burke 72
    Mike Henneman 72
38. Larry Andersen 71
    Terry Forster 71
    Dave Righetti 71
41. Bob Miller 70
42. Bryan Harvey 69
    Firpo Marberry 69
44. Gregg Olson 68
45. Duane Ward 67
46. Dick Hall 66
    Waite Hoyt 66
    Ron Reed 66
    Gerry Staley 66
50. 2 players tied 65

Adjusted Relievers' Runs

1. Hoyt Wilhelm 245
2. Rich Gossage 175
3. Dan Quisenberry 147
4. Kent Tekulve 142
5. Lee Smith 126
6. Bob Stanley 121
   Sparky Lyle 121
7. Rollie Fingers 120
8. Sparky Lyle 118
9. Bruce Sutter 117
10. John Hiller 115
11. Tug McGraw 113
12. Tom Henke 111
13. Lindy McDaniel 108
14. Mark Eichhorn 104
15. Mike Marshall 103
16. Greg Harris 100
17. Ellis Kinder 99
18. Dennis Eckersley 98
19. Clay Carroll 97
20. Gary Lavelle 96
21. John Franco 93
    Gene Garber 93
    Jeff Montgomery 93
    Jesse Orosco 93
25. Jeff Reardon 88
26. Tom Burgmeier 87
27. Don McMahon 85
28. Willie Hernandez 84
    Ron Perranoski 84
30. Stu Miller 83
31. Steve Farr 79
32. Terry Forster 78
33. Greg Minton 75
34. Ron Reed 74
35. Dave Smith 73
36. Larry Andersen 70
    Tim Burke 70
38. Mike Henneman 69
    Duane Ward 69
40. Bryan Harvey 68
41. Lefty Grove 67
42. Ted Abernathy 66
    Jay Howell 66
    Johnny Murphy 66
    Gregg Olson 66
46. Grant Jackson 64
    Gerry Staley 64
48. 4 players tied 63

Clutch Pitching Index

1	Ed Killian	116
	Bob Rhoads	116
	Ed Siever	116
4	Win Mercer	115
5	Chuck Finley	114
6	Ron Kline	113
	Bill Lee	113
	Will White	113
9	Al Benton	112
	Ed Lopat	112
	Bob Stanley	112
	Tom Zachary	112
13	Whitey Ford	111
	Preacher Roe	111
15	Frank Dwyer	110
	Max Lanier	110
	Bob Miller	110
	Gerry Staley	110
	Bill Wight	110
20	Steve Blass	109
	Bob Buhl	109
	Max Butcher	109
	Dan Casey	109
	Lefty Leifield	109
	Sal Maglie	109
	Mel Parnell	109
	Bob Shaw	109
	Geoff Zahn	109
29	Steve Barber	108
	Sheriff Blake	108
	Nixey Callahan	108
	Lefty Grove	108
	Carl Morton	108
	George Mullin	108
	Dizzy Trout	108
	Bob Veale	108
37	Nelson Briles	107
	Lloyd Brown	107
	Nig Cuppy	107
	Larry French	107
	Clark Griffith	107
	Claude Osteen	107
	Eddie Rommel	107
	Dutch Ruether	107
	Eddie Smith	107
	Zane Smith	107
	Dummy Taylor	107
	Steve Trout	107
	Mickey Welch	107
50	Jim Bagby	106
	Mark Baldwin	106
	Roger Craig	106
	Red Donahue	106
	Red Faber	106
	Dave Foutz	106
	Mel Harder	106
	Joe Haynes	106
	Guy Hecker	106
	Tommy John	106
	Jim McCormick	106
	Cal McLish	106
	Jeff Pfeffer	106
	Togie Pittinger	106
	Howie Pollet	106
	Nap Rucker	106
	Jim Scott	106
	Sherry Smith	106
	Sloppy Thurston	106
	John Tudor	106
	Rube Waddell	106
	Bucky Walters	106
72	Jack Curtis	105
	Murry Dickson	105
	Dick Ellsworth	105
	Wes Ferrell	105
	Fred Frankhouse	105
	Gene Garber	105
	Mike Garcia	105
	Ken Heintzelman	105
	Johnny Klippstein	105
	Frank Lary	105
	Thornton Lee	105
	Dutch Leonard	105
	Ted Lyons	105
	Bobby Mathews	105
	Tug McGraw	105
	Stu Miller	105
	Clarence Mitchell	105
	George Mogridge	105
	Shane Rawley	105
	Allie Reynolds	105
	Lee Richmond	105
	Johnny Sain	105
	Jim Slaton	105
	Al Smith	105
	George Suggs	105
	Jesse Tannehill	105
	Hippo Vaughn	105
	Lon Warneke	105
	Wilbur Wood	105

Pitcher Batting Runs

1	Red Ruffing	143
2	Bob Caruthers	111
3	Wes Ferrell	100
4	Walter Johnson	99
5	Red Lucas	98
6	George Uhle	92
7	Guy Hecker	90
	Bob Lemon	90
9	Jim Whitney	89
10	Warren Spahn	88
11	George Mullin	87
12	Don Newcombe	79
13	Babe Ruth	78
14	Schoolboy Rowe	76
15	Early Wynn	72
16	Bob Gibson	65
	Jack Stivetts	65
18	Carl Mays	64
19	Al Orth	63
20	Don Drysdale	60
21	Christy Mathewson	59
22	Gary Peters	57
	Bucky Walters	57
	Earl Wilson	57
25	Jesse Tannehill	55
26	Doc Crandall	54
	Jim Tobin	54
28	Burleigh Grimes	52
	Ad Gumbert	52
30	Claude Hendrix	50
	Tony Mullane	50
32	Joe Bush	49
	Steve Carlton	49
	Charlie Ferguson	49
35	Bob Forsch	48
	Scott Stratton	48
37	Don Larsen	46
38	Dave Foutz	45
	Vern Law	45
	Rick Rhoden	45
	Dutch Ruether	45
	Adonis Terry	45
43	Frank Killen	44
	Jack Scott	44
45	Tommy Byrne	41
	Jim Kaat	41
	Don Robinson	41
48	Charley Radbourn	40
	Johnny Sain	40
50	Wilbur Cooper	39
	Fred Hutchinson	39
52	Claude Osteen	38
	Sloppy Thurston	38
54	Dolf Luque	37
	Doc White	37
56	Jack Coombs	36
	Mickey McDermott	36
58	Ken Brett	35
	Clark Griffith	35
	Harvey Haddix	35
	Win Mercer	35
	Frank Smith	35
	Jack Taylor	35
64	Orel Hershiser	34
	Art Nehf	34
	Robin Roberts	34
	Rick Wise	34
68	Chief Bender	33
	Catfish Hunter	33
	Ben Sanders	33
71	Hooks Dauss	32
	Ted Lyons	32
	Al Maul	32
74	Ray Caldwell	31
	Dizzy Trout	31
	John Ward	31
	Joe Wood	31
78	Ed Brandt	30
	Lew Burdette	30
	Lefty Tyler	30
	Fernando Valenzuela	30
82	Dwight Gooden	29
	Jack Harshman	29
	Ed Lopat	29
	Jouett Meekin	29
	Camilo Pascual	29
	Juan Pizarro	29
88	Joe Nuxhall	28
	Tom Seaver	28
	Urban Shocker	28
91	Charlie Buffinton	27
	Whitey Ford	27
	Brickyard Kennedy	27
	Frank Kitson	27
	Bill Sherdel	27
	Lon Warneke	27
97	Jim Maloney	26
	Clarence Mitchell	26
	Blue Moon Odom	26
100	8 players tied	25

Pitcher Fielding Runs

1	Ed Walsh	83
2	Carl Mays	74
3	Christy Mathewson	68
4	Freddie Fitzsimmons	60
	Bob Lemon	60
6	Burleigh Grimes	58
7	Tommy John	55
8	Harry Howell	51
9	Harry Gumbert	50
10	John Clarkson	46
11	Bill Doak	43
12	Willis Hudlin	42
	Eddie Rommel	42
14	Greg Maddux	40
	Jack Quinn	40
16	Jim Galvin	39
	Rick Reuschel	39
	Bobby Shantz	39
19	Hooks Dauss	38
	Dizzy Trout	38
21	Jack Russell	36
	Mel Stottlemyre	36
23	Charlie Buffinton	35
	Johnny Schmitz	35
25	Nick Altrock	34
	Dennis Martinez	34
	Willie Sudhoff	34
28	Tony Mullane	33
29	Red Ames	32
	Murry Dickson	32
	Howard Ehmke	32
	Randy Jones	32
33	Pete Alexander	31
	Russ Christopher	31
	Curt Davis	31
	John Denny	31
37	Tommy Bond	30
	Addie Joss	30
	Hal Schumacher	30
40	Chick Fraser	29
	Gerry Staley	29
	Dave Stieb	29
	Fernando Valenzuela	29
44	Mike Boddicker	28
	Ben Cantwell	28
	Sid Hudson	28
	Matt Kilroy	28
	George Mullin	28
	Phil Niekro	28
	Ed Willett	28
51	Ted Abernathy	27
	Tom Burgmeier	27
	Spud Chandler	27
	Amos Rusie	27
	Frank Smith	27
	Bucky Walters	27
	Vic Willis	27
58	Nixey Callahan	26
	Whitey Ford	26
	Sherry Smith	26
61	Don Drysdale	25
	Larry Jackson	25
	Charlie Leibrandt	25
	Dan Quisenberry	25
65	Mike Caldwell	24
	Frank Corridon	24
	Ned Garvin	24
	Guy Hecker	24
	Orel Hershiser	24
	Dutch Leonard	24
	John Ward	24
	Doc White	24
73	Jean Dubuc	23
	Lindy McDaniel	23
	Cy Seymour	23
76	Tom Brewer	22
	Bill Hart	22
	Joe Horlen	22
	Carl Hubbell	22
	Jim McCormick	22
	Stu Miller	22
	Hal Newhouser	22
	Dan Petry	22
	Ed Reulbach	22
	Bob Stanley	22
	Kent Tekulve	22
87	Eldon Auker	21
	Joe Bush	21
	Benny Frey	21
	Sadie McMahon	21
	Frank Owen	21
	Gaylord Perry	21
	Bob Purkey	21
	Jack Taylor	21
	Lefty Tyler	21
96	12 players tied	20

Pitcher Batting Average

1	Jack Stivetts	.297
2	George Uhle	.289
3	Charlie Ferguson	.288
4	Win Mercer	.286
5	Doc Crandall	.285
6	Guy Hecker	.283
7	Bob Caruthers	.282
8	Red Lucas	.281
9	Wes Ferrell	.280
10	Dave Foutz	.276
11	Jack Scott	.275
	John Ward	.275
13	Scott Stratton	.274
14	Nixey Callahan	.273
	Ad Gumbert	.273
	Al Orth	.273
17	Don Newcombe	.271
18	Sloppy Thurston	.270
19	Red Ruffing	.269
20	Carl Mays	.268
21	Schoolboy Rowe	.263
22	George Mullin	.262
23	Kid Gleason	.261
	Brickyard Kennedy	.261
	Jim Whitney	.261
26	Dutch Ruether	.258
	Joe Shaute	.258
28	Lee Richmond	.257
29	Jesse Tannehill	.256
30	Joe Bush	.253
31	Clarence Mitchell	.252
	Jack Taylor	.252
33	Adonis Terry	.249
34	Ray Caldwell	.248
	Burleigh Grimes	.248
36	Amos Rusie	.247
37	Pete Donohue	.246
38	Charlie Buffinton	.245
	Johnny Sain	.245
40	Vern Kennedy	.244
41	Jouett Meekin	.243
	Tony Mullane	.243
	Elam Vangilder	.243
	Bucky Walters	.243
45	Don Larsen	.242
	Bob Smith	.242
47	Duke Esper	.241
	Pink Hawley	.241
	Claude Hendrix	.241
	Frank Killen	.241
51	Frank Kitson	.240
52	Wilbur Cooper	.239
53	Ed Crane	.238
	Rick Rhoden	.238
55	Tommy Bond	.236
	Ed Brandt	.236
	Jim McCormick	.236
58	Jack Coombs	.235
	Walter Johnson	.235
	Terry Larkin	.235
	Charley Radbourn	.235
62	Fritz Ostermueller	.234
63	Nig Cuppy	.233
	Clark Griffith	.233
	Ted Lyons	.233
	Sherry Smith	.233
67	Bob Lemon	.232
68	Ben Cantwell	.231
	Murry Dickson	.231
	Don Robinson	.231
71	Frank Dwyer	.230
	George Earnshaw	.230
	Jim Tobin	.230
74	Vic Aldridge	.229
75	George Bradley	.228
	Nels Potter	.228
77	George Haddock	.227
	Dolf Luque	.227
	Bill Swift	.227
80	Jim Bagby	.226
	Catfish Hunter	.226
	Kid Nichols	.226
	Ed Stein	.226
	Tom Zachary	.226
85	Dizzy Dean	.225
86	Frank Foreman	.224
	Fred Goldsmith	.224
	Mickey Welch	.224
89	Hal Carlson	.223
	Larry Corcoran	.223
	George Hemming	.223
	Bill Sherdel	.223
	Jack Taylor	.223
	Lon Warneke	.223
95	Matt Kilroy	.222
	Gary Peters	.222
97	Van Mungo	.221
98	Sid Hudson	.220
99	3 players tied	.219

Total Pitcher Index

#	Name	
1	Walter Johnson	90.5
2	Cy Young	79.9
3	Pete Alexander	64.9
4	Christy Mathewson	62.7
5	Lefty Grove	61.2
6	Kid Nichols	60.9
7	John Clarkson	48.7
8	Tom Seaver	48.2
9	Warren Spahn	47.0
10	Bob Gibson	44.0
11	Ed Walsh	43.3
12	Hal Newhouser	40.8
13	Hoyt Wilhelm	40.0
14	Carl Hubbell	39.2
15	Amos Rusie	38.9
16	Bob Lemon	37.4
17	Whitey Ford	37.2
	Tim Keefe	37.2
19	Roger Clemens	36.9
20	Ted Lyons	36.7
21	Carl Mays	36.1
22	Jim Palmer	35.5
23	Phil Niekro	35.4
24	Mordecai Brown	34.8
25	Dizzy Trout	34.5
26	Gaylord Perry	34.4
27	Don Drysdale	34.0
28	Steve Carlton	33.2
29	Tony Mullane	32.6
30	Wes Ferrell	32.3
31	Bert Blyleven	30.9
	Fergie Jenkins	30.9
33	Rich Gossage	30.2
34	Clark Griffith	29.7
35	Bob Caruthers	29.4
36	Juan Marichal	28.9
37	Dennis Eckersley	28.8
38	Tommy Bridges	28.7
	Charley Radbourn	28.7
40	Bucky Walters	28.6
41	Bob Feller	28.5
42	Jack Stivetts	28.2
43	Stan Coveleski	27.5
44	Dave Stieb	27.2
45	Red Faber	27.0
	Dazzy Vance	27.0
47	Eddie Plank	26.9
	Red Ruffing	26.9
49	Greg Maddux	26.5
50	Dolf Luque	26.3
51	Eddie Rommel	26.0
52	Eppa Rixey	25.9
53	Dutch Leonard	25.8
	Urban Shocker	25.8
55	Dan Quisenberry	25.7
56	Rick Reuschel	25.5
57	Harry Brecheen	25.4
	Addie Joss	25.4
59	Eddie Cicotte	25.2
60	Tommy John	25.0
61	Robin Roberts	24.9
62	Lee Smith	24.7
63	Rube Waddell	24.6
64	Kent Tekulve	24.3
	Joe Wood	24.3
66	Burleigh Grimes	24.0
67	Guy Hecker	23.9
68	John Franco	23.7
69	Jack Quinn	23.6
70	Billy Pierce	23.3
71	Silver King	23.2
72	Freddie Fitzsimmons	23.1
	Bret Saberhagen	23.1
74	Lon Warneke	22.7
75	Nig Cuppy	22.5
76	Dizzy Dean	22.2
77	Curt Davis	22.1
78	Vic Willis	22.0
79	Rollie Fingers	21.8
80	Orel Hershiser	21.5
	Jesse Tannehill	21.5
82	Tom Henke	21.3
83	Jim McCormick	21.2
84	Bobby Shantz	21.1
85	Mike Marshall	21.0
86	Nolan Ryan	20.8
	Bruce Sutter	20.8
88	Spud Chandler	20.6
	John Hiller	20.6
90	Charlie Buffinton	20.3
91	Mel Harder	20.0
92	Sparky Lyle	19.9
93	Wilbur Cooper	19.7
	Murry Dickson	19.7
95	Dave Foutz	19.6
96	Joe McGinnity	19.5
97	Jimmy Key	19.4
98	Doc White	19.1
99	Jim Kaat	19.0
100	Don Newcombe	18.9

Total Pitcher Index

#	Name	
101	Larry Jackson	18.8
102	Wilbur Wood	18.6
103	Sandy Koufax	18.5
	Red Lucas	18.5
105	Ron Guidry	18.3
106	Ed Lopat	18.1
	Mel Parnell	18.1
108	Lefty Gomez	17.9
	Hippo Vaughn	17.9
110	Ed Reulbach	17.7
	Jose Rijo	17.7
112	Bob Stanley	17.6
113	Ned Garver	17.4
	Schoolboy Rowe	17.4
115	Mel Stottlemyre	17.3
	Luis Tiant	17.3
117	Larry French	17.2
118	Andy Messersmith	17.1
	Babe Ruth	17.1
120	Dwight Gooden	17.0
	Stu Miller	17.0
	Jeff Montgomery	17.0
123	Noodles Hahn	16.9
	Thornton Lee	16.9
125	Gene Garber	16.7
	Jack Taylor	16.7
127	Early Wynn	16.6
128	Claude Passeau	16.5
129	Harry Howell	16.4
130	Doug Jones	16.3
	Max Lanier	16.3
	Dave Righetti	16.3
	Hal Schumacher	16.3
134	Jesse Orosco	16.1
135	Virgil Trucks	15.9
136	Sadie McMahon	15.8
137	Johnny Antonelli	15.7
	Ron Perranoski	15.7
	Deacon Phillippe	15.7
140	Ellis Kinder	15.4
141	Steve Rogers	15.3
142	John Tudor	15.2
143	Frank Viola	15.1
144	Babe Adams	15.0
	John Candelaria	15.0
	Charlie Hough	15.0
	Gary Lavelle	15.0
	Sam Leever	15.0
149	Frank Dwyer	14.8
	Lindy McDaniel	14.8
	Bob Shawkey	14.8
	Mickey Welch	14.8
153	Jim Whitney	14.7
154	Frank Linzy	14.6
155	Mark Eichhorn	14.5
	Mike Garcia	14.5
	Tug McGraw	14.5
	George Mullin	14.5
159	Claude Hendrix	14.4
	Waite Hoyt	14.4
161	David Cone	14.3
162	Bryan Harvey	14.2
163	Fred Hutchinson	14.1
	John Ward	14.1
165	Larry Corcoran	14.0
166	Frank Lary	13.9
167	Chief Bender	13.8
	Charlie Ferguson	13.8
	Nap Rucker	13.8
170	Bill Hutchison	13.7
	Sal Maglie	13.7
	Howie Pollet	13.7
173	Jim Bunning	13.6
	Don Sutton	13.6
175	Clay Carroll	13.5
	George Uhle	13.5
177	Tom Candiotti	13.4
	Mark Langston	13.4
179	Rick Aguilera	13.3
	Jim Maloney	13.3
	Frank Tanana	13.3
182	Jim Devlin	13.2
	Roy Face	13.2
	Claude Osteen	13.2
185	Doug Drabek	13.1
	Jerry Koosman	13.1
	Firpo Marberry	13.1
188	Steve Farr	13.0
	Jim Tobin	13.0
190	Mort Cooper	12.9
	Jim Galvin	12.9
	Frank Killen	12.9
193	Tom Burgmeier	12.8
	Van Mungo	12.8
	Gregg Olson	12.8
196	Curt Simmons	12.6
197	Willie Hernandez	12.5
198	Greg Minton	12.4
	Milt Pappas	12.4
200	Danny Darwin	12.3

Total Pitcher Index

#	Name	
	Dennis Martinez	12.3
	Sherry Smith	12.3
203	Will White	12.2
204	Mike Henneman	12.1
	Jon Matlack	12.1
206	Dave Smith	12.0
207	Ewell Blackwell	11.9
208	Kevin Appier	11.8
	Jake Weimer	11.8
210	Ted Breitenstein	11.7
211	Harvey Haddix	11.6
	Orval Overall	11.6
	Jeff Reardon	11.6
214	Chuck Finley	11.5
	Terry Forster	11.5
	Lefty Leifield	11.5
217	Johnny Sain	11.4
218	Al Brazle	11.3
219	Bob Rush	11.2
220	Jack Chesbro	11.1
	Gary Peters	11.1
222	Jim Kern	11.0
223	Russ Ford	10.9
	Jay Howell	10.9
	Camilo Pascual	10.9
226	Nixey Callahan	10.8
	Dean Chance	10.8
	Dick Radatz	10.8
	Fernando Valenzuela	10.8
230	Mike Boddicker	10.6
231	Charlie Root	10.5
	Sonny Siebert	10.5
	Al Worthington	10.5
234	Steve Howe	10.4
	Tex Hughson	10.4
	Matt Kilroy	10.4
	Charlie Leibrandt	10.4
238	Tim Burke	10.3
	Jeff Russell	10.3
	Ben Sanders	10.3
	Tom Zachary	10.3
242	Vida Blue	10.2
	Jim Brewer	10.2
	Don McMahon	10.2
	Johnny Murphy	10.2
246	Bob Ewing	10.1
	Jeff Pfeffer	10.1
	Rip Sewell	10.1
	Frank Sullivan	10.1
	Hooks Wiltse	10.1
251	Elton Chamberlain	10.0
	Joe Dobson	10.0
	Sam McDowell	10.0
	Fritz Ostermueller	10.0
	Todd Worrell	10.0
256	Hooks Dauss	9.9
	Bob Locker	9.9
	Win Mercer	9.9
259	Clint Brown	9.8
260	Art Nehf	9.7
	Jim Perry	9.7
	Duane Ward	9.7
263	Mickey McDermott	9.6
	Al Orth	9.6
265	Ned Garvin	9.5
	Monte Pearson	9.5
	Bobby Thigpen	9.5
268	Tippy Martinez	9.4
	Slim Sallee	9.4
	Gerry Staley	9.4
271	Mark Baldwin	9.3
	Teddy Higuera	9.3
	Jack McDowell	9.3
	Roger McDowell	9.3
	Jim Scott	9.3
276	Tom Glavine	9.2
	Larry Jansen	9.2
	Ed Morris	9.2
279	Howard Ehmke	9.1
280	Pink Hawley	9.0
	Bob Welch	9.0
282	Johnny Allen	8.9
	Al Benton	8.9
	Darold Knowles	8.9
	Randy Myers	8.9
	Dan Plesac	8.9
287	Steve Bedrosian	8.8
	Harry Coveleski	8.8
	Ray Kremer	8.8
	Johnny Rigney	8.8
291	Ted Abernathy	8.7
	Red Ames	8.7
	Larry Andersen	8.7
	Bill Hands	8.7
	Greg Harris	8.7
	Al McBean	8.7
	Jeff Tesreau	8.7
	John Wetteland	8.7
299	Watty Clark	8.6
300	2 players tied	8.5

Total Pitcher Index (alpha.)

Name	
Ted Abernathy	8.7
Babe Adams	15.0
Rick Aguilera	13.3
Pete Alexander	64.9
Johnny Allen	8.9
Red Ames	8.7
Larry Andersen	8.7
Johnny Antonelli	15.7
Kevin Appier	11.8
Mark Baldwin	9.3
Steve Bedrosian	8.8
Chief Bender	13.8
Al Benton	8.9
Ewell Blackwell	11.9
Vida Blue	10.2
Bert Blyleven	30.9
Mike Boddicker	10.6
Al Brazle	11.3
Harry Brecheen	25.4
Ted Breitenstein	11.7
Jim Brewer	10.2
Tommy Bridges	28.7
Clint Brown	9.8
Mordecai Brown	34.8
Charlie Buffinton	20.3
Jim Bunning	13.6
Tom Burgmeier	12.8
Tim Burke	10.3
Nixey Callahan	10.8
John Candelaria	15.0
Tom Candiotti	13.4
Steve Carlton	33.2
Clay Carroll	13.5
Bob Caruthers	29.4
Elton Chamberlain	10.0
Dean Chance	10.8
Spud Chandler	20.6
Jack Chesbro	11.1
Eddie Cicotte	25.2
Watty Clark	8.6
John Clarkson	48.7
Roger Clemens	36.9
David Cone	14.3
Wilbur Cooper	19.7
Mort Cooper	12.9
Larry Corcoran	14.0
Harry Coveleski	8.8
Stan Coveleski	27.5
Nig Cuppy	22.5
Danny Darwin	12.3
Hooks Dauss	9.9
Curt Davis	22.1
Dizzy Dean	22.2
Jim Devlin	13.2
Murry Dickson	19.7
Joe Dobson	10.0
Doug Drabek	13.1
Don Drysdale	34.0
Frank Dwyer	14.8
Dennis Eckersley	28.8
Howard Ehmke	9.1
Mark Eichhorn	14.5
Bob Ewing	10.1
Red Faber	27.0
Roy Face	13.2
Steve Farr	13.0
Bob Feller	28.5
Charlie Ferguson	13.8
Wes Ferrell	32.3
Rollie Fingers	21.8
Chuck Finley	11.5
Freddie Fitzsimmons	23.1
Whitey Ford	37.2
Russ Ford	10.9
Terry Forster	11.5
Dave Foutz	19.6
John Franco	23.7
Larry French	17.2
Jim Galvin	12.9
Gene Garber	16.7
Mike Garcia	14.5
Ned Garver	17.4
Ned Garvin	9.5
Bob Gibson	44.0
Tom Glavine	9.2
Lefty Gomez	17.9
Dwight Gooden	17.0
Rich Gossage	30.2
Clark Griffith	29.7
Burleigh Grimes	24.0
Lefty Grove	61.2
Ron Guidry	18.3
Harvey Haddix	11.6
Noodles Hahn	16.9
Bill Hands	8.7
Mel Harder	20.0
Greg Harris	8.7
Bryan Harvey	14.2
Pink Hawley	9.0
Guy Hecker	23.9

Total Pitcher Index (alpha.)

Claude Hendrix	14.4
Tom Henke	21.3
Mike Henneman	12.1
Willie Hernandez	12.5
Orel Hershiser	21.5
Teddy Higuera	9.3
John Hiller	20.6
Charlie Hough	15.0
Steve Howe	10.4
Harry Howell	16.4
Jay Howell	10.9
Waite Hoyt	14.4
Carl Hubbell	39.2
Tex Hughson	10.4
Fred Hutchinson	14.1
Bill Hutchison	13.7
Larry Jackson	18.8
Larry Jansen	9.2
Fergie Jenkins	30.9
Tommy John	25.0
Walter Johnson	90.5
Doug Jones	16.3
Addie Joss	25.4
Jim Kaat	19.0
Tim Keefe	37.2
Jim Kern	11.0
Jimmy Key	19.4
Frank Killen	12.9
Matt Kilroy	10.4
Ellis Kinder	15.4
Silver King	23.2
Darold Knowles	8.9
Jerry Koosman	13.1
Sandy Koufax	18.5
Ray Kremer	8.8
Mark Langston	13.4
Max Lanier	16.3
Frank Lary	13.9
Gary Lavelle	15.0
Thornton Lee	16.9
Sam Leever	15.0
Charlie Leibrandt	10.4
Lefty Leifield	11.5
Bob Lemon	37.4
Dutch Leonard	25.8
Frank Linzy	14.6
Bob Locker	9.9
Ed Lopat	18.1
Red Lucas	18.5
Dolf Luque	26.3
Sparky Lyle	19.9
Ted Lyons	36.7
Greg Maddux	26.5
Sal Maglie	13.7
Jim Maloney	13.3
Firpo Marberry	13.1
Juan Marichal	28.9
Mike Marshall	21.0
Tippy Martinez	9.4
Dennis Martinez	12.3
Christy Mathewson	62.7
Jon Matlack	12.1
Carl Mays	36.1
Al McBean	8.7
Jim McCormick	21.2
Lindy McDaniel	14.8
Mickey McDermott	9.6
Jack McDowell	9.3
Roger McDowell	9.3
Sam McDowell	10.0
Joe McGinnity	19.5
Tug McGraw	14.5
Don McMahon	10.2
Sadie McMahon	15.8
Win Mercer	9.9
Andy Messersmith	17.1
Stu Miller	17.0
Greg Minton	12.4
Jeff Montgomery	17.0
Ed Morris	9.2
Tony Mullane	32.6
George Mullin	14.5
Van Mungo	12.8
Johnny Murphy	10.2
Randy Myers	8.9
Art Nehf	9.7
Don Newcombe	18.9
Hal Newhouser	40.8
Kid Nichols	60.9
Phil Niekro	35.4
Gregg Olson	12.8
Jesse Orosco	16.1
Al Orth	9.6
Claude Osteen	13.2
Fritz Ostermueller	10.0
Orval Overall	11.6
Jim Palmer	35.5
Milt Pappas	12.4
Mel Parnell	18.1
Camilo Pascual	10.9

Total Pitcher Index (alpha.)

Claude Passeau	16.5
Monte Pearson	9.5
Ron Perranoski	15.7
Gaylord Perry	34.4
Jim Perry	9.7
Gary Peters	11.1
Jeff Pfeffer	10.1
Deacon Phillippe	15.7
Billy Pierce	23.3
Eddie Plank	26.9
Dan Plesac	8.9
Howie Pollet	13.7
Jack Quinn	23.6
Dan Quisenberry	25.7
Dick Radatz	10.8
Charley Radbourn	28.7
Jeff Reardon	11.6
Ed Reulbach	17.7
Rick Reuschel	25.5
Dave Righetti	16.3
Johnny Rigney	8.8
Jose Rijo	17.7
Eppa Rixey	25.9
Robin Roberts	24.9
Steve Rogers	15.3
Eddie Rommel	26.0
Charlie Root	10.5
Schoolboy Rowe	17.4
Nap Rucker	13.8
Red Ruffing	26.9
Bob Rush	11.2
Amos Rusie	38.9
Jeff Russell	10.3
Babe Ruth	17.1
Nolan Ryan	20.8
Bret Saberhagen	23.1
Johnny Sain	11.4
Slim Sallee	9.4
Ben Sanders	10.3
Hal Schumacher	16.3
Jim Scott	9.3
Tom Seaver	48.2
Rip Sewell	10.1
Bobby Shantz	21.1
Bob Shawkey	14.8
Urban Shocker	25.8
Sonny Siebert	10.5
Curt Simmons	12.6
Dave Smith	12.0
Lee Smith	24.7
Sherry Smith	12.3
Warren Spahn	47.0
Gerry Staley	9.4
Bob Stanley	17.6
Dave Stieb	27.2
Jack Stivetts	28.2
Mel Stottlemyre	17.3
Frank Sullivan	10.1
Bruce Sutter	20.8
Don Sutton	13.6
Frank Tanana	13.3
Jesse Tannehill	21.5
Jack Taylor	16.7
Kent Tekulve	24.3
Jeff Tesreau	8.7
Bobby Thigpen	9.5
Luis Tiant	17.3
Jim Tobin	13.0
Dizzy Trout	34.5
Virgil Trucks	15.9
John Tudor	15.2
George Uhle	13.5
Fernando Valenzuela	10.8
Dazzy Vance	27.0
Hippo Vaughn	17.9
Frank Viola	15.1
Rube Waddell	24.6
Ed Walsh	43.3
Bucky Walters	28.6
John Ward	14.1
Duane Ward	9.7
Lon Warneke	22.7
Jake Weimer	11.8
Mickey Welch	14.8
Bob Welch	9.0
John Wetteland	8.7
Doc White	19.1
Will White	12.2
Jim Whitney	14.7
Hoyt Wilhelm	40.0
Vic Willis	22.0
Hooks Wiltse	10.1
Joe Wood	24.3
Wilbur Wood	18.6
Todd Worrell	10.0
Al Worthington	10.5
Early Wynn	16.6
Cy Young	79.9
Tom Zachary	10.3

Total Pitcher Index (by era)

1876-1892

1	John Clarkson	48.7
2	Tim Keefe	37.2
3	Tony Mullane	32.6
4	Bob Caruthers	29.4
5	Charley Radbourn	28.7
6	Jack Stivetts	28.2
7	Guy Hecker	23.9
8	Silver King	23.2
9	Jim McCormick	21.2
10	Charlie Buffinton	20.3
11	Dave Foutz	19.6
12	Sadie McMahon	15.8
13	Mickey Welch	14.8
14	Jim Whitney	14.7
15	John Ward	14.1
16	Larry Corcoran	14.0
17	Charlie Ferguson	13.8
18	Bill Hutchison	13.7
19	Jim Devlin	13.2
20	Jim Galvin	12.9
21	Will White	12.2
22	Matt Kilroy	10.4
23	Ben Sanders	10.3
24	Elton Chamberlain	10.0
25	Mark Baldwin	9.3

1893-1919

1	Walter Johnson	90.5
2	Cy Young	79.9
3	Pete Alexander	64.9
4	Christy Mathewson	62.7
5	Kid Nichols	60.9
6	Ed Walsh	43.3
7	Amos Rusie	38.9
8	Mordecai Brown	34.8
9	Clark Griffith	29.7
10	Eddie Plank	26.9
11	Addie Joss	25.4
12	Eddie Cicotte	25.2
13	Rube Waddell	24.6
14	Joe Wood	24.3
15	Nig Cuppy	22.5
16	Vic Willis	22.0
17	Jesse Tannehill	21.5
18	Joe McGinnity	19.5
19	Doc White	19.1
20	Hippo Vaughn	17.9
21	Ed Reulbach	17.7
22	Babe Ruth	17.1
23	Noodles Hahn	16.9
24	Jack Taylor	16.7
25	Harry Howell	16.4

1920-1941

1	Lefty Grove	61.2
2	Carl Hubbell	39.2
3	Ted Lyons	36.7
4	Carl Mays	36.1
5	Wes Ferrell	32.3
6	Tommy Bridges	28.7
7	Bucky Walters	28.6
8	Stan Coveleski	27.5
9	Red Faber	27.0
	Dazzy Vance	27.0
11	Red Ruffing	26.9
12	Dolf Luque	26.3
13	Eddie Rommel	26.0
14	Eppa Rixey	25.9
15	Urban Shocker	25.8
16	Burleigh Grimes	24.0
17	Jack Quinn	23.6
18	Freddie Fitzsimmons	23.1
19	Lon Warneke	22.7
20	Dizzy Dean	22.2
21	Curt Davis	22.1
22	Mel Harder	20.0
23	Wilbur Cooper	19.7
24	Red Lucas	18.5
25	Lefty Gomez	17.9

Total Pitcher Index (by era)

1942-1960

1	Warren Spahn	47.0
2	Hal Newhouser	40.8
3	Hoyt Wilhelm	40.0
4	Bob Lemon	37.4
5	Whitey Ford	37.2
6	Dizzy Trout	34.5
7	Bob Feller	28.5
8	Dutch Leonard	25.8
9	Harry Brecheen	25.4
10	Robin Roberts	24.9
11	Billy Pierce	23.3
12	Bobby Shantz	21.1
13	Spud Chandler	20.6
14	Murry Dickson	19.7
15	Don Newcombe	18.9
16	Ed Lopat	18.1
	Mel Parnell	18.1
18	Ned Garver	17.4
19	Stu Miller	17.0
20	Early Wynn	16.6
21	Max Lanier	16.3
22	Virgil Trucks	15.9
23	Johnny Antonelli	15.7
24	Ellis Kinder	15.4
25	Mike Garcia	14.5

1961-1976

1	Tom Seaver	48.2
2	Bob Gibson	44.0
3	Jim Palmer	35.5
4	Phil Niekro	35.4
5	Gaylord Perry	34.4
6	Don Drysdale	34.0
7	Steve Carlton	33.2
8	Fergie Jenkins	30.9
9	Juan Marichal	28.9
10	Tommy John	25.0
11	Rollie Fingers	21.8
12	Mike Marshall	21.0
13	John Hiller	20.6
14	Sparky Lyle	19.9
15	Jim Kaat	19.0
16	Larry Jackson	18.8
17	Wilbur Wood	18.6
18	Sandy Koufax	18.5
19	Mel Stottlemyre	17.3
	Luis Tiant	17.3
21	Andy Messersmith	17.1
22	Ron Perranoski	15.7
23	Lindy McDaniel	14.8
24	Frank Linzy	14.6
25	Tug McGraw	14.5

1977-1994

1	Roger Clemens	36.9
2	Bert Blyleven	30.9
3	Rich Gossage	30.2
4	Dennis Eckersley	28.8
5	Dave Stieb	27.2
6	Greg Maddux	26.5
7	Dan Quisenberry	25.7
8	Rick Reuschel	25.5
9	Lee Smith	24.7
10	Kent Tekulve	24.3
11	John Franco	23.7
12	Bret Saberhagen	23.1
13	Orel Hershiser	21.5
14	Tom Henke	21.3
15	Nolan Ryan	20.8
	Bruce Sutter	20.8
17	Jimmy Key	19.4
18	Ron Guidry	18.3
19	Jose Rijo	17.7
20	Bob Stanley	17.6
21	Dwight Gooden	17.0
	Jeff Montgomery	17.0
23	Gene Garber	16.7
24	Doug Jones	16.3
	Dave Righetti	16.3

Total Baseball Ranking

1	Babe Ruth	124.7
2	Nap Lajoie	94.3
3	Willie Mays	92.2
4	Ty Cobb	91.2
5	Walter Johnson	90.1
6	Hank Aaron	89.8
7	Tris Speaker	86.5
8	Ted Williams	85.7
9	Honus Wagner	81.3
10	Rogers Hornsby	81.1
11	Cy Young	79.9
12	Mike Schmidt	78.4
13	Mickey Mantle	76.1
14	Rickey Henderson	74.6
15	Stan Musial	70.5
16	Eddie Collins	69.7
17	Frank Robinson	69.0
18	Lou Gehrig	65.7
19	Pete Alexander	64.9
20	Christy Mathewson	62.7
	Mel Ott	62.7
22	Lefty Grove	61.2
23	Kid Nichols	60.9
24	Joe Morgan	56.3
25	Jimmie Foxx	54.3
26	Eddie Mathews	51.6
27	Bill Dahlen	51.4
28	Tim Raines	51.0
29	George Davis	50.0
30	Barry Bonds	49.4
31	John Clarkson	48.7
32	Tom Seaver	48.2
33	Warren Spahn	47.0
34	Joe DiMaggio	46.9
35	Carl Yastrzemski	45.5
36	Al Kaline	44.6
37	Wade Boggs	44.4
	Charlie Gehringer	44.4
39	Ed Delahanty	44.3
40	Bobby Grich	44.1
41	Bob Gibson	44.0
42	Ed Walsh	43.3
43	Robin Yount	43.1
44	Ozzie Smith	43.0
45	Roberto Clemente	42.9
46	Reggie Jackson	42.8
47	Roger Connor	42.7
48	Lou Boudreau	41.3
49	Hal Newhouser	40.8
50	Luke Appling	40.7
	Bobby Wallace	40.7
52	Dan Brouthers	40.6
53	Gabby Hartnett	40.1
	Bid McPhee	40.1
55	Hoyt Wilhelm	40.0
56	Dave Winfield	39.7
57	Ron Santo	39.5
58	Joe Cronin	39.4
59	Carl Hubbell	39.2
	Cal Ripken	39.2
	Arky Vaughan	39.2
62	Frankie Frisch	39.1
63	George Brett	39.0
	Bobby Doerr	39.0
65	Amos Rusie	38.9
66	Ryne Sandberg	38.8
67	Tony Gwynn	38.5
68	Joe Jackson	37.5
69	Whitey Ford	37.2
	Tim Keefe	37.2
71	Roger Clemens	36.9
	Bob Lemon	36.9
73	Ted Lyons	36.7
74	Willie McCovey	36.5
75	Bill Mazeroski	36.3
76	Yogi Berra	36.2
	Jack Glasscock	36.2
	Johnny Mize	36.2
79	Carl Mays	36.1
	Paul Waner	36.1
81	Bob Johnson	35.6
	Eddie Murray	35.6
83	Jim Palmer	35.5
84	Phil Niekro	35.4
	Bill Dickey	35.4
86	Dick Allen	35.3
	Dave Bancroft	35.3
88	Paul Molitor	35.2
89	Reggie Smith	35.0
90	Mordecai Brown	34.8
91	Darrell Evans	34.6
92	Dizzy Trout	34.5
93	Gaylord Perry	34.4
	Keith Hernandez	34.4
	Joe Sewell	34.4
96	Don Drysdale	34.0
97	Frank Baker	33.8
98	Steve Carlton	33.2
	Jim Wynn	33.2
100	Willie Stargell	32.8

Total Baseball Ranking

101	Wes Ferrell	32.4
	Harry Heilmann	32.4
103	Jackie Robinson	31.8
104	Billy Herman	31.7
105	Bob Caruthers	31.4
	Rod Carew	31.4
	Mickey Cochrane	31.4
108	Tony Mullane	31.1
	Jack Clark	31.1
	Andre Dawson	31.1
	Billy Williams	31.1
112	Bert Blyleven	30.9
	Fergie Jenkins	30.9
114	Dwight Evans	30.4
115	Rich Gossage	30.2
	Richie Ashburn	30.2
	Sam Crawford	30.2
118	Cupid Childs	30.0
	Hank Greenberg	30.0
120	Cap Anson	29.9
121	Bobby Bonds	29.6
	Gary Carter	29.6
123	Buck Ewing	29.5
124	Clark Griffith	29.0
125	Juan Marichal	28.9
	Ralph Kiner	28.9
127	Dennis Eckersley	28.8
	Jose Cruz	28.8
129	Tommy Bridges	28.7
	Elmer Flick	28.7
131	Fred Clarke	28.6
132	Bob Feller	28.5
133	Sam Thompson	28.4
134	Cesar Cedeno	28.3
135	Joe Gordon	28.2
136	Dick Bartell	27.9
137	Barry Larkin	27.6
	Rusty Staub	27.6
139	Stan Coveleski	27.5
	Norm Cash	27.5
141	Kirby Puckett	27.4
142	Dave Stieb	27.2
	Fred Dunlap	27.2
	Stan Hack	27.2
145	Joe Medwick	27.1
146	Red Faber	27.0
	Dazzy Vance	27.0
	Heinie Groh	27.0
	Jim Rice	27.0
	Hardy Richardson	27.0
151	Eddie Plank	26.9
	Pete Browning	26.9
	Darryl Strawberry	26.9
154	Red Ruffing	26.8
155	Sherry Magee	26.6
156	Greg Maddux	26.5
157	Bucky Walters	26.4
	Jesse Burkett	26.4
	Billy Hamilton	26.4
	Harmon Killebrew	26.4
161	Dolf Luque	26.3
	Jack Stivetts	26.3
163	Charley Radbourn	26.2
	Hughie Jennings	26.2
165	Goose Goslin	26.1
166	Eddie Rommel	26.0
	Minnie Minoso	26.0
168	Eppa Rixey	25.9
	Ernie Banks	25.9
	Art Fletcher	25.9
171	Dutch Leonard	25.8
	Urban Shocker	25.8
173	Dan Quisenberry	25.7
174	Rocky Colavito	25.6
	Al Simmons	25.6
176	Rick Reuschel	25.5
177	Harry Brecheen	25.4
	Addie Joss	25.4
179	Eddie Cicotte	25.2
180	Tommy John	25.0
181	Robin Roberts	24.9
	Bill Terry	24.9
183	Lenny Dykstra	24.8
	Tony Oliva	24.8
185	Lee Smith	24.7
186	Rube Waddell	24.6
187	Zack Wheat	24.5
	Lou Whitaker	24.5
189	King Kelly	24.4
190	Kent Tekulve	24.3
	Johnny Bench	24.3
192	Travis Jackson	24.2
193	Burleigh Grimes	24.0
	Carlton Fisk	24.0
	Jack Fournier	24.0
	George Sisler	24.0
	Alan Trammell	24.0
198	John Franco	23.7
199	Jack Quinn	23.6
200	Charlie Keller	23.5

Total Baseball Ranking

201	Jimmy Collins	23.4
202	Billy Pierce	23.3
203	Silver King	23.2
204	Freddie Fitzsimmons	23.1
	Bret Saberhagen	23.1
	Willie Randolph	23.1
207	Max Carey	23.0
	Dave Parker	23.0
	Joe Tinker	23.0
210	Joe Wood	22.9
	Buddy Bell	22.9
212	Roy Thomas	22.8
213	Lon Warneke	22.7
	Jake Beckley	22.7
	Harlond Clift	22.7
216	Nig Cuppy	22.5
	Jose Canseco	22.5
218	George Foster	22.3
	Ed Konetchy	22.3
	Chet Lemon	22.3
	Fred Lynn	22.3
	Duke Snider	22.3
223	Dizzy Dean	22.2
	Wally Berger	22.2
225	Curt Davis	22.1
	Brett Butler	22.1
227	Vic Willis	22.0
228	Ron Cey	21.9
	Fred Pfeffer	21.9
	John Ward	21.9
231	Rollie Fingers	21.8
232	Roy Campanella	21.6
233	Orel Hershiser	21.5
	Chuck Klein	21.5
235	Graig Nettles	21.4
236	Guy Hecker	21.3
	Tom Henke	21.3
	Frank Howard	21.3
	Harry Stovey	21.3
	Roy White	21.3
241	Jim McCormick	21.2
	Larry Doby	21.2
243	Bobby Shantz	21.1
244	Mike Marshall	21.0
	Andy Van Slyke	21.0
246	Ken Griffey	20.9
	Kevin Mitchell	20.9
	Ken Singleton	20.9
	Fred Tenney	20.9
250	Nolan Ryan	20.8
	Bruce Sutter	20.8
	Will Clark	20.8
	Pie Traynor	20.8
254	Charley Jones	20.7
255	Spud Chandler	20.6
	John Hiller	20.6
	Frank Chance	20.6
	Art Devlin	20.6
	Jim Fregosi	20.6
260	Mike Griffin	20.5
	Frank Thomas	20.5
262	Jesse Tannehill	20.4
	Del Pratt	20.4
264	Glenn Hubbard	20.2
	Joe Kelley	20.2
266	Mel Harder	20.0
	Pete Rose	20.0
268	Sparky Lyle	19.9
269	Roger Bresnahan	19.8
	Denny Lyons	19.8
	Brooks Robinson	19.8
272	Wilbur Cooper	19.7
	Murry Dickson	19.7
274	Eric Davis	19.6
	Vern Stephens	19.6
	Joe Torre	19.6
277	Joe McGinnity	19.5
278	Jimmy Key	19.4
279	Dale Murphy	19.3
	Amos Otis	19.3
	Jimmy Sheckard	19.3
282	Charlie Bennett	19.2
283	Jim Kaat	19.0
	Bill Joyce	19.0
	Fred McGriff	19.0
	Bill Nicholson	19.0
287	Don Newcombe	18.9
	Gavvy Cravath	18.9
	Bob Elliott	18.9
290	Larry Jackson	18.8
291	Wilbur Wood	18.6
	Ken Boyer	18.6
	Brian Downing	18.6
294	Sandy Koufax	18.5
295	Eddie Stanky	18.4
296	Ron Guidry	18.3
	Wally Schang	18.3
298	Miller Huggins	18.2
299	Ed Lopat	18.1
	Mel Parnell	18.1

Total Baseball Ranking

	Roy Cullenbine	18.1
302	Gene Alley	18.0
303	Lefty Gomez	17.9
	Hippo Vaughn	17.9
	Rico Carty	17.9
306	Red Lucas	17.8
	Ferris Fain	17.8
308	Ed Reulbach	17.7
	Jose Rijo	17.7
	Doc White	17.7
311	Bob Stanley	17.6
	Earl Averill	17.6
313	Ned Garver	17.4
	Schoolboy Rowe	17.4
	Tommy Leach	17.4
316	Mel Stottlemyre	17.3
	Luis Tiant	17.3
	Babe Herman	17.3
	Johnny Logan	17.3
	Ernie Lombardi	17.3
321	Larry French	17.2
	Paul Hines	17.2
	Ken Williams	17.2
324	Andy Messersmith	17.1
	Tony Fernandez	17.1
326	Dwight Gooden	17.0
	Stu Miller	17.0
	Jeff Montgomery	17.0
329	Noodles Hahn	16.9
	Thornton Lee	16.9
	Tony Lazzeri	16.9
332	Gil McDougald	16.8
	Ted Simmons	16.8
334	Gene Garber	16.7
	Jack Taylor	16.7
	Orlando Cepeda	16.7
	Pedro Guerrero	16.7
338	Early Wynn	16.6
339	Claude Passeau	16.5
340	Jesse Barfield	16.4
	Jeff Heath	16.4
	Dwayne Murphy	16.4
343	Doug Jones	16.3
	Max Lanier	16.3
	Dave Righetti	16.3
	Hal Schumacher	16.3
	Enos Slaughter	16.3
	Danny Tartabull	16.3
349	Cy Seymour	16.2
	Kirk Gibson	16.2
	George Gore	16.2
	Cy Seymour	16.2
353	Jesse Orosco	16.1
	John McGraw	16.1
	Jim O'Rourke	16.1
	Jimmy Williams	16.1
357	Virgil Trucks	15.9
358	Sadie McMahon	15.8
	Kiki Cuyler	15.8
	Phil Rizzuto	15.8
	Chief Zimmer	15.8
362	Johnny Antonelli	15.7
	Ron Perranoski	15.7
	Deacon Phillippe	15.7
	Mike Hargrove	15.7
	Robby Thompson	15.7
367	Davey Johnson	15.6
	Jocko Milligan	15.6
	Hack Wilson	15.6
370	Ray Chapman	15.5
371	Ellis Kinder	15.4
	Bobby Bonilla	15.4
	Elmer Smith	15.4
374	Steve Rogers	15.3
	Jeff Bagwell	15.3
	Thurman Munson	15.3
	Gene Tenace	15.3
378	John Tudor	15.2
379	Frank Viola	15.1
	Sid Gordon	15.1
381	Babe Adams	15.0
	John Candelaria	15.0
	Charlie Hough	15.0
	Gary Lavelle	15.0
	Sam Leever	15.0
	Mark Belanger	15.0
	Bobby Knoop	15.0
388	Charlie Buffinton	14.9
	Henry Larkin	14.9
	Boog Powell	14.9
391	Frank Dwyer	14.8
	Lindy McDaniel	14.8
	Bob Shawkey	14.8
	Mickey Welch	14.8
	Benny Kauff	14.8
	Mike Scioscia	14.8
	Bobby Veach	14.8
398	Sixto Lezcano	14.7
399	Frank Linzy	14.6
	Augie Galan	14.6

Total Baseball Ranking

	Greg Luzinski	14.6
	Pee Wee Reese	14.6
403	Mark Eichhorn	14.5
	Mike Garcia	14.5
	Tug McGraw	14.5
	Lave Cross	14.5
	Duke Farrell	14.5
	Tommy Henrich	14.5
409	Claude Hendrix	14.4
	Waite Hoyt	14.4
	Kevin McReynolds	14.4
412	David Cone	14.3
	Bob Allison	14.3
414	Bryan Harvey	14.2
	Ron Hansen	14.2
416	Johnny Callison	14.1
417	Fred Hutchinson	14.0
	George Mullin	14.0
419	Harry Howell	13.9
	Frank Lary	13.9
	Rafael Palmeiro	13.9
	Jimmy Ryan	13.9
423	Chief Bender	13.8
	Charlie Ferguson	13.8
	Nap Rucker	13.8
	Harold Baines	13.8
427	Bill Hutchison	13.7
	Sal Maglie	13.7
	Howie Pollet	13.7
	Gil Hodges	13.7
	Roy Smalley	13.7
432	Jim Bunning	13.6
	Don Sutton	13.6
	Ben Chapman	13.6
	Willie Kamm	13.6
436	Clay Carroll	13.5
	George Uhle	13.5
	Fred Carroll	13.5
	Tommy Holmes	13.5
	Kip Selbach	13.5
	George Van Haltren	13.5
	Richie Zisk	13.5
443	Tom Candiotti	13.4
	Mark Langston	13.4
	Chief Meyers	13.4
	Al Oliver	13.4
447	Rick Aguilera	13.3
	Jim Maloney	13.3
	Frank Tanana	13.3
	Roger Peckinpaugh	13.3
	George Stone	13.3
452	Jim Devlin	13.2
	Roy Face	13.2
	Claude Osteen	13.2
	Bill Freehan	13.2
	Dave Orr	13.2
457	Doug Drabek	13.1
	Jerry Koosman	13.1
	Firpo Marberry	13.1
	Doug DeCinces	13.1
	Johnny Evers	13.1
	Rabbit Maranville	13.1
	Edd Roush	13.1
464	Steve Farr	13.0
	Jim Tobin	13.0
	Bobby Murcer	13.0
	Red Smith	13.0
	John Titus	13.0
	Larry Walker	13.0
470	Mort Cooper	12.9
	Jim Galvin	12.9
	Frank Killen	12.9
	Jim Whitney	12.9
	Don Mattingly	12.9
	Terry Pendleton	12.9
476	Tom Burgmeier	12.8
	Van Mungo	12.8
	Gregg Olson	12.8
	Kal Daniels	12.8
480	Dave Foutz	12.7
	Lou Brock	12.7
	Dolph Camilli	12.7
	Jack Clements	12.7
	Kid Elberfeld	12.7
	Harry Hooper	12.7
	Billy Nash	12.7
	Roy Sievers	12.7
488	Curt Simmons	12.6
	Clete Boyer	12.6
	Deacon McGuire	12.6
	Riggs Stephenson	12.6
492	Willie Hernandez	12.5
	Chick Hafey	12.5
	Matt Williams	12.5
495	7 players tied	12.4

Total Baseball Rank (alpha.)

Hank Aaron	89.8
Babe Adams	15.0
Rick Aguilera	13.3
Pete Alexander	64.9
Dick Allen	35.3
Gene Alley	18.0
Bob Allison	14.3
Cap Anson	29.9
Johnny Antonelli	15.7
Luke Appling	40.7
Richie Ashburn	30.2
Earl Averill	17.6
Jeff Bagwell	15.3
Harold Baines	13.8
Frank Baker	33.8
Dave Bancroft	35.3
Ernie Banks	25.9
Jesse Barfield	16.4
Dick Bartell	27.9
Jake Beckley	22.7
Mark Belanger	15.0
Buddy Bell	22.9
Johnny Bench	24.3
Chief Bender	13.8
Charlie Bennett	19.2
Wally Berger	22.2
Yogi Berra	36.2
Bert Blyleven	30.9
Wade Boggs	44.4
Barry Bonds	49.4
Bobby Bonds	29.6
Bobby Bonilla	15.4
Lou Boudreau	41.3
Clete Boyer	12.6
Ken Boyer	18.6
Harry Brecheen	25.4
Roger Bresnahan	19.8
George Brett	39.0
Tommy Bridges	28.7
Lou Brock	12.7
Dan Brouthers	40.6
Mordecai Brown	34.8
Pete Browning	26.9
Charlie Buffinton	14.9
Jim Bunning	13.6
Tom Burgmeier	12.8
Jesse Burkett	26.4
Brett Butler	22.1
Johnny Callison	14.1
Dolph Camilli	12.7
Roy Campanella	21.6
John Candelaria	15.0
Tom Candiotti	13.4
Jose Canseco	22.5
Rod Carew	31.4
Max Carey	23.0
Steve Carlton	33.2
Clay Carroll	13.5
Fred Carroll	13.5
Gary Carter	29.6
Rico Carty	17.9
Bob Caruthers	31.4
Norm Cash	27.5
Cesar Cedeno	28.3
Orlando Cepeda	16.7
Ron Cey	21.9
Frank Chance	20.6
Spud Chandler	20.6
Ray Chapman	15.5
Ben Chapman	13.6
Cupid Childs	30.0
Eddie Cicotte	25.2
Jack Clark	31.1
Will Clark	20.8
Fred Clarke	28.6
John Clarkson	48.7
Roger Clemens	36.9
Roberto Clemente	42.9
Jack Clements	12.7
Harlond Clift	22.7
Ty Cobb	91.2
Mickey Cochrane	31.4
Rocky Colavito	25.6
Eddie Collins	69.7
Jimmy Collins	23.4
David Cone	14.3
Roger Connor	42.7
Wilbur Cooper	19.7
Mort Cooper	12.9
Stan Coveleski	27.5
Gavvy Cravath	18.9
Sam Crawford	30.2
Joe Cronin	39.4
Lave Cross	14.5
Jose Cruz	28.8
Roy Cullenbine	18.1
Nig Cuppy	22.5
Kiki Cuyler	15.8
Bill Dahlen	51.4
Kal Daniels	12.8

Total Baseball Rank (alpha.)

Curt Davis	22.1
Eric Davis	19.6
George Davis	50.0
Andre Dawson	31.1
Dizzy Dean	22.2
Doug DeCinces	13.1
Ed Delahanty	44.3
Jim Devlin	13.2
Art Devlin	20.6
Bill Dickey	35.4
Murry Dickson	19.7
Joe DiMaggio	46.9
Larry Doby	21.2
Bobby Doerr	39.0
Brian Downing	18.6
Doug Drabek	13.1
Don Drysdale	34.0
Fred Dunlap	27.2
Frank Dwyer	14.8
Lenny Dykstra	24.8
Dennis Eckersley	28.8
Mark Eichhorn	14.5
Kid Elberfeld	12.7
Bob Elliott	18.9
Darrell Evans	34.6
Dwight Evans	30.4
Johnny Evers	13.1
Buck Ewing	29.5
Red Faber	27.0
Roy Face	13.2
Ferris Fain	17.8
Steve Farr	13.0
Duke Farrell	14.5
Bob Feller	28.5
Charlie Ferguson	13.8
Tony Fernandez	17.1
Wes Ferrell	32.4
Rollie Fingers	21.8
Carlton Fisk	24.0
Freddie Fitzsimmons	23.1
Art Fletcher	25.9
Elmer Flick	28.7
Whitey Ford	37.2
George Foster	22.3
Jack Fournier	24.0
Dave Foutz	12.7
Jimmie Foxx	54.3
John Franco	23.7
Bill Freehan	13.2
Jim Fregosi	20.6
Larry French	17.2
Frankie Frisch	39.1
Augie Galan	14.6
Jim Galvin	12.9
Gene Garber	16.7
Mike Garcia	14.5
Ned Garver	17.4
Lou Gehrig	65.7
Charlie Gehringer	44.4
Bob Gibson	44.0
Kirk Gibson	16.2
Jack Glasscock	36.2
Lefty Gomez	17.9
Dwight Gooden	17.0
Joe Gordon	28.2
Sid Gordon	15.1
George Gore	16.2
Goose Goslin	26.1
Rich Gossage	30.2
Hank Greenberg	30.0
Bobby Grich	44.1
Ken Griffey	20.9
Mike Griffin	20.5
Clark Griffith	29.0
Burleigh Grimes	24.0
Heinie Groh	27.0
Lefty Grove	61.2
Pedro Guerrero	16.7
Ron Guidry	18.3
Tony Gwynn	38.5
Stan Hack	27.2
Chick Hafey	12.5
Noodles Hahn	16.9
Billy Hamilton	26.4
Ron Hansen	14.2
Mel Harder	20.0
Mike Hargrove	15.7
Gabby Hartnett	40.1
Bryan Harvey	14.2
Jeff Heath	16.4
Guy Hecker	21.3
Harry Heilmann	32.4
Rickey Henderson	74.6
Claude Hendrix	14.4
Tom Henke	21.3
Tommy Henrich	14.5
Babe Herman	17.3
Billy Herman	31.7
Willie Hernandez	12.5
Keith Hernandez	34.4

Total Baseball Rank (alpha.)

Orel Hershiser	21.5
John Hiller	20.6
Paul Hines	17.2
Gil Hodges	13.7
Tommy Holmes	13.5
Harry Hooper	12.7
Rogers Hornsby	81.1
Charlie Hough	15.0
Frank Howard	21.3
Harry Howell	13.9
Waite Hoyt	14.4
Glenn Hubbard	20.2
Carl Hubbell	39.2
Miller Huggins	18.2
Fred Hutchinson	14.0
Bill Hutchison	13.7
Larry Jackson	18.8
Joe Jackson	37.5
Reggie Jackson	42.8
Travis Jackson	24.2
Fergie Jenkins	30.9
Hughie Jennings	26.2
Tommy John	25.0
Walter Johnson	90.1
Davey Johnson	15.6
Bob Johnson	35.6
Doug Jones	16.3
Charley Jones	20.7
Addie Joss	25.4
Bill Joyce	19.0
Jim Kaat	19.0
Al Kaline	44.6
Willie Kamm	13.6
Benny Kauff	14.8
Tim Keefe	37.2
Charlie Keller	23.5
Joe Kelley	20.2
King Kelly	24.4
Jimmy Key	19.4
Harmon Killebrew	26.4
Frank Killen	12.9
Ellis Kinder	15.4
Ralph Kiner	28.9
Silver King	23.2
Chuck Klein	21.5
Bobby Knoop	15.0
Ed Konetchy	22.3
Jerry Koosman	13.1
Sandy Koufax	18.5
Nap Lajoie	94.3
Mark Langston	13.4
Max Lanier	16.3
Barry Larkin	27.6
Henry Larkin	14.9
Frank Lary	13.9
Gary Lavelle	15.0
Tony Lazzeri	16.9
Tommy Leach	17.4
Thornton Lee	16.9
Sam Leever	15.0
Bob Lemon	36.9
Chet Lemon	22.3
Dutch Leonard	25.8
Sixto Lezcano	14.7
Frank Linzy	14.6
Johnny Logan	17.3
Ernie Lombardi	17.3
Ed Lopat	18.1
Red Lucas	17.8
Dolf Luque	26.3
Greg Luzinski	14.6
Sparky Lyle	19.9
Fred Lynn	22.3
Ted Lyons	36.7
Denny Lyons	19.8
Greg Maddux	26.5
Sherry Magee	26.6
Sal Maglie	13.7
Jim Maloney	13.3
Mickey Mantle	76.1
Rabbit Maranville	13.1
Firpo Marberry	13.1
Juan Marichal	28.9
Mike Marshall	21.0
Eddie Mathews	51.6
Christy Mathewson	62.7
Don Mattingly	12.9
Carl Mays	36.1
Willie Mays	92.2
Bill Mazeroski	36.3
Jim McCormick	21.2
Willie McCovey	36.5
Lindy McDaniel	14.8
Gil McDougald	16.8
Joe McGinnity	19.5
Tug McGraw	14.5
John McGraw	16.1
Fred McGriff	19.0
Deacon McGuire	12.6
Sadie McMahon	15.8

Total Baseball Rank (alpha.)

Bid McPhee	40.1
Kevin McReynolds	14.4
Joe Medwick	27.1
Andy Messersmith	17.1
Chief Meyers	13.4
Stu Miller	17.0
Jocko Milligan	15.6
Minnie Minoso	26.0
Kevin Mitchell	20.9
Johnny Mize	36.2
Paul Molitor	35.2
Jeff Montgomery	17.0
Joe Morgan	56.3
Tony Mullane	31.1
George Mullin	14.0
Van Mungo	12.8
Thurman Munson	15.3
Bobby Murcer	13.0
Dale Murphy	19.3
Dwayne Murphy	16.4
Eddie Murray	35.6
Stan Musial	70.5
Billy Nash	12.7
Graig Nettles	21.4
Don Newcombe	18.9
Hal Newhouser	40.8
Kid Nichols	60.9
Bill Nicholson	19.0
Phil Niekro	35.4
Jim O'Rourke	16.1
Tony Oliva	24.8
Al Oliver	13.4
Gregg Olson	12.8
Jesse Orosco	16.1
Dave Orr	13.2
Claude Osteen	13.2
Amos Otis	19.3
Mel Ott	62.7
Rafael Palmeiro	13.9
Jim Palmer	35.5
Dave Parker	23.0
Mel Parnell	18.1
Claude Passeau	16.5
Roger Peckinpaugh	13.3
Terry Pendleton	12.9
Ron Perranoski	15.7
Gaylord Perry	34.4
Fred Pfeffer	21.9
Deacon Phillippe	15.7
Billy Pierce	23.3
Eddie Plank	26.9
Howie Pollet	13.7
Boog Powell	14.9
Del Pratt	20.4
Kirby Puckett	27.4
Jack Quinn	23.6
Dan Quisenberry	25.7
Charley Radbourn	26.2
Tim Raines	51.0
Willie Randolph	23.1
Pee Wee Reese	14.6
Ed Reulbach	17.7
Rick Reuschel	25.5
Jim Rice	27.0
Hardy Richardson	27.0
Dave Righetti	16.3
Jose Rijo	17.7
Cal Ripken	39.2
Eppa Rixey	25.9
Phil Rizzuto	15.8
Robin Roberts	24.9
Brooks Robinson	19.8
Frank Robinson	69.0
Jackie Robinson	31.8
Steve Rogers	15.3
Eddie Rommel	26.0
Pete Rose	20.0
Edd Roush	13.1
Schoolboy Rowe	17.4
Nap Rucker	13.8
Red Ruffing	26.8
Amos Rusie	38.9
Babe Ruth	124.7
Nolan Ryan	20.8
Jimmy Ryan	13.9
Bret Saberhagen	23.1
Ryne Sandberg	38.8
Ron Santo	39.5
Wally Schang	18.3
Mike Schmidt	78.4
Hal Schumacher	16.3
Mike Scioscia	14.8
Tom Seaver	48.2
Kip Selbach	13.5
Joe Sewell	34.4
Cy Seymour	16.2
Cy Seymour	16.2
Bobby Shantz	21.1
Bob Shawkey	14.8
Jimmy Sheckard	19.3

Total Baseball Rank (alpha.)

Urban Shocker	25.8
Roy Sievers	12.7
Curt Simmons	12.6
Al Simmons	25.6
Ted Simmons	16.8
Ken Singleton	20.9
George Sisler	24.0
Enos Slaughter	16.3
Roy Smalley	13.7
Lee Smith	24.7
Reggie Smith	35.0
Elmer Smith	15.4
Red Smith	13.0
Ozzie Smith	43.0
Duke Snider	22.3
Warren Spahn	47.0
Tris Speaker	86.5
Eddie Stanky	18.4
Bob Stanley	17.6
Willie Stargell	32.8
Rusty Staub	27.6
Vern Stephens	19.6
Riggs Stephenson	12.6
Dave Stieb	27.2
Jack Stivetts	26.3
George Stone	13.3
Mel Stottlemyre	17.3
Harry Stovey	21.3
Darryl Strawberry	26.9
Bruce Sutter	20.8
Don Sutton	13.6
Frank Tanana	13.3
Jesse Tannehill	20.4
Danny Tartabull	16.3
Jack Taylor	16.7
Kent Tekulve	24.3
Gene Tenace	15.3
Fred Tenney	20.9
Bill Terry	24.9
Frank Thomas	20.5
Roy Thomas	22.8
Robby Thompson	15.7
Sam Thompson	28.4
Luis Tiant	17.3
Joe Tinker	23.0
John Titus	13.0
Jim Tobin	13.0
Joe Torre	19.6
Alan Trammell	24.0
Pie Traynor	20.8
Dizzy Trout	34.5
Virgil Trucks	15.9
John Tudor	15.2
George Uhle	13.5
Dazzy Vance	27.0
George Van Haltren	13.5
Andy Van Slyke	21.0
Arky Vaughan	39.2
Hippo Vaughn	17.9
Bobby Veach	14.8
Frank Viola	15.1
Rube Waddell	24.6
Honus Wagner	81.3
Larry Walker	13.0
Bobby Wallace	40.7
Ed Walsh	43.3
Bucky Walters	26.4
Paul Waner	36.1
John Ward	21.9
Lon Warneke	22.7
Mickey Welch	14.8
Zack Wheat	24.5
Lou Whitaker	24.5
Doc White	17.7
Roy White	21.3
Jim Whitney	12.9
Hoyt Wilhelm	40.0
Billy Williams	31.1
Jimmy Williams	16.1
Ken Williams	17.2
Matt Williams	12.5
Ted Williams	85.7
Vic Willis	22.0
Hack Wilson	15.6
Dave Winfield	39.7
Joe Wood	22.9
Wilbur Wood	18.6
Early Wynn	16.6
Jim Wynn	33.2
Carl Yastrzemski	45.5
Cy Young	79.9
Robin Yount	43.1
Chief Zimmer	15.8
Richie Zisk	13.5

Total Baseball Rank (by era)

1876-1892

1	John Clarkson	48.7
2	Roger Connor	42.7
3	Dan Brouthers	40.6
4	Bid McPhee	40.1
5	Tim Keefe	37.2
6	Jack Glasscock	36.2
7	Bob Caruthers	31.4
8	Tony Mullane	31.1
9	Cap Anson	29.9
10	Buck Ewing	29.5
11	Sam Thompson	28.4
12	Fred Dunlap	27.2
13	Hardy Richardson	27.0
14	Pete Browning	26.9
15	Jack Stivetts	26.3
16	Charley Radbourn	26.2
17	King Kelly	24.4
18	Silver King	23.2
19	Fred Pfeffer	21.9
	John Ward	21.9
21	Guy Hecker	21.3
	Harry Stovey	21.3
23	Jim McCormick	21.2
24	Charley Jones	20.7
25	Denny Lyons	19.8

1893-1919

1	Nap Lajoie	94.3
2	Ty Cobb	91.2
3	Walter Johnson	90.1
4	Tris Speaker	86.5
5	Honus Wagner	81.3
6	Cy Young	79.9
7	Eddie Collins	69.7
8	Pete Alexander	64.9
9	Christy Mathewson	62.7
10	Kid Nichols	60.9
11	Bill Dahlen	51.4
12	George Davis	50.0
13	Ed Delahanty	44.3
14	Ed Walsh	43.3
15	Bobby Wallace	40.7
16	Amos Rusie	38.9
17	Joe Jackson	37.5
18	Mordecai Brown	34.8
19	Frank Baker	33.8
20	Sam Crawford	30.2
21	Cupid Childs	30.0
22	Clark Griffith	29.0
23	Elmer Flick	28.7
24	Fred Clarke	28.6
25	Heinie Groh	27.0

1920-1941

1	Babe Ruth	124.7
2	Rogers Hornsby	81.1
3	Lou Gehrig	65.7
4	Mel Ott	62.7
5	Lefty Grove	61.2
6	Jimmie Foxx	54.3
7	Charlie Gehringer	44.4
8	Luke Appling	40.7
9	Gabby Hartnett	40.1
10	Joe Cronin	39.4
11	Carl Hubbell	39.2
	Arky Vaughan	39.2
13	Frankie Frisch	39.1
14	Ted Lyons	36.7
15	Carl Mays	36.1
	Paul Waner	36.1
17	Bob Johnson	35.6
18	Bill Dickey	35.4
19	Dave Bancroft	35.3
20	Joe Sewell	34.4
21	Wes Ferrell	32.4
	Harry Heilmann	32.4
23	Billy Herman	31.7
24	Mickey Cochrane	31.4
25	Hank Greenberg	30.0

Total Baseball Rank (by era)

1942-1960

1	Ted Williams	85.7
2	Mickey Mantle	76.1
3	Stan Musial	70.5
4	Eddie Mathews	51.6
5	Warren Spahn	47.0
6	Joe DiMaggio	46.9
7	Lou Boudreau	41.3
8	Hal Newhouser	40.8
9	Hoyt Wilhelm	40.0
10	Bobby Doerr	39.0
11	Whitey Ford	37.2
12	Bob Lemon	36.9
13	Yogi Berra	36.2
	Johnny Mize	36.2
15	Dizzy Trout	34.5
16	Jackie Robinson	31.8
17	Richie Ashburn	30.2
18	Ralph Kiner	28.9
19	Bob Feller	28.5
20	Joe Gordon	28.2
21	Minnie Minoso	26.0
22	Dutch Leonard	25.8
23	Harry Brecheen	25.4
24	Robin Roberts	24.9
25	Charlie Keller	23.5

1961-1976

1	Willie Mays	92.2
2	Hank Aaron	89.8
3	Frank Robinson	69.0
4	Joe Morgan	56.3
5	Tom Seaver	48.2
6	Carl Yastrzemski	45.5
7	Al Kaline	44.6
8	Bob Gibson	44.0
9	Roberto Clemente	42.9
10	Ron Santo	39.5
11	Willie McCovey	36.5
12	Bill Mazeroski	36.3
13	Jim Palmer	35.5
14	Phil Niekro	35.4
15	Dick Allen	35.3
16	Reggie Smith	35.0
17	Gaylord Perry	34.4
18	Don Drysdale	34.0
19	Steve Carlton	33.2
	Jim Wynn	33.2
21	Willie Stargell	32.8
22	Rod Carew	31.4
23	Billy Williams	31.1
24	Fergie Jenkins	30.9
25	Bobby Bonds	29.6

1977-1994

1	Mike Schmidt	78.4
2	Rickey Henderson	74.6
3	Tim Raines	51.0
4	Barry Bonds	49.4
5	Wade Boggs	44.4
6	Bobby Grich	44.1
7	Robin Yount	43.1
8	Ozzie Smith	43.0
9	Reggie Jackson	42.8
10	Dave Winfield	39.7
11	Cal Ripken	39.2
12	George Brett	39.0
13	Ryne Sandberg	38.8
14	Tony Gwynn	38.5
15	Roger Clemens	36.9
16	Eddie Murray	35.6
17	Paul Molitor	35.2
18	Darrell Evans	34.6
19	Keith Hernandez	34.4
20	Jack Clark	31.1
	Andre Dawson	31.1
22	Bert Blyleven	30.9
23	Dwight Evans	30.4
24	Rich Gossage	30.2
25	Gary Carter	29.6

At Bats

1	Willie Wilson, 1980	705
2	Juan Samuel, 1984	701
3	Dave Cash, 1975	699
4	Matty Alou, 1969	698
5	Woody Jensen, 1936	696
6	Maury Wills, 1962	695
	Omar Moreno, 1979	695
8	Bobby Richardson, 1962	692
9	Kirby Puckett, 1985	691
10	Lou Brock, 1967	689
	Sandy Alomar, 1971	689
12	Dave Cash, 1974	687
	Tony Fernandez, 1986	687
14	Horace Clarke, 1970	686
15	Lloyd Waner, 1931	681
	Jo-Jo Moore, 1935	681
17	Pete Rose, 1973	680
	Frank Taveras, 1979	680
	Kirby Puckett, 1986	680
20	Harvey Kuenn, 1953	679
	Curt Flood, 1964	679
	Bobby Richardson, 1964	679
23	Dick Groat, 1962	678
24	Matty Alou, 1970	677
	Jim Rice, 1978	677
	Don Mattingly, 1986	677
27	Felix Millan, 1975	676
	Omar Moreno, 1980	676
29	Rennie Stennett, 1974	673
	Bill Buckner, 1985	673
31	Rabbit Maranville, 1922	672
	Tony Oliva, 1964	672
	Sandy Alomar, 1970	672
	Garry Templeton, 1979	672
35	Jack Tobin, 1921	671
36	Al Simmons, 1932	670
	Pete Rose, 1965	670
	Buddy Bell, 1979	670
39	Vada Pinson, 1965	669
	Larry Bowa, 1974	669
41	Buddy Lewis, 1937	668
	Brooks Robinson, 1961	668
	Ralph Garr, 1973	668
44	Carl Furillo, 1951	667
45	Billy Herman, 1935	666
	Zoilo Versalles, 1965	666
	Felipe Alou, 1966	666
	Dave Cash, 1976	666
	Ron LeFlore, 1978	666
	Paul Molitor, 1982	666
51	Tommy Davis, 1962	665
	Pete Rose, 1976	665
	Paul Molitor, 1991	665
54	Taylor Douthit, 1930	664
	Bobby Richardson, 1965	664
	Don Kessinger, 1969	664
	Lou Brock, 1970	664
58	Jake Wood, 1961	663
	Bill Virdon, 1962	663
	Bobby Bonds, 1970	663
	Rick Burleson, 1977	663
	Cal Ripken, 1983	663
	Juan Samuel, 1985	663
	Joe Carter, 1986	663
65	Lloyd Waner, 1929	662
	Hughie Critz, 1930	662
	Richie Ashburn, 1949	662
	Granny Hamner, 1949	662
	Bobby Richardson, 1961	662
	Curt Flood, 1963	662
	Felipe Alou, 1968	662
	Pete Rose, 1975	662
73	Doc Cramer, 1933	661
	Doc Cramer, 1940	661
	Ken Hubbs, 1962	661
	Cecil Cooper, 1983	661
	Ruben Sierra, 1991	661
78	Tom Brown, 1892	660
	Doc Cramer, 1941	660
	Lou Brock, 1968	660
	Enos Cabell, 1978	660
82	Lloyd Waner, 1928	659
	Hughie Critz, 1932	659
	Red Schoendienst, 1947	659
	Billy Moran, 1962	659
	Zoilo Versalles, 1964	659
	Luis Aparicio, 1966	659
	Steve Garvey, 1975	659
	Warren Cromartie, 1979	659
	Travis Fryman, 1992	659
91	Heinie Manush, 1933	658
	Doc Cramer, 1938	658
	Bill White, 1963	658
	Dave Cash, 1978	658
	Steve Garvey, 1980	658
	Julio Franco, 1984	658
97	5 players tied	657

Runs

1	Billy Hamilton, 1894	192
2	Tom Brown, 1891	177
	Babe Ruth, 1921	177
4	Tip O'Neill, 1887	167
	Lou Gehrig, 1936	167
6	Billy Hamilton, 1895	166
7	Willie Keeler, 1894	165
	Joe Kelley, 1894	165
9	Arlie Latham, 1887	163
	Babe Ruth, 1928	163
	Lou Gehrig, 1931	163
12	Willie Keeler, 1895	162
13	Hugh Duffy, 1890	161
14	Fred Dunlap, 1884	160
	Hugh Duffy, 1894	160
	Jesse Burkett, 1896	160
17	Hughie Jennings, 1895	159
18	Bobby Lowe, 1894	158
	Babe Ruth, 1920	158
	Babe Ruth, 1927	158
	Chuck Klein, 1930	158
22	John McGraw, 1894	156
	Rogers Hornsby, 1929	156
24	King Kelly, 1886	155
	Kiki Cuyler, 1930	155
26	Dan Brouthers, 1887	153
	Jesse Burkett, 1895	153
	Willie Keeler, 1896	153
29	Arlie Latham, 1886	152
	Mike Griffin, 1889	152
	Harry Stovey, 1889	152
	Billy Hamilton, 1896	152
	Billy Hamilton, 1897	152
	Lefty O'Doul, 1929	152
	Woody English, 1930	152
	Al Simmons, 1930	152
	Chuck Klein, 1932	152
38	Babe Ruth, 1923	151
	Jimmie Foxx, 1932	151
	Joe DiMaggio, 1937	151
41	George Gore, 1886	150
	Babe Ruth, 1930	150
	Ted Williams, 1949	150
44	Herman Long, 1893	149
	Bill Dahlen, 1894	149
	Ed Delahanty, 1895	149
	Lou Gehrig, 1927	149
	Babe Ruth, 1931	149
49	Hub Collins, 1890	148
	Jake Stenzel, 1894	148
	Joe Kelley, 1895	148
	Joe Kelley, 1896	148
53	Mike Tiernan, 1889	147
	Hugh Duffy, 1893	147
	Ed Delahanty, 1894	147
	Ty Cobb, 1911	147
57	Darby O'Brien, 1889	146
	Tom Brown, 1890	146
	Hack Wilson, 1930	146
	Rickey Henderson, 1985	146
61	Jesse Burkett, 1893	145
	Cupid Childs, 1893	145
	Ed Delahanty, 1893	145
	Patsy Donovan, 1894	145
	Willie Keeler, 1897	145
	Nap Lajoie, 1901	145
	Harlond Clift, 1936	145
68	Hugh Duffy, 1889	144
	Billy Hamilton, 1889	144
	Ty Cobb, 1915	144
	Kiki Cuyler, 1925	144
	Charlie Gehringer, 1930	144
	Al Simmons, 1932	144
	Charlie Gehringer, 1934	144
	Hank Greenberg, 1938	144
76	Cupid Childs, 1894	143
	John McGraw, 1898	143
	Babe Ruth, 1924	143
	Babe Herman, 1930	143
	Lou Gehrig, 1930	143
	Earle Combs, 1932	143
	Red Rolfe, 1937	143
	Lenny Dykstra, 1993	143
84	Mike Griffin, 1887	142
	Harry Stovey, 1891	142
	Jesse Burkett, 1901	142
	Paul Waner, 1928	142
	Ted Williams, 1946	142
89	Billy Hamilton, 1891	141
	Rogers Hornsby, 1922	141
	Ted Williams, 1942	141
92	Tom Poorman, 1887	140
	Jimmy Ryan, 1889	140
	Jim McTamany, 1890	140
	Mike Griffin, 1895	140
	Willie Keeler, 1899	140
	John McGraw, 1899	140
	Max Carey, 1922	140
	Earl Averill, 1931	140
100	9 players tied	139

Runs per Game

1876-1892

1	Ross Barnes, 1876	1.91
2	Fred Dunlap, 1884	1.58
3	George Gore, 1890	1.42
4	Tip O'Neill, 1887	1.35
5	King Kelly, 1886	1.31
6	Tom Brown, 1891	1.29
7	George Gore, 1886	1.27
8	Dan Brouthers, 1887	1.24
9	Orator Shaffer, 1884	1.23
10	Mike Tiernan, 1889	1.20
11	Harry Stovey, 1890	1.20
12	Arlie Latham, 1887	1.20
13	Harry Stovey, 1884	1.19
14	George Gore, 1882	1.18
15	George Gore, 1881	1.18

1893-1919

1	Billy Hamilton, 1894	1.49
2	Billy Hamilton, 1895	1.35
3	Billy Hamilton, 1893	1.34
4	Herman Long, 1894	1.31
5	Ed Delahanty, 1894	1.29
6	Ed Delahanty, 1895	1.28
7	Hugh Duffy, 1894	1.28
8	Willie Keeler, 1894	1.28
	Joe Kelley, 1894	1.28
10	John McGraw, 1894	1.26
11	Willie Keeler, 1895	1.24
12	Bill Dahlen, 1894	1.23
13	Jimmy Ryan, 1894	1.22
14	Willie Keeler, 1896	1.21
15	Hughie Jennings, 1895	1.21

1920-1941

1	Babe Ruth, 1921	1.16
2	Babe Ruth, 1920	1.11
3	Al Simmons, 1930	1.10
4	Lou Gehrig, 1936	1.08
5	Babe Ruth, 1928	1.06
6	Lou Gehrig, 1931	1.05
7	Jimmie Foxx, 1939	1.05
8	Babe Ruth, 1927	1.05
9	Babe Ruth, 1930	1.03
10	Babe Ruth, 1931	1.03
11	Chuck Klein, 1930	1.01
12	Rogers Hornsby, 1929	1.00
	Joe DiMaggio, 1937	1.00
14	Kiki Cuyler, 1930	.99
15	Babe Ruth, 1923	.99

1942-1960

1	Ted Williams, 1949	.97
2	Ted Williams, 1946	.95
3	Tommy Henrich, 1948	.95
4	Ted Williams, 1942	.94
5	Dom DiMaggio, 1950	.93
6	Ted Williams, 1948	.91
7	Johnny Mize, 1947	.89
8	Eddie Joost, 1949	.89
9	Mickey Mantle, 1954	.88
10	Johnny Pesky, 1950	.88
11	Mickey Mantle, 1956	.88
12	Stan Musial, 1948	.87
13	Goody Rosen, 1945	.87
	Dom DiMaggio, 1949	.87
15	Johnny Pesky, 1948	.87

1961-1976

1	Mickey Mantle, 1961	.86
2	Bobby Bonds, 1970	.85
3	Billy Williams, 1970	.85
4	Willie Mays, 1961	.84
5	Frank Robinson, 1962	.83
6	Roger Maris, 1961	.82
7	Joe Morgan, 1972	.82
8	Bobby Bonds, 1973	.82
9	Hank Aaron, 1962	.81
10	Don Buford, 1971	.81
11	Reggie Jackson, 1969	.81
12	Jim Wynn, 1972	.81
13	Lou Brock, 1971	.80
14	Willie Mays, 1962	.80
	Pete Rose, 1976	.80

1977-1994

1	Rickey Henderson, 1985	1.02
2	Paul Molitor, 1987	.97
3	Jeff Bagwell, 1994	.95
4	Frank Thomas, 1994	.94
5	Kenny Lofton, 1994	.94
6	Eric Davis, 1987	.93
7	Lenny Dykstra, 1993	.89
8	Tim Raines, 1987	.88
9	Rickey Henderson, 1990	.88
10	Marquis Grissom, 1994	.87
11	Tim Raines, 1983	.85
12	Rickey Henderson, 1993	.85
13	Paul Molitor, 1982	.85
14	Rickey Henderson, 1986	.85
15	Albert Belle, 1994	.85

Hits

1	George Sisler, 1920	257
2	Lefty O'Doul, 1929	254
	Bill Terry, 1930	254
4	Al Simmons, 1925	253
5	Rogers Hornsby, 1922	250
	Chuck Klein, 1930	250
7	Ty Cobb, 1911	248
8	George Sisler, 1922	246
9	Heinie Manush, 1928	241
	Babe Herman, 1930	241
11	Jesse Burkett, 1896	240
	Wade Boggs, 1985	240
13	Willie Keeler, 1897	239
	Rod Carew, 1977	239
15	Ed Delahanty, 1899	238
	Don Mattingly, 1986	238
17	Hugh Duffy, 1894	237
	Harry Heilmann, 1921	237
	Paul Waner, 1927	237
	Joe Medwick, 1937	237
21	Jack Tobin, 1921	236
22	Rogers Hornsby, 1921	235
23	Lloyd Waner, 1929	234
	Kirby Puckett, 1988	234
25	Joe Jackson, 1911	233
26	Nap Lajoie, 1901	232
	Earl Averill, 1936	232
28	Earle Combs, 1927	231
	Freddy Lindstrom, 1928	231
	Freddy Lindstrom, 1930	231
	Matty Alou, 1969	231
32	Stan Musial, 1948	230
	Tommy Davis, 1962	230
	Joe Torre, 1971	230
	Pete Rose, 1973	230
	Willie Wilson, 1980	230
37	Rogers Hornsby, 1929	229
38	Kiki Cuyler, 1930	228
	Stan Musial, 1946	228
40	Nap Lajoie, 1910	227
	Rogers Hornsby, 1924	227
	Jim Bottomley, 1925	227
	Sam Rice, 1925	227
	Billy Herman, 1935	227
	Charlie Gehringer, 1936	227
46	Jesse Burkett, 1901	226
	Joe Jackson, 1912	226
	Ty Cobb, 1912	226
	Bill Terry, 1929	226
	Chuck Klein, 1932	226
51	Tip O'Neill, 1887	225
	Jesse Burkett, 1895	225
	Ty Cobb, 1917	225
	Harry Heilmann, 1925	225
	Johnny Hodapp, 1930	225
	Bill Terry, 1932	225
57	Eddie Collins, 1920	224
	George Sisler, 1925	224
	Joe Medwick, 1935	224
	Tommy Holmes, 1945	224
61	Frankie Frisch, 1923	223
	Lloyd Waner, 1927	223
	Paul Waner, 1928	223
	Chuck Klein, 1933	223
	Joe Medwick, 1936	223
	Hank Aaron, 1959	223
	Kirby Puckett, 1986	223
68	Sam Thompson, 1893	222
	Tris Speaker, 1912	222
	Charlie Jamieson, 1923	222
71	Jesse Burkett, 1899	221
	Zack Wheat, 1925	221
	Lloyd Waner, 1928	221
	Heinie Manush, 1933	221
	Richie Ashburn, 1951	221
76	Pete Browning, 1887	220
	Billy Hamilton, 1894	220
	Kiki Cuyler, 1925	220
	Lou Gehrig, 1930	220
	Stan Musial, 1943	220
81	Ed Delahanty, 1893	219
	Willie Keeler, 1894	219
	Jimmy Williams, 1899	219
	Cy Seymour, 1905	219
	Chuck Klein, 1929	219
	Lefty O'Doul, 1932	219
	Paul Waner, 1937	219
	Ralph Garr, 1971	219
	Cecil Cooper, 1980	219
90	12 players tied	218

Doubles

1	Earl Webb, 1931	67
2	George Burns, 1926	64
	Joe Medwick, 1936	64
4	Hank Greenberg, 1934	63
5	Paul Waner, 1932	62
6	Charlie Gehringer, 1936	60
7	Tris Speaker, 1923	59
	Chuck Klein, 1930	59
9	Billy Herman, 1935	57
	Billy Herman, 1936	57
11	Joe Medwick, 1937	56
	George Kell, 1950	56
13	Ed Delahanty, 1899	55
	Gee Walker, 1936	55
15	Hal McRae, 1977	54
	John Olerud, 1993	54
17	Tris Speaker, 1912	53
	Al Simmons, 1926	53
	Paul Waner, 1936	53
	Stan Musial, 1953	53
	Don Mattingly, 1986	53
22	Tip O'Neill, 1887	52
	Tris Speaker, 1921	52
	Tris Speaker, 1926	52
	Lou Gehrig, 1927	52
	Johnny Frederick, 1929	52
	Enos Slaughter, 1939	52
28	Hugh Duffy, 1894	51
	Nap Lajoie, 1910	51
	Baby Doll Jacobson, 1926	51
	George Burns, 1927	51
	Johnny Hodapp, 1930	51
	Beau Bell, 1937	51
	Joe Cronin, 1938	51
	Stan Musial, 1944	51
	Mickey Vernon, 1946	51
	Frank Robinson, 1962	51
	Pete Rose, 1978	51
	Wade Boggs, 1989	51
40	Tris Speaker, 1920	50
	Harry Heilmann, 1927	50
	Paul Waner, 1928	50
	Kiki Cuyler, 1930	50
	Chuck Klein, 1932	50
	Charlie Gehringer, 1934	50
	Odell Hale, 1936	50
	Ben Chapman, 1936	50
	Hank Greenberg, 1940	50
	Stan Musial, 1946	50
	Stan Spence, 1946	50
51	Ned Williamson, 1883	49
	Ed Delahanty, 1895	49
	Nap Lajoie, 1904	49
	George Sisler, 1920	49
	Heinie Manush, 1930	49
	Riggs Stephenson, 1932	49
	Hank Greenberg, 1937	49
	Robin Yount, 1980	49
	Rafael Palmeiro, 1991	49
60	Joe Kelley, 1894	48
	Nap Lajoie, 1901	48
	Nap Lajoie, 1906	48
	Tris Speaker, 1922	48
	Joe Sewell, 1927	48
	Babe Herman, 1930	48
	Dick Bartell, 1932	48
	Earl Averill, 1934	48
	Wally Moses, 1937	48
	Joe Medwick, 1939	48
	Stan Musial, 1943	48
	Keith Hernandez, 1979	48
	Don Mattingly, 1985	48
73	Harry Davis, 1905	47
	Ty Cobb, 1911	47
	George Burns, 1923	47
	Lou Gehrig, 1926	47
	Bob Meusel, 1927	47
	Lou Gehrig, 1928	47
	Heinie Manush, 1928	47
	Rogers Hornsby, 1929	47
	Chick Hafey, 1929	47
	Adam Comorosky, 1930	47
	Ed Morgan, 1930	47
	Charlie Gehringer, 1930	47
	Dale Alexander, 1931	47
	Eric McNair, 1932	47
	Joe Vosmik, 1935	47
	Joe Vosmik, 1937	47
	Joe Medwick, 1938	47
	Tommy Holmes, 1945	47
	Vada Pinson, 1959	47
	Wes Parker, 1970	47
	Pete Rose, 1975	47
	Fred Lynn, 1975	47
	Cal Ripken, 1983	47
	Wade Boggs, 1986	47
97	27 players tied	46

Triples

1	Chief Wilson, 1912	36
2	Dave Orr, 1886	31
	Heinie Reitz, 1894	31
4	Perry Werden, 1893	29
5	Harry Davis, 1897	28
6	George Davis, 1893	27
	Sam Thompson, 1894	27
	Jimmy Williams, 1899	27
9	John Reilly, 1890	26
	George Treadway, 1894	26
	Joe Jackson, 1912	26
	Sam Crawford, 1914	26
	Kiki Cuyler, 1925	26
14	Roger Connor, 1894	25
	Buck Freeman, 1899	25
	Sam Crawford, 1903	25
	Larry Doyle, 1911	25
	Tom Long, 1915	25
19	Ed McKean, 1893	24
	Ty Cobb, 1911	24
	Ty Cobb, 1917	24
22	Harry Stovey, 1884	23
	Sam Thompson, 1887	23
	Elmer Smith, 1893	23
	Dan Brouthers, 1894	23
	Nap Lajoie, 1897	23
	Ty Cobb, 1912	23
	Sam Crawford, 1913	23
	Earle Combs, 1927	23
	Adam Comorosky, 1930	23
	Dale Mitchell, 1949	23
32	Roger Connor, 1887	22
	Bid McPhee, 1890	22
	Jake Beckley, 1890	22
	Joe Visner, 1890	22
	Willie Keeler, 1894	22
	Kip Selbach, 1895	22
	John Anderson, 1898	22
	Honus Wagner, 1900	22
	Tommy Leach, 1902	22
	Sam Crawford, 1902	22
	Bill Bradley, 1903	22
	Elmer Flick, 1906	22
	Mike Mitchell, 1911	22
	Birdie Cree, 1911	22
	Tris Speaker, 1913	22
	Hy Myers, 1920	22
	Jake Daubert, 1922	22
	Paul Waner, 1926	22
	Earle Combs, 1930	22
	Snuffy Stirnweiss, 1945	22
52	Dave Orr, 1885	21
	Mike Tiernan, 1890	21
	Billy Shindle, 1890	21
	Tom Brown, 1891	21
	Ed Delahanty, 1892	21
	Sam Thompson, 1895	21
	Mike Tiernan, 1895	21
	Tom McCreery, 1896	21
	George Van Haltren, 1896	21
	Bobby Wallace, 1897	21
	Jimmy Williams, 1901	21
	Bill Keister, 1901	21
	Jimmy Williams, 1902	21
	Cy Seymour, 1905	21
	Frank Schulte, 1911	21
	Frank Baker, 1912	21
	Sam Crawford, 1912	21
	Vic Saier, 1913	21
	Joe Jackson, 1916	21
	Edd Roush, 1924	21
	Earle Combs, 1928	21
	Willie Wilson, 1985	21
74	36 players tied	20

Triples (by era)

1876-1892

1	Dave Orr, 1886	31
2	John Reilly, 1890	26
3	Harry Stovey, 1884	23
	Sam Thompson, 1887	23
5	Roger Connor, 1887	22
	Bid McPhee, 1890	22
	Jake Beckley, 1890	22
	Joe Visner, 1890	22
9	Dave Orr, 1885	21
	Mike Tiernan, 1890	21
	Billy Shindle, 1890	21
	Tom Brown, 1891	21
	Ed Delahanty, 1892	21
14	10 players tied	20

1893-1919

1	Chief Wilson, 1912	36
2	Heinie Reitz, 1894	31
3	Perry Werden, 1893	29
4	Harry Davis, 1897	28
5	George Davis, 1893	27
	Sam Thompson, 1894	27
	Jimmy Williams, 1899	27
8	George Treadway, 1894	26
	Joe Jackson, 1912	26
	Sam Crawford, 1914	26
11	Roger Connor, 1894	25
	Buck Freeman, 1899	25
	Sam Crawford, 1903	25
	Larry Doyle, 1911	25
	Tom Long, 1915	25

1920-1941

1	Kiki Cuyler, 1925	26
2	Earle Combs, 1927	23
	Adam Comorosky, 1930	23
4	Hy Myers, 1920	22
	Jake Daubert, 1922	22
	Paul Waner, 1926	22
	Earle Combs, 1930	22
8	Edd Roush, 1924	21
	Earle Combs, 1928	21
10	12 players tied	20

1942-1960

1	Dale Mitchell, 1949	23
2	Snuffy Stirnweiss, 1945	22
3	Stan Musial, 1943	20
	Stan Musial, 1946	20
	Willie Mays, 1957	20
6	Johnny Barrett, 1944	19
7	Stan Musial, 1948	18
	Minnie Minoso, 1954	18
9	Enos Slaughter, 1942	17
	Jim Gilliam, 1953	17
11	6 players tied	16

1961-1976

1	Ralph Garr, 1974	17
2	Johnny Callison, 1965	16
	Willie Davis, 1970	16
4	Gino Cimoli, 1962	15
5	Jake Wood, 1961	14
	Vada Pinson, 1963	14
	Dick Allen, 1965	14
	Roberto Clemente, 1965	14
	Donn Clendenon, 1965	14
	Lou Brock, 1968	14
	Don Kessinger, 1970	14
	Roger Metzger, 1973	14
	George Brett, 1976	14
14	10 players tied	13

1977-1994

1	Willie Wilson, 1985	21
2	George Brett, 1979	20
3	Garry Templeton, 1979	19
	Juan Samuel, 1984	19
	Ryne Sandberg, 1984	19
6	Garry Templeton, 1977	18
	Willie McGee, 1985	18
8	Tony Fernandez, 1990	17
9	Rod Carew, 1977	16
	Paul Molitor, 1979	16
11	11 players tied	15

Home Runs

1	Roger Maris, 1961	61
2	Babe Ruth, 1927	60
3	Babe Ruth, 1921	59
4	Jimmie Foxx, 1932	58
	Hank Greenberg, 1938	58
6	Hack Wilson, 1930	56
7	Babe Ruth, 1920	54
	Babe Ruth, 1928	54
	Ralph Kiner, 1949	54
	Mickey Mantle, 1961	54
11	Mickey Mantle, 1956	52
	Willie Mays, 1965	52
	George Foster, 1977	52
14	Ralph Kiner, 1947	51
	Johnny Mize, 1947	51
	Willie Mays, 1955	51
	Cecil Fielder, 1990	51
18	Jimmie Foxx, 1938	50
19	Babe Ruth, 1930	49
	Lou Gehrig, 1934	49
	Lou Gehrig, 1936	49
	Ted Kluszewski, 1954	49
	Willie Mays, 1962	49
	Harmon Killebrew, 1964	49
	Frank Robinson, 1966	49
	Harmon Killebrew, 1969	49
	Andre Dawson, 1987	49
	Mark McGwire, 1987	49
29	Jimmie Foxx, 1933	48
	Harmon Killebrew, 1962	48
	Frank Howard, 1969	48
	Willie Stargell, 1971	48
	Dave Kingman, 1979	48
	Mike Schmidt, 1980	48
35	Babe Ruth, 1926	47
	Lou Gehrig, 1927	47
	Ralph Kiner, 1950	47
	Eddie Mathews, 1953	47
	Ted Kluszewski, 1955	47
	Ernie Banks, 1958	47
	Willie Mays, 1964	47
	Reggie Jackson, 1969	47
	Hank Aaron, 1971	47
	George Bell, 1987	47
	Kevin Mitchell, 1989	47
46	Babe Ruth, 1924	46
	Babe Ruth, 1929	46
	Babe Ruth, 1931	46
	Lou Gehrig, 1931	46
	Joe DiMaggio, 1937	46
	Eddie Mathews, 1959	46
	Orlando Cepeda, 1961	46
	Jim Gentile, 1961	46
	Harmon Killebrew, 1961	46
	Jim Rice, 1978	46
	Barry Bonds, 1993	46
	Juan Gonzalez, 1993	46
58	Ernie Banks, 1959	45
	Rocky Colavito, 1961	45
	Hank Aaron, 1962	45
	Harmon Killebrew, 1963	45
	Willie McCovey, 1969	45
	Johnny Bench, 1970	45
	Mike Schmidt, 1979	45
	Gorman Thomas, 1979	45
	Ken Griffey, 1993	45
67	Jimmie Foxx, 1934	44
	Hank Greenberg, 1946	44
	Ernie Banks, 1955	44
	Hank Aaron, 1957	44
	Willie McCovey, 1963	44
	Hank Aaron, 1963	44
	Hank Aaron, 1966	44
	Harmon Killebrew, 1967	44
	Carl Yastrzemski, 1967	44
	Frank Howard, 1968	44
	Hank Aaron, 1969	44
	Frank Howard, 1970	44
	Willie Stargell, 1973	44
	Dale Murphy, 1987	44
	Jose Canseco, 1991	44
	Cecil Fielder, 1991	44
83	Chuck Klein, 1929	43
	Johnny Mize, 1940	43
	Ted Williams, 1949	43
	Al Rosen, 1953	43
	Duke Snider, 1956	43
	Ernie Banks, 1957	43
	Davey Johnson, 1973	43
	Tony Armas, 1984	43
	Juan Gonzalez, 1992	43
	Matt Williams, 1994	43
93	16 players tied	42

Home Runs (by era)

1876-1892

1	Ned Williamson, 1884	27
2	Fred Pfeffer, 1884	25
3	Abner Dalrymple, 1884 ...	22
4	Cap Anson, 1884........	21
5	Sam Thompson, 1889	20
6	Billy O'Brien, 1887	19
	Bug Holliday, 1889	19
	Harry Stovey, 1889	19
9	Jerry Denny, 1889	18
10	Roger Connor, 1887	17
	Jimmy Ryan, 1889......	17
12	5 players tied	16

1893-1919

1	Babe Ruth, 1919	29
2	Buck Freeman, 1899	25
3	Gavvy Cravath, 1915	24
4	Frank Schulte, 1911	21
5	Ed Delahanty, 1893	19
	Gavvy Cravath, 1913	19
	Gavvy Cravath, 1914	19
8	Hugh Duffy, 1894	18
	Sam Thompson, 1895 ...	18
	Fred Luderus, 1913	18
	Vic Saier, 1914........	18
12	5 players tied	17

1920-1941

1	Babe Ruth, 1927	60
2	Babe Ruth, 1921	59
3	Jimmie Foxx, 1932	58
	Hank Greenberg, 1938 ..	58
5	Hack Wilson, 1930	56
6	Babe Ruth, 1920	54
	Babe Ruth, 1928	54
8	Jimmie Foxx, 1938	50
9	Babe Ruth, 1930	49
	Lou Gehrig, 1934	49
	Lou Gehrig, 1936.......	49
12	Jimmie Foxx, 1933	48
13	Babe Ruth, 1926	47
	Lou Gehrig, 1927	47
15	5 players tied	46

1942-1960

1	Ralph Kiner, 1949	54
2	Mickey Mantle, 1956.....	52
3	Ralph Kiner, 1947	51
	Johnny Mize, 1947	51
	Willie Mays, 1955	51
6	Ted Kluszewski, 1954	49
7	Ralph Kiner, 1950	47
	Eddie Mathews, 1953 ...	47
	Ted Kluszewski, 1955 ...	47
	Ernie Banks, 1958	47
11	Eddie Mathews, 1959 ...	46
12	Ernie Banks, 1959	45
13	Hank Greenberg, 1946 ..	44
	Ernie Banks, 1955	44
	Hank Aaron, 1957	44

1961-1976

1	Roger Maris, 1961.......	61
2	Mickey Mantle, 1961.....	54
3	Willie Mays, 1965	52
4	Willie Mays, 1962	49
	Harmon Killebrew, 1964 ..	49
	Frank Robinson, 1966....	49
	Harmon Killebrew, 1969 ..	49
8	Harmon Killebrew, 1962 ..	48
	Frank Howard, 1969	48
	Willie Stargell, 1971......	48
11	Willie Mays, 1964	47
	Reggie Jackson, 1969 ...	47
	Hank Aaron, 1971	47
14	3 players tied	46

1977-1994

1	George Foster, 1977	52
2	Cecil Fielder, 1990	51
3	Andre Dawson, 1987.....	49
	Mark McGwire, 1987.....	49
5	Dave Kingman, 1979	48
	Mike Schmidt, 1980	48
7	George Bell, 1987	47
	Kevin Mitchell, 1989	47
9	Jim Rice, 1978.........	46
	Barry Bonds, 1993	46
	Juan Gonzalez, 1993	46
12	Mike Schmidt, 1979	45
	Gorman Thomas, 1979 ...	45
	Ken Griffey, 1993	45
15	3 players tied	44

Home Run Percentage

1	Babe Ruth, 1920	11.79
2	Babe Ruth, 1927	11.11
3	Babe Ruth, 1921	10.93
4	Mickey Mantle, 1961.....	10.51
5	Hank Greenberg, 1938 ...	10.43
6	Roger Maris, 1961.......	10.34
7	Babe Ruth, 1928	10.07
8	Jimmie Foxx, 1932	9.91
9	Ralph Kiner, 1949	9.84
10	Mickey Mantle, 1956.....	9.76
11	Jeff Bagwell, 1994......	9.75
12	Kevin Mitchell, 1994	9.68
13	Matt Williams, 1994......	9.66
14	Hack Wilson, 1930	9.57
15	Frank Thomas, 1994.....	9.52
16	Babe Ruth, 1926	9.49
	Hank Aaron, 1971	9.49
18	Jim Gentile, 1961	9.47
19	Barry Bonds, 1994......	9.46
20	Babe Ruth, 1930	9.46
21	Willie Stargell, 1971.....	9.39
22	Willie Mays, 1965	9.32
23	Ken Griffey, 1994	9.24
24	Babe Ruth, 1929	9.22
25	Boog Powell, 1964	9.20
26	Willie McCovey, 1969	9.16
27	Ted Williams, 1957	9.05
28	Ralph Kiner, 1947	9.03
29	Dave Kingman, 1979.....	9.02
30	Mark McGwire, 1992	8.99
31	Babe Ruth, 1932	8.97
32	Cecil Fielder, 1990	8.90
33	Jimmie Foxx, 1938	8.85
34	Harmon Killebrew, 1969 ..	8.83
35	Mark McGwire, 1987.....	8.80
36	Willie Mays, 1955	8.79
37	Mike Schmidt, 1980	8.76
38	Mike Schmidt, 1981	8.76
39	Harmon Killebrew, 1963 ..	8.74
	Albert Belle, 1994......	8.74
41	Johnny Mize, 1947	8.70
42	Babe Ruth, 1924	8.70
	Harmon Killebrew, 1962 ..	8.70
44	Kevin Mitchell, 1989	8.66
45	Babe Ruth, 1922	8.62
46	Babe Ruth, 1931	8.61
47	Ralph Kiner, 1950	8.59
48	Juan Gonzalez, 1993	8.58
49	Reggie Jackson, 1969 ...	8.56
50	Ted Kluszewski, 1954	8.55
51	Barry Bonds, 1993	8.53
52	Frank Robinson, 1966....	8.51
53	Harmon Killebrew, 1961 ..	8.50
54	Harmon Killebrew, 1964 ..	8.49
55	Lou Gehrig, 1934........	8.46
	Lou Gehrig, 1936........	8.46
57	George Foster, 1977	8.46
58	Willie Stargell, 1973.....	8.43
59	Hank Greenberg, 1946 ...	8.41
60	Eddie Mathews, 1954	8.40
61	Gary Sheffield, 1994.....	8.39
62	Rocky Colavito, 1958	8.38
63	Jimmie Foxx, 1933	8.38
64	Joe Adcock, 1956	8.37
65	Jack Clark, 1987	8.35
66	Mike Schmidt, 1979	8.32
67	Eddie Mathews, 1955	8.22
68	Jimmie Foxx, 1934	8.16
69	Willie Mays, 1964	8.13
70	Eddie Mathews, 1953	8.12
71	Ted Williams, 1941	8.11
72	Frank Howard, 1969	8.11
73	Mickey Mantle, 1958.....	8.09
74	Gorman Thomas, 1979 ...	8.08
75	Lou Gehrig, 1927........	8.05
76	Harmon Killebrew, 1967 ..	8.04
	Hank Aaron, 1969	8.04
78	Fred McGriff, 1994......	8.02
79	Reggie Jackson, 1980 ...	7.98
80	Mickey Mantle, 1962.....	7.96
81	Duke Snider, 1956......	7.93
82	Darrell Evans, 1985	7.92
83	Ralph Kiner, 1951	7.91
84	Roy Campanella, 1953 ...	7.90
85	Willie Mays, 1962	7.89
	Andre Dawson, 1987.....	7.89
87	Hank Sauer, 1954	7.88
88	Willie McCovey, 1970	7.88
89	Duke Snider, 1957......	7.87
90	Orlando Cepeda, 1961 ...	7.86
91	Babe Ruth, 1923	7.85
92	Roger Maris, 1960......	7.82
93	Duke Snider, 1955......	7.81
94	Dave Kingman, 1976.....	7.81
	Eric Davis, 1987.......	7.81
96	Willie McCovey, 1963	7.80
97	Harmon Killebrew, 1970 ..	7.78
98	Frank Howard, 1970	7.77
	Dale Murphy, 1987	7.77
100	Eddie Mathews, 1959 ...	7.74

Home Run Pct.(by era)

1876-1892

1	Ned Williamson, 1884	6.47
2	Fred Pfeffer, 1884	5.35
3	Cap Anson, 1884.......	4.42
4	Abner Dalrymple, 1884 ...	4.22
5	Billy O'Brien, 1887......	4.19
6	Sam Thompson, 1889 ...	3.75
7	Roger Connor, 1887	3.61
8	Dan Brouthers, 1884	3.52
9	Harry Stovey, 1889	3.42
10	Bug Holliday, 1889	3.37
11	Fred Pfeffer, 1887	3.34
12	Harry Stovey, 1883	3.33
13	Charlie Duffee, 1889	3.14
14	Jerry Denny, 1889	3.11
15	Dan Brouthers, 1881	2.96

1893-1919

1	Babe Ruth, 1919	6.71
2	Bill Joyce, 1894	4.79
3	Gavvy Cravath, 1915	4.60
4	Jack Clements, 1893	4.52
5	Buck Freeman, 1899	4.25
6	Gavvy Cravath, 1914	3.81
7	Jim Canavan, 1894	3.65
8	Frank Schulte, 1911	3.64
9	Gavvy Cravath, 1913	3.62
10	Bill Joyce, 1895	3.59
11	Sherry Magee, 1911	3.37
12	Vic Saier, 1914.......	3.35
13	Sam Thompson, 1895 ...	3.35
14	Hugh Duffy, 1894	3.34
15	Ed Delahanty, 1893	3.19

1920-1941

1	Babe Ruth, 1920	11.79
2	Babe Ruth, 1927	11.11
3	Babe Ruth, 1921	10.93
4	Hank Greenberg, 1938 ...	10.43
5	Babe Ruth, 1928	10.07
6	Jimmie Foxx, 1932	9.91
7	Hack Wilson, 1930	9.57
8	Babe Ruth, 1926	9.49
9	Babe Ruth, 1930	9.46
10	Babe Ruth, 1929	9.22
11	Babe Ruth, 1932	8.97
12	Jimmie Foxx, 1938	8.85
13	Babe Ruth, 1924	8.70
14	Babe Ruth, 1922	8.62
15	Babe Ruth, 1931	8.61

1942-1960

1	Ralph Kiner, 1949	9.84
2	Mickey Mantle, 1956.....	9.76
3	Ted Williams, 1957	9.05
4	Ralph Kiner, 1947	9.03
5	Willie Mays, 1955	8.79
6	Johnny Mize, 1947	8.70
7	Ralph Kiner, 1950	8.59
8	Ted Kluszewski, 1954 ...	8.55
9	Hank Greenberg, 1946 ...	8.41
10	Eddie Mathews, 1954 ...	8.40
11	Rocky Colavito, 1958	8.38
12	Joe Adcock, 1956	8.37
13	Eddie Mathews, 1955 ...	8.22
14	Eddie Mathews, 1953 ...	8.12
15	Mickey Mantle, 1958.....	8.09

1961-1976

1	Mickey Mantle, 1961.....	10.51
2	Roger Maris, 1961.......	10.34
3	Hank Aaron, 1971	9.49
4	Jim Gentile, 1961	9.47
5	Willie Stargell, 1971.....	9.39
6	Willie Mays, 1965	9.32
7	Boog Powell, 1964	9.20
8	Willie McCovey, 1969	9.16
9	Harmon Killebrew, 1969 ..	8.83
10	Harmon Killebrew, 1963 ..	8.74
11	Harmon Killebrew, 1962 ..	8.70
12	Reggie Jackson, 1969 ...	8.56
13	Frank Robinson, 1966....	8.51
14	Harmon Killebrew, 1961 ..	8.50
15	Harmon Killebrew, 1964 ..	8.49

1977-1994

1	Jeff Bagwell, 1994......	9.75
2	Kevin Mitchell, 1994	9.68
3	Matt Williams, 1994......	9.66
4	Frank Thomas, 1994.....	9.52
5	Barry Bonds, 1994......	9.46
6	Ken Griffey, 1994	9.24
7	Dave Kingman, 1979.....	9.02
8	Mark McGwire, 1992	8.99
9	Cecil Fielder, 1990	8.90
10	Mark McGwire, 1987.....	8.80
11	Mike Schmidt, 1980	8.76
12	Mike Schmidt, 1981	8.76
13	Albert Belle, 1994......	8.74
14	Kevin Mitchell, 1989	8.66
15	Juan Gonzalez, 1993	8.58

Total Bases

1	Babe Ruth, 1921	457
2	Rogers Hornsby, 1922 ...	450
3	Lou Gehrig, 1927	447
4	Chuck Klein, 1930	445
5	Jimmie Foxx, 1932	438
6	Stan Musial, 1948	429
7	Hack Wilson, 1930	423
8	Chuck Klein, 1932	420
9	Lou Gehrig, 1930	419
10	Joe DiMaggio, 1937	418
11	Babe Ruth, 1927	417
12	Babe Herman, 1930	416
13	Lou Gehrig, 1931	410
14	Rogers Hornsby, 1929 ...	409
	Lou Gehrig, 1934.......	409
16	Joe Medwick, 1937	406
	Jim Rice, 1978..........	406
18	Chuck Klein, 1929	405
	Hal Trosky, 1936.......	405
20	Jimmie Foxx, 1933	403
	Lou Gehrig, 1936.......	403
22	Hank Aaron, 1959	400
23	George Sisler, 1920.....	399
	Babe Ruth, 1923	399
25	Jimmie Foxx, 1938	398
26	Lefty O'Doul, 1929	397
	Hank Greenberg, 1937 ...	397
28	Al Simmons, 1925	392
	Bill Terry, 1930........	392
	Al Simmons, 1930	392
31	Babe Ruth, 1924	391
32	Hank Greenberg, 1935 ...	389
33	Babe Ruth, 1920	388
	George Foster, 1977	388
	Don Mattingly, 1986	388
36	Earl Averill, 1936.......	385
37	Hank Greenberg, 1940 ...	384
38	Stan Musial, 1949	382
	Willie Mays, 1955	382
	Willie Mays, 1962	382
	Jim Rice, 1977.........	382
42	Rogers Hornsby, 1925 ...	381
43	Babe Ruth, 1928	380
	Hank Greenberg, 1938 ...	380
	Frank Robinson, 1962....	380
46	Babe Ruth, 1930	379
	Ernie Banks, 1958	379
48	Rogers Hornsby, 1921 ...	378
	Duke Snider, 1954......	378
50	Willie Mays, 1954	377
51	Mickey Mantle, 1956.....	376
52	Hugh Duffy, 1894	374
	Babe Ruth, 1931	374
	Hal Trosky, 1934.......	374
	Tony Oliva, 1964	374
56	Rogers Hornsby, 1924 ...	373
	Al Simmons, 1929	373
	Bill Terry, 1932........	373
	Billy Williams, 1970	373
60	Lou Gehrig, 1932	370
	Duke Snider, 1953......	370
	Hank Aaron, 1963	370
	Don Mattingly, 1985	370
64	Kiki Cuyler, 1925	369
	Ripper Collins, 1934	369
	Jimmie Foxx, 1936	369
	Hank Aaron, 1957	369
	Jim Rice, 1979..........	369
	George Bell, 1987	369
70	Johnny Mize, 1940	368
	Ted Williams, 1949	368
	Ted Kluszewski, 1954 ...	368
	Cal Ripken, 1991	368
74	Ty Cobb, 1911	367
	Ken Williams, 1922	367
	Heinie Manush, 1928	367
	Al Simmons, 1932	367
	Joe Medwick, 1936	367
	Joe DiMaggio, 1936	367
	Tommy Holmes, 1945 ...	367
	Al Rosen, 1953	367
	Frank Robinson, 1966....	367
	Robin Yount, 1982	367
84	Lou Gehrig, 1937	366
	Stan Musial, 1946	366
	Willie Mays, 1957	366
	Roger Maris, 1961	366
	Hank Aaron, 1962	366
89	Harry Heilmann, 1921 ...	365
	Babe Ruth, 1926	365
	Chuck Klein, 1933	365
	Joe Medwick, 1935	365
	Kirby Puckett, 1986	365
	Barry Bonds, 1993	365
95	Lou Gehrig, 1928........	364
96	Dale Alexander, 1929 ...	363
	Eddie Mathews, 1953 ...	363
	George Brett, 1979	363
99	Jim Bottomley, 1928	362
100	4 players tied	361

Runs Batted In

1	Hack Wilson, 1930	190
2	Lou Gehrig, 1931	184
3	Hank Greenberg, 1937	183
4	Lou Gehrig, 1927	175
	Jimmie Foxx, 1938	175
6	Lou Gehrig, 1930	174
7	Babe Ruth, 1921	171
8	Chuck Klein, 1930	170
	Hank Greenberg, 1935	170
10	Jimmie Foxx, 1932	169
11	Joe DiMaggio, 1937	167
12	Sam Thompson, 1887	166
13	Sam Thompson, 1895	165
	Al Simmons, 1930	165
	Lou Gehrig, 1934	165
16	Babe Ruth, 1927	164
17	Babe Ruth, 1931	163
	Jimmie Foxx, 1933	163
19	Hal Trosky, 1936	162
20	Hack Wilson, 1929	159
	Lou Gehrig, 1937	159
	Ted Williams, 1949	159
	Vern Stephens, 1949	159
24	Al Simmons, 1929	157
25	Jimmie Foxx, 1930	156
26	Ken Williams, 1922	155
	Joe DiMaggio, 1948	155
28	Babe Ruth, 1929	154
	Joe Medwick, 1937	154
30	Babe Ruth, 1930	153
	Tommy Davis, 1962	153
32	Rogers Hornsby, 1922	152
	Lou Gehrig, 1936	152
34	Mel Ott, 1929	151
	Lou Gehrig, 1932	151
	Al Simmons, 1932	151
37	Hank Greenberg, 1940	150
38	Rogers Hornsby, 1929	149
	George Foster, 1977	149
40	Johnny Bench, 1970	148
41	Cap Anson, 1886	147
42	Hardy Richardson, 1890	146
	Ed Delahanty, 1893	146
	Babe Ruth, 1926	146
	Hank Greenberg, 1938	146
46	Hugh Duffy, 1894	145
	Chuck Klein, 1929	145
	Ted Williams, 1939	145
	Al Rosen, 1953	145
	Don Mattingly, 1985	145
51	Walt Dropo, 1950	144
	Vern Stephens, 1950	144
53	Rogers Hornsby, 1925	143
	Earl Averill, 1931	143
	Don Hurst, 1932	143
	Jimmie Foxx, 1936	143
	Ernie Banks, 1959	143
58	Lou Gehrig, 1928	142
	Babe Ruth, 1928	142
	Hal Trosky, 1934	142
	Roy Campanella, 1953	142
	Orlando Cepeda, 1961	142
	Roger Maris, 1961	142
64	Sam Thompson, 1894	141
	Ted Kluszewski, 1954	141
	Jim Gentile, 1961	141
	Willie Mays, 1962	141
68	Joe DiMaggio, 1938	140
	Rocky Colavito, 1961	140
	Harmon Killebrew, 1969	140
71	Harry Heilmann, 1921	139
	Lou Gehrig, 1933	139
	Hank Greenberg, 1934	139
	Jim Rice, 1978	139
	Don Baylor, 1979	139
76	Bob Meusel, 1925	138
	Goose Goslin, 1930	138
	Joe Medwick, 1936	138
	Zeke Bonura, 1936	138
	Johnny Mize, 1947	138
81	Ed Delahanty, 1899	137
	Babe Ruth, 1920	137
	Jim Bottomley, 1929	137
	Dale Alexander, 1929	137
	Chuck Klein, 1932	137
	Babe Ruth, 1932	137
	Johnny Mize, 1940	137
	Ted Williams, 1942	137
	Vern Stephens, 1948	137
	Joe Torre, 1971	137
	Andre Dawson, 1987	137
92	George Davis, 1897	136
	George Kelly, 1924	136
	Jim Bottomley, 1928	136
	Ed Morgan, 1930	136
	Duke Snider, 1955	136
	Frank Robinson, 1962	136
98	5 players tied	135

Runs Batted In per Game

1	Sam Thompson, 1894	1.42
2	Sam Thompson, 1895	1.39
3	Sam Thompson, 1887	1.31
4	Hack Wilson, 1930	1.23
5	Al Simmons, 1930	1.20
6	Hank Greenberg, 1937	1.19
7	Lou Gehrig, 1931	1.19
8	Cap Anson, 1886	1.18
9	Jimmie Foxx, 1938	1.17
10	Hugh Duffy, 1894	1.16
11	Dave Orr, 1890	1.16
12	Ed Delahanty, 1894	1.15
13	Babe Ruth, 1929	1.14
14	Lou Gehrig, 1930	1.13
15	Lou Gehrig, 1927	1.13
16	Babe Ruth, 1921	1.13
17	Babe Ruth, 1931	1.12
18	Hardy Richardson, 1890	1.12
19	Hank Greenberg, 1935	1.12
20	Ed Delahanty, 1893	1.11
21	Joe DiMaggio, 1937	1.11
22	Al Simmons, 1929	1.10
23	Jimmie Foxx, 1932	1.10
24	Jimmie Foxx, 1933	1.09
25	Chuck Klein, 1930	1.09
26	Babe Ruth, 1927	1.09
27	Oyster Burns, 1890	1.08
28	Hal Trosky, 1936	1.07
29	Lou Gehrig, 1934	1.07
30	Ed McKean, 1893	1.06
31	Hack Wilson, 1929	1.06
32	Walt Dropo, 1950	1.06
33	Babe Ruth, 1930	1.06
34	Jeff Bagwell, 1994	1.05
35	Buck Ewing, 1893	1.05
36	Lave Cross, 1894	1.05
37	Joe DiMaggio, 1939	1.05
38	George Davis, 1897	1.05
39	Dan Brouthers, 1894	1.04
40	Kirby Puckett, 1994	1.04
41	Rogers Hornsby, 1925	1.04
42	Jim O'Rourke, 1890	1.04
43	Babe Ruth, 1932	1.03
44	Ted Williams, 1949	1.03
	Vern Stephens, 1949	1.03
46	Ed Delahanty, 1896	1.02
47	Steve Brodie, 1895	1.02
	Joe Kelley, 1895	1.02
49	Jimmie Foxx, 1930	1.02
50	Hank Greenberg, 1940	1.01
51	Ken Williams, 1922	1.01
	Joe DiMaggio, 1948	1.01
53	Lou Gehrig, 1937	1.01
54	Cap Anson, 1882	1.01
55	George Decker, 1894	1.01
56	George Brett, 1980	1.01
57	Joe DiMaggio, 1940	1.01
58	Mel Ott, 1929	1.01
59	Nap Lajoie, 1897	1.00
	Al Simmons, 1931	1.00
61	Roger Connor, 1889	.99
62	Tommy McCarthy, 1894	.99
63	Jake Beckley, 1890	.99
64	Dan Brouthers, 1883	.99
65	Joe Medwick, 1937	.99
66	Rogers Hornsby, 1922	.99
67	Roy Campanella, 1953	.99
68	Jimmy Collins, 1897	.99
69	Ed McKean, 1894	.98
70	Bug Holliday, 1894	.98
71	Lou Gehrig, 1936	.98
72	Al Simmons, 1932	.98
73	Walt Wilmot, 1894	.98
74	Cap Anson, 1881	.98
75	Chuck Klein, 1929	.97
	Ted Williams, 1939	.97
77	Heinie Reitz, 1894	.97
78	Lou Gehrig, 1932	.97
79	Vern Stephens, 1950	.97
80	Joe DiMaggio, 1938	.97
81	Babe Ruth, 1920	.96
82	Cap Anson, 1885	.96
83	Hugh Duffy, 1897	.96
84	Sam Thompson, 1893	.96
85	Billy Nash, 1893	.96
86	Babe Ruth, 1926	.96
87	Harry Heilmann, 1929	.96
88	Tommy McCarthy, 1893	.96
89	Rogers Hornsby, 1929	.96
90	Hughie Jennings, 1895	.95
	Nap Lajoie, 1901	.95
92	Don Hurst, 1932	.95
93	Albert Belle, 1994	.95
94	Jim Gentile, 1961	.95
95	Jack Doyle, 1894	.95
96	Bill Dickey, 1937	.95
97	Ted Kluszewski, 1954	.95
98	George Kelly, 1924	.94
99	George Foster, 1977	.94
100	Hank Greenberg, 1938	.94

Walks

1	Babe Ruth, 1923	170
2	Ted Williams, 1947	162
	Ted Williams, 1949	162
4	Ted Williams, 1946	156
5	Eddie Yost, 1956	151
6	Eddie Joost, 1949	149
7	Babe Ruth, 1920	148
	Eddie Stanky, 1945	148
	Jim Wynn, 1969	148
10	Jimmy Sheckard, 1911	147
11	Mickey Mantle, 1957	146
12	Ted Williams, 1941	145
	Ted Williams, 1942	145
	Harmon Killebrew, 1969	145
15	Babe Ruth, 1921	144
	Babe Ruth, 1926	144
	Eddie Stanky, 1950	144
	Ted Williams, 1951	144
19	Babe Ruth, 1924	142
20	Eddie Yost, 1950	141
21	Babe Ruth, 1927	138
	Frank Thomas, 1991	138
23	Eddie Stanky, 1946	137
	Roy Cullenbine, 1947	137
	Ralph Kiner, 1951	137
	Willie McCovey, 1970	137
27	Jack Crooks, 1892	136
	Babe Ruth, 1930	136
	Ferris Fain, 1949	136
	Ted Williams, 1954	136
	Jack Clark, 1987	136
32	Babe Ruth, 1928	135
	Eddie Yost, 1959	135
34	Ferris Fain, 1950	133
35	Lou Gehrig, 1935	132
	Frank Howard, 1970	132
	Joe Morgan, 1975	132
	Jack Clark, 1989	132
	Tony Phillips, 1993	132
40	Bob Elliott, 1948	131
	Eddie Yost, 1954	131
	Harmon Killebrew, 1967	131
43	Babe Ruth, 1932	130
	Lou Gehrig, 1936	130
45	Eddie Yost, 1952	129
	Mickey Mantle, 1958	129
	Lenny Dykstra, 1993	129
48	Max Bishop, 1929	128
	Max Bishop, 1930	128
	Babe Ruth, 1931	128
	Harmon Killebrew, 1970	128
	Carl Yastrzemski, 1970	128
	Mike Schmidt, 1983	128
54	Lu Blue, 1931	127
	Lou Gehrig, 1937	127
	Eddie Stanky, 1951	127
	Jim Wynn, 1976	127
	Barry Bonds, 1992	127
59	Billy Hamilton, 1894	126
	Lu Blue, 1929	126
	Ted Williams, 1948	126
	Eddie Yost, 1951	126
	Mickey Mantle, 1961	126
	Darrell Evans, 1974	126
	Rickey Henderson, 1989	126
	Barry Bonds, 1993	126
67	Richie Ashburn, 1954	125
	Eddie Yost, 1960	125
	Gene Tenace, 1977	125
	Wade Boggs, 1988	125
71	John McGraw, 1899	124
	Norm Cash, 1961	124
	Eddie Mathews, 1963	124
	Darrell Evans, 1973	124
75	Bill Joyce, 1890	123
	Eddie Yost, 1953	123
	Ken Singleton, 1973	123
78	Jimmy Sheckard, 1912	122
	Lou Gehrig, 1929	122
	Luke Appling, 1935	122
	Ralph Kiner, 1950	122
	Eddie Joost, 1952	122
	Mickey Mantle, 1962	122
	John Mayberry, 1973	122
	Mickey Tettleton, 1992	122
	Frank Thomas, 1992	122
87	Jack Crooks, 1893	121
	Topsy Hartsel, 1905	121
	Roy Cullenbine, 1941	121
	Luke Appling, 1949	121
	Willie McCovey, 1969	121
	Darrell Porter, 1979	121
	Von Hayes, 1987	121
94	Cupid Childs, 1893	120
	Eddie Lake, 1947	120
	Joe Morgan, 1974	120
	Mike Schmidt, 1979	120
	Rickey Henderson, 1993	120
99	14 players tied	119

Strikeouts

1	Bobby Bonds, 1970	189
2	Bobby Bonds, 1969	187
3	Rob Deer, 1987	186
4	Pete Incaviglia, 1986	185
5	Cecil Fielder, 1990	182
6	Mike Schmidt, 1975	180
7	Rob Deer, 1986	179
8	Dave Nicholson, 1963	175
	Gorman Thomas, 1979	175
	Jose Canseco, 1986	175
	Rob Deer, 1991	175
12	Jim Presley, 1986	172
	Bo Jackson, 1989	172
14	Reggie Jackson, 1968	171
15	Gorman Thomas, 1980	170
16	Andres Galarraga, 1990	169
	Rob Deer, 1993	169
18	Juan Samuel, 1984	168
	Pete Incaviglia, 1987	168
20	Gary Alexander, 1978	166
	Steve Balboni, 1985	166
	Cory Snyder, 1987	166
23	Donn Clendenon, 1968	163
24	Butch Hobson, 1977	162
	Juan Samuel, 1987	162
26	Dick Allen, 1968	161
	Reggie Jackson, 1971	161
28	Mickey Tettleton, 1990	160
29	Bo Jackson, 1987	158
	Andres Galarraga, 1989	158
	Rob Deer, 1989	158
	Jose Canseco, 1990	158
33	Danny Tartabull, 1986	157
	Jose Canseco, 1987	157
	Jim Presley, 1987	157
36	Tommie Agee, 1970	156
	Dave Kingman, 1982	156
	Reggie Jackson, 1982	156
	Tony Armas, 1984	156
	Danny Tartabull, 1993	156
41	Frank Howard, 1967	155
	Jeff Burroughs, 1975	155
43	Willie Stargell, 1971	154
	Larry Parrish, 1987	154
	Dean Palmer, 1992	154
	Dean Palmer, 1993	154
47	Dave Kingman, 1975	153
	Andres Galarraga, 1988	153
	Rob Deer, 1988	153
	Pete Incaviglia, 1988	153
51	George Scott, 1966	152
	Larry Hisle, 1969	152
	Jose Canseco, 1991	152
54	Don Lock, 1963	151
	Greg Luzinski, 1975	151
	Juan Samuel, 1988	151
	Delino DeShields, 1991	151
	Cecil Fielder, 1991	151
	Cecil Fielder, 1992	151
60	Dick Allen, 1965	150
	Nate Colbert, 1970	150
	Ron Kittle, 1983	150
	Jesse Barfield, 1989	150
	Jesse Barfield, 1990	150
	Sammy Sosa, 1990	150
66	Billy Grabarkewitz, 1970	149
	Mike Schmidt, 1976	149
	Fred McGriff, 1988	149
	Travis Fryman, 1991	149
70	Bobby Bonds, 1973	148
	Mike Schmidt, 1983	148
	Gorman Thomas, 1983	148
	Bobby Kelly, 1990	148
74	Rob Deer, 1990	147
	Ray Lankford, 1992	147
	Cory Snyder, 1993	147
77	Deron Johnson, 1971	146
	Nate Colbert, 1973	146
	Steve Balboni, 1986	146
	Jesse Barfield, 1986	146
	Bo Jackson, 1988	146
	Pete Incaviglia, 1990	146
	Jay Buhner, 1992	146
84	Lee May, 1972	145
	Bobby Darwin, 1972	145
	Dale Murphy, 1978	145
	Jack Clark, 1989	145
88	Dick Stuart, 1963	144
	Bobby Knoop, 1966	144
	Dick Allen, 1969	144
	Travis Fryman, 1992	144
	Jay Buhner, 1993	144
93	Dave Kingman, 1977	143
	Nelson Mathews, 1964	143
	Byron Browne, 1966	143
	Rick Monday, 1968	143
	Gorman Thomas, 1982	143
	Jesse Barfield, 1985	143
	Juan Gonzalez, 1992	143
100	8 players tied	142

At Bats per Strikeout

1876-1892

1	Mike McGeary, 1876	276.0
2	Cap Anson, 1878	261.0
3	John Peters, 1876	158.0
4	John Clapp, 1876	149.0
5	Joe Start, 1877	135.5
6	Joe Start, 1876	132.0
7	Levi Meyerle, 1876	128.0
8	Jim Holdsworth, 1876	120.5
9	Lon Knight, 1876	120.0
10	Ezra Sutton, 1876	118.0
11	Bobby Mathews, 1876	109.0
12	Paul Hines, 1876	101.7
13	Deacon White, 1876	101.0
14	Al Spalding, 1876	97.3
15	Davy Force, 1876	95.7

1893-1919

1	Jack Doyle, 1894	140.7
2	John Ward, 1893	117.6
3	Willie Keeler, 1894	98.3
4	Joe Quinn, 1895	90.5
5	John Ward, 1894	90.0
6	Joe Quinn, 1893	78.1
7	Lave Cross, 1894	75.6
8	Steve Brodie, 1894	71.6
9	Jack Glasscock, 1893	69.7
10	Lave Cross, 1895	66.9
11	Ed McKean, 1896	63.4
12	Dummy Hoy, 1893	62.7
13	Patsy Donovan, 1893	62.4
14	Farmer Vaughn, 1896	61.9
15	Willie Keeler, 1896	60.4

1920-1941

1	Joe Sewell, 1932	167.7
2	Joe Sewell, 1925	152.0
3	Joe Sewell, 1929	144.5
4	Joe Sewell, 1933	131.0
5	Charlie Hollocher, 1922	118.4
6	Stuffy McInnis, 1922	107.4
7	Stuffy McInnis, 1924	96.8
8	Joe Sewell, 1926	96.3
9	Joe Sewell, 1927	81.3
10	Pie Traynor, 1929	77.1
11	Sam Rice, 1929	68.4
12	Tris Speaker, 1927	65.4
13	Joe Sewell, 1928	65.3
14	Sam Rice, 1925	64.9
15	Stuffy McInnis, 1921	64.9

1942-1960

1	Tommy Holmes, 1945	70.7
2	Emil Verban, 1947	67.5
3	Lou Boudreau, 1948	62.2
4	Dale Mitchell, 1949	58.2
5	Tommy Holmes, 1944	57.4
6	Dale Mitchell, 1952	56.8
7	Nellie Fox, 1958	56.6
8	Tommy Holmes, 1942	55.8
9	Jimmy Brown, 1942	55.1
10	Nellie Fox, 1951	54.9
11	Lou Boudreau, 1947	53.8
12	Nellie Fox, 1954	52.6
13	Harvey Kuenn, 1954	50.5
14	Don Mueller, 1955	50.4
15	Yogi Berra, 1950	49.8

1961-1976

1	Nellie Fox, 1962	51.8
2	Dave Cash, 1976	51.2
3	Nellie Fox, 1961	50.5
4	Matty Alou, 1970	37.6
5	Felix Millan, 1974	37.0
6	Vic Power, 1961	35.2
7	Nellie Fox, 1964	34.0
8	Glenn Beckert, 1968	32.2
9	Nellie Fox, 1963	31.7
10	Felix Millan, 1973	29.0
11	Bobby Richardson, 1962	28.8
12	Bobby Richardson, 1961	28.8
13	Bobby Richardson, 1963	28.6
14	Felix Millan, 1976	27.9
15	Glenn Beckert, 1972	27.9

1977-1994

1	Tim Foli, 1979	38.0
2	Felix Fermin, 1993	34.3
3	Tony Gwynn, 1992	32.5
4	Bill Buckner, 1980	32.1
5	Tim Foli, 1981	31.6
6	Ozzie Smith, 1993	30.3
7	Bob Bailor, 1978	29.6
8	Rich Dauer, 1980	29.3
9	Tony Gwynn, 1991	27.9
10	Tony Gwynn, 1984	26.3
11	Bill Buckner, 1981	26.3
12	Tony Gwynn, 1993	25.7
13	Bill Buckner, 1982	25.3
14	Bill Buckner, 1986	25.2
15	Tony Gwynn, 1990	24.9

Strikeout Percentage

1876-1892

1	Frank Meinke, 1884	26.10
2	Jim Galvin, 1883	24.53
3	Sam Wise, 1884	24.41
4	Jim Galvin, 1879	21.13
5	Charlie Bastian, 1885	21.08
6	Will White, 1878	20.81
7	Silver Flint, 1883	20.78
8	John Morrill, 1884	19.86
9	John Morrill, 1885	19.80
10	Charlie Bastian, 1886	19.57
11	Jim Lillie, 1886	19.23
12	Will White, 1879	19.05
13	John Morrill, 1886	18.84
14	Sam Wise, 1883	18.23
15	Bill Crowley, 1884	18.18

1893-1919

1	Gus Williams, 1914	24.05
2	Grover Gilmore, 1914	20.38
3	Gavvy Cravath, 1916	19.87
4	Ed McDonald, 1912	19.83
5	Art Wilson, 1914	18.18
6	Gavvy Cravath, 1912	17.66
7	Cozy Dolan, 1914	17.58
8	Max Carey, 1911	17.56
9	Danny Moeller, 1913	17.49
10	Doug Baird, 1915	17.19
11	Al Boucher, 1914	17.05
12	Wally Pipp, 1915	16.91
13	Joe Agler, 1914	16.85
14	Ray Powell, 1919	16.81
15	Cy Williams, 1917	16.67

1920-1941

1	Vince DiMaggio, 1938	24.81
2	Vince DiMaggio, 1937	22.52
3	Chet Ross, 1940	22.32
4	Dolph Camilli, 1941	21.74
5	Joe Orengo, 1940	21.69
6	Jimmie Foxx, 1941	21.15
7	Boze Berger, 1935	21.04
8	Jimmie Foxx, 1936	20.34
9	Dolph Camilli, 1938	19.84
10	Babe Ruth, 1922	19.70
11	Babe Ruth, 1933	19.61
12	Jimmy Dykes, 1922	19.56
13	Hank Greenberg, 1939	19.00
14	Vince DiMaggio, 1941	18.94
15	Dolph Camilli, 1939	18.94

1942-1960

1	Pancho Herrera, 1960	26.56
2	Jim Lemon, 1956	25.65
3	Dick Stuart, 1960	24.43
4	Frank Howard, 1960	24.11
5	Harmon Killebrew, 1960	23.98
6	Jim Lemon, 1958	23.95
7	Mickey Mantle, 1960	23.72
8	Larry Doby, 1953	23.59
9	Pat Seerey, 1945	23.43
10	Mickey Mantle, 1959	23.29
11	Mickey Mantle, 1958	23.12
12	Wally Post, 1956	23.01
13	Woodie Held, 1959	22.48
14	Gil Hodges, 1959	22.28
15	Norm Zauchin, 1955	22.01

1961-1976

1	Dave Nicholson, 1963	38.98
2	Dick Allen, 1969	32.88
3	Mike Schmidt, 1975	32.03
4	Reggie Jackson, 1970	31.69
5	Larry Hisle, 1969	31.54
6	Reggie Jackson, 1968	30.92
7	Dick Allen, 1968	30.90
8	Dave Kingman, 1975	30.48
9	Willie Stargell, 1971	30.14
10	Bobby Bonds, 1969	30.06
11	Frank Howard, 1967	29.87
12	Rick Monday, 1968	29.67
13	Dave Kingman, 1972	29.66
14	Willie Mays, 1971	29.50
15	Jim Wynn, 1969	28.69

1977-1994

1	Rob Deer, 1987	39.24
2	Rob Deer, 1991	39.06
3	Rob Deer, 1986	38.41
4	Rob Deer, 1993	36.27
5	Mickey Tettleton, 1990	36.04
6	Pete Incaviglia, 1986	34.26
7	Rob Deer, 1989	33.91
8	Rob Deer, 1990	33.41
9	Bo Jackson, 1989	33.40
10	Gary Alexander, 1978	33.33
11	Jack Clark, 1987	33.17
12	Pete Incaviglia, 1987	33.01
13	Jose Canseco, 1990	32.85
14	Jack Clark, 1989	31.87
15	Cecil Fielder, 1990	31.76

Batting Average

1	Hugh Duffy, 1894	.440
2	Tip O'Neill, 1887	.435
3	Ross Barnes, 1876	.429
4	Nap Lajoie, 1901	.426
5	Willie Keeler, 1897	.424
6	Rogers Hornsby, 1924	.424
7	George Sisler, 1922	.420
8	Ty Cobb, 1911	.420
9	Fred Dunlap, 1884	.412
10	Ed Delahanty, 1899	.410
11	Jesse Burkett, 1896	.410
12	Jesse Burkett, 1895	.409
13	Ty Cobb, 1912	.409
14	Joe Jackson, 1911	.408
15	Sam Thompson, 1894	.407
16	George Sisler, 1920	.407
17	Ed Delahanty, 1894	.407
18	Ted Williams, 1941	.406
19	Billy Hamilton, 1894	.404
20	Ed Delahanty, 1895	.404
21	Rogers Hornsby, 1925	.403
22	Harry Heilmann, 1923	.403
23	Pete Browning, 1887	.402
24	Rogers Hornsby, 1922	.401
25	Bill Terry, 1930	.401
26	Hughie Jennings, 1896	.401
27	Ty Cobb, 1922	.401
28	Cap Anson, 1881	.399
29	Lefty O'Doul, 1929	.398
30	Harry Heilmann, 1927	.398
31	Rogers Hornsby, 1921	.397
32	Ed Delahanty, 1896	.397
33	Jesse Burkett, 1899	.396
34	Joe Jackson, 1912	.395
35	Tony Gwynn, 1994	.394
36	Harry Heilmann, 1921	.394
37	Babe Ruth, 1923	.393
38	Harry Heilmann, 1925	.393
39	Babe Herman, 1930	.393
40	Joe Kelley, 1894	.393
41	Sam Thompson, 1895	.392
42	John McGraw, 1899	.391
43	Ty Cobb, 1913	.390
44	Fred Clarke, 1897	.390
45	Al Simmons, 1931	.390
46	George Brett, 1980	.390
47	Tris Speaker, 1925	.389
48	Bill Lange, 1895	.389
49	Billy Hamilton, 1895	.389
50	Ty Cobb, 1921	.389
51	Ted Williams, 1957	.388
52	King Kelly, 1886	.388
53	Rod Carew, 1977	.388
54	Luke Appling, 1936	.388
55	Tris Speaker, 1920	.388
56	Deacon White, 1877	.387
57	Al Simmons, 1925	.387
58	Rogers Hornsby, 1928	.387
59	Tris Speaker, 1916	.386
60	Willie Keeler, 1896	.386
61	Chuck Klein, 1930	.386
62	Lave Cross, 1894	.386
	Hughie Jennings, 1895	.386
64	Willie Keeler, 1898	.385
65	Arky Vaughan, 1935	.385
66	Rogers Hornsby, 1923	.384
67	Ty Cobb, 1919	.384
68	Nap Lajoie, 1910	.384
69	Ty Cobb, 1910	.383
70	Jesse Burkett, 1897	.383
71	Tris Speaker, 1912	.383
72	Ty Cobb, 1917	.383
73	Lefty O'Doul, 1930	.383
74	Joe Jackson, 1920	.382
75	Ty Cobb, 1918	.382
76	Honus Wagner, 1900	.381
77	Babe Herman, 1929	.381
78	Joe DiMaggio, 1939	.381
79	Al Simmons, 1930	.381
80	Paul Waner, 1927	.380
81	Rogers Hornsby, 1929	.380
82	Billy Hamilton, 1893	.380
83	Tris Speaker, 1923	.380
84	Goose Goslin, 1928	.379
85	Freddy Lindstrom, 1930	.379
86	Willie Keeler, 1899	.379
87	Lou Gehrig, 1930	.379
88	John Cassidy, 1877	.378
89	Pete Browning, 1882	.378
90	Ty Cobb, 1925	.378
91	Babe Ruth, 1924	.378
92	Sam Crawford, 1911	.378
93	Tris Speaker, 1922	.378
94	Earl Averill, 1936	.378
95	Babe Ruth, 1921	.378
96	Heinie Manush, 1928	.378
97	Heinie Manush, 1926	.378
98	Ed Delahanty, 1897	.377
99	Willie Keeler, 1895	.377
100	Ty Cobb, 1909	.377

Batting Average (by era)

1876-1892

1	Tip O'Neill, 1887	.435
2	Ross Barnes, 1876	.429
3	Fred Dunlap, 1884	.412
4	Pete Browning, 1887	.402
5	Cap Anson, 1881	.399
6	King Kelly, 1886	.388
7	Deacon White, 1877	.387
8	John Cassidy, 1877	.378
9	Pete Browning, 1882	.378
10	Dan Brouthers, 1883	.374
11	Pete Browning, 1890	.373
12	Dan Brouthers, 1889	.373
13	Dave Orr, 1890	.373
14	Sam Thompson, 1887	.372
15	Tommy Tucker, 1889	.372

1893-1919

1	Hugh Duffy, 1894	.440
2	Nap Lajoie, 1901	.426
3	Willie Keeler, 1897	.424
4	Ty Cobb, 1911	.420
5	Ed Delahanty, 1899	.410
6	Jesse Burkett, 1896	.410
7	Jesse Burkett, 1895	.409
8	Ty Cobb, 1912	.409
9	Joe Jackson, 1911	.408
10	Sam Thompson, 1894	.407
11	Ed Delahanty, 1894	.407
12	Billy Hamilton, 1894	.404
13	Ed Delahanty, 1895	.404
14	Hughie Jennings, 1896	.401
15	Ed Delahanty, 1896	.397

1920-1941

1	Rogers Hornsby, 1924	.424
2	George Sisler, 1922	.420
3	George Sisler, 1920	.407
4	Ted Williams, 1941	.406
5	Rogers Hornsby, 1925	.403
6	Harry Heilmann, 1923	.403
7	Rogers Hornsby, 1922	.401
8	Bill Terry, 1930	.401
9	Ty Cobb, 1922	.401
10	Lefty O'Doul, 1929	.398
11	Harry Heilmann, 1927	.398
12	Rogers Hornsby, 1921	.397
13	Harry Heilmann, 1921	.394
14	Babe Ruth, 1923	.393
15	Harry Heilmann, 1925	.393

1942-1960

1	Ted Williams, 1957	.388
2	Stan Musial, 1948	.376
3	Ted Williams, 1948	.369
4	Stan Musial, 1946	.365
5	Mickey Mantle, 1957	.365
6	Harry Walker, 1947	.363
7	Dixie Walker, 1944	.357
8	Stan Musial, 1943	.357
9	Ted Williams, 1942	.356
10	Phil Cavarretta, 1945	.355
11	Lou Boudreau, 1948	.355
12	Stan Musial, 1951	.355
13	Hank Aaron, 1959	.355
14	Billy Goodman, 1950	.354
15	Harvey Kuenn, 1959	.353

1961-1976

1	Rico Carty, 1970	.366
2	Rod Carew, 1974	.364
3	Joe Torre, 1971	.363
4	Norm Cash, 1961	.361
5	Rod Carew, 1975	.359
6	Roberto Clemente, 1967	.357
7	Bill Madlock, 1975	.354
8	Ralph Garr, 1974	.353
9	Roberto Clemente, 1961	.351
10	Rod Carew, 1973	.350
11	Pete Rose, 1969	.348
12	Tommy Davis, 1962	.346
13	Roberto Clemente, 1969	.345
14	Ralph Garr, 1971	.343
15	Vada Pinson, 1961	.343

1977-1994

1	Tony Gwynn, 1994	.394
2	George Brett, 1980	.390
3	Rod Carew, 1977	.388
4	Andres Galarraga, 1993	.370
5	Tony Gwynn, 1987	.370
6	Wade Boggs, 1985	.368
7	Jeff Bagwell, 1994	.368
8	Wade Boggs, 1988	.366
9	Wade Boggs, 1987	.363
10	John Olerud, 1993	.363
11	Wade Boggs, 1983	.361
12	Paul O'Neill, 1994	.359
13	Tony Gwynn, 1993	.358
14	Wade Boggs, 1986	.357
15	Albert Belle, 1994	.357

Batting Average (by position)

First Base

1	George Sisler, 1922	.420
2	George Sisler, 1920	.407
3	Bill Terry, 1930	.401
4	Cap Anson, 1881	.399
5	Rod Carew, 1977	.388
6	Lou Gehrig, 1930	.379
7	Dan Brouthers, 1883	.374
8	Lou Gehrig, 1928	.374
9	Lou Gehrig, 1927	.373
10	Dan Brouthers, 1889	.373

Second Base

1	Ross Barnes, 1876	.429
2	Nap Lajoie, 1901	.426
3	Rogers Hornsby, 1924	.424
4	Fred Dunlap, 1884	.412
5	Rogers Hornsby, 1925	.403
6	Rogers Hornsby, 1922	.401
7	Rogers Hornsby, 1921	.397
8	Rogers Hornsby, 1928	.387
9	Nap Lajoie, 1910	.384
10	Rogers Hornsby, 1929	.380

Shortstop

1	Hughie Jennings, 1896	.401
2	Luke Appling, 1936	.388
3	Hughie Jennings, 1895	.386
4	Arky Vaughan, 1935	.385
5	Honus Wagner, 1905	.363
6	Hughie Jennings, 1897	.355
7	Honus Wagner, 1903	.355
8	Honus Wagner, 1908	.354
9	Honus Wagner, 1907	.350
10	Honus Wagner, 1904	.349

Third Base

1	John McGraw, 1899	.391
2	George Brett, 1980	.390
3	Lave Cross, 1894	.386
4	Freddy Lindstrom, 1930	.379
5	Heinie Zimmerman, 1912	.372
6	John McGraw, 1895	.369
7	Wade Boggs, 1985	.368
8	Denny Lyons, 1887	.367
9	Wade Boggs, 1988	.366
10	Pie Traynor, 1930	.366

Outfield

1	Hugh Duffy, 1894	.440
2	Tip O'Neill, 1887	.435
3	Willie Keeler, 1897	.424
4	Ty Cobb, 1911	.420
5	Ty Cobb, 1912	.410
6	Ed Delahanty, 1899	.410
7	Jesse Burkett, 1896	.410
8	Jesse Burkett, 1895	.409
9	Joe Jackson, 1911	.408
10	Sam Thompson, 1894	.407
11	Ed Delahanty, 1894	.407
12	Ted Williams, 1941	.406
13	Billy Hamilton, 1894	.404
14	Ed Delahanty, 1895	.404
15	Harry Heilmann, 1923	.403
16	Pete Browning, 1887	.402
17	Ty Cobb, 1922	.401
18	Lefty O'Doul, 1929	.399
19	Harry Heilmann, 1927	.398
20	Ed Delahanty, 1896	.397

Catcher

1	Cal McVey, 1877	.368
2	Mickey Cochrane, 1930	.357
3	Wilbert Robinson, 1894	.353
4	Spud Davis, 1933	.349
5	Mickey Cochrane, 1931	.349
6	Ernie Lombardi, 1938	.342
7	Gabby Hartnett, 1930	.339
8	Mickey Cochrane, 1927	.338
9	Ted Simmons, 1975	.332
10	Bill Dickey, 1937	.332

Relative Batting Average

1	Ross Barnes, 1876	1.608
2	Tip O'Neill, 1887	1.564
3	Nap Lajoie, 1910	1.537
4	Ty Cobb, 1910	1.534
5	Pete Browning, 1882	1.526
6	Cap Anson, 1881	1.512
7	King Kelly, 1886	1.508
8	Roger Connor, 1885	1.506
9	Tris Speaker, 1916	1.506
10	Ty Cobb, 1917	1.501
11	Ty Cobb, 1912	1.501
12	Nap Lajoie, 1901	1.501
13	Nap Lajoie, 1904	1.499
14	Ty Cobb, 1911	1.493
15	Ty Cobb, 1909	1.492
16	Ted Williams, 1957	1.476
17	Ty Cobb, 1913	1.475
18	Ted Williams, 1941	1.472
19	Ty Cobb, 1918	1.469
20	George Gore, 1880	1.462
21	Rogers Hornsby, 1924	1.461
22	Rod Carew, 1977	1.458
23	Dan Brouthers, 1885	1.455
24	Joe Jackson, 1911	1.452
25	Joe Jackson, 1912	1.451
26	Dan Brouthers, 1882	1.449
27	Dave Orr, 1884	1.448
28	George Brett, 1980	1.448
29	Ty Cobb, 1915	1.448
30	Pete Browning, 1887	1.446
31	Ty Cobb, 1916	1.445
32	Cap Anson, 1886	1.442
33	Pete Browning, 1885	1.439
34	Dan Brouthers, 1886	1.439
35	Tony Gwynn, 1994	1.436
36	Honus Wagner, 1908	1.434
37	George Sisler, 1922	1.433
38	Cap Anson, 1882	1.428
39	Cy Seymour, 1905	1.425
40	Willie Keeler, 1897	1.422
41	Ed Delahanty, 1899	1.414
42	Wade Boggs, 1988	1.413
43	King Kelly, 1884	1.411
44	Joe Jackson, 1913	1.411
45	Rod Carew, 1974	1.408
46	Wade Boggs, 1985	1.407
47	Tris Speaker, 1912	1.406
48	Deacon White, 1877	1.405
49	Dan Brouthers, 1883	1.402
50	Jimmy Wolf, 1890	1.401
51	Stan Musial, 1948	1.400
52	George Stone, 1906	1.400
53	Cap Anson, 1888	1.399
54	George Sisler, 1920	1.398
55	Joe Torre, 1971	1.397
56	Hugh Duffy, 1894	1.395
57	Stan Musial, 1946	1.393
58	Ed Swartwood, 1883	1.392
59	Ty Cobb, 1919	1.392
60	Rod Carew, 1975	1.391
61	Tommy Tucker, 1889	1.391
62	Nap Lajoie, 1906	1.390
63	John Reilly, 1884	1.389
64	Harry Heilmann, 1923	1.389
65	Mickey Mantle, 1957	1.388
66	Willie Keeler, 1898	1.387
67	Honus Wagner, 1907	1.387
68	Roberto Clemente, 1967	1.385
69	George Sisler, 1917	1.383
70	Jim O'Rourke, 1884	1.383
71	Pete Browning, 1886	1.382
72	Tris Speaker, 1917	1.380
73	Ezra Sutton, 1884	1.380
74	Ty Cobb, 1907	1.379
75	Hick Carpenter, 1882	1.379
76	Roger Connor, 1886	1.378
77	Jesse Burkett, 1896	1.378
78	Paul Hines, 1879	1.377
79	Tony Gwynn, 1987	1.375
80	Pete Browning, 1884	1.374
81	Tris Speaker, 1913	1.374
82	Kirby Puckett, 1988	1.374
83	John Cassidy, 1877	1.373
84	Honus Wagner, 1905	1.372
85	Dave Orr, 1886	1.372
86	Rico Carty, 1970	1.372
87	George Hall, 1876	1.372
88	Eddie Collins, 1909	1.370
89	Tip O'Neill, 1888	1.370
90	Wade Boggs, 1987	1.370
91	Ty Cobb, 1922	1.370
92	Dan Brouthers, 1889	1.370
93	Cap Anson, 1880	1.368
94	Norm Cash, 1961	1.368
95	Jesse Burkett, 1895	1.367
96	Andres Galarraga, 1993	1.366
97	Jesse Burkett, 1901	1.365
98	Hardy Richardson, 1886	1.365
99	Willie Keeler, 1904	1.365
100	Wade Boggs, 1986	1.365

On Base Percentage

1	Ted Williams, 1941	.551
2	John McGraw, 1899	.547
3	Babe Ruth, 1923	.545
4	Babe Ruth, 1920	.530
5	Ted Williams, 1957	.528
6	Billy Hamilton, 1894	.523
7	Ted Williams, 1954	.516
8	Babe Ruth, 1926	.516
9	Mickey Mantle, 1957	.515
10	Babe Ruth, 1924	.513
11	Babe Ruth, 1921	.512
12	Rogers Hornsby, 1924	.507
13	John McGraw, 1900	.505
14	Joe Kelley, 1894	.502
15	Hugh Duffy, 1894	.502
16	Ed Delahanty, 1895	.500
17	Ted Williams, 1942	.499
18	Ted Williams, 1947	.499
19	Rogers Hornsby, 1928	.498
20	Ted Williams, 1946	.497
21	Ted Williams, 1948	.497
22	Bill Joyce, 1894	.496
23	Babe Ruth, 1931	.495
24	Frank Thomas, 1994	.494
25	Babe Ruth, 1930	.493
26	Arky Vaughan, 1935	.491
27	Ted Williams, 1949	.490
28	Billy Hamilton, 1895	.490
29	Billy Hamilton, 1893	.490
30	Tip O'Neill, 1887	.490
31	Rogers Hornsby, 1925	.489
	Babe Ruth, 1932	.489
33	Norm Cash, 1961	.488
34	Mickey Mantle, 1962	.488
35	Babe Ruth, 1927	.487
36	Ty Cobb, 1915	.486
37	Jesse Burkett, 1895	.486
38	Tris Speaker, 1920	.483
39	King Kelly, 1886	.483
40	Harry Heilmann, 1923	.481
41	Wade Boggs, 1988	.480
42	Billy Hamilton, 1898	.480
43	Tris Speaker, 1925	.479
	Ted Williams, 1956	.479
45	Ed Delahanty, 1894	.478
46	John Olerud, 1993	.478
47	Lou Gehrig, 1936	.478
48	Billy Hamilton, 1896	.477
49	Cupid Childs, 1894	.475
50	John McGraw, 1898	.475
51	Harry Heilmann, 1927	.475
52	Tris Speaker, 1922	.474
53	Lou Gehrig, 1927	.474
54	Luke Appling, 1936	.474
55	Lou Gehrig, 1930	.473
56	Lou Gehrig, 1937	.473
57	Hughie Jennings, 1896	.472
58	Ed Delahanty, 1896	.472
59	John McGraw, 1897	.471
60	Joe Morgan, 1975	.471
61	Dan Brouthers, 1891	.471
62	Tris Speaker, 1916	.470
63	Bill Joyce, 1896	.470
64	Joe Kelley, 1896	.469
65	Tris Speaker, 1923	.469
66	Jimmie Foxx, 1932	.469
67	Jesse Burkett, 1897	.468
68	Ty Cobb, 1925	.468
69	Joe Jackson, 1911	.468
70	Lou Gehrig, 1928	.467
71	Ty Cobb, 1913	.467
72	George Sisler, 1922	.467
73	Mike Griffin, 1894	.467
74	Cupid Childs, 1896	.467
75	Mickey Mantle, 1956	.467
76	Wade Boggs, 1987	.467
77	Ty Cobb, 1911	.467
78	Dan Brouthers, 1890	.466
79	Lou Gehrig, 1935	.466
80	Lou Gehrig, 1934	.465
81	Lefty O'Doul, 1929	.465
82	Jimmie Foxx, 1939	.464
83	Tris Speaker, 1912	.464
84	Ed Delahanty, 1899	.464
85	Pete Browning, 1887	.464
86	Ted Williams, 1951	.464
87	Willie Keeler, 1897	.464
88	Paul O'Neill, 1994	.464
89	Bob Caruthers, 1887	.463
90	Barry Bonds, 1993	.463
91	Cupid Childs, 1893	.463
92	Jimmie Foxx, 1929	.463
93	Hughie Jennings, 1897	.463
94	Nap Lajoie, 1901	.463
95	Jesse Burkett, 1899	.463
96	Ross Barnes, 1876	.462
	Jimmie Foxx, 1938	.462
	Ted Williams, 1958	.462
99	Dan Brouthers, 1889	.462
100	Fred Clarke, 1897	.462

Slugging Average

1	Babe Ruth, 1920	.847
2	Babe Ruth, 1921	.846
3	Babe Ruth, 1927	.772
4	Lou Gehrig, 1927	.765
5	Babe Ruth, 1923	.764
6	Rogers Hornsby, 1925	.756
7	Jeff Bagwell, 1994	.750
8	Jimmie Foxx, 1932	.749
9	Babe Ruth, 1924	.739
10	Babe Ruth, 1926	.737
11	Ted Williams, 1941	.735
12	Babe Ruth, 1930	.732
13	Ted Williams, 1957	.731
14	Frank Thomas, 1994	.729
15	Hack Wilson, 1930	.723
16	Rogers Hornsby, 1922	.722
17	Lou Gehrig, 1930	.721
18	Albert Belle, 1994	.714
19	Babe Ruth, 1928	.709
20	Al Simmons, 1930	.708
21	Lou Gehrig, 1934	.706
22	Mickey Mantle, 1956	.705
23	Jimmie Foxx, 1938	.704
24	Jimmie Foxx, 1933	.703
25	Stan Musial, 1948	.702
26	Babe Ruth, 1931	.700
27	Babe Ruth, 1929	.697
28	Lou Gehrig, 1936	.696
29	Rogers Hornsby, 1924	.696
30	Hugh Duffy, 1894	.694
31	Jimmie Foxx, 1939	.694
32	Tip O'Neill, 1887	.691
33	Mickey Mantle, 1961	.687
34	Chuck Klein, 1930	.687
35	Sam Thompson, 1894	.686
36	Hank Greenberg, 1938	.683
37	Kevin Mitchell, 1994	.681
38	Rogers Hornsby, 1929	.679
39	Babe Herman, 1930	.678
40	Barry Bonds, 1993	.677
41	Ken Griffey, 1994	.674
42	Joe DiMaggio, 1937	.673
43	Babe Ruth, 1922	.672
44	Joe DiMaggio, 1939	.671
45	Hank Greenberg, 1940	.670
46	Hank Aaron, 1971	.669
47	Hank Greenberg, 1937	.668
48	Ted Williams, 1946	.667
49	Willie Mays, 1954	.667
50	Mickey Mantle, 1957	.665
51	George Brett, 1980	.664
52	Lou Gehrig, 1931	.662
53	Norm Cash, 1961	.662
54	Babe Ruth, 1932	.661
55	Willie Mays, 1955	.659
56	Ralph Kiner, 1949	.658
57	Chuck Klein, 1929	.657
58	Babe Ruth, 1919	.657
59	Willie McCovey, 1969	.656
60	Sam Thompson, 1895	.654
61	Jimmie Foxx, 1934	.653
62	Chick Hafey, 1930	.652
63	Ted Williams, 1949	.650
64	Bill Joyce, 1894	.648
65	Lou Gehrig, 1928	.648
66	Ted Williams, 1942	.648
67	Duke Snider, 1954	.647
68	Barry Bonds, 1994	.647
69	Chuck Klein, 1932	.646
70	Jim Gentile, 1961	.646
71	Willie Stargell, 1973	.646
72	Willie Mays, 1965	.645
73	Mike Schmidt, 1981	.644
74	Hal Trosky, 1936	.644
75	Nap Lajoie, 1901	.643
76	Joe DiMaggio, 1941	.643
77	Lou Gehrig, 1937	.643
78	Ted Kluszewski, 1954	.642
79	Al Simmons, 1929	.642
80	Joe Medwick, 1937	.641
81	Al Simmons, 1931	.641
82	Ralph Kiner, 1947	.639
83	Rogers Hornsby, 1921	.639
84	Frank Robinson, 1966	.637
85	Jimmie Foxx, 1930	.637
86	Fred Lynn, 1979	.637
87	Hank Aaron, 1959	.636
88	Johnny Mize, 1940	.636
89	Jimmie Foxx, 1935	.636
90	Kevin Mitchell, 1989	.635
91	Mel Ott, 1929	.635
92	Ted Williams, 1954	.635
93	Ted Williams, 1947	.634
94	Chick Hafey, 1929	.632
95	Juan Gonzalez, 1993	.632
96	George Sisler, 1920	.632
97	Rogers Hornsby, 1928	.632
98	Harry Heilmann, 1923	.632
	Dick Allen, 1966	.632
100	Ed Delahanty, 1896	.631

Production

	Player, Year	
1	Babe Ruth, 1920	1.378
2	Babe Ruth, 1921	1.358
3	Babe Ruth, 1923	1.309
4	Ted Williams, 1941	1.286
5	Babe Ruth, 1927	1.259
6	Ted Williams, 1957	1.259
7	Babe Ruth, 1926	1.253
8	Babe Ruth, 1924	1.252
9	Rogers Hornsby, 1925	1.245
10	Lou Gehrig, 1927	1.240
11	Babe Ruth, 1930	1.225
12	Frank Thomas, 1994	1.223
13	Jimmie Foxx, 1932	1.218
14	Jeff Bagwell, 1994	1.211
15	Rogers Hornsby, 1924	1.203
16	Hugh Duffy, 1894	1.196
17	Babe Ruth, 1931	1.195
18	Lou Gehrig, 1930	1.194
19	Rogers Hornsby, 1922	1.181
20	Tip O'Neill, 1887	1.180
21	Mickey Mantle, 1957	1.179
22	Hack Wilson, 1930	1.177
23	Lou Gehrig, 1936	1.174
24	Mickey Mantle, 1956	1.172
25	Lou Gehrig, 1934	1.172
26	Babe Ruth, 1928	1.170
27	Jimmie Foxx, 1938	1.166
28	Ted Williams, 1946	1.164
29	Jimmie Foxx, 1939	1.158
30	Albert Belle, 1994	1.156
31	Jimmie Foxx, 1933	1.153
32	Stan Musial, 1948	1.152
33	Ted Williams, 1954	1.151
34	Babe Ruth, 1932	1.150
35	Norm Cash, 1961	1.150
36	Ted Williams, 1942	1.147
37	Sam Thompson, 1894	1.145
38	Bill Joyce, 1894	1.143
39	Ted Williams, 1949	1.141
40	Barry Bonds, 1993	1.140
41	Rogers Hornsby, 1929	1.139
42	Mickey Mantle, 1961	1.138
43	Ted Williams, 1947	1.133
44	Babe Herman, 1930	1.132
45	Al Simmons, 1930	1.130
46	Rogers Hornsby, 1928	1.130
47	Babe Ruth, 1929	1.128
48	George Brett, 1980	1.124
49	Chuck Klein, 1930	1.123
50	Hank Greenberg, 1938	1.122
51	Joe DiMaggio, 1939	1.119
52	Kevin Mitchell, 1994	1.119
53	Ed Delahanty, 1895	1.117
54	Lou Gehrig, 1937	1.116
55	Lou Gehrig, 1928	1.115
56	Babe Ruth, 1919	1.114
57	Willie McCovey, 1969	1.114
58	Harry Heilmann, 1923	1.113
59	Ted Williams, 1948	1.112
60	Lou Gehrig, 1931	1.108
61	Nap Lajoie, 1901	1.106
62	Babe Ruth, 1922	1.106
63	Hank Greenberg, 1937	1.105
64	Joe Kelley, 1894	1.104
65	Hank Greenberg, 1940	1.103
66	Ed Delahanty, 1896	1.103
67	Jimmie Foxx, 1934	1.102
68	Arky Vaughan, 1935	1.098
69	Rogers Hornsby, 1921	1.097
70	Jimmie Foxx, 1935	1.096
71	Mickey Mantle, 1962	1.093
72	Harry Heilmann, 1927	1.091
73	Ralph Kiner, 1949	1.089
74	Jimmie Foxx, 1929	1.088
75	Ty Cobb, 1911	1.088
76	Lefty O'Doul, 1929	1.087
77	Rogers Hornsby, 1923	1.086
78	Al Simmons, 1931	1.085
79	Barry Bonds, 1992	1.085
80	Joe DiMaggio, 1937	1.085
81	Sam Thompson, 1895	1.085
82	Ted Williams, 1956	1.084
83	Mel Ott, 1929	1.084
84	Joe DiMaggio, 1941	1.083
85	Willie Mays, 1954	1.083
86	Mike Schmidt, 1981	1.083
87	Hank Aaron, 1971	1.082
88	George Sisler, 1920	1.082
89	Tris Speaker, 1922	1.080
90	Ralph Kiner, 1951	1.079
91	Tris Speaker, 1923	1.079
92	Ken Griffey, 1994	1.078
93	John Olerud, 1993	1.077
94	Barry Bonds, 1994	1.076
95	Jim Gentile, 1961	1.074
96	Duke Snider, 1954	1.074
97	Lou Gehrig, 1932	1.072
98	Bill Terry, 1930	1.071
99	Jimmie Foxx, 1936	1.071
100	Johnny Mize, 1939	1.070

Adjusted Production

	Player, Year	
1	Babe Ruth, 1920	252
2	Babe Ruth, 1923	238
3	Babe Ruth, 1921	236
4	Ted Williams, 1941	232
5	Babe Ruth, 1927	229
6	Pete Browning, 1882	229
7	Babe Ruth, 1926	228
8	Ted Williams, 1957	227
9	Lou Gehrig, 1927	224
10	Babe Ruth, 1919	224
11	Babe Ruth, 1931	223
12	Mickey Mantle, 1957	223
13	Rogers Hornsby, 1924	223
14	Ross Barnes, 1876	222
15	Babe Ruth, 1924	221
16	Babe Ruth, 1930	216
17	Ted Williams, 1942	214
18	Jeff Bagwell, 1994	213
19	Lou Gehrig, 1934	213
20	Mickey Mantle, 1956	213
21	Willie McCovey, 1969	212
22	Frank Thomas, 1994	212
23	Ted Williams, 1946	211
24	Mickey Mantle, 1961	210
25	Babe Ruth, 1928	210
26	Rogers Hornsby, 1922	210
27	Ty Cobb, 1917	210
28	George Hall, 1876	208
29	Rogers Hornsby, 1925	208
30	Lou Gehrig, 1930	207
31	Barry Bonds, 1993	207
32	Barry Bonds, 1992	207
33	Babe Ruth, 1932	206
34	Nap Lajoie, 1904	205
35	Tip O'Neill, 1887	205
36	Honus Wagner, 1908	205
37	Rogers Hornsby, 1928	204
38	Dan Brouthers, 1886	204
39	Ty Cobb, 1912	203
40	Jimmie Foxx, 1932	203
41	Roger Connor, 1885	203
42	George Brett, 1980	203
43	Ty Cobb, 1910	202
44	Frank Robinson, 1966	200
45	Jimmie Foxx, 1933	199
46	Ted Williams, 1947	199
47	Lou Gehrig, 1931	199
48	Dan Brouthers, 1885	199
49	Babe Ruth, 1929	199
50	Dick Allen, 1972	199
51	Norm Cash, 1961	198
52	Mickey Mantle, 1962	198
53	Dan Brouthers, 1882	198
54	Nap Lajoie, 1910	198
55	Dave Orr, 1885	197
56	Ed Swartwood, 1882	197
57	Lou Gehrig, 1928	197
58	Stan Musial, 1948	196
59	Ty Cobb, 1918	196
60	Ty Cobb, 1913	196
61	Nap Lajoie, 1901	196
62	Orator Shaffer, 1878	196
63	Mike Schmidt, 1981	195
64	George Stone, 1906	195
65	Dave Orr, 1884	195
66	Harry Heilmann, 1923	195
67	Kevin Mitchell, 1989	194
68	Lou Gehrig, 1936	193
69	Ed Delahanty, 1899	193
70	Ty Cobb, 1911	193
71	Ted Williams, 1954	193
72	Joe Jackson, 1911	192
73	Ed Delahanty, 1896	192
74	Rogers Hornsby, 1921	191
75	Ty Cobb, 1909	190
76	Joe Jackson, 1913	190
77	Rickey Henderson, 1990	190
78	Pete Browning, 1885	190
79	Hank Aaron, 1971	190
80	Reggie Jackson, 1969	190
81	Deacon White, 1877	190
82	Joe Jackson, 1912	190
83	Rogers Hornsby, 1920	190
84	Cap Anson, 1881	189
85	Jim Gentile, 1961	189
86	Cupid Childs, 1890	189
87	Carl Yastrzemski, 1967	189
88	Mickey Mantle, 1958	189
89	Frank Robinson, 1967	189
90	Willie Stargell, 1973	189
91	Willie Stargell, 1971	189
92	King Kelly, 1879	188
93	Jimmie Foxx, 1934	188
94	Hank Aaron, 1959	188
95	Roger Connor, 1882	188
96	Rogers Hornsby, 1923	188
97	Kevin Mitchell, 1994	187
98	Arky Vaughan, 1935	187
99	Ed Swartwood, 1883	187
100	Ted Williams, 1949	187

Batting Runs

	Player, Year	
1	Babe Ruth, 1921	119
2	Babe Ruth, 1923	119
3	Babe Ruth, 1920	113
4	Ted Williams, 1941	102
5	Lou Gehrig, 1927	101
6	Babe Ruth, 1924	101
7	Babe Ruth, 1927	101
8	Babe Ruth, 1926	97
9	Jimmie Foxx, 1932	97
10	Ted Williams, 1946	94
11	Rogers Hornsby, 1924	94
12	Ted Williams, 1942	93
13	Babe Ruth, 1931	92
14	Ted Williams, 1947	91
15	Stan Musial, 1948	90
16	Rogers Hornsby, 1922	90
17	Ted Williams, 1957	90
18	Babe Ruth, 1930	90
19	Mickey Mantle, 1957	89
20	Ted Williams, 1949	89
21	Lou Gehrig, 1930	88
22	Rogers Hornsby, 1925	87
23	Tip O'Neill, 1887	86
24	Norm Cash, 1961	86
25	Lou Gehrig, 1934	86
26	Babe Ruth, 1928	84
27	Mickey Mantle, 1956	83
28	Jimmie Foxx, 1933	83
29	Lou Gehrig, 1936	82
30	Barry Bonds, 1993	82
31	Lou Gehrig, 1931	80
32	Ty Cobb, 1911	78
33	Jimmie Foxx, 1938	78
34	Carl Yastrzemski, 1967	76
35	Mickey Mantle, 1961	76
36	Willie McCovey, 1969	76
37	Lou Gehrig, 1928	76
38	Hugh Duffy, 1894	76
39	Ted Williams, 1948	76
40	Hack Wilson, 1930	75
41	Rogers Hornsby, 1921	74
42	Ty Cobb, 1917	74
43	John Olerud, 1993	74
44	Rogers Hornsby, 1929	74
45	Nap Lajoie, 1901	74
46	Frank Robinson, 1966	74
47	Lou Gehrig, 1937	73
48	George Sisler, 1920	73
49	Tris Speaker, 1912	73
50	Rogers Hornsby, 1928	72
51	Stan Musial, 1949	72
52	Arky Vaughan, 1935	72
53	Barry Bonds, 1992	72
54	Joe Jackson, 1911	72
55	Carl Yastrzemski, 1970	72
56	Ty Cobb, 1915	72
57	Frank Thomas, 1994	71
58	Babe Ruth, 1932	71
59	Ted Williams, 1954	71
60	Tris Speaker, 1923	71
61	Stan Musial, 1946	71
62	Ralph Kiner, 1951	71
63	Harry Heilmann, 1923	71
64	Joe Jackson, 1912	70
65	Stan Musial, 1951	70
66	Ralph Kiner, 1949	70
67	Chuck Klein, 1933	69
68	Joe Medwick, 1937	69
69	Hank Greenberg, 1940	69
70	Johnny Mize, 1939	69
71	Babe Herman, 1930	69
72	Lou Gehrig, 1932	69
73	Lefty O'Doul, 1929	69
74	Nap Lajoie, 1910	68
75	Chuck Klein, 1932	68
76	Ty Cobb, 1910	68
77	Ed Delahanty, 1899	68
78	Chuck Klein, 1930	67
79	Jimmie Foxx, 1935	67
80	Hank Greenberg, 1937	67
81	Ty Cobb, 1912	67
82	Rod Carew, 1977	67
83	Frank Robinson, 1962	67
84	Wade Boggs, 1987	67
85	Babe Ruth, 1919	67
86	Jimmie Foxx, 1934	66
87	Ed Delahanty, 1895	66
88	Jimmie Foxx, 1939	66
89	Dick Allen, 1972	66
90	Hank Greenberg, 1938	66
91	Dan Brouthers, 1886	66
92	Frank Thomas, 1991	66
93	Wade Boggs, 1988	66
94	Tris Speaker, 1920	66
95	Harmon Killebrew, 1969	66
96	Joe Jackson, 1913	66
97	Stan Musial, 1943	66
98	Hank Aaron, 1971	65
99	Honus Wagner, 1908	65
100	George Brett, 1980	65

Adjusted Batting Runs

	Player, Year	
1	Babe Ruth, 1923	116
2	Babe Ruth, 1921	115
3	Lou Gehrig, 1927	107
4	Babe Ruth, 1920	107
5	Babe Ruth, 1927	106
6	Babe Ruth, 1931	102
7	Babe Ruth, 1924	101
8	Babe Ruth, 1926	100
9	Rogers Hornsby, 1922	99
10	Lou Gehrig, 1934	98
11	Babe Ruth, 1930	98
12	Ted Williams, 1941	98
13	Rogers Hornsby, 1924	97
14	Lou Gehrig, 1930	97
15	Mickey Mantle, 1957	91
16	Jimmie Foxx, 1932	90
17	Lou Gehrig, 1931	90
18	Babe Ruth, 1928	89
19	Lou Gehrig, 1936	89
20	Mickey Mantle, 1956	89
21	Barry Bonds, 1993	87
22	Ted Williams, 1942	87
23	Ted Williams, 1946	85
24	Mickey Mantle, 1961	84
25	Rogers Hornsby, 1925	83
26	Norm Cash, 1961	82
27	Ted Williams, 1957	82
28	Lou Gehrig, 1928	81
29	Jimmie Foxx, 1933	81
30	Stan Musial, 1948	81
31	Rogers Hornsby, 1928	80
32	Ted Williams, 1947	79
33	Babe Ruth, 1932	79
34	Willie McCovey, 1969	79
35	Rogers Hornsby, 1921	78
36	Lou Gehrig, 1932	77
37	Ted Williams, 1949	77
38	Frank Robinson, 1966	76
39	Hank Aaron, 1959	75
40	Ty Cobb, 1917	75
41	Hack Wilson, 1930	74
42	Babe Ruth, 1919	74
43	Rogers Hornsby, 1929	74
44	Harry Heilmann, 1923	74
45	John Olerud, 1993	74
46	Ed Delahanty, 1899	73
47	Barry Bonds, 1992	73
48	Frank Thomas, 1994	73
49	Lou Gehrig, 1937	72
50	Jimmie Foxx, 1934	72
51	Ty Cobb, 1912	72
52	Babe Ruth, 1929	71
53	Tris Speaker, 1923	71
54	Babe Herman, 1930	71
55	Ty Cobb, 1915	71
56	Jimmie Foxx, 1938	70
57	Joe Jackson, 1911	70
58	Lou Gehrig, 1935	70
59	Frank Thomas, 1991	69
60	Rod Carew, 1977	69
61	Mickey Mantle, 1958	69
62	Stan Musial, 1951	69
63	Lou Gehrig, 1933	68
64	George Sisler, 1920	68
65	Jimmie Foxx, 1935	68
66	Ted Williams, 1948	68
67	Reggie Jackson, 1969	68
68	Tip O'Neill, 1887	68
69	Rogers Hornsby, 1920	68
70	Jeff Bagwell, 1994	68
71	Nap Lajoie, 1901	67
72	Arky Vaughan, 1935	67
73	Al Rosen, 1953	67
74	Ed Delahanty, 1896	67
75	Ralph Kiner, 1951	67
76	Nap Lajoie, 1910	66
77	Joe DiMaggio, 1941	66
78	Ralph Kiner, 1949	66
79	Joe Medwick, 1937	66
80	Jesse Burkett, 1901	66
81	Kevin Mitchell, 1989	66
82	Ed Delahanty, 1895	66
83	Joe Jackson, 1912	66
84	Frank Thomas, 1993	66
85	Stan Musial, 1949	65
86	Carl Yastrzemski, 1967	65
87	Honus Wagner, 1908	65
88	Tris Speaker, 1912	65
89	Stan Musial, 1946	65
90	Billy Hamilton, 1894	65
91	Hank Aaron, 1963	64
92	Ty Cobb, 1915	64
93	Frank Thomas, 1992	64
94	Frank Howard, 1969	64
95	Eddie Mathews, 1953	64
96	George Brett, 1980	64
97	Jim Gentile, 1961	64
98	Hank Greenberg, 1937	64
99	Dick Allen, 1972	64
100	Willie McCovey, 1970	64

Batting Wins

1	Babe Ruth, 1923	11.5
2	Babe Ruth, 1921	11.1
3	Babe Ruth, 1920	11.0
4	Ted Williams, 1941	9.9
5	Ted Williams, 1946	9.9
6	Lou Gehrig, 1927	9.6
7	Babe Ruth, 1927	9.6
8	Babe Ruth, 1924	9.5
9	Ted Williams, 1942	9.5
10	Ted Williams, 1947	9.4
11	Babe Ruth, 1926	9.4
12	Rogers Hornsby, 1924	9.3
13	Ted Williams, 1957	9.3
14	Mickey Mantle, 1957	9.2
15	Stan Musial, 1948	9.0
16	Jimmie Foxx, 1932	8.9
17	Ted Williams, 1949	8.6
18	Norm Cash, 1961	8.5
19	Babe Ruth, 1931	8.5
20	Rogers Hornsby, 1922	8.5
21	Carl Yastrzemski, 1967	8.4
22	Ty Cobb, 1917	8.3
23	Barry Bonds, 1993	8.2
24	Rogers Hornsby, 1925	8.2
25	Mickey Mantle, 1956	8.2
26	Babe Ruth, 1928	8.1
27	Babe Ruth, 1930	8.1
28	Lou Gehrig, 1930	8.0
29	Willie McCovey, 1969	8.0
30	Lou Gehrig, 1934	8.0
31	Frank Robinson, 1966	7.9
32	Jimmie Foxx, 1933	7.8
33	Barry Bonds, 1992	7.7
34	Ty Cobb, 1911	7.7
35	Ty Cobb, 1915	7.6
36	Nap Lajoie, 1910	7.6
37	Mickey Mantle, 1961	7.6
38	Honus Wagner, 1908	7.5
39	Ty Cobb, 1910	7.5
40	Stan Musial, 1946	7.5
41	Dick Allen, 1972	7.5
42	Carl Yastrzemski, 1970	7.4
43	Lou Gehrig, 1931	7.4
44	Rogers Hornsby, 1921	7.3
45	Lou Gehrig, 1928	7.3
46	Ted Williams, 1948	7.3
47	Ted Williams, 1954	7.3
48	Chuck Klein, 1933	7.3
49	Tris Speaker, 1912	7.3
50	Lou Gehrig, 1936	7.3
51	John Olerud, 1993	7.2
52	Ty Cobb, 1909	7.2
53	Stan Musial, 1949	7.2
54	Tris Speaker, 1916	7.1
55	Ralph Kiner, 1951	7.1
56	George Sisler, 1920	7.1
57	Rogers Hornsby, 1928	7.1
58	Jimmie Foxx, 1938	7.1
59	Joe Jackson, 1911	7.1
60	Joe Jackson, 1912	7.0
61	Stan Musial, 1951	7.0
62	Tip O'Neill, 1887	7.0
63	Hank Aaron, 1971	7.0
64	Stan Musial, 1943	7.0
65	Arky Vaughan, 1935	7.0
66	Nap Lajoie, 1904	7.0
67	Joe Jackson, 1913	7.0
68	Babe Ruth, 1919	7.0
69	Ralph Kiner, 1949	6.9
70	Harmon Killebrew, 1967	6.9
71	Harmon Killebrew, 1969	6.9
72	Johnny Mize, 1939	6.9
73	Tris Speaker, 1923	6.9
74	Willie Mays, 1965	6.8
75	Harry Heilmann, 1923	6.8
76	Hank Aaron, 1963	6.8
77	Joe Medwick, 1937	6.8
78	Chuck Klein, 1932	6.7
79	Rogers Hornsby, 1929	6.7
80	Lou Gehrig, 1937	6.7
81	Cy Seymour, 1905	6.7
82	Ty Cobb, 1912	6.7
83	Rogers Hornsby, 1920	6.7
84	Joe Torre, 1971	6.7
85	Nap Lajoie, 1901	6.7
86	Hack Wilson, 1930	6.7
87	Rod Carew, 1977	6.7
88	Wade Boggs, 1988	6.7
89	Frank Robinson, 1962	6.6
90	Kevin Mitchell, 1989	6.6
91	Mickey Mantle, 1958	6.6
92	Carl Yastrzemski, 1968	6.6
93	Frank Thomas, 1991	6.6
94	Frank Thomas, 1994	6.6
95	Babe Ruth, 1932	6.6
96	Billy Williams, 1972	6.6
97	Joe Morgan, 1976	6.5
98	Reggie Jackson, 1969	6.5
99	Hank Greenberg, 1940	6.5
100	Johnny Mize, 1940	6.5

Adjusted Batting Wins

1	Babe Ruth, 1923	11.2
2	Babe Ruth, 1921	10.7
3	Babe Ruth, 1920	10.3
4	Lou Gehrig, 1927	10.1
5	Babe Ruth, 1927	10.1
6	Babe Ruth, 1926	9.7
7	Rogers Hornsby, 1924	9.6
8	Babe Ruth, 1924	9.5
9	Ted Williams, 1941	9.5
10	Babe Ruth, 1931	9.5
11	Mickey Mantle, 1957	9.4
12	Rogers Hornsby, 1922	9.3
13	Lou Gehrig, 1934	9.1
14	Ted Williams, 1946	8.9
15	Ted Williams, 1942	8.9
16	Babe Ruth, 1930	8.9
17	Lou Gehrig, 1930	8.8
18	Barry Bonds, 1993	8.7
19	Mickey Mantle, 1956	8.7
20	Babe Ruth, 1928	8.6
21	Ted Williams, 1957	8.4
22	Lou Gehrig, 1931	8.4
23	Mickey Mantle, 1961	8.4
24	Ty Cobb, 1917	8.3
25	Jimmie Foxx, 1932	8.3
26	Willie McCovey, 1969	8.3
27	Ted Williams, 1947	8.2
28	Frank Robinson, 1966	8.2
29	Norm Cash, 1961	8.1
30	Stan Musial, 1948	8.1
31	Barry Bonds, 1992	7.9
32	Rogers Hornsby, 1928	7.8
33	Lou Gehrig, 1928	7.8
34	Lou Gehrig, 1936	7.8
35	Rogers Hornsby, 1925	7.8
36	Babe Ruth, 1919	7.7
37	Rogers Hornsby, 1921	7.7
38	Jimmie Foxx, 1933	7.7
39	Hank Aaron, 1959	7.6
40	Honus Wagner, 1908	7.5
41	Ted Williams, 1949	7.5
42	Nap Lajoie, 1910	7.4
43	Babe Ruth, 1932	7.3
44	Rogers Hornsby, 1920	7.2
45	Dick Allen, 1972	7.2
46	Carl Yastrzemski, 1967	7.2
47	Ty Cobb, 1912	7.2
48	John Olerud, 1993	7.2
49	Mickey Mantle, 1958	7.2
50	Lou Gehrig, 1932	7.1
51	Harry Heilmann, 1923	7.1
52	Reggie Jackson, 1969	7.1
53	Nap Lajoie, 1904	7.1
54	Kevin Mitchell, 1989	7.0
55	Hank Aaron, 1963	7.0
56	Frank Thomas, 1991	7.0
57	George Stone, 1906	6.9
58	Ty Cobb, 1911	6.9
59	Stan Musial, 1951	6.9
60	Joe Jackson, 1911	6.9
61	Tris Speaker, 1923	6.9
62	Stan Musial, 1946	6.9
63	Rod Carew, 1977	6.9
64	Ty Cobb, 1915	6.8
65	Al Rosen, 1953	6.7
66	Babe Ruth, 1929	6.7
67	Rogers Hornsby, 1929	6.7
68	Frank Thomas, 1994	6.7
69	Jimmie Foxx, 1934	6.7
70	Frank Howard, 1969	6.7
71	Ralph Kiner, 1951	6.7
72	Ed Delahanty, 1899	6.7
73	Jeff Bagwell, 1994	6.6
74	Lou Gehrig, 1937	6.6
75	George Sisler, 1920	6.6
76	Ty Cobb, 1910	6.6
77	Ted Williams, 1948	6.6
78	Joe Jackson, 1912	6.6
79	Bobby Murcer, 1971	6.6
80	Joe Jackson, 1913	6.6
81	Ty Cobb, 1909	6.6
82	Harmon Killebrew, 1969	6.6
83	Lou Gehrig, 1935	6.6
84	Ralph Kiner, 1949	6.6
85	Hack Wilson, 1930	6.5
86	Frank Thomas, 1992	6.5
87	Arky Vaughan, 1935	6.5
88	Joe Medwick, 1937	6.5
89	Tris Speaker, 1912	6.5
90	Lou Gehrig, 1933	6.5
91	Stan Musial, 1949	6.5
92	Willie Mays, 1965	6.5
93	Jesse Burkett, 1901	6.5
94	Joe DiMaggio, 1941	6.4
95	Jimmie Foxx, 1935	6.4
96	Carl Yastrzemski, 1970	6.4
97	Rickey Henderson, 1990	6.4
98	Frank Thomas, 1993	6.4
99	George Brett, 1980	6.4
100	Jimmie Foxx, 1938	6.4

Runs Created

1	Babe Ruth, 1921	238
2	Babe Ruth, 1923	223
3	Hugh Duffy, 1894	217
4	Lou Gehrig, 1927	212
5	Babe Ruth, 1920	211
6	Babe Ruth, 1927	208
7	Jimmie Foxx, 1932	207
8	Billy Hamilton, 1894	207
9	Ty Cobb, 1911	207
10	Babe Ruth, 1924	205
11	Ted Williams, 1941	202
12	Rogers Hornsby, 1922	200
13	Lou Gehrig, 1936	199
14	Babe Ruth, 1926	196
15	Lou Gehrig, 1930	195
16	Lou Gehrig, 1934	195
17	Tip O'Neill, 1887	194
18	Ted Williams, 1949	193
19	Babe Ruth, 1931	192
20	Babe Ruth, 1930	191
21	Pete Browning, 1887	191
22	Stan Musial, 1948	191
23	Hack Wilson, 1930	189
24	Jimmie Foxx, 1938	189
25	Ted Williams, 1946	188
26	Mickey Mantle, 1956	188
27	Rogers Hornsby, 1925	187
28	Ted Williams, 1947	186
29	Rogers Hornsby, 1924	186
30	Chuck Klein, 1930	186
31	Lou Gehrig, 1931	185
32	Ted Williams, 1942	185
33	Jimmie Foxx, 1933	184
34	Rogers Hornsby, 1929	183
35	Babe Herman, 1930	183
36	Joe Kelley, 1894	182
37	Babe Ruth, 1928	182
38	Lou Gehrig, 1937	181
39	Lefty O'Doul, 1929	180
40	Nap Lajoie, 1901	179
41	Mickey Mantle, 1957	178
42	Billy Hamilton, 1895	178
43	Joe Kelley, 1896	178
44	Norm Cash, 1961	178
45	Hank Greenberg, 1937	178
46	Ed Delahanty, 1895	176
47	George Sisler, 1920	176
48	Willie Keeler, 1897	176
49	Ed Delahanty, 1899	175
50	Benny Kauff, 1914	175
51	Tris Speaker, 1912	175
52	Joe Jackson, 1911	175
53	Mickey Mantle, 1961	174
54	Stan Musial, 1949	173
55	Joe DiMaggio, 1937	173
56	Ty Cobb, 1912	173
57	Barry Bonds, 1993	172
58	Hank Greenberg, 1938	172
59	Ted Williams, 1948	172
60	Chuck Klein, 1932	171
61	Hank Greenberg, 1940	171
62	Ed Delahanty, 1896	170
63	Joe Medwick, 1937	170
64	Bill Terry, 1930	170
65	Stan Musial, 1951	169
66	Lou Gehrig, 1928	169
67	Rogers Hornsby, 1921	169
68	Earl Averill, 1936	168
69	Jimmie Foxx, 1936	168
70	Lou Gehrig, 1932	168
71	Sam Thompson, 1895	167
72	Ted Williams, 1957	167
73	Ed Delahanty, 1893	167
74	Jesse Burkett, 1896	166
75	Stan Musial, 1953	166
76	Joe Jackson, 1912	166
77	Tris Speaker, 1923	166
78	Jimmie Foxx, 1934	165
79	Ralph Kiner, 1951	165
80	Jake Stenzel, 1894	165
81	Jesse Burkett, 1895	165
82	Ty Cobb, 1917	164
83	Stan Musial, 1946	164
84	Ralph Kiner, 1949	163
85	Arky Vaughan, 1935	163
86	Jimmie Foxx, 1935	163
87	Al Simmons, 1930	163
88	Johnny Mize, 1939	162
89	Chuck Klein, 1933	162
90	George Sisler, 1922	162
91	Joe DiMaggio, 1941	162
92	Duke Snider, 1954	161
93	Hank Greenberg, 1935	161
94	Duke Snider, 1953	161
95	John Olerud, 1993	161
96	Bill Lange, 1895	160
97	Rod Carew, 1977	160
98	Denny Lyons, 1887	160
99	Frank Robinson, 1962	160
100	Harry Heilmann, 1923	160

Total Average

1	Babe Ruth, 1920	1.797
2	Babe Ruth, 1921	1.745
3	Ted Williams, 1941	1.688
4	Babe Ruth, 1923	1.683
5	Hugh Duffy, 1894	1.619
6	Babe Ruth, 1926	1.606
7	Billy Hamilton, 1894	1.605
8	John McGraw, 1899	1.601
9	Ted Williams, 1957	1.599
10	Babe Ruth, 1927	1.571
11	Babe Ruth, 1924	1.558
12	Rogers Hornsby, 1925	1.539
13	Mickey Mantle, 1957	1.534
14	Bill Joyce, 1894	1.528
15	Ed Delahanty, 1895	1.517
16	Tip O'Neill, 1887	1.514
17	Babe Ruth, 1930	1.509
18	Joe Kelley, 1894	1.503
19	Lou Gehrig, 1927	1.500
20	Babe Ruth, 1931	1.487
21	Ty Cobb, 1911	1.464
22	Frank Thomas, 1994	1.453
23	Ted Williams, 1954	1.452
24	Jimmie Foxx, 1932	1.451
25	Billy Hamilton, 1895	1.443
26	Babe Ruth, 1932	1.432
27	Ted Williams, 1946	1.431
28	Joe Kelley, 1896	1.430
29	Lou Gehrig, 1936	1.426
30	Mickey Mantle, 1956	1.426
31	Rogers Hornsby, 1924	1.424
32	Pete Browning, 1887	1.422
33	Jeff Bagwell, 1994	1.413
34	Hack Wilson, 1930	1.411
35	Rogers Hornsby, 1928	1.409
36	Sam Thompson, 1894	1.409
37	Ed Delahanty, 1896	1.405
38	Babe Ruth, 1928	1.405
39	Lou Gehrig, 1934	1.401
40	Ted Williams, 1942	1.394
41	Jimmie Foxx, 1938	1.392
42	Ted Williams, 1947	1.391
43	Lou Gehrig, 1930	1.389
44	Billy Hamilton, 1893	1.386
45	Mickey Mantle, 1962	1.385
46	Mickey Mantle, 1961	1.384
47	Bill Lange, 1895	1.373
48	Bob Caruthers, 1887	1.368
49	King Kelly, 1886	1.366
50	Babe Ruth, 1919	1.358
51	Norm Cash, 1961	1.358
52	Rogers Hornsby, 1922	1.353
53	Babe Herman, 1930	1.351
54	Jimmie Foxx, 1933	1.348
55	Ted Williams, 1948	1.347
56	Ted Williams, 1949	1.347
57	Lou Gehrig, 1937	1.339
58	Barry Bonds, 1993	1.339
59	Rogers Hornsby, 1929	1.338
60	Barry Bonds, 1992	1.335
61	Nap Lajoie, 1901	1.327
62	Ty Cobb, 1912	1.321
63	Ty Cobb, 1910	1.321
64	Jake Stenzel, 1894	1.320
65	Joe Morgan, 1976	1.319
66	Arky Vaughan, 1935	1.317
67	Billy Hamilton, 1896	1.316
68	Ty Cobb, 1913	1.310
69	Jimmie Foxx, 1934	1.310
70	Tris Speaker, 1912	1.310
71	Joe Jackson, 1911	1.308
72	Bill Joyce, 1896	1.306
73	Hank Greenberg, 1938	1.306
74	Albert Belle, 1994	1.304
75	Jimmie Foxx, 1939	1.304
76	Stan Musial, 1948	1.298
77	Willie McCovey, 1969	1.296
78	Ed Delahanty, 1894	1.290
79	Joe Kelley, 1895	1.289
80	Jimmie Foxx, 1935	1.288
81	Babe Ruth, 1929	1.288
82	Harry Heilmann, 1923	1.288
83	Mel Ott, 1929	1.287
84	Joe Morgan, 1975	1.279
85	Benny Kauff, 1914	1.278
86	Hank Greenberg, 1937	1.277
87	Chuck Klein, 1930	1.274
88	Al Simmons, 1930	1.272
89	Tris Speaker, 1922	1.272
90	Fred Clarke, 1897	1.272
91	Billy Hamilton, 1891	1.270
92	Sam Thompson, 1895	1.269
93	Lou Gehrig, 1931	1.267
94	Harry Heilmann, 1927	1.265
95	Jesse Burkett, 1895	1.265
96	Hughie Jennings, 1896	1.263
97	Billy Hamilton, 1898	1.262
98	Willie Keeler, 1897	1.262
99	Jimmie Foxx, 1929	1.261
100	John McGraw, 1900	1.260

Runs Produced

1	Lou Gehrig, 1931	301
2	Babe Ruth, 1921	289
3	Chuck Klein, 1930	288
4	Hugh Duffy, 1894	287
5	Al Simmons, 1930	281
6	Hughie Jennings, 1895	280
	Hack Wilson, 1930	280
	Hank Greenberg, 1937	280
9	Sam Thompson, 1895	278
10	Lou Gehrig, 1927	277
11	Kiki Cuyler, 1930	276
	Lou Gehrig, 1930	276
13	Billy Hamilton, 1894	275
14	Ed Delahanty, 1894	274
15	Sam Thompson, 1887	273
16	Ed Delahanty, 1893	272
	Joe Kelley, 1895	272
	Joe DiMaggio, 1937	272
19	Joe Kelley, 1894	270
	Lou Gehrig, 1936	270
21	Ty Cobb, 1911	266
	Rogers Hornsby, 1929	266
	Babe Ruth, 1931	266
	Ted Williams, 1949	266
25	Jimmie Foxx, 1938	264
26	Ed Delahanty, 1899	263
27	Babe Ruth, 1927	262
	Jimmie Foxx, 1932	262
29	Al Simmons, 1932	260
	Lou Gehrig, 1937	260
31	Hardy Richardson, 1890	259
	Hugh Duffy, 1893	259
	Walt Wilmot, 1894	259
34	Dan Brouthers, 1894	256
	Bobby Lowe, 1894	256
	Jake Stenzel, 1894	256
	Nap Lajoie, 1901	256
38	Hack Wilson, 1929	255
	Lou Gehrig, 1932	255
	Hank Greenberg, 1935	255
41	Cap Anson, 1886	254
	Willie Keeler, 1894	254
	Lou Gehrig, 1928	254
	Babe Ruth, 1930	254
45	Harry Stovey, 1889	252
46	Rogers Hornsby, 1922	251
	Babe Ruth, 1928	251
	Earl Averill, 1931	251
	Chuck Klein, 1932	251
50	Charlie Gehringer, 1934	250
51	Hugh Duffy, 1897	248
52	John McGraw, 1894	247
	Mel Ott, 1929	247
54	Hughie Jennings, 1896	246
	Tris Speaker, 1923	246
	Jimmie Foxx, 1930	246
	Zeke Bonura, 1936	246
	Tommy Davis, 1962	246
59	Sam Thompson, 1893	245
	Bill Terry, 1930	245
	Lou Gehrig, 1933	245
	Charlie Gehringer, 1936	245
	Ted Williams, 1939	245
64	Tom Brown, 1891	244
	Steve Brodie, 1894	244
	Ed Delahanty, 1895	244
	Ed Delahanty, 1896	244
	Ken Williams, 1922	244
	Lou Gehrig, 1934	244
	Hal Trosky, 1936	244
71	Dan Brouthers, 1887	242
	Ed McKean, 1895	242
	Lefty O'Doul, 1929	242
	Ted Williams, 1942	242
75	Lave Cross, 1894	241
	Bill Dahlen, 1894	241
	Babe Ruth, 1920	241
	Babe Ruth, 1923	241
79	Dan Brouthers, 1892	240
	Joe Kelley, 1896	240
	Ty Cobb, 1915	240
	George Sisler, 1920	240
	Joe Cronin, 1930	240
	Jimmie Foxx, 1933	240
85	Hughie Jennings, 1894	239
	Vern Stephens, 1950	239
87	George Davis, 1897	238
	Babe Ruth, 1926	238
	Babe Herman, 1930	238
	Hank Greenberg, 1940	238
91	Rogers Hornsby, 1925	237
	Al Simmons, 1929	237
	Joe DiMaggio, 1938	237
94	8 players tied	236

Clutch Hitting Index

1	Cap Anson, 1880	178
2	Tom Herr, 1987	172
3	Ed Abbaticchio, 1907	166
4	Bill McClellan, 1878	165
	Ed McKean, 1892	165
6	Lon Knight, 1881	164
7	Jack Barry, 1913	163
8	George Stovall, 1911	163
9	John Sullivan, 1943	162
10	Tom Herr, 1985	161
11	Fred Hartman, 1902	160
12	Cookie Lavagetto, 1941	160
13	Cap Anson, 1886	158
14	Sherry Magee, 1918	158
15	John Gochnauer, 1903	155
16	Tommy Davis, 1969	155
17	Maurice Van Robays, 1940	154
18	George Davis, 1906	154
19	Art Devlin, 1904	154
20	Frank LaPorte, 1910	154
21	Jack Rowe, 1888	153
22	Pete Hotaling, 1888	153
23	John Ward, 1888	153
24	Sam Crawford, 1910	153
25	Johnny Berardino, 1941	152
26	Jackie Hayes, 1937	152
27	Rebel Oakes, 1915	152
28	Bill Harbidge, 1878	151
	Frank LaPorte, 1914	151
30	Possum Whitted, 1920	151
31	Heinie Reitz, 1896	151
32	Earl Sheely, 1931	151
33	Joe Gerhardt, 1879	150
	Socks Seybold, 1907	150
35	Oyster Burns, 1890	150
36	Cy Seymour, 1908	150
37	Tom Burns, 1888	150
38	Joe Battin, 1876	150
39	Norm Larker, 1960	149
40	Earl Sheely, 1924	149
41	Chick Galloway, 1925	149
42	Vic Wertz, 1960	149
43	Sam Thompson, 1887	149
44	Hugh Duffy, 1896	148
45	Cap Anson, 1893	148
46	Roger Connor, 1884	148
47	Farmer Vaughn, 1893	148
	Bill Brubaker, 1936	148
49	Pie Traynor, 1928	147
50	Reddy Mack, 1889	147
	Larry Kopf, 1920	147
52	Pete Hotaling, 1880	147
53	Fred Pfeffer, 1882	147
54	Doc Gessler, 1911	147
55	Stuffy McInnis, 1914	147
56	Heinie Zimmerman, 1917	146
57	Bill Dahlen, 1904	146
58	Bill Holbert, 1882	146
59	Deacon White, 1885	146
60	Ned Williamson, 1885	146
	Clyde Barnhart, 1925	146
62	Jimmy Brown, 1942	146
63	Nap Lajoie, 1901	145
64	Cap Anson, 1881	145
65	Cap Anson, 1885	145
	Cap Anson, 1890	145
67	Dave Foutz, 1889	145
68	Bill Mowrey, 1916	145
69	Roy McMillan, 1956	145
70	Joe Kelley, 1898	145
71	Larry Gardner, 1920	144
72	Lave Cross, 1903	144
73	Jose Cardenal, 1971	144
74	Ty Cobb, 1907	143
75	Cap Anson, 1882	143
	Ed Delahanty, 1900	143
77	Hal Chase, 1909	143
78	Cal McVey, 1879	143
	Ferris Fain, 1949	143
80	Jim O'Rourke, 1887	143
	Kirby Puckett, 1994	143
82	John Ward, 1881	143
	Maurice Van Robays, 1941	143
	Joe Medwick, 1942	143
85	Eddie Collins, 1919	143
	Bobby Veach, 1922	143
87	Bill Hague, 1878	142
	Ron Fairly, 1964	142
89	Ross Youngs, 1921	142
90	Bob Ferguson, 1877	142
91	Monte Cross, 1900	142
	Milt Stock, 1921	142
	Enos Slaughter, 1953	142
94	Deacon White, 1876	142
95	Fred Pfeffer, 1892	142
96	Cupid Childs, 1895	141
97	Cap Anson, 1896	141
	Tommy Corcoran, 1903	141
99	King Kelly, 1880	141
	Ty Cobb, 1908	141

Isolated Power

1	Babe Ruth, 1920	.472
2	Babe Ruth, 1921	.469
3	Babe Ruth, 1927	.417
4	Lou Gehrig, 1927	.392
5	Babe Ruth, 1928	.386
6	Jimmie Foxx, 1932	.385
7	Jeff Bagwell, 1994	.382
8	Frank Thomas, 1994	.376
9	Babe Ruth, 1930	.373
10	Babe Ruth, 1923	.372
11	Mickey Mantle, 1961	.370
12	Hank Greenberg, 1938	.369
13	Hack Wilson, 1930	.368
14	Babe Ruth, 1926	.366
15	Babe Ruth, 1924	.361
16	Babe Ruth, 1922	.357
17	Albert Belle, 1994	.357
18	Jimmie Foxx, 1938	.356
19	Kevin Mitchell, 1994	.355
20	Rogers Hornsby, 1925	.353
21	Mickey Mantle, 1956	.353
22	Babe Ruth, 1929	.353
23	Ken Griffey, 1994	.351
24	Roger Maris, 1961	.351
25	Ralph Kiner, 1949	.348
26	Jimmie Foxx, 1933	.347
27	Willie Stargell, 1973	.347
28	Kevin Mitchell, 1989	.344
29	Lou Gehrig, 1934	.344
30	Jim Gentile, 1961	.344
31	Ted Williams, 1957	.343
32	Lou Gehrig, 1930	.343
33	Lou Gehrig, 1936	.342
34	Hank Aaron, 1971	.341
35	Barry Bonds, 1993	.341
36	Willie Mays, 1955	.340
37	Matt Williams, 1994	.339
38	Mike Schmidt, 1980	.338
39	Willie McCovey, 1969	.336
40	Babe Ruth, 1919	.336
41	Barry Bonds, 1994	.335
42	Jimmie Foxx, 1939	.334
43	Reggie Jackson, 1969	.333
44	Willie Stargell, 1971	.333
45	Hank Greenberg, 1937	.332
46	Hank Greenberg, 1940	.330
47	Ted Williams, 1941	.329
48	Mark McGwire, 1987	.329
49	Willie Mays, 1965	.328
50	Babe Ruth, 1931	.328
51	Mike Schmidt, 1981	.328
52	Hank Greenberg, 1946	.327
53	Joe DiMaggio, 1937	.327
54	Al Simmons, 1930	.327
55	Stan Musial, 1948	.326
56	Ralph Kiner, 1947	.326
57	Dave Kingman, 1979	.325
58	Ted Williams, 1946	.325
59	Eddie Mathews, 1953	.325
60	Willie McCovey, 1970	.323
61	Juan Gonzalez, 1993	.323
62	Willie Mays, 1954	.322
63	Lou Gehrig, 1931	.321
64	Johnny Mize, 1940	.321
65	Frank Robinson, 1966	.321
66	Rogers Hornsby, 1922	.321
67	Duke Snider, 1955	.320
68	Babe Ruth, 1932	.319
69	Jimmie Foxx, 1934	.319
70	Ralph Kiner, 1951	.318
71	Ralph Kiner, 1950	.318
72	Harmon Killebrew, 1961	.318
73	Bob Hamelin, 1994	.317
74	Rocky Colavito, 1958	.317
75	Mark McGwire, 1992	.317
76	Chick Hafey, 1930	.316
77	Boog Powell, 1964	.316
78	Ted Kluszewski, 1954	.316
79	Dick Allen, 1966	.315
80	Cecil Fielder, 1990	.314
81	Eddie Mathews, 1954	.313
82	Duke Snider, 1957	.313
83	Barry Bonds, 1992	.313
84	Eddie Mathews, 1955	.313
85	Johnny Mize, 1947	.312
86	Willie Mays, 1964	.311
87	Willie Mays, 1962	.311
88	George Foster, 1977	.311
89	Mike Schmidt, 1979	.311
90	Jack Clark, 1987	.310
91	Hank Greenberg, 1939	.310
92	Harmon Killebrew, 1969	.308
93	Ken Griffey, 1993	.308
94	Gary Sheffield, 1994	.307
95	Ted Williams, 1949	.307
96	Hank Aaron, 1969	.307
97	Duke Snider, 1954	.307
98	Mel Ott, 1929	.306
99	Duke Snider, 1956	.306
100	Joe Adcock, 1956	.306

Extra Base Hits

1	Babe Ruth, 1921	119
2	Lou Gehrig, 1927	117
3	Chuck Klein, 1930	107
4	Chuck Klein, 1932	103
	Hank Greenberg, 1937	103
	Stan Musial, 1948	103
7	Rogers Hornsby, 1922	102
8	Lou Gehrig, 1930	100
	Jimmie Foxx, 1932	100
10	Babe Ruth, 1920	99
	Babe Ruth, 1923	99
	Hank Greenberg, 1940	99
13	Hank Greenberg, 1935	98
14	Babe Ruth, 1927	97
	Hack Wilson, 1930	97
	Joe Medwick, 1937	97
17	Hank Greenberg, 1934	96
	Hal Trosky, 1936	96
	Joe DiMaggio, 1937	96
20	Lou Gehrig, 1934	95
	Joe Medwick, 1936	95
22	Rogers Hornsby, 1929	94
	Chuck Klein, 1929	94
	Babe Herman, 1930	94
	Jimmie Foxx, 1933	94
26	Jim Bottomley, 1928	93
	Al Simmons, 1930	93
	Lou Gehrig, 1936	93
29	Babe Ruth, 1924	92
	Lou Gehrig, 1931	92
	Jimmie Foxx, 1938	92
	Stan Musial, 1953	92
	Hank Aaron, 1959	92
	Frank Robinson, 1962	92
35	Babe Ruth, 1928	91
36	Rogers Hornsby, 1925	90
	Stan Musial, 1949	90
	Willie Mays, 1962	90
	Willie Stargell, 1973	90
40	Hal Trosky, 1934	89
	Duke Snider, 1954	89
42	Joe DiMaggio, 1936	88
	Barry Bonds, 1993	88
44	Tris Speaker, 1923	87
	Kiki Cuyler, 1925	87
	Lou Gehrig, 1928	87
	Ripper Collins, 1934	87
	Charlie Gehringer, 1936	87
	Johnny Mize, 1940	87
	Willie Mays, 1954	87
	Robin Yount, 1982	87
	Kevin Mitchell, 1989	87
53	George Sisler, 1920	86
	Babe Ruth, 1930	86
	Wally Moses, 1937	86
	Johnny Mize, 1939	86
	Ted Williams, 1939	86
	Stan Musial, 1946	86
	Eddie Mathews, 1953	86
	Reggie Jackson, 1969	86
	Hal McRae, 1977	86
	Jim Rice, 1978	86
	Don Mattingly, 1985	86
	Don Mattingly, 1986	86
	Ken Griffey, 1993	86
66	Tip O'Neill, 1887	85
	Hugh Duffy, 1894	85
	Chick Hafey, 1929	85
	Goose Goslin, 1930	85
	Lou Gehrig, 1932	85
	Lou Gehrig, 1933	85
	Earl Averill, 1934	85
	Hank Greenberg, 1938	85
	Rudy York, 1940	85
	Ted Williams, 1949	85
	Stan Musial, 1954	85
	Frank Robinson, 1966	85
	George Foster, 1977	85
	George Brett, 1979	85
	Cal Ripken, 1991	85
81	Sam Thompson, 1895	84
	Ken Williams, 1922	84
	Al Simmons, 1929	84
	Ed Morgan, 1930	84
	Earl Webb, 1931	84
	Joe DiMaggio, 1941	84
	Duke Snider, 1953	84
	Tony Oliva, 1964	84
	Johnny Bench, 1970	84
	Jim Rice, 1979	84
91	11 players tied	83

Pinch Hits

1	Jose Morales, 1976	25
2	Dave Philley, 1961	24
	Vic Davalillo, 1970	24
	Rusty Staub, 1983	24
	Gerald Perry, 1993	24
6	Sam Leslie, 1932	22
	Red Schoendienst, 1962	22
	Wallace Johnson, 1988	22
9	Doc Miller, 1913	21
	Peanuts Lowrey, 1953	21
	Smoky Burgess, 1966	21
	Merv Rettenmund, 1977	21
13	Ed Coleman, 1936	20
	Frenchy Bordagaray, 1938	20
	Joe Frazier, 1954	20
	Smoky Burgess, 1965	20
	Ken Boswell, 1976	20
	Jerry Turner, 1978	20
	Thad Bosley, 1985	20
	Chris Chambliss, 1986	20

Pinch Hit Average
(30 at-bats minimum)

1	Ed Kranepool, 1974	.486
2	Smead Jolley, 1931	.467
3	Frenchy Bordagaray, 1938	.465
4	Rick Miller, 1983	.457
5	Jose Pagan, 1969	.452
6	Elmer Valo, 1955	.452
7	Gates Brown, 1968	.450
8	Ted Easterly, 1912	.433
	Milt Thompson, 1985	.433
	Randy Bush, 1986	.433
11	Joe Cronin, 1943	.429
	Don Dillard, 1961	.429
13	Candy Maldonado, 1986	.425
14	Richie Ashburn, 1962	.419
	Dick Williams, 1962	.419
16	Merritt Ranew, 1963	.415
	Carl Taylor, 1969	.415
18	Kurt Bevacqua, 1983	.412
19	Jerry Turner, 1978	.408
20	Bob Bowman, 1958	.406
	Chico Walker, 1991	.406
	Sid Bream, 1994	.406
23	Frankie Baumholtz, 1955	.405
24	6 players tied	.400

Pinch Hit Home Runs

1	Johnny Frederick, 1932	6
2	Joe Cronin, 1943	5
	Butch Nieman, 1945	5
	Gene Freese, 1959	5
	Jerry Lynch, 1961	5
	Cliff Johnson, 1974	5
	Lee Lacy, 1978	5
	Jerry Turner, 1978	5
9	Ernie Lombardi, 1946	4
	Del Wilber, 1953	4
	Bill Taylor, 1955	4
	Bob Thurman, 1957	4
	Rip Repulski, 1958	4
	George Crowe, 1959	4
	George Crowe, 1960	4
	Johnny Blanchard, 1961	4
	Carl Sawatski, 1961	4
	Jerry Lynch, 1963	4
	Don Mincher, 1964	4
	Hal Breeden, 1973	4
	Mike Ivie, 1978	4
	Del Unser, 1979	4
	Jeff Burroughs, 1982	4
	Danny Heep, 1983	4
	Candy Maldonado, 1986	4
	Mark Carreon, 1989	4
	Tommy Gregg, 1990	4
	Ernest Riles, 1990	4
	Howard Johnson, 1994	4

Total Player Rating / 150g

1	Babe Ruth, 1923	10.46
2	Mike Schmidt, 1981	10.29
3	Fred Dunlap, 1884	10.25
4	Pete Browning, 1882	10.22
5	Nap Lajoie, 1901	10.19
6	Jeff Bagwell, 1994	10.09
7	Nap Lajoie, 1901	10.08
8	Barry Bonds, 1992	9.86
9	Babe Ruth, 1921	9.28
10	Babe Ruth, 1927	9.14
11	Babe Ruth, 1920	9.08
12	Rickey Henderson, 1990	9.04
13	Mickey Mantle, 1957	8.96
14	Rogers Hornsby, 1924	8.92
15	Mickey Mantle, 1956	8.70
16	Cal Ripken, 1984	8.43
17	Ross Barnes, 1876	8.41
18	Nap Lajoie, 1906	8.39
	Ty Cobb, 1917	8.39
20	Babe Ruth, 1924	8.33
21	Barry Bonds, 1993	8.30
22	Babe Ruth, 1926	8.29
23	Ted Williams, 1941	8.29
24	Rogers Hornsby, 1922	8.28
25	George Brett, 1980	8.21
26	Fred Pfeffer, 1884	8.17
27	Rogers Hornsby, 1920	8.15
28	Ted Williams, 1942	8.10
29	Ted Williams, 1957	8.07
30	Eric Davis, 1987	8.02
31	Nap Lajoie, 1910	8.02
32	Cupid Childs, 1890	7.98
33	Rogers Hornsby, 1917	7.97
34	Ted Williams, 1946	7.90
35	Mickey Mantle, 1961	7.84
36	Lou Gehrig, 1927	7.84
37	Lou Boudreau, 1944	7.80
38	Tris Speaker, 1913	7.77
39	Rickey Henderson, 1985	7.76
40	Hughie Jennings, 1896	7.73
41	Nap Lajoie, 1904	7.71
42	Honus Wagner, 1906	7.71
43	Cal Ripken, 1991	7.69
44	Willie Mays, 1955	7.60
45	King Kelly, 1879	7.60
	George Sisler, 1920	7.60
	Lou Gehrig, 1934	7.60
48	Babe Ruth, 1930	7.55
	Babe Ruth, 1931	7.55
50	Tris Speaker, 1912	7.55
51	Cupid Childs, 1896	7.50
52	Nap Lajoie, 1908	7.45
53	Honus Wagner, 1905	7.45
54	Barry Bonds, 1994	7.37
55	Nap Lajoie, 1900	7.35
56	Honus Wagner, 1903	7.33
57	Jack Glasscock, 1882	7.32
58	Ed Delahanty, 1896	7.32
59	Mike Schmidt, 1980	7.30
60	Ty Cobb, 1911	7.29
	Joe Morgan, 1975	7.29
62	Andre Dawson, 1981	7.28
63	Babe Ruth, 1919	7.27
64	Ron Santo, 1966	7.26
65	Nap Lajoie, 1907	7.23
66	Rickey Henderson, 1981	7.22
67	Tris Speaker, 1914	7.22
68	Ty Cobb, 1910	7.18
69	Ed Delahanty, 1893	7.16
70	Frankie Frisch, 1927	7.16
71	Barry Bonds, 1990	7.15
72	Dick Bartell, 1937	7.15
73	Joe DiMaggio, 1939	7.13
74	Buddy Bell, 1981	7.11
75	W Jones, 1877	7.11
	Snuffy Stirnweiss, 1945	7.11
	Willie Mays, 1958	7.11
78	Barry Larkin, 1991	7.07
79	Robin Yount, 1981	7.03
80	Willie Mays, 1965	6.97
81	George Sisler, 1922	6.97
82	Harlond Clift, 1937	6.97
	George Brett, 1985	6.97
84	Honus Wagner, 1908	6.95
85	Bobby Wallace, 1901	6.94
86	Joe Jackson, 1911	6.94
87	Hughie Jennings, 1897	6.92
	Rogers Hornsby, 1929	6.92
	Ted Williams, 1947	6.92
90	Rogers Hornsby, 1921	6.92
	Snuffy Stirnweiss, 1944	6.92
92	Joe DiMaggio, 1941	6.91
93	Orator Shaffer, 1878	6.90
94	Pedro Guerrero, 1985	6.90
95	Bob Ferguson, 1878	6.89
96	Hughie Jennings, 1895	6.87
97	Eddie Collins, 1910	6.86
98	Ty Cobb, 1912	6.86
99	Honus Wagner, 1912	6.83
100	2 players tied	6.82

Stolen Bases

1	Hugh Nicol, 1887	138
2	Rickey Henderson, 1982	130
3	Arlie Latham, 1887	129
4	Lou Brock, 1974	118
5	Charlie Comiskey, 1887	117
6	John Ward, 1887	111
	Billy Hamilton, 1889	111
	Billy Hamilton, 1891	111
9	Vince Coleman, 1985	110
10	Arlie Latham, 1888	109
	Vince Coleman, 1987	109
12	Rickey Henderson, 1983	108
13	Vince Coleman, 1986	107
14	Tom Brown, 1891	106
15	Maury Wills, 1962	104
16	Pete Browning, 1887	103
	Hugh Nicol, 1888	103
18	Jim Fogarty, 1887	102
	Billy Hamilton, 1890	102
20	Rickey Henderson, 1980	100
21	Jim Fogarty, 1889	99
22	Billy Hamilton, 1894	98
23	Harry Stovey, 1890	97
	Billy Hamilton, 1895	97
	Ron LeFlore, 1980	97
26	Ty Cobb, 1915	96
	Omar Moreno, 1980	96
28	Bid McPhee, 1887	95
	Curt Welch, 1888	95
30	Mike Griffin, 1887	94
	Maury Wills, 1965	94
32	Tommy McCarthy, 1888	93
	Rickey Henderson, 1988	93
34	Darby O'Brien, 1889	91
35	Tim Raines, 1983	90
36	Curt Welch, 1887	89
	Herman Long, 1889	89
38	Tom Poorman, 1887	88
	Blondie Purcell, 1887	88
	John Ward, 1892	88
	Clyde Milan, 1912	88
42	Harry Stovey, 1888	87
	Arlie Latham, 1891	87
	Joe Kelley, 1896	87
	Rickey Henderson, 1986	87
46	Cub Stricker, 1887	86
47	Tommy Tucker, 1887	85
	Hub Collins, 1890	85
	Hugh Duffy, 1891	85
50	King Kelly, 1887	84
	Chippy McGarr, 1887	84
	Billy Sunday, 1890	84
	Bill Lange, 1896	84
54	Tommy McCarthy, 1890	83
	Billy Hamilton, 1896	83
	Ty Cobb, 1911	83
	Willie Wilson, 1979	83
58	Dummy Hoy, 1888	82
	John Reilly, 1888	82
60	Eddie Collins, 1910	81
	Vince Coleman, 1988	81
62	Emmett Seery, 1888	80
	Hugh Nicol, 1889	80
	Bob Bescher, 1911	80
	Rickey Henderson, 1985	80
	Eric Davis, 1986	80
67	Tom Brown, 1890	79
	Dave Collins, 1980	79
	Willie Wilson, 1980	79
70	Hugh Duffy, 1890	78
	Tom Brown, 1892	78
	John McGraw, 1894	78
	Ron LeFlore, 1979	78
	Tim Raines, 1982	78
	Marquis Grissom, 1992	78
76	Ted Scheffler, 1890	77
	Jimmy Sheckard, 1899	77
	Davey Lopes, 1975	77
	Omar Moreno, 1979	77
	Rudy Law, 1983	77
	Rickey Henderson, 1989	77
	Vince Coleman, 1990	77
83	Ed McKean, 1887	76
	Walt Wilmot, 1890	76
	Dusty Miller, 1896	76
	Ty Cobb, 1909	76
	Marquis Grissom, 1991	76
88	Yank Robinson, 1887	75
	George Van Haltren, 1891	75
	Clyde Milan, 1913	75
	Benny Kauff, 1914	75
	Billy North, 1976	75
	Tim Raines, 1984	75
94	Frank Fennelly, 1887	74
	Harry Stovey, 1887	74
	Walt Wilmot, 1894	74
	Fritz Maisel, 1914	74
	Lou Brock, 1966	74
99	7 players tied	73

Stolen Base Average

1	Kevin McReynolds, 1988	100.0
	Paul Molitor, 1994	100.0
3	Brady Anderson, 1994	96.9
4	Max Carey, 1922	96.2
5	Ken Griffey, 1980	95.8
6	Stan Javier, 1988	95.2
7	Amos Otis, 1970	94.3
8	Jack Perconte, 1985	93.9
9	Miguel Dilone, 1984	93.1
	Bob Dernier, 1986	93.1
11	Kirk Gibson, 1990	92.9
	Barry Larkin, 1994	92.9
13	Don Baylor, 1972	92.3
	Oddibe McDowell, 1987	92.3
15	Davey Lopes, 1985	92.2
16	Eric Davis, 1988	92.1
17	Henry Cotto, 1992	92.0
18	Bobby Bonds, 1969	91.8
	Davey Lopes, 1978	91.8
20	Davey Lopes, 1979	91.7
	Marquis Grissom, 1990	91.7
22	Jim Wynn, 1965	91.5
23	Larry Bowa, 1977	91.4
24	Ryne Sandberg, 1987	91.3
	Alan Trammell, 1987	91.3
26	Jerry Mumphrey, 1980	91.2
27	Tom Herr, 1985	91.2
28	Jack Smith, 1925	90.9
	Davey Lopes, 1981	90.9
	Tim Raines, 1987	90.9
31	Craig Biggio, 1994	90.7
32	Willie Wilson, 1984	90.4
33	Bake McBride, 1978	90.3
34	Devon White, 1992	90.2
35	Henry Cotto, 1988	90.0
36	Devon White, 1993	89.5
37	Mitchell Page, 1977	89.4
38	Tommy Harper, 1971	89.3
	Rick Manning, 1981	89.3
	Eric Davis, 1987	89.3
41	Maury Wills, 1962	88.9
	Jake Wood, 1962	88.9
	Tommy Harper, 1964	88.9
	Enzo Hernandez, 1972	88.9
	Dusty Baker, 1973	88.9
	Lee Lacy, 1981	88.9
	Rickey Henderson, 1985	88.9
48	Willie Wilson, 1980	88.8
49	Tim Raines, 1985	88.6
	Tim Raines, 1986	88.6

Stolen Base Runs

1	Vince Coleman, 1986	24
2	Maury Wills, 1962	23
3	Rickey Henderson, 1983	21
4	Rickey Henderson, 1988	20
5	Vince Coleman, 1987	20
6	Tim Raines, 1983	19
7	Vince Coleman, 1985	18
	Rickey Henderson, 1985	18
9	Willie Wilson, 1979	18
	Ron LeFlore, 1980	18
	Willie Wilson, 1980	18
12	Eric Davis, 1986	17
13	Tim Raines, 1984	17
14	Davey Lopes, 1975	16
	Rudy Law, 1983	16
16	Lou Brock, 1974	16
	Tim Raines, 1985	16
	Tim Raines, 1986	16
	Marquis Grissom, 1992	16
20	Rickey Henderson, 1986	15
21	Ron LeFlore, 1979	15
22	Tim Raines, 1981	15
	Rickey Henderson, 1989	15
24	Rickey Henderson, 1980	14
25	Max Carey, 1922	14
	Joe Morgan, 1975	14
27	Bert Campaneris, 1969	14
	Tim Raines, 1982	14
	Rickey Henderson, 1982	14
30	Vince Coleman, 1989	14
	Rickey Henderson, 1990	14
32	Davey Lopes, 1976	13
	Willie Wilson, 1983	13
	Vince Coleman, 1990	13
35	Mickey Rivers, 1975	13
	Joe Morgan, 1976	13
	Jerry Mumphrey, 1980	13
	Juan Samuel, 1984	13
	Marquis Grissom, 1991	13
	Kenny Lofton, 1992	13
	Kenny Lofton, 1993	13
42	Fritz Maisel, 1914	12
	Alan Wiggins, 1983	12
	Tim Raines, 1987	12
45	Julio Cruz, 1978	12
	Davey Lopes, 1985	12
	Ozzie Smith, 1988	12
48	4 players tied	11

Stolen Base Wins

1	Vince Coleman, 1986	2.5
2	Maury Wills, 1962	2.3
3	Rickey Henderson, 1983	2.1
4	Rickey Henderson, 1988	2.0
5	Tim Raines, 1983	1.9
6	Vince Coleman, 1987	1.9
7	Vince Coleman, 1985	1.9
8	Ron LeFlore, 1980	1.9
9	Eric Davis, 1986	1.8
10	Rickey Henderson, 1985	1.8
11	Willie Wilson, 1980	1.8
12	Tim Raines, 1984	1.7
13	Willie Wilson, 1979	1.7
14	Marquis Grissom, 1992	1.7
15	Davey Lopes, 1975	1.7
16	Tim Raines, 1985	1.6
17	Lou Brock, 1974	1.6
18	Tim Raines, 1986	1.6
19	Rudy Law, 1983	1.6
20	Tim Raines, 1981	1.6
21	Rickey Henderson, 1986	1.5
22	Rickey Henderson, 1989	1.5
23	Joe Morgan, 1975	1.5
24	Ron LeFlore, 1979	1.5
25	Tim Raines, 1982	1.4
26	Bert Campaneris, 1969	1.4
27	Vince Coleman, 1989	1.4
28	Rickey Henderson, 1980	1.4
29	Rickey Henderson, 1982	1.4
30	Rickey Henderson, 1990	1.4
31	Davey Lopes, 1976	1.4
32	Joe Morgan, 1976	1.3
33	Jerry Mumphrey, 1980	1.3
34	Max Carey, 1922	1.3
35	Vince Coleman, 1990	1.3
36	Fritz Maisel, 1914	1.3
37	Juan Samuel, 1984	1.3
38	Marquis Grissom, 1991	1.3
39	Lou Brock, 1968	1.3
40	Willie Wilson, 1983	1.3
41	Mickey Rivers, 1975	1.3
42	Kenny Lofton, 1992	1.3
43	Ozzie Smith, 1988	1.3
44	Alan Wiggins, 1983	1.3
45	Davey Lopes, 1985	1.2
46	Kenny Lofton, 1993	1.2
47	Julio Cruz, 1978	1.2
48	Lou Brock, 1966	1.2
49	Tim Raines, 1987	1.2
50	Davey Lopes, 1978	1.2

Fielding Average

First Base

1	Steve Garvey, 1984	1.000
2	Stuffy McInnis, 1921	.999
3	Frank McCormick, 1946	.999
4	Steve Garvey, 1981	.999
5	Jim Spencer, 1973	.999
6	Wes Parker, 1968	.999
7	Eddie Murray, 1981	.999
8	Hal Morris, 1992	.999
9	Jim Spencer, 1976	.998
10	Jim Spencer, 1981	.998

Second Base

1	Bobby Grich, 1985	.997
2	Jose Oquendo, 1990	.996
3	Ryne Sandberg, 1991	.995
4	Jody Reed, 1994	.995
5	Rob Wilfong, 1980	.995
6	Bobby Grich, 1973	.995
7	Frank White, 1988	.994
8	Mark Lemke, 1994	.994
9	Jose Oquendo, 1989	.994
10	Jerry Adair, 1964	.994

Shortstop

1	Cal Ripken, 1990	.996
2	Tony Fernandez, 1989	.992
3	Larry Bowa, 1979	.991
4	Ed Brinkman, 1972	.990
5	Cal Ripken, 1989	.990
6	Spike Owen, 1990	.989
7	Omar Vizquel, 1992	.989
8	Tony Fernandez, 1990	.989
9	Dick Schofield, 1992	.988
10	Ozzie Smith, 1991	.987

Third Base

1	Tony Fernandez, 1994	.991
2	Don Money, 1974	.989
3	Hank Majeski, 1947	.988
4	Aurelio Rodriguez, 1978	.987
5	Willie Kamm, 1933	.984
6	Steve Buechele, 1991	.983
7	George Kell, 1946	.983
8	Heinie Groh, 1924	.983
9	Carney Lansford, 1979	.983
10	Gary Gaetti, 1994	.982

Outfield

1	Danny Litwhiler, 1942	1.000
	Willard Marshall, 1951	1.000
	Tony Gonzalez, 1962	1.000
	Don Demeter, 1963	1.000
	Rocky Colavito, 1965	1.000
	Curt Flood, 1966	1.000
	Johnny Callison, 1968	1.000
	Mickey Stanley, 1968	1.000
	Ken Harrelson, 1968	1.000
	Ken Berry, 1969	1.000
	Mickey Stanley, 1970	1.000
	Roy White, 1971	1.000
	Al Kaline, 1971	1.000
	Ken Berry, 1972	1.000
	Carl Yastrzemski, 1977	1.000
	Terry Puhl, 1979	1.000
	Gary Roenicke, 1980	1.000
	Ken Landreaux, 1981	1.000
	Terry Puhl, 1981	1.000
	Ken Singleton, 1981	1.000
	Brian Downing, 1982	1.000
	John Lowenstein, 1982	1.000
	Brian Downing, 1984	1.000
	Brett Butler, 1991	1.000
	Darryl Hamilton, 1992	1.000
	Brett Butler, 1993	1.000
	Darren Lewis, 1993	1.000
	Tim Raines, 1993	1.000
	Lance Johnson, 1994	1.000
	Milt Thompson, 1994	1.000

Catcher

1	Spud Davis, 1939	1.000
	Buddy Rosar, 1946	1.000
	Lou Berberet, 1957	1.000
	Pete Daley, 1957	1.000
	Yogi Berra, 1958	1.000
	Rick Cerone, 1988	1.000
7	Tom Pagnozzi, 1992	.999
8	Joe Azcue, 1967	.999
9	Wes Westrum, 1950	.999
10	Terry Steinbach, 1994	.998

Pitcher (92 chances accepted)

1	Kid Nichols, 1896	1.000
	Frank Owen, 1904	1.000
	Mordecai Brown, 1908	1.000
	Pete Alexander, 1913	1.000
	Walter Johnson, 1913	1.000
	Eppa Rixey, 1917	1.000
	Walter Johnson, 1917	1.000
	Hal Schumacher, 1935	1.000
	Larry Jackson, 1964	1.000
	Randy Jones, 1976	1.000
	Greg Maddux, 1990	1.000

Total Chances per Game

First Base

1	Joe Gerhardt, 1876	13.28
2	Jiggs Donahue, 1907	12.73
3	Oscar Walker, 1879	12.60
4	Joe Start, 1876	12.54
5	Tim Murnane, 1878	12.52
6	Joe Start, 1879	12.49
7	Jake Goodman, 1878	12.45
8	Herman Dehlman, 1876	12.36
9	Phil Todt, 1926	12.36
10	Joe Start, 1877	12.35

Second Base

1	Thorny Hawkes, 1879	8.44
2	Chick Fulmer, 1879	8.34
3	Jack Burdock, 1878	8.30
4	Ed Somerville, 1876	8.28
5	Joe Gerhardt, 1877	8.12
6	Fred Pfeffer, 1884	8.08
7	Jack Burdock, 1879	7.88
8	Joe Quest, 1878	7.81
9	Pop Smith, 1885	7.74
10	Joe Quest, 1879	7.73

Shortstop

1	Herman Long, 1889	7.27
2	Hughie Jennings, 1895	7.16
3	Dave Bancroft, 1918	7.14
4	Phil Tomney, 1889	7.12
5	George Davis, 1899	7.08
6	Hughie Jennings, 1896	7.07
7	Hughie Jennings, 1897	7.03
8	Bobby Wallace, 1901	6.97
9	Monte Cross, 1897	6.97
10	Bill Dahlen, 1895	6.93

Third Base

1	Al Nichols, 1876	5.81
2	Bob Ferguson, 1877	5.61
3	Jumbo Davis, 1888	5.13
4	Cap Anson, 1876	5.03
5	George Bradley, 1880	4.93
6	Billy Shindle, 1892	4.93
7	Jack Gleason, 1882	4.90
8	Bill Bradley, 1900	4.87
9	Will Foley, 1877	4.79
10	Levi Meyerle, 1876	4.78

Outfield

1	Fred Treacey, 1876	4.39
2	Redleg Snyder, 1876	3.84
3	harley Jones, 1877	3.77
4	Taylor Douthit, 1928	3.68
5	Mike Mansell, 1879	3.64
6	Richie Ashburn, 1951	3.64
7	Chet Lemon, 1977	3.60
8	Thurman Tucker, 1944	3.58
9	Kirby Puckett, 1984	3.57
10	Irv Noren, 1951	3.53
11	Richie Ashburn, 1949	3.49
12	Carden Gillenwater, 1945	3.46
13	Taylor Douthit, 1926	3.43
14	Sam West, 1935	3.41
15	Richie Ashburn, 1956	3.40
16	Dom DiMaggio, 1948	3.39
17	Richie Ashburn, 1957	3.38
18	Lloyd Waner, 1932	3.37
19	Lloyd Waner, 1931	3.37
20	Richie Ashburn, 1958	3.36

Catcher

1	Bill Holbert, 1883	10.63
2	Sam Trott, 1884	10.35
3	Bill Holbert, 1884	9.51
4	Jocko Milligan, 1884	9.40
5	Mert Hackett, 1884	9.35
6	Barney Gilligan, 1884	9.30
7	Mike Hines, 1883	9.27
8	George Baker, 1884	8.99
9	Jocko Milligan, 1885	8.82
10	Lew Brown, 1877	8.65

Pitcher

1	Harry Howell, 1905	5.42
2	Harry Howell, 1904	5.12
3	Will White, 1882	4.76
4	Ed Walsh, 1907	4.75
5	George Mullin, 1904	4.53
6	Tony Mullane, 1882	4.38
7	Red Donahue, 1902	4.37
8	Nick Altrock, 1905	4.37
9	Harry Howell, 1906	4.34
10	Jack Katoll, 1902	4.31

Chances Accepted per Game

First Base

1	Jiggs Donahue, 1907	12.65
2	Joe Gerhardt, 1876	12.54
3	Phil Todt, 1926	12.21
4	Joe Start, 1879	12.15
5	George Burns, 1914	12.10
6	Stuffy McInnis, 1918	12.10
7	George Stovall, 1908	12.08
8	George Kelly, 1920	12.01
9	Joe Start, 1878	12.00
10	Oscar Walker, 1879	11.92

Second Base

1	Jack Burdock, 1878	7.62
2	Thorny Hawkes, 1879	7.56
3	Chick Fulmer, 1879	7.55
4	Fred Pfeffer, 1884	7.29
5	Joe Gerhardt, 1877	7.21
6	Ed Somerville, 1876	7.20
7	Jack Burdock, 1879	7.18
8	Joe Quest, 1879	7.16
9	Pop Smith, 1885	7.13
10	Bid McPhee, 1886	7.09

Shortstop

1	Hughie Jennings, 1895	6.73
2	George Davis, 1899	6.69
3	Dave Bancroft, 1918	6.62
4	Hughie Jennings, 1896	6.56
5	Hughie Jennings, 1897	6.55
6	Rabbit Maranville, 1919	6.48
7	Bobby Wallace, 1901	6.48
8	Monte Cross, 1897	6.41
9	Dave Bancroft, 1920	6.40
10	George Davis, 1900	6.39

Third Base

1	Bob Ferguson, 1877	4.71
2	Al Nichols, 1876	4.53
3	Billy Shindle, 1892	4.34
4	Jumbo Davis, 1888	4.33
5	Bill Bradley, 1900	4.29
6	Cap Anson, 1876	4.27
7	George Bradley, 1880	4.23
8	Joe Battin, 1883	4.17
9	Bill Hague, 1878	4.16
10	Billy Shindle, 1888	4.13

Outfield

1	Fred Treacey, 1876	3.70
2	Taylor Douthit, 1928	3.62
3	Richie Ashburn, 1951	3.59
4	Thurman Tucker, 1944	3.55
5	Kirby Puckett, 1984	3.55
6	Chet Lemon, 1977	3.52
7	Irv Noren, 1951	3.45
8	Richie Ashburn, 1949	3.42
9	Carden Gillenwater, 1945	3.39
10	Sam West, 1935	3.38
11	Richie Ashburn, 1956	3.34
12	Richie Ashburn, 1957	3.33
13	Dom DiMaggio, 1948	3.33
14	Lloyd Waner, 1932	3.32
15	Jim Busby, 1953	3.31
16	Richie Ashburn, 1958	3.31
17	Jim Busby, 1952	3.31
18	Richie Ashburn, 1953	3.29
19	Lloyd Waner, 1931	3.29
20	Dwayne Murphy, 1980	3.29

Catcher

1	Bill Holbert, 1883	9.78
2	Sam Trott, 1884	9.63
3	Jocko Milligan, 1884	8.83
4	Bill Holbert, 1884	8.75
5	Mert Hackett, 1884	8.68
6	Barney Gilligan, 1884	8.63
7	Duffy Dyer, 1972	8.25
8	Jocko Milligan, 1885	8.25
9	Mike Hines, 1883	8.22
10	George Baker, 1884	8.06

Pitcher

1	Harry Howell, 1905	5.24
2	Harry Howell, 1904	4.97
3	Ed Walsh, 1907	4.68
4	Will White, 1882	4.56
5	Nick Altrock, 1905	4.32
6	George Mullin, 1904	4.24
7	Tony Mullane, 1882	4.20
8	Willie Sudhoff, 1904	4.19
9	Red Donahue, 1902	4.14
10	Nick Altrock, 1904	4.13

Putouts

First Base

1	Jiggs Donahue, 1907	1846
2	George Kelly, 1920	1759
3	Phil Todt, 1926	1755
4	Wally Pipp, 1926	1710
5	Jiggs Donahue, 1906	1697
6	Candy LaChance, 1904	1691
7	Tom Jones, 1907	1687
8	Ernie Banks, 1965	1682
9	Wally Pipp, 1922	1667
10	Lou Gehrig, 1927	1662

Second Base

1	Bid McPhee, 1886	529
2	Bobby Grich, 1974	484
3	Bucky Harris, 1922	483
4	Nellie Fox, 1956	478
5	Lou Bierbauer, 1889	472
6	Billy Herman, 1933	466
7	Bill Wambsganss, 1924	463
8	Cub Stricker, 1887	461
9	Buddy Myer, 1935	460
10	Bill Sweeney, 1912	459

Shortstop

1	Hughie Jennings, 1895	425
	Donie Bush, 1914	425
3	Joe Cassidy, 1905	408
4	Rabbit Maranville, 1914	407
5	Dave Bancroft, 1922	405
	Eddie Miller, 1940	405
7	Monte Cross, 1898	404
8	Dave Bancroft, 1921	396
9	Mickey Doolan, 1906	395
10	Buck Weaver, 1913	392

Third Base

1	Denny Lyons, 1887	255
2	Jimmy Williams, 1899	251
	Jimmy Collins, 1900	251
4	Jimmy Collins, 1898	243
	Willie Kamm, 1928	243
6	Willie Kamm, 1927	236
7	Frank Baker, 1913	233
8	Bill Coughlin, 1901	232
9	Ernie Courtney, 1905	229
10	Jimmy Austin, 1911	228

Outfield

1	Taylor Douthit, 1928	547
2	Richie Ashburn, 1951	538
3	Richie Ashburn, 1949	514
4	Chet Lemon, 1977	512
5	Dwayne Murphy, 1980	507
6	Dom DiMaggio, 1948	503
	Richie Ashburn, 1956	503
8	Richie Ashburn, 1957	502
9	Richie Ashburn, 1953	496
10	Richie Ashburn, 1958	495
11	Jim Busby, 1954	491
12	Omar Moreno, 1979	490
13	Baby Doll Jacobson, 1924	488
	Bobby Thomson, 1949	488
	Al Bumbry, 1980	488
16	Lloyd Waner, 1931	484
17	Richie Ashburn, 1954	483
18	Jim Busby, 1953	482
	Willie Wilson, 1980	482
20	Omar Moreno, 1980	479

Catcher

1	Johnny Edwards, 1969	1135
2	Johnny Edwards, 1963	1008
3	Darren Daulton, 1993	981
4	Randy Hundley, 1969	978
5	Tony Pena, 1983	976
6	Bill Freehan, 1968	971
7	Gary Carter, 1985	956
8	Gary Carter, 1982	954
9	Bill Freehan, 1967	950
10	Johnny Bench, 1968	942

Pitcher

1	Dave Foutz, 1886	57
2	Tony Mullane, 1882	54
3	George Bradley, 1876	50
	Guy Hecker, 1884	50
5	Mike Boddicker, 1984	49
6	Larry Corcoran, 1884	47
7	Al Spalding, 1876	45
	Ted Breitenstein, 1895	45
9	Jim Devlin, 1876	44
	Dave Foutz, 1887	44
	Bill Hutchison, 1890	44

Putouts per Game

First Base

1	Joe Gerhardt, 1876	12.30
2	Joe Start, 1879	11.98
3	Joe Start, 1878	11.79
4	Jiggs Donahue, 1907	11.76
5	Joe Start, 1877	11.73
6	Herman Dehlman, 1876	11.72
7	Joe Start, 1880	11.63
8	Jake Goodman, 1878	11.55
9	George Burns, 1914	11.53
10	Oscar Walker, 1879	11.50

Second Base

1	Jack Burdock, 1878	4.08
2	Jack Burdock, 1880	3.81
3	Bid McPhee, 1886	3.78
4	Bid McPhee, 1884	3.71
5	Joe Quest, 1878	3.68
6	Cub Stricker, 1887	3.66
7	Lou Bierbauer, 1889	3.63
8	Jack Burdock, 1879	3.61
9	Chick Fulmer, 1879	3.59
10	Bob Ferguson, 1880	3.59

Shortstop

1	Hughie Jennings, 1895	3.24
2	Dave Bancroft, 1918	2.97
3	Hughie Jennings, 1896	2.90
4	Hughie Jennings, 1897	2.89
5	George Davis, 1898	2.88
6	George Davis, 1899	2.88
7	Rabbit Maranville, 1919	2.76
8	Honus Wagner, 1913	2.75
9	Kid Elberfeld, 1901	2.74
10	Buck Weaver, 1914	2.74

Third Base

1	Al Nichols, 1876	2.16
2	Cap Anson, 1876	2.05
3	Hick Carpenter, 1880	2.03
4	Bob Ferguson, 1877	1.95
5	Denny Lyons, 1887	1.86
6	Patsy Tebeau, 1890	1.85
7	Cap Anson, 1877	1.85
8	Joe Battin, 1876	1.83
9	Jerry Denny, 1883	1.82
10	Frank Hankinson, 1881	1.80

Outfield

1	Taylor Douthit, 1928	3.55
2	Fred Treacey, 1876	3.54
3	Richie Ashburn, 1951	3.49
4	Thurman Tucker, 1944	3.45
5	Chet Lemon, 1977	3.44
6	Kirby Puckett, 1984	3.42
7	Richie Ashburn, 1949	3.34
8	Irv Noren, 1951	3.33
9	Sam West, 1935	3.33
10	Jim Busby, 1952	3.28
11	Richie Ashburn, 1956	3.27
12	Richie Ashburn, 1958	3.26
13	Lloyd Waner, 1932	3.25
14	Dom DiMaggio, 1948	3.25
15	Carden Gillenwater, 1945	3.22
16	Richie Ashburn, 1957	3.22
17	Jim Busby, 1953	3.21
18	Baby Doll Jacobson, 1924	3.21
19	Dwayne Murphy, 1980	3.21
20	Taylor Douthit, 1926	3.19

Catcher

1	Sam Trott, 1884	8.18
2	Bill Holbert, 1883	7.75
3	Duffy Dyer, 1972	7.58
4	Johnny Edwards, 1969	7.52
5	Barney Gilligan, 1884	7.47
6	Javy Lopez, 1994	7.45
7	Johnny Romano, 1964	7.44
8	Johnny Edwards, 1964	7.42
9	Joe Azcue, 1967	7.40
10	Johnny Roseboro, 1960	7.36

Pitcher

1	Mike Boddicker, 1984	1.44
2	Oil Can Boyd, 1985	1.20
3	Nick Altrock, 1904	1.13
4	Greg Maddux, 1990	1.11
5	Dave Foutz, 1887	1.10
6	Dwight Gooden, 1986	1.09
7	Dan Petry, 1984	1.09
8	Greg Maddux, 1993	1.08
9	Nat Hudson, 1888	1.08
	Al Nipper, 1986	1.08

Assists

First Base

1	Bill Buckner, 1985	184
2	Mark Grace, 1990	180
3	Mark Grace, 1991	167
4	Sid Bream, 1986	166
5	Bill Buckner, 1983	161
6	Bill Buckner, 1982	159
7	Bill Buckner, 1986	157
8	Mickey Vernon, 1949	155
9	Fred Tenney, 1905	152
	Eddie Murray, 1985	152

Second Base

1	Frankie Frisch, 1927	641
2	Hughie Critz, 1926	588
3	Rogers Hornsby, 1927	582
4	Ski Melillo, 1930	572
5	Ryne Sandberg, 1983	571
6	Rabbit Maranville, 1924	568
7	Frank Parkinson, 1922	562
8	Tony Cuccinello, 1936	559
9	Johnny Hodapp, 1930	557
10	Lou Bierbauer, 1892	555

Shortstop

1	Ozzie Smith, 1980	621
2	Glenn Wright, 1924	601
3	Dave Bancroft, 1920	598
4	Tommy Thevenow, 1926	597
5	Ivan DeJesus, 1977	595
6	Cal Ripken, 1984	583
7	Whitey Wietelmann, 1943	581
8	Dave Bancroft, 1922	579
9	Rabbit Maranville, 1914	574
10	Don Kessinger, 1968	573

Third Base

1	Graig Nettles, 1971	412
2	Graig Nettles, 1973	410
	Brooks Robinson, 1974	410
4	Harlond Clift, 1937	405
	Brooks Robinson, 1967	405
6	Mike Schmidt, 1974	404
7	Doug DeCinces, 1982	399
8	Clete Boyer, 1962	396
	Mike Schmidt, 1977	396
	Buddy Bell, 1982	396

Outfield

1	Orator Shaffer, 1879	50
2	Hugh Nicol, 1884	48
3	Hardy Richardson, 1881	45
4	Tommy McCarthy, 1888	44
	Chuck Klein, 1930	44
6	Charlie Duffee, 1889	43
	Jimmy Bannon, 1894	43
8	Jim Fogarty, 1889	42
9	Orator Shaffer, 1883	41
	Jim Lillie, 1884	41
11	Jim Fogarty, 1887	39
	Tom Brown, 1893	39
	Mike Mitchell, 1907	39
14	King Kelly, 1883	38
	Harry Stovey, 1889	38
	Tommy McCarthy, 1889	38
17	Jack Manning, 1883	37
	Tom Brown, 1892	37
19	Lon Knight, 1884	36
	Jimmy Ryan, 1889	36
	Jack McGeachy, 1889	36
	Jimmy Sheckard, 1903	36

Catcher

1	Bill Rariden, 1915	238
2	Bill Rariden, 1914	215
3	Pat Moran, 1903	214
4	Oscar Stanage, 1911	212
	Art Wilson, 1914	212
6	Gabby Street, 1909	210
7	Frank Snyder, 1915	204
8	George Gibson, 1910	203
9	Bill Bergen, 1909	202
	Claude Berry, 1914	202

Pitcher

1	Ed Walsh, 1907	227
2	Will White, 1882	223
3	Ed Walsh, 1908	190
4	Harry Howell, 1905	178
5	Tony Mullane, 1882	177
6	John Clarkson, 1885	174
7	John Clarkson, 1889	172
8	Jack Chesbro, 1904	166
9	George Mullin, 1904	163
10	Ed Walsh, 1911	160

Assists per Game

First Base
1. Mark Grace, 1990 .... 1.18
2. Bill Buckner, 1986 .... 1.14
3. Bill Buckner, 1985 .... 1.14
4. Bill Buckner, 1983 .... 1.12
5. Jeff Bagwell, 1994 .... 1.10
6. Sid Bream, 1986 .... 1.08
7. Eric Karros, 1994 .... 1.08
8. Cecil Fielder, 1994 .... 1.06
9. Ferris Fain, 1951 .... 1.05
10. Mark Grace, 1991 .... 1.04

Second Base
1. Joe Gerhardt, 1877 ...... 4.28
2. Frankie Frisch, 1927 ...... 4.19
3. Thorny Hawkes, 1879 .... 4.13
4. Hughie Critz, 1933 ...... 4.07
5. Frank Parkinson, 1922 ... 4.04
6. Joe Quest, 1879 .... 3.99
7. Chick Fulmer, 1879 ..... 3.96
8. Ed Somerville, 1876 ..... 3.92
9. Ski Melillo, 1930 .... 3.86
10. Glenn Hubbard, 1985 .... 3.85

Shortstop
1. Germany Smith, 1885 .... 4.21
2. Arthur Irwin, 1880 .... 4.13
3. Art Fletcher, 1919 ...... 4.10
4. Bill Dahlen, 1895 .... 4.09
5. Phil Tomney, 1889 ...... 4.05
6. Bobby Wallace, 1901 .... 4.04
7. Jack Glasscock, 1887 ... 4.04
8. Germany Smith, 1892 .... 4.04
9. Henry Easterday, 1888 ... 3.99
10. Dave Bancroft, 1920 .... 3.99

Third Base
1. Jumbo Davis, 1888 ...... 2.96
2. Buddy Bell, 1981 .... 2.93
3. George Bradley, 1880 .... 2.89
4. Bill Hague, 1878 .... 2.85
5. Billy Shindle, 1892 ..... 2.85
6. Bob Ferguson, 1877 ..... 2.77
7. Ned Williamson, 1879 .... 2.76
8. Arlie Latham, 1884 ..... 2.75
9. Bill Bradley, 1900 ...... 2.75
10. Arlie Latham, 1891 ..... 2.74

Outfield
1. Orator Shaffer, 1879 .... 0.69
2. Hardy Richardson, 1881 .. 0.57
3. Hugh Nicol, 1884 .... 0.55
4. King Kelly, 1878 .... 0.51
5. John Cassidy, 1878 ..... 0.50
   King Kelly, 1880 .... 0.50
7. Bill Hallett, 1883 ...... 0.46
8. Jake Evans, 1882 ...... 0.46
9. Orator Shaffer, 1878 .... 0.44
10. Dick Higham, 1878 ..... 0.44
11. Orator Shaffer, 1883 .... 0.43
12. King Kelly, 1881 .... 0.43
13. Orator Shaffer, 1880 .... 0.42
14. Jake Evans, 1879 ...... 0.42
15. Jack Manning, 1883 .... 0.38
16. Jake Evans, 1881 ...... 0.37
17. Jimmy Wolf, 1883 ...... 0.37
18. Hugh Nicol, 1883 ...... 0.37
19. Jim Lillie, 1884 .... 0.36
20. Buttercup Dickerson, 1883 0.36

Catcher
1. Bill Holbert, 1884 .... 2.41
2. Tom Daly, 1887 .... 2.31
3. Bill Holbert, 1882 ...... 2.14
4. Pop Snyder, 1884 .... 2.08
5. Bill Holbert, 1883 ...... 2.03
6. Buck Ewing, 1881 ...... 2.02
7. Pat Moran, 1903 .... 2.00
8. Charlie Reipschlager, 1885 1.98
9. Connie Mack, 1888 ...... 1.92
10. King Kelly, 1888 .... 1.92

Pitcher
1. Harry Howell, 1905 ...... 4.68
2. Harry Howell, 1904 ...... 4.21
3. Will White, 1882 .... 4.13
4. Ed Walsh, 1907 .... 4.05
5. Willie Sudhoff, 1904 ..... 3.85
6. Red Donahue, 1902 ..... 3.71
7. George Mullin, 1904 ..... 3.62
8. Frank Owen, 1904 ...... 3.51
9. Carl Mays, 1918 .... 3.49
10. Nick Altrock, 1905 .... 3.47

Double Plays

First Base
1. Ferris Fain, 1949 194
2. Ferris Fain, 1950 192
3. Donn Clendenon, 1966 ... 182
4. Ron Jackson, 1979 175
5. Gil Hodges, 1951 171
6. Mickey Vernon, 1949 168
7. Ted Kluszewski, 1954 166
8. Rudy York, 1944 163
9. Donn Clendenon, 1965 ... 161
   Rod Carew, 1977 161

Second Base
1. Bill Mazeroski, 1966 161
2. Jerry Priddy, 1950 150
3. Bill Mazeroski, 1961 144
4. Nellie Fox, 1957 141
   Dave Cash, 1974 141
6. Buddy Myer, 1935 138
   Bill Mazeroski, 1962 138
   Carlos Baerga, 1992 138
9. Jerry Coleman, 1950 137
   Jackie Robinson, 1951 ... 137
   Red Schoendienst, 1954 . 137

Shortstop
1. Rick Burleson, 1980 147
2. Roy Smalley, 1979 144
3. Bobby Wine, 1970 137
4. Lou Boudreau, 1944 134
5. Spike Owen, 1986 133
6. Rafael Ramirez, 1982 ... 130
7. Roy McMillan, 1954 129
8. Hod Ford, 1928 128
   Vern Stephens, 1949 128
   Gene Alley, 1966 128

Third Base
1. Graig Nettles, 1971 54
2. Harlond Clift, 1937 50
3. Johnny Pesky, 1949 48
   Paul Molitor, 1982 48
5. Sammy Hale, 1927 46
   Clete Boyer, 1965 46
   Gary Gaetti, 1983 46
8. Eddie Yost, 1950 45
   Frank Malzone, 1961 45
   Darrell Evans, 1974 45

Outfield
1. Happy Felsch, 1919 15
2. Jimmy Sheckard, 1899 ... 14
3. Tom Brown, 1893 13
4. Tom Brown, 1886 12
   Tommy McCarthy, 1888 .. 12
   Jimmy Bannon, 1894 12
   Mike Griffin, 1895 12
   Danny Green, 1899 12
   Cy Seymour, 1905....... 12
   Ginger Beaumont, 1907 .. 12
   Ty Cobb, 1907 12
   Tris Speaker, 1909 12
   Jimmy Sheckard, 1911 ... 12
   Tris Speaker, 1914 12
   Mel Ott, 1929 12
16. Sam Thompson, 1886 ... 11
    Tommy McCarthy, 1889 .. 11
    Billy Sunday, 1890 11
    Sam Thompson, 1896 ... 11
    Fielder Jones, 1902 11
    Jimmy Sebring, 1903 ... 11
    Phil Geier, 1904 11
    Ben Koehler, 1905...... 11
    Burt Shotton, 1913 11
    Chief Wilson, 1914 11

Catcher
1. Steve O'Neill, 1916 36
2. Frankie Hayes, 1945 29
3. Ray Schalk, 1916 25
   Yogi Berra, 1951 25
5. Jack Lapp, 1915 23
   Muddy Ruel, 1924 23
   Tom Haller, 1968 23
8. Steve O'Neill, 1914 22
   Bob O'Farrell, 1922 22
10. Gabby Hartnett, 1927 ... 21
    Wes Westrum, 1950 21

Pitcher
1. Bob Lemon, 1953 15
2. Eddie Rommel, 1924 12
   Curt Davis, 1934 12
   Randy Jones, 1976 12
5. Scott Perry, 1919 11
   Tom Rogers, 1919 11
   Art Nehf, 1920 11
   Burleigh Grimes, 1925 ... 11
   Gene Bearden, 1948 11
10. 10 players tied 10

Fielding Runs

1. Glenn Hubbard, 1985 .... 61.8
2. Danny Richardson, 1892 . 57.6
3. Bill Mazeroski, 1963 ..... 56.7
4. Rabbit Maranville, 1914 .. 51.8
5. Freddie Maguire, 1928 ... 50.5
6. Nap Lajoie, 1908 .... 49.3
7. Danny Richardson, 1891 . 49.1
8. Frankie Frisch, 1927 ..... 48.6
9. Hughie Critz, 1933 ...... 46.5
10. George Davis, 1899...... 46.3
11. Fred Pfeffer, 1884 ...... 45.5
12. Nap Lajoie, 1907 .... 45.0
13. Dick Bartell, 1936 ...... 44.8
14. Ozzie Guillen, 1988 ..... 42.6
15. Dave Shean, 1910 ...... 42.5
    Lee Tannehill, 1911 ..... 42.5
17. Cupid Childs, 1896 ...... 42.4
18. Graig Nettles, 1971 ..... 42.3
19. Joe Gerhardt, 1890 ..... 41.5
20. Bid McPhee, 1889 ...... 41.1
    Bill Mazeroski, 1962 .... 41.1
    Ryne Sandberg, 1983 ... 41.1
23. Harlond Clift, 1937 ..... 41.0
    Glenn Hubbard, 1986 ... 41.0
25. Bill Mazeroski, 1966 .... 40.8
    Ozzie Smith, 1980 ...... 40.8
27. Nap Lajoie, 1903 .... 40.1
28. Germany Smith, 1885 ... 39.9
29. Lee Tannehill, 1906 ..... 39.6
30. Arlie Latham, 1884 ..... 39.5
31. John Kerins, 1886 ...... 39.0
    Dave Bancroft, 1920 .... 39.0
33. Bobby Wallace, 1899 ... 38.8
    Cal Ripken, 1984 .... 38.8
35. Bob Allen, 1890 .... 38.6
36. Fred Pfeffer, 1888 ...... 38.3
37. Everett Scott, 1921 ..... 38.1
38. Bill Dahlen, 1908 .... 37.5
    Dick Bartell, 1937 ...... 37.5
    Dal Maxvill, 1970 .... 37.5
41. Bobby Knoop, 1964 ..... 37.2
42. Al Weis, 1966 .... 36.9
43. Billy Shindle, 1888 ..... 36.8
44. Tim Wallach, 1985 ..... 36.7
45. Lou Bierbauer, 1889 .... 36.6
46. Miller Huggins, 1905 .... 36.2
    Clete Boyer, 1962 ...... 36.2
48. Tommy Leach, 1904 .... 35.8
    Ivan DeJesus, 1977 ..... 35.8
50. Hughie Jennings, 1895 .. 35.7
51. Bill Dahlen, 1895 .... 35.6
    Harry Steinfeldt, 1900 ... 35.6
53. Jack Glasscock, 1889 ... 35.5
    Billy Shindle, 1892 ..... 35.5
55. Bill Holbert, 1883 ...... 35.4
56. Freddie Patek, 1973 .... 35.3
57. Bobby Knoop, 1970 ..... 35.1
58. Jack Glasscock, 1887 ... 35.0
59. Chet Lemon, 1977 ..... 34.9
60. Jimmy Bloodworth, 1941 . 34.7
61. George Davis, 1898 ..... 34.6
62. Buddy Bell, 1982 .... 34.4
63. Hughie Jennings, 1896 .. 34.2
    Doc Lavan, 1916 .... 34.2
65. Art Fletcher, 1915 ...... 34.1
66. Bid McPhee, 1893 ...... 34.0
    Shorty Fuller, 1895 ..... 34.0
68. Bill Mazeroski, 1964 .... 33.9
69. Mark Belanger, 1978 .... 33.8
70. Eddie Collins, 1910 ..... 33.7
    Gene Alley, 1970 .... 33.7
72. Buck Weaver, 1913 ..... 33.6
73. Lave Cross, 1895 .... 33.5
    John Farrell, 1902 ...... 33.5
    Donie Bush, 1914 ...... 33.5
    Leo Cardenas, 1969 .... 33.5
77. Pop Smith, 1885 .... 33.2
78. Hughie Jennings, 1894 .. 33.1
    Joe Cassidy, 1905 ...... 33.1
    Ski Melillo, 1931 .... 33.1
    Roy Smalley, 1979 ..... 33.1
    Ozzie Smith, 1982 ...... 33.1
83. Mickey Doolan, 1915 ... 33.0
84. Tom Daly, 1887 .... 32.9
    Red Schoendienst, 1952 . 32.9
    Red Schoendienst, 1954 . 32.9
87. George McBride, 1908 ... 32.8
88. Lave Cross, 1899 .... 32.7
89. Don Zimmer, 1958 ..... 32.6
90. Dave Parker, 1977 ..... 32.5
91. Richie Ashburn, 1957 ... 32.4
92. Richie Ashburn, 1951 ... 32.3
    Marty Barrett, 1987 ..... 32.3
94. Herman Long, 1889 .... 32.2
95. Germany Smith, 1887 ... 32.0
    Wally Gerber, 1928 ..... 32.0
    Bucky Dent, 1979 ...... 32.0
98. Nap Lajoie, 1906 .... 31.9
    Spike Owen, 1986 ...... 31.9
100. Pep Young, 1938 ...... 31.8

Fielding Runs

First Base
1. Mark Grace, 1990 27
2. Bill Buckner, 1985 25
3. Chick Gandil, 1914 24
4. Sid Bream, 1986 24
5. Fred Tenney, 1905 22
6. Bill Buckner, 1983 22
7. Vic Power, 1960 21
8. Sid Bream, 1988 21
9. Jiggs Donahue, 1907 ... 21
10. Jake Beckley, 1892 21

Second Base
1. Glenn Hubbard, 1985 62
2. Bill Mazeroski, 1963 57
3. Freddie Maguire, 1928 ... 50
4. Frankie Frisch, 1927 49
5. Nap Lajoie, 1908 48
6. Hughie Critz, 1933 46
7. Fred Pfeffer, 1884 46
8. Danny Richardson, 1891 . 44
9. Nap Lajoie, 1907 43
10. Dave Shean, 1910 42

Shortstop
1. Rabbit Maranville, 1914 .. 52
2. George Davis, 1899 46
3. Dick Bartell, 1936 45
4. Ozzie Guillen, 1988 43
5. Ozzie Smith, 1980 41
6. Germany Smith, 1885 ... 40
7. Dave Bancroft, 1920 39
8. Cal Ripken, 1984 39
9. Bob Allen, 1890 39
10. Everett Scott, 1921 38

Third Base
1. Graig Nettles, 1971 42
2. Harlond Clift, 1937 41
3. Arlie Latham, 1884 40
4. Billy Shindle, 1892 38
5. Billy Shindle, 1888 37
6. Tim Wallach, 1985 37
7. Clete Boyer, 1962 36
8. Tommy Leach, 1904 36
9. Buddy Bell, 1982 35
10. Lave Cross, 1895 33

Outfield
1. Chet Lemon, 1977 35
2. Dave Parker, 1977 33
3. Richie Ashburn, 1957 ... 32
4. Richie Ashburn, 1951 ... 32
5. Jim Fogarty, 1887 32
6. Kirby Puckett, 1984 30
7. Tommy McCarthy, 1888 . 30
8. Max Carey, 1916 30
9. Eric Davis, 1987........ 28
10. Tris Speaker, 1914 28
11. Omar Moreno, 1980 27
12. Tom Brown, 1893 27
13. Garry Maddox, 1979 ... 27
14. Carl Yastrzemski, 1964 .. 27
15. Gerald Young, 1989 26
16. Ed Delahanty, 1893 26
17. Gary Ward, 1983 26
18. Richie Ashburn, 1953 ... 26
19. Mike Griffin, 1891 26
20. Richie Ashburn, 1956 ... 25

Catcher
1. Bill Holbert, 1883 37
2. Tom Daly, 1887 32
3. Duke Farrell, 1894 30
4. Pop Snyder, 1884 26
5. Connie Mack, 1892 25
6. Pop Snyder, 1879 25
7. George Mitterwald, 1970 . 24
8. Jim Hegan, 1950 24
9. Duke Farrell, 1890 24
10. Rollie Hemsley, 1934 24

Pitcher
1. Ed Walsh, 1907 22
2. Harry Howell, 1905 18
3. Ed Walsh, 1911 15
4. Ed Walsh, 1908 14
5. Will White, 1882 13
6. John Clarkson, 1889 11
7. Sadie McMahon, 1890 .. 11
8. Tony Mullane, 1882 11
9. Carl Mays, 1926 10
10. Frank Smith, 1909 10

Fielding Wins

#	Player	Value
1	Glenn Hubbard, 1985	6.5
2	Bill Mazeroski, 1963	6.2
3	Nap Lajoie, 1908	5.6
4	Rabbit Maranville, 1914	5.6
5	Danny Richardson, 1892	5.3
6	Nap Lajoie, 1907	5.0
7	Freddie Maguire, 1928	4.9
8	Hughie Critz, 1933	4.9
9	Frankie Frisch, 1927	4.8
10	Graig Nettles, 1971	4.6
11	Dave Shean, 1910	4.5
12	Danny Richardson, 1891	4.4
13	Dick Bartell, 1936	4.4
14	Lee Tannehill, 1906	4.4
15	Bill Dahlen, 1908	4.3
16	Ozzie Smith, 1980	4.3
17	Ozzie Guillen, 1988	4.3
18	Ryne Sandberg, 1983	4.3
19	Bill Mazeroski, 1966	4.3
20	Glenn Hubbard, 1986	4.3
21	George Davis, 1899	4.2
22	Dave Bancroft, 1920	4.2
23	Lee Tannehill, 1911	4.2
24	Nap Lajoie, 1903	4.2
25	Bill Mazeroski, 1962	4.1
26	Fred Pfeffer, 1884	4.1
27	Al Weis, 1966	4.0
28	Bobby Knoop, 1964	3.9
29	Cal Ripken, 1984	3.9
30	Tim Wallach, 1985	3.9
31	Doc Lavan, 1916	3.8
32	Art Fletcher, 1915	3.8
33	Tommy Leach, 1904	3.8
34	Harland Clift, 1937	3.8
35	Fred Pfeffer, 1888	3.8
36	Miller Huggins, 1905	3.8
37	Eddie Collins, 1910	3.7
38	Dal Maxvill, 1970	3.7
39	George McBride, 1908	3.7
40	Dick Bartell, 1937	3.7
41	Donie Bush, 1914	3.7
42	Joe Gerhardt, 1890	3.6
43	Bobby Knoop, 1970	3.6
44	Clete Boyer, 1962	3.6
45	Joe Cassidy, 1905	3.6
46	Ivan DeJesus, 1977	3.6
47	Freddie Patek, 1973	3.6
48	Heinie Wagner, 1908	3.6
49	Arlie Latham, 1884	3.6
50	Cupid Childs, 1896	3.6
51	Germany Smith, 1885	3.6
52	Bill Mazeroski, 1964	3.6
53	Buck Weaver, 1913	3.6
54	Everett Scott, 1921	3.6
55	Mickey Doolan, 1915	3.6
56	John Farrell, 1902	3.5
57	Joe Tinker, 1908	3.5
58	Bobby Wallace, 1899	3.5
59	Leo Cardenas, 1969	3.5
60	Nap Lajoie, 1906	3.5
61	Mark Belanger, 1978	3.5
62	Ozzie Smith, 1982	3.5
63	Bid McPhee, 1889	3.5
64	Chet Lemon, 1977	3.5
65	Buddy Bell, 1982	3.4
66	Buck Herzog, 1915	3.4
67	Bob Allen, 1890	3.4
68	John Kerins, 1886	3.4
69	Max Carey, 1916	3.4
70	Red Schoendienst, 1952	3.4
71	Brooks Robinson, 1967	3.4
72	Billy Shindle, 1888	3.4
73	Horace Clarke, 1968	3.4
74	Nap Lajoie, 1916	3.4
75	Jimmy Bloodworth, 1941	3.4
76	Gene Alley, 1970	3.4
77	Freddie Patek, 1972	3.4
78	Ron Santo, 1967	3.3
79	Johnny Evers, 1904	3.3
80	Buck Herzog, 1914	3.3
81	Richie Ashburn, 1957	3.3
82	Dave Parker, 1977	3.3
83	Don Zimmer, 1958	3.3
84	Billy Shindle, 1892	3.3
85	Red Schoendienst, 1954	3.3
86	Harry Steinfeldt, 1900	3.3
87	Bruno Betzel, 1916	3.2
88	Richie Ashburn, 1951	3.2
89	George Davis, 1898	3.2
90	Roy Smalley, 1979	3.2
91	Terry Pendleton, 1989	3.2
92	Ed Brinkman, 1970	3.2
93	Pep Young, 1938	3.2
94	Rabbit Maranville, 1919	3.2
95	Zoilo Versalles, 1962	3.2
96	Dave Bancroft, 1917	3.2
97	Buddy Bell, 1981	3.1
98	Johnny Evers, 1907	3.1
99	Spike Owen, 1986	3.1
100	Billy Jurges, 1932	3.1

Total Player Rating

#	Player	Value
1	Babe Ruth, 1923	10.6
2	Babe Ruth, 1921	9.4
3	Babe Ruth, 1927	9.2
	Barry Bonds, 1992	9.2
5	Cal Ripken, 1984	9.1
6	Nap Lajoie, 1901	8.9
7	Barry Bonds, 1993	8.8
8	Mickey Mantle, 1956	8.7
9	Babe Ruth, 1920	8.6
	Mickey Mantle, 1957	8.6
11	Nap Lajoie, 1906	8.5
	Nap Lajoie, 1910	8.5
	Ty Cobb, 1917	8.5
	Rogers Hornsby, 1922	8.5
	Rogers Hornsby, 1924	8.5
	Babe Ruth, 1924	8.5
17	Nap Lajoie, 1903	8.4
	Babe Ruth, 1926	8.4
19	Cal Ripken, 1991	8.3
20	Rickey Henderson, 1990	8.2
21	Rogers Hornsby, 1920	8.1
	Lou Gehrig, 1927	8.1
	Ted Williams, 1942	8.1
24	Mickey Mantle, 1961	8.0
25	Ted Williams, 1941	7.9
	Ted Williams, 1946	7.9
27	Nap Lajoie, 1908	7.8
	George Sisler, 1920	7.8
	Lou Gehrig, 1934	7.8
	Lou Boudreau, 1944	7.8
31	Tris Speaker, 1912	7.7
	Rogers Hornsby, 1917	7.7
	Willie Mays, 1955	7.7
34	Tris Speaker, 1914	7.6
35	Ron Santo, 1966	7.5
36	Rickey Henderson, 1985	7.4
	Jeff Bagwell, 1994	7.4
38	Honus Wagner, 1905	7.3
	Honus Wagner, 1906	7.3
	Tris Speaker, 1913	7.3
	Frankie Frisch, 1927	7.3
	Babe Ruth, 1930	7.3
	Babe Ruth, 1931	7.3
	Willie Mays, 1965	7.3
	Ron Santo, 1967	7.3
	Carl Yastrzemski, 1967	7.3
	Mike Schmidt, 1980	7.3
48	Nap Lajoie, 1904	7.2
	Rogers Hornsby, 1929	7.2
	Harland Clift, 1937	7.2
	Snuffy Stirnweiss, 1945	7.2
	Ted Williams, 1947	7.2
	Willie Mays, 1958	7.2
	George Brett, 1985	7.2
	Barry Bonds, 1990	7.2
56	Ty Cobb, 1911	7.1
	Rogers Hornsby, 1921	7.1
	Snuffy Stirnweiss, 1944	7.1
	Ted Williams, 1957	7.1
	Norm Cash, 1961	7.1
	Joe Morgan, 1975	7.1
62	Honus Wagner, 1908	7.0
	Eddie Collins, 1910	7.0
	Babe Ruth, 1928	7.0
	Mike Schmidt, 1981	7.0
	Robin Yount, 1982	7.0
	Kevin Mitchell, 1989	7.0
68	Fred Dunlap, 1884	6.9
	Joe Jackson, 1912	6.9
	Rogers Hornsby, 1927	6.9
	Lou Gehrig, 1930	6.9
	Lou Boudreau, 1948	6.9
	Rico Petrocelli, 1969	6.9
	Mike Schmidt, 1974	6.9
	Eric Davis, 1987	6.9
76	Joe Jackson, 1911	6.8
	Jackie Robinson, 1951	6.8
78	Cupid Childs, 1890	6.7
	Hughie Jennings, 1896	6.7
	Ty Cobb, 1910	6.7
	Joe Cronin, 1930	6.7
	Jimmie Foxx, 1933	6.7
	Lou Boudreau, 1943	6.7
	Ted Williams, 1949	6.7
	Willie Mays, 1954	6.7
	Frank Robinson, 1966	6.7
	Mike Schmidt, 1977	6.7
	Cal Ripken, 1983	6.7
89	Cupid Childs, 1896	6.6
	Nap Lajoie, 1907	6.6
	Honus Wagner, 1912	6.6
	George Sisler, 1922	6.6
	Hank Aaron, 1959	6.6
	Willie Mays, 1963	6.6
	Carl Yastrzemski, 1968	6.6
	Reggie Jackson, 1969	6.6
	Rickey Henderson, 1980	6.6
	Tim Raines, 1985	6.6
	Tony Gwynn, 1987	6.6
100	6 players tied	6.5

Total Player Rating (alpha.)

Player	Value
Hank Aaron, 1959	6.6
Jeff Bagwell, 1994	7.4
Barry Bonds, 1990	7.2
Barry Bonds, 1992	9.2
Barry Bonds, 1993	8.8
Lou Boudreau, 1943	6.7
Lou Boudreau, 1944	7.8
Lou Boudreau, 1948	6.9
George Brett, 1985	7.2
Norm Cash, 1961	7.1
Cupid Childs, 1890	6.7
Cupid Childs, 1896	6.6
Harland Clift, 1937	7.2
Ty Cobb, 1910	6.7
Ty Cobb, 1911	7.1
Ty Cobb, 1917	8.5
Eddie Collins, 1910	7.0
Joe Cronin, 1930	6.7
Eric Davis, 1987	6.9
Fred Dunlap, 1884	6.9
Jimmie Foxx, 1933	6.7
Frankie Frisch, 1927	7.3
Lou Gehrig, 1927	8.1
Lou Gehrig, 1930	6.9
Lou Gehrig, 1934	7.8
Tony Gwynn, 1987	6.6
Rickey Henderson, 1980	6.6
Rickey Henderson, 1985	7.4
Rickey Henderson, 1990	8.2
Rogers Hornsby, 1917	7.7
Rogers Hornsby, 1920	8.1
Rogers Hornsby, 1921	7.1
Rogers Hornsby, 1922	8.5
Rogers Hornsby, 1924	8.5
Rogers Hornsby, 1927	6.9
Rogers Hornsby, 1929	7.2
Joe Jackson, 1911	6.8
Joe Jackson, 1912	6.9
Reggie Jackson, 1969	6.6
Hughie Jennings, 1896	6.7
Nap Lajoie, 1901	8.9
Nap Lajoie, 1903	8.4
Nap Lajoie, 1904	7.2
Nap Lajoie, 1906	8.5
Nap Lajoie, 1907	6.6
Nap Lajoie, 1908	7.8
Nap Lajoie, 1910	8.5
Mickey Mantle, 1956	8.7
Mickey Mantle, 1957	8.6
Mickey Mantle, 1961	8.0
Willie Mays, 1954	6.7
Willie Mays, 1955	7.7
Willie Mays, 1958	7.2
Willie Mays, 1963	6.6
Willie Mays, 1965	7.3
Kevin Mitchell, 1989	7.0
Joe Morgan, 1975	7.1
Rico Petrocelli, 1969	6.9
Tim Raines, 1985	6.6
Cal Ripken, 1983	6.7
Cal Ripken, 1984	9.1
Cal Ripken, 1991	8.3
Jackie Robinson, 1951	6.8
Frank Robinson, 1966	6.7
Babe Ruth, 1920	8.6
Babe Ruth, 1921	9.4
Babe Ruth, 1923	10.6
Babe Ruth, 1924	8.5
Babe Ruth, 1926	8.4
Babe Ruth, 1927	9.2
Babe Ruth, 1928	7.0
Babe Ruth, 1930	7.3
Babe Ruth, 1931	7.3
Ron Santo, 1966	7.5
Ron Santo, 1967	7.3
Mike Schmidt, 1974	6.9
Mike Schmidt, 1977	6.7
Mike Schmidt, 1980	7.3
Mike Schmidt, 1981	7.0
George Sisler, 1920	7.8
George Sisler, 1922	6.6
Tris Speaker, 1912	7.7
Tris Speaker, 1913	7.3
Tris Speaker, 1914	7.6
Snuffy Stirnweiss, 1944	7.1
Snuffy Stirnweiss, 1945	7.2
Honus Wagner, 1905	7.3
Honus Wagner, 1906	7.3
Honus Wagner, 1908	7.0
Honus Wagner, 1912	6.6
Ted Williams, 1941	7.9
Ted Williams, 1942	8.1
Ted Williams, 1946	7.9
Ted Williams, 1947	7.2
Ted Williams, 1949	6.7
Ted Williams, 1957	7.1
Carl Yastrzemski, 1967	7.3
Carl Yastrzemski, 1968	6.6
Robin Yount, 1982	7.0

Total Player Rating (by era)

1876-1892

#	Player	Value
1	Fred Dunlap, 1884	6.9
2	Cupid Childs, 1890	6.7
3	Fred Pfeffer, 1884	6.1
	Dan Brouthers, 1892	6.1
5	Jack Glasscock, 1889	5.9
6	Billy Nash, 1888	4.9
	Harry Stovey, 1889	4.9
	Jack Glasscock, 1890	4.9
9	Hardy Richardson, 1886	4.8
	Denny Lyons, 1890	4.8
11	Pete Browning, 1882	4.7
	Ned Williamson, 1884	4.7
	Tip O'Neill, 1887	4.7
14	3 players tied	4.6

1893-1919

#	Player	Value
1	Nap Lajoie, 1901	8.9
2	Nap Lajoie, 1906	8.5
	Nap Lajoie, 1910	8.5
	Ty Cobb, 1917	8.5
5	Nap Lajoie, 1903	8.4
6	Nap Lajoie, 1908	7.8
7	Tris Speaker, 1912	7.7
	Rogers Hornsby, 1917	7.7
9	Tris Speaker, 1914	7.6
10	Honus Wagner, 1905	7.3
	Honus Wagner, 1906	7.3
	Tris Speaker, 1913	7.3
13	Nap Lajoie, 1904	7.2
14	Ty Cobb, 1911	7.1
15	2 players tied	7.0

1920-1941

#	Player	Value
1	Babe Ruth, 1923	10.6
2	Babe Ruth, 1921	9.4
3	Babe Ruth, 1927	9.2
4	Babe Ruth, 1920	8.6
5	Rogers Hornsby, 1922	8.5
	Rogers Hornsby, 1924	8.5
	Babe Ruth, 1924	8.5
8	Babe Ruth, 1926	8.4
9	Rogers Hornsby, 1920	8.1
	Lou Gehrig, 1927	8.1
11	Ted Williams, 1941	7.9
12	George Sisler, 1920	7.8
	Lou Gehrig, 1934	7.8
14	3 players tied	7.3

1942-1960

#	Player	Value
1	Mickey Mantle, 1956	8.7
2	Mickey Mantle, 1957	8.6
3	Ted Williams, 1942	8.1
4	Ted Williams, 1946	7.9
5	Lou Boudreau, 1944	7.8
6	Willie Mays, 1955	7.7
7	Snuffy Stirnweiss, 1945	7.2
	Ted Williams, 1947	7.2
	Willie Mays, 1958	7.2
10	Snuffy Stirnweiss, 1944	7.1
	Ted Williams, 1957	7.1
12	Lou Boudreau, 1948	6.9
13	Jackie Robinson, 1951	6.8
14	3 players tied	6.7

1961-1976

#	Player	Value
1	Mickey Mantle, 1961	8.0
2	Ron Santo, 1966	7.5
3	Willie Mays, 1965	7.3
	Ron Santo, 1967	7.3
	Carl Yastrzemski, 1967	7.3
6	Norm Cash, 1961	7.1
	Joe Morgan, 1975	7.1
8	Rico Petrocelli, 1969	6.9
	Mike Schmidt, 1974	6.9
10	Frank Robinson, 1966	6.7
11	Willie Mays, 1963	6.6
	Carl Yastrzemski, 1968	6.6
	Reggie Jackson, 1969	6.6
14	3 players tied	6.5

1977-1994

#	Player	Value
1	Barry Bonds, 1992	9.2
2	Cal Ripken, 1984	9.1
3	Barry Bonds, 1993	8.8
4	Cal Ripken, 1991	8.3
5	Rickey Henderson, 1990	8.2
6	Rickey Henderson, 1985	7.4
	Jeff Bagwell, 1994	7.4
8	Mike Schmidt, 1980	7.3
9	George Brett, 1985	7.2
	Barry Bonds, 1990	7.2
11	Mike Schmidt, 1981	7.0
	Robin Yount, 1982	7.0
	Kevin Mitchell, 1989	7.0
14	Eric Davis, 1987	6.9
15	2 players tied	6.7

Wins

1	Charley Radbourn, 1884	59
2	John Clarkson, 1885	53
3	Guy Hecker, 1884	52
4	John Clarkson, 1889	49
5	Charley Radbourn, 1883	48
	Charlie Buffinton, 1884	48
7	Al Spalding, 1876	47
	John Ward, 1879	47
9	Jim Galvin, 1883	46
	Jim Galvin, 1884	46
	Matt Kilroy, 1887	46
12	George Bradley, 1876	45
	Jim McCormick, 1880	45
	Silver King, 1888	45
15	Mickey Welch, 1885	44
	Bill Hutchison, 1891	44
17	Billy Taylor, 1884	43
	Tommy Bond, 1879	43
	Will White, 1879	43
	Larry Corcoran, 1880	43
	Will White, 1883	43
22	Lady Baldwin, 1886	42
	Tim Keefe, 1886	42
	Bill Hutchison, 1890	42
25	Charlie Sweeney, 1884	41
	Tim Keefe, 1883	41
	Dave Foutz, 1886	41
	Ed Morris, 1886	41
	Jack Chesbro, 1904	41
30	Jim McCormick, 1884	40
	Tommy Bond, 1877	40
	Tommy Bond, 1878	40
	Will White, 1882	40
	Bill Sweeney, 1884	40
	Bob Caruthers, 1885	40
	Bob Caruthers, 1889	40
	Ed Walsh, 1908	40
38	John Ward, 1880	39
	Mickey Welch, 1884	39
	Ed Morris, 1885	39
41	Toad Ramsey, 1886	38
	John Clarkson, 1887	38
	Kid Gleason, 1890	38
44	Jim Galvin, 1879	37
	Jim Whitney, 1883	37
	Tim Keefe, 1884	37
	Jack Lynch, 1884	37
	Toad Ramsey, 1887	37
	Bill Hutchison, 1892	37
	Christy Mathewson, 1908	37
51	Jim McCormick, 1882	36
	Tony Mullane, 1884	36
	John Clarkson, 1886	36
	Sadie McMahon, 1890	36
	Cy Young, 1892	36
	Frank Killen, 1893	36
	Amos Rusie, 1894	36
	Walter Johnson, 1913	36
59	Jim Devlin, 1877	35
	Tony Mullane, 1883	35
	Larry Corcoran, 1884	35
	Tim Keefe, 1887	35
	Tim Keefe, 1888	35
	Ed Seward, 1888	35
	Silver King, 1889	35
	Sadie McMahon, 1891	35
	Kid Nichols, 1892	35
	Jack Stivetts, 1892	35
	Cy Young, 1895	35
	Joe McGinnity, 1904	35
71	Mickey Welch, 1880	34
	Larry Corcoran, 1883	34
	Ed Morris, 1884	34
	Will White, 1884	34
	Elmer Smith, 1887	34
	Scott Stratton, 1890	34
	Mark Baldwin, 1890	34
	George Haddock, 1891	34
	Kid Nichols, 1893	34
	Cy Young, 1893	34
	Joe Wood, 1912	34
82	Charley Radbourn, 1882	33
	Dave Foutz, 1885	33
	Henry Porter, 1885	33
	Mickey Welch, 1886	33
	Tony Mullane, 1886	33
	John Clarkson, 1888	33
	John Clarkson, 1891	33
	Amos Rusie, 1891	33
	Jack Stivetts, 1891	33
	Amos Rusie, 1893	33
	Jouett Meekin, 1894	33
	Cy Young, 1901	33
	Christy Mathewson, 1904	33
	Walter Johnson, 1912	33
	Pete Alexander, 1916	33
97	9 players tied	32

Wins (by era)

1876-1892

1	Charley Radbourn, 1884	59
2	John Clarkson, 1885	53
3	Guy Hecker, 1884	52
4	John Clarkson, 1889	49
5	Charley Radbourn, 1883	48
	Charlie Buffinton, 1884	48
7	Al Spalding, 1876	47
	John Ward, 1879	47
9	Jim Galvin, 1883	46
	Jim Galvin, 1884	46
	Matt Kilroy, 1887	46
12	George Bradley, 1876	45
	Jim McCormick, 1880	45
	Silver King, 1888	45
15	2 players tied	44

1893-1919

1	Jack Chesbro, 1904	41
2	Ed Walsh, 1908	40
3	Christy Mathewson, 1908	37
4	Frank Killen, 1893	36
	Amos Rusie, 1894	36
	Walter Johnson, 1913	36
7	Cy Young, 1895	35
	Joe McGinnity, 1904	35
9	Kid Nichols, 1893	34
	Cy Young, 1893	34
	Joe Wood, 1912	34
12	6 players tied	33

1920-1941

1	Jim Bagby, 1920	31
	Lefty Grove, 1931	31
3	Dizzy Dean, 1934	30
4	Dazzy Vance, 1924	28
	Lefty Grove, 1930	28
	Dizzy Dean, 1935	28
7	Pete Alexander, 1920	27
	Carl Mays, 1921	27
	Urban Shocker, 1921	27
	Eddie Rommel, 1922	27
	Dolf Luque, 1923	27
	George Uhle, 1926	27
	Bucky Walters, 1939	27
	Robert Feller, 1940	27
15	7 players tied	26

1942-1960

1	Hal Newhouser, 1944	29
2	Robin Roberts, 1952	28
3	Dizzy Trout, 1944	27
	Don Newcombe, 1956	27
5	Hal Newhouser, 1946	26
	Robert Feller, 1946	26
7	Hal Newhouser, 1945	25
	Dave Ferriss, 1946	25
	Mel Parnell, 1949	25
10	Johnny Sain, 1948	24
	Bobby Shantz, 1952	24
12	13 players tied	23

1961-1976

1	Denny McLain, 1968	31
2	Sandy Koufax, 1966	27
	Steve Carlton, 1972	27
4	Sandy Koufax, 1965	26
	Juan Marichal, 1968	26
6	Whitey Ford, 1961	25
	Don Drysdale, 1962	25
	Sandy Koufax, 1963	25
	Juan Marichal, 1963	25
	Juan Marichal, 1966	25
	Jim Kaat, 1966	25
	Tom Seaver, 1969	25
	Mickey Lolich, 1971	25
	Catfish Hunter, 1974	25
	Fergie Jenkins, 1974	25

1977-1994

1	Bob Welch, 1990	27
2	Ron Guidry, 1978	25
	Steve Stone, 1980	25
4	Steve Carlton, 1980	24
	La Marr Hoyt, 1983	24
	Dwight Gooden, 1985	24
	Roger Clemens, 1986	24
	Frank Viola, 1988	24
9	Steve Carlton, 1977	23
	Mike Flanagan, 1979	23
	Steve Carlton, 1982	23
	Orel Hershiser, 1988	23
	Danny Jackson, 1988	23
	Bret Saberhagen, 1989	23
15	10 players tied	22

Losses

1	John Coleman, 1883	48
2	Will White, 1880	42
3	Larry McKeon, 1884	41
4	George Bradley, 1879	40
	Jim McCormick, 1879	40
6	Henry Porter, 1888	37
	Kid Carsey, 1891	37
	George Cobb, 1892	37
9	Stump Weidman, 1886	36
	Bill Hutchison, 1892	36
11	Jim Devlin, 1876	35
	Jim Galvin, 1880	35
	Fleury Sullivan, 1884	35
	Adonis Terry, 1884	35
	Hardie Henderson, 1885	35
	Red Donahue, 1897	35
17	Bobby Mathews, 1876	34
	Bob Barr, 1884	34
	Matt Kilroy, 1886	34
	Al Mays, 1887	34
	Mark Baldwin, 1889	34
	Amos Rusie, 1890	34
23	Hardie Henderson, 1883	33
	Dupee Shaw, 1884	33
	Harry McCormick, 1879	33
	Jim Whitney, 1881	33
	Lee Richmond, 1882	33
	Frank Mountain, 1883	33
	Jersey Bakely, 1888	33
30	Lee Richmond, 1880	32
	John Harkins, 1884	32
	Jim Whitney, 1885	32
	Jim Whitney, 1886	32
34	Sam Weaver, 1878	31
	Will White, 1879	31
	Charley Radbourn, 1886	31
	Dupee Shaw, 1886	31
	Billy Crowell, 1887	31
	Amos Rusie, 1892	31
40	Mickey Welch, 1880	30
	Jim McCormick, 1881	30
	Jim McCormick, 1882	30
	Jersey Bakely, 1884	30
	Jack Lynch, 1886	30
	Phenomenal Smith, 1887	30
	Toad Ramsey, 1888	30
	John Ewing, 1889	30
	Ed Beatin, 1890	30
	Ted Breitenstein, 1895	30
	Jim Hughey, 1899	30
51	Tommy Bond, 1880	29
	Jim Galvin, 1883	29
	John Healy, 1887	29
	Hank O'Day, 1888	29
	Bert Cunningham, 1888	29
	Red Ehret, 1889	29
	Silver King, 1891	29
	Bill Hart, 1896	29
	Jack Taylor, 1898	29
	Vic Willis, 1905	29
61	Jim McCormick, 1880	28
	Doc Landis, 1882	28
	Hank O'Day, 1884	28
	Hugh Daily, 1884	28
	Al Mays, 1886	28
	Gus Weyhing, 1887	28
	Mark Baldwin, 1891	28
	Duke Esper, 1893	28
	Bill Hill, 1896	28
70	Jim Galvin, 1879	27
	Tim Keefe, 1881	27
	Tim Keefe, 1883	27
	Charlie Buffinton, 1885	27
	Tony Mullane, 1886	27
	Toad Ramsey, 1886	27
	Toad Ramsey, 1887	27
	Park Swartzel, 1889	27
	Phil Knell, 1891	27
	Mark Baldwin, 1892	27
	Pink Hawley, 1894	27
	Chick Fraser, 1896	27
	Bill Hart, 1897	27
	Willie Sudhoff, 1898	27
	Bill Carrick, 1899	27
	Dummy Taylor, 1901	27
	George Bell, 1910	27
	Paul Derringer, 1933	27
88	21 players tied	26

Winning Percentage

1	Roy Face, 1959	.947
2	Ron Guidry, 1978	.893
3	Freddie Fitzsimmons, 1940	.889
4	Lefty Grove, 1931	.886
5	Preacher Roe, 1951	.880
6	Fred Goldsmith, 1880	.875
7	Joe Wood, 1912	.872
8	David Cone, 1988	.870
9	Orel Hershiser, 1985	.864
10	Bill Donovan, 1907	.862
	Whitey Ford, 1961	.862
12	Dwight Gooden, 1985	.857
	Roger Clemens, 1986	.857
14	Chief Bender, 1914	.850
15	Lefty Grove, 1930	.848
16	Tom Hughes, 1916	.842
	Emil Yde, 1924	.842
	Schoolboy Rowe, 1940	.842
	Sandy Consuegra, 1954	.842
	Ralph Terry, 1961	.842
	Ron Perranoski, 1963	.842
22	Lefty Gomez, 1934	.839
23	Bill Hoffer, 1895	.838
	Denny McLain, 1968	.838
25	Walter Johnson, 1913	.837
26	King Cole, 1910	.833
	Spud Chandler, 1943	.833
	Sandy Koufax, 1963	.833
29	Charley Radbourn, 1884	.831
30	Ed Reulbach, 1906	.826
	Elmer Riddle, 1941	.826
32	Jim Hughes, 1899	.824
	Jack Chesbro, 1902	.824
	Dazzy Vance, 1924	.824
35	Chief Bender, 1910	.821
	Bob Purkey, 1962	.821
37	Sal Maglie, 1950	.818
	Bob Welch, 1990	.818
	Mark Portugal, 1993	.818
40	Joe McGinnity, 1904	.814
41	Mordecai Brown, 1906	.813
	Russ Ford, 1910	.813
	Eddie Plank, 1912	.813
	Carl Hubbell, 1936	.813
45	Dizzy Dean, 1934	.811
46	Ed Reulbach, 1907	.810
	Doc Crandall, 1910	.810
	Johnny Allen, 1932	.810
	Ted Wilks, 1944	.810
	Phil Niekro, 1982	.810
	Jimmy Key, 1994	.810
52	Alvin Crowder, 1928	.808
	Bobo Newsom, 1940	.808
	Tiny Bonham, 1942	.808
	Larry Jansen, 1947	.808
	Dave McNally, 1971	.808
	Catfish Hunter, 1973	.808
58	Christy Mathewson, 1909	.806
	Howie Camnitz, 1909	.806
	Dave Ferriss, 1946	.806
	Juan Marichal, 1966	.806
62	Eddie Cicotte, 1919	.806
63	Mickey Welch, 1885	.800
	Ed Doheny, 1902	.800
	Sam Leever, 1905	.800
	Bert Humphries, 1913	.800
	Stan Coveleski, 1925	.800
	Firpo Marberry, 1931	.800
	Robin Roberts, 1952	.800
	Ed Lopat, 1953	.800
	Don Newcombe, 1955	.800
	Jim Palmer, 1969	.800
	John Candelaria, 1977	.800
	Larry Gura, 1978	.800
	Tommy Greene, 1993	.800
76	Al Spalding, 1876	.797
77	Don Newcombe, 1956	.794
78	Jocko Flynn, 1886	.793
	Ellis Kinder, 1949	.793
	Sal Maglie, 1951	.793
	Bret Saberhagen, 1989	.793
82	Dutch Leonard, 1914	.792
	Sandy Koufax, 1964	.792
	Wally Bunker, 1964	.792
85	Fred Klobedanz, 1897	.788
	Bill James, 1914	.788
	Joe Bush, 1922	.788
88	Jouett Meekin, 1894	.786
	Lon Warneke, 1932	.786
	Tex Hughson, 1942	.786
	Ron Guidry, 1985	.786
	Doug Drabek, 1990	.786
	Tom Glavine, 1993	.786
94	Bob Caruthers, 1889	.784
95	George Mullin, 1909	.784
96	9 players tied	.783

Winning Percentage (by era)

1876-1892
1	Fred Goldsmith, 1880	.875
2	Charley Radbourn, 1884	.831
3	Mickey Welch, 1885	.800
4	Al Spalding, 1876	.797
5	Jocko Flynn, 1886	.793
6	Bob Caruthers, 1889	.784
7	Jack Manning, 1876	.783
8	Will White, 1882	.769
	Charlie Ferguson, 1886	.769
10	John Clarkson, 1885	.768
11	Lady Baldwin, 1886	.764
12	Bob Caruthers, 1887	.763
	Charlie Buffinton, 1891	.763
14	George Haddock, 1891	.756
15	Bob Caruthers, 1885	.755

1893-1919
1	Joe Wood, 1912	.872
2	Bill Donovan, 1907	.862
3	Chief Bender, 1914	.850
4	Tom Hughes, 1916	.842
5	Bill Hoffer, 1895	.838
6	Walter Johnson, 1913	.837
7	King Cole, 1910	.833
8	Ed Reulbach, 1906	.826
9	Jim Hughes, 1899	.824
	Jack Chesbro, 1902	.824
11	Chief Bender, 1910	.821
12	Joe McGinnity, 1904	.814
13	Mordecai Brown, 1906	.813
	Russ Ford, 1910	.813
	Eddie Plank, 1912	.813

1920-1941
1	Freddie Fitzsimmons, 1940	.889
2	Lefty Grove, 1931	.886
3	Lefty Grove, 1930	.848
4	Emil Yde, 1924	.842
	Schoolboy Rowe, 1940	.842
6	Lefty Gomez, 1934	.839
7	Elmer Riddle, 1941	.826
8	Dazzy Vance, 1924	.824
9	Carl Hubbell, 1936	.813
10	Dizzy Dean, 1934	.811
11	Johnny Allen, 1932	.810
12	Alvin Crowder, 1928	.808
	Bobo Newsom, 1940	.808
14	Stan Coveleski, 1925	.800
	Firpo Marberry, 1931	.800

1942-1960
1	Roy Face, 1959	.947
2	Preacher Roe, 1951	.880
3	Sandy Consuegra, 1954	.842
4	Spud Chandler, 1943	.833
5	Sal Maglie, 1950	.818
6	Ted Wilks, 1944	.810
7	Tiny Bonham, 1942	.808
	Larry Jansen, 1947	.808
9	Dave Ferriss, 1946	.806
10	Robin Roberts, 1952	.800
	Ed Lopat, 1953	.800
	Don Newcombe, 1955	.800
13	Don Newcombe, 1956	.794
14	Ellis Kinder, 1949	.793
	Sal Maglie, 1951	.793

1961-1976
1	Whitey Ford, 1961	.862
2	Ralph Terry, 1961	.842
	Ron Perranoski, 1963	.842
4	Denny McLain, 1968	.838
5	Sandy Koufax, 1963	.833
6	Bob Purkey, 1962	.821
7	Dave McNally, 1971	.808
	Catfish Hunter, 1973	.808
9	Juan Marichal, 1966	.806
10	Jim Palmer, 1969	.800
11	Sandy Koufax, 1964	.792
	Wally Bunker, 1964	.792
13	Johnny Podres, 1961	.783
14	Tom Seaver, 1969	.781
15	2 players tied	.774

1977-1994
1	Ron Guidry, 1978	.893
2	David Cone, 1988	.870
3	Orel Hershiser, 1985	.864
4	Dwight Gooden, 1985	.857
	Roger Clemens, 1986	.857
6	Bob Welch, 1990	.818
	Mark Portugal, 1993	.818
8	Phil Niekro, 1982	.810
	Jimmy Key, 1994	.810
10	John Candelaria, 1977	.800
	Larry Gura, 1980	.800
	Tommy Greene, 1993	.800
13	Bret Saberhagen, 1989	.793
14	3 players tied	.786

Games

1	Mike Marshall, 1974	106
2	Kent Tekulve, 1979	94
3	Mike Marshall, 1973	92
4	Kent Tekulve, 1978	91
5	Wayne Granger, 1969	90
	Mike Marshall, 1979	90
	Kent Tekulve, 1987	90
8	Mark Eichhorn, 1987	89
9	Wilbur Wood, 1968	88
10	Rob Murphy, 1987	87
11	Kent Tekulve, 1982	85
	Frank Williams, 1987	85
	Mitch Williams, 1987	85
14	Ted Abernathy, 1965	84
	Enrique Romo, 1979	84
	Dick Tidrow, 1980	84
	Dan Quisenberry, 1985	84
18	Ken Sanders, 1971	83
	Craig Lefferts, 1986	83
20	Eddie Fisher, 1965	82
	Bill Campbell, 1983	82
	Juan Agosto, 1990	82
23	John Wyatt, 1964	81
	Dale Murray, 1976	81
	Jeff Robinson, 1987	81
	Duane Ward, 1991	81
	Joe Boever, 1992	81
	Kenny Rogers, 1992	81
	Mike Jackson, 1993	81
30	Mudcat Grant, 1970	80
	Pedro Borbon, 1973	80
	Willie Hernandez, 1984	80
	Mitch Williams, 1986	80
	Doug Jones, 1992	80
	Greg Harris, 1993	80
36	Dick Radatz, 1964	79
	Duane Ward, 1992	79
38	Hal Woodeshick, 1965	78
	Ted Abernathy, 1968	78
	Bill Campbell, 1976	78
	Rollie Fingers, 1977	78
	Tom Hume, 1980	78
	Kent Tekulve, 1980	78
	Greg Minton, 1982	78
	Ed Vande Berg, 1982	78
	Ted Power, 1984	78
	Tim Burke, 1985	78
	Lance McCullers, 1987	78
49	Dick Tidrow, 1979	77
	Bob Locker, 1967	77
	Wilbur Wood, 1970	77
	Charlie Hough, 1976	77
	Butch Metzger, 1976	77
	Rick Camp, 1980	77
	Gary Lavelle, 1984	77
	Mark Davis, 1985	77
	Craig Lefferts, 1987	77
	Bobby Thigpen, 1990	77
	Barry Jones, 1991	77
	Xavier Hernandez, 1992	77
	Mike Perez, 1992	77
62	Will White, 1879	76
	Jim Galvin, 1883	76
	Charley Radbourn, 1883	76
	Wilbur Wood, 1969	76
	Ron Herbel, 1970	76
	Larry Hardy, 1974	76
	Rollie Fingers, 1974	76
	Dan Spillner, 1977	76
	Dave Tomlin, 1977	76
	Sid Monge, 1979	76
	Rod Scurry, 1982	76
	Tippy Martinez, 1982	76
	Kent Tekulve, 1983	76
	Ed Vande Berg, 1985	76
	Rob Murphy, 1988	76
	Mitch Williams, 1989	76
	Chuck Crim, 1989	76
	Jeff Innis, 1992	76
	Rod Beck, 1993	76
	David West, 1993	76
82	Charley Radbourn, 1884	75
	Guy Hecker, 1884	75
	Bill Hutchison, 1892	75
	Ron Perranoski, 1969	75
	Rollie Fingers, 1975	75
	Butch Metzger, 1977	75
	Dan Quisenberry, 1980	75
	Willie Hernandez, 1982	75
	Jeff Reardon, 1982	75
	Roger McDowell, 1986	75
	Todd Worrell, 1987	75
	Juan Agosto, 1988	75
	Jeff Robinson, 1988	75
	Paul Assenmacher, 1991	75
96	22 players tied	74

Games (by era)

1876-1892
1	Will White, 1879	76
	Jim Galvin, 1883	76
	Charley Radbourn, 1883	76
4	Charley Radbourn, 1884	75
	Guy Hecker, 1884	75
	Bill Hutchison, 1892	75
7	Jim McCormick, 1880	74
	Lee Richmond, 1880	74
9	John Clarkson, 1889	73
10	Jim Galvin, 1884	72
11	Bill Hutchison, 1890	71
12	John Ward, 1879	70
	John Ward, 1880	70
	John Clarkson, 1885	70
15	Matt Kilroy, 1887	69

1893-1919
1	Ed Walsh, 1908	66
2	Ed Walsh, 1912	62
3	Dave Davenport, 1916	59
4	Amos Rusie, 1893	56
	Ted Breitenstein, 1894	56
	Pink Hawley, 1895	56
	Ed Walsh, 1907	56
	Christy Mathewson, 1908	56
	Ed Walsh, 1911	56
	Reb Russell, 1916	56
11	Frank Killen, 1893	55
	Joe McGinnity, 1903	55
	Jack Chesbro, 1904	55
	Dave Davenport, 1915	55
15	3 players tied	54

1920-1941
1	Firpo Marberry, 1926	64
2	Clint Brown, 1939	61
3	Garland Braxton, 1927	58
	Russ Van Atta, 1935	58
5	Eddie Rommel, 1923	56
	Firpo Marberry, 1927	56
	Hugh Mulcahy, 1937	56
8	Firpo Marberry, 1925	55
	Bump Hadley, 1931	55
	Jim Walkup, 1935	55
11	George Uhle, 1923	54
	Firpo Marberry, 1932	54
	Jack Russell, 1934	54
	Chubby Dean, 1939	54
	Clyde Shoun, 1940	54

1942-1960
1	Jim Konstanty, 1950	74
2	Hoyt Wilhelm, 1952	71
3	Ace Adams, 1943	70
	Mike Fornieles, 1960	70
5	Ellis Kinder, 1953	69
	Don Elston, 1958	69
7	Hoyt Wilhelm, 1953	68
	Roy Face, 1956	68
	Roy Face, 1960	68
10	Andy Karl, 1945	67
	Turk Lown, 1957	67
	Gerry Staley, 1959	67
13	6 players tied	65

1961-1976
1	Mike Marshall, 1974	106
2	Mike Marshall, 1973	92
3	Wayne Granger, 1969	90
4	Wilbur Wood, 1968	88
5	Ted Abernathy, 1965	84
6	Ken Sanders, 1971	83
7	Eddie Fisher, 1965	82
8	John Wyatt, 1964	81
	Dale Murray, 1976	81
10	Mudcat Grant, 1970	80
	Pedro Borbon, 1973	80
12	Dick Radatz, 1964	79
13	Hal Woodeshick, 1965	78
	Ted Abernathy, 1968	78
	Bill Campbell, 1976	78

1977-1994
1	Kent Tekulve, 1979	94
2	Kent Tekulve, 1978	91
3	Mike Marshall, 1979	90
	Kent Tekulve, 1987	90
5	Mark Eichhorn, 1987	89
6	Rob Murphy, 1987	87
7	Kent Tekulve, 1982	85
	Frank Williams, 1987	85
	Mitch Williams, 1987	85
10	Enrique Romo, 1979	84
	Dick Tidrow, 1980	84
	Dan Quisenberry, 1985	84
13	Craig Lefferts, 1986	83
14	Bill Campbell, 1983	82
	Juan Agosto, 1990	82

Games Started

1	Will White, 1879	75
	Jim Galvin, 1883	75
3	Jim McCormick, 1880	74
4	Charley Radbourn, 1884	73
	Guy Hecker, 1884	73
6	Jim Galvin, 1884	72
	John Clarkson, 1889	72
8	Bill Hutchison, 1892	71
9	John Clarkson, 1885	70
10	Matt Kilroy, 1887	69
11	Jim Devlin, 1876	68
	Charley Radbourn, 1883	68
	Tim Keefe, 1883	68
	Matt Kilroy, 1886	68
15	John Ward, 1880	67
	Jim McCormick, 1882	67
	Charlie Buffinton, 1884	67
	Toad Ramsey, 1886	67
19	Dupee Shaw, 1884	66
	Jim Galvin, 1879	66
	Lee Richmond, 1880	66
	Bill Hutchison, 1890	66
23	Jim McCormick, 1884	65
	Mickey Welch, 1884	65
	Tony Mullane, 1884	65
	Silver King, 1888	65
27	George Bradley, 1876	64
	Tommy Bond, 1879	64
	Mickey Welch, 1880	64
	Will White, 1883	64
	Tim Keefe, 1886	64
	Toad Ramsey, 1887	64
33	Jim Whitney, 1881	63
	Ed Morris, 1885	63
	Ed Morris, 1886	63
	Amos Rusie, 1890	63
37	Will White, 1880	62
38	Jim Devlin, 1877	61
	John Coleman, 1883	61
	Hardie Henderson, 1885	61
	Jersey Bakely, 1888	61
	Amos Rusie, 1892	61
43	Al Spalding, 1876	60
	Jim McCormick, 1879	60
	John Ward, 1879	60
	Larry Corcoran, 1880	60
	Larry McKeon, 1884	60
	Bill Sweeney, 1884	60
49	Billy Taylor, 1884	59
	Tommy Bond, 1878	59
	Frank Mountain, 1883	59
	Larry Corcoran, 1884	59
	Mickey Welch, 1886	59
	John Clarkson, 1887	59
	Mark Baldwin, 1889	59
56	Tommy Bond, 1877	58
	Terry Larkin, 1879	58
	Jim McCormick, 1881	58
	Hugh Daily, 1884	58
	Charley Radbourn, 1886	58
	Bill Hutchison, 1891	58
	Sadie McMahon, 1891	58
63	Tommy Bond, 1880	57
	Tim Keefe, 1884	57
	Dave Foutz, 1886	57
	Ed Seward, 1888	57
	Sadie McMahon, 1890	57
	Mark Baldwin, 1890	57
	Amos Rusie, 1891	57
70	Charlie Sweeney, 1884	56
	Bobby Mathews, 1876	56
	Terry Larkin, 1877	56
	Terry Larkin, 1878	56
	Jim Whitney, 1883	56
	Lady Baldwin, 1886	56
	Tony Mullane, 1886	56
	Tim Keefe, 1887	56
	Matt Kilroy, 1889	56
	Silver King, 1890	56
	Jack Stivetts, 1891	56
81	George Derby, 1881	55
	Tony Mullane, 1882	55
	Adonis Terry, 1884	55
	Mickey Welch, 1885	55
	John Clarkson, 1886	55
	Phenomenal Smith, 1887	55
	Gus Weyhing, 1887	55
	Ed Morris, 1888	55
	Kid Gleason, 1890	55
90	George Bradley, 1879	54
	Harry McCormick, 1879	54
	Jim Galvin, 1880	54
	Will White, 1882	54
	Jack Lynch, 1884	54
	Henry Porter, 1885	54
	John Clarkson, 1888	54
	Henry Porter, 1888	54
	Ed Beatin, 1890	54
	Bob Barr, 1890	54
100	8 players tied	53

Games Started (by era)

1876-1892

1	Will White, 1879	75
	Jim Galvin, 1883	75
3	Jim McCormick, 1880	74
4	Charley Radbourn, 1884	73
	Guy Hecker, 1884	73
6	Jim Galvin, 1884	72
	John Clarkson, 1889	72
8	Bill Hutchison, 1892	71
9	John Clarkson, 1885	70
10	Matt Kilroy, 1887	69
11	Jim Devlin, 1876	68
	Charley Radbourn, 1883	68
	Tim Keefe, 1883	68
	Matt Kilroy, 1886	68
15	4 players tied	67

1893-1919

1	Amos Rusie, 1893	52
2	Jack Chesbro, 1904	51
3	Ted Breitenstein, 1894	50
	Amos Rusie, 1894	50
	Ted Breitenstein, 1895	50
	Pink Hawley, 1895	50
	Frank Killen, 1896	50
8	Ed Walsh, 1908	49
9	Frank Killen, 1893	48
	Jouett Meekin, 1894	48
	Joe McGinnity, 1903	48
12	Cy Young, 1894	47
	Amos Rusie, 1895	47
	Jack Taylor, 1898	47
15	8 players tied	46

1920-1941

1	George Uhle, 1923	44
2	Pete Alexander, 1920	40
	Stan Coveleski, 1921	40
	George Uhle, 1922	40
	George Caster, 1938	40
	Bobo Newsom, 1938	40
	Robert Feller, 1941	40
8	Red Faber, 1920	39
	Red Faber, 1921	39
	Hooks Dauss, 1923	39
	Howard Ehmke, 1923	39
	George Earnshaw, 1930	39
	Alvin Crowder, 1932	39
	Kirby Higbe, 1941	39
15	24 players tied	38

1942-1960

1	Robert Feller, 1946	42
	Bob Friend, 1956	42
3	Bill Voiselle, 1944	41
	Robin Roberts, 1953	41
5	Dizzy Trout, 1944	40
6	Johnny Sain, 1948	39
	Robin Roberts, 1950	39
	Warren Spahn, 1950	39
	Vern Bickford, 1950	39
	Robin Roberts, 1951	39
	Ron Kline, 1956	39
	Lew Burdette, 1959	39
13	10 players tied	38

1961-1976

1	Wilbur Wood, 1972	49
2	Wilbur Wood, 1973	48
3	Mickey Lolich, 1971	45
4	Wilbur Wood, 1975	43
5	Don Drysdale, 1963	42
	Jack Sanford, 1963	42
	Don Drysdale, 1965	42
	Jim Kaat, 1965	42
	Fergie Jenkins, 1969	42
	Wilbur Wood, 1971	42
	Stan Bahnsen, 1973	42
	Mickey Lolich, 1973	42
	Wilbur Wood, 1974	42
14	22 players tied	41

1977-1994

1	Phil Niekro, 1979	44
2	Phil Niekro, 1977	43
3	Phil Niekro, 1978	42
4	Steve Rogers, 1977	40
	Mike Flanagan, 1978	40
	Dennis Leonard, 1978	40
	Jim Clancy, 1982	40
	Charlie Hough, 1987	40
9	9 players tied	39

Complete Games

1	Will White, 1879	75
2	Charley Radbourn, 1884	73
3	Jim McCormick, 1880	72
	Jim Galvin, 1883	72
	Guy Hecker, 1884	72
6	Jim Galvin, 1884	71
7	Tim Keefe, 1883	68
	John Clarkson, 1885	68
	John Clarkson, 1889	68
10	Bill Hutchison, 1892	67
11	Jim Devlin, 1876	66
	Charley Radbourn, 1883	66
	Matt Kilroy, 1886	66
	Toad Ramsey, 1886	66
	Matt Kilroy, 1887	66
16	Jim Galvin, 1884	65
	Jim McCormick, 1882	65
	Bill Hutchison, 1890	65
19	Mickey Welch, 1880	64
	Will White, 1883	64
	Tony Mullane, 1884	64
	Silver King, 1888	64
23	Jim McCormick, 1884	63
	George Bradley, 1876	63
	Charlie Buffinton, 1884	63
	Ed Morris, 1885	63
	Ed Morris, 1886	63
28	Mickey Welch, 1884	62
	Tim Keefe, 1886	62
30	Jim Devlin, 1877	61
	Toad Ramsey, 1887	61
32	Dupee Shaw, 1884	60
	Jersey Bakely, 1888	60
34	Billy Taylor, 1884	59
	Tommy Bond, 1879	59
	Jim McCormick, 1879	59
	John Ward, 1880	59
	John Coleman, 1883	59
	Larry McKeon, 1884	59
	Hardie Henderson, 1885	59
41	Tommy Bond, 1877	58
	John Ward, 1879	58
	Will White, 1880	58
	Bill Sweeney, 1884	58
	Amos Rusie, 1892	58
46	Tommy Bond, 1878	57
	Terry Larkin, 1879	57
	Larry Corcoran, 1880	57
	Lee Richmond, 1880	57
	Jim McCormick, 1881	57
	Jim Whitney, 1881	57
	Frank Mountain, 1883	57
	Larry Corcoran, 1884	57
	Charley Radbourn, 1886	57
	Ed Seward, 1888	57
56	Terry Larkin, 1878	56
	Tim Keefe, 1884	56
	Hugh Daily, 1884	56
	Mickey Welch, 1886	56
	John Clarkson, 1887	56
	Amos Rusie, 1890	56
	Bill Hutchison, 1891	56
63	Bobby Mathews, 1876	55
	Terry Larkin, 1877	55
	George Derby, 1881	55
	Mickey Welch, 1885	55
	Lady Baldwin, 1886	55
	Dave Foutz, 1886	55
	Tony Mullane, 1886	55
	Matt Kilroy, 1889	55
	Sadie McMahon, 1890	55
72	Jim Whitney, 1883	54
	Jack Lynch, 1884	54
	Adonis Terry, 1884	54
	Tim Keefe, 1887	54
	Phenomenal Smith, 1887	54
	Ed Morris, 1888	54
	Mark Baldwin, 1889	54
	Kid Gleason, 1890	54
	Mark Baldwin, 1890	54
81	Charlie Sweeney, 1884	53
	Al Spalding, 1876	53
	George Bradley, 1879	53
	Bob Caruthers, 1885	53
	Henry Porter, 1885	53
	Gus Weyhing, 1887	53
	John Clarkson, 1888	53
	Henry Porter, 1888	53
	Ed Beatin, 1890	53
	Sadie McMahon, 1891	53
91	Will White, 1878	52
	Will White, 1882	52
	Will White, 1884	52
	Ed Seward, 1887	52
	Bob Barr, 1890	52
	Amos Rusie, 1891	52
97	6 players tied	51

Complete Games (by era)

1876-1892

1	Will White, 1879	75
2	Charley Radbourn, 1884	73
3	Jim McCormick, 1880	72
	Jim Galvin, 1883	72
	Guy Hecker, 1884	72
6	Jim Galvin, 1884	71
7	Tim Keefe, 1883	68
	John Clarkson, 1885	68
	John Clarkson, 1889	68
10	Bill Hutchison, 1892	67
11	Jim Devlin, 1876	66
	Charley Radbourn, 1883	66
	Matt Kilroy, 1886	66
	Toad Ramsey, 1886	66
	Matt Kilroy, 1887	66

1893-1919

1	Amos Rusie, 1893	50
2	Jack Chesbro, 1904	48
3	Ted Breitenstein, 1894	46
	Ted Breitenstein, 1895	46
5	Amos Rusie, 1894	45
	Vic Willis, 1902	45
7	Cy Young, 1894	44
	Pink Hawley, 1895	44
	Frank Killen, 1896	44
	Joe McGinnity, 1903	44
11	Kid Nichols, 1893	43
12	7 players tied	42

1920-1941

1	Pete Alexander, 1920	33
	Burleigh Grimes, 1923	33
3	Red Faber, 1921	32
	George Uhle, 1926	32
5	Red Faber, 1922	31
	Wes Ferrell, 1935	31
	Bobo Newsom, 1938	31
	Bucky Walters, 1939	31
	Robert Feller, 1940	31
10	8 players tied	30

1942-1960

1	Robert Feller, 1946	36
2	Dizzy Trout, 1944	33
	Robin Roberts, 1953	33
4	Robin Roberts, 1952	30
5	Hal Newhouser, 1945	29
	Hal Newhouser, 1946	29
	Robin Roberts, 1954	29
8	Jim Tobin, 1942	28
	Jim Tobin, 1944	28
	Johnny Sain, 1948	28
	Bob Lemon, 1952	28
12	Bucky Walters, 1944	27
	Mel Parnell, 1949	27
	Vern Bickford, 1950	27
	Bobby Shantz, 1952	27

1961-1976

1	Juan Marichal, 1968	30
	Fergie Jenkins, 1971	30
	Steve Carlton, 1972	30
	Catfish Hunter, 1975	30
5	Mickey Lolich, 1971	29
	Gaylord Perry, 1972	29
	Gaylord Perry, 1973	29
	Fergie Jenkins, 1974	29
9	Bob Gibson, 1968	28
	Denny McLain, 1968	28
	Bob Gibson, 1969	28
	Gaylord Perry, 1974	28
13	4 players tied	27

1977-1994

1	Rick Langford, 1980	28
2	Mike Norris, 1980	24
	Bert Blyleven, 1985	24
4	Mike Caldwell, 1978	23
	Phil Niekro, 1979	23
6	Jim Palmer, 1977	22
	Nolan Ryan, 1977	22
	Phil Niekro, 1978	22
9	Wayne Garland, 1977	21
	Dennis Leonard, 1977	21
	Ron Guidry, 1983	21
12	6 players tied	20

Shutouts

1	George Bradley, 1876	16
	Pete Alexander, 1916	16
3	Jack Coombs, 1910	13
	Bob Gibson, 1968	13
5	Jim Galvin, 1884	12
	Ed Morris, 1886	12
	Pete Alexander, 1915	12
8	Tommy Bond, 1879	11
	Charley Radbourn, 1884	11
	Dave Foutz, 1886	11
	Christy Mathewson, 1908	11
	Ed Walsh, 1908	11
	Walter Johnson, 1913	11
	Sandy Koufax, 1963	11
	Dean Chance, 1964	11
16	Jim McCormick, 1884	10
	John Clarkson, 1885	10
	Cy Young, 1904	10
	Ed Walsh, 1906	10
	Joe Wood, 1912	10
	Dave Davenport, 1915	10
	Carl Hubbell, 1933	10
	Mort Cooper, 1942	10
	Robert Feller, 1946	10
	Bob Lemon, 1948	10
	Juan Marichal, 1965	10
	Jim Palmer, 1975	10
	John Tudor, 1985	10
29	Tommy Bond, 1878	9
	George Derby, 1881	9
	Cy Young, 1892	9
	Joe McGinnity, 1904	9
	Mordecai Brown, 1906	9
	Addie Joss, 1906	9
	Mordecai Brown, 1908	9
	Addie Joss, 1908	9
	Orval Overall, 1909	9
	Pete Alexander, 1913	9
	Walter Johnson, 1914	9
	Cy Falkenberg, 1914	9
	Babe Ruth, 1916	9
	Stan Coveleski, 1917	9
	Pete Alexander, 1919	9
	Bill Lee, 1938	9
	Bob Porterfield, 1953	9
	Luis Tiant, 1968	9
	Denny McLain, 1969	9
	Don Sutton, 1972	9
	Nolan Ryan, 1972	9
	Bert Blyleven, 1973	9
	Ron Guidry, 1978	9
52	Al Spalding, 1876	8
	John Ward, 1880	8
	Will White, 1882	8
	Charlie Buffinton, 1884	8
	Tim Keefe, 1888	8
	Ben Sanders, 1888	8
	John Clarkson, 1889	8
	Christy Mathewson, 1902	8
	Jack Chesbro, 1902	8
	Rube Waddell, 1904	8
	Christy Mathewson, 1905	8
	Ed Killian, 1905	8
	Lefty Leifield, 1906	8
	Rube Waddell, 1906	8
	Orval Overall, 1907	8
	Christy Mathewson, 1907	8
	Eddie Plank, 1907	8
	Mordecai Brown, 1909	8
	Christy Mathewson, 1909	8
	Ed Walsh, 1909	8
	Russ Ford, 1910	8
	Walter Johnson, 1910	8
	Reb Russell, 1913	8
	Jeff Tesreau, 1914	8
	Al Mamaux, 1915	8
	Jeff Tesreau, 1915	8
	Joe Bush, 1916	8
	Pete Alexander, 1917	8
	Jim Bagby, 1917	8
	Walter Johnson, 1917	8
	Hippo Vaughn, 1918	8
	Walter Johnson, 1918	8
	Carl Mays, 1918	8
	Babe Adams, 1920	8
	Hal Newhouser, 1945	8
	Steve Barber, 1961	8
	Camilo Pascual, 1961	8
	Whitey Ford, 1964	8
	Sandy Koufax, 1965	8
	Don Drysdale, 1968	8
	Juan Marichal, 1969	8
	Vida Blue, 1971	8
	Steve Carlton, 1972	8
	Wilbur Wood, 1972	8
	Fernando Valenzuela, 1981	8
	Dwight Gooden, 1985	8
	Orel Hershiser, 1988	8
	Roger Clemens, 1988	8
	Tim Belcher, 1989	8

Saves

	Player, Year	
1	Bobby Thigpen, 1990	57
2	Randy Myers, 1993	53
3	Dennis Eckersley, 1992	51
4	Dennis Eckersley, 1990	48
	Rod Beck, 1993	48
6	Lee Smith, 1991	47
7	Lee Smith, 1993	46
	Dave Righetti, 1986	46
	Bryan Harvey, 1991	46
10	Dan Quisenberry, 1983	45
	Bruce Sutter, 1984	45
	Dennis Eckersley, 1988	45
	Bryan Harvey, 1993	45
	Jeff Montgomery, 1993	45
	Duane Ward, 1993	45
16	Dan Quisenberry, 1984	44
	Mark Davis, 1989	44
18	Doug Jones, 1990	43
	Dennis Eckersley, 1991	43
	Lee Smith, 1992	43
	John Wetteland, 1993	43
	Mitch Williams, 1993	43
23	Jeff Reardon, 1988	42
	Rick Aguilera, 1991	42
25	Jeff Reardon, 1985	41
	Rick Aguilera, 1992	41
27	Steve Bedrosian, 1987	40
	Jeff Reardon, 1991	40
	Tom Henke, 1993	40
30	John Franco, 1988	39
	Jeff Montgomery, 1992	39
32	John Hiller, 1973	38
	Jeff Russell, 1989	38
	Randy Myers, 1992	38
	Roberto Hernandez, 1993	38
36	Clay Carroll, 1972	37
	Rollie Fingers, 1978	37
	Bruce Sutter, 1979	37
	Dan Quisenberry, 1985	37
	Doug Jones, 1988	37
	Gregg Olson, 1990	37
	John Wetteland, 1992	37
43	Bruce Sutter, 1982	36
	Bill Caudill, 1984	36
	Todd Worrell, 1986	36
	Lee Smith, 1987	36
	Mitch Williams, 1989	36
	Dave Righetti, 1990	36
	Doug Jones, 1992	36
	Gregg Olson, 1992	36
	Dennis Eckersley, 1993	36
52	Wayne Granger, 1970	35
	Sparky Lyle, 1972	35
	Rollie Fingers, 1977	35
	Dan Quisenberry, 1982	35
	Jeff Reardon, 1986	35
57	Ron Perranoski, 1970	34
	Don Aase, 1986	34
	Tom Henke, 1987	34
	Jim Gott, 1988	34
	Bobby Thigpen, 1988	34
	Bobby Thigpen, 1989	34
	Tom Henke, 1992	34
	Rick Aguilera, 1993	34
65	Rich Gossage, 1980	33
	Dan Quisenberry, 1980	33
	Bob Stanley, 1983	33
	Lee Smith, 1984	33
	Lee Smith, 1985	33
	Dave Smith, 1986	33
	Todd Worrell, 1987	33
	Dennis Eckersley, 1989	33
	Dan Plesac, 1989	33
	Mike Schooler, 1989	33
	John Franco, 1990	33
	Jeff Montgomery, 1991	33
	Jeff Russell, 1993	33
	Lee Smith, 1994	33
79	Jack Aker, 1966	32
	Mike Marshall, 1979	32
	Willie Hernandez, 1984	32
	Bob James, 1985	32
	John Franco, 1987	32
	Todd Worrell, 1988	32
	John Franco, 1989	32
	Doug Jones, 1989	32
	Rick Aguilera, 1990	32
	Tom Henke, 1990	32
	Tom Henke, 1991	32
90	20 players tied	31

Innings Pitched

	Player, Year	
1	Will White, 1879	680.0
2	Charley Radbourn, 1884	678.2
3	Guy Hecker, 1884	670.2
4	Jim McCormick, 1880	657.2
5	Jim Galvin, 1883	656.1
6	Jim Galvin, 1884	636.1
7	Charley Radbourn, 1883	632.1
8	Bill Hutchison, 1892	627.0
9	John Clarkson, 1885	623.0
10	Jim Devlin, 1876	622.0
11	John Clarkson, 1889	620.0
12	Tim Keefe, 1883	619.0
13	Bill Hutchison, 1890	603.0
14	Jim McCormick, 1882	595.2
15	John Ward, 1880	595.0
16	Jim Galvin, 1879	593.0
17	Lee Richmond, 1880	590.2
18	Matt Kilroy, 1887	589.1
19	Toad Ramsey, 1886	588.2
20	John Ward, 1879	587.0
	Charlie Buffinton, 1884	587.0
22	Silver King, 1888	585.2
23	Matt Kilroy, 1886	583.0
24	Ed Morris, 1885	581.0
25	Will White, 1883	577.0
26	Mickey Welch, 1880	574.0
27	George Bradley, 1876	573.0
28	Jim McCormick, 1884	569.0
29	Tony Mullane, 1884	567.0
30	Toad Ramsey, 1887	561.0
	Bill Hutchison, 1891	561.0
32	Jim Devlin, 1877	559.0
33	Mickey Welch, 1884	557.1
34	Tommy Bond, 1879	555.1
	Ed Morris, 1886	555.1
36	Jim Whitney, 1881	552.1
37	Amos Rusie, 1890	548.2
38	Jim McCormick, 1879	546.1
39	Dupee Shaw, 1884	543.1
40	Hardie Henderson, 1885	539.1
41	John Coleman, 1883	538.1
42	Bill Sweeney, 1884	538.0
43	Larry Corcoran, 1880	536.1
44	Tim Keefe, 1886	535.0
45	Tommy Bond, 1878	532.2
	Jersey Bakely, 1888	532.2
47	Amos Rusie, 1892	532.0
48	Tony Mullane, 1886	529.2
49	Al Spalding, 1876	528.2
50	Jim McCormick, 1881	526.0
51	Billy Taylor, 1884	523.0
	John Clarkson, 1887	523.0
53	Tommy Bond, 1877	521.0
54	Ed Seward, 1888	518.2
55	Will White, 1880	517.1
56	Larry Corcoran, 1884	516.2
57	Bobby Mathews, 1876	516.0
58	Jim Whitney, 1883	514.0
59	Mark Baldwin, 1889	513.2
60	Terry Larkin, 1879	513.1
61	Larry McKeon, 1884	512.0
62	Charley Radbourn, 1886	509.1
63	Sadie McMahon, 1890	509.0
64	Terry Larkin, 1878	506.0
	Kid Gleason, 1890	506.0
66	Dave Foutz, 1886	504.0
67	Frank Mountain, 1883	503.0
	Sadie McMahon, 1891	503.0
69	Terry Larkin, 1877	501.0
	Mark Baldwin, 1890	501.0
71	Hugh Daily, 1884	500.2
72	Amos Rusie, 1891	500.1
73	Mickey Welch, 1886	500.0
74	Jack Lynch, 1884	496.0
75	George Derby, 1881	494.2
76	Bob Barr, 1890	493.1
77	Tommy Bond, 1880	493.0
78	Charlie Sweeney, 1884	492.0
	Mickey Welch, 1885	492.0
80	Phenomenal Smith, 1887	491.1
81	George Bradley, 1879	487.0
	Lady Baldwin, 1886	487.0
83	John Clarkson, 1888	483.1
84	Tim Keefe, 1884	482.2
85	Bob Caruthers, 1885	482.1
86	Amos Rusie, 1893	482.0
87	Henry Porter, 1885	481.2
88	Matt Kilroy, 1889	480.2
89	Will White, 1882	480.0
	Guy Hecker, 1885	480.0
	Ed Morris, 1888	480.0
92	Tim Keefe, 1887	476.2
93	Adonis Terry, 1884	476.0
94	Ed Beatin, 1890	474.1
95	Jim Galvin, 1881	474.0
	Charley Radbourn, 1882	474.0
	Henry Porter, 1888	474.0
98	Larry Corcoran, 1883	473.2
99	Ed Seward, 1887	470.2
100	Gus Weyhing, 1892	469.2

Innings Pitched (by era)

1876-1892

	Player, Year	
1	Will White, 1879	680.0
2	Charley Radbourn, 1884	678.2
3	Guy Hecker, 1884	670.2
4	Jim McCormick, 1880	657.2
5	Jim Galvin, 1883	656.1
6	Jim Galvin, 1884	636.1
7	Charley Radbourn, 1883	632.1
8	Bill Hutchison, 1892	627.0
9	John Clarkson, 1885	623.0
10	Jim Devlin, 1876	622.0
11	John Clarkson, 1889	620.0
12	Tim Keefe, 1883	619.0
13	Bill Hutchison, 1890	603.0
14	Jim McCormick, 1882	595.2
15	John Ward, 1880	595.0

1893-1919

	Player, Year	
1	Amos Rusie, 1893	482.0
2	Ed Walsh, 1908	464.0
3	Jack Chesbro, 1904	454.2
4	Ted Breitenstein, 1894	447.1
5	Pink Hawley, 1895	444.1
6	Amos Rusie, 1894	444.0
7	Joe McGinnity, 1903	434.0
8	Frank Killen, 1896	432.1
9	Ted Breitenstein, 1895	429.2
10	Kid Nichols, 1893	425.0
11	Cy Young, 1893	422.2
12	Ed Walsh, 1907	422.1
13	Frank Killen, 1893	415.0
14	Cy Young, 1896	414.1
15	Vic Willis, 1902	410.0

1920-1941

	Player, Year	
1	Pete Alexander, 1920	363.1
2	George Uhle, 1923	357.2
3	Red Faber, 1922	352.0
4	Urban Shocker, 1922	348.0
5	Robert Feller, 1941	343.0
6	Jim Bagby, 1920	339.2
7	Carl Mays, 1921	336.2
8	Red Faber, 1921	330.2
	Burleigh Grimes, 1928	330.2
10	Bobo Newsom, 1938	329.2
11	Wilbur Cooper, 1920	327.0
	Wilbur Cooper, 1921	327.0
	Burleigh Grimes, 1923	327.0
	Alvin Crowder, 1932	327.0
15	Urban Shocker, 1921	326.2

1942-1960

	Player, Year	
1	Robert Feller, 1946	371.1
2	Dizzy Trout, 1944	352.1
3	Robin Roberts, 1953	346.2
4	Robin Roberts, 1954	336.2
5	Robin Roberts, 1952	330.0
6	Robin Roberts, 1951	315.0
7	Johnny Sain, 1948	314.2
8	Bob Friend, 1956	314.1
9	Hal Newhouser, 1945	313.1
10	Bill Voiselle, 1944	312.2
11	Hal Newhouser, 1944	312.1
12	Vern Bickford, 1950	311.2
13	Warren Spahn, 1951	310.2
14	Bob Lemon, 1952	309.2
15	Robin Roberts, 1955	305.0

1961-1976

	Player, Year	
1	Wilbur Wood, 1972	376.2
2	Mickey Lolich, 1971	376.0
3	Wilbur Wood, 1973	359.1
4	Steve Carlton, 1972	346.1
5	Gaylord Perry, 1973	344.0
6	Gaylord Perry, 1972	342.2
7	Denny McLain, 1968	336.0
8	Sandy Koufax, 1965	335.2
9	Wilbur Wood, 1971	334.0
10	Nolan Ryan, 1974	332.2
11	Gaylord Perry, 1970	328.2
12	Fergie Jenkins, 1974	328.1
13	Catfish Hunter, 1975	328.0
14	Mickey Lolich, 1972	327.1
15	2 players tied	326.0

1977-1994

	Player, Year	
1	Phil Niekro, 1979	342.0
2	Phil Niekro, 1978	334.1
3	Phil Niekro, 1977	330.1
4	Jim Palmer, 1977	319.0
5	Steve Carlton, 1980	304.0
6	Dave Goltz, 1977	303.0
7	Steve Rogers, 1977	301.2
8	Nolan Ryan, 1977	299.0
9	Jim Palmer, 1978	296.0
10	Steve Carlton, 1982	295.2
11	Dennis Leonard, 1978	294.2
12	Jack Morris, 1983	293.2
	Bert Blyleven, 1985	293.2
14	Mike Caldwell, 1978	293.1
15	Dennis Leonard, 1977	292.2

Hits per Game

	Player, Year	
1	Nolan Ryan, 1972	5.26
2	Luis Tiant, 1968	5.30
3	Nolan Ryan, 1991	5.31
4	Ed Reulbach, 1906	5.33
5	Dutch Leonard, 1914	5.57
6	Carl Lundgren, 1907	5.65
7	Sid Fernandez, 1985	5.71
8	Tommy Byrne, 1949	5.74
9	Dave McNally, 1968	5.77
10	Sandy Koufax, 1965	5.79
11	Russ Ford, 1910	5.83
12	Al Downing, 1963	5.84
13	Herb Score, 1956	5.85
14	Bob Gibson, 1968	5.85
15	Sam McDowell, 1965	5.87
16	Ed Walsh, 1910	5.89
17	Mike Scott, 1986	5.95
18	Mario Soto, 1980	5.96
19	Floyd Youmans, 1986	5.96
20	Nolan Ryan, 1977	5.96
21	Nolan Ryan, 1974	5.98
22	Nolan Ryan, 1981	5.98
23	Nolan Ryan, 1989	6.02
24	Sam McDowell, 1966	6.02
25	Vida Blue, 1971	6.03
26	Walter Johnson, 1913	6.03
27	Nolan Ryan, 1990	6.04
28	Pete Alexander, 1915	6.05
29	Sam McDowell, 1968	6.06
30	Joe Horlen, 1964	6.07
31	Andy Messersmith, 1969	6.08
32	Tim Keefe, 1880	6.09
33	Nolan Ryan, 1989	6.09
34	Stan Coveleski, 1917	6.09
35	Catfish Hunter, 1972	6.09
36	Nolan Ryan, 1976	6.11
37	Sid Fernandez, 1988	6.11
38	Bob Turley, 1957	6.12
39	Bob Turley, 1955	6.13
40	Don Sutton, 1972	6.14
41	Nolan Ryan, 1983	6.14
42	Ron Guidry, 1978	6.15
43	Mordecai Brown, 1908	6.17
44	Sandy Koufax, 1963	6.19
45	Jack Pfiester, 1906	6.21
46	Sandy Koufax, 1964	6.22
47	Roger Nelson, 1972	6.23
48	Herb Score, 1955	6.26
49	Cy Morgan, 1909	6.26
50	Dean Chance, 1964	6.27
51	Christy Mathewson, 1909	6.28
	J.R. Richard, 1978	6.28
53	Art Fromme, 1909	6.28
54	Walter Johnson, 1912	6.32
55	Jack Coombs, 1910	6.32
56	Rube Waddell, 1905	6.33
57	Vean Gregg, 1911	6.33
58	Jeff Robinson, 1988	6.33
59	Larry Cheney, 1916	6.33
60	Sonny Siebert, 1968	6.33
61	Allie Reynolds, 1943	6.34
62	Roger Clemens, 1986	6.34
63	Willie Mitchell, 1913	6.35
64	Jose DeLeon, 1989	6.36
65	Pascual Perez, 1988	6.37
66	Walter Johnson, 1910	6.37
67	Dave Boswell, 1966	6.38
68	Harry Krause, 1909	6.38
69	Dutch Leonard, 1915	6.38
70	Eddie Cicotte, 1917	6.39
71	Wayne Simpson, 1970	6.39
72	Babe Ruth, 1916	6.40
73	Spec Shea, 1947	6.40
74	Jim Bibby, 1973	6.42
75	Ed Reulbach, 1905	6.42
76	Gaylord Perry, 1974	6.42
77	Eddie Fisher, 1965	6.42
78	Addie Joss, 1908	6.42
79	Mordecai Brown, 1906	6.43
80	Luis Tiant, 1972	6.44
81	Frank Smith, 1908	6.44
82	Dwight Gooden, 1985	6.44
83	Orval Overall, 1909	6.44
84	Sid Fernandez, 1989	6.44
85	Denny McLain, 1968	6.46
86	Mordecai Brown, 1909	6.46
87	Ray Caldwell, 1914	6.46
88	Fred Toney, 1915	6.47
89	Gary Peters, 1967	6.47
90	Bob Turley, 1954	6.48
91	Ed Walsh, 1909	6.49
92	Guy Hecker, 1882	6.49
93	Frank Smith, 1910	6.49
94	Tom Seaver, 1981	6.49
95	Al Mamaux, 1915	6.51
96	Claude Hendrix, 1914	6.51
	Jim Palmer, 1969	6.51
98	Sam Jones, 1955	6.52
99	Bobby Bolin, 1968	6.52
100	Randy Johnson, 1993	6.52

Hits per Game (by era)

1876-1892

1	Tim Keefe, 1880	6.09
2	Guy Hecker, 1882	6.49
3	Tim Keefe, 1888	6.57
4	Charlie Sweeney, 1884	6.59
5	Adonis Terry, 1888	6.69
6	Silver King, 1888	6.72
7	Frank Knauss, 1890	6.73
8	Ed Seward, 1888	6.73
9	Tim Keefe, 1885	6.75
10	Tony Mullane, 1892	6.77
11	Larry Corcoran, 1880	6.78
12	Mickey Welch, 1885	6.80
13	Cannonball Titcomb, 1888	6.81
14	Toad Ramsey, 1886	6.83
15	Amos Rusie, 1892	6.85

1893-1919

1	Ed Reulbach, 1906	5.33
2	Dutch Leonard, 1914	5.57
3	Carl Lundgren, 1907	5.65
4	Russ Ford, 1910	5.83
5	Ed Walsh, 1910	5.89
6	Walter Johnson, 1913	6.03
7	Pete Alexander, 1915	6.05
8	Stan Coveleski, 1917	6.09
9	Mordecai Brown, 1908	6.17
10	Jack Pfiester, 1906	6.21
11	Cy Morgan, 1909	6.26
12	Christy Mathewson, 1909	6.28
13	Art Fromme, 1909	6.28
14	Walter Johnson, 1912	6.32
15	Jack Coombs, 1910	6.32

1920-1941

1	Johnny Vander Meer, 1941	6.84
2	Robert Feller, 1940	6.88
3	Robert Feller, 1939	6.89
4	Hal Schumacher, 1933	6.92
5	Dazzy Vance, 1924	6.95
6	Whit Wyatt, 1941	6.96
7	Bucky Walters, 1939	7.05
8	Johnny Vander Meer, 1938	7.07
9	Bucky Walters, 1940	7.11
10	Lefty Gomez, 1934	7.13
11	Ernie White, 1941	7.24
12	Dazzy Vance, 1928	7.26
13	Bump Hadley, 1931	7.26
14	Dolf Luque, 1920	7.28
15	Robert Feller, 1938	7.29

1942-1960

1	Tommy Byrne, 1949	5.74
2	Herb Score, 1956	5.85
3	Bob Turley, 1957	6.12
4	Bob Turley, 1955	6.13
5	Herb Score, 1955	6.26
6	Allie Reynolds, 1943	6.34
7	Spec Shea, 1947	6.40
8	Bob Turley, 1954	6.48
9	Sam Jones, 1955	6.52
10	Bob Turley, 1958	6.53
11	Hal Newhouser, 1946	6.61
12	Johnny Niggeling, 1943	6.66
13	Don Larsen, 1956	6.66
14	Whitey Ford, 1955	6.67
15	Mort Cooper, 1942	6.69

1961-1976

1	Nolan Ryan, 1972	5.26
2	Luis Tiant, 1968	5.30
3	Dave McNally, 1968	5.77
4	Sandy Koufax, 1965	5.79
5	Al Downing, 1963	5.84
6	Bob Gibson, 1968	5.85
7	Sam McDowell, 1965	5.87
8	Nolan Ryan, 1974	5.98
9	Sam McDowell, 1966	6.02
10	Vida Blue, 1971	6.03
11	Sam McDowell, 1968	6.06
12	Joe Horlen, 1964	6.07
13	Andy Messersmith, 1969	6.08
14	Catfish Hunter, 1972	6.09
15	Nolan Ryan, 1976	6.11

1977-1994

1	Nolan Ryan, 1991	5.31
2	Sid Fernandez, 1985	5.71
3	Mike Scott, 1986	5.95
4	Mario Soto, 1980	5.96
5	Floyd Youmans, 1986	5.96
6	Nolan Ryan, 1977	5.96
7	Nolan Ryan, 1981	5.98
8	Nolan Ryan, 1986	6.02
9	Nolan Ryan, 1990	6.04
10	Nolan Ryan, 1989	6.09
11	Sid Fernandez, 1988	6.11
12	Nolan Ryan, 1983	6.14
13	Ron Guidry, 1978	6.15
14	J.R. Richard, 1978	6.28
15	Jeff Robinson, 1988	6.33

Home Runs Allowed

1	Bert Blyleven, 1986	50
2	Robin Roberts, 1956	46
	Bert Blyleven, 1987	46
4	Pedro Ramos, 1957	43
5	Denny McLain, 1966	42
6	Robin Roberts, 1955	41
	Phil Niekro, 1979	41
8	Bill Gullickson, 1987	40
	Robin Roberts, 1957	40
	Ralph Terry, 1962	40
	Orlando Pena, 1964	40
	Phil Niekro, 1970	40
	Fergie Jenkins, 1979	40
	Jack Morris, 1986	40
15	Murry Dickson, 1948	39
	Pedro Ramos, 1961	39
	Jim Perry, 1971	39
	Catfish Hunter, 1973	39
	Jack Morris, 1987	39
20	Warren Hacker, 1955	38
	Pedro Ramos, 1958	38
	Lew Burdette, 1959	38
	Jim Bunning, 1963	38
	Don Sutton, 1970	38
	Mickey Lolich, 1974	38
	Matt Keough, 1982	38
	Floyd Bannister, 1987	38
	Don Sutton, 1987	38
	Curt Young, 1987	38
30	Jim Bunning, 1959	37
	Earl Wilson, 1964	37
	Luis Tiant, 1969	37
	Fergie Jenkins, 1975	37
	Jack Morris, 1982	37
	Dan Petry, 1983	37
	Frank Viola, 1986	37
37	Dennis Rasmussen, 1987	36
	Larry Jansen, 1949	36
	Art Mahaffey, 1962	36
	Pete Richert, 1966	36
	Mickey Lolich, 1971	36
	Ed Whitson, 1987	36
	Charlie Hough, 1987	36
	Tom Browning, 1988	36
45	Larry Corcoran, 1884	35
	Warren Hacker, 1953	35
	Robin Roberts, 1954	35
	Don Newcombe, 1955	35
	Jim Perry, 1960	35
	Roger Craig, 1962	35
	Robin Roberts, 1963	35
	Sammy Ellis, 1966	35
	Denny McLain, 1967	35
	Fergie Jenkins, 1973	35
	Mickey Lolich, 1973	35
	Mike Caldwell, 1983	35
	Mike Smithson, 1984	35
	Scott McGregor, 1986	35
	Scott Bankhead, 1987	35
	Bruce Hurst, 1987	35
	Bill Gullickson, 1992	35
	Mike Moore, 1993	35
63	Preacher Roe, 1950	34
	Johnny Sain, 1950	34
	Ken Raffensberger, 1950	34
	Robin Roberts, 1959	34
	Paul Foytack, 1959	34
	Juan Marichal, 1962	34
	Dick Ellsworth, 1964	34
	Bill Monbouquette, 1964	34
	Bob Gibson, 1965	34
	Mudcat Grant, 1965	34
	Earl Wilson, 1967	34
	Catfish Hunter, 1969	34
	Mike Cuellar, 1970	34
	Gaylord Perry, 1973	34
	Rick Wise, 1975	34
	Frank Viola, 1983	34
	Danny Darwin, 1985	34
	Scott McGregor, 1985	34
	Ken Schrom, 1986	34
	Don Carman, 1987	34
	Mike Witt, 1987	34
84	Don Newcombe, 1956	33
	Camilo Pascual, 1956	33
	Jim Bunning, 1957	33
	Billy Pierce, 1958	33
	Mike McCormick, 1961	33
	Gene Conley, 1961	33
	Phil Regan, 1963	33
	Phil Ortega, 1965	33
	Jim Merritt, 1969	33
	Lew Krausse, 1970	33
	Jerry Garvin, 1977	33
	Dennis Leonard, 1979	33
	Bill Travers, 1979	33
	Rick Langford, 1982	33
	Ken Dixon, 1986	33
	Willie Fraser, 1988	33
	Greg Harris, 1993	33

Home Runs Allowed (by era)

1876-1892

1	Larry Corcoran, 1884	35
2	Charlie Getzien, 1889	27
3	Bill Hutchison, 1891	26
4	Charlie Getzien, 1887	24
	John Healy, 1887	24
6	Jim Galvin, 1884	23
	Mark Baldwin, 1887	23
	Lev Shreve, 1888	23
9	Billy Serad, 1884	21
	John Clarkson, 1885	21
	Park Swartzel, 1889	21
	George Cobb, 1892	21
13	8 players tied	20

1893-1919

1	Frank Dwyer, 1894	27
	Jack Stivetts, 1894	27
3	Kid Nichols, 1894	23
4	Harry Staley, 1893	22
	Kid Carsey, 1894	22
6	Ted Breitenstein, 1894	21
7	Jack Stivetts, 1896	20
8	Tom Parrott, 1894	19
	Cy Young, 1894	19
10	Kid Gleason, 1893	18
	Al Orth, 1902	18
12	5 players tied	17

1920-1941

1	Lon Warneke, 1937	32
2	Phil Collins, 1934	30
	Bobo Newsom, 1938	30
4	Ray Kremer, 1930	29
	Lynn Nelson, 1938	29
6	George Earnshaw, 1932	28
	George Earnshaw, 1934	28
8	Roy Mahaffey, 1932	27
	Carl Hubbell, 1935	27
	Luke Hamlin, 1939	27
	Lynn Nelson, 1939	27
	Johnny Marcum, 1939	27
13	Freddie Fitzsimmons, 1930	26
	Gordon Rhodes, 1936	26
	Nels Potter, 1939	26

1942-1960

1	Robin Roberts, 1956	46
2	Pedro Ramos, 1957	43
3	Robin Roberts, 1955	41
4	Robin Roberts, 1957	40
5	Murry Dickson, 1948	39
6	Warren Hacker, 1955	38
	Pedro Ramos, 1958	38
	Lew Burdette, 1959	38
9	Jim Bunning, 1959	37
10	Larry Jansen, 1949	36
11	Warren Hacker, 1953	35
	Robin Roberts, 1954	35
	Don Newcombe, 1955	35
	Jim Perry, 1960	35
15	5 players tied	34

1961-1976

1	Denny McLain, 1966	42
2	Ralph Terry, 1962	40
	Orlando Pena, 1964	40
	Phil Niekro, 1970	40
5	Pedro Ramos, 1961	39
	Jim Perry, 1971	39
	Catfish Hunter, 1973	39
8	Jim Bunning, 1963	38
	Don Sutton, 1970	38
	Mickey Lolich, 1974	38
11	Earl Wilson, 1964	37
	Luis Tiant, 1969	37
	Fergie Jenkins, 1975	37
14	3 players tied	36

1977-1994

1	Bert Blyleven, 1986	50
2	Bert Blyleven, 1987	46
3	Phil Niekro, 1979	41
4	Bill Gullickson, 1987	40
	Fergie Jenkins, 1979	40
	Jack Morris, 1986	40
7	Jack Morris, 1987	39
8	Matt Keough, 1982	38
	Floyd Bannister, 1987	38
	Don Sutton, 1987	38
	Curt Young, 1987	38
12	Jack Morris, 1982	37
	Dan Petry, 1983	37
	Frank Viola, 1986	37
15	3 players tied	36

Walks

1	Amos Rusie, 1890	289
2	Mark Baldwin, 1889	274
3	Amos Rusie, 1892	267
4	Amos Rusie, 1891	262
5	Mark Baldwin, 1890	249
6	Jack Stivetts, 1891	232
7	Mark Baldwin, 1891	227
8	Phil Knell, 1891	226
9	Bob Barr, 1890	219
10	Amos Rusie, 1893	218
11	Cy Seymour, 1898	213
12	Gus Weyhing, 1889	212
13	Ed Crane, 1890	210
14	Robert Feller, 1938	208
15	Toad Ramsey, 1886	207
16	Elton Chamberlain, 1891	206
17	Mike Morrison, 1887	205
18	Henry Gruber, 1890	204
	Nolan Ryan, 1977	204
20	Ed Crane, 1891	203
	John Clarkson, 1889	203
22	Nolan Ryan, 1974	202
23	Bert Cunningham, 1890	201
24	Amos Rusie, 1894	200
25	Bill Hutchison, 1890	199
26	Mark Baldwin, 1892	194
	Robert Feller, 1941	194
28	Bobo Newsom, 1938	192
29	Ted Breitenstein, 1894	191
30	Ed Crane, 1892	189
	Tony Mullane, 1893	189
32	Tony Mullane, 1891	187
	Bill Hutchison, 1892	187
	Kid Gleason, 1893	187
35	Ed Beatin, 1890	186
36	Sam Jones, 1955	185
37	Tom Vickery, 1890	184
38	Nolan Ryan, 1976	183
39	Matt Kilroy, 1886	182
	Frank Killen, 1892	182
41	Willie McGill, 1893	181
	Bob Harmon, 1911	181
	Bob Turley, 1954	181
44	Jack Stivetts, 1890	179
	Gus Weyhing, 1890	179
	Tommy Byrne, 1949	179
47	Bill Hutchison, 1891	178
	Ted Breitenstein, 1895	178
49	Bob Turley, 1955	177
50	Phenomenal Smith, 1887	176
	George Hemming, 1893	176
52	Silver King, 1892	174
53	Jack Stivetts, 1892	171
	Jouett Meekin, 1894	171
	Bump Hadley, 1932	171
56	Elton Chamberlain, 1892	170
	Ed Stein, 1894	170
	Cy Seymour, 1899	170
59	Willie McGill, 1891	168
	Gus Weyhing, 1892	168
	Brickyard Kennedy, 1893	168
	Elmer Myers, 1916	168
63	Toad Ramsey, 1887	167
	Gus Weyhing, 1887	167
	Darby O'Brien, 1889	167
	Kid Gleason, 1890	167
	Bill Daley, 1890	167
	Bobo Newsom, 1937	167
69	Tony Mullane, 1886	166
	Sadie McMahon, 1890	166
	Phil Knell, 1890	166
	Chick Fraser, 1896	166
73	Elton Chamberlain, 1889	165
	Dan Casey, 1890	165
	Kid Gleason, 1891	165
	Weldon Wyckoff, 1915	165
77	Cy Seymour, 1897	164
	Earl Moore, 1911	164
	Phil Niekro, 1977	164
80	Mickey Welch, 1886	163
	Silver King, 1891	163
	Hank O'Day, 1890	163
	George Haddock, 1892	163
84	Johnny Vander Meer, 1943	162
	Nolan Ryan, 1973	162
86	John Sowders, 1890	161
	Kid Carsey, 1891	161
	Gus Weyhing, 1891	161
89	Tommy Byrne, 1950	160
90	George Hemming, 1894	159
	Amos Rusie, 1895	159
	Marty O'Toole, 1912	159
93	Joe Coleman, 1974	158
94	Matt Kilroy, 1887	157
	Bert Cunningham, 1888	157
	Pink Hawley, 1896	157
	Grover Lowdermilk, 1915	157
	Nolan Ryan, 1972	157
99	5 players tied	156

Fewest Walks/Game (by era)

1876-1892
1	George Zettlein, 1876	0.23
2	Cherokee Fisher, 1876	0.24
3	George Bradley, 1880	0.28
4	Tommy Bond, 1876	0.29
5	Tommy Bond, 1879	0.39
6	Bobby Mathews, 1876	0.42
7	Guy Hecker, 1882	0.43
8	Dale Williams, 1876	0.43
9	Al Spalding, 1876	0.44
10	Jim Galvin, 1879	0.47
11	George Bradley, 1879	0.48
12	Sam Weaver, 1878	0.49
13	Terry Larkin, 1879	0.53
14	Jim Devlin, 1876	0.54
15	Denny Driscoll, 1882	0.54

1893-1919
1	Christy Mathewson, 1913	0.62
2	Christy Mathewson, 1914	0.66
3	Cy Young, 1904	0.69
4	Cy Young, 1906	0.78
5	Babe Adams, 1919	0.79
6	Slim Sallee, 1919	0.79
7	Slim Sallee, 1918	0.82
8	Addie Joss, 1908	0.83
9	Cy Young, 1905	0.84
10	Deacon Phillippe, 1902	0.86
11	Cy Young, 1901	0.90
12	Deacon Phillippe, 1903	0.90
13	Christy Mathewson, 1908	0.97
14	Christy Mathewson, 1915	0.97
15	Jesse Tannehill, 1902	0.97

1920-1941
1	Babe Adams, 1920	0.62
2	Red Lucas, 1933	0.74
3	Babe Adams, 1922	0.79
4	Pete Alexander, 1923	0.89
5	Babe Adams, 1921	1.01
6	Paul Derringer, 1939	1.05
7	Carl Hubbell, 1934	1.06
8	Bill Swift, 1932	1.09
9	Pete Alexander, 1925	1.11
10	Herb Pennock, 1930	1.15
11	Red Lucas, 1932	1.17
12	Pete Alexander, 1921	1.18
13	Watty Clark, 1935	1.22
14	Pete Donohue, 1926	1.23
15	Pete Alexander, 1922	1.25

1942-1960
1	Tiny Bonham, 1942	0.96
2	Don Newcombe, 1959	1.09
3	Tiny Bonham, 1945	1.10
4	Lew Burdette, 1960	1.14
5	Lew Burdette, 1959	1.18
6	Robin Roberts, 1956	1.21
7	Robin Roberts, 1959	1.22
8	Robin Roberts, 1952	1.23
9	Hal Brown, 1960	1.25
10	Ray Prim, 1945	1.25
11	Robin Roberts, 1960	1.29
12	Fred Hutchinson, 1951	1.29
13	Ted Lyons, 1942	1.30
14	Schoolboy Rowe, 1943	1.31
15	Vern Law, 1960	1.33

1961-1976
1	Gary Nolan, 1976	1.02
2	Fergie Jenkins, 1971	1.02
3	Juan Marichal, 1966	1.05
4	Lew Burdette, 1961	1.09
5	Jim Merritt, 1967	1.19
6	Vern Law, 1966	1.22
7	Dick Donovan, 1963	1.22
8	Fritz Peterson, 1968	1.23
9	Fergie Jenkins, 1974	1.23
10	Gary Nolan, 1975	1.24
11	Ralph Terry, 1965	1.25
12	Bill Hands, 1968	1.25
13	Jim Kaat, 1976	1.27
14	Juan Marichal, 1968	1.27
15	Catfish Hunter, 1974	1.30

1977-1994
1	Bret Saberhagen, 1994	0.66
2	Bob Tewksbury, 1992	0.77
3	Bob Tewksbury, 1993	0.84
4	La Marr Hoyt, 1985	0.86
5	Dennis Eckersley, 1985	1.01
6	La Marr Hoyt, 1983	1.07
7	Jimmy Key, 1989	1.13
8	Zane Smith, 1991	1.14
9	Greg Swindell, 1991	1.17
10	Scott McGregor, 1979	1.19
11	Rick Honeycutt, 1981	1.20
12	Scott Sanderson, 1991	1.25
13	Bob Tewksbury, 1994	1.27
14	Ed Lynch, 1985	1.27
15	Greg Maddux, 1994	1.38

Strikeouts

1	Matt Kilroy, 1886	513
2	Toad Ramsey, 1886	499
3	Hugh Daily, 1884	483
4	Dupee Shaw, 1884	451
5	Charley Radbourn, 1884	441
6	Charlie Buffinton, 1884	417
7	Guy Hecker, 1884	385
8	Nolan Ryan, 1973	383
9	Sandy Koufax, 1965	382
10	Bill Sweeney, 1884	374
11	Jim Galvin, 1884	369
12	Mark Baldwin, 1889	368
13	Nolan Ryan, 1974	367
14	Tim Keefe, 1883	359
15	Toad Ramsey, 1887	355
16	Rube Waddell, 1904	349
17	Robert Feller, 1946	348
18	Hardie Henderson, 1884	346
19	Jim Whitney, 1883	345
	Mickey Welch, 1884	345
21	Jim McCormick, 1884	343
22	Amos Rusie, 1890	341
	Nolan Ryan, 1977	341
24	Charlie Sweeney, 1884	337
	Amos Rusie, 1891	337
26	Tim Keefe, 1888	335
27	Nolan Ryan, 1972	329
28	Nolan Ryan, 1976	327
29	Ed Morris, 1886	326
30	Tony Mullane, 1884	325
	Sam McDowell, 1965	325
32	Lady Baldwin, 1886	323
33	Tim Keefe, 1884	317
	Sandy Koufax, 1966	317
35	Bill Hutchison, 1892	316
36	Charley Radbourn, 1883	315
37	John Clarkson, 1886	313
	Walter Johnson, 1910	313
	J.R. Richard, 1979	313
40	Steve Carlton, 1972	310
41	Larry McKeon, 1884	308
	John Clarkson, 1885	308
	Mickey Lolich, 1971	308
	Randy Johnson, 1993	308
45	Sandy Koufax, 1963	306
	Mike Scott, 1986	306
47	Sam McDowell, 1970	304
48	Walter Johnson, 1912	303
	J.R. Richard, 1978	303
50	Ed Morris, 1884	302
	Rube Waddell, 1903	302
52	Vida Blue, 1971	301
	Nolan Ryan, 1989	301
54	Ed Morris, 1885	298
55	Tim Keefe, 1886	297
56	Jack Lynch, 1884	292
57	Sadie McMahon, 1890	291
	Roger Clemens, 1988	291
59	Bill Hutchison, 1890	289
	Jack Stivetts, 1890	289
	Tom Seaver, 1971	289
62	Amos Rusie, 1892	288
63	Rube Waddell, 1905	287
64	Bobby Mathews, 1884	286
	Bobby Mathews, 1885	286
	Steve Carlton, 1980	286
	Steve Carlton, 1982	286
68	Billy Taylor, 1884	284
	John Clarkson, 1889	284
70	Dave Foutz, 1884	283
	Sam McDowell, 1968	283
	Tom Seaver, 1970	283
73	Denny McLain, 1968	280
74	Jim Galvin, 1883	279
	Sam McDowell, 1969	279
76	Bob Veale, 1965	276
	Dwight Gooden, 1984	276
78	Hal Newhouser, 1946	275
	Steve Carlton, 1983	275
80	Bob Gibson, 1970	274
	Fergie Jenkins, 1970	274
	Mario Soto, 1982	274
83	Fergie Jenkins, 1969	273
84	Larry Corcoran, 1884	272
	Mickey Welch, 1886	272
	Ed Seward, 1888	272
87	Mickey Lolich, 1969	271
88	Jim Whitney, 1884	270
	Bob Gibson, 1965	270
	Nolan Ryan, 1987	270
91	Ed Walsh, 1908	269
	Sandy Koufax, 1961	269
	Bob Gibson, 1969	269
	Frank Tanana, 1975	269
95	Larry Corcoran, 1880	268
	Bill Wise, 1884	268
	Jim Bunning, 1965	268
	Bob Gibson, 1968	268
	Dwight Gooden, 1985	268
100	Christy Mathewson, 1903	267

Strikeouts (by era)

1876-1892
1	Matt Kilroy, 1886	513
2	Toad Ramsey, 1886	499
3	Hugh Daily, 1884	483
4	Dupee Shaw, 1884	451
5	Charley Radbourn, 1884	441
6	Charlie Buffinton, 1884	417
7	Guy Hecker, 1884	385
8	Bill Sweeney, 1884	374
9	Jim Galvin, 1884	369
10	Mark Baldwin, 1889	368
11	Tim Keefe, 1883	359
12	Toad Ramsey, 1887	355
13	Hardie Henderson, 1884	346
14	Jim Whitney, 1883	345
	Mickey Welch, 1884	345

1893-1919
1	Rube Waddell, 1904	349
2	Walter Johnson, 1910	313
3	Walter Johnson, 1912	303
4	Rube Waddell, 1903	302
5	Rube Waddell, 1905	287
6	Ed Walsh, 1908	269
7	Christy Mathewson, 1903	267
8	Christy Mathewson, 1908	259
9	Ed Walsh, 1910	258
	Joe Wood, 1912	258
11	Ed Walsh, 1911	255
12	Ed Walsh, 1912	254
13	Walter Johnson, 1913	243
14	Pete Alexander, 1915	241

1920-1941
1	Dazzy Vance, 1924	262
2	Robert Feller, 1940	261
3	Robert Feller, 1941	260
4	Robert Feller, 1939	246
5	Robert Feller, 1938	240
6	Van Mungo, 1936	238
7	Bobo Newsom, 1938	226
8	Dazzy Vance, 1925	221
9	Lefty Grove, 1930	209
10	Johnny Vander Meer, 1941	202
11	Dazzy Vance, 1928	200
12	Dizzy Dean, 1933	199
13	Dazzy Vance, 1923	197
14	Dizzy Dean, 1934	195
	Dizzy Dean, 1936	195

1942-1960
1	Robert Feller, 1946	348
2	Hal Newhouser, 1946	275
3	Herb Score, 1956	263
4	Don Drysdale, 1960	246
5	Herb Score, 1955	245
6	Don Drysdale, 1959	242
7	Sam Jones, 1958	225
8	Hal Newhouser, 1945	212
9	Bob Turley, 1955	210
10	Sam Jones, 1959	209
11	Jim Bunning, 1959	201
	Jim Bunning, 1960	201
13	Robin Roberts, 1953	198
	Sam Jones, 1955	198
15	Sandy Koufax, 1960	197

1961-1976
1	Nolan Ryan, 1973	383
2	Sandy Koufax, 1965	382
3	Nolan Ryan, 1974	367
4	Nolan Ryan, 1972	329
5	Nolan Ryan, 1976	327
6	Sam McDowell, 1965	325
7	Sandy Koufax, 1966	317
8	Steve Carlton, 1972	310
9	Mickey Lolich, 1971	308
10	Sandy Koufax, 1963	306
11	Sam McDowell, 1970	304
12	Vida Blue, 1971	301
13	Tom Seaver, 1971	289
14	Sam McDowell, 1968	283
	Tom Seaver, 1970	283

1977-1994
1	Nolan Ryan, 1977	341
2	J.R. Richard, 1979	313
3	Randy Johnson, 1993	308
4	Mike Scott, 1986	306
5	J.R. Richard, 1978	303
6	Nolan Ryan, 1989	301
7	Roger Clemens, 1988	291
8	Steve Carlton, 1980	286
	Steve Carlton, 1982	286
10	Dwight Gooden, 1984	276
11	Steve Carlton, 1983	275
12	Mario Soto, 1982	274
13	Nolan Ryan, 1987	270
14	Dwight Gooden, 1985	268
15	2 players tied	262

Strikeouts per Game

1	Nolan Ryan, 1987	11.48
2	Dwight Gooden, 1984	11.39
3	Nolan Ryan, 1989	11.32
4	Randy Johnson, 1993	10.86
5	Sam McDowell, 1965	10.71
6	Randy Johnson, 1994	10.67
7	Nolan Ryan, 1973	10.57
8	Nolan Ryan, 1991	10.56
9	Sandy Koufax, 1962	10.55
10	Nolan Ryan, 1972	10.43
11	Sam McDowell, 1966	10.42
12	Nolan Ryan, 1976	10.35
13	Randy Johnson, 1992	10.31
14	Nolan Ryan, 1977	10.26
15	Sandy Koufax, 1965	10.24
16	Nolan Ryan, 1990	10.24
17	Randy Johnson, 1991	10.19
18	Sandy Koufax, 1960	10.13
19	Mike Scott, 1986	10.00
20	Nolan Ryan, 1978	9.97
21	Nolan Ryan, 1974	9.93
22	Roger Clemens, 1988	9.92
23	David Cone, 1990	9.91
24	J.R. Richard, 1978	9.90
25	Andy Benes, 1994	9.87
26	Nolan Ryan, 1986	9.81
27	Herb Score, 1955	9.70
28	Nolan Ryan, 1984	9.65
29	J.R. Richard, 1979	9.64
30	Mario Soto, 1982	9.57
31	Tom Griffin, 1969	9.56
32	Jim Maloney, 1963	9.53
33	Sid Fernandez, 1985	9.51
34	Herb Score, 1956	9.49
35	Sandy Koufax, 1961	9.47
36	Sam McDowell, 1968	9.47
37	David Cone, 1992	9.41
38	Frank Tanana, 1975	9.41
39	Don Wilson, 1969	9.40
40	Bob Veale, 1965	9.34
41	Nolan Ryan, 1988	9.33
42	David Cone, 1991	9.32
43	Luis Tiant, 1967	9.22
44	Mark Langston, 1986	9.21
45	Luis Tiant, 1968	9.20
46	Dave Boswell, 1966	9.19
47	Sam McDowell, 1964	9.19
48	Sonny Siebert, 1965	9.11
49	Sid Fernandez, 1988	9.10
50	Tom Seaver, 1971	9.08
51	Sid Fernandez, 1990	9.08
52	Dennis Eckersley, 1976	9.03
53	Nolan Ryan, 1979	9.01
54	Sandy Koufax, 1964	9.00
55	Sam McDowell, 1967	8.99
56	Sam McDowell, 1970	8.97
57	Bobby Witt, 1990	8.96
58	Jose Rijo, 1994	8.93
59	Jim Maloney, 1964	8.92
60	Jose Rijo, 1988	8.89
61	Roger Clemens, 1994	8.86
62	Sandy Koufax, 1963	8.86
63	Pedro Martinez, 1994	8.83
64	Sandy Koufax, 1966	8.83
65	Sam McDowell, 1969	8.81
66	Sid Fernandez, 1986	8.81
67	Nolan Ryan, 1982	8.81
68	Tom Seaver, 1970	8.76
69	Al Downing, 1963	8.76
70	Bob Moose, 1969	8.74
71	Steve Carlton, 1983	8.73
72	Dwight Gooden, 1985	8.72
73	Steve Carlton, 1982	8.71
74	Juan Pizarro, 1961	8.69
75	Mickey Lolich, 1969	8.69
76	Vida Blue, 1971	8.68
77	Hugh Daily, 1884	8.68
78	Mark Langston, 1987	8.67
79	Bob Johnson, 1970	8.66
80	Jim Maloney, 1966	8.65
81	Dwight Gooden, 1990	8.63
82	Bruce Hurst, 1986	8.62
83	Mario Soto, 1980	8.61
84	Jim Maloney, 1965	8.60
85	Ramon Martinez, 1990	8.56
86	Tom Seaver, 1972	8.55
87	Dick Selma, 1969	8.54
88	Bob Veale, 1969	8.49
89	Steve Carlton, 1981	8.48
90	Steve Carlton, 1980	8.47
91	Mike Scott, 1987	8.47
92	Mark Langston, 1989	8.46
93	Floyd Bannister, 1985	8.46
94	Hal Newhouser, 1946	8.46
95	Nolan Ryan, 1981	8.46
96	Nolan Ryan, 1975	8.45
97	Tom Gordon, 1989	8.45
98	Robert Feller, 1946	8.43
99	Roger Clemens, 1986	8.43
100	Fernando Valenzuela, 1981	8.42

Strikeouts per Game (by era)

1876-1892

1	Hugh Daily, 1884	8.68
2	Matt Kilroy, 1886	7.92
3	Charlie Gagus, 1884	7.92
4	John Clarkson, 1884	7.78
5	Toad Ramsey, 1886	7.63
6	Dupee Shaw, 1884	7.47
7	Jim Whitney, 1884	7.23
8	Mike Dorgan, 1884	7.17
9	James Burke, 1884	7.13
10	Hardie Henderson, 1884	7.09
11	Tim Keefe, 1888	6.94
12	Bob Black, 1884	6.80
13	Lady Baldwin, 1885	6.78
14	Jack Stivetts, 1889	6.71
15	Toad Ramsey, 1890	6.63

1893-1919

1	Rube Waddell, 1903	8.39
2	Rube Waddell, 1904	8.20
3	Rube Waddell, 1905	7.86
4	Rube Marquard, 1911	7.68
5	Walter Johnson, 1910	7.61
6	Joe Wood, 1911	7.54
7	Walter Johnson, 1912	7.39
8	Rube Waddell, 1907	7.33
9	Rube Waddell, 1908	7.31
10	Dutch Leonard, 1914	7.05
11	Red Ames, 1906	6.90
12	Rube Waddell, 1902	6.84
13	Red Ames, 1905	6.78
14	Joe Wood, 1912	6.75
15	Orval Overall, 1908	6.68

1920-1941

1	Johnny Vander Meer, 1941	8.03
2	Robert Feller, 1938	7.78
3	Dazzy Vance, 1924	7.65
4	Dazzy Vance, 1925	7.50
5	Robert Feller, 1939	7.46
6	Dazzy Vance, 1926	7.46
7	Robert Feller, 1940	7.33
8	Van Mungo, 1936	6.87
9	Robert Feller, 1941	6.82
10	Van Mungo, 1937	6.82
11	Lefty Grove, 1926	6.77
12	Bill Hallahan, 1930	6.71
13	George Earnshaw, 1928	6.65
14	Red Ruffing, 1932	6.60
15	Lefty Grove, 1930	6.46

1942-1960

1	Sandy Koufax, 1960	10.13
2	Herb Score, 1955	9.70
3	Herb Score, 1956	9.49
4	Hal Newhouser, 1946	8.46
5	Robert Feller, 1946	8.43
6	Sam Jones, 1956	8.40
7	Herb Score, 1959	8.23
8	Don Drysdale, 1960	8.23
9	Sam Jones, 1958	8.10
10	Don Drysdale, 1959	8.05
11	Bob Turley, 1957	7.76
12	Camilo Pascual, 1956	7.73
13	Bob Turley, 1955	7.66
14	Stan Williams, 1960	7.60
15	Sam Jones, 1957	7.59

1961-1976

1	Sam McDowell, 1965	10.71
2	Nolan Ryan, 1973	10.57
3	Sandy Koufax, 1962	10.55
4	Nolan Ryan, 1972	10.43
5	Sam McDowell, 1966	10.42
6	Nolan Ryan, 1976	10.35
7	Sandy Koufax, 1965	10.24
8	Nolan Ryan, 1974	9.93
9	Tom Griffin, 1969	9.56
10	Jim Maloney, 1963	9.53
11	Sandy Koufax, 1961	9.47
12	Sam McDowell, 1968	9.47
13	Frank Tanana, 1975	9.41
14	Don Wilson, 1969	9.40
15	Bob Veale, 1965	9.34

1977-1994

1	Nolan Ryan, 1987	11.48
2	Dwight Gooden, 1984	11.39
3	Nolan Ryan, 1989	11.32
4	Randy Johnson, 1993	10.86
5	Randy Johnson, 1994	10.67
6	Nolan Ryan, 1991	10.56
7	Randy Johnson, 1992	10.31
8	Nolan Ryan, 1977	10.26
9	Nolan Ryan, 1990	10.24
10	Nolan Ryan, 1991	10.19
11	Mike Scott, 1986	10.00
12	Nolan Ryan, 1978	9.97
13	Roger Clemens, 1988	9.92
14	David Cone, 1990	9.91
15	J.R. Richard, 1978	9.90

Ratio

1	Guy Hecker, 1882	6.92
2	Walter Johnson, 1913	7.26
3	Addie Joss, 1908	7.31
4	Charlie Sweeney, 1884	7.35
5	Christy Mathewson, 1909	7.45
6	Ed Walsh, 1910	7.47
7	George Bradley, 1880	7.53
8	Tim Keefe, 1880	7.54
9	Christy Mathewson, 1908	7.60
10	Henry Boyle, 1884	7.68
11	Mordecai Brown, 1908	7.72
12	Denny Driscoll, 1882	7.79
13	Pete Alexander, 1915	7.82
14	Sandy Koufax, 1965	7.83
15	Juan Marichal, 1966	7.88
16	Bob Gibson, 1968	7.89
17	Roger Nelson, 1972	7.89
18	Dave McNally, 1968	7.91
19	Ed Walsh, 1908	7.91
20	Sandy Koufax, 1963	7.96
21	Luis Tiant, 1968	7.98
22	George Bradley, 1876	7.98
23	Jim Whitney, 1884	8.01
24	Guy Hecker, 1884	8.02
25	Cy Young, 1905	8.03
26	Mordecai Brown, 1909	8.04
27	Cy Young, 1908	8.07
28	Tommy Bond, 1876	8.12
29	Babe Adams, 1919	8.17
30	Russ Ford, 1910	8.17
31	John Ward, 1880	8.26
32	Lady Baldwin, 1885	8.28
33	Eddie Cicotte, 1917	8.28
34	Dutch Leonard, 1914	8.29
35	Charley Radbourn, 1884	8.30
36	Denny McLain, 1968	8.30
37	Catfish Hunter, 1972	8.32
38	Doc White, 1906	8.33
39	Greg Maddux, 1994	8.33
40	Silver King, 1888	8.34
41	Pete Alexander, 1919	8.35
42	Juan Marichal, 1965	8.35
43	Don Sutton, 1972	8.35
44	Sandy Koufax, 1964	8.35
45	Ed Morris, 1884	8.36
46	Mike Scott, 1986	8.37
47	Christy Mathewson, 1905	8.42
48	Larry Corcoran, 1880	8.44
49	Addie Joss, 1906	8.49
50	Reb Russell, 1916	8.51
51	Cy Young, 1904	8.53
52	Mordecai Brown, 1906	8.53
53	Walter Johnson, 1910	8.54
54	Ron Guidry, 1978	8.55
55	Claude Hendrix, 1914	8.55
56	Walter Johnson, 1912	8.56
57	Warren Hacker, 1952	8.56
58	Bill Burns, 1908	8.56
59	Jack Lynch, 1884	8.56
60	Jack Chesbro, 1904	8.57
61	John Clarkson, 1885	8.58
62	Joe Horlen, 1964	8.59
63	Ed Walsh, 1909	8.60
64	Perry Werden, 1884	8.60
65	Chief Bender, 1910	8.60
66	John Tudor, 1985	8.61
67	Addie Joss, 1909	8.64
68	Tom Seaver, 1971	8.64
69	Russ Ford, 1914	8.66
70	Tim Keefe, 1883	8.67
71	Bill Bernhard, 1902	8.68
72	Tim Keefe, 1888	8.68
73	Vida Blue, 1971	8.68
74	Charlie Buffinton, 1888	8.70
75	Lady Baldwin, 1886	8.70
76	Larry Corcoran, 1882	8.70
77	Frank Smith, 1908	8.71
78	Tony Mullane, 1883	8.71
79	Bret Saberhagen, 1989	8.71
80	Christy Mathewson, 1907	8.71
81	Joe Horlen, 1967	8.72
82	Jim Devlin, 1876	8.73
83	Tim Keefe, 1884	8.73
84	Frank Smith, 1909	8.73
85	Mordecai Brown, 1907	8.73
86	Charlie Getzien, 1884	8.74
87	Dwight Gooden, 1985	8.75
88	Fred Anderson, 1917	8.78
89	Charlie Ferguson, 1886	8.78
90	Dick Hughes, 1967	8.78
91	Ray Caldwell, 1914	8.79
92	Walter Johnson, 1918	8.81
93	Turk Farrell, 1963	8.81
94	Pascual Perez, 1988	8.81
95	Charley Radbourn, 1883	8.81
96	Addie Joss, 1903	8.82
97	Dick Rudolph, 1916	8.86
98	Chief Bender, 1908	8.86
99	Fred Goldsmith, 1880	8.86
100	Roger Clemens, 1986	8.86

Earned Run Average

1	Tim Keefe, 1880	0.86
2	Dutch Leonard, 1914	0.96
3	Mordecai Brown, 1906	1.04
4	Bob Gibson, 1968	1.12
5	Christy Mathewson, 1909	1.14
6	Walter Johnson, 1913	1.14
7	Jack Pfiester, 1907	1.15
8	Addie Joss, 1908	1.16
9	Carl Lundgren, 1907	1.17
10	Denny Driscoll, 1882	1.21
11	Pete Alexander, 1915	1.22
12	George Bradley, 1876	1.23
13	Cy Young, 1908	1.26
14	Ed Walsh, 1910	1.27
15	Walter Johnson, 1918	1.27
16	Christy Mathewson, 1905	1.28
17	Guy Hecker, 1882	1.30
18	Jack Coombs, 1910	1.30
19	Mordecai Brown, 1909	1.31
20	Jack Taylor, 1902	1.33
21	Walter Johnson, 1910	1.36
22	George Bradley, 1880	1.38
23	Charley Radbourn, 1884	1.38
24	Walter Johnson, 1912	1.39
25	Mordecai Brown, 1907	1.39
26	Harry Krause, 1909	1.39
27	Ed Walsh, 1909	1.41
28	Ed Walsh, 1908	1.42
29	Ed Reulbach, 1905	1.42
30	Orval Overall, 1909	1.42
31	Christy Mathewson, 1908	1.43
32	Fred Anderson, 1917	1.44
33	Mordecai Brown, 1908	1.47
34	Rube Waddell, 1905	1.48
35	Joe Wood, 1915	1.49
36	Walter Johnson, 1919	1.49
37	Jack Pfiester, 1906	1.51
38	John Ward, 1878	1.51
39	Harry McCormick, 1882	1.52
40	Doc White, 1906	1.52
41	George McQuillan, 1908	1.53
42	Dwight Gooden, 1985	1.53
43	Eddie Cicotte, 1917	1.53
44	Will White, 1882	1.54
45	Cy Morgan, 1910	1.55
46	Pete Alexander, 1916	1.55
47	Walter Johnson, 1915	1.55
48	Howie Camnitz, 1908	1.56
49	Greg Maddux, 1994	1.56
50	Jim Devlin, 1876	1.56
51	Tim Keefe, 1885	1.58
52	Fred Toney, 1915	1.58
53	Eddie Cicotte, 1913	1.58
54	Rube Marquard, 1916	1.58
55	Chief Bender, 1910	1.58
56	Barney Pelty, 1906	1.59
57	Addie Joss, 1904	1.59
58	Ed Walsh, 1907	1.60
59	Luis Tiant, 1968	1.60
60	Joe McGinnity, 1904	1.61
61	Ray Collins, 1910	1.62
62	Rube Waddell, 1904	1.62
63	Howie Camnitz, 1909	1.62
64	Cy Young, 1901	1.62
65	Spud Chandler, 1943	1.64
66	Ernie Shore, 1914	1.64
67	Silver King, 1888	1.64
68	Ed Summers, 1908	1.64
69	Dean Chance, 1964	1.65
70	Walter Johnson, 1908	1.65
71	Ed Reulbach, 1906	1.65
72	Russ Ford, 1910	1.65
73	Chief Bender, 1909	1.66
74	Sam Leever, 1907	1.66
75	Carl Hubbell, 1933	1.66
76	Mickey Welch, 1885	1.66
77	Candy Cummings, 1876	1.67
78	Joe Wood, 1910	1.68
79	Tommy Bond, 1876	1.68
80	Orval Overall, 1907	1.68
81	Ed Reulbach, 1907	1.69
82	Claude Hendrix, 1914	1.69
83	Bill Burns, 1908	1.69
84	Nolan Ryan, 1981	1.69
85	Jim McCormick, 1878	1.69
86	Rube Foster, 1914	1.70
87	Charlie Sweeney, 1884	1.70
88	Addie Joss, 1909	1.71
89	Ed Killian, 1909	1.71
90	Walter Johnson, 1914	1.72
91	Ned Garvin, 1904	1.72
92	Doc White, 1909	1.72
93	Bill Doak, 1914	1.72
94	Addie Joss, 1906	1.72
	Pete Alexander, 1919	1.72
96	Sandy Koufax, 1966	1.73
97	Bob Ewing, 1907	1.73
98	Vic Willis, 1906	1.73
99	Sandy Koufax, 1964	1.74
100	Hippo Vaughn, 1918	1.74

Earned Run Average (by era)

1876-1892

1	Tim Keefe, 1880	0.86
2	Denny Driscoll, 1882	1.21
3	George Bradley, 1876	1.23
4	Guy Hecker, 1882	1.30
5	George Bradley, 1880	1.38
6	Charley Radbourn, 1884	1.38
7	John Ward, 1878	1.51
8	Harry McCormick, 1882	1.52
9	Will White, 1882	1.54
10	Jim Devlin, 1876	1.56
11	Tim Keefe, 1885	1.58
12	Silver King, 1888	1.64
13	Mickey Welch, 1885	1.66
14	Candy Cummings, 1876	1.67
15	Tommy Bond, 1876	1.68

1893-1919

1	Dutch Leonard, 1914	0.96
2	Mordecai Brown, 1906	1.04
3	Christy Mathewson, 1909	1.14
4	Walter Johnson, 1913	1.14
5	Jack Pfiester, 1907	1.15
6	Addie Joss, 1908	1.16
7	Carl Lundgren, 1907	1.17
8	Pete Alexander, 1915	1.22
9	Cy Young, 1908	1.26
10	Ed Walsh, 1910	1.27
11	Walter Johnson, 1918	1.27
12	Christy Mathewson, 1905	1.28
13	Jack Coombs, 1910	1.30
14	Mordecai Brown, 1909	1.31
15	Jack Taylor, 1902	1.33

1920-1941

1	Carl Hubbell, 1933	1.66
2	Pete Alexander, 1920	1.91
3	Dolf Luque, 1923	1.93
4	Lon Warneke, 1933	2.00
5	Lefty Grove, 1931	2.06
6	Dazzy Vance, 1928	2.09
7	Babe Adams, 1920	2.16
8	Hal Schumacher, 1933	2.16
9	Dazzy Vance, 1924	2.16
10	Burleigh Grimes, 1920	2.22
11	Elmer Riddle, 1941	2.24
12	Bill Walker, 1931	2.26
13	Wilcy Moore, 1927	2.28
14	Bucky Walters, 1939	2.29
15	Carl Hubbell, 1934	2.30

1942-1960

1	Spud Chandler, 1943	1.64
2	Mort Cooper, 1942	1.78
3	Hal Newhouser, 1945	1.81
4	Max Lanier, 1943	1.90
5	Hal Newhouser, 1946	1.94
6	Billy Pierce, 1955	1.97
7	Whitey Ford, 1958	2.01
8	Al Benton, 1945	2.02
9	Allie Reynolds, 1952	2.06
10	Ted Lyons, 1942	2.10
11	Howie Pollet, 1946	2.10
12	Spud Chandler, 1946	2.10
13	Warren Spahn, 1953	2.10
14	Dizzy Trout, 1944	2.12
15	Roger Wolff, 1945	2.12

1961-1976

1	Bob Gibson, 1968	1.12
2	Luis Tiant, 1968	1.60
3	Dean Chance, 1964	1.65
4	Sandy Koufax, 1966	1.73
5	Sandy Koufax, 1964	1.74
6	Tom Seaver, 1971	1.76
7	Sam McDowell, 1968	1.81
8	Vida Blue, 1971	1.82
9	Phil Niekro, 1967	1.87
10	Joe Horlen, 1964	1.88
11	Sandy Koufax, 1963	1.88
12	Luis Tiant, 1972	1.91
13	Wilbur Wood, 1971	1.91
14	Gaylord Perry, 1972	1.92
15	Dave McNally, 1968	1.95

1977-1994

1	Dwight Gooden, 1985	1.53
2	Greg Maddux, 1994	1.56
3	Nolan Ryan, 1981	1.69
4	Ron Guidry, 1978	1.74
5	John Tudor, 1985	1.93
6	Roger Clemens, 1990	1.93
7	Orel Hershiser, 1985	2.03
8	Bill Swift, 1992	2.08
9	Bret Saberhagen, 1989	2.16
10	Bob Tewksbury, 1992	2.16
11	Joe Magrane, 1988	2.18
12	Greg Maddux, 1992	2.18
13	Bob Knepper, 1981	2.18
14	Don Sutton, 1980	2.20
15	Danny Darwin, 1990	2.21

Adjusted Earned Run Average

1	Tim Keefe, 1880	294
2	Dutch Leonard, 1914	280
3	Greg Maddux, 1994	266
4	Walter Johnson, 1913	258
5	Bob Gibson, 1968	258
6	Mordecai Brown, 1906	254
7	Walter Johnson, 1912	240
8	Christy Mathewson, 1905	230
9	Dwight Gooden, 1985	226
10	Pete Alexander, 1915	225
11	Christy Mathewson, 1909	224
12	Lefty Grove, 1931	218
13	Cy Young, 1901	217
14	Jack Pfiester, 1907	216
15	Denny Driscoll, 1882	216
16	Walter Johnson, 1919	216
17	Walter Johnson, 1918	215
18	Carl Lundgren, 1907	213
19	Roger Clemens, 1990	211
20	Ed Reulbach, 1905	210
21	Ron Guidry, 1978	208
22	Addie Joss, 1908	206
23	Charley Radbourn, 1884	205
24	Jack Taylor, 1902	203
25	Billy Pierce, 1955	201
26	Dolf Luque, 1923	200
27	Dean Chance, 1964	199
28	Silver King, 1888	198
29	Spud Chandler, 1943	197
30	Al Maul, 1895	196
31	Cy Young, 1908	195
32	Nolan Ryan, 1981	195
33	Hal Newhouser, 1945	194
34	Mordecai Brown, 1909	194
35	Tom Seaver, 1971	194
36	Carl Hubbell, 1933	193
37	Mort Cooper, 1942	193
38	Walter Johnson, 1915	191
39	Monty Stratton, 1937	191
40	Guy Hecker, 1882	191
41	Lefty Gomez, 1937	191
42	Sandy Koufax, 1966	191
43	Ed Siever, 1902	191
44	Clark Griffith, 1898	191
45	Dazzy Vance, 1928	190
46	Lefty Grove, 1936	189
47	Ed Walsh, 1910	189
48	Vean Gregg, 1911	189
49	Amos Rusie, 1894	189
50	Hal Newhouser, 1946	189
51	Dazzy Vance, 1930	188
52	Billy Rhines, 1896	188
53	Wilbur Wood, 1971	188
54	Jack Stivetts, 1889	188
55	Joe Wood, 1915	187
56	Warren Spahn, 1953	187
57	Sandy Koufax, 1964	187
58	Lefty Grove, 1939	186
59	Eddie Cicotte, 1913	185
60	Luis Tiant, 1968	185
61	Lefty Grove, 1930	184
62	Hank Aguirre, 1962	184
63	Joe Horlen, 1964	184
64	Henry Boyle, 1886	184
65	Vida Blue, 1971	183
66	Walter Johnson, 1910	183
67	John Tudor, 1985	183
68	Harry Brecheen, 1948	183
69	Jack Coombs, 1910	183
70	Billy Rhines, 1890	182
71	Steve Carlton, 1972	182
72	Fred Toney, 1915	182
73	Johnny Allen, 1937	181
74	Roger Clemens, 1994	180
75	Rube Waddell, 1905	180
76	Mordecai Brown, 1907	179
77	Orval Overall, 1909	179
78	Rube Waddell, 1902	179
79	Kevin Appier, 1993	179
80	Joe Wood, 1912	178
81	Bret Saberhagen, 1989	178
82	Phil Niekro, 1967	178
83	Max Lanier, 1943	177
84	Fred Anderson, 1917	177
85	David Cone, 1994	176
86	Cy Young, 1892	176
87	Johnny Antonelli, 1954	176
88	Whitey Ford, 1958	176
89	Lefty Grove, 1935	176
90	Jack Pfiester, 1906	175
91	Eddie Cicotte, 1919	175
92	Roger Clemens, 1992	175
93	Mel Harder, 1934	174
94	Lefty Gomez, 1934	174
95	Harry McCormick, 1882	174
96	Al Benton, 1945	174
97	George Bradley, 1876	174
98	Tom Seaver, 1973	174
99	Jim Devlin, 1876	174
100	Eddie Cicotte, 1917	174

Adjusted ERA (by era)

1876-1892

1	Tim Keefe, 1880	294
2	Denny Driscoll, 1882	216
3	Charley Radbourn, 1884	205
4	Silver King, 1888	198
5	Guy Hecker, 1882	191
6	Jack Stivetts, 1889	188
7	Henry Boyle, 1886	184
8	Billy Rhines, 1890	182
9	Cy Young, 1892	176
10	Harry McCormick, 1882	174
11	George Bradley, 1876	174
12	Jim Devlin, 1876	174
13	Will White, 1882	172
14	Guy Hecker, 1884	172
15	Jim McCormick, 1883	171

1893-1919

1	Dutch Leonard, 1914	280
2	Walter Johnson, 1913	258
3	Mordecai Brown, 1906	254
4	Walter Johnson, 1912	240
5	Christy Mathewson, 1905	230
6	Pete Alexander, 1915	225
7	Christy Mathewson, 1909	224
8	Cy Young, 1901	217
9	Jack Pfiester, 1907	216
10	Walter Johnson, 1919	216
11	Walter Johnson, 1918	215
12	Carl Lundgren, 1907	213
13	Ed Reulbach, 1905	210
14	Addie Joss, 1908	206
15	Jack Taylor, 1902	203

1920-1941

1	Lefty Grove, 1931	218
2	Dolf Luque, 1923	200
3	Carl Hubbell, 1933	193
4	Monty Stratton, 1937	191
5	Lefty Gomez, 1937	191
6	Dazzy Vance, 1928	190
7	Lefty Grove, 1936	189
8	Dazzy Vance, 1930	188
9	Lefty Grove, 1939	186
10	Lefty Grove, 1930	184
11	Johnny Allen, 1937	181
12	Lefty Grove, 1935	176
13	Mel Harder, 1934	174
14	Lefty Gomez, 1934	174
15	Dazzy Vance, 1924	173

1942-1960

1	Billy Pierce, 1955	201
2	Spud Chandler, 1943	197
3	Hal Newhouser, 1945	194
4	Mort Cooper, 1942	193
5	Hal Newhouser, 1946	189
6	Warren Spahn, 1953	187
7	Harry Brecheen, 1948	183
8	Max Lanier, 1943	177
9	Johnny Antonelli, 1954	176
10	Whitey Ford, 1958	176
11	Al Benton, 1945	174
12	Hoyt Wilhelm, 1959	173
13	Ted Lyons, 1942	172

1961-1976

1	Bob Gibson, 1968	258
2	Dean Chance, 1964	199
3	Tom Seaver, 1971	194
4	Sandy Koufax, 1966	191
5	Wilbur Wood, 1971	188
6	Sandy Koufax, 1964	187
7	Luis Tiant, 1968	185
8	Hank Aguirre, 1962	184
9	Joe Horlen, 1964	184
10	Vida Blue, 1971	183
11	Steve Carlton, 1972	182
12	Phil Niekro, 1967	178
13	Tom Seaver, 1973	174
14	Whitey Ford, 1964	170
15	Juan Marichal, 1965	169

1977-1994

1	Greg Maddux, 1994	266
2	Dwight Gooden, 1985	226
3	Roger Clemens, 1990	211
4	Ron Guidry, 1978	208
5	Nolan Ryan, 1981	195
6	John Tudor, 1985	183
7	Roger Clemens, 1994	180
8	Kevin Appier, 1993	179
9	Bret Saberhagen, 1989	178
10	David Cone, 1994	176
11	Roger Clemens, 1992	175
12	Orel Hershiser, 1985	171
13	John Candelaria, 1977	170
14	Greg Maddux, 1993	170
15	Dave Stieb, 1985	170

Pitching Runs

1	Amos Rusie, 1894	125.7
2	Charley Radbourn, 1884	120.9
3	Guy Hecker, 1884	108.0
4	Silver King, 1888	92.3
5	John Clarkson, 1889	88.7
6	Cy Young, 1901	84.2
7	Matt Kilroy, 1887	80.4
8	Pink Hawley, 1895	79.1
9	Walter Johnson, 1912	79.1
10	Silver King, 1890	78.9
11	Will White, 1883	77.7
12	Amos Rusie, 1893	76.9
13	Charley Radbourn, 1883	76.5
14	Dave Foutz, 1886	75.2
15	Lefty Grove, 1931	74.5
16	Dolf Luque, 1923	74.2
17	Jouett Meekin, 1894	73.9
18	Scott Stratton, 1890	72.3
19	Billy Rhines, 1890	72.2
20	Lefty Gomez, 1937	70.9
21	Jim Galvin, 1884	69.8
22	Walter Johnson, 1913	68.8
23	George Bradley, 1876	68.8
24	Cy Young, 1892	68.5
25	Kid Nichols, 1897	68.4
26	Lefty Grove, 1930	68.4
27	Dazzy Vance, 1930	67.9
28	Lefty Gomez, 1934	67.7
29	Elmer Smith, 1887	67.6
30	Sandy Koufax, 1966	67.5
31	John Clarkson, 1885	67.1
32	Red Faber, 1921	66.4
33	Toad Ramsey, 1886	65.7
34	Christy Mathewson, 1905	65.0
35	Warren Spahn, 1953	64.5
36	Pete Alexander, 1915	64.1
37	Kid Nichols, 1898	63.5
38	Amos Rusie, 1897	63.5
39	Kid Nichols, 1896	63.5
40	Ted Breitenstein, 1893	63.4
41	Dwight Gooden, 1985	63.4
42	Kid Nichols, 1890	63.2
43	Mickey Welch, 1885	63.1
44	Bob Gibson, 1968	63.1
45	Bob Caruthers, 1885	63.1
46	Robert Feller, 1940	63.0
47	Lefty Grove, 1936	62.8
48	Cy Young, 1894	62.7
49	Clark Griffith, 1898	62.6
50	Cy Young, 1895	62.5
51	Ed Morris, 1886	61.9
52	Amos Rusie, 1890	61.6
53	Ron Guidry, 1978	61.4
54	Carl Hubbell, 1934	61.3
55	Will White, 1882	61.3
56	Cy Young, 1893	61.1
57	Dean Chance, 1964	61.1
58	Tim Keefe, 1885	61.1
59	Cy Young, 1902	60.8
60	Jim Palmer, 1975	60.6
61	Ed Seward, 1888	60.5
62	Greg Maddux, 1994	59.5
63	Thornton Lee, 1941	59.4
64	Dazzy Vance, 1928	59.3
65	Robin Roberts, 1953	59.1
66	Charlie Ferguson, 1886	58.6
67	Dazzy Vance, 1924	58.5
68	Robert Feller, 1939	58.3
69	Bill Hutchison, 1890	58.2
70	Lady Baldwin, 1886	58.2
71	Bucky Walters, 1939	57.8
72	Kid Nichols, 1895	57.8
73	Carl Hubbell, 1936	57.8
74	John Clarkson, 1887	57.7
75	Ed Morris, 1885	57.7
76	Jesse Duryea, 1889	57.5
77	Carl Hubbell, 1933	57.5
78	Wilbur Wood, 1971	57.4
79	Guy Hecker, 1885	57.2
80	Tony Mullane, 1883	57.0
81	Vida Blue, 1971	57.0
82	Steve Carlton, 1972	56.9
83	Walter Johnson, 1919	56.1
84	Sandy Koufax, 1965	56.0
85	Warren Spahn, 1947	55.7
86	Tim Keefe, 1885	55.3
87	Win Mercer, 1894	55.0
88	Bill Hoffer, 1895	54.9
89	Walter Johnson, 1918	54.6
90	Robert Feller, 1946	54.5
91	Charlie Buffinton, 1884	54.5
92	Kid Nichols, 1893	54.3
93	Tom Seaver, 1971	54.3
94	Hal Newhouser, 1945	54.2
95	Joe Wood, 1912	53.9
96	Toad Ramsey, 1887	53.8
97	Charlie Sweeney, 1884	53.7
98	Mel Harder, 1934	53.6
99	Matt Kilroy, 1889	53.6
100	Tim Keefe, 1888	53.5

Adjusted Pitching Runs

1	Amos Rusie, 1894	121.7
2	Charley Radbourn, 1884	108.9
3	Silver King, 1888	105.2
4	John Clarkson, 1889	98.9
5	Guy Hecker, 1884	95.9
6	Silver King, 1890	84.5
7	John Clarkson, 1885	82.2
8	Jim Galvin, 1884	81.9
9	John Clarkson, 1887	81.8
10	Walter Johnson, 1912	79.8
11	Jim Devlin, 1876	79.7
12	Cy Young, 1901	78.6
13	Lefty Grove, 1931	78.2
14	Toad Ramsey, 1886	78.1
15	Amos Rusie, 1893	76.4
16	Kid Nichols, 1897	74.9
17	Dave Foutz, 1886	74.6
18	Will White, 1883	74.1
19	Cy Young, 1892	73.7
20	Charley Radbourn, 1883	72.7
21	Kid Nichols, 1890	71.8
22	Billy Rhines, 1890	71.7
23	Cy Young, 1893	71.4
24	Scott Stratton, 1890	71.4
25	Kid Nichols, 1895	71.3
26	Cy Young, 1895	70.9
27	Kid Nichols, 1896	70.9
28	Lefty Grove, 1936	70.6
29	Jouett Meekin, 1894	70.3
30	Elmer Smith, 1887	69.9
31	Walter Johnson, 1913	69.6
32	Dolf Luque, 1923	69.3
33	Lefty Grove, 1930	69.1
34	Cy Young, 1894	69.0
35	Matt Kilroy, 1887	67.4
36	Kid Nichols, 1898	67.3
37	Kid Nichols, 1893	67.1
38	Tony Mullane, 1883	66.3
39	Dazzy Vance, 1930	66.2
40	Ted Breitenstein, 1893	66.2
41	Pink Hawley, 1895	66.2
42	Jack Stivetts, 1891	65.7
43	Lefty Gomez, 1937	65.5
44	Jim Devlin, 1877	65.5
45	Red Faber, 1921	64.6
46	Bob Caruthers, 1885	64.3
47	Bill Hutchison, 1890	64.2
48	John Clarkson, 1886	64.0
49	Tim Keefe, 1883	63.8
50	Pete Alexander, 1915	63.7
51	Vic Willis, 1899	63.4
52	Christy Mathewson, 1905	62.3
53	Wilbur Wood, 1971	62.2
54	Steve Carlton, 1972	62.2
55	Lefty Grove, 1935	61.9
56	Clark Griffith, 1898	61.6
57	Cy Young, 1902	60.8
58	Jesse Duryea, 1889	60.1
59	Bob Gibson, 1968	60.0
60	Cy Young, 1896	59.9
61	Kid Nichols, 1891	59.8
62	Toad Ramsey, 1887	59.7
63	Dan Casey, 1887	59.5
64	Hal Newhouser, 1945	59.4
65	Dwight Gooden, 1985	59.2
66	Elton Chamberlain, 1889	59.0
67	Will White, 1882	58.8
68	Dazzy Vance, 1928	58.8
69	Matt Kilroy, 1889	58.7
70	Lady Baldwin, 1886	58.3
71	Charlie Ferguson, 1886	58.1
72	Greg Maddux, 1994	58.1
73	Ed Morris, 1886	58.0
74	Amos Rusie, 1897	57.9
75	Mark Baldwin, 1890	57.8
76	George Bradley, 1876	57.8
77	Thornton Lee, 1941	57.7
78	Kid Gleason, 1890	57.5
79	Amos Rusie, 1890	57.5
80	Cy Young, 1899	57.4
81	Ron Guidry, 1978	57.1
82	Robert Feller, 1940	57.1
83	Joe Wood, 1912	57.0
84	Nig Cuppy, 1895	56.7
85	Dizzy Trout, 1944	56.6
86	Bobo Newsom, 1940	56.5
87	Nig Cuppy, 1896	56.5
88	Sandy Koufax, 1966	56.3
89	Ed Seward, 1888	56.2
90	Robin Roberts, 1953	56.1
91	Tony Mullane, 1884	56.1
92	Guy Hecker, 1885	56.0
93	Hal Newhouser, 1946	55.8
94	Ed Morris, 1885	55.8
95	Walter Johnson, 1919	55.5
96	Silver King, 1889	55.1
97	Mel Harder, 1934	55.0
98	Mickey Welch, 1885	54.8
99	Bucky Walters, 1939	54.8
100	Lefty Grove, 1932	54.6

Pitching Wins

#	Player	
1	Charley Radbourn, 1884	10.8
2	Guy Hecker, 1884	9.9
3	Amos Rusie, 1894	9.6
4	Silver King, 1888	8.5
5	Walter Johnson, 1912	7.9
6	John Clarkson, 1889	7.7
7	Cy Young, 1901	7.6
8	Walter Johnson, 1913	7.3
9	Bob Gibson, 1968	7.2
10	Dolf Luque, 1923	7.1
11	Pete Alexander, 1915	7.1
12	Sandy Koufax, 1966	7.1
13	Lefty Grove, 1931	6.9
14	Will White, 1883	6.8
15	Christy Mathewson, 1905	6.7
16	Charley Radbourn, 1883	6.7
17	Dwight Gooden, 1985	6.7
18	Dave Foutz, 1886	6.6
19	Lefty Gomez, 1937	6.5
20	Matt Kilroy, 1887	6.5
21	Dean Chance, 1964	6.4
22	Billy Rhines, 1890	6.4
23	Pink Hawley, 1895	6.4
24	Scott Stratton, 1890	6.4
25	Cy Young, 1892	6.3
26	Ron Guidry, 1978	6.3
27	John Clarkson, 1885	6.3
28	Amos Rusie, 1893	6.3
29	Lefty Gomez, 1934	6.3
30	Silver King, 1890	6.3
31	Jim Galvin, 1884	6.2
32	Warren Spahn, 1953	6.2
33	Red Faber, 1921	6.2
34	Jim Palmer, 1975	6.2
35	Lefty Grove, 1930	6.2
36	Wilbur Wood, 1971	6.2
37	Vida Blue, 1971	6.1
38	Steve Carlton, 1972	6.1
39	Walter Johnson, 1918	6.1
40	Carl Hubbell, 1933	6.1
41	George Bradley, 1876	6.1
42	Dazzy Vance, 1930	6.0
43	Carl Hubbell, 1934	6.0
44	Robert Feller, 1940	5.9
45	Kid Nichols, 1898	5.9
46	Mickey Welch, 1885	5.9
47	Sandy Koufax, 1965	5.9
48	Walter Johnson, 1919	5.9
49	Kid Nichols, 1897	5.9
50	Greg Maddux, 1994	5.9
51	Clark Griffith, 1898	5.8
52	Tom Seaver, 1971	5.8
53	Dazzy Vance, 1924	5.8
54	Hal Newhouser, 1945	5.8
55	Dazzy Vance, 1928	5.8
56	Bucky Walters, 1939	5.8
57	Cy Young, 1902	5.8
58	Toad Ramsey, 1886	5.8
59	Thornton Lee, 1941	5.8
60	Ed Walsh, 1908	5.8
61	Ed Walsh, 1910	5.7
62	Robert Feller, 1946	5.7
63	Robin Roberts, 1953	5.7
64	Bob Caruthers, 1885	5.7
65	Jouett Meekin, 1894	5.7
66	Carl Hubbell, 1936	5.6
67	Will White, 1882	5.6
68	Kid Nichols, 1890	5.6
69	Ed Seward, 1888	5.6
70	Lefty Grove, 1936	5.5
71	Jack Taylor, 1902	5.5
72	Walter Johnson, 1915	5.5
73	Warren Spahn, 1947	5.5
74	Amos Rusie, 1890	5.5
75	Elmer Smith, 1887	5.5
76	Mordecai Brown, 1906	5.5
77	Amos Rusie, 1897	5.4
78	Ed Morris, 1886	5.4
79	Mordecai Brown, 1909	5.4
80	Joe McGinnity, 1904	5.4
81	Dizzy Trout, 1944	5.4
82	Joe Wood, 1912	5.4
83	Kid Nichols, 1896	5.4
84	Tim Keefe, 1883	5.4
85	Robert Feller, 1939	5.4
86	Hal Newhouser, 1946	5.3
87	John Tudor, 1985	5.3
88	Ed Reulbach, 1905	5.3
89	Jack Coombs, 1910	5.3
90	Tom Seaver, 1973	5.3
91	Pete Alexander, 1920	5.3
92	Charlie Ferguson, 1886	5.3
93	Walter Johnson, 1910	5.3
94	Pete Alexander, 1916	5.3
95	Sandy Koufax, 1963	5.3
96	Lady Baldwin, 1886	5.3
97	Tim Keefe, 1888	5.2
98	Juan Marichal, 1969	5.2
99	Tim Keefe, 1885	5.2
100	Ted Breitenstein, 1893	5.2

Adjusted Pitching Wins

#	Player	
1	Charley Radbourn, 1884	9.7
2	Silver King, 1888	9.7
3	Amos Rusie, 1894	9.3
4	Guy Hecker, 1884	8.8
5	John Clarkson, 1889	8.6
6	Walter Johnson, 1912	8.0
7	John Clarkson, 1885	7.7
8	Walter Johnson, 1913	7.4
9	Jim Galvin, 1884	7.3
10	Lefty Grove, 1931	7.3
11	Cy Young, 1901	7.1
12	Pete Alexander, 1915	7.1
13	Jim Devlin, 1876	7.0
14	John Clarkson, 1887	6.9
15	Bob Gibson, 1968	6.9
16	Toad Ramsey, 1886	6.8
17	Cy Young, 1892	6.8
18	Silver King, 1890	6.7
19	Wilbur Wood, 1971	6.7
20	Steve Carlton, 1972	6.7
21	Dolf Luque, 1923	6.7
22	Dave Foutz, 1886	6.5
23	Will White, 1883	6.5
24	Christy Mathewson, 1905	6.5
25	Kid Nichols, 1897	6.4
26	Kid Nichols, 1890	6.4
27	Billy Rhines, 1890	6.4
28	Hal Newhouser, 1945	6.4
29	Charley Radbourn, 1883	6.3
30	Kid Nichols, 1898	6.3
31	Scott Stratton, 1890	6.3
32	Amos Rusie, 1893	6.3
33	Lefty Grove, 1930	6.3
34	Lefty Grove, 1936	6.2
35	Dwight Gooden, 1985	6.2
36	Red Faber, 1921	6.0
37	Kid Nichols, 1896	6.0
38	Lefty Gomez, 1937	6.0
39	Dizzy Trout, 1944	6.0
40	Sandy Koufax, 1966	5.9
41	Walter Johnson, 1918	5.9
42	Ron Guidry, 1978	5.9
43	Cy Young, 1893	5.9
44	Hal Newhouser, 1946	5.8
45	Dazzy Vance, 1930	5.8
46	Jim Devlin, 1877	5.8
47	Tony Mullane, 1883	5.8
48	Walter Johnson, 1919	5.8
49	Lefty Grove, 1935	5.8
50	John Clarkson, 1886	5.8
51	Bob Caruthers, 1885	5.8
52	Kid Nichols, 1895	5.8
53	Cy Young, 1902	5.8
54	Clark Griffith, 1898	5.8
55	Dazzy Vance, 1928	5.7
56	Vic Willis, 1899	5.7
57	Cy Young, 1895	5.7
58	Greg Maddux, 1994	5.7
59	Joe Wood, 1912	5.7
60	Bill Hutchison, 1890	5.7
61	Elmer Smith, 1887	5.7
62	Jack Stivetts, 1891	5.7
63	Vida Blue, 1971	5.7
64	Walter Johnson, 1915	5.6
65	Gaylord Perry, 1972	5.6
66	Carl Hubbell, 1933	5.6
67	Tom Seaver, 1971	5.6
68	Tim Keefe, 1883	5.6
69	Pete Alexander, 1920	5.6
70	Thornton Lee, 1941	5.6
71	Roger Clemens, 1990	5.5
72	Kid Nichols, 1893	5.5
73	Bucky Walters, 1939	5.5
74	Mordecai Brown, 1906	5.5
75	Mort Cooper, 1942	5.5
76	Matt Kilroy, 1887	5.5
77	Pete Alexander, 1916	5.4
78	Ed Breitenstein, 1893	5.4
79	Robin Roberts, 1953	5.4
80	Will White, 1882	5.4
81	Dazzy Vance, 1924	5.4
82	Robert Feller, 1940	5.4
83	Jouett Meekin, 1894	5.4
84	Bill Hands, 1969	5.4
85	Pink Hawley, 1895	5.4
86	Joe McGinnity, 1904	5.3
87	Kid Nichols, 1891	5.3
88	Bobo Newsom, 1940	5.3
89	Dean Chance, 1964	5.3
90	Carl Hubbell, 1934	5.3
91	Bert Blyleven, 1973	5.3
92	Dizzy Dean, 1934	5.3
93	Cy Young, 1894	5.3
94	Ed Walsh, 1908	5.3
95	Lady Baldwin, 1886	5.3
96	Curt Davis, 1934	5.3
97	Ed Reulbach, 1905	5.3
98	Charlie Ferguson, 1886	5.3
99	Carl Hubbell, 1936	5.2
100	Jack Taylor, 1902	5.2

Opponents' Batting Average

#	Player	
1	Luis Tiant, 1968	.168
2	Nolan Ryan, 1972	.171
3	Nolan Ryan, 1991	.172
4	Ed Reulbach, 1906	.175
5	Sandy Koufax, 1965	.179
6	Dutch Leonard, 1914	.180
7	Sid Fernandez, 1985	.181
8	Dave McNally, 1968	.182
9	Tommy Byrne, 1949	.183
10	Al Downing, 1963	.184
11	Bob Gibson, 1968	.184
12	Sam McDowell, 1965	.185
13	Carl Lundgren, 1907	.185
14	Herb Score, 1956	.186
15	Mike Scott, 1986	.186
16	Tim Keefe, 1880	.187
17	Nolan Ryan, 1989	.187
18	Ed Walsh, 1910	.187
19	Mario Soto, 1980	.187
20	Walter Johnson, 1913	.187
21	Nolan Ryan, 1981	.188
22	Russ Ford, 1910	.188
23	Nolan Ryan, 1986	.188
24	Nolan Ryan, 1990	.188
25	Guy Hecker, 1882	.188
26	Floyd Youmans, 1986	.188
27	Sam McDowell, 1966	.188
28	Sandy Koufax, 1963	.189
29	Sam McDowell, 1968	.189
30	Don Sutton, 1972	.189
31	Catfish Hunter, 1972	.189
32	Vida Blue, 1971	.189
33	Nolan Ryan, 1974	.190
34	Andy Messersmith, 1969	.190
35	Joe Horlen, 1964	.190
36	Sid Fernandez, 1988	.191
37	Pete Alexander, 1915	.191
38	Sandy Koufax, 1964	.191
39	Bob Turley, 1955	.193
40	Nolan Ryan, 1977	.193
41	Charlie Sweeney, 1884	.193
42	Fred Beebe, 1908	.193
43	Ron Guidry, 1978	.193
44	Stan Coveleski, 1917	.194
45	Bob Turley, 1957	.194
46	Herb Score, 1955	.194
47	Jack Pfiester, 1906	.194
48	Mordecai Brown, 1908	.195
49	Nolan Ryan, 1976	.195
50	Nolan Ryan, 1983	.195
51	Dean Chance, 1964	.195
52	Roger Clemens, 1986	.195
53	Tim Keefe, 1888	.196
54	Walter Johnson, 1912	.196
55	Roger Nelson, 1972	.196
56	J.R. Richard, 1978	.196
57	Pascual Perez, 1988	.196
58	Jeff Robinson, 1988	.197
59	Lady Baldwin, 1885	.197
60	Jose DeLeon, 1989	.197
61	Dave Boswell, 1968	.197
62	Sandy Koufax, 1962	.197
63	Addie Joss, 1908	.197
64	Sonny Siebert, 1968	.198
65	Sid Fernandez, 1989	.198
66	Toad Ramsey, 1886	.198
67	Larry Cheney, 1916	.198
68	Wayne Simpson, 1970	.198
69	Orval Overall, 1909	.198
70	Gary Peters, 1967	.199
71	Larry Corcoran, 1880	.199
72	Willie Mitchell, 1913	.199
73	Rube Waddell, 1905	.199
74	Adonis Terry, 1888	.199
75	Nolan Ryan, 1987	.199
76	Mordecai Brown, 1904	.199
77	Christy Mathewson, 1909	.200
78	Denny McLain, 1968	.200
79	Larry Corcoran, 1882	.200
80	Bobby Bolin, 1968	.200
	Jim Palmer, 1969	.200
	Sid Fernandez, 1990	.200
83	Silver King, 1888	.200
84	Christy Mathewson, 1908	.200
85	Spec Shea, 1947	.200
86	Ed Seward, 1888	.200
87	Tony Mullane, 1892	.201
88	Art Fromme, 1909	.201
89	Babe Ruth, 1916	.201
90	Dwight Gooden, 1985	.201
91	Cannonball Titcomb, 1888	.201
92	Curt Schilling, 1992	.201
93	Hal Newhouser, 1946	.201
94	Ed Reulbach, 1905	.201
95	Jack Coombs, 1910	.201
96	Frank Knauss, 1890	.201
97	Dwight Gooden, 1984	.202
98	Jim Maloney, 1963	.202
99	Cy Morgan, 1909	.202
100	Mordecai Brown, 1909	.202

Opponents' On Base Pct.

#	Player	
1	Guy Hecker, 1882	.198
2	Charlie Sweeney, 1884	.211
3	Henry Boyle, 1884	.215
4	George Bradley, 1880	.217
5	Walter Johnson, 1913	.217
6	Denny Driscoll, 1882	.218
7	Addie Joss, 1908	.218
8	Tim Keefe, 1880	.222
9	Jim Whitney, 1884	.223
10	George Bradley, 1876	.224
11	Christy Mathewson, 1908	.225
12	Guy Hecker, 1884	.226
13	Ed Walsh, 1910	.226
14	Tommy Bond, 1876	.227
15	Lady Baldwin, 1885	.228
16	Sandy Koufax, 1965	.228
17	Christy Mathewson, 1909	.228
18	Sandy Koufax, 1963	.230
19	Juan Marichal, 1966	.230
20	John Ward, 1880	.232
21	Mordecai Brown, 1908	.232
22	Ed Walsh, 1908	.232
23	Luis Tiant, 1968	.233
24	Bob Gibson, 1968	.233
25	Pete Alexander, 1915	.234
26	Dave McNally, 1968	.234
27	Larry Corcoran, 1882	.234
28	Charley Radbourn, 1884	.234
29	Ed Morris, 1884	.234
30	Jim Devlin, 1876	.235
31	Perry Werden, 1884	.235
32	Jack Lynch, 1884	.236
33	Larry Corcoran, 1880	.236
34	Roger Nelson, 1972	.236
35	Charlie Getzien, 1884	.237
36	Tim Keefe, 1883	.237
37	Silver King, 1888	.237
38	Tony Mullane, 1883	.238
39	John Clarkson, 1885	.239
40	Mordecai Brown, 1909	.239
41	Fred Corey, 1880	.239
42	Juan Marichal, 1965	.240
43	Tim Keefe, 1884	.240
44	Cy Young, 1905	.240
45	Cy Young, 1908	.240
46	Don Sutton, 1972	.240
47	Babe Adams, 1919	.241
48	Sandy Koufax, 1964	.241
49	Catfish Hunter, 1972	.242
50	Pete Conway, 1888	.243
51	Harry McCormick, 1882	.243
52	Denny McLain, 1968	.243
53	Tim Keefe, 1888	.243
54	Lady Baldwin, 1886	.243
55	Mike Scott, 1986	.244
56	Charley Radbourn, 1883	.244
57	Will White, 1883	.244
58	Charlie Ferguson, 1886	.244
59	Charlie Buffinton, 1888	.244
60	Will White, 1882	.244
61	Charlie Buffinton, 1884	.244
62	Russ Ford, 1910	.245
63	Pete Alexander, 1919	.245
64	Christy Mathewson, 1905	.245
65	Greg Maddux, 1994	.245
66	Dutch Leonard, 1914	.246
67	Bobby Mathews, 1882	.246
68	Jim Galvin, 1884	.246
69	Charley Radbourn, 1882	.246
70	Sam Weaver, 1878	.247
71	Christy Mathewson, 1907	.247
72	Charlie Gagus, 1884	.247
73	Warren Hacker, 1952	.247
74	Jim McCormick, 1880	.247
75	Ed Morris, 1885	.247
76	Dupee Shaw, 1884	.247
77	Fred Goldsmith, 1880	.247
78	Eddie Cicotte, 1917	.248
79	Walter Johnson, 1912	.248
80	Doc White, 1906	.249
81	John Clarkson, 1889	.249
82	Jumbo McGinnis, 1883	.249
83	John Tudor, 1985	.249
84	Henry Gruber, 1888	.249
85	Ron Guidry, 1978	.250
86	Hugh Daily, 1884	.250
87	Joe Horlen, 1964	.250
88	Terry Larkin, 1879	.250
89	John Ward, 1879	.250
90	Billy Taylor, 1884	.251
91	John Ward, 1878	.251
92	Candy Cummings, 1876	.251
93	Jim Whitney, 1883	.251
94	Cy Young, 1904	.251
95	Claude Hendrix, 1914	.251
96	Dick Burns, 1884	.252
97	Jack Chesbro, 1904	.252
98	Vida Blue, 1971	.252
99	Mordecai Brown, 1906	.252
100	Addie Joss, 1906	.252

Wins Above Team

1	George Bradley, 1876	22.5
2	Will White, 1879	21.5
3	Charley Radbourn, 1884	20.1
4	Jim McCormick, 1880	19.4
5	Guy Hecker, 1884	18.0
6	Jim Galvin, 1883	17.6
7	Jim Devlin, 1877	17.5
8	Charley Radbourn, 1883	15.7
9	Matt Kilroy, 1887	15.4
10	Jim Galvin, 1884	15.1
11	Jim Devlin, 1876	15.0
12	Charlie Buffinton, 1884	14.9
13	Walter Johnson, 1913	14.7
14	Jim McCormick, 1884	14.6
15	Jack Chesbro, 1904	14.0
16	Tony Mullane, 1884	13.9
17	Sadie McMahon, 1890	13.4
18	Will White, 1882	13.1
19	Ed Morris, 1885	12.9
20	Joe Wood, 1912	12.8
21	Bill Sweeney, 1884	12.7
	Ed Walsh, 1908	12.7
23	John Clarkson, 1889	12.1
24	Tommy Bond, 1879	12.0
25	Lefty Grove, 1931	11.8
26	Steve Carlton, 1972	11.7
27	Cy Young, 1901	11.6
28	Bill Hutchison, 1891	11.4
	Denny McLain, 1968	11.4
30	Terry Larkin, 1878	11.2
	Mickey Welch, 1884	11.2
	Bob Caruthers, 1889	11.2
33	Henry Porter, 1885	11.0
	Bill Hoffer, 1895	11.0
	Christy Mathewson, 1908	11.0
36	Cy Young, 1902	10.9
37	Cy Young, 1895	10.7
38	Dazzy Vance, 1924	10.6
	Robin Roberts, 1952	10.6
	Ron Guidry, 1978	10.6
41	Bobby Mathews, 1876	10.5
	Dizzy Dean, 1934	10.5
43	Toad Ramsey, 1886	10.2
	Cy Young, 1892	10.2
	Joe McGinnity, 1904	10.2
	Eddie Rommel, 1922	10.2
47	Lefty Grove, 1930	10.1
48	Ed Morris, 1886	10.0
	Bill Donovan, 1907	10.0
50	Frank Mountain, 1883	9.9
	Eddie Cicotte, 1919	9.9
	Lefty Gomez, 1934	9.9
53	Kid Gleason, 1890	9.8
	Pete Alexander, 1915	9.8
	Hal Newhouser, 1944	9.8
56	Bobby Mathews, 1885	9.7
	Russ Ford, 1910	9.7
	Roger Clemens, 1986	9.7
59	Charlie Ferguson, 1886	9.6
	Pete Conway, 1888	9.6
	Eddie Plank, 1912	9.6
62	Pete Alexander, 1916	9.5
	Carl Hubbell, 1936	9.5
	Dwight Gooden, 1985	9.5
65	Jouett Meekin, 1894	9.4
	Walter Johnson, 1912	9.4
	Claude Hendrix, 1914	9.4
68	Joe McGinnity, 1900	9.3
	Sandy Koufax, 1963	9.3
70	Bert Cunningham, 1898	9.2
	Walter Johnson, 1911	9.2
	Bobby Shantz, 1952	9.2
	Don Newcombe, 1956	9.2
	Juan Marichal, 1966	9.2
	Bob Gibson, 1970	9.2
	Bob Welch, 1990	9.2
77	Tim Keefe, 1888	9.1
	Whitey Ford, 1961	9.1
79	Jim McCormick, 1882	9.0
	Cy Young, 1893	9.0
	Preacher Roe, 1951	9.0
82	Frank Killen, 1892	8.9
	Red Faber, 1921	8.9
84	Tim Keefe, 1883	8.8
	Tim Keefe, 1887	8.8
	Christy Mathewson, 1909	8.8
	Dolf Luque, 1923	8.8
88	Lee Richmond, 1881	8.7
	Frank Killen, 1893	8.7
	Jim Hughes, 1899	8.7
	Juan Marichal, 1963	8.7
	Juan Marichal, 1968	8.7
93	Jim McCormick, 1883	8.6
	Lefty Grove, 1933	8.6
	Robert Feller, 1946	8.6
	Roy Face, 1959	8.6
97	7 players tied	8.5

Wins Above League

1	Charley Radbourn, 1884	45.2
2	Guy Hecker, 1884	44.8
3	Charley Radbourn, 1883	42.8
4	Silver King, 1888	42.7
5	John Clarkson, 1889	42.6
6	John Clarkson, 1885	42.2
7	Jim Galvin, 1884	41.3
8	Jim Galvin, 1883	40.4
9	Bill Hutchison, 1892	40.3
10	Jim McCormick, 1880	40.1
11	Tim Keefe, 1883	39.6
12	Jim Devlin, 1876	39.5
13	Will White, 1879	39.4
14	Toad Ramsey, 1886	39.3
15	Bill Hutchison, 1890	39.2
16	Will White, 1883	39.0
17	Matt Kilroy, 1887	38.0
18	George Bradley, 1876	37.1
19	Toad Ramsey, 1887	36.8
20	Amos Rusie, 1890	36.6
21	Ed Morris, 1885	36.5
22	John Clarkson, 1887	36.4
23	Charlie Buffinton, 1884	36.3
24	Tony Mullane, 1884	36.1
25	Jim Devlin, 1877	35.8
26	Jim McCormick, 1884	35.6
27	Ed Morris, 1886	35.6
28	Jim McCormick, 1882	35.6
29	Dave Foutz, 1886	35.0
30	Lee Richmond, 1880	34.9
31	Tim Keefe, 1886	34.5
32	John Ward, 1880	34.5
33	Bill Hutchison, 1891	34.4
34	John Ward, 1879	34.3
35	Jim Galvin, 1879	34.0
36	Sadie McMahon, 1891	34.0
37	Tommy Bond, 1879	34.0
38	Amos Rusie, 1894	33.8
39	Mark Baldwin, 1890	33.6
40	Billy Taylor, 1884	33.5
41	Jim Whitney, 1883	33.3
42	Amos Rusie, 1893	33.3
43	Jack Stivetts, 1891	33.2
44	Dupee Shaw, 1884	33.1
45	Al Spalding, 1876	33.1
46	Jim Whitney, 1881	33.0
47	Amos Rusie, 1892	32.9
48	Ed Walsh, 1908	32.8
49	Lady Baldwin, 1886	32.8
50	Larry Corcoran, 1884	32.7
51	Silver King, 1890	32.7
52	Mickey Welch, 1885	32.7
53	Mickey Welch, 1884	32.6
54	Kid Gleason, 1890	32.6
55	Charlie Sweeney, 1884	32.3
56	John Clarkson, 1886	32.3
57	Bob Caruthers, 1885	32.3
58	Ed Seward, 1888	32.2
59	Tommy Bond, 1877	32.1
60	Matt Kilroy, 1889	32.0
61	Will White, 1880	31.9
62	Mickey Welch, 1880	31.9
63	Pink Hawley, 1895	31.9
64	Matt Kilroy, 1886	31.8
65	Guy Hecker, 1885	31.5
66	Jack Chesbro, 1904	31.5
67	Sadie McMahon, 1890	31.5
68	Will White, 1882	31.4
69	Larry Corcoran, 1880	31.2
70	Tim Keefe, 1884	31.2
71	George Derby, 1881	31.2
72	Tommy Bond, 1878	31.2
73	Elmer Smith, 1887	31.2
74	Bill Sweeney, 1884	31.0
75	Cy Young, 1893	30.9
76	Tony Mullane, 1883	30.8
77	Cy Young, 1892	30.8
78	Jesse Duryea, 1889	30.6
79	Mark Baldwin, 1889	30.6
80	Walter Johnson, 1912	30.5
81	Jim McCormick, 1879	30.4
82	Hardie Henderson, 1885	30.4
83	Scott Stratton, 1890	30.3
84	Larry Corcoran, 1883	30.2
85	Silver King, 1889	30.2
86	Charley Radbourn, 1886	30.0
87	Charley Radbourn, 1882	30.0
88	John Clarkson, 1891	29.9
89	Tim Keefe, 1887	29.9
90	Phil Knell, 1891	29.9
91	Tony Mullane, 1882	29.8
92	Joe McGinnity, 1903	29.8
93	Amos Rusie, 1891	29.7
94	Jersey Bakely, 1888	29.6
95	Kid Nichols, 1893	29.5
96	Henry Porter, 1885	29.5
97	Kid Nichols, 1890	29.4
98	Gus Weyhing, 1892	29.3
99	Tony Mullane, 1886	29.1
100	Gus Weyhing, 1889	29.0

Relief Games

1	Mike Marshall, 1974	106
2	Kent Tekulve, 1979	94
3	Mike Marshall, 1973	92
4	Kent Tekulve, 1978	91
5	Wayne Granger, 1969	90
	Kent Tekulve, 1987	90
7	Mike Marshall, 1979	89
	Mark Eichhorn, 1987	89
9	Rob Murphy, 1987	87
10	Wilbur Wood, 1968	86
11	Kent Tekulve, 1982	85
	Frank Williams, 1987	85
13	Ted Abernathy, 1965	84
	Enrique Romo, 1979	84
	Dick Tidrow, 1980	84
	Dan Quisenberry, 1985	84
	Mitch Williams, 1987	84
18	Ken Sanders, 1971	83
	Craig Lefferts, 1986	83
20	Eddie Fisher, 1965	82
	Bill Campbell, 1983	82
	Juan Agosto, 1990	82
23	John Wyatt, 1964	81
	Dale Murray, 1976	81
	Jeff Robinson, 1987	81
	Duane Ward, 1991	81
	Joe Boever, 1992	81
	Kenny Rogers, 1992	81
	Mike Jackson, 1993	81
30	Mudcat Grant, 1970	80
	Pedro Borbon, 1973	80
	Willie Hernandez, 1984	80
	Mitch Williams, 1986	80
	Doug Jones, 1992	80
	Greg Harris, 1993	80
36	Dick Radatz, 1964	79
	Duane Ward, 1992	79
38	Hal Woodeshick, 1965	78
	Ted Abernathy, 1968	78
	Bill Campbell, 1976	78
	Rollie Fingers, 1977	78
	Tom Hume, 1980	78
	Kent Tekulve, 1980	78
	Greg Minton, 1982	78
	Ed Vande Berg, 1982	78
	Ted Power, 1984	78
	Tim Burke, 1985	78
	Lance McCullers, 1987	78
49	12 players tied	77

Relief Wins

1	Roy Face, 1959	18
2	John Hiller, 1974	17
	Bill Campbell, 1976	17
4	Jim Konstanty, 1950	16
	Ron Perranoski, 1963	16
	Dick Radatz, 1964	16
	Tom Johnson, 1977	16
8	Mace Brown, 1938	15
	Hoyt Wilhelm, 1952	15
	Luis Arroyo, 1961	15
	Dick Radatz, 1963	15
	Eddie Fisher, 1965	15
	Mike Marshall, 1974	15
	Dale Murray, 1975	15
15	Joe Page, 1947	14
	Joe Black, 1952	14
	Hersh Freeman, 1956	14
	Stu Miller, 1961	14
	Stu Miller, 1965	14
	Phil Regan, 1966	14
	Frank Linzy, 1969	14
	Mike Marshall, 1972	14
	Mike Marshall, 1973	14
	Ron Davis, 1979	14
	Mark Clear, 1982	14
	Jim Slaton, 1983	14
	Roger McDowell, 1986	14
	Mark Eichhorn, 1986	14
29	Dick Tidrow, 1979	13
	Earl Caldwell, 1946	13
	Joe Page, 1949	13
	Clyde King, 1951	13
	Lindy McDaniel, 1959	13
	Larry Sherry, 1960	13
	Gerry Staley, 1960	13
	Lindy McDaniel, 1963	13
	Al Hrabosky, 1975	13
	Rollie Fingers, 1976	13
	Bill Campbell, 1977	13
	Sparky Lyle, 1977	13
	Gary Lavelle, 1978	13
	Bob Stanley, 1978	13
	Ron Reed, 1979	13
	Jim Kern, 1979	13
	Aurelio Lopez, 1980	13
	Jesse Orosco, 1983	13
	Rich Gossage, 1983	13
48	30 players tied	12

Relief Losses

1	Gene Garber, 1979	16
2	Darold Knowles, 1970	14
	John Hiller, 1974	14
	Mike Marshall, 1975	14
	Mike Marshall, 1979	14
6	Wilbur Wood, 1970	13
	Rollie Fingers, 1978	13
	Skip Lockwood, 1978	13
9	Roy Face, 1956	12
	Roy Face, 1961	12
	Ken Sanders, 1971	12
	Mike Marshall, 1974	12
	Gene Garber, 1975	12
	Jim Willoughby, 1976	12
	Charlie Hough, 1977	12
	Mike Marshall, 1978	12
	Kent Tekulve, 1980	12
	Ken Howell, 1986	12
	Roger Mason, 1993	12
20	Nels Potter, 1949	11
	Frank Funk, 1961	11
	Dick Radatz, 1965	11
	Frank Linzy, 1966	11
	Wilbur Wood, 1968	11
	Wilbur Wood, 1969	11
	Mike Marshall, 1973	11
	Rollie Fingers, 1976	11
	Rich Gossage, 1978	11
	Dave Heaverlo, 1979	11
	Mark Clear, 1980	11
	Greg Minton, 1983	11
	Ron Davis, 1984	11
	Mark Davis, 1985	11
	Joe Boever, 1989	11
35	45 players tied	10

Relief Innings Pitched

1	Mike Marshall, 1974	208.1
2	Mike Marshall, 1973	179.0
3	Bob Stanley, 1982	168.1
4	Bill Campbell, 1976	167.2
5	Andy Karl, 1945	166.2
6	Eddie Fisher, 1965	165.1
7	Hoyt Wilhelm, 1952	159.1
8	Dick Radatz, 1964	157.0
	Mark Eichhorn, 1986	157.0
10	Jim Konstanty, 1950	152.0
11	John Hiller, 1974	150.0
12	Tom Johnson, 1977	146.2
13	Garland Braxton, 1927	146.0
14	Bob Stanley, 1983	145.1
15	Hoyt Wilhelm, 1953	145.0
	Wilbur Wood, 1968	145.0
17	Allan Russell, 1923	144.2
	Wayne Granger, 1969	144.2
19	Steve Foucault, 1974	144.1
20	Hoyt Wilhelm, 1965	144.0
21	Jim Kern, 1979	143.0
22	Charlie Hough, 1976	142.2
23	Rich Gossage, 1975	141.2
24	Mike Marshall, 1979	140.2
25	Sammy Stewart, 1983	140.1
	Willie Hernandez, 1984	140.1
27	Bill Campbell, 1977	140.0
28	Jack Lamabe, 1963	139.2
29	Pedro Borbon, 1974	139.0
	Dan Quisenberry, 1983	139.0
31	Lindy McDaniel, 1973	138.1
32	Aurelio Lopez, 1984	137.2
33	Clay Carroll, 1966	137.1
34	Sparky Lyle, 1977	137.0
	Tom Hume, 1980	137.0
36	Dan Quisenberry, 1982	136.2
37	Ted Abernathy, 1965	136.1
	Ken Sanders, 1971	136.1
	Doug Corbett, 1980	136.1
40	Mudcat Grant, 1970	135.1
	Joe Page, 1949	135.1
42	Clay Carroll, 1968	135.0
	Kent Tekulve, 1978	135.0
44	Ted Abernathy, 1968	134.2
	Phil Regan, 1968	134.2
	Rollie Fingers, 1976	134.2
47	Bill Henry, 1959	134.1
	Dick Selma, 1970	134.1
	Rich Gossage, 1978	134.1
	Kent Tekulve, 1979	134.1

Relief Points

1	Bobby Thigpen, 1990	116
2	Dennis Eckersley, 1992	115
3	Randy Myers, 1993	106
4	Lee Smith, 1991	103
5	Dennis Eckersley, 1990	102
6	Rod Beck, 1993	101
	John Wetteland, 1993	101
8	Dave Righetti, 1986	100
9	Jeff Montgomery, 1993	99
10	Dan Quisenberry, 1983	97
	Dan Quisenberry, 1984	97
12	Dennis Eckersley, 1988	96
13	Bruce Sutter, 1984	93
	Mark Davis, 1989	93
15	Lee Smith, 1993	92
	Dennis Eckersley, 1991	92
	Bryan Harvey, 1991	92
18	John Hiller, 1973	91
	Doug Jones, 1990	91
	Duane Ward, 1993	91
21	Steve Bedrosian, 1987	87
	Rick Aguilera, 1991	87
	Bryan Harvey, 1993	87
24	Doug Jones, 1992	86
25	Lee Smith, 1992	85
	Mitch Williams, 1993	85
	Tom Henke, 1993	85
28	John Franco, 1988	84
	Jeff Reardon, 1988	84
	Jeff Russell, 1989	84
31	Luis Arroyo, 1961	83
	Sparky Lyle, 1972	83
	Dan Quisenberry, 1980	83
	Bill Caudill, 1984	83
35	Clay Carroll, 1972	82
	Bruce Sutter, 1982	82
37	Dick Radatz, 1964	81
	Dan Quisenberry, 1982	81
	Dan Quisenberry, 1985	81
	Gregg Olson, 1990	81
41	Bruce Sutter, 1979	80
	Todd Worrell, 1986	80
	Rick Aguilera, 1992	80
44	Mike Marshall, 1973	79
	Bill Campbell, 1977	79
	Jim Kern, 1979	79
	Willie Hernandez, 1984	79
	Mitch Williams, 1991	79
49	4 players tied	78

Relief Ranking

1	Jim Kern, 1979	65.0
2	John Hiller, 1973	64.9
3	John Wetteland, 1993	63.7
4	Rich Gossage, 1977	62.5
5	Lindy McDaniel, 1960	57.5
6	Mike Marshall, 1979	56.2
7	Mark Eichhorn, 1986	56.2
8	Dennis Eckersley, 1990	55.8
9	Bruce Sutter, 1977	54.0
10	Jeff Montgomery, 1993	53.8
11	Ellis Kinder, 1953	53.6
12	Jesse Orosco, 1983	52.2
13	Donnie Moore, 1985	51.9
14	Bill Caudill, 1982	51.9
15	Dick Radatz, 1964	50.4
16	Bob James, 1985	50.4
17	Sid Monge, 1979	49.5
18	Dick Radatz, 1963	49.4
19	Bobby Thigpen, 1990	48.3
20	Rich Gossage, 1975	47.7
21	Doug Corbett, 1980	46.9
22	Dan Quisenberry, 1985	46.9
23	Mike Marshall, 1972	46.8
24	Bill Campbell, 1977	45.5
25	Lee Smith, 1983	45.4
26	Bryan Harvey, 1993	45.2
27	Roy Face, 1962	45.2
28	Dave Righetti, 1986	45.1
29	Al Hrabosky, 1975	44.9
30	Bruce Sutter, 1984	44.8
31	Rich Gossage, 1978	44.7
32	Bryan Harvey, 1991	43.8
33	John Franco, 1988	43.8
34	Todd Worrell, 1986	43.5
35	Sparky Lyle, 1977	43.4
36	Dan Spillner, 1982	43.2
37	Tom Murphy, 1974	42.9
38	Stu Miller, 1965	42.7
39	Doug Jones, 1992	42.2
40	Ken Sanders, 1971	41.6
41	Luis Arroyo, 1961	41.6
42	Ron Perranoski, 1969	41.3
43	Dan Quisenberry, 1983	41.0
44	Hoyt Wilhelm, 1964	40.7
45	Doug Jones, 1989	40.4
46	Joe Page, 1949	40.3
47	Bruce Sutter, 1979	40.3
48	Willie Hernandez, 1984	39.9
49	Jim Brewer, 1972	39.8
50	Mike Henneman, 1988	39.8

Relievers' Runs

1	Mark Eichhorn, 1986	42.8
2	Jim Kern, 1979	42.0
3	Rich Gossage, 1977	33.8
4	John Hiller, 1973	33.1
5	Dan Quisenberry, 1983	32.7
6	Willie Hernandez, 1984	32.2
7	Doug Corbett, 1980	31.1
8	Bruce Sutter, 1977	30.6
9	Rich Gossage, 1975	30.5
10	Tim Burke, 1987	29.3
11	Sparky Lyle, 1977	28.8
12	Lindy McDaniel, 1960	28.6
13	Bob Lee, 1964	28.4
14	Mudcat Grant, 1970	28.3
15	Garland Braxton, 1927	28.2
16	Bruce Sutter, 1984	27.9
17	Mike Marshall, 1974	27.7
18	Dennis Eckersley, 1990	26.8
19	Sid Monge, 1979	26.4
20	Jesse Orosco, 1983	26.3
21	Hoyt Wilhelm, 1965	26.3
22	Rich Gossage, 1978	26.2
23	Phil Regan, 1966	25.8
24	Jeff Montgomery, 1989	25.7
25	Ellis Kinder, 1953	25.5
26	Aurelio Lopez, 1979	25.5
27	Donnie Moore, 1985	25.5
28	Dan Quisenberry, 1985	25.4
29	John Wetteland, 1993	25.3
30	Ellis Kinder, 1951	25.1
31	Jim Konstanty, 1950	25.0
32	Ted Abernathy, 1967	24.9
33	Mike Marshall, 1979	24.9
34	Sparky Lyle, 1974	24.8
35	Bob James, 1985	24.7
36	Rollie Fingers, 1973	24.5
37	Gary Lavelle, 1977	24.4
38	Dick Radatz, 1963	24.4
39	Hoyt Wilhelm, 1954	24.4
40	Joe Black, 1952	24.2
41	Greg Minton, 1982	24.2
42	Luis Arroyo, 1961	24.2
43	Joe Page, 1949	24.1
44	Dick Radatz, 1962	24.0
45	Hoyt Wilhelm, 1964	23.9
46	Todd Frohwirth, 1991	23.8
47	Dan Spillner, 1982	23.5
48	Tom Murphy, 1974	23.4
49	Ken Sanders, 1971	23.4
50	Dick Radatz, 1964	23.2

Adjusted Relievers' Runs

1	Mark Eichhorn, 1986	43.6
2	Jim Kern, 1979	40.9
3	John Hiller, 1973	36.9
4	Bruce Sutter, 1977	36.3
5	Doug Corbett, 1980	36.0
6	Rich Gossage, 1977	34.9
7	Dan Quisenberry, 1983	32.9
8	Lindy McDaniel, 1960	32.5
9	Rich Gossage, 1975	32.0
10	Willie Hernandez, 1984	31.1
11	Tim Burke, 1987	30.5
12	Ellis Kinder, 1951	29.3
13	Ted Abernathy, 1967	29.3
14	Ellis Kinder, 1953	28.0
15	Mike Marshall, 1979	27.4
16	Dick Radatz, 1964	27.3
17	Aurelio Lopez, 1979	27.0
18	Sparky Lyle, 1977	27.0
19	Sid Monge, 1979	26.9
20	Bob James, 1985	26.8
21	Dick Radatz, 1963	26.7
22	John Wetteland, 1993	26.5
23	Jesse Orosco, 1983	26.3
24	Bruce Sutter, 1984	26.3
25	Dick Radatz, 1962	26.2
26	Mudcat Grant, 1970	25.6
27	Dan Quisenberry, 1985	25.6
28	Jeff Montgomery, 1989	25.3
29	Dennis Eckersley, 1990	25.3
30	Donnie Moore, 1985	25.0
31	Lee Smith, 1983	24.5
32	Gary Lavelle, 1977	24.4
33	Tom Burgmeier, 1980	24.4
34	Bob Lee, 1964	24.3
35	Bob Stanley, 1983	24.2
36	Andy McGaffigan, 1987	24.2
37	Greg Minton, 1982	24.1
38	Rich Gossage, 1978	24.0
39	Duane Ward, 1992	24.0
40	Rob Dibble, 1990	23.9
41	Hoyt Wilhelm, 1954	23.9
42	Tug McGraw, 1980	23.9
43	Bill Campbell, 1977	23.8
44	Dick Hyde, 1958	23.7
45	Dan Spillner, 1982	23.6
46	Ken Sanders, 1971	23.5
47	Clay Carroll, 1966	23.5
48	Tom Murphy, 1974	23.4
49	Jim Konstanty, 1950	23.4
50	Bill Caudill, 1980	23.3

Percent of Team Wins (by era)

1876-1892

1	Will White, 1879	100.0
	Bobby Mathews, 1876	100.0
	Jim Devlin, 1877	100.0
	Jim Devlin, 1876	100.0
	George Bradley, 1876	100.0
6	Tommy Bond, 1878	97.6
7	Terry Larkin, 1878	96.7
8	Jim McCormick, 1880	95.7
9	Tommy Bond, 1877	95.2
10	Terry Larkin, 1877	93.5
11	Al Spalding, 1876	90.4
	Jim Galvin, 1883	88.5
13	Will White, 1880	85.7
	Jim McCormick, 1882	85.7
15	Mickey Welch, 1880	82.9

1893-1919

1	Ted Breitenstein, 1895	48.7
2	Amos Rusie, 1893	48.5
3	Ted Breitenstein, 1894	48.2
4	Cy Young, 1893	46.6
5	Ed Walsh, 1908	45.5
	Frank Killen, 1896	45.5
7	Ted Breitenstein, 1896	45.0
8	Jack Chesbro, 1904	44.6
9	Frank Killen, 1893	44.4
10	Pink Hawley, 1895	43.7
11	Win Mercer, 1896	43.1
12	Noodles Hahn, 1901	42.3
13	Cy Young, 1901	41.8
14	Cy Young, 1895	41.6
15	Cy Young, 1902	41.6

1920-1941

1	Eddie Rommel, 1922	41.5
2	Red Faber, 1921	40.3
3	Buck Newsom, 1938	36.4
4	Jimmy Ring, 1923	36.0
	Pete Alexander, 1920	36.0
6	Ted Lyons, 1930	35.5
7	Curt Davis, 1934	33.9
8	Urban Shocker, 1921	33.3
	Bob Feller, 1941	33.3
	Ed Morris, 1928	33.3
11	Howard Ehmke, 1923	32.8
12	Dazzy Vance, 1925	32.4
	Paul Derringer, 1935	32.4
14	Wes Ferrell, 1935	32.1
15	George Uhle, 1923	31.7

1942-1960

1	Ned Garver, 1951	38.5
2	Bob Feller, 1946	38.2
3	Murry Dickson, 1952	33.3
4	Robin Roberts, 1952	32.2
5	Bill Voiselle, 1944	31.3
6	Murry Dickson, 1951	31.3
7	Phil Marchildon, 1942	30.9
8	Dizzy Trout, 1944	30.7
9	Robin Roberts, 1954	30.7
10	Bobby Shantz, 1952	30.4
11	Ewell Blackwell, 1947	30.1
12	Robin Roberts, 1955	29.9
13	Johnny Antonelli, 1956	29.9
14	Dave Ferriss, 1945	29.6
15	2 players tied	29.0

1961-1976

1	Steve Carlton, 1972	45.8
2	Gaylord Perry, 1972	33.3
3	Nolan Ryan, 1974	32.4
4	Larry Jackson, 1964	31.6
5	Wilbur Wood, 1973	31.2
6	Bob Gibson, 1970	30.3
7	Randy Jones, 1976	30.1
8	Denny McLain, 1968	30.1
9	Fergie Jenkins, 1974	29.8
10	Juan Marichal, 1968	29.5
11	Sam McDowell, 1969	29.0
12	Fergie Jenkins, 1971	28.9
13	Steve Busby, 1974	28.6
14	Sandy Koufax, 1966	28.4
15	Juan Marichal, 1963	28.4

1977-1994

1	Phil Niekro, 1979	31.8
2	Dave Stieb, 1981	29.7
3	Fernando Valenzuela, 1986	28.8
4	Phil Niekro, 1978	27.5
5	Kevin Brown, 1992	27.3
6	Randy Johnson, 1994	26.5
7	Mike Norris, 1980	26.5
8	Danny Jackson, 1988	26.4
9	Steve Carlton, 1980	26.4
	Frank Viola, 1988	26.4
11	Ross Grimsley, 1978	26.3
12	Phil Niekro, 1977	26.2
13	Bob Welch, 1990	26.2
14	Dennis Leonard, 1981	26.0
15	Teddy Higuera, 1986	26.0

Clutch Pitching Index

1	Doc White, 1904	152.8
2	Mordecai Brown, 1903	152.7
3	Ned Garvin, 1904	152.6
4	Jim McCormick, 1878	152.3
5	Max Lanier, 1943	150.8
6	Pete Schneider, 1917	145.4
7	Sammy Stewart, 1981	144.8
8	Ed Killian, 1907	144.5
9	Carl Lundgren, 1902	144.0
10	Bill Burns, 1909	142.4
11	Cy Morgan, 1910	142.1
12	Ed Summers, 1908	142.0
13	Andy Coakley, 1905	141.7
14	Fred Olmstead, 1910	141.6
	Ben Tincup, 1914	141.6
16	Dick Rudolph, 1919	141.2
17	Sherry Smith, 1919	141.1
18	Mal Eason, 1902	140.9
19	Fred Blanding, 1913	140.8
20	Charlie Hodnett, 1884	140.3
21	Ed Poole, 1902	139.7
22	Ed Willett, 1908	139.6
23	Bert Humphries, 1915	139.5
24	Doug Rau, 1976	139.2
25	Sloppy Thurston, 1923	139.0
26	Vic Willis, 1906	138.7
	Al Benton, 1945	138.7
	Al Brazle, 1947	138.7
29	Dummy Taylor, 1902	138.2
30	Allan Anderson, 1988	137.8
31	Mark Baldwin, 1888	137.4
32	Al Maul, 1895	137.0
33	Bob Rhoads, 1906	136.8
34	Mike Sullivan, 1892	136.3
35	Spud Chandler, 1942	136.2
	Chuck Finley, 1990	136.2
37	Red Faber, 1917	135.9
38	King Cole, 1910	135.8
39	Clark Griffith, 1898	135.4
40	Bob Buhl, 1957	134.8
	John Tudor, 1988	134.8
42	Doug Rau, 1978	134.5
43	Stu Miller, 1959	134.4
44	Win Mercer, 1894	134.3
45	Ken Chase, 1940	134.2
	Dutch Leonard, 1948	134.2
47	Andy Coakley, 1908	134.1
48	Ed Siever, 1904	133.9
	Joe McGinnity, 1908	133.9
50	Mike Marshall, 1973	133.7
51	Ned Garvin, 1902	133.4
52	Joe Horlen, 1968	133.1
53	Eddie Plank, 1911	132.9
54	Art Nehf, 1928	132.8
55	Charlie Chech, 1905	132.7
56	Andy Coakley, 1907	132.6
57	Gene Bearden, 1948	132.3
	Hoyt Wilhelm, 1959	132.3
59	Win Mercer, 1897	132.1
	Stan Baumgartner, 1924	132.1
61	Ed Killian, 1909	131.9
	Bump Hadley, 1939	131.9
63	Lew Brockett, 1909	131.8
64	Jim Abbott, 1992	131.7
65	Jose DeLeon, 1991	131.5
66	Steve Blass, 1972	131.3
67	Chick Fraser, 1900	131.2
68	Don Schwall, 1961	131.1
69	Mike O'Neill, 1904	131.0
70	Ted Lyons, 1942	130.9
	Bobby Shantz, 1957	130.9
72	Tony Mullane, 1890	130.7
73	Rick Honeycutt, 1983	130.6
	Lon Warneke, 1933	130.6
	Pete Vuckovich, 1982	130.6
	Bill Swift, 1992	130.6
77	Bill Lee, 1978	130.5
78	Bill Bernhard, 1904	130.4
79	Hal McKain, 1929	130.3
	Bill Krueger, 1991	130.3
81	Larry Pape, 1911	130.2
	Hi Bithorn, 1942	130.2
	John Cerutti, 1989	130.2
84	Vean Gregg, 1913	130.0
85	Brickyard Kennedy, 1899	129.9
	Rollie Naylor, 1920	129.9
87	Earl Moore, 1911	129.6
	Ruben Gomez, 1954	129.6
	Larry McWilliams, 1984	129.6
90	Jim Galvin, 1886	129.5
	Wilson Alvarez, 1993	129.5
92	Lefty Weinert, 1922	129.4
93	Harry Moran, 1915	129.3
	Ned Garver, 1948	129.3
95	Tom Hughes, 1912	129.2
	Clarence Mitchell, 1929	129.2
	Atley Donald, 1944	129.2
	Joe Hatten, 1946	129.2
99	Bill Walker, 1929	129.1
	John Denny, 1976	129.1

Pitcher Batting Runs

	Player	
1	Guy Hecker, 1884	26.2
2	Bob Caruthers, 1886	24.5
3	Jim Whitney, 1882	22.3
4	Wes Ferrell, 1935	21.5
5	Don Drysdale, 1965	20.2
6	Don Newcombe, 1955	20.1
7	Bob Caruthers, 1887	20.1
8	Guy Hecker, 1886	19.4
9	Jim Whitney, 1883	18.1
10	Wes Ferrell, 1931	17.8
11	Charlie Ferguson, 1885	16.8
12	Tony Mullane, 1884	16.7
13	Schoolboy Rowe, 1943	16.7
14	George Uhle, 1923	16.4
15	Babe Ruth, 1917	16.3
16	Scott Stratton, 1890	16.1
17	Warren Spahn, 1958	16.0
18	Walter Johnson, 1925	15.9
19	Bob Caruthers, 1889	15.8
20	Red Ruffing, 1930	15.6
21	Bob Lemon, 1950	15.6
22	Don Newcombe, 1959	15.1
23	Jack Stivetts, 1892	15.1
24	Jack Stivetts, 1890	14.9
25	Jack Bentley, 1923	14.8
26	John Ward, 1879	14.7
27	Bob Lemon, 1949	14.7
28	Red Lucas, 1930	14.7
29	Claude Hendrix, 1912	14.6
30	Babe Ruth, 1915	14.5
31	Dave Foutz, 1887	14.3
32	Charlie Ferguson, 1887	14.2
33	Jim Tobin, 1942	14.0
34	Frank Killen, 1893	13.9
35	Red Ruffing, 1936	13.8
36	Pete Conway, 1888	13.8
37	Red Lucas, 1932	13.7
38	Robin Roberts, 1955	13.6
39	Terry Larkin, 1878	13.6
40	Elam Vangilder, 1922	13.4
41	Babe Ruth, 1916	13.1
42	Scott Stratton, 1888	13.1
43	Joe Bush, 1924	13.0
44	Adonis Terry, 1890	13.0
45	Jack Coombs, 1911	12.9
46	Pink Hawley, 1895	12.9
47	Clark Griffith, 1901	12.8
48	Bucky Walters, 1939	12.7
49	Bob Lemon, 1948	12.6
50	Red Lucas, 1933	12.5
51	Schoolboy Rowe, 1935	12.5
52	Red Ruffing, 1932	12.5
53	Doc Crandall, 1915	12.4
54	Cy Young, 1903	12.3
55	Curt Davis, 1939	12.3
56	Red Ruffing, 1935	12.2
57	Bob Gibson, 1970	12.2
58	Red Ruffing, 1928	12.2
59	Ad Gumbert, 1891	12.1
60	Catfish Hunter, 1971	12.1
61	Wes Ferrell, 1936	11.9
62	Dizzy Trout, 1944	11.9
63	Joe Bowman, 1939	11.8
64	Charley Radbourn, 1883	11.8
65	Billy Taylor, 1884	11.8
66	Fergie Jenkins, 1971	11.7
67	Johnny Sain, 1947	11.7
68	Dutch Ruether, 1921	11.6
69	Erv Brame, 1929	11.5
70	Babe Ruth, 1918	11.5
71	Jouett Meekin, 1896	11.5
72	Jack Stivetts, 1896	11.5
73	George Mullin, 1904	11.3
74	Adonis Terry, 1889	11.3
75	Charlie Ferguson, 1886	11.2
76	Schoolboy Rowe, 1934	11.2
77	George Van Haltren, 1888	11.1
78	Carl Mays, 1921	11.0
79	Guy Hecker, 1887	11.0
80	Jim Whitney, 1881	11.0
81	Tim Keefe, 1884	10.9
82	Mickey Welch, 1880	10.9
83	Red Lucas, 1931	10.9
84	Dave Ferriss, 1945	10.9
85	Ad Gumbert, 1889	10.8
86	Bob Caruthers, 1891	10.8
87	Charlie Buffinton, 1884	10.8
88	Red Ruffing, 1941	10.8
89	Erv Brame, 1930	10.8
90	Red Lucas, 1929	10.7
91	Jim Whitney, 1887	10.7
92	Jack Stivetts, 1894	10.7
93	Tom Parrott, 1895	10.7
94	Fred Hutchinson, 1947	10.7
95	Joe Wood, 1912	10.6
96	Frank Foreman, 1891	10.6
97	Burleigh Grimes, 1928	10.6
98	Burleigh Grimes, 1920	10.5
99	Blue Moon Odom, 1969	10.5
100	Matt Kilroy, 1889	10.4

Pitcher Fielding Runs

	Player	
1	Ed Walsh, 1907	21.6
2	Harry Howell, 1905	17.7
3	Ed Walsh, 1911	14.8
4	Ed Walsh, 1908	13.6
5	Will White, 1882	12.9
6	John Clarkson, 1889	11.3
7	Tony Mullane, 1882	10.7
	Sadie McMahon, 1890	10.7
9	Carl Mays, 1926	10.1
10	Frank Smith, 1909	10.0
11	Tommy Bond, 1880	9.8
12	Mike Morrison, 1887	9.7
	Ed Walsh, 1910	9.7
14	Christy Mathewson, 1908	9.6
15	Tony Mullane, 1884	9.5
	Matt Kilroy, 1887	9.5
	Charlie Buffinton, 1888	9.5
18	Harry Howell, 1904	9.4
19	Ed Scott, 1900	9.1
	Elmer Stricklett, 1906	9.1
	Carl Mays, 1916	9.1
	Carl Mays, 1918	9.1
	Curt Davis, 1934	9.1
24	John Clarkson, 1887	9.0
	Elmer Stricklett, 1905	9.0
26	Hooks Dauss, 1915	8.9
27	Addie Joss, 1907	8.6
	Gene Packard, 1914	8.6
29	Park Swartzel, 1889	8.5
	Bucky Walters, 1936	8.5
31	Jack Taylor, 1898	8.4
	Nick Altrock, 1905	8.4
	Hooks Dauss, 1920	8.4
	Wilcy Moore, 1927	8.4
	Bob Lemon, 1948	8.4
36	Cy Seymour, 1898	8.3
	Randy Jones, 1976	8.3
38	Harry Howell, 1907	8.2
	Burleigh Grimes, 1925	8.2
40	Matt Kilroy, 1889	8.1
	George Mullin, 1904	8.1
	Carl Mays, 1924	8.1
	Eddie Rommel, 1924	8.1
44	Fred Newman, 1965	8.0
45	Cy Young, 1895	7.9
	Cy Young, 1896	7.9
	Bob Lemon, 1953	7.9
	Mel Stottlemyre, 1969	7.9
49	John Clarkson, 1885	7.8
	Jim Galvin, 1887	7.8
	Carl Mays, 1917	7.8
	Freddie Fitzsimmons, 1931	7.8
	Harry Gumbert, 1938	7.8
	John Denny, 1978	7.8
55	Amos Rusie, 1894	7.7
	Joe Wood, 1912	7.7
	Mel Harder, 1933	7.7
	Harry Gumbert, 1937	7.7
	Russ Christopher, 1943	7.7
60	Larry McKeon, 1884	7.6
	Cy Seymour, 1897	7.6
	Ed Walsh, 1906	7.6
63	Willie Sudhoff, 1898	7.5
	Christy Mathewson, 1901	7.5
	Ned Garvin, 1903	7.5
	Jean Dubuc, 1913	7.5
	Greg Maddux, 1990	7.5
68	Harry Howell, 1906	7.4
	Christy Mathewson, 1911	7.4
	Carl Hubbell, 1933	7.4
71	Tommy Bond, 1879	7.3
	Charlie Buffinton, 1887	7.3
	Bob Caruthers, 1887	7.3
	Bill Doak, 1915	7.3
75	Jim Galvin, 1881	7.2
	Eddie Cicotte, 1913	7.2
	Russ Christopher, 1945	7.2
78	Jim Galvin, 1884	7.1
	Ed Walsh, 1912	7.1
	Harry Coveleski, 1914	7.1
81	George Mullin, 1905	7.0
	Doc White, 1908	7.0
	Red Ames, 1909	7.0
	Hal Schumacher, 1935	7.0
85	Guy Hecker, 1884	6.9
	Dave Foutz, 1885	6.9
	Red Donahue, 1902	6.9
	Elmer Stricklett, 1907	6.9
	Lefty Tyler, 1913	6.9
	Gene Krapp, 1915	6.9
	Larry Jackson, 1964	6.9
92	Jim McCormick, 1883	6.8
	Larry Corcoran, 1884	6.8
	Cy Young, 1894	6.8
	Vic Willis, 1904	6.8
	Christy Mathewson, 1910	6.8
	Pete Alexander, 1915	6.8
	Ted Wingfield, 1925	6.8
	Jim Tobin, 1944	6.8
100	8 players tied	6.7

Total Pitcher Index

	Player	
1	Guy Hecker, 1884	12.6
2	Silver King, 1888	11.4
3	Walter Johnson, 1912	11.2
4	Amos Rusie, 1894	11.0
5	Walter Johnson, 1913	10.9
6	John Clarkson, 1889	10.1
7	Charley Radbourn, 1884	9.8
8	Christy Mathewson, 1905	9.6
9	Dizzy Trout, 1944	9.1
10	John Clarkson, 1885	8.9
	Scott Stratton, 1890	8.9
12	Lefty Grove, 1931	8.7
13	Joe Wood, 1912	8.6
	Pete Alexander, 1915	8.6
15	Bucky Walters, 1939	8.5
16	Charley Radbourn, 1883	8.4
17	John Clarkson, 1887	8.3
	Cy Young, 1901	8.3
19	Dave Foutz, 1886	8.1
	Ed Walsh, 1908	8.1
21	Curt Davis, 1934	7.8
	Hal Newhouser, 1945	7.8
23	Tony Mullane, 1884	7.7
	Jack Stivetts, 1891	7.7
	Walter Johnson, 1915	7.7
26	Walter Johnson, 1918	7.6
27	Carl Hubbell, 1933	7.5
28	Pink Hawley, 1895	7.4
	Dolf Luque, 1923	7.4
	Steve Carlton, 1972	7.4
31	Jim Devlin, 1876	7.3
	Will White, 1882	7.3
	Matt Kilroy, 1887	7.3
	Kid Nichols, 1897	7.3
	Christy Mathewson, 1908	7.3
	Walter Johnson, 1914	7.3
	Pete Alexander, 1916	7.3
	Lefty Grove, 1930	7.3
	Bob Gibson, 1968	7.3
	Dwight Gooden, 1985	7.3
41	Amos Rusie, 1893	7.2
	Walter Johnson, 1919	7.2
	Wes Ferrell, 1935	7.2
44	Silver King, 1890	7.1
	Ed Walsh, 1910	7.1
	Pete Alexander, 1920	7.1
	Hal Newhouser, 1946	7.1
	Greg Maddux, 1994	7.1
49	Cy Young, 1895	7.0
	Christy Mathewson, 1909	7.0
	Red Faber, 1921	7.0
	Dazzy Vance, 1928	7.0
	Lefty Grove, 1936	7.0
	Gaylord Perry, 1972	7.0
55	Matt Kilroy, 1889	6.9
	Amos Rusie, 1890	6.9
	Kid Nichols, 1898	6.9
	Jack Chesbro, 1904	6.9
59	Jim Galvin, 1884	6.8
	Bob Caruthers, 1886	6.8
	Mordecai Brown, 1906	6.8
	Bob Lemon, 1948	6.8
63	Jesse Duryea, 1889	6.7
	Kid Nichols, 1890	6.7
	Christy Mathewson, 1911	6.7
	John Hiller, 1973	6.7
	Jim Kern, 1979	6.7
	Roger Clemens, 1990	6.7
69	Tim Keefe, 1883	6.6
	Will White, 1883	6.6
	Bob Caruthers, 1885	6.6
	Guy Hecker, 1885	6.6
	Cy Young, 1892	6.6
	Kid Nichols, 1896	6.6
	Ed Walsh, 1912	6.6
	Dazzy Vance, 1930	6.6
	Thornton Lee, 1941	6.6
	Warren Spahn, 1953	6.6
	Wilbur Wood, 1971	6.6
	Rich Gossage, 1977	6.6
81	John Clarkson, 1886	6.5
	Charlie Ferguson, 1886	6.5
	Toad Ramsey, 1886	6.5
	Billy Rhines, 1890	6.5
	Joe Wood, 1911	6.5
	Lefty Gomez, 1937	6.5
	Hal Newhouser, 1944	6.5
	Tom Seaver, 1971	6.5
	John Wetteland, 1993	6.5
90	Cy Young, 1893	6.4
	Cy Young, 1896	6.4
	Ed Walsh, 1907	6.4
	Walter Johnson, 1911	6.4
	Dizzy Dean, 1934	6.4
	Mel Harder, 1934	6.4
	Lefty Grove, 1935	6.4
	Fergie Jenkins, 1971	6.4
98	Charlie Sweeney, 1884	6.3
	Jack Taylor, 1902	6.3
100	8 players tied	6.2

Total Pitcher Index (alpha.)

Player	
Pete Alexander, 1915	8.6
Pete Alexander, 1916	7.3
Pete Alexander, 1920	7.1
Mordecai Brown, 1906	6.8
Steve Carlton, 1972	7.4
Bob Caruthers, 1885	6.6
Bob Caruthers, 1886	6.8
Jack Chesbro, 1904	6.9
John Clarkson, 1885	8.9
John Clarkson, 1886	6.5
John Clarkson, 1887	8.3
John Clarkson, 1889	10.1
Roger Clemens, 1990	6.7
Curt Davis, 1934	7.8
Dizzy Dean, 1934	6.4
Jim Devlin, 1876	7.3
Jesse Duryea, 1889	6.7
Red Faber, 1921	7.0
Charlie Ferguson, 1886	6.5
Wes Ferrell, 1935	7.2
Dave Foutz, 1886	8.1
Jim Galvin, 1884	6.8
Bob Gibson, 1968	7.3
Lefty Gomez, 1937	6.5
Dwight Gooden, 1985	7.3
Rich Gossage, 1977	6.6
Lefty Grove, 1930	7.3
Lefty Grove, 1931	8.7
Lefty Grove, 1935	6.4
Lefty Grove, 1936	7.0
Mel Harder, 1934	6.4
Pink Hawley, 1895	7.4
Guy Hecker, 1884	12.6
Guy Hecker, 1885	6.6
John Hiller, 1973	6.7
Carl Hubbell, 1933	7.5
Fergie Jenkins, 1971	6.4
Walter Johnson, 1911	6.4
Walter Johnson, 1912	11.2
Walter Johnson, 1913	10.9
Walter Johnson, 1914	7.3
Walter Johnson, 1915	7.7
Walter Johnson, 1918	7.6
Walter Johnson, 1919	7.2
Tim Keefe, 1883	6.6
Jim Kern, 1979	6.7
Matt Kilroy, 1887	7.3
Matt Kilroy, 1889	6.9
Silver King, 1888	11.4
Silver King, 1890	7.1
Thornton Lee, 1941	6.6
Bob Lemon, 1948	6.8
Dolf Luque, 1923	7.4
Greg Maddux, 1994	7.1
Christy Mathewson, 1905	9.6
Christy Mathewson, 1908	7.3
Christy Mathewson, 1909	7.0
Christy Mathewson, 1911	6.7
Tony Mullane, 1884	7.7
Hal Newhouser, 1944	6.5
Hal Newhouser, 1945	7.8
Hal Newhouser, 1946	7.1
Kid Nichols, 1890	6.7
Kid Nichols, 1896	6.6
Kid Nichols, 1897	7.3
Kid Nichols, 1898	6.9
Gaylord Perry, 1972	7.0
Charley Radbourn, 1883	8.4
Charley Radbourn, 1884	9.8
Toad Ramsey, 1886	6.5
Billy Rhines, 1890	6.5
Amos Rusie, 1890	6.9
Amos Rusie, 1893	7.2
Amos Rusie, 1894	11.0
Tom Seaver, 1971	6.5
Warren Spahn, 1953	6.6
Jack Stivetts, 1891	7.7
Scott Stratton, 1890	8.9
Charlie Sweeney, 1884	6.3
Jack Taylor, 1902	6.3
Dizzy Trout, 1944	9.1
Dazzy Vance, 1928	7.0
Dazzy Vance, 1930	6.6
Ed Walsh, 1907	6.4
Ed Walsh, 1908	8.1
Ed Walsh, 1910	7.1
Ed Walsh, 1912	6.6
Bucky Walters, 1939	8.5
John Wetteland, 1993	6.5
Will White, 1882	7.3
Will White, 1883	6.6
Joe Wood, 1911	6.5
Joe Wood, 1912	8.6
Wilbur Wood, 1971	6.6
Cy Young, 1892	6.6
Cy Young, 1893	6.4
Cy Young, 1895	7.0
Cy Young, 1896	6.4
Cy Young, 1901	8.3

Total Pitcher Index (by era)

1876-1892

1	Guy Hecker, 1884	12.6
2	Silver King, 1888	11.4
3	John Clarkson, 1889	10.1
4	Charley Radbourn, 1884	9.8
5	John Clarkson, 1885	8.9
	Scott Stratton, 1890	8.9
7	Charley Radbourn, 1883	8.4
8	John Clarkson, 1887	8.3
9	Dave Foutz, 1886	8.1
10	Tony Mullane, 1884	7.7
	Jack Stivetts, 1891	7.7
12	Jim Devlin, 1876	7.3
	Will White, 1882	7.3
	Matt Kilroy, 1887	7.3
15	Silver King, 1890	7.1

1893-1919

1	Walter Johnson, 1912	11.2
2	Amos Rusie, 1894	11.0
3	Walter Johnson, 1913	10.9
4	Christy Mathewson, 1905	9.6
5	Joe Wood, 1912	8.6
	Pete Alexander, 1915	8.6
7	Cy Young, 1901	8.3
8	Ed Walsh, 1908	8.1
9	Walter Johnson, 1915	7.7
10	Walter Johnson, 1918	7.6
11	Pink Hawley, 1895	7.4
12	Kid Nichols, 1897	7.3
	Christy Mathewson, 1908	7.3
	Walter Johnson, 1914	7.3
	Pete Alexander, 1916	7.3

1920-1941

1	Lefty Grove, 1931	8.7
2	Bucky Walters, 1939	8.5
3	Curt Davis, 1934	7.8
4	Carl Hubbell, 1933	7.5
5	Dolf Luque, 1923	7.4
6	Lefty Grove, 1930	7.3
7	Wes Ferrell, 1935	7.2
8	Pete Alexander, 1920	7.1
9	Red Faber, 1921	7.0
	Dazzy Vance, 1928	7.0
	Lefty Grove, 1936	7.0
12	Dazzy Vance, 1930	6.6
	Thornton Lee, 1941	6.6
14	Lefty Gomez, 1937	6.5
15	3 players tied	6.4

1942-1960

1	Dizzy Trout, 1944	9.1
2	Hal Newhouser, 1945	7.8
3	Hal Newhouser, 1946	7.1
4	Bob Lemon, 1948	6.8
5	Warren Spahn, 1953	6.6
6	Hal Newhouser, 1944	6.5
7	Robin Roberts, 1953	6.1
8	Johnny Sain, 1946	5.9
	Ellis Kinder, 1953	5.9
10	Spud Chandler, 1943	5.7
	Bob Lemon, 1949	5.7
	Ned Garver, 1950	5.7
13	5 players tied	5.5

1961-1976

1	Steve Carlton, 1972	7.4
2	Bob Gibson, 1968	7.3
3	Gaylord Perry, 1972	7.0
4	John Hiller, 1973	6.7
5	Wilbur Wood, 1971	6.6
6	Tom Seaver, 1971	6.5
7	Fergie Jenkins, 1971	6.4
8	Jim Palmer, 1975	6.1
9	Juan Marichal, 1965	6.0
	Bob Gibson, 1969	6.0
11	Juan Marichal, 1966	5.8
12	Bert Blyleven, 1973	5.7
13	Tom Seaver, 1969	5.6
14	Bill Hands, 1969	5.5
15	3 players tied	5.4

1977-1994

1	Dwight Gooden, 1985	7.3
2	Greg Maddux, 1994	7.1
3	Jim Kern, 1979	6.7
	Roger Clemens, 1990	6.7
5	Rich Gossage, 1977	6.6
6	John Wetteland, 1993	6.5
7	Ron Guidry, 1978	6.2
	Greg Maddux, 1992	6.2
9	Greg Maddux, 1993	6.1
10	Steve Carlton, 1977	6.0
	Jesse Orosco, 1983	6.0
12	Dennis Eckersley, 1990	5.9
13	4 players tied	5.8

Total Baseball Ranking

1	Guy Hecker, 1884	12.6
2	Silver King, 1888	11.4
3	Walter Johnson, 1912	11.2
4	Amos Rusie, 1894	11.0
5	Walter Johnson, 1913	10.9
6	Babe Ruth, 1923	10.6
7	John Clarkson, 1889	10.1
8	Charley Radbourn, 1884	9.8
9	Christy Mathewson, 1905	9.6
10	Babe Ruth, 1921	9.4
11	Babe Ruth, 1927	9.2
	Barry Bonds, 1992	9.2
13	Dizzy Trout, 1944	9.1
	Cal Ripken, 1984	9.1
15	John Clarkson, 1885	8.9
	Scott Stratton, 1890	8.9
	Nap Lajoie, 1901	8.9
18	Barry Bonds, 1993	8.8
19	Lefty Grove, 1931	8.7
	Mickey Mantle, 1956	8.7
21	Joe Wood, 1912	8.6
	Pete Alexander, 1915	8.6
	Babe Ruth, 1920	8.6
	Mickey Mantle, 1957	8.6
25	Bucky Walters, 1939	8.5
	Nap Lajoie, 1906	8.5
	Nap Lajoie, 1910	8.5
	Ty Cobb, 1917	8.5
	Rogers Hornsby, 1922	8.5
	Rogers Hornsby, 1924	8.5
	Babe Ruth, 1924	8.5
32	Charley Radbourn, 1883	8.4
	Nap Lajoie, 1903	8.4
	Babe Ruth, 1926	8.4
35	John Clarkson, 1887	8.3
	Cy Young, 1901	8.3
	Cal Ripken, 1991	8.3
38	Rickey Henderson, 1990	8.2
39	Dave Foutz, 1886	8.1
	Ed Walsh, 1908	8.1
	Rogers Hornsby, 1920	8.1
	Lou Gehrig, 1927	8.1
	Ted Williams, 1942	8.1
44	Mickey Mantle, 1961	8.0
45	Ted Williams, 1941	7.9
	Ted Williams, 1946	7.9
47	Curt Davis, 1934	7.8
	Hal Newhouser, 1945	7.8
	Nap Lajoie, 1908	7.8
	George Sisler, 1920	7.8
	Lou Gehrig, 1934	7.8
	Lou Boudreau, 1944	7.8
53	Tony Mullane, 1884	7.7
	Jack Stivetts, 1891	7.7
	Walter Johnson, 1915	7.7
	Tris Speaker, 1912	7.7
	Rogers Hornsby, 1917	7.7
	Willie Mays, 1955	7.7
59	Walter Johnson, 1918	7.6
	Tris Speaker, 1914	7.6
61	Carl Hubbell, 1933	7.5
	Ron Santo, 1966	7.5
63	Pink Hawley, 1895	7.4
	Dolf Luque, 1923	7.4
	Steve Carlton, 1972	7.4
	Rickey Henderson, 1985	7.4
	Jeff Bagwell, 1994	7.4
68	Jim Devlin, 1876	7.3
	Will White, 1882	7.3
	Matt Kilroy, 1887	7.3
	Kid Nichols, 1897	7.3
	Christy Mathewson, 1908	7.3
	Walter Johnson, 1914	7.3
	Pete Alexander, 1916	7.3
	Lefty Grove, 1930	7.3
	Bob Gibson, 1968	7.3
	Dwight Gooden, 1985	7.3
	Honus Wagner, 1905	7.3
	Honus Wagner, 1906	7.3
	Tris Speaker, 1913	7.3
	Frankie Frisch, 1927	7.3
	Babe Ruth, 1930	7.3
	Babe Ruth, 1931	7.3
	Willie Mays, 1965	7.3
	Ron Santo, 1967	7.3
	Carl Yastrzemski, 1967	7.3
	Mike Schmidt, 1980	7.3
88	Amos Rusie, 1893	7.2
	Walter Johnson, 1919	7.2
	Wes Ferrell, 1935	7.2
	Nap Lajoie, 1904	7.2
	Rogers Hornsby, 1929	7.2
	Harlond Clift, 1937	7.2
	Snuffy Stirnweiss, 1945	7.2
	Ted Williams, 1947	7.2
	Willie Mays, 1958	7.2
	George Brett, 1985	7.2
	Barry Bonds, 1990	7.2
99	11 players tied	7.1

Total Baseball Rank (alpha.)

Pete Alexander, 1915	8.6
Pete Alexander, 1916	7.3
Jeff Bagwell, 1994	7.4
Barry Bonds, 1990	7.2
Barry Bonds, 1992	9.2
Barry Bonds, 1993	8.8
Lou Boudreau, 1944	7.8
George Brett, 1985	7.2
Steve Carlton, 1972	7.4
John Clarkson, 1885	8.9
John Clarkson, 1887	8.3
John Clarkson, 1889	10.1
Harlond Clift, 1937	7.2
Ty Cobb, 1917	8.5
Curt Davis, 1934	7.8
Jim Devlin, 1876	7.3
Wes Ferrell, 1935	7.2
Dave Foutz, 1886	8.1
Frankie Frisch, 1927	7.3
Lou Gehrig, 1927	8.1
Lou Gehrig, 1934	7.8
Bob Gibson, 1968	7.3
Dwight Gooden, 1985	7.3
Lefty Grove, 1930	7.3
Lefty Grove, 1931	8.7
Pink Hawley, 1895	7.4
Guy Hecker, 1884	12.6
Rickey Henderson, 1985	7.4
Rickey Henderson, 1990	8.2
Rogers Hornsby, 1917	7.7
Rogers Hornsby, 1920	8.1
Rogers Hornsby, 1922	8.5
Rogers Hornsby, 1924	8.5
Rogers Hornsby, 1929	7.2
Carl Hubbell, 1933	7.5
Walter Johnson, 1912	11.2
Walter Johnson, 1913	10.9
Walter Johnson, 1914	7.3
Walter Johnson, 1915	7.7
Walter Johnson, 1918	7.6
Walter Johnson, 1919	7.2
Matt Kilroy, 1887	7.3
Silver King, 1888	11.4
Nap Lajoie, 1901	8.9
Nap Lajoie, 1903	8.4
Nap Lajoie, 1904	7.2
Nap Lajoie, 1906	8.5
Nap Lajoie, 1908	7.8
Nap Lajoie, 1910	8.5
Dolf Luque, 1923	7.4
Mickey Mantle, 1956	8.7
Mickey Mantle, 1957	8.6
Mickey Mantle, 1961	8.0
Christy Mathewson, 1905	9.6
Christy Mathewson, 1908	7.3
Willie Mays, 1955	7.7
Willie Mays, 1958	7.2
Willie Mays, 1965	7.3
Tony Mullane, 1884	7.7
Hal Newhouser, 1945	7.8
Kid Nichols, 1897	7.3
Charley Radbourn, 1883	8.4
Charley Radbourn, 1884	9.8
Cal Ripken, 1984	9.1
Cal Ripken, 1991	8.3
Amos Rusie, 1893	7.2
Amos Rusie, 1894	11.0
Babe Ruth, 1920	8.6
Babe Ruth, 1921	9.4
Babe Ruth, 1923	10.6
Babe Ruth, 1924	8.5
Babe Ruth, 1926	8.4
Babe Ruth, 1927	9.2
Babe Ruth, 1930	7.3
Babe Ruth, 1931	7.3
Ron Santo, 1966	7.5
Ron Santo, 1967	7.3
Mike Schmidt, 1980	7.3
George Sisler, 1920	7.8
Tris Speaker, 1912	7.7
Tris Speaker, 1913	7.3
Tris Speaker, 1914	7.6
Snuffy Stirnweiss, 1945	7.2
Jack Stivetts, 1891	7.7
Scott Stratton, 1890	8.9
Dizzy Trout, 1944	9.1
Honus Wagner, 1905	7.3
Honus Wagner, 1906	7.3
Ed Walsh, 1908	8.1
Bucky Walters, 1939	8.5
Will White, 1882	7.3
Ted Williams, 1941	7.9
Ted Williams, 1942	8.1
Ted Williams, 1946	7.9
Ted Williams, 1947	7.2
Joe Wood, 1912	8.6
Carl Yastrzemski, 1967	7.3
Cy Young, 1901	8.3

Total Baseball Rank (by era)

1876-1892

1	Guy Hecker, 1884	12.6
2	Silver King, 1888	11.4
3	John Clarkson, 1889	10.1
4	Charley Radbourn, 1884	9.8
5	John Clarkson, 1885	8.9
	Scott Stratton, 1890	8.9
7	Charley Radbourn, 1883	8.4
8	John Clarkson, 1887	8.3
9	Dave Foutz, 1886	8.1
10	Tony Mullane, 1884	7.7
	Jack Stivetts, 1891	7.7
12	Jim Devlin, 1876	7.3
	Will White, 1882	7.3
	Matt Kilroy, 1887	7.3
15	Silver King, 1890	7.1

1893-1919

1	Walter Johnson, 1912	11.2
2	Amos Rusie, 1894	11.0
3	Walter Johnson, 1913	10.9
4	Christy Mathewson, 1905	9.6
5	Nap Lajoie, 1901	8.9
6	Joe Wood, 1912	8.6
	Pete Alexander, 1915	8.6
8	Nap Lajoie, 1906	8.5
	Nap Lajoie, 1910	8.5
	Ty Cobb, 1917	8.5
11	Nap Lajoie, 1903	8.4
12	Cy Young, 1901	8.3
13	Ed Walsh, 1908	8.1
14	Nap Lajoie, 1908	7.8
15	3 players tied	7.7

1920-1941

1	Babe Ruth, 1923	10.6
2	Babe Ruth, 1921	9.4
3	Babe Ruth, 1927	9.2
4	Lefty Grove, 1931	8.7
5	Babe Ruth, 1920	8.6
6	Bucky Walters, 1939	8.5
	Rogers Hornsby, 1922	8.5
	Rogers Hornsby, 1924	8.5
	Babe Ruth, 1924	8.5
10	Babe Ruth, 1926	8.4
11	Rogers Hornsby, 1920	8.1
	Lou Gehrig, 1927	8.1
13	Ted Williams, 1941	7.9
14	3 players tied	7.8

1942-1960

1	Dizzy Trout, 1944	9.1
2	Mickey Mantle, 1956	8.7
3	Mickey Mantle, 1957	8.6
4	Ted Williams, 1942	8.1
5	Ted Williams, 1946	7.9
6	Hal Newhouser, 1945	7.8
	Lou Boudreau, 1944	7.8
8	Willie Mays, 1955	7.7
9	Snuffy Stirnweiss, 1945	7.2
	Ted Williams, 1947	7.2
	Willie Mays, 1958	7.2
12	Hal Newhouser, 1946	7.1
	Snuffy Stirnweiss, 1944	7.1
	Ted Williams, 1957	7.1
15	Lou Boudreau, 1948	6.9

1961-1976

1	Mickey Mantle, 1961	8.0
2	Ron Santo, 1966	7.5
3	Steve Carlton, 1972	7.4
4	Bob Gibson, 1968	7.3
	Willie Mays, 1965	7.3
	Ron Santo, 1967	7.3
	Carl Yastrzemski, 1967	7.3
8	Norm Cash, 1961	7.1
	Joe Morgan, 1975	7.1
10	Gaylord Perry, 1972	7.0
11	Rico Petrocelli, 1969	6.9
	Mike Schmidt, 1974	6.9
13	John Hiller, 1973	6.7
	Frank Robinson, 1966	6.7
15	4 players tied	6.6

1977-1994

1	Barry Bonds, 1992	9.2
2	Cal Ripken, 1984	9.1
3	Barry Bonds, 1993	8.8
4	Cal Ripken, 1991	8.3
5	Rickey Henderson, 1990	8.2
6	Rickey Henderson, 1985	7.4
	Jeff Bagwell, 1994	7.4
8	Dwight Gooden, 1985	7.3
	Mike Schmidt, 1980	7.3
10	George Brett, 1985	7.2
	Barry Bonds, 1990	7.2
12	Greg Maddux, 1994	7.1
13	Mike Schmidt, 1985	7.0
	Robin Yount, 1982	7.0
	Kevin Mitchell, 1989	7.0

Manager Roster

This section details the managerial record of every man who ever held the reins of a major league club from 1871 through 1994. For many years, the assignment of wins and losses was thought a relatively simple task—almost as simple as identifying the managers themselves. In recent years, however, Richard Topp and Robert Tiemann wondered how it was that "managers" who never set foot on the field to lead their charges or even accompanied their clubs on road trips could be regarded as managers at all, at least in the commonly understood sense of field manager rather than business manager. Topp and Tiemann wondered how John McGraw, for example, could be credited as manager of the New York Giants for all of 1924 when a knee injury kept him from the bench for seven weeks: Somebody else must have run the team, they figured, so why not credit that man as interim manager?

That there were record-keeping errors in the 1870s or even the early 1900s may strike the average fan as unsurprising, but the incorrect assignment of decisions to helmsmen has been characteristic of every decade, up to and including the 1990s. Tiemann and Topp undertook a complete review of managerial records dating back to the National Association and found that the records published in previous baseball encyclopedias were wrong—so wrong that they had to be refigured from scratch. Here are the criteria they established for their groundbreaking study:

1. *Definition* A manager is the person designated by the club ownership to run the club on the field.

2. *Absences* When the regular manager is unable to be with the team for 30 or more days, the assistant in charge during his absence should be credited with the team's record from the time the absence begins until the regular manager returns to active duty.

3. *Interim manager* When a manager is removed, either by resignation or by being fired, and his designated replacement is not present to replace him, the assistant temporarily in charge of the team shall be credited with the team's record during the interim.

4. *Head coaches* From 1961 through 1964, the Chicago Cubs had a "panel of coaches" rather than a single manager. One of these coaches was designated *head coach* for a period of time; and that coach is credited with the team's record during his term as head coach.

5. *Captains* During the early years of professional baseball, the man who had the title of "manager" often served merely as the club's business manager, while the captain (a player) was responsible for the team on the field. Some captains were also managers. Each ambiguous situation is judged according to its particular circumstances, but in general the captain, rather than the manager, is credited with the team's record if the manager did not travel with the team or did not have previous baseball experience.

6. *Suspended games* If a game was suspended when one man was managing the team and was completed on a later date when another man was managing, the second manager is credited if the game was suspended before five innings were completed. If the game was suspended after five or more innings were played, then:

(a) credit the first manager with a win if the team was leading at the point of suspension and maintained the lead to win the game; or

(b) credit the first manager with a loss if the team was losing at the point of suspension and remained behind to lose the game; or

(c) credit the second manager with a win (or tie) if the team was losing at the point of suspension but came back to tie the score or win the game; or

(d) credit the second manager with a loss if the team was winning at the point of suspension but then lost the lead and/or game; or

(e) credit the second manager with the win or loss if the score was tied at the point of suspension.

7. *Protested games* If a protest was granted and the game was ordered resumed from the point of protest, then the same rules used for suspended games apply. If a protested game of at least five innings' duration was ordered replayed in its entirety, then no win or loss is credited, but both managers are credited with a no-decision game.

8. *Forfeited games* All forfeited games are counted as games managed, even if the game did not start or if it did not go five innings.

9. *Split seasons* In 1892 the National League played a split season, the winners meeting for the championship. In 1981, because of a players' strike, the National and American Leagues played split seasons. The managers' totals will have entries for each half-season.

10. *Replacement clubs* In the American Association (1882–1891), there were three instances in which one club dropped out and was replaced by another club. In 1884 Richmond replaced Washington; in 1890 Baltimore replaced Brooklyn; and in 1891 Milwaukee replaced Cincinnati. In each case, the new club inherited the old club's record. Therefore, the manager of the new club is credited with starting in the position (standing) in which the old club finished.

In the Union Association (1884), when a new club

replaced an old one, the new club started with a 0–0 record rather than inheriting the old club's record, except in the case of the Chicago franchise, which moved to Pittsburgh. Therefore, all such Union Association managers are credited with a finish as if their teams had begun their season at the beginning of the league season. The finish for each manager is his club's standing in the eight-team league when (a) he left the job, (b) his club dropped out of the league, or (c) his club finished the season. The clubs that dropped out were Altoona (replaced by Kansas City); Philadelphia (replaced by Wilmington); Wilmington (replaced by St. Paul); and Pittsburgh (replaced by Milwaukee).

In a typical entry in the Manager Roster (a hypothetical entry has been created below), the column marked STANDING will, in cases where a team has had only one manager throughout the year, show the team's final standing (in the example below, see the entry for 1972). In the case of a manager who began the season but was replaced midway, however, the figure on the left of the column shows the team's standing when he departed and the figure on the right shows the team's final standing (in the example below, see the entry for 1976). In the case of a manager who finished the season but did not begin it, the team's standing when he took over is shown on the left and the final standing on the right (see the entry for 1978). In the case of a manager who began when the season was already under way but who failed to finish, the figure on the left of the column shows the team's standing when he took over; the middle figure shows the team's standing when he departed; and a third figure shows the team's final standing (see the entry for 1977). The figure in the next column represents the number of wins predicted by the team's runs scored and runs allowed, with about ten extra runs being required for each win beyond .500. Last, the number of wins in the A-E column, which may be a positive figure or a negative figure, reflects the extent to which a manager may have stretched (or hindered) his available talent. The bottom line of a manager's entry provides his career totals, beginning at the left with the number of years, full or partial, in which he managed a major league club. The symbols shown in the sample entry are explained after the example.

Whenever a manager served two or more teams in the same year, the totals for each club are shown separately (see the entry above for 1973). The split seasons of 1892 and 1981 are indicated with separate records for each half. A figure to the right of the year indicates first half or second half (see entry above for 1981).

TM/L   Team and League

G   Games managed (including ties)

W   Wins

L   Losses

PCT   Percentage of games won

M/Y   Manager/Year (The latter figure indicates how many managers the team employed that year, while the former indicates the chronological position of the manager whose entry it is; "2/5," for example, would mean that this manager was the second of the team's five managers during that year.)

W-EXP   Expected Wins   Calculated for the team based on its actual runs scored and allowed, not its predicted runs scored and runs allowed. A team that allows exactly as many runs as it scores is predicted to play .500 ball. The equation for expected wins is:

$$\frac{(\text{Runs Scored} - \text{Runs Allowed})}{\text{Runs Per Win}} + \frac{(\text{Wins} + \text{Losses})}{2}$$

A-E   Actual Wins Minus Expected Wins (A measure of the extent to which a team outperformed or underperformed its talent; for a single season or two a high figure may be attributable to chance, but over time one must credit good managing.)

E   Eastern Division

W   Western Division

*   Indicates playing manager; for vital statistics, consult the player or pitcher register

▲   Tied for first place, involved in league or division playoff

●   Tied for position in standings

♦   League Championship Series win

★   World Series win

The team and league abbreviations used in this section can be found on the last page of the book.

YEAR	TM/L	G	W	L	PCT	STANDING			M/Y	W-EXP	A-E
Blow, Josiah H. "Joe"											
1969	Det-A*	134	71	63	.530	3 E	3 E		1/2	66.8	4.2
1971	Tex-A*	23	9	14	.391	6 W	6 W		3/3	12.0	-3.0
1972	Tex-A	161	84	76	.525	2 W				79.1	4.9
1973	Tex-A	95	44	51	.463	4 W	3 W		1/2	44.2	-0.2
1973	NY-A	56	30	26	.535	3 E	3 E		2/2	28.7	1.3
1974	NY-A	159	97	62	.610	★ ♦ 1 E				82.8	14.2
1975	NY-A	162	100	62	.617	♦ 1 E				90.0	10.0
1976	NY-A	94	52	42	.553	3 E	▲ ♦ E		1/3	53.8	-1.8
1977	Bos-A	95	55	40	.579	4 E	4 E	2 E	2/3	50.4	4.6
1978	Oak-A	152	83	69	.546	5 W	● 2W		2/2	75.2	7.8
1979	Oak-A	60	37	23	.617	1 W	2 W		1/2	33.0	4.0
1980	Oak-A	49	27	22	.551	2 W	3 W		2/2	27.4	-0.4
1981(1)	Oak-A	62	24	38	.387	6 W				32.4	-7.6
1981(2)	Oak-A	100	44	56	.440	5 W				57.0	-13.0
1982	NY-A	162	91	71	.562	3 E				81.5	10.5
1983	NY-A	145	91	54	.628	7 E	2 E		2/2	84.0	7.0
		14	1709	939	769	.550				898.3	42.5

Adair, Marion Danne "Bill"

YEAR	TM/L	G	W	L	PCT	STANDING			M/Y	W-EXP	A-E
1970	Chi-A	10	4	6	.400	6 W	6 W	6 W	2/3	3.8	0.2

Adcock, Joseph Wilbur "Joe"

YEAR	TM/L	G	W	L	PCT	STANDING			M/Y	W-EXP	A-E
1967	Cle-A	162	75	87	.463	8				75.0	0.0

Addy, Robert Edward "Bob"

YEAR	TM/L	G	W	L	PCT	STANDING			M/Y	W-EXP	A-E
1875	Phi-n*	7	3	4	.429	4	5		2/2	4.3	-1.3
1877	Cin-N*	24	5	19	.208	6	6	6	2/3	5.3	-0.3
2		31	8	23	.258						-1.6

Allen, Robert Gilman "Bob"

YEAR	TM/L	G	W	L	PCT	STANDING			M/Y	W-EXP	A-E
1890	Phi-N*	35	25	10	.714	3	2	3	4/5	20.2	4.8
1900	Cin-N*	144	62	77	.446	7				65.5	-3.5
2		179	87	87	.500						1.3

Alou, Felipe Rojas

YEAR	TM/L	G	W	L	PCT	STANDING			M/Y	W-EXP	A-E
1992	Mon-N	125	70	55	.560	4 E	2 E		2/2	68.1	1.9
1993	Mon-N	163	94	68	.580	2 E				86.1	7.9
1994	Mon-N	114	74	40	.649	1 E				70.0	4.0
3		402	238	163	.594						13.8

Alston, Walter Emmons

YEAR	TM/L	G	W	L	PCT	STANDING			M/Y	W-EXP	A-E
1954	Bro-N	154	92	62	.597	2				80.6	11.4
1955	Bro-N	154	98	55	.641	★1				96.4	1.6
1956	Bro-N	154	93	61	.604	1				89.2	3.8
1957	Bro-N	154	84	70	.545	3				87.3	-3.3
1958	LA-N	154	71	83	.461	7				67.8	3.2
1959	LA-N	156	88	68	.564	▲★1				81.5	6.5
1960	LA-N	154	82	72	.532	4				84.3	-2.3
1961	LA-N	154	89	65	.578	2				80.7	8.3
1962	LA-N	165	102	63	.618	▲2				96.7	5.3
1963	LA-N	163	99	63	.611	★1				91.0	8.0
1964	LA-N	164	80	82	.494	●6				85.7	-5.7
1965	LA-N	162	97	65	.599	★1				90.9	6.1
1966	LA-N	162	95	67	.586	1				94.4	0.6
1967	LA-N	162	73	89	.451	8				72.3	0.7
1968	LA-N	162	76	86	.469	●7				76.2	-0.2
1969	LA-N	162	85	77	.525	4 W				90.2	-5.2
1970	LA-N	161	87	74	.540	2 W				87.0	-0.0
1971	LA-N	162	89	73	.549	2 W				89.2	-0.2
1972	LA-N	155	85	70	.548	3 W				83.9	1.1
1973	LA-N	162	95	66	.590	2 W				92.4	2.6
1974	LA-N	162	102	60	.630	♦1 W				105.6	-3.6
1975	LA-N	162	88	74	.543	2 W				93.7	-5.7
1976	LA-N	158	90	68	.570	2 W	2 W		1/2	86.1	3.9
23		3658	2040	1613	.558						36.8

Altobelli, Joseph "Joe"

YEAR	TM/L	G	W	L	PCT	STANDING			M/Y	W-EXP	A-E
1977	SF-N	162	75	87	.463	4 W				77.1	-2.1
1978	SF-N	162	89	73	.549	3 W				83.1	5.9
1979	SF-N	140	61	79	.436	4 W	4 W		1/2	63.1	-2.1
1983	Bal-A	162	98	64	.605	★1 E				95.7	2.3
1984	Bal-A	162	85	77	.525	5 E				82.5	2.5
1985	Bal-A	55	29	26	.527	4 E	4 E		1/3	29.3	-0.3
1991	Chi-N	1	0	1	.000	4 E	5 E	4 E	2/3	0.5	-0.5
7		844	437	407	.518						5.8

Amalfitano, John Joseph "Joey"

YEAR	TM/L	G	W	L	PCT	STANDING			M/Y	W-EXP	A-E
1979	Chi-N	7	2	5	.286	5 E	5 E		2/2	3.5	-1.5
1980	Chi-N	72	26	46	.361	6 E	6 E		2/2	30.7	-4.7
1981(1)	Chi-N	54	15	37	.288	6 E					
(2)	Chi-N	52	23	28	.451	5 E				39.5	-1.5
3		185	66	116	.363						-7.8

Anderson, George Lee "Sparky"

YEAR	TM/L	G	W	L	PCT	STANDING			M/Y	W-EXP	A-E
1970	Cin-N	162	102	60	.630	♦1 W				90.4	11.6
1971	Cin-N	162	79	83	.488	●4 W				81.6	-2.6
1972	Cin-N	154	95	59	.617	♦1 W				92.7	2.3
1973	Cin-N	162	99	63	.611	1 W				93.4	5.6
1974	Cin-N	163	98	64	.605	2 W				95.8	2.2
1975	Cin-N	162	108	54	.667	★1 W				106.7	1.3
1976	Cin-N	162	102	60	.630	★1 W				103.2	-1.2
1977	Cin-N	162	88	74	.543	2 W				88.5	-0.5
1978	Cin-N	161	92	69	.571	2 W				82.7	9.3
1979	Det-A	106	56	50	.528	5 E	5 E		3/3	55.1	0.9
1980	Det-A	163	84	78	.519	5 E				88.0	-4.0
1981(1)	Det-A	57	31	26	.544	4 E					
(2)	Det-A	52	29	23	.558	●2 E				57.0	3.0
1982	Det-A	162	83	79	.512	4 E				85.5	-2.5
1983	Det-A	162	92	70	.568	2 E				92.0	0.0
1984	Det-A	162	104	58	.642	★1 E				99.5	4.5
1985	Det-A	161	84	77	.522	3 E				84.6	-0.6
1986	Det-A	162	87	75	.537	3 E				89.2	-2.2
1987	Det-A	162	98	64	.605	1 E				96.2	1.8
1988	Det-A	162	88	74	.543	2 E				85.7	2.3
1989	Det-A	162	59	103	.364	7 E				60.9	-1.9
1990	Det-A	162	79	83	.488	3 E				80.6	-1.6
1991	Det-A	162	84	78	.519	●2 E				83.2	0.8
1992	Det-A	162	75	87	.463	6 E				80.7	-5.7
1993	Det-A	162	85	77	.525	●3 E				86.7	-1.7
1994	Det-A	115	53	62	.461	5 E				55.8	-2.8
25		3886	2134	1750	.549						18.2

Anson, Adrian Constantine "Cap"

YEAR	TM/L	G	W	L	PCT	STANDING			M/Y	W-EXP	A-E
1875	Ath-n*	8	4	2	.667	2	2		2/2	4.9	-0.9
1879	Chi-N*	64	41	21	.661	2	4		1/2	32.9	8.1
1880	Chi-N*	86	67	17	.798	1				63.0	4.0
1881	Chi-N*	84	56	28	.667	1				57.4	-1.4
1882	Chi-N*	84	55	29	.655	1				64.3	-9.3
1883	Chi-N*	98	59	39	.602	2				60.8	-1.8
1884	Chi-N*	113	62	50	.554	●4				71.5	-9.5
1885	Chi-N*	113	87	25	.777	1				88.1	-1.1
1886	Chi-N*	126	90	34	.726	1				92.5	-2.5
1887	Chi-N*	127	71	50	.587	3				68.9	2.1
1888	Chi-N*	136	77	58	.570	2				74.5	2.5
1889	Chi-N*	136	67	65	.508	3				70.5	-3.5
1890	Chi-N*	139	84	53	.613	2				82.5	1.5
1891	Chi-N*	137	82	53	.607	2				76.6	5.4
1892(1)	Chi-N*	71	31	39	.443	8					
(2)	Chi-N*	76	39	37	.513	7				63.2	6.8
1893	Chi-N*	128	56	71	.441	9				59.8	-3.8
1894	Chi-N*	137	57	75	.432	8				64.1	-7.1
1895	Chi-N*	133	72	58	.554	4				66.0	6.0
1896	Chi-N*	132	71	57	.555	5				65.4	5.6
1897	Chi-N*	138	59	73	.447	9				60.7	-1.7
1898	NY-N	22	9	13	.409	6	7	7	2/3	11.5	-2.5
21		2288	1296	947	.578						-3.2

Appling, Lucius Benjamin "Luke"

YEAR	TM/L	G	W	L	PCT	STANDING			M/Y	W-EXP	A-E
1967	KC-A	40	10	30	.250	10	10		2/2	16.5	-6.5

Armour, William Clark "Bill"

YEAR	TM/L	G	W	L	PCT	STANDING			M/Y	W-EXP	A-E
1902	Cle-A	137	69	67	.507	5				69.8	-0.8
1903	Cle-A	140	77	63	.550	3				76.1	0.9
1904	Cle-A	154	86	65	.570	4				93.8	-7.8
1905	Det-A	154	79	74	.516	3				66.5	12.5
1906	Det-A	151	71	78	.477	6				65.6	5.4
5		736	382	347	.524						10.3

Aspromonte, Kenneth Joseph "Ken"

YEAR	TM/L	G	W	L	PCT	STANDING			M/Y	W-EXP	A-E
1972	Cle-A	156	72	84	.462	5 E				72.4	-0.4
1973	Cle-A	162	71	91	.438	6 E				66.6	4.4
1974	Cle-A	162	77	85	.475	4 E				77.7	-0.7
3		480	220	260	.458						3.3

Austin, James Philip "Jimmy"

YEAR	TM/L	G	W	L	PCT	STANDING			M/Y	W-EXP	A-E
1913	StL-A*	8	2	6	.250	7	7	8	2/3	3.3	-1.3
1918	StL-A*	16	7	9	.438	6	6	5	2/3	7.7	-0.7
1923	StL-A*	51	22	29	.431	3	5		2/2	24.4	-2.4
3		75	31	44	.413						-4.5

Baker, Delmer David "Del"

YEAR	TM/L	G	W	L	PCT	STANDING			M/Y	W-EXP	A-E
1933	Det-A	2	2	0	1.000	5	5		2/2	1.0	1.0
1936	Det-A	34	18	16	.529	3	4	2	2/3	18.0	0.0
1937	Det-A	54	34	20	.630	3	3	2	2/5	29.9	4.1
	Det-A	10	7	3	.700	2	2		4/5	5.5	1.5
1938	Det-A	57	37	19	.661	5	4		2/2	30.2	6.8
1939	Det-A	155	81	73	.526	5				85.1	-4.1
1940	Det-A	155	90	64	.584	1				92.9	-2.9
1941	Det-A	155	75	79	.487	●4				71.4	3.6
1942	Det-A	156	73	81	.474	5				77.2	-4.2
1960	Bos-A	7	2	5	.286	8	8	7	2/3	3.0	-1.0
9		785	419	360	.538						4.7

Baker, Johnnie B "Dusty"

YEAR	TM/L	G	W	L	PCT	STANDING			M/Y	W-EXP	A-E
1993	SF-N	162	103	59	.636	2 W				98.3	4.7
1994	SF-N	115	55	60	.478	2 W				57.9	-2.9
2		277	158	119	.570						1.8

Bamberger, George Irvin

YEAR	TM/L	G	W	L	PCT	STANDING			M/Y	W-EXP	A-E
1978	Mil-A	162	93	69	.574	3 E				96.4	-3.4
1979	Mil-A	161	95	66	.590	2 E				88.8	6.2
1980	Mil-A	92	47	45	.511	4 E	4 E	3 E	2/3	53.2	-6.2
1982	NY-N	162	65	97	.401	6 E				69.1	-4.1
1983	NY-N	46	16	30	.348	6 E	6 E		1/2	19.8	-3.8
1985	Mil-A	161	71	90	.441	6 E				69.5	1.5
1986	Mil-A	152	71	81	.467	6 E	6 E		1/2	69.6	1.4
7		936	458	478	.489						-8.3

Bancroft, David James "Dave"

YEAR	TM/L	G	W	L	PCT	STANDING			M/Y	W-EXP	A-E
1924	Bos-N*	154	53	100	.346	8				47.8	5.2
1925	Bos-N*	153	70	83	.458	5				67.5	2.5
1926	Bos-N*	153	66	86	.434	7				66.4	-0.4
1927	Bos-N*	155	60	94	.390	7				65.1	-5.1
4		615	249	363	.407						2.2

Bancroft, Frank Carter

YEAR	TM/L	G	W	L	PCT	STANDING			M/Y	W-EXP	A-E
1880	Wor-N	85	40	43	.482	5				45.7	-5.7
1881	Det-N	84	41	43	.488	4				42.9	-1.9
1882	Det-N	86	42	41	.506	6				34.0	8.0
1883	Cle-N	100	55	42	.567	4				51.8	3.2
1884	Pro-N	114	84	28	.750	1				83.3	0.7
1885	Pro-N	110	53	57	.482	4				46.0	7.0
1887	Phi-a	55	26	29	.473	6	5		1/2	27.6	-1.6
1889	Ind-N	68	25	43	.368	7	7		1/2	30.8	-5.8
1902	Cin-N	16	9	7	.563	6	6	4	2/3	8.8	0.2
9		718	375	333	.530						4.1

Barkley, Samuel E. "Sam"

YEAR	TM/L	G	W	L	PCT	STANDING			M/Y	W-EXP	A-E
1888	KC-a*	58	21	36	.368	8	8	8	2/3	16.2	4.8

Barnie, William Harrison "Billy"

YEAR	TM/L	G	W	L	PCT	STANDING			M/Y	W-EXP	A-E
1883	Bal-a*	96	28	68	.292	8				25.1	2.9

YEAR	TM/L	G	W	L	PCT	STANDING			M/Y	W-EXP	A-E
1884	Bal-a	109	63	43	.594	6				64.1	-1.1
1885	Bal-a	110	41	68	.376	8				41.7	-0.7
1886	Bal-a	139	48	83	.366	8				42.4	5.6
1887	Bal-a	141	77	58	.570	3				77.0	0.0
1888	Bal-a	139	57	80	.416	5				56.8	0.2
1889	Bal-a	139	70	65	.519	5				67.1	2.9
1890	Bal-a	38	15	19	.441	8				16.0	-1.0
1891	Bal-a	139	71	64	.526	3				72.0	-1.0
1892(1)	Was-N	2	0	2	.000	●11	7		1/2	0.8	-0.8
1893	Lou-N	126	50	75	.400	11				47.6	2.4
1894	Lou-N	131	36	94	.277	12				39.3	-3.3
1897	Bro-N	136	61	71	.462	●6				62.3	-1.3
1898	Bro-N	35	15	20	.429	9	10		1/3	13.5	1.5
		14	1480	632	810	.438					6.1

Barrow, Edward Grant "Ed"

YEAR	TM/L	G	W	L	PCT	STANDING			M/Y	W-EXP	A-E
1903	Det-A	137	65	71	.478	5				71.0	-6.0
1904	Det-A	84	32	46	.410	7	7		1/2	31.9	0.1
1918	Bos-A	126	75	51	.595	★1				73.8	1.2
1919	Bos-A	138	66	71	.482	6				69.8	-3.8
1920	Bos-A	154	72	81	.471	5				71.6	0.4
		5	639	310	320	.492					-8.1

Barry, John Joseph "Jack"

YEAR	TM/L	G	W	L	PCT	STANDING	M/Y	W-EXP	A-E
1917	Bos-A*	157	90	62	.592	2		88.0	2.0

Battin, Joseph V. "Joe"

YEAR	TM/L	G	W	L	PCT	STANDING			M/Y	W-EXP	A-E
1883	Pit-a*	13	2	11	.154	7	7		3/3	4.2	-2.2
1884	Pit-a*	13	6	7	.462	11	10	10	3/5	2.9	3.1
	Pit-U*	6	1	5	.167	5	5		1/2	2.7	-1.7
		2	32	9	23	.281					-0.9

Bauer, Henry Albert "Hank"

YEAR	TM/L	G	W	L	PCT	STANDING			M/Y	W-EXP	A-E
1961	KC-A*	102	35	67	.343	8	●9		2/2	39.9	-4.9
1962	KC-A	162	72	90	.444	9				72.2	-0.2
1964	Bal-A	163	97	65	.599	3				93.2	3.8
1965	Bal-A	162	94	68	.580	3				87.9	6.1
1966	Bal-A	160	97	63	.606	★1				95.9	1.1
1967	Bal-A	161	76	85	.472	●6				87.2	-11.2
1968	Bal-A	80	43	37	.538	3	2		1/2	44.7	-1.7
1969	Oak-A	149	80	69	.537	2 W	2 W		1/2	80.3	-0.3
		8	1139	594	544	.522					-7.2

Baylor, Donald Edward "Don"

YEAR	TM/L	G	W	L	PCT	STANDING	M/Y	W-EXP	A-E
1993	Col-N	162	67	95	.414	6 W		61.8	5.2
1994	Col-N	117	53	64	.453	3 W		52.4	0.6
		2	279	120	159	.430			5.8

Benjamin, John W.

YEAR	TM/L	G	W	L	PCT	STANDING	M/Y	W-EXP	A-E
1873	Res-n	23	2	21	.087	8		-3.0	5.0

Benson, Vernon Adair "Vern"

YEAR	TM/L	G	W	L	PCT	STANDING			M/Y	W-EXP	A-E
1977	Atl-N	1	1	0	1.000	6 W	6 W	6 W	3/4	0.4	0.6

Berra, Lawrence Peter "Yogi"

YEAR	TM/L	G	W	L	PCT	STANDING			M/Y	W-EXP	A-E
1964	NY-A	164	99	63	.611	1				97.3	1.7
1972	NY-N	156	83	73	.532	3 E				72.4	10.6
1973	NY-N	161	82	79	.509	♦1 E				82.7	-0.7
1974	NY-N	162	71	91	.438	5 E				72.9	-1.9
1975	NY-N	109	56	53	.514	3 E	●3E		1/2	56.0	-0.0
1984	NY-A	162	87	75	.537	3 E				89.0	-2.0
1985	NY-A	16	6	10	.375	7 E	2 E		1/2	9.7	-3.7
		7	930	484	444	.522					4.0

Bezdek, Hugo Frank

YEAR	TM/L	G	W	L	PCT	STANDING			M/Y	W-EXP	A-E
1917	Pit-N	91	30	59	.337	8	8		3/3	35.8	-5.8
1918	Pit-N	126	65	60	.520	4				68.6	-3.6
1919	Pit-N	139	71	68	.511	4				70.2	0.8
		3	356	166	187	.470					-8.6

Bickerson

YEAR	TM/L	G	W	L	PCT	STANDING		M/Y	W-EXP	A-E
1884	Was-a	1	0	1	.000	12	12	2/2	0.2	-0.2

Birmingham, Joseph Leo "Joe"

YEAR	TM/L	G	W	L	PCT	STANDING			M/Y	W-EXP	A-E
1912	Cle-A*	28	21	7	.750	6	5		2/2	13.9	7.1
1913	Cle-A*	155	86	66	.566	3				86.6	-0.6
1914	Cle-A*	157	51	102	.333	8				58.3	-7.3
1915	Cle-A	28	12	16	.429	6	7		1/2	11.4	0.6
		4	368	170	191	.471					-0.2

Bissonette, Adelphia Louis "Del"

YEAR	TM/L	G	W	L	PCT	STANDING			M/Y	W-EXP	A-E
1945	Bos-N	60	25	34	.424	7	6		2/2	29.2	-4.2

Blackburne, Russell Aubrey "Lena"

YEAR	TM/L	G	W	L	PCT	STANDING			M/Y	W-EXP	A-E
1928	Chi-A	80	40	40	.500	6	5		2/2	36.4	3.6
1929	Chi-A*	152	59	93	.388	7				59.8	-0.8
		2	232	99	133	.427					2.8

Blades, Francis Raymond "Ray"

YEAR	TM/L	G	W	L	PCT	STANDING			M/Y	W-EXP	A-E
1939	StL-N	155	92	61	.601	2				91.0	1.0
1940	StL-N	39	14	24	.368	6	3		1/3	20.2	-6.2
1948	Bro-N	1	1	0	1.000	5	5	3	2/3	0.5	0.5
		3	195	107	85	.557					-4.7

Blair, Walter Allen "Walter"

YEAR	TM/L	G	W	L	PCT	STANDING			M/Y	W-EXP	A-E
1915	Buf-F*	2	1	1	.500	8	8	6	2/3	0.9	0.1

Bluege, Oswald Louis "Ossie"

YEAR	TM/L	G	W	L	PCT	STANDING	M/Y	W-EXP	A-E
1943	Was-A	153	84	69	.549	2		83.9	0.1
1944	Was-A	154	64	90	.416	8		69.4	-5.4
1945	Was-A	156	87	67	.565	2		83.5	3.5
1946	Was-A	155	76	78	.494	4		66.9	9.1
1947	Was-A	154	64	90	.416	7		57.5	6.5
		5	772	375	394	.488			13.7

Bond, Thomas Henry "Tommy"

YEAR	TM/L	G	W	L	PCT	STANDING			M/Y	W-EXP	A-E
1882	Wor-N*	6	2	4	.333	8	8	8	2/3	1.3	0.7

Boros, Stephen "Steve"

YEAR	TM/L	G	W	L	PCT	STANDING		M/Y	W-EXP	A-E
1983	Oak-A	162	74	88	.457	4 W			73.7	0.3
1984	Oak-A	44	20	24	.455	5 W	4 W	1/2	20.5	-0.5
1986	SD-N	162	74	88	.457	4 W			74.1	-0.1
		3	368	168	200	.457				-0.3

Bottomley, James Leroy "Jim"

YEAR	TM/L	G	W	L	PCT	STANDING			M/Y	W-EXP	A-E
1937	StL-A*	78	21	56	.273	7	8		2/2	24.7	-3.7

Boudreau, Louis "Lou"

YEAR	TM/L	G	W	L	PCT	STANDING	M/Y	W-EXP	A-E
1942	Cle-A*	156	75	79	.487	4		69.7	5.3
1943	Cle-A*	153	82	71	.536	3		79.0	3.0
1944	Cle-A*	155	72	82	.468	●5		73.5	-1.5
1945	Cle-A*	147	73	72	.503	5		73.5	-0.5
1946	Cle-A*	156	68	86	.442	6		66.0	2.0
1947	Cle-A*	157	80	74	.519	4		87.4	-7.4
1948	Cle-A*	156	97	58	.626	▲★1		104.7	-7.7
1949	Cle-A*	154	89	65	.578	3		87.6	1.4
1950	Cle-A*	155	92	62	.597	4		91.9	0.1
1952	Bos-A*	154	76	78	.494	6		78.0	-2.0
1953	Bos-A	153	84	69	.549	4		79.0	5.0
1954	Bos-A	156	69	85	.448	4		74.2	-5.2
1955	KC-A	155	63	91	.409	6		51.1	11.9
1956	KC-A	154	52	102	.338	8		56.3	-4.3
1957	KC-A	104	36	67	.350	8	7 1/2	41.2	-5.2
1960	Chi-N	139	54	83	.394	7	7 2/2	55.9	-1.9
		16	2404	1162	1224	.487			-6.9

Bowa, Lawrence Robert "Larry"

YEAR	TM/L	G	W	L	PCT	STANDING			M/Y	W-EXP	A-E
1987	SD-N	162	65	97	.401	6 W				71.4	-6.4
1988	SD-N	46	16	30	.348	5 W	3 W		1/2	23.3	-7.3
		2	208	81	127	.389					-13.8

Bowerman, Frank Eugene "Frank"

YEAR	TM/L	G	W	L	PCT	STANDING			M/Y	W-EXP	A-E
1909	Bos-N*	76	22	54	.289	8	8		1/2	24.2	-2.2

Boyd, William J. "Bill"

YEAR	TM/L	G	W	L	PCT	STANDING			M/Y	W-EXP	A-E
1875	Atl-n*	2	0	2	.000	12	12		2/2	-0.2	0.2

Boyer, Kenton Lloyd "Ken"

YEAR	TM/L	G	W	L	PCT	STANDING			M/Y	W-EXP	A-E
1978	StL-N	143	62	81	.434	6 E	5 E		3/3	66.1	-4.1
1979	StL-N	163	86	76	.531	3 E				84.9	1.1
1980	StL-N	51	18	33	.353	6 E	4 E		1/4	26.4	-8.4
		3	357	166	190	.466					-11.3

Bradley, William Joseph "Bill"

YEAR	TM/L	G	W	L	PCT	STANDING			M/Y	W-EXP	A-E
1905	Cle-A*	41	20	21	.488	●1	2	5	2/3	19.9	0.1
1914	Bro-F*	157	77	77	.500	5				75.5	1.5
		2	198	97	98	.497					1.6

Bragan, Robert Randall "Bobby"

YEAR	TM/L	G	W	L	PCT	STANDING			M/Y	W-EXP	A-E
1956	Pit-N	157	66	88	.429	7				70.1	-4.1
1957	Pit-N	104	36	67	.350	7	●7		1/2	43.8	-7.8
1958	Cle-A	67	31	36	.463	6	4		1/2	36.1	-5.1
1963	Mil-N	163	84	78	.519	6				88.9	-4.9
1964	Mil-N	162	88	74	.543	5				86.7	1.3
1965	Mil-N	162	86	76	.531	5				88.8	-2.8
1966	Atl-N	112	52	59	.468	7	5		1/2	62.3	-10.3
		7	927	443	478	.481					-33.8

Bresnahan, Roger Philip

YEAR	TM/L	G	W	L	PCT	STANDING	M/Y	W-EXP	A-E
1909	StL-N*	154	54	98	.355	7		60.8	-6.8
1910	StL-N*	153	63	90	.412	7		68.5	-5.5
1911	StL-N*	158	75	74	.503	5		67.1	7.9
1912	StL-N*	153	63	90	.412	6		60.1	2.9
1915	Chi-N*	157	73	80	.477	4		71.1	1.9
		5	775	328	432	.432			0.5

Bristol, James David "Dave"

YEAR	TM/L	G	W	L	PCT	STANDING			M/Y	W-EXP	A-E
1966	Cin-N	77	39	38	.506	8	7		2/2	38.0	1.0
1967	Cin-N	162	87	75	.537	4				85.6	1.4
1968	Cin-N	163	83	79	.512	4				82.8	0.2
1969	Cin-N	163	89	73	.549	3 W				83.9	5.1
1970	Mil-A	163	65	97	.401	●4 W				66.7	-1.7
1971	Mil-A	161	69	92	.429	6 W				72.1	-3.1
1972	Mil-A	30	10	20	.333	6 E	6 E		1/3	12.8	-2.8
1976	Atl-N	162	70	92	.432	6 W				72.6	-2.6
1977	Atl-N	29	8	21	.276	6 W	6 W		1/4	10.8	-2.8
	Atl-N	131	52	79	.397	6 W	6 W		4/4	48.6	3.4
1979	SF-N	22	10	12	.455	4 W	4 W		2/2	9.9	0.1
1980	SF-N	161	75	86	.466	5 W				73.8	1.2
		11	1424	657	764	.462					-0.5

Brown, Freeman

YEAR	TM/L	G	W	L	PCT	STANDING			M/Y	W-EXP	A-E
1882	Wor-N	41	9	32	.220	8	8		1/3	9.1	-0.1

Brown, Mordecai Peter Centennial "Three Finger"

YEAR	TM/L	G	W	L	PCT	STANDING			M/Y	W-EXP	A-E
1914	StL-F*	114	50	63	.442	7	8		1/2	46.1	3.9

Brown, Thomas T. "Tom"

YEAR	TM/L	G	W	L	PCT	STANDING			M/Y	W-EXP	A-E
1897	Was-N*	99	52	46	.531	11	●6		2/2	48.2	3.8
1898	Was-N*	38	12	26	.316	11	11		1/4	13.6	-1.6
		2	137	64	72	.471					2.2

Brucker, Earle Francis Sr

YEAR	TM/L	G	W	L	PCT	STANDING			M/Y	W-EXP	A-E
1952	Cin-N	5	3	2	.600	7	7	6	2/3	2.4	0.6

Buckenberger, Albert C. "Al"

YEAR	TM/L	G	W	L	PCT	STANDING			M/Y	W-EXP	A-E
1889	Col-a	140	60	78	.435	6				56.5	3.5
1890	Col-a	80	39	41	.488	5	2		1/3	51.9	-12.9
1892(1)	Pit-N	29	15	14	.517	7	6		1/2		
(2)	Pit-N	66	38	27	.585	10	4		2/2	47.3	5.7
1893	Pit-N	131	81	48	.628	2				81.3	-0.3
1894	Pit-N	110	53	55	.491	7	7		1/2	52.9	0.1
1895	StL-N	50	16	34	.320	11	11		1/4	16.0	-0.0
1902	Bos-N	142	73	64	.533	3				74.6	-1.6
1903	Bos-N	140	58	80	.420	6				57.0	1.0
1904	Bos-N	155	55	98	.359	7				49.1	5.9
9		1043	488	539	.475						1.3

Buffinton, Charles G. "Charlie"

YEAR	TM/L	G	W	L	PCT	STANDING			M/Y	W-EXP	A-E
1890	Phi-P	116	61	54	.530	5	5		2/2	63.6	-2.6

Burdock, John Joseph "Jack"

YEAR	TM/L	G	W	L	PCT	STANDING			M/Y	W-EXP	A-E
1883	Bos-N	54	30	24	.556	4	1		1/2	37.4	-7.4

Burke, James Timothy "Jimmy"

YEAR	TM/L	G	W	L	PCT	STANDING			M/Y	W-EXP	A-E
1905	StL-N	90	34	56	.378	7	6	6	2/3	32.8	1.2
1918	StL-A	61	29	31	.483	6	5		3/3	28.8	0.2
1919	StL-A	140	67	72	.482	5				65.9	1.1
1920	StL-A	154	76	77	.497	4				79.4	-3.4
4		445	206	236	.466						-0.9

Burnham, George Walter "Watch"

YEAR	TM/L	G	W	L	PCT	STANDING			M/Y	W-EXP	A-E
1887	Ind-N	28	6	22	.214	8			1/3	7.7	-1.7

Burns, Thomas Everett "Tom"

YEAR	TM/L	G	W	L	PCT	STANDING			M/Y	W-EXP	A-E
1892(1)	Pit-N	47	22	25	.468	7	6		2/2		
(2)	Pit-N	13	5	7	.417	10	4		1/2	29.7	-2.7
1898	Chi-N	152	85	65	.567	4				89.2	-4.2
1899	Chi-N	152	75	73	.507	8				78.6	-3.6
3		364	187	170	.524						-10.5

Burwell, William Edwin "Bill"

YEAR	TM/L	G	W	L	PCT	STANDING			M/Y	W-EXP	A-E
1947	Pit-N	1	1	0	1.000	8	●7		2/2	0.5	0.5

Bush, Owen Joseph "Donie"

YEAR	TM/L	G	W	L	PCT	STANDING			M/Y	W-EXP	A-E
1923	Was-A	155	75	78	.490	4				73.9	1.1
1927	Pit-N	156	94	60	.610	1				92.4	1.6
1928	Pit-N	152	85	67	.559	4				88.5	-3.5
1929	Pit-N	119	67	51	.568	2	2		1/2	67.7	-0.7
1930	Chi-A	154	62	92	.403	7				62.6	-0.6
1931	Chi-A	156	56	97	.366	8				54.8	1.2
1933	Cin-N	153	58	94	.382	8				59.8	-1.8
7		1045	497	539	.480						-2.7

Butler, Ormond Hook

YEAR	TM/L	G	W	L	PCT	STANDING			M/Y	W-EXP	A-E
1883	Pit-a	53	17	36	.321	6	6	7	2/3	17.3	-0.3

Byrne, Charles H. "Charlie"

YEAR	TM/L	G	W	L	PCT	STANDING			M/Y	W-EXP	A-E
1885	Bro-a	75	38	37	.507	7	●5		2/2	36.0	2.0
1886	Bro-a	141	76	61	.555	3				68.5	7.5
1887	Bro-a	138	60	74	.448	6				65.8	-5.8
3		354	174	172	.503						3.7

Callahan, James Joseph "Jim"

YEAR	TM/L	G	W	L	PCT	STANDING			M/Y	W-EXP	A-E
1903	Chi-A	138	60	77	.438	7				58.3	1.7
1904	Chi-A	42	23	18	.561	4	3		1/2	24.1	-1.1
1912	Chi-A	158	78	76	.506	4				76.1	1.9
1913	Chi-A	153	78	74	.513	5				74.8	3.2
1914	Chi-A	157	70	84	.455	●6				68.5	1.5
1916	Pit-N	157	65	89	.422	6				65.3	-0.3
1917	Pit-N	61	20	40	.333	8	8		1/3	24.1	-4.1
7		866	394	458	.462						2.8

Cammeyer, William Henry "Bill"

YEAR	TM/L	G	W	L	PCT	STANDING			M/Y	W-EXP	A-E
1876	NY-N	57	21	35	.375	6				14.7	6.3

Campau, Charles Columbus "Count"

YEAR	TM/L	G	W	L	PCT	STANDING			M/Y	W-EXP	A-E
1890	StL-a	42	27	14	.659	5	2	3	4/6	24.1	2.9

Cantillon, Joseph D. "Joe"

YEAR	TM/L	G	W	L	PCT	STANDING			M/Y	W-EXP	A-E
1907	Was-A	154	49	102	.325	8				55.6	-6.6
1908	Was-A	155	67	85	.441	7				69.0	-2.7
1909	Was-A	156	42	110	.276	8				43.9	-1.9
3		465	158	297	.347						-10.4

Carey, Max George

YEAR	TM/L	G	W	L	PCT	STANDING			M/Y	W-EXP	A-E
1932	Bro-N	154	81	73	.526	3				77.5	3.5
1933	Bro-N	157	65	88	.425	6				68.4	-3.4
2		311	146	161	.476						0.1

Carey, Thomas John "Tom"

YEAR	TM/L	G	W	L	PCT	STANDING			M/Y	W-EXP	A-E
1873	Bal-n	24	14	9	.609	3	3		2/2	16.9	-2.9
1874	Mut-n	25	13	12	.520	2	2		1/2	16.4	-3.4
2		49	27	21	.563						-6.3

Carrigan, William Francis "Bill"

YEAR	TM/L	G	W	L	PCT	STANDING			M/Y	W-EXP	A-E
1913	Bos-A	70	40	30	.571	5	4		2/2	36.0	4.0
1914	Bos-A	159	91	62	.595	2				85.5	5.5
1915	Bos-A	155	101	50	.669	★1				94.1	6.9
1916	Bos-A	156	91	63	.591	★1				85.2	5.8
1927	Bos-A	154	51	103	.331	8				51.7	-0.7
1928	Bos-A	154	57	96	.373	8				58.2	-1.2
1929	Bos-A	155	58	96	.377	8				57.3	0.7
7		1003	489	500	.494						21.0

Caruthers, Robert Lee "Bob"

YEAR	TM/L	G	W	L	PCT	STANDING			M/Y	W-EXP	A-E
1892(2)	StL-N	50	16	32	.333	12	11		3/3	17.5	-1.5

Cavarretta, Philip Joseph "Phil"

YEAR	TM/L	G	W	L	PCT	STANDING			M/Y	W-EXP	A-E
1951	Chi-N	74	27	47	.365	7	8		2/2	30.4	-3.4
1952	Chi-N	155	77	77	.500	5				76.7	0.3
1953	Chi-N	155	65	89	.422	7				57.3	7.7
3		384	169	213	.442						4.6

Caylor, Oliver Perry "O.P."

YEAR	TM/L	G	W	L	PCT	STANDING			M/Y	W-EXP	A-E
1885	Cin-a	112	63	49	.563	2				62.1	0.9
1886	Cin-a	141	65	73	.471	5				70.5	-5.5
1887	NY-a	100	35	60	.368	7	7		3/3	27.6	7.4
3		353	163	182	.472						2.7

Chance, Frank Leroy

YEAR	TM/L	G	W	L	PCT	STANDING			M/Y	W-EXP	A-E
1905	Chi-N	90	55	33	.625	4	3		2/2	58.5	-3.5
1906	Chi-N	155	116	36	.763	1				112.7	3.3
1907	Chi-N	155	107	45	.704	★1				98.1	8.9
1908	Chi-N	158	99	55	.643	★1				95.7	3.3
1909	Chi-N	155	104	49	.680	2				105.1	-1.1
1910	Chi-N	154	104	50	.675	1				99.8	4.2
1911	Chi-N	158	92	62	.597	2				92.3	-0.3
1912	Chi-N	153	91	59	.607	3				83.6	7.4
1913	NY-A	153	57	94	.377	7				60.6	-3.6
1914	NY-A	137	60	74	.448	7	●6		1/2	65.7	-5.7
1923	Bos-A	154	61	91	.401	8				53.6	7.4
11		1622	946	648	.593						20.3

Chapman, John Curtis "Jack"

YEAR	TM/L	G	W	L	PCT	STANDING			M/Y	W-EXP	A-E
1876	Lou-N	69	30	36	.455	5				26.6	3.4
1877	Lou-N	61	35	25	.583	2				34.8	0.2
1878	Mil-N	61	15	45	.250	6				18.0	-3.0
1882	Wor-N	37	7	30	.189	8	8		3/3	8.2	-1.2
1883	Det-N	101	40	58	.408	7				37.9	2.1
1884	Det-N	114	28	84	.250	8				28.9	-0.9
1885	Buf-N	88	31	57	.352	7	7		2/2	25.3	5.7
1889	Lou-a	7	1	6	.143	8	8		4/4	1.5	-0.5
1890	Lou-a	136	88	44	.667	1				87.5	0.5
1891	Lou-a	141	55	84	.396	7				53.7	1.3
1892(1)	Lou-a	54	21	33	.389	10	11		1/2	21.6	-0.6
11		869	351	502	.411						7.0

Chapman, William Benjamin "Ben"

YEAR	TM/L	G	W	L	PCT	STANDING			M/Y	W-EXP	A-E
1945	Phi-N	85	28	57	.329	8	8		2/2	25.2	2.8
1946	Phi-N	155	69	85	.448	5				61.8	7.2
1947	Phi-N	155	62	92	.403	●7				66.8	-4.8
1948	Phi-N	79	37	42	.468	7	6		1/3	32.2	4.8
4		474	196	276	.415						10.1

Chase, Harold Homer "Hal"

YEAR	TM/L	G	W	L	PCT	STANDING			M/Y	W-EXP	A-E
1910	NY-A	14	10	4	.714	3	2		2/2	7.7	2.3
1911	NY-A	153	76	76	.500	6				72.0	4.0
2		167	86	80	.518						6.3

Clapp, John Edgar

YEAR	TM/L	G	W	L	PCT	STANDING			M/Y	W-EXP	A-E
1872	Man-n	24	5	19	.208	8				4.1	0.9
1878	Ind-N	63	24	36	.400	5				26.7	-2.7
1879	Buf-N	79	46	32	.590	3				41.8	4.2
1880	Cin-N	82	21	59	.262	8				22.6	-1.6
1881	Cle-N	74	32	41	.438	6	7		2/2	34.6	-2.6
1883	NY-N	98	46	50	.479	6				43.8	2.2
6		420	174	237	.423						0.3

Clarke, Fred Clifford

YEAR	TM/L	G	W	L	PCT	STANDING			M/Y	W-EXP	A-E
1897	Lou-N	92	35	54	.393	9	11		2/2	32.9	2.1
1898	Lou-N	154	70	81	.464	9				65.6	4.4
1899	Lou-N	156	75	77	.493	9				80.9	-5.9
1900	Pit-N	140	79	60	.568	2				81.2	-2.2
1901	Pit-N	140	90	49	.647	1				93.2	-3.2
1902	Pit-N	142	103	36	.741	1				103.9	-0.9
1903	Pit-N	141	91	49	.650	1				87.1	3.9
1904	Pit-N	156	87	66	.569	4				85.2	1.8
1905	Pit-N	155	96	57	.627	2				89.3	6.7
1906	Pit-N	154	93	60	.608	3				93.7	-0.7
1907	Pit-N	157	91	63	.591	2				90.8	0.2
1908	Pit-N	155	98	56	.636	●2				90.3	7.7
1909	Pit-N	154	110	42	.724	★1				103.6	6.4
1910	Pit-N	154	86	67	.562	3				84.9	1.1
1911	Pit-N	156	85	69	.552	3				96.4	-11.4
1912	Pit-N	153	93	58	.616	2				94.5	-1.5
1913	Pit-N	155	78	71	.523	4				83.8	-5.8
1914	Pit-N	158	69	85	.448	7				72.7	-3.7
1915	Pit-N	157	73	81	.474	5				81.2	-8.2
19		2829	1602	1181	.576						-9.3

Clements, John J. "Jack"

YEAR	TM/L	G	W	L	PCT	STANDING			M/Y	W-EXP	A-E
1890	Phi-N	19	13	6	.684	1	2	3	2/5	11.0	2.0

Clinton, James Lawrence "Jim"

YEAR	TM/L	G	W	L	PCT	STANDING			M/Y	W-EXP	A-E
1872	Eck-n	11	0	11	.000	10	9		1/2	-1.2	1.2

Cobb, Tyrus Raymond "Ty"

YEAR	TM/L	G	W	L	PCT	STANDING			M/Y	W-EXP	A-E
1921	Det-A	154	71	82	.464	6				79.3	-8.3
1922	Det-A	155	79	75	.513	3				80.4	-1.4
1923	Det-A	155	83	71	.539	2				85.5	-2.5
1924	Det-A	156	86	68	.558	3				81.9	4.1
1925	Det-A	156	81	73	.526	4				83.7	-2.7

YEAR	TM/L	G	W	L	PCT	STANDING	M/Y	W-EXP	A-E
1926	Det-A*	157	79	75	.513	6		73.5	5.5
	6	933	479	444	.519				-5.3

Cochrane, Gordon Stanley "Mickey"

YEAR	TM/L	G	W	L	PCT	STANDING	M/Y	W-EXP	A-E
1934	Det-A*	154	101	53	.656	1		99.8	1.2
1935	Det-A*	152	93	58	.616	★1		99.1	-6.1
1936	Det-A*	53	29	24	.547	3 2	1/3	28.0	1.0
	Det-A*	67	36	31	.537	4 2	3/3	35.4	0.6
1937	Det-A*	29	16	13	.552	3 2	1/5	16.1	-0.1
	Det-A*	47	26	20	.565	3 2 2	3/5	25.5	0.5
1938	Det-A	98	47	51	.480	5 4	1/2	52.9	-5.9
	5	600	348	250	.582				-8.8

Cohen, Andrew Howard "Andy"

YEAR	TM/L	G	W	L	PCT	STANDING	M/Y	W-EXP	A-E
1960	Phi-N	1	1	0	1.000	●6 ●4 8	2/3	0.4	0.6

Coleman, Gerald Francis "Jerry"

YEAR	TM/L	G	W	L	PCT	STANDING	M/Y	W-EXP	A-E
1980	SD-N	163	73	89	.451	6 W		74.2	-1.2

Coleman, Robert Hunter "Bob"

YEAR	TM/L	G	W	L	PCT	STANDING	M/Y	W-EXP	A-E
1943	Bos-N	46	21	25	.457	6 6	1/2	18.0	3.0
1944	Bos-N	155	65	89	.422	6		68.5	-3.5
1945	Bos-N	94	42	51	.452	7 6	1/2	46.1	-4.1
	3	295	128	165	.437				-4.6

Collins, Edward Trowbridge Sr. "Eddie"

YEAR	TM/L	G	W	L	PCT	STANDING	M/Y	W-EXP	A-E
1924	Chi-A*	27	14	13	.519	6	3/4	12.4	1.6
1925	Chi-A*	154	79	75	.513	5		80.8	-1.8
1926	Chi-A*	155	81	72	.529	5		83.0	-2.0
	3	336	174	160	.521				-2.3

Collins, James Joseph "Jimmy"

YEAR	TM/L	G	W	L	PCT	STANDING	M/Y	W-EXP	A-E
1901	Bos-A*	138	79	57	.581	2		82.4	-3.4
1902	Bos-A*	138	77	60	.562	3		74.8	2.2
1903	Bos-A*	141	91	47	.659	★1		89.9	1.1
1904	Bos-A*	157	95	59	.617	1		93.3	1.7
1905	Bos-A*	153	78	74	.513	4		77.6	0.4
1906	Bos-A*	115	35	79	.307	8 8	1/2	37.3	-2.3
	6	842	455	376	.548				-0.4

Collins, John Francis "Shano"

YEAR	TM/L	G	W	L	PCT	STANDING	M/Y	W-EXP	A-E
1931	Bos-A	153	62	90	.408	6		58.8	3.2
1932	Bos-A	55	11	44	.200	8 8	1/2	15.4	-4.4
	2	208	73	134	.353				-1.2

Collins, Terry Lee

YEAR	TM/L	G	W	L	PCT	STANDING	M/Y	W-EXP	A-E
1994	Hou-N	115	66	49	.574	2 C		67.1	-1.1

Comiskey, Charles Albert "Charlie"

YEAR	TM/L	G	W	L	PCT	STANDING	M/Y	W-EXP	A-E
1883	StL-a*	19	12	7	.632	2 2	2/2	12.1	-0.1
1884	StL-a*	25	16	7	.696	5 4	2/2	13.8	2.2
1885	StL-a*	112	79	33	.705	1		76.3	2.7
1886	StL-a*	139	93	46	.669	1		101.3	-8.3
1887	StL-a*	138	95	40	.704	1		97.5	-2.5
1888	StL-a*	137	92	43	.681	1		95.7	-3.7
1889	StL-a*	141	89	46	.659	2		91.9	-1.9
1890	Chi-P*	138	75	62	.547	4		78.5	-3.5
1891	StL-a*	141	86	52	.623	2		88.1	-2.1
1892(1)	Cin-N*	77	44	31	.587	4			
(2)	Cin-N*	78	38	37	.507	8		78.4	3.6
1893	Cin-N*	131	65	63	.508	●6		59.2	5.8
1894	Cin-N*	134	55	75	.423	10		51.5	3.5
	12	1410	839	542	.608				-4.3

Connor, Roger

YEAR	TM/L	G	W	L	PCT	STANDING	M/Y	W-EXP	A-E
1896	StL-N*	46	8	37	.178	11 11 11	4/5	12.3	-4.3

Cooke, Allen Lindsey "Dusty"

YEAR	TM/L	G	W	L	PCT	STANDING	M/Y	W-EXP	A-E
1948	Phi-N	13	6	6	.500	7 6 6	2/3	4.9	1.1

Coombs, John Wesley "Jack"

YEAR	TM/L	G	W	L	PCT	STANDING	M/Y	W-EXP	A-E
1919	Phi-N	63	18	44	.290	8 8	1/2	22.3	-4.3

Cooney, John Walter "Johnny"

YEAR	TM/L	G	W	L	PCT	STANDING	M/Y	W-EXP	A-E
1949	Bos-N	46	20	25	.444	4 4	2/2	22.1	-2.1

Corrales, Patrick "Pat"

YEAR	TM/L	G	W	L	PCT	STANDING	M/Y	W-EXP	A-E
1978	Tex-A	1	1	0	1.000	●2 W ●2W	2/2	0.5	0.5
1979	Tex-A	162	83	79	.512	3 W		86.2	-3.2
1980	Tex-A	163	76	85	.472	4 W		80.9	-4.9
1982	Phi-N	162	89	73	.549	2 E		82.1	6.9
1983	Phi-N	86	43	42	.506	1 E ♦1E	1/2	45.9	-2.9
	Cle-A	62	30	32	.484	7 E 7 E	2/2	27.9	2.1
1984	Cle-A	163	75	87	.463	6 E		80.5	-5.5
1985	Cle-A	162	60	102	.370	7 E		68.4	-8.4
1986	Cle-A	163	84	78	.519	5 E		80.1	3.9
1987	Cle-A	87	31	56	.356	7 E 7 E	1/2	32.8	-1.8
	9	1211	572	634	.474				-13.2

Corriden, John Michael Sr. "Red"

YEAR	TM/L	G	W	L	PCT	STANDING	M/Y	W-EXP	A-E
1950	Chi-A	125	52	72	.419	8 6	2/2	51.9	0.1

Cottier, Charles Keith "Chuck"

YEAR	TM/L	G	W	L	PCT	STANDING	M/Y	W-EXP	A-E
1984	Sea-A	27	15	12	.556	7 W ●5W	2/2	12.0	3.0
1985	Sea-A	162	74	88	.457	6 W		71.4	2.6
1986	Sea-A	28	9	19	.321	6 W 7 W	1/3	12.0	-3.0
	3	217	98	119	.452				2.6

Cox, Robert Joseph "Bobby"

YEAR	TM/L	G	W	L	PCT	STANDING	M/Y	W-EXP	A-E
1978	Atl-N	162	69	93	.426	6 W		65.4	3.6
1979	Atl-N	160	66	94	.412	6 W		70.6	-4.6
1980	Atl-N	161	81	80	.503	4 W		77.3	3.7
1981(1)	Atl-N	55	25	29	.463	4 W			
(2)	Atl-N	52	25	27	.481	5 W		50.7	-0.7
1982	Tor-A	162	78	84	.481	●6 E		75.8	2.2
1983	Tor-A	162	89	73	.549	4 E		87.8	1.2
1984	Tor-A	163	89	73	.549	2 E		86.4	2.6
1985	Tor-A	161	99	62	.615	1 E		98.2	0.8
1990	Atl-N	97	40	57	.412	6 W 6 W	2/2	40.3	-0.3
1991	Atl-N	162	94	68	.580	♦1 W		91.7	2.3
1992	Atl-N	162	98	64	.605	♦1 W		93.2	4.8
1993	Atl-N	162	104	58	.642	1 W		102.8	1.2
1994	Atl-N	114	68	46	.596	2 E		66.6	1.4
	13	1935	1025	908	.530				18.1

Craft, Harry Francis

YEAR	TM/L	G	W	L	PCT	STANDING	M/Y	W-EXP	A-E
1957	KC-A	50	23	27	.460	8 7	2/2	20.0	3.0
1958	KC-A	156	73	81	.474	7		69.8	3.2
1959	KC-A	154	66	88	.429	7		69.3	-3.3
1961	Chi-N	12	4	8	.333	●6 7 7	2/9	5.2	-1.2
	Chi-N	4	3	1	.750	7 7 7	5/9	1.7	1.3
1962	Hou-N	162	64	96	.400	8		66.8	-2.8
1963	Hou-N	162	66	96	.407	9		60.8	5.2
1964	Hou-N	149	61	88	.409	9 9	1/2	60.6	0.4
	7	849	360	485	.426				6.0

Craig, Roger Lee

YEAR	TM/L	G	W	L	PCT	STANDING	M/Y	W-EXP	A-E
1978	SD-N	162	84	78	.519	4 W		80.2	3.8
1979	SD-N	161	68	93	.422	5 W		72.2	-4.2
1985	SF-N	18	6	12	.333	6 W 6 W	2/2	7.6	-1.6
1986	SF-N	162	83	79	.512	3 W		89.4	-6.4
1987	SF-N	162	90	72	.556	1 W		92.4	-2.4
1988	SF-N	162	83	79	.512	4 W		85.7	-2.7
1989	SF-N	162	92	70	.568	♦1 W		91.5	0.5
1990	SF-N	162	85	77	.525	3 W		81.9	3.1
1991	SF-N	162	75	87	.463	4 W		76.0	-1.0
1992	SF-N	162	72	90	.444	5 W		73.0	-1.0
	10	1475	738	737	.500				-11.9

Crandall, Delmar Wesley "Del"

YEAR	TM/L	G	W	L	PCT	STANDING	M/Y	W-EXP	A-E
1972	Mil-A	124	54	70	.435	6 E 6 E	3/3	52.8	1.2
1973	Mil-A	162	74	88	.457	5 E		78.7	-4.7
1974	Mil-A	162	76	86	.469	5 E		79.6	-3.9
1975	Mil-A	161	67	94	.416	5 E 5 E	1/2	68.9	-1.9
1983	Sea-A	89	34	55	.382	7 W 7 W	2/2	33.9	0.1
1984	Sea-A	135	59	76	.437	7 W ●5W	1/2	59.8	-0.8
	6	833	364	469	.437				-9.7

Crane, Samuel Newhall "Sam"

YEAR	TM/L	G	W	L	PCT	STANDING	M/Y	W-EXP	A-E
1880	Buf-N*	84	24	58	.293	7		24.6	-0.6
1884	Cin-U*	70	49	21	.700	5 3	2/2	49.2	-0.2
	2		73	79	.480				-0.8

Cravath, Clifford Carlton "Gavvy"

YEAR	TM/L	G	W	L	PCT	STANDING	M/Y	W-EXP	A-E
1919	Phi-N*	75	29	46	.387	8 8	2/2	27.0	2.0
1920	Phi-N*	153	62	91	.405	8		61.0	1.0
	2	228	91	137	.399				2.9

Craver, William H. "Bill"

YEAR	TM/L	G	W	L	PCT	STANDING	M/Y	W-EXP	A-E
1871	Tro-n*	25	12	12	.500	7 6	2/2	11.4	0.6
1872	Bal-n*	41	27	13	.675	2 2	1/2	29.6	-2.6
1874	Phi-n*	58	29	29	.500	4		32.6	-3.6
1875	Cen-n*	14	2	12	.143	11		1.7	0.3
	4	138	70	66	.515				-5.3

Creamer, George W.

YEAR	TM/L	G	W	L	PCT	STANDING	M/Y	W-EXP	A-E
1884	Pit-a*	8	0	8	.000	10 10 10	4/5	1.8	-1.8

Cronin, Joseph Edward "Joe"

YEAR	TM/L	G	W	L	PCT	STANDING	M/Y	W-EXP	A-E
1933	Was-A*	153	99	53	.651	1		93.6	5.4
1934	Was-A*	155	66	86	.434	7		68.7	-2.7
1935	Bos-A*	154	78	75	.510	4		75.1	2.9
1936	Bos-A*	155	74	80	.481	6		78.0	-4.0
1937	Bos-A*	154	80	72	.526	5		80.3	-0.3
1938	Bos-A*	150	88	61	.591	2		88.1	-0.1
1939	Bos-A*	152	89	62	.589	2		84.1	4.9
1940	Bos-A*	154	82	72	.532	●4		81.2	0.8
1941	Bos-A*	155	84	70	.545	2		87.7	-3.7
1942	Bos-A*	152	93	59	.612	2		92.8	0.2
1943	Bos-A*	155	68	84	.447	7		71.2	-3.2
1944	Bos-A*	156	77	77	.500	4		83.3	-6.3
1945	Bos-A*	157	71	83	.461	7		69.1	1.9
1946	Bos-A*	156	104	50	.675	1		96.9	7.1
1947	Bos-A	157	83	71	.539	3		82.1	0.9
	15	2315	1236	1055	.540				3.7

Crooks, John Charles

YEAR	TM/L	G	W	L	PCT	STANDING	M/Y	W-EXP	A-E
1892(1)	StL-N*	47	24	22	.522	11 9	3/3		
(2)	StL-N*	15	3	11	.214	12 11	1/3	21.9	5.1

Cross, Lafayette Napoleon "Lave"

YEAR	TM/L	G	W	L	PCT	STANDING	M/Y	W-EXP	A-E
1899	Cle-N*	38	8	30	.211	12 12	1/2	3.3	4.7

Cubbage, Michael Lee "Mike"

YEAR	TM/L	G	W	L	PCT	STANDING	M/Y	W-EXP	A-E
1991	NY-N	7	3	4	.429	3 E 5 E	2/2	3.5	-0.5

Curtis, Edwin R. "Ed"

YEAR	TM/L	G	W	L	PCT	STANDING	M/Y	W-EXP	A-E
1884	Alt-U	25	6	19	.240	6		1.7	4.3

Cushman, Charles H. "Charlie"

YEAR	TM/L	G	W	L	PCT	STANDING	M/Y	W-EXP	A-E
1891	Mil-a	36	21	15	.583	5		24.5	-3.5

YEAR	TM/L	G	W	L	PCT	STANDING			M/Y	W-EXP	A-E

Cuthbert, Edgar Edward "Ned"

YEAR	TM/L	G	W	L	PCT	STANDING			M/Y	W-EXP	A-E
1882	StL-a*	80	37	43	.463	5				31.3	5.7

Dahlen, William Frederick "Bill"

YEAR	TM/L	G	W	L	PCT	STANDING			M/Y	W-EXP	A-E
1910	Bro-N*	156	64	90	.416	6				62.9	1.1
1911	Bro-N*	154	64	86	.427	7				62.1	1.9
1912	Bro-N	153	58	95	.379	7				66.3	-8.3
1913	Bro-N	152	65	84	.436	6				72.6	-7.6
4		615	251	355	.414						-12.9

Dark, Alvin Ralph

YEAR	TM/L	G	W	L	PCT	STANDING			M/Y	W-EXP	A-E
1961	SF-N	155	85	69	.552	3				88.7	-3.7
1962	SF-N	165	103	62	.624	▲1				100.8	2.2
1963	SF-N	162	88	74	.543	3				89.7	-1.7
1964	SF-N	162	90	72	.556	4				88.5	1.5
1966	KC-A	160	74	86	.463	7				70.8	3.2
1967	KC-A	121	52	69	.430	10	10		1/2	50.0	2.0
1968	Cle-A	162	86	75	.534	3				81.9	4.1
1969	Cle-A	161	62	99	.385	6 E				65.2	-3.2
1970	Cle-A	162	76	86	.469	5 E				78.3	-2.3
1971	Cle-A	103	42	61	.408	6 E	6 E		1/2	37.7	4.3
1974	Oak-A	162	90	72	.556	★1 W				96.0	-6.0
1975	Oak-A	162	98	64	.605	1 W				96.7	1.3
1977	SD-N	113	48	65	.425	4 W	5 W		3/3	46.8	1.2
13		1950	994	954	.510						2.9

Davenport, James Houston "Jim"

YEAR	TM/L	G	W	L	PCT	STANDING			M/Y	W-EXP	A-E
1985	SF-N	144	56	88	.389	6 W	6 W		1/2	60.6	-4.6

Davidson, Mordecai H.

YEAR	TM/L	G	W	L	PCT	STANDING			M/Y	W-EXP	A-E
1888	Lou-a	3	1	2	.333	8	8	7	2/4	1.1	-0.1
	Lou-a	90	34	52	.395	8	7		4/4	32.7	1.3

Davis, George Stacey

YEAR	TM/L	G	W	L	PCT	STANDING			M/Y	W-EXP	A-E
1895	NY-N*	33	16	17	.485	8	9		1/3	16.9	-0.9
1900	NY-N*	78	39	37	.513	8	8		2/2	32.5	6.5
1901	NY-N*	141	52	85	.380	7				47.6	4.4
3		252	107	139	.435						10.0

Davis, Harry H

YEAR	TM/L	G	W	L	PCT	STANDING			M/Y	W-EXP	A-E
1912	Cle-A*	127	54	71	.432	6	5		1/2	62.2	-8.2

Davis, Virgil Lawrence "Spud"

YEAR	TM/L	G	W	L	PCT	STANDING			M/Y	W-EXP	A-E
1946	Pit-N	3	1	2	.333	7	7		2/2	1.3	-0.3

Day, John B.

YEAR	TM/L	G	W	L	PCT	STANDING			M/Y	W-EXP	A-E
1899	NY-N	66	29	35	.453	9	10		1/2	26.9	2.1

Deane, John Henry "Harry"

YEAR	TM/L	G	W	L	PCT	STANDING			M/Y	W-EXP	A-E
1871	Kek-n*	5	2	3	.400	7	8			0.6	1.4

Dent, Russell Earl "Bucky"

YEAR	TM/L	G	W	L	PCT	STANDING			M/Y	W-EXP	A-E
1989	NY-A	40	18	22	.450	6 E	5 E		2/2	17.7	0.3
1990	NY-A	49	18	31	.367	7 E	7 E		1/2	19.9	-1.9
2		89	36	53	.404						-1.6

Dickey, William Malcolm "Bill"

YEAR	TM/L	G	W	L	PCT	STANDING			M/Y	W-EXP	A-E
1946	NY-A*	105	57	48	.543	2	3	3	2/3	62.4	-5.4

Diddlebock, Henry H. "Harry"

YEAR	TM/L	G	W	L	PCT	STANDING			M/Y	W-EXP	A-E
1896	StL-N	17	7	10	.412	10	11		1/5	4.6	2.4

Doby, Lawrence Eugene "Larry"

YEAR	TM/L	G	W	L	PCT	STANDING			M/Y	W-EXP	A-E
1978	Chi-A	87	37	50	.425	5 W	5 W		2/2	38.1	-1.1

Donovan, Patrick Joseph "Patsy"

YEAR	TM/L	G	W	L	PCT	STANDING			M/Y	W-EXP	A-E
1897	Pit-N*	135	60	71	.458	8				51.2	8.8
1899	Pit-N*	131	69	58	.543	10	7		2/2	69.0	0.0
1901	StL-N*	142	76	64	.543	4				79.6	-3.6
1902	StL-N*	140	56	78	.418	6				48.8	7.2
1903	StL-N*	139	43	94	.314	8				40.0	3.0
1904	Was-A*	139	37	97	.276	8	8		2/2	37.3	-0.3
1906	Bro-N*	153	66	86	.434	5				61.7	4.3
1907	Bro-N*	153	65	83	.439	5				64.9	0.1
1908	Bro-N	154	53	101	.344	7				59.7	-6.7
1910	Bos-A	158	81	72	.529	4				84.5	-3.5
1911	Bos-A	153	78	75	.510	5				80.3	-2.3
11		1597	684	879	.438						6.9

Donovan, William Edward "Bill"

YEAR	TM/L	G	W	L	PCT	STANDING			M/Y	W-EXP	A-E
1915	NY-A*	154	69	83	.454	5				75.6	-6.6
1916	NY-A*	156	80	74	.519	4				78.8	1.2
1917	NY-A	155	71	82	.464	6				72.6	-1.6
1921	Phi-N	87	25	62	.287	8	8		1/2	27.3	-2.3
4		552	245	301	.449						-9.3

Dooin, Charles Sebastian "Red"

YEAR	TM/L	G	W	L	PCT	STANDING			M/Y	W-EXP	A-E
1910	Phi-N*	157	78	75	.510	4				80.1	-2.1
1911	Phi-N*	153	79	73	.520	4				74.9	4.1
1912	Phi-N*	152	73	79	.480	5				74.2	-1.2
1913	Phi-N*	159	88	63	.583	2				81.4	6.6
1914	Phi-N*	154	74	80	.481	6				73.3	0.7
5		775	392	370	.514						8.0

Dorgan, Michael Cornelius "Mike"

YEAR	TM/L	G	W	L	PCT	STANDING			M/Y	W-EXP	A-E
1879	Syr-N*	43	17	26	.395	6	7		1/3	10.9	6.1
1880	Pro-N*	39	26	12	.684	3	2		3/3	24.7	1.3
1881	Wor-N*	56	24	32	.429	7	8		1/2	22.9	1.1
3		138	67	70	.489						8.6

Dowd, Thomas Jefferson "Tom"

YEAR	TM/L	G	W	L	PCT	STANDING			M/Y	W-EXP	A-E
1896	StL-N*	63	25	38	.397	11	11		5/5	17.2	7.8
1897	StL-N*	29	6	22	.214	12	12		1/4	5.1	0.9
2		92	31	60	.341						8.8

Doyle, John Joseph "Jack"

YEAR	TM/L	G	W	L	PCT	STANDING			M/Y	W-EXP	A-E
1895	NY-N*	64	32	31	.508	8	9	9	2/3	32.2	-0.2
1898	Was-N*	17	8	9	.471	11	10	11	2/4	6.1	1.9
2		81	40	40	.500						1.7

Dressen, Charles Walter "Chuck"

YEAR	TM/L	G	W	L	PCT	STANDING			M/Y	W-EXP	A-E
1934	Cin-N	60	21	39	.350	8	8		3/3	21.7	-0.7
1935	Cin-N	154	68	85	.444	6				64.0	4.0
1936	Cin-N	154	74	80	.481	5				73.3	0.7
1937	Cin-N	130	51	78	.395	8	8		1/2	56.3	-5.3
1951	Bro-N	158	97	60	.618	▲2				96.2	0.8
1952	Bro-N	155	96	57	.627	1				93.8	2.2
1953	Bro-N	155	105	49	.682	1				101.5	3.5
1955	Was-A	154	53	101	.344	8				57.9	-4.9
1956	Was-A	155	59	95	.383	7				51.4	7.6
1957	Was-A	20	4	16	.200	8	8		1/2	7.4	-3.4
1960	Mil-N	154	88	66	.571	2				83.6	4.4
1961	Mil-N	130	71	58	.550	3	4		1/2	69.2	1.8
1963	Det-A	102	55	47	.539	9	●5		2/2	50.8	4.2
1964	Det-A	163	85	77	.525	4				83.2	1.8
1965	Det-A	120	65	55	.542	3	4		2/2	66.2	-1.2
1966	Det-A	26	16	10	.615	3	3		1/3	13.3	2.7
16		1990	1008	973	.509						18.2

Duffy, Hugh

YEAR	TM/L	G	W	L	PCT	STANDING			M/Y	W-EXP	A-E
1901	Mil-A*	139	48	89	.350	8				51.2	-3.2
1904	Phi-N*	155	52	100	.342	8				54.4	-2.4
1905	Phi-N*	155	83	69	.546	4				86.9	-3.9
1906	Phi-N*	154	71	82	.464	4				72.4	-1.4
1910	Chi-A	156	68	85	.444	6				73.8	-5.8
1911	Chi-A	154	77	74	.510	4				85.2	-8.2
1921	Bos-A	154	75	79	.487	5				74.2	0.8
1922	Bos-A	154	61	93	.396	8				59.8	1.2
8		1221	535	671	.444						-22.9

Dunlap, Frederick C. "Fred"

YEAR	TM/L	G	W	L	PCT	STANDING			M/Y	W-EXP	A-E
1882	Cle-N*	80	42	36	.538	8	5		2/2	38.2	3.8
1884	StL-U*	83	66	16	.805	1	1		2/2	70.3	-4.3
1885	StL-N*	50	21	29	.420	5	8		1/3	15.5	5.5
	StL-N*	22	9	11	.450	8	8		3/3	6.2	2.8
1889	Pit-N*	17	7	10	.412	6	7	5	2/3	7.6	-0.6
4		252	145	102	.587						7.1

Durocher, Leo Ernest

YEAR	TM/L	G	W	L	PCT	STANDING			M/Y	W-EXP	A-E
1939	Bro-N*	157	84	69	.549	3				82.9	1.1
1940	Bro-N*	156	88	65	.575	2				84.3	3.7
1941	Bro-N*	157	100	54	.649	1				99.2	0.8
1942	Bro-N	155	104	50	.675	2				101.5	2.5
1943	Bro-N*	153	81	72	.529	3				80.7	0.3
1944	Bro-N	155	63	91	.409	7				63.4	-0.4
1945	Bro-N	155	87	67	.565	3				83.8	3.2
1946	Bro-N	157	96	60	.615	▲2				91.8	4.2
1948	Bro-N	73	35	37	.486	5	3		1/3	39.6	-4.6
	NY-N	79	41	38	.519	4	5		2/2	43.3	-2.3
1949	NY-N	156	73	81	.474	5				81.3	-8.3
1950	NY-N	154	86	68	.558	3				86.2	-0.2
1951	NY-N	157	98	59	.624	▲1				92.5	5.5
1952	NY-N	154	92	62	.597	2				85.4	6.6
1953	NY-N	155	70	84	.455	5				79.0	-9.0
1954	NY-N	154	97	57	.630	★1				95.9	1.1
1955	NY-N	154	80	74	.519	3				79.9	0.1
1966	Chi-N	162	59	103	.364	10				64.5	-5.5
1967	Chi-N	162	87	74	.540	3				88.7	-1.7
1968	Chi-N	163	84	78	.519	3				81.1	2.9
1969	Chi-N	163	92	70	.568	2 E				92.4	-0.4
1970	Chi-N	162	84	78	.519	2 E				93.6	-9.6
1971	Chi-N	162	83	79	.512	●3 E				79.8	3.2
1972	Chi-N	91	46	44	.511	4 E	2 E		1/2	52.3	-6.3
	Hou-N	31	16	15	.516	2 W	2 W		3/3	17.0	-1.0
1973	Hou-N	162	82	80	.506	4 W				81.9	0.1
24		3739	2008	1709	.540						-14.0

Dwyer, John Francis "Frank"

YEAR	TM/L	G	W	L	PCT	STANDING			M/Y	W-EXP	A-E
1902	Det-A	137	52	83	.385	7				58.4	-6.4

Dyer, Edwin Hawley "Eddie"

YEAR	TM/L	G	W	L	PCT	STANDING			M/Y	W-EXP	A-E
1946	StL-N	156	98	58	.628	▲★1				95.7	2.3
1947	StL-N	156	89	65	.578	2				91.5	-2.5
1948	StL-N	155	85	69	.552	2				86.6	-1.6
1949	StL-N	157	96	58	.623	2				92.2	3.8
1950	StL-N	153	78	75	.510	5				78.8	-0.8
5		777	446	325	.578						1.2

Dykes, James Joseph "Jimmy"

YEAR	TM/L	G	W	L	PCT	STANDING			M/Y	W-EXP	A-E
1934	Chi-A*	138	49	88	.358	8	8		2/2	48.6	0.4
1935	Chi-A*	153	74	78	.487	5				74.8	-0.8
1936	Chi-A*	153	81	70	.536	3				79.6	1.4
1937	Chi-A*	154	86	68	.558	3				81.8	4.2
1938	Chi-A*	149	65	83	.439	6				69.9	-4.9
1939	Chi-A*	155	85	69	.552	4				78.7	6.3
1940	Chi-A	155	82	72	.532	●4				83.3	-1.3
1941	Chi-A	156	77	77	.500	3				75.9	1.1
1942	Chi-A	148	66	82	.446	6				66.3	-0.3

YEAR	TM/L	G	W	L	PCT	STANDING			M/Y	W-EXP	A-E
1943	Chi-A	155	82	72	.532	4				74.7	7.3
1944	Chi-A	154	71	83	.461	7				64.2	6.8
1945	Chi-A	150	71	78	.477	6				70.6	0.4
1946	Chi-A	30	10	20	.333	7	5		1/2	14.3	-4.3
1951	Phi-A	154	70	84	.455	6				76.1	-6.1
1952	Phi-A	155	79	75	.513	4				71.1	7.9
1953	Phi-A	157	59	95	.383	7				60.4	-1.4
1954	Bal-A	154	54	100	.351	7				56.7	-2.7
1958	Cin-N	41	24	17	.585	8	4		2/2	22.5	1.5
1959	Det-A	137	74	63	.540	8	4		2/2	66.8	7.2
1960	Det-A	96	44	52	.458	6	6		1/3	47.3	-3.3
	Cle-A	58	26	32	.448	4	4		3/3	28.0	-2.0
1961	Cle-A	160	77	83	.481	5	5		1/2	78.5	-1.5
	21	2962	1406	1541	.477						15.7

Ebbets, Charles Hercules "Charlie"

YEAR	TM/L	G	W	L	PCT	STANDING			M/Y	W-EXP	A-E
1898	Bro-N	110	38	68	.358	9	10		3/3	40.8	-2.8

Edwards, Howard Rodney "Doc"

YEAR	TM/L	G	W	L	PCT	STANDING			M/Y	W-EXP	A-E
1987	Cle-A	75	30	45	.400	7 E	7 E		2/2	28.3	1.7
1988	Cle-A	162	78	84	.481	6 E				74.4	3.6
1989	Cle-A	143	65	78	.455	6 E	6 E		1/2	66.7	-1.7
	3	380	173	207	.455						3.6

Elberfeld, Norman Arthur "Kid"

YEAR	TM/L	G	W	L	PCT	STANDING			M/Y	W-EXP	A-E
1908	NY-A*	98	27	71	.276	6	8		2/2	31.4	-4.4

Elia, Lee Constantine

YEAR	TM/L	G	W	L	PCT	STANDING			M/Y	W-EXP	A-E
1982	Chi-N	162	73	89	.451	5 E				77.6	-4.6
1983	Chi-N	123	54	69	.439	5 E	5 E		1/2	60.1	-6.1
1987	Phi-N	101	51	50	.505	5 E	●4E		2/2	47.6	3.4
1988	Phi-N	153	60	92	.395	6 E	6 E		1/2	62.5	-2.5
	4	539	238	300	.442						-9.8

Ellick, Joseph J. "Joe"

YEAR	TM/L	G	W	L	PCT	STANDING			M/Y	W-EXP	A-E
1884	Pit-U*	13	6	6	.500	5	5		2/2	5.4	0.6

Elliott, Robert Irving "Bob"

YEAR	TM/L	G	W	L	PCT	STANDING			M/Y	W-EXP	A-E
1960	KC-A	155	58	96	.377	8				62.8	-4.8

Ens, Jewel Winklemeyer

YEAR	TM/L	G	W	L	PCT	STANDING			M/Y	W-EXP	A-E
1929	Pit-N	35	21	14	.600	2	2		2/2	20.1	0.9
1930	Pit-N	154	80	74	.519	5				73.8	6.2
1931	Pit-N	155	75	79	.487	5				71.4	3.6
	3	344	176	167	.513						10.8

Ermer, Calvin Coolidge "Cal"

YEAR	TM/L	G	W	L	PCT	STANDING			M/Y	W-EXP	A-E
1967	Min-A	114	66	46	.589	6	●2		2/2	62.1	3.9
1968	Min-A	162	79	83	.488	7				82.8	-3.8
	2	276	145	129	.529						0.1

Essian, James Sarkis "Jim"

YEAR	TM/L	G	W	L	PCT	STANDING			M/Y	W-EXP	A-E
1991	Chi-N	122	59	63	.484	5 E	4 E		3/3	58.0	1.0

Esterbrook, Thomas Jefferson "Dude"

YEAR	TM/L	G	W	L	PCT	STANDING			M/Y	W-EXP	A-E
1889	Lou-a*	10	2	8	.200	7	8		1/4	2.2	-0.2

Evers, John Joseph "Johnny"

YEAR	TM/L	G	W	L	PCT	STANDING			M/Y	W-EXP	A-E
1913	Chi-N*	155	88	65	.575	3				85.6	2.4
1921	Chi-N	96	41	55	.427	6	7		1/2	41.6	-0.6
1924	Chi-A	21	10	11	.476	6			1/4	9.7	0.3
	Chi-A	103	41	61	.402	8			4/4	47.0	-6.0
	3	375	180	192	.484						-3.9

Ewing, William "Buck"

YEAR	TM/L	G	W	L	PCT	STANDING			M/Y	W-EXP	A-E
1890	NY-P*	132	74	57	.565	3				76.8	-2.8
1895	Cin-N*	132	66	64	.508	8				69.0	-3.0
1896	Cin-N*	128	77	50	.606	3				78.3	-1.3
1897	Cin-N*	134	76	56	.576	4				71.3	4.7
1898	Cin-N	157	92	60	.605	3				84.6	7.4
1899	Cin-N	157	83	67	.553	6				83.0	0.0
1900	NY-N	63	21	41	.339	8	8		1/2	26.5	-5.5
	7	903	489	395	.553						-0.5

Faatz, Jayson S. "Jay"

YEAR	TM/L	G	W	L	PCT	STANDING			M/Y	W-EXP	A-E
1890	Buf-P*	34	9	24	.273	8	8	8	2/3	8.6	0.4

Falk, Bibb August

YEAR	TM/L	G	W	L	PCT	STANDING			M/Y	W-EXP	A-E
1933	Cle-A	1	1	0	1.000	5	5	4	2/3	0.5	0.5

Fanning, William James "Jim"

YEAR	TM/L	G	W	L	PCT	STANDING			M/Y	W-EXP	A-E
1981(2)	Mon-N	27	16	11	.593	2 E	1 E		2/2	14.8	1.2
1982	Mon-N	162	86	76	.531	3 E				89.5	-3.5
1984	Mon-N	30	14	16	.467	5 E	5 E		2/2	15.2	-1.2
	3	219	116	103	.530						-3.5

Farrell, John A. "Jack"

YEAR	TM/L	G	W	L	PCT	STANDING			M/Y	W-EXP	A-E
1881	Pro-N*	51	24	27	.471	4	2		1/2	26.7	-2.7

Farrell, Major Kerby "Kerby"

YEAR	TM/L	G	W	L	PCT	STANDING			M/Y	W-EXP	A-E
1957	Cle-A	153	76	77	.497	6				72.5	3.5

Felske, John Frederick

YEAR	TM/L	G	W	L	PCT	STANDING			M/Y	W-EXP	A-E
1985	Phi-N	162	75	87	.463	5 E				80.4	-5.4
1986	Phi-N	161	86	75	.534	2 E				83.1	2.9
1987	Phi-N	61	29	32	.475	5 E	●4E		1/2	28.7	0.3
	3	384	190	194	.495						-2.2

Ferguson, Robert V. "Bob"

YEAR	TM/L	G	W	L	PCT	STANDING			M/Y	W-EXP	A-E
1871	Mut-n*	33	16	17	.485	4				15.7	0.3
1872	Atl-n*	37	9	28	.243	6				2.3	6.7
1873	Atl-n*	55	17	37	.315	6				13.5	3.5
1874	Atl-n*	56	22	33	.400	6				15.4	6.6
1875	Har-n*	86	54	28	.659	3				60.8	-6.8
1876	Har-N*	69	47	21	.691	3				49.9	-2.9
1877	Har-N*	60	31	27	.534	3				31.7	-0.7
1878	Chi-N*	61	30	30	.500	4				33.5	-3.5
1879	Tro-N*	30	7	22	.241	8	8		2/2	6.8	0.2
1880	Tro-N*	83	41	42	.494	4				37.1	3.9
1881	Tro-N*	85	39	45	.464	5				39.1	-0.1
1882	Tro-N*	85	35	48	.422	7				33.3	1.7
1883	Phi-N*	17	4	13	.235	8	8		1/2	2.1	1.9
1884	Pit-a*	42	11	31	.262	9	11	10	2/5	9.4	1.6
1886	NY-a	120	48	70	.407	8	7			47.7	0.3
1887	NY-a	30	6	24	.200	8	7		1/3	8.7	-2.7
	16	949	417	516	.447						9.8

Ferraro, Michael Dennis "Mike"

YEAR	TM/L	G	W	L	PCT	STANDING			M/Y	W-EXP	A-E
1983	Cle-A	100	40	60	.400	7 E	7 E		1/2	45.1	-5.1
1986	KC-A	74	36	38	.486	4 W	●3W		2/2	36.1	-0.1
	2	174	76	98	.437						-5.1

Fessenden, Wallace Clifton

YEAR	TM/L	G	W	L	PCT	STANDING			M/Y	W-EXP	A-E
1890	Syr-a	11	4	7	.364	7	7	6	2/3	4.5	-0.5

Fitzsimmons, Frederick Landis "Freddie"

YEAR	TM/L	G	W	L	PCT	STANDING			M/Y	W-EXP	A-E
1943	Phi-N	65	26	38	.406	7	7		2/2	27.4	-1.4
1944	Phi-N	154	61	92	.399	8				63.7	-2.7
1945	Phi-N	69	18	51	.261	8	8		1/2	20.4	-2.4
	3	288	105	181	.367						-6.5

Fletcher, Arthur "Art"

YEAR	TM/L	G	W	L	PCT	STANDING			M/Y	W-EXP	A-E
1923	Phi-N	155	50	104	.325	8				53.8	-3.8
1924	Phi-N	152	55	96	.364	7				59.1	-4.1
1925	Phi-N	153	68	85	.444	●6				66.0	2.0
1926	Phi-N	152	58	93	.384	8				55.7	2.3
1929	NY-A	11	6	5	.545	2	2		2/2	6.3	-0.3
	5	623	237	383	.382						-4.0

Flint, Frank Sylvester "Silver"

YEAR	TM/L	G	W	L	PCT	STANDING			M/Y	W-EXP	A-E
1879	Chi-N*	19	5	12	.294	2	4		2/2	9.0	-4.0

Fogarty, James G. "Jim"

YEAR	TM/L	G	W	L	PCT	STANDING			M/Y	W-EXP	A-E
1890	Phi-P*	16	7	9	.438	5	5		1/2	8.9	-1.9

Fogel, Horace S.

YEAR	TM/L	G	W	L	PCT	STANDING			M/Y	W-EXP	A-E
1887	Ind-N	70	20	49	.290	8	8		3/3	18.9	1.1
1902	NY-N	44	18	23	.439	4	8		1/3	14.1	3.9
	2	114	38	72	.345						5.0

Fohl, Leo Alexander "Lee"

YEAR	TM/L	G	W	L	PCT	STANDING			M/Y	W-EXP	A-E
1915	Cle-A	127	45	79	.363	6	7		2/2	50.6	-5.6
1916	Cle-A	157	77	77	.500	6				80.0	-3.0
1917	Cle-A	156	88	66	.571	3				81.6	6.4
1918	Cle-A	129	73	54	.575	2				69.8	3.2
1919	Cle-A	78	44	34	.564	3	2		1/2	44.7	-0.7
1921	StL-A	154	81	73	.526	3				76.1	4.9
1922	StL-A	154	93	61	.604	2				98.5	-5.5
1923	StL-A	103	52	49	.515	3	5		1/2	48.4	3.6
1924	Bos-A	157	67	87	.435	7				70.4	-3.4
1925	Bos-A	152	47	105	.309	8				49.5	-2.5
1926	Bos-A	154	46	107	.301	8				49.3	-3.3
	11	1521	713	792	.474						-5.8

Fonseca, Lewis Albert "Lew"

YEAR	TM/L	G	W	L	PCT	STANDING			M/Y	W-EXP	A-E
1932	Chi-A*	152	49	102	.325	7				54.0	-5.0
1933	Chi-A*	151	67	83	.447	6				62.5	4.5
1934	Chi-A	15	4	11	.267	8	8		1/2	5.3	-1.3
	3	318	120	196	.380						-1.8

Foutz, David Luther "Dave"

YEAR	TM/L	G	W	L	PCT	STANDING			M/Y	W-EXP	A-E
1893	Bro-N*	130	65	63	.508	●6				58.1	6.9
1894	Bro-N*	135	70	61	.534	5				66.6	3.4
1895	Bro-N*	134	71	60	.542	●5				68.3	2.7
1896	Bro-N*	133	58	73	.443	●9				59.0	-1.0
	4	532	264	257	.507						12.1

Fox, Charles Francis "Charlie"

YEAR	TM/L	G	W	L	PCT	STANDING			M/Y	W-EXP	A-E
1970	SF-N	120	67	53	.558	4 W	3 W		2/2	60.3	6.7
1971	SF-N	162	90	72	.556	1 W				87.4	2.6
1972	SF-N	155	69	86	.445	5 W				78.8	-9.8
1973	SF-N	162	88	74	.543	3 W				84.7	3.3
1974	SF-N	76	34	42	.447	5 W	5 W		1/2	33.7	0.3
1976	Mon-N	34	12	22	.353	6 E	6 E		2/2	12.4	-0.4
1983	Chi-N	39	17	22	.436	5 E	5 E		2/2	19.1	-2.1
	7	748	377	371	.504						0.5

Franks, Herman Louis

YEAR	TM/L	G	W	L	PCT	STANDING			M/Y	W-EXP	A-E
1965	SF-N	163	95	67	.586	2				90.5	4.5
1966	SF-N	161	93	68	.578	2				85.7	7.3
1967	SF-N	162	91	71	.562	2				92.1	-1.1
1968	SF-N	163	88	74	.543	2				89.0	-1.0
1977	Chi-N	162	81	81	.500	4 E				76.3	4.7
1978	Chi-N	162	79	83	.488	3 E				74.8	4.2
1979	Chi-N	155	78	77	.503	5 E	5 E		1/2	77.4	0.6
	7	1128	605	521	.537						19.2

Frazer, George Kasson

YEAR	TM/L	G	W	L	PCT	STANDING			M/Y	W-EXP	A-E
1890	Syr-a	71	31	40	.437	7	6		1/3	29.0	2.0
	Syr-a	46	20	25	.444	7	6		3/3	18.4	1.6

Frazier, Joseph Filmore "Joe"

YEAR	TM/L	G	W	L	PCT	STANDING			M/Y	W-EXP	A-E
1976	NY-N	162	86	76	.531	3 E				89.7	-3.7

YEAR	TM/L	G	W	L	PCT	STANDING			M/Y	W-EXP	A-E
1977	NY-N	45	15	30	.333	6 E	6 E		1/2	20.2	-5.2
	2	207	101	106	.488						-8.9

Fregosi, James Louis "Jim"

YEAR	TM/L	G	W	L	PCT	STANDING			M/Y	W-EXP	A-E
1978	Cal-A	117	62	55	.530	3 W	●2W		2/2	60.4	1.6
1979	Cal-A	162	88	74	.543	1 W				90.3	-2.3
1980	Cal-A	160	65	95	.406	6 W				70.3	-5.3
1981(1)	Cal-A	47	22	25	.468	4 W	4 W		1/2	24.5	-2.5
1986	Chi-A	96	45	51	.469	5 W	5 W		3/3	44.6	0.4
1987	Chi-A	162	77	85	.475	5 W				81.2	-4.2
1988	Chi-A	161	71	90	.441	5 W				67.6	3.4
1991	Phi-N	149	74	75	.497	6 E	3 E		2/2	69.5	4.5
1992	Phi-N	162	70	92	.432	6 E				77.8	-7.8
1993	Phi-N	162	97	65	.599	♦1 E				94.0	3.0
1994	Phi-N	115	54	61	.470	4 E				59.9	-5.9
	11	1493	725	768	.486						-15.2

Frey, James Gottfried "Jim"

YEAR	TM/L	G	W	L	PCT	STANDING			M/Y	W-EXP	A-E
1980	KC-A	162	97	65	.599	♦1 W				92.3	4.7
1981(1)	KC-A	50	20	30	.400	5 W				92.3	4.7
(2)	KC-A	20	10	10	.500	●2 W	1 W		1/2	34.4	-4.4
1984	Chi-N	161	96	65	.596	1 E				91.0	5.0
1985	Chi-N	162	77	84	.478	4 E				76.1	0.9
1986	Chi-N	56	23	33	.411	5 E	5 E		1/3	24.5	-1.5
	5	611	323	287	.530						4.6

Frisch, Frank Francis "Frankie"

YEAR	TM/L	G	W	L	PCT	STANDING			M/Y	W-EXP	A-E
1933	StL-N*	63	36	26	.581	5	5		2/2	34.3	1.7
1934	StL-N*	154	95	58	.621	★1				90.5	4.5
1935	StL-N*	154	96	58	.623	2				96.9	-0.9
1936	StL-N*	155	87	67	.565	●2				77.1	9.9
1937	StL-N*	157	81	73	.526	4				82.4	-1.4
1938	StL-N	139	63	72	.467	6	6		1/2	67.9	-4.9
1940	Pit-N	156	78	76	.506	4				79.4	-1.4
1941	Pit-N	156	81	73	.526	4				81.8	-0.8
1942	Pit-N	151	66	81	.449	5				68.6	-2.6
1943	Pit-N	157	80	74	.519	4				83.7	-3.7
1944	Pit-N	158	90	63	.588	2				84.7	5.3
1945	Pit-N	155	82	72	.532	4				83.6	-1.6
1946	Pit-N	152	62	89	.411	7	7		1/2	63.3	-1.3
1949	Chi-N	104	42	62	.404	7	8		2/2	39.8	2.2
1950	Chi-N	154	64	89	.418	7				63.7	0.3
1951	Chi-N	81	35	45	.438	7	8		1/2	32.9	2.1
	16	2246	1138	1078	.514						7.3

Fuchs, Emil Edmund "Judge"

YEAR	TM/L	G	W	L	PCT	STANDING			M/Y	W-EXP	A-E
1929	Bos-N	154	56	98	.364	8				56.2	-0.2

Gaffney, John H.

YEAR	TM/L	G	W	L	PCT	STANDING			M/Y	W-EXP	A-E
1886	Was-N	43	15	25	.375	8			2/2	9.0	6.0
1887	Was-N	126	46	76	.377	7				41.6	4.4
	2	169	61	101	.377						10.4

Galvin, James Francis "Jim"

YEAR	TM/L	G	W	L	PCT	STANDING			M/Y	W-EXP	A-E
1885	Buf-N*	24	7	17	.292	7	7		1/2	6.9	0.1

Ganzel, John Henry

YEAR	TM/L	G	W	L	PCT	STANDING			M/Y	W-EXP	A-E
1908	Cin-N*	155	73	81	.474	5				70.6	2.4
1915	Bro-F	35	17	18	.486	7			2/2	16.9	0.1
	2	190	90	99	.476						2.5

Garcia, David "Dave"

YEAR	TM/L	G	W	L	PCT	STANDING			M/Y	W-EXP	A-E
1977	Cal-A	81	35	46	.432	5 W	5 W		2/2	39.5	-4.5
1978	Cal-A	45	25	20	.556	3 W	●2W		1/2	23.2	1.8
1979	Cle-A	66	38	28	.576	6 E	6 E		2/2	31.2	6.8
1980	Cle-A	160	79	81	.494	6 E				73.3	5.7
1981(1)	Cle-A	50	26	24	.520	6 E					
(2)	Cle-A	53	26	27	.491	5 E				50.4	1.6
1982	Cle-A	162	78	84	.481	●6 E				74.4	3.6
	6	617	307	310	.498						14.9

Gardner, William Frederick "Billy"

YEAR	TM/L	G	W	L	PCT	STANDING			M/Y	W-EXP	A-E
1981(1)	Min-A	20	6	14	.300	6 W	7 W		2/2		
(2)	Min-A	53	24	29	.453	4 W				28.8	1.2
1982	Min-A	162	60	102	.370	7 W				64.9	-4.9
1983	Min-A	162	70	92	.432	5 W				70.0	0.0
1984	Min-A	162	81	81	.500	2 W				80.8	0.2
1985	Min-A	62	27	35	.435	6 W	4 W		1/2	28.1	-1.1
1987	KC-A	126	62	64	.492	4 W	2 W		1/2	64.9	-2.9
	6	747	330	417	.442						-7.4

Garner, Philip Mason "Phil"

YEAR	TM/L	G	W	L	PCT	STANDING			M/Y	W-EXP	A-E
1992	Mil-A	162	92	70	.568	2 E				95.2	-3.2
1993	Mil-A	162	69	93	.426	7 E				75.2	-6.2
1994	Mil-A	115	53	62	.461	5 C				53.8	-0.8
	3	439	214	225	.487						-10.2

Gaston, Clarence Edwin "Cito"

YEAR	TM/L	G	W	L	PCT	STANDING			M/Y	W-EXP	A-E
1989	Tor-A	126	77	49	.611	6 E	1 E		2/2	69.4	7.6
1990	Tor-A	162	86	76	.531	2 E				91.7	-5.7
1991	Tor-A	120	66	54	.550	1 E	1 E		1/3	64.9	1.1
	Tor-A	9	6	3	.667	1 E	1 E		3/3	4.9	1.1
1992	Tor-A	162	96	66	.593	★1 E				90.8	5.2
1993	Tor-A	162	95	67	.586	★1 E				91.1	3.9
1994	Tor-A	115	55	60	.478	3 E				56.3	-1.9
	6	856	481	375	.562						12.1

Gerhardt, John Joseph "Joe"

YEAR	TM/L	G	W	L	PCT	STANDING			M/Y	W-EXP	A-E
1883	Lou-a*	98	52	45	.536	5				48.7	3.3

YEAR	TM/L	G	W	L	PCT	STANDING			M/Y	W-EXP	A-E
1890	StL-a*	38	20	16	.556	2	3		6/6	21.1	-1.1
	2	136	72	61	.541						2.2

Gessler, Harry Homer "Doc"

YEAR	TM/L	G	W	L	PCT	STANDING			M/Y	W-EXP	A-E
1914	Pit-F	11	3	8	.273	8	7		1/2	4.8	-1.8

Gibson, George C. "Moon"

YEAR	TM/L	G	W	L	PCT	STANDING			M/Y	W-EXP	A-E
1920	Pit-N	155	79	75	.513	4				74.5	4.5
1921	Pit-N	154	90	63	.588	2				86.6	3.4
1922	Pit-N	65	32	33	.492	5	●3		1/2	37.6	-5.6
1925	Chi-N	26	12	14	.462	7	8		3/3	12.2	-0.2
1932	Pit-N	154	86	68	.558	2				76.0	10.0
1933	Pit-N	154	87	67	.565	2				82.0	5.0
1934	Pit-N	51	27	24	.529	4	5		1/2	26.2	0.8
	7	759	413	344	.546						17.9

Gifford, James H. "Jim"

YEAR	TM/L	G	W	L	PCT	STANDING			M/Y	W-EXP	A-E
1884	Ind-a	87	25	60	.294	10	11		1/2	21.5	3.5
1885	NY-a	108	44	64	.407	7				39.5	4.5
1886	NY-a	17	5	12	.294	8	7		1/2	6.9	-1.9
	3	212	74	136	.352						6.1

Glasscock, John Wesley "Jack"

YEAR	TM/L	G	W	L	PCT	STANDING			M/Y	W-EXP	A-E
1889	Ind-N*	67	34	32	.515	7	7		2/2	29.9	4.1
1892(1)	StL-N*	4	1	3	.250	10	9		1/3	1.5	-0.5
	2	71	35	35	.500						3.6

Gleason, William J. "Kid"

YEAR	TM/L	G	W	L	PCT	STANDING			M/Y	W-EXP	A-E
1919	Chi-A	140	88	52	.629	1				83.6	4.4
1920	Chi-A	154	96	58	.623	2				89.6	6.4
1921	Chi-A	154	62	92	.403	7				60.4	1.6
1922	Chi-A	155	77	77	.500	5				77.0	0.0
1923	Chi-A	156	69	85	.448	7				72.1	-3.1
	5	759	392	364	.519						9.3

Gomez, Pedro W. "Preston"

YEAR	TM/L	G	W	L	PCT	STANDING			M/Y	W-EXP	A-E
1969	SD-N	162	52	110	.321	6 W				50.5	1.5
1970	SD-N	162	63	99	.389	6 W				70.3	-7.3
1971	SD-N	161	61	100	.379	6 W				66.2	-5.2
1972	SD-N	11	4	7	.364	4 W	6 W		1/2	4.1	-0.1
1974	Hou-N	162	81	81	.500	4 W				83.2	-2.2
1975	Hou-N	127	47	80	.370	6 W	6 W		1/2	59.7	-12.7
1980	Chi-N	90	38	52	.422	6 E	6 E		1/2	38.4	-0.4
	7	875	346	529	.395						-26.5

Gonzalez, Miguel Angel "Mike"

YEAR	TM/L	G	W	L	PCT	STANDING			M/Y	W-EXP	A-E
1938	StL-N	17	8	8	.500	6	6		2/2	8.0	-0.0
1940	StL-N	6	1	5	.167	6	7	3	2/3	3.2	-2.2
	2	23	9	13	.409						-2.2

Gordon, Joseph Lowell "Joe"

YEAR	TM/L	G	W	L	PCT	STANDING			M/Y	W-EXP	A-E
1958	Cle-A	86	46	40	.535	6	4		2/2	46.4	-0.4
1959	Cle-A	154	89	65	.578	2				86.9	2.1
1960	Cle-A	95	49	46	.516	4	4		1/3	45.9	3.1
	Det-A	57	26	31	.456	6	6		3/3	28.1	-2.1
1961	KC-A	60	26	33	.441	8	●9		1/2	23.1	2.9
1969	KC-A	163	69	93	.426	4 W				70.1	-1.1
	5	615	305	308	.498						4.6

Gore, George F.

YEAR	TM/L	G	W	L	PCT	STANDING			M/Y	W-EXP	A-E
1892(2)	StL-N*	16	6	9	.400	12	12	11	1/3	5.5	0.5

Goryl, John Albert "Johnny"

YEAR	TM/L	G	W	L	PCT	STANDING			M/Y	W-EXP	A-E
1980	Min-A	36	23	13	.639	4 W	3 W		2/2	16.8	6.2
1981(1)	Min-A	37	11	25	.306	6 W	7 W		1/2	14.2	-3.2
	2	73	34	38	.472						3.0

Gould, Charles Harvey "Charlie"

YEAR	TM/L	G	W	L	PCT	STANDING			M/Y	W-EXP	A-E
1875	NH-n*	23	2	21	.087	11	8		1/3	1.9	0.1
1876	Cin-N*	65	9	56	.138	8				3.6	5.4
	2	88	11	77	.125						5.5

Gowdy, Henry Morgan "Hank"

YEAR	TM/L	G	W	L	PCT	STANDING			M/Y	W-EXP	A-E
1946	Cin-N	4	3	1	.750	6	6		2/2	1.9	1.1

Graffen, Samuel Mason "Mase"

YEAR	TM/L	G	W	L	PCT	STANDING			M/Y	W-EXP	A-E
1876	StL-N	56	39	17	.696	2	2		1/2	41.3	-2.3

Grammas, Alexander Peter "Alex"

YEAR	TM/L	G	W	L	PCT	STANDING			M/Y	W-EXP	A-E
1969	Pit-N	5	4	1	.800	3 E	3 E		2/2	2.7	1.3
1976	Mil-A	161	66	95	.410	6 E				71.3	-5.3
1977	Mil-A	162	67	95	.414	6 E				68.2	-1.2
	3	328	137	191	.418						-5.1

Green, George Dallas "Dallas"

YEAR	TM/L	G	W	L	PCT	STANDING			M/Y	W-EXP	A-E
1979	Phi-N	30	19	11	.633	5 E	4 E		2/2	14.3	4.7
1980	Phi-N	162	91	71	.562	★1 E				90.2	0.8
1981(1)	Phi-N	55	34	21	.618	1 E					
(2)	Phi-N	52	25	27	.481	3 E				55.4	3.6
1989	NY-A	121	56	65	.463	6 E	5 E		1/2	53.5	2.5
1993	NY-N	124	46	78	.371	7 E	7 E		2/2	56.4	-10.4
1994	NY-N	113	55	58	.487	3 E				54.5	0.5
	6	657	326	331	.496						1.6

Griffin, Michael Joseph "Mike"

YEAR	TM/L	G	W	L	PCT	STANDING			M/Y	W-EXP	A-E
1898	Bro-N*	4	1	3	.250	9	9	10	2/3	1.5	-0.5

Griffin, Tobias Charles "Sandy"

YEAR	TM/L	G	W	L	PCT	STANDING			M/Y	W-EXP	A-E
1891	Was-a*	6	2	4	.333	8	8		4/4	1.6	0.4

Griffith, Clark Calvin

YEAR	TM/L	G	W	L	PCT	STANDING			M/Y	W-EXP	A-E
1901	Chi-A*	137	83	53	.610	1				85.3	-2.3

YEAR	TM/L	G	W	L	PCT	STANDING			M/Y	W-EXP	A-E
1902	Chi-A*	138	74	60	.552	4				74.2	-0.2
1903	NY-A*	136	72	62	.537	4				67.6	4.4
1904	NY-A*	155	92	59	.609	2				83.5	8.5
1905	NY-A*	152	71	78	.477	6				70.7	0.3
1906	NY-A*	155	90	61	.596	2				86.5	3.5
1907	NY-A*	152	70	78	.473	5				67.8	2.2
1908	NY-A	57	24	32	.429	6	8		1/2	17.9	6.1
1909	Cin-N*	157	77	76	.503	4				77.3	-0.3
1910	Cin-N*	156	75	79	.487	5				70.4	4.6
1911	Cin-N	159	70	83	.458	6				74.1	-4.1
1912	Was-A*	154	91	61	.599	2				88.3	2.7
1913	Was-A*	155	90	64	.584	2				80.8	9.2
1914	Was-A*	158	81	73	.526	3				83.1	-2.1
1915	Was-A	155	85	68	.556	4				85.4	-0.4
1916	Was-A	159	76	77	.497	7				75.7	0.3
1917	Was-A	158	74	79	.484	5				73.9	0.1
1918	Was-A	130	72	56	.563	3				69.7	2.3
1919	Was-A	142	56	84	.400	7				66.0	-10.0
1920	Was-A	153	68	84	.447	6				68.5	-0.5
20		2918	1491	1367	.522						24.4

Grimes, Burleigh Arland

YEAR	TM/L	G	W	L	PCT	STANDING			M/Y	W-EXP	A-E
1937	Bro-N	155	62	91	.405	6				60.9	1.1
1938	Bro-N	151	69	80	.463	7				73.9	-4.9
2		306	131	171	.434						-3.8

Grimm, Charles John "Charlie"

YEAR	TM/L	G	W	L	PCT	STANDING			M/Y	W-EXP	A-E
1932	Chi-N*	55	37	18	.673	2	1		2/2	30.6	6.4
1933	Chi-N*	154	86	68	.558	3				88.9	-2.9
1934	Chi-N*	152	86	65	.570	3				82.2	3.8
1935	Chi-N*	154	100	54	.649	1				101.5	-1.5
1936	Chi-N*	154	87	67	.565	●2				92.4	-5.4
1937	Chi-N	154	93	61	.604	2				89.4	3.6
1938	Chi-N	81	45	36	.556	3	1		1/2	46.8	-1.8
1944	Chi-N	146	74	69	.517	8	4		3/3	74.6	-0.6
1945	Chi-N	155	98	56	.636	1				98.3	-0.3
1946	Chi-N	155	82	71	.536	3				81.3	0.7
1947	Chi-N	155	69	85	.448	6				60.9	8.1
1948	Chi-N	155	64	90	.416	8				65.7	-1.7
1949	Chi-N	50	19	31	.380	7	8		1/2	19.1	-0.1
1952	Bos-N	120	51	67	.432	7	7		2/2	52.2	-1.2
1953	Mil-N	157	92	62	.597	2				92.4	-0.4
1954	Mil-N	154	89	65	.578	3				89.1	-0.1
1955	Mil-N	154	85	69	.552	2				84.4	0.6
1956	Mil-N	46	24	22	.522	5	2		1/2	27.4	-3.4
1960	Chi-N	17	6	11	.353	7	7		1/2	6.9	-0.9
19		2368	1287	1067	.547						2.8

Groh, Henry Knight "Heinie"

YEAR	TM/L	G	W	L	PCT	STANDING			M/Y	W-EXP	A-E
1918	Cin-N*	10	7	3	.700	4	3		2/2	5.3	1.7

Gutteridge, Donald Joseph "Don"

YEAR	TM/L	G	W	L	PCT	STANDING			M/Y	W-EXP	A-E
1969	Chi-A	145	60	85	.414	4 W	5 W		2/2	63.4	-3.4
1970	Chi-A	136	49	87	.360	6 W	6 W		1/3	52.1	-3.1
2		281	109	172	.388						-6.5

Haas, George Edwin "Eddie"

YEAR	TM/L	G	W	L	PCT	STANDING			M/Y	W-EXP	A-E
1985	Atl-N	121	50	71	.413	5 W	5 W		1/2	49.2	0.8

Hack, Stanley Camfield "Stan"

YEAR	TM/L	G	W	L	PCT	STANDING			M/Y	W-EXP	A-E
1954	Chi-N	154	64	90	.416	7				70.6	-6.6
1955	Chi-N	154	72	81	.471	6				67.6	4.4
1956	Chi-N	157	60	94	.390	8				65.4	-5.4
1958	StL-N	10	3	7	.300	5	●5		2/2	4.4	-1.4
4		475	199	272	.423						-9.1

Hackett, Charles M. "Charlie"

YEAR	TM/L	G	W	L	PCT	STANDING			M/Y	W-EXP	A-E
1884	Cle-N	113	35	77	.313	7				32.0	3.0
1885	Bro-a	37	15	22	.405	7	●5		1/2	17.7	-2.7
2		150	50	99	.336						0.3

Hallman, William Wilson "Bill"

YEAR	TM/L	G	W	L	PCT	STANDING			M/Y	W-EXP	A-E
1897	StL-N*	50	13	36	.265	12	12	12	3/4	8.9	4.1

Haney, Fred Girard

YEAR	TM/L	G	W	L	PCT	STANDING			M/Y	W-EXP	A-E
1939	StL-A	156	43	111	.279	8				50.1	-7.1
1940	StL-A	156	67	87	.435	6				65.4	1.6
1941	StL-A	44	15	29	.341	7	●6		1/2	20.4	-5.4
1953	Pit-N	154	50	104	.325	8				51.6	-1.6
1954	Pit-N	154	53	101	.344	8				48.4	4.6
1955	Pit-N	154	60	94	.390	8				55.8	4.2
1956	Mil-N	109	68	40	.630	5	2		2/2	64.3	3.7
1957	Mil-N	155	95	59	.617	★1				93.0	2.0
1958	Mil-N	154	92	62	.597	1				91.3	0.7
1959	Mil-N	157	86	70	.551	▲2				88.3	-2.3
10		1393	629	757	.454						0.4

Hanlon, Edward Hugh "Ned"

YEAR	TM/L	G	W	L	PCT	STANDING			M/Y	W-EXP	A-E
1889	Pit-N*	46	26	18	.591	7	5		3/3	19.8	6.2
1890	Pit-P*	131	60	68	.469	6				59.3	0.7
1891	Pit-N*	78	31	47	.397	8	8		1/2	35.5	-4.5
1892(1)	Bal-N*	56	17	39	.304	12	12		3/3		
(2)	Bal-N*	77	26	46	.361	10				45.7	-2.7
1893	Bal-N	130	60	70	.462	8				59.0	1.0
1894	Bal-N	129	89	39	.695	1				90.9	-1.9
1895	Bal-N	132	87	43	.669	1				95.8	-8.8
1896	Bal-N	132	90	39	.698	1				92.7	-2.7

YEAR	TM/L	G	W	L	PCT	STANDING			M/Y	W-EXP	A-E
1897	Bal-N	136	90	40	.692	2				90.1	-0.1
1898	Bal-N	154	96	53	.644	2				103.8	-7.8
1899	Bro-N	150	101	47	.682	1				95.8	5.2
1900	Bro-N	142	82	54	.603	1				76.6	5.4
1901	Bro-N	137	79	57	.581	3				81.8	-2.8
1902	Bro-N	141	75	63	.543	2				73.9	1.1
1903	Bro-N	139	70	66	.515	5				66.6	3.4
1904	Bro-N	154	56	97	.366	6				63.4	-7.4
1905	Bro-N	155	48	104	.316	8				45.0	3.0
1906	Cin-N	155	64	87	.424	6				70.0	-6.0
1907	Cin-N	156	66	87	.431	6				77.3	-11.3
19		2530	1313	1164	.530						-29.8

Harder, Melvin Leroy "Mel"

YEAR	TM/L	G	W	L	PCT	STANDING			M/Y	W-EXP	A-E
1961	Cle-A	1	1	0	1.000	5	5		2/2	0.5	0.5
1962	Cle-A	2	2	0	1.000	6	6		2/2	0.9	1.1
2		3	3	0	1.000						1.6

Hargrove, Dudley Michael "Mike"

YEAR	TM/L	G	W	L	PCT	STANDING			M/Y	W-EXP	A-E
1991	Cle-A	85	32	53	.376	7 E	7 E		2/2	32.5	-0.5
1992	Cle-A	162	76	86	.469	●4 E				73.7	2.3
1993	Cle-A	162	76	86	.469	6 E				78.8	-2.8
1994	Cle-A	113	66	47	.584	2 C				67.1	-1.1
4		522	250	272	.479						-2.1

Harrah, Colbert Dale "Toby"

YEAR	TM/L	G	W	L	PCT	STANDING			M/Y	W-EXP	A-E
1992	Tex-A	76	32	44	.421	3 W	4 W		2/2	34.6	-2.6

Harrelson, Derrel Mc Kinley "Bud"

YEAR	TM/L	G	W	L	PCT	STANDING			M/Y	W-EXP	A-E
1990	NY-N	120	71	49	.592	4 E	2 E		2/2	72.3	-1.3
1991	NY-N	154	74	80	.481	3 E	5 E		1/2	76.4	-2.4
2		274	145	129	.529						-3.7

Harris, Chalmer Luman "Lum"

YEAR	TM/L	G	W	L	PCT	STANDING			M/Y	W-EXP	A-E
1961	Bal-A	27	17	10	.630	3	3		2/2	15.3	1.7
1964	Hou-N	13	5	8	.385	9	9		2/2	5.3	-0.3
1965	Hou-N	162	65	97	.401	9				65.8	-0.8
1968	Atl-N	163	81	81	.500	5				76.9	4.1
1969	Atl-N	162	93	69	.574	1 W				87.3	5.7
1970	Atl-N	162	76	86	.469	5 W				77.5	-1.5
1971	Atl-N	162	82	80	.506	3 W				75.2	6.8
1972	Atl-N	105	47	57	.452	4 W	4 W		1/2	45.0	2.0
8		956	466	488	.488						17.7

Harris, Stanley Raymond "Bucky"

YEAR	TM/L	G	W	L	PCT	STANDING			M/Y	W-EXP	A-E
1924	Was-A*	156	92	62	.597	★1				91.4	0.6
1925	Was-A*	152	96	55	.636	1				90.7	5.3
1926	Was-A*	152	81	69	.540	4				78.8	2.2
1927	Was-A*	157	85	69	.552	3				82.0	3.0
1928	Was-A*	155	75	79	.487	4				78.3	-3.3
1929	Det-A*	155	70	84	.455	6				76.8	-6.8
1930	Det-A	154	75	79	.487	5				72.4	2.6
1931	Det-A*	154	61	93	.396	7				59.1	1.9
1932	Det-A	153	76	75	.503	5				76.6	-0.6
1933	Det-A	153	73	79	.480	5	5		1/2	74.9	-1.9
1934	Bos-A	153	76	76	.500	4				80.2	-4.2
1935	Was-A	154	67	86	.438	6				69.3	-2.3
1936	Was-A	153	82	71	.536	4				84.6	-2.6
1937	Was-A	158	73	80	.477	6				68.6	4.4
1938	Was-A	152	75	76	.497	5				70.2	4.8
1939	Was-A	153	65	87	.428	6				66.9	-1.9
1940	Was-A	154	64	90	.416	7				62.9	1.1
1941	Was-A	156	70	84	.455	●6				70.3	-0.3
1942	Was-A	151	62	89	.411	7				59.7	2.3
1943	Phi-N	92	38	52	.422	7	7		1/2	38.5	-0.5
1947	NY-A	155	97	57	.630	★1				99.9	-2.9
1948	NY-A	154	94	60	.610	3				98.6	-4.6
1950	Was-A	155	67	87	.435	5				65.1	1.9
1951	Was-A	154	62	92	.403	7				68.0	-6.0
1952	Was-A	157	78	76	.506	5				75.9	2.1
1953	Was-A	152	76	76	.500	5				83.5	-7.5
1954	Was-A	155	66	88	.429	6				72.1	-6.1
1955	Det-A	154	79	75	.513	5				88.5	-9.5
1956	Det-A	155	82	72	.532	5				85.7	-3.7
29		4408	2157	2218	.493						-32.5

Hart, James Aristotle "Jim"

YEAR	TM/L	G	W	L	PCT	STANDING			M/Y	W-EXP	A-E
1885	Lou-a	112	53	59	.473	●5				52.8	0.2
1886	Lou-a	138	66	70	.485	4				70.4	-4.4
1889	Bos-N	133	83	45	.648	2				82.2	0.8
3		383	202	174	.537						-3.4

Hart, John Henry

YEAR	TM/L	G	W	L	PCT	STANDING			M/Y	W-EXP	A-E
1989	Cle-A	19	8	11	.421	6 E	6 E		2/2	8.9	-0.9

Hartnett, Charles Leo "Gabby"

YEAR	TM/L	G	W	L	PCT	STANDING			M/Y	W-EXP	A-E
1938	Chi-N*	73	44	27	.620	3	1		2/2	41.0	3.0
1939	Chi-N*	156	84	70	.545	4				81.6	2.4
1940	Chi-N*	154	75	79	.487	5				81.6	-6.6
3		383	203	176	.536						-1.2

Hartsfield, Roy Thomas

YEAR	TM/L	G	W	L	PCT	STANDING			M/Y	W-EXP	A-E
1977	Tor-A	161	54	107	.335	7 E				58.6	-4.6
1978	Tor-A	161	59	102	.366	7 E				61.4	-2.4
1979	Tor-A	162	53	109	.327	7 E				56.2	-3.2
3		484	166	318	.343						-10.3

Hastings, Winfield Scott "Scott"

YEAR	TM/L	G	W	L	PCT	STANDING			M/Y	W-EXP	A-E
1871	Rok-n*	25	4	21	.160	9				8.8	-4.8
1872	Cle-n*	20	6	14	.300	5	7			5.1	0.9
2		45	10	35	.222						-3.9

Hatfield, John Van Buren

YEAR	TM/L	G	W	L	PCT	STANDING			M/Y	W-EXP	A-E
1872	Mut-n*	40	24	14	.632	4	3		2/2	27.6	-3.6
1873	Mut-n*	28	11	17	.393	5	4		1/2	15.6	-4.6
2		68	35	31	.530						-8.1

Hatton, Grady Edgebert

YEAR	TM/L	G	W	L	PCT	STANDING			M/Y	W-EXP	A-E
1966	Hou-N	163	72	90	.444	8				72.2	-0.2
1967	Hou-N	162	69	93	.426	9				69.0	-0.0
1968	Hou-N	61	23	38	.377	10	10		1/2	27.1	-4.1
3		386	164	221	.426						-4.3

Hecker, Guy Jackson

YEAR	TM/L	G	W	L	PCT	STANDING			M/Y	W-EXP	A-E
1890	Pit-N*	138	23	113	.169	8				15.5	7.5

Heffner, Donald Henry "Don"

YEAR	TM/L	G	W	L	PCT	STANDING			M/Y	W-EXP	A-E
1966	Cin-N	83	37	46	.446	8			1/2	41.0	-4.0

Heilbroner, Louis Wilbur "Louie"

YEAR	TM/L	G	W	L	PCT	STANDING			M/Y	W-EXP	A-E
1900	StL-N	50	23	25	.479	7	●5		2/2	23.9	-0.9

Helms, Tommy Vann

YEAR	TM/L	G	W	L	PCT	STANDING			M/Y	W-EXP	A-E
1988	Cin-N	27	12	15	.444	4 W	4 W	2 W	2/3	14.3	-2.3
1989	Cin-N	37	16	21	.432	●4 W	5 W		2/2	17.1	-1.1
2		64	28	36	.438						-3.4

Hemus, Solomon Joseph "Solly"

YEAR	TM/L	G	W	L	PCT	STANDING			M/Y	W-EXP	A-E
1959	StL-N*	154	71	83	.461	7				68.5	2.5
1960	StL-N	155	86	68	.558	3				79.4	6.6
1961	StL-N	75	33	41	.446	6	5		1/2	38.7	-5.7
3		384	190	192	.497						3.3

Henderson, William C. "Bill"

YEAR	TM/L	G	W	L	PCT	STANDING			M/Y	W-EXP	A-E
1884	Bal-U	106	58	47	.552	4				55.5	2.5

Hendricks, John Charles "Jack"

YEAR	TM/L	G	W	L	PCT	STANDING			M/Y	W-EXP	A-E
1918	StL-N	133	51	78	.395	8				56.5	-5.5
1924	Cin-N	153	83	70	.542	4				83.9	-0.9
1925	Cin-N	153	80	73	.523	3				81.3	-1.3
1926	Cin-N	157	87	67	.565	2				86.7	0.3
1927	Cin-N	153	75	78	.490	5				75.5	-0.5
1928	Cin-N	153	78	74	.513	5				72.1	5.9
1929	Cin-N	155	66	88	.429	7				69.7	-3.7
7		1057	520	528	.496						-5.7

Hengle, Edward S. "Ed"

YEAR	TM/L	G	W	L	PCT	STANDING			M/Y	W-EXP	A-E
1884	Chi-U	74	34	39	.466	5				41.3	-0.3

Herman, William Jennings Bryan "Billy"

YEAR	TM/L	G	W	L	PCT	STANDING			M/Y	W-EXP	A-E
1947	Pit-N*	155	61	92	.399	8	●7		1/2	69.6	-8.6
1964	Bos-A	2	2	0	1.000	8	8		2/2	0.9	1.1
1965	Bos-A	162	62	100	.383	9				68.8	-6.8
1966	Bos-A	146	64	82	.438	9	9		1/2	66.0	-2.0
4		465	189	274	.408						-16.3

Herzog, Charles Lincoln "Buck"

YEAR	TM/L	G	W	L	PCT	STANDING			M/Y	W-EXP	A-E
1914	Cin-N*	157	60	94	.390	8				63.8	-3.8
1915	Cin-N*	160	71	83	.461	7				69.1	1.9
1916	Cin-N*	84	34	49	.410	8	●7		1/3	34.7	-0.7
3		401	165	226	.422						-2.6

Herzog, Dorrel Norman Elvert "Whitey"

YEAR	TM/L	G	W	L	PCT	STANDING			M/Y	W-EXP	A-E
1973	Tex-A	138	47	91	.341	6 W	6 W		1/3	49.9	-2.9
1974	Cal-A	4	2	2	.500	6 W	6 W	6 W	2/3	1.9	0.1
1975	KC-A	66	41	25	.621	2 W	2 W		2/2	35.6	5.4
1976	KC-A	162	90	72	.556	1 W				91.7	-1.7
1977	KC-A	162	102	60	.630	1 W				98.0	4.0
1978	KC-A	162	92	70	.568	1 W				92.2	-0.2
1979	KC-A	162	85	77	.525	2 W				84.3	0.7
1980	StL-N	73	38	35	.521	6 E 5 E 4 E			3/4	37.8	0.2
1981(1)	StL-N	51	30	20	.600	2 E					
(2)	StL-N	52	29	23	.558	2 E				55.8	3.2
1982	StL-N	162	92	70	.568	★1 E				89.1	2.9
1983	StL-N	162	79	83	.488	4 E				77.8	1.2
1984	StL-N	162	84	78	.519	3 E				81.7	2.3
1985	StL-N	162	101	61	.623	♦1 E				99.4	1.6
1986	StL-N	161	79	82	.491	3 E				79.4	-0.4
1987	StL-N	162	95	67	.586	♦1 E				91.4	3.6
1988	StL-N	162	76	86	.469	5 E				75.0	1.0
1989	StL-N	164	86	76	.531	3 E				83.6	2.4
1990	StL-N	80	33	47	.412	6 E	6 E		1/3	34.8	-1.8
18		2409	1281	1125	.532						21.6

Hewett, Walter F.

YEAR	TM/L	G	W	L	PCT	STANDING			M/Y	W-EXP	A-E
1888	Was-N	40	10	29	.256	8	8		1/2	12.2	-2.2

Hicks, Nathaniel Woodhull "Nat"

YEAR	TM/L	G	W	L	PCT	STANDING			M/Y	W-EXP	A-E
1875	Mut-n*	71	30	38	.441	7				25.1	4.9

Higgins, Michael Franklin "Pinky"

YEAR	TM/L	G	W	L	PCT	STANDING			M/Y	W-EXP	A-E
1955	Bos-A	154	84	70	.545	4				87.2	-3.2
1956	Bos-A	155	84	70	.545	4				79.8	4.2
1957	Bos-A	154	82	72	.532	3				82.3	-0.3
1958	Bos-A	155	79	75	.513	3				77.6	1.4
1959	Bos-A	73	31	42	.425	8	8		1/3	32.9	-6.9
1960	Bos-A	105	48	57	.457	8	7		3/3	44.7	3.3
1961	Bos-A	163	76	86	.469	6				74.8	1.2
1962	Bos-A	160	76	84	.475	8				75.1	0.9
8		1119	560	556	.502						0.6

Higham, Richard "Dick"

YEAR	TM/L	G	W	L	PCT	STANDING			M/Y	W-EXP	A-E
1874	Mut-n*	40	29	11	.725	2	2		2/2	26.2	2.8

Himsl, Avitus Bernard "Vedie"

YEAR	TM/L	G	W	L	PCT	STANDING			M/Y	W-EXP	A-E
1961	Chi-N	11	5	6	.455	6	●6		1/9	4.7	0.3
	Chi-N	17	5	12	.294	7	7	7	3/9	7.3	-2.3
	Chi-N	4	0	3	.000	7	7	7	6/9	1.3	-1.3

Hitchcock, William Clyde "Billy"

YEAR	TM/L	G	W	L	PCT	STANDING			M/Y	W-EXP	A-E
1960	Det-A	1	1	0	1.000	6	6	6	2/3	0.5	0.5
1962	Bal-A	162	77	85	.475	7				78.1	-1.1
1963	Bal-A	162	86	76	.531	4				83.5	2.5
1966	Atl-N	51	33	18	.647	7	5		2/2	28.6	4.4
1967	Atl-N	159	77	82	.484	7	7		1/2	78.6	-1.6
5		535	274	261	.512						4.8

Hobson, Clell Lavern "Butch"

YEAR	TM/L	G	W	L	PCT	STANDING			M/Y	W-EXP	A-E
1992	Bos-A	162	73	89	.451	7 E				73.5	-0.5
1993	Bos-A	162	80	82	.494	5 E				79.8	0.2
1994	Bos-A	115	54	61	.470	4 E				51.0	3.0
3		439	207	232	.472						2.7

Hodges, Gilbert Raymond "Gil"

YEAR	TM/L	G	W	L	PCT	STANDING			M/Y	W-EXP	A-E
1963	Was-N	121	42	79	.347	10	10		3/3	42.6	-0.6
1964	Was-N	162	62	100	.383	9				64.7	-2.7
1965	Was-N	162	70	92	.432	8				67.3	2.7
1966	Was-N	159	71	88	.447	8				68.4	2.6
1967	Was-N	161	76	85	.472	●6				70.9	5.1
1968	NY-N	163	73	89	.451	9				77.8	-4.8
1969	NY-N	162	100	62	.617	★1 E				91.1	8.9
1970	NY-N	162	83	79	.512	3 E				87.8	-4.8
1971	NY-N	162	83	79	.512	●3 E				85.3	-2.3
9		1414	660	753	.467						4.1

Hoey, Frederick C. "Fred"

YEAR	TM/L	G	W	L	PCT	STANDING			M/Y	W-EXP	A-E
1899	NY-N	87	31	55	.360	9	10		2/2	36.2	-5.2

Holbert, William H. "Bill"

YEAR	TM/L	G	W	L	PCT	STANDING			M/Y	W-EXP	A-E
1879	Syr-N*	1	0	1	.000	6	6	7	2/3	0.3	-0.3

Hollingshead, John Samuel "Holly"

YEAR	TM/L	G	W	L	PCT	STANDING			M/Y	W-EXP	A-E
1875	Was-n*	20	4	16	.200	8	10		1/2	-2.4	6.4
1884	Was-a	62	12	50	.194	12	12		1/2	10.8	1.2
2		82	16	66	.195						7.6

Holmes, Thomas Francis "Tommy"

YEAR	TM/L	G	W	L	PCT	STANDING			M/Y	W-EXP	A-E
1951	Bos-N*	95	48	47	.505	5	4		2/2	51.3	-3.3
1952	Bos-N	35	13	22	.371	7	7		1/2	15.5	-2.5
2		130	61	69	.469						-5.8

Hornsby, Rogers

YEAR	TM/L	G	W	L	PCT	STANDING			M/Y	W-EXP	A-E
1925	StL-N*	115	64	51	.557	8	4		2/2	62.0	2.0
1926	StL-N*	156	89	65	.578	★1				90.5	-1.5
1927	NY-N*	33	22	10	.688	4	3		2/2	17.9	4.1
1928	Bos-N*	122	39	83	.320	7	7		2/2	42.2	-3.2
1930	Chi-N*	4	4	0	1.000	2	2		2/2	2.3	1.7
1931	Chi-N*	156	84	70	.545	3				88.3	-4.3
1932	Chi-N*	99	53	46	.535	2	1		1/2	55.2	-2.2
1933	StL-A*	54	19	33	.365	8	8		3/3	21.0	-2.0
1934	StL-A*	154	67	85	.441	6				63.8	3.2
1935	StL-A*	155	65	87	.428	7				56.5	8.5
1936	StL-A*	155	57	95	.375	7				53.5	3.5
1937	StL-A*	78	25	52	.325	7	8		1/2	24.7	0.3
1952	StL-A	51	22	29	.431	8	7		1/2	21.1	0.9
	Cin-N	51	27	24	.529	7	6		3/3	24.0	3.0
1953	Cin-N	147	64	82	.438	6	6		1/2	66.2	-2.2
14		1530	701	812	.463						11.9

Houk, Ralph George "Ralph"

YEAR	TM/L	G	W	L	PCT	STANDING			M/Y	W-EXP	A-E
1961	NY-A	163	109	53	.673	★1				102.7	6.3
1962	NY-A	162	96	66	.593	★1				94.5	1.5
1963	NY-A	161	104	57	.646	1				98.4	5.6
1966	NY-A	140	66	73	.475	10	10		2/2	69.4	-3.4
1967	NY-A	163	72	90	.444	9				69.8	2.2
1968	NY-A	164	83	79	.512	5				81.6	1.4
1969	NY-A	162	80	81	.497	5 E				77.7	2.3
1970	NY-A	163	93	69	.574	2 E				88.2	4.8
1971	NY-A	162	82	80	.506	4 E				81.7	0.3
1972	NY-A	155	79	76	.510	4 E				80.9	-1.9
1973	NY-A	162	80	82	.494	4 E				84.3	-4.3
1974	Det-A	162	72	90	.444	6 E				65.8	6.2
1975	Det-A	159	57	102	.358	6 E				57.3	-0.3
1976	Det-A	161	74	87	.460	5 E				70.0	4.0
1977	Det-A	162	74	88	.457	4 E				77.3	-3.3
1978	Det-A	162	86	76	.531	5 E				87.3	-1.3
1981(1)	Bos-A	56	30	26	.536	5 E					
(2)	Bos-A	52	29	23	.558	●2 E				57.7	1.3
1982	Bos-A	162	89	73	.549	3 E				85.0	4.0
1983	Bos-A	162	78	84	.481	6 E				76.0	2.0
1984	Bos-A	162	86	76	.531	4 E				85.4	0.6
20		3157	1619	1531	.514						27.8

Howard, Frank Oliver

YEAR	TM/L	G	W	L	PCT	STANDING			M/Y	W-EXP	A-E
1981(1)	SD-N	56	23	33	.411	6 W					
(2)	SD-N	54	18	36	.333	6 W				47.1	-6.1
1983	NY-N	116	52	64	.448	6 E	6 E		2/2	49.9	2.1

YEAR	TM/L	G	W	L	PCT	STANDING			M/Y	W-EXP	A-E
	2	226	93	133	.412						-4.0
Howe, Arthur Henry "Art"											
1989	Hou-N	162	86	76	.531	3 W				78.7	7.3
1990	Hou-N	162	75	87	.463	●4 W				72.0	3.0
1991	Hou-N	162	65	97	.401	6 W				69.2	-4.2
1992	Hou-N	162	81	81	.500	4 W				74.6	6.4
1993	Hou-N	162	85	77	.525	3 W				90.0	-5.0
5		810	392	418	.484						7.6
Howley, Daniel Philip "Dan"											
1927	StL-A	155	59	94	.386	7				59.8	-0.8
1928	StL-A	154	82	72	.532	3				79.9	2.1
1929	StL-A	154	79	73	.520	4				78.0	1.0
1930	Cin-N	154	59	95	.383	7				58.7	0.3
1931	Cin-N	154	58	96	.377	8				61.7	-3.7
1932	Cin-N	155	60	94	.390	8				62.4	-2.4
6		926	397	524	.431						-3.5
Howser, Richard Dalton "Dick"											
1978	NY-A	1	0	1	.000	3 E	4 E	▲★E	2/3	0.6	-0.6
1980	NY-A	162	103	59	.636	1 E				96.7	6.3
1981(2)	KC-A	33	20	13	.606	●2 W	1 W		2/2	16.2	3.8
1982	KC-A	162	90	72	.556	2 W				87.6	2.4
1983	KC-A	163	79	83	.488	2 W				73.9	5.1
1984	KC-A	162	84	78	.519	1 W				79.7	4.3
1985	KC-A	162	91	71	.562	★1 W				86.0	5.0
1986	KC-A	88	40	48	.455	4 W	●3W		1/2	42.9	-2.9
8		933	507	425	.544						23.4
Huff, George A.											
1907	Bos-A	8	2	6	.250	●4	6	7	2/4	3.4	-1.4
Huggins, Miller James											
1913	StL-N*	153	51	99	.340	8				51.5	-0.5
1914	StL-N*	157	81	72	.529	3				78.5	2.5
1915	StL-N*	157	72	81	.471	6				75.3	-3.3
1916	StL-N*	153	60	93	.392	●7				59.4	0.6
1917	StL-N	154	82	70	.539	3				72.0	10.0
1918	NY-A	126	60	63	.488	4				63.4	-3.4
1919	NY-A	141	80	59	.576	3				77.3	2.7
1920	NY-A	154	95	59	.617	3				97.3	-2.3
1921	NY-A	153	98	55	.641	1				98.4	-0.4
1922	NY-A	154	94	60	.610	1				91.1	2.9
1923	NY-A	152	98	54	.645	★1				95.6	2.4
1924	NY-A	153	89	63	.586	2				88.7	0.3
1925	NY-A	156	69	85	.448	7				70.4	-1.4
1926	NY-A	155	91	63	.591	1				89.7	1.3
1927	NY-A	155	110	44	.714	★1				112.4	-2.4
1928	NY-A	154	101	53	.656	★1				96.6	4.4
1929	NY-A	143	82	61	.573	2	2		1/2	82.0	0.0
17		2570	1413	1134	.555						13.5
Hunter, Gordon William "Billy"											
1977	Tex-A	93	60	33	.645	5 W	2 W		4/4	52.9	7.1
1978	Tex-A	161	86	75	.534	●2 W	●2W		1/2	86.8	-0.8
2		254	146	108	.575						6.4
Hurst, Timothy Carroll "Tim"											
1898	StL-N	154	39	111	.260	12				40.6	-1.6
Hutchinson, Frederick Charles "Fred"											
1952	Det-A*	83	27	55	.329	8	8		2/2	31.0	-4.0
1953	Det-A*	158	60	94	.390	6				55.6	4.4
1954	Det-A	155	68	86	.442	5				68.5	-0.5
1956	StL-N	156	76	78	.494	4				75.0	1.0
1957	StL-N	154	87	67	.565	2				84.1	2.9
1958	StL-N	144	69	75	.479	5	●5		1/2	63.9	5.1
1959	Cin-N	74	39	35	.527	7	●5		2/2	38.2	0.8
1960	Cin-N	154	67	87	.435	6				71.7	-4.7
1961	Cin-N	154	93	61	.604	1				82.7	10.3
1962	Cin-N	162	98	64	.605	3				92.6	5.4
1963	Cin-N	162	86	76	.531	5				86.9	-0.9
1964	Cin-N	100	54	45	.545	3	●2		1/4	55.8	-1.8
	Cin-N	10	6	4	.600	4	3	●2	3/4	5.6	0.4
12		1666	830	827	.501						18.5
Irwin, Arthur Albert											
1889	Was-N*	76	28	45	.384	8	8		2/2	23.2	4.8
1891	Bos-a*	139	93	42	.689	1				97.8	-4.8
1892(1)	Was-N	74	35	39	.473	●11	7		2/2		
(2)	Was-N	34	11	21	.344	11	12		1/2	44.0	2.0
1894	Phi-N*	132	71	57	.555	4				77.1	-6.1
1895	Phi-N	133	78	53	.595	3				74.0	4.0
1896	NY-N	90	36	53	.404	10	7		1/2	45.0	-9.0
1898	Was-N	30	10	19	.345	11	11		4/4	10.4	-0.4
1899	Was-N	155	54	98	.355	11				54.4	-0.4
8		863	416	427	.493						-9.9
Jennings, Hugh Ambrose "Hughie"											
1907	Det-A*	153	92	58	.613	1				92.2	-0.2
1908	Det-A	154	90	63	.588	1				87.3	2.7
1909	Det-A*	158	98	54	.645	1				95.2	2.8
1910	Det-A	155	86	68	.558	3				87.2	-1.2
1911	Det-A	154	89	65	.578	2				82.1	6.9
1912	Det-A*	154	69	84	.451	6				71.0	-2.0
1913	Det-A	153	66	87	.431	6				67.2	-1.2
1914	Det-A	157	80	73	.523	4				76.2	3.8
1915	Det-A	156	100	54	.649	2				95.3	4.7
1916	Det-A	155	87	67	.565	3				84.9	2.1
1917	Det-A	155	78	75	.510	4				83.1	-5.1
1918	Det-A*	128	55	71	.437	7				54.4	0.6
1919	Det-A	140	80	60	.571	4				74.1	5.9
1920	Det-A	155	61	93	.396	7				59.5	1.5
1924	NY-N	44	32	12	.727	3	1	1	2/3	28.0	4.0
1925	NY-N	32	21	11	.656	1	1	2	2/3	16.7	4.3
16		2203	1184	995	.543						29.7
Johnson, Darrell Dean											
1974	Bos-A	162	84	78	.519	3 E				84.6	-0.6
1975	Bos-A	160	95	65	.594	♦1 E				88.5	6.5
1976	Bos-A	86	41	45	.477	5 E	3 E		1/2	46.1	-5.1
1977	Sea-A	162	64	98	.395	6 W				58.1	5.9
1978	Sea-A	160	56	104	.350	7 W				58.1	-2.1
1979	Sea-A	162	67	95	.414	6 W				70.4	-3.4
1980	Sea-A	105	39	65	.375	6 W	7 W		1/2	40.0	-1.0
1982	Tex-A	66	26	40	.394	6 W	6 W		2/2	26.2	-0.2
8		1063	472	590	.444						0.1
Johnson, David Allen "Davey"											
1984	NY-N	162	90	72	.556	2 E				78.5	11.5
1985	NY-N	162	98	64	.605	2 E				94.6	3.4
1986	NY-N	162	108	54	.667	★1 E				102.2	5.8
1987	NY-N	162	92	70	.568	2 E				93.2	-1.2
1988	NY-N	160	100	60	.625	1 E				98.5	1.5
1989	NY-N	162	87	75	.537	2 E				90.4	-3.4
1990	NY-N	42	20	22	.476	4 E	2 E		1/2	25.3	-5.3
1993	Cin-N	118	53	65	.449	5 W	5 W		2/2	54.5	-1.5
1994	Cin-N	115	66	48	.579	1 C				68.5	-2.5
9		1245	714	530	.574						8.2
Johnson, Roy J											
1944	Chi-N	1	0	1	.000	8	8	4	2/3	0.5	-0.5
Johnson, Walter Perry											
1929	Was-A	153	71	81	.467	5				71.6	-0.6
1930	Was-A	154	94	60	.610	2				96.0	-2.0
1931	Was-A	156	92	62	.597	3				91.5	0.5
1932	Was-A	154	93	61	.604	3				88.7	4.3
1933	Cle-A	99	48	51	.485	5	4		3/3	48.5	-0.5
1934	Cle-A	154	85	69	.552	3				81.8	3.2
1935	Cle-A	96	46	48	.489	5	3		1/2	49.2	-3.2
7		966	529	432	.550						1.7
Jones, Fielder Allison											
1904	Chi-A*	114	66	47	.584	4	3		2/2	66.4	-0.4
1905	Chi-A*	158	92	60	.605	2				94.6	-2.6
1906	Chi-A*	154	93	58	.616	★1				88.3	4.7
1907	Chi-A*	157	87	64	.576	3				88.7	-1.7
1908	Chi-A*	156	88	64	.579	3				83.9	4.1
1914	StL-F*	40	12	26	.316	7	8		2/2	15.5	-3.5
1915	StL-F*	159	87	67	.565	2				88.9	-1.9
1916	StL-A	158	79	75	.513	5				81.8	-2.8
1917	StL-A	155	57	97	.370	7				57.9	-0.9
1918	StL-A	46	22	24	.478	6	5		1/3	22.1	-0.1
10		1297	683	582	.540						-5.0
Joost, Edwin David "Eddie"											
1954	Phi-A*	156	51	103	.331	8				43.8	7.2
Joyce, William Michael "Bill"											
1896	NY-N*	43	28	14	.667	10	7		2/2	21.2	6.8
1897	NY-N*	138	83	48	.634	3				83.1	-0.1
1898	NY-N*	43	22	21	.512	6	7		1/3	22.5	-0.5
	NY-N*	92	46	39	.541	7	7		3/3	44.4	1.6
3		316	179	122	.595						7.7
Jurges, William Frederick "Billy"											
1959	Bos-A	80	44	36	.550	8	5		3/3	41.5	2.5
1960	Bos-A	42	15	27	.357	8	7		1/3	17.9	-2.9
2		122	59	63	.484						-0.4
Kasko, Edward Michael "Eddie"											
1970	Bos-A	162	87	75	.537	3 E				87.3	-0.3
1971	Bos-A	162	85	77	.525	3 E				83.5	1.5
1972	Bos-A	155	85	70	.548	2 E				79.6	5.4
1973	Bos-A	161	89	73	.547	2 E	2 E		1/2	89.8	-1.8
4		640	345	295	.539						4.8
Keane, John Joseph "Johnny"											
1961	StL-N	80	47	33	.587	6	5		2/2	41.8	5.2
1962	StL-N	163	84	78	.519	6				92.1	-8.1
1963	StL-N	162	93	69	.574	2				93.3	-0.3
1964	StL-N	162	93	69	.574	★1				87.5	5.5
1965	NY-A	162	77	85	.475	6				81.8	-4.8
1966	NY-A	20	4	16	.200	10	10		1/2	10.0	-6.0
5		749	398	350	.532						-8.5
Kelley, Joseph James "Joe"											
1902	Cin-N*	60	34	26	.567	6	4		3/3	33.0	1.0
1903	Cin-N*	141	74	65	.532	4				79.8	-5.8
1904	Cin-N*	157	88	65	.575	3				92.3	-4.3
1905	Cin-N*	155	79	74	.516	5				80.2	-1.2
1908	Bos-N*	156	63	91	.409	6				67.6	-4.6
5		669	338	321	.513						-14.8

YEAR	TM/L	G	W	L	PCT	STANDING			M/Y	W-EXP	A-E
Kelly, Jay Thomas "Tom"											
1986	Min-A	23	12	11	.522	7 W	6 W		2/2	10.2	1.8
1987	Min-A	162	85	77	.525	★1 W				79.1	5.9
1988	Min-A	162	91	71	.562	2 W				89.8	1.2
1989	Min-A	162	80	82	.494	5 W				81.2	-1.2
1990	Min-A	162	74	88	.457	7 W				74.6	-0.6
1991	Min-A	162	95	67	.586	★1 W				93.5	1.5
1992	Min-A	162	90	72	.556	2 W				90.6	-0.6
1993	Min-A	162	71	91	.438	●5 W				67.6	3.4
1994	Min-A	113	53	60	.469	4 C				48.1	4.9
	9	1270	651	619	.513						16.4
Kelly, John O.											
1887	Lou-a	139	76	60	.559	4				76.5	-0.5
1888	Lou-a	39	10	29	.256	8	7		1/4	14.8	-4.8
	2	178	86	89	.491						-5.3
Kelly, Michael Joseph "King"											
1887	Bos-N*	95	49	43	.533	5	5		1/2	48.5	0.5
1890	Bos-P*	133	81	48	.628	1				82.9	-1.9
1891	Cin-a*	102	43	57	.430	6				41.7	1.3
	3	330	173	148	.539						-0.1
Kennedy, James C. "Jim"											
1890	Bro-a	100	26	73	.263	8				28.8	-2.8
Kennedy, Kevin Curtis											
1993	Tex-A	162	86	76	.531	2 W				89.1	-3.1
1994	Tex-A	114	52	62	.456	1 W				49.6	2.4
	2	276	138	138	.500						-0.6
Kennedy, Robert Daniel "Bob"											
1963	Chi-N	162	82	80	.506	7				80.1	1.9
1964	Chi-N	162	76	86	.469	8				73.3	2.7
1965	Chi-N	58	24	32	.429	9	8		1/2	24.8	-0.8
1968	Oak-A	163	82	80	.506	6				83.9	-1.9
	4	545	264	278	.487						1.9
Kerins, John Nelson											
1888	Lou-a*	7	3	4	.429	8	8	7	3/4	2.7	0.3
1890	StL-a*	17	9	8	.529	4	4	3	2/6	10.0	-1.0
	2	24	12	12	.500						-0.6
Kessinger, Donald Eulon "Don"											
1979	Chi-A	106	46	60	.434	5 W	5 W		1/2	51.8	-5.8
Killefer, William Lavier "Bill"											
1921	Chi-N*	57	23	34	.404	6	7		2/2	24.7	-1.7
1922	Chi-N	156	80	74	.519	5				73.5	6.5
1923	Chi-N	154	83	71	.539	4				82.1	0.9
1924	Chi-N	154	81	72	.529	5				76.4	4.6
1925	Chi-N	75	33	42	.440	7	8		1/3	35.2	-2.2
1930	StL-A	154	64	90	.416	6				64.6	-0.6
1931	StL-A	154	63	91	.409	5				63.2	-0.2
1932	StL-A	154	63	91	.409	6				62.1	0.9
1933	StL-A	91	34	57	.374	8	8		1/3	36.7	-2.7
	9	1149	524	622	.457						5.6
King, Clyde Edward											
1969	SF-N	162	90	72	.556	2 W				89.0	1.0
1970	SF-N	42	19	23	.452	4 W	3 W		1/2	21.1	-2.1
1974	Atl-N	64	38	25	.603	4 W	3 W		2/2	35.7	2.3
1975	Atl-N	134	58	76	.433	5 W			1/2	53.4	4.6
1982	NY-A	62	29	33	.468	●5 E	5 E		3/3	30.7	-1.7
	5	464	234	229	.505						4.1
Kittridge, Malachi J.											
1904	Was-A*	18	1	16	.059	8	8		1/2	4.7	-3.7
Klein, Louis Frank "Lou"											
1961	Chi-N	11	5	6	.455	7	7	7	8/9	4.7	0.3
1962	Chi-N	30	12	18	.400	9	9	9	2/3	11.4	0.6
1965	Chi-N	106	48	58	.453	9	8		2/2	47.0	1.0
	3	147	65	82	.442						1.9
Kling, John "Johnny"											
1912	Bos-N*	155	52	101	.340	8				60.6	-8.6
Knabe, Franz Otto "Otto"											
1914	Bal-F*	160	84	70	.545	3				78.8	5.2
1915	Bal-F*	155	47	107	.305	8				55.4	-8.4
	2	315	131	177	.425						-3.2
Knight, Alonzo P. "Lon"											
1883	Phi-a*	98	66	32	.673	1				63.4	2.6
1884	Phi-a*	109	61	46	.570	7				67.1	-6.1
	2	207	127	78	.620						-3.5
Knoop, Robert Frank "Bobby"											
1994	Cal-A	2	1	1	.500	3 W	2 W	4 W	2/3	0.8	0.2
Krol, John Thomas "Jack"											
1978	StL-N	2	1	1	.500	6 E	6 E	5 E	2/3	0.9	0.1
1980	StL-N	1	0	1	.000	6 E	6 E	4 E	2/4	0.5	-0.5
	2	3	1	2	.333						-0.4
Kuehl, Karl Otto											
1976	Mon-N	128	43	85	.336	6 E	6 E		1/2	46.8	-3.8
Kuenn, Harvey Edward											
1975	Mil-A	1	1	0	1.000	5 E	5 E		2/2	0.4	0.6
1982	Mil-A	116	72	43	.626	5 E	◆1 E		2/2	69.3	2.7

YEAR	TM/L	G	W	L	PCT	STANDING			M/Y	W-EXP	A-E
1983	Mil-A	162	87	75	.537	5 E				86.6	0.4
	3	279	160	118	.576						3.7
Kuhel, Joseph Anthony "Joe"											
1948	Was-A	154	56	97	.366	7				54.6	1.4
1949	Was-A	154	50	104	.325	8				49.3	0.7
	2	308	106	201	.345						2.1
Lachemann, Marcel Ernest											
1994	Cal-A	74	30	44	.405	2 W	4 W		3/3	30.0	-0.0
Lachemann, Rene George											
1981(1)	Sea-A	33	15	18	.455	7 W	6 W		2/2		
(2)	Sea-A	52	23	29	.442	5 W				34.9	3.1
1982	Sea-A	162	76	86	.469	4 W				74.7	1.3
1983	Sea-A	73	26	47	.356	7 W	7 W		1/2	27.8	-1.8
1984	Mil-A	161	67	94	.416	7 E				71.0	-4.0
1993	Fla-N	162	64	98	.395	6 E				65.9	-1.9
1994	Fla-N	115	51	54	.486	5 E				46.7	4.3
	6	758	322	426	.430						1.0
Lajoie, Napoleon "Nap"											
1905	Cle-A*	58	37	21	.638	●1	5		1/3	28.2	8.8
	Cle-A*	56	19	36	.345	2	5		3/3	26.7	-7.7
1906	Cle-A*	157	89	64	.582	3				96.6	-7.6
1907	Cle-A*	158	85	67	.559	4				76.6	8.4
1908	Cle-A*	157	90	64	.584	2				90.0	-0.0
1909	Cle-A*	114	57	57	.500	4	6		1/2	53.6	3.4
	5	700	377	309	.550						5.3
Lake, Frederick Lovett "Fred"											
1908	Bos-A	40	22	17	.564	6	5		2/2	21.0	1.0
1909	Bos-A	152	88	63	.583	3				80.6	7.4
1910	Bos-N*	157	53	100	.346	8				54.1	-1.1
	3	349	163	180	.475						7.3
Lamont, Gene William											
1992	Chi-A	162	86	76	.531	3 W				85.9	0.1
1993	Chi-A	162	94	68	.580	1 W				92.3	1.7
1994	Chi-A	113	67	46	.593	1 C				69.3	-2.3
	3	437	247	190	.565						-0.4
Lanier, Harold Clifton "Hal"											
1986	Hou-N	162	96	66	.593	1 W				90.3	5.7
1987	Hou-N	162	76	86	.469	3 W				77.9	-1.9
1988	Hou-N	162	82	80	.506	5 W				79.5	2.5
	3	486	254	232	.523						6.4
Larkin, Henry E. "Ted"											
1890	Cle-P*	79	34	45	.430	7	7		1/2	30.9	3.1
LaRussa, Anthony "Tony"											
1979	Chi-A	54	27	27	.500	5 W	5 W		2/2	26.4	0.6
1980	Chi-A	162	70	90	.438	5 W				65.8	4.2
1981(1)	Chi-A	53	31	22	.585	3 W					
(2)	Chi-A	53	23	30	.434	6 W				58.5	-4.5
1982	Chi-A	162	87	75	.537	3 W				88.5	-1.5
1983	Chi-A	162	99	63	.611	1 W				96.0	3.0
1984	Chi-A	162	74	88	.457	●5 W				75.2	-1.2
1985	Chi-A	163	85	77	.525	3 W				82.6	2.4
1986	Chi-A	64	26	38	.406	6 W	5 W		1/3	29.7	-3.7
	Oak-A	79	45	34	.570	7 W	●3 W		3/3	38.1	6.9
1987	Oak-A	162	81	81	.500	3 W				82.6	-1.6
1988	Oak-A	162	104	58	.642	◆1 W				99.2	4.8
1989	Oak-A	162	99	63	.611	★1 W				95.5	3.5
1990	Oak-A	162	103	59	.636	◆1 W				98.2	4.8
1991	Oak-A	162	84	78	.519	4 W				79.4	4.6
1992	Oak-A	162	96	66	.593	1 W				88.4	7.6
1993	Oak-A	162	68	94	.420	7 W				68.3	-0.3
1994	Oak-A	114	51	63	.447	2 W				53.2	-2.2
	16	2362	1253	1106	.531						27.2
Lasorda, Thomas Charles "Tom"											
1976	LA-N	4	2	2	.500	2 W	2 W		2/2	2.2	-0.2
1977	LA-N	162	98	64	.605	◆1 W				100.4	-2.4
1978	LA-N	162	95	67	.586	◆1 W				97.3	-2.3
1979	LA-N	162	79	83	.488	3 W				83.2	-4.2
1980	LA-N	163	92	71	.564	▲2 W				89.3	2.7
1981(1)	LA-N	57	36	21	.632	★1 W					
(2)	LA-N	53	27	26	.509	4 W				65.4	-2.4
1982	LA-N	162	88	74	.543	2 W				89.4	-1.4
1983	LA-N	163	91	71	.562	1 W				85.9	5.1
1984	LA-N	162	79	83	.488	4 W				78.8	0.2
1985	LA-N	162	95	67	.586	1 W				92.1	2.9
1986	LA-N	162	73	89	.451	5 W				76.7	-3.7
1987	LA-N	162	73	89	.451	4 W				76.8	-3.8
1988	LA-N	162	94	67	.584	★1 W				89.9	4.1
1989	LA-N	160	77	83	.481	4 W				82.1	-5.1
1990	LA-N	162	86	76	.531	2 W				85.4	0.6
1991	LA-N	162	93	69	.574	2 W				91.9	1.1
1992	LA-N	162	63	99	.389	6 W				71.2	-8.2
1993	LA-N	162	81	81	.500	4 W				82.4	-1.4
1994	LA-N	114	58	56	.509	1 W				59.3	-1.3
	19	2820	1480	1338	.525						-19.4
Latham, George Warren "Juice"											
1875	NH-n*	18	4	14	.222	11	8	8	2/3	1.5	2.5
1882	Phi-a*	75	41	34	.547	2				39.1	1.9

YEAR	TM/L	G	W	L	PCT	STANDING	M/Y	W-EXP	A-E
	2	93	45	48	.484				4.4

Latham, Walter Arlington "Arlie"

YEAR	TM/L	G	W	L	PCT	STANDING	M/Y	W-EXP	A-E
1896	StL-N*	3	0	3	.000	10 10 11	2/5	0.8	-0.8

Lavagetto, Harry Arthur "Cookie"

YEAR	TM/L	G	W	L	PCT	STANDING	M/Y	W-EXP	A-E
1957	Was-A	134	51	83	.381	8 8	2/2	49.3	1.7
1958	Was-A	156	61	93	.396	8		56.8	4.2
1959	Was-A	154	63	91	.409	8		68.6	-5.6
1960	Was-A	154	73	81	.474	5		74.6	-1.6
1961	Min-A	49	19	30	.388	8 7	1/4	22.4	-3.4
	Min-A	10	4	6	.400	9 9 7	3/4	4.6	-0.6
5		657	271	384	.414				-5.3

Leadley, Robert H. "Bob"

YEAR	TM/L	G	W	L	PCT	STANDING	M/Y	W-EXP	A-E
1888	Det-N	40	19	19	.500	3 5	2/2	21.5	-2.5
1890	Cle-N	58	23	33	.411	7 7	2/2	20.2	2.8
1891	Cle-N	68	34	34	.500	4 5	1/2	31.8	2.2
3		166	76	86	.469				2.5

Lefebvre, James Kenneth "Jim"

YEAR	TM/L	G	W	L	PCT	STANDING	M/Y	W-EXP	A-E
1989	Sea-A	162	73	89	.451	6 W		77.6	-4.6
1990	Sea-A	162	77	85	.475	5 W		76.8	0.2
1991	Sea-A	162	83	79	.512	5 W		83.9	-0.9
1992	Chi-N	162	78	84	.481	4 E		77.6	0.4
1993	Chi-N	163	84	78	.519	4 E		80.9	3.1
5		811	395	415	.488				-1.7

Lemon, James Robert "Jim"

YEAR	TM/L	G	W	L	PCT	STANDING	M/Y	W-EXP	A-E
1968	Was-A	161	65	96	.404	10		64.9	0.1

Lemon, Robert Granville "Bob"

YEAR	TM/L	G	W	L	PCT	STANDING	M/Y	W-EXP	A-E
1970	KC-A	110	46	64	.418	5 W ●4W	2/2	48.3	-2.3
1971	KC-A	161	85	76	.528	2 W		84.6	0.4
1972	KC-A	154	76	78	.494	4 W		80.9	-4.9
1977	Chi-A	162	90	72	.556	3 W		87.9	2.1
1978	Chi-A	74	34	40	.459	5 W 5 W	1/2	32.4	1.6
	NY-A	68	48	20	.706	4 E ▲★E	3/3	40.7	7.3
1979	NY-A	65	34	31	.523	4 E 4 E	1/2	35.0	-1.0
1981(2)	NY-A	25	11	14	.440	4 E 6 E	2/2	14.5	-3.5
1982	NY-A	14	6	8	.429	●4E 5 E	1/3	6.9	-0.9
8		833	430	403	.516				-1.4

Lennon, William F. "Bill"

YEAR	TM/L	G	W	L	PCT	STANDING	M/Y	W-EXP	A-E
1871	Kek-n*	14	5	9	.357	7 8	1/2	1.8	3.2

Leyland, James Richard "Jim"

YEAR	TM/L	G	W	L	PCT	STANDING	M/Y	W-EXP	A-E
1986	Pit-N	162	64	98	.395	6 E		77.2	-13.2
1987	Pit-N	162	80	82	.494	●4 E		78.9	1.1
1988	Pit-N	160	85	75	.531	2 E		83.7	1.3
1989	Pit-N	164	74	88	.457	5 E		76.4	-2.4
1990	Pit-N	162	95	67	.586	1 E		92.8	2.2
1991	Pit-N	162	98	64	.605	1 E		94.9	3.1
1992	Pit-N	162	96	66	.593	1 E		91.4	4.6
1993	Pit-N	162	75	87	.463	5 E		71.3	3.7
1994	Pit-N	114	53	61	.465	●3 C		45.7	7.3
9		1410	720	688	.511				7.6

Leyva, Nicolas Tomas "Nick"

YEAR	TM/L	G	W	L	PCT	STANDING	M/Y	W-EXP	A-E
1989	Phi-N	163	67	95	.414	6 E		70.0	-3.0
1990	Phi-N	162	77	85	.475	●4 E		72.5	4.5
1991	Phi-N	13	4	9	.308	6 E 3 E	1/2	6.1	-2.1
3		338	148	189	.439				-0.5

Lillis, Robert Perry "Bob"

YEAR	TM/L	G	W	L	PCT	STANDING	M/Y	W-EXP	A-E
1982	Hou-N	51	28	23	.549	5 W 5 W	2/2	23.7	4.3
1983	Hou-N	162	85	77	.525	3 W		80.7	4.3
1984	Hou-N	162	80	82	.494	●2 W		87.6	-7.6
1985	Hou-N	162	83	79	.512	●3 W		82.5	0.5
4		537	276	261	.514				1.5

Lipon, John Joseph "Johnny"

YEAR	TM/L	G	W	L	PCT	STANDING	M/Y	W-EXP	A-E
1971	Cle-A	59	18	41	.305	6 E 6 E	2/2	21.6	-3.6

Lobert, John Bernard "Hans"

YEAR	TM/L	G	W	L	PCT	STANDING	M/Y	W-EXP	A-E
1938	Phi-N	2	0	2	.000	8 8	2/2	0.6	-0.6
1942	Phi-N	151	42	109	.278	8		40.8	1.2
2		153	42	111	.275				0.6

Lockman, Carroll Walter "Whitey"

YEAR	TM/L	G	W	L	PCT	STANDING	M/Y	W-EXP	A-E
1972	Chi-N	65	39	26	.600	4 E 2 E	2/2	37.7	1.3
1973	Chi-N	161	77	84	.478	5 E		76.1	0.9
1974	Chi-N	93	41	52	.441	5 E 6 E	1/2	37.6	3.4
3		319	157	162	.492				5.5

Loftus, Thomas Joseph "Tom"

YEAR	TM/L	G	W	L	PCT	STANDING	M/Y	W-EXP	A-E
1884	Mil-U	12	8	4	.667	2		8.1	-0.1
1888	Cle-a	71	30	38	.441	8 6	2/2	25.3	4.7
1889	Cle-N	136	61	72	.459	6		60.5	0.5
1890	Cin-N	134	77	55	.583	4		77.2	-0.2
1891	Cin-N	138	56	81	.409	7		55.1	0.9
1900	Chi-N	146	65	75	.464	●5		58.7	6.3
1901	Chi-N	140	53	86	.381	6		57.5	-4.5
1902	Was-A	138	61	75	.449	6		60.4	0.6
1903	Was-A	140	43	94	.314	8		41.7	1.3
9		1055	454	580	.439				9.6

Lopat, Edmund Walter "Ed"

YEAR	TM/L	G	W	L	PCT	STANDING	M/Y	W-EXP	A-E
1963	KC-A	162	73	89	.451	8		71.6	1.4
1964	KC-A	52	17	35	.327	10 10	1/2	19.1	-2.1

YEAR	TM/L	G	W	L	PCT	STANDING	M/Y	W-EXP	A-E
	2	214	90	124	.421				-0.7

Lopez, Alfonso Ramon "Al"

YEAR	TM/L	G	W	L	PCT	STANDING	M/Y	W-EXP	A-E
1951	Cle-A	155	93	61	.604	2		87.6	5.4
1952	Cle-A	155	93	61	.604	2		92.8	0.2
1953	Cle-A	155	92	62	.597	2		91.3	0.7
1954	Cle-A	156	111	43	.721	1		102.7	8.3
1955	Cle-A	154	93	61	.604	2		87.0	6.0
1956	Cle-A	155	88	66	.571	2		90.6	-2.6
1957	Chi-A	155	90	64	.584	2		91.8	-1.8
1958	Chi-A	155	82	72	.532	2		79.0	3.0
1959	Chi-A	156	94	60	.610	1		85.6	8.4
1960	Chi-A	154	87	67	.565	3		89.5	-2.5
1961	Chi-A	163	86	76	.531	4		84.9	1.1
1962	Chi-A	162	85	77	.525	5		86.1	-1.1
1963	Chi-A	162	94	68	.580	2		96.2	-2.2
1964	Chi-A	162	98	64	.605	2		96.9	1.1
1965	Chi-A	162	95	67	.586	2		91.1	3.9
1968	Chi-A	11	6	5	.545	9 9 ●8	3/5	5.0	1.0
	Chi-A	36	15	21	.417	9 ●8	5/5	16.3	-1.3
1969	Chi-A	17	8	9	.471	4 W 5 W	1/2	7.4	0.6
17		2425	1410	1004	.584				28.3

Lord, Harry Donald

YEAR	TM/L	G	W	L	PCT	STANDING	M/Y	W-EXP	A-E
1915	Buf-F*	110	60	49	.550	8 6	3/3	49.9	10.1

Lowe, Robert Lincoln "Bobby"

YEAR	TM/L	G	W	L	PCT	STANDING	M/Y	W-EXP	A-E
1904	Det-A*	78	30	44	.405	7 7	2/2	30.3	-0.3

Lucchesi, Frank Joseph

YEAR	TM/L	G	W	L	PCT	STANDING	M/Y	W-EXP	A-E
1970	Phi-N	161	73	88	.453	5 E		66.3	6.7
1971	Phi-N	162	67	95	.414	6 E		66.9	0.1
1972	Phi-N	76	26	50	.342	6 E 6 E	1/2	30.9	-4.9
1975	Tex-A	67	35	32	.522	4 W 3 W	2/2	32.7	2.3
1976	Tex-A	162	76	86	.469	●4W		77.1	-1.1
1977	Tex-A	62	31	31	.500	●3 W 2 W	1/4	35.3	-4.3
1987	Chi-N	25	8	17	.320	5 E 6 E	2/2	11.3	-3.3
7		715	316	399	.442				-4.4

Lumley, Harry G

YEAR	TM/L	G	W	L	PCT	STANDING	M/Y	W-EXP	A-E
1909	Bro-N*	155	55	98	.359	6		55.6	-0.6

Lyons, Theodore Amar "Ted"

YEAR	TM/L	G	W	L	PCT	STANDING	M/Y	W-EXP	A-E
1946	Chi-A	125	64	60	.516	7 5	2/2	59.1	4.9
1947	Chi-A	155	70	84	.455	6		65.4	4.6
1948	Chi-A	154	51	101	.336	8		50.4	0.6
3		434	185	245	.430				10.1

Mack, Cornelius Alexander "Connie"

YEAR	TM/L	G	W	L	PCT	STANDING	M/Y	W-EXP	A-E
1894	Pit-N*	23	12	10	.545	7 7	2/2	10.8	1.2
1895	Pit-N*	135	71	61	.538	7		68.1	2.9
1896	Pit-N*	131	66	63	.512	6		68.5	-2.5
1901	Phi-A	137	74	62	.544	4		71.9	2.1
1902	Phi-A	137	83	53	.610	1		81.0	2.0
1903	Phi-A	137	75	60	.556	2		75.7	-0.7
1904	Phi-A	155	81	70	.536	5		81.7	-0.7
1905	Phi-A	152	92	56	.622	1		88.5	3.5
1906	Phi-A	149	78	67	.538	4		74.5	3.5
1907	Phi-A	150	88	57	.607	2		80.4	7.6
1908	Phi-A	157	68	85	.444	6		67.7	0.3
1909	Phi-A	153	95	58	.621	2		99.5	-4.5
1910	Phi-A	155	102	48	.680	★1		101.0	1.0
1911	Phi-A	152	101	50	.669	★1		100.7	0.3
1912	Phi-A	153	90	62	.592	3		87.8	2.2
1913	Phi-A	153	96	57	.627	★1		96.6	-0.6
1914	Phi-A	158	99	53	.651	1		99.2	-0.2
1915	Phi-A	154	43	109	.283	8		42.3	0.7
1916	Phi-A	154	36	117	.235	8		41.5	-5.5
1917	Phi-A	154	55	98	.359	8		59.2	-4.2
1918	Phi-A	130	52	76	.406	8		50.0	2.0
1919	Phi-A	140	36	104	.257	8		40.8	-4.8
1920	Phi-A	156	48	106	.312	8		49.3	-1.3
1921	Phi-A	155	53	100	.346	8		54.0	-1.0
1922	Phi-A	155	65	89	.422	7		65.1	-0.1
1923	Phi-A	153	69	83	.454	6		66.2	2.8
1924	Phi-A	152	71	81	.467	5		67.0	4.0
1925	Phi-A	153	88	64	.579	2		87.1	0.9
1926	Phi-A	150	83	67	.553	3		86.1	-3.1
1927	Phi-A	155	91	63	.591	2		87.9	3.1
1928	Phi-A	153	98	55	.641	2		97.4	0.6
1929	Phi-A	151	104	46	.693	★1		102.1	1.9
1930	Phi-A	154	102	52	.662	★1		95.0	7.0
1931	Phi-A	153	107	45	.704	1		98.4	8.6
1932	Phi-A	154	94	60	.610	2		97.5	-3.5
1933	Phi-A	152	79	72	.523	3		77.5	1.5
1934	Phi-A	153	68	82	.453	5		68.1	-0.1
1935	Phi-A	149	58	91	.389	8		59.8	-1.8
1936	Phi-A	154	53	100	.346	8		47.1	5.9
1937	Phi-A	120	39	80	.328	7 7	1/2	48.0	-9.0
1938	Phi-A	154	53	99	.349	8		55.1	-2.1
1939	Phi-A	62	25	37	.403	6 7	1/2	19.7	5.3
1940	Phi-A	154	54	100	.351	8		55.9	-1.9
1941	Phi-A	154	64	90	.416	8		65.0	-1.0
1942	Phi-A	154	55	99	.357	8		51.5	3.5
1943	Phi-A	155	49	105	.318	8		53.4	-4.4
1944	Phi-A	155	72	82	.468	●5		69.3	2.7

YEAR	TM/L	G	W	L	PCT	STANDING	M/Y	W-EXP	A-E
1945	Phi-A	153	52	98	.347	8		59.1	-7.1
1946	Phi-A	155	49	105	.318	8		60.8	-11.8
1947	Phi-A	156	78	76	.506	5		79.0	-1.0
1948	Phi-A	154	84	70	.545	4		76.4	7.6
1949	Phi-A	154	81	73	.526	5		77.1	3.9
1950	Phi-A	154	52	102	.338	8		54.3	-2.3
	53	7755	3731	3948	.486				13.6

Mack, Dennis Joseph "Denny"

YEAR	TM/L	G	W	L	PCT	STANDING	M/Y	W-EXP	A-E
1882	Lou-a*	80	42	38	.525	3		48.7	-6.7

Mack, Earle Thaddeus

YEAR	TM/L	G	W	L	PCT	STANDING	M/Y	W-EXP	A-E
1937	Phi-A	34	15	17	.469	7 7	2/2	12.9	2.1
1939	Phi-A	91	30	60	.333	6 7	2/2	28.6	1.4
	2	125	45	77	.369				3.5

Macullar, James F. "Jimmy"

YEAR	TM/L	G	W	L	PCT	STANDING	M/Y	W-EXP	A-E
1879	Syr-N*	27	5	21	.192	6 7	3/3	6.6	-1.6

Magee, Leo Christopher "Lee"

YEAR	TM/L	G	W	L	PCT	STANDING	M/Y	W-EXP	A-E
1915	Bro-F*	118	53	64	.453	7 7	1/2	56.5	-3.5

Malone, Ferguson G. "Fergy"

YEAR	TM/L	G	W	L	PCT	STANDING	M/Y	W-EXP	A-E
1873	Phi-n*	10	8	2	.800	2 2	1/2	6.8	1.2
1874	Chi-n*	36	18	18	.500	4 5	1/2	15.1	2.9
1884	Phi-U*	67	21	46	.313	7		23.1	-2.1
	3	113	47	66	.416				2.0

Manning, James H. "Jimmy"

YEAR	TM/L	G	W	L	PCT	STANDING	M/Y	W-EXP	A-E
1901	Was-A	138	61	73	.455	6		58.3	2.7

Manning, John E. "Jack"

YEAR	TM/L	G	W	L	PCT	STANDING	M/Y	W-EXP	A-E
1877	Cin-N*	20	7	12	.368	6 6	3/3	4.2	2.8

Maranville, Walter James Vincent "Rabbit"

YEAR	TM/L	G	W	L	PCT	STANDING	M/Y	W-EXP	A-E
1925	Bro-F*	53	23	30	.434	7 7 8	2/3	24.8	-1.8

Marion, Martin Whitford "Marty"

YEAR	TM/L	G	W	L	PCT	STANDING	M/Y	W-EXP	A-E
1951	StL-N	155	81	73	.526	3		78.2	2.8
1952	StL-A*	104	42	61	.408	8 7	2/2	42.7	-0.7
1953	StL-A*	154	54	100	.351	8		54.3	-0.3
1954	Chi-A	9	3	6	.333	3 3	2/2	5.7	-2.7
1955	Chi-A	155	91	63	.591	3		94.5	-3.5
1956	Chi-A	154	85	69	.552	3		91.1	-6.1
	6	731	356	372	.489				-10.5

Marshall, Rufus James "Jim"

YEAR	TM/L	G	W	L	PCT	STANDING	M/Y	W-EXP	A-E
1974	Chi-N	69	25	44	.362	5 E 6 E	2/2	27.9	-2.9
1975	Chi-N	162	75	87	.463	●5 E		69.8	5.2
1976	Chi-N	162	75	87	.463	4 E		68.8	6.2
1979	Oak-A	162	54	108	.333	7 W		52.0	2.0
	4	555	229	326	.413				10.5

Martin, Alfred Manuel "Billy"

YEAR	TM/L	G	W	L	PCT	STANDING	M/Y	W-EXP	A-E
1969	Min-A	162	97	65	.599	1 W		98.5	-1.5
1971	Det-A	162	91	71	.562	2 E		86.8	4.2
1972	Det-A	156	86	70	.551	1 E		83.0	3.0
1973	Det-A	134	71	63	.530	3 E 3 E	1/2	64.2	6.8
	Tex-A	23	9	14	.391	6 W 6 W	3/3	8.3	0.7
1974	Tex-A	161	84	76	.525	2 W		79.2	4.8
1975	Tex-A	95	44	51	.463	4 W 3 W	1/2	46.4	-2.4
	NY-A	56	30	26	.536	3 E 3 E	2/2	31.5	-1.5
1976	NY-A	159	97	62	.610	♦1 E		95.7	1.3
1977	NY-A	162	100	62	.617	★1 E		98.9	1.1
1978	NY-A	94	52	42	.553	3 E ▲★E	1/3	56.3	-4.3
1979	NY-A	95	55	40	.579	4 E 4 E	2/2	51.2	3.8
1980	Oak-A	162	83	79	.512	2 W		85.6	-2.6
1981(1)	Oak-A	60	37	23	.617	1 W			
(2)	Oak-A	49	27	22	.551	2 W		60.4	3.6
1982	Oak-A	162	68	94	.420	5 W		68.4	-0.4
1983	NY-A	162	91	71	.562	3 E		87.7	3.3
1985	NY-A	145	91	54	.628	7 E 2 E	2/2	88.4	2.6
1988	NY-A	68	40	28	.588	2 E 5 E	1/2	35.0	5.0
	16	2267	1253	1013	.553				27.5

Martinez, Orlando [Oliva] "Marty"

YEAR	TM/L	G	W	L	PCT	STANDING	M/Y	W-EXP	A-E
1986	Sea-A	1	0	1	.000	6 W 6 W 7 W	2/3	0.4	-0.4

Mason, Charles E. "Charlie"

YEAR	TM/L	G	W	L	PCT	STANDING	M/Y	W-EXP	A-E
1887	Phi-a	82	38	40	.487	6 5	2/2	39.1	-1.1

Mathews, Edwin Lee "Eddie"

YEAR	TM/L	G	W	L	PCT	STANDING	M/Y	W-EXP	A-E
1972	Atl-N	50	23	27	.460	4 W 4 W	2/2	21.6	1.4
1973	Atl-N	162	76	85	.472	5 W		82.9	-6.9
1974	Atl-N	99	50	49	.505	4 W 3 W	1/2	56.1	-6.1
	3	311	149	161	.481				-11.6

Mathewson, Christopher "Christy"

YEAR	TM/L	G	W	L	PCT	STANDING	M/Y	W-EXP	A-E
1916	Cin-N*	69	25	43	.368	8 ●7	3/3	28.4	-3.4
1917	Cin-N	157	78	76	.506	4		75.9	2.1
1918	Cin-N	120	61	57	.517	4 3	1/2	62.3	-1.3
	3	346	164	176	.482				-2.7

Mattick, Robert James "Bobby"

YEAR	TM/L	G	W	L	PCT	STANDING	M/Y	W-EXP	A-E
1980	Tor-A	162	67	95	.414	7 E		66.8	0.2
1981(1)	Tor-A	58	16	42	.276	7 E			
(2)	Tor-A	48	21	27	.438	7 E		38.0	-1.0
	2	268	104	164	.388				-0.8

Mauch, Gene William

YEAR	TM/L	G	W	L	PCT	STANDING	M/Y	W-EXP	A-E
1960	Phi-N	152	58	94	.382	●4 8	3/3	60.8	-2.8
1961	Phi-N	155	47	107	.305	8		55.7	-8.7
1962	Phi-N	161	81	80	.503	7		75.1	5.9
1963	Phi-N	162	87	75	.537	4		88.0	-1.0
1964	Phi-N	162	92	70	.568	●2		87.4	4.6
1965	Phi-N	162	85	76	.528	6		79.1	5.9
1966	Phi-N	162	87	75	.537	4		86.9	0.1
1967	Phi-N	162	82	80	.506	5		84.4	-2.4
1968	Phi-N	54	27	27	.500	●6 ●7	1/3	24.3	2.7
1969	Mon-N	162	52	110	.321	6 E		59.5	-7.5
1970	Mon-N	162	73	89	.451	6 E		69.1	3.9
1971	Mon-N	162	71	90	.441	5 E		69.4	1.6
1972	Mon-N	156	70	86	.449	5 E		67.3	2.7
1973	Mon-N	162	79	83	.488	4 E		77.5	1.5
1974	Mon-N	161	79	82	.491	4 E		81.0	-2.0
1975	Mon-N	162	75	87	.463	●5 E		71.5	3.5
1976	Min-A	162	85	77	.525	3 W		84.9	0.1
1977	Min-A	161	84	77	.522	4 W		89.0	-5.0
1978	Min-A	162	73	89	.451	4 W		79.8	-6.8
1979	Min-A	162	82	80	.506	4 W		84.9	-2.9
1980	Min-A	125	54	71	.432	4 W 3 W	1/2	58.2	-4.2
1981(1)	Cal-A	13	9	4	.692	4 W 4 W	2/2		
(2)	Cal-A	50	20	30	.400	7 W		32.9	-3.9
1982	Cal-A	162	93	69	.574	1 W		95.3	-2.3
1985	Cal-A	162	90	72	.556	2 W		83.9	6.1
1986	Cal-A	162	92	70	.568	1 W		91.2	0.8
1987	Cal-A	162	75	87	.463	●6 W		77.8	-2.8
	26	3942	1902	2037	.483				-12.9

McAleer, James Robert "Jimmy"

YEAR	TM/L	G	W	L	PCT	STANDING	M/Y	W-EXP	A-E
1901	Cle-A*	138	55	82	.401	7		53.1	0.9
1902	StL-A*	140	78	58	.574	2		69.2	8.8
1903	StL-A	139	65	74	.468	6		66.7	-1.7
1904	StL-A	156	65	87	.428	6		62.0	3.0
1905	StL-A	156	54	99	.353	6		65.6	-11.6
1906	StL-A	154	76	73	.510	5		81.4	-5.4
1907	StL-A*	155	69	83	.454	6		74.5	-5.5
1908	StL-A	155	83	69	.546	4		83.1	-0.1
1909	StL-A	154	61	89	.407	7		59.3	1.7
1910	Was-A	157	66	85	.437	7		69.8	-3.8
1911	Was-A	154	64	90	.416	7		62.9	1.1
	11	1658	736	889	.453				-12.8

McBride, George Florian

YEAR	TM/L	G	W	L	PCT	STANDING	M/Y	W-EXP	A-E
1921	Was-A	154	80	73	.523	4		73.2	6.8

McBride, James Dickson "Dick"

YEAR	TM/L	G	W	L	PCT	STANDING	M/Y	W-EXP	A-E
1871	Ath-n*	28	21	7	.750	1		20.9	0.1
1872	Ath-n*	47	30	14	.682	4		35.1	-5.1
1873	Ath-n*	52	28	23	.549	5		30.7	-2.7
1874	Ath-n*	56	33	23	.589	3		35.2	-2.4
1875	Ath-n*	69	49	18	.731	2 2	1/2	55.1	-6.1
	5	252	161	85	.654				-16.0

McCallister, John "Jack"

YEAR	TM/L	G	W	L	PCT	STANDING	M/Y	W-EXP	A-E
1927	Cle-A	153	66	87	.431	6		66.9	-0.9

McCarthy, Joseph Vincent "Joe"

YEAR	TM/L	G	W	L	PCT	STANDING	M/Y	W-EXP	A-E
1926	Chi-N	155	82	72	.532	4		85.3	-3.3
1927	Chi-N	153	85	68	.556	4		85.3	-0.3
1928	Chi-N	154	91	63	.591	3		87.1	3.9
1929	Chi-N	156	98	54	.645	1		96.1	1.9
1930	Chi-N	152	86	64	.573	2 2	1/2	85.8	0.2
1931	NY-A	155	94	59	.614	2		103.3	-9.3
1932	NY-A	156	107	47	.695	★1		102.1	4.9
1933	NY-A	152	91	59	.607	2		89.3	1.7
1934	NY-A	154	94	60	.610	2		93.6	0.4
1935	NY-A	149	89	60	.597	2		92.4	-3.4
1936	NY-A	155	102	51	.667	★1		105.9	-3.9
1937	NY-A	157	102	52	.662	★1		105.5	-3.5
1938	NY-A	157	99	53	.651	★1		99.5	-0.5
1939	NY-A	152	106	45	.702	★1		114.5	-8.5
1940	NY-A	155	88	66	.571	3		91.1	-3.1
1941	NY-A	156	101	53	.656	★1		96.5	4.5
1942	NY-A	154	103	51	.669	1		107.3	-4.3
1943	NY-A	155	98	56	.636	★1		90.6	7.4
1944	NY-A	154	83	71	.539	3		82.9	0.1
1945	NY-A	152	81	71	.533	4		83.2	-2.2
1946	NY-A	35	22	13	.629	2 3	1/3	20.8	1.2
1948	Bos-A	155	96	59	.619	▲2		94.8	1.2
1949	Bos-A	155	96	58	.623	2		98.6	-2.6
1950	Bos-A	59	31	28	.525	4 3	1/2	36.9	-5.9
	24	3487	2125	1333	.615				-23.6

McCarthy, Thomas Francis "Tommy"

YEAR	TM/L	G	W	L	PCT	STANDING	M/Y	W-EXP	A-E
1890	StL-a*	22	11	11	.500	4 3	1/6	12.9	-1.9
	StL-a*	5	4	1	.800	2 2 3	5/6	2.9	1.1

McCloskey, John Joseph

YEAR	TM/L	G	W	L	PCT	STANDING	M/Y	W-EXP	A-E
1895	Lou-N	133	35	96	.267	12		33.4	1.6
1896	Lou-N	19	2	17	.105	12 12	1/2	5.2	-3.2
1906	StL-N	154	52	98	.347	7		59.5	-7.5
1907	StL-N	155	52	101	.340	8		54.5	-2.5
1908	StL-N	154	49	105	.318	8		46.9	2.1
	5	615	190	417	.313				-9.5

McCormick, James "Jim"

YEAR	TM/L	G	W	L	PCT	STANDING	M/Y	W-EXP	A-E
1879	Cle-N*	82	27	55	.329	6		27.5	-0.5

YEAR	TM/L	G	W	L	PCT	STANDING	M/Y	W-EXP	A-E
1880	Cle-N*	85	47	37	.560	3		47.1	-0.1
1882	Cle-N*	4	0	4	.000	8 5	1/2	2.0	-2.0
	3	171	74	96	.435				-2.6
McGaha, Fred Melvin "Mel"									
1962	Cle-A	160	78	82	.488	6 6	1/2	73.7	4.3
1964	KC-A	111	40	70	.364	10 10	2/2	40.3	-0.3
1965	KC-A	26	5	21	.192	10 10	1/2	10.2	-5.2
	3	297	123	173	.416				-1.2
McGeary, Michael Henry "Mike"									
1875	Phi-n*	63	34	27	.557	4 5	1/2	37.8	-3.8
1880	Pro-N*	16	8	7	.533	4 2	1/3	9.7	-1.7
1881	Cle-N*	11	4	7	.364	6 7	1/2	5.2	-1.2
	3	90	46	41	.529				-6.7
McGraw, John Joseph									
1899	Bal-N*	152	86	62	.581	4		86.9	-0.9
1901	Bal-A*	135	68	65	.511	5		67.4	0.6
1902	Bal-A*	58	26	31	.456	7 8	1/2	23.5	2.5
	NY-N*	65	25	38	.397	8 8	3/3	21.7	3.3
1903	NY-N*	142	84	55	.604	2		85.6	-1.6
1904	NY-N*	158	106	47	.693	1		105.4	0.6
1905	NY-N*	155	105	48	.686	★1		105.2	-0.2
1906	NY-N*	153	96	56	.632	2		88.7	7.3
1907	NY-N	155	82	71	.536	4		83.8	-1.8
1908	NY-N	157	98	56	.636	●2		99.1	-1.1
1909	NY-N	158	92	61	.601	3		85.0	7.0
1910	NY-N	155	91	63	.591	2		92.4	-1.4
1911	NY-N	154	99	54	.647	1		98.6	0.4
1912	NY-N	154	103	48	.682	1		100.6	2.4
1913	NY-N	156	101	51	.664	1		94.3	6.7
1914	NY-N	156	84	70	.545	2		87.2	-3.2
1915	NY-N	155	69	83	.454	8		71.1	-2.1
1916	NY-N	155	86	66	.566	4		86.5	-0.5
1917	NY-N	158	98	56	.636	1		97.3	0.7
1918	NY-N	124	71	53	.573	2		69.3	1.7
1919	NY-N	140	87	53	.621	2		84.6	2.4
1920	NY-N	155	86	68	.558	2		91.8	-5.8
1921	NY-N	153	94	59	.614	★1		96.1	-2.1
1922	NY-N	156	93	61	.604	★1		95.7	-2.7
1923	NY-N	153	95	58	.621	1		93.1	1.9
1924	NY-N	29	16	13	.552	3 1	1/3	18.4	-2.4
	NY-N	81	45	35	.563	1 1	3/3	50.9	-5.9
1925	NY-N	14	10	4	.714	1 2	1/3	7.3	2.7
	NY-N	106	55	51	.519	1 2	3/3	55.3	-0.3
1926	NY-N	151	74	77	.490	5		75.0	-1.0
1927	NY-N	122	70	52	.574	4 3	1/2	68.3	3.7
1928	NY-N	155	93	61	.604	2		92.1	0.9
1929	NY-N	152	84	67	.556	3		92.9	-8.9
1930	NY-N	154	87	67	.565	3		89.8	-2.8
1931	NY-N	153	87	65	.572	2		93.0	-6.0
1932	NY-N	40	17	23	.425	8 ●6	1/2	21.2	-4.2
	33	4769	2763	1948	.586				-12.0
McGuire, James Thomas "Deacon"									
1898	Was-N*	70	21	47	.309	10 11 11	3/4	24.3	-3.3
1907	Bos-A*	112	45	61	.425	8 7	4/4	45.2	-0.2
1908	Bos-A*	115	53	62	.461	6 5	1/2	61.8	-8.8
1909	Cle-A	41	14	25	.359	4 6	2/2	18.3	-4.3
1910	Cle-A*	161	71	81	.467	5		64.0	7.0
1911	Cle-A	17	6	11	.353	7 3	1/2	8.3	-2.3
	6	516	210	287	.423				-12.0
McGunnigle, William Henry "Bill"									
1888	Bro-a	143	88	52	.629	2		87.0	1.0
1889	Bro-a	140	94	43	.686	2		93.4	-0.4
1890	Bro-N	129	86	43	.667	1		87.7	-1.7
1891	Pit-N	59	24	33	.421	8 8	2/2	25.9	-1.9
1896	Lou-N	115	36	76	.321	12 12	2/2	30.9	5.1
	5	586	328	247	.570				2.1
McInnis, John Phalen "Stuffy"									
1927	Phi-N*	155	51	103	.331	8		55.9	-4.9
McKechnie, William Boyd "Bill"									
1915	New-F*	102	54	45	.545	6 5	2/2	51.2	2.8
1922	Pit-N	90	53	36	.596	5 ●3	2/2	51.5	1.5
1923	Pit-N	154	87	67	.565	3		85.7	1.3
1924	Pit-N	153	90	63	.588	3		90.4	-0.4
1925	Pit-N	153	95	58	.621	★1		94.6	0.4
1926	Pit-N	157	84	69	.549	3		84.4	-0.4
1928	StL-N	154	95	59	.617	1		93.8	1.2
1929	StL-N	63	34	29	.540	4 4	3/3	32.5	1.5
1930	Bos-N	154	70	84	.455	6		63.5	6.5
1931	Bos-N	156	64	90	.416	7		61.2	2.8
1932	Bos-N	155	77	77	.500	5		76.4	0.6
1933	Bos-N	156	83	71	.539	4		79.4	3.6
1934	Bos-N	152	78	73	.517	4		72.4	5.6
1935	Bos-N	153	38	115	.248	8		49.3	-11.3
1936	Bos-N	157	71	83	.461	6		68.4	2.6
1937	Bos-N	152	79	73	.520	5		78.5	0.5
1938	Cin-N	151	82	68	.547	4		83.9	-1.9
1939	Cin-N	156	97	57	.630	1		94.5	2.5
1940	Cin-N	155	100	53	.654	★1		95.5	4.5
1941	Cin-N	154	88	66	.571	3		82.6	5.4
1942	Cin-N	154	76	76	.500	4		74.0	2.0
1943	Cin-N	155	87	67	.565	2		84.2	2.8
1944	Cin-N	155	89	65	.578	3		81.0	8.0
1945	Cin-N	154	61	93	.396	7		60.2	0.8
1946	Cin-N	152	64	86	.427	6 6	1/2	69.8	-5.8
	25	3647	1896	1723	.524				37.3
McKeon, John Aloysius "Jack"									
1973	KC-A	162	88	74	.543	2 W		81.3	6.7
1974	KC-A	162	77	85	.475	5 W		81.5	-4.5
1975	KC-A	96	50	46	.521	2 W 2 W	1/2	51.7	-1.7
1977	Oak-A	53	26	27	.491	●5 W 7 W	1/2	21.6	4.4
1978	Oak-A	123	45	78	.366	1 W 6 W	2/2	48.4	-3.4
1988	SD-N	115	67	48	.583	5 W 3 W	2/2	58.4	8.6
1989	SD-N	162	89	73	.549	2 W		82.7	6.3
1990	SD-N	80	37	43	.463	4 W 5 W	1/2	40.0	-3.0
	8	953	479	474	.503				13.4
McKinnon, Alexander J. "Alex"									
1885	StL-N*	39	6	32	.158	5 8 8	2/3	11.8	-5.8
McKnight, Dennis Hamar "Denny"									
1884	Pit-a	12	4	8	.333	9 10	1/5	2.7	1.3
McManus, George									
1876	StL-N	8	6	2	.750	2 2	2/2	5.9	0.1
1877	StL-N	60	28	32	.467	4		26.8	1.2
	2	68	34	34	.500				1.3
McManus, Martin Joseph "Marty"									
1932	Bos-A*	99	32	67	.323	8	2/2	27.8	4.2
1933	Bos-A*	149	63	86	.423	7		68.9	-5.9
	2	248	95	153	.383				-1.7
McMillan, Roy David									
1972	Mil-A	2	1	1	.500	6 E 6 E 6 E	2/3	0.9	0.1
1975	NY-N	53	26	27	.491	3 E ●3E	2/2	27.2	-1.2
	2	55	27	28	.491				-1.1
McNamara, John Francis									
1969	Oak-A	13	8	5	.615	2 W 2 W	2/2	7.0	1.0
1970	Oak-A	162	89	73	.549	2 W		90.1	-1.1
1974	SD-N	162	60	102	.370	6 W		51.2	8.8
1975	SD-N	162	71	91	.438	4 W		66.8	4.2
1976	SD-N	162	73	89	.451	5 W		71.0	2.0
1977	SD-N	48	20	28	.417	4 W 5 W	1/3	19.9	0.1
1979	Cin-N	161	90	71	.559	1 W		89.4	0.6
1980	Cin-N	163	89	73	.549	3 W		84.8	4.2
1981(1)	Cin-N	56	35	21	.625	2 W			
(2)	Cin-N	52	31	21	.596	2 W		56.5	9.5
1982	Cin-N	92	34	58	.370	6 W 6 W	1/2	38.8	-4.8
1983	Cal-A	162	70	92	.432	●5 W		75.4	-5.4
1984	Cal-A	162	81	81	.500	●2 W		80.9	0.1
1985	Bos-A	163	81	81	.500	5 E		88.9	-7.9
1986	Bos-A	161	95	66	.590	♦1 E		90.2	4.8
1987	Bos-A	162	78	84	.481	5 E		82.6	-4.6
1988	Bos-A	85	43	42	.506	4 E 1 E	1/2	48.9	-5.9
1990	Cle-A	162	77	85	.475	4 E		80.5	-3.5
1991	Cle-A	77	25	52	.325	7 E 7 E	2/2	29.4	-4.4
	18	2367	1150	1215	.486				-2.2
McPhee, John Alexander "Bid"									
1901	Cin-N	142	52	87	.374	8		44.8	7.2
1902	Cin-N	65	27	37	.422	6 4	1/3	35.2	-8.2
	2	207	79	124	.389				-0.9
McRae, Harold Abraham "Hal"									
1991	KC-A	124	66	58	.532	7 W 6 W	3/3	62.4	3.6
1992	KC-A	162	72	90	.444	●5 W		74.9	-2.9
1993	KC-A	162	84	78	.519	3 W		79.0	5.0
1994	KC-A	115	64	51	.557	3 C		61.6	2.4
	4	563	286	277	.508				8.1
McVey, Calvin Alexander "Cal"									
1873	Bal-n*	32	19	13	.594	2 3	1/2	23.5	-4.5
1878	Cin-N*	61	37	23	.617	2		34.9	2.1
1879	Cin-N*	63	34	28	.548	4 5	2/2	32.4	1.6
	3	156	90	64	.584				-0.9
Mele, Sabath Anthony "Sam"									
1961	Min-A	7	2	5	.286	8 9 7	2/4	3.2	-1.2
	Min-A	95	45	49	.479	9 7	4/4	42.9	2.1
1962	Min-A	163	91	71	.562	2		89.4	1.6
1963	Min-A	161	91	70	.565	3		97.5	-6.5
1964	Min-A	163	79	83	.488	●6		87.0	-8.0
1965	Min-A	162	102	60	.630	1		98.9	3.1
1966	Min-A	162	89	73	.549	2		89.9	-0.9
1967	Min-A	50	25	25	.500	6 ●2	1/2	27.7	-2.7
	7	963	524	436	.546				-12.4
Melillo, Oscar Donald "Ski"									
1938	StL-A	10	2	7	.222	7 7	2/2	3.4	-1.4
Merrill, Carl Harrison "Stump"									
1990	NY-A	113	49	64	.434	7 E 7 E	2/2	45.9	3.1
1991	NY-A	162	71	91	.438	5 E		70.7	0.3
	2	275	120	155	.436				3.4
Metro, Charles "Charlie"									
1962	Chi-N	112	43	69	.384	9 9	3/3	42.5	0.5

YEAR	TM/L	G	W	L	PCT	STANDING	M/Y	W-EXP	A-E
1970	KC-A	52	19	33	.365	5 W ●4 W	1/2	22.8	-3.8
	2	164	62	102	.378				-3.3

Meyer, William Adam "Billy"

YEAR	TM/L	G	W	L	PCT	STANDING	M/Y	W-EXP	A-E
1948	Pit-N	156	83	71	.539	4		77.7	5.3
1949	Pit-N	154	71	83	.461	6		69.3	1.7
1950	Pit-N	154	57	96	.373	8		59.8	-2.8
1951	Pit-N	155	64	90	.416	7		62.1	1.9
1952	Pit-N	155	42	112	.273	8		48.3	-6.3
	5	774	317	452	.412				-0.2

Michael, Eugene Richard "Gene"

YEAR	TM/L	G	W	L	PCT	STANDING	M/Y	W-EXP	A-E
1981(1)	NY-A	56	34	22	.607	◆1 E			
(2)	NY-A	26	14	12	.538	4 E 6 E	1/2	47.7	0.3
1982	NY-A	86	44	42	.512	●4 E ●5 E 5 E	2/3	42.6	1.4
1986	Chi-N	102	46	56	.451	5 E 5 E	3/3	44.6	1.4
1987	Chi-N	136	68	68	.500	5 E 6 E	1/2	61.3	6.7
	4	406	206	200	.507				9.7

Milan, Jesse Clyde "Clyde"

YEAR	TM/L	G	W	L	PCT	STANDING	M/Y	W-EXP	A-E
1922	Was-A*	154	69	85	.448	6		71.3	-2.3

Miller, George Frederick

YEAR	TM/L	G	W	L	PCT	STANDING	M/Y	W-EXP	A-E
1894	StL-N*	133	56	76	.424	9		50.8	5.2

Miller, Joseph Wick "Joe"

YEAR	TM/L	G	W	L	PCT	STANDING	M/Y	W-EXP	A-E
1872	Nat-n*	11	0	11	.000	11		-1.2	1.2

Miller, Raymond Roger "Ray"

YEAR	TM/L	G	W	L	PCT	STANDING	M/Y	W-EXP	A-E
1985	Min-A	100	50	50	.500	6 W 4 W	2/2	45.3	4.7
1986	Min-A	139	59	80	.424	7 W 6 W	1/2	61.4	-2.4
	2	239	109	130	.456				2.3

Mills, Colonel Buster "Buster"

YEAR	TM/L	G	W	L	PCT	STANDING	M/Y	W-EXP	A-E
1953	Cin-N	8	4	4	.500	6 6	2/2	3.6	0.4

Mills, Everett

YEAR	TM/L	G	W	L	PCT	STANDING	M/Y	W-EXP	A-E
1872	Bal-n*	17	8	6	.571	2 2	2/2	10.3	-2.3

Mitchell, Frederick Francis "Fred"

YEAR	TM/L	G	W	L	PCT	STANDING	M/Y	W-EXP	A-E
1917	Chi-N	157	74	80	.481	5		75.3	-1.3
1918	Chi-N	131	84	45	.651	1		80.8	3.2
1919	Chi-N	140	75	65	.536	3		75.7	-0.7
1920	Chi-N	154	75	79	.487	●5		75.3	-0.3
1921	Bos-N	153	79	74	.516	4		78.9	0.1
1922	Bos-N	154	53	100	.346	8		54.2	-1.2
1923	Bos-N	155	54	100	.351	7		61.0	-7.0
	7	1044	494	543	.476				-7.2

Moore, Jackie Spencer

YEAR	TM/L	G	W	L	PCT	STANDING	M/Y	W-EXP	A-E
1984	Oak-A	118	57	61	.483	5 W 4 W	2/2	54.9	2.1
1985	Oak-A	162	77	85	.475	●4 W		78.1	-1.1
1986	Oak-A	73	29	44	.397	●6 W ●3 W	1/3	35.2	-6.2
	3	353	163	190	.462				-5.2

Moore, Terry Bluford

YEAR	TM/L	G	W	L	PCT	STANDING	M/Y	W-EXP	A-E
1954	Phi-N	77	35	42	.455	3 4	2/2	40.8	-5.8

Moran, Patrick Joseph "Pat"

YEAR	TM/L	G	W	L	PCT	STANDING	M/Y	W-EXP	A-E
1915	Phi-N	153	90	62	.592	1		90.4	-0.4
1916	Phi-N	154	91	62	.595	2		87.0	4.0
1917	Phi-N	155	87	65	.572	2		84.8	2.2
1918	Phi-N	125	55	68	.447	6		53.1	1.9
1919	Cin-N	140	96	44	.686	★1		90.0	6.0
1920	Cin-N	154	82	71	.536	3		84.0	-2.0
1921	Cin-N	153	70	83	.458	6		73.3	-3.3
1922	Cin-N	156	86	68	.558	2		85.8	0.2
1923	Cin-N	154	91	63	.591	2		85.0	6.0
	9	1344	748	586	.561				14.6

Morgan, Joseph Michael "Joe"

YEAR	TM/L	G	W	L	PCT	STANDING	M/Y	W-EXP	A-E
1988	Bos-A	77	46	31	.597	4 E 1 E	2/2	44.3	1.7
1989	Bos-A	162	83	79	.512	3 E		84.8	-1.8
1990	Bos-A	162	88	74	.543	1 E		84.6	3.4
1991	Bos-A	162	84	78	.519	●2 E		82.9	1.1
	4	563	301	262	.535				4.3

Moriarty, George Joseph

YEAR	TM/L	G	W	L	PCT	STANDING	M/Y	W-EXP	A-E
1927	Det-A	156	82	71	.536	4		80.2	1.8
1928	Det-A	154	68	86	.442	6		71.3	-3.3
	2	310	150	157	.489				-1.5

Morrill, John Francis

YEAR	TM/L	G	W	L	PCT	STANDING	M/Y	W-EXP	A-E
1882	Bos-N*	85	45	39	.536	●3		47.4	-2.4
1883	Bos-N*	44	33	11	.750	4 1	2/2	30.5	2.5
1884	Bos-N*	116	73	38	.658	2		76.1	-3.1
1885	Bos-N*	113	46	66	.411	5		50.2	-4.2
1886	Bos-N*	118	56	61	.479	5		58.1	-2.1
1887	Bos-N*	32	12	17	.414	5 5	2/2	15.3	-3.3
1888	Bos-N*	137	70	64	.522	4		71.9	-1.9
1889	Was-N*	51	13	38	.255	8 8	1/2	16.2	-3.2
	8	696	348	334	.510				-17.7

Morton, Charles Hazen "Charlie"

YEAR	TM/L	G	W	L	PCT	STANDING	M/Y	W-EXP	A-E
1884	Tol-a*	110	46	58	.442	8		41.4	4.6
1885	Det-N*	38	7	31	.184	8 6	1/2	16.7	-9.7
1890	Tol-a	134	68	64	.515	4		70.6	-2.6
	3	282	121	153	.442				-7.8

Moses, Felix I.

YEAR	TM/L	G	W	L	PCT	STANDING	M/Y	W-EXP	A-E
1884	Ric-a	46	12	30	.286	12		11.8	0.2

Moss, John Lester "Les"

YEAR	TM/L	G	W	L	PCT	STANDING	M/Y	W-EXP	A-E
1968	Chi-A	2	0	2	.000	9 9 ●8	2/5	0.9	-0.9
	Chi-A	34	12	22	.353	9 9 ●8	4/5	15.4	-3.4
1979	Det-A	53	27	26	.509	5 E 5 E	1/3	27.5	-0.5
	2	89	39	50	.438				-4.8

Murnane, Timothy Hayes "Tim"

YEAR	TM/L	G	W	L	PCT	STANDING	M/Y	W-EXP	A-E
1884	Bos-U*	111	58	51	.532	5		61.6	-3.6

Murray, William Jeremiah "Billy"

YEAR	TM/L	G	W	L	PCT	STANDING	M/Y	W-EXP	A-E
1907	Phi-N	149	83	64	.565	3		77.7	5.3
1908	Phi-N	155	83	71	.539	4		84.2	-1.2
1909	Phi-N	154	74	79	.484	5		76.3	-2.3
	3	458	240	214	.529				1.9

Murtaugh, Daniel Edward "Danny"

YEAR	TM/L	G	W	L	PCT	STANDING	M/Y	W-EXP	A-E
1957	Pit-N	51	26	25	.510	7 ●7	2/2	21.7	4.3
1958	Pit-N	154	84	70	.545	2		82.7	1.3
1959	Pit-N	155	78	76	.506	4		74.0	4.0
1960	Pit-N	155	95	59	.617	★1		91.5	3.5
1961	Pit-N	154	75	79	.487	6		78.9	-3.9
1962	Pit-N	161	93	68	.578	4		88.8	4.2
1963	Pit-N	162	74	88	.457	8		77.9	-3.9
1964	Pit-N	162	80	82	.494	●6		83.9	-3.9
1967	Pit-N	79	39	39	.500	6 6	2/2	38.3	0.7
1970	Pit-N	162	89	73	.549	1 E		87.7	1.3
1971	Pit-N	162	97	65	.599	★1 E		100.4	-3.4
1973	Pit-N	26	13	13	.500	2 E 3 E	2/2	13.2	-0.2
1974	Pit-N	162	88	74	.543	1 E		90.6	-2.6
1975	Pit-N	161	92	69	.571	1 E		96.2	-4.2
1976	Pit-N	162	92	70	.568	2 E		89.1	2.9
	15	2068	1115	950	.540				0.2

Mutrie, James J. "Jim"

YEAR	TM/L	G	W	L	PCT	STANDING	M/Y	W-EXP	A-E
1883	NY-a	97	54	42	.563	4		57.1	-3.1
1884	NY-a	112	75	32	.701	1		82.5	-7.5
1885	NY-N	112	85	27	.759	2		87.3	-2.3
1886	NY-N	124	75	44	.630	3		72.2	2.8
1887	NY-N	129	68	55	.553	4		69.6	-1.6
1888	NY-N	138	84	47	.641	1		84.3	-0.3
1889	NY-N	131	83	43	.659	1		82.2	0.8
1890	NY-N	135	63	68	.481	6		66.9	-3.9
1891	NY-N	136	71	61	.538	3		69.9	1.1
	9	1114	658	419	.611				-14.1

Myatt, George Edward "George"

YEAR	TM/L	G	W	L	PCT	STANDING	M/Y	W-EXP	A-E
1968	Phi-N	1	1	0	1.000	●6 5 ●7	2/3	0.5	0.5
1969	Phi-N	54	19	35	.352	5 E 5 E	2/2	23.6	-4.6
	2	55	20	35	.364				-4.0

Myers, Henry C.

YEAR	TM/L	G	W	L	PCT	STANDING	M/Y	W-EXP	A-E
1882	Bal-a*	74	19	54	.260	6		14.2	4.8

Nash, William Mitchell "Billy"

YEAR	TM/L	G	W	L	PCT	STANDING	M/Y	W-EXP	A-E
1896	Phi-N*	130	62	68	.477	8		64.9	-2.9

Neun, John Henry "Johnny"

YEAR	TM/L	G	W	L	PCT	STANDING	M/Y	W-EXP	A-E
1946	NY-A	14	8	6	.571	3 3	3/3	8.3	-0.3
1947	Cin-N	154	73	81	.474	5		69.7	3.3
1948	Cin-N	100	44	56	.440	7 7	1/2	39.1	4.9
	3	268	125	143	.466				7.8

Newman, Jeffrey Lynn "Jeff"

YEAR	TM/L	G	W	L	PCT	STANDING	M/Y	W-EXP	A-E
1986	Oak-A	10	2	8	.200	●6 W 7 W ●3 W	2/3	4.8	-2.8

Nichols, Charles Augustus "Kid"

YEAR	TM/L	G	W	L	PCT	STANDING	M/Y	W-EXP	A-E
1904	StL-N*	155	75	79	.487	5		77.8	-2.8
1905	StL-N*	14	5	9	.357	7 6	1/3	5.1	-0.1
	2	169	80	88	.476				-2.9

Nicol, Hugh

YEAR	TM/L	G	W	L	PCT	STANDING	M/Y	W-EXP	A-E
1897	StL-N	40	8	32	.200	12 12 12	2/4	7.3	0.7

Nixon, Russell Eugene "Russ"

YEAR	TM/L	G	W	L	PCT	STANDING	M/Y	W-EXP	A-E
1982	Cin-N	70	27	43	.386	6 W 6 W	2/2	29.5	-2.5
1983	Cin-N	162	74	88	.457	6 W		71.9	2.1
1988	Atl-N	121	42	79	.347	6 W 6 W	2/2	45.7	-3.7
1989	Atl-N	161	63	97	.394	6 W		69.7	-6.7
1990	Atl-N	65	25	40	.385	6 W 6 W	1/2	27.0	-2.0
	5	579	231	347	.400				-12.8

Norman, Henry Willis Patrick "Bill"

YEAR	TM/L	G	W	L	PCT	STANDING	M/Y	W-EXP	A-E
1958	Det-A	105	56	49	.533	8 5	2/2	56.3	-0.3
1959	Det-A	17	2	15	.118	8 4	1/2	8.3	-6.3
	2	122	58	64	.475				-6.6

Oakes, Ennis Telfair "Rebel"

YEAR	TM/L	G	W	L	PCT	STANDING	M/Y	W-EXP	A-E
1914	Pit-F*	143	61	78	.439	8 7	2/2	60.6	0.4
1915	Pit-F*	156	86	67	.562	3		84.1	1.9
	2	299	147	145	.503				2.3

Oates, Johnny Lane

YEAR	TM/L	G	W	L	PCT	STANDING	M/Y	W-EXP	A-E
1991	Bal-A	125	54	71	.432	7 E 6 E	2/2	54.1	-0.1
1992	Bal-A	162	89	73	.549	3 E		86.1	2.9
1993	Bal-A	162	85	77	.525	●3 E		85.0	-0.0
1994	Bal-A	112	63	49	.563	2 E		64.9	-1.9
	4	561	291	270	.519				1.0

O'Connor, John Joseph "Jack"

YEAR	TM/L	G	W	L	PCT	STANDING	M/Y	W-EXP	A-E
1910	StL-A*	158	47	107	.305	8		45.1	1.9

O'Day, Henry Francis "Hank"

YEAR	TM/L	G	W	L	PCT	STANDING			M/Y	W-EXP	A-E
1912	Cin-N	155	75	78	.490	4				69.9	5.1
1914	Chi-N	156	78	76	.506	4				73.5	4.5
2		311	153	154	.498						9.6

O'Farrell, Robert Arthur "Bob"

YEAR	TM/L	G	W	L	PCT	STANDING			M/Y	W-EXP	A-E
1927	StL-N*	153	92	61	.601	2				85.3	6.7
1934	Cin-N*	91	30	60	.333	8	8		1/3	32.5	-2.5
2		244	122	121	.502						4.2

O'Leary, Daniel "Dan"

YEAR	TM/L	G	W	L	PCT	STANDING			M/Y	W-EXP	A-E
1884	Cin-U*	35	20	15	.571	5	3		1/2	24.6	-4.6

O'Neill, Stephen Francis "Steve"

YEAR	TM/L	G	W	L	PCT	STANDING			M/Y	W-EXP	A-E
1935	Cle-A	60	36	23	.610	5	3		2/2	30.9	5.1
1936	Cle-A	157	80	74	.519	5				82.3	-2.3
1937	Cle-A	156	83	71	.539	4				81.6	1.4
1943	Det-A	155	78	76	.506	5				84.8	-6.8
1944	Det-A	156	88	66	.571	2				85.2	2.8
1945	Det-A	155	88	65	.575	★1				83.8	4.2
1946	Det-A	155	92	62	.597	2				91.4	0.6
1947	Det-A	158	85	69	.552	2				84.4	0.6
1948	Det-A	154	78	76	.506	5				74.4	3.6
1950	Bos-A	95	63	32	.663	4	3		2/2	59.5	3.5
1951	Bos-A	154	87	67	.565	3				84.5	2.5
1952	Phi-N	91	59	32	.648	6	4		2/2	52.1	6.9
1953	Phi-N	156	83	71	.539	●3				82.0	1.0
1954	Phi-N	77	40	37	.519	3	4		1/2	40.8	-0.8
14		1879	1040	821	.559						22.2

Onslow, John James "Jack"

YEAR	TM/L	G	W	L	PCT	STANDING			M/Y	W-EXP	A-E
1949	Chi-A	154	63	91	.409	6				68.1	-5.1
1950	Chi-A	31	8	22	.267	8	6		1/2	12.6	-4.6
2		185	71	113	.386						-9.7

O'Rourke, James Henry "Jim"

YEAR	TM/L	G	W	L	PCT	STANDING			M/Y	W-EXP	A-E
1881	Buf-N*	83	45	38	.542	3				40.9	4.1
1882	Buf-N*	84	45	39	.536	●3				45.5	-0.5
1883	Buf-N*	98	52	45	.536	5				51.8	0.2
1884	Buf-N*	115	64	47	.577	3				62.0	0.2
1893	Was-N*	130	40	89	.310	12				39.2	0.8
5		510	246	258	.488						6.7

Orr, David L. "Dave"

YEAR	TM/L	G	W	L	PCT	STANDING			M/Y	W-EXP	A-E
1887	NY-a*	8	3	5	.375	8	7	7	2/3	2.3	0.7

Ott, Melvin Thomas "Mel"

YEAR	TM/L	G	W	L	PCT	STANDING			M/Y	W-EXP	A-E
1942	NY-N*	154	85	67	.559	3				83.8	1.2
1943	NY-N*	156	55	98	.359	8				60.2	-5.2
1944	NY-N*	155	67	87	.435	5				68.1	-1.1
1945	NY-N*	154	78	74	.513	5				72.8	5.2
1946	NY-N*	154	61	93	.396	8				69.5	-8.5
1947	NY-N*	155	81	73	.526	4				83.5	-2.5
1948	NY-N	76	37	38	.493	4	5		1/2	41.1	-4.1
7		1004	464	530	.467						-14.9

Owens, Paul Francis

YEAR	TM/L	G	W	L	PCT	STANDING			M/Y	W-EXP	A-E
1972	Phi-N	80	33	47	.412	6 E	6 E		2/2	32.5	0.5
1983	Phi-N	77	47	30	.610	1 E	♦1E		2/2	41.5	5.5
1984	Phi-N	162	81	81	.500	4 E				84.1	-3.1
3		319	161	158	.505						2.9

Ozark, Daniel Leonard "Danny"

YEAR	TM/L	G	W	L	PCT	STANDING			M/Y	W-EXP	A-E
1973	Phi-N	162	71	91	.438	6 E				73.2	-2.2
1974	Phi-N	162	80	82	.494	3 E				78.4	1.6
1975	Phi-N	162	86	76	.531	2 E				85.1	0.9
1976	Phi-N	162	101	61	.623	1 E				103.3	-2.3
1977	Phi-N	162	101	61	.623	1 E				98.6	2.4
1978	Phi-N	162	90	72	.556	1 E				94.0	-1.0
1979	Phi-N	133	65	67	.492	5 E	4 E		1/2	63.1	1.9
1984	SF-N	56	24	32	.429	6 W	6 W		2/2	23.7	0.3
8		1161	618	542	.533						-1.4

Pabor, Charles Henry "Charlie"

YEAR	TM/L	G	W	L	PCT	STANDING			M/Y	W-EXP	A-E
1871	Cle-n*	29	10	19	.345	7				8.4	1.6
1875	Atl-n*	42	2	40	.048	12	12		1/2	-3.3	5.3
	NH-n*	6	1	5	.167	8	8		3/3	0.5	0.5
2		77	13	64	.169						7.5

Parker, Francis James "Salty"

YEAR	TM/L	G	W	L	PCT	STANDING			M/Y	W-EXP	A-E
1967	NY-N	11	4	7	.364	10	10		2/2	4.2	-0.2
1972	Hou-N	1	1	0	1.000	2 W	2 W		2/3	0.5	0.5
2		12	5	7	.417						0.3

Parks, William Robert "Bill"

YEAR	TM/L	G	W	L	PCT	STANDING			M/Y	W-EXP	A-E
1875	Was-n*	8	1	7	.125	8	10		2/2	-1.0	2.0

Pearce, Richard J. "Dickey"

YEAR	TM/L	G	W	L	PCT	STANDING			M/Y	W-EXP	A-E
1872	Mut-n*	16	10	6	.625	4	3		1/2	11.6	-1.6
1875	StL-n*	72	39	29	.574	4				35.6	3.4
2		88	49	35	.583						1.8

Peckinpaugh, Roger Thorpe

YEAR	TM/L	G	W	L	PCT	STANDING			M/Y	W-EXP	A-E
1914	NY-A*	20	10	10	.500	7	●6		2/2	9.8	0.2
1928	Cle-A	152	62	92	.403	7				62.0	0.0
1929	Cle-A	152	81	71	.533	3				74.2	6.8
1930	Cle-A	154	81	73	.526	4				74.8	6.2
1931	Cle-A	155	78	76	.506	4				81.7	-3.7
1932	Cle-A	153	87	65	.572	4				85.1	1.9
1933	Cle-A	51	26	25	.510	5	4		1/3	25.0	1.0
1941	Cle-A	155	75	79	.487	●4				77.9	-2.9
8		995	500	491	.505						9.5

Perez, Atanasio "Tony"

YEAR	TM/L	G	W	L	PCT	STANDING			M/Y	W-EXP	A-E
1993	Cin-N	44	20	24	.455	5 W	5 W		1/2	20.3	-0.3

Perkins, Ralph Foster "Cy"

YEAR	TM/L	G	W	L	PCT	STANDING			M/Y	W-EXP	A-E
1937	Det-A	15	6	9	.400	2	2		5/5	8.3	-2.3

Pesky, John Michael "Johnny"

YEAR	TM/L	G	W	L	PCT	STANDING			M/Y	W-EXP	A-E
1963	Bos-A	161	76	85	.472	7				76.6	-0.6
1964	Bos-A	160	70	90	.438	8	8		1/2	69.7	0.3
1980	Bos-A	5	1	4	.200	3 E	4 E		2/2	2.5	-1.5
3		326	147	179	.451						-1.8

Pfeffer, Nathaniel Frederick "Fred"

YEAR	TM/L	G	W	L	PCT	STANDING			M/Y	W-EXP	A-E
1892(1)	Lou-N*	23	9	14	.391	10	11		2/2		
(2)	Lou-N*	77	33	42	.440	9				39.2	2.8

Phelan, Lewis G. "Lew"

YEAR	TM/L	G	W	L	PCT	STANDING			M/Y	W-EXP	A-E
1895	StL-N	45	11	30	.268	11	11		4/4	13.1	-2.1

Phillips, Harold Ross "Lefty"

YEAR	TM/L	G	W	L	PCT	STANDING			M/Y	W-EXP	A-E
1969	Cal-A	124	60	63	.488	6 W	3 W		2/2	51.0	9.0
1970	Cal-A	162	86	76	.531	3 W				81.1	4.9
1971	Cal-A	162	76	86	.469	4 W				73.5	2.5
3		448	222	225	.497						16.4

Phillips, Horace B.

YEAR	TM/L	G	W	L	PCT	STANDING			M/Y	W-EXP	A-E
1879	Tro-N	47	12	34	.261	8	8		1/2	10.8	1.2
1883	Col-a	97	32	65	.330	6				32.4	-0.4
1884	Pit-a	35	9	24	.273	10	10		5/5	7.4	1.6
1885	Pit-a	111	56	55	.505	3				56.3	-0.3
1886	Pit-a	140	80	57	.584	2				83.7	-3.7
1887	Pit-N	125	55	69	.444	6				50.3	4.7
1888	Pit-N	139	66	68	.493	6				62.1	3.9
1889	Pit-N	71	28	43	.394	6	5		1/3	31.9	-3.9
8		765	338	415	.449						3.1

Phillips, William Corcoran "Bill"

YEAR	TM/L	G	W	L	PCT	STANDING			M/Y	W-EXP	A-E
1914	Ind-F	157	88	65	.575	1				90.6	-2.6
1915	New-F	53	26	27	.491	6	5		1/2	27.4	-1.4
2		210	114	92	.553						-4.0

Pike, Lipman Emanuel "Lip"

YEAR	TM/L	G	W	L	PCT	STANDING			M/Y	W-EXP	A-E
1871	Tro-n*	4	1	3	.250	7	6		1/2	1.9	-0.9
1874	Har-n*	54	17	37	.315	7				19.0	-3.0
1877	Cin-N*	14	3	11	.214	6	6		1/3	3.1	-0.1
3		72	21	51	.292						-4.0

Piniella, Louis Victor "Lou"

YEAR	TM/L	G	W	L	PCT	STANDING			M/Y	W-EXP	A-E
1986	NY-A	162	90	72	.556	2 E				86.8	3.2
1987	NY-A	162	89	73	.549	4 E				83.9	5.1
1988	NY-A	93	45	48	.484	2 E	5 E		2/2	47.9	-2.9
1990	Cin-N	162	91	71	.562	★1 W				91.2	-0.2
1991	Cin-N	162	74	88	.457	5 W				80.8	-6.8
1992	Cin-N	162	90	72	.556	2 W				86.5	3.5
1993	Sea-A	162	82	80	.506	4 W				81.3	0.7
1994	Sea-A	112	49	63	.438	3 W				51.7	-2.7
8		1177	610	567	.518						0.0

Plummer, William Francis "Bill"

YEAR	TM/L	G	W	L	PCT	STANDING			M/Y	W-EXP	A-E
1992	Sea-A	162	64	98	.395	7 W				69.1	-5.1

Popowski, Edward Joseph "Eddie"

YEAR	TM/L	G	W	L	PCT	STANDING			M/Y	W-EXP	A-E
1969	Bos-A	9	5	4	.556	3 E	3 E		2/2	4.5	0.5
1973	Bos-A	1	1	0	1.000	2 E	2 E		2/2	0.6	0.4
2		10	6	4	.600						0.9

Porter, Matthew S. "Matt"

YEAR	TM/L	G	W	L	PCT	STANDING			M/Y	W-EXP	A-E
1884	KC-U*	16	3	13	.188	8	8	8	2/3	2.5	0.5

Powers, Patrick Thomas "Pat"

YEAR	TM/L	G	W	L	PCT	STANDING			M/Y	W-EXP	A-E
1890	Roc-a	133	63	63	.500	5				62.8	0.2
1892(1)	NY-N	74	31	43	.419	10					
(2)	NY-N	79	40	37	.519	6				74.1	-3.1
2		286	134	143	.484						-2.9

Pratt, Albert George "Al"

YEAR	TM/L	G	W	L	PCT	STANDING			M/Y	W-EXP	A-E
1882	Pit-a	79	39	39	.500	4				39.9	-0.9
1883	Pit-a	32	12	20	.375	6	7		1/3	10.4	1.6
2		111	51	59	.464						0.6

Price, James L. "Jim"

YEAR	TM/L	G	W	L	PCT	STANDING			M/Y	W-EXP	A-E
1884	NY-N	100	56	42	.571	4	●4		1/2	54.5	1.5

Prothro, James Thompson "Doc"

YEAR	TM/L	G	W	L	PCT	STANDING			M/Y	W-EXP	A-E
1939	Phi-N	152	45	106	.298	8				45.6	-0.6
1940	Phi-N	153	50	103	.327	8				49.6	0.4
1941	Phi-N	155	43	111	.279	8				46.7	-3.7
3		460	138	320	.301						-3.9

Purcell, William Aloysius "Blondie"

YEAR	TM/L	G	W	L	PCT	STANDING			M/Y	W-EXP	A-E
1883	Phi-N	82	13	68	.160	8	8		2/2	10.0	3.0

Quilici, Francis Ralph "Frank"

YEAR	TM/L	G	W	L	PCT	STANDING			M/Y	W-EXP	A-E
1972	Min-A	84	43	43	.488	3 W	3 W		2/2	42.1	-1.1
1973	Min-A	162	81	81	.500	3 W				85.6	-4.6
1974	Min-A	163	82	80	.506	3 W				81.4	0.6
1975	Min-A	159	76	83	.478	4 W				78.3	-2.3
4		568	280	287	.494						-7.5

Quinn, Joseph J. "Joe"

YEAR	TM/L	G	W	L	PCT	STANDING	M/Y	W-EXP	A-E
1895	StL-N*	40	11	28	.282	11 11 11	3/4	12.5	-1.5
1899	Cle-N*	116	12	104	.103	12 12	2/2	10.0	2.0
2		156	23	132	.148				0.6

Rader, Douglas Lee "Doug"

YEAR	TM/L	G	W	L	PCT	STANDING	M/Y	W-EXP	A-E
1983	Tex-A	163	77	85	.475	3 W		84.3	-7.3
1984	Tex-A	161	69	92	.429	7 W		74.5	-5.5
1985	Tex-A	32	9	23	.281	7 W 7 W	1/2	12.6	-3.6
1986	Chi-A	2	1	1	.500	6 W 5 W 5 W	2/3	0.9	0.1
1989	Cal-A	162	91	71	.562	3 W		90.8	0.2
1990	Cal-A	162	80	82	.494	4 W		79.4	0.6
1991	Cal-A	124	61	63	.492	7 W 7 W	1/2	62.3	-1.3
7		806	388	417	.482				-16.9

Rapp, Vernon Fred "Vern"

YEAR	TM/L	G	W	L	PCT	STANDING	M/Y	W-EXP	A-E
1977	StL-N	162	83	79	.512	3 E		86.0	-3.0
1978	StL-N	17	6	11	.353	6 E 5 E	1/3	7.9	-1.9
1984	Cin-N	121	51	70	.421	5 W 5 W	1/2	51.3	-0.3
3		300	140	160	.467				-5.1

Reach, Alfred James "Al"

YEAR	TM/L	G	W	L	PCT	STANDING	M/Y	W-EXP	A-E
1890	Phi-N	11	4	7	.364	2 3 3	3/5	6.4	-2.4

Rice, Delbert "Del"

YEAR	TM/L	G	W	L	PCT	STANDING	M/Y	W-EXP	A-E
1972	Cal-A	155	75	80	.484	5 W		68.1	6.9

Richards, Paul Rapier

YEAR	TM/L	G	W	L	PCT	STANDING	M/Y	W-EXP	A-E
1951	Chi-A	155	81	73	.526	4		84.1	-3.1
1952	Chi-A	156	81	73	.526	3		81.6	-0.6
1953	Chi-A	156	89	65	.578	3		89.8	-0.8
1954	Chi-A	146	91	54	.628	3 3	1/2	91.5	-0.5
1955	Bal-A	156	57	97	.370	7		54.7	2.3
1956	Bal-A	154	69	85	.448	6		63.0	6.0
1957	Bal-A	154	76	76	.500	5		77.0	-1.0
1958	Bal-A	154	74	79	.484	6		70.4	3.6
1959	Bal-A	155	74	80	.481	6		69.4	4.6
1960	Bal-A	154	89	65	.578	2		84.9	4.1
1961	Bal-A	136	78	57	.578	3 3	1/2	76.7	1.3
1976	Chi-A	161	64	97	.398	6 W		63.9	0.1
12		1837	923	901	.506				15.9

Richardson, Daniel "Danny"

YEAR	TM/L	G	W	L	PCT	STANDING	M/Y	W-EXP	A-E
1892(2)	Was-N*	43	12	31	.279	11 12	2/2	17.9	-5.9

Rickey, Wesley Branch "Branch"

YEAR	TM/L	G	W	L	PCT	STANDING	M/Y	W-EXP	A-E
1913	StL-A	12	5	6	.455	7 8	3/3	4.6	0.4
1914	StL-A*	159	71	82	.464	5		66.2	4.8
1915	StL-A	159	63	91	.409	6		59.6	3.4
1919	StL-N	138	54	83	.394	7		58.7	-4.7
1920	StL-N	155	75	79	.487	●5		76.3	-1.3
1921	StL-N	154	87	66	.569	3		88.8	-1.8
1922	StL-N	154	85	69	.552	●3		81.0	4.0
1923	StL-N	154	79	74	.516	5		77.9	1.1
1924	StL-N	154	65	89	.422	6		76.0	-11.0
1925	StL-N	38	13	25	.342	8 4	1/2	20.5	-7.5
10		1277	597	664	.473				-12.6

Riddoch, Gregory Lee "Greg"

YEAR	TM/L	G	W	L	PCT	STANDING	M/Y	W-EXP	A-E
1990	SD-N	82	38	44	.463	4 W 5 W	2/2	41.0	-3.0
1991	SD-N	162	84	78	.519	3 W		79.9	4.1
1992	SD-N	150	78	72	.520	3 W 3 W	1/2	73.1	4.9
3		394	200	194	.508				6.0

Riggleman, James David "Jim"

YEAR	TM/L	G	W	L	PCT	STANDING	M/Y	W-EXP	A-E
1992	SD-N	12	4	8	.333	3 W 4 W	2/2	5.8	-1.8
1993	SD-N	162	61	101	.377	7 W		71.7	-10.7
1994	SD-N	117	47	70	.402	4 W		53.2	-6.2
3		291	112	179	.385				-18.7

Rigney, William Joseph "Bill"

YEAR	TM/L	G	W	L	PCT	STANDING	M/Y	W-EXP	A-E
1956	NY-N	154	67	87	.435	6		65.1	1.9
1957	NY-N	154	69	85	.448	6		71.1	-2.1
1958	SF-N	154	80	74	.519	3		79.9	0.1
1959	SF-N	154	83	71	.539	3		86.4	-3.4
1960	SF-N	58	33	25	.569	2 5	1/2	30.6	2.4
1961	LA-A	162	70	91	.435	8		76.6	-6.6
1962	LA-A	162	86	76	.531	3		82.2	3.8
1963	LA-A	161	70	91	.435	9		73.7	-3.2
1964	LA-A	162	82	80	.506	5		80.2	1.8
1965	Cal-A	162	75	87	.463	7		76.2	-1.2
1966	Cal-A	162	80	82	.494	6		76.8	3.2
1967	Cal-A	161	84	77	.522	5		78.3	5.7
1968	Cal-A	162	67	95	.414	8		67.6	-0.6
1969	Cal-A	39	11	28	.282	6 W 3 W	1/2	16.2	-5.2
1970	Min-A	162	98	64	.605	1 W		95.5	2.5
1971	Min-A	160	74	86	.463	5 W		78.3	-4.3
1972	Min-A	70	36	34	.514	3 W 3 W	1/2	35.1	0.9
1976	SF-N	162	74	88	.457	4 W		71.3	2.7
18		2561	1239	1321	.484				-2.0

Ripken, Calvin Edwin Sr. "Cal"

YEAR	TM/L	G	W	L	PCT	STANDING	M/Y	W-EXP	A-E
1985	Bal-A	1	1	0	1.000	4 E 4 E 4 E	2/3	0.5	0.5
1987	Bal-A	162	67	95	.414	6 E		66.6	0.4
1988	Bal-A	6	0	6	.000	7 E 7 E	1/2	2.1	-2.1
3		169	68	101	.402				-1.2

Robinson, Frank

YEAR	TM/L	G	W	L	PCT	STANDING	M/Y	W-EXP	A-E
1975	Cle-A*	159	79	80	.497	4 E		78.0	1.0
1976	Cle-A*	159	81	78	.509	4 E		79.5	1.5
1977	Cle-A	57	26	31	.456	5 E 5 E	1/2	26.2	-0.2
1981(1)	SF-N	59	27	32	.458	5 W			
(2)	SF-N	52	29	23	.558	3 W		56.9	-0.9
1982	SF-N	162	87	75	.537	3 W		79.6	7.4
1983	SF-N	162	79	83	.488	5 W		80.0	-1.0
1984	SF-N	106	42	64	.396	6 W 6 W	1/2	44.9	-2.9
1988	Bal-A	155	54	101	.348	7 E 7 E	2/2	53.6	0.4
1989	Bal-A	162	87	75	.537	2 E		83.3	3.7
1990	Bal-A	162	76	85	.472	5 E		77.5	-1.5
1991	Bal-A	37	13	24	.351	7 E 6 E	1/2	16.0	-3.0
11		1432	680	751	.475				4.6

Robinson, Wilbert

YEAR	TM/L	G	W	L	PCT	STANDING	M/Y	W-EXP	A-E
1902	Bal-A*	83	24	57	.296	7 8	2/2	33.5	-9.5
1914	Bro-N	154	75	79	.487	5		77.4	-2.4
1915	Bro-N	154	80	72	.526	3		73.3	6.7
1916	Bro-N	156	94	60	.610	1		90.1	3.9
1917	Bro-N	156	70	81	.464	7		70.0	-0.0
1918	Bro-N	127	57	69	.452	5		50.9	6.1
1919	Bro-N	141	69	71	.493	5		71.3	-2.3
1920	Bro-N	155	93	61	.604	1		91.3	1.7
1921	Bro-N	152	77	75	.507	5		74.6	2.4
1922	Bro-N	155	76	78	.494	6		75.9	0.1
1923	Bro-N	155	76	78	.494	6		78.2	-2.2
1924	Bro-N	154	92	62	.597	2		81.2	10.8
1925	Bro-N	153	68	85	.444	●6		69.2	-1.2
1926	Bro-N	155	71	82	.464	6		68.1	2.9
1927	Bro-N	154	65	88	.425	6		68.0	-3.0
1928	Bro-N	155	77	76	.503	6		79.1	-2.1
1929	Bro-N	153	70	83	.458	6		64.3	5.7
1930	Bro-N	154	86	68	.558	4		89.3	-3.3
1931	Bro-N	153	79	73	.520	4		76.8	2.2
19		2819	1399	1398	.500				16.4

Robison, Matthew Stanley "Stanley"

YEAR	TM/L	G	W	L	PCT	STANDING	M/Y	W-EXP	A-E
1905	StL-N	50	19	31	.380	6 6	3/3	18.2	0.8

Rodgers, Robert Leroy "Buck"

YEAR	TM/L	G	W	L	PCT	STANDING	M/Y	W-EXP	A-E
1980	Mil-A	47	26	21	.553	2 E 3 E	1/3	27.2	-1.2
		23	13	10	.565	4 E 3 E	3/3	13.3	-0.3
1981(1)	Mil-A	56	31	25	.554	3 E			
(2)	Mil-A	53	31	22	.585	1 E		58.0	4.0
1982	Mil-A	47	23	24	.489	5 E ◆1E	1/2	28.3	-5.3
1985	Mon-N	161	84	77	.522	3 E		80.2	3.8
1986	Mon-N	161	78	83	.484	4 E		75.2	2.8
1987	Mon-N	162	91	71	.562	3 E		83.1	7.9
1988	Mon-N	163	81	81	.500	3 E		84.9	-3.9
1989	Mon-N	162	81	81	.500	4 E		81.2	-0.2
1990	Mon-N	162	85	77	.525	3 E		87.9	-2.9
1991	Mon-N	49	20	29	.408	6 E 6 E	1/2	22.0	-2.0
	Cal-A	38	20	18	.526	7 W 7 W	2/2	19.1	0.9
1992	Cal-A	39	19	20	.487	5 W ●5W	1/3	17.1	1.9
	Cal-A	34	14	20	.412	5 W ●5W	3/3	14.9	-0.9
1993	Cal-A	162	71	91	.438	●5W		72.4	-1.4
1994	Cal-A	39	16	23	.410	3 W 4 W	1/3	15.8	0.2
13		1558	784	773	.504				3.4

Rogers, James F. "Jim"

YEAR	TM/L	G	W	L	PCT	STANDING	M/Y	W-EXP	A-E
1897	Lou-N*	44	17	24	.415	9 11	1/2	15.2	1.8

Rojas, Octavio Victor "Cookie"

YEAR	TM/L	G	W	L	PCT	STANDING	M/Y	W-EXP	A-E
1988	Cal-A	154	75	79	.487	4 W 4 W	1/2	71.6	3.4

Rolfe, Robert Abial "Red"

YEAR	TM/L	G	W	L	PCT	STANDING	M/Y	W-EXP	A-E
1949	Det-A	155	87	67	.565	4		86.6	0.4
1950	Det-A	157	95	59	.617	2		88.8	6.2
1951	Det-A	154	73	81	.474	5		71.5	1.5
1952	Det-A	73	23	49	.319	8 8	1/2	27.2	-4.2
4		539	278	256	.521				3.9

Rose, Peter Edward "Pete"

YEAR	TM/L	G	W	L	PCT	STANDING	M/Y	W-EXP	A-E
1984	Cin-N*	41	19	22	.463	5 W 5 W	2/2	17.4	1.6
1985	Cin-N*	162	89	72	.553	2 W		81.6	7.4
1986	Cin-N*	162	86	76	.531	2 W		82.5	3.5
1987	Cin-N	162	84	78	.519	2 W		84.0	-0.0
1988	Cin-N	23	11	12	.478	4 W 2 W	1/3	12.2	-1.2
	Cin-N	111	64	47	.577	4 W 2 W	3/3	58.9	5.1
1989	Cin-N	125	59	66	.472	●4 W 5 W	1/2	57.7	1.3
6		786	412	373	.525				17.7

Roseman, James John "Chief"

YEAR	TM/L	G	W	L	PCT	STANDING	M/Y	W-EXP	A-E
1890	StL-a*	15	7	8	.467	4 5 3	3/6	8.8	-1.8

Rowe, David E. "Dave"

YEAR	TM/L	G	W	L	PCT	STANDING	M/Y	W-EXP	A-E
1886	KC-N*	126	30	91	.248	7		26.1	3.9
1888	KC-a*	50	14	36	.280	8 8	1/3	14.2	-0.2
2		176	44	127	.257				3.7

Rowe, John Charles "Jack"

YEAR	TM/L	G	W	L	PCT	STANDING	M/Y	W-EXP	A-E
1890	Buf-P*	81	22	58	.275	8 8	1/3	20.9	1.1
	Buf-P*	19	5	14	.263	8 8	3/3	5.0	0.0

Rowland, Clarence Henry "Pants"

YEAR	TM/L	G	W	L	PCT	STANDING	M/Y	W-EXP	A-E
1915	Chi-A	156	93	61	.604	3		99.2	-6.2
1916	Chi-A	155	89	65	.578	2		88.7	0.3
1917	Chi-A	156	100	54	.649	★1		98.5	1.5
1918	Chi-A	124	57	67	.460	6		63.2	-6.2

YEAR	TM/L	G	W	L	PCT	STANDING			M/Y	W-EXP	A-E
	4	591	339	247	.578						-10.6

Ruel, Herold Dominic "Muddy"

YEAR	TM/L	G	W	L	PCT	STANDING			M/Y	W-EXP	A-E
1947	StL-A	154	59	95	.383	8				58.5	0.5

Runnells, Thomas William "Tom"

YEAR	TM/L	G	W	L	PCT	STANDING			M/Y	W-EXP	A-E
1991	Mon-N	112	51	61	.455	6 E	6 E		2/2	50.3	0.7
1992	Mon-N	37	17	20	.459	4 E	2 E		1/2	20.2	-3.2
2		149	68	81	.456						-2.4

Runnels, James Edward "Pete"

YEAR	TM/L	G	W	L	PCT	STANDING			M/Y	W-EXP	A-E
1966	Bos-A	16	8	8	.500	9	9		2/2	7.2	0.8

Ryan, Cornelius Joseph "Connie"

YEAR	TM/L	G	W	L	PCT	STANDING			M/Y	W-EXP	A-E
1975	Atl-N	27	9	18	.333	5 W	5 W		2/2	10.8	-1.8
1977	Tex-A	6	2	4	.333	3 W	5 W	2 W	3/4	3.4	-1.4
2		33	11	22	.333						-3.2

Sawyer, Edwin Milby "Eddie"

YEAR	TM/L	G	W	L	PCT	STANDING			M/Y	W-EXP	A-E
1948	Phi-N	63	23	40	.365	6	6		3/3	25.7	-2.7
1949	Phi-N	154	81	73	.526	3				76.4	4.6
1950	Phi-N	157	91	63	.591	1				87.0	4.0
1951	Phi-N	154	73	81	.474	5				77.4	-4.4
1952	Phi-N	63	28	35	.444	6	4		1/2	36.1	-8.1
1958	Phi-N	70	30	40	.429	8	8		2/2	30.6	-0.6
1959	Phi-N	155	64	90	.416	8				64.1	-0.1
1960	Phi-N	1	0	1	.000	●6	8		1/3	0.4	-0.4
8		817	390	423	.480						-7.7

Scanlon, Michael B. "Mike"

YEAR	TM/L	G	W	L	PCT	STANDING			M/Y	W-EXP	A-E
1884	Was-U	114	47	65	.420	6				46.3	0.7
1886	Was-N	82	13	67	.162	8	8		1/2	18.0	-5.0
2		196	60	132	.313						-4.3

Schaefer, Robert Wald "Bob"

YEAR	TM/L	G	W	L	PCT	STANDING			M/Y	W-EXP	A-E
1991	KC-A	1	1	0	1.000	7 W	7 W	6 W	2/3	0.5	0.5

Schalk, Raymond William "Ray"

YEAR	TM/L	G	W	L	PCT	STANDING			M/Y	W-EXP	A-E
1927	Chi-A*	153	70	83	.458	5				71.9	-1.9
1928	Chi-A*	75	32	42	.432	6	5		1/2	33.7	-1.7
2		228	102	125	.449						-3.6

Scheffing, Robert Boden "Bob"

YEAR	TM/L	G	W	L	PCT	STANDING			M/Y	W-EXP	A-E
1957	Chi-N	156	62	92	.403	●7				67.4	-5.4
1958	Chi-N	154	72	82	.468	●5				75.4	-3.4
1959	Chi-N	155	74	80	.481	●5				75.5	-1.5
1961	Det-A	163	101	61	.623	2				97.7	3.3
1962	Det-A	161	85	76	.528	4				87.1	-2.1
1963	Det-A	60	24	36	.400	9	●5		1/2	29.9	-5.9
6		849	418	427	.495						-15.1

Schlafly, Harry Linton "Larry"

YEAR	TM/L	G	W	L	PCT	STANDING			M/Y	W-EXP	A-E
1914	Buf-F*	156	80	71	.530	4				77.4	2.6
1915	Buf-F	41	13	28	.317	8	6		1/3	18.8	-5.8
2		197	93	99	.484						-3.2

Schmelz, Gustavius Heinrich "Gus"

YEAR	TM/L	G	W	L	PCT	STANDING			M/Y	W-EXP	A-E
1884	Col-a	110	69	39	.639	2				66.3	2.7
1886	StL-N	126	43	79	.352	6				45.3	-2.3
1887	Cin-a	136	81	54	.600	2				80.2	0.8
1888	Cin-a	137	80	54	.597	4				78.1	1.9
1889	Cin-a	141	76	63	.547	4				80.7	-4.7
1890	Cle-N	78	21	55	.276	7	7		1/2	27.4	-6.4
	Col-a	57	38	13	.745	5	2		2/3	33.1	4.9
1891	Col-a	138	61	76	.445	6				61.6	-0.6
1894	Was-N	132	45	87	.341	11				47.5	-2.5
1895	Was-N	133	43	85	.336	10				47.2	-4.2
1896	Was-N	133	58	73	.443	●9				57.0	1.0
1897	Was-N	36	9	25	.265	11	●6		1/2	16.7	-7.7
11		1357	624	703	.470						-17.2

Schoendienst, Albert Fred "Red"

YEAR	TM/L	G	W	L	PCT	STANDING			M/Y	W-EXP	A-E
1965	StL-N	162	80	81	.497	7				83.9	-3.9
1966	StL-N	162	83	79	.512	6				80.3	2.7
1967	StL-N	161	101	60	.627	★1				95.3	5.7
1968	StL-N	162	97	65	.599	1				94.1	2.9
1969	StL-N	162	87	75	.537	4 E				87.2	-0.2
1970	StL-N	162	76	86	.469	4 E				80.7	-4.7
1971	StL-N	163	90	72	.556	2 E				85.0	5.0
1972	StL-N	156	75	81	.481	4 E				74.5	0.5
1973	StL-N	162	81	81	.500	2 E				85.3	-4.3
1974	StL-N	161	86	75	.534	2 E				84.1	1.9
1975	StL-N	163	82	80	.506	●3 E				78.2	3.8
1976	StL-N	162	72	90	.444	5 E				76.6	-4.6
1980	StL-N	37	18	19	.486	5 E	4 E		4/4	19.1	-1.1
1990	StL-N	24	13	11	.542	6 E	6 E	6 E	2/3	10.4	2.6
14		1999	1041	955	.522						6.2

Schultz, Joseph Charles Jr. "Joe"

YEAR	TM/L	G	W	L	PCT	STANDING			M/Y	W-EXP	A-E
1969	Sea-A	163	64	98	.395	6 W				64.8	-0.8
1973	Det-A	28	14	14	.500	3 E	3 E		2/2	13.4	0.6
2		191	78	112	.411						-0.3

Selee, Frank Gibson

YEAR	TM/L	G	W	L	PCT	STANDING			M/Y	W-EXP	A-E
1890	Bos-N	134	76	57	.571	5				82.5	-6.5
1891	Bos-N	140	87	51	.630	1				86.3	0.7
1892(1)	Bos-N	75	52	22	.703	1					
(2)	Bos-N	77	50	26	.658	2				95.3	6.7
1893	Bos-N	131	86	43	.667	1				81.7	4.3
1894	Bos-N	133	83	49	.629	3				82.0	1.0
1895	Bos-N	133	71	60	.542	●5				72.2	-1.2
1896	Bos-N	132	74	57	.565	4				74.0	0.0
1897	Bos-N	135	93	39	.705	1				96.5	-3.5
1898	Bos-N	152	102	47	.685	1				99.3	2.7
1899	Bos-N	153	95	57	.625	2				96.4	-1.4
1900	Bos-N	142	66	72	.478	4				72.6	-6.6
1901	Bos-N	140	69	69	.500	5				66.3	2.7
1902	Chi-N	143	68	69	.496	5				71.7	-3.7
1903	Chi-N	139	82	56	.594	3				78.4	3.6
1904	Chi-N	156	93	60	.608	2				85.7	7.3
1905	Chi-N	65	37	28	.569	4	3		1/2	43.2	-6.2
16		2180	1284	862	.598						-0.1

Sewell, James Luther "Luke"

YEAR	TM/L	G	W	L	PCT	STANDING			M/Y	W-EXP	A-E
1941	StL-A	113	55	55	.500	7	●6		2/2	51.1	3.9
1942	StL-A*	151	82	69	.543	3				84.8	-2.8
1943	StL-A	153	72	80	.474	6				75.1	-3.1
1944	StL-A	154	89	65	.578	1				87.1	1.9
1945	StL-A	154	81	70	.536	3				80.9	0.1
1946	StL-A	125	53	71	.427	7	7		1/2	54.6	-1.6
1949	Cin-N	3	1	2	.333	7	7		2/2	1.2	-0.2
1950	Cin-N	153	66	87	.431	6				68.5	-2.5
1951	Cin-N	155	68	86	.442	6				65.5	2.5
1952	Cin-N	98	39	59	.398	7	6		1/3	46.1	-7.1
10		1259	606	644	.485						-9.0

Shannon, Daniel W. "Dan"

YEAR	TM/L	G	W	L	PCT	STANDING			M/Y	W-EXP	A-E
1889	Lou-a*	58	10	46	.179	8	8	8	3/4	12.1	-2.1
1891	Was-a*	51	15	34	.306	7	8	8	3/4	13.0	2.0
2		109	25	80	.238						-0.1

Sharsig, William A. "Bill"

YEAR	TM/L	G	W	L	PCT	STANDING			M/Y	W-EXP	A-E
1886	Phi-a	41	22	17	.564	6	6		2/2	15.3	6.7
1888	Phi-a	137	81	52	.609	3				88.1	-7.1
1889	Phi-a	138	75	58	.564	3				74.5	0.5
1890	Phi-a	132	54	78	.409	7				45.4	8.6
1891	Phi-a	18	6	11	.353	7	4		1/2	8.8	-2.8
5		466	238	216	.524						5.9

Shawkey, James Robert "Bob"

YEAR	TM/L	G	W	L	PCT	STANDING			M/Y	W-EXP	A-E
1930	NY-A	154	86	68	.558	3				90.8	-4.8

Sheehan, Thomas Clancy "Tom"

YEAR	TM/L	G	W	L	PCT	STANDING			M/Y	W-EXP	A-E
1960	SF-N	98	46	50	.479	2	5		2/2	50.6	-4.6

Shepard, Lawrence William "Larry"

YEAR	TM/L	G	W	L	PCT	STANDING			M/Y	W-EXP	A-E
1968	Pit-N	163	80	82	.494	6				86.9	-6.9
1969	Pit-N	157	84	73	.535	3 E	3 E		1/2	85.8	-1.8
2		320	164	155	.514						-8.6

Sherry, Norman Burt "Norm"

YEAR	TM/L	G	W	L	PCT	STANDING			M/Y	W-EXP	A-E
1976	Cal-A	66	37	29	.561	6 W	●4 W		2/2	29.3	7.7
1977	Cal-A	81	39	42	.481	5 W	5 W		1/2	39.5	-0.5
2		147	76	71	.517						7.2

Shettsline, William Joseph "Bill"

YEAR	TM/L	G	W	L	PCT	STANDING			M/Y	W-EXP	A-E
1898	Phi-N	104	59	44	.573	●8	6		2/2	54.0	5.0
1899	Phi-N	154	94	58	.618	3				91.8	2.2
1900	Phi-N	141	75	63	.543	3				70.6	4.4
1901	Phi-N	140	83	57	.593	2				82.8	0.2
1902	Phi-N	138	56	81	.409	7				51.2	4.8
5		677	367	303	.548						16.6

Shotton, Burton Edwin "Burt"

YEAR	TM/L	G	W	L	PCT	STANDING			M/Y	W-EXP	A-E
1928	Phi-N	152	43	109	.283	8				48.7	-5.7
1929	Phi-N	154	71	82	.464	5				65.1	5.9
1930	Phi-N	156	52	102	.338	8				56.4	-4.4
1931	Phi-N	155	66	88	.429	6				63.2	2.8
1932	Phi-N	154	78	76	.506	4				81.4	-3.4
1933	Phi-N	152	60	92	.395	7				60.7	-0.7
1934	Cin-N	1	1	0	1.000	8	8	8	2/3	0.4	0.6
1947	Bro-N	153	92	60	.605	●1	1		2/2	86.3	5.7
1948	Bro-N	81	48	33	.593	5	3		3/3	44.5	3.5
1949	Bro-N	156	97	57	.630	1				98.8	-1.8
1950	Bro-N	155	89	65	.578	2				88.6	0.4
11		1469	697	764	.477						3.0

Showalter, William Nathaniel "Buck"

YEAR	TM/L	G	W	L	PCT	STANDING			M/Y	W-EXP	A-E
1992	NY-A	162	76	86	.469	●4 E				79.7	-3.7
1993	NY-A	162	88	74	.543	2 E				86.8	1.2
1994	NY-A	113	70	43	.619	1 E				69.0	1.0
3		437	234	203	.535						-1.5

Silvestri, Kenneth Joseph "Ken"

YEAR	TM/L	G	W	L	PCT	STANDING			M/Y	W-EXP	A-E
1967	Atl-N	3	0	3	.000	7	7		2/2	1.5	-1.5

Simmons, Joseph S. "Joe"

YEAR	TM/L	G	W	L	PCT	STANDING			M/Y	W-EXP	A-E
1875	Wes-n*	13	1	12	.077	13				2.5	-1.5
1884	Wil-U	18	2	16	.111	8				0.8	1.2
2		31	3	28	.097						-0.2

Simmons, Lewis "Lew"

YEAR	TM/L	G	W	L	PCT	STANDING			M/Y	W-EXP	A-E
1886	Phi-a	98	41	55	.427	6	6		1/2	37.7	3.3

Sisler, George Harold

YEAR	TM/L	G	W	L	PCT	STANDING			M/Y	W-EXP	A-E
1924	StL-A*	153	74	78	.487	4				72.3	1.7
1925	StL-A*	154	82	71	.536	3				76.0	6.0
1926	StL-A*	155	62	92	.403	7				61.4	0.6
3		462	218	241	.475						8.3

Sisler, Richard Allan "Dick"

YEAR	TM/L	G	W	L	PCT	STANDING			M/Y	W-EXP	A-E
1964	Cin-N	6	3	3	.500	3	4	●2	2/4	3.4	-0.4
	Cin-N	47	29	18	.617	3	●2		4/4	26.5	2.5
1965	Cin-N	162	89	73	.549	4				92.8	-3.8
	2	215	121	94	.563						-1.7

Skaff, Francis Michael "Frank"

YEAR	TM/L	G	W	L	PCT	STANDING			M/Y	W-EXP	A-E
1966	Det-A	79	40	39	.506	2	3		3/3	40.5	-0.5

Skinner, Robert Ralph "Bob"

YEAR	TM/L	G	W	L	PCT	STANDING			M/Y	W-EXP	A-E
1968	Phi-N	107	48	59	.449	5	●7		3/3	48.2	-0.2
1969	Phi-N	108	44	64	.407	5 E	5 E		1/2	47.2	-3.2
1977	SD-N	1	1	0	1.000	4 W	4 W	5 W	2/3	0.4	0.6
	3	216	93	123	.431						-2.7

Slattery, John Terrence "Jack"

YEAR	TM/L	G	W	L	PCT	STANDING			M/Y	W-EXP	A-E
1928	Bos-N	31	11	20	.355	7	7		1/2	10.7	0.3

Smith, Edward Mayo "Mayo"

YEAR	TM/L	G	W	L	PCT	STANDING			M/Y	W-EXP	A-E
1955	Phi-N	154	77	77	.500	4				77.9	-0.9
1956	Phi-N	154	71	83	.461	5				70.0	1.0
1957	Phi-N	156	77	77	.500	5				73.5	3.5
1958	Phi-N	84	39	45	.464	8	8		1/2	36.7	2.3
1959	Cin-N	80	35	45	.438	7	●5		1/2	41.3	-6.3
1967	Det-A	163	91	71	.562	●2				91.3	-0.3
1968	Det-A	164	103	59	.636	★1				101.2	1.8
1969	Det-A	162	90	72	.556	2 E				91.6	-1.6
1970	Det-A	162	79	83	.488	4 E				74.4	4.6
	9	1279	662	612	.520						4.0

Smith, George Henry "Heinie"

YEAR	TM/L	G	W	L	PCT	STANDING			M/Y	W-EXP	A-E
1902	NY-N*	32	5	27	.156	4	8	8	2/3	11.0	-6.0

Smith, Harry Thomas

YEAR	TM/L	G	W	L	PCT	STANDING			M/Y	W-EXP	A-E
1909	Bos-N*	79	23	54	.299	8	8		2/2	24.6	-1.6

Smith, William J. "Bill"

YEAR	TM/L	G	W	L	PCT	STANDING			M/Y	W-EXP	A-E
1873	Mar-n*	5	0	5	.000	9				-3.9	3.9

Snyder, Charles N. "Pop"

YEAR	TM/L	G	W	L	PCT	STANDING			M/Y	W-EXP	A-E
1882	Cin-a*	80	55	25	.688	1				61.6	-6.6
1883	Cin-a*	98	61	37	.622	3				71.6	-10.6
1884	Cin-a*	40	24	14	.632	5	5		2/2	26.5	-2.5
1891	Was-a*	70	23	46	.333	6	7	8	2/4	18.3	4.7
	4	288	163	122	.572						-14.9

Snyder, James Robert "Jim"

YEAR	TM/L	G	W	L	PCT	STANDING			M/Y	W-EXP	A-E
1988	Sea-A	105	45	60	.429	6 W	7 W		2/2	47.2	-2.2

Sothoron, Allen Sutton

YEAR	TM/L	G	W	L	PCT	STANDING			M/Y	W-EXP	A-E
1933	StL-A	8	2	6	.250	8	8	8	2/3	3.2	-1.2

Southworth, William Harrison "Billy"

YEAR	TM/L	G	W	L	PCT	STANDING			M/Y	W-EXP	A-E
1929	StL-N*	90	43	45	.489	4	4		1/3	45.3	-2.3
1940	StL-N	111	69	40	.633	7	3		3/3	57.9	11.1
1941	StL-N	155	97	56	.634	2				91.4	5.6
1942	StL-N	156	106	48	.688	★1				106.1	-0.1
1943	StL-N	157	105	49	.682	1				99.6	5.4
1944	StL-N	157	105	49	.682	★1				106.8	-1.8
1945	StL-N	155	95	59	.617	2				94.7	0.3
1946	Bos-N	154	81	72	.529	4				80.5	0.5
1947	Bos-N	154	86	68	.558	3				85.1	0.9
1948	Bos-N	154	91	62	.595	1				92.4	-1.4
1949	Bos-N	111	55	54	.505	4	4		1/2	53.6	1.4
1950	Bos-N	156	83	71	.539	4				81.7	1.3
1951	Bos-N	60	28	31	.475	5	4		1/2	31.8	-3.8
	13	1770	1044	704	.597						17.1

Spalding, Albert Goodwill "Al"

YEAR	TM/L	G	W	L	PCT	STANDING			M/Y	W-EXP	A-E
1876	Chi-N*	66	52	14	.788	1				63.1	-11.1
1877	Chi-N*	60	26	33	.441	5				28.7	-2.7
	2	126	78	47	.624						-13.9

Speaker, Tristram E "Tris"

YEAR	TM/L	G	W	L	PCT	STANDING			M/Y	W-EXP	A-E
1919	Cle-A*	61	40	21	.656	3	2		2/2	35.0	5.0
1920	Cle-A*	154	98	56	.636	★1				97.7	0.3
1921	Cle-A*	154	94	60	.610	2				96.6	-2.6
1922	Cle-A*	155	78	76	.506	4				72.4	5.6
1923	Cle-A*	153	82	71	.536	3				89.5	-7.5
1924	Cle-A*	153	67	86	.438	6				71.0	-4.0
1925	Cle-A*	155	70	84	.455	6				73.7	-3.7
1926	Cle-A*	154	88	66	.571	2				89.8	-1.8
	8	1139	617	520	.543						-8.7

Spence, Harrison L. "Harry"

YEAR	TM/L	G	W	L	PCT	STANDING			M/Y	W-EXP	A-E
1888	Ind-N	136	50	85	.370	7				55.2	-5.2

Stahl, Charles Sylvester "Chick"

YEAR	TM/L	G	W	L	PCT	STANDING			M/Y	W-EXP	A-E
1906	Bos-A*	40	14	26	.350	8	8		2/2	13.1	0.9

Stahl, Garland "Jake"

YEAR	TM/L	G	W	L	PCT	STANDING			M/Y	W-EXP	A-E
1905	Was-A*	154	64	87	.424	7				68.6	-4.6
1906	Was-A*	151	55	95	.367	7				59.3	-4.3
1912	Bos-A*	154	105	47	.691	★1				101.9	3.1
1913	Bos-A*	81	39	41	.488	5	4		1/2	41.2	-2.2
	4	540	263	270	.493						-8.0

Stallings, George Tweedy

YEAR	TM/L	G	W	L	PCT	STANDING			M/Y	W-EXP	A-E
1897	Phi-N*	134	55	77	.417	10				62.5	-7.5
1898	Phi-N*	46	19	27	.413	●8	6		1/2	24.1	-5.1
1901	Det-A	136	74	61	.548	3				71.8	2.2
1909	NY-A	153	74	77	.490	5				75.8	-1.8
1910	NY-A	142	78	59	.569	3	2		1/2	75.3	2.7
1913	Bos-N	154	69	82	.457	5				70.5	-1.5
1914	Bos-N	158	94	59	.614	★1				88.3	5.7
1915	Bos-N	157	83	69	.546	2				80.1	2.9
1916	Bos-N	158	89	63	.586	3				86.6	2.4
1917	Bos-N	158	72	81	.471	6				74.7	-2.7
1918	Bos-N	124	53	71	.427	7				57.0	-4.0
1919	Bos-N	140	57	82	.410	6				58.6	-1.6
1920	Bos-N	153	62	90	.408	7				60.2	1.8
	13	1813	879	898	.495						-6.7

Stanky, Edward Raymond "Eddie"

YEAR	TM/L	G	W	L	PCT	STANDING			M/Y	W-EXP	A-E
1952	StL-N*	154	88	66	.571	3				81.8	6.2
1953	StL-N*	157	83	71	.539	●3				82.4	0.6
1954	StL-N	154	72	82	.468	6				77.8	-5.8
1955	StL-N	36	17	19	.472	5	7		1/2	15.6	1.4
1966	Chi-A	163	83	79	.512	4				87.6	-4.6
1967	Chi-A	162	89	73	.549	4				85.8	3.2
1968	Chi-A	79	34	45	.430	9	8		1/5	35.7	-1.7
1977	Tex-A	1	1	0	1.000	●3 W	3 W	2 W	2/4	0.6	0.4
	8	906	467	435	.518						-0.3

Start, Joseph "Joe"

YEAR	TM/L	G	W	L	PCT	STANDING			M/Y	W-EXP	A-E
1873	Mut-n*	25	18	7	.720	5	4		2/2	13.9	4.1

Stengel, Charles Dillon "Casey"

YEAR	TM/L	G	W	L	PCT	STANDING			M/Y	W-EXP	A-E
1934	Bro-N	153	71	81	.467	6				71.6	-0.6
1935	Bro-N	154	70	83	.458	5				71.1	-1.1
1936	Bro-N	156	67	87	.435	7				68.0	-1.0
1938	Bos-N	153	77	75	.507	5				69.8	7.2
1939	Bos-N	152	63	88	.417	7				66.3	-3.3
1940	Bos-N	152	65	87	.428	7				63.8	1.2
1941	Bos-N	156	62	92	.403	7				63.8	-1.8
1942	Bos-N	150	59	89	.399	7				60.0	-1.0
1943	Bos-N	107	47	60	.439	6	6		2/2	41.9	5.1
1949	NY-A	155	97	57	.630	★1				95.7	1.3
1950	NY-A	155	98	56	.636	★1				97.8	0.2
1951	NY-A	154	98	56	.636	★1				94.5	3.5
1952	NY-A	154	95	59	.617	★1				94.7	0.3
1953	NY-A	151	99	52	.656	★1				101.0	-2.0
1954	NY-A	155	103	51	.669	2				101.4	1.6
1955	NY-A	154	96	58	.623	1				96.7	-0.7
1956	NY-A	154	97	57	.630	★1				98.8	-1.8
1957	NY-A	154	98	56	.636	1				96.8	1.2
1958	NY-A	155	92	62	.597	★1				95.6	-3.6
1959	NY-A	155	79	75	.513	3				81.1	-2.1
1960	NY-A	155	97	57	.630	1				89.0	8.0
1962	NY-N	161	40	120	.250	10				48.1	-8.1
1963	NY-N	162	51	111	.315	10				51.8	-0.8
1964	NY-N	163	53	109	.327	10				59.4	-6.4
1965	NY-N	96	31	64	.326	10	10		1/2	31.1	-0.1
	25	3766	1905	1842	.508						-4.8

Stovall, George Thomas

YEAR	TM/L	G	W	L	PCT	STANDING			M/Y	W-EXP	A-E
1911	Cle-A*	139	74	62	.544	7	3		2/2	66.1	7.9
1912	StL-A*	117	41	74	.357	8	7		2/2	41.1	-0.1
1913	StL-A*	135	50	84	.373	7	8		1/3	56.1	-6.1
1914	KC-F*	154	67	84	.444	6				71.5	-4.5
1915	KC-F*	153	81	72	.529	4				76.1	4.9
	5	698	313	376	.454						2.1

Stovey, Harry Duffield

YEAR	TM/L	G	W	L	PCT	STANDING			M/Y	W-EXP	A-E
1881	Wor-N*	27	8	18	.308	7	8		2/2	10.6	-2.6
1885	Phi-a*	113	55	57	.491	4				62.1	-7.1
	2	140	63	75	.457						-9.7

Street, Charles Evard "Gabby"

YEAR	TM/L	G	W	L	PCT	STANDING			M/Y	W-EXP	A-E
1929	StL-N	1	1	0	1.000	4	4	4	2/3	0.5	0.5
1930	StL-N	154	92	62	.597	1				96.4	-4.4
1931	StL-N*	154	101	53	.656	★1				96.8	4.2
1932	StL-N	156	72	82	.468	●6				73.7	-1.7
1933	StL-N	91	46	45	.505	5	5		1/2	50.3	-4.3
1938	StL-A	146	53	90	.371	7	7		1/2	53.9	-0.9
	6	702	365	332	.524						-6.6

Stricker, John A. "Cub"

YEAR	TM/L	G	W	L	PCT	STANDING			M/Y	W-EXP	A-E
1892(1)	StL-N*	23	6	17	.261	10	11	9	2/3	8.4	-2.4

Strickland, George Bevan

YEAR	TM/L	G	W	L	PCT	STANDING			M/Y	W-EXP	A-E
1964	Cle-A	73	33	39	.458	8	●6		1/2	35.8	-2.8
1966	Cle-A	39	15	24	.385	3	5		2/2	19.2	-4.2
	2	112	48	63	.432						-7.0

Stubing, Lawrence George "Moose"

YEAR	TM/L	G	W	L	PCT	STANDING			M/Y	W-EXP	A-E
1988	Cal-A	8	0	8	.000	4 W	4 W		2/2	3.7	-3.7

Sukeforth, Clyde Leroy

YEAR	TM/L	G	W	L	PCT	STANDING			M/Y	W-EXP	A-E
1947	Bro-N	2	2	0	1.000	●1	1		1/2	1.1	0.9

Sullivan, Haywood Cooper

YEAR	TM/L	G	W	L	PCT	STANDING			M/Y	W-EXP	A-E
1965	KC-A	136	54	82	.397	10	10			53.1	0.9

Sullivan, James Patrick "Pat"

YEAR	TM/L	G	W	L	PCT	STANDING			M/Y	W-EXP	A-E
1890	Col-a	3	2	1	.667	5	5	2	3/3	1.9	0.1

Sullivan, Timothy Paul "Ted"

YEAR	TM/L	G	W	L	PCT	STANDING			M/Y	W-EXP	A-E
1883	StL-a	79	53	26	.671	2	2		1/2	50.3	2.7
1884	StL-U	31	28	3	.903	1	1		1/2	26.6	1.4
	KC-U*	62	13	46	.220	8	8		3/3	9.1	3.9

YEAR	TM/L	G	W	L	PCT	STANDING			M/Y	W-EXP	A-E
1888	Was-N	96	38	57	.400	8	8		2/2	29.8	8.2
3		268	132	132	.500						16.2

Sullivan, William Joseph Sr. "Billy"

YEAR	TM/L	G	W	L	PCT	STANDING			M/Y	W-EXP	A-E
1909	Chi-A*	159	78	74	.513	4				79.6	-1.6

Sweasy, Charles James "Charlie"

YEAR	TM/L	G	W	L	PCT	STANDING			M/Y	W-EXP	A-E
1875	RS-n*	19	4	15	.211	9				0.6	3.4

Swift, Robert Virgil "Bob"

YEAR	TM/L	G	W	L	PCT	STANDING			M/Y	W-EXP	A-E
1965	Det-A	42	24	18	.571	3	4		1/2	23.2	0.8
1966	Det-A	57	32	25	.561	3	2	3	2/3	29.2	2.8
2		99	56	43	.566						3.6

Tanner, Charles William "Chuck"

YEAR	TM/L	G	W	L	PCT	STANDING			M/Y	W-EXP	A-E
1970	Chi-A	16	3	13	.188	6 W	6 W		3/3	6.1	-3.1
1971	Chi-A	162	79	83	.488	3 W				83.2	-4.2
1972	Chi-A	154	87	67	.565	2 W				80.1	6.9
1973	Chi-A	162	77	85	.475	5 W				75.5	1.5
1974	Chi-A	163	80	80	.500	4 W				76.2	3.8
1975	Chi-A	161	75	86	.466	5 W				75.5	-0.5
1976	Oak-A	161	87	74	.540	2 W				89.8	-2.8
1977	Pit-N	162	96	66	.593	2 E				88.0	8.0
1978	Pit-N	161	88	73	.547	2 E				85.4	2.6
1979	Pit-N	163	98	64	.605	★1 E				94.4	3.6
1980	Pit-N	162	83	79	.512	3 E				83.1	-0.1
1981(1)	Pit-N	49	25	23	.521	4 E					
(2)	Pit-N	54	21	33	.389	6 E				49.1	-3.1
1982	Pit-N	162	84	78	.519	4 E				83.8	0.2
1983	Pit-N	162	84	78	.519	2 E				82.2	1.8
1984	Pit-N	162	75	87	.463	6 E				86.3	-11.3
1985	Pit-N	161	57	104	.354	6 E				65.6	-8.6
1986	Atl-N	161	72	89	.447	6 W				69.7	2.3
1987	Atl-N	161	69	92	.429	5 W				72.6	-3.6
1988	Atl-N	39	12	27	.308	6 W	6 W		1/2	14.7	-2.7
19		2738	1352	1381	.495						-9.6

Tappe, Elvin Walter "El"

YEAR	TM/L	G	W	L	PCT	STANDING			M/Y	W-EXP	A-E
1961	Chi-N	2	2	0	1.000	7	7	7	4/9	0.9	1.1
	Chi-N	79	35	43	.449	7	7		7/9	33.5	1.5
	Chi-N	16	5	11	.313	7	7		9/9	6.9	-1.9
1962	Chi-N	20	4	16	.200	9	9		1/3	7.6	-3.6
2		117	46	70	.397						-2.9

Taylor, George J.

YEAR	TM/L	G	W	L	PCT	STANDING			M/Y	W-EXP	A-E
1884	Bro-a	109	40	64	.385	9				36.3	3.7

Taylor, James Wren "Zack"

YEAR	TM/L	G	W	L	PCT	STANDING			M/Y	W-EXP	A-E
1946	StL-A	31	13	17	.433	7	7		2/2	13.2	-0.2
1948	StL-A	155	59	94	.386	6				59.4	-0.4
1949	StL-A	155	53	101	.344	7				53.9	-0.9
1950	StL-A	154	58	96	.377	7				55.4	2.6
1951	StL-A	154	52	102	.338	8				50.9	1.1
5		649	235	410	.364						2.2

Tebbetts, George Robert "Birdie"

YEAR	TM/L	G	W	L	PCT	STANDING			M/Y	W-EXP	A-E
1954	Cin-N	154	74	80	.481	5				73.7	0.3
1955	Cin-N	154	75	79	.487	5				84.5	-9.5
1956	Cin-N	155	91	63	.591	3				88.5	2.5
1957	Cin-N	154	80	74	.519	4				73.8	6.2
1958	Cin-N	113	52	61	.460	8	4		1/2	62.1	-10.1
1961	Mil-N	25	12	13	.480	3	4		2/2	13.4	-1.4
1962	Mil-N	162	86	76	.531	5				87.6	-1.6
1963	Cle-A	162	79	83	.488	●5				74.0	5.0
1964	Cle-A	91	46	44	.511	8	●6		2/2	44.8	1.2
1965	Cle-A	162	87	75	.537	5				86.3	0.7
1966	Cle-A	123	66	57	.537	3	5		1/2	60.5	5.5
11		1455	748	705	.515						-1.3

Tebeau, Oliver Wendell "Patsy"

YEAR	TM/L	G	W	L	PCT	STANDING			M/Y	W-EXP	A-E
1890	Cle-P*	52	21	30	.412	7	7		2/2	20.0	1.0
1891	Cle-N*	73	31	40	.437	4	5		2/2	33.2	-2.2
1892(1)	Cle-N*	74	40	33	.548	5					
(2)	Cle-N*	79	53	23	.697	1				97.9	-4.9
1893	Cle-N*	129	73	55	.570	3				75.0	-2.0
1894	Cle-N*	130	68	61	.527	6				67.4	0.6
1895	Cle-N*	132	84	46	.646	2				81.7	2.3
1896	Cle-N*	135	80	48	.625	2				81.2	-1.2
1897	Cle-N*	132	69	62	.527	5				73.9	-4.9
1898	Cle-N*	156	81	68	.544	5				79.2	1.8
1899	StL-N*	155	84	67	.556	5				83.1	0.9
1900	StL-N*	92	42	50	.457	7	●5		1/2	45.8	-3.8
11		1339	726	583	.555						-12.2

Tenace, Fury Gene "Gene"

YEAR	TM/L	G	W	L	PCT	STANDING			M/Y	W-EXP	A-E
1991	Tor-A	33	19	14	.576	1 E	1 E	1 E	2/3	17.8	1.2

Tenney, Frederick "Fred"

YEAR	TM/L	G	W	L	PCT	STANDING			M/Y	W-EXP	A-E
1905	Bos-N*	156	51	103	.331	7				48.3	2.7
1906	Bos-N*	152	49	102	.325	8				48.1	0.9
1907	Bos-N*	152	58	90	.392	7				57.7	0.3
1911	Bos-N*	154	44	107	.291	8				46.4	-2.4
4		616	202	402	.334						1.5

Terry, William Harold "Bill"

YEAR	TM/L	G	W	L	PCT	STANDING			M/Y	W-EXP	A-E
1932	NY-N*	114	55	59	.482	8	●6		2/2	60.5	-5.5
1933	NY-N*	156	91	61	.599	★1				89.4	1.6
1934	NY-N*	153	93	60	.608	2				94.4	-1.4
1935	NY-N*	156	91	62	.595	3				85.9	5.1
1936	NY-N*	154	92	62	.597	1				89.2	2.8
1937	NY-N	152	95	57	.625	1				89.2	5.8
1938	NY-N	152	83	67	.553	3				81.9	1.1
1939	NY-N	151	77	74	.510	5				77.3	-0.3
1940	NY-N	152	72	80	.474	6				76.4	-4.4
1941	NY-N	156	74	79	.484	5				72.6	1.4
10		1496	823	661	.555						6.3

Thomas, Frederick L. "Fred"

YEAR	TM/L	G	W	L	PCT	STANDING			M/Y	W-EXP	A-E
1887	Ind-N	29	11	18	.379	8	8	8	2/3	7.9	3.1

Thompson, Andrew M. "A. M."

YEAR	TM/L	G	W	L	PCT	STANDING			M/Y	W-EXP	A-E
1884	Stp-U	9	2	6	.250	7				0.7	1.3

Tighe, John Thomas "Jack"

YEAR	TM/L	G	W	L	PCT	STANDING			M/Y	W-EXP	A-E
1957	Det-A	154	78	76	.506	4				77.0	1.0
1958	Det-A	49	21	28	.429	8	5		1/2	26.3	-5.3
2		203	99	104	.488						-4.3

Tinker, Joseph Bert "Joe"

YEAR	TM/L	G	W	L	PCT	STANDING			M/Y	W-EXP	A-E
1913	Cin-N*	156	64	89	.418	7				65.2	-1.2
1914	Chi-F*	158	87	67	.565	2				88.6	-1.6
1915	Chi-F*	156	86	66	.566	1				87.1	-1.1
1916	Chi-N*	156	67	86	.438	5				74.1	-7.1
4		626	304	308	.497						-10.9

Torborg, Jeffrey Allen "Jeff"

YEAR	TM/L	G	W	L	PCT	STANDING			M/Y	W-EXP	A-E
1977	Cle-A	104	45	59	.433	5 E	5 E		2/2	47.9	-2.9
1978	Cle-A	159	69	90	.434	6 E				73.8	-4.8
1979	Cle-A	95	43	52	.453	6 E	6 E		1/2	44.9	-1.9
1989	Chi-A	161	69	92	.429	7 W				74.8	-5.8
1990	Chi-A	162	94	68	.580	2 W				86.2	7.8
1991	Chi-A	162	87	75	.537	2 W				88.8	-1.8
1992	NY-N	162	72	90	.444	5 E				75.2	-3.2
1993	NY-N	38	13	25	.342	7 E	7 E		1/2	17.3	-4.3
8		1043	492	551	.472						-16.8

Torre, Joseph Paul "Joe"

YEAR	TM/L	G	W	L	PCT	STANDING			M/Y	W-EXP	A-E
1977	NY-N*	117	49	68	.419	6 E	6 E		2/2	52.6	-3.6
1978	NY-N	162	66	96	.407	6 E				72.2	-6.2
1979	NY-N	163	63	99	.389	6 E				69.0	-6.0
1980	NY-N	162	67	95	.414	5 E				71.4	-4.4
1981(1)	NY-N	52	17	34	.333	5 E					
(2)	NY-N	53	24	28	.462	4 E				42.3	-1.3
1982	Atl-N	162	89	73	.549	1 W				84.7	4.3
1983	Atl-N	162	88	74	.543	2 W				91.9	-3.9
1984	Atl-N	162	80	82	.494	●2 W				78.6	1.4
1990	StL-N	58	24	34	.414	6 E	6 E		3/3	25.2	-1.2
1991	StL-N	162	84	78	.519	2 E				81.3	2.7
1992	StL-N	162	83	79	.512	3 E				83.9	-0.9
1993	StL-N	162	87	75	.537	3 E				82.4	4.6
1994	StL-N	115	53	61	.465	●3 C				48.9	4.1
13		1854	874	976	.472						-10.3

Tracewski, Richard Joseph "Dick"

YEAR	TM/L	G	W	L	PCT	STANDING			M/Y	W-EXP	A-E
1979	Det-A	2	2	0	1.000	5 E	5 E	5 E	2/3	1.0	1.0

Traynor, Harold Joseph "Pie"

YEAR	TM/L	G	W	L	PCT	STANDING			M/Y	W-EXP	A-E
1934	Pit-N*	100	47	52	.475	4	5		2/2	50.9	-3.9
1935	Pit-N*	153	86	67	.562	4				86.1	-0.1
1936	Pit-N	156	84	70	.545	4				85.3	-1.3
1937	Pit-N*	154	86	68	.558	3				82.9	3.1
1938	Pit-N	152	86	64	.573	2				82.8	3.2
1939	Pit-N	153	68	85	.444	6				71.0	-3.0
6		868	457	406	.530						-1.9

Trebelhorn, Thomas Lynn "Tom"

YEAR	TM/L	G	W	L	PCT	STANDING			M/Y	W-EXP	A-E
1986	Mil-A	9	6	3	.667	6 E	6 E		2/2	4.1	1.9
1987	Mil-A	162	91	71	.562	3 E				85.2	5.8
1988	Mil-A	162	87	75	.537	●3 E				88.0	-1.0
1989	Mil-A	162	81	81	.500	4 E				83.9	-2.9
1990	Mil-A	162	74	88	.457	6 E				78.2	-4.2
1991	Mil-A	162	83	79	.512	3 E				86.3	-3.3
1994	Chi-N	113	49	64	.434	5 C				51.7	-2.7
7		932	471	461	.505						-6.4

Trott, Samuel W. "Sam"

YEAR	TM/L	G	W	L	PCT	STANDING			M/Y	W-EXP	A-E
1891	Was-a	12	4	7	.364	6	9		1/4	2.9	1.1

Turner, Robert Edward "Ted"

YEAR	TM/L	G	W	L	PCT	STANDING			M/Y	W-EXP	A-E
1977	Atl-N	1	0	1	.000	6 W	6 W	6 W	2/4	0.4	-0.4

Unglaub, Robert Alexander "Bob"

YEAR	TM/L	G	W	L	PCT	STANDING			M/Y	W-EXP	A-E
1907	Bos-A*	29	9	20	.310	6	8	7	3/4	12.4	-3.4

Valentine, Robert John "Bobby"

YEAR	TM/L	G	W	L	PCT	STANDING			M/Y	W-EXP	A-E
1985	Tex-A	129	53	76	.411	7 W	7 W		2/2	50.8	2.2
1986	Tex-A	162	87	75	.537	2 W				83.7	3.3
1987	Tex-A	162	75	87	.463	●6 W				78.6	-3.6
1988	Tex-A	161	70	91	.435	6 W				70.4	-0.4
1989	Tex-A	162	83	79	.512	4 W				79.1	3.9
1990	Tex-A	162	83	79	.512	3 W				78.9	4.1
1991	Tex-A	162	85	77	.525	3 W				82.4	2.6
1992	Tex-A	86	45	41	.523	3 W	4 W		1/2	39.2	5.8
8		1186	581	605	.490						17.8

Van Haltren, George Edward

YEAR	TM/L	G	W	L	PCT	STANDING			M/Y	W-EXP	A-E
1892(1)	Bal-N*	11	1	10	.091	12	12		1/3	3.9	-2.9

Vernon, James Barton "Mickey"

YEAR	TM/L	G	W	L	PCT	STANDING			M/Y	W-EXP	A-E
1961	Was-A	161	61	100	.379	●9				64.4	-3.4
1962	Was-A	162	60	101	.373	10				68.2	-8.2
1963	Was-A	40	14	26	.350	10	10		1/3	14.1	-0.1
3		363	135	227	.373						-11.7

Virdon, William Charles "Bill"

YEAR	TM/L	G	W	L	PCT	STANDING			M/Y	W-EXP	A-E
1972	Pit-N	155	96	59	.619	1 E				96.8	-0.8
1973	Pit-N	136	67	69	.493	2 E	3 E		1/2	68.9	-1.9
1974	NY-A	162	89	73	.549	2 E				86.1	2.9
1975	NY-A	104	53	51	.510	3 E	3 E		1/2	58.4	-5.4
	Hou-N	35	17	17	.500	6 W	6 W		2/2	16.0	1.0
1976	Hou-N	162	80	82	.494	3 W				77.6	2.4
1977	Hou-N	162	81	81	.500	3 W				84.1	-3.1
1978	Hou-N	162	74	88	.457	5 W				77.9	-3.9
1979	Hou-N	162	89	73	.549	2 W				81.1	7.9
1980	Hou-N	163	93	70	.571	▲1 W				86.8	6.2
1981(1)	Hou-N	57	28	29	.491	3 W					
(2)	Hou-N	53	33	20	.623	1 W				62.4	-1.4
1982	Hou-N	111	49	62	.441	5 W	5 W		1/2	51.6	-2.6
1983	Mon-N	163	82	80	.506	3 E				84.3	-2.3
1984	Mon-N	131	64	67	.489	5 E	5 E		1/2	66.2	-2.2
13		1918	995	921	.519						-3.2

Vitt, Oscar Joseph "Ossie"

YEAR	TM/L	G	W	L	PCT	STANDING			M/Y	W-EXP	A-E
1938	Cle-A	153	86	66	.566	3				82.0	4.0
1939	Cle-A	154	87	67	.565	3				86.3	0.7
1940	Cle-A	155	89	65	.578	2				84.4	4.6
3		462	262	198	.570						9.3

Von Der Ahe, Christian Frederick Wilhelm "Chris"

YEAR	TM/L	G	W	L	PCT	STANDING			M/Y	W-EXP	A-E
1895	StL-N	1	1	0	1.000	11	11	11	2/4	0.3	0.7
1896	StL-N	2	0	2	.000	10	11	11	3/5	0.5	-0.5
1897	StL-N	14	2	12	.143	12	12		4/4	2.5	-0.5
3		17	3	14	.176						-0.4

Vukovich, John Christopher

YEAR	TM/L	G	W	L	PCT	STANDING			M/Y	W-EXP	A-E
1986	Chi-N	2	1	1	.500	5 E	5 E	5 E	2/3	0.9	0.1
1988	Phi-N	9	5	4	.556	6 E	6 E		2/2	3.7	1.3
2		11	6	5	.545						1.4

Wagner, Charles F. "Heinie"

YEAR	TM/L	G	W	L	PCT	STANDING			M/Y	W-EXP	A-E
1930	Bos-A	154	52	102	.338	8				57.1	-5.1

Wagner, John Peter "Honus"

YEAR	TM/L	G	W	L	PCT	STANDING			M/Y	W-EXP	A-E
1917	Pit-N*	5	1	4	.200	8	8	8	2/3	2.0	-1.0

Walker, Harry William

YEAR	TM/L	G	W	L	PCT	STANDING			M/Y	W-EXP	A-E
1955	StL-N*	118	51	67	.432	5	7		2/2	51.2	-0.2
1965	Pit-N	163	90	72	.556	3				91.3	-1.3
1966	Pit-N	162	92	70	.568	3				93.0	-1.0
1967	Pit-N	84	42	42	.500	6	6		1/2	41.2	0.8
1968	Hou-N	101	49	52	.485	10	10		2/2	44.9	4.1
1969	Hou-N	162	81	81	.500	5 W				81.8	-0.8
1970	Hou-N	162	79	83	.488	4 W				79.1	-0.1
1971	Hou-N	162	79	83	.488	●4 W				83.0	-4.0
1972	Hou-N	121	67	54	.554	2 W	2 W		1/3	66.3	0.7
9		1235	630	604	.511						-1.9

Wallace, Roderick John "Bobby"

YEAR	TM/L	G	W	L	PCT	STANDING			M/Y	W-EXP	A-E
1911	StL-A*	152	45	107	.296	8				51.6	-6.6
1912	StL-A*	40	12	28	.308	8	7		1/2	13.9	-1.9
1937	Cin-N	25	5	20	.200	8	8		2/2	10.9	-5.9
3		217	62	154	.287						-14.4

Walsh, Edward Augustine "Ed"

YEAR	TM/L	G	W	L	PCT	STANDING			M/Y	W-EXP	A-E
1924	Chi-A	3	1	2	.333	6			2/4	1.4	-0.4

Walsh, Michael John "Mike"

YEAR	TM/L	G	W	L	PCT	STANDING			M/Y	W-EXP	A-E
1884	Lou-a	110	68	40	.630	3				68.7	-0.7

Walters, William Henry "Bucky"

YEAR	TM/L	G	W	L	PCT	STANDING			M/Y	W-EXP	A-E
1948	Cin-N*	53	20	33	.377	7	7		2/2	20.7	-0.7
1949	Cin-N	153	61	90	.404	7	7		1/2	61.4	-0.4
2		206	81	123	.397						-1.2

Waltz, John J.

YEAR	TM/L	G	W	L	PCT	STANDING			M/Y	W-EXP	A-E
1892(1)	Bal-N	8	2	6	.250	12	12	12	2/3	2.9	-0.9

Ward, John Montgomery "Monte"

YEAR	TM/L	G	W	L	PCT	STANDING			M/Y	W-EXP	A-E
1880	Pro-N*	32	18	13	.581	4	3	2	2/3	20.1	-2.1
1884	NY-N*	16	6	8	.429	4	●4		2/2	7.8	-1.8
1890	Bro-P*	133	76	56	.576	2				71.7	4.3
1891	Bro-N*	137	61	76	.445	6				63.6	-2.6
1892(1)	Bro-N*	78	51	26	.662	2					
(2)	Bro-N*	80	44	33	.571	3				95.7	-0.7
1893	NY-N*	136	68	64	.515	5				73.9	-5.9
1894	NY-N*	139	88	44	.667	2				78.8	9.2
7		751	412	320	.563						0.4

Wathan, John David

YEAR	TM/L	G	W	L	PCT	STANDING			M/Y	W-EXP	A-E
1987	KC-A	36	21	15	.583	4 W	2 W		2/2	18.5	2.5
1988	KC-A	161	84	77	.522	3 W				86.3	-2.3
1989	KC-A	162	92	70	.568	2 W				86.8	5.2
1990	KC-A	161	75	86	.466	6 W				80.3	-5.3
1991	KC-A	37	15	22	.405	7 W				18.6	-3.6
1992	Cal-A	89	39	50	.438	5 W	5 W	●5W	2/3	39.0	-0.0
6		646	326	320	.505						-3.6

Watkins, Harvey L.

YEAR	TM/L	G	W	L	PCT	STANDING			M/Y	W-EXP	A-E
1895	NY-N	35	18	17	.514	9	9		3/3	17.9	0.1

Watkins, William Henry "Bill"

YEAR	TM/L	G	W	L	PCT	STANDING			M/Y	W-EXP	A-E
1884	Ind-a*	23	4	18	.182	10	11		2/2	5.6	-1.6
1885	Det-N	70	34	36	.486	8	6		2/2	30.8	3.2
1886	Det-N	126	87	36	.707	2				88.0	-1.0
1887	Det-N	127	79	45	.637	1				83.0	-4.0
1888	Det-N	94	49	44	.527	3	5		1/2	52.7	-3.7
	KC-a	25	8	17	.320	8	8		3/3	7.1	0.9
1889	KC-a	139	55	82	.401	7				53.9	1.1
1893	StL-N	135	57	75	.432	10				58.6	-1.6
1898	Pit-N	151	72	76	.486	8				67.9	4.1
1899	Pit-N	24	7	15	.318	10	7		1/2	11.9	-4.9
9		914	452	444	.504						-7.6

Weaver, Earl Sidney

YEAR	TM/L	G	W	L	PCT	STANDING			M/Y	W-EXP	A-E
1968	Bal-A	82	48	34	.585	3	2		2/2	45.8	2.2
1969	Bal-A	162	109	53	.673	♦1 E				108.8	0.2
1970	Bal-A	162	108	54	.667	★1 E				103.5	4.5
1971	Bal-A	158	101	57	.639	♦1 E				101.4	-0.4
1972	Bal-A	154	80	74	.519	3 E				87.8	-7.8
1973	Bal-A	162	97	65	.599	1 E				101.3	-4.3
1974	Bal-A	162	91	71	.562	1 E				86.0	5.0
1975	Bal-A	159	90	69	.566	2 E				93.4	-3.4
1976	Bal-A	162	88	74	.543	2 E				83.3	4.7
1977	Bal-A	161	97	64	.602	●2 E				87.3	9.7
1978	Bal-A	161	90	71	.559	4 E				83.3	6.7
1979	Bal-A	159	102	57	.642	♦1 E				97.6	4.4
1980	Bal-A	162	100	62	.617	2 E				97.6	2.4
1981(1)	Bal-A	54	31	23	.574	2 E					
(2)	Bal-A	51	28	23	.549	4 E				51.7	7.3
1982	Bal-A	163	94	68	.580	2 E				89.7	4.3
1985	Bal-A	105	53	52	.505	4 E	4 E		3/3	55.9	-2.9
1986	Bal-A	162	73	89	.451	7 E				75.8	-2.8
17		2541	1480	1060	.583						29.9

Westrum, Wesley Noreen "Wes"

YEAR	TM/L	G	W	L	PCT	STANDING			M/Y	W-EXP	A-E
1965	NY-N	68	19	48	.284	10	10		2/2	21.9	-2.9
1966	NY-N	161	66	95	.410	9				62.5	3.5
1967	NY-N	151	57	94	.377	10	10		1/2	57.4	-0.4
1974	SF-N	86	38	48	.442	5 W	5 W		2/2	38.1	-0.1
1975	SF-N	161	80	81	.497	3 W				79.2	0.8
5		627	260	366	.415						0.9

Wheeler, Harry Eugene

YEAR	TM/L	G	W	L	PCT	STANDING			M/Y	W-EXP	A-E
1884	KC-U*	4	0	4	.000	8	8		1/3	0.6	-0.6

White, James Laurie "Deacon"

YEAR	TM/L	G	W	L	PCT	STANDING			M/Y	W-EXP	A-E
1872	Cle-n*	2	0	2	.000	5	7		2/2	0.5	-0.5
1879	Cin-N*	18	9	9	.500	4	5		1/2	9.4	-0.4
2		20	9	11	.450						-0.9

White, Joyner Clifford "Jo-Jo"

YEAR	TM/L	G	W	L	PCT	STANDING			M/Y	W-EXP	A-E
1960	Cle-A	1	1	0	1.000	4	4	4	2/3	0.5	0.5

White, William Henry "Will"

YEAR	TM/L	G	W	L	PCT	STANDING			M/Y	W-EXP	A-E
1884	Cin-a*	72	44	27	.620	5			1/2	49.6	-5.6

White, William Warren "Warren"

YEAR	TM/L	G	W	L	PCT	STANDING			M/Y	W-EXP	A-E
1874	Bal-n*	47	9	38	.191	8				2.4	6.6

Wilber, Delbert Quentin "Del"

YEAR	TM/L	G	W	L	PCT	STANDING			M/Y	W-EXP	A-E
1973	Tex-A	1	1	0	1.000	6 W	6 W	6 W	2/3	0.4	0.6

Wilhelm, Irvin Key "Kaiser"

YEAR	TM/L	G	W	L	PCT	STANDING			M/Y	W-EXP	A-E
1921	Phi-N*	67	26	41	.388	8	8		2/2	21.0	5.0
1922	Phi-N	154	57	96	.373	7				59.9	-2.9
2		221	83	137	.377						2.1

Williams, James A. "Jimmy"

YEAR	TM/L	G	W	L	PCT	STANDING			M/Y	W-EXP	A-E
1884	StL-a	85	51	33	.607	5	4		1/2	50.5	0.5
1887	Cle-a	133	39	92	.298	8				34.6	4.4
1888	Cle-a	64	20	44	.313	8	6		1/2	23.8	-3.8
3		282	110	169	.394						1.1

Williams, James Francis "Jimy"

YEAR	TM/L	G	W	L	PCT	STANDING			M/Y	W-EXP	A-E
1986	Tor-A	163	86	76	.531	4 E				88.4	-2.4
1987	Tor-A	162	96	66	.593	2 E				99.7	-3.7
1988	Tor-A	162	87	75	.537	●3 E				89.3	-2.3
1989	Tor-A	36	12	24	.333	6 E	1 E		1/2	19.8	-7.8
4		523	281	241	.538						-16.3

Williams, Richard Hirschfeld "Dick"

YEAR	TM/L	G	W	L	PCT	STANDING			M/Y	W-EXP	A-E
1967	Bos-A	162	92	70	.568	1				92.3	-0.3
1968	Bos-A	162	86	76	.531	4				81.3	4.7
1969	Bos-A	153	82	71	.536	3 E	3 E		1/2	77.2	4.8
1971	Oak-A	161	101	60	.627	1 W				94.1	6.9
1972	Oak-A	155	93	62	.600	★1 W				94.4	-1.4
1973	Oak-A	162	94	68	.580	★1 W				95.7	-1.7
1974	Cal-A	84	36	48	.429	6 W	6 W		3/3	39.8	-3.8
1975	Cal-A	161	72	89	.447	6 W				70.7	1.3
1976	Cal-A	96	39	57	.406	6 W	●4W		1/2	42.7	-3.7
1977	Mon-N	162	75	87	.463	5 E				73.8	1.2
1978	Mon-N	162	76	86	.469	4 E				83.4	-7.4
1979	Mon-N	160	95	65	.594	2 E				92.7	2.3
1980	Mon-N	162	90	72	.556	2 E				87.8	2.2
1981(1)	Mon-N	55	30	25	.545	3 E					
(2)	Mon-N	26	14	12	.538	2 E	1 E		1/2	44.5	-0.5

YEAR	TM/L	G	W	L	PCT	STANDING			M/Y	W-EXP	A-E
1982	SD-N	162	81	81	.500	4 W				82.8	-1.8
1983	SD-N	163	81	81	.500	4 W				81.0	0.0
1984	SD-N	162	92	70	.568	♦1 W				86.5	5.5
1985	SD-N	162	83	79	.512	●3 W				84.0	-1.0
1986	Sea-A	133	58	75	.436	6 W	7 W		3/3	57.2	0.8
1987	Sea-A	162	78	84	.481	4 W				77.0	1.0
1988	Sea-A	56	23	33	.411	6 W	7 W		1/2	25.2	-2.2
21		3023	1571	1451	.520						7.0

Williams, Theodore Samuel "Ted"

YEAR	TM/L	G	W	L	PCT	STANDING			M/Y	W-EXP	A-E
1969	Was-A	162	86	76	.531	4 E				86.2	-0.2
1970	Was-A	162	70	92	.432	6 E				74.4	-4.4
1971	Was-A	159	63	96	.396	5 E				66.1	-3.1
1972	Tex-A	154	54	100	.351	6 W				58.2	-4.2
4		637	273	364	.429						-11.8

Wills, Maurice Morning "Maury"

YEAR	TM/L	G	W	L	PCT	STANDING			M/Y	W-EXP	A-E
1980	Sea-A	58	20	38	.345	6 W	7 W		2/2	22.3	-2.3
1981(1)	Sea-A	25	6	18	.250	7 W	6 W		1/2	9.9	-3.9
2		83	26	56	.317						-6.2

Wilson, James "Jimmie"

YEAR	TM/L	G	W	L	PCT	STANDING			M/Y	W-EXP	A-E
1934	Phi-N*	149	56	93	.376	7				63.1	-7.1
1935	Phi-N*	156	64	89	.418	7				58.8	5.2
1936	Phi-N*	154	54	100	.351	8				63.2	-9.2
1937	Phi-N*	155	61	92	.399	7				62.9	-1.9
1938	Phi-N*	149	45	103	.304	8	8		1/2	45.7	-0.7
1941	Chi-N	155	70	84	.455	6				76.6	-6.6
1942	Chi-N	155	68	86	.442	6				69.2	-1.2
1943	Chi-N	154	74	79	.484	5				79.9	-5.9
1944	Chi-N	10	1	9	.100	8	4		1/3	5.2	-4.2
9		1237	493	735	.401						-31.7

Wine, Robert Paul Sr. "Bobby"

YEAR	TM/L	G	W	L	PCT	STANDING			M/Y	W-EXP	A-E
1985	Atl-N	41	16	25	.390	5 W	5 W		2/2	16.7	-0.7

Wingo, Ivey Brown

YEAR	TM/L	G	W	L	PCT	STANDING			M/Y	W-EXP	A-E
1916	Cin-N*	2	1	1	.500	8	8	●7	2/3	0.8	0.2

Winkles, Bobby Brooks

YEAR	TM/L	G	W	L	PCT	STANDING			M/Y	W-EXP	A-E
1973	Cal-A	162	79	83	.488	4 W				78.0	1.0
1974	Cal-A	75	30	44	.405	6 W	6 W		1/3	35.1	-5.1
1977	Oak-A	108	37	71	.343	●5 W	7 W		2/2	44.0	-7.0
1978	Oak-A	39	24	15	.615	1 W	6 W		1/2	15.3	8.7
4		384	170	213	.444						-2.5

Wolf, William Van Winkle "Chicken"

YEAR	TM/L	G	W	L	PCT	STANDING			M/Y	W-EXP	A-E
1889	Lou-a*	65	14	51	.215	8	8	8	2/4	14.0	-0.0

Wolverton, Harry Sterling

YEAR	TM/L	G	W	L	PCT	STANDING			M/Y	W-EXP	A-E
1912	NY-A*	153	50	102	.329	8				55.5	-5.5

Wood, George A.

YEAR	TM/L	G	W	L	PCT	STANDING			M/Y	W-EXP	A-E
1891	Phi-a*	125	67	55	.549	7	4		2/2	62.8	4.2

Wood, James Leon "Jimmy"

YEAR	TM/L	G	W	L	PCT	STANDING			M/Y	W-EXP	A-E
1871	Chi-n*	28	19	9	.679	2				18.2	0.8
1872	Tro-n*	25	15	10	.600	5				18.2	-3.2
	Eck-n*	18	3	15	.167	10	9		2/2	-2.0	5.0
1873	Phi-n*	43	28	15	.651	2	2		2/2	29.1	-1.1
1874	Chi-n	23	10	13	.435	4	5		2/2	9.6	0.4
1875	Chi-n	69	30	37	.448	6				30.2	-0.2
5		206	105	99	.515						1.7

Wright, Alfred Hector "Al"

YEAR	TM/L	G	W	L	PCT	STANDING			M/Y	W-EXP	A-E
1876	Phi-N	60	14	45	.237	7				17.5	-3.5

Wright, George

YEAR	TM/L	G	W	L	PCT	STANDING			M/Y	W-EXP	A-E
1879	Pro-N*	85	59	25	.702	1				64.9	-5.9

Wright, William Henry "Harry"

YEAR	TM/L	G	W	L	PCT	STANDING			M/Y	W-EXP	A-E
1871	Bos-n*	31	20	10	.667	3				21.2	-1.2
1872	Bos-n*	48	39	8	.830	1				45.0	-6.0
1873	Bos-n*	60	43	16	.729	1				48.2	-5.2
1874	Bos-n*	71	52	18	.743	1				58.9	-6.9
1875	Bos-n*	82	71	8	.899	1				78.2	-7.2
1876	Bos-N*	70	39	31	.557	4				36.7	2.3
1877	Bos-N*	61	42	18	.700	1				44.0	-2.0
1878	Bos-N	60	41	19	.683	1				35.7	5.3
1879	Bos-N	84	54	30	.643	2				61.5	-7.5
1880	Bos-N	86	40	44	.476	6				38.2	1.8
1881	Bos-N	83	38	45	.458	6				35.4	2.6
1882	Pro-N	84	52	32	.619	2				52.3	-0.3
1883	Pro-N	98	58	40	.592	3				67.1	-9.1
1884	Phi-N	113	39	73	.348	6				32.3	6.7
1885	Phi-N	111	56	54	.509	3				55.2	0.8
1886	Phi-N	119	71	43	.623	4				69.0	2.0
1887	Phi-N	128	75	48	.610	2				78.4	-3.4
1888	Phi-N	132	69	61	.531	3				67.8	1.2
1889	Phi-N	130	63	64	.496	3				63.0	0.0
1890	Phi-N	22	14	8	.636	1	3		1/5	12.7	1.3
	Phi-N	46	22	23	.489	2	3		5/5	26.0	-4.0
1891	Phi-N	138	68	69	.496	4				67.0	1.0
1892(1)	Phi-N	77	46	30	.605	3				92.6	-5.6
(2)	Phi-N	78	41	36	.532	5				78.2	-6.2
1893	Phi-N	133	72	57	.558	4					-39.7
23		2145	1225	885	.581						

York, Preston Rudolph "Rudy"

YEAR	TM/L	G	W	L	PCT	STANDING			M/Y	W-EXP	A-E
1959	Bos-A	1	0	1	.000	8	8	5	2/3	0.5	-0.5

York, Thomas J. "Tom"

YEAR	TM/L	G	W	L	PCT	STANDING			M/Y	W-EXP	A-E
1878	Pro-N*	62	33	27	.550	3				31.4	1.6
1881	Pro-N*	34	23	10	.697	4	2		2/2	17.3	5.7
2		96	56	37	.602						7.3

Yost, Edward Frederick "Eddie"

YEAR	TM/L	G	W	L	PCT	STANDING			M/Y	W-EXP	A-E
1963	Was-A	1	0	1	.000	10	10	10	2/3	0.4	-0.4

Young, Denton True "Cy"

YEAR	TM/L	G	W	L	PCT	STANDING			M/Y	W-EXP	A-E
1907	Bos-A*	6	3	3	.500	●4	7		1/4	2.6	0.4

Young, Nicholas Ephraim "Nick"

YEAR	TM/L	G	W	L	PCT	STANDING			M/Y	W-EXP	A-E
1871	Oly-n	32	15	15	.500	5				15.5	-0.5
1872	Oly-n	9	2	7	.222	10				-1.1	3.1
1873	Was-n	39	8	31	.205	7				5.8	2.2
3		80	25	53	.321						4.7

Zimmer, Charles Louis "Chief"

YEAR	TM/L	G	W	L	PCT	STANDING			M/Y	W-EXP	A-E
1903	Phi-N*	139	49	86	.363	7				55.9	-6.9

Zimmer, Donald William "Don"

YEAR	TM/L	G	W	L	PCT	STANDING			M/Y	W-EXP	A-E
1972	SD-N	142	54	88	.380	4 W	6 W		2/2	53.0	1.0
1973	SD-N	162	60	102	.370	6 W				57.6	2.4
1976	Bos-A	76	42	34	.553	5 E	3 E		2/2	40.7	1.3
1977	Bos-A	161	97	64	.602	●2 E				94.6	2.4
1978	Bos-A	163	99	64	.607	▲2 E				95.5	3.5
1979	Bos-A	160	91	69	.569	3 E				92.5	-1.5
1980	Bos-A	155	82	73	.529	3 E	4 E		1/2	76.6	5.4
1981(1)	Tex-A	55	33	22	.600	2 W					
(2)	Tex-A	50	24	26	.480	3 W				59.2	-2.2
1982	Tex-A	96	38	58	.396	6 W	6 W		1/2	38.2	-0.2
1988	Chi-N	163	77	85	.475	4 E				77.5	-0.5
1989	Chi-N	162	93	69	.574	1 E				89.3	3.7
1990	Chi-N	162	77	85	.475	●4 E				72.6	4.4
1991	Chi-N	37	18	19	.486	4 E	4 E		1/3	17.6	0.4
13		1744	885	858	.508						20.1

Biographical Data for Managers Not Appearing in the Player/Pitcher Registers

BILL ADAIR   Adair, Marion Danne   b: 2/10/13, Mobile, Ala.

BILL ARMOUR   Armour, William Clark   b: 9/3/1869, Homestead, Pa.   d: 12/2/22, Minneapolis, Minn.

FRANK BANCROFT   Bancroft, Frank Carter   b: 5/9/1846, Lancaster, Mass.   d: 3/30/21, Cincinnati, Ohio

ED BARROW   Barrow, Edward Grant "Cousin Ed"   b: 5/10/1868, Springfield, Ill.   d: 12/15/53, Port Chester, N.Y.

JOHN BENJAMIN   Benjamin, John W.   b: 1835, Elizabeth, N.J.   d: 11/14/1895, Elizabeth, N.J.

HUGO BEZDEK   Bezdek, Hugo Frank   b: 4/1/1884, Prague, Czechoslovakia   d: 9/19/52, Atlantic City, N.J.

BICKERSON   Bickerson

DAVE BRISTOL   Bristol, James David   b: 6/23/33, Macon, Ga.

FREEMAN BROWN   Brown, Freeman   b: 1/31/1845, Hubbardstown, Mass   d: 12/27/16, Worcester, Mass.

AL BUCKENBERGER   Buckenberger, Albert C.   b: 1/31/1861, Detroit, Mich.   d: 7/1/17, Syracuse, N.Y.

GEORGE BURNHAM   Burnham, George Walter "Watch"   b: 5/20/1860, Albion, Mich.   d: 11/18/02, Detroit, Mich.

ORMOND BUTLER   Butler, Ormond Hook   b: 11/1854, West Virginia   d: 9/12/15, Mt.Hope, Md.

CHARLIE BYRNE   Byrne, Charles H.   b: 9/1843, New York, N.Y.   d: 1/4/1898, New York, N.Y.

BILL CAMMEYER   Cammeyer, William Henry   b: 3/20/1821, New York, N.Y.   d: 9/4/1898, New York, N.Y.

JOE CANTILLON   Cantillon, Joseph D. "Pongo Joe"   b: 8/19/1861, Janesville, Wis.   d: 1/31/30, Hickman, Ky.

O. P. CAYLOR   Caylor, Oliver Perry   b: 12/17/1849, Near Dayton, Ohio   d: 10/19/1897, Winona, Minn.

TERRY COLLINS   Collins, Terry Lee   b: 5/27/49, Midland, Mich.

ED CURTIS   Curtis, Edwin R.

CHARLIE CUSHMAN   Cushman, Charles H.   b: 5/25/1850, New York, N.Y.   d: 6/29/09, Milwaukee, Wis.

MORDECAI DAVIDSON   Davidson, Mordecai H.   b: 11/30/1846, Port Washington, O   d: 9/6/40, Louisville, Ky.

JOHN DAY   Day, John B.   b: 9/23/47, Colchester, Mass.   d: 1/25/25, Cliffside, N.J.

HARRY DIDDLEBOCK Diddlebock, Henry H. b: 6/27/1854, Philadelphia, Pa. d: 2/5/1900, Philadelphia, Pa.
CHARLIE EBBETS Ebbets, Charles Hercules b: 10/29/1859, New York, N.Y. d: 4/18/25, New York, N.Y.
WALLACE FESSENDEN Fessenden, Wallace Clifton b: 10/5/1860, Windham, N.H.
HORACE FOGEL Fogel, Horace S. b: 3/2/1861, Macungie, Pa. d: 11/15/28, Philadelphia, Pa.
GEORGE FRAZER Frazer, George Kasson b: 1/7/1861, Syracuse, N.Y. d: 2/5/13, Philadelphia, Pa.
JIM FREY Frey, James Gottfried b: 5/26/31, Cleveland, Ohio
JUDGE FUCHS Fuchs, Emil Edwin b: 4/17/1878, Hamburg, Germany d: 12/5/61, Boston, Mass.
JOHN GAFFNEY Gaffney, John H. b: 6/29/1855, Roxbury, Mass. d: 8/8/13, New York, N.Y.
DAVE GARCIA Garcia, David b: 9/15/20, E.St.Louis, Mo.
JIM GIFFORD Gifford, James H. b: 10/18/1845, Warren, N.Y. d: 12/19/01, Columbus, Ohio
MASE GRAFFEN Graffen, Samuel Mason b: 1845, Philadelphia, Pa. d: 11/18/1883, Silver City, N.Mex
CHARLIE HACKETT Hackett, Charles M. b: 1855, Lee, Mass. d: 8/1/1898, Holyoke, Mass.
JIM HART Hart, James Aristotle b: 7/10/1855, Fairview, Pa. d: 7/18/19, Chicago, Ill.
JOHN HART Hart, John Henry (born John Henry Reen) b: 7/21/48, Tampa, Fla.
LOUIE HEILBRONER Heilbroner, Louis Wilbur b: 7/4/1861, Ft.Wayne, Ind. d: 12/21/33, Ft.Wayne, Ind.
BILL HENDERSON Henderson, William C.
ED HENGLE Hengle, Edward Siegfried b: Chicago, Ill. d: 11/4/27, Norwich, England
WALTER HEWETT Hewett, Walter F. b: 1861, Washington, D.C. d: 10/7/44, Washington, D.C.
VEDIE HIMSL Himsl, Avitus Bernard b: 4/2/17, Plevna, Mont.
FRED HOEY Hoey, Frederick Chamberlain b: 1866, New York, N.Y. d: 12/7/33, Paris, France
GEORGE HUFF Huff, George A. "Gee" b: 6/11/1872, Champaign, Ill. d: 10/1/36, Champaign, Ill.
TIM HURST Hurst, Timothy Carroll b: 6/30/1865, Ashland, Pa. d: 6/4/15, Pottsville, Pa.
JOHNNY KEANE Keane, John Joseph b: 11/3/11, St.Louis, Mo. d: 1/6/67, Houston, Tex.
JIM KENNEDY Kennedy, James C. b: 1867, New York, N.Y. d: 4/20/04, Brighton Beach, N.Y.
KEVIN KENNEDY Kennedy, Kevin Curtis b: 9/26/54, Los Angeles, Cal.
JACK KROL Krol, John Thomas b: 7/5/36, Chicago, Ill. d: 5/30/94, Winston-Salem, N.C.
KARL KUEHL Kuehl, Karl Otto b: 9/5/37, Monterey Park, Cal.
BOB LEADLEY Leadley, Robert H. b: 1858, Brooklyn, N.Y.
JIM LEYLAND Leyland, James Richard b: 12/15/44, Toledo, Ohio
NICK LEYVA Leyva, Nicholas Tomas b: 8/16/53, Ontario, Cal.
FRANK LUCCHESI Lucchesi, Frank Joseph b: 4/24/27, San Francisco, Cal.
JACK McCALLISTER McCallister, John b: 1/19/1879, Marietta, Ohio d: 10/18/46, Columbus, Ohio
JOE McCARTHY McCarthy, Joseph Vincent "Marse Joe" b: 4/21/1887, Philadelphia, Pa. d: 1/13/78, Buffalo, N.Y.
JOHN McCLOSKEY McCloskey, John Joseph "Honest John" b: 4/4/1862, Louisville, Ky. d: 11/17/40, Louisville, Ky.
MEL McGAHA McGaha, Fred Melvin b: 9/26/26, Bastrop, La.
JACK McKEON McKeon, John Aloysius b: 11/23/30, South Amboy, N.J.
DENNY McKNIGHT McKnight, Dennis Hamar b: 1847, Pittsburgh, Pa. d: 5/5/1900, Pittsburgh, Pa.
GEORGE McMANUS McManus, George b: 1846, Ireland d: 10/2/18, New York, N.Y.
JOHN McNAMARA McNamara, John Francis b: 6/4/32, Sacramento, Cal.
STUMP MERRILL Merrill, Carl Harrison b: 2/25/44, Brunswick, Me.
RAY MILLER Miller, Raymond Roger b: 4/30/45, Takoma Park, Md.
FELIX MOSES Moses, Felix I. b: Richmond, Va.
BILLY MURRAY Murray, William Jeremiah b: 4/13/1864, Peabody, Mass. d: 3/25/37, Youngstown, Ohio
JIM MUTRIE Mutrie, James J. "Truthful Jim" b: 6/13/1851, Chelsea, Mass. d: 1/24/38, New York, N.Y.
PAUL OWENS Owens, Paul Francis b: 2/7/24, Salamanca, N.Y.
DANNY OZARK Ozark, Daniel Leonard (born Daniel Leonard Orzechowski) b: 11/26/23, Buffalo, N.Y.
LEW PHELAN Phelan, Lewis G.
LEFTY PHILLIPS Phillips, Harold Ross b: 6/16/19, Los Angeles, Cal. d: 6/12/72, Fullerton, Cal.
HORACE PHILLIPS Phillips, Horace B. b: 5/14/1853, Salem, Ohio
EDDIE POPOWSKI Popowski, Edward Joseph b: 8/20/13, Sayerville, N.J.
PAT POWERS Powers, Patrick Thomas b: 6/27/1860, Trenton, N.J. d: 8/29/25, Belmar, N.J.
JIM PRICE Price, James L. b: 1847, New York, N.Y. d: 10/6/31, Chicago, Ill.
VERN RAPP Rapp, Vernon Fred b: 5/11/28, St.Louis, Mo.
GREG RIDDOCH Riddoch, Gregory Lee b: 7/17/45, Greeley, Colo.
JIM RIGGLEMAN Riggleman, James David b: 11/9/52, Fort Dix, N.J.
CAL RIPKEN Ripken, Calvin Edwin Sr. b: 12/17/35, Aberdeen, Md.
STAN ROBISON Robison, Matthew Stanley b: 3/30/1859, Pittsburgh, Pa. d: 3/24/11, Cleveland, Ohio
PANTS ROWLAND Rowland, Clarence Henry b: 2/12/1879, Platteville, Wis. d: 5/17/69, Chicago, Ill.
EDDIE SAWYER Sawyer, Edwin Milby b: 9/10/10, Westerly, R.I.
MIKE SCANLON Scanlon, Michael B. b: 1847, Cork, Ireland d: 1/18/29, Washington, D.C.
BOB SCHAEFER Schaefer, Robert Walden b: 5/22/44, Putnam, Conn. 5'11", 180 lbs. Deb: 5/22/91 M
GUS SCHMELZ Schmelz, Gustavius Heinrich b: 9/26/1850, Columbus, Ohio d: 10/13/25, Columbus, Ohio
FRANK SELEE Selee, Frank Gibson b: 10/26/1859, Amherst, N.Y. d: 7/5/09, Denver, Colo.
BILL SHARSIG Sharsig, William A. b: 1855, Philadelphia, Pa. d: 2/1/02, Philadelphia, Pa.
LARRY SHEPARD Shepard, Lawrence William b: 4/3/19, Lakewood, Ohio
BILL SHETTSLINE Shettsline, William Joseph b: 10/25/1863, Philadelphia, Pa. d: 2/22/33, Philadelphia, Pa.
BUCK SHOWALTER Showalter, William Nathaniel b: 5/23/56, DeFuniak Springs, Fla.
LEW SIMMONS Simmons, Lewis b: 8/27/1838, New Castle, Pa. d: 9/2/11, Jamestown, Pa.
HARRY SPENCE Spence, Harrison L. b: 1858, Virginia d: 5/17/08, Chicago, Ill.
PAT SULLIVAN Sullivan, James Patrick d: 5/22/1898,
GEORGE TAYLOR Taylor, George J. b: 11/22/1853, New York
FRED THOMAS Thomas, Frederick L. b: Indiana
JACK TIGHE Tighe, John Thomas b: 8/9/13, Kearny, N.J.
TOM TREBELHORN Trebelhorn, Thomas Lynn b: 1/27/48, Portland, Ore.
TED TURNER Turner, Robert Edward b: 11/19/38, Cincinnati, Ohio
CHRIS VonDER AHE Von Der Ahe, Christian Frederick Wilhelm b: 10/7/1851, Hille, Germany d: 6/5/13, St.Louis, Mo.
MIKE WALSH Walsh, Michael John b: 4/29/1850, Ireland d: 2/2/29, Louisville, Ky.
JOHN WALTZ Waltz, John J.
HARVEY WATKINS Watkins, Harvey L.
EARL WEAVER Weaver, Earl Sidney b: 8/14/30, St.Louis, Mo.
JIMMY WILLIAMS Williams, James Andrews b: 1/3/1848, Columbus, Ohio d: 10/24/18, N.Hempstead, N.Y.
BOBBY WINKLES Winkles, Bobby Brooks b: 3/11/30, Tuckerman, Ark.
AL WRIGHT Wright, Alfred Hector b: 3/30/1842, Cedar Grove, N.J. d: 4/20/05, New York, N.Y.
NICK YOUNG Young, Nicholas Ephraim b: 9/12/1840, Fort Johnson, N.Y. d: 10/31/16, Washington, D.C.

The Coach Roster

In an age of ever greater specialization in baseball, coaches have become increasingly important to the successful management of a team. The need for such assistance did not occur to any manager until John McGraw took on Arlie Latham as baseball's first full-time coach in 1909; today, teams employ separate coaches for first base, third base, pitching, the bullpen, hitting, baserunning, strength, conditioning, and more. Some coaches, like Charlie Lau and Roger Craig, have achieved fame exceeding that of the managers under whom they served. But coaches leave no statistical trail by which to track them. Players and pitchers have official records, and so do managers, but the accomplishments of coaches (and umpires) have until now resided largely in memory.

In the first edition of *Total Baseball,* the Coach Roster that follows represented a first attempt in a baseball encyclopedia to recognize these foot soldiers, who too often serve as scapegoats when a team fails but are invisible when it succeeds. We offered the roster in full knowledge that there were gaps and probably gaffes in our research; we hoped that our readers would advise us of omissions so that we could improve this roster in future editions of *Total Baseball*—and they have. We owe particular thanks to Bob Hoie and Walt Wilson. An additional feature, besides the inclusion of many new names, is full biographical data for all coaches who did not play at the major-league level and so are absent from the Registers.

The principal sources of the data herein are, for 1921–1939, the *Baseball Blue Book*; for 1940–1981, *The Sporting News Dope Book of 1961,* the *Baseball Register*, and for years since 1982, the *American League Red Book* and the *National League Green Book.* We have done our best to reconcile the many differences among the lists. The team and league abbreviations used in the Coach Roster are found on the final page of this book.

Aaron, Tommie Lee Atl-N 1979-83
Abbott, Spencer Was-A 1935
Adair, James A. "Jimmy" Chi-A 1951-52, Bal-A 1957-61, Hou-N 1962-65
Adair, K. Jerry Oak-A 1972-74, Cal-A 1975
Adair, Marion D. "Bill" Mil-N 1962, Atl-N 1967, Chi-A 1970, Mon-N 1976
Adair, M. Richard "Rick" Cle-A 1992-93
Adams, Charles D. "Red" LA-N 1969-80
Adams, Robert H. "Bobby" Chi-N 1961-64
Aguirre, Henry J. "Hank" Chi-N 1972-74
Aker, Jackie D. "Jack" Cle-A 1985-87
Alfonso, Carlos SF-N 1992
Allenson, Gary M. Bos-A 1992-94
Alomar, Santos C. "Sandy" SD-N 1986-90
Alou, Felipe R. Mon-N 1979-80, 1984, 1992
Alou, Jesus M. R. Hou-N 1979
Altobelli, Joseph S. "Joe" NY-A 1981-82, 1986, Chi-N 1988-91
Altrock, Nicholas "Nick" Was-A 1912-53
Amalfitano, J. Joseph "Joey" Chi-N 1967-71, SF-N 1972-75, SD-N 1976-77, Chi-N 1978-80, Cin-N 1982, LA-N 1983-94
Amaro, Ruben Phi-N 1980-81, Chi-N 1983-86
Anderson, George L. "Sparky" SD-N 1969
Appling, Lucius B. "Luke" Det-A 1960, Cle-A 1960-61, Bal-A 1963, KC-A 1964-67, Chi-A 1970-71
Auferio, Anthony P. "Tony" StL-N 1973
Austin, James P. "Jimmy" StL-A 1923-32, Chi-A 1933-40
Babe, Loren R. NY-A 1967, Chi-A 1980-81, 1983
Bader, Lore V. Bos-N 1926
Bailor, Robert M. "Bob" Tor-A 1992-94
Baker, Delmer D. "Del" Det-A 1933-38, Cle-A 1943-44, Bos-A 1945-48, 1953-60
Baker, Eugene W. "Gene" Pit-N 1963
Baker, Floyd W. Min-A 1961-64
Baker, Johnnie B "Dusty" SF-N 1988-92
Baker, William P. "Bill" Chi-N 1950
Bamberger, George I. Bal-A 1968-77
Bancroft, David J. "Dave" NY-N 1930-32
Bando, Salvatore L. "Sal" Mil-A 1980-81
Banks, Ernest "Ernie" Chi-N 1967-69, 1972-73
Bartell, Richard W. "Dick" NY-N 1946, Det-A 1949-52, Cin-N 1954-55
Bartirome, Anthony J. "Tony" Atl-N 1986-88
Basgall, Romanus "Monty" LA-N 1973-86
Bassler, John L. "Johnny" Cle-A 1938-40, StL-A 1941
Baylor, Don E. Mil-A 1990-91, StL-N 1992
Bauer, Henry A. "Hank" Bal-A 1963
Beauchamp, James E. "Jim" Atl-N 1991-94
Bearnarth, Lawrence D. "Larry" Mon-N 1976, 1985-91, Col-N 1993-94
Beck, Walter W. "Boom-Boom" Was-A 1957-59
Becker, Joseph E. "Joe" Bro-N 1955-57, LA-N 1958-64, StL-N 1965-66, Chi-N 1967-70
Bedell, Howard W. "Howie" KC-A 1984, SE-A 1988
Bell, David G. "Buddy" Cle-A 1994
Bender, Charles A. "Chief" Chi-A 1925-26, NY-N 1931, Phi-A 1951-53
Bengough, Bernard O. "Benny" Was-A 1940-43, Bos-N 1944-45, Phi-N 1946-58
Benson, Vernon A. "Vern" Chi-A 1961-64, NY-A 1965-66, Cin-N 1966-69, StL-N 1970-75, Atl-N 1976-77, SF-N 1980
Berardino, John "Johnny" StL-A 1951
Berardino, Richard J. "Dick" Bos-A 1989-91
Berg, Morris "Moe" Bos-A 1940-41
Beringer, Carroll J. "C. B." LA-N 1967-72, Phi-N 1973-78
Berra, Lawrence P. "Yogi" NY-A 1963, NY-N 1965-71, NY-A 1976-83, Hou-N 1986-89
Berres, Raymond F. "Ray" Chi-A 1949-66, 1968-69
Berry, Charles F. "Charlie" Phi-A 1936-40
Bevington, Terry Paul Chi-A 1989-94
Biagini, Gregory P. "Greg" Bal-A 1992-94
Bissonette, Adelphia L. "Del" Bos-N 1945, Pit-N 1946
Blackburn, Wayne C. Det-A 1963-64
Blackburne, Russell A. "Lena" Chi-A 1927-28, StL-A 1930, Phi-A 1933-40, 1942-43
Blades, F. Raymond "Ray" StL-N 1930-32, Cin-N 1942, Bro-N 1947-48, StL-N 1951, Chi-N 1953-56
Blaylock, Gary N. KC-A 1984-87
Bloomfield, Gordon L. "Jack" SD-N 1974, Chi-N 1975-76
Bluege, Oswald L. "Ossie" Was-A 1940-42
Bochy, Bruce D. SD-N 1993-94
Bonds, Bobby L. Cle-A 1984-87, SF-N 1993-94
Boone, Robert R. "Bob" Cin-N 1994

Boros, Stephen "Steve" KC-A 1975-79, Mon-N 1981-82, KC-A 1993-94
Bosman, Richard A. "Dick" Chi-A 1986-87, Bal-A 1992-94
Bottomley, James L. "Jim" StL-A 1937
Bowa, Lawrence R. "Larry" Phi-N 1988-94
Boyer, Cletis L. "Clete" Oak-A 1980-85, NY-A 1988, 1992-94
Boyer, Cloyd V. NY-A 1975, 1977, Atl-N 1978-81, KC-A 1982-83
Boyer, Kenton L. "Ken" StL-N 1971-72
Bragan, James A. "Jimmy" Cin-N 1967-69, Mon-N 1970-72, Mil-A 1976-77
Bragan, Robert R. "Bobby" LA-N 1960, Hou-N 1962
Braun, Stephen R. "Steve" StL-N 1990
Brecheen, Harry D. Bal-A 1954-67
Breeden, H. Scott Cin-N 1986-89
Brenly, Robert E. "Bob" SF-N 1992-94
Bresnahan, Roger P. NY-N 1925-28, Det-N 1930-31
Brewer, James T. "Jim" Mon-N 1977-79
Bridges, Everett L. "Rocky" LA-N 1962-63, Cal-A 1968-71, SF-N 1985
Bridges, Thomas J. "Tommy" Det-A 1946, Cin-N 1951
Brinkman, Edwin A. "Ed" Det-A 1979, SD-N 1981, Chi-A 1983-88
Bristol, J. David "Dave" Cin-N 1966, Mon-N 1973-75, SF-N 1978-79, Phi-N 1982-85, 1988, Cin-N 1989, 1993
Brown, H. Harold "Hal" Bal-A 1964
Brown, Jackie G. Tex-A 1979-82, Chi-A 1992-94
Brown, James R. "Jimmy" Bos-N 1949-51
Brown, Mace S. Bos-A 1965
Brown, William J. "Gates" Det-A 1978-84
Brucker, Earle F., Sr. Phi-A 1941-49, StL-A 1950, Cin-N 1952
Bryant, Claiborne H. "Clay" LA-N 1961, Cle-A 1967, 1974
Bryant, Donald R. "Don" Bos-A 1974-76, Sea-A 1977-80
Buford, Donald A. "Don" SF-N 1981-84, Bal-A 1994
Bumbry, Alonza B. "Al" Bos-A 1988-93
Burdette, S. Lewis "Lew" Atl-N 1972-73
Burgess, Thomas R. "Tom" NY-N 1977, Atl-N 1978
Burgmeier, Thomas H. "Tom" KC-A 1991
Burke, James T. "Jimmy" Det-A 1914-17, Bos-A 1921-23, Chi-N 1926-30, NY-A 1931-33
Burkett, Jesse C. NY-N 1921
Burleson, Richard P. "Rick" Oak-A 1991, Bos-A 1992-93
Burns, George J. NY-N 1931
Burns, John I. "Jack" Bos-A 1955-59
Burris, B. Ray Mil-A 1990-91, Tex-A 1992
Burwell, William E. "Bill" Bos-A 1944, Pit-N 1947-48, 1958-62
Busby, James F. "Jim" Bal-A 1961, Hou-N 1962, 1963-67, Atl-N 1968-75, Chi-A 1976, Sea-A 1977-78
Butler, John S. "Johnny" Chi-A 1932
Butterfield, Brian J. NY-A 1994
Camacho, Joseph G. "Joe" Was-A 1969-71, Tex-A 1972
Camilli, Douglas J. "Doug" Was-A 1968-69, Bos-A 1970-73
Cannizzaro, Christopher J. "Chris" Atl-N 1976-78
Cardenal, Jose R. D. Cin-N 1993, StL-N 1994
Carew, Rodney D. "Rod" Cal-A 1992-94
Carey, Max G. Pit-N 1930
Carey, Thomas F. "Tom" Bos-A 1946-47
Carisch, Frederick B. "Fred" Det-A 1923-24
Carnevale, Daniel J. "Danny" KC-A 1970
Carrion, Leonel S, Mon-N 1988
Carter, Richard J. "Dick" Phi-N 1959-60
Case, George W. Was-A 1961-63, Min-A 1968
Castro, William R. "Bill" Mil-A 1992-94
Cavarretta, Philip J. "Phil" Det-A 1961-63, NY-N 1978
Cepeda, Orlando M. Chi-A 1980
Chambliss, C. Christopher "Chris" NY-A 1988, StL-N 1993-94
Chandler, Spurgeon F. "Spud" KC-A 1957-58
Chapman, W. Benjamin "Ben" Cin-N 1952
Chesbro, John D. "Jack" Was-A 1924
Chiti, H. Dominic "Dom" Cle-A 1991-93
Cisco, Galen B. KC-A 1971-79, Mon-N 1980-84, SD-N 1985-87, Tor-A 1988, 1990-94
Clark, Ronald B. "Ron" Chi-A 1988-90, Sea-A 1991, Cle-A 1992-93
Clarke, Fred C. Pit-N 1925

Clarke, Thomas A. "Tommy" NY-N 1932-35, 1938
Clary, Ellis Was-A 1955-60, Tor-A 1989
Clear, E. Robert "Bob" Cal-A 1976-87
Clines, Eugene A. "Gene" Chi-N 1979-81, Hou-N 1988, Sea-A 1989-92, Mil-A 1993-94
Cloninger, Tony L. NY-A 1992-94
Cluck, Robert A. "Bob" Hou-N 1979, 1990-93
Clymer, William J. "Bill" Cin-N 1925
Cochrane, Gordon S. "Mickey" Phi-A 1950
Cohen, Andrew H. "Andy" Phi-N 1960
Colavito, Rocco D. "Rocky" Cle-A 1973, 1976-78, KC-A 1982-83
Cole, Richard R. "Dick" Chi-N 1961
Coleman, Joseph H. "Joe" Cal-A 1988-90, StL-N 1991-94
Coleman, Robert H. "Bob" Bos-A 1926, Det-A 1932, Bos-N 1943
Collins, David S "Dave" StL-N 1991-92
Collins, Edward T. "Eddie" Phi-A 1931-32
Collins, James A. "Ripper" Chi-N 1961-63
Collins, Terry L. Pit-N 1992-93
Combs, Earle B. NY-A 1936-44, StL-A 1947, Bos-A 1948-52, Phi-N 1954
Combs, Merrill R. "Merl" Tex-A 1974-75
Comer, Stephen M. "Steve" Cle-A 1987
Connor, Mark P. NY-A 1984-85, 1986-87, 1990-94
Connors, William J. "Billy" KC-A 1980-81, Chi-N 1982-86, Sea-A 1987-88, NY-A 1989-90, Chi-N 1991-93, NY-A 1994
Conroy, William E. "Wid" Phi-N 1922
Consolo, William A. "Billy" Det-A 1979-92
Cooke, Allen L. "Dusty" Phi-N 1948-52
Coombs, John W. "Jack" Det-A 1920
Cooney, John W. "Johnny" Bos-N 1940-42, 1946-49, 1950-52, Mil-N 1953-55, Chi-A 1957-64
Cooper, W. Walker StL-N 1957, KC-A 1960
Corrales, Patrick "Pat" Tex-A 1975-78, NY-A 1989, Atl-N 1990-94
Corriden, John M., Sr "Red" Chi-N 1932-40, Bro-N 1941-46, NY-A 1947-48, Chi-A 1950
Cottier, Charles K. "Chuck" NY-N 1979-81, Sea-A 1982-84, Chi-N 1988-94
Courtney, Clinton D. "Clint" Hou-N 1965
Cox, Larry E. Chi-N 1988-89
Cox, Robert J. "Bobby" NY-A 1977
Crabtree, Estel C. Cin-N 1943-44
Craft, Harry F. KC-A 1955-57, Chi-N 1960-61
Craig, Roger L. SD-N 1969-72, Hou-N 1974-75, SD-N 1976-77, Det-A 1980-84
Cramer, Roger M. "Doc" Det-A 1948, Chi-A 1951-53
Crandall, Delmar W. "Del" Cal-A 1977
Crandall, J. Otis "Doc" Pit-N 1931-34
Crandall, James M. "Jim" StL-A 1953
Cravath, Clifford C. "Gavvy" Phi-N 1923
Cresse, Mark E. LA-N 1977-94
Crosetti, Frank P. J. "Frankie" NY-A 1947-68, Sea-A 1969, Min-A 1970-71
Crowley, Terrence M. "Terry" Bal-A 1985-88, Min-A 1991-94
Cubbage, Michael L. "Mike" NY-N 1990-91, 1992-94
Cuccinello, Anthony F. "Tony" Cin-N 1949-51, Cle-A 1952-56, Chi-A 1957-66, Det-A 1967-68, Chi-A 1969
Culp, Benjamin B. "Benny" Phi-N 1946-47
Cunningham, Joseph R. "Joe" StL-N 1982
Cunningham, William A. "Bill" Chi-A 1932
Cuyler, Hazen S. "Kiki" Chi-N 1941-43, Bos-A 1949
Dahlgren, Ellsworth T. "Babe" KC-A 1964
Dal Canton, J. Bruce Chi-A 1978, Atl-N 1987-90
Daly, Thomas D. "Tom" Bos-A 1933-46
Dark, Alvin R. Chi-N 1965, 1977
Dauer, Richard F. "Rich" Cle-A 1990-91
Davenport, James H. "Jim" SF-N 1970, SD-N 1974-75, SF-N 1976-82, 1984, Phi-N 1986-87, Cle-A 1989
Davis, Harry H. Phi-A 1913-19
Davis, H. Thomas "Tommy" Sea-A 1981
Davis, R. Brandon "Brandy" Phi-N 1972
Davis, Virgil L. "Spud" Pit-N 1942-46, Chi-N 1950-53
Deal, Ellis F. "Cot" Cin-N 1959-60, Hou-N 1962-64, NY-A 1965, KC-A 1966-67, Cle-A 1970-71, Det-A 1973-74, Hou-N 1983-85
Dean, Jay H. "Dizzy" Chi-N 1941
DeMars, William L. "Billy" Phi-N 1969-81, Mon-N 1982-84, Cin-N 1985-87
DeMerritt, Martin G. "Marty" SF-N 1989
Demeter, Stephen "Steve" Pit-N 1985
Dent, Russell E. "Bucky" StL-N 1991-94
Detore, George F. Pit-N 1959

Devlin, Arthur M. "Art" Bos-N 1926, 1928
Dews, Robert W. "Bobby" Atl-N 1979-81, 1985
Dickey, William M. "Bill" NY-A 1949-57, 1960
Didier, Robert D. "Bob" Oak-A 1984-86,
  Sea-A 1989-90
DiMaggio, Joseph P. "Joe" Oak-A 1968-69
Dobson, Patrick E. "Pat" Mil-A 1982-84,
  SD-N 1988-90, KC-A 1991
Doby, Lawrence E. "Larry" Mon-N 1971-73,
  Cle-A 1974, Mon-N 1976, Chi-A 1977-78
Doerr, Robert P. "Bobby" Bos-A 1967-69,
  Tor-A 1977-81
Dolan, Albert J. "Cozy" NY-N 1922-24
Donnelly, Richard F. "Rich" Tex-A 1980,
  1983-85, Pit-N 1986-94
Donovan, William E. "Bill" Det-A 1918
Doolan, Michael J. "Mickey" Chi-N 1926-28,
  Cin-N 1930-32
Dorish, Harry "Fritz" Bos-A 1963, Atl-N 1968-71
Douglas, Otis W. Cin-N 1961-62
Down, Richard J. "Rick" Cal-A 1987-88,
  NY-A 1993-94
Drabowsky, Myron W. "Moe" Chi-A 1986,
  Chi-N 1994
Dressen, Charles W. "Chuck" Bro-N 1939-42,
  1943-46, NY-A 1947-48, LA-N 1958-59
Dubuc, Jean J. Det-A 1930-31
Duffy, Hugh Bos-A 1932
Dugey, Oscar J. Chi-N 1921-24
Duncan, David E. "Dave" Cle-A 1978-81,
  Sea-A 1982, Chi-A 1983-86, Oak-A 1986-94
Dunlop, Harry A. KC-A 1969-75, Chi-N 1976,
  Cin-N 1979-82, SD-N 1983-86
Durocher, Leo E. LA-N 1961-64
Dusan, Eugene P. "Gene" NY-N 1983
Dyer, Don R. "Duffy" Chi-N 1983, Mil-A 1989-94
Dykes, James J. "Jimmy" Phi-A 1949-50,
  Cin-N 1955-58, Pit-N 1959, Mil-N 1962,
  KC-A 1963-64
Earnshaw, George L. Phi-N 1949-50
Easler, Michael A. "Mike" Mil-A 1992,
  Bos-A 1993-94
Easter, L. Luke Cle-A 1969
Edwards, Howard R. "Doc" Phi-N 1970-72,
  Cle-A 1985-87, NY-N 1990-91
Egan, Arthur A. "Ben" Bro-N 1925, Chi-A 1926
Egan, Richard W. "Dick" Tex-A 1988-89
Elia, Lee C. Phi-N 1980-81, 1985-87, NY-A 1989,
  Sea-A 1993-94
Elliott, Robert I. "Bob" LA-A 1961
Ellis, Samuel J. "Sammy" NY-A 1982, 1983-84,
  1986, Chi-A 1989-91, Chi-N 1992, Sea-A 1993-94
Emery, Calvin W. "Cal" Chi-A 1988
Ens, Jewel L. Pit-N 1926-29, Det-A 1932,
  Cin-N 1933, Bos-N 1934, Pit-N 1935-39,
  Cin-N 1941
Ermer, Calvin C. "Cal" Bal-A 1962,
  Mil-A 1970-71, Oak-A 1977
Estrada, Charles L. "Chuck" Tex-A 1973,
  SD-N 1978-81, Cle-A 1983
Etchebarren, Andrew A. "Andy" Cal-A 1977,
  Mil-A 1985-91
Evans, Darrell W. NY-A 1990
Evans, Dwight M. Col-N 1994
Evers, John J. "Johnny" NY-N 1920,
  Chi-A 1922-23, Bos-N 1929-32
Evers, Walter A. "Hoot" Cle-A 1970
Ezell, Glenn W. Tex-A 1983-85, KC-A 1989-94
Faber, Urban C. "Red" Chi-A 1946-48
Fahey, William R. "Bill" SF-N 1986-91
Falk, Bibb A. Cle-A 1933, Bos-A 1934
Fanning, W. James "Jim" Atl-N 1967
Farrell, M. Kerby Chi-A 1966-69, Cle-A 1970-71
Felske, John F. Tor-A 1980-81, Phi-N 1984
Ferguson, Joseph V. "Joe" Tex-A 1986-87,
  LA-N 1988-89, 1992-93
Ferraro, Michael D. "Mike" NY-A 1979-82,
  KC-A 1984-86, NY-A 1987-88, 1989-91,
  Bal-A 1993
Ferrell, Richard B. "Rick" Was-A 1946-49,
  Det-A 1950-53
Ferrick, Thomas J. "Tom" Cin-N 1954-58,
  Phi-N 1959, Det-A 1960-63, KC-A 1964-65
Ferriss, David M. "Dave" Bos-A 1955-59
Fischer, William C. "Bill" Cin-N 1979-83,
  Bos-A 1985-91
Fitzgerald, Edward R. "Ed" Cle-A 1960,
  KC-A 1961, Min-A 1962-64
Fitzgerald, Joseph P. "Joe" Was-A 1947-56
Fitzpatrick, John A. Pit-N 1953-56,
  Mil-A 1958-59
Fitzsimmons, Frederick "Freddie" Bro-N 1942,
  Bos-N 1948, NY-N 1949-53, 1954-55,
  Chi-N 1957-59, KC-A 1960, Chi-N 1966
Fletcher, Arthur "Art" NY-A 1927-45

Flowers, D'Arcy R. "Jake" Pit-N 1940-45,
  Bos-N 1946, Cle-A 1951-52
Foley, Marvis E. "Marv" Chi-N 1994
Foli, Timothy J. "Tim" Tex-A 1986-87,
  Mil-A 1992-94
Foote, Barry C. Chi-A 1991, NY-N 1992-93
Ford, Edward C. "Whitey" NY-A 1964, 1968,
  1974-75
Fowler, J. Arthur "Art" LA-A 1964, Min-A 1969,
  Det-A 1971-73, Tex-A 1973-75, NY-A 1977-79,
  Oak-A 1980-82, NY-A 1983, 1988
Fox, Charles F. "Charlie" SF-N 1965-68,
  NY-A 1989
Fox, J. Nelson "Nellie" Hou-N 1965, 1966-67,
  Was-A 1968-71, Tex-A 1972
Foxx, James E. "Jimmie" Chi-N 1944
Franks, Herman L. NY-N 1949-55, SF-N 1958,
  1964, Chi-N 1970
Fraser, Charles C. "Chick" Pit-N 1923
Frey, James G. "Jim" Bal-A 1970-79,
  NY-N 1982-83
Friend, Owen L. KC-A 1969
Frisch, Frank F. "Frankie" NY-N 1949
Funk, Franklin R. "Frank" SF-N 1976,
  Sea-A 1980-81, 1983-84, KC-A 1988-90
Galan, August J. "Augie" Phi-A 1954
Galante, Matthew "Matt" Hou-N 1985-94
Gale, Richard B. "Rich" Bos-A 1992-93
Garcia, David "Dave" SD-N 1970-73,
  Cle-A 1975-78, Cal-A 1977, Cle-A 1979,
  Mil-A 1983-84
Gardenhire, Ronald C. "Ron" Min-A 1991-94
Gardner, William F. "Billy" Bos-A 1965-66,
  Mon-N 1977-78, Min-A 1981
Garner, Philip M. "Phil" Hou-N 1989-91
Garrett, H. Adrian KC-A 1988-92
Garrison, R. Ford Cin-N 1953
Gaston, Clarence E. "Cito" Tor-A 1982-89
Gebhard, Robert H. "Bob" Mon-N 1982
Gehringer, Charles L. "Charlie" Det-A 1942
Gernert, Richard E. "Dick" Tex-A 1975-76
Gharrity, E. Patrick "Patsy" Was-A 1929-32,
  Cle-A 1933-35
Gibson, George C. Was-A 1923, Chi-N 1925
Gibson, Robert "Bob" NY-N 1981, Atl-N 1982-84
Gilbert, Andrew "Andy" SF-N 1972-75
Gilliam, James W. "Jim" LA-N 1965-78
Gladding, Fred E. Det-A 1976-78
Gleason, William J. "Kid" Phi-N 1908-11,
  Chi-A 1912-14, 1916-17, Phi-A 1926-32
Gleeson, James J. "Jim" KC-A 1957, NY-A 1964
Glynn, Eugene P. "Gene" Col-N 1994
Gomez, Juan A. "Orlando" Tex-A 1991-92
Gomez, Pedro "Preston" LA-N 1965-68,
  Hou-N 1973, StL-N 1976, LA-N 1977-79,
  Cal-A 1981-84
Gonzalez, Miguel A. "Mike" StL-N 1934-46
Gooch, John B. "Johnny" Pit-N 1937-39
Goodman, William D. "Billy" Atl-N 1968-70
Gordon, Joseph L. "Joe" Det-A 1956
Goryl, John A. "Johnny" Min-A 1968-69,
  1979-80, Cle-A 1982-88
Gowdy, Henry M. "Hank" Bos-N 1929-37,
  Cin-N 1938-42, 1945-46, NY-N 1947-48
Graff, Milton E. "Milt" Pit-N 1985
Grammas, Alexander P. "Alex" Pit-N 1965-69,
  Cin-N 1970-75, 1978, Atl-N 1979, Det-A 1980-91
Griffey, G. Kenneth Sr. "Ken" Sea-A 1993-94
Grimes, Burleigh A. KC-A 1955
Grimm, Charles J. "Charlie" Chi-N 1941,
  1961-62
Grissom, Marvin E. "Marv" LA-A 1961-65,
  Cal-A 1966, Chi-A 1967-68, Cal-A 1969,
  Min-A 1970-71, Chi-N 1975-76, Cal-A 1977-78
Grodzicki, John "Johnny" Det-A 1979
Guerrero, Epifanio O. "Epy" Tor-A 1981
Gullett, Donald E. "Don" Cin-N 1993-94
Gustine, Frank W. "Frankie" Pit-N 1950
Gutteridge, Donald J. "Don" Chi-A 1955-66,
  1968-69
Haas, G. Edward "Eddie" Atl-N 1974-77, 1984
Haas, George W. "Mule" Chi-A 1940-46
Hack, Stanley C. "Stan" StL-N 1957-58
Hacker, Richard W. "Rich" StL-N 1986-90,
  Tor-A 1991-94
Haddix, Harvey NY-N 1966-67, Cin-N 1969,
  Bos-A 1971, Cle-A 1975-78, Pit-N 1979-84
Haines, Jesse J. Bro-N 1938
Hairston, Samuel "Sammy" Chi-A 1978
Haller, Thomas F. "Tom" SF-N 1977-79
Hamilton, Steve A. Det-A 1975
Hancken, Morris M. "Buddy" Hou-N 1968-72
Haney, Fred G. Mil-N 1956
Haney, W. Larry Mil-A 1978-91
Hansen, Guy C. KC-A 1991-93

Hansen, Roger C. Sea-A 1992
Hansen, Ronald L. "Ron" Mil-A 1980-83,
  Mon-N 1985-89
Harder, Melvin L. "Mel" Cle-A 1947, 1948-63,
  NY-N 1964, Chi-N 1965, Cin-N 1966-68,
  KC-A 1969
Hargrove, D. Michael "Mike" Cle-A 1990-91
Harmon, Thomas "Tom" Chi-N 1982
Harper, Tommy Bos-A 1980-84, Mon-N 1990-94
Harrah, Colbert D. "Toby" Tex-A 1989-92
Harrelson, Derrel M. "Bud" NY-N 1982, 1985-90
Harris, C. Luman "Lum" Chi-A 1951-54,
  Bal-A 1955-61, Hou-N 1962-64
Hart, John H. Bal-A 1988
Hartenstein, Charles O. "Chuck" Cle-A 1979,
  Mil-A 1987-89
Hartley, Grover A. Cle-A 1928-30, Pit-N 1931-33,
  StL-A 1934-36, NY-N 1946
Hartnett, Charles L. "Gabby" Chi-N 1938,
  NY-N 1941, KC-A 1965
Hartsfield, Roy T. LA-A 1969-72, Atl-N 1973
Hassey, Ronald W. "Ron" Col-N 1993-94
Hatcher, Michael V. "Mickey" Tex-A 1993-94
Hatfield, Fred J. Det-A 1977-78
Hatton, Grady E. Chi-N 1960, Hou-N 1973-74
Haynes, Joseph W. "Joe" Was-A 1953-55
Hayworth, Raymond H. "Ray" Bro-N 1945,
  Chi-N 1955
Hebner, Richard J. "Richie" Bos-A 1989-91
Heffner, Donald H. "Don" KC-A 1958-60,
  Det-A 1961, NY-N 1964-65, Cal-A 1967-68
Hegan, James E. "Jim" NY-A 1960-73,
  Det-A 1974-78, NY-A 1979-80
Heilmann, Harry E. Cin-N 1932
Heist, Alfred M. "Al" Hou-N 1966-67, SD-N 1980
Helms, Tommy V. Tex-A 1981-82, Cin-N 1983-89
Hemsley, Ralston B. "Rollie" Phi-A 1954,
  Was-A 1961-62
Hemus, Solomon J. "Solly" NY-N 1962-63,
  Cle-A 1964-65
Henderson, Stephen C. "Steve" Hou-N 1994
Hendricks, Elrod J. Bal-A 1978-94
Henrich, Thomas D. "Tommy" NY-A 1951,
  NY-N 1957, Det-A 1958-59
Herman, Floyd C. "Babe" Pit-N 1951
Herman, William J. "Billy" Bro-N 1952-57,
  Mil-N 1958-59, Bos-A 1960-64, Cal-A 1967,
  SD-N 1978-79
Hernandez, Carlo A "Chuck" Cal-A 1992-94
Herndon, Larry D. Det-A 1992-94
Herzog, Dorrel N. "Whitey" KC-A 1965,
  NY-N 1966, Cal-A 1974-75
Hiatt, Jack E Chi-N 1981
High, Andrew A. "Andy" Bro-N 1937-38
Hill, Marc K. Hou-N 1988, NY-A 1991
Hill, Perry W. Tex-A 1992-94
Hiller, Charles J. "Chuck" Tex-A 1973,
  KC-A 1976-79, StL-N 1981-83, SF-N 1985,
  NY-N 1990
Hilton, J. David "Dave" Mil-A 1987-88
Himsl, Avitus B. "Vedie" Chi-N 1960-64
Hinchman, William W. "Bill" Pit-N 1923
Hines, Benjamin T. "Ben" Sea-A 1984,
  LA-N 1986, 1988-93, Hou-N 1994
Hines, Bruce E. Cal-A 1991
Hisle, Larry E. Tor-A 1992-94
Hitchcock, William C. "Billy" Det-A 1955-60,
  Atl-N 1966
Hoak, Donald A. "Don" Phi-N 1967
Hofman, Robert G. "Bobby" KC-A 1966-67,
  Was-A 1968, Oak-A 1969-70, Cle-A 1971-72,
  Oak-A 1974-75, 1978
Hofmann, Fred StL-A 1938-49, 1951
Holke, Walter H. StL-A 1940
Hollingsworth, Albert W. "Al" StL-N 1957-58
Holt, Golden D. "Goldie" Pit-N 1948-50,
  Chi-N 1961-64
Holmberg, Dennis Tor-A 1994
Holmquist, Douglas L. "Doug" NY-A 1984, 1985
Hopp, John L. "Johnny" Det-A 1954, StL-N 1956
Hornsby, Rogers Chi-N 1958-59, NY-N 1962
Horton, Willie W. NY-A 1985, Chi-A 1986
Hoscheit, Vernard A. "Vern" Bal-A 1968,
  Oak-A 1969-74, Cal-A 1976, NY-N 1984-87
Houk, Ralph G. NY-A 1954, 1958-60
House, Thomas R. "Tom" Tex-A 1985-92
Howard, Elston G. NY-A 1969-79
Howard, Frank O. Mil-A 1977-80, NY-A 1982-83,
  1984, Mil-A 1985-86, Sea-A 1987-88, NY-A 1989,
  1991-92, NY-N 1994
Howe, Arthur H. "Art" Tex-A 1985-88
Howley, Daniel P. "Dan" Det-A 1919,
  Det-A 1921-22
Howser, Richard D. "Dick" NY-A 1969-78

Hriniak, Walter J. "Walt" Mon-N 1974-75,
Bos-A 1977-88, Chi-A 1989-94
Hudlin, G. Willis Det-A 1957-59
Hubbard, John H. "Jack" StL-N 1993
Hudson, Sidney C. "Sid" Was-A 1961-65,
1968-71, Tex-A 1972, 1975-78
Hulswitt, Rudolph E. "Rudy" Bos-A 1931-33
Hundley, C. Randolph "Randy" Chi-N 1977
Hunter, Frederick C. "Newt" Phi-N 1928-31,
1933
Hunter, G. William "Billy" Bal-A 1964-77
Isaac, Luis Cle-A 1987-91, 1994
Jackson, Alvin N. "Al" Bos-A 1977-79,
Bal-A 1989-91
Jackson, Grant D. Pit-N 1984-85, Cin-N 1994
Jackson, Roland T. "Sonny" Atl-N 1982-83
Jackson, Travis C. NY-N 1939-40, 1947-48
Jansen, Lawrence J. "Larry" NY-N 1954,
SF-N 1961-71, Chi-N 1972-73
Jaramillo, Rudolph "Rudy" Hou-N 1990-93
Jennings, Hugh A. "Hughie" NY-N 1921-25
Johnson, Darrell D. StL-N 1960-61, Bal-A 1962,
Bos-A 1968-69, Tex-A 1981-82, NY-N 1993
Johnson, Deron R. Cal-A 1979-80, NY-N 1981,
Phi-N 1982-84, Sea-A 1985-86, Chi-A 1987,
Cal-A 1989-91
Johnson, Roy J Chi-N 1935-39, 1944-53
Johnson, Sylvester W. "Syl" Phi-N 1937-40
Johnson, Timothy E. "Tim" Mon-N 1993-94
Johnston, James H. "Jimmy" Bro-N 1931
Jones, Clarence W. Atl-N 1985, 1988-94
Jones, Gordon B. Hou-N 1966-67
Jones, Grover W. "Deacon" Hou-N 1976-82,
SD-N 1984-87
Jones, Lynn M. KC-A 1991-92
Jones, Joseph C. "Joe" KC-A 1987, 1992
Jonnard, Clarence J. "Bubber" Phi-N 1935,
NY-N 1942-46
Judge, Joseph I. "Joe" Was-A 1945-46
Jurges, William F. "Billy" Chi-N 1947-48,
Was-A 1956-59
Kaat, James L. "Jim" Cin-N 1984-85
Kahn, Louis "Lou" StL-N 1955
Katt, Raymond F. "Ray" StL-N 1959-60,
Cle-A 1962
Kaufmann, Anthony C. "Tony" StL-N 1947-50
Keane, John J. "Johnny" StL-N 1959-61
Keefe, David E. "Dave" Phi-A 1940-49
Keely, Robert W. "Bob" Bos-N 1946-52,
Mil-N 1953-57
Kelleher, Michael D. "Mick" Pit-N 1986
Keller, Charles E. "Charlie" NY-A 1957, 1959
Kelley, Joseph J. "Joe" Bro-N 1926
Kelly, Bernard F. "Mike" Chi-A 1930-31,
Chi-N 1934, Bos-N 1937-39, Pit-N 1940-41
Kelly, George L. Cin-N 1935-37, Bos-N 1938-43,
Cin-N 1947-48
Kelly, J. Thomas "Tom" Min-A 1983-86
Kennedy, Kevin Mon-N 1992
Kennedy, Robert D. "Bob" Chi-N 1962-64,
Atl-N 1967
Kerr, John F. Was-A 1935
Kerrigan, Joseph T. "Joe" Mon-N 1983-86,
1992-94
Killefer, William L. "Bill" StL-N 1926,
StL-A 1927-29, Bro-N 1939, Phi-N 1942
Kim, Wendell K. SF-N 1989-94
Kimm, Bruce E. Cin-N 1984-88, Pit-N 1989,
SD-N 1991-92
King, Clyde E. Cin-N 1959, Pit-N 1965-67,
NY-A 1978, 1981, 1988
Kison, Bruce E. KC-A 1992-94
Kissell, George M. StL-N 1969-75
Kittle, Hubert M. "Hub" Hou-N 1971-75,
StL-N 1981-83
Klein, Charles H. "Chuck" Phi-N 1942-45
Klein, Louis F. "Lou" Chi-N 1960-65
Kluszewski, Theodore B. "Ted" Cin-N 1970-78
Knight, C. Ray Cin-N 1993-94
Knoop, Robert F. "Bobby" Chi-A 1977-78,
Cal-A 1979-94
Knowles, Darold D. StL-N 1983, Phi-N 1989-90
Koenig, Fred Carl Cal-A 1970-71, StL-N 1976,
Tex-A 1977-82, Chi-N 1983, Cle-A 1985-86
Kress, Ralph "Red" Det-A 1940, NY-N 1946-49,
Cle-A 1953-60, LA-A 1961, NY-N 1962
Krol, John T. "Jack" StL-N 1977-80,
SD-N 1981-86
Krug, Everett B. "Chris" SD-N 1969
Kuehl, Karl O. Min-A 1977-82
Kuenn, Harvey E. Mil-A 1971-82
Kuntz, Russell J. "Rusty" Sea-A 1989-92
Kusnyer, Arthur W. "Art" Chi-A 1980-87,
Oak-A 1989-94

Lachemann, Marcel E. Cal-A 1984-92,
Fla-N 1993-94
Lachemann, Rene G. Bos-A 1985-86,
Oak-A 1987-92
Lakeman, Albert W. "Al" Bos-A 1963-64,
1967-69
Lamont, Gene W. Pit-N 1986-91
Land, Grover C. Pit-N 1914, Cin-N 1925-28,
Chi-N 1929
Landestoy, Rafael S. Mon-N 1989
Landrith, Hobert N. "Hobie" Was-A 1964
Lanier, Harold C. "Hal" StL-N 1981-85,
Phi-N 1990-91
LaRoche, David E. "Dave" Chi-A 1989-91,
NY-N 1992-93
LaRussa, Anthony "Tony" Chi-A 1978
Lasorda, Thomas C. "Tommy" LA-N 1973-76
Latham, W. Arlington "Arlie" Cin-N 1900,
NY-N 1909
Lau, Charles R. "Charley" Bal-A 1969,
Oak-A 1970, KC-A 1971-74, 1975-78,
NY-A 1979-81, Chi-A 1982-83
Lauder, William "Billy" Chi-A 1925
Lavagetto, Harry A. "Cookie" Bro-N 1951-53,
Was-A 1955-57, NY-N 1962-63, SF-N 1964-67
Law, Vernon S. "Vern" Pit-N 1968-69
Lazzeri, Anthony M. "Tony" Chi-N 1938
Lefebvre, James K. "Jim" LA-N 1978-79,
SF-N 1980-82, Oak-A 1987-88, 1994
Leifield, Albert P. "Lefty" StL-A 1920-23,
Bos-A 1924-26, Det-A 1927-28
Lemon, James R. "Jim" Min-A 1965-67, 1981-84
Lemon, Robert G. "Bob" Cle-A 1960,
Phi-N 1961, Cal-A 1967-68, KC-A 1970,
NY-A 1976
Lenhardt, Donald E. "Don" Bos-A 1970-73
Leonard, Emil J. "Dutch" Chi-N 1954-56
Leppert, Donald G. "Don" Pit-N 1968-76,
Tor-A 1977-79, Hou-N 1980-85
Lett, James C. "Jim" Cin-N 1988-89
Levy, Leonard "Len" Pit-N 1957-63
Lewis, George E. "Duffy" Bos-N 1931-35
Lewis, Johnny J. StL-N 1973-76, 1985-89
Leyland, James R. "Jim" Chi-A 1982-85
Leyva, Nicolas T. "Nick" StL-N 1984-88,
Tor-A 1993-94
Lillis, Robert P. "Bob" Hou-N 1967, 1973-82,
SF-N 1986-94
Linares, Julio Hou-N 1994
Lipon, John J. "Johnny" Cle-A 1968-71
Litwhiler, Daniel W. "Danny" Cin-N 1951
Llenas, Winston E. Tor-A 1988
Lobe, William C. "Bill" Cle-A 1951-56
Lobert, John B. "Hans" NY-N 1928,
Phi-N 1934-41, Cin-N 1943-44
Lockman, Carroll W. "Whitey" Cin-N 1960,
SF-N 1961-64, Chi-N 1966
Lodigiani, Dario A. KC-A 1961-62
Lollar, J. Sherman "Sherm" Bal-A 1964-67,
Oak-A 1968
Long, R. Dale NY-A 1963
Lonnett, Joseph P. "Joe" Chi-A 1971-75,
Oak-A 1976, Pit-N 1977-84
Lopat, Edmund W. "Ed" NY-A 1960, Min-A 1961,
KC-A 1962
Lopes, David E. "Davey" Tex-A 1988-91,
Bal-A 1992-94
Lowe, Q. V. "Q. V." Chi-N 1972
Lowrey, Harry L. "Peanuts" Phi-N 1960-66,
SF-N 1967-68, Mon-N 1969, Chi-N 1970-71,
Cal-A 1972, Chi-N 1977-79, 1981
Lucchesi, Frank J. Tex-A 1974-75, 1979-80
Lum, Michael K. "Mike" Chi-A 1985,
KC-A 1988-89
Lumpe, Jerry D. Oak-A 1971
Lund, Donald A. "Don" Det-A 1957-58
Luque, Adolfo "Dolf" NY-N 1935-38, 1941-45
Lutz, R. Joseph "Joe" Cle-A 1971-73
Luzinski, Gregory M. "Greg" Oak-A 1993
Lyons, Edward H. "Eddie" Min-A 1976
Lyons, Theodore A. "Ted" Det-A 1949-53,
Bro-N 1954
Macha, Kenneth E. "Ken" Mon-N 1986-91,
Cal-A 1992-94
Mack, Earle T. Phi-A 1924-50
MacKenzie, H. Gordon "Gordy" KC-A 1980-81,
Chi-N 1982, SF-N 1986-88, Cle-A 1991
Maglie, Salvatore A. "Sal" Bos-A 1960-62,
1966-67, Sea-A 1969
Mahoney, James T. "Jim" Chi-A 1972-76,
Sea-A 1985-86
Majtyka, LeRoy W. "Roy" Atl-N 1988-90
Malmberg, Harry W. Bos-A 1963-64
Maloof, Jack G. SD-N 1990
Maltzberger, Gordon R. Min-A 1962-64

Mancuso, August R. "Gus" Cin-N 1950
Mansolino, Doug Chi-A 1992-94
Mantle, Mickey C. NY-A 1970
Manuel, Charles F. "Charlie" Cle-A 1988-89,
1994
Manuel, Jerry Mon-N 1991-94
Manush, Henry E. "Heinie" Was-A 1953-54
Marion, Martin W. "Marty" StL-A 1952,
Chi-A 1954
Marshall, R. James "Jim" Chi-N 1974
Martin, Alfred M. "Billy" Min-A 1965-68,
Tex-A 1974
Martin, Fred T. Chi-N 1961-64, Chi-A 1979
Martin, John L. "Pepper" Chi-N 1956
Martin, Joseph C. "J. C." Chi-N 1974
Martinez, Jose KC-A 1980-87, Chi-N 1988-94
Martinez, Orlando "Marty" Sea-A 1984-86, 1992
Mathews, Edwin L. "Eddie" Atl-N 1971-72
Mathews, Henry "Harry" Cle-A 1926-27,
NY-A 1929
Mathews, Rick R. Col-N 1993
Mathewson, Christopher "Christy"
NY-N 1919-21
Maxvill, C. Dallan "Dal" Oak-A 1975, NY-N 1978,
StL-N 1979-80, Atl-N 1982-84
May, Lee A. KC-A 1984-86, Cin-N 1988-89,
KC-A 1992-93
May, Milton S. "Milt" Pit-N 1987-94
Mayberry, John C. KC-A 1989-90
Mayo, Edward J. "Eddie" Bos-A 1951,
Phi-N 1952-54
Mays, Willie H. NY-N 1974-79
Mazeroski, William S. "Bill" Pit-N 1973,
Sea-A 1979-80
Mazzone, Leo D. Atl-N 1985, 1990-94
McBride, George F. Det-A 1925-26, 1929
McBride, Kenneth F. "Ken" Mil-A 1975
McCallister, John "Jack" Cle-A 1920-26,
Bos-A 1930
McClure, Robert C. "Bob" Fla-N 1994
McCormick, Frank A. Cin-N 1956-57
McCrabb, Lester W. "Les" Phi-A 1950-54
McCraw, Tommy L. Cle-A 1975, 1979-82,
SF-N 1983-85, Bal-A 1989-91, NY-N 1992-94
McCullough, Clyde E. Was-A 1960, Min-A 1961,
NY-N 1963, SD-N 1982
McDermott, Maurice J. "Mickey" Cal-A 1968
McDonnell, Robert A. "Maje" Phi-N 1951-57
McGaha, F. Melvin "Mel" Cle-A 1961,
KC-A 1963-64, Hou-N 1968-70
McGinnity, Joseph J. "Joe" Bro-N 1926
McGuire, James T. "Deacon" Det-A 1911-16
McKay, David L. "Dave" Oak-A 1984-94
McKechnie, William B. "Bill" Pit-N 1922,
StL-N 1927, Cle-A 1947-49, Bos-A 1952-53
McKee, J. R. Pit-N 1947
McKeon, John A. "Jack" Oak-A 1978
McLaren, John L. Tor-A 1986-90, Bos-A 1991,
Cin-N 1992, Sea-A 1993-94
McLish, Calvin C. "Cal" Phi-N 1965-66,
Mon-N 1969-75, Mil-N 1976-82
McMahon, Donald J. "Don" SF-N 1973-75,
Min-A 1976-77, SF-N 1980-82, Cle-A 1983-85
McMillan, Roy D. Mil-A 1970-72, NY-N 1973-76
McNamara, John F. Oak-A 1968-69,
SF-N 1971-73, Cal-A 1978
McNeely, G. Earl StL-A 1931, Was-A 1936-37
McNertney, Gerald E. "Jerry" Bos-A 1988
McRae, Harold A. "Hal" KC-A 1987,
Mon-N 1990-91
Mejias, Samuel E. "Sammy" Sea-A 1993-94
Mele, Sabath A. "Sam" Was-A 1959-60,
Min-A 1961
Melillo, Oscar D. "Ski" StL-A 1938,
Cle-A 1939-40, 1942, 1945-48, 1950,
Bos-A 1952-53, KC-A 1955-56
Mendoza, C. Rigoberto "Minnie" Bal-A 1988
Menke, Denis J. Tor-A 1980-81, Hou-N 1983-88,
Phi-N 1989-94
Merkle, Frederick C. "Fred" NY-A 1925-26
Merrill, Carl H. "Stump" NY-A 1985, 1986-87
Metro, Charles "Charlie" Chi-N 1962,
Chi-A 1965, Oak-A 1982
Meusel, Emil F. "Irish" NY-N 1930
Meyer, Bernhard "Benny" Phi-N 1924-26,
Det-A 1928-30
Meyer, Russell C. "Russ" Or "Monk" NY-A 1992
Michael, Eugene R. "Gene" NY-A 1976-77,
1978, 1984-86, 1988, 1989
Milan, J. Clyde Was-A 1928-29, 1938-52
Miley, David A. "Dave" Cin-N 1993
Miller, Dyar K Chi-A 1987-88
Miller, Edmund J. "Bing" Bos-A 1937,
Det-A 1938-41, Chi-A 1942-49, Phi-A 1950-53
Miller, L. Otto Bro-N 1926-36

Miller, Raymond R. "Ray" Bal-A 1978-85, Pit-N 1987-94

Miller, Robert L. "Bob" Tor-A 1977-79, SF-N 1985

Milliken, Robert F. "Bob" StL-N 1965-70, 1976

Mills, Arthur G. "Art" Det-A 1944-48

Mills, C. Buster Cle-A 1946, Chi-A 1947-50, Cin-N 1953, Bos-A 1954

Minoso, S. Orestes "Minnie" Chi-A 1976-78, 1980-81

Mitchell, Clarence E. NY-N 1932-33

Mitchell, Frederick F. "Fred" Bos-N 1914-16

Mitterwald, George E. Oak-A 1979-82, NY-A 1988

Mize, John R. "Johnny" KC-A 1961

Monbouquette, William C. "Bill" NY-N 1982-83, NY-A 1985

Monchak, Alex "Al" Chi-A 1971-75, Oak-A 1976, Pit-N 1977-84, Atl-N 1986-88

Moon, Wallace W. "Wally" SD-N 1969

Moore, Jackie S. Mil-A 1970-72, Tex-A 1973-74, 1975-76, Tor-A 1977-79, Tex-A 1980, Oak-A 1981-84, Mon-N 1987-89, Cin-N 1990-92, Tex-A 1993-94

Moore, Terry B. StL-N 1949-52, 1956-58

Morales, Jose M. SF-N 1986-88, Cle-A 1990-93

Morales, Richard A. "Rich" Atl-N 1986-87

Morgan, Joseph M. "Joe" Pit-N 1972, Bos-A 1985-88

Morgan, Tom S. Cal-A 1972-74, SD-N 1975, NY-A 1979, Cal-A 1981-83

Morgan, Vernon T. "Vern" Min-A 1969-75

Moses, Wallace "Wally" Phi-A 1952-54, Phi-N 1955-58, Cin-N 1959-60, NY-A 1961-62, 1966, Det-A 1967-70

Moss, J. Lester "Les" Chi-A 1967-68, 1969-70, Chi-A 1981, Hou-N 1982-84, 1985-89

Mota, Manuel R. "Manny" LA-N 1980-89

Motton, Curtell H. "Curt" Bal-A 1991

Mozzali, Maurice J. "Mo" StL-N 1977-78

Mueller, Ray C. NY-N 1956, Chi-N 1957

Muffett, Billy A. StL-N 1967-70, Cal-A 1974-77, Det-A 1985-94

Mulcahy, Hugh N. Chi-A 1970

Mull, Jack L. SF-N 1985

Mulleavy, Gregory T. "Greg" Bro-N 1957, LA-N 1958-60, 1962-64

Mullin, Patrick J. "Pat" Det-A 1963-66, Cle-A 1967, Mon-N 1979-81

Murphy, Daniel F. "Danny" Phi-A 1921-24, Phi-N 1927

Murtaugh, Daniel E. "Danny" Pit-N 1956-57

Muser, Anthony J. "Tony" Mil-A 1985-89, Chi-N 1993-94

Myatt, George E. Was-A 1950-54, Chi-A 1955-56, Chi-N 1957-59, Mil-N 1960-61, Det-A 1962-63, Phi-N 1964-72

Napoleon, Edward G. "Ed" Cle-A 1983-85, KC-A 1987-88, Hou-N 1989, NY-A 1992-93

Naragon, Harold R. "Hal" Min-A 1963-66, Det-A 1967-69

Narron, Jerry A. Bal-A 1993-94

Narron, Samuel "Sam" Pit-N 1952-64

Neale, A. Earle "Greasy" StL-N 1929

Nelson, David E. "Dave" Chi-A 1981-84, Cle-A 1992-94

Nettles, Graig NY-A 1991

Neun, John H. "Johnny" NY-A 1944-46

Newman, Jeffrey L. "Jeff" Oak-A 1986, Cle-A 1992-94

Niarhos, C. Gus KC-A 1962-64

Niehoff, J. Albert "Bert" NY-N 1929

Nixon, Russell E. "Russ" Cin-N 1976-82, Mon-N 1984-85, Atl-N 1986-87, Sea-A 1992

Noren, Irving A. "Irv" Oak-A 1971-74, Chi-N 1975

Norman, H. Willis P. "Bill" StL-A 1952-53

Northey, Ronald J. "Ron" Pit-N 1961-63

Nossek, Joseph R. "Joe" Mil-A 1973-75, Min-A 1976, Cle-A 1977-81, KC-A 1982-83, Chi-A 1984-85, 1986, 1991-94

Nottle, Edward W. "Ed" Oak-A 1983

Oates, Johnny L. Chi-A 1984-87, Bal-A 1989-91

O'Brien, Edward J. "Eddie" Sea-A 1969

Oceak, Frank J. Pit-N 1958-64, Cin-N 1965, Pit-N 1970-72

O'Connell, Daniel F. "Danny" Was-A 1963-64

O'Connor, Patrick F. "Paddy" NY-A 1918-21

Oester, Ronald J. "Ron" Cin-N 1993

Okrie, Leonard J. "Len" Bos-A 1961-62, 1965-66, Det-A 1970

Oldis, Robert C. "Bob" Phi-N 1964-66, Min-A 1968, Mon-N 1969

O'Leary, Charles T. "Charley" StL-N 1913, NY-A 1921-30, Chi-N 1931-33, StL-A 1934-37

Oliva, Pedro "Tony" Min-A 1976-78, 1985-91

Oliveras, Max Cal-A 1994

Oliver, David J. "Dave" Tex-A 1987-94

Oliver, Thomas N. "Tom" Phi-A 1951-53, Bal-A 1954

Olson, Ivan M. "Ivy" Bro-N 1924, 1930-31, NY-N 1932

O'Neil, G. Michael "Mickey" Cle-A 1930

O'Neil, John S. "Buck" Chi-N 1962

O'Neill, Stephen F. "Steve" Cle-A 1935, Det-A 1941, Cle-A 1949, Bos-A 1950

Onslow, John J. "Jack" Pit-N 1925-26, Was-A 1927, StL-N 1928, Phi-N 1931-32, Bos-A 1934

Osborn, Donald E. "Don" Pit-N 1963-64, 1970-72, 1974-76

Osteen, Claude W. StL-N 1977-80, Phi-N 1982-88, Tex-A 1993-94

Otero, Regino J. "Regie" Cin-N 1959-65, Cle-A 1966

Otis, Amos J. SD-N 1988-90, Col-N 1993

Ott, N. Edward "Ed" Hou-N 1989-93

Overmire, Frank "Stubby" Det-A 1963-66

Owen, Arnold M. "Mickey" Bos-A 1955-56

Owens, James P. "Jim" Hou-N 1967-72

Ozark, Daniel L. "Danny" LA-N 1965-72, 1980-82, SF-N 1983-84

Pacheco, Antonio A. "Tony" Cle-A 1974, Hou-N 1976-79, 1982

Paepke, Jack LA-A 1961-64, Cal-A 1965-66

Pafko, Andrew "Andy" Mil-N 1960-62

Pagan, Jose A. Pit-N 1974-78

Page, Philippe R. "Phil" Cin-N 1947-52

Paige, Leroy R. "Satchell" Atl-N 1968-69

Parker, Francis J. "Salty" SF-N 1958-61, Cle-A 1962, LA-A 1964, Cal-A 1965-66, NY-N 1967, Hou-N 1968-72, Cal-A 1973-74

Pascual, Camilo A. Min-A 1978-80

Patterson, Henry J. C. "Hank" Bos-A 1932

Pattin, Martin W. "Marty" Tor-A 1989

Paul, Michael G. "Mike" Oak-A 1987-88, Sea-A 1989-91, Oak-A 1993

Pavlick, Gregory M. "Greg" NY-N 1985-86, 1988-91, 1994

Peitz, Henry C. "Heinie" StL-N 1913

Pennock, Herbert J. "Herb" Bos-A 1936-39

Pepitone, Joseph A. "Joe" NY-A 1982

Perez, Atanacio R. "Tony" Cin-N 1987-92

Perkins, Ralph F. "Cy" NY-A 1932-33, Det-A 1934-39, Phi-N 1946-54

Perlozzo, Samuel B. "Sam" NY-N 1987-89, Cin-N 1990-92, Sea-A 1993-94

Perranoski, Ronald P. "Ron" LA-N 1981-94

Pesky, John M. "Johnny" Pit-N 1965-67, Bos-A 1975-84

Peterson, Eric H. "Rick" Pit-N 1984-85

Pfister, George E. Bro-N 1952

Phillips, Harold R. "Lefty" LA-N 1965-68, Cal-A 1969

Phillips, Richard E. "Dick" SD-N 1980

Picciolo, Robert M. "Rob" SD-N 1990-94

Piche, Ronald J. "Ron" Mon-N 1976

Picinich, Valentine J. "Val" Cin-N 1934

Piersall, James A. "Jimmy" Tex-A 1975

Pignatano, Joseph B. "Joe" Was-A 1965-67, NY-N 1968-81, Atl-N 1982-85

Piniella, Louis V. "Lou" NY-A 1984-85

Pinson, Vada E. Sea-A 1977-80, Chi-A 1981, Sea-A 1982-83, Det-A 1985-91, Fla-N 1993-94

Pitler, Jacob A. "Jake" Bro-N 1947-57

Pitts, Gaylen R. StL-N 1991-94

Plaza, Ronald C. "Ron" Sea-A 1969, Cin-N 1978-83, Oak-A 1986

Plummer, William F. "Bill" Sea-A 1982-83, 1988-91, Col-N 1993

Podres, John J. "Johnny" SD-N 1973, Bos-A 1980, Min-A 1981-85, Phi-N 1991-94

Pole, Richard H. "Dick" Chi-N 1988-91, SF-N 1993-94

Pollet, Howard J. "Howie" StL-N 1959-64, Hou-N 1965

Popowski, Edward J. "Eddie" Bos-A 1967-76

Posedel, William J. "Bill" Pit-N 1949-53, StL-N 1954-57, Phi-N 1958, SF-N 1959-60, Oak-A 1968-72, SD-N 1974

Pujols, Luis B. Mon-N 1993-94

Queen, Melvin D. "Mel" Cle-A 1982

Quilici, Francis R. "Frank" Min-A 1971-72

Quirk, James P. "Jamie" StL-N 1984, KC-A 1994

Rader, Douglas L. "Doug" SD-N 1978-79, Chi-A 1986-87, Oak-A 1992, Fla-N 1993-94

Radison, Daniel J. "Dan" SD-N 1993-94

Ragan, D. C. Patrick "Pat" Phi-N 1924

Randall, Robert L. "Bobby" Min-A 1980

Randolph, Willie L. NA-Y 1994

Rapp, Vernon F. "Vern" Mon-N 1979-83

Reberger, Frank B. Cal-A 1991, Fla-N 1993-94

Redys, Edward "Ed" StL-A 1950-51

Reese, Harold H. "Pee Wee" LA-N 1959

Reese, James M. "Jimmie" Cal-A 1973-94

Regan, Philip R. "Phil" Sea-A 1984-86, Cle-A 1994

Reiser, Harold P. "Pete" LA-N 1960-64, Chi-N 1966-69, Cal-A 1970-71, Chi-N 1972-73

Renick, W. Richard "Rick" KC-A 1981, Mon-N 1985-86, Min-A 1987-90

Resinger, Grover S. Atl-N 1966, Chi-A 1967-68, Det-A 1969-70, Cal-A 1975-76

Rettenmund, Mervin W. "Merv" Cal-A 1980-82, Tex-A 1983-85, Oak-A 1989-90, SD-N 1991-94

Reyes, Benjamin "Cananea" Sea-A 1981

Reynolds, Tommie D Oak-A 1989-94

Rice, Delbert "Del" StL-N 1959, LA-A 1962-64, Cal-A 1965-66, Cle-A 1967

Rice, James E. "Jim" Bos-A 1994

Ricketts, David W. "Dave" Pit-N 1971-73, StL-N 1974-75, 1978-91

Riddle, John L. "Johnny" Pit-N 1948-50, StL-N 1952-55, Mil-N 1956-57, Cin-N 1958, Phi-N 1959

Riddoch, Gregory L. "Greg" SD-N 1987-90

Riggleman, James D. "Jim" StL-N 1989-90

Rigney, William J. "Bill" SD-N 1975

Ripken, Calvin E., Sr. "Cal" Bal-A 1976-86, 1989-92

Rippelmeyer, Raymond R. "Ray" Phi-N 1970-78

Roarke, Michael T. "Mike" Det-A 1965-66, Cal-A 1967-69, Det-A 1970, Chi-N 1978-80, StL-N 1984-90, SD-N 1991-93, Bos-A 1994

Roberts, David W. "Dave" Cle-A 1987

Roberts, Melvin H. "Mel" Phi-N 1992-94

Robertson, Sherrard A. "Sherry" Min-A 1970

Robinson, Brooks C. Bal-A 1977

Robinson, Dewey E. Chi-A 1993-94

Robinson, Frank Cal-A 1977, Bal-A 1978-80, 1985-87

Robinson, Warren G. "Sheriff" NY-N 1964, 1965-67, 1972

Robinson, Wilbert NY-N 1911-13

Robinson, William H. "Bill" NY-N 1984-89

Robinson, W. Edward "Eddie" Bal-A 1957-59

Robson, Thomas J. "Tom" Tex-A 1986-92

Rodgers, Robert L. "Bob" Min-A 1970-74, SF-N 1976, Mil-A 1978-80

Rojas, Octavio V. "Cookie" Chi-N 1978-81, Fla-N 1993-94

Rolfe, Robert A. "Red" NY-A 1946

Rommel, Edwin A. "Eddie" Phi-A 1933-34

Roof, Eugene L.'Gene" Det-A 1992-94

Roof, Phillip A. "Phil" SD-N 1978, Sea-A 1983-88, Chi-N 1990-91

Root, Charles H. "Charlie" Chi-N 1951-53, Mil-N 1956-57, Chi-N 1960

Roseboro, John J. Was-A 1970-71, Cal-A 1972-74

Rosenbaum, Glen O. Chi-A 1973-75, 1986-88

Roth, Francis C. "Frank" Pit-N 1917, NY-A 1921-22, Cle-A 1923-25, Chi-A 1927

Rothschild, Lawrence L. "Larry" Cin-N 1990-93

Roush, Edd J Cin-N 1938

Rowe, Donald H. "Don" Chi-A 1988, Mil-A 1992-94

Rowe, Kenneth D. "Ken" Bal-A 1985-86

Rowe, Lynwood T. "Schoolboy" Det-A 1954-55

Rowe, Ralph E. Min-A 1972-75, Bal-A 1981-84

Royster, Jeron K. "Jerry" Col-N 1993

Ruberto, John E. "Sonny" StL-N 1977-78

Rudi, Joseph O. "Joe" Oak-A 1986-87

Rudolph, Richard "Dick" Bos-N 1921-27

Ruel, Herold D. "Muddy" Chi-A 1935-45, Cle-A 1948-50

Ruffing, Charles H. "Red" NY-A 1962

Runnels, James E. "Pete" Bos-A 1965-66

Runnells, Thomas W. "Tom" Mon-N 1990-91

Russell, William E. "Bill" LA-N 1987-91, 1994

Ruth, George H. "Babe" Bro-N 1938

Ryan, Cornelius J. "Connie" Mil-N 1957, Atl-N 1971, 1973-75, Tex-A 1977-79

Ryan, John B. "Jack" Bos-A 1923-27

Ryan, Michael J. "Mike" Phi-N 1980-89

Ryba, Dominic J. "Mike" StL-N 1951-54

Sain, John F. "Johnny" KC-A 1959, NY-A 1961-63, Min-A 1965-66, Det-A 1967-69, Chi-A 1971-75, Atl-N 1977, 1985-86

Sanford, John A. "Jack" Cle-A 1968-69

Sandt, Thomas J. "Tommy" Pit-N 1987-94

Sarni, William F. "Bill" NY-N 1957

Sauer, Henry J. "Hank" SF-N 1959

Saul, James A. "Jim" Chi-N 1975-76, Oak-A 1979

Scarborough, Ray W. Bal-A 1968

Schacht, Alexander "Al"   Was-A 1925-34,
  Bos-A 1935-36
Schaefer, Robert W. "Bob"   KC-A 1988-91
Schaffer, Jimmie R. "Jim"   Tex-A 1978,
  KC-A 1980-88
Schalk, Raymond W. "Ray"   Chi-A 1930-31
Schang, Walter H. "Wally"   Cle-A 1936-38
Scheffing, Robert B. "Bob"   StL-A 1952-53,
  Chi-N 1954-55, Mil-N 1960
Scherger, George R.   Cin-N 1970-78, 1982-86
Schoendienst, Albert F. "Red"   StL-N 1961-64,
  Oak-A 1977-78, StL-N 1979-89
Schreiber, Paul F.   NY-A 1942, Bos-A 1947-58
Schueler, Ronald R. "Ron"   Chi-A 1979-82,
  Oak-A 1983-84, Pit-N 1986
Schulte, John C. "Johnny"   Chi-N 1933,
  NY-A 1934-48, Bos-A 1949-50
Schultz, George W. "Barney"   StL-N 1971-75,
  Chi-N 1977
Schultz, Joseph C., Jr. "Joe"   StL-A 1949,
  StL-N 1963-68, KC-A 1970, Det-A 1971-76
Seminick, Andrew W. "Andy"   Phi-N 1957-58,
  1967-69
Sewell, J. Luther "Luke"   Cle-A 1939-41,
  Cin-N 1949
Sewell, Joseph W. "Joe"   NY-A 1934-35
Sewell, Truett B. "Rip"   Pit-N 1948
Shanks, Howard S. "Howie"   Cle-A 1928-32
Shaughnessy, Francis J. "Shag"   Det-A 1928
Shaw, Robert J. "Bob"   Mil-A 1973
Shawkey, J. Robert "Bob"   NY-A 1929
Shea, Mervyn D. "Merv"   Det-A 1939-42,
  Phi-N 1944-45, Chi-N 1949
Sheehan, Thomas C. "Tom"   Cin-N 1935-37,
  Bos-N 1944
Shellenback, Frank V.   StL-A 1939,
  Bos-A 1940-44, Det-A 1946-47, NY-N 1949-55
Shellenback, James P. "Jim"   Min-A 1983
Shepard, Robert E. "Bert"   Was-A 1946
Shepard, Lawrence W. "Larry"   Phi-N 1967,
  Cin-N 1970-78, SF-N 1979
Sherry, Lawrence "Larry"   Pit-N 1977-78,
  Cal-A 1979-80
Sherry, Norman B. "Norm"   Cal-A 1970-71, 1976,
  Mon-N 1978-81, SD-N 1982-84, SF-N 1986-91
Shore, Raymond E. "Ray"   Cin-N 1963-67
Shotton, Burton E. "Burt"   StL-A 1923-25,
  Cin-N 1934, Cle-A 1942-45
Showalter, William N. "Buck"   NY-A 1990-91
Siebert, Wilfred C. "Sonny"   SD-N 1994
Sievers, Roy E.   Cin-N 1966
Silvera, Charles A. "Charlie"   Min-A 1969,
  Det-A 1971-73, Tex-A 1973-75
Silvestri, Kenneth J. "Ken"   Phi-N 1959-60,
  Mil-N 1963-65, Atl-N 1966-75, Chi-A 1976, 1982
Simmons, Aloysius H. "Al"   Phi-A 1940-42,
  1944-49, Cle-A 1950-51
Sisler, George H.   Bos-N 1930
Sisler, Richard A. "Dick"   Cin-N 1961-64,
  StL-N 1966-70, SD-N 1975-76, NY-N 1979-80
Sisti, Sebastian D. "Sibby"   Mil-N 1954,
  Sea-A 1969
Skaff, Francis M. "Frank"   Bal-A 1954,
  Det-A 1965-66, 1971
Skinner, Robert R. "Bob"   SD-N 1970-73,
  Pit-N 1974-76, SD-N 1977, Cal-A 1978,
  Pit-N 1979-85, Atl-N 1986-88
Slattery, John T. "Jack"   Bos-N 1918-19
Slider, Rachel W. "Rac"   Bos-A 1987-90
Smith, Alfred J. "Al"   NY-N 1933
Smith, Billy F.   Tor-A 1984-88
Smith, C. Reginald "Reggie"   LA-N 1994
Smith, Harold R. "Hal"   StL-N 1962,
  Pit-N 1965-67, Cin-N 1968-69, Mil-N 1976-77
Smith, Richard P. "Red"   Chi-A 1945-48
Snitker, Brian G.   Atl-N 1985, 1988-90
Snyder, Francis E. "Frank"   NY-N 1933-41
Snyder, James R. "Jim"   Chi-N 1987,
  Sea-A 1988, SD-N 1991-92
Sommers, Dennis J. "Denny"   NY-N 1977-78,
  Cle-A 1980-85, SD-N 1988-90
Sothoron, Allen S.   StL-N 1927-28, StL-A 1932-33
Southworth, William H. "Billy"   NY-N 1933
Spahn, Warren E.   NY-N 1965, Cle-A 1972-73
Spalding, Charles H. "Dick"   Phi-N 1934-36,
  Chi-N 1941-43
Spangler, Albert D. "Al"   Chi-N 1970-71, 1974
Sparks, Joseph C. "Joe"   Chi-A 1979,
  Cin-N 1984, Mon-N 1989, NY-A 1990
Spencer, H. Thomas "Tom"   Cle-A 1988-89,
  NY-N 1991, Hou-N 1992-93
Squires, Michael L. "Mike"   Tor-A 1989-91,
  Chi-A 1992
Staller, George W.   Bal-A 1962, 1969-75

Stanage, Oscar H.   Pit-N 1927-31
Stange, A. Lee   Bos-A 1969, 1972-74,
  Min-A 1975, Oak-A 1977-79, Bos-A 1981-84
Stanky, Edward R. "Eddie"   Cle-A 1957-58
Stanley, Frederick B. "Fred"   Mil-A 1991
Stargell, Wilver D. "Willie"   Pit-N 1985,
  Atl-N 1986-88
Starrette, Herman P. "Herm"   Atl-N 1974-76,
  SF-N 1977-78, Phi-N 1979-81, SF-N 1983-84,
  Mil-A 1985-86, Chi-N 1987, Bal-A 1988
Staub, Daniel J. "Rusty"   NY-N 1982
Stearns, John H.   NY-A 1989
Stelmaszek, Richard J. "Rick"   Min-A 1981-94
Stengel, Charles D. "Casey"   Bro-N 1932-33
Stevens, Edward L. "Ed"   SD-N 1981
Stock, Milton J. "Milt"   Chi-N 1944-48,
  Bro-N 1949-50, Pit-N 1951-52
Stock, Wesley G. "Wes"   KC-A 1967,
  Mil-N 1970-72, Oak-A 1972-76, Sea-A 1977-81,
  Oak-A 1984-86
Stottlemyre, Melvin L. "Mel"   NY-N 1984-93,
  Hou-N 1994
Stratton, Monty F.   Chi-A 1939-41
Street, Charles E. "Gabby"   StL-N 1929,
  StL-A 1937
Strickland, George B.   Min-A 1962,
  Cle-A 1963-69, KC-A 1970-72
Stubing, Lawrence G. "Moose"   Cal-A 1985-88,
  1989-90
Such, Richard S. "Dick"   Tex-A 1983-85,
  Min-A 1985-94
Sugden, Joseph "Joe"   StL-N 1921-25,
  Phi-N 1926-27
Sukeforth, Clyde L.   Bro-N 1943-51,
  Pit-N 1952-57
Sullivan, John P.   KC-A 1979, Atl-N 1980-81,
  Tor-A 1982-93
Summers, John J. "Champ"   NY-A 1989-90
Susce, George C. M.   Cle-A 1941-47, 1948-49,
  Bos-A 1950-54, KC-A 1955-56, Mil-N 1958-59,
  Was-A 1961-67, 1969-71, Tex-A 1972
Sweeney, William J. "Bill"   Det-A 1947-48
Sweet, Ricky J. "Rick"   Sea-A 1984
Swift, Robert V. "Bob"   Det-A 1953-54,
  KC-A 1957-59, Was-A 1960, Det-A 1963-66
Swisher, Steven E. "Steve"   NY-N 1993
Tannehill, Jesse N.   Phi-N 1920
Tappe, Elvin W. "El"   Chi-N 1958-63
Taylor, Antonio N. "Tony"   Phi-N 1977-79,
  1988-89
Taylor, James W. "Zack"   Bro-N 1936,
  StL-A 1941-46, Pit-N 1947
Temple, John E. "Johnny"   Cin-N 1964
Tenace, F. Gene   Hou-N 1986-87, Tor-A 1990-94
Terwilliger, W. Wayne   Was-A 1969-71,
  Tex-A 1972, 1981-85, Min-A 1986-94
Testa, Nicholas "Nick"   SF-N 1958
Thomas, George H.   Bos-A 1970
Thomas, Ira F.   Phi-A 1914-17, 1925-26
Thomas, J. Leroy "Lee"   StL-N 1972, 1983
Thomas, Roy A.   StL-N 1922
Thompson, Charles L. "Tim"   StL-N 1981
Tiefenauer, Bobby G.   Phi-N 1979
Tighe, John T. "Jack"   Det-A 1942, 1955-56
Tincup, A. Ben   Bro-N 1940
Tobin, John T. "Jack"   StL-A 1949-51
Tolan, Robert "Bobby"   SD-N 1980-83,
  Sea-A 1987
Torborg, Jeffrey A. "Jeff"   Cle-A 1975-77,
  NY-A 1979-88
Torchia, Anthony L. "Tony"   Bos-A 1985
Torgeson, C. Earl   NY-A 1961
Torres, Hector E.   Tor-A 1991
Tracewski, Richard J. "Dick"   Det-A 1972-94
Trebelhorn, Thomas L. "Tom"   Mil-A 1984, 1986,
  Chi-N 1992-93
Trucks, Virgil O.   Pit-N 1963
Turley, Robert L. "Bob"   Bos-A 1964
Turner, James R. "Jim"   NY-A 1949-59,
  Cin-N 1961-65, NY-A 1966-73
Turner, Terrence L. "Terry"   StL-N 1924
Uhle, George E.   Cle-A 1936-37, Chi-N 1940,
  Was-A 1944
Unser, Delbert B. "Del"   Phi-N 1985-88
Upshaw, Willie C.   Tex-A 1993-94
Valentine, Robert J. "Bobby"   NY-N 1983-85,
  Cin-N 1993
Valo, Elmer W.   Cle-A 1963-64
Van Ornum, John C.   SF-N 1980-84
Vernon, James B. "Mickey"   Pit-N 1960, 1964,
  StL-N 1965, Mon-N 1977-78, NY-A 1982
Vincent, Albert L. "Al"   Det-A 1943-44,
  Bal-A 1955-59, Phi-N 1961-63, KC-A 1966-67
Virdon, William C. "Bill"   Pit-N 1968-71, 1986

Virgil, Osvaldo Jose Sr. "Ozzie"   SF-N 1969-72,
  1974-75, Mon-N 1976-81, SD-N 1982-85,
  Sea-A 1986-88
Vukovich, John C.   Chi-N 1982-87, Phi-N 1988,
  1989-94
Wagner, Charles F. "Heinie"   Bos-A 1916-19,
  1927-29
Wagner, Charles T. "Charley"   Bos-A 1970
Wagner, John P. "Honus"   Pit-N 1933-51
Walker, Albert B. "Rube"   LA-N 1958,
  Was-A 1965-67, NY-N 1968-81, Atl-N 1982-84
Walker, Fred "Dixie"   StL-N 1953, 1955,
  Mil-N 1963-65
Walker, Gerald H. "Gee"   Cin-N 1946
Walker, Harry W.   StL-N 1959-62
Walker, Jerry A.   NY-A 1981-82, Hou-N 1983-85
Walker, Verlon L.   Chi-N 1961-70
Wallace, Roderick J. "Bobby"   Cin-N 1926
Walls, R. Lee   Oak-A 1979-82, NY-A 1983
Walsh, Edward A. "Ed"   Chi-A 1923-25, 1928-30
Walters, William H. "Bucky"   Bos-N 1950-52,
  Mil-N 1953-55, NY-N 1956-57
Walton, James R. "Jim"   Mil-A 1973-75
Waner, Paul G.   Phi-N 1965
Ward, John F. "Jay"   NY-A 1987, Mon-N 1991-92
Ward, Peter T. "Pete"   Atl-N 1978
Wares, Clyde E. "Buzzy"   StL-N 1930-35,
  1937-52
Warner, Harry C.   Tor-A 1977-79, 1980,
  Mil-A 1981-82
Warthen, Daniel D. "Dan"   Sea-A 1991-92
Wathan, John D.   KC-A 1986, Cal-A 1992-93,
  Bos-A 1994
Watson, Robert J. "Bob"   Oak-A 1986-88
Weaver, Earl S.   Bal-A 1968
Webb, William J. "Billy"   Chi-A 1935-39
Werle, William G. "Bill"   SF-N 1966
West, Samuel F. "Sam"   Was-A 1947-49
Westrum, Wesley N. "Wes"   SF-N 1958-63,
  NY-N 1964-65, SF-N 1968-71
Whisenant, T. Peter "Pete"   Cin-N 1961-62
White, Ernest D. "Ernie"   Bos-N 1947-48,
  NY-N 1963
White, Frank   Bos-A 1994
White, Joyner C. "Jo-Jo"   Cle-A 1958-60,
  Det-A 1960, KC-A 1961-62, Mil-N 1963-65,
  Atl-N 1966, KC-A 1969
White, Roy H.   NY-A 1983-84, 1986
Whitehill, Earl O.   Cle-A 1941, Phi-N 1943
Whitmer, Daniel C. "Dan"   Det-A 1992-94
Widmar, Albert J. "Al"   Phi-N 1962-64, 1968-69,
  Mil-A 1973-74, Tor-A 1980-88, 1989
Wietelmann, William F. "Whitey"   Cin-N 1966-67,
  SD-N 1969-79
Wilber, Delbert Q. "Del"   Chi-A 1955-56,
  Was-A 1970, Tex-A 1973
Wiley, Mark E.   Bal-A 1987, Cle-A 1988-91
Wilhelm, Irvin K. "Kaiser"   Phi-N 1921
Wilks, Theodore "Ted"   Cle-A 1960, KC-A 1961
Williams, Billy L.   Chi-N 1980-82, Oak-A 1983-85,
  Chi-N 1986-87
Williams, Dan   Cle-A 1993
Williams, David C. "Davey"   NY-N 1956-57
Williams, Donald E. "Don"   SD-N 1977-80
Williams, Donald R. "Spin"   Pit-N 1994
Williams, James B. "Jimmy"   Hou-N 1975,
  Bal-A 1981-87
Williams, James F. "Jimy"   Tor-A 1980-85,
  Atl-N 1990-94
Williams, Otto G.   Det-A 1925, StL-N 1926,
  StL-A 1927, Cin-N 1930
Williams, Richard H. "Dick"   Mon-N 1970
Williams, Stanley W. "Stan"   Bos-A 1975-76,
  Chi-A 1977-78, NY-A 1980-81, 1982, Cin-N 1984,
  NY-A 1987, 1989, Cin-N 1990-91
Williams, Walter A. "Walt"   Chi-A 1988
Wilson, James "Jimmy"   Cin-N 1939-40, 1944-46
Wiltse, George L. "Hooks"   NY-A 1925
Wine, Robert P. Sr. "Bobby"   Phi-N 1972-83,
  Atl-N 1985, 1988-90, NY-N 1993-94
Winegarner, Ralph L.   StL-A 1948-51
Wingo, Ivey B.   Cin-N 1928-29, 1936
Winkles, Bobby B.   Cal-A 1972, Oak-A 1974-75,
  SF-N 1976-77, Chi-A 1979-81, Mon-N 1986-88
Wolgamot, C. Earl   Cle-A 1931-33
Woodall, C. Lawrence "Larry"   Bos-A 1942-48
Woodling, Eugene R. "Gene"   Bal-A 1964-67
Worthington, Allan F. "Al"   Min-A 1972-73
Wright, Melvin J. "Mel"   Cin-N 1963-64, 1971,
  Pit-N 1973, NY-A 1974-75, Hou-N 1976-82
Wyatt, J. Whitlow "Whit"   Phi-N 1955-57,
  Mil-N 1958-65, Atl-N 1966-67
Wynn, Early   Cle-A 1964-66, Min-A 1967-69
York, P. Rudolph "Rudy"   Bos-A 1959-62

Yost, Edward F. "Eddie" LA-A 1962,
   Was-A 1963-67, NY-N 1968-76, Bos-A 1977-84
Youngblood, Joel R. Cin-N 1994
Zarilla, Allen L. "Al" Was-A 1971
Zeller, Barton W. "Bart" StL-N 1970

Zimmer, Donald W. "Don" Mon-N 1971,
   SD-N 1972, Bos-A 1974-76, NY-A 1983,
   Chi-N 1984-86, NY-A 1986, SF-N 1987,
   Bos-A 1992, Col-N 1993-94

Zimmer, Thomas J. "Tom" StL-N 1976
Zimmerman, Gerald R. "Gerry" Min-A 1967,
   Mon-N 1969-75, Min-A 1976-80
Zwilling, Edward H. "Dutch" Cle-A 1941

Biographical Data for Coaches Not Appearing in the Player/Pitcher Registers or Manager Roster

SPENCER ABBOTT Abbott, Spencer Arthur b: 8/27/1877, Chicago, Ill. d: 12/18/51, Washington, D.C. BL/TL, (1B)
RICK ADAIR Adair, Michael Richard b: 1/19/58, Spartanburg, S.Car. BL/TL, 6', 185 lbs. (P)
CARLOS ALFONSO Alfonso, Carlos b: 12/18/50, Havana, Cuba BR/TR, 6'2", 205 lbs. (P)
TONY AUFERIO Auferio, Anthony Patrick b: 6/13/47, Orange, N.J. BR/TR, 5'10", 185 lbs. (3B)
DICK BERARDINO Berardino, Richard J. b: 7/2/37, Cambridge, Mass. BR/TR, 6'1", 190 lbs. (OF)
C. B. BERINGER Beringer, Carroll James b: 8/14/28, Bellwood, Neb. BR/TR, 6', 195 lbs. (P)
TERRY BEVINGTON Bevington, Terry Paul b: 7/7/56, Akron, Ohio BR/TR, 6'2", 190 lbs. (C)
GREG BIAGINI Biagini, Gregory Peter b: 5/12/52, Chicago, Ill. BB/TR, 6'2", 205 lbs. (1B-OF)
WAYNE BLACKBURN Blackburn, Wayne Clark b: 7/10/16, Mt.Joy, Ohio BL/TR, 5'10", 165 lbs. (OF-3B-2B)
JACK BLOOMFIELD Bloomfield, Gordon Leigh b: 8/7/32, Monti Alto, Tex. BL/TR, 6'2", 185 lbs. (2B)
JIMMY BRAGAN Bragan, James Alton b: 3/12/29, Birmingham, Ala. BR/TR, 6', 198 lbs. (2B) (Brother of Bobby Bragan)
SCOTT BREEDEN Breeden, Harold Scott b: 9/17/37, Charlottesville, Va. BR/TR, 6'2", 210 lbs. (P)
JOE CAMACHO Camacho, Joseph Gomes b: 5/29/28, New Bedford, Mass. BR/TR, 6', 185 lbs. (SS-2B)
DANNY CARNEVALE Carnevale, Daniel Joseph b: 2/8/18, Buffalo, N.Y. BR/TR, 6', 195 lbs. (SS)
LEONEL CARRION Carrion, Leonel Santiago (Matheus) b: 2/15/52, Maracaibo, Venez. BR/TR, 5'11", 185 lbs. (OF)
DICK CARTER Carter, Richard Joseph b: 8/31/16, Philadelphia, Pa. d: 9/11/69, Philadelphia, Pa. BR/TR, 5'10", 190 lbs. (P-OF)
DOM CHITI Chiti, Harry Dominic b: 12/10/58, Independence, Mo. BL/TL, 6'2", 200 lbs. (P)
BOB CLEAR Clear, Elwood Robert b: 12/14/27, Denver, Colo. BR/TR, 5'10", 170 lbs. (P)
BOB CLUCK Cluck, Robert Alton b: 1/10/46, San Diego, Cal. BL/TL, 6'2", 195 lbs. (P)
TERRY COLLINS Collins, Terry Lee b: 5/7/49, Midland, Mich. BR/TR, 5'8", 160 lbs. (2B)
MARK CONNOR Connor, Mark Peter b: 5/27/49, Brooklyn, N.Y. BR/TR, 6'3", 195 lbs. (P)
JIMMIE CRANDALL Crandall, James Mark b: 12/7/12, Wadena, Ind. BB/TR, 5'11", 190 lbs. (P-C) (Son of Doc Crandall)
MARK CRESSE Cresse, Mark Emery b: 9/21/51, St.Albans, N.Y. BR/TR, 6'3", 220 lbs. (C)
MARTY DeMERRITT DeMerritt, Martin Gordon b: 3/4/53, San Francisco, Cal. BR/TR, 6'2.5", 205 lbs. (P)
BOBBY DEWS Dews, Robert Walter b: 3/23/38, Clinton, Iowa BR/TR, 6'1", 175 lbs. (SS)
RICH DONNELLY Donnelly, Richard Francis b: 8/3/46, Steubenville, Ohio BL/TR, 6', 185 lbs. (C)
OTIS DOUGLAS Douglas, Otis W. b: 7/25/11, Reedville, Va. d: 3/21/89, Kilmarnock, Va. BR/TR, 6'1", 230 lbs. (DNP)
RICK DOWN Down, Richard John b: 12/14/50, Wyandotte, Mich. BR/TR, 5'11", 220 lbs. (OF)
HARRY DUNLOP Dunlop, Harry Alexander b: 9/6/33, Sacramento, Cal. BL/TR, 6'3", 200 lbs. (C)
GENE DUSAN Dusan, Eugene Paul b: 11/9/49, Los Angeles, Cal. BB/TR, 6', 200 lbs. (C)
GLENN EZZELL Ezzell, Glenn Wayne b: 10/29/44, Kentwood, La. BR/TR, 6', 190 lbs. (C)
JOE FITZGERALD Fitzgerald, Joseph Patrick b: 3/17/1897, Washington, D.C. d: 8/29/67, Orlando, Fla. BR/TR, 5'11", 200 lbs. (C)
JOHN FITZPATRICK Fitzpatrick, John Arthur b: 3/19/04, LaSalle, Ill. BR/TR, 6'1.5", 185 lbs. (C)
MATT GALANTE Galante, Matthew Joseph b: 3/2/44, Brooklyn, N.Y. BR/TR, 5'6", 175 lbs. (2B)
ORLANDO GOMEZ Gomez, Juan Alejandro b: 6/24/46, Juana Diaz, P.R. BR/TR, 6', 190 lbs. (C)
EPY GUERRERO Guerrero, Epifanio Obdulio (Abud) b: 1/3/42, Santo Domingo, D.R. BR/TR, 5'11", 168 lbs. (OF) (Brother of Mario Guerrero)
GUY HANSEN Hansen, Guy Christopher b: 11/12/47, Los Angeles, Cal. BR/TR, 6', 170 lbs. (P)
ROGER HANSEN Hansen, Roger Christian b: 8/28/61, Johnstown, Pa. BR/TR, 6', 200 lbs. (C)
TOM HARMON Harmon, Thomas Harold b: 12/16/48, Lubbock, Tex. BR/TR, 5'11", 185 lbs. (C)
CHUCK HERNANDEZ Hernandez, Carlo Amado b: 11/11/60, Tampa, Fla. BL/TL, 6'3", 200 lbs. (P)
PERRY HILL Hill, Perry Wendell b: 3/19/52, Salina, Kan. BR/TR, 5'10", 170 lbs. (2B)
BEN HINES Hines, Benjamin Thortan b: 11/7/35, Yeager, Okla. BR/TR, 5'11", 205 lbs. (3B-C) (Father of Bruce Hines)
BRUCE HINES Hines, Bruce Edwin b: 11/7/57, Pomona, Cal. BB/TR, 5'10", 180 lbs. (2B) (Son of Ben Hines)
DOUG HOLMQUIST Holmquist, Douglas Leonard b: 10/4/41, Bridgeport, Conn. d: 2/27/88, Altamonte Springs, Fla. BR/TR, 6'2", 195 lbs. (C)
GOLDIE HOLT Holt, Golden Desmond b: 3/22/02, Enlo, Tex. d: 6/11/91, Sherman Oaks, Cal. BR/TR, 5'7.5", 165 lbs. (3B-OF-2B)
VERN HOSCHEIT Hoscheit, Vernard Arthur b: 4/1/22, Brunswick, Neb. BR/TR, 5'9", 185 lbs. (C)
JACK HUBBARD Hubbard, John H. b: 10/4/50, Rock Hall, Md. BR/TR, 5'11", 175 lbs. (DNP)
LUIS ISAAC Isaac, Luis (Aponte) b: 6/19/46, Rio Piedras, P.R. BR/TR, 5'11.5", 195 lbs. (C)
RUDY JARAMILLO Jaramillo, Rudolph b: 9/20/50, Beeville, Tex. BL/TR, 5'11", 180 lbs. (OF)
JOE JONES Jones, Joseph Carmack b: 12/13/41, Lebanon, Tenn. BR/TR, 5'9", 155 lbs. (2B)
LOU KAHN Kahn, Louis b: 12/4/16, St.Louis, Mo. BR/TR, 5'11", 195 lbs. (C)
MIKE KELLY Kelly, Bernard Francis b: 5/1/1896, Indianapolis, Ind. d: 10/23/68, Indianapolis, Ind. BR/TR, 6', 198 lbs. (1B)
WENDELL KIM Kim, Wendell Kealohapauloe b: 3/9/51, Honolulu, Hawaii BR/TR, 5'5", 160 lbs. (2B)
GEORGE KISSELL Kissell, George Marshall b: 9/9/21, Watertown, N.Y. BR/TR, 5'8", 175 lbs. (3B)
HUB KITTLE Kittle, Hubert Milton b: 2/19/17, Los Angeles, Cal. BR/TR, 6'1", 195 lbs. (P)
FRED KOENIG Koenig, Fred Carl b: 4/27/31, St.Louis, Mo. d: 1/12/93, Wagoner, Okla. BR/TR, 6'3", 200 lbs. (1B-3B)
JIM LETT Lett, James Curtis b: 1/3/51, Charleston, W.Va. BR/TR, 6'2", 185 lbs. (3B)
LENNY LEVY Levy, Leonard Howard b: 6/11/13, Pittsburgh, Pa. d: 2/2/93, Palm Desert, Cal. BR/TR, 5'10.5", 190 lbs. (C)
BILL LOBE Lobe, William Charles b: 3/24/12, Cleveland, Ohio d: 1/7/69, Cleveland, Ohio BR/TR, 5'9.5", 178 lbs. (C)
Q. V. LOWE Lowe, Q. V. b: 1/15/45, Red Level, Ala. BR/TR, 6'1", 185 lbs. (P)
ROY MAJTYKA Majtyka, Le Roy W. b: 6/1/39, Buffalo, N.Y. BR/TR, 5'11", 170 lbs. (2B)
JACK MALOOF Maloof, Jack Garth b: 10/12/49, Redlands, Cal. BL/TL, 6', 175 lbs. (1B-OF)
DOUG MANSOLINO Mansolino, Douglas b: 9/20/56, Plainfield, N.J. BR/TR, 5'7", 155 lbs. (IF)
HARRY MATHEWS Mathews, Henry
RICK MATHEWS Mathews, Rick Ray b: 10/9/47, Centerville, Iowa B?/T?, 5'11", 180 lbs. (P)
LEO MAZZONE Mazzone, Leo David b: 10/16/48, Keyser, W.Va. BL/TL, 5'10", 185 lbs. (P)
MAJE McDONNELL McDonnell, Robert A. b: 7/20/20, Philadelphia, Pa. BR/TR, 5'6", 135 lbs. (P)
J. R. McKEE McKee, John R.
JOHN McLAREN McLaren, John Lowell b: 9/29/51, Galveston, Tex. BR/TR, 6', 200 lbs. (C)
DAVE MILEY Miley, David Allen b: 4/3/62, Tampa, Fla. BL/TR, 6'3", 220 lbs. (C)
MO MOZZALI Mozzali, Maurice Joseph b: 12/12/22, Louisville, Ky. d: 3/2/87, Lakeland, Fla. BL/TL, 5'10", 160 lbs. (1B)
JACK MULL Mull, Jack Leroy b: 9/29/43, Chambersburg, Pa. BR/TR, 5'10", 188 lbs. (C)
ED NAPOLEON Napoleon, Edward George b: 9/17/37, Baltimore, Md. BR/TR, 5'8", 165 lbs. (OF-3B-1B)
ED NOTTLE Nottle, Edward William b: 10/22/39, Philadelphia, Pa. BR/TR, 5'10", 180 lbs. (P)
FRANK OCEAK Oceak, Frank John "Fez" b: 9/8/12, Pocahontas, Va. d: 3/19/83, Johnstown, Pa. BR/TR, 5'9", 172 lbs. (2B)
BUCK O'NEIL O'Neil, John Jordan b: 11/13/11, Carrabelle, Fla. BR/TR, 6'2", 190 lbs. (1B)
DON OSBORN Osborn, Donald Edwin b: 6/3/08, Sandpoint, Idaho d: 3/23/79, Torrance, Cal. BR/TR, 6', 185 lbs. (P)
TONY PACHECO Pacheco, Antonio Aristides b: 8/9/27, Havana, Cuba d: 8/7/86, Miami, Fla. BR/TR, 6', 190 lbs. (2B)
JACK PAEPKE Paepke, Jack b: 8/28/22, Provo, Utah BR/TR, 6'2.5", 220 lbs. (C-P) (Father of Dennis Paepke)
GREG PAVLICK Pavlick, Gregory Michael b: 3/10/50, Washington, D.C. BR/TR, 6'3", 205 lbs. (P)
RICK PETERSON Peterson, Eric Harding b: 10/30/54, Brunswick, N.J. BL/TL, 6', 175 lbs. (P) (Son of Harding Peterson)
RON PLAZA Plaza, Ronald Charles b: 8/24/34, Passaic, N.J. BR/TR, 6', 180 lbs. (3B)
DAN RADISON Radison, Daniel J. b: 8/24/50, St.Louis, Mo. BR/TR, 6'2", 190 lbs. (C)
ED REDYS Redys, Edward b: 6/23/21, Detroit, Mich. BR/TR, 6', 185 lbs. (P)
GROVER RESINGER Resinger, Grover S b: 10/20/15, St.Louis, Mo. d: 1/11/86, St.Louis, Mo. BR/TR, 5'9", 180 lbs. (3B)
CANANEA REYES Reyes, Benjamin (Chavez) b: 2/18/37, Nacosari, Sonora, Mexico d: 11/11/91, Hermosillo, Mexico BR/TR, 5'10", 180 lbs. (OF)

MEL ROBERTS Roberts, Melvin Henry   b: 1/18/43, Abington, Pa.   BR/TR, 6', 180 lbs.   (OF)
DEWEY ROBINSON Robinson, Dewey Everett   b: 4/28/55, Evanston, Ill.   BR/TR, 6', 190 lbs.   (P)
SHERIFF ROBINSON Robinson, Warren Grant   b: 9/8/21, Cambridge, Md.   BR/TR, 6'1", 195 lbs.   (C)
GLEN ROSENBAUM Rosenbaum, Glen Otis   b: 6/14/36, Union Mills, Ind.   BR/TR, 5'11", 180 lbs.   (P)
RALPH ROWE Rowe, Ralph Emanuel   b: 7/14/24, Newberry, S.C.   BL/TR, 5'6", 160 lbs.   (OF)
JIM SAUL Saul, James Allen   b: 11/24/39, Bristol, Va.   BL/TR, 6'3", 210 lbs.   (C)
GEORGE SCHERGER Scherger, George Richard   b: 11/20/20, Dickinson, N.D.   BR/TR, 5'8", 183 lbs.   (2B)
RAC SLIDER Slider, Rachel W.   b: 12/23/33, Simms, Tex.   BL/TR, 5'8", 160 lbs.   (SS)
BILLY SMITH Smith, Billy Franklin   b: 1/14/30, High Point, N.C.   BL/TL, 5'9", 160 lbs.   (1B-OF)
BRIAN SNITKER Snitker, Brian Gerald   b: 10/17/55, Decatur, Ill.   BR/TR, 6'1", 192 lbs.   (C)
DENNY SOMMERS Sommers, Dennis James   b: 7/12/40, New London, Wis.   BL/TR, 6'2", 205 lbs.   (C)
JOE SPARKS Sparks, Joseph Everett   b: 3/15/38, McComas, W.Va.   BL/TR, 6', 195 lbs.   (3B-2B)
TONY TORCHIA Torchia, Anthony Lewis   b: 12/13/43, Chicago, Ill.   BR/TL, 5'10", 180 lbs.   (1B-OF)
JOHN VanORNUM Van Ornum, John Clayton   b: 10/20/39, Pasadena, Cal.   BR/TR, 5'11", 175 lbs.   (C)
AL VINCENT Vincent, Albert Linder   b: 12/23/06, Birmingham, Ala.   BR/TR, 5'9.5", 170 lbs.   (2B)
VERLON WALKER Walker, Verlon Lee "Rube"   b: 3/7/29, Lenoir, N.C.   d: 3/24/71, Chicago, Ill.   BL/TR, 6', 210 lbs.   (C) (Brother of Rube Walker)
JIM WALTON Walton, James Robert   b: 9/5/35, Shattuck, Okla.   BR/TR, 6'2", 190 lbs.   (P)
HARRY WARNER Warner, Harry Clinton   b: 12/11/28, Reeders, Pa.   BL/TR, 6'2", 215 lbs.   (1B)
DANA WILLIAMS Williams, Dana   b: 3/20/63, Weirton, W.Va.   BR/TR, 5'10", 170 lbs.   (OF)
DON WILLIAMS Williams, Donald Ellis   b: 12/24/37, Paragould, Ark.   BR/TR, 5'10", 185 lbs.   (SS)
JIMMY WILLIAMS Williams, James Bernard   b: 5/15/26, Toronto, Ont., Can.   BR/TR, 5'10", 180 lbs.   (OF)
EARL WOLGAMOT Wolgamot, Clinton Earl   b: 12/21/1895, Fairbank, Iowa   d: 4/25/70, Independence, Iowa   BR/TR, 5'8", 155 lbs.   (C)
TOM ZIMMER Zimmer, Thomas Jeffrey   b: 6/30/52, Mobile, Ala.   BR/TR, 5'8", 165 lbs.   (C) (Son of Don Zimmer)

The Umpire Roster

The men in blue have been rebuked and scorned since the Knickerbockers cavorted on the Elysian Fields of Hoboken. The first to incur an umpire's wrath in return was Knickerbocker player Davis, fined six cents for swearing, perhaps understandably since his team was being trounced by the New York Club, 23–1. The name of the umpire in that historic game of June 19, 1846—the first match game under Alexander Cartwright's new rules—was not recorded. Ever since, a handful of researchers have scrambled to find out who umpired the league games of baseball's early history.

Larry Gerlach, who knows more about umpires and umpiring than anybody, has created the Umpire Roster that follows. The basis of his roster is the list compiled by S. C. Thompson in the 1930s and 1940s, but his research has corrected several errors and omissions in that list and has scrupulously brought the umpire roster up to date. In *Total Baseball 1* he hoped that "by the next edition we will have finished a complete re-study of the umpire roster. . . . I am going to try to fashion a biographical encyclopedia of major league umpires—vital statistics; minor and major league service; All-Star, World Series, Playoff games; special achievements; and so on. One of the more frustrating things about the Turkin/Thompson roster (and even ours) is how years of service are noted in terms of seasons; it really is misleading to identify someone as working from 1980–1987 when he may have broken into the majors on September 24, 1980."

The data presented here does not meet those lofty goals, but it is vastly increased and improved, as well as reorganized. Umpires are now divided not only by league but also by: regular, league-employed umpires; substitutes; player-umpires, pressed into emergency service; and those subs used during the recent strikes. New leads continue to flow in, especially about the early days, when umpires were not assigned by the leagues but were supplied by the teams, recruited from among the fans in attendance (this explains why so many given names are lacking for pre-1900 arbiters), or, not infrequently, plucked from the team's reserve players. A feature unique to *Total Baseball* is the identification of substitute umpires in the National Association years 1871-75. An instance of this last practice occurred as late as 1935, when Chicago White Sox outfielder Jocko Conlan was recruited to fill in for umpire Red Ormsby in a game between the Sox and the St. Louis Browns. Conlan, of course, went on to a Hall of Fame career as a man in blue.

Let's call the roll.

REGULAR UMPIRES

National Association (1871-75)

Avery, C. Hamilton 1875
Beardslee, John J. 1871
Blodgett, C. W. 1875
Boardman, Frederick "Fred" 1875
Bomeisler, Theodore 1871-73
Boyd, William J. "Bill" 1875
Burdock, John J. "Jack" 1872-74
Carey, Thomas J. "Tom" 1874
Clapp, John E. 1874-75
Cone, J. Frederick "Fred" 1875
Daniels, Charles F. 1874-75
Dehlman, Herman J. 1874
Dole, Lester C. 1875
Ferguson, Robert V. "Bob" 1872-73, 1875
Fulmer, Charles J. "Chick" 1873
Heubel, George A. 1875
Hodges, Amory G. 1874-75
Holly, Samuel J. "Sam" 1871
Lennon, William F. "Bill" 1871-72, 1873-74
Mack, Dennis J. "Denny" 1875
Martin, Alphonse C. "Phonney" 1875
Mathews, Robert T. "Bobby" 1873-75
McLean, William H. "Billy" 1874-75
Mills, Charles "Charlie" 1872-73
Patterson, Daniel T. "Dan" 1874
Rogers, M. Mortimer "Mort" 1871
Sensenderfer, John P. J. "Count" 1874
Swandell, J. Martin "Marty" 1872-73
Tate, William 1874
Walsh, Michael F. "Mike" 1875
Young, Nicholas E. "Nick" 1871-75

National League (1876-)

Andrews, G. Edward "Ed" 1895, 1898-99
Baker, William P. "Bill" 1957
Ballanfant, E. Lee 1936-57
Barlick, Albert J. "Al" 1940-43, 1946-55, 1958-71
Barnes, Ronald "Ron" 1990-94
Barnie, William S. "Billy" 1892
Barr, George M. 1932-49
Barron, Mark E. 1992-94
Battin, Joseph V. "Joe" 1891
Bausewine, George 1905
Behle, Frank 1901
Bell, Wally 1992-94
Betts, William G. 1894-96, 1898-99
Betz, Edwin J. 1961
Boggess, Lynton R. "Dusty" 1944-48, 1950-62
Boles, Charles 1877
Bond, Thomas H. "Tommy" 1883, 1885
Bonin, Gregory "Greg" 1986-94
Bradley, George H. "Foghorn" 1879-83
Brady, Jackson 1887
Bransfield, William E. "Kitty" 1917
Bredburg, George W. 1877
Brennan, John E. "Jack" 1899

Brennan, William T. "Bill" 1909-13, 1921
Brocklander, Fred W. 1979-90
Brown, Thomas T. "Tom" 1898-99, 1901-02
Bunce, Joshua 1877
Burkhart, W. Kenneth "Ken" 1957-73
Burnham, George W. 1883, 1889, 1895
Burns, John S. 1884
Burns, Thomas E. "Tom" 1892
Burns, Thomas P. "Oyster" 1899
Burtis, L. W. 1876-77
Bush, Garnet C. 1911-12
Byron, William J. "Bill" or "Lord" 1913-19
Callahan, Edward J. 1881
Campbell, Daniel "Dan" 1894-96
Campbell, William M. "Bick" 1939-40
Cantillon, Joseph D. "Joe" 1902
Carpenter, William B. "Bill" 1897, 1904, 1906-07
Chapman, John C. "Jack" 1880
Chipman, Harry F. 1883, 1885
Clarke, Robert M. "Bob" 1930-31
Cockill, George W. 1915
Colgan, Harry W. 1901
Colosi, Nicholas "Nick" 1968-82
Conahan, — 1896
Cone, J. F. "Fred" 1877
Conlan, John B. "Jocko" 1941-64
Connolly, John M. 1886
Connolly, Thomas H. "Tommy" 1898-1900
Conway, John H. 1906
Crandall, Robert 1877
Crawford, Gerald J. "Jerry" 1976-94
Crawford, Henry C. "Shag" 1956-75
Cross, John A. 1878
Cunningham, Elmer E. "Bert" 1901
Curry, Wesley "Wes" 1885-86, 1889, 1898
Cusack, Stephen P. 1909
Cushman, Charles H. "Charley" 1885, 1898
Cuzzi, Phil 1991-93
Dailey, John J. 1882
Dale, Jerry P. 1970-85
Daniels, Charles F. 1876, 1878-80, 1887-88
Danley, Kerwin 1991-94
Darling, Gary R. 1988-94
Dascoli, Frank 1948-62
Davidson, David L. "Satch" 1969-84
Davidson, Robert A. "Bob" 1983-94
Davis, Gerald "Gerry" 1985-94
Decker, Stewart M. 1883-85, 1888
Delmore, Victor "Vic" 1956-59
DeMuth, Dana A. 1986-94
Derr, Doll 1923
Devinney, P. H. "Dan" 1877
Dezelan, Frank J. 1966-68, 1969-71
Dixon, Hal N. 1953-59
Donatelli, August J. "Augie" 1950-73
Donnelly, Charles H. 1931-32
Donohue, Michael R. 1930
Doscher, John H. Sr. "Herm" 1880-81, 1887
Doyle, John J. "Jack" 1911
Ducharme, — 1876-77
Dunn, Thomas P. "Tom" 1939-46
Dunnigan, Joseph 1881-82
Dwyer, J. Francis "Frank" 1899, 1901

Eagan, John J. 1878, 1886
Eason, Malcolm W. "Mal" 1902, 1910-16
Ellick, Joseph J. "Joe" 1886
Emslie, Robert D. "Bob" 1891-1924
Engel, Robert A. "Bob" 1965-90
Engeln, William R. "Bill" 1952-56
Ferguson, Robert V. "Bob" 1879, 1884-85
Fessenden, Wallace C. "Wally" 1889-90
Fields, Stephen H. "Steve" 1979-82
Finneran, William F. 1911-12, 1923-24
Forman, Allen S. "Al" 1961-65
Fountain, Edward G. 1879
Frary, Ralph 1911
Froemming, Bruce N. 1971-94
Fulmer, Charles J. "Chick" 1886
Furlong, William E. "Bill" 1878-79, 1883-84
Fyfe, Lee C. 1920
Gaffney, John H. 1884-86, 1891-94, 1899-1900
Galvin, James F. "Jim" 1895
Gibbons, Brian 1994
Gillean, Thomas 1879-80
Goetz, Lawrence J. "Larry" 1936-57
Gore, Arthur J. "Artie" 1947-56
Gorman, Brian 1991-94
Gorman, Thomas D. "Tom" 1951-76
Gregg, Eric E. 1977-91, 1993-94
Guglielmo, A. Augie 1952
Gunning, Thomas F. "Tom" 1887
Guthrie, William J. "Bill" 1913-15
Hallion, Thomas F. "Tom" 1986-94
Harris, Lannie D. 1979-85
Harrison, Peter A. "Pete" 1916-20
Hart, Eugene F. "Bob" 1920-29
Hart, William F. "Bill" 1914-15
Harvey, H. Douglas "Doug" 1962-77, 1979-92
Hautz, Charles A. "Charlie" 1876, 1879
Henderson, J. Harding "Hardie" 1895-96
Hengle, Edward S. "Ed" 1887
Henline, Walter J. "Butch" 1945-48
Hernandez, Angel 1991-94
Heuble, George A. 1876
Heydler, John A. 1898
Higham, Richard "Dick" 1881-82
Hirschbeck, Mark 1988-94
Hoagland, Willard A. 1894
Hodges, A. D. 1876
Hohn, William J. "Bill" 1987-94
Holland, John A. 1887
Holliday, James W. "Bug" 1903
Holmes, Howard 1921
Hornung, M. Joseph "Joe" 1893, 1896
Hunt, John T. 1895, 1898-99
Hurst, Timothy C. "Tim" 1891-97, 1900, 1903
Irwin, Arthur A. 1902
Jackowski, William A. "Bill" 1952-68
Jeffers, W. W. 1881
Jevne, Frederick "Fred" 1895
Johnson, Henry S. "Steamboat" 1914

Johnstone, James E. "Jim" 1903-12
Jorda, Louis D. "Lou" 1927-31, 1940-52
Julian, Joseph O. 1878
Kane, Stephen J. 1909-10
Keefe, Timothy J. "Tim" 1894-96
Kellogg, Jeffery "Jeff" 1991-94
Kelly, John O. 1882, 1888, 1897
Kennedy, Charles 1904
Kenney, John 1877
Kibler, John W. 1963-89
Klem, William J. "Bill" 1905-41
Knight, Alonzo P. "Lon" 1889
Landes, Stanley A. "Stan" 1955-72
Lane, Frank H. 1883
Latham, W. Arlington "Arlie" 1899, 1902
Layne, Jerry B. 1989-94
Libby, Stephen A. 1880
Lincoln, Frederick H. 1914, 1917
Long, "Robert "Bob" 1992
Long, William H. "Billy" 1895
Lynch, Thomas J. "Tom" 1888-99
Macullar, James F. "Jimmy" 1892
Magee, Sherwood R. "Sherry" 1928
Magerkurth, George L. 1929-47
Mahoney, Michael J. 1892
Malone, Ferguson G. "Fergy" 1884
Manassau, Alfred S. "Al" 1899
Marsh, Randall G. "Randy" 1983-94
Mathews, Robert T. "Bobby" 1880
McCafferty, Charles 1921, 1923
McCormick, William J. "Barry" 1919-29
McDermott, Michael J. "Sandy" 1890, 1897
McDonald, James F. 1895, 1897-99
McElwee, Harvey 1877
McFarland, Horace 1896-97
McGarr, James B. "Chippy" 1899
McGrew, Harry T. "Ted" 1930-31, 1933-34
McLaughlin, Edward J. 1929
McLaughlin, Michael 1893
McLaughlin, Peter J. 1924-28
McLean, William H. "Billy" 1876, 1878-80, 1882-84
McQuaid, John H. "Jack" 1889-94
McSherry, John P. 1971-94
Miller, George E. 1879
Mitchell, Charles 1892
Montague, Edward M. "Ed" 1976-94
Moran, August "Augie" 1903-04, 1910, 1918
Moran, Charles B. "Charlie" 1917-39
Mullin, John 1909
Nash, William M. "Billy" 1901
O'Connor, Arthur 1914
O'Day, Henry F. "Hank" 1895, 1897-1911, 1913, 1915-27
Odlin, Albert F. 1883
O'Hara, — 1915
Olsen, Andrew H. "Andy" 1968-81
O'Rourke, James H. "Jim" 1894
Orth, Albert L. "Al" 1912-17
O'Sullivan, John J. 1922
Owens, Clarence B. "Brick" 1908, 1912-13

Pallone, David M. "Dave" 1979-88
Parker, George L. 1936-38
Pearce, Richard J. "Dicky" 1878, 1882
Pears, Frank 1897, 1905
Pelekoudas, Christos G. "Chris" 1960-75
Pfirman, Charles H. "Cy" 1922-36
Pierce, Grayson S. "Gracie" 1886-87
Pinelli, Ralph A. "Babe" 1935-56
Poncino, Larry L. 1986-88, 1991-94
Potter, Scott 1991-94
Powell, Cornelius J. "Jack" 1923-24, 1933
Power, Charles B. 1902
Powers, Philip J. "Phil" 1879, 1881, 1886-91
Pratt, Albert G. "Al" 1879
Pratt, Thomas J. "Tom" 1886
Pryor, J. Paul 1961-81
Pulli, Frank V. 1972-94
Quest, Joseph L. "Joe" 1886-87
Quick, James E. "Jim" 1976-94
Quigley, Ernest C. "Ernie" 1913-37
Quinn, Joseph C. "Joe" 1882
Rapuano, Edward "Ed" 1990-94
Reardon, John E. "Beans" 1926-49
Reliford, Charles "Charlie" 1989-94
Rennert, Laurence H. "Dutch" 1973-92
Rieker, Richard "Rich" 1992-94
Rigler, Charles "Cy" 1906-22, 1924-35
Riley, William J. 1880
Rippley, T. Steven "Steve" 1985-94
Robb, Douglas W. "Scotty" 1948-52
Roberts, Leonard W. "Lenny" 1953-55
Rudderham, John E. 1908
Runge, Paul E. 1973-94
Ryan, Walter 1946
Scott, James "Jim" 1930-31
Sears, John W. "Ziggy" 1934-45
Secory, Frank E. 1952-70
Sentelle, Leopold T. "Paul" 1922-23
Seward, Edward W. "Ed" 1893
Seward, George E. 1876, 1878
Sheridan, John F. "Jack" 1892, 1896-97
Smith, Charles M. "Pop" 1881
Smith, Vincent A. "Vinnie" 1957-65
Smith, William W. "Billy" 1898-99
Snyder, Charles N. "Pop" 1892-93, 1898-1901
Stage, Charles W. "Billy" 1894
Stambaugh, Calvin G. 1877-78
Stark, Albert D. "Dolly" 1928-35, 1937-39, 1942
Steiner, Melvin J. "Mel" 1961-72
Steinfeldt, Harry M. 1905
Stello, Richard J. "Dick" 1969-87
Sternburg, Paul 1909
Stewart, William J. "Bill" 1933-54
Stockdale, M. J. 1915
Strief, George A. 1890
Sudol, Edward L. "Ed" 1957-77
Sullivan, David F. "Dave" 1882, 1885

Sullivan, Jeremiah "Jerry" 1887
Sullivan, T. P. 1880
Summer, James G. 1877
Swartwood, C. Edward "Ed" 1894, 1898-1900
Sweeney, James M. "Jim" 1924-26
Tata, Terry A. 1973-94
Terry, William H. "Adonis" 1900
Tilden, Otis 1880
Tremblay, Richard H. "Dick" 1971
Truby, Harry G. 1909
Valentine, John G. 1887-88
Van Court, Eugene 1884
Vanover, Larry 1991, 1993-94
Vargo, Edward P. "Ed" 1960-83
Venzon, Anthony "Tony" 1957-71
Walker, William E. 1876-77
Walsh, Francis D. "Frank" 1961-63
Walsh, Michael F. "Mike" 1876, 1878, 1880
Warneke, Lonnie "Lon" 1949-55
Warner, Albert "Al" 1898-1900
Weidman, George E. "Stump" 1896
Wendelstedt, Harry H. 1966-94
West, Joseph H. "Joe" 1976, 1978-94
Westervelt, Frederick E. 1922
Weyer, Lee H. 1961, 1963-88
White, Gideon F. 1878
Wickham, Daniel "Dan" 1990-92
Wilbur, Charles E. 1879
Williams, Arthur "Art" 1972-77
Williams, Charles H. "Charlie" 1978, 1983-94
Williams, William G. "Bill" 1963-87
Wilson, Frank 1922-28
Wilson, John A. 1887
Winters, Michael J. "Mike" 1990-94
Wise, Samuel W. "Sam" 1889, 1893
Wood, George A. 1898
York, Thomas J. "Tom" 1886
Young, Joseph 1879
Zacharias, Thomas 1890
Zimmer, Charles L. "Chief" 1904

American Association (1882-91)

Barnum, George W. 1890
Bauers, Albert J. "Al" 1887
Becannon, William H. 1883
Bradley, George H. "Foghorn" 1886
Brennan, John E. "Jack" 1884
Butler, Ormond H. 1883
Carey, Thomas J. "Tom" 1882
Clinton, James L. "Jim" 1886
Connell, Terence G. 1884, 1890
Connelly, John M. 1885, 1887
Connelly, William 1884
Curry, Wesley "Wes" 1887, 1890
Cuthbert, Edgar E. "Ned" 1887
Dailey, John J. 1884
Daniels, Charles F. 1883-85, 1889
Davis, James J. "Jumbo" 1891
Devinney, P. H. "Dan" 1884
Doscher, John H. Sr. "Herm" 1888, 1890

Dyler, John F. 1884
Emslie, Robert D. "Bob" 1890
Ferguson, Robert V. "Bob" 1886-89, 1891
Gaffney, John H. 1888-89
Gleason, William G. "Bill" 1891
Goldsmith, Frederick E. "Fred" 1888-89
Griffith, E. A. 1884
Hautz, Charles A. "Charlie" 1882
Hecker, Guy J. 1889
Holland, John A. 1884
Holland, Willard A. 1889
Hurley, Daniel "Dan" 1887
Jennings, Alfred J. "Al" 1887
Jones, Charles W. "Charley" 1890
Kelly, John O. 1883-86
Kerins, John A. "Jack" 1889-91
Knight, Alonzo P. "Lon" 1887
Lawler, John F. 1884
Macullar, James F. "Jimmy" 1891
Mack, Dennis J. "Denny" 1886
Magner, John T. 1883
Mahoney, Michael J. 1891
Mathews, Robert T. "Bobby" 1891
McLaughlin, Thomas 1891
McLean, William H. "Billy" 1885
McNichol, Robert T. 1883
McQuaid, John H. "Jack" 1886-88
Morton, Charles H. "Charlie" 1886
O'Brien, Frank 1890
Peoples, James E. "Jimmy" 1890
Pike, Lipman. E. "Lip" 1889
Pratt, Albert G. "Al" 1883
Quinn, A. J. 1886
Riley, William J. 1882
Ross, Robert T. 1882
Seward, George E. 1884
Simmons, Joseph S. "Joe" 1882
Smith, Charles M. "Pop" 1882
Snyder, Charles N. "Pop" 1891
Sommer, Benjamin F. 1883
Sullivan, Jeremiah "Jerry" 1887
Sullivan, Theodore P. "Ted" 1887
Taylor, Walter 1890
Toole, Stephen J. "Steve" 1890
Tunnison, William 1885-86
Valentine, John G. 1884-87
Walsh, Michael F. "Mike" 1882-83, 1885-86
York, Thomas J. "Tom" 1886
Young, Benjamin F. "Ben" 1886

Union Association (1884)

Crawford, Alexander 1884
Devinney, P. H. "Dan" 1884
Dutton, Patrick J. 1884
Hengle, Emory J. "Moxie" 1884
Holland, John A. 1884
Hooper, Michael H. 1884
Jennings, Alfred "Al" 1884
Jordan, William H. "Bill" 1884
Mapledoram, Blake A. 1884
McCaffrey, Harry 1884
Seward, George E. 1884
Stearns, D. Eckford "Ecky" 1884
Sullivan, David F. "Dave" 1884

Players League (1890)

Barnes, Roscoe C. "Ross" 1890
Ferguson, Robert V. "Bob" 1890
Gaffney, John H. 1890
Gunning, Thomas F. "Tom" 1890
Holbert, William H. "Bill" 1890
Jones, Charles W. "Charley" 1890
Knight, Alonzo P. "Lon" 1890
Leach, Henry 1890
Matthews, John 1890
Pierce, Grayson S. "Gracie" 1890
Sheridan, John F. "Jack" 1890
Snyder, Charles N. "Pop" 1890

American League (1901-)

Adams, John H. 1903
Anthony, G. Merlyn 1969-75
Ashford, Emmett L. 1966-70
Avants, Nick R. 1969-71
Barrett, Ted 1994
Barnett, Lawrence R. "Larry" 1968-94
Barry, Daniel "Dan" 1928
Basil, Stephen J. "Steve" 1936-42
Bean, Ed 1994
Berry, Charles F. "Charlie" 1942-62
Betts, William G. 1901
Boyer, James M. "Jim" 1944-50
Bremigan, Nicholas G. "Nick" 1974-88
Brinkman, Joseph N. "Joe" 1973-94
Campbell, William M. "Bick" 1928-31
Cantillon, Joseph D. "Joe" 1901
Carrigan, H. Sam 1961-65
Carpenter, William B. "Bill" 1904
Caruthers, Robert L. "Bob" 1902-03
Cederstrom, Gary 1989-94
Chill, Oliver P. "Ollie" 1914-16, 1919-22
Chylak, Nestor L. 1954-78
Clark, Alan M. "Al" 1976-94
Coble, G. Drew 1983-94
Colliflower, James H. 1910
Connolly, Thomas H. "Tommy" 1901-31
Connor, Thomas "Tom" 1905-06
Cooney, Terrance J. "Terry" 1975-92
Cousins, Derryl 1979-94
Craft, Terry 1989-94
Culbreth, Fielding 1993-94
Deegan, William E. J. "Bill" 1970-80
Denkinger, Donald A. "Don" 1968-94
DiMuro, Louis J. "Lou" 1963-80
Dinneen, William H. "Bill" 1909-37
Donnelly, Charles H. 1934-35
Doyle, Walter J. 1963
Drummond, Calvin T. "Cal" 1960-69
Duffy, James F. "Jim" 1951-55
Dwyer, J. Francis "Frank" 1904
Egan, John J. "Rip" 1903, 1908-14
Eldridge, Clarence E. 1914-15
Evans, James B. "Jim" 1971-94
Evans, William G. "Billy" 1906-27

Ferguson, Charles A. 1913
Flaherty, John F. "Red" 1953-73
Ford, R. Dale 1975-94
Frantz, Arthur F. "Art" 1969-77
Friel, William E. "Bill" 1920
Froese, Grover A. 1952-53
Garcia, Richard R. "Rich" 1975-94
Geisel, Harry C. 1925-42
Goetz, Russell L. "Russ" 1968-83
Grieve, William T. T. "Bill" 1938-55
Guthrie, William J. "Bill" 1922, 1928-32
Haller, William E. "Bill" 1961, 1963-82
Hart, Robert F. "Bertie" 1912-13
Hart, William F. "Bill" 1901
Haskell, John E. 1901
Hassett, James E. 1903
Hayes, Gerald 1925-26
Hendry, Eugene "Ted" 1978-94
Henrichs, Jeff 1993
Hickox, Edward "Ed" 1990-94
Hildebrand, George A. 1912-34
Hirschbeck, John F. 1984-94
Holmes, Howard E. "Ducky" 1923-24
Honochick, G. James "Jim" 1949-73
Hubbard, R. Cal 1936-51, 1954-62
Hurley, Edwin H. "Eddie" 1947-65
Hurst, Timothy C. "Tim" 1905-09
Johnson, Mark S. 1984-94
Johnston, Charles E. 1936-37
Johnstone, James E. "Jim" 1902
Jones, Nicholas I. "Red" 1944-49
Joyce, James A. "Jim" 1989-94
Kaiser, Kenneth J. "Ken" 1977-94
Kelly, Thomas B. 1905
Kerin, John 1909-10
King, Charles F. 1904
Kinnamon, William E. "Bill" 1960-69
Kolls, Louis C. "Lou" 1933-40
Kosc, Gregory J. "Greg" 1976-94
Kunkel, William G. "Bill" 1968-84
Linsalata, Joseph N. "Joe" 1961-62
Luciano, Ronald M. "Ron" 1968-80
Maloney, George P. 1969-83
Manassau, Alfred S. "Al" 1901
Marberry, Frederick "Firpo" 1935
McCarthy, John "Jack" 1905
McClelland, Timothy R. "Tim" 1984-94
McCormick, William J. "Barry" 1917
McCoy, Larry S. 1970-94
McGowan, William A. "Bill" 1925-54
McGreevy, Edward 1912-13
McKean, James G. "Jim" 1974-94
McKinley, William F. "Bill" 1946-65
Meriwether, Julius "Chuck" 1988-94
Merrill, E. Durwood 1977-94
Morgenweck, Henry C. "Hank" 1972-75

Moriarty, George J. 1917-26, 1929-40
Morrison, Daniel G. "Dan" 1984-94
Mullaney, Dominic J. 1915
Mullin, John 1911-12
Nallin, Richard F. "Dick" 1915-33
Napp, Larry A. 1951-74
Neudecker, Jerome A. "Jerry" 1965-85
O'Brien, Joseph "Joe" 1912, 1914
Odom, James C. "Jim" 1965-74
O'Donnell, James M. "Jake" 1968-71
O'Loughlin, Francis H. "Silk" 1902-18
O'Nora, Brian 1992-94
Ormsby, Emmett T. "Red" 1923-41
Owens, Clarence B. "Brick" 1916-37
Palermo, Stephen M. "Steve" 1977-91
Paparella, Joseph J. "Joe" 1946-65
Parker, Harley P. 1911
Parks, Dallas F. 1979-83
Passarella, Arthur M. "Art" 1941-42, 1945-53
Perrine, Fred "Bull" 1909-12
Phillips, David R. "Dave" 1971-94
Pipgras, George W. 1938-46
Quinn, John A. 1935-42
Reed, Rick A. 1984-94
Reilly, Michael E. "Mike" 1978-94
Rice, John L. 1955-73
Robb, Douglas W. "Scotty" 1952-53
Rodriguez, Armando H. 1974-75
Roe, John "Rocky" 1982-94
Rommel, Edwin A. "Eddie" 1938-59
Rowland, Clarence H. "Pants" 1923-27
Rue, Joseph W. "Joe" 1938-47
Runge, Edward P. "Ed" 1954-70
Salerno, Alexander J. "Al" 1961-68
Schwarts, Harry C. 1960-62
Scott, Dale A. 1986-94
Sheridan, John F. "Jack" 1901-14
Shulock, John R. 1979-94
Smith, W. Alaric "Al" 1960-65
Soar, A. Henry "Hank" 1950-73
Spenn, Frederick C. "Fred" 1979-80
Springstead, Martin J. "Marty" 1965-86
Stafford, John H. "Jack" 1907
Stevens, John W. "Johnny" 1948-71
Stewart, Ernest D. 1941-45
Stewart, Robert W. "Bob" 1959-70
Summers, William R. "Bill" 1933-59
Tabacchi, Frank T. 1956-59
Tschida, Timothy J. "Tim" 1986-94
Umont, Frank W. 1954-73
Valentine, William T. "Bill" 1963-68
Van Graflan, Roy 1927-33
Voltaggio, Vito H. "Vic" 1977-94
Wallace, Roderick J. "Bobby" 1915-16
Walsh, Edward A. "Ed" 1922
Weafer, Harold L. "Hal" 1943-47
Welke, Timothy J. "Tim" 1985-94

Westervelt, Frederick E.
1911-12
Wilson, Frank 1921-22
Winans, Mark 1994
Young, Larry E. 1985-94

Federal League (1914-15)

Anderson, Oliver O. "Ollie"
1914
Brennan, William T. "Bill"
1914-15
Bush, Garnet C. 1914
Corcoran, Thomas W.
"Tommy" 1915
Cross, Montford M.
"Monte" 1914
Cusack, Stephen P. 1914
Finneran, William E. 1915
Fyfe, Louis 1915
Goeckel, E. 1914
Howell, H. Harry 1915
Johnstone, James E. "Jim"
1915
Kane, Stephen J. 1914
Langden, Joseph 1915
Mannassau, Alfred S. "Al"
1914
McCormick, William J.
"Barry" 1914-15
Mullin, John 1915
O'Brien, Joseph "Joe"
1915
Quisser, —, 1914
Shannon, William P.
"Spike" 1914-15
Stocksdale, Otis H. 1915
Van Sickle, Charles F. 1914
Westervelt, Frederick E.
1915
Wilhelm, Irving K. "Kaiser"
1915

SUBSTITUTE UMPIRES

National Association
(1871-75)

Addy, Robert E. "Bob"
1875
Allison, Andrew K. "Andy"
1872, 1874
Allison, Arthur A. "Art" 1872
Allison, Douglas L. "Doug"
1872-73, 1875
Alston, David 1871-72,
1875
Annan, William H. 1873
Arnold, Willis S. "Billy"
1875
Avery, C. Hamilton 1874
Barlow, Thomas H. "Tom"
1875
Barnes, Roscoe C. "Ross"
1874
Barrett, William "Bill" 1872,
1874
Barron, James "Jim" 1875
Barrows, Franklin L.
"Frank" 1872
Battin, Joseph V. "Joe"
1874
Beals, Thomas L. "Tommy"
1872, 1874-75
Beardslee, John J. 1872-73
Bechtel, George A. 1874
Beck, W. S. 1872
Berthrong, Hnery W.
"Harry" 1872
Bielaski, Oscar 1874-75
Bigelow, W. J. 1875
Birdsall, David S. "Dave"
1873-74
Blair, William J. 1873
Boake, John L. 1871
Bomeisler, Theodore
1874-75
Bond, Thomas H.'Tommy'
1875
Bonse, Nicholas 1871
Boyd, William J. "Bill" 1873
Bradley, George H.
"Foghorn" 1875
Brainard, Asa 1872, 1875
Briggs, Warren R. 1874
Brown, William 1872, 1875
Bruce, D. W. 1875

Buck, William F. 1871
Bunce, Frederick L. "Fred"
1874
Bunce, H. C. 1872
Bush, Archibald M. "Archie"
1871
Carey, Thomas J. "Tom"
1873, 1875
Carpenter, John R. 1874
Cassidy, John P. 1875
Cavanaugh, J. H. "Harry"
1875
Chandler, Moses E.
1872-1875
Chapman, John C. "Jack"
1871, 1873-74
Clifton, — 1872
Clinton, James L. "Jim"
1873, 1875
Colby, — 1873
Collins, Daniel T. "Dan"
1875
Cone, J. Frederick "Fred"
1873-74
Cope, Elias 1871
Craver, William H. "Bill"
1873
Cuthbert, Edgar E. "Ned"
1875
Daubney, Thomas 1871
David, L. N. 1874
Dawson, Mort 1871
Deane, J. Henry "Harry"
1871, 1874
Dehlman, Herman J. 1873,
1875
Demorest, D. P. 1872-73
Dobson, H. A. 1871
Dornlach, D. E. 1872
Draper, John H. 1871
Ellis, William R. 1871-72,
1875
English, John W. 1874-75
Erby, Frederick 1872
Evans, George 1872
Fellows, T. E. 1871
Ferguson, Robert V. "Bob"
1871, 1874
Fisher, William C.
"Cherokee" 1871, 1875
Foley, Thomas J. "Tom"
1874-75
Force, David W. "Davy"
1873
Fulmer, Charles J. "Chick"
1872, 1874-75
Garrigan, Charles 1873
Geer, William H. "Billy"
1874-75
Gerhardt, Joseph J. "Joe"
1875
Glenn, John W. 1874
Glover, Frank 1873
Goodwin, J. Cheever
1871-72
Gould, Charles H. "Charlie"
1874-75
Graham, J. S. 1871-72
Halback, A. C. N. 1871,
1873-75
Hall, George W. 1873-75
Hall, James "Jim" 1872-73
Hall, N. Samuel 1873
Hanna, Dr. 1872
Hastings, W. Scott 1871-74
Hatfield, John V. B.
1872-73
Hayhurst, E. Hicks 1875
Haynie, James L. 1871
Hegeman, William H. 1871
Helm, J. 1871-72
Higham, Richard "Dick"
1872-75
Hodes, Charles "Charlie"
1874
Hooper, Michael H. "Mike"
1872-74
Hosworth, —, 1872-74
Hough, Pliny 1875
Howard, Charles 1872
Jennings, Alfred J. "Al"
1873
Johns, William R. 1873
Kahn, S. L. 1875
Keerl, George W. 1872
Kenney, John 1872
Kent, John 1875
Knight, George H. 1875

Kohler, Henry C. 1873
Lamb, Henry W. "Harry"
1875
Laughlin, Benjamin "Ben"
1873
Leonard, Andrew J. "Andy"
1872-73, 1875
Leonard, J. 1872
Leroy, Isaac 1871
Locke, Marshall 1873-74
Lovett, James D. 1871
Lowell, John A. 1872-73
Lush, M. R. 1873
MacDiarmed, Thomas 1872
Mack, Dennis J. "Denny"
1873-74
Malone, — 1875
Malone, Ferguson G.
"Fergy" 1875
Martin, Alphonse C.
"Phonney" 1871, 1873
Martin, Lewis G. 1871,
1873-74
Mathews, Robert T.
"Bobby" 1871
Mawny, J. H. 1871
Maxwell, Cortez "Corty"
1875
Mays, — 1871
McCrea, — 1872
McDonald, James F. 1872
McGeary, Michael H. 1872,
1875
McLean, Harry C. 1871,
1873
McLean, William H. "Billy"
1872-73
McMahon, William 1871
McMullin, John F. 1874
McVey, Calvin A. "Cal"
1871, 1873, 1875
Meacham, — 1875
Miller, Joseph W. "Joe"
1872-73
Mills, Charles "Charlie"
1871
Mincher, Edward J. "Ed"
1872, 1875
Mincher, William E. 1875
Mitchell, Franklin B.
1874-75
Murnane, Timothy H. "Tim"
1873-75
Nelson, John W. "Candy"
1872
Nichols, A. N. 1871
Norton, Frank P. 1872
O'Brien, P. 1875
Pabor, Charles H. "Charlie"
1875
Parks, William R. "Bill"
1875
Patterson, Daniel T. "Dan"
1872
Peak, Frank 1871
Pearson, S. W. 1872
Phelps, Cornelius C. "Neal"
1874
Pike, Jacob Emanuel "Jay"
1875
Porter, — 1874
Powers, W. 1872-73, 1875
Pratt, Thomas J. "Tom"
1871-73
Quinn, — 1875
Radcliff, John Y. 1873
Ramsey, R. 1875
Rastall, Joseph H. 1872
Reach, Albert J. 1872-75
Reed, Hugh 1871, 1873-74
Remsen, John J. "Jack"
1873-74
Robinson, A. Valentine
"Val" 1872
Robinson, Miley 1873
Rockwell, Horace T. 1874
Rogers, George R. 1871-72
Ryan, John J. 1872, 1875
Sawyer, Dent 1871
Schafer, Harry C. 1875
Schrader, Louis 1875
Schuester, John A.
1874-75
Scofield, John W. 1871
Sears, John K. 1873
Selman, Frank C. 1873
Sensenderfer, John P. J.
"Count" 1872-73, 1875

Simmons, Joseph S. "Joe"
1871, 1873-74
Smith, Eb 1872
Smith, George 1872
Snyder, Charles N. "Pop"
1875
Stahl, George 1875
Stanwood, —, 1872-73
Stires, Garrett "Gat" 1875
Stophlet, J. 1871
Sutton, Ezra B. 1875
Swandell, J. Martin "Marty"
1871, 1874
Sweasy, Charles J.
"Charlie" 1871, 1873-74
Tighe, Edward 1871
Treacey, Frederick S.
"Fred" 1871, 1873, 1875
Tyler, Columbus T. 1871-73
Urell, M. E. 1873
Van Delft, —, 1875
Voltz, Edward "Ed" 1871-72
Walk, Frank 1871
Wardell, — 1874
Waterman, Frederick A.
"Fred" 1873
Weaver, Charles 1873
Weigel, William H. 1873-74
White, Horatio S. 1873
White, W. Warren 1874
White, William H. "Will"
1875
Wiggins, — 1875
Wildey, John 1871
Willard, Gardner 1871
Wirth, Adam 1872, 1875
Wood, James B. "Jimmy"
1871
Wright, W. Harrison "Harry"
1875
York, Thomas J. "Tom"
1874

National League (1876-)

Adams, James 1897
Allen, Hezekiah "Ham"
1876
Ayers, —, 1876
Baker, Charles 1884
Barker, Alfred L. 1881
Barnie, William S. "Billy"
1882
Barnum, George W. 1896
Barton, — 1876
Battin, Joseph V. "Joe"
1895
Beard, Oliver P. "Ollie"
1894
Becannon, James M.
"Buck" 1885
Behle, Frank 1895-96
Berger, Frederick 1886
Bigelow, —, 1877
Bittman, Henry P. "Red"
1892, 1894-95, 1897
Blakiston, Robert J. "Bob"
1884
Blodgett, C. W. 1876
Bradley, George H.
"Foghorn" 1877
Brady, —, 1877
Bredburg, George W.
1878-79
Brennan, John E. "Jack"
1887
Brockway, John 1877,
1879
Bullymore, Charles L. 1882
Burke, — 1892
Burlingame, Frank A. 1878
Burnham, George W.
1886-87
Campbell, Al 1886
Campbell, Daniel "Dan"
1897
Carsey, Wilfred "Kid" 1901
Caruthers, Robert L. "Bob"
1886, 1893
Chandler, Moses E. 1876
Chapman, John C. "Jack"
1876, 1882
Chill, Oliver P. "Ollie" 1916
Cheppy, John T. 1876
Chipman, Harry F. 1886
Clack, Robert H. "Bobby"
1897
Cohen, —, 1893

Colgan, Harry W. 1899
Collins, Daniel T. "Dan"
1876
Cone, J. F. "Fred" 1876
Connell, Terence G. 1885,
1887
Connolly, John M. 1885,
1887, 1892-93
Cook, W. H. 1879
Crandall, Robert 1876,
1878
Crane, Edward N. "Ed"
1893
Crane, Samuel N. "Sam"
1879, 1887
Cray, P. C. 1893
Cross, John A. 1876
Cudworth, Al 1880
Curren, Peter 1876
Cushman, Charles H.
"Charley" 1894
Daniels, —, 1885
Deane, J. Henry "Harry"
1876, 1878
Devinney, P. H. "Dan" 1876
Doscher, John H. Sr.
"Herm" 1879
Draper, John H. 1877
Dunlap, Frederick C. "Fred"
1879
Dyler, John F. 1892, 1897
Eagan, John J. 1879
Earle, William M. "Billy"
1892
Eason, Malcolm W. "Mal"
1901
Evans, Jacob "Jake" 1886
Fenno, Norman 1876
Fisher, William C.
"Cherokee" 1876
Flaherty, —, 1882
Flaherty, Patrick J. "Patsy"
07
Flynn, John A. "Jocko"
1893
Fouser, William C. 1876
Fulmer, Charles J. "Chick"
1881
Furlong, William E. "Bill"
1877, 1880, 1888
Gaffney, John H. 1887,
1898
Galvin, James F. "Jim"
1886
Ganzel, Charles W.
"Charlie" 1901
Gifford, James H. 1881
Gillean, Thomas 1881
Gleason, John D. 1877
Gleason, William G. "Bill"
1877
Glenn, John W. 1880
Goldsmith, Frederick E.
"Fred" 1886
Graves, Frank M. 1895
Griffiths, — 1884
Gross, Edward M. 1881
Guinney, Daniel 1882
Hardie, Louis W. "Lou"
1887
Hartley, John "Jack" 1894
Hastings, W. Scott 1877
Hatfield, John V. B. 1876
Hawes, William A. 1880-82
Hegeman, William H. 1881
Hernon, Thomas H. "Tom"
1894
Heydler, John A. 1895-97
Hickey, James L. 1882
Hodges, A. D. 1877
Hogan, —, 1897
Hogriever, George C. 1893
Hornung, M. Joseph "Joe"
1892
Howard, C. F. 1884
Hurll, George 1876
Hurst, Timothy C. "Tim"
1904
Jevne, Frederick "Fred"
1892, 1894
Jose, —, 1889
Joyce, C. E. 1879
Kane, Stephen J. 1906
Keefe, Timothy J. "Tim"
1893
Keenan, James W. "Jim"
1893
Kelley, J. P. 1879

Kelley, W. W. 1877
Kelly, John O. 1884-85
Kennedy, — 1893
Kennedy, Michael J. 1884
Kenney, John 1876
Kerins, John A. "Jack" 1888
Kipp, Eden 1881
Kling, William "Bill" 1892
Klusman, William F. "Billy" 1893
Knight, Alonzo P. "Lon" 1876, 1888
Lally, Bud 1896
Lanigan, Charles 1908
Latham, W. Arlington "Arlie" 1900
Laughlin, —, 1876
Lawler, Michael H. 1882
Leary, — 1879
Libby, Stephen A. 1879
Long, William H. "Billy" 1893, 1897
Lynch, F. G. 1892
Lynch, Thomas J. "Tom" 1902
Maddox, Charles 1882
Malone, Ferguson G. "Fergy" 1892
Maloney, James "Jim" 1893
Manning, James H. "Jim" 1893
Manning, John E. "Jack" 1881
Mapledoram, Blake A. 1886
Martin, Alphonse C. "Phonney" 1876
Mason, Charles E. "Charlie" 1876
Mathews, Robert T. "Bobby" 1876
Mayer, — 1893
McCaffrey, Harry 1885-86
McCrum, — 1892
McGee, — 1876
McGinnis, —, 1910
McGinty, — 1897
McKinney, — 1883
McLeod, — 1895
McMullen, John F. 1876
Meagher, John 1877
Meals, Gerald W. "Jerry" 1992-94
Mears, Charles W. 1894
Medart, William 1876-77
Megrue, Cliff 1876
Mills, Abraham G. 1877
Montague, — 1877
Morrill, John F. 1891, 1896
Morris, Edward 1895, 1897
Morris, John S. 1876
Muir, Thomas 1876
Mullane, Anthony J. "Tony" 1897
Mullen, Peter C. 1893
Murnane, Timothy H. "Tim" 1886
Murphy, Henry 1880
Murphy, Martin W. 1886
Murray, Jeremiah J. "Miah" 1894, 1900, 1905, 1910
Myers, Henry C. 1890
Nicol, Hugh N. 1894
O'Brien, William 1876
O'Day, Henry F. "Hank" 1896
Orr, David L. "Dave" 1891
Osborne, William 1876
Pfeffer, Nathaniel F. "Nate" 1897
Phelan, — 1896
Pierce, — 1893
Pierce, Grayson C. "Gracie" 1892
Pike, Lipman E. "Lip" 1890
Power, Charles B. 1893-95
Pratt, Albert G. "Al" 1880, 1887
Quincy, W. 1893
Quinn, Joseph C. "Joe" 1881
Quinn, P. J. 1876
Quinn, William H. "Billy" 1887, 1889
Redheffer, — 1895
Reid, William A. 1882
Reilly, Charles 1880

Remsen, John J. "Jack" 1880
Rhodes, Eugene A. 1887
Richards, J. E. 1880
Ritchie, F. 1876
Rocap, Adam 1876
Roll, — 1876
Rowe, John C. "Jack" 1881
Rudderham, Francis F. "Frank" 1907
Say, Louis I. "Lou" 1879
Schofield, J. W. 1879
Schurer, — 1896
Seward, Edward W. "Ed" 1892
Seward, George E. 1877
Shepard, W. L. 1879
Sheridan, John F. "Jack" 1893
Sick, — 1884
Simmons, Joseph S. "Joe" 1876
Skelly, — 1880
Skinner, S. A. 1886
Smith, — 1876
Sneeden, — 1895
Snodd, Carey 1877
Snyder, Charles N. "Pop" 1895
Sommers, Joseph A. "Joe" 1893
Stack, W. Edward "Eddie" 1934
Stafford, John H. "Jack" 1906
Stage, Charles W. "Billy" 1895
Stambaugh, Calvin G. 1879
Strief, George A. 1880
Sullivan, — 1889
Sullivan, David F. "Dave" 1883, 1887-88
Summer, James G. 1876, 1878
Supple, William N. 1906
Sutton, Ezra B. 1876
Sweasy, Charles J. "Charlie" 1879
Tilden, Otis 1876
Tindall, — 1890
Toole, Stephen J. "Steve" 1888
Tuthill, Benjamin "Ben" 1895
Twitchell, Lawrence G. "Larry" 1894
Wade, Ben F. 1879-80
Walker, William E. 1878
Walsh, Michael F. "Mike" 1879
Walters, —, 1892-93
Walton, G. W. 1876
Warren, L. B. 1876
Wash, Frank 1877
Weeden, —, 1889-90
West, — 1885
West, George 1878
West, Milton D. "Buck" 1890
White, Gideon F. 1876-77
White, W. Warren 1876
Williams, Elisha A. "Dale" 1876
Wilson, William G. "Bill" 1892-93
Witham, C. B. 1879
Wolf, William V. "Jimmy" 1893, 1895-97
Wood, George A. 1899
Wood, James B. "Jimmy" 1876
Wright, W. Harrison "Harry" 1885
Wycoff, — 1892

American Association (1882-91)

Arnold, Frank W. 1889
Austin, Ed 1890
Barnie, William S. "Billy" 1882, 1884, 1887, 1889
Battin, Joseph V. "Joe" 1882, 1886
Bauers, Albert J. "Al" 1890
Bell, Frank G. 1889
Bittman, Henry P. "Red" 1889

Blogg, Wesley C. "Wes" 1886
Bloom, — 1887
Bond, Thomas H. "Tommy" 1891
Burdock, John J. "Jack" 1887
Burkalow, Isaac 1888
Burns, — 1882
Butler, Charles 1889
Butler, Ormond H. 1886
Campbell, Daniel "Dan" 1890
Carlin, William J. "Billy" 1885, 1888-89
Connell, J. 1885
Connell, Terence G. 1885-86, 1889
Cornell, — 1884
Crandall, Robert 1882
Creighton, — 1889-90
Critchley, Morris A. "Morrie" 1884-85
Curry, Frank 1884, 1886
Cuthbert, Edgar E. "Ned" 1888
Dailey, John J. 1889
Daniels, Lawrence 1887
Devine, W. James "Jim" 1890
Devinney, P. H. "Dan" 1887
Devlin, Charles "Charlie" 1888
Dolan, Thomas J. "Tom" 1890-91
Dow, Clarence 1891
Dugan, — 1887
Duke, Martin F. 1890
Dunlevy, Hugh 1887
Dyler, John F. 1883, 1885-86
Ellick, Joseph J. "Joe" 1888-89
Ewing, William "Buck" 1882
Fell, — 1885
Fountain, Henry V. 1888
Galvin, James F. "Jim" 1885
Geer, William H. "Billy" 1885
Gill, Thomas H. "Tommy" 1886
Helburn, Hugo 1887
Henderson, J. Harding "Hardie" 1889
Hengle, Edward S. "Ed" 1889
Hicks, Nathaniel W. "Nat" 1885
Holliday, James W. "Bug" 1888
Irwin, — 1882
Irwin, John 1885
Jennings, Alfred J. "Al" 1882, 1884-85, 1889
Julian, Joseph O. 1888
Kelly, John O. 1887
Kelly, William 1884
Kleinbacker, —, 1886
Levis, Charles H. "Charlie" 1882
Lilly, J. 1884
Little, — 1884
Loughlin, —, 1885
Loughlin, William 1882
Lyons, Toby A. 1891
Lyston, William E. 1890
Magner, John T. 1882, 1884, 1887
Malone, J. R. 1888
Marshall, — 1887
Mathews, Robert T. "Bobby" 1888
McCartney, Joseph 1882
McCormick, —, 1888
McGee, Patrick 1882, 1884
McGinnis, George W. "Jumbo" 1888-89
McIntosh, — 1882
McLaughlin, William 1882
McLean, William H. "Billy" 1882, 1889-90
McQuade, James H. 1891
McSorley, John B. "Trick" 1888
Medart, William 1887
Miller, Charles A. 1884
Mitchell, — 1887

Morgan, Henry W. 1884
Morton, Charles H. "Charlie" 1884
Mullen, Peter C. 1891
O'Dea, Lawrence 1890
Paasch, William 1887-89
Parker, — 1887
Phillips, Horace B. 1882
Pierce, Grayson S. "Gracie" 1884
Pike, Lipman. E. "Lip" 1887
Pratt, Albert G. "Al" 1886
Quinn, William H. "Billy" 1884-85
Ramsey, Dick 1887
Reeder, James E. 1884
Reising, Charles 1882
Rice, — 1885
Riley, William J. 1885
Robb, John 1886
Ross, Robert T. 1884
Ruhl, Gus 1882
Ryan, John 1882
Selman, Frank C. 1882
Sherman, Sharon L. "Shang" 1890
Simpson, Lew 1882
Skinner, —, 1884, 1886
Smith, George 1887
Sneed, Jonathon L. 1885
Sullivan, David F. "Dave" 1884
Talbot, — 1887
Tinney, — 1882
Walsh, Michael F. "Mike" 1887-88
West, — 1885, 1887
Wood, George A. 1886
Wright, — 1884
Young, Benjamin F. "Ben" 1887
Young, Joseph 1890

Union Association (1884)

Adler, — 1884
Burlingame, F. A. 1884
Donovan, E. S. 1884
Furlong, William E. "Bill" 1884
Hudson, Vincent D. 1884
Lee, Thomas F. 1884
McGunningle, William H. "Bill" 1884
McManaway, D. 1884
McMinimum, Dennis 1884
Montgomery, — 1884
Powers, Charles B. 1884
Timblin, — 1884
Torry, — 1884

American League (1901-)

Betts, William G. 1903
Brown, Thomas T. "Tom" 1907
Egan, John J. "Rip" 1907
Kennedy, — 1910
Kerin, John 1908
Kerins, John A. "Jack" 1903
Mace, Harry L. 1903
Pears, Frank 1903
Quigley, Ernest C. "Ernie" 1906
Terry, William H. "Adonis" 1901

Federal League (1914-15)

Murphy, J. A. 1914

ACTIVE PLAYERS WHO UMPIRED

National League (1876-)

Abbey, Charles S. "Charlie" 1897
Abbott, Frederick H. "Fred" 1905
Andrews, G. Edward "Ed" 1889
Arundel, John T. "Tug" 1888
Baker, Philip "Phil" 1889

Baldwin, Marcus E. "Mark" 1892
Bannon, James H. "Jimmy" 1894
Beatin, Ebenezer "Ed" 1889
Beck, Erwin T. "Erve" 1902
Beckley, Jacob P. "Jake" 1906
Beebe, Fred L. 1907
Berger, John H. "Tun" 1891
Bonner, Frank J. 1894
Boyle, Henry J. 1886
Boyle, John A. "Jack" 1892, 1897
Breitenstein, Theodore P. "Ted" 1900
Briody, Charles F. "Fatty" 1881
Brown, Samuel W. "Sam" 1907
Brown, Willard 1891
Buelow, Charles J. "Charlie" 1901
Buffinton, Charles G. "Charlie" 1883, 1888-89, 1892
Burdock, John J. "Jack" 1881
Burns, Thomas P. "Oyster" 1895
Bushong, Albert J. "Doc" 1880, 1890
Butler, Richard H. "Dick" 1897
Carrick, William M. "Bill" 1900
Carroll, Frederick H. "Fred" 1887
Carsey, Wilfred "Kid" 1894, 1896
Caruthers, Robert L. "Bob" 1891
Casey, Daniel M. "Dan" 1888
Caskin, Edward J. "Ed" 1884
Cassidy, John P. 1882
Chamberlain, Elton P. 1894
Chance, Frank L. 1902
Clack, Robert H. "Bobby" 1876
Clarke, Arthur F. "Artie" 1890
Clarke, William J. "Boileryard" 1893-94, 1896
Clarkson, Arthur H. "Dad" 1893-96
Clarkson, John G. 1888, 1892-93
Clements, John J. "Jack" 1892
Coleman, John F. 1884
Coogan, Daniel G. "Dan" 1895
Cooney, John W. "Johnny" 1941
Crane, Edward N. "Ed" 1892
Crane, Samuel N. "Sam" 1886, 1890
Crolius, Frederick J. "Fred" 1901
Cronin, John J. "Jack" 1902-03
Cross, Lafayette N. "Lave" 1892
Culler, Richard B. "Dick" 1947
Cunningham, Elmer E. "Bert" 1896-97, 1900
Cuppy, George M. 1894
Cusick, Andrew D. "Tony" 1886-87
Daily, Cornelius F. "Con" 1886, 1891, 1894, 1896
Daly, Thomas P. "Tom" 1901
Darling, Conrad "Dell" 1887
Dealy, Patrick E. "Pat" 1886
Dexter, Charles D. "Charlie" 1896-97
Donahue, Francis R. "Red" 1897
Donahue, Timothy C. "Tim" 1895-96
Donlin, Michael J. "Mike" 1900

Donnelly, James B. "Jim" 1896
Donovan, William E. "Bill" 1902
Dooin, Charles S. "Red" 1904
Douglass, William B. "Klondike" 1903
Dowse, Thomas J. "Tom" 1890
Duggleby, William J. "Bill" 1905
Dwyer, J. Francis "Frank" 1889, 1893-94, 1896-97
Earle, William M. "Billy" 1894
Ehret, Philip S. "Phil" 1892, 1895-97
Farrell, Charles A. "Duke" 1901-02
Ferguson, Charles J. "Charlie" 1886
Fitzsimmons, Frederick "Freddie" 1941
Flaherty, Patrick J. "Patsy" 1904
Force, David W. "Davy" 1881
Foreman, Francis I. "Frank" 1895
Foreman, John D. "Brownie" 1896
Foster, Clarence F. "Pop" 1900
Freeman, John F. "Buck" 1900
Galvin, James F. "Jim" 1881, 1887, 1889
Gardner, James A. "Jim" 1899
George, William M. "Bill" 1889
German, Lester S. "Les" 1895
Gleason, William J. "Kid" 1890, 1892
Grady, Michael W. "Mike" 1895
Graves, Frank M. 1886
Griffith, Clark C. 1894-95
Grim, John H. 1892, 1895-96
Gruber, Henry J. 1889
Gumbert, Addison C. "Ad" 1892, 1895
Gunning, Thomas F. "Tom" 1884-85
Gunson, Joseph B. "Joe" 1892
Hackett, Mortimer M. "Mert" 1886
Haddock, George S. 1889
Hallman, William W. "Bill" 1903
Hanlon, Edward H. "Ned" 1892
Hart, William F. "Bill" 1896-97
Hatfield, Gilbert "Gil" 1889
Healy, John J. 1887
Hemming, George E. 1895-96
Hines, Michael P. "Mike" 1884
Holliday, James W. "Bug" 1897
Howe, John "Shorty" 1890
Hurst, Timothy C. "Tim" 1898
Hyatt, R. Hamilton "Ham" 1912
Irwin, Arthur A. 1881
Jacklitsch, Fred L. 1901
Jennings, Hugh A. "Hughie" 1893, 1900
Johnson, Sylvester "Syl" 1934
Jones, Henry M. 1890
Kahoe, Michael J. "Mike" 1905
Karger, Edwin "Ed" 1906
Keefe, Timothy J. "Tim" 1880-82, 1884-85, 1887, 1892
Keeler, William H. "Willie" 1910
Kellum, Winford A. "Win" 1905

Kelly, Michael J. "King" 1892-93
Killen, Frank B. 1896-97
Kinslow, Thomas F. "Tom" 1892
Kittridge, Malachi J. 1890, 1899
Kitson, Frank R. 1902
Klein, Charles H. "Chuck" 1942
Kling, John G. "Johnny" 1901
Knell, Philip H. "Phil" 1895
Knowles, James "Jimmy" 1892
Krieg, William F. "Bill" 1887
Leever, Samuel W. "Sam" 1900, 1904
Lindeman, Vivian A. "Vive" 1907
Lundgren, Carl L. 1905-06
Maloney, William A. "Billy" 1902
Manning, James H. "Jim" 1886
Mathews, Robert T. "Bobby" 1882
Mathewson, Christopher "Christy" 1901, 1907
McAleer, James R. "Jim" 1893
McAllister, Lewis W. "Sport" 1899
McCarthy, Thomas F. M. "Tommy" 1896
McCauley, Allen A. "Al" 1890
McCauley, Patrick M. "Pat" 1896
McCormick, James "Jim" 1885
McFarland, Edward W. "Ed" 1896
McGarr, James B. "Chippy" 1895
McGinnity, Joseph J. "Joe" 1900
McGuire, James T. "Deacon" 1886, 1894, 1896-97, 1901
McKinnon, Alexander J. "Alex" 1886
McMahon, John J. "Sadie" 1893
Meekin, Jouette 1895-96
Menefee, John "Jock" 1903
Mertes, Samuel B. "Sam" 1905
Miller, George F. "Doggie" 1893, 1896
Miller, Joseph H. 1884
Miller, L. Otto 1934
Moran, Patrick J. "Pat" 1901
Mullane, Anthony J. "Tony" 1893
Mulvey, Joseph H. "Joe" 1895
Murphy, Morgan E. 1893, 1896, 1898
Murphy, William H. "Yale" 1895, 1897
Murray, Jeremiah J. "Miah" 1895
Myers, George D. 1886
Needham, Thomas J. "Tom" 1904, 1907
Newton, Eustace J. "Doc" 1902
Nichols, Charles A. "Kid" 1900-01
Nolan, Edward S. "The Only" 1881
Noonan, Peter J. "Pete" 1906-07
O'Brien, John F. "Darby" 1889
O'Connor, John J. "Jack" 1893, 1901
O'Day, Henry F. "Hank" 1888-89
O'Neill, Michael J. "Mike" 1904
O'Rourke, James H. "Jim" 1893
Orth, Albert L. "Al" 1901
Overall, Orval 1905, 1910

Peitz, Henry C. "Heinie" 1901, 1906
Phelps, Edward J. "Ed" 1912
Phillippe, Charles L. "Deacon" 1903
Quinn, Joseph J. "Joe" 1894, 1896
Reilly, Charles T. "Charlie" 1892, 1894-95
Reitz, Henry P. "Heinie" 1892
Rhines, William P. "Billy" 1891, 1896
Richardson, A. Harding "Hardie" 1892
Richmond, J. Lee 1883
Robinson, Wilbert 1898
Ryan, James E. "Jimmy" 1892
Sanders, A. Bennett "Ben" 1889
Schmidt, Henry M. 1903
Schriver, William F. "Pop" 1901
Serad, William I. "Billy" 1884
Smith, A. Edgar 1883
Smith, Edgar E. 1890
Smith, George H. "Heinie" 1901
Smith, Harry T. 1903
Smith, William E. "Bill" 1886
Sommers, Joseph A. "Joe" 1889
Staley, Harry E. 1892, 1895
Stearns, D. Eckford "Ecky" 1881
Stein, Edward F. "Ed" 1890, 1894, 1896
Stivetts, John C. "Jack" 1894
Stocksdale, Otis H. 1895
Stricker, John A. "Cub" 1892
Stricklett, Elmer E. 1907
Sugden, Joseph "Joe" 1897
Sullivan, James E. "Jim" 1896
Sullivan, Martin C. "Marty" 1889
Sullivan, Michael J. "Mike" 1897
Sullivan, Thomas J. "Sleeper" 1881
Sutcliffe, Elmer E. "Sy" 1889, 1892
Tannehill, Jesse N. 1897, 1901-02
Tate, Edward C. "Pop" 1888
Taylor, John B. "Jack" 1899
Taylor, John W. "Jack" 1901, 1905
Tener, John K. 1889
Terry, William H. "Adonis" 1892, 1895-96
Tiernan, Michael J. "Mike" 1895
Vaughn, Harry F. "Farmer" 1892, 1899
Viau, Leon "Lee" 1891
Vickery, Thomas G. "Tom" 1890
Walker, Thomas W. "Tom" 1905
Wall, Joseph F. "Joe" 1901
Wallace, Roderick J. "Bobby" 1895
Walters, William H. "Bucky" 1942, 1947
Ward, John M. "Monte" 1888
Warneke, Lonnie "Lon" 1940
Warner, John J. "Jack" 1896-97, 1901, 1903
Weaver, William B. "Farmer" 1893
Weimer, Jacob W. "Jake" 1905, 1907
Welch, Michael F. "Mickey" 1881-82, 1885-86, 1888
Weyhing, August "Gus" 1899-1900
Whistler, Lewis "Lew" 1891

White, Guy H. "Doc" 1901-02
White, James L. "Deacon" 1880
Whitney, James E. "Jim" 1884, 1886
Wilhelm, Irving K. "Kaiser" 1904-05
Williamson, Edward N. "Ned" 1878, 1880
Willis, Victor G. "Vic" 1903
Wilmot, Walter R. "Walt" 1897
Wilson, Frank A. "Zeke" 1896, 1899
Wilson, James "Jimmie" 1940
Wilson, Parke A. 1894-96, 1899
Wilson, William G. "Bill" 1890
Wright, W. Harrison "Harry" 1876-77
Yeager, George J. 1901
Young, Denton T. "Cy" 1896
Young, Irving M. "Irv" 1905, 1907
Zimmer, Charles L. "Chief" 1889, 1901

American Association (1882-91)

Baldwin, Clarence G. "Kid" 1887
Becannon, James M. "Buck" 1884
Bond, Thomas H. "Tommy" 1884
Booth, Amos S. 1882
Boyle, John A. "Jack" 1888
Brennan, John G. "Jack" 1888
Briody, Charles F. "Fatty" 1888
Burns, Thomas P. "Oyster" 1888
Bushong, Albert J. "Doc" 1888-89
Carlin, William J. "Billy" 1886
Carsey, Wilfred "Kid" 1891
Cassidy, John P. 1884
Chamberlain, Elton P. 1887, 1891
Cross, Lafayette N. "Lave" 1889
Crowell, William T. "Billy" 1888
Darling, Conrad "Dell" 1891
Donahue, James A. "Jim" 1888
Easton, John S. "Jack" 1891
Ehret, Philip S. "Phil" 1890
Ewing, John 1889
Fulmer, Charles J. "Chick" 1888
Galvin, James F. "Jim" 1886
Ganzel, Charles W. "Charlie" 1886
Goldsby, Walton H. "Walt" 1888
Greenwood, William F. "Bill" 1884
Griffith, Clark C. 1891
Gunning, Thomas F. "Tom" 1888-89
Healy, John J. 1890
Hecker, Guy J. 1888
Herr, Edward J. "Ed" 1888
Higgins, William E. "Bill" 1890
Holbert, William H. "Bill" 1888
Johnston, Richard F. "Dick" 1884
Keefe, Timothy J. "Tim" 1884
Keenan, James W. "Jim" 1887-88
Kilroy, Matthew A. "Matt" 1887
Kirby, John F. 1888
Knell, Philip H. "Phil" 1891

Latham, George W. "Juice" 1884
Lynch, John H. "Jack" 1884
Macullar, James F. "Jimmy" 1886
Mattimore, Michael J. "Mike" 1888
Mays, Albert C. "Al" 1887
McCarthy, Thomas F. M. "Tommy" 1889
McKelvy, Russell E. "Russ" 1882
McMahon, John J. "Sadie" 1890
McSorley, John B. "Trick" 1884
Merrill, Edward M. "Ed" 1884
Mountain, Frank H. 1884
Mullane, Anthony J. "Tony" 1888
Murphy, Joseph A. "Joe" 1887
O'Brien, William D. "Darby" 1887-88
O'Connor, John J. "Jack" 1889
O'Day, Henry F. "Hank" 1884
Peoples, James E. "Jimmy" 1888-89
Pierce, Grayson S. "Gracie" 1882
Sage, Harry 1890
Serad, William I. "Billy" 1888
Smith, Charles M. "Pop" 1886
Smith, Frederick C. "Fred" 1890
Smith, John F. "Phenomenal" 1888
Snyder, Charles N. "Pop" 1886
Sommer, Joseph J. "Joe" 1888
Sprague, Charles W. "Charlie" 1890
Stivetts, John C. "Jack" 1891
Sweeney, Charles J. "Charley" 1887
Sylvester, Louis J. "Lou" 1888
Terry, William H. "Adonis" 1884, 1888
Townsend, George H. 1890
Traffley, William F. "Bill" 1884
Vaughn, Harry F. "Farmer" 1891
Weyhing, August "Gus" 1891
Wheeler, Harry E. 1882
Wood, George A. 1891
Zimmer, Charles L. "Chief" 1888

Union Association (1884)

Bradley, George W. 1884
Callahan, Edward J. "Ed" 1884
Carroll, Patrick "Pat" 1884
Cuthbert, Edgar E. "Ned" 1884
Kelly, John F. 1884
McLaughlin, James C. "Jim" 1884
Oberbeck, Henry A. 1884
Wheeler, Harry E. 1884
Williams, Washington J. "Wash" 1884

Players League (1890)

Bakely, Edward E. "Ed" 1890
Carney, John J. 1890
Comiskey, Charles A. "Charlie" 1890
Daily, Cornelius F. "Con" 1890
Gumbert, Addison C. "Ad" 1890
Haddock, George S. 1890
Hallman, William W. "Bill" 1890

Keefe, Timothy J. "Tim" 1890
Kelly, Michael J. "King" 1890
Madden, Michael J. "Kid" 1890
Milligan, John "Jocko" 1890
O'Day, Henry F. "Hank" 1890
Tener, John K. 1890

American League (1901-)

Altrock, Nicholas "Nick" 1907
Bejma, Alojzy F. "Ollie" 1935
Bender, Charles A. "Chief" 1907
Bernhard, William H. "Bill" 1903, 1907
Beville, H. Monte 1903-04
Blankenship, Clifford D. "Cliff" 1907
Buelow, Frederick W. "Fritz" 1906
Callahan, James J. "Nixey" 1901
Conlan, John B. "Jocko" 1935
Coughlin, William P. "Bill" 1904
Cronin, John J. "Jack" 1901
Davis, Harry H. 1903
Dinneen, William H. "Bill" 1907
Donahue, Francis R. "Red" 1903, 1906
Donovan, William E. "Bill" 1903, 1906
Drill, Lewis L. "Lew" 1903-04
Flaherty, Patrick J. "Patsy" 1903
Foreman, Francis I. "Frank" 1901
Grady, Michael W. "Mike" 1901
Griffith, Clark C. 1903
Harris, Joseph W. "Joe" 1906
Hickman, Charles T. "Charlie" 1907
Howell, H. Harry 1904, 1906-07
Kittridge, Malachi J. 1905-06
Leahy, Thomas J. "Tom" 1901
Leppert, Donald G. "Don" 1978
Lowe, Robert L. "Bobby" 1905
McAllister, Lewis W. "Sport" 1901-02
McGuire, James T> "Deacon" 1905
Moore, Earl A. 1903
O'Brien, Peter J. "Pete" 1907
Patten, Case L. 1903
Pelty, Barney 1906
Powers, Michael R. "Mike" 1902
Schmidt, Charles "Boss" 1907
Schreckengost, Ossee F. 1903
Siever, Edward T. "Ed" 1901
Warner, John J. "Jack" 1908
White, Guy H. "Doc" 1903
Winter, George L. 1903, 1905

Young, Denton T. "Cy" 1903
Zimmerman, Gerald R. "Jerry" 1978

UMPIRES DURING STRIKES

National League (1876-)

Anderson, Lewis E. "Andy" 1978-79
Andress, William J. "Bill" 1979
Baird, John 1979
Ballino, Frank 1991
Barston, Michael "Mike" 1979
Baswell, Jack S. 1979
Beck, Robert "Bob" 1979
Bendekovits, Joseph "Joe" 1979
Betcher, Ralph A. 1976
Blandford, Fred 1970
Bovey, Terry R. 1979, 1984
Bruns, Randy 1991
Campagna, Frank J. 1979, 1984
Cavenaugh, Richard P. "Dick" 1979, 1984
Cohen, Alfred A. "Al" 1976
Cote, Emilien 1979
Cuneo, James "Jim" 1978-79
Deniston, Shannon W. "Shan" 1978
Dierking, Roger A. 1978
Edwards, Larry 1978
Fick, Jerry D. 1978-79
Fisher, Frank 1979, 1984
Fleming, Thomas E. "Tom" 1979
Floras, John 1991
Fowler, A. Wheeler 1978
Freels, Robert L. "Bob" 1979
Gisondi, Tony 1991
Graham, Scott 1991
Grimsley, John 1970
Grinder, Scott 1976
Grooms, Roger C. 1979
Grygiel, George R. 1970
Guckert, Elmer 1976
Hadry, Merrill A. 1979
Hamil, Ray 1979
Hansen, Howard 1978-79
Hantak, H. Robert "Bob" 1979
Henry, William E. "Bill" 1979
Holoka, Mike 1991
Hutson, Ronald "Ron" 1979
January, Don 1991
Jeffers, Ronald L. "Ron" 1979
Jones, James "Jim" 1979
Jumper, Howard 1979
Lauzon, Jacques 1979
Lawson, William R. "Bill" 1979
Loeber, Gerald G. "Jerry" 1979
Lospitalier, Philip A. "Phil" 1979
Lupo, Charles "Charlie" 1978-79
Maher, Robert J. "Bob" 1979, 1984
Martine, Bruce 1991
Mauer, Boyd 1978-79
Melton, David "Dave" 1978
Miller, Marvin G. "Bud" 1979
Mills, Greg 1979
Morgenweck, Henry C. "Hank" 1970

Mrvos, Joseph S. "Joe" 1979
Myers, Joseph "Joe" 1979
Negri, Peter "Pete" 1979
Nelson, Robert "Bob" 1979, 1991
Norris, Edward E. "Ed" 1978-79
Oliger, Edward C. "Ed" 1979
Patch, Tony D. 1978-79
Perez, J. Ray 1979
Pomponi, Joseph L. "Joe" 1979, 1984
Rains, James "Jim" 1978-79
Riccio, Dennis R. 1979
Riccio, L. Leonard "Len" 1979
Roth, Roy 1978-79
Rountree, Henry J. "Hank" 1978-79
Schaller, Cliff 1978-79
Schleyer, John 1979
Schratz, Joseph "Joe" 1979
Schroeder, Robert L. "Bobby" 1978-79
Scott, James "Jim" 1978-79
Sharkey, Michael E. "Mick" 1978-79
Sharp, Robert C. "Bob" 1979
Siroka, Harold L. 1979
Slattery, Donald L. "Don" 1979
Slickenmeyer, David W. "Dave" 1979, 1984
Smail, Harry F. 1979
Spange, John 1991
Spinelli, Michel 1979
Stansell, B. Jack 1979
Stewart, John 1979, 1984
Strey, Murray W. 1978-79
Telford, Thomas "Tom" 1979
Tillman, Henry T. "Hank" 1978-79
Treitel, Leslie J. "Les" 1978-79
Tremblay, Richard H. "Dick" 1979
Urlage, Richard C. "Dick" 1979, 1991
Waller, James "Jim" 1979
Williams, Dale 1978-79
Willman, Bob 1991

American League (1901-)

Arata, Mark 1991
Berry, Charles F. "Charlie" 1970
Bible, Jonathan D. "Jon" 1984
Bishop, Homer L. 1979
Borga, Steven A. "Steve" 1979
Briscese, Michael L. "Mike" 1979
Brown, Buddy Lee "Bud" 1979
Brown, Douglas D. "Doug" 1979
Brown, Jeff 1978-79
Camp, John W. 1979
Campbell, Robert "Bob" 1979
Clegg, Richard "Dick" 1979
Clement, Robert F. "Bob" 1978-79
Contant, Alan 1978-79
Cossey, Douglas C. "Doug" 1978-79, 1984

Cuneo, James "Jim" 1979
Cristal, W. Randle "Randy" 1984
Davidson, Dale F. 1979
Deegan, William E. J. "Bill" 1970, 1984, 1991
DeFlesco, Pete 1991
Denny, Richard 1984
Dreke, Roy 1979
Driscoll, Joseph M. "Joe" 1978
Dunne, James "Jim" 1978-79
Easley, Harold L. 1979
Eshelman, George R. 1979
Evans, Jeff 1991
Farmer, Michael "Mike" 1979
Farnsworth, Harry 1979
Feaser, Richard L. "Dick" 1979
Fitzpatrick, Michael N. "Mike" 1979
Follmer, William A. "Bill" 1979
Forman, Allen S. "Al" 1978-79
Fuchs, Lester 1978-79
Gallagher, Lawrence E. "Larry" 1979
George, Edward "Ed" 1979
Giard, Robert "Bob" 1978
Gustafson, G. David "Dave" 1978
Hafner, William F. "Bill" 1979
Hadry, Merrill A. 1979
Harvey, Randy 1991
Heitzer, Richard "Dick" 1979
Henry, William E. "Bill" 1979
Higgins, John 1991
Ivory, William J. "Bill" 1979
Jackson, Charles L. 1979
James, John F. "Johnny" 1978-79
Jones, Robert G. "Bob" 1979, 1984
Jordan, Harold E. 1984
Kavulich, Joseph "Joe" 1978-79
Keister, R. Wayne 1978-79
Kelly, Eugene C. "Gene" 1979
Kimball, Shawn 1991
Kirby, Kenneth "Ken" 1979
Klein, Gus 1991
Knauss, Jim 1991
LaPierre, Richard 1979
Laude, William F. "Bill" 1978-79
Lazar, Richard R. "Richie" 1978-79
Levet, Jay 1979
Loeber, Gerald G. "Jerry" 1979
Lospitalier, Philip A. "Phil" 1979
Lupo, Charles "Charlie" 1979
Mabbot, Frederick J. "Fred" 1979
Mackin, John F. 1979
Marino, James H. "Jimmy" 1979
Mauer, Boyd 1979
McDougall, Scott 1991
McNally, James "Jim" 1979
Merritt, Clarence 1979
Miller, Gale 1979
Miller, John A. "Jack" 1979
Moyer, Robert "Bob" 1979
Mulcahy, James "Jim" 1979

Murray, Ed 1991
Nelson, Richard "Dick" 1979
Nothhnagel, Carl L. 1984
Novack, Lester A. "Les" 1979
O'Brien, James D. "Jim" 1979
O'Connor, James "Jim" 1978-79
O'Connor, Thomas M. "Tom" 1979
O'Dell, Mikel R. "Mike" 1984
Panas, Richard J. "Rich" 1978-79
Parks, Dallas F. 1991
Patch, Tony D. 1979
Perez, David A. "Dave" 1979
Phipps, George H. "Jerry" 1978-79
Pratt, Lester 1979
Purduski, Al J. 1979
Ravashiere, Thomas "Tom" 1979
Riccio, L. Leonard "Len" 1979
Rice, Robert W. "Bob" 1979
Robinson, William N. "Bill" 1978-79
Roesner, Robert A. "Bob" 1978-79
Roth, Roy 1979
Rountree, Henry J. "Hank" 1991
Runchey, Richard D. "Dick" 1979, 1984
Satchell, Darold L. 1970
Sawchuk, Joseph W. "Joe" 1978-79
Scheel, Alfred M. "Al" 1979
Schirmer, Donald A. "Don" 1979
Schulte, Donald E. "Don" 1979
Shaw, A. Duane 1979
Shewmake, James B. "Jim" 1978
Siroka, Harold L. 1979
Slattery, Donald L. "Don" 1979
Slickenmeyer, David W. "Dave" 1979, 1991
Spenn, Frederick C. "Fred" 1991
Sprincz, William "Bill" 1978-79
Stevens, John W. "Johnny" 1970
Sweeney, George P. 1979
Swenson, Charles H. 1979
Taylor, Joe Bob 1979
Terlop, Russell F. "Russ" 1979
Theilander, Theodore "Ted" 1979
Thompson, Michael G. "Mike" 1978-79
Tillman, Henry T. "Hank" 1979
Trimmer, Harry 1979
Turner, Leo I. 1978
Urchak, Woody J. 1978-79
Uremovich, Jim 1991
Williams, Dale 1979
Zirbel, Lawrence A. "Larry" 1979, 1984
Zivic, Richard J. "Dick" 1984
Zuccaro, Amerigo J. "Rico" 1978-79

The Owners and Officials Roster

Although Major League Baseball began in 1871 with the National Association, it is undeniable that with the founding of the National League in 1876 something dramatic occurred that altered forevermore the character of professional baseball: the division of the game into two classes, labor and management.

The National Association of Professional Base Ball Players was an outgrowth of the amateur association of the same name, in which baseball clubs were formed as organizations devoted to social intercourse and fraternal competition. Amateur clubs were organized along the same lines as today's Elks or Odd Fellows, with elected officials and dues-paying members. As players of special skill were invited into these clubs, their dues might be forgiven or "emoluments" offered—no-show jobs or under-the-table payments. The abuses of the amateur system of the mid-1860s led to the declaration by several clubs of their openly professional status; players would sometimes draw salaries and as often would share in gate receipts. By the end of the decade gambling and game-fixing were rife.

Despite the formation of the National Association, these evils continued largely unabated into the 1870s. A monopolization of talent, largely in Boston, rendered Western clubs uncompetitive, and spectator rowdyism spawned by gambling interest, and the open sale of hard liquor burdened the new league. Clubs were admitted into the NA for paltry fees and fulfilled their schedules half-heartedly. Some of the member clubs had active presidents who functioned much as owners later would; other clubs were "cooperative nines," managed by the players themselves; still others were hybrids, born of civic boosterism. By 1876, the odd amalgam of the NA, presided over by Brooklyn Atlantics star Bob Ferguson, was failing.

Thus in 1876 William Hulbert, president of the Chicago club, combined with seven other team representatives to form the National League, a circuit run entirely by owners. Since then, fan interest has focused on the players, of course, and to a lesser extent on the managers, coaches, and umpires. But it can be said with some justice that while the on-field personnel and personalities "are" the game, it is the club owners, presidents, and league officials who make the game possible and ensure its continuity.

The Owners and Officials Roster that follows represents a first attempt in a baseball encyclopedia to recognize these individuals. As we did with the Coach Roster in the first edition of *Total Baseball*, we offered this section in *Total Baseball*'s second and third editions with the full knowledge that there were gaps and probably gaffes in our research; we hope that our readers will advise us of omissions so that we can continue to improve the roster in future editions. (The names of National Association club presidents and officials are listed below despite our understanding that these individuals were, by and large, not owners in the sense used after 1876.)

For prose accounts of the history of owners and officials, see the essays by John Thorn and by David Pietrusza.

Commissioners, Major League Baseball

1920–1944	Kenesaw M. Landis
1945–1951	Albert B. Chandler
1951–1965	Ford C. Frick
1965–1968	William D. Eckert
1969–1984	Bowie K. Kuhn
1984–1989	Peter Ueberroth
1989	A. Bartlett Giamatti
1989–1992	Francis T. Vincent, Jr.

National Association

Association President

1871	James W. Kerns
1872–1875	Robert W. Ferguson

Club Presidents and/or NA Convention Delegates

Baltimore Lord Baltimores

1872	—
1873	R. C. Hall
1874	C. A. Hadel

Baltimore Marylands

1873	W. J. Smith

Boston Red Stockings

1871	Ivers Whitney Adams
1872	Col. Charles H. Porter
1873–1875	Nathan Taylor Appolonio

Brooklyn Atlantics

1872–1873	Robert W. Ferguson
1874	—
1875	B. Van Delft

Brooklyn Eckfords

1872	William H. Ray

Chicago White Stockings

1871	J. M. Thatcher
1874	Mr. Gassette
	George W. Gage
1875	William A. Hulbert

Cleveland Forest City

1871	J. F. Evans
1872	H. C. Doolittle

Elizabeth Resolutes

1873	Charles N. Garrighan

Fort Wayne Kekiongas

1871	George J. E. Mayers

Hartford Dark Blues

1874	G. B. Hubbell
1875	Morgan G. Bulkeley

Keokuk Westerns

1875	W. Trimble

Middletown Mansfields

1872	B. Douglass, Jr.
	T. W. Ratcliff

New Haven Elm City

1875	W. S. Arnold

New York Mutuals

1871–1872	Alexander V. Davidson
1873	Robert Mathews
1874	Alexander V. Davidson
1875	William H. Cammeyer

Philadelphia Athletics

1871	James W. Kerns
1872–1873	E. H. Hayhurst
1874	D. F. Houston
1875	George W. Thompson
	C. Spering

Philadelphia White Stockings

1873	Frank McBride
1874	D. L. Reid
1875	George Concannon

Philadelphia Centennials

1875	E. H. Hayhurst

Rockford Forest City

1871	Hiram Waldo

St. Louis Brown Stockings

1875	C. O. Bishop

St. Louis Red Stockings

1875	A. Blong

Troy Haymakers

1871	J. W. Scofield
1872	C. C. Clark

Washington Nationals

1872	Mr. Millar
	R. Hough

Washington Olympics

1871	Nicholas E. Young
1872	Mr. Pike

Washington

1873	Nicholas E. Young
1875	D. W. Bruce
	A. F. Childs

National League

Presidents

1876	Morgan G. Bulkeley
1877–1882	William A. Hulbert
1882	Arthur H. Soden
1883–1884	Abraham G. Mills
1885–1902	Nicholas E. Young
1903–1909	Harry C. Pulliam
1909	John A. Heydler
1910–1913	Thomas J. Lynch
1913–1918	John K. Tener
1918–1934	John A. Heydler
1934–1951	Ford C. Frick
1951–1969	Warren C. Giles
1970–1986	Charles S. Feeney
1986–1989	A. Bartlett Giamatti
1989–1994	William White
1994–	Leonard Coleman

Vice Presidents

1929–1932	Barney Dreyfuss
1933–1936	Charles A. Stoneham
1936–1947	Samuel Breadon
1947–1966	Philip K. Wrigley
1966–1969	Horace C. Stoneham
1970–1986	John J. McHale
1987–	Phyllis Collins

Club Presidents

Atlanta

1966	John J. McHale
1967–1972	William C. Bartholomay
1973–1975	Daniel J. Donahue
1976–1986	R. E. (Ted) Turner
1987–	William C. Bartholomay (Ch. of Bd.)

Baltimore

1892	Harry B. Von der Horst
1893–1899	Edward H. Hanlon

Boston (to Milwaukee)

1876	Nathan Taylor Appolonio
1907–1909	George B. Dovey
1909–1910	John S. Dovey
1911	W. Hepburn Russell
1912	John M. Ward
1913–1915	James E. Gaffney
1916–1918	Percy D. Haughton
1919–1922	George W. Grant
1923	Christopher Mathewson
1924	J. A. Robert Quinn
1925	Christopher Mathewson
1926	J. A. Robert Quinn
1927–1935	Emil E. Fuchs
1936–44	J. A. Robert Quinn
1945–1952	Louis R. Perini

Brooklyn (to L.A.)

1890–1897	Charles H. Byrne
1898–1925	Charles H. Ebbets
1925	Edward J. McKeever
1925–1929	Wilbert Robinson
1930–1932	Frank B. York
1933–1938	Stephen W. McKeever
1939–1942	Leland S. MacPhail, Sr.
1943–1950	W. Branch Rickey
1950–1957	Walter F. O'Malley

Buffalo

1879–1880	E. B. Smith
1880	John B. Sage
1881–1885	Josiah Jewett

Chicago

1876–1881	William A. Hulbert
1882–1891	Albert G. Spalding
1892–1905	James A. Hart
1906–1913	Charles W. Murphy
1914–1915	Charles H. Thomas
1916–1918	Charles H. Weeghman
1919	Fred F. Mitchell
1919–1933	William L. Veeck, Sr.
1934	William M. Walker
1934–1977	Philip K. Wrigley
1977–1981	William J. Hagenah, Jr.
1982–1983	Andrew J. McKenna (Ch. of Bd.)
1984	James E. Finks (Pres./CEO)
1985–1987	Dallas Green
1988	John W. Madigan (Ch. of Bd.)
1989–	Stanton Cook (Ch. of Bd.)

Cincinnati

1876–1877	Josiah L. Keck
1878–1879	J. Wayne Neff
1880	Justus Thorner

Cincinnati

1890	Aaron A. Stern
1891–1902	John T. Brush
1902–1927	August Herrmann
1928–1929	C. J. McDiarmid
1930–1933	Sidney Weil
1934–1946	Powel Crosley, Jr.
1946–1951	Warren C. Giles
1951–1961	Powel Crosley, Jr.
1961–1966	William O. DeWitt
1967–1973	Francis L. Dale
1973–1978	Robert L. Howsam
1979–1983	Richard Wagner
1984–1985	Robert L. Howsam (Pres./CEO)
1986–	Marge Schott (Gen. Partner/Pres.)

Cleveland

1879–1881	J. Ford Evans
1882–1884	C. H. Bulkley

Cleveland

1889–1898	Frank D. Robison
1899	M. Stanley Robison

Colorado

1992	John Antonucci (Ch./CEO)
1993–	Jerry McMorris (Ch./CEO/Pres.)

Detroit

1881–1884	William G. Thompson
1885–1886	Joseph H. Marsh
1887–1888	Fred K. Stearns
1888	Charles W. Smith

Florida

1992	Wayne Huizenga (Chairman)

Hartford

1876–1877	Morgan G. Bulkeley

Houston

1962	Craig Cullinan, Jr.
1963–1971	Roy Hofheinz
1972–1973	Reuben W. Askanase
1974–1975	T. H. Neyland
1976	Sidney L. Shlenker
1976–1980	Talbot M. Smith
1981–1985	Albert L. Rosen
1986–1987	Dick Wagner
1988	Fred Stanley
1980–1992	Dr. John J. McMullen (Ch. of Bd.)
1992–	Drayton McLane, Jr. (Ch. of Bd./CEO)

Indianapolis

1878	William D. Perritt

Indianapolis

1887–1889	John T. Brush

Kansas City

1886	Joseph J. Heim

Los Angeles

1958–1969	Walter F. O'Malley
1970–	Peter O'Malley (Pres.)

Louisville

1876–1877	Walter N. Haldeman

Louisville

1892	T. Hunt Stucky
1893–1896	Fred Drexler
1897–1899	Harry C. Pulliam
1899	Barney Dreyfuss

Milwaukee

1878	J. R. Kaine

Milwaukee Braves (to Atlanta Braves)

1953–1956	Louis R. Perini
1957–1961	Joseph F. Cairnes
1962–1966	John J. McHale

Montreal Expos

1969–1986	John J. McHale
1987–1992	Claude R. Brochu (Pres./CEO)
1969–1991	Charles R. Bronfman (Ch. of Bd.)
1992–	Jacques Menard (Ch. of Bd.)

Mutual Club (N.Y.)

1876	William H. Cammeyer

New York Giants (to San Francisco)

1883–1892	John B. Day
1893–1894	C. C. Van Cott
1895–1902	Andrew Freedman
1903–1912	John T. Brush
1912–1918	Harry N. Hempstead
1919–1935	Charles A. Stoneham
1936–1957	Horace C. Stoneham

New York Mets

1962–1966	George M. Weiss
1967	Vaughan P. Devine
1968–1975	Mrs. Joan W. Payson
1976–1979	Mrs. Lorinda de Roulet
1980–	Fred Wilpon (Pres./CEO)

Philadelphia Athletics

1876	Thomas J. Smith

Philadelphia Phillies

1883–1902	Alfred J. Reach
1903–1904	James Potter
1905–1908	William J. Shettsline
1909	Israel W. Durham
1909–1912	Horace S. Fogel
1912	Alfred D. Wiler
1913	William H. Locke
1913–1930	William F. Baker
1931–1932	L. Charles Ruch
1933–1942	Gerald P. Nugent
1943	William D. Cox
1943–1972	Robert M. Carpenter, Jr.
1973–1981	Robert M. Carpenter III
1982–	Bill Giles (Pres./CEO)

Pittsburgh

1887–1890	William A. Nimick
1891	J. Palmer O'Neill
1892	William C. Temple
1893	Albert C. Buckenberger
1894–1897	William W. Kerr
1898	William H. Watkins
1899	William W. Kerr
1900–1932	Barney Dreyfuss
1932–1946	William E. Benswanger
1946–1950	Frank E. McKinney
1951–1969	John W. Galbreath
1970–1985	Daniel M. Galbreath
1986–1987	Malcolm Prine
1988–1990	Carl Barger
1988–1991	Douglas D. Danforth (Chairman/CEO)
1992	Vincent Sarni (Pres./CEO)
1992–	Mark Sauer (Pres./CEO)

Providence

1878	John D. Thurston
1879–1881	Henry J. Root
1882–1883	Henry B. Winship
1884–1885	Henry J. Root

St. Louis Brown Stockings

1876–1877	John R. Lucas

St. Louis Maroons

1885–1886	Henry V. Lucas

St. Louis Cardinals

1892–1897	Chris Von der Ahe
1898	Benjamin S. Muckenfuss
1899–1906	Frank D. Robison
1907–1910	M. Stanley Robison
1911–1912	E. A. Steininger
1912	James C. Jones

1913–1916	Schuyler P. Britton
1916	Mrs. Schuyler P. Britton
1917–1919	W. Branch Rickey
1920–1947	Samuel Breadon
1947–1949	Robert E. Hannegan
1949–1952	Fred M. Saigh, Jr.
1953–1989	August A. Busch, Jr.
1990–1991	Fred L. Kuhlmann (Pres./CEO)
1992–	Stuart Meyer (Pres./CEO)

San Diego

1969–1977	Emil J. Bavasi
1977–1980	Ray A. Kroc
1981–1983	Ray A. Kroc (owner)
1980–1987	Ballard F. Smith, Jr.
1988	Chub Feeney
1990	Dick Freeman
1984–1990	Joan Kroc (owner)
1991–1994	Tom Werner (Prin. Owner/Ch.)

San Francisco

1958–1975	Horace C. Stoneham
1976–1985	Robert A. Lurie
1976–1990	Robert A. Lurie (owner)
1986–1992	Al Rosen
1993–	Peter A. Magowan

Syracuse

1879	Hamilton S. White

Troy

1879–1880	Gardner Earl
1881–1882	A. L. Hotchkin
1882	Francis N. Mann

Washington

1886–1888	Robert C. Hewitt
1889	Walter F. Hewitt

Washington

1892–1899	George W. Wagner

Worcester

1880–1882	Elbert B. Pratt

American Association

League Presidents

1882–1885	H. D. McKnight
1886–1889	Wheeler C. Wyckoff
1890	Zach Phelps
1891	Louis Kramer
	Ed Renau
	Zach Phelps

Club Presidents

Baltimore

1882	H. C. Myers (?)
1883	William Barnie (?)
1884	H. T. Houck
1885–1887	William Barnie
1888	Harry Von der Horst
1889	William Barnie
1891	Harry Von der Horst

Boston

1891	Charles A. Prince

Brooklyn

1884–1889	Charles H. Byrne

Brooklyn–Baltimore

1890	James M. Kennedy
	Wm. Barnie (?)

Cincinnati

1882	Justus Thorner
1883–1884	Aaron S. Stern
1885	George L. Herancourt
1886	John Hauck
1887–1889	Aaron S. Stern

Cincinnati-Milwaukee

1891	Albert Johnson

Cleveland

1887–1888	Frank Robison

Columbus

1883–1884	H. T. Crittendon (?)
1889–1891	Conrad Born, Jr.

Indianapolis

1884	Joseph Schwabacher

Kansas City

1888	Joseph J. Heim
1889	John W. Speas

Louisville

1882–1883	J. H. Pank
1884	William L. Jackson, Jr.
1885–1887	Zach Phelps
1888	W. L. Lyons
1889	M. H. Davidson
1890	Lawrence S. Parsons
1891	Julian B. Hart

New York

1883–1884	John B. Day
1885	Frank Rhouer
1886–1887	Erastus Wiman

Philadelphia

1882	Lew Simmons (?)
1883–1886	William Sharsig
1887	Lew Simmons
1888–1890	H. C. Pennypacker
1891	J. Earle Wagner

Pittsburgh

1882–1883	H. D. McKnight
1884	E. E. Converse
1885–1886	William A. Nimick

Richmond

1884	W. C. Seddon

Rochester

1890	Henry Brinker

St. Louis

1882–1891	Chris Von der Ahe

Syracuse

1890	George K. Frazier

Toledo

1884	W. J. Colburn
1890	V. H. Ketcham

Washington

1884	L. Moxley
1891	H. B. Bennett

Union Association

League Presidents

1883	H. B. Bennett
	Henry V. Lucas
1883–1885	Henry V. Lucas

Club Presidents

Altoona

1884	W. W. Rich

Baltimore

1884	J. W. Lowe

Boston

1884	Frank E. Winslow

Chicago-Pittsburgh

1884	A. H. Henderson

Cincinnati

1884	Justus Thorner

Kansas City

1884	Americus V. McKim

Milwaukee

1884	Charles Kippen (?)

Philadelphia

1884	Thomas J. Pratt

St. Louis

1884	H. V. Lucas

St. Paul

1884	A. M. Thompson (?)

Washington

1884	H. B. Bennett

Wilmington

1884	John T. West

Players League

League President

1890	Col. Edward A. McAlpin

Club Presidents

Boston

1890	Col. Charles H. Porter

Brooklyn
1890	Wendell Goodwin

Buffalo
1890	Moses Shire

Chicago
1890	John Addison

Cleveland
1890	Albert L. Johnson

New York
1890	Cornelius Van Cott

Philadelphia
1890	H. M. Love

Pittsburgh
1890	William McCallin

American League

Presidents
1901–1927	B. Bancroft Johnson
1927–1931	Ernest S. Barnard
1931–1959	William Harridge
1959–1973	Joseph E. Cronin
1974–1984	Leland S. MacPhail, Jr.
1984–1994	Robert W. Brown, M.D.
1994–	Gene Budig

Vice Presidents
1901–1916	Charles W. Somers
1917–1919	Charles A. Comiskey
1921–1935	Frank J. Navin
1935–1938	Jacob Ruppert
1939–1955	Clark C. Griffith
1955–1976	Thomas A. Yawkey
1976–1982	Calvin R. Griffith
1983–1984	Calvin R. Griffith
	John Fetzer
	Gene Autry
1985	John Fetzer and Gene Autry
1986–1989	Calvin R. Griffith
	John Fetzer
	Gene Autry
1990	John Fetzer and Gene Autry
1991	Jean Yawkey and Gene Autry
1992–	Gene Autry

Club Presidents

Baltimore (to New York)
1901	Sidney W. Frank
1902	John J. Mahon

Baltimore
1954–1955	Clarence W. Miles
1956–1959	James Keelty, Jr.
1960–1965	Leland S. MacPhail, Jr.
1966–1979	Jerold C. Hoffberger (Ch. of Bd.)
1980–1982	Jerold C. Hoffberger (as Pres.)
1983–1988	Edward B. Williams (Ch. of Bd./Pres.)
1989–1992	Lawrence Lucchino
1994–	Peter Angelos Managing Gen. Partner)

Boston
1901–1902	Charles W. Somers
1903–1904	Henry J. Killilea
1904–1911	John I. Taylor
1912–1913	James R. McAleer
1913–1916	Joseph J. Lannin
1917–1923	Harry H. Frazee
1923–1932	John A. Quinn
1933–1976	Thomas A. Yawkey
1977–1988	Jean R. Yawkey (majority owner)
1989–	John L. Harrington (General Partner)

California (includes Los Angeles, 1961–64)
1961–1974	Robert Reynolds
1975–1977	Arthur E. Patterson
1977–1990	Gene Autry (owner/president)
1990–	Richard M. Brown

Chicago
1901–1931	Charles A. Comiskey
1932–1939	J. Louis Comiskey
1940	Harry Grabiner (VP)
1941–1956	Mrs. Grace Comiskey
1957–1958	None
1959–1961	William L. Veeck, Jr.
1961–1969	Arthur C. Allyn, Jr.
1970–1975	John W. Allyn
1976–1980	William L. Veeck, Jr.
1981–	Jerry M. Reinsdorf (Chairman)

Cleveland
1901–1909	John F. Kilfoyl
1910–1915	Charles W. Somers
1916–1922	James C. Dunn
1922–1927	Ernest S. Barnard
1928–1946	Alva Bradley
1946–1949	William L. Veeck, Jr.
1950–1952	Ellis W. Ryan
1953–1962	Myron H. Wilson, Jr.
1963–1971	Gabriel H. Paul
1972–1975	Nick Mileti
1975–1977	Alva T. Bonda
1978–1983	F. J. (Steve) O'Neill
1983–1986	Patrick J. O'Neill (Chairman)
1978–1985	Gabriel H. Paul
1986	Peter Bavasi
1987–	Richard E. Jacobs (Ch. of Bd./CEO)

Detroit
1901	James D. Burns (Pres.)
1902–1903	Samuel F. Angus (Pres.)
1904–1907	William H. Yawkey (Pres.)
1908–1935	Frank J. Navin (Pres.)
1936–1952	Walter O. Briggs, Sr. (Pres.)
1952–1956	Walter O. Briggs, Jr. (Pres.)
1957	Frederick A. Knorr (Pres.)
1957–1959	Harvey R. Hansen (Pres.)
1960	William O. DeWitt (Pres.)
1961–1989	John E. Fetzer (Pres.)
1978–1989	James Campbell (Pres.)
1984–1990	Thomas S. Monaghan (Pres.)
1990–1992	Glenn E. (Bo) Schembechler (Pres.)
1992–	Michael Ilitch (Pres.)

Kansas City A's (to Oakland)
1955–1959	Arnold Johnson
1960	Parke Carroll (VP)
1961–1967	Charles O. Finley

Kansas City Royals
1969–1993	Ewing Kauffman (Ch. of Bd.)
1993–	David D. Glass (Ch./CEO)

Milwaukee (to St. Louis)
1901	Matthew Killilea

Milwaukee Brewers
1970–	Allan H. "Bud" Selig (Pres./CEO)

Minnesota
1961–1984	Calvin R. Griffith (Chairman/ Pres.)
1985–1986	Howard T. Fox, Jr.
1987–1989	Jerry Bell
1985–	Carl Pohlad (owner)

New York
1903–1906	Joseph W. Gordon
1903–1915	Frank J. Farrell and William S. Devery (owners)
1907–1914	Frank J. Farrell
1915–1938	Jacob Ruppert
1939–1944	Edward G. Barrow
1945–1947	Leland S. MacPhail, Sr.
1948–1966	Daniel R. Topping
1966–1973	Michael Burke
1973–1977	Gabriel H. Paul
1978–1980	Albert Rosen
1980–1990	George M. Steinbrenner (Ch. of Bd.)
1990–1991	Robert Nederlander (Man. Gen. Part.)
1992	Daniel McCarthy (Man. Gen. Part.)
1993–	George M. Steinbrenner (Prin. owner)

Oakland
1968–1980	Charles O. Finley
1981–1987	Roy Eisenhardt
1981–1990	Walter Haas (owner)
1990–	Walter J. Haas (Chairman/CEO)

Philadelphia (to Kansas City)
1901–1921	Benjamin F. Shibe
1922–1935	Thomas S. Shibe
1936	John D. Shibe
1937–1954	Connie Mack

Seattle Pilots (to Milwaukee)
1969	Dewey Soriano

Seattle Mariners
1977–1979	Danny Kaye and Lester Smith
1980–1983	Daniel F. O'Brien
1981–1989	George L. Argyros (Ch. of Bd./CEO)
1984–1989	Charles G. Armstrong
1990–1991	Jeff Smulyan (Ch. of Bd.)
1992–	John W. Ellis (Ch. of Bd./CEO)

St. Louis (to Baltimore)
1902	Ralph T. Orthwein
1903–1915	Robert L. Hedges
1916–1933	Philip D. Ball
1934–1936	Louis B. Von Weise
1937–1945	Donald L. Barnes
1946–1948	Richard C. Muckerman
1949–1951	William O. DeWitt
1951–1953	William L. Veeck, Jr.

Texas
1972–1974	Robert E. Short
1974	Robert W. Brown, M.D.
1975–1980	Bradford G. Corbett
1980–1987	Eddie Chiles (Owner/Ch. of Bd./CEO)
1984–1990	Michael H. Stone
1991–	J. Thomas Schieffer (Pres.)

Toronto
1977–1981	Peter Bavasi
1977–1988	R. Howard Webster (Ch. of Bd.)
1989–	Paul Beeston (Pres./CEO)

Washington (to Minnesota)
1901–1903	Frederick Postal
1904	Thomas J. Loftus
1904	Harry B. Lambert
1905–1912	Thomas C. Noyes
1920–1955	Clark C. Griffith
1956–1960	Calvin R. Griffith

Washington
1961–1962	Elwood R. Quesada
1963–1967	James M. Johnston (Ch. of Bd.)
1968	James H. Lemon (Ch. of Bd.)
1969–1971	Robert E. Short

Federal League

League President
1914–1915	James A. Gilmore

Club Presidents

Baltimore
1914–1915	Carrol W. Rasin

Brooklyn
1914–1915	Robert B. Ward

Buffalo
1914	Walter F. Mullen
	William E. Robertson
1915	William E. Robertson

Chicago
1914–1915	Charles A. Weeghman

Indianapolis
1914	J. E. Krause

Kansas City
1914	C. C. Madison
1915	Charles Baird
	Conrad H. Mann

Newark
1915	P. T. Powers
	Harry Sinclair

Pittsburgh
1914	John R. Barbour
1915	Edward W. Gwinner

St. Louis
1914	E. A. Steininger
1915	Lloyd H. Rickart

Negro Baseball Roster

Dick Clark and Larry Lester

In 1970 Robert Peterson wrote a pioneering book, *Only the Ball Was White,* that launched the serious study of black baseball in the years before Jackie Robinson broke the color line in 1947. Peterson was followed in that decade by John Holway's *Voices from the Great Black Baseball Leagues* and William Brashler's *Josh Gibson,* and in the 1980s by Jules Tygiel's *Baseball's Great Experiment: Jackie Robinson and His Legacy.* Recent years have produced further interesting work, from television documentaries to lavish pictorials to oral histories. You don't hear much argument anymore, as once was prevalent, about whether black stars like Satchel Paige or Buck Leonard, Oscar Charleston or Judy Johnson, truly belong in Baseball's Hall of Fame.

Underlying much of the good work that has come forth over the last two decades has been the diligent research of unheralded members of the Society for American Baseball Research (SABR), founded in 1971 by L. Robert Davids and fifteen other empassioned students of the game. Their early establishment of a Negro Leagues research committee spurred such valuable efforts as the compilation of team and individual statistics for many seasons of Negro League play; the dedication of a monument in honor of Bud Fowler, the nation's first profes-

sional black player; the founding of a Negro League Baseball Museum in Kansas City, Missouri; and the long, steady progress toward an encyclopedic research guide to black baseball, culminating in publication by SABR in 1994.

Part of that volume, edited by Larry Lester and Dick Clark, co-chairs of SABR's Negro Leagues Committee, is a massive revision of Robert Peterson's listing of black baseball players and officials up to 1950. (We also offer a smattering of names from the waning years of the Negro Leagues, 1951-55.) Lester and Clark, aided by other SABR members, have added players, corrected names and team affiliations, ranged earlier and later, broader and deeper, than Peterson's original work, and have provided us with an invaluable reference tool.

From vintage figures like Bud Fowler, Moses Fleetwood Walker and Billy Whyte to more recognizable names like Willie Mays, Henry Aaron, Larry Doby, Monte Irvin, and Ernie Banks; from Hall of Famers like Martin Dihigo and Ray Dandridge to storied figures like Cannonball Dick Redding and Bullet Joe Rogan, Turkey Stearnes and Oliver Marcelle, the shadows of legend are here. They were part of America's game; savor their names.

Aaron, Henry Louis (Hank), 1952 INF, Indianapolis Clowns

Aballi, —, 1930 P, Cuban Stars

Abbott, —, 1906-1908 P, OF, Cuban Giants, Genuine Cuban Giants

Abernathy, James, 1946-47 OF, Boston Blues, Indianapolis Clowns

Abreau, Eufemio [Abreu], 1920-34 C, 1B, OF, Cuban Stars (NNL), Cuban Stars (ECL)

Acosta, Jose, 1915 P, Long Branch N.J. Cubans

Adams, Emery (Ace), 1932-46 P, Memphis Red Sox, Baltimore Elite Giants, New York Black Yankees

Adams, (Packinghouse), 1938 3B, Kansas City Monarchs

Addison, J., 1910-11 C, Philadelphia Giants

Addison, K., 1911-12 3B, Philadelphia Giants, Pittsburgh Giants

Addison, T., 1911 SS, Philadelphia Giants

Adkins, Clarence, 1931 OF, Nashville Elite Giants

Adkins, Stacy, *see Stacy Atkins*

Agnew, Clyde, 1950 P, Baltimore Elite Giants

Ahrens, —, 1930 OF, P, Cuban Stars

Albrecht, R., 1928-29 P, Bacharach Giants

Albright, Thomas (Pistol Pete), 1936 P, New York Cubans

Albritton, Alexander (Alex), 1921-25 P, Baltimore Black Sox, Washington Potomacs, Hilldale, Bacharach Giants

Alderette, —, 1918 P, Cuban Stars (East)

Alexander, —, 1918-21 OF, 1B, 2B, Dayton Marcos, Chicago Giants, Columbus Buckeyes

Alexander, Calvin, 1922 P, New Orleans Crescent Stars

Alexander, (Chuffy), 1927-32 3B, OF, 1B, Birmingham Black Barons, Monroe Monarchs

Alexander, Freyl, 1912 pres, Homestead Grays

Alexander, Grover Cleveland (Buck), 1923-26 P, Chicago Giants, Detroit Stars, Indianapolis ABCs, Cleveland Elites

Alexander, (Hub), 1913 C, Chicago Giants

Alexander, Joe, 1950 C, Kansas City Monarchs

Alexander, Spencer, 1940-41 OF, Newark Eagles

Alexander, Ted (Red), 1940-49 P, Cleveland Bears, Chicago American Giants, Kansas City Monarchs, Birmingham Black Barons, Homestead Grays, New York Black Yankees

Alfonso, Angel, 1924-30 SS, 3B, 2B, Cuban Stars (NNL), Cuban Stars (ECL)

Allen, —, 1940,1943 OF, Birmingham Black Barons, New York Black Yankees

Allen, Clifford (Crooks, Clyde), 1932-38 P, Hilldale, Baltimore Black Sox, Homestead Grays, Memphis Red Sox, Philadelphia Stars

Allen, Dave, 1887 C, 1B, UTIL, Trenton Cuban Giants (Middle States Lg.), Pittsburgh Keystones

Allen, Homer, 1932 P, Monroe Monarchs

Allen, Hoses (Buster), 1942-47 P, UTIL, Jacksonville Red Caps, Cincinnati Clowns, Cincinnati-Indianapolis Clowns, Memphis Red Sox, Cleveland Buckeyes

Allen, M., 1919-22 2B, Lincoln Giants, Baltimore Black Sox

Allen, Newton Henry (Newt, Colt), 1922-47 2B, SS, OF, MGR, All Nations, Kansas City Monarchs, St. Louis Stars, Homestead Grays, Indianapolis Clowns

Allen, Todd, 1915-25 3B, MGR, Bowser's ABCs, Indianapolis ABCs, Chicago American Giants, Lincoln Giants

Allen, Toussaint L'Ouverture (Tom), 1914-26 1B, Havana Red Sox, Hilldale, Wilmington Potomacs, Newark Stars

Allen, William 1887 player, Cincinnati Browns

Allison, —, 1915-17,21,25 1B, 2B, C, Chicago Union Giants, Chicago American Giants, Nashville Elite Giants, Indianapolis ABCs

Almagro, Jorge, 1945 OF, Pittsburgh Crawfords

Almas, —, 1925 P, Cubans (NNL)

Almenteros, Juan Pablo, 1916 P, Cuban Stars

Almeyda, —, 1905 3B, All Cubans

Alonso, Rogelio, 1927-30 P, OF, Cuban Stars (NNL)

Alsop, Clifford, 1920-22 P, Kansas City Monarchs

Alston, Tom, 1948 1B, Greensboro (NC) Red Wings

Alvarez, Raul, 1924-33 P, Cuban Stars (NNL), Cuban Stars (East)

Amoros, Edmundo (Sandy), 1950 1B, OF, New York Cubans

Anas, A., 1935 P, New York Cubans

Anderson, —, 1908,1912 P, 3B, Cuban Giants

Anderson, Lewis , 1930-33 C, Chicago American Giants, Baltimore Black Sox

Anderson, Ralph, 1927,1932 OF, Nashville Elite Giants, Indianapolis ABCs, Homestead Grays

Anderson, Robert James (Bobby), 1915-25 SS, 2B, Peters' Union Giants, Chicago American Giants, Philadelphia Giants, Gilkerson's Union Giants, Chicago Giants

Anderson, Theodore (Bubbles), 1922-25 2B, C, Kansas City Monarchs, Birmingham Black Barons, Washington Potomacs, Wilmington Potomacs, Indianapolis ABCs

Anderson, William, 1927,1930 OF, Nashville Elite Giants

Anderson, William (Bill), 1940-47 P, Brooklyn Royal Giants, Cuban Stars, New York Cubans, Philadelphia Stars

Andrews, Herman (Jabo), 1930-43 OF, P, 1B, MGR, Birmingham Black Barons, Memphis Red Sox, Indianapolis ABCs, Detroit Wolves, Homestead Grays, Columbus Blue Birds, Pittsburgh Crawfords, Washington Black Senators, Chicago American Giants, Jacksonville Red Caps, Cleveland Bears, Philadelphia Stars, New York Cubans

Andrews, (Pop), 1906-19 P, OF, 1B, 2B, Brooklyn Royal Giants, Pittsburgh Stars of Buffalo, Philadelphia Giants, Havana Red Sox

Anthony, Lavance (Pete), 1950 C, Houston Eagles, New York Cubans

Anthony, Thad, 1950 C, Baltimore Elite Giants

Arango, Luis, 1925-39 3B, 1B, Cuban Stars (NNL), New York Cubans

Archer, —, 1919-24 P, C, Lincoln Giants, Baltimore Black Sox, Philadelphia Giants

Arencibia, Eduardo, 1948 OF, New York Cubans

Arguelles, Martinano, *see Garay*

Ariosa, Homero Mario, 1947-49 OF, New York Cubans

Armentero, —, 1916 P, New York Cuban Stars

Armour, —, 1933 P, 3B, Detroit Stars

Armour, Alfred (Buddy), 1936-50 OF, SS, St. Louis Stars, Indianapolis ABCs, New Orleans-St. Louis Stars, Harrisburg- St.Louis Stars, Cleveland Buckeyes, Chicago American Giants, Homestead Grays

Armstead, James (Jimmie), 1938-49 P, OF, Indianapolis ABCs, St.Louis Stars, Baltimore Elite Giants, Philadelphia Stars

Arnet, —, 1921 P, Bacharach Giants

Arnold, Paul, 1926-36 OF, Brooklyn Royal Giants, Newark Dodgers, Bacharach Giants, Hilldale

Arthur, Robert, 1946 P, Pittsburgh Crawfords

Arumis, (Arumi), 1920 OF, 2B, Kansas City Monarchs

Asbury, —, 1918 P, Lincoln Giants

Ascanio, Carlos, 1946 1B, New York Black Yankees

Ash, Rudolph [Rudolph], 1920,1926 OF, P, Chicago American Giants, Newark Stars, Hilldale

Ashby, Earl, 1945-48 C, Cleveland Buckeyes, Birmingham Black Barons, Homestead Grays, Newark Eagles

Askew, Jesse, 1936 SS, St. Louis Stars

Ashport, , 1913 3B, Havana Red Sox

Atame, , 1920 P, Kansas City Monarchs

Atkins, Abe, 1923 SS, 3B, Toledo Tigers

Atkins, Joseph O. (Joe, Leroy) , 1946-47 3B, Pittsburgh Crawfords, Cleveland Buckeyes

Atkins, Stacy, 1950 P, Chicago American Giants

Augustine, Leon, 1923 umpire, NNL

Augustus, —, 1927 P, Memphis Red Sox

Austin, Frank Samuel (Junior), 1944-48 SS, Philadelphia Stars

Austin, John 1887 player, Cincinnati Browns

Austin, (Tank), 1930-32 P, Nashville Elite Giants, Birmingham Black Barons, Atlanta Black Crackers

Averett, —, 1943 OF, New York Black Yankees

Awkard, Russell, 1940-41 OF, Cuban Stars, Newark Eagles

Aylor, James 1887 player, Philadelphia Pythians

Bagley, —, 1937 C, Cincinnati Tigers

Bailey, —, 1910 C, Chicago Giants

Bailey, Alonza, 1935 P, Newark Dodgers

Bailey, Bob, 1932 OF, Hilldale

Bailey, D., 1916-28 OF, 3B, Lincoln Stars, Pennsylvania Red Caps of New York

Bailey, Otha William, 1950 C, Cleveland Buckeyes, Houston Eagles

Bailey, Percy (Bill), 1927-34 P, Baltimore Black Sox, Nashville Elite Giants, Detroit Stars, Cole's American Giants, New York Black Yankees

Baird, Thomas Y., 1938-50 officer, Kansas City Monarchs; booking agent for NAL exhibition games

Baker, Edgar, 1945-46 P, Memphis Red Sox, Cleveland Clippers (USL)

Baker, Eugene Walter (Gene), 1948-50 SS, Kansas City Monarchs

Baker, Henry, 1925-32 OF, Indianapolis ABCs, Dayton Marcos

Baker, Howard (Home Run), 1910 player, Leland Giants

Baker, Lamar, 1950 P, New York Black Yankees

Baker, Norman (Bud), 1937 P, Newark Eagles, New York Black Yankees

Baker, Rufus (Scoop), 1943-50 INF, C, OF, New York Black Yankees

Baker, Sammy, 1950 P, Chicago American Giants

Baker, Tom, 1940 P, Baltimore Elite Giants

Baker, W.B., 1937-38 bus. mgr, Atlanta Black Crackers

Baldwin, Robert , 1925-26 SS, 2B, Indianapolis ABCs, Cleveland Elites, Detroit Stars

Ball, George Walter (Georgia Rabbit), 1902-23 P, Cuban X Giants, Augusta, Georgia, Philadelphia Giants, Leland Giants, Chicago Giants, Chicago American Giants, St.Louis Giants, Mohawk Giants, Brooklyn Royal Giants, Chicago Union Giants, Milwaukee Giants, Lincoln Stars, Lincoln Giants

Ballard, —, 1910 P, Chicago Giants

Ballesteros, —, 1916 P, Long Branch Cubans

Ballestro, Miguel (Pedro Ballester), 1948 SS, New York Cubans

Ballew, —, 1930 P, Louisville White Sox

Bames, —, 1937 C, Birmingham Black Barons

Bankes, James, 1950 P, Baltimore Elite Giants

Bankhead, Daniel Robert (Dan), 1940-47 P, Chicago American Giants, Birmingham Black Barons, Memphis Red Sox

Bankhead, Fred, 1936-48 2B, 3B, 1B, Birmingham Black Barons, Memphis Red Sox

Bankhead, Garnett, 1948 P, Homestead Grays

Bankhead, Joe, 1948 P, Birmingham Black Barons

Bankhead, Samuel Howard (Sam), 1930-50 SS, OF, 2B, P, MGR, Birmingham Black Barons, Nashville Elite Giants, Pittsburgh Crawfords, Toledo Crawfords, Homestead Grays, Louisville Black Caps, Kansas City Monarchs

Banks, —, 1896 P, Cuban X Giants

Banks, —, 1930 2B, Hilldale

Banks, Earl, 1945 2B, Newark Eagles

Banks, Ernest (Ernie), 1950-53 SS, Kansas City Monarchs

Banks, G., 1914-17-P, Lincoln Giants, Philadelphia Giants

Banks, Johnny, 1950 P, Philadelphia Stars

Banks, S., 1915-19 C, Philadelphia Giants, Lincoln Giants

Banton, —, 1914 P, Chicago American Giants

Bapiste, —, 1923-24 OF, Bacharach Giants, Philadelphia Giants

Baranda, —, 1915-16 3B, OF, Long Branch N.J. Cubans, Jersey City Cubans

Barbee, Lamb (Bud, Barboo), 1937-49 P, 1B, MGR, New York Black Yankees, Cincinnati Clowns, Cincinnati-Indianapolis Clowns, Philadelphia Stars, Baltimore Elite Giants, Raleigh Tigers, Indianapolis Clowns

Barbee, Quincy (Bud), 1949 OF, Louisville Buckeyes, Kansas City Monarchs

Barber, (Bull), 1920,1925 2B, Hilldale, Kansas City Monarchs

Barber, John, 1946 OF, Pittsburgh Crawfords

Barber, Sam, 1943-50 P, Cleveland Clippers (USL), Cleveland Buckeyes,

Barbette, —, 1918 1B, Cuban Stars (East)

Barbour, Jess, 1910-1926 OF, 1B, 3B, Philadelphia Giants, Chicago American Giants, Bacharach Giants, Detroit Stars, Pittsburgh Keystones, Harrisburg Giants, St. Louis Giants, Indianapolis ABCs

Barcelo, —, 1921 P, Cuban Stars (East)

Barker, Marvin (Hack), 1935-50 OF, 2B, 3B, MGR, New York Black Yankees, Philadelphia Stars, Newark Dodgers, Bacharach Giants

Barkins, W.C., 1928 officer, Cleveland Stars

Barlow, Tom 1877 player, Mutuals of Washington

Barnes, —, 1906 3B, Philadelphia Giants

Barnes, —, 1925 P, Kansas City Monarchs

Barnes, Ed, 1937-40 P, Kansas City Monarchs, Baltimore Elite Giants

Barnes, Frank, 1947-50 P, Indianapolis ABCs, Kansas City Monarchs

Barnes, Harry (Tack Head), 1949 C, Memphis Red Sox

Barnes, John (Tubby, Fat), 1921-31,36-38 C, Cleveland Tate Stars, Cleveland Browns, Detroit Stars, St. Louis Stars, Cleveland Hornets, Cleveland Tigers, Memphis Red Sox, Toledo Tigers, Indianapolis ABCs, Birmingham Black Barons

Barnes, O., 1932 officer, New York Black Yankees

Barnes, Tobias, 1937 INF, Chicago American Giants

Barnes, V., 1940 OF, Kansas City Monarchs

Barnes, William (Jimmy, Bill), 1941-47 P, Baltimore Elite Giants, Memphis Red Sox, Indianapolis Clowns

Barnhill, David (Dave, Impo), 1939-49 P, New Orleans-St. Louis Stars, New York Cubans, Ethiopian Clowns

Barnhill, Herbert (Herb), 1938-46 C, Jacksonville Red Caps, Kansas City Monarchs, Chicago American Giants, Cleveland Bears

Baro, Bernardo, 1916-30 OF, 1B, P, Cuban Stars (East), Cuban Stars (NNL), New York Cuban Stars, Kansas City Monarchs

Barr, —, 1921-22 3B, SS, Kansas City Monarchs, Cuban Stars

Barrow, Wesley, 1945-47 MGR, New Orleans Black Pelicans, Nashville Cubs, Baltimore Elite Giants

Bartamino, —, 1904 MGR., All Cubans

Bartlett, Howard (Homer, Hop), 1913-25 P, Indianapolis ABCs, Kansas City Monarchs

Barton, Sherman 1896-1911 OF, 3B, Chicago Unions, Columbia Giants, Quaker Giants of New York, Cuban X Giants, St. Paul Gophers, Chicago Giants, Chicago Union Giants, Leland Giants Adrian (MI) Page Fence Giants, Algona (IA) Brownies

Bashum, —, 1932 C, Indianapolis ABCs

Baskin, William 1890-92 2B, Chicago Unions

Bass, Leroy (Red), 1938-40 C, Homestead Grays, Pittsburgh Crawfords

Bassett, Lloyd P. (Pepper), 1934-50 C, New Orleans Crescent Stars, Philadelphia Stars, Chicago American Giants, Pittsburgh Crawfords, Cincinnati Clowns, Cincinnati-Indianapolis Clowns, Birmingham Black Barons, Toledo Crawfords, Homestead Grays

Batson, —, 1908-09 OF, Genuine Cuban Giants, Philadelphia Giants

Battles, Ray, 1944-45 3B, Homestead Grays

Battle, William (Bill), 1947-49 P, Homestead Grays, Memphis Red Sox

Battles, —, 1924 INF, C, Harrisburg Giants

Batum, G.W. 1885 2B, Brooklyn Remsens

Bauchman, Harry, 1915-23 2B, SS, 1B, Chicago American Giants, Chicago Union Giants, Chicago Giants

Bauza, Marcelino, 1930 SS, Cuban Stars (NNL)

Bayliss, Henry J., 1948-50 INF, C, Chicago American Giants, Baltimore Elite Giants, Birmingham Black Barons

Baynard, Frank, 1917-28 OF, Pennsylvania Red Caps of New York, Newark Stars, Hilldale, Bacharach Giants, Havana Red Sox

Baxter, Al 1898 OF, Celeron Acme Colored Giants (Iron and Oil Lg.)

Bea, Bill, 1940 OF, New York Black Yankees, Philadelphia Stars

Beal, G. (Lefty), 1947 P, Newark Eagles

Bebley, —, 1925 P, Birmingham Black Barons

Bebop, Ralph (Spec), 1950 player, Indianapolis Clowns

Beckwith, John, 1917-38 SS, 3B, C, OF, MGR, Chicago Giants, Chicago American Giants, Baltimore Black Sox, Homestead Grays, Harrisburg Giants, Lincoln Giants, Bacharach Giants, New York Black Yankees, Newark Dodgers, Brooklyn Royal Giants, Newark Browns, Hilldale Daisies

Bejerano, Agustin, 1928-29-OF, Cuban Stars (ECL)

Bell, —, 1918 OF, Baltimore Black Sox

Bell, —, 1946 UTIL, Philadelphia Stars

Bell, Charles (Lefty), 1948 P, Homestead Grays

Bell, Clifford (Cliff, Cherry), 1921-31 P, Kansas City Monarchs, Memphis Red Sox, Cleveland Cubs

Bell, Frank 1888-91-OF, Cuban Giants, New York Gorhams(Middle States Lg.), Ansonia Cuban Giants (Connecticut St.Lg.), Philadelphia Giants

Bell, Fred (Lefty), 1922-27 P, OF, St. Louis Stars, Detroit Stars, Birmingham Black Barons, Toledo Tigers, Harrisburg Giants, Washington Potomacs

Bell, Herman, 1943-50 C, Birmingham Black Barons

Bell, James Thomas (Cool Papa), 1922-46 OF, P, St. Louis Stars, Pittsburgh Crawfords, Detroit Wolves, Kansas City Monarchs, Chicago American Giants, Memphis Red Sox, Homestead Grays

Bell, James (Steel Arm), 1933-40 C, Montgomery Grey Sox, Indianapolis Crawfords, Jacksonville Red Caps

Bell, Julian (Jute), 1923-30 P, Birmingham Black Barons, Memphis Red Sox, Detroit Stars

Bell, William, 1902-04 P, OF, Philadelphia Giants

Bell, William Sr. (W.), 1923-48 P, MGR, Kansas City Monarchs, Detroit Wolves, Homestead Grays, Pittsburgh Crawfords, Newark Dodgers, Newark Eagles, New York Black Yankees

Bell, William R. Jr.(Lefty), 1950 P, Kansas City Monarchs, Birmingham Black Barons

Benjamin, Jerry Charles, 1932-48 OF, Memphis Red Sox, Detroit Stars, Birmingham Black Barons, Homestead Grays, Toledo Crawfords, New York Cubans

Bennett, Bradford, 1940-46 OF, St. Louis Stars, New Orleans-St. Louis Stars, New York Black Yankees, Boston Blues

Bennett, Don, 1926,1932-34 2B, Dayton Marcos, Cleveland Cubs, Memphis Red Sox

Bennett, Frank, 1918 MGR, Bacharach Giants

Bennett, Jim, 1945-48 P, Cincinnati-Indianapolis Clowns, Indianapolis Clowns

Bennett, John, 1932 OF, Louisville Black Colonels

Bennett, Sam, 1911-25 OF, C, St. Louis Giants, St. Louis Stars

Bennette, George Clifford (Jew Baby), 1920-36 OF, C, Columbus Buckeyes, Memphis Red Sox, Indianapolis ABCs, Detroit Stars, Chicago Giants, Chicago Union Giants, Pittsburgh Keystones

Benning, —, 1937 2B, Indianapolis Athletics

Benson, —, 1940 P, Memphis Red Sox

Benson, Eugene (Gene, Spider), 1933-48 OF, Brooklyn Royal Giants Bacharach Giants, Pittsburgh Crawfords, Philadelphia Stars, Newark Eagles

Bention, see Gene Benson

Benton, —, 1950 P, Memphis Red Sox

Benvenuti, Julius, 1939 vice-pres, Chicago American Giants

Berkely, —, 1919 C, Hilldale

Berkley, —, 1941 P, New Orleans-St. Louis Stars

Bernal, Blacedo (Pablo), 1941 P, New York Cuban Stars

Bernard, —, 1911-17-C, OF, Pittsburgh Giants, Lincoln Stars, Cuban Giants, Philadelphia Giants, Lincoln Giants

Bernard, Pablo, 1949-50 2B, SS, Louisville Buckeyes, Cleveland Buckeyes

Berry, E., 1930 SS, 2B, Memphis Red Sox, Detroit Stars

Berry, John Paul, 1935-37,1945 P, 1B, Kansas City Monarchs, St. Louis Stars

Berry, R., 1947 P, Kansas City Monarchs

Bert, —, 1906 P, Cuban Giants

Best, R., 1904-06 P, Brooklyn Royal Giants, Cuban Giants

Betts, —, 1938 OF, Kansas City Monarchs

Betts, Russell B., 1950 P, Kansas City Monarchs

Beverie, —, 1939 3B, Baltimore Elite Giants

Beverly, Charles, 1924-36 P, Cleveland Browns, Birmingham Black Barons, Kansas City Monarchs, Cleveland Stars, Pittsburgh Crawfords, New Orleans Crescent Stars, Newark Eagles, Nashville Elite Giants, Philadelphia Stars

Beverly, William (Fireball), 1950 P, Houston Eagles

Bibbs, Rainey, 1933-44 2B, SS, 3B, Detroit Stars, Cincinnati Tigers, Chicago American Giants, Kansas City Monarchs, Indianapolis Crawfords, Chicago American Giants, Cleveland Buckeyes

Billings, —, 1948 C, Homestead Grays

Billings, William, 1921 P, Nashville Elite Giants

Billingsley, John, 1950 C, Memphis Red Sox

Billingsley, Sam, 1950 P, Memphis Red Sox

Binder, James (Jimmy), 1930-37 3B, 2B, Memphis Red Sox, Brooklyn Eagles, Indianapolis ABCs, Detroit Stars, Homestead Grays, Washington Elite Giants, Pittsburgh Crawfords

Binga, Jess E. 1887 player, Washington Capital Citys

Binga, William 1895-1910 3B, C, Page Fence Giants, Columbia Giants, Philadelphia Giants, St. Paul Gophers, Chicago Union Giants, Kansas City (KS) Giants, Adrian (Michigan State Lg.)

Bingham, (Bingo), 1910-21 OF, Chicago Union Giants, Chicago Giants, West Baden (Ind.) Sprudels

Biot, Charles (Charlie), 1939-41 OF, Newark Eagles, New York Black Yankees, Baltimore Elite Giants, Philadelphia Stars

Biran, —, 1916 INF, Chicago American Giants

Bissant, John, 1934-47 OF, P, 2B, Cole's American Giants, Chicago American Giants, Birmingham Black Barons, Chicago Brown Bombers

Bivins, —, 1948 P, Memphis Red Sox

Bix, —, 1921 P, St. Louis Giants

Black, —, 1926 P, Cleveland Elites

Black, Howard, 1928 INF, Brooklyn Cuban Giants

Black, Joseph (Joe), 1943-50 P, Baltimore Elite Giants

Blackburn, —, 1920 P, Kansas City Monarchs

Blackman, Clifford, 1937-41 P, Chicago American Giants, Birmingham Black Barons, Memphis Red Sox, New York Cubans, Indianapolis ABCs, Homestead Grays, New Orleans-St. Louis Stars

Blackman, Henry, 1920-24 3B, Indianapolis ABCs, Baltimore Black Sox

Blackstone, William 1887 player, Cincinnati Browns

Blackwell, Charles, 1915-29 OF, West Baden, Ind. Sprudels, Bowser's ABCs, Jewell's ABCs, St. Louis Giants, St. Louis Stars, Birmingham Black Barons, Indianapolis ABCs, Detroit Stars, Nashville Elite Giants

Blair, Garnet E. Sr, 1945-46 P, Homestead Grays

Blair, Lonnie J., 1949-50 P, 2B, Homestead Grays

Blake, Frank (Big Red), 1932-35 P, Baltimore Black Sox, New York Black Yankees, New York Cubans

Blakely, Bert, 1934 C, Cincinnati Tigers

Blanchard, Chester, 1926-33 SS, Dayton Marcos

Blanco, Carlos, 1938-41 1B, New York Cubans, Cuban Stars

Blanco, Heberto (Harry, Henny), 1941-42 2B, Cuban Stars, New New Cubans

Blatner, —, 1921 1B, OF, Kansas City Monarchs

Blavis, Fox, 1936 3B, Homestead Grays

Bleach, Larry, 1937 2B, Detroit Stars

Bledsoe, —, 1937 player, St. Louis Stars

Blount, John T. (Tenny), 1919-33 officer, Detroit Stars; vice- pres, NNL

Blueitt, Virgil, 1916-18,1937-49 2B, umpire, Chicago Union Giants, NAL

Blukoi, Frank, 1917,1920 2B, All Nations, Kansas City Monarchs

Boada, Lucas, 1921-24 P, OF, Cuban Stars (NNL) Cuban Stars (ECL)

Bobo, J., see James Leonard

Bobo, Willie, 1923-30 1B, All Nations, Kansas City Monarchs, St. Louis Stars, Nashville Elite Giants

Boggs, G., 1923-34 P, OF, Milwaukee Bears, Detroit Stars, Dayton Marcos, Cleveland Tigers

Bolden, Edward (Ed, Chief), 1910-50 officer, Hilldale, Darby Phantoms, Philadelphia Stars; officer, ECL, ANL, NNL

Bolden, L.W. 1885 player, Brooklyn Remsens

Bolden, Otto, 1910,1920 C, P, Leland Giants, Chicago Giants

Bond, Timothy, 1935-40 SS, 3B, Pittsburgh Crawfords, Newark Dodgers, Chicago American Giants

Bonds, —, 1927 C, Cleveland Hornets

Bonner, Robert, 1921-26 1B, C, 2B, Cleveland Tate Stars, St. Louis Stars, Toledo Stars, Cleveland Browns, Cleveland Elites

Booker, Billy 1898 2B, Celeron (NY) Acme Colored Giants (Iron and Oil Lg.)

Booker, Dan, 1909 P, Kansas City (MO) Royal Giants

Booker, James (Pete), 1905-17 C, 1B, Philadelphia Giants, Leland Giants, Lincoln Giants, Chicago American Giants, Chicago Giants, Mohawk Giants, Brooklyn Royal Giants

Boone, Alonzo D. (Buster), 1929-50 P, MGR, Cleveland Cubs, Birmingham Black Barons, Chicago American Giants, Cincinnati Buckeyes, Cleveland Buckeyes, Louisville Buckeyes, Memphis Red Sox, Cleveland Bears

Boone, Charles (Lefty), 1941-46 P, New Orleans-St. Louis Stars, Harrisburg-St. Louis Stars, Pittsburgh Crawfords, Cincinnati Buckeyes, Jacksonville Red Caps, Cleveland Buckeyes, Philadelphia Stars

Boone, Oscar, 1939-42 C, 1B, Indianapolis ABCs, Chicago American Giants, Birmingham Black Barons

Boone, Robert, 1923-28 umpire, NNL

Boone, Steve (Lefty), 1940 P, Memphis Red Sox

Borden, —, 1912 CF, Pittsburgh Giants

Borden, J., 1932-33 SS, UTIL, Birmingham Black Barons

Bordes, Ed, 1940 UTIL, Cleveland Bears

Borges, —, 1928 INF, Cuban Stars (NNL)

Borselo, [Borotto], 1921 P, C, Cuban Stars (East), All Cubans

Bostick, —, 1924 OF, St. Louis Giants

Bostock, Lyman Wesley Sr., 1940-49 1B, OF, Birmingham Black Barons, Chicago American Giants, New York Cubans

Boston, Bob, 1948 3B, Homestead Grays

Boswell, —, 1939 P, Toledo Crawfords

Bough, —, 1923 P, Milwaukee Bears

Bowe, Randolph (Bob, Lefty), 1938-40 P, Kansas City Monarchs, Chicago American Giants

Bowen, —, 1904 OF, Philadelphia Giants

Bowen, —, 1950 P, Indianapolis Clowns

Bowen, (Chuck), 1937-43 OF, Indianapolis Athletics, Chicago Brown Bombers

Bowers, —, 1887 OF, Philadelphia Pythians

Bowers, —, 1926 P, SS, Baltimore Black Sox

Bowers, Julius (Julie), 1947-1950 C, New York Black Yankees

Bowman, Emmett (Scotty), 1905-12 3B, P, C, SS, OF, Philadelphia Giants, Leland Giants, Brooklyn Royal Giants

Boyd, —, 1933 OF, Kansas City Monarchs

Boyd, Benjamin 1885-91 2B, OF, Argyle Hotel, Cuban Giants, York Cuban Giants (Eastern Interstate Lg.), Trenton Cuban Giants (Middle States Lg.), Ansonia Cuban Giants (Connecticut St.Lg.)

Boyd, Fred 1920-26 OF, Chicago American Giants, Cleveland Tate Stars

Boyd, James, 1946 P, Newark Eagles

Boyd, Lincoln, 1949 OF, Louisville Buckeyes

Boyd, Robert R. (Bob, Rope), 1947-50 1B, Memphis Red Sox

Bracken, Herb (Doc), 1940,1946-47 P, St. Louis Stars, Cleveland Buckeyes

Bradford, Charles, 1910-28 P, OF, 1B, coach, Pittsburgh Giants, Lincoln Giants, Philadelphia Giants

Bradford, William (Bill), 1938-43 OF, 2B, Indianapolis ABCs, St. Louis Stars, Memphis Red Sox, Birmingham Black Barons, New York Black Yankees, Chicago American Giants

Bradley, Frank (Red, Dick), 1937-43 P, Cincinnati Tigers, Kansas City Monarchs, Memphis Red Sox

Bradley, Phil, 1905-27 C, 1B, UTIL, Brooklyn Royal Giants, Lincoln Giants, Smart Set, Pittsburgh Colored Stars, Pittsburgh Stars of Buffalo, Mohawk Giants, Cuban Giants, Philadelphia Giants, Pop Watkins Stars

Brady, John 1887 player, Pittsburgh Keystones

Brady (Lefty), 1921 P, Cleveland Tate Stars

Bragana, Ramon, 1928-37,1947 P, OF, Cuban Stars (ECL), Stars of Cuba, New York Cubans, Cleveland Buckeyes

Bragg, Eugene, 1925 C, Chicago American Giants

Bragg, Jesse, 1908-19 3B, SS, 2B, Genuine Cuban Giants, Cuban Giants, Brooklyn Royal Giants, Mohawk Giants, Lincoln Giants, Philadelphia Giants, Pennsylvania Red Caps of NY

Braithwaite, Alonzo (Archie), 1944-48 OF, Newark Eagles, Philadelphia Stars

Bram, —, 1930 P, Hilldale

Brammell, —, 1932 C, Indianapolis ABCs

Branahan, J. Finis (Slim), 1922-27,1931 P, Cleveland Tate Stars, Harrisburg Giants, Detroit Stars, Cleveland Elites, Cleveland Hornets, St. Louis Stars, Toledo Tigers, Lincoln Giants, Indianapolis ABCs

Branham, (Slim), 1917-23 P, Jewell's ABCs, Toledo Tigers, Dayton Marcos, Cleveland Elites

Branham, Luther, 1949-50 INF, Birmingham Black Barons, Chicago American Giants

Brannigan, George, 1926-27 P, Cleveland Elites, Cleveland Hornets

Brantley, Ollie, 1950 P, Memphis Red Sox

Bray, James, 1922-31 C, OF, Chicago Giants, Chicago American Giants, Chicago Columbia Giants

Brazelton, John Clarkson [Clarkson], 1915-16 C, Chicago American Giants, Chicago Giants

Breda, Bill, 1950 OF, Kansas City Monarchs

Breen, W., 1935 OF, Pittsburgh Crawfords

Bremmer, Eugene (Gene), 1932-48 P, New Orleans Crescent Stars, Cincinnati Tigers, Memphis Red Sox, Kansas City Monarchs, Cincinnati Buckeyes, Cleveland Buckeyes

Brewer, Chester Arthur (Chet), 1925-48 P, Kansas City Monarchs, Washington Pilots, New York Cubans, Philadelphia Stars, Chicago American Giants, Cleveland Buckeyes

Brewer, Luther, 1918-21 1B, OF, Chicago Giants

Brewer, Sherwood (Sherry), 1949-50 OF, SS, Indianapolis Clowns

Brewster, Samuel, 1950 OF, Cleveland Buckeyes

Brewton, —, 1936 P, Birmingham Black Barons

Bridgefort, R., 1932 officer, Cleveland Cubs

Briggery, —, 1932 SS, Atlanta Black Crackers

Briggs, —, 1917 P, Indianapolis ABCs

Briggs, Otto, 1914-34 OF, MGR, West Baden Ind., Sprudels, Dayton Marcos, Hilldale, Quaker Giants, Bacharach Giants

Brigham, —, 1924 P, Harrisburg Giants

Bright, John M. 1888-1909 MGR, Cuban Giants

Brisker, William, 1950 gen mgr, Cleveland Buckeyes

Britt, Charles (Charlie), 1927-33 3B, Homestead Grays

Britt, George (Chippy) [Britton], 1920-44 P, C, INF, Dayton Marcos, Columbus Buckeyes, Baltimore Black Sox, Hilldale, Homestead Grays, Newark Dodgers, Columbus Elite Giants, Washington Black Senators, Jacksonville Red Caps, Brooklyn Royal Giants, Chicago American Giants, Detroit Wolves, Cleveland Buckeyes, Harrisburg Giants

Britton, John (Jack), 1940-50 3B, St. Louis Stars, Cincinnati Clowns, Birmingham Black Barons, Indianapolis Clowns

Broadnax, Willie (Broadway), 1928-29 P, OF, Memphis Red Sox

Brodnax, Maceo (Baby Boy), 1932 P, Kansas City Monarchs

Broiles, see Broyles

Brooks, —, 1887 player, Louisville Falls City

Brooks, Alex (Alvin), 1934-40 OF, New York Black Yankees, Brooklyn Royal Giants, Hilldale

Brooks, Ameal (Macon), 1929-47 C, OF, Chicago American Giants, Cleveland Cubs, Cole's American Giants, Columbus Blue Birds, Cincinnati Clowns, New York Black Yankees, Cuban Stars, New York Cubans, Homestead Grays, Newark Eagles

Brooks, Beattie, 1918-21 INF, C, Lincoln Giants, Brooklyn Royal Giants, Philadelphia Giants

Brooks, Charles, 1919-26 2B, P, OF, St. Louis Giants, St. Louis Stars, Homestead Grays, Dayton Marcos, Detroit Stars

Brooks, Chester, 1918-33 OF, Brooklyn Royal Giants

Brooks, E., 1936 P, Kansas City Monarchs

Brooks, Edward (Eddie), 1949-50 2B, Houston Eagles, Memphis Red Sox

Brooks, Gus 1894-95 OF, Page Fence Giants, Chicago Unions

Brooks, Irvin, 1919-27 P, UTIL, Brooklyn Royal Giants

Brooks, James 1887 player, Baltimore Lord Baltimores

Brooks, Jesse, 1934-37 3B, OF, Cleveland Red Sox, Kansas City Monarchs

Brooks, John O., 1942 P, Memphis Red Sox

Brooks, Moxie, 1945 P, Toledo Cubs (USL)

Brooks, Wallace, 1948 P, Baltimore Elite Giants

Broom, —, 1941-42 P, Jacksonville Red Caps

Broome, J.B., 1947 OF, New York Black Yankees

Browcow, —, 1905-06 2B, Brooklyn Royal Giants

Brown, —, 1890 UTIL, Lincoln (Neb) Giants

Brown, —, 1906-12 OF, Brooklyn Royal Giants

Brown, —, 1910 OF, West Baden (Ind.) Sprudels

Brown, A., 1923 C, Birmingham Black Barons

Brown, Arnold, 1921-22 SS, 2B, Hilldale, Bacharach Giants, Harrisburg Giants, Washington Braves

Brown, B., 1918 OF, Washington Red Caps

Brown, Barney, 1931-49 P, Cuban Stars (East & West), Philadelphia Stars, New York Black Yankees

Brown, Ben 1899-1900 P, OF, Genuine Cuban Giants

Brown, Benny, 1932 SS, Newark Stars

Brown, Charles 1886-87 P, Cuban Giants, Pittsburgh Keystones

Brown, Curtis, 1947,1950 1B, New York Black Yankees

Brown, David (Dave, Lefty), 1918-25 P, Chicago American Giants, Lincoln Giants

Brown, E., 1918 3B, Chicago Union Giants

Brown, Earl, 1923-26 P, OF, Lincoln Giants, Baltimore Black Sox, Harrisburg Giants

Brown, Edward, 1920-21 P, Detroit Stars, Indianapolis ABCs, Chicago Giants

Brown, Elias (Country), 1918-33 3B, 2B, OF, New York Bacharach Giants, Bacharach Giants, Brooklyn Royal Giants, Washington Potomacs, Wilmington Potomacs, Hilldale

Brown, Elmore (Scrappy), 1918-32 SS, Washington Red Caps, Lincoln Giants, Baltimore Black Sox, Brooklyn Royal Giants, Hilldale

Brown, F., 1918 2B, Chicago Union Giants

Brown, G., 1925-27 P, St. Louis Stars

Brown, George, 1915-28 OF, MGR, Jewell's ABCs, Indianapolis ABCs, St. Louis Giants, Dayton Marcos, Detroit Stars, Columbus Buckeyes, West Baden (Ind) Sprudels

Brown, George, 1939-42 OF, Ethiopian Clowns, Cincinnati Buckeyes, Cleveland Buckeyes

Brown, H., 1913-15 P, Mohawk Giants, Brooklyn Royal Giants

Brown, James (Jim), 1918-42 C, 1B, MGR, Chicago American Giants, Louisville Black Caps, Cole's American Giants, Minneapolis -

St. Paul Gophers, Chicago Columbia Giants, Cleveland Cubs

Brown, James Phillips, 1939-48 P, of Newark Eagles, Indianapolis Clowns

Brown, Jerome, 1949 INF, Houston Eagles

Brown, Jesse J. (Professor, Lefty), 1938-42 P, New York Black Yankees, Newark Eagles, Baltimore Elite Giants

Brown, Jim, see Willard Brown

Brown, John W., 1942-49 P, St. Louis Giants, Cleveland Buckeyes, Houston Eagles

Brown, L.A., 1926-27 officer, St. Louis Stars

Brown, Larry, 1919-49 C, MGR, Birmingham Black Barons, Pittsburgh Keystones, Indianapolis ABCs, Memphis Red Sox, Detroit Stars, Chicago American Giants, Lincoln Giants, New York Black Yankees, Cole's American Giants, Philadelphia Stars

Brown, Lawrence James (Lefty), 1933-37 P, Memphis Red Sox

Brown, M., 1918 OF, Bacharach Giants

Brown, Maywood, 1921-25 P, Indianapolis ABCs

Brown, Oliver, 1932 bus. mgr, Newark Browns

Brown, Oscar, 1939 C, Indianapolis ABCs, Baltimore Elite Giants

Brown, Ossie, 1934-39 P, OF, Cole's American Giants, Indianapolis Athletics, Indianapolis ABCs, St. Louis Stars

Brown, Ray, 1939-40 C, Brooklyn Royal Giants, Chicago American Giants

Brown, Raymond (Ray), 1930-48 P, OF, Dayton Marcos, Indianapolis ABCs, Detroit Wolves, Homestead Grays

Brown, Robert 1887 player, Boston Resolutes

Brown, Ronnie, 1943 1B, Harrisburg-St. Louis Stars

Brown, Roy, 1928,1931 P, OF, Kansas City Monarchs

Brown, T.J. (Tom), 1939-50 SS, 3B, Memphis Red Sox, Cleveland Buckeyes, Indianapolis Clowns, Harrisburg-St.Louis Stars

Brown, Theo, 1911 3B, Chicago Union Giants

Brown, Tom, 1917-19 P, Brooklyn Royal Giants, Chicago American Giants, Lincoln Giants

Brown, (Tute), 1918 3B, Washington Red Caps

Brown, Ulysses (Buster, Joe), 1937-42 C, OF, Newark Eagles, Jacksonville Red Caps, Cincinnati Buckeyes, Cleveland Buckeyes

Brown, W. (Mike), 1910-15 P, 1B, OF, Mohawk Giants, Philadelphia Giants, Cuban Giants

Brown, Walter S. 1887 MGR, pres, Pittsburgh Keystones, Lg. of Colored Base Ball Clubs

Brown, Willard Jesse, 1934-50 OF, SS, Monroe Monarchs, Kansas City Monarchs

Brown, William, 1906 asst MGR, Leland Giants

Brown, William H. 1887 player, Pittsburgh Keystones

Brown, William M., 1931-32 officer, Montgomery Grey Sox

Browne, (Hap), 1924 P, Cleveland Browns

Broyles, [Broiles], 1925-27 P, St. Louis Stars

Bruce, Clarence, 1947-48 2B, Homestead Grays

Bruce, Lloyd, 1940 P, Chicago American Giants

Bruton, Charles John (Jack) [Burton], 1928-41,1950 P, OF, INF, Cleveland Bears, Philadelphia Stars, New Orleans-St. Louis Stars, Birmingham Black Barons, Cleveland Buckeyes, New York Black Yankees

Bryant, Allen (Lefty), 1937-46 P, All Nations, Kansas City Monarchs, Memphis Red Sox

Bryant, Eddie, 1925-28 2B, Pennsylvania Red Caps of NY Harrisburg Giants

Bryant, Johnnie, 1950 OF, Cleveland Buckeyes

Bryant, R.B., 1937 SS, Memphis Red Sox

Bubbles, —, 1938 P, Atlanta Black Crackers

Buchanan, Chester (Buck), 1936-43 P, Philadelphia Stars, Bacharach Giants

Buchanan, Floyd (Buck), 1914 P, Hilldale

Buck, —, 1923 P, Birmingham Black Barons

Buckner, Harry 1896-1918 P, OF, Chicago Unions, Columbia Giants, Philadelphia Giants, Cuban X Giants, Brooklyn Royal Giants, Quaker Giants, Lincoln Giants, Smart Set, Chicago Giants, Mohawk Giants

Budbill, —, 1950 P, Houston Eagles

Buddles, —, 1925 INF, Chicago American Giants

Buford, (Black Bottom), 1927-34 3B, SS, 2B, Nashville Elite Giants, Cleveland Cubs, Detroit Stars, Louisville Red Caps, Birmingham Black Barons

Bumpus, Earl, 1944-48 P, OF, Kansas City Monarchs, Birmingham Black Barons, Chicago American Giants

Burbage, Knowlington O.(Buddy), 1929-43 OF, Hilldale, Pittsburgh Crawfords, Baltimore Black Sox, Bacharach Giants, Newark Dodgers, Homestead Grays, Washington Black Senators, Brooklyn Royal Giants, Philadelphia Stars

Burch, John Walter, 1931-46 C, 2B, SS, MGR, Bacharach Giants, Baltimore Black Sox, Cleveland Bears, St. Louis Stars, New Orleans-St. Louis Stars, Cincinnati Buckeyes, Cleveland Buckeyes, Chicago American Giants

Burdine, J., 1927-32 P, OF, Birmingham Black Barons, Memphis Red Sox

Burgee, Louis, 1910,1917 P, 2B, Hilldale

Burgess, —, 1942 P, Chicago American Giants

Burgett, —, 1920 OF, St. Louis Giants

Burgin, —, 1913 rf, Havana Red Sox

Burgin, Ralph, 1917-1943 2B, SS, 3B, OF, Hilldale, New York Black Yankees, Philadelphia Stars, Brooklyn Royal Giants Baltimore Black Sox, Pittsburgh Crawfords

Burgos, Jose Antonio, 1949-50 SS, Birmingham Black Barons

Burke, Billy, 1942 3B, Boston Royal Giants

Burke, Charles, 1937 SS, Indianapolis Athletics

Burke, Ernest, 1947-48 P, Baltimore Elite Giants

Burnett, Fred (Tex), 1922-46 C, 1B OF, coach, MGR, Pittsburgh Keystones, Indianapolis ABCs, Lincoln Giants, Harrisburg Giants, Brooklyn Royal Giants, New York Black Yankees, Baltimore Black Sox, Homestead Grays, Brooklyn Eagles, Newark Eagles, Pittsburgh Crawfords, Bacharach Giants, Nashville Cubs

Burnham, Willie (Bee), 1930-34 P, Monroe Monarchs

Burns, Pete 1890-1902 C, OF, Page Fence Giants, Columbia Giants Chicago Unions, Adrian (MI. St. Lg.), Algona (IA) Brownies

Burns, William (Bill, Willie), 1935-44 P, Memphis Red Sox, Cincinnati- Indianapolis Clowns, Newark Dodgers, Philadelphia Stars, Baltimore Elite Giants, Ethiopian Clowns Atlanta Black Crackers

Burrell, George 1884-85 P, C, Baltimore Atlantics

Burrell, —, 1918 OF, Baltimore Black Sox

Burris, Samuel (Speed), 1937-40 P, Memphis Red Sox, Birmingham Black Barons

Burton, see Charles Bruton

Busby, —, 1933 OF, Detroit Stars

Busby, Maurice (Lefty), 1920-21 P, Bacharach Giants, All Cubans, Baltimore Black Sox

Bush, —, 1946 P, Cleveland Buckeyes

Bustamente, Luis, 1905-12 SS, 2B, Cuban Stars, All Cubans

Buster, Herbert, 1943 INF, Chicago American Giants

Butler, —, 1917 OF, Lincoln Giants

Butler, —, 1937 3B, Pittsburgh Crawfords

Butler, Benjamin 1887 manager, New York Gorhams

Butler, (Doc), 1950 C, Memphis Red Sox

Butler, Frank 1894-95 OF, P, Chicago Unions

Butler, J. 1884 Philadelphia Mutual B.B.C.

Butler, (Sol), 1925 P, Kansas City Monarchs

Butts, Harry, 1949-50 P, Indianapolis Clowns

Butts, Thomas (Tommy, Pee Wee), 1938-50 SS, Atlanta Black Crackers, Indianapolis ABCs, Baltimore Elite Giants

Byas, Richard Thomas (Subby), 1931-42 C, 1B, OF, Kansas City Monarchs, Cole's American Giants, Chicago American Giants, Newark Dodgers, Memphis Red Sox

Byatt, see Charles Biot

Byers, Henry [Byus] 1887 2B, Pittsburgh Keystones

Byrd, —, 1921 1B, Chicago Giants

Byrd, James F., 1927-30 officer, Hilldale

Byrd, Prentice, 1934 officer, Cleveland Red Sox

Byrd, William (Bill), 1932-50 P, OF, Columbus Turfs, Columbus Blue Birds, Columbus Elite Giants, Washington Elite Giants, Baltimore Elite Giants, Nashville Elite Giants, Cleveland Red Sox

Caballero, Luis Perez [Luis Perez], 1948-50 3B, Indianapolis Clowns, New York Cubans

Cabrera, —, 1905 1B, All Cubans

Cabrera, Clemente (Sungo) [Carrera], 1938-41 2B, OF, 3B, New York Cubans, Cuban Stars

Cabrera, Lorenzo (Chiquitin), 1947-50 1B, New York Cubans

Cabrera, Luis Raul, 1948 P, Indianapolis Clowns

Cabrera, Rafael Villa, 1944-50 P, OF, Indianapolis Clowns, Birmingham Black Barons

Cade, Joe, 1929 P, OF, Bacharach Giants

Caffie, Joseph Clifford (Joe), 1950 OF, Cleveland Buckeyes

Cain, Marion (Sugar), 1937-49 P, Pittsburgh Crawfords, Brooklyn Royal Giants, Indianapolis Clowns, New York Black Yankees

Calderin, —, 1917-18, 1924 P, OF, Havana Stars, Cuban Stars (East)

Calderon, Benito, 1926-28 C, Cuban Stars (NNL), Homestead Grays

Caldwell, —, 1933 OF, Birmingham Black Barons

Caldwell, Frank, 1947 P, Cleveland Buckeyes

Calhan, Rowland, 1938 P, Washington Black Senators

Calhoun, Jim, 1923 2B, Toledo Tigers

Calhoun, Walter (Lefty), 1931-46 P, Birmingham Black Barons, Montgomery Grey Sox, Washington Black Senators, Pittsburgh Crawfords, Indianapolis ABCs, St. Louis Stars, New Orleans- St. Louis Stars, New York Black Yankees, Harrisburg-St. Louis Stars, Cleveland Buckeyes, Philadelphia Stars, Memphis Red Sox, Indianapolis Athletics, Louisville Black Colonels

Calhoun, Wesley, 1950 INF, OF, Cleveland Buckeyes

Call, F. 1884-85 INF, Baltimore Atlantics

Callis, J. Joseph 1887 manager, Baltimore Lord Baltimore

Calvo, Jacinto (Jack), 1913-15 OF, Long Branch, N.J. Cubans

Calvo, T., 1915-16 OF, Long Branch, N.J. Cubans, Jersey City Cubans

Cam, —, 1891 OF, Ansonia Cuban Giants (Connecticut St.Lg.)

Cambria, Joe, 1933 owner, officer, Baltimore Black Sox

Campanella, Roy, 1937-45 C, Baltimore Elite Giants

Campbell, Andrew, 1903-06 C, Leland Giants, Chicago Union Giants

Campbell, David (Dave), 1938-41 2B, New York Black Yankees, Philadelphia Stars

Campbell, Grant 1887-93 2B, OF, Chicago Unions

Campbell, Hunter, 1938-42 MGR, Officer, Ethiopian Clowns, Cincinnati Clowns

Campbell, Joe 1887-93 P, Chicago Unions

Campbell, Joe, 1922 OF, 3B, Pittsburgh Keystones

Campbell, Robert (Buddy), 1932 C, Cole's American Giants

Campbell, William (Zip), 1923-29 P, Washington Potomacs, Philadelphia Giants, Hilldale, Lincoln Giants, Richmond Giants

Campini, Joe, 1948 C, Baltimore Elite Giants

Campos, Manuel, 1905 MGR, Cuban Stars of Santiago

Campos, Tatica, 1915-23 P, OF, 1B, 2B, 3B, Cuban Stars, Cuban Stars (East), Cuban Stars (NNL)

Canada, James (Cat), 1936-45 1B, Birmingham Black Barons, Memphis Red Sox, Baltimore Elite Giants, Jacksonville Red Caps, Atlanta Black Crackers

Canizares, Avelino, 1945 SS, Cleveland Buckeyes

Cannady, Walter (Rev), 1921-45 2B, SS, OF, 3B, 1B, P, MGR, Columbus Buckeyes, Dayton Marcos, Cleveland Tate Stars, Homestead Grays, Harrisburg Giants, Hilldale, Lincoln Giants, Darby Daisies, Pittsburgh Crawfords, New York Black Yankees, Philadelphia Stars,

Brooklyn Royal Giants, Chicago American Giants, Cincinnati-Indianapolis Clowns, New York Cubans

Cannon, Richard (Speed Ball), 1928-34   P, St. Louis Stars, Nashville Elite Giants, Birmingham Black Barons, Louisville Red Caps, Cleveland Cubs, Louisville Blacks Caps

Caper, —, 1912   SS, Pittsburgh Giants

Capers, (Lefty), 1930-31   P, Louisville White Sox

Carabello, Esterio, 1939   OF, Cuban Stars

Card, Al 1887   player, Pittsburgh Keystones

Cardenas, P., 1924-27   C, OF, Cuban Stars (ECL), Cuban Stars (NNL)

Carey, [Carry], 1916-1921   3B, 2B, St. Louis Giants, Dayton Marcos

Carlisle, Matthew (Lick), 1931-46   2B, SS, Birmingham Black Barons, Montgomery Grey Sox, Memphis Red Sox, Homestead Grays, New Orleans Crescent Stars

Carlson, —, 1916   C, Chicago American Giants

Carlyle, Sylvester Junius, 1945   INF, Kansas City Monarchs

Carmichael, Luther, 1948   sec'y, NSL

Carpenter, —, 1923,1927   OF, Memphis Red Sox, Nashville Elite Giants

Carpenter, Clay, 1925-26   P, 3B, Baltimore Black Sox, Philadelphia Giants

Carr, —, 1890   OF, Lincoln (Neb) Giants

Carr, George Henry (Tank), 1912-1934   1B, 3B, OF, C, Los Angeles White Sox, Kansas City Monarchs, Hilldale, Bacharach Giants, Philadelphia Stars, Lincoln Giants

Carr, Wayne, 1920-28   P, St. Louis Giants, Indianapolis ABCs, Baltimore Black Sox, Washington Potomacs, Bacharach Giants, Wilmington Potomacs, Newark Stars, Brooklyn Royal Giants, Lincoln Giants

Carrera, *see Sungo Cabrera*

Carroll, Hal 1887   player, Cincinnati Browns

Carroll, (Sonny), 1950   P, Baltimore Elite Giants

Cary, —, 1927   P, Brooklyn Royal Giants

Carry, *see Carey*

Carswell, Frank, 1944-46   P, Cleveland Buckeyes

Carter, —, 1897-99   P, Cuban Giants

Carter, —, 1918   2B, Chicago Giants

Carter, Alfred, 1935   40-OF, UTIL, Pittsburgh Crawfords, New York Cuban Stars

Carter, Bill, 1948   P, Newark Eagles

Carter, (Bo), 1931   pres, Chattanooga Black Lookouts

Carter, Charles (Kid), 1902-13   P, Philadelphia Giants, Wilmington Giants, Brooklyn Royal Giants

Carter, Charles, 1943   P, Baltimore Elite Giants, Homestead Grays

Carter, Clifford, 1923-34   P, Baltimore Black Sox, Bacharach Giants, Harrisburg Giants, Philadelphia Tigers, Hilldale, Philadelphia Stars

Carter, Dr. A.B., 1933   vice-pres, NSL

Carter, Elmer (Willie), 1930-32   C, SS, 1B, Birmingham Black Barons

Carter, Ernest C. (Spoon, Whip), 1932-49   P, MGR, Pittsburgh Crawfords, Memphis Red Sox, Cleveland Red Sox, Toledo Crawfords, Indianapolis Crawfords, Newark Eagles, Philadelphia Stars, Homestead Grays, Birmingham Black Barons, Louisville Black Caps, Akron Tyrites, Cleveland Giants, Montgomery Dodgers

Carter, Frank, 1917   P, St. Louis Giants

Carter, Ike 1884   2B, St. Louis Black Stockings

Carter, Jimmy, 1938-39   P, Philadelphia Stars

Carter, Kenneth, 1950   C, Cleveland Buckeyes

Carter, Marlin Theodore (Mel, Pee Wee), 1933-50   3B, 2B, Cincinnati Tigers, Atlanta Black Crackers, Memphis Red Sox, Chicago American Giants

Carter, Paul (Nick), 1924-36   P, Hilldale, Darby Daisies, Philadelphia Stars, New York Black Yankees

Carter, Robert, 1947   P, Homestead Grays

Carter, William, 1920-22   C, Detroit Stars, Kansas City Monarchs

Carter, William, 1937,1943   3B, St. Louis Stars, Harrisburg- St. Louis Stars

Cartmill, Alfred Jr., 1949   2B, Kansas City Monarchs

Casey, Joe, 1920   P, St. Louis Giants

Casey, William (Mickey), 1930-43   C, MGR, Baltimore Black Sox, Bacharach Giants,

Philadelphia Stars, Washington Black Senators, New York Cubans, Cuban Stars, Baltimore Grays, New York Black Yankees, Hilldale

Cash, William Walker (Bill, Ready), 1943-50   C, OF, 3B, Philadelphia Stars

Cason, John, 1917-32   C, OF, 2B, SS, Brooklyn Royal Giants, Norfolk Stars, Hilldale, Lincoln Giants, Bacharach Giants, Baltimore Black Sox, Birmingham Black Barons, Havana Red Sox

Castillo, Julian, 1911-12   1B, All Cubans, Cuban Stars

Castone, William 1889-92   P, OF, Lincoln-Kearney (Nebraska State Lg.), Lincoln (Neb) Giants, Aspen (Colorado St.Lg.)

Castro, Antonio, 1929   C, Cuban Stars (East)

Cates, Joe (Rabbit), 1931-34   SS, Louisville White Sox, Louisville Red Caps

Cathey, Willis (Jim, Bill), 1948-50   P, Indianapolis Clowns

Cato, Harry 1887-96   2B, P, OF, SS, Cuban X Giants, Cuban Giants New York Gorhams (Middle States Lg.), Philadelphia Giants, Trenton (NJ) Cuban Giants

Caulfield, Fred, 1926   MGR, New Orleans Ads

Celada, —, 1928-29   SS, Cuban Stars (NNL)

Cepeda, Pedro Anibal (Perucho), 1941   OF, New York Cuban Stars

Cephus, Goldie, 1925-31,1938   OF, SS, Philadelphia Giants, Bacharach Giants, Birmingham Black Barons

Chacon, Pelayo, 1910-31   SS, MGR, Stars of Cuba, Cuban Stars, Havana Stars, Cuban Stars (ECL), Cuban Stars (NNL)

Chamberlain, 1889   1B, New York Gorhams (Middle States Lg.)

Chambers, Arthur (Rube), 1925-27   P, Lincoln Giants, Wilmington Potomacs

Chapman, Edward, 1927,1931   P, Detroit Stars, Chicago Columbia Giants

Chapman, J.W. 1887   player, Cincinnati Browns

Chapman, John 1887   player, Cincinnati Browns

Chapman, Roy Lee (Ray), 1949-50   P, New York Black Yankees

Charleston, —, 1942   C, Cincinnati Buckeyes

Charleston, Benny, 1930   OF, Homestead Grays

Charleston, Oscar Mckinley, 1915-50   OF, 1B, MGR, Bowser's ABCs, Indianapolis ABCs, Lincoln Stars, Chicago American Giants, St. Louis Giants, Harrisburg Giants, Hilldale, Homestead Grays, Pittsburgh Crawfords, Toledo Crawfords, Indianapolis Crawfords, Philadelphia Stars, Brooklyn Brown Dodgers,

Charleston, Porter, 1927-35   P, Hilldale, Darby Daisies, Philadelphia Stars

Charleston, (Red), 1921-32   C, Nashville Elite Giants, Birmingham Black Barons, Memphis Red Sox, Montgomery Grey Sox

Charter, William M.(Baby, Bill), 1933-34,1942-46   OF, 1B, C, 3B, Louisville Red Caps, Chicago American Giants, Detroit Black Sox

Chase, —, 1920,1923   OF, P, Detroit Stars, Chicago Giants, Toledo Tigers

Chatman, —, 1922   P, Cleveland Tate Stars

Chatman, Edgar, 1944-45   P, Memphis Red Sox

Chavous, —, 1895-96   P, OF, Adrian (MI) Page Fence Giants

Cheatham, —, 1930-34   P, Baltimore Black Sox, Pittsburgh Crawfords, Homestead Grays

Cherry, Hugh, 1949   officer, Houston Eagles

Chester, —, 1926   OF, Harrisburg Giants

Chestnut, Henry (Joe), 1950   P, Indianapolis Clowns, Philadelphia Stars

Childs, Andy, 1936-45   2B, P, Indianapolis Athletics, Memphis Red Sox, St. Louis Stars, Indianapolis ABCs

Chirban, Louis, 1950   P, Chicago American Giants

Chism, Elijah (Eli, Little Chis), 1937,1946-47   OF, St. Louis Stars, Birmingham Black Barons, Cleveland Buckeyes

Chretian, Ernest, 1950   OF, INF, Kansas City Monarchs, Philadelphia Stars

Christian, —, 1915   OF, Indianapolis ABCs

Christopher, Ted, 1949   C, New York Black Yankees

Christopher, Thadist (Thad), 1935-45   OF, 1B,

Newark Eagles, Pittsburgh Crawfords, New York Black Yankees, Cincinnati Buckeyes, Cincinnati Clowns, Cleveland Buckeyes, Toledo Crawfords, Homestead Grays, Nashville Elite Giants, Cincinnati Buckeyes, Ethiopian Clowns, Jacksonville Red Caps

Cisco, J. 1884   player, Philadelphia Mutual B.B.C.

Clarizio, Louis, 1950   OF, Chicago American Giants

Clark, —, 1887   player, Louisville Falls City

Clark, —, 1908   2B, Brooklyn Colored Giants

Clark, —, 1919   OF, Brooklyn Royal Giants

Clark, —, 1931   OF, Louisville White Sox

Clark, —, 1931   P, Kansas City Monarchs

Clark, Albert, 1919-26   P, Dayton Marcos, Cleveland Tate Stars, Pittsburgh Keystones, Indianapolis ABCs, Cleveland Browns, Memphis Red Sox

Clark, Chifian Cleveland, 1945-50   OF, New York Cubans

Clark, Dell, 1914-23   SS, Brooklyn Royal Giants, Indianapolis ABCs, Lincoln Giants, Washington Potomacs, St. Louis Giants

Clark, Harry (Lefty), 1922-25   P, Brooklyn Royal Giants, Hilldale Bacharach Giants

Clark, John L., 1932-46   bus. mgr, Pittsburgh Crawfords; public relations man, Homestead Grays; sec'y, NNL

Clark, Maceo (Marty), 1923-25   1B, P, Washington Potomacs Wilmington Potamacs, Indianapolis ABCs, Bacharach Giants

Clark, Milton J., Jr., 1937   sec'y, Chicago American Giants

Clark, Morten (Specs), 1910-23   SS, 3B, OF, Indianapolis ABCs, Baltimore Black Sox, West Baden (Ind.) Sprudels

Clark, Roy, 1934-35   P, Newark Dodgers

Clark, William (Eggie, Biff), 1928   OF, Memphis Red Sox

Clarke, (Allie), 1938   1B, 2B, C, OF, Washington Black Senators

Clarke, Robert (Kike, Eggie), 1922-48   C, MGR, Richmond Giants, Baltimore Black Sox, New York Black Yankees, Philadelphia Stars, Baltimore Elite Giants

Clarke, Vibert Ernesto (Webbo), 1946-50   P, Cleveland Buckeyes, Louisville Buckeyes, Memphis Red Sox

Clarkson, *see John Brazelton*

Clarkson, James Buster (Bus), 1937-50   SS, OF, 2B, Pittsburgh Crawfords, Toledo Crawfords, Indianapolis Crawfords, Newark Eagles, Philadelphia Stars, Baltimore Elite Giants

Clay, Albert (Alton), 1949-50   OF, New York Black Yankees

Clay, William (Lefty), 1932   P, Kansas City Monarchs

Clayton, Leroy Watkins (Zack), 1934-44   1B, C, Bacharach Giants, Cole's American Giants, Chicago American Giants, New York Black Yankees, Chicago Brown Bombers, Brooklyn Eagles

Claxton, James E., 1916,1932   P, Oakland Oaks (PCL), Cuban Stars

Cleage, Pete, 1936   umpire, NNL

Cleage, Ralph, 1924   OF, St. Louis Stars

Cleveland, Howard (Duke) [Duke], 1938-46   OF, Jacksonville Red Caps, Cleveland Bears, Cincinnati Buckeyes, Cleveland Buckeyes, Indianapolis Clowns

Clifford, Luther, 1948-50   C, OF, Homestead Grays

Clifton, Nat (Sweetwater), 1949   1B, Chicago American Giants

Clinton, —, 1917   3B, Bacharach Giants

Close, Herman 1887   manager, Philadelphia Pythians

Cobb, L.S.N., 1920-34   officer, St. Louis Giants, Birmingham Black Barons, Memphis Red Sox, Cleveland Elites; sec'y, NSL

Cobb, W., 1915-20,1928   C, OF, St. Louis Giants, Lincoln Giants, Jewell's ABCs, Indianapolis ABCs, St. Louis Stars

Cockerell, Phi, *see Cockrell*

Cockerham, Jimmy, 1939   1B, Indianapolis ABCs

Cockrell, Philip (Phil, Fish), 1913-46   P, OF, Havana Red Sox, Lincoln Giants, Hilldale, Darby Daisies, Bacharach Giants, Philadelphia Stars; umpire, NNL

Coffey, Marshall 1889   2B, Chicago Unions

Coffie, Cliffor, see Joe Caffie
Cohen, James C.(Jim, Fireball), 1948-50   P, Indianapolis Clowns
Coimbre, Francisco (Pancho, Al), 1940-44   OF, 2B, Cuban Stars, New York Cubans
Colas, Carlos (Charlie), 1941,1949-50   C, Cuban Stars, Memphis Red Sox
Colas, Jose Luis, 1947-50   OF, MGR, Memphis Red Sox
Cole, see Coley
Cole, Cecil, 1946   P, Newark Eagles
Cole, Ralph (Punjab, Askari), 1939-46   OF, Jacksonville Red Caps, Cleveland Bears, Cincinnati Clowns
Cole, Robert A., 1932-35   officer, Chicago American Giants; tres, NNL; vice-pres, NSL
Cole, William 1896-99   C, P, Cuban Giants
Coleman, Benny, 1950   P, Chicago American Giants
Coleman, Clarence, 1913-21,1926   P, C, OF, 1B, 2B, Chicago Giants, Chicago Union Giants, Indianapolis ABCs, Cleveland Tate Stars, St. Louis Giants, Columbus Buckeyes, Dayton Marcos, Lincoln Giants, All Nations, Bowser's ABCs
Coleman, Gilbert, 1928,1932   INF, OF, Brooklyn Cuban Giants, Bacharach Giants
Coleman, John 1885   OF, Brooklyn Remsens
Coleman, John, 1950   P, Baltimore Elite Giants
Coleman, Melvin, 1937-39   SS, C, Birmingham Black Barons, Ethiopian Clowns
Coley, —, 1923-24   P, Toledo Tigers, Kansas City Monarchs, Detroit Stars
Coley, —, 1931   OF, Nashville Elite Giants
Collier, —, 1928   C, Bacharach Giants
Colliers, Leonard, 1950   P, Cleveland Buckeyes
Collins, —, 1910-18   C, 1B, New York Black Sox, Brooklyn Royal Giants, Pennsylvania Red Caps of New York, Lincoln Giants, Pittsburgh Giants, Philadelphia Giants, Pittsburgh Stars of Buffalo
Collins, —, 1928   P, Baltimore Black Sox
Collins, —, 1936   P, New York Black Yankees
Collins, Eugene (Gene), 1947-50   P, OF, Kansas City Monarchs
Collins, George, 1921-33   OF, 2B, P, SS, New Orleans Crescent Stars, Milwaukee Bears, Toledo Tigers, Indianapolis ABCs, Nashville Elite Giants, New Orleans Caulfield Ads
Collins, Nat 1888-89   P, New York Gorhams (Middle States Lg.), Philadelphia Giants
Collins, Walter, 1947-48   P, Chicago American Giants, Memphis Red Sox
Collins, Willie, 1933   OF, Nashville Elite Giants
Collins, Willie P. (James), 1950   P, Birmingham Black Barons
Colzie, Jim, 1946-47   P, Cincinnati-Indianapolis Clowns, Indianapolis Clowns
Combs, A. Clark (Jack), 1922-26   P, Detroit Stars
Condon, Lafayette 1887   player, Louisville Falls Citys
Connors, John W., 1904-1922   owner, Officer, Brooklyn Royal Giants, Bacharach Giants
Cook, Howard (Johnny), 1937   P, Indianapolis Athletics
Cook, Walter 1886-88   officer, Cuban Giants
Cooke, James (Jay), 1932-33   P, Baltimore Black Sox, Bacharach Giants
Cooley, Walter, 1931   C, 3B, Birmingham Black Barons
Cooper, Alex, 1928   OF, Philadelphia Tigers, Harrisburg Giants
Cooper, Alfred (Army), 1923-32   P, Kansas City Monarchs, Cleveland Stars
Cooper, Andy (Lefty), 1920-41   P, MGR, Detroit Stars, Chicago American Giants, St. Louis Stars, Kansas City Monarchs
Cooper, Anthony (Ant), 1928-35,1941   SS, 2B, OF, Birmingham Black Barons, Cleveland Stars, Baltimore Black Sox, Cleveland Red Sox, Louisville Red Sox, Pittsburgh Crawfords, Newark Dodgers, Homestead Grays, New York Black Yankees
Cooper, C. 1884   player, Philadelphia Mutual B.B.C.
Cooper, (Chief), 1928   umpire, NNL
Cooper, Daltie, 1921-40   P, Nashville Elite Giants, Indianapolis ABCs, Harrisburg Giants, Lincoln Giants, Hilldale, Bacharach Giants,

Homestead Grays, Baltimore Black Sox, Newark Eagles, Washington Potomacs
Cooper, E., 1916-1924   1B, OF, Lincoln Stars, Cleveland Tate Stars, St. Louis Giants
Cooper, James, 1938,1946-47   P, Atlanta Black Crackers, New York Black Yankees, Newark Eagles
Cooper, Ray, 1928-29   P, Hilldale
Cooper, Sam, 1926-34   P, Harrisburg Giants, Baltimore Black Sox, Bacharach Giants, Homestead Grays
Cooper, Thomas (Tom), 1947-50   C, OF, 1B, Kansas City Monarchs
Cooper, W.T. (Bill, Thomas), 1938-46   C, Atlanta Black Crackers, Philadelphia Stars, New York Black Yankees
Copeland, L., 1935   INF, Brooklyn Eagles
Corbett, Charles, 1921-28   P, Pittsburgh Keystones, Indianapolis ABCs, Harrisburg Giants, Hilldale
Corcoran, Tom, 1942   P, Homestead Grays
Cordova, (Pete), 1921-23   3B, SS, Kansas City Monarchs, Cleveland Tate Stars, Toledo Tigers
Cornelius, William McKinley (Willie, Sug), 1928-46   P, Nashville Elite Giants, Memphis Red Sox, Chicago American Giants, Cole's American Giants, Birmingham Black Barons, Cleveland Elites
Cornett, Harry, 1913   C, Indianapolis ABCs
Correa, Marcelino (Cho-Cho Cuco), 1926-36   SS, Cuban Stars (NNL), Cuban Stars (East), New York Cubans
Cortez, Aurelio, 1928-31   C, Cuban Stars (NNL), Cuban Stars (East)
Cosa, —, 1932   OF, Memphis Red Sox
Costello, —, 1911   1B, All Cubans
Cottman, Darby 1887-93   3B, Chicago Unions
Cotton, see Robert A. Williams
Cotton, James, 1945   officer, Chattanooga Choo Choos
Cottrell, —, 1923   C, Hilldale
Cowan, Eddie, 1919   SS, Cleveland Tate Stars
Cowan, Johnnie, 1934-50   3B, 2B, Birmingham Black Barons, Cleveland Buckeyes, Memphis Red Sox, Cincinnati Buckeyes
Cowans, Russ, 1942   sec'y, Negro Baseball Lg. of America
Cox, Comer Lane (Hannibal), 1930-31-OF, Nashville Elite Giants, Cleveland Cubs
Cox, M.D. Alphonse, 1938-43   P, Memphis Red Sox, Jacksonville Red Caps, Cleveland Bears
Cox, Roosevelt, 1937-43   3B, 2B, SS, Detroit Stars, Kansas City Monarchs, New York Cubans, Cuban Stars, Ethiopian Clowns
Cox, Tom (Lefty), 1930-32   P, Lincoln Giants, Cleveland Cubs
Cozart, Haywood (Harry, Big Train), 1939-43   P, Newark Eagles
Craig, Charles, 1926-28   P, Lincoln Giants, Brooklyn Cuban Giants, Harrisburg Giants, Homestead Grays
Craig, Dick, 1940   1B, Indianapolis Crawfords
Craig, Homer, 1935   P, Newark Stars
Craig, John, 1935-46   umpire, NNL
Craig, Joseph (Joe), 1940,1946   1B, OF, Indianapolis Crawfords, Philadelphia Stars
Crain, A.C. 1887   player, Baltimore Lord Baltimores
Crawford, John, 1943   umpire, NNL
Crawford, Sam, 1910-38   P, MGR, coach, New York Black Sox, Chicago Giants, Chicago American Giants, Chicago Union Giants, Detroit Stars, Kansas City Monarchs, Brooklyn Royal Giants, Birmingham Black Barons, Chicago Columbia Giants, Cole's American Giants, Indianapolis Athletics, St. Louis Stars, Cleveland Tate Stars
Crawford, Willie Walker, 1934   OF, Birmingham Black Barons
Creacy, A.D. (Dewey), 1924-40   3B, Kansas City Monarchs, St. Louis Stars, Detroit Wolves, Washington Pilots, Columbus Blue Birds, Cleveland Giants, Philadelphia Stars, Brooklyn Royal Giants
Creek, Willie, 1924,1930-32   C, SS, Washington Potomacs, Brooklyn Royal Giants
Crelin, Wilbur C., 1926   officer, Newark Stars
Crespo, Alejandro Rogelio, 1918-33   2B, 3B, Cuban Stars (East), Cuban Stars of Havana
Crespo, Alejandro (Alex, Home Run), 1940-46   OF, Cuban Stars, New York Cubans

Crockett, Frank, 1916-23   OF, Bacharach Giants, Brooklyn Royal Giants, Norfolk Stars
Cromartie, Leroy, 1945   2B, Cincinnati-Indianapolis Clowns
Cross, Bennie 1887   OF, Boston Resolutes
Cross, Norman, 1932-36   P, Cole's American Giants
Crowder, —, 1920   P, Lincoln Stars
Crowe, George, 1947-49-1B, INF, New York Cubans, New York Black Yankees
Croxton, —, 1908-09   P, C, Cuban Giants
Crudup, Zeke, 1925-26   P, Philadelphia Giants
Crue, Martin (Matty), 1942-48   P, New York Cubans, Homestead Grays
Crumbie, Ralph, 1946   C, Pittsburgh Crawfords
Crumbley, Alex, 1937-38   OF, New York Black Yankees, Atlanta Black Crackers, Pittsburgh Crawfords, Washington Black Senators
Crump, James, 1920-38   2B, Norfolk Giants, Hilldale, Philadelphia Giants, Norfolk Stars; umpire, NNL
Crump, Willis, 1916-23   OF, 2B, Bacharach Giants
Crutchfield, John William (Jimmie), 1930-45   OF, Birmingham Black Barons, Indianapolis ABCs, Pittsburgh Crawfords, Newark Eagles, Toledo Crawfords, Indianapolis Crawfords, Chicago American Giants, Cleveland Buckeyes
Cruz, —, 1930   P, Cuban Stars
Cuella, Jose Luis, 1945   OF, Pittsburgh Crawfords
Cuerira, Basilo, 1921-22   P, OF, All Cubans, Cuban Stars (NNL)
Culver, [Culcra], 1916-22   3B, SS, OF, Pittsburgh Stars of Buffalo Penn Red Caps of NY, Cuban Stars (NNL)
Cumming, Hugh S. 1887   player, Baltimore Lord Baltimores
Cummings, —, 1932   C, Louisville Black Caps
Cummings, Napoleon (Chance), 1916-29   1B, 2B, Bacharach Giants, Hilldale, Norfolk Stars, Madison Stars
Cunningham, —, 1917-20   SS, St. Louis Giants, Dayton Marcos
Cunningham, —, 1926-27   2B, Pennsylvania Red Caps of NY
Cunningham, —, 1934   OF, Baltimore Black Sox
Cunningham, H. (Rounder), 1918-31   SS, Montgomery Grey Sox
Cunningham, Harry (Baby), 1930-37   P, Memphis Red Sox, Birmingham Black Barons
Cunningham, Larry, 1950   P, Memphis Red Sox, Houston Eagles
Cunningham, Marion (Daddy), 1921-26   1B, MGR, Memphis Red Sox, Montgomery Grey Sox
Cunningham, Robert (Slim), 1950   P, Cleveland Buckeyes
Curley, Earl C., 1925   OF, Memphis Red Sox
Currie, Reuben (Rube, Black Snake), 1919-32   P, Chicago Unions, Kansas City Monarchs, Hilldale, Chicago American Giants, Detroit Stars, Cleveland Red Sox, Baltimore Black Sox
Curry, Homer (Goose), 1928-50   OF, P, MGR, Memphis Red Sox, Washington Elite Giants, New York Black Yankees, Newark Eagles, Baltimore Elite Giants, Philadelphia Stars, Nashville Elite Giants, Cleveland Tigers, Indianapolis Athletics
Curry, Oscar J. 1887   P, Cuban Giants
Curtis, see Curtiss Ricks
Curtis, —, 1932   C, Louisville Black Caps
Curtis, Harry 1898   MGR, Celeron Acme Colored Giants (Iron and Oil Lg.)
Cyrus, Herb, see Herb Souell
Dabney, Milton 1885-96   OF, P, Argyle Hotel, Cuban X Giants, Cuban Giants
Dailey, James, 1948   P, Baltimore Elite Giants
Dallard, William (Eggie), 1920-33   1B, OF, C, 2B, Wilmington Potomacs, Baltimore Black Sox, Bacharach Giants, Hilldale, Quaker Giants, Darby Daisies, Philadelphia Stars, Washington Potomacs, Madison Stars, Pennsylvania Giants
Dallas, Porter (Big Boy), 1929-32   3B, Birmingham Black Barons, Monroe Monarchs
Dalton, Rossie, 1940   UTIL, Chicago American Giants, Birmingham Black Barons
Dandridge, John, 1949   P, Houston Eagles

Dandridge, (Ping) [Dandy], 1917-20 INF, P, Havana Red Sox, Lincoln Giants, St.Louis Giants

Dandridge, Raymond Emmett (Hooks, Squatty), 1933-49 3B, 2B, SS, Detroit Stars, Nashville Elite Giants, Newark Dodgers, Newark Eagles, New York Cubans

Dandridge, Troy Rasmussen (Dan), 1926-29 3B, SS, Chicago Giants, Dayton Marcos

Daniels, Eddie, 1946-47 P, New York Cubans

Daniels, Fred, 1919-28 P, St. Louis Giants, Hilldale, Birmingham Black Barons, Lincoln Giants, Nashville Elite Giants

Daniels, Hammond, 1924-26 officer, Bacharach Giants

Daniels, James George (Jim, Schoolboy), 1943 P, Birmingham Black Barons

Daniels, Leon (Pepper), 1921-35 C, 1B, Detroit Stars, Harrisburg Giants, Cuban Stars, Brooklyn Eagles, Bacharach Giants, Chicago Columbia Giants

Darden, Clarence, 1938 3B, Atlanta Black Crackers

Darden, Floyd, 1950 2B, OF, Baltimore Elite Giants

Davenport, Lloyd (Bear Man, Ducky), 1934-49 OF, MGR, Monroe Monarchs, Philadelphia Stars, Cincinnati Tigers, Memphis Red Sox, Birmingham Black Barons, Chicago American Giants, Cleveland Buckeyes, Pittsburgh Crawfords, Louisville Buckeyes, Jacksonville Red Caps, New Orleans Crescent Stars

Davidson, Charles (Specks), 1939-40,1946-49 P, New York Black Yankees, Brooklyn Royal Giants, Baltimore Elite Giants, Memphis Red Sox

Davis, —, 1934 OF, Kansas City Monarchs

Davis, A. 1886-91 OF, MGR, Boston Resolutes, New York Gorhams

Davis, A.L., 1924-25 SS, OF, Indianapolis ABCs

Davis, Albert, 1927-37 P, Detroit Stars, Baltimore Black Sox

Davis, (Big Boy), 1932 P, Indianapolis ABCs

Davis, Dwight, 1930 P, Detroit Stars

Davis, Earl (Hawk), 1927-36 2B, Indianapolis ABCs, Bacharach Giants, Newark Browns, Hilldale, Philadelphia Giants

Davis, Edward A. (Eddie, Peanuts, Nyasses), 1939-50 P, Ethiopian Clowns, Cincinnati Clowns, Cincinnati-Indianapolis Clowns, Indianapolis Clowns

Davis, (Goldie, Red), 1924-25 P, OF, Indianapolis ABCs

Davis, Hy, 1934 1B, Hilldale, Newark Dodgers

Davis, Jack, 1922-25 3B, Bacharach Giants, Philadelphia Giants

Davis, James, 1920 P, Chicago Giants, Lincoln Giants

Davis, John, 1903-10 P, Leland Giants, Cuban Giants, Philadelphia Giants, Chicago Union Giants, Cuban Stars, Algona (IA) Brownies

Davis, John Howard (Cherokee), 1941-50 OF, P, Newark Eagles, Houston Eagles

Davis, Lee, 1945 P, Kansas City Monarchs

Davis, Lorenzo (Piper), 1942-50 1B, 2B, SS, MGR, Birmingham Black Barons

Davis, Martin Luther, 1945 P, Chicago American Giants

Davis, Nathaniel, 1947-50 1B, New York Black Yankees, Philadelphia Stars

Davis, (Quack), 1913 player, Indianapolis ABCs

Davis, Robert (Butch), 1947-50 OF, Baltimore Elite Giants

Davis, Roosevelt (Rosey, Duro), 1924-45 P, St. Lous Stars, Columbus Blue Birds, Pittsburgh Crawfords, New York Black Yankees, Philadelphia Stars, Memphis Red Sox, Brooklyn Royal Giants, Baltimore Elite Giants, Chicago Brown Bombers, Cincinnati Clowns, Cincinnati-Indianapolis Clowns, Cleveland Buckeyes, Indianapolis ABCs, Newark Eagles

Davis, Ross (Satchel), 1943-47 P, Cleveland Buckeyes, Boston Blues (USL)

Davis, S., 1935 OF, Brooklyn Eagles

Davis, Saul Henry (Rareback), 1921-31 3B, 2B, SS, Birmingham Black Barons, Cleveland Tigers, Memphis Red Sox, Chicago American Giants, Detroit Stars, Columbus Buckeyes

Davis, Spencer (Babe), 1937-48 SS, OF, 3B, MGR, Atlanta Black Crackers, Indianapolis

ABCs, New York Black Yankees, Winston-Salem Giants, Memphis Red Sox

Davis, Walter (Steel Arm), 1923-34 OF, 1B, P, Detroit Stars, Chicago American Giants, Chicago Columbia Giants, Cole's American Giants, Nashville Elite Giants

Davis, William, 1937-40 3B, OF, St. Louis Stars, Indianapolis ABCs, Memphis Red Sox, Atlanta Black Crackers

Davis, William N. (Bill), 1945-47 P, Philadelphia Stars

Davis, Willie, 1945 officer, Mobile Black Shippers

Dawson, —, 1908 P, New York Colored Giants

Dawson, Johnny, 1938-42 C, Memphis Red Sox, Kansas City Monarchs Chicago American Giants, Birmingham Black Barons

Dawson, Leroy, 1946 MGR., Philadelphia Stars

Day, Eddie 1898 SS, Celeron Acme Colored Giants (Iron and Oil Lg.)

Day, Guy 1885 C, Argyle Hotel

Day, Leon, 1934-50 P, Bacharach Giants, Brooklyn Eagles, Newark Eagles, Baltimore Elite Giants

Day, Wilson C. (Connie), 1920-32,1939 2B, 3B, SS, manager, Indianapolis ABCs, Baltimore Black Sox, Harrisburg Giants, Bacharach Giants

Dean, Bob, 1937-40 P, St. Louis Stars

Dean, Charlie, 1947 P, New York Black Yankees

Dean, Jimmy, 1949-50 P, Philadelphia Stars

Dean, Nelson, 1925-32 P, Kansas City Monarchs, Cleveland Hornets, Cleveland Tigers, Detroit Stars, Cleveland Stars, Memphis Red Sox, Birmingham Black Barons

Dean, Robert, 1925-33 3B, 2B, Lincoln Giants, Pennsylvania Red Caps of New York

Deane, Alpheus, 1947 P, New York Black Yankees

Deas, James Alvin (Yank), 1916-28 C, Bacharach Giants, Pennsylvania Giants, Lincoln Giants, Hilldale, Richmond Giants, Philadelphia Giants

Deberry, C.I. (Charlie), 1948 MGR, Greensboro Red Wings; vice- pres, Negro American Association

Debran, Roy, 1940 OF, New York Black Yankees

Decker, Charles (Dusty), 1932-38 INF, MGR, Indianapolis ABCs, Montgomery Grey Sox, Detroit Stars, Memphis Red Sox, Louisville Black Colonels

Decuir, Lionel, 1939-40 C, Kansas City Monarchs

Dedeaux, Russ, 1941,1946 P, Newark Eagles, New York Black Yankees

Delgado, Felix Rafael (Felle), 1941 OF, 1B, Cuban Stars

Delugo, —, 1935 P, New York Cubans

Demeza, —, 1905 P, All Cubans

Demoss, Elwood (Bingo), 1905-43 2B, SS, P, MGR, Topeka Giants, Kansas City, Kan., Giants, Oklahoma Giants, Indianapolis ABCs, Chicago American Giants, Detroit Stars, Cleveland Giants, Chicago Brown Bombers, Bowser's ABCs, All Cubans

Dennard, Dick, 1945 player, Toledo Cubs (USL)

Dennis, Wesley L. (Doc), 1943-48 1B, OF, Baltimore Elite Giants, Philadelphia Stars

Dent, Carl J., 1950 SS, Indianapolis Clowns

Derrick, L.B., 1925-26 officer, Detroit Stars

Despert, Denny, 1914-16 OF, Lincoln Giants, Brooklyn Royal Giants, Philadelphia Giants

Devean, —, 1908 C, New York Colored Giants

Devers, —, 1950 P, Houston Eagles

Devoe, —, 1905-18 C, Philadelphia Giants, Chicago Giants

Devoe, J.R., 1922 bus. mgr, Cleveland Tate Stars

Devon, —, 1933 OF, Philadelphia Stars

Dewberry, William, 1904 C, Chicago Union Giants

Dewear, —, 1923 C, Kansas City Monarchs

Dewitt, Fred, 1925-30 1B, INF, Kansas City Monarchs, Memphis Red Sox, Hilldale

Dewitt, S.R., 1917-30 3B, Dayton Giants, Dayton Marcos, Indianapolis ABCs, Columbus Buckeyes, Toledo Tigers, Kansas City Monarchs, Cleveland Tigers, Hilldale

Dial, Kermit, 1933-40 2B, P, Columbus Blue

Birds, Cole's American Giants, Detroit Stars, Cincinnati Buckeyes

Dials, Alonzo Odem (Lou), 1925-36 1B, OF, Detroit Stars Chicago American Giants, Memphis Red Sox, Hilldale, Cleveland Giants Homestead Grays, Akron Tyrites, Birmingham Black Barons

Diamond, (Lefty), *see Robert Pipkin*

Diaz, Fernando, *see Fernando Diaz Pedroso*

Diaz, Heliodoro (Yoyo), 1926-39 P, 1B, OF, Cuban Stars (NNL), New York Cubans (East)

Diaz, Pablo Mesa, 1930-35 C, 1B, Cuban Stars (NNL), Cuban Stars (East), New York Cubans

Diaz, Pedro (Manny), *see Fernando Diaz Pedroso*

Dibut, Pedro, 1923 P, Cubans (NNL)

Dickins, —, 1945 P, Cincinnati Clowns

Dickerson, John Fount (Babe), 1950 P, Homestead Grays, Chicago American Giants

Dickerson, Lou, 1921 P, Hilldale

Dickey, John (Steel Arm), 1921-22 P, Montgomery Grey Sox, St. Louis Stars, St. Louis Giants

Dieckert, —, 1943 3B, Cuban Stars

Dihigo, Martin, 1923-1945 2B, P, OF, SS, 3B, 1B, C, MGR, Cuban Stars (East), New York Cubans, Homestead Grays, Hilldale, Darby Daisies

Dillard, —, 1927 P, Lincoln Giants

Dilworth, Arthur, 1916-18 P, OF, C, Bacharach Giants, Hilldale, Lincoln Giants

Dimes, —, 1926,1933 OF, Dayton Marcos, Akron

Direaux, Jimmy [Direux], 1937-39 P, Washington Elite Giants, Baltimore Elite Giants

Dismukes, William (Dizzy), 1910-50 P, MGR, NNL sec'y, club sec'y, Philadelphia Giants, Brooklyn Royal Giants, Mohawk Giants, Indianapolis ABCs, Chicago American Giants, Dayton Marcos, Pittsburgh Keystones, Memphis Red Sox, St. Louis Stars, Cincinnati Dismukes, Detroit Wolves, Homestead Grays, Columbus Blue Birds, Birmingham Black Barons, Kansas City Monarchs, West Baden (Ind.) Sprudels, Lincoln Giants

Dixon, —, 1915-16 P, Chicago American Giants, Chicago Giants

Dixon, Eddie Lee (Ed), 1938-39 P, Atlanta Black Crackers, Indianapolis ABCs, Baltimore Elite Giants

Dixon, George (Tubby), 1917-31 C, Chicago American Giants, Indianapolis ABCs, Birmingham Black Barons, Cleveland Hornets, Cleveland Tigers, Cleveland Cubs

Dixon, Glenn, 1937 OF, P, St. Louis Stars

Dixon, Herbert Albert (Rap), 1922-37 P, MGR., Harrisburg Giants, Baltimore Black Sox, Chicago American Giants, Hilldale Darby Daisies, Pittsburgh Crawfords, Philadelphia Stars, Brooklyn Eagles, Homestead Grays, New York Cubans, Washington Potomacs

Dixon, John Robert (Johnny Bob), 1927-34 P, SS, Cleveland Tigers, Detroit Stars, Cuban Stars, Cleveland Giants, Cleveland Red Sox, Indianapolis ABCs

Dixon, John, 1950 P, Chicago American Giants, Birmingham Black Barons

Dixon, Paul Perry (Dick), 1931-38 OF, Bacharachs Giants, Baltimore Black Sox, Washington Pilots, New York Cubans, Philadelphia Stars

Dixon, Tom, 1932-36 C, P, Baltimore Black Sox, Bacharach Giants, Hilldale

Dobbins, Nat, 1921 P, SS, Hilldale

Doby, Lawrence Eugene (Larry) [Larry Walker], 1942-47 2B, Newark Eagles

Dominguez, —, 1925 P, Cuban Stars (NNL)

Donaldson, John Wesley, 1916-34 P, OF, All Nations, Los Angeles White Sox, Chicago Giants, Indianapolis ABCs, Kansas City Monarchs, Detroit Stars, Brooklyn Royal Giants, Donaldson All-Stars, Lincoln Giants

Donaldson, W.W. (Billy), 1923-37 umpire, NNL

Donoso, Lino Galata, 1947-49 P, New York Cubans

Dorsey, F.T. 1884-85 OF, Baltimore Lord Baltimore

Dougherty, Charles (Pat), 1909-15 P, Leland Giants, Chicago American Giants, Chicago Giants

Dougherty, Lon, 1935 P, Brooklyn Eagles

Douglas, Eddie, 1922 OF, St. Louis Stars

Douglas, George 1885,1891 OF, P, Brooklyn Remsens, Ansonia Cuban Giants (Connecticut St.Lg.)

Douglas, Jesse Warren, 1937-50 INF, OF, Kansas City Monarchs, Birmingham Black Barons, Chicago American Giants, Memphis Red Sox

Douglass, Edward (Eddie), 1918-29 1B, MGR, Brooklyn Royal Giants, Lincoln Giants

Dow, —, 1911 P, Philadelphia Giants

Downer, Fred, 1921-22 OF, Pittsburgh Keystones, Baltimore Black Sox

Downs, Ellsworth 1887 player, Cincinnati Browns

Downs, McKinley (Bunny), 1915-43 2B, SS, 3B, MGR, St. Louis Giants, Bacharach Giants, Hilldale, Brooklyn Royal Giants, Brooklyn Cuban Giants, Philadelphia Tigers, Cincinnati Clowns, Indianapolis ABCs, West Baden (Ind.) Sprudels, Louisville Sox, Harrisburg Giants, Richmond Giants

Drake, Andrew, 1930-32 C, P, Birmingham Black Barons, Chattanooga Black Lookouts, Cole's American Giants, Nashville Elite Giants, Louisville Red Sox

Drake, Reynaldo Verdes, 1945-50 OF, Cincinnati-Indianapolis Clowns, Indianapolis Clowns

Drake, William P. (Plunk), 1916-30 P, St. Louis Giants, St. Louis Stars, Kansas City Monarchs, Indianapolis ABCs, Detroit Stars

Dreke, Valentin, 1919-28 OF, Cuban Stars of Havana, Cuban Stars (NNL)

Drew, John M., 1931-32 officer, Darby Daisies, Hilldale

Drew, P., 1939 OF, P, Indianapolis ABCs

Drummer, —, 1948 P, Newark Eagles

Duany, Claro, 1944-47 OF, New York Cubans

Dubisson, D.J., 1932 officer; Little Rock Grays

Ducey, —, 1924-26 INF, OF, St. Louis Giants, Dayton Marcos

Duckett, Mahlon Newton (John, Mal), 1940-49 3B, 2B, SS, Philadelphia Stars, Homestead Grays

Ducy, Eddie, 1947 2B, Homestead Grays

Dudley, C.A., 1920-23 OF, St. Louis Giants, St. Louis Stars

Dudley, Edward, 1925-28-P, Lincoln Giants, Brooklyn Royal Giants, Philadelphia Tigers

Duff, Ernest, 1925-32 OF, Indianapolis ABCs, Cleveland Elites, Cleveland Hornets, Cleveland Tigers, Cuban Stars

Duffy, Bill, 1947 C, Kansas City Monarchs

Dukes, Tommy, 1928-45 C, 3B, Chicago American Giants, Memphis Red Sox, Nashville Elite Giants, Columbus Elite Giants, Homestead Grays, Toledo Crawfords, Indianapolis Crawfords Birmingham Black Barons, Cuban Stars (East)

Dula, Louis, 1933-38 P, Cincinnati Tigers, Homestead Grays

Dumas, Jim, 1940-41 P, Memphis Red Sox

Dumpson, Bill, 1950 P, Indianapolis Clowns, Philadelphia Stars

Dunbar, Ashby, 1909-19 OF, Brooklyn Royal Giants, Lincoln Stars, Indianapolis ABCs, Pennsylvania Red Caps of New York, Lincoln Giants, Louisville Sox, Mohawk Giants

Dunbar, Frank, 1908 OF, Philadelphia Giants

Dunbar, (Vet), 1937 INF, C, Memphis Red Sox, Indianapolis Athletics

Duncan, Charlie (Scottie), 1938-40 P, Atlanta Black Crackers, Indianapolis ABCs, St. Louis Stars

Duncan, Frank (Pete), 1909-28 OF, MGR, Philadelphia Giants, Leland Giants, Chicago American Giants, Detroit Stars, Chicago Giants, Toledo Tigers, Cleveland Elites, Cleveland Hornets, Cleveland Tigers, Milwaukee Bears

Duncan, Frank Jr., 1920-48 C, OF, MGR, Chicago Giants, Kansas City Monarchs, New York Black Yankees, Pittsburgh Crawfords, Homestead Grays, New York Cubans, Chicago American Giants

Duncan, Frank, III, 1941,1945-46 P, Kansas City Monarchs, Baltimore Elite Giants

Duncan, Joe, 1927 C, Bacharachs Giants

Duncan, Melvin L., 1949-50 P, Kansas City Monarchs

Duncan, Warren, 1922-1927 C, OF, Bacharach Giants

Dunkin, Ishkooda (Stringbean), 1937 P, Pittsburgh Crawfords

Dunlap, Herman, 1936-39 OF, Chicago American Giants

Dunn, Alphonse (Blue), 1937-43 1B, OF, Detroit Stars, New York Cubans, Birmingham Black Barons, Ethiopian Clowns

Dunn, Joseph (Jake), 1930-41 SS, OF, 2B, MGR, Detroit Stars, Washington Pilots, Nashville Elite Giants, Baltimore Black Sox, Philadelphia Stars

Dunn, Willie, 1942 P, Jacksonville Red Caps

Durant, —, 1932 OF, Washington Pilots, Baltimore Black Sox, Hilldale

Durvant, —, 1923 P, Cuban Stars (NNL)

Dwight, Edward Joseph (Eddie, Pee Wee), 1924-37 OF, Indianapolis ABCs, Kansas City Monarchs, Gilkerson's Union Giants

Dykes, A., 1929 2B, Birmingham Black Barons

Dykes, John, 1932 officer, Washington Pilots

Dyll, Frank R., 1950 SS, Chicago American Giants

Dysoin, Major, 1950 SS, New York Black Yankees

Earle, Charles Babcock (Frank, Peles), 1906-19 OF, P, MGR, Wilmington Giants, Cuban Giants, Philadelphia Giants, Brooklyn Royal Giants, Lincoln Giants, Bacharach Giants, Pennsylvania Red Caps of NY

Easley, —, 1936 OF, Memphis Red Sox

Easte, —, 1923 P, Hilldale

Easter, Luscious (Luke), 1946-48 OF, 1B, Cincinnati Crescents, Homestead Grays

Easterling, Howard, 1936-49 3B, SS, 2B, Cincinnati Tigers, Chicago American Giants, Homestead Grays, New York Cubans

Eatmon, [Eaton], 1937-38 P, Birmingham Black Barons

Echevarria, Rafael, 1938 2B, New York Cubans

Echols, Jim, 1943 P, Atlanta Black Crackers

Echols, Joe, 1939 OF, Newark Eagles

Eckelson, Juan [Ekelson], 1925 P, Cuban Stars (NNL)

Edsall, George 1898 OF, Celeron Acme Colored Giants (Iron and Oil Lg.)

Edwards, Chancellor (Jack, Pep), 1928 C, Cleveland Tigers

Edwards, Frank Nutinous (Teannie)-1936-37 2B, C, St. Louis Stars

Edwards, James, 1919 C, Bacharach Giants

Edwards, Jesse (Johnny), 1923-31 2B, OF, P, Nashville Elite Giants, Birmingham Black Barons, Memphis Red Sox, Detroit Stars

Edwards, Osee, 1950 CF, New York Black Yankees

Edwards, Smokey, 1913-18 P, OF, Mohawk Giants, Lincoln Stars, Pennsylvania Red Caps of New York

Edwards, William, 1944 P, Kansas City Monarchs

Eggleston, Macajah Marchand (Mack, Egg), 1917-34 C, OF, 3B, Dayton Giants, Dayton Marcos, Detroit Stars, Indianapolis ABCs, Washington Potomacs, Columbus Buckeyes, Wilmington Potomacs, Harrisburg Giants, Baltimore Black Sox, Bacharach Giants, New York Black Yankees, Washington Pilots, Homestead Grays, Nashville Elite Giants, Lincoln Giants

Eggleston, William 1885 SS, Argyle Hotel

Ekelson, see Eckelson

Elam, James (Ed) [Elan], 1943 P, INF, Newark Eagles

Ellerbe, Lacey, 1950 UTIL, Baltimore Elite Giants

Ellis, Albert, 1950 P, Cleveland Buckeyes

Ellis, James, 1921-1925 1B, 3B, Memphis Red Sox, Dayton Marcos, Nashville Elite Giants, Cleveland Browns

Ellis, (Rocky, Rube), 1925-42 P, OF, Hilldale, Philadelphia Stars, Homestead Grays, Jacksonville Red Caps, Baltimore Grays Bacharach Giants, Birmingham Black Barons

Else, Harry (Speedy), 1931-40 C, Monroe Monarchs, Kansas City Monarchs, Chicago American Giants, New Orleans Black Creoles

Embry, William R. (Cap), 1923 umpire, NNL

Emery, Jack, 1908-16-P, OF, Brooklyn Colored Giants, Philadelphia Giants, Smart Set, Pittsburgh Colored Stars, Pittsburgh Stars of Buffalo

Emmett, —, 1924 P, Indianapolis ABCs

Emory, —, 1887-89 C, 1B, New York Gorhams (Middle States Lg.), Philadelphia Pythians

English, H.D., 1932 officer, Monroe Monarchs

English, Louis, 1929-34 C, OF, Louisville White Sox, Louisville Black Caps, Louisville Red Caps, Nashville Elite Giants, Detroit Stars

Ervin, Willie, 1948 P, New York Black Yankees

Erye, John, see John Frye

Espenosia, —, 1947 P, Indianapolis Clowns

Estenza, —, 1927-28 P, OF, 3B, C, Cuban Stars (NNL)

Estrada, Oscar, 1924-25,1931 P, OF, Cuban Stars (ECL), Cuban Stars (West)

Etchegoyen, Carlos, 1930-32 OF, 3B, Cuban Stars (East)

Evans, —, 1918 2B, Baltimore Black Sox

Evans, Charles Alexander, 1921-27 P, Bacharach Giants, Penn Red Caps of NY, Baltimore Black Sox

Evans, Clarence, 1949 P, Homestead Grays

Evans, Felix (Chin), 1934-49 P, OF, Atlanta Black Crackers, Indianapolis ABCs, Memphis Red Sox, Birmingham Black Barons Baltimore Elite Giants, St. Louis Stars

Evans, Frank, 1915 player, Kansas City Giants

Evans, Frank, 1950 OF, Cleveland Buckeyes

Evans, George 1887 player, New York Gorhams

Evans, John 1887-88 player, New York Gorhams

Evans, Robert (Bob), 1934-43 P, Newark Dodgers, Newark Eagles, Jacksonville Red Caps, New York Black Yankees, Philadelphia Stars

Evans, Ulysses (Cowboy), 1933,1943 P, Louisville Red Caps, Cincinnati Clowns, Chicago Brown Bombers

Evans, William, 1903 C, OF, Philadelphia Giants

Evans, William Demont II (Bill, Happy, Grey Ghost), 1924-36 OF, SS, 3B, P, Chicago American Giants, Brooklyn Royal Giants, Dayton Marcos, Cleveland Hornets, St. Louis Stars, Indianapolis ABCs, Homestead Grays, Washington Pilots, Detroit Wolves, Cincinnati Tigers, Memphis Red Sox

Evans, W. P., 1920-24 OF, P, Baltimore Black Sox, Chicago American Giants, Lincoln Stars

Everett, —, 1927 SS, Kansas City Monarchs, Detroit Stars

Everett, Curtis, 1950 C, OF, Kansas City Monarchs

Everett, Dean, 1929 P, Lincoln Giants

Everett, James W., 1931-43 P, OF, Pennsylvania Red Caps of New York, Cincinnati Clowns, Newark Browns, Memphis Red Sox

Ewell, Wilmer, 1925-34 C, Indianapolis ABCs, Cincinnati Tigers

Ewing, William Monroe (Buck), 1920-30 C, Chicago American Giants, Columbus Buckeyes, Indianapolis ABCs, Homestead Grays, Lincoln Giants, Cleveland Tate Stars

Eyers, Henry, see Henry Byers

Fabelo, Julian, 1916-23 INF, OF, Cuban Stars (East), Havana Stars, New York Cuban Stars

Fabre, Isidro, 1918-39 P, OF, Cuban Stars (ECL), Cuban Stars (NNL), New York Cubans, All Cubans

Fabors, Thomas, 1942 P, Baltimore Elite Giants

Fagan, Gervis, 1942-43 INF, Memphis Red Sox, Jacksonville Red Caps, Philadelphia Stars

Fagan, R.W. (Bob), 1920-23 2B, Kansas City Monarchs, St. Louis Stars

Falling, John, 1947 P, New York Black Yankees

Fanell, —, 1950 P, Baltimore Elite Giants

Farmer, Greene Jr., 1942-47 OF, Cincinnati Clowns, New York Cubans, New York Black Yankees, Jacksonville Red Caps

Farrell, Jack, 1934 owner, Baltimore Black Sox

Farrell, Luther [Luther], 1920-34 P, OF, Bacharach Giants, Lincoln Giants, New York Black Yankees, Chicago Giants, Chicago American Giants, Lincoln Giants, Hilldale, St. Louis Stars, Gilkerson's Union Giants

Favors, —, 1947 UTIL, Kansas City Monarchs

Felder, James, 1948 SS, Indianapolis Clowns

Felder, Kendall (Buck), 1944-46 3B, Memphis

Red Sox, Chicago American Giants, Birmingham Black Barons,

Felder, William (Benny), 1946-48 SS, Newark Eagles, Indianapolis Clowns

Fellows, —, 1937 P, C, Birmingham Black Barons

Fennar, Albertus A. (Al, Cleffie), 1932 SS, Brooklyn Royal Giants

Fern, —, 1920 P, Kansas City Monarchs

Fernandez, Bernard, 1938-39,1948-49 P, Atlanta Black Crackers, Jacksonville Red Caps, New York Cubans, New York Black Yankees

Fernandez, Jose Maria Sr, 1916-50 C, 1B, MGR, Havana Stars, Cuban Stars (East), New York Cubans, Chicago American Giants, New York Cuban Stars

Fernandez, Jose M. Jr. (Pepe), 1948-50 C, New York Cubans

Fernandez, Renaldo, 1950 OF, New York Cubans

Fernandez, Rodolfo, 1916,1923 P, Cuban Stars, Cuban Stars (NNL)

Fernandez, Rodolfo (Rudy, Ven Pordios), 1932-46 P, New York Cubans, Cuban Stars, New York Black Yankees

Fernandez, T., 1941 P, Cuban Stars

Ferrell, Leroy Howard, 1948-50 P, Baltimore Elite Giants

Ferrell, W.E., 1918 1B, Pennsylvania Giants

Ferrell, Willie (Truehart, Red), 1937-43 P, Homestead Grays, Chicago American Giants, Cincinnati Clowns, Birmingham Black Barons, Jacksonville Red Caps, Cleveland Bears

Ferrer, Efigenio (Coco, Al), 1946-48 2B, SS, Indianapolis Clowns

Ferrer, Pedro, 1922-25 2B, Cuban Stars (ECL)

Fiall, George, 1920-29 SS, 3B, Lincoln Giants, Harrisburg Giants, Baltimore Black Sox, Birmingham Black Barons, Penn Red Caps of NY

Fiall, Tom, 1917-25,1931 OF, C, 3B, Cuban Giants, Brooklyn Royal Giants, Lincoln Giants, Hilldale, Pennsylvania Red Caps of New York

Fields, —, 1918-26 P, Chicago American Giants, Cleveland Browns, St. Louis Giants, Dayton Marcos, Cleveland Elites

Fields, Benny, 1930-36 2B, OF, Memphis Red Sox, Cleveland Cubs, Birmingham Black Barons

Fields, Clifford Peter, 1950 OF, Chicago American Giants

Fields, Wilmer Leon Sr.(Red, Bill), 1940-50 P, 3B, OF, Homestead Grays

Fifer, —, 1921 P, Indianapolis ABCs

Figarola, Jose, 1910-16 C, 1B, Stars of Cuba, Cuban Stars

Figueroa, Enrique (Tite), 1946 P, Baltimore Elite Giants

Figueroa, Jose Antonio (Tito), 1940,1946 P, Baltimore Elite Giants, New York Cubans

Fillmore, Joe, 1941-50 P, Philadelphia Stars, Baltimore Grays

Fine, Charlie, see Charles Harmon

Finch, Rayford, 1949-50 P, Cleveland Buckeyes, Louisville Buckeyes

Finch, Robert [Fitch], 1926 P, Lincoln Giants

Findell, Thomas 1887 player, Washington Capital City

Finley, Thomas (Tom), 1923-33 3B, C, Bacharach Giants, Lincoln Giants, Brooklyn Royal Giants, Pennsylvania Red Caps of New York, Darby Daisies, New York Black Yankees, Baltimore Black Sox, Philadelphia Stars, Wilmington Potomacs, Washington Potomacs

Finner, John, 1919-25 P, St. Louis Giants, St. Louis Stars, Milwaukee Bears, Birmingham Black Barons

Finney, Ed, 1948-50 3B, Baltimore Elite Giants

Fisher, —, 1909-10 P, Philadelphia Giants

Fisher, —, 1932 P, Columbus Turfs

Fisher, A. 1884 player, Philadelphia Mutual B.B.C.

Fisher, F. 1884 player, Philadelphia Mutual B.B.C.

Fisher, George, 1922-23 OF, Richmond Giants, Harrisburg Giants

Fisher, W. —, 1884 player, Philadelphia Mutual B.B.C.

Fishue, Pete (The Wonder) 1886 C, New York Gorhams

Fleet, Joseph, 1930 P, Chicago American Giants

Fleming, Buddy, see Fleming Reedy

Flemming, Frank, 1946 P, Cleveland Buckeyes

Flood, Jess, 1919 C, Cleveland Tate Stars

Flourney, —, 1950 P, Cleveland Buckeyes

Flournoy, Fred, 1928 C, Brooklyn Cuban Giants, Penn Red Caps of NY

Flournoy, Willis (Pud), 1919-33 P, Hilldale, Brooklyn Royal Giants, Baltimore Black Sox, Bacharach Giants

Flowers, Johnny (Jake), 1941-43 INF, New York Black Yankees

Floyd, —, 1935-37 P, Brooklyn Eagles, Indianapolis Athletics

Floyd, J.J., 1932 officer, Little Rock Greys

Footes, Robert 1895-1909 C, Chicago Unions, Philadelphia Giants, Brooklyn Royal Giants, Chicago Union Giants

Forbes, —, 1886-88 OF, 3B, Cuban Giants, Philadelphia Pythians

Forbes, Frank, 1929-43 umpire; bus. mgr, New York Cubans; NNL promoter

Forbes, Joe, 1913-27 SS, 3B, OF, Lincoln Giants, Pennsylvania Red Caps of New York, Bacharach Giants, Brooklyn Royal Giants, Lincoln Stars, Philadelphia Giants

Force, William, 1921-30 P, Detroit Stars, Baltimore Black Sox, Brooklyn Royal Giants

Ford, (Bubber), 1947 officer, Jacksonville Eagles

Ford, C., 1918 P, Pennsylvania Giants

Ford, Carl, 1947 officer, Shreveport Tigers

Ford, Frank, 1915-18 C, Pennsylvania Giants, Hilldale

Ford, James (Jimmy), 1931-45 3B, 2B, Memphis Red Sox, St. Louis Stars, New Orleans-St. Louis Stars, New York Black Yankees, Cincinnati Clowns, Philadelphia Stars, Baltimore Elite Giants, Harrisburg-St.Louis Stars, Washington Black Senators

Ford, Roy, 1918-25 2B, Baltimore Black Sox, Harrisburg Giants

Foreman, —, 1921 SS, Hilldale

Foreman, F.Slyvester (Hooks), 1921-33 C, P, Kansas City Monarchs, Indianapolis ABCs, Washington Pilots, Milwaukee Bears. Homestead Grays

Foreman, Zack, 1920 P, Kansas City Monarchs

Forest, Charles, 1920 player, St. Louis Giants

Forkins, Marty, 1931 officer, New York Black Yankees

Formenthal, Pedro, 1947-50 OF, Memphis Red Sox

Forrest, —, 1917-28 OF, C, Havana Red Sox, Lincoln Giants, Philadelphia Giants

Forrest, Joe, 1949 P, New York Black Yankees

Forrest, Percy (Pete), 1938-49 P, Chicago American Giants, Newark Eagles, New York Black Yankees, Indianapolis Clowns

Foster, Albert (Red), 1910 1B, Kansas City, Kan., Giants

Foster, Andrew (Rube), 1902-26 P, MGR, Chicago Union Giants, Cuban X Giants, Philadelphia Giants, Leland Giants, Chicago American Giants; founder and pres, tres, NNL

Foster, Jim, 1945 officer, Chicago Brown Bombers

Foster, Leland, 1932-36 P, Monroe Monarchs

Foster, Leonard, 1938 INF, Atlanta Black Crackers

Foster, Willie Hendrick (Bill), 1923-37 P, MGR, Memphis Red Sox, Chicago American Giants, Homestead Grays, Kansas City Monarchs, Cole's American Giants, Birmingham Black Barons, Pittsburgh Crawfords

Foulke, —, 1912 rf, Cuban Giants

Fowler, J.W. (Bud) (real name John Jackson) 1872-1899 2B, P, OF, 3B, C, SS, MGR, New Castle, Pa.; Stillwater (Northwestern Lg.); Keokuk and Topeka (Western Lg.); Binghamton (International Lg.); Crawfordsville, Terre Haute, and Galesburg (Central Interstate Lg.); Lafayette, Indiana; Greenville (Michigan Lg.); Sterling and Davenport (Illinois-Iowa Lg.); Evansville, New York Gorhams, All-American Black Tourists, Page Fence Giants Adrian (Michigan St. Lg.), Lansing (Michigan St. Lg.) Lynn (Int. Ass.), Lincoln-Kearney (Neb. St. Lg.), Galesburg (Ill-Iowa Lg.), Burlington (Ill-Iowa Lg.), Pueblo (Colorado Lg.) Worcester (New England Assn.), Santa Fe (New Mexico Lg.), Montpelier (Vermont Lg.)

Fowlkes, Erwin, 1947-48 SS, Chicago American Giants, Homestead Grays

Fowlkes, Samuel, 1950 P, Kansas City Monarchs, Cleveland Buckeyes

Fox, Orange 1887 rf, Chicago Unions

Francis, Del, 1917-20 2B, Indianapolis ABCs

Francis, William (Billy, Brodie), 1906-25 3B, SS, Wilmington Giants, Cuban Giants, Philadelphia Giants, Lincoln Giants, Chicago American Giants, Hilldale, Bacharach Giants, Cleveland Browns, Chicago Giants

Franklin, —, 1908 SS, Brooklyn Colored Giants

Franklin, William B. 1887 manager, Louisville Falls City

Frazier, Albert Edwin (Cool Papa), 1932-40 2B, 3B, Montgomery Grey Sox, Jacksonville Red Caps, Cleveland Bears

Freeman, Bill, 1925,1933 P, Indianapolis ABCs, Cuban Stars

Freeman, Charlie, 1916,1927-30 player, Officer, Hilldale

Freeman, William 1888-89 3B, Chicago Unions

Freihofer, William, 1906 pres, International Lg. of Independent Professional Base Ball Clubs

Friely, —, 1922 2B, Bacharach Giants

Frye, John H. (Jack) 1883-96 1B, C, P, OF, Cuban Giants, Reading, Pa (Interstate Lg.), Lewiston (Penn. St. Lg.), York Cuban Giants (Eastern Interstate Lg.), Trenton Cuban Giants (Middle States Lg.), Ansonia Cuban Giants (Connecticut St. Lg.), New York Gorhams

Fulcur, Robert, 1940 P, Chicago American Giants, Birmingham Black Barons

Fuller, Jimmy, 1912-20 C, Cuban Giants, Bacharach Giants, Philadelphia Giants

Fuller, W.W. (Chick), 1908-19 SS, 2B, Bacharach Giants, Cuban Giants, Pennsylvania Giants, Cleveland Tate Stars, Hilldale Brooklyn Colored Giants, New York Colored Giants, Pennsylvania Red Caps of NY

Fumes, —, 1925-30 OF, Cuban Stars (NNL), Cuban Stars (East)

Gadsden, Gus, 1932 OF, Hilldale

Gaichey, —, 1948 P, Memphis Red Sox

Gaideria, —, 1918 P, Cuban Stars

Gaines, Jonas George (Lefty), 1937-50 P, Newark Eagles, Baltimore Elite Giants, Philadelphia Stars, Washington Elite Giants

Gaines, Willie, 1950 P, Philadelphia Stars

Galata, Domingo, 1949 P, New York Cubans

Galata, Raul, 1949-50 P, Indianapolis Clowns, New York Cubans

Gales, —, 1931 1B, Detroit Stars

Galey, —, 1897 1B, OF, Cuban Giants

Gallardy, —, 1906 OF, Cuban Giants

Galloway, Bill 1899-06 OF, 2B, Cuban X Giants, Cuban Giants, Woodstock (Canadian Lg.)

Galvez, Cuneo, 1928-32 P, Cuban Stars (NNL), Cuban Stars (East)

Gamble, —, 1921 P, Columbus Buckeyes

Gans, Robert Edward (Jude, Judy), 1910-38 OF, P, MGR, Cuban Giants, Smart Set, Lincoln Giants, Chicago American Giants, Chicago Giants, Lincoln Stars, Mohawk Giants; umpire, East- West Lg., NNL

Gant, —, 1887 3B, Pittsburgh Keystones

Gantz, see Domingo Gomez

Garay, Martiniano Arguelles (Jose) [Arguelles], 1948-50-OF, P, New York Cubans

Garcia, Antonio, 1909-12 C, 1B, Cuban Stars, All Cubans

Garcia, Atires (Angel), 1945-50 P, Cincinnati-Indianapolis Clowns, Indianapolis Clowns

Garcia, John, 1904 C, Cuban Giants

Garcia, Manuel (Cocaina), 1926-36 P, OF, Cuban Stars (NNL), New York Cubans

Garcia, Romando (Chano), 1926-27 2B, Bacharach Giants, Lincoln Giants

Garcia, Silvio, 1940-47 INF, Cuban Stars, New York Cubans

Gardner, —, 1920-23,1926 OF, Toledo Tigers, St. Louis Stars, Dayton Marcos

Gardner, Floyd (Jelly), 1919-1933 OF, 1B, Detroit Stars, Chicago American Giants, Lincoln Giants, Homestead Grays

Gardner, James (Chappy), 1908-17 2B, 3B,

Brooklyn Royal Giants, Havana Red Sox, Cuban Giants, Brooklyn Colored Giants

Gardner, Kenneth (Ping, Steel Arm), 1918-32 P, Washington Red Caps, Brooklyn Royal Giants, Hilldale, Philadelphia Royal Stars, Lincoln Giants, Harrisburg Giants, Bacharach Giants, Cleveland Tigers, Baltimore Black Sox, Newark Browns

Garey, —, 1925 C, Cuban Stars (NNL)

Garmer, 1886 3B, New York Gorhams

Garner, Horace Charles, 1949 OF, Indianapolis Clowns

Garren, —, 1905 C, All Cubans

Garrett, Al H. 1899-1900 manager, Columbia Giants

Garrett, Frank 1887 player, Louisville Falls Citys

Garrett, Soloman, 1950 2B, New York Black Yankees

Garrett, William, 1943 officer, New York Black Yankees

Garrido, Gil, 1945-46 INF, New York Cubans

Garrison, Robert, 1909 P, St. Paul Gophers

Garrison, Ross 1889-97 SS, 3B, York Cuban Giants (Eastern Interstate Lg.), New York Gorhams (Middle States Lg.), Cuban Giants

Garvin, Leedell, 1942 P, Philadelphia Stars

Gary, Charles, 1948-50 3B, Homestead Grays

Gaston, —, 1921 SS, Hilldale

Gaston, Robert (Rab Roy), 1932-49 C, Homestead Grays

Gatewood, Bill, 1905-28 P, MGR, Cuban X Giants, Philadelphia Giants, Brooklyn Royal Giants, Leland Giants, Chicago Giants, Chicago American Giants, St. Louis Giants, Detroit Stars, St. Louis Stars, Toledo Tigers, Albany, Ga. Giants, Birmingham Black Barons, Memphis Red Sox, Milwaukee Bears, Lincoln Giants

Gatewood, Ernest, 1914-27 C, 1B, Lincoln Giants, Brookyn Royal Giants, Bacharach Giants, Harrisburg Giants, Lincoln Stars

Gavin, —, 1935 P, Brooklyn Eagles

Gay, Herbert, 1929-30 P, OF, Chicago American Giants, Birmingham Black Barons, Baltimore Black Sox

Gay, W. —, 1929 P, Chicago American Giants

Gee, Richard (Rich), 1922-29 C, OF, Lincoln Giants, New Orleans Crescent Stars

Gee, Tom, 1925-26 C, Lincoln Giants, Newark Stars

George, John, 1921-25 SS, New Orleans Crescent Stars, Chicago Giants, Harrisburg Giants, Chicago American Giants, Bacharach Giants, New Orleans Caulfield Ads

Gerald, Alphonso [Gerrard], 1945-49 OF, INF, New York Black Yankees, Chicago American Giants, Indianapolis Clowns

Getty, —, 1936 C, Bacharach Giants

Gholston, Bert E., 1923-43 umpire, NNL, East-West Lg.

Gibbons, —, 1923 3B, Harrisburg Giants

Gibbons, Walter Lee, 1948-49 P, Indianapolis Clowns

Gibson, B., 1927 P, Cleveland Hornets

Gibson, Jerry A., 1936-43 OF, P, Cincinnati Tigers, Cincinnati Clowns, Cincinnati Buckeyes

Gibson, Joshua (Josh) Sr, 1930-46 C, OF, Homestead Grays, Pittsburgh Crawfords

Gibson, Joshua, Jr., 1949-50 INF, Homestead Grays

Gibson, Ted, 1940-41 INF, P, Columbus Buckeyes, Chicago American Giants, Cincinnati Buckeyes

Gibson, Welda H., 1949-50 P, Houston Eagles

Gilcrest, Dennis, 1931-35 C, 2B, Indianapolis ABCs, Columbus Blue Birds, Cleveland Red Sox, Brooklyn Eagles

Gilers, —, 1928 OF, Birmingham Black Barons

Giles, George Franklin, 1927-38 1B, Kansas City Monarchs, St. Louis Stars, Brooklyn Eagles, New York Black Yankees, Philadelphia Stars, Detroit Wolves, Homestead Grays, Pittsburgh Crawfords, Baltimore Black Sox

Gill, William, 1931-37 1B, 3B, OF, Detroit Stars, Louisville Red Caps, Indianapolis Athletics, Homestead Grays

Gillard, (Hamp), 1909-14 P, St. Louis Giants, Chicago American Giants, West Baden (In) Sprudels, Birmingham Giants

Gillard, Luther (Pen) [Gilyard], 1934-42 OF, 1B, Memphis Red Sox, Chicago American

Giants, Indianapolis Crawfords, Birmingham Black Barons, St. Louis Stars, Kansas City Monarchs

Gillespie, H. 1887 player, Louisville Falls Citys

Gillespie, Henry, 1917-34 P, OF, Pennsylvania Giants, Hilldale, Lincoln Giants, Bacharach Giants, Philadelphia Tigers, Quaker Giants, New York Black Yankees, Baltimore Black Sox Harrisburg Giants, Madison Stars

Gillespie, Murray (Lefty), 1930-32 P, Memphis Red Sox, Nashville Elite Giants, Monroe Monarchs

Gilliam, James (Junior), 1945-50 2B, Nashville Black Vols, Baltimore Elite Giants

Gilmore, Quincy Jordan, 1922-37 bus MGR, Kansas City Monarchs; sec'y, tres, NNL; pres, Texas-Oklahoma-Louisiana Lg.

Gilmore, (Speed), 1926-28 P, Lincoln Giants

Gilyard, Luther, *see Luther Gillard*

Gipson, Alvin (Bubber, Skeet), 1941-50 P, Chicago American Giants, Birmingham Black Barons, Houston Eagles

Gisentaner, Willie (Lefty), 1921-36 P, OF, Columbus Buckeyes, Washington Potomacs, Kansas City Monarchs, Harrisburg Giants, Newark Stars, Lincoln Giants, Cuban Stars (East), Louisville White Sox, Pittsburgh Crawfords, Nashville Elite Giants, Louisville Red Caps, Homestead Grays, Louisville Black Caps, Chicago American Giants, Philadelphia Giants

Givens, —, 1927 SS, Cleveland Hornets

Givens, Oscar, 1946-48 SS, Newark Eagles

Gladney, —, 1932 SS, Indianapolis ABCs

Gladstone, Granville, 1950 OF, Indianapolis Clowns

Glass, Carl Lee (Butch), 1923-36 P, MGR, Memphis Red Sox, Cincinnati Tigers, St. Louis Stars, Birmingham Black Barons, Chicago American Giants, Kansas City Monarchs, Louisville White Sox

Glenn, Hubert (Country), 1945-49 P, New York Black Yankees, Brooklyn Brown Dodgers, Indianapolis Clowns

Glenn, Oscar, 1937-38 3B, Atlanta Black Crackers

Glenn, Stanley Rudolf (Doc), 1943-50 C, P, Philadelphia Stars

Glover, Thomas (Lefty), 1934-45 P, Birmingham Black Barons, Cleveland Red Sox, New Orleans Black Pelicans, Washington Elite Giants, Memphis Red Sox, Baltimore Elite Giants, Columbus Elite Giants

Godinez, Manuel, 1946-49 P, Cincinnati-Indianapolis Clowns, Indianapolis Clowns

Goines, Charles, 1915 C, Indianapolis ABCs

Goins, —, 1932 P, Montgomery Grey Sox

Golden, Clyde, 1948-50 P, Newark Eagles, Houston Eagles, Cleveland Buckeyes

Goldie, —, 1926-28 1B, Indianapolis ABCs, Cleveland Tigers, Cleveland Elites, Cleveland Hornets

Goliath, Fred, 1920 OF, Chicago Giants

Gomez, David, 1925-28,1932 P, Cuban Stars (NNL)

Gomez, Domingo (Harry), 1926-29 C, Harrisburg Giants, Philadelphia Tigers, Baltimore Black Sox

Gomez, Joe, 1932-33 P, Bacharach Giants

Gomez, Sijo [Sijo], 1929 C, P, Cuban Stars (East)

Gonzales, A., 1910-12 P, Cuban Stars

Gonzalez, Gervasio (Strike), 1910-17 1B, C, Cuban Stars, Long Branch Cubans

Gonzalez, Luis (Chicho), 1910 P, Cuban Stars

Gonzalez, Miguel Angel Cordero (Mike), 1911-14 C, 1B, Cuban Stars

Gonzalez, Rene, 1950 OF, New York Cubans

Good, —, 1890 OF, York Cuban Giants (Eastern Interstate Lg.)

Good, —, 1916 C, OF, Lincoln Stars

Good, Cleveland, 1937 P, Newark Eagles

Gooden, Ernest (Pud), 1922-23 2B, 3B, Pittsburgh Keystones, Toledo Tigers, Chicago American Giants, Cleveland Tate Stars

Goodgame, John, 1917 P, Chicago Giants

Goodman, —, 1928 OF, Harrisburg Giants

Goodrich, Joe, 1923-26 2B, SS, 3B, Washington Potomacs, Philadelphia Giants, Wilmington Potomacs, Harrisburg Giants

Goodson, M.E., 1932 officer, New York Black Yankees

Gordon, —, 1905-11 SS, 3B, Genuine Cuban Giants, Cuban Giants

Gordon, —, 1915 OF, Indianapolis ABCs

Gordon, Charles William (Charlie, Flash), 1940 OF, New York Black Yankees

Gordon, Harold, 1950 P, Chicago American Giants

Gordon, Herman, 1920-24 P, OF, 2B, Toledo Tigers, Birmingham Black Barons, Kansas City Monarchs, St. Louis Stars, Cleveland Browns

Gorham, —, 1911 rf, Philadelphia Giants

Goshay, Samuel, 1949 OF, Kansas City Monarchs

Gottlieb, Eddie, 1936-50 officer, Philadelphia Stars; sec'y, NNL; promoter and booking agent, Owner

Gould, John (Willie, Hal), 1947-48 P, Philadelphia Stars

Govantes, Manuel, 1909-10 2B, OF, Cuban Stars, Stars of Cuba

Govern, S.K. (Siki) 1887-88,1896 MGR, Cuban Giants

Grace, Arthur 1889 P, 1B, Champaign (Ill.-Ind. Lg.)

Grace, Ellsworth, 1950 2B, New York Black Yankees

Grace, Willie, 1942-50 OF, Cincinnati Buckeyes, Cleveland Buckeyes, Louisville Buckeyes, Houston Eagles

Grady, —, 1924 P, Washington Potomacs

Graham, Dennis, 1918-31 OF, Washington Red Caps, Bacharach Giants, St. Louis Stars, Homestead Grays, Pittsburgh Crawfords

Graham, Vasco 1895-99 C, OF, Lansing, Michigan, Colored Capital All-Americans, Page Fence Giants, Adrian (Michigan St. Lg.) Dubuque (IA), Cuban Giants

Gransberry, Bill, 1929 OF, 1B, Chicago American Giants, Chicago Giants

Grant, Art, 1920-22 C, Baltimore Black Sox, Richmond Giants

Grant, Charles 1896-1913 2B, Page Fence Giants, Columbia Giants, Cuban X Giants, Philadelphia Giants, New York Black Sox, Lincoln Giants

Grant, Frank 1886-1905 2B, SS, Meriden (Eastern Lg.); Buffalo (International Lg.); Cuban Giants, Harrisburg (Eastern Interstate Lg.); Lansing, Michigan, Colored Capital All-Americans, New York Gorhams (Middle States Lg.), Ansonia Cuban Giants (Connecticut St.Lg.), Trenton Cuban Giants (Middle States Lg.), Philadelphia Giants

Grant, Leroy, 1911-25 1B, Chicago American Giants, Lincoln Giants, Indianapolis ABCs, Cleveland Browns, Mohawk Giants

Graves, Bob, 1932-37 P, OF, Indianapolis ABCs, Indianapolis Athletics

Graves, Lawrence, 1923 P, Harrisburg Giants

Graves, Whitt, 1950 P, Indianapolis Clowns

Gray, —, 1931 3B, Nashville Elite Giants

Gray, Chesley (Chester), 1940-45 C, St. Louis Stars, New York Black Yankees, Harrisburg-St. Louis Stars, Kansas City Monarchs, Toledo Cubs (USL)

Gray, G.E. (Willie, Dolly) [Grey], 1920-33-OF, P, Cleveland Tate Stars, Homestead Grays, Lincoln Giants, Pennnsylvania Red Caps of New York, Dayton Marcos, Pittsburgh Keystones, Newark Stars

Gray, Roosevelt (Chappy), 1920-23 1B, P, Cleveland Tate Stars, Toledo Tigers, Dayton Marcos, Kansas City Monarchs

Gray, William 1884-87 OF, Baltimore Atlantics, Baltimore Lord Baltimores

Greason, William Henry (Willie, Bill), 1948-50 P, Birmingham Black Barons

Green, —, 1920 P, Detroit Stars

Green, —, 1939-41 P, Cleveland Bears, Memphis Red Sox

Green, —, 1940 2B, Philadelphia Stars

Green, Alvin, 1950 INF, Baltimore Elite Giants

Green, Charles (Joe), 1902-31 MGR, OF, Leland Giants, Chicago Giants, Chicago American Giants, Union Giants, Columbia Giants

Green, Curtis, 1923-26 1B, OF, Birmingham Black Barons, Brooklyn Cuban Giants

Green, Dave, 1950 OF, Baltimore Elite Giants

Green, Henryene P., 1949-50 owner, Baltimore Elite Giants

Green, James [Greene], 1950 3B, New York Black Yankees

Green, Julius, 1929-30 OF, Memphis Red Sox, Detroit Stars

Green, Leslie (Chin), 1939-46 OF, St. Louis Stars, New York Black Yankees, Memphis Red Sox

Green, Peter (Ed), 1908-20 OF, P, Pittsburgh Giants Lincoln Stars, Brooklyn Royal Giants, Brooklyn Colored Giants

Green, Vernon (Fat, Baby), 1921,1942-49 C, officer, Nashville Giants, Baltimore Elite Giants

Green, William, 1915-23 3B, OF, Chicago Giants, Chicago Union Giants

Green, Willie, 1910-12 C, P, Pittsburgh Giants, St. Louis Giants

Greene, James Elbert (Joe) [James Green], 1932-48 C, Kansas City Monarchs, Cleveland Buckeyes, Atlanta Black Crackers, Homestead Grays

Greene, Walter, 1928 OF, 1B, Brooklyn Cuban Giants, Bacharach Giants

Greene, Will, 1912 P, Pittsburgh Giants

Greenidge, Victor (Slicker), 1941-45 P, Cuban Stars, New York Cubans

Greenlee, William Augustus (Gus,Big Red), 1931-45 officer, Pittsburgh Crawfords; founder and pres, second NNL; founder, United States Baseball Lg.

Greer, J.B., 1939-42 officer, Cleveland Bears, Knoxville Red Caps, Jacksonville Red Caps

Gregory, —, 1940 P, Birmingham Black Barons

Grey, William, see G.E. Gray

Greyer, George, 1918-22 1B, Baltimore Black Sox

Grier, Claude (Red), 1924-28 P, Wilmington Potomacs, Bacharach Giants, Washington Potomacs

Griffin, C.B. (Clarence), 1933-35 OF, Columbus Blue Birds, Cleveland Red Sox, Brooklyn Eagles, Columbus Elite Giants

Griffin, James (Horse), 1912-21 2B, Cuban Giants, Nashville Elite Giants, Pittsburgh Giants, Philadelphia Giants

Griffin, Robert, 1931-37 P, Chicago Columbia Giants, St. Louis Stars

Griffith, Robert Lee (Big Bill, Schoolboy), 1934-49 P, Nashville Elite Giants, Columbus Elite Giants, Washington Elite Giants, Baltimore Elite Giants, New York Black Yankees, Philadelphia Stars

Griggs, Wiley Lee (Willie), 1948-50 3B, INF, Birmingham Black Barons, Houston Eagles, Cleveland Buckeyes

Grimes, —, 1943 OF, P, Cleveland Buckeyes, Harrisburg-St. Louis Stars

Grimm, —, 1921 OF, Bacharach Giants

Gross, Ben, Jr. 1887 OF, Pittsburgh Keystones

Guerra, Juan, 1910-24 OF, 1B, C, Stars of Cuba, Cuban Stars (NNL), New York Cuban Stars, Cuban Stars

Guerra, Marcelino, 1916 1B, Cuban Stars

Guilbe, Felix, 1946 OF, Baltimore Elite Giants

Guilbe, Juan, 1940-47 P, OF, Cuban Stars, Baltimore Elite Giants, Indianapolis Clowns

Guiterrez, Luis (Joe), 1926 OF, Cuban Stars (NNL)

Guiwn, Jefferson, 1943-45 C, Cleveland Buckeyes

Gulley, Napoleon, 1943-47 P, Cleveland Buckeyes, Newark Eagles

Gurley, James, 1922-32 OF, P, 1B, St. Louis Stars, Memphis Red Sox, Chicago American Giants, Montgomery Grey Sox, Nashville Elite Giants, Birmingham Black Barons, Indianapolis ABCs, Cleveland Hornets, Harrisburg Giants

Guy, Wesley, 1927-29 P, Chicago Giants

Hackett, —, 1932 P, Washington Pilots

Hackley, Albert 1887-96 OF, INF, Chicago Unions

Haddad, —, 1931 P, OF (House of David) Cubans

Hadley, (Red), 1937-38 C, OF, Atlanta Black Crackers

Haines, —, 1920 P, Indianapolis ABCs

Hairston, Harold (Hal), 1946-47 P, Homestead Grays

Hairston, Napoleon, 1938-40 OF, Pittsburgh Crawfords, Indianapolis Crawfords, Toledo Crawfords

Hairston, (Rap), 1934 player, Newark Dodgers

Hairston, Samuel (Sam), 1945-50 C, 3B,

Cincinnati-Indianapolis Clowns, Indianapolis Clowns

Hairstone, J.Burke (J.B.), 1918-22-MGR, OF, C, Baltimore Black Sox, Bacharach Giants

Hale, (Red), 1937-39 SS, Detroit Stars, Chicago American Giants

Haley, —, 1923 P, Detroit Stars

Haley, (Red), 1928 2B, Chicago American Giants, Birmingham Black Barons

Hall, —, 1887 2B, Philadelphia Pythians

Hall, —, 1921-23 P, St. Louis Giants, Milwaukee Bears, Detroit Stars

Hall, (Bad News), 1937-40 3B, Indianapolis Athletics, Indianapolis Crawfords

Hall, Blainey, 1913-26 OF, Mohawk Giants, Lincoln Giants, Philadelphia Giants, Baltimore Black Sox

Hall, Horace G., 1933-42 officer, Chicago American Giants; vice pres, NAL

Hall, Joseph W., 1945 officer, Hilldale Club of Philadelphia

Hall, Perry, 1926-47 3B, OF, Memphis Red Sox, Cleveland Tigers, Chicago Giants, Indianapolis Athletics, Chicago Columbia Giants, Birmingham Black Barons, Detroit Stars

Hall, Sellers Mckee (Sell), 1916-20 P, Pittsburgh Colored Giants, Homestead Grays, Chicago American Giants

Hamilton, —, 1886 2B, New York Gorhams

Hamilton, —, 1921-24 P, Kansas City Monarchs, Cleveland Browns, St. Louis Stars, Bacharach Giants

Hamilton, George, 1923-29 C, Memphis Red Sox, Birmingham Black Barons

Hamilton, J.C. (John, Ed), 1940-42 P, Homestead Grays

Hamilton, J.H. (John), 1924-27 3B, INF, Washington Potomacs, Birmingham Black Barons, Indianapolis ABCs, Cleveland Elites, Wilmington Potomacs

Hamilton, Jim, 1946 SS, Kansas City Monarchs

Hamilton, L., 1923-25 2B, OF, Memphis Red Sox, Birmingham Black Barons

Hamilton, Theron B., 1934 vice pres, Homestead Grays

Hammond, Don, 1923-24 3B, SS, Cleveland Tate Stars, Cleveland Browns, Toledo Tigers

Hampton, Eppie, 1925-38 C, P, Memphis Red Sox, Washington Pilots, New Orleans Crescent Stars, Birmingham Black Barons, Cleveland Tigers

Hampton, Lewis, 1921-28 P, Columbus Buckeyes, Indianapolis ABCs, Bacharach Giants, Washington Potomacs, Lincoln Giants, Detroit Stars

Hampton, Wade, 1918-23 P, Pennsylvania Giants, Hilldale

Hancock, Art, 1926-27 1B, OF, Cleveland Elites, Cleveland Hornets

Hancock, Charles Winston (Charley), 1921 C, St. Louis Giants

Hancock, W. 1885 player, Brooklyn Remsens

Handy, George, 1947-49 INF, Memphis Red Sox, Houston Eagles

Handy, William Oscar (Bill,Buck), 1910-27 2B, SS, 3B, New York Black Sox, Brooklyn Royal Giants, St. Louis Giants, Lincoln Giants, Bacharach Giants, Philadelphia Royal Giants

Hanks, —, 1908 C, Brooklyn Colored Giants

Hannibal, —, 1914-17 OF, Bowser's ABCs, Indianapolis ABCs

Hannibal, Leo Jack, 1932,1937-38 P, Indianapolis ABCs, Indianapolis Athletics, Homestead Grays

Hannon, —, 1908-10 OF, 3B, Pop Watkins Stars, Philadelphia Giants, St.Louis Giants

Hanson, —, 1915 SS, Chicago American Giants

Hanson, Harry, 1926 vice pres, NSL

Harden, James, 1947 P, Homestead Grays

Harden, John H., 1939-48 officer, Atlanta Black Crackers, Indianapolis ABCs, New York Black Yankees; tres, NSL

Harden, Lovell (Big Pitch), 1943-45 P, Cleveland Buckeyes

Hardiman, —, 1937 P, St. Louis Stars

Harding, A. Hallie, 1926-31 SS, 2B, 3B, Indianapolis ABCs, Detroit Stars, Kansas City Monarchs, Chicago Columbia Giants, Bacharach Giants, Baltimore Black Sox

Harding, Roy, 1937 P, Philadelphia Stars

Harding, Tom, 1940 OF, Indianapolis Crawfords

Hardy, Arthur Wesley (Art), 1906-12 P, Topeka Giants, Kansas City, Kansas, Giants

Hardy, (Doc), 1950 INF, Cleveland Buckeyes

Hardy, Paul James, 1931-47 C, Montgomery Grey Sox, Detroit Stars, Birmingham Black Barons, Baltimore Elite Giants, Columbus Elite Giants, Chicago American Giants, Kansas City Monarchs, Memphis Red Sox

Hardy, Walter, 1945-50 SS, 2B, New York Black Yankees, New York Cubans

Hargett, —, 1918 P, Hilldale

Hargett, Yook 1887 player, Philadelphia Pythians

Harland, Bill, 1929 P, Lincoln Giants

Harmon, Charles (Chuck) [Charlie Fine], 1947 OF, Indianapolis Clowns

Harness, Robert Marseilles (O), 1927-28 P, Chicago Giants

Harney, George, 1923-31 P, Chicago Giants, Chicago Columbia Giants, Chicago American Giants

Harper, —, 1910 P, Leland Giants

Harper, (Chick), 1920-25 SS, OF, P, Hilldale, Norfolk Stars, Kansas City Monarchs, Detroit Stars

Harper, David (Dave), 1943-45 OF, P, Kansas City Monarchs, Philadelphia Stars

Harper, John, 1922-26 P, Bacharach Giants, Lincoln Giants, Richmond Giants

Harper, Walter, 1923,1929-31 1B, C, Chicago American Giants, Birmingham Black Barons, Chicago Columbia Giants

Harps, Fred, 1928 INF, Brooklyn Cuban Giants

Harris, —, 1919 OF, Lincoln Giants

Harris, —, 1921 P, Indianapolis ABCs, Columbus Buckeyes, Chicago American Giants

Harris, —, 1927 1B, Lincoln Giants

Harris, Ananias, 1921-23 P, Brooklyn Royal Giants, Hilldale, Harrisburg Giants

Harris, Andy, 1917-26 3B, MGR, Hilldale, Pennsylvania Giants, Pennsylvania Red Caps of New York, Newark Stars, Pittsburgh Stars of Buffalo

Harris, Bill, 1930-32 C, Memphis Red Sox, Indianapolis ABCs, Monroe Monarchs

Harris, Charlie, 1943 INF, Cincinnati Clowns, Chicago Brown Bombers

Harris, Chick (Popsickle, Moocha), 1931-36 OF, 1B, Detroit Wolves, Kansas City Monarchs, New Orleans Crescent Stars, Cleveland Stars

Harris, Curtis (Popeye), 1931-40 2B, SS, 1B, C, Pittsburgh Crawfords, Philadelphia Stars, Kansas City Monarchs

Harris, Dixon, 1932 player, Homestead Grays

Harris, E. 1884 player, Philadelphia Mutual B.B.C.

Harris, Elander Victor (Vic), 1923-50 OF, MGR, coach, Cleveland Tate Stars, Cleveland Browns, Chicago American Giants, Homestead Grays, Pittsburgh Crawfords, Baltimore Elite Giants, Birmingham Black Barons, Toledo Tigers, Detroit Wolves

Harris, Frank 1885 P, Argyle Hotel

Harris, George, 1932-33 2B, Louisville Black Caps, Louisville Red Caps

Harris, H.B., 1919 bus. mgr, Brooklyn Royal Giants

Harris, Henry, 1928-34 SS, Memphis Red Sox, Louisville Black Caps, Baltimore Black Sox

Harris, Isaiah, 1949-50 P, Memphis Red Sox

Harris, J. (Sonny), 1936-1942 OF, INF, Cincinnati Buckeyes, Cincinnati Tigers, Cleveland Buckeyes

Harris, James 1884-87 OF, Baltimore Atlantics, Baltimore Lord Baltimores

Harris, Joseph 1887 player, Boston Resolutes

Harris, (Lefty), 1941 P, Cuban Stars

Harris, Nathan (Nate), 1901-11 2B, OF, Philadelphia Giants, Leland Giants, Chicago Giants, Cuban Giants, Columbia Giants

Harris, Neal (Nate), 1931 OF, 3B, Pittsburgh Crawfords

Harris, Raymond M. (MO), 1916-43 2B, OF, Homestead Grays; umpire, East-West Lg., NNL

Harris, Robert (Bob), 1935 ph., Pittsburgh Crawfords

Harris, Roger, 1942 INF, Birmingham Black Barons

Harris, Sam, 1932 OF, Monroe Monarchs

Harris, Samuel, 1940 P, Chicago American Giants, Birmingham Black Barons

Harris, Tommy, 1946-49 C, Cleveland Buckeyes, Louisville Buckeyes

Harris, Virgil, 1936-37 P, OF, 2B, Cincinnati Tigers

Harris, William (Bill), 1930-31 OF, Pittsburgh Crawfords

Harris, Wilmer, 1945-50 P, Philadelphia Stars

Harris, Win, 1922-28 1B, SS, Homestead Grays

Harrison, —, 1915-16 1B, West Baden (Ind.) Sprudels, Bowser's ABCs

Harrison, Abraham 1885-97 SS, Philadelphia Orions, Argyle Hotel, Cuban Giants, Trenton Cuban Giants (Middle States Lg.), York Cuban Giants (Eastern Interstate Lg.)

Harrison, Tomlini, 1927-30 P, St. Louis Stars, Kansas City Monarchs

Harriston, Clyde, 1944 INF, Birmingham Black Barons, Cincinnati-Indianapolis Clowns

Hart, —, 1887 C, Pittsburgh Keystones

Hart, Frank 1884 SS, St. Louis Black Stockings

Hartley, (Hop), 1925 P, Kansas City Monarchs

Harvey, —, 1937 SS, Philadelphia Stars

Harvey, B.T., 1950 sec'y, NSL

Harvey, Charles, 1950 SS, Cleveland Buckeyes

Harvey, David William (Bill), 1932-45 P, Memphis Red Sox, Pittsburgh Crawfords, Baltimore Elite Giants, Cleveland Red Sox, Toledo Crawfords, Indianapolis Crawfords, Cleveland Giants

Harvey, Frank, 1912-24 P, OF, St. Louis Giants, Brooklyn Royal Giants, Lincoln Stars, Lincoln Giants, Bacharach Giants, Philadelphia Giants

Harvey, Robert A. (Bob), 1943-50 OF, Newark Eagles, Houston Eagles

Haslett, Claude, 1936-37 P, Memphis Red Sox, Indianapolis Athletics

Havis, Chester, 1947 P, Memphis Red Sox

Hawk, —, 1905 C, Brooklyn Royal Giants

Hawks, —, 1913 3B, Philadelphia Giants

Hawkins, Lemuel (Hawk), 1919-28 1B, OF, Los Angeles White Sox, Kansas City Monarchs, Chicago Giants, Chicago American Giants

Hawley, —, 1932 C, Memphis Red Sox

Hayes, —, 1912-13 C, OF, SS, Pittsburgh Giants, Philadelphia Giants, Newark Red Sox

Hayes, Buddy, 1916-24 C, Chicago American Giants, Indianapolis ABCs, Pittsburgh Keystones, Cleveland Browns, St. Louis Giants, Milwaukee Bears, Toledo Tigers

Hayes, Burnalle James (Bun), 1929-35 P, Baltimore Black Sox, Washington Pilots, Chicago American Giants, Newark Dodgers, Brooklyn Eagles

Hayes, Jimmy, 1949 C, Kansas City Monarchs

Hayes, John William, 1934-50 C, Newark Dodgers, Newark Eagles, New York Black Yankees, Boston Blues, Baltimore Elite Giants

Hayes, John W., 1940 SS, 2B, Philadelphia Stars, St. Louis Stars

Hayes, Thomas H. Jr., 1939-50 officer, Birmingham Black Barons; vice pres, NAL

Hayes, Wilbur, 1942-50 off., g.m., Cincinnati Buckeyes, Cleveland Buckeyes; sergeant-at-arms, NAL

Hayman, Charles (Bugs), 1909-16 P, 1B, Philadelphia Giants

Haynes, Sammy, 1943-45 C, Kansas City Monarchs

Haynes, Bill (Willie), 1921-24 P, Dallas Giants, Hilldale, Harrisburg Giants, Baltimore Black Sox, Bacharach Giants

Haywood, Albert (Buster), 1935-50 C, MGR, Birmingham Black Barons, New York Cubans, Cincinnati-Indianapolis Clowns, Indianapolis Clowns, Cincinnati Clowns, Memphis Red Sox, Brooklyn Eagles

Heard, Jehosie, 1947-50 P, Birmingham Black Barons, Memphis Red Sox, Houston Eagles

Heat, —, 1941 P, Cuban Stars

Heffner, Arthur, 1947-49 OF, New York Black Yankees, Philadelphia Stars

Henderson, —, 1925 C, Birmingham Black Barons

Henderson, Armour, 1915 P, Mohawk Giants

Henderson, Arthur Chauncey (Rats), 1922-31 P, Richmond Giants, Bacharach Giants, Detroit Stars

Henderson, Ben, 1936-37 P, St. Louis Stars, Birmingham Black Barons

Henderson, Curtis (Curt), 1936-42 SS, 3B, Philadelphia Stars New York Black Yankees, Washington Black Senators, Toledo Crawfords, Indianapolis Crawfords, Chicago American Giants Homestead Grays

Henderson, George (Rube), 1921-23 OF, 3B, P, Cleveland Tate Stars, Toledo Tigers, Detroit Stars

Henderson, H. (Long), 1932 1B, Nashville Elite Giants

Henderson, Lenon, 1930-33 3B, SS, Nashville Elite Giants, Birmingham Black Barons, Montgomery Grey Sox, Louisville Black Caps, Indianapolis ABCs

Henderson, Louis, 1925 P, OF, Bacharach Giants

Henderson, Neal, 1949 OF, Kansas City Monarchs

Hendricks, —, 1918,1922 P, OF, Lincoln Giants,Baltimore Black Sox

Hendrix, Stokes, 1934 P, Nashville Elite Giants

Henry, Alfred, 1950 OF, Baltimore Elite Giants

Henry, Charles (Charlie), 1922-42 P, MGR, Hilldale, Harrisburg Giants, Detroit Stars, Bacharach Giants, Detroit Black Sox, Louisville Black Colonels

Henry, Joe, 1950 2B, Memphis Red Sox

Henry, Leo (Preacher), 1938-47 P, Jacksonville Red Caps, Cleveland Bears, Cincinnati Clowns, Indianapolis Clowns

Henry, Otis, 1931-37 2B, 3B, Memphis Red Sox, Monroe Monarchs, Indianapolis Athletics

Hensley, Logan (Eggie, Slap), 1923-39 P, St. Louis Stars, Toledo Tigers, Indianapolis ABCs, Detroit Stars, Cleveland Giants, Chicago American Giants, Cleveland Tate Stars, Cleveland Browns

Herbert, 1894 OF, Pawtucket (New England Lg.)

Heredia, Ramon (Napoleon), 1939-45 3B, SS, Cuban Stars, New York Cubans

Herman, see Herman Andrews

Hernandez, Jose, 1920-22 P, OF, Cuban Stars (NNL)

Hernandez, Ramon, 1929-30 3B, Cuban Stars (NNL)

Hernandez, Ricardo (Chico), 1909-14 2B, 3B, Cuban Stars, All Cubans

Herrera, Ramon (Paito), 1916-28 2B, 3B, Jersey City Cubans, Cuban Stars (NNL), Cuban Stars (ECL), Long Branch Cubans

Herring, —, 1920 3B, St. Louis Giants

Herron, Robert Lee, 1950 OF, Houston Eagles

Heslip, Jesse, 1945 pres; Toledo Cubs (USL)

Hewitt, Joe, 1910-32 SS, OF, 2B, MGR, St. Louis Giants, Brooklyn Royal Giants, Lincoln Giants, Philadelphia Giants, Detroit Stars, Chicago American Giants, St. Louis Stars, Cleveland Cubs, Dayton Marcos, Milwaukee Bears, Birmingham Black Barons, Nashville Elite Giants

Heywood, Charlie (Dobie), 1925-26 P, Lincoln Giants

Hicks, Eugene (Jimmy), 1940-41 P, Homestead Grays, New York Cuban Stars

Hicks, Wesley, 1927-31 OF, Chicago American Giants, Memphis Red Sox, Kansas City Monarchs

Hidalgo, Heliodoro, 1910-12 OF, 3B, Stars of Cuba, Cuban Stars, All Cubans

Higdon, Barney, 1943 P, Cincinnati Clowns

Higgins, Robert (Bob) 1887-88 P, Syracuse (International Lg.)

Higgins, N. 1887 C, Columbus (Ohio St. Lg.)

Hightower, —, 1890 1B, Lincoln (Neb) Giants

Hill, Ben, 1943,1946 P, Philadelphia Stars, Pittsburgh Crawfords

Hill, C. (Lefty), 1914-24 OF, P, Chicago Union Giants, Dayton Marcos, Detroit Stars, St. Louis Giants, Chicago American Giants

Hill, Herb, 1949 OF, P, Philadelphia Stars

Hill, J. Preston (Pete), 1904-25 OF, 2B, MGR, bus. mgr, Philadelphia Giants, Leland Giants, Chicago American Giants, Detroit Stars, Milwaukee Bears, Baltimore Black Sox, Cuban X Giants

Hill, Jimmy (Lefty, Squab), 1938-45 P, Albany (NY) Black Sox, Newark Eagles

Hill, John, 1900-05 3B, SS, Genuine Cuban Giants, Philadelphia Giants, Cuban X Giants

Hill, Johnson (Fred), 1920-28 2B, 3B, OF, St. Louis Giants, Detroit Stars, Milwaukee Bears, Brooklyn Royal Giants

Hill, Jonathan, 1937 OF, P, Atlanta Black Crackers, St. Louis Stars

Hill, Samuel (Sam), 1937,1947-48 OF, 1B, Detroit Stars, Chicago American Giants,

Hill, W.R., 1885 SS, Brooklyn Remsens

Hines, John, 1924-34 C, OF, Chicago American Giants, Cole's American Giants

Hinson, Frank, 1896 P, Cuban X Giants

Hinton, Roland (Archie, Charlie), 1945-46 P, INF, Baltimore Elite Giants

Hitchman, —, 1925 3B, Indianapolis ABCs

Hoagland, F.B., 1885 sec'y, Brooklyn Remsens

Hoard, —, 1921 P, Kansas City Monarchs

Hobgood, Frederick (Lefty, John) [Hopgood], 1941-46-P, UTIL, Newark Eagles, New York Black Yankees

Hobson, Charles (Johnny [Hopson]), 1922-25 P, SS, OF, Lincoln Giants, Bacharach Giants, Richmond Giants

Hocker, Bruce, 1914-20 1B, OF, Bowser's ABCs, Lincoln Stars Dayton Marcos, Louisville White Sox, Chicago American Giants, Hilldale

Hodges, William (Jimmy), 1918-25 P, Lincoln Giants, Baltimore Black Sox

Hoke, (Bud), 1945 player, Toledo Cubs (USL)

Holcomb, —, 1923 P, Detroit Stars

Holland, —, 1921 1B, Hilldale

Holland, Elvis William (Bill), 1920-41 P, MGR, Detroit Stars, Chicago American Giants, Lincoln Giants, Brooklyn Royal Giants, New York Black Yankees, Philadelphia Stars

Holland, William (Billy) 1894-1908,1923 P, OF, 3B, Page Fence Giants, Chicago Unions, Brooklyn Royal Giants, Leland Giants, Pop Watkins Stars, Algona (IA) Brownies; umpire, NNL

Holliday, Charles Dourcher (Flit), 1938 OF, P, Atlanta Black Crackers

Hollingsworth, Curtis, 1947,1950 P, Birmingham Black Barons

Hollins, —, 1936 P, Birmingham Black Barons

Holloway, Christopher Columbus (Crush), 1921-39 OF, Indianapolis ABCs, Baltimore Black Sox, Hilldale, Detroit Stars, Bacharach Giants, Brooklyn Eagles, New York Black Yankees

Holmes, Benjamin F. (Ben) 1885-89 3B, Argyle Hotel, Cuban Giants, Trenton Cuban Giants (Middle States Lg.)

Holmes, Eddie, 1932 P, Baltimore Black Sox

Holmes, Frank (Sonny), 1929-38 P, Bacharach Giants, Philadelphia Stars, Lincoln Giants, Washington Elite Giants, Washington Black Senators

Holmes, Leroy Thomas (Phillie), 1935-45 SS, Jacksonville Red Caps, Cleveland Bears, Atlanta Black Crackers, Kansas City Monarchs, Cincinnati-Indianapolis Clowns, New York Black Yankees, Brooklyn Eagles

Holsey, Robert J. (Frog), 1928-32 P, Chicago American Giants, Chicago Columbia Giants, Cleveland Cubs, Nashville Elite Giants

Holt, Johnny, 1922-23 OF, Pittsburgh Keystones, Toledo Tigers

Holt, Joseph, 1928 OF, Brooklyn Cuban Giants

Holtz, Eddie, 1920-24 2B, SS, St. Louis Giants, Chicago American Giants, St. Louis Stars, Lincoln Giants

Hood, Dozier Charles, 1945 C, Kansas City Monarchs

Hoods, William, see William Woods

Hooker, see Bruce Hocker

Hooker, Leniel Charlie (Len, Elbow), 1940-49 P, Newark Eagles, Houston Eagles

Hopkins, George 1890-99 P, 2B, Chicago Unions, Adrian Page Fence Giants

Hopwood, —, 1928 OF, Kansas City Monarchs

Hordy, J.H. 1887 player, Baltimore Lord Baltimores

Horn, —, 1925 2B, Birmingham Black Barons

Horn, William (Will) 1896-1905 P, Chicago Unions, Philadelphia Giants, Leland Giants

Horne, William (Billie), 1938-46 SS, 2B, Monroe Monarchs, Chicago American Giants, Cincinnati Buckeyes, Cleveland Buckeyes, Harrisburg-St.Louis Stars

Horns, James J. 1887 player, Boston Resolutes

Hoskins, David Taylor (Dave), 1942-49 OF, P, Cincinnati Clowns, Chicago American Giants, Homestead Grays, Louisville Buckeyes

Hoskins, William (Bill), 1937-46 OF, Detroit Stars, Memphis Red Sox, Baltimore Elite Giants, New York Black Yankees, St. Louis Stars, Kansas City Monarchs

House, Charles (Red), 1937,1942 3B, Detroit Stars, Detroit Black Sox

Houston, —, 1910 C, SS, West Baden (Ind) Sprudels

Houston, —, 1920 P, 2B, Indianapolis ABCs, Kansas City Monarchs

Houston, Bill, 1941-42 P, Homestead Grays

Houston, Nathanial (Jess), 1930-39 P, INF, Memphis Red Sox, Cincinnatitigers, Chicago American Giants

Hovley, —, 1932 P, Nashville Elite Giants

Howard, —, 1897-99 UTIL, Cuban Giants, Cuban X Giants

Howard, —, 1921-23,1927 P, 3B, Detroit Stars, Indianapolis ABCs, Memphis Red Sox, Cleveland Hornets

Howard, —, 1920-29 SS, P, Norfolk Giants, Harrisburg Giants, Baltimore Black Sox, Lincoln Stars, Norfolk Stars

Howard, Carl, 1935 OF, Pittsburgh Crawfords

Howard, Carranza (Schoolboy), 1941-50 P, Cuban Stars, New York Cubans, Indianapolis Clowns, New York Black Yankees

Howard, Elston, 1948-50 OF, C, Kansas City Monarchs

Howard, Herb, 1948 P, OF, Kansas City Monarchs

Howard, Herman (Red), 1932-46 P, Atlanta Black Crackers, Memphis Red Sox, Washington Elite Giants, Indianapolis Athletics, Jacksonville Red Caps, Indianapolis ABCs, Chicago American Giants, Birmingham Black Barons, Little Rock Black Travelers, Cleveland Bears

Howard, William (Bill), 1931-33 1B, 3B, Birmingham Black Barons

Howell, —, 1908 OF, Brooklyn Royal Giants

Howell, Henry, 1918-21 P, Pennsylvania Giants, Bacharach Giants, Pennsylvania Red Caps of New York, Brooklyn Royal Giants

Hubbard, Dehart, 1934-37,1942 official, sec'y, Cincinnati Tigers, Cleveland-Cincinnati Buckeyes

Hubbard, Jesse James (Mountain), 1919-34 P, OF, Bacharach Giants, Brooklyn Royal Giants, Baltimore Black Sox, Hilldale, Homestead Grays, New York Black Yankees

Hubbard, Larry, 1946 UTIL, Kansas City Monarchs

Huber, —, 1930-31 C, OF, Memphis Red Sox, Nashville Elite Giants, Birmingham Black Barons

Huber, John Marshall [Hubert], 1939-50 P, C, Ethiopian Clowns, Chicago American Giants, Birmingham Black Barons, Cincinnati Clowns, Memphis Red Sox, Philadelphia Stars

Hubert, Willie (Bubber), 1939-46 P, Newark Eagles, Baltimore Elite Giants, Cincinnati Buckeyes, Baltimore Grays, Homestead Grays, Pittsburgh Crawfords, Brooklyn Brown Dodgers, Philadelphia Stars, Cleveland Buckeyes, New York Black Yankees

Hudson, —, 1908 OF, Brooklyn Colored Giants

Hudson, Charles (Keen Legs), 1923,1930 P, Milwaukee Bears, Louisville White Sox

Hudson, William, 1937-42 P, Cincinnati Tigers, Chicago American Giants

Hudspeth, Robert (Highpockets), 1920-32 1B, Indianapolis ABCs, Columbus Buckeyes, Bacharach Giants, Lincoln Giants, Brooklyn Royal Giants, Hilldale, New York Black Yankees

Hueston, William C., 1926-31 pres, NNL

Huff, Eddie, 1923-32 C, OF, MGR, Bacharach Giants, Dayton Marcos

Hughbanks, [Hubanks] 1890 2B, Lincoln (Neb) Giants

Hughes, A., 1927 OF, Kansas City Monarchs

Hughes, Charley, 1931-38 2B, Cleveland Red Sox, Columbus Blue Birds, Washington Black Senators, Washington Pilots, Pittsburgh Crawfords

Hughes, Frank, 1937 P, Indianapolis Athletics

Hughes, Lee, 1950 P, Kansas City Monarchs

Hughes, Robert, 1931 P, Louisville White Sox

Hughes, Samuel Thomas (Sammy T.), 1930-46 2B, Louisville White Sox, Nashville Elite Giants, Homestead Grays, Columbus Elite Giants, Washington Elite Giants, Baltimore Elite Giants, Washington Pilots

Humber, Tom (Charlie), 1945,1950 2B, Newark Eagles, Baltimore Elite Giants

Humes, John, 1937 P, Newark Eagles

Humphries, —, 1936-37 OF, Atlanta Black Crackers, Memphis Red Sox

Hundley, Johnny Lee, 1943 C, OF, Cleveland Buckeyes

Hungo, —, 1916 1B, Long Branch Cubans

Hunt, Grover, 1946 C, Chicago American Giants

Hunt, Leonard (Len), 1949-50 OF, Kansas City Monarchs

Hunter, Bertrum (Nate), 1931-36 P, St. Louis Stars, Detroit Wolves, Pittsburgh Crawfords, Kansas City Monarchs, Philadelphia Stars, Homestead Grays

Hunter, Eugene, 1924 P, Memphis Red Sox, Cleveland Browns

Hunter, Willie, 1933 P, Akron Black Tyrites

Hutchinson, Fred (Hutch, Puggey), 1910-25 SS, 3B, 2B, Leland Giants, Chicago American Giants, Indianapolis ABCs, Bacharach Giants, Bowser's ABCs

Hutchinson, Willie (Ace), 1939-50 P, Kansas City Monarchs, Memphis Red Sox

Hutt, —, 1920-24 1B, OF, Dayton Marcos, Toledo Tigers, St. Louis Giants

Hyde, —, 1927-30 OF, 2B, Memphis Red Sox, Birmingham Black Barons

Hyde, Cowan F. (Bubba), 1937-50 OF, 2B, Cincinnati Tigers, Memphis Red Sox, Chicago American Giants, Indianapolis Athletics, Houston Eagles

Hyde, Harry 1896-1904 3B, 1B, Chicago Unions, Chicago Union Giants

Ingersoll, —, 1905 2B, Brooklyn Royal Giants

Ingram, Alfred, 1942 P, Jacksonville Red Caps

Irvin, Irwin (Bill), 1906,1919 3B, OF,MGR, Leland Giants, Cleveland Tate Stars

Irvin, Monford Merrill (Monte), 1937-48 OF, SS, 3B, Newark Eagles

Israel, Clarence Charles (Pint), 1940-47 3B, 2B, Newark Eagles, Homestead Grays

Israel, Elbert, 1950 INF, Philadelphia Stars

Ivory, —, 1936 P, 1B, Chicago American Giants

Jackman, Bill (Earl, Cannon Ball), 1925-42 P, Lincoln Giants, Philadelphia Giants, Quaker Giants, Brooklyn Eagles, Boston Royal Giants

Jackson, —, 1915 SS, Chicago Giants

Jackson, —, 1916-26 C, OF, Pennsylvania Red Caps of New York, Lincoln Giants, Newark Stars, Lincoln Stars, Philadelphia Giants

Jackson, —, 1921 P, Indianapolis ABCs

Jackson, —, 1931 P, Brooklyn Royal Giants

Jackson, —, 1932 OF, C, Indianapolis ABCs

Jackson, A. Matthew, 1932-34 3B, SS, Montgomery Grey Sox, Birmingham Black Barons, Cincinnati Tigers

Jackson, Andrew (Andy), 1888-99 3B, New York Gorhams, Cuban Giants, Lansing, (Mi) Colored Capital All-Americans, Cuban X Giants, York Cuban Giants (Eastern Interstate Lg.), New York Gorhams (Middle States Lg.)

Jackson, B. (Bozo), 1945 3B, Homestead Grays

Jackson, C., 1929 3B, Homestead Grays

Jackson, Carlton, 1928 officer, Harrisburg Giants

Jackson, Dallas, 1950 2B, INF, Cleveland Buckeyes

Jackson, Daniel M. (Dan, Hatchet), 1949 OF, Homestead Grays

Jackson, Edgar S., 1937 C, Memphis Red Sox

Jackson, F., 1887 officer, Brooklyn Remsens

Jackson, (Gen) 1947 OF, P, Baltimore Elite Giants

Jackson, George, 1886-87 P, OF, Philadelphia Pythians, Trenton Cuban Giants (Middle States Lg.)

Jackson, George, 1950 INF, New York Black Yankees

Jackson, (Gumbo), 1922 3B, New Orleans Crescent Stars

Jackson, Jack, 1927-28 OF, Bacharach Giants, Baltimore Black Sox

Jackson, Jackie, 1950 OF, Homestead Grays

Jackson, John W. Jr. (Stony), 1950 P, Houston Eagles

Jackson, (Lefty), 1926 P, Philadelphia Giants

Jackson, Lester E., 1938-41 P, OF, Newark Eagles, New York Black Yankees

Jackson, Norman (Jelly), 1934-45 SS, 2B, Cleveland Red Sox, Homestead Grays, Washington Elite Giants

Jackson, Oscar, 1887-96 OF, 1B, New York Gorhams, Cuban Giants, Cuban X Giants, York Cuban Giants (Eastern Interstate Lg.), Philadelphia Giants

Jackson, R.B., 1931-50 pres, vice pres, NSL; officer, owner, Nashville Black Vols, Nashville Cubs

Jackson, R.R. (Major), 1889 manager, Chicago Unions

Jackson, R.T., 1928-31 officer, Birmingham Black Barons; pres, NSL

Jackson, Randolph, 1887 2B, Oswego (International Lg.)

Jackson, Richard, 1921-31 2B, SS, 3B, Bacharach Giants, Harrisburg Giants, Baltimore Black Sox, Hilldale

Jackson, Robert (Bob), 1887-96 C, 1B, OF, New York Gorhams, Cuban X Giants, Ansonia Cuban Giants (Connecticut St. Lg.)

Jackson, Robert, 1897-1900 C, Chicago Unions

Jackson, Robert R.(Major), 1939-42 commissioner, NAL

Jackson, Rufus (Sonnyman), 1934-49 pres, tres, Homestead Grays

Jackson, Sam, 1887 player, Pittsburgh Keystones

Jackson, Sam, 1926 C, Cleveland Elites

Jackson, Samuel, 1942-47 P, 1B, Chicago American Giants

Jackson, Stanford, 1923-31 OF, SS, 3B, 2B, Memphis Red Sox, Chicago American Giants, Chicago Columbia Giants, Birmingham Black Barons

Jackson, Tom, 1924-31 P, St. Louis Stars, Cleveland Tigers, Nashville Elite Giants, Memphis Red Sox, Louisville White Sox

Jackson, Thomas, 1916-28 officer, Bacharach Giants

Jackson, Verdell, 1950 P, Memphis Red Sox

Jackson, W. (Big Train), 1938-40 P, Kansas City Monarchs, Memphis Red Sox

Jackson, William, 1890-1906 OF, C, 2B, Cuban Giants, Cuban X Giants, York Cuban Giants (Eastern Interstate Lg.), Ansonia Cuban Giants (Connecticut St.Lg.)

Jackson, William (Ashes), 1910-17 3B, Kansas City, (KS) Giants, Kansas City Royal Giants

Jamerson, Londell (Tincy), 1950 P, Kansas City Monarchs

James, —, 1896 P, Cuban X Giants

James, —, 1925 P, Cuban Stars (ECL)

James, J., 1912 1B, Smart Set

James, Livingston (Tice, Winky, Tarzan), 1939-42-SS, Ethiopian Clowns, Cincinnati Buckeyes, Cincinnati Clowns, Chicago American Giants, Cleveland Buckeyes

James, W. (Gus, Nux), 1905-20 2B, C, OF, Philadelphia Giants, Smart Set, Mohawk N.Y. Giants, Lincoln Giants, Bacharach Giants, Brooklyn Royal Giants, Pop Watkins Stars, Pittsburgh Stars of Buffalo

James, William, 1887 player, Philadelphia Pythians

Jameson, —, 1932-35 P, Newark Dodgers, Homestead Grays

Jamison, Caesar, 1923-32 umpire, NNL, East-West Lg.

Jamison, Eddie, 1950 C, Cleveland Buckeyes

Jarmon, Don, 1933 P, Columbus Blue Birds

Jasper, —, 1932 P, Birmingham Black Barons

Jauron —, 1928 P, Cleveland Tigers

Jefferson, Edward L. (Eddie), 1945-47 P, Philadelphia Stars

Jefferson, George Leo (Jeff), 1942-50 P, Jacksonville Red Caps, Cleveland Buckeyes, Louisville Buckeyes

Jefferson, R., 1939 3B, P, Indianapolis ABCs

Jefferson, Ralph, 1918-26 OF, Indianapolis ABCs, Bacharach Giants, Philadelphia Royal Stars, Washington Potomacs, Philadelphia Giants, Peter's Chicago Union Giants

Jefferson, Willie, 1937-50 P, Cincinnati Tigers,

Memphis Red Sox, Cincinniati Buckeyes, Cleveland Buckeyes

Jeffreys, Frank, 1917-20 OF, 2B, Chicago Giants

Jeffries, E., 1922 C, Chicago Giants

Jeffries, Harry, 1920-48 3B, C, SS, 1B, MGR, Chicago Giants, Chicago American Giants, Detroit Stars, Cleveland Tigers, Chicago Columbia Giants, Bacharach Giants, Knoxville Giants, Toledo Tigers, Baltimore Black Sox, Harrisburg Giants, Baltimore Panthers, Cleveland Browns

Jeffries, James C., 1914-31 P, OF, Indianapolis ABCs, Baltimore Black Sox, Birmingham Black Barons, Harrisburg Giants

Jeffries, Jeff, 1940 P, Brooklyn Royal Giants

Jeffries, M., 1925,1932 3B, Baltimore Black Sox, Hilldale

Jenkins, —, 1924 P, Washington Potomacs

Jenkins, Clarence (Barney), 1925-29 C, Philadelphia Giants, Detroit Stars

Jenkins, Clarence R. (Fats), 1920-40 OF, MGR, Lincoln Giants, Harrisburg Giants, Bacharach Giants, Baltimore Black Sox, New York Black Yankees, Philadelphia Stars, Brooklyn Eagles, Brooklyn Royal Giants, Pittsburgh Crawfords, Toledo Crawfords, Penn Red Caps of NY

Jenkins, Horace, 1914-25 OF, P, Chicago American Giants, Chicago Giants, Chicago Unions Giants

Jenkins, James Edward (Pee Wee), 1944-50 P, Cincinnati- Indianapolis Clowns, New York Cubans

Jenkins, Tom, 1916,1928 player, sec'y, Hilldale

Jennings, Thurman (Jack), 1915-27 2B, SS, OF, Chicago Giants

Jessie, W., 1887 player, Louisville Falls City

Jessup, Gentry, 1940-49 P, Chicago American Giants, Birmingham Black Barons

Jethroe, Samuel (Sam, The Jet), 1942-48 OF, Cincinnati Buckeyes, Cleveland Buckeyes

Jewell, Warner, 1917-26 owner, officer, Jewell's ABCs, Indianapolis ABCs

Jimenez, Bienvenido (Hooks), 1915-29 2B, Cuban Stars (NNL), Cuban Stars (ECL), Cuban Stars

Jimenez, E., 1920-21 OF, Philadelphia Giants, Cuban Stars (NNL)

Johnson, —, 1886 OF, New York Gorhams

Johnson, —, 1922 OF, Detroit Stars

Johnson, A., 1914-17 2B, 3B, Lincoln Stars

Johnson, A. (Sampson), 1914-22 C, Bacharach Giants, Pittsburgh Giants, Pennsylvania Giants, Homestead Grays, Philadelphia Giants

Johnson, Al, 1938-40 P, Baltimore Elite Giants, Washington Black Senators

Johnson, Allen, 1942-46 officer, owner, St. Louis Stars, New York Black Yankees, Harrisburg-St. Louis Stars, Boston Blues

Johnson, B. (Monk), 1917-26 1B, 2B, P, OF, Pennsylvania Red Caps of New York, Lincoln Giants

Johnson, B., 1940 SS, Brooklyn Royal Giants

Johnson, Ben, 1916-23 P, Bacharach Giants

Johnson, Bert, see Bert Johnston

Johnson, Bill, 1933 3B, Akron Tyrites

Johnson, Bill (Willie), 1938-39 C, New York Black Yankees, Chicago American Giants

Johnson, Byron (Mex), 1937-39 SS, Kansas City Monarchs

Johnson, C., see G. Claude Johnson

Johnson, Cecil (Sess), 1918-28 1B, 3B, SS, P, Hilldale, Philadelphia Tigers, Philadelphia Royal Stars, Baltimore Black Sox, Newark Stars, Norfolk Stars

Johnson, Charles, 1949-50 3B, Cleveland Buckeyes, Memphis Red Sox

Johnson, Charles B., 1925-26 officer, Bacharach Giants

Johnson, Clifford Jr. (Cliff, Connie), 1940-50 P, Indianapolis Crawfords, Kansas City Monarchs

Johnson, Curtis, 1950 P, Kansas City Monarchs

Johnson, D. (Dud), 1914-19 OF, SS, 2B, Philadelphia Giants, Brooklyn Royal Giants

Johnson, Dan (Shang), 1916-21 P, Bacharach Giants, Brooklyn Royal Giants, Lincoln Giants, Hilldale, Indianapolis ABCs

Johnson, Ernest (Schoolboy), 1949-50 P, OF, Kansas City Monarchs

Johnson, Frank, 1932-37 OF,MGR, Monroe Monarchs, Memphis Red Sox

Johnson, Fred, 1946 P, Pittsburgh Crawfords

Johnson, G. Claude (Hooks), 1921-32 3B, 2B, SS, P, Baltimore Black Sox, Harrisburg Giants, Detroit Stars, Birmingham Black Barons, Memphis Red Sox, Cleveland Tate Stars, Hilldale

Johnson, George (Chappie), 1896-1939 C, 1B, MGR Columbia Giants, Chicago Unions Giants, Brooklyn Royal Giants, Leland Giants, Chicago Giants, St. Louis Giants, Dayton Chappies, Custer's Baseball Club of Columbus, Philadelphia Royal Stars, Norfolk Stars, Algona (IA) Brownies, Adrian Page Fence Giants, Mohawk Giants, Philadelphia Giants, Pennsylvania Red Caps of N.Y., Chappie Johnson's Stars

Johnson, George Washington (Dibo), 1909-28 OF, Fort Worth Wonders, Kansas City, Kan., Giants, Brooklyn Royal Giants, Hilldale, Lincoln Giants, Philadelphia Tigers, Bacharach Giants

Johnson, Grant (Home Run), 1894-1921 SS, 2B, MGR, Page Fence Giants, Columbia Giants, Brooklyn Royal Giants, Cuban X Giants, Philadelphia Giants, Lincoln Giants, Lincoln Stars, Pittsburgh Colored Stars, Pittsburgh Stars of Buffalo, Chicago Unions, Findlay, Ohio, Mohawk Giants, Brooklyn Colored Giants

Johnson, H. (Hamp), 1933-34,1946 OF, Birmingham Black Barons

Johnson, Harry A., 1886-89 2B, OF, C, Cuban Giants, Trenton Cuban Giants (Middle States Lg.)

Johnson, J. (Lefty), 1929-33 1B, P, OF, Memphis Red Sox

Johnson, Jack (Topeka Jack), 1903-04,1909-10 1B, OF, Philadelphia Giants, Kansas City (Mo.) Royal Giants, Kansas City, Kansas Giants

Johnson, Jack, 1938-40 3B, Homestead Grays, Toledo Crawfords, Cincinnati Buckeyes

Johnson, James, 1898 RF, C, Adrian Page Fence Giants

Johnson, James (J.D.), 1950 P, Philadelphia Stars

Johnson, Jim, 1932-34 SS, Hilldale, Bacharach Giants

Johnson, Jimmy (Slim), 1939-43 P, Toledo Crawfords, Indianapolis Crawfords, Philadelphia Stars

Johnson, Jimmy (Jeep), 1946-47 SS, Pittsburgh Crawfords, Homestead Grays

Johnson, Joe, 1884-85 P, C, Baltimore Atlantics

Johnson, John (Johnny), 1938-46 P, Birmingham Black Barons, Homestead Grays, New York Black Yankees, Newark Eagles, Baltimore Elite Giants

Johnson, John, 1950 UTIL, New York Cubans

Johnson, John B., 1925-28 pres, MGR, Brooklyn Cuban Giants

Johnson, Rev. John H., 1947-48 pres, NNL

Johnson, John Wesley (Smokey), 1922-28 P, Cleveland Tate Stars, Cleveland Elites, Cleveland Browns, Lincoln Giants

Johnson, Johnny, 1943 P, Cleveland Buckeyes

Johnson, Joseph, 1937 officer, Indianapolis Athletics

Johnson, Joshua (Josh, Brute), 1934-42 C, P, OF, Cincinnati Tigers, Homestead Grays, New York Black Yankees, Brooklyn Royal Giants

Johnson, Judy, see Johnson, William J

Johnson, Junior, 1899-1906 1B, C, Columbia Giants, Philadelphia Giants, Quaker Giants, Brooklyn Royal Giants

Johnson, L., 1948 P, Kansas City Monarchs

Johnson, Leaman, 1941-45 SS, INF, Memphis Red Sox, Newark Eagles, Birmingham Black Barons, New York Black Yankees

Johnson, Lee, 1941 C, Birmingham Black Barons

Johnson, Leonard, 1947-48 P, Chicago American Giants

Johnson, Leroy, 1950 P, Birmingham Black Barons

Johnson, Louis (Dicta), 1911-25 P, MGR, coach, Twin City Gophers, Chicago American

Giants, Indianapolis ABCs, Detroit Stars, Toledo Tigers, Pittsburgh Keystones, Milwaukee Bears, Bowser's ABCs

Johnson, M., see B. (Monk) Johnson

Johnson, (Monk), see B. (Monk) Johnson

Johnson, Nate, 1922-24 P, Bacharach Giants, Cleveland Browns, Brooklyn Royal Giants, Harrisburg Giants

Johnson, Othello, 1916-22 P, OF, Bacharach Giants, Brooklyn Royal Giants, Philadelphia Giants, Lincoln Giants, Penn Red Caps of NY

Johnson, Oscar (Heavy), 1922-33 OF, C, 2B, Kansas City Monarchs, Baltimore Black Sox, Harrisburg Giants, Cleveland Tigers, Memphis Red Sox, Dayton Marcos

Johnson, (Pee Wee), 1939 2B, Newark Eagles

Johnson, Pearley (Tubby, Peter), 1920-27, 1942 P, OF, INF, Baltimore Black Sox, Boston Royal Giants

Johnson, R., 1932 OF, Washington Pilots

Johnson, Ralph, 1940-41,1945 P, Philadelphia Stars

Johnson, Ralph, 1950 SS, Indianapolis Clowns

Johnson, (Rat), 1909 player, St. Paul Gophers

Johnson, Ray, 1923 OF, St. Louis Stars

Johnson, Richard, 1887-90 C, OF, Zanesville (Ohio State Lg.), Tri-State Lg.), Springfield and Peoria (Central Interstate Lg.)

Johnson, Robert (Bob), 1928 INF, Brooklyn Cuban Giants, Philadelphia Tigers

Johnson, Robert, 1939-40 OF, New York Black Yankees

Johnson, Robert, 1944 P, Kansas City Monarchs

Johnson, Roy (Bubbles), 1920-22 1B, 2B, St. Louis Giants, Kansas City Monarchs

Johnson, Rudolph, 1950 OF, Cleveland Buckeyes

Johnson, S., see Cecil Johnson

Johnson, Tom (Tommy), 1937-42 P, St. Louis Stars, Chicago American Giants

Johnson, Thomas (Tommy), 1914-25 P, Indianapolis ABCs, Chicago American Giants, Pittsburgh Keystones;umpire, NNL

Johnson, Tommy F., 1950 P, Indianapolis Clowns

Johnson, W., 1944-45 P, Memphis Red Sox

Johnson, W., 1925 see William H. Johnson

Johnson, W., 1928 see Wade Johnston

Johnson, William H. (Wise, Bill, Big C.), 1920-33 C, OF, MGR, Homestead Grays, Hilldale, Philadelphia Tigers, Pennsylvania Red Caps of New York, Wilmington Potomacs, Harrisburg Giants, Washington Potomacs, Dayton Marcos

Johnson, William Julius (Judy), 1918-38 3B, SS, MGR, Hilldale, Homestead Grays, Darby Daisies, Pittsburgh Crawfords

Johnston, Bert (Bucky) [Johnson], 1933-38 OF, Newark Dodgers, Baltimore Black Sox, Birmingham Black Barons

Johnston, C., 1916 2B, Lincoln Stars

Johnston, Tom, 1923 umpire, NNL

Johnston, Wade [Johnson], 1920-33 OF, P, Cleveland Tate Stars, Kansas City Monarchs, Baltimore Black Sox, Detroit Stars, Pennsylvania Red Caps of NY

Johnstone, —, 1912-13 C, Pittsburgh Giants, Philadelphia Giants

Jones, —, 1912 P, Cuban Giants

Jones, —, 1920-21 SS, Indianapolis ABCs

Jones, Abe, 1887-94 C, manager, Chicago Unions

Jones, Albert Alonzo, 1944-46 P, Chicago American Giants, Memphis Red Sox

Jones, Alvin, 1928 officer, Harrisburg Giants

Jones, Archie, 1939 P, New York Cubans

Jones, Arthur Brown (Mutt, Dump), 1925,1934 P, Birmingham Black Barons

Jones, B., 1934 OF, C, Cleveland Red Sox

Jones, Ben, 1950 SS, New York Black Yankees

Jones, Bert, 1896-1903 P, OF, Chicago Unions, Atchison (Kansas St. Lg.), Algona (IA) Brownies

Jones, Charles, 1950 3B, Cleveland Buckeyes

Jones, Clinton Jr. (Casey), 1944-50 C, Memphis Red Sox

Jones, Collins (Collis), 1943-44 UTIL, Cincinnati Clowns, Birmingham Black Barons

Jones, (Country), 1932-33 2B, C, Brooklyn Royal Giants

Jones, Curtis, 1946 P, Cleveland Buckeyes

Jones, D., 1884 player, Philadelphia Mutual B.B.C.

Jones, Edward, 1915-29 C, Chicago American Giants, Chicago Giants, Bacharach Giants

Jones, Ernest (Mint), 1937-41 1B, Jacksonville Red Caps, Cleveland Bears, Philadelphia Stars

Jones, Eugene, 1943 P, Homestead Grays, Baltimore Elite Giants

Jones, Fate, 1950 OF, Birmingham Black Barons

Jones, Hurley, 1931 P, Birmingham Black Barons

Jones, James, 1949-50 OF, 1B, Philadelphia Stars

Jones, John, 1922-34 OF, 1B, Detroit Stars, Memphis Red Sox, Indianapolis ABCs

Jones, Lee, 1908-22 OF, Brooklyn Colored Giants, Brooklyn Royal Giants, Dallas Giants

Jones, Ollie, 1919 3B, St. Louis Giants

Jones, Paul, 1949-50 P, Louisville Buckeyes, Cleveland Buckeyes

Jones, Reuben, 1918-49 OF, MGR, Dallas Giants, Birmingham Black Barons, Indianapolis ABCs, Chicago American Giants, Little Rock Black Travelers, Memphis Red Sox, Houston Eagles

Jones, Robert Leo (Fox), 1933-34 OF, Memphis Red Sox

Jones, Sam (Red, Sad Sam), 1946-48 P, Homestead Grays, Cleveland Buckeyes

Jones, Stuart (Slim, Country), 1933-38 P, Baltimore Black Sox, Philadelphia Stars

Jones, Tom (Pete), 1946 C, Philadelphia Stars

Jones, W., 1934 OF, Birmingham Black Barons

Jones, William (Fox), 1915-30 C, P, Chicago American Giants, Chicago Giants, Bacharach Giants, Hilldale, Chicago Union Giants

Jones, Willis (Will), 1895-1911 SS, OF, Chicago Unions, Leland Giants, Chicago Union Giants, Algona (IA) Brownies

Jordan, Henry (Hen), 1921-25 C, OF, Harrisburg Giants, Pittsburg Stars of Buffalo, Baltimore Black Sox

Jordan, Larnie, 1936-42 SS, Philadelphia Stars, New York Black Yankees, Brooklyn Royal Giants, Bacharach Giants

Jordan, Maynard, 1950 OF, Houston Eagles

Jordan, Robert, 1896-1906 C, 1B, Cuban Giants, Cuban X Giants, Philadelphia Giants

Jordan William F., 1899 MGR, Baltimore Giants

Jordan, Willie, 1933,1938 P, Chicago American Giants, Louisville Black Colonels

Joseph, Walter Lee (Newt), 1922-39 3B, 2B, MGR, Kansas City Monarchs, Birmingham Black Barons, Satchel Paige's All- Stars

Josephs, William, 1924-25 SS, Birmingham Black Barons, Cleveland Browns

Joyner, William, 1893-1902 SS, Chicago Unions, Chicago Union Giants

Juanelo, see Juanelo Mirabel

Juillo, —, 1940 P, Cuban Stars

Juncos, Jose, 1912-21 P, Cuban Stars (East)

Jupiter, —, 1887 P, Cuban Giants

Juran, B., 1923 P, Birmingham Black Barons

Juran, Eli, 1923-1926 P,Birmingham Black Barons, Newark Stars

Justice, Charles P. (Charley), 1933,1937 P, Akron Tyrites, Detroit Stars

Kaiser, Cecil, 1945-49 P, Pittsburgh Crawfords, Homestead Grays

Keene, —, 1915 3B, West Baden (Ind.) Sprudels, Bowser's ABCs

Keeton, Eugene, 1921-26 P, Dayton Marcos, Cleveland Tate Stars, Indianapolis ABCs

Keck, D.J., 1948 tres, Negro American Association

Keenan, James J., 1919-30 bus. mgr, Lincoln Giants; sec'y-tres, ECL

Keigeri, —, 1887 player, Louisville Falls City

Kelley, Holland, 1942 gen. sec'y, United States Lg.

Kelley, Palmer, 1916-18 P, Chicago Giants, Chicago Union Giants

Kelley, Richard A. (Charles), 1889-91 1B, 2B, SS, Danville (Illinois- Indiana Lg.); Jamestown (Pennsylvania-New York Lg.)

Kellman, Edric (Leon), 1946-50 3B, Cleveland Buckeyes, Louisville Buckeyes, Memphis Red Sox

Kelly, —, 1900-08 SS, OF, 3B, Genuine Cuban Giants, Famous Cuban Giants, New York Colored Giants

Kelly, —, 1941 P, Jacksonville Red Caps

Kelly, (Lefty), see Kelly Searcy

Kelly, Walter, 1950 P, Cleveland Buckeyes

Kelly, William, 1898 3B, Celeron Acme Colored Giants (Iron and Oil Lg.)

Kelly, William, 1945-47-C, New York Black Yankees, Homestead Grays

Kemp, —, 1943 C, New York Black Yankees

Kemp, Ed, 1914-28 OF, Philadelphia Royal Giants, Norfolk Stars, Norfolk Giants, Baltimore Black Sox, Lincoln Giants

Kemp, George, 1917 OF, Hilldale

Kemp, James, 1937-39 2B, Atlanta Black Crackers, Jacksonville Red Caps, Indianapolis ABCs

Kemp, John, 1923-28 OF, Memphis Red Sox, Birmingham Black Barons

Kendall, —, 1920,1925 2B, Lincoln Giants

Kendricks, L.H. (Willie), 1943 P, Atlanta Black Crackers

Kennard, Dan, 1915-25 C, Indianapolis ABCs, Chicago American Giants, St. Louis Giants, Lincoln Giants, St. Louis Stars, Detroit Stars

Kennedy, —, 1926 SS, Lincoln Giants

Kennedy, Ernest D., 1950 INF, Memphis Red Sox

Kennedy, Walter, 1950 OF, Chicago American Giants

Kenner, —, 1921,1928 SS, 2B, Hilldale, Washington Grays

Kent, Richard, 1922-31 officer, St. Louis Stars

Kenyon, Harry C., 1919-29 P, 2B, OF, MGR, Brooklyn Royal Giants, Hilldale, Indianpolis ABCs, Chicago American Giants, Lincoln Giants, Detroit Stars, Kansas City Monarchs, Memphis Red Sox

Kerner, J., 1931-33 OF, Columbus Blue Birds, Detroit Stars, Indianapolis ABCs

Key, Ludie, 1934 pres, Birmingham Black Barons

Keyes, Garvin, 1943 INF, Philadelphia Stars

Keyes, Robert, 1944-46 P, Memphis Red Sox

Keyes, Steve (Youngie, Zeke, Khora), 1940-48 P, Memphis Red Sox, Philadelphia Stars, Indianapolis Crawfords, Cincinnati Clowns

Keys, —, 1950 P, Houston Eagles

Keys, Dr. George B., 1922-32 officer, St. Louis Stars; officer, NNL

Kimbro, Arthur (Jess, Ted), 1915-18 3B, 2B, Bowser's ABCs, St. Louis Giants, Lincoln Giants, Louisville Sox

Kimbro, Henry Allen (Kimmie), 1937-50 OF, MGR, Washington Elite Giants, Baltimore Elite Giants, New York Black Yankees

Kimbro, (Howdy), 1945 P, Pittsburgh Crawfords

Kimbrough, Jim, 1945-48 P, Philadelphia Stars, Homestead Grays

Kimbrough, Larry Nathaniel (Schoolboy), 1942-46 P, Philadelphia Stars

Kinard, Roosevelt, 1932 3B, Washington Pilots

Kincaide, C.J., 1945-47 officer, NSL

Kincannon, Harry, 1930-39 P, Pittsburgh Crawfords, Philadelphia Stars, New York Black Yankees, Washington Black Senators, Toledo Crawfords

Kindle, William (Bill), 1911-20 SS, 2B, OF, Brooklyn Royal Giants, Indianapolis ABCs, Chicago American Giants, Lincoln Stars, Lincoln Giants

King, Brendan, 1943 P, Cincinnati Clowns

King, Clarence (Charley, Pijo), 1947-50 OF, Birmingham Black Barons

King, Leonard, 1921 OF, Kansas City Monarchs

King, Wilbur, 1944-47 SS, 2B Memphis Red Sox, Cleveland Buckeyes, Chicago American Giants, Homestead Grays

King, William, 1890-92 SS, Chicago Unions

Kinkeide, John, 1887 player, Louisville Falls City

Kirby, —, 1928 P, Cleveland Tigers

Kirksey, —, 1926 C, Dayton Marcos

Klepp, Eddie, 1946 P, Cleveland Buckeyes

Knight, —, 1921 OF, Detroit Stars

Knight, —, 1922 1B, Baltimore Black Sox

Knight, H., 1930 P, Chicago American Giants

Knox, Elwood C., 1920 co-drafter of constitution, NNL

Kranson, Floyd Arthur [Kranston], 1936-41

P, Kansas City Monarchs, Memphis Red Sox, Chicago American Giants

Krider, J. Monroe [Kreiter], 1890 MGR, Cuban Giants (Colored Monarchs of York, Pa., Eastern Interstate Lg.)

Kyle, Andy, 1922 OF, P, Baltimore Black Sox, Bacharach Giants

Lackey, Obie Ezekiel [Obie], 1927-43 SS, 2B, P, 3B, Philadelphia Giants, Hilldale, Bacharach Giants, Pittsburgh Crawfords, Homestead Grays, Baltimore Black Sox, Philadelphia Stars, Brooklyn Royal Giants, New York Black Yankees

Lacy, Raymond, 1949-50 OF, Houston Eagles

Lain, William, 1911 3B, Chicago Giants

Lair, —, 1925 OF, Pennsylvania Red Caps of New York

Lamar, Clarence (Lemon), 1937-42 SS, 2B, St. Louis Stars, Cleveland Bears, Jacksonville Red Caps, Indianapolis ABCs, Birmingham Black Barons

Lamar, E.B., Jr., 1895-1926 MGR, club officer, booker, Cuban X Giants, Cuban Stars, Bacharach Giants, Harrisburg Giants, Brooklyn Cuban Giants

Lamarque, James H.(Jim, Lefty), 1942-50 P, Kansas City Monarchs

Lamberto, —, 1929 OF, Cuban Stars (ECL)

Land, —, 1908-13 OF, 1B, New York Colored Giants, Cuban Giants, Smart Set, Mohawk Giants

Landers, John, 1917 P, Indianapolis ABCs

Landers, Robert Henry, 1949 P, Kansas City Monarchs

Lane, —, 1911 SS, Chicago American Giants

Lane, Alto, 1929-34 P, Memphis Red Sox, Indianapolis ABCs, Cincinnati Tigers, Louisville White Sox, Kansas City Monarchs

Lane, Isaac S., 1917-22 OF, 3B, P, Dayton Giants, Dayton Marcos, Columbus Buckeyes, Detroit Stars

Lang, John F., 1885-86 MGR, Argyle Hotel, Cuban Giants

Langford, (Ad), 1912-20 P, OF, St. Louis Giants, Lincoln Stars, Brooklyn Royal Giants, Pennsylvania Red Caps of New York, Lincoln Giants, Mohawk Giants

Langram, —, 1939 2B, OF, Kansas City Monarchs

Langrum, Dr. E.L., 1934 officer, Cleveland Red Sox

Lanier, A.S., 1921 officer, Cuban Stars (NNL)

Lansing, Wilbur, 1948-49 P, Newark Eagles, Houston Eagles

Lantiqua, Enrique, 1935 C, New York Cubans

Lanuza, Pedro, 1931-32 C, Cuban Stars, House of David Cubans

Larrinago, Perez, 1946 2B, SS, Cleveland Buckeyes

Latimer, —, 1921 P, Indianapolis ABCs

Lattimore, —, 1929-33 C, Baltimore Black Sox, Brooklyn Royal Giants, Columbus Blue Birds

Lau, —, 1927 P, Cubans (ECL)

Laurent, Milfred Stephen (Milt, Rick), 1929-35 3B, 1B, OF, 2B, C, Memphis Red Sox, Cleveland Cubs, Birmingham Black Barons, Nashville Elite Giants, New Orleans Crescent Stars

Lavelle, —, 1908-12 C, 1B, Genuine Cuban Giants, Cuban Giants, Cuban Stars

Lavera, —, 1919 C, Cuban Stars

Lawson, L.B. (Flash), 1940 P, Philadelphia Stars

Lawyer, —, 1913 rf, Mohawk Giants

Layton, Obie, 1931 P, Hilldale

Lazaga, Agipito, 1916-22 OF, P, Cuban Stars (NNL), New York Cuban Stars

Leak, Curtis, A., 1940-48 officer, New York Black Yankees; sec'y, NNL

Leary, —, 1920-25 3B, Dayton Marcos, Penn Red Caps of NY

Lebeaux, —, 1936 SS, 2B, Chicago American Giants

Leblanc, —, 1915 SS, Lincoln Giants

Leblanc, Julio (Jose), 1919-21 P, OF, Cuban Stars (NNL)

Lee, Dick, 1917-18 OF, Chicago Union Giants

Lee, Fred, 1915 OF, Kansas City Giants

Lee, Holsey Scranton (Scrip), 1920-43 P, OF, 1B, Norfolk Stars, Philadelphia Stars, Hilldale, Norfolk Giants, Richmond Giants, Baltimore

Black Sox, Bacharach Giants, Cleveland Red Sox, Philadelphia Giants; umpire, NNL

Lee, Lown, 1909   P, Kansas City Royal Giants

Lee, William, 1888   SS, Chicago Unions

Leftwich, John (Hymie), 1945   P, Homestead Grays

Legrove, —, 1937   OF, Indianapolis Athletics

Leland, Frank C., 1887-1912   OF, MGR, Washington Capital Citys, Chicago Union Giants, Leland Giants, Chicago Giants

Lemon, see Clarence Lamar

Lenox, —, 1943   1B, New York Black Yankees

Leon, —, 1917-18   OF, P, Cuban Stars (East)

Leon, Isidore, 1948   OF, New York Cubans

Leonard, James (Bobo), 1919-32   P, OF, 1B, Cleveland Tate Stars, Cleveland Browns, Cleveland Tigers, Cleveland Hornets, Toledo Tigers, Chicago American Giants, Bacharach Giants, Lincoln Giants, Baltimore Black Sox, Homestead Grays, Pennsylvania Red Caps of New York

Leonard, Walter Fenner (Buck), 1933-50   1B, OF, Brooklyn Royal Giants, Homestead Grays

Lerue, —, 1921   C, Detroit Stars

Lester, —, 1932   P, Nashville Elite Giants

Lett, Roger, 1943   P, Cincinnati Clowns

Lettlers, George, 1887   player, Washington Capital Citys

Leuschner, W.A. (Bill), 1940-43   booking agent; officer, New York Black Yankees

Levis, Oscar [Oscal], 1921-32   P, Cuban Stars (East), Hilldale, Darby Daisies, Baltimore Black Sox, All Cubans

Lewis, —, 1887   player, Boston Resolutes

Lewis, —, 1923   P, Indianapolis ABCs

Lewis, A.D., 1937-38   1B, Birmingham Black Barons, Louisville Black Colonels

Lewis, Bernard, 1943   P, Atlanta Black Crackers

Lewis, Cary B., 1920   co-drafter, constitution of NNL; sec'y, NNL

Lewis, Charles (Babe), 1926   SS, Lincoln Giants, Philadelphia Giants

Lewis, Clarence (Foots), 1931-37   SS, Memphis Red Sox, Cleveland Red Sox, Nashville Elite Giants, Pittsburgh Crawfords, Akron Tyrites, Cleveland Giants

Lewis, F., 1932   P, Montgomery Grey Sox

Lewis, George (Peaches), 1917-22   P, Lincoln Giants, Bacharach Giants

Lewis, Grover, 1928   3B, Homestead Grays

Lewis, Henry N., 1943-45   MGR, officer, owner, Atlanta Black Crackers, Knoxville Black Smokies

Lewis, Ira F., 1922   sec'y, Pittsburgh Keystones

Lewis, Jerome, 1910   1B, West Baden (Ind.) Sprudels

Lewis, Jim (Slim), 1943,1947   P, Chicago Brown Bombers, New York Black Yankees

Lewis, Joseph Herman (Sleepy), 1919-34,1946   C, 3B,MGR, Baltimore Black Sox, Washington Potomacs, Homestead Grays, Hilldale, Lincoln Giants, Quaker Giants, Darby Daisies, Bacharach Giants, Norfolk-Newport News Royals

Lewis, Milton, 1922-28   2B, 1B,UTIL, Wilmington Potomacs, Bacharach Giants, Richmond Giants, Harrisburg Giants, Philadelphia Giants

Lewis, R.S. (Bubbles), 1923-28   officer, Memphis Red Sox; vice pres, NNL

Lewis, Rufus (Lew), 1936-50   P, Pittsburgh Crawfords, Newark Eagles, Houston Eagles

Lewis, (Tuck), 1916   2B, Chicago Giants

Liggons, James, 1932-34   P, OF, Monroe Monarchs, Memphis Red Sox, Little Rock Black Travelers

Lightner, —, 1920,1932   P, Kansas City Monarchs, Cole's American Giants

Ligon, Rufus, 1944-45   P, Memphis Red Sox

Lillard, Joe, 1932-37   P, OF, C, Cole's American Giants, Chicago American Giants, Cincinnati Tigers

Lillie, —, 1925   UTIL, Birmingham Black Barons

Linares, Abel, 1911-12   owner, pres., All Cubans, Cuban Stars

Linares, Rogelio (Ice Cream), 1940-46   1B, OF, Cuban Stars, New York Cubans

Lincoln, —, 1890-95   3B, Lincoln (Neb) Giants, Adrian Page Fence Giants

Linder, —, 1922   P, Kansas City Monarchs

Lindsay, Bill, 1910-15   P, Kansas City, Kansas,

Giants, Leland Giants, Chicago American Giants

Lindsay, Charles Clarence, 1920-34   SS, Richmond Giants, Bacharach Giants, Baltimore Black Sox, Wilmington Potomacs, Penn Red Caps of New York, Lincoln Giants, Philadelphia Giants

Lindsay, James, 1943   INF, Birmingham Black Barons

Lindsay, Leonard (Yahoodi), 1942-46   1B, P, 3B, Cincinnati Clowns, Birmingham Black Barons, Indianapolis Clowns

Lindsay, Merf, 1910   OF, Kansas City (Kan) Giants

Lindsay, P., 1910   1B, OF, Kansas City (Kan) Giants

Lindsay, Robert (Frog), 1910-17   SS, Kansas City, (Kan.), Giants

Lindsey, —, 1912   OF, Lincoln Giants

Lindsey, Ben, 1929   SS, Bacharach Giants

Lindsey, Bill, 1924-26   SS, 2B, OF, Washington Potomacs, Lincoln Giants, Dayton Marcos

Lindsey, James, 1887   OF, Pittsburgh Keystones

Lindsey, Robert, 1931   P, OF, 1B, Indianapolis ABCs

Linton, Benjamin, 1945   officer, Detroit Giants

Lisby, —, 1934   P, Newark Dodgers, Bacharach Giants

Listach, Nora [Listash], 1940-41   OF, Birmingham Black Barons, Cincinnati Buckeyes

Little, William, 1937-50   officer, Chicago American Giants

Littles, Ben, 1947-50   OF, Homestead Grays, New York Black Yankees, Philadelphia Stars

Livingston, Curtis, 1950   OF, Cleveland Buckeyes

Livingston, L.D. (Lee, Goo Goo), 1928-32   OF, Kansas City Monarchs, New York Black Yankees, Pittsburgh Crawfords, Pennsylvania Red Caps of NY

Lloyd, John Henry (Pop), 1905-32   SS, 1B, 2B, C, MGR, Macon Acmes, Cuban X Giants, Philadelphia Giants, Leland Giants, Lincoln Giants, Chicago American Giants, Brooklyn Royal Giants, Columbus Buckeyes, Bacharach Giants, Hilldale, New York Black Yankees, Lincoln Stars, Kansas City Monarchs

Locke, Clarence Virgil, 1945-48   P, 1B, Chicago American Giants

Locke, Eddie, 1943-50   P, 3B, Cincinnati Clowns, Kansas City Monarchs, New York Black Yankees

Lockett, Lester (Buck), 1937-50   2B, 3B, OF, Chicago American Giants, Birmingham Black Barons, Cincinnati-Indianapolis Clowns, Baltimore Elite Giants, Memphis Red Sox, St.Louis Stars, Cincinnati Buckeyes

Lockett, Monroe, 1938   P, Indianapolis ABCs

Lockett, Willie, 1938   OF, Indianapolis ABCs

Lockhart, A.J., 1925-26   P, 3B, Wilmington Potomacs, Philadelphia Giants

Lockhart, G. Hubert (Joe), 1923-29   P, Bacharach Giants, Chicago American Giants, Wilmington Potomacs

Loftin, Louis Santop, see Santop, Louis

Logan, Carl, 1940   INF, Philadelphia Stars

Logan, Fred, 1950   OF, New York Black Yankees

Logan, Nick, 1920-25   P, Baltimore Black Sox

Londo, Julius, 1909   player, St. Paul Gophers

Long, —, 1920-26   OF, Detroit Stars, Indianapolis ABCs

Long, (Buck), 1950   C, Memphis Red Sox

Long, Emory (Bang), 1932-40,1945   3B, OF, Atlanta Black Crackers, Chicago American Giants, Indianapolis Athletics, Philadelphia Stars, Kansas City Monarchs, Washington Black Senators

Long, Ernest S., 1948-50   P, Cleveland Buckeyes, Louisville Buckeyes

Longest, Bernell, 1942-47   2B, Chicago Brown Bombers, Chicago American Giants

Longest, Jimmy, 1942   1B, Chicago Brown Bombers

Longley, Wayman (Red, Ray), 1932-50   2B, OF, SS, C, 1B, 3B, Memphis Red Sox, Chicago American Giants, Little Rock Black Travelers

Longware, —, 1920   2B, 3B, OF, Detroit Stars

Looney, Charlie, 1933,1938   2B, Akron Tyrites, Louisville Black Colonels

Lopez, Cando, 1920-35   OF, 3B, Cuban Stars (NNL), New York Cubans

Lopez, Justo, 1939   1B, Cuban Stars

Lopez, Pedro, 1938-39   OF, Cuban Stars

Lopez, Raul, 1948-50   P, New York Cubans

Lopez, Vidal, 1923-39   P, Cuban Stars (ECL), Cuban Stars (NNL)

Lorenzo, Jesus, 1928-30   P, Cuban Stars (NNL)

Lott, Benjamin (Benny, Honey), 1949-50-2B, 3B, Indianapolis Clowns, New York Black Yankees

Lott, Raymond (Ray), 1950   OF, Philadelphia Stars

Louden, Louis Oliver (Tommy, Lou), 1942-50   C, New York Cubans, Cuban Stars

Love, William Andy, 1930-31,1945   C, OF, Detroit Stars, Memphis Red Sox, Toledo Cubs (USL)

Loving, J.G., 1887   player, Washington Capital Citys

Lowe, William M., 1921-31   3B, SS, 2B, OF, MGR, Indianapolis ABCs, Detroit Stars, Memphis Red Sox, Chattanooga Black Lookouts, Nashville Elite Giants

Lowell, —, 1924   P, Bacharach Giants

Lucas, Miles (Pepe), 1919-20,1925-27   P, OF, Cuban Stars of Havana, Cuban Stars (East), New Orleans Crescent Stars, Harrisburg Giants

Lucas, (Scotty), 1928   officer, Philadelphia Tigers

Lugo, Levingelo (Leo), 1944-46   OF, Cincinnati-Indianapolis Clowns, Indianapolis Clowns

Lundy, Richard (Dick), 1916-48   SS, 3B, 2B, MGR, Bacharach Giants, Lincoln Giants, Hilldale, Baltimore Black Sox, Philadelphia Stars, Newark Dodgers, New York Cubans, Newark Eagles, Jacksonville Eagles, Brooklyn Royal Giants, Havana Red Sox

Luque, Adolfo (Dolf), 1912-13   P, OF, Cuban Stars, Long Branch (NJ) Cubans

Luther, see Luther Farrell

Lyda, —, 1932   P, Coles American Giants

Lyles, John, 1932-43   OF, SS, 2B, 3B, C, Homestead Grays, Indianapolis ABCs, Cleveland Bears, St. Louis Stars, Chicago American Giants, Cincinnati Buckeyes, Cleveland Buckeyes, Indianapolis Clowns, New Orleans-St. Louis Stars

Lynch, Thomas, 1917-18   OF, Indianapolis ABCs, Dayton Marcos

Lynn, —, 1917   P, Jewell's ABCs

Lyons, —, 1950   P, Cleveland Buckeyes

Lyons, Bennie, 1917-18   1B, Jewell's ABCs, Dayton Marcos

Lyons, Chase, 1899-1905   P, Genuine Cuban Giants, Cuban Giants

Lyons, Granville, 1931-42   1B, P, Nashville Elite Giants, Louisville Black Caps, Detroit Stars, Louisville Red Caps, Philadelphia Stars, Memphis Red Sox, Baltimore Black Sox

Lyons, James (Jimmie), 1910-32   OF, MGR, Lincoln Giants, St. Louis Giants, Chicago Giants, Brooklyn Royal Giants, Indianapolis ABCs, Chicago American Giants, Detroit Stars, Cleveland Browns, Louisville Black Caps, Washington Potomacs Bowser's ABCs

Lytle, Clarence, 1901-06   P, Chicago Union Giants, Leland Giants

Mack, John H., 1945   P, Kansas City Monarchs

Mack, Paul, 1916-17   OF, 3B, Bacharach Giants, Jersey City Colored Giants

Mack, Robert, 1945   P, New York Black Yankees

Mackey, Raleigh (Biz), 1918-47   C, SS, 3B, MGR, San Antonio Giants, Indianapolis ABCs, Hilldale, Darby Daisies, Philadelphia Stars, Washington Elite Giants, Baltimore Elite Giants, Newark Eagles, Newark Dodgers, Nashville Elite Giants

Macklin, —, 1924-29   3B, OF, Chicago Giants

Maddix, Raydell (Ray, Bo), 1949-50   P, Indianapolis Clowns

Maddox, (One Wing), 1923—, P, OF, Birmingham Black Barons

Madert, —, 1917   2B, Chicago Giants

Madison, Robert, 1935-42   P, OF, 3B, Kansas City Monarchs, Memphis Red Sox, Indianapolis Athletics, Birmingham Black Barons

Magrinat, Hector (Kako), 1909-16 OF, Cuban Stars, All Cubans

Mainor, Hank, 1950 P, Baltimore Elite Giants

Mahoney, Tony, 1920-23 P, Norfolk Giants, Indianapolis ABCs, Baltimore Black Sox, Brooklyn Royal Giants, Norfolk Stars

Mahoney, Ulysses, 1944 P, Philadelphia Stars

Maison, J., 1887 player, Pittsburgh Keystones

Makell, Frank, 1944-49 C, Newark Eagles, Baltimore Elite Giants

Malarcher, David Julius (Cap, Gentleman Dave), 1916-34 3B, OF, 2B, MGR, Indianapolis ABCs, Detroit Stars, Chicago American Giants, Cole's American Giants, Chicago Columbia Giants

Malloy, [Mallory], 1918-21 OF, Pennsylvania Red Caps of New York, Nashville Elite Giants

Malone, William H., 1887-97 P, 1B, 3B, OF, Cuban Giants, Pittsburgh Keystones, New York Gorhams (Middle States Lg.), Page Fence Giants, York Cuban Giants (Eastern Interstate Lg.), Trenton Cuban Giants (Middle States Lg.), Philadelphia Pythians

Manella, see Manolo

Manese, E., 1923-26 2B, Detroit Stars, Kansas City Monarchs, Indianapolis ABCs

Mangrum, —, 1948 OF, New York Cubans

Manley, Abraham (Abe), 1935-46 officer, Brooklyn Eagles, Newark Eagles; vice pres, tres, NNL

Manley, Effa (Mrs. Abraham), 1935-48 officer, Brooklyn Eagles, Newark Eagles, sec'y; NNL

Mann, —, 1918 1B, Chicago Union Giants

Manning, —, 1932 1B, Montgomery Grey Sox

Manning, John, 1902 OF, Philadelphia Giants

Manning, Maxwell (Max), 1939-49 P, Newark Eagles, Houston Eagles

Manolo, [Manella, Manno], 1916-24 1B, P, Cuban Stars (East & West)

Manuel, (Clown), 1940 OF, Cleveland Bears

Mapp, Dick, 1942 SS, Boston Royal Giants

Mara, Candido, 1948 3B, Memphis Red Sox

Maravale, —, 1923 P, Cuban Stars (ECL)

Marcel, Everett (Sam, Ziggy, Joe), 1939-48 C, Chicago American Giants, Newark Eagles, Baltimore Elite Giants, New York Black Yankees, Kansas City Monarchs

Marcelle, Oliver H. (Ghost) [Marcel, Marcell], 1918-32 3B, SS, Brooklyn Royal Giants, Bacharach Giants, Lincoln Giants, Detroit Stars, Baltimore Black Sox

Marcello, —, 1921 P, Cuban Stars (NNL)

Markham, John Matthew [Marcum], 1930-45 P, Kansas City Monarchs, Monroe Monarchs, Birmingham Black Barons

Markham, Melvin, 1935-36 P, Brooklyn Eagles, Newark Eagles

Marlotica, —, 1911 OF, All Cubans

Marquez, Luis Angel Canena, 1945-48 SS, 2B, 3B, OF, New York Black Yankees, Homestead Grays, Baltimore Elite Giants

Marsans, Armando, 1923 OF, Cuban Stars

Marsellas, David, Jr., 1941 C, New York Black Yankees

Marsh, Lorenzo, 1950 C, Cleveland Buckeyes

Marshall, Jack, 1920-29 P, Chicago American Giants, Detroit Stars, Kansas City Monarchs

Marshall, Robert W. (Bobby), 1909-11 1B, MGR, St. Paul Gophers, Leland Giants, Twin City Gophers, Chicago Giants

Marshall, William James (Jack, Boisy), 1926-44 2B, 3B, 1B, Dayton Marcos, Gilkerson's Union Giants, Chicago Columbia Giants, Cole's American Giants, Chicago American Giants, Philadelphia Stars, Cincinnati-Indianapolis Clowns, Kansas City Monarchs

Martin, Alexander, 1932 officer, Cleveland Cubs

Martin, Dr. A.T., 1923-50 officer, Memphis Red Sox

Martin, Dr. B.B., 1933-50 officer, Memphis Red Sox; officer, NSL

Martin, Dr. John B., 1929-50 officer, Memphis Red Sox, Chicago American Giants; pres, Negro Dixie Lg., NSL, NAL

Martin, Dr. William S., 1927-50 officer, Memphis Red Sox; pres, NSL, officer, NAL

Martin, R., 1885 P, Argyle Hotel

Martin, William (Stack), 1925-28 OF, 1B, C, Indianapolis ABCs, Detroit Stars, Dayton Marcos, Wilmington Potomacs

Martinez, C., 1928 C, Cubans (NNL)

Martinez, Francisco, 1939 P, Cuban Stars

Martinez, Horacio (Rabbit), 1935-47 SS, 3B, New York Cubans, Cuban Stars

Martinez, Pasquel, 1920-28 P, Cuban Stars (NNL), Cuban Stars (East)

Martini, Jose, 1928 P, Cubans (NNL)

Marvarez, Fernando, 1945 INF, Pittsburgh Crawfords

Marvin, Alfred, 1938 P, Kansas City Monarchs

Marvray, Charles, 1949-50 OF, Louisville Buckeyes, Cleveland Buckeyes

Mason, —, 1927 3B, INF, Baltimore Black Sox

Mason, Charles (Corporal), 1922-29 P, P, Richmond Giants, Bacharach Giants, Lincoln Giants, Newark Stars, Homestead Grays

Mason, Jim, 1932-34 1B, OF, Cuban Stars (ECL), Cubans (NNL), Memphis Red Sox, Washington Pilots

Massey, —, 1930 OF, Louisville White Sox

Massip, Armando, 1920-30 1B, OF, Cuban Stars (ECL), Washington Pilots, Memphis Red Sox

Matchett, Jack, 1940-45 P, Kansas City Monarchs

Mathew, —, 1946 OF, Memphis Red Sox

Mathis, Verdell Sr. (Lefty), 1940-50 P, OF, 1B, Memphis Red Sox, Philadelphia Stars

Matlock, Leroy, 1929-42 P, St. Louis Stars, Detroit Wolves, Washington Pilots, Homestead Grays, Pittsburgh Crawfords, New York Cubans

Matthews, Clifford, 1945 officer, owner, New Orleans Black Pelicans

Matthews, Dell, 1904-05 P, OF, Chicago Union Giants, Leland Giants

Matthews, Dick, 1932-33 P, Monroe Monarchs, New Orleans Crescent Stars

Matthews, Francis Oliver (Fran), 1938-45 1B, Newark Eagles, Boston Royal Giants, Baltimore Elite Giants, New York Cubans

Matthews, Jack, 1923 3B, Toledo Tigers

Matthews, Jesse, 1942 INF, Birmingham Black Barons

Matthews, John, 1919-33 officer, Dayton Marcos

Matthews, William Clarence, 1905-10 SS, 2B, Burlington (Vermont Lg.); New York Black Sox

Maupin, Frank, 1890-92 C, 3B, Lincoln (Neb) Giants, Plattsmouth (Nebraska St. Lg.)

Maxwell, —, 1914 OF, Chicago American Giants

Maxwell, Zearlee (Jiggs), 1931-38 3B, 2B, Monroe Monarchs, Memphis Red Sox

Mayari, —, 1923 1B, Cuban Stars (ECL)

Mayers, George, see George Meyers

Mayfield, Fred, 1887 player, Louisville Falls City

Mayo, George (Hot Stuff), 1911-17, 1928 1B, OF, officer, Pittsburgh Giants, Pittsburgh Colored Stars, Hilldale, Pittsburgh Stars of Buffalo

Mays, —, 1937 P, St. Louis Stars, Memphis Red Sox

Mays, Dave, 1937 OF, Kansas City Monarchs

Mays, Willie, 1948-50 OF, Birmingham Black Barons

Mayweather, Eldridge (Chillie, Ed), 1934-46 1B, Monroe Monarchs, Kansas City Monarchs, St. Louis Stars, New Orleans-St. Louis Stars, New York Black Yankees, Boston Blues, Brooklyn Eagles

Mayweather, Elliott, 1928-29 P, Memphis Red Sox

Maywood, —, 1917-19 P, Lincoln Giants

Mazaar, Robert, 1945 officer, Hilldale Club of Philadelphia

McAdoo, Dudley (Tully), 1907-24 1B, Topeka Giants, Kansas City, Kan., Giants, St. Louis Giants, St. Louis Stars, Cleveland Browns, Chicago American Giants

McAllister, Frank (Chip, Bud), 1938-46 P, Indianapolis ABCs, St. Louis Stars, New Orleans-St. Louis Stars, New York Black Yankees, Harrisburg-St. Louis Stars, Brooklyn Brown Dodgers, Cleveland Clippers (USL)

McAllister, George, 1923-34 1B, Birmingham Black Barons, Chicago American Giants, Indianapolis ABCs, Memphis Red Sox, Homestead Grays, Cleveland Red Sox, Detroit Stars

McAllister, Mike, 1921 OF, Kansas City Monarchs

McBride, Fred, 1931-40 1B, OF, Indianapolis

ABCs, Chicago American Giants, Birmingham Black Barons

McCabb, —, 1923 P, St. Louis Stars

McCall, (Butch), 1936-38 1B, Chicago American Giants, Birmingham Black Barons, Indianapolis Athletics

McCall, Henry, 1945 OF, Chicago American Giants

McCall, William (Bill), 1922-31 P, Pittsburgh Keystones, Birmingham Black Barons, Kansas City Monarchs, Chicago American Giants, Indianapolis ABCs, Detroit Stars, Toledo Tigers, Cleveland Tigers

McCampbell, Ernest, 1915 player, Kansas City Giants

McCampbell, Tom, 1915 player, Kansas City Giants

McCarey, Willie, 1943-45 P, Cleveland Buckeyes

McCarthy, C.H., 1921 pres, Southeastern Negro Lg.

McCauley, —, 1930 P, Nashville Elite Giants

McClain, Bill, 1933 P, Columbus Blue Birds

McClain, Edward (Boots) [Mclain], 1920-26 INF, P, Dayton Marcos, Cleveland Tate Stars, Toledo Tigers, Cleveland Browns, Detroit Stars, Indianapolis ABCs, Columbus Buckeyes

McClinic, Nathaniel (Nath), 1946-48 OF, Cleveland Buckeyes

McClellan, Dan, 1903-30 P, MGR, Cuban X Giants, Philadelphia Giants, Smart Set, Lincoln Giants, Quaker Giants, Washington Potomacs, Wilmington Potomacs

McClelland, Dr. J.W., 1922 officer, St. Louis Stars

McClure, Robert (Bob), 1920-30 P, Indianapolis ABCs, Cleveland Tate Stars, Baltimore Black Sox, Bacharach Giants, Brooklyn Royal Giants, Toledo Tigers

McClure, Will, 1947 officer, Chattanooga Choo Choos

McCord, Clinton Hill Jr. (Butch), 1947-50 INF, 1B, Baltimore Elite Giants, Chicago American Giants

McCoy, Frank (Chink), 1931-43 C, Newark Stars, Newark Dodgers, Harrisburg-St. Louis Stars

McCoy, Roy, 1932 officer, Washington Pilots

McCoy, Walter, 1945-48 P, Chicago American Giants

McCrary, George, 1943 P, New York Black Yankees

McCreary, Fred, 1938-49 umpire, NNL

McCurine, James, 1946-48 OF, Chicago American Giants

McDaniels, Booker Taliaferro, 1940-49 P, OF, Kansas City Monarchs, Memphis Red Sox

McDaniels, Fred, 1940-50 OF, Memphis Red Sox, Kansas City Monarchs

McDevitt, John J., 1922 officer, Baltimore Black Sox

McDonald, Earl, 1938 officer, Washington Black Senators

McDonald, Luther (Vet), 1927-37 P, St. Louis Stars, Chicago American Giants, Chicago Columbia Giants, Cole's American Giants, Detroit Stars, Memphis Red Sox

McDonald, Webster (Mac), 1918-45 P, MGR, Philadelphia Giants, Richmond Giants, Chicago American Giants, Hilldale, Darby Daisies, Washington Pilots, Philadelphia Stars, Wilmington Potomacs, Detroit Stars, Homestead Grays, Lincoln Giants, Norfolk Stars

McDonnel, —, 1921 P, Bacharach Giants

McDougal, Lemuel (Lem), 1917-20 P, Chicago American Giants, Indianapolis ABCs, Chicago Giants

McDuffie, Terris, 1930-45 P, Of Birmingham Black Barons, Baltimore Black Sox, New York Black Yankees, Newark Eagles, Homestead Grays, Philadelphia Stars, Newark Dodgers, Brooklyn Eagles, Pennsylvania Red Caps

McFall, —, 1940 OF, Cincinnati Buckeyes

McFarland, John, 1944-47 P, New York Black Yankees

McGee, Horace, 1887 manager, Cincinnati Browns

McGowan, Curtis, 1950 P, Memphis Red Sox

McGowan, Malcolm, 1923-41 owner, officer, Bacharach Giants

McHaskell, J.C., 1927-29 1B, Memphis Red Sox

McHenry, Henry (Cream), 1930-50 P, Kansas City Monarchs, New York Black Yankees, Philadelphia Stars, Indianapolis Clowns, Pennsylvania Red Caps

McIntosh, Jimmy, 1937 C, Detroit Stars

McIntyre, B., 1924 P, Memphis Red Sox

McKamey, —, 1946 SS, Kansas City Monarchs

McKeg, —, 1897 SS, Cuban Giants

McKelvin, Fred [Mckellam], 1942 P, Cincinnati Buckeyes, Cleveland Buckeyes

McKenzie, Herbert, 1950 C, New York Black Yankees

McKinley, —, 1940 P, Chicago American Giants

McKinnis, Gread (Lefty), 1941-49 P, Birmingham Black Barons, Chicago American Giants, Pittsburgh Crawfords

McLain, see Edward McClain

McLaughlin, —, 1917-1919 P, 1B, OF, Jewell's ABCs, Lincoln Giants

McLaurin, Felix, 1942-49 OF, Jacksonville Red Caps, Birmingham Black Barons, New York Black Yankees, Chicago American Giants

McLawn, —, 1948 C, Newark Eagles

McMahon, Jess, 1911-14 officer, Lincoln Giants

McMahon, Rod, 1911-14 officer, Lincoln Giants

McMeans, Willie, 1945 P, Chicago American Giants

McMillan, Earl, 1923 OF, Toledo Tigers

McMullin, Clarence [Mccullin], 1945-49 OF, Kansas City Monarchs, Houston Eagles

McMurray, William, 1909-22 C, St. Paul Gophers, St. Louis Giants

McNair, Hurley Allen (Bugger), 1912-42 OF, Chicago Giants, Gilkerson's Union Giants, Chicago American Giants, Detroit Stars, Chicago Union Giants, Kansas City Monarchs, Cincinnati Tigers, All Nations; umpire, NAL

McNeal, Clyde, 1945-50 SS, Chicago American Giants

McNeil, —, 1918-20 1B, C, Dayton Marcos

McNeil, William (Red), 1930-33 OF, P, Louisville White Sox, Louisville Black Caps, Nashville Elite Giants, Louisville Red Caps

McQueen, Pete, 1932,1937-45 OF, Memphis Red Sox, New York Black Yankees, Little Rock Black Travelers

McReynolds, —, 1916 OF, P, Bowser's ABCs, Indianapolis ABCs

Meade, (Chick), 1916-22 3B, SS, OF, Pittsburgh Colored Stars, Hilldale, Pittsburgh Stars of Buffalo, Bacharach Giants, Baltimore Black Sox, Harrisburg Giants, Indianapolis ABCs

Meadows, Helburn, 1934 OF, Cincinnati Tigers

Means, Lewis, 1920-27 2B, 1B, C, Bacharach Giants, Birmingham Black Barons

Means, Thomas, 1900-04 P, Chicago Unions, Chicago Union Giants

Meckling, S., 1909 C, Kansas City Royal Giants

Mederos, Jesus (Frank), 1911-20 P, OF, All Cubans, Bacharach Giants

Medina, Lazarus (Lazaro) [Chapman], 1944-46 P, Cincinnati- Indianapolis Clowns, Indianapolis Clowns

Medina, Pedro, 1905 C, Cuban Stars of Santiago

Medley, Calvin, 1946 P, New York Black Yankees

Medros, —, 1910 P, Cuban Stars

Mellito, see Emilio Navarro

Mellix, George Ralph (Lefty), 1922-34,1946 P, MGR, Homestead Grays, Newark Browns, Brooklyn Brown Dodgers

Mello, Harry, 1946 INF, Chicago American Giants

Melton, —, 1916 P, St. Louis Giants

Melton, Elbert, 1928-29 OF, Brooklyn Cuban Giants, Lincoln Giants, Baltimore Black Sox

Mendez, Jose De La Caridad (Joe), 1908-26 P, SS, 3B, 2B, MGR, Cuban Stars, Stars of Cuba, All Nations, Los Angeles White Sox, Chicago American Giants, Detroit Stars, Kansas City Monarchs

Mendieta, Inocente, 1912-13 2B, Cuban Stars, Long Branch (NJ) Cubans

Meredith, Buford (Geetchie), 1923-31 SS, 2B,

Birmingham Black Barons, Nashville Elite Giants, Memphis Red Sox

Merchant, Henry L. (Speed), 1940-50 P, OF, Chicago American Giants, Cincinnati-Indianapolis Clowns, Indianapolis Clowns

Merritt, B., 1905-17 P, Brooklyn Royal Giants, Lincoln Giants

Merritt, Schute, 1934-35 UTIL, Newark Dodgers

Mesa, Andres Anares, 1948 OF, Indianapolis Clowns

Mesa, Pablo, 1921-27 OF, Cuban Stars (ECL)

Metz, —, 1939 player, Kansas City Monarchs

Meyers, C., 1908 LF, Brooklyn Colored Giants

Meyers, George (Deacon) [Myers, Mayers], 1921-26 P, 1B, St. Louis Stars, Dayton Marcos, St. Louis Giants, Toledo Tigers

Meyers, L., 1908 2B, Brooklyn Colored Giants

Miarka, Stanley V., 1950 2B, P, Chicago American Giants

Mickey, James, 1940 SS, 3B, Chicago American Giants, Birmingham Black Barons

Mickey, John, 1898 P, Celeron Acme Colored Giants (Iron and Oil Lg.)

Miles, —, 1940 P, Cincinnati Buckeyes

Miles, John (Jack, Mule, Sonny Boy), 1934-38 OF, 3B, Chicago American Giants, Philadelphia Stars

Miles, Willie, 1923-27 OF, 1B, 3B, Toledo Tigers,Memphis Red Sox Cleveland Tate Stars, Cleveland Browns, Cleveland Elites, Cleveland Hornets, Homestead Grays

Miles, Zell, 1946-49 OF, 3B, Chicago American Giants

Miller, —, 1911-20 C, Pittsburgh Giants, Dayton Marcos

Miller, —, 1934 2B, Cincinnati Tigers

Miller, —, 1934 SS, New Orleans Crescent Stars

Miller, A., 1927 OF, Memphis Red Sox, Birmingham Black Barons

Miller, Bob (Ruby), 1923-28 2B, 3B, Memphis Red Sox, Birmingham Black Barons

Miller, Dempsey (Dimp), 1926-45 P, MGR, Cleveland Hornets, Cleveland Tigers, Nashville Elite Giants, Detroit Stars, Detroit Giants, Cleveland Cubs, Birmingham Black Barons, Memphis Red Sox, Kansas City Monarchs

Miller, Eddie (Buck), 1924-31 P, SS, 3B, Chicago American Giants, Indianapolis ABCs, Homestead Grays, Chicago Columbia Giants

Miller, Eugene, 1909 OF, St. Paul Gophers

Miller, Frank, 1887-97 P, OF, Pittsburgh Keystones, Cuban Giants, Cuban X Giants, New York Gorhams (Middle States Lg.), Philadelphia Giants

Miller, Henry Joseph (Hank), 1938-49 P, Philadelphia Stars

Miller, Jasper, 1930,1940 P, Memphis Red Sox

Miller, Joe, 1895-03 P, OF, Page Fence Giants, Columbia Giants, Adrian (Michigan State Lg), Chicago Union Giants

Miller, L., 1912-23 3B, 2B, Smart Set, Lincoln Giants, Lincoln Stars, Brooklyn Royal Giants, Bacharach Giants, Baltimore Black Sox

Miller, Leroy (Flash), 1935-43 SS, 2B, Newark Dodgers, New York Black Yankees

Miller, Ned, 1937 1B, Indianapolis Athletics

Miller, Percy, 1921-33 P, OF, St. Louis Stars, St. Louis Giants, Nashville Elite Giants, Chicago Giants, Kansas City Monarchs

Miller, Pleas (Hub), 1913-16 P, West Baden, (Ind) Sprudels, St. Louis Giants

Miller, W., 1940 P, Chicago American Giants

Milliner, Eugene J., 1903-10 OF, Chicago Union Giants, St. Paul Gophers, Kansas City Royal Giants

Millon, Herald, 1946-47 UTIL, Chicago American Giants

Mills, Charles A., 1909-24 officer, St. Louis Giants, St. Louis Black Sox

Milton, C., 1933-34 INF, Cleveland Red Sox, Columbus Blue Birds

Milton, Edward, 1926-28 OF, 2B, Cleveland Elites

Milton, Henry, 1932-43 OF, Chicago Giants, Indianapolis ABCs, Chicago American Giants, Brooklyn Royal Giants, Kansas City Monarchs, New York Black Yankees, Brooklyn Eagles

Mimms, —, 1932 P, Columbus Turfs

Mincey, —, 1939 P, Philadelphia Stars

Minor, George, 1944-49 OF, Chicago American Giants, Cleveland Buckeyes, Louisville Buckeyes

Minoso, Saturnino Orestes Arrieta Armas (Minnie), 1945-48 3B, New York Cubans

Mirabel, Juanelo, 1922-32,1949-50 P, pres, Cuban Stars (ECL) New York Cubans

Mirable, Autorio, 1939-40 C, New York Cuban Stars

Miraka, Stanley, see Stanley Miarka

Mirall, —, 1930 3B, Brooklyn Royal Giants

Miranda, P., 1916 player, Cuban Stars

Miro, Pedro, 1945-48 2B, New York Cubans

Missouri, Jim, 1937-41 P, Philadelphia Stars

Mitchell, —, 1901 C, Chicago Union Giants

Mitchell, —, 1914 P, Pittsburgh Giants

Mitchell, A., 1884 player, Philadelphia Mutual B.B.C.

Mitchell, Alonzo (Fluke, Hooks), 1921-41 MGR, 1B, P, club officer, Jacksonville Red Caps, Cleveland Bears, Atlanta Black Crackers, Jacksonville Red Caps, Indianapolis ABCs, Baltimore Black Sox, Bacharach Giants, Harrisburg Giants, Birmingham Black Barons, Akron Tyrites

Mitchell, Arthur Harold, 1939 INF, New York Black Yankees

Mitchell, Bob, 1950 P, Cleveland Buckeyes

Mitchell, (Bud), 1929-34 OF, P, C, Hilldale, Darby Daisies, Bacharach Giants

Mitchell, Charlie, 1942 C, Boston Royal Giants

Mitchell, George, 1925-49 P, MGR, bus. mgr, Chicago American Giants, Indianapolis ABCs, Montgomery Grey Sox, Cleveland Cubs, Mounds City, Illinois, Blues (became Indianapolis ABCs), St. Louis Stars, New Orleans-St. Louis Stars, New York Black Yankees, Harrisburg-St. Louis Stars, Houston Eagles, Cleveland Stars, Detroit Stars, Kansas City Monarchs

Mitchell, John, 1932 C, OF, Montgomery Grey Sox

Mitchell, Leonard Otto, 1930-31 2B, Birmingham Black Barons, Louisville White Sox

Mitchell, Robert, 1923-24 C, OF, St. Louis Stars, Birmingham Black Barons

Moles, (Lefty), 1935 P, Philadelphia Stars

Molina, —, 1929-30 P, Cuban Stars (NNL)

Molina, Agustin (Tinti), 1907-31 1B, OF, C, MGR., Officer, Cuban Stars, Cuban Stars (NNL)

Mollett, —, 1913-16 2B, SS, Mohawk Giants, Lincoln Stars

Molloy, —, 1922 P, Bacharach Giants

Mongin, Sam, 1908-27 3B, 2B, Brooklyn Royal Giants, Lincoln Stars, Lincoln Giants, Bacharach Giants, St. Louis Giants Baltimore Black Sox, Philadelphia Giants

Monceville, [Monchile], —, 1930-31 OF, Cuban Stars (East & West)

Monroe, Al, 1937 sec'y, NAL

Monroe, Bill, 1920,1927 3B, SS, Pittsburgh Stars of Buffalo Baltimore Black Sox

Monroe, William (Bill), 1896-1914 2B, 3B, Chicago Unions, Philadelphia Giants, Brooklyn Royal Giants, Chicago American Giants, Cuban X Giants

Montalvo, Estaban, 1923-28 1B, OF, Cuban Stars (NNL) New York Cubans

Montgomery, A.G., 1926 sec'y, NSL

Montgomery, Lou, 1942 P, OF, INF, Cincinnati Clowns

Moody, —, 1931 SS, Memphis Red Sox

Moody, —, 1940 P, Birmingham Black Barons

Moody, Lee, 1944-47 1B, Kansas City Monarchs

Moody, Willis, 1921-29 OF, Pittsburgh Keystones, Homestead Grays

Moore, Charles, 1943 umpire, NNL

Moore, Clarence Lee (C.L., Cool Breeze), 1945-48 MGR., Officer, owner, Asheville Blues; pres. Negro American Association

Moore, Excell, 1950 P, Cleveland Buckeyes

Moore, Harry W. (Mike), 1894-1912 OF, 1B, 3B, Chicago Unions, Algona (IA) Brownies, Cuban X Giants, Philadelphia Giants, Leland Giants, Chicago Giants, Lincoln Giants

Moore, Henry L., 1937-38 officer, St. Louis Stars, Birmingham Black Barons

Moore, James (Red), 1936-40 1B, Newark

Eagles, Atlanta Black Crackers, Baltimore Elite Giants, Indianapolis ABCs

Moore, John, 1929   SS, Birmingham Black Barons

Moore, L., 1910-20   OF, St. Louis Giants, Bowser's ABCs, West Baden (Ind.) Sprudels, Lincoln Giants, Louisville Sox

Moore, N., 1920-24   OF, Detroit Stars

Moore, P.D., 1932   C, Monroe Monarchs

Moore, Ralph (Squire, Roy, Square), 1921-28   P, 1B, Memphis Red Sox, Kansas City Monarchs, Cleveland Hornets, Cleveland Tigers, Cleveland Tate Stars, Birmingham Black Barons

Moore, Shirley, 1915   P, Bowser's ABCs, Louisville Sox

Moore, Walter (Dobie), 1920-26   SS, OF, Kansas City Monarchs

Moorhead, Albert, 1925-32   C, Chicago Giants, Cleveland Cubs

Morales, Ismael, 1932   OF, Cuban Stars

Moran, Francisco, 1911   OF, Cuban Stars, All Cubans

Morefield, Fred, 1945-46   OF, Pittsburgh Crawfords

Morehead, Albert, 1943   C, Birmingham Black Barons, Chicago Brown Bombers

Moreland, Nate, 1940-45   P, Baltimore Elite Giants, Kansas City Monarchs

Morgan, —, 1928   OF, Birmingham Black Barons

Morgan, John. L. (Pepper), 1937   OF, Memphis Red Sox, Indianapolis Athletics

Morgan, William (Wild Bill), 1945-48   P, Memphis Red Sox, Baltimore Elite Giants, Birmingham Black Barons

Morin, Eugenio, 1910-23   2B, 3B, C, Cuban Stars, Cuban Stars (NNL)

Morney, Leroy, 1931-44   SS, 3B, 2B, Monroe Monarchs, Columbus Blue Birds, Cleveland Giants, Pittsburgh Crawfords, Columbus Elite Giants, Washington Elite Giants, New York Black Yankees, Philadelphia Stars, Chicago American Giants, Birmingham Black Barons, Cincinnati Clowns, Toledo Crawfords, Homestead Grays, Nashville Elite Giants

Morris, Al, 1927-30   OF, 2B, Nashville Elite Giants, Louisville White Sox

Morris, Barney (Big Ad), 1932-48   P, Monroe Monarchs, Pittsburgh Crawfords, Cuban Stars, New York Cubans, Toledo Crawfords, New Orleans Stars

Morris, F.B., 1948   sec'y, Negro American Association

Morris, Harold (Yellowhorse), 1924-36   P, Kansas City Monarchs, Detroit Stars, Chicago American Giants, Monroe Monarchs

Morrison, Jimmy, 1930   UTIL, Memphis Red Sox

Morrison, W., 1925   1B, Cleveland Browns

Mortin, R., 1885   P, Argyle Giants

Morton, —, 1917   2B, Havana Red Sox

Morton, Ferdinand Q., 1935-38   commissioner, NNL

Morton, John, 1935   OF, Brooklyn Eagles

Morton, Sidney Douglas (Sy), 1940-47   SS, 2B, Philadelphia Stars, Pittsburgh Crawfords, Chicago American Giants

Moseley, Beauregard F., 1910-11   officer, Leland Giants

Moses, —, 1938-40   P, Kansas City Monarchs

Mosley, —, 1934-35   P, New Orleans Crescent Stars, Homestead Grays

Mosley, William, 1928-33   officer, Detroit Stars

Moss, Porter (Ankle Ball), 1934-44   P, Cincinnati Tigers, Memphis Red Sox

Mothell, Carroll Ray (Dink), 1920-34   OF, 2B, 1B, SS, C, All Nations, Kansas City Monarchs, Cleveland Stars, Chicago American Giants

Mott, —, 1931   3B, Birmingham Black Barons

Mullen, A., 1928   OF, Birmingham Black Barons

Mungin, J., 1925-27   P, Baltimore Black Sox, Harrisburg Giants

Munoz, Joseito (Joe), 1909-16   P, OF, Cuban Stars, Stars of Cuba, Jersey City Cubans, Long Branch Cubans

Munroe, Elmer, 1942   P, Boston Royal Giants

Munroe, William, *see William Monroe*

Murdock, —, 1924   P, Indianapolis ABCs

Murphy, —, 1908   CF, Brooklyn Colored Giants

Murphy, —, 1915   OF, Chicago American Giants

Murphy, —, 1922   P, Kansas City Monarchs

Murphy, Al, 1936-37   P, Indianapolis Athletics, Birmingham Black Barons, Cincinnati Tigers

Murray, Charles, 1949-50   player, Cleveland Buckeyes

Murray, Mitchell, 1920-32   C, Indianapolis ABCs, Dayton Marcos, Cleveland Tate Stars, Toledo Tigers, St. Louis Stars, Chicago American Giants

Muse, B., 1922,1934   P, New Orleans Crescent Stars, Hilldale, Monroe Monarchs

Myers, —, 1908-10   SS, Pop Watkins Stars, Brooklyn Royal Giants

Nance, —, 1929   SS, Chicago American Giants

Napier, Euthumn (Eudie), 1935-50   C, Homestead Grays, Pittsburgh Crawfords

Napoleon, Lawrence (Larry), 1946-47   P, Kansas City Monarchs

Naranjo, Pedro, 1950   P, Indianapolis Clowns

Nash, William, 1928-34   P, OF, Birmingham Black Barons, Memphis Red Sox, Nashville Elite Giants

Navarrete, Ramundo, 1950   P, New York Cubans

Navarro, Emilio (Millito), 1928-29   INF, Cuban Stars (East)

Navarro, Raymond Raul, 1945-46   OF, INF, C, Cincinnati-Indianapolis Clowns, Indianapolis Clowns

Neal, George, 1910-11   2B, Chicago Giants, Kansas City Kan. Giants

Nears, (Red), 1940   C, OF, Memphis Red Sox

Neely, —, 1932-33   P, Louisville Black Caps, Cuban Stars

Neil, Ray, 1942-50   2B, Cincinnati Clowns, Indianapolis Clowns

Nelson, Clyde, 1939,1943-49   3B, 2B, 1B, OF, Chicago Brown Bombers, Chicago American Giants, Cleveland Buckeyes, Indianapolis Clowns, Indianapolis ABCs

Nelson, Everett (Ace), 1922,1931-33   P, Montgomery Grey Sox, Detroit Stars

Nelson, John, 1887-1903   P, OF, New York Gorhams, Cuban Giants, Cuban X Giants, Philadelphia Giants, Philadelphia Gorhams, (Middle States Lg.) Ansonia Cuban Giants (Connecticut St. Lg.), Trenton Cuban Giants (Middle States Lg.), Adrian Page Fence Giants

Nesbit, Dr. E.E., 1929   officer, Memphis Red Sox

Nestor, S. Jace, 1926   OF, Lincoln Giants

Newberry, Henry, 1947   P, Chicago American Giants

Newberry, James Lee (Jimmie), 1943-50   P, Birmingham Black Barons

Newberry, Richard, 1947   SS, Chicago American Giants

Newcombe, Donald (Don), 1944-45   P, Newark Eagles

Newkirk, Alexander (Alex), 1946-49   P, New York Black Yankees, New York Cubans

Newman, —, 1940   P, Memphis Red Sox

Newsome, Omer, 1923-29   P, Indianapolis ABCs, Washington Potomacs, Detroit Stars, Dayton Marcos, Memphis Red Sox, Wilmington Potomacs

Newson, —, 1940   OF, Newark Eagles

Nichols, Charles, 1885   OF, Argyle Hotel

Nichols, William, 1936   P, Newark Eagles

Nirsa, —, 1923   OF, Cuban Stars

Nix, —, 1939   P, Brooklyn Royal Giants

Nixon, —, 1940-41   OF, Birmingham Black Barons

Noble, Carlos, 1950   P, New York Cubans

Noble, Juan (John, Gyp), 1949-50   P, New York Cubans

Noble, Rafael Miguel (Ray, Sam), 1945-50   C, New York Cubans

Noel, Eddie, 1921   P, Nashville Elite Giants

Nolan, —, 1916-17   C, St. Louis Giants, Kansas City Colored Giants

Norman, Alton (Ed), 1920-26   SS, Lincoln Giants, Cleveland Elites

Norman, (Bud, Ace), 1940   P, Indianapolis Crawfords

Norman, Garrett, 1923   OF, Memphis Red Sox

Norman, Jim, 1909   INF, Kansas City, Kansas, Giants

Norman, William (Shin), 1906-10   P, Leland Giants, Union Giants

Norris, (Slim), 1930   3B, Louisville White Sox

Norwood, C.H., 1887   player, Philadelphia Pythians

Norwood, Walter, 1933   officer, Detroit Stars

Nunley, Beauford, 1934   1B, Memphis Red Sox

Nuttall, H. (Bill), 1924-26   P, Lincoln Giants, Bacharach Giants

Nutter, Isaac H., 1927-28   officer, Bacharach Giants, pres., Eastern Lg.

O'Bryant, Willie [O'Brien], 1932   SS, OF, Washington Pilots

O'Dell, John Wesley, 1949-50   P, Houston Eagles

Oden, J. Webb, 1927-32   SS, OF, Birmingham Black Barons, Knoxville Giants, Louisville Black Caps, Memphis Red Sox

O'Farrell, Orlando, 1949   SS, Indianapolis Clowns, Philadelphia Stars

Offert, Mose, 1925-26   P, Indianapolis ABCs

Oldham, Jimmy, 1920-23   P, St. Louis Giants, St. Louis Stars

Oliver, James (Pee Wee), 1943-46   SS, Cincinnati-indianapolis Clowns, Birmingham Black Barons, Indianapolis Clowns

Oliver, John, 1885   3B, Brooklyn Remsens

Oliver, John Henry, 1945-46   SS, Memphis Red Sox, Cleveland Buckeyes

Oliver, Leonard E., 1913   SS, Philadelphia Giants

Oliver, Martin, 1930-34   C, OF, Birmingham Black Barons, Louisville Black Caps, Memphis Red Sox

Oms, Alejandro (Walla Walla), 1917-35   OF, Cuban Stars (ECL), New York Cubans, All Cubans

O'Neil, John Jordan (Buck), 1937-55   1B, MGR, Memphis Red Sox, Kansas City Monarchs

O'Neill, —, 1910   P, West Baden (Ind.) Sprudels

O'Neill, Charles, 1921-23   C, Columbus Buckeyes, Bacharach Giants, Toledo Tigers, Chicago American Giants

Ora, Clarence, 1932   OF, Cleveland Cubs

Orange, Grady, 1925-31   SS, 2B, 3B, Birmingham Black Barons, Kansas City Monarchs, Detroit Stars, Cleveland Tigers

Ormes, A.W., 1911   player, Leland Giants

Ortiz, Julio Arango (Ortie, Bill), 1944-45   OF, SS, Cincinnati- Indianapolis Clowns, Kansas City Monarchs

Ortiz, Rafaelito, 1948   P, Chicago American Giants

Osborne, —, 1905   P, Philadelphia Giants

Oscal, *see Oscar Levis*

Osley, —, 1938   P, Birmingham Black Barons

Osorio, Alberto, 1949   P, Louisville Buckeyes

Otis, Amos, 1921   OF, Nashville Elite Giants

Ousley, Guy C., 1931-32   SS, 2B, 3B, Chicago Columbia Giants, Cleveland Cubs, Memphis Red Sox

Overton, Albert, 1937   P, Philadelphia Stars

Overton, John, 1925   officer, Indianapolis ABCs

Owens, —, 1934,1937   P, Newark Dodgers, Newark Eagles

Owens, A., 1928   SS, Cleveland Tigers

Owens, Albert, 1930-31   P, Nashville Elite Giants

Owens, Aubrey, 1920-25   P, Indianapolis ABCs, Chicago American Giants, New Orleans Caulfield Ads, Chicago Giants

Owens, Dewitt, 1936-39   OF, 2B, Birmingham Black Barons, Indianapolis ABCs

Owens, Jackson, 1950   P, Chicago American Giants

Owens, Raymond (Smokey, Kankol), 1939-42   P, OF, Cleveland Bears, Cleveland Buckeyes, New Orleans-St. Louis Stars, Cincinnati Clowns, Cincinnati Buckeyes, Jacksonville Red Caps

Owens, W.E., 1887   player, Cincinnati Browns

Owens, W. Oscar, 1913-31   P, 1B, OF, Homestead Grays, Indianapolis ABCs, Pittsburgh Keystones

Owens, William John (Willie), 1923-33   SS, 2B, P, Washington Potomacs, Chicago American Giants, Indianapolis ABCs, Dayton Marcos, Birmingham Black Barons, Memphis Red Sox, Detroit Stars, Cleveland Elites, Harrisburg Giants, Brooklyn Royal Giants, Wilmington Potomacs

Pace, —, 1930   OF, Nashville Elite Giants

Pace, Benjamin (Brother), 1922   C, Pittsburgh Keystones, Homestead Grays

Padrone, Juan Luis, 1909-26   P, 2B, OF,

Cuban Stars (ECL), Smart Set, Long Branch (NJ) Cubans, Chicago American Giants, Lincoln Giants, Cuban Stars (NNL), Indianapolis ABCs, Brooklyn Royal Giants, Birmingham Black Barons, All Cubans

Page, Allen, 1945-50   vice pres, tres, NSL; officer, New Orleans Creoles; promoter

Page, R., 1925   officer, Indianapolis ABCs

Page, Theodore Roosevelt (Ted), 1926-37 OF, 1B, Newark Stars, Homestead Grays, Pittsburgh Crawfords, New York Black Yankees, Newark Eagles, Philadelphia Stars, Brooklyn Royal Giants, Baltimore Black Sox, Quaker Giants, Brooklyn Eagles

Pages, Pedro, 1939,1947   OF, New York Cubans

Paige, Leroy (Satchel), 1926-50   P, Chattanoogo Black Lookouts, Birmingham Black Barons, Cleveland Cubs, Pittsburgh Crawfords, Kansas City Monarchs, New York Black Yankees, Satchel Paige's All-Stars, Philadelphia Stars, Memphis Red Sox, Baltimore Black Sox

Paine, Henry, 1884   OF, Brooklyn Remsens

Paine, John, 1887   OF, Philadelphia Pythians

Palm, Robert Clarence (Spoony), 1927-46   C, Birmingham Black Barons, St. Louis Stars, Detroit Stars, Cleveland Giants, Homestead Grays, Brooklyh Eagles, New York Black Yankees, Philadelphia Stars, Cole's American Giants, Akron Tyrites, Pittsburgh Crawfords

Palma, —, 1930   P, Cuban Stars (NNL)

Palmer, Earl, 1918-19   OF, Chicago Union Giants, Lincoln Giants

Palmer, Curtis, 1949-50   OF, New York Black Yankees

Palmer, James, 1887   UTIL, New York Gorhams

Palmer, Leon, 1926,1930   OF, Dayton Marcos, Louisville White Sox

Panier, —, 1917-20   P, Cuban Giants, Philadelphia Giants

Pape, Ed, 1946   OF, Homestead Grays

Pardee, —, 1925   C, Birmingham Black Barons

Pareda, H. (Monk, Pastor), 1910-21   P, 1B, Stars of Cuba, Cuban Stars, Cuban Stars (NNL)

Parego, George A. [Parago], 1885-88   P, OF, 1B, Argyle Hotel, Cuban Giants, Trenton Cuban Giants (Middle States Lg.), Cuban Stars

Parker, —, 1890-1908   OF, Genuine Cuban Giants, Chicago Unions, New York Colored Giants

Parker, —, 1921-23   1B, OF, Pittsburgh Stars of Buffalo, Baltimore Black Sox, Memphis Red Sox

Parker, Jack, 1938   INF, Pittsburgh Crawfords

Parker, (Sonny), 1942-43   P, Chicago Brown Bombers, Kansas City Monarchs, Harrisburg-St.Louis Stars

Parker, Thomas (Tom, Big Train), 1929-48   P, OF, MGR, Memphis Red Sox, Indianapolis ABCs, Monroe Monarchs, Homestead Grays, New Orleans-St. Louis Stars, New York Black Yankees, Harrisburg-St. Louis Stars, New York Cubans, Boston Blues, Indianapolis Athletics, Nashville Elite Giants, Columbus Elite Giants

Parker, Willie (Lefty), 1918-20   P, Lincoln Giants, Baltimore Black Sox

Parkinson, (Parky, 1950   P, Houston Eagles

Parks, Charles Edison (Charlie, Hunky), 1940-47   C, Newark Eagles

Parks, John, 1939-47   C, OF, New York Black Yankees, Newark Eagles

Parks, Joseph B., 1909-19   OF, C, SS, Cuban Giants, Philadelphia Giants, Brooklyn Royal Giants, Pennsylvania Red Caps of New York

Parks, Sam, 1945   officer, Memphis Grey Sox

Parks, William (Bubber), 1910-20   SS, 2B, OF, Chicago Giants, Lincoln Giants, Chicago American Giants, Lincoln Giants, Pennsylvania Red Caps of New York, Philadelphia Giants

Parnell, Roy (Red), 1926-50   OF, 1B, MGR, Birmingham Black Barons, Monroe Monarchs, New Orleans Crescent Stars, Columbus Elite Giants, Philadelphia Stars, Pittsburgh Crawfords, Houston Eagles, Nashville Elite Giants, New York Cubans Stars

Parpetti, Augustin, 1909-23   1B, OF, Cuban Stars, Kansas City Monarchs, Bacharach Giants, Richmong Giants

Parris, Jonathan Clyde (The Dude), 1946-49

1B, 3B, OF, New York Black Yankees, Louisville Buckeyes

Parson, —, 1908   P, Genuine Cuban Giants

Parsons, A.S., 1895-97   MGR, Adrian (MI) Page Fence Giants

Partlow, Roy (Silent Roy), 1934-50   P, Cincinnati Tigers, Memphis Red Sox, Homestead Grays, Philadelphia Stars

Passon, Harry, 1934   officer, Bacharach Giants

Pastoria, —, 1924   P, Cuban Stars (NNL)

Pate, Archie, 1909,1917   OF, St. Paul Gophers, Chicago Giants

Patterson, —, 1886   OF, New York Gorhams

Patterson, —, 1941-43   OF, C, New York Black Yankees

Patterson, Andrew L. (Pat), 1934-49   2B, 3B, OF, Pennsylvania Red Caps Cleveland Red Sox, Pittsburgh Crawfords, Kansas City Monarchs, Philadelphia Stars, Newark Eagles, Houston Eagles

Patterson, Gabriel, 1945-50   OF, Pittsburgh Crawfords, Homestead Grays, New York Black Yankees, Philadelphia Stars

Patterson, John W. (Pat), 1890-1906   2B, OF, SS, MGR, Lincoln (Nebraska) Giants, Page Fence Giants, Columbia Giants of Chicago, Philadelphia Giants, Cuban X Giants, Cuban Giants, Quaker Giants, of New York, Brooklyn Royal Giants, Chicago Union Giants, Plattsmouth (Nebraska St. Lg.)

Patterson, Roy (Willie), 1950   C, New York Cubans

Patterson, William B., 1914-25   MGR, Houston Black Buffaloes, Austin Senators, Birmingham Black Barons

Patton, —, 1909   OF, P, Philadelphia Giants

Patton, —, 1926   P, St. Louis Stars

Paul, —, 1908   SS, Brooklyn Colored Giants

Payne, —, 1926-31   2B, P, Brooklyn Royal Giants, Newark Stars, Philadelphia Giants

Payne, —, 1928   OF, Birmingham Black Barons

Payne, Andrew H. (Jap), 1902-22   OF, Philadelphia Giants, Cuban X Giants, Leland Giants, Chicago American Giants, Chicago Union Giants, New York Central Red Caps, Brooklyn Royal Giants, Pennsylvania Red Caps of NY, Lincoln Stars

Payne, Ernest (Rusty), 1937,1940   OF, Cincinnati Tigers, Indianapolis Crawfords

Payne, James, 1887   OF, Baltimore Lord Baltimore, Cuban Giants

Payne, Tom, 1933   OF, Homestead Grays, Baltimore Black Sox

Payne, William (Doc), 1898   OF, Celeron Acme Colored Giants (Iron and Oil Lg.)

Peace, Warren, 1945-48   P, Newark Eagles

Peacock, —, 1933   3B, Homestead Grays

Peak, Rufus, 1931   officer, Detroit Stars

Pearson, Frank (Ivy, Wahoo), 1945-50   P, Memphis Red Sox, Chicago American Giants

Pearson, Jimmy, 1949   P, New York Cubans

Pearson, Leonard Curtis (Lennie, Hoss), 1937-50   OF, 3B, SS, 1B, MGR, Newark Eagles, Baltimore Elite Giants, St. Louis Stars

Peatross, Maurice, 1947   1B, Homestead Grays

Pedemonte, —, 1926   P, 3B, OF, Cuban Stars (NNL)

Pedroso, Eustaquio, 1910-30   P, OF, 1B, C, Cuban Stars, All Cubans, Cuban Stars (ECL), Cuban Stars (NNL)

Pedroso, [Fernando Diaz] (El Bicho), 1945-50-INF, OF, New York Cubans

Peebles, A.J., 1933   officer, Columbus Blue Birds

Peeks, A.J., 1932   officer, Atlanta Black Crackers

Peeples, Nathaniel, 1950   C, Kansas City Monarchs, Indianapolis Clowns

Peete, Charles, 1950   OF, Indianapolis Clowns

Pelham, William (Don), 1933-38   SS, OF, Bacharach Giants, Atlanta Black Crackers

Pellas, —, 1923   P, Cuban Stars (NNL)

Pena, —, 1929   C, 1B, Cuban Stars (NNL)

Pendleton, James (Jim), 1948   SS, Chicago American Giants

Pennington, —, 1929   P, Nashville Elite Giants

Pennington, Arthur David (Art, Superman), 1940-50   OF, 1B, 2B, Chicago American Giants, Pittsburgh Crawfords

Penno, Dan, 1893-1896   P, OF, 2B, Cuban Giants, Cuban X Giants

Penoy, —, 1932   C, Pennsylvania Red Caps

Perdue, Frank M., 1920-34   pres, NSL; officer, Birmingham Black Barons

Pereira, Jose (Pepin), 1947   P, Baltimore Elite Giants

Perez, Javier (Blue), 1942-45   3B, New York Cubans, Cuban Stars

Perez, Jose (Pepin), 1911-37   P, 1B, C, 2B, SS, 3B, Cuban Stars (ECL), Cuban Stars (NNL), Harrisburg Giants, Bacharach Giants, Hilldale, New York Cubans, Homestead Grays, Brooklyn Eagles, Madison Stars

Perez, Luis, see Luis Perez Caballero

Perkins, William George (Bill), 1928-48   C, OF, MGR, Birmingham Black Barons, Cleveland Cubs, Pittsburgh Crawfords, Cleveland Stars, Philadelphia Stars, Baltimore Elite Giants, New York Black Yankees, Homestead Grays

Perry, Alonzo Thomas, 1940-50   P, 1B, Homestead Grays, Birmingham Black Barons

Perry, Carlisle (Carl), 1921-26   2B, 3B, SS, Detroit Stars, Bacharach Giants, Washington Potomacs, Lincoln Giants, Cleveland Browns, Baltimore Black Sox, Indianapolis ABCs, Hilldale, Cleveland Tate Stars, Richmond Giants, Norfolk Giants

Perry, Don, 1921-27   1B, Madison Stars, Washington Braves, Harrisburg Giants

Perry, Ed, 1887   player, Washington Capital City

Perry, Hank, 1926,1934   P, Hilldale, Newark Dodgers

Pervis, —, 1932,1937   P, Monroe Monarchs, Birmingham Black Barons

Peters, Frank, 1916-23   SS, Chicago Union Giants, Peters Union Giants

Peters, William S., 1887-1923   1B, owner, MGR, Chicago Unions, Peters Union Giants

Peterson, Harvey (Pete), 1931-36,1946   OF, P, INF, Montgomery Grey Sox, Birmingham Black Barons, Memphis Red Sox, Cincinnati Tigers, Cleveland Clippers(USL)

Peterson, L., 1885   1B, Brooklyn Remsens

Petricola, —, 1924   P, Cuban Stars (NNL)

Pettus, William Thomas (Zack), 1909-23   C, 1B, 2B, SS, MGR, Kansas City Giants, Leland Giants, Chicago Giants, Lincoln Stars, Lincoln Giants, St. Louis Giants, Hilldale, Bacharach Giants, Richmond Giants, Harrisburg Giants, Brooklyn Royal Giants

Petway, —, 1931-32   SS, 2B, Nashville Elite Giants, Birmingham Black Barons, Louisville Black Caps

Petway, Bruce, 1906-25   C, OF, MGR, Leland Giants, Brooklyn Royal Giants, Philadelphia Giants, Chicago American Giants, Detroit Stars

Petway, Howard, 1906   P, Leland Giants

Petway, Sherley (Charlie), 1937-44   C, MGR, Detroit Stars, Chicago Brown Bombers, Cleveland Buckeyes

Pfiffer, —, 1937   3B, St. Louis Stars

Phillips, —, 1921-23   SS, 2B, Nashville Elite Giants, Detroit Stars

Phillips, —, 1927   P, Birmingham Black Barons

Phillips, John, 1939   P, Baltimore Elite Giants

Phillips, Norris, 1942-43   P, Kansas City Monarchs, Memphis Red Sox

Pierce, Herbert, 1925-26   C, Homestead Grays

Pierce, Leonard, 1924-27   P, Wilmington Potomacs, Philadelphia Giants

Pierce, Steve, 1925-28   officer, Detroit Stars

Pierce, William H. (Bill), 1910-32   1B, C, OF, Philadelphia Giants, Chicago American Giants, Lincoln Stars, Lincoln Giants, Pennsylvania Red Caps of New York, Bacharach Giants, Norfolk Giants, Detroit Stars, Baltimore Black Sox, Homestead Grays, Mohawk Giants; umpire, East-West Lg.

Pierson, 1937, see Len Pearson

Pierson, —, 1933   3B, Homestead Grays

Pierre, Joseph, 1950   INF, Kansas City Monarchs

Pierre, Rogers, 1939   P, Chicago American Giants

Pigg, Leonard, 1947-50   C, Indianapolis Clowns, Cleveland Buckeyes

Pillot, Guillermo Luis (Guillo), 1941-43   P, New York Black Yankees, Cincinnati Clowns

Piloto, Jose, 1949-50   P, Memphis Red Sox

Pinder, Eddie (Potato), 1914-16   OF, Hilldale

Pinder, Fred, 1910-17   SS, Hilldale

Pinder, George (Monk), 1910   OF, Hilldale

Pinkston, Al, 1936   1B, St. Louis Stars

Pipkin, Robert (Lefty, Black Diamond), 1928-33, 1942 P, Birmingham Black Barons, Cleveland Cubs, New Orleans Crescent Stars

Pitts, Curtis, 1950 C, Chicago American Giants, Cleveland Buckeyes

Pitts, Ed, 1940 C, Philadelphia Stars

Pla, —, 1933 P, Cuban Stars

Pluno, —, 1887 player, Boston Resolutes

Poindexter, Robert, 1924-29 P, 1B, Birmingham Black Barons, Chicago American Giants, Memphis Red Sox

Poinsette, Robert, 1939 OF, P, New York Black Yankees, Toledo Crawfords

Pointer, Robert Lee, 1950 P, Kansas City Monarchs

Pointter, —, 1887 P, 3B, Binghamton, N.Y. (Int. Lg.)

Polanco, Rafael (Ralph), 1942 P, Philadelphia Stars

Poles, E. (Possum, Googles), 1922-28 SS, 3B, Baltimore Black Sox, Harrisburg Giants

Poles, Spottswood (Spot), 1909-23 OF, Philadelphia Giants, Lincoln Giants, Brooklyn Royal Giants, Lincoln Stars, Hilldale, Bacharach Giants, Richmond Giants

Pollard, —, 1936 OF, St. Louis Stars

Pollard, Nat, 1946-50 P, Birmingham Black Barons

Pollock, Syd, 1926-50 off.,owner, Havana Red Sox, Cuban House of David, Cuban Stars, Ethiopian Clowns, Cincinnati Clowns, Indianapolis Clowns

Pompez, Alexandro (Alex), 1922-50 officer, Cuban Stars (ECL), New York Cubans; vice-pres, NNL

Pontello, —, 1927 P, Cuban Stars (ECL)

Poole, Claude, 1945-46 P, New York Black Yankees

Pope, A., 1948 OF, Homestead Grays

Pope, Dave, 1946 UTIL, Homestead Grays

Pope, Edgar, 1938 OF, Atlanta Black Crackers

Pope, James, 1931-32 P, Louisville White Sox, Montgomery Grey Sox

Pope, Willie (Bill), 1947-48 P, Homestead Grays

Porsee, —, 1921 P, St. Louis Giants

Porter, Andrew (Andy, Pullman), 1932-50 P, Cleveland Cubs, Nashville Elite Giants, Washington Elite Giants, Baltimore Elite Giants, Indianapolis Clowns, Columbus Elite Giants, Louisville White Sox, Newark Eagles

Portuando, Bartolo, 1916-27 3B, 1B, Cuban Stars, Kansas City Monarchs, Cuban Stars (ECL), New York Cuban Stars

Posey, Cumberland Willis (Cum), 1911-46 OF, officer, Homestead Grays, Detroit Wolves; founder, East-West Lg.; sec'y, tres, NNL

Posey, Seward Hayes (See, Sea), 1911-48 officer, bus. mgr, Homestead Grays

Postell, —, 1934 2B, Cincinnati Tigers

Potter, —, 1921 C, Kansas City Monarchs

Potter, D., 1932 OF, Atlanta Black Crackers

Powell, —, 1914-15 P, Lincoln Giants

Powell, Edward D. (Eddie, Big Red, Boche), 1936-38 C, New York Black Yankees, Washington Black Senators, New York Cubans

Powell, Elvin (Shoeless), 1931 2B, Memphis Red Sox

Powell, J.J., 1931 officer, Little Rock Black Travelers

Powell, Melvin (Putt), 1930-43 P, OF, Cole's American Giants, Chicago American Giants, Chicago Brown Bombers, Chicago Columbia Giants

Powell, Richard D. (Dick), 1938-52 officer, owner, Baltimore Elite Giants, Nashville Elite Giants

Powell, Russell, 1914-21 C, 2B, Indianapolis ABCs

Powell, William H. (Bill), 1947-50 P, Birmingham Black Barons

Powell, Willie Ernest (Wee Willie, Piggy), 1925-35 P, Chicago American Giants, Detroit Stars, Cole's American Giants, Cleveland Red Sox, Akron Tyrites

Presby, —, 1945 P, Chicago Brown Bombers

Presswood, Henry, 1948-50 SS, Cleveland Buckeyes

Preston, Albert, 1943-1949 P, New York Black Yankees

Preston, Robert, 1950 P, Baltimore Elite Giants

Price, —, 1922 OF, Pittsburgh Keystones

Price, Marvin, 1950 1B, Cleveland Buckeyes, Chicago American Giants

Prichett, W., 1921 P, Hilldale

Prim, Randolph, 1926 P, Kansas City Monarchs

Prim, William, 1905 C, Leland Giants

Primm, —, 1910 C, St. Louis Giants

Pritchett, Wilbur, 1924-32 P, Harrisburg Giants, Baltimore Black Sox, Brooklyn Royal Giants, Hilldale, Bacharach Giants

Proctor, James (Cub), 1884-87 P, C, Baltimore Atlantics, Baltimore Lord Baltimores

Pryor, —, 1916-17 P, Indianapolis ABCs, St. Louis Giants, Jewell's ABCs, Bowser's ABCs

Pryor, Anderson, 1922-33 2B, SS, Milwaukee Bears, Detroit Stars, Memphis Red Sox, New Orleans Crescent Stars,

Pryor, Bill, 1927-31 P, Memphis Red Sox, Detroit Stars

Pryor, Edward, 1925-27 2B, Lincoln Giants, Penn Red Caps of NY

Pryor, Wes, 1910-13 3B, Leland Giants, Chicago American Giants, St. Louis Giants, Chicago Giants, Mohawk Giants, Brooklyn Royal Giants

Pugh, Johnny, 1912-22 3B, 2B, OF, Mohawk Giants, Brooklyn Royal Giants, Philadelphia Giants, Bacharach Giants, Harrisburg Giants, Lincoln Giants, Lincoln Stars

Pulamino, —, 1905 OF, All Cubans

Pullen, C. Neil, 1920-27 C, Brooklyn Royal Giants, Kansas City Monarchs, Baltimore Black Sox, Lincoln Giants

Pulliam, Arthur (Chick), 1909-15 C, Kansas City (KS) Giants, Kansas City (MO) Royal Giants

Purcell, Herman, 1944-47 3B, P, Cleveland Buckeyes, Memphis Red Sox

Purgen, —, 1920-21 SS, Madison Stars, Hilldale

Quinones, Thomas Plancharon, 1946-47 P, Indianapolis Clowns

Quintana, Busta, 1928-34 INF, Cuban Stars (NNL), Newark Dodgers

Radcliff, Alexander (Alex), 1926-46 SS, 3B, Chicago Giants, Cole's American Giants, Chicago American Giants, New York Cubans, Kansas City Monarchs, Cincinnati-Indianapolis Clowns, Memphis Red Sox, Dayton Marcos, Birmingham Black Barons

Radcliffe, Theodore R. (Double Duty), 1928-50 C, P, MGR, Detroit Stars, St. Louis Stars, Pittsburgh Crawfords, Homestead Grays, Columbus Blue Birds, New York Black Yankees, Brooklyn Eagles, Cincinnati Tigers, Memphis Red Sox, Birmingham Black Barons, Chicago American Giants, Louisville Buckeyes, Kansas City Monarchs

Raggs, Harry, *see Harry Roberts*

Ragland, Hurland, 1920-21 P, Indianapolis ABCs, Kansas City Monarchs, Columbus Buckeyes, Dayton Marcos

Raine, J., 1884-85 OF, Baltimore Atlantics

Ramirez, Ramiro (Rome), 1916-48 OF, MGR, Cuban Stars, Havana Stars, Cuban Stars (East), All Cubans, Bacharach Giants, Baltimore Black Sox, Havana Red Sox, Cuban House of David, Indianapolis Clowns, Brooklyn Royal Giants, New York Cuban Stars, Richmond Giants

Ramos, —, 1912 P, Cuban Stars, Long Branch (NJ) Cubans

Ramos, Jose (Cheo), 1921-29 OF, All Cubans, Cuban Stars (ECL)

Ramsay, William, 1889 OF, Chicago Unions

Randolph, Andrew G., 1882-88 1B, OF, Argyle Hotel, Trenton (NJ) Cuban Giants, Boston Resolutes, Active of Philadelphia

Rankin, Bill (Bullets, Shorty), 1923-27 P, C, Washington Potomacs, Richmond Giants, Philadelphia Giants

Rankin, George, 1887 player, Cincinnati Browns

Ransom, Joe, 1926 C, Cleveland Elites

Rawlins, —, 1905 OF, Cuban Giants

Ray, John, 1932-45 OF, Montgomery Grey Sox, Birmingham Black Barons, Cleveland Bears, Jacksonville Red Caps, Cincinnati-Indianapolis Clowns, Kansas City Monarchs, Pittsburgh Crawfords

Ray, Otto C. (Jaybird), 1920-24 P, C, OF, Kansas City Monarchs, Chicago Giants, St. Louis Stars, Cleveland Tate Stars, Cleveland Browns, Toledo Tigers

Ray, Richard, 1943 INF, OF, Chicago Brown Bombers

Ray, Thomas, 1887 player, New York Gorhams

Reavis, W., 1920-32 P, Lincoln Giants, Pennsylvania Red Caps of New York

Rector, Cornelius (Connie), 1920-44 P, Hilldale, Brooklyn Royal Giants, Lincoln Giants, New York Black Yankees, New York Cubans

Redd, Eugene, 1922-23 3B, Pittsburgh Keystones, Milwaukee Bears New Orleans Crescent Stars, Kansas City Monarchs

Redd, Ulysses A. (Hickey), 1940-41 SS, Chicago American Giants, Birmingham Black Barons

Redding, Richard (Dick, Cannonball), 1911-38 P, OF, MGR, Lincoln Giants, Lincoln Stars, Indianapolis ABCs, Chicago American Giants, Brooklyn Royal Giants, Bacharach Giants

Reddon, Bob, 1919 P, Cleveland Tate Stars

Redmon, Tom, 1911 player, Leland Giants

Redus, Wilson, 1924-40 OF, MGR, coach, St. Louis Stars, Cleveland Stars, Columbus Blue Birds, Cleveland Giants, Kansas City Monarchs, Cleveland Red Sox, Chicago American Giants, Cleveland Browns, Indianapolis ABCs

Redwine, —, 1926 P, Cleveland Elites

Reed, Ambrose, 1922-32 OF, 2B, 1B, 3B, Bacharach Giants, Hilldale, Pittsburgh Crawfords, Atlanta Black Crackers, Homestead Grays

Reed, Andrew, 1917-21 3B, OF, Chicago Union Giants, Detroit Stars, Chicago Giants

Reed, Curtis, 1937 OF, St. Louis Stars

Reed, John, 1934-42 P, Cole's American Giants, Indianapolis ABCs, Chicago American Giants, Chicago Brown Bombers, Atlanta Black Crackers, Indianapolis Athletics, St. Louis Stars

Reedy, Fleming (Buddy), 1950 3B, Baltimore Elite Giants

Reel, Jimmy, 1923 OF, Toledo Tigers

Reese, —, 1910 P, Cuban Giants

Reese, James, 1934-35 P, Cleveland Red Sox, Brooklyn Eagles

Reese, John E., 1918-31 OF, Bacharach Giants, Hilldale, Chicago American Giants, Detroit Stars, Toledo Tigers, St. Louis Stars

Reeves, —, 1908 CF, Brooklyn Colored Giants

Reeves, —, 1929 C, Hilldale

Reeves, Donald, 1937-41 1B, OF, Atlanta Black Crackers, Indianapolis ABCs, Chicago American Giants

Reeves, John, 1890-92 3B, OF, Lincoln (Neb) Giants, Plattsmouth (Nebraska St. Lg.)

Reggie, —, 1921 P, Indianapolis ABCs

Reid, Porter, 1949 OF, Houston Eagles

Rena, *see Pena*

Renfro, William, 1887 P, Binghamton, N.Y. (Int. Lg.)

Renfroe, Othello Nelson Sr. (Chico, Chappy), 1945-50 OF, C, SS, Kansas City Monarchs, Cleveland Buckeyes, Indianapolis Clowns

Reveria, Charlie, 1939 3B, Baltimore Elite Giants

Reynolds, —, 1946 1B, Birmingham Black Barons

Reynolds, Jimmy, 1940,1946 3B, Indianapolis Crawfords, Cleveland Buckeyes

Reynolds, Joe, 1935 P, Philadelphia Stars

Reynolds, Louis Thomas (Lou), 1897-99-OF, 1B, Chicago Columbia Giants, Chicago Unions

Reynolds, William Ernest (Bill), 1948-50 2B, SS, Cleveland Buckeyes, Louisville Buckeyes

Rhoades, Cornelius (Neal), 1910-18-C, OF, Bowser's ABCs, Hilldale

Rhodes, Claude (Dusty), 1931-33 P, Louisville Black Caps, Columbus Blue Birds, Chattanoogna Black Lookouts

Rhodes, Harry, 1942-50 P, 1B, Chicago American Giants

Rice, Miller, 1934-37 OF, Cincinnati Tigers

Rich, —, 1924 3B, St. Louis Giants

Richardson, —, 1908 OF, Brooklyn Colored Giants

Richardson, Bob (Johnny), 1949-50 SS, Homestead Grays

Richardson, Dewey, 1922 C, Hilldale

Richardson, Earl, 1943 SS, Newark Eagles

Richardson, Eugene (Gene), 1947-50   P, Kansas City Monarchs

Richardson, George, 1901-03   SS, Chicago Union Giants, Algona (IA) Brownies

Richardson, George, 1925   officer, Detroit Stars

Richardson, Glemby (Glenn), 1946-49   2B, New York Black Yankees

Richardson, Henry (Long Tom), 1921-38   P, OF, Baltimore Black Sox, Washington Pilots, Bacharach Giants, Washington Black Senators, Pittsburgh Crawfords, Cuban Stars, Richmond Giants

Richardson, Jim, 1939   P, New York Black Yankees

Richardson, John, 1924-25   P, Birmingham Black Barons

Richardson, Vicial, 1946   SS, Cleveland Buckeyes

Ricks, Curtiss, 1921-26-OF, P, 1B, Dayton Marcos, Cleveland Tate Stars, Indianapolis ABCs, Chicago American Giants, Cleveland Browns

Ricks, Napoleon, 1887   player, Louisville Falls City

Ricks, Pender, 1924-28-1B, Philadelphia Giants, Harrisburg Giants

Ricks, William (Bill), 1944-50   P, Philadelphia Stars

Riddick, Vernon, 1939-41   SS, Newark Eagles

Riddle, Marshall Lewis (Jit), 1936-43   2B, SS, Indianapolis ABCs, St. Louis Stars, New Orleans-St. Louis Stars, Cleveland Buckeyes, Jacksonville Red Caps

Ridgely, (Buck), 1919-23   SS, Lincoln Giants, Baltimore Black Sox, Harrisburg Giants

Ridley, Jack, 1927-34   OF, 1B, Nashville Elite Giants, Cleveland Cubs, Louisville Red Caps

Rigal, —, 1922-27   SS, 3B, Cuban Stars (NNL)

Riggins, Orville, 1920-35   SS, 3B, 2B, MGR, Detroit Stars, Cleveland Hornets, Homestead Grays, Lincoln Giants, New York Black Yankees, Brooklyn Royal Giants, Chicago American Giants

Rigney, H.G. (Hank), 1939-45   officer, Toledo Crawfords, Indianapolis Crawfords, Toledo Cubs (USL)

Rile, Edward (Ed, Huck), 1920-33   P, 1B, Indianapolis ABCs, Chicago American Giants, Lincoln Giants, Columbus Buckeyes, Detroit Stars, Cole's American Giants, Brooklyn Royal Giants, Kansas City Monarchs

Riley, Jim (Jack), 1945   2B, Birmingham Black Barons

Rims, —, 1920   P, Bacharach Giants

Rios, Herman, 1915-24   3B, SS, Cuban Stars (NNL), Havana Stars, Cuban Stars

Risley, —, 1922-23   3B, Baltimore Black Sox, Washington Potomacs

Ritchey, John F., 1947   C, Chicago American Giants

Rivas, —, 1917-18   2B, Cuban Stars (East)

Rivera, Nenene Aniceto, 1933   P, INF, Cuban Stars

Rivero, Carlos (Charley), 1939,1943-44   SS, 3B, Cuban Stars, New York Black Yankees, Baltimore Elite Giants

Rivers, Bill (Rivera), 1944   OF, Kansas City Monarchs

Rivers, Dewey(Deep), 1926,1933   OF, Hilldale, Baltimore Black Sox

Roberson, (Charley), 1934   SS, Nashville Elite Giants

Roberts, —, 1931   C, Chicago Columbia Giants

Roberts, Charley, 1938   P, Washington Black Senators

Roberts, Curtis B., 1947-50   3B, 2B, Kansas City Monarchs

Roberts, Elihu, 1916-20   OF, Bacharach Giants, Hilldale

Roberts, Harry (Raggs), 1920-32   OF, C, Norfolk Giants, Baltimore Black Sox, Harrisburg Giants, Homestead Grays, Chicago Columbia Giants, Pittsburgh Crawfords, Norfolk Stars

Roberts, J.D., 1918-24   SS, 3B, 2B, Pennsylvania Giants, Hilldale, Bacharach Giants, Richmond Giants

Roberts, Leroy (Roy, Everready), 1916-34   P, Bacharach Giants, Columbus Buckeyes, Brooklyn Royal Giants, Lincoln Giants, Hilldale, Cleveland Giants, Cleveland Red Sox, Madison Stars

Roberts, P., 1903   2B, Chicago Union Giants

Roberts, Sarah Mutt, 1937-39   P, Philadelphia Stars, Nashville Elite Giants, Baltimore Elite Giants

Roberts, Tom (Speck), 1937-45   P, Homestead Grays, New York Black Yankees, Newark Eagles, Philadelphia Stars, Washington Black Senators

Robertson, Bobbie, *see William Robinson*

Robertson, Charles, 1921-25   P, Birmingham Black Barons, St. Louis Stars, New Orleans Caulfield Ads

Robinson, —, 1943   C, New York Black Yankees

Robinson, Al, 1905-12   1B, P, Brooklyn Royal Giants, New York Black Sox

Robinson, Bill (Bojangles), 1931   officer, New York Stars (Black Yankees)

Robinson, (Black Diamond), 1886   1B, New York Gorhams

Robinson, Bob, 1905   C, Leland Giants

Robinson, Bobby (Robbie), 1939-40,1945   UTIL, 3B, St. Louis Stars, Homestead Grays

Robinson, Charles, 1939   OF, Chicago American Giants

Robinson, Cornelius Randall (Neil), 1936-50   OF, SS, Cincinnati Tigers, Homestead Grays, Memphis Red Sox

Robinson, Edward, 1931   OF, Louisville White Sox

Robinson, George (Sis), 1918   P, Bacharach Giants

Robinson, George, 1924   officer, Washington Potomacs

Robinson, Henry Frazier (Sloe, Hank), 1942-50   C, Baltimore Grays, Baltimore Elite Giants, Kansas City Monarchs

Robinson, J., 1905-10   OF, Kansas City, Kan. Giants, Brooklyn Royal Giants

Robinson, J., 1938-39   3B, Indianapolis ABCs, St. Louis Stars

Robinson, Jack Roosevelt (Jackie), 1945   SS, Kansas City Monarchs

Robinson, Jacob, 1946-47   3B, Chicago American Giants

Robinson, James (Black Rusie), 1894-1906   P, Lansing, Michigan, Colored Capital All-Americans, Cuban Giants, Cuban X Giants, Brooklyn Royal Giants, Pawtucket (New Eng. Lg.)

Robinson, Johnny, 1930,1942   INF, OF, Memphis Red Sox, Detroit Black Sox

Robinson, Joshua, 1939   OF, New York Black Yankees

Robinson, Kenneth, 1931,1939   2B, 3B, OF, Brooklyn Royal Giants, Newark Eagles

Robinson, Neil, *see Cornelius Robinson*

Robinson, Newt, *see Walter Robinson*

Robinson, Norman Wayne (Bobby, Norm), 1939-50   OF, SS, 3B, Baltimore Elite Giants, Birmingham Black Barons

Robinson, Ray (Not Sugar), 1941-47   P, Newark Eagles, Cincinnati Giants, Philadelphia Stars, Cleveland Buckeyes

Robinson, Richmond, 1883-86   OF, St.Louis Black Stockings Trenton (NJ) Cuban Giants,

Robinson, Walter William (Newt, Bill), 1925-31   SS, Hilldale, Lincoln Giants, Harrisburg Giants, New York Black Yankees

Robinson, Walter (Skindown), 1940-42   2B, Cleveland Bears, Jacksonville Red Caps

Robinson, William (Bobbie), 1925-34   3B, SS, Indianapolis ABCs, Cleveland Elites, Memphis Red Sox, Detroit Stars, Cleveland Stars, Cleveland Red Sox, Birmingham Black Barons

Rochelle, Clarence, 1944   P, Kansas City Monarchs

Roddy, B.M., 1926   pres, NSL

Rodgers, Silvester Clifford (Speedie), 1949-50   P, Baltimore Elite Giants

Rodriquez, —, 1915   P, Cuban Stars

Rodriguez, Antonio, 1939   P, Cuban Stars

Rodriguez, Antonio Hector, 1944   3B, New York Cubans

Rodriguez, B.Conrado, 1922,1927-29   P, OF, Cuban Stars (NNL)

Rodriguez, Benvienido, 1948   OF, C, Chicago American Giants

Rodriguez, Herrado, *see Antonio Hector Rodriguez*

Rodriguez, Jose, 1915-29   C, Cuban Stars, Cuban Stars (East), Detroit Stars, Kansas City Monarchs, Cuban Stars (NNL), All Cubans

Rodriquez, Oscar, 1935   MGR., Havana Red Sox

Rodoud, —, 1921   C, Cuban Stars (East)

Roesink, John, 1925-30   officer, owner, Detroit Stars

Rogan, Wilber (Bullet Joe), 1917-46   P, OF, 1B, 2B, 3B, SS, MGR, Kansas City Colored Giants, All Nations, Los Angeles White Sox, Kansas City Monarchs; umpire, NAL

Rogers, —, 1900   P, Genuine Cuban Giants

Rogers, Pierre, 1934-39   P, Cincinnati Tigers, Chicago American Giants, Ethiopian Clowns

Rogers, Sid, 1887   player, Cincinnati Browns

Rogers, William Nathaniel (Nat), 1923-45   OF, 1B, 3B, C, Harrisburg Giants, Brooklyn Royal Giants, Memphis Red Sox, Chicago Columbia Giants, Cole's American Giants, Chicago American Giants, Birmingham Black Barons, Kansas City Monarchs

Rojo, Julio, 1916-38   C, 3B, Cuban Stars, Havana Stars, Bacharach Giants, Baltimore Black Sox, Cuban Stars of Havana, Lincoln Giants, New York Cuban Stars

Rolls, Charles, 1911   player, Leland Giants

Romanach, —, 1916   SS, Long Branch Cubans

Romby, Robert L. (Bob), 1946-50   P, Baltimore Elite Giants

Ronsell, —, 1928-31   OF, Birmingham Black Barons, Memphis Red Sox, Nashville Elite Giants

Roque, Jacinto (Battling Siki), 1928-29   OF, Cuban Stars (NNL)

Rose, Cecil, 1924   P, St. Louis Stars

Rose, Haywood, 1907   C, Leland Giants

Roselle, Basilio [Rosselle, Rosello], 1926-35   P, Cuban Stars (NNL), Cuban Stars (ECL), New York Cubans

Ross, Alex, 1887-1889   3B, OF, Greenville (Northern Mich. Lg.), and (Michigan St. Lg.)

Ross, —, 1918   P, Indianapolis ABCs

Ross, Arthur, 1903-05   P, Chicago Union Giants, Leland Giants

Ross, Dick, 1925   OF, St. Louis Stars

Ross, Harold, 1922-25   P, Indianapolis ABCs, Washington Potomacs, Chicago American Giants, Cleveland Browns

Ross, Jerry, 1926   P, Cleveland Elites

Ross, Sam, 1923   P, Hilldale, Harrisburg Giants

Ross, William, 1924-30   P, St. Louis Stars, Cleveland Hornets, Chicago American Giants, Homestead Grays

Rossiter, George, 1922-31   officer, owner, Baltimore Black Sox

Roth, Herman Joseph (Bobby), 1921-25   C, New Orleans Crescent Stars, Chicago American Giants, Milwaukee Bears, Detroit Stars, Birmingham Black Barons

Rotoret, —, 1950   P, New York Cubans

Rovira, Jaime, 1911   3B, All Cubans

Rowe, —, 1932   P, Nashville Elite Giants

Rowe, William (Schoolboy), 1943-45   P, Chicago Brown Bombers, Pittsburgh Crawfords, Cleveland Buckeyes

Royall, Joseph John, 1937-42   P, OF, Indianapolis Athletics, Jacksonville Red Caps, New York Black Yankees, Cleveland Bears

Ruffin, Charles Leon (Lassas), 1935-50   P, MGR, Newark Eagles, Pittsburgh Crawfords, Philadelphia Stars, Houston Eagles, Brooklyn Eagles, Toledo Crawfords

Ruiz, Antonio (Perez), 1944   P, Cincinnati-Indianapolis Clowns

Ruiz, Silvino (Poppa), 1928-42   P, Cuban Stars (ECL), New York Cubans

Rush, Joe, 1923-26   officer, Birmingham Black Barons; sec'y, NNL; pres, NSL

Ruson, —, 1931   SS, Brooklyn Royal Giants

Russ, Pythias, 1925-29   C, SS, Chicago American Giants, Memphis Red Sox

Russell, 1929-31, *see Ronsell*

Russell, —, 1933   P, Brooklyn Royal Giants

Russell, 1940   *see Russell Awkard*

Russell, Aaron A., 1913-20   3B, Homestead Grays

Russell, Branch L., 1922-33   3B, OF, Kansas City Monarchs, St. Louis Stars, Cleveland Stars, Cleveland Cubs

Russell, E., 1924-26   3B, OF, Harrisburg Giants, Dayton Marcos

Russell, Frank (Junior), 1943-49   2B, OF, Baltimore Elite Giants

Russell, John Henry (Pistol), 1923-34   2B, 3B, Memphis Red Sox, St. Louis Stars,

Indianapolis ABCs, Pittsburgh Crawfords, Detroit Wolves, Cleveland Red Sox

Russell, Thomas, 1950 P, Cleveland Buckeyes

Rutledge, —, 1921 P, Dayton Marcos

Ryan, Merven J. (Red), 1915-31 P, Pittsburgh Stars of Buffalo, Brooklyn Royal Giants, Hilldale, Harrisburg Giants, Bacharach Giants, Baltimore Black Sox, Lincoln Stars, Newark Browns, Lincoln Giants, New York Black Yankees

Saabin, —, 1927 P, Cuban Stars (ECL)

Sadler, William A.(Bill, Bubby), 1935-38 SS, Brooklyn Eagles, Washington Black Senators

St. Thomas, Larry, 1943,1947 C, Newark Eagles, New York Black Yankees

Salas, Wilfredo, 1948 P, New York Cubans

Salazar, Lazaro, 1924-36 OF, P, 1B, Cuban Stars (NNL), New York Cubans

Salazar, Santos, 1945 UTIL, New York Cubans

Salmon, Harry, 1923-35 P, Birmingham Black Barons, Homestead Grays, Memphis Red Sox, Detroit Wolves

Salters, Edward, 1937 OF, Detroit Stars

Salvat, —, 1924-25 P, Cuban Stars (ECL)

Sama, Pablo, 1950 3B, Indianapolis Clowns

Sampson, —, 1899-1905 P, OF, Genuine Cuban Giants, Cuban Giants

Sampson, Eddie (Leo), 1941-43 OF, Birmingham Black Barons

Sampson, John, 1942 OF, New York Cubans

Sampson, Ormond Leonard, 1932-38 SS, Atlanta Black Crackers, Brooklyn Royal Giants, Newark Dodgers

Sampson, Sam, 1940-41 2B, OF, Cleveland Bears, Jacksonville Red Caps

Sampson, Thomas (Tommy, Toots), 1938-48 2B, 1B, MGR, Chicago American Giants, Birmingham Black Barons, New York Cubans

Samuels, —, 1940 P, Philadelphia Stars

San, Pedro Alejandro (Eli), 1926-28 P, Cuban Stars (ECL)

Sanchez, —, 1913 OF, 1B, Philadelphia Giants

Sanchez, Amando, 1948 P, Memphis Red Sox

Sanders, Willie, 1936 P, Memphis Red Sox

Sanderson, Johnny, 1947 SS, Kansas City Monarchs

Sands, Sam (Piggy), 1950 SS, Indianapolis Clowns

Santa Cruz, Eugenio (Santa), 1909-10 OF, Cuban Stars

Santaella, Anastacio (Juan, Tacho), 1935-36 2B, SS, New York Cubans

Santiago, Carlos Manuel, 1946 2B, New York Cubans

Santiago, Jose Guillermo, 1947-48 P, SS, New York Cubans

Santop, Louis (Top)   (real name Louis Santop Loftin), 1909-26 C, OF, MGR, Fort Worth Wonders, Oklahoma Monarchs, Philadelphia Giants, Lincoln Giants, Chicago American Giants, Lincoln Stars, Brooklyn Royal Giants, Hilldale

Saperstein, A.M. (Abe), 1932-50 booking agent; officer, Cleveland Cubs, Cincinnati Clowns, Chicago American Giants; pres, Negro Midwestern Lg., West Coast Negro Baseball Association

Sarvis, Andrew (Smoky), 1939-42 P, Cleveland Bears, Jacksonville Red Caps

Satterfield, —, 1905-11 2B, SS, Cuban Giants, Genuine Cuban Giants, Brooklyn Royal Giants

Saunders, —, 1925-28 C, 3B, Pennsylvania Red Caps of NY

Saunders, Bob, 1926-37 2B, SS, P, Kansas City Monarchs, Detroit Stars, Bacharach Giants, Monroe Monarchs, Louisville Red Caps, Cleveland Hornets, Memphis Red Sox

Saunders, Leo, 1940 P, SS, Chicago American Giants, Birmingham Black Barons

Saunders, William, 1887 player, Pittsburgh Keystones

Saunders, William, 1950 C, Baltimore Elite Giants

Savage, —, 1925 P, Bacharach Giants, Wilmington Potomacs

Savage, Artie, 1932 officer, Cleveland Stars

Savage, Bill (Junior), 1940 P, Memphis Red Sox

Sawyer, Carl, 1924 2B, Detroit Stars

Saxon, Thomas (Lefty), 1942 P, New York Cubans

Saylor, Alfred (Greyhound), 1940-45 P, 1B, C,

Birmingham Black Barons, Cincinnati Buckeyes

Scales, George (Tubby), 1920-48 2B, 3B, OF, SS, MGR, St. Louis Giants, St. Louis Stars, Lincoln Giants, Newark Stars, Homestead Grays, New York Black Yankees, Philadelphia Stars, Baltimore Elite Giants, Pittsburgh Keystones

Scantlebury, Patricio Athelstan (Pat), 1944-50 P, New York Cubans

Schiff, —, 1908 LF, Genuine Cuban Giants

Schlichter, H. Walter, 1902-10 officer,MGR, Philadelphia Giants; pres, National Associaton of Colored Base Ball Clubs of the United States and Cuba

Schorling, John M., 1911-27 officer, Chicago American Giants

Scotland, —, 1914-17 OF, Chicago Union Giants, Indianapolis ABCs, Bowser's ABCs, Louisville Sox

Scott, —, 1916 P, Chicago Giants

Scott, —, 1920 C, Detroit Stars

Scott, —, 1937 P, Birmingham Black Barons

Scott, —, 1940 P, Cincinnati Buckeyes

Scott, C.L., 1915 player, Mohawk Giants

Scott, Charles, 1919-20 OF, St. Louis Giants

Scott, Elisha, 1920 co-drafter, constitution of NNL

Scott, Frank, 1887-94 2B, SS, Chicago Unions

Scott, Jimmy, 1950 P, Memphis Red Sox

Scott, John, 1944-50 OF, 1B, Birmingham Black Barons, Kansas City Monarchs, Louisville Buckeyes, Chicago American Giants, Philadelphia Stars

Scott, Joseph (Joe), 1947-50 1B, Birmingham Black Barons, Chicago American Giants

Scott, Joseph Burt (Joe), 1944-49 OF, Memphis Red Sox

Scott, Robert, 1920-27 OF, Brooklyn Royal Giants, Lincoln Giants Hilldale

Scott, Robert, 1950 P, New York Black Yankees

Scott, William, 1932 officer, Louisville Black Caps

Scott, William Jr. (Bill), 1950 OF, Philadelphia Stars

Scott, Willie Lee (Joe), 1927-34 1B, Memphis Red Sox, Louisville White Sox, Indianapolis ABCs, Columbus Blue Birds, Homestead Grays, Chicago American Giants

Scragg, Jesse, 1915 P, Philadelphia Giants

Scroggins, John, 1947 P, Kansas City Monarchs

Scruggs, Robert, 1950 P, Cleveland Buckeyes

Scruggs, William C. (Willie), 1949-50 P, Louisville Buckeyes, Cleveland Buckeyes, Houston Eagles, Birmingham Black Barons

Scudder, —, 1887 C, Philadelphia Pythians

Seagraves, —, 1937 OF, Indianapolis Athletics

Seagraves, Samuel, 1946 C, Chicago American Giants

Searcy, Kelly (Lefty), 1950 P, Baltimore Elite Giants, Memphis Red Sox

Seay, Richard William (Dick, Erkie), 1925-47 2B, SS, Pennsylvania Red Caps of New York, Newark Stars, Baltimore Black Sox, Brooklyn Royal Giants, Philadelphia Stars, Pittsburgh Crawfords, Newark Eagles, New York Black Yankees

Segula, —, 1921-23 P, New Orleans Caulfield Ads, Milwaukee Bears

Selden, William H., 1887-99 P, OF, Boston Resolutes, Cuban Giants, New York Gorhams (Middle States Lg.), Lansing, Michigan Colored Capital All-Americans, Cuban X Giants, Trenton Cuban Giants (Middle States Lg.), York Cuban Giants (Eastern Interstate Lg.)

Seldom, —, 1910-14 SS, Chicago Giants, Indianapolis ABCs

Seller, see George Suttles

Semler, James (Soldier Boy), 1932-48 officer, New York Black Yankees

Serrell, William C. (Bonnie, Barney), 1942-50 2B, 3B, Kansas City Monarchs

Seruby, —, 1888 OF, Cuban X Giants

Seto, —, 1929 OF, Cuban Stars (ECL)

Shackleford, John G., 1924-45 3B, 2B, Cleveland Browns, Chicago American Giants, Birmingham Black Barons, Harrisburg Giants, pres, United States Lg.

Shamberg, —, 1938 player, Atlanta Black Crackers

Shanks, Hank, 1927 1B, Birmingham Black Barons

Shannon, —, 1932 OF, Pittsburgh Crawfords

Sharpe, —, 1923 SS, St. Louis Stars

Sharpe, Robert (Pepper), 1943-49 P, OF, Memphis Red Sox, Chicago American Giants, Chicago Brown Bombers

Shartz, —, 1911 C, Philadelphia Giants

Shaw, —, 1920 OF, St. Louis Giants

Shaw, R., 1897 P, Page Fence Giants, Chicago Unions

Shaw, Theodore (Ted), 1927-31 P, Chicago American Giants, Detroit Stars, Memphis Red Sox

Shawler, —, 1909 OF, Leland Giants

Sheffey, Doug, 1910 P, Hilldale

Shelby, Hiawatha, 1946 OF, Indianapolis Clowns

Shelton, —, 1920 C, Dayton Marcos

Shelton, —, 1943 OF, Harrisburg-St. Louis Stars

Shepard, Fred, 1945-48 P, UTIL, Birmingham Black Barons, Chicago American Giants

Sheppard, Ray, 1924-32 SS, Birmingham Black Barons, Detroit Wolves, Homestead Grays, Detroit Stars, Kansas City Monarchs Monroe Monarchs, Indianapolis ABCs

Sheppard, Samuel (Sam), 1887-1926 player, New York Gorhams; officer, St. Louis Stars, owner, Cleveland Elites

Sheppard, William, 1922-24 P, Kansas City Monarchs, Memphis Red Sox

Sherkliff, Ed, 1931 P, Hilldale

Shields, —, 1916 P, Lincoln Giants

Shields, Charlie (Lefty), 1941-45 P, Chicago American Giants, Homestead Grays, New York Cubans

Shields, Jimmy, 1928-29 P, Bacharach Giants

Shipp, Jesse, 1908-12 P, Brooklyn Royal Giants, New York Colored Giants

Shirley, —, 1914 OF, Brooklyn Royal Giants

Shively, George, 1914-25 Indianapolis ABCs, Bacharach Giants, Washington Potomacs, Bowser's ABCs, Brooklyn Royal Giants

Shropshire, —, 1937 C, St. Louis Stars

Sibley, —, 1913 P, Indianapolis ABCs

Siebert, —, 1937 OF, St. Louis Stars

Sierra, Felipe, 1921-32 SS, 2B, 3B, OF, All Cubans, Cuban Stars (NNL)

Sigenero, —, 1940 P, Cuban Stars

Sijo, see Sijo Gomez

Siki, Roque, 1931-32 OF, Cuban Stars, Cuban House of David

Silva, Pedro, 1921-22 P, OF, All Cubans, Cuban Stars (NNL)

Silvers, —, 1933 INF, Philadelphia Stars

Simerson, —, 1936 P, St. Louis Stars

Simmons, —, 1926 P, Lincoln Giants

Simmons, Hubert, 1950 P, Baltimore Elite Giants

Simmons, J.R., 1887 player, Baltimore Lord Baltimores

Simmons, R.S., 1943-49 officer, Chicago American Giants; sec'y, NAL

Simms, Willie (Bill, Simmy), 1934-43 OF, Monroe Monarchs, Cincinnati Tigers, Kansas City Monarchs, Chicago American Giants

Simpson, —, 1933 1B, OF, Cleveland Giants, Baltimore Black Sox, Akron Tyrites

Simpson, Harry (Suitcase), 1946-48 OF, Philadelphia Stars

Simpson, Herbert, 1942 OF, Birmingham Black Barons

Simpson, James, 1887 OF, Philadelphia Pythians

Simpson, Lawrence, 1916-20 P, OF, Chicago Union Giants, Chicago Giants, Bowser's ABCs

Sinclair, Harry, 1931 sec'y, NNL

Sinelan, —, 1932 3B, Bacharach Giants

Singer, Orville (Red), 1921-32 OF, INF, Lincoln Giants, Cleveland Browns, Cleveland Tigers, Cleveland Cubs, Cleveland Stars

Singleton, —, 1896 C, Cuban X Giants

Singleton, —, 1946 P, Cleveland Buckeyes

Singlong, —, 1929 2B, OF, Nashville Elite Giants

Sis —, 1934 OF, New Orleans Crescent Stars

Sisco, —, 1913 LF, Philadelphia Giants

Skinner, A., 1910,1917 C, UTIL, Leland Giants, Kansas City Colored Giants

Skinner, —, 1948 C, Newark Eagles

Slaughter, C., 1884-85 INF, Baltimore Atlantics

Slawson, —, 1916   3B, 2B, Lincoln Stars

Sloan, Robert, 1919-21   OF, Brooklyn Royal Giants

Smallwood, Dewitt Mark (Woody), 1950-1952   OF, Philadelphia Stars, New York Black Yankees, Birmingham Black Barons, Indianapolis Clowns.

Smallwood, Louis, 1923-29   2B, Milwaukee Bears, Chicago Giants

Smart, —, 1932   P, Indianapolis ABCs

Smaulding, Owen, 1927-28   P, Kansas City Monarchs, Cleveland Tigers, Chicago American Giants, Birmingham Black Barons

Smith, —, 1897   1B, Cuban Giants

Smith, —, 1908   OF, New York Colored Giants

Smith, —, 1925   C, St. Louis Stars

Smith, —, 1927   OF, Memphis Red Sox

Smith, Alphonse Eugene (Al, Fuzzy), 1946-48   OF, SS, Cleveland Buckeyes

Smith, B.B.H. (Babe), 1887   P, New York Gorhams

Smith, (Buster), 1932-33   P, 1B, Birmingham Black Barons

Smith, C., 1931   1B, Chicago Columbia Giants

Smith, C., 1933-38   C, Birmingham Black Barons

Smith, Charles (Chino), 1924-31   OF, 2B, Philadelphia Giants, Brooklyn Royal Giants, Lincoln Giants

Smith, Charlie, 1938   INF, Washington Black Senators

Smith, Clarence, 1921-33   OF, MGR, Columbus Buckeyes, Detroit Stars, Birmingham Black Barons, Baltimore Black Sox, Cleveland Cubs, Bacharach Giants

Smith, Cleveland (Cleo), 1922-28   2B, 3B, SS, Baltimore Black Sox, Lincoln Giants, Homestead Grays, Philadelphia Tigers, Harrisburg Giants

Smith, Clyde (Carl, Boots), 1938   3B, Pittsburgh Crawfords

Smith, D., 1945-46   P, Philadelphia Stars, Homestead Grays

Smith, Dode, 1942   P, Cincinnati Buckeyes, Cleveland Buckeyes

Smith, Douglas, 1943   officer, Baltimore Elite Giants

Smith, Ed, 1887   player, Boston Resolutes

Smith, Ernest, 1934-40   C, Monroe Monarchs, Chicago American Giants

Smith, Eugene (Genie), 1939-50   P, St. Louis Stars, New Orleans- St. Louis Stars, New York Black Yankees, Homestead Grays, Cleveland Buckeyes, Louisville Buckeyes, Chicago American Giants, Kansas City Monarchs, Ethiopian Clowns

Smith, Eugene, 1942-46   3B, Jacksonville Red Caps, Cincinnati Buckeyes, Cleveland Buckeyes, Indianapolis Clowns

Smith, F. (Lefty), 1922-24   P, Richmond Giants, Baltimore Black Sox

Smith, Ford, see John Ford Smith

Smith, Fred, 1946   C, Kansas City Monarchs

Smith, G., 1941   P, Kansas City Monarchs

Smith, George C., 1956-57   2B, Indianapolis Clowns

Smith, H., 1922-32   P, Washington Potomacs, Baltimore Black Sox, Bacharach Giants, Homestead Grays

Smith, Harry, 1902-05   1B, OF, Philadelphia Giants

Smith, Harvey, 1938   P, Pittsburgh Crawfords

Smith, Henry, 1942-47   2B, SS, Jacksonville Red Caps, Chicago American Giants, Cincinnati Clowns, Cincinnati-Indianapolis Clowns, New York Black Yankees, Indianapolis Clowns

Smith, Hilton Lee, 1932-48   P, New Orleans Black Creoles, Monroe Monarchs, Kansas City Monarchs

Smith, Hy, 1885   OF, Brooklyn Remsens

Smith, J., 1922-28   2B, SS, Brooklyn Royal Giants, Harrisburg Giants, Bacharach Giants

Smith, James, 1903-06   3B, INF, Cuban X Giants, Leland Giants, Chicago Union Giants

Smith, James, 1925,1930   SS, Detroit Stars

Smith, John Ford (Lefty, Gerinomo), 1939-50   OF, P, Indianapolis Crawfords, Chicago American Giants, New York Black Yankees, Kansas City Monarchs

Smith, L., 1922-23   OF, Baltimore Black Sox

Smith, L., 1942   C, Jacksonville Red Caps

Smith, (Lefty), 1920-21   P, OF, Kansas City Monarchs

Smith, (Lefty), 1940-43   see John Ford Smith

Smith, Mance, 1944   OF, Kansas City Monarchs

Smith, Marshall (Darknight), 1920-24   P, Baltimore Black Sox, Homestead Grays, Richmond Giants, Madison Stars

Smith, Milt, 1949-50   INF, Philadelphia Stars

Smith, O.H., 1885   P, Brooklyn Remsens

Smith, Oliver (Ollie), 1945   P, Cincinnati-Indianapolis Clowns

Smith, P., 1939   P, St. Louis Stars

Smith, Pete, 1937   OF, Pittsburgh Crawfords

Smith, Quincy, 1943-45   OF, Cleveland Buckeyes, Birmingham Black Barons

Smith, R., 1912-15   P, OF, Lincoln Giants

Smith, Robert (Bob), 1930-44   C, 3B, Birmingham Black Barons, Memphis Red Sox, Cincinnati Tigers, St. Louis Stars, New Orleans-St. Louis Stars, Chicago American Giants, Pittsburgh Crawfords, Cleveland Cubs

Smith, Taylor, 1948-49   P, Chicago American Giants

Smith, Theolic (Fireball), 1936-49   P, Pittsburgh Crawfords, St. Louis Stars, New Orleans-St. Louis Stars, Cleveland Buckeyes, Kansas City Monarchs, Toledo Crawfords, Chicago American Giants

Smith, W., 1921,1925   SS, P, Hilldale, Lincoln Giants

Smith, Wardell, 1946   P, Chicago American Giants

Smith, William, 1938   2B, SS, Newark Eagles

Smith, William T. (Big Bill), 1888-1913   C, OF,MGR, Genuine Cuban Giants, Cuban X Giants, Philadelphia Giants, Brooklyn Royal Giants, Mohawk Giants, Chicago Unions

Smith, Willie D., 1948   P, Homestead Grays

Smith, Wyman, 1920-25   OF, Baltimore Black Sox

Smoot, —, 1886   SS, New York Gorhams

Snaer, Lucian, 1923   umpire, NNL

Snead, Sylvester, 1939-46   OF, 2B, SS, Ethiopian Clowns, Kansas City Monarchs, Cincinnati Clowns, New York Black Yankees

Sneed, Eddie (Lefty), 1940-42   P, Birmingham Black Barons

Sneeden, —, 1894   OF, Cuban Giants

Snow, Felton (Skipper), 1931-47   3B, 2B, MGR, Louisville White Sox, Louisville Black Caps, Nashville Elite Giants, Columbus Elite Giants, Washington Elite Giants, Baltimore Elite Giants, Nashville Cubs, New Orleans Crescent Stars

Snowden, —, 1933   P, Detroit Stars

Snyder, —, 1943   OF, New York Cubans

Sockard, see Stockard

Soldero, —, 1932   P, Cuban Stars

Solis, L., 1928-34   2B, 3B, Cuban Stars (East)

Soss, Ramon, 1948   C, Homestead Grays

Sostre, Francisco, 1947   P, New York Cubans

Souell, Herbert [Herb Cyrus], 1940-50   INF, Kansas City Monarchs

Southall, John, 1898   C, Celeron Acme Colored Giants (Iron and Oil Lg.)

Southy, —, 1921   SS, Lincoln Giants

Sowell, Clyde, 1948   P, Baltimore Elite Giants

Sparks, Joe, 1937-40   2B, SS, St. Louis Stars, Chicago American Giants

Sparrow, Roy W., 1938   officer, Washington Black Senators

Spearman, Alvin, 1950   P, Chicago American Giants

Spearman, Charles, 1919-31   C, 2B, 3B, SS, Brooklyn Royal Giants, Cleveland Elites, Homestead Grays, Lincoln Giants, Pennsylvania Red Caps of New York

Spearman, Clyde (Splo), 1932-46   OF, Pittsburgh Crawfords, New York Black Yankees, New York Cubans, Newark Eagles, Philadelphia Stars, Chicago American Giants, Birmingham Black Barons

Spearman, Henry (Jake, Splo), 1932-46   3B, 1B, Homestead Grays, Pittsburgh Crawfords, Washington Black Senators, New York Black Yankees, Baltimore Elite Giants, Philadelphia Stars, Newark Eagles

Spearman, William, 1923-29   P, Memphis Red Sox, Cleveland Elites, Cleveland Hornets, Nashville Elite Giants, St. Louis Stars

Spedden, Charles P., 1922-31   officer, owner, Baltimore Black Sox

Spencer, —, 1921-22   OF, Pittsburgh Keystones

Spencer, J.C., see Joseph Spencer

Spencer, Joseph B., 1942-48   2B, SS, Birmingham Black Barons, Homestead Grays, Pittsburgh Crawfords, New York Cubans, Baltimore Elite Giants, New York Black Yankees

Spencer, (Pee Wee), 1933-40,1945   C, 3B, Chicago American Giants, Toledo Crawfords, Indianapolis Crawfords, Toledo Cubs (USL)

Spencer, Willie, 1941   OF, Birmingham Black Barons

Spencer, Zack, 1931-33   P, Chicago Columbia Giants, Columbus Blue Birds, Detroit Stars, Cleveland Cubs

Spike, —, 1923   P, Washington Potomacs

Spotsville, Roy (Bill), 1950   P, Houston Eagles

Stamps, Hulan (Lefty), 1924-28   P, Memphis Red Sox, Indianapolis ABCs

Stanley, John Wesley (Neck), 1928-49   P, Bacharach Giants, Lincoln Giants, Quaker Giants, Brooklyn Royal Giants, Baltimore Black Sox, New York Black Yankees, New York Cubans, Philadelphia Stars, Hilldale

Staples, John, 1921   MGR, Montgomery Grey Sox

Starks, James, 1938-46   1B,New York Black Yankees, Harrisburg- St. Louis Stars

Stark, L., 1887   player, Cincinnati Browns

Starks, Leslie, 1927,1934-35   OF, Memphis Red Sox, Kansas City Monarchs, Newark Dodgers

Starks, Otis (Lefty), 1919-1932   P, Hilldale, Chicago American Giants, Brooklyn Royal Giants, Lincoln Giants, Bacharach Giants, Newark Stars, St. Louis Giants

Starmand, —, 1887   OF, Pittsburgh Keystones

Stearnes, Norman Thomas (Turkey), 1920-42,45   OF,Nashville Giants, Montgomery Grey Sox, Detroit Stars, Lincoln Giants, Cole's American Giants, Chicago American Giants, Philadelphia Stars, Kansas City Monarchs, Detroit Black Sox, Toledo Cubs (USL)

Stedgrass, —, 1937   P, Memphis Red Sox

Steel, Harry, 1938   P, Indianapolis ABCs

Steele, Edward (Ed, Stainless), 1941-50   OF, Birmingham Black Barons

Stephens, see Frank Stevens

Stephens, Paul Eugene (Jake) [Stevens], 1921-37   SS, Hilldale, Philadelphia Giants, Homestead Grays, Pittsburgh Crawfords, Philadelphia Stars, New York Black Yankees

Stephens, Joe (Junior), 1949-50   P, New York Black Yankees

Sterman, Tom, 1909,1915   OF, Kansas City Giants

Stevens, —, 1927-29   C, Detroit Stars

Stevens, —, 1929   P, Bacharach Giants

Stevens, —, 1950   P, Houston Eagles

Stevens, Frank, 1921-27   P, OF, 1B, Chicago American Giants, Indianapolis ABCs, Cleveland Hornets, Toledo Tigers, St. Louis Stars

Stevens, (Jake), see Stephens

Stevens, Jim, 1933   2B, Philadelphia Stars

Stevens, L., see Frank Stevens

Stevenson, (Lefty), 1925-28   P, OF, Cleveland Tigers, Indianapolis ABCs, Birmingham Black Barons

Stevenson, Willie, 1940,1943   P, Homestead Grays

Stewart, —, 1920-23   P, SS, St. Louis Giants, St. Louis Stars

Stewart, Artis, 1950   P, Cleveland Buckeyes

Stewart, Frank, 1936-40   P, Washington Elite Giants, Indianapolis ABCs, Memphis Red Sox

Stewart, Leoniel, 1940-42   P, OF, Newark Eagles, Birmingham Black Barons

Stewart, Leslie, 1922   C, Philadelphia Giants

Stewart, Manuel, 1946-47   3B, Baltimore Elite Giants

Stewart, Riley A. Sr., 1947-50   P, Chicago American Giants, New York Cubans

Stewart, W., 1946   P, Memphis Red Sox

Stiles, Norris, 1950   P, Cleveland Buckeyes

Still, Bobby, 1887   player, Philadelphia Pythians

Still, Joe, 1887   player, Philadelphia Pythians

Stinson, C.P., 1887   player, Philadelphia Pythians

Stitler, —, 1922   P, Bacharach Giants

Stockard, Theodore, 1927-28–SS, 3B, Cleveland Hornets, Cleveland Tigers

Stockley, Lawrence, 1950   OF, New York Black Yankees

Stone, Ed, 1931-50   OF, Bacharach Giants, Brooklyn Eagles, Newark Eagles, Philadelphia Stars, Pittsburgh Crawfords, New York Black Yankees

Stovall, —, 1924   P, Cleveland Browns

Stovall, Fred, 1930-35   officer, Monroe Monarchs

Stovey, George Washington, 1886-96   P, OF, Jersey City (Eastern Lg.); Newark (International Lg.); Cuban Giants, New York Gorhams (Middle States Lg.), Cuban X Giants, Worcester (Northeastern Lg.), Ansonia Cuban Giants Connecticut St. Lg.), Troy (NY St. Lg.), York Cuban Giants (Eastern Interstate Lg.), Trenton Cuban Giants (Middle States Lg.)

Stratton, Felton, 1930   C, Hilldale

Stratton, Leroy, 1920-33   SS, 3B, 2B, MGR, Nashville Giants, Milwaukee Bears, Birmingham Black Barons, Chicago American Giants, Nashville Elite Giants

Streeter, Samuel (Sam, Lefty), 1920-35   P, Montgomery Grey Sox, Atlanta Black Crackers, Chicago American Giants, Bacharach Giants, Lincoln Giants, Birmingham Black Barons, Homestead Grays, Cleveland Cubs, Pittsburgh Crawfords

Streets, Albert, 1925   INF, Chicago American Giants

Strickland, —, 1924   P, Indianapolis ABCs

Strong, Fulton, 1922-23   P, Cleveland Tate Stars, Chicago American Giants New Orleans Crescent Stars, Milwaukee Bears

Strong, Henry, 1936   SS, Chicago American Giants

Strong, Joseph Talton (Joe, Baby Face, J.T.), 1922-37   P, Hilldale, St. Louis Stars, Homestead Grays, Baltimore Black Sox

Strong, Nathanial Colvin (Nat), 1908-34   booking agent; officer, Brooklyn Royal Giants, New York Black Yankees, Cuban Stars

Strong, Othello L., 1949-50   P, Chicago American Giants

Strong, T.R. (Ted), 1937-48   OF, INF, MGR, Indianapolis Athletics, Indianapolis ABCs, Kansas City Monarchs, Indianapolis Clowns

Strothers, C.W., 1924-27   officer, Harrisburg Giants

Strothers, Tim Samuel (Sam), 1908-18   C, 1B, 2B, Leland Giants, Chicago American Giants, Chicago Giants, Chicago Union Giants, West Baden (Ind.) Sprudels

Stuart, —, 1900   SS, Cuban X Giants

Stuart, Joe, 1884-85   P, C, Brooklyn Atlantics

Stubblefield, —, 1948   P, Kansas City Monarchs

Sturdeven, Mark, 1916,1928   player, treasurer, Hilldale

Suarez, —, 1916-21   P, Cuban Stars, Havana Stars, Cuban Stars of Havana, Cuban Stars (NNL), New York Cuban Stars

Sullivan, —, 1918   OF, Chicago Union Giants

Sullivan, —, 1937   P, Birmingham Black Barons

Summerall, William (Big, Red), 1936-40   P, St. Louis Stars, Memphis Red Sox

Summers, Lonnie, 1938-49   OF, C, Baltimore Elite Giants, Chicago American Giants

Summers, Smith (Tack), 1923-29   OF, Toledo Tigers, Cleveland Browns, Cleveland Elites, Cleveland Hornets, Cleveland Tigers, Chicago American Giants

Susini, Antonio, 1921   2B, SS, All Cubans

Sunkett, Pete (Golden), 1943-45   P, Philadelphia Stars

Suttles, Earl, 1950   1B, Cleveland Buckeyes

Suttles, George (Mule), 1918-48   1B, OF, Birmingham Black Barons, St. Louis Stars, Detroit Wolves, Washington Pilots, Chicago American Giants, Cole's American Giants, Newark Eagles, New York Black Yankees, Bacharach Giants Baltimore Black Sox; umpire

Sutton, Leroy, 1941-45   P, New Orleans-St. Louis Stars, Chicago American Giants, Cincinnati-Indianapolis Clowns

Swan, —, 1933   SS, Akron

Swancy, —, 1924   P, Indianapolis ABCs

Sweatt, George Alexander (Never, Sharkey), 1921-28   3B, 2B, OF, Chicago Giants,

Kansas City Monarchs, Chicago American Giants

Sykes, Franklin J.(Doc), 1915-26   P, Lincoln Stars, Hilldale, Baltimore Black Sox, Brooklyn Royal Giants

Sykes, Melvin, 1926   OF, Hilldale

Sykes, Joe (Siki), 1942   OF, Cincinnati Clowns

Taborn, Earl, 1946-50   C, Kansas City Monarchs

Talbert, Dangerfield, 1900-11   3B, Leland Giants, Chicago Giants Cuban X Giants, Chicago Unions, Algona, (IA) Brownies

Talbert, James, 1947-48   C, Chicago American Giants

Talley, —, 1934   P, New York Black Yankees

Tapley, John R., 1933   3B, Akron Tyrites

Tapley, Townsend, 1933   SS, Akron Tyrites

Tate, —, 1914   P, Lincoln Giants

Tate, George, 1918-22   officer, Cleveland Tate Stars; vice pres, NNL

Tate, Roosevelt (Speed), 1931-37   OF, Birmingham Black Barons, Nashville Elite Giants, Memphis Red Sox, Cincinnati Tigers, Knoxville, Louisville White Sox, Chicago American Giants

Tatum, Reece (Goose), 1941-49   OF, 1B, Birmingham Black Barons, Minneapolis-St. Paul Gophers, Cincinnati Clowns, Cincinnati-Indianapolis Clowns, Indianapolis Clowns

Taylor, Alfred, 1933   1B, Akron Tyrites

Taylor, Benjamin, 1947   P, New York Black Yankees

Taylor, Benjamin H. (Ben), 1910-40   1B, MGR, Chicago American Giants, Indianapolis ABCs, St. Louis Giants, Bacharach Giants, Washington Potomacs, Harrisburg Giants, Baltimore Black Sox, Baltimore Stars, Brooklyn Eagles, Washington Black Senators, New York Cubans, West Baden (Ind.) Sprudels, Washington Pilots, Hilldale, Lincoln Giants

Taylor, (Big), see John Taylor

Taylor, Charles Ishum (C.I.), 1904-22   MGR, Birmingham Giants, West Baden (Ind.) Sprudels, Indianapolis ABCs; vice pres, NNL

Taylor, Mrs. C.I., 1922-24   officer, Indianapolis ABCs

Taylor, Cyrus G., 1924-25   OF, Lincoln Giants, Harrisburg Giants

Taylor, George, 1889-06   1B, C, INF, OF, Aspen (Colo. St. Lg.), Denver (Colorado St. Lg.)Page Fence Giants, Chicago Union Giants, Leland Giants, Beatrice (Neb. St. Lg.), Lincoln (Neb) Giants

Taylor, H.C., 1887   player, Boston Resolutes

Taylor, James Allen (Candy Jim), 1904-48   3B, 2B, MGR, Birmingham Giants, St. Paul Gophers, Leland Giants, Indianapolis ABCs, St. Louis Giants, Chicago American Giants, Dayton Marcos, Cleveland Tate Stars, St. Louis Stars, Cleveland Elites, Memphis Red Sox, Detroit Stars, Nashville Elite Giants, Columbus Elite Giants, Homestead Grays, Baltimore Elite Giants, Bowser's ABCs, Toledo Tigers, Louisville Sox, Chicago Giants; vice chairman, NNL

Taylor, Jim, 1896   OF, Cuban Giants

Taylor, John (Big, Red), 1920-28   Chicago Giants, Lincoln Giants, Kansas City Monarchs, Penn Red Caps of NY

Taylor, John (Johnny, Schoolboy), 1935-45   P, New York Cubans, Cuban Stars, Pittsburgh Crawfords, Toledo Crawfords, Homestead Grays

Taylor, Johnathan Boyce (Steel Arm Johnny), 1903-21   P, St. Paul Gophers, Leland Giants, Chicago Giants, St. Louis Giants, Lincoln Giants, Indianapolis ABCs, Bowser's ABCs, West Baden (Ind.) Sprudels, Birmingham Giants, Louisville Sox, Bacharach Giants, Hilldale

Taylor, Johnny, 1943-45   OF, Birmingham Black Barons

Taylor, Joe C., 1949-50   C, Chicago American Giants

Taylor, Leroy R., 1925-36   OF, Chicago American Giants, Indianapolis ABCs, Kansas City Monarchs, Detroit Wolves, Homestead Grays, Cleveland Red Sox, Detroit Stars

Taylor, O., 1935   P, Columbus Elite Giants

Taylor, Olan (Jelly), 1934-46   1B, C, MGR, Cincinnati Tigers, Memphis Red Sox, Birmingham Black Barons

Taylor, Raymond, 1931-46   C, Memphis Red Sox, Cincinnati Buckeyes Columbus Buckeyes, Kansas City Monarchs, Cleveland Clippers (USL), New York Black Yankees, New Orleans-St. Louis Stars, Cleveland Buckeyes

Taylor, (Rip), 1931   player, Hilldale

Taylor, Robert (Lightning), 1938-42   C, Indianapolis ABCs, St. Louis Stars, New York Black Yankees

Taylor, S., 1912-31   P, MGR, St. Louis Giants, Little Rock Black Travelers

Taylor, (Shine), 1939   OF, Toledo Crawfords

Taylor, Zachary, 1937   P, Memphis Red Sox

Teasley, Ron, 1945   OF, 1B, Toledo Cubs (USL)

Tenney, William, 1910   C, Kansas City, (KS) Giants

Teran, Recurvon (Julio), 1916-24   2B, 3B, Cuban Stars (East), Cuban Stars of Havana, Cuban Stars (NNL), New York Cuban Stars

Terrell, Lawrence, 1924-25   P, Detroit Stars

Terrell, S.M., 1928   officer, Cleveland Stars

Terrill, Windsor. W., 1887-96   SS,UTIL, Boston Resolutes, Cuban X Giants, York Cuban Giants (Eastern Interstate Lg.), Ansonia Cuban Giants (Connecticut St. Lg.)

Terry, John, 1931-36   2B, 3B, Indianapolis ABCs, Homestead Grays, Cincinnati Tigers

Tevera, —, 1924   2B, Cuban Stars (NNL)

Thomas, —, 1904,1911   1B, P, Philadelphia Giants

Thomas, —, 1919-20   1B, Pennsylvania Red Caps of NY

Thomas, A., 1909-11   P, OF, Brooklyn Royal Giants

Thomas, Alfred (Buck), 1944-49   P, Chicago American Giants

Thomas, Arthur, 1886-91   C, 1B, OF, Cuban Giants, New York Gorhams, Trenton Cuban Giants (Middle States Lg.), York Cuban Giants (Eastern Interstate Lg.)

Thomas, (Boy), see Herb Thomas

Thomas, Charley, 1918-22   C, Baltimore Black Sox

Thomas, Clinton Cyrus (Clint, Hawk), 1920-38   OF, 2B, Brooklyn Royal Giants, Columbus Buckeyes, Detroit Stars, Hilldale, Bacharach Giants, Lincoln Giants, Darby Daisies, New York Black Yankees, Newark Eagles, Philadelphia Stars

Thomas, Dan, 1921-28   2B, Indianapolis ABCs, St. Louis Stars, Kansas City Monarchs, Cleveland Hornets, Memphis Red Sox

Thomas, Dan, 1936-40   OF, P, Jacksonville Red Caps, Chicago American Giants, Birmingham Black Barons, Cincinnati Tigers

Thomas, David (Showboat), 1923-46   1B, OF, MGR, Montgomery Grey Sox, Birmingham Black Barons, Baltimore Black Sox, New York Black Yankees, New York Cubans, Washington Black Senators, Brooklyn Royal Giants

Thomas, Hazel, 1935   P, Chicago American Giants

Thomas, Henry, 1931   OF, New York Black Yankees

Thomas, Herb (Boy, Lefty), 1929-30   P, Lincoln Giants, Hilldale

Thomas, J., 1887   player, Louisville Falls City

Thomas, J., 1932,1937   SS, Indianapolis ABCs, Detroit Stars

Thomas, J., 1946-47   OF, Birmingham Black Barons

Thomas, Jack (Jules), 1911-31   OF, Brooklyn Royal Giants, Lincoln Giants, Pennsylvania Red Caps of New York

Thomas, Jerome, 1887   player, Washington Capital City

Thomas, John, 1950   P, Cleveland Buckeyes

Thomas, L., 1928-30   C, OF, 1B, Birmingham Black Barons, Nashville Elite Giants

Thomas, Lacey, 1934-39–P, OF, Jacksonville Red Caps, Cleveland Bears

Thomas, M., 1919   P, Lincoln Giants

Thomas, Nelson, 1947   P, Newark Eagles

Thomas, Orel (Little Dean), 1937   P, Detroit Stars

Thomas, Walter Lewis, 1937-47   P, OF, Detroit Stars, Kansas City Monarchs, Memphis Red Sox, Birmingham Black Barons

Thomas, William, 1943   OF, Chicago Brown Bombers

Thomason, Charles (Charlie), 1941-44   OF, Newark Eagles

Tompkins, —, 1920   OF, Dayton Marcos

Thompson, —, 1906 P, Cuban Giants

Thompson, —, 1916-20 P, 1B, Lincoln Stars, Pittsburgh Stars of Buffalo, Detroit Stars, Lincoln Giants, Penn Red Caps of NY

Thompson —, 1917 1B, Cuban Giants, Pittsburgh Stars of Buffalo

Thompson, —, 1933 P, Cuban Giants

Thompson, (Buddy), 1942 C, Chicago Brown Bombers

Thompson, (Copperknee), 1942 INF, Cincinnati Clowns, Minneapolis-St. Paul Gophers

Thompson, Frank, 1885 organizer, Argyle Hotel, Cuban Giants

Thompson, Frank (Groundhog), 1945-50 P, Birmingham Black Barons, Homestead Grays, Memphis Red Sox

Thompson, Harold, 1949 P, Kansas City Monarchs

Thompson, Henry Curtis, 1943-48 OF, 2B, SS, Kansas City Monarchs

Thompson, James (Sandy), 1920-32 OF, C, 1B, Dayton Marcos, Milwaukee Bears, Birmingham Black Barons, Chicago American Giants, Chicago Columbia Giants, Cole's American Giants

Thompson, Jimmy, 1945 umpire, NAL

Thompson, Lloyd P., 1910-16,1922-30 OF, SS, Officer, Hilldale

Thompson, Marshall, 1887 manager, Boston Resolutes

Thompson, Samuel Tommy (Sad Sam, Long Tom), 1931-42 P, Kansas City Monarchs, Indianapolis ABCs, Detroit Stars, Columbus Elite Giants, Philadelphia Stars, Chicago American Giants, Monroe Monarchs, Nashville Elite Giants

Thompson, Sammy (Runt), 1937-38 2B,Memphis Red Sox, Little Rock Black Travelers, Cleveland Bears, Atlanta Black Crackers

Thompson, Wade, 1923-26 P, Harrisburg Giants, Richmond Giants

Thompson, Will, 1949-50 P, Philadelphia Stars

Thompson, William, 1887-1900 C, Louisville Falls City, Genuine Cuban Giants

Thornton, Charles, 1887 player, Pittsburgh Keystones

Thornton, H., 1931 OF, Memphis Red Sox

Thornton, Jack, 1932-37 P, 2B, 1B, Atlanta Black Crackers

Thornton, Jesse, 1937 officer, Indianapolis Athletics

Thorpe, Clarence Jim, 1928 P, Hilldale

Thurman, —, 1937 1B, St. Louis Stars

Thurman, Jim, 1932-33-P, OF, Louisville Black Caps, Columbus Blue Birds

Thurman, Robert Burns, 1946-49 P, Homestead Grays, Kansas City Monarchs

Thurston, —, 1938 P, Birmingham Black Barons

Thurston, Bobby, 1911 OF, Chicago Giants

Tiant, Luis Sr. (Lefty), 1930-47 P, Cuban Stars (NNL), New York Cubans, Cuban House of David

Tindle, Levy, 1933 officer, Detroit Stars

Tinker, Harold (Hooks), 1931 OF, Pittsburgh Crawfords

Titus, James, 1937 officer, Detroit Stars

Tolbert, —, 1946 P, New York Black Yankees

Toles, Ted (Lefty), 1946 P, Pittsburgh Crawfords

Tomm, —, 1917-18 OF, Brooklyn Royal Giants, Philadelphia Giants, Bacharach Giants

Toney, Albert, 1901-16 SS, 2B, OF, Chicago Union Giants, Leland Giants, Chicago American Giants, Chicago Giants, Algona (IA) Brownies

Torres, —, 1916 C, Long Branch Cubans

Torres, Armando, 1939 P, Cuban Stars

Torriente, Christobel; see below

Torriente, Cristobal (Carlos) [Torrienti], 1914-32 OF, P, Cuban Stars, Chicago American Giants, Kansas City Monarchs, Detroit Stars, Gilkerson's Union Giants, Atlanta Black Crackers, Cleveland Cubs

Torrin, —, 1920 P, St. Louis Giants

Town, see Tomm

Trabue, —, 1924 P, Indianapolis ABCs

Trammel, Nat, 1930-32 1B, Birmingham Black Barons, Brooklyn Royal Giants

Trawick, Joe, 1950 2B, Cleveland Buckeyes

Treadwell, Harold, 1919-28 P, Brooklyn Royal Giants, Bacharach Giants, Harrisburg Giants, Chicago American Giants, Indianapolis ABCs, Dayton Marcos, Detroit Stars, Cleveland Browns, Lincoln Giants

Treadway, —, 1939-40 P, Kansas City Monarchs, Toledo Crawfords

Trealkill, Clarence, Harvey [Trilkill], 1929-31 SS, OF, Nashville Elite Giants

Trent, Theodore (Ted), 1927-39 P, St. Louis Stars, Detroit Wolves, Homestead Grays, Cole's American Giants, Chicago American Giants, Washington Pilots, New York Black Yankees

Trice, Robert (Bill), 1948-50 P, OF, Homestead Grays

Trimble, William E., 1927-32 officer, Chicago American Giants

Triplett, —, 1917-18 OF, Hilldale

Trouppe, Quincy Thomas (Big Train), 1930-49 C, OF, P, MGR, St. Louis Stars, Detroit Wolves, Homestead Grays, Kansas City Monarchs, Chicago American Giants, Indianapolis ABCs, Cleveland Buckeyes, New York Cubans

Troy, Donald, 1944-45 P, Baltimore Elite Giants

Trusty, Job, 1896 3B, Cuban Giants

Trusty, Shepard (Shep), 1885-89 P, OF, Philadelphia Orions, Argyle Hotel, Cuban Giants, Trenton Cuban Giants (Middle States Lg.)

Tucker, Henry, 1916-22 OF, officer, Bacharach Giants

Tucker, Orval, 1930,1942 2B, Baltimore Black Sox, Hilldale, Boston Royal Giants

Tugerson, Leander, 1950 P, Indianapolis Clowns

Turner, —, 1908 2B, New York Colored Giants

Turner, —, 1930 1B, Kansas City Monarchs

Turner, B., 1916-17 1B, Chicago Union Giants, Chicago Giants, All Nations

Turner, Bob, 1946,1950 C, Kansas City Monarchs, Houston Eagles

Turner, E.C. (Pop), 1925-37 3B, SS, Brooklyn Royal Giants, Homestead Grays, Birmingham Black Barons, Cleveland Cubs, Cole's American Giants New York Black Yankees; umpire, NNL

Turner, Etwood, 1923 OF, Toledo Tigers

Turner, Henry (Flash), 1938-43 C, 2B, 1B, OF, Jacksonville Red Caps, Cleveland Bears, Harrisburg-St. Louis Stars

Turner, J.O., 1887 player, Philadelphia Pythians

Turner, (Little Lefty), 1940-42 1B, Indianapolis Crawfords, Baltimore Elite Giants

Turner, Oliver, 1943 P, Chicago Brown Bombers

Turner, Thomas, 1947 1B, Chicago American Giants

Turner, (Tuck), 1919,1923,1928 P, Chicago American Giants, St. Louis Stars

Turnstall, Willie, 1950 P, Cleveland Buckeyes

Tut, Richard (King), 1943-50 1B, Cincinnati Clowns, Indianapolis Clowns

Tye, Dan, 1930-36 3B, SS, P, Memphis Red Sox, Cincinnati Tigers

Tyler, Charles H., 1934-35 officer, Newark Dodgers

Tyler, Edward, 1926-28 P, Brooklyn Cuban Giants, Hilldale, St.Louis Stars

Tyler, Eugene, 1942-43 C, INF, Chicago Brown Bombers, Kansas City Monarchs

Tyler, Roy, 1925-27 P, OF, Chicago American Giants, Cleveland Hornets

Tyler, William (Steel Arm), 1925-32 P, Memphis Red Sox, Detroit Stars, Kansas City Monarchs, Cole's American Giants

Tyms, —, 1923 OF, Chicago American Giants

Tyree, Ruby, 1916-24 P, All Nations, Chicago American Giants, Chicago Brown Bombers, Cleveland Browns

Tyson, Armand Cupree (Cap), 1936-40 C, Birmingham Black Barons

Tyus, Julius Jr, 1947 P, Philadelphia Stars

Underhill, Bob, 1924 P, Hilldale

Underwood, Ely, 1937 OF, Detroit Stars

Underwood, Ray, 1937 P, Detroit Stars

Vactor, John, 1887-88 player, Philadelphia Pythians, New York Gorhams

Valdes, Fermin, 1944 2B, Cincinnati-Indianapolis Clowns

Valdes, Rogelio, 1911 OF, All Cubans

Valdez, Strico (Swat), 1931-39 2B, SS, Cuban Stars, Atlanta Black Crackers, New York Cubans

Valdez, Tony, 1910-20 OF, P, Stars of Cuba, Cuban Stars (NNL)

Valentine, —, 1915-18 OF, Hilldale, Philadelphia Giants

Valos, —, 1917 3B, Cuban Giants

Van Buren, —, 1931 OF, Memphis Red Sox

Vance, Columbus, 1927-34 P, Birmingham Black Barons, Homestead Grays, Detroit Wolves, Detroit Stars, Indianapolis ABCs

Vandever, Bobby, 1944 INF, Kansas City Monarchs

Van Dyke, Fred, 1895-97 P, OF, Page Fence Giants

Vargas, —, 1927-31 SS, Cuban Stars (ECL), Cuban Stars (West)

Vargas, Juan Esteban (Tetelo) [Jose], 1927-44 OF, SS, Cuban Stars (ECL) Cuban Stars (NNL), Cuban Stars, New York Cubans

Vargas, Guillermo, 1949 OF, New York Cubans

Vargas, Roberto Enrique, 1948 P, Chicago American Giants

Varona, Gilberto, 1950 1B, Memphis Red Sox

Varona, Orlando Clemente [Verona], 1948-50 SS, Memphis Red Sox

Vasquez, Armando, 1944-48 UTIL, Cincinnati-Indianapolis Clowns, Indianapolis Clowns, New York Cubans

Vaughn, Harold, 1926-27 OF, Kansas City Monarchs

Vaughn, Joe, 1931 sec'y, NSL

Vaughn, Ray (Slim), 1934 P, Newark Dodgers, Newark Browns

Veal, —, 1931 P, OF, Birmingham Black Barons

Velasquez, Jose Luis, 1948 P, Indianapolis Clowns

Velasquez, Laru, 1948-50 P, Indianapolis Clowns

Veney, Jerome, 1908-17 OF, MGR, Homestead Grays

Ventura, —, 1929 P, Cuban Stars (NNL)

Vernal, (Sleepy), 1941 P, New York Cuban Stars

Verona, Orlando, see Orlando Varona

Victory, George M., 1919-20 officer, Pennsylvania Giants

Vierira, Chris, 1949 OF, New York Black Yankees

Villa, Roberto (Bobby), 1910-22 OF, 2B, Stars of Cuba, Cuban Stars, All Cubans, Cuban Stars (NNL)

Villafane, Vicente, 1947 UTIL, Indianapolis Clowns

Villodas, Luis, 1946-47 C, Baltimore Elite Giants

Vincent, Irving B. (Lefty), 1934-35 P, Pittsburgh Crawfords

Vines, Eddie, 1940 P, 3B, Chicago American Giants, Birmingham Black Barons

Vivens, —, 1929 P, St. Louis Stars

Waddy, Irving (Lefty), 1932-33 P, Indianapolis ABCs, Detroit Stars

Wade, Lee, 1909-19 P, OF, 1B, Cuban Giants, Philadelphia Giants, St. Louis Giants, Lincoln Giants, Chicago American Giants, Lincoln Stars, Brooklyn Royal Giants, Pennsylvania Red Caps of New York

Wagner, Bill, 1921-27 SS, 2B, MGR, Lincoln Giants, Brooklyn Royal Giants

Wagner, J., 1927 2B, 1B, Bacharach Giants, Hilldale

Waite, Arnold, 1936-37 P, Homestead Grays, Washington Elite Giants

Wakefield, Bert, 1895-1902,1915 1B, 2B, Chicago Unions, Kansas City Giants, Salina and Emporia (Kansas St. Lg.), Algona (IA) Brownies

Waldon, (Allie, Ollie), 1944 OF, Chicago American Giants

Walker, —, 1904 C, Brooklyn Royal Giants

Walker, A., 1923,1927 P, Milwaukee Bears, Kansas City Monarchs

Walker, A.M., 1937 MGR, Birmingham Black Barons

Walker, Casey, 1935-37-C, Newark Dodgers, Indianapolis Athletics

Walker, Charlie, 1930-34 officer, Homestead Grays

Walker, Edsall (Big), 1933-47 P, Albany (NY)

Black Sox, Mohawk Giants, Homestead Grays, Philadelphia Stars

Walker, George T. (Little, Schoolboy), 1937-50 P, Homestead Grays, Kansas City Monarchs

Walker, H., 1932 C, Monroe Monarchs

Walker, Jack, 1940-43 P, Newark Eagles, Philadelphia Stars, Harrisburg-St. Louis Stars

Walker, Jesse (Hoss, Deuce, Aussa), 1929-50 SS, 3B, MGR, Officer Bacharach Giants, Cleveland Cubs, Nashville Elite Giants, Washington Elite Giants, Baltimore Elite Giants, New York Black Yankees, Birmingham Black Barons, Cincinnati Clowns, Cincinnati-Indianapolis Clowns, Nashville Cubs, Indianapolis Clowns, Columbus Elite Giants

Walker, Larry, *see Larry Doby*

Walker, Moses Fleetwood (Fleet), 1883-89 C, OF, 1B, Toledo (Northwestern Lg. and American Association); Cleveland (Western Lg.); Waterbury southern New England and Eastern Lg.s); Newark and Syracuse (International Lg.)

Walker, Moses L., 1928-31 officer, Detroit Stars

Walker, Pete (Lottie), 1923-26 P, OF, 2B, 3B, Homestead Grays

Walker, R.A., 1887 player, Boston Resolutes

Walker, Robert Taylor (R.T.), 1945-49 P, Homestead Grays

Walker, Tom (Tony), 1945 P, Baltimore Elite Giants

Walker, W., 1931-32 OF, Monroe Monarchs

Walker, Weldy Wilberforce, 1884-87 OF, C, 2B, Toledo (American Association); Akron (Ohio State Lg.); Pittsburgh Keystones, Cleveland (Western Lg.)

Wallace, —, 1940 2B, Cincinnati Buckeyes

Wallace, Felix (Dick), 1906-21 SS, 2B, 3B, MGR, St. Paul Gophers, Leland Giants, St. Louis Giants, Bacharach Giants, Lincoln Giants, Cuban Giants, Hilldale

Wallace, Jack, 1926-31 3B, 2B, Bacharach Giants, Cleveland Cubs, Philadelphia Giants

Wallace, James, 1949 C, Houston Eagles

Waller, —, 1906 SS, Cuban Giants

Waller, George, 1943 INF, Chicago Brown Bombers

Walls, Eddie [Wall], 1925-26 P, St. Louis Stars, Cleveland Hornets, Cleveland Elites

Walls, (Greenie), 1941-42 umpire

Walsh, —, 1916 2B, Bacharach Giants

Walters, —, 1923-24 P, Milwaukee Bears, Cleveland Browns

Walton, —, 1948 UTIL, Indianapolis Clowns

Walton, (Fuzzy), 1938 OF, Pittsburgh Crawfords

Ward, Britt, 1944 C, Kansas City Monarchs

Ward, C. (Pinky), 1924-35 OF, Memphis Red Sox, Chicago Columbia Giants, Louisville Black Caps, Cincinnati Tigers, Birmingham Black Barons, Brooklyn Eagles, Indianapolis ABCs Bacharach Giants

Ward, Ira, 1922-27 SS, 1B, Chicago Giants

Ware, Joe (Showboat), 1921,1932-36 OF, Nashville Elite Giants Cleveland Stars, Cleveland Giants, Memphis Red Sox, Akron Tyrites, Pittsburgh Crawfords, Newark Dodgers

Ware, Archie V., 1940-50 1B, Chicago American Giants, Kansas City Monarchs, Cleveland Buckeyes, Louisville Buckeyes, Indianapolis Clowns, Cincinnati Buckeyes

Ware, William, 1924-26 1B, Chicago American Giants

Warfield, Francis Xavier (Frank), 1915-32 2B, SS, 3B, MGR, St. Louis Giants, Indianapolis ABCs, Kansas City Monarchs, Detroit Stars, Hilldale, Baltimore Black Sox, Washington Pilots, Bowser's ABCs

Warmack, —, 1910 1B, St. Louis Giants

Warmack, Sam, 1922-38 OF, Richmond Giants, Hilldale, Bacharach Giants, Louisville Black Colonels

Warren, Cicero, 1946-47 P, Homestead Grays

Warren, Jesse, 1940-47 2B, 3B, P, Memphis Red Sox, New Orleans- St. Louis Stars, Birmingham Black Barons, Chicago American Giants

Warrick, —, 1905 P, Brooklyn Royal Giants

Washington, —, 1929 C, Nashville Elite Giants

Washington, Edgar (Ed, Blue), 1915-20 P, 1B, Chicago American Giants, Kansas City Monarchs

Washington, I. (Jap), 1922-37 3B, 1B, OF, Pittsburgh Keystones, Homestead Grays, Pittsburgh Crawfords, Newark Browns; umpire, NNL

Washington, Isaac, 1928 officer, Bacharach Giants

Washington, John G. (Johnny), 1933-50 1B, 3B, Montgomery Grey Sox, Birmingham Black Barons, Pittsburgh Crawfords, New York Black Yankees, Baltimore Elite Giants, Houston Eagles

Washington, L., 1884-85 SS, Baltimore Atlantics

Washington, Lafayette (Fay), 1940-45 P, Chicago American Giants, Birmingham Black Barons, Cincinnati-Indianapolis Clowns, Kansas City Monarchs, St. Louis Stars, New Orleans-St. Louis Stars

Washington, Lawrence, 1945 1B, New York Black Yankees

Washington, Namon, 1920-31 OF, SS, C, Indianapolis ABCs, Hilldale, Brooklyn Cuban Giants, Philadelphia Tigers, Lincoln Giants, Brooklyn Royal Giants

Washington, Peter (Pete), 1923-35 OF, Washington Potomacs, Wilmington Potomacs, Baltimore Black Sox, Philadelphia Stars, Lincoln Giants

Washington, Tom, 1904-10 C, OF, Philadelphia Giants, Chicago Giants, Pittsburgh Giants

Waters, —, 1887 player, Boston Resolutes

Waters, Dick, 1916 MGR, St. Louis Giants

Waters, Theodore (Ted), 1920-1928-P, OF, Chicago Giants, Hilldale, Philadelphia Tigers

Watkins, F. (Pop), 1899-1922 1B, C, MGR, Genuine Cuban Giants, Cuban Giants, Havana Red Sox, Pop Watkins Stars

Watkins, G.C., 1937 officer, Indianapolis Athletics

Watkins, Murray (Skeeter), 1943-50 3B, Newark Eagles, Philadelphia Stars

Watkins, Richard, 1950 INF, Memphis Red Sox

Watson, Amos, 1945-50 P, Cincinnati-Indianapolis Clowns, Baltimore Elite Giants, New York Cubans, Indianapolis Clowns, Kansas City Monarchs

Watson, David, 1923 P, Birmingham Black Barons

Watson, Everett, 1931 officer, Detroit Stars

Watson, George Johnny, 1922-26 OF, Detroit Stars

Watson, Jimmy, 1950 P, New York Cubans

Watson, William, 1925-26,1931 OF, Brooklyn Royal Giants, Bacharach Giants, Penn Red Caps of NY

Watters, —, 1916 INF, Chicago Giants

Watts, Andrew (Sonny, Big Six), 1946-50 INF, Cleveland Buckeyes, Birmingham Black Barons

Watts, Eddie, 1924-27 2B, 1B, St. Louis Stars, Cleveland Hornets, Cleveland Elites

Watts, Herman (Lefty), 1941-42 P, Jacksonville Red Caps, Cincinnati Buckeyes, Cleveland Buckeyes, New York Black Yankees

Watts, Jack, 1913-19 C, Louisville Cubs, Chicago American Giants, Indianapolis ABCs, Dayton Marcos, Bowser's ABCs

Watts, Richard (Dick), 1949-50 P, Birmingham Black Barons

Webb, —, 1917-19 P, Lincoln Giants

Webb, James (Baby), 1910 C, Leland Giants

Webb, Normal (Tweed), 1926,1931 INF, Ft. Wayne Pirates, St.Louis Pullmans

Webster, Charles, 1950 OF, Birmingham Black Barons

Webster, Daniel Jim (Double Duty), 1933-37 C, P, Detroit Stars, Kansas City Monarchs

Webster, William (West, Specks), 1912-26 C, 1B, OF, St. Louis Giants, Chicago Giants, Brooklyn Royal Giants, Mohawk Giants, Lincoln Giants, Hilldale, Detroit Stars, Dayton Marcos, Brooklyn Cuban Giants, Jewell's ABCs, Bacharach Giants

Weeks, E., 1918-24 2B, 3B, Pennsylvania Giants, Harrisburg Giants, Pittsburgh Stars of Buffalo, Brooklyn Royal Giants, Hilldale

Weeks, William, 1922 officer, Bacharach Giants

Weems, —, 1936 OF, Memphis Red Sox

Welch, Wingfield Scott (Moe), 1918-49 MGR, player, New Orleans Black Pelicans, Monroe

Monarchs, Shreveport Giants, Cincinnati Buckeyes, Birmingham Black Barons, Cincinnati Crescents, New York Cubans, Chicago American Giants

Wells, —, 1918 2B, C, Lincoln Giants, Pennsylvania Giants

Wells, I., 1948 P, Memphis Red Sox

Wells, Willie Brooks, 1944-50 SS, Memphis Red Sox

Wells, Willie James (The Devil, Chico), 1924-49 SS, 3B, MGR, St. Louis Stars, Detroit Wolves, Kansas City Monarchs, Chicago American Giants, Cole's American Giants, Newark Eagles, Memphis Red Sox, New York Black Yankees, Baltimore Elite Giants, Indianapolis Clowns, Homestead Grays

Welmaker, Roy Horace (Snook), 1932-45 P, Atlanta Black Crackers, Homestead Grays, Philadelphia Stars

Wesley, Charles (Connie), 1921-30 OF, 2B, manager, Columbus Buckeyes, Pittsburgh Keystones, Indianapolis ABCs, Memphis Red Sox, Birmingham Black Barons, St. Louis Stars, Louisville White Sox, Louisville Red Caps

Wesley, Edgar, 1918-31 1B, Detroit Stars, Cleveland Hornets, Bacharach Giants, Chicago American Giants, Harrisburg Giants

Wesson, Les, 1949 P, New York Black Yankees

West, C., *see James West*

West, Charlie, 1942 OF, Birmingham Black Barons

West, James (Jim), 1930-47 1B, Birmingham Black Barons, Cleveland Cubs, Memphis Red Sox, Nashville Elite Giants, Columbus Elite Giants, Washington Elite Giants, Baltimore Elite Giants, Philadelphia Stars, New York Black Yankees

West, Ollie Ernest, 1942-46 P, Chicago American Giants, Pittsburgh Crawfords, Birmingham Black Barons, Homestead Grays

Weston, —, 1930 P, Hilldale

Weston, Issac (Deacon), 1949 P, Louisville Buckeyes

Weyman, J.B., 1887 player, Baltimore Lord Baltimores

Wharton, —, 1923 OF, Kansas City Monarchs

Whatley, David (Speed), 1936-46 OF, Birmingham Black Barons, Homestead Grays, Pittsburgh Crawfords, Cleveland Bears, Jacksonville Red Caps

Wheeler, Joe (Jodie), 1922-28 P, Bacharach Giants, Baltimore Black Sox, Brooklyn Cuban Giants, Wilmington Potomacs

Wheeler, Sam, 1948 OF, New York Cubans

White, —, 1913 P, Mohawk Giants

White, Artemis (Art), 1948 P, Indianapolis Clowns

White, Arthur, 1934 P, Newark Dodgers

White, Burlin, 1915-42 C, MGR, West Baden (Ind.) Sprudels, Bacharach Giants, Lincoln Giants, Philadelphia Royal Stars, Harrisburg Giants, Philadelphia Giants, Quaker Giants, Cuban Stars, Boston Royal Giants, Bowser's ABCs, Hilldale, Madison Stars

White, Butler, 1920-23 1B, Chicago Giants

White, Chaney, 1920-36 OF, Hilldale, Bacharach Giants, Wilmington Potomacs, Quaker Giants, Homestead Grays, Darby Daisies, Philadelphia Stars, Baltimore Black Sox, New York Cubans

White, Charles, 1950 3B, Philadelphia Stars

White, Clarence (Red), 1928-32 P, Nashville Elite Giants, Memphis Red Sox, Louisville White Sox, Monroe Monarchs

White, Edward, 1944 P, Homestead Grays

White, Eugene, 1935-36 3B, Brooklyn Eagles, Newark Eagles

White, Henry (Lefty), 1940 P, Cleveland Bears

White, (Ladd), 1947-48 P, Memphis Red Sox

White, Lawrence (Eugene), 1950 INF, Chicago American Giants

White, M., 1886-87 P, New York Gorhams

White, R.W., 1887 player, Washington Capital Citys, Cuban Giants

White, (Red), *see Clarence White*

White, Robert, 1922-23 2B, 3B, Pittsburgh Keystones, Toledo Tigers, St. Louis Stars

White, Sol, 1887-1926 2B, 3B, OF, 1B, MGR, coach, bus. mgr, Pittsburgh Keystones, Washington Capital Citys, Wheeling (Ohio State Lg.); New York Gorhams (Middle States

Lg.), York Monarchs (Eastern Interstate Lg.); York Cuban Giants (Eastern Interstate Lg.), Genuine Cuban Giants, Fort Wayne (Western Interstate Lg.); Page Fence Giants, Cuban X Giants, Columbia Giants, Philadelphia Giants, Lincoln Giants, Quaker Giants, Cleveland Browns, Newark Stars, Philadelphia Gorhams, Ansonia Cuban Giants (Connecticut St. Lg.)

White, Zarlie, 1934   OF, Monroe Monarchs

Whitfield, (Lefty), 1950   P, Baltimore Elite Giants

Whitlock, —, 1926   1B, Dayton Marcos

Whitney, —, 1942   P, OF, New York Black Yankees

Whitworth, Richard, 1915-24   P, Chicago American Giants, Chicago Giants, Hilldale

Whyte, William T. (Billy), 1883-1894   P, OF, Cuban Giants, York Cuban Giants (Eastern Interstate Lg.), Trenton Cuban Giants (Middle States Lg.), St.Louis Black Stockings, Boston Resolutes

Wickware, Frank (Smiley, Smokey), 1910-25   P, Leland Giants, St. Louis Giants, Philadelphia Giants, Mohawk Giants, Lincoln Stars, Chicago American Giants, Chicago Giants, Brooklyn Royal Giants, Detroit Stars, Norfolk Stars, Lincoln Giants, Jewell ABCs, Indianapolis ABCs

Wiggins, —, 1920   SS, Chicago American Giants

Wiggins, Bob, 1942   SS, Chicago Brown Bombers

Wiggins, Joe, 1930-34   3B, Nashville Elite Giants, Bacharach Giants, Baltimore Black Sox

Wigware, —, 1930   SS, 3B, Nashville Elite Giants

Wilbert, Art (Mofike), 1942   OF, Cincinnati Clowns, Minneapolis- St. Paul Gophers

Wilds, —, 1892   C, Stockton (California Lg.)

Wiley, F., 1920-27   2B, P, OF, Lincoln Giants, Pennsylvania Red Caps of New York

Wiley, Joe, 1947-50   3B, 2B, Baltimore Elite Giants, Memphis Red Sox

Wiley, Wabishaw Spencer (Doc), 1910-23   C, 1B, OF, Brooklyn Royal Giants, Lincoln Giants, Philadelphia Giants, West Baden (Ind.) Sprudels, Mohawk Giants

Wilkes, Barron D., 1919   officer, New York Bacharach Giants

Wilkes, James E. (Jimmy), 1945-50   OF, Newark Eagles, Houston Eagles

Wilkins, Wesley, 1910-15   OF, Kansas City, Kansas, Giants

Wilkinson, James Leslie (J.L.), 1909-48   officer, All Nations, Kansas City Monarchs; sec'y, NNL; tres, NAL

Willas, S., 1887   player, New York Gorhams

Willburn, —, 1926   P, Baltimore Black Sox

Willett, Pete, 1923-28   SS, OF, Lincoln Giants, Cleveland Browns, Cleveland Tigers, Homestead Grays

Williams, —, 1939   C, Indianapolis ABCs

Williams, A., 1916-18   P, OF, 2B, Brooklyn Royal Giants

Williams, A.D., 1925   officer, Indianapolis ABCs

Williams, A.N., 1922   officer, Pittsburgh Keystones

Williams, Albert, 1943-45   P, Newark Eagles

Williams, Andrew (Stringbean), 1915-25   P, MGR, St. Louis Giants, Pennsylvania Red Caps of New York, Indianapolis ABCs, Chicago American Giants, Dayton Marcos, Bacharach Giants, Brooklyn Royal Giants, Washington Potomacs

Williams, B., 1931-32,1939   OF, Montgomery Grey Sox, Indianapolis ABCs

Williams, Bert, 1923   officer, Philadelphia Giants

Williams, Bilbo (Biggie), 1942-43   OF, Chicago Brown Bombers, Baltimore Elite Giants

Williams, Bill, 1894-1900   P, Genuine Cuban Giants, Cuban X Giants

Williams, C., 1885   MGR, Brooklyn Remsens

Williams, Charles, 1887   player, Boston Resolutes

Williams, Charles Arthur, 1924-31   SS, 2B, Memphis Red Sox, Chicago American Giants, Indianapolis ABCs, Chicago Columbia Giants

Williams, Charles Henry (Lefty), 1915-34   P, Homestead Grays

Williams, Charley, 1945   P, Toledo Cubs (USL)

Williams, Chester, Arthur, 1930-43   SS, 2B,

Memphis Red Sox, Pittsburgh Crawfords, Homestead Grays, Philadelphia Stars, Chicago American Giants, Toledo Crawfords

Williams, Clarence, 1886-1912   C, SS, 3B, OF,MGR, Cuban Giants, New York Gorhams, Cuban X Giants, Philadelphia Giants, Lansing, Michigan Colored Capital All-Americans, Smart Set, Ansonia Cuban Giants (Connecticut St. Lg.), Trenton Cuban Giants, (Middle States Lg.) Harrisburg (Eastern Interstate Lg.)

Williams, Clarence, 1938-40   P, OF, Baltimore Elite Giants, Washington Black Senators

Williams, Clyde (Lefty), 1947-50   P, Cleveland Buckeyes

Williams, (Cotton), see Robert Williams

Williams, Craig (Stringbean), 1928   P, Brooklyn Cuban Giants

Williams, (Curly), see Willie Williams

Williams, E.J., 1887   player, Washington Capital Citys

Williams, Elbert, 1931-34   P, Louisville White Sox, Monroe Monarchs

Williams, Eli (Eddie), 1943-45   OF, Harrisburg-St. Louis Stars, Kansas City Monarchs

Williams, F., 1927   OF, Birmingham Black Barons

Williams, Felix (Jeff), 1950   2B, Houston Eagles, Kansas City Monarchs

Williams, Frank (Shorty), 1942-46   OF, Homestead Grays

Williams, Fred, 1922-25   C, Washington Potomacs, Harrisburg Giants, Brooklyn Royal Giants, Indianapolis ABCs

Williams, G., 1939   UTIL, Baltimore Elite Giants

Williams, George, 1885-1902   2B, 1B, 3B Philadelphia Orions, Argyle Hotel, Cuban Giants, New York Gorhams, Cuban X Giants, York Cuban Giants (Eastern Interstate Lg.), Trenton Cuban Giants (Middle States Lg.)

Williams, George, 1928   SS, 3B, Cleveland Tigers

Williams, Gerard, 1921-25   SS, Indianapolis ABCs, Homestead Grays, Lincoln Giants

Williams, Graham H., 1929-34   P, Homestead Grays, Monroe Monarchs, New Orleans Crescent Stars

Williams, Hank, 1911-13   3B, 2B, 1B, Mohawk Giants, Brooklyn Royal Giants

Williams, Harry, 1918-22   3B, Baltimore Black Sox

Williams, Harry, 1931-50   3B, 2B, SS, MGR, Pittsburgh Crawfords, Toledo Crawfords, Baltimore Black Sox, Homestead Grays, Brooklyn Eagles, Newark Eagles, New York Black Yankees, Harrisburg-St. Louis Stars, Baltimore Elite Giants, New York Cubans, New Orleans Creoles

Williams, Henry (Flick), 1922-31   C, Kansas City Monarchs, St. Louis Stars, Indianapolis ABCs

Williams, James, 1885   C, Brooklyn Remsens

Williams, James (Jim), 1937-48   OF, MGR, Homestead Grays, Toledo Crawfords, Cleveland Bears, New York Black Yankees, New York Cubans, Birmingham Black Barons, Durham Eagles, Atlanta Black Crackers

Williams, Jesse, 1942-47   C, UTIL, Cleveland Buckeyes

Williams, Jesse Horace (Bill), 1939-50   SS, 3B, Kansas City Monarchs, Indianapolis Clowns

Williams, Jim (Bullet), 1929-32   P, Nashville Elite Giants, Cleveland Cubs, Detroit Wolves

Williams, Jim, 1934-37   OF, 1B, Newark Dodgers, New York Black Yankees, Philadelphia Stars

Williams, Joe, 1941   SS, Homestead Grays

Williams, Joe, 1946   OF, New York Black Yankees

Williams, John (Big Boy), 1926-38   OF, P, 1B, St. Louis Stars, Indianapolis ABCs, Detroit Stars, Homestead Grays, Dayton Marcos, Columbus Elite Giants, Jacksonville Red Caps

Williams, John, 1948   1B, Chicago American Giants

Williams, Johnny, 1943-48   P, Chicago Brown Bombers, Cincinnati- Indianapolis Clowns, Indianapolis Clowns

Williams, Joseph (Cyclone, Smokey Joe), 1905-1932   P, MGR, San Antonio Bronchos, Leland Giants, Chicago Giants, Lincoln Giants,

Chicago American Giants, Bacharach Giants, Brooklyn Royal Giants, Homestead Grays, Detroit Wolves, Hilldale, Mohawk Giants

Williams, L., 1905-09   OF, Cuban Giants

Williams, L.C., 1939-42   OF, Ethiopian Clowns, New York Cubans

Williams, L.R., 1931   officer, Cleveland Stars

Williams, Lem, 1923   umpire, NNL

Williams, Lemuel, 1937-39   P, St.Louis Stars, Chicago American Giants

Williams, Len, 1950   INF, OF, Indianapolis Clowns

Williams, Leroy, 1947-50   SS, 2B, Newark Eagles, Kansas City Monarchs

Williams, M., 1931   SS, Pittsburgh Crawfords

Williams, M., 1939   P, Baltimore Elite Giants

Williams, Marvin, 1943-50   2B, Philadelphia Stars

Williams, Mathis (Matt), 1921-23   SS, 3B, Pittsburgh Keystones, Cleveland Tate Stars

Williams, Morris, 1920-21   P, Indianapolis ABCs

Williams, Nish (Zeke, Nate), 1927-39   C, OF, 3B, 1B, Nashville Elite Giants, Cleveland Cubs, Columbus Elite Giants, Washington Elite Giants, Birmingham Black Barons, Indianapolis ABCs, Atlanta Black Crackers

Williams, Norm, 1930   OF, Nashville Elite Giants

Williams, Phil (Pete), 1931-39   2B, Baltimore Black Sox, Toledo Crawfords, Jacksonville Red Caps

Williams, Poindexter, 1920-33   C, MGR, Chicago American Giants, Detroit Stars, Kansas City Monarchs, Birmingham Black Barons, Louisville White Sox, Nashville Elite Giants, Homestead Grays

Williams, Ray, 1933-39   P, New York Black Yankees

Williams, Ray, 1950   P, OF, New York Black Yankees

Williams, (Red), 1926   SS, Indianapolis ABCs

Williams, Robert A. (Cotton), 1943-50   P, INF, Newark Eagles, Houston Eagles

Williams, Robert Lawns (Bobby), 1918-45   SS, 2B, 3B, MGR, Chicago American Giants, Indianapolis ABCs, Homestead Grays, Pittsburgh Crawfords, Cleveland Red Sox, Cleveland Tigers, Columbus Blue Birds, Akron, Cleveland Giants

Williams, Roy K., 1931-41   P, Pittsburgh Crawfords, Columbus Blue Birds, Baltimore Black Sox, Brooklyn Royal Giants, Brooklyn Eagles, Philadelphia Stars, New York Black Yankees, Baltimore Elite Giants, Homestead Grays

Williams, S., 1914-18   P, Brooklyn Royal Giants, Philadelphia Giants

Williams, S. (Al), 1945   P, Newark Eagles

Williams, Samuel C. (Sam), 1947-50   P, Birmingham Black Barons

Williams, Solomon (Sol), 1884-85   OF, Baltimore Atlantics

Williams, Stuart, 1950   2B, Cleveland Buckeyes

Williams, T., 1896-05   C, OF, Cuban X Giants

Williams, Thomas (Tom), 1916-25   P, Bacharach Giants, Chicago American Giants, Lincoln Giants, Brooklyn Royal Giants, Hilldale, Chicago Giants, Detroit Stars

Williams, V., 1929   C, St.Louis Stars

Williams, Walter, 1898   P, Celeron Acme Colored Giants (Iron and Oil Lg.)

Williams, Walter, 1939   P, Newark Eagles

Williams, Wil, 1902   1B, St. Cloud, (Minn.)

Williams, (Willie), 1929-33   SS, 2B, Bacharach Giants, Brooklyn Royal Giants

Williams, Willie, 1937-41   P, Washington Elite Giants, Baltimore Elite Giants, Birmingham Black Barons

Williams, Willie C. (Curley), 1945-50   3B, SS, Newark Eagles, Houston Eagles

Williams, Wilmore, 1943   OF, Newark Eagles

Williams, Woodrow, 1933   P, Akron Tyrites

Williams, (Zeke), see Nish Williams

Willis, Jim (Cannonball), 1927-39   P, Birmingham Black Barons, Nashville Elite Giants, Cleveland Cubs, Philadelphia Stars, Columbus Elite Giants, Washington Elite Giants, Baltimore Elite Giants

Willis, S., 1887   player, New York Gorhams

Wills, —, 1911   3B, Brooklyn Royal Giants

Wilmore, Alfred (Apple), 1947-50 P, Philadelphia Stars, Baltimore Elite Giants

Wilson, —, 1917 SS, Bacharach Giants

Wilson, —, 1927 C, Harrisburg Giants

Wilson, —, 1950 P, Cleveland Buckeyes

Wilson, Alec, 1939 OF, New York Black Yankees

Wilson, Andrew, 1922-27 OF, P, New Orleans Crescent Stars, Milwaukee Bears, Chicago Giants

Wilson, Arthur Lee (Artie), 1940,1944-48 SS, Birmingham Black Barons

Wilson, Benjamin (Benny), 1923-28 OF, Lincoln Giants, Pennsylvania Red Caps of New York

Wilson, Bill, 1948 3B, Newark Eagles

Wilson, Carter (Coltie), 1920-23 OF, Gilkerson's Union Giants, Peters' Union Giants, Chicago Giants

Wilson, Charles, 1917-22 P, OF, Dayton Giants, Dayton Marcos Columbus Buckeyes, Detroit Stars

Wilson, Charles, 1948-49 OF, 3B, Indianapolis Clowns

Wilson, Daniel Richard (Dan), 1937-47 OF, 3B, 2B, SS, Pittsburgh Crawfords, St. Louis Stars, New Orleans-St. Louis Stars, New York Black Yankees, Harrisburg-St. Louis Stars, Homestead Grays, Philadelphia Stars

Wilson, Ed, 1896-1905 1B, OF, Cuban X Giants, Lansing, Michigan, Colored Capital All-Americans, Adrian (MI) Page Fence Giants

Wilson, Edward, 1898 P, Celeron Acme Colored Giants (Iron and Oil Lg.)

Wilson, Elmer, 1921-26 2B, 3B, Dayton Marcos, Detroit Stars, St. Louis Stars

Wilson, Emmett Dabney, 1937-46 OF, Pittsburgh Crawfords, Cincinnati Buckeyes, Cleveland Buckeyes, Cincinnati Clowns, Boston Blues

Wilson, Felton, 1937 C, Detroit Stars

Wilson, Fietman, 1932-33 P, C, Akron Tyrites, Cleveland Stars

Wilson, Fred (Sardo),1938-45 OF, P, MGR, New York Black Yankees, Newark Eagles, Cincinnati Clowns, Cincinnati-Indianapolis Clowns

Wilson, George H., 1895-1905 P, OF, Page Fence Giants, Columbia Giants, Chicago Union Giants, Adrian (Michigan St. Lg.)

Wilson, George, 1922 OF, New Orleans Crescent Stars

Wilson, Harvey, 1939 INF, Toledo Crawfords

Wilson, Herb, 1928-29 P, Kansas City Monarchs

Wilson, J.H., 1887 player, Baltimore Lord Baltimore

Wilson, James (Chubby), 1929 OF, Bacharach Giants

Wilson, James, 1940 OF, 2B, Indianapolis Crawfords

Wilson, James, 1947 P, Memphis Red Sox

Wilson, Jay, 1945-1948 SS, Birmingham Black Barons

Wilson, John E. (Johnny), 1948-49 OF, Chicago American Giants

Wilson, Joseph, 1887 player, Washington Capital Citys

Wilson, Judson Ernest (Jud, Bojum), 1922-45 3B, 1B, 2B, MGR, Baltimore Black Sox, Homestead Grays, Philadelphia Stars, Pittsburgh Crawfords

Wilson, (Lefty), see Woodrow Wilson

Wilson, Percy Lawrance, 1922-24 1B, OF, New Orleans Crescent Stars, Milwaukee Bears

Wilson, Pete, 1924 1B, Baltimore Black Sox

Wilson, Ray, 1902-10 1B, Cuban X Giants, Philadelphia Giants

Wilson, Robert (Bob), 1947-50 3B, Newark Eagles, Houston Eagles

Wilson, Thomas T. (Tom), 1918-47 officer, Nashville Standard Giants, Nashville Elite Giants, Cleveland Cubs, Baltimore Elite Giants; vice-chairman, tres, pres, NNL; sec'y, pres, NSL

Wilson, W. Rollo, 1929-34 sec'y, ANL; commissioner, NNL

Wilson, William H., 1887 SS, Pittsburgh Keystones

Wilson, Woodrow (Lefty), 1931,1936-40 P, Kansas City Monarchs, Memphis Red Sox, Baltimore Elite Giants, New York Cubans

Wingfield, —, 1920-23,1931 2B, OF, SS, P, Dayton Marcos Detroit Stars, Toledo Tigers, Memphis Red Sox

Wingo, (Doc), 1944 C, Kansas City Monarchs

Winkle, —, 1946 3B, Indianapolis Clowns

Winston, —, 1929-32 P, OF, Chicago Giants, Chicago Columbia Giants, Atlanta Black Crackers, Detroit Stars

Winston, Clarence (Bobby), 1905-23 OF, Philadelphia Giants, Leland Giants, Chicago Giants, Cuban X Giants

Winters, Jesse (Nip), 1919-33 P, Norfolk Stars, Bacharach Giants, Norfolk Giants, Hilldale, Philadelphia Stars, Harrisburg Giants, Lincoln Giants, Darby Daisies, Newark Browns, Washington Pilots, Baltimore Black Sox

Wise, Russell, 1940 1B, Indianapolis Crawfords

Wisher, —, 1923 OF, Harrisburg Giants

Witherspoon, Lester, 1948-49 P, OF, Indianapolis Clowns, Homestead Grays

Wolfolk, Lewis, 1923-24 P, Chicago American Giants

Womack, James, 1923-33 1B, Cleveland Tigers, Indianapolis ABCs, Cuban Stars (NNL), Columbus Turfs, Columbus Blue Birds, Baltimore Black Sox, Richmond Giants

Woodard, —, 1928 INF, Cleveland Tigers

Wood, —, 1897 OF, Adrian Page Fence Giants

Woods, —, 1916 P, Chicago American Giants

Woods, (Doggy), 1904 P, Gray Eagle (Minn.)

Woods, Ed, 1891-98 P, 1B, Ansonia Cuban Giants (Connecticut St. Lg.), Chicago Unions

Woods, Parnell, 1933-49 3B, MGR, Birmingham Black Barons, Cleveland Bears, Jacksonville Red Caps, Cincinnati Buckeyes, Cleveland Buckeyes, Louisville Buckeyes, Philadelphia Stars

Woods, Sam (Buddy), 1946-50 P, Cleveland Buckeyes, Memphis Red Sox

Woods, William, 1887 SS, Philadelphia Pythians

Woods, William J., 1919-26 OF, Brooklyn Royal Giants, Indianapolis ABCs, Columbus Buckeyes, St. Louis Stars, Washington Potomacs, Bacharach Giants, Chicago American Giants, St. Louis Giants

Woolridge, Edward, 1926-28 SS, 1B, OF, Cleveland Elites, Cleveland Tigers

Wright, —, 1908 1B, Brooklyn Colored Giants

Wright, —, 1915 C, Chicago American Giants

Wright, —, 1946 3B, New York Cubans

Wright, Burnis (Bill), 1932-45 OF, Nashville Elite Giants, Columbus Elite Giants, Washington Elite Giants, Baltimore Elite Giants, Philadelphia Stars

Wright, Charley, 1931 P, Birmingham Black Barons

Wright, Clarence (Buggy), 1898 1B, Celeron Acme Colored Giants (Iron and Oil Lg.)

Wright, Ernest (Ernie), 1941-49 off., owner, Cleveland White Sox, Cincinnati Buckeyes, Cleveland Buckeyes; vice-pres, NAL

Wright, George (Ed), 1905-13 SS, 2B, Quaker Giants, Brooklyn Royal Giants, Leland Giants, Chicago Giants, Lincoln Giants

Wright, Henry, 1928-35 P, Nashville Elite Giants, Cleveland Cubs, Columbus Elite Giants, Birmingham Black Barons

Wright, Henry L. Jr. (Red), 1948 C, Baltimore Elite Giants

Wright, Howard, 1933 P, Nashville Elite Giants

Wright, John Richard (Needle Nose), 1937-48 P, Newark Eagles, Indianapolis Crawfords, Pittsburgh Crawfords, Homestead Grays, Toledo Crawfords

Wright, L., 1932 OF, Nashville Elite Giants

Wright, Zollie, 1931-43 OF, Memphis Red Sox, Monroe Monarchs, New Orleans Crescent Stars, Columbus Elite Giants, Washington Elite Giants, Washington Black Senators, New York Black Yankees, Philadelphia Stars

Wyatt, —, 1929 C, Detroit Stars

Wyatt, David (Dave), 1896-1920 OF, 2B, SS, Chicago Unions, Chicago Union Giants; co-drafter, constitution of NNL

Wyatt, Ralph Arthur (Pepper), 1941-46 SS, Chicago American Giants, Homestead Grays, Cleveland Buckeyes

Wylie, Ensloe, 1944-47 P, Kansas City Monarchs, Memphis Red Sox

Wynder, Clarence, 1950 C, Cleveland Buckeyes

Wynn, Calvin, 1949 OF, Louisville Buckeyes

Wynn, Willie, 1944-50 C, Newark Eagles, New York Cubans

Yancy, —, 1911 CF, Philadelphia Giants

Yancey, William James (Bill, Yank), 1923-36 SS, Philadelphia Giants, Hilldale, Philadelphia Tigers, Lincoln Giants, Darby Daisies, New York Black Yankees, Brooklyn Eagles, Philadelphia Stars, New York Cubans, Bacharach Giants

Yarbrough, —, 1932 C, Atlanta Black Crackers

Yokeley, Laymon Samuel (Norman), 1926-38 P, Baltimore Black Sox, Bacharach Giants, Philadelphia Stars, Washington Black Senators, Brooklyn Eagles

Yokum, —, 1922 P, Kansas City Monarchs

York, Jim, 1919-23 C, OF, Norfolk Stars, Hilldale, Bacharach Giants

Young, Berdell, 1922-28 OF, Bacharach Giants, Lincoln Giants

Young, Bob, 1950 INF, Cleveland Buckeyes

Young, Edward (Pep), 1936-47 C, 1B, 3B, Chicago American Giants, Kansas City Monarchs, Homestead Grays

Young, Frank A. (Fay), 1939-48 sec'y, NAL

Young, John, 1923-24-P, St. Louis Stars, Memphis Red Sox

Young, Leandy, 1944-45 OF, Birmingham Black Barons, Kansas City Monarchs

Young, Maurice (Doolittle), 1927 P, Kansas City Monarchs

Young, Norman Harvey, 1941-44 SS, Baltimore Elite Giants, Cleveland Buckeyes, New York Black Yankees

Young, Roy, 1942-45 umpire, NAL

Young, Thomas Jefferson (T.J., Tom), 1926-41 C, Kansas City Monarchs, St. Louis Stars, Detroit Wolves, New York Cubans, Pittsburgh Crawfords, Homestead Grays, Newark Eagles

Young, Dr. W.H., 1949-50 officer, Houston Eagles

Young, Wilbur, 1945 P, Birmingham Black Barons

Young, William P. (Pep), 1919-34 C, Homestead Grays

Young, William, 1927 P, Kansas City Monarchs

Yvanes, Armando, 1949-50 SS, New York Cubans

Zapp, James (Zipper), 1948-50 OF, Birmingham Black Barons, Baltimore Elite Giants

Zapp, Stephen, 1946 INF, Baltimore Elite Giants

Ziegler, William (Doc), 1927-29 OF, Chicago Giants

Zimmerman, George, 1887 player, Pittsburgh Keystones

Zomphier, Charles (Zomp), 1926-31 2B, 3B, SS, Cleveland Elites, Cleveland Hornets, Cleveland Tigers, Memphis Red Sox, Cleveland Cubs, Birmingham Black Barons, St. Louis Stars, Cuban Stars (NNL); umpire NAL

All-American Girls Baseball League Register

Barbara Gregorich and Debra A. Shattuck

The All American Girls Baseball League began in 1943, when World War II called men to the front, threatened the viability of major league baseball, and decimated many minor leagues. Under the leadership of Chicago Cubs owner Philip K. Wrigley, four teams embarked upon an ambitious 108-game schedule.

For further details about the AAGBL, see "Women in Baseball," earlier in this volume. For a key to the abbreviations in the statistical headings, consult The Player Register and The Pitcher Register of major league baseball. Below are the AAGBL cities, the abbreviations employed in this Register, and their year(s) of operation:

BC	*Battle Creek 1951-52*	Min	*Minneapolis 1944*
Chi	*Chicago 1948*	Mus	*Muskegon 1946-49, 1953*
FW	*Fort Wayne 1945-54*	Peo	*Peoria 1946-51*
GR	*Grand Rapids 1945-54*	Rac	*Racine 1943-50*
Kal	*Kalamazoo 1950-54*	Rck	*Rockford 1943-54*
Ken	*Kenosha 1943-51*	SB	*South Bend 1943-54*
Mil	*Milwaukee 1944*	Spg	*Springfield 1948*

For readers who know little about the players of the AAGBL, we present capsule biographies of the league's twenty greatest stars. We wanted to: (a) choose at least one player at each of the nine positions; (b) take into account the most commanding statistics; (c) credit career longevity; and (d) factor in intangibles such as leadership and reliability.

Although both of the authors of this entry have written extensively on women's baseball, the AAGBL has as yet inspired no definitive history, encyclopedia, or general literature evaluating players. Other writers evaluating the same evidence might well select other players.

That said, the list below gives a picture not only of the twenty players and their place in AAGBL history but also a sense of the quality of league play, its evolution from underhand to overhand pitching, the commitment and professionalism of the players, and the excitement of each season's pennant race.

Mary "Bonnie" Baker *Catcher/Infielder. Born July 10, 1918. All-Star 1943, 1946.* Back in Saskatchewan, Bonnie Baker's eight brothers and sisters were all catchers, so it stood to reason that Baker would become one too. She came to the AAGBL in the spring of 1943. Her husband was fighting overseas, but she promised him she would quit playing ball when he came home. A member of the South Bend Blue Sox, Baker, a former model, was often chosen to pose for publicity photos and act as a spokesperson. Although she was easily the most recognized AAGBLer, glamour never stopped her from doing her job: in 1946, when Sophie Kurys set the all-time stolen bases record, and Dottie Kamenshek batted .316, Baker stole 94 bases and batted .286.

When her soldier husband returned home that year, she tried to give up baseball but it was in her blood. During the 1950 season, Baker was traded to the struggling Kalamazoo Lassies to act as player-manager—the only AAGBLer ever to be offered a management contract. The Lassies lost again (36-73), and, the following year, the league passed a ruling against female managers. Baker skipped the 1951 season to have a child, but returned in 1952 to play for the Lassies one more year.

Thelma "Tiby" Eisen *Outfielder. Born May 11, 1922. All-Star 1946.* Along with Dottie Wiltse, Alma "Gabby" Ziegler, Faye Dancer, and Gladys "Terrie" Davis, Eisen was one of the "California girls" who took the train east in 1944 to try out for Phil Wrigley's league. All five were signed to contracts and assigned to expansion teams—Wiltse, Dancer, and Davis going to the Minneapolis Millerettes and Ziegler and Eisen to the Milwaukee Chicks. Playing 107 games for manager Max Carey, rookie Eisen stole 91 bases to help the Chicks win the first of their first three championships. When the Chicks moved to Grand Rapids the next year, Eisen went with them, but, in the 1946 expansion, she was sent to the Peoria Redwings. Playing for the last-place Redwings, Eisen stole 128 bases.

In the middle of the following season, Eisen was traded to Fort Wayne, where she played until the end of her career. A wide-ranging center fielder, she is credited with 1,857 putouts in 959 games. Batting leadoff for the Daisies, she averaged over 70 stolen bases a year. In 1949 she was chosen as one of the AAGBLers to tour Central America.

Jean Faut *Pitcher/Third Baseman. Born January 17, 1925. Player of the Year, 1951, 1953.* As the league game evolved from softball to baseball, Jean Faut evolved from infielder to pitcher. Faut, who grew up throwing batting practice for a men's semipro team, was stationed at third base in 1946. When side-arm pitching was allowed later that year, along with underhand pitching, the righthander went to the mound and immediately stood out, going 8-3 with a 1.33 ERA, then compiling a 19-13 record the following year.

Overhand pitching arrived in 1948. Faut, who had married Karl Winsch, future manager of the South Bend Blue Sox, gave birth to her first child in March and continued to pitch under her maiden name. She pitched 34 games, going 16-11, played another 30 or so games at third base, and was an outstanding hitter as well.

Faut dominated league pitching from 1950 to 1953. On July 21, 1951, she pitched the league's first perfect overhand game, led her team to its first Shaughnessy Series victory, and was elected Player of the Year. Nearly invincible in 1952, she compiled a 20-2 record with a 0.93 ERA and led the Sox to a second championship. The following year she pitched her second perfect game and was again elected Player of the Year.

Betty Weaver (m. Foss)   *First Base/Third Base. Born May 10, 1929. Rookie of the Year, 1950. All-Star first baseman, Player of the Year, 1952.* In 1950 Foss persuaded her husband to let her try out for the AAGBL and convinced her parents to let her take along her fourteen-year-old sister, Joanne, who had also grown up playing baseball in Metropolis, Illinois.

Foss joined the Fort Wayne Daisies in 1950. By midseason the 5'10" 175-pound third baseman was hailed as "the most sensational rookie in the game's history." Batting lefthanded, she shattered the league batting record of .316 by 30 points in her rookie year. For five consecutive years, either Foss or her sister Joanne held the batting title. In her sophomore season, Foss was switched to first base and lived up to the promise of her rookie year by batting .368, the highest mark in AAGBL history until her sister topped it in 1954. In 1952 her .331 average was second to Joanne's .344, but Betty was elected Player of the Year, beating Jean Faut by one vote.

As league attendance declined, the owners sought to attract more fans by making the game more challenging. In 1953 the basepaths were lengthened from 72 feet to 75 and the pitcher's mound from 55 feet to 56, the first such changes since 1949. Betty Foss was a star to the end, batting .352 in 1954, the final year of the AAGBL.

Rose Gacioch   *Outfielder/Pitcher/Utility Infielder. Born August 31, 1915. Played on all four of Rockford's championship teams. Voted All-Star pitcher, 1952, 1954, All-Star utility infielder, 1953.* Gacioch is unique among AAGBL players. Versatile enough to be chosen both an All-Star pitcher and infielder, she also set a record for outfield assists.

In 1934 the eighteen-year-old Gacioch was chosen by Maud Nelson, renowned nineteenth century Bloomer Girl, to barnstorm with the All-Star Rangers as an outfielder and pitcher. Ten years later, she joined the AAGBL and was its second oldest player. Outlasting the oldest and many of the youngest, she played league ball for eleven years. When she didn't pitch, Gacioch was usually in the lineup as an infielder, playing third base or first, because of her prowess at bat. Even at the age of thirty-eight she was good enough to bat .304.

Gacioch performed indifferently as a South Bend Blue Sox rookie in 1944, and in 1945 the club's president traded her to the Rockford Peaches, an incident which so angered the Board of Directors and manager that they passed a resolution restricting the president's functions. In Rockford Gacioch played right field, where she made 31 assists in 1945, setting a league record (which two years later she and Doris Sams tied). She led the league with 44 RBIs, as the Peaches won their first crown.

Gacioch batted .262 in 1946 and led the league with 9 triples. In 1948 manager Bill Allington took a calculated risk and converted her into a pitcher. She was the league's only 20-game winner in 1951, going 20-7 with a 1.68 ERA. Two years later she threw a seven-inning no-hitter against South Bend.

When the league folded, Gacioch took up bowling, once winning the national doubles championship.

Dorothy "Snookie" Harrell (m. Doyle)   *Shortstop. Born February 4, 1924. Selected All-Star shortstop four consecutive years, 1947-50.* Nicknamed "Snookie" shortly after birth in imitation of an older boy cousin named "Snooky," Harrell received a catcher's mitt and baseball uniform when she was five years old, but it was as a shortstop that Harrell made her mark.

Assigned to the Rockford Peaches in 1944, she played the position exclusively from 1944-52, except for 1951, when she played semipro softball. Hailed as a natural for her fielding at

short, Harrell also helped the Peaches with her bat, usually ranking as the shortstop with the highest batting average.

In the 1945 playoffs, Dottie Kamenshek, Rose Gacioch, Harrell and Jo Lenard supplied the hits that gave Rockford its first championship. Harrell had the most hits (13) in the 1948 playoff series, helping the Peaches win their second championship, and they repeated in 1949; after the season she got married and played thereafter as Snookie Harrell Doyle.

The Peaches tried for an unprecedented third consecutive championship (fourth overall) in 1950. In the pivotal fifth game of that seven-game series, Doyle drew a walk in the top of the tenth, eventually advanced to third, and, as part of a double steal, stole home with the winning run.

At the end of the 1952 season, she retired and went to college, graduating as a physical education teacher.

Dottie "Kammie" Kamenshek   *First Baseman. Born December 21, 1925. Won back-to-back batting titles 1946-47. Selected to seven All-Star teams, 1943, 1946-51.* Considered the AAGBL's best all-round player, the tireless and dedicated Kamenshek studied major leaguers as they hit and fielded. Wally Pipp considered her "the fanciest-fielding first baseman I've ever seen, man or woman." The lefthanded Kamenshek was an outstanding bunter and contact hitter, placing the ball where she wanted down either baseline, particularly in the league's dead-ball days. In 3,736 lifetime at bats, she struck out only 81 times and led the league in fewest strikeouts four seasons. (The Fort Lauderdale club of the Florida International Baseball league, a men's minor-league circuit, offered to buy Kamenshek's contract but was turned down.)

In her ten-year career with the Rockford Peaches, Kamenshek led the league twice in batting before the introduction of the livelier ball, hitting .316 in 1946 and .306 in 1947. Wearing a back brace her last two years of play, she still hit .345 in 1951 and stole 63 bases.

A team player who could sacrifice or go for the fence, depending on the game situation, Kamenshek helped Rockford win four championships. After the Peaches fell apart in the sixth game of the 1950 series, losing 8-0 to the Daisies, she rallied her teammates to win the final game, slapping out two singles, a triple, a homer, and driving in five runs.

Kamenshek went on to earn a degree in physical therapy

Jackie Kelley   *Utility Player. Born November 11, 1926. Died 1988. All Star, 1950.* A true utility player, Kelley did indeed play every position on the diamond, including catcher and pitcher. In her career, she played 80 games in the outfield, 20 at first, 43 at second, 58 at third, 21 at short, 52 behind the plate, and 53 on the mound.

Kelley came to the league in 1947 with her good friend, Alice Pollitt. Assigned to Rockford, Pollitt played third base; Kelly, assigned to South Bend, played any position. The following year, Kelley was with the Chicago Colleens, who lasted less than a month before lack of fan interest forced them to become barnstormers. Rescued from the Colleens in 1949, she was assigned to the Peoria Redwings, a team with little depth. Midseason, she was traded to the Rockford Peaches.

A member of the 1950 Peaches, Kelley helped win Rockford's fourth championship when she replaced the injured Pollitt at third base. With the series tied at two games and momentum favoring the Daisies, Kelley drove in the tie-breaking run in the top of the tenth, then combined with Snookie Doyle on a double steal in which Doyle scored the winning run. In the seventh game, Kelley doubled twice and drove in two runs.

After retiring from baseball at the end of the 1953 season, Kelley joined the Marines, got married, and raised a family.

Sophie Kurys   *Second Baseman. Born May 14, 1925. Holds AAGBL records for stolen bases in a season (201) and career (1,114). Player of the Year, 1946. All-Star, 1946-49.* Sophie

Kurys was nothing short of sensational in getting on base, stealing bases, and scoring runs. Joining the Racine Belles in 1943 and batting leadoff, the eighteen-year-old native of Flint, Michigan, stole 44 bases, a warmup for what would follow. In 1944 she stole a record-breaking 166 bases in 116 games— seven of them in one game.

When the AAGBL lengthened the basepaths from 68 feet to 72 after the 1945 season, experts predicted that the 166 record might be unbreakable, but Kurys proved them wrong the very next year: in 203 stolen base attempts, the "Flint Flash" was successful 201 times. She also set four other league records that year: scoring 117 runs; scoring five runs in one game; walking 93 times; and compiling a .973 fielding average at second base. Not surprisingly, she was named Player of the Year.

Kurys also scored the winning run in the sixth and final game of the 1946 World Series. The Belles came to bat in the bottom of the fourteenth inning of a scoreless tie; Kurys led off with a single and stole second. With teammate Betty Trezza at bat, she broke for third; Trezza singled through the drawn-in infield, and Kurys headed home, sliding under the tag. Racine fans stormed the field and carried the second baseman off on their shoulders. After baseball, Kurys worked in electrical manufacturing.

June Peppas *First baseman/Pitcher. Born June 16, 1929. All-Star first baseman, 1953.* Fort Wayne native June Peppas pitched softball in her home town and dreamed of playing for the AAGBL Daisies. However, when she finally made the team in 1948, overhand pitching had replaced underhand. Peppas couldn't master it, going 4-12 with a 4.62 ERA.

At the plate, though, the lefthanded Peppas racked up a healthy .264 average her first year. In 1951 she played in 108 games and batted .285 for Kalamazoo. In need of pitching, the Lassies tried her on the mound, where she went 1-7 with a 4.58 ERA. In 1952 and 1953, she played first base exclusively.

Peppas had her best season in 1954, when she batted .333 and took the mound 13 times, going 6-4. In the last league World Series, she drove in four runs and also pitched and won the final game.

She played a significant role in AAGBL history when, in 1981, she put out the first league newsletter. That initial act, in turn, created the reunions and conventions that resulted in the formation of the AAGPBL Players Association and the preservation of the league's heritage.

Ruth Richard *Catcher/Outfielder. Born September 20, 1928. All-Star catcher, 1949-54.* Joining the Grand Rapids Chicks in 1947, Richard played 47 games and was traded to the Peaches the following season. In Rockford she developed into a formidable catcher. During her tenure there, sportswriters selected her to the All-Star team as catcher six consecutive seasons.

Richard was one of a handful of players chosen to tour Central America in 1949. In Nicaragua, Costa Rica, Panama, and Venezuela, two AAGBL teams played exhibition games in an unsuccessful attempt to establish winter-league teams there.

In Rockford, Richard, who played on the championship Peaches teams of 1948-50, often caught in both ends of a doubleheader. In the last game of the 1950 regular season, she snagged her spikes and broke her ankle. During the second game of the Shaughnessy Series playoffs, fans took up a collection and gave the injured Richard $602 as she watched the Peaches win their third consecutive championship.

When the AAGBL disbanded, Richard was picked as one of the twelve players to tour with Allington's All Americans. She played for the barnstormers from 1955 through 1957.

Doris Sams *Outfielder/Pitcher. Born February 2, 1927. Batting champion, 1949; Player of the Year, 1947, 1949.* Assigned to the perennial underdog Muskegon Lassies in 1946, righthander Sams took the mound 25 times, posting an 8-9 record and a 3.78 ERA while batting .274 in 42 games. Recognizing

her batting ability, manager Bill Wambsganss played her in the outfield in 1947. Her .280 mark was the third highest in the league, and she tied Rose Gacioch's record of 31 outfield assists in a season. Sent to the mound 19 times, she posted an 11-4 record with a 0.98 ERA, pitching a perfect underhand game (the third such in league history) against the Fort Wayne Daisies on August 18, 1947. For her outstanding performance, the sophomore player was elected Player of the Year.

In 1949 Sams won the batting championship with a .279 mark and took the mound 28 times, posting a 15-10 record with a 1.58 ERA. These feats earned her another Player of the Year.

When the Muskegon Lassies moved to Kalamazoo in 1950, Sams connected with overhand pitching to bat over .300 for four seasons. Her overhand delivery, though, wasn't equal to her underhand style: she went 12-13 in 1950 and 0-1 the following year, her last as a pitcher. Setting a new league record with 12 home runs in 1952, Sams batted .314. At the end of the 1953 season, she retired, never having played for the championship. The next year, the Lassies upset the mighty Fort Wayne Daisies to win the World Series, a year too late for Sams.

Dottie Schroeder *Shortstop. Born April 11, 1928. Only woman to play all twelve years of AAGBL ball. All-Star, 1952-54.* Schroeder was fifteen years old when she tried out for Phil Wrigley's new league and made the cut. Assigned to the South Bend Blue Sox in 1943, she played in the AAGBL's very first game and in almost every game thereafter.

Starting out as a .180 hitter, Schroeder improved slowly, batting .245 in 1952 and .304 in 1954. She turned 31 double plays in 1944, a league record that stood for years. Long before the Sox became contenders (1945), Schroeder was traded to the Kenosha Comets, who seldom left the basement.

Highly visible on the field (5'8" and wearing long braids), Schroeder was traded to Fort Wayne in 1947. In her six seasons as the Daisies shortstop, she participated in many playoffs but never played for a championship. Before the 1953 season, however, just when the Daisies seemed unbeatable, Schroeder was traded to the hapless Kalamazoo Lassies. There she finished out her career, helping the Lassies upset the Daisies for the final league championship by driving in the winning run in the AAGBL's final game.

When the league folded, Schroeder toured with Allington's All Americans. After their last season, in 1957, she retired and went to work for a cap and gown factory in Champaign, Illinois.

Fern Shollenberger *Third Baseman. Birthday Unknown. Died 1977. All-Star, 1950-54.* Like her teammate Audrey Wagner, Fern Shollenberger played for the Kenosha Comets, a team that never won a championship. She took over third base for Kenosha in 1946 and stayed with the Comets until 1954.

During the AAGBL's twelve-year existence, All-Star teams were chosen ten times (1943, 1946-54). Three different players were chosen as third base All-Stars in the first five selections, but for the last five, Shollenberger was a nearly unanimous selection. Shollenberger's development at third base was evident by 1948, when she set two new records for third base—a .946 fielding percentage and 23 double plays. From then on, she only got better as the Comets, first in fielding but last in wins, sought a division title.

At the end of the 1951 season, the city of Kenosha could no longer support the Comets, and the team, one of the original four, folded. Shollenberger moved on, not to a contender such as the Blue Sox or Daisies, but to the Kalamazoo Lassies, themselves the remnants of the Muskegon Lassies.

On Christmas Eve of 1977, Shollenberger was killed in a car crash. Because she played for underdog teams and did not live to see the AAGBL rediscovered by baseball fans, she has received almost no notice since her death. Nevertheless, those who played with or against her consider Fern Shollenberger the finest third baseman of the AAGBL.

Audrey Wagner *Outfielder. Born December 27, 1927. Died 1985. Player of the Year, 1948.* Coming to the AAGBL in the spring of 1943 at the age of fifteen, Wagner was assigned to the Kenosha Comets. Hitting a league-respectable .230, she helped the Comets advance to the AAGBL's first world series, which was won, however, by the Racine Belles. The next two years saw the righthanded hitter struggle at the plate with averages under .200, but in 1946 Wagner graduated from high school and batted .281.

A premed student, Wagner took her hitting as seriously as she took the medical profession, spending hours alone at batting practice each morning. With the introduction of sidearm pitching in 1947, her average soared to .305. Although she lost the batting championship (by one percentage point) to Dottie Kamenshek, Wagner led the league in hits (119), doubles (25), RBIs (53) and home runs (7).

When overhand pitching arrived in 1948, twenty-year-old Wagner won the batting title with .312, leading the league with 130 hits. Her selection as Player of the Year in 1948 marked the start of a new kind of league ball, one in which hitting would come to dominate pitching.

At the end of the 1949 season Wagner retired from the AAGBL, later establishing a medical practice.

Joanne Weaver *Outfielder. Born 1936. First (and last) of the league's .400 hitters. All-Star, 1952. Player of the Year, 1954.* As a fourteen-year-old, Jo Weaver accompanied her older sister, Betty Weaver Foss, to try out with the Fort Wayne Daisies and made the team. Although she is credited with being a utility player for the Daisies in 1950, she had no plate appearances. The following year she appeared in 48 games and hit .276. In 1952 the sixteen-year-old hit her stride; in 314 at-bats, she led the league with a .344 average, outdoing her older sister's .331.

For three consecutive years, "Joltin' Jo" won the league batting crown, hitting .346 in 1953. In the league's last year, the kid broke .400, setting an unequaled record of .429. The six-foot, 145-pound righthanded hitter also led the league with 143 hits, 29 home runs, and 79 stolen bases.

When the league disbanded, Weaver was still only eighteen years old. She toured with Allington's All Americans in 1955, then went to work in Fort Wayne.

Dottie Wiltse (m. Collins) *Pitcher. Born September 23, 1923. Twenty-game winner four straight years.* Condemned to pitch for a team that would place last (and later be told to leave town), Dottie Wiltse started 38 times for the expansion Minneapolis Millerettes in 1944. She had a 20-16 record, striking out 205 in the process to lead the league (while also setting an unenviable record of 44 hit batters).

Wiltse grew up on fast-pitch softball in southern California, pitching for championship teams when she was thirteen, and she could throw a wider variety of underhand pitches than most league pitchers. When the Millerettes moved to more hospitable Fort Wayne in 1945, changing their name to the Daisies, Wiltse went 29-10 and pitched an amazing 17 shutouts. After pitching and winning both ends of a doubleheader, she met baseball fan Harvey Collins, whom she married in the spring of 1946.

Pitching under her married name, Dottie continued to win. In 1946 she struck out 294 (16 in one game against Peoria) and went 22-20. When sidearm pitching was introduced the following year, her record was 20-14. She pitched the 1948 season while pregnant, taking a leave of absence in her fifth month. Making a comeback in 1950, Collins pitched overhand, going 13-8. She retired at the end of the 1950 season with a lifetime ERA of 1.83.

In Fort Wayne she went to work for the *Baseball Blue Book* and took up golf, becoming a city champion.

Joanne Winter *Pitcher. Born November 24, 1924. Shares record for wins in a season (33); holds record for consecutive shutout innings (63); All-Star, 1946, 1948.* Joanne Winter, who spent eight years with the Racine Belles, is the only pitcher to post the highest number of wins in both the underhand and overhand years of the AAGBL. In her initial three years with the league, few would have predicted this of the 5'8" righthander. Her 11-11 record of 1943 did the Belles no harm as they went on to win the AAGBL's first world championship, but Winter struggled for the next two years, leading the league in losses in 1944 (23) and 1945 (22).

In 1946 she came back to pitch in 46 games, posting a 33-10 record with a 1.19 ERA (tying Connie Wisniewski for most wins). Pitching underhand, Winter set an all-time league record of 63 consecutive shutout innings. That year, in the sixth and final inning of the Shaughnessy Series—a contest many call the most exciting game ever played in the AAGBL—Winter went the distance and then some, pitching 14 innings of scoreless ball against Rockford and helping the Belles win the championship.

When the league switched to sidearm in 1947, Winter continued her underhand delivery, going 22-13. Seeing the inevitability of overhand pitching, she spent the offseason learning it. In 1948 Winter pitched 329 innings, with 248 strikeouts. She went 25-12 that year, with an ERA of 1.18 (tying Alice Haylett for most wins). After the Belles played their last season in 1950, Winter quit the AAGBL and moved to Arizona, where she became a golf pro.

Connie Wisniewski *Pitcher/Outfielder. Born February 18, 1922. Shares AAGBL record for wins in a season (33). Player of the Year, 1945. All-Star pitcher 1946, All-Star outfielder 1948, 1949, 1951.* A former softball player from Detroit, righthander Wisniewski signed with the AAGBL in 1944. After going 5-0 for the Milwaukee Chicks, she injured her knee. Wearing a knee brace for the remainder of the season, she compiled a 23-10 record, leading all pitchers with a .697 winning percentage.

Managed by Max Carey, the Chicks (70-45) faced the Kenosha Comets in the championship series. Rookie Wisniewski won four games of the best-of-seven series, propelling the Chicks to the first of three world championships.

The following year the Chicks relocated to Grand Rapids. Wisniewski posed a 32-11 record, a 0.81 ERA, the year's best winning percentage (.744), and was selected as the league's first Player of the Year. In 1946 she went 33-9.

With the advent of sidearm pitching in 1947, Wisniewski struggled to a 16-14 record. When overhand pitching arrived, she took the mound only eight times, going 3-4. Luckily, manager Johnny Rawlings saw that the lefthanded Wisniewski was better at hitting overhand pitching. He put her in the outfield, where she batted .289 and was elected to the All-Star team. In 1951 she hit .326, third highest average of the season. She retired at the end of the 1952 season.

Alma Ziegler *Second base/Pitcher. Born January 9, 1921. Player of the Year, 1950.* The AAGBL did not recruit players from California until 1944, when twenty-three-year-old Alma Ziegler and four others boarded a train for Chicago. Assigned to the Chicks in 1944, Ziegler played for the franchise eleven years, until the league folded in 1954.

A hitless wonder with a lifetime batting average of .173, Ziegler never batted .200 until 1954, when she managed to hit that figure exactly. On the diamond, though, she was an inspiration, participating in each of the Chicks' three world championships. Elected team captain every year from 1944-54, she was a sparkplug who yelled directions on every play, earning her the nickname, "Gabby."

With her strong arm, Ziegler was a natural pitcher. In the first year of overhand she went 9-6 with a 1.21 ERA. In 1950, she took the mound 35 times, compiling a 19-7 record and a 1.38 ERA, earning her the Player of the Year Award. When the league was dissolved, Ziegler returned to California, where she became a court reporter.

YEAR	TEAM	G	AB	R	H	2B	3B	HR	RBI	BB	SO	SB	AVG	PRO+	BR
Abbott, Velma - 3B															
1946	Ken-Peo-Rck	60	169	15	30	0	2	0	5	11	15	15	.178	68	-8
1947	FW	89	269	27	38	2	2	1	15	27	28	18	.141	71	-10
Total	2	149	438	42	68	2	4	1	20	38	43	33	.155	70	-18
Adams, Evelyn - SS															
1946	FW-GR	39	86	6	12	1	1	0	1	6	20	4	.140	49	-6
Albright, Eileen - 3B															
1948	Chi	65	142	9	20	3	0	0	4	19	24	9	.141	62	-6
Alderfer, Gertrude															
1950	Kal														
Allard, Beatrice - P															
1949	Mus	19	20	1	4	1	1	0	1	3	8	0	.200	202	1
Allen, Agnes - P															
1951	Kal-BC	27	36	4	6	0	0	0	1	5	5	0	.167	14	-4
1952	Kal	56	161	15	26	6	0	0	10	6	13	6	.161	44	-13
1953	Kal	38	70	12	13	0	1	0	2	6	7	1	.186	62	-4
Total	3	121	267	31	45	6	1	0	13	12	25	7	.169	45	-21
Allen, Doreen Betty (see Petryna)															
Alspaugh, Melba - OF															
1948	FW-Rck	51	135	17	25	1	0	0	9	10	26	18	.185	71	-3
1949	Mus-Rck	61	162	24	34	0	0	0	10	19	20	22	.210	100	2
Total	2	112	297	41	59	1	0	0	19	29	46	40	.199	87	-1
Alvares, Isabel - OF															
1951	FW-BC	17	21	1	2	1	0	0	1	1	2	0	.095	10	-3
1953	Kal	53	123	4	24	4	0	0	12	7	9	0	.195	65	-8
1954	GR-FW	23	68	6	13	2	0	0	2	2	5	3	.191	29	-7
Total	3	93	212	11	39	7	0	0	15	10	16	3	.184	46	-18
Anderson, Janet - OF															
1946	Ken	36	75	5	13	0	2	0	2	10	12	2	.173	100	-2
Anderson, Vivian - 3B															
1944	Mil	11	34	3	5	0	0	0	1	6	1	1	.147	63	-1
Applegren, Amy Irene - P															
1944	Rck	43	99	10	25	2	0	0	7	13	6	3	.253	141	2
1945	Rck	30	73	8	15	1	0	0	5	4	0	6	.205	109	1
1946	Mus	30	66	10	17	0	1	0	7	5	3	1	.258	135	0
1947	Mus	27	75	3	18	2	0	0	3	7	11	1	.240	137	1
1948	Mus	49	133	13	23	1	0	0	8	15	14	8	.173	72	-4
1949	Mus-Rck	30	69	5	13	1	0	0	4	5	10	1	.188	84	-2
1950	Rck	45	134	18	30	2	0	0	12	8	4	5	.224	100	-3
1951	Rck	31	73	7	15	1	0	0	5	5	7	1	.205	71	-3
1952	Rck	105	364	47	92	7	0	1	29	28	31	24	.253	104	-1
1953	SB	76	277	24	67	5	1	0	24	21	17	24	.242	98	-1
Total	10	466	1363	145	315	22	4	1	104	111	103	74	.231	103	-11
Arbour, Beatrice															
1947	Rac	1	1		0								.000	-99	-0
Armato, Angie - 2B															
1953	Kal	27	26	5	2	0	0	0	2	8	6	1	.077	20	-2
Armstrong, Charlotte - P															
1944	SB	43	120	4	16	1	0	0	7	11	15	3	.133	34	-10
1945	SB	47	129	6	21	1	0	0	5	8	0	14	.163	81	-1
Total	2	90	249	10	37	2	0	0	12	19	15	17	.149	58	-11
Arnold, Lenna - P															
1946	FW	6	14		3								.214	60	-1
1948	SB	20	21	1	3	0	1	0	0	5	2	0	.143	131	-0
1949	SB	16	29	2	3	1	0	0	2	2	2	0	.103	27	-3
Total	3	42	64	3	9	1	1	0	2	7	4	0	.141	37	-4
Arnold, Louise - P															
1951	SB	20	35	5	5	0	0	0	2	9	2	0	.143	52	-2
1952	SB	16	20	1	2	0	0	0	1	1	2	0	.100	-7	-2
Total	2	36	55	6	7	0	0	0	3	10	4	0	.127	32	-4
Baker, Mary Bonnie - C/2B															
1943	SB	73	256	45	64	7	2	1	31	24	6	46	.250	128	6
1944	SB	109	373	45	88	1	4	0	41	49	20	92	.236	131	15
1945	SB	110	394	49	93	6	5	0	7	21	1	17	.236	164	18
1946	SB	94	325	63	93	4	2	0	31	61	19	94	.286	171	32
1947	SB	106	369	54	80	5	1	0	20	40	32	58	.217	119	9
1948	SB	126	468	62	109	3	4	0	29	56	33	56	.233	125	11
1949	SB	111	408	58	88	4	2	0	25	50	38	68	.216	116	10
1950	SB-Kal	99	349	43	85	7	0	0	26	37	23	37	.244	99	-0
1952	Kal	102	366	43	76	7	0	0	20	38	22	20	.208	74	-12
Total	9	930	3308	465	776	44	20	1	230	376	194	488	.235	124	89
Baker, Phyllis - P															
1953	Mus	30	79	1	14	0	0	0	3	0	12	0	.177	18	-8
1954	SB-FW	22	48	3	5	0	0	1	4	3	11	0	.104	11	-7
Total	2	52	127	4	19	0	0	1	7	3	23	0	.150	14	-15
Ballingall, Chris - OF															
1953	Mus	72	188	14	34	3	1	1	13	30	52	4	.181	83	-6
1954	Kal	90	285	54	69	6	0	17	40	53	56	0	.242	171	7
Total	2	162	473	68	103	9	1	18	53	83	108	4	.218	140	1
Barbaze, Barbara - OF															
1948	Spg	80	223	19	43	2	0	0	16	24	29	23	.193	93	-3
Barker, Lois - OF															
1950	GR	32	64	4	8	0	0	0	3	6	15	0	.125	14	-6
Barnett, Charlene - 2B															
1947	FW	33	78	7	9	0	0	0	4	3	10	0	.115	3	-8
1948	Chi	126	448	48	74	7	5	1	19	67	59	29	.165	96	-8
1949	Rck	104	359	30	57	6	0	0	13	42	37	30	.159	67	-12
1950	Rck	92	331	35	73	3	2	0	29	32	22	30	.221	84	-7
Total	4	355	1216	120	213	16	7	1	65	144	128	89	.175	79	-35
Barney, Edith															
1948	GR	4	4		0								.000	-99	-1
Barr, Doris - P															
1943	SB	65	134	14	36	7	1	0	18	16	11	8	.269	153	4
1944	SB	32	55	3	7	0	0	0	6	6	15	4	.127	27	-4
1945	SB-Rac	44	104	8	23	1	0	0	2	5	0	11	.221	121	2
1946	Rac	21	39	6	5	0	0	0	1	6	9	1	.128	35	-3
1947	Rac	33	60	7	10	1	2	0	4	20	14	0	.167	167	3
1948	Spg	73	174	14	40	4	5	0	10	28	20	6	.230	169	6
1949	Mus	40	70	6	5	0	0	0	3	16	23	2	.071	15	-5
1950	Peo-Kal	30	41	3	10	2	0	0	3	3	6	0	.244	120	-0
Total	8	338	677	61	136	15	8	0	47	100	98	32	.201	121	3
Barringer, Patricia															
1947	Mus	1	1		0								.000	-99	-0
Batikis, Anastasia															
1945	Rac	5	11		0								.000	-99	-2
Battaglia, Fern - 2B															
1951	BC		60	5	10	1	0	0	4	6	8	4	.167	52	-3
Baumgartner, Mary "Wimpy" - C															
1950	SB-Kal	36	74	5	13	2	0	0	5	9	22	3	.176	66	-3
1951	SB	24	44	2	9	0	0	0	3	6	5	1	.205	69	-2
1949	Peo	15	22	1	2	1	0	0	0	1	9	0	.091	19	-2
1952	SB	34	50	7	5	0	0	0	0	20	15	2	.100	49	-1
1953	SB	90	262	26	49	8	0	0	22	38	48	6	.187	78	-9
1954	SB	81	226	26	42	5	1	4	19	42	33	12	.186	85	-10
Total	6	280	678	67	120	16	1	4	49	116	132	24	.177	75	-27
Beans, Charlene															
1952	GR														
Beare, Kathryn - C															
1946	FW	24	45	1	5	0	0	0	0	6	3	0	.111	18	-4
Becker, Donna															
1951	Kal														
Bell, Virginia - P															
1948	Spg	1	4		2								.500	280	1
Bennett, Catherine - P															
1943	Ken-SB	32	77	5	16	1	1	0	9	3	3	1	.208	77	-4
1944	SB	34	78	3	4	1	0	0	3	4	8	3	.051	-31	-11
Total	2	66	155	8	20	2	1	0	12	7	11	4	.129	26	-16
Berger, Barbara - C															
1950	Rac	11	17	2	3	0	0	0	1	3		1	.176	33	-1
Berger, Joan - 2B/SS															
1951	Rck	48	155	20	30	2	1	0	15	18	20	4	.194	75	-7
1952	Rck	109	382	54	96	5	6	1	33	39	34	24	.251	125	5
1953	Rck	103	368	56	91	8	3	1	28	44	16	31	.247	120	4
1954	Rck	85	289	43	81	12	2	2	22	18	5	19	.280	108	-4
Total	4	345	1194	173	298	27	12	4	98	119	75	78	.250	112	-1
Berger, Margaret - P															
1943	SB	47	113	10	22	1	0	0	14	3	3	1	.195	56	-7
1944	SB	41	109	5	12	0	0	0	4	2	3	1	.110	-10	-14
Total	2	88	222	15	34	1	0	0	18	9	6	2	.153	26	-21
Bergmann, Erma - P															
1946	Mus	50	141	13	36	5	1	1	7	9	16	2	.255	160	2
1947	Mus	28	76	5	14	1	1	0	6	5	6	2	.184	95	-2
1948	Spg	34	87	6	11	1	0	0	6	9	17	1	.126	38	-6
1949	Rac	32	80	2	17	2	0	0	1	5	7	1	.213	101	-2
1950	Rac	33	81	10	15	0	0	0	9	9	5	1	.185	57	-7
1951	BC	42	87	3	18	2	0	0	10	3	5	0	.207	67	-5
Total	6	219	552	39	111	11	2	1	39	40	56	7	.201	92	-18
Beschorner, Mary - OF															
1949	GR	36	85	5	14	2	1	0	4	2	19	3	.165	72	-5
1950	Peo	49	133	7	20	3	0	0	10	10	22	1	.150	34	-12
Total	2	85	218	12	34	5	1	0	14	12	41	4	.156	47	-17
Bevis, Muriel - OF															
1950	Ken	56	165	13	35	4	2	1	13	5	38	4	.212	101	-5
Bird, Nelda - P															
1945	SB	41	117	10	19	1	2	0	3	5	0	19	.162	97	-0
Bittner, Jaynne - P															
1947	SB	9	16		3								.188	48	-1
1948	Mus	21	58	3	4	1	0	0	0	3	14	1	.069	-5	-7
1949	GR	28	41	3	3	1	0	0	1	7	14	0	.073	27	-3
1950	GR	21	40	3	5	1	0	0	3	9		0	.125	25	-4
1951	GR	23	70	12	13	0	0	0	5	4	10	1	.186	47	-5
1952	GR-FW	28	71	5	9	0	0	0	4	4		0	.127	2	-8
1953	FW	30	74	5	12	1	0	0	4	8	22	1	.162	42	-5
1954	GR	29	38	7	6	1	0	0	3	5	7	0	.158	30	-4
Total	8	189	408	38	55	5	0	0	17	34	80	3	.135	21	-37
Blair, Maybelle															
1948	Peo	1	1		0								.000	-99	-0
Blaski, Alice - OF															
1953	FW	47	162	33	32	1	2	2	14	24	16	22	.198	109	1
1954	FW	45	144	35	37	4	2	3	17	34	18	1	.257	145	5
Total	2	92	306	68	69	5	4	5	31	58	34	23	.225	127	5
Bleiler, Audrey - 3B															
1950	SB	23	43	5	4	0	0	0	3	6	11	0	.093	2	-5
1951	SB	64	168	22	34	3	3	0	21	21	19	6	.202	100	-4

YEAR	TEAM	G	AB	R	H	2B	3B	HR	RBI	BB	SO	SB	AVG	PRO+	BR
1952	SB	16	50	4	9	1	0	0	6	6	12	3	.180	60	-2
Total	3	103	261	31	47	4	3	0	30	33	42	9	.180	76	-11

■ Blumetta, Kay - P

YEAR	TEAM	G	AB	R	H	2B	3B	HR	RBI	BB	SO	SB	AVG	PRO+	BR
1944	Mil-Min	33	82	7	9	1	0	0	7	16	19	4	.110	46	-5
1945	GR	23	67	6	7	0	0	0	6	0	2	23	.104	12	-2
1946	Peo	43	113	11	13	0	0	0	6	8	27	3	.115	10	-11
1947	Peo-FW	27	62	3	10	1	0	0	2	4	9	1	.161	59	-3
1948	FW	30	80	7	9	0	0	0	4	5	19	2	.112	3	-8
1949	FW	27	70	2	10	0	0	0	4	5	20	0	.143	31	-5
1950	FW	23	55	2	5	0	0	0	1	5	10	1	.091	-15	-7
1951	Kal	33	61	3	9	1	0	0	2	5	17	1	.148	32	-5
1952	Kal	21	55	1	11	1	0	0	1	3	10	0	.200	62	-3
1953	Kal	23	59	3	8	1	0	0	6	1	13	0	.136	6	-7
1954	Kal	20	36	5	11	1	0	0	5	2	9	0	.306	95	-1
Total	11	303	740	50	102	6	0	0	44	54	155	35	.138	28	-59

■ Borg, Lorraine - C

YEAR	TEAM	G	AB	R	H	2B	3B	HR	RBI	BB	SO	SB	AVG	PRO+	BR
1944	Min	23	83	7	11	0	0	0	2	7	5	2	.133	25	-7

■ Born, Ruth - P

YEAR	TEAM	G	AB	R	H	2B	3B	HR	RBI	BB	SO	SB	AVG	PRO+	BR
1943	SB	11	18	1	2	0	0	0	3	2	1	0	.111	5	-2

■ Boyce, Ethel

YEAR	TEAM	G	AB	R	H	2B	3B	HR	RBI	BB	SO	SB	AVG	PRO+	BR
1946	Ken	5	3	0										.000	-99	-1

■ Briggs, Rita - C

YEAR	TEAM	G	AB	R	H	2B	3B	HR	RBI	BB	SO	SB	AVG	PRO+	BR
1947	Rck	79	270	26	58	3	1	1	15	25	28	26	.215	119	2
1948	Rck-Chi	128	425	39	85	6	7	0	37	47	38	43	.200	116	1
1949	Rac-Peo	8	30		9								.300	134	0
1949	SB	64	191	23	40	1	0	0	21	16	16	22	.209	91	-1
1950	Peo	104	338	39	73	9	1	1	26	47	22	14	.216	102	-4
1951	Peo	106	363	57	100	6	1	0	44	55	9	29	.275	132	12
1952	BC	111	384	36	71	8	0	1	29	37	14	20	.185	65	-18
1953	FW	80	234	28	54	6	0	0	22	45	6	19	.231	111	5
1954	FW	77	230	26	49	3	0	3	33	46	12	13	.213	84	-7
Total	9	757	2465	274	539	42	10	6	227	318	145	186	.219	100	-10

■ Briggs, Wilma - OF

YEAR	TEAM	G	AB	R	H	2B	3B	HR	RBI	BB	SO	SB	AVG	PRO+	BR
1948	FW	67	193	14	44	0	6	1	15	42	19	2	.228	177	9
1949	FW	109	362	38	73	2	5	1	23	56	30	15	.202	128	5
1950	FW	107	396	69	109	13	1	3	38	79	31	29	.275	161	23
1951	FW	102	385	64	106	12	2	1	43	58	23	32	.275	150	16
1952	FW	105	399	46	102	16	4	3	50	44	46	1	.256	145	6
1953	FW	109	404	75	104	14	5	9	59	59	32	33	.257	181	21
1954	SB	92	317	69	95	7	1	25	73	42	33	16	.300	228	25
Total	7	691	2456	375	633	64	24	43	301	380	214	128	.258	167	106

■ Brown, Patricia
1951 BC

■ Brumfield, Delores - 1B/2B

YEAR	TEAM	G	AB	R	H	2B	3B	HR	RBI	BB	SO	SB	AVG	PRO+	BR
1947	SB	39	103	8	12	0	0	0	4	15	15	6	.117	36	-6
1948	Ken	86	261	18	37	3	0	0	17	28	60	18	.142	45	-15
1949	Ken	80	274	27	58	4	3	0	26	30	26	20	.212	121	1
1950	Ken	108	409	58	108	14	7	1	37	44	23	29	.264	148	11
1951	Ken	66	216	23	59	14	3	0	27	31	15	13	.273	175	11
1952	FW	88	293	33	64	13	1	1	23	48	22	10	.218	118	1
1953	FW	66	211	48	70	13	3	2	26	51	15	11	.332	234	26
Total	7	533	1767	215	408	61	17	4	160	247	176	107	.231	134	30

■ Bryson, Marion - P

YEAR	TEAM	G	AB	R	H	2B	3B	HR	RBI	BB	SO	SB	AVG	PRO+	BR
1946	Peo	15	18	0	2	0	0	0	0	2	3	1	.111	26	-1

■ Buckley, Jean - OF

YEAR	TEAM	G	AB	R	H	2B	3B	HR	RBI	BB	SO	SB	AVG	PRO+	BR
1950	Ken	71	222	23	46	6	4	2	22	13	28	5	.207	116	-6
1951	Ken	88	288	23	57	6	1	1	31	31	50	14	.198	87	-8
1952	Rck	96	317	31	62	8	1	4	35	22	61	14	.196	92	-12
Total	3	255	827	77	165	20	6	7	88	66	139	33	.200	97	-26

■ Bureker, Geraldine - OF

YEAR	TEAM	G	AB	R	H	2B	3B	HR	RBI	BB	SO	SB	AVG	PRO+	BR
1948	Rac	28	57	5	8	0	0	0	2	9	9	2	.140	47	-3

■ Burkovich, Shirley

YEAR	TEAM	G	AB	R	H	2B	3B	HR	RBI	BB	SO	SB	AVG	PRO+	BR
1951	Rck	17	28	2	2	0	0	0	0	2	7	0	.071	-32	-4

■ Burmeister, Eileen - OF

YEAR	TEAM	G	AB	R	H	2B	3B	HR	RBI	BB	SO	SB	AVG	PRO+	BR
1943	Rck	105	377	39	72	8	7	0	41	36	30	12	.191	93	-14
1944	Rck	62	194	18	41	2	4	0	19	26	16	15	.211	134	1
Total	2	167	571	57	113	10	11	0	60	62	46	27	.198	106	-13

■ Butcher, Mary - P

YEAR	TEAM	G	AB	R	H	2B	3B	HR	RBI	BB	SO	SB	AVG	PRO+	BR
1945	Ken-GR	5	2	0										.000	-99	-0
1946	GR	1	2	0										.000	-99	-0
Total	2	6	4	0										.000	-99	-1

■ Callaghan, Helen (m. Candaele 1949) - OF

YEAR	TEAM	G	AB	R	H	2B	3B	HR	RBI	BB	SO	SB	AVG	PRO+	BR
1944	Min	111	397	81	114	5	4	3	17	73	39	112	.287	199	42
1945	FW	111	408	77	122	17	4	3	12	29	4	34	.299	247	46
1946	FW	112	399	70	85	10	3	1	26	73	61	114	.213	135	21
1948	FW	54	178	21	34	3	4	0	13	23	27	36	.191	125	4
1949	Ken	107	374	50	94	9	5	0	32	50	59	65	.251	166	22
Total	5	495	1756	299	449	44	20	7	100	248	190	361	.256	180	135

■ Callaghan, Margaret - 3B/2B

YEAR	TEAM	G	AB	R	H	2B	3B	HR	RBI	BB	SO	SB	AVG	PRO+	BR
1944	Min	47	154	19	28	1	0	0	10	20	18	20	.182	81	-3
1945	FW	99	280	34	55	1	1	1	11	17	3	45	.196	135	16
1946	FW	111	340	72	64	2	3	1	11	88	52	80	.188	127	20
1947	FW	104	324	40	65	2	1	0	23	61	63	57	.201	121	1
1948	FW	112	391	44	73	2	3	0	27	49	72	42	.187	98	1
1949	SB	62	160	26	27	3	0	0	16	26	33	24	.169	89	1
1950	Peo	30	70	5	11	1	0	0	5	20	8	14	.157	75	1
1951	Peo-BC	107	339	40	80	6	1	0	34	53	38	26	.236	114	15
Total	8	672	2058	280	403	18	9	2	137	334	277	308	.196	111	55

■ Callow, Eleanor - OF

YEAR	TEAM	G	AB	R	H	2B	3B	HR	RBI	BB	SO	SB	AVG	PRO+	BR
1947	Peo	51	143	18	35	5	2	0	14	3	11	7	.245	149	1
1948	Chi-Rck	114	387	43	97	6	15	6	52	23	38	19	.251	210	16
1949	Rck	105	387	34	88	3	11	2	36	26	29	25	.227	156	6
1950	Rck	109	409	47	105	12	11	7	56	33	29	24	.257	178	13
1951	Rck	106	380	66	124	16	10	4	84	49	23	40	.326	229	38
1952	Rck	107	400	56	101	14	6	8	49	42	25	39	.253	170	16
1953	Rck	100	386	58	117	23	4	8	58	39	19	37	.303	214	30
1954	Rck	86	273	59	89	9	1	20	58	50	18	23	.326	244	33
Total	8	778	2765	381	756	88	60	55	407	265	192	214	.273	197	151

■ Candaele, Helen (see Callaghan)

■ Carey, Mary - 3B/2B

YEAR	TEAM	G	AB	R	H	2B	3B	HR	RBI	BB	SO	SB	AVG	PRO+	BR
1946	Ken	103	310	32	47	3	0	0	20	17	38	42	.152	39	-19
1947	Peo	67	194	17	35	1	0	0	16	17	14	12	.180	72	-6
1948	Peo	122	428	49	76	6	3	0	29	50	53	37	.178	85	-10
1949	Peo	97	330	21	54	3	1	1	22	25	24	17	.164	68	-15
1950	Peo	109	412	54	97	12	2	0	24	45	40	37	.235	107	-0
1951	Peo	102	374	47	66	8	2	1	22	36	30	27	.176	69	-18
1952	Kal	65	196	23	41	1	0	0	9	18	15	5	.209	63	-9
1953	Kal-Mus-Rck	91	311	22	54	2	1	0	17	32	21	13	.174	48	-19
1954	SB	84	252	16	53	5	0	0	17	23	20	8	.210	47	-20
Total	9	840	2807	281	523	41	9	2	169	263	255	198	.186	68	-116

■ Carver, Virginia - P

YEAR	TEAM	G	AB	R	H	2B	3B	HR	RBI	BB	SO	SB	AVG	PRO+	BR
1953	SB														
1954	FW	32	75	7	13	0	0	0	7	9	23	0	.173	27	-8
Total	2	32	75	7	13	0	0	0	7	9	23	0	.173	27	-8

▣ Carveth, Betty - P

YEAR	TEAM	G	AB	R	H	2B	3B	HR	RBI	BB	SO	SB	AVG	PRO+	BR
1945	Rck-FW	21	47	2	7	0	1	0	2	1	0	4	.149	89	-1

■ Castillo, Ysora - 3B

YEAR	TEAM	G	AB	R	H	2B	3B	HR	RBI	BB	SO	SB	AVG	PRO+	BR
1950	Kal	96	207	20	28	6	2	0	14	52	39	6	.135	80	-5
1951	Kal-Ken	83	192	18	23	1	0	0	9	50	31	2	.120	43	-10
Total	2	179	399	38	51	7	2	0	23	102	70	8	.128	63	-15

■ Chapman, Dorothy (see Maguire)

■ Chester, Bea - 2B

YEAR	TEAM	G	AB	R	H	2B	3B	HR	RBI	BB	SO	SB	AVG	PRO+	BR
1943	SB	18	58	6	11	2	1	0	5	7	8	6	.190	102	-1
1944	Rck	11	42	4	9	0	1	0	4	6	8	1	.214	133	-0
Total	2	29	100	10	20	2	2	0	9	13	16	7	.200	114	-1

■ Christ, Dorothy

YEAR	TEAM	G	AB	R	H	2B	3B	HR	RBI	BB	SO	SB	AVG	PRO+	BR
1948	SB	1	0	0										.000	-99	0

■ Cindric, Ann

YEAR	TEAM	G	AB	R	H	2B	3B	HR	RBI	BB	SO	SB	AVG	PRO+	BR
1948	Mus	3	10		1									.100	-24	-1

■ Cione, Jean - P/1B

YEAR	TEAM	G	AB	R	H	2B	3B	HR	RBI	BB	SO	SB	AVG	PRO+	BR
1945	Rck	20	45	2	4	0	0	0	2	1	0	10	.089	11	-2
1946	Peo	106	343	32	59	2	5	0	23	42	53	24	.172	88	-10
1947	Rck-Ken	65	163	15	27	1	5	1	11	8	38	10	.166	113	-4
1948	Ken	60	173	14	29	3	4	1	14	20	55	5	.168	118	-3
1949	Ken	84	245	24	54	3	7	0	27	23	42	16	.220	147	3
1950	Ken	79	268	29	67	7	3	1	37	17	39	10	.250	124	-1
1951	Ken	80	292	31	71	11	0	1	34	17	27	10	.243	114	-4
1952	BC	94	320	43	88	17	2	0	32	45	31	7	.275	152	11
1953	Mus	96	356	27	87	15	1	0	41	32	34	4	.244	114	-11
1954	Rck	74	242	23	62	8	0	4	27	23	24	0	.256	106	-7
Total	10	758	2447	240	548	67	27	8	248	228	343	96	.224	117	-19

■ Clapp, Louise
1954 SB-GR

■ Coben, Muriel - P

YEAR	TEAM	G	AB	R	H	2B	3B	HR	RBI	BB	SO	SB	AVG	PRO+	BR
1943	SB-Rck	34	70	6	10	0	0	0	4	2	6	4	.143	12	-7

■ Colacito, Lucille - C

YEAR	TEAM	G	AB	R	H	2B	3B	HR	RBI	BB	SO	SB	AVG	PRO+	BR
1944	Ken	85	268	23	48	7	0	1	22	24	28	21	.179	89	-10
1945	Ken	68	177	14	25	2	0	1	2	6	0	22	.141	68	-5
Total	2	153	445	37	73	9	0	2	24	30	28	43	.164	81	-14

■ Collins, Dottie (see Wiltse)

■ Cook, Clara - P

YEAR	TEAM	G	AB	R	H	2B	3B	HR	RBI	BB	SO	SB	AVG	PRO+	BR
1943	Ken	36	80	7	14	2	0	0	7	12	6	3	.175	71	-4
1944	Ken-Mil	13	22	2	2	0	0	0	2	5	4	1	.091	28	-2
Total	2	49	102	9	16	2	0	0	9	17	10	4	.157	62	-5

■ Cook, Donna - P

YEAR	TEAM	G	AB	R	H	2B	3B	HR	RBI	BB	SO	SB	AVG	PRO+	BR
1946	Mus	78	231	18	36	2	3	0	14	20	16	4	.156	69	-13
1947	Mus	48	134	6	23	1	0	0	7	4	8	4	.172	53	-8
1948	Chi-Mus-FW	41	81	8	10	0	0	0	6	14	13	6	.123	38	-4
1949	FW	30	67	5	13	3	1	0	5	12	5	3	.194	148	1
1950	GR	11	19	2	4	0	1	0	1	2	2	0	.211	141	0
1951	BC	102	358	18	67	6	1	0	17	20	18	11	.187	60	-22
1952	BC	62	207	27	51	5	3	0	11	9	16	13	.246	112	-1
1953	Mus-SB	53	131	12	26	2	0	0	10	14	5	6	.198	69	-5
1954	Rck	55	152	10	33	4	0	2	11	14	9	2	.217	77	-9
Total	9	480	1380	108	263	23	9	2	82	109	92	49	.191	76	-61

■ Cook, Doris - OF

YEAR	TEAM	G	AB	R	H	2B	3B	HR	RBI	BB	SO	SB	AVG	PRO+	BR
1951	Kal	18	32	5	3	0	0	0	4	8	5	1	.094	26	-2
1952	Kal	55	152	10	18	1	0	0	6	13	20	0	.118	11	-16
1953	Kal-SB	36	66	4	11	0	0	0	4	8	8	0	.167	39	-5
Total	3	109	250	19	32	1	0	0	14	29	33	1	.128	21	-23

■ Cook, Dorothy

YEAR	TEAM	G	AB	R	H	2B	3B	HR	RBI	BB	SO	SB	AVG	PRO+	BR
1946	FW-Rck	14	24	0	0	0	0	0	2	5	5	1	.000	-33	-3

■ Cooper, Bonnie
1952 BC

■ Cordes, Gloria - P

YEAR	TEAM	G	AB	R	H	2B	3B	HR	RBI	BB	SO	SB	AVG	PRO+	BR
1950	Kal-Rac	28	45	0	1	0	0	0	2	4	10	0	.022	-60	-8
1951	BC-Kal	26	61	6	8	0	0	0	5	7	11	2	.131	21	-5
1952	Kal	28	79	9	16	3	0	0	5	3	16	0	.203	68	-5
1953	Kal	29	76	4	9	0	0	0	1	7	14	0	.118	2	-9

YEAR	TEAM	G	AB	R	H	2B	3B	HR	RBI	BB	SO	SB	AVG	PRO+	BR
1954	Kal	28	62	4	8	1	0	0	1	8	21	0	.129	9	-8
Total	5	139	323	23	42	4	0	0	14	29	72	2	.130	14	-35

■ Cornett, Betty Jane - 3B

YEAR	TEAM	G	AB	R	H	2B	3B	HR	RBI	BB	SO	SB	AVG	PRO+	BR
1951	BC-Kal	47	114	10	15	2	0	0	6	18	30	7	.132	40	-8

■ Courtney, Patricia

| 1950 | GR | 10 | 17 | 3 | 1 | 0 | 0 | 0 | 0 | 3 | 8 | 0 | .059 | -16 | -2 |

■ Cramer, Peggy

| 1954 | SB | | | | | | | | | | | | | | |

■ Crawley, Pauline - OF

1946	Peo	20	81	7	7	0	0	0	4	4	9	2	.086	-17	-10
1951	BC	105	337	33	60	2	2	0	21	29	35	19	.178	55	-19
Total	2	125	418	40	67	2	2	0	25	33	44	21	.160	42	-30

■ Crews, Mary (see Nesbitt)

■ Crigler, Idona - 3B

| 1947 | SB | 20 | 65 | 2 | 9 | 0 | 0 | 0 | 0 | 5 | 7 | 0 | .138 | 36 | -4 |

■ Crites, Shirley - 3B

| 1953 | FW | 47 | 132 | 15 | 17 | 3 | 1 | 0 | 11 | 15 | 17 | 7 | .129 | 43 | -10 |

■ Dabbs, Sarah Mavis

| 1947 | FW | 12 | 22 | 0 | 2 | 0 | 0 | 0 | 1 | 2 | 1 | 1 | .091 | -0 | -2 |

■ Daetweiler, Louella - C

| 1944 | Rck | 33 | 76 | 4 | 6 | 0 | 0 | 0 | 8 | 6 | 3 | 4 | .079 | -9 | -9 |

■ Dailey, Mary - OF

1950	SB-Peo	54	159	16	22	2	1	0	10	15	25	1	.138	36	-14
1951	SB-BC-Peo	63	155	8	29	2	0	0	6	19	23	9	.187	66	-6
Total	2	117	314	24	51	4	1	0	16	34	48	10	.162	51	-20

■ Damaschke, Dorothy

| 1945 | Rac | 1 | 2 | 0 | | | | | | | | | .000 | -99 | -0 |

■ Dancer, Faye - OF

1944	Min	96	329	58	90	6	5	2	48	53	24	63	.274	195	26
1945	FW	108	343	44	67	7	1	3	22	29	5	38	.195	150	16
1946	FW	110	368	56	92	11	5	1	43	52	22	68	.250	167	21
1947	FW-Peo	106	380	51	90	11	1	2	26	43	30	71	.237	155	19
1948	Peo	122	459	89	109	10	2	6	34	55	79	102	.237	164	28
1950	Peo	49	193	25	40	8	0	2	13	12	30	19	.207	105	-4
Total	6	591	2072	323	488	53	14	16	186	244	190	361	.236	160	107

■ D'Angelo, Josephine - OF

1943	SB	104	358	62	79	9	2	2	38	55	3	53	.221	123	8
1944	SB	40	141	11	21	0	0	0	9	12	8	9	.149	37	-10
Total	2	144	499	73	100	9	2	2	47	67	11	62	.200	101	-2

■ Danhauser, Marnie - 1B

1943	Rac	61	162	18	27	2	1	0	21	8	11	6	.167	44	-13
1944	Rac	109	329	34	49	0	0	0	34	35	16	27	.149	48	-19
1945	Rac	110	335	25	31	0	0	0	21	10	3	20	.093	2	-28
1946	Rac	113	387	35	76	3	3	2	41	31	21	20	.196	100	-9
1947	Rac	112	364	21	45	0	0	1	20	27	28	15	.124	31	-25
1948	Rac	125	390	24	65	10	6	0	38	32	48	9	.167	93	-14
1949	Rac	98	290	10	32	1	0	0	12	13	45	5	.110	8	-28
Total	7	728	2257	167	325	16	10	3	187	156	172	102	.144	51	-137

■ Daniels, Audrey (see Haines)

■ Danz, Shirley - OF

| 1950 | Rac | 23 | 55 | 4 | 8 | 0 | 0 | 0 | 1 | 4 | 18 | 1 | .145 | 20 | -5 |

■ Dapkus, Eleanor - OF/P

1943	Rac	89	309	65	68	6	5	10	42	30	36	25	.220	169	5
1944	Rac	103	362	48	99	10	4	5	56	34	17	46	.273	199	20
1945	Rac	100	345	26	79	9	2	0	7	37	3	21	.229	168	22
1946	Rac	112	403	49	102	6	9	8	57	51	36	25	.253	203	20
1947	Rac	112	398	25	86	7	5	2	41	35	59	16	.216	139	3
1948	Rac	116	411	39	83	5	6	4	46	43	57	18	.202	131	-1
1949	Rac	68	155	11	35	3	1	0	16	16	18	1	.226	129	1
1950	Rac	75	166	13	31	4	4	1	21	21	28	2	.187	111	-4
Total	8	775	2549	276	583	50	36	30	286	267	254	154	.229	162	64

■ Davis, Gladys - SS

1943	Rck	102	349	78	116	7	10	4	58	52	9	53	.332	228	40
1944	Rck-Mil	80	277	42	68	4	1	1	34	38	24	63	.245	148	14
1946	Mus	58	193	22	39	8	0	0	31	23	22	21	.202	110	-1
Total	3	240	819	142	223	19	11	5	123	113	55	137	.272	176	53

■ DeCambra, Alice - 2B

1946	FW	101	314	21	58	2	0	0	11	28	11	18	.185	68	-13
1947	FW-Peo	98	307	35	57	3	0	0	12	17	16	24	.186	74	-9
1948	Peo	121	392	46	74	8	1	0	30	49	26	34	.189	96	-4
1949	Peo	101	352	32	72	4	3	0	26	25	18	24	.205	100	-6
1950	Peo-Kal	69	213	18	52	12	2	0	26	19	5	7	.244	132	-0
Total	5	490	1578	152	313	29	6	0	105	138	76	107	.198	92	-32

■ Deegan, Mildred - 2B/P

1943	Rck	29	97	8	20	1	2	0	17	8	8	6	.206	96	-3
1944	Rck	104	353	45	82	5	5	1	39	38	19	47	.232	145	8
1945	Rck	102	346	47	72	9	5	1	13	34	3	19	.208	170	19
1946	Rck	87	272	31	58	6	5	2	25	23	12	11	.213	140	-1
1947	Rck-Ken	55	131	14	28	4	5	0	8	8	8	4	.214	171	2
1948	Ken-Spg	49	124	6	26	6	1	0	11	9	9	0	.210	135	-0
1949	FW	41	90	8	15	7	0	0	4	13	9	1	.167	134	0
1950	FW	39	94	10	29	8	1	1	12	11	10	0	.309	219	7
1951	FW-Peo	27	53	6	9	2	0	0	2	4	6	0	.170	67	-3
1952	Rck														
Total	10	533	1560		339								.217	98	28

■ Degner, Betty

| 1949 | Mus | 2 | 5 | | 1 | | | | | | | | .200 | 56 | -0 |

■ DelMonico, Lena (see Surkowski)

■ DeMarco

YEAR	TEAM	G	AB	R	H	2B	3B	HR	RBI	BB	SO	SB	AVG	PRO+	BR
1954	Kal														

■ Dennert, Pauline

| 1947 | Mus | 3 | 4 | 0 | | | | | | | | | .000 | -99 | -1 |

■ DeNoble, Jerre - OF

| 1947 | Peo | 21 | 28 | 3 | 3 | 1 | 0 | 0 | 0 | 3 | 11 | 4 | .107 | 44 | -1 |

■ Denton, Mona - P

1946	SB	3	5	1									.200	50	-0
1947	Ken	26	51	3	10	1	1	0	2	2	19	1	.196	117	-1
Total	2	29	56	3	11	1	1	0	2	2	19	1	.196	97	-1

■ Deschaine, Alice (see Pollit)

■ Descombes, Jeanie - P

1953	GR														
1954	GR	22	39	4	7	0	0	0	3	6	3	0	.179	32	-4
Total	2	22	39	4	7	0	0	0	3	6	3	0	.179	32	-4

■ DeShone, Nancy

| 1948 | SB | 1 | 2 | 0 | | | | | | | | | .000 | -99 | -0 |

■ Dokish, Juanita - 2B

| 1954 | Rck | 27 | 44 | 5 | 5 | 0 | 0 | 0 | 2 | 10 | 14 | 0 | .114 | 12 | -5 |

■ Donahue, Terry - C/3B

1946	Peo	95	274	29	42	0	1	0	14	32	38	28	.153	55	-12
1947	Peo	49	115	12	19	1	0	0	4	11	10	3	.165	73	-4
1948	Peo	71	174	17	17	1	1	0	18	32	31	7	.098	48	-8
1949	Peo	72	159	9	14	1	0	0	14	48	28	6	.088	52	-4
Total	4	287	722	67	92	3	2	0	50	123	107	44	.127	56	-27

■ Dougal

| 1953 | Mus | | | | | | | | | | | | | | |

■ Downs, Dorothea

| 1945 | SB | 3 | 5 | 0 | | | | | | | | | .000 | -99 | -1 |

■ Doyle, Cartha - SS

| 1947 | Rck | 59 | 166 | 5 | 28 | 4 | 0 | 0 | 7 | 5 | 24 | 2 | .169 | 63 | -9 |

■ Doyle, Dorothy (see Harrell)

■ Drinkwater, Maxine - 1B

| 1954 | SB | 45 | 95 | 8 | 14 | 0 | 0 | 0 | 4 | 12 | 22 | 1 | .147 | 10 | -12 |

■ Dunn, Gertrude - SS

1951	SB-BC	45	151	14	28	3	1	0	10	27	9	6	.185	86	-4
1952	SB	95	326	35	77	15	2	0	21	31	14	13	.236	116	-1
1953	SB	112	438	46	122	17	1	0	36	33	13	20	.279	130	7
1954	SB	92	311	59	93	14	1	6	38	47	10	25	.299	149	13
Total	4	344	1226	154	320	49	5	6	105	138	46	70	.261	126	14

■ Dusanko, Julianna - 3B

| 1944 | Min-Rac | 76 | 246 | 21 | 41 | 3 | 2 | 0 | 16 | 21 | 26 | 29 | .167 | 72 | -11 |

■ Dwojak, Loretta - OF

| 1944 | Min-SB | 63 | 174 | 19 | 35 | 4 | 2 | 0 | 19 | 18 | 17 | 18 | .201 | 115 | -2 |

■ Earp, Mildred - P

1947	GR	35	89	2	13	1	0	0	2	4	17	1	.146	38	-6
1948	GR	35	94	7	11	3	1	0	9	11	13	0	.117	64	-6
1949	GR	27	74	1	13	0	0	0	5	10	11	1	.176	71	-2
1950	GR	12	21	0	1	0	0	0	1	6	6	1	.048	7	-2
Total	4	109	278	10	38	4	1	0	17	31	47	3	.137	53	-17

■ Eisen, Thelma "Tiby" - OF

1944	Mil	107	392	55	80	6	3	1	41	28	12	91	.204	105	0
1945	GR	108	392	44	94	16	1	1	13	34	1	15	.240	178	21
1946	Peo	99	363	68	93	9	3	2	30	52	10	128	.256	177	32
1947	Peo-FW	111	425	49	92	5	1	3	26	26	13	52	.216	120	3
1948	FW	121	464	67	102	5	4	1	30	29	25	88	.220	116	8
1949	FW	109	424	59	78	7	0	3	18	36	31	57	.184	95	-5
1950	FW	106	432	87	103	20	3	0	19	55	27	75	.238	127	13
1951	FW	104	399	88	78	17	1	0	21	73	14	88	.195	103	7
1952	FW	106	415	77	110	6	1	0	22	35	17	54	.265	107	6
Total	9	971	3706	594	830	85	23	11	220	368	150	648	.224	124	84

■ Emerson, June - OF

1948	Spg	47	110	8	20	1	0	0	5	16	10	6	.182	88	-1
1949	Peo	21	49	3	6	1	0	0	0	15	6	1	.122	84	-0
Total	2	68	159	11	26	2	0	0	5	31	16	7	.164	87	-1

■ Emry, Betty - SS/P

1945	Rac	96	280	13	40	1	0	0	14	19	2	28	.143	62	-6
1946	Rac	36	85	11	14	0	0	0	5	17	14	6	.165	70	-2
Total	2	132	365	24	54	1	0	0	19	36	16	34	.148	64	-8

■ English, Madeline - 3B

1943	Rac	101	359	69	79	0	4	0	23	33	21	75	.220	86	-2
1944	Rac	112	371	50	45	2	3	0	21	61	37	65	.121	54	-15
1945	Rac	99	349	33	54	1	2	0	17	16	3	41	.155	81	-2
1946	Rac	75	257	21	55	1	1	1	21	24	19	39	.214	100	-1
1947	Rac	103	335	31	44	2	1	0	30	36	49	47	.131	52	-13
1948	Rac	121	400	41	64	4	6	0	24	49	72	60	.160	85	-6
1949	Rac	111	364	28	61	6	5	0	21	45	44	26	.168	97	-6
1950	Rac	110	382	60	80	10	6	4	41	65	32	61	.209	135	12
Total	8	832	2817	333	482	26	28	6	198	329	277	414	.171	88	-32

■ Erickson, Louise - P

1948	Rac	3	3	1									.333	154	0
1949	Rck	26	76	3	13	2	0	0	4	7	12	0	.171	77	-3
1950	Rck	37	88	11	21	0	0	0	4	6	13	0	.239	75	-3
Total	3	66	167	14	35	2	0	0	8	13	25	0	.210	73	-7

■ Fabac, Elizabeth - 2B

| 1945 | Ken | 105 | 356 | 41 | 71 | 2 | 2 | 0 | 11 | 14 | 3 | 31 | .199 | 115 | 6 |

YEAR	TEAM	G	AB	R	H	2B	3B	HR	RBI	BB	SO	SB	AVG	PRO+	BR
1946	Ken	3	7		2								.286	114	-0
1947	Ken	90	294	32	39	0	0	1	18	33	25	40	.133	48	-11
1948	Ken	123	445	68	85	5	3	0	15	68	58	43	.191	102	1
Total	4	321	1102	141	197	7	5	1	44	115	86	114	.179	91	-4

■ Faralla, Lillian - P

YEAR	TEAM	G	AB	R	H	2B	3B	HR	RBI	BB	SO	SB	AVG	PRO+	BR
1946	Peo	55	138	8	25	1	0	0	13	14	28	12	.181	73	-4
1947	FW	32	68	7	19	3	2	0	4	1	8	7	.279	212	4
1948	SB	66	169	5	38	3	0	0	16	14	23	2	.225	104	-3
1949	SB	38	90	6	20	0	0	0	6	11	7	1	.222	107	0
1950	SB-Kal	48	85	6	17	2	0	2	16	7	16	1	.200	114	-3
1951	SB	27	57	11	8	1	1	1	8	16	17	2	.140	121	0
Total	6	266	607	43	127	10	3	3	63	63	99	25	.209	112	-5

■ Farrow, Elizabeth - P

YEAR	TEAM	G	AB	R	H	2B	3B	HR	RBI	BB	SO	SB	AVG	PRO+	BR
1944	Rck-Min	20	36	1	6	1	0	0	1	2	3	0	.167	64	-3

■ Faut, Jean - P/3B

YEAR	TEAM	G	AB	R	H	2B	3B	HR	RBI	BB	SO	SB	AVG	PRO+	BR
1946	SB	101	344	37	61	2	2	2	40	58	21	38	.177	100	-2
1947	SB	56	123	8	29	3	3	0	11	18	15	5	.236	177	5
1948	SB	50	104	6	24	2	0	0	7	12	10	1	.231	121	0
1949	SB	53	117	14	34	7	0	0	21	12	10	12	.291	194	8
1950	SB	76	198	23	43	7	2	0	26	31	12	15	.217	116	1
1951	SB	62	178	29	46	6	0	2	28	23	11	9	.258	147	4
1952	SB	73	230	30	67	12	0	0	32	27	11	15	.291	150	10
1953	SB	98	316	33	87	11	1	4	38	49	10	17	.275	164	16
Total	8	569	1610	180	391	50	8	8	203	230	100	112	.243	141	43

■ Ferguson, Dorothy (m. Key 1949) - OF

YEAR	TEAM	G	AB	R	H	2B	3B	HR	RBI	BB	SO	SB	AVG	PRO+	BR
1945	Rck	37	84	5	11	2	0	0	1	4	0	14	.131	67	-1
1946	Peo-Rck	80	235	43	43	0	2	0	15	42	27	39	.183	97	3
1947	Rck	112	367	51	61	2	1	0	20	52	39	71	.166	88	4
1948	Rck	123	419	73	64	6	0	0	16	76	62	73	.153	78	0
1949	Rck	100	346	51	62	6	2	0	20	59	52	56	.179	106	6
1950	Rck	102	364	61	85	5	4	0	27	43	34	36	.234	107	1
1951	Rck	107	370	91	80	6	0	1	27	67	32	91	.216	106	14
1952	Rck	108	354	54	86	8	4	1	41	38	27	46	.243	123	8
1953	Rck	101	400	56	83	8	1	0	21	43	30	29	.207	78	-11
1954	Rck	77	277	35	70	6	0	0	8	26	16	14	.253	72	-11
Total	10	947	3216	520	645	49	14	2	196	450	319	469	.201	94	13

■ Ferguson, Fern - P

YEAR	TEAM	G	AB	R	H	2B	3B	HR	RBI	BB	SO	SB	AVG	PRO+	BR
1945	Rac	3	4		1								.250	103	-0

■ Figlo, Josephine

YEAR	TEAM	G	AB	R	H	2B	3B	HR	RBI	BB	SO	SB	AVG	PRO+	BR
1944	Rac-Mil	15	34	7	2	1	0	0	3	4	13	4	.059	8	-3

■ Filarski, Helen - 3B

YEAR	TEAM	G	AB	R	H	2B	3B	HR	RBI	BB	SO	SB	AVG	PRO+	BR
1945	Rck	99	324	44	56	7	1	0	17	25	1	30	.173	116	8
1946	Rck	77	231	33	42	5	3	1	23	43	14	23	.182	124	2
1947	Peo-Ken	72	227	22	42	3	1	0	12	35	21	14	.185	105	0
1948	SB	101	324	29	58	1	1	0	29	48	29	18	.179	80	-7
1949	SB	92	290	31	60	3	3	0	26	30	28	19	.207	112	-1
1950	SB	93	287	30	60	6	6	0	26	44	15	13	.209	114	-1
Total	6	534	1683	189	318	25	15	1	133	225	108	117	.189	108	2

■ Fischer, Alva Jo - SS/P

YEAR	TEAM	G	AB	R	H	2B	3B	HR	RBI	BB	SO	SB	AVG	PRO+	BR
1945	Rck	17	33	3	6	0	6	0	1	2	0	7	.182	375	5
1946	Mus	42	97	11	30	5	1	0	11	11	7	1	.309	207	6
1947	Mus	112	361	22	73	7	3	0	35	31	23	28	.202	113	-1
1948	Mus	107	353	31	89	10	1	0	36	26	22	14	.252	138	5
1949	Mus	109	384	24	76	2	1	0	47	33	30	22	.198	85	-9
Total	5	387	1228	91	274	24	12	0	130	103	82	72	.223	127	7

■ Fisher, Lorraine, - OF/P

YEAR	TEAM	G	AB	R	H	2B	3B	HR	RBI	BB	SO	SB	AVG	PRO+	BR
1947	Rck	51	129	7	15	1	1	0	9	7	14	2	.116	29	-11
1948	GR	54	143	18	23	1	0	0	7	14	11	4	.161	53	-8
1949	GR	26	55	4	7	0	0	0	2	7	5	1	.127	37	-3
Total	3	131	327	29	45	2	1	0	18	28	30	7	.138	41	-22

■ Florreich, Lois - P/3B

YEAR	TEAM	G	AB	R	H	2B	3B	HR	RBI	BB	SO	SB	AVG	PRO+	BR
1943	SB	89	351	61	81	9	6	4	43	27	62	57	.231	138	5
1944	SB	99	366	49	65	4	6	1	25	54	50	113	.178	112	8
1945	SB-Ken	67	217	28	39	4	1	0	2	23	0	24	.180	115	5
1946	Ken	78	231	26	54	1	7	0	21	27	28	19	.234	151	5
1947	Rck	55	153	8	29	2	1	0	12	11	11	18	.190	92	-2
1948	Rck	41	106	5	10	2	0	0	1	13	24	1	.094	19	-10
1949	Rck	29	95	7	8	1	0	0	5	9	20	9	.084	1	-9
1950	Rck	46	114	15	28	8	1	1	9	10	18	4	.246	157	1
Total	8	504	1633	199	314	31	22	6	118	174	213	245	.192	114	4

■ Folder, Rose - OF

YEAR	TEAM	G	AB	R	H	2B	3B	HR	RBI	BB	SO	SB	AVG	PRO+	BR
1944	Ken	71	207	23	54	1	3	1	24	13	6	7	.261	155	2

■ Foss, Anita - 2B

YEAR	TEAM	G	AB	R	H	2B	3B	HR	RBI	BB	SO	SB	AVG	PRO+	BR
1948	Mus-GR	25	49	5	6	1	0	0	5	14	11	5	.122	77	-0
1949	Rck-Mus	3	2		0								.000	-99	-0
Total	2	28	51		6								.118	58	-0

■ Foss, Betty (née Weaver) - 1B

YEAR	TEAM	G	AB	R	H	2B	3B	HR	RBI	BB	SO	SB	AVG	PRO+	BR
1950	FW	96	361	64	125	24	3	5	61	43	46	64	.346	234	44
1951	FW	94	342	77	126	34	2	4	58	48	34	60	.368	271	51
1952	FW	106	414	81	137	26	17	4	74	53	40	56	.331	254	51
1953	FW	110	449	99	144	20	8	5	65	28	35	80	.321	203	39
1954	FW	92	332	80	117	13	0	14	54	27	21	34	.352	201	30
Total	5	498	1898	401	649	117	30	32	312	199	176	294	.342	230	214

■ Fox, Helen (see Nicol)

■ Francis, Betty - OF

YEAR	TEAM	G	AB	R	H	2B	3B	HR	RBI	BB	SO	SB	AVG	PRO+	BR
1949	Mus	9	23		1								.043	-66	-4
1950	Kal	56	129	15	33	2	1	1	10	17	12	5	.256	134	2
1951	Kal	97	325	42	75	8	0	0	20	49	14	21	.231	105	-0
1952	Kal	99	329	20	69	8	0	0	14	42	18	4	.210	84	-9
1953	Kal	78	212	31	48	7	0	0	23	16	10	5	.226	107	0
1954	SB	90	300	49	105	13	2	8	58	41	22	7	.350	189	23
Total	6	429	1318	157	331	38	3	9	125	185	76	42	.251	122	12

■ Francisco, Philomena - OF

YEAR	TEAM	G	AB	R	H	2B	3B	HR	RBI	BB	SO	SB	AVG	PRO+	BR
1945	GR	21	39	6	6	1	0	0	0	1	0	6	.154	107	1
1946	GR	98	342	34	77	9	2	2	53	38	33	21	.225	138	3
1947	GR	32	98	13	16	2	1	0	5	12	13	6	.163	98	-1
1948	Rac	114	398	34	81	11	2	4	35	47	36	45	.204	137	7
Total	4	265	877	87	180	23	5	6	93	98	82	78	.205	132	10

■ Frank, Edna - C

YEAR	TEAM	G	AB	R	H	2B	3B	HR	RBI	BB	SO	SB	AVG	PRO+	BR
1944	Min-Rac	16	46	1	5	0	0	0	2	1	4	1	.109	-10	-6

■ Franks, Hermine

YEAR	TEAM	G	AB	R	H	2B	3B	HR	RBI	BB	SO	SB	AVG	PRO+	BR
1946	Ken	1	1		0								.000	-99	-0

■ Fritz, Betty Jane - OF

YEAR	TEAM	G	AB	R	H	2B	3B	HR	RBI	BB	SO	SB	AVG	PRO+	BR
1943	Rck	98	348	38	73	4	1	0	43	9	16	29	.210	62	-18

■ Froning, Mary - OF

YEAR	TEAM	G	AB	R	H	2B	3B	HR	RBI	BB	SO	SB	AVG	PRO+	BR
1951	SB														
1952	SB-BC	13	25	1	2	0	0	0	1	1	5	0	.080	-36	-4
1953	SB	111	375	50	78	8	0	0	26	46	49	32	.208	80	-8
1954	SB	85	251	44	58	10	0	3	26	16	29	26	.231	83	-11
Total	4	209	651	95	138	18	0	3	46	62	83	58	.212	77	-23

■ Gacioch, Rose - OF/P

YEAR	TEAM	G	AB	R	H	2B	3B	HR	RBI	BB	SO	SB	AVG	PRO+	BR
1944	SB	98	348	29	56	2	2	0	37	25	13	27	.161	57	-21
1945	Rck	105	374	34	79	8	2	0	21	44	2	23	.211	136	10
1946	Rck	111	405	56	106	14	9	1	57	27	19	52	.262	176	15
1947	Rck	100	338	23	87	5	3	1	31	25	20	31	.257	155	11
1948	Rck	121	426	41	102	11	3	1	44	39	28	18	.239	143	7
1949	Rck	90	281	19	57	3	0	0	34	25	15	3	.203	99	-6
1950	Rck	61	156	9	41	5	2	0	18	12	8	2	.263	130	0
1951	Rck	40	109	11	32	3	0	0	15	3	5	1	.294	163	2
1952	Rck	47	121	8	26	6	1	0	11	7	11	2	.215	101	-4
1953	Rck	75	179	13	51	4	6	2	18	12	10	1	.285	183	6
1954	Rck	79	217	27	66	8	1	13	45	8	10	5	.304	199	8
Total	11	927	2954	270	703	69	34	18	329	227	141	165	.238	140	29

■ Galdonik, Barbara

YEAR	TEAM	G	AB	R	H	2B	3B	HR	RBI	BB	SO	SB	AVG	PRO+	BR
1951	BC														

■ Gallegos, Luisa - P

YEAR	TEAM	G	AB	R	H	2B	3B	HR	RBI	BB	SO	SB	AVG	PRO+	BR
1948	Peo-SB	29	36	3	3	0	0	0	1	2	11	2	.083	-20	-4

■ Ganote, Gertrude - 1B

YEAR	TEAM	G	AB	R	H	2B	3B	HR	RBI	BB	SO	SB	AVG	PRO+	BR
1944	Ken	97	338	35	45	3	2	0	11	42	60	24	.133	53	-21
1945	SB	81	287	26	55	5	2	0	12	19	1	32	.192	118	5
Total	2	178	625	61	100	8	4	0	23	61	61	56	.160	82	-16

■ Garman, Ann - 1B

YEAR	TEAM	G	AB	R	H	2B	3B	HR	RBI	BB	SO	SB	AVG	PRO+	BR
1953	SB	21	65	5	10	0	0	0	7	13	13	1	.154	47	-3

■ Gasby

YEAR	TEAM	G	AB	R	H	2B	3B	HR	RBI	BB	SO	SB	AVG	PRO+	BR
1953	GR														

■ Gascon, Eileen - OF

YEAR	TEAM	G	AB	R	H	2B	3B	HR	RBI	BB	SO	SB	AVG	PRO+	BR
1951	GR-BC-Peo	27	87	12	16	2	0	0	4	16	22	7	.184	81	-1

■ Gates, Barbara - P

YEAR	TEAM	G	AB	R	H	2B	3B	HR	RBI	BB	SO	SB	AVG	PRO+	BR
1953	GR-SB	17	19	1	2	0	0	0	1	4	8	1	.105	19	-1
1954	FW														
Total	2	17	19		2								.105	19	-1

■ Geissinger, Jean - 2B

YEAR	TEAM	G	AB	R	H	2B	3B	HR	RBI	BB	SO	SB	AVG	PRO+	BR
1951	FW	22	67	8	13	1	0	2	7	4	14	0	.194	127	-1
1952	FW-GR	108	407	41	114	16	5	5	56	17	63	15	.280	163	10
1953	FW	105	397	50	117	21	10	8	81	30	47	28	.295	219	27
1954	FW	93	313	78	118	17	2	26	91	45	41	17	.377	295	49
Total	4	328	1184	177	362	55	17	41	235	96	165	60	.306	219	85

■ George, Gene - C

YEAR	TEAM	G	AB	R	H	2B	3B	HR	RBI	BB	SO	SB	AVG	PRO+	BR
1948	Mus	15	13	1	2	0	0	0	2	0	4	0	.154	17	-1

■ Georges, Beulah - P

YEAR	TEAM	G	AB	R	H	2B	3B	HR	RBI	BB	SO	SB	AVG	PRO+	BR
1948	Chi-FW	10	16	2	2	0	0	0	0	2	6	0	.125	42	-1

■ Gilchrist, Jean

YEAR	TEAM	G	AB	R	H	2B	3B	HR	RBI	BB	SO	SB	AVG	PRO+	BR
1946	Peo	3	6		1								.167	25	-1

■ Goldsmith, Bethany - P

YEAR	TEAM	G	AB	R	H	2B	3B	HR	RBI	BB	SO	SB	AVG	PRO+	BR
1948	Ken	31	82	7	9	2	0	0	3	11	13	3	.110	40	-6
1949	Ken	29	60	11	11	0	0	0	8	6	9	1	.183	69	-2
1950	Ken	27	70	6	14	0	0	0	4	1	7	0	.200	41	-5
Total	3	87	212	24	34	2	0	0	15	18	29	4	.160	48	-13

■ Gosbee, Ann - 2B

YEAR	TEAM	G	AB	R	H	2B	3B	HR	RBI	BB	SO	SB	AVG	PRO+	BR
1953	GR	18	33	5	3	0	0	0	0	3	6	0	.091	-8	-4
1954	Rck-GR	57	85	17	13	0	0	0	7	22	5	1	.153	38	-7
Total	2	75	118	22	16	0	0	0	7	25	11	1	.136	27	-11

■ Graham, Mary Lou - P

YEAR	TEAM	G	AB	R	H	2B	3B	HR	RBI	BB	SO	SB	AVG	PRO+	BR
1953	SB														

■ Grant, Olga - OF

YEAR	TEAM	G	AB	R	H	2B	3B	HR	RBI	BB	SO	SB	AVG	PRO+	BR
1944	Mil	21	73	6	18	1	0	0	6	7	6	9	.247	128	1

■ Green, Dorothy - C

YEAR	TEAM	G	AB	R	H	2B	3B	HR	RBI	BB	SO	SB	AVG	PRO+	BR
1943	Rck	48	128	12	21	0	0	1	4	12	35	0	.164	54	-9
1944	Rck	98	290	33	42	3	3	0	20	45	49	23	.145	76	-11
1945	Rck	44	117	13	17	5	0	0	3	5	2	9	.145	90	-2
1946	Rck	76	206	14	24	1	2	0	13	32	31	16	.117	45	-13
1947	Rck	14	26	1	3	0	0	0	1	2	3	0	.115	25	-2
Total	5	280	767	73	107	9	5	1	41	96	120	48	.140	64	-37

■ Guest, Geraldine

YEAR	TEAM	G	AB	R	H	2B	3B	HR	RBI	BB	SO	SB	AVG	PRO+	BR
1951	Peo	26	42	5	5	0	0	0	2	3	12	1	.119	-1	-5

■ Gutz, Julie - C

YEAR	TEAM	G	AB	R	H	2B	3B	HR	RBI	BB	SO	SB	AVG	PRO+	BR
1948	Spg	83	223	11	34	0	3	0	8	14	35	4	.152	57	-14
1949	Mus	40	121	6	16	3	1	0	9	8	23	5	.132	55	-8
1950	Ken	112	365	45	74	10	1	0	27	41	36	5	.203	91	-11
Total	3	235	709	62	124	13	5	1	44	63	94	14	.175	75	-32

Habben, Carol - OF/3B

YEAR	TEAM	G	AB	R	H	2B	3B	HR	RBI	BB	SO	SB	AVG	PRO+	BR
1951	Rck	10	26	1	1	0	0	0	1	1	7	0	.038	-63	-5
1952	Rck														
1953	Rck	82	242	18	47	5	1	0	18	14	41	5	.194	73	-10
1954	Kal	98	308	45	85	5	1	15	46	42	41	8	.276	168	10
Total	4	190	576	64	133	10	2	15	65	57	89	13	.231	123	-5

Hageman, Johanna - 1B

YEAR	TEAM	G	AB	R	H	2B	3B	HR	RBI	BB	SO	SB	AVG	PRO+	BR
1943	SB	108	378	47	85	10	6	1	45	50	28	24	.225	127	1
1944	SB	116	365	24	52	2	0	0	28	52	39	23	.142	52	-20
1945	Ken	96	273	8	32	2	0	0	10	9	0	20	.117	37	-14
Total	3	320	1016	79	169	14	6	1	83	111	67	67	.166	79	-33

Haine, Audrey (m. Daniels 1951) - P

YEAR	TEAM	G	AB	R	H	2B	3B	HR	RBI	BB	SO	SB	AVG	PRO+	BR
1944	Min	34	86	3	13	2	0	0	4	4	8	5	.151	50	-6
1945	FW	37	85	14	14	2	0	0	3	6	2	5	.165	100	0
1946	FW-GR	30	79	5	12	0	0	0	5	4	7	1	.152	31	-7
1947	GR-Peo	29	69	8	19	2	0	0	5	6	4	1	.275	164	2
1948	Peo	33	79	8	11	1	0	0	5	5	11	1	.139	33	-6
1951	Rck	11	28	3	5	1	1	0	4	1	4	0	.179	110	-1
Total	6	174	426	41	74	8	1	0	26	26	36	13	.174	71	-18

Haines, Martha

YEAR	TEAM	G	AB	R	H	2B	3B	HR	RBI	BB	SO	SB	AVG	PRO+	BR
1947	Ken	1	1	0										.000	-99	-0

Harnett, Ann - 3B/OF/C

YEAR	TEAM	G	AB	R	H	2B	3B	HR	RBI	BB	SO	SB	AVG	PRO+	BR
1943	Ken	101	387	54	105	10	10	6	69	19	7	15	.271	179	9
1944	Ken	98	351	41	87	8	8	1	45	23	9	18	.248	164	4
1945	Ken	99	322	22	65	5	5	0	8	25	0	13	.202	141	7
1946	Ken	16	58	4	13	3	1	0	3	2	6	5	.224	140	-0
1947	Peo	110	414	47	84	8	4	0	29	23	18	13	.203	108	-7
Total	5	424	1532	168	354	34	28	7	154	92	40	64	.231	148	12

Harney, Elsie - P

YEAR	TEAM	G	AB	R	H	2B	3B	HR	RBI	BB	SO	SB	AVG	PRO+	BR
1943	Ken	44	116	13	20	0	1	0	5	7	15	5	.172	35	-9
1944	Ken	35	89	9	10	0	0	0	8	10	10	2	.112	20	-8
1945	Ken	43	99	7	12	0	1	0	4	4	0	10	.121	41	-5
1946	Ken-FW	34	89	8	16	0	0	0	10	12	11	0	.180	70	-4
1947	FW	17	32	0	0	0	0	0	0	1	10	0	.000	-89	-6
Total	5	173	425	37	58	0	2	0	27	34	46	17	.136	32	-32

Harrell, Dorothy "Snookie" (m. Doyle 1949) - SS

YEAR	TEAM	G	AB	R	H	2B	3B	HR	RBI	BB	SO	SB	AVG	PRO+	BR
1944	Rck	93	322	24	57	4	2	0	14	22	10	18	.177	73	-16
1945	Rck	92	310	36	74	6	5	2	18	27	0	8	.239	189	17
1946	Rck	88	301	34	64	6	2	0	26	28	9	28	.213	108	-2
1947	Rck	99	351	31	71	6	5	1	41	24	18	34	.202	123	1
1948	Rck	116	414	52	104	9	7	1	58	48	21	45	.251	167	19
1949	Rck	111	431	40	95	3	5	0	50	25	7	39	.220	112	-1
1950	Rck	107	431	45	119	16	10	3	63	18	10	23	.276	165	10
1952	Rck	93	362	40	83	6	1	2	27	13	12	18	.229	86	-12
Total	8	799	2922	302	667	56	37	9	297	205	87	213	.228	129	15

Hasham, Josephine - P

YEAR	TEAM	G	AB	R	H	2B	3B	HR	RBI	BB	SO	SB	AVG	PRO+	BR
1948	Mus-Peo	34	73	2	13	0	0	0	7	4	6	0	.178	57	-4
1949	SB	35	69	1	11	1	0	0	6	10	10	1	.159	75	-2
1950	Peo	32	80	7	8	0	0	0	4	5	12	0	.100	-10	-10
1951	Peo	50	94	4	24	5	0	0	7	14	5	0	.255	140	2
1952	BC	81	158	6	35	2	0	0	21	8	3	1	.222	70	-7
1953	Mus	62	112	6	27	3	0	1	13	7	5	1	.241	111	-2
1954	Rck-GR	37	43	3	15	1	0	3	9	3	1	0	.349	229	3
Total	7	331	629	29	133	12	0	4	67	51	42	3	.211	90	-21

Hatzell, Beverly - P

YEAR	TEAM	G	AB	R	H	2B	3B	HR	RBI	BB	SO	SB	AVG	PRO+	BR
1950	Rac	26	37	3	3	0	0	0	1	6	13	0	.081	11	-3
1951	BC-Peo	24	35	4	2	0	0	0	2	5	9	1	.057	-12	-4
Total	2	50	72	7	5	0	0	0	3	11	22	1	.069	-0	-7

Havlish, Jean - SS

YEAR	TEAM	G	AB	R	H	2B	3B	HR	RBI	BB	SO	SB	AVG	PRO+	BR
1951	Kal														
1952	FW														
1953	FW	104	344	35	65	4	0	0	22	35	40	14	.189	60	-16
1954	FW	89	276	39	70	13	0	4	36	46	16	9	.254	120	0
Total	4	193	620	74	135	17	0	4	58	81	56	23	.218	89	-16

Haylett, Alice - P

YEAR	TEAM	G	AB	R	H	2B	3B	HR	RBI	BB	SO	SB	AVG	PRO+	BR
1946	GR	41	104	9	23	1	1	0	5	8	11	1	.221	111	-2
1947	GR	31	90	6	17	4	0	0	12	3	7	1	.189	99	-3
1948	GR	33	93	7	13	0	0	0	3	12	7	2	.140	42	-6
1949	GR	32	83	7	11	1	1	0	5	7	5	0	.133	54	-6
Total	4	137	370	29	64	6	2	0	25	30	30	2	.173	78	-16

Headin, Irene - P

YEAR	TEAM	G	AB	R	H	2B	3B	HR	RBI	BB	SO	SB	AVG	PRO+	BR
1945	SB	1	0	0										.000	-99	0

Heafner, Ruby - C

YEAR	TEAM	G	AB	R	H	2B	3B	HR	RBI	BB	SO	SB	AVG	PRO+	BR
1946	Rck	47	128	16	18	1	2	0	8	23	24	6	.141	78	-5
1947	FW	65	198	14	34	7	0	0	14	20	36	5	.172	95	-4
1948	FW	59	156	9	25	1	0	0	8	15	33	3	.160	58	-8
1949	FW	50	146	5	25	2	1	0	7	11	18	4	.171	76	-6
1950	Rac	65	204	19	43	3	1	0	17	22	28	4	.211	82	-7
1951	BC	56	127	20	26	3	0	0	3	33	15	6	.205	108	-2
Total	6	342	959	83	171	17	4	0	57	124	154	28	.178	84	-28

Healy, Dorothy - OF

YEAR	TEAM	G	AB	R	H	2B	3B	HR	RBI	BB	SO	SB	AVG	PRO+	BR
1948	Chi	12	41	2	5	1	0	0	7	4	2	0	.122	43	-3

Heim, Kay - C

YEAR	TEAM	G	AB	R	H	2B	3B	HR	RBI	BB	SO	SB	AVG	PRO+	BR
1943	Ken	25	77	8	9	0	1	0	3	8	6	6	.117	11	-8
1944	Ken	33	105	9	19	0	0	1	10	5	8	19	.181	73	-4
Total	2	58	182	17	28	0	1	1	16	8	14	25	.154	45	-12

Hickey, Lillian - OF

YEAR	TEAM	G	AB	R	H	2B	3B	HR	RBI	BB	SO	SB	AVG	PRO+	BR
1946	Ken	21	61	3	13	0	0	1	1	3	13	1	.213	68	-3

Hickson, Irene - C

YEAR	TEAM	G	AB	R	H	2B	3B	HR	RBI	BB	SO	SB	AVG	PRO+	BR
1943	Rac	68	193	62	54	4	4	1	24	34	16	68	.280	178	21
1944	Rac	85	325	52	47	1	0	0	9	35	15	76	.145	47	-11
1945	Rac	97	318	36	55	5	1	0	5	21	4	33	.173	107	5
1946	Rac	46	147	34	28	1	1	1	12	39	7	41	.190	132	10
1947	Rac	101	309	34	47	6	2	0	21	42	23	49	.152	92	1
1948	Rac	97	287	37	47	3	5	0	16	51	48	23	.164	105	-0
1949	Rac	83	210	23	27	3	1	0	8	42	24	16	.129	71	-5
1950	Rac	33	64	17	11	0	0	1	9	25	7	5	.172	120	3
1951	Ken	11	23	1	5	0	0	0	5	5	0	2	.217	92	0
Total	9	621	1876	296	321	23	14	3	109	294	144	313	.171	101	24

Hill

YEAR	TEAM	G	AB	R	H	2B	3B	HR	RBI	BB	SO	SB	AVG	PRO+	BR
1952	SB														

Hill, Joyce (m. Westerman 1951) - C/1B

YEAR	TEAM	G	AB	R	H	2B	3B	HR	RBI	BB	SO	SB	AVG	PRO+	BR
1945	GR	9	18	2										.111	-10	-2
1946	SB-FW	21	57	6	7	0	0	0	3	9	12	7	.123	36	-3
1947	Peo	90	251	24	57	5	2	0	19	36	26	16	.227	148	9
1948	Peo-Rac	89	252	29	47	6	5	0	28	43	37	18	.187	131	4
1949	Rac	64	121	16	23	1	2	0	12	32	12	4	.190	138	5
1950	Peo	70	197	26	50	4	2	0	19	45	29	4	.254	140	8
1951	Peo	102	355	51	86	13	3	0	50	68	19	20	.242	138	11
1952	SB	86	264	39	73	5	0	0	36	59	14	12	.277	138	14
Total	8	531	1515	191	345	34	14	0	167	292	149	81	.228	133	44

Hlavaty, Lillian - OF

YEAR	TEAM	G	AB	R	H	2B	3B	HR	RBI	BB	SO	SB	AVG	PRO+	BR
1951	Rck	47	127	13	24	3	0	0	5	20	34	7	.189	78	-4

Hoffman, Barbara - 3B

YEAR	TEAM	G	AB	R	H	2B	3B	HR	RBI	BB	SO	SB	AVG	PRO+	BR
1951	SB	46	137	20	29	2	3	0	11	25	20	9	.212	123	2
1952	SB	49	134	11	23	3	1	1	11	20	30	3	.172	85	-5
Total	2	95	271	31	52	5	4	1	22	45	50	12	.192	104	-3

Hoffman, Nadine

YEAR	TEAM	G	AB	R	H	2B	3B	HR	RBI	BB	SO	SB	AVG	PRO+	BR
1946	Peo	2	4	0										.000	-99	-1

Hohlmayer, Alice - 1B

YEAR	TEAM	G	AB	R	H	2B	3B	HR	RBI	BB	SO	SB	AVG	PRO+	BR
1946	Ken	110	372	24	83	10	6	0	33	24	63	21	.223	129	-3
1947	Ken	90	298	24	62	7	6	0	24	22	47	8	.208	138	1
1948	Ken	81	243	10	35	4	1	1	17	28	30	2	.144	69	-13
1949	Mus	98	310	13	55	3	1	0	18	39	23	10	.177	83	-8
1950	Kal-Peo	63	158	6	38	5	0	2	28	18	19	1	.241	131	0
1951	Peo	44	105	8	28	6	1	0	8	7	10	1	.267	150	7
Total	6	486	1486	85	301	35	15	3	128	138	192	43	.203	113	-21

Holda, Mary - 2B

YEAR	TEAM	G	AB	R	H	2B	3B	HR	RBI	BB	SO	SB	AVG	PRO+	BR
1943	SB	29	73	9	15	0	0	0	6	4	11	8	.205	53	-4

Holderness, Joan - OF

YEAR	TEAM	G	AB	R	H	2B	3B	HR	RBI	BB	SO	SB	AVG	PRO+	BR
1949	Ken	34	48	2	8	0	0	0	8	2	8	1	.167	42	-3
1950	Ken-GR	62	175	10	26	1	1	0	10	20	10	3	.149	39	-14
1951	GR-BC	23	61	1	9	1	0	0	10	8	3	0	.148	42	-5
Total	3	119	284	13	43	2	1	0	28	30	21	4	.151	40	-21

Holgerson, Margaret (played as Silvestri 1949-52) - P

YEAR	TEAM	G	AB	R	H	2B	3B	HR	RBI	BB	SO	SB	AVG	PRO+	BR
1946	Rck	61	158	17	30	0	0	0	7	4	1	21	.190	52	-8
1947	Rck	40	111	8	22	0	3	0	7	5	10	5	.198	116	-2
1948	Rck	38	93	4	10	0	2	0	9	5	13	1	.108	32	-9
1949	Rck-Mus	17	41	0	6	0	0	0	1	2	3	1	.146	34	-3
1950	Mus-GR	39	80	6	14	0	0	0	8	4	4	0	.175	30	-7
1951	GR	30	78	9	14	0	0	0	5	4	1	1	.179	41	-6
1952	GR	27	61	3	11	1	1	0	7	0	2	1	.180	56	-5
Total	7	252	622	47	107	1	6	0	44	24	34	30	.172	54	-38

Holle, Mable - OF

YEAR	TEAM	G	AB	R	H	2B	3B	HR	RBI	BB	SO	SB	AVG	PRO+	BR
1943	SB	90	332	37	66	3	1	0	21	22	33	24	.199	64	-16

Hoover, Alice

YEAR	TEAM	G	AB	R	H	2B	3B	HR	RBI	BB	SO	SB	AVG	PRO+	BR
1948	FW	6	4	0										.000	-99	-1

Horstman, Katie - 3B/P

YEAR	TEAM	G	AB	R	H	2B	3B	HR	RBI	BB	SO	SB	AVG	PRO+	BR
1951	FW	38	117	13	30	6	0	1	13	6	18	3	.256	137	-0
1952	FW	90	312	36	78	11	5	2	36	28	20	3	.250	143	3
1953	FW	94	329	47	96	12	7	4	46	37	13	14	.292	191	19
1954	FW	86	299	68	98	13	2	16	55	33	10	8	.328	217	24
Total	4	308	1057	164	302	42	14	23	150	104	61	28	.286	180	45

Hosbein, Marion

YEAR	TEAM	G	AB	R	H	2B	3B	HR	RBI	BB	SO	SB	AVG	PRO+	BR
1954	SB														

Huff, Anna (see Kunkel)

Hunter, Dorothy - 1B

YEAR	TEAM	G	AB	R	H	2B	3B	HR	RBI	BB	SO	SB	AVG	PRO+	BR
1943	Rac	82	254	27	57	6	5	1	28	16	18	9	.224	120	-5

Hutchison, Anna May - P/C

YEAR	TEAM	G	AB	R	H	2B	3B	HR	RBI	BB	SO	SB	AVG	PRO+	BR
1944	Rac	52	115	7	22	2	0	0	9	2	11	1	.191	65	-8
1945	Rac	24	55	2	7	1	2	0	0	2	0	4	.127	101	-2
1946	Rac	52	144	11	16	1	0	0	9	16	15	3	.111	20	-13
1947	Rac	44	123	5	18	1	0	0	5	5	11	1	.146	37	-9
1948	Rac	14	21	0	4	0	0	0	3	1	0	0	.190	58	-1
1949	Mus	26	53	1	11	0	0	0	3	2	6	0	.208	77	-2
1951	Ken														
Total	7	212	511		78								.153	36	-35

Jackson, Lillian - OF

YEAR	TEAM	G	AB	R	H	2B	3B	HR	RBI	BB	SO	SB	AVG	PRO+	BR
1944	Min	58	179	23	36	1	2	0	19	13	11	24	.201	95	-3
1945	FW	62	188	24	23	1	0	1	2	12	2	28	.122	55	-6
Total	2	120	367	47	59	2	2	1	21	25	13	52	.161	75	-9

Jacobs, Jane - P

YEAR	TEAM	G	AB	R	H	2B	3B	HR	RBI	BB	SO	SB	AVG	PRO+	BR
1944	Rac	31	79	3	7	0	0	0	4	4	9	0	.089	-13	-9
1945	Rac	21	43	2	7	0	3	1	1	4	2	6	.163	234	3
1946	Peo	23	58	1	6	0	0	0	1	4	10	1	.103	6	-6
1947	Rac	13	24	1	4	0	0	0	0	2	4	0	.167	32	-2
Total	4	88	204	7	24	0	3	1	6	12	25	16	.118	49	-14

Jacobs, Janet - SS

YEAR	TEAM	G	AB	R	H	2B	3B	HR	RBI	BB	SO	SB	AVG	PRO+	BR
1945	Rac	38	100	6	17	1	0	2	3	7	1	15	.170	137	3

Jameson, Janet

YEAR	TEAM	G	AB	R	H	2B	3B	HR	RBI	BB	SO	SB	AVG	PRO+	BR
1948	SB	1	1	0									.000	-99	-0

Jameson, Shirley - OF

YEAR	TEAM	G	AB	R	H	2B	3B	HR	RBI	BB	SO	SB	AVG	PRO+	BR
1943	Ken	105	399	111	108	6	10	4	32	66	7	126	.271	179	37
1944	Ken	85	288	64	73	4	2	2	23	78	6	119	.253	184	37
1945	Ken	91	307	41	58	4	4	1	5	9	2	13	.189	148	12
1946	Ken	104	374	62	74	2	3	1	9	68	12	98	.198	111	12
Total	4	385	1368	278	313	16	19	8	69	221	27	356	.229	156	98

Janssen, Frances - P

YEAR	TEAM	G	AB	R	H	2B	3B	HR	RBI	BB	SO	SB	AVG	PRO+	BR
1948	GR	11	20	2	5	0	0	0	4	2	4	0	.250	114	-0
1950	Peo-Kal-FW	19	33	0	6	1	0	0	0	1	6	0	.182	49	-3
1951	FW-BC-Kal	26	52	4	6	2	0	0	1	4	8	0	.115	24	-6
1952	BC														
Total	4	56	105		17								.162	29	-8

Jaykoski, Joan - OF

YEAR	TEAM	G	AB	R	H	2B	3B	HR	RBI	BB	SO	SB	AVG	PRO+	BR
1951	Ken	30	42	5	9	0	0	0	5	9	12	2	.214	97	1
1952	GR	15	41	2	1	0	0	0	0	5	7	0	.024	-50	-7
Total	2	45	83	7	10	0	0	0	5	14	19	2	.120	26	-6

Jenkins, Marilyn - C

YEAR	TEAM	G	AB	R	H	2B	3B	HR	RBI	BB	SO	SB	AVG	PRO+	BR
1952	GR	19	30	1	4	1	0	0	2	3	6	0	.133	42	-2
1953	GR	69	203	17	42	4	2	0	13	22	25	9	.207	88	-5
1954	GR	53	132	20	24	3	0	1	18	25	12	2	.182	63	-8
Total	3	141	365	38	70	8	2	1	33	50	43	11	.192	74	-16

Jewitt, Christine - OF

YEAR	TEAM	G	AB	R	H	2B	3B	HR	RBI	BB	SO	SB	AVG	PRO+	BR
1948	Ken	117	430	46	93	7	4	3	35	27	50	51	.216	126	3
1949	Ken-Peo	85	247	24	51	0	0	0	15	16	23	17	.206	83	-5
Total	2	202	677	70	144	7	4	3	50	43	73	68	.213	111	-2

Jinright, Migdalia (see Perez)

Jochum, Betsy - OF

YEAR	TEAM	G	AB	R	H	2B	3B	HR	RBI	BB	SO	SB	AVG	PRO+	BR
1943	SB	101	439	70	120	12	7	1	35	27	21	66	.273	143	12
1944	SB	112	433	72	128	5	1	2	23	40	16	127	.296	171	33
1945	SB	110	388	40	92	6	5	1	10	36	1	18	.237	171	19
1946	SB	110	400	64	100	7	7	2	63	44	10	73	.250	162	18
1947	SB	105	402	36	85	11	5	0	42	17	15	44	.211	121	-0
1948	SB	107	339	25	66	2	4	1	33	16	24	23	.195	91	-10
Total	6	645	2401	307	591	43	29	7	206	180	87	351	.246	145	72

Jogerst, Donna - P

YEAR	TEAM	G	AB	R	H	2B	3B	HR	RBI	BB	SO	SB	AVG	PRO+	BR
1952	Rck														

Johnson, Arleene - 3B

YEAR	TEAM	G	AB	R	H	2B	3B	HR	RBI	BB	SO	SB	AVG	PRO+	BR
1945	FW	15	18	2	4	0	1	0	0	0	0	7	.222	183	1
1946	Mus	112	393	35	64	5	6	0	31	35	67	38	.163	80	-15
1947	Mus	112	345	32	57	5	0	2	22	34	73	34	.165	85	-7
1948	FW-Mus	115	373	34	58	4	6	1	38	43	77	51	.155	86	-8
Total	4	354	1129	103	183	14	13	3	91	112	217	130	.162	85	-29

Jones, Doris

YEAR	TEAM	G	AB	R	H	2B	3B	HR	RBI	BB	SO	SB	AVG	PRO+	BR
1945	SB	6	15	0									.000	-99	-3

Jones, Marguerite - P

YEAR	TEAM	G	AB	R	H	2B	3B	HR	RBI	BB	SO	SB	AVG	PRO+	BR
1944	Min-Rck	33	68	4	11	1	1	0	6	7	20	1	.162	84	-4

Jones, Marilyn - C

YEAR	TEAM	G	AB	R	H	2B	3B	HR	RBI	BB	SO	SB	AVG	PRO+	BR
1948	Ken	25	50	4	2	0	0	0	2	5	11	0	.040	-34	-7
1949	FW	3	3	0									.000	-99	-1
1950	Rck	31	69	7	14	0	0	0	6	7	12	2	.203	65	-1
1951	Rck-BC	58	139	13	24	3	0	0	6	17	19	2	.173	64	-7
1952	BC	37	65	3	6	2	0	0	3	10	20	0	.092	22	-6
1953	Mus	37	87	7	17	1	0	0	3	14	12	0	.195	73	-3
1954	FW	31	68	9	13	1	0	0	8	13	5	0	.191	57	-4
Total	7	222	481	43	76	7	0	0	28	66	79	4	.158	49	-31

Junor, Daisy - OF

YEAR	TEAM	G	AB	R	H	2B	3B	HR	RBI	BB	SO	SB	AVG	PRO+	BR
1946	SB	99	322	30	60	6	1	0	22	21	35	33	.186	76	-12
1947	SB	90	248	17	33	2	1	0	14	16	41	17	.133	41	-15
1948	SB-Spg	98	248	23	31	2	1	0	15	26	49	19	.125	38	-16
1949	FW	9	29		5								.172	35	-2
Total	4	296	847		129								.152	40	-45

Jurgensmeier, Margaret

YEAR	TEAM	G	AB	R	H	2B	3B	HR	RBI	BB	SO	SB	AVG	PRO+	BR
1951	Rck														

Kabick, Josephine - P

YEAR	TEAM	G	AB	R	H	2B	3B	HR	RBI	BB	SO	SB	AVG	PRO+	BR
1944	Mil	46	128	9	22	0	2	0	12	6	14	4	.172	70	-8
1945	GR	35	99	6	12	4	0	0	6	4	0	15	.121	54	-4
1946	GR-Ken	40	114	5	19	2	0	0	3	2	8	0	.167	45	-9
1947	Peo	31	80	2	10	1	0	0	1	3	13	2	.125	24	-7
Total	4	152	421	22	63	7	2	0	22	15	35	21	.150	51	-28

Kamenshek, Dorothy - 1B

YEAR	TEAM	G	AB	R	H	2B	3B	HR	RBI	BB	SO	SB	AVG	PRO+	BR
1943	Rck	101	395	58	107	6	3	3	39	33	6	42	.271	138	8
1944	Rck	113	447	60	115	8	5	1	23	34	6	74	.257	151	13
1945	Rck	109	419	80	115	11	2	0	6	26	1	8	.274	189	27
1946	Rck	107	408	78	129	7	1	1	22	39	10	109	.316	180	36
1947	Rck	101	366	52	112	10	8	6	32	35	6	66	.306	257	40
1948	Rck	124	448	89	128	8	5	2	35	72	14	94	.286	192	43
1949	Rck	111	385	62	98	8	4	0	25	89	8	69	.255	178	35
1950	Rck	94	341	64	114	14	3	0	26	59	9	39	.334	193	34
1951	Rck	97	339	90	117	12	9	0	34	80	7	63	.345	230	50
1953	Rck	55	188	34	55	5	1	0	18	27	7	15	.293	146	9
Total	10	1012	3736	667	1090	89	41	13	260	494	74	579	.292	186	294

Kaufman, Joan - 3B

YEAR	TEAM	G	AB	R	H	2B	3B	HR	RBI	BB	SO	SB	AVG	PRO+	BR
1954	Rck	43	97	3	13	3	0	0	5	9	13	0	.134	12	-13

Kazmierczak, Marie - OF

YEAR	TEAM	G	AB	R	H	2B	3B	HR	RBI	BB	SO	SB	AVG	PRO+	BR
1944	Mil-Rac-Ken	16	31	3	1	0	0	0	2	4	4	2	.032	-37	-4

Keagle, Merle "Pat" - OF/SS

YEAR	TEAM	G	AB	R	H	2B	3B	HR	RBI	BB	SO	SB	AVG	PRO+	BR
1944	Mil	109	406	72	107	7	5	7	47	45	21	122	.264	197	32
1946	GR	112	409	69	116	15	4	2	59	47	24	107	.284	189	34
1948	GR	116	423	75	106	11	9	3	27	61	41	85	.251	193	35
Total	3	337	1238	216	329	33	18	12	133	153	86	314	.266	193	101

Keller

YEAR	TEAM	G	AB	R	H	2B	3B	HR	RBI	BB	SO	SB	AVG	PRO+	BR
1951	Kal														

Kelley, Jackie - OF/3B

YEAR	TEAM	G	AB	R	H	2B	3B	HR	RBI	BB	SO	SB	AVG	PRO+	BR
1947	SB	44	107	7	19	3	2	0	13	9	28	4	.178	114	-2
1948	Chi	54	145	7	20	1	2	0	6	11	27	5	.138	53	-10
1949	Rck-Peo	41	117	5	19	3	0	0	5	5	16	8	.162	63	-6
1950	Rck	69	217	31	49	7	3	2	18	22	16	13	.226	132	0
1951	Rck	107	380	37	85	14	6	2	52	33	33	31	.224	130	1
1952	Rck	42	122	12	22	5	4	0	15	13	17	3	.180	115	-3
1953	Rck	69	219	13	56	9	2	1	22	12	29	6	.256	131	-0
Total	7	426	1307	112	270	42	19	5	131	105	166	70	.207	115	-19

Kellogg, Vivian - 1B

YEAR	TEAM	G	AB	R	H	2B	3B	HR	RBI	BB	SO	SB	AVG	PRO+	BR
1944	Min	111	382	20	77	8	7	3	46	16	16	13	.202	128	-11
1945	FW	107	383	31	82	10	6	1	9	38	2	17	.214	158	10
1946	FW	89	324	25	62	6	5	0	31	18	15	8	.191	95	-13
1947	FW	100	354	18	73	10	6	0	23	17	19	21	.206	128	-2
1947	SB	1	4		1								.250	98	-0
1948	FW	126	472	52	117	9	9	0	43	39	39	19	.248	152	8
1949	FW	107	397	36	98	10	3	1	34	29	24	10	.247	150	7
1950	FW	107	397	37	91	13	3	3	49	27	26	9	.229	116	-7
Total	8	748	2713	219	601	66	39	8	235	184	141	97	.222	133	-8

Kemmerer, Beatrice

YEAR	TEAM	G	AB	R	H	2B	3B	HR	RBI	BB	SO	SB	AVG	PRO+	BR
1951	SB														

Kerrigan, Margarita

YEAR	TEAM	G	AB	R	H	2B	3B	HR	RBI	BB	SO	SB	AVG	PRO+	BR
1951	Rck														

Kerwin, Irene - 1B

YEAR	TEAM	G	AB	R	H	2B	3B	HR	RBI	BB	SO	SB	AVG	PRO+	BR
1949	Peo	27	73	2	10	0	0	0	1	7	12	2	.137	39	-4

Ketola, Helen - 3B

YEAR	TEAM	G	AB	R	H	2B	3B	HR	RBI	BB	SO	SB	AVG	PRO+	BR
1950	FW	31	61	8	8	0	0	0	9	11	14	0	.131	30	-5

Key, Dorothy (see Ferguson)

Keyes, Erma - OF

YEAR	TEAM	G	AB	R	H	2B	3B	HR	RBI	BB	SO	SB	AVG	PRO+	BR
1951	BC-Peo	89	316	23	67	0	0	0	23	20	23	7	.212	63	-16

Kidd, Glenna Sue - P

YEAR	TEAM	G	AB	R	H	2B	3B	HR	RBI	BB	SO	SB	AVG	PRO+	BR
1950	Mus-Peo-SB	26	49	5	10	2	0	0	1	5	3	0	.204	86	-2
1951	SB-BC	29	64	8	10	1	0	0	3	10	4	1	.156	58	-3
1952	SB	30	80	8	15	1	0	0	6	5	6	0	.188	48	-6
1953	SB	66	198	17	37	4	0	0	17	12	16	1	.187	52	-14
1954	SB	60	172	18	41	3	0	5	32	7	11	2	.238	97	-9
Total	5	211	563	56	113	11	0	5	59	39	40	4	.201	70	-33

Kimball, Mary Ellen

YEAR	TEAM	G	AB	R	H	2B	3B	HR	RBI	BB	SO	SB	AVG	PRO+	BR
1948	Rac	2	4	0									.000	-99	-1

King

YEAR	TEAM	G	AB	R	H	2B	3B	HR	RBI	BB	SO	SB	AVG	PRO+	BR
1951	Ken														

Kissel, Audrey - 2B

YEAR	TEAM	G	AB	R	H	2B	3B	HR	RBI	BB	SO	SB	AVG	PRO+	BR
1944	Min	102	360	47	68	1	3	1	19	32	12	47	.189	90	-8

Kline, Maxine - P

YEAR	TEAM	G	AB	R	H	2B	3B	HR	RBI	BB	SO	SB	AVG	PRO+	BR
1948	FW	25	56	3	9	1	1	0	4	7	3	0	.161	100	-1
1949	FW	28	82	10	19	1	1	0	4	14	3	5	.232	146	3
1950	FW	37	111	15	24	8	0	1	10	7	5	0	.216	129	-2
1951	FW	26	79	9	19	3	0	0	3	6	4	1	.241	108	-1
1952	FW	28	89	9	14	1	0	0	5	6	6	1	.157	31	-8
1953	FW	37	90	8	14	4	0	0	6	9	1	1	.156	59	-6
1954	FW	38	85	13	16	3	0	2	8	7	3	0	.188	81	-6
Total	7	219	592	67	115	21	2	3	40	56	25	8	.194	92	-22

Klosowski, Delores - 1B

YEAR	TEAM	G	AB	R	H	2B	3B	HR	RBI	BB	SO	SB	AVG	PRO+	BR
1944	Mil	20	72	6	16	1	0	0	12	7	6	10	.222	105	-0
1945	SB	19	65	2	11	1	4	0	3	4	0	9	.169	180	2
Total	2	39	137	8	27	2	4	0	15	11	6	19	.197	140	2

Knezovich, Ruby - C

YEAR	TEAM	G	AB	R	H	2B	3B	HR	RBI	BB	SO	SB	AVG	PRO+	BR
1944	Rac	17	41	4	6	0	0	0	2	3	3	1	.146	33	-3

Kobuczewski, Theresa - P

YEAR	TEAM	G	AB	R	H	2B	3B	HR	RBI	BB	SO	SB	AVG	PRO+	BR
1946	Ken	21	45	3	10	0	0	0	3	3	9	1	.222	83	-2
1947	Ken-FW	31	79	12	20	1	0	1	3	2	3	5	.253	147	1
1948	Mus	2	3	0									.000	-99	-1
Total	3	54	127		30								.236	93	-1

Koehn, Phyllis - OF/P

YEAR	TEAM	G	AB	R	H	2B	3B	HR	RBI	BB	SO	SB	AVG	PRO+	BR
1943	Ken	95	353	56	84	9	6	4	52	14	21	37	.238	135	-1
1944	Ken	114	428	62	91	6	6	1	42	15	13	50	.213	114	-7
1945	Ken-SB	115	408	32	95	5	3	1	4	43	0	19	.233	154	16
1946	SB	48	151	11	24	5	1	0	4	8	15	1	.159	67	-11
1947	SB	49	128	4	20	1	3	0	11	7	13	1	.156	82	-6
1948	SB-Peo-Rac	79	256	22	41	6	2	0	21	14	39	9	.160	67	-15
1949	Rac-FW	30	56	1	9	2	0	0	1	4	5	0	.161	72	-3
1950	GR	57	166	11	26	3	0	0	11	11	18	3	.157	36	-14
Total	8	587	1946	199	390	37	21	6	156	116	124	120	.200	106	-40

Kotil, Arlene - 1B

YEAR	TEAM	G	AB	R	H	2B	3B	HR	RBI	BB	SO	SB	AVG	PRO+	BR
1950	Mus-SB	83	244	21	50	5	1	0	21	30	64	10	.205	85	-7
1951	SB														
Total	2	83	244		50								.205	66	-7

Kotowicz, Irene - P/OF

YEAR	TEAM	G	AB	R	H	2B	3B	HR	RBI	BB	SO	SB	AVG	PRO+	BR
1945	Rck	52	154	14	25	2	0	0	6	12	0	15	.162	91	1
1946	FW	37	121	12	23	3	0	0	8	15	4	9	.190	90	-3
1947	FW-Ken	23	55	2	7	1	0	0	2	4	4	0	.127	36	-4
1948	Rac	39	106	4	9	0	1	0	7	6	14	0	.085	-5	-13
1949	Rac	26	61	8	6	0	1	0	3	8	11	2	.098	41	-4
1950	Rac	11	21	5	3	0	0	0	0	3	4	1	.143	30	-2
Total	6	188	518	45	73	6	2	0	26	48	37	27	.141	58	-25

YEAR	TEAM	G	AB	R	H	2B	3B	HR	RBI	BB	SO	SB	AVG	PRO+	BR
Krick, Jaynne - P/3B															
1948	Spg-SB	52	131	13	25	2	0	0	9	15	26	1	.191	94	-2
1949	SB	5	9		2								.222	74	-0
1951	BC-Peo	83	267	20	56	6	1	0	21	22	44	2	.210	84	-10
1952	GR	54	117	13	19	0	1	0	6	8	17	0	.162	42	-9
1953	GR														
Total	5	194	524		102								.195	61	-22
Kruckel, Marie - OF															
1946	SB	5			0								.000	-99	-2
1947	FW	23	60	3	4	0	0	0	3	7	13	4	.067	-7	-6
1948	SB-Mus	22	48	4	8	0	0	0	5	3	7	2	.167	44	-3
1949	Mus	48	119	9	23	1	1	0	8	32	15	1	.193	127	3
Total	4	98	236	16	35	1	1	0	16	42	35	7	.148	70	-7
Kunkel, Anna (m. Hough 1951)															
1950	SB														
1951	Peo														
Kurys, Sophie - 2B															
1943	Rac	106	383	60	104	8	7	3	59	28	21	44	.272	155	11
1944	Rac	116	394	87	96	7	3	1	60	69	32	166	.244	158	37
1945	Rac	105	347	73	83	6	2	1	19	15	5	27	.239	176	25
1946	Rac	113	392	117	112	5	6	3	33	93	31	201	.286	209	65
1947	Rac	112	432	81	99	8	6	2	19	49	31	142	.229	159	31
1948	Rac	124	444	97	112	12	5	3	22	81	21	172	.252	187	53
1949	Rac	111	416	70	102	3	3	2	26	59	19	137	.245	155	34
1950	Rac	110	424	95	130	22	6	7	42	68	18	120	.307	219	54
1952	BC	17	66	8	21	0	1	0	3	6	4	17	.318	148	5
Total	9	914	3298	688	859	71	39	22	283	468	182	1026	.260	178	315
Ladd, Jean															
1951	Ken														
Lake															
1953	Mus														
Lawson, Mary - OF															
1946	Peo	25	57	3	6	2	0	0	1	1	3	1	.105	15	-6
Leduc, Noella - P															
1951	Peo														
1952	BC	34	59	3	10	3	0	0	2	2	12	1	.169	54	-5
1953	Mus	59	90	12	13	1	0	0	4	5	16	1	.144	18	-9
1954	FW	51	118	18	29	2	0	2	15	16	17	2	.246	99	-3
Total	4	144	267	33	52	6	0	2	21	23	45	4	.195	65	-17
Lee, Annabelle - P															
1944	Min	59	147	15	25	2	0	0	9	20	4	9	.170	78	-5
1945	FW	31	74	4	7	2	0	0	6	6	1	6	.095	43	-4
1946	Peo	44	98	8	14	2	0	0	2	23	7	6	.143	79	-2
1947	Peo-GR	24	50	2	9	0	0	0	1	5	5	4	.180	80	-1
1948	FW	30	69	3	10	0	0	0	1	9	6	1	.145	47	-4
1949	Peo	25	51	4	5	1	0	0	1	12	3	1	.098	53	-2
1950	Peo	17	21	0	5	0	0	0	0	3	0	0	.238	90	-0
Total	7	230	510	36	75	7	0	0	20	78	26	29	.147	68	-17
Lee, Dolores - P															
1952	Rck														
1953	Rck	48	145	13	22	0	2	0	2	5	18	8	.152	30	-13
1954	Rck	45	101	7	17	0	0	0	7	5	3	1	.168	7	-13
Total	3	93	246	20	39	0	2	0	9	10	21	9	.159	19	-26
Lenard, Jo - OF															
1944	Rck	101	356	52	75	8	10	0	34	40	11	68	.211	148	8
1945	Rck	95	330	42	56	3	1	0	10	24	2	17	.170	94	-1
1946	Mus	83	273	34	51	5	2	0	25	50	19	60	.187	107	6
1947	Mus	111	391	58	102	10	1	0	38	39	30	83	.261	159	25
1948	Mus	120	421	70	89	10	6	0	56	50	57	64	.211	128	8
1949	Mus-Peo	110	383	41	79	4	2	0	29	43	25	44	.206	105	1
1950	Ken	110	389	52	101	9	4	1	51	59	19	53	.260	137	15
1951	Ken	100	333	43	75	4	2	0	32	68	16	46	.225	111	9
1952	SB	104	351	49	91	15	0	0	47	59	24	47	.259	133	15
1953	SB	66	193	24	37	5	0	0	15	39	16	19	.192	87	-1
Total	10	1000	3420	465	756	73	28	1	337	471	219	501	.221	123	86
Leonard, Rhoda															
1946	FW	9	21		2								.095	-29	-3
Lessing, Ruth "Tex" - C															
1944	Min	57	198	13	35	1	0	0	11	16	14	22	.177	61	-9
1945	FW	110	342	32	42	2	1	1	14	31	3	50	.123	71	-3
1946	GR	112	367	43	79	10	1	0	35	38	52	20	.215	121	-1
1947	GR	111	396	24	81	9	3	0	42	32	26	19	.205	115	-2
1948	GR	125	417	43	86	7	2	0	36	56	33	22	.206	109	-1
1949	GR	44	120	9	28	2	0	0	9	21	9	2	.233	137	3
Total	6	559	1840	164	351	31	7	2	147	194	137	135	.191	102	-13
Lester, Mary Louise - 2B															
1943	Ken	94	319	41	64	4	3	0	31	43	26	23	.201	90	-7
1944	Ken-SB	18	26	2	0	0	0	0	2	7	3	2	.000	-27	-3
Total	2	112	345	43	64	4	3	0	33	50	29	25	.186	82	-10
Liebrich, Barbara															
1948	Rck	3	4		1								.250	90	-0
Lionikis, Irene															
1948	GR	2	4		0								.000	-99	-1
Little, Alta - P															
1947	Mus	7	10		1								.100	-21	-1
1948	FW	9	37		5								.135	3	-4
Total	2	16	47		6								.128	-2	-5
Little, Olive - P															
1943	Rck	45	110	10	16	0	0	0	6	8	9	4	.145	20	-10
1945	Rck	34	110	6	18	3	2	0	5	9	0	16	.164	120	1

YEAR	TEAM	G	AB	R	H	2B	3B	HR	RBI	BB	SO	SB	AVG	PRO+	BR
1946	Rck	34	74	6	9	1	0	0	4	10	7	1	.122	36	-6
Total	3	113	294	22	43	4	2	0	15	27	16	21	.146	59	-15
Lobrovich, Clara - OF															
1947	Ken-Rck	81	258	22	54	3	2	0	21	23	27	15	.209	115	1
Lonetto, Sarah - OF/P															
1947	Rac	22	61	0	7	0	0	0	0	1	12	2	.115	-4	-6
1948	Mus	53	109	21	20	2	1	1	4	18	14	4	.183	127	0
1949	Mus	27	56	4	5	0	0	0	1	1	11	2	.089	-25	-7
Total	3	102	226	25	32	2	1	1	5	20	37	8	.142	58	-13
Lovell, Jean - C															
1948	Rck	52	151	6	33	1	0	0	8	4	19	3	.219	88	-4
1949	Rck	26	64	5	10	2	0	0	4	8	8	1	.156	81	-2
1950	Kal	94	289	22	64	8	2	1	30	36	22	4	.221	109	-4
1951	Kal-Ken	91	278	27	60	14	2	0	31	36	27	2	.216	118	-3
1952	Kal	55	142	10	35	5	2	1	12	11	16	0	.246	135	-0
1953	Kal	70	193	18	39	4	0	2	20	20	16	1	.202	91	-7
1954	Kal	82	259	43	74	5	0	21	69	25	25	0	.286	215	12
Total	7	470	1376	131	315	39	6	25	174	140	133	11	.229	131	-9
Lovett, Frances															
1946	Peo	1	2		0								.000	-99	-0
Luckey, Lillian - P															
1946	SB	8	15		2								.133	-0	-2
Luhtala, Shirley - 1B															
1950	Rac														
1951	BC-Rck	30	96	6	16	1	0	0	5	7	13	1	.167	38	-8
Total	2	30	96	6	16	1	0	0	5	7	13	1	.167	38	-8
Luna, Betty - P/OF															
1944	Rck	29	72	3	8	1	0	0	1	7	2	3	.111	23	-7
1945	SB	42	120	8	30	7	2	1	4	3	3	15	.250	218	8
1946	SB	48	116	9	24	1	3	0	12	12	11	2	.207	123	-2
1947	Rck	47	117	11	25	3	1	0	17	5	6	2	.214	114	-2
1948	Chi	97	257	22	61	7	6	1	26	28	32	24	.237	170	9
1949	FW	95	320	32	63	5	1	1	26	38	28	17	.197	107	-2
1950	FW-Kal	104	376	42	89	18	3	2	50	36	30	19	.237	131	0
Total	7	462	1378	127	300	42	16	5	136	129	112	82	.218	132	5
Machado, Helene - OF															
1946	Peo	73	252	13	46	7	1	0	14	11	9	6	.183	76	-14
1947	FW	90	301	26	67	6	3	0	23	24	23	27	.223	136	6
Total	2	163	553	39	113	13	4	0	37	35	32	33	.204	108	-8
MacLean, Lucella - C															
1943	SB	70	228	30	47	4	1	0	22	22	9	44	.206	82	-3
1944	SB	31	66	4	13	0	0	0	3	6	8	21	.197	74	0
Total	2	101	294	34	60	4	1	0	25	28	17	65	.204	81	-3
Maguire, Dorothy (m. Chapman 1948) - C															
1943	Rac	70	219	34	59	4	0	0	33	11	7	29	.269	135	4
1944	Mil	109	361	40	69	2	5	1	29	24	14	53	.191	97	-8
1945	GR	99	327	35	52	6	1	0	15	20	5	28	.159	96	0
1946	Mus	101	340	42	74	7	4	1	47	47	18	57	.218	137	11
1947	Mus	75	232	28	50	6	1	0	24	22	14	27	.216	126	4
1948	Mus	124	373	40	58	4	3	0	1	30	56	58	47	.155	70	-8
1949	Mus	17	54	3	8	1	0	0	2	5	10	3	.148	59	-3
Total	7	595	1906	222	370	30	15	3	180	185	126	244	.194	106	1
Mahon, Elizabeth "Lib" - OF															
1944	Min-Ken	107	341	43	72	6	2	3	38	60	18	31	.211	144	7
1945	SB	80	260	28	64	4	4	0	6	21	2	16	.246	176	15
1946	SB	112	399	90	110	7	7	1	72	64	15	114	.276	183	37
1947	SB	83	299	26	70	5	8	0	23	15	12	22	.234	155	5
1948	SB	117	422	59	109	12	4	2	65	48	26	38	.258	168	18
1949	SB	106	396	62	97	16	3	0	60	40	18	66	.245	158	18
1950	SB	69	256	23	63	11	1	1	37	19	15	17	.246	123	-0
1951	SB	104	364	69	98	14	5	1	68	60	19	53	.269	164	22
1952	SB	59	166	32	38	9	0	0	16	27	11	13	.229	121	3
Total	9	837	2903	432	721	84	34	8	385	354	136	370	.248	157	124
Mahoney, Marie - OF															
1947	SB	47	147	14	30	3	7	1	13	6	23	13	.204	187	4
1948	SB-FW	56	107	17	15	0	0	0	1	10	18	14	.140	32	-6
Total	2	103	254	31	45	3	7	1	14	16	41	27	.177	120	-2
Malach, Kay															
1947	FW	1	1		0								.000	-99	-0
Mandella, Lenora - P															
1951	Peo	17	27	1	3	2	0	0	4	2	10	0	.111	59	-2
Mansfield, Marie - P/OF															
1950	Rck	77	208	19	29	1	0	0	9	24	48	7	.139	30	-16
1951	GR	41	102	14	13	1	0	0	8	16	17	4	.127	36	-7
1952	Rck-BC	40	83	3	11	2	0	0	4	5	14	0	.133	28	-8
1953	Rck	53	124	11	22	3	1	0	11	13	30	1	.177	70	-7
1954	Rck	42	106	7	16	3	0	0	6	11	31	1	.151	24	-13
Total	5	253	623	54	91	10	1	0	38	69	140	13	.146	37	-50
Marks, Gloria - P															
1943	Rac	33	68	9	18	4	2	1	7	11	2		.265	208	3
Marlowe, Jean - P															
1948	Spg	32	83	4	9	1	1	0	2	10	24	2	.108	42	-6
1949	Ken	98	305	25	67	6	4	1	17	31	68	16	.220	139	3
1950	Ken	42	109	11	23	1	1	0	10	10	24	4	.211	103	-2
1951	Ken	66	178	17	31	4	0	0	16	31	27	4	.174	73	-6
1952	Kal	35	86	12	25	4	0	3	12	10	9	2	.291	212	6
1954	Kal	41	77	14	12	1	1	0	6	15	14	0	.156	96	-2
Total	6	314	838	83	167	17	6	7	68	117	166	28	.199	113	-7
Marrero, Mirtha - P															
1948	Chi	30	73	5	17	1	0	0	3	4	13	0	.233	107	-1

YEAR	TEAM	G	AB	R	H	2B	3B	HR	RBI	BB	SO	SB	AVG	PRO+	BR
1950	Kal	34	58	3	9	3	0	0	1	10	22	1	.155	87	-1
1951	FW	29	76	9	14	5	0	0	6	13	13	0	.184	107	-1
1952	BC	32	60	4	11	1	0	0	3	6	5	0	.183	56	-4
1953	Mus	10	11	2	2	0	0	0	1	2	5	1	.182	61	-0
Total	5	135	278	23	53	10	0	0	14	35	58	2	.191	90	-8

■ Marsh, Doris

1945	FW	3	5	0									.000	-99	-1

■ Marshall, Theda - 1B

1947	SB	113	362	27	51	10	5	0	31	24	79	27	.141	79	-14
1948	SB-Chi	125	392	26	55	6	4	0	17	36	60	7	.140	61	-23
Total	2	238	754	53	106	16	9	0	48	60	139	34	.141	69	-38

■ Mason, Pat

1953 GR

■ Matlock, Ruth - P

1950	FW	21	36	5	13	1	0	0	2	8	3	0	.361	199	4

■ Mattson, Jacquelin - C

1951	Ken	22	51	6	5	0	0	0	3	7	7	1	.098	1	-6

■ Matuzewski, Joan - OF

1953	SB	28	99	15	16	2	1	0	2	15	14	3	.162	70	-4

■ Mayer, Alice - OF

1948	SB	37	90	6	19	0	2	0	13	7	15	9	.211	118	0

■ McCarty, Mary - OF

1951	Peo	72	207	20	35	6	2	0	24	20	49	9	.169	71	-11

■ McCormick, Judy - P

1954 SB

■ McCreary, Ethel - OF

1943	Ken	71	231	29	58	6	1	1	36	18	7	11	.251	122	-0

■ McKenna, Betty - 3B

1951	FW-BC-Peo	61	159	20	24	6	1	0	14	45	32	9	.151	95	-0
1952	BC	11	26	2	2	0	0	0	2	7	0		.077	-28	-4
1953	Mus	94	293	31	63	8	1	0	28	48	38	16	.215	101	-1
Total	3	166	478	53	89	14	2	0	42	95	77	25	.186	93	-5

■ McKinley, Therese - OF

1949	Mus	37	101	10	10	0	0	0	4	9	18	7	.099	10	-8

■ Meacham, Mildred - 1B

1947	FW-Rac	2	2	0									.000	-99	-0
1948	Spg	95	289	26	52	4	3	0	10	32	37	24	.180	97	-3
Total	2	97	291	26	52	4	3	0	10	32	37	24	.179	95	-4

■ Measner, Hazel

1946	Rck	1	1	0									.000	-99	-0

■ Meier, Naomi "Sally" - OF

1946	Rck	103	374	44	93	2	2	1	49	23	26	33	.249	121	1
1947	Rck-FW	92	308	27	47	3	2	1	18	25	38	16	.153	74	-12
1948	Peo-Chi	127	450	54	100	5	3	0	47	39	63	55	.222	111	3
1949	Rac-Mus	107	354	30	83	3	3	0	32	44	43	29	.234	134	9
1950	Kal-FW	94	326	41	85	5	0	1	36	32	40	34	.261	112	4
1951	FW	21	75	12	18	3	0	0	14	8	8	8	.240	113	0
1952	FW-BC	55	163	13	41	6	2	0	11	11	13	6	.252	123	-0
1953	Mus	111	406	44	93	6	2	1	27	37	46	25	.229	94	-7
Total	8	710	2456	265	560	33	14	4	234	219	277	206	.228	109	-2

■ Melin, Berith - OF

1943	Rck	56	146	7	23	2	2	0	4	5	25	4	.158	45	-13

■ Menheer, Marie

1945	Rac	1	3	0									.000	-99	-1

■ Metesch, Bernice

1948	Rck	2	3	0									.000	-99	-1

■ Metrolis, Norma - C

1946	Mus	15	32	2	6	0	0	0	1	2	2	2	.188	77	-1
1947	Rac	18	47	2	7	0	0	0	2	4	4	2	.149	48	-2
1948	SB	12	25	2	4	0	0	0	2	3	1	2	.160	53	-1
1949	SB-Peo	15	27	1	4	0	0	0	3	4	4	1	.148	53	-1
1950	FW														
Total	5	60	131		21								.160	57	-5

■ Meyer, Anna

1944	Ken-Min	17	28	3	3	0	0	0	1	5	7	3	.107	29	-2

■ Meyer, Rita "Slats" (m. Moellering 1949) - SS

1946	Peo	103	339	26	57	0	3	0	19	22	32	19	.168	59	-20
1947	Peo	83	257	18	58	4	2	1	30	13	16	5	.226	127	-1
1948	Peo	122	457	49	106	12	1	2	68	31	32	45	.232	126	2
1949	Peo	91	332	28	63	8	1	0	23	17	16	7	.190	86	-13
Total	4	399	1385	121	284	24	7	3	140	83	96	76	.205	100	-31

■ Michelson, Darlene - OF

1943	Ken	47	161	18	22	1	2	0	29	19	20	10	.137	43	-12
1945	SB	3	4		1								.250	103	-0
Total	2	50	165		23								.139	52	-12

■ Middleton, Ruth - OF

1951	BC														
1952	BC	86	160	16	22	3	0	0	10	24	32	6	.138	40	-11
1953	Mus	36	72	9	9	0	0	0	2	7	9	2	.125	11	-7
Total	3	122	232	25	31	3	0	0	12	31	41	8	.134	31	-18

■ Miller, Polly

1948	Ken	1	0	0									.000	-99	0

■ Moczynski, Betty - OF

1943	Rck	59	208	15	36	1	2	1	27	17	13	13	.173	64	-12

■ Moellering, Rita (see Meyer)

■ Moffet, Jane - C/OF

1951	Kal	94	312	35	64	11	1	0	23	33	38	23	.205	91	-8
1952	Kal-BC	56	151	13	33	2	3	0	14	14	15	8	.219	101	-2
Total	2	150	463	48	97	13	4	0	37	47	53	31	.210	94	-10

■ Montalbano, Rose - 2B

1951	SB														
1952	BC-SB	12	32	5	6	1	0	0	7	5	10	0	.188	90	-0
1953	SB-Mus	26	63	8	15	1	0	0	2	10	10	3	.238	104	0
Total	3	38	95	13	21	2	0	0	9	15	20	3	.221	99	-0

■ Montgomery, Dorothy - 2B

1945	Rac	7	17		3								.176	43	-1
1946	Mus	26	53	5	11	0	0	0	2	7	3	3	.208	86	-1
Total	2	33	70	5	14	0	0	0	2	7	3	3	.200	46	-2

■ Moon, Dorothy - P

1946	Rck	18	30	2	5	0	1	0	2	0	6	0	.167	75	-2

■ Mooney, Georgette (see Vincent)

■ Moore, Dolores - 2B

1953	GR	56	156	11	31	3	0	0	18	13	20	4	.199	67	-7
1954	GR	93	321	35	83	5	0	3	39	20	19	6	.259	80	-15
Total	2	149	477	46	114	8	0	3	57	33	39	10	.239	76	-22

■ Moore, Elleanor - P

1951	Kal-FW	30	68	3	12	2	0	0	5	3	9	0	.176	51	-5
1952	FW-GR	29	52	5	10	1	0	0	3	2	5	0	.192	50	-4
1953	GR	41	91	13	21	2	1	0	13	7	18	0	.231	99	-2
1954	GR	53	104	16	39	1	5	1	13	6	5	1	.375	191	7
Total	4	153	315	37	82	6	6	1	34	18	37	1	.260	116	-5

■ Moore, Evelyn

1951 Kal

■ Moore, Mary Ann - 2B

1948	Rck	8	18		4								.222	69	-1
1952	BC	42	88	11	13	1	0	0	0	20	31	5	.148	57	-3
Total	2	50	106	11	17	1	0	0	0	20	31	5	.160	36	-4

■ Moraty, Mary - P

1946	FW	6	11		2								.182	36	-1

■ Morris, Carolyn - P

1944	Rck	46	126	9	18	1	2	0	8	13	28	4	.143	67	-8
1945	Rck	43	118	12	17	0	0	0	4	7	2	29	.144	48	-2
1946	Rck	49	122	4	23	1	1	0	11	14	18	2	.189	88	-4
Total	3	138	366	25	58	2	3	0	23	34	48	35	.158	68	-14

■ Mudge, Nancy - 2B

1949	FW	2	0		0								.000	-99	0
1951	Kal	85	251	32	42	6	0	0	17	35	61	17	.167	63	-11
1952	Kal-BC	61	153	22	23	2	0	0	4	33	54	8	.150	56	-6
1953	Mus	104	337	58	53	4	3	1	12	68	66	39	.157	74	-8
1954	Kal	98	353	74	82	13	0	7	22	68	52	33	.232	114	1
Total	5	350	1094	186	200	25	3	8	55	204	233	97	.183	83	-24

■ Mueller, Dorothy - P

1947	Peo	53	122	10	22	1	3	0	7	2	11	0	.180	95	-5
1948	Peo	35	102	7	18	1	2	0	8	10	15	1	.176	97	-3
1949	Peo	38	90	6	16	2	0	0	5	6	13	0	.178	76	-4
1950	SB	29	80	5	16	0	0	0	6	11	11	1	.200	65	-3
1951	SB	75	229	18	54	9	0	0	30	22	34	5	.236	109	-3
1952	SB	47	152	17	38	11	1	2	8	8	23	1	.250	160	1
1953	GR	41	81	5	17	3	0	0	8	7	7	0	.210	86	-3
Total	7	318	856	68	181	27	6	2	85	66	114	8	.211	106	-21

■ Naum, Dorothy - C/SS/P

1946	SB	31	72	13	14	0	0	0	8	10	10	12	.194	84	-0
1947	Ken	83	232	26	48	0	0	0	9	28	13	22	.207	98	1
1948	Ken	104	311	23	54	2	0	0	9	39	16	31	.174	72	-7
1949	Ken	81	172	23	27	3	0	0	13	28	11	22	.157	76	-2
1950	Ken	74	191	25	40	4	1	0	11	21	12	10	.209	86	-5
1951	Ken	103	331	30	60	5	2	0	13	52	18	23	.181	76	-10
1952	Kal	70	237	24	36	2	0	0	6	39	11	7	.152	46	-13
1953	Kal	32	74	10	14	2	0	0	3	8	2	0	.189	68	-4
Total	8	578	1620	184	293	18	3	0	72	225	93	127	.181	74	-41

■ Neal, Doris - 3B

1948	Spg	122	406	27	62	5	6	0	28	47	62	23	.153	79	-15
1949	GR	58	178	11	14	2	0	0	11	24	19	4	.079	9	-16
Total	2	180	584	38	76	7	6	0	39	71	81	27	.130	58	-31

■ Nearing, Merna

1943	Ken	7	8	1	0	0	0	0	0	0	3	0	.000	-99	-2

■ Nelson, Dodie - OF

1944	Rck	99	373	51	86	5	1	1	23	36	28	70	.231	125	8

■ Nelson, Helen - C

1943	Rck	83	214	36	45	4	0	0	20	35	16	15	.210	93	-2

■ Nelson, Mary

1954 FW

■ Nesbitt, Mary (m. Crews 1944, m. Wisham 1947) - P/1B

1943	Rac	73	186	34	52	7	4	2	29	20	7	27	.280	187	11
1944	Rac	74	168	14	37	5	3	2	23	24	13	10	.220	179	5
1945	Rac	66	135	20	43	2	2	0	1	11	1	11	.319	234	16
1947	Peo	110	399	47	104	9	11	3	43	32	32	34	.261	204	22
1948	Peo	126	438	69	128	24	12	3	58	82	41	64	.292	255	53
1950	Peo	49	162	25	55	8	4	3	22	34	13	14	.340	261	23
Total	6	498	1488	209	419	55	36	13	176	203	107	160	.282	224	130

■ Nicol, Helen (m. Fox 1945) - P

1943	Ken	62	154	15	34	3	5	2	18	9	8	8	.221	146	-1
1944	Ken	40	96	9	13	0	0	1	6	3	7	4	.135	40	-9

YEAR	TEAM	G	AB	R	H	2B	3B	HR	RBI	BB	SO	SB	AVG	PRO+	BR
1945	Ken	46	126	4	10	0	1	0	5	3	0	11	.079	-8	-12
1946	Ken	51	100	6	20	1	0	0	6	5	7	2	.200	75	-5
1947	Ken-Rck	26	56	3	7	1	0	0	0	2	8	1	.125	24	-5
1948	Rck	32	88	7	11	0	1	0	1	2	15	1	.125	19	-9
1949	Rck	26	69	3	14	2	0	0	4	3	13	1	.203	96	-2
1950	Rck	28	77	9	12	0	0	1	8	3	16	1	.156	40	-7
1951	Rck	28	83	7	12	1	1	0	2	2	12	0	.145	32	-8
1952	Rck	15	43	3	4	1	0	0	1	0	8	0	.093	-23	-7
Total	10	354	892	66	137	9	8	4	51	32	94	29	.154	55	-64

■ Niemiec, Dolly - 3B

YEAR	TEAM	G	AB	R	H	2B	3B	HR	RBI	BB	SO	SB	AVG	PRO+	BR
1950	GR	49	147	12	25	3	0	0	4	12	24	1	.170	50	-10
1951	GR-BC	29	65	8	6	0	0	0	6	12	7	0	.092	7	-7
Total	2	78	212	20	31	3	0	0	10	24	31	1	.146	37	-17

■ Nogay

YEAR	TEAM
1951	Kal

■ Nordquist, Helen - P/OF

YEAR	TEAM	G	AB	R	H	2B	3B	HR	RBI	BB	SO	SB	AVG	PRO+	BR
1951	Ken	82	240	23	38	7	4	1	12	22	40	7	.158	79	-14
1952	Rck	22	38	4	4	0	0	0	3	6	8	1	.105	14	-3
1953	Rck	21	43	2	5	0	0	0	0	2	6	1	.116	-4	-5
1954	SB	52	113	14	35	7	0	3	16	16	16	2	.310	174	6
Total	4	177	434	43	82	14	4	4	31	46	70	11	.189	94	-16

■ Normine, Cynthia

YEAR	TEAM
1950	Rck

■ Norris, Donna

YEAR	TEAM	G	AB	R	H	2B	3B	HR	RBI	BB	SO	SB	AVG	PRO+	BR
1953	FW-SB	16	36	3	3	1	0	0	2	1	13	0	.083	-18	-5

■ O'Brian, Penny - OF

YEAR	TEAM	G	AB	R	H	2B	3B	HR	RBI	BB	SO	SB	AVG	PRO+	BR
1945	FW	83	282	34	61	0	0	1	14	23	1	46	.216	118	9

■ O'Brien, Eileen

YEAR	TEAM	G	AB	R	H	AVG	PRO+	BR
1946	Mus	5	18		2	.111	-17	-2

■ O'Dowd, Anna Mae - C

YEAR	TEAM	G	AB	R	H	2B	3B	HR	RBI	BB	SO	SB	AVG	PRO+	BR
1949	Ken	3	1	0									.000	-99	-0
1950	Kal-Rac	41	106	6	23	2	0	0	10	9	7	1	.217	79	-4
1951	BC	26	68	7	9	1	0	0	5	7	8	0	.132	28	-6
Total	3	70	175	13	32	3	0	0	15	16	15	1	.183	58	-11

■ Ogden, Joanne - 2B

YEAR	TEAM	G	AB	R	H	2B	3B	HR	RBI	BB	SO	SB	AVG	PRO+	BR
1953	SB	42	87	11	22	2	0	0	5	4	9	6	.253	96	-1

■ O'Hara, Janice - OF/P

YEAR	TEAM	G	AB	R	H	2B	3B	HR	RBI	BB	SO	SB	AVG	PRO+	BR
1943	Ken	97	337	46	63	3	5	0	28	24	19	19	.187	72	-18
1944	Ken	95	321	31	49	3	0	1	26	30	16	37	.153	61	-15
1945	Ken	88	247	18	37	1	0	0	14	16	4	16	.150	66	-6
1946	Ken	66	168	15	25	2	0	0	10	8	18	6	.149	38	-13
1947	Ken	51	110	8	19	3	0	0	8	7	5	7	.173	122	-2
1948	Ken	25	47	2	5	0	0	0	2	5	6	2	.106	10	-4
1949	Ken	17	37	0	3	1	0	0	2	0	2	0	.081	-16	-5
Total	7	439	1267	120	201	13	8	1	90	90	70	87	.159	63	-63

■ Olinger, Marilyn - SS

YEAR	TEAM	G	AB	R	H	2B	3B	HR	RBI	BB	SO	SB	AVG	PRO+	BR
1948	Chi-GR	121	408	34	68	6	2	2	28	36	51	22	.167	86	-12
1949	GR	113	432	51	92	11	1	1	18	43	25	21	.213	122	1
1950	GR	113	396	78	89	7	1	1	21	58	25	35	.225	106	3
1951	GR	106	401	82	107	3	2	0	18	46	9	49	.267	122	12
1952	GR	47	173	22	35	1	1	0	10	18	1	14	.202	73	-5
1953	GR	99	365	67	88	6	0	0	20	54	16	56	.241	105	8
Total	6	599	2175	334	479	34	7	4	115	255	127	197	.220	105	8

■ Ortman, Dorothy - P

YEAR	TEAM	G	AB	R	H	2B	3B	HR	RBI	BB	SO	SB	AVG	PRO+	BR
1944	Rac	16	34	3	2	0	0	0	5	7	7	3	.059	1	-3

■ Overleese, Jo Anne - 2B

YEAR	TEAM	G	AB	R	H	2B	3B	HR	RBI	BB	SO	SB	AVG	PRO+	BR
1946	Mus-Peo	54	174	13	31	4	1	0	15	25	21	6	.178	100	-3

■ Paire, Lavonne "Pepper" - C/SS

YEAR	TEAM	G	AB	R	H	2B	3B	HR	RBI	BB	SO	SB	AVG	PRO+	BR
1944	Min	60	220	28	53	8	2	0	20	20	8	5	.241	151	2
1945	FW	111	392	29	77	6	0	0	14	39	4	6	.196	119	5
1946	Rac	101	383	31	91	10	4	0	59	33	15	13	.238	134	0
1947	Rac	112	430	35	97	14	0	0	50	29	17	18	.226	124	0
1948	GR	114	377	24	70	8	4	0	27	34	36	2	.186	98	-11
1949	GR	110	371	21	76	2	3	0	37	46	11	12	.205	110	-1
1950	GR	110	370	35	92	16	0	1	70	35	10	15	.249	122	9
1951	GR	81	261	21	69	6	2	1	56	38	5	5	.264	146	8
1952	GR-FW	67	200	13	46	3	0	0	18	17	2	0	.230	85	-5
1953	FW	60	160	14	42	6	0	0	24	19	7	2	.262	124	9
Total	10	926	3164	251	713	79	15	2	375	310	115	78	.225	121	0

■ Palesch, Shirley - OF

YEAR	TEAM	G	AB	R	H	2B	3B	HR	RBI	BB	SO	SB	AVG	PRO+	BR
1949	Rac	8	13		1								.077	-40	-2
1950	Rck-GR	10	25	0	1	0	0	0	2	1	4	0	.040	-62	-5
Total	2	18	38	0	2	0	0	0	2	1	4	0	.053	-73	-7

■ Panos, Vickie - OF

YEAR	TEAM	G	AB	R	H	2B	3B	HR	RBI	BB	SO	SB	AVG	PRO+	BR
1944	SB-Mil	114	403	84	106	1	0	0	31	66	25	141	.263	141	31

■ Parks, Barbara - 2B

YEAR	TEAM	G	AB	R	H	2B	3B	HR	RBI	BB	SO	SB	AVG	PRO+	BR
1950	Ken														
1951	Ken	26	72	4	6	0	0	0	2	4	13	1	.083	-28	-11
Total	2	26	72	4	6	0	0	0	2	4	13	1	.083	-28	-11

■ Parsons, Sue - P

YEAR	TEAM	G	AB	R	H	2B	3B	HR	RBI	BB	SO	SB	AVG	PRO+	BR
1953	Rck	19	51	3	4	1	0	0	3	0	12	0	.078	-35	-8
1954	Rck	34	55	3	3	1	0	0		3	11	0	.055	-41	-11
Total	2	53	106	6	7	2	0	0	3	3	23	0	.066	-39	-20

■ Payne, Barbara - SS/2B

YEAR	TEAM	G	AB	R	H	2B	3B	HR	RBI	BB	SO	SB	AVG	PRO+	BR
1950	Kal	100	299	19	57	8	1	0	16	20	45	6	.191	67	-17
1951	Kal-BC-Rck	94	294	38	51	4	5	0	33	42	57	11	.173	84	-10
Total	2	194	593	57	108	12	6	0	49	62	102	17	.182	75	-27

■ Pearson, Dolly - SS

YEAR	TEAM	G	AB	R	H	2B	3B	HR	RBI	BB	SO	SB	AVG	PRO+	BR
1948	Mus	82	233	15	35	3	2	0	12	23	54	10	.150	65	-11

YEAR	TEAM	G	AB	R	H	2B	3B	HR	RBI	BB	SO	SB	AVG	PRO+	BR
1949	Peo	30	74	4	16	3	1	0	4	11	10	1	.216	153	1
1950	Rac	110	400	41	94	5	4	0	47	47	31	14	.235	105	-3
1951	BC-Kal	100	346	38	64	9	5	0	37	42	28	19	.185	90	-11
1952	Kal	44	138	11	28	3	1	0	11	17	5	5	.203	85	-4
1953	SB	90	297	38	55	8	1	0	29	69	25	11	.185	93	-2
1954	GR	85	272	68	89	5	0	18	57	70	30	10	.327	229	33
Total	7	541	1760	215	381	36	14	18	197	279	183	70	.216	119	3

■ Peppas, June - 1B/P

YEAR	TEAM	G	AB	R	H	2B	3B	HR	RBI	BB	SO	SB	AVG	PRO+	BR
1948	FW	20	53	5	14	1	1	2	9	1	8	0	.264	234	2
1949	FW-Rac	50	121	9	14	2	1	0	7	12	26	3	.116	42	-9
1950	Rac	109	395	34	106	11	5	4	52	45	39	8	.268	158	11
1951	BC-Kal	108	382	46	109	11	4	1	35	48	36	26	.285	158	17
1952	Kal	108	412	38	108	12	0	0	36	31	20	8	.262	110	-2
1953	Kal	108	417	46	113	10	3	0	33	37	19	10	.271	125	3
1954	Kal	98	366	75	122	4	0	16	49	37	30	15	.333	178	20
Total	7	601	2146	253	586	51	14	23	221	211	178	70	.273	142	43

■ Perez, Migdalia "Mickey" (m. Jinright 1952) - P

YEAR	TEAM	G	AB	R	H	2B	3B	HR	RBI	BB	SO	SB	AVG	PRO+	BR
1948	Chi	35	82	6	6	0	0	0	2	8	11	2	.073	-13	-9
1951	BC	45	92	11	8	0	0	0	4	25	13	1	.087	20	-7
1952	BC-Rck	33	66	5	14	1	0	0	7	4	6	0	.212	65	-3
1953	Rck	34	71	6	5	0	0	0	1	7	4	0	.070	-27	-10
1954	Rck	25	56	1	10	0	0	0	2	6	2	0	.179	22	-6
Total	5	172	367	29	43	1	0	0	16	50	36	3	.117	14	-36

■ Perkins, Joy

YEAR	TEAM
1953	SB

■ Perlick, Edythe - OF

YEAR	TEAM	G	AB	R	H	2B	3B	HR	RBI	BB	SO	SB	AVG	PRO+	BR
1943	Rac	84	310	56	83	10	4	1	42	22	10	55	.268	143	9
1944	Rac	116	423	51	97	7	2	2	63	30	9	52	.229	127	2
1945	Rac	107	389	47	83	4	7	2	14	41	5	14	.213	162	13
1946	Rac	112	431	72	99	6	4	6	56	37	17	88	.230	151	13
1947	Rac	112	436	62	104	11	6	2	39	21	19	83	.239	156	16
1948	Rac	111	415	55	101	11	3	2	51	39	28	82	.243	150	18
1949	Rac	99	364	38	93	3	9	2	41	33	18	44	.255	180	18
1950	Rac	110	409	64	101	10	7	3	59	34	23	33	.247	136	4
Total	8	851	3177	445	761	62	46	18	365	257	129	451	.240	150	94

■ Peters, Marjorie - P

YEAR	TEAM	G	AB	R	H	2B	3B	HR	RBI	BB	SO	SB	AVG	PRO+	BR
1943	Rck	60	125	24	25	1	2	1	9	6	10	19	.200	91	-4
1944	Rck	10	23	3	6	0	0	0	0	3	4	2	.261	130	0
Total	2	70	148	27	31	1	2	1	9	9	14	21	.209	96	-3

■ Peterson, Betty Jean

YEAR	TEAM
1953	Mus

■ Petras, Ernestine "Teeny" - SS

YEAR	TEAM	G	AB	R	H	2B	3B	HR	RBI	BB	SO	SB	AVG	PRO+	BR
1944	Mil	32	82	7	8	1	0	0	8	7	5	10	.098	12	-7
1945	GR	110	359	31	58	3	1	0	14	29	5	38	.162	80	-4
1946	GR	112	355	38	68	5	1	0	34	31	27	53	.192	86	-5
1947	GR	112	394	45	69	6	3	0	25	29	31	51	.175	88	-6
1948	GR-Chi	108	349	59	76	7	0	0	32	53	32	86	.218	121	16
1949	Ken	111	378	59	74	4	3	0	17	68	32	73	.196	118	14
1950	Ken	104	381	57	88	8	4	0	23	59	38	52	.231	115	8
1951	BC	53	170	24	36	7	1	0	10	33	24	22	.212	119	4
1952	BC	92	322	38	75	14	1	0	18	40	22	42	.233	114	5
Total	9	834	2790	358	552	55	14	0	181	349	216	427	.198	102	24

■ Petryna, Doreen Betty (m. Allen 1949) - 3B

YEAR	TEAM	G	AB	R	H	2B	3B	HR	RBI	BB	SO	SB	AVG	PRO+	BR
1948	GR	25	61	6	7	0	0	0	2	7	8	2	.115	26	-4
1949	FW	97	300	15	43	4	0	0	18	29	34	10	.143	49	-18
Total	2	122	361	21	50	4	0	0	20	36	42	12	.139	45	-22

■ Pieper, Marge - OF/SS

YEAR	TEAM	G	AB	R	H	2B	3B	HR	RBI	BB	SO	SB	AVG	PRO+	BR
1946	FW	83	289	22	50	8	4	1	24	18	18	14	.173	95	-12
1947	FW-Ken	109	369	33	83	11	5	5	38	34	30	31	.225	178	13
1948	Ken-Chi	107	369	42	70	7	1	0	37	53	35	57	.190	98	2
1949	FW-Rac	69	221	18	36	3	2	0	14	31	16	21	.163	88	-3
1950	Ken-Peo	91	304	40	63	12	3	3	27	38	24	19	.207	124	-1
1951	Peo-BC	76	244	31	62	16	3	1	29	33	9	18	.254	168	10
1952	BC	91	304	44	77	11	8	4	47	38	33	11	.253	178	13
1953	Mus	92	314	26	72	8	4	3	38	41	26	10	.229	132	2
Total	8	718	2414	256	513	76	30	17	254	286	191	181	.213	135	22

■ Pirok, Pauline - SS/3B

YEAR	TEAM	G	AB	R	H	2B	3B	HR	RBI	BB	SO	SB	AVG	PRO+	BR
1943	Ken	88	333	59	78	6	1	0	33	33	15	37	.234	99	-2
1944	Ken	112	404	73	94	10	3	0	38	46	11	75	.233	136	11
1945	Ken-SB	106	355	37	58	5	1	0	5	18	0	29	.163	95	0
1946	SB	21	71	5	14	0	0	0	2	5	7	15	.197	69	-1
1947	SB	113	400	51	77	6	4	0	17	24	21	53	.192	102	-2
1948	SB	119	413	37	90	5	4	0	19	32	51	16	.218	109	-5
Total	6	559	1976	262	411	32	13	0	114	158	105	225	.208	107	1

■ Podolski, Bertha

YEAR	TEAM	G	AB	R	H	AVG	PRO+	BR
1946	FW	3	9		2	.222	66	-1

■ Pollitt, Alice (m. Deschaine 1952) - 3B

YEAR	TEAM	G	AB	R	H	2B	3B	HR	RBI	BB	SO	SB	AVG	PRO+	BR
1947	Rck	18	39	1	3	0	0	0	1	3	5	2	.077	-15	-4
1948	Rck	116	376	33	71	4	0	0	31	22	45	12	.189	90	-12
1949	Rck	106	385	23	81	5	4	0	27	17	32	30	.210	105	-5
1950	Rck	65	240	21	67	3	7	3	37	10	16	25	.279	168	8
1951	Rck	105	405	40	121	7	9	4	45	36	50	61	.299	183	27
1952	Rck	108	418	45	113	8	6	1	34	22	27	35	.270	128	6
1953	Rck	88	314	39	99	14	5	0	39	29	9	16	.315	177	17
Total	7	606	2177	250	555	41	35	8	214	139	184	181	.255	139	36

■ Pratt, Mary - P

YEAR	TEAM	G	AB	R	H	2B	3B	HR	RBI	BB	SO	SB	AVG	PRO+	BR
1943	Rck	24	51	4	12	0	0	0	1	4	8	1	.235	78	-2
1944	Rck-Ken	45	103	7	13	0	0	0	6	7	7	4	.126	19	-10
1945	Ken	27	46	3	8	0	1	0	3	4	2	1	.174	123	2
1946	Rck	14	19	0	0	0	0	0	0	1	2	1	.000	-83	-4
1947	Rck	4	10	0									.000	-99	-2
Total	5	114	229	33									.144	35	-15

Pryer, Charlene "Shorty" - 2B/OF

YEAR	TEAM	G	AB	R	H	2B	3B	HR	RBI	BB	SO	SB	AVG	PRO+	BR
1946	Mus	108	381	64	77	9	0	0	18	51	33	45	.202	105	1
1947	Mus	108	422	51	105	3	2	1	20	22	23	76	.249	134	15
1948	Mus	112	408	70	107	5	3	1	29	56	41	58	.262	157	22
1949	Mus	76	277	56	65	2	2	1	10	38	16	68	.235	143	16
1950	Mus-SB	112	427	75	115	11	1	0	25	51	41	75	.269	130	19
1951	SB	109	426	106	133	8	3	0	32	40	39	129	.312	155	35
1952	SB	79	293	41	70	6	1	0	18	23	21	59	.239	96	3
Total	7	704	2634	463	672	44	12	3	152	281	214	510	.255	133	111

Redman, Magdalen - C

YEAR	TEAM	G	AB	R	H	2B	3B	HR	RBI	BB	SO	SB	AVG	PRO+	BR
1948	Ken	49	121	6	12	1	0	0	4	9	26	3	.099	5	-12
1949	Ken	66	134	15	20	1	0	0	3	27	16	2	.149	72	-3
1950	GR	35	77	7	10	1	0	0	5	8	11	1	.130	24	-7
1951	GR	31	96	3	10	1	0	0	8	14	7	1	.104	13	-10
1952	GR	43	114	7	25	1	0	0	4	16	14	2	.219	82	-3
1953	GR	70	199	13	37	4	0	0	19	33	15	1	.186	74	-7
1954	GR	75	177	39	44	6	2	2	20	55	12	0	.249	135	6
Total	7	369	918	90	158	15	2	2	63	162	101	10	.172	71	-36

Reeser, Sara - 1B

YEAR	TEAM	G	AB	R	H	2B	3B	HR	RBI	BB	SO	SB	AVG	PRO+	BR
1946	Mus	110	382	53	79	2	2	1	39	62	37	45	.207	111	4
1947	Mus	110	398	36	92	6	3	0	21	30	25	36	.231	128	6
1948	Mus	110	372	42	83	6	1	0	28	55	32	30	.223	119	5
1950	Kal	12	25	3	2	0	0	0	0	2	3	1	.080	-25	-3
Total	4	342	1177	134	256	14	6	1	88	149	97	112	.218	116	11

Rehrer, Rita

YEAR	TEAM	G	AB	R	H	2B	3B	HR	RBI	BB	SO	SB	AVG	PRO+	BR
1946	Peo	1	3	0									.000	-99	-1

Reid

1954 Rck

Reid, Dorice - OF

YEAR	TEAM	G	AB	R	H	2B	3B	HR	RBI	BB	SO	SB	AVG	PRO+	BR
1948	Chi	50	115	3	16	1	1	0	4	12	36	6	.139	55	-6
1949	GR	99	307	23	49	3	1	0	23	38	32	16	.160	75	-3
1950	GR	107	392	59	78	6	3	0	28	60	43	36	.199	88	-5
1951	GR	67	212	23	27	1	0	0	5	20	34	11	.127	18	-19
Total	4	323	1026	108	170	11	5	0	60	130	145	69	.166	66	-39

Reis, Ruth

1952 Rck

Reynolds, Mary - OF/3B/P

YEAR	TEAM	G	AB	R	H	2B	3B	HR	RBI	BB	SO	SB	AVG	PRO+	BR
1946	Peo	90	254	18	59	5	4	0	28	35	23	9	.232	144	4
1947	Peo	113	400	40	98	17	5	1	42	39	29	7	.245	177	13
1948	Peo	119	390	42	83	7	4	0	43	67	60	11	.213	132	7
1949	Peo	104	344	28	68	8	4	0	29	53	17	2	.198	128	2
1950	Peo	57	103	15	24	3	1	0	9	22	14	1	.233	131	2
Total	5	483	1491	143	332	40	18	1	151	216	143	30	.223	145	28

Richard, Ruth - C

YEAR	TEAM	G	AB	R	H	2B	3B	HR	RBI	BB	SO	SB	AVG	PRO+	BR
1947	GR	47	147	5	26	3	1	0	7	4	13	2	.177	82	-6
1948	Rck	110	363	30	61	9	5	1	35	25	24	11	.168	95	-14
1949	Rck	84	265	23	45	0	0	1	20	27	14	11	.170	71	-9
1950	Rck	95	315	29	79	11	6	1	28	25	13	12	.251	139	2
1951	Rck	99	368	34	102	7	3	0	60	18	19	6	.277	127	1
1952	Rck	106	394	41	112	14	5	3	46	13	12	9	.284	151	6
1953	Rck	92	341	33	86	11	0	2	48	15	9	7	.252	113	-5
1954	Rck	92	325	42	97	12	0	7	43	15	5	14	.298	130	0
Total	8	725	2518	237	608	67	20	15	287	142	109	72	.241	119	-25

Ricketts, Joyce - OF

YEAR	TEAM	G	AB	R	H	2B	3B	HR	RBI	BB	SO	SB	AVG	PRO+	BR
1953	GR	114	417	48	120	19	5	5	71	43	18	12	.288	181	19
1954	GR	93	290	63	92	14	4	15	72	66	21	2	.317	229	31
Total	2	207	707	111	212	33	9	20	143	109	39	14	.300	203	50

Rini, Mary - P

YEAR	TEAM	G	AB	R	H	2B	3B	HR	RBI	BB	SO	SB	AVG	PRO+	BR
1945	Ken	23	39	1	0	0	0	0	0	0	0	12	.000	-91	-5
1946	Mus	2	0	0									.000	-99	0
Total	2	25	39	0									.000	-91	-5

Risinger, Earlene - P

YEAR	TEAM	G	AB	R	H	2B	3B	HR	RBI	BB	SO	SB	AVG	PRO+	BR
1948	Spg	22	36	1	2	0	0	0	0	6	10	0	.056	-5	-4
1949	GR	30	82	4	10	0	1	0	1	3	10	0	.122	25	-8
1950	GR	32	88	6	21	1	0	0	6	3	4	1	.239	80	-3
1951	GR	24	63	4	10	1	0	0	5	3	9	0	.159	38	-5
1952	GR	27	66	4	10	0	0	0	3	7	0		.152	16	-7
1953	GR	30	79	8	16	1	0	0	8	5	8	1	.203	58	-5
1954	GR	23	53	3	11	1	0	0	4	6	2	0	.208	52	-4
Total	7	188	467	30	80	4	1	0	28	29	50	2	.171	43	-35

Rohrer, Kay - C

YEAR	TEAM	G	AB	R	H	2B	3B	HR	RBI	BB	SO	SB	AVG	PRO+	BR
1945	Rck	100	327	34	78	8	1	2	17	26	1	9	.239	173	16

Romatowski, Jenny - C

YEAR	TEAM	G	AB	R	H	2B	3B	HR	RBI	BB	SO	SB	AVG	PRO+	BR
1946	SB	10	9	0	0	0	0	0	0	1	3	0	.000	-66	-2
1947	Rck	80	220	15	27	0	0	0	6	12	25	9	.123	22	-17
1948	Rac-Chi	89	242	15	51	4	0	0	27	28	29	8	.211	108	-0
1949	Peo	5	18	4									.222	74	-1
1950	SB	46	134	11	28	2	0	0	9	12	11	4	.209	75	-5
1951	Kal	89	304	19	59	5	1	0	21	13	19	4	.194	61	-19
1952	Kal	68	224	13	50	5	0	0	18	8	15	3	.223	72	-10
1953	Kal	80	263	19	57	3	1	0	21	11	6	6	.217	69	-13
1954	Kal	68	225	23	58	2	1	6	26	12	6	0	.258	106	-8
Total	9	535	1639	115	334	21	3	6	128	97	114	31	.204	72	-76

Rommelaere, Martha - OF

YEAR	TEAM	G	AB	R	H	2B	3B	HR	RBI	BB	SO	SB	AVG	PRO+	BR
1950	Ken	30	80	7	15	0	0	0	7	10	12	8	.188	54	-3

Roth, Elaine - OF/P

YEAR	TEAM	G	AB	R	H	2B	3B	HR	RBI	BB	SO	SB	AVG	PRO+	BR
1948	Peo	16	17	5	4	1	0	0	2	1	0	4	.235	149	0
1948	Peo	39	104	11	16	0	0	0	3	6	22	3	.154	33	-8
1949	Peo	25	58	0	5	0	0	0	1	0	10	0	.086	-33	-8
1949	Peo	91	322	32	52	2	0	0	13	34	21	16	.161	62	-13
1950	Kal	107	386	55	78	4	4	0	21	64	20	64	.202	91	1
1950	SB	26	50	4	5	1	0	0	2	7	6	1	.100	14	-5
1951	Kal	34	54	6	6	1	0	0	2	4	9	2	.111	7	-6
Total	7	338	991	113	166	9	4	0	44	116	88	90	.168	62	-38

Roth, Eilaine - P/OF

YEAR	TEAM	G	AB	R	H	2B	3B	HR	RBI	BB	SO	SB	AVG	PRO+	BR
1951	Kal	79	207	24	52	5	3	0	16	22	16	16	.251	132	4
1952	Kal	21	24	1	3	0	0	0	1	3	3	0	.125	14	-2
1953	Kal	26	26	4	5	0	0	0	4	3	2	0	.192	54	-1
1954	Kal	26	54	6	12	0	0	0	0	6	11	0	.222	46	-4
Total	4	152	311	35	72	5	3	0	21	34	32	16	.232	98	-4

Rotvig, Barbara - P

YEAR	TEAM	G	AB	R	H	2B	3B	HR	RBI	BB	SO	SB	AVG	PRO+	BR
1948	Ken	30	72	5	8	0	0	0	2	8	16	0	.111	18	-6
1949	Ken	32	58	2	3	0	0	0	3	10	14	2	.052	-8	-6
1951	Ken	29	64	8	17	2	0	0	5	9	8	0	.266	132	1
Total	3	91	194	15	28	2	0	0	10	27	38	2	.144	52	-11

Rountree, Mary - C

YEAR	TEAM	G	AB	R	H	2B	3B	HR	RBI	BB	SO	SB	AVG	PRO+	BR
1946	Peo	87	291	22	63	1	2	0	41	41	21	27	.216	111	2
1947	FW	53	148	10	31	2	3	0	9	13	7	12	.209	135	2
1948	FW	84	251	19	41	3	0	0	18	40	20	20	.163	76	-5
1949	FW	65	182	12	41	2	0	0	16	29	14	16	.225	122	4
1950	FW	25	63	12	13	1	0	0	9	5	5	0	.206	67	-3
1951	FW	43	98	16	25	3	0	0	8	20	9	9	.255	134	4
1952	FW-GR	65	178	14	36	2	1	0	5	18	10	5	.202	76	-6
Total	7	422	1211	105	250	14	6	0	107	166	86	89	.206	102	-2

Roy, Patricia - 1B

YEAR	TEAM	G	AB	R	H	2B	3B	HR	RBI	BB	SO	SB	AVG	PRO+	BR
1954	FW	14	38	0	3	0	0	0	2	0	9	0	.079	-56	-8

Roylance, Juanita

YEAR	TEAM	G	AB	R	H	2B	3B	HR	RBI	BB	SO	SB	AVG	PRO+	BR
1946	Mus	6	15	1									.067	-50	-2

Ruhnke, Irene (m. Sanvitis 1947) - 2B

YEAR	TEAM	G	AB	R	H	2B	3B	HR	RBI	BB	SO	SB	AVG	PRO+	BR
1943	Rck	77	285	54	72	5	5	1	36	14	12	22	.253	127	-0
1944	Rck-Min	90	296	21	57	3	4	0	26	23	20	28	.193	98	-8
1945	FW	90	290	22	45	8	0	0	14	16	2	17	.155	82	-7
1946	FW	107	389	37	75	5	6	1	50	30	27	24	.193	101	-11
1947	Rck	21	67	3	11	1	1	0	2	3	4	3	.164	78	-3
Total	5	385	1327	137	260	22	16	2	128	86	65	94	.196	102	-29

Ruiz, Gloria - OF

YEAR	TEAM	G	AB	R	H	2B	3B	HR	RBI	BB	SO	SB	AVG	PRO+	BR
1948	Peo	52	126	8	12	0	0	0	8	19	26	10	.095	25	-8

Rukavina, Terry - 2B

YEAR	TEAM	G	AB	R	H	2B	3B	HR	RBI	BB	SO	SB	AVG	PRO+	BR
1951	Kal	48	87	3	10	0	0	0	2	4	15	1	.115	-10	-11
1953	Kal	99	269	31	48	7	1	1	21	27	57	5	.178	72	-14
Total	2	147	356	34	58	7	1	1	23	31	72	6	.163	53	-25

Rumsey, Janet - P

YEAR	TEAM	G	AB	R	H	2B	3B	HR	RBI	BB	SO	SB	AVG	PRO+	BR
1951	SB-BC	20	34	1	3	1	0	0	1	8	10	0	.088	33	-3
1952	SB	26	51	3	6	0	0	0	3	1	15	0	.118	-17	-7
1953	SB	36	83	5	12	0	0	0	5	9	12	0	.145	23	-8
1954	SB	33	75	7	20	2	0	0	4	2	10	1	.267	68	-4
Total	4	115	243	16	41	3	0	0	13	20	47	1	.169	33	-22

Russell, Betty

YEAR	TEAM	G	AB	R	H	2B	3B	HR	RBI	BB	SO	SB	AVG	PRO+	BR
1946	Rac	12	28	0	4	1	0	0	1	0	3	0	.143	34	-3

Russo, Margaret - SS

YEAR	TEAM	G	AB	R	H	2B	3B	HR	RBI	BB	SO	SB	AVG	PRO+	BR
1950	Peo	93	266	14	35	2	1	0	23	42	46	6	.132	37	-20
1951	Peo	106	368	66	91	6	4	2	51	44	27	22	.247	134	7
1952	BC	100	320	39	71	13	3	1	28	52	21	14	.222	127	5
1953	Mus	112	402	65	91	9	9	2	29	55	33	45	.226	134	9
1954	Rck	90	284	67	89	9	2	10	35	58	20	17	.313	187	24
Total	5	501	1640	251	377	39	19	15	166	251	147	104	.230	128	25

Sachetti, Toni

1954 FW

Salisbury

1953 SB

Sams, Doris - OF/P

YEAR	TEAM	G	AB	R	H	2B	3B	HR	RBI	BB	SO	SB	AVG	PRO+	BR
1946	Mus	42	106	15	29	1	0	0	9	15	4	6	.274	142	3
1947	Mus	107	346	31	97	9	5	0	41	28	33	40	.280	187	21
1948	Mus	117	409	57	105	6	7	3	59	39	41	23	.257	172	15
1949	Mus	109	408	35	114	6	1	0	35	12	39	29	.279	141	8
1950	Kal	94	279	42	84	15	3	4	31	27	19	11	.301	197	16
1951	Kal	97	356	40	109	16	2	2	33	29	21	19	.306	174	16
1952	Kal	109	408	47	128	25	3	12	57	43	23	15	.314	233	35
1953	Kal	46	173	23	54	4	2	1	21	14	11	11	.312	173	11
Total	8	721	2485	290	720	82	23	22	286	214	194	154	.290	182	124

Sands, Sarah Jane - OF

YEAR	TEAM	G	AB	R	H	2B	3B	HR	RBI	BB	SO	SB	AVG	PRO+	BR
1953	Rck	76	234	23	50	1	0	0	15	4	39	4	.214	50	-15
1954	Rck	60	180	14	37	4	0	1	14	9	9	5	.206	48	-16
Total	2	136	414	37	87	5	0	1	29	13	48	9	.210	49	-31

Sanvitis (see Ruhnke)

Satterfield, Doris - OF

YEAR	TEAM	G	AB	R	H	2B	3B	HR	RBI	BB	SO	SB	AVG	PRO+	BR
1947	GR	12	21	1	1	0	0	0	1	2	4	0	.048	-18	-2
1948	GR	125	452	45	111	10	6	1	61	30	22	40	.246	148	10
1949	GR	113	421	42	109	22	8	2	58	27	15	15	.259	197	15
1950	GR	113	432	68	120	16	8	4	54	32	24	38	.278	168	16
1951	GR	105	401	64	112	19	2	6	62	37	13	36	.279	168	16
1952	GR	103	386	43	110	14	7	0	51	24	13	40	.285	150	13
1953	GR	112	404	58	119	16	4	0	79	47	30	40	.295	158	21
Total	7	683	2517	321	682	90	42	9	366	199	124	209	.271	163	88

Schacter, Blanche

YEAR	TEAM	G	AB	R	H	2B	3B	HR	RBI	BB	SO	SB	AVG	PRO+	BR
1948	Ken	9	25	1									.040	-70	-4

Schatz, Joan - OF

YEAR	TEAM	G	AB	R	H	2B	3B	HR	RBI	BB	SO	SB	AVG	PRO+	BR
1952	Kal	13	43	4	8	0	0	0		2	6	4	.186	35	-3

Scheer, Edna - P

YEAR	TEAM	G	AB	R	H	2B	3B	HR	RBI	BB	SO	SB	AVG	PRO+	BR
1950	Rck	18	28	5	8	1	0	0	1	4	11	0	.286	148	1

Schillace, Clara - OF

YEAR	TEAM	G	AB	R	H	2B	3B	HR	RBI	BB	SO	SB	AVG	PRO+	BR
1943	Rac	102	350	65	88	7	3	1	38	50	18	40	.251	131	9
1944	Rac	112	374	65	78	3	3	0	30	38	21	58	.209	104	-1
1945	Rac	105	357	31	66	3	0	1	15	26	5	27	.185	121	11
1946	Rac	98	310	40	50	2	4	0	18	47	31	21	.161	83	-9
Total 4		417	1391	201	282	15	10	2	101	161	75	146	.203	111	9

Schmidt, Marilyn

YEAR	TEAM	G	AB	R	H	2B	3B	HR	RBI	BB	SO	SB	AVG	PRO+	BR
1952	Rck														

Schmidt, Violet

YEAR	TEAM	G	AB	R	H	2B	3B	HR	RBI	BB	SO	SB	AVG	PRO+	BR
1946	FW-Rck	4	3		1								.333	149	0

Schofield, June - SS/3B

YEAR	TEAM	G	AB	R	H	2B	3B	HR	RBI	BB	SO	SB	AVG	PRO+	BR
1948	Spg	125	440	40	104	12	9	2	49	46	44	29	.236	168	15
1949	Peo-Mus	109	378	18	86	7	3	0	27	47	39	9	.228	135	5
Total 2		234	818	58	190	19	12	2	76	93	83	38	.232	153	20

Schroeder, Dorothy - SS

YEAR	TEAM	G	AB	R	H	2B	3B	HR	RBI	BB	SO	SB	AVG	PRO+	BR
1943	SB	98	298	44	56	4	2	1	31	56	51	39	.188	97	0
1944	SB	116	328	50	59	1	2	1	24	58	50	70	.180	106	7
1945	SB-Ken	94	312	33	60	2	8	2	8	19	1	62	.192	163	19
1946	Ken	110	334	31	56	3	1	0	14	54	6	24	.168	80	8
1947	Ken-FW	100	344	40	59	3	0	0	19	37	48	32	.172	93	-4
1948	FW	125	418	41	71	5	3	0	43	57	69	30	.170	88	-7
1949	FW	104	346	36	72	4	4	0	31	55	40	14	.208	128	5
1950	FW	107	371	52	78	15	3	6	58	60	48	22	.210	138	5
1951	FW	85	285	39	57	9	2	4	45	58	50	17	.200	136	5
1952	FW	102	392	67	96	12	5	6	43	60	52	5	.245	158	11
1953	Kal	110	389	76	111	12	0	6	39	80	54	10	.285	177	26
1954	Kal	98	312	63	95	8	0	17	65	27	41	11	.304	186	14
Total 12		1249	4129	572	870	79	33	42	420	621	510	336	.211	131	74

Schulze, Shirley - OF

YEAR	TEAM	G	AB	R	H	2B	3B	HR	RBI	BB	SO	SB	AVG	PRO+	BR
1944	Mil	15	44	5	8	0	0	0	2	6	4	7	.182	83	-0

Schweigerdt, Gloria - P

YEAR	TEAM	G	AB	R	H	2B	3B	HR	RBI	BB	SO	SB	AVG	PRO+	BR
1951	GR-BC	15	23	3	6	1	0	0	2	1	6	0	.261	125	-0
1952	BC	39	64	3	5	2	0	0	4	2	17	1	.078	-11	-9
Total 2		54	87	6	11	3	0	0	6	3	23	1	.126	25	-9

Scott, Patricia - P

YEAR	TEAM	G	AB	R	H	2B	3B	HR	RBI	BB	SO	SB	AVG	PRO+	BR
1951	FW	27	84	12	12	2	0	0	4	3	6	0	.143	25	-9
1952	FW	27	79	4	19	3	0	0	4	3	3	0	.241	93	-3
1953	FW	37	98	14	26	5	1	0	13	2	4	0	.265	131	-1
Total 3		91	261	30	57	10	1	0	21	8	13	0	.218	86	-12

Shero, Doris - OF

YEAR	TEAM	G	AB	R	H	2B	3B	HR	RBI	BB	SO	SB	AVG	PRO+	BR
1950	Rac	83	194	14	18	0	0	0	9	21	27	10	.093	3	-20
1951	BC	14	40	5	4	0	0	0	4	4	5	6	.100	10	-3
Total 2		97	234	19	22	0	0	0	13	25	32	16	.094	4	-23

Shinen, Dorothy - OF

YEAR	TEAM	G	AB	R	H	2B	3B	HR	RBI	BB	SO	SB	AVG	PRO+	BR
1945	Ken	36	83	4	12	1	2	0	3	5	0	7	.145	97	-2

Shinen, Kay - 3B

YEAR	TEAM	G	AB	R	H	2B	3B	HR	RBI	BB	SO	SB	AVG	PRO+	BR
1945	Ken	98	333	23	56	3	0	1	8	20	1	14	.168	86	-6

Shively, Twila - OF/1B

YEAR	TEAM	G	AB	R	H	2B	3B	HR	RBI	BB	SO	SB	AVG	PRO+	BR
1945	GR	106	372	42	73	7	2	1	18	23	2	53	.196	131	12
1946	GR	111	409	78	101	9	4	1	45	56	37	75	.247	151	19
1947	GR	104	369	42	76	9	2	1	27	30	51	51	.206	120	4
1948	Chi-Peo	75	263	37	41	3	3	0	14	55	58	36	.156	95	1
1949	Peo	109	347	31	65	4	4	0	21	58	59	18	.187	112	1
1950	Peo	109	381	44	73	10	5	1	36	51	64	29	.192	98	-7
Total 6		614	2141	274	429	42	20	4	161	273	271	262	.200	119	29

Shollenberger, Fern - 3B

YEAR	TEAM	G	AB	R	H	2B	3B	HR	RBI	BB	SO	SB	AVG	PRO+	BR
1946	Ken	94	342	35	77	0	3	0	24	26	16	35	.225	101	-3
1947	Ken	81	273	19	45	3	1	0	10	15	13	18	.165	63	-12
1948	Ken	127	466	47	98	5	4	0	17	33	44	24	.210	99	-9
1949	Ken	111	370	32	66	7	2	1	18	32	26	32	.178	90	-9
1950	Ken	112	417	48	106	8	2	0	31	32	22	28	.254	106	-2
1951	Ken	105	382	48	97	11	1	0	21	41	16	21	.254	118	5
1952	Kal	86	316	32	72	7	1	0	29	18	18	11	.228	85	-10
1953	Kal	107	388	42	75	12	3	0	23	34	15	6	.193	80	-18
1954	Kal	95	332	47	89	8	0	8	58	38	12	6	.268	121	-3
Total 9		918	3286	350	725	61	17	9	231	269	182	181	.221	97	-64

Silvestri, Margaret (see Holgerson)

Sindelar, Joan - OF

YEAR	TEAM	G	AB	R	H	2B	3B	HR	RBI	BB	SO	SB	AVG	PRO+	BR
1950	Kal														
1951	Kal	45	73	10	9	4	1	0	2	17	24	1	.123	89	-3
1952	Kal														
1953	Kal	81	246	25	55	4	0	2	14	27	40	3	.224	101	-4
Total 4		126	319	35	64	8	1	2	16	44	64	4	.201	99	-7

Sloan, Frances

YEAR	TEAM	G	AB	R	H	2B	3B	HR	RBI	BB	SO	SB	AVG	PRO+	BR
1946	GR	3	0		0								.000	-99	0

Smith, Charlotte - SS/2B

YEAR	TEAM	G	AB	R	H	2B	3B	HR	RBI	BB	SO	SB	AVG	PRO+	BR
1943	Rac	53	149	36	47	1	0	0	18	12	6	54	.315	138	12
1944	Rac	77	204	21	38	1	2	0	15	27	12	39	.186	96	-0
Total 2		130	353	57	85	2	2	0	33	39	18	93	.241	115	12

Smith, Colleen - 3B

YEAR	TEAM	G	AB	R	H	2B	3B	HR	RBI	BB	SO	SB	AVG	PRO+	BR
1949	GR	40	98	7	18	1	0	0	4	7	11	3	.184	72	-4

Smith, Helen

YEAR	TEAM	G	AB	R	H	2B	3B	HR	RBI	BB	SO	SB	AVG	PRO+	BR
1946	Rck	2	6		3								.500	274	1
1947	Ken	5	8		1								.125	-1	-1
Total 2		7	14		4								.286	121	-0

Smith, Jean - OF

YEAR	TEAM	G	AB	R	H	2B	3B	HR	RBI	BB	SO	SB	AVG	PRO+	BR
1948	Ken-FW	104	310	36	52	5	5	1	22	55	58	15	.168	114	-1
1949	FW	25	67	10	10	2	2	1	11	17	14	7	.149	173	3
1950	Peo	89	267	36	58	10	3	0	14	36	44	12	.217	115	-1

YEAR	TEAM	G	AB	R	H	2B	3B	HR	RBI	BB	SO	SB	AVG	PRO+	BR
1951	Peo	93	305	50	71	10	2	0	30	45	17	38	.233	124	8
1952	GR	69	194	28	38	6	1	1	18	21	11	21	.196	97	-2
1953	GR	114	401	86	91	20	5	1	23	71	27	73	.227	141	18
1954	GR	93	309	74	78	14	0	9	56	88	17	28	.252	156	19
Total 7		587	1853	320	398	67	18	13	174	333	188	194	.215	130	44

Smith, Marjean - OF

YEAR	TEAM	G	AB	R	H	2B	3B	HR	RBI	BB	SO	SB	AVG	PRO+	BR
1948	GR	22	52	8	10	2	0	0	2	6	6	2	.192	103	-1

Smith, Shirley - 2B

YEAR	TEAM	G	AB	R	H	2B	3B	HR	RBI	BB	SO	SB	AVG	PRO+	BR
1947	Peo	61	171	14	26	1	0	0	6	21	19	8	.152	63	-6

Sopkovic, Kay - C

YEAR	TEAM	G	AB	R	H	2B	3B	HR	RBI	BB	SO	SB	AVG	PRO+	BR
1945	SB	12	15	0	1	0	0	0	0	1	1	1	.067	-25	-2

Sowers, Barbara - OF

YEAR	TEAM	G	AB	R	H	2B	3B	HR	RBI	BB	SO	SB	AVG	PRO+	BR
1953	Mus	70	166	16	34	3	1	1	15	21	28	5	.205	99	-3
1954	GR	70	197	35	56	8	1	3	34	57	26	7	.284	155	13
Total 2		140	363	51	90	11	2	4	49	78	54	12	.248	132	11

Steck, Elma

YEAR	TEAM	G	AB	R	H	2B	3B	HR	RBI	BB	SO	SB	AVG	PRO+	BR
1948	Peo	11	17	1	1	0	0	0	1	1	7	1	.059	-37	-2
1949	Rck	6	16		1								.063	-51	-2
Total 2		17	33		2								.061	-44	-5

Stefani, Margaret - 2B

YEAR	TEAM	G	AB	R	H	2B	3B	HR	RBI	BB	SO	SB	AVG	PRO+	BR
1943	SB	107	397	87	99	6	11	4	55	71	5	90	.249	172	28
1944	SB	116	400	57	87	4	5	0	46	66	7	83	.218	131	13
1945	SB	105	337	39	78	13	8	1	7	39	0	7	.231	222	32
1946	SB	112	370	70	83	5	1	8	53	80	15	79	.224	160	24
1947	SB	99	337	34	80	7	1	2	38	33	13	27	.237	151	11
1948	Rck	103	317	30	62	6	4	0	25	52	18	8	.196	123	2
Total 6		642	2158	317	489	41	37	8	224	341	58	294	.227	160	110

Stephens, Ruby - P

YEAR	TEAM	G	AB	R	H	2B	3B	HR	RBI	BB	SO	SB	AVG	PRO+	BR
1946	Rac	7	9		0								.000	-99	-2
1947	SB	33	61	6	11	2	0	0	3	9	17	0	.180	109	-1
1948	Spg-Ken	37	80	6	14	0	0	0	2	8	10	4	.175	62	-3
1949	Ken	33	65	8	9	1	0	0	5	8	15	2	.138	52	-4
1950	Ken	29	72	13	16	0	0	0	8	10	12	0	.222	79	-2
1951	Ken	18	31	1	3	0	0	0	3	4	1	1	.097	5	-3
Total 6		157	318	34	53	3	0	0	21	39	55	7	.167	62	-14

Stevenson, Emily - OF

YEAR	TEAM	G	AB	R	H	2B	3B	HR	RBI	BB	SO	SB	AVG	PRO+	BR
1944	Mil	32	74	12	12	0	0	0	5	12	8	3	.162	65	-3

Stevenson, Rosemary

YEAR	TEAM	G	AB	R	H	2B	3B	HR	RBI	BB	SO	SB	AVG	PRO+	BR
1954	GR	32	82	15	19	3	0	3	9	4	27	3	.232	118	-3

Stocker, Jeanette

YEAR	TEAM	G	AB	R	H	2B	3B	HR	RBI	BB	SO	SB	AVG	PRO+	BR
1946	Ken	3	3		0								.000	-99	-1

Stoll, Nancy Jane "Jeep" - OF

YEAR	TEAM	G	AB	R	H	2B	3B	HR	RBI	BB	SO	SB	AVG	PRO+	BR
1946	Peo	58	164	13	23	2	0	0	14	20	25	12	.140	52	-9
1947	GR	71	203	16	33	2	4	0	12	40	41	21	.163	122	4
1948	Spg	116	413	61	79	8	3	0	18	59	33	55	.191	106	3
1949	SB	99	341	50	79	3	1	0	28	49	17	42	.232	127	11
1950	SB	99	350	40	95	14	2	1	50	44	13	71	.271	148	11
1951	SB	101	347	46	93	15	2	0	47	51	20	26	.268	148	13
1952	SB	86	316	45	95	23	3	1	60	40	17	21	.301	188	21
1953	Kal	110	396	37	122	18	0	3	65	47	20	14	.308	172	21
1954	Kal	34	106	11	32	3	0	0	18	17	3	8	.302	110	2
Total 9		774	2636	319	651	88	15	5	312	367	189	216	.247	139	77

Stolze, Dorothy - 2B/OF

YEAR	TEAM	G	AB	R	H	2B	3B	HR	RBI	BB	SO	SB	AVG	PRO+	BR
1946	Mus	81	273	31	53	4	1	0	34	31	15	33	.194	92	-3
1947	Mus	103	383	44	83	5	0	0	22	24	18	65	.217	103	4
1948	Mus	121	467	62	113	2	3	0	29	26	29	67	.242	111	4
1949	Mus-Rac	108	399	32	65	4	0	0	29	29	16	47	.163	55	-16
1950	Peo	106	415	44	101	8	4	1	32	27	18	28	.243	108	-5
1951	Peo	105	404	62	90	9	1	0	27	49	18	37	.223	97	-3
1952	GR	81	308	34	74	4	4	0	19	22	11	23	.240	102	-2
Total 7		705	2649	309	579	36	13	1	192	208	125	300	.219	96	-23

Stone, Lucille - SS

YEAR	TEAM	G	AB	R	H	2B	3B	HR	RBI	BB	SO	SB	AVG	PRO+	BR
1945	Rac-SB	19	50	1	2	0	0	0	0	2	0	12	.040	-14	-3

Stovroff, Shirley - C

YEAR	TEAM	G	AB	R	H	2B	3B	HR	RBI	BB	SO	SB	AVG	PRO+	BR
1948	Spg-SB	100	279	13	44	0	0	0	20	46	46	8	.158	63	-10
1949	SB	77	199	22	38	4	1	0	12	29	33	8	.191	108	-1
1950	SB	85	228	20	45	6	0	0	18	25	35	7	.197	74	-10
1951	SB	100	304	37	81	19	0	0	54	56	33	25	.266	158	16
1952	SB	93	296	46	74	10	2	1	39	75	23	8	.250	150	16
Total 5		455	1306	138	282	39	3	1	143	231	170	56	.216	116	11

Studnicka, Mary Lou - P

YEAR	TEAM	G	AB	R	H	2B	3B	HR	RBI	BB	SO	SB	AVG	PRO+	BR
1951	GR	26	63	3	8	0	0	0	2	9		1	.127	-1	-8
1952	GR	31	62	6	18	0	0	0	10	7	7	0	.290	116	1
1953	GR	30	64	1	8	0	0	0	3	0	9	1	.125	-17	-9
Total 3		87	189	10	34	0	0	0	15	9	25	1	.180	34	-16

Stuhr, Beverly - OF

YEAR	TEAM	G	AB	R	H	2B	3B	HR	RBI	BB	SO	SB	AVG	PRO+	BR
1949	Peo	8	14		4								.286	123	-0
1950	Rac	19	34	4	3	0	0	0	1	6	9	3	.088	8	-3
Total 2		27	48	4	7	0	0	0	1	6	9	3	.146	-18	-3

Surkowski, Anne - OF

YEAR	TEAM	G	AB	R	H	2B	3B	HR	RBI	BB	SO	SB	AVG	PRO+	BR
1945	SB	21	39	5	4	0	0	0	2	1	2	1	.103	14	-2

Surkowski, Lee (m. DelMonico 1948) - OF

YEAR	TEAM	G	AB	R	H	2B	3B	HR	RBI	BB	SO	SB	AVG	PRO+	BR
1944	SB	100	335	32	71	7	4	3	29	36	24	37	.212	144	4
1945	SB	106	349	42	73	8	4	1	8	28	4	34	.209	151	13
1946	SB-Rck	82	256	21	51	4	3	1	28	21	31	11	.199	112	-5
1948	FW	63	226	33	42	2	5	0	20	23	34	16	.186	111	-2
Total 4		351	1166	128	237	21	16	5	85	108	93	98	.203	133	10

Sutherland, Shirley

YEAR	TEAM	G	AB	R	H	2B	3B	HR	RBI	BB	SO	SB	AVG	PRO+	BR
1951	BC-GR														

Taylor, Eunice - C

YEAR	TEAM	G	AB	R	H	2B	3B	HR	RBI	BB	SO	SB	AVG	PRO+	BR
1951	Ken	38	114	5	22	1	1	0	10	4	11	1	.193	60	-8

Taylor, Mary - OF

YEAR	TEAM	G	AB	R	H	2B	3B	HR	RBI	BB	SO	SB	AVG	PRO+	BR
1953	FW	46	160	30	38	4	0	4	19	12	25	9	.237	144	2
1954	Kal	33	87	12	24	0	0	0	9	11	13	1	.276	77	-3
Total	2	79	247	42	62	4	0	4	28	23	38	10	.251	116	-1

Teillet, Yolande

YEAR	TEAM	G	AB	R	H	2B	3B	HR	RBI	BB	SO	SB	AVG	PRO+	BR
1945	FW	10	13	2	3	0	0	0	0	3	0	2	.231	165	1
1946	GR	5	6		1								.167	25	-1
1947	Ken	2	3		1								.333	164	0
Total	3	17	22		5								.227	131	1

Terkowski, Georgia

YEAR	TEAM	G	AB	R	H	2B	3B	HR	RBI	BB	SO	SB	AVG	PRO+	BR
1952	Rck	17	35	6	6	1	1	0	3	1	13	5	.171	89	-1

Terry, Betty

YEAR	TEAM	G	AB	R	H	2B	3B	HR	RBI	BB	SO	SB	AVG	PRO+	BR
1946	Peo	8	19		3								.158	18	-2

Tetro, Barbara

YEAR	TEAM	G	AB	R	H	2B	3B	HR	RBI	BB	SO	SB	AVG	PRO+	BR
1948	GR	1	0		0								.000	-99	0

Tetzlaff, Doris - 3B

YEAR	TEAM	G	AB	R	H	2B	3B	HR	RBI	BB	SO	SB	AVG	PRO+	BR
1944	Mil	102	345	62	73	3	4	3	42	47	32	101	.212	140	15
1945	GR	110	378	43	72	9	2	0	7	24	1	51	.190	144	23
1946	GR	112	382	57	76	4	0	1	34	74	46	57	.199	108	7
1947	GR	89	285	27	51	4	2	0	18	46	22	31	.179	108	3
1948	Chi-FW	121	392	44	75	5	7	0	27	82	74	30	.191	130	10
1949	Mus	91	274	34	44	4	0	0	16	68	37	28	.161	96	4
1950	FW														
1952	FW														
Total	8	625	2056		391								.190	98	62

Tezak, Virginia

YEAR	TEAM	G	AB	R	H	2B	3B	HR	RBI	BB	SO	SB	AVG	PRO+	BR
1948	Rac	4	7		0								.000	-99	-1

Thatcher
1951 BC

Thomas, Mava Lee
1951 FW

Thompson, Anna Jane - P

YEAR	TEAM	G	AB	R	H	2B	3B	HR	RBI	BB	SO	SB	AVG	PRO+	BR
1943	Rac	32	85	5	13	2	1	1	4	1	29	2	.153	69	-7

Thompson, Barbara

YEAR	TEAM	G	AB	R	H	2B	3B	HR	RBI	BB	SO	SB	AVG	PRO+	BR
1951	Rck	18	49	6	10	0	0	0	3	10	11	4	.204	85	-0
1952	Rck														
Total	2	18	49		10								.204	85	-0

Thompson, Viola - P

YEAR	TEAM	G	AB	R	H	2B	3B	HR	RBI	BB	SO	SB	AVG	PRO+	BR
1944	Mil	33	67	6	8	0	0	0	7	11	12	1	.119	44	-4
1945	GR	34	77	2	8	0	0	0	5	2	1	14	.104	35	-2
1946	SB	31	66	3	4	0	0	0	3	16	10	0	.061	10	-6
1947	SB	1	1		0								.000	-99	-0
Total	4	99	211		20								.095	29	-12

Tognatti, Alice - OF

YEAR	TEAM	G	AB	R	H	2B	3B	HR	RBI	BB	SO	SB	AVG	PRO+	BR
1946	FW	21	45	2	3	0	0	0	1	5	24	2	.067	-19	-6

Torrison, Loraine "Peggy" - P

YEAR	TEAM	G	AB	R	H	2B	3B	HR	RBI	BB	SO	SB	AVG	PRO+	BR
1944	Min	16	54	7	9	0	1	0	5	9	8	1	.167	96	-2

Trezza, Betty - SS/OF/2B

YEAR	TEAM	G	AB	R	H	2B	3B	HR	RBI	BB	SO	SB	AVG	PRO+	BR
1944	Min	64	194	25	21	1	0	2	16	29	16	48	.108	50	-8
1945	FW-SB	86	276	28	31	2	0	0	21	16	0	36	.112	48	-8
1946	Rac	111	422	58	74	6	8	0	43	52	42	65	.175	99	-5
1947	Rac	112	433	51	68	4	3	1	27	27	36	66	.157	67	-13
1948	Rac	126	469	67	85	4	4	1	27	44	55	64	.181	88	-7
1949	Rac	110	387	47	76	6	8	1	27	53	34	53	.196	135	8
1950	Rac	108	385	55	89	6	5	1	35	44	22	53	.231	111	3
Total	7	717	2566	331	444	29	28	6	196	265	205	385	.173	91	-30

Tucker, Elizabeth "Betty" - P

YEAR	TEAM	G	AB	R	H	2B	3B	HR	RBI	BB	SO	SB	AVG	PRO+	BR
1946	Peo	38	48	8	10	0	1	0	0	4	12	0	.208	106	-1
1947	FW-Rck-GR	21	28	3	2	0	0	0	1	2	8	5	.071	-21	-3
1948	Chi	48	86	15	18	1	0	0	5	10	19	11	.209	101	1
1949	Peo	16	37	3	7	1	0	0	3	9	8	0	.189	121	1
Total	4	123	199	29	37	2	1	0	9	25	47	16	.186	90	-3

Tysver, Joan
1950 GR
1951 Rck

Vanderlip, Dolly - P

YEAR	TEAM	G	AB	R	H	2B	3B	HR	RBI	BB	SO	SB	AVG	PRO+	BR
1952	FW	10	14	0	1	0	0	0	1	3	7	0	.071	13	-1
1953	FW	14	12	3	0	0	0	0	0	3	3	0	.000	-37	-2
1954	SB	19	43	4	8	0	0	0	6	8	9	0	.186	41	-3
Total	3	43	69	7	9	0	0	0	7	14	19	0	.130	24	-6

Ventura, Virginia - 1B

YEAR	TEAM	G	AB	R	H	2B	3B	HR	RBI	BB	SO	SB	AVG	PRO+	BR
1953	Rck	11	27	1	2	0	0	0	0	2	8	0	.074	-30	-4

Villa, Margaret - 2B/SS/C

YEAR	TEAM	G	AB	R	H	2B	3B	HR	RBI	BB	SO	SB	AVG	PRO+	BR
1946	Ken	108	355	52	70	5	1	3	33	72	30	44	.197	126	8
1947	Ken	105	353	45	71	3	6	1	30	52	32	36	.201	138	9
1948	Ken	119	405	54	77	6	8	1	31	71	40	36	.190	133	8
1949	Ken	111	387	53	79	6	3	0	36	65	29	54	.204	122	10
1950	Ken	94	332	45	85	12	3	0	38	42	20	30	.256	133	8
Total	5	537	1832	249	382	32	21	5	168	302	151	200	.209	130	44

Vincent, Georgette "Jetty" (m. Mooney 1952) - P

YEAR	TEAM	G	AB	R	H	2B	3B	HR	RBI	BB	SO	SB	AVG	PRO+	BR
1947	Rac	4	7		0								.000	-99	-1
1948	Rac	21	36	8	4	0	0	0	3		6		.111	22	-3
1949	SB	17	15	0	0	0	0		2	0			.000	-99	-3
1950	SB	40	107	9	20	0	0	0	5	12	13	8	.187	57	-4
1951	SB	34	58	9	9	1	2	0	5	7	4	7	.155	90	-2
1952	SB	36	71	9	12	2	1	0	9	9	8	3	.169	77	-3

YEAR	TEAM	G	AB	R	H	2B	3B	HR	RBI	BB	SO	SB	AVG	PRO+	BR
1954	SB														
Total	7	152	294		45								.153	35	-16

Violetta, Karen
1953 GR

Vonderau, Kathryn - C

YEAR	TEAM	G	AB	R	H	2B	3B	HR	RBI	BB	SO	SB	AVG	PRO+	BR
1946	FW	98	289	13	43	2	2	0	30	26	28	4	.149	52	-20
1947	Mus	45	148	9	29	3	0	0	9	5	8	5	.196	82	-5
1948	Chi-Peo	82	265	18	46	3	4	0	11	21	31	2	.174	83	-12
1949	Peo-Mus	86	252	19	44	4	1	0	13	28	37	4	.175	87	-7
1950	FW	90	295	23	57	4	0	0	25	29	44	4	.193	66	-14
1951	FW	74	249	24	55	12	0	0	32	26	29	1	.221	108	-5
1952	FW	66	219	20	46	8	2	1	20	13	20	1	.210	99	-8
1953	Mus	101	321	21	65	6	0	0	29	33	21	3	.202	70	-14
Total	8	642	2038	147	385	42	9	1	169	181	218	24	.189	79	-85

Voyce, Inez - 1B

YEAR	TEAM	G	AB	R	H	2B	3B	HR	RBI	BB	SO	SB	AVG	PRO+	BR
1946	SB	104	329	31	69	6	3	2	43	64	22	32	.210	143	11
1947	GR	113	383	27	82	5	4	1	45	30	15	19	.214	128	2
1948	GR	126	436	46	99	9	2	1	52	66	29	31	.227	136	11
1949	GR	113	374	51	96	6	0	3	53	67	9	22	.257	171	22
1950	GR	113	380	53	111	14	5	3	66	72	23	13	.292	187	27
1951	GR	106	372	43	106	14	5	2	49	59	12	10	.285	179	21
1952	GR	107	390	57	115	16	3	10	54	47	14	19	.295	204	27
1953	GR	112	383	55	103	11	4	6	60	75	20	22	.269	177	24
Total	8	894	3047	363	781	81	26	28	422	480	144	168	.256	167	145

Vukovich. Frances
1951 BC

Weddell, Helen - 2B/3B

YEAR	TEAM	G	AB	R	H	2B	3B	HR	RBI	BB	SO	SB	AVG	PRO+	BR
1950	Rck	54	149	11	14	3	0	0	12	17	37	3	.094	5	-17
1951	Rck-BC	69	217	25	32	2	0	0	17	24	36	6	.147	36	-17
Total	2	123	366	36	46	5	0	0	29	41	73	9	.126	23	-34

Waggott
1952 BC

Wagner, Audrey - OF

YEAR	TEAM	G	AB	R	H	2B	3B	HR	RBI	BB	SO	SB	AVG	PRO+	BR
1943	Ken	73	257	30	59	3	10	4	27	26	35	17	.230	169	5
1944	Ken	90	317	34	60	5	4	0	26	23	28	24	.189	96	-11
1945	Ken	101	343	26	68	5	9	2	13	26	2	22	.198	167	12
1946	Ken	109	392	53	110	15	5	9	53	40	29	32	.281	230	29
1947	Ken	107	390	48	119	25	9	7	53	32	25	39	.305	288	42
1948	Ken	117	417	70	130	16	14	4	56	56	31	53	.312	264	48
1949	Ken	97	348	28	81	8	4	3	40	48	55	23	.233	169	14
Total	7	694	2464	289	627	77	55	29	268	251	205	215	.254	204	140

Wagoner, Betty - OF

YEAR	TEAM	G	AB	R	H	2B	3B	HR	RBI	BB	SO	SB	AVG	PRO+	BR
1948	Mus-SB	84	248	42	69	2	1	0	11	42	42	7	.278	163	14
1949	Mus-SB	114	382	58	87	4	1	0	26	87	36	64	.228	139	23
1950	SB	106	388	61	115	11	3	0	39	64	22	37	.296	158	24
1951	SB	110	375	77	102	9	3	0	41	63	20	50	.272	145	20
1952	SB	97	353	64	104	7	4	0	27	64	16	40	.295	157	25
1953	SB	107	352	42	84	9	2	0	32	63	5	19	.239	118	6
1954	SB	48	150	23	48	12	0	0	15	20	4	4	.320	142	5
Total	7	666	2248	367	609	54	14	0	191	403	145	221	.271	145	116

Walker, Nellie Jean

YEAR	TEAM	G	AB	R	H	2B	3B	HR	RBI	BB	SO	SB	AVG	PRO+	BR
1945	SB	2	2		0								.000	-99	-0

Walmsley, Thelma

YEAR	TEAM	G	AB	R	H	2B	3B	HR	RBI	BB	SO	SB	AVG	PRO+	BR
1946	Rac	6	16		0								.000	-99	-3

Walulik, Helen - P

YEAR	TEAM	G	AB	R	H	2B	3B	HR	RBI	BB	SO	SB	AVG	PRO+	BR
1948	Mus-FW	18	25	1	3	0	0	1	4	2	4	1	.120	119	-1
1950	Kal	49	106	10	17	1	0	0	6	1	9	4	.160	19	-11
Total	2	67	131	11	20	1	0	1	10	3	13	5	.153	37	-11

Wanless, Betty - 3B

YEAR	TEAM	G	AB	R	H	2B	3B	HR	RBI	BB	SO	SB	AVG	PRO+	BR
1953	GR	85	306	49	76	10	1	3	35	27	39	48	.248	130	7
1954	SB	86	321	75	88	13	2	15	47	29	32	26	.274	173	11
Total	2	171	627	124	164	23	3	18	82	56	71	74	.262	154	18

Warfel, Betty - 3B

YEAR	TEAM	G	AB	R	H	2B	3B	HR	RBI	BB	SO	SB	AVG	PRO+	BR
1948	Rck	70	193	16	32	3	0	1	15	21	37	10	.166	81	-6
1949	Rck	25	58	6	4	0	0	0	1	8	17	3	.069	-7	-6
Total	2	95	251	22	36	3	0	1	16	29	54	13	.143	61	-12

Warren, Nancy - P

YEAR	TEAM	G	AB	R	H	2B	3B	HR	RBI	BB	SO	SB	AVG	PRO+	BR
1946	Mus	39	116	12	18	1	2	0	3	15	14	3	.155	79	-5
1947	Mus	31	81	6	16	1	0	0	5	1	10	2	.198	70	-4
1948	Mus-Chi	32	62	5	11	1	0	0	3	3	4	1	.177	60	-4
1949	Peo	27	61	5	8	0	0	0	5	9	3	0	.131	48	-3
1950	Peo	32	81	5	10	0	0	0	6	5	11	0	.123	-1	-10
1951	Peo-FW	27	64	5	10	0	0	0	0	9	15	1	.156	39	-5
1952	FW	28	82	9	18	2	1	0	9	7	8	1	.220	96	-2
1953	Mus	27	66	4	5	0	0	0	2	6	11	0	.076	-25	-10
1954	Kal	26	56	4	8	3	0	0	4	5	9	0	.143	28	-7
Total	9	269	669	55	104	8	3	0	37	60	85	8	.155	46	-49

Warwick, Mildred - 3B/2B

YEAR	TEAM	G	AB	R	H	2B	3B	HR	RBI	BB	SO	SB	AVG	PRO+	BR
1943	Rck	92	354	62	93	5	7	1	30	19	7	34	.263	132	2
1944	Rck	97	342	45	71	4	2	1	37	35	17	69	.208	111	3
Total	2	189	696	107	164	9	9	2	67	54	24	103	.236	122	5

Watson, Marion

YEAR	TEAM	G	AB	R	H	2B	3B	HR	RBI	BB	SO	SB	AVG	PRO+	BR
1946	Peo	8	11		0								.000	-99	-2

Wawryshyn, Evelyn - 2B

YEAR	TEAM	G	AB	R	H	2B	3B	HR	RBI	BB	SO	SB	AVG	PRO+	BR
1946	Ken-Mus	73	235	29	51	2	2	0	18	16	21	24	.217	102	-3
1947	Mus	36	93	10	22	2	2	0	7	7	4	2	.237	159	2
1948	Spg	118	435	58	114	4	4	0	30	32	39	66	.262	140	15
1949	FW	109	391	47	98	8	6	0	34	38	52	64	.251	158	18
1950	FW	104	399	71	124	13	2	1	50	36	38	65	.311	160	24
1951	FW	104	390	60	108	8	0	0	54	48	18	50	.277	128	13
Total	6	544	1943	275	517	37	16	1	193	177	175	273	.266	142	70

Weaver, Jean - 3B

YEAR	TEAM	G	AB	R	H	2B	3B	HR	RBI	BB	SO	SB	AVG	PRO+	BR
1950	FW														
1951	FW	87	312	39	77	4	2	2	31	16	42	31	.247	114	-0
1952	FW	55	160	21	36	9	3	0	19	8	17	8	.225	124	-2
1953	FW	30	48	11	15	2	1	0	5	1	3	2	.313	168	1
Total	4	172	520	71	128	15	6	2	55	25	62	41	.246	122	-1

Weaver, Joanne - OF

YEAR	TEAM	G	AB	R	H	2B	3B	HR	RBI	BB	SO	SB	AVG	PRO+	BR
1951	FW	48	163	23	45	8	2	1	21	15	16	6	.276	171	6
1952	FW	84	314	58	108	10	5	3	50	23	23	19	.344	205	26
1953	FW	104	410	79	142	18	6	5	76	23	26	70	.346	215	40
1954	FW	93	333	109	143	16	4	29	87	32	24	79	.429	329	73
Total	4	329	1220	269	438	52	17	38	234	93	89	174	.359	242	145

Weddle, Mary - 3B

YEAR	TEAM	G	AB	R	H	2B	3B	HR	RBI	BB	SO	SB	AVG	PRO+	BR
1954	FW	76	241	39	52	6	2	2	21	38	37	5	.216	86	-10

Weeks, Rossey

YEAR	TEAM	G	AB	R	H	2B	3B	HR	RBI	BB	SO	SB	AVG	PRO+	BR
1947	Rck	7	17		1								.059	-53	-3

Wegman, Marie - 3B/2B

YEAR	TEAM	G	AB	R	H	2B	3B	HR	RBI	BB	SO	SB	AVG	PRO+	BR
1947	Rck	101	297	19	52	4	1	1	10	24	43	18	.175	87	-8
1948	FW	36	86	3	8	0	1	0	6	13	19	2	.093	28	-7
1949	Mus	60	165	12	23	1	0	0	8	22	26	9	.139	48	-8
1950	GR	94	286	26	67	9	1	0	27	43	31	22	.234	113	2
Total	4	291	834	60	150	14	3	1	51	102	119	51	.180	84	-20

Weierman, Shirley Ann - 3B

YEAR	TEAM	G	AB	R	H	2B	3B	HR	RBI	BB	SO	SB	AVG	PRO+	BR
1953	FW														
1954	FW	11	28	0	5	0	0	0	0	1	12	0	.179	7	-4
Total	2	11	28	0	5	0	0	0	0	1	12	0	.179	7	-4

Wenzell, Margaret - OF/2B

YEAR	TEAM	G	AB	R	H	2B	3B	HR	RBI	BB	SO	SB	AVG	PRO+	BR
1945	GR	34	93	10	16	2	4	0	1	11	1	15	.172	191	8
1946	Mus	8	26		7								.269	101	-1
1947	Peo-FW	31	72	4	7	1	0	0	0	14	13	11	.097	44	-2
1948	Spg	104	346	30	58	3	4	1	19	55	39	33	.168	97	-3
1949	Rac-FW	70	220	22	40	3	1	0	13	29	17	27	.182	95	-0
1950	Kal-Rac	73	184	28	34	0	1	0	14	31	21	14	.185	68	-6
1951	Kal-BC	108	381	43	81	10	7	0	41	53	36	25	.213	117	-1
1952	BC-SB	84	259	28	56	6	6	0	20	27	16	21	.216	111	-2
1953	SB	45	96	14	17	5	1	0	10	28	13	10	.177	121	3
Total	9	557	1677	179	316	30	24	1	118	248	156	156	.188	102	-3

Westerman, Helen - C

YEAR	TEAM	G	AB	R	H	2B	3B	HR	RBI	BB	SO	SB	AVG	PRO+	BR
1943	Ken	82	263	36	48	3	1	0	21	15	14	20	.183	52	-17

Westerman, Joyce (see Hill)

Whalen, Dorothy - C

YEAR	TEAM	G	AB	R	H	2B	3B	HR	RBI	BB	SO	SB	AVG	PRO+	BR
1948	Spg	49	111	9	17	2	0	0	5	14	13	11	.153	70	-3

Whiteman, Vera - 2B

YEAR	TEAM	G	AB	R	H	2B	3B	HR	RBI	BB	SO	SB	AVG	PRO+	BR
1946	GR	16	45	6	6	0	0	0	2	6	9	3	.133	39	-3

Whiting, Betty - 1B

YEAR	TEAM	G	AB	R	H	2B	3B	HR	RBI	BB	SO	SB	AVG	PRO+	BR
1944	Mil	114	371	41	75	6	5	0	34	50	31	53	.202	123	4
1945	GR	103	358	36	63	4	0	0	19	14	16	17	.176	89	-4
1946	GR	112	374	41	67	8	1	0	24	34	34	27	.179	76	-15
1947	FW	110	356	31	56	6	1	1	19	34	30	31	.157	83	-8
1948	Chi-SB	120	338	33	62	6	5	1	20	67	55	17	.183	137	10
1949	SB	93	254	25	49	7	3	0	40	48	45	7	.193	145	9
1950	SB-Kal	92	285	36	59	15	0	1	25	54	33	4	.207	122	2
1951	Kal-BC	95	269	30	51	8	0	0	28	55	28	16	.190	93	-2
1952	BC	104	342	38	79	4	1	0	28	43	30	14	.231	94	-3
Total	9	943	2947	311	561	64	16	3	237	399	302	186	.190	106	-6

Wicken, Elizabeth - OF

YEAR	TEAM	G	AB	R	H	2B	3B	HR	RBI	BB	SO	SB	AVG	PRO+	BR
1945	GR	89	319	22	60	7	4	0	3	28	2	31	.188	139	11
1946	Mus-GR	28	88	10	14	5	1	0	6	13	16	8	.159	112	-2
Total	2	117	407	32	74	12	5	0	9	41	18	39	.182	133	9

Wigiser, Margaret - OF

YEAR	TEAM	G	AB	R	H	2B	3B	HR	RBI	BB	SO	SB	AVG	PRO+	BR
1944	Min-Rck	78	273	30	58	1	4	2	38	26	25	29	.212	128	-0
1945	Rck	86	309	39	77	8	2	2	5	35	2	17	.249	193	22
1946	Rck	39	118	11	24	1	2	0	15	8	5	12	.203	102	-2
Total	3	203	700	80	159	10	8	4	58	69	32	58	.227	152	19

Wiley, Janet - 1B

YEAR	TEAM	G	AB	R	H	2B	3B	HR	RBI	BB	SO	SB	AVG	PRO+	BR
1950	SB	40	97	5	13	1	1	0	7	12	28	1	.134	46	-7
1951	SB	74	181	21	40	3	1	0	13	16	26	3	.221	90	-6
1952	SB														
1953	Rck	33	102	5	21	1	0	0	5	3	15	3	.206	53	-6
Total	4	147	380	31	74	5	2	0	25	31	69	7	.195	69	-19

Williams, Ruth - P

YEAR	TEAM	G	AB	R	H	2B	3B	HR	RBI	BB	SO	SB	AVG	PRO+	BR
1946	FW	6	5	0									.000	-99	-1
1947	SB	26	59	2	8	0	0	0	1	6	12	2	.136	41	-3
1948	SB	23	55	1	7	0	0	0	4	4	9	1	.127	17	-5
1949	SB	25	48	3	8	0	0	0	5	3	14	1	.167	52	-3
1950	SB-Kal	20	34	3	4	0	0	0	0	4	12	0	.118	8	-4
1951	Kal	26	45	4	6	0	0	0	2	7	12	2	.133	27	-3
1952	Kal	23	52	3	8	0	0	0	5	5	13	0	.154	26	-5
1953	Kal	22	40	5	3	0	0	0	1	10	12	1	.075	8	-4
Total	8	171	338	21	44	0	0	0	15	39	84	7	.130	25	-27

Wilson, Dodie - OF

YEAR	TEAM	G	AB	R	H	2B	3B	HR	RBI	BB	SO	SB	AVG	PRO+	BR
1947	Peo	79	230	17	50	1	1	0	23	21	22	16	.217	111	1

Wilson, Verna

YEAR	TEAM	G	AB	R	H	2B	3B	HR	RBI	BB	SO	SB	AVG	PRO+	BR
1946	Rck	1	1	0									.000	-99	-0

Wiltse, Dottie (m. Collins 1946) - P

YEAR	TEAM	G	AB	R	H	2B	3B	HR	RBI	BB	SO	SB	AVG	PRO+	BR
1944	Min	41	107	5	13	0	0	0	4	12	20	2	.121	24	-10
1945	FW	46	113	9	12	0	0	0	14	5	0	35	.106	57	0
1946	FW	51	113	13	12	2	1	0	6	26	34	2	.106	60	-6
1947	FW	40	85	5	2	0	0	0	1	11	30	2	.024	-34	-10
1948	FW	24	48	3	5	0	0	0	3	11	26	0	.104	45	-2
1950	FW	26	57	2	8	0	0	0	3	8	13	0	.140	27	-5
Total	6	228	523	37	52	5	1	0	31	73	123	41	.099	33	-33

Wind, Dottie - SS

YEAR	TEAM	G	AB	R	H	2B	3B	HR	RBI	BB	SO	SB	AVG	PRO+	BR
1943	Rac	88	321	56	82	4	7	2	44	18	15	36	.255	137	4
1944	Rac	56	208	29	50	4	4	0	19	17	7	28	.240	148	4
Total	2	144	529	85	132	8	11	2	63	35	22	64	.250	141	7

Wingrove, Elsie - OF

YEAR	TEAM	G	AB	R	H	2B	3B	HR	RBI	BB	SO	SB	AVG	PRO+	BR
1946	FW-GR	38	110	10	23	2	1	0	7	5	17	5	.209	97	-4
1947	GR	81	243	20	41	5	0	0	8	15	23	14	.169	68	-10
Total	2	119	353	30	64	7	1	0	15	20	40	19	.181	77	-14

Winslow

YEAR	TEAM	G	AB	R	H	2B	3B	HR	RBI	BB	SO	SB	AVG	PRO+	BR
1953	SB														

Winter, Joanne - P

YEAR	TEAM	G	AB	R	H	2B	3B	HR	RBI	BB	SO	SB	AVG	PRO+	BR
1943	Rac	31	83	9	21	0	0	1	12	4	7	7	.253	107	-1
1944	Rac	50	127	14	21	2	0	0	12	17	9	12	.165	76	-4
1945	Rac	45	118	4	14	1	2	0	4	3	0	14	.119	61	-5
1946	Rac	51	115	22	25	1	3	1	12	24	13	7	.217	168	4
1947	Rac	42	105	8	17	3	0	0	8	15	16	4	.162	88	-2
1948	Rac	39	100	8	12	1	0	1	6	23	23	3	.120	77	-3
1949	Rac	32	66	4	6	0	0	0	4	14	15	0	.091	25	-4
1950	Rac	38	76	8	17	2	0	1	8	5	8	0	.224	112	-2
Total	8	328	790	77	133	10	5	4	66	105	91	47	.168	93	-16

Wirth, Senaida "Shoo Shoo" - SS

YEAR	TEAM	G	AB	R	H	2B	3B	HR	RBI	BB	SO	SB	AVG	PRO+	BR
1946	SB	107	372	65	91	4	1	0	27	61	22	89	.245	133	20
1947	SB	73	229	35	52	0	1	0	5	42	20	32	.227	135	11
1948	SB	113	399	60	96	6	4	0	26	42	37	36	.241	136	9
1949	SB	113	389	62	89	1	0	1	40	55	38	66	.229	123	15
1950	SB	105	384	61	103	9	2	1	49	49	20	67	.268	134	17
1951	SB	105	347	77	95	6	4	0	54	64	23	69	.274	149	24
Total	6	616	2120	360	526	26	12	2	201	313	160	359	.248	135	96

Wisham, Mary (see Nesbitt)

Wisniewski, Connie - P/OF

YEAR	TEAM	G	AB	R	H	2B	3B	HR	RBI	BB	SO	SB	AVG	PRO+	BR
1944	Mil	39	111	6	17	2	3	0	9	11	10	5	.153	99	-5
1945	GR	54	138	18	27	1	1	0	6	17	1	12	.196	133	6
1946	GR	55	136	20	34	5	1	0	16	15	11	7	.250	152	3
1947	GR	62	189	19	55	9	4	0	24	26	12	10	.291	230	16
1948	GR	124	439	70	127	20	2	7	66	68	30	60	.289	229	44
1949	GR	112	406	64	113	13	7	0	32	56	27	41	.278	198	29
1951	GR	105	386	78	126	15	9	0	42	48	31	22	.326	204	32
1952	GR	105	360	64	96	14	3	0	25	55	33	35	.267	142	15
Total	8	656	2165	339	595	79	30	7	220	296	155	192	.275	186	140

Wood, Loita - P

YEAR	TEAM	G	AB	R	H	2B	3B	HR	RBI	BB	SO	SB	AVG	PRO+	BR
1950	FW														

Wood, Mary - OF

YEAR	TEAM	G	AB	R	H	2B	3B	HR	RBI	BB	SO	SB	AVG	PRO+	BR
1946	Peo	88	269	23	52	5	3	0	13	36	36	33	.193	106	-1
1947	Ken	70	211	13	27	1	0	0	6	28	41	26	.128	46	-8
Total	2	158	480	36	79	6	3	0	19	64	77	59	.165	80	-9

Wood, Trois - P

YEAR	TEAM	G	AB	R	H	2B	3B	HR	RBI	BB	SO	SB	AVG	PRO+	BR
1951	Ken	30	72	4	10	1	0	0	4	5	16	0	.139	21	-7

Wright, Sadie

YEAR	TEAM	G	AB	R	H	2B	3B	HR	RBI	BB	SO	SB	AVG	PRO+	BR
1951	BC														

Wronski, Sylvia - P

YEAR	TEAM	G	AB	R	H	2B	3B	HR	RBI	BB	SO	SB	AVG	PRO+	BR
1944	Mil	13	20	1	1	0	0	0	0	2	10	3	.050	-32	-2
1945	BC	4	2	0									.000	-99	-0
Total	2	17	22	0	1								.045	-37	-3

Yahr, Betty - OF

YEAR	TEAM	G	AB	R	H	2B	3B	HR	RBI	BB	SO	SB	AVG	PRO+	BR
1946	Rck	22	76	11	13	1	1	0	8	12	12	2	.171	96	-2

Young, Ruth - P

YEAR	TEAM	G	AB	R	H	2B	3B	HR	RBI	BB	SO	SB	AVG	PRO+	BR
1951	BC														

Youngberg, Renae - 3B

YEAR	TEAM	G	AB	R	H	2B	3B	HR	RBI	BB	SO	SB	AVG	PRO+	BR
1951	GR	98	338	26	68	7	2	0	31	18	33	5	.201	72	-19
1952	GR	86	287	27	48	8	2	0	24	24	20	12	.167	61	-16
1953	Mus-SB-GR	72	234	24	52	7	0	0	18	39	9	6	.222	102	-1
1954	GR	85	282	50	76	6	1	8	50	43	17	13	.270	136	4
Total	4	341	1141	127	244	28	5	8	123	124	79	36	.214	94	-32

Youngen, Lois - OF/C

YEAR	TEAM	G	AB	R	H	2B	3B	HR	RBI	BB	SO	SB	AVG	PRO+	BR
1951	Ken-FW														
1952	FW	11	16	2	5	0	0	0	0	0	1	0	.313	120	0
1953	SB	40	101	10	19	1	0	0	9	19	7	1	.188	72	-3
1954	FW-SB	65	208	27	59	7	0	1	35	27	14	2	.284	108	-1
Total	4	116	325	39	83	8	0	1	44	46	22	3	.255	99	-4

Ziegler, Alma - 2B/P

YEAR	TEAM	G	AB	R	H	2B	3B	HR	RBI	BB	SO	SB	AVG	PRO+	BR
1944	Mil	115	324	51	62	2	1	0	25	72	29	77	.191	110	12
1945	GR	103	365	35	51	3	0	0	16	15	3	26	.140	65	-9
1946	GR	101	344	60	52	7	0	0	27	65	26	55	.151	79	-2
1947	GR	112	388	55	71	4	0	0	8	62	36	67	.183	98	7
1948	GR	126	454	61	77	8	0	1	33	61	44	38	.170	86	-7
1949	GR	113	370	58	67	0	2	0	18	87	12	34	.181	106	9
1950	GR	111	322	37	56	4	0	0	23	70	19	19	.174	74	-6
1951	GR	106	340	35	58	10	4	0	35	52	16	20	.171	89	-9
1952	GR	85	249	20	49	2	1	0	16	33	9	7	.197	72	-8
1953	GR	96	250	37	42	4	0	0	18	55	23	17	.168	72	-5
1954	GR	86	215	33	43	3	0	2	21	38	9	5	.200	70	-11
Total	11	1154	3621	482	628	47	8	3	240	610	226	365	.173	84	-30

Ziemak, Frances - P

YEAR	TEAM	G	AB	R	H	2B	3B	HR	RBI	BB	SO	SB	AVG	PRO+	BR
1951	Peo														

Zonia, Violet

YEAR	TEAM	G	AB	R	H	2B	3B	HR	RBI	BB	SO	SB	AVG	PRO+	BR
1948	Spg	1	1	0									.000	-99	-0

Zurowski, Agnes - P

YEAR	TEAM	G	AB	R	H	2B	3B	HR	RBI	BB	SO	SB	AVG	PRO+	BR
1945	Rac-FW	4	5	0									.000	-99	-1

YEAR	TEAM	G	W	L	PCT	IP	H	R	BB	SO	ERA	ERA+	PR
● Albright, Eileen													
1948	Chi	4	0	4	.000	22	17	11	19	10	2.45	92	-1
● Allard, Beatrice													
1949	Mus	19	2	2	.500	59	48	26	49	15	2.75	75	-4
● Allen, Agnes													
1951	Kal-BC	24	3	10	.231	100	86	94	126	51	6.21	45	-38
1952	Kal	12	1	7	.125	66	74	56	57	33	6.00	42	-25
1953	Kal	24	10	9	.526	158	130	85	113	50	3.70	71	-19
Total	3	60	14	26	.350	324	290	235	296	134	4.94	54	-82
● Alvarez, Isabel													
1951	FW-BC	13	2	0	1.000	34	41	29	26	7	3.71	75	-4
● Anderson, Janet													
1946	Ken	10	0	6	.000	36	45	49	30	8	7.75	31	-21
● Applegren, Amy Irene													
1944	Rck	36	16	15	.516	250	168	123	128	56	2.77	92	-6
1945	Rck	29	13	11	.542	214	132	81	130	27	2.44	79	-12
1946	Mus	28	8	18	.308	197	134	90	126	62	2.79	86	-9
1947	Mus	27	16	10	.615	220	113	41	81	62	1.06	182	21
1948	Mus	29	15	12	.556	210	110	64	117	129	1.76	128	12
1949	Mus-Rck	20	5	12	.294	131	78	54	124	64	3.09	67	-15
1950	Rck	21	9	10	.474	132	104	76	83	68	3.75	74	-14
1951	Rck	15	4	10	.286	94	66	57	91	33	4.21	66	-15
1952	Rck	1	0	0	.000	3							
Total	9	206	86	98	.467	1451	905	586	880	501	2.52	91	-38
● Armstrong, Charlotte													
1944	SB	39	21	15	.583	321	231	99	71	68	1.51	168	37
1945	SB	46	18	22	.450	355	280	137	83	91	1.98	98	-2
Total	2	85	39	37	.513	676	511	236	154	159	1.76	126	35
● Arnold, Lenna													
1946	FW	6	2	4	.333	40	37	32	23	1	4.50	53	-9
1948	SB	20	4	4	.500	82	64	48	32	17	4.06	55	-1
1949	SB	16	5	2	.714	91	72	32	32	17	2.27	91	-2
1951	SB	20	10	2	.833	117	106	54	35	28	2.62	106	2
1952	SB	16	4	8	.333	76	83	49	18	13	3.43	74	-8
Total	5	78	25	20	.556	406	362	215	140	76	3.17	77	-34
● Baker, Phyllis													
1953	Mus	28	7	12	.368	188	161	84	88	36	3.21	82	-12
1954	SB-FW	22	5	11	.313	129	145	89	78	30	4.81	75	-17
Total	2	50	12	23	.343	317	306	173	166	66	3.86	79	-29
● Barr, Doris													
1943	SB	32	15	13	.536	254	199	123	151	63	2.91	104	4
1944	SB	29	8	11	.421	148	72	61	141	62	2.98	85	-7
1945	SB-Rac	31	20	8	.714	252	144	66	168	104	1.71	113	6
1946	Rac	21	6	9	.400	119	77	73	109	53	3.86	62	-19
1947	Rac	30	14	12	.538	219	144	78	91	96	2.26	86	-8
1948	Spg	30	7	19	.269	208	150	104	113	116	2.68	84	-10
1949	Mus	27	8	13	.381	191	141	82	108	53	2.40	86	-7
1950	Peo-Kal	18	1	11	.083	83	94	73	78	25	6.51	43	-34
Total	8	218	79	96	.451	1474	1021	660	959	572	2.80	83	-77
● Becker, Donna													
1951	Kal	3	0	0	.000	3							
● Bell, Virginia													
1948	Spg	1	0	0	.000	8	6	10	8	4	7.88	29	-5
● Bennett, Catherine													
1943	Ken-SB	31	8	13	.381	190	179	140	69	53	3.79	80	-16
1944	SB	34	14	9	.609	229	185	81	44	69	2.04	124	13
Total	2	65	22	22	.500	419	364	221	113	122	2.84	97	-3
● Berger, Joan													
1952	Rck	1	0	0	.000	0							
● Berger, Margaret													
1943	SB	47	25	13	.658	306	207	103	70	112	1.91	158	38
1944	SB	41	21	17	.553	315	188	84	64	92	1.57	162	34
Total	2	88	46	30	.605	621	395	187	134	204	1.74	160	72
● Bergman, Erma													
1946	Mus	35	15	16	.484	263	195	119	94	62	2.05	116	10
1947	Mus	27	11	10	.524	207	137	74	71	47	1.74	112	5
1948	Spg	32	9	19	.321	236	190	127	85	77	3.05	74	-21
1949	Rac	32	11	14	.440	225	156	80	71	42	2.08	99	-1
1950	Rac	29	11	14	.440	208	173	108	68	51	2.68	103	2
1951	BC	27	7	18	.280	200	195	119	73	59	3.92	71	-25
Total	6	182	64	91	.413	1339	1046	627	462	338	2.56	92	-30
● Bevis, Muriel													
1950	Ken	7	1	2	.333	29	30	27	25	5	6.83	41	-13
● Bird, Nelda													
1945	SB	31	13	17	.433	223	135	117	160	128	2.70	71	-19
● Bittner, Jayne													
1947	SB	8	1	2	.333	35	35	15	8	8	1.54	126	2
1948	Mus	21	9	9	.500	152	148	69	81	29	2.55	88	-5
1949	GR	26	4	10	.286	131	94	70	72	31	3.44	60	-20
1950	GR	20	5	10	.333	119	136	96	77	55	5.60	49	-37
1951	GR	23	15	8	.652	183	128	76	78	57	2.95	94	-4
1952	GR-FW	25	11	12	.478	178	163	92	111	93	3.34	76	-16
1953	FW	30	16	7	.696	209	149	89	128	75	2.45	108	4
1954	GR	24	5	11	.313	119	120	92	92	45	5.07	71	-19
Total	8	177	66	69	.489	1126	973	599	647	359	3.38	78	-95
● Blumetta, Kay													
1944	Min	5	0	0	.000	0							
1945	GR	4	1	2	.333	18	15	21	25	2	6.00	32	-8
1946	Peo	26	11	12	.478	209	117	65	74	137	1.72	139	16
1947	Peo-FW	27	9	14	.391	193	171	79	69	105	2.80	69	-18
1948	FW	30	14	13	.519	238	157	81	117	100	2.16	104	3
1949	FW	27	9	16	.360	217	145	72	71	102	1.99	103	2
1950	FW	23	9	12	.429	170	135	76	103	63	2.33	119	8
1951	Kal	24	8	11	.421	151	114	59	62	65	2.74	101	0
1952	Kal	21	8	11	.421	170	138	71	55	54	2.54	100	-0
1953	Kal	23	10	9	.526	164	149	58	52	29	1.98	134	12
1954	Kal	19	5	5	.500	83	107	77	51	16	5.86	62	-21
Total	11	229	84	105	.444	1613	1248	659	679	673	2.48	99	-7
● Born, Ruth													
1943	SB	11	4	5	.444	68	61	47	47	6	3.57	85	-4
● Brown, Patricia													
1951	BC	1	0	0	.000	2							
● Bryson, Marion													
1946	Peo	14	0	8	.000	71	74	60	36	11	5.32	45	-23
● Burkovich, Shirley													
1951	Rck	3	0	0	.000	2							
● Butcher, Mary													
1945	Ken-GR	1	0	0	.000	8							
● Callow, Eleanor													
1952	Rck	3	0	1	.000	11	11	8	15	3	5.73	44	-4
1953	Rck	1	0	1	.000	4	5	4	3	0	4.50	59	-1
Total	2	4	0	2	.000	15	16	12	18	3	5.40	48	-5
● Carver, Virginia													
1954	FW	17	5	7	.417	80	102	91	70	12	8.78	41	-46
● Carveth, Betty													
1945	Rck-FW	21	4	11	.267	138	116	57	47	24	2.28	85	-5
● Cione, Jean													
1947	Rck-Ken	37	19	14	.576	271	146	80	73	98	1.30	150	19
1948	Ken	31	12	13	.480	229	142	83	80	75	1.85	122	10
1949	Ken	32	15	10	.600	223	151	58	87	80	1.57	131	12
1950	Ken	32	18	10	.643	243	204	108	114	72	2.96	93	-5
1951	Ken	18	5	9	.357	127	109	64	52	41	3.90	71	-16
1952	BC	9	2	5	.286	50	49	27	16	21	3.24	78	-4
1953	Mus	1	1	0	1.000	5	7	4	2	1	5.40	49	-2
1954	Rck	10	4	4	.500	52	51	41	38	24	5.02	72	-8
Total	8	170	76	65	.539	1200	859	465	462	412	2.32	102	7
● Clapp, Louise													
1954	GR-SB	3	0	0	.000	5							
● Coben, Muriel													
1943	SB-Rck	37	4	16	.200	193	218	150	55	43	4.76	64	-37
● Collins, Dottie (see Wiltse)													
● Cook, Clara													
1943	Rck-Ken	30	6	17	.261	204	213	177	52	26	4.41	69	-31
1944	Ken-Mil	9	2	2	.500	45	42	24	16	7	3.40	75	-4
Total	2	39	8	19	.296	249	255	201	68	33	4.23	70	-36
● Cook, Donna													
1947	Mus	25	14	8	.636	178	101	49	58	54	1.42	137	10
1948	Chi-Mus-FW	20	4	9	.308	116	84	64	107	67	4.03	56	-23
1949	FW	22	9	9	.500	153	111	55	99	75	1.94	106	2
1950	GR	4	0	2	.000	18	24	25	20	9	10.00	28	-14
1951	BC	17	1	7	.125	78	71	53	66	33	4.38	63	-14
1953	SB	7	0	2	.000	16	24	35	33	5	12.94	20	-18
1954	Rck	4	0	0	.000	7							
Total	7	99	28	37	.431	566	415	281	383	243	3.08	71	-56
● Cook, Doris													
1951	Kal	8	0	1	.000	22	16	19	19	5	5.73	48	-7
1953	Kal-SB	9	0	2	.000	30	36	34	36	3	8.40	31	-19
Total	2	17	0	3	.000	52	52	53	55	8	7.27	37	-26
● Cordes, Gloria													
1950	Kal-Rac	25	5	10	.333	119	122	77	76	23	3.63	76	-11
1951	BC-Kal	26	3	15	.167	179	168	110	96	70	3.52	79	-15
1952	Kal	24	16	8	.667	213	156	68	52	84	1.44	177	26
1953	Kal	29	13	11	.542	218	165	78	74	106	1.98	133	16
1954	Kal	24	12	7	.632	145	139	89	63	86	4.59	79	-16
Total	5	128	49	51	.490	874	750	422	361	369	2.82	100	0
● Cornett, Betty Jane													
1951	BC	2	0	1	.000	8	15	12	12	4	11.25	25	-8
● Crews, Mary (see Nesbitt)													
● Dailey, Mary													
1951	Peo	3	1	0	1.000	15	18	12	10	5	6.00	46	-5
● Dancer, Faye													
1944	Min	2	0	0	.000	0							
1945	FW	1	0	0	.000	3							
1946	FW	21	10	9	.526	148	111	67	59	38	1.95	123	7
1947	Peo	4	1	2	.333	26	32	15	11	5	4.15	47	-6
Total	4	28	11	11	.500	177	143	82	70	43	2.24	104	2
● Daniels, Audrey (see Haine)													
● Dapkus, Eleanor													
1947	Rac	5	0	3	.000	55	32	17	27	23	2.45	79	-3
1948	Rac	39	24	9	.727	297	172	75	104	191	1.55	146	23
1949	Rac	27	14	11	.522	208	162	75	74	71	2.25	92	-4
1950	Rac	31	17	11	.607	229	162	65	63	112	1.81	153	24
Total	4	102	53	34	.609	789	528	232	268	397	1.87	125	40
● DeCambra, Alice													
1946	FW	16	6	5	.583	93	87	40	17	9	2.81	85	-4
1947	FW-Peo	14	4	3	.571	70	67	41	19	17	4.24	46	-18
1950	Peo	1	0	0	.000	2							
Total	3	31	11	8	.579	165	154	81	36	26	3.38	65	-22
● Deegan, Mildred													
1946	Rck	21	10	5	.667	139	78	67	55	47	2.46	97	-1

YEAR	TEAM	G	W	L	PCT	IP	H	R	BB	SO	ERA	ERA+	PR
1947	Rck-Ken	21	8	9	.471	133	103	61	63	61	2.30	84	-5
1948	Ken-Spg	29	12	15	.444	237	152	91	89	115	2.13	106	3
1949	FW	28	16	11	.593	234	153	73	87	82	1.77	116	8
1950	FW	29	16	9	.640	220	161	80	134	75	2.17	128	15
1951	FW-Peo	17	4	9	.308	110	102	69	81	29	3.44	81	-8
1952	Rck	1	0	1	.000	8	6	3	5	3	2.25	113	0
Total	7	146	66	59	.528	1081	755	444	514	412	2.26	104	11

● Denton, Mona

YEAR	TEAM	G	W	L	PCT	IP	H	R	BB	SO	ERA	ERA+	PR
1946	SB	3	0	1	.000	13	15	15	4	2	6.92	35	-7
1947	Ken	23	1	10	.091	112	108	75	35	20	3.54	55	-20
Total	2	26	1	11	.083	125	123	90	39	22	3.89	51	-26

● Descombes, Jeanie

YEAR	TEAM	G	W	L	PCT	IP	H	R	BB	SO	ERA	ERA+	PR
1953	GR	7	0	1	.000	17	21	22	24	5	7.41	36	-9
1954	GR	22	10	8	.556	117	119	72	70	63	5.00	72	-18
Total	2	29	10	9	.526	134	140	94	94	68	5.31	66	-27

● Earp, Mildred

YEAR	TEAM	G	W	L	PCT	IP	H	R	BB	SO	ERA	ERA+	PR
1947	GR	35	20	8	.714	280	172	30	32	192	0.68	287	39
1948	GR	34	15	14	.517	282	180	70	60	166	1.31	172	30
1949	GR	27	14	10	.583	216	162	61	48	143	1.83	112	5
1950	GR	12	5	6	.455	82	62	34	35	33	2.52	110	2
Total	4	108	54	38	.587	860	576	195	175	534	1.35	159	77

● Eisen, Thelma "Tiby"

YEAR	TEAM	G	W	L	PCT	IP	H	R	BB	SO	ERA	ERA+	PR
1948	FW	1	0	0	.000	7	5	4	6	1	5.14	44	-2

● Emry, Betty

YEAR	TEAM	G	W	L	PCT	IP	H	R	BB	SO	ERA	ERA+	PR
1946	Rac	15	7	4	.636	91	65	39	24	16	2.18	110	2

● Erickson, Louise

YEAR	TEAM	G	W	L	PCT	IP	H	R	BB	SO	ERA	ERA+	PR
1948	Rac	3	1	0	1.000	11	11	7	4	3	5.73	39	-4
1949	Rck	25	17	6	.739	216	145	44	61	39	1.54	134	12
1950	Rck	27	16	10	.615	221	187	82	57	88	2.52	110	6
Total	3	55	34	16	.680	448	343	133	122	130	2.13	113	14

● Faralla, Lillian

YEAR	TEAM	G	W	L	PCT	IP	H	R	BB	SO	ERA	ERA+	PR
1946	Peo	2	0	1	.000	4	7	8	6	2	11.25	21	-4
1947	FW	22	3	12	.200	123	87	53	56	26	1.98	98	-0
1948	SB	34	10	20	.333	267	170	86	86	75	1.99	113	8
1949	SB	34	19	9	.679	245	148	48	107	40	1.36	152	19
1950	GR-Kal	28	8	10	.444	170	164	82	82	40	3.12	89	-7
1951	SB	22	15	4	.789	170	130	53	61	57	1.85	149	17
Total	6	142	55	56	.495	979	706	330	398	240	2.04	115	33

● Farrow, Elizabeth

YEAR	TEAM	G	W	L	PCT	IP	H	R	BB	SO	ERA	ERA+	PR
1944	Rck-Min	19	1	12	.077	99	72	93	85	16	5.64	45	-34

● Faut, Jean

YEAR	TEAM	G	W	L	PCT	IP	H	R	BB	SO	ERA	ERA+	PR
1946	SB	12	8	3	.727	81	53	20	21	21	1.33	179	10
1947	SB	44	19	13	.594	298	179	56	67	97	1.15	169	26
1948	SB	34	16	11	.593	250	156	68	113	165	1.44	156	23
1949	SB	34	24	8	.750	261	136	47	118	120	1.10	187	28
1950	SB	36	21	9	.700	290	175	64	104	118	1.12	248	53
1951	SB	23	15	7	.682	190	121	43	65	135	1.33	209	30
1952	SB	23	20	7	.909	184	111	31	42	114	0.93	273	33
1953	SB	29	17	11	.607	226	162	74	59	143	1.51	174	28
Total	8	235	140	64	.686	1780	1093	403	589	913	1.23	195	231

● Ferguson, Dorothy (m. Key 1949)

YEAR	TEAM	G	W	L	PCT	IP	H	R	BB	SO	ERA	ERA+	PR
1945	Rck	1	0	0	.000	1							
1950	Rck	1	0	0	.000	1							
1951	Rck	2	0	2	.000	9	11	14	14	3	10.00	28	-7
1953	Rck	1	0	0	.000	2							
Total	4	5	0	2	.000	13	11	14	14	3	6.92	40	-6

● Ferguson, Fern

YEAR	TEAM	G	W	L	PCT	IP	H	R	BB	SO	ERA	ERA+	PR
1945	Rac	1	0	0	.000	11	12	10	9	0	4.91	39	-4

● Fischer, Alva Jo

YEAR	TEAM	G	W	L	PCT	IP	H	R	BB	SO	ERA	ERA+	PR
1945	SB	16	4	7	.364	98	78	52	73	33	3.77	51	-20
1946	Mus	29	11	16	.407	224	171	106	131	58	2.77	86	-10
1948	Mus	21	9	7	.563	129	78	39	37	55	1.47	154	11
1949	Mus	25	10	7	.588	157	92	42	55	86	1.78	116	5
Total	4	91	34	37	.479	608	419	239	296	232	2.40	92	-13

● Fisher, Lorraine

YEAR	TEAM	G	W	L	PCT	IP	H	R	BB	SO	ERA	ERA+	PR
1947	Rck	13	4	4	.500	69	44	22	20	24	2.35	83	-3
1948	GR	32	16	11	.593	230	177	97	138	61	2.82	80	-15
1949	GR	25	13	11	.542	161	110	68	92	42	2.18	94	-2
Total	3	70	33	26	.559	460	331	187	250	127	2.52	85	-20

● Florreich, Lois

YEAR	TEAM	G	W	L	PCT	IP	H	R	BB	SO	ERA	ERA+	PR
1946	Ken	33	9	16	.360	244	171	124	101	72	2.40	100	-0
1947	Rck	35	13	19	.406	257	132	70	102	90	1.68	115	7
1948	Rck	36	22	10	.688	282	157	60	87	231	1.18	191	34
1949	Rck	29	22	7	.759	269	104	33	94	210	0.67	308	42
1950	Rck	32	20	8	.714	252	144	56	65	171	1.18	235	45
Total	5	165	86	60	.589	1304	708	343	449	774	1.40	162	127

● Folder, Rose

YEAR	TEAM	G	W	L	PCT	IP	H	R	BB	SO	ERA	ERA+	PR
1944	Ken	14	2	7	.222	73	75	67	49	15	5.67	45	-25

● Foss, Anita

YEAR	TEAM	G	W	L	PCT	IP	H	R	BB	SO	ERA	ERA+	PR
1949	Mus	3	0	0	.000	6							

● Foss, Betty

YEAR	TEAM	G	W	L	PCT	IP	H	R	BB	SO	ERA	ERA+	PR
1950	FW	2	0	1	.000	1	2	7	5	1	54.00	5	-6

● Fox, Helen (see Nicol)

● Froning, Mary

YEAR	TEAM	G	W	L	PCT	IP	H	R	BB	SO	ERA	ERA+	PR
1951	SB	1	0	0	.000	1							
1954	SB	5	1	2	.333	12	10	14	16	4	6.00	60	-3
Total	2	6	1	2	.333	13	10	14	16	4	5.54	65	-3

● Gacioch, Rose

YEAR	TEAM	G	W	L	PCT	IP	H	R	BB	SO	ERA	ERA+	PR
1946	Rck	4	2	2	.500	34	35	26	20	12	4.50	53	-8
1947	Rck	1	0	0	.000	0							
1948	Rck	21	14	5	.737	175	121	59	52	64	2.21	102	1
1949	Rck	14	9	2	.818	91	63	26	33	23	1.68	123	4
1950	Rck-GR	23	7	9	.438	162	152	74	92	38	3.56	78	-14
1951	Rck	29	20	7	.741	231	153	59	63	48	1.68	165	28
1952	Rck	31	20	10	.667	259	200	82	40	48	1.88	135	19
1953	Rck	29	15	12	.556	229	208	106	69	48	2.67	99	-1
1954	Rck	22	7	15	.318	152	186	113	43	45	4.68	77	-18
Total	9	174	94	62	.603	1333	1118	545	412	326	2.60	103	11

● Gallegos, Luisa

YEAR	TEAM	G	W	L	PCT	IP	H	R	BB	SO	ERA	ERA+	PR
1948	Peo-SB	16	2	6	.250	73	46	55	76	37	5.79	39	-29

● Ganote, Gertrude

YEAR	TEAM	G	W	L	PCT	IP	H	R	BB	SO	ERA	ERA+	PR
1944	Ken	12	4	6	.400	91	76	45	48	13	3.26	78	-7
1945	SB	10	2	2	.500	53	47	31	32	7	4.42	44	-15
Total	2	22	6	8	.429	144	123	76	80	20	3.69	63	-22

● Gates, Barbara

YEAR	TEAM	G	W	L	PCT	IP	H	R	BB	SO	ERA	ERA+	PR
1953	GR-SB	16	1	3	.250	55	51	54	59	19	6.71	39	-25
1954	FW	3	0	1	.000	2	2	8	10	1	27.00	13	-5
Total	2	19	1	4	.200	57	53	62	69	20	7.42	36	-30

● Geissinger, Jean

YEAR	TEAM	G	W	L	PCT	IP	H	R	BB	SO	ERA	ERA+	PR
1954	FW	5	0	0	.000	10							

● Georges, Beulah

YEAR	TEAM	G	W	L	PCT	IP	H	R	BB	SO	ERA	ERA+	PR
1948	Chi-FW	10	0	4	.000	48	57	38	28	5	5.63	40	-18

● Goldsmith, Bethany

YEAR	TEAM	G	W	L	PCT	IP	H	R	BB	SO	ERA	ERA+	PR
1948	Ken	31	14	14	.500	245	135	71	99	117	1.62	139	17
1949	Ken	29	8	11	.421	179	113	79	110	49	3.17	65	-22
1950	Ken	27	12	9	.571	198	162	101	123	80	3.68	75	-20
Total	3	87	34	34	.500	622	410	251	332	246	2.72	87	-25

● Graham, Mary Lou

YEAR	TEAM	G	W	L	PCT	IP	H	R	BB	SO	ERA	ERA+	PR
1953	SB	6	0	0	.000	8							

● Habben, Carol

YEAR	TEAM	G	W	L	PCT	IP	H	R	BB	SO	ERA	ERA+	PR
1954	Kal	2	0	0	.000	4							

● Haine, Audrey (m. Daniels 1951)

YEAR	TEAM	G	W	L	PCT	IP	H	R	BB	SO	ERA	ERA+	PR
1944	Min	34	8	20	.286	230	190	171	209	115	4.85	52	-59
1945	FW	32	16	10	.615	223	159	98	156	101	2.46	78	-13
1946	FW-GR	30	14	11	.560	208	130	120	236	120	4.11	58	-40
1947	GR-Peo	28	13	12	.520	199	139	96	82	58	2.89	67	-21
1948	Peo	33	17	14	.548	228	179	116	100	82	2.92	77	-17
1951	Rck	10	4	3	.571	66	54	37	52	17	3.82	73	-8
Total	6	167	72	70	.507	1154	851	638	835	493	3.48	65	158

● Harnett, Ann

YEAR	TEAM	G	W	L	PCT	IP	H	R	BB	SO	ERA	ERA+	PR
1947	Peo	1	0	0	.000	0							

● Harney, Elsie

YEAR	TEAM	G	W	L	PCT	IP	H	R	BB	SO	ERA	ERA+	PR
1943	Ken	45	19	19	.500	304	282	167	104	102	2.93	103	3
1944	Ken	34	18	14	.563	262	175	114	115	88	2.23	114	9
1945	Ken	43	14	22	.389	301	201	125	121	91	2.60	74	-22
1946	Ken-FW	33	10	20	.333	255	219	143	116	61	2.93	82	-15
1947	FW	17	2	10	.167	107	114	61	43	24	3.79	51	-22
Total	5	172	63	85	.426	1229	991	610	499	366	2.78	87	-47

● Hasham, Josephine

YEAR	TEAM	G	W	L	PCT	IP	H	R	BB	SO	ERA	ERA+	PR
1948	Mus-Peo	10	0	6	.000	63	46	22	26	22	2.14	105	1
1949	SB	23	12	8	.600	169	134	58	81	45	2.02	102	1
1950	Peo	32	8	19	.296	226	213	119	64	88	3.38	82	-15
1951	Peo	30	13	15	.464	218	220	108	107	43	3.10	89	-8
1952	BC	33	12	14	.462	222	195	94	74	36	2.51	101	1
1953	Mus	31	8	19	.296	206	224	119	66	22	3.71	71	-25
1954	Rck	20	5	7	.417	60	94	54	22	14	7.05	51	-23
Total	7	179	58	88	.397	1164	1126	574	440	270	3.15	83	-69

● Hatzell, Beverly

YEAR	TEAM	G	W	L	PCT	IP	H	R	BB	SO	ERA	ERA+	PR
1950	Rac	19	4	7	.364	102	86	72	83	35	4.85	57	-24
1951	BC-Peo	20	1	14	.067	105	111	103	97	38	5.66	49	-34
Total	2	39	5	21	.192	207	197	175	180	73	5.26	53	-57

● Hayiett, Alice

YEAR	TEAM	G	W	L	PCT	IP	H	R	BB	SO	ERA	ERA+	PR
1946	GR	38	17	21	.447	297	203	119	191	113	2.97	80	-19
1947	GR	31	19	11	.633	258	169	78	67	92	1.95	99	-0
1948	GR	32	25	5	.833	269	169	36	67	114	0.77	292	44
1949	GR	27	9	10	.474	220	149	70	80	71	1.88	109	4
Total	4	128	70	47	.598	1044	690	303	405	390	1.92	113	29

● Headin, Irene

YEAR	TEAM	G	W	L	PCT	IP	H	R	BB	SO	ERA	ERA+	PR
1945	SB	1	0	0	.000	1							

● Heafner, Ruby

YEAR	TEAM	G	W	L	PCT	IP	H	R	BB	SO	ERA	ERA+	PR
1948	FW	2	0	1	.000	2	6	6	0	0	13.50	17	-3

● Hohlmayer, Alice

YEAR	TEAM	G	W	L	PCT	IP	H	R	BB	SO	ERA	ERA+	PR
1947	Ken	16	7	6	.538	129	105	37	12	16	1.88	103	1
1948	Ken	13	4	4	.500	80	70	34	21	23	2.36	95	-1
1949	Mus	7	0	1	.000	22	22	12	7	7	3.68	56	-4
1950	Kal-Peo	24	7	10	.412	139	152	89	53	34	4.01	69	-19
1951	Peo	29	15	11	.577	209	184	74	48	46	2.02	137	17
Total	5	89	33	32	.508	579	533	246	141	126	2.58	96	-6

● Holgerson, Margaret (played as Silvestri 1949-52)

YEAR	TEAM	G	W	L	PCT	IP	H	R	BB	SO	ERA	ERA+	PR
1946	Rck	5	2	2	.500	33	18	7	11	8	1.09	219	5
1947	Rck	27	9	15	.375	201	138	80	77	48	2.42	80	-11
1948	Rck	37	16	15	.516	277	143	71	108	194	1.92	117	10
1949	Rck-Mus	17	5	10	.333	132	85	39	47	47	1.70	121	5
1950	Mus-GR	33	14	12	.538	230	185	84	70	100	2.00	139	20
1951	GR	25	16	6	.727	200	120	45	77	123	1.53	181	28
1952	GR	24	14	9	.609	168	138	65	81	78	2.36	108	3
Total	7	168	76	69	.524	1241	832	393	497	599	1.97	122	60

● Horstman, Katie

YEAR	TEAM	G	W	L	PCT	IP	H	R	BB	SO	ERA	ERA+	PR
1951	FW-Ken	6	3	0	1.000	23	15	10	14	9	2.35	118	1
1952	FW	10	5	2	.714	65	45	24	31	28	2.35	108	1
1953	FW	17	11	5	.688	124	92	44	46	57	2.32	114	4

YEAR	TEAM	G	W	L	PCT	IP	H	R	BB	SO	ERA	ERA+	PR
1954	FW	16	10	4	.714	101	90	51	31	46	2.85	127	9
Total	4	49	29	11	.725	313	242	129	122	140	2.50	118	15

● Hutchison, Anna May

YEAR	TEAM	G	W	L	PCT	IP	H	R	BB	SO	ERA	ERA+	PR
1946	Rac	51	26	14	.650	288	204	89	69	102	1.59	150	25
1947	Rac	44	27	13	.675	360	230	77	72	120	1.38	141	23
1948	Rac	14	3	6	.333	76	79	41	37	16	3.67	61	-12
1949	Mus	25	8	12	.400	161	126	58	74	19	2.35	88	-5
1951	Ken	4	1	2	.333	24	20	14	13	2	4.88	57	-6
Total	5	138	65	47	.580	909	659	279	265	259	1.90	113	25

● Jacobs, Jane

YEAR	TEAM	G	W	L	PCT	IP	H	R	BB	SO	ERA	ERA+	PR
1944	Rac	31	9	16	.360	230	251	113	65	16	2.82	90	-7
1945	Rac	21	7	9	.438	125	137	68	30	9	2.88	67	-13
1946	Peo	23	6	12	.333	164	147	80	63	21	2.14	112	5
1947	Peo	13	2	6	.250	71	46	31	31	6	2.92	67	-8
Total	4	88	24	43	.358	590	581	292	189	52	2.65	87	-23

● Janssen, Frances

YEAR	TEAM	G	W	L	PCT	IP	H	R	BB	SO	ERA	ERA+	PR
1948	GR	11	4	4	.500	61	63	35	24	7	3.98	56	-12
1950	Peo-Kal-FW	19	3	3	.500	93	96	63	51	14	3.87	72	-11
1951	FW-Peo	26	6	10	.375	145	131	69	57	43	2.67	104	2
1952	BC	5	0	1	.000	18	18	11	11	3	5.00	51	-5
Total	4	61	13	18	.419	317	308	178	143	67	3.41	78	-26

● Jaykoski, Joan

YEAR	TEAM	G	W	L	PCT	IP	H	R	BB	SO	ERA	ERA+	PR
1951	Ken	10	1	3	.250	30	32	42	44	4	7.80	36	-17

● Jinright, Migdalia (see Perez)

● Jochum, Betsy

YEAR	TEAM	G	W	L	PCT	IP	H	R	BB	SO	ERA	ERA+	PR
1948	SB	29	14	13	.519	215	154	61	58	103	1.51	149	18

● Jogerst, Donna

YEAR	TEAM	G	W	L	PCT	IP	H	R	BB	SO	ERA	ERA+	PR
1952	Rck	1	0	0	.000	1							

● Jones, Marguerite

YEAR	TEAM	G	W	L	PCT	IP	H	R	BB	SO	ERA	ERA+	PR
1944	Min-Rck	28	6	12	.333	175	150	96	24	1	3.70	69	-23

● Jones, Marilyn

YEAR	TEAM	G	W	L	PCT	IP	H	R	BB	SO	ERA	ERA+	PR
1952	BC	17	9	7	.563	128	94	35	69	46	1.69	151	12
1953	Mus	30	14	11	.560	218	186	92	125	86	2.56	103	2
1954	FW	22	8	8	.500	131	135	86	65	59	4.26	85	-9
Total	3	69	31	26	.544	477	415	213	259	191	2.79	103	5

● Jurgensmeier, Margaret

YEAR	TEAM	G	W	L	PCT	IP	H	R	BB	SO	ERA	ERA+	PR
1951	Rck	9	1	1	.500	26	23	31	37	7	7.96	35	-15

● Kabick, Josephine

YEAR	TEAM	G	W	L	PCT	IP	H	R	BB	SO	ERA	ERA+	PR
1944	Mil	45	26	19	.578	366	270	158	147	81	2.66	96	-5
1945	GR	35	16	18	.471	292	204	91	113	33	1.85	104	3
1946	GR-Ken	40	19	19	.500	324	283	131	72	53	2.39	100	0
1947	Peo	31	13	16	.448	231	191	101	71	78	2.34	83	-10
Total	4	151	74	72	.507	1213	948	481	403	245	2.33	96	-12

● Keagle, Merle "Pat"

YEAR	TEAM	G	W	L	PCT	IP	H	R	BB	SO	ERA	ERA+	PR
1946	GR	6	3	2	.600	51	41	13	15	14	1.94	123	3
1948	GR	10	4	3	.571	51	32	33	51	8	3.71	61	-8
Total	2	16	7	5	.583	102	73	46	66	22	2.82	82	-6

● Kelley, Jackie

YEAR	TEAM	G	W	L	PCT	IP	H	R	BB	SO	ERA	ERA+	PR
1950	Rck	7	0	1	.000	9	9	11	18	8	9.00	31	-6
1951	Rck	6	1	1	.500	29	18	15	24	8	2.79	99	-0
1952	Rck	27	12	11	.522	209	178	91	132	73	2.89	88	-8
1953	Rck	13	2	5	.286	63	54	40	42	26	4.86	54	-16
Total	4	53	15	18	.455	310	259	157	216	115	3.45	75	-30

● Kerrigan, Marguerite

YEAR	TEAM	G	W	L	PCT	IP	H	R	BB	SO	ERA	ERA+	PR
1951	Rck	1	0	0	.000	1							

● Key, Dorothy (see Ferguson)

● Kidd, Glenna Sue

YEAR	TEAM	G	W	L	PCT	IP	H	R	BB	SO	ERA	ERA+	PR
1950	Mus	26	1	10	.091	141	148	75	30	39	2.94	94	-3
1951	SB-BC	19	11	7	.611	136	119	55	37	50	2.51	110	4
1952	SB	23	13	7	.650	189	154	65	30	64	2.00	127	11
1953	SB	31	13	15	.464	258	225	94	51	67	2.37	111	8
1954		18	9	6	.600	133	142	64	37	50	2.91	124	10
Total	5	117	47	45	.511	857	788	353	185	270	2.49	113	31

● Kline, Maxine

YEAR	TEAM	G	W	L	PCT	IP	H	R	BB	SO	ERA	ERA+	PR
1948	FW	24	8	13	.381	164	127	70	41	45	2.58	87	-6
1949	FW	28	14	11	.560	229	141	66	60	57	1.93	107	3
1950	FW	33	23	9	.719	266	241	96	72	87	2.44	114	10
1951	FW	24	18	4	.818	194	141	67	56	69	1.95	142	18
1952	FW	28	19	7	.731	238	189	69	48	70	1.93	132	16
1953	FW	31	16	14	.533	246	225	88	60	76	2.49	106	4
1954	FW	28	18	7	.720	181	180	82	52	91	3.23	112	8
Total	7	196	116	65	.641	1518	1244	538	389	495	2.34	113	53

● Kobuczewski, Theresa

YEAR	TEAM	G	W	L	PCT	IP	H	R	BB	SO	ERA	ERA+	PR
1946	Ken	21	3	9	.250	123	96	65	44	56	2.71	88	-4
1947	Ken-FW	30	11	15	.423	208	158	95	64	47	2.42	80	-11
Total	2	51	14	24	.368	331	254	160	108	103	2.53	83	-16

● Koehn, Phyllis

YEAR	TEAM	G	W	L	PCT	IP	H	R	BB	SO	ERA	ERA+	PR
1945	SB	7	2	4	.333	52	32	28	26	6	1.90	101	0
1946	SB	39	22	15	.595	309	233	132	131	64	2.48	97	3
1947	SB	34	16	16	.500	265	191	98	76	73	2.17	89	-7
1948	SB-Peo-Rac	21	6	8	.429	128	97	67	87	60	3.02	74	-11
1949	Rac-FW	22	2	11	.154	126	78	68	93	31	3.43	60	-19
1950	GR	1	0	0	.000	6							
Total	6	124	48	54	.471	886	631	393	413	234	2.55	85	-38

● Kotowicz, Irene

YEAR	TEAM	G	W	L	PCT	IP	H	R	BB	SO	ERA	ERA+	PR
1947	FW-Ken	23	8	10	.444	162	120	69	64	30	2.61	74	-12
1948	Chi	37	18	17	.514	296	193	109	167	197	2.71	83	-15
1949	Rac	25	8	15	.348	190	144	74	109	69	2.32	89	-6
1950	Rac	11	0	5	.000	54	46	47	73	19	4.67	59	-11
Total	4	96	34	47	.420	702	503	299	413	315	2.73	79	-44

● Krick, Jaynie

YEAR	TEAM	G	W	L	PCT	IP	H	R	BB	SO	ERA	ERA+	PR
1948	SB	13	2	6	.250	59	47	44	60	22	4.12	55	-12
1949	SB	5	2	1	.667	25	20	20	26	10	1.44	143	2
1951	BC-Peo	19	2	7	.222	107	104	79	47	38	4.12	67	-16
1952	GR	21	2	7	.222	117	104	55	48	38	2.69	94	-2
1953	GR	3	0	1	.000	7	11	9	8	1	3.86	68	-1
Total	5	61	8	22	.267	315	286	207	189	97	3.37	75	-30

● Kruckel, Marie

YEAR	TEAM	G	W	L	PCT	IP	H	R	BB	SO	ERA	ERA+	PR
1948	SB-Mus	19	9	4	.692	120	83	45	41	19	1.65	136	8
1949	Mus	15	1	7	.125	85	82	41	23	8	2.75	75	-7
Total	2	34	10	11	.476	205	165	86	64	27	2.11	103	1

● Kurys, Sophie

YEAR	TEAM	G	W	L	PCT	IP	H	R	BB	SO	ERA	ERA+	PR
1950	Rac	1	0	0	.000	2							

● Leduc, Noella

YEAR	TEAM	G	W	L	PCT	IP	H	R	BB	SO	ERA	ERA+	PR
1952	BC	19	3	4	.429	81	79	37	24	5	3.11	82	-5
1953	Mus	24	3	9	.250	97	104	75	50	19	5.10	52	-27
1954	FW	24	9	10	.474	125	148	106	72	42	6.05	60	-34
Total	3	67	15	23	.395	303	331	218	146	66	4.96	61	-65

● Lee, Annabelle

YEAR	TEAM	G	W	L	PCT	IP	H	R	BB	SO	ERA	ERA+	PR
1944	Min	29	11	14	.440	211	175	96	69	56	2.43	104	3
1945	FW	31	13	16	.448	243	162	67	49	54	1.56	124	10
1946	Peo	37	12	23	.343	266	233	134	71	82	2.74	87	-10
1947	Peo-GR	24	9	11	.450	165	140	61	37	29	2.24	87	-5
1948	FW	27	10	14	.417	208	155	78	87	74	2.25	100	0
1949	Peo	21	5	14	.263	161	152	82	76	58	2.18	94	-2
1950	Peo	17	3	4	.429	68	56	25	26	28	2.51	110	2
Total	7	186	63	96	.396	1322	1073	543	415	381	2.25	99	-3

● Lee, Dolores

YEAR	TEAM	G	W	L	PCT	IP	H	R	BB	SO	ERA	ERA+	PR
1952	Rck	5	1	2	.333	26	24	12	12	6	3.46	73	-3
1953	Rck	26	12	10	.545	193	175	84	63	30	2.24	118	9
1954	Rck	22	10	10	.500	152	141	81	93	94	3.91	93	-5
Total	3	53	23	22	.511	371	340	177	168	130	3.01	101	1

● Little, Alta

YEAR	TEAM	G	W	L	PCT	IP	H	R	BB	SO	ERA	ERA+	PR
1947	Mus	1	0	0	.000	0							

● Little, Olive

YEAR	TEAM	G	W	L	PCT	IP	H	R	BB	SO	ERA	ERA+	PR
1943	Rck	44	21	15	.583	288	201	137	112	151	2.56	118	15
1945	Rck	34	22	11	.667	295	182	94	140	142	1.68	115	8
1946	Rck	34	14	17	.452	247	167	108	131	88	2.51	95	-3
Total	3	112	57	43	.570	830	550	339	383	381	2.23	110	20

● Lonetto, Sarah

YEAR	TEAM	G	W	L	PCT	IP	H	R	BB	SO	ERA	ERA+	PR
1948	Mus	17	3	9	.250	97	88	48	57	12	2.78	81	-6
1949	Mus	3	0	0	.000	12							
Total	2	20	3	9	.250	109	88	48	57	12	2.48	91	-3

● Lovell, Jean

YEAR	TEAM	G	W	L	PCT	IP	H	R	BB	SO	ERA	ERA+	PR
1948	Rck	9	3	4	.429	54	54	39	29	9	4.00	56	-11
1951	Kal-Ken	8	0	6	.000	48	49	44	31	8	5.25	53	-13
1954	Kal	1	0	0	.000	1							
Total	3	18	3	10	.231	103	103	83	60	17	4.54	55	-23

● Lovett, Frances

YEAR	TEAM	G	W	L	PCT	IP	H	R	BB	SO	ERA	ERA+	PR
1946	Peo	1	0	1	.000	7	13	12	2	0	10.29	23	-6

● Luckey, Lillian

YEAR	TEAM	G	W	L	PCT	IP	H	R	BB	SO	ERA	ERA+	PR
1946	SB	8	2	4	.333	54	51	37	48	10	3.50	68	-7

● Luna, Betty

YEAR	TEAM	G	W	L	PCT	IP	H	R	BB	SO	ERA	ERA+	PR
1944	Rck	27	12	13	.480	207	141	93	85	63	2.61	97	-2
1945	SB	30	14	15	.483	230	141	68	66	77	1.53	126	10
1946	SB	41	23	13	.639	298	199	102	126	93	2.30	104	3
1947	Rck	29	11	14	.440	234	142	59	81	75	1.65	117	7
1948	Chi	25	12	9	.571	171	97	55	117	98	1.95	116	6
1949	FW	10	2	6	.250	67	48	52	49	24	3.90	53	-14
Total	6	162	74	70	.514	1207	768	429	524	430	2.12	104	11

● Maguire, Dorothy

YEAR	TEAM	G	W	L	PCT	IP	H	R	BB	SO	ERA	ERA+	PR
1945	GR	1	0	0	.000	4							

● Mandella, Lenora

YEAR	TEAM	G	W	L	PCT	IP	H	R	BB	SO	ERA	ERA+	PR
1951	Peo	17	3	4	.429	80	75	66	71	23	4.28	65	-13

● Mansfield, Marie

YEAR	TEAM	G	W	L	PCT	IP	H	R	BB	SO	ERA	ERA+	PR
1951	Rck	30	16	8	.667	202	126	94	150	121	2.85	97	-2
1952	Rck-BC	24	3	14	.176	122	95	81	128	53	4.94	51	-33
1953	Rck	24	10	12	.455	188	135	91	151	143	2.82	93	-4
1954	Rck	14	5	8	.385	99	68	55	76	52	3.27	111	4
Total	4	92	34	42	.447	611	424	321	505	369	3.33	85	-34

● Marks, Gloria

YEAR	TEAM	G	W	L	PCT	IP	H	R	BB	SO	ERA	ERA+	PR
1943	Rac	29	11	9	.550	166	145	125	117	29	4.07	75	-19

● Marlowe, Jean

YEAR	TEAM	G	W	L	PCT	IP	H	R	BB	SO	ERA	ERA+	PR
1948	Spg	31	7	22	.241	236	212	141	60	42	3.66	61	-37
1949	Ken	17	7	7	.500	108	83	42	49	11	2.67	77	-7
1950	Ken	25	12	12	.500	201	160	66	64	51	2.42	115	8
1951	Ken	28	12	15	.444	211	171	89	86	116	2.52	110	6
1952	Kal	21	10	11	.476	172	150	77	77	60	3.24	78	-13
1954	Kal	23	8	12	.400	147	165	109	114	43	4.78	76	-19
Total	6	145	56	79	.415	1075	941	524	450	323	3.19	84	-63

● Marrero, Mirtha

YEAR	TEAM	G	W	L	PCT	IP	H	R	BB	SO	ERA	ERA+	PR
1948	Chi	29	4	21	.160	211	178	122	113	49	3.75	60	-35
1950	Kal	30	7	17	.292	186	164	108	98	78	3.73	74	-20
1951	FW	29	17	8	.680	213	177	90	94	87	2.24	124	13
1952	BC	23	4	14	.222	138	142	85	63	33	3.59	71	-16
1953	Mus	8	0	2	.000	26	32	32	28	5	7.27	36	-13
Total	5	119	32	62	.340	774	693	437	396	252	3.42	76	-72

● Marsh, Doris

YEAR	TEAM	G	W	L	PCT	IP	H	R	BB	SO	ERA	ERA+	PR
1945	FW	3	0	2	.000	17	18	10	8	2	3.18	61	-2

● Matlock, Ruth

YEAR	TEAM	G	W	L	PCT	IP	H	R	BB	SO	ERA	ERA+	PR
1950	FW	14	0	4	.000	61	37	34	65	6	3.54	78	-5

YEAR	TEAM	G	W	L	PCT	IP	H	R	BB	SO	ERA	ERA+	PR
● McCormick, Judy													
1954	SB	1	0	0	.000	4							
● Menheer, Marie													
1945	Rac	1	0	0	.000	6							
● Meyer, Rita "Slats"													
1947	Peo	13	3	6	.333	75	45	41	48	56	3.12	62	-10
● Moon, Dorothy													
1946	Rck	15	2	6	.250	63	64	66	64	17	7.00	34	-32
● Mooney, Georgette (see Vincent)													
● Moore, Elleanor													
1951	Kal-FW	29	6	14	.300	176	162	86	69	65	2.86	97	-2
1952	FW-GR	28	6	12	.333	143	126	73	45	59	3.08	82	-9
1953	GR	30	17	7	.708	221	168	76	106	119	2.00	132	16
1954	GR	24	14	7	.667	163	150	80	84	53	3.31	109	6
Total	4	111	43	40	.518	703	606	315	304	296	2.74	105	11
● Moore, Mary Ann													
1948	Rck	8	2	3	.400	45	31	23	40	5	4.00	56	-9
● Moraty, Mary													
1946	FW	6	0	2	.000	28	34	24	22	5	4.82	50	-8
● Morris, Carolyn													
1944	Rck	44	23	18	.561	343	189	116	133	112	2.15	118	15
1945	Rck	42	28	12	.700	333	163	68	55	119	1.08	179	31
1946	Rck	48	29	13	.690	356	204	82	98	240	1.42	169	39
Total	3	134	80	43	.650	1032	556	266	286	471	1.55	148	85
● Mueller, Dorothy													
1947	Peo	48	21	13	.618	312	187	88	75	112	1.41	137	18
1948	Peo	32	21	9	.700	267	140	61	79	181	1.11	202	34
1949	Peo	26	7	16	.304	219	146	73	53	114	1.89	109	4
1950	SB	27	16	9	.640	221	185	82	53	90	2.48	112	7
1951	SB	13	10	2	.833	104	89	21	19	40	1.56	178	14
1952	SB	12	5	7	.417	104	85	39	25	38	1.82	140	8
1953	GR	28	12	7	.632	182	142	71	62	82	2.67	99	-1
Total	7	186	92	63	.594	1409	974	435	366	657	1.80	130	85
● Naum, Dorothy													
1950	Ken	19	6	4	.600	94	59	37	40	38	2.39	116	4
1951	Ken	12	5	4	.556	79	44	16	38	27	1.14	243	14
1952	Kal	8	2	4	.333	68	67	33	17	20	1.99	128	4
1953	Kal	25	14	7	.667	198	171	69	54	75	2.18	121	10
Total	4	64	27	19	.587	439	341	155	149	160	2.01	133	33
● Nearing, Merna													
1943	Ken	5	0	1	.000	19	31	22	13	0	7.11	43	-9
● Nesbitt, Mary (m. Crews 1944)													
1943	Rac	47	26	13	.667	308	220	132	97	85	2.63	115	14
1944	Rac	45	23	17	.575	343	225	137	190	106	2.73	93	-7
1945	Rac	37	16	19	.457	284	208	111	101	58	1.87	103	2
Total	3	129	65	49	.570	935	653	380	388	249	2.44	103	8
● Nicol, Helen (m. Fox 1945)													
1943	Ken	47	31	8	.795	348	219	115	108	220	1.81	167	47
1944	Ken	32	17	11	.607	243	119	57	83	136	0.93	274	44
1945	Ken	46	24	19	.558	357	203	98	145	220	1.34	144	24
1946	Ken	33	15	17	.469	231	147	79	147	137	2.10	114	7
1947	Ken-Rck	26	6	16	.273	175	135	74	99	90	2.62	74	-13
1948	Rck	32	17	13	.567	252	204	107	81	52	2.61	86	-10
1949	Rck	26	13	8	.619	212	101	35	65	70	0.98	211	26
1950	Rck	28	14	12	.538	218	158	78	67	60	1.98	140	19
1951	Rck	28	18	7	.720	214	174	79	69	67	2.57	108	5
1952	Rck	15	8	7	.533	132	119	56	31	24	2.80	91	-4
Total	10	313	163	118	.580	2382	1579	778	895	1076	1.89	129	144
● Nordquist, Helen													
1952	Rck	17	3	7	.300	86	77	68	80	20	4.50	56	-19
1953	Rck	12	1	4	.200	46	40	40	55	20	3.91	67	-7
1954	SB	15	2	9	.182	77	105	89	54	17	7.36	49	-32
Total	3	44	6	20	.231	209	222	197	189	57	5.43	55	-57
● O'Hara, Janice													
1943	Ken	3	1	0	1.000	14	11	7	6	0	3.21	94	-0
1944	Ken	4	0	0	.000	0							
1947	Ken	21	6	8	.429	118	122	58	33	20	3.51	55	-21
1948	Ken	20	4	6	.400	104	80	51	62	38	3.20	70	-11
1949	Ken	11	2	3	.400	60	57	36	39	23	4.65	44	-17
Total	5	59	13	17	.433	296	270	152	140	81	3.62	59	-49
● Ortman, Dorothy													
1944	Rac	15	6	8	.429	99	94	53	47	5	3.36	76	-9
● Paire, Lavonne "Pepper"													
1950	GR	1	0	0	.000	7							
1952	FW	3	0	0	.000	3							
1953	FW	3	1	0	1.000	11	17	4	7	2	2.45	108	0
Total	3	7	1	0	1.000	21	17	4	7	2	1.29	205	3
● Parsons, Sue													
1953	Rck	1	0	0	.000	2							
1954	Rck	17	0	2	.000	52	58	45	68	7	5.88	62	-13
Total	2	18	0	2	.000	54	58	45	68	7	5.67	64	-12
● Payne, Barbara													
1951		1	0	0	.000	2							
● Pearson, Dolly													
1953	SB	5	0	2	.000	11	14	14	11	1	9.00	29	-8
● Peppas, June													
1948	FW	16	4	12	.250	113	107	70	91	39	4.62	49	-30
1949	FW-Rac	12	3	4	.429	68	45	29	35	10	2.25	92	-1
1950	Rac	11	4	4	.500	67	63	41	41	21	4.57	61	-13
1951	BC-Kal	11	1	7	.125	57	63	44	31	20	4.58	60	-11
1954	Kal	13	6	4	.600	65	62	38	44	28	3.32	109	2
Total	5	63	18	31	.367	370	340	222	242	118	3.94	67	-54
● Perez, Migdalia "Mickey" (m. Jinright 1952)													
1948	Chi	32	10	17	.370	240	220	111	62	22	2.55	88	-8
1951	BC	32	13	16	.448	237	241	118	50	25	3.00	92	-6
1952	BC	33	11	12	.478	208	214	78	41	25	2.34	109	5
1953	Rck	34	12	14	.462	220	204	101	42	15	2.25	117	10
1954	Rck	24	11	11	.500	164	197	98	51	29	3.73	97	-2
Total	5	155	57	70	.449	1069	1076	506	246	116	2.73	99	-2
● Peters, Marjorie													
1943	Rck	39	12	19	.387	270	272	161	58	27	3.10	98	-2
1944	Rck	9	1	5	.167	70	75	42	12	8	3.34	76	-6
Total	2	48	13	24	.351	340	347	203	70	35	3.15	93	-8
● Pieper, Marge													
1948	Chi	4	0	1	.000	15	7	12	10	10	2.40	94	-0
1951	Peo	3	1	1	.500	13	18	21	18	4	11.77	24	-13
1953	Mus	1	0	0	.000	5							
Total	3	8	1	2	.333	33	25	33	28	14	5.73	44	-12
● Pirok, Pauline													
1947	SB	3	0	0	.000	0							
● Podolski, Bertha													
1946	FW	2	1	1	.500	17	12	5	13	1	1.59	150	2
● Pratt, Mary													
1943	Rck	24	5	11	.313	150	157	97	38	8	3.96	77	-16
1944	Rck-Ken	41	21	15	.583	303	207	133	90	26	2.50	102	2
1945	Ken	27	1	16	.059	158	131	95	66	14	3.99	48	-36
1946	Rck	14	1	7	.125	69	79	48	38	6	4.83	50	-19
1947	Rck	4	0	2	.000	27	28	23	8	1	6.33	31	-13
Total	7	110	28	51	.354	707	602	396	240	55	3.51	70	-82
● Reis, Ruth													
1952	Rck	3	0	1	.000	4	7	14	9	1	24.75	10	-10
● Reynolds, Mary													
1946	Peo	13	3	9	.250	91	68	38	29	21	2.37	101	0
1947	Peo	3	0	3	.000	17	16	7	6	2	2.65	73	-1
1948	Peo	18	9	6	.600	135	97	50	44	44	2.27	99	-0
1949	Peo	12	6	6	.500	93	79	40	29	21	2.90	71	-9
1950	Peo	33	12	14	.462	221	194	91	53	106	2.85	97	-2
Total	5	79	30	38	.441	557	454	226	162	194	2.63	93	-12
● Richard, Ruth													
1947	GR	3	0	0	.000	0							
● Rini, Mary													
1945	Ken	23	2	12	.143	112	103	76	48	15	3.62	53	-21
● Risinger, Earlene													
1948	Spg	22	3	8	.273	129	91	68	62	69	3.35	67	-16
1949	GR	30	15	12	.556	234	146	90	143	116	2.35	88	-7
1950	GR	31	14	13	.519	231	201	76	87	90	2.38	117	10
1951	GR	24	9	9	.500	177	116	66	77	65	2.14	130	12
1952	GR	27	10	15	.400	192	150	72	97	82	2.34	108	4
1953	GR	30	15	10	.600	231	151	66	95	121	1.75	151	23
1954	GR	23	7	13	.350	153	170	87	58	38	4.06	89	-7
Total	7	187	73	80	.477	1347	1025	525	619	581	2.51	105	19
● Rohrer, Kay													
1945	Rck	1	0	0	.000	0							
● Roth, Elaine													
1948	Peo	39	18	15	.545	291	225	113	60	81	2.38	94	-4
1949	Peo	24	4	12	.250	151	146	77	29	15	2.92	71	-14
1950	SB	23	7	13	.350	151	140	80	39	47	3.28	84	-9
1951	Kal	30	5	9	.357	137	136	84	54	43	4.01	69	-19
Total	4	116	34	49	.410	730	647	354	182	186	2.98	81	-46
● Roth, Eilaine													
1952	Kal	19	2	6	.250	70	68	40	18	9	2.83	90	-2
1953	Kal	25	4	2	.667	82	76	32	20	14	2.30	115	3
1954	Kal	24	5	12	.294	146	153	75	40	29	3.14	115	8
Total	3	68	11	20	.355	298	297	147	78	52	2.84	109	9
● Rotvig, Barbara													
1948	Ken	30	11	16	.407	209	159	99	96	99	2.84	79	-14
1949	Ken	32	11	15	.423	209	137	86	117	97	2.33	89	-6
1951	Ken	20	6	10	.375	133	79	57	93	93	2.57	108	3
Total	3	82	28	41	.406	551	375	242	306	289	2.58	89	-17
● Rumsey, Janet													
1951	SB-BC	19	4	8	.333	107	92	55	48	45	2.52	110	3
1952	SB	26	9	10	.474	178	157	62	47	65	2.22	114	6
1953	SB	35	11	19	.367	249	205	97	102	86	2.42	109	6
1954	SB	25	15	6	.714	169	131	55	65	89	2.18	166	27
Total	4	105	39	43	.476	703	585	269	262	285	2.33	123	42
● Sams, Doris													
1946	Mus	25	8	9	.471	169	148	109	102	31	3.78	63	-26
1947	Mus	19	11	4	.733	138	81	26	28	34	0.98	198	15
1948	Mus	32	18	10	.643	268	159	64	97	117	1.54	146	21
1949	Mus	28	15	10	.600	211	121	59	90	81	1.58	131	11
1950	Kal	29	12	13	.480	218	197	87	83	109	2.60	107	4
1952	Kal	1	0	1	.000	3	13	11	1	2	30.00	8	-9
Total	6	134	64	47	.577	1007	719	356	401	374	2.16	107	16
● Satterfield, Doris													
1947	GR	1	0	0	.000	0							
● Scheer, Edna													
1950	Rck	18	3	1	.750	71	63	52	66	21	5.58	50	-22
● Schofield, June													
1948	Spg	1	0	1	.000	1	4	8		1	36.00	6	-4

YEAR	TEAM	G	W	L	PCT	IP	H	R	BB	SO	ERA	ERA+	PR
Schroeder, Dorothy													
1948	FW	2	0	2	.000	17	14	11	6	7	3.18	71	-2
1950	FW	1	0	0	.000	1							
Total	2	3	0	2	.000	18	14	11	6	7	3.00	75	-2
Schweigert, Gloria													
1951	GR-BC	14	4	6	.400	76	63	39	36	25	2.72	102	0
1952	BC	28	10	10	.500	180	167	75	82	44	2.95	86	-8
Total	2	42	14	16	.467	256	230	114	118	69	2.88	90	-8
Scott, Patricia													
1951	FW	26	15	7	.682	190	153	65	57	62	2.13	130	13
1952	FW	26	17	7	.708	202	175	65	50	60	2.05	124	11
1953	FW	32	16	12	.571	238	224	102	67	65	3.06	86	-11
Total	3	84	48	26	.649	630	552	232	174	187	2.46	108	13
Silvestri, Margaret (see Holgerson)													
Smith, Jean													
1949	FW	3	0	1	.000	8	5	3	3	2	3.38	61	-1
1950	Peo	4	2	0	1.000	5	7	3	6	0	1.80	154	1
1951	Peo	18	7	7	.500	111	75	48	91	28	2.92	95	-2
1952	GR	14	1	2	.333	48	50	38	29	15	5.44	47	-15
Total	4	39	10	10	.500	172	137	92	129	45	3.61	74	-18
Stephens, Ruby													
1946	Rac	7	2	1	.667	34	27	30	21	6	5.03	48	-10
1947	SB	31	9	15	.375	194	162	86	70	25	2.88	67	-20
1948	Spg-Ken	36	20	11	.645	241	159	79	68	114	1.87	121	10
1949	Ken	32	13	9	.591	195	131	51	55	51	1.38	149	15
1950	Ken	29	15	9	.625	211	170	78	93	70	2.73	101	1
1951	Ken	15	3	8	.273	86	78	56	31	39	3.77	74	-10
Total	6	150	62	53	.539	961	727	380	338	305	2.44	95	-14
Studnicka, Mary Lou													
1951	GR	23	15	5	.750	164	120	72	72	72	2.36	117	7
1952	GR	28	11	12	.478	185	177	81	70	70	2.53	100	0
1953	GR	27	12	13	.480	176	150	79	84	54	2.56	103	2
Total	3	78	38	30	.559	525	447	232	226	196	2.49	106	9
Thompson, Anna Jane													
1943	Rac	32	11	15	.423	223	237	159	64	28	3.47	87	-11
Thompson, Viola													
1944	Mil	33	15	12	.556	222	217	120	73	27	2.88	88	-8
1945	GR	34	11	19	.367	260	209	91	93	20	1.90	101	1
1946	SB	31	15	6	.714	202	195	104	62	14	2.90	83	-11
1947	SB	1	0	0	.000	0							
Total	4	99	41	37	.526	684	621	315	228	61	2.51	90	-19
Tucker, Elizabeth "Betty"													
1946	Peo	22	1	12	.077	125	108	85	64	20	3.38	71	-14
1947	FW-Rck-GR	16	0	12	.000	92	88	63	36	18	3.72	52	-18
1948	Chi	33	11	17	.393	238	162	106	112	90	2.68	84	-12
1949	Peo	16	4	8	.333	118	108	51	35	25	2.67	77	-8
Total	4	87	16	49	.246	573	466	305	247	153	3.00	73	-51
Tysver, Joan													
1950	GR	1	0	1	.000	8	11	10	11	3	10.13	27	-7
1951	Rck	9	0	2	.000	32	40	42	37	4	9.28	30	-23
Total	2	10	0	3	.000	40	51	52	48	7	9.45	29	-30
Vanderlip, Dolly													
1952	FW	10	0	4	.000	39	25	26	35	11	3.92	65	-6
1953	FW	14	2	2	.500	50	40	25	32	14	2.88	92	-1
1954	SB	19	11	6	.647	120	122	53	65	39	2.40	151	16
Total	3	43	13	12	.520	209	187	104	132	64	2.80	114	9
Vincent, Georgette "Jetty" (m. Mooney 1952)													
1948	Rac	15	5	2	.714	59	41	34	59	28	3.66	61	-9
1949	SB	11	3	2	.600	36	20	18	34	13	3.50	59	-6
1950	SB	21	8	12	.400	153	125	82	105	72	3.12	89	-6
1951	SB	23	13	9	.591	171	113	62	88	113	2.42	114	7
1952	SB	24	8	8	.500	160	140	69	68	65	2.36	108	3
1954	SB	3	1	1	.500	21	18	18	20	8	5.57	65	-5
Total	6	97	38	34	.528	600	457	283	374	299	2.88	92	-16
Voyce, Inez													
1948	GR	4	1	1	.500	21	20	8	5	0	3.43	66	-3
Vukovich, Frances													
1951	BC	5	0	3	.000	16	8	18	16	3	5.06	55	-4
Waggott													
1952	BC	1	0	0	.000	1							
Wagner, Audrey													
1943	Ken	5	1	2	.333	30	36	23	7	5	3.30	92	-1
1947	Ken	2	0	0	.000	0							
Total	2	7	1	2	.333	30	36	23	7	5	3.30	92	-1
Wagoner, Betty													
1950	SB	4	0	3	.000	24	22	12	18	9	4.13	67	-4
1951	SB	1	0	0	.000	1							
1952	SB	9	5	2	.714	55	53	31	31	15	4.25	60	-10
1953	SB	19	4	13	.235	149	150	84	106	60	3.02	87	-6
1954	SB	9	4	4	.500	58	59	42	38	34	4.66	78	-7
Total	5	42	13	22	.371	287	284	169	193	118	3.67	77	-27
Walulik, Helen													
1948	Mus-FW	17	2	6	.250	91	71	42	44	29	3.07	73	-8
1950	Kal	15	2	4	.333	57	56	40	44	17	3.63	76	-5
Total	2	32	4	10	.286	148	127	82	88	46	3.28	77	-14
Warfel, Betty													
1948	Rck	6	1	0	1.000	17	7	6	11	5	1.06	213	2

YEAR	TEAM	G	W	L	PCT	IP	H	R	BB	SO	ERA	ERA+	PR
1949	Rck	14	5	5	.500	79	50	30	37	13	2.96	70	-8
Total	2	20	6	5	.545	96	57	36	48	18	2.63	80	-6
Warren, Nancy													
1946	Mus	11	4	6	.400	85	60	33	25	40	2.12	113	3
1947	Mus	31	17	11	.607	223	142	54	25	93	1.13	172	20
1948	Mus-Chi	23	12	5	.706	161	103	47	52	86	1.45	155	14
1949	Peo	27	10	16	.385	192	135	92	63	79	3.00	69	-20
1950	Peo	32	13	13	.500	228	198	82	53	86	2.37	117	10
1951	Peo-FW	27	10	10	.500	188	146	67	63	79	2.20	126	12
1952	FW	27	17	7	.708	219	189	87	53	91	2.14	119	10
1953	Mus	28	6	17	.261	200	195	107	71	100	2.70	98	-1
1954	Kal	26	12	9	.571	151	155	98	70	63	4.65	78	-17
Total	9	232	101	94	.518	1647	1323	667	475	717	2.37	107	30
Weaver, Jean													
1950	FW	1	0	0	.000	0							
1952	FW	5	0	2	.000	14	24	31	24	10	12.86	20	-16
1953	FW	20	7	1	.875	92	60	43	76	41	2.64	100	-0
Total	3	26	7	3	.700	106	84	74	100	51	3.99	66	-16
Weaver, Joanne													
1951	FW	1	0	0	.000	2							
1952	FW	1	0	0	.000	1							
Total	2	2	0	0	.000	3	0	0	0	0	0.00	0	0
Weddle, Mary													
1954	FW	15	3	1	.750	47	23	30	60	21	3.83	95	-1
Wegman, Marie													
1948	FW	3	0	0	.000	11	13	11	9	5	6.55	34	-5
Williams, Ruth													
1947	SB	25	12	8	.600	180	115	51	50	48	1.70	114	5
1948	SB	23	10	10	.500	160	126	53	66	55	2.25	100	0
1949	SB	25	10	6	.625	170	119	48	60	41	1.64	126	8
1950	SB-Peo-Kal	19	5	10	.333	121	122	68	59	40	3.57	78	-11
1951	Kal	25	10	11	.476	156	117	47	45	59	1.96	141	14
1952	Kal	23	10	12	.455	174	156	71	52	41	2.48	102	1
1953	Kal	22	8	12	.400	153	124	65	63	31	2.12	125	9
Total	7	162	65	69	.485	1114	879	403	395	315	2.19	110	26
Wiltse, Dottie (m. Collins 1946)													
1944	Min	38	20	16	.556	297	156	107	130	205	1.88	135	22
1945	FW	46	29	10	.744	345	132	58	111	293	0.83	231	42
1946	FW	49	22	20	.524	357	215	122	187	294	2.32	103	3
1947	FW	40	20	14	.588	292	156	57	88	244	1.33	146	20
1948	FW	24	13	8	.619	175	121	60	62	101	2.01	112	5
1950	FW	26	13	8	.619	169	132	84	95	68	3.46	80	-13
Total	6	223	117	76	.606	1635	912	488	673	1205	1.83	124	78
Wiley, Janet													
1953	Rck	1	0	0	.000	0							
Winter, Joanne													
1943	Rac	29	11	11	.500	200	201	121	47	13	2.57	118	10
1944	Rac	40	15	23	.395	310	276	172	133	52	2.96	86	-15
1945	Rac	34	7	22	.241	256	209	125	77	35	2.53	76	-17
1946	Rac	46	33	10	.767	349	199	82	132	183	1.19	201	47
1947	Rac	38	22	13	.629	297	222	93	122	121	2.06	94	-4
1948	Rac	38	25	12	.676	329	49	67	86	248	1.18	191	39
1949	Rac	32	11	13	.458	228	156	84	95	72	2.17	95	-3
1950	Rac	30	9	11	.450	190	158	78	67	46	2.46	112	6
Total	8	287	133	115	.536	2159	1470	822	759	770	2.06	113	64
Wisniewski, Connie													
1944	Mil	36	23	10	.697	291	200	88	47	49	2.23	114	10
1945	GR	46	32	11	.744	391	206	64	61	82	0.81	240	49
1946	GR	48	33	9	.786	366	235	71	59	79	0.96	249	58
1947	GR	32	16	14	.533	264	223	82	49	44	2.15	90	-6
1948	GR	8	3	4	.429	62	60	31	29	12	2.47	91	-2
Total	5	170	107	48	.690	1374	924	336	245	266	1.48	148	110
Wood, Loita													
1950	FW	2	0	0	.000	1							
Wood, Trois													
1951	Ken	24	3	16	.158	165	166	116	96	37	4.75	58	-36
Wronski, Sylvia													
1944	Mil	13	4	2	.667	53	44	33	30	2	3.06	83	-3
1945	GR	4	0	0	.000	11							
Total	2	17	4	2	.667	64	44	33	30	2	2.53	100	0
Young													
1951	BC	2	0	0	.000	3							
Youngberg, Renae													
1954	GR	1	0	0	.000	6							
Ziegler, Alma													
1948	GR	18	9	6	.600	119	76	21	24	49	1.21	186	14
1949	GR	5	2	1	.667	31	26	7	8	4	1.16	177	3
1950	GR	35	19	7	.731	235	173	49	33	84	1.38	201	36
1951	GR	22	14	8	.636	171	112	38	38	62	1.26	219	29
1952	GR	12	3	4	.429	72	77	34	9	7	2.50	102	0
1953	GR	17	8	4	.667	116	98	43	28	28	3.03	87	-5
1954	GR	17	5	4	.556	95	115	58	36	16	3.98	91	-4
Total	7	126	60	34	.638	839	677	250	176	250	1.94	141	73
Ziemak, Frances													
1951	Peo	2	0	1	.000	9	7	10	9	2	6.00	46	-3
Zurowski, Agnes													
1945	Rac	4	0	1	.000	12	26	19	9	2	12.75	15	-14

APPENDIXES

Rules and Scoring

Dennis Bingham and Thomas R. Heitz

The chronologies presented here trace the evolution of baseball's playing and scoring rules from those governing the first properly organized baseball club (1845) to the present major league clubs (through 1994).

Playing Rules

As a starting point, the rules of the 1845 Knickerbocker Base Ball Club of New York City are provided. During earlier decades, rules had been published for popular bat-and-ball and baserunning games played by eighteenth- and early nineteenth-century youths (indeed, some basic baseball principles can be traced back for centuries), but the codified Knickerbocker rules serve as a direct link to the rules of today. Their rules were the model for the hundreds of organized amateur clubs that sprang up in the 1850s. Following the 1845 rules is an outline listing the significant rule changes made in the next eleven years.

This brief outline illustrates how little the rules had changed in more than a decade.

In 1857, however, several baseball clubs, led by the old Knickerbockers, held a convention with the purpose of changing the rules to make baseball less a mere recreation and more a "scientific and manly" exercise and competition. At this convention, the club delegates greatly expanded, refined, clarified, and polished the rule book. The following year, the baseball clubs held another convention, made some rule changes, and formed themselves into a permanent body—the National Association of Base Ball Players. Although these baseball clubs were composed primarily of amateurs, their rule book became the core of every rule book for every baseball league that followed. The 1857 rules are set forth in their entirety and are followed by changes to the rules under annual headings through 1994.

The work of the Nineteenth Century Committee of the Society for American Baseball Research (SABR) was instrumental in compiling these chronologies.

The first major league, the National Association of Professional Base-Ball Players, was formed in 1871 and used essentially the same rule book as its predecessor. In 1876 the National League dethroned the professional players' association and adopted their rule book, with their amendments to the rules noted under that year's heading.

Rule differences for subsequent major leagues are also listed in the chronology and are noted under the annual heading in which they were introduced, e.g. Union Association (1884) and Players League (1890).

In most cases, the actual text of a new rule or change has been taken verbatim from original sources. However, to reduce verbiage, the references to section numbering and headings, which have varied widely over the years, have been deleted along with other extraneous spacing and punctuation. In many cases, primarily in the early years, the wording has been slightly changed to convey the meaning of the rule more clearly. In a few cases the technical wording of complex rules has been summarized for ease of reading. Researchers requiring precise quotations of rules are advised to consult original sources, e.g., the *Spalding* and *Reach Baseball Guides*.

Headings have been added to each of the changes under the annual headings to assist the reader. By consulting the index and headings, readers may follow the evolution of any one particular rule through the years.

The chronology does not include *all* changes to the playing rules—only those of significance and substance. Numerous minor changes in wording not affecting meaning, or changes in punctuation and spelling which had no purpose other than grammatical correctness, have been ignored. Also, the chronology includes only those rules and regulations found in the official baseball rule book, not those found in other baseball documents such as league constitutions and the Basic Agreement. Thus rules and subject matter that may have been dropped from the early rule books, such as those concerning player eligibility and discipline, may still govern baseball for years later but had been inserted in the league's constitution.

In some instances, significant rule changes affecting umpires and little-used rules regarding suspended games or batting out of order have been summarized or simply alluded to in the interests of brevity. The scoring rules are presented in a separate section of this appendix because of their length and special interest.

Baseball's rules continue to evolve in the twentieth century despite the perception of many that "the game remains pretty much the same as it always has been." The most far-reaching revision of baseball's playing rules came in 1950 when the entire code was virtually rewritten. Additional changes and refinements were added throughout the 1950s, and it is the rules of 1950 for the most part that we use today.

The rules of baseball are commonly considered the means of keeping the game in that delicate balance between offense and defense with neither side enjoying a marked advantage. This balance is the dynamic force of competition, which drives the game and ultimately creates interest and motivation for players and spectators alike.

But changes to the playing rules can also be categorized in terms of response to various social, economic, and technological factors as well as to the need for competitive balance. For example, when the uncouth language of hard-bitten nineteenth-century players became offensive to female rooters, appropriate rules were adopted (in an attempt) to modify player behavior. Likewise, gloves were introduced gradually in the 1870s and 1880s to protect the players' catching hands from injury. However, when glove design clearly departed from the goal of protection and extended to aiding in the catching process, effectively making the glove an extension of the hand, it became necessary to invoke standards for gloves in the rules.

In terms of competitive balance, perhaps the most striking evolution is that of the pitching rules, which have undergone a remarkable transformation from the days of simple underhanded hurling from a boxlike enclosure to today's complex series of physical motions from which almost any deviation is likely to elicit a call of "balk."

In many cases, the introduction of a playing rule followed several years of development on the field of play. Like state and federal legislative bodies, baseball's rule-making authorities are often slow to respond to changing conditions or perhaps justifiably cautious about making such changes before the effects are fully understood. For example, there is no mention of pitching mounds in the playing rules until 1903, when the maximum elevation was fixed at 15 inches. However, pitching mounds were in general use many years prior to 1903 and may have come into vogue as early as the 1880s. The lifting of restrictions on the angle of pitching delivery in 1884 made overhanded throwing legal, and it was not long before the hurlers realized the mechanical advantages of stepping off a short incline as they directed the ball toward the plate. Presumably, by 1903 the lack of uniformity in certain parks had become a problem, and so the rules set a standard.

Another point that should be kept in mind while reading this chronology is that just because a particular rule is "in the book" doesn't necessarily mean that it was (or is) always enforced.

The researcher is advised to scan the Index to Playing Rule Changes prior to consulting the chronology.

Scoring Rules

The chronology presented after that of the playing rules traces the evolution of professional baseball's scoring rules from 1877 through 1994.

Clubs, sportswriters, and fans had been keeping score and compiling statistics for decades, but the scoring rules of 1877 are presented as a starting point, in their entirety, because they are the first official scoring rules included in the rule book. Thereafter changes to the scoring rules are noted under annual headings.

In most cases, as with the playing rules, the actual text of a new scoring rule or change has been taken verbatim from original sources.

The scoring rules are at the heart of baseball's accountability to itself and to the millions of fans who follow the game day by day. Through the use of these rules the daily performance of players and teams is described and measured in a uniform and meaningful way. Baseball is unique in publishing the performance records of its key personnel, and in so doing it subjects the individual, the team, and its management to the scrutiny and judgment of anyone who has the price of a daily newspaper.

Like the playing rules, they have evolved from a rather primitive code to a complex, legalistic document. The scoring rules have been transformed over the decades from the simple recording of hits, outs, errors, and assists in the 1870s into a highly technical set of rules and guidelines used to record every significant offensive and defensive event that transpires on the field of play.

While the collection of such statistics as "caught stealing" did not commence until later years, still baseball's major performance records can be traced in an unbroken skein well back into the nineteenth century. As a result, no other professional sport can claim such a rich resource of historical statistics.

The researcher is advised to scan the Index to Scoring Rule Changes prior to consulting the chronology.

Playing Rules for 1845

1. Members must strictly observe the time agreed upon for exercise, and be punctual in their attendance.
2. When assembled for exercise, the President, or in his absence the Vice-President, shall appoint an Umpire, who shall keep the game in a book provided for that purpose, and note all violations of the By-Laws and Rules during the time of exercise.
3. The presiding officer shall designate two members as Cap-

tains, who shall retire and make the match to be played, observing at the same time that the players put opposite to each other should be as nearly equal as possible; the choice of sides to be then tossed for, and the first in hand to be decided in like manner.
4. The bases shall be from "home" to second base, forty-two paces; from first to third base, forty-two paces, equidistant.
5. No stump match shall be played on a regular day of exercise.
6. If there should not be a sufficient number of members of the Club present at the time agreed upon to commence exercise, gentlemen not members may be chosen in to make up the match, which shall not be broken up to take in members that may afterwards appear; but, in all cases, members shall have the preference, when present, at the making of a match.
7. If members appear after the game is commenced they may be chosen in if mutually agreed upon.
8. The game to consist of twenty-one counts, or aces; but at the conclusion an equal number of hands must be played.
9. The ball must be pitched, and not thrown, for the bat.
10. A ball knocked out of the field, or outside the range of the first or third base, is foul.
11. Three balls being struck at and missed and the last one caught, is a hand out; if not caught is considered fair, and the striker bound to run.
12. If a ball be struck, or tipped, and caught, either flying or on the first bound, it is a hand out.
13. A player running the bases shall be out, if the ball is in the hands of an adversary on the base, or the runner is touched with it before he makes his base; it being understood, however, that in no instance is a ball to be thrown at him.
14. A player running who shall prevent an adversary from catching or getting the ball before making his base, is a hand out.
15. Three hands out, all out.
16. Players must take their strike in regular turn.
17. All disputes and differences relative to the game, to be decided by the Umpire, from which there is no appeal.
18. No ace or base can be made on a foul strike.
19. A runner cannot be put out in making one base, when a balk is made by the pitcher.
20. But one base allowed when a ball bounds out of the field when struck.

Rule Changes 1846–56

In 1848 a rule was amended declaring that the batter-runner was out if the ball was held on first base before he reached it; previously, the rule applied the situation to *all* bases. By 1852, the captains of each club had been given the authority to position each player in the field, which could not be changed without their consent, and that each club member would take turns as umpire.

The 1854 rule book included the following: "When a fair ball is struck and the striker not put out, the first base must be vacated as well as the next base or bases if similarly occupied; players may be put out, under these circumstances, in the same manner as when running to first base." In other words, the force out had been introduced.

The dimensions of the ball had also been established—from 5½ to 6 ounces in weight and from 2¾ to 3½ inches in diameter. A player was also now called out if he *intentionally* prevented an opponent from catching the ball.

A major rule change was made in 1857 when it was determined that nine complete innings would constitute a game rather than the first team to score 21 runs at the end of equal innings.

Playing Rules for 1857

Section 1. Ball. The ball must weigh not less than 6 nor more than 6¼ ounces avoirdupois. It must measure not less than 10 nor more than 10¼ inches in circumference. It must be composed of India rubber and yarn, and covered with leather. It shall be furnished by the challenging club, and become the property of the winning club as a trophy of victory.

Section 2. Bat. The bat must be round and must not exceed 2½ half inches in diameter in the thickest part. It must be made of wood and may be of any length to suit the striker.

Section 3. Bases. The bases must be four in number, placed at equal distances from each other, and securely fastened upon the four corners of a square whose sides are respectively thirty yards. They must be so constructed as to be distinctly seen by the umpires and referees, and must cover a space equal to one square foot of surface. The first, second, and third bases shall be canvas bags, painted white, and filled with sand or sawdust; the home base and pitcher's points to be each marked with a flat circular iron plate, painted or enameled white.

Section 4. Bases/Position. The base from which the ball is struck shall be designated the home base and must be directly opposite the second base; the first base must always be that upon the right hand, and the third base that upon the left hand side of the striker when occupying the position at the home base.

Section 5. Pitcher/Position. The pitcher's position shall be designated by a line four yards in length, drawn at right angles to a line from home to the second base, having its center upon that line, at a fixed iron plate placed at a point 15 yards from the home base.

Section 6. Pitcher/Delivery. The ball must be pitched, not jerked or thrown, to the bat; and whenever the pitcher draws back his hand, with the apparent purpose or pretension to deliver the ball, he shall so deliver it. The pitcher must deliver the ball as near as possible over the center of the home base, and must have neither foot in advance of the line at the time of delivering the ball; and if he fails in either of these particulars, then it shall be declared a balk.

Section 7. Balk. When a balk is made by the pitcher, every player running the bases is entitled to one base without being put out.

Section 8. Fair/Foul balls. If the ball, from a stroke of the bat, is caught behind the range of home and the first base or home and the third base, without having touched the ground, or first touches the ground behind those bases, it shall be termed foul and must be so declared by the umpire unasked. If the ball first touches the ground, either upon or in front of the range of those bases, it shall be considered fair.

Section 9. Run scored. A player making the home base shall be entitled to score one run.

Section 10. Strikeout. If three balls are struck at and missed, and the last one is not caught either flying or upon the first bound, it shall be considered fair and the striker must attempt to make his run.

Section 11. Batter/Caught foul. The striker is out if a foul ball is caught, either before touching the ground or upon the first bound;

Section 12. Strikeout. Or if three balls are struck at and missed, and the last is caught either before touching the ground or upon the first bound;

Section 13. Batter/Caught fair fly. Or if a fair ball is struck, and the ball is caught without having touched the ground or upon the first bound;

Section 14. Batter/Out at first. Or if a fair ball is struck, and the ball is held by an adversary on the first base before the striker touches the base;

Section 15. Batter/Tagged. Or if, at any time, he is touched by the ball while in play in the hands of an adversary, without some part of his person being on a base.

Section 16. Runner/Advancing. No ace nor base can be made upon a foul ball, nor when a fair ball has been caught without having touched the ground; and the ball shall, in both instances, be considered dead and not in play until it shall first have been settled in the hands of the pitcher. When a fair ball has been caught without having touched the ground, the players running the bases shall have the privilege of returning to them.

Section 17. Batter/Position. Players must stand on a line drawn through the center of the home base, not exceeding in length three feet from either side thereof, and such lines shall be parallel with the line occupied by the pitcher. They shall strike in regular rotation and, after the first inning is played, the turn commences with the player who stands on the list next to the one who lost the third hand.

Section 18. Runner/Forced. Players must take their bases in the order of striking; and when a fair ball is struck, and not caught flying nor on the first bound, the first base must be vacated, as also the second and third bases if they are occupied at the same time. Players may be put out upon any base, under these circumstances, in the same manner as the striker when running to the first base.

Section 19. Runner/Out of baseline. Players running the bases must, as far as possible, keep upon the direct line between the bases; and should any player run three feet out of this line, for the purpose of avoiding the ball in the hands of an adversary, he shall be declared out.

Section 20. Interference/Offensive. Any player who shall intentionally prevent an adversary from catching or fielding the ball, shall be declared out.

Section 21. Obstruction. If the player is prevented from making a base by the intentional obstruction of an adversary, he shall be entitled to that base and not be put out.

Section 22. Fielder/Illegal act. If any adversary stops the ball with his hat or cap, or takes it from the hands of a party not engaged in the game, no player can be put out unless the ball shall first have been settled in the hands of the pitcher.

Section 23. Catch. If a ball, from the strike of a bat, is held under any other circumstances than as enumerated in Section 22, and without having touched the ground more than once, the striker is out.

Section 24. Run scored. If two hands are already out, no player running home at the time a ball is struck can make an ace if the striker is put out.

Section 25. Game/Inning. An inning must be concluded at the time the third hand is put out.

Section 26. Game. The game shall consist of nine innings to each side, when, should the number of runs be equal, the innings shall be continued until a majority of runs, upon an equal number of innings shall be declared, which shall conclude the game.

Section 27. Player/Eligible substitute, positions. In playing all matches, nine players from each club shall constitute a full field, and they must have been regular members of the club which they represent, for thirty days prior to the match. No changes or substitution shall be made after the game has been commenced, unless for reason of illness or injury. Positions of players shall be determined by captains previously appointed for that purpose by the respective clubs.

Section 28. Player/Eligible. Any player holding membership in more than one club at the same time shall not be permitted to play in the matches of either club.

Section 29. Umpire/Duties. The umpire in all matches shall take care that the regulations respecting the ball, bats, bases, and the pitcher's and striker's positions are strictly observed. They shall be the judge of fair and unfair play, and shall determine all differences which may occur during the game; they shall take especial care to declare all fair balls and balks immediately on their occurrence. They shall together select a referee from whose decision—in case of a disagreement—there shall be no appeal.

Section 30. Gambling/Substitute. No person engaged in a match, either as umpire, referee, or player, shall be directly or indirectly interested in any bet upon the game. Neither umpire, referee, nor player shall be changed during a match, unless with the consent of both parties, except for a violation of this law and except as provided in Section 27, and then the referee may dismiss any transgressor.

Section 31. Game/Legal. The umpires and referee in any match shall determine when play shall be suspended; and if the game cannot be concluded, it shall be decided by the last even innings, provided five innings have been played, and the party having the greatest number of runs shall be declared the winner.

Section 32. Ground rules. Clubs may adopt such rules respecting balls knocked beyond or outside the bounds of the field, as the circumstances of the ground may demand, and these rules shall govern all matches played upon the ground, provided that they are distinctly made known to every player and umpire and the referee previous to the commencement of the game.

Section 33. Interference. No person shall be permitted to approach or to speak with the referee, umpires, scorers, or players, or in any manner to interrupt or interfere during the progress of the game, unless by special request of the umpires or referee.

Section 34. Umpire. No person shall be permitted to act as umpire or referee in any match, unless he shall be a member of a base ball club governed by these rules.

Section 35. Game/Start, forfeit. Whenever a match shall have been determined upon between two clubs, play shall be called at the exact hour appointed; and should either party fail to produce their players within fifteen minutes thereafter, the party so failing shall admit a defeat.

Section 36. Ineligible players. No person who may be in arrears to any club he may have belonged to previous to the one he is then a member of shall be competent to play in a match unless such arrears are paid.

Section 37. Calling strikes. Should a striker stand at the bat without striking at good balls repeatedly pitched to him, for the purpose of delaying the game or of giving advantage to a player, the umpire, after warning him, shall call one strike, and if he persists in such action, two and three strikes. When three strikes are called, he shall be subject to the same rules as if he had struck at the three balls.

Chronology of Rule Changes 1858–1994

1858

Pitcher/delivery The pitcher must deliver the ball as near as possible over the center of the plate and for the striker.

Player/Eligible No person who may be in arrears to any club he may have belonged to previous to the one he is then a member of shall be competent to play in a match unless such arrears are paid.

Runner/Returning Players running the bases shall return to them following foul balls and fair balls caught on the fly, and shall not be put out in so running unless the ball has been first pitched to the striker.

Strike Zone Should a striker stand at the bat without striking at good balls repeatedly pitched to him, for the purpose of delaying the game or of giving advantage to a player, the umpire, after warning him, shall call one strike; and if he persists in such action, two and three strikes. When three strikes are called, he shall be subject to the same rules as if he had struck at three balls.

Umpire The umpire in all matches shall take care that the regulations respecting the ball, bat, bases, and the pitcher's and striker's positions are strictly observed. He shall keep a record of the game in a book prepared for the purpose. He shall be the judge of fair and unfair play, and shall determine all disputes and differences which may occur during the game. He shall take especial care to declare all foul balls and balks immediately upon occurrence, unasked, and in a district and audible manner.

Note: All references to a "referee" and "umpires" in the plural sense have been deleted. The game is now under control of a single umpire, rather than a tribunal.

Umpire/Scorer In all matches, the umpire shall be selected by the captains of the respective sides, and shall perform all duties enumerated in Section 29, except recording the game, which shall be done by two scorers, one of whom shall be appointed by each of the contending clubs.

Note: "Section 29" is the paragraph under the heading "Umpire" above. Also, the rules prohibiting gambling and requiring participants to be members of a baseball club now applied to scorers as well as umpires and players.

1859

Ball The ball must weigh 5¾ to 6 ounces and measure 9¾ to 10 inches in circumference.

Player/Eligible No person who receives compensation for his services as a player shall be competent to play in any match.

Game/Number Every match shall be decided by a single game.

Note: In previous years, a series of games often determined the winner of a "match."

Runner/Advancing Caught fly balls which do not touch the ground are no longer considered dead balls.

Note: With this amendment it was understood that runners, following caught fly balls, could now advance after returning to their original base. This, however, was not as yet written into the rules.

1860

Game/Number Every match shall be decided by a single game unless otherwise mutually agreed upon by the contesting clubs.

Runner/Returning Runners, returning to their bases following foul balls and caught fly balls not touching the ground, may be put out in the same manner as the batter when running to first base.

Note: At the 1857 meeting of baseball clubs, the progressive Knickerbockers proposed that in order to retire the batter the ball must be caught on the fly and not on one bounce. It became a hotly debated topic during the next several conventions but, although it gained more support each year, the "fly rule" continued to be defeated when put to a vote. In 1860, however, the "fly game" was allowed if both contesting clubs agreed. This concession was not officially written into the rule book.

1861

Ball The ball must weigh 5½ to 5¾ ounces and measure 9½ to 9¾ inches in circumference.

Foul Ball If the ball, from the stroke of the bat, first touches the ground, the person of a player, or any object behind the range of home and first or home and third base, it shall be a foul ball.

Grounds A line connecting home and first base and home and third base shall be marked by chalk, or other suitable material, so as to be distinctly seen by the umpire.

Runner Players running the bases must make them in the following order: first, second, third, and home, and in returning must reverse this order.

Umpire The umpire, before leaving the grounds, must declare the winning club and record his decision in the scorebooks of the two clubs.

1862

There were no changes to the playing rules this year.

1863

Base on Balls When three "balls" have been called, the striker is entitled to first base, and each player occupying a base is entitled to one base without being put out.

Note: In actuality it took more than three balls to be awarded first base; see 1863, *Strike Zone*.

Pitcher/Delivery If the pitcher, at the time of delivery, has either foot off the ground or in advance of the front line of his position, it shall be declared a balk.

Pitcher/Position The pitcher's position shall be two lines, each twelve feet in length, with the front line forty-five feet and the back line forty-eight feet distant from home base.

Note: This introduces the pitcher's box, which replaces the single twelve-foot line.

Runner/Advancing Runners, after returning to their respective bases, may advance immediately after a fair fly ball has been settled in the hands of a fielder.

Note: This put into words what had been understood for the past four years; see 1859 rule.

Runner/Bases Each runner must touch each base in making the circuit.

Note: Runners were previously allowed to go around or near the bases.

Strike Zone Should the pitcher repeatedly fail to deliver "fair" balls, for the purpose of delaying the game or for any cause, the umpire, after warning him, shall call one "ball"; and if the pitcher persists, two and three balls.

1864

There were no changes to the playing rules this year.

1865

Batter/Caught Foul A batted ball in foul territory must be caught on the fly to be declared an out.

Note: The "fly game" has been adopted; fair balls caught on one bounce are no longer outs.

Interference/Spectator If a ball is stopped by any person not engaged in the game, no player may be put out unless the ball has first been settled in the hands of the pitcher.

Umpire The umpire is no longer responsible for keeping a record of the game in the scorebook.

Note: This amendment corrects a contradiction in earlier rule books in which one rule held the umpire responsible for keeping score and another rule instructed the umpire not to perform the duty.

1866

Bases First, second, and third bases shall be canvas bags, painted white and filled with some soft material.

Game/Legal Any game played in contravention of National Association rules shall be considered null and void and shall not be counted in the list of games won or lost; unless a game is delayed by rain beyond the appointed start. Any game may be put off by mutual consent of the two clubs. No game shall be commenced in the rain.

Game/Number Every game shall be decided by the best two games out of three, unless a single game is mutually agreed upon by the two clubs.

Pitcher/Position The back line of the pitcher's box is moved back one foot, increasing the length to 4 feet while remaining 12 feet in width.

1867

Batter/Position The batter, when in the act of striking, shall not step forward or backward but must stand on the three-foot line drawn through the center of home base.

Batter-Runner The batter shall be considered a baserunner as soon as he hits a fair ball.

Dead Ball Any pitch on which a "balk" or "ball" has been called is considered a dead ball, and the batter cannot be put out if he hits such a ball. Dead balls are returned to play when the ball has been settled in the hands of the pitcher while he stands within the pitcher's box.

Forfeited Game A club failing to produce their players within thirty minutes of the start of the game shall admit a defeat. The opposing club receives a win and is entitled to nine runs, and the game is counted in the list of games played. The game shall not be forfeited if the club fails to play because of the recent death of one of its members and there hasn't been sufficient time to notify the opposing club.

Pitcher/Delivery The pitcher must deliver the ball as near as possible over the center of home base and fairly for the striker.

The ball must be pitched, not jerked or thrown, to the bat. The ball shall be considered jerked if the pitcher's arm touches his person when the arm is swung forward to deliver the ball; and it is a throw if the arm is bent at the elbow at an angle from the body or horizontally from the shoulder when the arm is swung forward in delivery. A pitched ball is one delivered with arm straight and swinging perpendicularly and free from the body.

Note: The word *perpendicular* was used in the rule but the word *parallel* was intended. This error would be repeated for several years.

Pitcher/Position The pitcher's box is reduced in size to six feet in width and four feet in length.

Player/Eligible All players who play baseball for money, place, or emolument are regarded as professional players and shall not take part in any game. Any club giving compensation to a player or having knowledge that one of their players is playing for compensation shall be expelled from the National Association. Any club engaging in a game with an expelled club shall also forfeit membership.

Run Scored If there are two outs, no player can score a run if the batter is put out by a legal catch, forced between home and first base, or the ball is held by an adversary on first base before the batter reaches it.

Strikeout The batter is out if three balls are swung at and missed and the last one is caught either on the fly or on the first bound; provided the pitches are not those on which "balks" or "balls" have been called, or if the batter swings for the purpose of willfully striking out.

Strike Zone All pitches striking the ground in front of home base, over the head of the batter, or to the side opposite to that which the batter swings from, shall be considered unfair "balls."

Substitute An umpire, scorer, or player shall not be changed during a game except for reason of illness or injury and with the consent of both clubs; or when the umpire dismisses a transgressor for violation of the rules.

Umpire The umpire must declare when a player is out and in what position and manner.

Note: For example, if a batter is out on a caught fly to center, the umpire must yell, "Striker is out on the fly by the center fielder." This rule lasted only one year.

1868

Ball The ball must weigh from 5 to 5¼ ounces and measure from 9¼ to 9½ inches in circumference.

The challenging club must furnish a ball with the size, weight, and maker's name on it.

Bases The base-bag shall be considered the base and not the part to which it is or should be fastened.

Note: This rule was dropped in 1876.

The home plate and pitcher's points must be flat plates, painted white.

Bat The bat shall not exceed forty inches in length.

Batter/Position The batter, when about to strike the ball, must stand astride the three-foot line which is drawn through the center of home base and parallel with the front line of the pitcher's box.

The batter must not take any backward step when striking at the ball. The penalty is the calling of "foul strike," and when three such strikes are called, the batter is out. The batter is also out if he hits such a "strike" and the ball is caught, either fair or foul. No base may be run, but the baserunner is allowed to return to his base without being put out.

Catch If a fair ball is held by a fielder before touching the ground after it has rebounded from the hands or person of another player, it shall be considered a catch. A foul ball, if similarly held but touches the ground once, is also a catch.

Dead Ball No base may be run or player put out on a dead ball. If the batter hits a pitch on which a "balk" or "ball" has been called, no "strike" or foul ball shall be called, or a player put out; except bases may be taken on balks and calls of ball three.

Forfeited Game Any club failing to take their positions within five minutes after the umpire calls "play" shall forfeit the game.

Game/Rain No game shall be started when rain is falling and no game shall be continued when rain has fallen for five minutes.

Game/Scheduled When a challenge has been accepted for a series of games, each of the three games must be played at least within fifteen days of the previous game. The first game is played on the grounds of the challenger, the second game on the grounds of the challenged, and the third game, if necessary, on grounds mutually agreed upon. When a first-nine match is to be played, the clubs must play their recognized first nine, as far as practicable.

Note: This rule was dropped the next season.

Game/"Time" When the umpire calls "play," the game must begin at once. When the umpire calls "time," play shall be suspended until he calls "play" again. When the umpire "calls" a game, it shall end, but when he merely suspends play for any stated period, it may be resumed at the point at which it was suspended, provided it does not extend to the next day.

Obstruction If a runner is prevented from making a base by the intentional obstruction of an adversary, he shall be entitled to that base and not be put out. Any obstruction that could readily have been avoided shall be considered intentional.

Pitcher/Delivery The pitcher is no longer required to keep both feet on the ground when delivering the ball.

Player Every player taking part in a regular match game, no matter how many innings have been played, shall be, in the meaning of these rules, considered a member of the club with which he plays.

Runner/Bases If a runner fails to touch each base, he shall be declared out unless he returns to the base before the ball is held on it.

Run Scored When there are two outs, no runner may score if the batter is put out.

Substitute No player may be substituted after the third inning except in cases of illness and injury.

Umpire/Decisions Only the captain of each club is allowed to appeal for the reversal of a decision by the umpire. No decision by the umpire shall be reversed by the testimony of any player; and no decision whatever shall be reversed except for a palpable infringement of the rules, and then only on an appeal by the captain.

Umpire/Scorer The umpire shall require that the game be recorded by a scorer for each of the contesting clubs.

Note: This rule was dropped from the rule book in 1874.

1869

Ball In the first and third games of a series the ball shall be furnished by the challenging club, and in the second game by the challenged club.

Base on Balls When the batter is awarded first base after three called balls, no other runner shall take a base unless he is obliged to vacate the base he occupies.

Bat The bat shall not exceed forty-two inches in length.

Batter/Fails to Bat Any player failing to take his turn at bat, unless for reason of illness or injury or by consent of the opposing captain, shall be declared out.

Note: In 1870, the rule was amended: Any player failing to bat "after the umpire has called for the striker . . . shall be declared out."

Catch It is not a catch if the ball is caught after touching any object [fence, building, tree] other than a player, even if the ball does not touch the ground.

Club/Eligible Any club willfully infringing any rule shall be suspended for a period not to exceed one year for the first offense, and expulsion from membership for the second offense, after trial by the judiciary committee.

Forfeited Game No game shall be forfeited because of the failure of the umpire to discharge his duties or for failing to declare the winning club of a match.

There must be at least a two-day notice for postponement of a game because of the death of a club member or the club is liable to forfeit.

Game/Drawn If the score is tied at the end of nine innings, the captains may mutually agree to consider the game a draw. In case of no such agreement, the club refusing to continue play shall forfeit the ball.

Game/Winner If the game cannot be continued, it shall be decided by the score of the last equal innings and the club having the greater number of runs is the winner; unless one club has completed their inning and the other club has exceeded their opponent's score in their uncompleted inning, in which case the club with the higher score is the winner. But no game shall be considered as played unless five innings on each side have been completed.

Pitcher/Delivery When about to deliver the ball or at the actual time of delivery, the pitcher cannot have either foot outside the pitcher's box.

Pitcher/Position The pitcher's box is enlarged to a six-foot square.

Player/Eligible Players must not have been members of any other National Association club (college clubs excepted) for sixty days immediately prior to the game.

All players who play baseball for money or who at any time receive compensation for their services as players shall be considered professional players; and all others shall be regarded as amateur players.

Note: This rule officially recognized two distinct classes of players—professional and amateur—and permitted the participation of professional players.

Runner/Forced No baserunner shall be forced to vacate a base unless as provided in these rules.

Note: This amendment prevented a runner, not forced to vacate his own base, from forcing another to vacate his base. For example, if a runner attempts to steal third base, changes his mind before reaching third, and returns to second base to find the runner from first now standing on the bag, the original runner still has the right to the base.

Run Scored   When there are two outs, no runner may score a run if the batter or player running the bases is put out before touching first base.

Strike Zone   Balls and strikes may not be called unless there has first been issued a warning and they may not be called until the pitch has crossed the plate. All "balls" *must* be called by the umpire after the pitcher has been warned of the penalty. One warning for each batter shall suffice.

Substitute/Runner   No player shall be allowed to have a substitute run the bases for him except in cases of illness or injury.

1870

Ball   The challenged club must supply the means of ascertaining the size and weight of the ball furnished by the other club.

Note: This rule was dropped in 1871 and replaced with the previous rule requiring the challenging club to furnish a ball on which its size, weight, and the name of the manufacturer is stamped.

Base on Balls   Any player awarded a base on balls is allowed to advance, at his own risk, beyond the base awarded him.

Note: This rule was inexplicably left out of the 1871 rule book but was back in 1872.

Dead Ball   Called "balls" not hit by the batter are no longer dead balls, and any base can be run or player put out on such pitches.

Fair Ball   If the ball, from the stroke of the bat, first touches the ground, the person of a player or any other object, either upon or in front of the foul lines, it shall be declared a fair ball.

Forfeited Game   All games in which any rule is infringed shall be considered forfeited games and shall be recorded as games won by a score of 9 to 0 against the club infringing the rules.

No forfeit shall be declared if a club fails to play a game because of the recent death of one of its members.

Note: The requirement of two days notice has been dropped.

Grounds   The lines of the batter's and pitcher's positions must be marked with chalk or other suitable material so as to be distinctly seen by the umpire.

Runner/Forced   The moment the player running to first base is out, other baserunners previously forced to vacate their bases shall cease to be forced and may return to their bases.

Note: In 1872 the rule was amended and clarified that runners could still be put out in returning to their base.

Strike Zone   The umpire no longer issues a warning before calling a pitch, but "balls" and "strikes" may not be called on the first pitch delivered.

All pitches which are not within the fair reach of the striker, such as pitches over the striker's head, on the ground in front of home base, to the side opposite to that the batsman strikes from, or which hit the striker while he is standing in his proper position, are considered unfair "balls" and must be called whenever delivered (except for the first pitch).

Umpire/Decisions   No decision given by the umpire shall be reversed by the testimony of any player, and the umpire shall not be guided in his decisions by any such testimony.

1871

The rule book is adopted by the National Association of Professional Base-Ball Players.

Ball   The ball must weigh from 5 to 5¼ ounces and must measure exactly 9¼ inches in circumference.

Batter/Position   The batter must stand at least one foot from home base and astride the three-foot line drawn through the center of home base. When striking at the ball, he may take a forward step but must keep one foot behind the line.

Dead Ball   It is a dead ball whenever a pitch touches the umpire, or is accidentally stopped by him.

Game/Legal   Under no circumstances shall a game be considered played unless five innings have been completed. Should darkness or rain prevent the continuing of the game before the end of the fifth inning, the umpire shall declare "no game."

Note: This made clearer what had long been understood by most.

Grounds   No fence may be erected within ninety feet of home base, unless the fence marks the boundary line of the field. Baserunners are entitled to one base whenever the ball passes the catcher and touches a fence located closer than ninety feet behind home base.

Pitcher/Delivery   The penalty for pitches thrown, jerked, or delivered other than with a straight arm swinging perpendicular [parallel] to the body shall be the calling of a "ball." If, after a warning by the umpire, three men are awarded first base in one inning on such called balls, the game shall be declared a forfeit.

Player/Eligible   Players who have been constitutionally expelled from another club for dishonorable conduct shall not be permitted to play in any game played during the year they were expelled.

Player/Position   The fielders may take any position in the field their captain may choose to assign them.

Note: This rule made it clear that the captains could position their players anywhere in the field they wished, including foul territory. The rule, with an obvious omission, was rectified in 1874 with the added phrase, "with the exception of the pitcher, who must occupy his appointed position."

Runner/Advancing   Baserunners, on caught fly balls, may advance after they return to their original base after the ball has been settled momentarily in the hands of the pitcher. Baserunners shall not be entitled to any base touched after a fair fly ball has been hit and prior to the catch being made.

Runner/Fielder   When a fielder, holding the ball, tags a runner who is off a base but the ball is knocked out of his hand by the runner, the runner is still out.

Runner/Overrunning First   A baserunner touching and overrunning first base shall be allowed to return at once to the base without being put out, provided he does not attempt to make second base.

Strike Zone   The batter is allowed to call for either a "high" or "low" pitch, and the pitcher must deliver the ball as required. A "high" ball is one pitched between the waist and the shoulder of the batter; a "low" ball is one pitched between the knee and the waist. Should the batter refuse to swing at balls pitched over the home base and within the specified reach of the bat, it shall be a called "strike." All pitches over the home base that are between the batter's knee and shoulder are considered "fair" pitches.

No strike shall be called when the pitch is struck at for the purpose of willfully striking out.

Note: This sentence was deleted from the rules in 1874.

No strike shall be called on the first pitch delivered unless the batter swings at the pitch.

Note: This one was dropped in 1875.

Substitute/Runner   No player shall be allowed to have a substitute run the bases for him, except for illness or injury, unless by special consent of the opposing captain.

1872

Ball The ball must weigh from 5 to 5¼ ounces and measure from 9 to 9¼ inches in circumference.

Note: These are the dimensions of today's ball.

The ball shall contain one ounce of vulcanized rubber in mold form.

If the ball becomes ripped, out of shape, or, in the umpire's opinion, unfit for play, the umpire shall call for a new ball at the end of a complete inning.

Bases Home base shall be made of white marble or stone and fixed in the ground so as to be even with the surface.

Bat A batter shall be privileged to use his own private bat exclusively. No player of the opposing club shall have any claim to the use of the bat except by consent of the owner.

Note: This rule was dropped in 1874.

Batter/Illegal Act The batter is out if he willfully "balks" [interferes with] the catcher.

Batter/Position When striking at the ball, the batter is allowed to make a backward step as well as a forward step as long as he keeps one foot on either side of the line.

Coach The umpire shall require members of the side at bat to remain a reasonable distance (at least fifteen feet) from the foul lines while directing the movements of baserunners to prevent the interference of fielders. If a club persists in infringing this rule, the umpire shall declare a forfeit.

Dead Balls Foul balls are dead and are not in play until the ball has been settled in the hands of the pitcher, no matter in what part of the field the pitcher may happen to be.

Forfeited Game It is not a forfeit if a club fails to play because of the death of a club member or because of an unavoidable accident.

Note: This rule was dropped in 1876.

Game/Drawn Clubs are no longer allowed to mutually agree to call a game a draw. Drawn games may only be declared if, after five or more innings, the game is prevented from being continued because of darkness, rain, or other cause, and the score is equal on the even innings played.

Game/Rain Should rain begin to fall during a game, the umpire must promptly note the time and should the rain continue to fall for five minutes, the umpire shall suspend play and the game shall not continue until, in the umpire's opinion, the ground is fit for fair fielding.

Interference/Offensive Any player who designedly [*willfully and intentionally* are used in subsequent years] lets the ball hit him or kicks the ball while at bat or running the bases, thus preventing an opponent from holding or fielding the ball, shall be declared out. Any baserunner who, in any way, prevents a fielder from catching a batted fly ball, fair or foul, shall be called out.

Pitcher/Delivery The pitcher must deliver the ball while within the lines of his position and must remain within them until the ball has left his hand. He shall not make any motion to deliver the ball while outside the box.

Whenever the pitcher delivers the pitch with an overhand or roundarm throw, the umpire shall call a "foul balk." Should the pitcher persist in such action, the umpire, after warning him of the penalty, shall declare the game forfeited. Baserunners are awarded one base on "foul balks" as on any other balk.

Note: This rule legalized the jerk, wrist snap, and bent-elbow deliveries and, thus, the curveball. It was now legal for the pitcher to snap his wrist as long as he kept his hand, while in the forward motion, below the hip.

Pitcher/Position Iron plates must be placed at each end of the front line of the pitcher's box.

Player/Eligible Any player who has willfully broken a written engagement to a club shall not be eligible to play in any game during the year the engagement was made. No engagement shall be considered binding unless made in writing and signed by at least two witnesses. This rule shall be binding unless rescinded by the judiciary committee.

Runner/Overrunning First A runner may overrun first base without being put out if, after touching first, he runs straight down the line or to the right of the bag. Should he turn to the left or attempt to make second base, he shall be at risk of being put out.

Strike Zone All pitches that come within one foot of the batter shall be called "balls."

All pitches that are sent in over home base at the height called for by the batter and are not delivered with an overhand throw or round-arm delivery as in cricket are "fair" pitches. Should the batter fail to call either a "high" or "low" pitch, no "ball" shall be called for "fair" pitches.

A "low" ball is a pitch between the waist of the batter and one foot from the ground.

Substitute/Runner No player shall be allowed a substitute in running the bases, except for illness or injury, unless by special consent of the opposing captain; and in such case the captain shall select the player to run as substitute.

Umpire/Duties The umpire is required to call all foul balls, while the ball is still in the air, as soon as he sees the ball is falling in foul territory.

Umpire/Replacing The umpire shall not be changed during the game, unless with the consent of both captains, except for illness or injury or for violation of the rules.

1873

Interference/Spectator If a ball is stopped in any way by a person not engaged in the game, no player can be put out until the ball has been first settled in the hands of the pitcher while he stands within the lines of his position.

Fielder/Illegal Act If a fielder stops the ball with his hat or cap, no player can be put out and each baserunner shall be entitled to one base.

1874

Ball The yarn used in the composition of the ball must be woolen.

The visiting club furnishes the ball for a series of games; the home team when only a single game is played.

Base Home base must have one corner facing the pitcher's position.

Base on Balls Note: In 1874 there were two classifications of base on balls. See explanation under *Strike Zone*.

Bat The bat must be made wholly of wood.

Note: This made it clear that the bat must be made entirely of wood. Any metal or other material on it renders it illegal.

Batter/Fails to Bat Any batter refusing to bat within three minutes after the umpire has called for him shall be declared out.

Batter/Position The batter's position shall be a space on either side of home base, six feet long by three feet wide, which extends three feet in front and three feet behind the line drawn through the center of home base, and its nearest line one foot from home base. Batters must stand within this position when in the act of striking the ball.

Note: This introduces the batter's box.

Batter/Runner　When the batsman has fairly struck a fair ball, he shall vacate his position and is considered a baserunner until he is put out or scores his run.

Batting Order　The batsmen must take their positions in the order in which they are named on the scorebook.

Any batsman failing to take his position in the order of striking, unless by reason of illness or injury or by consent of the opposing captain, shall be declared out, unless the error is discovered before a fair ball has been hit or the batter is put out.

Catch　Should the umpire be unable to see whether a catch has been fairly made, he shall be privileged to appeal to the bystanders and render his decision according to the fairest testimony at command.

Coach/Offensive Team　The umpire shall require members of the batting side, who are not at bat or running the bases, to keep at a distance of at least fifty feet from the foul lines, or farther if the umpire desires. The captain and one assistant only are permitted to approach the foul lines, and not nearer than fifteen feet, to coach baserunners. If a club persists in infringing this rule, the umpire shall declare a forfeit.

Dead Ball　All pitches that touch the striker's bat without being swung at, or touch the batter while he is standing in his box, or which hit the umpire, shall be considered dead balls. No base shall be run or run scored on such balls. Pitches that strike the umpire are not dead balls unless the ball passes the catcher.

Should the batter swing at or hit any pitch on which a "ball" has been called, the umpire shall disregard his call and render his decision on the swing or hit made. It is not a dead ball.

Fielder/Illegal Act　Should any fielder stop the ball with his hat, cap, or any other part of his dress, the umpire shall call "dead ball" and the ball shall not be in play again until the umpire calls "ball in play." Baserunners are entitled to the base they were running for.

Forfeited Game　Any game in which the umpire declares any section of these rules to have been willfully violated, he shall at once declare the game a forfeit.

Gambling　Any player who shall, in any way, be interested in any bet or wager on the game in which he takes part, either as umpire, player, or scorer, or who purchases or has purchased for him any "pool" or chance, sold or given away, on the game in which he takes part, he shall be dishonorably expelled from both his club and the association [league in 1876]. Umpires, players, and scorers who have wagers on any other association [league] game shall be suspended for the season.

Ground Rules　Before calling "play," the umpire shall ask the home field captain whether there are any special ground rules and shall take note of such rules and see that they are enforced, provided they do not conflict with any regular rules of the game. Should the umpire not be notified of any ground rules, the rules shall not be enforced.

Note: This last sentence was dropped from the 1876 rule book.

Grounds　The foul ball lines shall be unlimited in length and shall run from the center of home base through the center of first and third bases to the foul ball posts, which shall be located at the boundary of the field and within the range of home and first base, and home and third base. Said lines shall be marked from base to base with chalk, or some other white substance, so as to be plainly seen by the umpire.

Interference/Spectator　Should the ball be willfully stopped by any outside person not engaged in the game, the ball shall be dead until settled in the hands of the pitcher while standing in his box. Baserunners at the time shall be entitled to the base they were running for.

Pitcher/Delivery　The ball must be delivered with the arm swinging nearly perpendicular [parallel] to the side of the body.

Should the pitcher deliver the ball by an overhand throw, outward swing of the arm, roundarm bowling, or any other swing other than nearly perpendicular to the body, it shall be a "foul balk." When a foul balk is called, the umpire shall warn the pitcher of the penalty and should three foul balks be called in one inning, the umpire shall declare a forfeit.

If the pitcher makes any motion to deliver the ball and fails to do so—except if the ball is accidentally dropped—the umpire shall call a balk.

Pitcher/Position　Each corner of the pitcher's box must be marked by a flat six-inch square iron plate.

Player/Eligible　Players must not have been members of any other club in the association for sixty days prior to the date of the game, unless their previous club has disbanded and their contract with such club has been canceled.

The rules of 1874 also include other rules concerning contracts including disciplinary actions for players who violate them.

Runner　A player running the bases shall be considered holding a base—entitled to occupy it—until he has regularly touched the next base in order.

Note: This new rule is inaccurate because it neglects to mention the important exception of runners forced off their base. This correction would not be made until 1880.

Runner/Foul Ball　In the case of a foul ball, the baserunner returning to touch the base must remain on it until the ball is held by the pitcher, no matter in what part of the field the pitcher happens to be.

Runner/Overrunning First　The batter may overrun first base without risk of being put out provided he makes no attempt to run to second base and returns at once to first base.

Run Scored　No run shall score unless the home base is touched before three players have been put out; and if the third player is put out before reaching first base, the run shall not be scored.

Spectators　No person not engaged in the game shall be permitted to occupy any position within the lines of the field, or in any way interrupt the umpire during the game.

Strike Zone　There are now two classifications of unfair pitches: "balls" and "wide balls."

"Balls" are pitches not at the height called for by the batter ("high" or "low") or are not exactly over home base. "Wide balls" are pitches that are out of the reach of the striker's bat, such as those that hit the ground or the batter, or are over the batter's head. The umpire shall call every third "ball." When three "balls" [actually nine pitches] have been called, the batter is awarded first base. With the exception of the first pitch, all "wides" are called in the order of their delivery. When three "wides" have been called, the batter is awarded first base.

Note: When you consider that one type of base on balls required three (and sometimes four) pitches, while another required nine pitches—not to mention calling strikes—it's no wonder they started paying the unfortunate umpire of 1874. "Wide balls" as a special classification of unfair pitches lasted only one year and was dropped from the rule book in 1875.

Substitute　No player not in position on the field or ready to bat after the close of the third inning and before the start of the fourth, shall be substituted for another player, except in running the bases.

Substitute/Runner　A player serving as substitute for another in running the bases must cross the batter's position in front of home base, and must not start to run until the batter strikes at the ball.

Note: This clarified the position in which the substitute runner must stand. In previous years, substitute runners often ran behind the batter and interfered with the catcher.

Umpire/Decisions   The umpire shall render no decision except when appealed to by a player, unless expressly required to do so by the rules of the game, as in calling "balls," etc.

No player shall be permitted to converse with the umpire during the game, except to make a legal appeal for his decision in giving a player out.

No decision by the umpire on any point of play in baserunning shall be reversed upon the testimony of any player. But if it is shown by the two captains that the umpire has misinterpreted the rules or has given an erroneous decision, the umpire shall be allowed to reverse his decision.

Umpire/Payment   The umpire may receive compensation for his services as the clubs deem advisable, provided he receives the same amount from both clubs.

Note: This was dropped from the rule book in 1876.

Umpire/Replacing   The umpire shall not be changed during the game, except for illness or injury, or by consent of both captains if the umpire has willfully violated the written rules of the game.

Should the umpire fail to enforce any section of the rules or should he interpret the rules other than the express letter of the rule, he shall cease to be eligible to act in the position and shall at once be dismissed.

Note: This last paragraph was dropped from the 1876 rule book.

1875

Ball   When the ball becomes out of shape, cut or ripped to expose the yarn, or in any way injured to be unfit for fair use, the umpire, at the close of an even inning at the request of either captain, shall call for a new ball.

Base   The corner of home base facing the pitcher's position must touch the intersection of the foul lines.

Note: This places home base entirely in foul territory.

Base on Balls   See *Strike Zone*.

Batter/Position   The batsman's position is six feet long by three feet wide, extending two feet in front of and four feet behind the center of home base. Its nearest line is one foot from home base.

Note: With the placement of home base in foul territory, the batter's box has also been moved back.

Should the batter step outside the batter's box while striking the ball, the umpire shall call "foul strike," and two such foul strikes shall put the batter out. All baserunners are allowed to return to their original base.

Game/Rain   After rain has fallen for five minutes, the umpire shall suspend play at the request of either captain.

Strike Zone   All pitches not over home base or at the height called for by the batter are considered unfair "balls." Every third consecutive "ball" must be called by the umpire. When three "balls" [nine pitches] have been called, the batter is awarded first base.

Note: The term *wide balls* has been dropped from the rule book. In 1876, the word *consecutive* was dropped.

Umpire   The umpire shall not enter the infield while the ball is in play.

1876

The National League is founded and adopts the rule book.

Ball   In all regular match games, the balls are furnished by the home club. Should any ball used in a game prove, on examination by the umpire, to be illegal in size, weight, or materials,

balls of the same manufacture shall not be used thereafter in regular match games.

The rubber used in the composition of the ball must weigh not more than one ounce.

Should the ball be lost during a game, the umpire, at the expiration of five minutes, shall call for a new ball.

Batter/Position   If the batter steps outside the batter's box when he strikes at the ball, the umpire shall call "foul balk and out" and baserunners shall return to their original base.

Fielder/Illegal Act   Baserunners are entitled to two bases for any fair hit ball stopped or caught by a fielder with his hat, cap, or any part of his dress. The ball is dead.

Foul Ball   See *Runner/Advancing*.

Game/Rain   If a game cannot be concluded, it shall be decided by the score of the last equal innings played, unless one club has completed an inning and the other club has equaled or exceeded their opponent's score in an incomplete inning, in which case the game shall be decided by the total score.

Obstruction   If a baserunner is prevented from making a base by the obstruction of an adversary, he shall be entitled to that base and shall not be put out.

Pitcher/Delivery   It shall be a balk if the pitcher unnecessarily delays the game by not delivering the ball.

Player/Eligible   Many rules and regulations concerning eligibility of players, contracts, and disciplinary actions are removed from the rule book.

Player/Illegal Act   No manager, captain, or player shall address the audience except in case of necessary explanation. Any manager, captain, or player who uses abusive, threatening, or improper language to the audience shall be punished by suspension from play for twenty days and forfeiture of his salary for such period.

Rules   No section of these rules shall be construed as conflicting with or affecting any article of the league's constitution.

Runner/Advancing   Following caught fly balls, runners may advance after returning to their original base. On all other foul balls, including foul balls caught on one bounce, runners may not advance but may return to their original base without being put out.

Run Scored   If the third out is forced out or is put out before reaching first base, no run shall be scored.

Strikeout   Should the batter, with two strikes, not swing at the next "good ball," the umpire shall not call a "strike" but warn him by calling "good ball." But should the batter swing and miss or fail to swing at the next good ball, "three strikes" must be called and the batter must run to first as in the case of hitting a fair ball.

Strike Zone   The batsman, on taking his position, must call for a "high," "low," or "fair" pitch, and the umpire shall notify the pitcher to deliver the ball as required; such call cannot be changed after the first pitch is delivered.

Substitute   No player taking part in the game shall be replaced by another after the start of the fourth inning, except in running the bases.

Umpire   No player shall be permitted to converse with the umpire during the game, except the two captains and then only to appeal a misinterpretation of the rules or an erroneous decision.

1877

Ball   No ball is to be used except those furnished by the secretary of the league.

Bases First, second, and third bases must cover a space equal to 15 inches square.

Home base is to be placed entirely into fair territory with two of its sides forming part of the foul lines.

Batter/Fails to Bat Any batsman who fails to take his position at bat within one minute after the umpire has called for him shall be out.

Batter/Position The batter's box is six feet long by three feet wide with the line of home base running through its center.

Note: This arrangement permitted a batter to stand three feet in front of or three feet behind home base.

Coach See *Grounds*.

Foul/Fair Balls A batted ball striking in foul territory and then in fair is fair; a batted ball striking fair and then foul is foul.

Game The home club shall first take the bat.

Game/Rain Should rain continue to fall for 10 minutes (following suspension of play) the game shall terminate.

Grounds Lines parallel to the foul lines and 15 feet back are to be drawn to delineate a boundary for the captain and one assistant to coach baserunners. Lines parallel to the foul lines and 50 feet back are to be drawn to delineate a boundary for players on the batting side.

Note: In the rules of 1880, these lines are referred to as the "Captain's Lines" and the "Players' Lines" respectively.

Interference/Offensive When a fielder occupies the basepath in the act of fielding a ball, the baserunner shall run out of the path and behind the fielder to avoid interference.

A baserunner struck by a batted ball is out.

A baserunner, from home to first base, shall not run inside the foul line or more than three feet outside of it, or he shall be declared out.

Player/Expulsion Any player who shall, in any way, be interested in any bet or wager on any league game or who shall purchase or have purchased for him any "pool" or chance, sold or given away, shall be expelled.

The club is entitled to the best services of the player, and players who become indifferent or careless in play or who become unable to render satisfactory service to the club from any cause may have their salaries suspended or their contracts canceled.

Players conspiring against the interest of their clubs or who "manifest a disposition" to obstruct club management may be expelled.

Note: These three rules were removed from the rule book in 1878.

Runner/Fielder A baserunner who knocks the ball out of the hand of a fielder while in the act of running to a base is no longer out.

Strike Zone A "low" pitch is one thrown belt high or below the belt and above the knee. A "high" pitch is one above the belt to the shoulder.

A ball pitched and called "dead" by reason of having struck the umpire shall be counted as one of nine called balls entitling the batter to a base if it is also an "unfair" ball.

Substitute No substitution is to be made after the start of the second inning except in cases of illness or injury.

1878

Batting Order The batsmen must take their positions in the order in which they are directed by their captain, and after each player has had one time at bat, the order established shall not be changed during the game.

Batter/Position The batter must actually hit the ball while

outside the batter's box to commit a "foul strike" and be called out.

Game The club that bats first shall be determined by the two captains.

Grounds The foul lines shall be continued to the limits of the field beyond and back of home base. This triangular area shall be for the exclusive use of the catcher, umpire, and batsman; and no offensive player (except the batsman) shall occupy it.

Note: In the rules of 1880, these lines are referred to as the "Catcher's Lines."

Pitcher/Delivery The pitcher's hand must pass below the waist in delivering the ball.

Substitute/Runner No player shall be allowed a substitute in running the bases except for illness or injury incurred in the game then being played, and then such substitute shall take the player's place only after the latter has reached first base.

1879

Ball The "Spalding League Ball" is adopted as the official ball, which is indicated in the footnotes of some rule books.

Base on Balls Note: The amount of unfair pitches is still the same for the awarding of a base on balls but, to everyone's delight, the terminology is finally changed from "every third ball must be called" to "every ball must be called." The result is the same, nine "balls" and the batter is awarded first base.

Batter/Caught Foul A batted ball in foul territory must be caught on the fly to be declared an out.

Note: This rule was dropped in 1880 but was again added in 1883.

Batting Order After the first inning, the first striker in each inning shall be the batsman whose name follows that of the last man who has completed his turn (time) at bat in the preceding inning.

Pitcher/Delivery The pitcher, when taking his position to deliver the ball, must face the batter.

Pitcher/Illegal Act If a pitcher delivers the ball to intentionally strike the batter, in the judgment of the umpire, the umpire shall fine the pitcher not less than $10 nor more than $50.

Pitcher/Position The pitcher's box is now four feet wide and six feet long.

Strikeout The batter is out after three strikes if the ball is caught before touching the ground.

1880

Appeal/Runner A baserunner who fails to touch intervening bases when returning to a base shall not be declared out unless the opposing captain appeals to the umpire before the pitcher delivers the ball to the batter.

Base on Balls A base on balls is awarded to the batter when eight balls have been called by the umpire.

Grounds The ground must be an enclosed field sufficient in size to enable each player to play in his position as required by the rules.

Interference/Offensive No run can be scored if a baserunner is declared out for being hit with a fair hit batted ball.

Runner/Returning The baserunner is out if he fails to return to the base he occupied after a foul fly has been caught and the runner is touched with the ball or the ball is returned to the base the runner occupied before he returns.

Strikeout The batter becomes a runner immediately when three strikes have been called by the umpire.

Umpire No player except the captain or his assistant shall address the umpire concerning any point of play. Violators are subject to a fine.

1881

Base on Balls A batter is awarded first base after seven balls are called by the umpire.

Forfeited Game Every club shall furnish sufficient police force upon its own grounds to preserve order. In the event of a crowd entering the field during the progress of a game, and interfering with play in any manner, the visiting club may refuse to play further until the field is cleared; if the ground is not cleared within 15 minutes, the visiting club is entitled to a forfeit by a score of 9–0, regardless of the number of innings played.

Pitcher/Position The pitcher's box is to be fifty feet from the center of home base.

Security See *Forfeited Game.*

Spectators No person shall be allowed upon any part of the field during the progress of the game, in addition to the nine players on each side and the umpire, except such officers of the law who are present in uniform to preserve the peace.

Strikeout The batter, on a called third strike, is no longer given a warning of "good ball" by the umpire. (See 1876 *Strikeout*)

Substitute A substitute is not permitted unless a player is disabled by injury or illness in the game being played.

Substitute/Runner A player shall not have a substitute run the bases for him.

Umpire/Decisions The umpire shall *not* reverse his decision on any point of play upon the testimony of any player or bystander.

1882

The American Association begins its first season and makes several modifications to the rule book to meet its own needs and wants. Among the rules not included in the AA rule book are the prohibition of liquor being sold on club grounds, and the fining of pitchers who, in the umpire's judgment, purposely hit batters with pitched balls. Other changes and amendments particular to the AA are noted below.

Ball Should the ball become so injured as to be unfit for fair use in the opinion of the umpire, on being appealed to by either captain, a new ball shall be called for by the umpire at the end of an even inning.
Note: The AA's rule doesn't require an appeal by a captain.

Ball (American Association) The ball must be stamped "American Association." Each ball shall be enclosed in a paper box and sealed by the manufacturer. The seal shall not be broken except by the umpire in the presence of the two captains after "play" has been called.
Note: The AA selected the Mahn Sporting Company's ball as its official ball.

Batter The two players following the batsman, in the order in which they are named on the scorebook, must be ready with bat in hand to promptly take their position as batsmen.
Note: This rule was not adopted by the AA.

Game/"Time" The umpire shall suspend play for an accident to himself or a player; but in case of an accident to a fielder, time shall not be called until the ball is returned and held by the pitcher standing in his position.
Note: The AA rule book does not include this important exception.

Grounds/Bench The players' bench must be furnished by the home club and placed on a portion of the ground outside the players' lines. It must be twelve feet in length and fastened to the ground. Bat racks sufficient in size to hold twenty bats are to be adjacent to the players' bench.
Note: This is not in the AA rule book.

Grounds/Three-Foot Line The three-foot line area, in which the batter-runner must run to avoid interference, must be marked on the field.
Note: The rules of the AA do not require the actual markings.

Interference/Offensive A baserunner is out if he obstructs a fielder attempting to field a batted ball; provided that if two or more fielders attempt to field the ball and the runner comes in contact with one of them, the umpire shall determine which fielder is entitled to the benefit of the rule and shall not call the runner out for coming in contact with the other fielder.
Note: This provision isn't included in the AA rules.
The batter is out if he plainly attempts to hinder the catcher from catching the ball, without effort to make a fair hit.
Note: Not outlined in the AA rules.

Interference/Spectator A "blocked ball" is a batted or thrown ball that is stopped or handled by any person not engaged in the game. Whenever a block is called, baserunners may run the bases without being put out until the ball is returned to and held by the pitcher standing in his position. Exception: When the person not engaged in the game retains possession of the ball or throws or kicks it beyond reach of fielders, the umpire should call time and require baserunners to stop at the last base touched by them.
Note: The AA does not use the term *blocked ball* and uses the following rule for spectator interference: "If a batted or thrown ball is stopped by any person not engaged in the game, the ball shall not be considered in play until it is held by the pitcher standing in his position. The baserunner shall be entitled to take one base."

Spectators Spectators hissing or hooting at the umpire are to be promptly ejected from the grounds.

1883

Ball In calling for a new ball, replacing one unfit for fair play, the umpire may call for one "at once" and does not have to wait until the end of the inning.
Note: The AA here still requires the umpire to wait until the close of an inning before calling for a new ball.

Ball (American Association) The ball must be manufactured by A. J. Reach, according to the specifications, and stamped "American Association."
Note: The Mahn ball was found unsatisfactory.

Batter/Caught Foul A batted ball in foul territory must be caught on the fly to be declared an out.
Note: Foul balls caught on one bounce are no longer outs. The AA refuses to go along with the rule and continues with the one-bound foul flyout.

Batting Order The batter is out if he fails to take his position at bat in the order of batting, unless the error is discovered and the proper batsman takes his position before a fair hit has been made. In such case, the "balls" and "strikes" called will be counted in the time at bat of the proper batsman.
Note: This last sentence is not included in the AA rule book.

Pitcher/Delivery A fair ball is a ball delivered by the pitcher, while wholly within the lines of his position, and while facing the batsman and his hand, in delivering the ball, must not pass above the line of his shoulder.
When the umpire has called two "foul balks," the batter and all baserunners are awarded one base. Three foul balks in one inning no longer constitutes a forfeited game.
Note: The AA discards the term "foul balk."

Runner/Overrunning First In the American Association a runner touching and overrunning first base is at risk of being put out while off the base if he turns to the left from the foul line while returning to the bag.

Runner/Returning   A baserunner who fails to return to his base at a run following a foul ball is liable to be put out by being touched by the ball while off his base.

Substitute/Runner   The American Association allows a substitute to run the bases for a player if the player is injured in the game being played and the opposing club consents to the use of a substitute runner.

Umpire   Umpires are to be salaried employees.

1884

In 1884 the Union Association became operational and adopted virtually the same rule book used by the American Association. The few exceptions include the additional rule requiring foul balls to be caught on the fly to record an out, and the Wright & Ditson ball as the league's official ball. The Union Association folded after one season.

Base on Balls   The batter is awarded a base on balls after six balls have been called by the umpire. Note: The AA and UA retain the seven-ball base on balls.

Bat Boy/Girl   The American Association allows "a person to take charge of the bats of each club" to be on the playing field.
   Note: Not in the UA rule book.

Fair/Foul Balls   When a batted ball passes outside the grounds, the umpire shall declare it fair should it disappear within, or foul should it disappear outside of the range of the foul lines.
   Note: This is not found in the AA and UA rule books.

Hit by Pitch   The American Association adds the following rule: If a batsman be solidly hit by a ball from the pitcher when he evidently cannot avoid the same, he shall be given his base by the umpire.
   Note: The AA is the first league to award a batter first base for being hit with a pitch; not in the UA rule book.

Pitcher/Delivery   All restrictions on the delivery of the ball are lifted except that the pitcher must be entirely within the lines of his position and must face the batter.
   Note: The overhanded delivery was thus permitted for the first time. The AA and UA kept the shoulder-high delivery.

1885

Bases   The home base may be made of white rubber or stone.
   Note: In the AA, home base must be made of white rubber only.

Bat   The handle of the bat may be wound with twine not to exceed 18 inches from the end.
   Note: No such rule in the AA rule book.
   The bat must be round except that a portion of the surface on one side may be flat.
   Note: The AA nixed this one also.

Batter/Caught Foul   In a special midseason meeting held on June 7, 1885, the American Association adopts the rule that a foul ball must be caught on the fly to be declared an out.

Batter/Position   The batter's box is now six feet long by four feet wide with its nearest line six inches from home base.
   Note: The AA keeps the six by three foot box that is one foot from the plate.

Game   The American Association gives the option of which club bats first to the home team captain.

Grounds/Fence   A fair batted ball that goes over the fence at a distance less than 210 feet from home base shall entitle the batsman to two bases. A distinctive line shall be marked on the fence at this point.

Note: This is not in the AA rule book.

Grounds/Three-Foot Line   The American Association requires the marking of the three-foot area in which the batsman must run to avoid interference.

Home Run/Double   See *Grounds/Fence*.

Pitcher/Delivery   The pitcher must have both feet touching the ground while making any one of the series of motions he is accustomed to make in the delivery of the ball. A violation of this rule shall be a "foul balk" and two foul balks shall entitle the batter and each runner to one base.
   Note: At a special National League meeting held on June 7, 1885, this rule was dropped. The term "foul balk" was also dropped from the rules. (The AA never required its pitchers to keep both feet on the ground during delivery.) However, in a special meeting of their own, also held on June 7, the AA adopted the rule allowing the overhand delivery, conforming with the NL rule.
   A balk is made whenever the pitcher, when about to deliver the ball to the bat while standing in his position, makes any one of the series of actions he habitually makes in delivery, and he fails to deliver the ball to the bat.

Uniforms (American Association)   Every club shall be required to adopt a neat and attractive uniform for its players, and shall at all times be required to present the same upon the field in a clean and attractive condition.

1886

Ball   Should the ball be knocked outside of the enclosure or lost during the game, the umpire shall call at once for another ball.

Base on Balls   The NL increases the number to seven balls for the awarding of a base on balls. The AA drops the number to six balls.

Bat/Handle   A granulated substance may be applied to the bat handle not to exceed 18 inches from the end.

Batter/Position   The batter's box is returned to the six foot long by three foot wide area, one foot from home base.

Pitcher/Delivery   The pitcher is no longer required to keep both feet on the ground while delivering the ball.
   Note: The term "foul balk" is dropped from the rules.

Pitcher/Position   The pitcher's lines must be straight lines forming a box seven feet long by four feet wide.

1887

The National League and the American Association agree to be governed by the same rule book after several rules are rewritten.

Ball   In all games, the ball or balls played with shall be furnished by the home club, and the last ball in play becomes the property of the winning club. Each ball to be used in championship games shall be examined, measured, and weighed by the Secretary of the Association, enclosed in a paper box, and sealed with the seal of the Secretary, which seal shall not be broken except by the umpire in the presence of the captains of the two contesting nines after play has been called.
   Note: The Spalding and Reach balls respectively remain the official balls of the National League and the American Association.
   For each championship game, two balls shall be furnished by the home club to the umpire for use. When the ball in play is batted over the fence or stands, onto foul ground out of sight of the players, the other ball shall be immediately put into play by the umpire. As often as one of the two in use shall be lost, a new one must be substituted, so that the umpire may at all times, after the game begins, have two for use. The moment the umpire

delivers the alternate ball to the catcher or pitcher, it comes into play, and shall not be exchanged until it, in turn, passes out of sight onto foul ground.

Base on Balls The batter is entitled to one base when five balls have been called by the umpire.

Bases Home base must be made of whitened rubber.

Second base shall be upon its corner of the infield, and the center of the first and third bases shall be on lines running to and from second base and 7½ inches from the foul lines, providing that each base shall be entirely within the foul lines.

Note: This placed first and third bases, for the first time, entirely as they are today. However, a careful reading of the 1887 rule above reveals that the precise description actually places first and third base 7½ inches farther toward the outfield than they are today, and thus not entirely within the 90-foot square. In fact, the bases were never placed as outlined in the poorly written rule, and some years later the rule was modified to reflect its intent.

Batter/Position The batter's box is again made four feet wide by six feet long.

Coach/Position The captain's or coacher's lines must be 15 feet from and parallel with the foul lines and should commence 75 feet distant from the catcher's line. Should the captain or coacher willfully fail to remain in said bounds, he shall be fined by the umpire $5 for each such offense, except upon an appeal by the captain from the umpire's decision upon a misinterpretation of the rules.

The captains and coachers are restricted in coaching to the baserunner only, and are not allowed to address any remarks except to the baserunner, and then only in words of necessary direction; no player shall use language which will, in any manner, refer to or reflect upon a player of the opposing club or the audience. To enforce the above, the captain of the opposing side may call the attention of the umpire to the offense and upon a repetition of the same the club shall be debarred from further coaching during the game.

Foul Ball See last paragraph under *Strike Zone*.

Game The choice of innings is given to the home team captain.

No game is to be begun later than two hours before sunset.

The players of each club in a match game shall be nine in number, and in no case shall less than nine men be allowed to play on each side.

Game/Rain The home club captain shall be the sole judge of the fitness of the ground for beginning a game after rain.

Game/"Time" The umpire may call "timeout" to enforce order in case of annoyance from spectators.

Grounds/Foul Lines The foul lines must be drawn in straight lines from the outer corner of home base along the outer edges of the first and third bases to the boundaries of the ground.

Note: Also see *Coach* for "Coacher's Lines."

Hit by Pitch The batter is entitled to take first base if his person or clothing is hit by a ball from the pitcher, unless in the umpire's opinion he intentionally permitted himself to be hit.

Interference/Offensive The baserunner is out if he intentionally interferes with a thrown ball.

Pitcher/Delivery The pitcher shall take his position facing the batsman, with both feet squarely on the ground, the right foot on the rear line of the "box," his left foot in advance of the right, and to the left of an imaginary line from his right foot to the center of the home base. He shall not raise his right foot, unless in the act of delivering the ball, nor make more than one step in such delivery. He shall hold the ball, before delivery, fairly in front of his body, and in sight of the umpire. In the case of a

lefthanded pitcher, the above words "left" and "right" are to be reversed. When the pitcher feigns to throw the ball to a base, he must resume the above position and pause momentarily before delivering the ball to the bat.

Any motion made by the pitcher to deliver the ball to the bat without delivering it is a balk, and shall be held to include any and every accustomed motion with the hands, arms, or feet, or position of the body assumed by the pitcher in his delivery of the ball, and any motion calculated to deceive a baserunner, except the ball be accidentally dropped.

It is a balk if the ball be held by the pitcher so long as to delay the game unnecessarily. It is a balk if the pitcher makes any motion to deliver the ball to the bat when any part of his person is upon grounds outside of the lines of his position, including all preliminary motions with the hands, arms, and feet. The batter becomes a baserunner after any illegal delivery of a ball by the pitcher.

Pitcher/Position The pitcher's box is now 5½ feet long by four feet wide.

Player/Illegal Act No umpire, manager, captain, or player shall address the audience during the progress of a game, except in case of necessary explanation.

Runner/Overrunning First If the baserunner overruns first base and turns to his left from the foul line, he may be put out in returning to the base or in attempting to advance.

Runner/Returning Baserunners need not return to their bags on the run following a foul ball etc., provided they do not unnecessarily delay the game.

Spectators No person shall be allowed upon any part of the field during the progress of a game, in addition to the players in uniform, the manager on each side, and the umpire; except such officers of the law as may be present in uniform, and such officials of the home club as may be necessary to preserve the peace.

Strikeout The batter is out after four strikes are declared by the umpire.

Strike Zone The batter can no longer call for a "high" or "low" pitch.

A "fair" ball (strike) is defined as a legally pitched ball that passes over home base "not lower than the batsman's knee, nor higher than his shoulder."

A strike is called when the batter makes any obvious attempt to make a foul hit.

Umpire/Decisions No one except the captains of the contending teams can question an umpire's decision; no player other than a captain can approach or address the umpire unless required to do so. Violators may be fined $10.

The umpire cannot reverse his decision by the testimony of a player or spectator. However, the umpire may consult a player on the question before rendering his decision.

Uniforms/Shoes Every club shall be required to adopt uniforms for its players. Each player shall be required to present himself upon the field during the game in a neat and clean condition, but no player shall attach anything to the sole or heel of his shoes other than the ordinary baseball shoe plate.

1888

Interference/Offensive If a fair hit ball strikes the baserunner before touching a fielder, the runner shall be declared out—however, in such case, no base shall be run unless forced by the batter becoming a baserunner, and no run shall be scored.

Note: In 1890, the rule was amended with the additional phrase, "and no other baserunner put out." This clarified that the batter could not be thrown out nor any possible double play could be made on such a play.

Strikeout   The batter is out after three strikes are declared by the umpire.

The batter is out if, while making the third strike, the ball hits his person or clothing.

1889

Base on Balls   A batter is entitled to take first base when four balls have been called by the umpire.

Foul Tip   A foul tip is defined as a foul hit not rising above the batter's head and caught by the catcher playing within 10 feet of home base. In the case of a foul tip, the batter is not out and any baserunners may return to their bases without being put out.

Pitcher/Delivery   The pitcher shall take his position facing the batsman with both feet square on the ground, one foot on the rear line of the "box." He shall not raise either foot, unless in the act of delivering the ball, nor make more than one step in such delivery. He shall hold the ball, before the delivery fairly in front of his body, and in sight of the umpire. When the pitcher feigns to throw the ball to a base, he must resume the above position and pause momentarily before delivering the ball to the bat.

Substitute   One player, whose name shall be printed on the scorecard as an extra player, may be substituted at the end of any complete inning by either club, but the player retired shall not thereafter participate in the game. In addition thereto, a substitute may be allowed at any time in place of a player disabled in the game then being played, by reason of illness or injury, of the nature and extent of which the umpire shall be the sole judge.

Substitute/Runner   The baserunner shall not have a substitute run for him, except by consent of the captains of the contesting teams.

1890

In 1890, the Players League was in operation for its one and only season, for which they adopted the rule book and made several modifications.

Ball   The Players League used the "Keefe ball" as its official ball.

Ball/Defacing   At no time shall the ball be intentionally discolored by rubbing it with the soil or otherwise.

Note: This rule was not in the Players League rule book.

Forfeited Game (Players League)   If a club fails to begin play within one minute after the umpire calls "play" at the start of the game, unless such delay is unavoidable, the game shall be declared a forfeit.

If the club fails to resume play within five minutes after the umpire has called "play" (following suspension of play), the game shall be declared a forfeit.

Note: The NL and AA rule book allowed for just the opposite before declaring a forfeit—five minutes at the start of the game, one minute after suspended play.

Pitcher/Delivery   The Players League deleted the following line from its rule book: "He [the pitcher] shall not raise either foot, unless in the act of delivering the ball."

Note: See 1889 *Pitcher/Delivery*.

Pitcher/Position (Players League)   The pitcher's lines must be six feet long by four feet wide, its forward line distant fifty-one feet from the center of home base. Each corner of the "box" must be marked by a wooden peg.

The NL and AA require the pitcher's points to be flat, round, rubber plates, six inches in diameter.

Substitute   Two players, whose names shall be printed on the scorecard as extra players, may be substituted at any time by either club, but no player so retired shall thereafter participate in the game.

Note: The Players League applied this rule but required the substitution to be made at the end of a complete inning.

Umpire (Players League)   There shall be two umpires at every championship game; one shall stand behind the bat and the other shall stand in the field.

Note: Leave it to the players to understand the importance of having at least two umpires on the field of play.

1891

Substitute   Each team is required to have one or more substitutes available.

1892

Coach   A team is permitted to have not more than two coaches who may be one player participating in the game and any other player under contract to the club.

Coachers are not to use language which in any manner refers to or reflects upon spectators.

Dead/Live Ball   A legally delivered fair ball that touches the bat of the batter in his position shall be considered a batted ball and in play.

Forfeited Game   A forfeit shall be declared if a team resorts to dilatory practices in order to gain time, for the purpose of having the game called on account of darkness or rain or for any reason whatsoever.

Game   "No Game" shall be declared by the umpire if he shall terminate play on account of rain or darkness before five innings on each side are completed, except in a case when the game is called, the club second at bat shall have more runs at the end of its fourth inning than the club first at bat made in its five innings, then the umpire shall award the game to the club having made the greatest number of runs, and it shall be a game and be so counted in the championship record.

Grounds/Fence   A fair batted ball that goes over the fence shall entitle the batter to a home run; except that should it go over the fence at a distance less than 235 feet from home base, the batter is entitled to only two bases. A distinctive line is to be marked on the fence showing the required point.

Hit by Pitch   The batter becomes a baserunner if, while he be a batsman, his person—excepting hands or forearm, which makes it a dead ball—or clothing be hit by a ball from the pitcher, unless, in the opinion of the umpire, he intentionally permits himself to be so hit.

Home Run/Double   See *Grounds/Fence*.

Interference/Offensive   The batter is out if he attempts to hinder the catcher from fielding or throwing the ball by stepping outside the lines of his position or otherwise obstructing or interfering with the catcher.

Player/Bench   Players' benches must be located at least 25 feet back of the players' lines.

1893

Bat   The bat must be made wholly of hard wood except that the handle may be wound with twine, or a granulated substance applied, not to exceed 18 inches from the end. It must be round, not to exceed 2½ inches in diameter in the thickest part, and must not exceed 42 inches in length.

Note: Bats with a flat side are now illegal.

Batting Order   The batsmen must take their positions within the batsmen's lines in the order in which they are named in the batting order, which batting order must be submitted by the captains of the opposing teams to the umpire before the game, and when approved by him this batting order must be followed except in the case of a substitute player, in which case the substitute must take the place of the original player in the batting order. After the first inning the first striker (batter) in each inning shall be the batsman whose name follows that of the last man who has completed his turn—time at bat—in the preceding inning.

Pitcher/Delivery The pitcher shall take his position facing the batter with both feet square on the ground, and in front of the pitcher's plate but in the act of delivering the ball one foot must be in contact with the pitcher's plate.

A balk is any motion in delivering the ball to the bat by the pitcher while not in the required position.

Pitcher/Position The pitcher's boundary shall be marked by a white rubber plate 12 inches long and 4 inches wide so fixed in the ground as to be even with the surface at the distance of 60 feet 6 inches from the outer corner of the home plate, so that a line drawn from the center of the home base and the center of the second base shall give 6 inches on either side.

1894

Foul Ball See *Strike Zone.*

Grounds Detailed directions are included in the rules of 1894 for laying out a baseball diamond.

Strike Zone A strike is called when the batter makes a foul hit, other than a foul tip, while attempting a bunt hit that falls or rolls upon foul ground between home base and first or third bases.

1895

Bat The bat cannot exceed 2¾ inches in diameter.

Batting Order The batsman is out if he fails to take his position at the bat in his order of batting, unless the error be discovered and the proper batsman takes his position before a time "at bat" recorded; and in such case the balls and strikes called must be counted in the time "at bat" of the proper batsman, and only the proper batsman shall be declared out. This rule shall not take effect unless the out is declared before the ball is delivered to the succeeding batsman, and no runs shall be scored or bases run, and further, no outs shall be counted other than that of the proper batsman.

Foul Tip A strike is called when a ball is tipped by the batter and caught by the catcher within the 10-foot lines.

Glove The catcher and first baseman are permitted to wear a glove or mitt of any size, shape or weight. All other players are restricted to the use of a glove or mitt weighing not over 10 ounces, and measuring in circumference around the palm of the hand not over 14 inches.

Infield Fly The batter is out if he hits a fly ball that can be handled by an infielder while first and second bases are occupied, or first, second, and third, with only one out. If the third strike is called (on attempted bunt in foul territory) the umpire shall declare infield or outfield hit.

Pitcher/Position The pitcher's plate is enlarged to 24 by 6 inches.

Strike Zone See *Foul Tip.*

Umpire Umpires may assess fines of $25 to $100 for specified misconduct by players.

1896

Ball The home club shall have at least a dozen regulation balls on the field ready for use on the call of the umpire during each game.

Game/Rain The choice of innings shall be given to the captain of the home club, who shall also be the sole judge of the fitness of the ground for beginning a game after rain, but after play has been called by the umpire he alone shall be the judge as to the fitness of the ground for resuming play after the game has been suspended on account of rain.

Pitcher/Delivery The pitcher is no longer required to hold the ball before the delivery fairly in front of his body and in the sight of the umpire.

Player/Bench No one is to occupy the players' bench under any circumstances except the club president, managers, and players in uniform.

Player/Illegal Act Players guilty of indecent or vulgar language or conduct shall be removed from the game and fined $25.

Umpire Umpires may assess fines of $5 to $10 for specified misconduct; repeat violators are to be fined $25.

1897

Ball/Defaced At no time shall the ball be intentionally discolored by rubbing it with the soil or otherwise. In the event of a new ball being intentionally discolored, or otherwise injured by a player, the umpire shall, upon appeal from the captain of the opposite side, forthwith demand the return of that ball and shall substitute another new ball and impose a fine of $5 upon the offending player.

Bunt A bunt hit is a ball delivered by the pitcher to the batsman who, while standing within the lines of his position, makes a deliberate attempt to hit the ball so slowly within the infield that it cannot be fielded in time to retire the batsman. If such a bunt hit goes to foul ground a strike shall be called by the umpire.

Defense/Illegal Act See *Ball/Defacing.*

Fair/Foul Ball A fair hit is a ball batted by the batsman—while he is standing within the lines of his position—that first touches "fair" ground, or the person of a player or the umpire while standing on fair ground, and then settles on fair ground before passing the line of first or third base.

A foul hit is a similarly batted ball that first touches "foul" ground or the person of a player or the umpire while standing on foul ground.

Should such "fair hit" ball bound or roll to foul ground before passing the line of first or third base and settle on foul ground, it shall be declared by the umpire a foul ball.

Should such "foul hit" ball bound or roll to fair ground and settle there before passing the line of first or third base, it shall be declared by the umpire a "fair ball."

Foul Tip A foul tip is a ball batted by the batsman while standing within the lines of his position that goes foul sharp from the bat to the catcher's hands.

Obstruction The baserunner shall be entitled, without being put out, to take a base in the following cases: (1) If he be prevented from making a base by the obstruction of an adversary, unless the latter be a fielder having the ball in his hand ready to meet the baserunner; (2) If the fielder stop or catch a batted ball with his hat or any part of his uniform except his gloved hand.

Runner/Bases The baserunner must touch each base in regular order, viz., first, second, third, and home bases, and when obliged to return (except on a foul hit) must retouch the base or bases in reverse order. He shall only be considered as holding a base after touching it, and shall then be entitled to hold such base until he has legally touched the next base in order or has been legally forced to vacate it for a succeeding baserunner. However, no baserunner shall score a run to count in the game until the baserunner preceding him in the batting list (provided there has been such a baserunner who has not been put out in that inning) shall have first touched home base without being put out.

Substitute In every championship game, each side shall be

required to have present on the field, in uniform, a sufficient number of substitute players to carry out the provision which requires that not less than nine players shall occupy the field in any inning of a game.

Umpire   The umpire shall not address the spectators at any time, except in case of necessary explanation of misunderstood decision or points of play.

Umpire/Decisions   No decision, rendered by the umpire, shall be reversed by him in which the question of an error of judgment is alone involved.

Should the umpire render any decision based on an illegal interpretation of any rule of the game, the same shall be reversed on the appeal of either of the two captains, but not otherwise.

1898

Batting Order   The batsman is out if he fails to take his position at the bat in his order of batting, unless the error be discovered and the proper batsman takes his position before a time "at bat" is recorded, and, in such case, the balls and strikes called must be counted in the time "at bat" of the proper batsman, and only the proper batsman shall be declared out, and no runs shall be scored or bases run because of any act of the improper batsman. Provided, this rule shall not take effect unless the out is declared before the ball is delivered to the succeeding batsman. Should the batsman declared out by this rule be sufficient to retire the side, the proper batsman the next inning is the player who would have come to bat had the players been out by ordinary play.

Pitcher/Delivery   A balk shall be: (1) Any motion made by the pitcher to deliver the ball to the bat without delivering it; (2) Any delivery of the ball to the bat while his pivot foot is not in contact with the pitcher's plate; (3) Any motion in delivering the ball to the bat by the pitcher while not in the position required by the rules; (4) The holding of the ball by the pitcher so long as, in the opinion of the umpire, to delay the game unnecessarily; (5) Standing in position and making any motion to pitch without having the ball in his possession, except in the case of a "block ball"; (6) The making of any motion the pitcher habitually makes in his method of delivery, without his immediately delivering the ball to the bat; (7) If the pitcher feigns to throw the ball to a base and does not resume his legal position and pause momentarily before delivering the ball to the bat. When the pitcher feigns to throw the ball to a base he must resume the required position and pause momentarily before delivering the ball to the bat.

Player/Illegal Act   Players in uniform shall not be permitted to occupy seats in the stands or to stand among the spectators.

Umpire   The rules of 1898 describe in detail the responsibilities of each umpire in games where two umpires are assigned.

1899

Catcher/Position   The catcher must stand within the lines of his position whenever the pitcher delivers the ball to the bat.

Foul Tip   A foul tip by the batter, caught by the catcher while standing within the lines of his position is a strike.

Game   If the umpire calls "Game" on account of darkness or rain at any time after five innings have been completed, the score shall be that of the last equal innings played, but if the side second at bat shall have scored in an unequal number of innings or before the completion of its unfinished inning one or more runs than the side first at bat, the score of the game shall be the total number of runs made.

Interference/Defensive   The batter becomes a baserunner if the catcher interferes with him, preventing him from striking the ball.

Pitcher/Delivery   In addition to the rules for "balk" promulgated in 1898, the rules of 1899 state: A balk shall be: (1) The throwing of the ball by the pitcher to any base to catch the baserunner without first stepping directly towards said base immediately before throwing the ball; (2) Any delivery of the ball to the bat by the pitcher while his pivot foot is not in contact with the pitcher's plate, and he is not facing the batsman; (3) If the pitcher delivers the ball to the bat when the catcher is standing outside the lines of the catcher's position as defined by the rules.

The batter becomes a baserunner when a balk is called by the umpire.

Player/Bench   The players' benches must be furnished by the home club and placed upon a portion of the ground not less than 25 feet outside of the players' lines. One such bench shall be for the exclusive use of the visiting club, and one for the exclusive use of the home club. The benches must be covered by a roof and closed at the back and each end; a space, however, not more than six inches wide may be left just under the roof for ventilation. All players of the side at bat must be seated on their bench, except such as are legally assigned to coach baserunners, and also the batsman, except when called to the bat by the umpire, and under no circumstances shall the umpire permit any person, except managers and players in uniform to occupy seats on the benches.

Strike Zone   See *Foul Tip*.

Substitute   In any championship game, each side shall be required to have present on the field, in uniform, conforming to the suits worn by their teammates, a sufficient number of substitute players to carry out the provision which requires that not less than nine players shall occupy the field in any innings of a game.

Uniforms   Every club shall adopt uniforms for its players, and the suit of each team shall conform in color and style. No player who shall attach anything to the sole or heel of his shoes other than the ordinary baseball shoe plate, or who shall appear in a uniform not conforming to the suits of the other members of his team, shall be permitted to take part in the game.

1900

Bases   The shape of home base is changed from a 12-inch square to a five-sided shape, 17 inches wide.

Pitcher/Delivery   The batter does not become a runner when the pitcher balks in throwing to pick off a runner on the bases.

Any motion made by the pitcher to deliver the ball to the bat or to first base without delivering it is a balk.

Note: This rule previously specified "any base."

1901

The American League begins operation and adopts the rule book with only a few modifications.

Catcher/Position   The catcher must stand within the lines of his position whenever the pitcher delivers the ball to the bat and within 10 feet of the home base.

Note: This rule was adopted by the National League in 1901. The American League adopted the rule in 1902.

Foul Ball   A foul hit ball not caught on the fly is a strike unless two strikes have already been called.

Note: This rule was used by the National League in 1901 and 1902. The American League adopted the rule in 1903. See 1902 summary for further elaboration of this rule by the National League.

A "bunt hit" which sends the ball to foul ground either directly or by bounding or rolling from fair ground to foul ground and which settles on foul ground is a strike.

Infield Fly   The batter is out if he hits a fly ball that can be handled by an infielder while first and second bases are occupied, or first, second, and third, unless two hands are out. In such case the umpire shall, as soon as the ball is hit, declare infield or outfield hit.

Pitcher/Delivery If the ball is thrown by the pitcher to any player other than the catcher (except to retire a baserunner) and the batsman is standing in his proper position ready to strike at a pitched ball, each ball so delivered shall be called a ball.

The umpire shall call a ball on the pitcher each time he delays the game by failing to deliver the ball to the batsman when in position for a longer period than 20 seconds.

Strike See *Foul Ball*.

1902

Foul Ball The batter is out if after two strikes have been called he obviously attempts to make a foul hit.

Hit by Pitch The batsman becomes a baserunner if while he be a batsman, without making any attempt to strike at the ball, his person or clothing be hit by a ball from the pitcher, unless in the opinion of the umpire he plainly avoids making any effort to get out of the way of the ball from the pitcher and thereby permits himself to be so hit.

Pitcher/Delivery The umpire shall call a ball on the pitcher each time he delays the game by failing to deliver the ball to the batsman when in position for a longer period than 20 seconds, excepting that in the case of the first batsman in each inning, the pitcher may occupy not more than one minute in delivering [warm-up pitches] not to exceed five balls to a baseman.

If the ball is thrown by the pitcher to any player other than the catcher (except to retire a baserunner) after the batter is standing in his position ready to strike at a pitched ball each ball so delivered will be called a ball.

Strike/Strikeout See *Foul Ball*.

1903

Pitcher/Position The pitcher's box shall be no more than 15 inches higher than the baselines and home plate. The baselines and home plate shall be on a perfect level, and the slope from the pitcher's box towards the baselines and home plate shall be gradual.

Note: In 1904, the phrase "pitcher's box" was deleted from this rule and replaced by the phrase "pitcher's plate."

Umpire The rules of 1903 contain an extensive reorganization and rewriting of the rules pertaining to umpires.

1904

Ball Two regulation balls of the make adopted by the league of which the contesting clubs are members shall be delivered by the home club to the umpire at or before the hour for the commencement of a championship game. If the ball first placed in play be batted or thrown out of the grounds or into one of the stands for spectators or, in the judgment of the umpire, become unfit for play from any cause, the umpire shall at once deliver the alternate ball to the pitcher and another legal ball shall be supplied to him, so that he shall at all times have in his control one or more alternate balls to substitute for the ball in play in any of the contingencies above set forth. Provided, however, that all balls batted or thrown out of the ground or into a stand, shall, when returned to the field, be given into the custody of the umpire immediately and become alternate balls, and so long as he has in his possession two or more alternate balls, he shall not call for a new ball to replace a ball that has gone out of play. The alternate balls shall become the ball in play in the order in which they were delivered to the umpire.

Bunt A bunt hit is a legally batted ball, not swung at, but met with the bat and tapped slowly within the infield by the batsman

with the expectation of reaching first base before the ball can be fielded to that base. If the attempt to bunt result in a foul, a strike shall be called by the umpire.

Coach/Illegal Act The baserunner is out if, before two hands are out and while third base is occupied, the coacher stationed near that base shall run in the direction of home base on or near the baseline while a fielder is making or trying to make a play on a batted ball not caught on the fly, or on a thrown ball, and thereby draws a throw to home base. The baserunner entitled to third base shall be declared out by the umpire for the coacher's interference with and prevention of the legitimate play.

Note: In 1914, the words "on a fly ball" were inserted in this rule.

Dead/Live Ball Immediately upon the delivery to him of the alternate ball by the umpire, the pitcher shall take his position and on the call of "Play," by the umpire, it shall become the ball in play. Provided, however, that play shall not be resumed with the alternate ball when a fair batted ball or a ball thrown by a fielder goes out of the ground or into a stand for spectators until the baserunners have completed the circuit of the bases unless compelled to stop at second or third base in compliance with a ground rule.

Grounds/Fences To obviate the necessity for ground rules, the shortest distance from a fence or stand on fair territory to home base should be 235 feet and from home base to the grandstand 90 feet.

Interference/Offensive The baserunner is out if one or more members of the team at bat stand or collect at or around a base for which a baserunner is trying, thereby confusing the fielding side and adding to the difficulty of making such play. The baserunner shall be declared out for the interference of his teammate or teammates.

The players of the side at bat must speedily abandon their bench and hasten to another part of the field when by remaining upon or near it they or any of them would interfere with a fielder in an attempt to catch or handle a thrown ball.

Player The players of each club, actively engaged in a game at one time, shall be nine in number, one of whom shall act as captain; and in no case shall more or less than nine men be allowed to play on a side in a game.

Note: The previous rule read, "in no case shall less than nine men be allowed to play."

Runner The baserunner is out if he touch home base before a baserunner preceding him in the batting order, if there be such preceding baserunner, lose his right to third base.

Uniform Every club shall adopt two uniforms for its players, one to be worn in games at home and the other in games abroad, and the suits of each of the uniforms of a team shall conform in color and style.

1905

There were no changes in the playing rules this year.

1906

Bunt A bunt hit is a legally batted ball, not swung at, but met with the bat and tapped slowly within the infield by the batsman. If the attempt to bunt result in a foul not legally caught, a strike shall be called by the umpire.

Game/Rain The choice of innings shall be given to the captain of the home club, who shall be the sole judge of the fitness of the ground for beginning a game after a rain; but, after play has been called by the umpire, he alone shall be the judge as to the fitness of the ground for resuming play after the game has been suspended on account of rain, and when time is so called the groundskeeper and sufficient assistants shall be under the control of the umpire for the purpose of putting the ground in proper shape for play, under penalty of forfeiture of the game by the home team.

Ground/Foul Lines Foul lines are to be clearly visible from any part of the diamond, and no wood or other hard substance shall be used in the construction of such lines.

1907

Ball/Defaced In the event of a ball being intentionally discolored by rubbing it with the soil or otherwise by any player except the pitcher, or otherwise damaged by any player, the umpire shall, upon appeal by the captain of the opposite side, forthwith demand the return of that ball and substitute for it another legal ball and impose a fine of $5 on the offending player.

Batter/Awarded Bases The baserunner shall be entitled to advance one base without liability to be put out if, while the batsman, he becomes a baserunner by reason of "four balls" or for being hit by a pitched ball, or for being interfered with by the catcher in striking at a pitched ball.

Batter/Position The batter is out if he steps from one batsman's box to the other after the pitcher has taken his position.

Batter/Runner The batter becomes a baserunner if a fair hit ball strike the person or clothing of the umpire or a baserunner on fair ground.

Defense/Illegal Act See *Ball/Defaced.*

Game/Legal If the umpire calls a game at any time after five innings have been completed, the score shall be that of the last equal innings played, except that if the side second at bat shall have scored in an unequal number of innings, or before the completion of the unfinished inning, at least one run more than the side first at bat, the score of the game shall be the total number of runs each team has made.

Game/Rain If the game be called by the umpire on account of darkness, rain, fire, panic, or for other cause which puts patrons or players in peril, the game shall terminate.

Interference/Offensive The baserunner is out if with one or no one out and a baserunner on third base, the batsman interferes with a play being made at home plate.

See also *Batter/Runner.*

Interference/Umpire See *Batter/Runner.*

Pitcher/Delivery A fairly delivered ball is a ball pitched or thrown to the bat by the pitcher while standing in his position and facing the batsman that passes over any portion of the home base, before touching the ground, not lower than the batsman's knee, nor higher than his shoulder. For every such fairly delivered ball, the umpire shall call one strike.

An unfairly delivered ball is a ball delivered to the bat by the pitcher while standing in his position and facing the batsman that does not pass over any portion of the home base between the batsman's shoulder and knees, or that touches the ground before passing home base, unless struck at by the batsman. For every unfairly delivered ball the umpire shall call one ball.

Runner/Illegal Act The baserunner is out if he passes a baserunner who is caught between two bases. He shall be declared out immediately upon passing the preceding baserunner.

1908

Ball/Defacing The rule prohibiting the discoloring of the ball by rubbing it with the soil was amended to include the pitcher as well as all players.

1909

Dead/Live Ball In case of a foul strike, foul hit ball not legally caught, dead ball, interference with the fielder or batsman, or a fair hit ball touching a baserunner, the ball shall not be consid-

ered in play until it be held by the pitcher standing in his position and the umpire shall have called "Play."

Fair/Foul Ball A fair hit is a legally batted ball that settles on fair ground between home and first base or between home and third base or that is on fair ground when bounding to the outfield past first or third base or that first falls on fair territory beyond first or third base or that, while on or over fair ground, touches the person of the umpire or a player.

A foul hit is a legally batted ball that settles on foul territory between home and first base or home and third base or that bounds past first or third base in foul territory or that falls on foul territory beyond first or third base or while on or over foul ground, touches the person of the umpire or a player.

Ground Rules Before the commencement of a game the umpire shall see that the rules governing all the materials of the game are strictly observed. He shall ask the captain of the home club whether there are any special ground rules, and if there be, he shall acquaint himself with them, advise the captain of the visiting team of their scope, and see that each is duly enforced, provided that it does not conflict with any of these rules, and are acceptable to the captain of the visiting team. If the latter object to a proposed ground rule, the umpire shall have authority to adopt or reject it.

Pitcher When the umpire announces the pitcher prior to commencement of the game, the player announced must pitch until the first batsman has either been put out or has reached first base.

Player/Ejected In the event of removal of player or manager by the umpire, he shall go direct to the club house and remain there during progress of the game, or leave the grounds; and a failure to do so will warrant a forfeiture of the game by the umpire.

Relief Pitcher In event of the pitcher being taken from the game by either manager or captain, the player substituted for him shall continue to pitch until the batsman then at bat has either been put out or has reached first base.

1910

Batter/Awarded Bases The baserunner shall be entitled, without liability to be put out, to advance a base if, while the batsman, he becomes a baserunner by reason of "four balls" or for being hit by a pitched ball, or if a fair hit ball strike the person or clothing of the umpire or a baserunner on fair ground.

Batter/Position The batter is out if he steps from one batsman's box to the other while the pitcher is in his position ready to pitch.

An illegally batted ball is a ball batted by the batsman when either or both of his feet are upon the ground outside the lines of the batsman's position.

Note: This rule replaced the term "foul strike."

Batting Order The batting order of each team must be on the scorecard and must be delivered before the game by its captain to the umpire at home plate, who shall submit it to the inspection of the captain of the other side. The batting order delivered to the umpire must be followed throughout the game unless a player be substituted for another, in which case the substitute must take the place in the batting order of the retired player.

Dead/Live Ball In case of an illegally batted ball, a balk, foul hit ball not legally caught, dead ball, interference with the fielder or batsman, or a fair hit ball striking a baserunner or umpire before touching a fielder, the ball shall not be considered in play until it be held by the pitcher standing in his position, and the umpire shall have called "Play."

Fielder/Illegal Act If the fielder stop or catch a batted ball with his cap, glove, or any part of his uniform, while detached from its proper place on his person, the runner or runners shall be entitled to three bases.

Ground Rules/Spectators In case of spectators overflowing on the playing field, the home captain shall make special ground rules to cover balls batted or thrown into the crowd, provided such rules be acceptable to the captain of the visiting club. If the latter object, then the umpire shall have full authority to make and enforce such special rules, and he shall announce the scope of same to the spectators.

Interference/Offensive The baserunner shall return to his base without liability to be put out if the umpire declares the batsman or another baserunner out for interference.

Interference/Umpire If a thrown or pitched ball strike the person or clothing of an umpire on foul ground the ball shall be considered in play and the runner or runners shall be entitled to all the bases they can make.

The baserunner shall return to his base without liability to be put out if the umpire be struck by a fair hit ball before touching a fielder; in which case no base shall be run unless necessitated by the batsman becoming a baserunner, and no run shall be scored unless all the bases are occupied.

Pitcher/Delivery An unfairly delivered ball is a ball delivered to the bat by the pitcher while standing in his position and facing the batsman that does not pass over any portion of the home base between the batsman's shoulder and knees, or that touches the ground before passing home base, unless struck at by the batsman; or, with the bases unoccupied, any ball delivered by the pitcher while either foot is not in contact with the pitcher's plate. For every unfairly delivered ball the umpire shall call one ball.

Player/Position The players of the team not at bat may be stationed at any points of the field on fair ground their captain may elect, regardless of their respective positions, except that the pitcher, while in the act of delivering the ball to the bat must take his position as defined in the rules and the catcher likewise must be within the lines of his position and within 10 feet of home base whenever the pitcher delivers the ball to the bat.

Relief Pitcher In event of the pitcher being taken from his position by either manager or captain, the player substituted for him shall continue to pitch until the batsman then at bat has either been put out or has reached first base.

Runner/Awarded Bases In all cases where there are no spectators on the playing field, and where a thrown ball goes into a stand for spectators, or over or through any fence surrounding the playing field, into the players' bench (whether the ball rebounds into the field or not), the runner or runners shall be entitled to two bases. The umpire in awarding such bases shall be governed by the position of the runner or runners at the time the throw is made.

Substitute Whenever one player is substituted for another, whether as batsman, baserunner, or fielder, the captain of the side making the change must immediately notify the umpire, who in turn must announce the same to the spectators. A fine of $5 shall be assessed by the umpire against the captain for each violation of this rule, and the president of the League shall impose a similar fine against the umpire who, after having been notified of a change, fails to make proper announcement. Play shall be suspended while announcement is being made, and the player substituted shall become actively engaged in the game immediately upon his captain's notice of the change to the umpire.

Umpire The rules of 1910 contain new provisions for umpires and describe the respective duties of the Umpire-in-Chief and the Field Umpire.

1911

Ball Cork-center balls are used for the first time as regulation balls in all games.

1912-13

There were no changes in the playing rules in these years.

1914

The Federal League begins operation and adopts virtually the entire rule book. The Victor Sporting Goods Company provides the new league's official ball. The Federal League folded after the 1915 season.

Ball League presidents are no longer required to examine, measure, and weigh baseballs for use in championship games.

Coach A coach may address words of assistance and direction to the baserunners and to the batter.

Coach/Illegal Acts If, while third base is occupied, the coacher stationed near that base shall run in the direction of home base on or near the base line while a fielder is making or trying to make a play on a batted ball not caught on the fly or on a thrown ball or a fly ball [see note below], and thereby draws a throw to home base, the baserunner entitled to third base shall be declared out by the umpire for the coacher's interference with and prevention of the legitimate play.

Note: This rule was first adopted in 1904 but did not include the phrase "or a fly ball."

If a coach at third base touch or hold a baserunner at third base or a baserunner who is rounding third base for home plate, such baserunner is out.

Fielder/Illegal Acts The baserunner is entitled to advance a base without liability to be put out if the fielder stop or catch a batted ball or a thrown ball with his cap, glove, or any part of his uniform, while detached from its proper place on his person, the runner or runners shall be entitled to three bases if a batted ball or to two bases if a thrown ball.

Home Run/Double See *Runner/Bases*.

Interference/Offensive The batter is out if he obstructs or interferes with the catcher except when he does so with a runner on third base (with one out or no one out) in which case the baserunner is out.

Interference/Umpire The baserunner shall return to his base without liability to be put out if the person or clothing of the umpire, while stationed back of the bat, interfere with the catcher in an attempt to throw.

The baserunner is entitled to advance a base if a thrown or pitched ball strike the person or clothing of an umpire. The ball shall be considered in play and the baserunner or runners shall be entitled to all the bases they can make.

Note: Under the previous rule only balls striking the umpire in foul territory entitled the baserunner to advance.

Pitcher/Delivery The pitcher is permitted to have his feet on top of the pitcher's plate or in front of the plate preliminary to pitching.

Runner/Awarded Bases In all cases where there are no spectators on the playing field, and where a thrown ball goes into a stand for spectators or over or through any fence surrounding the playing field or into the players' bench (whether the ball rebounds into the field or not) or remains in the meshes of a wire screen protecting the spectators, the runner or runners shall be entitled to two bases. The umpire in awarding such bases shall be governed by the position of the runner or runners at the time the throw is made.

Runner/Bases A batter who hits a home run or a ground-rule double must touch all of the bases in regular order.

1915–19
There were no changes in the playing rules in these years.

1920

Ball The President of the League of which the contesting clubs are members shall specify the number of baseballs which the home club must deliver to the umpire prior to the hour set for the commencement of a championship game, and all of such baseballs shall be of the regulation make adopted by the league.

The seal on boxes of new balls is not to be broken by the umpire except prior to game time and for the purpose of inspecting the ball and removing the gloss therefrom.

Ball Defacing In event of the ball being intentionally discolored by any player, either by rubbing it with the soil, or by applying rosin, paraffin, licorice, or any other foreign substance to it, or otherwise intentionally damaging or roughening the same with sandpaper or emery paper, or other substance, the umpire shall forthwith demand the return of that ball and substitute for it another legal ball, and the offending player shall be disbarred from further participation in the game. If, however, the umpire cannot detect the violator of this rule, and the ball is delivered to the bat by the pitcher, then the latter shall be at once removed from the game, and as an additional penalty shall be automatically suspended for a period of 10 days.

At no time during the progress of the game shall the pitcher be allowed to: (1) Apply a foreign substance of any kind to the ball; (2) Expectorate either on the ball or his glove; (3) Rub the ball on his glove, person, or clothing; (4) Deface the ball in any manner; (5) or to deliver what is called the "shine" ball, "spit" ball, "mud" ball, or "emery" ball. For violation of any part of this rule the umpire shall at once order the pitcher from the game, and in addition he shall be automatically suspended for a period of 10 days, on notice from the president of the League.

Note: In adopting the foregoing rule against "freak" deliveries on February 9, 1920, it was understood and agreed that all bona fide spitball pitchers would be certified to the respective presidents of the National and American leagues at least 10 days prior to April 14, 1920, and that the pitchers so certified would be exempt from the operation of the rule, as far as it related to the spitball only.

Batter/Awarded Bases The baserunner shall be entitled to advance one base if, while the batsman, he becomes a baserunner by reason of "four balls" or for being hit by a pitched ball or for being interfered with by the catcher in striking at a pitched ball or if a fair hit ball strike the person or clothing of the umpire or a baserunner on fair ground before touching a fielder. Provided, that if a fair hit ball strike the umpire after having passed a fielder or having been touched by a fielder, the ball shall be considered in play. Also, if a fair hit ball strike the umpire on foul ground, the ball shall be in play.

Catcher/Position It shall be illegal for the catcher to leave his natural position immediately and directly back of the plate for the purpose of aiding the pitcher to intentionally give a base on balls to a batsman. If the catcher shall move out of position prior to the time of the ball leaving the pitcher's hand, all runners on bases shall be entitled to advance one base.

Also see *Interference/Defensive*.

Coach See *Interference/Offensive*.

Dead Ball The baserunner shall return to his base without liability to be put out if the umpire declares a dead ball, unless it also be the fourth unfair ball, and he be thereby forced to take the next base as provided in the rules. Provided, such fourth unfair ball shall not be called if the umpire declare the ball "dead" because of a pitched ball accidentally hitting the bat.

Fair/Foul Ball A fair or foul fly must be judged according to the relative position of the ball and the foul line, and not as to whether the fielder is on fair or foul ground at the time he touches the ball.

Fielder See *Runner Tagged*.

Force Out A force out can be made only when a baserunner legally loses the right to the base he occupies by reason of the batsman becoming a baserunner, and he is thereby obliged to advance.

Game/Doubleheader Whenever necessity demands that two games be played in one afternoon, the first game shall be the regularly scheduled game for that day.

Game/Drawn A drawn game shall be declared by the umpire if the score is equal on the last even inning played when he terminates play in accordance with the rules after five or more equal innings have been played by each team. But if the side that went second to bat is at bat when the game is terminated, and has scored the same number of runs as the other side, the umpire shall declare the game drawn without regard to the score of the last equal inning. Provided, that if the side last at bat shall, before the completion of the fifth inning, equal the score made by the opposing side in five complete innings then the game shall be declared as legally drawn, and the individual and team averages shall be incorporated in the Official Playing Records.

Game/Legal "No Game" shall be declared by the umpire if he terminates play in accordance with the rules before five innings are completed by each team. Provided, however, that if the club second at bat shall have made more runs at the end of its fourth inning, or before the completion of its fifth inning, than the club first at bat made in five completed innings of a game so terminated, the umpire shall award the game to the club having made the greater number of runs, and it shall count as a legal game in the championship record.

Game/"Time" The rules of 1920 contain several new provisions governing the calling of "Time" by the umpire, the most important of which is the following: That in case of an accident to a player or players in attempting to make a play on either a batted or a thrown ball, "Time" shall not be called until, in the judgment of the umpire, no further play is possible.

Hit by Pitch A "dead" ball is a ball delivered to the bat by the pitcher, not struck at by the batsman, that touches any part of the batsman's person or clothing while he is standing in his position or a wildly pitched ball which the batsman plainly makes an attempt to dodge to avoid being hit, but which ball accidentally hits his bat.

Home Run/Game-Ending If a batsman, in the last half of the final inning of any game, hit a home run over the fence or into a stand, all runners on the bases at the time, as well as the batsman, shall be entitled to score, and in such event all bases must be touched in order, and the final score of the game shall be the total number of runs made.

Infield Fly If, before two hands are out, while first and second or first, second, and third bases are occupied, he hit a fair fly ball, other than a line drive, that can be handled by an infielder, the batter is out. In such case, the umpire shall, as soon as the ball be hit, declare it an infield or outfield hit; but the runners may be off their bases or advance at the risk of the ball being caught, the same as on any other fly ball. Provided, that, with first and second bases occupied, with less than two out, any attempt to bunt which results in a fair fly ball shall not be regarded as an infield fly.

Interference/Defensive In the event a baserunner is trying to score from third base on a pitched ball or the "squeeze" play, a "balk" and also an "interference" should be called if the catcher runs out in front of the plate to catch the ball; the runner shall be allowed to score and the batsman entitled to first base. The same penalties must be imposed in case the catcher pushes the batsman out of the way or tips his bat.

Interference/Offensive The baserunner is out if, in the judgment of the umpire, the coacher at third base by touching or holding the runner physically assists him in returning to or leaving third base. The runner, however, should not be declared out if no play is being made.

The baserunner shall be entitled to advance one base if a thrown ball strike a coacher on foul ground and the ball shall be considered in play. Provided, that if in the opinion of the umpire the coacher intentionally interfere with such thrown ball, the runner or runners must return to the last bases touched, and the coacher penalized by removal from the playing field.

The baserunner is *not* out if a fair hit ball goes through an infielder, and hits a runner immediately back of him. The umpire must be convinced that the ball passed through the infield and that no other infielder had the chance to make a play on the ball. If, in the judgment of the umpire, the runner deliberately and intentionally kicks such a hit ball, on which the infielder has missed a play, then the runner must be called out for interference.

Interference/Umpire See *Batter/Awarded Bases.*

Pitcher/Delivery The following prohibitions were added to the previous balk rule in 1920:

A balk shall be: Making any motion to pitch while standing in his position without having the ball in his possession; or, regardless of whether he makes any motion to pitch or not, if the pitcher takes a legal position on the rubber without the ball in his possession, or if he takes a position off the rubber and feints to deliver the ball to the bat.

A balk shall be: After the pitcher has taken position, with both hands holding the ball in front of him, he cannot take either hand off the ball except in the act of delivering the ball to the batsman or in throwing to bases.

A balk shall be: If, with one or more runners on bases, the pitcher, in the act of delivering the ball to the batsman or in throwing to first base, drop the ball, either intentionally or accidentally, the umpire shall call it a "balk" and advance runner or runners. No penalty shall be imposed if, with no one on bases, the pitcher drop the ball while delivering it to the batsman.

If the pitcher steps off the rubber, after being in position, for the purpose either of drying his hands or rubbing his eyes, or for other reasons, and it is a legitimate action not understood or interpreted by the umpire to deceive the baserunner, then the umpire shall call "Time."

In case a balk is called, the ball shall be considered "dead" when announcement is made, and no play can be made until the runner or runners reach the base or bases to which they are entitled.

If, with no one on base, the pitcher deliver the ball while off the rubber, the umpire shall call a "ball" whether it goes over the plate fair or not. If, however, the batsman strikes at such illegally delivered ball it counts either for a strike or whatever play may follow.

Pitcher/Illegal Act See *Ball/Defacing.*

Player/Position The players of the team not at bat may be stationed at any points of the field on fair ground their captain may elect, regardless of their respective positions, except that the pitcher, while in the act of delivering the ball to the bat must take his position and the catcher must be within the lines of his position, and within 10 feet of home base, whenever the pitcher delivers the ball to the bat; nor shall the catcher leave his natural position immediately and directly back of the plate for the purpose of aiding the pitcher to intentionally give a base on balls to a batsman.

Runner/Advancing A baserunner who holds his base on a fly ball shall have the right to advance the moment such fly ball touches the hands of a fielder.

Runner/Bases The failure of a preceding runner to touch a base (and who is declared out therefore) shall not affect the status of a succeeding runner who touches each base in proper order.

Runner/Illegal Act A baserunner having acquired legal title to a base cannot run bases in reverse order for the purpose either of confusing the fielders or making a travesty of the game. A runner violating this rule is out if touched with the ball, or the ball held on the base said runner was entitled to hold.

Runner/Returning In case a runner is being run down between bases, and the following runner occupies the same base the first runner has left, the second man cannot be put out while holding said base. If the first runner, however, returns safely to the base he left, and both runners are then occupying the same base, the second runner is the man out, if touched with the ball.

Runner/Tagged The baserunner is out if at any time while the ball is in play, he be touched by the ball in the hands of a fielder, unless some part of his person be touching the base he is entitled to occupy; provided, however, that the ball be held by the fielder after touching him, unless the baserunner deliberately knock it out of his hand. The ball must be firmly held by the fielder after touching the runner. The ball cannot be juggled, even though the fielder may retain possession of the ball and prevent same from dropping to the ground.

Substitute When a substitution is made but no announcement of the substitution is made as required by the rules the substitute will nevertheless be considered in the game as follows: if a pitcher, when he takes his place on the rubber; if a batter, when he takes his place in the batsman's box; if a fielder, when he takes the place of the fielder substituted for; if a runner, when the substitute replaces him on the base he is holding, and any play made by such unannounced substitute shall be legal under the rules.

Umpire The rules of 1920 contain various new provisions governing umpires and their respective duties.

1921

Pitcher Note: By concurrent action of the National and American leagues taken at their respective annual meetings held in New York in December 1920, it was agreed that all bona fide spitball pitchers then remaining in the National and American leagues be exempt from the operation of the rule against the use of the spitball during the balance of their major league careers. The pitchers so exempted were: National League—William Doak, Phil Douglas, Dana Fillingim, Ray Fisher, Marvin Goodwin, Burleigh Grimes, Clarence Mitchell, and Richard Rudolph (8). American League—A. W. Ayers, Ray Caldwell, Stanley Coveleskie, Urban Faber, H. B. Leonard, Jack Quinn, Allan Russell, Urban Shocker, and Allan Sothoron (9).

1922–25

There were no changes to the playing rules in these years.

1926

Batter/Awarded Bases A fair batted ball that goes over the fence or into a stand shall entitle the batsman to a home run, unless it should pass out of the ground or into a stand at a distance less than 250 feet from the home base, in which case the batsman shall be entitled to two bases only. In either event the batsman must touch the bases in regular order. The point at which a fence or stand is less than 250 feet from the home base shall be plainly indicated by a white or black sign or mark for the umpire's guidance.

Pitcher/Legal Act   Under the supervision and control of the umpire, the pitcher may use to dry his hands a small, finely meshed sealed bag containing powdered rosin, furnished by the League.

Note: This rule was first adopted by the National League only.

1927–30

There were no changes to the playing rules in these years.

1931

Batter   The rules of 1931 provide new wording for the rule governing when the batter is out without changing the substance of the rule.

Batter/Awarded Bases   A fair hit ball that bounds into a stand or over a fence shall be a two-base hit.

Note: There is no reference to distance in this rule and any fair hit ball bounding over the fence or into the stand is a two-base hit.

Coach   See *Interference/Offensive*.

Dead Ball   The rules of 1931 merge two previous rules governing dead balls in one differently worded rule without changing the substance of the old rules.

Fair/Foul Ball   When a batted ball passes outside the playing field the umpire shall decide it fair or foul according to where it leaves the playing field.

Game   The rules of 1931 merge four previous rules governing regulation games in one differently worded rule without changing the substance of the old rules.

Game/Legal   "No game" shall be declared by the umpire if he terminates play in accordance with the rules before five innings have been completed by each team; but if the team last at bat is at bat in the last half of the fifth inning and has equaled before the completion of that inning the score of the side first at bat, the umpire shall declare the game "legally drawn" in accordance with the rules. If the team second at bat shall have made more runs at the end of its fourth inning or before the completion of its fifth inning, than the team first at bat has made in five completed innings of a game so terminated, the umpire shall award the game to the team having made the greater number of runs, and it shall count as a legal game in the championship record.

Glove/Pitcher   The pitcher's glove must be uniform in color.

Interference/Offensive   The players or coaches of the side at bat must immediately vacate any space occupied by them if it is needed by a fielder attempting to handle a batted or thrown ball.

The baserunner is out if, in running the last half of the distance from home base to first base, while the ball is being fielded to first base, he run outside the three-foot lines, and, in the opinion of the umpire, interferes with the fielder taking the throw at first base; except that he may run outside the three-foot lines to avoid a fielder attempting to field a batted ball.

Obstruction   The baserunner shall advance one base if he be prevented from making a base by the obstruction of a fielder, except when a fielder is trying to field a batted ball unless the latter has the ball in his hand ready to touch the baserunner. The ball is still in play so far as other baserunners are concerned.

Pitcher/Delivery   Preliminary to pitching, the pitcher shall take his position facing the batsman, with both feet squarely on the ground and on top of the pitcher's plate, or one foot on top of the pitcher's plate and the other foot in contact with same, or one foot in front of the pitcher's plate and the other foot on top of same, and in the act of delivering the ball to the batsman he must keep one foot in contact with the pitcher's plate. He shall not raise either foot until in the act of delivering the ball to the batsman, or in throwing to a base; nor may he make more than one step in such delivery. With a runner on first base or on second base, the pitcher must face the batsman with both hands holding the ball in front of him. If he indulges in a preliminary stretch by raising his arms above his head or out in front, he must return to a natural pitcher's position and stop before starting his delivery of the ball to the batsman.

Runner/Awarded Bases   In all cases where there are no spectators on the playing field and where a thrown ball goes into a stand for spectators or over or through any fence surrounding the playing field or into the players' bench (whether the ball rebounds into the field or not) or remains in the meshes of a wire screen protecting the spectators, the runner or runners shall be entitled to two bases. When the throw is made by an infielder, the umpire, in awarding such bases, shall be governed by the position of the runner or runners at the time the ball was pitched; when the throw is made by an outfielder, the award shall be governed by the position of the runner or runners at the time the throw was made.

The baserunner shall advance one base without liability to be put out if a ball delivered by the pitcher pass the catcher and touch any fence or building within 60 feet of the home base. The ball shall be dead in such case.

Runner/Bases   The baserunner is out if, when advancing bases or obliged to return to a base while the ball is in play, he fail to touch the intervening base or bases, if any, in the regular or reverse order, as the case may be, he may be put out by the ball being held by a fielder on any base he failed to touch or by being touched by the ball in the hand of a fielder in the same manner as in running to first base; provided, that the baserunner shall not be out in such case if the ball be delivered to the bat by the pitcher before the fielder hold it on said base or touch the baserunner with it; however, after a fly ball other than a foul tip be legally caught by a fielder, the baserunner who complies with this rule can only be retired by the ball being held by a fielder on the base occupied by the runner when such ball was batted or by being touched by the ball in the hand of the fielder.

The failure of a preceding runner to touch a base (and who is declared out therefore) shall not affect the status of a succeeding runner who touches each base in proper order; except that, after two are out, a succeeding runner cannot score a run when a preceding runner is declared out for failing to touch a base as provided in the rules. This exception also applies to a batsman who hits the ball out of the playing field for an apparent home run.

Substitute   Substitutions shall not be in effect until the manager or captain of the team making the change notifies the umpire.

Substitute/Runner   The manager or the captain of the opposing team must consent before a runner can be substituted for another baserunner.

Note: Previously this rule referred only to the captain. Throughout the rules of 1931, wherever authority or decision-making authority is granted to the captain, the words "or manager" have been added.

Uniform   Glass buttons or polished metal must not be used on a uniform.

1932–38

There were no changes to the playing rules in these years.

1939

Batter/Caught Fly   The baserunner is out if, having made a fair hit while batsman, such fair hit ball be caught by a fielder before touching the ground or any object other than a fielder; provided, it be not caught in a fielder's hat, cap, protector, pocket, or other part of his uniform.

Fielder/Drops Fly Ball   If, before two are out, while first and second or first, second, and third bases are occupied, an outfielder, in the judgment of the umpire, intentionally drops a fly ball or a line drive, he shall immediately rule the ball has been caught.

Note: Baserunners are obliged to "tag up" after the out has been declared before they can advance.

Gloves   The catcher may wear a leather glove or mitt of any size, shape or weight.

The first baseman may wear a leather glove or mitt not more than 12 inches from top to bottom and not more than 8 inches wide across the palm, with thumb and palm connected by leather lacing of not more than 4 inches from thumb to palm, which lacing shall not be enlarged, extended or reinforced by any process or material whatever.

Every other player is restricted to the use of a leather glove weighing not over 10 ounces and measuring not over 14 inches around the palm. The pitcher's glove must be uniform in color.

Pitcher/Delivery   Preliminary to pitching, the pitcher shall take his position facing the batsman with both feet squarely on the ground, but his pivot foot must be on or in front in contact with the pitcher's plate; his other foot may be directly behind or in front (not on the side) of the pitcher's plate, and in the act of delivering the ball to the batsman he must keep one foot in contact with the pitcher's plate. He shall not raise either foot until in the act of delivering the ball to the batsman or in throwing to a base; nor may he make more than one step in such delivery. With a runner on first base or second base, the pitcher must face the batsman with both hands holding the ball in front of him. If he indulges in a preliminary stretch by raising his arms above his head or out in front, he must return to a natural pitcher's position and stop before starting his delivery of the ball to the batsman.

Note: After the pitcher takes legal position for delivery of the ball to the batsman, he can take but one step and that must be forward.

A balk will be called (entitling the runner or runners to advance one base) if the pitcher makes any delivery of the ball to the bat while his pivot foot is back of and not in contact with the pitcher's plate.

1940

Bat   The bat must be made entirely of hardwood in one piece.

Coach   No fines are to be assessed for violations of the coaching rules.

Dead Ball   A batted or thrown ball touched, stopped, or handled by a person not engaged in the game is dead and not in play. If a fair hit, the batsman making the hit shall be entitled to two bases and each baserunner shall be entitled to advance two bases. If a thrown ball, each baserunner shall be entitled to advance in accordance with the rules governing a thrown ball.

Note: This rule replaces the rule regarding "blocked balls."

Fielder   See *Runner/Tagged.*

Fielder/Drops Fly Ball   See *Runner/Advancing.*

Foul Ball   A foul hit is a legally batted ball that settles on foul territory between home and first base or home and third base or that bounds past first or third base on or over foul territory or that falls on foul territory beyond first or third base or, while on or over foul ground, touches the person of the umpire or a player or any object foreign to the natural ground. A foul fly must be judged according to the relative position of the ball and the foul line, and not as to whether the fielder is on foul or fair ground at the time he touches the ball.

Game/Doubleheader   No club or clubs shall engage in more than two championship games within a period of one day.

Game/Start   No inning of any night game shall be started after 11:50 P.M. standard time.

Grounds   The ball ground must be enclosed. To obviate the necessity for ground rules, the shortest distance from a fence or stand on fair territory to the home base should be 250 feet and from home base to the grandstand 60 feet.

Grounds/Foul Lines   The foul lines are to be continued until they reach the boundary lines of the ground and not less than 10 feet above the top of the fence or stand. The foul lines are to be made, on the playing field, of lime, chalk, or other powder or paint.

Infield Fly   The batter is out if, before two are out, while first and second or first, second, and third bases are occupied, he hit a fair fly ball, other than a line drive, that can reasonably be caught by an infielder. In such case, the umpire shall declare it an infield fly. However, the runners may be off their bases or advance at the risk of the ball being caught, the same as on any other fly ball; but if hit by the ball while standing on base, that baserunner shall not be called out, but the ball is dead and the batsman shall be called out and if the baserunner be hit while off base, both that baserunner and the batsman shall be called out and the ball is dead. Provided, that, with first and second bases occupied or first, second, and third bases occupied, with less than two out, any attempt to bunt which results in a fair fly ball shall not be regarded as an infield fly.

Interference/Defensive   The batter becomes a baserunner if the catcher interferes with him, unless he makes a safe hit.

The baserunner is entitled to advance one base if the catcher interferes with the batsman while a baserunner is attempting to steal a base.

Interference/Offensive   If one or more members of the team at bat stand or collect at or around a base for which a baserunner is trying, thereby confusing the team in the field and adding to the difficulty of making such play or if a batsman or baserunner who has just been retired obstructs or interferes with any following play being made on a baserunner, the baserunner shall be declared out for the interference of his teammate or teammates.

The baserunner is out if, after having hit or bunted a ball to fair territory, his bat again hits the ball on or over fair territory and deflects its course. Other baserunners cannot advance.

Pitcher/Delivery   Preliminary to pitching, the pitcher shall take his position facing the batsman with his pivot foot always on or in front of and in contact with the pitcher's plate. In the act of delivering the ball to the batsman, the pitcher's other foot is free, except that he cannot step to either side of the pitcher's plate. He shall not raise either foot until in the act of delivering the ball to the batsman or in throwing to a base. With a runner on first or second base, the pitcher must face the batsman with both hands holding the ball in front of him. If he raises his arms above his head or out in front he must return to a natural pitcher's position and stop before starting the delivery of the ball to the batsman.

Note: After pitcher takes legal position for delivery of ball to batsman, he may take one step backward and one step forward, but not to either side.

It is a balk if the pitcher, in the act of delivering the ball to the batsman or in throwing to first base, drop the ball, either intentionally or accidentally.

Note: With no one on base, it is not a balk if the pitcher drops the ball while delivering it to the batsman.

A balk (entitling the runner or runners to advance one base) shall be called for: (1) Throwing the ball by the pitcher to any base to catch the baserunner without first stepping directly toward such base in the act of making such throw; or throwing or feinting to throw to an unoccupied base; (2) Making any motion of the arm, shoulder, hip, knee, foot, or body the pitcher habitually makes in his method of delivery, without immediately delivering the ball to the bat.

Runner/Advancing   A baserunner who holds his base on a fly ball shall have the right to advance the moment such fly ball touches the person or uniform of a fielder.

The baserunner may "tag up" and advance if, before two are out, while first, or first and second, or first, second, and third bases are occupied, any player, in the judgment of the umpire, intentionally drops a fly ball or a line drive, the umpire shall immediately rule the ball has been caught.

Runner/Awarded Bases   In all cases where there are no spectators on the playing field, and where a thrown ball goes into a stand for spectators, or over or through any fence surrounding the playing field, or into the players' bench (whether the ball rebounds into the field or not), or remains in the meshes of a wire screen protecting the spectators, the runner or runners shall be entitled to two bases. When a first throw made by an infielder, the umpire, in awarding such bases, shall be governed by the position of the runner or runners at the time the ball was pitched; when the throw is made by an outfielder or is the result of any following plays or attempted plays, the award shall be governed by the position of the runner or runners at the time the last throw was made.

Runner/Overrunning First   The baserunner is permitted to "overslide" as well as overrun first base without liability to be put out.

Runner/Tagged   The baserunner is out if at any time while the ball is in play, he be touched by the ball in the hand of a fielder, unless some part of his person be touching the base he is entitled to occupy; provided, however, that the ball be held by the fielder after touching him, unless the baserunner deliberately knock it out of his hand. The ball must be firmly held by the fielder after touching the runner. The ball cannot be juggled, even though the fielder may regain possession of the ball and prevent same from dropping to the ground.

Note: The previous rule read: "even though the fielder may *retain* possession of the ball."

Trainer   Trainers are permitted to occupy the players' bench.

Trainer/Umpire   Umpires are given authority over trainers.

Umpire   The rules of 1940 describe the procedures to be used when more than two umpires are assigned.

The Umpire-in-Chief is to make all decisions regarding batters.

1941

There were no changes to the playing rules this year.

1942

Game/Start   No inning of any night game shall be started after 12:50 A.M. war time.

1943–48

There were no changes to the playing rules in these years.

1949

Catcher/Position   The catcher must stand with both feet inside the catcher's lines until the ball leaves the pitcher's hand.

Coach   First base coaches as well as third base coaches must refrain from touching or holding the runner physically or the runner is out.

Foul/Fair Ball   A foul fly must be judged according to the relative position of the ball and the foul line, including the foul pole, and not as to whether the fielder is on foul or fair ground at the time he touches the ball.

Game/Start   No inning of any night game shall be started after 12:50 A.M. local city time.

Pitcher/Delivery   No balk can be committed with all bases empty.

Player/Illegal Act   No manager, captain, coach, or player shall address the spectators before or during a game except in reply to a request for information about the progress or state of the game or to give the name of a player.

1950

Bases   The home plate and the pitcher's plate shall be of whitened rubber, anchored in the ground, even with its surface. The home plate, with beveled edges, shall be level with the baselines. The pitcher's plate shall be on an 18-foot-diameter mound, exactly 15 inches above the level of home plate. The plate shall be placed six inches from the front of a two-foot by five-foot leveled area atop the mound. The slope from the pitcher's plate to the baselines shall be gradual.

First, second, and third bases shall be approved bags of white canvas, securely anchored in the ground. They shall be 15 inches square and not less than three, nor more than five inches thick and shall be filled with soft material.

Bat   The bat shall be round, not over 2¾ inches in diameter at the thickest part, not more than 42 inches in length, and entirely of hard, solid wood in one piece. Twine may be wound around it or a granulated substance applied to it, for a distance of 18 inches from the end of the handle, but not elsewhere.

Batter/Awarded Bases   Each runner including the batter-runner may, without liability of being put out, advance to home base, scoring a run, if a fair ball goes over the field fence in flight and he touch all bases legally; or if a fair ball which, in the umpire's judgment, would have cleared the field fence in flight, is deflected by the act of a defensive player in throwing his glove, cap, or any article of his apparel, the runner shall be awarded a home run.

The rules of 1950 include various new provisions for baserunners when balls are hit or thrown into the stands.

The batter becomes a baserunner when a fair ball, after touching the ground, bounds into the stands or passes through or under a fence or through or under a scoreboard or through or under shrubbery or vines on the fence, in which case the batter and the baserunners shall be entitled to advance two bases.

The batter becomes a baserunner when any fair ball which, either before or after striking the ground, passes through or under a fence or through or under a scoreboard or through any opening in the fence or scoreboard or through or under shrubbery or vines on the fence, in which case the batter and the baserunners shall be entitled to two bases.

The batter becomes a baserunner when any bounding fair ball is deflected by the fielder into the stands or over or under a fence on fair or foul ground, in which case the batter and all baserunners shall be entitled to advance two bases.

The batter becomes a baserunner when any fair fly ball is deflected by the fielder into the stands or over the fence into foul territory, in which case the batter shall be entitled to advance to second base; but if deflected into the stands or over the fence in fair territory, the batter shall be entitled to a home run.

Batter/Illegal Act   The batter is out for illegal action when he fails to take his position in the batter's box promptly. If he persists in unwarranted delay in taking his position the umpire shall direct the pitcher to deliver the ball to the bat and every such pitch shall be called "strike" by the umpire. If he enters the batter's box in the interval between any such pitches, the ball and strike count shall continue regularly, but if he has not entered the batter's box when three strikes are called he shall be declared "out."

Catch   A catch is the act of a defensive player in receiving, and holding firmly in his hand or glove, a batted or thrown ball. It is not a catch, however, if simultaneously or immediately following his contact with the ball, he collide with a player or with a wall or if he fall down, and as a result of such collision or falling, drops the ball. If the player has made the catch and drops the ball while in the act of making a throw following the catch, the ball shall be adjudged to have been caught. In establishing the validity of the catch, the player shall hold the ball long enough to prove that he has complete control of the ball and that his release of the ball is voluntary and intentional.

Dead/Live Ball   See *Game/"Time."*

Definitions   Rule Two of the rules of 1950 includes the definitions of 69 baseball terms as used in the rules. Several of the key definitions are quoted throughout this year's rule entries.

Fair Territory   Fair territory is that part of the playing field within, and including the first and third baselines, from home base to the bottom of the playing field fence and perpendicularly upwards. All foul lines are in fair territory.

Foul Tip   A foul tip is a ball batted by the batter that goes sharp and direct from the bat to the catcher's hands and is legally caught. It is not a foul tip unless caught and any foul tip that is caught is a strike, and the ball is in play. It is not a catch if it is a rebound from any part of the catcher's equipment other than the catcher's glove or hand.

Game   Baseball is a game between two teams of nine players, each with adequate substitutes, coaches, and trainers, under direction of a manager, played in accordance with these rules, under jurisdiction of an umpire or umpires on an enclosed field.

The object of each team is to win by scoring the more runs.

A game consists of nine innings, except as otherwise provided, and an inning is that portion of the game during which each team shall play both offensively and defensively.

The winner of the game shall be that team which shall have scored, in accordance with these rules, the greater number of runs at the conclusion of a regulation game.

Game/Doubleheader   The rules of 1950 include a series of new provisions governing the conduct of doubleheaders.

Game/Rain   The manager of the home team shall be the sole judge of the fitness of the playing field for the beginning of any game other than the second game of a doubleheader. Exception: Any league may permanently authorize its president to suspend the application of this rule as to that league during the closing weeks of its championship season in order to ensure that the championship is decided each year on its merits. When the postponement of, and possible failure to play, a game in the final series of a championship season between any two teams might affect the final standing of any club in the league, the president, on appeal from any league member, may assume the authority granted the home team manager by this rule.

Game/Start   The players of the home team shall take their defensive positions, the first batter of the visiting team shall take his position in the batter's box, the umpire shall call "Play," and the game shall proceed.

The rules of 1950 include a series of new provisions governing the preliminaries before championship games.

Game/"Time"   The ball is dead when the umpire-in-chief suspends play by calling "Time" when a manager requests "Time" for a substitution or for conference with his player.

The ball is dead when the umpire-in-chief suspends play by calling "Time" when a fielder, after catching a fly ball, falls into a bench, dugout, or stand or falls across ropes into a crowd (when spectators are on the field), and baserunners may advance one base without liability to be put out.

Note: If player after making the catch steps into the dugout

but does not fall, the ball is alive and in play and runners may advance at their own peril.

After the umpire calls "Play" the ball is alive and in play and remains alive and in play until for legal cause, or at the umpire's call of "Time" suspending play, the ball becomes dead. While the ball is dead no player may be put out, no bases may be run, and no runs may be scored, except that runners may advance as legally provided.

Glove/Fielder   Each player, other than the first baseman and the catcher, is restricted to the use of a leather glove not more than twelve inches long nor more than eight inches wide, measured from the base of the thumb crotch to the outside edge of the glove. The space between the thumb and the forefinger shall not exceed 4½ inches at the top nor more than 3½ inches at the base of the thumb crotch. The webbing may be standard leather or lacing and shall not be enlarged, extended, or reinforced by any process or materials whatever. The webbing cannot be constructed of wound or wrapped lacing to make a net type of trap. The glove may be of any weight.

Glove/First Baseman   The first baseman may wear a leather glove or mitt not more than 12 inches long from top to bottom and not more than eight inches wide across the palm, measured from base of thumb crotch to outer edge of the mitt. The space between the thumb section and the finger section of the mitt shall not exceed four inches at the top of the mitt and 3½ inches at the base of the thumb crotch. The mitt shall be constructed so that this space is permanently fixed and cannot be enlarged, extended, widened, or deepened by the use of any materials or process whatever. The web of the mitt shall measure not more than five inches from its top to the base of the thumb crotch. The web may be either a lacing, lacing through leather tunnels, or a center piece of leather which may be an extension of the palm connected to the mitt with lacing and constructed so that it will not exceed the above-mentioned measurements. The webbing cannot be constructed of wound or wrapped lacing or deepened to make a net type of trap.

Glove/Pitcher   The pitcher's glove shall be uniform in color and cannot be white or gray.

Home Run   See *Batter/Awarded Bases.*

Infield Fly   An infield fly is an out called by the umpire on the batter—if, before two are out, while first and second or first, second, and third bases are occupied, he hit a fair fly ball, other than a line drive, that in the judgment of the umpire can reasonably be caught by an infielder. Where a defensive player who normally plays in the outfield places himself in the infield, he shall for the purpose of the infield fly rule be considered an infielder. In such case, the umpire shall declare it an infield fly. However, the runners may be off their bases or advance at the risk of the ball being caught, the same as on any other fly ball. If a runner is hit by the ball while standing on base, he shall not be called out, but the ball is dead and the batter shall be called out; but if a baserunner is hit while off base, both he and the batter shall be called out and the ball is dead. Provided, that, with first and second bases occupied, or first, second, and third bases occupied, before two are out, any attempt to bunt which results in a fair fly ball shall not be regarded as an infield fly.

Interference/Offensive   The rules of 1950 include several new provisions describing the circumstances under which a baserunner is out for interference.

The batter is out when a preceding runner shall, in the umpire's judgment, intentionally interfere with the play of a defensive player who is attempting to catch a thrown ball or to throw the ball in an attempt to complete any play.

The batter is out when with two out, a runner on third base, and two strikes on the batter, the runner attempts to steal home base on a legal pitch and the ball strikes the runner in the strike zone. The umpire shall call "strike three," the batter is out and the run shall not count; with less than two out the umpire shall call "strike three," the ball is dead, and the run counts.

The batter is out when after striking or bunting the ball he intentionally strikes the ball a second time, or strikes it with a thrown bat or deflects its course in any manner while running to first base. The ball is dead and no runners may advance. If the runner drops his bat and the ball rolls against the bat and, in the umpire's judgment, there was no intention to interfere with the course of the ball, the ball is alive and in play.

Obstruction   A batter who has become a runner is entitled to unimpeded progress as he advances around the bases. Whenever a defensive player impedes the runner in any way, unless he is attempting to field a batted ball or has the ball in his possession, the umpire shall call "obstruction," the ball shall remain in play, and all runners shall be permitted to advance, without liability to be put out, to the bases which, in the judgment of the umpire, the runners would have reached had obstruction not been called.

In a "run-down" play, if the runner's progress is impeded by any defensive player who does not have the ball in his possession, the umpire shall call "obstruction" and the runner shall be entitled to occupy the base he is attempting to reach when the obstruction occurred.

Pitcher/Delivery   There are two legal pitching positions: The "Wind-up" position and the "Set" position. Either position may be used at any time.

Pivot Foot   The pitcher's pivot foot is that foot which is in contact with the pitcher's plate as he delivers the pitch.

Set Position   Set position is the pitcher's position when he stands facing the batter with his entire pivot foot on or in front of and in contact with, and not off the end of the pitcher's plate, and his other foot in front of the pitcher's plate, holding the ball in both hands in front of his body and coming to a complete stop of at least one second.

Wind-up Position   Wind-up position is the pitcher's position when he stands facing the batter, his pivot foot on or in front of and touching the pitcher's plate, and the other foot free.

From the set position, the pitcher may deliver the ball to the batter, throw to a base, or step backward off the pitcher's plate with his pivot foot. Before assuming set position the pitcher may elect to make any natural preliminary motion such as that known as "the stretch." But if he so elects, he must come to set position before delivering the ball to the batter. After assuming set position, any natural motion associated with his delivery of the ball to the batter commits him to the pitch without alteration or interruption.

If there is a runner or runners it is a balk if the pitcher delivers the pitch from "set position" without coming to a stop of one full second.

Pitcher/Illegal Act   The pitcher shall not be allowed to pitch at a batter's head, and if, in the umpire's opinion, such violation occurs, he shall call "Time" and warn the pitcher and the manager of the defensive team that another such pitch will mean the immediate expulsion of the pitcher from the game. If such pitch is repeated, the umpire shall inflict the penalty as follows: The pitcher shall be removed from the game and from the grounds. The president of the League shall impose such fine and suspension as his judgment warrants.

See also *Pitcher/Uniform*.

Pitcher/Illegal Pitches   If the pitcher makes an illegal pitch with the bases unoccupied it shall be called a ball, unless the batter shall make a fair hit or reaches first base on an error or otherwise.

The pitcher shall not be allowed to pitch the "quick return ball." Whenever such pitch is attempted the umpire shall call "Time." If the offense is repeated the umpire shall call each such repeated offense a "ball," unless the batter reaches first base on a fair hit, an error, or otherwise, and no other runner is forced by his reaching first base, in which case the play proceeds.

Pitcher-Infielder   If the pitcher removes his pivot foot from contact with the pitcher's plate by stepping backward with that foot, he thereby becomes an infielder and, if his subsequent throw to a base, when off the pitcher's plate, goes into a stand or over, through, or under a fence or into a bench or dugout (whether the ball rebounds or not) or remains in the meshes of a wire screen protecting the spectators, the ball is dead and all runners shall be entitled to advance two bases.

Pitcher/Pick-Off   At any time during the pitcher's preliminary movements and until his natural pitching motion commits him to the pitch, he may throw to any base provided he step directly toward such base before making the throw.

Pitcher/Position   See *Bases* for pitcher's plate.

Pitcher/Uniform   The pitcher shall not be allowed to wear a garment with ragged, frayed or slit sleeves, and shall not be permitted to attach tape or other material of a color different from his uniform or glove to his glove or clothing.

Pitcher/Warm-Ups   When a pitcher takes his position at the beginning of each inning or when he relieves another pitcher, he shall be permitted to pitch not to exceed eight preparatory pitches to his catcher during which play shall be suspended. Such preparatory pitches shall not consume more than one minute of time.

Player/Illegal Acts   Players in uniform shall not address nor mingle with spectators, nor sit in the stands before or during a game. No manager, captain, coacher, or player shall address any spectator before or during a game. Players of opposing teams shall not fraternize at any time while in uniform. Penalty: The president of the league shall impose fines for violation of this rule at his discretion.

No manager, player, substitute, coacher, trainer, or batboy shall at any time, whether from the bench, the coacher's box, or on the playing field, or elsewhere call "Time," or employ any other word or phrase while the ball is alive and in play for the obvious purpose of confusing an umpire or an opposing player.

Except the batter, or a runner attempting to score, no offensive player shall cross the catcher's lines when the ball is in play.

Runner/Out   The baserunner is out if, after he has acquired legal possession of a base, he or that base is tagged while he is running the bases in reverse order for the purpose of confusing the defense or making a travesty of the game. No runner may advance in this situation in the event of an error on this play by the defensive team.

The baserunner is out if, in running or sliding for home base, he fails to touch home base and makes no attempt to return to the base, when a defensive player holds the ball in his hand while touching home base and appeals to the umpire for the decision.

Strike Zone   The strike zone is that space over home plate which is between the batter's armpits and the top of his knees when he assumes his natural stance.

Substitute   A player or players may be substituted during a game at any time the ball is dead. A substituted player shall bat in the replaced player's position in the team's batting order. A player once removed from a game shall not re-enter that game. If a substitute enters the game in place of a manager, the manager may thereafter go to the coaching lines at his discretion. When two or more substitute players of the defensive team enter the game at the same time, the manager, or his designated representative, shall, immediately before they take their position as defensive players, designate to the umpire-in-chief such players' positions in the team's batting order and the umpire-in-chief shall so notify the official scorer. If this information is not immediately given to the umpire-in-chief, he shall have authority to designate the substitutes' places in the batting order.

Substitute/Runner   A player whose name is on his team's batting order may not become a substitute runner for another member of his team.

Umpire Each umpire is the representative of the president of the league, the president of the National Association and the Commissioner of Baseball.

The umpire-in-chief shall enforce the rules from the moment he receives the batting order from the manager of the home team until termination of the game. This shall include control of ground crews, newsmen, and photographers, and any other persons whose duties require their presence upon the field.

1951–53

There were no changes to the playing rules in these years.

1954

Bat The bat shall be a smooth, rounded stick not more than 2¾ inches in diameter at the thickest part and not more than 42 inches in length. The bat shall be one piece of solid wood or formed from a block of wood consisting of two or more pieces of wood bonded together with an adhesive in such a way that the grain direction of all pieces is essentially parallel to the length of the bat. Any such laminated bat shall contain only wood or adhesive, except for a clear finish.

For a distance of 18 inches from the end by which the bat is gripped, it may be roughened or wrapped with tape or twine.

Note: Approval of the laminated bat is experimental for the 1954 season, and no laminated bat shall be used in a professional game until the manufacturer has secured approval from the Rules Committee of his design and method of manufacture. In giving or withholding such approval, the Rules Committee will be guided by comparison of the laminated bat with one-piece solid wood bats. Laminated bats which are inferior to one-piece solid wood bats in safety or durability will not be approved. A design or method of manufacture which produces a "loaded" or "freak" type of bat or which produces a substantially greater reaction or distance factor than one-piece solid wood bats will not be approved.

Batter/Illegal Act See *Interference/Offensive*.

Catch A catch is the act of a fielder in getting secure possession in his hand or glove of a ball in flight and firmly holding it; providing he does not use his cap, protector, pocket, or any other part of his uniform in getting possession.

Dead/Live Ball See *Game/"Time."*

Definitions Rules Two and Three of the rules of 1954 contain several new definitions of baseball terms as used in the rules.

Fielder/Drops Fly Ball The batter is out when, with less than two out and first, first and second, first and third, or first, second, and third bases occupied, a fielder intentionally drops a fair fly ball or line drive. Runners need not re-touch and may advance at their own peril.

Fielder/Illegal Act No fielder shall take a position in the batter's line of vision, and with deliberate unsportsmanlike intent, act in a manner to distract the batter.

Game The rules of 1954 contain a series of new provisions governing suspended games.

Game/"Time" After the umpire calls "Play" the ball is alive and in play and remains alive and in play until for legal cause, or at the umpire's call of "Time" suspending play, the ball becomes dead. While the ball is dead no player may be put out, no bases may be run, and no runs may be scored, except that runners may advance one or more bases as the result of acts which occurred while the ball was alive (such as, but not limited to, a balk, an overthrow, interference, or a home run or other fair hit out of the playing field).

Gloves/Equipment Members of the offensive team shall carry all gloves and other equipment off the field and to the dugout while their team is at bat. No equipment shall be left lying on the field, either in fair or foul territory.

Interference/Defensive Defensive interference is an illegal act by a fielder which hinders or prevents a batter from hitting a pitch.

Interference/Offensive The batter is out after hitting or bunting a fair ball, when his bat hits the ball a second time in fair territory. The ball is dead and no runners may advance. If the batter-runner drops his bat and the ball rolls against the bat in fair territory and, in the umpire's judgment, there was no intention to interfere with the course of the ball, the ball is alive and in play.

The batter is out after hitting or bunting a foul ball, when he intentionally deflects the course of the ball in any manner while running to first base. The ball is dead and no runners may advance.

The batter is out when his fair ball touches him before touching a fielder.

It is interference by a batter or runner when he intentionally deflects the course of a foul ball in any manner.

Interference/Spectator The batter is out when spectator interference clearly prevents a fielder from catching his fly ball.

Spectator interference occurs when a spectator reaches out of the stands, or goes on the playing field and touches a live ball. When there is spectator interference with any thrown ball, except a throw by the pitcher, the ball shall be dead at the moment of interference and the umpire shall impose such penalties as in his opinion will nullify the act of interference.

Pitcher/Delivery In the event a balk is called, the ball is dead, and each runner shall advance one base without liability to be put out unless the batter hits the pitch on which the balk is made, in which case the manager of the offensive team may elect to accept either the balk penalty or the result of the batter's action.

Pitcher/Illegal Pitch A quick return pitch is a pitch made with obvious intent to catch a batter off balance.

Pitcher/Starter The pitcher named in the batting order handed the umpire-in-chief shall pitch to the first batter or any substitute batter until the batter is put out or reaches first base, unless the pitcher sustains injury or illness which, in the judgment of the umpire-in-chief, incapacitates him from pitching further.

If the pitcher is replaced, the substitute pitcher shall pitch to the batter then at bat, or any substitute batter, until such batter is retired or reaches first base, or until the offensive team is retired, unless the substitute pitcher sustains injury or illness which, in the umpire-in-chief's judgment, incapacitates him for further play as a pitcher.

Relief Pitcher See above, *Pitcher/Starter*.

Runner The rules of 1954 include several new provisions awarding baserunners additional bases in various circumstances.

Squeeze Play Squeeze play is a term to designate a play when a team, with a runner on third base, attempts to score that runner by means of a bunt.

Triple Play A triple play is a play by the defense in which three offensive players are legally put out as a result of continuous action, providing there is no error between the putouts.

Umpire The umpire's authority to act in legal manner on all matters pertaining to a game shall not be questioned. The umpire shall have power to make decisions on any points not specifically covered in the rules.

Wild Pitch A wild pitch is one so high, so low, or so wide of the plate that it cannot be handled with ordinary effort by the catcher.

1955

Ball   The ball shall be a sphere formed by yarn wound around a small core of cork, rubber or similar material, covered with two strips of white horsehide, tightly stitched together. It shall weigh not less than 5 nor more than 5¼ ounces avoirdupois and measure not less than 9 nor more than 9¼ inches in circumference.

Batter/Position (Illegal)   An illegally batted ball is one hit by the batter with one or both feet outside of the batter's box.

Batting Order   The umpire-in-chief shall make certain that the original and copies of the respective batting orders are identical, and then tender a copy of each batting order to the opposing manager. The copy retained by the umpire shall be the official batting order. The tender of the batting order by the umpire shall establish the batting orders. Thereafter, no substitutions shall be made by either manager, except as provided in the rules.

Catcher/Position   The catcher shall stand with both feet within the lines of the catcher's box, directly back of the plate, until the ball leaves the pitcher's hand. The intent of this rule is to deter the giving of intentional bases on balls. If the catcher has either foot outside his box when the pitcher delivers the ball, it is a balk.

Dead/Live Ball   See *Game/"Time."*

Interference/Defensive   The batter becomes a runner and is entitled to first base when the catcher or any other fielder interferes with him, unless the batter reaches first base on a hit, an error, or otherwise, and all other runners advance at least one base, in which case the play proceeds without reference to the interference.

Interference/Offensive   It is interference by a batter or runner when any member or members of the offensive team stand or gather around any base to which a runner is advancing, to confuse, hinder, or add to the difficulty of the fielders. Such runner shall be declared out for the interference of his teammate or teammates.

It is interference by a batter or runner when any batter or runner who has just been retired hinders or impedes any following play being made on a runner. Such runner shall be declared out for the interference of his teammate.

Forfeited Game   A game shall be forfeited in favor of the opposing team when a team is unable or refuses to place nine players on the field.

Game   The rules of 1955 include new provisions for determining a suspended game and its resumption.

Game/Rain   The manager of the home team shall be the sole judge as to whether a game shall be started because of unsuitable weather conditions or the unfit condition of the playing field, except for the second game of a doubleheader.

Game/"Time"   The ball becomes dead when the umpire-in-chief suspends play by calling "Time" when an accident incapacitates a player or umpire, or if it is necessary to remove a player or spectator from the grounds. The umpire shall not call "Time" because of an accident to player or umpire during a play, until in his judgment, no further action is possible in that play, unless an accident to a runner is such as to prevent him from proceeding to a base to which he is legally entitled, as on a home run hit out of the playing field, or an award of one or more bases, in which case a substitute runner shall be permitted to complete the play.

Pitcher/Delivery   When the bases are unoccupied, the pitcher shall deliver the ball to the batter within 20 seconds after taking his pitching position. Each time the pitcher delays the game by violating this rule, the umpire shall call "Ball."

1956

There were no changes to the playing rules this year.

1957

The rules of 1957 contain new wording and explanation for the rules governing a batter who bats out of order.

Ball/Defacing   See *Pitcher/Illegal Act.*

Batter/Position   The batter shall take his position in the batter's box promptly when it is his time at bat.

The batter shall not leave his position in the batter's box after the pitcher comes to the Set Position, or starts his windup. Penalty: If the pitcher pitches, the umpire shall call "Ball" or "Strike," as the case may be.

Catcher/Position   When the ball is put in play at the start of or during a game, all fielders other than the catcher shall be on fair territory. The catcher shall station himself directly back of the plate. He may leave his position at any time to catch a pitch or make a play except that when the batter is being given an intentional base on balls, the catcher must stand with both feet within the lines of the catcher's box until the ball leaves the pitcher's hand. Penalty: Balk.

Coach   The offensive team shall station two coaches on the field during its term at bat, one near first base and one near third base. Failure to place two coaches on the field shall subject the manager to fine or suspension or both by the league president.

Coaches shall be limited to two in number and shall (1) be in team uniform; (2) remain within the coach's box at all times; and (3) address players of their own team only. Penalty: The offending coach shall be removed from the game, and shall leave the playing field.

Game   When the winning run is scored in the last half-inning of a regulation game, or in the last half of an extra inning, as the result of a base on balls, hit batsman, or any other play with the bases full which forces the runner on third to advance, the umpire shall not declare the game ended until the runner forced to advance from third has touched home base and the batter-runner has touched first base. Penalty: If the runner on third refuses to advance to and touch home base in a reasonable time, the umpire shall disallow the run, call out the offending player, and order the game resumed. If, with less than two out, the batter-runner refuses to advance to and touch first base, the run shall count, but the offending player shall be called out.

The rules of 1957 include a rewording of the rules governing suspended games and the resumption of suspended games.

Game/Doubleheader   A league may adopt a rule providing that one game of a doubleheader shall be seven innings in length. In such games, any of these rules applying to the ninth inning shall apply to the seventh inning.

The second game of a doubleheader shall start 20 minutes after the first game is completed, unless a longer interval (not to exceed 30 minutes) is declared by the umpire-in-chief and announced to the opposing managers at the end of the first game. Exception: If the league president has approved a request of the home club for a longer interval between games for some special event, the umpire-in-chief shall declare such longer interval and announce it to the opposing managers. The umpire-in-chief of the first game shall be the timekeeper controlling the interval between games.

Hit by Pitch   The batter becomes a runner and is entitled to first base without liability to be put out (provided he advances to and touches first base) when he is touched by a pitched ball which he is not attempting to hit unless: (1) The ball is in the strike zone when it touches the batter, or (2) The batter makes no attempt to avoid being touched by the ball.

Note: If the ball is in the strike zone when it touches the batter, it shall be called a strike, whether or not the batter tries to avoid the ball. If the ball is outside the strike zone when it touches the batter, it shall be called a ball if he makes no attempt to avoid being touched.

Infield Fly   An infield fly is a fair fly ball (not including a line drive nor an attempted bunt) which can be caught by an infielder with ordinary effort when first and second, or first, second, and third bases are occupied, before two are out. The pitcher, catcher, and any outfielder who stations himself in the infield on the play shall be considered infielders for the purpose of this rule.

When it seems apparent that a batted ball will be an infield fly, the umpire shall immediately declare "Infield Fly" for the benefit of the runners. If the ball is near the baselines, the umpire shall declare "Infield Fly, if Fair."

The ball is alive and runners may advance at the risk of the ball being caught, or re-touch and advance after the ball is touched, the same as on any fly ball. If the hit becomes a foul ball, it is treated the same as any foul.

Note: If a declared infield fly is allowed to fall untouched to the ground, and bounces foul, it is a foul ball. If a declared infield fly falls untouched to the ground outside the baseline, and bounces fair, it is an infield fly.

Interference/Defensive   If, with a runner on third base and trying to score by means of a squeeze play or a steal, the catcher or any other fielder steps on, or in front of home base without possession of the ball, or touches the batter or his bat, the pitcher shall be charged with a balk, the batter shall be awarded first base on the interference, and the ball is dead.

Each runner, other than the batter, may without liability to be put out, advance one base when he is attempting to steal a base, if the batter is interfered with by the catcher or any other fielder.

Note: When a runner is entitled to a base without liability to be put out, while the ball is in play, or under any rule in which the ball is in play after the runner reaches the base to which he is entitled, and the runner fails to touch the base to which he is entitled before attempting to advance to the next base, the runner shall forfeit his exemption from liability to be put out, and he may be put out by tagging the base or by tagging the runner before he returns to the missed base.

Obstruction   In a rundown play, if the runner is obstructed by any fielder who does not have the ball in his possession (unless the fielder is in the act of fielding the ball), the umpire shall call "Obstruction" and the runner shall be entitled to occupy the base he is attempting to reach when the obstruction occurs. If such base is held by a following runner, any following runner forced to vacate his base by the obstructed runner's return shall be permitted to return to his last-held base without liability to be put out.

Pitcher/Delivery   When the bases are unoccupied, the pitcher shall deliver the ball to the batter within 20 seconds after he receives the ball. Each time the pitcher delays the game by violating this rule, the umpire shall call "Ball."

Note: The intent of this rule is to avoid unnecessary delays. The umpire shall insist that the catcher return the ball promptly to the pitcher, and that the pitcher take his position on the rubber promptly. Obvious delay by the pitcher should instantly be penalized by the umpire.

If there is a runner or runners it is a balk if the pitcher, while giving an intentional base on balls, pitches when the catcher is not in the catcher's box.

If there is a runner or runners it is a balk if the pitcher makes an illegal pitch.

Pitcher/Illegal Act   The pitcher shall not (1) apply a foreign substance of any kind to the ball; (2) expectorate either on the ball or his glove; (3) rub the ball on his glove, person, or clothing; (4) deface the ball in any manner; (5) deliver what is called the "shine" ball, "spit" ball, "mud" ball or "emery" ball.

The pitcher, of course, is allowed to rub the ball between his bare hands. Penalty: For violation of any part of this rule, the umpire shall immediately disqualify the pitcher, and the league president shall suspend the pitcher for a period of 10 days. If a pitch is delivered in violation of this rule, it shall be treated as an illegal pitch.

Player/Illegal Act   Players in uniform shall not address nor mingle with spectators, nor sit in the stands before, during, or after a game. No manager, captain, coach, or player shall address any spectator before or during a game.

Players of opposing teams shall not fraternize at any time while in uniform. Penalty: The league president shall impose fines for violation of this rule at his discretion.

Player/Position   See *Catcher/Position*.

Relief Pitcher   If an improper substitution is made for the pitcher, the umpire shall direct the proper pitcher to return to the game until the provisions of this rule are fulfilled. If the improper pitcher is permitted to pitch, any play that results is legal. The improper pitcher becomes the proper pitcher as soon as he makes his first pitch to the batter, or as soon as any runner is retired.

Strike Zone   A strike is a legal pitch when so called by the umpire which (a) is struck at by the batter and is missed; (b) enters the strike zone in flight and is not struck at; (c) is fouled by the batter when he has less than two strikes; (d) is bunted foul; (e) touches the batter as he strikes at it; (f) touches the batter in flight in the strike zone; or (g) becomes a foul tip. Note: (f) was added to the former rule and definition.

Touch/Definition   To touch a player or umpire is to touch any part of his body, clothing, or his equipment.

Umpire   Each umpire has authority to disqualify any player, coach, manager, or substitute for objecting to decisions or for unsportsmanlike conduct or language, and to remove such disqualified person from the playing field. If an umpire disqualifies a player while a play is in progress, the disqualification shall not take effect until no further action is possible in that play.

Each umpire has authority at his discretion to remove from the playing field (1) any person whose duties permit his presence on the field, such as ground-crew members, ushers, photographers, newsmen, broadcasting-crew members, etc., or (2) any spectator or other person not authorized to be on the playing field.

Umpire/Decisions   If different decisions should be made on one play by different umpires, the umpire-in-chief shall call all the umpires into consultation, with no manager or player present. After consultation, the umpire-in-chief (unless another umpire may have been designated by the league president) shall determine which decision shall prevail, based on which umpire was in best position and which decision was most likely correct. Play shall proceed as if only the final decision had been made.

1958

Appeal/Runner   Any runner shall be called out, on appeal, when (a) after a fly ball is caught, he fails to re-touch his base before he or his base is tagged; (b) with the ball in play, while advancing or returning to a base, he fails to touch each base in order before he, or a missed base is tagged; (c) he overruns or overslides first base and fails to return to the base immediately, and he or the base is tagged; (d) he fails to touch home base and makes no attempt to return to that base, and home base is tagged. Any appeal under this rule must be made before the next legal pitch. If the violation occurs during a play which ends a half-inning, the appeal must be made before the defensive team leaves the field.

Note: Appeal plays may require an umpire to recognize an apparent "fourth out." If the third out is made during a play in which an appeal play is sustained on another runner, the appeal play decision takes precedence in determining the out. If there is more than one appeal during a play that ends a half-inning, the defense may elect to take the out that gives it the advantage. If the third out on appeal is a force play or failure of the batter-runner to touch first base, no runs can score on the play. Otherwise runs made before the appeal is sustained shall count. For the purposes of this rule, the defensive team has "left the field" when the pitchers and all infielders have left fair territory on their way to the bench or clubhouse.

1959

Grounds   Any playing field constructed by a professional club after June 1, 1958, shall provide a minimum distance of 325 feet from home base to the nearest fence, stand, or other obstruction on the right and left field foul lines, and a minimum distance of 400 feet to the center field fence. No existing playing fields shall be remodeled after June 1, 1958, in such manner as to reduce the distance from home base to the foul poles and to the center field fence below the minimum distances.

Interference/Spectator   When there is spectator interference with any thrown ball, the ball shall be dead at the moment of interference, and the umpire shall impose such penalties as in his opinion will nullify the act of interference.

Runner/Awarded Bases   The runner is entitled to advance one base, if a ball, pitched to the batter, or thrown by the pitcher from his position on the pitcher's plate to a base to catch a runner, goes into a stand, or players' bench, or over or through a field fence or backstop. The ball is dead.

Note: If such a wild pitch is ball four, the batter-runner is entitled to first base only.

Each runner, including the batter-runner, may advance two bases, if a fair ball bounces or is deflected into the stands outside the first or third base foul lines; or if it goes through or under a field fence, or through or under a scoreboard, or through or under shrubbery or vines on the fence; or if it sticks in such fence, scoreboard, shrubbery, or vines.

1960–62

There were no changes to the playing rules in these years.

1963

Interference/Offensive   Offensive interference is an act by the team at bat which interferes with, obstructs, impedes, hinders, or confuses any fielder attempting to make a play. If the umpire declares the batter, batter-runner, or a runner out for interference, all other runners shall return to the last base that was, in the judgment of the umpire, legally touched at the time of the interference.

Pitcher/Delivery   Wind-up Position   The pitcher shall stand facing the batter, his entire pivot foot on, or in front of and touching and not off the end of the pitcher's plate, and the other foot free. From this position any natural movement associated with his delivery of the ball to the batter commits him to the pitch without interruption or alteration. He shall not raise either foot from the ground, except that in his actual delivery of the ball to the batter, he may take one step backward, and one step forward with his free foot.

Note: When a pitcher holds the ball with both hands in front of his body, with his entire pivot foot on, or in front of and touching but not off the end of the pitcher's plate, and his other foot free, he will be considered in a Windup Position.

If there is a runner, or runners, it is a balk when the pitcher, after coming to a legal pitching position, removes one hand from the ball other than in an actual pitch, or in throwing to a base.

Pitcher/Warm-Up Pitches   When a pitcher takes his position at the beginning of each inning, or when he relieves another pitcher, he shall be permitted to pitch not to exceed eight preparatory pitches to his catcher during which play shall be suspended. A league by its own action may limit the number of preparatory pitches to less than eight preparatory pitches. Such preparatory pitches shall not consume more than one minute of time. If a sudden emergency causes a pitcher to be summoned into the game without any opportunity to warm up, the umpire-in-chief shall allow him as many pitches as the umpire deems necessary.

Runner   A runner acquires the right to an unoccupied base when he touches it before he is out. He is then entitled to it until he is put out, or forced to vacate it for another runner.

Unless two are out, the status of a following runner is not affected by a preceding runner's failure to touch or re-touch a base. If, upon appeal, the preceding runner is the third out, no runners following him shall score. If such third out is the result of a force play, neither preceding nor following runners shall score.

Strike Zone   The strike zone is that space over home plate which is between the top of the batter's shoulders and his knees when he assumes his natural stance. The umpire shall determine the strike zone according to the batter's usual stance when he swings at a pitch.

1964

Bat   No colored bat may be used in a professional game unless approved by the rules committee.

Interference/Defensive   The batter becomes a runner and is entitled to first base when the catcher or any fielder interferes with him. If a play follows the interference, the manager of the offense may advise the plate umpire that he elects to decline the interference penalty and accept the play. Such election shall be made immediately at the end of the play. However, if the batter reaches first base on a hit, an error, a base on balls, a hit batsman, or otherwise, and all other runners advance at least one base, the play proceeds without reference to the interference.

Interference/Offensive   It is interference by a batter or a runner when a batter-runner willfully and deliberately interferes with a batted ball or a fielder in the act of fielding a batted ball, with the obvious intent to break up a double play. The ball is dead. The umpire shall call the batter-runner out for interference and also call out the next preceding runner for the action of his teammate. In no event may bases be run or runs scored because of such action by a runner.

It is interference by a batter or a runner when, in the judgment of the umpire, a baserunner willfully and deliberately interferes with a batted ball or a fielder in the act of fielding a batted ball with the obvious intent to break up a double play. The ball is dead. The umpire shall call the runner out for interference and also call out the batter-runner because of the action of his teammate. In no event may bases be run or runs scored because of such action by a runner.

Pitcher/Delivery   The Set Position   Set Position shall be indicated by the pitcher when he stands facing the batter with his entire pivot foot on, or in front of, and in contact with, and not off the end of the pitcher's plate, and his other foot in front of the pitcher's plate, holding the ball in both hands in front of his body and coming to a complete stop. From such Set Position he may deliver the ball to the batter, throw to a base or step backward off the pitcher's plate with his pivot foot. Before assuming Set Position, the pitcher may elect to make any natural preliminary motion such as that known as "the stretch." But, if he so elects, he shall come to Set Position before delivering the ball to the batter. After assuming Set Position any natural motion associated with his delivery of the ball to the batter commits him to the pitch without alteration or interruption.

Uniforms   Any part of an undershirt exposed to view shall be of a uniform solid color for all players on a team. Any player other than the pitcher may have numbers, letters, insignia attached to the sleeve of an undershirt.

1965

Glove/Catcher The catcher may wear a leather glove or mitt no more than 38 inches in circumference, nor more than 15½ inches from top to bottom. Such limits shall include all lacing and any leather band or facing attached to the outer edge of the mitt. The space between the thumb section and the finger section of the mitt shall not exceed six inches at the top of the mitt and four inches at the base of the thumb crotch. The web shall measure not more than seven inches across the top or more than six inches from its top to the base of the thumb crotch. The web may be either a lacing or lacing through leather tunnels, or a center piece of leather which may be an extension of the palm, connected to the mitt with lacing and constructed so that it will not exceed any of the above mentioned requirements. The glove may be of any weight.

Interference/Offensive It is interference by a batter or runner if a batter-runner willfully and deliberately interferes with a batted ball or a fielder in the act of fielding a batted ball.

Runner/Bases Any runner shall be called out, on appeal, when with the ball in play, while advancing or returning to a base, he fails to touch each base in order before he, or a missed base, is tagged. Approved Ruling: (1) No runner may return to touch a missed base after a following runner has scored. (2) When the ball is dead, no runner may return to touch a missed base or one he has left after he has advanced to and touched a base beyond the missed base.

1966

There were no changes to the playing rules this year.

1967

Catch A catch is the act of a fielder in getting secure possession in his hand or glove of a ball in flight and firmly holding it; providing he does not use his cap, protector, pocket, or any other part of his uniform in getting possession. It is not a catch, however, if simultaneously or immediately following his contact with the ball, he collides with a player, or with a wall, or if he falls down, and as a result of such collision or falling, drops the ball. It is not a catch if a fielder touches a fly ball which then hits a member of the offensive team or an umpire and then is caught by another defensive player. If the fielder has made the catch and drops the ball while in the act of making a throw following the catch, the ball shall be adjudged to have been caught. In establishing the validity of the catch, the fielder shall hold the ball long enough to prove that he has complete control of the ball and that his release of the ball is voluntary and intentional.

Coach/Manager See *Pitcher/Visits.*

Interference/Offensive It is interference by a batter or runner when, in the judgment of the umpire, a batter-runner willfully and deliberately interferes with a batted ball or a fielder in the act of fielding a batted ball, with the obvious intent to break up a double play. The ball is dead. The umpire shall call the batter-runner out for interference and shall also call out the runner who had advanced closest to the home plate regardless where the double play might have been possible. In no event shall bases be run because of such interference.

The players, coaches, or any member of an offensive team shall vacate any space (including both dugouts) needed by a fielder who is attempting to field a batted or thrown ball. Penalty: Interference shall be called and the batter or runner on whom the play is being made shall be declared out.

The batter becomes a runner when a fair ball, after having passed a fielder other than the pitcher, or after having been touched by a fielder, including the pitcher, shall touch an umpire or runner on fair territory.

Interference/Umpire See above, *Interference/Offensive.*

Pitcher/Delivery Pitchers shall take signs from the catcher while standing on the rubber.

The ball becomes dead and runners advance one base, or return to their bases, without liability to be put out when a balk is committed.

Pitcher/Visits A professional league shall adopt the following rule pertaining to the visit of the manager or coach to the pitcher: (a) This rule limits the number of trips a manager or coach may make to any one pitcher in any one inning; (b) A second trip to the same pitcher in the same inning will cause the pitcher's automatic removal; (c) The manager or coach is prohibited from making a second visit to the mound while the same batter is at bat; but (d) If a pinch-hitter is substituted for this batter, the manager or coach may make a second visit to the mound, but must remove the pitcher.

A manager or coach is considered to have concluded his visit to the mound when he leaves the 18-foot circle surrounding the pitcher's rubber.

Runner A runner acquires the right to an unoccupied base when he touches it before he is out. He is then entitled to it until he is put out, or forced to vacate it for another runner legally entitled to that base.

1968

Ball/Defaced See *Pitcher/Illegal Act.*

Coach See *Interference/Offensive.*

Interference/Offensive The ball becomes dead and runners advance one base or return to their bases without liability to be put out when a base coach intentionally interferes with a thrown ball. Runners return to the base last legally touched.

Pitcher/Illegal Act The pitcher shall not (1) bring his pitching hand in contact with his mouth or lips. Penalty: For violating this part of this rule the umpire shall warn the pitcher and if this action is repeated the umpire shall immediately disqualify the pitcher; (2) apply a foreign substance of any kind to the ball; (3) expectorate on the ball, his pitching hand, or his glove; (4) rub the ball on his glove, person, or clothing; (5) deface the ball in any manner; (6) deliver what is called the "shine" ball, "spit" ball, "mud" ball, or "emery" ball. The pitcher, of course, is allowed to rub the ball between his bare hands. Penalty: For violation of any part of this rule the umpire shall immediately disqualify the pitcher.

1969

Game A game called at the end of a completed inning with the score tied after nine innings shall be a suspended game.

Pitcher/Position The pitcher's plate shall be 10 inches above the level of home plate. The degree of slope from a point six inches in front of the pitcher's plate to a point six feet toward home plate shall be one inch to one foot, and such degree of slope shall be uniform. The leveled area atop the mound is enlarged to 34 inches by feet, with the added 10 inches placed behind the pitcher's plate.

Runner/Advancing Any runner is out when he fails to re-touch his base after a fair or foul ball is legally caught before he or his base is tagged by a fielder. He shall not be called out for failure to re-touch his base after the first following pitch, or any play or attempted play. This is an appeal play.

Strike Zone The strike zone is that space over home plate which is between the batter's armpits and the top of his knees when he assumes his natural stance. The umpire shall determine the strike zone according to the batter's usual stance when he swings at a pitch.

1970

There were no changes to the playing rules this year.

1971

Helmet   All players shall use some type of protective helmet while at bat.

1972

Appeal   An appeal is not to be interpreted as a play or an attempted play.

   Successive appeals may not be made on a runner at the same base. If the defensive team on its first appeal errs, a request for a second appeal on the same runner at the same base shall not be allowed by the umpire.

Game/Suspended   A game may be suspended to be completed at a future date by reason of light failure or malfunction of a mechanical field device, e.g., automatic tarpaulin or water-removal equipment.

1973

Designated Hitter   Any league may elect to use the Designated Hitter (DH) rule as follows: (1) A hitter may be designated to bat for the starting pitcher and all subsequent pitchers in any game without otherwise affecting the status of the pitcher or pitcher in the game. A DH for the pitcher must be selected prior to the game and must be included in the lineup cards presented to the umpire-in-chief; (2) It is not mandatory that a club designate a hitter for the pitcher, but failure to do so prior to the game precludes the use of a DH for that game; (3) Pinch hitters for a DH may be used. Any substitute hitter for a DH becomes the DH. A replaced DH shall not re-enter the game in any capacity; (4) The DH may be used defensively, continuing to bat in the same position in the batting order, but the pitcher must then bat in the place of the substituted defensive player, unless more than one substitution is made, and the manager then must designate their spots in the batting order; (5) A runner may be substituted for the DH and the runner assumes the role of DH; (6) A DH is "locked" into the batting order. No multiple substitutions may be made that will alter the batting rotation of the DH; (7) Once the game-pitcher is switched from the mound to a defensive position this move shall terminate the DH role for the remainder of the game; (8) Once the game-pitcher bats for the DH this move shall terminate the DH's role for the remainder of the game. The game pitcher may only pinch-hit for the DH; (9) Once a DH assumes a defensive position this move shall terminate the DH role for the remainder of the game.

   Note: The DH rule was adopted only by the American League.

Game   In all protested games, the decision of the league president shall be final.

1974

Ball/Defaced   See *Pitcher/Illegal Act*.

Helmet   All players are required to wear batting helmets with ear flaps.

Pitcher/Illegal Act   If, in his judgment, the umpire determines that a foreign substance has been applied to the ball, he shall (a) call the pitch a ball, warn the pitcher and have announced by the public address system the reason for the action; (b) in the case of a second offense by the same pitcher any time later in the game, the pitcher shall be disqualified from the game and may additionally be subject to such action as may be imposed by the league office; (c) if a play follows the violation called by the umpire, the manager of the offensive team may advise the plate umpire that he elects to decline the penalty and accept the play.

Such election shall be made immediately at the end of the play. However, if a batter reaches first base on a hit, an error, a base on balls, a hit batsman, or otherwise, and no other runner is put out before advancing at least one base, the play shall proceed without reference to the violation; (d) even though the offense elects to take the play, the violation shall be recognized and the penalties in (a) and (b) will still be in effect; (e) the umpire shall be the sole judge on whether any portion of this rule has been violated.

1975

Ball   The ball can be covered with white cowhide as well as horsehide.

Bat   Cupped Bats   An indentation in the end of the bat up to one inch in depth is permitted and may be no wider than two inches and no less than one inch in diameter. The indentation must be curved with no foreign substance added.

Bat/Illegal   A batter is out for illegal action when he hits a fair ball with a filled, doctored, or flat-surfaced bat in which event he shall be immediately ejected from the game and suspended by his league president for three days.

Fielder/Drops Fly Ball   A batter is out when an infielder intentionally drops a fair fly ball or line drive, with first, first and second, first and third, or first, second, and third bases occupied before two are out. The ball is dead and runner or runners shall return to their original base or bases. Approved Ruling: In this situation, the batter is not out if the infielder permits the ball to drop untouched to the ground, except when the infield fly rule applies.

Game   A game may be suspended if local law prohibits the use of lights and it is too dark to continue.

Infield Fly   See *Fielder/Drops Fly Ball*.

Pitcher/Illegal Act   The pitcher shall not have on his person, or in his possession, any foreign substance. For such infraction of this section the penalty shall be immediate ejection from the game.

Runner/Advancing   Any runner shall be called out, on appeal, when after a fly ball is caught, he fails to re-touch his original base before he or his original base is tagged.

Runner/Awarded Bases   Each runner, including the batter-runner, may advance one base if a ball, pitched to the batter, or thrown by the pitcher from his position on the pitcher's plate to a base to catch a runner, goes into a stand or a bench, or over or through a field fence or backstop. The ball is dead. Approved Ruling: When a wild pitch or passed ball goes through or by the catcher, or deflects off the catcher, and goes directly into the dugout, stands, above the break, or any area where the ball is dead, the awarding of bases shall be one base. One base shall also be awarded if the pitcher, while in contact with the rubber, throws to a base, and the throw goes directly into the stands or into any area where the ball is dead.

   If, however, the pitched or thrown ball goes through or by the catcher or through the fielder, and remains on the playing field, and is subsequently kicked or deflected into the dugout, stands or other area where the ball is dead, the awarding of bases shall be two bases from position of runners at the time of the pitch or throw.

1976

Bat   The bat handle, for not more than 18 inches from the end, may be covered or treated with any material (including pine tar) to improve the grip. Any such material, including pine tar, which extends past the 18-inch limitation, in the umpire's judgment, shall cause the bat to be removed from the game. No such material shall improve the reaction or distance factor of the bat.

Bat/Illegal   The batter is out for illegal action when he uses or attempts to use a bat that, in the umpire's judgment, has been altered or tampered with in such a way to improve the distance factor or cause an unusual reaction on the baseball. This includes, bats that are filled, flat-surfaced, nailed, hollowed, grooved, or covered with a substance such as paraffin, wax, etc. No advancement on the bases will be allowed and any out or outs made during a play shall stand. In addition to being called out, the player shall be ejected from the game and may be subject to additional penalties as determined by the league president.

Designated Hitter A Designated Hitter (DH) may not pinch run.

Once a pinch hitter bats for any player in the batting order and then enters the game to pitch, this move shall terminate the DH role for the remainder of the game.

A substitute for the DH need not be announced until it is the DH's turn to bat.

Player/Illegal Act No manager, player, substitute, coach, trainer, or batboy shall at any time, whether from the bench, the coach's box or on the playing field, or elsewhere make intentional contact with the umpire in any manner.

Umpire See *Player/Illegal Act.*

Uniform/Shoes No player shall attach anything to the heel or toe of his shoe other than the ordinary shoe plate or toe plate. Shoes with pointed spikes similar to golf or track shoes shall not be worn.

1977

There were no changes to the playing rules this year.

1978

Designated Hitter In the event of interleague competition between clubs of leagues using the Designated Hitter rule and clubs of leagues not using the Designated Hitter rule, the rule will be used as follows: (1) In exhibition games, the rule will be used or not used as is the practice of the home team; (2) In All-Star Games, the rule will only be used if both teams and both leagues so agree; (3) In World Series play, the rule will be used every other year. It will not be used in 1977, but will be used in 1978, etc.

Pitcher/Illegal Act The pitcher shall not intentionally pitch at the batter. If, in the umpire's judgment, such a violation occurs, the umpire shall warn the pitcher and his manager that another such pitch will mean immediate expulsion of the pitcher. At the same time the umpire shall warn the opposing manager that such an infraction by his pitcher shall result in that pitcher's expulsion. If, in the umpire's judgment, there is another such pitch during the game by any pitcher, the umpire shall eject the pitcher from the game. If, in the umpire's judgment circumstances warrant, one or both teams may be officially "warned" prior to the game or an actual violation during the game in progress. League presidents may take additional action under the rules.

Note: To pitch at a batter's head is unsportsmanlike and highly dangerous. It should be—and is—condemned by everybody. Umpires should act without hesitation in enforcement of this rule.

1979

There were no changes to the playing rules this year.

1980

Game The rules of 1980 include several amendments to the rules governing suspended games and protested games.

Substitute/Fielder If no announcement of a substitution is made, the substitute shall be considered as having entered the game when, if a fielder, he reaches the position usually occupied by the fielder he has replaced and play commences.

1981

Designated Hitter The Designated Hitter (DH) named in the starting lineup must come to bat at least one time, unless the opposing club changes pitchers.

1982

Pitcher Under extreme cold weather conditions a pitcher may warm his throwing hand by blowing on it provided that both managers and umpires have agreed to this before the game begins.

1983

Helmet All players shall use some type of protective helmet while at bat. All players in National Association Leagues shall wear a double ear-flap helmet while at bat. All players entering the major leagues commencing with the 1983 championship season and every succeeding season thereafter must wear a single ear-flap helmet (or at the player's option, a double ear-flap helmet), except those players who were in the major leagues during the 1982 season, and who, as recorded in that season, objected to wearing a single ear-flap helmet. If the umpire observes any violation of these rules, he shall direct the violation to be corrected. If the violation is not corrected within a reasonable time, in the umpire's judgment, the umpire shall eject the offender from the game.

1984

Bat The bat handle, for not more than 18 inches from its end, may be covered or treated with any material or substance to improve the grip. Any such material or substance, which extends past the 18-inch limitation, shall cause the bat to be removed from the game.

1985

Uniform No part of the uniform shall include patches or designs relating to commercial advertisements.

A league may provide that the uniforms of its member teams include the names of its players on their backs. Any name other than the last name of the player must be approved by the league president. If adopted, all uniforms for a team must have the names of its players.

1986

Designated Hitter The Designated Hitter (DH) rule will be used or not used in World Series or exhibition games according to the practice of the home team.

1987

There were no changes to the playing rules this year.

1988

Bases Home base shall be marked by a five-sided slab of whitened rubber. It shall be a 17-inch square with two of the corners removed so that one edge is 17 inches long, two adjacent sides are 8½ inches and the remaining two sides are 12 inches and set at an angle to make a point. It shall be set in the ground with the point at the intersection of the lines extending from home base to first base and to third base; with the 17-inch edge facing the pitcher's plate, and the two 12-inch edges coinciding with the first and third baselines. The top edges of home base shall be beveled and the base shall be fixed in the ground level with the ground surface.

Helmet All catchers shall wear a catcher's protective helmet, while fielding their position.

All bat/ballboys or girls shall wear a protective helmet while performing their duties.

Pitcher/Delivery   The Set Position   Preparatory to coming to a set position, the pitcher shall have one hand by his side.

Set Position is assumed by the pitcher when he stands facing the batter with his entire pivot foot on, and parallel to, the pitcher's plate, or in front of, parallel to, and in contact with, the pitcher's plate. The non-pivot foot must be on the ground in front of the pitcher's plate. The pitcher must hold the ball in both hands in front of his body and come to a single complete and discernible stop before throwing the ball. A complete stop shall not be construed as occurring because of a change in direction of the hands and arms.

From such set position he must deliver the ball to the batter, throw to a base, or step backward off the pitcher's plate with his pivot foot.

Before assuming set position, the pitcher may elect to make any natural preliminary motion such as that known as "the stretch." But if he so elects, he shall come to a set position before delivering the ball to the batter. After assuming set position, any natural motion associated with his delivery of the ball to the batter commits him to the pitch without alteration or interruption.

The pitcher, following his stretch, must (a) hold the ball in both hands in front of his body and (b) come to a complete and discernible stop, with both feet on the ground. This must be enforced. Umpires should watch this closely, and should immediately call a "balk" for any violation.

Pitcher/Illegal Act   The pitcher shall not intentionally pitch at the batter. If, in the umpire's judgment, such a violation occurs, the umpire may elect either to: (1) expel the pitcher, or the manager and the pitcher, from the game, or; (2) may warn the pitcher and the manager of both teams that another such pitch will result in the immediate expulsion of that pitcher (or a replacement) and the manager. If, in the umpire's judgment, and circumstances warrant, both teams may be officially "warned" prior to the game or at any time during the game. League presidents may take additional action under the rules.

1989

Bat   The bat shall be a smooth, *round* stick not more than 2¾ inches in diameter at the thickest part and not more than 42 inches in length. The bat shall be one piece of solid wood.

Note: No laminated or experimental bats shall be used in a professional game (either championship or exhibition games) until the manufacturer has secured approval from the Rules Committee of his design and methods of manufacture.

Pitcher/Delivery   The Set Position   Set Position shall be indicated by the pitcher when he stands facing the batter with his entire pivot foot on, or in front of, and in contact with, and not off the end of the pitcher's plate, and his other foot in front of the pitcher's plate, holding the ball in both hands in front of his body and coming to a complete stop. From such Set Position he may deliver the ball to the batter, throw to a base, or step backward off the pitcher's plate with his pivot foot. Before assuming Set Position, the pitcher may elect to make any natural preliminary motion such as that known as "the stretch." But if he so elects, he shall come to Set Position before delivering the ball to the batter. After assuming Set Position, any natural motion associated with his delivery of the ball to the batter commits him to the pitch without alteration or interruption.

Preparatory to coming to a set position, the pitcher shall have one hand on his side; from this position he shall go to his set position as defined above without interruption and in one continuous motion.

The whole width of the foot in contact with the rubber must be on the rubber. A pitcher cannot pitch from off the end of the rubber with just the side of his foot touching the rubber.

The pitcher, following his stretch, must (a) hold the ball in both hands in front of his body and (b) come to a complete stop. This must be enforced. Umpires should watch this closely.

Pitchers are constantly attempting to "beat the rule" in their efforts to hold runners on bases and in cases where the pitcher fails to make a complete "stop" called for in the rules, the umpire should immediately call a "balk."

1990–1994

There were no changes to the playing rules in these years.

Index to Playing Rule Changes 1845–1994

Note: Dates shown following an entry refer to the year a rule change or amendment was adopted. Rule changes and summaries of rules are to be found in the chronology.

Catch, definition of legal 1845; 1857; 1868; 1869; 1874; 1879; 1883; 1885; 1950; 1954; 1967

Catcher 1878; 1882; 1892; 1895; 1899; 1901; 1907; 1920; 1939; 1940; 1949; 1950; 1954; 1955; 1957; 1963; 1964; 1965; 1967; 1975; 1988

Catcher's Box 1878; 1901

Catcher's interference (See Interference by catcher)

Catcher's mitt (See Glove, restrictions on)

Club, eligible 1867; 1869

Coaches, number of required 1957

Coach hit by thrown ball (See also Interference by coach) 1920

Coach, no fines for rule violations to be assessed to 1940

Coach required to be in uniform 1957

Coach, restrictions on 1872; 1874; 1887; 1892; 1904; 1914; 1920; 1940; 1949; 1957; 1967

Coach's Box 1872; 1874; 1877; 1887

Coach's interference (See Interference by coach)

Coach, use of offensive language by 1887, 1892

Contract, player's 1872; 1874; 1876; 1877

Darkness (See Game, delayed or terminated)

Dead Ball 1857; 1867; 1868; 1871; 1874; 1876; 1909; 1910; 1920; 1931; 1940; 1950; 1954; 1955; 1957; 1959; 1964; 1965; 1967; 1968; 1975

Death of player prevents game 1867; 1869; 1870; 1872

Defensive interference, definition of (See also Interference) 1964

Definitions of terms used in rules as special section 1950

Designated Hitter (DH) rule 1973; 1976; 1978; 1980; 1986

Dimensions of field (See Grounds, layout of)

Doubleheader 1920; 1940; 1950; 1957

Dugout, bench, player's area 1877; 1882; 1892; 1896; 1899; 1904; 1950

Emery Ball (See Pitcher, freak deliveries by)

Equipment, while at bat removal from field of 1954

Fair and Foul Balls 1845; 1857; 1861; 1867; 1870; 1876; 1877; 1884; 1887; 1894; 1897; 1901; 1904; 1906; 1909; 1910; 1920; 1931; 1940

Fair territory, definition of 1950

Fences on grounds 1871; 1885; 1892; 1904; 1940; 1959

Fielder distracting batter 1954

Fielder, legal catch by (See Catch, definition of legal)

First baseman's mitt (See Glove, restrictions on)

Force out (See also Runner forced to vacate base) 1846-56; 1857; 1920; 1958; 1963

Forfeited game 1857; 1868; 1869; 1870; 1872; 1874; 1881; 1890; 1892; 1906; 1909; 1955

Foul fly 1845; 1876; 1879; 1883; 1885; 1940; 1949

Foul lines 1861; 1874; 1876; 1877; 1887; 1906; 1940; 1950

Foul tip 1889; 1895; 1897; 1899; 1950

Gambling 1857; 1874; 1877

Game, "called" (no game) 1857; 1868; 1871; 1892; 1920; 1931

Game, choice of innings 1845; 1877; 1878; 1885; 1887; 1896; 1906

Game, commencement of 1866; 1868; 1887; 1896; 1906; 1940; 1942; 1949; 1950

Game, complete (official) 1845; 1857; 1859; 1860; 1866; 1868; 1869; 1871; 1876; 1892; 1907; 1920; 1931; 1957

Game, delayed or terminated (rain, darkness, locust, etc.) 1866; 1868; 1871; 1872; 1875; 1876; 1877; 1887; 1892; 1899; 1906; 1907; 1950

Game, drawn (tie game) 1869; 1872; 1876; 1920; 1931; 1969

Game of baseball defined 1950

Game, preliminaries 1845; 1857; 1874; 1893; 1904; 1909; 1910; 1940; 1950; 1955

Game, suspended 1907; 1931; 1954; 1957; 1969; 1972; 1975; 1980

Game winner defined 1845; 1857; 1869; 1876; 1892; 1899; 1907; 1920; 1931; 1950; 1957

Glass buttons or polished metal not to be used on uniforms 1931

Gloves, restrictions on 1895; 1931; 1939; 1950; 1965

Gloves, while at bat removal from field of 1954

"Ground rule" double 1885; 1892; 1914; 1926; 1931

Ground rules 1858; 1874; 1876; 1904; 1909; 1910; 1940

Grounds, fitness of (See also League President, Manager or Umpire as judge of fitness of grounds) 1872; 1880; 1887; 1896; 1906; 1950; 1955

Groundskeeper/Grounds Crew 1906; 1950; 1957

Grounds, layout of 1845; 1857; 1861; 1870; 1871; 1875; 1874; 1877; 1878; 1880; 1882; 1885; 1887; 1892; 1894; 1904; 1940; 1959

Helmet, bat/ballboys and girls 1988

Helmet, batter 1971; 1974; 1983

Helmet, catcher 1988

Hit by Pitch 1884; 1887; 1888; 1892; 1902; 1907; 1910; 1920; 1957

Home Base (plate) (See Base, Home)

Home run 1885; 1892; 1914; 1920; 1926; 1931; 1950; 1955

Illegally batted ball (See Batter out of batter's box)

Infield fly rule 1895; 1901; 1920; 1940; 1950; 1954; 1957; 1975

Inning, definition of 1845; 1857; 1950

Interference by batter 1845; 1846-56; 1857; 1872; 1877; 1882; 1892; 1907; 1910; 1914; 1931; 1950; 1954; 1955; 1965; 1967

Interference by catcher 1899; 1907; 1920; 1940; 1954; 1955; 1957; 1964

Interference by coach 1904; 1914; 1920; 1931; 1967; 1968

Interference by fielder 1954; 1955; 1957; 1964

Interference by retired runner 1940; 1955

Interference by runner 1845; 1846-56; 1857; 1872; 1880; 1882; 1887; 1888; 1910; 1920; 1931; 1940; 1950; 1954; 1955; 1963; 1964; 1965; 1967

Interference by spectators 1857; 1865; 1873; 1874; 1881; 1882; 1954; 1959

Interference by teammates 1867; 1904; 1931; 1940; 1950; 1955

Interference by umpire 1877; 1907; 1910; 1914; 1920; 1967

League President as judge of fitness of ground 1950

Malfunction of mechanical field devices 1972

Manager appealing for new ball 1875; 1882

Manager appealing to or addressing umpire (See Umpire, addressing the)

Manager as coach (See Coach, restrictions on)

Manager as judge of fitness of ground 1887

Manager may elect balk penalty or result of play 1954

Manager may elect freak delivery penalty or result of play 1974

Manager may elect interference penalty or result of play 1964

Manager's authority to call game a draw 1869

Manager's authority to position players 1846-56; 1857; 1858; 1871

Manager's choice of innings (See Game, choice of innings)

Manager's consent to replace umpire 1872; 1875

Manager selects opponent's substitute runner 1872; 1883; 1889

Mud Ball (See Pitcher, freak deliveries by)

Newsmen and photographers 1950; 1957

No changes in the playing rules 1862; 1864; 1905; 1912; 1913; 1915; 1916; 1917; 1918; 1919; 1921; 1922; 1923; 1924; 1925; 1927; 1928; 1930; 1932; 1933; 1934; 1935; 1936; 1937; 1938; 1941; 1943; 1944; 1945; 1946; 1947; 1948; 1951; 1952; 1953; 1956; 1960; 1961; 1962; 1966; 1970; 1977; 1979; 1987; 1990; 1991; 1992; 1993; 1994.

Objective of baseball club 1950

Obstruction 1857; 1868; 1876; 1897; 1931; 1950; 1957

Offensive interference, definition of (See also Interference) 1963

Pitcher allowed to warm up 1902; 1950; 1963

Pitcher attempting pickoff 1898; 1899; 1900; 1901; 1902; 1950; 1959; 1963; 1975

Pitcher, delivery by 1845; 1857; 1863; 1867; 1868; 1869; 1871; 1872; 1874; 1876; 1878; 1879; 1883; 1884; 1885; 1887; 1889; 1890; 1893; 1898; 1899; 1900; 1901;1902; 1904; 1910;

Scoring Rules for 1877

Batting

Section 1. The first item in the tabulated score, after the player's name and position, shall be the number of times he has been at bat during the game. Any time or times where the player has been sent to base on called balls shall not be included in this column.

Section 2. In the second column should be set down the runs made by each player.

Section 3. In the third column should be placed the first-base hits made by each player. A base hit should be scored in the following cases:

When the ball from the bat strikes the ground between the foul lines and out of the reach of the fielders.

When a hit is partially or wholly stopped by a fielder in motion, but such player cannot recover himself in time to handle the ball before the striker reaches first base.

When the ball is hit so sharply to an infielder that he cannot handle it in time to put out a man. In case of doubt over this class of hits, score a base hit and exempt the fielder from the charge of an error.

When a ball is hit so slowly toward a fielder that he cannot reach it before the batsman is safe.

Section 4. In the fourth column should be placed to the credit of each player the total bases made off his hits. The unit, or base, consists in getting from any one base to any other base without being put out, and the striker is to be credited not only with the number of bases which he himself makes after a hit, but, in addition, with those safely made by every other player who is on base at the time he runs toward first. It should be understood that a base or bases made off an error of a fielder count toward the score of the player who ran from home base toward first base when the error was made. All the bases made off such error, whether by the striker or by some other player then on base, shall go to the credit of the striker. The striker shall be credited with a base when he is sent to base on called balls, and, in addition, with all the bases made by other players who may be advanced on the play under the rules.

A base or bases shall be given to the runner for a successful steal, whether made on an error of his opponents, or without error.

Bases shall not be given to a striker when any player, other than himself, shall be put out on his strike.

Fielding

Section 5. The number of opponents put out by each player shall be set down in the fifth column. Where a striker is given out by the umpire for a foul strike or because he struck out of his turn, the putout shall be scored to the catcher.

Section 6. The number of times a player assists shall be set down in the sixth column. An assist should be given to each player who handles the ball in a runout or other play of the kind.

An assist should be given to the pitcher when a batsman fails to hit the ball on the third strike.

An assist should be given to the pitcher in each case where the batsman is declared out for making a foul strike or striking out of turn.

An assist should be given to a player who makes a play in time to put a runner out, even if the player who should complete the play fails, through no fault of the player assisting.

An assist should not be given to a player who muffs the ball, or allows it to bound off his body toward a player who then assists or puts out a player.

And, generally, an assist should be given to each player who handles the ball from the time it leaves the bat until it reaches the player who makes the putout, or in case of a thrown ball, to each player who throws or handles it cleanly, and in such way that a putout results, or would result, if no error were made by the receiver.

Section 7. An error should be given for each misplay, which allows the striker or baserunner to make one or more bases, when perfect play would have insured his being put out. In scoring errors off batted balls, see Sec. 3 of this Article.

Chronology of Scoring Rules 1878–1994

1878

Assist An assist is no longer denied a player who has a ball bounce off him toward a player who then makes the play.

On-Base In the fourth column should be placed to the credit of each player the number of times he reaches first base during the game, whether upon hits, errors, called balls, or in any other way he is not put out.

Total Bases The statistic crediting players with total bases is dropped from the rule book (Section 4 in 1877).

1879

There were no changes to the scoring rules this year.

1880

Base Hit Score a base hit when a ball is hit so slowly toward a fielder that he cannot handle it in time to put out a man.

Total Bases In the fourth column should be placed to the credit of each player the total bases run during the game. In scoring "bases run" where a player has reached first base as the result of the putting out of another player, such first base shall not be credited to the striker as one of the bases run by him.

Total Chances In the seventh column should be placed the "total chances offered" to retire players, which should include each perfect play, as well as each misplay or failure to accept a chance to retire a batsman or baserunner. "Chances offered" should not include "passed balls," "called balls," or "wild pitches." In scoring "chances offered" off batted balls, see Sec. 3 of the Scoring Rules.

Note: This rule does not appear in the scoring rules following 1880.

1881

Total Bases In the fourth column should be placed to the credit of each player the total bases made by him off his hits.

1882

In 1882 the American Association was founded, adopted the

rule book, and made the following addition and deletion for their scoring rules:

Assist (American Association) An assist should be given to the pitcher on every chance offered to the catcher for a putout on a foul ball.

Total Bases (American Association) Total bases were not credited to the player's record.

1883

Assist (American Association) The pitcher is no longer credited with an assist when the batsman fails to hit the ball on the third strike, or when the batsman is declared out for making a foul strike or for striking out of turn.

Assist (American Association) An assist should be given to the pitcher when a batsman fails to hit the ball on the third strike.

An assist should be given to the pitcher in each case where the batsman is declared out for making a foul strike, or striking out of turn. Such assistance is to be placed in the summary of the score.

Note: These two rules were dropped by the AA in 1884.

Error An error should be given to the pitcher when the batsman is given first base on "called balls."

Scoring Summary In the summary of the game should be credited to the pitcher the number of times a batsman fails to hit the ball on the third strike.

Scoring Summary (American Association) The summary shall contain: (1) The number of earned runs made by each side; (2) The number of two-base hits made by each player; (3) The number of three-base hits made by each player; (4) The number of home runs made by each player; (5) The number of men on each side left on bases; (6) The number of double and triple plays made by each side; (7) The number of men struck out by each pitcher; (8) The number of men given base on balls by each pitcher; (9) The number of passed balls by each catcher; (10) The number of wild pitches by each pitcher; (11) The time of game; (12) The name of the umpire.

1884

In 1884 the Union Association was formed and adopted the same scoring rules used by the American Association, with the exception that the new league credited assists to the pitcher for strikeouts, batters called out for batting out of turn, and batters striking the ball while out of the batter's box. The Union Association existed for one season.

Scoring Summary (American Association) The number of men given bases from being hit by pitched balls is added to the summary.

Note: The Union Association did not include this in their summary.

Strikeout (American Association) A strikeout should be given to the pitcher when a batsman fails to hit the ball on the third strike, and in each case where the batsman is declared out for making a foul strike, or striking out of turn.

1885

Assist An assist shall be given the pitcher when the batsman fails to hit the ball on the third strike, and the same shall also be entered in the summary under the head of "struck out."

Note: This rule was dropped in 1889.

Error Wild pitches and passed balls shall be charged to the pitcher and catcher respectively in the error column, and shall also appear in the summary.

Note: This rule was dropped in 1886.

Error (American Association) An error shall be given for each misplay which allows the striker or baserunner to make one

or more bases, when perfect play would have insured his being put out; except that wild pitches, bases on called balls, bases on the batsman being struck by a pitched ball, balks, and passed balls shall not be included in said column.

Note: The National League adopted this rule in 1887 and added the term "illegal pitched ball" to the exceptions. The phrase "bases on called balls" was deleted from the exceptions in 1888 only.

1886

Stolen Base Bases stolen by players shall appear to their credit in the summary of the game.

1887

In 1887 the National League and the American Association agreed to use the same scoring rules.

Assist An assist shall be given the pitcher when the batsman fails to hit the ball on the fourth [third in 1888] strike, and the same shall be entered in the summary under the head of "struck out."

Note: This rule was dropped in 1889.

Base Hit A base hit is to be scored when the batsman is awarded a base on balls.

Note: This rule was dropped in 1888.

Scoring Summary The summary shall contain: (1) The number of earned runs made by each side; (2) The number of two-base hits made by each player; (3) The number of three-base hits made by each player; (4) The number of home runs made by each player; (5) The number of double and triple plays made by each side, with the names of the players assisting in the same; (6) The number of men given bases on called balls by each pitcher; (7) The number of men given bases from being hit by pitched balls; (8) The number of passed balls by each catcher; (9) The number of wild pitches by each pitcher; (10) The time of the game; (11) The name of the umpire.

Stolen Base In the fourth column shall be scored bases stolen, and shall include every base made after first base has been reached by a baserunner, except those made by reason of, or with the aid of, a "battery" error, or by batting, "balks" or by being forced off. In short, shall include all bases made by a "clean steal," or through a wild throw or muff of the ball by a fielder who is directly trying to put the baserunner out while attempting to steal a base.

Time at Bat The first item in the tabulated score, after the player's name and position, shall be the number of times he has been at bat during the game. Any time or times where the player has been sent to base by being hit by a pitched ball or by the pitcher's illegal delivery, shall not be included in this column.

1888

Base Hit In all cases where a baserunner is retired by being hit by a batted ball, the batsman should be credited with a base hit.

That when a player reaches first base through an error of judgment such as two fielders allowing the ball to drop between them, the batter shall not be credited with a base hit, nor the fielder charged with an error, but it shall be scored as an unaccepted chance, and the batter shall be charged with a time at the bat.

Note: This rule was dropped in 1889.

Earned Run An earned run shall be scored every time the player reaches the home base unaided by errors before chances have been offered to retire the side, but bases on balls, though summarized as errors, shall be credited as factors in earned runs.

Note: This rule was deleted in 1898 but reappears in 1917. Also see 1912.

Stolen Base In the fourth column shall be scored bases stolen, and shall be governed as follows: Any attempt to steal a base must go to the credit of the baserunner, but any manifest error is to be charged to the fielder making the same. If the baserunner advances another base he shall not be credited with a stolen base, and the fielder allowing the advancement is also to be charged with an error. If a baserunner makes a start and a battery error is made, the runner secures the credit of a stolen base, and the battery error is scored against the player making it. Should a baserunner overrun a base and then be put out, he should receive the credit for the stolen base.

Time at Bat The first item in the tabulated score, after the player's name and position, shall be the number of times he has been at bat during the game. At any time or times where the player has been sent to base by being hit by a pitched ball, by the pitcher's illegal delivery, or by a base on balls shall not be included in this column.

1889

Base Hit A base hit should be scored when a batted ball hits the person or clothing of the umpire as provided in the playing rules.

Earned Run An earned run shall be scored every time the player reaches the home base unaided by errors before chances have been offered to retire the side.
Note: See entries under 1888, 1912, and 1917.

Sacrifice In the fourth column shall be placed sacrifice hits, which shall be credited to the batsman, who when but one man is out advances a runner on base on a fly to the outfield or a ground hit, which results in putting out the batsman, or would so result if handled without error.

Scoring Summary The number of bases stolen is added to the scoring summary.

1890

Assist Assistances on strikes are not to be included in the record of fielding assistances.

Earned Run Earned runs should be charged against the pitcher only on the basis of base hits made off the pitching, and should not include stolen bases or bases scored in any other way.

1891

Scoring Summary The number of runs batted in by base hits by each batsman is added to the scoring summary.

1892

Stolen Base The following sentence is added to the 1888 rule for scoring stolen bases: If a baserunner advances a base on a fly out, or gains two bases on a single base hit, or an infield out, or attempted out, he shall be credited with a stolen base, provided there is a possible chance and a palpable attempt made to retire him.
Note: This sentence was dropped from the rule in 1897.

1893

There were no changes to the scoring rules this year.

1894

Sacrifice A sacrifice hit is to be credited to the batsman who advances a runner with no one out or one out by a bunt sacrifice which results in putting out the batsman.
Note: Previously the rule applied only with one out. See 1889.

Time at Bat The batter is not charged with a time at bat for a sacrifice hit purposely made to the infield which advances a runner without resulting in a putout except to the batsman.

1895–6

There were no changes to the scoring rules in these years.

1897

Earned Run An earned run shall be scored every time the player reaches the home base by the aid of base hits only before chances have been offered to retire the side.
Note: See entries under 1888, 1912 and 1917.

Sacrifice In the fourth column shall be placed the sacrifice hits, which shall be credited to the batsman who, when no one is out or when but one man is out, advances a runner a base by a bunt hit, which results in putting out the batsman, or would so result if the ball were handled without error.

Scoring Summary The summary shall contain: (1) The number of earned runs made off each pitcher; (2) The number of two-base hits made by each player; (3) The number of three-base hits made by each player; (4) The number of home runs made by each player; (5) The number of bases stolen by each player; (6) The number of double and triple plays made by each side and the names of the players assisting in the same; (7) The number of men given bases on called balls by each pitcher and the names of the players who were thus given bases; (8) The number of men given bases from being hit by pitched balls by each pitcher and the names of the players who are thus given bases; (9) The number of men struck out by each pitcher and the names of the players struck out; (10) The number of passed balls by each catcher; (11) The number of wild pitches by each pitcher; (12) The number of baserunners left on bases by each side; (13) The number of innings each pitcher played; (14) The number of base hits made off each pitcher; (15) The number of bases on balls given by each pitcher; (16) The number of batsmen hit by each pitcher; (17) The number of batsmen struck out by each pitcher [Note: This requirement apparently duplicates Sec. 9 above]; (18) The number of baserunners of each side who reached first base by fielding errors; (19) The time it took to play the game; (20) The condition of the weather; (21) The condition of the playing field; (22) The name of the umpire.

Stolen Base The rule regarding stolen bases is now the same as that used between 1888 through 1891. Additional language adopted in 1892 and included through 1896 has been deleted. See 1892.

Time at Bat The first item in the tabulated score, after the player's name and position, shall be the number of times he has been at bat during the game. The time or times when the player has been sent to base by being hit by a pitched ball, by the pitcher's illegal delivery, or by a base on balls, or has made a sacrifice hit which was manifestly intentional, shall not be included in this column.

1898

Assist Assists should be credited to every player who handles the ball in the play which results in a baserunner being called out for interference or for running out of line.

Base Hit A base hit should be scored when a ball is hit with such force to an infielder that he cannot handle it in time to put out the batsman. In case of doubt over this class of hits, score a base hit and exempt the fielder from the charge of an error.
In no case shall a base hit be scored when a baserunner has been forced out by the play.

Error An error shall be given in the seventh column for each misplay which allows the striker or baserunner to make one or more bases when perfect play would have insured his being put out, except that "wild pitches," "bases on balls," bases on the batsman being struck by a "pitched ball," or in case of illegal pitched balls, balks and passed balls, all of which comprise battery errors, shall not be included in said column. In scoring errors of batted balls see Sec. 3 of this rule.
An error shall not be scored against the catcher for a wild

throw to prevent a stolen base, unless the baserunner advances an extra base because of the error.

No error shall be scored against an infielder who attempts to complete a double play, unless the throw is so wild that an additional base is gained.

Putout The number of opponents put out by each player shall be set down in the fifth column. Where a batsman is given out by the umpire for a foul strike, or where the batsman fails to bat in proper order, the putout shall be scored to the catcher. In all cases of "out" for interference, running out of line, or infield fly dropped, the "out" should be credited to the player who would have made the play but for the action of the baserunner or batsman.

Scoring Summary The summary shall contain: (1) The score made in each inning of the game; (2) The number of bases stolen by each player; (3) The number of two-base hits made by each player; (4) The number of three-base hits made by each player; (5) The number of home runs made by each player; (6) The number of double and triple plays made by each side and the names of the players assisting in the same; (7) The number of innings each pitcher pitched in; (8) The number of base hits made off each pitcher; (9) The number of times the pitcher strikes out the opposing batsmen; (10) The number of times the pitcher gives bases on balls; (11) The number of wild pitches charged to the pitcher; (12) The number of times the pitcher hits batsmen with pitched ball; (13) The number of passed balls by each catcher; (14) The time of the game; (15) The names and positions of each umpire.

Stolen Base A stolen base shall be credited to the baserunner whenever he reaches the base he attempts to steal unaided by a fielding or by a battery error or a hit by the batsman.

Time at Bat The first item in the tabulated score, after the player's name and position, shall be the number of times he has been at bat during the game. No time at bat shall be scored if the batsman be hit by a pitched ball while standing in his position, and after trying to avoid being so hit, or in case of the pitcher's illegal delivery of the ball to the bat which gives the batsman his base, or when he intentionally hits the ball to the field, purposely to be put out, or if he is given first base on called balls.

1899–1903

There were no changes to the scoring rules in these years.

1904

Assist The number of times, if any, each player assists in putting out an opponent shall be set down in the sixth column. An assist should be given to each player who handles the ball in aiding in a run-out or any other play of the kind, except the one who completes it.

Note: The rule remains unchanged except to clarify that the fielder completing a run-down play by making the putout is not to be credited with an assist even if he handled the ball prior to receiving it again to make the putout. But see the entry under 1910.

Base Hit A base hit should be scored when the ball is hit so slowly toward a fielder that he cannot handle it in time to put out the batsman or force out a baserunner.

Note: The phrase "or force out a baserunner" has been added to the original rule. See 1878.

Error An error shall be given in the seventh column for each misplay which prolongs the time at bat of the batsman or allows a baserunner to make one or more bases when perfect play would have insured his being put out. But a wild pitch, a base on balls, a base awarded to a batsman by being struck by a pitched ball, an illegal pitch, a balk and a passed ball, each of which is a battery and not a fielding error, shall not be included in the seventh column.

In case a baserunner advance a base through the failure of a baseman to stop or try to stop a ball accurately thrown to his base, he shall be charged with an error and not the player who made such throw, provided there were occasion for it. If such throw be made to second base, the scorer shall determine whether the second baseman or shortstop shall be charged with an error.

Putout The number of opponents, if any, put out by each player shall be set down in the fifth column. Where the batsman is given out by the umpire for a foul strike, or fails to bat in proper order, the putout shall be scored to the catcher. In cases of the baserunner being declared "out" for interference, running out of line, or on an infield fly, the "out" should be credited to the player who would have made the play but for the action of the baserunner or the announcement of the umpire.

Note: The phrase "or the announcement of the umpire" has been added in place of "or batsman." See 1898.

Sacrifice In the fourth column shall be placed the sacrifice hits. A sacrifice hit shall be credited to the batsman who, when no one is out or when but one man is out, advances a runner a base by a bunt hit, which results in the batsman being put out before reaching first, or would so result if it were handled without error.

Note: The phrase "before reaching first" has been added to the rule. See 1889.

Scoring Summary The scoring summary is to include the total runs by each side as well as the score made in each inning.

Stolen Base A stolen base shall be credited to the baserunner whenever he advances a base unaided by a base hit, a putout, a fielding or a battery error.

Time at Bat The first item in the tabulated score, after the player's name and position, shall be the number of times he has been at bat during the game, but the exceptions made in rule 82 must not be included.

Note: See rule 82 below.

"A Time at Bat" is the term at-bat of a batsman. It begins when he takes his position, and continues until he is put out or becomes a baserunner. But a time at bat shall not be charged against a batsman who is awarded first base by the umpire for being hit by a pitched ball or for the illegal delivery of the pitcher, or on called balls, or when he makes a sacrifice hit.

1905–06

There were no changes to the scoring rules in these years.

1907

Base Hit In all cases where a baserunner is retired by being hit by a batted ball, unless batted by himself, the batsman should be credited with a base hit.

Game Played All appearances by a player in a championship game count as a game played in the American League, which prior to 1907 had not so credited the appearances of pinch hitters, pinch runners, and defensive substitutes in most cases. See 1912 for National League.

1908

Sacrifice A sacrifice hit shall be credited to the batsman who, when no one is out or when but one man is out, advances a runner a base by a bunt hit, which results in the batsman being put out before reaching first, or would so result if it were handled without error. A sacrifice hit shall also be credited to a batsman who, when no one is out or when but one man is out, hits a fly ball that is caught but results in a run being scored.

1909

Double Play A double play shall mean any two continuous putouts that take place between the time the ball leaves the pitcher's hands until it is returned to him again standing in the pitcher's box.

Error In case a runner advances a base through the failure of a baseman to stop or try to stop a ball accurately thrown to his base, the latter shall be charged with an error and not the player who made such throw, provided there was occasion for it. If such throw be made to second base, the scorer shall determine whether the second baseman or shortstop shall be charged with an error.

An error shall be given in the sixth column for each misplay which prolongs the time at bat of the batsman or allows a baserunner to make one or more bases when perfect play would have insured his being put out. But a base on balls, a base awarded to a batsman by being struck by a pitched ball, an illegal pitch, a balk, a passed ball or wild pitch, unless such wild pitch or passed ball be on the third strike and allow the batter to reach first base, shall not be included in the sixth column. In case of a wild pitch or a passed ball allowing the batter to reach first base, the pitcher or the catcher, as the case may be, shall be charged with an error.

In event of a fielder dropping a fly but recovering the ball in time to force a batter at another base, he shall be exempted from an error, the play being scored as a "force-out."

Putout The number of opponents, if any, put out by each player shall be set down in the fourth column. Where the batsman is given out by the umpire for a foul strike, or fails to bat in proper order, or is declared out on third bunt strike, the putout shall be scored to the catcher. In cases of the baserunner being declared "out" for interference, running out of line, or on an infield fly, the "out" should be credited to the player who would have made the play but for the action of the baserunner or the announcement of the umpire.

Sacrifice A sacrifice hit shall be credited to the batsman who, when no one is out or when but one man is out, advances a runner a base by a bunt hit, which results in the batsman being put out before reaching first, or would so result if it were handled without error. A sacrifice hit shall also be credited to a batsman who, when no one is out or when but one man is out, hits a fly ball that is caught but results in a run being scored, or would in the judgment of the scorer so result if caught.

Scoring Summary The summary shall contain: (1) The score made in each inning of the game and the total runs of each side in the game; (2) The number of stolen bases, if any, by each player; (3) The number of sacrifice hits, if any, made by each player; (4) The number of sacrifice flies, if any, made by each player; (5) The number of two-base hits, if any, made by each player; (6) The number of three-base hits, if any, made by each player; (7) The number of home runs, if any, made by each player; (8) The number of double and triple plays, if any, made by each club and the players participating in same; (9) The number of innings each pitcher pitched in; (10) The number of base hits, if any, made off each pitcher and the number of legal at-bats scored against each pitcher; (11) The number of times, if any, the pitcher strikes out the opposing batsmen; (12) The number of times, if any, the pitcher gives bases on balls; (13) The number of wild pitches, if any, charged against the pitcher; (14) The number of times, if any, the pitcher hits a batsman with a pitched ball, the name or names of the batsman or batsmen so hit to be given; (15) The number of passed balls by each catcher; (16) The time of the game; (17) The name of the umpires.

Stolen Base A stolen base shall be credited to the baserunner whenever he advances a base unaided by a base hit, a putout, a fielding or a battery error, subject to the following exceptions: (1) In event of a double steal being attempted from bases one and two to bases two and three, where either is thrown out, the other shall not be credited with a stolen base; (2) In event of a baserunner being touched out after sliding over a base, he shall

not be regarded as having stolen the base in question; (3) In event of a baserunner making his start to steal a base prior to a battery error, he shall be credited with a stolen base; (4) In event of a palpable muff of a ball thrown by the catcher, when the baserunner is clearly blocked, the infielder making the muff shall be charged with an error and the baserunner shall not be credited with a stolen base.

1910

Assist The number of times, if any, each player assists in putting out an opponent shall be set down in the fifth column. An assist should be given to each player who handles the ball in aiding in a run-out or any other play of the kind, even though he complete the play by making the putout.

Note: Compare to the 1904 rule.

Error An error shall be given in the sixth column for each misplay which prolongs the time at bat of the batsman or allows a baserunner to make one or more bases when perfect play would have insured his being put out. But a base on balls, a base awarded to a batsman by being struck by a pitched ball, a balk, a passed ball, or wild pitch shall not be included in the sixth column.

Passed Ball A passed ball is a legally delivered ball that the catcher should hold or control with ordinary effort, but his failure to do so enables the batsman, who becomes a baserunner on such pitched ball, to reach first base or a baserunner to advance.

Stolen Base In event of a double or triple steal being attempted, where either runner is thrown out, the other or others shall not be credited with a stolen base.

Wild Pitch A wild pitch is a legally delivered ball, so high, low or wide of the plate that the catcher cannot or does not stop and control it with ordinary effort, and as a result the batsman, who becomes a baserunner on such pitched ball, reaches first base or a baserunner advances.

1911

There were no changes to the scoring rules this year.

1912

Earned Run An earned run is charged to the pitcher every time a player scores by the aid of safe hits, sacrifice hits, bases on balls, hit batters, wild pitches, and balks before fielding chances have been offered to retire the side.

Note: This rule is not included in the scoring rules for 1912 but earned runs were compiled in the official pitching records of the National League (1912) and American League (1913). The earned run scoring rule does not appear in the scoring rules until 1917.

Game Played All appearances by a player in a championship game count as a game played in the National League, which prior to 1912 had not so credited the appearances of pinch hitters, pinch runners, and defensive substitutes, with certain exceptions.

1913

There were no changes to the scoring rules this year.

1914

Assist The number of times, if any, each player assists in putting out an opponent shall be set down in the fifth column. One assist and no more shall be given to each player who handles the ball in aiding in a run-out or any other play of the kind even though he complete the play by making the putout.

Note: Compare to 1910 and 1904.

Base Hit A base hit should be scored when the ball from the bat strikes the ground on or within the foul lines and out of reach of the fielders, provided the batter reaches first base safely.

When a fielder, after handling a batted ball, elects to try to retire a baserunner instead of the batter, the play is known as a "fielder's choice." In case the runner is retired, or would be retired but for an error, the batter shall be charged with a time at bat, but no hit. If the runner is not retired, and no error is made, the batter shall be charged with a time at bat, but no hit, provided he swung at the ball, and shall be credited with a sacrifice hit, provided he bunted the ball; if, however, in the judgment of the scorer, the batter could not have been retired at first base by perfect fielding, he shall be credited with a base hit.

Error   In event of a baserunner making his start to steal a base prior to a battery error, he shall be credited with a stolen base and the battery error shall also be charged.

An error shall not be scored against the catcher or an infielder who attempts to complete a double play, unless the throw be so wild that an additional base be gained. This, however, does not exempt from an error a player who drops a thrown ball when by holding it he would have completed a double play.

An error shall be given in the sixth column for each misplay which prolongs the time at bat of the batsman or prolongs the life of the baserunner or allows a baserunner to make one or more bases when perfect play would have insured his being put out. But a base on balls, a base awarded to a batsman by being struck with a pitched ball, a balk, a passed ball, or wild pitch shall not be included in the sixth column.

Note: The phrase "or prolongs the life of the baserunner" has been added to the existing rule.

Fielder's Choice   See *Base Hit.*

Sacrifice   A sacrifice hit shall also be credited to a batsman who, when no one is out or when but one man is out, hits a fly ball that is caught but results in a run being scored on the catch, or would in the judgment of the scorer so result if caught.

1915–16

There were no changes to the scoring rules in these years.

1917

Earned Run   A run earned off the pitcher shall be scored every time a player reaches home base by the aid of safe hits, sacrifice hits, stolen bases, bases on balls, hit batsmen, wild pitches, and balks, before fielding chances have been offered to retire the side.

The pitcher shall be given the benefit of doubt whenever fielding errors are made and in determining the base to which a runner should have been held with perfect support on part of fielders. A fielding error made by the pitcher shall be considered the same as any other fielding error. No run can be earned that scores as a result of the batsman having reached first base on a fielding error or passed ball; nor can any run be earned after the fielding side has failed to accept chances offered to retire the side.

Percentage   To determine the pitcher's percentage for the season, the total number of runs earned off his pitching shall be divided by the total number of innings he has pitched; then multiplied by nine, to find his average effectiveness for a complete game.

1918–19

There were no changes to the scoring rules in these years.

1920

Error   An error shall be charged to the first baseman if, on receiving a throw in ample time to retire the batsman, he fail to touch first base.

An error shall be charged to the catcher if he drop a third strike, allowing the runner to reach first base; except this rule is not to apply in case of a wild pitch.

Game Ending Hit   If, in the last half of the final inning, with the winning run on base, the batsman drives home that run, credit shall be given him for as many bases on his hit as the runner advances; except, however, that in case of the batsman driving a fair ball out of the playing field, he shall receive credit for a home run.

Percentage   To determine the percentage of games won and lost, divide the total number of games won and lost into the number won.

To determine batting averages, divide the total "Times at Bat" into the total number of base hits.

To determine fielding averages, divide the total of putouts, assists, and errors into the total of putouts and assists.

In all cases where the remaining fraction is one-half or over, a point is added to the average.

Sacrifice   A sacrifice hit shall also be credited to a batsman who, when no one is out or when but one man is out, hits a fly ball that is caught but results in a run being scored on the catch, or would in the judgment of the scorer so result if caught; but no distinction shall be made in the summary as between bunted or fly-ball sacrifices.

Scoring Summary   The scoring summary is to include sacrifice flies (within the category of sacrifice hits) and the number of runs batted in by each batsman.

Stolen Base   No stolen base shall be credited to a runner who is allowed to advance without any effort being made to stop him.

Wild Pitch   See *Error*, second paragraph.

1921–25

There were no changes to the scoring rules in these years.

1926

Error   See *Wild Pitch.*

Passed Ball   The catcher shall be charged with a passed ball when a baserunner is enabled to advance by the catcher's failure to hold or control a legally delivered ball that should have been held or controlled with ordinary effort.

Sacrifice Fly   Awarded if any runner is advanced.

Wild Pitch   An error shall be charged to the pitcher if he make a wild pitch for the third strike, and the batsman reach first base; in such case the pitcher shall not have credit for a strikeout.

A wild pitch is a legally delivered ball, so high, low, or wide of the plate that the catcher cannot or does not stop and control it with ordinary effort, and as a result the batsman reaches first base or a baserunner advances.

1927–30

There were no changes to the scoring rules in these years.

1931

Assist   Credit an assist to a player who, by deflecting a batted ball with his glove or any part of his body, aids in retiring the batsman or another baserunner.

Credit an assist to each player who handles and throws the ball in such a way that a putout would have resulted except for the error of a teammate.

Do not credit an assist to a fielder who makes a bad throw, even when a runner trying to advance on it is subsequently retired. A play that follows an error is a new play and the player making an error is not entitled to an assist unless he takes part in the new play.

Do not credit an assist to the pitcher when, in legally delivering the ball to the batsman, he helps to retire a runner attempting to steal home.

Base Hit A base hit shall be scored in the following cases: (1) When a fair hit is made, as defined in the Playing Rules, and the batsman reaches first base safely; (2) When a fair hit ball is partially or wholly stopped by a fielder in motion, but such player cannot recover himself in time to field the ball to first before the batsman reaches that base, or to some other base in time to force out another runner; (3) When a ball is hit with such force to an infielder or pitcher that he cannot handle it in time to put out the batsman or force out a baserunner; except when the ball is recovered by another fielder in time to retire the batsman or force out a baserunner. In case of doubt over this kind of hit, a base hit should be scored and the fielder be exempted from the charge of an error.

Earned Run A run earned off the pitcher shall be scored every time a player reaches home base by the aid of safe hits, sacrifice hits, stolen bases, putouts, bases on balls, hit batsman, wild pitches, or balks, before fielding chances have been offered to retire the side.

The pitcher shall be given the benefit of doubt whenever fielding errors are made and in determining the base to which a runner should have been held with perfect support on part of fielders. A fielding error made by the pitcher shall be considered the same as any other fielding error. No run can be earned that scores as a result of the batsman having reached first base on a catcher's interference, a fielding error, or passed ball; nor can any run be earned after the fielding side has failed to accept chances offered to retire the side.

Note: The phrase "catcher's interference" has been added to the prior rule. See entry for 1917.

Error An error, but not a passed ball, shall be charged to the catcher if he drops or misses a third strike, allowing the batsman to reach first base. Credit the pitcher with a strikeout.

An error shall be charged to the first baseman (or the pitcher or second baseman when covering first base) if, on receiving a throw in ample time to retire the batsman, he does not touch first base as required by rule. The same rule shall be followed with respect to any fielder covering any other base on a force play.

Forfeited Game In a regulation game which the umpire shall declare forfeited after four and one-half innings have been played, all individual and team averages shall be incorporated in the official playing records.

Game-Ending Hit If, in the last half of the final inning, with the winning run on base, the batsman drives home that run, credit shall be given him for as many bases as, in the judgment of the official scorer, he would have made under normal conditions; the number, however, not to exceed the number of bases advanced by the runner; except when the batsman drives a fair ball out of the playing field, he shall receive credit for a home run, provided he legally touches each base in proper order.

Hit by Pitch When a batsman is hit by what would have been the fourth called ball, it shall be scored as a "hit by pitcher."

Passed Ball See *Error*.

Percentage In determining averages where the remaining fraction is one-half or over, a full point is to be added to the average.

Putout The number of opponents, if any, put out by each player shall be set down in the fourth column. When the batsman is called out by the umpire for an illegally batted ball, or for a foul third strike bunt, or for being hit by his own batted ball, or for interference with the catcher, or for failing to bat in proper turn, the putout shall be credited to the catcher. When a baserunner is declared out on an infield fly, the putout shall be credited to the player who would have made the play except for the action of the runner or the announcement of the umpire. When a

baserunner is declared out because of being hit by a batted ball, the putout shall be credited to the fielder nearest to the ball at the time of the occurrence.

Run Batted In Runs batted in should include runs scored on safe hits (including home runs), sacrifice hits, infield outs, and when the run is forced over by reason of batsman becoming a baserunner. With less than two out, if an error is made on a play on which a runner from third would ordinarily score, credit the batsman with a run batted in.

Sacrifice Rule Awarding of sacrifice flies is abolished.

Stolen Base In the event of a palpable muff of a ball thrown by the catcher, when, in the judgment of the scorer, the baserunner would have been out if the ball had been held, the infielder making the muff shall be charged with an error and the baserunner shall not be credited with a stolen base.

When a wild pitch or a passed ball occurs after a runner has started to steal, do not credit the runner with a stolen base but charge the wild pitch or passed ball.

Do not give a stolen base to a runner who has started to steal and the pitcher balks.

Time at Bat A "Time at Bat" is the term at bat of a batsman. It begins when he takes his position, and continues until he is put out or becomes a baserunner. But a time at bat shall not be charged against a batsman who is awarded first base by the umpire for being hit by a pitched ball, or on called balls, or when he makes a sacrifice hit, or for interference by the catcher.

Note: This rule is Rule 69, Sec. 5, of the Playing Rules.

The first item in the tabulated score, after the player's name and position, shall be the number of times he has been at bat during the game, but the exceptions made in Rule 69, Sec. 5, must not be included.

Note: See above entry for Rule 69, Sec. 5.

Wild Pitch A wild pitch is a legally delivered ball, so high, low, or wide of the plate that the catcher cannot or does not stop and control it with ordinary effort, and as a result the batsman reaches first base or a baserunner advances. Any pitched ball that strikes the ground before reaching the home plate and passes the catcher, allowing runners to advance, shall be scored as a wild pitch.

1932–38

There were no changes to the scoring rules in these years.

1939

Base Hit/Value In event of a batsman oversliding second or third bases and being tagged by the opposing fielder when said batsman is attempting to stretch a single into a two-base hit or a two-base hit into a three-base hit, the play should be scored the same as when a baserunner attempts to steal, overslides the base and is tagged out. In other words, the batsman oversliding second base and is tagged out shall be credited only with a single, while one who overslides third base and is tagged out shall be credited only with a two-base hit.

Earned Run A wild pitch which is a third strike is to be used in determining earned runs charged to the pitcher.

Run Batted In The batsman shall not be credited with driving in a run when a runner scores as he hits into a force infield double play or a double play in which the first baseman picks up a fair hit ground ball, touches first base and then throws to second retiring the runner who had been on first, said runner not being forced, has to be tagged out.

Sacrifice A sacrifice hit also shall be credited to the batsman who, when no one is out or when but one man is out, hits a fly ball that is caught but which results in a baserunner scoring, or would have scored a runner if said fly ball had not been dropped for an error, in the judgment of the scorer; but no distinction shall be made in the summary as between bunted or fly ball sacrifices.

1940

Base Hit   In all cases where a baserunner is retired by being hit by a batted ball, unless batted by himself, the batsman should be credited with a base hit, except if the runner is hit by an infield fly, the play should be scored as provided in the Playing Rules (Sec. 8 of Rule 44).

Earned Run   A run earned off the pitcher shall be scored every time a player reaches home base by the aid of safe hits, sacrifice hits, stolen bases, putouts, bases on balls, hit batsman, wild pitches, or balks, even though the wild pitch be a third strike, before fielding chances have been offered to retire the team. The preceding pitcher, and not a relieving pitcher shall be charged with runs scored by any runners on base when such relief pitcher entered the game. The relieving pitcher shall not be charged with his first batsman reaching first base if such batsman had any advantage because of poor pitching by the preceding pitcher. With the count two or three balls and one or no strikes, or three balls and two strikes, charge preceding pitcher if batsman reaches first base, but credit relieving pitcher if batsman is retired. With count one or two balls and two strikes, charge relieving pitcher if batsman reaches first base and credit him if batsman is retired.

Forfeited Game   In a regulation game which the umpire shall declare forfeited after four and one-half innings have been played, all individual and team averages shall be incorporated in the official playing records, except that no pitcher shall be credited with a victory or charged with a loss in said game.

1941–49

There were no changes to the scoring rules in these years.

1950

Assist   An assist shall be credited to each player who throws or deflects a batted or thrown ball in such a way that a putout results, or would have resulted except for a subsequent error by a teammate, but only one assist and no more shall be credited to each player who throws or deflects the ball in a rundown play which results in a putout, or would have resulted in a putout, except for a subsequent error.

Credit an assist to each player who throws or deflects the ball during a play which results in a baserunner being called out for interference, or for running out of line.

Do not credit an assist to a pitcher when, in legally delivering the ball to a batter, he helps to retire a baserunner attempting to steal home.

Situations will arise in which a wild throw shall be scored as an assist and not as an error while on some plays a wild throw shall be scored both as an assist and as an error.

Note: The scoring rules for 1950 then present four detailed examples illustrating the application of the assist provisions.

Base Hit   A base hit shall be scored under these circumstances: (1) When a batter reaches first base (or any succeeding base) safely on a legally batted ball which settles on fair ground or strikes a fence behind fair ground before being touched by a fielder, or which clears a fence behind fair territory; (2) When a batter reaches first base after hitting a ball with such force, or so slowly, that the pitcher or fielder attempting to make a play with it has no opportunity to do so; (3) When a batter reaches first base safely on a batted ball which strikes either first base, second, or third base before being touched by a fielder and bounces away from the reach of the fielder; (4) When a batter reaches first base safely on a legally batted ball which has not been touched by a fielder and which is in fair territory when it bounds into the outfield unless in the scorer's judgment it could have been handled with ordinary effort; (5) When a legally

batted ball which has not been touched by a fielder becomes "dead" by reason of touching the person or clothing of a runner or umpire, except that when a runner is called out for having been struck by an "infield fly" the batter shall not be credited with a hit; (6) When, in the scorer's judgment, the batter could not have been retired at first base by perfect fielding, when the fielder fails in an attempt to retire a preceding baserunner; (7) Always give the batter the benefit of the doubt. A safe course to follow being to score a hit when exceptionally good fielding of a batted ball fails to result in a putout; (8) In no case shall a base hit be scored when a runner is forced out by a batted ball, or would have been forced out except for a fielding error. Nor shall a hit be scored when an infield batted ball results in another runner, who is attempting to advance one base, being retired, whether forced out or not; (9) Score the play as a "fielder's choice" when a fielder uses a batted ball to retire a preceding baserunner, or would have retired one with ordinary effort except for a fielding error, charging the batter with time at bat, but no hit.

Base Hit/Value   Whether a safe hit shall be scored as a one-base hit, two-base hit or a three-base hit when no error or putout results shall be determined as follows:

It is a one-base hit if the batter stops at first base; it is a two-base hit if the batter stops at second base; it is a three-base hit if the batter stops at third base, but note this exception: the batter must, if attempting to take two or three bases on a safe hit by sliding, hold the last base to which he advances. If he overslides and is tagged out before getting back to the base safely he shall be given credit for only as many bases as he safely attained. If he overslides second base and is tagged out he shall be given a one-base hit; if he overslides third base and is tagged out, he shall be given a two-base hit. If he runs past second base after reaching that base on his feet, attempts to return and is tagged out, he shall be given credit for a two-base hit. If he runs past third base after reaching that base on his feet, attempts to return and is tagged out, he shall be given credit for a three-base hit.

If a batter is awarded three bases on a batted or bunted ball because a fielder has touched the ball with his glove, cap, or any other part of his uniform while such article is detached from its proper place on his person, the scorer's judgment shall dictate whether the batter shall be given credit for a one-base hit, a two-base hit, a three-base hit, or a home run. If the scorer believes the fielder could have, by ordinary effort, kept the hit from being good for more than one, two, or three bases he shall score it as a one-base hit or as a two-base hit or as a three-base hit and charge the fielder with an error. If, however, the scorer believes the hit would have been a legitimate home run, despite illegal use of equipment, he shall so score it if the batter touches all bases in the proper order.

In no instance shall the batter be credited with a two-base hit or a three-base hit if he fail to advance a preceding runner whose advance is necessary to permit the batter to reach second or third base. Example: Runner on first, batter makes a long hit and reaches second but runner is thrown out at third. Score a one-base hit and credit batter with reaching second on the play.

Should a batter, after making a safe hit, be called out for having failed to touch a base, the last base he reached safely shall determine if his hit is scored as a one-base hit, a two-base hit, or a three-base hit. If he is called out for missing second base, the hit shall be scored as a one-base hit. If he is called out for missing third base, his hit shall be scored as a two-base hit. If he is tagged out after missing home base, his hit shall be scored as a three-base hit. If he is called out for missing first base, he shall be charged with a time at bat but no hit.

When a batter ends a game with a safe hit, other than a home run, which drives in as many runs as are necessary to put his team in the lead, he shall be credited with only as many bases on his hit as are advanced by the runner who scores the winning run, and then only if the batter runs out his hit for as many bases as are advanced by the runner who scores the winning run, touching each base in the proper order.

If a batter ends a game with a home run out of the playing field and touches all the bases in their proper order, his run, and also the runs of all other runners who were on base when the home run was hit, shall count in the final score even though this gives the team last at bat a winning margin in excess of one run.

Base on Balls A base on balls shall be scored whenever a batter is awarded first base by the umpire because of four balls having been pitched outside the strike zone, but when the fourth such ball strike the batter it shall be scored as a "hit batter."

Championship To be eligible for the individual batting championship of any minor league, a player must have appeared in at least two-thirds of the games played by his team. Thus, if a team plays 154 games, a player must appear in 102 games. If his team plays 150 games he must appear in 100. If his team plays 140 games he must appear in 93, etc.

To be eligible for the individual batting championship of a major league, a player must be credited with at least 400 official "times at bat."

Double Play A double play is any two successive putouts which take place between the time a ball leaves a pitcher's hand and is returned to him while he is standing in the pitcher's box.

Earned Run An earned run is a run for which the pitching is held accountable.

An earned run shall be scored every time a player reaches home base by the aid of safe hits, sacrifices, stolen bases, putouts, bases on balls, hit batters, balks, or wild pitches (even though a wild pitch be a third strike which enables a batter to reach first base), before fielding chances have been offered to retire the offensive team.

Since a wild pitch on which a batter reaches first base is the pitcher's fault, solely, even though it is scored as a fielding error, it shall be disregarded as an error and considered as a wild pitch in computing earned runs and is the only instance in which an error is so disregarded.

In computing earned runs, any type of fielding error made by a pitcher (other than the one mentioned in the preceding two paragraphs) shall be considered in the same light as an error by any other fielder.

Whenever a fielding error occurs the pitcher shall be given the benefit of the doubt in determining to which bases any baserunners would have advanced had the fielding by the defensive team been errorless.

No run can be earned which scores as a result of a batter having reached first base safely because of a catcher's interference, or because of any fielding error, except a wild pitch.

When pitchers are changed during an inning, the preceding pitcher, and not the relieving pitcher, shall be charged with any earned or unearned runs scored by any runners on base when such relief pitcher entered the game. There is, however, this exception: If the action of any batter to whom the relieving pitcher pitches results in the retirement of a runner left on base by the preceding pitcher, the batter whose action resulted in the retirement of that runner shall be considered as having been left on base by the preceding pitcher and any run scored by such runner shall be charged to the preceding pitcher.

A relieving pitcher shall not be held accountable for the first batter to whom he pitches reaching first base if that batter had a decided advantage because of ineffective pitching by the pitcher whom the relieving pitcher succeeded. Thus, if the count is two or three balls and one or no strikes, or if the count is three balls and two strikes when pitchers are changed, and the batter reaches first base safely, charge that batter to the pitcher who was replaced. If such a batter is retired, or would have been retired except for a fielding error, the batter shall be credited to the relieving pitcher. Likewise, if such a batter hits into a force-out or into a fielder's choice on which a runner is retired, or would have been retired

except for a fielding error, credit the action of such a batter to the relieving pitcher. (The foregoing sentence is not to be construed as affecting or conflicting with the exception noted.) If pitchers are changed when the count is two balls and one or no strikes, or one ball and one or no strikes, the relieving pitcher shall be held accountable for whatever the batter does.

Error An error shall be scored for each misplay (fumble, muff, or wild throw) which prolongs the time at bat of a batter, or which prolongs the life of a runner, or which permits a runner to advance one or more bases when perfect play would have resulted in the batter or the runner being retired.

Certain misplays by the catcher and pitcher known as "passed balls" and "wild pitches" are not errors but items for the summary and are defined elsewhere in these rules.

Errors are not charged when a batter is awarded first base because of a base on balls, or for being struck by a pitched ball, or if a runner, or runners, advance because of a passed ball or because of the pitcher making a balk or a wild pitch, except: If a batter swings at a wild pitch for his third strike and thereby is enabled to reach first base, it shall be scored as a strikeout and also as an error for the pitcher and not a wild pitch; when a catcher muffs a third strike, thereby permitting a batter to reach first base, it shall be scored as an error for the catcher, not a passed ball, and as a strikeout.

No error shall be charged against the catcher or any other player for making a wild throw in attempting to prevent a stolen base or any other advance by a runner, unless the scorer is convinced such wild throw permitted the runner to advance one or more bases. If the wild throw permits a runner to advance an extra base, or bases, one error shall be charged to the player making the wild throw.

When any player throws wildly in attempting to complete a double play, or a triple play, no error shall be scored unless the throw is so wild that at least one additional base be gained. However, if a fielder muff a thrown ball which, if held, would have completed a double play or a triple play, score an error for the player who drops the ball.

An error shall be scored against any player who, on receiving a thrown ball in ample time to retire a batter or any other baserunner on a force play, does not touch the base as required by the rules.

When a runner advances because of the failure of a fielder to stop, or try to stop, an accurately thrown ball, the fielder failing to stop the ball shall be charged with an error and not the player making the throw, provided there was occasion for the throw. If such throw be made to second base the scorer shall determine whether it was the duty of the second baseman or the shortstop to stop the ball, and he shall charge the error to the negligent player.

No error shall be scored if any fielder, after dropping a fly ball, a line drive or a thrown ball recovers the ball in time to force out a runner at another base.

Accurately directed throws, especially from the outfield, which strike a baserunner or an umpire, or which take an unnatural bounce and permit a baserunner or baserunners to advance, shall be scored as errors for the player making the throw, even though it appears to be doing an injustice to the thrower. Every base advanced by a baserunner must be accounted for.

Game-Ending Hit See last two paragraphs, *Base Hit/Value*.

Hit by Pitch See *Base on Balls*.

Innings Pitched In giving a pitcher credit for the number of innings pitched divide each inning into three parts. Thus, if a pitcher is replaced, with one opponent out, in the sixth inning the pitcher so replaced shall be credited with having pitched $5\frac{1}{3}$ innings. If a pitcher is replaced with none out in the opposing team's sixth inning he shall be credited with having pitched 5 innings and a notation made to the effect that there were none out in the sixth inning.

Passed Ball A catcher shall be charged with a passed ball when a runner, or runners, advance because of the catcher's failure to hold or to control a legally pitched ball which should have been held or controlled with ordinary effort.

Percentage To determine a pitcher's earned run prevention average for a season, the total number of earned runs charged against his pitching shall be divided by the total number of innings he has pitched, then multiplied by nine to find his average effectiveness for a complete game.

(a) To determine the percentage of games won and lost divide the total number of games won and lost into the number won.

(b) To determine a batting average, divide the total "times at bat" into the total number of safe hits.

(c) To determine a slugging percentage, divide the total "times at bat" into the total bases of all safe hits.

(d) To determine a fielding average, divide the total of putouts, assists, and errors into the total of putouts and assists.

Putout A putout shall be recorded each time a defensive player catches a fly ball, whether fair or foul, a line drive or a thrown ball which retires a batter or runner, or when a fielder tags a runner with the ball when the runner is off the base to which he legally is entitled.

Automatic putouts shall be credited to the catcher as follows: (1) When a batter is called out by the umpire for an illegally batted ball; when a batter is called out by the umpire for bunting foul for his third strike; when a batter is called out by an umpire for being struck by his own batted ball; when a batter is called out by an umpire for interfering with the catcher; when a batter is called out by an umpire for failing to bat in his proper turn. (Note exception in 10.14 (a).) (2) Other automatic putouts shall be credited as follows: (3) When a batter is called out on an infield fly which is not caught, the putout shall be credited to the fielder whom the scorer believes could have made the putout; (4) When a runner is called out for being struck by a fair ball (including an infield fly) the putout shall be credited to the fielder nearest the ball; (5) When a runner is declared out by an umpire for running out of line to avoid being tagged by the ball in the hands of a fielder, the putout shall be credited to the fielder whom the runner avoided; (6) When a runner is declared out by the umpire for having interfered with a fielder, credit the putout to the fielder with whom the runner interfered, unless the fielder was in the act of throwing the ball when interfered with, in which case the putout shall be credited to the fielder for whom the throw was intended, and the fielder whose throw was interfered with shall be credited with an assist.

Relief Pitcher See last two paragraphs, *Earned Run*.

Runs Batted In A run batted in is a run which reaches home base safely because of a safe hit, sacrifice hit, infield putout or outfield putout, or which is forced over home plate by reason of the batter being struck by a pitched ball, or being awarded a base on balls, or being awarded first base because of interference by the catcher. If a batter hit a home run with the bases empty, score both a home run and a run batted in. If, with less than two out, an error is made on a play on which a runner from third base ordinarily would score and does score, credit the batter with a run batted in.

The batter shall not be credited with a run batted in if a run scores when he hits into a force double play, or into a double play in which the first baseman fields a fair hit ground ball, touches first base ahead of the batter for an out, then throws to second or third base, retiring a second runner who has to be tagged.

Sacrifice Score a sacrifice if, with less than two out, the batter advances one or more runners with a bunt and is retired at first base, or would have been retired except for a fielding error. In case a runner is forced out at any base on a bunt, it shall be scored as a time at bat but no sacrifice.

Scorer The scorer is an actual official of the game he is scoring, is an accredited representative of the league, is entitled to the respect and dignity of his office and shall be accorded full protection by the president of the league.

The scorer shall report to the President of the league any indignity expressed by manager, player, club employee or club official in the course of, or as the result of, the discharge of his duties.

To promote uniformity in keeping the records of championship games, scorers shall conform to the instructions of this scoring code.

Scoring Summary In making a box score of a game, each player's name and the fielding position or positions he has played shall be listed in the order in which he batted, or would have batted if the game ends before he gets to bat, followed by a tabulated record of each player's batting and fielding. (a) The first column shall show the number of times each player batted during the game, but no time at bat shall be charged against a player when he is awarded first base on four called balls, for being hit by a pitched ball, or because of being interfered with by the catcher, or for being obstructed by the catcher or any other player, while en route to first base. A sacrifice also exempts a player from being charged with a time at bat. (b) The second column shall show the number of runs, if any, made by each player. (c) The third column shall show the number of safe hits, if any, made by each player. (d) The fourth column shall show the number of putouts, if any, made by each player. (e) The fifth column shall show the number of fielding assists, if any, made by each player. (f) The sixth column shall show the number of fielding errors, if any, made by each player. (g) All players inserted into each team's lineup as substitute batters or substitute runners shall be so designated by special symbols plus notations at the bottom of their team's tabulated record. The symbols a, b, c, d, etc., are recommended. It also is recommended that the notations should describe what the extra batters did, such as—a-Singled for _____ in sixth inning; b-Flied out for _____ in third inning; c-Forced _____ for _____ in seventh inning; d-Grounded out for _____ in ninth inning. (h) The score by innings of each team follows the box score tabulations and precedes the summary in which should be listed the following items in this order: (1) Runs batted in; (2) Two-base hits; (3) Three-base hits; (4) Home runs, together with the names of the pitchers off whom hit; (5) Stolen bases; (6) Sacrifices; (7) Double plays; (8) Triple plays; (9) Number of runners left on base by each team; (10) Number of bases on balls issued by each pitcher; (11) Number of batters struck out by each pitcher. These shall be listed as "strikeouts"; (12) Number of hits and runs (also earned runs) allowed by each pitcher (if one or both teams use more than one pitcher), together with the number of innings pitched by each pitcher. If a team uses only one pitcher, list the number of earned runs he allowed; (13) The names of any hit batters together with the names of the pitchers who hit them, if a team uses more than one pitcher; (14) The number of wild pitches made; (15) The number of passed balls made by the catchers; (16) The name of the winning pitcher, if the winning team uses more than one pitcher; (17) The name of the losing pitcher, if the losing team uses more than one pitcher; (18) The names of the umpires, listed in this order: (a) plate umpire; (b) first base umpire; (c) second base umpire; (d) third base umpire; (19) The time of game with any delays for rain, fog, snow, light failure or violent wind storm deducted; (20) All individual and team records of any forfeited or tied game which has reached or exceeded legal length when ended shall become a part of the official averages except that no pitcher shall be credited with a victory or charged with a defeat; (21) A box score is in balance (or proved) when the total of a team's times at bat, bases on balls received, hit batters, sacrifices and batters awarded first base because of interference or obstruction equals the total of that team's runs, players left on base, and the other team's putouts.

Stolen Base A stolen base shall be credited to a runner whenever he advances one base unaided by a base hit, a putout, a forceout, a fielder's choice, a passed ball, a wild pitch or a balk, subject to the following exceptions:

If a double or triple steal is attempted and one runner is thrown out before reaching and holding the base he is attempting to steal, no other runner shall be credited with a stolen base;

A runner who is touched out after oversliding a base shall not be regarded as having stolen that base.

If it is the scorer's judgment that a palpable muff of a thrown ball prevents a runner who is attempting to steal from being retired, it shall be scored as an error for the player muffing the throw, an assist for the player throwing the ball, and not a stolen base.

No stolen base shall be scored when a runner advances solely because of the defensive team's indifference to his advancement.

If a runner advances while the defensive team, unsuccessfully, is attempting to retire another runner who, in attempting to steal, evades being put out in a rundown play and returns to the base he originally occupied, a stolen base shall be credited to the runner who so advances.

If a runner has started for a succeeding base before the pitcher delivers the ball and the pitch results in a wild pitch or a passed ball, credit the runner with a stolen base with this exception: If another runner also advances because of the pitch becoming a wild pitch or passed ball, the wild pitch or passed ball also shall be scored.

If a runner, attempting to steal, is well advanced toward the base he is attempting to steal and a balk is called on the pitcher, credit the runner with a stolen base and do not score the balk unless another runner who is not attempting to steal is advanced by the balk.

Note: This paragraph was dropped in 1951.

Squeeze Play "Squeeze play" is the term designating a play when a team, with a runner on third base, attempts to score that runner by means of a bunt. It also is a "squeeze play" if an attempt is made to score a runner from second base by means of a bunt.

Strikeout A strikeout shall be scored whenever a pitcher delivers three legal pitches at which the batter swings and misses, or which the umpire decrees are strikes even though the batter may reach first base safely after the third strike by reason of a wild pitch or the catcher's failure to hold the ball.

A strikeout shall be scored whenever a batter bunts foul when there are two strikes against him, except that should the bunt result in a foul fly caught by the catcher or any other player it shall not be scored as a strikeout but as a regular foul-fly putout.

When a batter goes out of the game with two strikes against him and the substitute batter completes a strikeout, score it as a strikeout for the first batter. If the substitute batter completes the turn at bat in any other manner, score the action as having been that of the substitute batter.

Substitute Batter See last paragraph, *Strikeout.*

Triple Play A triple play is any three successive putouts which take place between the time a ball leaves a pitcher's hand and is returned to him while he is standing in the pitcher's box.

Wild Pitch A wild pitch shall be scored when a legally delivered ball is so high, or so wide, or so low that the catcher does not stop and control the ball by ordinary effort and, as a result, a runner, or runners, advance.

Any legally pitched ball which strikes the ground before reaching home plate and passes the catcher, permitting a runner, or runners, to advance shall be scored as a wild pitch.

Winning and Losing Pitcher Determining the winning and losing pitcher of a game often calls for much careful consideration.

Do not give the starting pitcher credit for a game won, even if the score is in his favor, unless he has pitched at least five innings when replaced.

The five-inning rule to determine a winning pitcher shall be in effect for all games of six or more innings. When a game is called after five innings of play the starting pitcher must have pitched at least four innings to be credited with the victory. If the starting pitcher is replaced (except in a five-inning game) before he has pitched five complete innings when his team is ahead, remains ahead to win, and more than one relief pitcher is used by his team, the scorer shall credit the victory (as among all relieving pitchers) to the pitcher whom the scorer considers to have done the most effective pitching. If, in a five-inning game, the starting pitcher is replaced before pitching four complete innings when his team is ahead, remains ahead to win, and more than one relief pitcher is used by his team, the scorer shall credit the victory (as among all relieving pitchers) to the pitcher whom the scorer considers to have done the most effective pitching.

Regardless of how many innings the first pitcher has pitched, he shall be charged with the loss of the game if he is replaced when his team is behind in the score, and his team thereafter fails to either tie the score or gain the lead.

If a pitcher retires from the game for a substitute batter, or a substitute runner, after pitching five or more innings and his team scores enough runs in the inning in which he is replaced to take the lead, those runs shall be credited to his benefit. Thus, if a pitcher is removed for a substitute batter or a substitute baserunner in any inning after the pitcher has pitched at least five complete innings and during the inning in which he is removed his team assumes the lead, he shall be credited with the victory if his team remains ahead until the finish of the game.

Examples: If the pitcher of the team first at bat is removed in the first half of the sixth inning for a substitute batter, or a substitute runner, and his team gains the lead in that inning and the relieving pitcher holds the lead through the last half of the ninth inning, the pitcher who was removed shall be credited with the victory; if the pitcher of the team last at bat is removed in the last half of the fifth inning for a substitute batter, or a substitute runner, and his team gains the lead in that inning with the relieving pitcher holding the lead through the ninth inning, the pitcher who was removed shall be credited with the victory.

1951

Base Hit When a batter apparently hits safely and a runner who is obliged to advance by reason of the batter becoming a baserunner misses touching the first base to which he is advancing and is called out on appeal, charge the batter with a time at bat but no hit.

Caught Stealing When records are kept of players caught stealing by catchers, credit the catcher with preventing a stolen base each time he traps a runner off any base with a thrown ball and, as a result of such throw, the runner is retired or would have been except for a subsequent error by any fielder, including the catcher. Runners who are retired in rundown plays started by the catcher trapping a runner off any base, or whose baserunning life is prolonged by an error after they have been trapped off base by the catcher, are to be included among those prevented from stealing by the catcher.

Championship To be designated as the leader of his league's pitchers in the minimum average number of earned runs allowed, a pitcher is required to pitch at least as many innings as the number of games scheduled for each team in his league. (This would be 154 innings in a major league.)

Error If a batter is awarded first base by an umpire because of interference by the catcher, charge the catcher with an error; if an umpire awards a runner or runners one or more bases because of interference or obstruction by any defensive player, charge the player who committed the interference or obstruction with one error, no matter how many bases the runner or runners are advanced.

An error is to be charged when a fielder, in violation of the playing rules, touches a thrown ball with his cap, glove, or uniform while such article is detached from its proper place.

Sacrifice   Score a sacrifice if, with less than two out, the batter advances one or more runners with a bunt and is retired at first base, or would have been retired except for a fielding error. In case a runner is forced out at any base on a bunt, it shall be scored as a time at bat but no sacrifice. Also score a sacrifice if, with less than two out, the fielders handle a bunted ball without error in attempting to force a preceding runner but fail to do so. Exception: When such an attempt is made to turn a bunt into a force-out of a preceding runner and fails and it is the scorer's judgment that perfect play would not have retired the batter at first base, it shall be scored as a one-base hit and not as a sacrifice.

Shutout   No pitcher shall be credited with pitching a shutout unless he pitches the complete game. When two or more pitchers combine to pitch a shutout, a notation to that effect should be included in the league's official pitching records.

Stolen Base   See *Caught Stealing*; also see 1950 *Stolen Base* entry.

Time at Bat   See *Base Hit*.

Winning and Losing Pitcher   Determining the winning and losing pitcher of a game in which a team uses more than one pitcher often calls for careful consideration. Scorers can be guided by these rules: (1) Credit the starting pitcher with a game won only if he has pitched at least five complete innings and his team not only is in the lead when he is replaced but remains in the lead the remainder of the game; (2) They "must pitch five complete innings" rule in respect to the starting pitcher shall be in effect for all games of six or more innings. When a game is ended after five innings of play the starting pitcher must have pitched at least four complete innings to be credited with a victory. As stated in 10.16 (a), the starting pitcher in a five-inning game can be credited with a victory only if his team is in the lead when he is replaced (after pitching at least four complete innings) and his team remains in the lead to the finish of the game; (3) Except in a five-inning game (when they "must pitch at least four complete innings" rule applies) if the winning team uses more than two pitchers and the starting pitcher has not pitched at least five complete innings the victory shall be awarded one of the relieving pitchers on this basis: (a) Once the opposing team assumes the lead, all pitchers who have pitched for the winning team up to that point are excluded from being credited with the victory with the exception that if the pitcher against whose pitching the opposing team gained the lead continues to pitch until his team regains the lead which it holds to the finish of the game that pitcher would be the winning pitcher; (b) If, after the starting pitcher is replaced before pitching at least five complete innings, the opposing team does not tie the score or take the lead, credit the victory to the relief pitcher deemed by the scorer to have done the most effective pitching; (c) Whenever the score is tied, the game becomes a new contest insofar as determining the winning and losing pitchers are concerned; (d) With one exception, no pitcher can be credited with a victory unless he is the pitcher of record when his team assumes a lead and maintains the lead to the finish of the game; (e) The exception to the foregoing is: Do not credit a game won to a relief pitcher who pitches briefly and ineffectively and is the pitcher of record when his team assumes a lead which it maintains over a period of innings to the finish of the game. If a succeeding relief pitcher pitches effectively in helping to main-

tain his team in the lead credit such relief pitcher with the victory.

Championship   The individual batting champion of any league shall be the player with the highest batting average, if he is credited with as many or more times at bat as the number of games scheduled for one club in his league during the season, multiplied by 2.6. However, if there is any player in a league with fewer than the required number of times at bat whose average would be the highest if he were charged with this required at-bat total, then that player shall be awarded the batting championship.

Putout   When a runner is declared out by an umpire for running out of line to avoid being tagged by the ball in the hands of a fielder, the putout shall be credited to the fielder whom the runner avoided; when a runner is called out for passing another runner, credit the putout to the fielder nearest the spot at which the violation took place.

There were no changes to the scoring rules this year.

Double Play   A double play is a play by the defense in which two offensive players are legally put out as a result of continuous action, providing there is no error between putouts.

Sacrifice   The following section was added to the rule regarding sacrifice bunts and flies: Also score a sacrifice if, with less than two out, the batter hits a fair fly ball which is caught, and a runner scores after the catch, or is dropped for an error, and a runner scores, if in the scorer's judgment, the runner could have scored after the catch had the fly been caught.

Scorer   To promote uniformity in keeping the records of championship games, scorers shall conform to the instructions of this scoring code, but in no case shall the scorer's decisions conflict with the playing rules.

Scoring Summary   Sacrifice flies and bunts are to be listed separately in the scoring summary.

Assist   Mere ineffective contact with the ball shall not be considered an assist. "Deflect" shall mean to slow down or change the direction of the ball and thereby effectively assist in retiring a batter or runner.

Do not credit an assist to the pitcher when, as the result of a legal pitch caught by the catcher, a runner is retired, as when the catcher picks a runner off base, throws out a runner trying to steal or tags a runner trying to steal home.

Do not credit an assist to a fielder whose wild throw permits a runner to advance, even though the runner subsequently is retired as a result of a continuous play. A play which follows an error is a new play, and the player making an error is not entitled to an assist unless he takes part in the new play.

Base Hit   A base hit shall be scored when a batter reaches first base safely on a fair ball which takes an unnatural bounce so that a fielder cannot handle it with ordinary effort, or which strikes the pitcher's plate or any base (including home plate) before being touched by a fielder and bounces so that a fielder cannot handle it with ordinary effort.

A base hit shall be scored when the fielder throws to another base in an unsuccessful attempt to retire a preceding runner, and in the scorer's judgment the batter-runner would not have been retired at first base by perfect fielding.

A base hit shall not be scored when a fielder fails in an attempt to retire a preceding runner, and in the scorer's judgment the batter-runner could have been retired at first base.

A base hit shall not be scored when a fielder handles a batted ball and retires a preceding runner, or would have retired one with ordinary effort except for a fielding error. Charge the batter with a time at bat but no hit.

Note: This shall not apply if the fielder merely looks toward or feints toward another base before attempting to make the putout at first base.

Base Hit/Value Whether a safe hit shall be scored as a one-base hit, two-base hit, or three-base hit when no error or putout results, shall be determined as follows: When, with one or more runners on base, the batter advances more than one base on a safe hit and the defensive team makes an attempt to retire a preceding runner, the scorer shall determine whether the batter made a legitimate two-base hit or three-base hit, or whether he advanced beyond first base on the fielder's choice.

Note: The rules of 1955 include a series of examples to illustrate the application of this rule for the guidance of the scorer.

When the batter attempts to make a two-base hit or a three-base hit by sliding, he must hold the last base to which he advances. If he overslides and is tagged out before getting back to the base safely, he shall be credited with only as many bases as he attained safely. If he overslides second base and is tagged out, he shall be credited with a one-base hit; if he overslides third base and is tagged out he shall be credited with a two-base hit.

Note: If the batter overruns second or third base and is tagged out trying to return, he shall be credited with the last base he touched. If he runs past second base after reaching that base on his feet, attempts to return and is tagged out, he shall be credited with a two-base hit. If he runs past third base after reaching that base on his feet, attempts to return and is tagged out, he shall be credited with a three-base hit.

Subject to provisions of the playing rules, when the batter ends a game with a safe hit which drives in as many runs as are necessary to put his team in the lead, he shall be credited with only as many bases on his hit as are advanced by the runner who scores the winning run, and then only if the batter runs out his hit for as many bases as are advanced by the runner who scores the winning run, touching each base in proper order.

Note: Apply this rule even when the batter is theoretically entitled to more bases because of being awarded an "automatic" extra-base hit under various provisions of the playing rules.

Base on Balls A base on balls shall be scored whenever a batter is awarded first base because of four balls having been pitched outside the strike zone, but when the fourth such ball strikes the batter it shall be scored as a "hit batter."

Note: The scoring rules contain detailed instructions for charging runners who receive a base on balls when the pitcher is changed in mid-batter.

Batter/Out of Turn When a player bats out of turn, and is put out, and the proper batter is called out before the ball is pitched to the next batter, charge the proper batter with a time at bat and score the putout and any assists the same as if the correct batting order had been followed. If an improper batter becomes a runner by reason of a hit, error, fielder's choice, hit batter, base on balls, interference or obstruction, and the proper batter is called out for having missed his turn at bat, charge the proper batter with a time at bat, credit the putout to the catcher, and ignore everything entering into the improper batter's safe arrival on base. If more than one batter bats out of turn in succession, score all plays just as they occur, skipping the turn at bat of the player or players who first missed batting in the proper order.

Box Score A box score is in balance (or proved) when the total of the team's times at bat, bases on balls received, hit batters, sacrifice bunts, sacrifice flies, and batters awarded first base because of interference or obstruction, equals the total of that team's runs, players left on base, and the opposing team's putouts.

Caught Stealing Do not credit the catcher with a man "caught stealing" when he traps a runner off base after fielding a batted ball or on any play started by another fielder.

Championship The individual fielding champions shall be the fielders with the highest fielding average at each position, subject to the following: (1) A catcher must have participated as a catcher in at least 90 games (80 games in leagues playing schedules of 140 games or less); (2) An infielder or outfielder must have participated at his position in at least 100 games (90 games in leagues playing schedules of 140 games or less); (3) A pitcher must have pitched in at least as many innings as the number of games scheduled for each club in his league that season.

Earned Run The scoring rules of 1955 contain detailed provisions for charging runners and runs to starting pitchers and relief pitchers where pitching changes are made in mid-batter.

No run can be earned which scores as a result of the batter reaching first base (1) on a hit or otherwise after his time at bat is prolonged by a muffed foul fly; (2) because of interference or obstruction; or (3) because of any fielding error, except for a wild pitch charged as an error.

Error Slow handling of the ball which does not involve mechanical misplay shall not be construed as an error.

An error shall be charged against any fielder when he muffs a foul fly, to prolong the time at bat of the batter, whether the batter subsequently reaches first base or is retired.

If a runner advances on a throw by a fielder, and in the scorer's judgment there was no occasion for the throw, an error shall be charged to the fielder making the unnecessary throw.

An error shall be charged against any fielder whose throw takes an unnatural bounce, or strikes a base or the pitcher's plate, or strikes a runner, a fielder or an umpire, thereby permitting any runner to advance.

Note: Apply this rule even when it appears to be an injustice to a fielder whose throw was accurately directed. Every base advanced by a runner must be accounted for.

When an umpire awards the batter or any runner or runners one or more bases because of interference or obstruction, charge the fielder who committed the interference or obstruction with one error, no matter how many bases the batter, or runner or runners, may be advanced.

No error shall be charged against the catcher when he makes a wild throw in attempting to prevent a stolen base, unless such wild throw permits the base stealer to advance one or more extra bases, or in the scorer's judgment permits another runner to advance one or more bases. Charge only one error on such a wild throw, regardless of the number of bases advanced by the runner or runners.

No error shall be charged against any fielder when he makes a wild throw in attempting to prevent a runner's advance, unless in the scorer's judgment such wild throw permits the runner to advance beyond the base he would have reached had the throw not been wild, or permits any other runner to advance one or more bases beyond the base he would have reached had the throw not been wild. Charge only one error on such wild throw, regardless of the number of bases advanced by the runner or runners.

See also *Wild Pitch*.

Fielder's choice Fielder's choice is the act of a fielder who handles a fair grounder and, instead of throwing to first base to retire the batter-runner, throws to another base in an attempt to retire a preceding runner. The term is also used by scorers (1) to account for the advance of the batter-runner who takes one or more extra bases when the fielder who handles his safe hit attempts to retire a preceding runner; and (2) to account for the advance of a runner (other than by stolen base or error) while a fielder is attempting to retire another runner.

Note: This definition appears in the Playing Rules for 1955.

Game-Ending Hit   See last paragraph, *Base Hit/Value*.

Putout   When a runner is called out for running the bases in reverse order, credit the putout to the fielder covering the base he left in starting his reverse run. Do not credit any assist on such plays.

When the batter-runner is called out because of interference by a preceding runner, credit the putout to the first baseman. If the fielder interfered with was in the act of throwing the ball, credit him with an assist, but credit only one assist on any one play.

Run Batted In   A run batted in is a run which reaches home base safely because of a safe hit, a sacrifice bunt, a sacrifice fly, a putout via a foul fly, an infield putout, or a fielder's choice; or which is forced over home plate by reason of the batter being struck by a pitched ball, or being awarded a base on balls, or being awarded first base because of interference or obstruction. If a batter hits a home run always score the home run as a run batted in. Also count all other runs which score ahead of the batter who hit the home run as runs batted in. If, with less than two out, an error is made on a play on which a runner from third base ordinarily would score and does score, credit the batter with a run batted in.

Sacrifice   Score a sacrifice bunt when, with less than two outs, the fielders handle a bunted ball without error in an unsuccessful attempt to retire a preceding runner advancing one base. Exception: When an attempt to turn a bunt into a putout of a preceding runner fails, and in the scorer's judgment perfect play would not have retired the batter at first base, the batter shall be credited with a one-base hit and not a sacrifice.

Do not score a sacrifice bunt when a runner is retired attempting to advance one base on a bunt. Charge the batter with a time at bat.

Scorer   The Official Scorer shall keep records of each game as outlined in the scoring rules. He shall have sole authority to make all decisions involving judgment, such as whether a batter's advance to first base is the result of a hit or an error. In no event shall a scorer make a decision conflicting with the Official Playing Rules or with an umpire's decision.

Scoring Summary   The scoring summary shall contain: (1) Number of runners left on base by each team. This total shall include all runners who get on base by any means and who do not score and are not put out. Include in this total a batter-runner whose batted ball results in another runner being retired for the third out; (2) Total number of bases on balls issued by each pitcher and a separate listing of the number of intentional bases on balls issued by each pitcher.

The scoring rules of 1955 also include detailed instructions for notations to the tabulated game records. It is recommended that letters a, b, c, d, etc., be used in the notations as symbols for substitute batters and that numerals 1, 2, 3, 4, etc., be used as symbols for substitute runners. Also the instructions detail notations needed when a substitute is announced but removed for another substitute before he actually enters the game.

Stolen Base   A stolen base shall be credited to a runner whenever he advances one base unaided by a base hit, a putout, an error, a force-out, a fielder's choice, a passed ball, a wild pitch or a balk, subject to the following: When a runner, attempting to steal, evades being put out in a rundown play and advances to the next base without the aid of an error, credit the runner with a stolen base. If another runner also advances on the play, credit both runners with stolen bases. If a runner advances while another runner, attempting to steal, evades being put out in a rundown play and returns safely, without the aid of an error, to

the base he originally occupied, credit a stolen base to the runner who advances.

Strikeout   A strikeout shall be scored whenever a pitcher delivers three legal pitches at which the batter swings and misses, or which the umpire decrees are strikes. A strikeout shall be scored even though the batter reaches first base safely after the third strike because of an error by the pitcher or catcher as defined in the scoring rules.

Wild Pitch   When the batter's fourth called ball is a wild pitch and as a result (1) the batter-runner advances to a base beyond first base; (2) any runner, forced to advance by reason of the batter becoming a runner, advances more than one base; or (3) any runner, not forced to advance by reason of the batter becoming a runner, advances one or more bases, score the base on balls and also an error for the pitcher and do not score a wild pitch.

When the batter swings at a wild pitch for his third strike and thereby is enabled to reach first base, score a strikeout and also an error for the pitcher, and do not score a wild pitch.

When the batter swings at a wild pitch for his third strike or when the catcher muffs a third strike, if the catcher recovers the ball and throws out the batter-runner trying to reach first base, but another runner or runners advance, score the strikeout and error the same as if the batter had reached first base. Credit an assist to the catcher, and a putout to the fielder taking the throw at first base.

Winning and Losing Pitcher   In some non-championship games (such as the Major League All-Star Game) it is provided in advance that each pitcher shall work a stated number of innings, usually two or three. In such games, it is customary to credit the victory to the pitcher of record, whether starter or reliever, when the winning team takes a lead which it maintains to the end of the game, unless such pitcher is knocked out after the winning team has a commanding lead, and the scorer believes a subsequent pitcher is entitled to credit for the victory.

1956

Base Hit   A base hit should be scored when the fielder unsuccessfully attempts to retire a preceding runner, and, in the scorer's judgment, the batter-runner would not have been retired at first base by perfect fielding.

Also see *Time at Bat*.

Run Batted In   The batter shall not be credited with a run batted in if a run scores when he grounds into a force double play, or grounds into a double play in which the first out is made at first base and the second out made by tagging a runner who was originally forced, attempting to advance one base.

Time at Bat   When a fielder handles a batted ball and retires a preceding runner who is attempting to advance one base, or would have retired one with ordinary effort except for a fielding error, charge the batter with a time at bat but no hit.

1957

Base Hit   A base hit shall be scored when a batter reaches first base safely on a fair ball hit with such force, or so slowly, that any fielder attempting to make a play with it has no opportunity to do so.

Note: A hit shall be scored if the fielder attempting to handle the ball cannot make a play, even if such fielder deflects the ball from or cuts off another fielder who could have retired a runner.

Also see *Time at Bat*.

Championship   To assure uniformity in establishing the batting, pitching and fielding championship of professional leagues, such champions shall meet the following minimum performance standards: The individual batting champion shall be the player with the highest batting average, provided he is credited with as many or more total appearances at the plate in league championship games as the number of games scheduled for each club in the league that season, multiplied by 3.1. Total appearances at the plate shall include official times at bat, plus bases on balls, times hit by pitcher, sacrifice hits, sacrifice flies and times awarded first base because of interference or obstruction.

Earned Run   An earned run shall be scored every time a runner reaches home base by the aid of safe hits, sacrifice bunts, a sacrifice fly, stolen bases, putouts, fielder's choices, bases on balls, hit batters, balks or wild pitches (including a wild pitch on third strike which permits a batter to reach first base) before fielding chances have been offered to retire the offensive team.

Note: A wild pitch is solely the pitcher's fault, and contributes to an earned run just as a base on balls or a balk.

No run can be earned which scores as a result of the batter reaching base (1) on a hit or otherwise after his time at bat is prolonged by a muffed foul fly; (2) because of interference or obstruction; or (3) because of any fielding error.

An error by the pitcher is treated exactly the same as an error by any other fielder in computing earned runs.

Error   No error shall be charged to any fielder who permits a foul fly to fall safe with a runner on third base before two are out, if in the scorer's judgment the fielder deliberately refuses the catch in order that the runner on third shall not score after the catch.

Because the pitcher and catcher handle the ball much more than other fielders, certain misplays on pitched balls are called "wild pitches" and "passed balls," and are defined elsewhere in the scoring rules. No error shall be charged when a wild pitch or passed ball is scored. No error shall be charged when the batter is awarded first base on four called balls or because he was touched by a pitched ball, or when he reaches first base as the result of a wild pitch or passed ball. When the third strike is a wild pitch, permitting the batter to reach first base, score a strikeout and a wild pitch. When the third strike is a passed ball, permitting the batter to reach first base, score a strikeout and a passed ball.

Passed Ball   See second paragraph, *Error*.

Run Batted In   Scorer's judgment must determine whether a run batted in shall be credited for a run which scores when a fielder holds the ball, or throws to a wrong base. Ordinarily, if the runner keeps going, credit a run batted in; if the runner stops and takes off again when he notices the misplay, credit the run as scored on a fielder's choice.

Scorer   The league president shall appoint an official scorer for each league championship game. The official scorer shall observe the game from a position in the press box. The scorer shall have sole authority to make all decisions involving judgment, such as whether a batter's advance to first base is the result of a hit or an error. He shall communicate such decisions to the press box and broadcasting booths by hand signals or over the press box loudspeaker system, and shall advise the public address announcer of such decisions if requested.

After each game, including drawn, forfeited and called games, the scorer shall prepare a report, on a form prescribed by the league president, listing the date of the game, where it was played, the names of the competing clubs and the umpires, the full score of the game, and all records of individual players compiled according to the system specified in these Official Scoring Rules. He shall forward this report to the league office within 36 hours after the game ends. He shall forward the report of any suspended game within 36 hours after the game has been completed, or after it becomes an official game because it cannot be completed, as provided by the Official Playing Rules.

To achieve uniformity in keeping the records of championship games, the scorer shall conform strictly to the Official Scoring Rules.

If the teams change sides before three men are put out, the scorer shall immediately inform the umpire of the mistake.

If the game is protested or suspended, the scorer shall make note of the exact situation at the time of the protest or suspension, including the score, the number of outs, the position of any runners, and the ball and strike count on the batter.

Note: It is important that a suspended game resume with exactly the same situation as existed at the time of suspension. If a protested game is ordered replayed from the point of protest, it must be resumed with exactly the situation that existed just before the protested play.

The scorer shall not make any decision conflicting with the Official Playing Rules or with an umpire's decision.

The scorer shall not call the attention of the umpire or of any member of either team to the fact that a player is batting out of turn.

The scorer is an official representative of the league, and is entitled to the respect and dignity of his office, and shall be accorded full protection by the league president. The scorer shall report to the president any indignity expressed by any manager, player, club employee or club officer in the course of, or as the result of, the discharge of his duties.

The umpire-in-chief shall inform the official scorer of the official batting order, and any changes in the lineups and batting order, on request.

Wild Pitch   See second paragraph, *Error*.

Winning and Losing Pitcher   Regardless of how many innings the first pitcher has pitched, he shall be charged with the loss of the game if he is replaced when his team is behind in the score, and his team thereafter fails either to tie the score or gain the lead.

1958

Championship   The individual fielding champions shall be the fielders with the highest fielding average at each position, provided: (1) A catcher must have participated as a catcher in at least one-half the number of games scheduled for each club in his league that season; (2) An infielder or outfielder must have participated at his position in at least two-thirds of the number of games scheduled for each club in his league that season; (3) A pitcher must have pitched at least as many innings as the number of games scheduled for each club in his league that season.

Percentage   To compute the pitcher's earned run average, multiply the total earned runs charged against his pitching by 9, and divide the result by the total number of innings he pitched.

Sacrifice   Score a sacrifice fly when, before two are out, the batter hits a fair fly ball which: (1) is caught, and a runner scores after the catch, or (2) is dropped, and a runner scores, if, in the scorer's judgment, the runner could have scored after the catch had the fly been caught.

Note: Score a sacrifice fly in accordance with the scoring rules even though another runner is forced out by reason of the batter becoming a runner.

1959–64

There were no changes to the scoring rules in these years.

1965

Championship   To qualify for the fielding championship at his position a pitcher must have pitched at least as many innings as the number of games scheduled for each club in his league that season. Exception: If another pitcher has a fielding average as high or higher, and has handled more total chances in a lesser number of innings, he shall be the fielding champion.

1966

There were no changes to the scoring rules this year.

1967

Championship The individual batting champion shall be the player with the highest batting average, provided he is credited with as many or more total appearances at the plate in league championship games as the number of games scheduled for each club in his league that season, multiplied by 3.1. Exception: However, if there is any player with fewer than the required number of plate appearances whose average would be highest if he were charged with the required number of plate appearances or official at-bats, then that player shall be awarded the batting championship.

Error Mental mistakes or misjudgments are not to be scored as errors unless specifically covered in the rules.

No error shall be charged against any fielder when, after fumbling a ground ball or dropping a fly ball, a line drive or a thrown ball, he recovers the ball in time to force out a runner at any base.

Sacrifice Do not score a sacrifice bunt when, in the judgment of the scorer, the batter is bunting for a base hit and not solely for the purpose of advancing a runner or runners. Charge the batter with a time at bat.

Note: In applying this rule always give the batter the benefit of the doubt.

Stolen Base When a runner, attempting to steal, or after being picked off base, evades being put out in a rundown play and advances to the next base without the aid of an error, credit the runner with a stolen base. If another runner also advances on the play, credit both runners with stolen bases. If a runner advances while another runner, attempting to steal, evades being put out in a rundown play and returns safely, without the aid of an error, to the base he originally occupied, credit a stolen base to the runner who advances.

1968

There were no changes to the scoring rules this year.

1969

Double Play/Triple Play Credit participation in the double play or triple play to each fielder who earns a putout or an assist when two or three players are put out between the time a pitch is delivered and the time the ball next becomes dead or is next in possession of the pitcher in pitching position, unless an error or misplay intervenes between putouts.

Note: Credit the double play or triple play also if an appeal play after the ball is in possession of the pitcher results in an additional putout.

Earned Run An earned run is a run for which the pitcher is held accountable. In determining earned runs, the inning should be reconstructed without the errors and passed balls, and the benefit of the doubt should always be given to the pitcher in determining which bases would have been reached by errorless play.

When pitchers are changed during an inning, the relief pitcher shall not have the benefit of previous chances for outs not accepted in determining earned runs.

Note: It is the intent of this rule to prevent relief pitchers from not being charged with earned runs for which they are solely responsible.

Error When an umpire awards the batter or any runner or runners one or more bases because of interference or obstruction, charge the fielder who committed the interference or obstruction with one error, no matter how many bases the batter, or runner or runners, may be advanced.

Note: Do not charge an error if obstruction does not change the play in the opinion of the scorer.

Relief Pitcher See *Earned Run*, second paragraph.

Sacrifice Do not score a sacrifice bunt when, in the judgment of the scorer, the batter is bunting *primarily* for a base hit and not for the purpose of advancing a runner or runners. Charge the batter with a time at bat.

Note: In applying this rule always give the batter the benefit of the doubt.

Note: The rule is the same as that appearing in the 1967 scoring rules with the addition of the word *primarily*.

Save Credit a save to a relief pitcher who enters a game with his team in the lead if he holds the lead the remainder of the game, provided he is not credited with the victory. A relief pitcher cannot be credited with a save if he does not finish the game unless he is removed for a pinch hitter or pinch runner. When more than one relief pitcher qualifies for a save under the provisions of this rule, credit the save to the relief pitcher judged by the scorer to have been the most effective. Only one save can be credited in any game.

1970–72

There were no changes to the scoring rules in these years.

1973

Save A pitcher shall be credited with a save when, in entering a game as a relief pitcher, he finds the potential tying or winning run either on base or at the plate or pitches at least three or more effective innings and, in either case, preserves the lead.

1974

Hitting/Playing Streaks A consecutive hitting streak shall not be terminated if the plate appearance results in a base on balls, hit batsman, defensive interference or a sacrifice bunt.

A sacrifice fly shall terminate the streak.

A consecutive-game hitting streak shall not be terminated if all the player's plate appearances (one or more) result in a base on balls, hit batsman, defensive interference or a sacrifice bunt. The streak shall terminate if the player has a sacrifice fly and no hit.

A consecutive-game playing streak shall be extended if the player plays one half-inning on defense, or if he completes a time at bat by reaching base or being put out. A pinch-running appearance only shall not extend the streak. If a player is ejected from a game by an umpire before he can comply with the requirements of this rule, his streak shall continue.

Suspended Game For the purpose of the scoring rules, all performances in the completion of a suspended game shall be considered as occurring on the original date of the game.

1975

Sacrifice Score a sacrifice fly when, before two are out, the batter hits a fly ball or a line drive handled by an outfielder or an infielder running in the outfield which: (1) is caught, and a runner scores after the catch, or (2) is dropped, and a runner scores, if in the scorer's judgment the runner could have scored after the catch had the fly been caught.

Note: Score a sacrifice fly in accordance with the scoring rules even though another runner is forced out by reason of the batter becoming a runner.

Save Credit a pitcher with a save when he meets all three of the following conditions: (1) He is the finishing pitcher in a game won by his club; and (2) He is not the winning pitcher; and (3) He qualifies under one of the following conditions: (a) He enters the game with a lead of no more than three runs and pitches for at least one inning; or (b) He enters the game with the potential tying run either on base, or at bat, or on deck (that is, the potential tying run is either already on base or is one of the first two batsmen he faces); or (c) He pitches effectively for at least three innings. No more than one save may be credited in each game.

1976

Base on Balls See *Strikeout*.

Earned Run An earned run is a run for which the pitcher is held accountable. In determining earned runs, the inning should be reconstructed without the errors (which includes catcher's interference) and passed balls, and the benefit of the doubt should always be given to the pitcher in determining which bases would have been reached by errorless play.

When pitchers are changed during an inning, the relief pitcher shall not be charged with any run (earned or unearned) scored by a runner who was on base at the time he entered the game, nor for runs scored by any runner who reaches base on a fielder's choice which puts out a runner left on base by the preceding pitcher.

Note: It is the intent of this rule to charge each pitcher with the number of runners he put on base, rather than with the individual runners. When a pitcher puts runners on base and is relieved, he shall be charged with all runs subsequently scored up to and including the number of runners he left on base when he left the game, unless such runners are put out without action by the batter, i.e., caught stealing, picked off base, or called out for interference when a batter-runner does not reach first base on the play. Exception: The pitcher walks batter A and is relieved. The relief pitcher allows B to single, but runner A is out trying for third. Runner B takes second on the throw. Batter C singles, scoring runner B. Charge the run to the relief pitcher rather than the preceding pitcher.

Game Played When a player listed in the starting lineup for the visiting club is substituted for before he plays defensively, he shall not receive credit in the defensive statistics (fielding), unless he actually plays that position during a game. All such players, however, shall be credited with one game played (in batting statistics) as long as they are announced into the game or listed on the official lineup card.

Percentage For purposes of earned run average calculations and innings pitched totals, innings pitched shall be rounded off to the nearest whole inning. Examples: 200⅓ innings becomes 200; 200⅔ becomes 201.

Note: This standard was changed in 1982 and fractions were no longer rounded off but counted for their full value. Also see rule addition under 1981.

Relief Pitcher See *Earned Run*, second paragraph.

Scoring Summary The name of a pitcher credited with a save is to be shown on the scoring summary.

Strikeout When the batter leaves the game with two strikes against him, and the substitute batter completes a strikeout, charge the strikeout and the time at bat to the first batter. If the substitute batter completes the turn at bat in any other manner, including a base on balls, score the action as having been that of the substitute batter.

Substitute Batter See *Strikeout*.

1977

Base on Balls Intentional base on balls shall be scored when the pitcher makes no attempt to throw the last pitch to the batter into the strike zone but purposely throws the ball wide to the catcher outside the catcher's box.

1978

There were no changes to the scoring rules this year.

1979

Caught Stealing A runner shall be charged as "caught stealing" if he is put out, or would have been put out by errorless play, when he (1) tries to steal; (2) is picked off a base and tries

to advance (any move toward the next base shall be considered an attempt to advance); (3) overslides while stealing.

Note: In those instances where a pitched ball eludes the catcher and the runner is put out trying to advance, no caught stealing shall be charged.

Earned Run An earned run is a run for which the pitcher is held accountable. In determining earned runs, the inning should be reconstructed without the errors (which include catcher's interference) and passed balls, and the benefit of the doubt should always be given to the pitcher in determining which bases would have been reached by errorless play. For the purpose of determining earned runs, an intentional base on balls, regardless of the circumstances, shall be construed in exactly the same manner as any other base on balls.

Scorer The official scorer must make all decisions concerning judgment calls within twenty-four (24) hours after a game has been officially concluded. No judgment decision shall be changed thereafter except, upon immediate application to the league president, the scorer may request a change, citing the reasons for such. In all cases the official scorer is not permitted to make a scoring decision which is in conflict with the scoring rules.

1980

Run Batted In Game-winning RBI is credited for the RBI that gives a club the lead it never relinquishes.

Note: There does not have to be a game-winning RBI in every game and all game-winning RBIs must conform to the scoring rule governing RBIs.

1981

Percentage For purposes of earned run average calculations and innings pitched totals, do not round off the fraction where a pitcher has only ⅓ of an inning for the entire season. In such cases carry his total for innings pitched as ⅓.

1982

Percentage Earned run averages shall be calculated on the basis of total innings pitched, including fractional innings. Example: 9⅓ innings pitched and three earned runs is an earned run average of 2.89 (3 ER times 9 divided by 9⅓ equals 2.89).

1983

Championship The individual batting champion or slugging champion shall be the player with the highest batting average or slugging percentage, provided he is credited with as many or more total appearances at the plate in League championship games as the number of games scheduled for each club in his League that season, multiplied by 3.1 in the case of a major league player. Exception: However, if there is any player with fewer than the required number of plate appearances or official at-bats, but who, when credited with an out for each of his deficient at-bats, still has the highest average, then that player shall be awarded the batting championship or slugging championship.

1984

Percentage To compute on-base percentage, divide the total of hits, all bases on balls, and hit by pitch, by the total of at-bats, all bases on balls, hit by pitch, and sacrifice flies.

Note: For the purpose of computing on-base percentage, ignore being awarded first base on interference or obstruction.

1985–88

There were no changes to the scoring rules this year.

1989

Run Batted In The game-winning RBI is dropped from the rule book.

Game Scores, 1982-94

Robert L. Tiemann and Arnold Braunstein

This new feature in *Total Baseball* should prove invaluable to researchers and fans alike. What *was* the score of that game ten years ago, the one in which your son or daughter first set foot in a major league park? How many games did the fledgling Colorado Rockies take from the Atlanta Braves in their inaugural year? What were the scores of the Giants' crucial season-ending series with Dodgers that same year?

It's all here, day by day, and coded in a simple fashion that will enable the reader to identify the date, the score, the winner, the loser, and the site of the game. The four-digit date in column one represents month and day, so that "0509" stands for May 9, "1002" stands for October 2, and so on. The visiting team is always listed first, and so is the visitor's score. As an additional finding aid, an asterisk (*) between the run totals indicates a victory by the visitor, while a dash (–) indicates a win for the host. In rare instances, an equal sign (=) indicates a tie game, ruled complete and not resumed at a later date. A pound sign (#) indicates a suspended game that was completed later. The second games of doubleheaders may be easily spotted by looking for blanks in column one, then reading across.

Note that for all the years shown, the American League has had fourteen teams, thus yielding up to seven games on a given day. The National League had twelve teams in 1969-93, explaining why the column for "Game 7" is blank for the years 1982-92. In future editions of *Total Baseball,* we will provide game scores for earlier periods.

American League

◆1982◆	GAME 1		GAME 2		GAME 3		GAME 4		GAME 5		GAME 6		GAME 7	
0405	KC-BAL	5-13												
0406	SEA-MIN	11*7	CAL-OAK	2-3										
0407	SEA-MIN	5-7	CAL-OAK	7*0										
0408	SEA-MIN	1-4	CAL-OAK	8*6										
0409	CAL-MIN	1-2	SEA-OAK	3-5	DET-KC	2-4	MIL-TOR	15*4						
0410	CAL-MIN	8*1	TEX-CLE	8*3	DET-KC	2-5	MIL-TOR	2-3	BOS-BAL	2*0				
									BOS-BAL	3-5				
0411	TEX-CLE	1-13	DET-KC	2*1	CAL-MIN	1-3	MIL-TOR	14*5	BOS-BAL	6*0	CHI-NY	7*6	SEA-OAK	6*3
											CHI-NY	2*0	SEA-OAK	1-3
0412	CHI-BOS	3*2	NY-TEX	10*7	DET-TOR	5-9								
0413	SEA-CAL	3#3	NY-TEX	6*3	DET-TOR	4*2	MIL-CLE	9*8	BAL-KC	5-6	OAK-MIN	8*3		
0414	SEA-CAL	3-4	NY-TEX	1-4	DET-TOR	4-5	MIL-CLE	2-6	BAL-KC	3-4	OAK-MIN	7*5	CHI-BOS	5*4
	SEA-CAL	1-2												
0415	SEA-CAL	2-3	CHI-BOS	8*4	MIL-CLE	1-8	TOR-DET	2-4	OAK-MIN	5-11				
0416	MIN-CAL	2-4	TOR-BOS	2*0	KC-CLE	3*1	NY-DET	10*2	TEX-MIL	4*1	OAK-SEA	0-5		
0417	MIN-CAL	2-6	TOR-BOS	4-5	KC-CLE	12*10	NY-DET	3-5	TEX-MIL	5*3	OAK-SEA	10*3	BAL-CHI	1-3
													BAL-CHI	6-10
0418	TOR-BOS	3-4	MIN-CAL	2-5	KC-CLE	2-8	NY-DET	2-5	TEX-MIL	9*6	OAK-SEA	3-4	BAL-CHI	4-6
0419	TOR-BOS	5*4	MIN-OAK	5*2			KC-DET	2-3			CAL-SEA	3*1		
0420	BAL-BOS	3-8	MIN-OAK	3-4	NY-CHI	11*2	KC-DET	0-8	CLE-TEX	9*4	CAL-SEA	4-6		
0421	BAL-BOS	5-6	MIN-OAK	2-5	NY-CHI	1*0	KC-DET	1-4	CLE-TEX	2-4	CAL-SEA	3-5	TOR-MIL	1-3
0422	DET-NY	3*1							CLE-TEX	4*3	MIN-SEA	4-8	TOR-MIL	0-7
0423	DET-NY	9*1	CHI-BAL	4*2	OAK-CAL	2-7	CLE-KC	6-11	MIL-TEX	2*1	MIN-SEA	12*4	BOS-TOR	5*4
0424	DET-NY	7*2	CHI-BAL	4-7	OAK-CAL	2-4	CLE-KC	1-5	MIL-TEX	4*1	MIN-SEA	2-3	BOS-TOR	8*7
0425	DET-NY	1-3	CHI-BAL	1-2	OAK-CAL	1-5	CLE-KC	3-6	MIL-TEX	11*6	MIN-SEA	4-5	BOS-TOR	5*4
0426	BOS-CHI	3*2												
	BOS-CHI	5*0												
0427	KC-BOS	5-7	SEA-CLE	7*4	CHI-MIL	11*2	DET-MIN	5*2	CAL-NY	3*1	TEX-TOR	4-8		
0428	KC-BOS	8*5	SEA-CLE	1-6	CHI-MIL	1-2	DET-MIN	2-4	CAL-NY	0-6	TEX-TOR	4-6	OAK-BAL	6*2
													OAK-BAL	1-5
0429	DET-CHI	2-3	SEA-CLE	1-5	TOR-KC	7*0	CAL-NY	2*0					OAK-BAL	9*6
0430	DET-CHI	6*4	OAK-CLE	8*0	TOR-KC	7-8	SEA-NY	6*3	TEX-BOS	1-7	MIL-MIN	4-7	CAL-BAL	4-9
0501	DET-CHI	5*2	OAK-CLE	8*2	TOR-KC	7-8	SEA-NY	1-5	TEX-BOS	5-6	MIL-MIN	6*5	CAL-BAL	6*4
0502	DET-CHI	3-10	OAK-CLE	5*2	TOR-KC	7*5	SEA-NY	2-4	TEX-BOS	0-6	MIL-MIN	11*4	CAL-BAL	4-6
0503	KC-MIL	3*2	CAL-CLE	5*4			OAK-NY	5*2	MIN-BOS	2-6			SEA-BAL	0-6
0504	KC-MIL	5-9	CAL-CLE	5-6	TOR-CHI	3-4	OAK-NY	9*7	MIN-BOS	3-5	TEX-DET	3-4	SEA-BAL	4*3
0505	KC-MIL	3*2			TOR-CHI	1-4			MIN-BOS	3*2	TEX-DET	4-6		
0506	MIN-MIL	3-6	BAL-CAL	9*2	CLE-OAK	2-4	NY-SEA	3-7	BOS-TEX	5*2				
0507	MIN-MIL	1-4	BAL-CAL	5*3	CLE-OAK	15*6	NY-SEA	2-5	BOS-TEX	0-1	CHI-DET	8*5	KC-TOR	4-6
0508	MIN-MIL	1-12	BAL-CAL	2-7	CLE-OAK	8*5	NY-SEA	9*4	BOS-TEX	2*1	CHI-DET	7*4	KC-TOR	1-2
0509	MIN-MIL	2-6	BAL-CAL	4-8	CLE-OAK	14*2	NY-SEA	3*0	BOS-TEX	1*0	CHI-DET	4*3	KC-TOR	0-2
0510	MIL-KC	2-3	NY-CAL	1-2	BAL-OAK	6-7	CLE-SEA	4-6	DET-TEX	3*1	BOS-MIN	9*5	CHI-TOR	6*3
0511	MIL-KC	3-17	NY-CAL	3*2	BAL-OAK	7*1	CLE-SEA	5*4			BOS-MIN	6-10	CHI-TOR	4-9
0512	MIL-KC	7-9	NY-CAL	6*5	BAL-OAK	4-5	CLE-SEA	8*5			BOS-MIN	4*1	CHI-TOR	9*2
0513	BOS-KC	2-11	CLE-CAL	2-3	NY-OAK	6*4	BAL-SEA	3*1	MIL-CHI	2-13	MIN-DET	2-6	TOR-TEX	3-4
0514			CLE-CAL	2-5	NY-OAK	7*4	BAL-SEA	11*4	MIL-CHI	2*1	MIN-DET	2-4	TOR-TEX	3-4
0515	BOS-KC	10*5	CLE-CAL	6-9	NY-OAK	3-7	BAL-SEA	2-3	MIL-CHI	8*3	MIN-DET	4-5	TOR-TEX	5*2
0516	BOS-KC	0-5	CLE-CAL	0-3	NY-OAK	6-7	BAL-SEA	5*4	MIL-CHI	1-6	MIN-DET	6-7	TOR-TEX	1-2
0517	NY-KC	0-7							TEX-CHI	6-8				
0518	NY-KC	6*2	MIN-BAL	8*7	SEA-BOS	3*0	TOR-CLE	5-6	TEX-CHI	2-10	OAK-DET	9-11	CAL-MIL	4*1
0519	NY-KC	3*2	MIN-BAL	2-4	SEA-BOS	5-6	TOR-CLE	8*5	TEX-CHI	5-6	OAK-DET	3-6	CAL-MIL	7*2
0520			MIN-BAL	0-6	SEA-BOS	2-11	TOR-CLE	2*0			OAK-DET	3-11	CAL-MIL	1-4
0521	CLE-CHI	2-3	TEX-KC	0-3	OAK-BOS	7-8	MIN-NY	1-12	BAL-TOR	3*0	CAL-DET	9*7	SEA-MIL	1-4
0522	CLE-CHI	3-7	TEX-KC	3*1	OAK-BOS	4-7	MIN-NY	0-1	BAL-TOR	6*0	CAL-DET	1-5	SEA-MIL	7*1

♦1982♦	GAME 1	GAME 2	GAME 3	GAME 4	GAME 5	GAME 6	GAME 7
0523	CLE-CHI 6*4	TEX-KC 3-5	OAK-BOS 0-6	MIN-NY 2-4	BAL-TOR 1-7	CAL-DET 7*2	SEA-MIL 6*5
0524	KC-CHI 1-3	CLE-MIN 9*2			BAL-TOR 7*5		
0525	KC-CHI 7*4	CLE-MIN 7*0	CAL-BOS 10*2	OAK-MIL 10*5	TOR-NY 0-8	DET-SEA 6-7	BAL-TEX 10*3
0526	KC-CHI 5-7	CLE-MIN 2*1		OAK-MIL 7*2	TOR-NY 7*0	DET-SEA 2-4	BAL-TEX 3-5
0527	MIL-CAL 4*3					BOS-SEA 6-10	BAL-TEX 6*0
0528	MIL-CAL 5-6	CHI-CLE 2-5	NY-MIN 10*5	DET-OAK 6*4		BOS-SEA 3*2	KC-TEX 2-8
0529	MIL-CAL 4-5	CHI-CLE 2-5	NY-MIN 6*4	DET-OAK 7*4	TOR-BAL 1-3	BOS-SEA 2-4	KC-TEX 14*1
					TOR-BAL 11*10		
0530	MIL-CAL 7*3	CHI-CLE 2-4	NY-MIN 8*6	BOS-SEA 1-2	TOR-BAL 6*0	KC-TEX 1-8	DET-OAK 5*2
							DET-OAK 3-10
0531	TEX-BAL 7-8	DET-CAL 4*3	MIN-CLE 4-9	CHI-KC 4-11	MIL-SEA 4-5	NY-TOR 4-5	BOS-OAK 5*2
0601		DET-CAL 2*1	MIN-CLE 4-6	CHI-KC 3-4	MIL-SEA 2*1	NY-TOR 2-5	BOS-OAK 2-3
0602	TEX-BAL 4*1	DET-CAL 5*4	MIN-CLE 2-4	CHI-KC 6-7	MIL-SEA 5*2	NY-TOR 12*6	BOS-OAK 0-5
0603						NY-TOR 1-3	
0604	BOS-CAL 11*4	SEA-DET 4*0	BAL-MIN 0-6	KC-NY 4*3	MIL-OAK 10*1	CLE-TOR 6*3	CHI-TEX 3-4
0605	BOS-CAL 7*2		BAL-MIN 3*1		MIL-OAK 11*3		CHI-TEX 2*1
0606	BOS-CAL 5*1	SEA-DET 2-10	BAL-MIN 7*5	KC-NY 14*1	MIL-OAK 7*2	CLE-TOR 1-5	CHI-TEX 4-5
						CLE-TOR 7*5	
0607	OAK-CHI 5-6	BAL-MIL 7*2	KC-MIN 5*4	SEA-TEX 6*0		CLE-TOR 3-7	
0608	OAK-CHI 4-5	BAL-MIL 9*4	KC-MIN 9*4	SEA-TEX 2*1	NY-BOS 3-4	CAL-TOR 11*4	CLE-DET 3-8
0609	OAK-CHI 5*4	BAL-MIL 8*3	KC-MIN 8*5	SEA-TEX 4*3	NY-BOS 2-3	CAL-TOR 4-5	CLE-DET 1-2
							CLE-DET 3#4
0610	NY-BOS 5*3	CAL-CHI 6-7	BAL-MIL 7-9	KC-MIN 7-8		OAK-TOR 1-2	
0611	CLE-BOS 2-6	CAL-CHI 6*5	DET-MIL 6-8	NY-BAL 4-9	SEA-KC 2-3	OAK-TOR 8*1	MIN-TEX 3-4
0612	CLE-BOS 4-6	CAL-CHI 3*0	DET-MIL 7*3	NY-BAL 3-5	SEA-KC 3*2	OAK-TOR 7*5	MIN-TEX 4-10
0613		CAL-CHI 7*4	DET-MIL 5-13		SEA-KC 7*1	OAK-TOR 4*2	
0614	MIL-BAL 4-9	BOS-NY 1-5	TEX-SEA 0-4	DET-CLE 0-5	MIN-KC 0-3		
				DET-CLE 1-2			
0615	MIL-BAL 6*3	TOR-CAL 2*0	MIN-KC 4-7	BOS-NY 4-5	CHI-OAK 7*0	TEX-SEA 5*2	
0616	MIL-BAL 22	TOR-CAL 1-7	MIN-KC 5*2	BOS-NY 1-4	CHI-OAK 7*6	TEX-SEA 2-7	
0617	BOS-CLE 6*3	TOR-CAL 8-10	MIL-DET 3*2		CHI-OAK 11*7	TEX-SEA 5*1	
0618	BOS-CLE 3-10	CHI-CAL 2-7	MIL-DET 5*2	TEX-MIN 3*2	TOR-OAK 6*4	KC-SEA 4*1	BAL-NY 4*1
0619	BOS-CLE 7*3	CHI-CAL 7*6	MIL-DET 10*3	TEX-MIN 6*3	TOR-OAK 3*1	KC-SEA 3-10	BAL-NY 3-4
0620	BOS-CLE 4-5	CHI-CAL 1-3	MIL-DET 7*5	TEX-MIN 1-4	TOR-OAK 3*2	KC-SEA 7*5	BAL-NY 5*3
0621	BAL-CLE 7*0	TEX-CAL 2-10	DET-BOS 1-5	MIN-CHI 4-5	KC-OAK 3-4	TOR-SEA 4-5	NY-MIL 2-6
0622	BAL-CLE 6-8	TEX-CAL 4*0	DET-BOS 4-5	MIN-CHI 5-6	KC-OAK 2*1	TOR-SEA 5-6	NY-MIL 2-3
0623	BAL-CLE 3*1	TEX-CAL 3-5	DET-BOS 4-10	MIN-CHI 6*3	KC-OAK 1*0	TOR-SEA 5*3	NY-MIL 3*2
0624	DET-BAL 7*1	KC-CAL 2-7	CLE-NY 5*2	OAK-TEX 1-2			
0625	DET-BAL 2-5	KC-CAL 8*6	CLE-NY 3-11	OAK-TEX 6*2	MIL-BOS 9*3	CHI-SEA 0-1	
0626	DET-BAL 1-4	KC-CAL 5-6	CLE-NY 3-4	OAK-TEX 2-5	MIL-BOS 11*10	CHI-SEA 13*3	MIN-TOR 4*3
0627	DET-BAL 1-13	KC-CAL 1-9	CLE-NY 4*3	OAK-TEX 4-10	MIL-BOS 7*5	CHI-SEA 5-6	MIN-TOR 2-3
0628	OAK-KC 8*4	CHI-MIN 8*7			MIL-BOS 7-9		
0629	OAK-KC 2-7	CHI-MIN 5-12	CLE-BAL 9*2	BOS-DET 4*2	MIL-NY 11*4	CAL-TEX 2*1	SEA-TOR 4*3
0630	OAK-KC 4*0	CHI-MIN 3-4	CLE-BAL 9*0	BOS-DET 3-12	MIL-NY 9*7	CAL-TEX 3-5	SEA-TOR 10*4
0701		CHI-MIN 2-9	CLE-BAL 6*2	BOS-DET 4-5	MIL-NY 3-5	CAL-TEX 2-7	SEA-TOR 4*3
0702	NY-CLE 3*1	TOR-MIN 9*4	CAL-KC 2-7	BAL-DET 5*4	BOS-MIL 5-14	TEX-OAK 7*0	
0703	NY-CLE 10*6	TOR-MIN 1-2	CAL-KC 2-6	BAL-DET 8*3	BOS-MIL 0-7	TEX-OAK 3-5	SEA-CHI 6-7
0704	NY-CLE 3*2	TOR-MIN 3-4	CAL-KC 1-6	BAL-DET 1-6	BOS-MIL 4*1	TEX-OAK 11*4	SEA-CHI 3*1
0705	BAL-CAL 8*5	NY-SEA 4-5	BOS-KC 4*3	MIN-DET 5*3	TOR-TEX 2-3	CLE-OAK 0-2	MIL-CHI 10*4
			BOS-KC 3-4				
0706	BAL-CAL 3*2	MIN-DET 6-11	BOS-KC 2-6	CLE-OAK 3-7	NY-SEA 4*3	TOR-TEX 4*3	
0707	CLE-CAL 8*6	DET-CHI 0-7	TOR-KC 1-3	NY-OAK 5*3	BAL-SEA 7-8	BOS-TEX 8*5	MIN-MIL 11*8
0708	CLE-CAL 1-5	DET-CHI 2-3	TOR-KC 5*4	NY-OAK 3-6	BAL-SEA 3-4	BOS-TEX 3*0	MIN-MIL 3*0
0709	NY-CAL 1-4	MIN-BOS 4*1	CHI-TOR 6-7	BAL-OAK 7*5	CLE-SEA 7*4	DET-TEX 2-3	KC-MIL 6-9
						DET-TEX 1-3	
0710	MIN-BOS 4-5	NY-CAL 6-12	KC-MIL 0-7	BAL-OAK 1-3	CLE-SEA 7*1	DET-TEX 5-6	CHI-TOR 6*5
						DET-TEX 6*0	
0711	MIN-BOS 7*3	NY-CAL 1-2	KC-MIL 5-8	BAL-OAK 8*7	CLE-SEA 4*3	DET-TEX 3*2	CHI-TOR 16*7
0715	KC-BOS 3-5	SEA-BAL 2-3	CHI-MIL 4-8	CAL-CLE 8*2	DET-MIN 18*2	OAK-NY 1-2	TEX-TOR 1-5
			CHI-MIL 4-5				
0716	SEA-BAL 6*0	KC-BOS 3-7	CHI-MIL 3-5	CAL-CLE 15*0	DET-MIN 6*3	OAK-NY 2-6	TEX-TOR 3-11
0717	SEA-BAL 4-8	KC-BOS 4-8	CHI-MIL 2-5	CAL-CLE 4-10	DET-MIN 8*4	OAK-NY 1-4	TEX-TOR 3-11
0718	SEA-BAL 3-4	KC-BOS 9*0	CHI-MIL 3-9	CAL-CLE 4-5	DET-MIN 1-6	SEA-NY 3-7	TEX-TOR 4-5
0719	CAL-BAL 6*5	TEX-BOS 5-9	CHI-DET 6*0	OAK-CLE 1-4	MIL-MIN 4-6	SEA-NY 3-5	KC-TOR 2-4
0720	CAL-BAL 7*4		CHI-DET 0-1	OAK-CLE 6*4	MIL-MIN 3-5	SEA-NY 6*5	KC-TOR 2-9
0721	CAL-BAL 7-8	TEX-BOS 6*3	CHI-DET 9*3	OAK-CLE 6*4	MIL-MIN 10*4	SEA-NY 6*5	KC-TOR 9*7
		TEX-BOS 1-6					
0722	TOR-CHI 2-3	TEX-NY 3-4		SEA-CLE 3-4	TEX-DET 3*1	MIL-KC 3-4	BOS-MIN 4-8
0723	TOR-CHI 7*1	CAL-NY 3-6	OAK-BAL 1-2	SEA-CLE 9*0	TEX-DET 1-3	MIL-KC 7*4	BOS-MIN 3-5
0724	TOR-CHI 8*1	CAL-NY 5-6	OAK-BAL 4-5	SEA-CLE 3-5	TEX-DET 2-7	MIL-KC 4-6	BOS-MIN 5*0
					TEX-DET 6-7		
0725	TOR-CHI 3-5	CAL-NY 6*4	OAK-BAL 2-6				
0726	CHI-BAL 2-6	TOR-BOS 2-3	OAK-CAL 11*8	KC-CLE 8*1	DET-NY 5*3	MIN-SEA 10*4	MIL-TEX 1-3
0727	CHI-BAL 3-5	TOR-BOS 3*1	OAK-CAL 7-8	KC-CLE 8*1	DET-NY 5-6	MIN-SEA 7-9	MIL-TEX 8*2
0728	CHI-BAL 1-2	TOR-BOS 7-9	OAK-CAL 1-13	KC-CLE 2-4	DET-NY 7-8	MIN-SEA 2-6	MIL-TEX 3*2
0729	BOS-CHI 7*3	BAL-KC 2-7	SEA-CAL 1-3	CLE-MIL 5*1	MIN-OAK 0-5		DET-TOR 5-6
0730	BOS-CHI 6-9	BAL-KC 3-4	SEA-CAL 0-2	CLE-MIL 7*2	MIN-OAK 3-4	NY-TEX 4*0	DET-TOR 0-1
0731	BOS-CHI 5-7	BAL-KC 0-2	SEA-CAL 9*3	CLE-MIL 2-4	MIN-OAK 2-3	NY-TEX 2-3	DET-TOR 8*5
0801	BOS-CHI 2-4	BAL-KC 2-4	SEA-CAL 4-9	CLE-MIL 4*1	MIN-OAK 8*7	NY-TEX 2-4	
				CLE-MIL 2-7			
0802	BOS-BAL 5*2	MIN-CAL 9*7	TEX-CLE 2-6	DET-KC 5-6	SEA-OAK 5-6	MIL-TOR 4-9	
0803	BOS-BAL 2-7	MIN-CAL 5*4	TEX-CLE 0-2	DET-KC 5-6	SEA-OAK 3*2	MIL-TOR 7*4	CHI-NY 1*0
	BOS-BAL 7*6		TEX-CLE 5*4				CHI-NY 14*2
0804	BOS-BAL 2-4	MIN-CAL 6-8	TEX-CLE 4-8	DET-KC 7*1	MIL-TOR 8*0	SEA-OAK 5*2	CHI-NY 2-6
						SEA-OAK 3-8	CHI-NY 7*0
0805	KC-BAL 1-5	MIN-CAL 8*6	TOR-DET 2-5				TEX-NY 7*2
			TOR-DET 4-7				
0806	CHI-BOS 6*3	MIL-CLE 5*2	TOR-DET 0-6	OAK-MIN 4*1	TEX-NY 0-6	CAL-SEA 11*9	KC-BAL 3*1
							KC-BAL 4*0
0807	CHI-BOS 7*3	MIL-CLE 3-4	TOR-DET 7*4	OAK-MIN 7*1	TEX-NY 1-9	CAL-SEA 3*1	KC-BAL 5-6
0808	CHI-BOS 6-12	MIL-CLE 7*6	TOR-DET 7*4	OAK-MIN 5*2	TEX-NY 6*4	CAL-SEA 9*5	KC-BAL 6-10
			TOR-DET 7*4		TEX-NY 5-8		
0809	BAL-CHI 5-9	CLE-KC 2-12	NY-DET 9*7	TEX-MIL 1-9	OAK-SEA 9*4	BOS-TOR 2-4	
0810	BAL-CHI 4-9	CLE-KC 1-5	NY-DET 1-10	TEX-MIL 3-11	OAK-SEA 2-4	BOS-TOR 0-4	CAL-MIN 2-5
0811	BAL-CHI 1-4	CLE-KC 0-8	NY-DET 2-3	TEX-MIL 6*3	OAK-SEA 4-7	BOS-TOR 3-4	CAL-MIN 6*3
0812	NY-CHI 1-2			TOR-MIL 1-7			CAL-MIN 3*1
				TOR-MIL 3-4			
0813	BAL-BOS 2-5	NY-CHI 4*3	KC-DET 1-10	TOR-MIL 1-3	SEA-MIN 1-3	CAL-OAK 9*0	CLE-TEX 7-8
0814	BAL-BOS 5*2	NY-CHI 0-6	KC-DET 1*0	TOR-MIL 4*2	SEA-MIN 3*1	CAL-OAK 1-10	CLE-TEX 2-3
0815	BAL-BOS 0-8	NY-CHI 4-6	KC-DET 6*1	TOR-MIL 1-3	SEA-MIN 10*2	CAL-OAK 2-3	CLE-TEX 6*4
0816	BAL-BOS 4-9	CLE-TOR 1-2	SEA-DET 1-3	KC-NY 0-2		CAL-OAK 8*4	CHI-TEX 6*1
				KC-NY 3-4			
0817	BOS-CAL 2-10	BAL-MIN 8*4	MIL-OAK 6-10	KC-NY 8*4	CHI-TEX 3-4	SEA-DET 5*4	CLE-TOR 6*5
						SEA-DET 2-3	CLE-TOR 9*5
0818	BOS-CAL 4*1	BAL-MIN 5-6	KC-NY 2-9	MIL-OAK 2-3	CHI-TEX 1-11	SEA-DET 2-7	
0819	BOS-CAL 5-8	BAL-MIN 3-9	CHI-KC 0-3	MIL-OAK 10*6			
0820	DET-CAL 8*6	MIN-CLE 5-7	CHI-KC 5-13	BOS-OAK 3-4	TOR-NY 2-4	MIL-SEA 6*5	BAL-TEX 4*2

♦1982♦	GAME 1	GAME 2	GAME 3	GAME 4	GAME 5	GAME 6	GAME 7
0821	DET-CAL 1-13	MIN-CLE 4*3	CHI-KC 3-4	BOS-OAK 5-12	TOR-NY 3*1	MIL-SEA 3*2	BAL-TEX 8*6
0822	DET-CAL 5-6	MIN-CLE 3-4	CHI-KC 12*3	BOS-OAK 4*2	TOR-NY 1-3	MIL-SEA 8*5	BAL-TEX 10*3
0823	MIL-CAL 3-5	CHI-CLE 4-5		DET-OAK 5*1	TOR-NY 3-4	BOS-SEA 4*3	KC-TEX 2-5
0824	MIL-CAL 7*3	CHI-CLE 7-14	TOR-BAL 3-7	DET-OAK 0-3	MIN-NY 5*0	BOS-SEA 5*4	KC-TEX 5*3
0825		CHI-CLE 5*1	TOR-BAL 3-8		MIN-NY 1-8		KC-TEX 4*3
0826	OAK-MIL 3-10	DET-SEA 4-5	TOR-BAL 5-12	CAL-BOS 10*1	MIN-NY 2-7		KC-TEX 5*3
				CAL-BOS 3-4			
0827	KC-CHI 7*1	OAK-MIL 4-5	CLE-MIN 3-5	CAL-BOS 7*6	DET-SEA 6*1	NY-TOR 3-10	TEX-BAL 1-3
							TEX-BAL 4*3
0828	CAL-BOS 6-7	KC-CHI 10*1	OAK-MIL 7*6	CLE-MIN 0-10	DET-SEA 3-4	NY-TOR 2-3	TEX-BAL 3-8
0829	CAL-BOS 3-9	KC-CHI 7*4	OAK-MIL 1-8	CLE-MIN 3-6	DET-SEA 6*2	NY-TOR 8*2	TEX-BAL 2-3
0830	OAK-BOS 7-9	CLE-CHI 1-4	SEA-MIL 3*2	NY-MIN 8*2	TEX-KC 3-8	BAL-TOR 6*3	
0831	OAK-BOS 0-4	CLE-CHI 6-14	SEA-MIL 2-8	NY-MIN 3*1	TEX-KC 6*0	BAL-TOR 1*0	CAL-DET 11*0
0901	OAK-BOS 4-7	CLE-CHI 0-6	SEA-MIL 3-7	NY-MIN 2-7	TEX-KC 7*3	BAL-TOR 5*2	CAL-DET 3-5
0902		TEX-CHI 5-6	CLE-MIL 1-2				CAL-DET 3-6
			CLE-MIL 4*2				
0903	MIN-BAL 2-4	SEA-BOS 8-10	CAL-MIL 5*2	TEX-CHI 5-7	TOR-CLE 2-3	OAK-DET 3-6	NY-KC 3-5
0904	MIN-BAL 0-3	SEA-BOS 4*3	CAL-MIL 2-8	TEX-CHI 3-4	TOR-CLE 3-4	OAK-DET 4*3	NY-KC 3*2
0905	MIN-BAL 4-5	SEA-BOS 5-6	CAL-MIL 5-8	TEX-CHI 10*7	TOR-CLE 6*5	OAK-DET 1-8	NY-KC 18*7
0906	CHI-CAL 6-8	BAL-NY 8*2	DET-MIL 6*5	TOR-OAK 3*1	BOS-CLE 10*3	KC-SEA 2-6	MIN-TEX 3-4
							MIN-TEX 7-11
0907	CHI-CAL 7*4	BOS-CLE 4-5	DET-MIL 0-4	BAL-NY 7*2	TOR-OAK 2*1	KC-SEA 2-5	MIN-TEX 8*1
0908	CHI-CAL 5*3	BOS-CLE 0-2	DET-MIL 7-9	BAL-NY 5-10	TOR-OAK 6*5	KC-SEA 6*2	MIN-TEX 0-2
0909		BAL-CLE 0-3		MIL-NY 4-5			
0910	DET-BOS 6*4	BAL-CLE 3*2	TOR-CAL 2-6	MIL-NY 5*3	MIN-KC 5*0	CHI-OAK 9*3	SEA-TEX 5*2
0911	DET-BOS 3-13	BAL-CLE 8*1	TOR-CAL 1-4	MIL-NY 2-14	MIN-KC 3-9	CHI-OAK 2*0	SEA-TEX 2-5
0912	DET-BOS 7-10	BAL-CLE 0-3	TOR-CAL 2-3	MIL-NY 8-9	MIN-KC 7-18	CHI-OAK 2-4	SEA-TEX 1*0
0913	CLE-BOS 3*1	NY-BAL 7-8	CAL-CHI 6*4	MIL-DET 3-4	SEA-KC 0-8	TEX-MIN 0-2	
	CLE-BOS 4*3						
0914	CLE-BOS 1-12	CAL-CHI 7*0	MIL-DET 6*3	SEA-KC 2-5	TEX-MIN 2-3	NY-BAL 4-5	
						NY-BAL 3-5	
0915	CLE-BOS 7*4	CAL-CHI 3-8	MIL-DET 5*3	SEA-KC 4-5	TEX-MIN 2-10	NY-BAL 5-8	OAK-TOR 2-3
							OAK-TOR 11-12
0916	NY-BAL 1-3	OAK-CHI 3-6	BOS-DET 2-4	SEA-KC 4*2	TEX-MIN 8*2		CAL-TOR 1-2
0917	CLE-BAL 5*3	NY-MIL 0-14	BOS-DET 1-5	TEX-SEA 0-6	KC-MIN 4-5		CAL-TOR 2-6
0918	CLE-BAL 2-5	NY-MIL 4-6	BOS-DET 6*2	TEX-SEA 10*4	KC-MIN 5-11	OAK-CHI 2*1	CAL-TOR 8*6
						OAK-CHI 5*4	
0919	CLE-BAL 2-4	BOS-DET 6*4	NY-MIL 1-14	KC-MIN 4-9	TEX-SEA 7-9	OAK-CHI 3-8	CAL-TOR 5*1
0920	DET-BAL 1-3	KC-CAL 2-3	BOS-MIL 2-5	TOR-MIN 3-5	CHI-SEA 2-5	TEX-OAK 10*3	
0921	DET-BAL 11*1	KC-CAL 1-2	BOS-MIL 4*3	TOR-MIN 5*1	CHI-SEA 4-5	TEX-OAK 1-6	CLE-NY 9*8
							CLE-NY 2-6
0922	KC-CAL 5-8	BOS-MIL 1-3	TOR-MIN 3*2	TEX-OAK 3-5	CHI-SEA 4-8		CLE-NY 5*0
0923	DET-BAL 10*5	CAL-TEX 4-5			CHI-SEA 12*4		
0924	NY-BOS 2-4	CAL-TEX 10*1	MIN-CHI 2-3	CLE-DET 3-4	TOR-SEA 2-3	BAL-MIL 6-15	KC-OAK 7*4
				CLE-DET 6*2			
0925	NY-BOS 6*2	MIN-CHI 1-13	BAL-MIL 7*2	CLE-DET 0-4	KC-OAK 3-10	TOR-SEA 0-7	CAL-TEX 6*5
0926	NY-BOS 2-5	MIN-CHI 2*1	BAL-MIL 5*2	CLE-DET 4*3	KC-OAK 4-5	TOR-SEA 6*2	CAL-TEX 5-7
0927	NY-BOS 10*3	SEA-CHI 8*4	CAL-KC 3*2				OAK-TEX 1-4
		SEA-CHI 1-4					
0928	MIL-BOS 9*3	SEA-CHI 1-3	NY-CLE 6*4	BAL-DET 6-9	CAL-KC 4-5	OAK-TEX 5*4	MIN-TOR 0-3
							MIN-TOR 3-4
0929	MIL-BOS 6*3	SEA-CHI 5-6	NY-CLE 13*6	BAL-DET 2-3	CAL-KC 5-6	OAK-TEX 3-5	MIN-TOR 8*0
0930	MIL-BOS 4-9		NY-CLE 7*5	BAL-DET 6*5	OAK-KC 4-11		MIN-TOR 4-6
1001	TEX-CAL 0-4	CHI-MIN 2-3	DET-CLE 3-4	BOS-NY 3*2	OAK-KC 7-12	MIL-BAL 3-8	SEA-TOR 0-2
			DET-CLE 4*2			MIL-BAL 1-7	
1002	TEX-CAL 4-6	OAK-KC 4-5	DET-CLE 0-2	CHI-MIN 5*3	BOS-NY 5*0	MIL-BAL 3-11	SEA-TOR 0-3
			DET-CLE 4*1				
1003	MIL-BAL 10*2	TEX-CAL 6-7	DET-CLE 9*1	OAK-KC 6*3	CHI-MIN 6*1	BOS-NY 5*3	SEA-TOR 2-5

♦1983♦	GAME 1	GAME 2	GAME 3	GAME 4	GAME 5	GAME 6	GAME 7
0404	KC-BAL 7*2	CLE-OAK 8*5	CHI-TEX 3-5				
0405	TOR-BOS 7*1	MIL-CAL 2-3	CHI-TEX 1-4	DET-MIN 11*3	NY-SEA 4-5		
0406	KC-BAL 3-4	MIL-CAL 3-4	CHI-TEX 1-4	DET-MIN 9*5	NY-SEA 2-6	CLE-OAK 3-5	
0407	TOR-BOS 4-7	MIL-CAL 5*3		DET-MIN 4-5	NY-SEA 8*1	CLE-OAK 9*1	
0408	CHI-DET 6*3	BOS-TEX 8*5			MIN-SEA 5*4	CAL-OAK 3-5	
0409	BAL-CLE 4-8	BOS-TEX 3-10	MIL-KC 2-5	NY-TOR 4-7	MIN-SEA 2-3	CAL-OAK 10*2	
0410	BAL-CLE 13*2	BOS-TEX 7-9	MIL-KC 9*5	NY-TOR 3*0	MIN-SEA 6*3	CAL-OAK 4-11	CHI-DET 7*5
0411	SEA-CAL 1-6		BOS-KC 2-6				
0412	SEA-CAL 8*1	BAL-CHI 10*8	BOS-KC 1-5	TEX-CLE 2*1	DET-NY 13*2	MIN-OAK 3-4	MIL-TOR 6*5
0413	SEA-CAL 1-6		BOS-KC 18*4	TEX-CLE 3-4	DET-NY 7*5	MIN-OAK 4-5	MIL-TOR 2-7
0414	BAL-CHI 11-12	OAK-SEA 5*3			DET-NY 3-6		MIL-TOR 5*4
0415	DET-CHI 6*0	OAK-SEA 1-5	TEX-BOS 1-4	KC-MIL 4*3	TOR-NY 6*5	CAL-MIN 8*2	
0416	DET-CHI 1-3	OAK-SEA 5*2	TEX-BOS 1-2	CLE-BAL 0-2		CAL-MIN 9*5	
				CLE-BAL 7*4			
0417	TEX-BOS 1*0	DET-CHI 1-6	KC-MIL 3-6	CLE-BAL 1-6	CAL-MIN 8-11	TOR-NY 5-7	OAK-SEA 7*4
0418	MIL-BOS 14*0	OAK-CAL 5*3		CLE-BAL 1-4	SEA-MIN 5-8	TOR-NY 0-3	
0419	NY-CHI 3-13	CLE-TOR 7-9		TEX-BAL 2-4	SEA-MIN 2-6		
0420	NY-CHI 6*4	CLE-TOR 1-4	MIL-BOS 4-5	TEX-BAL 11*2	SEA-MIN 2-11	KC-DET 8*7	
0421	OAK-CAL 2-6			TEX-BAL 2-3	SEA-MIN 2*0		
	OAK-CAL 5-6						
0422	BAL-CAL 5-6	CHI-CLE 1-5	SEA-DET 0-4	TOR-KC 5-6	MIN-NY 5*3	BOS-OAK 3*1	MIL-TEX 2-3
0423	BAL-CAL 3*1	CHI-CLE 3-6	SEA-DET 0-4	TOR-KC 5*4	MIN-NY 4-7		MIL-TEX 3*0
0424	BAL-CAL 3-7	CHI-CLE 9*3	SEA-DET 2-4	TOR-KC 1-7	BOS-OAK 4*2		MIL-TEX 3*1
0425	MIN-NY 1-2						
0426	KC-NY 10*4	MIN-CLE 1-7	CHI-MIL 3-4	BAL-OAK 3-4	BOS-SEA 6-7	TOR-TEX 1-2	
0427	KC-NY 0-6	MIN-CLE 5*3	CHI-MIL 6*2	BAL-OAK 6*0	BOS-SEA 2*1	TOR-TEX 3*2	DET-CAL 3-13
0429	CLE-KC 5-6	MIL-MIN 4-7	CHI-TOR 9*3	DET-OAK 4-5	BAL-SEA 9*1	NY-TEX 3-8	BOS-CAL 6*5
0430	CLE-KC 5*1	MIL-MIN 7-9			BAL-SEA 2-6	NY-TEX 3-6	BOS-CAL 1-4
0501	CLE-KC 2*1	MIL-MIN 8*4	CHI-TOR 0-8	DET-OAK 3-8	BAL-SEA 8*2	NY-TEX 8*4	BOS-CAL 10*9
				DET-OAK 0-2			
0502	MIL-CHI 8*4	NY-KC 1-4	TEX-TOR 5-6	CAL-BAL 2-4	OAK-BOS 1-3	CLE-MIN 3*1	DET-SEA 2*1
0503	MIL-CHI 6-7	NY-KC 2-5	TEX-TOR 7*2	CAL-BAL 16*8	OAK-BOS 1-7	CLE-MIN 11*7	DET-SEA 1-5
0504	MIL-CHI 2-3	NY-KC 8*1	TEX-TOR 1-7			CLE-MIN 7*5	
0505							
0506	OAK-BAL 2-9	SEA-BOS 4-6	CLE-CHI 3-8	CAL-DET 4*2	TEX-MIL 9*4	NY-MIN 8*4	KC-TOR 1-6
0507	OAK-BAL 6-8	SEA-BOS 0-8	CLE-CHI 6*5	CAL-DET 6*5		NY-MIN 8*7	KC-TOR 4-7
0508	OAK-BAL 1*0	SEA-BOS 4*2	CLE-CHI 13*6	CAL-DET 1-5	TEX-MIL 3-6	NY-MIN 5-6	KC-TOR 6*1
0509	SEA-BAL 6*4	CAL-BOS 2-8	TOR-CLE 6*1				
0510	SEA-BAL 2-13	CAL-BOS 6*5	KC-CLE 1-4	OAK-DET 3-4	MIN-MIL 1-4	TEX-NY 4*2	
0511	SEA-BAL 0-1	CAL-BOS 3*1	KC-CLE 0-2	OAK-DET 2-5	MIN-MIL 1-4	TEX-NY 3*1	TOR-CHI 3*1
0512			TOR-CLE 6*3	OAK-DET 11*4	BOS-MIL 5*3		
0513	MIN-CAL 5*4	DET-KC 2-5	TOR-CLE 1-5	CHI-NY 1-3	SEA-OAK 2-9	BAL-TEX 8*1	
0514	MIN-CAL 2*1	DET-KC 11*10	TOR-CLE 8*1	CHI-NY 5-8	SEA-OAK 4*1	BAL-TEX 14*11	BOS-MIL 7-8
0515	MIN-CAL 8*6	DET-KC 6*4		CHI-NY 7*3	SEA-OAK 0-3	BAL-TEX 1-2	BOS-MIL 6*1
0516	NY-DET 7*0	OAK-MIN 7*6				CLE-TEX 1-3	TOR-MIL 2*1
0517	NY-DET 7*5	OAK-MIN 7*6	KC-BOS 1-4	CAL-SEA 3*1	CHI-BAL 2-7	CLE-TEX 5-6	TOR-MIL 6-9
					CHI-BAL 0-5		

♦1983♦	GAME 1		GAME 2		GAME 3		GAME 4		GAME 5		GAME 6		GAME 7	
0518	KC-BOS	2*1	NY-DET	6*4	TOR-MIL	6-7	OAK-MIN	5-16	CHI-BAL	0-1	CAL-SEA	1-2	CLE-TEX	2-3
0519	MIN-BOS	1-4	TEX-DET	1-2	BAL-TOR	2*1					CAL-SEA	0-1		
0520	MIN-BOS	10*4	TEX-DET	4*0	BAL-TOR	5-7	CLE-CAL	4-5	CHI-KC	9*6	MIL-SEA	4*3	NY-OAK	4-8
0521	MIN-BOS	4-11	TEX-DET	3-5	BAL-TOR	0-6	CLE-CAL	9*3	CHI-KC	4-8	MIL-SEA	4-5	NY-OAK	1*0
0522	MIN-BOS	4*3	TEX-DET	5-12	BAL-TOR	0-5	CLE-CAL	0-9	CHI-KC	11*3	MIL-SEA	6*0	NY-OAK	4*2
0523	MIN-BAL	12*4	BOS-CHI	6*4	DET-TOR	0-4	NY-CAL	0-3	TEX-KC	2-5	CLE-SEA	2-3	MIL-OAK	4-5
0524	MIN-BAL	6*1	BOS-CHI	4-12	DET-TOR	6-7	NY-CAL	1-7	TEX-KC	22	CLE-SEA	6*4	MIL-OAK	7-8
0525	MIN-BAL	7*4	BOS-CHI	2*0	DET-TOR	6*2	NY-CAL	1-7	TEX-KC	2-5	CLE-SEA	1-2	MIL-OAK	7*6
0526			TEX-CHI	3*1	BOS-TOR	7*2			BAL-KC	2-8				
0527	CAL-CLE	5*4	TEX-CHI	2-3	BOS-TOR	2*0	SEA-MIL	7*5	BAL-KC	7*4	OAK-NY	2-4	MIN-DET	4-7
													MIN-DET	1-2
0528	TEX-CHI	3-8	CAL-CLE	7*4	BAL-KC	1*0	SEA-MIL	4*3	OAK-NY	2-5	BOS-TOR	5-9	MIN-DET	1-6
0529	TEX-CHI	3-8	CAL-CLE	6*4	BAL-KC	0-4	SEA-MIL	6*4	OAK-NY	0-5	BOS-TOR	1-6	MIN-DET	6-7
0530	CHI-BOS	6*4	CAL-CLE	5-6	BAL-MIN	6*1	OAK-MIL	3-6	OAK-NY	5-10			TOR-DET	6*4
0531	CHI-BOS	1-2	SEA-CLE	2-5	BAL-MIN	3-10	OAK-MIL	2-5	CAL-NY	3-5	KC-TEX	6*5		
0601	CHI-BOS	8*3	SEA-CLE	2-5	BAL-MIN	6*3	OAK-MIL	7*5	CAL-NY	0-3	KC-TEX	4-7	TOR-DET	1-3
0602	KC-CHI	3-6	SEA-CLE	1-3			OAK-MIL	1-4	CAL-NY	9*8			TOR-DET	6*1
0603	KC-CHI	0-2	TOR-BAL	2-3	BOS-MIN	6*3	CAL-MIL	3*0	SEA-NY	5*0	DET-TEX	12*1		
0604	KC-CHI	7*1	TOR-BAL	4-6	BOS-MIN	8*6	CAL-MIL	8*3	SEA-NY	5*4	DET-TEX	2-5	OAK-CLE	6*3
0605	KC-CHI	7*5	TOR-BAL	5*2	BOS-MIN	4-10	CAL-MIL	4-5	SEA-NY	8*7	DET-TEX	5*4	OAK-CLE	8*3
	KC-CHI	2-5											OAK-CLE	9*2
0606	TOR-BAL	1-8	DET-BOS	11*6	CAL-MIL	7-9	SEA-NY	2-6						
0607	MIL-BAL	4-6	DET-BOS	4*2	CHI-CAL	12*11	CLE-NY	2*1	MIN-KC	4-9	TOR-OAK	3-5	TEX-SEA	10*0
0608	MIL-BAL	3-7	DET-BOS	6*3	CHI-CAL	4-7	CLE-NY	5-6	MIN-KC	2-9	TOR-OAK	5*2	TEX-SEA	1*0
0609	MIL-BAL	7-10	DET-BOS	8*2	CHI-CAL	2-3			MIN-KC	5-6	TOR-OAK	1-3	TEX-SEA	2-3
0610	CLE-DET	1-7	BAL-BOS	3*0	TOR-CAL	3-5	NY-MIL	7*1	TEX-MIN	4*2	CHI-OAK	1-2	KC-SEA	2*0
0611	CLE-DET	9*1	BAL-BOS	10*6	TOR-CAL	3*2	NY-MIL	2-6	TEX-MIN	11*0	CHI-OAK	4-5	KC-SEA	4*1
0612	CLE-DET	1-4	BAL-BOS	6-7	TOR-CAL	6*5	NY-MIL	5-6	TEX-MIN	4*3	CHI-OAK	12*10	KC-SEA	1-8
	CLE-DET	1-3									CHI-OAK	8*1		
0613	CAL-CHI	7*4	NY-CLE	0-9	BAL-MIL	3*2	KC-MIN	4-9	SEA-TEX	2-5				
0614	BOS-DET	6*2	NY-CLE	6-9	OAK-TOR	7-13	KC-MIN	1-8	SEA-TEX	1-7				
0615	BOS-DET	2-4	NY-CLE	8*5	OAK-TOR	10*1	KC-MIN	2-6	SEA-TEX	6*4	CAL-CHI	2-5	BAL-MIL	11*8
0616	BOS-DET	2-10	NY-CLE	8*1	OAK-TOR	1-9			MIN-TEX	4*3			BAL-MIL	1-2
0617	BOS-BAL	5*3	DET-CLE	11*4	CAL-TOR	3-6	OAK-CHI	3-6	MIN-TEX	1-10	SEA-KC	1-3	MIL-NY	2-7
0618	BOS-BAL	3*2	DET-CLE	8-12	CAL-TOR	7*6	OAK-CHI	3*1	MIN-TEX	8*4	SEA-KC	5-6	MIL-NY	4-5
0619	BOS-BAL	3-6	DET-CLE	2-7	CAL-TOR	1-6	OAK-CHI	0-1	MIN-TEX	1-4	SEA-KC	2-4	MIL-NY	3-8
0620	CLE-BOS	3-6	MIL-DET	1-4	MIN-TOR	1-2	SEA-CHI	3-7	CAL-TEX	10*9	OAK-KC	7*2		
0621	CLE-BOS	3*1	MIL-DET	10*3	MIN-TOR	3-8	SEA-CHI	2-4	CAL-TEX	2-3	OAK-KC	2-4	NY-BAL	2-5
0622	CLE-BOS	9*4	MIL-DET	2-6	MIN-TOR	4*3	SEA-CHI	3-6	CAL-TEX	1-9	OAK-KC	6-7	NY-BAL	5*2
0623	CLE-BOS	5*4	TOR-SEA	5*4			MIN-CHI	6-8			CAL-KC	7*2		
0624	NY-BOS	4-5	TOR-SEA	4*2	DET-BAL	9*0	MIN-CHI	5*1	CLE-MIL	2-6	CAL-KC	3-11	OAK-TEX	5-6
													OAK-TEX	2-6
0625	DET-BAL	9*3	NY-BOS	4*1	MIN-CHI	3-8	CAL-KC	9*2	CLE-MIL	2-7	TOR-SEA	2-5	OAK-TEX	3-8
0626	DET-BAL	1-3	NY-BOS	5-12	MIN-CHI	7-9			CLE-MIL	3-4	TOR-SEA	19*7	OAK-TEX	1-4
0627	TEX-CAL	0-8	BAL-NY	1-7	KC-OAK	1-7					CHI-SEA	7*4		
0628	TEX-CAL	3*1	BOS-CLE	11*3	KC-OAK	3-4	DET-MIL	5*4	TOR-MIN	2-5	CHI-SEA	2-6		
0629	TEX-CAL	1-2	BOS-CLE	3-5	KC-OAK	6-11	DET-MIL	3-4	TOR-MIN	4*2	CHI-SEA	5*3	BAL-NY	0-7
			BOS-CLE	11*10										
0630	TEX-CAL	4*2	DET-MIL	1-4	TOR-MIN	11*3	BAL-NY	3-4	KC-OAK	7*4				
0701	KC-CAL	6-7	MIL-CLE	11*10	CHI-MIN	3-6	BOS-NY	8-12	TEX-OAK	8*5	BAL-DET	9*5	SEA-TOR	11*2
0702	KC-CAL	5*3	MIL-CLE	6*5	CHI-MIN	4*2	BOS-NY	10*4	TEX-OAK	13*3	BAL-DET	7*2	SEA-TOR	6-7
0703	KC-CAL	2-5	MIL-CLE	2-5	CHI-MIN	3-4	BOS-NY	7*3	TEX-OAK	16*4	BAL-DET	1-10	SEA-TOR	4*1
0704	KC-CAL	5*1	MIL-CLE	8*3	CHI-MIN	12*6	BOS-NY	0-4	TEX-OAK	3-4				
0708	SEA-BAL	3*0	CAL-BOS	9*3	CLE-MIN	10*4	MIL-CHI	4*3	OAK-DET	2-3	NY-KC	9*2	TEX-TOR	5-8
0709	SEA-BAL	3*2	CAL-BOS	3-10	CLE-MIN	2-3	MIL-CHI	3*1	OAK-DET	3*1	NY-KC	2-3	TEX-TOR	1-5
0710	SEA-BAL	0-2	CAL-BOS	5*3	CLE-MIN	4-6	MIL-CHI	12*9	OAK-DET	3-5	NY-KC	6*4	TEX-TOR	4-6
0711	OAK-BAL	6-7	SEA-BOS	5-6	NY-MIN	2-4	CLE-CHI	2-9	CAL-DET	6-12	TOR-KC	7*4	MIL-TEX	4-5
0712	OAK-BAL	1-3	SEA-BOS	3*2	NY-MIN	4*3	CLE-CHI	0-8	CAL-DET	4-5	TOR-KC	9*6	MIL-TEX	9*2
0713	OAK-BAL	2-6	SEA-BOS	6*4	NY-MIN	1-6	CLE-CHI	1-5	CAL-DET	1-7	TOR-KC	4-5	MIL-TEX	6*2
0714	CAL-BAL	1-5	OAK-BOS	4-9	KC-CLE	8*0	TOR-CHI	8*0	MIN-MIL	1-5	TEX-NY	11*2	DET-SEA	4*2
0715	CAL-BAL	4-10	OAK-BOS	7-10	KC-CLE	10*0	TOR-CHI	3*2	MIN-MIL	3-6	TEX-NY	5-7	DET-SEA	2-7
0716	CAL-BAL	8*5	OAK-BOS	12*5	KC-CLE	3-17	TOR-CHI	7*5	MIN-MIL	0-5	TEX-NY	1-3	DET-SEA	0-1
0717	CAL-BAL	1-11	OAK-BOS	13*9	KC-CLE	7*2	TOR-CHI	2-3	MIN-MIL	6-10	TEX-NY	6-8	DET-SEA	8*1
0718	BOS-CAL	7*2	DET-OAK	4*2	CHI-CLE	5*3	KC-TOR	2-8	TEX-MIL	3-4	MIN-NY	2-4	BAL-SEA	9*4
									TEX-MIL	4-5				
0719	BOS-CAL	1-6	CHI-CLE	4-5	MIN-NY	0-4	DET-OAK	4*3	TEX-MIL	3*1	BAL-SEA	8*1	KC-TOR	6*2
0720	BOS-CAL	6*4	CHI-CLE	8*2	MIN-NY	4-6	DET-OAK	2-9	TEX-MIL	3-4	BAL-SEA	4*2	KC-TOR	14*8
0721	DET-CAL	5*1	TOR-TEX	2-3			BAL-OAK	7-9	CHI-MIL	6-7	BOS-SEA	14*13		
	DET-CAL	2-3												
0722	DET-CAL	13*11	MIN-CLE	5-8	CHI-MIL	2*1	BAL-OAK	3-4	BOS-SEA	5*4	TOR-TEX	10*5	KC-NY	6-7
													KC-NY	3*2
0723	DET-CAL	7*2	MIN-CLE	5*2	CHI-MIL	7-8	BAL-OAK	7*3	BOS-SEA	0-5	TOR-TEX	3*2	KC-NY	1-5
0724	DET-CAL	4*3	MIN-CLE	7*5	CHI-MIL	7-8	BAL-OAK	4*3	BOS-SEA	6*0	TOR-TEX	0-3	KC-NY	2#4
			MIN-CLE	5*4										
0725	BAL-CAL	2-5	CLE-KC	1-6	MIL-MIN	3-17	BOS-OAK	3*0	NY-TEX	6*5	CHI-TOR	7*4		
0726	BAL-CAL	5*4	CLE-KC	2*0	MIL-MIN	5-6	BOS-OAK	2-9	NY-TEX	5*0	CHI-TOR	4-6	SEA-DET	3-8
							BOS-OAK	5*3			CHI-TOR	4*3		
0727	BAL-CAL	10*4	SEA-DET	5*3	CLE-KC	4-5	BOS-OAK	6-7	MIL-MIN	13*9	CHI-TOR	11*3	NY-TEX	4*3
0728			SEA-DET	1-6										
0729	TEX-BAL	6-8	KC-DET	1#10	MIL-BOS	11*5	OAK-CAL	5*2	NY-CHI	2-7	SEA-MIN	3-4	CLE-TOR	2-4
0730	TEX-BAL	4-7	KC-DET	1-10	MIL-BOS	5-10	OAK-CAL	13*8	NY-CHI	1-5	SEA-MIN	7*3	CLE-TOR	5-6
			KC-DET	1-4			OAK-CAL	2*1						
0731	TEX-BAL	0-6	KC-DET	6-8	MIL-BOS	7*5	OAK-CAL	0-4	NY-CHI	12*6	SEA-MIN	3*2	CLE-TOR	16*11
			KC-DET	7*5										
0801	MIL-BOS	6*2	KC-DET	2-3	NY-CHI	1-4	OAK-SEA	4*3	CLE-TOR	6*0	CAL-MIN	12*6		
											CAL-MIN	0-7		
0802	DET-CHI	5-7	OAK-SEA	12-15	BOS-TEX	6*5	BAL-CLE	1-3	KC-MIL	1-5	CAL-MIN	2*1	NY-TOR	9-10
							BAL-CLE	3-4	KC-MIL	2-3			NY-TOR	6-13
0803	DET-CHI	6*3	CAL-MIN	7*5	OAK-SEA	6*1	BAL-CLE	8*2	KC-MIL	8*5	BOS-TEX	5*4	NY-TOR	2-6
0804	DET-CHI	2-4	OAK-MIN	3-4	CAL-SEA	5-11	BAL-CLE	4*3	KC-MIL	6*2	BOS-TEX	1-6	NY-TOR	3*1
0805	CHI-BAL	4-5	OAK-MIN	3*2	CAL-SEA	1-3	TEX-CLE	2*0	TOR-MIL	0-7	BOS-KC	5*4	DET-NY	3-12
0806	CHI-BAL	6*4	OAK-MIN	6*4	CAL-SEA	1-2	TEX-CLE	6*1	TOR-MIL	0-3	BOS-KC	0-4	DET-NY	3-13
0807	CHI-BAL	4*3	OAK-MIN	6*0	CAL-SEA	4*3	TEX-CLE	4*3	TOR-MIL	6-9	BOS-KC	0-1	DET-NY	8*5
							TEX-CLE	0-7						
0808	CLE-BAL	9*4	TEX-BOS	12*7	MIN-CAL	4*2	SEA-OAK	1-2	CHI-DET	5*4	MIL-KC	4-5	TOR-NY	3-8
									CHI-DET	2-7	MIL-KC	8*5	TOR-NY	3-11
0809	CLE-BAL	4*3	TEX-BOS	4-6	MIN-CAL	2-8	SEA-OAK	6-7	CHI-DET	6*5	MIL-KC	2-8	TOR-NY	8*0
0810	CLE-BAL	4*3	TEX-BOS	2-4	MIN-CAL	4*1	SEA-OAK	7*5			MIL-KC	4*0	TOR-NY	3-8
0811	BAL-CHI	3-9	NY-DET	6*5	MIL-TOR	6*4	MIN-OAK	0-6						
0812	BAL-CHI	1-2	NY-DET	6-7	MIL-TOR	4-5	MIN-OAK	5*3	SEA-CAL	7*6	CLE-TEX	2-6		
0813	BAL-CHI	5*2	NY-DET	3-6	MIL-TOR	1-3	MIN-OAK	7*3	SEA-CAL	5-10	CLE-TEX	3-4	KC-BOS	5*4
													KC-BOS	3-12
0814	SEA-CAL	2-7	BAL-CHI	2*1	NY-DET	4*1	MIN-OAK	0-6	CLE-TEX	3*0	MIL-TOR	3-4	KC-BOS	3-4
													KC-BOS	6*3
0815	TOR-CLE	3*2	DET-KC	4-6	BOS-MIL	0-2	CHI-NY	1*0	CAL-OAK	0-5	MIN-SEA	7*4	BAL-TEX	6*4
0816	TOR-CLE	2-3	DET-KC	7-18	BOS-MIL	3-4	CHI-NY	5*3	CAL-OAK	0-4	MIN-SEA	5*1	BAL-TEX	0-2
	TOR-CLE	9*6												

◆1983◆	GAME 1	GAME 2	GAME 3	GAME 4	GAME 5	GAME 6	GAME 7
0817	TOR-CLE 6*5	DET-KC 10*4	CHI-NY 7*5	CAL-OAK 6*5	MIN-SEA 7*4	BAL-TEX 4*2	BOS-MIL 3-4 / BOS-MIL 1-5
0818	KC-NY 5*4						
0819	CAL-NY 6-11	TOR-BOS 8*7	SEA-CLE 5-6	OAK-MIL 9*1	DET-MIN 5*1	KC-BAL 4-5 / KC-BAL 1-3	CHI-TEX 3*2 / CHI-TEX 6*1
0820	TOR-BOS 2-5	SEA-CLE 2-3	OAK-MIL 1-3	DET-MIN 9*1	CAL-NY 2-6	KC-BAL 1-6	CHI-TEX 1-6
0821	TOR-BOS 7*3	SEA-CLE 7*2	OAK-MIL 1-7	DET-MIN 3-4	CAL-NY 1-2	KC-BAL 8*3	CHI-TEX 3*1
0822	TOR-BOS 2-4	CAL-CLE 7*3	SEA-MIL 2-3	CHI-KC 3*1	OAK-NY 3*2		DET-TEX 1-3
0823	TOR-BAL 9*3	CAL-CLE 5*2	SEA-MIL 5*0	CHI-KC 2-10	OAK-NY 9*3	BOS-MIN 2-3	DET-TEX 2*0
0824	TOR-BAL 4-7	OAK-CLE 0-1 / OAK-CLE 2-4	CAL-MIL 0-1	CHI-KC 4*3	SEA-NY 3-6	BOS-MIN 7-8	DET-TEX 5*2
0825	TOR-BAL 1-2	OAK-CLE 6*0	CHI-DET 1-10	CAL-MIL 0-7	BOS-MIN 2-5	SEA-NY 4-7	TEX-KC 1-3 / TEX-KC 4-5
0826	MIN-BAL 0-9	NY-CAL 3*2	BOS-CHI 3*1	TOR-DET 3-4	MIL-OAK 3-4	CLE-SEA 4*1	TEX-KC 3-8
0827	MIN-BAL 3-5	NY-CAL 6-7	BOS-CHI 1-2	TOR-DET 7*4	MIL-OAK 2-5	CLE-SEA 3-6	TEX-KC 0-2
0828	MIN-BAL 4-11	NY-CAL 7*3	BOS-CHI 2-6	TOR-DET 2-4	MIL-OAK 4*2	CLE-SEA 5*2	TEX-KC 1*0
0829	BOS-TOR 1-5 / BOS-TOR 8*7	CLE-CAL 6*4	TEX-CHI 1-2	MIN-DET 5*4		MIL-SEA 1-2	BAL-KC 9*2
0830	BOS-TOR 5*4	CLE-CAL 6-10	TEX-CHI 0-5	MIN-DET 3-4	BAL-KC 12*4	NY-OAK 8*5	MIL-SEA 3*2
0831	BAL-TOR 10*2	CLE-CAL 7*5	KC-CHI 3-7	TEX-DET 5*1		NY-OAK 6*4	MIL-SEA 1-4
0901	BAL-TOR 3-5	MIN-BOS 11*0 / MIN-BOS 3-9	KC-CHI 0-12	TEX-DET 0-5		NY-OAK 0-2	
0902	MIL-CAL 5-6	CHI-BOS 1-5	BAL-MIN 1*0	CLE-OAK 4*2	NY-SEA 5*4	KC-TEX 0-7	DET-TOR 9*8 / DET-TOR 7-8
0903	CHI-BOS 9*6	MIL-CAL 4*3	BAL-MIN 13*0	CLE-OAK 13*6	NY-SEA 5*3	KC-TEX 5*0 / KC-TEX 1-8	DET-TOR 7*4
0904	CHI-BOS 2-6	MIL-CAL 3-5	BAL-MIN 9*6	CLE-OAK 9*2	NY-SEA 4*3	KC-TEX 2-3	DET-TOR 3-6
0905	BOS-BAL 2*0	OAK-CHI 1-11	DET-CLE 2-3	SEA-KC 1-3	NY-MIL 1-3	MIN-TEX 3-7	CAL-TOR 0-7
0906	BOS-BAL 1-8	OAK-CHI 6-7		SEA-KC 3*1	NY-MIL 3-6	MIN-TEX 5*3	CAL-TOR 4-6
0907	BOS-BAL 2-5	OAK-CHI 7-8	DET-CLE 1-7 / DET-CLE 7*3	SEA-KC 2-3	NY-MIL 11*5	MIN-TEX 0-3	CAL-TOR 9*6
0908	CAL-CHI 5-8	NY-MIL 6*5					
0909	CAL-CHI 0-11	DET-MIL 1-2 / DET-MIL 2*1	BOS-CLE 6*4	KC-MIN 6-7	BAL-NY 3-5	TEX-SEA 4-6	OAK-TOR 7*5
0910	CAL-CHI 6-7	DET-MIL 4*0	BOS-CLE 6-8	KC-MIN 3-6	TEX-SEA 2-4	OAK-TOR 5-7	BAL-NY 8*4 / BAL-NY 3*1
0911	CAL-CHI 4-5	BOS-CLE 4*1	DET-MIL 6*4	KC-MIN 3*1	TEX-SEA 2*1	OAK-TOR 6-16	BAL-NY 5*3
0912	CLE-DET 1-5						MIL-NY 0-1
0913	CLE-DET 2-3	KC-CAL 4*3	CHI-MIN 5*1	TEX-OAK 5-6	TOR-SEA 6*4	BAL-BOS 7*4 / BAL-BOS 7*1	MIL-NY 1-2
0914	KC-CAL 1*0	CLE-DET 0-5	CHI-MIN 0-1	MIL-NY 1-4	TEX-OAK 4*2	BAL-BOS 5*0	TOR-SEA 4*3
0915	SEA-CHI 0-12		TOR-MIN 2-6		TEX-OAK 6*5	BAL-BOS 1-7	
0916	SEA-CHI 0-7	MIL-BAL 1-8	TOR-MIN 4-11	TEX-CAL 6-8	OAK-KC 5-6	DET-BOS 1-6	
0917	SEA-CHI 3-4	MIL-BAL 4-5	TOR-MIN 13*3	TEX-CAL 5*2	OAK-KC 1-10	DET-BOS 2-3	NY-CLE 6-7
0918	SEA-CHI 0-6	MIL-BAL 9-10		TEX-CAL 7*6	OAK-KC 6*2	DET-BOS 9*6	NY-CLE 6-10 / NY-CLE 13*8
0919	MIL-BAL 7-8	NY-BOS 3-5	MIN-CHI 7*5	SEA-TOR 9*6	CAL-KC 4-8 / CAL-KC 6-7		
0920	NY-BOS 3*2	MIL-CLE 11*7	BAL-DET 1-14	OAK-TEX 2-3	CAL-KC 6*4	SEA-TOR 3-7	
0921	NY-BOS 1-3	MIL-CLE 10*7	BAL-DET 6*0 / BAL-DET 7*3	OAK-TEX 2-4	CAL-KC 3*0	SEA-TOR 3-4	MIN-CHI 1-2 / MIN-CHI 6-7
0922	CHI-CAL 3*2	MIL-CLE 5-9	BAL-DET 4-5	MIN-KC 2*1	SEA-TEX 2-5		
0923	CHI-CAL 2*1	BAL-MIL 4*2	BOS-DET 0-7	MIN-KC 2-3	SEA-TEX 1-2	CLE-NY 4-7	TOR-OAK 0-2
0924	CHI-CAL 2*0	BAL-MIL 2-5	BOS-DET 5*3	MIN-KC 4-12	SEA-TEX 2*0	CLE-NY 1-9	TOR-OAK 1-2
0925	CHI-CAL 8*5	BAL-MIL 5*1	BOS-DET 2-3	MIN-KC 7*1	SEA-TEX 2*1	CLE-NY 4-6	TOR-OAK 8*6
0926	TOR-CAL 3*2	KC-SEA 6*2				CLE-NY 7*0	
0927	TOR-CAL 1-7	KC-SEA 0-4	DET-BAL 9*2	CLE-MIL 4-8	TEX-MIN 6*1	BOS-NY 2-7	CHI-OAK 4-5
0928	TOR-CAL 5*3	KC-SEA 11*8	DET-BAL 9*5	CLE-MIL 4-6	TEX-MIN 0-3	BOS-NY 3*2	CHI-OAK 5*3
0929		KC-SEA 4-5	DET-BAL 9*4	CLE-MIL 4*2	TEX-MIN 0-2	BOS-NY 3-4	CHI-OAK 0-3
0930	CLE-BOS 0-10	CHI-SEA 9*4	NY-BAL 6*4 / NY-BAL 2-3	MIL-DET 6*2	CAL-TEX 3-4	MIN-TOR 0-8	
1001	CLE-BOS 3*1	MIL-DET 10*1	NY-BAL 5*4	CHI-SEA 9*3	CAL-TEX 6*5	MIN-TOR 3-4	KC-OAK 4*1 / KC-OAK 7*3
1002	NY-BAL 0-2	CLE-BOS 1-3	MIL-DET 7*4	CHI-SEA 3*0	CAL-TEX 2*0	MIN-TOR 9*3	KC-OAK 4-8

◆1984◆	GAME 1	GAME 2	GAME 3	GAME 4	GAME 5	GAME 6	GAME 7
0402	CHI-BAL 5*2	BOS-CAL 1-2					
0403	NY-KC 2-4	DET-MIN 8*1					
0404	NY-KC 4*3	BOS-CAL 2*1	MIL-OAK 5-6	CLE-TEX 9*1			
0405	NY-KC 4-15	BOS-CAL 7*4	MIL-OAK 3-4	TOR-SEA 2-3			
0406	CLE-KC 2*0	TOR-CAL 11*5	BAL-MIN 4-9	MIL-SEA 3-6	NY-TEX 6-7	DET-CHI 3*2	BOS-OAK 1-3
0407		TOR-CAL 3*1	BAL-MIN 4-13	MIL-SEA 2-3	NY-TEX 5-8	DET-CHI 4*0	BOS-OAK 3*0
0408	CLE-KC 4-5	TOR-CAL 3-4	BAL-MIN 3-7	MIL-SEA 4-5	NY-TEX 4*3	DET-CHI 7*3	BOS-OAK 2-14
0409							TOR-OAK 3-4
0410	KC-BAL 3-6	MIL-CAL 10*1	CLE-CHI 3-7	TEX-DET 1-5	MIN-NY 1-4	BOS-SEA 1-5	TOR-OAK 3*0
0411	KC-BAL 5*2	MIL-CAL 5-9	CLE-CHI 1-6			BOS-SEA 4-5	
0412	TEX-DET 4-9	MIN-NY 3*0	CAL-OAK 3*2				
0413	DET-BOS 13*9	CHI-NY 5*3	CAL-OAK 1-2	MIL-KC 3-6	SEA-MIN 3-4	TOR-TEX 3*2	
0414	BAL-CLE 2-8		CAL-OAK 3-4	MIL-KC 8*4	SEA-MIN 3-4	TOR-TEX 2-6	
0415	BAL-CLE 6*5	CHI-NY 1-2	CAL-OAK 12*8	MIL-KC 3*2	SEA-MIN 5*4	TOR-TEX 2*1	
0416	BAL-CLE 3-4	OAK-SEA 9*6			CAL-MIN 2-9		
0417	TEX-BOS 8*4	OAK-SEA 6*2	CHI-MIL 3-7	BAL-TOR 2-3	CAL-MIN 6*3		
0418	TEX-BOS 4*3	OAK-SEA 4*3	NY-CLE 5*0	BAL-TOR 1-7	CAL-MIN 9*2	KC-DET 3-4	
0419	TEX-BOS 7*4	CHI-MIL 3*1		BAL-TOR 1-2		KC-DET 5*2	
0420	OAK-BOS 1-3	SEA-MIL 5*0	MIN-BAL 2-4	CAL-TOR 10*6	KC-CLE 6*4	CHI-DET 2-3	TEX-NY 1-4
0421	OAK-BOS 5*2	SEA-MIL 2-6	MIN-BAL 3-5	CAL-TOR 8*4	KC-CLE 2-3	CHI-DET 1-4	TEX-NY 1*0
0422	OAK-BOS 8-12		MIN-BAL 6*1	CAL-TOR 9*6		CHI-DET 1-9	TEX-NY 4*0
0423	CAL-BOS 0-2	BAL-CHI 6-7	TEX-CLE 1-3	SEA-TOR 5-8			
0424	CAL-BOS 8*7	BAL-CHI 8*3	OAK-MIL 2-3	SEA-TOR 4*2	KC-NY 0-4	MIN-DET 5-6 / MIN-DET 3-4	
0425	SEA-BOS 1-2	CHI-CLE 2-9	BAL-KC 2-3	CAL-MIL 5*1	NY-MIN 6-8	DET-TEX 9*4	OAK-TOR 0-11
0426	SEA-BOS 6*5	CHI-CLE 4-5	BAL-KC 11*3	CAL-MIL 1-2	NY-MIN 2-4	DET-TEX 7*5	OAK-TOR 7*4
0427	TEX-BAL 3-4	SEA-CAL 3-9	TOR-KC 1*0	BOS-CHI 5*3	CLE-DET 8*4	MIL-NY 12*0	MIN-OAK 3-5
0428	TEX-BAL 1-6	SEA-CAL 1-10	TOR-KC 6*0	BOS-CHI 8*7	CLE-DET 2-6	MIL-NY 8*0	MIN-OAK 0-7
0429	TEX-BAL 2-3	SEA-CAL 9*6		BOS-CHI 4-6	CLE-DET 1-6	MIL-NY 5-6	MIN-OAK 5*2 / MIN-OAK 0-3
0430	CLE-BAL 3-6	SEA-CAL 1-8	NY-CHI 3-5	BOS-DET 2-11	KC-MIL 3*0	MIN-SEA 8-11	TEX-TOR 4-10
0501	CLE-BAL 0-3	OAK-CAL 1-4	NY-CHI 5-7	BOS-DET 5*4 / BOS-DET 1*0		MIN-SEA 8*6	TEX-TOR 4*1 / TEX-TOR 6-7
0502	CLE-BAL 9*7	OAK-CAL 7*6	NY-CHI 0-3				
0503	KC-MIL 5-6						
0504	NY-MIL 0-1	CHI-BOS 5*3	DET-CLE 9*2	OAK-MIN 1-3	CAL-SEA 4*1	BAL-TEX 2*0	KC-TOR 3-4
0505	NY-MIL 1-2	CHI-BOS 8*5	DET-CLE 6*5	OAK-MIN 4-5	CAL-SEA 3*1	BAL-TEX 7*5	KC-TOR 1-10
0506	NY-MIL 8*4	CHI-BOS 1-3	DET-CLE 6*5	OAK-MIN 3-4	CAL-SEA 1-3	BAL-TEX 6*1	KC-TOR 1-2
0507	MIN-CAL 11*1	MIL-CHI 7*3	DET-KC 10*3	CLE-NY 2-5	SEA-OAK 5-6		
0508	MIN-CAL 5*0	MIL-CHI 3#3	DET-KC 5*2	BOS-TEX 3-4	SEA-OAK 2-3		

◆1984◆	GAME 1	GAME 2	GAME 3	GAME 4	GAME 5	GAME 6	GAME 7
0509	MIN-CAL 5*2	MIL-CHI 6-7	DET-KC 3*1	BOS-TEX 2*0	SEA-OAK 4*1	CLE-NY 4-11	TOR-BAL 4-7
		MIL-CHI 4-5					TOR-BAL 3-7
0510	CLE-NY 6-7	TEX-CHI 6-8					TOR-BAL 4*3
0511	SEA-NY 4*3	TEX-CHI 6*1	CAL-DET 2-8	BOS-KC 4-6	MIN-MIL 1-4		OAK-BAL 3-4
0512	SEA-NY 5*0	TEX-CHI 6*4	CAL-DET 4*2	BOS-KC 0-3	MIN-MIL 4*2	TOR-CLE 4-8	OAK-BAL 12*2
0513	SEA-NY 0-7	TEX-CHI 1-8		BOS-KC 1-5	MIN-MIL 1-4	TOR-CLE 44	OAK-BAL 1-5
						BOS-CLE 6*1	CAL-BAL 1-4
0514	OAK-NY 1-3	KC-CHI 0-2	SEA-DET 5-7			BOS-CLE 5-7	CAL-BAL 5*2
0515	OAK-NY 6-9	KC-CHI 2-3	SEA-DET 4-6	TEX-MIL 2-3	TOR-MIN 5*2	BOS-CLE 5*2	CAL-BAL 0-5
0516	OAK-NY 6-7	KC-CHI 7*6	SEA-DET 1-10	TEX-MIL 1-5	TOR-MIN 8*7	BOS-CLE 11*10	
0517	CHI-TOR 2-3			TEX-MIL 4*1			
0518	CHI-TOR 3-4	SEA-BAL 1-4	OAK-DET 4-8	CLE-MIL 8*4	TEX-KC 2*1	BOS-MIN 3-8	CAL-NY 4*3
0519	CHI-TOR 0-1	SEA-BAL 6*5	OAK-DET 4*2	CLE-MIL 1-6	TEX-KC 2-6	BOS-MIN 0-7	CAL-NY 4*0
0520	CHI-TOR 3*0	SEA-BAL 1-5	OAK-DET 3-4	CLE-MIL 3*2	TEX-KC 3*2	BOS-MIN 5*4	CAL-NY 3*0
0521	MIN-TOR 2-3	CLE-BOS 3-6			CHI-KC 8*4		
0522	MIN-TOR 2-3	CLE-BOS 1-7	DET-CAL 3*1	BAL-OAK 4-6	CHI-KC 6-7	NY-SEA 3-5	MIL-TEX 7*1
0523	MIN-TOR 1-4	CLE-BOS 5*4	DET-CAL 4*2	BAL-OAK 9*5	CHI-KC 0-1	NY-SEA 3*0	MIL-TEX 1-6
0524			DET-CAL 5*1	BAL-OAK 2-3		NY-SEA 2*0	MIL-TEX 3-4
0525	KC-BOS 8*5	MIL-MIN 4-7	BAL-CAL 2-10	NY-OAK 7-10	CLE-TOR 1-5	DET-SEA 3-7	CHI-TEX 0-11
0526	KC-BOS 11*7	MIL-MIN 6-7	BAL-CAL 9*5	NY-OAK 8*4	CLE-TOR 1-2	DET-SEA 5-9	CHI-TEX 5*1
0527	KC-BOS 0-6	MIL-MIN 5*4	BAL-CAL 8*0	NY-OAK 1-7	CLE-TOR 1-6	DET-SEA 1-6	CHI-TEX 3-11
					CLE-TOR 5-6		
0528	NY-CAL 2-6	DET-OAK 6*2	BAL-SEA 7*4	KC-TEX 6*1			
0529	NY-CAL 5-6	DET-OAK 5-8	BAL-SEA 3*2	KC-TEX 7*5	TOR-CHI 1-8	MIL-CLE 5*3	
0530	NY-CAL 10*1	DET-OAK 2*1	BAL-SEA 8*2	KC-TEX 3-7	TOR-CHI 2*1	MIL-CLE 1-9	MIN-BOS 0-2
						MIL-CLE 3*2	
0531	KC-MIN 2-7						
0601	KC-MIN 7*1	OAK-CHI 4-6	CAL-CLE 5*2	BAL-DET 2-14	BOS-MIL 3*1	SEA-TEX 5*3	NY-TOR 2-10
0602	KC-MIN 7*6	OAK-CHI 6*3	CAL-CLE 6*4	BAL-DET 5*0	BOS-MIL 6*3	SEA-TEX 10*7	NY-TOR 8-9
0603	KC-MIN 5*2	OAK-CHI 2-3	CAL-CLE 7*4	BAL-DET 2*1	BOS-MIL 6*3	SEA-TEX 10*4	NY-TOR 15*2
0604	TEX-MIN 2-6	CAL-CHI 4-6	OAK-CLE 7*3	TOR-DET 8*4	MIL-BAL 3*1	SEA-KC 7*1	BOS-NY 3-8
0605	TEX-MIN 2*1	CAL-CHI 6*1	OAK-CLE 4*2	TOR-DET 8*4	MIL-BAL 8*3	SEA-KC 3-4	BOS-NY 5*4
0606	TEX-MIN 1-2	CAL-CHI 0-4	OAK-CLE 6-7	TOR-DET 6*3	MIL-BAL 0-3	SEA-KC 2-5	BOS-NY 5*3
0607	TEX-MIN 4-5	CAL-CHI 10-11	MIL-BOS 6*3	TOR-DET 3-5		SEA-KC 8-9	
0608	DET-BAL 3*2	MIN-CHI 1-6	MIL-BOS 3-11	SEA-CLE 3-4	TOR-NY 3-4	OAK-TEX 4-8	
0609	DET-BAL 0-4	MIN-CHI 4-8	MIL-BOS 6-15	SEA-CLE 7-8	TOR-NY 1-2	OAK-TEX 3-4	CAL-KC 4*1
0610	DET-BAL 10*4	MIN-CHI 12*5	MIL-BOS 4-5	SEA-CLE 1-3	TOR-NY 3-5	OAK-TEX 1-3	CAL-KC 2*0
	DET-BAL 8*0			SEA-CLE 4*3			
0611	NY-BOS 6-9	BAL-MIL 3*1	OAK-TEX 3-6	DET-TEX 5*4			
0612	NY-BOS 8-9	BAL-MIL 5*4	MIN-TEX 2-6	DET-TOR 3-12	CHI-CAL 2-3	CLE-OAK 11*5	KC-SEA 2-3
0613	NY-BOS 4*2	BAL-MIL 1-6	MIN-TEX 0-3	DET-TOR 3-7	CHI-CAL 2*1	CLE-OAK 1-3	KC-SEA 6*4
0614	NY-BOS 12*11	BAL-MIL 2-3	MIN-TEX 3*2		CHI-CAL 3-9	CLE-OAK 6-7	KC-SEA 1-4
0615	MIN-KC 3*0	DET-MIL 3*2	BAL-NY 2*1	BOS-TOR 3-4	CLE-CAL 2-5	CHI-OAK 1-2	TEX-SEA 3-4
0616	MIN-KC 6*1	DET-MIL 6*0	BAL-NY 3-8	BOS-TOR 0-7	CLE-CAL 2-7	CHI-OAK 2-6	TEX-SEA 5*1
0617	MIN-KC 3*1	DET-MIL 7*4	BAL-NY 6*2	BOS-TOR 3-5	CLE-CAL 4*3	CHI-OAK 9*4	TEX-SEA 2-5
					TEX-CAL 6*2	KC-OAK 2-10	CHI-SEA 8*4
0618	NY-DET 2*1						
0619	NY-DET 6-7	BAL-BOS 9*7	CLE-MIN 7*4	MIL-TOR 6*5	TEX-CAL 4*2	KC-OAK 6*2	CHI-SEA 2-8
0620	NY-DET 6-9	BAL-BOS 4*1	CLE-MIN 2-8	MIL-TOR 5*4	TEX-CAL 3*2	KC-OAK 1-8	CHI-SEA 5*4
0621	MIL-DET 4*3	TOR-BOS 5*2	CLE-MIN 7*0	NY-BAL 5*3			
0622	MIL-DET 3-7	TOR-BOS 1-8	CHI-MIN 8*6	NY-BAL 4-5	KC-CAL 1-8	TEX-OAK 4*0	CLE-SEA 13*3
0623	MIL-DET 1-5	TOR-BOS 9*3	CHI-MIN 3-4	NY-BAL 5*4	KC-CAL 6*5	TEX-OAK 1-5	CLE-SEA 11*4
0624	MIL-DET 1-7	TOR-BOS 3-5	CHI-MIN 2-3		KC-CAL 3*2	TEX-OAK 2-4	CLE-SEA 5*0
0625	BOS-BAL 7*4	SEA-CHI 6*1	OAK-KC 0-16	DET-NY 3-7	CAL-TEX 4-5	TOR-MIL 1-2	
						TOR-MIL 4-9	
0626	BOS-BAL 5*2	SEA-CHI 5*0	MIN-CLE 8*3	DET-NY 9*7	CAL-TEX 3*2	TOR-MIL 3-6	OAK-KC 8*4
							OAK-KC 6*1
0627	BOS-BAL 1-3	SEA-CHI 7-9	MIN-CLE 4-6	TOR-MIL 1-5	DET-NY 4-5	CAL-TEX 2*1	OAK-KC 9*5
0628	SEA-BOS 6-9	BAL-CHI 2*0	TEX-CLE 10*6	CAL-MIL 7*3	OAK-TOR 6-9		
			TEX-CLE 2-7				
0629	SEA-BOS 5*3	BAL-CHI 1-2	TEX-CLE 12-13	NY-KC 2-3	CAL-MIL 0-1	OAK-TOR 2*1	MIN-DET 5*3
							MIN-DET 5-7
0630	SEA-BOS 2*1	BAL-CHI 4-5	TEX-CLE 2*1	NY-KC 2-6	CAL-MIL 2*0	OAK-TOR 1-6	MIN-DET 3-4
0701	SEA-BOS 1*0	BAL-CHI 8*3	TEX-CLE 5-13	NY-KC 0-8	CAL-MIL 7*6	OAK-TOR 6-7	MIN-DET 9*0
0702	OAK-BOS 9*6	DET-CHI 1-7	KC-CLE 9*3	BAL-MIN 4-6	SEA-MIL 2-3	CAL-TOR 6*3	NY-TEX 6-7
			KC-CLE 4*3		SEA-MIL 4-6		
0703	OAK-BOS 5-6	DET-CHI 5-9	KC-CLE 3-15	BAL-MIN 1-3	SEA-MIL 6-11	NY-TEX 5*4	CAL-TOR 0-4
0704	OAK-BOS 9-13	DET-CHI 2-8	KC-CLE 4*0	BAL-MIN 6*4	SEA-MIL 2-4	NY-TEX 5*0	CAL-TOR 3-6
0705	CAL-BOS 7-12	CLE-CHI 6-7		NY-MIN 4-5	OAK-MIL 5-7	DET-TEX 7*4	SEA-TOR 8-10
0706	CAL-BOS 7-8	CLE-CHI 6-11	KC-BAL 6*2	NY-MIN 4-9	OAK-MIL 7*6	DET-TEX 3-5	SEA-TOR 2-9
					OAK-MIL 11*0		
0707	CLE-CHI 2-4	NY-MIN 11*4	DET-TEX 5*2	SEA-TOR 8*4	OAK-MIL 8*2	KC-BAL 2-6	
						KC-BAL 0-8	
0708	CLE-CHI 8-9	OAK-MIL 4*1	NY-MIN 3-4	DET-TEX 7-9	SEA-TOR 7*1	KC-BAL 6*1	CAL-BOS 2-3
							CAL-BOS 4*0
0712	MIL-CAL 2-5	DET-MIN 2-4	KC-NY 2-5	TOR-OAK 4-7	BOS-SEA 2-3	CLE-TEX 2-7	CHI-BAL 1-2
							CHI-BAL 0-3
0713	MIL-CAL 5*4	DET-MIN 5*3	TOR-OAK 6*3	BOS-SEA 9*5	CLE-TEX 5*0	KC-NY 1-7	CHI-BAL 5-7
						KC-NY 1-8	
0714	CHI-BAL 3*2	MIL-CAL 1-2	DET-MIN 6*5	TOR-OAK 2*1	BOS-SEA 4-5	KC-NY 1-4	CLE-TEX 5*0
0715	CHI-BAL 4-6	MIL-CAL 6-7	DET-MIN 6*2	TOR-OAK 6*3	BOS-SEA 11*3	KC-NY 1-4	CLE-TEX 5*4
0716	MIN-BAL 1-3	TOR-CAL 0-3	CHI-DET 1-7	BOS-OAK 4*1	MIL-SEA 2-11	TEX-NY 8-9	CLE-KC 1-3
0717	MIN-BAL 1-3	TOR-CAL 3-5	CHI-DET 2-3	BOS-OAK 6*1	MIL-SEA 1-3	TEX-NY 10*4	CLE-KC 9*7
							CLE-KC 6*2
0718	MIN-BAL 3*1	TOR-CAL 8*2	CHI-DET 10*6	TEX-NY 1-3	BOS-OAK 2-7	MIL-SEA 5*2	CLE-KC 2*1
0719	CHI-CLE 3*0		TEX-DET 2-9	MIN-NY 2*1	MIL-OAK 1-4	TOR-SEA 8*1	BAL-KC 3-6
0720	CHI-CLE 3-6	BOS-CAL 4*3	TEX-DET 1-3	MIN-NY 3-4	MIL-OAK 9*7	TOR-SEA 12*7	BAL-KC 3-4
0721	CHI-CLE 4*3	BOS-CAL 16*4	TEX-DET 6-7	MIN-NY 5*2	MIL-OAK 7*4	TOR-SEA 3-9	BAL-KC 4*3
0722	CHI-CLE 1-4	BOS-CAL 3*0	TEX-DET 0-2	MIN-NY 5-6	MIL-OAK 4-5	TOR-SEA 5*3	BAL-KC 4-8
0723	DET-CLE 4*1	SEA-CAL 1-7	NY-MIL 4-6	OAK-MIN 4-14	BAL-TEX 9*5		TOR-KC 8-9
							TOR-KC 2-7
0724	CHI-BOS 2-3	SEA-CAL 4*3	DET-CLE 9*5	NY-MIL 1-2	OAK-MIN 4-6	BAL-TEX 2-3	TOR-KC 4-5
0725	CHI-BOS 2-3	SEA-CAL 0-1	DET-CLE 1-4	NY-MIL 3*0	OAK-MIN 1*0	BAL-TEX 3*1	TOR-KC 4-5
0726	CHI-BOS 0-7						
0727	CLE-BAL 3-4	NY-CHI 8*6	CAL-MIN 0-2	OAK-SEA 2-12	TEX-TOR 4*2	BOS-DET 1-9	KC-MIL 12*8
						BOS-DET 4*0	KC-MIL 1-3
0728	CLE-BAL 6*3	NY-CHI 3*2	CAL-MIN 1-6	OAK-SEA 1-2	TEX-TOR 5*4	BOS-DET 3*2	KC-MIL 2-3
0729	CLE-BAL 1-3	NY-CHI 4-5	CAL-MIN 5-6	OAK-SEA 1-4	TEX-TOR 2-6	BOS-DET 0-3	KC-MIL 5*1
0730	TEX-BAL 5*1	BOS-CHI 0-7	SEA-MIN 5-9	MIL-NY 3-4	KC-TOR 7*4	CAL-OAK 5*4	
0731	TEX-BAL 7*6	BOS-CHI 14*4	SEA-MIN 2-9	MIL-NY 4-7	KC-TOR 5-6	CAL-OAK 7*3	CLE-DET 1-5
							CLE-DET 6*4
0801	TEX-BAL 2-7	BOS-CHI 3-5	SEA-MIN 5*1	MIL-NY 3-7	CAL-OAK 6*4	KC-TOR 1-4	CLE-DET 4*2
0802	MIN-CAL 2-14			MIL-NY 4-6			CLE-DET 1-2
0803	MIN-CAL 4*2	TOR-BAL 5*2	TEX-BOS 4*3	CLE-NY 0-9	CHI-MIL 5*1	SEA-OAK 3-5	KC-DET 9*6
				CLE-NY 2-3		SEA-OAK 7-11	
0804	TOR-BAL 6*2	TEX-BOS 2-5	MIN-CAL 2-4	CLE-NY 5-8	KC-DET 9*5	SEA-OAK 2-4	CHI-MIL 7*3
0805	TOR-BAL 4*3	TEX-BOS 2-4	MIN-CAL 4*2	CLE-NY 0-4	KC-DET 5*4	SEA-OAK 4-5	CHI-MIL 7*0
					KC-DET 4*0		

♦1984♦	GAME 1	GAME 2	GAME 3	GAME 4	GAME 5	GAME 6	GAME 7
0806	BAL-CLE 4*2	CHI-MIL 5*3	MIN-OAK 7*4	CAL-SEA 8*4	TOR-TEX 4-5	DET-BOS 9*7 / 2-10	
0807	BAL-CLE 4-5	MIL-KC 5-8	MIN-OAK 2*1	CAL-SEA 7*6	TOR-TEX 6-7	DET-BOS 7-12 / 7*5	CHI-NY 6*3 / 0-7
0808	BAL-CLE 7*4	MIL-KC 3*2	MIN-OAK 0-5	CAL-SEA 2-7	TOR-TEX 7*2	DET-BOS 0-8	CHI-NY 5*4
0809	BAL-CLE 5-7	MIL-KC 4-5	OAK-CAL 5*4	MIN-SEA 5-6	BOS-TEX 3-7		CHI-NY 6-7
0810	NY-CLE 6*4 / 10*1	DET-KC 5*4	OAK-CAL 7*6	MIN-SEA 13*7	BOS-TEX 4-8	MIL-CHI 4*2	BAL-TOR 0-2
0811	NY-CLE 10*1	OAK-CAL 3*2	MIL-CHI 10*5	DET-KC 9*5	MIN-SEA 4-5	BOS-TEX 5*4	BAL-TOR 2-3
0812	NY-CLE 0-6	OAK-CAL 9-10	MIL-CHI 8*1	DET-KC 8*4	MIN-SEA 3*0	BOS-TEX 3*2	BAL-TOR 5*4
0813	NY-CLE 5-6	MIL-MIN 1-5	TEX-CHI 3-5	BOS-KC 1-6			BAL-TOR 2*1
0814	TOR-CLE 8*1 / 9*5	MIL-MIN 2-3	TEX-CHI 9*3	BOS-KC 8*2	OAK-BAL 4*3	SEA-NY 2*1	CAL-DET 6*4 / 12*1
0815	TOR-CLE 1-16 / 3-4	OAK-BAL 6*1	TEX-CHI 6*5	BOS-KC 8-13	MIL-MIN 8*4	SEA-NY 2-3	CAL-DET 3-8
0816	TOR-CLE 5-6	OAK-BAL 8*1	MIN-BOS 5-7	CAL-DET 7-8	SEA-NY 5*4	KC-TEX 6*3	
0817	MIL-CLE 3-5	CAL-BAL 5-6	MIN-BOS 6*5	SEA-DET 2-6	OAK-NY 7*3	KC-TEX 6-8	TOR-CHI 4*3
0818		CAL-BAL 0-1	MIN-BOS 6*4 / 3*1	SEA-DET 3-4	OAK-NY 0-8	KC-TEX 5*4	TOR-CHI 6-7
0819	CAL-BAL 4-10	TOR-CHI 7*4	MIN-BOS 4-5	SEA-DET 4*1	OAK-NY 6-9	KC-TEX 4-6	MIL-CLE 6-8 / 1-2
0820	SEA-BAL 4-5	KC-BOS 8*5	OAK-DET 1-14	CAL-NY 4-8	CHI-TEX 7*5		
0821	SEA-BAL 4*3	KC-BOS 1-11	OAK-DET 6-12	CAL-NY 2-8	CHI-TEX 3-4	CLE-TOR 3*1	
0822	SEA-BAL 0-4	KC-BOS 6*2	OAK-DET 4-11	CAL-NY 2*1	CHI-TEX 1-3	CLE-TOR 13*3	MIN-MIL 5*2 / 4*3
0823	CLE-TOR 1-6						MIN-MIL 2-5
0824	CLE-BOS 6-7	DET-CAL 3-5	CHI-KC 2-5	TOR-MIN 6*2	BAL-OAK 4*2	NY-SEA 6*4	TEX-MIL 10*3
0825	CLE-BOS 6-11	DET-CAL 5*1	CHI-KC 3*0	TOR-MIN 4-5	BAL-OAK 4-5	NY-SEA 14*1	TEX-MIL 6-7
0826	CLE-BOS 2-4	DET-CAL 12*6	CHI-KC 5-6	TOR-MIN 2*1	BAL-OAK 13*6	NY-SEA 7*2	TEX-MIL 3-6
0827		BAL-CAL 7*6	CHI-KC 4-7	TOR-MIN 5*2	NY-OAK 8*7		CLE-MIL 7*1
0828	DET-SEA 5*4	BAL-CAL 2-4	TEX-KC 6*0	BOS-MIN 1-2	NY-OAK 3-4	CHI-TOR 6-7	CLE-MIL 8*5
0829	DET-SEA 1-5	BAL-CAL 5-7	TEX-KC 1-4	BOS-MIN 4*0	NY-OAK 4*1	CHI-TOR 8*5	CLE-MIL 5*2
0830	DET-SEA 1-2	TOR-CHI 4*3	TEX-KC 4*3	BOS-MIN 9*3			CLE-MIL 6-7
0831	BAL-SEA 11*7	KC-CHI 3*1	NY-CAL 3-4	BOS-CLE 8*7	DET-OAK 6-7	MIL-TEX 6-7	MIN-TOR 0-7
0901	BAL-SEA 9-10	KC-CHI 1-6	NY-CAL 6-11	BOS-CLE 4*1	DET-OAK 5-7	MIL-TEX 4-8	MIN-TOR 4-12
0902	BAL-SEA 4*3	KC-CHI 6*4	NY-CAL 5*3	BOS-CLE 3-8	DET-OAK 6*3		MIN-TOR 0-6
0903	BAL-DET 7*4	OAK-CHI 8*2	MIN-KC 4*1	CAL-CLE 5-6	BOS-MIL 8*5	TOR-NY 0-2	SEA-TEX 7*3
0904	BAL-DET 4*1	OAK-CHI 2-12	MIN-KC 1-4	CAL-CLE 5*3	BOS-MIL 3*1	TOR-NY 6*4	SEA-TEX 6*3
0905	BAL-DET 0-1	OAK-CHI 5*4	MIN-KC 1-4	CAL-CLE 11*4	BOS-MIL 5-7	TOR-NY 3-4	SEA-TEX 6*5
0906		OAK-CHI 3-7					
0907	MIL-BAL 10*8	CAL-CHI 16*8	NY-BOS 4*2	OAK-CLE 2-13	SEA-KC 4-5	TEX-MIN 3-7	DET-TOR 7*4
0908	MIL-BAL 3-5	CAL-CHI 6*5	NY-BOS 12*6	OAK-CLE 9*5	SEA-KC 4-5	TEX-MIN 4-5	DET-TOR 10*4
0909	MIL-BAL 0-4	CAL-CHI 2-8	NY-BOS 1-10	OAK-CLE 5-7	SEA-KC 5-6	TEX-MIN 9*3	DET-TOR 7*2
0910	DET-BAL 1-3	CHI-OAK 0-1	MIL-BOS 7*4	TEX-SEA 3-7		KC-MIN 3-7	NY-TOR 6*2
0911	DET-BAL 9*2	CHI-OAK 1-4	MIL-BOS 14*6	TEX-SEA 3-4	CLE-CAL 4*2	KC-MIN 1-5	NY-TOR 3-10
0912	DET-BAL 1-3	CHI-OAK 4*2	MIL-BOS 4-5	TEX-SEA 8*1	CLE-CAL 7*1	KC-MIN 3*2	NY-TOR 1-2
0913				TEX-SEA 9*7	CLE-CAL 3-7		NY-TOR 6*1
0914	TOR-DET 7*2	BAL-MIL 2-4	BOS-NY 1-7	KC-SEA 1-2	CHI-CAL 0-5	CLE-OAK 6*1	MIN-TEX 2-9
0915	TOR-DET 1-2	BAL-MIL 0-7	BOS-NY 4*3	KC-SEA 8*5	CHI-CAL 2-11	CLE-OAK 6*3	MIN-TEX 1*0
0916	TOR-DET 3-8	BAL-MIL 11*8	BOS-NY 5*3	KC-SEA 4*2	CHI-CAL 2-4	CLE-OAK 8*4	MIN-TEX 2*0
0917	MIL-DET 3-7	CHI-MIN 7*3	BAL-NY 7-12	CLE-SEA 2-3	KC-CAL 10*1	TEX-OAK 3-5	BOS-TOR 4-5
0918	MIL-DET 0-3	CHI-MIN 5*3	BAL-NY 2-10	CLE-SEA 3-6	KC-CAL 10*0	TEX-OAK 2-5	BOS-TOR 10*3
0919	MIL-DET 2-4	CHI-MIN 7*3	BAL-NY 5-6	CLE-SEA 3-4	KC-CAL 3-4	TEX-OAK 7-8	BOS-TOR 10*4
0920	BOS-BAL 1-15	CHI-MIN 4-5			KC-CAL 0-2		MIL-TOR 4-6
0921	BOS-BAL 8*0	CLE-MIN 3-7	SEA-CHI 5*1	NY-DET 5*3	TEX-CAL 4-5	OAK-KC 4-7	MIL-TOR 5*1
0922	BOS-BAL 4*2	CLE-MIN 1-4	SEA-CHI 7*1	NY-DET 0-6	TEX-CAL 9*7	OAK-KC 2-4	MIL-TOR 1-2
0923	BOS-BAL 6*2	CLE-MIN 1-5	SEA-CHI 0-4	NY-DET 1-4	TEX-CAL 2*1	OAK-KC 5*1	MIL-TOR 8*5
0924	NY-BAL 1-8 / 6-7	TOR-BOS 9*8	MIN-CHI 8*4	DET-MIL 7*3	OAK-TEX 10*6	CAL-KC 0-4 / 4-12	
0925	NY-BAL 6*5	TOR-BOS 6-14	MIN-CHI 4-8	SEA-CLE 5-13	DET-MIL 9*1	CAL-KC 5-6	OAK-TEX 7*5
0926	NY-BAL 3*1	TOR-BOS 8*4	MIN-CHI 3-9	SEA-CLE 0-1	DET-MIL 5-7	CAL-KC 2*0	OAK-TEX 7*5
0927	DET-NY 1-2	BAL-BOS 3-4	CHI-SEA 2-7	MIN-CLE 3-4			CAL-TEX 1-2
0928	DET-NY 4*2	BAL-BOS 4-5	CHI-SEA 1-7	MIN-CLE 10-11	TOR-MIL 3-4	KC-OAK 6*5	CAL-TEX 1-4
0929	DET-NY 11*3	BAL-BOS 6*3	CHI-SEA 6*2	MIN-CLE 4-6	TOR-MIL 5*4	KC-OAK 2-6	CAL-TEX 4*0
0930	DET-NY 2-9	BAL-BOS 5*3	CHI-SEA 3-5	MIN-CLE 4-7	TOR-MIL 0-4	KC-OAK 2-8	CAL-TEX 1*0

♦1985♦	GAME 1	GAME 2	GAME 3	GAME 4	GAME 5	GAME 6	GAME 7
0408	TEX-BAL 2-4	NY-BOS 2-9	CLE-DET 4-5	TOR-KC 1-2			
0409	MIN-CAL 6*2	CHI-MIL 4*2	OAK-SEA 3-6				
0410	MIN-CAL 6*3	TEX-BAL 1-7	OAK-SEA 4-5	NY-BOS 5-14	CLE-DET 1-8	TOR-KC 1*0	
0411	MIN-CAL 3-4	CHI-MIL 1-8	OAK-SEA 6-14	NY-BOS 4-6	CLE-DET 10-11	TOR-KC 4*3	
0412	TOR-BAL 2-7	CAL-OAK 6-15	MIN-SEA 1-2	MIL-TEX 11*6			
0413	TOR-BAL 7-8	CAL-OAK 6*1	MIN-SEA 7-8	MIL-TEX 6*5	CHI-BOS 2-7	NY-CLE 6*3	DET-KC 3*1
0414	TOR-BAL 5*3	CAL-OAK 1-8	MIN-SEA 1-5	MIL-TEX 8*1	CHI-BOS 11*6	NY-CLE 2*1	DET-KC 5*1
0415	CAL-MIN 5*0	SEA-OAK 4-7			CHI-BOS 6*5		
0416	BAL-CLE 3-6	SEA-OAK 7-9	MIL-DET 1-2	BOS-KC 0-2	CHI-NY 4-5	TEX-TOR 9*4	
0417	BAL-CLE 6*3	SEA-OAK 4-8	MIL-DET 2*0	BOS-KC 1-6	CAL-MIN 4*3	TEX-TOR 1-3	
0418	BAL-CLE 5-11	CHI-NY 2-3		BOS-KC 4*3	CAL-MIN 9*8	TEX-TOR 2-4	
0419	SEA-CAL 1-9	CLE-NY 2*1	BOS-CHI 1-8	KC-DET 9*2	TEX-MIL 4*1	BAL-TOR 5-6	MIN-OAK 2-4
0420	SEA-CAL 3*2	CLE-NY 2-5	BOS-CHI 12*8	KC-DET 3-4	TEX-MIL 5*1	BAL-TOR 2-3	MIN-OAK 2-6
0421	SEA-CAL 2-9	CLE-NY 3*0	BOS-CHI 2-7	KC-DET 3*2	TEX-MIL 5*2	BAL-TOR 3*2	MIN-OAK 2*0
0422	OAK-CAL 1-6	DET-CLE 4-6	MIL-CHI 4*2	SEA-MIN 5-9	BAL-TEX 1-6	KC-TOR 2*0	
0423	OAK-CAL 14*9	DET-CLE 4*3	MIL-CHI 5-6	SEA-MIN 2-4	BAL-TEX 11*1	KC-TOR 7*6	BOS-NY 5*4
0424	OAK-CAL 6*4	DET-CLE 6-7	MIL-CHI 3*2	SEA-MIN 0-10	BAL-TEX 2*1	KC-TOR 2-10	BOS-NY 7*6
0425	CLE-BAL 1-7	DET-MIL 7-11	CAL-SEA 3*0	OAK-MIN 4-5			BOS-NY 1-5
0426	CLE-BAL 3-6	DET-MIL 1*0	CAL-SEA 11*3	OAK-MIN 7-8	KC-BOS 2-5	NY-CHI 2-4	TOR-TEX 6*5
0427	CLE-BAL 10*4	DET-MIL 3*2	CAL-SEA 6*1	OAK-MIN 6-8	KC-BOS 5*4	NY-CHI 4-5	TOR-TEX 9*8
0428	CLE-BAL 7-8	DET-MIL 5*0	CAL-SEA 2*1	OAK-MIN 1-10	KC-BOS 5*2	NY-CHI 1-6	TOR-TEX 3*1
0429	BOS-CAL 6-7	CLE-KC 2-3	MIL-SEA 7-9	TOR-OAK 2*1			NY-TEX 5-7
0430	BOS-CAL 2-3	CLE-KC 1-5	MIL-SEA 3-4	TOR-OAK 4*3	CHI-BAL 7-9	MIN-DET 11*2	NY-TEX 4-8
0501	TOR-CAL 6*3	CLE-KC 6*5	BOS-SEA 0-7	MIL-OAK 7*4	CHI-BAL 1-3	MIN-DET 7*3	NY-TEX 5*1
0502	TOR-CAL 2-3		BOS-SEA 2*1	MIL-OAK 4-5			
0503	MIL-CAL 7*0	TEX-CLE 0-4	TOR-SEA 5*4	BOS-OAK 10*0	CHI-DET 7*1	BAL-MIN 8*7	KC-NY 1-7
0504	MIL-CAL 3-4	TEX-CLE 1-3	TOR-SEA 1-8	BOS-OAK 5*4	CHI-DET 1-7	BAL-MIN 6-8	KC-NY 2-5
0505	MIL-CAL 1-5	TEX-CLE 7*2	TOR-SEA 1-4	BOS-OAK 3-6	CHI-DET 3-4	BAL-MIN 10*5	KC-NY 2-6
0507	CAL-BOS 4-6	CHI-CLE 7*4	BAL-KC 4*2	SEA-MIL 2-5	DET-TEX 10*1	NY-MIN 6-8	OAK-TOR 1-10
0508	CAL-BOS 1-6	CHI-CLE 4*0	BAL-KC 8-9	SEA-MIL 4*2	DET-TEX 4*1	NY-MIN 6-8	OAK-TOR 6*4
0510	OAK-BOS 5-6	MIN-BAL 5-6	NY-KC 5*4	CAL-MIL 5*4	CLE-TEX 2-5	DET-CHI 3*1	SEA-TOR 3-8
0511	OAK-BOS 12*1	MIN-BAL 2-4	NY-KC 11*3	CAL-MIL 6*5	CLE-TEX 4*1	DET-CHI 4-7	SEA-TOR 2-4
0512	OAK-BOS 5*3	MIN-BAL 7*3	NY-KC 5-6	CAL-MIL 4-7	CLE-TEX 6*0	DET-CHI 0-8	SEA-TOR 5-9
0513	TEX-DET 4-7	KC-BAL 5*2	MIN-NY 8-9			CLE-CHI 0-8	
0514	TEX-DET 1-4	KC-BAL 5*3	MIN-NY 7-10	SEA-BOS 5*0	OAK-MIL 6*3	CLE-CHI 1-2	CAL-TOR 3-6
0515	KC-CLE 5*1	DET-MIN 4-5	TEX-NY 5-6	SEA-BOS 7*1	OAK-MIL 19*3	BAL-CHI 2-5	CAL-TOR 9*6
0516	KC-CLE 7*1	DET-MIN 5-7	TEX-NY 5-6			BAL-CHI 3*1	
0517	BOS-CLE 5*0	TOR-MIN 6-7	NY-CAL 6*0	KC-MIL 3*0	DET-OAK 10*2	TEX-CHI 2-4	BAL-SEA 11*3
0518	BOS-CLE 1-4	TOR-MIN 3*1	NY-CAL 6*1	KC-MIL 2-7	DET-OAK 9*6	TEX-CHI 7*2	BAL-SEA 6*4
0519	BOS-CLE 1-2	TOR-MIN 2-8	NY-CAL 1-4	KC-MIL 10-11	DET-OAK 7-9	TEX-CHI 1-5	BAL-SEA 2*1

♦1985♦	GAME 1	GAME 2	GAME 3	GAME 4	GAME 5	GAME 6	GAME 7
0520	KC-TEX 7-8	BOS-MIN 2-5	DET-CAL 2-7	CHI-TOR 1-6			
0521	KC-TEX 5*0	BOS-MIN 9*1	DET-CAL 1-2	CHI-TOR 3-4		BAL-OAK 2-3	NY-SEA 11*1
0522	KC-TEX 6*3	BOS-MIN 4*3	DET-CAL 3*2	CHI-TOR 0-10		BAL-OAK 3*0	NY-SEA 1-4
0523	BOS-TEX 6-7				TOR-CLE 6*5	BAL-OAK 2-4	NY-SEA 4-6
0524	BOS-TEX 0-1	BAL-CAL 4*3	CHI-KC 4-8	MIN-MIL 2-5	TOR-CLE 7*6	NY-OAK 10*3	DET-SEA 4*3
0525	BOS-TEX 3-10	BAL-CAL 3-5	CHI-KC 0-3	MIN-MIL 7-9	TOR-CLE 10*7	NY-OAK 7-8	DET-SEA 3*2
0526	BOS-TEX 3-5	BAL-CAL 4-10	CHI-KC 2-3	MIN-MIL 3-5	TOR-CLE 6*5	NY-OAK 13*1	DET-SEA 6*0
0527	MIN-BOS 2-9	BAL-CAL 6*4	TEX-KC 2-4	CLE-MIL 8*0		NY-OAK 1-2	DET-SEA 2-5
0528	TOR-CHI 6*1		TEX-KC 6*1	CLE-MIL 2-3			
0529	TOR-CHI 5-8	SEA-BAL 5*4	TEX-KC 2-6	CLE-MIL 2-7	MIN-BOS 0-7		CAL-NY 2-7
0530	KC-CHI 3-4	SEA-BAL 2-8			MIN-BOS 7-8	OAK-DET 4*2	CAL-NY 1-3
0531	KC-CHI 3-8	OAK-BAL 2-9	MIL-MIN 6*4	CLE-TOR 2-7	TEX-BOS 3*1	OAK-DET 2-3	SEA-NY 3-8
0601	KC-CHI 7-8	OAK-BAL 3*1	MIL-MIN 7*2	CLE-TOR 0-6	TEX-BOS 0-6	CAL-DET 6*3	SEA-NY 2-8
0602	KC-CHI 1-4	OAK-BAL 1-10	MIL-MIN 4-5	CLE-TOR 5*4	TEX-BOS 3-12	CAL-DET 9*2	SEA-NY 7*6
				CLE-TOR 2-5			
0603	CAL-BAL 5-7	CLE-BOS 5-6	SEA-DET 9*8	OAK-NY 2-5	CHI-TEX 3-7	CAL-DET 3-4	
0604	CAL-BAL 6*5	CLE-BOS 0-5	SEA-DET 7*6	OAK-NY 2*0	CHI-TEX 3-7	MIL-KC 3-4	MIN-TOR 2-9
0605	CAL-BAL 0-4		SEA-DET 2-5			MIL-KC 10*2	MIN-TOR 0-5
0606	SEA-CLE 1-9	NY-MIL 1-5	CHI-TEX 4*3				DET-TOR 0-2
0607	SEA-CLE 6*4	NY-MIL 9-10	BOS-BAL 8*4	KC-CAL 6*0	CHI-MIN 3-6	TEX-OAK 4*2	DET-TOR 2-9
0608	SEA-CLE 8-12	NY-MIL 2*1	BOS-BAL 2*1	KC-CAL 4*1	CHI-MIN 3*1	TEX-OAK 5-6	DET-TOR 10*1
0609	SEA-CLE 10*6	NY-MIL 4-9	BOS-BAL 12*0	KC-CAL 0-1	CHI-MIN 5*1	TEX-OAK 8*4	DET-TOR 8*3
						TEX-OAK 5-6	
0610	MIL-BOS 2-4	TEX-CAL 1-8	MIN-CLE 6*4	BAL-DET 7-8	TOR-NY 2-4	KC-OAK 1-2	CHI-SEA 9*4
0611	MIL-BOS 5*3	TEX-CAL 6*4			TOR-NY 4*1	KC-OAK 3-4	CHI-SEA 7*1
0612	MIL-BOS 2-7	TEX-CAL 2-3	BAL-DET 2-6		TOR-NY 3*2	KC-OAK 3*2	CHI-SEA 6*3
0613	TOR-BOS 7-8	CHI-CAL 1-2	MIL-BAL 3-8	MIN-TEX 7*5			KC-SEA 4*3
0614	TOR-BOS 1-4	CHI-CAL 4*2	MIL-BAL 3-9	MIN-TEX 2-4	OAK-CLE 1-6	DET-NY 4*0	KC-SEA 5-13
0615	TOR-BOS 5-7	CHI-CAL 3*2	MIL-BAL 5-7	MIN-TEX 2-11	OAK-CLE 8*6	DET-NY 10*8	KC-SEA 1-2
0616	TOR-BOS 6-7	CHI-CAL 1-3	MIL-BAL 1-9	MIN-TEX 4*1	OAK-CLE 3*2	DET-NY 1-2	KC-SEA 1-2
					OAK-CLE 11*6		
0617	NY-BAL 10*0	BOS-DET 3*2	MIN-KC 3-10	TOR-MIL 1-2		CAL-CLE 7*3	
0618	NY-BAL 6*4	BOS-DET 8-9	MIN-KC 1-10	TOR-MIL 1-4	OAK-CHI 3-4	CAL-CLE 0-2	SEA-TEX 5-8
0619	NY-BAL 10*0	BOS-DET 3-9	MIN-KC 2-3	TOR-MIL 5*1	OAK-CHI 7-8	CAL-CLE 4*0	SEA-TEX 4-5
0620	BOS-DET 5-6	NY-DET 9-10	MIN-KC 11*8		OAK-CHI 12*1		SEA-TEX 11*3
0621	BOS-TOR 2-7	NY-DET 4-6	BAL-MIL 10-13	TEX-MIN 2-3	CAL-CHI 5*2	CLE-OAK 1-9	
0622	BOS-TOR 5*3	NY-DET 4*0	BAL-MIL 3*2	TEX-MIN 2-3	CAL-CHI 6*3	CLE-OAK 4-6	SEA-KC 2*1
0623	BOS-TOR 1-8	NY-DET 1-3	BAL-MIL 2-6	TEX-MIN 11*1	CAL-CHI 11*1	CLE-OAK 3-9	SEA-KC 8*2
0624	DET-BOS 2-9	CLE-CAL 2*1	BAL-NY 4-5	KC-MIN 12*6	TEX-SEA 0-2	CHI-OAK 7*1	
0625	DET-BOS 3*0	CLE-CAL 3-7	BAL-NY 4-7	KC-MIN 3*0	TEX-SEA 1-2	CHI-OAK 4-5	MIL-TOR 1-7
0626	DET-BOS 3*0	CLE-CAL 6-10	BAL-NY 3-4	KC-MIN 1-2	TEX-SEA 4-5	CHI-OAK 0-10	MIL-TOR 5*4
0627							MIL-TOR 3-7
0628	BAL-BOS 1-6	MIN-CHI 5*4	TOR-DET 2*0	CAL-KC 4-5	MIL-NY 2-5	CLE-SEA 6-8	OAK-TEX 5-7
0629	BAL-BOS 16*4	MIN-CHI 1*0	TOR-DET 0-8	CAL-KC 7*1	MIL-NY 6*0	CLE-SEA 2-3	OAK-TEX 7*6
0630	BAL-BOS 3*0	MIN-CHI 4*3	TOR-DET 6*5	CAL-KC 1-3	MIL-NY 7*5	CLE-SEA 7*3	OAK-TEX 7*4
0701	DET-BAL 7*1	SEA-CHI 3*1	BOS-MIL 1-5	OAK-KC 4*3	CLE-MIN 5*2	NY-TOR 4*1	CAL-TEX 5-10
0702	DET-BAL 4-5	SEA-CHI 4-12	BOS-MIL 3-4	OAK-KC 1-10	CLE-MIN 7-8	NY-TOR 5*3	CAL-TEX 7*2
0703	DET-BAL 4*3	SEA-CHI 5*1	BOS-MIL 9*0	OAK-KC 0-3	CLE-MIN 0-7	NY-TOR 2-3	CAL-TEX 3*2
0704	BOS-CAL 4-5	CHI-CLE 5*0	MIN-NY 2-3	BAL-KC 5*3	TOR-OAK 2-3	MIL-SEA 2-3	DET-TEX 1-4
0705	BOS-CAL 4-13	CHI-CLE 8*3	MIN-NY 3-6	BAL-KC 6*3	TOR-OAK 8*2	MIL-SEA 6-7	DET-TEX 1-3
0706	BOS-CAL 7*5	CHI-CLE 6*4		BAL-KC 8*3	TOR-OAK 1-5	MIL-SEA 3-5	DET-TEX 4*3
0707	BOS-CAL 3-8	CHI-CLE 3-10	MIN-NY 2-3	BAL-KC 4-8	TOR-OAK 8*2	MIL-SEA 2*1	DET-TEX 5*3
			MIN-NY 2-14				
0708	MIN-BAL 7*4	MIL-CAL 2-3	KC-NY 5*2	TEX-CLE 0-4	CHI-DET 9*4	BOS-OAK 2*1	TOR-SEA 4*0
0709	MIN-BAL 6-11	MIL-CAL 4-5	KC-NY 4-6	TEX-CLE 2-7	CHI-DET 5-6	BOS-OAK 6*3	TOR-SEA 9*4
0710	MIN-BAL 2*1	MIL-CAL 1-2	KC-NY 5-6	TEX-CLE 4*1	CHI-DET 1-8	BOS-OAK 4-5	TOR-SEA 11*1
0711	CHI-BAL 6-7	TOR-CAL 5*3	TEX-NY 7-11	KC-CLE 1*0	MIN-DET 5*1	MIL-OAK 3-9	BOS-SEA 7*1
0712	CHI-BAL 3-10	TOR-CAL 3-5	TEX-NY 0-6	KC-CLE 4-5	MIN-DET 3*2	MIL-OAK 5*3	BOS-SEA 5*4
0713	CHI-BAL 10*8	TOR-CAL 3-4	TEX-NY 1-3	KC-CLE 5*1	MIN-DET 6*4	MIL-OAK 0-2	BOS-SEA 5-6
0714	CHI-BAL 5*3	TOR-CAL 3-5	TEX-NY 1-7	KC-CLE 9*5	MIN-DET 0-8	MIL-OAK 2-11	BOS-SEA 6*2
0718	KC-BAL 3-8	CAL-BOS 4-5	CLE-CHI 0-10	SEA-MIL 5*2	TEX-DET 3*2	NY-MIN 4-8	OAK-TOR 6*4
0719	KC-BAL 10*3	CAL-BOS 3*2	CLE-CHI 0-1	SEA-MIL 7-9	TEX-DET 2*1	NY-MIN 6*4	OAK-TOR 1-5
0720	KC-BAL 7*5	CAL-BOS 5*3	CLE-CHI 6-8	SEA-MIL 13*10	TEX-DET 5-6	NY-MIN 8*3	OAK-TOR 5*1
0721	KC-BAL 4-6	CAL-BOS 4-8	CLE-CHI 4*3	SEA-MIL 4-5	TEX-DET 4-5	NY-MIN 5*2	OAK-TOR 4-11
0722	NY-KC 4-5	OAK-BOS 4-6	DET-CHI 4-9	CAL-MIL 3-16	CLE-TEX 1-2	BAL-MIN 4-5	SEA-TOR 1-3
0723	NY-KC 2-5	OAK-BOS 2-3	DET-CHI 3-5	CAL-MIL 2*0	CLE-TEX 4-8	BAL-MIN 2-5	SEA-TOR 2-4
0724	NY-KC 3-5	OAK-BOS 5-6	DET-CHI 5*4	CAL-MIL 8*4	CLE-TEX 8*4	BAL-MIN 4*2	SEA-TOR 1-3
0725		SEA-BOS 3-5	BAL-CHI 5*1	OAK-MIL 11*2		DET-MIN 7*2	
0726	CLE-KC 1-7	SEA-BOS 2-6	BAL-CHI 8-9	OAK-MIL 7*3	NY-TEX 8-9	DET-MIN 5-6	CAL-TOR 0-7
0727	CLE-KC 3-6	SEA-BOS 10*3	BAL-CHI 9*1	OAK-MIL 3-4	NY-TEX 14*2	DET-MIN 4-11	CAL-TOR 3-8
0728	CLE-KC 4-7	SEA-BOS 7*2	BAL-CHI 6*1	OAK-MIL 5*2	NY-TEX 2-8	DET-MIN 3*2	CAL-TOR 1-5
0729	TOR-BAL 4*3	NY-CLE 8*2	KC-DET 4*2	TEX-MIL 2-3	MIN-SEA 6-8		
0730	TOR-BAL 3-4	NY-CLE 8*5	KC-DET 7-11	TEX-MIL 3-6	MIN-SEA 12*4	CHI-BOS 7*5	CAL-OAK 4-5
		NY-CLE 2-3					
0731	TOR-BAL 5*3	NY-CLE 5-6	CHI-BOS 11	KC-DET 5*2	TEX-MIL 2-5	CAL-OAK 8*5	MIN-SEA 3-12
0801	TOR-BAL 9*3	NY-CLE 1-9	CHI-BOS 7*2			CAL-OAK 1-3	
			CHI-BOS 3-4				
0802	MIN-CAL 1-3	BAL-CLE 8*6	MIL-DET 1-4	BOS-KC 3-4		SEA-OAK 1-3	
0803	MIN-CAL 4-5	BAL-CLE 4-10	MIL-DET 3-9	BOS-KC 5*4		SEA-OAK 6*2	
0804	MIN-CAL 5-6	BAL-CLE 5*4	MIL-DET 4-7	BOS-KC 6*5		SEA-OAK 3-5	
			MIL-DET 14*4				
0805	SEA-CAL 1-3	DET-KC 8*4	CHI-MIN 3-7	MIN-OAK 1-5			
0808	CAL-MIN 2-4	DET-KC 3-10	CLE-NY 1-8	OAK-SEA 11*2	BOS-CHI 6-7	MIL-TEX 7*4	BAL-TOR 2-7
		DET-KC 4-6	CLE-NY 6-7		BOS-CHI 6*1	MIL-TEX 3*1	
0809	NY-BOS 10*6	TOR-KC 2-4	DET-CLE 2-4	CAL-MIN 1-6	MIL-CHI 8*7	BAL-TEX 2-5	BAL-TOR 4-7
0810	NY-BOS 7*3	TOR-KC 3-4	DET-CLE 5*4	CAL-MIN 9*1	MIL-CHI 5*2	BAL-TEX 9*8	OAK-SEA 6*4
0811	NY-BOS 5*3	TOR-KC 5*3	DET-CLE 2-7	CAL-MIN 12*0	MIL-CHI 1-4	BAL-TEX 1-4	OAK-SEA 11*5
0812	KC-BOS 3*2	CLE-BAL 8*5	DET-MIL 3-4	OAK-MIN 3-4	NY-CHI 10*4	TOR-TEX 4-5	OAK-SEA 6-9
				OAK-MIN 4-5			CAL-SEA 5-6
0813	CLE-BAL 4-8	KC-BOS 6*3	NY-CHI 3-4	OAK-MIN 1-8	DET-MIL 5*4	TOR-TEX 5*3	CAL-SEA 4*3
0814	CLE-BAL 4-8	KC-BOS 3-16	NY-CHI 10*7	OAK-MIN 5*0	DET-MIL 4*3	TOR-TEX 4*1	CAL-SEA 4-11
				OAK-MIN 7*4			CAL-SEA 3*1
0815	TEX-BAL 1-9	CLE-DET 7*6	CHI-MIL 5-7	SEA-MIN 5-14		OAK-CAL 2-5	KC-TOR 4*2
0816	TEX-BAL 2-4	CLE-DET 2-3	CHI-MIL 2-3	SEA-MIN 6*5	OAK-CAL 2-5	BOS-NY 4-5	KC-TOR 4*2
0817	TEX-BAL 2-9	CLE-DET 5-7	CHI-MIL 12*7	SEA-MIN 0-2	OAK-CAL 5-9	BOS-NY 1-3	KC-TOR 6-10
0818		CLE-DET 0-4	CHI-MIL 8*4	SEA-MIN 7*2	OAK-CAL 4*3	BOS-NY 2-4	
0819	TEX-BAL 2-9	TOR-CLE 3-5	MIN-MIL 1-4	DET-KC 1-2	OAK-CAL 4-5	DET-OAK 4*1	BAL-SEA 3-4
0820	TEX-BOS 3*1	TOR-CLE 3*2	MIN-MIL 2-3	KC-CHI 1-2	NY-CAL 8*5	DET-OAK 3-4	BAL-SEA 11*8
0821	TEX-BOS 5*3	TOR-CLE 2-5	MIN-MIL 2-3	KC-CHI 2*1	NY-CAL 13*10	DET-OAK 3-4	BAL-SEA 0-4
				KC-CHI 7*3	NY-CAL 2-3	DET-OAK 5*3	
0822	TEX-BOS 4-8			TOR-CHI 6*3		BAL-OAK 7*2	
				TOR-CHI 10*3			
0823	MIN-BOS 5*2	MIL-CLE 5-10	TEX-KC 4*3	TOR-CHI 6*3	DET-CAL 6-7	BAL-OAK 7*2	NY-SEA 3*1
				TOR-CHI 10*3			
0824	MIN-BOS 1*0	DET-CAL 13*2	TEX-KC 2-8	TOR-CHI 6*3	BAL-OAK 4*3	NY-SEA 4*3	
0825	MIL-CLE 2-6	DET-CAL 1-7	TEX-KC 7*3	TOR-CHI 3-5	BAL-OAK 4-10	NY-SEA 8*5	
	MIL-CLE 0-2						
0826	MIL-CLE 3-4	BAL-CAL 17*3	BOS-CHI 6-7	TEX-KC 2-9	TOR-MIN 4*3	NY-OAK 2-3	DET-SEA 6*3
	MIL-CLE 8*3						

Game Scores, 1982-94

◆1985◆

	GAME 1	GAME 2	GAME 3	GAME 4	GAME 5	GAME 6	GAME 7
0827	BOS-CLE 2-6	BAL-CAL 3-7	TEX-CHI 4-7	KC-MIL 5-8	TOR-MIN 8*0	NY-OAK 0-3	DET-SEA 1-3
0828	BOS-CLE 4-7		TEX-CHI 1-5	KC-MIL 8*2	TOR-MIN 5-6		
0829	BOS-CLE 17*2	SEA-BAL 0-7	TEX-CHI 5-6	OAK-DET 2-3	CAL-NY 0-4		
0830	CLE-MIL 6-9	SEA-BAL 0-6	BOS-MIN 7*3	OAK-DET 8*3	CAL-NY 4*1	KC-TEX 1-4	CHI-TOR 3-5
0831	CLE-MIL 8-10	SEA-BAL 6*0	BOS-MIN 5-6	OAK-DET 1-4	CAL-NY 4-10	KC-TEX 4-6	CHI-TOR 2-6
			BOS-MIN 4-5				
0901	SEA-BAL 10*2	OAK-DET 3-14	BOS-MIN 10*3	CLE-MIL 11*4	CAL-NY 3-5	KC-TEX 3-5	CHI-TOR 4*1
0902	OAK-BAL 4-12	CAL-DET 11*1	MIL-MIN 1-6	CHI-KC 2-3	SEA-NY 7-8	BOS-TEX 11*2	CLE-TOR 2-3
0903	OAK-BAL 3*2	CAL-DET 8-14	MIL-MIN 3-4	CHI-KC 2-3	SEA-NY 3-6	BOS-TEX 6*4	
0904	OAK-BAL 1-6	CAL-DET 5*2	MIL-MIN 11*10	CHI-KC 5-6	SEA-NY 3-4	CLE-TOR 5*4	
0905	CHI-TEX 11*4	CLE-BOS 6-13		MIL-KC 1-4	OAK-NY 3-7	MIN-TOR 0-7	
		CLE-BOS 9*5					
0906	CAL-BAL 2-6	SEA-DET 8*4	OAK-NY 4-8	CHI-TEX 12*1	MIN-TOR 3-8	MIL-KC 3-4	
						MIL-KC 1-7	
0907	CAL-BAL 3-4	SEA-DET 12*5	OAK-NY 2-3	CHI-TEX 3*2	MIN-TOR 6*3	MIL-KC 4-7	CLE-BOS 9-11
							CLE-BOS 4-7
0908	CAL-BAL 7*4	SEA-DET 6*2	MIL-KC 11-13	OAK-NY 6-9	CHI-TEX 7*6	MIN-TOR 9-10	CLE-BOS 1-8
0909	KC-CAL 1-7	MIN-CHI 5*0	NY-MIL 9*4	TEX-OAK 3*1	CLE-SEA 7-8	DET-TOR 3-5	
0910	KC-CAL 6*0	MIN-CHI 2-7	NY-MIL 13*10	TEX-OAK 3-10	CLE-SEA 8*5	DET-TOR 1-2	BAL-BOS 7*5
							BAL-BOS 3-5
0911	KC-CAL 2*1	MIN-CHI 0-5	NY-MIL 3-4	TEX-OAK 6*3	CLE-SEA 5-9	DET-TOR 2-3	BAL-BOS 1-4
0912	TEX-CAL 3-5	MIN-CHI 2-4	TOR-NY 5-7		KC-OAK 5*2	CHI-SEA 6*1	BAL-BOS 3*1
0913	TEX-CAL 0-2	BAL-DET 6*4	TOR-NY 3*2	BOS-MIL 3-6			MIN-CLE 2-3
							MIN-CLE 3*1
0914	TEX-CAL 8*5	BOS-MIL 10*8	TOR-NY 7*4	KC-OAK 2*1	CHI-SEA 5-6	BAL-DET 3-10	MIN-CLE 9-11
						BAL-DET 5*4	MIN-CLE 5*3
0915	TEX-CAL 4-12	BOS-MIL 4*2	TOR-NY 8*5	CHI-SEA 6*3	KC-OAK 2-4	BAL-DET 1-4	MIN-CLE 5*2
					KC-OAK 7*2		
0916	BAL-DET 14*7	SEA-KC 5*1	BOS-MIL 3-5	TEX-MIN 6-7	CLE-NY 9*5		OAK-CLE 8-15
0917	NY-DET 1-9	SEA-KC 7*0	MIL-BAL 0-6	TEX-MIN 2-7	TOR-BOS 5-6	CAL-CHI 2-5	OAK-CLE 1*0
0918	NY-DET 2-5	SEA-KC 6*0	MIL-BAL 1-6	TEX-MIN 3-4	TOR-BOS 1-13	CAL-CHI 9*3	
						CAL-CHI 8*0	
0919	NY-DET 3-10	SEA-KC 6*4	MIL-BAL 5*2			OAK-CHI 4-10	MIL-TOR 5-7
0920	DET-BOS 6*2	MIN-KC 1-5	NY-BAL 2-4	CLE-CAL 5-7	SEA-TEX 9-10	OAK-CHI 8*3	MIL-TOR 1-2
0921	DET-BOS 6-7	MIN-KC 5-6	NY-BAL 5*2	CLE-CAL 3-12	SEA-TEX 2-7	OAK-CHI 5-7	MIL-TOR 2*1
0922	DET-BOS 2-6	MIN-KC 7*3	NY-BAL 5*4	CLE-CAL 9-10	SEA-TEX 0-6		MIL-TOR 1-5
0923	DET-BOS 2*1	CLE-OAK 7-8		CHI-CAL 6*5	SEA-TEX 4-11		BOS-TOR 2-6
0924	BAL-MIL 6-10	CLE-OAK 8-10	DET-NY 9*1	CHI-CAL 8*1	MIN-TEX 0-5	KC-SEA 2-5	BOS-TOR 4*2
0925	BAL-MIL 0-3	CLE-OAK 7*2	DET-NY 2-10	CHI-CAL 4-7	MIN-TEX 5*1	KC-SEA 5*4	BOS-TOR 4*1
0926	BAL-MIL 9*1	CHI-OAK 11*7			MIN-TEX 0-2	KC-SEA 5*2	
0927	TOR-MIL 5*1	CHI-OAK 4*3	CAL-CLE 3-7	BOS-DET 1-5	KC-MIN 1-4	TEX-SEA 0-6	
0928	TOR-MIL 6*1	CHI-OAK 4-7	CAL-CLE 5-7	BOS-DET 2*0	KC-MIN 3-5	TEX-SEA 2-3	BAL-NY 5-6
0929	TOR-MIL 13*5	CHI-OAK 3*0	CAL-CLE 9*3	BOS-DET 8*4	KC-MIN 3-6	TEX-SEA 5*2	BAL-NY 0-4
							BAL-NY 2-9
0930	CAL-KC 1-3	CHI-MIN 1-7	OAK-TEX 3-5				BAL-NY 4-5
1001	CAL-KC 4*2	CHI-MIN 12*6	OAK-TEX 2-3	BOS-BAL 10*3	SEA-CLE 3-9	TOR-DET 1-6	MIL-NY 1-6
1002	CAL-KC 0-4	CHI-MIN 1-3	OAK-TEX 14*3		SEA-CLE 2-12	TOR-DET 2-4	MIL-NY 1*0
1003	CAL-KC 1-4	SEA-CHI 5*4	BOS-BAL 6*2			TOR-DET 0-2	MIL-NY 0-3
			BOS-BAL 8-9				
1004	MIL-BOS 8*7	SEA-CHI 5-7	DET-BAL 2-5	OAK-KC 2-4	CLE-MIN 8*6	CAL-TEX 0-6	NY-TOR 4*3
1005	MIL-BOS 3*2	SEA-CHI 4-10	DET-BAL 6*7	OAK-KC 4-5	CLE-MIN 2-8	CAL-TEX 3*1	NY-TOR 1-5
1006	MIL-BOS 9*6	SEA-CHI 2-3	DET-BAL 11*3	OAK-KC 9*3	CLE-MIN 2-4	CAL-TEX 6*5	NY-TOR 8*0

◆1986◆

	GAME 1	GAME 2	GAME 3	GAME 4	GAME 5	GAME 6	GAME 7
0407	BOS-DET 5-6	MIL-CHI 5*3	CLE-BAL 6*4				
0408	KC-NY 2-4	MIN-OAK 3*2	CAL-SEA 4-8	TOR-TEX 3-6			
0409	KC-NY 7*4	MIN-OAK 5*4	CAL-SEA 9*5	TOR-TEX 3*1	CLE-BAL 3-4	MIL-CHI 4*3	BOS-DET 5-6
0410	KC-NY 5-6	MIN-OAK 0-3	CAL-SEA 2-5	TOR-TEX 11*10	CLE-BAL 1-5	MIL-CHI 8*5	BOS-DET 4*2
0411	MIL-NY 2-3	CAL-OAK 10*3	DET-CLE 7*2	BAL-TEX 4-5	TOR-KC 6*2	BOS-CHI 7*2	SEA-MIN 1-5
0412	MIL-NY 3-7	CAL-OAK 9*3	DET-CLE 2-6	BAL-TEX 1-2	TOR-KC 0-1	BOS-CHI 1-3	SEA-MIN 10*4
0413	MIL-NY 2-3	CAL-OAK 7-11	DET-CLE 2-8	BAL-TEX 3*2	TOR-KC 4-7	BOS-CHI 12*2	SEA-MIN 4*2
0414	KC-BOS 8*2	SEA-CAL 6-7	TEX-MIL 10*1	BAL-TOR 2*1		DET-CHI 10*8	OAK-MIN 7*6
0415	NY-CLE 6*2	SEA-CAL 9*4					OAK-MIN 8*2
0416	KC-BOS 1*0	SEA-CAL 0-4	DET-CHI 4-10				OAK-MIN 5-7
0417	KC-BOS 2-6	MIN-CAL 4*1	DET-CHI 10*6	NY-CLE 4-6	TEX-MIL 7*5	BAL-TOR 5*3	
						BAL-TOR 4-7	
0418	TEX-BAL 12*3	CHI-BOS 1-2	MIN-CAL 5-6	CLE-DET 1-6	NY-MIL 5-6	KC-TOR 6*4	OAK-SEA 4*1
0419	TEX-BAL 4-10	CHI-BOS 2-3	MIN-CAL 4-5	CLE-DET 8*6	NY-MIL 3-4	KC-TOR 5-6	OAK-SEA 7*2
0420	TEX-BAL 1-6	CHI-BOS 2-6	MIN-CAL 5-8		NY-MIL 5*4	KC-TOR 6*4	OAK-SEA 9*3
0421	BAL-CLE 0-7	DET-BOS 5*4	OAK-CAL 6*2	NY-KC 8*4		TEX-TOR 6-7	MIN-SEA 5*2
0422	BAL-CLE 5*2	DET-BOS 4-6	OAK-CAL 1-5	NY-KC 5*1	CHI-MIL 5*4	TEX-TOR 10*1	MIN-SEA 7*1
0423	BAL-CLE 1-5	DET-BOS 3*1	OAK-CAL 0-5	NY-KC 2*1	CHI-MIL 2*1	TEX-TOR 9*8	MIN-SEA 3-4
0424	CLE-NY 1-2	SEA-OAK 3*1					
0425	CLE-NY 3-10	SEA-OAK 2-11	TOR-BAL 2*1	CHI-DET 9*7	BOS-KC 0-6	CAL-MIN 4-7	MIL-TEX 11*1
0426	CLE-NY 5-7	SEA-OAK 3-5	TOR-BAL 5-11	CHI-DET 5*4	BOS-KC 6*1	CAL-MIN 7*6	MIL-TEX 10*2
0427	CLE-NY 9*7	SEA-OAK 0-1	TOR-BAL 8*0	CHI-DET 1-4		CAL-MIN 8*7	MIL-TEX 2-6
0429	MIN-NY 11-14	SEA-BOS 1-3	BAL-CHI 8*1	KC-DET 1-2	OAK-MIL 4-5	CAL-TOR 4*3	CLE-TEX 6*5
0430	MIN-NY 2-3	SEA-BOS 4-9	BAL-CHI 6-8	KC-DET 7*3	OAK-MIL 1-5	CAL-TOR 4-6	CLE-TEX 6*4
0501	MIN-NY 7*4	SEA-BOS 2-12			OAK-MIL 7*2	CAL-TOR 7*4	
0502	TEX-NY 7*0	OAK-BOS 4*1	CLE-CHI 7*5	MIN-DET 10*1	CAL-MIL 4-5	SEA-TOR 3*2	BAL-KC 0-5
0503	TEX-NY 4-9	OAK-BOS 3-4	CLE-CHI 8*7	MIN-DET 4-7	CAL-MIL 3-4	SEA-TOR 4*2	BAL-KC 3*2
0504	TEX-NY 4*3	OAK-BOS 1-4	CLE-CHI 6*4	MIN-DET 1-4	CAL-MIL 3-5	SEA-TOR 2-3	BAL-KC 1-11
0505	KC-CLE 4-5	CAL-BOS 0-3	NY-CHI 4*1	DET-TEX 10*3	SEA-MIL 1-3	OAK-TOR 6-10	
0506	KC-CLE 1-6	CAL-BOS 6*2	NY-CHI 10*6	DET-TEX 2-4	SEA-MIL 0-10	OAK-TOR 17*3	BAL-MIN 5*3
0507	KC-CLE 1-7	TOR-CAL 2-6	NY-CHI 5*1	DET-TEX 1-2	MIL-OAK 6-7	BOS-SEA 11*5	BAL-MIN 2-5
0508		TOR-CAL 7*6			MIL-OAK 1-2	BOS-SEA 4*2	
0509	KC-BAL 7*4	MIL-CAL 16*5	CHI-CLE 4*3	DET-MIN 7-8	BOS-OAK 9*6	TOR-SEA 3-13	
0510	KC-BAL 2-5	MIL-CAL 4*2	CHI-CLE 4*0	DET-MIN 2-12	BOS-OAK 4*2	TOR-SEA 7-8	NY-TEX 4*3
0511	KC-BAL 3-4	MIL-CAL 1-5	CHI-CLE 5*4	DET-MIN 4*1	BOS-OAK 6*5	TOR-SEA 4*3	NY-TEX 3-6
							NY-TEX 1-9
0512	CHI-BAL 3-4	BOS-CAL 1-7	TEX-CLE 19*2	DET-KC 5-6	NY-MIN 9*8	TOR-OAK 5*3	MIL-SEA 0-6
0513	CHI-BAL 1-3	BOS-CAL 4-5	TEX-CLE 2-3	DET-KC 2-4	NY-MIN 6*4	TOR-OAK 3-6	MIL-SEA 5-8
0514	MIN-BAL 3-8	BOS-CAL 8*5	TEX-DET 2-8	CLE-KC 0-5	CHI-NY 3*2	TOR-OAK 4-9	MIL-SEA 9*6
0515	MIN-BAL 3-5		TEX-DET 8*1	CLE-KC 3-6	CHI-NY 8*1		
0516	OAK-BAL 8*4	TEX-BOS 4*1	CAL-DET 11*1	KC-CHI 2-4	SEA-NY 7*3	MIN-MIL 6-7	CLE-TOR 6-7
0517	OAK-BAL 2-8	TEX-BOS 2-8	CAL-DET 4-10	KC-CHI 6-7	SEA-NY 6-11	MIN-MIL 1-4	CLE-TOR 5-11
0518	OAK-BAL 4-13	TEX-BOS 4-5		KC-CHI 1-5	SEA-NY 3-11	MIN-MIL 5*3	CLE-TOR 2-10
							CLE-TOR 6*4
0519	KC-TEX 6*4	MIN-BOS 7-8					
0520	KC-TEX 0-4	MIN-BOS 7-17	CAL-BAL 6*4	TOR-CHI 1-2	SEA-DET 0-12	CLE-MIL 9-12	OAK-NY 2*1
0521	KC-TEX 1-2	MIN-BOS 2-3	CAL-BAL 1-2	TOR-CHI 4-5	SEA-DET 4-6	CLE-MIL 4*2	OAK-NY 4-10
0522	KC-TEX 5*4		CAL-BAL 3-6	TOR-CHI 5*0	SEA-DET 5*3	CLE-MIL 5*4	OAK-NY 3-4
0523	BOS-TEX 2*1	TOR-CLE 1-3	CHI-KC 4*1	MIL-MIN 7-8	OAK-DET 5*1	BAL-SEA 7*5	CAL-NY 5-10
0524	BOS-TEX 2-3	TOR-CLE 9*6	CHI-KC 6-7	MIL-MIN 6*3	OAK-DET 1-4	BAL-SEA 5*4	CAL-NY 6-7
0525	BOS-TEX 7*1	TOR-CLE 8*1	CHI-KC 1-2	MIL-MIN 3-4	OAK-DET 1-2	BAL-SEA 6*3	CAL-NY 5-8
0526	CHI-TEX 2-7	BOS-CLE 5*3	MIL-KC 4*0	TOR-MIN 1-9	OAK-DET 4-5	BAL-SEA 6-7	CAL-NY 8*7
0527	CHI-TEX 3-6	BOS-CLE 2*0	MIL-KC 9*1	TOR-MIN 6-7			
0528	CHI-TEX 3-6	BOS-CLE 13*7	MIL-KC 3-4	TOR-MIN 14*8	DET-CAL 4*1	BAL-OAK 9*5	NY-SEA 6*5
0529		MIL-CLE 11*7			DET-CAL 7*4	BAL-OAK 8*6	NY-SEA 2*0

♦1986♦	GAME 1	GAME 2	GAME 3	GAME 4	GAME 5	GAME 6	GAME 7
0530	TEX-KC 2-12	MIL-CLE 2-3	BOS-MIN 5-13	CHI-TOR 0-6	BAL-CAL 3*0	NY-OAK 3-6	DET-SEA 7-8
0531	TEX-KC 1-8	MIL-CLE 7-9	BOS-MIN 7*2	CHI-TOR 3-4	BAL-CAL 0-2	NY-OAK 3-4	DET-SEA 4-7
0601	TEX-KC 3-5		BOS-MIN 6*3	CHI-TOR 6*4	BAL-CAL 4-7	NY-OAK 7*1	DET-SEA 1-9
0602	CLE-BOS 1-3	TEX-CHI 1*0	KC-MIL 2-7	MIN-TOR 1-3	NY-CAL 7-8	DET-OAK 1-7	
0603	CLE-BOS 1-5	TEX-CHI 4*1	KC-MIL 4*1	MIN-TOR 5-6	NY-CAL 2-4	DET-OAK 4-6	SEA-BAL 2-4
0604	CLE-BOS 4-6	TEX-CHI 5*2	KC-MIL 8*6	MIN-TOR 10*4	NY-CAL 11*0	DET-OAK 8*5	SEA-BAL 5*1
0605	CAL-CLE 0-3	OAK-CHI 5-7	BOS-MIL 5-7	MIN-KC 2-8			SEA-BAL 1-7
0606	CAL-CLE 8*2	OAK-CHI 4-6	BOS-MIL 3*0	MIN-KC 1-6		BAL-NY 5*2	SEA-TEX 5-6
0607	CAL-CLE 4-11	OAK-CHI 3-10	BOS-MIL 0-3	MIN-KC 4*1	TOR-DET 1-2	BAL-NY 7*5	SEA-TEX 5-7
0608	OAK-CHI 5-8	TOR-DET 4*2	MIN-KC 5*2	BOS-MIL 3-7	BAL-NY 18*9		SEA-TEX 2-3
0609	CAL-CHI 3*0	NY-DET 9*7	SEA-KC 5*3	BAL-MIL 2-3	OAK-CLE 5-6		SEA-TEX 4-5
0610	CAL-CHI 3-7	NY-DET 6*3	SEA-KC 5-9	BAL-MIL 3-6	OAK-CLE 7-8	TEX-MIN 2-3	BOS-TOR 1-5
0611	CAL-CHI 12*11	NY-DET 3-9	SEA-KC 12*2	BAL-MIL 4*3	OAK-CLE 4-7	TEX-MIN 14*10	BOS-TOR 4*3
0612	NY-BAL 7*5	KC-CAL 2-3	CHI-SEA 8*4			TEX-MIN 6*2	BOS-TOR 3*2
0613	NY-BAL 3*1	KC-CAL 10*2	CHI-SEA 10-11	MIL-BOS 3-5	MIN-CLE 2-11	TEX-OAK 2*1	DET-TOR 0-9
0614	NY-BAL 4*2	KC-CAL 5-6	CHI-SEA 3-7	MIL-BOS 2*0	MIN-CLE 9*3	TEX-OAK 2-3	DET-TOR 10*5
0615	NY-BAL 3-4	KC-CAL 6*5	CHI-SEA 5-10	MIL-BOS 7*3	MIN-CLE 7*3	TEX-OAK 2-9	DET-TOR 5-6
0616	DET-BAL 5*4	TEX-CAL 1-2	TOR-MIL 9*2	BOS-NY 10*1		KC-OAK 3*2	DET-TOR 6-9
0617	DET-BAL 6*3	TEX-CAL 0-4	TOR-MIL 2*1	BOS-NY 7*6	SEA-CLE 5*2	KC-OAK 2*1	
0618	DET-BAL 6*1	TEX-CAL 1-5	TOR-MIL 1-3	BOS-NY 5*2	SEA-CLE 1-5	KC-OAK 0-1	CHI-MIN 1-4
0619	DET-BAL 7*5	OAK-TEX 2-3	NY-TOR 9-10		SEA-CLE 1-8		CHI-MIN 9-10
0620	BAL-BOS 14*3	OAK-TEX 7-10	NY-TOR 10*8	SEA-CHI 5*3	CAL-KC 6*2	DET-MIL 0-1	CHI-MIN 9*8
0621	BAL-BOS 2-7	OAK-TEX 2-3	NY-TOR 4*2	SEA-CHI 6-7	CAL-KC 4*3	DET-MIL 4*3	CLE-MIN 8-9
0622	BAL-BOS 4*0	OAK-TEX 4-5	NY-TOR 1-15	SEA-CHI 4-10	CAL-KC 4-7	DET-MIL 4-5	CLE-MIN 7*5
0623	NY-BOS 11*3	CAL-TEX 6*4	MIL-TOR 5*3	MIN-CHI 2-11	OAK-CLE 3-6	DET-SEA 8*6	CLE-MIN 4*1
0624	NY-BOS 8*1	CAL-TEX 12*3	MIL-TOR 0-8	MIN-CHI 2*1	OAK-KC 8*4	CLE-SEA 7-8	
0625	NY-BOS 4-5	CAL-TEX 7*1	MIL-TOR 1-5	MIN-CHI 3-4	OAK-KC 4-5	CLE-SEA 1-8	BAL-DET 2*1
0626					OAK-KC 2-9	TEX-SEA 10*3	BAL-DET 2-11
0627	BOS-BAL 5*3	CLE-CAL 6*3	KC-MIN 4-6	TOR-NY 14*7	CHI-OAK 6-8	TEX-SEA 5-6	BAL-DET 3-8
0628	BOS-BAL 7*3	CLE-CAL 3-9	KC-MIN 2-7	TOR-NY 7*4	CHI-OAK 4*1	TEX-SEA 5*2	MIL-DET 2-4
0629	BOS-BAL 8*3	CLE-CAL 6*4	KC-MIN 4-9	TOR-NY 6*3	CHI-OAK 6*5	TEX-SEA 3-9	MIL-DET 5-8
							MIL-DET 5-9
							MIL-DET 3*1
0630	MIL-BAL 2-5	TOR-BOS 9-10	CHI-CAL 4*3	DET-NY 2-3	CLE-OAK 8*3	KC-SEA 2-3	MIN-TEX 5-2
0701	MIL-BAL 3-7	TOR-BOS 7-9	CHI-CAL 5*3	DET-NY 4-5	CLE-OAK 9*0	KC-SEA 5-8	MIN-TEX 0-5
0702	MIL-BAL 1*0	TOR-BOS 4*2	CHI-CAL 3-4	DET-NY 8*3	CLE-OAK 7*3	KC-SEA 3-5	MIN-TEX 2-10
0703	BAL-MIN 7-11	TOR-BOS 8*5		DET-NY 5-9			
0704	BAL-MIN 12*7	SEA-BOS 5-6	NY-CHI 1-2	KC-CLE 3-10	OAK-MIL 4-5		
0705	BAL-MIN 6-7	SEA-BOS 9*5	NY-CHI 8*0	KC-CLE 5-10	OAK-MIL 1-2	DET-TEX 1-2	CAL-TOR 9*1
0706	BAL-MIN 1*0	SEA-BOS 3-7	NY-CHI 2-5	KC-CLE 0-5	OAK-MIL 6*3	DET-TEX 3-9	CAL-TOR 3-7
0707	DET-MIN 8-10	OAK-BOS 6*4	CLE-CHI 3-4	BAL-KC 8*1	CAL-MIL 3*1	DET-TEX 5*2	CAL-TOR 8*2
0708	DET-MIN 5*1	OAK-BOS 7-8	CLE-CHI 2-6	BAL-KC 8*4	CAL-MIL 14*3	NY-TEX 14*3	SEA-TOR 5-7
0709	DET-MIN 7*0	OAK-BOS 6-7	CLE-CHI 6*3	BAL-KC 0-3	CAL-MIL 6*1	NY-TEX 1-6	SEA-TOR 8*5
0710	NY-MIN 11*1	CAL-BOS 7-8	BAL-CHI 5*3	TEX-CLE 6-9	SEA-MIL 4*1	NY-TEX 5*4	SEA-TOR 5-6
0711	NY-MIN 9*3	CAL-BOS 5*0	BAL-CHI 4*2	TEX-CLE 2-7	SEA-MIL 9*3	DET-KC 3-4	OAK-TOR 4-8
						DET-KC 8*7	OAK-TOR 5-6
0712	CAL-BOS 2-3	BAL-CHI 3-6	TEX-CLE 11*6	SEA-MIL 15*9	NY-MIN 8*0	DET-KC 4-7	OAK-TOR 5*3
0713	CAL-BOS 12*3	BAL-CHI 0-7	TEX-CLE 5*3	SEA-MIL 0-5	NY-MIN 0-5	DET-KC 5*0	OAK-TOR 10*5
0717	MIN-BAL 2-6	TOR-CAL 8*5	TEX-DET 1-2	CHI-NY 4-5	BOS-SEA 4-5	CLE-KC 1-5	MIL-OAK 1-6
0718	MIN-BAL 7*3	TOR-CAL 2*0	TEX-DET 0-5	CHI-NY 4-8	BOS-SEA 4-10	CLE-KC 3*2	MIL-OAK 2-3
0719	MIN-BAL 0-1	TOR-CAL 3-9	TEX-DET 3-5	CHI-NY 8*3	BOS-SEA 9*4	CLE-KC 6*4	MIL-OAK 7*2
0720	MIN-BAL 3-8	TOR-CAL 6*3	TEX-DET 0-4	CHI-NY 8*0	BOS-SEA 5-8	CLE-KC 5-8	MIL-OAK 2-4
0721	KC-BAL 6*1	MIL-CAL 5*3	CHI-CLE 2-5	MIN-DET 1*0	TEX-NY 4-8	TOR-SEA 8*3	BOS-OAK 2-5
0722	KC-BAL 4-5	MIL-CAL 6*2	CHI-CLE 4-8	MIN-DET 0-3	TEX-NY 1-9	TOR-SEA 7-8	BOS-OAK 2-4
0723	KC-BAL 7*3	MIL-CAL 2-3	CHI-CLE 2-7	MIN-DET 2-12	TEX-NY 2-3	TOR-SEA 6*2	BOS-OAK 2-9
0724	CHI-BAL 6-12	CLE-TEX 3-7		KC-DET 1*0			
0725	CHI-BAL 2-6	CLE-TEX 5-7	BOS-CAL 8*1	KC-DET 2-9	MIN-NY 9*5	TOR-OAK 5-6	
0726	CHI-BAL 1-2	CLE-TEX 5-8	BOS-CAL 1-4	KC-DET 3-4	MIN-NY 8*4	TOR-OAK 0-2	MIL-SEA 4*2
0727	CHI-BAL 3-11	CLE-TEX 8*3	BOS-CAL 0-3	KC-DET 5*4	MIN-NY 1-4	TOR-OAK 0-1	MIL-SEA 2-5
0728	BOS-CHI 3*1	BAL-TEX 4*3	DET-CLE 5*1	TOR-KC 6*0	NY-MIL 4-5	CAL-OAK 6*3	MIL-SEA 8*1
0729	BOS-CHI 1-4	BAL-TEX 5-6	DET-CLE 6*3	TOR-KC 5*2	NY-MIL 4-6	CAL-OAK 2-4	SEA-MIN 5-6
0730	BOS-CHI 2-7	BAL-TEX 3-5	DET-CLE 11*3	TOR-KC 7*2	NY-MIL 0-5	CAL-OAK 6*2	SEA-MIN 2-4
0731			DET-CLE 7-8		TEX-MIL 7*2	CAL-OAK 8*5	SEA-MIN 4*2
					TEX-MIL 8*6		
0801	KC-BOS 3-5	DET-CHI 5*4	OAK-MIN 1-10	CAL-SEA 3*2	TEX-MIL 8-9	BAL-TOR 7*3	NY-CLE 3-4
							NY-CLE 5*3
0802	KC-BOS 13*2	DET-CHI 3-5		OAK-MIN 0-8		BAL-TOR 5*2	NY-CLE 5-6
0803	KC-BOS 3-5	DET-CHI 1-10	TEX-MIL 7*6	OAK-MIN 5*4	CAL-SEA 3-7	BAL-TOR 4-6	
0804	CHI-BOS 1*0	MIL-NY 5*4		CAL-MIN 5-6	CAL-SEA 3-6	BAL-TOR 12*2	NY-CLE 12*8
0805	CHI-BOS 3*1	MIL-NY 2*1	TEX-BAL 2-9	CAL-MIN 13*1	OAK-SEA 8-9	KC-TOR 8*6	CLE-DET 5-6
							CLE-DET 9-11
0806	TEX-BAL 13*11	CHI-BOS 0-9	CAL-MIN 2-5	MIL-NY 3-5	OAK-SEA 7*5	KC-TOR 0-8	
0807	TEX-BAL 9*8	SEA-CAL 3-4	CLE-DET 1-15	MIL-NY 10*2		KC-TOR 4-5	
			CLE-DET 2-6				
0808	CLE-BAL 3*0	SEA-CAL 4-6	BOS-DET 6*1	CHI-MIL 12*6	KC-NY 0-2	MIN-OAK 2-5	TOR-TEX 7-9
0809	CLE-BAL 8*2	SEA-CAL 0-5	BOS-DET 8*7	CHI-MIL 0-1	KC-NY 2-3	MIN-OAK 9*2	TOR-TEX 6-7
0810	CLE-BAL 6*3	SEA-CAL 0-4	BOS-DET 9*6	CHI-MIL 4-5	KC-NY 13*3	MIN-OAK 2-6	TOR-TEX 8*7
						MIN-OAK 5-6	
0811	TOR-BAL 1-3	MIN-CAL 2*0	BOS-DET 0-5	CHI-MIL 6*1	CLE-NY 5-6	SEA-OAK 6*4	BOS-KC 1-5
							BOS-KC 5-6
0812	TOR-BAL 3*0	MIN-CAL 4-5	CHI-DET 3-7	MIL-TEX 7*2	CLE-NY 4-6	SEA-OAK 2-3	BOS-KC 5*2
0813	TOR-BAL 6-7	MIN-CAL 6*2	CHI-DET 2-5	CLE-NY 0-4	SEA-OAK 1-4	MIL-TEX 4-5	BOS-KC 11*6
0814	BAL-CLE 12*2	MIN-CAL 14*1	CHI-DET 8*2			MIL-TEX 2-8	
0815	BAL-CLE 2-3	MIN-SEA 0-1	DET-BOS 5-8	OAK-CAL 4-6	MIL-CHI 4*3	TEX-TOR 1-6	NY-KC 7*4
0816	BAL-CLE 1-2	MIN-SEA 6-7	DET-BOS 12*6	OAK-CAL 2-5	MIL-CHI 6*5	TEX-TOR 1-13	NY-KC 2-4
0817	BAL-CLE 6-11	MIN-SEA 1-11	DET-BOS 5-7	OAK-CAL 3-7	MIL-CHI 4-7	TEX-TOR 7-8	NY-KC 0-5
0818	MIL-CLE 4-10	BOS-MIN 3*1					
0819	MIL-CLE 5*3	BOS-MIN 1-5	OAK-BAL 4*1	TEX-KC 8-9	SEA-NY 7*3	CHI-TOR 1-5	CAL-DET 5*2
							CAL-DET 3-8
0820	MIL-CLE 6*3	TEX-KC 7*1	BOS-MIN 9*1	SEA-NY 2-5	CHI-TOR 1-4		CAL-DET 0-3
0821	BOS-CLE 24*5	TEX-KC 3-4			CHI-TOR 4*3		CAL-DET 6*1
0822	BOS-CLE 6*3	CAL-BAL 7-8	KC-MIL 4*2	TOR-MIN 3-4	OAK-NY 2-3	CHI-TEX 3-11	SEA-DET 1-4
0823	BOS-CLE 4-5	CAL-BAL 2-4	KC-MIL 4-8	TOR-MIN 7*4	OAK-NY 2*1	CHI-TEX 1-3	SEA-DET 0-14
0824	BOS-CLE 2-5	CAL-BAL 4*3	KC-MIL 2-3	TOR-MIN 7*5	OAK-NY 11*4	CHI-TEX 2-3	SEA-DET 3*1
0825	KC-CHI 2*0		MIN-MIL 5-6	BAL-SEA 2-5	CAL-NY 5*3	BOS-TEX 2-4	OAK-DET 8*4
0826	KC-CHI 6*1	TOR-CLE 66	MIN-MIL 7*5	BAL-SEA 1-4	CAL-NY 2*0	BOS-TEX 8*1	OAK-DET 7-8
0827	KC-CHI 1-3	TOR-CLE 3*2				BOS-TEX 1-4	
		TOR-CLE 6*3					
0828	DET-CAL 2-4	TOR-CLE 9*1	TEX-CHI 2-6	MIN-MIL 6*2	NY-SEA 4*2	BAL-OAK 4-5	
						BAL-OAK 7-8	
0829	CLE-BOS 7*3	DET-CAL 12-13	TEX-CHI 5*2	MIL-KC 3*1	NY-SEA 13*12	BAL-OAK 3-4	MIN-TOR 5-6
						BAL-OAK 0-4	
0830	CLE-BOS 3-7	DET-CAL 4-5	TEX-CHI 6*2	MIL-KC 1-10	MIN-TOR 1-8	BAL-OAK 5*4	NY-SEA 0-1
							NY-SEA 3*0
0831	CLE-BOS 3-4	DET-CAL 3-5	TEX-CHI 1-3	MIL-KC 1-6	BAL-OAK 0-7	MIN-TOR 5-7	NY-SEA 2-6
0901	TEX-BOS 4-6	BAL-CAL 9*3	MIL-MIN 3-9	CHI-KC 4*0	NY-OAK 8-9	CLE-TOR 4-5	DET-SEA 6*5

◆1986◆

	GAME 1	GAME 2	GAME 3	GAME 4	GAME 5	GAME 6	GAME 7
0902	TEX-BOS 6-8	BAL-CAL 1-10	MIL-MIN 0-4	CHI-KC 3*0	NY-OAK 9*8	CLE-TOR 9*5	DET-SEA 7*5
0903	TEX-BOS 3-4	BAL-CAL 2-5	MIL-MIN 5-11	CHI-KC 1-2	NY-OAK 3-5	CLE-TOR 1-3	DET-SEA 2-3
0904	CLE-MIL 15*4			CHI-KC 0-1			
0905	CLE-MIL 13*5	SEA-BAL 8*2	MIN-BOS 2-12	NY-CAL 7*4	TOR-CHI 0-5	DET-OAK 9*4	KC-TEX 6-7
0906	CLE-MIL 17*9	SEA-BAL 6*2	MIN-BOS 2-3	NY-CAL 2-9	TOR-CHI 4*0	DET-OAK 4-5	KC-TEX 4-6
0907	CLE-MIL 2-7	SEA-BAL 0-8	MIN-BOS 0-9	NY-CAL 2-7	TOR-CHI 3-4	DET-OAK 4-8	KC-TEX 5*2
0908	MIN-KC 0-5	BOS-BAL 9*3					
0909	MIN-KC 3-11	BOS-BAL 7*5	OAK-CHI 1-4	CAL-CLE 8*1	MIL-DET 3*1	SEA-TEX 3*1	NY-TOR 3*1
0910		BOS-BAL 9*4	OAK-CHI 6*2	CAL-CLE 7*6	MIL-DET 7-11	SEA-TEX 2-3	
0911	SEA-KC 6-7	BOS-BAL 6-8	OAK-CHI 2*1	TEX-MIN 2-6	MIL-DET 0-8	NY-TOR 3*1	
						NY-TOR 7*5	
0912	CAL-CHI 2-3	OAK-CLE 3-9	BAL-DET 3-5	SEA-KC 4*2	TOR-MIL 1-4	TEX-MIN 2-4	BOS-NY 7*2
0913	CAL-CHI 3*2	OAK-CLE 6-8	BAL-DET 2-7	SEA-KC 4-5	TOR-MIL 7*1	TEX-MIN 14*1	BOS-NY 6-11
0914	CAL-CHI 1-3	OAK-CLE 2-5	BAL-DET 0-7	SEA-KC 3-10	TOR-MIL 0-5	TEX-MIN 6-7	BOS-NY 5-11
0915	CAL-CHI 6*5	MIN-CLE 0-4	TEX-OAK 6*2		TOR-MIL 5*2		BAL-NY 3-5
0916	KC-CAL 5-6	MIN-CLE 7*3	TEX-OAK 10*6	CHI-SEA 0-7	DET-TOR 4-6	MIL-BOS 1-2	BAL-NY 1-8
						MIL-BOS 3-9	
0917	KC-CAL 1-3	MIN-CLE 2-5	BAL-NY 8*3	TEX-OAK 4*0	CHI-SEA 3*0	MIL-BOS 1-4	DET-TOR 8*6
					CHI-SEA 6*4	MIL-BOS 1-7	
0918	KC-CAL 3-18						
0919	CHI-CAL 7*1	MIL-BAL 1-3	NY-DET 3-8	CLE-OAK 1-5	KC-SEA 5-6	MIN-TEX 1-4	BOS-TOR 4-6
0920	CHI-CAL 7-8	MIL-BAL 3-4	NY-DET 5*2	CLE-OAK 6*5	KC-SEA 0-3	MIN-TEX 3*2	BOS-TOR 2-5
0921	CHI-CAL 0-3	MIL-BAL 5*4	NY-DET 1-3	CLE-OAK 2-4	KC-SEA 8*1	MIN-TEX 1-2	BOS-TOR 3*2
0922	CLE-CAL 3-4	NY-BAL 4*2	TOR-DET 1-2	CHI-OAK 3-5	TEX-SEA 2*0	KC-MIN 1-2	
	CLE-CAL 7*0						
0923	CLE-CAL 5*2	NY-BAL 5*3	TOR-DET 6*3	BOS-MIL 5-8	KC-MIN 2-9	CHI-OAK 3-4	TEX-SEA 12*6
0924		NY-BAL 4*1	TOR-DET 8*2		KC-MIN 2*1	CHI-OAK 2-4	TEX-SEA 4-5
0925	CLE-CAL 3-6	BAL-MIL 3-9	TOR-DET 4*2		KC-MIN 8*1		
0926	TEX-CAL 3-8	BAL-MIL 0-2	TOR-BOS 1*0	DET-NY 3*2	CLE-SEA 9*7		
0927	TEX-CAL 1*0	BAL-MIL 7*0	TOR-BOS 0-2	DET-NY 1*0	CLE-SEA 12*4	MIN-CHI 2-5	OAK-KC 6*3
						MIN-CHI 3-4	OAK-KC 9*6
0928	TOR-BOS 3-12	TEX-CAL 4*3	BAL-MIL 2-10	DET-NY 2-10	CLE-SEA 5*4	MIN-CHI 6*1	OAK-KC 2-6
0929	BAL-BOS 5-7	CLE-MIN 5-6	OAK-TEX 0-3	TOR-NY 1-8			CAL-KC 1-2
0930	BAL-BOS 6*3	CLE-MIN 9-10	OAK-TEX 5-9	TOR-NY 2-5	DET-MIL 0-5	SEA-CHI 4-5	CAL-KC 8*4
						SEA-CHI 4-5	
1001	BAL-BOS 7-11	CAL-KC 0-2	DET-MIL 2*1	CLE-MIN 12*3	TOR-NY 3*0	SEA-CHI 1-3	OAK-TEX 9*7
1002	NY-BOS 6*1		DET-MIL 2*1	CHI-MIN 8*4			CAL-TEX 9-10
1003	DET-BAL 6*3	SEA-CLE 5-6	KC-OAK 8*4	CHI-MIN 2-9	MIL-TOR 4*1		CAL-TEX 1-6
1004	DET-BAL 11*4	SEA-CLE 5-6	KC-OAK 2*0	CHI-MIN 3-7	NY-BOS 5*3		CAL-TEX 2*0
					NY-BOS 3*1		
1005	DET-BAL 6*3	SEA-CLE 2-4	CHI-MIN 0-3	KC-OAK 0-6	NY-BOS 7*0	CAL-TEX 4-7	MIL-TOR 2*1
							MIL-TOR 4*3

◆1987◆

	GAME 1	GAME 2	GAME 3	GAME 4	GAME 5	GAME 6	GAME 7
0406	TEX-BAL 1-2	NY-DET 2*1	CHI-KC 5*4	BOS-MIL 1-5			CLE-TOR 3-7
0407	SEA-CAL 1-7	OAK-MIN 4-5					CLE-TOR 1-5
0408	SEA-CAL 1-7	OAK-MIN 1-4	TEX-BAL 6*4	NY-DET 6*5	CHI-KC 3-9	BOS-MIL 2-3	CLE-TOR 14*3
0409	SEA-CAL 7*2	OAK-MIN 4-5	TEX-BAL 6-8	NY-DET 3-9	CHI-KC 6*0	BOS-MIL 11-12	MIL-TEX 11*8
0410	TOR-BOS 0-3	DET-CHI 11*4	BAL-CLE 12*11	CAL-OAK 6*4	NY-KC 1-13	MIN-SEA 8*1	MIL-TEX 8*6
0411	TOR-BOS 11*1	DET-CHI 7*1	BAL-CLE 7*3	CAL-OAK 6*3	NY-KC 15*2	MIN-SEA 5-6	MIL-TEX 7*5
0412	TOR-BOS 3-8	DET-CHI 7*1	BAL-CLE 7*1	CAL-OAK 1-7	NY-KC 2-8	MIN-SEA 8*5	
						CAL-SEA 5*3	
0413	MIL-BAL 6*3	CLE-NY 3-11		MIN-OAK 3-6			CHI-TOR 3-4
0414	MIL-BAL 7*4	CLE-NY 6-10	TEX-BOS 1-4	MIN-OAK 9*8	DET-KC 1-10	CAL-SEA 4-6	CHI-TOR 5*0
0415	MIL-BAL 7*0	CLE-NY 3-4	TEX-BOS 4-5	MIN-OAK 5*2	DET-KC 1-2	CAL-SEA 4*0	BOS-TOR 2-4
						OAK-SEA 5-6	
0416						OAK-SEA 2-4	BOS-TOR 5-10
0417	CLE-BAL 1-4	MIN-CAL 1-2	CHI-DET 1-3	TEX-MIL 2-10		OAK-SEA 7*5	BOS-TOR 6*4
0418	CLE-BAL 3-16	MIN-CAL 0-1	CHI-DET 2-3	TEX-MIL 3-4	KC-NY 6-7	OAK-SEA 1-8	BOS-TOR 4*1
0419	CLE-BAL 3*0	MIN-CAL 6*5	CHI-DET 7*2	TEX-MIL 4-6	KC-NY 0-5		
	CLE-BAL 8*7				KC-NY 0-1		
0420	KC-BOS 10*2	OAK-CAL 10*5	MIL-CHI 5*4	TOR-CLE 8*7	DET-NY 2-8	SEA-MIN 5-13	
0421	KC-BOS 0-8	OAK-CAL 5-8	MIL-CHI 1-7	TOR-CLE 0-5	DET-NY 1-3	SEA-MIN 1-6	BAL-TEX 4-6
0422	KC-BOS 0-1	OAK-CAL 7*6		TOR-CLE 6*3	DET-NY 1-4	SEA-MIN 4*3	BAL-TEX 3*2
				NY-CLE 5*4		CAL-MIN 7*3	BAL-TEX 4-9
0423							
0424	TOR-CHI 4*2	KC-DET 7*3	BAL-MIL 4-6	NY-CLE 5-6	SEA-OAK 6*3	CAL-MIN 8*1	BOS-TEX 4-6
0425	TOR-CHI 4-5	KC-DET 2-13	BAL-MIL 2-8	NY-CLE 1-2	SEA-OAK 3-7	CAL-MIN 7-8	BOS-TEX 1-2
0426	TOR-CHI 5*2	KC-DET 6*1	BAL-MIL 3-5	NY-CLE 14*2	SEA-OAK 8*5	CAL-MIN 5-10	BOS-TEX 3-5
					BOS-OAK 2-5		
0427	MIL-CAL 10*7	DET-SEA 2-5			BOS-OAK 1-7	NY-TEX 1-3	MIN-TOR 1-5
0428	MIL-CAL 5-10	DET-SEA 4-6	CHI-CLE 0-1	BAL-KC 3*0	MIL-OAK 8*7	NY-TEX 7-8	MIN-TOR 1-8
					MIL-OAK 1-4		
0429	DET-CAL 2*1	BOS-SEA 11*5	CHI-CLE 5-6	BAL-KC 4-5	DET-OAK 1-2	NY-MIN 4-7	TEX-TOR 2-3
0430	DET-CAL 12*4	BOS-SEA 2-11		CLE-KC 2*0	DET-OAK 2-3	NY-MIN 6*4	TEX-TOR 8-9
0501	BOS-CAL 12*3	MIL-SEA 10*8	CHI-BAL 5*1	CLE-KC 2*0	DET-OAK 0-2	NY-MIN 3-4	TEX-TOR 1-3
0502	BOS-CAL 2-4	MIL-SEA 6*4	CHI-BAL 7*3	CLE-KC 4-5			
0503	BOS-CAL 4-11	MIL-SEA 3-7	CHI-BAL 4*3	CLE-KC 1-2			
0504	NY-CHI 6*1						
0505	NY-CHI 0-2	OAK-BOS 0-6	SEA-DET 7*5	TOR-KC 4-6	CAL-MIL 2*0	BAL-MIN 5*4	CLE-TEX 5-6
0506	NY-CHI 4*1	OAK-BOS 2-6	SEA-DET 5-7	TOR-KC 3-6	CAL-MIL 3*0	BAL-MIN 6*0	CLE-TEX 2-7
						BAL-MIN 2-5	
0507							
0508	CAL-BOS 4-6	BAL-CHI 7*6	KC-CLE 9*6	OAK-DET 7*2	SEA-MIL 4*3	MIN-NY 7-11	TOR-TEX 7*4
0509	CAL-BOS 8*1	BAL-CHI 15*6	KC-CLE 4*0	OAK-DET 8*7	SEA-MIL 8*2	MIN-NY 2*0	TOR-TEX 15*4
0510	CAL-BOS 0-7	BAL-CHI 6*4	KC-CLE 2-4	OAK-DET 6-7	SEA-MIL 5*1	MIN-NY 1-6	TOR-TEX 8-9
0511	SEA-BOS 4*3	MIN-BAL 10*4	TEX-CLE 6*3	CAL-DET 5*1	KC-TOR 0-4	CHI-NY 2-3	
0512	SEA-BOS 2-3	MIN-BAL 7-10	TEX-CLE 6*1	CAL-DET 2-15	KC-TOR 3*1	CHI-NY 4-5	OAK-MIL 10*8
0513	SEA-BOS 5*4	KC-BAL 8*7	CLE-CHI 7*5	CAL-DET 7-10	TOR-MIN 7*0	TEX-NY 8*6	OAK-MIL 8*2
		KC-BAL 3-4	CLE-CHI 3-4		TOR-MIN 16*4	TEX-NY 1-9	
0514							
0515	BAL-CAL 6-7	CLE-DET 3-4	TEX-CHI 0-5	MIL-KC 3-4	BOS-MIN 1-3	TOR-OAK 3*2	NY-SEA 7*3
0516	BAL-CAL 4*2	CLE-DET 3-5	TEX-CHI 7*2	MIL-KC 0-13	BOS-MIN 6*1	TOR-OAK 3-10	NY-SEA 8-10
0517	BAL-CAL 3*2	CLE-DET 4-8	TEX-CHI 5-8	MIL-KC 2-3	BOS-MIN 8-10	TOR-OAK 0-3	NY-SEA 8*3
0518	TOR-CAL 12*0	DET-TEX 6*3		BOS-KC 2-4		NY-OAK 2*1	BAL-SEA 6*0
0519	TOR-CAL 1-2	DET-TEX 8-10	MIN-CLE 3-4	BOS-KC 1-4	CHI-MIL 5*1	NY-OAK 2-4	BAL-SEA 15*4
0520	TOR-CAL 4-5	DET-TEX 6*4	MIN-CLE 8*2	BOS-KC 7*1	CHI-MIL 1-5	NY-OAK 5-7	BAL-SEA 2-6
			MIN-CLE 3-6				
0521							
0522	CHI-BOS 4*3	NY-CAL 7*2	CLE-MIL 2-4	DET-MIN 3*2	BAL-OAK 10*6	TOR-SEA 7*5	KC-TEX 8*1
0523	CHI-BOS 9*1	NY-CAL 3*0	CLE-MIL 6*2	DET-MIN 5-7	BAL-OAK 5*4	TOR-SEA 6*2	KC-TEX 4-6
0524	CHI-BOS 4*1	NY-CAL 10*8	CLE-MIL 5*3	DET-MIN 7*2	BAL-OAK 4*3	TOR-SEA 2-5	KC-TEX 5*2
0525	CLE-BOS 6-10	NY-CAL 6*3	KC-CHI 6*1	TEX-DET 5-8	BAL-OAK 4*3	TOR-SEA 6*5	
0526	CLE-BOS 5-6	MIL-MIN 2-4	KC-CHI 5*4	TEX-DET 7-8			
0527	CLE-BOS 0-1	MIL-MIN 2-7	KC-CHI 2-3	TEX-DET 3-4	CAL-BAL 6-8	SEA-NY 6*5	OAK-TOR 4*1
0528	CLE-BOS 8-12	MIL-MIN 1-13			CAL-BAL 7-8	SEA-NY 2-5	OAK-TOR 4*3
0529	BOS-CHI 6-8	MIL-CLE 6-9	MIN-DET 7-15	TEX-KC 16*5	SEA-BAL 7*3	OAK-NY 13*5	CAL-TOR 1-3
0530	BOS-CHI 2-3	MIL-CLE 6*5		TEX-KC 7-12	SEA-BAL 12*0	OAK-NY 4*3	CAL-TOR 3-4
0531	BOS-CHI 10*9	MIL-CLE 7*1	MIN-DET 9*5	TEX-KC 3*2	SEA-BAL 8*5	OAK-NY 5-9	CAL-TOR 2-7
			MIN-DET 11*3				
0601	OAK-BAL 9*6	MIN-BOS 9*5	DET-CLE 6-9	KC-MIL 2-3	CAL-NY 9*2	CHI-TEX 9-11	SEA-TOR 2*0
0602	OAK-BAL 2-9	MIN-BOS 5-6		KC-MIL 3-14	CAL-NY 2-3	CHI-TEX 15*5	SEA-TOR 3-4
0603	OAK-BAL 7*3	MIN-BOS 6-7	DET-CLE 15*3	KC-MIL 2-4	CAL-NY 3-9	CHI-TEX 3-14	SEA-TOR 2-7
0604	CHI-CAL 2-3	DET-BOS 5-8	KC-SEA 6*1	NY-MIL 3-9			
0605	CHI-CAL 4-6	DET-BOS 4*2	KC-SEA 2-7	NY-MIL 13*1	TEX-MIN 15*9	CLE-OAK 4*3	BAL-TOR 2-6
0606	CHI-CAL 1-2	DET-BOS 5*3	KC-SEA 5*2	NY-MIL 6-7	TEX-MIN 2-3	CLE-OAK 4-6	BAL-TOR 5-8

♦1987♦	GAME 1	GAME 2	GAME 3	GAME 4	GAME 5	GAME 6	GAME 7
0607	CHI-CAL 4*0	DET-BOS 18*8	KC-SEA 9*1	NY-MIL 5*3	TEX-MIN 4-7	CLE-OAK 12*2	BAL-TOR 2-3
0608	CLE-CAL 2*0	BOS-BAL 6*2	TEX-SEA 0-6	TOR-NY 11*0	KC-MIN 3-5	CHI-OAK 3-9	
0609	CLE-CAL 5-6	BOS-BAL 2*1	TEX-SEA 3*0	TOR-NY 7*2	KC-MIN 2-5	CHI-OAK 3-8	MIL-DET 5-8
0610	CLE-CAL 7-10	BOS-BAL 15*4	TEX-SEA 9*5	TOR-NY 4*1	KC-MIN 3-4	CHI-OAK 2-5	MIL-DET 8*5
0611		TOR-BAL 8*6					MIL-DET 8*5
0612	CAL-KC 0-1	TOR-BAL 8*5	MIL-NY 3-8	CLE-SEA 10*6	OAK-TEX 6*1	MIN-CHI 5*2	BOS-DET 4-11
						MIN-CHI 7*4	
0613	TOR-BAL 8*2	BOS-DET 4-6	CAL-KC 4*0	MIL-NY 1-4	CLE-SEA 6*1	MIN-CHI 2-6	OAK-TEX 10*8
0614	TOR-BAL 5-8	BOS-DET 1-2	CAL-KC 12*0	MIL-NY 6*4	CLE-SEA 3-4	MIN-CHI 6*3	OAK-TEX 1-5
0615	TEX-CAL 9*7	MIN-MIL 5*0	OAK-KC 7*6	BAL-NY 2-9	CHI-SEA 2-8	DET-TOR 2*1	
0616	TEX-CAL 5*4	MIN-MIL 7*3	OAK-KC 11*1	BAL-NY 5-6	CHI-SEA 6-8	DET-TOR 4-10	BOS-CLE 7-8
0617	TEX-CAL 1-6	MIN-MIL 5-8	OAK-KC 5-10	BAL-NY 3-4	CHI-SEA 0-2	DET-TOR 3*2	BOS-CLE 4*0
0618	KC-CAL 10*4			BAL-NY 3-6		MIL-TOR 6*3	BOS-CLE 5-7
0619	KC-CAL 2*0	DET-BAL 5*3	NY-BOS 10*5	CHI-MIN 6-7	TEX-OAK 4*2	MIL-TOR 6-15	SEA-CLE 7*4
0620	KC-CAL 8*4	DET-BAL 4*9	NY-BOS 4-9	CHI-MIN 10*5	TEX-OAK 7*6	MIL-TOR 3*2	SEA-CLE 2-9
0621	KC-CAL 0-8	DET-BAL 5-9	NY-BOS 2-4	CHI-MIN 6-8	TEX-OAK 3-7	MIL-TOR 6-7	SEA-CLE 5*0
		DET-BAL 9*3			TEX-OAK 13*3		
0622	MIL-BOS 2-5	NY-BAL 7*3	SEA-CHI 3*0	TOR-DET 0-2	KC-OAK 1-4		CLE-MIN 4-9
0623	MIL-BOS 5-9	NY-BAL 2*1	SEA-CHI 3-13	TOR-DET 8*7	KC-OAK 4*0	CAL-TEX 7*3	CLE-MIN 8-14
0624	MIL-BOS 7-8	NY-BAL 0-4	SEA-CHI 10*7	TOR-DET 5*3	KC-OAK 2-4	CAL-TEX 8*6	
0625						CAL-TEX 4*1	CLE-MIN 3-4
0626	CAL-CHI 3*1	OAK-CLE 5*0	BAL-DET 0-9	SEA-KC 5*1	TOR-MIL 5-10	BOS-NY 11-12	MIN-TEX 0-1
0627	CAL-CHI 3*1	OAK-CLE 13*3	BAL-DET 4*2	SEA-KC 0-6	TOR-MIL 8*1	BOS-NY 1-9	MIN-TEX 6-11
0628	CAL-CHI 13*3	OAK-CLE 10*0	BAL-DET 7-8	SEA-KC 3-8	TOR-MIL 5-11	BOS-NY 6*2	MIN-TEX 2-7
0629	OAK-CHI 2-5	CAL-CLE 11*4	BAL-BOS 3-14	MIN-KC 2-3	DET-MIL 11*1	NY-TOR 15*14	MIN-TEX 3-6
0630	OAK-CHI 3-12	CAL-CLE 1-2	BAL-BOS 9-13	MIN-KC 3*1	DET-MIL 8*5	NY-TOR 4*0	SEA-TEX 3-4
0701	OAK-CHI 3-5	CAL-CLE 10*5	BAL-BOS 2-6	MIN-KC 3-4	DET-MIL 2-13	NY-TOR 6*1	SEA-TEX 5*2
0702	MIL-CAL 7-9	CHI-CLE 1-2	BOS-OAK 3-5	MIN-KC 3-10	DET-SEA 2-5		SEA-TEX 3-7
0703	MIL-CAL 6*4	CHI-CLE 14*9	BOS-OAK 2*0	TOR-KC 4-6	DET-SEA 5*2	BAL-MIN 5-6	TEX-NY 9*0
				TOR-KC 4-5			TEX-NY 1-3
0704	MIL-CAL 2*1	CHI-CLE 3*2	BAL-MIN 1-4	TOR-KC 1-9	BOS-OAK 5-9	DET-SEA 7*3	TEX-NY 3-4
0705	MIL-CAL 3-4	CHI-CLE 17*0	BAL-MIN 3-4	TOR-KC 3-4	BOS-OAK 3-6	DET-SEA 7*5	TEX-NY 10*4
0706	BOS-CAL 7-10	KC-CLE 7-9	CHI-BAL 1-4	TEX-TOR 4-6	DET-OAK 3-5	MIL-SEA 2-3	MIN-NY 2*0
0707	BOS-CAL 4-9	KC-CLE 4-6	CHI-BAL 9*3	TEX-TOR 2-6	DET-OAK 6*4	MIL-SEA 5-9	MIN-NY 7-12
0708	BOS-CAL 3-5	KC-CLE 8-9	CHI-BAL 5-6	TEX-TOR 2-5	DET-OAK 9*5	MIL-SEA 2-5	MIN-NY 4-13
0709	DET-CAL 2-5	CLE-TEX 10*4	MIN-BAL 3*1	KC-TOR 1-7	MIL-OAK 8*3	BOS-SEA 5-11	CHI-NY 6*3
0710	DET-CAL 9*4	CLE-TEX 4-10	MIN-BAL 12-13	KC-TOR 0-7	MIL-OAK 3-7	BOS-SEA 7*4	CHI-NY 5-9
0711	DET-CAL 12*5	CLE-TEX 2-6	MIN-BAL 2*1	KC-TOR 2*1	MIL-OAK 5-6	BOS-SEA 10*4	CHI-NY 5*2
0712	DET-CAL 4-5	CLE-TEX 6-7	MIN-BAL 0-5	KC-TOR 2-3	MIL-OAK 4*3	BOS-SEA 1-6	CHI-NY 2-6
0716	OAK-BOS 6*3	NY-TEX 12*3	CLE-CHI 4*3	SEA-DET 2-3	BAL-KC 5*4	CAL-MIL 4-6	TOR-MIN 5*2
0717	OAK-BOS 11*6	NY-TEX 8*4	CLE-CHI 3-4	SEA-DET 0-7	BAL-KC 3*1	CAL-MIL 2-12	TOR-MIN 2-3
0718	OAK-BOS 3-5	NY-TEX 2-7	CLE-CHI 6-10	SEA-DET 6-10	BAL-KC 11*7	CAL-MIL 12*6	TOR-MIN 7*5
0719	OAK-BOS 5*3	NY-TEX 3-20	CLE-CHI 7-9	SEA-DET 5*4	BAL-KC 5*1	CAL-MIL 8*5	TOR-MIN 6-7
0720	CAL-BOS 3*2	TOR-TEX 5*3	BAL-CHI 4*1	OAK-DET 4-5	CLE-KC 9*5	SEA-MIL 11-13	NY-MIN 7*1
0721	CAL-BOS 0-3	TOR-TEX 4-6	BAL-CHI 11*6	OAK-DET 4-5	CLE-KC 2-3	SEA-MIL 4-6	NY-MIN 1-2
0722	CAL-BOS 6*5	TOR-TEX 3-5	BAL-CHI 10*5	OAK-DET 10*1	CLE-KC 1-5	SEA-MIL 2*1	NY-MIN 1-3
0723	KC-BAL 1-2	TEX-CLE 2-4	MIN-TOR 3-4		OAK-MIL 5-12		
0724	KC-BAL 1-3	TEX-CLE 6*3	MIN-TOR 6-8	SEA-BOS 4-5	NY-CHI 2-5	OAK-MIL 2-10	CAL-DET 3-6
0725	KC-BAL 3-4	TEX-CLE 7*3	MIN-TOR 13*9	SEA-BOS 5-11	NY-CHI 2-3	OAK-MIL 13*4	CAL-DET 4-5
0726	KC-BAL 4*0	TEX-CLE 11*3	MIN-TOR 2-4	SEA-BOS 1-11	NY-CHI 5*2	OAK-MIL 4-7	CAL-DET 2-6
0727	CAL-OAK 1-6	MIN-SEA 4*3	BOS-TOR 8-10	MIL-TEX 4-5			CHI-DET 1-4
0728	CAL-OAK 9*2	MIN-SEA 1-6	BOS-TOR 1-6	MIL-TEX 9*2	BAL-CLE 3-4	KC-NY 1-2	CHI-DET 1-3
0729	CAL-OAK 5*4	MIN-SEA 3-8	BOS-TOR 6*5	MIL-TEX 9*8	BAL-CLE 7*4	KC-NY 0-4	CHI-DET 4*0
0730	CHI-MIL 1-6				BAL-CLE 4-6	KC-NY 3-6	
0731	CHI-MIL 8*6	SEA-CAL 2-8	BOS-KC 4*0	MIN-OAK 5*3	BAL-TEX 8*4	DET-NY 5-6	CLE-TOR 3-8
0801	CHI-MIL 3*2	SEA-CAL 3-4	BOS-KC 0-4	MIN-OAK 2-3	BAL-TEX 7*1	DET-NY 10*5	CLE-TOR 3*0
0802	CHI-MIL 7*3	SEA-CAL 5*4	BOS-KC 5-13	MIN-OAK 5-6	BAL-TEX 2-5	DET-NY 5-8	CLE-TOR 5-11
0803	TOR-CHI 14*5	MIN-CAL 11*3	NY-CLE 0-2	SEA-OAK 4*3	BOS-TEX 11*2	KC-DET 4*2	
0804	TOR-CHI 4*1	MIN-CAL 3-12	NY-CLE 3-15	SEA-OAK 3-9	BOS-TEX 8*6	KC-DET 8*4	BAL-MIL 8-9
0805	TOR-CHI 3*2	MIN-CAL 1-6	NY-CLE 1-6	SEA-OAK 1-3	BOS-TEX 8-9	KC-DET 2-4	BAL-MIL 1-5
0806	OAK-MIN 4-9	CAL-SEA 4-15	TOR-CLE 5-14			NY-DET 5-12	BAL-MIL 8-11
0807	OAK-MIN 4-9	CAL-SEA 0-14	TOR-CLE 15*1	TEX-BAL 2-9	KC-BOS 3-4	NY-DET 0-8	MIL-CHI 7*4
0808	OAK-MIN 2-9	CAL-SEA 3-5	TOR-CLE 1-3	TEX-BAL 11*5	KC-BOS 3-8	NY-DET 7*0	MIL-CHI 5*3
							MIL-CHI 6-8
0809	TEX-BAL 4-5	KC-BOS 8*3	TOR-CLE 5*1	NY-DET 4-15	OAK-MIN 5-7	CAL-SEA 7*5	MIL-CHI 8*4
0810	CLE-BAL 3-4	TOR-BOS 1-9	NY-KC 1-10	TEX-MIL 3-4		OAK-SEA 15*4	DET-CHI 4-5
0811	CLE-BAL 6*3	TOR-BOS 8*3	NY-KC 5-8	TEX-MIL 7*1	CAL-MIN 2-7	OAK-SEA 2-8	DET-CHI 9*6
0812	CLE-BAL 8*6	TOR-BOS 10*4	NY-KC 1-2	TEX-MIL 12*3	CAL-MIN 8*2	OAK-SEA 3-4	DET-CHI 8*7
0813	MIL-BAL 4-5	CHI-TOR 10*3	DET-KC 4*1		CAL-MIN 5*1		
0814	MIL-BAL 6*2	CHI-TOR 2-3	DET-KC 5-7	OAK-CAL 7*6	SEA-MIN 3-6	CLE-NY 6*5	TEX-BOS 3-9
0815	MIL-BAL 1-2	OAK-CAL 13*3	DET-KC 8*4	SEA-MIN 4-14	CLE-NY 2-11	CHI-TOR 1*0	TEX-BOS 9*4
0816	MIL-BAL 6*2	OAK-CAL 9*6	DET-KC 10*6	SEA-MIN 1-5	CLE-NY 1*0	CHI-TOR 4-6	TEX-BOS 6-7
0817	BOS-CHI 1-2	OAK-CAL 4-6	MIL-CLE 5*3	SEA-MIN 2-4	KC-TEX 7*6		TEX-BOS 2-12
0818	BOS-CHI 14*8	BAL-CAL 4*1	MIL-CLE 8-9	MIN-DET 2-11	KC-TEX 1-3	TOR-OAK 2*1	
0819	BOS-CHI 3-8	BAL-CAL 2*1	MIL-CLE 13*2	MIN-DET 1-7	KC-TEX 11*6	TOR-OAK 3-7	NY-SEA 4*3
0820		BAL-CAL 4*2	MIL-CLE 14*2	MIN-DET 0-8	CHI-TEX 1-5	TOR-OAK 7*6	NY-SEA 8*0
0821	MIN-BOS 3-11	TOR-CAL 1-5	DET-CLE 4-12	KC-MIL 0*3	CHI-TEX 5*1	NY-OAK 4-6	NY-SEA 3-4
			DET-CLE 3-8				BAL-SEA 2-3
0822	MIN-BOS 5-6	TOR-CAL 2*0	DET-CLE 8*6	KC-MIL 8*7	NY-OAK 0-6	BAL-SEA 6-14	CHI-TEX 6-8
0823	MIN-BOS 4-6	TOR-CAL 2-5	DET-CLE 4*3	KC-MIL 5-10	NY-OAK 4*0	BAL-SEA 6*5	CHI-TEX 8*1
0824	CHI-BOS 6*3	NY-CAL 3*2	TEX-KC 4*2	DET-MIN 4-5	BAL-OAK 3-7	TOR-SEA 7*3	CLE-MIL 9-10
0825	CHI-BOS 3-7	NY-CAL 1-5	TEX-KC 15*8	DET-MIN 5*4	BAL-OAK 7-9	TOR-SEA 6*3	CLE-MIL 0-1
0826	CHI-BOS 5*3		TEX-KC 0-3	DET-MIN 10*8			CLE-MIL 3-4
0827	CAL-BAL 5-9	OAK-TOR 4-9	TEX-KC 2-3				
0828	CAL-BAL 5-6	OAK-TOR 3*2	KC-CHI 9*3	TEX-DET 5*3	SEA-NY 10*4		MIN-MIL 0-1
0829	CAL-BAL 6*5	OAK-TOR 6*5	KC-CHI 2-7	TEX-DET 1-4	SEA-NY 7*1	BOS-CLE 2-7	MIN-MIL 12*3
					SEA-NY 2-4	BOS-CLE 1-2	
0830	CAL-BAL 6*2	KC-CHI 11*7	TEX-DET 0-7	MIN-MIL 10*6	SEA-NY 1-4	BOS-CLE 7*3	OAK-TOR 3-13
0831	SEA-BAL 3-4	KC-CHI 3-5	CLE-DET 7*2		OAK-NY 1-4		CAL-TOR 8*7
0901	SEA-BAL 5*0	TEX-CHI 6*4	CLE-DET 5-6	MIL-KC 2*0	OAK-NY 8*3	BOS-MIN 9*0	CAL-TOR 3-4
0902	SEA-BAL 8*6	TEX-CHI 0-5	CLE-DET 1-2	MIL-KC 3*2	OAK-NY 2-3	BOS-MIN 4-5	CAL-TOR 6-7
0903		TEX-CHI 2-5	CLE-DET 1-3	MIL-KC 8*2		BOS-MIN 1-2	
0904	OAK-BAL 2-5	CLE-BOS 2-5	CAL-NY 4-8	CHI-KC 2-6	DET-TEX 11*2	MIL-MIN 1-2	SEA-TOR 5-6
0905	OAK-BAL 7*2	CLE-BOS 15*2	CAL-NY 6-7	CHI-KC 2-4	DET-TEX 7-8	MIL-MIN 1-2	SEA-TOR 0-3
0906	OAK-BAL 6-7	CLE-BOS 3*1	CAL-NY 3*1	CHI-KC 6*5	DET-TEX 3-9	MIL-MIN 6*0	SEA-TOR 2-3
0907	DET-BAL 12*4	NY-BOS 9*5	KC-CAL 5*2	SEA-CLE 6*4	TOR-MIL 5*3	CHI-MIN 1-8	TEX-OAK 1-2
0908		NY-BOS 6-8	KC-CAL 4*2	SEA-CLE 7*0	TOR-MIL 4-6	CHI-MIN 4*3	TEX-OAK 12*1
0909	DET-BAL 7*4	NY-BOS 3-5		SEA-CLE 9*4	TOR-MIL 4-6	CHI-MIN 1-2	TEX-OAK 7-11
	DET-BAL 6*0						
0910	BAL-BOS 4-5	TEX-CAL 7-8	DET-MIL 3-4	KC-OAK 2-3			
0911	BAL-BOS 3-9	TEX-CAL 7*2	DET-MIL 2-5	KC-OAK 9*0		CHI-SEA 5*1	NY-TOR 5-6
0912	BAL-BOS 3-4	TEX-CAL 4*3	DET-MIL 2-11	KC-OAK 10*7	MIN-CLE 13*10	CHI-SEA 2-12	NY-TOR 1-13
0913		TEX-CAL 8*2	DET-MIL 5*1	KC-OAK 6*5	MIN-CLE 4-5	CHI-SEA 7*3	NY-TOR 0-7
0914	MIN-CHI 2-8	BOS-DET 0-3	CAL-KC 5-8	MIL-NY 6*4	OAK-TEX 1-2	CLE-SEA 11*8	BAL-TOR 3-18
0915	MIN-CHI 2-6	BOS-DET 8-9	CAL-KC 7*1	MIL-NY 3-4	OAK-TEX 6*5	CLE-SEA 4*2	BAL-TOR 2-6

♦1987♦

	GAME 1	GAME 2	GAME 3	GAME 4	GAME 5	GAME 6	GAME 7
0916	MIN-CHI 10-13	BOS-DET 1-4	CAL-KC 6*4	MIL-NY 5*4	OAK-TEX 1-4	CLE-SEA 3-5	BAL-TOR 0-7
0917	SEA-CHI 8-9		CAL-KC 6-7	TOR-NY 5-6		CAL-TEX 1-5	
0918	SEA-CHI 1*0	MIL-DET 6-7	OAK-KC 4*0	TOR-NY 6*3	CLE-MIN 4-9		BOS-BAL 4-9
							BOS-BAL 10*7
0919	SEA-CHI 8-10	MIL-DET 2-5	OAK-KC 9*5	CLE-MIN 1-3	TOR-NY 2-4	CAL-TEX 3-4	BOS-BAL 5*1
0920	SEA-CHI 3-5	MIL-DET 11*4	OAK-KC 7*6	CLE-MIN 2-3	TOR-NY 6*2	CAL-TEX 1-2	BOS-BAL 6*3
							TOR-BAL 2*1
0921	DET-BOS 4-9	CHI-CAL 5*3	OAK-CLE 3-6	KC-SEA 1-5			TOR-BAL 8*4
0922	DET-BOS 8*5	CHI-CAL 3-5	OAK-CLE 10*2	KC-SEA 4*3	TEX-MIN 4-6	NY-MIL 2-7	
						NY-MIL 10*8	
0923	TOR-BAL 6*1	DET-BOS 4*0	CHI-CAL 6-10	OAK-CLE 6-8	TEX-MIN 2-4	NY-MIL 7-8	KC-SEA 9*0
					TEX-MIN 0-4	BOS-MIL 6-7	
0924	CHI-OAK 4*2	DET-TOR 3-4		CAL-CLE 5-7	KC-MIN 6*4	BOS-MIL 9*2	TEX-SEA 3-12
0925	CHI-OAK 2*1	DET-TOR 2-3	NY-BAL 8*4	CAL-CLE 10-11	KC-MIN 7*4	BOS-MIL 2-3	TEX-SEA 1-2
0926	CHI-OAK 3*2	DET-TOR 9-10	NY-BAL 2*0	CAL-CLE 11*8	KC-MIN 1-8	BOS-MIL 6-9	TEX-SEA 3-5
0927	CHI-OAK 5*0	DET-TOR 3*2	NY-BAL 5-9	SEA-KC 5*1	MIN-TEX 5*3		
0928	BAL-DET 3*0	MIL-TOR 6*4	SEA-KC 3-6	BOS-NY 0-6	MIN-TEX 5-7	CAL-CHI 0-1	CLE-OAK 4-5
0929	BAL-DET 1-10	MIL-TOR 5*3	SEA-KC 3-7	BOS-NY 7*0	MIN-TEX 1-2	CAL-CHI 2-5	CLE-OAK 3-4
0930	BAL-DET 7*3	MIL-TOR 5*2		BOS-NY 7*5	SEA-TEX 8*6	CAL-CHI 3-6	CLE-OAK 5-9
1001	BAL-DET 5-9			BAL-NY 1-3	SEA-TEX 5*4	OAK-CHI 4*3	MIN-KC 3-6
1002	TOR-DET 3-4	MIL-BOS 2-3	CLE-CAL 4-10	BAL-NY 2-6	SEA-TEX 6*4	OAK-CHI 1-17	MIN-KC 2-4
1003	TOR-DET 2-3	MIL-BOS 8*4	CLE-CAL 5-12	BAL-NY 4*2	SEA-TEX 7*4	OAK-CHI 2-5	MIN-KC 1-10
1004	TOR-DET 0-1	MIL-BOS 0-4	CLE-CAL 10*6				

♦1988♦

	GAME 1	GAME 2	GAME 3	GAME 4	GAME 5	GAME 6	GAME 7
0404	MIL-BAL 12*0	DET-BOS 5*3	SEA-OAK 1-4		CLE-TEX 3-4	CAL-CHI 5-8	TOR-KC 5*3
			SEA-OAK 0-6				
0405	MIN-NY 0-8		SEA-OAK 6*5	DET-BOS 5-6	CAL-CHI 4*2	TOR-KC 11*4	CLE-TEX 5*1
				DET-BOS 11*6	CAL-CHI 1-2	TOR-KC 4-7	CLE-TEX 4*1
0406	MIN-NY 3-5				SEA-CHI 2-3	DET-KC 2-3	BOS-TEX 4*0
0407							
0408	OAK-CAL 8*2	BAL-CLE 0-3	TOR-MIN 3-6	MIL-NY 4-6	SEA-CHI 2-3	DET-KC 11*4	BOS-TEX 2*1
0409	OAK-CAL 8*6	BAL-CLE 1-12	TOR-MIN 10*0	MIL-NY 1-4	SEA-CHI 7*4	DET-KC 1-8	BOS-TEX 1-4
0410	OAK-CAL 4-6	BAL-CLE 3-6	TOR-MIN 2-4	MIL-NY 6-7			
0411	NY-TOR 9-17	BAL-CLE 2-7		TEX-BOS 3*2		CHI-CAL 6-15	OAK-SEA 4-6
0412	NY-TOR 12*3	MIN-CLE 7*6	KC-BAL 6*1	MIL-BOS 1-3	CHI-CAL 2-5		OAK-SEA 12*7
0413	NY-TOR 5*1	MIN-CLE 3-6	KC-BAL 9*3	MIL-BOS 3-6	TEX-DET 2*1		OAK-SEA 5*4
0414	NY-TOR 7*3	MIN-CLE 1-3	KC-BAL 4*3	MIL-BOS 0-2			CAL-SEA 5*3
0415	NY-MIL 7*1	CHI-OAK 11*3	CLE-BAL 3*2	TEX-BOS 3*2	KC-DET 2-4	MIN-TOR 3*2	CAL-SEA 6-7
0416	NY-MIL 2-9	CHI-OAK 5*1	CLE-BAL 1*0	TEX-BOS 2*0	KC-DET 6-8	MIN-TOR 0-2	CAL-SEA 7*4
0417	NY-MIL 3-6	CHI-OAK 7*6	CLE-BAL 4*1	TEX-BOS 2-15	KC-DET 3-4		CHI-SEA 4*0
0418	NY-MIN 18*5	CAL-OAK 4-5		BAL-MIL 5-9	BOS-DET 7*3	KC-TOR 3-12	CHI-SEA 7*2
0419	NY-MIN 7*6	CAL-OAK 3-8	TEX-CLE 3*0	BAL-MIL 6-8		KC-TOR 0-3	CHI-SEA 7*2
0420	NY-MIN 7*6	CAL-OAK 8-9	TEX-CLE 1-2	BAL-MIL 1-7			
0421	SEA-CAL 6-11	OAK-CHI 6*3	BOS-DET 12*3	BAL-MIL 1-7			
0422	SEA-CAL 7*4	OAK-CHI 5-7	BAL-KC 1-13	CLE-MIN 11*6	TOR-NY 6*4	DET-TEX 5*3	
0423	SEA-CAL 11*4	OAK-CHI 3*2	BAL-KC 3-4	CLE-MIN 10*2	TOR-NY 3*2	DET-TEX 7*6	
0424	SEA-CAL 4*2	OAK-CHI 5*3	BAL-KC 1-3	CLE-MIN 7-13	TOR-NY 3-5	DET-TEX 2-4	BOS-MIL 4*0
							BOS-MIL 5*1
0425							
0426	SEA-CLE 6-12	CAL-DET 0-6	BAL-MIN 2-4	KC-NY 4-5	MIL-TEX 1-3	OAK-TOR 6*1	
0427	SEA-CLE 4-6	CAL-DET 4*3	BAL-MIN 6-7	KC-NY 3*1	MIL-TEX 4*3	OAK-TOR 5*3	
0428	SEA-CLE 3*1	CAL-DET 1-2	BAL-MIN 6-7	KC-NY 6*3	BOS-CHI 0-6	OAK-TOR 6*2	
0429	MIN-BOS 5-6	SEA-DET 6-9	KC-MIL 7*2	TEX-NY 1-2	BAL-CHI 9*0	CAL-TOR 9*5	
0430	MIN-BOS 3-8	SEA-DET 3-4	KC-MIL 1-4	TEX-NY 3-15	BAL-CHI 1-4	CAL-TOR 6*1	OAK-CLE 11*3
0501	MIN-BOS 2*0	SEA-DET 2*0	KC-MIL 6-10	TEX-NY 5*1	BAL-CHI 3-7	CAL-TOR 4-6	OAK-CLE 8*4
0502	KC-BOS 2*0	OAK-DET 4*2	MIN-MIL 3-4	TEX-BAL 4-9	NY-CHI 6*4	TOR-SEA 5-7	CAL-CLE 0-3
0503	KC-BOS 9*3	OAK-DET 8*2	MIN-MIL 3-4	TEX-BAL 4*2	NY-CHI 4*1	TOR-SEA 9*2	CAL-CLE 8*4
0504	CHI-BOS 6*2	DET-CAL 1*0	TEX-MIL 5-6	MIN-BAL 3-4	NY-KC 4*3	CLE-SEA 4-5	TOR-OAK 2-3
0505	CHI-BOS 3-16	DET-CAL 8*5	TEX-MIL 1-9		NY-KC 5*3	CLE-SEA 2-7	TOR-OAK 5-8
0506	BOS-MIN 0-5	TOR-CAL 3*2	NY-TEX 6-7		MIL-KC 8*4		
0507	BOS-MIN 2-5	TOR-CAL 9*4	NY-TEX 2-3	CHI-BAL 11*7	MIL-KC 4*2	DET-SEA 6-7	CLE-OAK 3-14
0508	BOS-MIN 10*6	TOR-CAL 1-8	NY-TEX 8-10	CHI-BAL 5-6	MIL-KC 6*2	DET-SEA 9*3	CLE-OAK 1-5
				CHI-BAL 3*0	BOS-KC 2*0		DET-OAK 1-3
0509	MIL-MIN 9*6	CLE-CAL 1-2		BAL-TEX 5-13	BOS-KC 2-7	SEA-TOR 4*2	DET-OAK 8*2
0510	MIL-MIN 3-9	CLE-CAL 7*1	CHI-NY 3-17	BAL-TEX 0-8		SEA-TOR 3-9	DET-OAK 8*4
0511	MIL-MIN 1-2	CLE-CAL 4*3	CHI-NY 2-12	BAL-TEX 1-2		SEA-TOR 2-8	
0512	CLE-MIL 8*1					MIN-TEX 0-7	CAL-NY 5*4
0513	CLE-MIL 4*3	OAK-BAL 1-4	SEA-BOS 8-14	KC-TEX 1-2	TOR-CHI 1-4	MIN-DET 7*0	CAL-NY 2-6
0514	CLE-MIL 6*4	OAK-BAL 8*0	SEA-BOS 0-3	KC-TEX 3-6	TOR-CHI 5-7	MIN-DET 10*2	CAL-NY 2-9
0515	CLE-MIL 5-9	OAK-BAL 7*4	SEA-BOS 11*7	KC-TEX 5*4	TOR-CHI 5-6		SEA-NY 1-3
0516	DET-MIL 1-3		OAK-BOS 3*0	KC-TEX 7*6	TOR-CHI 5*1		SEA-NY 6*2
0517	DET-MIL 8*4	CHI-CLE 2-6	OAK-BOS 12*7	KC-MIN 5-6	TEX-TOR 7*6		
0518	DET-MIL 3*1	CHI-CLE 1-2	OAK-BOS 1-4	KC-MIN 8*2	TEX-TOR 4*0	CAL-BAL 7-8	
0519		CHI-CLE 0-1		KC-MIN 14*1		CAL-BAL 2*1	
						CAL-BAL 9*6	
0520	CAL-BOS 4*2	DET-CHI 14*6	CLE-KC 3-4	TOR-MIL 3*1	OAK-NY 11*3	SEA-BAL 3*2	MIN-TEX 0-3
0521	CAL-BOS 4-8	DET-CHI 3*1	CLE-KC 9*5	TOR-MIL 4*0	OAK-NY 2-3	SEA-BAL 1-3	MIN-TEX 15*5
0522	CAL-BOS 4-12	DET-CHI 3*1	CLE-KC 8*7	TOR-MIL 1-7	OAK-NY 0-2	SEA-BAL 2-7	MIN-TEX 4*2
0523	NY-CAL 5*2	CLE-CHI 2-3	MIN-KC 7*5	TOR-MIL 7-9	BAL-OAK 7*3	BOS-SEA 3-14	TOR-TEX 13*2
0524	NY-CAL 5*3	CLE-CHI 4*3	MIN-KC 6*5	MIL-DET 7*0	BAL-OAK 0-6	BOS-SEA 1-14	TOR-TEX 1-5
0525	NY-CAL 4*2	CLE-CHI 5*2	MIN-KC 4*2	MIL-DET 3-4	BAL-OAK 1-8	BOS-SEA 4*0	TOR-TEX 7-8
				MIL-DET 3-4			
0526							CHI-TOR 3-4
0527	BAL-CAL 2-4	MIL-CLE 3*2	TEX-KC 3*2	DET-MIN 1-7	BOS-OAK 2-3	NY-SEA 5*1	CHI-TOR 3*2
0528	BAL-CAL 0-5	MIL-CLE 2*0	TEX-KC 6-8	DET-MIN 2-5	BOS-OAK 5-7	NY-SEA 1-6	CHI-TOR 2-4
0529	BAL-CAL 3*2	MIL-CLE 7*2	TEX-KC 1-12	DET-MIN 3-6	BOS-OAK 4-5	NY-SEA 7*3	MIL-TOR 4*1
				TEX-MIN 6*1	NY-OAK 2-3	BAL-SEA 1-4	MIL-TOR 0-9
0530	BOS-CAL 5*2	KC-CLE 1-4		TEX-MIN 6-8	NY-OAK 5*0	BAL-SEA 12*5	MIL-TOR 2-7
0531	BOS-CAL 4*3	KC-CLE 6*3	CHI-DET 10*1	TEX-MIN 1-7	NY-OAK 3-4	BAL-SEA 3-4	
0601		KC-CLE 4-5	CHI-DET 3-9	CAL-MIL 4-9			
0602	TOR-BOS 5*4	TEX-CHI 10*2	SEA-KC 0-3	CAL-MIL 2-8	NY-BAL 4*0	CLE-DET 6*3	OAK-MIN 8*5
0603	TOR-BOS 6*3	TEX-CHI 9*3	SEA-KC 1-3	CAL-MIL 3-4	NY-BAL 6-7	CLE-DET 2-5	OAK-MIN 6*4
0604	TOR-BOS 10*2	TEX-CHI 3-4	SEA-KC 3-4	CAL-MIL 6*5	NY-BAL 9*2	CLE-DET 2-6	OAK-MIN 3-4
0605	TOR-BOS 12*4	TEX-CHI 4-5	SEA-KC 3-7	OAK-KC 0-2	BOS-NY 3*2	MIL-SEA 0-2	CAL-TEX 4-6
0606	TOR-CLE 3-6	MIN-CHI 9*4	OAK-KC 0-6	BOS-NY 3-4	DET-BAL 2-5	MIL-SEA 4-5	CAL-TEX 1*0
0607	TOR-CLE 3-5	MIN-CHI 8-10	OAK-KC 4-5	BOS-NY 4*3	DET-BAL 3-4	MIL-SEA 8*7	CAL-TEX 5*2
0608	TOR-CLE 2-4	MIN-CHI 5*2		BOS-NY 4*3	DET-BAL 12*4	MIN-SEA 7*5	OAK-TEX 2-5
0609	DET-CLE 6*2					MIN-SEA 3*1	OAK-TEX 7*6
0610	DET-CLE 2*1	KC-CAL 0-1	MIL-CHI 0-1	BAL-NY 5*3	BOS-TOR 0-3	MIN-SEA 2-3	OAK-TEX 13*4
0611	DET-CLE 11*3	KC-CAL 7*0	MIL-CHI 3-5	BAL-NY 6-8	BOS-TOR 3-4	MIN-SEA 6-2	OAK-TEX 13*4
0612	DET-CLE 6*4	KC-CAL 6*4	MIL-CHI 16*2	BAL-NY 5-6	BOS-TOR 8*2	MIN-SEA 6*2	OAK-TEX 2-3
0613	NY-BOS 12*6	KC-CAL 5*3	BAL-DET 6*4	SEA-MIL 1-3	CLE-TOR 8*6	CHI-MIN 4*1	
0614	NY-BOS 3-7	TEX-CAL 0-3	BAL-DET 3-9	SEA-MIL 1-5	CLE-TOR 2-3	CHI-MIN 1-3	KC-OAK 2*1
0615	NY-BOS 3-8	TEX-CAL 6*3	BAL-DET 0-1	SEA-MIL 1-5	CLE-TOR 3-15	CHI-MIN 1-5	KC-OAK 2*0
				CHI-MIL 3*1			KC-OAK 9*5
0616	BOS-BAL 4-8	TEX-CAL 0-3	TOR-DET 13*5	CHI-MIL 2-7	CAL-KC 9*7	SEA-MIN 1-4	TEX-OAK 6-7
0617	BOS-BAL 4-6	NY-CLE 4*3	TOR-DET 5-12	CHI-MIL 3-6	CAL-KC 6*3	SEA-MIN 2-6	TEX-OAK 1-2
0618	BOS-BAL 5*0	NY-CLE 6*3	TOR-DET 1-6	CHI-MIL 5*0	CAL-KC 5*0	SEA-MIN 5*4	TEX-OAK 5*4
0619	BOS-BAL 15*7	NY-CLE 3-11	TOR-DET 6*4	OAK-MIL 5*4	SEA-TEX 3-4	CAL-MIN 6*5	BAL-TOR 2-5
0620	KC-CHI 3-5	BOS-CLE 14*7	NY-DET 1-2	OAK-MIL 4*2	SEA-TEX 0-6	CAL-MIN 5*4	BAL-TOR 4*2
0621	KC-CHI 6*2	BOS-CLE 10*6	NY-DET 6-7	OAK-MIL 6*2	SEA-TEX 3*2	CAL-MIN 1-3	BAL-TOR 2-4
0622	KC-CHI 4-5	BOS-CLE 1-3	NY-DET 2-3				BAL-TOR 2-5
0623	CLE-NY 3-4						

♦1988♦	GAME 1	GAME 2	GAME 3	GAME 4	GAME 5	GAME 6	GAME 7
0624	CLE-NY 7*5	BAL-BOS 6*2	MIL-CAL 5*4	MIN-OAK 11*5	KC-SEA 0-7	CHI-TEX 2-5	DET-TOR 3-6
0625	CLE-NY 1-4	BAL-BOS 3-10	MIL-CAL 3-7	MIN-OAK 3-4	KC-SEA 7*3	CHI-TEX 10*5	DET-TOR 7*2
0626	CLE-NY 3-4	BAL-BOS 1-10	MIL-CAL 2-4	MIN-OAK 11*0	KC-SEA 0-8	CHI-TEX 7*5	DET-TOR 1-4
				MIN-OAK 5*0			
0627	TOR-BAL 2-6	CLE-BOS 5-9	MIN-CAL 7-16	MIL-OAK 4-5	CHI-KC 1-2	DET-NY 6*3	TEX-SEA 3-6
0628	TOR-BAL 0-7	CLE-BOS 1-6	MIN-CAL 8*2	MIL-OAK 4*1	CHI-KC 4*3	DET-NY 6*1	TEX-SEA 6*0
0629	TOR-BAL 4*2	CLE-BOS 1-5	MIN-CAL 1-2	MIL-OAK 2-7	CHI-KC 8-9	DET-NY 3-7	TEX-SEA 1*0
0630	NY-CHI 5*3						
0701	NY-CHI 1-2	SEA-CLE 11*3	CAL-DET 0-11	BOS-KC 7-8	MIN-MIL 5*4	BAL-TEX 7*1	OAK-TOR 2*1
0702	NY-CHI 4*0	SEA-CLE 7-10	CAL-DET 1-6	BOS-KC 1-3	MIN-MIL 8*2	BAL-TEX 7*4	OAK-TOR 11*3
0703	NY-CHI 3-4	SEA-CLE 7*6	CAL-DET 10*4	BOS-KC 2-3	MIN-MIL 3-4	BAL-TEX 1-13	OAK-TOR 9*8
0704	BAL-CHI 1-5	OAK-CLE 4*2	SEA-DET 3-5	BOS-KC 9*2	MIN-MIL 3*1	NY-TEX 13*2	CAL-TOR 11*6
0705	BAL-CHI 5*1	OAK-CLE 0-3	SEA-DET 5*4	MIL-KC 3*1	BOS-MIN 4-6	NY-TEX 5*3	CAL-TOR 1-4
		OAK-CLE 2-4					
0706	BAL-CHI 1-4	OAK-CLE 6-8	SEA-DET 6-7	MIL-KC 4*2	BOS-MIN 1-8	NY-TEX 2-4	
0707	TEX-BAL 0-6	CAL-CLE 7*1	OAK-DET 1-8	MIL-KC 3-7	BOS-MIN 4*3		
0708	TEX-BAL 8*5	CAL-CLE 10*6	OAK-DET 3*2	KC-NY 4*0	MIL-MIN 5*3	SEA-TOR 2-3	BOS-CHI 5-6
0709	TEX-BAL 1-4	CAL-CLE 8*5	OAK-DET 3-4	MIL-MIN 5*4	KC-NY 3-5	SEA-TOR 9*3	BOS-CHI 10*7
							BOS-CHI 8*2
0710	TEX-BAL 1-2	CAL-CLE 7*5	OAK-DET 8*2	MIL-MIN 3*2	KC-NY 5*3	SEA-TOR 0-5	BOS-CHI 1-4
0714	MIN-BAL 1-7	DET-CAL 0-2	TOR-OAK 7*1	CLE-SEA 1-3	CHI-NY 5-7	MIL-TEX 6*2	
	MIN-BAL 8*2						
0715	MIN-BAL 4*2	DET-CAL 4-6	CHI-NY 3-5	TOR-OAK 1*0	CLE-SEA 5-8	MIL-TEX 4*2	KC-BOS 1-3
							KC-BOS 4-7
0716	MIN-BAL 4*3	DET-CAL 10*1	CHI-NY 7*4	TOR-OAK 1-4	CLE-SEA 8*2	MIL-TEX 4*3	KC-BOS 6-7
0717	MIN-BAL 7*2	DET-CAL 0-4	CHI-NY 3-7	TOR-OAK 9*6	CLE-SEA 7*4	MIL-TEX 0-3	KC-BOS 8-10
0718	KC-MIL 1-6	TOR-CAL 12*2	TEX-NY 2-7	CLE-OAK 2-7	DET-SEA 12*3		MIN-MIL 5-6
0719	KC-MIL 1-3	TOR-CAL 7*6	TEX-NY 7*2	CLE-OAK 2-4	DET-SEA 6-9	CHI-BAL 4-6	MIN-BOS 0-5
				CLE-OAK 6-9		CHI-BAL 2*0	
0720	MIN-BOS 7-9	TOR-CAL 6-7	KC-MIL 4*0	CLE-OAK 5*4	DET-SEA 12*5		
0721	CHI-BOS 1-6	NY-KC 1-6	TEX-MIL 1-6		TOR-SEA 2-6		
0722	CHI-BOS 3-4	NY-KC 9*8	TEX-MIL 1-2	CLE-CAL 4-7	TOR-SEA 9-10	BAL-MIN 1-6	DET-OAK 1-4
0723	CHI-BOS 5-11	NY-KC 5-6	TEX-MIL 7*4	CLE-CAL 4-5	TOR-SEA 5*2	BAL-MIN 11*8	DET-OAK 1-4
0724	CHI-BOS 2-3	NY-KC 10*8	TEX-MIL 6*4	CLE-CAL 9*2	TOR-SEA 6*0	BAL-MIN 1-6	DET-OAK 0-1
						TOR-MIN 4-5	
0725	SEA-CHI 5-6	MIL-NY 2-3	BOS-TEX 2*0	OAK-CAL 1-2		TOR-MIN 3-6	KC-DET 1-2
0726	SEA-CHI 0-1	MIL-NY 2-3	BOS-TEX 8-9	OAK-CAL 6*2	BAL-CLE 3-7	TOR-MIN 4*1	KC-DET 1-3
0727	SEA-CHI 1-6	MIL-NY 3-16	BOS-TEX 10*7	OAK-CAL 8-9	BAL-CLE 2-12		KC-DET 1-7
0728	CAL-CHI 7*6	MIL-NY 6*1		NY-TOR 1-7	BAL-CLE 5*2		TEX-DET 2-3
0729	CAL-CHI 4*2	KC-BAL	OAK-SEA 3-5	NY-TOR 1-7	MIN-CLE 0-7	MIL-BOS 4-6	TEX-DET 2*1
						MIL-BOS 4-5	
0730	KC-BAL 8*7	CAL-CHI 15*14	MIN-CLE 4*2	OAK-SEA 5*2	NY-TOR 3*1	MIL-BOS 2-3	TEX-DET 0-3
0731	KC-BAL 4*1	CAL-CHI 7*5	MIN-CLE 12*4	OAK-SEA 6*2	NY-TOR 6*3	MIL-BOS 0-5	TEX-DET 1-5
				CAL-SEA 8*4	MIN-TOR 1-3		
0801	DET-KC 3-5	OAK-CHI 10*2		CAL-SEA 8*4	MIN-TOR 1-3		
0802	DET-KC 1*0	OAK-CHI 5-7	CLE-BAL 2-5	CAL-SEA 10*2	MIN-TOR 1-11	TEX-BOS 2-7	NY-MIL 5-11
0803	DET-KC 1-2	OAK-CHI 4*3	CLE-BAL 3-8	CAL-SEA 7-8	MIN-TOR 8*3	TEX-BOS 4-5	NY-MIL 5-6
					MIN-TOR 2*1		
0804	BOS-DET 6-11	SEA-OAK 0-2	CLE-BAL 0-5		KC-TOR 6-7	CHI-CAL 5-6	MIN-NY 7*5
0805	BOS-DET 1-3	SEA-OAK 1-4	MIL-BAL 1-4	CLE-TEX 4-8		CHI-CAL 5*4	MIN-NY 11*2
	BOS-DET 2-3		MIL-BAL 3*1				
0806	BOS-DET 2-4	SEA-OAK 4-5	MIL-BAL 2-7	CLE-TEX 5*3	KC-TOR 11*1	CHI-CAL 5-7	MIN-NY 3-5
0807	BOS-DET 3*0	SEA-OAK 12*7	MIL-BAL 7*2	CLE-TEX 0-2	KC-TOR 5*1	CHI-CAL 6*3	MIN-NY 1-5
0808	CLE-MIN 2-7	CHI-OAK 5-9		DET-TEX 3*2	KC-TOR 1-5	SEA-CAL 4*3	
0809	CLE-MIN 3-4	CHI-OAK 1-8	BAL-KC 4-5	DET-TEX 2-6	TOR-NY 6*3	SEA-CAL 4*1	BOS-MIL 2-3
							BOS-MIL 5*1
0810	SEA-CAL 1-2	BAL-KC 3-4	CLE-MIN 4-10	TOR-NY 5*0	CHI-OAK 1-2	DET-TEX 2*1	BOS-MIL 3-8
							BOS-MIL 0-4
0811	TEX-CLE 5*4	BAL-KC 5-6	CHI-SEA 4*3	TOR-NY 6*5	CAL-OAK 2-7		BAL-MIL 3-8
0812	TEX-CLE 3-6	TOR-KC 3*2	CHI-SEA 7*2	DET-BOS 4-9	CAL-OAK 0-4	NY-MIN 6*4	BAL-MIL 5*0
0813	TEX-CLE 12*3	TOR-KC 2*0	CHI-SEA 7*4	DET-BOS 4-16	CAL-OAK 2-6	NY-MIN 2-12	BAL-MIL 11*9
0814	TEX-CLE 0-3	TOR-KC 0-6	CHI-SEA 0-11	DET-BOS 18*6	CAL-OAK 6*4	NY-MIN 9*6	BAL-MIL 1-4
							BAL-MIL 1-4
0815	MIN-DET 2*1	TEX-KC 3-12		SEA-BOS 7*0	TOR-CHI 4-5	MIL-CLE 5-6	CAL-NY 15*6
0816	MIN-DET 4*1	TEX-KC 5*4	OAK-BAL 6*3	SEA-BOS 2-7	TOR-CHI 1-5	MIL-CLE 7-11	CAL-NY 7-11
0817	MIN-DET 2*1	TEX-KC 6-9	OAK-BAL 10*4	SEA-BOS 6*1		MIL-CLE 3-4	CAL-NY 7*1
0818	CHI-DET 4-6	TEX-MIN 4*2	OAK-BAL 1-10	OAK-BOS 6*1		KC-CLE 2-4	SEA-NY 3-5
							SEA-NY 6*1
0819	CHI-DET 4-5	TEX-MIN 5*0	CAL-BAL 1-3	OAK-BOS 6-7	MIL-TOR 7*4	KC-CLE 2-4	SEA-NY 7*1
0820	CAL-BAL 2-3	OAK-BOS 5-7	KC-CLE 4*2	CHI-DET 1-2	TEX-MIN 3*2	MIL-TOR 8*1	SEA-NY 9*5
0821	CAL-BAL 3*2	OAK-BOS 5*4	KC-CLE 3*1	CHI-DET 0-5	TEX-MIN 2-12	MIL-TOR 4-8	SEA-NY 4*2
0822	SEA-BAL 7*3	CAL-BOS 2-6	CLE-MIL 3-7	KC-TEX 5-9	DET-MIN 0-7	CHI-TOR 3-6	OAK-NY 9*2
0823		CAL-BOS 2-10	CLE-MIL 6*2	KC-TEX 11*7	DET-MIN 5-7	CHI-TOR 2-7	OAK-NY 4-5
0824	SEA-BAL 3-4	CAL-BOS 4*3	CLE-MIL 7*2	KC-TEX 4-7	DET-MIN 2-8	CHI-TOR 6*4	OAK-NY 6-7
	SEA-BAL 3-4						
0825	NY-MIL 1-4						
0826	DET-MIL 3*2	NY-CAL 6-7	CLE-CHI 7*6	MIN-KC 3-4	BAL-OAK 5-8	BOS-SEA 5*3	TOR-TEX 1-5
0827	DET-MIL 5-6	NY-CAL 0-12	CLE-CHI 1-4	MIN-KC 1-4	BAL-OAK 1-5	BOS-SEA 3-5	TOR-TEX 3-5
0828	DET-MIL 10-12	NY-CAL 2-13	CLE-CHI 5*4	MIN-KC 3-12	BAL-OAK 2*1	BOS-SEA 7*2	TOR-TEX 6*5
0829	TOR-MIL 6*1	BAL-CAL 2-4	DET-CHI 2-3	CLE-KC 3-6	BOS-OAK 1-3	NY-SEA 6-9	MIN-TEX 3*2
0830	TOR-MIL 2-6	BAL-CAL 5*2	DET-CHI 1-4	CLE-KC 4*1	BOS-OAK 0-1	NY-SEA 1-7	MIN-TEX 6-8
0831	TOR-MIL 4*2	BAL-CAL 5-6	DET-CHI 9*3	CLE-KC 0-1	BOS-OAK 2-7	NY-SEA 4*1	MIN-TEX 10*1
0901	MIL-DET 6*2	BOS-CAL 4*2	KC-MIN 5*2	TEX-TOR 1-5			
0902	MIL-DET 5*0	BOS-CAL 2-3	KC-MIN 3-6	TEX-TOR 6-7	CHI-CLE 3-4	NY-OAK 4*1	BAL-SEA 4*3
0903	MIL-DET 7*3	BOS-CAL 1-2	KC-MIN 6-8	TEX-TOR 4-7	CHI-CLE 2-3	NY-OAK 4-5	BAL-SEA 0-1
0904	MIL-DET 6*1	BOS-CAL 6*5	KC-MIN 3*2	TEX-TOR 7-9	CHI-CLE 5*2	NY-OAK 2-11	BAL-SEA 6*4
0905	BOS-BAL 4*1	TOR-DET 5*4	CAL-KC 4*2	CHI-MIL 2-5	SEA-MIN 0-2	CLE-NY 11*4	OAK-TEX 11*4
0906	BOS-BAL 6*1	TOR-DET 7*3	CAL-KC 2-3		SEA-MIN 8*3	CLE-NY 1*0	OAK-TEX 1-3
0907	BOS-BAL 3-4	TOR-DET 3-4	CAL-KC 2-4	CHI-MIL 7*2	SEA-MIN 2*1	CLE-NY 5*4	OAK-TEX 6*3
0908			OAK-KC 5*1			DET-NY 4-7	CAL-TEX 4*3
0909	TOR-BAL 8*1	CLE-BOS 4-7	OAK-KC 14*6	MIN-CHI 1*0	SEA-MIL 1-2	DET-NY 4-9	CAL-TEX 5*3
0910	TOR-BAL 4-7	CLE-BOS 0-6	OAK-KC 4-9	MIN-CHI 6*5	SEA-MIL 1-3	DET-NY 4-9	CAL-TEX 2-3
0911	TOR-BAL 2-4	CLE-BOS 4*2	OAK-KC 8*7	MIN-CHI 2-3	SEA-MIL 3-5	DET-NY 4-5	CAL-TEX 3-8
0912	NY-CLE 6-8	BAL-BOS 1-6	MIN-SEA 1-3	MIL-CHI 1*0	DET-TOR 6*5		
0913	NY-CLE 5*4	BAL-BOS 4-6	MIN-SEA 2*1	MIL-CHI 4*0	DET-TOR 1-9	KC-CAL 4*3	TEX-OAK 1-2
0914	NY-CLE 7*5	BAL-BOS 3-4	MIN-SEA 0-2	MIL-CHI 4*2	DET-TOR 2-3	KC-CAL 4*2	TEX-OAK 9*1
0915	CHI-MIN 3-10	NY-BOS 5*3			CLE-TOR 0-3	KC-CAL 2*1	TEX-OAK 2-6
0916	CHI-MIN 4-5	NY-BOS 4-7	BAL-DET 7-8	MIL-SEA 5*1	CLE-TOR 3-4	TEX-CAL 2-7	KC-OAK 3*0
0917	CHI-MIN 1-3	NY-BOS 1-3	BAL-DET 3-7	MIL-SEA 0-11	CLE-TOR 12*3	TEX-CAL 7*4	KC-OAK 2-3
0918	CHI-MIN 8*5	NY-BOS 4-9	BAL-DET 2*0	MIL-SEA 10*2	CLE-TOR 0-4	TEX-CAL 5*2	KC-OAK 2-3
0919	BAL-NY 2-3	CHI-TEX 7*3	CLE-DET 4*3	KC-SEA 0-4	BOS-MIL 4-5	MIL-CAL 4*2	MIN-OAK 3-5
0920	BAL-NY 1-7	CHI-TEX 1-4	CLE-DET 1-3	KC-SEA 10-11	BOS-TOR 13*2	MIL-CAL 6*5	MIN-OAK 3-12
0921	BAL-NY 2-3	CHI-TEX 6*1	CLE-DET 2-3	KC-SEA 5*4	BOS-TOR 0-1	MIL-CAL 10*3	MIN-OAK 3-6
						MIN-CAL 6*2	
0922	DET-BAL 7*4						
0923	DET-BAL 4-5	KC-CHI 0-2	TOR-CLE 4*2	OAK-MIL 9*8	BOS-NY 10*9	MIN-CAL 7*1	
0924		KC-CHI 6*2	TOR-CLE 1*0	OAK-MIL 5*2	BOS-NY 4-5	MIN-CAL 3*2	SEA-TEX 2-3
0925	DET-BAL 2*1	KC-CHI 5-6	TOR-CLE 3-4	OAK-MIL 2-4	BOS-NY 6*0	MIN-CAL 6*2	SEA-TEX 3*0
	DET-BAL 7*4						
0926	NY-BAL 5*4	TOR-BOS 11*1	TEX-CHI 5*3	DET-CLE 6*3	SEA-KC 0-5		SEA-TEX 8*5
0927	NY-BAL 5*1	TOR-BOS 15*9	TEX-CHI 2-3	DET-CLE 0-4	SEA-KC 10*3	CAL-MIL 5-6	OAK-MIN 0-5

◆1988◆	GAME 1	GAME 2	GAME 3	GAME 4	GAME 5	GAME 6	GAME 7
0928	NY-BAL 0-2	TOR-BOS 1*0	TEX-CHI 2-3	DET-CLE 2-4		CAL-MIL 3-4	OAK-MIN 5*2
							OAK-MIN 6*2
0929	NY-BAL 5*1	CHI-KC 6-7	TEX-SEA 1-5	BOS-CLE 12*0			CAL-MIN 6*2
0930	NY-DET 2-6	CHI-KC 2-4	TEX-SEA 11*6	BOS-CLE 2-4	MIL-OAK 1-7	BAL-TOR 0-4	CAL-MIN 5-8
1001	NY-DET 5-6	CHI-KC 3*0	TEX-SEA 3-4	BOS-CLE 0-1	MIL-OAK 8*3	BAL-TOR 3-7	CAL-MIN 5-10
1002	NY-DET 3-4	CHI-KC 5*1	TEX-SEA 7*2	BOS-CLE 5-6	MIL-OAK 0-4	BAL-TOR 3-9	CAL-MIN 2-3

◆1989◆	GAME 1	GAME 2	GAME 3	GAME 4	GAME 5	GAME 6	GAME 7
0403	BOS-BAL 4-5	TOR-KC 4*3		MIL-CLE 1-2	SEA-OAK 2-3		
0404	CHI-CAL 9*2	NY-MIN 4*2					
0405	CHI-CAL 2-6	NY-MIN 2-12	DET-TEX 0-4	SEA-OAK 1-11			
0406	CHI-CAL 3*2	NY-MIN 1-7	TOR-KC 1-2	SEA-OAK 3-11	BOS-BAL 4-6	MIL-CLE 3*0	DET-TEX 4-5
0407	SEA-CAL 1-2	BAL-MIN 3-8	TOR-KC 2-3	CHI-OAK 7*1	MIL-DET 3-10	CLE-NY 4*2	TOR-TEX 10*9
0408	SEA-CAL 7*0	BAL-MIN 5-6	BOS-KC 1-2	CHI-OAK 7*4	MIL-DET 5*2	CLE-NY 11*1	TOR-TEX 4-5
0409	SEA-CAL 5-13	BAL-MIN 8*1	BOS-KC 8*6	CHI-OAK 2-4		CLE-NY 4*3	TOR-TEX 2-3
0410	OAK-CAL 4*0	CLE-BOS 2-5	BAL-KC 0-3	TEX-MIL 6*4	CHI-SEA 8*0	TOR-NY 8*0	
0411	OAK-CAL 1-7	MIN-DET 14*0	BAL-KC 5-6		CHI-SEA 8*6	TOR-NY 11*6	
0412	OAK-CAL 0-5	CLE-BOS 10*6	BAL-KC 5*4	TEX-MIL 8*1	CHI-SEA 1-9	TOR-NY 3-5	
0413	OAK-CAL 5*0	CLE-BOS 1-9	MIN-DET 0-3	TEX-MIL 6*1			
0414	OAK-CHI 7*4	BAL-BOS 4-7	TEX-DET 4*2	CLE-MIL 4-8	MIN-NY 5-8	CAL-SEA 5-9	KC-TOR 0-3
0415	OAK-CHI 4-7	BAL-BOS 12*4	TEX-DET 4*1	CLE-MIL 1-5		CAL-SEA 9*2	KC-TOR 10*5
0416	OAK-CHI 3*2	MIN-NY 9*4	TEX-DET 9*6	CLE-MIL 3-4		CAL-SEA 10*0	KC-TOR 8-15
0417	CAL-CHI 3*0	BAL-BOS 4-6	MIL-TEX 8*1			OAK-SEA 2-7	NY-TOR 7*2
0418	KC-BAL 7*4	DET-MIN 8-9	MIL-TEX 2-6		BOS-CLE 8*4	OAK-SEA 5*3	NY-TOR 2*0
0419	KC-BAL 5-6	DET-MIN 3*2	MIL-TEX 1-5	CAL-CHI 7*2	BOS-CLE 5*2	OAK-SEA 7*5	NY-TOR 4*2
				SEA-CHI 5*2			
0420	KC-BAL 0-2	DET-MIN 2-7		SEA-CHI 11*1	NY-CLE 5-6	CAL-OAK 6-10	TEX-TOR 3-6
0421	MIN-BAL 7*1	KC-BOS 7*4	DET-MIL 1-2	SEA-CHI 11*1	NY-CLE 1-3	CAL-OAK 3-4	TEX-TOR 2-4
0422	MIN-BAL 1-4	KC-BOS 7*3	DET-MIL 6*3	SEA-CHI 0-1	NY-CLE 5*0	CAL-OAK 0-2	TEX-TOR 4*1
0423	MIN-BAL 0-3	KC-BOS 10*0	DET-MIL 11*3	SEA-CHI 10*6	NY-CLE 6*3	TOR-OAK 4-5	
0424	BAL-CAL 2-3	SEA-DET 2-3	MIN-MIL 4-5		TEX-CLE 11*7	TOR-OAK 1-3	NY-KC 3-5
0425	BAL-CAL 8*1	SEA-DET 2-5	MIN-MIL 4-10	CHI-BOS 0-11	TEX-CLE 4*2	BAL-OAK 2*1	NY-KC 3-5
0426	DET-CAL 0-1	TOR-SEA 6-7	MIN-MIL 0-12	CHI-BOS 4-5		BAL-OAK 4-9	NY-KC 3*2
0427	DET-CAL 3-10	TOR-SEA 6*1		CHI-BOS 3*1		DET-OAK 1-2	MIL-KC 1-8
0428	TOR-CAL 0-9	BAL-SEA 5-11	CLE-MIN 9*7	CHI-NY 1-2	BOS-TEX 6#6	DET-OAK 2-3	MIL-KC 3-4
0429	TOR-CAL 3-4	BAL-SEA 3-4	CLE-MIN 4*1	CHI-NY 2-8	BOS-TEX 6-7	DET-OAK 7*2	BAL-SEA 4*3
0430	BOS-TEX 1-2	TOR-CAL 0-1	MIL-KC 0-2	CLE-MIN 1-2	CHI-NY 2-5		
	BOS-TEX 8*5						
0501	CLE-TEX 11*1	MIL-CHI 0-6	BOS-MIN 13*6	DET-SEA 3-5	CAL-BAL 3-4	KC-NY 5*3	OAK-TOR 8*5
0502	CLE-TEX 8*3	MIL-CHI 1-6	BOS-MIN 4*2	DET-SEA 2-7	CAL-BAL 2*0	KC-CLE 2-6	OAK-TOR 0-2
0503	NY-TEX 1-4	BOS-CHI 8*4	MIL-MIN 7*2	DET-SEA 2-3		KC-CLE 1-3	CAL-TOR 3*2
0504	NY-TEX 11*7	BOS-CHI 4-5	MIL-MIN 3*2			MIN-CLE 3*2	CAL-TOR 5*3
0505	TEX-BOS 6-7	NY-CHI 7*5	OAK-DET 5*3	KC-MIL 5*4	SEA-BAL 2*1		CAL-TOR 5*4
					SEA-BAL 6*5		
0506	TEX-BOS 0-7	NY-CHI 5*2	OAK-DET 3-6	KC-MIL 0-1	SEA-BAL 5*3		
0507	TEX-BOS 5-9	NY-CHI 2-6	OAK-DET 5*4	KC-MIL 2-8		MIN-CLE 4-5	
						MIN-CLE 1-12	
0508	OAK-BAL 6*1	MIN-BOS 4*2	CAL-DET 9*2	TEX-NY 13*2	SEA-TOR 4*3	CHI-MIL 10*1	
0509	CLE-KC 1-3	MIN-BOS 2-6	CAL-DET 5*1	TEX-NY 3-5	SEA-TOR 2-3	CHI-MIL 12*2	
0510	CLE-KC 2-3		CAL-DET 2-3				
0511	TEX-KC 6*3	OAK-BAL 2-6	NY-CAL 5*2	DET-CLE 6*3	TOR-MIN 5-6	MIL-OAK 4-5	BOS-SEA 2*0
0512	TEX-KC 3-4	CHI-BAL 6-9	NY-CAL 1-6	DET-CLE 1-3	TOR-MIN 8-10	MIL-OAK 3-4	BOS-SEA 6-14
0513	TEX-KC 1-4	CHI-BAL 8*2	NY-CAL 0-5	DET-CLE 3-8	TOR-MIN 1-13	MIL-OAK 2*1	BOS-SEA 3-4
0514	TEX-KC 2-6	CHI-BAL 8*5	NY-CAL 3-4		KC-MIN 4*3	MIL-OAK 2-12	
0515	CHI-DET 2-3	CLE-TOR 3-5			KC-MIN 8*1		
0516	CHI-DET 7-9	CLE-TOR 6-7	BOS-CAL 2-7	MIL-SEA 5-6	KC-MIN 3-4	NY-OAK 3*2	BAL-TEX 8*2
0517	CHI-DET 10*7	CLE-TOR 6*3	BOS-CAL 0-5	MIL-SEA 9*6		NY-OAK 3-8	MIN-TEX 5-6
			BOS-CAL 5*2	MIL-SEA 5-9		NY-OAK 2-6	
0518	CLE-BAL 2-3			NY-SEA 9*5	KC-DET 0-2	BOS-OAK 7*4	MIN-TEX 2-4
0519	CLE-BAL 4*1	TOR-CHI 9*3	MIL-CAL 1-3	NY-SEA 4-6	KC-DET 1-2	BOS-OAK 3-6	MIN-TEX 19*3
0520	CLE-BAL 1-5	TOR-CHI 11*1	MIL-CAL 5*3	NY-SEA 6*2	KC-DET 2-4	BOS-OAK 4-5	MIN-TEX 6*1
0521	CLE-BAL 2*0	TOR-CHI 9*3	MIL-CAL 9-12		CLE-DET 7*3		KC-TEX 1-4
0522	MIN-TOR 6*2	BAL-CHI 5*1			CLE-DET 2-7		KC-TEX 8-10
0523	MIN-TOR 1-2	BAL-CHI 9*3	SEA-BOS 5-6	OAK-MIL 1-9	CLE-DET 1-2	CAL-NY 11*4	KC-TEX 6*4
0524	MIN-TOR 10*4	BAL-CHI 8*0	SEA-BOS 5-6	OAK-MIL 1-4	CLE-DET 5-9	CAL-NY 6-8	
0525			SEA-BOS 0-10	OAK-MIL 1-4			CHI-TOR 3-11
0526	BAL-CLE 5*2	DET-KC 3-6	CAL-BOS 5*0	SEA-MIN 7*2	TEX-MIN 5*3	OAK-NY 4*0	CHI-TOR 5*3
0527	BAL-CLE 5*1	DET-KC 1-5		SEA-MIN 2-3	TEX-MIN 5*3	OAK-NY 3*0	CHI-TOR 5-7
0528	BAL-CLE 0-1	DET-KC 5-9	CAL-BOS 3*0	SEA-MIL 4-6	TEX-MIN 8*6	OAK-NY 4*3	DET-CHI 4*2
0529	TOR-CLE 3-5	MIN-KC 1-7	OAK-BOS 2-3	CAL-MIL 12*3	TEX-BAL 1-6	SEA-NY 3-6	DET-CHI 10*3
0530	TOR-CLE 2-6	MIN-KC 7*1	OAK-BOS 4*2	CAL-MIL 3*2	TEX-BAL 2-6	SEA-NY 3*2	DET-CHI 4*3
0531	TOR-CLE 4-7	MIN-KC 7*1	OAK-BOS 3-4	CAL-MIL 1-4	TEX-BAL 5-8	SEA-NY 5-9	
0601	BAL-DET 8*3	TEX-SEA 2-3		NY-MIL 0-5		MIN-CHI 8*0	CLE-OAK 5*3
0602	BAL-DET 4*1	TEX-SEA 9*5	TOR-BOS 7*2	NY-MIL 3*2		MIN-CHI 5*4	CLE-OAK 0-7
0603	BAL-DET 4*2	TEX-SEA 6*1	TOR-BOS 10*2	NY-MIL 0-2		MIN-CHI 1-2	
0604	TOR-BOS 13*11	KC-CAL 1-5	BAL-DET 7*4	NY-MIL 12*9	MIN-OAK 2*1	MIN-CHI 1-2	TEX-SEA 1-2
0605	BAL-NY 16*3	CLE-CAL 7*3	BOS-DET 5*2	CHI-TEX 2-4	MIN-OAK 0-1	MIL-TOR 5*3	KC-SEA 5*3
0606	BAL-NY 0-4	CLE-CAL 1-2	BOS-DET 1-5	CHI-TEX 1-3	MIN-OAK 2-3	MIL-TOR 6*4	KC-SEA 2-5
0607		CLE-CAL 1*0	BOS-DET 6*1	CHI-TEX 6*4		MIL-TOR 2-4	KC-SEA 9*6
0608	MIL-BAL 6*2	BOS-NY 7-8		CHI-TEX 7-11	CHI-MIN 8*3	DET-TOR 0-2	
0609	MIL-BAL 1-7	SEA-CLE 4-5	CAL-KC 1-6	OAK-TEX 8-11	CHI-MIN 8-11	DET-TOR 11*8	BOS-NY 14*8
0610	MIL-BAL 6*0	SEA-CLE 3*1	CAL-KC 4-5	OAK-TEX 5*1	CHI-MIN 2-5	DET-TOR 0-4	BOS-NY 2-4
0611	MIL-BAL 3*1	SEA-CLE 6*3	CAL-KC 3-5	OAK-TEX 5*1			BOS-NY 7-8
0612	CLE-CHI 3-5	OAK-KC 1-2	CAL-TEX 0-4	DET-TOR 4-5	TOR-MIL 4*3	SEA-MIN 3-4	
0613	CLE-CHI 9*6	OAK-KC 3-5	NY-BAL 2-5	DET-BOS 7-8	TOR-MIL 6*1	SEA-MIN 8-10	CAL-TEX 1-5
0614	CLE-CHI 1-3	OAK-KC 2*1	NY-BAL 2*1	DET-BOS 7*3			CAL-TEX 3-6
0615	NY-BAL 2-3	KC-CLE 5*4	TOR-MIL 4-6	SEA-MIN 9*5		SEA-TOR 3-4	TEX-NY 3-8
0616	OAK-BAL 7*5	KC-CLE 0-1	BOS-CHI 2*0	MIL-MIN 8*6	CAL-DET 9*4		TEX-NY 1-6
	OAK-BAL 1-5						
0617	OAK-BAL 2-4	BOS-CHI 6*1	KC-CLE 3-4	CAL-DET 6*3	MIL-MIN 3-7	SEA-TOR 2-3	TEX-NY 3-5
0618	OAK-BAL 2-4	BOS-CHI 7*4	KC-CLE 1-4	CAL-DET 3*1	MIL-MIN 6-8	SEA-TOR 8*2	TEX-NY 5*2
0619	TOR-CAL 8*1	BOS-CHI 2-8	DET-OAK 6*4	BAL-SEA 9*5	MIL-MIN 11*8	KC-MIL 8*2	CHI-NY 13*6
0620	TOR-CAL 6*2	TEX-BOS 3-6	DET-OAK 4-6	BAL-SEA 8*6	MIN-CLE 7*4	KC-MIL 6*0	CHI-NY 7*3
0621	TOR-CAL 6*1	TEX-BOS 10*3	DET-OAK 3-6	BAL-SEA 8*6	MIN-CLE 5*1		CHI-NY 7-10
0622	BAL-CAL 6*5	TEX-BOS 9*1	TOR-OAK 4*2	NY-KC 0-3	MIN-CLE 9*8	KC-MIL 5-17	
0623	BAL-CAL 1-5	MIN-BOS 10*0	TOR-OAK 10*8		DET-SEA 5*4	CHI-MIL 6*4	CLE-TEX 0-4
						CHI-MIL 5*3	
0624	BAL-CAL 3-8	NY-KC 12*5	TOR-OAK 1-7	DET-SEA 1-3	CLE-TEX 7*3	CLE-TEX 2-4	MIN-BOS 2-6
							MIN-BOS 2-11
0625	BAL-CAL 6-7	NY-KC 5*4	CHI-MIL 1-3	DET-SEA 3-6	DET-SEA 3-5	CLE-TEX 4*3	MIN-BOS 7*0
0626	OAK-MIN 3-4				NY-DET 5-6	SEA-KC 8*0	BOS-MIL 4-5
0627	OAK-MIN 5-11	TOR-BAL 6-16	TEX-CHI 5*1	CAL-CLE 2*1	NY-DET 5-6	SEA-KC 7-12	BOS-MIL 5-12
0628	OAK-MIN 0-2	TOR-BAL 1-2	TEX-CHI 10*5	CAL-CLE 5-6	NY-DET 7*6		BOS-MIL 2*1
0629	CAL-MIN 10*3	TOR-BAL 11*1	KC-CHI 5-12	SEA-TEX 2*0	SEA-TEX 4*3		BOS-TOR 3*1
0630	CAL-MIN 7*2	DET-BAL 16*5	KC-CHI 6*3	SEA-TEX 4*3	OAK-CLE 5*0	MIL-NY 1-5	BOS-TOR 3*1
0701	CAL-MIN 6*1	DET-BAL 1-8	KC-CHI 4-6	SEA-TEX 0-1	OAK-CLE 6*4	MIL-NY 10*2	BOS-TOR 3*1
0702	CAL-MIN 1-2	DET-BAL 7*3	KC-CHI 3-7		OAK-CLE 11*3		BOS-TOR 4*1

♦1989♦	GAME 1	GAME 2	GAME 3	GAME 4	GAME 5	GAME 6	GAME 7
0703	TEX-CAL 2-5	DET-BAL 4-11	KC-OAK 0-1		CHI-CLE 2-4	MIL-NY 8*5	BOS-TOR 2-3
0704	TEX-CAL 2-5	MIL-BOS 4*3	KC-OAK 10*1	MIN-SEA 2-3	CHI-CLE 2-3	DET-NY 0-1	BAL-TOR 8*0
0705	TEX-CAL 1-2		KC-OAK 12*9	MIN-SEA 3-7	CHI-CLE 2-4	DET-NY 0-9	BAL-TOR 5*4
0706	TEX-CAL 3*0	MIL-BOS 4-5	KC-OAK 1-3	MIN-SEA 5-7		DET-NY 5-6	BAL-TOR 1-4
0707	MIN-CAL 2-5	NY-BOS 4-6	TEX-OAK 6*3	CLE-SEA 4*3	TOR-DET 6*4	CHI-KC 2-4	BAL-MIL 4-6
0708	MIN-CAL 1-4	NY-BOS 7*5	TEX-OAK 5*4	CLE-SEA 3-4	TOR-DET 8*3	CHI-KC 4-5	BAL-MIL 5*2
0709	MIN-CAL 3-9	NY-BOS 5-10	TEX-OAK 1-7	CLE-SEA 0-8	TOR-DET 2*0	CHI-KC 4-5	BAL-MIL 2-7
0713	CAL-BAL 13*5	MIL-CHI 4-5	TEX-CLE 9*3	BOS-MIN 3*1	SEA-DET 5*4	KC-NY 0-6	OAK-TOR 11*7
0714	CAL-BAL 4-6	MIL-CHI 4-6	TEX-CLE 5-11	BOS-MIN 5*0	SEA-DET 13*0	KC-NY 14*5	OAK-TOR 1-4
						KC-NY 7-9	
0715	CAL-BAL 9-11	MIL-CHI 1-2	TEX-CLE 1-7	SEA-DET 9*3	BOS-MIN 2-3	KC-NY 7*1	OAK-TOR 1-6
0716	CAL-BAL 2-3	MIL-CHI 0-2	TEX-CLE 5-11	SEA-DET 5-8	BOS-MIN 3-4	KC-NY 1-10	OAK-TOR 6*2
0717	SEA-BAL 4-8	NY-CHI 3-7	MIL-KC 2-3	OAK-DET 1-2	CLE-MIN 2-5	BOS-TEX 6-12	CAL-TOR 4-6
0718	SEA-BAL 3-4	OAK-DET 7*2	MIL-KC 4-9	CLE-MIN 4-5	BOS-TEX 1-8		CAL-TOR 4-5
0719	SEA-BAL 7*0	NY-CHI 5-11	MIL-KC 7*1	CLE-MIN 10*1	BOS-TEX 4*0		CAL-TOR 1*0
0720	DET-CAL 3-4	BAL-OAK 2-5	CLE-KC 4*0	TOR-SEA 2-5	NY-TEX 2-6		
0721	DET-CAL 7-8	BAL-OAK 2-3	CLE-KC 1-6	TOR-SEA 8*1	NY-TEX 2-5	CHI-BOS 1*0	MIN-MIL 3-5
0722	DET-CAL 4-5	BAL-OAK 1-3	CLE-KC 1*0	TOR-SEA 7*1	NY-TEX 1-2	CHI-BOS 10*6	MIN-MIL 6*1
0723	DET-CAL 2-3	BAL-OAK 2-3	CLE-KC 17*5	TOR-SEA 2-5	NY-TEX 4-5	CHI-BOS 2-8	MIN-MIL 1-4
0724	SEA-CHI 4-5	CAL-OAK 5*4	NY-CLE 3-7		TOR-TEX 6*3		DET-MIL 0-10
0725	SEA-CHI 6-7	CAL-OAK 4*0	NY-CLE 5*1	KC-BOS 0-10	TOR-TEX 4*0	BAL-MIN 3-9	DET-MIL 7*2
0726	SEA-CHI 3-5	CAL-OAK 5-9	NY-CLE 7-9	KC-BOS 7*4	TOR-TEX 1-11	BAL-MIN 4-5	DET-MIL 2-3
0727	CHI-CAL 5-8			KC-BOS 2-7		BAL-MIN 6-10	DET-MIL 1-11
0728	CHI-CAL 5-6	BAL-KC 4*3	TOR-NY 6*2	SEA-OAK 7-8	MIL-TEX 15*3	BOS-CLE 2-3	MIN-DET 4-6
						BOS-CLE 1-2	MIN-DET 7*3
0729	CHI-CAL 1-2	BAL-KC 0-5	TOR-NY 2-7	SEA-OAK 14*6	MIL-TEX 8*2	BOS-CLE 5*0	MIN-DET 2-3
0730	CHI-CAL 3*2	BAL-KC 6-7	TOR-NY 6-7	SEA-OAK 3-5	MIL-TEX 3-9	BOS-CLE 5*2	MIN-DET 14*3
0731	BAL-BOS 6-9	CLE-MIL 1-6	TOR-NY 6*5	CHI-OAK 2-3	CAL-SEA 5-6		
0801	BAL-BOS 3-5	CLE-MIL 2-4	MIN-NY 5*4	CHI-OAK 0-2	CAL-SEA 1-8	TEX-DET 4*3	KC-TOR 2*1
	BAL-BOS 2-6						
0802	BAL-BOS 9*8	TEX-DET 4-6	CLE-MIL 1*0	CHI-OAK 0-2	CAL-SEA 7*0	KC-TOR 0-8	MIN-NY 6-7
							MIN-NY 4*3
0803	CLE-BOS 4*2	TEX-DET 6-9	CHI-OAK 6*4	CAL-SEA 6*0	KC-TOR 5*0		MIN-NY 1-8
0804	CLE-BOS 4*3	TEX-BAL 6*4	DET-CHI 4-5	OAK-SEA 5*3	NY-TOR 1-2	CAL-MIL 6*2	KC-MIN 1-5
0805	CLE-BOS 2-10	TEX-BAL 2-5	DET-CHI 6-7	OAK-SEA 5-11	NY-TOR 5*4	CAL-MIL 2-5	KC-MIN 4-6
0806	CLE-BOS 4-6	TEX-BAL 2-3	DET-CHI 4*3	OAK-SEA 2*1	NY-TOR 5-6	CAL-MIL 6*0	KC-MIN 3*2
0807	BOS-KC 4-6	MIN-BAL 4*2	CLE-NY 0-9	OAK-SEA 1-5	TEX-TOR 1-2	MIL-DET 3-5	
						MIL-DET 5*2	
0808	MIN-BAL 1-6	SEA-CAL 6*4	OAK-CHI 3*2	BOS-KC 1-8	CLE-NY 3*1	MIL-DET 3-6	TEX-TOR 0-7
0809	MIN-BAL 7*0	SEA-CAL 1-4	OAK-CHI 2-3	BOS-KC 6*2	CLE-NY 7*4	MIL-DET 6*1	TEX-TOR 4*3
0810	MIL-CLE 10*3	SEA-CAL 3*2	OAK-CHI 4*1	DET-TEX 1-4	NY-MIN 11*3	CHI-SEA 9*6	BOS-BAL 6*4
0811	MIL-CLE 0-5	OAK-CAL 5*0	TOR-KC 2-6	DET-TEX 3-7			BOS-BAL 1-4
	MIL-CLE 8*7						
0812	MIL-CLE 5*1	OAK-CAL 8*3	TOR-KC 2*0	NY-MIN 3-6	CHI-SEA 3-4	DET-TEX 6*5	BOS-BAL 10*8
0813	MIL-CLE 5*4	OAK-CAL 3-4	TOR-KC 3-8	NY-MIN 9*7	CHI-SEA 6*4	DET-TEX 4*2	BOS-BAL 1-6
0814	TOR-BOS 4*2	MIN-CAL 6*3	KC-CHI 3-4	BAL-DET 4*1	NY-MIL 4-5		
0815	TOR-BOS 7*2	MIN-CAL 2-3	KC-CHI 10*6	BAL-DET 2*0	NY-MIL 0-1	CLE-OAK 2-5	TEX-SEA 0-2
0816	TOR-BOS 7*3	MIN-CAL 3-7	KC-CHI 5*4	BAL-DET 0-4	NY-MIL 1-6	CLE-OAK 6*3	TEX-SEA 3*1
0817	TOR-BAL 6-11		TEX-CHI 1-6	NY-DET 2*1	BOS-MIL 4-8	CLE-OAK 0-1	KC-SEA 4*2
0818	TOR-BAL 9*2	CLE-CAL 5-6	TEX-CHI 6*5	NY-DET 3-7	BOS-MIL 2-5	MIN-OAK 4*3	KC-SEA 3*1
0819	TOR-BAL 5*1	CLE-CAL 4-7	TEX-CHI 7*6	NY-DET 4-5	BOS-MIL 3*1	MIN-OAK 4-5	KC-SEA 13*5
0820	TOR-BAL 2-7	CLE-CAL 0-1	TEX-CHI 7*1	NY-DET 6-7	BOS-MIL 3-6	MIN-OAK 0-5	KC-SEA 5*4
0821	MIL-BAL 0-5	CAL-KC 2-4	BOS-NY 4-6	OAK-DET 6*1			
0822	MIL-BAL 2-4	CAL-KC 2-4	BOS-NY 4*3	SEA-CLE 2-3	CHI-MIN 10*2	OAK-TEX 2*0	DET-TOR 2-3
0823	MIL-BAL 1-3	CAL-KC 4-6	BOS-NY 4*1	SEA-CLE 3-5	CHI-MIN 7-8	OAK-TEX 5*4	DET-TOR 4-11
0824		CAL-KC 5*0	BAL-NY 1-5	SEA-CLE 2-5	CHI-MIN 4-6	OAK-TEX 2-6	DET-TOR 3-11
			BAL-NY 9*2				
0825	CHI-CLE 5*4	OAK-KC 1-3	BAL-NY 3*1	SEA-MIN 1-2	CAL-TEX 4*1	MIL-TOR 1-3	DET-BOS 2-4
							DET-BOS 3-11
0826	CHI-CLE 4*3	OAK-KC 0-2	SEA-MIN 0-1	BAL-NY 6*4	CAL-TEX 2-3	MIL-TOR 0-7	DET-BOS 2-5
0827	CHI-CLE 9*3	OAK-KC 6*0	SEA-MIN 5-8	BAL-NY 8*5	CAL-TEX 5*4	MIL-TOR 4-5	DET-BOS 1-7
0828			SEA-MIN 4-5	OAK-NY 7*3		MIL-TOR 8*2	DET-BOS 3-6
0829	BAL-CLE 1-3	DET-KC 8-12	TEX-MIN 4*2	OAK-NY 19*5	SEA-MIL 5*3	CHI-TOR 2-3	CAL-BOS 4-8
							CAL-BOS 5-13
0830	BAL-CLE 7*4	DET-KC 1-6	SEA-MIL 7*3	TEX-MIN 3-7	OAK-NY 5-8	CHI-TOR 1-2	CAL-BOS 4*0
0831	BAL-CLE 0-11	DET-KC 0-3	SEA-MIL 1-6	TEX-MIN 6-8		CHI-TOR 1-5	CAL-BOS 2-5
0901	BAL-CHI 1-10	CLE-DET 1-2	OAK-MIL 5-6	CAL-NY 5-11	KC-TEX 5*3	MIN-TOR 3-7	SEA-BOS 7*2
0902	BAL-CHI 2*1	CLE-DET 4-10	OAK-MIL 7*2	CAL-NY 1-2	KC-TEX 3-6	MIN-TOR 2-4	SEA-BOS 5-6
0903	BAL-CHI 2-4	CLE-DET 3-12	OAK-MIL 5*0	CAL-NY 2-5	KC-TEX 13*2	MIN-TOR 9*4	SEA-BOS 3*2
0904	TOR-CHI 5*2	KC-DET 1-5	CLE-BAL 4-5	MIL-CAL 4-8	MIN-TEX 5-8	BOS-OAK 8*5	
0905	TOR-CHI 6*1	KC-DET 2-10	CLE-BAL 1-3	MIL-CAL 7*4	MIN-TEX 8*4	BOS-OAK 1-13	NY-SEA 12*2
0906	TOR-CHI 4*2	KC-DET 5-11	CLE-BAL 9*0	MIL-CAL 7*1	MIN-TEX 2-3	BOS-OAK 5-7	NY-SEA 5*3
0907	TOR-CLE 12*4				BAL-TEX 8*3		NY-SEA 6*4
					BAL-TEX 9*6		
0908	BOS-CAL 1-2	TOR-CLE 4-5	CHI-DET 5-7	MIN-KC 0-6	BAL-TEX 1-3	NY-OAK 5*1	MIL-SEA 7*3
0909	BOS-CAL 5-8	TOR-CLE 7*5	CHI-DET 13*3	MIN-KC 1-3	BAL-TEX 4*2	NY-OAK 0-7	MIL-SEA 7*3
0910	BOS-CAL 1-2	TOR-CLE 5*4	CHI-DET 5-6	MIN-KC 8*2	BAL-TEX 1-8	NY-OAK 2-6	MIL-SEA 7*1
0911	CHI-BAL 3-6			MIN-KC 1-6			BOS-SEA 1-2
0912	CHI-BAL 11*1	NY-CAL 6-7	DET-CLE 0-1	TEX-KC 5-6	TOR-MIN 2-8	MIL-OAK 7*6	BOS-SEA 3-5
0913	CHI-BAL 3*0	NY-CAL 3-4	DET-CLE 3*1	TEX-KC 2-3	TOR-MIN 2-3	MIL-OAK 6-7	BOS-SEA 4-7
0914			DET-CLE 0-4	TEX-KC 10*4	TOR-MIN 0-2		
0915	KC-BAL 2-5	OAK-BOS 2-7	TEX-MIL 2-6	SEA-NY 3*1	DET-MIN 4-8	CLE-TOR 2-5	CAL-CHI 1-3
							CAL-CHI 2*1
0916	KC-BAL 5-7	OAK-BOS 2-5	TEX-MIL 3-5	DET-MIN 7-8	SEA-NY 1-4	CLE-TOR 2-3	CAL-CHI 1-2
0917	KC-BAL 7*0	OAK-BOS 6-7	TEX-MIL 4*2	DET-MIN 9*2	SEA-NY 3*0	CLE-TOR 1-2	CAL-CHI 6*3
0918	OAK-CLE 4*2	CHI-KC 4*2	SEA-TEX 2-5	CAL-MIN 6*3		BOS-TOR 6*3	
0919	OAK-CLE 5*1	CHI-KC 3-5	SEA-TEX 3-5	CAL-MIN 7*3	DET-BAL 2-6	BOS-TOR 5-6	
0920	OAK-CLE 8*6	CHI-KC 7*2	SEA-TEX 2-3	CAL-MIN 9*1	DET-BAL 2-9	BOS-TOR 10*3	
0921	CAL-CLE 4-5	MIL-NY 14*1	SEA-TEX 8*3	OAK-MIN 2*1			
		MIL-NY 4-5					
0922	NY-BAL 5*4	BOS-DET 9*7	TOR-MIL 7*3	OAK-MIN 5*2	CHI-TEX 9*6	SEA-KC 2-9	
						SEA-KC 2*0	
0923	NY-BAL 2-10	BOS-DET 6*1	TOR-MIL 1-4	OAK-MIN 3-5	CHI-TEX 4-6	SEA-KC 8*0	CAL-CLE 3-4
							CAL-CLE 2-6
0924	NY-BAL 2*0	BOS-DET 4*2	SEA-KC 1-4	TOR-MIL 3-8	OAK-MIN 9*3	CHI-TEX 4-5	CAL-CLE 4-5
0925	NY-BOS 4-7	TOR-DET 2*0	MIN-CHI 2-10	BAL-MIL 5*3	TEX-OAK 3*2	KC-CAL 4*0	CLE-SEA 2-3
0926	NY-BOS 5-9	TOR-DET 3-4	MIN-CHI 7*1	BAL-MIL 3-7	TEX-OAK 3-4	KC-CAL 8*3	CLE-SEA 4*1
0927	NY-BOS 3*0	TOR-DET 8*1	MIN-CHI 6*1	BAL-MIL 4*0	TEX-OAK 0-5	KC-CAL 0-2	CLE-SEA 2-6
0928	MIL-BOS 6-12				TEX-OAK 3-5	KC-OAK 3-4	MIN-SEA 10*7
0929	MIL-BOS 4-5	CLE-CHI 1-2	DET-NY 1-5	BAL-TOR 1-2	KC-OAK 3-4	TEX-CAL 5*0	MIN-SEA 1-2
0930	MIL-BOS 3*1	CLE-CHI 2-8	DET-NY 2-9	BAL-TOR 3-4	KC-OAK 6*1	TEX-CAL 2*0	MIN-SEA 1-2
1001	MIL-BOS 1-5	CLE-CHI 1*0	DET-NY 5*3	BAL-TOR 7*5	KC-OAK 3-4	TEX-CAL 3-4	MIN-SEA 1-3

♦1990♦	GAME 1	GAME 2	GAME 3	GAME 4	GAME 5	GAME 6	GAME 7
0409	DET-BOS 2-5	MIL-CHI 1-2	BAL-KC 7*6	TOR-TEX 2-4	MIN-OAK 3-8	SEA-CAL 7*4	
0410	DET-BOS 2-4	CHI-MIL 5*3	TEX-TOR 1-2		MIN-OAK 3-5	SEA-CAL 0-7	

♦1990♦	GAME 1	GAME 2	GAME 3	GAME 4	GAME 5	GAME 6	GAME 7
0411	DET-BOS 2-3	BAL-KC 1-2	TEX-TOR 11*5		MIN-OAK 3*0	SEA-CAL 0-1	
						MIN-CAL 1-3	
0412	BOS-DET 7-11	CLE-NY 4-6	TEX-TOR 1-7		TOR-KC 3*1	MIN-CAL 7*4	OAK-SEA 15*7
0413	BAL-DET 6-10	TEX-NY 0-3	MIL-BOS 9*5	CLE-CHI 6*2	TOR-KC 1-3	MIN-CAL 5-7	OAK-SEA 5*2
0414	BAL-DET 7*4	TEX-NY 8*4	MIL-BOS 3-4	CLE-CHI 4-9	TOR-KC 5*4	MIN-CAL 1-4	OAK-SEA 3*0
0415	BAL-DET 4-6	TEX-NY 1-3		CLE-CHI 1-4			MIN-SEA 3-6
0416	MIL-BOS 18*0	BAL-TOR 2-4			CLE-KC 6*3	MIL-TEX 2-6	MIN-SEA 6*5
0417	OAK-CAL 7*5	BAL-TOR 2-8	BOS-CHI 1-2	NY-DET 4*1	CLE-KC 2-4	MIL-TEX 11*6	MIN-SEA 4*3
0418	OAK-CAL 3*1	BAL-TOR 8*5	BOS-CHI 7*5	NY-DET 4-8	CLE-KC 0-7	MIL-TEX 11*0	
0419	DET-BAL 2-4	NY-CLE 0-1	SEA-OAK 2-5		KC-TOR 6-17	NY-TEX 5-6	
0420	DET-BAL 0-6	BOS-MIL 0-5	SEA-OAK 6*1	CAL-MIN 1-13	KC-TOR 1-5	NY-TEX 6-9	CHI-CLE 4-8
0421	DET-BAL 3*2	BOS-MIL 0-2	SEA-OAK 6-7	CAL-MIN 0-8	KC-TOR 7*1	NY-TEX 4-10	CHI-CLE 2-5
0422	DET-BAL 2-3	BOS-MIL 4*2	SEA-OAK 5*2	CAL-MIN 5*2	CLE-TOR 9-12		
0423	KC-BAL 5-8			DET-MIN 6*3	CLE-TOR 3-4	SEA-NY 2-6	CHI-TEX 4-5
0424	OAK-BAL 7*1	CAL-BOS 2-4	KC-MIL 3-7	DET-MIN 4-16	CLE-TOR 3-5	SEA-NY 5*2	CHI-TEX 5*4
0425	OAK-BAL 4*3	CAL-BOS 3*1	KC-MIL 0-1	DET-MIN 6*4	CLE-TOR 4*3	SEA-NY 6*2	CHI-TEX 0-1
0426	OAK-BAL 6*4	CAL-BOS 4-5	KC-MIL 2-3				TEX-KC 7*6
0427	SEA-BAL 4*3	OAK-BOS 6-7	TOR-CHI 1-6	MIN-CLE 2-7	MIL-DET 9*6	CAL-NY 4-5	TEX-KC 9*2
0428	SEA-BAL 4*3	OAK-BOS 3-12	TOR-CHI 4-5	MIN-CLE 0-3	MIL-DET 5-13	CAL-NY 2-3	TEX-KC 2-5
0429	SEA-BAL 4-5	OAK-BOS 1*0	TOR-CHI 3-10	MIN-CLE 4-6	MIL-DET 6*1	CAL-NY 4*3	
0430	CAL-BAL 1-2	SEA-BOS 0-11	TEX-CHI 4-5	TOR-CLE 10*4	MIL-DET 6*1	OAK-NY 6*0	MIL-KC 6*4
0501	CAL-BAL 7*1	SEA-BOS 2-8	TEX-CHI 1-5	TOR-CLE 4*3	MIN-DET 9*5	OAK-NY 4*2	
0502	CAL-BAL 3*0	SEA-BOS 9*2	TEX-CHI 6*3	TOR-CLE 0-3	MIN-DET 8*2	OAK-NY 2*0	
0503	MIL-KC 9*5	CAL-SEA 8-10			MIN-DET 3*1	CLE-NY 10*5	
0504	CHI-KC 5*4	BAL-SEA 9*8	NY-CAL 5*2	BOS-OAK 3-8	DET-TOR 3*1		
0505	CHI-KC 6*0	BAL-SEA 2-5	NY-CAL 11*3	BOS-OAK 5*1	DET-TOR 1-5	TEX-CLE 9*5	MIN-MIL 9*5
0506	CHI-KC 6-7	BAL-SEA 4-5	NY-CAL 4*2	BOS-OAK 2-4	DET-TOR 7-11	TEX-CLE 5-9	MIN-MIL 4*0
						TEX-CLE 0-3	
0507	BAL-CAL 6*5	DET-MIL 4-5	NY-OAK 1-5	BOS-SEA 5*4	CHI-TOR 1-6	KC-CLE 4*2	
0508	BAL-CAL 0-6	DET-MIL 5-7	NY-OAK 0-5	BOS-SEA 1-2	CHI-TOR 4*1	CLE-MIN 5-6	KC-TEX 10*5
0509	BAL-CAL 9*1	DET-MIL 2*1	NY-OAK 1-2	BOS-SEA 4*1	CHI-TOR 3-4	CLE-MIN 7*3	KC-TEX 3-9
0510	TOR-DET 5-10			CAL-SEA 2-5		CLE-MIN 2-3	KC-TEX 6*2
0511	TOR-DET 4*2	BOS-CAL 3*2	KC-CHI 4-6	NY-SEA 8*5	BAL-OAK 0-5	MIL-MIN 6*3	CLE-TEX 5*4
				NY-SEA 4*1	BAL-OAK 3*2	MIL-MIN 2-5	CLE-TEX 1-2
0512		BOS-CAL 7*1	KC-CHI 3-6			MIL-MIN 6-8	CLE-TEX 4*1
0513	TOR-DET 6*3	BOS-CAL 4-8	KC-CHI 3-4	NY-SEA 5-10	BAL-OAK 4*1		
0514	TOR-DET 8*3	BOS-KC 5-9				OAK-MIN 2-6	
0515	BAL-CHI 2-3	OAK-CLE 4-5	CAL-MIL 8*3	MIN-NY 3-7	DET-TEX 3*2	SEA-TOR 4*3	
0516	BAL-CHI 2-4	OAK-CLE 7*6	CAL-MIL 5-13	BOS-KC 7*1	DET-TEX 12*0	SEA-TOR 4*2	
0517	BAL-CHI 3-7	MIN-NY 4*1	CAL-MIL 3-6		DET-TEX 7*5	SEA-TOR 14*6	
0518	DET-CHI 8*2	KC-NY 4*1	OAK-MIL 0-5	TEX-BAL 1-13	MIN-BOS 6*0	CAL-TOR 4*2	SEA-CLE 0-5
0519	DET-CHI 6*4	KC-NY 4-5	OAK-MIL 9*1	TEX-BAL 5*3	MIN-BOS 1-13	CAL-TOR 11*9	SEA-CLE 3-4
0520	DET-CHI 3*2	KC-NY 4*3	OAK-MIL 2-5	TEX-BAL 0-4	MIN-BOS 5*4	CAL-TOR 1-5	SEA-CLE 8*7
0521	KC-DET 6-11	CHI-NY 6*5	SEA-MIL 9*4	MIN-BAL 7*3	TEX-BOS 2-4	OAK-TOR 4*1	CAL-CLE 5*3
0522	KC-DET 9*8	CHI-NY 2-5	SEA-MIL 2-3	MIN-BAL 2-10	TEX-BOS 5*4	OAK-TOR 5*4	CAL-CLE 8*3
0523	TEX-DET 1-5	TOR-CAL 4-5	NY-MIN 12*0	CHI-BAL 6*3	KC-BOS 4*1	MIL-OAK 5-12	CLE-SEA 1-4
0524	TEX-DET 3*2	TOR-CAL 3-4	NY-MIN 4-5	CHI-BAL 5*3	KC-BOS 1-4	MIL-OAK 1-13	CLE-SEA 5*3
0525	CHI-DET 1-2	MIL-CAL 4-5	BOS-MIN 0-16	NY-KC 6*3	BAL-TEX 12*2	CLE-OAK 2-5	TOR-SEA 3*1
0526	CHI-DET 10*4	MIL-CAL 3-10	BOS-MIN 5-6	NY-KC 4-9	BAL-TEX 7*5	CLE-OAK 3-6	TOR-SEA 11*4
0527	CHI-DET 2*1	MIL-CAL 3-7	BOS-MIN 1-3	NY-KC 2-6	BAL-TEX 9*2		TOR-SEA 5*1
0528	NY-CHI 1-2	CLE-CAL 3*0	BAL-MIN 4-6	DET-KC 2-3	BOS-TEX 4*3	TOR-OAK 1*0	MIL-SEA 3-4
0529	NY-CHI 4-5	CLE-CAL 1-2	BAL-MIN 5*1	DET-KC 3-5	BOS-TEX 2*1	TOR-OAK 2*1	MIL-SEA 5*3
0530	NY-CHI 2-5	CLE-CAL 4*2	BAL-MIN 3-12	DET-KC 3-4	BOS-TEX 3-4	TOR-OAK 5-8	MIL-SEA 1-2
0531	MIN-CHI 3*2			OAK-KC 6*4			
0601	MIN-CHI 1-2	BOS-CLE 4*3	BAL-NY 3-4	OAK-KC 4*3	DET-SEA 9*7	CAL-TEX 4*3	MIL-TOR 7*1
0602	MIN-CHI 2*1	BOS-CLE 5-7	BAL-NY 4*2	OAK-KC 4-10	DET-SEA 0-2	CAL-TEX 3-6	MIL-TOR 7*6
0603	MIN-CHI 2-5	BOS-CLE 8*2	BAL-NY 4*3	OAK-KC 2-8	DET-SEA 2*0	CAL-TEX 0-1	MIL-TOR 4-7
0604	NY-BOS 3-5	BAL-MIL 6*4	SEA-CHI 10*6	DET-CLE 6*2	CAL-KC 6*4	OAK-TEX 7*4	MIN-TOR 3-7
0605	NY-BOS 8-9	BAL-MIL 4-6	SEA-CHI 0-5	DET-CLE 6*4	CAL-KC 6*2	OAK-TEX 5*4	MIN-TOR 12*5
0606	NY-BOS 1-4	BAL-MIL 8*7	SEA-CHI 2*1	DET-CLE 8*0	CAL-KC 2*1	OAK-TEX 1-3	MIN-TOR 3-10
0607	NY-BOS 0-3	BAL-MIL 5*2	NY-BAL 4-5	TEX-CAL 10*6	CHI-MIN 3*2	KC-OAK 1-3	SEA-DET 5*2
							SEA-DET 3-6
0608	CLE-BOS 3-4	TOR-MIL 11*5			CHI-MIN 4*2	KC-OAK 0-5	SEA-DET 5*2
0609	NY-BAL 1-10	CLE-CAL 6-11	TEX-CAL 3-8	TOR-MIL 7*3	CHI-MIN 5*3	KC-OAK 2-3	SEA-DET 3-4
0610	NY-BAL 5*2	CLE-BOS 4*0	TEX-CAL 2*1	TOR-MIL 13*5	TEX-OAK 5*0		
0611	CHI-SEA 3*1	CLE-BOS 4*3	KC-CAL 2-3	TOR-MIL 1-4	TOR-MIN 5*4	TEX-OAK 6*5	BOS-NY 4-5
0612	CHI-SEA 2-5	MIL-BAL 3-4	KC-CAL 0-3	CLE-DET 7*3	TOR-MIN 10*1	TEX-OAK 2-3	BOS-NY 4*1
0613	CHI-SEA 11*2	MIL-BAL 7*2	KC-CAL 11*4	CLE-DET 4-5	TOR-MIN 7*1		BOS-NY 1-3
0614	TEX-SEA 4-5	MIL-BAL 8*5	OAK-CHI 3-7	CLE-DET 3-7	MIL-CLE 3-5	MIN-KC 1-5	TOR-NY 5*4
0615	TEX-SEA 4*3	BOS-BAL 4*3	OAK-CHI 5*4	CAL-DET 1-2	MIL-CLE 9-10	MIN-KC 3-5	TOR-NY 2*1
0616	TEX-SEA 0-5	BOS-BAL 6*3	OAK-CHI 12*3	CAL-DET 2-6	MIL-CLE 4-12	MIN-KC 4*1	TOR-NY 8*1
0617	TEX-SEA 3-6	BOS-BAL 6*5	OAK-CHI 5*2	CAL-DET 7*3	MIN-TEX 1-7	SEA-KC 2-6	
0618	NY-MIL 2-4	BOS-BAL 2-7	CAL-CHI 4*1	OAK-DET 2-7	MIN-TEX 4-5	SEA-KC 1-2	BOS-TOR 4*2
0619	NY-MIL 5*1	BAL-CLE 4-5	CAL-CHI 5*3	OAK-DET 6-7	MIN-TEX 0-8	SEA-KC 3*2	BOS-TOR 0-11
0620	NY-MIL 5*4	BAL-CLE 3*1	CAL-CHI 1-2	OAK-DET 12*7			NY-TOR 7*6
0621	DET-CAL 4-6	BAL-CLE 3-4	KC-MIN 14*4	CLE-MIL 7-9	CHI-OAK 5*0	SEA-TEX 2-5	NY-TOR 8*7
0622	DET-CAL 0-1	BAL-BOS 3-4	KC-MIN 2-3	CLE-MIL 1-11	CHI-OAK 5*3	SEA-TEX 8*6	NY-TOR 4-8
0623	DET-CAL 9*4	BAL-BOS 3-4	KC-MIN 1-5	CLE-MIL 9*5	CHI-OAK 3*2	SEA-TEX 11*5	NY-TOR 3-8
0624	DET-CAL 2-10	BAL-BOS 0-2	KC-MIN 11*2	CLE-MIL 10*5	DET-OAK 3-4		
0625	CHI-CAL 2*0	TOR-BOS 8-10	TEX-MIN 1-9	CLE-BAL 5*3	DET-OAK 2-3	MIL-NY 2-8	KC-SEA 4*1
0626	CHI-CAL 11*9	TOR-BOS 0-3	TEX-MIN 4-5	CLE-BAL 3-6	DET-OAK 5*4	MIL-NY 5*4	KC-SEA 2-3
0627	CHI-CAL 5*2	TOR-BOS 5-9	TEX-MIN 9*2	CLE-BAL 7*4		MIL-NY 2-3	KC-SEA 4-6
0628		TOR-BOS 3-4	TEX-MIN 8*6				MIL-SEA 2-4
0629	NY-CHI 0-1	TEX-BOS 4*3	BAL-MIN 6*2	CAL-CLE 7*2	DET-KC 2-3	OAK-TOR 5*0	MIL-SEA 2-6
0630	NY-CHI 10*7	TEX-BOS 6*5	BAL-MIN 6*0	CAL-CLE 1-4	DET-KC 5*3	OAK-TOR 9*4	MIL-SEA 5-6
0701	NY-CHI 0-4	TEX-BOS 4-15	BAL-MIN 3-4	CAL-CLE 3-5	DET-KC 9*4	OAK-TOR 3-4	
0702	DET-CHI 4-5	TEX-BOS 3*2		CAL-CLE 2*1	NY-KC 5-11	OAK-TOR 3*2	
0703	DET-CHI 13*7	OAK-MIL 5*0	BOS-MIN 3-7	SEA-CLE 4-9	NY-KC 1-6	CAL-TOR 2-5	BAL-TEX 2-7
0704	DET-CHI 10*7	OAK-MIL 1-7	BOS-MIN 4*3	SEA-CLE 3*2	NY-KC 6-13	CAL-TOR 2-4	BAL-TEX 9*4
0705	KC-DET 15*3	OAK-MIL 3-4	BOS-MIN 4*7	SEA-CLE 4*1		CAL-TOR 2-9	BAL-TEX 2-3
0706	KC-DET 0-4	CAL-MIL 9*8	BAL-CHI 2-4	OAK-CLE 1-6	MIN-NY 2*0	SEA-TOR 0-1	BOS-TEX 0-4
				OAK-CLE 12*1	MIN-NY 3-5		
0707	BAL-CHI 4*1	KC-DET 4*0	CAL-MIL 4*3	OAK-CLE 0-1	MIN-NY 4-5	BOS-TEX 4-7	SEA-TOR 2-4
0708	BAL-CHI 8*6	KC-DET 4-10	CAL-MIL 7-20	OAK-CLE 8*3	MIN-NY 6*3	BOS-TEX 3-4	SEA-TOR 6*3
0711	MIL-CHI 12*9	KC-CAL 11*7	OAK-MIN 11*7	CAL-SEA 1-2			
0712	TOR-CAL 5*0	TEX-DET 11*1	CHI-NY 8*0	CLE-SEA 5*4	MIL-OAK 3-5	KC-BOS 5*3	MIN-BAL 5-8
0713	TOR-CAL 0-2	TEX-DET 7*6	CHI-NY 3*2	CLE-SEA 13*7	MIL-OAK 2*0		MIN-BAL 3*1
0714	TOR-CAL 7-8	TEX-DET 5*3	CHI-NY 8*7	MIL-OAK 1-3	CLE-SEA 3*0	KC-BOS 2*1	MIN-BAL 2-3
						KC-BOS 7-8	
0715	MIN-BAL 10*3	TOR-CAL 2-3	TEX-DET 2-3	CHI-NY 8*5	MIL-OAK 1-4	CLE-OAK 0-3	CLE-SEA 0-7
0716	TEX-BAL 6-7	MIL-CAL 3*1	CHI-DET 4-5	KC-NY 2-3	CLE-OAK 4*2	MIN-BOS 3*2	TOR-SEA 4*3
0717	TEX-BAL 3-5	MIL-CAL 1-8	CHI-DET 7*3	KC-NY 10*7	CLE-OAK 1-4	MIN-BOS 0-1	TOR-SEA 5-7
0718	TEX-BAL 7*1	MIL-CAL 3*2	CHI-DET 7*5	KC-NY 3-5	CLE-OAK 2-5	MIN-BOS 4-5	TOR-SEA 2-5
0719	CHI-BAL 1-4	BOS-DET 0-1	SEA-MIL 0-4	NY-MIN 2*1	TOR-OAK 8*6	DET-TEX 3-5	BOS-KC 0-5
0720	CHI-BAL 2-3	CLE-CAL 4-9	SEA-MIL 6*4	NY-MIN 1-2			BOS-KC 3*1
0721	CHI-BAL 0-2	CLE-CAL 2-5	SEA-MIL 3-10	NY-MIN 1-2	TOR-OAK 2*1	DET-TEX 8*1	BOS-KC 2-4

♦1990♦

Date	GAME 1	GAME 2	GAME 3	GAME 4	GAME 5	GAME 6	GAME 7
0722	CHI-BAL 3-9	CLE-CAL 8*1	SEA-MIL 4*3	NY-MIN 10*6	TOR-OAK 0-3	DET-TEX 3-5	BOS-KC 1-2
0723	CLE-CHI 1-3	BAL-DET 13*3	BOS-MIL 0-13		CAL-OAK 6-7	NY-TEX 2-3	
0724	CLE-CHI 3-8	BAL-DET 2-8	BOS-MIL 5-6	SEA-MIN 8*2	CAL-OAK 3-5	NY-TEX 1-4	KC-TOR 5*3
0725	CLE-CHI 6*1	BAL-DET 3-4	BOS-MIL 2*0	SEA-MIN 0-6	CAL-OAK 3-13	NY-TEX 7-9	KC-TOR 6*1
0726		BOS-DET 4-10		SEA-MIN 6*4	CAL-OAK 4*2		KC-TOR 5-7
0727	MIL-CHI 4-7	BOS-DET 1*0	BAL-KC 9*2	OAK-MIN 4-9	CAL-SEA 1-8	NY-CLE 3*0	TEX-TOR 0-1
						NY-CLE 4*1	
0728	MIL-CHI 4-5	BOS-DET 9-17	CAL-SEA 1-2	TEX-TOR 3*2	BAL-KC 9-10	NY-CLE 1-2	OAK-MIN 4*1
					BAL-KC 3*1		
0729	MIL-CHI 9*8	BOS-DET 13*3	CAL-SEA 6*2	TEX-TOR 8-10	BAL-KC 4*1	NY-CLE 8*5	OAK-MIN 4-9
						NY-CLE 4*3	OAK-MIN 5-6
0730	TOR-BAL 9*2	CHI-BOS 0-3	TEX-MIL 3*1	CAL-MIN 3-7	DET-NY 2-6	KC-CLE 7*6	SEA-OAK 2-6
0731	TOR-BAL 4-6	CHI-BOS 2-7	TEX-MIL 11*3	CAL-MIN 13*2	DET-NY 4-10	KC-CLE 8*4	SEA-OAK 7*2
0801	TOR-BAL 7*4	CHI-BOS 5-9	TEX-MIL 8*2	CAL-MIN 11*5	DET-NY 15*4	KC-CLE 1-4	SEA-OAK 0-1
0802	KC-BAL 1-5	OAK-CAL 7*5	CHI-MIL 4*2	MIN-SEA 2-7	DET-NY 6*5	TOR-TEX 4-5	
			CHI-MIL 4*2				
0803	KC-BAL 1-14	DET-BOS 5-14	CHI-MIL 6*2	OAK-CAL 8*6	CLE-NY 4-6	MIN-SEA 6*2	TOR-TEX 1-9
0804	KC-BAL 9*1	DET-BOS 1-3	CHI-MIL 9*6	OAK-CAL 4-14	CLE-NY 17*3	MIN-SEA 3-4	TOR-TEX 2-3
0805		DET-BOS 7*2	CHI-MIL 6*1	OAK-CAL 4*1	CLE-NY 3-5	MIN-SEA 0-4	TOR-TEX 6*4
0806	CHI-KC 4-5	MIL-MIN 6*0			CLE-NY 1-2		TOR-TEX 3-4
0807	CHI-KC 5*3	MIL-MIN 5*3	BOS-CAL 6*3	TEX-CLE 4-8	BAL-OAK 2-3	NY-SEA 3*1	DET-TOR 5-11
0808	CHI-KC 1-5	MIL-MIN 2-4	BOS-CAL 6-8	TEX-CLE 3-5	BAL-OAK 4*1	NY-SEA 6*4	DET-TOR 3-8
0809	CHI-KC 3-5		BOS-CAL 14*3	TEX-CLE 13*5	BAL-OAK 2-5	NY-SEA 1*0	DET-TOR 5*4
0810	MIL-KC 5-6	TEX-CHI 2-5	BAL-CAL 1-2	DET-CLE 2-5	NY-OAK 0-3	BOS-SEA 1-4	MIN-TOR 7*3
	MIL-KC 4-9	TEX-CHI 1-5					
0811	MIL-KC 11*5	TEX-CHI 7*5	BAL-CAL 4-12	DET-CLE 4-13	NY-OAK 1-10	BOS-SEA 4*2	MIN-TOR 4-7
0812	MIL-KC 1-7		BAL-CAL 11*6	DET-CLE 5-9	NY-OAK 1-6	BOS-SEA 7*2	MIN-TOR 5*4
0813	TEX-KC 3-5	TOR-CHI 4*3	NY-CAL 2-4	DET-CLE 2-6	BOS-OAK 0-4	BAL-SEA 3*2	
0814	TEX-KC 0-1	TOR-CHI 12*4	NY-CAL 5-9	MIN-CLE 5*4	BOS-OAK 2*0	BAL-SEA 1-7	MIL-DET 7*6
0815	TEX-KC 2*1	TOR-CHI 3-4	NY-CAL 1-8	MIN-CLE 4-5	BOS-OAK 2-6	BAL-SEA 0-2	MIL-DET 7*3
0816					MIN-CLE 5-7		MIL-DET 8*4
0817	OAK-BAL 8*3	CAL-BOS 1*0	KC-MIL 1-2	TOR-MIN 5*1	SEA-NY 2-3	CHI-TEX 0-1	CLE-DET 0-3
						CHI-TEX 4*2	
0818	OAK-BAL 3*1	CAL-BOS 4*3	CLE-DET 3-6	KC-MIL 10*1	TOR-MIN 3*0	CHI-TEX 3-8	SEA-NY 0-6
0819	OAK-BAL 2-3	CAL-BOS 1-4		KC-MIL 2-7	TOR-MIN 9*1	CHI-TEX 4*2	SEA-NY 1-3
0820	OAK-CHI 1-11	BAL-BOS 1-2	CAL-DET 5*3	CLE-MIL 3-4	MIN-KC 1-7	SEA-TEX 5-6	TOR-NY 5-6
0821	OAK-CHI 1-4	BAL-BOS 9*5	CAL-DET 2-6	CLE-MIL 5-6	MIN-KC 7-8	SEA-TEX 4*3	TOR-NY 2-3
0822	OAK-CHI 7*1	BAL-BOS 2-13	CAL-DET 4-7	CLE-MIL 4*2	MIN-KC 2-6	SEA-TEX 4-5	TOR-NY 2-4
0823	CAL-CHI 2-4	BOS-TOR 3-4			SEA-KC 1-4		MIL-NY 8*2
0824	CAL-CHI 2-5	BOS-TOR 2*0	CLE-BAL 4-5	OAK-DET 6*4	SEA-KC 3-4	MIN-TEX 0-2	MIL-NY 1*0
0825	CAL-CHI 3*2	BOS-TOR 1*0	CLE-BAL 11*5	OAK-DET 4-14	SEA-KC 6*3	MIN-TEX 8*5	MIL-NY 5*3
0826	CAL-CHI 4*1	BOS-TOR 1*0	CLE-BAL 8*3	OAK-DET 3-7	SEA-KC 2-8	MIN-TEX 0-1	MIL-NY 3-4
0827	TEX-CAL 3-7	MIL-TOR 4*2	NY-BAL 4*2	BOS-CLE 12*4	CHI-MIN 0-7		
0828	TEX-CAL 0-2	MIL-TOR 6*2	NY-BAL 11*3	BOS-CLE 6*5	CHI-MIN 6-12	KC-OAK 2-3	DET-SEA 3-4
0829	TEX-CAL 2-9	MIL-TOR 3-7	NY-BAL 3*2	BOS-CLE 7*1	CHI-MIN 1-6	KC-OAK 6*0	DET-SEA 4*2
0830			NY-BAL 1-6	BOS-CLE 9*2	CHI-MIN 4*3	KC-OAK 5-6	DET-SEA 3*2
0831	NY-BOS 3-7	CHI-CAL 6*5	BAL-MIL 1-4	TOR-CLE 12*8	DET-MIN 12*6	TEX-OAK 2-4	KC-SEA 2-5
0901	NY-BOS 1-15	CHI-CAL 9*5	BAL-MIL 3-4	TOR-CLE 8*0	DET-MIN 9*5	TEX-OAK 3*2	KC-SEA 0-3
0902	NY-BOS 1-7	CHI-CAL 0-1	BAL-MIL 2-4	TOR-CLE 3*0	DET-MIN 3-4	TEX-OAK 3-4	KC-SEA 8*0
0903	OAK-BOS 9*5	SEA-BAL 6*2	MIN-MIL 6*0	KC-CHI 2-4	TOR-DET 0-5	CAL-NY 7*0	CLE-TEX 2-6
			MIN-MIL 9*5				
0904	SEA-BAL 7*2	OAK-BOS 6*2	MIN-MIL 7*1	KC-CHI 3-6	TOR-DET 1-3	CLE-TEX 7*5	
0905	SEA-BAL 9*5	OAK-BOS 10*0	MIN-MIL 4-7	KC-CHI 0-3	TOR-DET 7*3	CLE-TEX 2-3	CAL-NY 1-2
0906					CLE-DET 6*0	KC-TEX 1-12	CAL-NY 1-2
0907	CAL-BAL 2-6	SEA-BOS 4-5	DET-MIL 5-6	CLE-MIN 0-2	CHI-TOR 1-3	KC-TEX 4-9	OAK-NY 7*1
0908	CAL-BAL 4-5	SEA-BOS 2-10	DET-MIL 2-5	CLE-MIN 1-6	CHI-TOR 0-3	KC-TEX 1-2	OAK-NY 5*2
0909	CAL-BAL 1-3	SEA-BOS 3*1	DET-MIL 5*0	CLE-MIN 12*9	CHI-TOR 1-6	KC-TEX 5-6	OAK-NY 7*3
0910	DET-BAL 8*0	MIL-BOS 4-5	MIN-CAL 1-3	TOR-KC 6*1	OAK-SEA 2-5	CHI-CLE 2-3	TEX-NY 1*0
		MIL-BOS 6*1				CHI-CLE 6*2	
0911	DET-BAL 2*1	MIL-BOS 4*2	MIN-CAL 0-9	TOR-KC 8*4	TEX-NY 4-5	CHI-CLE 3-4	OAK-SEA 10*2
0912	DET-BAL 1-2	MIL-BOS 1-6	MIN-CAL 1-6	TOR-KC 5*4	TEX-NY 5*4	CHI-CLE 2-12	OAK-SEA 9*3
0913	BOS-CHI 6-9	NY-DET 7*3	SEA-CAL 1-7	MIN-OAK 3*1	BAL-TOR 5*3		
0914	BOS-CHI 0-4	NY-DET 5*2	SEA-CAL 5-7	MIN-OAK 1-9	BAL-TOR 7-8	CLE-KC 6*4	MIL-TEX 1-2
0915	BOS-CHI 4-7	NY-DET 3-4	SEA-CAL 7*2	MIN-OAK 1-4	BAL-TOR 3-4	CLE-KC 14*6	MIL-TEX 3-6
0916	BOS-CHI 2-4	NY-DET 2-5	SEA-CAL 5*3	MIN-OAK 4-5	BAL-TOR 5-6	CLE-KC 6-9	MIL-TEX 5*3
0917	BOS-BAL 7*3	MIL-CLE 2-4	KC-MIN 1*0	CHI-OAK 7*0	NY-TOR 4-6	TEX-SEA 10*4	
0918	BOS-BAL 1-4	MIL-CLE 3-8	KC-MIN 4-10	CHI-OAK 8*2	NY-TOR 2-3	TEX-SEA 3-7	DET-CAL 3*2
0919	BOS-BAL 4-8	MIL-CLE 3-6	KC-MIN 0-1	CHI-OAK 3-7	NY-TOR 6-7	TEX-SEA 6*5	DET-CAL 12*5
						CHI-SEA 3-4	
0920	CLE-NY 12*7						
0921	BOS-NY 3*0	MIL-BAL 3-5	CAL-KC 12*5	TEX-MIN 2*1	DET-OAK 5-6	CHI-SEA 5*4	CLE-TOR 2*1
0922	BOS-NY 2-5	MIL-BAL 2-3	CAL-KC 3-4	TEX-MIN 0-2	DET-OAK 1-5	CHI-SEA 14*5	CLE-TOR 5*2
0923	BOS-NY 4-5	MIL-BAL 1-2	CAL-KC 0-4	TEX-MIN 4-6	DET-OAK 6*0	CHI-SEA 2*1	CLE-TOR 4-5
0924	BAL-NY 6*3	TOR-MIL 9*5	OAK-KC 3-10	CAL-TEX 3*2		MIN-CHI 4*3	SEA-DET 1-4
0925	BAL-NY 3-15	TOR-MIL 4-8	OAK-KC 5*0	CAL-TEX 8*2	CLE-BOS 5*2	MIN-CHI 1-3	SEA-DET 8*4
0926	BAL-NY 2-4	TOR-MIL 0-6	OAK-KC 3*2	CAL-TEX 2-6	CLE-BOS 2-7	MIL-CHI 4-6	BOS-DET 3*2
0927	KC-CAL 6-7	BAL-CLE 5*2		OAK-TEX 6-8			
0928	KC-CAL 2*1	BAL-CLE 2*0	TOR-BOS 6-7	OAK-TEX 4*1	NY-MIL 7*2	SEA-CHI 13*4	MIN-DET 1-3
0929	KC-CAL 9*6		TOR-BOS 5-7	OAK-TEX 7*3	NY-MIL 1-8	SEA-CHI 2-5	MIN-DET 2*0
0930	KC-CAL 2*1	BAL-CLE 6*3	TOR-BOS 10*5	OAK-TEX 7*2	NY-MIL 7*2	SEA-CHI 1-2	MIN-DET 0-1
		BAL-CLE 3-7					
1001	TOR-BAL 3-6	CHI-BOS 3-4	TEX-MIL 4*2	SEA-MIN 5-7	DET-NY 2*0	CAL-OAK 2*0	
1002	TOR-BAL 2*1	CHI-BOS 3*2	TEX-MIL 0-1	SEA-MIN 3*0	DET-NY 1-4	CAL-OAK 4-6	KC-CLE 3-13
1003	TOR-BAL 2-3	CHI-BOS 1-3	TEX-MIL 3-6	SEA-MIN 4-7	DET-NY 10*3	CAL-OAK 11*6	KC-CLE 2-5

♦1991♦

Date	GAME 1	GAME 2	GAME 3	GAME 4	GAME 5	GAME 6	GAME 7
0408	CHI-BAL 9*1	NY-DET 4-6	CLE-KC 2-4	MIL-TEX 5*4	BOS-TOR 6*2		
0409	MIN-OAK 2-7	CAL-SEA 3*2	CLE-KC 2*1		BOS-TOR 3-4		
0410	MIN-OAK 4*1	CAL-SEA 5*3	CLE-KC 0-1		BOS-TOR 3-5	NY-DET 4*0	
0411	MIN-OAK 0-3	CAL-SEA 5*0	CLE-BOS 6*4	CHI-BAL 2*0	MIL-TOR 3-7	NY-DET 5-11	MIL-TEX 6*0
0412	SEA-OAK 1-6	NY-KC 5*2	CAL-MIN 0-6		MIL-TOR 4-5	CHI-DET 4*1	
0413	SEA-OAK 2-4	NY-KC 9*8	CAL-MIN 15*9	BAL-TEX 11*4	MIL-TOR 7*3	CHI-DET 4*1	
0414	SEA-OAK 6-7	NY-KC 3-5	CAL-MIN 9*4	BAL-TEX 3-15	MIL-TOR 0-9		CLE-BOS 0-4
0415	OAK-CAL 5*2	TOR-DET 4*3	BAL-MIL 7*2	CHI-NY 6*5	MIN-SEA 4-8		CLE-BOS 6*0
0416	OAK-CAL 8*5	TOR-DET 2-6	TEX-CLE 3*1	CHI-NY 4*3	MIN-SEA 0-3		CLE-BOS 1*0
0417	OAK-CAL 3*1	TOR-DET 4-5	BAL-MIL 3-7	CHI-NY 1-10	MIN-SEA 3-4		KC-BOS 2-5
0418	OAK-CAL 1-7	DET-CHI 16*0	BAL-MIL 3-4	TEX-CLE 7*0			KC-BOS 2-6
0419	MIN-CAL 0-2	TEX-BAL 0-5	TOR-MIL 5*2	KC-NY 1-3			KC-BOS 0-1
0420	MIN-CAL 1-2	TEX-BAL 1*0	TOR-MIL 4*2	KC-NY 5*2	OAK-SEA 7-11		
0421	MIN-CAL 4*3		TOR-MIL 8-11		OAK-SEA 2-3	DET-CHI 2*1	BOS-CLE 2*1
					OAK-SEA 2-7	DET-CHI 4-5	
0422	SEA-CAL 4*3	TOR-BOS 4-6	KC-CHI 4-10	OAK-MIN 2-3	DET-NY 10*5	BAL-CHI 7-8	
0423	SEA-CAL 2*0	TOR-BOS 0-3	KC-CLE 6*0	OAK-MIN 7*5	DET-NY 0-5	BAL-CHI 4-10	TEX-MIL 6*5
0424	SEA-CAL 5-9	TOR-BOS 6*1	KC-CLE 4*2	OAK-MIN 4-7		BAL-CHI 5*1	TEX-MIL 8*2
0425	DET-TOR 2-3				SEA-MIN 3-4		TEX-MIL 1-9
0426	DET-TOR 4-5	MIL-BAL 5*4	NY-CHI 3*2	SEA-MIN 0-6	BOS-KC 3-5	CAL-OAK 1-4	CLE-TEX 5*2
0427	DET-TOR 4*2	MIL-BAL 5*2	NY-CHI 9-14	SEA-MIN 2-7	BOS-KC 6*4	CAL-OAK 3-4	CLE-TEX 1-4
0428	DET-TOR 6-9	MIL-BAL 4-5	NY-CHI 1-4	SEA-MIN 2-8	BOS-KC 2*1	CAL-OAK 3-7	CLE-TEX 4*2
0429		SEA-BAL 10*1			DET-KC 3*1		

♦1991♦	GAME 1	GAME 2	GAME 3	GAME 4	GAME 5	GAME 6	GAME 7
0430	CLE-CAL 5-6	SEA-BAL 6*3	CHI-MIL 2-8	BOS-MIN 7*5	DET-KC 13*7	NY-OAK 3-7	TOR-TEX 5-8
0501	CLE-CAL 5*1	SEA-BAL 1-2	CHI-MIL 9-10	BOS-MIN 0-1	DET-KC 6*4	NY-OAK 4-7	TOR-TEX 0-3
0502			MIN-MIL 1-5		TOR-KC 3*1		
0503	BAL-CAL 2*0	BOS-CHI 7*2	MIN-MIL 5-6	TEX-DET 6-7	TOR-KC 5*1	CLE-OAK 3-4	NY-SEA 5*0
0504	BAL-CAL 3-6	BOS-CHI 4*0	MIN-MIL 7*4	TEX-DET 6*5	TOR-KC 5-6	CLE-OAK 20*6	NY-SEA 2-3
0505	BAL-CAL 4-6	BOS-CHI 9*1	MIN-MIL 5*2	TEX-DET 7-8	TOR-KC 3*0	CLE-OAK 15*6	NY-SEA 4-5
0506	BAL-CAL 7*0						NY-SEA 2-4
0507	NY-CAL 4-7	MIN-BOS 9*3	MIL-CHI 1-2	KC-DET 4-5	BAL-OAK 3-11	TEX-TOR 3*2	CLE-SEA 6-7
0508	NY-CAL 10*5	MIN-BOS 3-8	MIL-CHI 1-2	KC-DET 3-7	BAL-OAK 3-9	TEX-TOR 2-4	CLE-SEA 2-6
0509	DET-MIN 3*0	TEX-BOS 4-8				CHI-TOR 0-2	
0510	DET-MIN 2-5	TEX-BOS 3-5	CAL-CLE 12*2	KC-MIL 2*1	OAK-NY 3-5	CHI-TOR 5*3	BAL-SEA 1-3
0511	DET-MIN 4-5	TEX-BOS 4-5	CAL-CLE 2*1	KC-MIL 4*2	OAK-NY 10*2	CHI-TOR 2-5	BAL-SEA 11*5
0512	DET-MIN 3-8	TEX-BOS 12*5	CAL-CLE 1-4	KC-MIL 6*4	OAK-NY 6-10	CHI-TOR 2-4	BAL-SEA 4-5
0513	DET-TEX 1-8	CHI-BOS 4*3	CAL-CLE 9*5		OAK-NY 3-6	KC-TOR 2-4	
0514	DET-TEX 3-5	CHI-BOS 1-4	SEA-CLE 2*1	OAK-BAL 1-6	CAL-NY 1-7	KC-TOR 1-4	MIL-MIN 1-5
0515	DET-TEX 4-5	CHI-BOS 6-9	SEA-CLE 6*4	OAK-BAL 6*3	CAL-NY 10*2	KC-TOR 6*4	MIL-MIN 4*2
0516			SEA-CLE 3*1	OAK-BAL 11*5	CAL-NY 7*0		MIL-MIN 6*3
0517	TOR-CHI 3-5	MIN-DET 8*1	OAK-CLE 6-11	CAL-BAL 1-5	SEA-NY 1*0	MIL-KC 7*5	BOS-TEX 4-6
0518	TOR-CHI 9*2	MIN-DET 4*1	OAK-CLE 3*0	CAL-BAL 4*2	SEA-NY 4*1	MIL-KC 4-7	BOS-TEX 5-13
0519	TOR-CHI 4-5	MIN-DET 3-8	OAK-CLE 9*4	CAL-BAL 10*2	SEA-NY 2-3	MIL-KC 4*2	BOS-TEX 4-12
0520	MIL-BOS 0-3	BAL-DET 5-11	NY-CLE 1-3	CHI-CAL 3-6	TOR-OAK 1*0	SEA-KC 8*6	TEX-MIN 6*5
0521	MIL-BOS 6-10	BAL-DET 5*4	NY-CLE 2-5	CHI-CAL 2-4	TOR-OAK 11*7	SEA-KC 3-4	TEX-MIN 5*2
0522	MIL-BOS 0-4	BAL-DET 5-9	NY-CLE 8*1	CHI-CAL 5*3	TOR-OAK 1-2	SEA-KC 1-3	TEX-MIN 10*6
0523	CLE-MIL 3-7	BOS-DET 3-5			CHI-OAK 11*1		KC-MIN 7*3
0524	CLE-MIL 0-1	BOS-DET 10*9	NY-BAL 7*1	TOR-CAL 3*2	CHI-OAK 5-6	TEX-SEA 7*3	KC-MIN 11*2
0525	CLE-MIL 5*4	BOS-DET 2-3	NY-BAL 6*5	TOR-CAL 0-5	CHI-OAK 3-5	TEX-SEA 8*6	KC-MIN 5*1
0526	CLE-MIL 6-7	BOS-DET 4-9	NY-BAL 2*1	TOR-CAL 2-6	CHI-OAK 2-6	TEX-SEA 6*4	
0527	DET-MIL 15*9	BOS-NY 5-6	CLE-BAL 3*2	MIN-TEX 4-11		KC-SEA 6*3	
0528	DET-MIL 2-15	BOS-NY 6*2	CLE-BAL 2-5	MIN-TEX 3*0	CAL-CHI 5-6	KC-SEA 6*5	OAK-TOR 8*4
0529	DET-MIL 2-6	BOS-NY 0-7	CLE-BAL 1-2	MIN-TEX 9*1	CAL-CHI 8*4	KC-SEA 0-8	OAK-TOR 3-8
0530	BAL-BOS 9*3	MIN-CAL 4*2		SEA-TEX 11*4	CAL-CHI 7*6		OAK-TOR 8*6
0531	BAL-BOS 2-7	MIN-KC 1-4	DET-CLE 9-11	SEA-TEX 6-7	OAK-CHI 4-5	MIL-NY 2-3	CAL-TOR 1-5
0601	BAL-BOS 3*1	MIN-KC 8*4	DET-CLE 1-3	SEA-TEX 12*8	OAK-CHI 7*4	MIL-NY 6*3	CAL-TOR 11*8
0602	BAL-BOS 5*1	MIN-KC 4*1	DET-CLE 2-3		OAK-CHI 3-4	MIL-NY 4-7	CAL-TOR 7*2
0603	BAL-MIN 2-3		DET-CLE 0-2		OAK-CHI 5*3	TOR-NY 5*3	
0604	BAL-MIN 3-4	BOS-CAL 0-3	CHI-CLE 4*1	SEA-DET 8*6	TEX-KC 1-4	TOR-NY 3-5	MIL-OAK 3-4
0605	BAL-MIN 3-4	BOS-CAL 2-7	CHI-CLE 1-2	SEA-DET 1-7	TEX-KC 2-3	TOR-NY 4*1	MIL-OAK 4-6
0606	TOR-BAL 4-6	BOS-CAL 2-3	CHI-CLE 2*1	SEA-DET 3-4	TEX-KC 3-4		MIL-OAK 8-9
0607	TOR-BAL 4-6	DET-CAL 5*0	CLE-MIN 0-2	TEX-NY 4-5	CHI-KC 2*0	MIL-SEA 1-2	BOS-OAK 3*1
0608	TOR-BAL 8*4	DET-CAL 4*3	CLE-MIN 1-2	TEX-NY 7-10	CHI-KC 14*7	MIL-SEA 2-6	BOS-OAK 8*1
0609	TOR-BAL 3*2	DET-CAL 3-7	CLE-MIN 2-9	TEX-NY 4-6	CHI-KC 8*2	MIL-SEA 1-6	BOS-OAK 0-8
0610	CHI-TEX 3*2	MIL-CAL 7*2	CLE-MIN 5-8			BOS-SEA 6*2	DET-OAK 6-12
0611	CHI-TEX 0-2	MIL-CAL 3-4	NY-MIN 3-5	KC-BAL 11*0	TOR-CLE 1-2	BOS-SEA 8*5	DET-OAK 5*1
0612	CHI-TEX 2-4	MIL-CAL 8*0	NY-MIN 3-6	KC-BAL 9*8	TOR-CLE 1*0	BOS-SEA 3-5	DET-OAK 1-3
0613	CHI-TEX 4-8		NY-MIN 3-10	KC-BAL 6*4	TOR-CLE 1*0	DET-SEA 5-6	
0614	NY-TEX 4-8	CAL-BOS 4-9	KC-CHI 3-9	BAL-TOR 1-9	MIN-CLE 7*0	DET-SEA 5*1	OAK-MIL 4-6
0615	NY-TEX 3-4	CAL-BOS 3-13	KC-CHI 5*3	BAL-TOR 8*4	MIN-CLE 11*7	DET-SEA 2-15	OAK-MIL 7*3
0616	CAL-BOS 0-2	KC-CHI 9*4	MIN-CLE 4*2	DET-SEA 7*3	NY-TEX 3-4	BAL-TOR 13*8	OAK-MIL 7-11
0617	CAL-BOS 4*2	MIN-BAL 5-6			KC-TEX 9-10		OAK-MIL 0-5
0618	SEA-BOS 2*1	MIN-BAL 9*2	CLE-CHI 5-6	OAK-DET 0-2	KC-TEX 12*5	NY-TOR 4*2	CAL-MIL 6-10
0619	SEA-BOS 4*3	MIN-BAL 8*4	CLE-CHI 4*3	OAK-DET 5*4	KC-TEX 15*2	NY-TOR 3*0	CAL-MIL 4*1
0620	OAK-BOS 7-8	BAL-KC 2-3	TEX-CHI 7*3	CAL-DET 7*5		NY-TOR 1-6	SEA-MIL 0-4
0621	OAK-BOS 2-3	MIN-NY 5*4	TEX-CHI 5-6	CAL-DET 2-9		CLE-TOR 4-8	SEA-MIL 5*1
0622	OAK-BOS 5-9	MIN-NY 4*3	TEX-CHI 1-3	CAL-DET 10*3	BAL-KC 1*0	CLE-TOR 0-4	SEA-MIL 5*0
0623	OAK-BOS 4*2	MIN-NY 2-11	TEX-CHI 5-6	CAL-DET 3-4	BAL-KC 9*8	CLE-TOR 1-3	SEA-MIL 2-5
0624		MIN-NY 5*0	SEA-CHI 2-6		CAL-KC 9*4	CLE-TOR 3-4	TEX-OAK 6*1
0625	NY-BOS 6*4	BAL-CLE 5*3	SEA-CHI 0-4	MIL-DET 11*3	CAL-KC 4*2	TOR-MIN 6-8	TEX-OAK 8*1
0626	NY-BOS 5*1	BAL-CLE 4-10	SEA-CHI 5*4	MIL-DET 7-8	CAL-KC 10*5	TOR-MIN 5*2	TEX-OAK 9*6
0627	NY-BOS 8*0	BAL-CLE 7*2	SEA-CHI 2-5	MIL-DET 9*3		TOR-MIN 1*0	TEX-OAK 7*3
0628	BOS-BAL 9*3	TEX-CAL 8-10	NY-MIL 2-5	CLE-DET 1-7	SEA-TOR 3*1	CHI-MIN 4*2	KC-OAK 11*0
0629	BOS-BAL 3-7	TEX-CAL 7*4	NY-MIL 9*8	CLE-DET 4-9	SEA-TOR 0-4	CHI-MIN 8*4	KC-OAK 3-6
0630	BOS-BAL 4-6	TEX-CAL 2*1	NY-MIL 8*6	CLE-DET 0-4	SEA-TOR 1-6	CHI-MIN 0-3	KC-OAK 2-3
0701	DET-BAL 2-10	TEX-CAL 2-6	BOS-MIL 6*0	CLE-NY 2-6	SEA-TOR 3-4	CHI-MIN 5*4	KC-OAK 7*3
0702	DET-BAL 4*3	KC-CAL 3-10	BOS-MIL 14*4	CLE-NY 5-8	MIN-TOR 3-4	CHI-SEA 3*2	OAK-TEX 6-9
0703	DET-BAL 8*2	KC-CAL 3-4	BOS-MIL 5*3	CLE-NY 2-3	MIN-TOR 1*0	CHI-SEA 2-3	OAK-TEX 5*0
0704	DET-BOS 6*1	KC-CAL 12*5	MIL-CLE 0-3	BAL-NY 2-3	OAK-KC 9*3	TOR-SEA 2*1	OAK-TEX 4-5
0705	DET-BOS 1-10	MIN-CHI 2-4	MIL-CLE 4*2	BAL-NY 7*4	OAK-KC 9*7	TOR-SEA 4*3	CAL-TEX 0-8
0706	DET-BOS 4-7	MIN-CHI 5*4	MIL-CLE 0-2	BAL-NY 5-13	OAK-KC 5-7	TOR-SEA 5*2	CAL-TEX 3-4
0707	DET-BOS 7*6	MIN-CHI 30*4	MIL-CLE 10*6	BAL-NY 5*3	BAL-OAK 1-6	CLE-SEA 0-6	CAL-TEX 0-7
0711	NY-CAL 2*0	KC-DET 9*5	CHI-MIL 1-5	BOS-MIN 3-7	BAL-OAK 6*3	CLE-SEA 0-7	TEX-TOR 0-2
0712	NY-CAL 2*1	KC-DET 3-6	CHI-MIL 8*6	BOS-MIN 4-5	BAL-OAK 2*0	CLE-SEA 6*3	TEX-TOR 2-6
0713	NY-CAL 2*0	KC-DET 5-8	CHI-MIL 2-8	BOS-MIN 1-3	BAL-OAK 2-3	CLE-SEA 3-14	TEX-TOR 2-3
0714	NY-CAL 2-10	KC-DET 18*4	CHI-MIL 15*1	BOS-MIN 9-3	CLE-OAK 1-6	NY-SEA 1-5	TOR-KC 5*3
0715	BAL-CAL 2*1	TEX-DET 7-8	MIN-MIL 11*7	BOS-CHI 1-7	CLE-OAK 6-7	NY-SEA 0-5	TOR-KC 1-2
0716	BAL-CAL 1-2	TEX-DET 5-6	MIN-MIL 3-4	BOS-CHI 2*0	CLE-OAK 2*1		BAL-KC 8-9
0717		TEX-DET 4-6	SEA-MIL 1-6	BOS-CHI 4*2			BAL-KC 1-5
0718	MIN-BOS 11*3	CLE-CAL 4-5	SEA-MIL 12*0	TOR-TEX 4*0	NY-OAK 3*2	MIL-CHI 3-14	DET-KC 17*0
0719	MIN-BOS 3*2	CLE-CAL 4*2	SEA-BAL 1-4	TOR-TEX 7*2	NY-OAK 3*0	MIL-CHI 6-7	DET-KC 4-8
0720	MIN-BOS 5*0	CLE-CAL 4*1	SEA-BAL 5*1	TOR-TEX 6-11	NY-OAK 5*1	MIL-CHI 2*1	DET-KC 4-8
0721	MIN-BOS 14*1	CLE-CAL 5*2	SEA-BAL 6*4	TOR-TEX 5-6	NY-OAK 2-4	MIL-CHI 4-5	
0722				TOR-TEX 1-2			
0723	CAL-BAL 5*4	OAK-CLE 10*7	MIN-DET 3-6	BOS-TEX 4-5	MIL-KC 7-8	TOR-CHI 2-3	SEA-NY 6*1
0724	CAL-BAL 2-5	OAK-CLE 8*4	MIN-DET 8*4	BOS-TEX 2*1	MIL-KC 4-7	TOR-CHI 1-7	SEA-NY 2-10
0725	CAL-BAL 4-8	OAK-CLE 7-8	MIN-DET 9*3		MIL-KC 0-2		SEA-NY 6*3; CAL-NY 5*1
0726	OAK-BAL 12*9	SEA-CLE 7*4	MIL-MIN 3-6	DET-TEX 3*2	KC-TOR 5-6	CHI-BOS 10*8	CAL-NY 10-12
0727	OAK-BAL 9*1	SEA-CLE 1-6	MIL-MIN 4-7	DET-TEX 5-8	KC-TOR 5*2	CHI-BOS 7*4	
0728	OAK-BAL 4*3	SEA-CLE 6*5	MIL-MIN 11*2	CAL-NY 8*4	DET-TEX 6-10	CHI-BOS 5*2; TEX-BOS 7*2	KC-TOR 10*4
0729	BAL-SEA 9*3	CAL-CLE 10*2	DET-MIN 3-6	OAK-NY 10*8	KC-MIL 3-9	TEX-BOS 6-11	CHI-TOR 12*4
0730	BAL-SEA 2-8	CAL-CLE 4*2	DET-MIN 7-9	OAK-NY 6*5	KC-MIL 5*4	OAK-BOS 10-11	CHI-TOR 8*7
0731	BAL-SEA 4*2	TEX-CHI 8-10	CAL-DET 1-3	MIN-NY 12*3	KC-MIL 6*5	OAK-BOS 4*2	CLE-TOR 1-3
0801		TEX-CHI 2-13	CAL-DET 3-5	MIN-NY 3-8	TEX-MIL 15*1	TOR-BOS 3-5	CLE-TOR 5-7
0802	SEA-CAL 4*3	BAL-CHI 3*0	NY-DET 3-7	KC-CLE 6*4	TEX-MIL 14*5	TOR-BOS 1-4	MIN-OAK 1-3
0803	SEA-CAL 9*3	BAL-CHI 6*3	NY-DET 6-7	KC-CLE 1-3	TEX-MIL 2-3	TOR-BOS 2*1	MIN-OAK 8*6
0804	SEA-CAL 5*2	BAL-CHI 0-1	NY-DET 7-8	KC-CLE 2*0	CLE-TEX 5*0		MIN-OAK 6*2
0805	MIN-CAL 7*4	MIL-BAL 6*5	NY-DET 7*5	BOS-KC 3-5	CLE-TEX 8-10	DET-TOR 1-2	SEA-OAK 0-3
0806	MIN-CAL 7*4	MIL-BAL 5-13	NY-CHI 5-14	BOS-KC 0-6	CLE-TEX 10-12	DET-TOR 2-5	SEA-OAK 0-3
0807	MIN-CAL 1-8	MIL-BAL 4*2	NY-CHI 2-10	BOS-KC 0-2		DET-TOR 4*0	SEA-OAK 1-6
0808		MIL-BAL 6*4	NY-CHI 6*4			BOS-TOR 12*7	
0809	OAK-CAL 5*4	CHI-BAL 7*4	CLE-KC 2-4	MIN-SEA 5*2	MIL-TEX 10*8	BOS-TOR 7*1	DET-NY 5*1
0810	OAK-CAL 3*1	CHI-BAL 6*4	CLE-KC 1*0	MIN-SEA 0-8	MIL-TEX 5*2		DET-NY 4*0
0811	CHI-BAL 7*0	OAK-CAL 3*2	CLE-KC 2-3	MIN-SEA 5*2	MIL-TEX 4-5	BOS-TOR 9*6	DET-NY 6-12
0812	CHI-BAL 4-5	CAL-MIN 3-4	OAK-SEA 3-6	MIL-TEX 14*7	BOS-TOR 11*8		DET-NY 8-10

◆1991◆

	GAME 1	GAME 2	GAME 3	GAME 4	GAME 5	GAME 6	GAME 7
0813	TEX-BAL 3-4	CAL-MIN 8*3	OAK-SEA 2-5	BOS-CLE 6-8	CHI-DET 9-11	TOR-MIL 4-5	KC-NY 5*0
	TEX-BAL 7-8			BOS-CLE 7*5	CHI-DET 3-4		KC-NY 8*1
0814	TEX-BAL 2-10	TOR-MIL 3-5	CAL-MIN 7*4	BOS-CLE 2*1	CHI-DET 9*8	OAK-SEA 0-4	KC-NY 5*1
0815	TEX-BAL 2-9	TOR-MIL 4*1	CAL-MIN 9*1	BOS-CLE 6*2	CHI-DET 4-6	OAK-SEA 6-8	KC-NY 1-5
0816	KC-BOS 2-3	BAL-MIL 5-8	OAK-MIN 4-5	TEX-CLE 5*3	TOR-DET 2-5	CAL-SEA 3-5	CHI-NY 5-6
				TEX-CLE 9-13			
0817	KC-BOS 4*3	TOR-DET 7*5	BAL-MIL 6-7	TEX-CLE 2*0	OAK-MIN 4-12	CHI-NY 2-4	CAL-SEA 4*1
0818	KC-BOS 1-5	TOR-DET 4*2	BAL-MIL 1-2	TEX-CLE 9*4	OAK-MIN 4-6	CHI-NY 11*3	CAL-SEA 4*3
0819	DET-CHI 3*2	NY-KC 6*2	BAL-TEX 1-4		OAK-MIN 8*7		CAL-SEA 1-7
0820	DET-CHI 5*0	NY-KC 7*3	BAL-TEX 8*6	CAL-OAK 2-3	SEA-MIN 5-10	MIL-TOR 1-3	
0821	DET-CHI 12*9	NY-KC 4-7	BAL-TEX 4*3	CAL-OAK 0-2	SEA-MIN 1-9	MIL-TOR 3*0	CLE-BOS 5-13
							CLE-BOS 4-5
0822	TEX-KC 4*2	SEA-MIN 4-5	CAL-OAK 1-2	MIL-TOR 8*7			CLE-BOS 6-7
0823	TEX-KC 6*1	MIN-BAL 13*4	MIL-OAK 13*4	NY-TOR 5-6	BOS-CAL 1-4	CHI-CLE 3-4	SEA-DET 6-8
0824	TEX-KC 1-8	MIN-BAL 5*2	MIL-OAK 7*0	NY-TOR 6*5	BOS-CAL 0-1	CHI-CLE 1-2	SEA-DET 2-7
0825	TEX-KC 8*4	MIN-BAL 3-7	MIL-OAK 8*2	NY-TOR 7-11	BOS-CAL 5-9	CHI-CLE 0-3	SEA-DET 3-4
0826	CHI-KC 0-7	TOR-BAL 5*2	BOS-OAK 3*0	TEX-NY 10*2	DET-CAL 5*1	MIN-CLE 5*3	MIL-SEA 4-5
0827	CHI-KC 2-3	TOR-BAL 6*1	BOS-OAK 6*4	TEX-NY 7*2	DET-CAL 2-4	MIN-CLE 1-2	MIL-SEA 4-6
0828	CHI-KC 6*7	TOR-BAL 3*0	BOS-OAK 3-9	TEX-NY 1-5	DET-CAL 0-1	MIN-CLE 4*2	MIL-SEA 6-7
				TEX-NY 6*2			
0829	CLE-CHI 2-7						
0830	CLE-CHI 3*2	CAL-MIL 2-6	BAL-MIN 11*5	TOR-NY 2-9	DET-OAK 3-6	BOS-SEA 3*2	KC-TEX 2-6
0831	CLE-CHI 5-10	CAL-MIL 2-8	BAL-MIN 2-5	TOR-NY 5*0	DET-OAK 8-9	BOS-SEA 4*1	KC-TEX 3*2
0901	CLE-CHI 1-6	CAL-MIL 1-3	BAL-MIN 3-14	TOR-NY 2-4	DET-OAK 5*2	BOS-SEA 13*2	KC-TEX 4-6
0902	KC-CHI 1-5	CAL-MIL 7*6	CLE-MIN 3-9	BAL-TOR 4-5		DET-SEA 12*5	NY-TEX 2-7
0903	KC-CHI 8*0	OAK-MIL 3-5	CAL-BOS 2*0	BAL-TOR 8*4		DET-SEA 0-1	NY-TEX 1-5
0904	KC-CHI 1-4	OAK-MIL 0-2	CAL-BOS 0-2	BAL-TOR 1-3	CLE-MIN 8*4		NY-TEX 3*2
0905	KC-CHI 2-11	TOR-CLE 13*1	SEA-BOS 3-4	OAK-DET 4*1			
0906	KC-BAL 6-9	TOR-CLE 7*4	SEA-BOS 5-6	OAK-DET 2-11	MIL-CAL 1-2	NY-MIN 1-3	CHI-TEX 11*6
0907	KC-BAL 7*4	TOR-CLE 4*1	SEA-BOS 10-11	OAK-DET 3*1	MIL-CAL 0-1	NY-MIN 2-3	CHI-TEX 11*6
0908	KC-BAL 3*2	TOR-CLE 11*5	SEA-BOS 6-17	OAK-DET 7*4	MIL-CAL 0-1	NY-MIN 5-6	CHI-TEX 6-7
0909	NY-BAL 0-8	BOS-CLE 4*3	MIN-KC 10*4	CHI-OAK 7*1	TEX-CAL 2-4		
0910	NY-BAL 3-6	BOS-DET 4*0	MIN-KC 7*2	CHI-OAK 3*1	TEX-CAL 6*1	CLE-MIL 5*2	SEA-TOR 5*4
0911	NY-BAL 2-4	BOS-DET 2-8	MIN-KC 1-4	CHI-OAK 5-6	TEX-CAL 11*9		SEA-TOR 7*3
0912	CLE-BAL 6*5	DET-MIL 0-7	BOS-NY 7*2	MIN-TEX 3-4	CHI-CAL 4-7		
0913	CLE-BAL 4-5	DET-MIL 3*2	BOS-NY 5*4	MIN-TEX 7*3	CHI-CAL 1*0		OAK-TOR 6-7
0914	CLE-BAL 6*5	DET-MIL 6*4	BOS-NY 1-3	MIN-TEX 0-3	CHI-CAL 2-3	SEA-KC 2-3	OAK-TOR 0-6
						SEA-KC 4*3	
0915	CLE-BAL 3-4	DET-MIL 3-5	BOS-NY 5*4	MIN-TEX 2-4	CHI-CAL 9*2	SEA-KC 14*7	OAK-TOR 10*5
0916	BAL-BOS 9*2	KC-MIN 0-9	MIL-NY 5*4	TOR-SEA 5-6			
0917	BAL-BOS 3-4	KC-MIN 4*1	MIL-NY 2*0	TOR-SEA 4-5	OAK-CHI 0-1	DET-CLE 1-3	CAL-TEX 7*2
0918	BAL-BOS 5-7	KC-MIN 10*4	MIL-NY 1-2	TOR-SEA 5*3	OAK-CHI 0-6	DET-CLE 2-3	
0919	CAL-TEX 3-10			KC-SEA 5-10			
	CAL-TEX 5*2						
0920	NY-BOS 0-2	CAL-CHI 2-3	BAL-CLE 2*1	MIL-DET 8*5	TEX-MIN 4-6	TOR-OAK 5-6	KC-SEA 3*0
0921	NY-BOS 1-12	CAL-CHI 4*3	BAL-CLE 1-10	MIL-DET 5*2	TEX-MIN 4-8	TOR-OAK 0-4	KC-SEA 1-4
0922	NY-BOS 7*5	CAL-CHI 4*2	BAL-CLE 1-2	MIL-DET 9*5	TEX-MIN 4-9	TOR-OAK 3*2	KC-SEA 2*1
0923	BOS-BAL 3-4	TOR-CAL 9-10	NY-MIL 9*8	CLE-DET 1-2		KC-OAK 6-7	TEX-SEA 11*4
0924	CHI-MIN 2-9	TOR-CAL 3*0	NY-MIL 4-5	CLE-DET 2-7		KC-OAK 5*4	TEX-SEA 8*7
0925	CHI-MIN 6*1	TOR-CAL 7*2	NY-MIL 8*6	CLE-DET 6*4		KC-OAK 4-8	TEX-SEA 7*1
0926	BOS-BAL 2*1	CAL-KC 2-3	NY-MIL 2-6	CLE-DET 5-6		TEX-OAK 0-10	
	BOS-BAL 5-6						
0927	SEA-CHI 10*8	NY-CLE 3*0	BAL-DET 9*7	CAL-KC 1-4	BOS-MIL 5-7	TEX-OAK 3*0	MIN-TOR 2-7
0928	SEA-CHI 2-5	NY-CLE 4-5	BAL-DET 4-5	CAL-KC 4*3	BOS-MIL 1-4	TEX-OAK 6*3	MIN-TOR 5*0
0929	SEA-CHI 2*1	NY-CLE 2-5	BAL-DET 7*4	CAL-KC 6*4	BOS-MIL 4-5	TEX-OAK 5-19	MIN-TOR 1-2
0930	MIN-CHI 8*3	NY-CLE 3*0	BAL-DET 3-8	OAK-KC 4-8	BOS-MIL 9*8	SEA-TEX 3*2	CAL-TOR 2*1
						SEA-TEX 0-2	
1001	DET-BOS 8*5	MIN-CHI 3*2	MIL-CLE 11*0	OAK-KC 4*0	BAL-NY 2-3	SEA-TEX 8*1	CAL-TOR 2-5
			MIL-CLE 2-6				
1002	DET-BOS 3-5	OAK-KC 5-16	MIL-CLE 11*4	BAL-NY 3-4	SEA-TEX 4*3	CAL-TOR 5-6	
1003	DET-BOS 10*5	MIN-CHI 2-3	MIL-CLE 9*3	BAL-NY 6-9	MIN-CHI 12-13		
1004	MIL-BOS 3*2	DET-BAL 4*2	KC-CAL 2-6	CLE-NY 3*2	TOR-MIN 4*1	CHI-SEA 4-6	OAK-TEX 3-4
1005	MIL-BOS 13*4	DET-BAL 3-7	KC-CAL 1-5	CLE-NY 7*5	TOR-MIN 1-3	CHI-SEA 0-10	OAK-TEX 12*5
1006	MIL-BOS 6*3	DET-BAL 7*1	KC-CAL 1-3	CLE-NY 4-7	TOR-MIN 3*2	CHI-SEA 3*2	OAK-TEX 2-4

◆1992◆

	GAME 1	GAME 2	GAME 3	GAME 4	GAME 5	GAME 6	GAME 7
0406	TOR-DET 4*2	CLE-BAL 0-2	MIN-MIL 4*2	KC-OAK 3-5		TEX-SEA 12*10	
0407	CHI-CAL 10*4	BOS-NY 3-4				TEX-SEA 4*0	
0408	CHI-CAL 4*3	CLE-BAL 4*0	TOR-DET 10*9	MIN-MIL 5-9	KC-OAK 3-4	TEX-SEA 13*1	
0409	CHI-CAL 7*6	CLE-BAL 0-2	TOR-DET 3*1	MIN-MIL 3*1	KC-OAK 2-5	TEX-SEA 9*1	BOS-NY 2-3
0410	MIL-CAL 5*4	TEX-MIN 1-7	NY-DET 7*3	BAL-TOR 3-4	CHI-OAK 0-4	KC-SEA 3-9	
0411	MIL-CAL 1-4	TEX-MIN 10*8	NY-DET 8*1	BAL-TOR 2-7	CHI-OAK 6-7	KC-SEA 0-1	BOS-CLE 7*5
0412	MIL-CAL 9-13	TEX-MIN 4*3	NY-DET 5*1	BAL-TOR 1-3	CHI-OAK 6*4	KC-SEA 1-2	BOS-CLE 1-2
							BOS-CLE 3*0
0413	BAL-BOS 8*6	SEA-CHI 0-1	OAK-KC 6*1	CAL-TEX 3*0	NY-TOR 5*2		DET-CLE 7*5
0414	MIL-MIN 11*1		OAK-KC 1-3	CAL-TEX 8*1	NY-TOR 6-12		DET-CLE 7-8
0415	MIL-MIN 7*4	BAL-BOS 5-6	OAK-KC 10*6	CAL-TEX 2-3	NY-TOR 0-2	SEA-CHI 6*0	DET-CLE 8*1
0416			OAK-KC 1*0	CAL-TEX 3*2	NY-TOR 6-7	SEA-CHI 4-5	DET-CLE 13*4
0417	DET-BAL 0-8	TOR-BOS 0-1	CAL-KC 8*1	OAK-TEX 5-6		MIN-CHI 7*0	CLE-NY 11*1
0418	DET-BAL 1-6	TOR-BOS 2*1	CAL-KC 5*3	OAK-TEX 5*3	SEA-MIL 5*3	MIN-CHI 3-4	CLE-NY 0-14
0419	DET-BAL 2-3	TOR-BOS 4-5		OAK-TEX 4-6	SEA-MIL 12*9	MIN-CHI 1-4	CLE-NY 3-5
0420	DET-BAL 4-12	TOR-BOS 6*4	CAL-OAK 3-4	MIN-SEA 0-2			CLE-NY 3*1
0421	NY-CHI 4*3	BAL-MIN 10*4	CAL-OAK 3*2	MIN-SEA 5*2		DET-TEX 4*2	CLE-TOR 1-2
0422	NY-CHI 4*3	BAL-KC 2*1	CAL-OAK 4-10	MIN-SEA 8*1		DET-TEX 12*8	CLE-TOR 7*2
0423	BOS-MIL 2-3	BAL-KC 8*1		MIN-SEA 2-3		DET-TEX 11*5	CLE-TOR 8-13
0424	TEX-BOS 1-3	SEA-CAL 7*2	MIL-CLE 5*0	CHI-DET 9*1	OAK-MIN 5-6	BAL-NY 0-5	KC-TOR 3-4
0425		SEA-CAL 10*6			OAK-MIN 8*4	BAL-NY 9*2	KC-TOR 4-6
0426	TEX-BOS 3*1	SEA-CAL 5-7	MIL-CLE 9*4	CHI-DET 7*6	OAK-MIN 4-8	BAL-NY 1-3	KC-TOR 9*0
	TEX-BOS 4*2		MIL-CLE 1-3				
0427	BAL-MIN 1-4	TEX-NY 7-8					
0428	BAL-MIN 10*5	TEX-NY 1*0	CHI-BOS 3-6	OAK-CLE 3*1	SEA-DET 1-4	KC-MIL 3*2	CAL-TOR 9*5
0429	BAL-MIN 5*4	TEX-NY 5*1	CHI-BOS 1-6	OAK-CLE 2-5		KC-MIL 3-5	CAL-TOR 0-1
0430	TEX-CHI 1-12	OAK-DET 10*6		CAL-CLE 8*5		TOR-MIL 2-3	
0501	TEX-CHI 8*4	OAK-DET 7*6	SEA-BAL 1-15	CAL-CLE 7*5	KC-BOS 5-6	TOR-MIL 3-4	MIN-NY 3-5
0502	TEX-CHI 4*1	OAK-DET 3-5	SEA-BAL 2-4	CAL-CLE 2-3	KC-BOS 6-7	TOR-MIL 4-5	MIN-NY 7*6
0503	TEX-CHI 3-5	OAK-DET 4-8	SEA-BAL 6-8	CAL-CLE 6*3	KC-BOS 5*2	TOR-MIL 4*1	MIN-NY 4*2
0504	MIL-CHI 0-7	CAL-DET 2-6	TEX-BAL 5-8	KC-CLE 11*6	MIN-BOS 6*1	TOR-OAK 7*3	NY-SEA 3-5
0505	MIL-CHI 2-12	CAL-DET 1-2	TEX-BAL 5*3	KC-CLE 6-8	MIN-BOS 1-4	TOR-OAK 5*1	NY-SEA 4-7
0506	BOS-CHI 5-7	NY-CAL 2-3	MIN-BAL 2-6	MIL-KC 5*3	CLE-TEX 7*2	DET-OAK 2-5	TOR-SEA 12*4
0507	BOS-CHI 6*7	NY-CAL 0-6	MIN-BAL 4-5	MIL-KC 4-6	CLE-TEX 8*7	DET-OAK 2-6	TOR-SEA 8*7
0508	CLE-MIN 4-7	TOR-CAL 1-4	CHI-BAL 4*3	BOS-KC 1-2	MIL-TEX 2-3	NY-OAK 6-8	DET-SEA 7*6
0509	CLE-MIN 5-10	TOR-CAL 1-2	CHI-BAL 2-5	BOS-KC 5*0	MIL-TEX 4-5	NY-OAK 2-5	DET-SEA 13*0
0510	CLE-MIN 6-10	TOR-CAL 4*1	CHI-BAL 5*2	BOS-KC 10*6	MIL-TEX 6*2	NY-OAK 3-5	DET-SEA 2-6
0512	BOS-MIN 3-6	DET-CAL 4*2	CHI-MIL 2-6	CLE-KC 0-3	BAL-TEX 5*1	SEA-NY 1-3	OAK-TOR 0-3
0513	BOS-MIN 3-4	DET-CAL 5-7	CHI-MIL 1*0	CLE-KC 3-5	BAL-TEX 4*2	SEA-NY 4-12	OAK-TOR 1-4
0514							SEA-TOR 4-5
0515	CAL-BOS 0-3	BAL-CHI 2*0	MIN-CLE 0-5	DET-KC 8*2	TEX-MIL 3-5	OAK-NY 2-3	SEA-TOR 2*1
0516	CAL-BOS 0-3	BAL-CHI 7*2	MIN-CLE 8*6	DET-KC 7*2	TEX-MIL 4-5	OAK-NY 6*3	SEA-TOR 7*6
0517	CAL-BOS 3*1	BAL-CHI 10-14	MIN-CLE 9*5	DET-KC 1-2	TEX-MIL 2*1	OAK-NY 2-11	SEA-TOR 3*2

♦1992♦	GAME 1	GAME 2	GAME 3	GAME 4	GAME 5	GAME 6	GAME 7
0518	SEA-BOS 2-3	KC-CHI 6*1	TEX-CLE 3*2	OAK-BAL 8*4	MIL-DET 9*1	CAL-NY 2-7	MIN-TOR 6*2
0519	SEA-BOS 5-7	KC-CHI 1-2	TEX-CLE 8*7	OAK-BAL 5*3	MIL-DET 0-3	CAL-NY 4-5	MIN-TOR 7*1
0520	SEA-BOS 4-6	KC-CHI 7*2	TEX-CLE 1*0	OAK-BAL 4*2	MIL-DET 3-4	CAL-NY 2-3	MIN-TOR 7-8
					MIL-DET 7*3		
0521	KC-TEX 7*5						
0522	KC-TEX 7-10	CAL-BAL 3-5	OAK-BOS 5*3	TOR-CHI 6*2	MIN-DET 3-6	MIL-NY 10*9	CLE-SEA 1-2
0523	KC-TEX 2-4	CAL-BAL 6*2	OAK-BOS 1-5	TOR-CHI 2-5	MIN-DET 6*5	MIL-NY 5*4	CLE-SEA 5*4
0524	KC-TEX 3-4	CAL-BAL 4-6	OAK-BOS 4*0	TOR-CHI 1-8	MIN-DET 15*0	MIL-NY 7-8	CLE-SEA 4-5
						MIL-NY 10-13	BAL-SEA 3-7
0525	CLE-OAK 10*6						BAL-SEA 13*8
0526	CLE-OAK 1*0	BOS-CAL 4*1	KC-DET 1-8	NY-MIN 5*4	CHI-TEX 5-6	MIL-TOR 4-5	BAL-SEA 1-7
0527	CLE-OAK 4*2	BOS-CAL 4*3	KC-DET 2-11	NY-MIN 1-5	CHI-TEX 3-4	MIL-TOR 8*4	
0528		BOS-CAL 2*1	KC-DET 5*1		CHI-TEX 2-4		
0529	TEX-KC 5*3	CLE-CAL 14*2	NY-MIL 3*8	DET-MIN 5-17	BAL-OAK 3-5	BOS-SEA 3-7	CHI-TOR 0-3
0530	TEX-KC 2-8	CLE-CAL 1-3	NY-MIL 8*1	DET-MIN 5-7	BAL-OAK 7*6	BOS-SEA 0-3	CHI-TOR 1-2
0531	TEX-KC 6-7	CLE-CAL 4*3	NY-MIL 1-2	DET-MIN 1-4	BAL-OAK 4*2	BOS-SEA 7*1	CHI-TOR 2-3
0601	CHI-KC 5*3	BAL-CAL 8*2	DET-MIL 2-6	TOR-MIN 5*3	BOS-OAK 7-10	NY-TEX 7*1	
0602	CHI-KC 1-2	BAL-CAL 4*2	DET-MIL 4-5	TOR-MIN 7*5	BOS-OAK 4-5	NY-TEX 2-8	SEA-CLE 3-4
0603	CHI-KC 1-3	BAL-CAL 3-4	DET-MIL 10*4	TOR-MIN 3-11	BOS-OAK 6-7	NY-TEX 3-4	SEA-CLE 3-8
0604	DET-NY 6*2					MIN-TEX 15*12	SEA-CLE 10*3
0605	TOR-BAL 0-1	OAK-CHI 10*3	SEA-KC 4-6	CAL-MIL 1-7		MIN-TEX 4-5	
0606	TOR-BAL 4*3	OAK-CHI 6*4	SEA-KC 3-4	CAL-MIL 3-4	CLE-BOS 1-5	MIN-TEX 6*1	DET-NY 6*2
					CLE-BOS 3*1		
0607	TOR-BAL 1-7	OAK-CHI 1-6	SEA-KC 1-4	CAL-MIL 3-10	CLE-BOS 0-4	DET-NY 5-6	MIN-TEX 4-5
0608	BOS-BAL 2-5	CAL-CHI 6-9	MIN-KC 6*9	OAK-MIL 2-9	CLE-DET 2-9	TOR-NY 16*3	SEA-TEX 3-14
0609	BOS-BAL 4*1	CAL-CHI 2-4	MIN-KC 4*2	OAK-MIL 6*1	CLE-DET 6*1	TOR-NY 2*1	SEA-TEX 2*1
0610	BOS-BAL 1-3	CAL-CHI 2-3	MIN-KC 6-7	OAK-MIL 5*2	CLE-DET 4*2	TOR-NY 10*3	SEA-TEX 3-5
					BAL-DET 7*5		
0611	BOS-TOR 0-4	CAL-CHI 4*0			BAL-DET 6*0	TEX-OAK 5-6	MIL-SEA 1-4
0612	BOS-TOR 5*0	KC-CAL 0-5	NY-CLE 0-3	CHI-MIN 1-5	BAL-DET 1-15	TEX-OAK 1-7	MIL-SEA 8*7
0613	BOS-TOR 5*3	KC-CAL 4-5	NY-CLE 4*1	CHI-MIN 4*2	BAL-DET 4-7	TEX-OAK 1-6	MIL-SEA 14*4
0614	BOS-TOR 2-6	KC-CAL 1-5	NY-CLE 4*3	CHI-MIN 7-8		MIL-OAK 2-3	CHI-SEA 1-4
0615	NY-BOS 0-1	TEX-CAL 5*2	BAL-CLE 6*5	KC-MIN 7*0		MIL-OAK 10*0	CHI-SEA 6-9
0616	NY-BOS 3-4	TEX-CAL 1-4	BAL-CLE 5-7	KC-MIN 7*5	DET-TOR 4*3	MIL-OAK 10*2	CHI-SEA 1-2
0617	NY-BOS 3-4	TEX-CAL 0-3	BAL-CLE 2-3	KC-MIN 2-4	DET-TOR 2-6		CHI-SEA 4-5
0618	NY-BOS 5*4	CLE-MIL 1-4		KC-MIN 1-3	DET-TOR 14*10		
0619	NY-BAL 7-10	CLE-MIL 5*3	OAK-CAL 12*8	SEA-MIN 1*0	DET-CHI 8*3	TOR-KC 4-11	BOS-TEX 1-4
0620	NY-BAL 9*5	CLE-MIL 1-4	OAK-CAL 0-10	SEA-MIN 3-5	DET-CHI 1-3	TOR-KC 6*1	BOS-TEX 1-4
0621	NY-BAL 8*2	CLE-MIL 2-4	OAK-CAL 2-4	SEA-MIN 0-5	DET-CHI 5-6	TOR-KC 0-2	BOS-TEX 2-3
0622	NY-BAL 4-5	BOS-DET 2-4	SEA-OAK 2-7	CAL-MIN 0-2	CLE-CHI 1-7		TOR-TEX 16*7
0623	NY-KC 1-2	BOS-DET 7-11	SEA-OAK 7-12	CAL-MIN 3-5	CLE-CHI 1-7	BAL-MIL 7*1	
0624	NY-KC 6*3	BOS-DET 1-5	SEA-OAK 2-7	CAL-MIN 0-11	CLE-CHI 3-4	BAL-MIL 8*4	TOR-TEX 3*2
						BAL-MIL 0-1	
0625	NY-KC 4*3	TEX-DET 5*2	MIN-OAK 1-5	CAL-SEA 4-13			CHI-NY 2*1
0626	KC-BAL 5-6	TEX-DET 4-5	MIN-OAK 4*3	CAL-SEA 10*1	MIL-BOS 4-8	TOR-CLE 6*1	CHI-NY 7-8
0627	KC-BAL 2*0	TEX-DET 10*8	MIN-OAK 12*2	CAL-SEA 2*1	MIL-BOS 7-8	TOR-CLE 4-6	CHI-NY 6*3
0628	KC-BAL 9*2	TEX-DET 8*4	MIN-OAK 10*2	CAL-SEA 2-9	MIL-BOS 9*3	TOR-CLE 6-7	KC-NY 7*3
0629	MIL-BAL 5*3	MIN-CAL 5*1	TEX-TOR 4-11	OAK-SEA 5*4	DET-BOS 8*3	CHI-CLE 9*6	KC-NY 0-6
0630	MIL-BAL 3-12	MIN-CAL 2*0	TEX-TOR 16*13	OAK-SEA 4*2	DET-BOS 5-8	CHI-CLE 4-5	KC-NY 6-7
0701	MIL-BAL 4-7	MIN-CAL 2*1	TEX-TOR 2-3	OAK-SEA 3*1	DET-BOS 4-6	CHI-CLE 8*5	
0702	BOS-CHI 3-8	MIL-KC 2-8					
0703	BOS-CHI 1-2	MIL-KC 7*3	OAK-CLE 1-8	SEA-DET 4-6	BAL-MIN 6*1	NY-TEX 9*6	CAL-TOR 1-10
				SEA-DET 11*0			
0704	BOS-CHI 2*1	OAK-CLE 1-8	BAL-MIN 2-3	SEA-DET 4*3	NY-TEX 1-4	CAL-TOR 6-8	
0705	BOS-CHI 2-4	OAK-CLE 5*2	BAL-MIN 1-2	SEA-DET 5-8	NY-TEX 5*4	CAL-TOR 2-6	MIL-KC 2*1
							MIL-KC 9*7
0706	CHI-BAL 3-4	KC-BOS 6*3	OAK-CLE 13*4	SEA-DET 2-5	MIN-NY 10*5	MIL-TEX 1-3	CAL-TOR 0-3
0707	CHI-BAL 8*4	KC-BOS 2-3	CAL-CLE 1-3	OAK-DET 2-3	MIN-NY 1-2	MIL-TEX 4*3	SEA-TOR 3-4
0708	CHI-BAL 3-5	KC-BOS 4-5	CAL-CLE 4-8	OAK-DET 3-6	MIN-NY 3*2	MIL-TEX 4*3	SEA-TOR 0-6
0709	MIN-BAL 2-4	CHI-BOS 10*3	KC-MIL 3*2	CAL-DET 4-5	SEA-NY 6-7	CLE-TEX 4-14	OAK-TOR 3-4
0710	MIN-BAL 5*2	CHI-BOS 5-6	KC-MIL 3*1	CAL-DET 6*1	SEA-NY 5*2	CLE-TEX 5-6	OAK-TOR 5*1
0711	MIN-BAL 6*5	CHI-BOS 2-11	KC-MIL 1-5	CAL-DET 2*1	SEA-NY 5*3	CLE-TEX 1-5	OAK-TOR 3*1
0712	MIN-BAL 9*4	CHI-BOS 0-3	KC-MIL 5*1	CAL-DET 5*4	SEA-NY 7*6	CLE-TEX 6*3	OAK-TOR 8*0
0716	NY-CAL 2-3	MIL-CHI 4-5	CLE-KC 2-3	BOS-MIN 6-7	DET-OAK 0-4	BAL-TEX 2-5	TOR-SEA 7*2
0717	NY-CAL 4*3	MIL-CHI 4*3	CLE-KC 3-4	BOS-MIN 2-3	DET-OAK 4*3	BAL-TEX 8*0	TOR-SEA 6-8
0718	NY-CAL 3-5	MIL-CHI 3*1	CLE-KC 1-4	BOS-MIN 1*0	DET-OAK 5*2	BAL-TEX 7*0	TOR-SEA 3*0
0719	NY-CAL 8*3	MIL-CHI 6*3	CLE-KC 4*3	BOS-MIN 5-7	DET-OAK 2-6	BAL-TEX 3*2	TOR-SEA 8*4
0720	TOR-CAL 3-5	BAL-CHI 5*2	BOS-KC 5*3	CLE-MIN 5*1	NY-OAK 1*0	TEX-MIL 4-5	DET-SEA 6*4
0721	TOR-CAL 9*5	BAL-CHI 7-10	BOS-KC 0-8	CLE-MIN 5*2	NY-OAK 5*1	TEX-MIL 6*3	DET-SEA 6*2
0722	TOR-CAL 4-5	BAL-CHI 5-7	BOS-KC 4-6	CLE-MIN 1-2	NY-OAK 5-8	TEX-MIL 1-4	DET-SEA 3*2
0723	DET-CAL 5*2	TEX-BAL 4*2	KC-CLE 0-1		TOR-OAK 9*3	CHI-MIL 6*2	NY-SEA 5*4
0724	DET-CAL 3-6	TEX-BAL 2-9	KC-CLE 8*3	MIN-BOS 5*0	TOR-OAK 5-6	CHI-MIL 2-3	NY-SEA 8*7
				MIN-BOS 4-5			
0725	TEX-BAL 10*8	DET-CAL 0-9	KC-CLE 5-6	MIN-BOS 3*2	CHI-MIL 0-3	TOR-OAK 0-6	NY-SEA 2-8
0726	TEX-BAL 6*2	DET-CAL 3-4	KC-CLE 1-2	MIN-BOS 8*2	CHI-MIL 4-15	TOR-OAK 1-9	NY-SEA 5-8
0727	OAK-MIN 9*1	SEA-CAL 0-3	MIL-CLE 4*0	TEX-BOS 5-7	CHI-DET 8*6	BAL-NY 5*2	KC-TOR 4-6
					CHI-DET 5*3		
0728	OAK-MIN 12*10	SEA-CAL 8*1	MIL-CLE 2-4	TEX-BOS 2*1	CHI-DET 8*6	BAL-NY 5*2	KC-TOR 5*2
0729	TEX-BOS 5-6	SEA-CAL 8*0	MIL-CLE 3-4	OAK-MIN 5*4	CHI-DET 8*6	BAL-NY 6*0	KC-TOR 0-3
0730		SEA-CAL 5-6		MIL-MIN 5*3		BAL-NY 3-6	KC-TOR 0-3
0731	BAL-BOS 4-7	SEA-CAL 6*3	DET-CLE 9*6	MIL-MIN 1-4	OAK-KC 5-6	CAL-TEX 5*3	NY-TOR 2-13
	BAL-BOS 4*3						
0801	BAL-BOS 9*3	SEA-CHI 1-8	DET-CLE 5-8	OAK-KC 4-8	MIL-MIN 6-9	CAL-TEX 6*1	NY-TOR 1-3
0802	BAL-BOS 2*1	SEA-CHI 4-7	DET-CLE 5*4	OAK-KC 8*4	MIL-MIN 0-5	CAL-TEX 1-5	NY-TOR 6-7
						OAK-TEX 4*1	
0803	TOR-BOS 1-7	DET-BAL 3-6	CLE-NY 8*6		CAL-KC 5*1	OAK-TEX 9*0	SEA-MIL 2-5
0804	TOR-BOS 4-9	DET-BAL 3-6	CLE-NY 3-4	MIN-CHI 11-19	CAL-KC 1-4		
0805	DET-BAL 0-4	TOR-BOS 5*4	MIN-CHI 5-9	SEA-MIL 1-8	CAL-KC 2-5	CLE-NY 4*3	OAK-TEX 4*3
0806	TOR-DET 15*11		MIN-CHI 3-5	SEA-MIL 2-4	CAL-KC 6-7	BOS-NY 3*1	OAK-TEX 2*0
0807	TOR-DET 2-7	CLE-BAL 5*4	CHI-CAL 1-3	KC-OAK 6-8	TEX-SEA 7*6	BOS-NY 5-7	
0808	TOR-DET 6-8	CLE-BAL 6*0	CHI-CAL 8*2	KC-OAK 3-5	TEX-SEA 7*3	BOS-NY 4*2	MIN-MIL 0-4
							MIN-MIL 3*1
0809	CLE-BAL 2-3	CHI-CAL 12*8	TOR-DET 2-9	BOS-NY 0-6	KC-OAK 5*2	TEX-SEA 5-6	MIN-MIL 2-4
0810	BOS-CLE 5-8	MIL-CAL 1-4	NY-DET 5-10	TEX-MIN 5-7	CHI-OAK 3-5	KC-SEA 1-3	BAL-TOR 4-8
0811	BOS-CLE 1-3	MIL-CAL 0-1	NY-DET 1-5	TEX-MIN 2-3	CHI-OAK 10*6	KC-SEA 9*6	BAL-TOR 3*0
0812	BOS-CLE 5-8	MIL-CAL 1-2	NY-DET 10*0	TEX-MIN 5-3	CHI-OAK 1-2	KC-SEA 3-6	BAL-TOR 11*4
0813	BOS-CLE 4*2			TEX-MIN 6*1	CAL-OAK 1-4		BAL-TOR 2-4
0814	TOR-CLE 9*5	NY-CHI 2-6	BAL-KC 3*1	BOS-MIL 7-8	CAL-OAK 2*1	MIN-SEA 9*6	DET-TEX 9*6
				BOS-MIL 0-1			
0815	NY-CHI 4*2	BAL-KC 4-5	CAL-OAK 5-9	BOS-MIL 3*1	MIN-SEA 2-3	DET-TEX 10*3	
0816	NY-CHI 2-4	BAL-KC 2-15	CAL-OAK 4-5	BOS-MIL 0-1	MIN-SEA 7-8	DET-TEX 6*0	TOR-CLE 2-4
							TOR-CLE 6*2
0817	NY-CHI 3-4	DET-KC 5-6		CAL-BOS 0-8	MIN-CLE 1-8	TOR-MIL 12*1	OAK-NY 3-7
0818	TEX-CHI 0-3	DET-KC 5*1	SEA-BAL 8*3	CAL-BOS 3-2	MIN-CLE 1-5	TOR-MIL 5-10	OAK-NY 3-14
0819	TEX-CHI 2-3	DET-KC 2-7	SEA-BAL 10*8	CAL-BOS 2*0	MIN-CLE 1-2	TOR-MIL 3-16	OAK-NY 8*6
0820	TEX-CHI 6*1		SEA-BAL 1-2	CAL-BOS 2-0	TEX-CLE 6-8	DET-MIL 2-3	CAL-NY 9*5
0821	KC-CHI 4*3	TOR-MIN 1-5	OAK-BAL 2-4	SEA-BOS 5*2	TEX-CLE 1-6	DET-MIL 1-5	CAL-NY 0-3
0822	KC-CHI 2-3	TOR-MIN 4*2	OAK-BAL 5*3	SEA-BOS 8-10	TEX-CLE 14*4	DET-MIL 3*2	CAL-NY 7*3
0823	KC-CHI 1-3	TOR-MIN 0-2	OAK-BAL 7*3	SEA-BOS 9*3			MIL-NY 8-9
0824	TOR-CHI 4-8	DET-MIN 6*2	CAL-BAL 5*2	OAK-BOS 9*3			
0825	TOR-CHI 3-6	DET-MIN 4*3	CAL-BAL 1-9	OAK-BOS 4-5	CLE-SEA 0-6	KC-TEX 2-6	MIL-NY 1-5

◆1992◆	GAME 1	GAME 2	GAME 3	GAME 4	GAME 5	GAME 6	GAME 7
0826	TOR-CHI 9*0	DET-MIN 0-1	CAL-BAL 4-6	OAK-BOS 1-2	CLE-SEA 6*3	KC-TEX 1-3	MIL-NY 3-4
0827	MIL-TOR 4-5	NY-MIN 5*0			CLE-SEA 2-6	KC-TEX 7*2	
0828	MIL-TOR 22*2	NY-MIN 3-4	BOS-CAL 7*1	KC-DET 2-4	BAL-SEA 4-6	CHI-TEX 1-4	
0829	MIL-TOR 7*2	NY-MIN 6*3	BOS-CAL 2-7	KC-DET 1-12	BAL-SEA 4*0	CHI-TEX 6*4	CLE-OAK 6-7
0830	MIL-TOR 3-5	NY-MIN 3-5	BOS-CAL 4*2	KC-DET 9*4	BAL-SEA 2*0	CHI-TEX 4-10	CLE-OAK 1-4
0831	CHI-TOR 2-9	TEX-KC 2-5	CLE-CAL 4*3	MIN-DET 5*3	BOS-SEA 2-15	NY-MIL 1-4	CLE-OAK 5-7
0901	CHI-TOR 3-9	TEX-KC 3-8	CLE-CAL 6-7	MIN-DET 5*4	BOS-SEA 3-4	NY-MIL 7*1	BAL-OAK 4*0
0902	CHI-TOR 3*2	TEX-KC 6*2	CLE-CAL 2-3	MIN-DET 4*2	BOS-SEA 5*3	NY-MIL 0-7	BAL-OAK 5*1
0903		CHI-KC 7*3					BAL-OAK 2*1
0904	BAL-CAL 8*7	CHI-KC 8*0	SEA-CLE 0-7	MIL-DET 6*3	TEX-NY 3-6	BOS-OAK 8*3	MIN-TOR 5-16
0905	BAL-CAL 4*1	CHI-KC 12*6	SEA-CLE 4-5	MIL-DET 10*3	TEX-NY 7*3	BOS-OAK 7*3	MIN-TOR 3-7
0906	BAL-CAL 2-5	CHI-KC 2-3	SEA-CLE 9-12	MIL-DET 2-6	TEX-NY 0-7	BOS-OAK 1-2	MIN-TOR 2-4
0907	OAK-CAL 2-3	TOR-KC 4-5	NY-BAL 6*2	CLE-MIL 0-2	SEA-MIN 2-4	BOS-TEX 3*0	
0908	OAK-CAL 14*2	TOR-KC 5*0	NY-BAL 16*4	CLE-MIL 3-7	SEA-MIN 4-8	BOS-TEX 1-6	DET-CHI 3-4
							DET-CHI 3-4
0909	NY-BAL 5*2	OAK-CAL 3*0	TOR-KC 1*0	CLE-MIL 5*4	SEA-MIN 2-6		DET-CHI 4-6
0910	SEA-OAK 4-6					BOS-TEX 2-3	DET-CHI 8*0
0911	SEA-OAK 3-4	MIL-BAL 2-3	DET-BOS 6-7	CAL-MIN 8*0	KC-NY 1-2	TOR-TEX 7*5	CLE-CHI 5*1
						TOR-TEX 3-4	
0912	MIL-BAL 5*0	DET-BOS 9*5	CLE-CHI 5*3	CAL-MIN 2-7	KC-NY 9-11	TOR-TEX 4*2	SEA-OAK 4-5
0913	MIL-BAL 3*1	DET-BOS 7*2	CLE-CHI 2*1	CAL-MIN 2-6	KC-NY 3*0	TOR-TEX 7*2	SEA-OAK 1-3
0914	KC-BAL 1-2	MIL-BOS 6*0	CLE-TOR 2*1		CHI-NY 8*6		MIN-OAK 2-3
0915	KC-BAL 1-2	MIL-BOS 7*2	CLE-TOR 4-5	TEX-DET 6*5	CHI-NY 4*2	CAL-SEA 9*0	MIN-OAK 1-2
0916	KC-BAL 0-3	MIL-BOS 1-2	CLE-TOR 6*3	TEX-DET 1-4	CHI-NY 9*6	CAL-SEA 2*1	MIN-OAK 2-4
0917	MIN-CAL 2*1	MIL-BOS 10*4	CLE-TOR 5-7				
0918	MIN-CAL 4*1	CHI-CLE 8*7	TEX-TOR 0-13	BOS-DET 3-10	NY-KC 2-3	BAL-MIL 4-12	OAK-SEA 7*4
0919	MIN-CAL 1-5	CHI-CLE 4-5	TEX-TOR 0-1	BOS-DET 2-3	NY-KC 4-7	BAL-MIL 1-4	OAK-SEA 4-6
0920	MIN-CAL 7*5	CHI-CLE 10*8	TEX-TOR 7*5	BOS-DET 5*4	NY-KC 10*4	BAL-MIL 3-9	OAK-SEA 4*2
0921	OAK-CHI 6*5			BOS-DET 5-6	SEA-KC 0-3	BAL-MIL 4*1	
0922	OAK-CHI 3-8	TOR-BAL 4*3	CLE-BOS 4*2	DET-NY 5-6	SEA-KC 0-3	CAL-MIL 2-3	MIN-TEX 1*0
				DET-NY 4-7			
0923	TOR-BAL 1-4	CLE-BOS 7*3	OAK-CHI 6-17	DET-NY 10*8	SEA-KC 6*1	CAL-MIL 0-3	MIN-TEX 3-5
0924	TOR-BAL 8*2	CLE-BOS 4-6	OAK-CHI 4*1	DET-NY 1-10	SEA-KC 0-2	CAL-MIL 0-4	
0925	CLE-DET 5-6	KC-MIN 4*3	CAL-CHI 5-6	TOR-NY 3*1	SEA-TEX 4*3	OAK-MIL 1-4	
0926	CLE-DET 7*4	KC-MIN 2-9	CAL-CHI 1*0	TOR-NY 1-2	SEA-TEX 8*4	OAK-MIL 1-2	BOS-BAL 7*3
							BOS-BAL 0-2
0927	CAL-CHI 2-3	CLE-DET 3-13	OAK-MIL 3-5	KC-MIN 0-4	TOR-NY 12*2	SEA-TEX 2-3	BOS-BAL 6*1
0928	KC-CAL 5-6	NY-CLE 4-6		CHI-MIN 9*4			BOS-BAL 3-7
0929	KC-CAL 2*0	NY-CLE 3-4	BAL-DET 7*2	CHI-MIN 4-5	TEX-OAK 0-5	MIL-SEA 7*4	BOS-TOR 2-5
0930	KC-CAL 4*0	NY-CLE 4*2	BAL-DET 2-4	CHI-MIN 4*3	TEX-OAK 7*3	MIL-SEA 4-7	BOS-TOR 1*0
1001	KC-CAL 2-5	BAL-CLE 3*2		CHI-MIN 6-9	TEX-OAK 4*3	MIL-SEA 7*2	
1002	TEX-CAL 3-6	BAL-CLE 5-8	NY-BOS 6*3	MIN-KC 5*1	MIL-OAK 3*2	CHI-SEA 0-2	DET-TOR 7-8
1003	TEX-CAL 2-4	BAL-CLE 7*1	NY-BOS 5-7	MIN-KC 6-7	MIL-OAK 3-10	CHI-SEA 2-7	DET-TOR 1-3
1004	TEX-CAL 9*5	BAL-CLE 4*3	NY-BOS 2-8	MIN-KC 6*0	MIL-OAK 1-7	CHI-SEA 3-4	DET-TOR 4-7

◆1993◆	GAME 1	GAME 2	GAME 3	GAME 4	GAME 5	GAME 6	GAME 7
0405	BOS-KC 3*1	DET-OAK 4-9	NY-CLE 9*1	TEX-BAL 7*4			
0406	CHI-MIN 10*5	MIL-CAL 1-3	TOR-SEA 1-8				
0407	CHI-MIN 1-6	MIL-CAL 3*2	TOR-SEA 2*0	TEX-BAL 3*1	BOS-KC 3*2	DET-OAK 7-12	NY-CLE 2-4
0408	CHI-MIN 9*4				BOS-KC 9*4	DET-OAK 3*2	NY-CLE 5-15
0409	BOS-TEX 1-3	DET-CAL 5-7	BAL-SEA 0-6	CLE-TOR 10-13	MIN-KC 8*7	MIL-OAK 6*5	NY-CHI 11*6
0410	BOS-TEX 10*2	DET-CAL 5*2	BAL-SEA 5*3	CLE-TOR 4-5	MIN-KC 3*2	MIL-OAK 3-4	NY-CHI 12*0
0411	BOS-TEX 1-4	DET-CAL 6-7	BAL-SEA 6-7	CLE-TOR 10*6	MIN-KC 1-2	MIL-OAK 2-8	NY-CHI 4-6
0412	BAL-TEX 3-6	CAL-MIL 12*5	KC-NY 1-4				MIN-CHI 3*2
0413	BAL-TEX 3-8	CLE-BOS 2-6	OAK-DET 4-20	SEA-TOR 5-6			MIN-CHI 0-4
0414	BAL-TEX 6*5	CLE-BOS 7-12	CAL-MIL 12*2	SEA-TOR 10*9	KC-NY 5-6		
0415	OAK-DET 2-3	CLE-BOS 3-4		SEA-TOR 1-3	KC-NY 5*4		
0416	SEA-DET 0-5	CHI-BOS 9*4	CAL-BAL 1-4	KC-MIN 3-4	TEX-NY 3-5	TOR-CLE 1-13	
0417	SEA-DET 3-20	CHI-BOS 1-5	CAL-BAL 7*5	KC-MIN 2-8	TEX-NY 9*0	TOR-CLE 8*1	OAK-MIL 3-6
0418	SEA-DET 7-8	CHI-BOS 0-4	CAL-BAL 3-4	KC-MIN 5*4	TEX-NY 12*2	TOR-CLE 5-6	OAK-MIL 0-8
0419	SEA-DET 10*6	CHI-BOS 0-6				TOR-CLE 7*1	
0420	TEX-SEA 1-3	BOS-SEA 5*2	CHI-BAL 2*1	MIL-MIN 0-10	CLE-CAL 2-7	NY-OAK 7-9	TOR-KC 2-8
0421	TEX-DET 4-5	BOS-SEA 0-5		MIL-MIN 10*8	CLE-CAL 6-7	NY-OAK 5*3	TOR-KC 5-6
0422		BOS-SEA 0-7	CHI-BAL 3*2	MIL-MIN 4-5	CLE-CAL 0-8	NY-OAK 5*1	TOR-KC 6*3
0423	CHI-TOR 5*4	NY-SEA 3-6	TEX-MIL 1-5	DET-MIN 12*4	BOS-CAL 1-4		BAL-KC 6-7
0424	CHI-TOR 4-10	NY-SEA 1*0	TEX-MIL 15*4	DET-MIN 17*1	BOS-CAL 5-8	CLE-OAK 10*3	BAL-KC 6*5
0425	CHI-TOR 0-1	NY-SEA 10*9	TEX-MIL 6*1	DET-MIN 16*5	BOS-CAL 1-2	CLE-OAK 6*0	BAL-KC 2-3
0426	TEX-TOR 6-8	CLE-SEA 3-6	MIN-MIL 3-10	BAL-CHI 0-7			DET-KC 5*3
0427	TEX-TOR 3-4	CLE-SEA 0-4	MIN-MIL 2-3	BAL-CHI 4-9	NY-CAL 5*0	BOS-OAK 2-7	DET-KC 3-4
0428	KC-TOR 5*3	CLE-SEA 0-4	DET-TEX 5-6	MIL-CHI 2-11	NY-CAL 2-3	BOS-OAK 3*1	MIN-BAL 4-8
0429	KC-TOR 0-8		DET-TEX 3*1	MIL-CHI 4-7			MIN-BAL 0-11
0430	CAL-BOS 1-6	MIN-DET 0-8	MIL-TEX 5*4	TOR-CHI 2-10	OAK-CLE 8*2	SEA-NY 0-3	KC-BAL 5-12
0501	CAL-BOS 1-3	MIN-DET 5*2	MIL-TEX 4*3	TOR-CHI 2-8	OAK-CLE 0-1	SEA-NY 2-6	KC-BAL 5*4
0502	CAL-BOS 3-4	MIN-DET 6*3	MIL-TEX 2-13	TOR-CHI 6*1	OAK-CLE 2-10	SEA-NY 2-3	KC-BAL 3-4
0503	SEA-BOS 2*0	BAL-MIN 3-4	MIL-TEX 2-9		CAL-CLE 4-5	OAK-NY 4*2	
0504	SEA-BOS 7*6	CHI-MIL 1-6	TOR-TEX 2-3	KC-DET 3-5	CAL-CLE 3-5	OAK-NY 2-4	
0505	OAK-BOS 1-3	CHI-MIL 3*1	TOR-TEX 1-7	KC-DET 4*3	SEA-CLE 2-3	CAL-NY 6*2	
0506	OAK-BOS 6*3	BAL-TOR 8-10			SEA-CLE 9*5	CAL-NY 3*1	BAL-MIN 3*0
0507	BOS-MIL 1*0	BAL-TOR 2-3	CLE-CHI 5-6	NY-DET 6-7	MIN-SEA 5*4	KC-CAL 2*1	
0508	BOS-MIL 3-6	BAL-TOR 6*3	CLE-CHI 7-10	NY-DET 10*8	MIN-SEA 2-7	KC-CAL 3-5	TEX-KC 4-9
0509	BOS-MIL 0-6	BAL-TOR 4*3	CLE-CHI 5-6	NY-DET 11*2	MIN-SEA 4-6	KC-CAL 4*2	
0510	BOS-BAL 1-2	TEX-OAK 7*4		NY-DET 1-2	CHI-SEA 13*2	MIN-CAL 13*3	TEX-KC 2*1
0511	BOS-BAL 4*0	TEX-OAK 0-6	DET-TOR 12*7	KC-CLE 7*6	CHI-SEA 3-4	MIN-CAL 3-5	MIL-NY 1-5
0512	BOS-BAL 2*0	TEX-OAK 7-8	DET-TOR 13*8	KC-CLE 2-6	CHI-SEA 6*5	MIN-CAL 5*2	MIL-NY 4*1
0513		TEX-OAK 9*5	DET-TOR 5-6	KC-CLE 7*3			MIL-NY 2-4
0514	BAL-DET 3-4	SEA-OAK 1-2	BOS-MIN 3-4	CHI-TEX 4*0	CLE-MIL 2-5	KC-CAL 2*1	TOR-NY 8*6
0515	BAL-DET 3-5	SEA-OAK 1-2	BOS-MIN 4-7	CHI-TEX 4-6	CLE-MIL 9*5	KC-CAL 3-5	TOR-NY 3-4
0516	BAL-DET 3*2	SEA-OAK 7*0	BOS-MIN 11*5	CHI-TEX 5-8	CLE-MIL 3-5	KC-CAL 4*2	TOR-NY 12*6
0517	CAL-CHI 11*4	CLE-BAL 2*0	NY-MIN 11*5	SEA-TEX 16*9	TOR-BOS 9*3		
0518	CAL-CHI 4-7	CLE-BAL 0-7	NY-MIN 5*3	SEA-TEX 2-3	DET-MIL 5*1	OAK-KC 1-6	
0519	CAL-CHI 2*0	CLE-BAL 3-6	NY-MIN 11*6	SEA-TEX 3-4	DET-MIL 8*6	OAK-KC 8-13	TOR-BOS 5-10
0520		CLE-BAL 3*1		SEA-TEX 7*4	DET-MIL 6*2	OAK-KC 4*1	TOR-BOS 4*3
0521	OAK-CHI 12*11	MIL-BAL 9*3	DET-CLE 5-10	CAL-TEX 4-6	MIN-TOR 2-11	SEA-KC 1-2	NY-BOS 2-7
0522	OAK-CHI 6*4	MIL-BAL 4-5	DET-CLE 5*1	CAL-TEX 2-4	MIN-TOR 0-7	SEA-KC 1-4	NY-BOS 7*3
0523	OAK-CHI 4-5	MIL-BAL 9*1	DET-CLE 4*2	CAL-TEX 6*2	MIN-TOR 1-2	SEA-KC 10*7	NY-BOS 2-5
0524	BAL-NY 8*6	BOS-DET 6*5	TEX-CLE 1*0	CAL-SEA 1-4	MIL-TOR 1-4		
0525	BAL-NY 0-1	BOS-DET 1-4	TEX-CLE 5*1	CAL-SEA 6*3	MIL-TOR 2-4	KC-CHI 3*2	MIN-OAK 1-3
0526	BAL-NY 6*2	BOS-DET 2-4	TEX-CLE 6-7	CAL-SEA 0-2	MIL-TOR 8*1	KC-CHI 4*3	MIN-OAK 12*11
0527	BAL-NY 4*3			CAL-SEA 5*0	MIL-TOR 9*3	KC-CHI 6*4	
0528	CHI-NY 0-4	BAL-CAL 4-8	CLE-MIN 6-7	DET-SEA 3-4	KC-MIL 1-5	TEX-BOS 1-4	TOR-OAK 2-3
0529	CHI-NY 2-8	BAL-CAL 3-6	CLE-MIN 3-9	DET-SEA 3*2	KC-MIL 6*5	TEX-BOS 1-15	TOR-OAK 5*4
0530	CHI-NY 3-6	BAL-CAL 5-7	CLE-MIN 2-8	DET-SEA 5-9	KC-MIL 2-8	TEX-BOS 5-6	TOR-OAK 13*11
0531	CLE-NY 2-8	TOR-CAL 1*0	TEX-MIN 1*0			KC-BOS 5*3	BAL-OAK 3*1
0601	CLE-NY 15*6	TOR-CAL 8*0	TEX-MIN 5-7	MIL-SEA 10*0	CHI-DET 4*2	KC-BOS 5-3	BAL-OAK 3-4
0602	CLE-NY 5-8	TOR-CAL 7*6	TEX-MIN 3-6	MIL-SEA 3-6	CHI-DET 10*1	KC-BOS 7*2	BAL-OAK 5*2
0603	MIL-KC				CHI-DET 3-5		
0604	MIL-KC 2-3	BOS-CHI 1*0	MIN-CLE 3*2	NY-TEX 3-5	CAL-DET 6*3	OAK-TOR 3-4	SEA-BAL 5-6

◆1993◆	GAME 1	GAME 2	GAME 3	GAME 4	GAME 5	GAME 6	GAME 7
0605	MIL-KC 8*2	BOS-CHI 3-11	MIN-CLE 6-7	NY-TEX 9*6	CAL-DET 1-5	OAK-TOR 5-9	SEA-BAL 3-5
0606	MIL-KC 7-8	BOS-CHI 3-4	MIN-CLE 5*4	NY-TEX 3-4	CAL-DET 4-11	OAK-TOR 10*3	SEA-BAL 2-5
0607	NY-KC 3-8	DET-CHI 3-7	SEA-MIL 3-5	MIN-TEX 2-8		CAL-TOR 2-4	OAK-BAL 2-3
0608	NY-KC 9*4	DET-CHI 6*4	SEA-MIL 1-2	MIN-TEX 3*2	BOS-CLE 4-5	CAL-TOR 6-14	OAK-BAL 4-6
0609	NY-KC 3-10	DET-CHI 7*4	SEA-MIL 6*1		BOS-CLE 2-3	CAL-TOR 6*4	OAK-BAL 4-7
0610	BAL-BOS 2-5	TOR-DET 3-5	NY-MIL 3*1	MIN-TEX 6*5			SEA-CAL 2-8
0611	BAL-BOS 16*4	TOR-DET 1-6	NY-MIL 5*4	CLE-TEX 8*3	CHI-KC 6*1	OAK-MIN 8-11	SEA-CAL 2*0
0612	BAL-BOS 5*1	TOR-DET 1-12	NY-MIL 1-9	CLE-TEX 10*9	CHI-KC 2*1	OAK-MIN 2-7	SEA-CAL 12*7
0613	BAL-BOS 2-4	TOR-DET 13*4	NY-MIL 9*5	CLE-TEX 1-5	CHI-KC 4-5	OAK-MIN 7*6	TEX-CAL 2-8
0614	BOS-NY 0-4	CLE-DET 3-7	BAL-MIL 8*5	CHI-OAK 3-7	KC-SEA 3-6	TOR-MIN 3-4	TEX-CAL 6*5
0615	BOS-NY 7-9	CLE-DET 4-10	BAL-MIL 4*2	CHI-OAK 4*0	KC-SEA 1-6	TOR-MIN 6*3	TEX-CAL 2-5
0616	BOS-NY 7*1	CLE-DET 8*2	BAL-MIL 2-7	CHI-OAK 4*0	KC-SEA 5*1	TOR-MIN 4*0	TEX-CAL 18*2
0617	MIN-NY 5-6	CLE-DET 5-9	BOS-TOR 0-7	CHI-OAK 2-5			CHI-CAL 8-9
0618	MIN-NY 0-5	MIL-DET 6*3	BOS-TOR 2-11	KC-OAK 9-10	TEX-SEA 2-3	BAL-CLE 4*1	CHI-CAL 4-5
0619	MIN-NY 4-8	MIL-DET 7-10	BOS-TOR 4-9	KC-OAK 3*0	TEX-SEA 5-6	BAL-CLE 0-3	CHI-CAL 11*6
0620	MIN-NY 0-8	MIL-DET 3-7	BOS-TOR 2-3	KC-OAK 1-4	TEX-SEA 2-13	BAL-CLE 6*3	
0621	CAL-KC 4*3	MIN-BOS 3-6	TEX-CHI 6-7		OAK-SEA 5*3	MIL-CLE 0-3	
0622	CAL-KC 3-5	MIN-BOS 1-4	TEX-CHI 2-3	DET-BAL 9-12	OAK-SEA 10*3	MIL-CLE 2-3	NY-TOR 4-5
0623	CAL-KC 8*7	MIN-BOS 1-3	TEX-CHI 4-7	DET-BAL 2-6	OAK-SEA 7-8	MIL-CLE 1-3	NY-TOR 4*3
0624	CAL-KC 1-7			DET-BAL 2-6	OAK-SEA 3*2	MIL-CLE 5*3	NY-TOR 2-7
0625	CAL-MIN 5-8	DET-BOS 2-8	SEA-CHI 3*2	NY-BAL 6-7	TOR-MIL 5-6	KC-CLE 1-6	
0626	CAL-MIN 4*0	DET-BOS 4-13	SEA-CHI 4-7	NY-BAL 10-12	TOR-MIL 3*2	KC-CLE 4-7	OAK-TEX 7-10
0627	CAL-MIN 0-2	DET-BOS 2-8	SEA-CHI 4-6	NY-BAL 9*5	TOR-MIL 5*4	KC-CLE 2-3	OAK-TEX 0-4
0628	SEA-MIN 4*1	MIL-BOS 3-4	DET-NY 2-8	TOR-BAL 7*2		CHI-CLE 0-2	KC-TEX 4*2
0629	SEA-MIN 5-7	MIL-BOS 7*6	DET-NY 3-4	TOR-BAL 2*1	CAL-OAK 7-8	CHI-CLE 2-8	KC-TEX 3-4
0630	SEA-MIN 5*3	MIL-BOS 2-12	DET-NY 0-7	TOR-BAL 0-6	CAL-OAK 4-5	CHI-CLE 4-5	KC-TEX 4-5
0701	SEA-MIN 6*1	BAL-CHI 1*0	TEX-DET 8*5	BOS-SEA 9*8	CAL-OAK 3-6		
0702	MIL-MIN 10-11	BAL-CHI 1-12	TEX-DET 4-6	BOS-SEA 6*5	NY-OAK 3-4	CLE-CAL 10*8	TOR-KC 2-3
0703	MIL-MIN 3*1	BAL-CHI 9*6	TEX-DET 11*5	BOS-SEA 6*0	NY-OAK 4-5	CLE-CAL 5*3	TOR-KC 2-3
0704	MIL-MIN 3-4	BAL-CHI 1-3	TEX-DET 8*6	BOS-SEA 6*0	NY-OAK 6-7	CLE-CAL 6-7	TOR-KC 1-3
0705	DET-MIN 3-13	CHI-TOR 4*3	TEX-MIL 5*4	NY-SEA 6*3	CLE-OAK 5-6	BOS-CAL 4*3	BAL-KC 1-7
					CLE-OAK 6*2		
0706	DET-MIN 4*1	CHI-TOR 1-5	TEX-MIL 11*1	NY-SEA 4-12	CLE-OAK 11*8	BOS-CAL 2-3	BAL-KC 8*0
0707	DET-MIN 8*4	CHI-TOR 5*2	TEX-MIL 6-7	NY-SEA 5-6	CLE-OAK 0-3	BOS-CAL 6-7	BAL-KC 8*3
0708	CHI-BAL 12*5	TEX-TOR 6*1	MIN-MIL 3-15		BOS-OAK 11*9	NY-CAL 3-4	DET-KC 5-6
0709	CHI-BAL 6-15	TEX-TOR 4*2	MIN-MIL 10*6	CLE-SEA 4-6	BOS-OAK 2-4	NY-CAL 3*2	DET-KC 10*5
0710	CHI-BAL 0-6	TEX-TOR 10*7	MIN-MIL 4-5	CLE-SEA 6-7	BOS-OAK 5*0	NY-CAL 2-4	DET-KC 9*8
0711	CHI-BAL 11*5	TEX-TOR 11*6	MIN-MIL 4-5	CLE-SEA 4-5	BOS-OAK 3*2	NY-CAL 2-3	DET-KC 2-6
0715	MIN-BAL 3-5	KC-TOR 2-7	CHI-MIL 6*4	CAL-CLE 3-7	DET-TEX 7-12	OAK-NY 8*3	SEA-BOS 3*2
0716	MIN-BAL 7-9	KC-TOR 7*3	CHI-MIL 4*3	CAL-CLE 2*1	DET-TEX 6-9	OAK-NY 3-10	SEA-BOS 3-5
0717	MIN-BAL 4*2	KC-TOR 5*4	CHI-MIL 9*4	CAL-CLE 0-3	DET-TEX 6*4	OAK-NY 5-9	SEA-BOS 3-4
0718	MIN-BAL 2-7	KC-TOR 3-4	CHI-MIL 3*1	CAL-CLE 1-2	DET-TEX 2*0	OAK-NY 6-13	SEA-BOS 6-7
0719	KC-BAL 5-6	MIN-DET 4*2	TOR-CHI 15*7	OAK-CLE 2-4	MIL-TEX 3-5	SEA-NY 2-8	CAL-BOS 6-8
0720	KC-BAL 0-7	MIN-DET 4*3	TOR-CHI 1-2	OAK-CLE 5-9	MIL-TEX 1-5	SEA-NY 9*5	CAL-BOS 1-2
0721	KC-BAL 8*6	MIN-DET 7*2	TOR-CHI 4*1	OAK-CLE 7*2		SEA-NY 10*3	CAL-BOS 1-4
0722	BAL-MIN 4-8	KC-DET 12*6	MIL-CHI 2-7	SEA-CLE 3*2	TOR-TEX 8*7	CAL-NY 1-12	OAK-BOS 7-9
0723	BAL-MIN 5*1	KC-DET 7*6	MIL-CHI 3*2	SEA-CLE 4-9	TOR-TEX 5-6	CAL-NY 2-5	OAK-BOS 5-6
0724	BAL-MIN 9*2	KC-DET 6*3	MIL-CHI 5-6	SEA-CLE 6*5	TOR-TEX 5*1	CAL-NY 3-5	OAK-BOS 3-5
0725	BAL-MIN 2-5	KC-DET 0-3	MIL-CHI 7*3	SEA-CLE 9-11	TOR-TEX 9*7	CAL-NY 8-9	OAK-BOS 1-8
0726	BOS-MIL 2-3	NY-DET 2-5	CLE-CHI 3-4	OAK-CAL 11*4	TEX-KC 3-12		
					TEX-KC 5-6		
0727	BOS-MIL 2-3	NY-DET 5*2	CLE-CHI 4-7	OAK-CAL 8-15	TEX-KC 1*0	BAL-TOR 5-6	MIN-SEA 8-10
0728	BOS-MIL 8*4	NY-DET 12*7	CLE-CHI 4-9	OAK-CAL 2-3	TEX-KC 10*3	BAL-TOR 4-5	MIN-SEA 5*1
0729	BOS-MIL 7*3			OAK-CAL 2*1	TEX-KC 4-9	DET-TOR 4-7	MIN-SEA 3-4
0730	BOS-BAL 8*7	MIL-NY 4-8	TEX-OAK 1-4	MIN-CAL 2-4	CLE-KC 0-3	DET-TOR 8*5	CHI-SEA 6*4
0731	BOS-BAL 0-4	MIL-NY 4-5	TEX-OAK 8*2	MIN-CAL 3-4	CLE-KC 6*4	DET-TOR 1-3	CHI-SEA 13*10
0801	BOS-BAL 2*1	MIL-NY 9*2	TEX-OAK 5-9	MIN-CAL 9*2	CLE-KC 9*5	DET-TOR 1-2	CHI-SEA 4*0
0802	MIL-BAL 5-7	TOR-NY 4*0	CHI-TEX 8-9			DET-CLE 4-9	SEA-OAK 5*4
0803	MIL-BAL 8-13	TOR-NY 8*6	CHI-TEX 11*6	KC-CAL 2-3	BOS-MIN 5*4	DET-CLE 8*3	SEA-OAK 4-5
0804	MIL-BAL 6-8	TOR-NY 2-6	CHI-TEX 2-5	KC-CAL 3*2	BOS-MIN 5*4	DET-CLE 4-8	SEA-OAK 3*2
0805	MIL-BAL 1-3	TOR-NY 4-5	CHI-TEX 1-7	KC-CAL 4-5	BOS-MIN 2*1		OAK-KC 5*2
0806	CLE-BAL 1-8	BOS-DET 1-5	SEA-TEX 3-5	CAL-CHI 7*3	NY-MIN 3-4	MIL-TOR 10-11	OAK-KC 2-5
0807	CLE-BAL 6-8	BOS-DET 4*1	SEA-TEX 2*1	CAL-CHI 4-6	NY-MIN 5-6	MIL-TOR 7*1	OAK-KC 3-4
0808	CLE-BAL 6-7	BOS-DET 1-5	SEA-TEX 1-7	CAL-CHI 2*1	NY-MIN 8*6	MIL-TOR 5*2	SEA-KC 6-7
0809		BAL-DET 4*1		OAK-CHI 4-5			SEA-KC 1-4
0810	CLE-MIL 4-5	BAL-DET 1-15	CAL-TEX 3-6	OAK-CHI 0-4	NY-BOS 0-5	MIN-TOR 3-6	SEA-KC 4*3
0811	CLE-MIL 7*5	BAL-DET 5-15	CAL-TEX 4*1	OAK-CHI 3*1	NY-BOS 8*3	MIN-TOR 2-4	
0812	CLE-MIL 8*6	BAL-DET 11-17	CAL-TEX 2-4	KC-CHI 4*2	NY-BOS 4*1	MIN-TOR 9*2	
0813	DET-MIL 1-6	BAL-NY 1-4	CAL-SEA 1-2	KC-CHI 4-5	TOR-BOS 3-5	MIN-OAK 5*2	TEX-CLE 3-6
	DET-MIL 1-7						
0814	DET-MIL 5*1	BAL-NY 2-4	CAL-SEA 2-7	KC-CHI 1-4	TOR-BOS 5*2	MIN-OAK 5*1	TEX-CLE 5-8
						MIN-OAK 6*2	
0815	DET-MIL 4-6	BAL-NY 0-1	CAL-SEA 14*2	KC-CHI 7*5	TOR-BOS 9*1	MIN-OAK 12*5	TEX-CLE 4*1
0816	DET-CAL 7*2		BAL-SEA 6-8			MIL-OAK 1-4	TOR-CLE 4*1
0817	DET-CAL 9*3	TEX-NY 4-11	BAL-SEA 3-5	KC-MIN 3*2	CHI-BOS 3*2	MIL-OAK 3-6	TOR-CLE 6*4
		TEX-NY 3*2					
0818	DET-CAL 8*6	TEX-NY 4*2	BAL-SEA 8*1	KC-MIN 5*2	CHI-BOS 0-5	MIL-OAK 1-2	TOR-CLE 7*6
0819	MIL-CAL 4-5			KC-MIN 4*2	CLE-BOS 5*1		
0820	MIL-CAL 7*2	KC-NY 2-7	OAK-DET 7*6	CHI-MIN 4*2	CLE-BOS 7*6	SEA-TOR 4*1	TEX-BAL 5-10
0821	MIL-CAL 6-7	KC-NY 2-3	OAK-DET 3-4	CHI-MIN 9*4	CLE-BOS 10*5	SEA-TOR 5*2	TEX-BAL 5-6
0822	MIL-CAL 7*5	KC-NY 7*0	OAK-DET 3-5	CHI-MIN 1*0	CLE-BOS 3*2	SEA-TOR 7-12	TEX-BAL 11*4
0823	MIN-KC 3*2	NY-CHI 6*5	OAK-DET 0-9			CLE-TOR 9*8	TEX-BAL 13*6
0824	MIN-KC 3-5	NY-CHI 2-4	SEA-DET 1-4	BOS-TEX 3-4	OAK-MIL 2-9	CLE-TOR 6-8	CAL-BAL 0-1
					OAK-MIL 6-7		
0825	MIN-KC 4*2	NY-CHI 7*5	SEA-DET 4-7	BOS-TEX 2-10	OAK-MIL 2-12	CLE-TOR 7-10	CAL-BAL 2*1
0826	MIN-KC 0-3	NY-CLE 4*0	TOR-SEA 3-6	BOS-TEX 3*1	OAK-MIL 3-5		CAL-BAL 4-9
0827	BOS-KC 5*0	NY-CLE 2-9	TOR-SEA 6-7	BAL-TEX 4-5	CAL-MIL 6-7	DET-OAK 13*4	MIN-CHI 3-7
					CAL-MIL 3-4		MIN-CHI 7*2
0828	BOS-KC 2*1	NY-CLE 4-8	TOR-SEA 1-2	BAL-TEX 1-11	CAL-MIL 6*2	DET-OAK 5*3	MIN-CHI 1-4
0829	BOS-KC 4-5	NY-CLE 14*8	TOR-SEA 6*2	BAL-TEX 6*3	CAL-MIL 6*1	DET-OAK 3-7	MIN-CHI 5-13
0830	TEX-BOS 3-7		DET-SEA 13*2		KC-MIL 1-2	TOR-OAK 4*2	MIN-CHI 1-4
0831	TEX-BOS 8*1	BAL-CAL 8*2	DET-SEA 4-5	CHI-NY 11*3	KC-MIL 6*5	TOR-OAK 3*2	CLE-MIN 6-15
0901	TEX-BOS 9*7	BAL-CAL 5*1	DET-SEA 3-9	CHI-NY 5*3	KC-MIL 1-7	TOR-OAK 8*3	CLE-MIN 12*7
0902		BAL-CAL 4*3	MIL-SEA 1-8	CHI-NY 1-7			CLE-MIN 4*3
0903	KC-BOS 5*1	TOR-CAL 7*4	MIL-SEA 7*4	CLE-NY 7*3	CHI-DET 8*6	BAL-OAK 5*4	TEX-MIN 5-9
0904	KC-BOS 4*2	TOR-CAL 2-4	MIL-SEA 1-6	CLE-NY 0-4	CHI-DET 11*2	BAL-OAK 6*3	TEX-MIN 6*4
0905	KC-BOS 5*2	TOR-CAL 1-5	MIL-SEA 2-3	CLE-NY 2-7	CHI-DET 5*3	BAL-OAK 9*2	TEX-MIN 3-8
0906	BOS-CHI 3*2	MIL-KC 3*2	NY-TEX 5-8	SEA-BAL 1-5			
0907	BOS-CHI 4*3	MIN-CLE 6*0	NY-TEX 4-5	SEA-BAL 3*2	CAL-DET 6-10	OAK-TOR 11*7	
0908	BOS-CHI 1-8	MIN-CLE 8-15	NY-TEX 1-4	SEA-BAL 3-6	CAL-DET 2-4	OAK-TOR 2*1	MIL-KC 2*1
0909		MIN-CLE 5*3			CAL-DET 6*0	OAK-TOR 7*4	
0910	DET-CHI 4*0	BOS-CLE 4-7	MIN-TEX 3-4	OAK-BAL 12*9	SEA-MIL 10*3	CAL-TOR 4-10	NY-KC 5-6
		BOS-CLE 5*4	MIN-TEX 2-3				
0911	DET-CHI 1-3	BOS-CLE 3-9	MIN-TEX 4-7	OAK-BAL 1-3	SEA-MIL 7*3	CAL-TOR 5-9	NY-KC 12*5
0912	DET-CHI 6*3	BOS-CLE 11*1	MIN-TEX 1-12	OAK-BAL 5-14	SEA-MIL 1-4	CAL-TOR 1-4	NY-KC 2-10
0913	BAL-BOS 4-6	OAK-MIN 7*2	CLE-TEX 1-12	SEA-CAL 10*1	NY-MIL 3*1		CHI-KC 0-9
0914	BAL-BOS 11*3	OAK-MIN 8*3	CLE-TEX 2*0	SEA-CAL 2-9	NY-MIL 12*5	TOR-DET 9*5	CHI-KC 8*3

♦1993♦

Date	GAME 1	GAME 2	GAME 3	GAME 4	GAME 5	GAME 6	GAME 7
0915	BAL-BOS 5-6	OAK-MIN 15*2	CLE-TEX 4-7	SEA-CAL 1-15	NY-MIL 5-15	TOR-DET 14*8	CHI-KC 10*6
0916	BOS-NY 6*4	OAK-MIN 4-5	KC-SEA 1-14				
0917	BOS-NY 4-5	TOR-MIN 4*2	KC-SEA 6*3	TEX-CAL 1-2	BAL-MIL 0-2	CLE-DET 3*1	CHI-OAK 8*0
0918	BOS-NY 3-4	TOR-MIN 5*1	KC-SEA 1*0	TEX-CAL 9*2	BAL-MIL 0-3	CLE-DET 6-7	CHI-OAK 2-3
0919	BOS-NY 8*3	TOR-MIN 10*0	KC-SEA 1-4	TEX-CAL 8-9	BAL-MIL 8*4	CLE-DET 12*2	CHI-OAK 3*1
0920	BAL-CLE 4-6		TEX-SEA 2*1	CHI-CAL 10*2		MIL-DET 3*1	KC-OAK 1-2
0921	BAL-CLE 7*6	BOS-TOR 0-5	TEX-SEA 0-8	CHI-CAL 0-8	MIN-NY 5*4	MIL-DET 7*4	KC-OAK 6-9
0922	BAL-CLE 2-4	BOS-TOR 7*5	TEX-SEA 4-7	CHI-CAL 1*0	MIN-NY 5*2	MIL-DET 4-8	KC-OAK 3*2
0923		BOS-TOR 1-5		CHI-CAL 7*1			KC-OAK 1-2
0924	MIL-CLE 11*8	NY-TOR 3-7	OAK-SEA 5*3	CAL-KC 2-7	DET-BAL 2*0	MIN-BOS 4-7	TEX-CHI 4-5
0925	MIL-CLE 2-6	NY-TOR 1-3	OAK-SEA 7*2	CAL-KC 6*2		MIN-BOS 9*7	
0926	MIL-CLE 4-6	NY-TOR 7*3	OAK-SEA 3*2	CAL-KC 8-9	DET-BAL 9*4	MIN-BOS 5*2	TEX-CHI 3-5
					DET-BAL 6*5		TEX-CHI 3*2
0927	CAL-MIN 3-11	TOR-MIL 2*0		CLE-KC 5-6	NY-BAL 9*1		SEA-CHI 2-4
0928	CAL-MIN 1-2	TOR-MIL 6*4	OAK-TEX 0-2	CLE-KC 3*2	NY-BAL 1-9	DET-BOS 6-11	SEA-CHI 5*2
			OAK-TEX 10*3			DET-BOS 7*6	
0929	CAL-MIN 2-3	TOR-MIL 9*6	OAK-TEX 6-11	CLE-KC 2-3	NY-BAL 8*3	DET-BOS 8*7	SEA-CHI 2-3
0930	CAL-MIN 3-4		OAK-TEX 2-6		TOR-BAL 6*2	DET-BOS 7*4	SEA-CHI 2*1
1001	SEA-MIN 8*2	CAL-OAK 2-7	KC-TEX 0-2	CHI-CLE 4*2	TOR-BAL 2-7	MIL-BOS 8*4	DET-NY 6-9
1002	SEA-MIN 7*3	CAL-OAK 6*2	KC-TEX 7*4	CHI-CLE 4*2	TOR-BAL 4-8	MIL-BOS 8*5	DET-NY 4*1
1003	SEA-MIN 2-7	CAL-OAK 7*3	KC-TEX 4*1	CHI-CLE 4*0	TOR-BAL 11*6	MIL-BOS 6*3	DET-NY 1-2

♦1994♦

Date	GAME 1	GAME 2	GAME 3	GAME 4	GAME 5	GAME 6	GAME 7
0404	CHI-TOR 3-7	DET-BOS 8-9	KC-BAL 3-6	SEA-CLE 3-4	TEX-NY 3-5		
0405	CHI-TOR 3-5	CAL-MIN 8*2	OAK-MIL 7-11				
0406	CHI-TOR 9*2	CAL-MIN 4*1	DET-BOS 4-5	KC-BAL 2-4			
0407	OAK-MIL 2-12	CAL-MIN 4-7	DET-BOS 6-9	SEA-CLE 2-6	TEX-NY 6-18		
0408	CAL-MIL 1-5	OAK-MIN 10*9	BOS-CHI 8*6	CLE-KC 8*3	DET-NY 0-4	SEA-TOR 2-8	TEX-BAL 7*5
0409	CAL-MIL 6*4	OAK-MIN 14*0	BOS-CHI 5-6		DET-NY 5*2	SEA-TOR 6-8	TEX-BAL 5-7
0410	CAL-MIL 4*1	OAK-MIN 15*5	BOS-CHI 0-8	CLE-KC 1-6	DET-NY 8*3	SEA-TOR 6-12	TEX-BAL 8*7
0411	BAL-DET 7*4	CLE-CAL 9*6	MIL-TEX 4*3	BOS-KC 8*5	MIN-SEA 8-9	TOR-OAK 14*5	
0412	NY-CHI 5-10	CLE-CAL 5*4		BOS-KC 22*11	MIN-SEA 0-12	TOR-OAK 4-8	
0413	NY-CHI 0-5	CLE-CAL 6*5	MIL-TEX 3-4	BOS-KC 1-2	MIN-SEA 9*6	TOR-OAK 7-8	BAL-DET 3-6
0414	NY-CHI 10*3	TOR-CAL 4-6	MIL-TEX 7*2			MIN-OAK 5*4	BAL-DET 3*1
0415	CHI-BOS 3-5	TOR-CAL 13-14	BAL-TEX 3-8	KC-CLE 2*1	MIL-SEA 1-9	MIN-OAK 8*7	NY-DET 7*5
0416		TOR-CAL 5*4	BAL-TEX 6*4	KC-CLE 12*9	MIL-SEA 1*0	MIN-OAK 3-8	NY-DET 4-5
0417	CHI-BOS 7*4	TOR-CAL 5*4	BAL-TEX 6*5	KC-CLE 8*3	MIL-SEA 3-8	MIN-OAK 1-5	NY-DET 8*6
0418	CHI-BOS 12*1						KC-DET 11*1
0419	OAK-BOS 5-13	CAL-BAL 3-4	CHI-MIL 6*2	CLE-MIN 7*6	SEA-NY 7*1	TEX-TOR 3-13	KC-DET 5-9
0420	OAK-BOS 0-2	CAL-BAL 8*2	CHI-MIL 8*6	CLE-MIN 5-6	SEA-NY 4-7	TEX-TOR 3-4	KC-DET 11*6
0421	OAK-BOS 5-6	CAL-BAL 11*8	CHI-MIL 4-6	CLE-MIN 10*6	SEA-NY 2-4		
0422	CAL-BOS 5-6	SEA-BAL 4-6	KC-MIL 8-9	CLE-TEX 3-7	OAK-NY 6-8	MIN-TOR 2-8	DET-CHI 2-7
0423	CAL-BOS 3-5	SEA-BAL 3-4	KC-MIL 2-3	CLE-TEX 10*9	OAK-NY 6-8	MIN-TOR 6-8	DET-CHI 3-9
0424	CAL-BOS 4-5	SEA-BAL 7*6	KC-MIL 0-7	CLE-TEX 12*7	OAK-NY 2-6	MIN-TOR 7*3	DET-CHI 7*6
0425	BOS-SEA 2-4	OAK-BAL 6-8	MIN-CLE 9*7	TOR-KC 3-4	CAL-NY 1-11		MIL-CHI 13*4
0426	BOS-SEA 3-4	OAK-BAL 4-10	MIN-CLE 3-11	TOR-KC 8*6	CAL-NY 6*3	DET-TEX 1-6	MIL-CHI 0-3
0427	NY-SEA 12*2	BAL-CAL 13*1	CHI-CLE 7-8	BOS-OAK 1*0	MIL-MIN 4*1	TOR-TEX 3-11	
0428	NY-SEA 0-6	BAL-CAL 4*2	CHI-CLE 5*3	BOS-OAK 4*1	MIL-MIN 12*2	TOR-TEX 0-1	DET-KC 4-13
0429	BAL-SEA 4-5	BOS-CAL 6*4	TEX-CLE 4-5	NY-OAK 10*6	TOR-MIN 12*7	CHI-DET 3-4	MIL-KC 4*3
0430	BAL-SEA 6*4	BOS-CAL 4*1	TEX-CLE 14*6	NY-OAK 7*5	TOR-MIN 9-11		MIL-KC 2-6
0501	BAL-SEA 0-6	BOS-CAL 10*1	TEX-CLE 5*4	NY-OAK 1-8	TOR-MIN 3-7	CHI-DET 5-8	MIL-KC 3-7
0502						TEX-DET 8-10	
0503	CLE-CHI 1-12	NY-CAL 6*5	KC-TOR 0-1	BAL-OAK 9*1	MIN-MIL 6-7	TEX-DET 7*2	SEA-BOS 6-7
0504	CLE-CHI 1-6	NY-CAL 6-7	KC-TOR 6*4	BAL-OAK 4*3	MIN-MIL 8*7	TEX-DET 7-14	SEA-BOS 2-4
0505			OAK-CAL 3-4	KC-TOR 11*9			
0506	KC-CHI 6*5	OAK-CAL 6-11	MIL-TOR 7*1	BOS-NY 1-3	CLE-BAL 4*2	SEA-DET 4-9	MIN-TEX 0-7
0507	KC-CHI 2-4	OAK-CAL 7*4	MIL-TOR 2-3	BOS-NY 5-6		SEA-DET 4-10	MIN-TEX 9*7
0508	KC-CHI 9*7	OAK-CAL 0-7	MIL-TOR 1-3	BOS-NY 4-8	CLE-BAL 6-8	SEA-DET 4*3	MIN-TEX 5*2
0509	SEA-CHI 3*2	MIL-BOS 7*4	MIN-KC 9*5	CLE-NY 3-4	TOR-BAL 1-4		CAL-TEX 3-11
0510	SEA-CHI 2-16	MIL-BOS 9*5	MIN-KC 7*4	CLE-NY 3-5	TOR-BAL 3-6	OAK-DET 2-10	CAL-TEX 8*6
0511	SEA-CHI 6-14	MIL-BOS 1-7	MIN-KC 0-9	CLE-NY 3-6	TOR-BAL 1-4	OAK-DET 2-6	CAL-TEX 13*1
0512		MIL-BOS 1-3		CLE-NY 6-7		OAK-DET 5-6	
0513	BAL-MIN 1-4	TOR-BOS 3-5	OAK-KC 6-16	CAL-SEA 11*1	DET-CLE 0-2	NY-MIL 10*4	CHI-TEX 7-11
0514	BAL-MIN 5-8	TOR-BOS 2-11	OAK-KC 5*4	CAL-SEA 7-10	DET-CLE 3-9	NY-MIL 6*2	CHI-TEX 2-5
0515	BAL-MIN 2-5		OAK-KC 6*2	CAL-SEA 5-9	DET-CLE 6-11	NY-MIL 12*1	CHI-TEX 9*6
0516	CHI-CAL 8*5	DET-TOR 2-7	TEX-SEA 11*7	KC-SEA 6*4			
0517	CHI-CAL 10*2	DET-TOR 13*6	TEX-OAK 8*7	KC-SEA 4*0	MIL-CLE 3-7	BOS-BAL 2-3	NY-MIN 4-5
0518	CHI-CAL 2-3	DET-TOR 3-9	TEX-OAK 6*2	KC-SEA 7*6	MIL-CLE 3-5	BOS-BAL 5*2	NY-MIN 5-13
			TEX-SEA 4-5		MIL-CLE 2-4	BOS-BAL 3*2	
0519	KC-CAL 4-5						
0520	KC-CAL 6-7	CLE-TOR 0-2	CHI-OAK 13*6	TEX-SEA 2-19	BAL-NY 1-5	MIL-DET 4-10	BOS-MIN 2-21
0521	KC-CAL 0-3	CLE-TOR 7-9	CHI-OAK 6*5	TEX-SEA 2-13	BAL-NY 4-5	MIL-DET 6-7	BOS-MIN 0-1
0522	KC-CAL 4*0	CLE-TOR 8*0	CHI-OAK 5*2	TEX-SEA 2-8	BAL-NY 6*5	MIL-DET 6-9	BOS-MIN 9*2
0523	BAL-MIL 5*3	CLE-TOR 5-6	SEA-OAK 5-7				
0524	BAL-MIL 13*5	CLE-BOS 5*3	SEA-OAK 1-10	MIN-CHI 3-5	TOR-NY 1-6	CAL-DET 8*5	TEX-KC 2*0
0525	BAL-MIL 6*3		SEA-OAK 1*0	MIN-CHI 1-12	TOR-NY 2-5	CAL-DET 7-9	TEX-KC 3-8
0526		CLE-BOS 5-13				CAL-DET 7*5	TEX-KC 1-3
0527	SEA-MIL 2-5	BOS-TEX 3-4	CAL-TOR 6*2	BAL-CHI 0-3	DET-MIN 2-5	OAK-CLE 2-3	NY-KC 5*2
0528	SEA-MIL 5-7	BOS-TEX 3*2	CAL-TOR 4-9	BAL-CHI 2-6	DET-MIN 9-10	OAK-CLE 2-4	NY-KC 5*3
0529	SEA-MIL 8-9	BOS-TEX 6-8	CAL-TOR 0-5	BAL-CHI 8*4	DET-MIN 5*1	OAK-CLE 5-7	NY-KC 6-10
0530	TEX-MIL 5*4	CHI-NY 7*2	OAK-TOR 6*2	DET-BAL 5*3	SEA-MIN 12*0	CAL-CLE 2-10	KC-BOS 5-6
0531	TEX-MIL 7*4	CHI-NY 1-10	OAK-TOR 7*2	DET-BAL 7*6	SEA-MIN 2-6		KC-BOS 9*7
0601	TEX-MIL 1-8	CHI-NY 5*4	OAK-TOR 9*5	DET-BAL 11*3	SEA-MIN 1-2	CAL-CLE 2-3	KC-BOS 2-4
0602				DET-BAL 5-11			
0603	CLE-OAK 9*5	KC-NY 7*4	MIL-CAL 4*3	CHI-BAL 4*2	MIN-DET 8-9	TOR-SEA 9*6	TEX-BOS 13*2
0604	CLE-OAK 8*2	KC-NY 4*3	MIL-CAL 7*6	CHI-BAL 7*1	MIN-DET 21*7	TOR-SEA 0-2	TEX-BOS 10*4
0605	CLE-OAK 8*1	KC-NY 3*1	MIL-CAL 1-3	CHI-BAL 5-8	MIN-DET 3-5	TOR-SEA 5*4	TEX-BOS 10*7
0606	MIL-OAK 9*6	BAL-KC 4*2	MIN-CAL 8*2	NY-TEX 17*7	BOS-DET 5-11	CLE-SEA 4-5	
0607	MIL-OAK 5-6	BAL-KC 3-7	MIN-CAL 8*6	NY-TEX 9-10	BOS-DET 5*1	CLE-SEA 5-9	TOR-CHI 9*5
0608	MIL-OAK 6*1	BAL-KC 6*4	MIN-CAL 4-5	NY-TEX 5-6	BOS-DET 5-14	CLE-SEA 5*3	TOR-CHI 2-3
0609	CHI-MIN 4-8	CLE-MIL 3-4	DET-CAL 7*4	KC-TEX 4-7	NY-TOR 5-7		
0610	CHI-MIN 6-8	CLE-MIL 6-7	DET-CAL 8*4	KC-TEX 2-3	NY-TOR 2-7	OAK-SEA 4*3	BAL-BOS 10*7
0611	CHI-MIN 0-6	CLE-MIL 1*0	DET-CAL 11*5	KC-TEX 4*3	NY-TOR 9*2	OAK-SEA 3-6	BAL-BOS 5*2
0612	CHI-MIN 2-6	CLE-MIL 12*6	DET-CAL 6-8	KC-TEX 7*2	NY-TOR 1-3	OAK-SEA 11*2	BAL-BOS 8*4
0613	CAL-KC 7-12	NY-BAL 3*1	OAK-CHI 0-1	SEA-TEX 9-17	TOR-CLE 3-7		MIN-BOS 5*2
0614	CAL-KC 1*0	NY-BAL 4*3	OAK-CHI 5*2	SEA-TEX 7*6	TOR-CLE 5-7	DET-MIL 10*8	MIN-BOS 5*4
0615	CAL-KC 3-4	NY-BAL 4-8	OAK-CHI 7*5	SEA-TEX 5*2	TOR-CLE 3-4	DET-MIL 7-11	MIN-BOS 7*5
0616	SEA-KC 1-4	NY-BAL 6*1	CAL-CHI 6*5	OAK-TEX 6*4	BOS-CLE 6-7	DET-MIL 4-5	
0617	SEA-KC 5*1	MIN-BAL 2-9	CAL-CHI 5*3	OAK-TEX 4*2	BOS-CLE 1-8	MIL-NY 8*1	TOR-DET 7*4
0618	SEA-KC 3*1	MIN-BAL 6-11	CAL-CHI 4*3	OAK-TEX 11*10	BOS-CLE 2-8	MIL-NY 2-4	TOR-DET 5-6
0619	SEA-KC 9-12	MIN-BAL 10*4	CAL-CHI 1-7	OAK-TEX 5*0	BOS-CLE 5-6	MIL-NY 10*7	TOR-DET 1-3
0620	BOS-TOR 4*1	MIL-BAL 6*5	TEX-CHI 12*6	SEA-CAL 5*0		MIN-NY 5-7	CLE-DET 7*1
0621	BOS-TOR 13*1	MIL-BAL 1-6	TEX-CHI 4-5	SEA-CAL 2-7	KC-OAK 2*0	MIN-NY 4-6	CLE-DET 5-7
0622	BOS-TOR 3*2	MIL-BAL 9*2	TEX-CHI 0-4	SEA-CAL 12*3	KC-OAK 10*1	MIN-NY 2-9	CLE-DET 9*6
0623	CHI-SEA 13*2				KC-OAK 0-4		
0624	CHI-SEA 6*2	BAL-TOR 5*1	BOS-MIL 4*3	TEX-CAL 2*1	DET-SEA 3-4	KC-MIN 1-4	
0625	CHI-SEA 2*1	BAL-TOR 4*1	BOS-MIL 10*8	TEX-CAL 7-12	DET-OAK 1-2	KC-MIN 4*1	NY-CLE 11*6

♦1994♦	GAME 1	GAME 2	GAME 3	GAME 4	GAME 5	GAME 6	GAME 7
0626	CHI-SEA 8*7	BAL-TOR 7*1	BOS-MIL 4-5	TEX-CAL 3-4	DET-OAK 5-10	KC-MIN 4-11	NY-CLE 12*11
0627	DET-SEA 11*1	NY-BOS 5*1	TOR-MIL 1-5		CAL-OAK 2-10	KC-MIN 2*1	BAL-CLE 7*6
0628	DET-SEA 4-6	NY-BOS 10*4	TOR-MIL 4-6	KC-CHI 4*3	CAL-OAK 0-3	TEX-MIN 10*6	BAL-CLE 8-9
0629	DET-SEA 4-9	NY-BOS 4*3	TOR-MIL 5*0	KC-CHI 6-7	CAL-OAK 0-1	TEX-MIN 11*10	BAL-CLE 7*6
0630		NY-BOS 5-6	TOR-MIL 2-9	KC-CHI 2-3		TEX-MIN 4-6	BAL-CLE 2-4
0701	CAL-BAL 7-14	OAK-BOS 6*3	SEA-NY 4*3	MIL-CHI 0-8	TOR-KC 3-4	DET-TEX 6-10	MIN-CLE 1-6
						DET-TEX 6-8	
0702	CAL-BAL 1*0	OAK-BOS 2-10	SEA-NY 12*6	MIL-CHI 0-5	TOR-KC 7*6	DET-TEX 6*1	MIN-CLE 1-9
0703	CAL-BAL 3-10	OAK-BOS 10*0	SEA-NY 2-5	MIL-CHI 9*2	TOR-KC 6-11	DET-TEX 3-5	MIN-CLE 9-10
0704	SEA-BAL 3-9	CAL-BOS 1-4	OAK-NY 4*0	MIL-CHI 2-3	TOR-KC 9*4	DET-TEX 3-4	MIN-CLE 1-7
0705	SEA-BAL 2-5	CAL-BOS 10*3	OAK-NY 8*7	TOR-MIN 14*3	MIL-KC 5-10	CLE-TEX 3-4	CHI-DET 2-6
							CHI-DET 6*4
0706	SEA-BAL 4-5	CAL-BOS 10*6	OAK-NY 4*2	TOR-MIN 4-5	MIL-KC 4*3	CLE-TEX 13*4	CHI-DET 6*2
0707	OAK-BAL 6*4	SEA-BOS 4*3	CAL-NY 2-5	TOR-MIN 4*3	MIL-KC 3-8	CLE-TEX 4-6	CHI-DET 9*5
0708	OAK-BAL 3-13	SEA-BOS 3-4	CAL-NY 3-4	CLE-MIN 6-8	CHI-MIL 9*5	KC-TOR 6*5	TEX-DET 3-7
0709	OAK-BAL 7-8	SEA-BOS 7*4	CAL-NY 10*5	CLE-MIN 4*3	CHI-MIL 11*7	KC-TOR 4-9	TEX-DET 10*4
0710	OAK-BAL 5*4	SEA-BOS 2-9	CAL-NY 9*6	CLE-MIN 9*1	CHI-MIL 7*2	KC-TOR 3-7	TEX-DET 5-6
0714	BAL-CAL 3*2	BOS-OAK 2*1	CLE-CHI 3-6	MIL-MIN 6*4	DET-KC 2-5	NY-SEA 13*8	TOR-TEX 3-7
0715	BAL-CAL 9*2	BOS-OAK 4*1	CLE-CHI 3*2	MIL-MIN 8*7	DET-KC 14*2	NY-SEA 10*8	TOR-TEX 7*5
					DET-KC 3-5		
0716	BAL-CAL 3-4	BOS-OAK 0-9	CLE-CHI 2*0	MIL-MIN 2-5	DET-KC 13*7	NY-SEA 9*3	TOR-TEX 2-4
0717	BAL-CAL 10*5	BOS-OAK 4*3	CLE-CHI 2-5	MIL-MIN 5*3	DET-KC 1-4	NY-SEA 14*4	TOR-TEX 3*1
0718	BOS-CAL 4-13	NY-OAK 5*3	DET-CHI 9-10	KC-MIL 2*0	MIN-TOR 4-7	BAL-SEA 5-7	TEX-CLE 6*5
0719	BOS-CAL 4-6	NY-OAK 2-6	DET-CHI 5-10	KC-MIL 3-4	MIN-TOR 2-4		TEX-CLE 3-12
0720	BOS-CAL 4-8	NY-OAK 1*0	DET-CHI 0-3	KC-MIL 1-11	MIN-TOR 2-9		TEX-CLE 13*11
0721	NY-CAL 11*7	BAL-OAK 3-4		MIN-MIL 3-9	TEX-TOR 3-9		CHI-CLE 6*5
0722	NY-CAL 12*3	BAL-OAK 5*4	KC-DET 2-5	MIN-MIL 6*5	TEX-TOR 2-3	SEA-BOS 6*3	CHI-CLE 8-9
0723	NY-CAL 7*2	BAL-OAK 3-6	KC-DET 4*1	MIN-MIL 5*1	TEX-TOR 1-9	SEA-BOS 5-6	CHI-CLE 2-11
						SEA-BOS 6*3	
0724	NY-CAL 6*4	BAL-OAK 6-7	KC-DET 6*4	MIN-MIL 10*6	TEX-TOR 2-4	SEA-BOS 2-8	CHI-CLE 4*2
0725	CHI-KC 4-6	MIN-TEX 4-7		BOS-NY 10*7	MIL-TOR 7*5	OAK-CAL 6*0	CLE-BAL 4-10
							CLE-BAL 9*2
0726	CHI-KC 2-3	MIN-TEX 7-8	SEA-DET 1-9	BOS-NY 3-4	MIL-TOR 5*0	OAK-CAL 11*3	
0727	CHI-KC 1-4	MIN-TEX 1*0	SEA-DET 1-3	BOS-NY 1*0	MIL-TOR 5*4		CLE-BAL 7*2
							CLE-BAL 5*2
0728	CHI-KC 3-5	CAL-TEX 0-4	SEA-DET 2-4				
0729	MIN-KC 3-5	CAL-TEX 3-5	OAK-DET 6*4	CLE-NY 2-5	MIL-BOS 2-7	SEA-CHI 4-5	TOR-BAL 4*3
0730	MIN-KC 4-5	CAL-TEX 14*4	OAK-DET 2-14	CLE-NY 5-6	MIL-BOS 5*1	SEA-CHI 2-4	TOR-BAL 5-7
0731	MIN-KC 5-9	CAL-TEX 4*3	OAK-DET 4-5	CLE-NY 1-4	MIL-BOS 1-8	SEA-CHI 1-8	TOR-BAL 6*4
0801	OAK-KC 2-4	BAL-MIN 1*0	DET-CLE 2-6	NY-MIL 8*3	TOR-BOS 6*2		
					TOR-BOS 3-4		
0802	OAK-KC 4-6	BAL-MIN 10*0	DET-CLE 12*9	NY-MIL 7*1	TOR-BOS 8*7	CHI-TEX 6*2	SEA-CAL 10*2
0803	OAK-KC 5-9	BAL-MIN 3-4	DET-CLE 4-7	NY-MIL 2*1	TOR-BOS 2-7	CHI-TEX 8-11	SEA-CAL 8*4
0804	OAK-KC 2-5	NY-MIN 9*2	DET-CLE 0-5	BAL-MIL 3-5	TOR-BOS 5*2	CHI-TEX 1-4	SEA-CAL 4*2
0805	SEA-KC 0-8	NY-MIN 12*3	DET-TOR 2-4	BAL-MIL 4*0	TEX-OAK 4-5		CHI-CAL 3-5
0806	SEA-KC 11*2	NY-MIN 4-10	DET-TOR 3*2	BAL-MIL 5*0	TEX-OAK 4-6	CLE-BOS 4-8	CHI-CAL 16*10
						CLE-BOS 7*0	
0807	SEA-KC 10*6	NY-MIN 6-7	DET-TOR 8*7	BAL-MIL 6*3	TEX-OAK 3-8	CLE-BOS 1-4	CHI-CAL 10*5
						CLE-BOS 15*10	
0808	BAL-NY 5-6	BOS-MIN 2-5	CLE-TOR 6*1	MIL-DET 12*4	CHI-OAK 2*1	SEA-TEX 14*4	KC-CAL 1-6
0809	BAL-NY 6*5	BOS-MIN 3-4	CLE-TOR 5-12	MIL-DET 4-10	CHI-OAK 2-4	SEA-TEX 8*5	KC-CAL 5*3
0810	BAL-NY 8*1	BOS-MIN 7-17	CLE-TOR 5*3	MIL-DET 0-4	CHI-OAK 4*3	SEA-TEX 3*2	KC-CAL 1-2
0811	TOR-NY 8*7			MIL-DET 10*5	SEA-OAK 8*1		

National League

♦1977♦	GAME 1	GAME 2	GAME 3	GAME 4	GAME 5	GAME 6	GAME 7
0406	SD-CIN 3-5						
0407	NY-CHI 5*3	SF-LA 1-5	STL-PIT 12*6				
0408	SD-CIN 3-6	ATL-HOU 2-3					
0409	SD-CIN 6*3	ATL-HOU 0-2	NY-CHI 8*6	SF-LA 2-8	MON-PHI 4*3	STL-PIT 8*2	
0410	SD-CIN 12*4	ATL-HOU 6*0	NY-CHI 2-5	SF-LA 8*4	MON-PHI 9*8	STL-PIT 8*7	
0411		CIN-HOU 3-4		ATL-LA 7*6	CHI-PHI 6*2		
0412	STL-NY 0-4	CIN-HOU 3-4	MON-PIT 1-2	ATL-LA 10-14	SF-SD 3-4		
0413	STL-NY 7*3	CIN-HOU 6-7	MON-PIT 0-3	ATL-LA 3-4	SF-SD 3*1	CHI-PHI 3*1	
0414	STL-NY 4*1				SF-SD 8*4		
0415	CHI-NY 8*4	HOU-ATL 3-4	PHI-MON 7*2	LA-SF 7*1	CIN-SD 9*5	PIT-STL 7*0	
0416	CHI-NY 1-4	HOU-ATL 3-4	PHI-MON 3-4	LA-SF 5*0	CIN-SD 4-5	PIT-STL 3*1	
0417	CHI-NY 0-6	HOU-ATL 4-5	PHI-MON 1-2	LA-SF 7*6	CIN-SD 4*1	PIT-STL 3-4	
0418	PHI-CHI 3*1	SD-ATL 12*6	PIT-MON 5-6	LA-CIN 7*3		NY-STL 2-3	
0419	PHI-CHI 7*5	SD-ATL 1-4	PIT-MON 0-6	SF-HOU 7*4		NY-STL 5*2	
0420	LA-CIN 3*1	SD-ATL 0-2	PIT-MON 8*6	SF-HOU 1*0		NY-STL 2-4	
0422	PIT-NY 4*3	LA-ATL 5-6	SF-MON 2-3	SD-HOU 4*2	STL-PHI 10*1		
0423	PIT-NY 6*5	LA-ATL 6*4	SF-MON 4*2	SD-HOU 7*2	STL-PHI 1-11	CIN-CHI 1-2	
				SD-HOU 11*8			
0424	LA-ATL 16*6	CIN-CHI 1-7	SF-MON 6*5	SD-HOU 8-9	STL-PHI 3-6		
0425	CIN-ATL 23*9	LA-SD 7*3	STL-CHI 1-4	PHI-PIT 0-5	HOU-SF 4*3		
0426	CIN-ATL 9*1	LA-SD 4*1	STL-CHI 21*3	PHI-PIT 3-7	HOU-SF 2-3	MON-NY 3*2	
0427	CIN-ATL 3*1	LA-SD 7*6			HOU-SF 3*1		
0428		LA-SD 7*5					
0429	CHI-CIN 2-3	NY-SD 9*2	MON-LA 0-4	HOU-PIT 11*3	PHI-SF 6*5	ATL-STL 2-5	
0430	CHI-CIN 0-8	NY-SD 4*1	MON-LA 4-6	HOU-PIT 0-10	PHI-SF 6*4	ATL-STL 4-5	
0501	CHI-CIN 4*1	NY-SD 8*2	MON-LA 6*2	HOU-PIT 7-9	PHI-SF 7*2	ATL-STL 0-8	
0502	STL-CIN 2-3	PHI-SD 3-4	NY-LA 1-3	PIT-ATL 11*1	MON-SF 3*2		
0503	HOU-CHI 0-9	PHI-SD 8*7	NY-LA 1-4	PIT-ATL 8*7	MON-SF 1-5	STL-CIN 8*1	
0504	HOU-CHI 5*4	PHI-SD 8*2	NY-LA 1-3	PIT-ATL 8*0	MON-SF 7*1		
0505	HOU-CHI 7-8	PHI-SD 8*5	NY-LA 2-7				
0506	ATL-CHI 2-7	MON-SD 4-6	PHI-LA 3-9	CIN-PIT 3-6	NY-SF 3-5	HOU-STL 1-4	
0507	ATL-CHI 4-11	MON-SD 7*6	PHI-LA 7*4	CIN-PIT 10-12	NY-SF 6*0	HOU-STL 3*1	
0508	ATL-CHI 3-6			CIN-PIT 4-6	NY-SF 2-4	HOU-STL 1-2	
					NY-SF 0-10		
0509	CHI-HOU 6*1	CIN-STL 5-6		SF-PHI 0-3	ATL-PIT 0-3		
					ATL-PIT 1-2		
0510	CHI-HOU 11*5	CIN-STL 2*1	LA-MON 3-4		ATL-PIT 1-2	SD-NY 6*3	
						SD-NY 4*3	
0511	CHI-HOU 2-8	LA-MON 5*1	SF-PHI 4*2	CIN-STL 5*1	ATL-PIT 1-2	SD-NY 5*2	
0512	LA-MON 8*2	SF-PHI 0-3	ATL-PIT 6*1	CIN-STL 1-10	PIT-HOU 0-3	LA-NY 0-3	
0513	CHI-MON 5*3	SD-PHI 4-5	STL-ATL 3*0	SF-CIN 4-6	PIT-HOU 6*2	LA-NY 5*4	
0514	CHI-MON 6*3	SD-PHI 5-9	STL-ATL 7*6	SF-CIN 4*3	PIT-HOU 3*1	LA-NY 4*3	
0515	CHI-MON 4*3	SD-PHI 2-5	STL-ATL 12-15	SF-CIN 2-6			
	CHI-MON 4*2						
0516	SD-CHI 6-9	LA-PHI 6-10	MON-ATL 6-9	PIT-CIN 3*0	STL-HOU 2-5	SF-NY 1-8	
0517	SD-CHI 6-23	LA-PHI 6*4	MON-ATL 8-10	PIT-CIN 3-8	STL-HOU 8*4	SF-NY 0-2	
0518		LA-PHI 6*4					
0519	SD-MON 5*2	LA-PIT 5-6	CHI-ATL 0-6		PHI-HOU 2-3	SF-NY 3-4	

◆1977◆	GAME 1	GAME 2	GAME 3	GAME 4	GAME 5	GAME 6	GAME 7
0520	SD-MON 12*4	LA-PIT 6*1	CHI-ATL 13*4	NY-CIN 2-6	PHI-HOU 2-5	SF-STL 7*5	
0521	SD-MON 11*8	LA-PIT 4*3	CHI-ATL 9*3	NY-CIN 7-8	PHI-HOU 7*4	SF-STL 5-8	
0522	SD-MON 1-3	LA-PIT 4-11	CHI-ATL 2-5	NY-CIN 1-8	PHI-HOU 6*3	SF-STL 2*0	
				NY-CIN 4*3			
0523	ATL-SD 6*5	SF-STL 7*2					
0524	ATL-SD 3-4	PHI-STL 5-8	MON-CHI 5*4	HOU-LA 2-4	NY-PIT 2-5		
0525	ATL-SD 5-6	PHI-STL 2*1	MON-CHI 3-7	HOU-LA 7*6	CIN-SF 5-6		
0526	ATL-SD 8*3	PHI-STL 3-4	MON-CHI 0-1	HOU-LA 3-4	CIN-SF 5-6		
0527	HOU-SD 4*3	MON-STL 3-7	PIT-CHI 2-4	CIN-LA 3-10	ATL-SF 3-4	NY-PHI 4-5	
0528	HOU-SD 5-6	MON-STL 5-7	PIT-CHI 3-6	CIN-LA 6*3	ATL-SF 2*1	NY-PHI 2-4	
0529	HOU-SD 2-3	MON-STL 14*4	PIT-CHI 2-3	CIN-LA 8*1	ATL-SF 2-3	NY-PHI 6-7	
0530	ATL-CIN 3-7	CHI-STL 0-14	LA-HOU 3-5	MON-NY 5*1	SD-SF 12*8	PIT-PHI 4-6	
				MON-NY 3*2	SD-SF 9*8		
0531	ATL-CIN 3-5	LA-HOU 2-5	PIT-HOU 5-6	MON-NY 2-6	SD-SF 4*2	CHI-STL 0-6	
0601	ATL-CIN 2-5	LA-HOU 6*2	PIT-PHI 3*0	NY-MON 6*4	SD-SF 0-2	CHI-STL 4*3	
0602	HOU-CIN 6*4			NY-MON 7*4			
0603	HOU-CIN 0-4	SD-LA 1*0	PHI-NY 1*0	STL-MON 0-2	CHI-PIT 0-5	SF-ATL 3-5	
						SF-ATL 7-8	
0604	HOU-CIN 8*1	SD-LA 4-9	STL-MON 7-8	PHI-NY 0-2	CHI-PIT 4*3	SF-ATL 1-7	
0605	HOU-CIN 4-14	SD-LA 2-4	STL-MON 5-7	PHI-NY 5-6	CHI-PIT 4-5	SF-ATL 10*9	
				PHI-NY 2-3			
0606	LA-CHI 1-3	ATL-MON 2-4	HOU-PHI 5-9	SF-PIT 3*1	SD-STL 3-4		
0607	LA-CHI 4-10	CIN-NY 0-8	HOU-PHI 8-9	SF-PIT 7*6	SD-STL 9*5		
0608	LA-CHI 4*2	CIN-NY 5*0	HOU-PHI 2-3	SF-PIT 3*2	SD-STL 0-3		
0609	SF-CHI 0-1	PHI-ATL 0-3			LA-STL 3-6	ATL-MON 0-6	
0610	SF-CHI 1-3	PHI-ATL 7*5	MON-CIN 1-13	NY-HOU 1-4	LA-STL 7-8	SD-PIT 7-10	
0611	SF-CHI 3-5	PHI-ATL 13*10	MON-CIN 6*4	NY-HOU 1-4	LA-STL 9*8	SD-PIT 4*1	
				NY-HOU 6*4			
0612	PHI-ATL 3-5	SF-CHI 5-6	LA-STL 2-5	NY-HOU 3*1	MON-CIN 6-7	SD-PIT 1-6	
					MON-CIN 8-14	SD-PIT 4-7	
0613	NY-ATL 7*1	MON-HOU 3*2			PHI-CIN 4-5		
0614	NY-ATL 5-8	MON-HOU 0-5	PIT-LA 2-3	CHI-SD 6*5	PHI-CIN 2-3	STL-SF 1-7	
0615	NY-ATL 6*5	MON-HOU 2*0	PIT-LA 1-10	CHI-SD 2*0	PHI-CIN 7-8	STL-SF 9*6	
0616	HOU-NY 3-4		PIT-LA 2-3	CHI-SD 6-8		STL-SF 1-5	
0617	HOU-NY 7*1	CIN-MON 9*4	CHI-LA 7*3	STL-SD 3-4	ATL-PHI 5-11	PIT-SF 3-4	
0618	HOU-NY 4*3	CIN-MON 6*0	CHI-LA 1-2	STL-SD 1-4	ATL-PHI 5-8	PIT-SF 5-7	
0619	HOU-NY 2-8	CIN-MON 4-8	CHI-LA 1-3	STL-SD 2-6	ATL-PHI 2-4	PIT-SF 0-8	
						PIT-SF 6-8	
0620	STL-LA 3-9	HOU-MON 6*3	CIN-PHI 4-10	PIT-SD 5*3		CHI-SF 10*9	
0621	STL-LA 4*3	HOU-MON 0-6	CIN-PHI 10*5	PIT-SD 9*2	ATL-NY 2-5	CHI-SF 8*2	
0622	STL-LA 1-12	HOU-MON 7*0	CIN-PHI 9-15	PIT-SD 3*1	ATL-NY 4*1	CHI-SF 4*2	
0624	SD-ATL 8-9	NY-CHI 0-5	LA-CIN 3*2	SF-HOU 5-6	MON-PIT 5-6	PHI-STL 1-7	
0625	SD-ATL 5-9	NY-CHI 4-5	LA-CIN 6-7	SF-HOU 3-4	MON-PIT 2-10	PHI-STL 2-3	
				SF-HOU 4*1			
0626	SD-ATL 5-8	NY-CHI 2-5	PHI-STL 2*0	SF-HOU 2*0	LA-CIN 4-5	MON-PIT 4-7	
					LA-CIN 9*3	MON-PIT 6*3	
0627	LA-ATL 2*1	SD-HOU 6-7	CHI-MON 4*3	PHI-NY 4*2	SF-CIN 14*9	PIT-STL 1-6	
0628	LA-ATL 3*2	SD-HOU 1-5	CHI-MON 4*2	PHI-NY 3*1	SF-CIN 4-11	PIT-STL 1-6	
						PIT-STL 3-13	
0629	LA-ATL 13*7	SF-CIN 4-5	SD-HOU 7*4	CHI-MON 0-5	PHI-NY 3-5	PIT-STL 9*1	
0630	LA-ATL 4-5	SF-CIN 5-11	PIT-PHI 1-8	NY-MON 4*3		CHI-STL 1-2	
0701	ATL-HOU 1-3	CIN-SD 2*1	PIT-PHI 6-7	NY-MON 5-6	LA-SF 10*5	CHI-STL 1-3	
				NY-MON 3-5			
0702	ATL-HOU 2*1	PIT-PHI 3-4	CIN-SD 6*3	NY-MON 3-4	LA-SF 10*3	CHI-STL 3-10	
0703	ATL-HOU 3-9	PIT-PHI 7-11	CIN-SD 7-8	NY-MON 2-4	LA-SF 10*7	CHI-STL 4*0	
0704	CIN-ATL 4-5	NY-PHI 1-3	HOU-SD 12*7	MON-CHI 19*3	LA-SF 4*0	STL-PIT 2-5	
				MON-CHI 7*6		STL-PIT 3-4	
0705	CIN-ATL 9*3	NY-PHI 1-12	HOU-SD 7-8	MON-CHI 9*8		STL-PIT 7*3	
0706	CIN-ATL 15*13	NY-PHI 3-5	HOU-LA 2*1	MON-CHI 6-8	SD-SF 7*5	STL-PIT 8-11	
0707		NY-PHI 4-6	HOU-LA 4-7	STL-CHI 0-2	SD-SF 1-5		
0708	CIN-HOU 8*5	MON-NY 5*4	SD-LA 3-5	STL-CHI 6-7	ATL-SF 2-3	PHI-PIT 7-8	
0709	CIN-HOU 3*1	MON-NY 5-7	SD-LA 2*1	STL-CHI 4*3	ATL-SF 4-5	PHI-PIT 8-9	
0710	CIN-HOU 5-6	MON-NY 1-2	SD-LA 7*5	STL-CHI 8*3	ATL-SF 2-5	PHI-PIT 1-5	
			SD-LA 5*4	STL-CHI 3-4	ATL-SF 5-12	PHI-PIT 10-12	
0711	CIN-HOU 0-2	PIT-MON 2-4	SF-SD 5*1				
0712	LA-HOU 8*0	PIT-MON 5*4	SF-SD 3-7	ATL-CIN 4*3	CHI-NY 2-4	STL-PHI 4-5	
0713	LA-HOU 2-3	PIT-MON 6*1	SF-SD 5*4	ATL-CIN 4*3	CHI-NY 2#1	STL-PHI 2-5	
0714	LA-HOU 3-4			ATL-CIN 1-7		STL-PHI 7*6	
0715	SF-ATL 2-3	STL-MON 6-7	LA-SD 3-5	HOU-CIN 3-8	PIT-NY 7*1	CHI-PHI 2-4	
					PIT-NY 1-6	CHI-PHI 2-9	
0716	SF-ATL 4*0	HOU-CIN 8*0	STL-MON 0-3	LA-SD 1*0	PIT-NY 3-5	CHI-PHI 9*8	
0717	SF-ATL 10-11	HOU-CIN 3*1	STL-MON 7-8	LA-SD 4*3	PIT-NY 3*1	CHI-PHI 2-4	
					PIT-NY 3-9		
0721	ATL-CHI 3-4	MON-LA 4*0	CIN-PIT 2-6	NY-SD 2-3	PHI-SF 9*6	HOU-STL 0-4	
0722	ATL-CHI 0-1	MON-LA 2*1	CIN-PIT 7-8	NY-SD 5*0	PHI-SF 2-6	HOU-STL 4*2	
0723	ATL-CHI 6*4	MON-LA 5*4	CIN-PIT 4-5	NY-SD 3-4	PHI-SF 6*3	HOU-STL 3-4	
0724	HOU-CHI 10*6	NY-LA 3-5	ATL-PIT 6-7	PHI-SD 7*4	MON-SF 0-3	CIN-STL 0-3	
	HOU-CHI 6*4				MON-SF 4-5		
0725	HOU-CHI 7-9	NY-LA 1*0	ATL-PIT 3-6	PHI-SD 6*4	MON-SF 8*3	CIN-STL 8-9	
0726	CIN-CHI 0-3	PHI-LA 1-5	HOU-PIT 2-3	MON-SD 3-4	NY-SF 8*3	ATL-STL 2-4	
		PHI-LA 5*1		MON-SD 5*2			
0727	HOU-PIT 2-3	PHI-LA 5-7	NY-SF 7*4	MON-SD 5-7	ATL-STL 3-5	CIN-CHI 6*2	
						CIN-CHI 1-5	
0728	PHI-LA 1-2	HOU-PIT 4-9	MON-SD 5*4	ATL-STL 0-3		CIN-CHI 15-16	
0729	PIT-ATL 3-5	CHI-HOU 0-1	LA-MON 4*1	SD-NY 1-4	SF-PHI 7*0	STL-CIN 5-6	
0730	PIT-ATL 10*6	CHI-HOU 3-11	LA-MON 7*4	SD-NY 8*6	SF-PHI 3-9	STL-CIN 10*3	
0731	PIT-ATL 3-8	CHI-HOU 4*1	LA-MON 8*2	SD-NY 9-10	SF-PHI 4-5	STL-CIN 4*1	
0801	STL-ATL 6*5	PIT-HOU 3-4	SF-MON 9*2	LA-NY 7-8		STL-CIN 2-6	
0802	STL-ATL 6*4	PIT-HOU 6*3	SF-MON 2-10	LA-NY 7*2		CHI-CIN 6-7	
0803	STL-ATL 5*1	PIT-HOU 0-3	SF-MON 2-4	LA-NY 3-4	SD-PHI 4*2	CHI-CIN 5*2	
0804	MON-ATL 2-5				SD-PHI 1-8	CHI-CIN 3-5	
					SD-PHI 1-2		
0805	MON-ATL 6*4	SD-CHI 11*8	STL-HOU 4-5	SF-NY 2-3	LA-PHI 3-8	PIT-CIN 12*1	
						PIT-CIN 10*6	
0806	MON-ATL 1-3	SD-CHI 5-10	SF-NY 7*3	LA-PHI 0-1	STL-HOU 3*1	PIT-CIN 3-8	
					STL-HOU 1-4		
0807	MON-ATL 2-6	PIT-CIN 0-6	SF-NY 7*4	LA-PHI 1-3	STL-HOU 5*2	SD-CHI 8*6	
						SD-CHI 4-9	
0808	CIN-LA 0-4	SD-MON 5-6	STL-NY 4*2	CHI-PIT 6-7	HOU-SF 3-4		
					HOU-SF 0-5		
0809	CIN-LA 4*0	SD-MON 8*3	STL-NY 1-4	CHI-PIT 4*1	HOU-SF 8*6	ATL-SD 6-8	
0810	CIN-LA 0-1	STL-NY 3*1	CHI-PIT 1-2	MON-PHI 1-6		ATL-SD 1-2	
				MON-PHI 1-6		ATL-SD 1-2	
0811	CIN-LA 5*4	NY-PIT 1-9	HOU-SF 7*5	MON-PHI 5-10		HOU-SD 4-5	
0812	ATL-LA 5*2	NY-PIT 2-3	CIN-SF 3-4	PHI-CHI 10*3	MON-STL 1-2		
		NY-PIT 5-6					
0813	PHI-CHI 10*7	NY-PIT 0-2	ATL-LA 0-11	CIN-SF 3*1	MON-STL 0-1		

♦1977♦	GAME 1	GAME 2	GAME 3	GAME 4	GAME 5	GAME 6	GAME 7
0814	PHI-CHI 10*2	NY-PIT 3-6	ATL-LA 0-1	CIN-SF 1-6	MON-STL 6*2	HOU-SD 6*3	
	PHI-CHI 4*2			CIN-SF 9*3			
0815	HOU-ATL 15*3	SD-CIN 0-3	SF-LA 6*3	NY-STL 7*4	PIT-CHI 5-6	PHI-MON 7*5	
0816	HOU-ATL 4*1	SD-CIN 1-5	SF-LA 2-3	NY-STL 5*1	PIT-CHI 2-4	PHI-MON 0-13	
0817	HOU-ATL 6-9	SD-CIN 7*4		NY-STL 0-2	PIT-CHI 7*6	PHI-MON 8*3	
0818	SF-LA 0-7						
0819	HOU-PHI 5-9	SF-PIT 1-6	SD-STL 4-12	CIN-NY 4*1	LA-CHI 2-6	ATL-MON 5*3	
				CIN-NY 4*3		ATL-MON 2-7	
0820	LA-CHI 4-5	HOU-PHI 4-5	SF-PIT 5*1	CIN-NY 8*2	SD-STL 1-7	ATL-MON 3-6	
0821	LA-CHI 5*1	HOU-PHI 3-7	SF-PIT 5*4	CIN-NY 5*1	SD-STL 7*0	ATL-MON 4-10	
0622	SF-CHI 2-3	PHI-ATL 5*4	SD-PIT 1*0	HOU-NY 1-2	LA-STL 6-8	MON-CIN 5*1	
0823	SF-CHI 4*3	PHI-ATL 3*2	SD-PIT 6-7	HOU-NY 1-2	LA-STL 1-2	MON-CIN 4*2	
0824	PHI-HOU 1-3	CHI-ATL 3-4	LA-PIT 2*1		SF-STL 2-3	NY-CIN 4-11	
0825	PHI-HOU 5-6	CHI-ATL 6-8	LA-PIT 1-2		SF-STL 4*2	NY-CIN 2-3	
0826	MON-HOU 5-6	NY-ATL 3-5	STL-LA 4-5	PIT-SD 3*1	CHI-SF 5*2	PHI-CIN 2-4	
0827	MON-HOU 0-4	NY-ATL 4-5	STL-LA 3-4	PIT-SD 4*0	CHI-SF 1-7	PHI-CIN 5-6	
0828	MON-HOU 2-7	NY-ATL 4-6	STL-LA 0-11	PIT-SD 10*1	CHI-SF 1-4	PHI-CIN 0-9	
0829	CIN-MON 2-7	ATL-PHI 2-3	CHI-LA 1-4	STL-SD 3-4			
0830	CIN-MON 4*3	ATL-PHI 2-11	CHI-LA 4*1	STL-SD 4-7	NY-HOU 2-6	PIT-SF 3*1	
0831	CIN-MON 6*0	ATL-PHI 1-6	CHI-LA 0-5	STL-SD 1-2	NY-HOU 2-5	PIT-SF 3-6	
0902	HOU-MON 5*2	CIN-PHI 0-3	PIT-LA 2-10	CHI-SD 0-5	ATL-NY 0-4	STL-SF 6*4	
					ATL-NY 3*2		
0903	PIT-LA 4-6	HOU-MON 1-5	CIN-PHI 3-9	CHI-SD 1-4	ATL-NY 1-9	STL-SF 5-6	
0904	PIT-LA 2-8	HOU-MON 7*1	CIN-PHI 5*2	CHI-SD 2*1	ATL-NY 7*5	STL-SF 8*2	
0905	SF-ATL 0-4	STL-CHI 2-4	CIN-HOU 1-5	LA-SD 0-1	MON-NY 4*3	PHI-PIT 1-3	
						PHI-PIT 11*1	
0906	SF-ATL 12*2	STL-CHI 3*1	CIN-HOU 3-8	MON-NY 3-5	LA-SD 3*2	PHI-PIT 4-5	
0907	LA-ATL 5*2	MON-CHI 4*2	SD-HOU 9*5	PHI-NY 6*2	SF-CIN 6*3	STL-PIT 4-5	
0908	LA-ATL 5*4	MON-CHI 2-3	SD-HOU 1-7	PHI-NY 8*2	SF-CIN 5-6	STL-PIT 5-9	
0909	SD-ATL 6-8	NY-CHI 8-10	SF-HOU 1-6	STL-PHI 4-11	LA-CIN 4*1	MON-PIT 2*1	
0910	SD-ATL 6-9	NY-CHI 7*2	SF-HOU 0-2	STL-PHI 1-3	LA-CIN 4-7	MON-PIT 4*2	
0911	SD-ATL 3-7	NY-CHI 7*3	SF-HOU 2*1	STL-PHI 5-6	LA-CIN 2-6	MON-PIT 4-10	
0912	SD-LA 6-7	NY-MON 4*3	ATL-SF 3*1	PIT-SD 2-6	HOU-CIN 7*2	CHI-STL 9-11	
0913	SD-LA 4-18	NY-MON 5-8	ATL-SF 7-8	PIT-PHI 2*0	HOU-CIN 13*4	CHI-STL 1-3	
0914	CIN-LA 9*8	CHI-MON 2-3	HOU-SF 2-3	NY-PHI 1*0	ATL-SD 4-6		
0915	CIN-LA 3*2	CHI-MON 4-5	HOU-SF 6*3	NY-PHI 2-8	ATL-SD 8*7	PIT-STL 4*3	
						PIT-STL 7-10	
0916	CHI-NY 5*2	ATL-LA 2-3	PIT-MON 0-5	HOU-SD 3-4	CIN-SF 5*3	PHI-STL 12*6	
0917	CHI-NY 6*3	ATL-LA 3-7	PIT-MON 6*3	HOU-SD 11*0	CIN-SF 8*6	PHI-STL 8*4	
	CHI-NY 4*3						
0918	CHI-NY 6*3	ATL-LA 9*8	PIT-MON 7*5	CIN-SF 2-3	PHI-STL 5-12		
	CHI-NY 0-6						
0920	PIT-NY 4*2	ATL-HOU 3-6	CHI-PHI 2-4	CIN-SD 4*0	LA-SF 3*1		
0921	PIT-NY 4*0	ATL-HOU 5*3	CHI-PHI 2*0	CIN-SD 3*2	LA-SF 4-5	STL-MON 2-4	
						STL-MON 8*2	
						STL-MON 0-2	
0922	ATL-HOU 8*4	CHI-PHI 5*3	CIN-SD 1-3			PHI-MON 6*1	
0923	LA-HOU 3-4	CIN-ATL 5*1	SF-SD 6*4	PIT-CHI 2*0	STL-NY 10*6	PHI-MON 1*0	
0924	LA-HOU 1*0	CIN-ATL 8*7	SF-SD 3*2	PIT-CHI 7*3		PHI-MON 8*5	
0925	LA-HOU 5*4	CIN-ATL 4*0	SF-SD 2-9	PIT-CHI 4*0			
0926	SF-LA 9*1	HOU-ATL 10-12	MON-STL 9*5	PHI-CHI 7-10	SD-CIN 3*1	NY-PIT 7*1	
0927	SF-LA 2-5	HOU-ATL 7*5	MON-STL 3-5	PHI-CHI 15*9	SD-CIN 0-8	NY-PIT 2-3	
0928	SF-LA 1-2	HOU-ATL 2*1	MON-STL 4*2	PHI-CHI 5*2		NY-PIT 2-5	
0929	HOU-LA 4*2	MON-PHI 7*2				CHI-PIT 1-3	
0930	HOU-LA 5-6	MON-PHI 4-9	ATL-CIN 1-7	SD-SF 5-7	NY-STL 2-7		
					NY-STL 6*3		
1001	ATL-CIN 2-6	HOU-LA 3-4	MON-PHI 6*5	SD-SF 4-13	NY-STL 8*4		
					NY-STL 2-4		
1002	ATL-CIN 6*3	HOU-LA 6*3	MON-PHI 3-5	SD-SF 3*1	NY-STL 6*4	CHI-PIT 1-5	
						CHI-PIT 2-3	

♦1978♦	GAME 1	GAME 2	GAME 3	GAME 4	GAME 5	GAME 6	GAME 7
0406	HOU-CIN 9-11			STL-PHI 5*1	CHI-PIT 0-1	SD-SF 3*2	
0407	HOU-CIN 4-5	LA-ATL 13*4	MON-NY 1-3	STL-PHI 0-7	CHI-PIT 3-4	SD-SF 0-6	
0408	HOU-CIN 1-2	LA-ATL 6*2	MON-NY 5-6	STL-PHI 3-12	CHI-PIT 4*3	SD-SF 5-7	
0409	HOU-CIN 3-9	LA-ATL 7*4	MON-NY 5-6				
			MON-NY 5*0				
0410	SD-ATL 7-8	LA-HOU 5*2	CHI-NY 0-6	PIT-STL 2-11			
0411	SD-ATL 3*2	LA-HOU 0-1	CHI-NY 4*2	SF-CIN 3*2	PIT-STL 1-5		
0412	MON-PHI 8*7	LA-HOU 10-11	CHI-NY 4*2	SF-CIN 3-12	PIT-STL 5-6		
0413				SF-CIN 6-7			
0414	PIT-CHI 4-5	CIN-HOU 8*4	ATL-LA 1-5	NY-MON 3*2	PHI-STL 4*3	SF-SD 3*2	
0415	PIT-CHI 13*10	CIN-HOU 1-6		NY-MON 3-4	PHI-STL 3*2		
0416	PIT-CHI 1-5	CIN-HOU 3-4	ATL-LA 0-8	NY-MON 1-4	PHI-STL 0-5	SF-SD 8*4	
0417	PHI-PIT 6*2	ATL-SF 1-5	CIN-LA 8*2		NY-STL 6*2		
0418	MON-CHI 1-2	ATL-SF 1*0	CIN-LA 11*3	HOU-SD 5*1	NY-STL 3*2		
0419	MON-CHI 8*6	ATL-SF 2*0	CIN-LA 4-5	HOU-SD 2*1	NY-STL 2*0		
0420			ATL-SD 0-2				
0421	NY-CHI 0-5	CIN-SF 0-3	HOU-LA 1-5	ATL-SD 3-9			
0422	NY-CHI 3*2	CIN-SF 5*4	HOU-LA 8*6	ATL-SD 0-2	STL-PIT 7-8	PHI-MON 3-7	
						PHI-MON 3-5	
0423	NY-CHI 2-3	HOU-LA 3-7	ATL-SD 4-5	CIN-SF 2*1	STL-PIT 7-14	PHI-MON 2-5	
					STL-PIT 4#5		
0424	SD-HOU 3-4	STL-MON 3-5	PIT-NY 4*2	CHI-PHI 2-12			
0425	SD-HOU 3-4	STL-MON 7*2	PIT-NY 2*1	CHI-PHI 0-7	SF-ATL 1-3	LA-CIN 4*2	
0426	SD-HOU 2*1	STL-MON 12*2	PIT-NY 1*0	CHI-PHI 4*2	SF-ATL 1-6	LA-CIN 14*4	
					SF-ATL 5*3		
0427							
0428	MON-HOU 6*3	CIN-NY 5*1	SD-PHI 2-3	SF-PIT 5*4	CHI-ATL 4*3	LA-STL 7*1	
0429	MON-HOU 1-3	CIN-NY 14*7	SD-PHI 2-7	SF-PIT 2-6	CHI-ATL 0-5	LA-STL 0-1	
0430	MON-HOU 2*1	CIN-NY 4-6	SD-PHI 4-11	SF-PIT 7*3	CHI-ATL 7*5	LA-STL 0-4	
0501	PHI-CIN 12*1			SD-PIT 4-7	NY-ATL 5-6	SF-STL 2*1	
0502	LA-CHI 4-5			SD-PIT 2*1	NY-ATL 4-5	SF-STL 0-9	
0503	LA-CHI 9*5	PHI-CIN 3-12	HOU-MON 3-10	SD-PIT 7*5		SF-STL 4*0	
0504	LA-CHI 4*1	NY-ATL 8*2					
0505	MON-CIN 4*3	HOU-ATL 2-5	NY-PHI 4-9	LA-PIT 7*2	SD-STL 2*1		
0506	MON-CIN 2-6	HOU-ATL 1-2	NY-PHI 2-7	LA-PIT 2-3	SD-STL 0-1	SF-CHI 2*1	
0507	MON-CIN 19*5		NY-PHI 5-8	LA-PIT 4-6	SD-STL 4-8	SF-CHI 2*1	
	MON-CIN 2-4						
0508	NY-CIN 3*2						
0509	NY-CIN 6-7	STL-LA 1-3	HOU-PHI 5*1	CHI-SD 8*5	PIT-SF 2-3	MON-ATL 2-3	
						MON-ATL 7*6	
0510	STL-LA 6*5	NY-MON 7*2	HOU-PHI 1-3	CHI-SD 0-1	PIT-SF 5*1		
0511	STL-LA 2*0	NY-MON 3*2	CIN-PHI 1-4	CHI-SD 4*3	PIT-SF 2-6		
0512	CHI-LA 9*7	ATL-MON 3-5	CIN-PHI 3*0	PIT-SD 4-6	STL-SF 3-9	HOU-NY 5*4	
0513	CHI-LA 2-5	ATL-MON 0-3	CIN-PHI 4*3	PIT-SD 5-6	STL-SF 6-7	HOU-NY 7*4	
0514	CHI-LA 10*7	ATL-MON 2*1	CIN-PHI 4-7	PIT-SD 1*0	STL-SF 4-5		
					STL-SF 3-4		
0515	PHI-HOU 0-5	PIT-LA 6-7	STL-SD 3-4				

♦1978♦	GAME 1	GAME 2	GAME 3	GAME 4	GAME 5	GAME 6	GAME 7
0516	PHI-HOU 1-6	PIT-LA 2-3	STL-SD 5-7	CIN-MON 5*1	CHI-SF 3-4		
0517	PHI-HOU 1-2	PIT-LA 1-10	STL-SD 2-5	CIN-MON 4-5	CHI-SF 5-9	ATL-NY 2*1	
						ATL-NY 1-3	
0518	PHI-HOU 8*5	CIN-MON 3*2				ATL-NY 7-8	
0519	ATL-HOU 0-6	PIT-MON 5*3	STL-CHI 2-6	SD-CIN 3-4	SF-LA 10*7	PHI-NY 3-4	
0520	ATL-HOU 0-13	PIT-MON 6*0	STL-CHI 2-10	SD-CIN 6-10	SF-LA 2-3	PHI-NY 9*4	
0521	ATL-HOU 6*4	PIT-MON 7*0	STL-CHI 2-3	SD-CIN 7*2	SF-LA 1-4	PHI-NY 5-6	
				SD-CIN 0-1			
0522	PIT-MON 2-5	LA-SD 8*1		ATL-CIN 0-10			
0523	NY-PIT 7*3	LA-SD 2-3	HOU-SF 2-3	ATL-CIN 6*4	MON-STL 4*1		
0524	NY-PIT 5-6	LA-SD 3-9	HOU-SF 0-2	ATL-CIN 4-5	MON-STL 0-2	PHI-CHI 4-6	
0525	NY-PIT 3*2		HOU-SF 1-9		MON-STL 11*2	PHI-CHI 1-5	
0526	MON-PIT 1-2	PHI-ATL 2-4	LA-SD 2-4	NY-HOU 4-5	CHI-STL 6*0	CIN-SD 3*1	
0527	MON-PIT 15*1	PHI-ATL 6*5	LA-SF 3*1	NY-HOU 9*7	CHI-STL 3*2	CIN-SD 5*2	
0528	MON-PIT 2-5	PHI-ATL 3-5	LA-SF 5-6	NY-HOU 4*1	CHI-STL 2*0	CIN-SD 1-3	
0529	SD-LA 6-9	CIN-ATL 7*5	CHI-MON 2-4	SF-HOU 8*1	PIT-PHI 3-4	STL-NY 2-7	
						STL-NY 6*2	
0530	CIN-ATL 3-4	SF-HOU 1*0	SD-LA 2-10	CHI-MON 4-7	PIT-PHI 1-6	STL-NY 8*2	
0531	CIN-ATL 10*4	SF-HOU 0-1	SD-LA 3*1	CHI-MON 1-9	PIT-PHI 2*1	STL-NY 5*4	
0602	ATL-CHI 1-2	STL-HOU 1-2	PIT-CIN 2-3	SF-MON 6*5	LA-PHI 2-4	SD-NY 5*4	
0603	ATL-CHI 6-8	STL-HOU 2-5	PIT-CIN 3-4	SF-MON 3-5	LA-PHI 1-5	SD-NY 2-3	
		STL-HOU 2*1					
0604	ATL-CHI 4-6	STL-HOU 4*2	PIT-CIN 4*1	SF-MON 3*2	SD-NY 5*2	LA-PHI 4-9	
0605	HOU-CHI 1-2	ATL-PIT 8*4	CIN-STL 2*1	SD-MON 3-4	LA-NY 8-9	SF-PHI 3-4	
0606	HOU-CHI 4-9	ATL-PIT 2-4	CIN-STL 1-4	SD-MON 0#2	LA-NY 8*2	SF-PHI 6-7	
0607	CIN-CHI 9*6		ATL-STL 6*0	SD-MON 0-4	LA-NY 2-3	SF-PHI 4-5	
				SD-MON 3-8			
0608	CIN-CHI 1-10	ATL-STL 0-2		LA-MON 1-4			
0609	SD-CHI 0-5	HOU-STL 11*7	SF-NY 2-3	LA-MON 9-10	ATL-PHI 1-6	CIN-PIT 9-11	
0610	SD-CHI 10*8	HOU-STL 12*5	SF-NY 2*1	LA-MON 5*4	ATL-PHI 2-6	CIN-PIT 6*4	
0611	SD-CHI 4-7	HOU-STL 3-5	SF-NY 7*5	LA-MON 11*4	ATL-PHI 4*0	CIN-PIT 1-3	
0612	STL-ATL 1-2	CHI-CIN 3*2	PIT-HOU 5-6	PHI-LA 5-6	NY-SD 2-3	MON-SF 0-1	
0613	STL-ATL 1-12	CHI-CIN 0-1	PIT-HOU 1-2	PHI-LA 3-5	NY-SD 3*2	MON-SF 5-9	
0614	STL-ATL 1-7	CHI-CIN 1-3	PIT-HOU 6*4	NY-LA 3-5	MON-SD 2-6	PHI-SF 1-2	
					MON-SD 0-1		
0615	NY-LA 0-3	PHI-SF 1-6			MON-SD 3*1		
0616	MON-LA 1-2	NY-SF 4-7	PIT-ATL 9*4	STL-CIN 0-4	PHI-SD 5*0	CHI-HOU 7*6	
0617	MON-LA 6*3	NY-SF 5*4	PIT-ATL 5*3	STL-CIN 5-6	PHI-SD 0-7	CHI-HOU 4-5	
0618	MON-LA 0-5	NY-SF 0-3	PIT-ATL 7-8	STL-CIN 2-4	PHI-SD 1-4	CHI-HOU 1-3	
		NY-SF 3-4					
0619	CHI-PIT 6*4						
0620	CHI-PIT 1-6	HOU-LA 5*3	MON-NY 0-3	STL-PHI 4*2	ATL-SD 5*3	CIN-SF 6*3	
0621	CHI-PIT 1-2	HOU-LA 4-5	MON-NY 2*1		ATL-SD 2*0	CIN-SF 0-3	
0622	STL-PHI 1-2	HOU-LA 4*3	MON-NY 2*0		ATL-SD 0-2	CIN-SF 5*0	
0623	CHI-PHI 1-6	CIN-LA 0-1	PIT-NY 2-3	MON-STL 4-8	HOU-SD 0-3	ATL-SF 0-9	
	CHI-PHI 1-6						
0624	CHI-PHI 2-6	CIN-LA 3-4	PIT-NY 7*4	HOU-SD 5-6	ATL-SF 1-2	MON-STL 2*0	
0625	CHI-PHI 2-4	CIN-LA 5*4	PIT-NY 4*0	HOU-SD 1-6	ATL-SF 3-9	MON-STL 5-7	
				HOU-SD 4-7			
0626	LA-ATL 2-5	NY-CHI 9-10	CIN-HOU 4*3	SF-SD 1-2	PHI-MON 1-5	STL-PIT 4-5	
						STL-PIT 8-11	
0627	LA-ATL 3*0	NY-CHI 7*2	CIN-HOU 4-7	PHI-MON 1*0	SF-SD 9*1	STL-PIT 2*0	
						STL-PIT 6*1	
0628	LA-ATL 3*2	NY-CHI 8-9	CIN-HOU 0-3	PHI-MON 7*5	SF-SD 4*2	STL-PIT 7*5	
					SF-SD 1-4		
0629	LA-ATL 7*3	PHI-CHI 9*3	CIN-HOU 0-5	NY-PIT 3-4			
0630	SF-ATL 9-10	PHI-CHI 0-2	SD-HOU 5*2	NY-PIT 6*5	STL-MON 2*1	LA-CIN 5*3	
	SF-ATL 5-10	PHI-CHI 6*5				LA-CIN 5*2	
0701	SF-ATL 15*4	PHI-CHI 2*1	STL-MON 2-3	NY-PIT 0-1	SD-HOU 2-9	LA-CIN 2*0	
					SD-HOU 9*3		
0702	SF-ATL 7-9	PHI-CHI 6*5	LA-CIN 6-7	STL-MON 5*4	SD-HOU 6*2		
				STL-MON 4*2			
0703	HOU-CIN 7-8	ATL-LA 4*2	MON-PIT 2*0	SD-SF 4*3	CHI-STL 6*2		
0704	HOU-CIN 3*1	ATL-LA 1-4	MON-PIT 1-3	SD-SF 7*5	CHI-STL 7*5	PHI-NY 0-4	
			MON-PIT 3-4			PHI-NY 3*2	
0705	HOU-CIN 1-2	ATL-LA 9*8	SD-SF 4-5	CHI-STL 5*1		PHI-NY 7*5	
0706	MON-PHI 6-7	ATL-LA 1-5	SD-SF 4-5	PIT-STL 2-3		CHI-NY 6-9	
0707	MON-PHI 7*4	SD-ATL 3-11	LA-HOU 7*4	PIT-STL 2*1	SF-CIN 7*6	CHI-NY 9*7	
					SF-CIN 1-2		
0708	CHI-NY 0-7	PIT-STL 0-4	SD-ATL 4-6	LA-HOU 7*1	SF-CIN 4*2	MON-PHI 3-6	
			SD-ATL 7*0	LA-HOU 7*5		MON-PHI 8*1	
0709	SF-CIN 2-8	CHI-NY 4*1	SD-ATL 2-5	LA-HOU 1-5	PIT-STL 6*1	MON-PHI 7-8	
0713	NY-CIN 4*2	SD-CHI 5*2	HOU-MON 0-6	SF-PIT 4*0	LA-STL 1-6		
0714	NY-CIN 3-6	SD-CHI 9*5	HOU-MON 4*3	SF-PIT 2-5	LA-STL 1-4	PHI-ATL 2-7	
			HOU-MON 5*4				
0715	PHI-ATL 2-3	SD-CHI 1-3	HOU-MON 0-8	NY-CIN 5-7	SF-PIT 6*5	LA-STL 2*1	
0716	PHI-ATL 4*2	LA-CHI 2-3	HOU-MON 1-6	NY-CIN 2-9	SD-PIT 2-3	SF-STL 4-9	
		LA-CHI 5*3			SD-PIT 6-10	SF-STL 6*0	
0717	MON-CIN 6-8	LA-CHI 4*3	PHI-HOU 1-2	NY-ATL 0-3	SD-PIT 7-8	SF-STL 9*7	
				NY-ATL 7*4			
0718	SF-CHI 6-7	MON-CIN 3*1	PHI-HOU 1-9	NY-ATL 3-4	LA-PIT 7*2	SD-STL 3*2	
0719	SF-CHI 7*4	CIN-PHI 7*2	ATL-MON 6-8	HOU-NY 8*3	LA-PIT 3-6	SD-STL 5*3	
	SF-CHI 5-7		ATL-MON 3*1	HOU-NY 1-2			
0720	SF-CHI 9#8	CIN-PHI 6-8	ATL-MON 3-7	HOU-NY 4-7	LA-PIT 6-7	SD-STL 2-3	
				HOU-NY 4-5			
0721	STL-LA 5-7	CIN-MON 10*3	CHI-SD 5*4	ATL-NY 3-12	PIT-SF 3*0	HOU-PHI 1-6	
						HOU-PHI 2-8	
0722	STL-LA 3-4	CIN-MON 2*1	ATL-NY 0-2	CHI-SD 2-4	PIT-SF 2-3	HOU-PHI 2-3	
0723	STL-LA 2*0	CIN-MON 5*4	ATL-NY 3*0	CHI-SD 4*3	PIT-SF 1-3	HOU-PHI 1-3	
0724	CHI-LA 2-3	MON-HOU 5-6	CIN-NY 5*3			HOU-PHI 2-13	
0725	CHI-LA 1-3	MON-HOU 2-3	CIN-NY 2-9	PIT-SD 1-2	STL-SF 2-3	ATL-PHI 5*1	
0726	CHI-LA 2-8	MON-HOU 0-5	CIN-NY 3-12	PIT-SD 5-6	STL-SF 2*1	ATL-PHI 4*0	
				PIT-SD 3-6		ATL-PHI 4*2	
0727		NY-HOU 3-8					
0728	PIT-LA 3-7	NY-HOU 3-4	SF-CHI 9*8	STL-SD 3-8	MON-ATL 4-6	PHI-CIN 12*2	
			CHI-SF 1*0		MON-ATL 4*1		
0729	PIT-LA 1-2	STL-SD 3-7	CHI-SF 5*3		MON-ATL 6-9	PHI-CIN 1-2	
0730	PIT-LA 5*3	STL-SD 2-3	CHI-SF 2-4	NY-HOU 3-4	MON-ATL 19*0	PHI-CIN 2-6	
			CHI-SF 0-1			PHI-CIN 3-5	
0731	CIN-ATL 3*2	SF-HOU 1-4	PIT-MON 2-3	NY-PHI 1-6	LA-SD 3-4		
0801	CIN-ATL 4-16	SF-HOU 2-4	PIT-MON 3-4	NY-PHI 5*1	LA-SD 0-1		
0802	CIN-ATL 6*2	SF-HOU 4*2	PIT-MON 3*0	NY-PHI 6-8	LA-SD 1-2	STL-CHI 2-4	
0803	LA-SF 4-5					STL-CHI 2-3	
						STL-CHI 2-3	
0804	LA-SF 1-2	HOU-ATL 2-7	SD-CIN 3*2	NY-STL 8*3	PHI-PIT 2*0	MON-CHI 4-6	
					PHI-PIT 2-5		
0805	MON-CHI 7*4	SD-CIN 1-7	LA-SF 2*0'	NY-STL 3-5	HOU-ATL 5*3		
					HOU-ATL 7*0		

♦1978♦	GAME 1	GAME 2	GAME 3	GAME 4	GAME 5	GAME 6	GAME 7
0806	SD-CIN 1-3	LA-SF 5*1	NY-STL 1-3	MON-CHI 2*1 MON-CHI 3-4	HOU-ATL 2-3	PHI-PIT 3*2 PHI-PIT 5*0	
0807	ATL-CIN 5*3	SD-LA 1-3	PHI-STL 3-6	PIT-CHI 4-5			
0808	ATL-CIN 6*5	SD-LA 2-3	PHI-STL 0-2 PHI-STL 2-6	PIT-CHI 9*5	NY-MON 1-6	HOU-SF 2-3	
0809	PIT-CHI 4-5	ATL-CIN 0-10	PHI-STL 6*3	SD-LA 0-3 SF-LA 2-12	NY-MON 10*3	HOU-SF 6*5	
0810	PIT-PHI 1-3	CIN-SD 3-15					
0811	PIT-PHI 4-15	CIN-SD 2*0	ATL-HOU 1*0	SF-LA 3-4	CHI-MON 0-1	STL-NY 4*1	
0812	PIT-PHI 1-10	CIN-SD 2-4	ATL-HOU 2-5	SF-LA 3*2	CHI-MON 3-4	STL-NY 5*1	
0813	PIT-PHI 7*3	CIN-SD 2-3	ATL-HOU 0-3	SF-LA 7*6	CHI-MON 2*1	STL-NY 6*1	
0814	ATL-CHI 7-13	CIN-PIT 4-7	HOU-STL 6*0				
0815	ATL-CHI 8-12	CIN-PIT 4*3	HOU-STL 5-11	SF-MON 3-4	SD-NY 1-3	LA-PHI 5*4	
0816	ATL-CHI 9*0	CIN-PIT 2-13	HOU-STL 4*2	SF-MON 0-1	SD-NY 2*1	LA-PHI 5*2	
0817	CIN-CHI 0-2	HOU-PIT 1-5 HOU-PIT 2-3	ATL-STL 3-4	SF-MON 3*0	SD-NY 9*2	LA-PHI 5*2	
0818	CIN-CHI 8*3	HOU-PIT 3-6	SD-MON 3*2	LA-NY 7*3	SF-PHI 6*5	ATL-STL 1-5	
0819	CIN-CHI 9*7	HOU-PIT 2-4	SD-MON 3*2	LA-NY 4-8	SF-PHI 0-3	ATL-STL 3*0	
0820	CIN-CHI 1-2	HOU-PIT 6*7 HOU-PIT 1-3	SD-MON 5*4	LA-NY 5*4	SF-PHI 3-5	ATL-STL 4-6	
0821	STL-CIN 14*9	CHI-HOU 3-8	LA-MON 2-4	SF-NY 4*2	SD-PHI 7*3		
0822	STL-CIN 4-5	CHI-HOU 1-2	PIT-ATL 3*1	SF-NY 7*4	SD-PHI 3-5		
0823	LA-MON 4*2	CHI-HOU 0-3	PIT-ATL 4*3	SF-NY 2*1	SD-PHI 6*5		
0824	STL-CIN 4*3	PHI-LA 4-5	PIT-ATL 5*1	NY-SD 6*3			
0825	CHI-CIN 5*2	PHI-LA 5-6	STL-ATL 11*10	NY-SD 2*1	PIT-HOU 5-7	MON-SF 8*5	
0826	CHI-CIN 8*6	PHI-LA 3*1	STL-ATL 9*4	NY-SD 1-2	PIT-HOU 2-7	MON-SF 1-4	
0827	CHI-CIN 7*1	PHI-LA 9*3	STL-ATL 14*3	NY-SD 0-3	PIT-HOU 8*5	MON-SF 2*1 MON-SF 2-11	
0828	CHI-ATL 3-4	PIT-CIN 3*1	MON-LA 0-4	PHI-SD 6*1			
0829	CHI-ATL 3-4	PIT-CIN 5*0	MON-LA 1-4	PHI-SD 9*5	STL-HOU 3-6	NY-SF 0-2	
0830	CHI-ATL 2-6		MON-LA 3-4	PHI-SD 6*5	STL-HOU 4*2	NY-SF 10*4	
0831	CIN-STL 11*6			MON-SD 1-6			
0901	CIN-STL 5*2	HOU-CHI 11-14	NY-LA 3-4	MON-SD 3*2	PHI-SF 3-4	ATL-PIT 3-8 ATL-PIT 0-3	
0902	HOU-CHI 8*5	MON-SD 3*2	PHI-SF 3*1	CIN-STL 6*3	NY-LA 2-3 NY-LA 5*3	ATL-PIT 3-4	
0903	ATL-PIT 3-6	CIN-STL 2-10	HOU-CHI 2-3 HOU-CHI 2-4	PHI-SF 1-4 PHI-SF 2-3	NY-LA 8*5		
0904	SD-ATL 8*4	CIN-HOU 6*3	MON-CHI 5*3 MON-CHI 6*5	SF-LA 4-5	NY-PIT 4-7 NY-PIT 0-7	PHI-STL 2-3 PHI-STL 10*2	
0905	SD-ATL 1-8	CIN-HOU 2-3	MON-CHI 10*8		NY-PIT 0-8		
0906	SD-ATL 5*3	SF-LA 2-9	PHI-CHI 8*1	NY-MON 2-8	PIT-STL 4*1		
0907	SF-ATL 5-6	SD-CIN 2-6	PHI-CHI 5*3	NY-MON 9*4	PIT-STL 4-5	LA-HOU 3*2	
0908	SF-ATL 8*5	SD-CIN 3*2	PIT-NY 2-3	CHI-MON 4*2	STL-PHI 0-1 STL-PHI 1-2	LA-HOU 0-5	
0909	LA-ATL 4-7	SF-CIN 3-6	SD-HOU 4-10	CHI-MON 6*3	STL-PHI 3-6	PIT-NY 1-4	
0910	LA-ATL 11*5	SF-CIN 1-8	SD-HOU 2-3	CHI-MON 6*3	STL-PHI 8*6	PIT-NY 9-11	
0911	ATL-SD 7*2	HOU-CIN 8-9	LA-SF 7*2	STL-MON 1-3	PIT-PHI 3-10	CHI-NY 9*4	
0912	ATL-SD 1-3	HOU-CIN 3-4	LA-SF 8*0	STL-MON 1-5	PIT-PHI 5*1		
0913	CIN-SD 2-6	HOU-LA 0-6	ATL-SF 5*3	MON-NY 4*3	CHI-PHI 2-6	STL-PIT 1-7	
0914	CIN-SD 1-8	HOU-LA 1-2	ATL-SF 4*1	MON-NY 6-7	CHI-PHI 5-11	STL-PIT 4-7	
0915	HOU-SD 8*4	ATL-LA 0-5	CIN-SF 6*1	STL-CHI 6*2	NY-PHI 5*4	MON-PIT 1-6	
0916	HOU-SD 1-2	ATL-LA 0-2	CIN-SF 2-3	STL-CHI 4*1	NY-PHI 1-2	MON-PIT 5-12	
0917	HOU-SD 1-3	ATL-LA 3*2	CIN-SF 7*1	STL-CHI 2-4	NY-PHI 2*0	MON-PIT 3-5	
0918		CIN-LA 4*0					
0919	PIT-CHI 12*11	CIN-LA 0-8	ATL-HOU 3*2	PHI-MON 2-5	SF-SD 1-4	NY-STL 3-5	
0920	PIT-CHI 1-5	CIN-LA 4*3	ATL-HOU 3*2	PHI-MON 4*2	SF-SD 6*3	NY-STL 7*6	
0921	PIT-CHI 3*2		ATL-HOU 0-2		SF-SD 1-5	NY-STL 2-6 CHI-STL 5*3	
0922	CIN-ATL 6*4	SD-LA 12*3	HOU-SF 0-2			CHI-STL 1-5	
0923	CIN-ATL 1-8	SD-LA 3-5	HOU-SF 2-3	PIT-MON 2-3	PHI-NY 1*0 PHI-NY 6*3		
0924	CIN-ATL 2*1	SD-LA 0-4	PIT-MON 0-4	CHI-STL 5*4	PHI-NY 8*2	HOU-SF 0-7 HOU-SF 4-6	
0925	STL-NY 3*0	MON-PHI 2-3	CHI-PIT 4-7		LA-CIN 4-6	SD-SF 4*1	
0926	STL-NY 1-3	MON-PHI 3-5 MON-PHI 3*0	CHI-PIT 2-5	HOU-ATL 2*0			
0927	HOU-ATL 4*0	MON-PHI 4-5	LA-CIN 3-5	CHI-PIT 3-8	SD-SF 0-1		
0928	HOU-ATL 4*3		LA-CIN 7-8				
0929	SF-HOU 2*1	LA-SD 1-3	ATL-CIN 2-7	MON-STL 7*5	NY-CHI 3*2 NY-CHI 4-5	PHI-PIT 4-5 PHI-PIT 1-2	
0930	ATL-CIN 0-4	SF-HOU 4-7	LA-SD 7*0	MON-STL 1-6	NY-CHI 5-7	PHI-PIT 10*8	
1001	ATL-CIN 8-10	SF-HOU 0-3	LA-SD 3-4	MON-STL 5*1	NY-CHI 5*3	PHI-PIT 3-5	

♦1979♦	GAME 1	GAME 2	GAME 3	GAME 4	GAME 5	GAME 6	GAME 7
0404	SF-CIN 11*5						
0405	NY-CHI 10*6	SD-LA 4*3					
0406	SF-CIN 7*2	SD-LA 1-10	ATL-HOU 1-2	MON-PIT 3*2	PHI-STL 1-8		
0407	SF-CIN 4*2	SD-LA 2-5	ATL-HOU 0-6	MON-PIT 6-7	PHI-STL 2-3	NY-CHI 9*4	
0408	SF-CIN 6-7	SD-LA 5-6	ATL-HOU 0-2	MON-PIT 5*4	PHI-STL 22		
0409	CIN-ATL 9*4		LA-HOU 2*1				
0410	CIN-ATL 4-6	MON-NY 3*2	LA-HOU 1-2	PIT-PHI 3-7	SD-SF 2-4	CHI-STL 0-7	
0411	CIN-ATL 9*5	MON-NY 3*2	LA-HOU 3-10	PIT-PHI 4-5	SD-SF 4*1		
0412	ATL-LA 10*2	PHI-NY 2-3	STL-PIT 1-3		SD-SF 3-4		
0413	ATL-LA 2*1	CIN-SD 4*2	STL-PIT 6-7		HOU-SF 7-8		
0414	ATL-LA 5-6	CIN-SD 2-3	STL-PIT 4-7	CHI-MON 0-2	HOU-SF 1-2		
0415	ATL-LA 11*4	CIN-SD 3-6 CIN-SD 7*5	STL-PIT 9*4	CHI-MON 5*1	HOU-SF 4*3 HOU-SF 9*1	PHI-NY 3*2 PHI-NY 6*3	
0416	HOU-LA 4*0	CHI-MON 0-2					
0417	HOU-LA 6-10	NY-MON 4-5	STL-CHI 3-5	ATL-CIN 4-7	PHI-PIT 13*2	SF-SD 3-4	
0418	HOU-LA 4*0	NY-MON 5-6	STL-CHI 3*2		PHI-PIT 3*2	SF-SD 6-7	
0419	ATL-CIN 0-2		STL-CHI 2-3			SF-SD 14*10	
0420	SD-ATL 7*4	PIT-HOU 4-5	MON-CHI 5-8	NY-PHI 0-8	LA-SF 2-3	CIN-STL 10*3	
0421	SD-ATL 9*5	PIT-HOU 4-5	MON-CHI 3-4	NY-PHI 0-3	LA-SF 2*1	CIN-STL 4*1	
0422	SD-ATL 7-8	PIT-HOU 2-3	MON-CHI 1-4	NY-PHI 4*2 LA-PHI 3-4	LA-SF 9*2	CIN-STL 3-4	
0423	STL-ATL 3*2						
0424	STL-ATL 6*5	PIT-CIN 9*2	SD-MON 1-5	LA-PHI 6-7	SF-NY 3-10		
0425	HOU-CHI 0-4	PIT-CIN 3*2	SD-MON 6-9	LA-PHI 4-5	SF-NY 0-2		
0426	HOU-CHI 6*2						
0427	CHI-ATL 2-3	STL-CIN 3-4	SF-MON 8-14	SD-PHI 0-2	HOU-PIT 9*8		
0428	CHI-ATL 2-7	STL-CIN 12*1	SF-MON 4-6	SD-PHI 5*0	LA-NY 3*1		
0429	CHI-ATL 6*5	STL-CIN 1-5	SF-MON 5-7	SD-PHI 3-4	LA-NY 8*3 LA-NY 3-6 SD-NY 3-4	HOU-PIT 5-10	
0430	LA-MON 4-8	SF-PHI 1-4	HOU-STL 6*5		SD-NY 10*5	ATL-PIT 5*2	
0501	LA-MON 3-7	SF-PHI 7*0	HOU-STL 6-7	CHI-CIN 5*1		ATL-PIT 2-10	
0502			HOU-STL 2-5	CHI-CIN 1-4			
0503	PHI-LA 2-5	MON-SD 2-10	HOU-STL 4*1	NY-SF 5-7			
0504	PHI-LA 5*2	MON-SD 12*1	PIT-STL 3-4	NY-SF 3-4	ATL-CHI 2-6	HOU-CIN 5-6	
0505	PHI-LA 11*0	MON-SD 3-6	PIT-STL 6*5	NY-SF 4-6	ATL-CHI 3-9	HOU-CIN 2-6	

♦1979♦	GAME 1	GAME 2	GAME 3	GAME 4	GAME 5	GAME 6	GAME 7
0506	PHI-LA 4*0	MON-SD 7*5	PIT-STL 2-4	NY-SF 5*4	ATL-CHI 13-14	HOU-CIN 5-17	
						HOU-CIN 8*2	
0507	PIT-ATL 4*2	NY-LA 2-5	PHI-SD 11*6				
0508	PIT-ATL 1-4	NY-LA 2-3	PHI-SD 9*8	CIN-CHI 8*7	STL-HOU 4*1	MON-SF 4*0	
0509	PIT-ATL 17*9	NY-LA 2-7	PHI-SD 2*0	CIN-CHI 7*4	STL-HOU 4-5	MON-SF 2-9	
0510		NY-LA 1-14	PHI-SD 3*2	CIN-CHI 7#7	STL-HOU 3*1	MON-SF 3*0	
0511	CIN-PIT 8*4	MON-LA 0-7	NY-SD 4*0	ATL-STL 3*0	CHI-HOU 5*3	PHI-SF 1-2	
0512	CIN-PIT 2-3	MON-LA 3-4	NY-SD 1-2	ATL-STL 6-7	CHI-HOU 3-11	PHI-SF 1-4	
					CHI-HOU 2*0		
0513	MON-LA 2-8	CIN-PIT 7*3	NY-SD 4-5	PHI-SF 12*3	CHI-HOU 0-3	ATL-STL 3-7	
0514	SD-CIN 4-7						
0515	SD-CIN 2*1	LA-ATL 5*4	PHI-CHI 1-7	SF-HOU 8*1	NY-PIT 3*0	MON-STL 0-1	
0516	SD-CIN 0-7	LA-ATL 2-3	PHI-CHI 13*0	SF-HOU 8*4	NY-PIT 3-4	MON-STL 0-2	
0517		LA-ATL 3-6	PHI-CHI 23*22	SF-HOU 3*0	NY-PIT 5-6	MON-STL 2#2	
0518	LA-CIN 6-7	SF-ATL 4-6	PIT-CHI 9*5	SD-HOU 2-3	MON-PHI 5*3		
0519	LA-CIN 4-5	SF-ATL 4*2	PIT-CHI 3*0	SD-HOU 4*2	MON-PHI 10*5		
		SF-ATL 7*6					
0520	PIT-CHI 6*5	SF-ATL 8*1	LA-CIN 6*4	STL-NY 7-8	MON-PHI 10*6	SD-HOU 0-1	
						SD-HOU 3-6	
0521	HOU-ATL 5-7	PIT-MON 4*2	STL-PHI 3-5	LA-SD 2-3			
0522	HOU-ATL 4*1	PIT-MON 3-6	STL-PHI 1-3	LA-SD 6-7	CHI-NY 2-4	CIN-SF 2-12	
0523	HOU-ATL 5-6	PIT-MON 0-3	STL-PHI 3*1	LA-SD 4*2		CIN-SF 5*0	
0524	CHI-NY 9*7					CIN-SF 1-2	
	CHI-NY 2-4						
0525	PIT-NY 33	CIN-LA 6-17	CHI-PHI 3*0	HOU-SD 1-2	ATL-SF 4-6		
0526	PIT-NY 8-10	CIN-LA 3*1	CHI-PHI 4*1	HOU-SD 9*0	ATL-SF 5*4		
0527	PIT-NY 2*1	CIN-LA 7-8	CHI-PHI 4-6	HOU-SD 4*2	ATL-SF 10*8	STL-MON 3-8	
0528	CIN-LA 3*2	PIT-NY 6*1	CHI-PHI 4*1	HOU-SD 4-5	ATL-SF 4*1	STL-MON 11*3	
0529	SF-LA 5-6	CIN-HOU 1-2	PHI-MON 0-9	ATL-SD 3-6	CHI-PIT 0-8	NY-STL 6*2	
				ATL-SD 2-3			
0530	CIN-HOU 3-6	SF-LA 5-6	PHI-MON 0-2	ATL-SD 2-10	CHI-PIT 2-9	NY-STL 3-7	
0531	CIN-HOU 0-3	SF-LA 10-12	PHI-MON 0-1	ATL-SD 1-3	CHI-PIT 3-4	NY-STL 6-9	
0601	MON-HOU 2-3	NY-ATL 5*4	SF-CHI 2-8	PHI-CIN 2-4	SD-PIT 8-9	LA-STL 7-8	
0602	MON-HOU 1-2	NY-ATL 6-7	SF-CHI 8*6	PHI-CIN 2-4	SD-PIT 3*1	LA-STL 5-12	
0603	MON-HOU 4-5	NY-ATL 9*4	SF-CHI 1-2	PHI-CIN 0-6	SD-PIT 0-7	LA-STL 4-6	
				PHI-CIN 2-12			
0604	MON-ATL 8*1	PHI-HOU 0-3	LA-PIT 4*2	NY-CIN 6*2			
0605	MON-ATL 1-4	PHI-HOU 8*0	LA-PIT 1-3	NY-CIN 1-6			
0606	MON-ATL 12*2	PHI-HOU 3-4	LA-PIT 4-5	NY-CIN 5*3	SD-CHI 11*3	SF-STL 4-5	
0607					SD-CHI 0-3	SF-STL 5-6	
					SD-CHI 3-4	SF-STL 12*10	
0608	MON-CIN 2-3	HOU-NY 5*0	ATL-PHI 11*5	SF-PIT 2-3	LA-CHI 11*4	SD-STL 8*7	
0609	MON-CIN 1-7	HOU-NY 0-4	ATL-PHI 3-9	SF-PIT 6*2	LA-CHI 3-5	SD-STL 4-7	
0610	MON-CIN 2-3	HOU-NY 5*3	ATL-PHI 10*3	SF-PIT 7*4	LA-CHI 3-10	SD-STL 2-3	
0611	STL-LA 9*7	CIN-NY 2-3	HOU-PHI 2-4	ATL-MON 5-6			
0612	STL-LA 3-9	CIN-NY 6-12	HOU-PHI 0-4	PIT-SD 3-6	CHI-SF 2-7		
0613	STL-LA 8-9	CIN-NY 4*1	HOU-PHI 4*3	PIT-SD 2-3	CHI-SF 3*2		
0614				PIT-SD 1-2	CHI-SF 8*6	ATL-MON 1-4	
0615	PIT-LA 6*2	ATL-NY 1-2	CIN-PHI 6*3	CHI-SD 3*2	STL-SF 6-9	ATL-MON 3-4	
0616	PIT-LA 6*3	ATL-NY 0-2	CIN-PHI 3-4	CHI-SD 5*2	STL-SF 1-6	HOU-MON 2*1	
0617	PIT-LA 5*1	ATL-NY 1#1	CIN-PHI 3-9	CHI-SD 8*5	STL-SF 4-7	HOU-MON 2-4	
0618	CHI-LA 3-7	PHI-ATL 5-10	NY-HOU 2-3	STL-SD 2-3		HOU-MON 3-19	
0619	CHI-LA 7*4	PHI-ATL 4-10	NY-HOU 1-3	STL-SD 7*2	PIT-SF 9*4	CIN-MON 3*2	
0620		PHI-ATL 10*4	NY-HOU 4-5	STL-SD 1-3	PIT-SF 8*5	CIN-MON 2-3	
0621		LA-ATL 6*4				CIN-MON 4-5	
0622	SF-CIN 3*2	LA-ATL 2-3	SD-HOU 1-2	PHI-MON 5-6	CHI-PIT 2-7	NY-STL 2-4	
0623	SF-CIN 5*2	LA-ATL 3-7	SD-HOU 2-3	PHI-MON 0-3	CHI-PIT 4*3		
0624	SF-CIN 7-8	LA-ATL 2-4	SD-HOU 1-4	PHI-MON 5*2	CHI-PIT 5*0	NY-STL 6*2	
0625	PHI-CHI 2-8	SD-LA 3-4	CIN-HOU 2*1	ATL-SF 6*1	PIT-NY 8*1	MON-STL 3*2	
			CIN-HOU 0-4		PIT-NY 0-4	MON-STL 8*2	
0626	PHI-CHI 5*3	SD-LA 5*1	CIN-HOU 5-6	ATL-SF 5-6	PIT-NY 2*1	MON-STL 5*3	
0627	PHI-CHI 4-11	CIN-LA 9*1	NY-PIT 12*9	HOU-SF 3-6	ATL-SD 1-2	MON-STL 0-5	
					ATL-SD 5*2		
0628	CIN-LA 2*1	NY-PIT 3*2	HOU-SF 6*5		ATL-SD 5-6		
0629	ATL-LA 5*2	MON-PIT 5-6	CIN-SF 4-6	PHI-STL 8*7	HOU-SD 4*1		
				PHI-STL 1-7			
0630	NY-CHI 9*8	ATL-LA 7*4	MON-PIT 5*3	PHI-STL 6*4	HOU-SD 3*0	CIN-SF 2*0	
0701	NY-CHI 4-5	ATL-LA 2*1		PHI-STL 7-13	HOU-SD 4*1	CIN-SF 1-2	
	NY-CHI 2-8			PHI-STL 1-2		CIN-SF 3-7	
0702	MON-CHI 5*0	NY-PHI 2-6	LA-SD 6*3	PIT-STL 5*4			
0703	MON-CHI 2-3	NY-PHI 2-4	LA-SD 2-3	PIT-STL 4*1	SF-ATL 2-5	HOU-CIN 3*2	
0704	MON-CHI 2*1	NY-PHI 0-1	LA-SD 0-6	PIT-STL 6*4	SF-ATL 6-7	HOU-CIN 3*2	
0705	MON-CHI 1-3	NY-PHI 3*2		PIT-STL 0-2	SF-ATL 4-5	HOU-CIN 4-5	
0706	HOU-CHI 4*2	SF-PHI 1-6	LA-MON 4-6	SD-NY 6*5	STL-ATL 9*5	PIT-CIN 1-2	
					STL-ATL 5*4		
0707	PIT-CIN 2-6	LA-MON 1-2	SD-NY 11*3	SF-PHI 8*6	STL-ATL 2-10	HOU-CHI 0-6	
						HOU-CHI 3-8	
0708	STL-ATL 5-6	LA-MON 8*6	SF-PHI 3-5	PIT-CIN 2-4	SD-NY 5*3	HOU-CHI 0-10	
				PIT-CIN 2*1	SD-NY 1-4		
0709	CHI-ATL 7*4	LA-MON 0-3	SF-PHI 2-4	STL-CIN 6*3			
0710	CHI-ATL 7*3	SF-MON 11*7	SD-PHI 5-6	STL-CIN 2-4	PIT-HOU 4*3	LA-NY 7*4	
0711	CHI-ATL 5-6	SF-MON 1*0	SD-PHI 7*3	STL-CIN 1-6	PIT-HOU 5*1	LA-NY 3-4	
0712		SF-MON 5*3	SD-PHI 3-4	CHI-CIN 10*8	PIT-HOU 5*3	LA-NY 5-12	
0713	PIT-ATL 4-13	SD-MON 7*5	LA-PHI 2-3	CHI-CIN 3*1	STL-HOU 1*0	SF-NY 6-7	
		SD-MON 7-10				SF-NY 2-5	
0714	PIT-ATL 5*1	SD-MON 5*1	CHI-CIN 1*0	STL-HOU 2-3	LA-PHI 7-10	SF-NY 2-3	
0715	PIT-ATL 7*3	SD-MON 0-4	CHI-CIN 1-7	STL-HOU 3*1	LA-PHI 3-10	SF-NY 4*0	
0719	ATL-CHI 8*2	MON-LA 3-7	NY-SD 1-3	PHI-SF 0-1	CIN-STL 16*4	HOU-PIT 5-9	
						HOU-PIT 2-4	
0720	ATL-CHI 2-10	MON-LA 5-6	NY-SD 1-2	PHI-SF 6*4	CIN-STL 3*0	HOU-PIT 3-9	
0721	ATL-CHI 2-3	MON-LA 7*2	NY-SD 2*1	PHI-SF 1-4	CIN-STL 3-12	HOU-PIT 5-6	
0722	CIN-CHI 12*1	NY-LA 3-4	PHI-SD 5*2	MON-SF 6-8	HOU-STL 7*6	ATL-PIT 4-5	
	CIN-CHI 4-8			MON-SF 15*5		ATL-PIT 2-3	
0723	CIN-CHI 8-9	NY-LA 1-3	PHI-SD 5-6	MON-SF 8*3	HOU-STL 3*2	ATL-PIT 1-7	
	CIN-CHI 1-2					ATL-PIT 8*0	
0724	CHI-HOU 1-6	PHI-LA 3-15	MON-SD 3-4	NY-SF 6*5	ATL-STL 3-7	CIN-PIT 6*5	
0725	CHI-HOU 4-6	PHI-LA 8-16	MON-SD 6*5	NY-SF 3*0	ATL-STL 13*4	CIN-PIT 6*5	
0726	LA-HOU 6*5	CHI-NY 9*2	SF-SD 6*2		ATL-STL 2-6	CIN-PIT 9*7	
0727	LA-HOU 11*7	CHI-NY 4*2	SF-SD 4*3	CIN-ATL 2*0	STL-PHI 5*0	PIT-MON 5*4	
						PIT-MON 9*1	
0728	LA-HOU 2-5	CHI-NY 4-6	STL-PHI 5*4	SF-SD 3-4	CIN-ATL 8*6	PIT-MON 5*3	
					CIN-ATL 5-8		
0729	LA-HOU 3-4	CHI-NY 0-4	STL-PHI 6*5	PIT-MON 3-5	CIN-ATL 9*4	SF-SD 4*2	
0730	SF-HOU 8*0	LA-CIN 4-9	CHI-PHI 4-5	STL-MON 7*2	NY-PIT 5-8		
				STL-MON 1-5			
0731	SD-ATL 10*3	LA-CIN 7*6	SF-HOU 4-6	STL-MON 0-5	CHI-PHI 1-4	NY-PIT 2*1	
0801	SD-ATL 4-5	LA-CIN 5-10	SF-HOU 4-5	CHI-MON 5-7	PHI-NY 9*6	STL-PIT 3-4	

♦1979♦	GAME 1	GAME 2	GAME 3	GAME 4	GAME 5	GAME 6	GAME 7
0802				CHI-MON 4-6	PHI-NY 7*4 PHI-NY 1-2	STL-PIT 5*4	
0803	STL-CHI 2-4	SD-CIN 6*4	ATL-HOU 1-4	SF-LA 3-11	NY-MON 6-10	PHI-PIT 3-6 PHI-PIT 1-5	
0804	STL-CHI 6-8	SD-CIN 1-7	SF-LA 3-4	NY-MON 3*2	ATL-HOU 3-4 ATL-HOU 2-6	PHI-PIT 0-4	
0805	SD-CIN 1-9	SF-LA 1-8	STL-CHI 2-3 STL-CHI 5*4	NY-MON 4*2 NY-MON 3-7	ATL-HOU 2-3	PHI-PIT 8-12 PHI-PIT 2-5	
0806	ATL-CIN 1-3	SF-LA 7*1				STL-NY 9*2	
0807	ATL-CIN 3*2	HOU-LA 8-10	PIT-CHI 2-15	MON-PHI 2-4	SD-SF 2-3	STL-NY 2*1	
0808	PIT-CHI 5*2	ATL-CIN 1-3	HOU-LA 4*1	MON-PHI 3-4	SD-SF 7-10	STL-NY 8*4	
0809	PIT-CHI 3-11	ATL-CIN 2-5	HOU-LA 3-4	MON-PHI 4-6	SD-SF 4*0	STL-NY 4*0	
0810	HOU-ATL 2*1	CIN-SD 2-3	CHI-STL 8-13 CHI-STL 3-5	PIT-PHI 3-4 PIT-PHI 3*2	LA-SF 9*0	MON-NY 1-7 MON-NY 6*5	
0811	LA-SF 7*4		CHI-STL 7*3	PIT-PHI 14*11		MON-NY 5*2	
0812	LA-SF 1-4	HOU-ATL 2-3	CHI-STL 5*3	CIN-SD 9*2 CIN-SD 4-5			
0813	MON-HOU 1-4	PIT-PHI 9*1	CHI-STL 2-3				
0814	MON-HOU 1-2	NY-ATL 18*5	LA-STL 9*0	SF-CHI 8*2	PHI-CIN 1-2	SD-PIT 1-7	
0815	MON-HOU 3*0	NY-ATL 6*3	LA-STL 6*5	SF-CHI 5-6	PHI-CIN 3*2	SD-PIT 1-5	
0816		NY-ATL 6*3	LA-STL 4*2	SF-CHI 4-14		SD-PIT 4-5	
0817	NY-CIN 3-4	PHI-HOU 5*2	SF-STL 0-3	SD-CHI 6-9	ATL-MON 0-1	LA-PIT 7*6	
0818	NY-CIN 3-4	PHI-HOU 1*0	SF-STL 4-5	SD-CHI 2-3	ATL-MON 1-2	LA-PIT 5*1	
0819	NY-CIN 5-6	PHI-HOU 3*2	SF-STL 0-4	SD-CHI 1-3	ATL-MON 1-5	LA-PIT 0-2	
0820	MON-CIN 5*2	HOU-NY 8*1	SD-STL 3-6	LA-CHI 1-2	ATL-PHI 5*2	SF-PIT 5-6	
0821	MON-CIN 2-3	HOU-NY 0#5	SD-STL 3*2	LA-CHI 4*2	ATL-PHI 5*4	SF-PIT 6*1	
0822	MON-CIN 2-7	HOU-NY 0-5 HOU-NY 3*1	SD-STL 5-8	LA-CHI 7*2	ATL-PHI 4*3	SF-PIT 6-8	
0824	MON-ATL 2*0	CIN-NY 1*0	STL-LA 12*5	HOU-PHI 3-5	PIT-SD 2-3	CHI-SF 4*1	
0825		CIN-NY 8*4	STL-LA 5*4	HOU-PHI 3*1	PIT-SD 4*3	CHI-SF 2-5	
0826		CIN-NY 8*0	STL-LA 1-4	HOU-PHI 4*1	PIT-SD 9*2	CHI-SF 4*1	
0827	HOU-MON 3*0	ATL-NY 1-2 ATL-NY 5*1	PIT-LA 2-4	CIN-PHI 4*2	CHI-SD 4-5		
0828	PIT-LA 4*1	ATL-NY 6*4	HOU-MON 6-7	CIN-PHI 5*2	CHI-SD 3*1	STL-SF 2*1	
0829	PIT-LA 4*1	ATL-NY 5*4	HOU-MON 3-5	CIN-PHI 7*6	CHI-SD 1-3	STL-SF 5*1 STL-SF 2-3	
0830	CHI-LA 4*1					PIT-SF 6*4	
0831	CHI-LA 4-6	PHI-ATL 6*2	NY-HOU 0-2	CIN-MON 7-8	STL-SD 8*7	PIT-SF 5*3	
0901	CHI-LA 4-5	PHI-ATL 6*4	NY-HOU 1-3	CIN-MON 2-7	STL-SD 5*3	PIT-SF 7*2 PIT-SF 5*3	
0902	PHI-ATL 2*1	NY-HOU 5*4	CHI-LA 2-6	CIN-MON 1-13	STL-SD 2*1	PIT-SF 5*3	
0903	CIN-ATL 6*5	LA-HOU 1*0	STL-CHI 2*1	NY-MON 2-7 NY-MON 5-6	SF-SD 0-3	PHI-PIT 2*0 PHI-PIT 3-7	
0904	CIN-ATL 6-7	STL-CHI 6*4	LA-HOU 4-9	NY-MON 1-5	SF-SD 3*1		
0905	LA-ATL 5*3	MON-CHI 4*3	SD-HOU 3-4	SF-CIN 5-6	PIT-STL 7*5	NY-PHI 5*3	
0906	LA-ATL 2-6	MON-CHI 1*0	SD-HOU 0-2	SF-CIN 3-12	PIT-STL 6-8	NY-PHI 1-2	
0907	SD-ATL 8*0	PHI-CHI 3-4	LA-CIN 6*5	SF-HOU 9*2	PIT-NY 6*4	MON-STL 4-5	
0908	SD-ATL 9*2	PHI-CHI 9*8	LA-CIN 1-4	SF-HOU 2*1	PIT-NY 2-3	MON-STL 7*2	
0909	SD-ATL 4*1	PHI-CHI 2-15	LA-CIN 3*1	SF-HOU 1-4	PIT-NY 6*5	MON-STL 4*1	
0911	SD-LA 3*1	STL-PIT 3-7	HOU-CIN 8-9	ATL-SF 2*1	PHI-NY 5*2	CHI-MON 6-8 CHI-MON 2-3	
0912	HOU-CIN 4-7	SD-LA 2-5	PHI-NY 4*0	STL-PIT 0-2	ATL-SF 3-4	CHI-MON 3-6	
0913		SD-LA 6-8	PHI-NY 2*1		ATL-SF 4*1	CHI-MON 3-4	
0914	CHI-PHI 2*0	CIN-LA 0-2	ATL-SD 10*7		HOU-SF 7*0	STL-MON 1-2	
0915	CHI-PHI 1-8	CIN-LA 2*1	ATL-SD 6*1	NY-PIT 4-5	HOU-SF 3-5	STL-MON 4*1	
0916	CIN-LA 2*0	CHI-PHI 3-4	NY-PIT 3*0	HOU-SF 1-2		STL-MON 4*3 STL-MON 1-5 PIT-MON 2*1	
0917	ATL-LA 4-9	HOU-SD 1*0	CIN-SF 4-7	PHI-STL 7*5	CHI-NY 2*0	PIT-MON 5*3	
0918	ATL-LA 1-6	HOU-SD 0-4	CIN-SF 1-3	PHI-STL 5*3	CHI-NY 2*1		
0919	ATL-HOU 6*5	SF-LA 2-7	CIN-SD 3*2	PIT-PHI 9*6 PIT-PHI 5-6	MON-NY 3*1 MON-NY 4*1	CHI-STL 3-6 CHI-STL 3*2	
0920	ATL-HOU 1-7	SF-LA 0-3	CIN-SD 8*5	PIT-PHI 1-2	MON-NY 6*3 MON-NY 2*0	CHI-STL 1-2	
0921	PIT-CHI 0-2	CIN-HOU 2-3	LA-SD 1-3		STL-NY 6*3	MON-PHI 8-9	
0922	PIT-CHI 4*1	CIN-HOU 1-4	LA-SD 8-10	SF-ATL 2-10	STL-NY 3*2 STL-NY 7*4	MON-PHI 8*2 MON-PHI 7*4	
0923	SF-ATL 2*1	PIT-CHI 6*0	CIN-HOU 7*1	LA-SD 5*2		MON-PHI 7*2	
0924	HOU-ATL 4-5 HOU-ATL 1-8	NY-CHI 3*1	MON-PIT 2-5 MON-PIT 7*6			STL-PHI 7*2	
0925	HOU-ATL 8*0	SD-CIN 8*2	MON-PIT 4-10	STL-PHI 4*1	LA-SF 11*2	NY-CHI 3-11 NY-CHI 4*3	
0926	HOU-ATL 4-9	SD-CIN 3-4	STL-PHI 5-11 STL-PIT 9*5	MON-PIT 1-10	LA-SF 8*4 LA-SF 3-5	NY-CHI 8*3	
0927				CHI-PIT 1-6	SD-SF 2*0	NY-STL 6*2	
0928	ATL-CIN 0-3	HOU-LA 5-6	PHI-MON 3*2			NY-STL 7*6	
0929	ATL-CIN 2*0	HOU-LA 3*0	PHI-MON 2-3	CHI-PIT 7*6	SD-SF 5-6	NY-STL 8*7	
0930	ATL-CIN 7*2	HOU-LA 3*2	PHI-MON 2*0	CHI-PIT 3-5	SD-SF 5*3	NY-STL 4*2	

♦1980♦	GAME 1	GAME 2	GAME 3	GAME 4	GAME 5	GAME 6	GAME 7
0409	ATL-CIN 0-9						
0410	LA-HOU 2-3	CHI-NY 2-5	SF-SD 4-6	PIT-STL 0-1			
0411	LA-HOU 6-10	CHI-NY 7*5	SF-SD 3-5	PIT-STL 4*3	ATL-CIN 0-6	MON-PHI 3-6	
0412	LA-HOU 6*5	CHI-NY 6*3	SF-SD 2-4	PIT-STL 7*2	ATL-CIN 4-5	MON-PHI 2-6	
0413	LA-HOU 2-4	CHI-NY 0-5	SF-SD 3*1	PIT-STL 3*0	ATL-CIN 0-5	MON-PHI 5*4	
0414	ATL-HOU 4-5	CHI-PIT 4-5	LA-SD 1-2		SF-CIN 5-6		
0415	ATL-HOU 2-6	MON-NY 7*3	LA-SD 5-9	PHI-STL 2-7	SF-CIN 3-8		
0416		MON-NY 2-3	LA-SD 10*4	PHI-STL 8*3	SF-CIN 3-5		
0417	CIN-ATL 4*1	NY-CHI 1-4	HOU-LA 4-6	STL-PIT 12*9	SD-SF 3-7		
0418	CIN-ATL 0-3	PHI-MON 5-7	HOU-LA 7*4	STL-PIT 10-12	SD-SF 2-5 SD-SF 3*0		
0419	CIN-ATL 6*1	NY-CHI 9-12	HOU-LA 2*0	PHI-MON 13*4	STL-PIT 2*1		
0420	CIN-ATL 5*3	NY-CHI 3-6	HOU-LA 2-4	PHI-MON 6-7	STL-PIT 3-6	SD-SF 1-5	
0421	CIN-HOU 6*5	NY-CHI 3*0	SF-LA 3-4	PIT-MON 7*1		STL-CHI 12-16	
0422	CIN-HOU 0-8	NY-PHI 8-14	SF-LA 0-6	PIT-MON 5*3	SD-ATL 2-3	STL-CHI 3*1	
0423	CIN-HOU 3*2	NY-PHI 3*2	SF-LA 0-4	PIT-MON 2-3	SD-ATL 1-2		
0424			SF-LA 2-5		SD-ATL 7-8		
0425	PIT-CHI 3-5	NY-HOU 4-7	SD-LA 3-6	STL-PHI 3*1	MON-ATL 7-8	CIN-SF 3-4	
0426	PIT-CHI 9*2	NY-HOU 0-6	SD-LA 3-4	STL-PHI 7*4	MON-ATL 4*3	CIN-SF 1-3	
0427		NY-HOU 3-4	SD-LA 1-3	STL-PHI 10*1	MON-ATL 3-6	CIN-SF 3*1	
0428	CHI-STL 4*2		MON-PIT 4-5	LA-SF 5*0			
0429	CHI-STL 6*4	HOU-CIN 3*0	MON-PIT 0-5	LA-SF 4*3			
0430	CHI-STL 2-8	HOU-CIN 5*1	MON-PIT 1-2		PHI-NY 0-2	ATL-SD 1-2	
0501		HOU-CIN 9*3			PHI-NY 2*1	ATL-SD 3-4	
0502	SF-MON 3-4	CHI-CIN 12*4	ATL-PIT 6*1	LA-PHI 5-9	SD-NY 1*0	HOU-STL 1-9	

◆1980◆	GAME 1		GAME 2		GAME 3		GAME 4		GAME 5		GAME 6		GAME 7
0503	SF-MON	3*2	CHI-CIN	7*1	ATL-PIT	3*1	LA-PHI	3-7	SD-NY	2*1	HOU-STL	4*2	
0504	SF-MON	8*4	CHI-CIN	2-3	ATL-PIT	4-13	LA-PHI	12*10	SD-NY	4*3	HOU-STL	4*2	
	SF-MON	4-6	CHI-CIN	4-5					SD-NY	2-6			
0505	HOU-MON	1-10	ATL-PHI	1-7	SF-STL	5-9			CIN-NY	2-3			
0506	HOU-MON	8*4	ATL-PHI	5-10	SF-STL	7-10	SD-CHI	4*0	CIN-NY	12*10	LA-PIT	1-2	
0507	HOU-MON	0-3			SF-STL	2-12	SD-CHI	4-7	CIN-NY	3*2	LA-PIT	6-7	
0508							SD-CHI	9*6					
0509	HOU-ATL	4-5	PHI-CIN	2-5	NY-MON	2*1	SF-CHI	6*3	PIT-SD	4*3	LA-STL	7-15	
0510	HOU-ATL	3*2	PHI-CIN	3-5	NY-MON	3-5	SF-CHI	9-15	PIT-SD	9*5	LA-STL	5*3	
0511	HOU-ATL	4-7	PHI-CIN	7*3			SF-CHI	3*0	PIT-SD	0-5	LA-STL	4*2	
0512	CHI-LA	1-2											
0513	CHI-LA	2-4	PHI-ATL	3-7	NY-CIN	4-15	MON-HOU	3*2	STL-SD	2-3	PIT-SF	0-5	
0514	CHI-LA	5*2	PHI-ATL	9*1	NY-CIN	7*6	MON-HOU	1*0	STL-SD	2*1	PIT-SF	3*2	
0515									STL-SD	1-2	PIT-SF	3*2	
0516	NY-ATL	5*3	PHI-HOU	3*0	PIT-LA	6-8	CIN-MON	1-2	CHI-SD	0-2	STL-SF	3-4	
0517			PHI-HOU	4*2	PIT-LA	1-3	CIN-MON	6-9	CHI-SD	2*1	STL-SF	2-4	
0518	NY-ATL	1-2	PHI-HOU	0-3	PIT-LA	0-2			CHI-SD	3-4	STL-SF	5-6	
	NY-ATL	2*1											
0519	STL-LA	1-5	ATL-MON	8-11	CIN-PHI	4-6							
0520	STL-LA	3-4	ATL-MON	1*0	CIN-PHI	7*6	HOU-NY	3*2	CHI-SF	0-2			
0521	STL-LA	3-5	ATL-MON	2-3	CIN-PHI	8-9	HOU-NY	1-5	CHI-SF	1-4	SD-PIT	3-4	
0522	HOU-NY	8*5									SD-PIT	2-3	
											SD-PIT	6*4	
0523	ATL-NY	1-2	LA-CHI	0-2	MON-CIN	7*4	HOU-PHI	0-3	SD-STL	2*0	SF-PIT	4-5	
0524	ATL-NY	4-5	LA-CHI	4*2	MON-CIN	0-2	HOU-PHI	4-5	SD-STL	8*4	SF-PIT	10*9	
0525	ATL-NY	0-3	LA-CHI	1-2	MON-CIN	7*4	HOU-PHI	2-6	SD-STL	11*5	SF-PIT	5*2	
0526	SF-ATL	1-2	MON-CHI	4*0	LA-CIN	4*0	PIT-PHI	6-7	NY-STL	5-8	SD-HOU	1-4	
					LA-CIN	4-5							
0527	SF-ATL	3-6	MON-CHI	2-4	LA-CIN	1-6	SD-HOU	3-4	PIT-PHI	3*2	NY-STL	9*5	
0528	SF-ATL	2-3	MON-CHI	3#3			SD-HOU	0-1	PIT-PHI	3-6	NY-STL	6*5	
0529	ATL-LA	0-3	CIN-SD	5*3					PIT-PHI	5*4			
0530	ATL-LA	4-8	CIN-SD	5*3	PHI-CHI	7-10	NY-PIT	5*1	HOU-SF	2-3	MON-STL	10*4	
0531	ATL-LA	6*5	CIN-SD	5-7	PHI-CHI	7*0	NY-PIT	0-5	HOU-SF	5*0	MON-STL	6-8	
0601	ATL-LA	9*5	CIN-SD	7*6	PHI-CHI	4-5	NY-PIT	3-13	HOU-SF	2-6	MON-STL	7*6	
0602	CIN-LA	2-3	HOU-SD	0-3	CHI-MON	7-8	PHI-PIT	3-9	ATL-SF	4*2			
0603	CIN-LA	1-5	HOU-SD	3*2	CHI-MON	5*2	PHI-PIT	3-4	ATL-SF	2-3	STL-NY	8*1	
0604	CIN-LA	5*4	HOU-SD	4*3	CHI-MON	1-8	PHI-PIT	4*3	ATL-SF	7*2	STL-NY	1*0	
0605					CHI-MON	0-2					STL-NY	1-2	
0606	LA-ATL	5*0	SD-CIN	2-4	STL-MON	2-7	SF-HOU	0-2	CHI-PHI	5-6	PIT-NY	4-9	
0607	LA-ATL	1-6	SD-CIN	6*1	STL-MON	1-2	SF-HOU	0-3	CHI-PHI	2-5	PIT-NY	5-6	
0608	LA-ATL	3*1	SD-CIN	0-1	STL-MON	4-6	SF-HOU	4-5	CHI-PHI	2*0	PIT-NY	4-6	
					STL-MON	4-9					PIT-NY	3*0	
0609	STL-ATL	8*5	SD-CIN	66	CHI-HOU	2-6	SF-PHI	3*1					
0610	STL-ATL	2-5	PIT-CIN	5*3	CHI-HOU	2-5	SF-PHI	3-4	SD-MON	4-8	LA-NY	4-5	
0611	STL-ATL	4*3	PIT-CIN	2-3	CHI-HOU	0-3	SF-PHI	7*4	SD-MON	6-7	LA-NY	2-6	
0612			PIT-CIN	10*6					SD-MON	1-9	LA-NY	5-6	
0613	ATL-CHI	7*6	SD-PHI	6-9	HOU-PIT	3-5	CIN-STL	5*2	LA-MON	3-4	SF-NY	3*1	
0614	ATL-CHI	5-10	SD-PHI	1-3	HOU-PIT	7*3	CIN-STL	3-4	LA-MON	8*0	SF-NY	6-7	
0615	ATL-CHI	1-4	SD-PHI	5-8	HOU-PIT	1-4	CIN-STL	9-10	LA-MON	1*0	SF-NY	3*0	
0616	HOU-CHI	2*1	PHI-LA	3*2	CIN-PIT	3-5	ATL-STL	6*3	NY-SD	2-3	MON-SF	1-5	
0617	HOU-CHI	7*1	PHI-LA	6*5	CIN-PIT	4*3	ATL-STL	2-3	NY-SD	1-2	MON-SF	2*1	
0618	CIN-CHI	0-7	MON-LA	7-8	STL-HOU	0-3	PIT-ATL	2-3	PHI-SD	5*1	NY-SF	5-8	
							PIT-ATL	4-5					
0619	CIN-CHI	2-5	STL-HOU	0-2	MON-LA	3-5	PIT-ATL	3-4	PHI-SD	3-4	NY-SF	3-4	
0620	STL-CIN	7*5	PIT-HOU	4-6	NY-LA	3-5	CHI-ATL	4*2	MON-SD	2-4	PHI-SF	1-5	
0621	STL-CIN	5-8	PIT-HOU	2-4	NY-LA	0-5	CHI-ATL	0-8	MON-SD	7*4	PHI-SF	3-9	
0622	STL-CIN	12*2	PIT-HOU	2*1	NY-LA	9*6	CHI-ATL	3*2	MON-SD	2*0	PHI-SF	4*3	
0623	PIT-STL	1-6	LA-HOU	3*0									
0624	PIT-STL	2-3	LA-HOU	4-5	NY-CHI	6*5	ATL-CIN	2-8	MON-PHI	7*6	SF-SD	3-5	
0625	PIT-STL	1-4	LA-HOU	9*2	NY-CHI	9*1	ATL-CIN	3-15	MON-PHI	1-2	SF-SD	3-7	
					NY-CHI	1-4							
0626	MON-PHI	1*0	SF-SD	2*1	NY-CHI	4*3							
0627	NY-PHI	3*2	ATL-SD	5*3	STL-CHI	3*2	CIN-HOU	4-5	PIT-MON	6*4	LA-SF	8*0	
0628	NY-PHI	2*1	ATL-SD	5*4	STL-CHI	8*6	CIN-HOU	8*5	PIT-MON	4*3	LA-SF	3-4	
	NY-PHI	5*4	ATL-SD	2-3	STL-CHI	1-2							
0629	NY-PHI	2-5	ATL-SD	4*2	STL-CHI	9*7	CIN-HOU	10-12	PIT-MON	1-4	LA-SF	3-4	
											LA-SF	3*0	
0630	HOU-ATL	4-5	SD-LA	4*3	PHI-MON	7*5	STL-PIT	4-5			CIN-SF	4-8	
0701	HOU-ATL	4-13	SD-LA	4*1	PHI-MON	5*4	STL-PIT	2-3	CHI-NY	4*3	CIN-SF	1-4	
0702	HOU-ATL	0-14	SD-LA	7-10	PHI-MON	1-6	STL-PIT	7*5	CHI-NY	1-3	CIN-SF	6*2	
0703	HOU-ATL	5*3	SD-LA	4-5	PHI-STL	2*1	CHI-PIT	3-5	MON-NY	2-7	CIN-SF	3-4	
					PHI-STL	8*1							
0704	SD-ATL	0-9	HOU-CIN	1-8	PHI-STL	0-1	SF-LA	0-4	MON-NY	5-9	CHI-PIT	4*2	
									MON-NY	6*5	CHI-PIT	2*1	
0705	SD-ATL	2-3	SF-LA	2-3	PHI-STL	1-6	HOU-CIN	6-8	MON-NY	5-7	CHI-PIT	4-5	
							HOU-CIN	2-3					
0706	SD-ATL	5-6	SF-LA	7*4	MON-NY	9*4	HOU-CIN	3*2	CHI-PIT	4-5	PHI-STL	8*3	
0710	CIN-ATL	8*6	HOU-LA	3-4	PIT-NY	0-2	STL-MON	5-6	CHI-PHI	3-5	SD-SF	2-9	
0711	CIN-ATL	5*3	HOU-LA	2-3	PIT-NY	4*2	STL-MON	5*3	CHI-PHI	2-3	SD-SF	3-7	
0712	ATL-HOU	5-9	LA-SD	2-3	STL-NY	8*6	CHI-MON	2-10	PIT-PHI	4-5	SF-CIN	7*4	
							CHI-MON	8*6			SF-CIN	10*7	
0713	PIT-PHI	7*3	LA-SD	3-4	ATL-HOU	5-6	CHI-MON	1-2	STL-NY	4-7	SF-CIN	2*0	
					ATL-HOU	1-6			STL-NY	4-10			
0714	SF-CIN	5*3	PIT-PHI	13*11	ATL-HOU	2*0	LA-SD	3-6					
0715	MON-CIN	7-11	NY-ATL	9*2	PHI-HOU	2-3	LA-CHI	6*2					
0716	MON-CIN	6*4	NY-ATL	2-5	PHI-HOU	4*2	LA-CHI	1-4	SF-PIT	1-3	SD-STL	0-3	
0717	MON-CIN	6*1	NY-ATL	6*0	PHI-HOU	2*1	LA-CHI	3*1	SF-PIT	2-3	SD-STL	3-15	
0718	NY-CIN	3-5	PHI-ATL	7*2	MON-HOU	5*4	SD-CHI	2*1	LA-PIT	4-6	SF-STL	8*7	
	NY-CIN	3-8											
0719	NY-CIN	13*3	SD-CHI	7-8	LA-PIT	3-7	SF-STL	7*4	PHI-ATL	2-5	MON-HOU	2-4	
									PHI-ATL	2-7	MON-HOU	5*2	
0720	SD-CHI	0-6	NY-CIN	3-4	SF-STL	1-2	LA-PIT	4*2	PHI-ATL	2-3	MON-HOU	3-4	
							LA-PIT	7-8					
0721	MON-ATL	8*6	SF-CHI	0#0	PHI-CIN	4-5	NY-HOU	2-3	LA-STL	2-5			
0722	MON-ATL	5-7	SF-CHI	2*0	PHI-CIN	2-3	NY-HOU	5-6	LA-STL	2-3	PIT-SD	4*3	
			SF-CHI	1-3									
0723	MON-ATL	5-6	SF-CHI	14*6	PHI-CIN	3-7	NY-HOU	4*3	PIT-SD	2-3	LA-STL	3-7	
0724									PIT-SD	7*1			
0725	CHI-LA	6-7	HOU-MON	9*8	CIN-NY	0-2	PIT-SF	5*1	STL-SD	3*2	ATL-PHI	4-5	
											ATL-PHI	3*0	
0726	CHI-LA	5*3	HOU-MON	1-2	CIN-NY	5*1	STL-SD	3-4	PIT-SF	3-4	ATL-PHI	3-6	
0727	CHI-LA	2-3	HOU-MON	6*3	CIN-NY	10*4	STL-SD	2-5	PIT-SF	6*4	ATL-PHI	4-17	
0728	PIT-LA	6*4	CIN-MON	3*2	ATL-NY	6*3	CHI-SD	2-4			HOU-PHI	3*2	
			CIN-MON	4-5									
0729	PIT-LA	2-10	CIN-MON	1-4	ATL-NY	1-2	HOU-PHI	6-9	CHI-SD	1-3	STL-SF	1-4	
0730	PIT-LA	0-3	CIN-MON	1-2	ATL-NY	0-3	HOU-PHI	4-6	CHI-SD	2-5	STL-SF	4*0	
0731											STL-SF	4-6	

◆1980◆	GAME 1		GAME 2		GAME 3		GAME 4		GAME 5		GAME 6		GAME 7
0801	STL-LA	1-2	ATL-MON	1-4	HOU-NY	4-5	CIN-PHI	1-3	SD-PIT	1*0	CHI-SF	5*3	
0802	STL-LA	2-3	ATL-MON	1-5	HOU-NY	3-5	CIN-PHI	2*0			CHI-SF	5-8	
0803	STL-LA	4*1	ATL-MON	5-6	HOU-NY	3*2	CIN-PHI	4-8	SD-PIT	5*2	CHI-SF	3*2	
									SD-PIT	4*1	CHI-SF	3*2	
0804	LA-ATL	5*3	SF-HOU	2-4	SD-CIN	1-7	NY-MON	3-4					
					SD-CIN	2-11	NY-MON	4*3					
0805	LA-ATL	4-6	PIT-CHI	3-11	SD-CIN	2-9	NY-MON	5-11	SF-HOU	9*3			
0806	LA-ATL	6*2	PIT-CHI	9*7	SD-CIN	3-4	NY-MON	1-4	SF-HOU	0-1	STL-PHI	14*0	
			PIT-CHI	2*0									
0807	LA-ATL	3-4	PIT-CHI	11*3	SD-HOU	5*1	NY-MON	7*1	STL-PHI	2-3			
0808	SF-ATL	3-7	MON-CHI	4-8	SD-HOU	5*3	LA-CIN	5-8	PHI-PIT	5-6	NY-STL	3*2	
			MON-CHI	5*2									
0809	SF-ATL	5*4	MON-CHI	1-3	LA-CIN	9*4	SD-HOU	5-9	PHI-PIT	1-4	NY-STL	6-9	
			MON-CHI	4*3									
0810	SF-ATL	1-3	MON-CHI	7*3	LA-CIN	7*1	SD-HOU	3*2	NY-STL	4*1	PHI-PIT	1-7	
											PHI-PIT	1-4	
0811	PHI-CHI	5-5	ATL-LA	3*2	CIN-SD	1*0	HOU-SF	4-5	MON-STL	0-16	NY-PIT	1-2	
0812	PHI-CHI	8*5	ATL-LA	7*6	CIN-SD	3*2	HOU-SF	0-2	MON-STL	4*0	NY-PIT	3*1	
	PHI-CHI	5*2											
0813	PHI-CHI	1-2	ATL-LA	2*0	NY-PIT	5*3	CIN-SD	4*3	HOU-SF	5-6	MON-STL	5-7	
0814	PHI-NY	8*1					HOU-SD	2*1	ATL-SF	1-5	CHI-STL	9-10	
0815	PHI-NY	8*0	CIN-LA	1-3	MON-PIT	3-7	HOU-SD	3*1	ATL-SF	8*2	CHI-STL	5*4	
0816	PHI-NY	11*6	CIN-LA	3*2	MON-PIT	0-5			ATL-SF	1-2	CHI-STL	9*4	
0817	PHI-NY	9*4	CIN-LA	6*2	MON-PIT	1-5	HOU-SD	5*0	ATL-SF	8*2	CHI-STL	6*2	
	PHI-NY	4*1			MON-PIT	4*2	HOU-SD	9*2					
0818	STL-CIN	10*1					LA-MON	3*2	SF-NY	5*4	SD-PHI	4-7	
0819	STL-CIN	2-4	CHI-ATL	4-5	PIT-HOU	2-5	LA-MON	5*1	SF-NY	2*1	SD-PHI	7*5	
0820	STL-CIN	3-4	CHI-ATL	5-9	PIT-HOU	1-5	LA-MON	5*4	SF-NY	1-5	SD-PHI	8-9	
0821			CHI-ATL	4-6	PIT-HOU	5-12	LA-NY	2-4	SF-PHI	4*3			
0822	PIT-CIN	4*2	STL-ATL	7*4	CHI-HOU	2-3	SD-MON	2-6	LA-NY	2-4	SF-PHI	6*2	
0823	PIT-CIN	2*1	STL-ATL	2-7	CHI-HOU	0-1	SD-MON	0-2	LA-NY	4*2	SF-PHI	1-7	
0824	PIT-CIN	5*2	STL-ATL	5-10	CHI-HOU	1-2	SD-MON	9-12	LA-NY	3*2	SF-PHI	8*4	
0825	CHI-CIN	0-2	ATL-PIT	8*6	HOU-STL	1-3	SF-MON	1-3			LA-PHI	8*4	
0826	CHI-CIN	4*2	ATL-PIT	4*2	HOU-STL	7*2	SD-NY	8*6			LA-PHI	3-4	
0827	SF-MON	1*0	ATL-PIT	7*4	HOU-STL	2-10	SD-NY	4*1					
0828	HOU-CHI	4*1	CIN-PIT	4*0	ATL-STL	2-11			PHI-SD	3*2	NY-SF	0-1	
0829	HOU-CHI	6*5	CIN-PIT	8*7	ATL-STL	4*3	MON-LA	4-5	PHI-SD	6*1	NY-SF	9*5	
0830	HOU-CHI	2*0	CIN-PIT	5*3	ATL-STL	3-5	MON-LA	3-4	PHI-SD	1-5			
0831	HOU-CHI	7-8	CIN-PIT	5*4	ATL-STL	6*2	MON-LA	0-2	PHI-SD	3-10	NY-SF	4-11	
							MON-LA	2-7			NY-SF	4-9	
0901	ATL-CHI	5*2	MON-SD	5*3	CIN-STL	8*1	NY-LA	2-5	HOU-PIT	10*4	PHI-SF	6*4	
									HOU-PIT	5-7			
0902	ATL-CHI	10*5	NY-LA	5-6	MON-SD	2*1	PHI-SF	2*1	CIN-STL	4-12			
0903	ATL-CHI	4*3	NY-LA	0-2	MON-SD	3-4	PHI-SF	4*3	CIN-STL	3-4	HOU-PIT	4-10	
0904			PHI-LA	3*2	NY-SD	2-3	MON-SF	4*0					
0905	PIT-ATL	4-7	PHI-LA	0-1	NY-SD	2-4	MON-SF	8*0	CIN-CHI	5*3	STL-HOU	7*5	
0906	PIT-ATL	2-3	PHI-LA	3-7	NY-SD	7-8	MON-SF	9*0	CIN-CHI	6*1	STL-HOU	5-9	
									CIN-CHI	4-6	STL-HOU	4-6	
0907	PIT-ATL	5-6	PHI-LA	0-6	NY-SD	2-5	MON-SF	3-6	CIN-CHI	4-6	STL-HOU	2*0	
0908	CIN-ATL	6*1	PIT-PHI	2-6	CHI-STL	6*2							
0909	CIN-ATL	7*1	PIT-PHI	4-5	CHI-STL	4-6	LA-HOU	4-5	NY-MON	0-3	SF-SD	5-12	
0910	CIN-ATL	3*0	PHI-NY	5*0	PIT-STL	7*6	LA-HOU	5-6	CHI-MON	2-4	SF-SD	2-4	
0911			PHI-NY	5*1	PIT-STL	2*1			CHI-MON	5-6			
0912	SD-ATL	2-6	CHI-NY	10*5	LA-CIN	5*2	SF-HOU	3-5	PIT-MON	0-1	STL-PHI	7*4	
											STL-PHI	5*0	
0913	SD-ATL	3-5	LA-CIN	3*2	SF-HOU	2-3	PIT-MON	4*0	CHI-NY	2-4	STL-PHI	1-2	
0914	SD-ATL	3-4	LA-CIN	3*1	SF-HOU	4-6	PIT-MON	0-4	CHI-NY	7-10	STL-PHI	4-8	
0915	LA-ATL	0-9	SF-CIN	2-6	SD-HOU	6*3	STL-CHI	5*1					
0916	LA-ATL	1-2	SF-CIN	8*1	SD-HOU	4*3	STL-CHI	5-6	PHI-PIT	2-3	MON-NY	5*3	
											MON-NY	4*2	
0917	STL-CHI	8*5	HOU-CIN	0-7	SD-LA	1-2	PHI-PIT	5*4	ATL-SF	0-2	MON-NY	2-5	
0918			HOU-CIN	10*2	SD-LA	3-7			ATL-SF	2*1			
0919	PHI-CHI	3-4	NY-PIT	3-4	CIN-LA	10*7	ATL-SD	4-7	HOU-SF	3-4	MON-STL	8-9	
0920	PHI-CHI	7*3	NY-PIT	9*6	CIN-LA	10*2	ATL-SD	2-3	HOU-SF	3*2	MON-STL	5*4	
0921	PHI-CHI	7*3	NY-PIT	4-9	CIN-LA	7*2	ATL-SD	5-8	HOU-SF	5*1	MON-STL	1-4	
0922	NY-CHI	2-3	MON-PIT	2-4	ATL-LA	7*2	HOU-SD	4*2	CIN-SF	3-7	PHI-STL	3*2	
0923	NY-CHI	5-6	MON-PIT	7*1	ATL-LA	2-4	HOU-SD	4-9	CIN-SF	2*1	PHI-STL	3-6	
0924	MON-CHI	8*4	STL-PIT	3-6	SF-LA	4-5	CIN-SD	7*6	HOU-ATL	2-4	NY-PHI	0-1	
0925	MON-CHI	4-5	STL-PIT	10*2	SF-LA	3*2	CIN-SD	5*3	HOU-ATL	4*2	NY-PHI	1-2	
0926	PIT-CHI	8-9	CIN-HOU	0-2	STL-NY	5*1	LA-SD	2-3	SF-ATL	3-5	MON-PHI	1-2	
0927	PIT-CHI	0-2	CIN-HOU	0-2	STL-NY	4*2	LA-SD	6*4	SF-ATL	2*1	MON-PHI	4*3	
0928	PIT-CHI	2-3	CIN-HOU	8*5	STL-NY	0-8	LA-SD	5-7			MON-PHI	8*3	
0929	STL-MON	2-5			PIT-NY	4-5					CHI-PHI	5-6	
0930	STL-MON	2-7	SD-CIN	3*2	PIT-NY	2-3	ATL-HOU	3-7	LA-SF	6*3	CHI-PHI	2-14	
1001	STL-MON	0-8	SD-CIN	1-2	PIT-NY	10*5	ATL-HOU	2-5	LA-SF	8*4	CHI-PHI	0-5	
1002							ATL-HOU	2-3	LA-SF	2-3	CHI-PHI	2-4	
1003	ATL-CIN	4*1	HOU-LA	2-3	PHI-MON	2*1	CHI-PIT	1-3	SD-SF	12*0	NY-STL	4-6	
1004	ATL-CIN	2-3	HOU-LA	1-2	PHI-MON	6*4	CHI-PIT	6*0	SD-SF	2-3	NY-STL	5*2	
1005	ATL-CIN	0-1	HOU-LA	3-4	PHI-MON	7-8	CHI-PIT	0-1	SD-SF	7*3	NY-STL	2-3	
1006			HOU-LA	7*1									

◆1981◆	GAME 1		GAME 2		GAME 3		GAME 4		GAME 5		GAME 6		GAME 7
0408	PHI-CIN	2-3											
0409	NY-CHI	2*0	HOU-LA	0-2	MON-PIT	6*5	SD-SF	4*1					
0410	CIN-ATL	3-5					SD-SF	4*2					
0411	CIN-ATL	3*2	NY-CHI	1-3	HOU-LA	4-7	SD-SF	0-2	PHI-STL	5*2			
0412	CIN-ATL	2-3	NY-CHI	2*1	HOU-LA	2-3	SD-SF	6-7	PHI-STL	3-7	MON-PIT	2-3	
0413	ATL-HOU	2*1	PIT-PHI	1-5	CIN-SD	7*1	LA-SF	4*3					
0414	ATL-HOU	2-8			CIN-SD	3*1	LA-SF	7*1					
0415	ATL-HOU	0-2	CHI-MON	4-5	CIN-SD	10*1	LA-SF	4*2	STL-NY	3-5	PIT-PHI	3-4	
0416			CHI-MON	0-7					STL-NY	5*1	PIT-PHI	3-5	
0417	SF-ATL	6*2	STL-CIN	9*5	PIT-HOU	4*3	LA-SD	2-3			CHI-PHI	2-6	
0418	SF-ATL	4*1	STL-CIN	10*4	PIT-HOU	6*3	LA-SD	2*0	MON-NY	5*3	CHI-PHI	3-4	
0419	SF-ATL	3-4			PIT-HOU	2*0	LA-SD	6*1	MON-NY	4*3	CHI-PHI	3-7	
									MON-NY	2-7			
0420	LA-HOU	5*2	PHI-MON	8-9	SF-SD	9*0	CHI-STL	1-6	ATL-CIN	10*1			
0421	LA-HOU	0-1	PHI-MON	3-10	SF-SD	1-3	CHI-STL	0-8	ATL-CIN	7*3	NY-PIT	22	
0422	LA-HOU	1*0	PHI-MON	3-4	SF-SD	0-4	CHI-STL	0-3					
0423	CIN-HOU	5*4	SD-LA	1-3	ATL-SF	7*3							
0424	CIN-HOU	3*0	SD-LA	6*5	ATL-SF	7*1	PHI-CHI	6*4	NY-MON	2-4	STL-PIT	5*1	
0425	CIN-HOU	2*1	SD-LA	1-2	ATL-SF	4*0	PHI-CHI	7*5	NY-MON	4-8	STL-PIT	3*2	
0426	CIN-HOU	0-1	SD-LA	2-3	ATL-SF	1-3	PHI-CHI	6*2	NY-MON	6-7			
					ATL-SF	5-8							
0427	SF-LA	0-5	MON-PHI	1-3			SD-CIN	2-11	PIT-NY	8*0			
0428	SF-LA	6*1	MON-PHI	6*3	HOU-ATL	2*1							

◆1981◆	GAME 1	GAME 2	GAME 3	GAME 4	GAME 5	GAME 6	GAME 7
0429	SF-LA 3*2	MON-PHI 2-6	HOU-ATL 5*4	SD-CIN 5-8	PIT-NY 10*0	STL-CHI 1-6	
						STL-CHI 22	
0430	HOU-ATL 5*1	SD-CIN 3-4	PIT-NY 7*4				
0501	ATL-CHI 2*1	LA-MON 8-9	SD-NY 4*2	HOU-PIT 5*3			
0502	ATL-CHI 2-5	LA-MON 4*0	SD-NY 2-6	HOU-PIT 4-5		SF-PHI 6*2	
						SF-PHI 1-3	
0503	ATL-CHI 9*7	LA-MON 6*1	HOU-PIT 3*1	CIN-STL 4-5	SD-NY 4*1	SF-PHI 5-7	
					SD-NY 4-7		
0504	HOU-CHI 5*4	LA-MON 3-4	SF-PHI 4-6	ATL-STL 9*6			
0505	HOU-CHI 4*3	SD-MON 3-4	LA-PHI 7-8	ATL-STL 1-4	SF-NY 9*7		
0506	HOU-CHI 1-2	SD-MON 13*5	LA-PHI 2*1	ATL-STL 10*2	SF-NY 6*4	PIT-CIN 8-9	
0507	HOU-CHI 6*0	SD-MON 1-2	LA-PHI 2*1	ATL-STL 4*3	SF-NY 2-3	PIT-CIN 3*1	
						PIT-CIN 7*1	
0508	CHI-ATL 3-4	SF-MON 4*3	LA-NY 1*0	SD-PHI 7-11	PIT-STL 4-5	HOU-CIN 0-4	
0509	CHI-ATL 7*3	SF-MON 8*2	LA-NY 4-7	SD-PHI 6-9	PIT-STL 0-13	HOU-CIN 5-9	
0510	CHI-ATL 55	SF-MON 5*1	LA-NY 5*3	SD-PHI 8*4	PIT-STL 8*2	HOU-CIN 7*5	
		SF-MON 0-4					
0511	PIT-ATL 2-3	HOU-CIN 5*0					
0512	PIT-ATL 0-2	CHI-CIN 1-2	STL-HOU 3*2	MON-LA 0-5	NY-SD 0-3	PHI-SF 0-4	
0513	PIT-ATL 7*5	CHI-CIN 3-8	STL-HOU 0-3	MON-LA 6-8	NY-SD 0-5	PHI-SF 2-5	
0514		CHI-CIN 1-6	STL-HOU 7*6	MON-LA 2-3	NY-SD 6-10	PHI-SF 3*1	
0515	STL-ATL 3-11	CIN-PIT 4*1	CHI-HOU 0-5	NY-LA 5-6	PHI-SD 2*1	MON-SF 2-4	
0516	STL-ATL 6*2	CIN-PIT 4*0	CHI-HOU 1-6	NY-LA 0-9	PHI-SD 1-2	MON-SF 5*0	
0517	STL-ATL 4*3	CIN-PIT 4*3	CHI-HOU 1-6	NY-LA 1-6	PHI-SD 6*3	MON-SF 4-5	
0518				PHI-LA 4*0	MON-SD 3*2	NY-SF 1-3	
0519	CIN-CHI 5*0	ATL-PIT 0-5	HOU-STL 12-15	PHI-LA 3*2	MON-SD 1-3	NY-SF 1-4	
0520	CIN-CHI 10*7	ATL-PIT 1-6	HOU-STL 4*3	PHI-LA 2-3	MON-SD 6*2	NY-SF 4*3	
0521	CIN-CHI 1-5		HOU-STL 1-3				
0522	MON-CHI 6*3	SD-ATL 5*2	NY-STL 9*3	LA-CIN 4*2	SF-HOU 6*3	PHI-PIT 1-3	
0523	MON-CHI 4-6	SD-ATL 6-7	NY-STL 2-8	LA-CIN 9*6	SF-HOU 3-5	PHI-PIT 6*4	
0524	MON-CHI 2-6	SD-ATL 7*5	NY-STL 3*1	LA-CIN 2-3	SF-HOU 2*1	PHI-PIT 1-7	
				LA-CIN 10*3			
0525	LA-ATL 7*1	PIT-CHI 9-10	SD-HOU 3-6	SF-CIN 3-6	STL-MON 3-5	PHI-NY 3-13	
0526		PIT-CHI 6*4	SD-HOU 0-1		STL-MON 3-4	PHI-NY 7*5	
0527	LA-ATL 2-3	PIT-CHI 3*2	SD-HOU 0-1	SF-CIN 2-3	STL-MON 1-4	PHI-NY 1-3	
0528	LA-ATL 4-9	PIT-CHI 9*4		SF-CIN 4-7			
0529	CIN-LA 2-5	PIT-MON 2-3	CHI-NY 1-6	STL-PHI 11*4	ATL-SD 7*1	HOU-SF 1-3	
0530	CIN-LA 9*1	PIT-MON 3*2	CHI-NY 10*3	STL-PHI 2-10	ATL-SD 1-11	HOU-SF 9*8	
0531	CIN-LA 4-16	PIT-MON 1-5	CHI-NY 2-3	STL-PHI 1-6	ATL-SD 1-5	HOU-SF 1-6	
0601	ATL-LA 2-5	MON-STL 2-4		NY-PHI 4-5		CIN-SF 8*5	
0602	ATL-LA 3*1	MON-STL 8*1	CHI-PIT 3-16	NY-PHI 7-9	HOU-SD 2*1	CIN-SF 7-15	
0603	ATL-LA 4*2	MON-STL 2-3	CHI-PIT 2-3	NY-PHI 6*2	HOU-SD 6*1	CIN-SF 6*2	
0604		MON-STL 1-4	CHI-PIT 4-5		HOU-SD 5-7		
0605	PHI-ATL 1-4	SD-STL 1-2	SF-PIT 5*3	LA-CHI 3-4	MON-CIN 3-6	NY-HOU 0-3	
0606	PHI-ATL 3*0	SD-STL 1-11	SF-PIT 6-7	LA-CHI 5-11	MON-CIN 3-9	NY-HOU 2-6	
0607	PHI-ATL 7*5	SD-STL 5*1	SF-PIT 2-3	LA-CHI 7*0	MON-CIN 0-2	NY-HOU 3*1	
0608	HOU-PHI						
0609	HOU-PHI 3-10	SF-CHI 0#2	ATL-MON 1-12	CIN-NY 8*4	SD-PIT 7*4	LA-STL 1-6	
0610	HOU-PHI 4-5	SF-CHI 4-7	ATL-MON 2-11	CIN-NY 2*0	SD-PIT 3*2	LA-STL 4*1	
0611		SF-CHI 1-6	ATL-MON 0-7	CIN-NY 5*2		LA-STL 1-2	
0810	CIN-LA 0-4	NY-CHI 7*5	PIT-MON 1-3	STL-PHI 7*3	ATL-SD 3*2	HOU-SF 6*5	
0811	CIN-LA 7*6	NY-CHI 4*2	PIT-MON 6*3	STL-PHI 5-6	ATL-SD 5*1	HOU-SF 2-3	
0812	CIN-LA 5-8	NY-CHI 7*4	MON-PIT 3*2	STL-PHI 11*3	ATL-SD 4*3	HOU-SF 5*4	
0813	ATL-LA 9*1	NY-CHI 1-6	MON-PIT 7*2	STL-PHI 5*2	HOU-SD 1-9		
0814	ATL-LA 0-5	STL-MON 3*1	PHI-NY 8*4	SF-CIN 4*0	HOU-SD 5*1		
				SF-CIN 6-7			
0815	PIT-CHI 3-4	ATL-LA 6*4	PHI-NY 1-3	SD-STL 1-2	SF-CIN 5*2	HOU-SD 5*0	
0816	PIT-CHI 4*3	ATL-LA 5-6	PHI-NY 2-5		SF-CIN 1-2	HOU-SD 3*0	
	PIT-CHI 4-6						
0817	LA-CHI 1-3	MON-HOU 6*2	SF-PIT 5*1	SD-STL 1-2			
0818	LA-CHI 5*0	MON-HOU 2-4	SF-PIT 4*2	SD-STL 4*3	NY-ATL 4*0	PHI-CIN 1-3	
0819	LA-CHI 3-4	MON-HOU 1-9	SF-PIT 3-7	SD-STL 6-7	NY-ATL 2-5	PHI-CIN 3-6	
0820					NY-ATL 4-6		
0821	SF-CHI 4*3	NY-CIN 0-2	HOU-PHI 4-5	LA-STL 4*0	MON-ATL 4*1	SD-PIT 2-4	
						SD-PIT 2-3	
0822	SF-CHI 2*1	NY-CIN 7*4	HOU-PHI 4-8	LA-STL 3*2	MON-ATL 5*4	SD-PIT 7*6	
					MON-ATL 1-9		
0823	SF-CHI 5-6	NY-CIN 3*2	HOU-PHI 0-6	SD-PIT 2-5	MON-ATL 1-2	LA-STL 7-11	
0824	SD-CHI 8-9	NY-CIN 0-2	ATL-PHI 5-7	LA-PIT 3*0		SF-STL 1-2	
0825	SD-CHI 3-4	CIN-MON 1-9	ATL-PHI 12*2	LA-PIT 9*7	HOU-NY 1-2	SF-STL 4*2	
0826	SD-CHI 7-9	CIN-MON 0-6	ATL-PHI 5*3	LA-PIT 16*6	HOU-NY 9*3	SF-STL 4-9	
0827	CHI-LA 0-6	CIN-MON 0-12	STL-SD 3*2	PIT-SF 4-5	HOU-NY 2-3		
0828	CHI-LA 1-6	ATL-MON 0-3	PHI-HOU 2-3	PIT-SF 1-5	CIN-NY 5*2		
0829	CHI-LA 3*1	ATL-MON 3-4	PHI-HOU 1-6	PIT-SF 3-8	CIN-NY 2-3	STL-SD 6*1	
			PHI-HOU 1-2			STL-SD 6*5	
0830	CHI-LA 2*1	ATL-MON 5*4	PHI-HOU 4-5	CIN-NY 6*3		STL-SD 6-9	
0831	PIT-LA 5*4	PHI-ATL 11*8	NY-HOU 1-6	MON-CIN 8-9		CHI-SD 1-4	
0901	PIT-LA 2-3	PHI-ATL 3*0	NY-HOU 2-3	MON-CIN 4*3	STL-SF 2-4	CHI-SD 2-3	
0902	PIT-LA 2-6	PHI-ATL 2-3	NY-HOU 0-8	MON-CIN 0-7	STL-SF 5*2	CHI-SD 4-5	
0903	STL-LA 5*3	HOU-MON 2*1	CIN-PHI 9*3		CHI-SF 0-12	PIT-SD 7*3	
0904	STL-LA 7*2	HOU-MON 5*0	CIN-PHI 6-7	ATL-NY 1-4	CHI-SF 2-3	PIT-SD 4-5	
0905	STL-LA 3-4	HOU-MON 2-5	CIN-PHI 4-5	ATL-NY 2-4	CHI-SF 8*2	PIT-SD 2*1	
0906	STL-LA 0-5	HOU-MON 4*3	CIN-PHI 5*4	ATL-NY 5*2	CHI-SF 0-3	PIT-SD 9*5	
0907	SF-LA 1-5	HOU-ATL 3*2	MON-PHI 5*4	SD-CIN 7-8	CHI-STL 10*0	NY-PIT 1-2	
						NY-PIT 4-5	
0908	HOU-ATL 2-3	SD-CIN 6*1	SF-LA 0-4	MON-PHI 5-10	CHI-STL 4*3	NY-PIT 3*1	
0909	HOU-ATL 0-9	SD-CIN 4-5	SF-LA 6*3	MON-PHI 8-11	CHI-STL 7*3	NY-PIT 5*3	
0911	SD-ATL 1-4	LA-CIN 2-3	MON-CHI 5-6	SF-HOU 0-6	NY-STL 2-4	PHI-PIT 8*0	
0912	SD-ATL 4-5	LA-CIN 5-6	MON-CHI 2*0	SF-HOU 2-5	NY-STL 2-4	PHI-PIT 2-6	
0913	SD-ATL 6*4	LA-CIN 4*2	MON-CHI 10*6	SF-HOU 0-3	NY-STL 2-4	PHI-PIT 2-3	
0914	LA-SD 10*5	ATL-SF 2-4		CIN-HOU 4*2			
0915	LA-SD 2-8	ATL-SF 5-6	PIT-CHI 8*2	CIN-HOU 4*0	STL-MON 3*2		
0916	ATL-LA 2-3	HOU-SD 5*2	CIN-SF 7-12	PHI-NY 3*1	STL-MON 3-4		
					STL-MON 7*1		
				PHI-NY 4-5	STL-MON 3-4		
0917	ATL-LA 0-2	HOU-SD 9*0	CIN-SF 1*0	PHI-NY 3*2	STL-MON 7*4		
0918	CIN-LA 5*4	ATL-SD 3*0	HOU-SF 2-5	STL-NY 1-8	CHI-MON 0-11	PIT-PHI 7*6	
0919	CIN-LA 7*3	ATL-SD 3-6	HOU-SF 8*1	STL-NY 2-6	CHI-MON 2*1	PIT-PHI 2-8	
0920	CIN-LA 5*1	ATL-SD 3*1	HOU-SF 7*3	STL-NY 6-7	CHI-MON 0-4	PIT-PHI 4-5	
0921	STL-CHI 2*0	CIN-SD 0-6		PIT-NY 3-4	PHI-MON 0-1		
0922	STL-CHI 3-4	CIN-SD 3*2	ATL-HOU 0-3	PIT-NY 5*3	PHI-MON 2-6	LA-SF 2-5	
0923	NY-CHI 1-2	CIN-SD 5*1	ATL-HOU 3*1	PHI-STL 9*4	PIT-MON 2-3	LA-SF 4-8	
0924	NY-CHI 9-10		ATL-HOU 3-5	PHI-STL 14*6	PIT-MON 1-7	LA-SF 7*3	
0925	PHI-CHI 9*2	CIN-ATL 10*2	LA-HOU 3*0	PIT-STL 5*4	NY-MON 3-6	SF-SD 3*0	
0926		CIN-ATL 2*0	LA-HOU 0-5	PIT-STL 3-5	NY-MON 2-4	SF-SD 6*5	
0927	PHI-CHI 5*2	CIN-ATL 4*2	LA-HOU 1-4	PIT-STL 5-7	NY-MON 2*1	SF-SD 7*3	
	PHI-CHI 0-14						

♦1981♦	GAME 1	GAME 2	GAME 3	GAME 4	GAME 5	GAME 6	GAME 7
0928	LA-ATL 1-2	SF-CIN 4*0	SD-HOU 1-2	NY-PHI 4-12	MON-STL 2-6	CHI-PIT 0-4	
						CHI-PIT 3*1	
0929	LA-ATL 5*3	SF-CIN 3-4	SD-HOU 2*1	NY-PHI 7*0	MON-STL 4-8	CHI-PIT 6-10	
0930	SF-ATL 2-9	HOU-CIN 2-5	SD-LA 2*0	STL-PHI 5-8	CHI-NY 1-2	MON-PIT 3*2	
1001	SF-ATL 6*2	HOU-CIN 8*1	SD-LA 1*0	STL-PHI 3*2	CHI-NY 22	MON-PIT 5*2	
1002		ATL-CIN 11*5	HOU-LA 1-6	CHI-PHI 7-9	MON-NY 3*0	STL-PIT 7-8	
1003	SD-SF 4*3	ATL-CIN 4*3	HOU-LA 2-7	CHI-PHI 8*4	MON-NY 5*4	STL-PIT 8*3	
	SD-SF 7*2						
1004	SD-SF 3-4	ATL-CIN 0-3	HOU-LA 5*3	MON-NY 1-2	CHI-PHI 1-2	STL-PIT 4*0	

♦1982♦	GAME 1	GAME 2	GAME 3	GAME 4	GAME 5	GAME 6	GAME 7
0405		CHI-CIN 3*2	ATL-SD 1*0				
0406	STL-HOU 14*3	SF-LA 3-4	ATL-SD 6*4	CHI-CIN 2-6			
0407	STL-HOU 2-3	SF-LA 2-9					
0408	STL-HOU 0-1	NY-PHI 7*2					
0409	HOU-ATL 2-6	MON-PHI 2*0	NY-CHI 0-5	SF-CIN 0-7	SD-LA 7*4		
0410	HOU-ATL 6-8	MON-PHI 11*3	NY-CHI 9*5	SF-CIN 7*5	SD-LA 0-6	PIT-STL 11*7	
0411	HOU-ATL 0-5	MON-PHI 0-1	NY-CHI 5*4	SF-CIN 6*1		PIT-STL 6-7	
0412	LA-HOU 1-2		NY-CHI 4-5	ATL-CIN 6*1		PIT-STL 4-5	
0413	LA-HOU 9*5	PHI-NY 2-5	STL-CHI 4*3	ATL-CIN 8*5	SD-SF 2-3	PIT-MON 4-5	
0414	LA-HOU 1-2	PHI-NY 1-8	STL-CHI 3*1	ATL-CIN 5*2	SD-SF 3*2	PIT-MON 4*3	
0415	LA-SD 0-2	PHI-NY 8*4	STL-CHI 6*1			PHI-STL 2-3	
0416	LA-SD 3-8	MON-NY 4*3	ATL-HOU 5*3	CHI-PIT 6-7	CIN-SF 1-6	PHI-STL 0-6	
0417	LA-SD 3-4	MON-NY 1-2	ATL-HOU 2*1	CHI-PIT 10*2	CIN-SF 8*2	PHI-STL 5-6	
0418	LA-SD 3-9	MON-NY 7*6	ATL-HOU 6*5	CHI-PIT 5*1	CIN-SF 2-4		
0419	SF-SD 6-13	HOU-LA 6*4	PHI-MON 2*0				
0420	SF-SD 4-8	HOU-LA 2-10	CIN-ATL 2-4	CHI-NY 2-3	STL-PIT 7*4		
0421	SF-SD 6-7	HOU-LA 0-6	CIN-ATL 3-4	CHI-NY 4-7	STL-PIT 6*2	PHI-MON 2-5	
0422			CIN-ATL 2*1				
0423	PIT-CHI 12*10	CIN-HOU 3-7	SD-ATL 6*3	NY-MON 4-5	STL-PHI 9*2	LA-SF 9*0	
0424	PIT-CHI 8*5	CIN-HOU 3*2	SD-ATL 6*4	NY-MON 1*0	STL-PHI 7*4	LA-SF 7*6	
0425	PIT-CHI 3-5	CIN-HOU 4*3		NY-MON 2-5	STL-PHI 4-8	LA-SF 3-6	
0426	PIT-ATL 6*4	HOU-STL 6*2					
0427	PIT-ATL 10*4	HOU-STL 3*0	CIN-CHI 6*3	PHI-LA 0-3	NY-SD 5-8	MON-SF 3*2	
0428	PIT-ATL 6-7	HOU-STL 4-5	CIN-CHI 0-6	PHI-LA 9*3	NY-SD 5*4	MON-SF 0-7	
0429	CHI-ATL 0-3	HOU-PIT 6-9		PHI-LA 2-4	NY-SD 0-6	MON-SF 3-7	
0430	CHI-ATL 0-1	HOU-PIT 4*3	STL-CIN 2-8	MON-LA 4*2	PHI-SD 3*1	NY-SF 4-5	
0501	CHI-ATL 5*1	HOU-PIT 6*3	STL-CIN 1-10	MON-LA 1-2	PHI-SD 6-9	NY-SF 3-6	
0502	CHI-ATL 3-10	HOU-PIT 6*2	STL-CIN 1-5	MON-LA 13*1	PHI-SD 3*0	NY-SF 3-4	
			STL-CIN 6*4			NY-SF 2*0	
						PHI-SF 5*3	
0503	NY-LA 6*3	ATL-PIT 10*4	MON-SD 8*2	CHI-STL 4-9		PHI-SF 9*4	
0504	NY-LA 1-2	ATL-PIT 4-8	MON-SD 3-7	CHI-STL 4-7	HOU-CIN 2-5		
0505		ATL-PIT 2-4		CHI-STL 6-7	HOU-CIN 8*7		
0506	LA-MON 3*2	SF-NY 5*3	SD-PHI 7-12				
0507	LA-MON 6*2	SF-NY 2-3	SD-PHI 2-5	HOU-CHI 6-12	PIT-CIN 0-5	ATL-STL 6*3	
0508	LA-MON 10*8	SF-NY 8*3	SD-PHI 1-5	HOU-CHI 2-3	PIT-CIN 4*2	ATL-STL 7-8	
0509	LA-MON 5*4	SF-NY 5-6	SD-PHI 6*0	HOU-CHI 3-6	PIT-CIN 6*3	ATL-STL 3*0	
0510	SF-MON 4-5	SD-NY 2-3	LA-PHI 8-9	PIT-HOU 3-7		CIN-STL 3*1	
0511	SF-MON 5*4	SD-NY 0-6	LA-PHI 8-9	PIT-HOU 2-4	ATL-CHI 4-6	CIN-STL 1-5	
0512	SF-MON 3*2		LA-PHI 3-11		ATL-CHI 6*3		
0513	SD-MON 5-6	STL-ATL 10*9	SF-PHI 1-8	CHI-HOU 5*0	LA-NY 2*1	CIN-PIT 2*1	
0514	SD-MON 7-8	STL-ATL 1-2	SF-PHI 0-2	CHI-HOU 6*3	LA-NY 4*1	CIN-PIT 7-8	
0515	SD-MON 6*2	STL-ATL 7*6	SF-PHI 3-5	CHI-HOU 1-4	LA-NY 4-6	CIN-PIT 9-12	
0516	SD-MON 8*2	STL-ATL 2-5	SF-PHI 1-6	CHI-HOU 2*1	LA-NY 4-13	CIN-PIT 3*1	
0517	ATL-MON 0-4		HOU-PHI 8*1		CIN-NY 7*2		
0518	ATL-MON 6*4	CHI-LA 1-2	HOU-PHI 2*1	STL-SD 2*0	CIN-NY 4-7	PIT-SF 1-2	
0519	ATL-MON 9*1	CHI-LA 1-4	HOU-PHI 5*3	STL-SD 4-5	CIN-NY 2-4	PIT-SF 2*1	
0520		CHI-LA 8*3		STL-SD 6*3		PIT-SF 1-3	
0521	PHI-ATL 6-7	STL-LA 6*3	MON-CIN 2*0	PIT-SD 5-7	NY-HOU 1-5	CHI-SF 6*4	
0522	PHI-ATL 5*2	STL-LA 2-3	MON-CIN 4*2	PIT-SD 3-12	NY-HOU 6*5	CHI-SF 2*1	
0523	PHI-ATL 2*1	STL-LA 0-5	MON-CIN 4*2	PIT-SD 4*2	NY-HOU 2*0	CHI-SF 3-4	
						CHI-SF 3-6	
0524	NY-ATL 5*3	PHI-CIN 9*1	MON-HOU 2*0	PIT-LA 9*3	CHI-SD 2-8	STL-SF 6*0	
0525	NY-ATL 2-10	PHI-CIN 3-4	MON-HOU 6*1	PIT-LA 2-5	CHI-SD 1-2	STL-SF 8*3	
0526	NY-ATL 6*4	PHI-CIN 0-2	MON-HOU 4*0	PIT-LA 2-3	CHI-SD 5*3	STL-SF 8*4	
0528	LA-CHI 3-4	CIN-MON 2-4	HOU-NY 8*3	SF-PIT 10*5	SD-STL 2-5		
0529	LA-CHI 2-3	CIN-MON 1-4	HOU-NY 5*2	SF-PIT 9*5	SD-STL 4*2	ATL-PHI 0-1	
0530	LA-CHI 7*0	CIN-MON 7*3	HOU-NY 5-9	SF-PIT 6-7	SD-STL 5-6	ATL-PHI 2-6	
0531	SD-CHI 9*7	HOU-MON 0-10	ATL-NY 4-10	LA-PIT 5*4	SF-STL 6-11	CIN-PHI 4-5	
0601	SD-CHI 9*1		ATL-NY 7*3	LA-PIT 1-3	SF-STL 4*3	CIN-PHI 4*1	
0602	SD-CHI 3*1	HOU-MON 6*4	ATL-NY 3*1	LA-PIT 7-8	SF-STL 0-1	CIN-PHI 2-4	
0603				MON-PIT 4-5			
0604	SF-CHI 4*3	NY-CIN 3-8	PHI-HOU 3-8	SD-PIT 5*4	LA-STL 2-5		
0605	SF-CHI 2*1	NY-CIN 2-6	PHI-HOU 5*3	MON-ATL 1-2	LA-STL 6*2		
0606	SF-CHI 5*3	NY-CIN 6-7	PHI-HOU 6-7	MON-ATL 6*3	LA-STL 5*3	SD-PIT 1-2	
0607	ATL-LA 4*3	STL-MON 2-3	PIT-NY 4*3	CHI-PHI 5-7	CIN-SD 5-6		
0608	ATL-LA 4*3	STL-MON 5*4	PIT-NY 6*2	CHI-PHI 2-5	CIN-SD 1-4	HOU-SF 3-7	
0609	ATL-LA 11*5	STL-MON 1-5	PIT-NY 2-3	CHI-PHI 2-4	CIN-SD 4*3	HOU-SF 6*1	
					HOU-SD 0-5		
0610	CIN-LA 3*2				HOU-SD 2-6	ATL-SF 5*3	
0611	CIN-LA 1-11	CHI-MON 8-9	STL-NY 7*3	PIT-PHI 1*0	HOU-SD 0-4	ATL-SF 10*5	
0612	CIN-LA 3-4	CHI-MON 5-7	STL-NY 2-6	PIT-PHI 9*2	HOU-SD 4-5	ATL-SF 1-2	
0613	CIN-LA 4*2	CHI-MON 3-5				ATL-SF 5*1	
0614	PHI-CHI 11-12	ATL-HOU 0-9	NY-PIT 2*1	LA-SD 4*3	MON-STL 1-2		
0615	PHI-CHI 5-8	ATL-HOU 7*0	NY-PIT 3-13	LA-SD 3*0	MON-STL 2-3	SF-CIN 4*3	
0616	PHI-CHI 6-7	ATL-HOU 5*4		LA-SD 6*0	MON-STL 8*3	SF-CIN 3-7	
0617	MON-CHI 8-12	PHI-PIT 4*3	SF-ATL 3-8	SD-HOU 2-7	NY-STL 5*3	SF-CIN 2-4	
0618	MON-CHI 4*0	PHI-PIT 8*3			NY-STL 4-5	LA-CIN 3*2	
					NY-STL 8*5	PHI-PIT 8*3	
0619	SF-ATL 9*4	MON-CHI 5*2	LA-CIN 2*1	SD-HOU 7*1	NY-STL 5*4	PHI-PIT 1-3	
0620	SF-ATL 5*3	MON-CHI 11*5	LA-CIN 4*2	SD-HOU 4-8	PHI-STL 5-7	CHI-PIT 3-4	
0621	SF-ATL 6-7	MON-NY 5*1	LA-CIN 2-10	SD-HOU 7*4	PHI-STL 2-3	CHI-PIT 2-9	
0622	LA-ATL 4*1	MON-NY 4*3	SD-CIN 5-7	SF-HOU 0-2	PHI-STL 7*1	CHI-PIT 6*5	
0623	LA-ATL 2-7	MON-NY 5*0	SD-CIN 4-5	SF-HOU 9*8	PHI-STL 10*2		
0624	LA-ATL 5*3	MON-NY 1-3	SD-CIN 7*6	LA-HOU 5-7	PIT-MON 4*3	NY-PHI 0-1	
					PIT-MON 9*7	NY-PHI 3-5	
0625	STL-CHI 3-5	SD-SF 3*2	ATL-CIN 5*2		PIT-MON 14*5	NY-PHI 3-4	
						NY-PHI 4-7	
0626	ATL-CIN 1-2	LA-HOU 4*1	SD-SF 7*6	STL-CHI 4*1		NY-PHI 3-8	
				STL-CHI 2*1			
0627	ATL-CIN 2*0	LA-HOU 7*3	PIT-MON 2-5	STL-CHI 2-4	SD-SF 1-7	STL-PHI 0-1	
				PIT-CHI 4-6	CIN-SF 1-7		
0628	HOU-ATL 6*2	SD-LA 4-6		PIT-CHI 3*1	CIN-SF 0-3	STL-PHI 15*3	
0629	HOU-ATL 5-6	SD-LA 7*5	NY-MON 5*4	PIT-CHI 7*3	CIN-SF 6*7	STL-PHI 3-6	
0630	HOU-ATL 4-5	SD-LA 1-5	NY-MON 1-4				
		SD-LA 6*4					
0701	PIT-CHI 5*2	NY-MON 2*1			MON-PIT 3-6	SF-SD 8*4	
0702	CIN-ATL 4-6	HOU-LA 4*1	PHI-NY 4-8	CHI-STL 4*3	MON-PIT 2-7	SF-SD 2-3	

◆1982◆	GAME 1		GAME 2		GAME 3		GAME 4		GAME 5		GAME 6		GAME 7
0703	CIN-ATL	2-4	HOU-LA	4-5	CHI-STL	2*1			MON-PIT	2-4	SF-SD	4*3	
0704	CIN-ATL	1-4	HOU-LA	3*0	CHI-STL	2-7	PHI-NY	9*7	MON-PIT	16*6	SF-SD	3-4	
							PHI-NY	7*2	MON-PIT	4-10			
0705	CHI-ATL	5-7	STL-CIN	6*5	SD-MON	8*6	LA-NY	4*1	HOU-PIT	6*4			
0706	CHI-ATL	7*2	STL-CIN	3*1	SD-MON	5*1	LA-NY	9*3	HOU-PIT	0-1	SF-PHI	3*1	
0707	STL-ATL	2-3	CHI-HOU	1-5	LA-MON	3*1	SF-NY	3*2	CIN-PIT	6*3	SF-PHI	2-3	
0708	STL-ATL	5*2	CHI-HOU	5*3	LA-MON	3-7	SF-NY	9*7	CIN-PIT	8-9	SD-PHI	5*3	
0709	PIT-ATL	4-6	STL-HOU	3*2	SF-MON	3*2	SD-NY	5*3	CIN-CHI	0-12	SD-PHI	5*3	
							SD-NY	3-6					
0710	PIT-ATL	6*1	STL-HOU	2-4	SF-MON	4-8	SD-NY	7-9	LA-PHI	2-4	CIN-CHI	0-1	
0711	PIT-ATL	3*1	STL-HOU	2-4	SF-MON	8*7	SD-NY	6*2	LA-PHI	3-4	CIN-CHI	5#5	
											CIN-CHI	6*5	
											CIN-CHI	2-9	
0715	PIT-HOU	5*1	NY-LA	5*2	MON-SD	6*2	PHI-SF	2*1	CIN-STL	7*3	ATL-CHI	11*4	
0716	PIT-HOU	2-4	NY-LA	6-7	MON-SD	4*3	PHI-SF	1*0	CIN-STL	4-6	ATL-CHI	3-4	
0717	PIT-HOU	3-4	NY-LA	5-6	MON-SD	4*1	PHI-SF	5*3	CIN-STL	2-4	ATL-CHI	9*4	
0718	PIT-HOU	2-4	NY-LA	8*3	MON-SD	9*2	PHI-SF	3-4	CIN-STL	5-6	ATL-CHI	4*2	
0719	PIT-CIN	5*4	MON-LA	1-2	PHI-SD	7*6			ATL-STL	4*1	HOU-CHI	5-6	
0720	PIT-CIN	3*1	MON-LA	1-10	PHI-SD	0-2	NY-SF	1-5	ATL-STL	8*6	HOU-CHI	3-5	
0721	PIT-CIN	3*2	MON-LA	4*1	PHI-SD	7*1	NY-SF	6*2	ATL-STL	0-8	HOU-CHI	2*1	
0723	CHI-CIN	7*5	PHI-LA	6*3	NY-SD	4-11	MON-SF	8*7	HOU-STL	2-6	ATL-PIT	0-6	
0724	CHI-CIN	2-3	PHI-LA	2-3	NY-SD	4*3	MON-SF	2-5	HOU-STL	1-5	ATL-PIT	4*3	
0725	CHI-CIN	1-2	PHI-LA	1*0	NY-SD	2-3	MON-SF	2-3	HOU-STL	3-4	ATL-PIT	0-8	
0726	CHI-CIN	2-4					LA-SF	1-6					
0727	MON-CHI	4*3	CIN-HOU	2-3	PHI-PIT	0-4	LA-SF	7*3	NY-STL	4-9	SD-ATL	2-9	
											SD-ATL	6-8	
0728	MON-CHI	5*3	CIN-HOU	2-4	PHI-PIT	4*3	LA-SF	2-6	NY-STL	5-7	SD-ATL	6-8	
0729	STL-MON	3-4	CIN-HOU	3-4	PIT-NY	4*1	CHI-PHI	2-3			SD-ATL	2-6	
0730	STL-MON	4-5	SF-HOU	1-3	PIT-NY	5*1	CHI-PHI	1-3	SD-CIN	2-4	LA-ATL	10*9	
											LA-ATL	8*2	
0731	STL-MON	10*1	PIT-NY	4-9	CHI-PHI	0-2	SD-CIN	5*4	SF-HOU	5*4	LA-ATL	3*0	
									SD-CIN	6*2	SF-HOU	0-5		
0801	LA-ATL	9*4	STL-MON	4-5	PIT-NY	4*3	SD-CIN	8*6	SF-HOU	4*2	CHI-PHI	7*2	
							LA-CIN	1-5	SD-HOU	4-6			
0802	SF-ATL	3-7	PIT-STL	4*2			LA-CIN	4*0	SD-HOU	6-7	MON-PHI	1-2	
0803	SF-ATL	6*3	PIT-STL	5*2	NY-CHI	0-5	LA-CIN	8*2	SD-HOU	5*2	MON-PHI	2-3	
0804	SF-ATL	3*2	PIT-STL	3-7	NY-CHI	7*4			HOU-SF	2-5	MON-PHI	4-5	
0805	ATL-LA	2-3			NY-CHI	1-5	CIN-SD	4*2	HOU-SF	6-7	MON-PHI	9*2	
0806	ATL-LA	4-5	MON-STL	5*3	PHI-CHI	2-4	CIN-SD	0-2	HOU-SF	6-7	NY-PIT	3-7	
									HOU-SF	3-8	NY-PIT	7*3		
0807	PHI-CHI	2-3	ATL-LA	6-7	CIN-SD	1-4	HOU-SF	2-9	MON-STL	5-9	NY-PIT	5*2	
0808	PHI-CHI	5-8	ATL-LA	0-2	CIN-SD	1-3	HOU-SF	2-3	MON-STL	2*1	NY-PIT	1-4	
							HOU-SF	3-8					
0809	CIN-LA	2-3	CHI-MON	9*2	STL-NY	7*2	ATL-SF	0-5	HOU-SD	4*3	PIT-PHI	3-4	
											PIT-PHI	9#6	
0810	CIN-LA	3-11	CHI-MON	5*3	STL-NY	7*2	HOU-SD	4*1	ATL-SF	2-3	PIT-PHI	9*6	
											PIT-PHI	5-9	
0811	CIN-LA	2*1	CHI-MON	0-3	HOU-SD	3*0	ATL-SF	6-8			PIT-PHI	1-4	
0812	SF-LA	2-6	PHI-MON	3-6	ATL-SD	2-8	CHI-NY	13*6	STL-PIT	3*2			
			PHI-MON	7-8									
0813	HOU-CIN	0-3	PHI-MON	2-3	SF-LA	1-6	CHI-NY	4-6	STL-PIT	4-7			
0814	HOU-CIN	2*0	PHI-MON	15*11	SF-LA	4*2	CHI-NY	7*4	STL-PIT	4*1	ATL-SD	4-7	
0815	HOU-CIN	7*3	PHI-MON	3*1	SF-LA	8*6	CHI-NY	4-5	STL-PIT	12*5	ATL-SD	6*5	
							CHI-NY	6*5	STL-PIT	5*2	ATL-SD	5-6	
0816	HOU-CIN	2-3											
0817	NY-CIN	2-9	LA-CHI	1#1	PHI-HOU	0-2	SF-PIT	1-4	SD-STL	2-3	MON-ATL	13*7	
											MON-ATL	3*2	
0818	LA-CHI	2*1	NY-CIN	6-7	PHI-HOU	5*3	SF-PIT	16*9	SD-STL	1-2	MON-ATL	12*2	
	LA-CHI	7*4											
0819	LA-CHI	2-8	MON-ATL	4-5	NY-CIN	1-3	PHI-HOU	6-7	SF-PIT	1-6	SD-STL	4*3	
0820	SD-CHI	2-3	NY-ATL	1-2	PHI-CIN	9*2	MON-HOU	3-4	LA-PIT	1*0	SF-STL	8*7	
0821	SD-CHI	2*0	NY-ATL	5-6	PHI-CIN	3-10	MON-HOU	3-5	LA-PIT	1-2	SF-STL	6-7	
0822	SD-CHI	7-8	NY-ATL	9-10	PHI-CIN	8*2	MON-HOU	5*0	LA-PIT	3-4	SF-STL	4-5	
0823	SF-CHI	5-8	PHI-ATL	3-4	MON-CIN	2-6	NY-HOU	0-2	SD-PIT	6-8	LA-STL	3-11	
									SD-PIT	5*3			
0824	PHI-ATL	7-9	SF-CHI	4-8	MON-CIN	5*1	NY-HOU	4-5	SD-PIT	5-6	LA-STL	5*2	
0825	PHI-ATL	11*9	SF-CHI	2-4	MON-CIN	0-1	NY-HOU	4-5	SD-PIT	6-7	LA-STL	11*3	
0826	HOU-MON	2-3											
	HOU-MON	3-5											
0827	CHI-LA	4-9	ATL-NY	9*8	CIN-PHI	8*1	STL-SD	2*1	PIT-SF	3*2			
0828	CHI-LA	1-7	ATL-NY	4*3	CIN-PHI	1-7	HOU-MON	2*0	PIT-SF	2-4			
0829	CHI-LA	7*2	ATL-NY	9*4	CIN-PHI	1-3	HOU-MON	3-5	PIT-SF	4*3	STL-SD	4-9	
											STL-SD	5*3	
											PIT-SD	1-2	
0830	STL-LA	3*2	CIN-MON	1-3	HOU-NY	4*2	ATL-PHI	1-6					
							ATL-PHI	11*9					
0831	STL-LA	1-4	CIN-MON	2*1	HOU-NY	4*0	ATL-PHI	3*0	PIT-SD	7*1	CHI-SF	3-4	
0901	STL-LA	6*5	CIN-MON	1-2	HOU-NY	1-5	ATL-PHI	4*0	PIT-SD	1-4	CHI-SF	7*6	
0903	PIT-LA	3*2	ATL-MON	4*3	CIN-NY	1*0	HOU-PHI	1-2	CHI-SD	0-3	STL-SF	2-3	
0904	PIT-LA	1*0	ATL-MON	1-4	CIN-NY	2-3	HOU-PHI	2-4	CHI-SD	1-4	STL-SF	4-5	
0905	PIT-LA	1-2	ATL-MON	1-2	CIN-NY	2-10	HOU-PHI	3-4	CHI-SD	5*1	STL-SF	1-5	
0906	SF-ATL	8*2	PHI-CHI	3-4	LA-CIN	7*2	SD-HOU	4*2	NY-PIT	1-6	MON-STL	0-1	
0907	SF-ATL	3*2	PHI-CHI	7*5	LA-CIN	8*4	SD-HOU	3-4	NY-PIT	5-9	MON-STL	7*4	
0908	LA-ATL	11-12	PHI-CHI	4*3	SD-CIN	9*4	SF-HOU	1-8	NY-PIT	9*1	MON-STL	0-1	
0909	LA-ATL	3-10			SD-CIN	4*1	SF-HOU	5*1					
0910	CIN-ATL	2-8	MON-CHI	7*2	PHI-HOU	7*5	LA-PIT	3*2	SF-SD	5*1	NY-STL	2*1	
0911	CIN-ATL	4*3	MON-CHI	10*6	PHI-PIT	9-10	LA-HOU	5*3	SF-SD	8*3	NY-STL	3-6	
0912	CIN-ATL	3*1	MON-CHI	11*3	PHI-PIT	2-4	LA-HOU	7*3			NY-STL	4*1	
0913	HOU-ATL	5*3	SD-LA	3-4	CHI-PIT	7*3	STL-PHI	0-2	CIN-SF	5*4			
0914	HOU-ATL	4*0	SD-LA	0-1	CHI-PIT	5-15	STL-PHI	2*0	CIN-SF	1-2	NY-MON	1-3	
0915	HOU-ATL	5*4	SD-LA	0-5	CHI-PIT	7*2	STL-PHI	8*0	CIN-SF	4-5	NY-MON	5-6	
0916									SD-SF	3-9	NY-MON	9*4	
0917	ATL-CIN	2-5	HOU-LA	2-9	PIT-PHI	4*2	STL-NY	3*2	SD-SF	4*2	CHI-MON	3*1	
							STL-NY	7*1					
0918	ATL-CIN	5*4	HOU-LA	2*0	CHI-MON	10*7	STL-NY	2*0	PIT-PHI	4-5	SD-SF	1-4	
							STL-NY	6*2					
0919	ATL-CIN	6*1	HOU-LA	4-5	CHI-MON	7*5	STL-NY	3*1	PIT-PHI	8*1	SD-SF	3-4	
0920	PIT-CHI	1-3	ATL-HOU	3-4	PHI-STL	1-4					MON-NY	1-2	
0921	PIT-CHI	0-1	ATL-HOU	3-5	PHI-STL	5*2	SF-CIN	5-6	LA-SD	0-3	MON-NY	1-2	
											MON-NY	5*1	
0922	NY-CHI	5*2	SF-CIN	2*0	ATL-HOU	2-3	PHI-MON	4-11	LA-SD	1-2	PIT-STL	1-2	
0923	NY-CHI	5*4	SF-CIN	11*7			PHI-MON	2*0			PIT-STL	5*3	
0924	SD-ATL	6-11	HOU-CIN	0-2	SF-LA	3*2	PIT-MON	4-6	PHI-NY	2*1	CHI-STL	1-3	
0925	SD-ATL	6-12	HOU-CIN	3*1	SF-LA	5*4	PIT-MON	4-9	PHI-NY	1-2	CHI-STL	1-5	
0926	SD-ATL	3*2	HOU-CIN	4*0	SF-LA	3*2	PIT-MON	3*0	PHI-NY	4-6	CHI-STL	6*1	
0927	CHI-PHI	8*1	HOU-SD	7*3	CIN-LA	6*1	STL-MON	4*2	PIT-NY	1-4	ATL-SF	7*0	
0928	CHI-PHI	2-3	HOU-SD	0-3	CIN-LA	4*3	STL-MON	4-5	PIT-NY	2-3	ATL-SF	8*3	
0929	MON-PHI	0-4	CIN-SD	2-3	ATL-LA	4*3	STL-PIT	3-7	CHI-NY	4*1	HOU-SF	1-6	
0930	MON-PHI	4-5	CIN-SD	6*4	ATL-LA	3-10	STL-PIT	2-7	CHI-NY	3*1	HOU-SF	6-7	

Game Scores, 1982-94

♦1982♦	GAME 1	GAME 2	GAME 3	GAME 4	GAME 5	GAME 6	GAME 7
1001	NY-PHI 1*0	ATL-SD 4*0	CIN-HOU 4*2	MON-PIT 8*5		LA-SF 4*0	
1002	NY-PHI 3-4	ATL-SD 4*2	CIN-HOU 2-4	MON-PIT 1-2	STL-CHI 4-8	LA-SF 15*2	
1003	NY-PHI 1-4	ATL-SD 1-5	CIN-HOU 0-3	MON-PIT 6*1	STL-CHI 5*4	LA-SF 3-5	

♦1983♦	GAME 1	GAME 2	GAME 3	GAME 4	GAME 5	GAME 6	GAME 7
0404	ATL-CIN 4-5						
0405	LA-HOU 16*7	PHI-NY 0-2	SD-SF 16*13	PIT-STL 7*1			
0406	LA-HOU 4*2	MON-CHI 3*0	SD-SF 5*3	ATL-CIN 5*1			
0407	PIT-HOU 3*2	MON-CHI 7*3	PHI-NY 2-6				
0408	PIT-HOU 5*3	SD-ATL 2-4	CHI-CIN 3-7	MON-LA 8*3	PHI-SF 2-3		
0409	PIT-HOU 1*0	SD-ATL 5-6	CHI-CIN 4-8	MON-LA 7*2	PHI-SF 5*4	STL-NY 5*0	
0410	PIT-HOU 10*8	SD-ATL 3-4	CHI-CIN 2-7	MON-LA 0-3	PHI-SF 10*2		
0411		SD-ATL 0-4	CHI-CIN 1-5	HOU-LA 3-4			
0412	CHI-MON 5*0	CIN-ATL 1-4	NY-PHI 3-4	HOU-LA 1-3	STL-PIT 4*3	SF-SD 6*5	
0413		CIN-ATL 1-6	NY-PHI 9-10	HOU-LA 3-5	STL-PIT 9*1	SF-SD 1-2	
0414	CHI-MON 3-4	NY-STL 1-7				SF-SD 4-6	
0415	MON-HOU 6-7	NY-STL 2-5	SD-LA 2-6	CIN-SF 3*1			
0416	MON-HOU 2*0	NY-STL 2-6	SD-LA 5-8	CIN-SF 8*3	ATL-PHI 4-8	CHI-PIT 6*5	
0417	MON-HOU 3-6		SD-LA 9*1	CIN-SF 0-3	ATL-PHI 3*1	CHI-PIT 0-7	
				CIN-SF 12*3			
0418	CHI-PHI 2-8	ATL-SD 3-10		LA-SF 4*3			
0419	CIN-HOU 5-6	ATL-SD 9*2					
0420	CIN-HOU 6*4	CHI-PHI 0-2	LA-SF 2-3	PIT-NY 0-6			
				PIT-NY 5-7			
0421	CIN-HOU 3-4	STL-MON 5-6	SF-CHI 2-7	MON-CIN 4*0	LA-PIT 4*2	SD-STL 4*1	
0422	PHI-HOU 6*3	NY-ATL 4-5	SF-CHI 5*0		LA-PIT 3*2	SD-STL 5-9	
0423	PHI-HOU 7*3		SF-CHI 1-5	NY-ATL 3-6		SD-STL 0-2	
0424	PHI-HOU 2-3	MON-CIN 5*4		NY-ATL 3-5			
0425	LA-STL 8*0		SD-CHI 10*8	NY-CIN 0-7	HOU-MON 2*0	SF-PIT 0-3	
0426	LA-STL 3*1	PHI-ATL 4-10	SD-CHI 4-5	NY-CIN 2*1	HOU-MON 4*2	SF-PIT 3*2	
0427	LA-STL 6-7	PHI-ATL 6*2	SD-CHI 3*1				
0428							
0429	CIN-MON 6-9	ATL-NY 5-6	LA-CHI 4*3	HOU-PHI 6*3	SF-STL 5#5		
0430	CIN-MON 4*3	ATL-NY 6*1	LA-CHI 2-7	HOU-PHI 0-8	SF-STL 5-6	SD-PIT 8*4	
					SF-STL 5*0	SD-PIT 1-2	
0501	LA-CHI 3*2	ATL-NY 2*1	HOU-PHI 3-11	CIN-MON 4-5	SF-STL 9-10		
				CIN-MON 6*3			
0502	PIT-LA 5*1	HOU-NY 3*2	CIN-PHI 5*2				
0503	PIT-LA 4-5	HOU-NY 7*4	CIN-PHI 7-13	ATL-MON 5*2	STL-SD 3-4	CHI-SF 4-5	
0504	PIT-LA 2-3	HOU-NY 4*3	CIN-PHI 4-9	ATL-MON 1-4	STL-SD 0-10	CHI-SF 4-7	
0505	HOU-ATL 3-6				STL-SD 4*3		
0506	HOU-ATL 6*0	STL-LA 10-16	PHI-MON 5*2	CIN-NY 4-7	CHI-SD 3*2	PIT-SF 1-2	
0507	HOU-ATL 1-10	STL-LA 3-5	PHI-MON 2-3	CIN-NY 7*5	CHI-SD 6*4	PIT-SF 1-5	
0508	HOU-ATL 3-4	STL-LA 4-6		CIN-NY 5-10	CHI-SD 3-5	PIT-SF 1-12	
					PIT-SD 5*3	STL-SF 4-5	
0509	MON-ATL 5*3	CHI-LA 3-4	NY-HOU 4-6		PIT-SD 1-4	STL-SF 8*4	
0510	MON-ATL 2-4	CHI-LA 3*2	NY-HOU 4-5	PHI-CIN 3*1			
0511	MON-ATL 8*5		NY-HOU 3*0	PHI-CIN 0-2			
0512	PHI-CHI 3-6	NY-PIT 2-6	ATL-HOU 3-4	SF-CIN 4*2	LA-SD 4*3	MON-STL 0-4	
0513	PHI-CHI 2-10	NY-PIT 1-2	ATL-HOU 2-5	SF-CIN 8*5	LA-SD 4-6	MON-STL 4-5	
0514		NY-PIT 6*2	ATL-HOU 4*3	SF-CIN 8*7	LA-SD 4*1	MON-STL 2-3	
0515	PHI-CHI 5*3		ATL-HOU 9*4	SF-CIN 5*2	LA-SD 3*2	MON-STL 2-4	
0516	NY-PIT 11*4						
0517	CIN-PIT 2*1	ATL-CHI 3-4	LA-MON 2-3	SD-NY 4-6	SF-PHI 1-2	HOU-STL 4-8	
0518	CIN-PIT 1-2	ATL-CHI 3-5	LA-MON 13*3	SD-NY 1-2	SF-PHI 8*1	HOU-STL 5-9	
				SD-NY 3*2			
0519							
0520	CIN-CHI 9*5	SF-MON 1-7	SD-PHI 5*0	LA-NY 0-4		ATL-STL 2*1	
0521	CIN-CHI 4-8	SF-MON 5*2			HOU-PIT 3-4	ATL-STL 4*1	
0522	CIN-CHI 4*3	SF-MON 0-2	LA-NY 5*0		HOU-PIT 6*4	ATL-STL 7*5	
0523	PIT-ATL 3-6	SD-MON 1-3	SF-NY 3-4	STL-CIN 1-2	CHI-HOU 2-3	LA-PHI 2*0	
0524	PIT-ATL 6*5	SD-MON 4-5	SF-NY 6*2	STL-CIN 7*1	CHI-HOU 5*4	LA-PHI 3*0	
0525	PIT-ATL 0-6	SD-MON 0-2	SF-NY 7*6	STL-CIN 7*2	CHI-HOU 0-1	LA-PHI 6*1	
0526	CHI-ATL 5*1	SF-LA 5*3		PIT-CIN 6*4	STL-HOU 5*3		
0527	CHI-ATL 8*6	SF-LA 6*3	MON-PHI 7*4	PIT-CIN 0-9	STL-HOU 3*1	NY-SD 0-4	
0528	CHI-ATL 4-6	SF-LA 0-5	MON-PHI 3-5	PIT-CIN 3-4	STL-HOU 2-9	NY-SD 4-5	
0529	CHI-ATL 2-6	SF-LA 6*4	MON-PHI 2-5	PIT-CIN 8*5	STL-HOU 7*3	NY-SD 3*2	
0530	HOU-CHI 9*7	PHI-LA 2-5	ATL-PIT 6-8	NY-SF 0-5	CIN-STL 1-9	MON-SD 4-5	
0531	HOU-CHI 12*10	PHI-LA 1-4	ATL-PIT 10*2	NY-SF 1-2	CIN-STL 2*1	MON-SD 3-5	
0601	HOU-CHI 2-3	PHI-LA 0-1	ATL-PIT 6*3	NY-SF 2-4	CIN-STL 3-8	MON-SD 8*6	
0602	PIT-CHI 2-3	NY-LA 4-5	STL-ATL 1-8	MON-SF 11*4		PHI-SD 1-4	
0603	PIT-CHI 3-9	NY-LA 5*2	STL-ATL 3-5	MON-SF 9*2	HOU-CIN 1-3	PHI-SD 5-8	
0604	PIT-CHI 2-5	NY-LA 1-2	STL-ATL 4-6	MON-SF 2-4	HOU-CIN 13*0	PHI-SD 4-5	
0605	PIT-CHI 1-3	NY-LA 4*2	STL-ATL 8*3	MON-SF 12*9	HOU-CIN 6*3	PHI-SD 2*1	
0607	NY-CHI 1-6	SF-HOU 2-4	LA-ATL 1-4	PIT-MON 3*2	SD-CIN 7*3	STL-PHI 2*1	
0608	NY-CHI 1-2	SF-HOU 0-1	LA-ATL 11*5	PIT-MON 4-5	SD-CIN 5*3	STL-PHI 4-7	
0609	NY-CHI 6*4	SF-HOU 0-3	LA-ATL 4*2	PIT-MON 6*3	SD-CIN 1-8	STL-PHI 5-6	
0610	STL-CHI 0-7	SD-HOU 1-2	SF-ATL 6*4	MON-NY 2-4	LA-CIN 2-3	PIT-PHI 4*3	
			SF-ATL 3-7				
0611	STL-CHI 5*4	LA-CIN 3*2	SF-ATL 7*6	SD-HOU 8*4	MON-NY 5*2	PIT-PHI 7-9	
0612	STL-CHI 3-6	LA-CIN 1-3	SF-ATL 2-3	SD-HOU 0-2	MON-NY 1-9	PIT-PHI 4-5	
0613	MON-PIT 3-4	LA-CIN 5*1	PHI-STL 6*2	SD-HOU 0-2	CHI-NY 7*3	HOU-SF 3*2	
0614	MON-PIT 7*3	ATL-LA 3-4	PHI-STL 4-5	CIN-SD 4*3	CHI-NY 3-4	HOU-SF 1-7	
0615	MON-PIT 7*4	ATL-LA 3*2	PHI-STL 6-7	CIN-SD 1-5	CHI-NY 7*4	HOU-SF 7*2	
0616		ATL-LA 1-6		CIN-SD 1-3			
0617	NY-MON 2-7	CIN-LA 0-1	PHI-PIT 1-2	HOU-SD 4*1	CHI-STL 2-7	ATL-SF 1-2	
0618	NY-MON 6*1	CIN-LA 3*2	PHI-PIT 6*4	HOU-SD 1-2	CHI-STL 10*1	ATL-SF 4-5	
0619	NY-MON 3-4	CIN-LA 1-5	PHI-PIT 14*2	HOU-SD 4-6	CHI-STL 4*1	ATL-SF 6-9	
0620	PHI-MON 0-5	SD-LA 4*1	CHI-PIT 4-5	ATL-HOU 7*1	STL-NY 3*1	CIN-SF 3-4	
			CHI-PIT 5-6		STL-NY 4-6		
0621	ATL-HOU 0-5	SD-LA 2*0	CHI-PIT 4-8	CIN-SF 6*5	STL-NY 6*0	PHI-MON 8*1	
						PHI-MON 4-5	
0622	ATL-HOU 3-4	SD-LA 5*2	CHI-PIT 2-5	CIN-SF 4*2	STL-NY 4-6	PHI-MON 0-4	
					STL-NY 1-2		
					STL-NY 5-7		
0623	SD-LA 7*5	PHI-MON 3-4	CHI-PIT 2-5			ATL-CIN 3*0	
						ATL-CIN 10*5	
0624	HOU-LA 2-7	CHI-MON 3-4	SD-SF 0-5	PIT-STL 8*2	PHI-NY 6*3	ATL-CIN 8*2	
0625	HOU-LA 1-2	CHI-MON 2*1	PHI-NY 4*2	SD-SF 3*2	PIT-STL 10*3	ATL-CIN 5*1	
0626	HOU-LA 9*7	CHI-MON 9*5	PHI-NY 8*4	SD-SF 0-2	PIT-STL 5*0		
			PHI-NY 1-5	SD-SF 3-4			
0627	ATL-CIN 2*1	CHI-MON 1-3	PIT-STL 6*1	PIT-CHI 7-8	MON-PHI 55	LA-SD 9*5	
0628	SF-CIN 4-5	HOU-ATL 4*3	NY-STL 10*1				
			NY-STL 1-8				
0629	HOU-ATL 1-11	PIT-CHI 0-5	NY-STL 3-4	SF-CIN 6-7	LA-SD 2-13	MON-PHI 5*2	
						MON-PHI 2-3	
0630	HOU-ATL 4-6	PIT-CHI 3-4	SF-CIN 5-15	LA-SD 6-7	NY-STL 1-6	MON-PHI 1-3	
0701	CIN-ATL 2-5	MON-CHI 5-7	LA-HOU 5*2	SF-SD 4*3	STL-PIT 13*6	NY-PHI 1-5	

◆1983◆	GAME 1	GAME 2	GAME 3	GAME 4	GAME 5	GAME 6	GAME 7
0702	CIN-ATL 2-4	MON-CHI 2-5	LA-HOU 1-3	SF-SD 4-5	STL-PIT 1-3	NY-PHI 5-6	
						NY-PHI 4*3	
0703	CIN-ATL 2*1	MON-CHI 4-7	LA-HOU 1-8	STL-PIT 4*3	SF-SD 1-4	NY-PHI 4-6	
0704	CIN-ATL 5-9	MON-CHI 6*3	LA-HOU 4-5	STL-PIT 2-7	SF-SD 3-4	NY-PHI 0-4	
		MON-CHI 4*2		STL-PIT 11*4			
0708	PHI-CIN 1-3	PIT-LA 4*3	ATL-MON 6*5	HOU-NY 6*3	STL-SD 2-3	CHI-SF 1-4	
0709	PHI-CIN 1-2	PIT-LA 3*0	ATL-MON 8*5	HOU-NY 7*3	STL-SD 12*4	CHI-SF 4*2	
0710	PHI-CIN 2*0	PIT-LA 3-10	ATL-MON 6-7	HOU-NY 5-7	STL-SD 4*2	CHI-SF 8-10	
						CHI-SF 2-4	
0711	PHI-CIN 11*7	STL-LA 6-7	ATL-MON 6*4	CHI-SD 5-6		PIT-SF 3*2	
0712	MON-HOU 5-7	STL-LA 1-3	CIN-NY 6*2	CHI-SD 3-5	ATL-PHI 1-4	PIT-SF 6*2	
					ATL-PHI 6-7		
0713	MON-HOU 4-9	STL-LA 6*5	CIN-NY 3*1	CHI-SD 4-5	ATL-PHI 5*2	PIT-SF 7*6	
0714	MON-HOU 0-3	CHI-LA 4-8	CIN-NY 4-7	PIT-SD 8*6	ATL-PHI 5*2	STL-SF 6*5	
0715	NY-HOU 0-6	CHI-LA 8*4	MON-ATL 3-9	PIT-SD 4*2	CIN-PHI 3*2	STL-SF 4-5	
0716	NY-HOU 1-3	CHI-LA 4-7	MON-ATL 3-6	PIT-SD 3*2	CIN-PHI 3-9	STL-SF 9*3	
0717	NY-HOU 3*1	CHI-LA 10*0	MON-ATL 3*1	PIT-SD 4*3	CIN-PHI 5*2	STL-SF 1-3	
0718			NY-ATL 4-7		HOU-PHI 8*2		
0719	SF-CHI 4*3	CIN-MON 5*2	NY-ATL 7-11	SD-STL 0-4	HOU-PHI 7*3	LA-PIT 1-4	
						LA-PIT 3*2	
0720	NY-ATL 3*2	SF-CHI 4*3	CIN-MON 4-6	HOU-PHI 3-10	SD-STL 5*4	LA-PIT 3-7	
0721	PHI-ATL 10*6	SF-CHI 2-3	HOU-MON 4-9	NY-CIN 1-6	SD-STL 4*2	LA-PIT 4-5	
0722	PHI-ATL 1-6	SD-CHI 3-7	HOU-MON 11*8	NY-CIN 3*2	LA-STL 9*4	SF-PIT 5*3	
0723	PHI-ATL 5-6	SD-CHI 4*2	HOU-MON 1-4	NY-CIN 3-7	LA-STL 10*5	SF-PIT 2-5	
0724	PHI-ATL 4-12	SD-CHI 2-5	HOU-MON 3-7	NY-CIN 2-4	LA-STL 0-3	SF-PIT 1-3	
						SF-PIT 8*5	
0725	LA-CHI 3-9	ATL-NY 4-5	SF-STL 4-9	MON-CIN 2-4		SD-PIT 3-6	
				MON-CIN 8*1			
0726	LA-CHI 5*2	PHI-HOU 1*0	ATL-NY 1-2	MON-CIN 5*0	SF-STL 5-6	SD-PIT 6*1	
						SD-PIT 5-10	
0727	LA-CHI 1-2	MON-CIN 6*3	PHI-HOU 3*1	ATL-NY 6*3	SF-STL 6-7	SD-PIT 1-10	
0728	STL-MON 3*2		PHI-HOU 6*5	PIT-NY 6*2			
	STL-MON 10*1						
0729	STL-MON 2-7	CIN-HOU 1-4	PIT-NY 2*1	CHI-PHI 2-3	LA-SF 2-5	ATL-SD 2*1	
						ATL-SD 5-6	
0730	CIN-HOU 3*2	STL-MON 3*2	PIT-NY 6*3	LA-SF 0-8	CHI-PHI 4*3	ATL-SD 5*2	
					CHI-PHI 3-4		
0731	CIN-HOU 2-9	STL-MON 5-6	ATL-SD 2-5	PIT-NY 6-7	CHI-PHI 2-5	LA-SF 2*1	
				PIT-NY 0-1		LA-SF 6-8	
0801	CIN-LA 4*2	CHI-PHI 1-2	HOU-SD 4-7			ATL-SF 8*3	
0802	CIN-LA 1-3	MON-NY 2-5	HOU-SD 4*2	PHI-PIT 3-10	CHI-STL 5*3	ATL-SF 3-7	
0803	CIN-LA 4-7	MON-NY 1-2	HOU-SD 1*0	PHI-PIT 2-7	CHI-STL 4*0	ATL-SF 6*4	
0804	CIN-LA 4*3	MON-NY 2*1	HOU-SD 2-4	PHI-PIT 5*1	CHI-STL 9*6	ATL-SF 8*1	
0805	ATL-LA 1-2	NY-CHI 9*4	CIN-SD 4*3	MON-PIT 7*1	PHI-STL 10*7	HOU-SF 1-7	
0806	ATL-LA 2-4	NY-CHI 4*1	CIN-SD 4-11	MON-PIT 7*3	PHI-STL 1*0	HOU-SF 4*2	
			CIN-SD 2-6				
0807	NY-CHI 6*4	ATL-LA 5*2	CIN-SD 5*3	MON-PIT 6*0	HOU-SF 2*1	PHI-STL 5*2	
0808	NY-MON 6*5	PIT-PHI 5-14					
0809	NY-MON 3-7	PIT-PHI 3*1	SF-ATL 2-7	STL-CHI 3-5	LA-CIN 4-5	SD-HOU 3*2	
0810	NY-MON 3-5	PIT-PHI 2-4	SF-ATL 7*4	STL-CHI 9*5	LA-CIN 2-9	SD-HOU 3-4	
0811			SF-ATL 4-6	STL-CHI 5-10	LA-CIN 4*3	SD-HOU 1-5	
0812	PIT-MON 6*3	CHI-NY 0-2	LA-ATL 5*3	STL-PHI 2-5	SD-CIN 5-6	SF-HOU 2-5	
0813	PIT-MON 2*0	CHI-NY 1-5	LA-ATL 7-8	STL-PHI 6*2	SD-CIN 1-3	SF-HOU 1-4	
0814	PIT-MON 5*3	CHI-NY 2-5	LA-ATL 5*4	STL-PHI 1-5	SD-CIN 10*9	SF-HOU 5*2	
0815	PHI-CHI 5*0	SF-LA 7*3	SD-ATL 4*0	NY-PIT 2-4	HOU-CIN 9*1	MON-STL 5*1	
0816	PHI-CHI 1-10	SF-LA 1-5	SD-ATL 3*2	NY-PIT 1-3	HOU-CIN 8*5	MON-STL 3-4	
	PHI-CHI 6*2						
0817	HOU-CIN 7*6	NY-LA 1-4	PHI-SD 4-5	MON-SF 12*5			
0818	ATL-CHI 0-3	CIN-PIT 6*5	PHI-SD 4*2	MON-SF 3-5	HOU-STL 4-5		
0819	ATL-CHI 5*3	CIN-PIT 2*1	MON-SD 5-6	NY-SF 7*6	HOU-STL 0-2	PHI-LA 0-3	
0820	ATL-CHI 9*2	CIN-PIT 0-4		NY-SF 7*2	HOU-STL 0-3	PHI-LA 3-4	
0821	ATL-CHI 11*9	CIN-PIT 6*4	MON-SD 3*0	NY-SF 4*3	HOU-STL 2-5	PHI-LA 0-6	
			MON-SD 2-5				
0822	CIN-CHI 0-2	MON-LA 1-4	NY-SD 3-4	PHI-SF 5-11			
0823	CIN-CHI 4*2	MON-LA 3-6	NY-SD 8*3	PHI-SF 1-3	ATL-STL 0-7	HOU-PIT 6*5	
						HOU-PIT 2*1	
0824	CIN-CHI 0-3	MON-LA 2-3	NY-SD 2-3	PHI-SF 3-5	ATL-STL 11*3	HOU-PIT 10*4	
0825					ATL-STL 1-2	HOU-PIT 3-5	
0826	STL-CIN 3-7	CHI-HOU 0-1	SD-MON 4-10	SF-NY 12*1	LA-PHI 1-4	ATL-PIT 1-9	
0827	STL-CIN 3*1	CHI-HOU 9*5	SD-MON 4-6	SF-NY 3-6	LA-PHI 6*1	ATL-PIT 0-2	
0828	STL-CIN 4-5	CHI-HOU 2-4	SD-MON 0-8	SF-NY 7*2	LA-PHI 8*3	ATL-PIT 2*1	
0829	PIT-CIN 2*1	STL-HOU 6*1	SF-MON 0-5	LA-NY 6*1	SD-PHI 6*5	CHI-ATL 7*5	
				LA-NY 7*3	SD-PHI 6-8		
0830	CHI-ATL 9*6	PIT-CIN 5*3	STL-HOU 1-3	LA-NY 2-3	SD-PHI 0-6	SF-MON 13*2	
				LA-NY 2*1	SD-PHI 7*5		
0831	STL-ATL 6*3	CHI-CIN 4-6	PIT-HOU 1-4	LA-NY 1-7	SD-PHI 3-4	SF-MON 3-4	
0901	STL-ATL 8*3	CHI-CIN 3*1	PIT-HOU 0-3		SF-PHI 2-4	LA-MON 3-8	
0902	PIT-ATL 4*1	HOU-CHI 6*5	SD-NY 3-7	CIN-STL 4*0	SF-PHI 3-5	LA-MON 4*1	
0903	PIT-ATL 6*2	HOU-CHI 3-9	SD-NY 3-4	CIN-STL 3*2	SF-PHI 5*4	LA-MON 4*0	
0904	PIT-ATL 5-6	HOU-CHI 7-9	SD-NY 7*5	CIN-STL 4-5	SF-PHI 10*4	LA-MON 2-3	
0905	HOU-ATL 5-7	SD-LA 5*2	PHI-NY 5-6	PIT-STL 4-7	CIN-SF 2-3	CHI-MON 3-7	
				PIT-STL 6-7			
0906	SD-LA 8*3	CHI-MON 2-8	PHI-NY 2*0	PIT-STL 5*0	CIN-SF 11*1		
0907	CIN-LA 3-7	CHI-MON 1-6	PHI-NY 6*1	PIT-STL 2-5	ATL-SF 1-2	HOU-SD 7-8	
0908	CIN-LA 2-5				ATL-SF 12*9	HOU-SD 3*2	
0909	ATL-LA 2-3	STL-CHI 6*5	NY-MON 5*4	PHI-PIT 4*3	HOU-SF 7*4	CIN-SD 2-8	
0910	ATL-LA 6*3	STL-CHI 5-8	NY-MON 9-10	PHI-PIT 5-6	HOU-SF 5*3		
0911	ATL-LA 6-7	STL-CHI 2*1	NY-MON 0-4	PHI-PIT 5*3	HOU-SF 2-3	CIN-SD 4*2	
0912	NY-PHI 1-2	MON-CHI 0-8		STL-PIT 5-7			
0913	NY-PHI 5*1	MON-CHI 5*2	ATL-CIN 0-6	STL-PIT 0-6	LA-HOU 5*1	SF-SD 3-4	
0914	MON-PHI 5-9	STL-NY 2*1	ATL-CIN 4-6	CHI-PIT 3-6	LA-HOU 2-4	SF-SD 4-7	
	MON-PHI 0-5						
0915	MON-PHI 4*1	LA-HOU 6*0	STL-NY 4-6	CHI-PIT 4-8			
0916	STL-PHI 2-3	SD-ATL 0-6	CHI-NY 7*4	MON-PIT 0-9	HOU-CIN 3-8	LA-SF 0-1	
0917	STL-PHI 1-4	SD-ATL 2*1	CHI-NY 7*6	MON-PIT 4-5	HOU-CIN 4*3	LA-SF 1-4	
0918	STL-PHI 3-5	SD-ATL 4*2	CHI-NY 6*5	MON-PIT 5*2	HOU-CIN 4*1	LA-SF 3-6	
0919	CHI-PHI 6-7	HOU-LA 2-9	PIT-NY 4-5	STL-MON 0-3		SD-SF 4*2	
				STL-MON 3-6			
0920	HOU-LA 15*2	PIT-NY 4*0	CHI-PHI 5-8	STL-MON 1-10	SD-SF 1-8		
0921	HOU-LA 1-2	PIT-CHI 6-7	NY-STL 3-9	CIN-ATL 1-9	SD-SF 4-5		
				CIN-ATL 4*3			
0922	PIT-CHI 8*2	NY-STL 2-3	PHI-MON 9*7				
			PHI-MON 7*1				
0923	LA-ATL 11*2	NY-CHI 1-4	PIT-MON 10*1	SD-CIN 11*8	SF-HOU 3*2	PHI-STL 6*2	
0924	LA-ATL 2-3	NY-CHI 7*6	PIT-MON 1*0	SD-CIN 2-3	SF-HOU 5-6	PHI-STL 9*6	
0925	LA-ATL 1-7	NY-CHI 7-11	PIT-MON 3-5	SD-CIN 2-5	SF-HOU 3*0	PHI-STL 6*5	
0926	SF-ATL 2-6	PHI-CHI 5*2		LA-CIN 12*9	SD-HOU 3-5	MON-STL 0-3	

♦1983♦	GAME 1	GAME 2	GAME 3	GAME 4	GAME 5	GAME 6	GAME 7
0927	SF-ATL 6*2	PHI-CHI 0-3	NY-PIT 4*3	LA-CIN 7*4	SD-HOU 5-8	MON-STL 10*4	
0928	LA-SD 44	PHI-CHI 13*6	NY-PIT 4*2	SF-CIN 4-5	ATL-HOU 3*1	MON-STL 4*0	
					ATL-HOU 1-5		
0929	SF-CIN 11*7	NY-PIT 2-4	LA-SD 1-7		ATL-HOU 5*4		
			LA-SD 1-4				
0930	CIN-HOU 2-3	SF-LA 3-4	ATL-SD 2-3	PIT-PHI 1-2	CHI-STL 2-9		
1001	CIN-HOU 6*4	SF-LA 4*1	ATL-SD 3-4	PIT-PHI 3-5	CHI-STL 2-3	MON-NY 4-5	
1002	CIN-HOU 2-3	SF-LA 4*3	ATL-SD 4*3	PIT-PHI 4*0	CHI-STL 6-9	MON-NY 0-1	
						MON-NY 4-5	

♦1984♦	GAME 1	GAME 2	GAME 3	GAME 4	GAME 5	GAME 6	GAME 7
0402	NY-CIN 1-8						
0403	PHI-ATL 5*0	MON-HOU 4*2	STL-LA 11*7	PIT-SD 1-5	CHI-SF 5*3		
0404	PHI-ATL 0-4	MON-HOU 2-8	NY-CIN 2*0				
0405	STL-LA 2-5	PIT-SD 6-8	CHI-SF 11*7				
0406	PIT-LA 3*1	CHI-SD 2-3	STL-SF 2*0	MON-ATL 8*5	PHI-CIN 8*4	NY-HOU 8*1	
0407	PIT-LA 3*0	CHI-SD 6-7	STL-SF 0-11	MON-ATL 7*2	PHI-CIN 9*1	NY-HOU 3*2	
0408	PIT-LA 5*2	CHI-SD 8*5	STL-SF 9*3	MON-ATL 2-6	PHI-CIN 7-8	NY-HOU 3*1	
					MON-CIN 6-9		
0409	CHI-LA 2-4				MON-CIN 6-8		
0410	NY-ATL 4*2	HOU-PHI 1-3	STL-SD 3-7	PIT-SF 3-4	MON-CIN 9*3		
0411	NY-ATL 6*1	HOU-PHI 6*7	STL-SD 5-7	PIT-SF 1-2		CHI-LA 1-2	
			ATL-SD 1-6				
0412							
0413	NY-CHI 2-11	CIN-HOU 0-1	ATL-SD 2-5	SF-LA 0-2	PHI-MON 1-5	PIT-STL 1-4	
0414	NY-CHI 2-5	CIN-HOU 1-9	ATL-SD 5*1	SF-LA 4-8	PHI-MON 4*3	PIT-STL 5-7	
0415		CIN-HOU 5-6	ATL-SD 4-6	SF-LA 8*6		PIT-STL 0-1	
0416		LA-HOU 5*4					
0417	MON-NY 10*0	LA-HOU 1*0	PHI-PIT 4*1	SD-SF 2*1			
0418	MON-NY 4-5	LA-HOU 0-3	PHI-PIT 3-6	ATL-CIN 5*4	STL-CHI 5*0		
					STL-CHI 1-6		
0419	SD-LA 0-4	MON-NY 6-7	CIN-SF 1-3		STL-CHI 1-6		
0420	SD-LA 2-8	HOU-ATL 7-8	CIN-SF 4-6	NY-PHI 3*1	PIT-CHI 4-5		
0421	SD-LA 9*6	HOU-ATL 4*3	CIN-SF 5*4	NY-PHI 2-12	PIT-CHI 8*5	MON-STL 6*3	
						MON-STL 4*0	
0422	HOU-ATL 3*1	SD-LA 7-15	NY-PHI 5-12	CIN-SF 5-9		MON-STL 4*2	
0423	NY-MON 4-6	HOU-LA 1-2	SF-SD 2-8			CHI-STL 6*2	
0424	CIN-ATL 2-4	HOU-LA 3-5	SF-SD 1-6	PIT-PHI 3*2		CHI-STL 3*2	
0425	CIN-ATL 4*3	HOU-LA 2-4	SF-SD 0-3	PIT-PHI 7-8	NY-MON 2*1	CHI-STL 5-7	
			LA-SD 6*5				
0426	CIN-ATL 1-2		LA-SD 1*0	STL-MON 8*2	PHI-NY 8*3	CHI-PIT 2-3	
0427	SF-CIN 3-9	ATL-HOU 6*0	LA-SD 1-5	STL-MON 6*1	PHI-NY 3-4	CHI-PIT 7*1	
0428	SF-CIN 6-7	ATL-HOU 5*3	LA-SD 6*0	STL-MON 2-6	PHI-NY 2-6	CHI-PIT 2*1	
0429	SF-CIN 1-8	ATL-HOU 5-8					
	SF-CIN 3-7						
0430	MON-PHI 5*2	STL-PIT 5*3	LA-SF 1*0		HOU-CIN 1-2	CHI-NY 1-8	
0501	MON-PHI 4-7	STL-PIT 10*5	LA-SF 3*2	SD-ATL 3*2	HOU-CIN 2-3	CHI-NY 3-4	
0502	MON-PHI 3*2	STL-PIT 3*1	LA-SF 3-4				
0503	SD-ATL 5-6	HOU-NY 0-2	CIN-PHI 9*5	SF-STL 2*0			
0504	SD-CHI 6-7	HOU-NY 10*6	CIN-PHI 2-11	SF-STL 7*0	ATL-MON 1-2	LA-PIT 7-8	
0505	SD-CHI 5-6	HOU-NY 10*1	CIN-PHI 5*3	SF-STL 3*2	ATL-MON 2*0	LA-PIT 6*4	
0506	SD-CHI 8*5				ATL-MON 9*8	LA-PIT 1-2	
					HOU-MON 1-4		
0507	SF-CHI 7-10	CIN-NY 11*2	ATL-PHI 8*6	LA-STL 1-5			
0508	SF-CHI 11-12		ATL-PHI 8*2	LA-STL 2*1			
0509	LA-CHI 0-7	PHI-HOU 1-7	CIN-MON 6*4	SD-STL 3*2	ATL-NY 1-3		
0510	LA-CHI 5*1	PHI-HOU 2-4	CIN-MON 2*1	SD-STL 0-7	ATL-NY 7*3	SF-PIT 2-4	
0511	PIT-ATL 2-4	CHI-HOU 1-3	STL-CIN 3-4	NY-LA 2*0	PHI-SD 6*4	MON-SF 7*5	
0512	PIT-ATL 3-4	CHI-HOU 5*4	STL-CIN 1-2	NY-LA 4*3	PHI-SD 3*2	MON-SF 7-8	
0513	PIT-ATL 8-9	CHI-HOU 0-1	STL-CIN 6*2	NY-LA 3-5	PHI-SD 8*3	MON-SF 3-4	
				PHI-LA 3*2	MON-SD 7*6		
0514	HOU-PIT 2-3						
0515	HOU-PIT 2-3	CHI-CIN 6*3	NY-SF 7*6	PHI-LA 12*1	MON-SD 6*4	ATL-STL 1-9	
0516	HOU-PIT 1*0	CHI-CIN 10*4	NY-SF 3-4	PHI-LA 7*2	MON-SD 6*2	ATL-STL 2-4	
		CHI-CIN 3-5			MON-SD 4-5	ATL-STL 7*2	
0517							
0518	HOU-CHI 6-7	MON-LA 5*4	ATL-PIT 0-6	PHI-SF 1*0	NY-SD 4-5	CIN-STL 3-5	
0519	HOU-CHI 4-5	MON-LA 1-5	ATL-PIT 4*2	PHI-SF 6*2	NY-SD 3-8	CIN-STL 1-9	
0520	HOU-CHI 3-10	MON-LA 2-3	ATL-PIT 5*1	PHI-SF 7*4	NY-SD 4*2	CIN-STL 2-3	
						HOU-STL 3*2	
0521						HOU-STL 4*3	
0522	SD-MON 2-3	SF-NY 5*4	LA-PHI 1-3	CIN-PIT 5*3		HOU-STL 4*0	
0523	SD-MON 2*1	SF-NY 3*2	LA-PHI 1*0	CIN-PIT 2-7	ATL-CHI 1-3		
0524			LA-PHI 3-4	CIN-PIT 1-5	ATL-CHI 7-10		
					ATL-CHI 5-7		
0525	STL-ATL 4-8	PIT-HOU 6*2	SF-MON 2-3	LA-NY 1-2	CIN-CHI 3*0	SD-PHI 7*3	
0526	STL-ATL 3-7	PIT-HOU 0-2	SF-MON 2-4	LA-NY 1-2	CIN-CHI 7*6	SD-PHI 2-7	
0527	STL-ATL 12*9	PIT-HOU 2*1	SF-MON 2-6	LA-NY 3*2	CIN-CHI 4*3	SD-PHI 4*0	
0528	STL-ATL 2-6	PIT-HOU 7*0	LA-MON 6*1	SD-NY 5*4			
0529	CHI-ATL 4-7	STL-HOU 0-1	PIT-CIN 4-5				
0530	CHI-ATL 6*4	STL-HOU 6*4	PIT-CIN 4-6	LA-MON 4*1	SF-PHI 2-3		
					CHI-PHI 2-10		
0531	STL-NY 5*2	MON-PIT 1-2	ATL-CIN 7*1		CHI-PHI 12*3	SD-SF 7-11	
0601	STL-NY 5*1	MON-PIT 2*0	ATL-CIN 4*2	HOU-LA 2-6			
			ATL-CIN 7*3				
0602	HOU-LA 9*3	STL-NY 2-5	ATL-CIN 9*3	CHI-PHI 2-3	MON-PIT 1-2	SD-SF 3*2	
0603	HOU-LA 5*3	STL-NY 1*0	ATL-CIN 4*0	CHI-PHI 11*2	MON-PIT 0-4	SD-SF 7*5	
						SD-SF 7*6	
0604	CIN-LA 3*1	NY-PIT 4*2	HOU-SD 0-3	PHI-STL 3-4		ATL-SF 2*1	
0605	CIN-LA 1-2	NY-PIT 3*0	HOU-SD 0-3	PHI-STL 3-5	CHI-MON 3*2	ATL-SF 8*3	
0606	CIN-LA 2-3	NY-PIT 2*1	HOU-SD 3-4	PHI-STL 3-4	CHI-MON 1-8	ATL-SF 5*4	
0607	ATL-LA 8*1		CIN-SD 12*1		CHI-MON 1-2	HOU-SF 14*5	
0608	ATL-LA 3-5	CHI-STL 4-5	CIN-SD 0-6	PIT-PHI 4-5	NY-MON 4*1	HOU-SF 4-5	
				PIT-PHI 1-2			
0609	ATL-LA 3-4	CIN-SD 2-12	HOU-SF 5-6	PIT-PHI 5-6	CHI-STL 5*0	NY-MON 5*3	
						NY-MON 6*5	
0610	ATL-LA 2-3	PIT-PHI 12*6	CIN-SD 5-7	HOU-SF 7*4	CHI-STL 2*0	NY-MON 2-3	
0611	SF-LA 8*4	STL-PHI 6*4	ATL-SD 4-5	MON-CHI 2*1	CIN-HOU 2-3	PIT-NY 1-3	
0612	SF-LA 7-8	STL-PHI 7*2	ATL-SD 6-7	MON-CHI 4-11	CIN-HOU 0-7	PIT-NY 6*3	
				MON-CHI 4-7	CIN-HOU 5*4	PIT-NY 0-2	
0613	SF-LA 10*5	STL-PHI 1-4					
0614	CIN-ATL 0-3	PIT-MON 3*2	SF-SD 5*2	PHI-CHI 11*2	LA-HOU 1-3	NY-STL 6*0	
0615	CIN-ATL 1-6	PIT-MON 0-1	SF-SD 2-3	PHI-CHI 5*2	LA-HOU 2-3	NY-STL 5*0	
0616	CIN-ATL 2*1	PIT-MON 2-3	SF-SD 6*3	PHI-CHI 8*2	LA-HOU 5-7	NY-STL 4*1	
0617	CIN-ATL 5-6	PIT-MON 3-5	SF-SD 5*3	PHI-CHI 9*7	LA-HOU 0-1	NY-STL 3-6	
0619	SF-ATL 6-11	STL-MON 3-6	LA-CIN 4-10	PHI-NY 6*4	SD-HOU 2*0	CHI-PIT 4-3	
0620	SF-ATL 5-6	STL-MON 2*0	LA-CIN 2-4	PHI-NY 4-7	SD-HOU 6*2	CHI-PIT 1-5	
0621	SF-ATL 5*3		LA-CIN 9*7	PHI-NY 7-10	SD-HOU 5-11	CHI-PIT 6-8	
0622	LA-ATL 10*4	STL-CHI 3-9	SD-CIN 7-8	MON-NY 2*1	SF-HOU 3-10	PHI-PIT 3-10	
						PHI-PIT 6-7	
0623	LA-ATL 10*2	STL-CHI 11-12	SD-CIN 5*2	SF-HOU 7*5	MON-NY 0-2	PHI-PIT 7*5	
0624	LA-ATL 5*2	STL-CHI 0-5	SD-CIN 8*3	SF-HOU 3-8	MON-NY 5*3	PHI-PIT 4*2	
0625	HOU-ATL 8*5	PIT-CHI 3*0	SD-LA 9*4	NY-PHI 10*5	CIN-SF 2*1	MON-STL 4-5	
	HOU-ATL 4-6						

◆1984◆	GAME 1	GAME 2	GAME 3	GAME 4	GAME 5	GAME 6	GAME 7
0626	HOU-ATL 10*5	SD-LA 5*0	NY-PHI 0-3	CIN-SF 4*2	MON-STL 3-6	PIT-CHI 9*0 PIT-CHI 8-9	
0627	HOU-ATL 4-6	SD-LA 4-5	NY-PHI 1-5	CIN-SF 9-14	MON-STL 4*2	PIT-CHI 7-8	
0628	ATL-NY 5*3	CHI-LA 5*3	HOU-PHI 7*6	PIT-SF 3-4	STL-SD 3-7		
0629	ATL-NY 5*3	CHI-LA 1-7	HOU-PHI 2-7	PIT-SF 0-3	STL-SD 5*0	MON-CIN 7*3	
0630		CHI-LA 14*4	HOU-PHI 7*0	PIT-SF 5-7	STL-SD 4*1	MON-CIN 1-4	
0701	ATL-NY 1-2 ATL-NY 2-3	CHI-LA 4*3	HOU-PHI 13*1	PIT-SF 4-7	STL-SD 1-3	MON-CIN 1-4	
0702	HOU-NY 2-4	MON-ATL 5*4	PIT-LA 4-5	CIN-PHI 0-4	CHI-SD 1-5		
0703	HOU-NY 3-4	MON-ATL 3-5	PIT-LA 6*0	CIN-PHI 6*5	CHI-SD 3*2	STL-SF 2-6	
0704	HOU-NY 10*5	MON-ATL 7*4	PIT-LA 0-9	CIN-PHI 5*4	CHI-SD 2*1	STL-SF 4*3 STL-SF 5*1	
0705	STL-LA 3*0	CIN-NY 3-4	ATL-PHI 0-1	PIT-SD 1-2	HOU-MON 2*1	CHI-SF 9*3	
0706	STL-LA 2-3	CIN-NY 0-1 CIN-NY 5-6	ATL-PHI 5*0	PIT-SD 3-7	HOU-MON 8*2 HOU-MON 5-7	CHI-SF 5*4	
0707	STL-LA 0-3	CIN-NY 4-14	ATL-PHI 5*2	PIT-SD 0-1	HOU-MON 3*2	CHI-SF 2-7	
0708	STL-LA 8*6	CIN-NY 3-7	ATL-PHI 0-7	PIT-SD 4*3	HOU-MON 5-8	CHI-SF 6*3	
0712	NY-ATL 8*6	LA-CHI 2-3	PHI-HOU 5*3	SF-PIT 3-6	CIN-MON 1-3	SD-STL 4*1	
0713	NY-ATL 5*4	LA-CHI 5-7	PHI-HOU 7*3	SF-PIT 2-8 SF-PIT 3-4	CIN-MON 2-7	SD-STL 4-7	
0714	NY-ATL 7*0	LA-CHI 8*0	PHI-HOU 4*3	SF-PIT 2-6	CIN-MON 2-6	SD-STL 6-7	
0715	NY-ATL 3-8	LA-CHI 1-4	PHI-HOU 2-3	SF-PIT 3-9	CIN-MON 3*2	SD-STL 6*1	
0716	PHI-CIN 7*2	SD-CHI 4*0	NY-HOU 13*3	LA-PIT 1-4	ATL-MON 1-3	SF-STL 7*6	
0717	PHI-CIN 4*3	SD-CHI 6*5	NY-HOU 2-3	LA-PIT 5*0	ATL-MON 0-2	SF-STL 7*2	
0718	PHI-CIN 7*5	SD-CHI 1-4	NY-HOU 2-3	LA-PIT 2-5	ATL-MON 3*2	SF-STL 4-8	
0719	NY-CIN 6-9	SF-CHI 4-6	MON-HOU 2-3	SD-PIT 1-5	PHI-ATL 9*1	LA-STL 10*0	
0720	NY-CIN 3*2	SF-CHI 3*2	MON-HOU 4-8	SD-PIT 3-4 SD-PIT 3*2	PHI-ATL 1-13	LA-STL 5-10	
0721	PHI-ATL 3-5	SF-CHI 3-4	NY-CIN 2*1	SD-PIT 6*4	MON-HOU 4*2	LA-STL 3*1	
0722	PHI-ATL 6*2	SF-CHI 11*5	NY-CIN 7*6	SD-PIT 5*1 SD-PIT 2-3	MON-HOU 1-6	LA-STL 6-7	
0723	STL-NY 3-4	CHI-PHI 3*2			CIN-SD 4*2	HOU-SF 10*3	
0724	STL-NY 8-9	CHI-PHI 2-3	ATL-LA 4*2	PIT-MON 12*5	CIN-SD 5-6	HOU-SF 3-7	
0725	STL-NY 3-9	CHI-PHI 9*4	ATL-LA 1-2	PIT-MON 3*1	CIN-SD 2-8	HOU-SF 2-3	
0726			ATL-LA 5*1	PIT-MON 4-5			
0727	CHI-NY 1-2	MON-PHI 6*1	CIN-LA 4*0	STL-PIT 3*2	HOU-SD 3-7	ATL-SF 0-6	
0728	CHI-NY 11*4	MON-PHI 4*1	CIN-LA 0-1	STL-PIT 5*1	HOU-SD 3*1 HOU-SD 0-1	ATL-SF 4*3	
0729	CIN-LA 0-1	MON-PHI 4-6	STL-PIT 4*3	ATL-SF 4*3	HOU-SD 0-9	CHI-NY 3*0 CHI-NY 5*1	
0730	PHI-CHI 2-3	ATL-HOU 3-4	MON-PIT 3*1	LA-SD 0-12	NY-STL 1-3		
0731	PHI-CHI 2*1	ATL-HOU 6*3	MON-PIT 3-5	LA-SD 0-1	NY-STL 3-6	SF-CIN 0-3	
0801	PHI-CHI 4-5	ATL-HOU 6*5	MON-PIT 0-4	LA-SD 3-4	NY-STL 2-11	SF-CIN 3-6	
0802	MON-CHI 2-3		NY-PIT 4-6		PHI-STL 3*2	SF-CIN 5*2	
0803	MON-CHI 6*5	SF-ATL 1-2	NY-PIT 4*1	SD-HOU 2-6	PHI-STL 3-4	LA-CIN 5*2	
0804	MON-CHI 1-4	SF-ATL 9*2	NY-PIT 4*3	SD-HOU 5*2	PHI-STL 2-3	LA-CIN 5*3	
0805	MON-CHI 3-4	SF-ATL 7*4	NY-PIT 3*1	SD-HOU 9*5	PHI-STL 6*3	LA-CIN 1-2	
0806	NY-CHI 3-9	LA-ATL 0-2	PHI-MON 4*1	SF-HOU 0-8	PIT-STL 3*2	SD-CIN 1*0	
0807	NY-CHI 6-8 NY-CHI 4-8	LA-ATL 2*1	PHI-MON 6*2 PHI-MON 2-3	SF-HOU 9*2	PIT-STL 1-2	SD-CIN 7-8	
0808	NY-CHI 6-7	LA-ATL 5*1	PHI-MON 1-3	SD-CIN 2-4	SF-HOU 6-7	PIT-STL 6*4	
0809	PIT-NY 11*0	LA-ATL 1*0	CHI-MON 0-1	SD-CIN 0-8	SF-HOU 0-6	STL-PHI 1-2	
0810	PIT-NY 4*1	SD-ATL 1-3 SD-ATL 10*4	CHI-MON 2-4	HOU-CIN 4-5 HOU-CIN 11*7	LA-SF 1-4	STL-PHI 3*0	
0811	CHI-MON 2*1	SD-ATL 4*1	PIT-NY 1-3	HOU-CIN 8*2	STL-PHI 1-6	LA-SF 4*2	
0812	CHI-MON 7*3	SD-ATL 3-5	PIT-NY 3-6	HOU-CIN 6*1		LA-SF 5*4	
0813	CHI-HOU 1-2	NY-LA 2-9	CIN-STL 3-5				
0814	CHI-HOU 6-7	NY-LA 4*0	CIN-STL 2-8	PIT-ATL 1-3	PHI-SD 2-3	MON-SF 7*6	
0815	CHI-HOU 2-6	NY-LA 3*2	CIN-STL 3*2	PIT-ATL 3-7	PHI-SD 3-4	MON-SF 8*3	
0816				PIT-ATL 5*2	PHI-SD 8*3	MON-SF 11*3	
0817	CHI-CIN 4-6	PHI-LA 1-2	HOU-PIT 7*4	ATL-STL 1-3	MON-SD 8*4	NY-SF 2*0	
0818	CHI-CIN 13*11	PHI-LA 6*5	HOU-PIT 5*0	ATL-STL 8*3		NY-SF 5-6	
0819	CHI-CIN 9*6	PHI-LA 6*3	HOU-PIT 4*3	ATL-STL 5-8	MON-SD 3*0	NY-SF 6-7 NY-SF 4*2	
0820	HOU-CHI 1-6	STL-CIN 9*7	MON-LA 3*1	ATL-PIT 4*1	NY-SD 1-3	PHI-SF 6*4	
0821	HOU-CHI 5-11	STL-CIN 1-4	MON-LA 3-4	ATL-PIT 4-5	NY-SD 4-7	PHI-SF 12*5	
0822	HOU-CHI 8*3	STL-CIN 6*3	MON-LA 5*3	ATL-PIT 2-7	NY-SD 5*2	PHI-SF 5-7	
0823	STL-HOU 6-9						
0824	STL-HOU 2-7	ATL-CHI 0-3	LA-PHI 5-6	CIN-PIT 2*0	SD-MON 1-4 SD-MON 5*4	SF-NY 7*6 SF-NY 6*5	
0825	ATL-CHI 3*2	STL-HOU 2-5	LA-PHI 7*4	CIN-PIT 3-5	SD-MON 4*3	SF-NY 5*4	
0826	ATL-CHI 0-5	STL-HOU 3*2	LA-PHI 8-10	CIN-PIT 1-7	SD-MON 2*1	SF-NY 6-11	
0827			SD-PHI 1-9		SF-MON 5*4	LA-NY 1-5	
0828	STL-ATL 5*3	PIT-HOU 2-3	SD-PHI 8-11	CIN-CHI 2-5 CIN-CHI 2-5	SF-MON 3*2	LA-NY 1-5	
0829	STL-ATL 10*6	PIT-HOU 4*2	SF-MON 4*3	CIN-CHI 2-7	LA-NY 2-3	SD-PHI 2*0	
0830	CHI-ATL 8*3	PIT-CIN 1-4	LA-MON 2-5			SF-PHI 6*5 SF-PHI 5-6	
0831	CHI-ATL 2-3	PIT-CIN 6*2	LA-MON 2-5	HOU-STL 5-7	SD-NY 5*1 SD-NY 0-4	SF-PHI 6*5	
0901	CHI-ATL 4*1	PIT-CIN 5-7	LA-MON 4*3	SF-PHI 7*2	SD-NY 4-7 SD-NY 6-10	HOU-STL 8*4	
0902	CHI-ATL 4*2	PIT-CIN 1-7	LA-MON 0-4	SF-PHI 3-8	SD-NY 2-3	HOU-STL 1-4	
0903	HOU-ATL 4-6	SD-LA 4*3	PIT-MON 3*0	CHI-PHI 4*3	CIN-SF 3-4	NY-STL 3-7	
0904	HOU-ATL 7-8	SD-LA 1-2	PIT-MON 5*3	CHI-PHI 7*2	CIN-SF 8*3	NY-STL 2-12	
0905	NY-PIT 4*2	ATL-LA 3-4	CHI-MON 1-3	CIN-SD 11-15	HOU-SF 4*1	PHI-STL 5-6	
0906	NY-PIT 0-2	ATL-LA 3*2	CHI-MON 4*1	CIN-SD 10*3	HOU-SF 14*2	PHI-STL 5-6	
0907	STL-PIT 1-4	CIN-LA 1*0	PHI-MON 1-7	HOU-SD 6*4	ATL-SF 4-5	CHI-NY 0-10	
0908	STL-PIT 9*2	CIN-LA 3-6	PHI-MON 0-4		ATL-SF 0-4	CHI-NY 6*0	
0909	STL-PIT 2*1	CIN-LA 5*1	PHI-MON 6*5	HOU-SD 4-8	ATL-SF 4-6	CHI-NY 1-5	
0910	MON-PIT 8*5	PHI-CHI 2-3	ATL-HOU 3*1			STL-NY 3*2	
0911	MON-PIT 1-5	PHI-CHI 6*3	ATL-HOU 6*4	SF-CIN 3-7	LA-SD 5*2	STL-NY 9*5	
0912	STL-PHI 1-3 STL-PHI 5-6	MON-CHI 5-11	ATL-HOU 4*1	SF-CIN 4-7	LA-SD 8*1	PIT-NY 0-2	
0913	STL-PHI 2-10	PIT-NY 14*4					
0914	MON-PHI 5-9	SF-ATL 3*0	NY-CHI 1-7	LA-CIN 6*5	SD-HOU 4*2	PIT-STL 8*7	
0915	MON-PHI 4*3	SF-ATL 1-4	NY-CHI 4-5	LA-CIN 5*2	SD-HOU 2-3	PIT-STL 3-8	
0916	MON-PHI 8*4	SF-ATL 5-7	NY-CHI 9*3	LA-CIN 7*5	SD-HOU 9-10	PIT-STL 7-8	
0917	NY-PHI 1-2	LA-ATL 9*0		SD-CIN 3*2	SF-HOU 3-5		
0918	NY-PHI 8*5	LA-ATL 5-6	PIT-CHI 6*2	SD-CIN 2*0	SF-HOU 4-5	MON-STL 7*4	
0919	NY-PHI 5-13	CIN-ATL 4*2	PIT-CHI 11*6	SF-SD 4-5	LA-HOU 3*1	MON-STL 0-1	
0920		CIN-ATL 3-9	PIT-CHI 7*6	SF-SD 4-5	LA-HOU 6*2	MON-STL 2-3	
0921	MON-NY 2-6	PHI-PIT 1-5	LA-SF 1-5	ATL-SD 3*1	CIN-HOU 5*2	CHI-STL 0-8	
0922	MON-NY 2-4	PHI-PIT 1-2	LA-SF 7-8	ATL-SD 5*2	CIN-HOU 2*1		
0923	MON-NY 1-6	PHI-PIT 2-4	LA-SF 1-2	ATL-SD 1-2	CIN-HOU 1-2	CHI-STL 8*1 CHI-STL 4*2	

◆1984◆

Date	GAME 1	GAME 2	GAME 3	GAME 4	GAME 5	GAME 6	GAME 7
0924	HOU-LA 1-5	STL-MON 1-2	PHI-NY 5-7	CHI-PIT 4*1	SD-SF 7*1 SD-SF 8*6		
0925	ATL-CIN 4*2	HOU-LA 12*6	STL-MON 6*4	PHI-NY 4-6	SD-SF 3-4	CHI-PIT 1-7	
0926	ATL-CIN 3-6	HOU-LA 3*1	STL-MON 5*0	PHI-NY 1-7	SD-SF 4*0	CHI-PIT 5*2	
0927	ATL-CIN 1-2		STL-MON 3-6				
0928	HOU-CIN 6*3	SD-ATL 4*2	NY-MON 0-7	STL-CHI 4*1	SF-LA 3-4		
0929	HOU-CIN 1-4	SD-ATL 6*2	NY-MON 8*4	STL-CHI 5-9	SF-LA 3-4	PIT-PHI 4*0	
0930	HOU-CIN 6-7	SD-ATL 3-4	NY-MON 4-5	STL-CHI 1-2	SF-LA 2-7	PIT-PHI 2*0 PIT-PHI 7*2	

◆1985◆

Date	GAME 1	GAME 2	GAME 3	GAME 4	GAME 5	GAME 6	GAME 7
0408	MON-CIN 1-4						
0409	PIT-CHI 1-2	LA-HOU 1-2	STL-NY 5-6	ATL-PHI 6*0	SD-SF 3-4		
0410	MON-CIN 4*1	LA-HOU 5*4			SD-SF 3*0		
0411	PIT-CHI 1-4	LA-HOU 4*3	STL-NY 1-2	ATL-PHI 6*3			
0412	MON-CHI 5*1	PHI-HOU 3-8	CIN-NY 0-1	SD-ATL 7*3	SF-LA 4*1	STL-PIT 4-6	
0413	MON-CHI 3-8	PHI-HOU 4*2	CIN-NY 1-2	SD-ATL 5-7	SF-LA 0-1	STL-PIT 3-4	
0414	MON-CHI 2-4	PHI-HOU 3-5	CIN-NY 0-4	SD-ATL 1-3	SF-LA 8*4	STL-PIT 10*4	
0415	PHI-CHI 1-2	SF-SD 3-8	MON-STL 1-6	CIN-ATL 9*8	HOU-LA 3-5	NY-PIT 1-4	
0416	PHI-CHI 0-1	SF-SD 1-2		CIN-ATL 2*1	HOU-LA 7*3	NY-PIT 2*1	
0417	PHI-CHI 4-5	MON-STL 2*1		CIN-ATL 6*1	HOU-LA 0-1	NY-PIT 10*6	
0418	SF-CIN 3-4	MON-STL 7*1	LA-SD 5*0				
0419	SF-CIN 2-4	PIT-STL 4-5	LA-SD 2-11	HOU-ATL 5-9	CHI-MON 3-5	NY-PHI 1*0	
0420	SF-CIN 1-2	PIT-STL 3-4	LA-SD 3-4	HOU-ATL 8*1	CHI-MON 0-4	NY-PHI 6-7	
0421	SF-CIN 0-1	PIT-STL 0-6	LA-SD 2*0	HOU-ATL 4*2	CHI-MON 4*0	NY-PHI 6-10	
0422	CIN-HOU 1-4	NY-STL 7*6	ATL-SD 3-5	CHI-PIT 3-5	PHI-MON 9*1	LA-SF 3*2	
0423	CIN-HOU 4-6	NY-STL 3-8	ATL-SD 4*2	CHI-PIT 5*0	PHI-MON 4-5	LA-SF 1-2	
0424	CIN-HOU 8*3	NY-STL 1-5	ATL-SD 1-3	CHI-PIT 5*2	PHI-MON 6-7	LA-SF 4*2	
0425	ATL-HOU 3*2	SD-LA 3-6			STL-MON 2-4	CIN-SF 3-7	
0426	ATL-HOU 2-3	SD-LA 0-2	PIT-NY 0-6	CHI-PHI 7*3	STL-MON 5-10	CIN-SF 6-7	
0427	ATL-HOU 8*2	SD-LA 4*3	PIT-NY 3*2	CHI-PHI 1-6	STL-MON 3-8	CIN-SF 2*1	
0428	ATL-HOU 1-2	SD-LA 1*0	PIT-NY 4-5	CHI-PHI 2-3	STL-MON 3-5	CIN-SF 1-2	
0429				MON-PHI 2-3			
0430	SF-CHI 1-3	ATL-CIN 8*4	HOU-NY 1-4	MON-PHI 0-11	SD-PIT 2-6	LA-STL 1-6	
0501	SF-CHI 3-4	ATL-CIN 17*9	HOU-NY 10*3	MON-PHI 3*2	SD-PIT 6*4	LA-STL 2*1	
0503	SD-CHI 6*5	NY-CIN 9*4	MON-ATL 9*2	HOU-PHI 2-3	LA-PIT 2-16	SF-STL 1-8	
0504	SD-CHI 8-12	NY-CIN 2-14	MON-ATL 9*3	HOU-PHI 5-7	LA-PIT 6*5	SF-STL 4-6	
0505	SD-CHI 2#4	NY-CIN 3*2	MON-ATL 1-6	HOU-PHI 4*3	LA-PIT 2-3	SF-STL 5*0	
0506	LA-CHI 5*4				SF-PIT 7*5	SD-STL 2-5	
0507	LA-CHI 2-4	HOU-MON 3*1	ATL-NY 3-5	CIN-PHI 2*0	SF-PIT 5*3	SD-STL 12*2	
0508	STL-LA 2-5	HOU-MON 0-1	ATL-NY 0-4	CIN-PHI 8*2	PIT-SD 2-12	CHI-SF 1*0	
0509	STL-LA 5*4				PIT-SD 0-1	CHI-SF 0-1	
0510	PIT-LA 0-1	HOU-CIN 2-5	ATL-MON 0-5	PHI-NY 0-5	CHI-SD 6*2	STL-SF 9*3	
0511	PIT-LA 5*2	HOU-CIN 10*7	ATL-MON 0-3	PHI-NY 0-4	CHI-SD 1-3	STL-SF 9*4	
0512	PIT-LA 0-2	HOU-CIN 10*5	ATL-MON 0-4	PHI-NY 2-3	CHI-SD 3-5	STL-SF 4-5	
0513	NY-ATL 0-1	PHI-CIN 3-7	MON-HOU 2-3				
0514	NY-ATL 3*1	PHI-CIN 7*1	MON-HOU 0-10	CHI-LA 8*3	STL-SD 2-6	PIT-SF 1-3	
0515	PHI-ATL 2-3	CIN-MON 2*1	NY-HOU 5*3	CHI-LA 3*2	STL-SD 14*4	PIT-SF 3*2	
0516	PHI-ATL 4*2	CIN-MON 4*2	NY-HOU 0-1				
0517	CHI-ATL 7*5	SD-MON 1-2	STL-HOU 8*6	SF-NY 2-3	LA-PHI 5-10	CIN-PIT 6*3	
0518	CHI-ATL 3-4	SD-MON 8*2	STL-HOU 5-6	SF-NY 8*2	LA-PHI 5-7	CIN-PIT 8*0	
0519	CHI-ATL 0-3	SD-MON 8*3	STL-HOU 3-7	SF-NY 2-3	LA-PHI 3*2	CIN-PIT 7*1	
0520	CIN-CHI 1-6	LA-MON 1-9	ATL-STL 0-14	SD-NY 2*0	SF-PHI 1-2	HOU-PIT 1-3	
0521	CIN-CHI 5*2	LA-MON 4*0	ATL-STL 3-6		SF-PHI 5-6	HOU-PIT 2-3	
0522	CIN-CHI 4-7	LA-MON 4*0	ATL-STL 3-5	SD-NY 5*4	SF-PHI 6*2	HOU-PIT 5*3	
0524	HOU-CHI 6*2	SF-MON 0-2	PIT-ATL 4*2	LA-NY 4*3	SD-PHI 1*0	STL-CIN 6-7	
0525	HOU-CHI 4-5	SF-MON 1-3	PIT-ATL 8*2	LA-NY 6*2	SD-PHI 4*1	STL-CIN 6*4	
0526	HOU-CHI 8-10	SF-MON 1-3	PIT-ATL 4-5	LA-NY 1-2	SD-PHI 7*2	STL-CIN 7*2	
0527	PIT-HOU 2-4	SF-MON 6*1		LA-NY 1-8	SD-PHI 9-10	CHI-CIN 4*3	
0528	PIT-HOU 4*3	STL-ATL 9*3	MON-SD 8*5			CHI-CIN 11-13	
0529	PIT-HOU 3-8	STL-ATL 3-5	MON-SD 2*1	PHI-LA 1-6	NY-SF 4*3	CHI-CIN 0-1	
0530		STL-ATL 6*0	MON-SD 4-5	PHI-LA 6*1	NY-SF 2*1		
0531	CHI-HOU 6*2	ATL-PIT 8*2	NY-SD 3-4	MON-LA 0-4	PHI-SF 3-4	CIN-STL 0-5	
0601	CHI-HOU 4*1	ATL-PIT 3-6	NY-SD 5*3	MON-LA 4*2	PHI-SF 1-2	CIN-STL 9*3	
0602	CHI-HOU 3-4	ATL-PIT 0-5	NY-SD 7*3	MON-LA 7-8	PHI-SF 1-3	CIN-STL 8*3	
0603			PHI-SD 3*2	NY-LA 4-5	MON-SF 4*2	HOU-STL 5-9	
0604	ATL-CHI 3-5	PIT-CIN 3-9	PHI-SD 5-6	NY-LA 4*1	MON-SF 1-5	HOU-STL 1-6	
0605	ATL-CHI 4*2	PIT-CIN 9-11	PHI-SD 1-3	NY-LA 1-2	MON-SF 6*0	HOU-STL 8*3	
0606	PIT-CHI 2-3						
0607	PIT-CHI 0-1	LA-ATL 7*2	SF-HOU 1-4	STL-NY 7*2	MON-PHI 3*1	SD-CIN 9*3 SD-CIN 3*2	
0608	LA-ATL 3-7	PIT-CHI 3-7	SF-HOU 1-4	STL-NY 1*0	MON-PHI 4*3	SD-CIN 4-7	
0609	LA-ATL 3-10	PIT-CHI 1-5	SF-HOU 0-5	STL-NY 1-6 STL-NY 8*2	MON-PHI 1-4	SD-CIN 5*3	
0610	SF-ATL 0-7	LA-CIN 7*4	SD-HOU 9*1	CHI-MON 5*4	NY-PHI 4-6	STL-PIT 6*1	
0611	SF-ATL 5*4		SD-HOU 0-11	CHI-MON 5*3	NY-PHI 7-26	STL-PIT 2-13	
0612	SF-ATL 2-5		SD-HOU 2-3	CHI-MON 0-2	NY-PHI 7*3		
0613	CIN-ATL 9*2	STL-PIT 2*1	SD-SF 3*0	CHI-MON 7-9	NY-PHI 4-5		
0614	CIN-ATL 4-6	PHI-PIT 2-3	SD-SF 4-5	NY-MON 4-5	STL-CHI 11*10	LA-HOU 10*2	
0615	CIN-ATL 6*5	PHI-PIT 13*3	SD-SF 1*0	NY-MON 2-3	STL-CHI 2*0	LA-HOU 3*0	
0616	CIN-ATL 6*5	PHI-PIT 3*2	SD-SF 3-7 SD-SF 4-5	NY-MON 2-7	STL-CHI 5*2	LA-HOU 9*0	
0617	HOU-ATL 4*3	SD-LA 3*2	CIN-SF 0-4	PIT-MON 5*2	CHI-NY 0-2		
0618	HOU-ATL 2-3	SD-LA 4*0	CIN-SF 6*1	PIT-MON 4*1	CHI-NY 1-5	PHI-STL 2-6	
0619	HOU-ATL 7*3	SD-LA 1-5	CIN-SF 2-5	PIT-MON 3-4	CHI-NY 0-1	PHI-STL 1*0	
0620	HOU-ATL 2*0	SF-SD 5-6		PIT-MON 2*1	CHI-NY 3-5	PHI-STL 0-5	
0621	HOU-LA 2-7	SF-SD 1-6	PIT-PHI 3-4	ATL-CIN 2-4 ATL-CIN 5*4	MON-NY 3-6	CHI-STL 5-7	
0622	HOU-LA 3-6	MON-NY 5*4	PIT-PHI 2-5	ATL-CIN 3-4	SF-SD 1-2	CHI-STL 1-2	
0623	HOU-LA 2-6	MON-NY 5*1	PIT-PHI 2-3	ATL-CIN 2*1	SF-SD 1-6	CHI-STL 0-7	
0624	HOU-LA 8*4						
0625	NY-CHI 3*2	SF-CIN 6-7	ATL-HOU 6*4	STL-PHI 1-3	MON-PIT 3*2	LA-SD 3*2	
0626	NY-CHI 3-7	SF-CIN 4-6	ATL-HOU 3*1	STL-PHI 4-6	MON-PIT 2-11	LA-SD 4-10	
0627	NY-CHI 2-4	SF-CIN 6-7	ATL-HOU 4*1	STL-PHI 4*3	MON-PIT 4*2	LA-SD 4-5	
0628	ATL-LA 11*2	PHI-MON 3-5	HOU-SF 3*1	NY-STL 2-3	CHI-PIT 5*0	CIN-SD 11*9	
0629	ATL-LA 2-3	PHI-MON 6*2	HOU-SF 8*1	NY-STL 0-6	CHI-PIT 5-6	CIN-SD 0-3	
0630	ATL-LA 3-4	PHI-MON 3*2	HOU-SF 6*2 HOU-SF 4-7	NY-STL 1-2	CHI-PIT 9*2	CIN-SD 3*2	
0701	CIN-LA 1-8	STL-MON 2-3	ATL-SF 4*1	PIT-NY 1*0	CHI-PHI 3*1	HOU-SD 5-6	
0702	CIN-LA 0-3	STL-MON 4*0	ATL-SF 3-8	PIT-NY 4-5	CHI-PHI 2-11	HOU-SD 3*2	
0703				PIT-NY 2-6	CHI-PHI 4*3		
0704	NY-ATL 16*13	SF-CHI 6*4	MON-HOU 9*3	SD-PIT 9*1	CIN-PHI 1-3	LA-STL 2-3	
0705	NY-ATL 6*1	SF-CHI 12*6	MON-HOU 2-4	SD-PIT 4-5	CIN-PHI 2-5	LA-STL 4*1	
0706		SF-CHI 6*4	MON-HOU 7-8	SD-PIT 7-8	CIN-PHI 4*2	LA-STL 8*3	
0707	NY-ATL 4*0 NY-ATL 8*5	SF-CHI 5-6	MON-HOU 6*3	SD-PIT 3*0	CIN-PHI 3*2	LA-STL 1-7	

♦1985♦	GAME 1	GAME 2	GAME 3	GAME 4	GAME 5	GAME 6	GAME 7
0708	MON-ATL 1-7	SD-CHI 3-6 / SD-CHI 8*4	NY-CIN 7*5	PHI-HOU 7*4	LA-PIT 4*3	SF-STL 1-6	
0709	MON-ATL 5*1	SD-CHI 3-7	NY-CIN 11*2	PHI-HOU 5*3	LA-PIT 8*3	SF-STL 1-3	
0710	MON-ATL 6*5	SD-CHI 3-4	NY-CIN 2*1	PHI-HOU 0-10	LA-PIT 5*4	SF-STL 3-7	
0711	PHI-ATL 2-3	LA-CHI 3*1	MON-CIN 0-2	NY-HOU 3-4	SF-PIT 4-6	SD-STL 0-6	
0712	PHI-ATL 4-7	LA-CHI 7*4	MON-CIN 4-5	NY-HOU 3*2	SF-PIT 1-3	SD-STL 2*0	
0713	PHI-ATL 5-13	LA-CHI 9*1	MON-CIN 6*3	NY-HOU 10*1	SF-PIT 4*1	SD-STL 3-7	
0714	PHI-ATL 3-12	LA-CHI 4-10	MON-CIN 4-5	NY-HOU 1*0	SF-PIT 7*3	SD-STL 1-2	
0718	STL-LA 1-2	HOU-MON 0-3	PHI-CIN 6*3	ATL-NY 6-7	PIT-SD 2-3	CHI-SF 0-1	
0719	STL-LA 2-5	HOU-MON 0-4	PHI-CIN 2-3	ATL-NY 1*0	PIT-SD 0-6	CHI-SF 4*3	
0720	STL-LA 0-3	HOU-MON 1-6	PHI-CIN 10*6	ATL-NY 4-16	PIT-SD 2-4	CHI-SF 2*1	
0721	STL-LA 4*2	HOU-MON 5*4	PHI-CIN 6-7	ATL-NY 10-15	PIT-SD 5*2	CHI-SF 1-2	
0722	PIT-LA 6*3	ATL-MON 7*1	HOU-PHI 6-7	CIN-NY 5*1	CHI-SD 5*3	STL-SF 4*3	
0723	PIT-LA 0-6	ATL-MON 2-4	HOU-PHI 6-12	CIN-NY 4*0	CHI-SD 8*1	STL-SF 6*3	
0724	PIT-LA 1-9	ATL-MON 1-3	HOU-PHI 1-3	CIN-NY 3*2	CHI-SD 4*3	STL-SF 4*0	
0725	CHI-LA 3-7	CIN-MON 0-1	ATL-PHI 3*2	HOU-NY 3-6	STL-SD 9*6	PIT-SF 3-4	
0726	CHI-LA 0-10	CIN-MON 7*6	ATL-PHI 6*4		STL-SD 2*1	PIT-SF 1-3	
0727	CHI-LA 4-5	CIN-MON 7*6	ATL-PHI 4-5	HOU-NY 4-16 / HOU-NY 3-7	STL-SD 0-2	PIT-SF 3-8	
0728	CHI-LA 9*2	CIN-MON 0-6	ATL-PHI 3-7	HOU-NY 12*4	STL-SD 4*2	PIT-SF 2-3	
0729	SF-LA 5-10			MON-NY 2-3			
0730	SF-LA 2-4	SD-ATL 5*4	STL-CHI 11*3	MON-NY 2-5	HOU-CIN 1-4	PHI-PIT 2*0	
0731	SF-LA 7*5	SD-ATL 4-5	STL-CHI 2-5	MON-NY 2-5	HOU-CIN 9*2	PHI-PIT 3-4	
0801		SD-ATL 6*0	STL-CHI 8-9		HOU-CIN 2-5	PHI-PIT 3*0	
0802	SD-HOU 9-12	SF-ATL 7-12	NY-CHI 1-2	PHI-STL 2-3	LA-CIN 5*3 / LA-CIN 2-5	MON-PIT 3*2	
0803	SF-ATL 7*5	NY-CHI 5*4	SD-HOU 3-4	MON-PIT 6*5	LA-CIN 2*0	PHI-STL 6*4	
0804	SF-ATL 4-5	NY-CHI 4*1	SD-HOU 1-2	MON-PIT 3-4	LA-CIN 4-5	PHI-STL 6*0	
0805	LA-ATL 6*1	NY-CHI 7*2	SF-HOU 5-7	MON-PIT 5*2	SD-CIN 7-8	PHI-STL 9*1	
0808	CIN-LA 6*5	NY-MON 14*7	PIT-PHI 3-7	HOU-SD 6*5	ATL-SF 2*0	CHI-STL 0-8	
0809	CIN-LA 1-3	PIT-MON 2-7	STL-PHI 5*4	HOU-SD 4-6 / HOU-SD 1-2	ATL-SF 6*5	CHI-NY 4-6	
0810	CIN-LA 1-2	PIT-MON 5-7	CHI-NY 3-8	ATL-SF 5-6	STL-PHI 5*4 / STL-PHI 13*4		
0811	CIN-LA 0-4	PIT-MON 5-6	CHI-NY 2-6	HOU-SD 7*2	STL-PHI 1-4	ATL-SF 7*4	
0812	ATL-LA 0-3	MON-CHI 7-8	PHI-NY 3-4	CIN-SD 0-2	PIT-STL 1-8		
0813	ATL-LA 1-2	MON-CHI 4*1	PHI-NY 2-4	CIN-SD 3*2	PIT-STL 5-6	HOU-SF 2-4	
0814	ATL-LA 0-5	MON-CHI 8*7	PHI-NY 2*1	CIN-SD 1-4		HOU-SF 7*5	
0815	ATL-LA 4-5	MON-CHI 7*3	PHI-NY 7-10	CIN-SD 5*4	PIT-STL 1-3 / PIT-STL 3-4	HOU-SF 4*1	
0816	PHI-CHI 5-6	CIN-HOU 4-5	NY-PIT 1-7	ATL-SD 3-6	MON-STL 1-6	LA-SF 5*1	
0817	PHI-CHI 10*4	CIN-HOU 8*0	NY-PIT 4*3		MON-STL 5*4	LA-SF 2-5	
0818	PHI-CHI 9*5	CIN-HOU 8*3	NY-PIT 0-5	ATL-SD 1-2 / ATL-SD 6*3	MON-STL 6*5	LA-SF 1-2	
0819	NY-MON 1*0						
0820	SD-MON 1*0	CHI-ATL 5*2	STL-HOU 2-17	SF-NY 0-3	LA-PHI 5*4	CIN-PIT 2-3	
0821	SD-MON 6*2	CHI-ATL 9*5	STL-HOU 7*4	SF-NY 3*2	LA-PHI 15*6	CIN-PIT 8*5	
0822	SD-MON 3*0	CHI-ATL 3*2	STL-HOU 2*1	SF-NY 0-7	LA-PHI 0-2	CIN-PIT 1-5	
0823	LA-MON 8*4	STL-ATL 6*2	CHI-CIN 2-3	SD-NY 6*1 / SD-NY 3*0	SF-PHI 4*1	HOU-PIT 2*0	
0824	STL-ATL 7*0	CHI-CIN 4*0	LA-MON 2-5	SD-NY 1-5	SF-PHI 2-9		
0825	STL-ATL 5*2	CHI-CIN 3-5	LA-MON 1-6	SD-NY 3-9	SF-PHI 5-14	HOU-PIT 3-9 / HOU-PIT 9-10	
0826	PIT-ATL 1-2	STL-CIN 3*0	CHI-HOU 10*4	SF-MON 7*4	LA-NY 6*1	SD-PHI 3-4	
0827	PIT-ATL 6-7	STL-CIN 6*4	CHI-HOU 4-11	SF-MON 6*1	LA-NY 2*1	SD-PHI 4*1	
0828	PIT-ATL 1-6	STL-CIN 6-7	CHI-HOU 0-3				
0829	ATL-CHI 9*6	PIT-CIN 0-6	PHI-LA 3*2	MON-SD 8*5	NY-SF 3-6		
0830	ATL-CHI 8*1	PIT-CIN 0-1	PHI-LA 5*2	HOU-STL 7*5	NY-SF 2*1		
0831	ATL-CHI 4-5	PIT-CIN 6*0	PHI-LA 5*0	HOU-STL 3*1	NY-SF 2-3	MON-SD 7*1	
0901	ATL-CHI 2-15	PIT-CIN 2-3	PHI-LA 4*1	HOU-STL 0-5	NY-SF 4*3	MON-SD 1-5	
0902	HOU-CHI 7*2	ATL-PIT 4-5	MON-LA 4-5	CIN-STL 4*1	PHI-SF 4*3	NY-SD 12*4	
0903	HOU-CHI 8*7	ATL-PIT 2*0	MON-LA 0-4	CIN-STL 4-6	PHI-SF 4*3	NY-SD 8*3	
0904	HOU-CHI 11*6	ATL-PIT 0-2	MON-LA 2-4	CIN-STL 3-4	PHI-SF 3-4	NY-SD 9*2	
0905	PIT-HOU 3-4			CHI-STL 1-6			
0906	PIT-HOU 3-4	CIN-CHI 7*5	NY-LA 2*0	ATL-STL 0-8	PHI-SD 2-3	MON-SF 3-8	
0907	PIT-HOU 7*1	CIN-CHI 7-9	NY-LA 6-7	ATL-STL 3*1	PHI-SD 2*0	MON-SF 7*1	
0908		CIN-CHI 55	NY-LA 4*3	ATL-STL 7*3	PHI-SD 9*7	MON-SF 9*6	
0909	LA-ATL 9*7	SD-CIN 1-2	SF-HOU 2*4	CHI-STL 3*1			
0910	LA-ATL 10*1 / LA-ATL 10*4	SD-CIN 3*2	SF-HOU 1-4	STL-NY 4-5	MON-PHI 2-5	CHI-PIT 1-2	
0911	LA-ATL 12*3	SD-CIN 0-2	STL-NY 1*0	MON-PHI 1-4	CHI-PIT 3*1	SF-HOU 11*4 / SF-HOU 9-10	
0912	LA-ATL 6-11	SD-CIN 1-2	STL-NY 6-7	MON-PHI 6*3	CHI-PIT 2-10	SF-HOU 2-5	
0913	SF-ATL 9*3	LA-CIN 8*2 / LA-CIN 5-6	STL-CHI 9*3	NY-MON 1-5 / NY-MON 7*2	PHI-PIT 6*3	SD-HOU 2-3	
0914	SF-ATL 3*1	LA-CIN 7*0	STL-CHI 5*4	NY-MON 1-5	SD-HOU 3-4	PHI-PIT 3-6	
0915	SF-ATL 1-4	LA-CIN 6-10	STL-CHI 5*1	NY-MON 6*2	SD-HOU 1-2	PHI-PIT 4-5	
0916	HOU-ATL 7*2	SF-CIN 6-7	PHI-NY 0-9	CHI-MON 5-8	LA-SD 2-4	STL-PIT 8*4 / STL-PIT 3*1	
0917	HOU-ATL 10*6	SF-CIN 1-6	CHI-MON 3*0	PHI-NY 5*1	LA-SD 7*1	STL-PIT 10*4	
0918	CIN-ATL 7*3	HOU-LA 7*2	PIT-MON 10*6	CHI-NY 2-4	STL-PHI 7*0	SD-SF 6-9	
0919	CIN-ATL 15*5	HOU-LA 6*5	PIT-MON 8*6	CHI-NY 1-5	STL-PHI 3-6	SD-SF 11*3	
0920	CIN-HOU 5*3	ATL-SD 1-11	MON-STL 3-5	PIT-NY 7*5	CHI-PHI 3*1	LA-SF 3-5	
0921	CIN-HOU 5-9	ATL-SD 0-1	MON-STL 6-7	PIT-NY 1-12	CHI-PHI 9*2	LA-SF 11*2	
0922	CIN-HOU 6*5	ATL-SD 7*5	MON-STL 5-6	PIT-NY 5*3	CHI-PHI 9*2	LA-SF 5*3	
0923	LA-HOU 5*3	SF-SD 7*2	PIT-STL 4-5	MON-CHI 10*7	NY-PHI 4*1		
0924	LA-HOU 7*2	SF-SD 3-4	PIT-STL 4-5	MON-CHI 17*15	NY-PHI 7*1	ATL-CIN 5-7	
0925	LA-HOU 4-6	SF-SD 4-7	PHI-STL 3-6	NY-CHI 4-5	MON-PIT 2-8	ATL-CIN 4*2	
0926			PHI-STL 0-5	NY-CHI 3*0		ATL-CIN 1-6	
0927	SD-ATL 10*1	SF-LA 2-6	NY-PIT 7-8	PHI-CHI 7-9		HOU-CIN 3-4	
0928	SD-ATL 6*5	SF-LA 1-3	NY-PIT 3*1	PHI-CHI 10-11	STL-MON 0-2 / STL-MON 4*2	HOU-CIN 2-5	
0929	SD-ATL 2-3	PHI-CHI 2-6	HOU-CIN 0-5	SF-LA 2-7	STL-MON 5-7	NY-PIT 9*7	
0930	ATL-HOU 6*3	CIN-SF 3-4		SD-LA 6*4			
1001	ATL-HOU 0-2	CIN-SF 7*6	PIT-CHI 3-4	SD-LA 3-10	NY-STL 1*0		
1002	CIN-SD 4-5	HOU-SF 7*2	PIT-CHI 9*4	ATL-LA 3-9	NY-STL 5*2	PHI-MON 1-3 / PHI-MON 3*2	
1003	PIT-CHI 5-13	ATL-LA 5*0	CIN-SD 4-9	HOU-SF 7*2	NY-STL 3-4	PHI-MON 8*7	
1004	MON-NY 4-9	CIN-LA 4*2	HOU-SD 3-4	ATL-SF 0-1	CHI-STL 2-4	PIT-PHI 7*2 / PIT-PHI 5-8	
1005	CIN-LA 1-3	MON-NY 8*3	HOU-SD 9*3	ATL-SF 1-7	CHI-STL 1-7	PIT-PHI 4*2 / PIT-PHI 5*0	
1006	CIN-LA 6*5	MON-NY 2*1	HOU-SD 6*4	ATL-SF 8*7	CHI-STL 8*2	PIT-PHI 0-5	

♦1986♦	GAME 1	GAME 2	GAME 3	GAME 4	GAME 5	GAME 6	GAME 7
0407	SD-LA 1-2	PHI-CIN 4-7					
0408	SD-LA 1*0	MON-ATL 0-6	SF-HOU 8*3	NY-PIT 4*2	CHI-STL 1-2		

◆1986◆	GAME 1		GAME 2		GAME 3		GAME 4		GAME 5		GAME 6		GAME 7
0409	SD-LA	0-1	PHI-CIN	5*3	SF-HOU	4*1							
0410	SD-LA	3*2	MON-ATL	6*3	SF-HOU	0-4	CHI-STL	2-4					
0411	SF-LA	9*8	NY-PHI	9*7	ATL-HOU	1-2	MON-STL	1-9	CHI-PIT	5*4	CIN-SD	3-4	
0412	SF-LA	7*6	NY-PHI	8-9	ATL-HOU	3-4	MON-STL	3-6	CHI-PIT	1-3	CIN-SD	3*2	
0413	SF-LA	2-3	NY-PHI	2-4	ATL-HOU	8*7	MON-STL	3*2	CHI-PIT	0-8	CIN-SD	6-7	
0414	STL-NY	6*2	PIT-PHI	3*1							LA-SD	3-4	
0415	CIN-ATL	5*3	CHI-MON	3-4	HOU-SF	8*3					LA-SD	1-2	
0416	CIN-ATL	5*3			HOU-SF	4*1					LA-SD	1-2	
0417	CHI-MON	7*6			SD-SF	1-4							
0418	STL-MON	4*2	LA-ATL	3-6	SD-SF	1-6	PIT-CHI	4*0	HOU-CIN	6*4	PHI-NY	2-5	
0419	STL-MON	9*6	LA-ATL	0-3	SD-SF	5-6	PIT-CHI	14*8	HOU-CIN	4*3	PHI-NY	2-3	
0420	STL-MON	0-2	LA-ATL	7*3	SD-SF	0-4	PIT-CHI	8#8	HOU-CIN	6*4	PHI-NY	0-8	
0421			HOU-ATL	2-8	LA-SF	1-5					PIT-NY	5-6	
0422	STL-CHI	2-3	HOU-ATL	3*2	LA-SF	3-10	PHI-MON	2-8			PIT-NY	1-7	
0423	STL-CHI	0-6	HOU-ATL	3*2	LA-SF	6*4	PHI-MON	5*4	SD-CIN	7*4			
0424	MON-CHI	5-7	CIN-HOU	3*0	ATL-LA	3-6	PHI-PIT	4*2	NY-STL	5*4			
0425	MON-CHI	4*2	CIN-HOU	1-3	ATL-LA	4*1	PHI-PIT	6*3	NY-STL	9*0	SF-SD	8-9	
0426	MON-CHI	4*2	CIN-HOU	0-1	ATL-LA	5*4	PHI-PIT	6*5	NY-STL	4*3	SF-SD	3*2	
0427	MON-CHI	10-12	CIN-HOU	0-6	ATL-LA	4-7	PHI-PIT	5-13	NY-STL	5*3	SF-SD	4-6	
0428	STL-SF	5*4			PIT-LA	1-2					CHI-SD	4*3	
0429	STL-SF	0-2	NY-ATL	10*5	PIT-LA	4-5	MON-CIN	7*4	HOU-PHI	4-12	CHI-SD	4-5	
0430	PIT-SF	5-6	NY-ATL	8*1	CHI-LA	0-4	MON-CIN	8*0	HOU-PHI	1*0	STL-SD	0-5	
0501	PIT-SF	6*2	NY-ATL	2-7	CHI-LA	0-4					STL-SD	3-4	
0502	CHI-SF	6*5	NY-CIN	8*7	STL-LA	2-3	HOU-MON	6*3	ATL-PHI	7*1	PIT-SD	4*0	
0503	CHI-SF	6*5	NY-CIN	4*1	STL-LA	0-3	HOU-MON	6-7	ATL-PHI	10*4	PIT-SD	7*6	
0504	CHI-SF	1-2	NY-CIN	7*2	STL-LA	3*1	HOU-MON	6-7	ATL-PHI	1-5	PIT-SD	5*2	
	CHI-SF	1-2											
0505	ATL-CIN	4*3	MON-PHI	6*4									
0506	ATL-CIN	0-2	MON-PHI	8*0	LA-CHI	6-7	HOU-NY	0-4	SF-PIT	7*2	SD-STL	3*2	
0507			MON-PHI	8*2	LA-CHI	8*4	HOU-NY	2-3	SF-PIT	7*5	SD-STL	3-4	
0508	ATL-CIN	10*5			LA-CHI	5-6			SF-PIT	2-8	SD-STL	3-13	
0509	PHI-ATL	7*6	LA-MON	4-8	SD-CHI	6*2	CIN-NY	1-2	HOU-PIT	3*2	SF-STL	2*1	
0510	PHI-ATL	1-3	LA-MON	2-3	SD-CHI	5-6	CIN-NY	1-5	HOU-PIT	6*3	SF-STL	3-6	
0511	PHI-ATL	2*1	LA-MON	3-4	SD-CHI	5-9	CIN-NY	3*2	HOU-PIT	3-4	SF-STL	3-4	
0512	PHI-HOU	5*1	CIN-MON	4*3			ATL-NY	0-1					
0513	PHI-HOU	2-3	CIN-MON	2-4	SF-CHI	6*5	ATL-NY	6*3	SD-PIT	4*2	LA-STL	6*5	
0514	NY-HOU	2-6	ATL-MON	2-3	SF-CHI	11*3	CIN-PHI	6-8	SD-PIT	10*4	LA-STL	8*3	
0515	NY-HOU	6*2	ATL-MON	7*4			CIN-PHI	6*5					
0516	CHI-HOU	6-9	STL-ATL	2-6	PIT-CIN	2-7	NY-LA	3-4	MON-SD	3*2	PHI-SF	3*0	
0517	CHI-HOU	1-5	STL-ATL	0-2	PIT-CIN	4*0	NY-LA	2-6	MON-SD	3-5	PHI-SF	7-12	
0518	CHI-HOU	5*2	STL-ATL	2-5	PIT-CIN	3-7	NY-LA	8*4	MON-SD	8*3	PHI-SF	1-4	
0520	PIT-HOU	4*2	CHI-ATL	3-8	CIN-STL	5*3	MON-LA	0-4	PHI-SD	3-4	NY-SF	2*1	
0521	PIT-HOU	2*1	CHI-ATL	8-9	CIN-STL	3-8	MON-LA	1-6	PHI-SD	2-7	NY-SF	7*4	
0522	PIT-HOU	0-4	CHI-ATL	0-2	CIN-STL	6*4	MON-LA	5*2	PHI-SD	2-6	NY-SF	2-10	
0523	HOU-CHI	1-4	CIN-PIT	12*9	ATL-STL	2-3	PHI-LA	8*2	NY-SD	4-7	MON-SF	4*3	
0524	HOU-CHI	3-4	CIN-PIT	4*2	ATL-STL	5-9	PHI-LA	0-6	NY-SD	5*4	MON-SF	7*4	
0525	HOU-CHI	3*1	CIN-PIT	7*4	ATL-STL	6*2	PHI-LA	2-5	NY-SD	4*2	MON-SF	3-11	
0526	CIN-CHI	6-9	ATL-PIT	9*4	HOU-STL	4*1	SD-MON	9*6					
0527	CIN-CHI	5*4	ATL-PIT	6*2	HOU-STL	5*4	SD-MON	4-5	LA-NY	1-8	SF-PHI	2-6	
0528	CIN-CHI	0-5	ATL-PIT	3-4	HOU-STL	4*3	SD-MON	10*1	LA-NY	2-4	SF-PHI	0-4	
0529									LA-NY	2-5	SF-PHI	4-5	
0530	ATL-CHI	1-6	STL-CIN	4-6	MON-HOU	1*0	LA-PIT	6*4	SF-NY	7-8	SD-PHI	0-2	
0531	ATL-CHI	8*4	STL-CIN	11*2	MON-HOU	3-4	LA-PIT	0-4	SF-NY	7*3	SD-PHI	0-1	
0601	ATL-CHI	3-7	STL-CIN	2*1	MON-HOU	4-8	LA-PIT	3-12	SF-NY	7*3	SD-PHI	5-16	
0602	PIT-ATL	9*2	CHI-CIN	8*6	STL-HOU	9*2			SD-NY	2-11	LA-PHI	2-13	
0603	PIT-ATL	5-8	CHI-CIN	3-5	STL-HOU	3*1	SF-MON	7*6	SD-NY	5*4	LA-PHI	11*4	
0604	PIT-ATL	12*3	CHI-CIN	0-2	STL-HOU	2-4	SF-MON	4*2	SD-NY	2-4	LA-PHI	7-8	
0605	HOU-LA	0-1	NY-PIT	7*0	ATL-SD	4*2	PHI-MON	7*3	CHI-STL	3-4			
0606	HOU-LA	2-3	NY-PIT	1-7	ATL-SD	2-3	PHI-MON	9-10	CHI-STL	9*3	CIN-SF	5*3	
			NY-PIT	10*4									
0607	HOU-LA	7*5	NY-PIT	6*4	PHI-MON	3*1	ATL-SD	4*2	CIN-SF	2-6	CHI-STL	2-3	
0608	HOU-LA	3*2	NY-PIT	4*3	PHI-MON	0-12	ATL-SD	1-4	CIN-SF	7*3	CHI-STL	14*2	
									CIN-SF	1-3			
0609	CIN-LA	5-6	PHI-NY	3*2	CHI-PIT	5-6	HOU-SD	5*3	MON-STL	5*4			
0610	CIN-LA	0-1	PHI-NY	4-8	CHI-PIT	4-6	HOU-SD	12*1	MON-STL	4*2	ATL-SF	0-3	
0611	CIN-LA	4-5	PHI-NY	3-5	CHI-PIT	3-5	HOU-SD	7-11	MON-STL	4*3	ATL-SF	2*1	
0612	SF-HOU	1-4											
0613	SF-HOU	3*1	CIN-ATL	2-3	PIT-NY	5-6	MON-PHI	1-2	LA-SD	6*2	STL-CHI	1*0	
											STL-CHI	2-3	
0614	CIN-ATL	2*1	SF-HOU	3-7	PIT-NY	1-5	MON-PHI	6-7	LA-SD	0-12	STL-CHI	1*0	
0615	CIN-ATL	9*7	SF-HOU	7*2	PIT-NY	1-4	MON-PHI	2*0	LA-SD	6*0	STL-CHI	3-4	
					PIT-NY	5-8							
0616	CIN-ATL	3-4	PHI-CHI	5-7	NY-MON	4*1	STL-PIT	4#1	SF-SD	0-4			
0617	LA-ATL	3-4	PHI-CHI	11*8	NY-MON	2-4	STL-PIT	7*2	SF-SD	5-8	HOU-CIN	4-5	
0618	LA-ATL	5*2	PHI-CHI	4-5	NY-MON	4-7	STL-PIT	4*2	SF-SD	6*3	HOU-CIN	2-3	
							STL-PIT	1-2					
0619	LA-ATL	9*4	HOU-CIN	6*2	PIT-MON	4*2	STL-PHI	3-5	SF-SD	3-8			
0620	SD-LA	5*4	ATL-CIN	4-6	PIT-MON	2-7	STL-PHI	9*2	CHI-NY	3-10	HOU-SF	1-3	
			ATL-CIN	5-8									
0621	SD-LA	8*7	ATL-CIN	7*6	PIT-MON	14*1	CHI-NY	8*6	STL-PHI	8*6	HOU-SF	1-2	
0622	SD-LA	5*4	ATL-CIN	2-5	PIT-MON	1-2	CHI-NY	2-4	STL-PHI	7*4	HOU-SF	2-4	
											HOU-SF	2-3	
0623	CIN-HOU	6-7	ATL-LA	6*5	MON-NY	5*4	CHI-PHI	1-19	PIT-STL	1-2	SD-SF	1-18	
0624	CIN-HOU	4-8	ATL-LA	2-6	MON-NY	6*2	CHI-PHI	6-7	PIT-STL	2-5	SD-SF	3*0	
0625	CIN-HOU	4*3	ATL-LA	3*2	MON-NY	2-5	CHI-PHI	10*7	PIT-STL	1-2	SD-SF	3*1	
0627	LA-HOU	0-5	SD-ATL	4-5	SF-CIN	7*6	MON-PIT	1-7	PHI-STL	2*1			
0628	LA-HOU	4-6	SD-ATL	3-5	SF-CIN	5*1	MON-PIT	3*2	PHI-STL	7*4	NY-CHI	5*2	
0629	LA-HOU	1-2	SD-ATL	1-3	SF-CIN	3-4	MON-PIT	6*4	PHI-STL	8*7	NY-CHI	7*4	
0630	SD-HOU	9*2	SF-ATL	1-5	LA-CIN	5-6	PHI-PIT	2-3	NY-STL	7*0	MON-CHI	4*3	
0701	SD-HOU	7*4	SF-ATL	9*6			PHI-PIT	5*4	NY-STL	2*1	MON-CHI	0#0	
0702	SD-HOU	1-8	SF-ATL	4-7	LA-CIN	3-4	PHI-PIT	3-4	NY-STL	4*3	MON-CHI	0-1	
											MON-CHI	4-5	
0703	MON-ATL	1-3	PIT-LA	3-6	HOU-NY	5-6	CIN-PHI	3-7	CHI-SD	1-4	STL-SF	0-1	
0704	MON-ATL	11*5	PIT-LA	6*4	HOU-NY	1-2	CIN-PHI	4*1	CHI-SD	1-2	STL-SF	1-6	
0705	MON-ATL	12*5	PIT-LA	5*0	HOU-NY	2*1	CIN-PHI	7*2	CHI-SD	3*2	STL-SF	7*4	
0706	MON-ATL	11*8	PIT-LA	3-4	HOU-NY	3-5	CIN-PHI	5-12	CHI-SD	1-2	STL-SF	3-8	
0707	HOU-MON	12*1	STL-LA	0-1	CIN-NY	7*6	ATL-PHI	3-7	PIT-SD	3*1			
0708	HOU-MON	4*1	STL-LA	1*0	CIN-NY	5*4	ATL-PHI	2-8	PIT-SD	2-4	CHI-SF	4*1	
0709	HOU-MON	1-2	STL-LA	2-8	CIN-NY	11*1	ATL-PHI	7*3	PIT-SD	6*4	CHI-SF	4*3	
0710	CIN-MON	6-8	CHI-LA	4-11	ATL-NY	1-5	PHI-HOU	4-11	STL-SD	3-4	PIT-SF	3-6	
0711	CIN-MON	3*2	CHI-LA	6*3	ATL-NY	0-11	PHI-HOU	4*1	STL-SD	4*2	PIT-SF	8*4	
0712	CIN-MON	2*0	CHI-LA	7*4	ATL-NY	1-10	PHI-HOU	4*2	STL-SD	4*2	PIT-SF	1-3	
0713	CIN-MON	3#2	CHI-LA	3-4	ATL-NY	0-2	PHI-HOU	5*4	STL-SD	6-13	PIT-SF	4-11	
0717	ATL-MON	2-4	SF-CHI	6*4	PHI-CIN	6-7	NY-HOU	13*2	SD-PIT	2*1	LA-STL	2-12	
0718	ATL-MON	4-5	SF-CHI	1-2	PHI-CIN	5-6	NY-HOU	0-3	SD-PIT	7-12	LA-STL	4*3	
0719	ATL-MON	7*2	SF-CHI	6-11	PHI-CIN	2-5	NY-HOU	4-5	SD-PIT	3-4	LA-STL	1-2	
0720			SF-CHI	5*4	PHI-CIN	9*3	NY-HOU	8-9	SD-PIT	2-4	LA-STL	7*2	

◆1986◆	GAME 1		GAME 2		GAME 3		GAME 4		GAME 5		GAME 6		GAME 7
0721	PHI-ATL	3*1	SD-CHI	1-6	NY-CIN	4*2	MON-HOU	7-8			SF-STL	3-8	
0722	PHI-ATL	5*4	SD-CHI	4-6	NY-CIN	6*3	MON-HOU	0-1	LA-PIT	4*3	SF-STL	7-10	
0723	PHI-ATL	4*2	SD-CHI	7*5	NY-CIN	3*2	MON-HOU	3-4	LA-PIT	6*5	SF-STL	3-4	
0724	CIN-MON	10*2	HOU-PHI	9*3					LA-PIT	9*2			
	MON-CIN	6*5											
0725	MON-CIN	2-9	LA-CHI	3-8	HOU-PHI	2-4	SF-PIT	7*3	SD-STL	2-3			
0726	MON-CIN	6-7	LA-CHI	4-9	HOU-PHI	2-3	SF-PIT	9*0	SD-STL	2-4	NY-ATL	3-4	
											NY-ATL	5-8	
0727	LA-CHI	13*11	MON-CIN	7-9	HOU-PHI	3*2	SF-PIT	0-7	SD-STL	2-3	NY-ATL	5*1	
0728	ATL-HOU	2-4	SF-LA	1-2	STL-PHI	3*1	PIT-MON	7*4	CHI-NY	2-9	CIN-SD	2-5	
0729	ATL-HOU	1*0	SF-LA	1-2	STL-PHI	7-12			CHI-NY	0-3	CIN-SD	1-2	
									CHI-NY	2*1			
0730	ATL-HOU	2-4	SF-LA	2-4	PIT-MON	2-3	STL-PHI	6*3	CHI-NY	4*3	CIN-SD	3-9	
0731	ATL-SF	2-3											
0801	ATL-SF	1-3	CIN-LA	5-9	MON-NY	1-3	CHI-PHI	3-4	STL-PIT	0-4	HOU-SD	6*3	
0802	ATL-SF	5-7	CIN-LA	1-7	MON-NY	1-4	CHI-PHI	2-12	STL-PIT	7*3	HOU-SD	5*4	
0803	ATL-SF	4*2	CIN-LA	1-2	MON-NY	3-4	CHI-PHI	2-6	STL-PIT	0-3	HOU-SD	1-5	
0804	CIN-SF	2*1	HOU-LA	3-7	NY-CHI	2-4	PHI-STL	1-5	MON-PIT	5*4	ATL-SD	4*1	
0805	CIN-SF	11*6	HOU-LA	10*2	NY-CHI	5-8	PHI-STL	4-7	MON-PIT	3*0	ATL-SD	3*2	
0806	CIN-SF	1-2	HOU-LA	4-7	NY-CHI	7*6	PHI-STL	1-2	MON-PIT	3*2	ATL-SD	4*2	
					NY-CHI	6#4							
0807	MON-PIT	5*4	PHI-STL	5-6	NY-CHI	7*6							
					NY-CHI	12*3							
0808	SF-ATL	6-7	SD-HOU	0-5	PHI-CHI	1-2	NY-MON	3-5	PIT-STL	1-3	LA-CIN	0-4	
											LA-CIN	1-5	
0809	SF-ATL	4*3	PHI-CHI	4*2	SD-HOU	2-6	NY-MON	10*8	PIT-STL	8*5	LA-CIN	2-6	
0810	SF-ATL	4*3	PHI-CHI	0-4	SD-HOU	5*3	NY-MON	7*2	PIT-STL	4-5	LA-CIN	5*0	
0811	SD-ATL	6-11	PIT-CHI	10*8	LA-HOU	6-7	STL-MON	5*4	NY-PHI	8*4	SF-CIN	13*4	
			PIT-CHI	10*7									
0812	SD-ATL	4*3	PIT-CHI	1-3	SF-CIN	2*1	LA-HOU	0-3	STL-MON	3-10	NY-PHI	1-3	
0813	SD-ATL	7-8	PIT-CHI	8-9	SF-CIN	6-8	LA-HOU	5*3	STL-MON	6*2	NY-PHI	4-8	
0814	SD-ATL	3-7	STL-NY	3-4	SF-CIN	0-2	LA-HOU	2-3	CHI-MON	4-5	PIT-PHI	7-8	
			STL-NY	5*1									
0815	HOU-ATL	3*0	STL-NY	4*2	LA-SF	1-5	SD-CIN	2-7	CHI-MON	2-5	PIT-PHI	6*5	
							SD-CIN	7*1	CHI-MON	1-5	PIT-PHI	2-3	
0816	HOU-ATL	7*4	STL-NY	3*1	LA-SF	6*5	SD-CIN	1-4	CHI-MON	5*0	PIT-PHI	6*1	
											PIT-PHI	0-6	
0817	HOU-ATL	3-4	SD-CIN	9*5	CHI-MON	2*1	LA-SF	2*0	STL-NY	2*1	PIT-PHI	1-5	
									STL-NY	2-9			
0818	SD-CIN	5-6	NY-LA	5*4	HOU-PIT	3*0							
0819	STL-CIN	1-6	NY-LA	6*4	HOU-PIT	1*0	ATL-CHI	7*2	MON-SD	1-7	PHI-SF	6*5	
0820	STL-CIN	1-3	NY-LA	7*5	HOU-PIT	1-4	ATL-CHI	8*3	MON-SD	2-3	PHI-SF	1*0	
0821	STL-CIN	4-9					ATL-CHI	5*2	MON-SD	0-6	PHI-SF	6-7	
0822	MON-LA	1-2	ATL-PIT	5-16	HOU-STL	5-6	CIN-CHI	2-3	PHI-SD	4*1	NY-SF	5*3	
0823	MON-LA	7*4	ATL-PIT	3-4	HOU-STL	1-7	CIN-CHI	7*3	PHI-SD	3-4	NY-SF	3*2	
0824	MON-LA	2-3	ATL-PIT	3-4	HOU-STL	5*1	CIN-CHI	7*1	PHI-SD	6*5	NY-SF	1-10	
0825	PHI-LA	1-3	CIN-PIT	5*4	ATL-STL	4*2	CHI-HOU	2-3	NY-SD	5*2	MON-SF	6*5	
0826	PHI-LA	6*4	CIN-PIT	5*4	ATL-STL	1-7	CHI-HOU	5*3	NY-SD	11*6	MON-SF	0-1	
0827	PHI-LA	2*1	CIN-PIT	9*5	ATL-STL	1-2	CHI-HOU	1-7	NY-SD	2-3	MON-SF	2-3	
0829	CHI-ATL	7*3	LA-NY	1-2	CIN-STL	2*0	PIT-HOU	2-3	SF-PHI	4-6	SD-MON	1-10	
0830	CHI-ATL	3-4	LA-NY	3-6	CIN-STL	2-5	PIT-HOU	13*3	SF-PHI	3-5	SD-MON	5*4	
											SD-MON	5*4	
0831	CHI-ATL	3-4	PIT-HOU	8*2	LA-NY	7*4	SF-PHI	3-4	CIN-STL	3-9	SD-MON	4*1	
0901	STL-ATL	5*2	HOU-CHI	6*4	SF-NY	2-5	SD-PHI	4-5	PIT-CIN	5-6	LA-MON	6-7	
0902	STL-ATL	2-4	HOU-CHI	4#4	SF-NY	4*3	SD-PHI	6*2	PIT-CIN	1-9	LA-MON	0-1	
0903	STL-ATL	5*3	HOU-CHI	8*7	SF-NY	2-4	SD-PHI	7*5	PIT-CIN	5*3	LA-MON	5*3	
			HOU-CHI	8*2									
0904	SF-MON	2-4											
0905	SF-MON	8*4	PIT-ATL	3-4	CHI-CIN	2-11	STL-HOU	8*5	LA-PHI	0-4			
0906	SF-MON	1-3	PIT-ATL	2-4	CHI-CIN	1-5	STL-HOU	6-7	LA-PHI	3*2	SD-NY	3-4	
0907	SF-MON	1*0	PIT-ATL	3*1	CHI-CIN	11*3	STL-HOU	3-6	LA-PHI	1-2	SD-NY	1-7	
											SD-NY	5-6	
0908	PHI-CHI	4-7	CIN-HOU	1-3	ATL-LA	0-7	STL-PIT	2-3	SD-SF	3-4	MON-NY	9*1	
0909	PHI-CHI	6-8	CIN-HOU	2-9	ATL-LA	5-9	STL-PIT	3*1	SD-SF	0-7	MON-NY	9*7	
0910	PHI-CHI	7-8	ATL-SD	4-9	HOU-LA	1-5	STL-PIT	4*3	CIN-SF	14*2	MON-NY	1-6	
0911			ATL-SD	1-9	HOU-LA	6-14			CIN-SF	1-2			
0912	NY-PHI	3-6	HOU-SD	5*3	CIN-LA	8*3	CHI-PIT	9*8	ATL-SF	2-11	MON-STL	4*3	
0913	NY-PHI	5-6	HOU-SD	3-4	CIN-LA	3*0	CHI-PIT	2-5	ATL-SF	4*1	MON-STL	5*1	
0914	NY-PHI	0-6	HOU-SD	2-3	CIN-LA	4*3	CHI-PIT	2-9	ATL-SF	6-7	MON-STL	2-10	
											NY-STL	0-1	
0915	PIT-PHI	0-5	CHI-MON	7*3	LA-ATL	1-3	HOU-CIN	6*1	SF-SD	4*1	NY-STL	4*2	
0916	PIT-PHI	5-9	CHI-MON	1-4	LA-ATL	1-4	HOU-CIN	6*1	SF-SD	4-5	CHI-NY	2-4	
0917	STL-PHI	8*5	PIT-MON	5-6									
			PIT-MON	4*1									
0918	LA-ATL	3-4	PIT-MON	3*1	HOU-CIN	5*3	CHI-NY	0-5	STL-PHI	3-4			
0919	SF-ATL	4*0	STL-MON	2-3	LA-CIN	9*7	PHI-NY	4*3	PIT-CHI	2-8	SD-HOU	4-5	
0920	SF-ATL	1-2	STL-MON	3*1	LA-CIN	5-9	PHI-NY	5-9	PIT-CHI	0-1	SD-HOU	6-10	
0921	SF-ATL	8*2	STL-MON	7*2	LA-CIN	4-8	PHI-NY	7*1	PIT-CHI	2-3	SD-HOU	5*0	
0922	SD-ATL	8-9	PHI-PIT	8*4	SF-CIN	10*7	STL-NY	2-5	MON-CHI	5*2	LA-HOU	9*2	
0923	SD-ATL	5*2	PHI-PIT	5-6	SF-CIN	5-6	STL-NY	1-9	MON-CHI	10*5	LA-HOU	0-4	
0924	PHI-STL	1-7	MON-PIT	1-2	ATL-CIN	1-4			NY-CHI	2-8	SF-HOU	0-6	
0925	PHI-STL	4-5	MON-PIT	8*4	ATL-CIN	4-6	SD-LA	3-4	NY-CHI	6*5	SF-HOU	0-2	
							SD-LA	7*6					
0926	HOU-ATL	4-5	PHI-MON	5*0	NY-PIT	3*1	CIN-SD	8*6	LA-SF	0-3	CHI-STL	4*1	
0927	HOU-ATL	4*0	PHI-MON	1*0	NY-PIT	4*2	CIN-SD	7*4	LA-SF	3-8	CHI-STL	5*3	
0928	HOU-ATL	2*0	PHI-MON	5*2	NY-PIT	4*1	CIN-SD	6*3	LA-SF	5-6	CHI-STL	1-4	
0929	CHI-PHI	8*3					LA-SD	10*0					
0930	CHI-PHI	2-9	CIN-ATL	7-8	NY-MON	0-1	LA-SD	8-11	HOU-SF	5-6	PIT-STL	3-5	
1001			CIN-ATL	6*5	NY-MON	6*4	LA-SD	2-3	HOU-SF	5*0	PIT-STL	4*3	
1002			CIN-ATL	6*4	NY-MON	8*2			HOU-SF	2*1	PIT-STL	5*1	
1003	SD-CIN	3-6	ATL-HOU	2-6	SF-LA	8*2	MON-PHI	6*5			PIT-NY	1-6	
1004	SD-CIN	7-10	ATL-HOU	2-3	SF-LA	1-2	MON-PHI	4-5	STL-CHI	7-8	PIT-NY	2-5	
1005	STL-CHI	1-8	SD-CIN	2*1	ATL-HOU	1-4	SF-LA	11*2	MON-PHI	1-2	PIT-NY	0-9	

◆1987◆	GAME 1		GAME 2		GAME 3		GAME 4		GAME 5		GAME 6		GAME 7
0406	SD-SF	3-4	MON-CIN	5-11	LA-HOU	3-4							
0407	SD-SF	3-4	PHI-ATL	0-6	LA-HOU	5-6	STL-CHI	9*3	PIT-NY	2-3			
0408	SD-SF	1-2	MON-CIN	2-7	LA-HOU	3-7							
0409	PHI-ATL	7-8	STL-CHI	4*2	SF-LA	8*1	PIT-NY	2-4					
0410	SD-CIN	3-6	MON-HOU	1-6	SF-LA	5*4	ATL-NY	3-6	CHI-PHI	4*3	STL-PIT	3-4	
0411	SD-CIN	1-5	MON-HOU	2-3	SF-LA	1-5	ATL-NY	4*3	CHI-PHI	9*1	STL-PIT	6*3	
0412	SD-CIN	5*2	MON-HOU	0-1	SF-LA	5-7	ATL-NY	12*4	CHI-PHI	8-9	STL-PIT	4-7	
0413	CIN-ATL	7*2	SF-SD	13*6	HOU-LA	2-4			CHI-PHI	5*2	STL-PIT	8*4	
0414	CIN-ATL	6*3	SF-SD	3*2	HOU-LA	2-3	MON-STL	9*4	NY-PHI	7*5			
0415	CIN-ATL	3-4	SF-SD	1*0	HOU-LA	4*0	PIT-CHI	3*1	NY-PHI	4*1			
0416	MON-STL	4*3	LA-SD	2-3			PIT-CHI	6*0	NY-PHI	9*3			
0417	NY-STL	3-4	LA-SD	5*3	HOU-CIN	8-9	MON-CHI	0-7	PHI-PIT	6*2	ATL-SF	2*0	

♦1987♦	GAME 1	GAME 2	GAME 3	GAME 4	GAME 5	GAME 6	GAME 7
0418	NY-STL 8-12	LA-SD 5*2	HOU-CIN 0-8	MON-CHI 4*2	PHI-PIT 8*6	ATL-SF 1-2	
0419	NY-STL 2-4	LA-SD 9*1	HOU-CIN 7*3	MON-CHI 3*1	PHI-PIT 2-5	ATL-SF 3-4	
			HOU-CIN 2-6				
0420	PHI-MON 4*3	NY-PIT 6-9	CIN-SD 12*3	LA-SF 3-4			
0421	ATL-HOU 6-7	NY-PIT 9*6	CIN-SD 2-3	LA-SF 11*8	CHI-STL 5*4		
0422	ATL-HOU 0-6	NY-PIT 8*7	CIN-SD 3-6	LA-SF 5*3	CHI-STL 5*4	PHI-MON 3-7	
0423	ATL-HOU 3-5		CIN-SD 3*2		CHI-STL 2-5	PHI-MON 5-6	
0424	CIN-HOU 4*3	SF-ATL 7*5	SD-LA 0-5	STL-NY 1-2		CHI-MON 6*4	
0425	CIN-HOU 3*0	SF-ATL 3-5	SD-LA 2-4	STL-NY 3*2	PIT-PHI 2-3	CHI-MON 9*4	
0426	CIN-HOU 11*3	SF-ATL 6*4	SD-LA 4*0	STL-NY 7*4	PIT-PHI 4-6	CHI-MON 7*1	
0427		SF-ATL 7*3		HOU-NY 11*1	MON-PHI 6*4		
0428	SF-CHI 6*2	ATL-CIN 7*3	LA-PIT 1-6	SD-STL 5*2	MON-PHI 7*1		
0429	SF-CHI 4-8	ATL-CIN 5*2	LA-PIT 10*2	SD-STL 6-10	MON-PHI 0-5	HOU-NY 1-2	
0430	SF-CHI 5*4	ATL-CIN 8-9	LA-PIT 4-5	SD-STL 4-5		MON-NY 3-11	
0501	SD-CHI 5-7	HOU-ATL 12*3	SF-PIT 2-4	LA-STL 4-5	CIN-PHI 8*5	MON-NY 6-7	
0502	SD-CHI 3-7	HOU-ATL 4-12	SF-PIT 0-1	LA-STL 7*6	CIN-PHI 3-8	MON-NY 11*7	
0503	SD-CHI 2-4	HOU-ATL 3-5			CIN-PHI 9*6	MON-NY 2*0	
0504	LA-CHI 4-5	MON-ATL 7-10	PIT-SD 5-9	SF-STL 10*7			
0505	LA-CHI 3*1	MON-ATL 6*4	PIT-SD 10*8	SF-STL 10*6	CIN-NY 2*0	HOU-PHI 5*1	
0506	PIT-LA 1-2	MON-ATL 6*2	STL-SD 3*0	CHI-SF 9*4	CIN-NY 2-3	HOU-PHI 3*2	
0507	PIT-LA 3-6		STL-SD 17*10	CHI-SF 1-11			
0508	STL-LA 5*1	NY-ATL 3-4	CHI-SD 6*3	PIT-SF 2-4	PHI-CIN 3-4	HOU-MON 3*0	
0509	STL-LA 2-4	NY-ATL 4-5	CHI-SD 5*2	PIT-SF 4*2	PHI-CIN 4*2	HOU-MON 1-3	
0510	STL-LA 6-7	NY-ATL 7-8	CHI-SD 2-14	PIT-SF 4*1	PHI-CIN 4*3	HOU-MON 2-6	
0511	CHI-LA 6*3	PHI-HOU 7*6			NY-CIN 2-12	ATL-MON 6-7	
0512	CHI-LA 0-7	PHI-HOU 2-5	SD-PIT 5-12	STL-SF 6*5	NY-CIN 6*2	ATL-MON 5*2	
0513	CHI-LA 5*0	NY-HOU 1-2	SD-PIT 5-9	STL-SF 7*6	ATL-PHI 10*5	CIN-MON 12*6	
0514		NY-HOU 4-5	SD-PIT 3-10		ATL-PHI 4-5	CIN-MON 10*9	
0515	SF-NY 3-8	CHI-HOU 3*1	ATL-PIT 9*3	CIN-STL 4-5	SD-PHI 4-7	LA-MON 3-6	
0516	SF-NY 5*4	CHI-HOU 2*1	ATL-PIT 10*8	CIN-STL 5-6	SD-PHI 0-9	LA-MON 3-10	
0517	SF-NY 4-6	CHI-HOU 6*4	ATL-PIT 5-6	CIN-STL 2-10	SD-PHI 6*5	LA-MON 3-8	
0518	SD-NY 7*5		HOU-PIT 4*1		LA-PHI 3-5	SF-MON 2-7	
0519	SD-NY 4-5	STL-ATL 5-6	HOU-PIT 2-5	CIN-CHI 2-9		SF-MON 6*2	
0520	SD-NY 3-10	STL-ATL 5*4	HOU-PIT 3-5	CIN-CHI 6*2		SF-MON 9*7	
0521	LA-PHI 3-6	STL-ATL 7*2		CIN-CHI 7-8			
0522	SF-PHI 2*1	PIT-CIN 4*1	STL-HOU 7*5	ATL-CHI 9*5	LA-NY 4-6	MON-SD 3-5	
0523	SF-PHI 8-9	PIT-CIN 3*2	STL-HOU 4*3	ATL-CHI 6-7	LA-NY 4*2	MON-SD 6*0	
0524	SF-PHI 6*3	PIT-CIN 7*2	STL-HOU 8*2	ATL-CHI 2-3	LA-NY 8*6	MON-SD 2*1	
0525	MON-LA 3*1	CHI-CIN 4-5	PIT-HOU 2-7	NY-SF 8*7	ATL-STL 14*5	PHI-SD 6*4	
0526	MON-LA 8*3	CHI-CIN 2-3	PIT-HOU 3-10	NY-SF 3*2	ATL-STL 5*4	PHI-SD 3*1	
0527	MON-LA 4-6	CHI-CIN 4*1	PIT-HOU 2-7	NY-SF 4*3		PHI-SD 6*4	
0528	ATL-STL 5-11						
0529	HOU-STL 2-8	CHI-ATL 5-6	PHI-LA 0-6	CIN-PIT 13*6	NY-SD 5*4	MON-SF 10*4	
0530	HOU-STL 2-3	CHI-ATL 11*6	PHI-LA 3*0	CIN-PIT 6*2	NY-SD 3*0	MON-SF 6*4	
0531	HOU-STL 8*7	CHI-ATL 1-2	PHI-LA 3*1	CIN-PIT 5*2	NY-SD 0-1	MON-SF 0-8	
0601	HOU-CHI 6*5	STL-CIN 8*6	NY-LA 5*2			PHI-SF 2-9	
0602	HOU-CHI 2-13	STL-CIN 2-3	NY-LA 3-6	PIT-ATL 4*1	SD-MON 2-6	PHI-SF 7*6	
0603	HOU-CHI 7-22	STL-CIN 4-6	NY-LA 2-5	PIT-ATL 4*1	SD-MON 3-4	PHI-SF 1-4	
0604	STL-CHI 3*1			PIT-ATL 3-8	SD-MON 5-8		
0605	STL-CHI 5*1	LA-CIN 6-8	SF-HOU 1-6	SD-ATL 10*3	PIT-NY 1-5	MON-PHI 6-7	
0606	STL-CHI 5-6	LA-CIN 2-5	SF-HOU 4*3	SD-ATL 5*3	PIT-NY 2-4	MON-PHI 3-4	
0607	STL-CHI 13*9	LA-CIN 13*7	SF-HOU 0-3	SD-ATL 12-13	PIT-NY 4-5	MON-PHI 1-3	
					PIT-NY 10*9		
0608	LA-ATL 6*3	NY-CHI 2-4	SF-CIN 6-7	SD-HOU 5*4	PIT-MON 1-7	STL-PHI 12*8	
0609	LA-ATL 5*3	NY-CHI 5-6	SF-CIN 10*2	SD-HOU 0-1	PIT-MON 8*1	STL-PHI 2-3	
0610	LA-ATL 1-7	NY-CHI 13*2	SF-CIN 9*4	SD-HOU 1-10	PIT-MON 3-4	STL-PHI 3*1	
0611	HOU-LA 1*0	SD-SF 0-1	ATL-CIN 6*4				
0612	HOU-LA 5*1	SD-SF 5*0	ATL-CIN 4*3	PHI-MON 6-13	NY-PIT 10*2	CHI-STL 1-4	
0613	HOU-LA 1-7	SD-SF 11*2	ATL-CIN 2-5	PHI-MON 5-7	NY-PIT 3-4	CHI-STL 2-9	
0614	HOU-LA 4*1	SD-SF 4*1	ATL-CIN 3-4	PHI-MON 11*6	NY-PIT 7*3	CHI-STL 2-3	
0615	PHI-CHI 3*2	CIN-HOU 0-4		NY-MON 0-4		PIT-STL 3*1	
0616	PHI-CHI 2-7	CIN-HOU 1-4	SF-ATL 2-7	NY-MON 7*3	LA-SD 2-3	PIT-STL 1-11	
0617	PHI-CHI 3-5	CIN-HOU 9*1	SF-ATL 1-6	NY-MON 1-9	LA-SD 7-8	PIT-STL 4*1	
0618	PHI-CHI 7-9	LA-HOU 6*4	CIN-ATL 8*4	NY-MON 10*7	SF-SD 1-3	PIT-STL 6-8	
0619	PIT-CHI 4*0	LA-HOU 2-3	CIN-ATL 5-16	PHI-NY 1-8	SF-SD 7*6	MON-STL 8*7	
0620	PIT-CHI 8*2	LA-HOU 2-3	CIN-ATL 6-8	PHI-NY 2-3	SF-SD 4-10	MON-STL 7*5	
0621	PIT-CHI 3-6	LA-HOU 1-6	CIN-ATL 6*5	PHI-NY 3-8	SF-SD 11*2	MON-STL 3-7	
0622	PIT-CHI 2-3						
0623	ATL-LA 2-3	CHI-NY 4*1	MON-PIT 8*2	HOU-SD 1-4	CIN-SF 4*1	PHI-STL 4*1	
0624	ATL-LA 4-5	CHI-NY 1-2	MON-PIT 6-9	HOU-SD 12*7	CIN-SF 5*4	PHI-STL 3-5	
0625	ATL-LA 1-2	CHI-NY 2-8	MON-PIT 7*2	HOU-SD 1-4	CIN-SF 6-7	PHI-STL 0-3	
0626	CIN-LA 6*0	STL-MON 1-5	CHI-PIT 2-5	ATL-SD 1-5	HOU-SF 9*6	NY-PHI 2-5	
0627	CIN-LA 3-4	STL-MON 15*5	CHI-PIT 0-7	ATL-SD 4-8	HOU-SF 6*5	NY-PHI 5*4	
0628	CIN-LA 2-4	STL-MON 7*6	CHI-PIT 2-6	ATL-SD 5*2	HOU-SF 4-8	NY-PHI 4-5	
0629	SD-LA 3*0	CHI-MON 9*5	STL-NY 8*7		ATL-SF 1*0	PIT-PHI 5-6	
						PIT-PHI 3-11	
0630	HOU-CIN 4-5	SD-LA 0-4	CHI-MON 4-5	STL-NY 2-3	ATL-SF 2-5	PIT-PHI 4-6	
0701	HOU-CIN 4-6	SD-LA 4*0	CHI-MON 1*0	STL-NY 6-9	ATL-SF 8*3	PIT-PHI 4-11	
0702	NY-CIN 5*0					HOU-PHI 7*6	
0703	NY-CIN 3-8	STL-ATL 9*1	SF-CHI 3*1	SD-MON 1-2	LA-PIT 0-6	HOU-PHI 1-2	
0704	NY-CIN 3-7	STL-ATL 3*0	SF-CHI 3-5	SD-MON 3-4	LA-PIT 2-4	HOU-PHI 3-9	
0705	NY-CIN 5-7	STL-ATL 4*1	SF-CHI 7*5	SD-MON 3*2	LA-PIT 6*1	HOU-PHI 8*2	
0706	PHI-CIN 9*6	MON-HOU 3-9	SD-CHI 0-7		SF-PIT 7*5		
					SF-PIT 7*4		
0707	SD-CHI 5-7	PHI-CIN 10*8	MON-HOU 2*0	NY-ATL 6*2	SF-PIT 4-6	LA-STL 4-5	
				NY-ATL 5*1		LA-STL 4-5	
0708	SD-CHI 8-12	PHI-CIN 7*2	MON-HOU 1*0	NY-ATL 3-5	SF-PIT 8*4	LA-STL 3-6	
						LA-STL 7-8	
0709	PHI-ATL 6-11	LA-CHI 5#12	MON-CIN 2-7	NY-HOU 3-4		SF-STL 6-7	
0710	PHI-ATL 5*2	LA-CHI 5-12	MON-CIN 5*1	NY-HOU 7*3	SD-PIT 5-6	SF-STL 5-7	
		LA-CHI 4#4					
0711	PHI-ATL 4-5	LA-CHI 5*4	MON-CIN 11*5	NY-HOU 9*6	SD-PIT 3*1	SF-STL 3*1	
		LA-CHI 0-7					
0712	PHI-ATL 3-9	LA-CHI 12*0	MON-CIN 4*2	NY-HOU 5*2	SD-PIT 2-4	SF-STL 2-3	
0716	PIT-LA 0-7	ATL-MON 0-2	CIN-NY 0-9	PHI-HOU 1-2	STL-SD 8-9	CHI-SF 4*1	
0717	PIT-LA 2-3	ATL-MON 4-5	CIN-NY 5*2	PHI-HOU 2*1	STL-SD 4*3	CHI-SF 5*1	
0718	PIT-LA 4*2	ATL-MON 2-3	CIN-NY 7*3	PHI-HOU 4*2	STL-SD 3-4	CHI-SF 2-9	
0719	PIT-LA 7*2	ATL-MON 1-2	CIN-NY 5-6	PHI-HOU 4*1	STL-SD 5*4	CHI-SF 3-4	
0720	CIN-PHI 10*6	HOU-MON 1-4	ATL-NY 2-9		CHI-SD 4-7	PIT-SF 7*6	
0721	CIN-PHI 4*3	HOU-MON 4*2	ATL-NY 8*3		CHI-SD 3-4	PIT-SF 0-7	
0722	CIN-PHI 3-5	HOU-MON 7*0	ATL-NY 3-4	STL-LA 6*1	CHI-SD 6*3	PIT-SF 4*0	
0723	ATL-PHI 1-5	CIN-MON 8*4		STL-LA 3*1	PIT-SD 1-2		
0724	ATL-PHI 5-11	CIN-MON 2-3	STL-SF 3-4	STL-LA 9*6	PIT-SD 3*2	HOU-NY 2-5	
				CHI-LA 6*4		HOU-NY 4-7	
0725	CHI-LA 2-7	CIN-MON 3-4	ATL-PHI 2*1	PIT-SD 9*3	STL-SF 4-5	HOU-NY 7*5	
0726	CHI-LA 6-7	CIN-MON 0-6	ATL-PHI 3-7	PIT-SD 4-7	STL-SF 3-6	HOU-NY 5*2	
					STL-SF 2-5		

♦1987♦	GAME 1		GAME 2		GAME 3		GAME 4		GAME 5		GAME 6		GAME 7
0727	SF-LA	5-6											
0728	SF-LA	2-4	HOU-ATL	1-6	MON-CHI	3-8	SD-CIN	7-8	PHI-PIT	5*2	NY-STL	6*4	
0729	SF-LA	16*2	HOU-ATL	3-5	MON-CHI	11*3	SD-CIN	5-15	PHI-PIT	4*3	NY-STL	6*4	
0730			HOU-ATL	8*5	MON-CHI	6*1	SD-CIN	12*8	PHI-PIT	1*0	NY-STL	5*3	
0731	SD-HOU	6*2	LA-ATL	9*5	PHI-CHI	8*5	SF-CIN	2-9	NY-MON	3-13	PIT-STL	3-4	
0801	SD-HOU	6*0	LA-ATL	5*2	PHI-CHI	3-5	SF-CIN	7*3	NY-MON	12*4	PIT-STL	6-7	
0802	SD-HOU	0-6	LA-ATL	5-10	PHI-CHI	2-3	SF-CIN	4-5	NY-MON	7*4	PIT-STL	1-9	
0803	SF-HOU	3-5	PHI-NY	2-3	CHI-PIT	4-6	LA-CIN	7*2	STL-MON	5*2			
0804	SF-HOU	4-5	PHI-NY	3-5	CHI-PIT	3*2	LA-CIN	4-10	STL-MON	5-10	SD-ATL	7-12	
0805	SF-HOU	5-6	PHI-NY	3-13	CHI-PIT	0-10	LA-CIN	3-6	STL-MON	1-2	SD-ATL	7*3	
0806	STL-PHI	5*2	CHI-NY	6-7	MON-PIT	6*3					SD-ATL	7*4	
0807	STL-PHI	5-15	CHI-NY	1-7	MON-PIT	3-9	ATL-LA	4*3	HOU-SD	1-7	CIN-SF	1-3	
0808	STL-PHI	9*5	CHI-NY	5*3	MON-PIT	2-5	ATL-LA	9*7	HOU-SD	3-4	CIN-SF	2-5	
0809	STL-PHI	7-8	CHI-NY	6*3	MON-PIT	3-4	ATL-LA	2-5	HOU-SD	3-4	CIN-SF	2-3	
											CIN-SF	2-5	
0810	CIN-LA	4*3	MON-NY	2*1	CHI-PHI	2-4	STL-PIT	6*0	ATL-SD	0-2	HOU-SF	5-6	
0811	CIN-LA	2-7	MON-NY	2-6	CHI-PHI	8-9	STL-PIT	6*5	ATL-SD	6-7	HOU-SF	7*3	
0812	CIN-LA	0-1	MON-NY	2-4	CHI-PHI	7-13	STL-PIT	0-11	ATL-SD	2*1	HOU-SF	1-8	
0813	CIN-LA	5*2	NY-CHI	5-7	PIT-MON	7-9	PHI-STL	4*2	ATL-SD	3-5	HOU-SF	6-7	
0814	ATL-HOU	4-8	NY-CHI	1-6	PIT-MON	3-4	PHI-STL	4-8	CIN-SD	2*0	LA-SF	4*3	
									CIN-SD	8-15			
0815	NY-CHI	3-7	ATL-HOU	0-8	PIT-MON	3-6	LA-SF	0-5	PHI-STL	5*2			
0816	NY-CHI	23*10	ATL-HOU	2-6	PIT-MON	7-10	LA-SF	0-1	PHI-STL	4*3	CIN-SD	2*0	
0817			ATL-HOU	2-11									
0818	CHI-ATL	5-9	STL-HOU	0-4	PIT-CIN	7*4	LA-MON	1-2	SF-NY	2-7	SD-PHI	9*4	
0819	CHI-ATL	9*1	STL-HOU	1-2	PIT-CIN	10*9	LA-MON	10*9	SF-NY	10*6	SD-PHI	5-6	
0820	CHI-ATL	4-13	STL-HOU	4-5	PIT-CIN	3-5	LA-MON	7*2	SF-NY	4-7	SD-PHI	2-10	
0821	PIT-ATL	4-5	HOU-CHI	5-7	STL-CIN	2*1	SF-MON	6*3	SD-NY	6*2	LA-PHI	1-2	
											LA-PHI	3-7	
0822	PIT-ATL	3-10	HOU-CHI	9*7	STL-CIN	9*7	SF-MON	4-5	SD-NY	8*3	LA-PHI	0-2	
0823	PIT-ATL	2-6	HOU-CHI	4*2	STL-CIN	12*6	SF-MON	5*3	SD-NY	2-9	LA-PHI	5*1	
0824	CIN-PIT	4-5	HOU-STL	5*2					LA-NY	0-1	SF-PHI	6*1	
0825	CIN-PIT	0-1	HOU-STL	1-7	MON-SD	1-5			LA-NY	3*1	SF-PHI	3*2	
0826	CIN-PIT	5-6	HOU-STL	4-5	MON-SD	6*5			LA-NY	2-3	SF-PHI	2*0	
0827	ATL-CHI	5*2			MON-SD	3*0							
	ATL-CHI	6-8											
0828	CHI-CIN	6*5	MON-LA	2*1	HOU-PIT	2-4	PHI-SD	8*1	NY-SF	4*0	ATL-STL	3-4	
0829	CHI-CIN	1-4	MON-LA	6*5	HOU-PIT	2-8	PHI-SD	1-3	NY-SF	1-9	ATL-STL	2-4	
0830	CHI-CIN	3*1	MON-LA	5*4	HOU-PIT	0-7	PHI-SD	1-6	NY-SF	5*3	ATL-STL	3-4	
0831	CHI-HOU	4*3	PHI-LA	4*2	ATL-PIT	3-7	NY-SD	6*5	MON-SF	0-5	CIN-STL	0-4	
0901	CHI-HOU	3*2	PHI-LA	7*5	ATL-PIT	4*0	NY-SD	9*1	MON-SF	4-14	CIN-STL	7*4	
0902	CHI-HOU	1-10	PHI-LA	6*2	ATL-PIT	0-2	NY-SD	4*3	MON-SF	7*3	CIN-STL	3*1	
0904	PIT-HOU	0-2	NY-LA	5*1	MON-ATL	4*3	CIN-CHI	4*3	PHI-SF	2-3	SD-STL	2-4	
0905	PIT-HOU	1-5	NY-LA	4*3	MON-ATL	4*1	CIN-CHI	10*5	PHI-SF	3-6	SD-STL	4*1	
0906	PIT-HOU	4*3	NY-LA	2-3	MON-ATL	5*2	CIN-CHI	1-3	PHI-SF	1-4	SD-STL	4-6	
0907	SF-HOU	2-4	LA-CIN	2*1	SD-ATL	11*4	PIT-CHI	3*2	STL-MON	2-9	PHI-NY	5*3	
0908	SF-HOU	6*4	LA-CIN	5*3	SD-ATL	2*4	PIT-CHI	4*1	STL-MON	1-4	PHI-NY	2-5	
0909	SF-HOU	2-4	LA-CIN	1-4	SD-ATL	2-3	PIT-CHI	4*3	STL-MON	3-8	PHI-NY	5-11	
0910	HOU-SD	7-8											
0911	HOU-SD	0-11	LA-ATL	5*2	MON-CHI	4-8	SF-CIN	3-4	STL-NY	6*4	PIT-PHI	4*2	
0912			LA-ATL	9-10	MON-CHI	7*1	SF-CIN	7*1	STL-NY	8*1	PIT-PHI	12*4	
0913	HOU-SD	2-10	LA-ATL	6*2	MON-CHI	2-5	SF-CIN	6*1	STL-NY	2-4	PIT-PHI	6*1	
0914	HOU-LA	8*1	CIN-ATL	2-3	MON-PIT	6*4	SD-SF	3-4	CHI-NY	5-6	STL-PHI	2-3	
0915	HOU-LA	2-3	CIN-ATL	21*6	MON-PIT	1-5	SD-SF	3-13	CHI-NY	4-12	STL-PHI	4*3	
0916	NY-MON	10*0	ATL-SD	0-3	STL-PIT	8*5	HOU-SF	1-7			CHI-PHI	5-8	
0917	NY-MON	1-4	ATL-SD	1-7	STL-PIT	0-1	HOU-SF	0-4	CIN-LA	3*2	CHI-PHI	3-4	
									CIN-LA	3-6			
0918	SD-HOU	2*1	PHI-MON	3-6	NY-PIT	9-10	CHI-STL	8*1	ATL-LA	4-7			
0919	SD-HOU	2*1	PHI-MON	4-12	NY-PIT	5*4	CHI-STL	3-5	ATL-LA	10*7	CIN-SF	1-5	
0920	SD-HOU	2-3	PHI-MON	4*1	NY-PIT	8-9	CHI-STL	2-10	ATL-LA	3-5	CIN-SF	10*6	
0921	NY-CHI	7*1	PIT-MON	5*2			PHI-STL	1-3			LA-SF	4*2	
0922	NY-CHI	2-6	PIT-MON	3-4	HOU-ATL	2-6	PHI-STL	2-3	SD-CIN	3-5	LA-SF	4*3	
0923	PHI-CHI	5*0	MON-NY	3-4	HOU-ATL	4-5	PIT-STL	2*0	SD-CIN	6*4	LA-SF	8-9	
0924	PHI-CHI	3*2	MON-NY	5*4	HOU-ATL	7-8	PIT-STL	4-5	SD-CIN	4-5			
0925	STL-CHI	1-2	PIT-NY	2-10	SF-ATL	9*2	SD-LA	3-5	HOU-CIN	1-4	MON-PHI	2-4	
0926	STL-CHI	5*3	PIT-NY	8*2	SF-ATL	5-10	SD-LA	1-3	HOU-CIN	5*3	MON-PHI	7*4	
0927	STL-CHI	3-7	PIT-NY	3-12	SF-ATL	15*6	SD-LA	3-4	HOU-CIN	2-4	MON-PHI	5*3	
0928	LA-HOU	5-11	SF-SD	5*4					ATL-CIN	5-6	NY-PHI	1*0	
0929	LA-HOU	6*1	SF-SD	5*3	MON-STL	0-1			ATL-CIN	4-5	NY-PHI	0-3	
					MON-STL	0-3							
0930	ATL-HOU	3*1	SF-LA	3*0	MON-STL	6*1	NY-PHI	3-4	CIN-SD	3*1	CHI-PIT	3-5	
											CHI-PIT	10*8	
1001	ATL-HOU	5-6	SF-LA	0-7	CIN-SD	4*3	MON-STL	2-8			CHI-PIT	3-12	
1002	CIN-HOU	12*7	CHI-MON	1-7	LA-SD	10*3	NY-STL	2-3	ATL-SF	6*4	PHI-PIT	4-6	
1003	CIN-HOU	4-6	CHI-MON	4-5	LA-SD	0-1	NY-STL	7*1	ATL-SF	3-6	PHI-PIT	5-10	
1004	CIN-HOU	2*1	CHI-MON	7*5	LA-SD	5*3	NY-STL	11*6	ATL-SF	4-5	PHI-PIT	2-4	

♦1988♦	GAME 1		GAME 2		GAME 3		GAME 4		GAME 5		GAME 6		GAME 7
0404	STL-CIN	4-5	NY-MON	10*6	SF-LA	5*1							
0405	CHI-ATL	10*9	SD-HOU	3-6	SF-LA	0-5							
0406	CHI-ATL	3*0	SD-HOU	1-5	NY-MON	1-5	PIT-PHI	5-6					
0407	LA-ATL	5*2	STL-CIN	1-8	NY-MON	8*5	SD-SF	1-6					
0408	LA-ATL	6*3	HOU-CIN	8*3	CHI-MON	6*4	SD-SF	1-5	NY-PHI	1-5	PIT-STL	4*3	
0409	LA-ATL	11*3	HOU-CIN	4-5	CHI-MON	6-10	SD-SF	1-3	NY-PHI	3-9	PIT-STL	0-3	
0410	LA-ATL	3*1	HOU-CIN	12*3	CHI-MON	10*7	SD-SF	6*4	NY-PHI	4*3	PIT-STL	5*3	
0411	PHI-PIT	1-5					CIN-SF	4*0			CHI-STL	6*1	
0412	HOU-ATL	8*3	MON-NY	0-3	LA-SD	3-5	CIN-SF	4*3			CHI-STL	5-7	
0413	HOU-ATL	4*0	PHI-PIT	0-7	LA-SD	4*3	CIN-SF	4-5			CHI-STL	3-4	
0414	CIN-HOU	3-9	PHI-PIT	2-4	LA-SD	0-2	MON-NY	0-1					
0415	CIN-HOU	4*2	PIT-CHI	0-6	SF-SD	8*3	STL-NY	4-6	ATL-LA	2-3	PHI-MON	4-6	
0416	CIN-HOU	8*2	PIT-CHI	4*0	SF-SD	1-2	STL-NY	4-6	ATL-LA	4-7	PHI-MON	1-2	
0417	CIN-HOU	3-5	PIT-CHI	12*7	SF-SD	9*4	STL-NY	2-3	ATL-LA	3*1	PHI-MON	2-5	
0418	SF-CIN	6*3					PHI-NY	10*7	SD-LA	0-6			
0419	SF-CIN	0-8	MON-CHI	9*1	ATL-HOU	5*4	PHI-NY	10*2	STL-PIT	0-3			
0420	SF-CIN	5*3	MON-CHI	5*1	ATL-HOU	0-1	PHI-NY	2-6	STL-PIT	1-8			
0421	SF-CIN	6-7	MON-CHI	2-6	ATL-HOU	0-8			STL-PIT	9*3			
0422	CIN-ATL	4*0	MON-PHI	0-2	HOU-SD	1-3	NY-STL	4*0	CHI-PIT	4-8			
0423	CIN-ATL	1-4	MON-PHI	33	HOU-SD	0-4	NY-STL	12*9	CHI-PIT	4-5	LA-SF	10*3	
0424			MON-PHI	3*1	HOU-SD	0-3	NY-STL	4-5	CHI-PIT	2-4	LA-SF	4*0	
0426	NY-ATL	13*4	PHI-HOU	1-3	STL-SD	4*0	CHI-LA	7*3	CIN-MON	5*2	PIT-SF	2*0	
0427	NY-ATL	5*2	PHI-HOU	2-3	STL-SD	2*1	CHI-LA	0-4	CIN-MON	0-1	PIT-SF	4-6	
0428					STL-SD	6*4	CHI-LA	5*1			PIT-SF	2*1	
0429	NY-CIN	5*4	MON-HOU	4-6	PIT-SD	3-6	STL-LA	4-6			CHI-SF	3-4	
0430	NY-CIN	6*5	MON-HOU	0-3	PIT-SD	5*1	STL-LA	5*2	ATL-PHI	5-7	CHI-SF	2*1	
0501	NY-CIN	11*0	MON-HOU	7*3	PIT-SD	4*2	STL-LA	9*0	ATL-PHI	9*5	CHI-SF	6-7	
0502	MON-CIN	2-3	ATL-NY	3*1	CHI-SD	5*2	PIT-LA	3-6	HOU-PHI	1-7	STL-SF	5*1	
0503	MON-CIN	4*3	ATL-NY	0-8	CHI-SD	13*5	PIT-LA	6-14	HOU-PHI	4*0	STL-SF	0-2	

◆1988◆	GAME 1	GAME 2	GAME 3	GAME 4	GAME 5	GAME 6	GAME 7
0504	PHI-CIN 1-3	HOU-NY 0-8	CHI-SD 6*3	PIT-LA 5-8	ATL-MON 7*5	STL-SF 5*3	
0505	PHI-CIN 4-10				ATL-MON 1-4		
0506	PHI-ATL 7*3	SF-CHI 2-3	CIN-NY 3-4	SD-PIT 1-4	HOU-MON 5-6	LA-STL 10*2	
0507	PHI-ATL 5-6	SF-CHI 2*1	CIN-NY 1-2	SD-PIT 3*2	HOU-MON 3-4	LA-STL 1-2	
0508	PHI-ATL 5*1	SF-CHI 7-13	CIN-NY 1-5	SD-PIT 2-6	HOU-MON 7*2	LA-STL 12*6	
0509	MON-ATL 8-9	NY-HOU 2-6	CIN-PHI 2*0	SF-PIT 8*6		SD-STL 1-7	
0510	MON-ATL 6*1	NY-HOU 5*2	CIN-PHI 10*1	SF-PIT 2-6	LA-CHI 6*5	SD-STL 1-5	
0511	MON-ATL 2-3	NY-HOU 9*8	CIN-PHI 3-4	LA-PIT 1-2	SD-CHI 0-1	SF-STL 5*4	
0512				LA-PIT 4-7	SD-CHI 1-2	SF-STL 12-13	
0513	CHI-HOU 2-8	PHI-LA 2*1	MON-SD 1-7	CIN-PHI 5-6	NY-SF 2-3	ATL-STL 5-7	
0514	CHI-HOU 1-3	PHI-LA 2-3	MON-SD 2-3	CIN-PIT 5*3	NY-SF 2-3	ATL-STL 7*5	
0515	CHI-HOU 2*1	PHI-LA 2-9	MON-SD 1-2	CIN-PIT 7*6	NY-SF 1-5	ATL-STL 6-7	
0516	PIT-HOU 2-9	ATL-CIN 2-4	NY-SD 7*4		PHI-SF 3*0		
0517	PIT-HOU 2-3	ATL-CIN 6*2	NY-SD 1*0	STL-CHI 3*0	PHI-SF 8*1	MON-LA 6*5	
0518	PIT-HOU 2-4	ATL-CIN 4-8	NY-SD 5*2	STL-CHI 4*1	PHI-SF 1-5	MON-LA 3*0	
0519			NY-SD 9*4	STL-CHI 5*1		MON-LA 0-2	
0520	CHI-CIN 2-7	ATL-PIT 3-10	PHI-SD 3-4	MON-SF 2-11	HOU-STL 5*3	NY-LA 5*2	
0521	CHI-CIN 11*6	ATL-PIT 3*7	PHI-SD 4*3	MON-SF 6*0	HOU-STL 4-7	NY-LA 4*0	
0522	CHI-CIN 5*1	ATL-PIT 6*4	PHI-SD 2-9	MON-SF 2-7	HOU-STL 2*1	NY-LA 5*2	
0523		HOU-PIT 3*0			CIN-STL 8*3		
0524	SD-MON 6-7	HOU-PIT 4-5	SF-NY 4*2	LA-PHI 2*1	CIN-STL 2-3	ATL-CHI 3*0	
						ATL-CHI 1-2	
0525	SD-MON 2-6	SF-NY 3-6	LA-PHI 4*0	HOU-PIT 3-4	CIN-STL 0-6	ATL-CHI 2*1	
0526	SD-MON 2-6	SF-NY 5*2	LA-PHI 10*8				
0527	LA-MON 5*2	SD-NY 2*0	SF-PHI 2-5	STL-ATL 5*2	HOU-CHI 2-3	PIT-CIN 3-5	
0528	LA-MON 2-3	SD-NY 1-5	SF-PHI 3-4	STL-ATL 1-5	HOU-CHI 7-14	PIT-CIN 5*2	
0529	LA-MON 2*1	SD-NY 6*3	SF-PHI 2-4	STL-ATL 3*1	HOU-CHI 7*1	PIT-CIN 4*2	
0530	SF-MON 2-3	LA-NY 4-5	SD-PHI 3-7	PIT-ATL 14*2	CIN-CHI 3-12	STL-HOU 4-5	
0531	SF-MON 9*2	LA-NY 4-5	SD-PHI 8*0	PIT-ATL 1-11	CIN-CHI 0-4	STL-HOU 9*7	
0601	SF-MON 2*1	LA-NY 4*3	SD-PHI 7-9	PIT-ATL 2-14	CIN-CHI 3-6	STL-HOU 3*2	
0602	MON-PIT 7*3	CHI-NY 1-2	STL-PHI 3*2				
0603	MON-PIT 1-2	CHI-NY 5*0	STL-PHI 5*4	CIN-LA 5-13	ATL-SD 5-7	HOU-SF 8*4	
0604	MON-PIT 7*3	CHI-NY 5-6	STL-PHI 8*1	CIN-LA 5*2	ATL-SD 5-6	HOU-SF 2-8	
0605	MON-PIT 3*2	CHI-NY 3-11	STL-PHI 3-6	CIN-LA 4-5	ATL-SD 3*1	HOU-SF 3-9	
0606	PHI-MON 5*4	NY-STL 6*2		HOU-LA 10*4	CIN-SD 12*0		
0607	PHI-MON 10*5	NY-STL 1-4	CHI-PIT 8*5	HOU-LA 5*2	CIN-SD 2-6	ATL-SF 0-5	
0608	PHI-MON 4-5	NY-STL 2-5	CHI-PIT 1-5	HOU-LA 1-11	CIN-SD 7*1	ATL-SF 4-6	
0609			CHI-PIT 3-4	HOU-LA 2-4	CIN-SD 1-3	ATL-SF 4-6	
0610	ATL-HOU 10*3	NY-MON 2-5	PHI-PIT 12*10	CHI-STL 7*3	LA-SD 3-4	CIN-SF 6-9	
0611	ATL-HOU 4-5	NY-MON 4-6	PHI-PIT 2-8	CHI-STL 2*0	LA-SD 1-2	CIN-SF 7*2	
0612	ATL-HOU 0-5	NY-MON 3-4	PHI-PIT 5*4	CHI-STL 4*3	LA-SD 2-5	CIN-SF 10*6	
0613	ATL-HOU 5-6	PIT-CHI 8*0	STL-NY 1-2	MON-PHI 2-5	SF-SD 3-7		
0614	LA-ATL 5*4	PIT-CHI 6*3	STL-NY 0-5	MON-PHI 9*0	SF-SD 5-8	HOU-CIN 1-7	
				MON-PHI 2-4			
0615	LA-ATL 7*5	PIT-CHI 4-7	HOU-CIN 3-5	MON-PHI 2-6	STL-NY 4-6	SF-SD 4*2	
0616	LA-ATL 2-9		HOU-CIN 7*4				
0617	HOU-ATL 3-4	MON-CHI 3-7	SF-CIN 0-6	PHI-NY 3*1	STL-PIT 7*3	SD-LA 7*4	
	HOU-ATL 5-6					SD-LA 4*3	
0618	HOU-ATL 14*7	MON-CHI 0-3	SF-CIN 2-3	PHI-NY 2-3	STL-PIT 6*3	SD-LA 0-3	
0619	HOU-ATL 6*4	MON-CHI 3-9	SF-CIN 5*3	PHI-NY 0-6	STL-PIT 2-3	SD-LA 2-12	
						SD-LA 4-5	
0620	CIN-HOU 2*1	STL-MON 2-3	PIT-NY 8*5	CHI-PHI 7*2	SD-SF 2*1	ATL-LA 3-7	
0621	CIN-HOU 1-3	STL-MON 0-7	PIT-NY 0-9	CHI-PHI 1-6	SD-SF 8*3	ATL-LA 1-2	
0622	CIN-HOU 1-5	STL-MON 2-6	PIT-NY 0-3	CHI-PHI 3-5	SD-SF 7-8	ATL-LA 4*1	
0623	NY-CHI 1-4	PIT-MON 6*4	PHI-STL 0-2				
0624	NY-CHI 8*3	PIT-MON 5*1	PHI-STL 7*6	SD-ATL 3-4	LA-CIN 5*3	SF-HOU 11*0	
0625	NY-CHI 2-5	PIT-MON 5*1	PHI-STL 1-4	SD-ATL 4-8	LA-CIN 6*4	SF-HOU 4*1	
0626	NY-CHI 3-6	PIT-MON 3*0	PHI-STL 7*5	SD-ATL 2*1	LA-CIN 9*6	SF-HOU 0-6	
0627	PHI-CHI 1-2	NY-PIT 6*3	MON-STL 6*3	SF-ATL 10*9	SD-CIN 9*2	LA-HOU 4*0	
0628	PHI-CHI 4-6	NY-PIT 5*2	MON-STL 4-5	SF-ATL 13*7	SD-CIN 3-4	LA-HOU 3-4	
0629	PHI-CHI 4*2	NY-PIT 8*7	MON-STL 3*2	SF-ATL 7*2	SD-CIN 3*2	LA-HOU 2*0	
0630	ATL-MON 0-6	HOU-NY 6-12			SD-CIN 3-4		
0701	ATL-MON 3-9	HOU-NY 2-3	CHI-LA 9*2	CIN-PHI 5*3	STL-SD 1-5	PIT-SF 5*2	
		HOU-NY 6*5					
0702	CHI-LA 1-8	HOU-NY 2-7	ATL-MON 5*4	CIN-PHI 3-5	STL-SD 5-7	PIT-SF 1-2	
0703	CHI-LA 2*1	HOU-NY 0-5	ATL-MON 2-9	CIN-PHI 3*2	STL-SD 5*4	PIT-SF 0-4	
0704	STL-LA 3-5	CIN-NY 5*1	PHI-LA 0-7	MON-HOU 7*4	PIT-SD 3*2	CHI-SF 3*2	
0705	STL-LA 3-6	CIN-NY 3*1	PHI-ATL 5-10	MON-HOU 4*3	PIT-SD 3*2	CHI-SF 0-9	
0706	STL-LA 3-7	CIN-NY 4-5	PHI-ATL 2-3	MON-HOU 4*2		CHI-SF 0-2	
0707	PHI-CIN 2-5	PIT-SD 2*0					
0708	PHI-CIN 1*0	CHI-SD 2-4	MON-ATL 7*1	NY-HOU 2-4	PIT-LA 4*3	STL-SF 0-1	
0709	PHI-CIN 3-6	CHI-SD 2*1	MON-ATL 9*4	NY-HOU 3-6	PIT-LA 8*2	STL-SF 2-21	
0710	PHI-CIN 4-5	CHI-SD 4*2	MON-ATL 4*2	NY-HOU 5-6	PIT-LA 7*2	STL-SF 1-2	
0714	CIN-MON 0-1	HOU-PHI 7*5	NY-ATL 9*8	SF-PIT 2-9	SD-STL 3*1	LA-CHI 1*0	
						LA-CHI 6*3	
0715	NY-ATL 3-4	CIN-MON 6*3	HOU-PHI 5*2	SF-PIT 5-8	SD-STL 7*3	LA-CHI 3*2	
0716	NY-ATL 3*2	CIN-MON 1-6	HOU-PHI 6-10	SF-PIT 1-10	SD-STL 2-3	LA-CHI 22	
0717	NY-ATL 4*2	CIN-MON 3*1	HOU-PHI 4-10	SF-PIT 4-5	SD-STL 3*1	LA-CHI 4*1	
						LA-CHI 5*2	
0718	NY-CIN 1-2	HOU-MON 6*1	LA-STL 1*0	ATL-PHI 9*8		SF-CHI 3-8	
				ATL-PHI 1-4			
0719	SF-CHI 3*1	NY-CIN 2-11	HOU-MON 4*3	ATL-PHI 4-6	LA-STL 2-3	SD-PIT 6*2	
						SD-PIT 5-9	
0720	SF-CHI 12*2	HOU-MON 3*2	ATL-PHI 3-4	LA-STL 7-8		SD-PIT 2-3	
0721	SD-CHI 3*1	MON-CIN 3*2	PHI-HOU 0-2	SF-STL 4-6		LA-PIT 2-3	
0722	SD-CHI 4-5	MON-CIN 1-4	PHI-HOU 3-5	SF-STL 2-4	ATL-NY 1-6	LA-PIT 4*2	
					ATL-NY 1-5		
0723	SD-CHI 2-3	MON-CIN 1*0	PHI-HOU 6-7	LA-PIT 6*2	ATL-NY 6*1	SF-STL 6*5	
0724	SD-CHI 2*1	MON-CIN 5*3	PHI-HOU 6*4	LA-PIT 2*1	ATL-NY 4*2	SF-STL 5*0	
0725	NY-PHI 2-3	LA-SF 1-3				PIT-STL 1-5	
0726	NY-PHI 7*5	LA-SF 7*3	CHI-MON 4-8	HOU-SD 1-5	CIN-ATL 3*2	PIT-STL 2*1	
		LA-SF 6*5			CIN-ATL 1-2		
0727	CHI-MON 4-5	LA-SF 1-2	NY-PHI 10*2	HOU-SD 4*1	CIN-ATL 3*2	PIT-STL 3*2	
0728	STL-MON 3-4		CHI-PHI 7*0	HOU-SD 3*2	CIN-ATL 5*2		
0729	STL-MON 7*5	HOU-LA 3*1	CHI-PHI 8*3	CIN-SD 3-5	PIT-NY 0-1	ATL-SF 3-5	
0730	STL-MON 1-2	HOU-LA 14*6	CHI-PHI 2-3	CIN-SD 2*0	PIT-NY 0-3	ATL-SF 1-2	
0731	STL-MON 0-2	HOU-LA 1-6	CHI-PHI 3-6	CIN-SD 5-8	PIT-NY 1-2	ATL-SF 2-4	
						ATL-SF 2-3	
						HOU-SF 1-4	
0801	CIN-LA 4*3	PIT-NY 7*2	ATL-SD 3-6			HOU-SF 13*10	
0802	CIN-LA 0-2	CHI-NY 5*0	ATL-SD 1-4	MON-PIT 2-3	PHI-STL 2*0	HOU-SF 3*2	
0803	CIN-LA 7*4	CHI-NY 3*1	ATL-SD 4*2	MON-PIT 6*4	PHI-STL 2-4		
0804		CHI-NY 4*3		MON-PIT 3*2	PHI-STL 2-9		
0805	SF-ATL 5-8	PHI-CHI 9*3	SD-CIN 7-10	NY-PIT 3*2	MON-STL 3*1	LA-HOU 4-6	
0806	SF-ATL 2-7	PHI-CHI 4-7	SD-CIN 4*1	NY-PIT 5*3	MON-STL 5*4	LA-HOU 5*3	
0807	SF-ATL 14*4	PHI-CHI 7*4	SD-CIN 6*2	NY-PIT 6*2	MON-STL 11*5	LA-HOU 2-4	
0808	SF-ATL 5*2			NY-PIT 0-1	MON-STL 2-4	LA-HOU 0-10	
0809	SD-ATL 5*1	NY-CHI 4-6	LA-CIN 0-6	PIT-MON 10*8	STL-PHI 7*3	SF-HOU 2-3	

♦1988♦	GAME 1		GAME 2		GAME 3		GAME 4		GAME 5		GAME 6		GAME 7
0810	SD-ATL	5*4	NY-CHI	5-6	LA-CIN	8*5	PIT-MON	4-5	STL-PHI	1*0	SF-HOU	5*0	
0811	SD-ATL	1-2	NY-CHI	9*6	LA-CIN	8-9	PIT-MON	6*1	STL-PHI	0-1	SF-HOU	6*0	
0812	SF-LA	3-7	STL-CHI	4*0	ATL-CIN	9*4	MON-NY	5*2	PIT-PHI	1-9	SD-HOU	4*3	
									PIT-PHI	4-6			
0813	STL-CHI	1-5	ATL-CIN	1-3	SD-HOU	0-1	SF-LA	1-2	PIT-PHI	10*4	MON-NY	7*4	
0814	STL-CHI	3-8	ATL-CIN	0-2	SD-HOU	6*1	SF-LA	15*4	PIT-PHI	9*8	MON-NY	3-4	
											MON-NY	2-4	
0815	SD-HOU	3-7	SF-LA	0-1	ATL-PIT	4*3							
0816	CHI-CIN	4-6	PHI-LA	5-7	ATL-PIT	2-4	MON-SD	2-6	NY-SF	13*6	HOU-STL	0-3	
0817	CHI-CIN	5*0	PHI-LA	2-7	ATL-PIT	1-2	MON-SD	2-4	NY-SF	0-4	HOU-STL	1*0	
0818	CHI-CIN	1-9	PHI-LA	0-4			MON-SD	4-5	NY-SF	1-4	HOU-STL	1-2	
0819	ATL-CHI	7-8	MON-LA	0-2	HOU-PIT	5*1	NY-SD	2-3	PHI-SF	2-6	CIN-STL	4-10	
0820	ATL-CHI	4-5	MON-LA	3-4	HOU-PIT	1-2			PHI-SF	3-4	CIN-STL	6*2	
0821	ATL-CHI	1*0	MON-LA	0-4	HOU-PIT	2*1	NY-SD	0-1	PHI-SF	3-6	CIN-STL	1-7	
0822	HOU-CHI	9*7	NY-LA	7*1	CIN-PIT	2*0	PHI-SD	6*5	MON-SF	2-3	ATL-STL	5*3	
0823	HOU-CHI	3-9	NY-LA	5*1	CIN-PIT	0*2	PHI-SD	1-9	MON-SF	2*1	ATL-STL	0-7	
0824	HOU-CHI	2-3	NY-LA	2*1	CIN-PIT	6*2	PHI-SD	2-5	MON-SF	7*5	ATL-STL	3-5	
0825	CHI-ATL	6*1	STL-CIN	1-4									
0826	CHI-ATL	0-4	STL-CIN	4*2	PIT-HOU	0-2	SD-MON	4*3	SF-NY	0-3	LA-PHI	7*2	
0827	CHI-ATL	5*0	STL-CIN	2-3	PIT-HOU	1-3	SD-MON	0-4	SF-NY	1-2	LA-PHI	4*2	
0828	CHI-ATL	2-4	STL-CIN	5*3	PIT-HOU	4*3	SD-MON	5*3	SF-NY	7*4	LA-PHI	5*0	
0829	STL-ATL	3*2	PIT-CIN	8*1	CHI-HOU	2*1	LA-MON	2*1	SD-NY	0-6	SF-PHI	0-3	
0830	STL-ATL	9*1	PIT-CIN	4-6	CHI-HOU	4-7	LA-MON	4*2	SD-NY	0-1	SF-PHI	5-7	
0831	STL-ATL	6*4	PIT-CIN	1-4	CHI-HOU	3*1	LA-MON	3-4	SD-NY	6*3	SF-PHI	3*2	
0902	PIT-ATL	1-2	CIN-CHI	6*5	STL-HOU	2*0	SF-MON	0-10	LA-NY	0-8	SD-PHI	7*4	
0903			CIN-CHI	6*4	STL-HOU	1-10	SF-MON	4-6	LA-NY	1-2	SD-PHI	5*2	
0904			CIN-CHI	17*0	STL-HOU	3-4	SF-MON	2-3					
0905	LA-ATL	3*0	PHI-CHI	3-14	CIN-HOU	0-3	NY-PIT	7*5	SD-SF	7*4	MON-STL	2-6	
			PHI-CHI	4*3									
0906	LA-ATL	1-2	PHI-CHI	3*2	CIN-HOU	10*3	NY-PIT	2-3	SD-SF	4*3	MON-STL	0-1	
0907	HOU-LA	1-4	NY-CHI	8-9	CIN-SD	0-1	MON-PIT	4-5	ATL-SF	4*1	PHI-STL	0-5	
0908	HOU-LA	2*1	NY-CHI	13*6	CIN-SD	2*1	MON-PIT	5*4	ATL-SF	2-3	PHI-STL	0-1	
0909	CIN-LA	5*2	NY-MON	7*3	ATL-SD	5*4	PHI-PIT	2-5	HOU-SF	4*3	CHI-STL	2-6	
0910	CIN-LA	0-5	NY-MON	6*0	ATL-SD	2-6	PHI-PIT	1-5	HOU-SF	2-3	CHI-STL	3-9	
0911	CIN-LA	3-5	NY-MON	3*0	ATL-SD	2-8	PHI-PIT	7*4	HOU-SF	4*1	CHI-STL	2-3	
0912	ATL-LA	4-5	STL-MON	2-14	SF-SD	4*2	PIT-NY	2-3	CHI-PHI	1-5			
0913	ATL-LA	0-2	STL-MON	1-7	SF-SD	4*1	PIT-NY	1*0	CHI-PHI	9*2	HOU-CIN	2-5	
0914	ATL-LA	0-1	PIT-MON	4*1	SF-SD	6*5	CHI-NY	1-3	STL-PHI	2-9	HOU-CIN	7*1	
0915			PIT-MON	4-9			CHI-NY	1-4	STL-PHI	3*1	HOU-CIN	5-7	
0916	STL-CHI	3*0	SF-HOU	5*4			MON-NY	3-4	PIT-PHI	7*5	LA-CIN	0-1	
0917	STL-CHI	4-6	SF-HOU	4*2	SD-ATL	9*4	MON-NY	2-6	PIT-PHI	7*2	LA-CIN	4*3	
					SD-ATL	3-6							
0918	STL-CHI	5*4	LA-CIN	2*0	SD-ATL	5-6	SF-HOU	10*3	MON-NY	3-5	PIT-PHI	5-6	
0919	PIT-STL	5*4	SD-CIN	2-7	SF-ATL	3-4	LA-HOU	1*0					
0920	PIT-STL	5*1	SD-CIN	2-7	SF-ATL	7*4	LA-HOU	6*0	PHI-NY	4-6	MON-CHI	4-5	
											MON-CHI	9*1	
0921	SF-CIN	1-5	ATL-HOU	0-1	PHI-NY	3-4	PIT-STL	5*0	SD-LA	9*3	MON-CHI	8*5	
									SD-LA	5-6			
0922	SF-CIN	1-3	ATL-HOU	2-3	PHI-NY	1-3			SD-LA	5*4			
0923	CIN-ATL	5*4	MON-PHI	3*2	CHI-PIT	5*3	HOU-SD	3-4	LA-SF	3*0	NY-STL	1-2	
0924	CIN-ATL	2*1	MON-PHI	1*0	CHI-PIT	2*1	HOU-SD	0-3	LA-SF	7*3	NY-STL	14*1	
0925	CIN-ATL	2*1	MON-PHI	5-8	CHI-PIT	4-7	HOU-SD	1-9	LA-SF	0-2	NY-STL	9*7	
0926	CHI-MON	2-3	NY-PHI	10*4	STL-PIT	7*1	LA-SD	3*2	CIN-SF	5*2			
0927	CHI-MON	5*3	NY-PHI	4-5	STL-PIT	2-3	LA-SD	4-8	CIN-SF	3-6	HOU-ATL	3*2	
0928	CHI-MON	3*1	NY-PHI	3-9	STL-PIT	2*1	LA-SD	1-2	CIN-SF	1-6	HOU-ATL	3-4	
											HOU-ATL	5*4	
0929	CHI-MON	4-5											
0930	PHI-MON	2*1	PIT-CHI	10*9	ATL-CIN	7-8	SD-HOU	5*1	SF-LA	4-6	STL-NY	2-4	
1001	PHI-MON	5*4	PIT-CHI	7-9	ATL-CIN	4*2	SD-HOU	6*3	SF-LA	1-2	STL-NY	3-6	
1002	PHI-MON	1-3	PIT-CHI	4-8	ATL-CIN	0-1	SD-HOU	5*1	SF-LA	1*0	STL-NY	5-7	

♦1989♦	GAME 1		GAME 2		GAME 3		GAME 4		GAME 5		GAME 6		GAME 7
0403	SF-SD	5*3			LA-CIN	4-6					STL-NY	4-8	
0404	SF-SD	8*3	PHI-CHI	4-5	ATL-HOU	3-10	PIT-MON	5-6					
0405	SF-SD	3-4	PHI-CHI	12*4	ATL-HOU	8*4	PIT-MON	3*0	LA-CIN	3-4	STL-NY	3*1	
0406			PHI-CHI	8*3	ATL-HOU	3*2	PIT-MON	2-3	LA-CIN	4*1			
0407	LA-ATL	1-6	PIT-CHI	5-6	SD-HOU	5*3	NY-MON	3-7	SF-CIN	3-4			
0408	STL-PHI	4-5	PIT-CHI	3-5	SD-HOU	2-6	NY-MON	2-3					
0409	STL-PHI	15*3	PIT-CHI	3-8	SD-HOU	5*0	NY-MON	2*1	LA-ATL	4*2	SF-CIN	9*1	
0410	MON-PHI	6-7	ATL-SD	2-5	CIN-HOU	8*3	LA-SF	7*4					
0411	MON-PHI	2-6	ATL-SD	2-3	CIN-HOU	3-5	LA-SF	3-8	STL-CHI	4-5	NY-PIT	3-4	
0412	MON-PHI	3-6	ATL-SD	5*0	CIN-HOU	3*1	LA-SF	1-3	STL-CHI	2-3			
0413	HOU-LA	4*2	ATL-SD	4*1	NY-PIT	2-4							
0414	HOU-LA	3*2	CIN-SD	5-6	MON-PIT	7*6	CHI-PHI	6*4	ATL-SF	5-7	NY-STL	9*4	
0415	HOU-LA	1-3	CIN-SD	6*3	MON-PIT	4-6			ATL-SF	0-1	NY-STL	2-3	
0416	HOU-LA	1-2	CIN-SD	5*0	MON-PIT	5*4	CHI-PHI	5*3	ATL-SF	7*2	NY-STL	3-5	
									ATL-SF	1-6			
0417	CIN-LA	3*2	CHI-MON	1-2	PHI-NY	2-5	PIT-STL	2-4	SD-SF	0-9			
0418	CIN-LA	0-6	CHI-MON	2-11	PHI-NY	7*1	PIT-STL	4*3	SD-SF	4*2	HOU-ATL	4-5	
0419	CIN-LA	0-3	CHI-MON	5*0	PHI-NY	2-4	PIT-STL	7*5	SD-SF	4*3	HOU-ATL	3-4	
0420	PHI-PIT	9*4			CHI-NY	3-4	MON-STL	2-5			HOU-ATL	4*3	
0421	PHI-PIT	3*2	HOU-CIN	7*0	CHI-NY	8*4	MON-STL	0-1	SF-LA	2-8	SD-ATL	5*3	
0422	PHI-PIT	3-4	HOU-CIN	4-5	CHI-NY	1-3	MON-STL	2-5	SF-LA	5*4	SD-ATL	1-5	
0423	PHI-PIT	4-6	HOU-CIN	5*2	CHI-NY	2-4	MON-STL	9*3	SF-LA	6-7	SD-ATL	4-9	
											SD-ATL	5*2	
0424	PHI-HOU	8*4											
0425	PHI-HOU	1-4	LA-CHI	4*0	MON-CIN	1-6	ATL-NY	1-2	SD-PIT	1*0	SF-STL	4*0	
0426	PHI-HOU	5-6	LA-CHI	3*1	MON-CIN	5-6	ATL-NY	1-6	SD-PIT	3*1	SF-STL	1-3	
0427			LA-CHI	0-1					SD-PIT	8*1	SF-STL	1-10	
0428	NY-HOU	7*3	SD-CHI	1-3	ATL-MON	4-10	CIN-PHI	3*0	SF-PIT	0-1	LA-STL	3-6	
0429	NY-HOU	5*1	SD-CHI	5*4	ATL-MON	7-9	CIN-PHI	0-8	SF-PIT	4*3	LA-STL	0-1	
0430	NY-HOU	6-7	SD-CHI	3-7	ATL-MON	6-9	CIN-PHI	5*3	SF-PIT	1-11	LA-STL	3-4	
0501	NY-ATL	3*1	PIT-LA	0-1	CIN-SD	19*6	STL-SD	6*0	CHI-SF	4*3			
0502	NY-ATL	7*1	PIT-LA	0-7	CIN-MON	4-6	STL-SD	1-7	CHI-SF	0-4	HOU-PHI	12*4	
0503	PHI-ATL	3-6	STL-LA	3-4	HOU-MON	5-6	CHI-SD	5*4	PIT-SF	5*3	CIN-NY	6*4	
0504	PHI-ATL	0-3	STL-LA	12*0	HOU-MON	5*4	CHI-SD	4*0	PIT-SF	3-6	CIN-NY	2-3	
0505	MON-ATL	1-6	CHI-LA	4*2	PHI-CIN	7*0	PIT-SD	4*2	STL-SF	3*1			
0506	MON-ATL	3-13	CHI-LA	4-7	PHI-CIN	4*1	PIT-SD	2-4	STL-SF	0-9	HOU-NY	1-2	
0507	MON-ATL	1-7	CHI-LA	4*2	PHI-CIN	5*0	PIT-SD	1-3	STL-SF	1-5	HOU-NY	5*0	
0508	MON-HOU	4*1			NY-CIN	0-3							
0509	MON-HOU	4*2	SF-CHI	4*2	NY-CIN	3*1	ATL-PHI	7*2	SD-STL	3-4			
0510	MON-HOU	10*1	SF-CHI	4*3	NY-CIN	11*4			SD-STL	1-3			
0511	ATL-PHI	8*3							SD-STL	5-6			
0512	LA-PHI	0-3	HOU-CHI	3*1	SF-MON	2*1	SD-NY	4*3	CIN-STL	5*0	ATL-PIT	2-10	
0513	LA-PHI	0-2	HOU-CHI	1*0	SF-MON	4-5	SD-NY	3-4	CIN-STL	3*2	ATL-PIT	3-8	
0514	LA-PHI	9*0	HOU-CHI	5*1	SF-MON	3-4	SD-NY	1-2	CIN-STL	5*2	ATL-PIT	5*2	
0515	SF-PHI	2-3	ATL-CHI	0-4	SD-MON	6*5	LA-NY	3*1	PIT-CIN	5-6			
0516	SF-PHI	13*5	ATL-CHI	3-4	SD-MON	5*2	STL-HOU	7-8	PIT-CIN	5*0			
0517	SF-PHI	6*0	ATL-CHI	0-4	SD-MON	6*5	STL-HOU	2-3	PIT-CIN	4-5	LA-NY	4*3	

♦1989♦	GAME 1	GAME 2	GAME 3	GAME 4	GAME 5	GAME 6	GAME 7
0518				STL-HOU 4*3		LA-NY 3-5	
0519	STL-ATL 2-3	CHI-CIN 8*2	LA-MON 8*0	PIT-HOU 0-3	SD-PHI 8*2	SF-NY 2-3	
0520	STL-ATL 1*0	CHI-CIN 7*3	LA-MON 3*2	PIT-HOU 4-5	SD-PHI 3*2	SF-NY 3*0	
0521	STL-ATL 6*1	CHI-CIN 2-7	LA-MON 1-3	PIT-HOU 17*5	SD-PHI 1-3	SF-NY 10*6	
0522				CHI-HOU 5*3			
0523	PIT-ATL 5*2	STL-CIN 4-6	PHI-LA 4*1	CHI-HOU 5*4	NY-SD 2-3	MON-SF 2-4	
0524	PIT-ATL 4*1	STL-CIN 1-5	PHI-LA 2-4	CHI-HOU 3*1	NY-SD 3*0	MON-SF 1*0	
0525	PIT-ATL 7*3		PHI-LA 6-7		NY-SD 1-2	MON-SF 2*0	
0526	CIN-CHI 10*8	HOU-PIT 4*2	NY-LA 8*2	ATL-STL 0-3	MON-SD 5*0	PHI-SF 1-6	
0527	CIN-CHI 3-5	HOU-PIT 5*4	NY-LA 1-2	ATL-STL 4*1	MON-SD 0-5	PHI-SF 2-6	
0528	CIN-CHI 1-6	HOU-PIT 9*2	NY-LA 3-4	ATL-STL 33	MON-SD 10*2	PHI-SF 5-8	
0529	CHI-ATL 1-2	CIN-PIT 3-12	MON-LA 3*2	HOU-STL 3*2	PHI-SD 0-1	NY-SF 2-3	
0530	CHI-ATL 3*2	CIN-PIT 0-2	MON-LA 5*4	HOU-STL 8*4	PHI-SD 3-9	NY-SF 3-10	
0531	CHI-ATL 2-3	CIN-PIT 4*3	MON-LA 4-9	HOU-STL 4*3	PHI-SD 1-2	NY-SF 3*1	
0601	LA-HOU 2-7						
0602	LA-HOU 0-1	SF-ATL 7*6	SD-CIN 4-9	PIT-NY 2-3	MON-PHI 2*1	CHI-STL 5*2	
0603	LA-HOU 4-5	SF-ATL 4*0	SD-CIN 2-6	PIT-NY 3-9	MON-PHI 7*5	CHI-STL 5-6	
0604	LA-HOU 6-7	SF-ATL 3-6	SD-CIN 3-5	PIT-NY 3-4	MON-PHI 7*4	CHI-STL 11*3	
0605	SD-HOU 10*2	LA-ATL 7*0	SF-CIN 11*8	NY-CHI 3-15	PIT-PHI 33	STL-MON 5*4	
		LA-ATL 5*2				SF-CIN 3-4	
0606	NY-CHI 4-8	LA-ATL 0-3	SD-HOU 7-8	STL-MON 2-3	PIT-PHI 4-9	SF-CIN 3*2	
0607	LA-ATL 5*4	NY-CHI 10*5	SD-HOU 2-3	STL-MON 5*2	PIT-PHI 5-7	SF-CIN 5-12	
0608		NY-CHI 4-5	SD-HOU 0-1	STL-MON 7*2	PIT-PHI 11-15	SF-CIN 2-3	
0609	CIN-LA 4*0	STL-CHI 1*0	ATL-HOU 5-6	PHI-MON 0-5	NY-PIT 3-4	SD-SF 2-12	
0610	CIN-LA 5*0	STL-CHI 6*0	ATL-HOU 0-1	PHI-MON 1-9	NY-PIT 5-6	SD-SF 0-1	
0611	CIN-LA 1-3	STL-CHI 10*7	ATL-HOU 6-10	PHI-MON 2-7	NY-PIT 6*1	SD-SF 1-3	
0612	CIN-LA 2-9	STL-CHI 3-10					
0613	HOU-LA 2-3	CHI-NY 4*2	PHI-PIT 10*2	CIN-SD 9*6	ATL-SF 2-3	MON-STL 2*0	
0614	HOU-LA 0-3	CHI-NY 0-2	PHI-PIT 4-6	CIN-SD 2-4	ATL-SF 1-10	MON-STL 0-10	
0615	HOU-LA 1-2	CHI-NY 3-4	PHI-PIT 6-7	CIN-SD 0-1	ATL-SF 2*1	MON-STL 3-4	
0616	ATL-LA 6*1	CHI-MON 5-8	NY-PHI 15*11	HOU-SD 3*1	CIN-SF 5*4	PIT-STL 2-6	
0617	ATL-LA 2*1	CHI-MON 3*2	NY-PHI 1*0	HOU-SD 1-2	CIN-SF 1-8	PIT-STL 7*2	
0618	ATL-LA 3-5	CHI-MON 5*4	NY-PHI 5-6	HOU-SD 5*2	CIN-SF 1-2	PIT-STL 12*4	
0619	MON-NY 3-5			LA-SD 1-5	HOU-SF 2-3		
0620	MON-NY 8*5	CHI-PIT 5*4	STL-PHI 6*4	LA-SD 0-2	HOU-SF 0-4		
			STL-PHI 5*3				
0621	MON-NY 0-2	CHI-PIT 1*0	LA-SD 6*2	HOU-SF 0-2	CIN-ATL 3-4		
					CIN-ATL 0-1		
0622	STL-PHI 2-11	CHI-PIT 8*0			CIN-ATL 6*1		
0623	MON-CHI 5*1	STL-PIT 3*2	LA-CIN 1-3	PHI-NY 3-9	HOU-ATL 5*2	SF-SD 8*7	
0624	MON-CHI 5*0	STL-PIT 2-5	LA-CIN 10*3	PHI-NY 2-4	HOU-ATL 4-5	SF-SD 3*1	
0625	MON-CHI 5*0	STL-PIT 3-5	LA-CIN 7*0	PHI-NY 1-5	HOU-ATL 12*6	SF-SD 7-10	
0626	PIT-CHI 2*1	SF-HOU 4*3	LA-CIN 3-5	NY-MON 1-5	PHI-STL 5*4		
0627	PIT-CHI 5*4	SF-HOU 5-7	ATL-CIN 3-9	NY-MON 2-3	PHI-STL 4*2	SD-LA 5*3	
0628	PIT-CHI 3*1	SF-HOU 3-7	ATL-CIN 4*3	NY-MON 3-4	PHI-STL 1-2	SD-LA 2*1	
0629	CHI-SF 2-12		ATL-CIN 2*1	HOU-MON 8*3		SD-LA 5*3	
0630	CHI-SF 6*4	SD-STL 3-4	NY-CIN 11*1	HOU-MON 1-6	ATL-PHI 2-4	PIT-LA 4*3	
					ATL-PHI 3*1		
0701	NY-CIN 2-6	PIT-LA 0-1	HOU-MON 4*1	CHI-SF 3*2	ATL-PHI 2-4	SD-STL 3-9	
0702	NY-CIN 7*2	PIT-LA 2-3	HOU-MON 2-13	CHI-SF 3-4	ATL-PHI 3*1	SD-STL 5*2	
0703	MON-ATL 3*0	PIT-LA 4*2	NY-HOU 3*1		CIN-PHI 1-2		
0704	MON-ATL 3-9	SD-CHI 1-5	NY-HOU 3-10	SF-PIT 3-5	CIN-PHI 2*1	LA-STL 1-2	
0705	MON-ATL 7*5	SD-CHI 3-5	NY-HOU 5-6	SF-PIT 6*4	CIN-PHI 2-3	LA-STL 2-3	
0706	PHI-ATL 4*0	SD-CHI 3-7	CIN-NY 10*2	SF-PIT 2*1		LA-STL 2-14	
0707	PHI-ATL 3-5	LA-CHI 4-6	CIN-NY 1-7	SD-PIT 0-3	MON-HOU 11*8	SF-STL 4-6	
0708	PHI-ATL 3-4	LA-CHI 8*2	CIN-NY 3-8	SD-PIT 2*0	MON-HOU 2-3	SF-STL 8*5	
0709	PHI-ATL 4*3	LA-CHI 4-11	CIN-NY 3-6	SD-PIT 5*3	MON-HOU 6*1	SF-STL 4-6	
0713	NY-ATL 5*1	MON-CIN 6*3	STL-LA 2-3	CHI-SD 7*3	PIT-SF 2-3	HOU-PHI 4-11	
						HOU-PHI 3*0	
0714	NY-ATL 2-3	MON-CIN 1*0	STL-LA 7*2	CHI-SD 4-7	PIT-SF 7*4	HOU-PHI 2-4	
0715	NY-ATL 6*4	MON-CIN 3-5	STL-LA 2*0	CHI-SD 2-3	PIT-SF 3-8	HOU-PHI 9*6	
0716	NY-ATL 2-6	MON-CIN 6*3	STL-LA 2-3	CHI-SD 3-4	PIT-SF 1-3		
0717	ATL-MON 2-5	PHI-CIN 4*1	CHI-LA 6*3	PIT-SD 4*1	STL-SF 4-8	HOU-NY 6*0	
						HOU-NY 12*3	
0718	PHI-CIN 6*5	CHI-LA 1-4	ATL-MON 7*6	PIT-SD 4-17	STL-SF 3-7	HOU-NY 0-9	
0719	PHI-CIN 9*4	CHI-LA 4*0	ATL-MON 3*2	PIT-SD 1-9	STL-SF 5-7	HOU-NY 2-8	
0720	SF-CHI 3-4		CIN-MON 1-4	STL-SD 7*1	LA-PIT 1-4	ATL-NY 1-4	
					LA-PIT 7*3		
0721	SF-CHI 4*3	PHI-HOU 2-4	CIN-MON 1-3	STL-SD 5*0		ATL-NY 4-6	
0722	SF-CHI 2-5	CIN-MON 5-6	ATL-NY 5-7	STL-SD 5*2	LA-PIT 8*4	PHI-HOU 0-1	
						PHI-HOU 3-4	
0723	SF-CHI 5-9	CIN-MON 4-12	ATL-NY 2-7	STL-SD 3*2	LA-PIT 4*3	PHI-HOU 2-3	
					LA-PIT 1-2		
0724	SF-ATL 2*0	PHI-MON 3-4	CHI-STL 3*2		LA-PIT 4-7		
0725	SF-ATL 5*4	PHI-MON 0-2	CHI-STL 4*2	SD-CIN 6*2	LA-HOU 6*0	PIT-NY 4*2	
0726	SF-ATL 4-5	PHI-MON 4*3	CHI-STL 0-2	SD-CIN 5*3	LA-HOU 2-6	PIT-NY 3*2	
0727	SF-ATL 1-10			SD-CIN 1-6	LA-HOU 7*0	PIT-NY 10*8	
0728	CIN-ATL 4*2	NY-CHI 5-6	STL-MON 2*0	LA-SD 1-2	SF-HOU 3*2	PIT-PHI 10*5	
						PIT-PHI 1-6	
0729	CIN-ATL 4*1	NY-CHI 3-10	SF-HOU 1-8	STL-MON 0-2	LA-SD 4-9	PIT-PHI 2-6	
0730	CIN-ATL 2-5	NY-CHI 4-6	SF-HOU 2-6	STL-MON 8*3	LA-SD 10*1	PIT-PHI 6-8	
0731	MON-PIT 4*2	NY-CHI 2-3				CHI-PHI 10*2	
						CHI-PHI 4-7	
0801	SD-ATL 5*2	HOU-CIN 5*0	SF-LA 5*2	MON-PIT 5*4	NY-STL 11*0	CHI-PHI 4*1	
0802	SD-ATL 9*7	HOU-CIN 2-5	SF-LA 4-7	MON-PIT 3*1	NY-STL 4*3	CHI-PHI 0-6	
0803	SD-ATL 6*5	HOU-CIN 2-18	SF-LA 3-6	MON-PIT 0-1	NY-STL 5-6	CHI-PHI 2*0	
0804	MON-NY 5-11	ATL-CIN 4-5	SD-LA 3-6	CHI-PIT 3*2	PHI-STL 3-2	HOU-SF 2-4	
0805	MON-NY 2-3	ATL-CIN 7*1	SD-LA 4*2	CHI-PIT 4*2	PHI-STL 7*3	HOU-SF 0-7	
0806	MON-NY 1-2	ATL-CIN 2-3	SD-LA 2-3	CHI-PIT 4-5	PHI-STL 4-5	HOU-SF 3*2	
0807	MON-CHI 2-5	NY-PHI 1-2	ATL-LA 1*0	STL-PIT 4*0	HOU-SD 2-5	CIN-SF 10*2	
0808	MON-CHI 2-4	NY-PHI 9*0	ATL-LA 2-10	STL-PIT 3-7	HOU-SD 12*3	CIN-SF 10*4	
0809	MON-CHI 0-3	NY-PHI 6*0	ATL-LA 6*3	STL-PIT 5*2	HOU-SD 1-2	CIN-SF 1-10	
0810	PHI-CHI 16*13	STL-NY 1-5			HOU-SD 3-13	CIN-SF 3-4	
		STL-NY 4-6					
0811	PHI-CHI 2-9	STL-NY 3*0	CIN-HOU 6*1	PIT-MON 1-4	LA-SF 2-10	ATL-SD 6*5	
						ATL-SD 0-2	
0812	PHI-CHI 7-9	CIN-HOU 5-6	PIT-MON 2-5	STL-NY 1-3	LA-SF 5*1	ATL-SD 5*4	
0813	PHI-CHI 5*3	CIN-HOU 5*0	PIT-MON 6*4	STL-NY 2-3	LA-SF 3*2		
0814	ATL-STL 4-7		PIT-MON 6*1				
	ATL-STL 2-5						
0815	ATL-STL 1-9	CHI-CIN 5*2	PIT-HOU 2-3	SF-MON 3*2	SD-NY 2-3	LA-PHI 6-7	
0816	ATL-STL 2-3	CHI-CIN 5*1	PIT-HOU 2-4	SF-MON 2-4	SD-NY 2-7	LA-PHI 2-6	
0817		CHI-CIN 3*2	PIT-HOU 3-5	SF-MON 10*5	SD-NY 6*2	LA-PHI 10*4	
0818	PIT-ATL 6-13	STL-CIN 2-6	CHI-HOU 5-6	SD-MON 2-5	LA-NY 2-3	SF-PHI 5*2	
		STL-CIN 3-8					
0819	PIT-ATL 3-4	STL-CIN 5*1	CHI-HOU 4-8	SD-MON 4-6	LA-NY 1-4	SF-PHI 0-1	

◆1989◆	GAME 1		GAME 2		GAME 3		GAME 4		GAME 5		GAME 6		GAME 7
0820	PIT-ATL	7*6	STL-CIN	8*1	CHI-HOU	4-8	SD-MON	5*2	LA-NY	5*4	SF-PHI	5*2	
0821	CIN-CHI	6*5					LA-MON	6*1	SF-NY	1-4	SD-PHI	8*2	
0822	CIN-CHI	7*2	STL-ATL	10*5	HOU-PIT	1-4	LA-MON	2-4	SF-NY	5*0	SD-PHI	2-4	
0823	CIN-CHI	8*5	STL-ATL	0-3	HOU-PIT	1-6	LA-MON	1*0	SF-NY	5*0	SD-PHI	7*3	
0824			STL-ATL	4*1	HOU-PIT	2-3							
0825	ATL-CHI	3-4	PIT-CIN	12*3	STL-HOU	7*4	PHI-LA	3*2	NY-SD	3-5	MON-SF	12*2	
0826	ATL-CHI	5*3	PIT-CIN	4-6	STL-HOU	5*3	PHI-LA	0-4	NY-SD	4-9	MON-SF	3-8	
0827	ATL-CHI	2-3	PIT-CIN	0-1	STL-HOU	3-6	PHI-LA	1-8	NY-SD	7-13	MON-SF	6*3	
0828	HOU-CHI	1-6	ATL-PIT	5*2	CIN-STL	2-3	NY-LA	1*0	MON-SD	4-9	PHI-SF	9*1	
0829	HOU-CHI	9-10	ATL-PIT	4-5	CIN-STL	2-4	NY-LA	2*1	MON-SD	1-2	PHI-SF	6*1	
0830	HOU-CHI	8*4	ATL-PIT	5-7	CIN-STL	2*0	NY-LA	9*3	MON-SD	5*1	PHI-SF	2-3	
0831									PHI-SD	1-5			
0901	CHI-ATL	1-5	MON-LA	0-2	CIN-PIT	11*5	NY-SF	1-7	HOU-STL	6*3			
0902	CHI-ATL	10*3	MON-LA	3-4	CIN-PIT	6*2	NY-SF	2-6	HOU-STL	5-13	PHI-SD	2-3	
0903	CHI-ATL	5-8	MON-LA	4*0	CIN-PIT	1-3	NY-SF	0-4	HOU-STL	3-4	PHI-SD	5-9	
0904	SD-ATL	10*9	SF-CIN	9*8	LA-HOU	7*5	CHI-NY	7*3	MON-STL	1-4	PIT-PHI	7*5	
0905	SD-ATL	7*5	SF-CIN	5-6	LA-HOU	2-3	CHI-NY	2-3	MON-STL	6*2	PIT-PHI	2-3	
0906	SF-ATL	7*2	LA-CIN	5-9	SD-HOU	3*2	STL-NY	3*2	PIT-MON	6-11	CHI-PHI	1-9	
0907	SF-ATL	7*5	LA-CIN	8*2	SD-HOU	1-2	STL-NY	1-13	PIT-MON	7*4	CHI-PHI	6*2	
0908	STL-CHI	11*8	ATL-CIN	1-5	SF-HOU	2-5	PIT-NY	2-7	PHI-MON	4*3	LA-SD	0-1	
0909	STL-CHI	2-3	ATL-CIN	2*1	SF-HOU	1-4	PIT-NY	8*5	PHI-MON	5-6	LA-SD	1-3	
0910	STL-CHI	1-4	ATL-CIN	4-5	SF-HOU	5*3	PIT-NY	4*1	PHI-MON	4*2	LA-SD	14*8	
0911	MON-CHI	3-4	CIN-LA	2-8	NY-PHI	5*2	ATL-SF	2-3	PIT-STL	3*1	HOU-SD	3-7	
0912	MON-CHI	0-2	CIN-LA	4-5	NY-PHI	1-2	ATL-SF	6*5	PIT-STL	5*2	HOU-SD	0-9	
0913	MON-CHI	1-3	HOU-LA	3*1	NY-PHI	10*4	CIN-SF	7-8	PIT-STL	00	ATL-SD	2-3	
0914			HOU-LA	11*3			CIN-SF	3-4	PIT-STL	4*3	ATL-SD	13*4	
0915	CIN-HOU	1-4	ATL-LA	0-5	NY-MON	5*0	SD-SF	5*3	CHI-PIT	7*2	STL-PHI	0-2	
											STL-PHI	7*6	
0916	CIN-HOU	1-3	ATL-LA	0-1	NY-MON	1-10	CHI-PIT	6-8					
0917	CIN-HOU	0-1	ATL-LA	3-4	NY-MON	0-1	CHI-PIT	0-2	STL-PHI	5-9	SD-SF	3-5	
									STL-PHI	2*0	SD-SF	6*1	
0918	NY-CHI	6-10	STL-MON	3*2	PHI-PIT	2-6							
0919	NY-CHI	5*2	STL-MON	5*0	PHI-PIT	2-4	HOU-ATL	0-3	SD-CIN	5*1	LA-SF	2-3	
0920	PHI-CHI	9*8	NY-STL	3-5	MON-PIT	1-9	HOU-ATL	7*6	SD-CIN	3*1	LA-SF	7-8	
0921	PHI-CHI	1-9	NY-STL	6*1	MON-PIT	6*5	HOU-ATL	0-3	SD-CIN	11*7	LA-SF	3-4	
0922	PIT-CHI	2-4	PHI-STL	1-2	SD-LA	1-2	CIN-ATL	8*3	MON-NY	2-3	HOU-SF	3*1	
0923	PIT-CHI	2-3	PHI-STL	5-11	SD-LA	7*1	CIN-ATL	11*5	MON-NY	6-13	HOU-SF	1-3	
0924	PIT-CHI	2-4	PHI-STL	1-2	SD-LA	1*0	CIN-ATL	2-6	MON-NY	6*5	HOU-SF	2-10	
0925	ATL-HOU	5*3	CHI-MON	3-4	SF-LA	2-5	STL-PIT	2-4	PHI-NY	2*1	CIN-SD	5*3	
0926	ATL-HOU	2-3	CHI-MON	3*2	SF-LA	1-2	STL-PIT	1-4	PHI-NY	0-3	CIN-SD	1-3	
0927	ATL-HOU	5*4	CHI-MON	7*2	SF-LA	0-1	STL-PIT	0-1	PHI-NY	5*3	CIN-SD	2*1	
0929	HOU-CIN	3-4	MON-PHI	0-2	CHI-STL	5-7	NY-PIT	6*2			SF-SD	7*2	
							NY-PIT	7*0					
0930	HOU-CIN	9*2	MON-PHI	3-6	SF-SD	5-11	NY-PIT	7*2	CHI-STL	6*4			
1001	HOU-CIN	2*0	MON-PHI	3-5	SF-SD	0-3	NY-PIT	7*3	CHI-STL	5*1	LA-ATL	3*1	

◆1990◆	GAME 1		GAME 2		GAME 3		GAME 4		GAME 5		GAME 6		GAME 7
0409	CIN-HOU	8*4	SD-LA	2-4	PIT-NY	12*3			MON-STL	5-6			
0410	CIN-HOU	3*2	PHI-CHI	1-2	LA-SD	1*0			MON-STL	2-4			
0411	CIN-HOU	5*0	PIT-NY	0-3	LA-SD	1-3	SF-ATL	8*0	MON-STL	6*4			
							SF-ATL	3-4					
0412	PIT-NY	6*2	LA-SD	6-8	PHI-CHI	5*4	SF-ATL	13*4					
					PHI-CHI	3-6							
0413	CIN-ATL	5*2	LA-HOU	6*1	NY-MON	4*1	STL-PHI	11*0	CHI-PIT	2*0	SD-SF	8*3	
0414			LA-HOU	3-7	NY-MON	5-6	STL-PHI	4*1	CHI-PIT	4*1	SD-SF	5*3	
0415	CIN-ATL	13*6	LA-HOU	5*4	NY-MON	1-3	STL-PHI	0-4	CHI-PIT	3-4	SD-SF	4*3	
0416	CIN-ATL	5*3	NY-CHI	10*1	PHI-MON	4-5	SF-LA	3*1	CHI-PIT	6*4			
0417	SD-CIN	1-2	ATL-HOU	8*3	PHI-MON	1-2	CHI-NY	8*6	STL-PIT	2-7	LA-SF	10*5	
0418	SD-CIN	7-11	ATL-HOU	5-10	PHI-MON	4*3	CHI-NY	8*5	STL-PIT	3*0	LA-SF	6*2	
0419	HOU-LA	3-7	MON-PHI	5*0	PIT-STL	5*1	CHI-NY	1-4					
0420	HOU-LA	4*2	PIT-CHI	9*4	PHI-STL	3*0	MON-NY	2*1	SF-SD	2-9			
0421	HOU-LA	6*5	PIT-CHI	4*3	PHI-STL	7*6	MON-NY	4-5	SF-SD	6*4	ATL-CIN	1-8	
0422	HOU-LA	0-2	PIT-CHI	3*2	PHI-STL	5*3	MON-NY	0-5	SF-SD	3*1	ATL-CIN	3*1	
0423					PIT-STL	4-7			SF-SD	3-13			
0424	MON-HOU	5*3	STL-LA	0-3	ATL-NY	1-2	CIN-PHI	3-6	CHI-SD	3-13	PIT-SF	4*1	
0425	MON-HOU	1*0	STL-LA	5*1	ATL-NY	5-8	CIN-PHI	12*7	CHI-SD	0-3	PIT-SF	7*4	
0426	HOU-ATL	3*0	STL-LA	7*1					CHI-SD	3*1	PIT-SF	2*1	
0427	PHI-ATL	7*1	CHI-LA	0-5	MON-CIN	2-3	NY-HOU	1*0	PIT-SD	9*4	STL-SF	3-12	
0428	PHI-ATL	2*1	CHI-LA	4-5	MON-CIN	4-6	NY-HOU	4-8	PIT-SD	4*3	STL-SF	5*0	
0429	PHI-ATL	1-3	CHI-LA	4*0	MON-CIN	6*3	NY-HOU	1-2	PIT-SD	10*1	STL-SF	7-9	
0430	NY-ATL	4-7	SF-LA	8*4	PHI-CIN	2-6	HOU-MON	4*2					
0501	NY-ATL	2-5	PIT-LA	1-4	PHI-CIN	4*2	HOU-MON	1-2	STL-SD	2*1	CHI-SF	7*4	
0502	CIN-NY	0-5	PIT-LA	2-6	HOU-PHI	4-14	ATL-MON	8*1	STL-SD	3-4	CHI-SF	9*6	
0503	CIN-NY	5*0			HOU-PHI	10*3	ATL-MON	4*1					
0504	CIN-STL	8*3			LA-PHI	3-8	SF-MON	4-5					
0505	CIN-STL	4*2	HOU-NY	9*5	LA-PHI	3*0	SF-MON	4*1	SD-CHI	2-3			
									SD-CHI	6*5			
0506	SF-MON	0-7	LA-PHI	5-9	CIN-STL	5*1	HOU-NY	4-7	SD-CHI	8*3	ATL-PIT	4-6	
							HOU-NY	6-7			ATL-PIT	2-4	
0507	ATL-CHI	9*8	SF-MON	6-7	CIN-STL	3*0	HOU-NY	1-7			SD-PIT	1-4	
0508	ATL-CHI	8-10	LA-MON	1-9	PHI-HOU	2-3	SF-NY	1-4			SD-PIT	2-10	
0509	ATL-CHI	0-4	LA-MON	3-5	PHI-HOU	10*1	SF-NY	4*2	SD-STL	5-11	CIN-PIT	2-6	
0510			LA-MON	2-8					SD-STL	9*1	CIN-PIT	10*4	
0511	CHI-CIN	5-7	LA-NY	4-9	SF-PHI	6-10	MON-SD	3-5	ATL-STL	2-5	HOU-PIT	3-4	
0512	CHI-CIN	4*2	LA-NY	0-7	SF-PHI	6*2	MON-SD	2-5	ATL-STL	3-4	HOU-PIT	1-3	
0513	CHI-CIN	9-13			SF-PHI	1-4	MON-SD	15*0	ATL-STL	3*1	HOU-PIT	1-5	
0514	PIT-CIN	3-5	CHI-ATL	2-3	MON-LA	2-3	PHI-SD	1-5	NY-SF	2-4			
0515	PIT-CIN	4-5	CHI-ATL	12*2	MON-LA	2-3	PHI-SD	2*1	NY-SF	5-6	HOU-STL	0-4	
0516			CHI-ATL	0-4	MON-LA	2-3	PHI-SD	6*5	NY-SF	3-4	HOU-STL	6-10	
0517	STL-CIN	3*0	PIT-ATL	1-6	CHI-HOU	4-5							
0518	STL-CIN	0-1	PIT-ATL	9*3	CHI-HOU	7*0	PHI-LA	2-4	NY-SD	3-6	MON-SF	2-7	
0519	STL-CIN	0-4	PIT-ATL	1-2	CHI-HOU	4*1	PHI-LA	15*12	NY-SD	6*4	MON-SF	7*4	
0520	STL-CIN	6*2	PIT-ATL	11-13	CHI-HOU	5*1	PHI-LA	3-6	NY-SD	1-3	MON-SF	6*5	
0521	CIN-CHI	4*3	STL-ATL	5-6	PIT-HOU	2-3	NY-LA	12*3			PHI-SF	5*2	
0522	CIN-CHI	1-2	STL-ATL	4*3	PIT-HOU	8*4	NY-LA	8*3	SD-MON	1-6	PHI-SF	4*2	
0523	LA-CHI	3*1	SF-STL	6*1	PIT-HOU	3-7			SD-MON	0-4			
0524	LA-CHI	15*6	SF-STL	2-3	SD-NY	5*4	ATL-PHI	4-8	CIN-MON	7*1			
0525	SF-PIT	9*8	LA-STL	4*1	SD-NY	5*4	ATL-PHI	4-5	CIN-MON	5*0			
0526	SF-PIT	4-10	LA-STL	8*0	SD-NY	0-11	ATL-PHI	12*3	CIN-MON	5*3	HOU-CHI	8*1	
											HOU-CHI	12*3	
0527	CIN-MON	3-5	SD-NY	8*4	ATL-PHI	6*1	SF-PIT	2-5	LA-STL	14*7	HOU-CHI	6-11	
0528	MON-ATL	4*1	STL-HOU	1-5	SD-PHI	9*5	LA-PIT	5-6			SF-CHI	1-5	
0529	NY-CIN	1-2	STL-HOU	3*2			LA-PIT	5-9			SF-CHI	6*2	
0530	MON-ATL	9*6	STL-HOU	1-5	SD-PHI	8*3	LA-PIT	3-5			SF-CHI	4*1	
0531	CIN-LA	1-2	ATL-SD	1-2	HOU-SF	5*3							
0601	CIN-LA	5*2	ATL-SD	16*11	HOU-SF	5-6	NY-PHI	4*0	MON-PIT	4*1	CHI-STL	4-6	
0602	CIN-LA	8*3	ATL-SD	0-9	HOU-SF	4-5	NY-PHI	4-5	MON-PIT	3-4	CHI-STL	7*6	

♦1990♦	GAME 1	GAME 2	GAME 3	GAME 4	GAME 5	GAME 6	GAME 7
0603	CIN-LA 2*0	ATL-SD 4*2	HOU-SF 3-7	NY-PHI 3-8	MON-PIT 4*3	CHI-STL 4-7	
0604	ATL-LA 0-6	HOU-SD 2-10	CIN-SF 1-10	MON-NY 5*3	CHI-PIT 2-6	PHI-STL 2-3	
0605	ATL-LA 6*4	HOU-SD 2-11	CIN-SF 1-6	MON-NY 5-6	CHI-PIT 5-6	PHI-STL 9*6	
0606	ATL-LA 5-7	HOU-SD 2-3	CIN-SF 1-6	MON-NY 3-4	CHI-PIT 1-6	PHI-STL 11-12	
0607	PHI-CHI 3*1	CIN-HOU 6*1	STL-MON 2-3	PIT-NY 5*4			
0608	PHI-CHI 2-15	CIN-HOU 1-3	STL-MON 2-18	PIT-NY 1-7	SF-ATL 23*8	LA-SD 6-12	
0609	PHI-CHI 3-4	CIN-HOU 1-4	STL-MON 1-3	PIT-NY 3-9	SF-ATL 3-5	LA-SD 5*4	
0610	PHI-CHI 5-7	CIN-HOU 2-4	STL-MON 5*3	PIT-NY 3-8	SF-ATL 9*3	LA-SD 1-2	
0611	NY-CHI 5-8	LA-HOU 3-5	PIT-STL 8*7	MON-PHI 5*0	SF-ATL 8*3		
				MON-PHI 3*2			
0612	NY-CHI 19*8	LA-HOU 4-5	SF-SD 7*2	MON-PHI 2-7	PIT-STL 6*3	ATL-CIN 8*3	
						ATL-CIN 3*2	
0613	LA-HOU 1-5	MON-PHI 4*3	SF-SD 6*0	PIT-STL 6*5	NY-CHI 15*10	ATL-CIN 4-13	
					NY-CHI 9*6		
0614	ATL-CIN 3-4	SF-SD 6*2	MON-STL 3*2				
0615	HOU-CIN 3-6	SD-LA 3*1	MON-STL 7*4	NY-PIT 7*5	ATL-SF 2-8	CHI-PHI 5-6	
						CHI-PHI 0-7	
0616	HOU-CIN 2-6	SD-LA 2-5	NY-PIT 6-11	ATL-SF 0-7	MON-STL 3-5	CHI-PHI 1-2	
0617	HOU-CIN 1-7	SD-LA 3-6	NY-PIT 4*3	ATL-SF 7-9	MON-STL 1-7	CHI-PHI 5*3	
0618	CHI-MON 1-5	HOU-LA 2-5		SD-SF 1-2			
0619	CHI-MON 2*1	HOU-LA 1-5	STL-NY 0-6	SD-SF 4*3	PIT-PHI 1-2	CIN-ATL 4*2	
						CIN-ATL 0-3	
0620	HOU-LA 2-3	CHI-MON 2-3	STL-NY 3-6	PIT-PHI 2-7	SD-SF 4*3	CIN-ATL 9*8	
0621						CIN-ATL 3-4	
0622	STL-CHI 7*0	LA-CIN 7*6	SF-HOU 4*3	PIT-MON 3-4	PHI-NY 1-5		
0623	STL-CHI 8*7	LA-CIN 6-11	SF-HOU 2-4	PIT-MON 1-6	PHI-NY 0-3	SD-ATL 7*5	
0624	STL-CHI 2-3	LA-CIN 6-10	SF-HOU 2-8	PIT-MON 5*3	PHI-NY 5-6	SD-ATL 10-11	
0625	MON-CHI 7*3	SF-CIN 2-5	SD-HOU 3-5	PHI-PIT 0-5	NY-STL 3*2	LA-ATL 5*2	
0626	MON-CHI 6*5	SF-CIN 2-3	SD-HOU 7*0	PHI-PIT 0-1	NY-STL 8*6	LA-ATL 2-4	
0627	MON-CHI 3-5	SF-CIN 8*3	SD-HOU 1-9	PHI-PIT 3-5	NY-STL 5*2	LA-ATL 0-4	
0628	MON-CHI 2-3	CIN-NY 4-5	SD-HOU 1-2		PIT-STL 1-5		
0629	STL-LA 0-6	CIN-NY 2-4	ATL-MON 4*2	HOU-PHI 0-2	CHI-SD 3*2	PIT-SF 3-7	
0630	STL-LA 6*5	CIN-NY 7*4	ATL-MON 7*6	HOU-PHI 8*3	CHI-SD 7*3	PIT-SF 4*3	
0701	STL-LA 6*5	CIN-NY 2-3	ATL-MON 1-5	HOU-PHI 4-8	CHI-SD 11*10	PIT-SF 8*5	
0702	CHI-LA 1-3		ATL-MON 6*3	HOU-PHI 1-5	PIT-SD 4*3	STL-SF 2-3	
0703	CHI-LA 6-7	HOU-NY J-12	CIN-MON 2*0	ATL-PHI 1-5	PIT-SD 5*3	STL-SF 0-4	
0704	CHI-LA 5*3	HOU-NY 4-7	CIN-MON 3-5	ATL-PHI 4*1	PIT-SD 4-5	STL-SF 2-9	
0705	PIT-LA 9*6	NY-ATL 9*8	HOU-MON 0-11	CIN-PHI 9*2	STL-SD 4*1		
0706	PIT-LA 6*3	NY-ATL 10*7	HOU-MON 2-3	CIN-PHI 4*1	STL-SD 5*3	CHI-SF 5*2	
0707	PIT-LA 2-4	NY-ATL 3-4	HOU-MON 1-3	CIN-PHI 5*0	STL-SD 1-3	CHI-SF 9-10	
0708	PIT-LA 7*2	NY-ATL 2*1	HOU-MON 5*3	CIN-PHI 3-4	STL-SD 4*1	CHI-SF 3-5	
						CHI-SF 4-10	
0712	MON-ATL 3*0	LA-CHI 6*3	PHI-HOU 4-7	SD-PIT 3-4	SF-STL 4*2	NY-CIN 10*3	
						NY-CIN 2-3	
0713	LA-CHI 5*2	PHI-HOU 4*2	SD-PIT 1-4	SF-STL 6*1		NY-CIN 2-4	
0714	LA-CHI 7*0	PHI-HOU 12*8	SD-PIT 4-8	SF-STL 1-2	MON-ATL 2-3	NY-CIN 6*3	
					MON-ATL 6*2		
0715	LA-CHI 1-5	NY-CIN 1-2	PHI-HOU 1-6	SD-PIT 4*1	MON-ATL 16*14	SF-STL 5*3	
0716	SD-CHI 3-4	MON-CIN 3-8	NY-HOU 1-6	SF-PIT 6*1	PHI-ATL 7*2	LA-STL 5*2	
0717	SD-CHI 2-7	MON-CIN 2-6	NY-HOU 6*2	SF-PIT 6*3	PHI-ATL 10-14	LA-STL 0-3	
0718	SD-CHI 2-4	MON-CIN 7-8	NY-HOU 0-1	SF-PIT 2-11	PHI-ATL 4*3	LA-STL 6*1	
0719	ATL-NY 2-6	PHI-CIN 5*2	MON-HOU 3-4			SD-STL 3-8	
0720	ATL-NY 1-6	PHI-CIN 1-5	MON-HOU 6-12	SF-CHI 4-5	LA-PIT 2-4	SD-STL 2-4	
0721	ATL-NY 2-4	PHI-CIN 1-6	MON-HOU 3*2	SF-CHI 2-3	LA-PIT 6*0	SD-STL 2-4	
0722	ATL-NY 3*2	PHI-CIN 6*2	MON-HOU 2-3	SF-CHI 2-4	LA-PIT 6-11	SD-STL 4-6	
0723	HOU-ATL 1-3	SF-LA 1-11	PIT-MON 0-5	NY-PHI 4-7	CIN-SD 9*2	CHI-STL 3*1	
0724	HOU-ATL 3-9	SF-LA 2-9	PIT-MON 5*3	NY-PHI 7*4	CIN-SD 0-10	CHI-STL 4-9	
	HOU-ATL 8-9						
0725	HOU-ATL 5*1	SF-LA 7*2	PIT-MON 7-8	NY-PHI 10*9	CHI-STL 0-9	CIN-SD 1-2	
						CIN-SD 4-10	
0726	ATL-LA 1-8	CHI-MON 2-3	PHI-PIT 12*4	CIN-SF 3-4	STL-NY 1-6	HOU-SD 2-8	
					STL-NY 3*1		
0727	ATL-LA 4-5	CHI-MON 2*0	PHI-PIT 5*3	HOU-SD 2-6	STL-NY 1-10	CIN-SF 3-4	
0728	ATL-LA 7-8	CHI-MON 10*7	PHI-PIT 4*3	HOU-SD 5*3	STL-NY 1*0	CIN-SF 2-3	
0729	ATL-LA 3-4	CHI-MON 2*1	PHI-PIT 1-2	HOU-SD 3-4	STL-NY 0-6	CIN-SF 0-4	
0730	CIN-LA 1-4			ATL-SD 4*3		HOU-SF 6*1	
0731	CIN-LA 5*2	PIT-CHI 9*1	NY-MON 4*3	ATL-SD 6-7	STL-PHI 4*2	HOU-SF 2-3	
0801	SF-LA 2*1	PIT-CHI 0-5	NY-MON 6*4	CIN-SD 6*3	STL-PHI 10-11		
0802	SD-CIN 8*5	PIT-CHI 8*5	NY-MON 5*1	ATL-HOU 1-3	STL-PHI 4*3	LA-SF 1-3	
0803	SD-CIN 3*2	MON-CHI 4-10	NY-STL 5*4	ATL-HOU 0-3	PIT-PHI 11*0	LA-SF 11*2	
0804	SD-CIN 7*3	MON-CHI 2-10	NY-STL 5-7	ATL-HOU 2-6	PIT-PHI 3*1	LA-SF 1-2	
0805	SD-CIN 2-6	MON-CHI 1-3	NY-STL 3-8	ATL-HOU 2-6	PIT-PHI 6-8	LA-SF 12*6	
0806			NY-STL 1-5	SF-HOU 1-4	PIT-PHI 10*1		
					PIT-PHI 4*3		
0807	STL-CHI 3-5	LA-CIN 0-1	SF-HOU 0-4	PHI-NY 9*0	MON-PIT 3-4	SD-ATL 7*2	
						SD-ATL 11*9	
0808	STL-CHI	LA-CIN 4*2	SF-HOU 8*4	PHI-NY 4-8	MON-PIT 6*2	SD-ATL 1-7	
0809	STL-CHI 3*1	LA-CIN 10*3		PHI-NY 4-5	MON-PIT 7*6	SD-ATL 7*0	
0810	SD-HOU 2*0	SF-CIN 0-7	PHI-MON 3-4	CHI-NY 1-5	STL-PIT 8*3	LA-ATL 2-3	
0811	SD-HOU 6*3	SF-CIN 4*2	PHI-MON 4-5	CHI-NY 6*3	STL-PIT 3*2	LA-ATL 6*4	
0812	SD-HOU 9*0	SF-CIN 4-6	PHI-MON 3-6	CHI-NY 10*2	STL-PIT 6*0	LA-ATL 7*3	
						LA-ATL 5-9	
0813	HOU-CHI 7*2	SF-CIN 5-6		CIN-STL 9*4	LA-NY 8-9	ATL-PIT 1-3	
0814	HOU-CHI 2-5	SF-PHI 3-4	MON-SD 8*3		LA-NY 2*1	ATL-PIT 4-6	
0815	HOU-CHI 8*4	SF-PHI 0-6	MON-SD 5*3	CIN-STL 3*1	LA-NY 3*2	ATL-PIT 8*1	
0816		SF-PHI 4-6	MON-SD 2-3	HOU-STL 4*2	LA-NY 1-4	ATL-PIT 3-4	
0817	ATL-CHI 0-7	MON-LA 6-7	PHI-SD 2*1	HOU-STL 0-5	NY-SF 2-3	PIT-CIN 7*1	
						PIT-CIN 4*3	
0818	ATL-CHI 17*6	MON-LA 2-3	PHI-SD 2-4	NY-SF 9*2	HOU-STL 3*2	PIT-CIN 3*1	
0819	ATL-CHI 4-5	MON-LA 2*1	PHI-SD 3*2	NY-SF 10*9	HOU-STL 3-7	PIT-CIN 6*3	
0820	HOU-PIT 1-7	PHI-LA 1-2	NY-SD 1-3	MON-SF 2-4	ATL-STL 2-7	CHI-CIN 3*1	
0821	HOU-PIT 2*1	PHI-LA 12*11	NY-SD 0-7	MON-SF 10*5	ATL-STL 7*2	CHI-CIN 1-8	
0822	HOU-PIT 2-4	PHI-LA 2-3	NY-SD 4*1	MON-SF 1-2	ATL-STL 2*1	CHI-CIN 1-4	
0823	CIN-PIT 3-9	NY-LA 2-4	HOU-ATL 8*3	PHI-SF 3-6			
0824	CIN-PIT 4*3	NY-LA 3*2	CHI-ATL 0-3	PHI-SF 2-13	STL-HOU 3*2	SD-MON 2*1	
0825	CIN-PIT 6*1	NY-LA 2-3	CHI-ATL 6*3	PHI-SF 2-4	STL-HOU 4-6	SD-MON 1-2	
0826	CIN-PIT 6*2	NY-LA 1-2	CHI-ATL 3-4	PHI-SF 5*1	STL-HOU 2-4	SD-MON 2-4	
0827						SD-MON 4*1	
0828	PIT-ATL 0-9	STL-CIN 1-2	CHI-HOU 5*2	SD-NY 0-4	LA-PHI 5*1	SF-MON 2-5	
0829	PIT-ATL 10*0	STL-CIN 9*1	CHI-HOU 0-1	SD-NY 1-2	LA-PHI 12*2	SF-MON 6*5	
0830	STL-ATL 5*3	CIN-CHI 6*5		SF-NY 2-12	LA-PHI 3*2		
0831	STL-ATL 1-4	CIN-CHI 3-4	PIT-HOU 2-3	SF-NY 3-4	SD-PHI 2-4	LA-MON 2-5	
0901	STL-ATL 3-4	CIN-CHI 8*1	PIT-HOU 1-2	SF-NY 5-6	SD-PHI 2-3	LA-MON 0-6	
					SD-PHI 1-2		
0902	STL-ATL 0-5	CIN-CHI 6*2	PIT-HOU 7*6	LA-MON 12*5	SD-PHI 9*1	SF-NY 6-10	
0903	CIN-ATL 6-8	HOU-LA 1-3	PHI-PIT 1-4	CHI-MON 2-3	SF-SD 5*4	NY-STL 9*3	
0904	CIN-ATL 4-7	HOU-LA 10*8	PHI-PIT 7-11	CHI-MON 3*1	SF-SD 6*4	NY-STL 0-1	

♦1990♦	GAME 1	GAME 2	GAME 3	GAME 4	GAME 5	GAME 6	GAME 7
0905	CHI-PHI 1-4	ATL-LA 6*2	NY-PIT 0-1 / NY-PIT 1-3	CIN-SF 5*3	HOU-SD 2-5	MON-STL 6*2	
0906	ATL-LA 0-5	CHI-PHI 5*2	NY-PIT 1-7	HOU-SD 0-3	CIN-SF 2-6	MON-STL 2-4	
0907	CIN-LA 1-3	NY-PHI 1-4	MON-PIT 4*1	ATL-SD 4*1	HOU-SF 2*1	STL-CHI 4*3	
0908	CIN-LA 8*4	NY-PHI 12*2	MON-PIT 1-6	ATL-SD 11*5	HOU-SF 1-2	STL-CHI 4-5	
0909	CIN-LA 4-6	NY-PHI 2-6	MON-PIT 9*5	ATL-SD 5-8	HOU-SF 1-5	STL-CHI 9*2	
0910	STL-NY 1-10	PIT-PHI 3*2		LA-SD 2-5	ATL-SF 6-7	MON-CHI 7*4	
0911	STL-NY 8-10	PIT-PHI 5*1	HOU-CIN 3-5	LA-SD 0-4	ATL-SF 0-2	MON-CHI 6-11	
0912	PIT-NY 1-2	STL-MON 2-6	HOU-CIN 3*1	LA-SD 10*3	ATL-SF 3-8	PHI-CHI 3-9	
0913	PIT-NY 3-6	STL-MON 6*4	HOU-CIN 5-7			PHI-CHI 5-6	
0914	PHI-NY 4*1	PIT-MON 2-4	LA-CIN 10*4	SD-ATL 3-7	SF-HOU 1-2	CHI-STL 6*2	
0915	PHI-NY 2-4	PIT-MON 3-4	LA-CIN 3*0	SD-ATL 5*3	SF-HOU 2-3	CHI-STL 6*2	
0916	PHI-NY 8*3	PIT-MON 1-4	LA-CIN 5-9	SD-ATL 9*4	SF-HOU 2-3	CHI-STL 8*4	
0917			SF-CIN 0-4	LA-ATL 5*2	SD-HOU 5*0		
0918	PIT-CHI 5-8	MON-NY 4*3	SF-CIN 5*3	LA-ATL 6*2	SD-HOU 8*1	PHI-STL 6*3	
0919	PIT-CHI 8*7	SD-LA 9*4		SF-ATL 1-5	CIN-HOU 2-5	PHI-STL 8*4	
0920	PIT-CHI 11*2	SD-LA 2-7	MON-NY 6*4 / MON-NY 2*0	SF-ATL 5*3	CIN-HOU 2-3	PHI-STL 4-5	
0921	HOU-ATL 4*3	NY-CHI 3-4	SF-LA 3-16	MON-PHI 4-5	STL-PIT 0-1	CIN-SD 10*1	
0922	HOU-ATL 1-3	NY-CHI 11*5	SF-LA 3-6	MON-PHI 2-3	STL-PIT 3*2	CIN-SD 6*4 / CIN-SD 9*5	
0923	HOU-ATL 0-3	NY-CHI 7*3	SF-LA 6*2	MON-PHI 1-2	STL-PIT 2-7	CIN-SD 9*2	
0924	LA-HOU 7*5	NY-CHI 3-4	SD-SF 1-3	MON-PHI 0-3			
0925	LA-HOU 3*1	ATL-CIN 10*0	SD-SF 1-3	STL-PHI 3*1	NY-MON 3*1	CHI-PIT 3-5	
0926	LA-HOU 1-10	ATL-CIN 2-5	SD-SF 6-7	STL-PHI 8*1	NY-MON 4*0	CHI-PIT 3-4	
0927		ATL-CIN 2-4		STL-PHI 3-4	NY-MON 6*0	CHI-PIT 7*1	
0928	ATL-HOU 1-2	SD-CIN 2*1	CHI-NY 1-7	LA-SF 6-7	PHI-MON 5*4	PIT-STL 6*4	
0929	ATL-HOU 0-9	SD-CIN 3*1	CHI-NY 3*2	LA-SF 3-4	PHI-MON 1-5	PIT-STL 8*0	
0930	ATL-HOU 2-6	SD-CIN 3*0	CHI-NY 6*5	LA-SF 2-8	PHI-MON 2*1	PIT-STL 2-0	
1001	SD-LA 1-2	HOU-CIN 3-4	CHI-PHI 6-7	ATL-SF 5*3	STL-MON 9-15	NY-PIT 4*1	
1002	SD-LA 7-8	HOU-CIN 2-3	CHI-PHI 3*1	ATL-SF 16*7	STL-MON 1-2	NY-PIT 4-9	
1003	SD-LA 7*3	HOU-CIN 3*2	CHI-PHI 4*3	ATL-SF 3-6	STL-MON 2-9	NY-PIT 6*3	

♦1991♦	GAME 1	GAME 2	GAME 3	GAME 4	GAME 5	GAME 6	GAME 7
0408	PHI-NY 1-2	HOU-CIN 2-6				MON-PIT 7*0	
0409	PHI-NY 1-2	STL-CHI 4*1	SF-SD 4-7			MON-PIT 3-4	
0410	PHI-NY 8*7	STL-CHI 0-2	SF-SD 3-4	LA-ATL 6*4	HOU-CIN 5-6	MON-PIT 3-6	
0411	MON-NY 3-6	STL-CHI 5*4	SF-SD 11*9	LA-ATL 4*2	HOU-CIN 4*1		
0412	MON-NY 4*3	PIT-CHI 3*1	SF-HOU 2-3	SD-LA 4*2	STL-PHI 4-11		
0413	MON-NY 3-5	PIT-CHI 3-7	SF-HOU 16*2	SD-LA 6*3	STL-PHI 2-4	ATL-CIN 7*5	
0414	MON-NY 1-7	PIT-CHI 4-6	SF-HOU 2-7	SD-LA 5*3	STL-PHI 11*7	ATL-CIN 12*1	
0415	HOU-ATL 3*1	PHI-CHI 4-5	STL-MON 5*4	NY-PIT 9*3	CIN-SD 2-3	LA-SF 2*1	
0416	HOU-ATL 4-10	PHI-CHI 3-4	STL-MON 1-4	NY-PIT 2-4	CIN-SD 1*0	LA-SF 6-8	
0417	HOU-ATL 4*3	PHI-CHI 1-4	STL-MON 0-1	NY-PIT 0-4	CIN-SD 5*1	LA-SF 6*2	
0418				CHI-PIT 3*2	LA-SD 5-10		
0419	CIN-ATL 8*3	NY-MON 1-2	HOU-SF 2-5	CHI-PIT 4-5	LA-SD 4*0	PHI-STL 1-3	
0420	CIN-ATL 3*0	NY-MON 3*1	HOU-SF 0-4	CHI-PIT 3-9	LA-SD 3-5	PHI-STL 1-12 / PHI-STL 6*5	
0421	CIN-ATL 2-3	NY-MON 9*5	CHI-PIT 12-13	LA-SD 6*0	HOU-SF 0-1 / SD-SF 7*5	PHI-STL 6-7	
0422	CIN-HOU 1-2	ATL-LA 7*1		NY-PHI 2*1	SD-SF 7*6	CHI-STL 2-3	
0423	CIN-HOU 3*1	ATL-LA 4*0	PIT-MON 7*3	NY-PHI 7*3	SD-SF 1-6	CHI-STL 2-4	
0424	CIN-HOU 0-1	ATL-LA 4-8	PIT-MON 2*1	NY-PHI 3-5		CHI-STL 1*0	
0425	CHI-CIN 4-6	SF-LA 1-7	PIT-MON 8*0	NY-PHI 3-5			
0426	CHI-CIN 1-3	SF-LA 0-9	ATL-HOU 7*2	SD-PHI 4*0	PIT-NY 0-2	MON-STL 0-4	
0427	CHI-CIN 8*3	SF-LA 4*3	ATL-HOU 2*1	SD-PHI 3-4	PIT-NY 10*1	MON-STL 1-2	
0428	CHI-CIN 3-4	SF-LA 3-7	ATL-HOU 0-2	SD-PHI 2-9	PIT-NY 7*3	MON-STL 9*6	
0429				SD-PHI 2-7		ATL-STL 3-4	
0430	HOU-CHI 3-10	PIT-CIN 3-4	LA-MON 0-1	SF-PHI 9-11	SD-NY 3-6	ATL-STL 3-5	
0501	HOU-CHI 8-11	PIT-CIN 6*4	LA-MON 3-9	SF-PHI 1-4	SD-NY 8*7	ATL-STL 5*4	
0503	CHI-ATL 2-5	STL-CIN 4*2	SD-MON 1-4	LA-PHI 7*1	SF-NY 0-3	HOU-PIT 0-1	
0504	CHI-ATL 2-4	STL-CIN 1-3	SD-MON 6*5	LA-PHI 3-4	SF-NY 4-6	HOU-PIT 8*3	
0505	CHI-ATL 9*6	STL-CIN 2-4	SD-MON 6*3	LA-PHI 3*2	SF-NY 2*0	HOU-PIT 6*4	
0506	CHI-HOU 4*3		SF-MON 4-10			CIN-PIT 1-3	
0507	CHI-HOU 4*3	STL-ATL 2-9	SF-MON 2-3	LA-NY 5-6	PHI-SD 2-4	CIN-PIT 2-7	
0508	CHI-HOU 2-4	STL-ATL 1-17	SF-MON 4-5	LA-NY 3*1	PHI-SD 5*2	CIN-PIT 2-7	
0509					PHI-SD 9*6		
0510	CIN-CHI 5-6	STL-HOU 7*5	PHI-LA 1-3	ATL-PIT 2-5	MON-SD 6*4	NY-SF 0-7	
0511	CIN-CHI 12*2	STL-HOU 1-6	PHI-LA 3*2	ATL-PIT 3*2	MON-SD 5*1	NY-SF 6*2	
0512	CIN-CHI 5*3	STL-HOU 7*3	PHI-LA 7*3	ATL-PIT 6*1	MON-SD 8*6	NY-SF 4*2	
0513	ATL-CHI 5*3	CIN-STL 0-1	MON-LA 3-8		NY-SD 2-5	PHI-SF 3*2	
0514	ATL-CHI 4-5	CIN-STL 3*1	MON-LA 2-6	PIT-HOU 6*3	NY-SD 6*1	PHI-SF 9*0	
0515	ATL-CHI 1-6	CIN-STL 2-8	MON-LA 3-4	PIT-HOU 8*7	NY-SD 7*1	PHI-SF 2-4	
0516				PIT-HOU 6*4		MON-SF 4-5	
0517	PIT-ATL 3-9	SD-CIN 3-7	NY-LA 4*2	CHI-PHI 0-1	HOU-STL 5*4	MON-SF 3*0	
0518		SD-CIN 5*2	NY-LA 3-4	CHI-PHI 2-5	HOU-STL 2-12	MON-SF 3*1	
0519	PIT-ATL 1-7	SD-CIN 3*2	NY-LA 5-7	CHI-PHI 2*1	HOU-STL 2-9	MON-SF 5*4	
0520	SD-ATL 7*3	LA-HOU 1-4					
0521	SD-ATL 1-4	LA-HOU 7*3	SF-CIN 2-3	PHI-MON 0-3	CHI-NY 6-8	STL-PIT 3-5	
0522	SD-ATL 7*2	LA-HOU 2-3	SF-CIN 4-9	PHI-MON 8*1	CHI-NY 5*2	STL-PIT 5*3	
0523	SD-ATL 11*10	LA-HOU 2*0	SF-CIN 2-6	PHI-MON 2*0	CHI-NY 4*3	STL-PIT 8*2	
0524	SF-ATL 2-3	SD-HOU 0-1	LA-CIN 11*3	MON-CHI 3-4	STL-NY 2-6	PHI-PIT 1-9	
0525	SF-ATL 7*6	SD-HOU 4*2	LA-CIN 8*1	MON-CHI 1-6	STL-NY 7*2	PHI-PIT 2-4	
0526	SF-ATL 10*6	SD-HOU 3-13	LA-CIN 0-3	MON-CHI 6-8	STL-NY 14*4	PHI-PIT 2-5	
0527	HOU-LA 1-4	MON-PHI 8*1	ATL-SD 3*1	NY-CHI 3*1	CIN-SF 3*2	PIT-STL 8*0	
0528	HOU-LA 2-8	MON-PHI 0-12	ATL-SD 8*6	NY-CHI 9*8	CIN-SF 2-6	PIT-STL 9*8	
0529	HOU-LA 8*2	MON-PHI 1-2	ATL-SD 5*1	NY-CHI 8*1	CIN-SF 1-6	PIT-STL 6*0	
0530	CIN-LA 7*2		HOU-SD 0-4		ATL-SF 7*2		
0531	CIN-LA 4-7	CHI-MON 7*2	HOU-SD 4-5	PIT-PHI 5*1	ATL-SF 5*2	NY-STL 10*5	
0601	CIN-LA 6*5	CHI-MON 2*1	HOU-SD 2-7	PIT-PHI 5*3	ATL-SF 2-8	NY-STL 5-6	
0602	CIN-LA 1-4	CHI-MON 4*3	HOU-SD 1-3	PIT-PHI 5*3	ATL-SF 1-2	NY-STL 1-3	
0604	PHI-ATL 5-9	SD-CHI 7*1	NY-CIN 4*2	MON-HOU 4*1	SF-PIT 5*3	LA-STL 2-3	
0605	PHI-ATL 12*11	SD-CHI 3*0	NY-CIN 10-11	MON-HOU 8*2	SF-PIT 3-7	LA-STL 2*0	
0606	PHI-ATL 4-9	SD-CHI 2-6	NY-CIN 3-5	MON-HOU 8-9	SF-PIT 6*3	LA-STL 1*0	
0607	MON-ATL 11*2	LA-CHI 3*2	PHI-CIN 5*4	NY-HOU 6*3	SD-PIT 0-1	SF-STL 5*2	
0608	MON-ATL 6-7	LA-CHI 3-4	PHI-CIN 4*1	NY-HOU 4*3	SD-PIT 11*0	SF-STL 2-3	
0609	MON-ATL 6-8	LA-CHI 6*3	PHI-CIN 3-6	NY-HOU 0-1	SD-PIT 5*3	SF-STL 3*2	
0610	MON-ATL 7*1	LA-CHI 13*5	PHI-CIN 3-9	NY-HOU 4-6	SD-PIT 3-5	SF-STL 2-3	
0611	CIN-MON 6*1	SF-CHI 8*6	ATL-NY 1-2	PHI-HOU 0-1	STL-SD 10*4		
0612	CIN-MON 9-10	SF-CHI 1-6	ATL-NY 6*1	PHI-HOU 2-3	STL-SD 2-7	LA-PIT 1-2	
0613	CIN-MON 3*2	SF-CHI 3-4	ATL-NY 3*2	PHI-HOU 5*4	STL-SD 12*1	LA-PIT 3*2	
0614	ATL-MON 1-2	STL-LA 1-2	HOU-NY 4*1	CIN-PHI 4*2	CHI-SD 7*3	PIT-SF 2-3	
0615	ATL-MON 0-2	STL-LA 5*4	HOU-NY 0-6	CIN-PHI 3*1	CHI-SD 2-6	PIT-SF 0-4	
0616	ATL-MON 6-7	STL-LA 2-7	HOU-NY 5*4	CIN-PHI 8*6	CHI-SD 2-4	PIT-SF 4*3	
0617	HOU-MON 2-3	CHI-LA 4-6	CIN-NY 6-10	ATL-PHI 3-7	PIT-SD 3*2	STL-SF 5*4	
0618	HOU-MON 4-5	CHI-LA 5-6	CIN-NY 5-7	ATL-PHI 4-8	PIT-SD 3*1	STL-SF 3*1	
0619	HOU-MON 1-3	CHI-LA 8-9	CIN-NY 7*6	ATL-PHI 9*2	PIT-SD 5-6	STL-SF 3*2	
0620	NY-ATL 9*7	PIT-LA 2-3	MON-CIN 1*0	HOU-PHI 3-7		CHI-SF 3-4	

♦1991♦	GAME 1		GAME 2		GAME 3		GAME 4		GAME 5		GAME 6		GAME 7
0621	NY-ATL	2-4	PIT-LA	5*1	MON-CIN	3-7	HOU-PHI	0-3	SD-STL	3-4	CHI-SF	2-4	
0622	NY-ATL	7*2	PIT-LA	1-4	MON-CIN	7*4	HOU-PHI	4*3	SD-STL	4*3	CHI-SF	3-6	
0623	NY-ATL	3-4	PIT-LA	0-2	MON-CIN	4-8	HOU-PHI	6*4	SD-STL	3*2	CHI-SF	1-2	
0624									SD-STL	4*1			
0625	SD-CIN	2-8	ATL-HOU	0-1	SF-LA	9*4	MON-NY	5-8	PHI-STL	9-10	CHI-PIT	5*1	
0626	SD-CIN	2-6	ATL-HOU	3*2	SF-LA	3*2	MON-NY	4-7	PHI-STL	1-14	CHI-PIT	6-7	
0627	SD-CIN	0-3	ATL-HOU	3*0			MON-NY	3-4	PHI-STL	2-4	CHI-PIT	3-4	
0628	HOU-CIN	5-8	LA-ATL	2-3	STL-CHI	14*6	PHI-NY	6*2	PIT-MON	6*1	SF-SD	3-5	
			LA-ATL	8*2									
0629	STL-CHI	4-6	LA-ATL	2*1	HOU-CIN	6*2	PIT-MON	2*1	PHI-NY	0-5	SF-SD	6*4	
0630	STL-CHI	4-7	LA-ATL	11*4	HOU-CIN	4-5	PIT-MON	2*1	PHI-NY	10*9	SF-SD	8*7	
0701	PIT-CHI	5-6	STL-PHI	1*0			NY-MON	4*2					
0702	PIT-CHI	13*4	STL-PHI	6*1	CIN-ATL	6*3	NY-MON	2*1	LA-SD	4*1	HOU-SF	8*4	
0703	PIT-CHI	11*7	STL-PHI	4*3	CIN-ATL	6-8	NY-MON	4*0	LA-SD	6*3	HOU-SF	9*0	
0704	PIT-CHI	8-9	STL-PHI	1-7	CIN-ATL	10*4	NY-MON	5*1	LA-SD	4-5	HOU-SF	14*6	
0705	CIN-HOU	1*0	NY-PHI	3*1	ATL-LA	4*1	MON-PIT	4*3	CHI-STL	5*1	SD-SF	4*2	
0706	CIN-HOU	0-3	NY-PHI	2*1	ATL-LA	6-7	MON-PIT	2*1	CHI-STL	12*2	SD-SF	1-4	
0707	CIN-HOU	3-7	NY-PHI	8*2	ATL-LA	3-5	MON-PIT	1-6	CHI-STL	7-8	SD-SF	0-3	
0711	STL-ATL	1-4	SF-PHI	2-3	HOU-CHI	6*4	PIT-CIN	10*6	LA-MON	2-3	SD-NY	3-4	
0712	STL-ATL	2-6	SF-PHI	0-1	HOU-CHI	2-5	PIT-CIN	7*2	LA-MON	5-6	SD-NY	3-6	
0713	STL-ATL	5-10	SF-PHI	7*5	HOU-CHI	3-4	PIT-CIN	5*2	LA-MON	2-3	SD-NY	1-3	
									LA-MON	4-7			
0714	STL-ATL	1-2	HOU-CHI	3-4	PIT-CIN	10*6	SD-NY	2*1	SF-PHI	17*5			
0715	CHI-ATL	6*4	SD-MON	0-3	STL-CIN	5*2	SF-NY	4*3	LA-PHI	8-9	HOU-PIT	0-8	
0716	CHI-ATL	5-8	SD-MON	4*3	STL-CIN	8*7	SF-NY	4-6	LA-PHI	1-3	HOU-PIT	4-6	
0717	CHI-ATL	2-12	SD-MON	7*5	STL-CIN	6*5	SF-NY	5-6	LA-PHI	2-4	HOU-PIT	10*2	
0718							SF-NY	10*5					
0719	CHI-HOU	2-5	SF-MON	0-6	CIN-PIT	2-7	LA-NY	2-6	PHI-SD	4*1	ATL-STL	8*3	
0720	CHI-HOU	6*0	SF-MON	5*3	CIN-PIT	3*2	LA-NY	11*7	PHI-SD	4*0	ATL-STL	1-2	
0721	CHI-HOU	4*2	SF-MON	3*2	CIN-PIT	0-6	LA-NY	4-9	PHI-SD	2-5	ATL-STL	5*1	
0722					ATL-PIT	7*3					HOU-STL	1-9	
0723	CIN-CHI	5-8	PHI-LA	5-6	ATL-PIT	3-12	MON-SD	1-2	NY-SF	2-4	HOU-STL	1-5	
0724	CIN-CHI	12*3	PHI-LA	1-2	ATL-PIT	4-7	MON-SD	8*2	NY-SF	4-8	HOU-STL	3-4	
0725	CIN-CHI	4-5	PHI-LA	0-5			MON-SD	5-6	NY-SF	1-8			
0726	ATL-CHI	6*2	MON-LA	0-1	PIT-HOU	8*1	NY-SD	2-8	PHI-SF	2-3	CIN-STL	1-5	
0727	ATL-CHI	5-7	MON-LA	0-7	PIT-HOU	11*5	NY-SD	4*0	PHI-SF	0-3	CIN-STL	13*1	
0728	ATL-CHI	2-6	MON-LA	2*0	PIT-HOU	7-9	NY-SD	0-2	PHI-SF	1-2	CIN-STL	2-3	
0729	PIT-ATL	5-7	NY-LA	5*1	STL-HOU	2-6			MON-SF	5-6			
	PIT-ATL	3-5											
0730	PIT-ATL	3-10	CHI-CIN	5-6	STL-HOU	5-7	NY-LA	1-3	SD-PHI	1-2	MON-SF	3-10	
0731	PIT-ATL	6-8	CHI-CIN	1-5	STL-HOU	5-9	NY-LA	3-6	SD-PHI	3-9			
0801	PHI-MON	4*1	SF-CIN	8*1	PIT-STL	3-6							
0802	PHI-MON	6*5	SF-CIN	4-5	PIT-STL	3-4	SD-ATL	13*3	LA-HOU	8-9	CHI-NY	4*2	
0803	PHI-MON	7*1	SF-CIN	7*3	PIT-STL	5-6	SD-ATL	3*2	LA-HOU	1-2	CHI-NY	9*2	
0804	PHI-MON	3*2	SF-CIN	4-6	PIT-STL	2*1	SD-ATL	7-9	LA-HOU	1-2	CHI-NY	8*3	
0805			LA-CIN	6-10			SF-ATL	2-5	SD-HOU	1-2	CHI-NY	7*2	
0806	CHI-PHI	2-6	LA-CIN	5*2	MON-STL	6-7	SF-ATL	6-10	SD-HOU	1-6	PIT-NY	3*1	
0807	CHI-PHI	4-5	LA-CIN	2*0	MON-STL	1*0	SF-ATL	1*0	SD-HOU	7*4	PIT-NY	1-7	
0808	CHI-PHI	1-11	LA-CIN	6*4			SF-ATL	8*1	SD-HOU	5*3	PIT-NY	3-4	
0809	MON-PHI	4-5	NY-CHI	4-5	STL-PIT	5*1	HOU-ATL	2-7	CIN-SD	5*1	LA-SF	0-1	
0810	MON-PHI	2-4	NY-CHI	2-6	STL-PIT	5-11	HOU-ATL	0-4	CIN-SD	0-1	LA-SF	3-4	
0811	MON-PHI	4-5	NY-CHI	2-3	STL-PIT	4-6	HOU-ATL	1-3	CIN-SD	0-13	LA-SF	3-4	
0812	MON-PHI	1-2	NY-CHI	2-3	STL-PIT	3-4	CIN-LA	2-3	HOU-SD	5-6	ATL-SF	2*1	
0813	NY-STL	4-7	MON-CHI	7*6	PHI-PIT	3-4	CIN-LA	4*3	HOU-SD	12*9	ATL-SF	9*2	
0814	NY-STL	4-5	MON-CHI	2*0	PHI-PIT	3-5	CIN-LA	1-4	HOU-SD	1-4	ATL-SF	3-8	
0815	NY-STL	1-4	MON-CHI	6-7	PHI-PIT	6*4	HOU-LA	6*1	ATL-SD	0-1	CIN-SF	1-4	
0816	STL-MON	4*2	PHI-CHI	1-9	NY-PIT	2-8	HOU-LA	1-4	ATL-SD	3*2	CIN-SF	5*0	
0817	STL-MON	0-3	PHI-CHI	5*2	NY-PIT	1-4	HOU-LA	7-8	ATL-SD	2*1	CIN-SF	7*0	
0818	STL-MON	4*1	PHI-CHI	6-7	NY-PIT	2-9	HOU-LA	8*4	ATL-SD	1-2	CIN-SF	4*3	
0819	CHI-MON	3*2					SD-LA	2-3					
0820	CHI-MON	2-4	ATL-CIN	2-8	ATL-CIN	5*1	SD-LA	4-6	SF-HOU	9*3	PIT-PHI	5-6	
0821	CHI-MON	3*1	ATL-CIN	10*9	STL-NY	7*3	SD-LA	5-9	SF-HOU	4-13	PIT-PHI	5-6	
					STL-NY	0-8							
0822	ATL-CIN	4*1	SF-HOU	11*8	STL-NY	0-6	PIT-PHI	3-4					
0823	PHI-ATL	2-4	MON-HOU	2-9	CIN-NY	6*1	SD-CHI	4-5	SF-PIT	0-8	LA-STL	1-2	
0824	PHI-ATL	6*5	MON-HOU	5*1	CIN-NY	7*0	SD-CHI	4*1	SF-PIT	5*1	LA-STL	3-7	
0825	PHI-ATL	6*5	MON-HOU	4*0	CIN-NY	1-2	SD-CHI	12*9	SF-PIT	3-8	LA-STL	2-5	
0826	MON-ATL	9-14	NY-HOU	6*4	PHI-CIN	4-5	LA-CHI	4*3	SD-PIT	7*5	SF-STL	6-7	
0827	MON-ATL	2-3	NY-HOU	3-8	PHI-CIN	2-4	LA-CHI	1-2	SD-PIT	2-5	SF-STL	4-5	
0828	NY-ATL	1-3	PIT-LA	6*4	MON-CIN	3-11	HOU-PHI	10-11	CHI-SF	8*6	SD-STL	2*1	
0829	NY-ATL	0-2	PIT-LA	4*1	MON-CIN	4-5	HOU-PHI	5*1	CHI-SF	5*4	SD-STL	1*0	
0830	HOU-MON	1-3	CHI-LA	0-2	NY-CIN	3*2	ATL-PHI	6*1	STL-SF	3-8	PIT-SD	4*1	
0831	HOU-MON	4-5	CHI-LA	2-3	NY-CIN	8*7	ATL-PHI	0-5	STL-SF	1-6	PIT-SD	3*2	
0901	HOU-MON	1-6	CHI-LA	3-12	NY-CIN	9*4	ATL-PHI	4-5	STL-SF	14*1	PIT-SD	4-7	
0902	ATL-MON	3-4	STL-LA	7*4	HOU-NY	3*0	CIN-PHI	5-8	PIT-SF	9*8	CHI-SD	10*8	
0903	ATL-MON	4*1	STL-LA	4-5	HOU-NY	1-6	CIN-PHI	8*5	PIT-SF	5*3	CHI-SD	1-4	
0904	ATL-MON	4-8	STL-LA	3-8	HOU-NY	8*3	CIN-PHI	5*1	PIT-SF	8*3	CHI-SD	1-5	
0905											STL-SD	1-3	
0906	SF-CHI	2-3	PHI-HOU	1-3	CIN-MON	1-4	ATL-NY	4*2	LA-PIT	4*3	STL-SD	2-6	
									LA-PIT	1-3			
0907	SF-CHI	1-2	PHI-HOU	0-6	CIN-MON	5-7	ATL-NY	6*1	LA-PIT	5*1	STL-SD	0-1	
0908	SF-CHI	4*3	PHI-HOU	5*0	CIN-MON	2-4	ATL-NY	7*5	LA-PIT	5*1			
0909	PIT-CHI	12*10	SD-HOU	3*0	SF-ATL	3-8	MON-NY	4*3	LA-CIN	10*4	PHI-STL	2-4	
0910	PIT-CHI	2-6	SD-HOU	7*6	SF-ATL	1-4	MON-NY	0-9	LA-CIN	0-6	PHI-STL	5*2	
0911	NY-CHI	4*1	LA-HOU	9*1	SD-ATL	0-1	MON-PHI	6*5	SF-CIN	4*2	PIT-STL	3*1	
0912	NY-CHI	6*3	LA-HOU	6*2	SD-ATL	1-5	MON-PHI	6*2	SF-CIN	3-7	PIT-STL	0-1	
0913	MON-CHI	3*2	SD-SF	13*2	LA-ATL	5*2	PIT-PHI	8*6	HOU-CIN	2-13	NY-STL	4*2	
0914	MON-CHI	5-7	SD-SF	3*1	LA-ATL	2-3	PIT-PHI	5*3	HOU-CIN	7*3	NY-STL	1-2	
0915	MON-CHI	6*5	SD-SF	2-7	LA-ATL	1-9	PIT-PHI	3-8	HOU-CIN	0-10	NY-STL	2-7	
0916	CIN-LA	5-6	ATL-SF	5-8	CHI-PIT	4-5	STL-PHI	3*0	HOU-SD	1-6			
0917	CIN-LA	3-5	ATL-SF	2-3	CHI-PIT	2-9	STL-PHI	2-4	HOU-SD	3*0	MON-NY	5*4	
											MON-NY	2-3	
0918	HOU-LA	4-5	MON-PHI	0-1	STL-PIT	5-6	ATL-SD	6*4	CIN-SF	2-7	CHI-NY	4*1	
0919	HOU-LA	3-4	MON-PHI	4-5	STL-PIT	1-5	ATL-SD	4*2	CIN-SF	1-4			
0920	ATL-LA	3*0	CIN-HOU	2-3	PHI-PIT	8*3	SF-SD	5-10	STL-NY	0-1			
0921	ATL-LA	1-2	CIN-HOU	4*1	PHI-PIT	0-7	SF-SD	2-3	STL-NY	3-5			
0922	ATL-LA	0-3	CIN-HOU	1-4	PHI-PIT	1-2	SF-SD	3-6	STL-NY	2*1	MON-CHI	6*2	
											MON-CHI	5*3	
0923	SF-HOU	0-8	MON-STL	1-10							PHI-CHI	3-10	
			MON-STL	5*1									
0924	PHI-CHI	4*2	MON-STL	3-4	SF-HOU	9*7	PIT-NY	10*8	LA-SD	5*2			
0925	PHI-CHI	5*4	MON-STL	7*2	SF-HOU	2*1	CIN-ATL	1-2	LA-SD	2-8	CIN-ATL	10*9	
0926	PIT-NY	4*3					CIN-ATL	8*0					
	PIT-NY	1-2											
0927	PHI-NY	4-6	SD-CIN	8*3	ATL-HOU	4*2	SF-LA	2-6	MON-PIT	12*8	CHI-STL	4-5	
0928	PHI-NY	6*2	SD-CIN	4*2	ATL-HOU	5*4	SF-LA	4*1	MON-PIT	3*2	CHI-STL	2-3	
0929	PHI-NY	3-4	SD-CIN	1-8	ATL-HOU	6*5	SF-LA	2-3	MON-PIT	3-6	CHI-STL	5*3	

◆1991◆	GAME 1	GAME 2	GAME 3	GAME 4	GAME 5	GAME 6	GAME 7
0930	CHI-PHI 5-6	ATL-CIN 4*0	HOU-SF 2*0	SD-LA 2-7	NY-PIT 5-6	MON-STL 1-11	
1001	CHI-PHI 5-6	ATL-CIN 7*6	HOU-SF 4-6	SD-LA 1-3	NY-PIT 1-2	MON-STL 1-3	
1002	CHI-PHI 1*0	ATL-CIN 6*3	HOU-SF 7*5	SD-LA 9*4	NY-PIT 9*6	MON-STL 4-6	
1004	NY-PHI 4-5	HOU-ATL 2-5	LA-SF 1-4	CIN-SD 2-3	MON-PIT 3*1		
1005	NY-PHI 0-1	HOU-ATL 2-5	LA-SF 0-4	CIN-SD 7-10	MON-PIT 3-4	STL-CHI 2-3	
						STL-CHI 5-7	
1006	HOU-ATL 8*3	NY-PHI 7*0	MON-PIT 0-7	CIN-SD 1-3	LA-SF 2*0	STL-CHI 3-7	

◆1992◆	GAME 1	GAME 2	GAME 3	GAME 4	GAME 5	GAME 6	GAME 7
0406	SD-CIN 4*3	SF-LA 8*1	MON-PIT 0-2	NY-STL 4*2			
0407	SD-CIN 2-4	SF-LA 0-3	ATL-HOU 2*0	NY-STL 2-9	CHI-PHI 4*3		
0408	SD-CIN 2*1	MON-PIT 2-4	ATL-HOU 3*1	NY-STL 7-15	CHI-PHI 3-11		
0409	SF-ATL 11*4	MON-PIT 8*3	CIN-HOU 5-6	NY-STL 7*1	CHI-PHI 1-7	LA-SD 6*3	
0410	SF-ATL 3-5	STL-CHI 2*1	CIN-HOU 8*5	MON-NY 4*0	PIT-PHI 3*2	LA-SD 3-8	
0411	SF-ATL 3*0	STL-CHI 1-5	CIN-HOU 1-2	MON-NY 9*2	PIT-PHI 4-7	LA-SD 2-3	
0412	SF-ATL 2-6	STL-CHI 2-4	CIN-HOU 5*4	MON-NY 8*2	PIT-PHI 6*1	LA-SD 4-5	
0413	ATL-CIN 4-5	STL-MON 3-8	LA-HOU 3-8	PHI-NY 3*2			
0414	ATL-CIN 4-5	STL-MON 3*1	LA-HOU 6*2	PHI-NY 5-8	CHI-PIT 2-3	SD-SF 4*0	
0415	ATL-CIN 1-3	STL-MON 4*2	LA-HOU 4-5	PHI-NY 2-7	CHI-PIT 2-7	SD-SF 5*3	
0416	ATL-LA 3*0					SD-SF 1-6	
0417	ATL-LA 5-7	SD-HOU 1-3	NY-MON 10*2	PHI-PIT 4-7		CIN-SF 3-7	
0418	ATL-LA 3-7	SD-HOU 2-4	NY-MON 6-8	PHI-PIT 2-9	CHI-STL 5*4	CIN-SF 3-7	
0419	ATL-LA 2-4	SD-HOU 0-1	NY-MON 11*6	PHI-PIT 0-11	CHI-STL 3-4	CIN-SF 2-8	
0420	CIN-LA 0-6	SF-HOU 2-3	PIT-MON 11*1	PHI-CHI 3-8	ATL-SD 10*4		
0421	CIN-LA 4*3	SF-HOU 6*2	PIT-MON 8*7	PHI-CHI 7*5	ATL-SD 2-4	STL-NY 2-4	
0422	CIN-LA 4*3	SF-HOU 1-3	PIT-MON 2*0	PHI-CHI 5-9	ATL-SD 4-9	STL-NY 2-3	
0423			PIT-MON 8*2	PHI-CHI 8*2		STL-NY 0-1	
0424	HOU-ATL 4*2	NY-PHI 3-4	CIN-SD 7*6	PIT-CHI 3*2	LA-SF 5*3	MON-STL 3-4	
0425	HOU-ATL 0-2	NY-PHI 3*2	CIN-SD 11*5	PIT-CHI 1*0	LA-SF 7*6	MON-STL 1-2	
0426	HOU-ATL 2-3	NY-PHI 4-5	CIN-SD 1-2	PIT-CHI 4-5	LA-SF 4-5	MON-STL 6*0	
0427	CHI-ATL 0-5	STL-LA 5*4	PHI-SD 12*9		MON-SF 1-2		
0428	CHI-ATL 0-1	STL-LA 2*1	PHI-SD 6-7	PIT-CIN 2-3	MON-SF 1-2	HOU-NY 0-4	
0429	CHI-ATL 0-8	PHI-LA 7*3	MON-SD 2-7	PIT-CIN 4*0	STL-SF 2*1	HOU-NY 0-1	
0430			MON-SD 9*3		STL-SF 3-9	HOU-NY 3-4	
0501	NY-ATL 8*7	CHI-CIN 0-4	STL-SD 5-7	PIT-HOU 4-10			
0502	NY-ATL 0-3	CHI-CIN 10*3	STL-SD 3*0	PIT-HOU 6*0	PHI-SF 1-2		
0503	NY-ATL 7*0	CHI-CIN 1-7	STL-SD 7*1	PIT-HOU 0-1	PHI-SF 12*3		
0504	ATL-CHI 6*1	CIN-PIT 5-12		NY-HOU 5*1			
0505	ATL-CHI 3-4	CIN-PIT 2-5	SD-MON 2-5	NY-HOU 4-5	LA-PHI 2-6	SF-STL 5-7	
0506	HOU-CHI 4-8	ATL-PIT 3-4	SD-MON 3-4	NY-CIN 3-5	LA-PHI 3*1	SF-STL 4-5	
0507	HOU-CHI 2-9	ATL-PIT 4*2		NY-CIN 2-4		SF-STL 2*0	
0508	CIN-CHI 10*7	HOU-PIT 3-6	SF-MON 6*3	LA-NY 3-4	SD-PHI 6*5	ATL-STL 2*1	
0509	CIN-CHI 1-3	HOU-PIT 0-3	SF-MON 3-9	LA-NY 2-5	SD-PHI 5*1	ATL-STL 11-12	
0510	CIN-CHI 6*0	HOU-PIT 6*4	SF-MON 8*3	LA-NY 0-3	SD-PHI 3-9	ATL-STL 5-6	
0511	CHI-HOU 1-2		LA-MON 5-6	SD-NY 4*2	SF-PHI 3-8	ATL-STL 3-8	
0512	CHI-HOU 3*2	PIT-ATL 2-4	LA-MON 2*0	SD-NY 3-7	SF-PHI 7*5	CIN-STL 4-6	
0513	CHI-HOU 8*3	PIT-ATL 11*10	LA-MON 1-5	SD-NY 7*0	SF-PHI 5*3	CIN-STL 2-4	
0514		PIT-ATL 4*3					
0515	PHI-CIN 8*0	MON-ATL 2-4	STL-HOU 7*5	NY-LA 4*1	SD-PIT 9*2	CHI-SF 5*3	
0516	PHI-CIN 5-6	MON-ATL 7*1	STL-HOU 2-3	NY-LA 0-2	SD-PIT 10*9	CHI-SF 0-2	
0517	PHI-CIN 5*4	MON-ATL 5*4	STL-HOU 7*5	NY-LA 3-6	SD-PIT 6*5	CHI-SF 4*3	
0518	CIN-MON 2*1	STL-ATL 1-5	HOU-PHI 4*2	CHI-LA 3*0	NY-SD 0-3		
0519	CIN-MON 7*4	STL-ATL 3-4	HOU-PHI 3-4	CHI-LA 2-5	NY-SD 8*0	PIT-SF 2-7	
0520	CIN-MON 5-6	STL-ATL 3-6	HOU-PHI 1-2	CHI-LA 3-5	NY-SD 6-12	PIT-SF 1-3	
0521					NY-SD 8*3	PIT-SF 0-1	
0522	PIT-LA 6*4	ATL-MON 1-7	CIN-PHI 2-8	HOU-STL 3*1	CHI-SD 0-2	NY-SF 6-7	
0523	PIT-LA 4-5	ATL-MON 6-7	CIN-PHI 10*0	HOU-STL 4-10	CHI-SD 7*2	NY-SF 6*3	
0524	PIT-LA 2*1	ATL-MON 2-4	CIN-PHI 8*3	HOU-STL 3-4	CHI-SD 6*4	NY-SF 6*0	
0525	CIN-NY 3*0	HOU-MON 10*8	ATL-PHI 1-4	LA-STL 5-6	PIT-SD 6-7		
0526	SF-CHI 3*2	HOU-MON 9*4	ATL-PHI 2-5	LA-STL 5*2	PIT-SD 3-6		
0527	SF-CHI 6*2	HOU-MON 5-8	ATL-PHI 9*3	LA-STL 9*2	PIT-SD 7-8	CIN-NY 1*0	
0528	SF-CHI 0-5						
0529	LA-CHI 1*0	MON-CIN 2-3	PHI-HOU 2*1	ATL-NY 5*1	SF-PIT 3-13	SD-STL 2*1	
0530	LA-CHI 3*2	MON-CIN 4-9	PHI-HOU 4-5	ATL-NY 6*1	SF-PIT 2-3	SD-STL 1-5	
0531	LA-CHI 6*2	MON-CIN 6*2	PHI-HOU 6*3		SF-PIT 5*3	SD-STL 10*0	
0601	SD-CHI 1-6	PHI-ATL 6-7	MON-HOU 7*1	SF-NY 1-14	LA-PIT 8*6		
0602	SD-CHI 2-3	PHI-ATL 3-5	MON-HOU 0-6	SF-NY 3-4	LA-PIT 0-1	STL-CIN 1-2	
0603	SD-CHI 5*1	PHI-ATL 4*1	MON-HOU 3-5		LA-PIT 5-6	STL-CIN 7-8	
0604	CIN-LA 4-7	HOU-SF 12*6			NY-PIT 2-7		
0605	CIN-LA 6*2	HOU-SF 5*4	CHI-MON 10*4	STL-PHI 5-7	NY-PIT 4-5	ATL-SD 3*2	
			CHI-MON 2-6				
0606	CIN-LA 5*4	STL-PHI 5-7	NY-PIT 15*1	ATL-SD 5*1	HOU-SF 6-12		
0607	CIN-LA 0-1	STL-PHI 5*4	NY-PIT 0-3	ATL-SD 9*4	HOU-SF 0-3	CHI-MON 2-3	
0608	ATL-LA 4*2	PIT-PHI 0-7	CHI-STL 5*2	HOU-SD 2-3	CIN-SF 4*1	NY-MON 0-6	
			CHI-STL 6*4				
0609	ATL-LA 2-3	NY-MON 6*5	CHI-STL 5-6	PIT-PHI 5*3	HOU-SD 4-5	CIN-SF 3*2	
0610	ATL-LA 2*1	NY-MON 2-8	CHI-STL 4*2	PIT-PHI 2*1	HOU-SD 1-5	CIN-SF 2-6	
0612	SD-ATL 4-6	MON-CHI 2-5	PHI-STL 8*5	LA-CIN 3-4	SF-HOU 3*2	PIT-NY 3*2	
0613	SD-ATL 2-4	MON-CHI 3-4	PHI-STL 1-4	LA-CIN 1-11	SF-HOU 1-4	PIT-NY 3*2	
0614	SD-ATL 2-4	MON-CHI 1-5	PHI-STL 2-5	LA-CIN 1-5	SF-HOU 7-15	PIT-NY 5*4	
0615	LA-ATL 0-2	STL-CHI 1-7	PHI-PIT 4*1	SF-CIN 5-7	SD-HOU 7*1	MON-NY 4*1	
0616	LA-ATL 8-9	STL-CHI 1-2	PHI-PIT 5-6	SF-CIN 3-5	SD-HOU 0-11	MON-NY 2-5	
0617	LA-ATL 3-4		PHI-PIT 2-8	SF-CIN 4-6	SD-HOU 5*0	MON-NY 5*2	
0618	CIN-ATL 7*5	CHI-PHI 3-4	MON-PIT 4*0	SD-SF 9*4		STL-NY 8*3	
0619	CIN-ATL 2-3	CHI-PHI 5*2	MON-PIT 2*1	SD-SF 3*2	LA-HOU 1-2	STL-NY 3-4	
0620	CIN-ATL 1-2	CHI-PHI 1-4	MON-PIT 4*3	SD-SF 1-3	LA-HOU 0-1	STL-NY 6*1	
0621	CIN-ATL 0-2	CHI-PHI 5*2	MON-PIT 4-5	SD-SF 0-1	LA-HOU 0-2	STL-NY 2-6	
0622	HOU-CIN 5*2	PHI-MON 5*3	STL-PIT 2-5	LA-SD 4*2		CHI-NY 2-8	
0623	HOU-CIN 6-10	PHI-MON 5*0	STL-PIT 4*1	LA-SD 4-8	SF-ATL 0-7	CHI-NY 1-4	
0624	HOU-CIN 6-9	PHI-MON 1-8	STL-PIT 4*1		SF-ATL 0-5	CHI-NY 2-3	
0625	HOU-LA 5-8	SF-SD 0-8				CHI-NY 9*2	
0626	HOU-LA 5-6	SF-SD 2-6	PHI-CHI 0-3	ATL-CIN 4-7	PIT-MON 2-6	NY-STL 3-4	
0627	HOU-LA 5*1	SF-SD 5*3	PHI-CHI 5*4	ATL-CIN 3-12	PIT-MON 12*4	NY-STL 2*1	
0628	HOU-LA 2-8	SF-SD 3-7	PHI-CHI 3-5	ATL-CIN 5-6	PIT-MON 0-9	NY-STL 2-3	
0629	SD-LA 5-6	CIN-HOU 3-4	NY-CHI 2-5	MON-PHI 4-5		PIT-STL 1-3	
0630	SD-LA 1-5	CIN-HOU 1-5	NY-CHI 1-3	MON-PHI 7*2	ATL-SF 4*3	PIT-STL 2*0	
0701	SD-LA 6*2	CIN-HOU 2-3	NY-CHI 6*4	MON-PHI 6*3	ATL-SF 1-2	PIT-STL 1*0	
0702	PHI-LA 4-9	CIN-PIT 2*1	MON-SD 3*2		STL-SF 1*0		
0703	PHI-LA 1-5	CIN-PIT 7*3	MON-SD 4-6	CHI-ATL 0-3	STL-SF 1-4		
	PHI-LA 0-2						
0704	PHI-LA 3*2	CHI-ATL 2-4	HOU-NY 3-5	CIN-PIT 5*2	MON-SD 3*2	STL-SF 1*0	
			HOU-NY 3*1				
0705	CHI-ATL 8*0	PHI-LA 9*3	HOU-NY 2*0	CIN-PIT 2*1	MON-SD 4*3	STL-SF 1-3	
0706	NY-ATL 3*1	MON-LA 3-8	CIN-CHI 6*2	HOU-PIT 0-1	STL-SD 4*0	PHI-SF 2-4	
		MON-LA 3-4					
0707	NY-ATL 5*4	MON-LA 4*1	CIN-CHI 3*2	HOU-PIT 3-5	STL-SD 6*3	PHI-SF 7-8	
		MON-LA 4*0				PHI-SF 6-10	

◆1992◆	GAME 1	GAME 2	GAME 3	GAME 4	GAME 5	GAME 6	GAME 7
0708	NY-ATL 1-2	MON-LA 0-1 / MON-LA 4*1	CIN-CHI 2-3	HOU-PIT 3*2	STL-SD 1*0	PHI-SF 3-4	
0709	ATL-CHI 2*0	STL-LA 1-2	PIT-CIN 2-5	NY-HOU 0-4	PHI-SD 1-3	MON-SF 6*5	
0710	ATL-CHI 4*0	STL-LA 3*1	PIT-CIN 4*0	NY-HOU 7*6	PHI-SD 7-8	MON-SF 3*2	
0711	ATL-CHI 3*1	STL-LA 4*1	PIT-CIN 9*3	NY-HOU 8*2	PHI-SD 2-3	MON-SF 0-3	
0712	ATL-CHI 7*4	STL-LA 0-9	PIT-CIN 7*6	NY-HOU 1-3	PHI-SD 2-8	MON-SF 0-4	
0716	SD-MON 4-7	SF-NY 6*4	STL-CIN 5*1	ATL-HOU 4*2	LA-PHI 7*5	CHI-PIT 1-2	
0717	SD-MON 0-3	SF-NY 0-1	STL-CIN 1-8	ATL-HOU 5*0	LA-PHI 3-11	CHI-PIT 2*1	
0718	SD-MON 10*3	SF-NY 0-3	STL-CIN 2-3	ATL-HOU 3*0	LA-PHI 3-14	CHI-PIT 0-4	
0719	SD-MON 9*2	SF-NY 4-8	STL-CIN 4-5	ATL-HOU 3*2	LA-PHI 5-6	CHI-PIT 4*2	
0720	SF-MON 1-2	LA-NY 9*2	CHI-CIN 2-5	PIT-HOU 8-11	SD-PHI 2*1		
0721	SF-MON 1-5	LA-NY 2-5	CHI-CIN 1*0	PIT-HOU 3-4	SD-PHI 4*3	ATL-STL 9*7	
0722	SF-MON 4*1	LA-NY 5-7	CHI-CIN 3*0	PIT-HOU 10*7	SD-PHI 0-4	ATL-STL 2*0	
0723						CIN-STL 2-3	
0724	PIT-ATL 3-4	CHI-HOU 1*0	LA-MON 3-4	SD-NY 0-3	SF-PHI 4-8	CIN-STL 2-8	
0725	PIT-ATL 0-1	CHI-HOU 2-3	LA-MON 1-4	SD-NY 2*0	SF-PHI 6*2	CIN-STL 9*1	
0726	PIT-ATL 5*4	CHI-HOU 8*5	LA-MON 3-4	SD-NY 1*0	SF-PHI 2-7	CIN-STL 7*6	
0727	HOU-ATL 5*1	PIT-CHI 2-3	CIN-SD 1-2	LA-SF 1-5	NY-PHI 0-5	MON-STL 6*4	
0728	HOU-ATL 7*5	PIT-CHI 1-11	CIN-SD 4*1	LA-SF 3-5	NY-PHI 8*6	MON-STL 7*4	
0729	HOU-ATL 3-5	PIT-CHI 4-6	CIN-SD 3-7	LA-SF 6*1	NY-PHI 3-6	MON-STL 1-4	
0730	SD-LA 5-6	PHI-MON 2-7	STL-PIT 0-4	ATL-SF 0-5			
0731	SD-LA 4*3	PHI-MON 2*0	STL-PIT 2-3	ATL-SF 3-4	HOU-CIN 1-6		
0801	SD-LA 2-7	PHI-MON 4*2	STL-PIT 1-4	ATL-SF 5*3	HOU-CIN 0-9	CHI-NY 0-3 / CHI-NY 6*1	
0802	HOU-CIN 5*4	SD-LA 1-4	PHI-MON 0-1	STL-PIT 1-2	ATL-SF 3*0 / ATL-SF 8*5	CHI-NY 2-4	
0803	HOU-CIN 0-4	CHI-MON 2-3	SF-SD 5-6	PHI-STL 1-2			
0804	CIN-ATL 5-7	CHI-MON 8*6	SF-SD 7*1	PHI-STL 5-9	HOU-LA 2-7	NY-PIT 2-3	
0805	CIN-ATL 1-5	CHI-MON 3-5	SF-SD 4-5	PHI-STL 4-5	HOU-LA 7*6	NY-PIT 2-6	
0806	CIN-ATL 3-5	NY-CHI 2-5	HOU-SD 5-7	PIT-STL 3*2	MON-PHI 7*4		
0807	LA-ATL 2-6	NY-CHI 1-9	HOU-SD 2-4	PIT-STL 5*1	MON-PHI 1-3	SF-CIN 3-4	
0808	LA-ATL 2-12	NY-CHI 3-4	HOU-SD 5-7	PIT-STL 2*1	MON-PHI 6*1	SF-CIN 3-4	
0809	LA-ATL 3-10	NY-CHI 2-6	HOU-SD 3-4	PIT-STL 7*5	MON-PHI 6*2	SF-CIN 7*1	
0810	LA-ATL 5*3	MON-CHI 11*0	PIT-NY 4*2	HOU-SF 1-4			
0811	SD-ATL 8*4	MON-CHI 3*2	PIT-NY 0-2	HOU-SF 6*3	LA-CIN 8*4	STL-PHI 7*6	
0812		MON-CHI 3*1	PIT-NY 7*6	HOU-SF 5*4	LA-CIN 2-3	STL-PHI 3*2	
0813	SD-ATL 3-4	HOU-CHI 4*3			LA-CIN 4*3		
0814	SF-LA 3*2	HOU-CHI 2-4	STL-MON 1-4	PHI-NY 6*2	SD-CIN 5*1	ATL-PIT 15*0	
0815	SF-LA 2*1	HOU-CHI 5*0	STL-MON 6*4	PHI-NY 4*3	SD-CIN 4-5	ATL-PIT 7*5	
0816	SF-LA 2*1	HOU-CHI 0-1	STL-MON 5*2		SD-CIN 2-12	ATL-PIT 2-4	
0817	SF-LA 0-2					ATL-PIT 5*4	
0818	NY-LA 0-4	ATL-MON 5*1	CIN-PHI 6*0 / CIN-PHI 1-6	CHI-SF 4*1	HOU-STL 7*6	SD-PIT 1-5	
0819	NY-LA 1-2	ATL-MON 4*2	CIN-PHI 3-9	SD-PIT 2-3	CHI-SF 1-9	HOU-STL 1-12	
0820	NY-LA 11*4	ATL-MON 2-3		SD-PIT 1-7	CHI-SF 6*5	HOU-STL 1-3	
0821	CHI-LA 3*2	CIN-MON 3-6	STL-ATL 5*2	HOU-PHI 6*1	PIT-SF 5-6		
0822	CHI-LA 5*4	CIN-MON 1-3	STL-ATL 2-3	HOU-PHI 14*9	PIT-SF 9*2	NY-SD 2-4	
0823	CHI-LA 4*2	CIN-MON 1*0	STL-ATL 8*3	HOU-PHI 3*1	PIT-SF 2-5	NY-SD 3-4	
0824	PIT-LA 4-5	PHI-CIN 5-8			NY-SF 4*1	CHI-SD 6*3	
0825	PIT-LA 10*3	PHI-CIN 1-7	MON-ATL 6*0	STL-HOU 5*3	NY-SF 2*1	CHI-SD 4-7	
0826	PIT-LA 2*0	PHI-CIN 3-4	MON-ATL 5*4	STL-HOU 5-6	NY-SF 5*3	CHI-SD 0-3	
0827				STL-HOU 1-5			
0828	SF-CHI 2-3	CIN-NY 3-4 / CIN-NY 1-12	ATL-PHI 3-7	MON-HOU 1-8	PIT-SD 6-11	LA-STL 0-1	
0829	SF-CHI 2-7	CIN-NY 5-6	MON-HOU 2-8	ATL-PHI 7*6	PIT-SD 3*2	LA-STL 2-3	
0830	SF-CHI 1-3	CIN-NY 3-4	MON-HOU 4*0	ATL-PHI 2-10	PIT-SD 6*3	LA-STL 0-3	
0831	LA-CHI 0-2	ATL-NY 8*6 / ATL-NY 7*5	PHI-HOU 2-9	MON-CIN 8*4		SD-STL 2-6	
0901	LA-CHI 5*4	ATL-NY 4*1	MON-CIN 5*2	PHI-HOU 3-5	SF-PIT 3-5	SD-STL 0-2	
0902	LA-CHI 1-5	ATL-NY 5-6	MON-CIN 7*3	PHI-HOU 2-3	SF-PIT 2-3	SD-STL 5*4	
0903	MON-ATL 11*2		NY-CIN 3-4		SF-PIT 3-9		
0904	PHI-ATL 2*1	SD-CHI 7*5	NY-CIN 5*2	HOU-MON 2-5	LA-PIT 5-6	SF-STL 4*3	
0905	PHI-ATL 5-6	SD-CHI 5*3	NY-CIN 5-6	HOU-MON 5*2	LA-PIT 1-6	SF-STL 0-4	
0906	PHI-ATL 3-4	SD-CHI 3*1	NY-CIN 1-6	HOU-MON 3*1	LA-PIT 7*5	SF-STL 3-5	
0907	LA-ATL 1-7	CIN-HOU 10*0	NY-PHI 6*3	STL-MON 8*7	CHI-PIT 6*5	SD-SF 7*5	
0908	LA-ATL 5-7	CIN-HOU 0-2	NY-PHI 1-2	STL-MON 1-6	CHI-PIT 2-5	SD-SF 5-6	
0909	CIN-ATL 7-12	SD-LA 1-4	NY-PHI 1-2	STL-MON 10*3	CHI-PIT 8-13	HOU-SF 6*4	
0910	CIN-ATL 2-3	SD-LA 3*1				HOU-SF 2-5	
0911	ATL-HOU 7*0	SF-LA 7*3	NY-MON 3-4	PIT-PHI 2-5	CIN-SD 4*1	CHI-STL 8*2	
0912	ATL-HOU 9*3	SF-LA 0-7	NY-MON 1-4	PIT-PHI 9*7	CIN-SD 7*4	CHI-STL 3-11	
0913	ATL-HOU 9*2	SF-LA 7*3	NY-MON 5-7	PIT-PHI 3-6	CIN-SD 1-3	CHI-STL 3-10	
0914	SF-HOU 0-5	NY-CHI 10*8		MON-PHI 2-5	LA-SD 5*4	PIT-STL 5*4	
0915	SF-HOU 6-9	NY-CHI 4*2	ATL-CIN 2-4	MON-PHI 3*0	LA-SD 6*3	PIT-STL 4*2	
0916	SF-HOU 1-3	PHI-CHI 9-14	ATL-CIN 3*2	STL-NY 10*4	LA-SD 1-3	MON-PIT 6*3	
0917		PHI-CHI 0-3	ATL-CIN 2-3	STL-NY 3*2		MON-PIT 2-3	
0918	HOU-ATL 13*3	STL-CHI 7-9	SD-CIN 2-4	MON-NY 10*4	LA-SF 11*4	PHI-PIT 2-5	
0919	HOU-ATL 3*2	STL-CHI 5-6 / STL-CHI 11*10	SD-CIN 2-5	MON-NY 5-7	LA-SF 0-3	PHI-PIT 0-3	
0920	HOU-ATL 1-16	STL-CHI 16*4	SD-CIN 1-6	MON-NY 0-1	PHI-PIT 2-3	LA-SF 2-3	
0921	ATL-LA 4*2	PHI-MON 9*2	SF-NY 7*1	CHI-NY 10*1	STL-PIT 1-0		
0922	ATL-LA 1-4	PHI-MON 5*2	SF-SD 1-2	CHI-NY 7-8	STL-PIT 5*4	HOU-CIN 3-6 / HOU-CIN 3-4	
0923	CIN-LA 3*0	PIT-MON 1-5	CHI-PHI 3-9	HOU-SD 7*6	ATL-SF 7*0	NY-STL 3*2	
0924	CIN-LA 8*4	PIT-MON 9*3	CHI-PHI 2-3	HOU-SD 1-7	ATL-SF 0-4	NY-STL 3-4	
0925	HOU-LA 4*3	CHI-MON 3-4	NY-PIT 2-3	ATL-SD 0-1	CIN-SF 4*2		
0926	HOU-LA 5*4	CHI-MON 0-12	NY-PIT 2-19	ATL-SD 2*1	CIN-SF 3-8	STL-PHI 1-3 / STL-PHI 0-10	
0927	HOU-LA 4*2	CHI-MON 0-1	NY-PIT 2-4	ATL-SD 2*1	CIN-SF 3*2	STL-PHI 8*1 / STL-PHI 5-6	
0928	PIT-CHI 10*3	PHI-NY 7*6 / PHI-NY 7*6	MON-STL 1-4				
0929	SF-ATL 0-6	PHI-NY 5*3	PIT-CHI 3*0	LA-CIN 5*0	SD-HOU 5-6	MON-STL 1-2	
0930	SF-ATL 1*0	PHI-NY 2-6	PIT-CHI 0-6	LA-CIN 1-3	SD-HOU 4-5	MON-STL 2-3	
1001	SF-ATL 5-6			LA-CIN 4*2	SD-HOU 3*2		
1002	SD-ATL 1-4 / SD-ATL 2-7	MON-CHI 1-3	PIT-NY 3-6	SF-CIN 4*1	LA-HOU 1-6	PHI-STL 1-2	
1003	SD-ATL 0-1	MON-CHI 3*1	SF-CIN 1-6	LA-HOU 2-3	PIT-NY 1-2	PHI-STL 3*2	
1004	SD-ATL 4*3	MON-CHI 2-3	SF-CIN 6*2	LA-HOU 0-3	PIT-NY 2*0	PHI-STL 3-6	

◆1993◆	GAME 1	GAME 2	GAME 3	GAME 4	GAME 5	GAME 6	GAME 7
0405	ATL-CHI 1*0	COL-NY 0-3	LA-FLA 3-6	MON-CIN 1-2	PHI-HOU 3*1		
0406	ATL-CHI 0-1	SD-PIT 4-9	LA-FLA 4*2	SF-STL 2*1	PHI-HOU 5*3		
0407	ATL-CHI 5*4	COL-NY 1-6	LA-FLA 4*2	SF-STL 2-6	PHI-HOU 6*3	MON-CIN 5*1	
0408	LA-ATL 1-6	SD-PIT 4-5		SF-STL 1-2		MON-CIN 14*11	
0409	LA-ATL 0-2	SF-PIT 5-6	SD-FLA 2*1	CIN-STL 2-8	CHI-PHI 11*7	HOU-NY 7*3	MON-COL 4-11
0410	LA-ATL 2*1	SF-PIT 12*5	SD-FLA 1-2	CIN-STL 1-2	CHI-PHI 4-5	HOU-NY 6*3	MON-COL 5-9
0411	LA-ATL 0-3	SF-PIT 4*3	SD-FLA 6*2	CIN-STL 4*3	CHI-PHI 0-3	HOU-NY 5*4	MON-COL 19*9

♦1993♦	GAME 1		GAME 2		GAME 3		GAME 4		GAME 5		GAME 6		GAME 7	
0412	CHI-ATL	5*1	FLA-SF	3-4	PIT-SD	4*2			CIN-PHI	4-5				
0413	CHI-ATL	2-3	FLA-SF	1-3	PIT-SD	6*4	HOU-MON	9*6	CIN-PHI	1-4	STL-LA	9*7	NY-COL	8*4
0414	CHI-ATL	6*0	FLA-SF	6*4	PIT-SD	11*7	HOU-MON	9*5	CIN-PHI	2-9	STL-LA	2*1	NY-COL	6*3
0415			ATL-SF	1-6	PIT-SD	5*4	HOU-MON	1-2			STL-LA	4*2	NY-COL	3-5
0416	FLA-HOU	3-9	ATL-SF	0-1	STL-SD	1-5	COL-MON	2-3	NY-CIN	3*1	PIT-LA	4-7	PHI-CHI	1-3
0417	FLA-HOU	9*4	ATL-SF	2*0	STL-SD	0-2	COL-MON	9*1	NY-CIN	4*1	PIT-LA	3-6	PHI-CHI	3-6
0418	FLA-HOU	0-3	ATL-SF	12-13	STL-SD	6-10	COL-MON	2-4	NY-CIN	2-3	PIT-LA	4-6	PHI-CHI	11*10
0420	ATL-FLA	5*4	CIN-PIT	5*0	COL-STL	5*0	LA-MON	3-7	SD-PHI	3-4	SF-NY	4*1	HOU-CHI	1-2
0421	ATL-FLA	7*4	CIN-PIT	8*7	COL-STL	11*2	LA-MON	4-6			SF-NY	0-10	HOU-CHI	2*0
0422	ATL-FLA	3-4	CIN-PIT	4-5	COL-STL	2-5	LA-MON	1-3	SD-PHI	2*1	SF-NY	13*4		
0423	FLA-COL	4-5	HOU-PIT	4*2	ATL-STL	3*1	SF-MON	2-7	LA-PHI	0-2	SD-NY	1-6	CIN-CHI	4-7
0424	FLA-COL	2*1	HOU-PIT	8*4	ATL-STL	11*0	SF-MON	1-6	LA-PHI	3-7	SD-NY	5*3	CIN-CHI	15*5
0425	FLA-COL	11*1	HOU-PIT	2-7	ATL-STL	3-7	SF-MON	4*1	LA-PHI	2-5	SD-NY	9*8	CIN-CHI	1-2
0426	CHI-COL	6*3	FLA-CIN	0-3	MON-SD	6*4	PIT-ATL	4*3	SF-PHI	8-9	STL-HOU	3*2		
0427	CHI-COL	2-11	FLA-CIN	4*3	MON-SD	1-4	PIT-ATL	6*2	SF-PHI	6*3	STL-HOU	2-9	LA-NY	4*1
0428	STL-COL	7*6	PIT-CIN	2-4	PHI-SD	5*3	FLA-ATL	3*1	MON-LA	1-6	CHI-HOU	1-6	NY-SF	3-4
0429	STL-COL	5*2			PHI-SD	5*3	FLA-ATL	6*5	MON-LA	7*3	CHI-HOU	4-5	NY-SF	5-10
0430	COL-FLA	6*2	CHI-CIN	7*3	NY-SD	6*7	STL-ATL	2-3	PHI-LA	7*6	PIT-HOU	2-11	MON-SF	2-5
0501	COL-FLA	6-7	CHI-CIN	4-9	NY-SD	3-5	STL-ATL	10*3	PHI-LA	1-5	PIT-HOU	3-7	MON-SF	3-7
0502	COL-FLA	2*1	CHI-CIN	4*3	NY-SD	3*2	STL-ATL	3-4	PHI-LA	9*1	PIT-HOU	6*2	MON-SF	3-4
0504	CIN-FLA	6-9	ATL-PIT	3*2	COL-CHI	14*13	HOU-STL	1-6	NY-LA	4-8	SD-MON	1-6	PHI-SF	4*3
0505	CIN-FLA	6*2	ATL-PIT	1-4	COL-CHI	2-3	HOU-STL	6*3	NY-LA	5-6	SD-MON	5-6	PHI-SF	2-11
0506	ATL-COL	13*3	CIN-HOU	5*4										
0507	ATL-COL	13*5	CIN-HOU	7*5	SD-CHI	2*1	FLA-NY	0-4	MON-PIT	1*0	STL-PHI	3-4	LA-SF	5-8
0508	ATL-COL	8*7	CIN-HOU	1-12	SD-CHI	6-8	FLA-NY	4*2	MON-PIT	9-10	STL-PHI	1-2	LA-SF	5*2
0509	ATL-COL	12*7	CIN-HOU	3-6	SD-CHI	5*4	FLA-NY	6*4	MON-PIT	5-6	STL-PHI	5-6	LA-SF	6*4
0510	SF-COL	4-7	ATL-HOU	2-5	LA-CHI	2-6	FLA-NY	0-1	SD-CIN	5-6	PIT-PHI	1-5		
0511	SF-COL	5*3	ATL-HOU	5*4	LA-CHI	1-2	FLA-MON	4-6	SD-CIN	2-4	PIT-PHI	8*4	NY-STL	4-7
0512	SF-COL	8*2	ATL-HOU	5*2	LA-CHI	9*3	FLA-MON	10*7	SD-CIN	2-3	PIT-PHI	1-4	NY-STL	5-6
0513	SF-COL	13*8					FLA-MON	4-5	SD-CIN	1-7			NY-STL	4*0
0514	PHI-ATL	7-10	LA-HOU	1-9	PIT-CHI	2-3	NY-MON	7-8	COL-CIN	5-13	SF-SD	1-3	FLA-STL	2-7
0515	PHI-ATL	3-5	LA-HOU	1-7	PIT-CHI	5-14	NY-MON	1-2	COL-CIN	3-5	SF-SD	3*0	FLA-STL	8*0
0516	PHI-ATL	5*4	LA-HOU	2-3	PIT-CHI	5*3	NY-MON	3-4	COL-CIN	2-14	SF-SD	9*4	FLA-STL	0-1
0517	MON-ATL	2-5	CIN-LA	4-5	HOU-SF	7-8	PHI-FLA	10*3	PIT-NY	9*4	COL-SD	0-4		
0518	MON-ATL	1*0	CIN-LA	1-9	HOU-SF	2-7	PHI-FLA	6*0	PIT-NY	10*8	COL-SD	2*1	CHI-STL	4*1
0519	MON-ATL	0-1	CIN-LA	2-5	HOU-SF	3-6	PHI-FLA	3-5	PIT-NY	4-6	COL-SD	3-7	CHI-STL	5*3
0520	MON-PHI	3-9			CIN-SF	1-6					COL-SD	4-5	CHI-STL	3-6
0521	MON-PHI	6*2	COL-LA	0-8	CIN-SF	0-3	CHI-FLA	3-5	ATL-NY	4*2	HOU-SD	2-3	STL-PIT	10*8
0522	MON-PHI	6*5	COL-LA	3-4	CIN-SF	6*2	CHI-FLA	2*1	ATL-NY	1-6	HOU-SD	4-9	STL-PIT	2-4
0523	MON-PHI	7-14	COL-LA	0-4	CIN-SF	2-3	CHI-FLA	2-4	ATL-NY	2*1	HOU-SD	9*7	STL-PIT	4*3
0524	NY-PHI	3-6	SD-LA	4-5	STL-MON	4*1								
0525	NY-PHI	2-4	SD-LA	9-10	STL-MON	2-4	ATL-CIN	5*0	COL-HOU	7*5	SF-CHI	5*4	FLA-PIT	0-2
0526	NY-PHI	5*4	SD-LA	3-8	STL-MON	0-6	ATL-CIN	0-4	COL-HOU	3*2	SF-CHI	2-4	FLA-PIT	5*4
0527							ATL-CIN	4-5	COL-HOU	0-8	SF-CHI	4-5	FLA-PIT	8-13
0528	CIN-NY	5*2	HOU-FLA	4-5	PHI-COL	15*9	SD-STL	2-3	SF-ATL	4-7	MON-CHI	22	LA-PIT	7*2
0529	CIN-NY	3-4	HOU-FLA	4*2	PHI-COL	6*0	SD-STL	7*4	SF-ATL	6*3	MON-CHI	5*4	LA-PIT	6*1
0530	CIN-NY	8*4	HOU-FLA	2*1	PHI-COL	18*1	SD-STL	4-10	SF-ATL	4*3	MON-CHI	2-5	LA-PIT	3-5
0531	MON-HOU	1-2	PHI-CIN	4-6	PIT-COL	2-6	LA-STL	5*1	SD-ATL	1-2	NY-CHI	9*5		
0601	MON-HOU	2*1	PHI-CIN	6*3	PIT-COL	8*6	LA-STL	11*6	SD-ATL	2*1	NY-CHI	3-8	SF-FLA	3-7
													SF-FLA	4*3
0602	MON-HOU	4-5	PHI-CIN	5*2	PIT-COL	5*3	LA-STL	4-5	SD-ATL	2-5	NY-CHI	11*3	SF-FLA	3*2
0603	CHI-MON	1-7	STL-CIN	9*2	PIT-SF	2*1			SD-ATL	12*4				
0604	CHI-MON	1-3	ATL-LA	4-5	PIT-SF	3*2	COL-PHI	2*1	FLA-SD	6*2	NY-HOU	2-7		
0605	CHI-MON	3-6	ATL-LA	1-5	PIT-SF	2-3	COL-PHI	2-6	FLA-SD	3*1	NY-HOU	5-7	STL-CIN	2-6
0606	CHI-MON	4*1	ATL-LA	2*0	PIT-SF	1-7	COL-PHI	7-11	FLA-SD	9*2	NY-HOU	4-5	STL-CIN	5*1
0607	CIN-MON	12*3	FLA-LA	5*3	CHI-NY	2-7	HOU-PHI	5-7	ATL-SD	4*0				
0608	CIN-MON	2-4	FLA-LA	1-2	CHI-NY	5*1	HOU-PHI	6*3	ATL-SD	4-5	COL-PIT	4*1	STL-SF	4-3
0609	CIN-MON	3*2			CHI-NY	8*3	HOU-PHI	0-8			COL-PIT	1-4	STL-SF	1-3
0610	CIN-ATL	3*1	MON-STL	4-7	PHI-NY	7*6	PIT-FLA	3-4	LA-SD	2-14				
0611	CIN-ATL	5-6	MON-STL	0-1	PHI-NY	5*2	PIT-FLA	3-11	LA-SD	4-15	HOU-COL	4-5	CHI-SF	2-7
0612	CIN-ATL	2-7	MON-STL	3-13	PHI-NY	3*0	PIT-FLA	2-5	LA-SD	6*4	HOU-COL	11-14	CHI-SF	4-5
0613	CIN-ATL	3*1	MON-STL	3*1	PHI-NY	5*3	PIT-FLA	2-5	LA-SD	2*1	HOU-COL	1-9	CHI-SF	3-5
0614	NY-ATL	7*4	PIT-STL	3-8	FLA-CHI	3-6	PHI-MON	10*3	SD-HOU	3*0	LA-COL	9*4	SF-CIN	5-10
0615	NY-ATL	1-2	PIT-STL	3-6	FLA-CHI	0-3	PHI-MON	4-8	SD-HOU	4-5	LA-COL	12*4	SF-CIN	6*5
0616	NY-ATL	2-5	PIT-STL	2-3	FLA-CHI	4-6	PHI-MON	3-4	SD-HOU	1-4	LA-COL	6-7	SF-CIN	5*1
0617	FLA-PHI	4*1	NY-PIT	2-6	STL-CHI	11*10			SF-HOU	5*0	SD-COL	11*1	LA-CIN	3-4
0618	FLA-PHI	3-7	NY-PIT	2-5	STL-CHI	3-8	ATL-MON	1-2	SF-HOU	10*3	SD-COL	3-17	LA-CIN	4-8
0619	FLA-PHI	2-5	NY-PIT	3-8	STL-CHI	6*4	ATL-MON	4*3	SF-HOU	8*5	SD-COL	1-3	LA-CIN	6*3
0620	FLA-PHI	2-5	NY-PIT	2-3	STL-CHI	7*4	ATL-MON	5*1						
0621	ATL-PHI	8*1	CHI-PIT	5*1	HOU-LA	0-7	MON-NY	3-8	SD-SF	3-8	CIN-COL	4-5	STL-FLA	4*3
0622	ATL-PHI	3-5	CHI-PIT	2-7	HOU-LA	5*1	MON-NY	6*3	SD-SF	2*1	CIN-COL	16*13	STL-FLA	5-7
0623	ATL-PHI	3-8	CHI-PIT	4-9	HOU-LA	5*3	MON-NY	4*3	SD-SF	2-6	CIN-COL	5-15	STL-FLA	4*3
0624	CIN-SD	6*4			HOU-LA	1*0			COL-SF	2-17				
0625	CIN-SD	6*2	PHI-PIT	8*6	CHI-LA	8*5	STL-NY	8*5	COL-SF	2-7	HOU-ATL	2-8	MON-FLA	1-3
0626	CIN-SD	0-2	PHI-PIT	2-4	CHI-LA	4-5	STL-NY	4*2	COL-SF	5*1	HOU-ATL	5-6	MON-FLA	4*2
0627	CIN-SD	7*1	PHI-PIT	3-4	CHI-LA	1-3	STL-NY	5*3	COL-SF	0-5	HOU-ATL	3*0	MON-FLA	2-9
0628	CHI-SD	4*3	PHI-STL	1-3	SF-LA	0-4	PIT-MON	9*5						
0629	CHI-SD	10*5	PHI-STL	13*10	SF-LA	3*1	PIT-MON	2-9	HOU-CIN	0-3	COL-ATL	4-6	NY-FLA	10*9
0630	CHI-SD	4*1	PHI-STL	3-9	SF-LA	3-5	PIT-MON	1-9	HOU-CIN	4-5	COL-ATL	2-3	NY-FLA	7*1
0701			PHI-STL	5-14			PIT-MON	5-7	HOU-CIN	8*1	COL-ATL	0-4	NY-FLA	5-7
0702	CHI-COL	11*8	SF-NY	3*1	STL-HOU	1-7	LA-MON	4*3	PIT-CIN	10*9	FLA-ATL	4*2	SD-PHI	5*2
										PIT-CIN	1-9			SD-PHI	5-6
0703	CHI-COL	4-5	SF-NY	3-6	STL-HOU	0-6	LA-MON	4-6	PIT-CIN	3-5	FLA-ATL	2-11	SD-PHI	6*4
0704	CHI-COL	1-3	SF-NY	10*8	STL-HOU	4-9	LA-MON	1*0	PIT-CIN	2-7	FLA-ATL	3-4	SD-PHI	4-8
0705	CHI-COL	10*1	SD-NY	12*7	STL-HOU	10*4	SF-MON	10*4	PIT-CIN	4-6	FLA-ATL	7-9	LA-PHI	7*5
0706	FLA-COL	3-8	SD-NY	7-9	PIT-HOU	10*3	SF-MON	13*5	ATL-STL	4-5	CIN-CHI	2-3	LA-PHI	6-7
0707	FLA-COL	5-6	SD-NY	2*0	PIT-HOU	5*2	SF-MON	0-3	ATL-STL	1-3	CIN-CHI	4*3	SF-PHI	13*2
0708	FLA-COL	2-3	LA-NY	11*8	PIT-HOU	4-10	SD-MON	4-5	ATL-STL	1-7	CIN-CHI	7*3		
			LA-NY	3-6											
0709	ATL-FLA	5*1	LA-NY	6*2	CIN-PIT	1-4	SD-MON	1-6	COL-STL	5*4	HOU-CHI	2-5	SF-PHI	15*8
0710	ATL-FLA	2-5	LA-NY	6-7	CIN-PIT	10*7	SD-MON	2-3	COL-STL	3-9	HOU-CHI	4*0	SF-PHI	3-8
											HOU-CHI	5*2			
0711	ATL-FLA	6*3	LA-NY	2*1	CIN-PIT	2-3	SD-MON	4-5	COL-STL	4*1	HOU-CHI	10*1	SF-PHI	10*2
0715	FLA-CIN	4-7	MON-LA	2-3	NY-SF	1-8	PHI-SD	2-5	HOU-STL	2-4	COL-CHI	0-1	PIT-ATL	0-4
0716	FLA-CIN	0-4	MON-LA	1-2	NY-SF	2-4	PHI-SD	3-5	HOU-STL	7*6	COL-CHI	2-8	PIT-ATL	2-3
0717	FLA-CIN	6*3	MON-LA	9*6	NY-SF	3*1	PHI-SD	2-4	HOU-STL	3-5	COL-CHI	1-5	PIT-ATL	4*3
0718	FLA-CIN	3-5	MON-LA	1-2	NY-SF	12*6	PHI-SD	6*3	HOU-STL	6-7	COL-CHI	2-12	PIT-ATL	0-2
0719	CHI-CIN	6*4	PHI-LA	7*5	MON-SF	2-6	NY-SD	2*1	COL-FLA	1-3	HOU-PIT	4*2	STL-ATL	4*0
0720	CHI-CIN	3-8	PHI-LA	8*2	MON-SF	3-8	NY-SD	1-4	COL-FLA	6*3	HOU-PIT	1-2	STL-ATL	5-8
0721	CHI-CIN	4*1	PHI-LA	7*0	MON-SF	4-5	NY-SD	3-2	COL-FLA	6*4	HOU-PIT	5*3	STL-ATL	2-14
0722	CHI-HOU	4-9	NY-LA	10*5	PHI-SF	1-4	MON-SD	10*5	CIN-FLA	7*3	ATL-PIT	7-8	STL-COL	6-7
0723	CHI-HOU	1-5	NY-LA	2-5	PHI-SF	2*1	MON-SD	5*0	CIN-FLA	3*2	ATL-PIT	6*2	STL-COL	13*11
0724	CHI-HOU	7*6	NY-LA	4-5	PHI-SF	4-5	MON-SD	4-11	CIN-FLA	0-2	ATL-PIT	11*6	STL-COL	8-9
0725	CHI-HOU	3*1	NY-LA	4*0	PHI-SF	2-5	MON-SD	5*4	CIN-FLA	3-7	ATL-PIT	13*1	STL-COL	5*4
0726	CIN-HOU	6*1	SD-CHI	6-9	LA-SF	15*1							ATL-COL	12*7
0727	CIN-HOU	5-6	SD-CHI	8*0	LA-SF	2-3	FLA-NY	3-4	STL-PHI	7-10	MON-PIT	8*6	ATL-COL	10*5
0728	CIN-HOU	2-4	SD-CHI	6-8	LA-SF	2*1	FLA-NY	4-5	STL-PHI	6-14	MON-PIT	2-3	ATL-COL	3*2

♦1993♦	GAME 1	GAME 2	GAME 3	GAME 4	GAME 5	GAME 6	GAME 7
0729	ATL-HOU 0-2			FLA-NY 2*1	STL-PHI 4-6	MON-PIT 3*2	
0730	ATL-HOU 4*1	LA-CHI 1-2	FLA-MON 1-11	NY-STL 2-3	PIT-PHI 4*2	SD-CIN 11*9	SF-COL 10*4
0731	ATL-HOU 4*3	LA-CHI 7*2	FLA-MON 5-6	NY-STL 10*3	PIT-PHI 2-10	SD-CIN 3-6	SF-COL 4*3
0801	ATL-HOU 3*2	LA-CHI 4-10	FLA-MON 5*4	NY-STL 10*3	PIT-PHI 4-5	SD-CIN 3*1	SF-COL 6*5
0802		PIT-CHI 10-12	NY-MON 4*3	FLA-STL 3-5		COL-CIN 2-6	
0803	LA-HOU 1-6	PIT-CHI 7*3	NY-MON 1-3	FLA-STL 1*0	PHI-ATL 5*3	COL-CIN 4-5	SF-SD 12*7
0804	LA-HOU 4*2	PIT-CHI 6*5	NY-MON 1-3	FLA-STL 2-10	PHI-ATL 8-9	COL-CIN 3-9	SF-SD 10-11
0805	LA-HOU 5*2	PIT-CHI 5*2	NY-MON 12*9	FLA-STL 6-16	PHI-ATL 10*4	COL-CIN 4-11	SF-SD 5*3
0806	CIN-LA 2-3	HOU-SF 3-4	PHI-FLA 3-4	CHI-STL 6*4	MON-ATL 8*2		COL-SD 3-6
							COL-SD 2-6
0807	CIN-LA 9*6	HOU-SF 6*5	PHI-FLA 8*7	CHI-STL 1-4	MON-ATL 5*3	PIT-NY 2*1	
						PIT-NY 8-10	
0808	CIN-LA 8*5	HOU-SF 4*1	PHI-FLA 5-6	CHI-STL 2*1	MON-ATL 2-3	PIT-NY 3*2	COL-SD 5*2
0809	COL-LA 3*2	CIN-SF 7-10	CHI-FLA 2-3	STL-PIT 7*3			HOU-SD 5*4
0810	COL-LA 4*2	CIN-SF 1-2	CHI-FLA 2-3	STL-PIT 4*2	MON-PHI 2-5	ATL-NY 3*2	HOU-SD 2-7
0811	COL-LA 3*2	CIN-SF 0-6	CHI-FLA 11-12	STL-PIT 6-8	MON-PHI 5-6	ATL-NY 4*2	HOU-SD 9*6
0812	COL-LA 4*1		CHI-FLA 5*1	STL-PIT 4-5	MON-PHI 4-7	ATL-NY 8*4	HOU-SD 5*3
0813	SD-LA 4*1	ATL-CIN 14*0	COL-HOU 5*3	FLA-PIT 3-8	NY-PHI 5-9	SF-CHI 4*1	STL-MON 3-4
0814	SD-LA 3-4	ATL-CIN 4*2	COL-HOU 0-9	FLA-PIT 8*3	NY-PHI 9*5	SF-CHI 2-3	STL-MON 2*0
0815	SD-LA 2-4	ATL-CIN 1*0	COL-HOU 4*3	FLA-PIT 3-4	NY-PHI 4-5	SF-CHI 9*7	STL-MON 1-7
0816		NY-CIN 6*2					
0817	LA-ATL 2-3	NY-CIN 0-6	FLA-HOU 0-4	SF-PIT 3-10	PHI-COL 10*7	MON-CHI 2-7	SD-STL 4-8
						MON-CHI 6*4	
0818	LA-ATL 4-5	NY-CIN 12*2	FLA-HOU 1-2	SF-PIT 9*6	PHI-COL 7*6	MON-CHI 0-2	SD-STL 0-4
0819	LA-ATL 7*5		FLA-HOU 3-8	SF-PIT 6*3	PHI-COL 5-6	MON-CHI 10*2	SD-STL 2-3
0820	FLA-SF 5*4	MON-CIN 2-4	PHI-HOU 6*4	PIT-SD 7*6		ATL-CHI 3-6	LA-STL 3*2
0821	FLA-SF 4-7	MON-CIN 6*3	PHI-HOU 2-3		NY-COL 3-4	ATL-CHI 6*3	LA-STL 8*4
					NY-COL 6-8		
0822	FLA-SF 6-7	MON-CIN 7*2	PHI-HOU 3-7	PIT-SD 10*5	NY-COL 3-4	ATL-CHI 4*3	LA-STL 3*0
0823	ATL-SF 5*3	CHI-MON 0-1	CIN-NY 6*2	STL-SD 5-7	COL-PHI 3*2	PIT-LA 1-6	
0824	ATL-SF 6*4	CHI-MON 6*5	CIN-NY 4-5	STL-SD 4-17	COL-PHI 2-4	PIT-LA 4-13	HOU-FLA 4*0
0825	ATL-SF 9*1	CHI-MON 3-7	CIN-NY 4*1	STL-SD 1-2	COL-PHI 5-8	PIT-LA 2*1	HOU-FLA 3*2
0826			COL-NY 1-7				HOU-FLA 4-5
0827	CHI-ATL 9*7	HOU-MON 1-3	COL-NY 2-3	SD-PIT 10*6	CIN-PHI 8*5	STL-LA 3*2	SF-FLA 4-7
0828	CHI-ATL 1-5	HOU-MON 3-7	COL-NY 7*5	SD-PIT 5*3	CIN-PHI 9*5	STL-LA 4*3	
0829	CHI-ATL 2-8	HOU-MON 2-3	COL-NY 6*1	SD-PIT 4-7	CIN-PHI 0-12	STL-LA 3-8	SF-FLA 9*3
				SD-PIT 11*0			
0830	CIN-STL 10*3	MON-COL 6*1	HOU-NY 4-5	PHI-CHI 6-10			SF-FLA 5*1
0831	CIN-STL 6-7	MON-COL 14*3	HOU-NY 10*2	PHI-CHI 7*0	LA-PIT 2-6	SF-ATL 2-8	SD-FLA 1-2
0901	CIN-STL 4-7	MON-COL 11*3	HOU-NY 3*2	PHI-CHI 4*1	LA-PIT 1-5	SF-ATL 3*2	SD-FLA 13*5
0902				NY-CHI 8*3	LA-PIT 4*0	SF-ATL 3-5	SD-FLA 2-8
0903	SF-STL 6*1	PIT-COL 6-7	MON-HOU 3*0	NY-CHI 3-4	PHI-CIN 14*2	SD-ATL 3-7	LA-FLA 5*4
0904	SF-STL 3*1	PIT-COL 4-10	MON-HOU 7*5	NY-CHI 8-9	PHI-CIN 5-6	SD-ATL 2-3	LA-FLA 9*4
0905	SF-STL 6*7	PIT-COL 1-4	MON-HOU 1-7	NY-CHI 1-2	PHI-CIN 5*3	SD-ATL 2-3	LA-FLA 3-4
0906	ATL-LA 1-2	CHI-PHI 7*6	NY-HOU 2-7	COL-MON 3-4	FLA-SD 2*0	PIT-SF 1-4	
0907	ATL-LA 1*0	CHI-PHI 5*4	NY-HOU 3-4	COL-MON 3-4	FLA-SD 4-6	PIT-SF 4*3	STL-CIN 13-14
							STL-CIN 15*2
0908	ATL-LA 8*2	CHI-PHI 8*5	NY-HOU 1-7	COL-MON 1-6	FLA-SD 2-3		STL-CIN 2-6
0909	FLA-LA 5-6	CHI-PHI 8-10	COL-PIT 10*7		ATL-SD 1*0	STL-SF 9*4	
0910	FLA-LA 2*1	HOU-PHI 2-6	COL-PIT 9*8	CIN-MON 3-4	ATL-SD 3*2	STL-SF 6*2	CHI-NY 12*10
0911	FLA-LA 3*2	HOU-PHI 4*1	COL-PIT 3*2	CIN-MON 2-4	ATL-SD 13*1	STL-SF 3*1	CHI-NY 4*3
0912	FLA-LA 0-1	HOU-PHI 9*2	COL-PIT 3-4	CIN-MON 2-3	ATL-SD 4-5	STL-SF 4*2	CHI-NY 0-5
0913					LA-SD 3-4	CHI-SF 6*5	PHI-NY 5*0
0914	CIN-ATL 3-10	MON-STL 12*9	PIT-FLA 1*0	HOU-COL 4-9	LA-SD 5*3	CHI-SF 8*1	PHI-NY 4-5
				HOU-COL 5-6			
0915	CIN-ATL 6-7	MON-STL 4-5	PIT-FLA 8*1	HOU-COL 4-6	LA-SD 5*4	CHI-SF 3*1	PHI-NY 6*3
0916	CIN-ATL 2-3	MON-STL 4*3	PIT-FLA 10*0	HOU-COL 3-6			
0917	NY-ATL 1-2	PIT-STL 2*1	FLA-CHI 2*0	LA-COL 3-12	PHI-MON 7-8	SD-HOU 0-3	SF-CIN 13*0
0918	NY-ATL 3*2	PIT-STL 1-8	FLA-CHI 5-6	LA-COL 9*0	PHI-MON 5*4	SD-HOU 2-4	SF-CIN 6*1
0919	NY-ATL 2-11	PIT-STL 5-6	FLA-CHI 2*1	LA-COL 5-8	PHI-MON 5-6	SD-HOU 6*3	SF-CIN 7*3
0920	FLA-PHI 1-7	NY-PIT 2-6	STL-CHI 5-6	SD-COL 11*7		SF-HOU 7*2	LA-CIN 5*2
0921	FLA-PHI 3-5	NY-PIT 4*3	STL-CHI 3-13	SD-COL 4-15	ATL-MON 18*5	SF-HOU 0-6	LA-CIN 5*3
0922	FLA-PHI 1-2	NY-PIT 6*5	STL-CHI 9-11	SD-COL 4-11	ATL-MON 1-6	SF-HOU 3*1	LA-CIN 3*1
0923					ATL-MON 6*3	SF-HOU 7*0	LA-CIN 2-11
0924	ATL-PHI 0-3	CHI-PIT 8*3	HOU-LA 2-9	CIN-COL 2-9	MON-NY 6*3	SD-SF 3-4	STL-FLA 9*5
0925	ATL-PHI 9*7		HOU-LA 12*4	CIN-COL 6*0	MON-NY 4*1	SD-SF 1-3	STL-FLA 1-2
0926	ATL-PHI 7*2	CHI-PIT 1-5	HOU-LA 5*4	CIN-COL 7-12	MON-NY 3-9	SD-SF 2-5	STL-FLA 10*7
		CHI-PIT 0-1					
0927		PHI-PIT 6*4	CHI-LA 7*3		STL-NY 4*3	SD-SF 4-8	MON-FLA 1-3
0928	CIN-SD 4-11	PHI-PIT 10*7	CHI-LA 5-6	HOU-ATL 5*2	STL-NY 1-6	COL-SF 4-6	MON-FLA 3*2
0929	CIN-SD 8*0	PHI-PIT 1-9	CHI-LA 6*1	HOU-ATL 3-6	STL-NY 0-1	COL-SF 5*3	MON-FLA 7*1
0930		PHI-PIT 0-5	SF-LA 3*1	HOU-ATL 10*8	STL-NY 2-3		MON-FLA 5*3
1001	CHI-SD 8*5	HOU-CIN 2*0	SF-LA 8*7	COL-ATL 4*2	PHI-STL 4*2	PIT-MON 3-6	NY-FLA 4*1
1002	CHI-SD 3-7	HOU-CIN 3*1	SF-LA 5*3	COL-ATL 1-10	PHI-STL 4-5	PIT-MON 4*2	NY-FLA 7*1
1003	CHI-SD 4*1	HOU-CIN 4-7	SF-LA 1-12	COL-ATL 3-5	PHI-STL 0-2	PIT-MON 1-3	NY-FLA 9*2

♦1994♦	GAME 1	GAME 2	GAME 3	GAME 4	GAME 5	GAME 6	GAME 7
0403	STL-CIN 6*4						
0404	STL-CIN 4-5	ATL-SD 4*1	MON-HOU 5-6	NY-CHI 12*8	PHI-COL 12*6	PIT-SF 0-8	
0405	FLA-LA 3-4	ATL-SD 5*1	MON-HOU 5*1	NY-CHI 6*2		PIT-SF 0-2	
0406	FLA-LA 2-3	ATL-SD 7*2	MON-HOU 9*3	NY-CHI 4*1	PHI-COL 7*5	PIT-SF 2-4	STL-CIN 88
0407	FLA-LA 1*0	ATL-SD 10*8			PHI-COL 13*8		
0408	ATL-LA 6*0	FLA-SD 0-4	NY-HOU 3-6	CHI-MON 4*0	COL-PIT 7*3		PHI-CIN 4-5
0409	ATL-LA 2*1	FLA-SD 15*1	NY-HOU 8*2	CHI-MON 4*3	COL-PIT 5-10	STL-SF 3-4	PHI-CIN 1-2
						STL-SF 5*1	
0410	ATL-LA 6*3	FLA-SD 8*5	NY-HOU 1-6	CHI-MON 2-8		STL-SF 2*1	PHI-CIN 5-7
0411	CHI-NY 9*5	COL-PHI 8*7		CIN-MON 9*4			
0412	HOU-FLA 7*2	LA-STL 7*3	SF-ATL 7*5	CIN-MON 7*1	SD-PIT 2-4		
0413	HOU-FLA 4*2	LA-STL 3-6	SF-ATL 3-6	CIN-MON 2-3	SD-PIT 2-3	COL-PHI 3-12	
0414	HOU-FLA 2-8	LA-STL 8-9	SF-ATL 1-6	CHI-NY 9-10	SD-PIT 2-4	COL-PHI 5*0	
0415	SF-STL 6*0	SD-STL 6-10	ATL-CHI 19*5	HOU-NY 8*1	LA-PIT 4-6	CIN-PHI 1-3	MON-COL 2-9
0416	SF-FLA 3-5	SD-STL 8*2	ATL-CHI 4*1	HOU-NY 1-9	LA-PIT 3-4	CIN-PHI 4-6	MON-COL 3-7
0417	SF-FLA 9*8	SD-STL 0-5	ATL-CHI 4*2	HOU-NY 2-4	LA-PIT 19*2	CIN-PHI 7*0	MON-COL 5-6
0418	MON-SF 1-2	NY-SD 3-6	STL-ATL 1-7			LA-PHI 4-5	FLA-COL 5*3
0419	MON-SF 4*3	NY-SD 4*3	STL-ATL 5*4	HOU-CHI 3*0	PIT-CIN 2-8	LA-PHI 8*7	FLA-COL 6*4
0420	PHI-SF 4*2	MON-SD 4*2	STL-ATL 8*3	HOU-CHI 7*5	PIT-CIN 4-5	NY-LA 5-6	FLA-COL 6-16
						NY-LA 3-13	
0421	PHI-SF 6*1	MON-SD 5*4					
0422	NY-SF 3*1	PHI-SD 5-6	PIT-ATL 5*2	HOU-STL 5-6	FLA-CIN 2-4	MON-LA 7*6	CHI-COL 9*2
0423	NY-SF 1-10	PHI-SD 2-8	PIT-ATL 6*1	HOU-STL 15*5	FLA-CIN 3*2	MON-LA 8*6	CHI-COL 2-8
0424	NY-SF 2-4	PHI-SD 5-6	PIT-ATL 0-3	HOU-STL 4-5	FLA-CIN 2-5	MON-LA 1-7	CHI-COL 12*4
0425	ATL-FLA 3-4	PIT-HOU 3-7		COL-STL 7*6	CHI-CIN 3-4		
0426	ATL-FLA 9*6	PIT-HOU 7*4	SD-NY 6*3	COL-STL 1-2	CHI-CIN 2-8	PHI-LA 3-4	SF-MON 3-7
0427	COL-FLA 2-3	CHI-HOU 5-8	SD-NY 2-3	CIN-PIT 1-3		PHI-LA 4-5	SF-MON 1-7
0428	COL-FLA 7-8	CHI-HOU 5*3		CIN-PIT 19*7			
0429	CIN-FLA 8*5	STL-HOU 3-4	LA-NY 4-6	ATL-PIT 5-8	COL-CHI 6*5	SF-PHI 3-6	SD-MON 1-3
0430	CIN-FLA 3-4	STL-HOU 5-15	LA-NY 12*10	ATL-PIT 1-2		SF-PHI 1*0	SD-MON 3-5
0501	CIN-FLA 4-9	STL-HOU 6*5	LA-NY 4-7	ATL-PIT 1-4	COL-CHI 6*2	SF-PHI 4-6	SD-MON 2-3

◆1994◆	GAME 1	GAME 2	GAME 3	GAME 4	GAME 5	GAME 6	GAME 7
0502			SF-NY 10*3		CIN-CHI 9*0	SD-PHI 2-7	LA-MON 5-10
0503	FLA-ATL 6*3	STL-COL 1-10	SF-NY 6*5	HOU-PIT 7*4	CIN-CHI 5*2	SD-PHI 8*3	LA-MON 10*4
0504	FLA-ATL 0-3	STL-COL 6*5	SF-NY 4-7	HOU-PIT 7*4	CIN-CHI 2-5		LA-MON 4-5
0505	HOU-CIN 8*6	LA-SF 9*6	NY-STL 8*1	PHI-FLA 0-5			
0506	HOU-CIN 3-4	LA-SF 1-2	NY-STL 2-3	PHI-FLA 5-9	CHI-PIT 10*1	COL-SD 0-8	MON-ATL 0-5
0507	HOU-CIN 7-11	LA-SF 3*2	NY-STL 1*0	PHI-FLA 7-8		COL-SD 1-2	MON-ATL 1-2
0508	HOU-CIN 5*0	LA-SF 4-5	NY-STL 3*2	PHI-FLA 9*2	CHI-PIT 2-9	COL-SD 1*0	MON-ATL 1*0
					CHI-PIT 3-9		
0509	HOU-LA 8-9	COL-SF 5-12	CHI-STL 6*3	PIT-FLA 9*5	NY-MON 5*4	CIN-SD 3*2	PHI-ATL 2-7
0510	HOU-LA 4-5	COL-SF 4*2	CHI-STL 6-7	PIT-FLA 0-1	NY-MON 3*2	CIN-SD 5*0	PHI-ATL 8-9
0511	HOU-LA 0-1	COL-SF 1-6	CHI-STL 2-3	PIT-FLA 5*1	NY-MON 3-4	CIN-SD 9*5	PHI-ATL 2-4
0512	PIT-PHI 4-6		CHI-STL 8*6				
0513	PIT-PHI 1-12	CIN-SF 5-9	ATL-NY 7*2	COL-HOU 2-4	STL-MON 1-9	FLA-CHI 4-6	SD-LA 4-5
0514	PIT-PHI 2-3	CIN-SF 1-3	ATL-NY 4-11	COL-HOU 4*2	STL-MON 6*3	FLA-CHI 6*4	SD-LA 1-7
0515	PIT-PHI 0-1	CIN-SF 9*6	ATL-NY 6*1	COL-HOU 4*0	STL-MON 8-9	FLA-CHI 3*0	SD-LA 1-7
0516	MON-PHI 4*1	LA-COL 9*2	FLA-NY 3*1	SF-HOU 2-3	STL-PIT 2-7	SD-CHI 2-4	
0517	MON-PHI 5-6	LA-COL 6-7	FLA-NY 3-4	SF-HOU 5*2	STL-PIT 2*0	SD-CHI 4-11	ATL-CIN 3-4
0518	MON-PHI 6*1	LA-COL 5*2	FLA-NY 4*3	SF-HOU 2-4	STL-PIT 4*3	SD-CHI 4-5	ATL-CIN 3*1
0519		LA-COL 8*2		SD-HOU 5-9			ATL-CIN 0-3
0520	NY-PHI 3-5	ATL-COL 7*1	STL-FLA 3*2	SD-HOU 1-2	MON-PIT 5*3	SF-CHI 1-2	LA-CIN 2-3
0521	NY-PHI 8-9	ATL-COL 5*4	STL-FLA 7*5	SD-HOU 2-4	MON-PIT 0-6	SF-CHI 10-12	LA-CIN 6*4
0522	NY-PHI 3-8	ATL-COL 8*3	STL-FLA 10*9	SD-HOU 7*6	MON-PIT 3*2	SF-CHI 5-6	LA-CIN 10*3
0523	CHI-LA 6*3	CIN-COL 3-8	MON-FLA 2-3	PHI-STL 11*3	SF-SD 0-4		
0524	CHI-LA 2*0	CIN-COL 7-11	MON-FLA 11*1	PHI-STL 4*0	SF-SD 3-6	HOU-ATL 8*0	NY-PIT 4*2
0525	CHI-LA 6-7	CIN-COL 2-3	MON-FLA 3*1	PHI-STL 5-10	SF-SD 5*2	HOU-ATL 5-6	NY-PIT 6*3
0526		CIN-COL 14*4			SF-SD 5*3	HOU-ATL 8*5	NY-PIT 10-11
0527	PIT-LA 5-6	CIN-NY 2-10	COL-MON 2-4	FLA-SF 3-4	STL-SD 6-8	CHI-ATL 4-5	HOU-PHI 4*2
0528	PIT-LA 7*2	CIN-NY 4-5	COL-MON 3*2	FLA-SF 3*2	STL-SD 0-4	CHI-ATL 9*2	HOU-PHI 7*5
0529	PIT-LA 3-4	CIN-NY 5-8	COL-MON 3-4	FLA-SF 1-3	STL-SD 2-7	CHI-ATL 4*2	HOU-PHI 2-4
0530	STL-LA 6*5	COL-NY 12*2	FLA-HOU 3-4	ATL-SF 4*3	PIT-SD 2-10	MON-CIN 3-7	PHI-CHI 7-8
0531	STL-LA 6*0	COL-NY 3*2	FLA-HOU 3-5	ATL-SF 6*3	PIT-SD 5-15	MON-CIN 4-5	PHI-CHI 8*7
0601	STL-LA 0-7	COL-NY 4*3	FLA-HOU 3*2	ATL-SF 1*0	PIT-SD 4-6	MON-CIN 10*9	PHI-CHI 4*2
0602							PHI-CHI 4*2
0603	LA-ATL 5-8	PIT-COL 4-6	PHI-HOU 2-4	SD-FLA 1-5	SF-STL 1-3	NY-CIN 4*3	MON-CHI 3*1
0604	LA-ATL 2-4	PIT-COL 4*3	PHI-HOU 1-5	SD-FLA 3-4	SF-STL 1-2	NY-CIN 5-8	MON-CHI 6*1
0605	LA-ATL 5-6	PIT-COL 4*3	PHI-HOU 2-4	SD-FLA 5-10	SF-STL 10*3	NY-CIN 6-9	MON-CHI 10*5
0606	SD-ATL 4*3	NY-COL 11*3	CHI-PHI 1-3	LA-FLA 10-11	HOU-MON 5-10	SF-PIT 4*3	
0607	SD-ATL 3-12	NY-COL 8-10	CHI-PHI 6-7	LA-FLA 2*0	HOU-MON 2-3	SF-PIT 3*2	CIN-STL 5*0
0608	SD-ATL 2-5	NY-COL 4-5	CHI-PHI 0-3	LA-FLA 4-5	HOU-MON 9*2	SF-PIT 1-3	CIN-STL 2-8
0609	COL-CIN 1-7	MON-NY 9*0	STL-PHI 2-6			FLA-PIT 1-3	
0610	COL-CIN 4-10	MON-NY 6*4	STL-PHI 4*3	ATL-HOU 5*2	LA-CHI 2*1	FLA-PIT 4-5	SD-SF 5*2
0611	COL-CIN 4-6	MON-NY 7*4	STL-PHI 7*4	ATL-HOU 6-7	LA-CHI 4-7	FLA-PIT 4-10	SD-SF 3*1
0612	COL-CIN 3*2	MON-NY 4-5	STL-PHI 2-7	ATL-HOU 3*1	LA-CHI 2*1	FLA-PIT 1-5	SD-SF 5*2
0613	CIN-LA 4-5	PHI-NY 3-4	COL-ATL 7*2	FLA-STL 1-2	PIT-MON 2-10		HOU-SF 4-5
0614	CIN-LA 2-5	PHI-NY 3*2	COL-ATL 1-3	FLA-STL 7*0	PIT-MON 7-12	CHI-SD 7*6	HOU-SF 7*4
0615	CIN-LA 4*2	PHI-NY 0-1	COL-ATL 0-4	FLA-STL 13*3	PIT-MON 2-13	CHI-SD 5*0	HOU-SF 7*2
0616	NY-FLA 2-4		COL-ATL 8-11	PIT-STL 7*5		CHI-SD 1-7	HOU-SF 6*3
0617	NY-FLA 5-6	COL-LA 13*5	CIN-ATL 5-6	PIT-STL 7*4	PHI-MON 10*8	HOU-SD 2-3	CHI-SF 1-6
0618	NY-FLA 11*3	COL-LA 9*3	CIN-ATL 16*0	PIT-STL 0-9	PHI-MON 8*4	HOU-SD 6*1	CHI-SF 6*4
0619	NY-FLA 6*1	COL-LA 3-7	CIN-ATL 12*4	PIT-STL 3-12	PHI-MON 13*0	HOU-SD 1-5	CHI-SF 10*6
0620	HOU-COL 5*4		NY-ATL 3-7	MON-STL 8*4		LA-SD 3*2	
0621	HOU-COL 0-8	CHI-FLA 7*2	NY-ATL 3-4	MON-STL 4-5	PHI-PIT 1-7	LA-SD 3-4	SF-CIN 1-2
0622	HOU-COL 5-14		NY-ATL 6*4	MON-STL 6*4	PHI-PIT 4-5	LA-SD 5-8	SF-CIN 3-4
0623		CHI-FLA 9*3					SF-CIN 5-7
0624	SF-COL 10*3	ATL-PHI 9*4	FLA-MON 0-9	LA-HOU 4-16	PIT-NY 9*4	STL-CHI 3*1	SD-CIN 2-3
0625	SF-COL 4-6	ATL-PHI 1-7	FLA-MON 3-7	LA-HOU 4*2	PIT-NY 3*1	STL-CHI 1-3	SD-CIN 6*0
0626	SF-COL 8*1	ATL-PHI 8-9	FLA-MON 6*1	LA-HOU 5*4	PIT-NY 7*3	STL-CHI 3*1	SD-CIN 4-12
0627	SD-COL 7-12	FLA-PHI 1-5	ATL-MON 2-7	CIN-HOU 6-7	STL-NY 9*8	PIT-CHI 1-2	SF-LA 3*2
0628	SD-COL 9-10	FLA-PHI 2*1	ATL-MON 7-8	CIN-HOU 5*3	STL-NY 8*6	PIT-CHI 6*5	SF-LA 4-7
	SD-COL 11*3						
0629	SD-COL 10*4	FLA-PHI 2-5	ATL-MON 6*2	CIN-HOU 1-3		PIT-CHI 5-6	SF-LA 2-6
0630	ATL-FLA 8*3	CIN-PIT 4-6	COL-STL 7-9	CHI-HOU 3-5	MON-SF 7*3	NY-SD 3*1	PHI-LA 3-4
0701	ATL-FLA 3-4	CIN-PIT 4*2	COL-STL 4-11	CHI-HOU 3*2	MON-SF 7-14	NY-SD 10*7	PHI-LA 3*0
0702	ATL-FLA 5*0	CIN-PIT 8*2	COL-STL 7*5	CHI-HOU 4-5	MON-SF 10*9	NY-SD 1-4	PHI-LA 3-9
0703	ATL-FLA 12*6	CIN-PIT 4*3	COL-STL 5*2	CHI-HOU 6-12	MON-SF 5-8	NY-SD 0-7	PHI-LA 1-3
0704	CIN-FLA 5*1	COL-CHI 3-4	HOU-STL 13*6		NY-SF 2*1	PHI-SD 10*4	MON-LA 5*1
		COL-CHI 4*2					
0705	CIN-FLA 9*4	COL-CHI 9*6	HOU-STL 3*1	PIT-ATL 3*1	NY-SF 4*2	PHI-SD 2-7	MON-LA 1-2
0706	CIN-FLA 3-4	COL-CHI 7*1	HOU-STL 7*6	PIT-ATL 3*1	NY-SF 4*1	PHI-SD 2-5	MON-LA 4*2
				PIT-ATL 2-4			
0707	COL-FLA 2*1	HOU-CHI 9*3	PIT-CIN 7-8		PHI-SF 4-5	MON-SD 7*0	NY-LA 3*0
0708	COL-FLA 2-5	HOU-CHI 5-6	PIT-CIN 4-12	STL-ATL 2*0	PHI-SF 2-3	MON-SD 14*0	NY-LA 2-3
0709	COL-FLA 2-4	HOU-CHI 3-7	PIT-CIN 3-5	STL-ATL 3-5	PHI-SF 2-3	MON-SD 5*1	NY-LA 3-8
0710	COL-FLA 4-6	HOU-CHI 5*3	PIT-CIN 7*6	STL-ATL 6*1	PHI-SF 1-2	MON-SD 8*2	NY-LA 5*1
0714	HOU-PIT 2-8	SF-MON 8*3	CHI-CIN 4*3	FLA-ATL 5*3	STL-COL 1-8		
0715	HOU-PIT 8-11	SF-MON 7*3	CHI-CIN 1-7	FLA-ATL 4-6	STL-COL 6-10	LA-PHI 3-4	SD-NY 3-7
						LA-PHI 3*2	SD-NY 2*1
0716	HOU-PIT 7*1	SF-MON 4*2	CHI-CIN 7*2	FLA-ATL 5-7	STL-COL 4-15	LA-PHI 6-10	SD-NY 4-5
0717	HOU-PIT 9*0	SF-MON 6*4	CHI-CIN 2-3	FLA-ATL 1-2	STL-COL 6-10	LA-PHI 7-9	SD-NY 10*1
0718	ATL-PIT 3*2	SD-MON 2-9	FLA-CIN 3-5	STL-HOU 12-15	CHI-COL 6*3	SF-PHI 7*5	LA-NY 7*6
0719	ATL-PIT 10-13	SD-MON 3-4	FLA-CIN 5-13	STL-HOU 10*0	CHI-COL 6*1	SF-PHI 2-5	LA-NY 4-7
0720	ATL-PIT 4-5	SD-MON 2-5	FLA-CIN 8*7	STL-HOU 0-2	CHI-COL 9*8	SF-PHI 9*2	LA-NY 4-5
0721	ATL-STL 3-6			PIT-HOU 6-13			
	ATL-STL 6*1						
0722	ATL-STL 0-5	LA-MON 2-8	CIN-CHI 6-7	PIT-HOU 4*1	FLA-COL 4*0	SD-PHI 3-4	SF-NY 3-6
	ATL-STL 2-3					SD-PHI 7*4	
0723	ATL-STL 8*5	LA-MON 0-2	CIN-CHI 3*1	PIT-HOU 0-11	FLA-COL 4-5	SD-PHI 7*1	SF-NY 4*2
0724	ATL-STL 8*5	LA-MON 4-7	CIN-CHI 0-13	PIT-HOU 1-13	FLA-COL 6*4	SD-PHI 3-5	SF-NY 8*1
0725	NY-STL 7*1	CHI-PIT 2-6	COL-SD 4*3	HOU-CIN 4-7	LA-SF 10*5	MON-ATL 6*4	PHI-FLA 8*1
0726	NY-STL 10*9	CHI-PIT 8*4	COL-SD 6*5	HOU-CIN 6*5	LA-SF 5-12	MON-ATL 5*3	PHI-FLA 10*8
0727	NY-STL 7*4	CHI-PIT 4-9	COL-SD 2-9	HOU-CIN 7*1	LA-SF 1-4	MON-ATL 1-4	PHI-FLA 3*1
0728		CHI-PIT 10*3	CIN-SD 2-3		COL-SF 5*1		
0729	CHI-STL 8*3	NY-PIT 4*1	CIN-SD 4*1	HOU-LA 5-7	COL-SF 4-8	PHI-ATL 2-5	MON-FLA 8*4
0730	CHI-STL 7-10	NY-PIT 2-3	CIN-SD 7*6	HOU-LA 1-6	COL-SF 4-6	PHI-ATL 5*2	MON-FLA 7*3
0731	CHI-STL 9*7	NY-PIT 6*4	CIN-SD 2*1	HOU-LA 1-7	COL-SF 4-9	PHI-ATL 5-9	MON-FLA 13*4
0801	ATL-NY 4*2	COL-HOU 8*3	FLA-CHI 5-8	SD-LA 5*4	CIN-SF 4*3	STL-MON 2-3	
0802	ATL-NY 1-4	COL-HOU 1-3	FLA-CHI 3*2	SD-LA 6-7	CIN-SF 9*7	STL-MON 4-5	PIT-PHI 3*2
0803	ATL-NY 2-3	COL-HOU 1-2	FLA-CHI 9*8	SD-LA 4*2	CIN-SF 17*4	STL-MON 3-8	PIT-PHI 0-7
0804		COL-HOU 2-6	FLA-CHI 5*1	SD-LA 0-1		STL-MON 7*3	PIT-PHI 7*4
0805	FLA-NY 7-10	SF-HOU 4-12	SD-CHI 4*2	ATL-CIN 16*6	LA-COL 5*4	STL-PIT 11*3	MON-PHI 5*0
0806	FLA-NY 4*3	SF-HOU 7-8	SD-CHI 1-7	ATL-CIN 2*1		STL-PIT 6*3	MON-PHI 6*4
0807	FLA-NY 2*0	SF-HOU 4-7	SD-CHI 5*1	ATL-CIN 2-3	LA-COL 6*2	STL-PIT 5-6	MON-PHI 6*4
0808	STL-FLA 11*1		SF-CHI 5*4	ATL-CIN 6*4	LA-COL 6-7	MON-PIT 3*2	NY-PHI 3*2
0809	STL-FLA 3-5	SD-HOU 4*3	SF-CHI 3*2	LA-CIN 3-5	ATL-COL 4*3	MON-PIT 4*3	NY-PHI 1-5
0810	STL-FLA 12*4	SD-HOU 1-3	SF-CHI 5*2	LA-CIN 6*3	ATL-COL 0-1	MON-PIT 4*0	NY-PHI 6*2
0811	STL-FLA 8*6	SD-HOU 8*6		LA-CIN 2*0	ATL-COL 13*0	MON-PIT 0-4	NY-PHI 1-2

Notes on Contributors

Paul Adomites was born and raised in Pittsburgh, and lives there now. He was publications director for the Society for American Baseball Research from 1987–1990. He is the founding editor of *The SABR Review of Books* and its successor, *The Cooperstown Review*.

Larry Amman was born and raised in the suburbs of Detroit. He graduated from Wayne State University with a B.A. in history and political science in 1967, then served in the U.S. Army Intelligence in Vietnam and Germany. Although he has lived in the Washington, D.C., area for the last ten years, the Detroit Tigers remain his favorite team. He has published several articles on the Tigers, and has compiled all their game-winning RBIs from 1901–1980. He is currently employed as a travel agent.

Dennis Bingham is a writer for the Chicago Police Department, a freelance cartoonist, and an umpire for several adult and youth baseball leagues in the Chicago area. (His umpiring partner is often his father, Bill, who taught him the rules.) Bingham served as a historical adviser for the movie *Eight Men Out*, in which he also played a bit part as umpire Billy Evans. He was associate editor of the SABR publication *Baseball in Chicago*. One of the three founding members of SABR's Umpires and Rules Committee, Bingham lives with his wife, Diane, and sons Sean, Kevin, and Dennis on Chicago's South Side.

Arnold Braunstein is a computer programmer who lives in Valley Cottage, New York. A longtime Yankee fan, he is a member of SABR and active in its Computerization Committee. Among the projects he has contributed to is the Tattersall-McConnell Home Run Log.

Bob Carroll, a former high school teacher, is a freelance writer and illustrator who lives in North Huntingdon, Pennsylvania. He is the founder and executive director of PFRA (the Professional Football Researchers Association) and a longtime member of SABR. He regularly writes and illustrates for *Oldtyme Baseball News*. His baseball books include *Baseball Between the Lies, The Whole Baseball Catalogue* (with John Thorn), *The Dodgers Trivia Book,* and *The Major League Way to Play Baseball.* Among his football credits are *The Hidden Game of Football* (with Pete Palmer and John Thorn) and *When the Grass Was Real.* His hobbies are listening to classical music, cleaning the Augean stables, and writing threatening letters.

Dick Clark, co-chairman of SABR's Negro Leagues Committee, was born and raised in Detroit and has been a lifelong Tiger fan. He has been active in Negro Leagues research for over ten years and has served as a consultant for numerous books on the subject. A resident of Ypsilanti, Michigan, he is the author of several articles on the Negro Leagues for *The Baseball Research Journal* and *The National Pastime.* With Larry Lester he edited *The Negro Leagues Book,* published by SABR in 1994.

Merritt Clifton edits *Animal People: News for People Who Care about Animals.* Clifton also is author of numerous works on "outlaw" baseball, especially as played in Quebec, Vermont, Japan, and Mexico, and *Relative Baseball,* a pioneering sabermetric study.

Don L. Daglow founded and is president of Stormfront Studios, Inc., which publishes the *Tony LaRussa Baseball* games on computer and on CD. He also designed or produced other games, such as *World Series Baseball, Earl Weaver Baseball, ESPN Baseball Tonight,* and *Microsoft Baseball for Windows.*

Bill Deane is a freelance baseball researcher and writer stationed near Cooperstown, New York, where he spent eight years as Senior Research Associate for the National Baseball Library & Archive. He has published two books and more than one hundred articles for such publications as *Street & Smith's Official Baseball Yearbook* and *USA Today Baseball Weekly,* and was a recipient of the 1989 SABR-Macmillan Baseball Research Award. Deane resides in Fly Creek, New York, with his wife, Pam, and daughter, Sarah.

Eddie Epstein is currently director of research and statistics for the Baltimore Orioles. In that capacity he evaluates professional talent, participates in the negotiation of major league player contracts, and provides information to the team's manager about upcoming opponents. His work has been published in Bill James' *The Baseball Book* and *Baseball Abstract, Sports Illustrated, USA Today Baseball Weekly,* and *The Sporting News.* A Baltimore native, Eddie earned a BA (1981) and an MA (1985) from the University of Delaware.

Bill Felber is executive editor of *The Manhattan Mercury* (Manhattan, Kansas). A native of Chicago, he is the author of several baseball books and articles, including most recently *125 Years of Professional Baseball.* His work has appeared in *The National Pastime, Baseball History,* and *The Encyclopedia of Major League Baseball Teams* (Meckler). He is a SABR member.

Myles E. Friedman is editor and vice president of Vanguard Publications, which has published the annual *Spring Training Baseball Yearbook* since 1988. He also publishes historical wall charts on baseball, football, and World Cup soccer.

Warner Fusselle is the voice behind numerous television and radio programs and films on the subject of baseball. He has worked with Mel Allen on *This Week in Baseball* since its inception in 1977. He continues to host ESPN's *Major League Baseball Magazine,* which he commenced in 1990. In addition to his baseball narration, Fusselle's play-by-play announcing can be heard on WABC Radio in New York City. He is the author of *Baseball . . . A Laughing Matter!* and has produced two albums of baseball music for Rhino Records: *Baseball's Greatest Hits* and *Baseball's Greatest Hits . . . Let's Play II.*

Cappy Gagnon joined SABR in 1977 and has written articles for its *Baseball Research Journal* on Roger Bresnahan, Ed Reulbach, and the subject of "batting eye." He served on the SABR Board of Directors for eight years, including two years as president. Additionally, he has written for the Greenwood Press *Baseball Biographical Encyclopedia, The Ballplayers, The Chronological History of Baseball, Baseball Digest,* and *Baseball Quarterly Review,* and is in the midst of writing *Anson to Yaz,* a book about the sixty-seven major leaguers who attended Notre Dame. Gagnon has been employed in law enforcement or executive protection since 1976.

Larry R. Gerlach is professor of American sports history at the University of Utah. He is a member of the editorial board of *Nine*, the board of directors of SABR, and chair of SABR's Umpires and Rules Committee. He has published numerous articles in journals and reference works, as well as *The Men in Blue: Conversations with Umpires*.

Mike Gershman is known among baseball fans for his series of *Baseball Card Engagement Books* and the *Baseball Stadium Postcard Albums*. *Diamonds*, his book about the evolution of the ballpark, was published by Houghton-Mifflin in the fall of 1993 and received both the SABR-Macmillan Award and the Casey Award. He is also, with John Thorn, the co-founder of the Total Sports Company.

Gary Gillette is the author of the annual *Great American Baseball Stat Book* and is working on his next book, *The Baseball Atlas*, for Facts on File. He served as executive director or chairman of Project Scoresheet in 1987–1992. The Baseball Workshop, over which he presides, continues the work of Project Scoresheet under license by collecting and publishing computerized play-by-play data for all major league games. Gillette also acts as a consultant in arbitration cases for several prominent player agents, and has written for *USA Today, USA Today Baseball Weekly, Baseball Today* magazine, and several daily newspapers. He provides baseball commentary for WHYY in Philadelphia and several Public Radio stations.

Barbara Gregorich is the author of *Woman at Play: The Story of Women in Baseball*, which received the 1993 SABR-Macmillan Award for best baseball research. Her novel, *She's on First*, is about the first woman to play in the big leagues. She has also created more than 150 educational workbooks and activity books for children.

Gary Hailey is a Philadelphia attorney and the author of "Anatomy of a Murder: The Federal League and the Courts," which appeared in the Spring 1985 issue of *The National Pastime*. He is a native of Joplin, Missouri, and a graduate of Rice University and Harvard Law School. Although he now realizes that he will never achieve his childhood ambition of playing center field for the New York Yankees, he still daydreams about one day being the Yankees' general counsel.

Donald Hall is the author of many books of verse, nineteen books of prose and anthologies, and editor for numerous publications. His poetry has won the National Book Critics Circle Award and the Robert Frost Medal of the Poetry Society of America. His most recent book of verse is *The Museum of Clear Ideas*.

Tom Heitz, born in Kansas City, Missouri, in 1940, has been a lifelong baseball fan. He learned the National Pastime from his father, a law professor and Little League coach, and from Harry Caray, the voice of the St. Louis Cardinals. Heitz received his formal education at the University of Kansas (B.A., 1962), the University of Missouri at Kansas City School of Law (J.D., 1965), and the University of Washington, where he studied library science under renowned law librarian Marian Gallagher. Heitz served as Librarian at the National Baseball Library & Archive from 1983 through 1994. He now writes and lectures on baseball subjects.

Bob Hoie has long been an active member of the Society for American Baseball Research, receiving the Society's Bob Davids Award for meritorious service in 1987. He has served as chairman of SABR's Minor League Committee, was a principal contributor to *Minor League Baseball Stars,* volumes 1, 2 and 3, and contributed to *The Encyclopedia of Minor League Baseball.* A native of Los Angeles and a fan of the Pacific Coast League Angels until their demise in 1957, Hoie recently retired after nearly thirty years as an urban planner for Los Angeles County.

John B. Holway has written for numerous magazines and newspapers, including *American Heritage, The Sporting News, The New York Times,* and the *Washington Post*. He is the author of *Voices from the Great Black Baseball Leagues, Blackball Stars, The Pitcher* with John Thorn, and *The Last .400 Hitter*. He has written about Ted Williams, whom he saw in 1941, the Negro leagues, which he saw in 1944, Japanese baseball, which he saw in 1948, and pitching, which he has spent a lifetime swinging at and missing. He won *Spitball* magazine's Casey Award and SABR's Bob Davids Award, both in 1990.

Frederick Ivor-Campbell turned to baseball research and writing after many years in religious publishing (editor/writer, Gospel Light Publications, California), public information (Barrington College, Rhode Island), and college teaching (English, at the University of Rhode Island and The King's College, New York). He has written baseball history and biography for several periodicals and reference works. Ivor-Campbell serves on the board of directors of the Society for American Baseball Research, and chairs SABR's Nineteenth Century Committee. He lives with his wife, Alma, in Warren, Rhode Island.

Clifford S. Kachline, following a stint as sports editor of the North Penn *Reporter* of Lansdale, Pennsylvania, joined the editorial staff of *The Sporting News* at age twenty-one in April 1943. He remained there for twenty-four years. Besides writing for *TSN,* for twenty years he was the compiler and editor of the *Official Baseball Guide* and *The Dope Book*. Kachline left *TSN* in May 1967 to become public relations director of the North American Soccer League; he then served as Baseball Hall of Fame historian (1969–1982), and then, until his retirement in 1985, as the first executive director of the Society for American Baseball Research.

Jack Kavanagh has given up the pretense of retirement for a writer's life in Rhode Island. His books have focused on such diverse subjects as Shoeless Joe Jackson and Robert E. Lee. He will celebrate his seventy-fifth birthday with his first adult, full-scale biography, a treatment of Walter Johnson (Diamond Communications). In progress for Salamander Books is *An Illustrated History of Baseball*. He enjoys his five nearby grandchildren and the health to sniff the roses while they bloom. He has wonderful memories of a fifty-year marriage to his late wife Sally.

Jack Lang has reported on major league baseball for half a century, starting in 1946 when he covered the Brooklyn Dodgers for the *Long Island Press*. His last thirteen years on the beat were for the *New York Daily News,* where he was the senior major league baseball writer in 1987, when he retired. In 1966 he began conducting the annual Hall of Fame election and was elected Secretary-Treasurer of the Baseball Writers Association of America, for whom he conducted the annual polls for the Most Valuable Player, Cy Young, Rookie, and Manager Awards. In 1987 Lang himself was elected to the Hall of Fame when he was named winner of the J.G. Taylor Spink Award for meritorious contributions to baseball writing.

Larry Lester is the research director and treasurer of the Negro Leagues Baseball Museum in Kansas City, Missouri. He is also the editor of their annual yearbook and quarterly newsletter, *Silhouettes*. As co-chairman of the Negro Leagues Committee of SABR, he edited, with Dick Clark, *The Negro Leagues Book,* published by SABR in 1994. Lester is a member of the Black Collectors Hall of Fame in Washington, D.C., and staff writer for *Black Ethnic Collectibles* magazine. He lives in Raytown, Missouri, with his wife Valcinia and three daughters, Tiffany, Marisa, and Erica Joi.

Philip J. Lowry is author of *Green Cathedrals*, the definitive study of all ballparks ever used for Major League and Negro League games since 1871, and of *Green Gridirons,* a similar study on all pro football stadiums. He has served on the Board of Directors and as Ballparks Chair and Negro Leagues Chair for SABR. Phil received B.A. and M.B.A. degrees from Harvard University, served in the U.S. Army airborne for six years as an infantry captain, and now resides in Minneapolis with his wife, Ellen, and their two young children, Evan and Megan.

Yoichi Nagata holds a B.A. from Osaka University in Japan and an M.A. from the University of Pennsylvania. He has been a freelance sports journalist, writing numerous articles on sports for Japanese magazines. He is an avid baseball fan of the now-defunct Nishitetsu Lions of Fukuoka and of the Philadelphia Phillies.

David Osinski has served as Executive Director of the International Baseball Foundation since 1994. Osinski, who holds an advanced degree in International Affairs from George Washington University, was National Coaching Director of the Australian Baseball Federation in 1981–86 and Executive Director of the International Baseball Association in 1986–94. In 1988 and 1992 he oversaw the planning and implementation of baseball competition for those years' summer Olympiads.

Joseph M. Overfield was born in 1916 in Buffalo, where he has lived all his life, except for three years in the Air Force in World War Two. Historian for the Buffalo Bisons and a member of the Buffalo Baseball Hall of Fame Committee, he wrote *100 Seasons of Buffalo Baseball* in 1985, and has written for *Baseball Digest, The Sporting News,* Buffalo's *Courier-Express* and *News, Niagara Frontier,* and SABR's *Baseball Research Journal* and *The National Pastime.* Overfield was honored in 1986 by SABR for his contributions to minor league history. He is now semiretired after fifty-one years with a Buffalo real-estate title firm.

Pete Palmer is the former editor of the Barnes *Official Encyclopedia of Baseball.* He began compiling his historical and analytical data in the mid-1960s, and from 1978–1987 he was chairman of SABR's statistical analysis committee. In that time he also served as a consultant for the Sports Information Center, the official statisticians of the American League. He was on the board of directors of Project Scoresheet. Palmer has contributed articles to *Sport, USA Today, Sports Heritage, The National Pastime,* and *Baseball Research Journal.* He is coauthor, with John Thorn, of *The Hidden Game of Baseball* and *The Official Major League Baseball Record Book;* with Thorn and Bob Carroll of *The Hidden Game of Football* and *The Football Abstract;* and with Thorn and Eliot Cohen of *The Baseball Annual 1990.* He won SABR's prestigious Bob Davids Award in 1989.

Douglas R. Pappas is an attorney in New York. He founded SABR's Business of Baseball Committee and serves as its chairman, as well as SABR's legal advisor. Baseball, in the form of the Amazing Mets, seduced him at age eight; the affair has now lasted a quarter century, through The University of Chicago (A.B. 1982) and The University of Michigan Law School (J.D. 1985).

David Pietrusza, president of the Society for American Baseball Research (SABR), is the author of *Minor Miracles: The Legends & Lures of Minor League Baseball; Major Leagues;* and *Baseball's Canadian-American League.* He has been a research consultant for *Ballparks of North America* and *All My Octobers* and a contributor to *Collier's Encyclopedia.* Pietrusza served as producer for the documentary *Local Heroes: Baseball on Capital Region Diamonds* for PBS-television station WMHT (Schenectady, NY) and as consultant for the Baseball Online segment of the PBS LearningLink system. A columnist for *Oldtyme Baseball News,* he has written for such other periodicals as *USA Today, Baseball Weekly, Baseball America, Elysian Fields Quarterly, The National Pastime, New Mexico Magazine,*

and *The Baseball Research Journal.* Pietrusza was also a writer for Microsoft's multimedia product *Complete Baseball.* A former member of the Amsterdam (N.Y.) City Council, he holds an M.A. in history and is also the author of *The End of the Cold War* and *The Battle of Normandy.*

Bruce L. Prentice was born and raised in Toronto, Ontario, Canada, and was a top amateur baseball player before turning to coaching and instruction. In the late 1970s he assisted the introduction of the first high school baseball programs in Canada. He was founder of Canada's first college baseball program at Seneca College in Toronto and was an area scout for the Blue Jays from 1980–1986. Prentice is the owner and operator of Proway Baseball Schools, the founder and long-time president of the Canadian Baseball Hall of Fame and Museum, and was instrumental in forming the World Baseball Hall of Fame in 1989.

Rob Ruck is the author of *Sandlot Seasons: Sport in Black Pittsburgh* and *The Tropic of Baseball: Baseball in the Dominican Republic,* a 1991 MacMillan–SABR Award Winner. He is currently developing *Kings on the Hill: Baseball's Forgotten Men,* a documentary on the Negro Leagues. He is on the faculty of the Center for Latin American Studies and the History Department at the University of Pittsburgh.

Tom Shieber is founder and chair of SABR's Pictorial History Committee. Born and raised in St. Louis, he was summer intern at *The Sporting News* in 1982-84. He was the recipient of the SABR-*USA Today Baseball Weekly* Award for best research presentation at the 1994 SABR National Convention. He currently operates a solar telescope at Mt. Wilson Observatory in southern California.

Allan Simpson is the founding editor of *Baseball America* and is recognized as the expert on baseball's amateur free-agent draft. *Baseball America* is based in Durham, North Carolina, and specializes in the coverage of all aspects of player development.

John Thorn is the author/editor of many baseball books, including *The Game for All America, The Armchair Books of Baseball, Ted Williams: Seasons of the Kid* (with Richard Ben Cramer and Mark Rucker), *The National Pastime, and The Relief Pitcher.* He coauthored *The Pitcher* with John Holway, and *The Hidden Game of Baseball* and *The Baseball Record Book* with Pete Palmer. With Palmer and Bob Carroll he also coauthored *The Hidden Game of Football* and *The Football Abstract.* He has written for several periodicals, among them *The Sporting News, Sport,* and *American Heritage.* Thorn was Senior Creative Consultant to *Baseball,* Ken Burns's nine-part film for the Public Broadcasting System, and serves as a consultant to the National Baseball Hall of Fame Committee on Baseball Veterans.

Robert L. Tiemann is chairman of the nineteenth-century research committee of the Society for American Baseball Research and is the author of *Cardinal Classics* and *Dodger Classics.* He heads a SABR research project that is reconstructing from newspaper play-by-play accounts much of the missing data for the National Association of 1871–1875. With Rich Topp, Tiemann shared a SABR award for his redevelopment of the Manager Roster as it appears in *Total Baseball,* and in 1992 won SABR's Bob Davids Award.

Jules Tygiel is a professor of history at San Francisco State University. He is the author of *Baseball's Great Experiment: Jackie Robinson and his Legacy* (Oxford University Press, 1983; Vintage Paperback edition, 1984) and has contributed articles to many periodicals.

Eduardo Valero, Chairman of the Latin America Committee of SABR, is also President of the Puerto Rico Professional Baseball Hall of Fame and the Puerto Rico Amateur Baseball Hall of Fame. A former Vice President of the Sportswriter Federation of

America and President of the Puerto Rico Professional Sports-writers Association, Valero is also a feature writer of the sports supplement of the daily newspaper *El Vocero de Puerto Rico*. Over the past thirty-five years he has covered major and minor league baseball, the Caribbean Baseball Series, the Olympics, and the Panamerican and Centroamerican Caribbean Games for newspapers, news agencies, and radio/TV stations.

Joseph M. Wayman, publisher and editor of *Grandstand Baseball Annual,* which he founded in 1985, has been the subject of a "SABR Salute," which commended him for his steadfast "investigative reporting of questionable baseball records." Several of his discoveries have been accepted as fact by *Total Baseball* and the Elias Sports Bureau and have resulted in a rewriting of the baseball record books. His writings have also appeared in the *Baseball Research Journal* and *Baseball Bulletin.*

With appreciation to these readers of *Total Baseball 1* who sent in corrections or made suggestions on how to improve the second edition:

Larry Amman, Ray Andreotti, Mel Bailey, Craig Barbarino, Edgar K. Beatty, James M. Beck, Joseph R. Bender, Robert Beukelher, John Booth, Jim Bostain, Therese R. Brown, J. Paul Browne, Bob Cambris, Kevin A. Carleton, Bob Carroll, Anthony M. Chieco, Ken Coleman, Steve Cooper, Owen Curtis, Clay Davenport, L. Robert Davids, Bill Deane, Harold Dellinger, Ted D. DeVries, Don Dewey, Raymond A. DiSanto, Sam Elfand, Don Elliott, John Emerson, Eddie Epstein, Kenneth Fink, Robert L. Franz, Andrew Fussner, Cam Gibson, Steven Goldberg, Ray Gonzalez, Dan Greenia, Bill Haber, Rod Hay, Bob Hoie, Fred Ivor-Campbell, Tom Jennings, Bill Jensen, Warren Johnson, Cliff Kachline, James Kaufman, Dave Kemp, Larry Kempster, Randall Kleinman, Jack Lang, Ron Liebman, Jerry Malloy, James F. Maxfield, Bob McConnell, Joe M. McGowan, David Molnar, George S. Moskal, Frank J. Mueller, Neil Munro, Thomas L. Nester, Dave Nichols, Tom O'Brien, Yoshio Ohno, S. Mark Parker, Paul E. Pennebaker, Peretz Perl, Dave Pietrusza, Mike Post, Jorgen Rasmussen, Allan Rausch, Andrew Richardson, John Rickert, John M. Roca, Winslow Rogers, Tom Ruane, Bill Rubenstein, David Schermer, Leon Schmerhold, John Schwartz, Alfred Secondi, Sy Siegel, Richard Siegelman, Al Smith, David M. Snyder, David Stephan, Mike Sparks, Lyle Spatz, Dean Sullivan, Isaac Thorn, Richard Topp, Stephen Toth, T. Brook Treakle III, Jim Troisi, Jim Tuttle, Jim

Vail, Cullen P. Vane, David Vincent, Joseph M. Wayman, Jim Weigand, Bernard Weisberger, Christopher Williams, Frank Williams, Joseph C. Williams, Ralph Winnie, Jim Wright, and Ed Yerha.

And to these readers of *Total Baseball II* who improved the third edition:

David Aceto, Tim Anderson, Andrew J. Balog, Robert Browning, Chuck Carey, Keith Carlson, Garrett M. Casey, Jim Conroy, Bob Davids, Bill Deane, Dennis DeValeria, Ted DiTullio, Robert Downer, Tom Dunken, Jules Egyrd, Eddie Epstein, Ken Fetterman, Bob Franzosa, Gary Gillette, Jay Gregory, Charlie Harville, Jeffrey Hatt, Ralph Horton, Jeff James, Darlene Kadlecik, Jerry Kahn, John Kenyon, Patrick Kinas, D.C. Larkin, II, Matthew Lesniewski, Morris Levin, Don Luce, Michael Lucich, Ed Luteran, Jeff Magalif, E.H. Marshall, Richard A. Marston, Ronald A. Mayer, John P. McBride, John McClaran, Randy Messel, Scott Messinger, Steve Moore, Neil Munro, John O'Malley, Ed Oswalt, Douglas R. Pappas, Richard Pardoe, Danny Radakovich, Matt Rapacz, Louis Rauco, Matt Reese, Eric Reinholdt, Dennis Repp, John Richards, Bob Richardson, John M. Roca, Seth D. Rodgers, Robert Schulz, John Schwartz, John Scott, Jamie Selko, Jim Smith, Dave Smith, Lewis J. Snyder, Lyle Spatz, Alan Steinberg, David Stephan, A.D. Suehsdorf, James Swetnam, Blair D. Tarr, Robert Tiemann, Harry L. Turtledove, Bill Wallace, Patrick K. Walsh, Joe Wayman, Jim Weigand, Frank Williams, Walt Wilson, and Edgar M. Wyatt.

This fourth edition has benefited from the comments of :

Tim Anderson, Arnie Braunstein, Chuck Carey, Bill Carle, Tim Cashion, Tom Chase, Ed Coen, Bob Davids, Bill Deane, Dan Dischley, Ted DiTullio, Jules Egyrd, Eddie Epstein, Bill French, Campbell Gibson, Gary Gillette, Herb Goldman, Albert A. Gunnell, Robert Kern, Joe Kinsman, Joe Klein, Joe Marchetto, Jeff Marcus, Bob McConnell, Randy Messell, Scott Messinger, Neil Munro, John O'Malley, Ed Oswalt, Doug Pappas, Jeffrey Platt, Frank Phelps, Bob Richardson, Win Rogers, Bob Rosiek, Jim Sargent, Robert Schulz, John Schwartz, Jamie Selko, Dave Smith, Jim Smith, David Stephan, Chuck Stevens, David Stone, Adie Suehsdorf, Bob Tiemann, David Vincent, Bill Way, Joe Wayman, Jim Weigand, Roy White, Alan Whitney, Frank Williams, Walt Wilson, and Ed Yerha.

Glossary of Statistical Terms

This Glossary contains definitions of the statistical terms and measures that may be unfamiliar to the average baseball fan or that represent what today might seem odd scoring practices. The Glossary will also be of value to the advanced fan who wishes to know more about the mathematical and theoretical foundations of certain statistics.

/A "Adjusted"; means that the statistic to the immediate left of this mark has been normalized to league average and adjusted for home park factor. Stats that are normalized in this book are Batting Runs, Production, Batting Average, On Base Percentage, Slugging Average, Earned Run Average, and Pitcher Runs.

Assist Although credited to pitchers on strikeouts in some of baseball's early years, not counted as such in this volume.

Assist Average Assists divided by games played. Stat created by Philadelphia baseball writer Al Wright in 1875.

At-Bats Charged to batters on sacrifice hits, 1889–1893; on sacrifice-fly situations, 1931–1938 and 1940–1953; bases on balls, 1876, 1887. However, we did not count at-bats for bases on balls.

Average and Over Early form of expressing averages for base hits, runs, and outs. The average of a batter with 23 hits in six games would be not 3.83 but 3–5 (an average of 3 with an overage, or remainder, of 5); borrowed from cricket.

Average Bases Allowed A pitcher's total bases allowed, divided by his innings pitched—what might be termed Opponents' Slugging Average. Created by Alfred P. Berry in 1951.

Average Batting (Pitching, Fielding) Skill The great philosophical as well as statistical puzzler: after one has normalized a player's performance to that of his league, how does one compare one season's league average with that of another far removed in time? Does a .266 batting average in the NL of 1902 mean the same thing as a .266 batting average in the AL of 1977?

Bases on Balls Counted as outs for batters in 1876 and as hits for batters in 1887, but as neither throughout this book. Awarded for a varying number of errant pitches since 1876, from nine in that year to the current four (standardized in 1889). (After 1887, the batter was no longer allowed to specify strike zone as waist to shoulders or waist to shins.)

Bases on Balls Percentage Batters' stat: most walks per 100 at-bats plus bases on balls.

Bases on Balls Per Game Game defined as nine innings; league-leading pitchers calculated on basis of lowest mark; computed as bases on balls times nine, divided by innings.

Base-Out Percentage Barry Codell's stat for measuring complete offensive performance, in which the elements of the numerator represent bases gained while the events in the denominator represent outs produced (sacrifices and sacrifice flies appear in both because they achieve both—gaining a base for the team while costing it an out). The formula:

$$\frac{\text{Total Bases} + \text{Walks} + \text{HBP} + \text{Steals} + \text{Sacrifices} + \text{Sacrifice Flies}}{\text{At-bats} - \text{Hits} + \text{Caught Stealing} + \text{GIDP} + \text{Sac.} + \text{Sac. Flies}}$$

(GIDP, in the equation above, stands for Grounded Into Double Play; HBP for Hit By Pitch.)

Batters Facing Pitcher Unavailable before 1903 in the National League. The 1903 and 1908 data was not published and has been reconstructed. BFP was unavailable for the American League of 1901-1907. Excepting the NL of 1876-1888 and the AA of 1882 and 1884-1887, for which John Tattersall calculated BFP from box scores, earlier years in both leagues have had their BFP constructed from available data in this manner: subtract league base hits from league at-bats, divide by league innings pitched, multiply by the pitcher's innings, and add his hits allowed, walks, hit by pitch, and sacrifice hits, if available. Abbreviated as BFP.

Batter's Park Factor The Park Factor shown in the batters' section of the team statistics in the Annual Record, Player Register, and Home-Road Statistics. Above 100 means batters benefited from playing half their games in a good hitting park. Abbreviated as BPF or, in what are clearly batters' stats (as in the Player Register) simply as PF. See entry for *Park Factor* for the computation.

Battery Errors In baseball's early years, wild pitches, passed balls, and hit batsmen were lumped together in the statistical summary of a game as *battery errors* and were charged against the fielding percentage of the pitcher or catcher. Such battery errors have been removed from individual and team stats for this book.

Batting Average Calculated as base hits divided by at-bats ever since its first appearance in print in 1874. In 1876 walks were counted as at-bats, and in 1887 they were counted as at-bats and as hits. For this book, batting averages are computed in uniform fashion throughout baseball history. Abbreviated in Part 2 of this volume as AVG, although it is also commonly abbreviated BA.

Batting Runs The Linear Weights measure of runs contributed *beyond* those of a league-average batter or team, such league average defined as zero. The formula depends upon the run values for each offensive event that resulted from Pete Palmer's 1978 computer simulation of all major league games played since 1901. Run values change marginally with changing conditions of play (an out costs a team more in a hitters' year, such as 1930, than in a pitchers' year, such as 1908), and they differ slightly up and down the batting order (a homer is not worth as much to the leadoff hitter as it is to the fifth-place batter; a walk is worth more for the man batting second than for the man batting eighth); however, these differences have been averaged out historically in the figures below.

$$\text{Runs} = (.47)1B + (.78)2B + (1.09)3B + (1.40)HR + (.33)(BB + HB) - (.25)(AB - H) - (.50)OOB$$

(An out is considered to be a hitless at-bat and its value is set so that the sum of all events times their frequency is zero, thus establishing zero as the baseline, or norm, for performance.)

Some events one might expect to see included in this formula but that do not appear are sacrifices, sacrifice hits, grounded into double plays, and reached on error. The last is not known for most years and in the official statistics is indistinguishable from outs on base (OOB). The sacrifice has values that essentially cancel one another, trading an out for an advanced base which, often as not, leaves the team in a situation with poorer run potential than it had before the sacrifice. The sacrifice fly has dubious run value because it is entirely dependent on a situation not under the batter's control: while a single or a walk or a hit by pitch always has potential run value, a long fly does not unless a man happens to be poised at third base. Last, the grounded into double play is to a far greater extent a function of one's place in the batting order than it is of poor speed or failure in the clutch, and thus it does not find a home in a formula applicable to all batters. It is no accident that Hank Aaron, who ran well for most of his long career and wasn't too shabby in the clutch, hit into more DPs than anyone else, nor that Roberto Clemente, Al Kaline, and Frank Robinson, who fit the same description, are also among the ten "worst" in this department.

The Batting Runs formula can be condensed by eliminating the components for steals, caught stealing, and outs on base. Outs on base (calculated as *Hits + Walks + Hit Batsman − Left on Base − Runs − Caught Stealing*) is meaningful only for teams, not individuals. We eliminate steals from the formula in those years in which caught-stealing figures are not available, but the surviving data for the early years indicate that few of the men with high base-stealing totals exceeded the break-even point of 66.7 percent by a margin large enough to produce even one additional Batting Win. A further condensation that we have used for our historical data, as indicated in the formula above, involves setting the value of a single at .47 runs and each extra base at .31, making a double .78, a triple 1.09, and a homer 1.40. (This tends to even out the fluctuations in run values for base hits and extra bases over time: a double, for example, was in fact worth .82 runs from 1901–1920, .80 runs from 1941–1960, and .77 runs from 1961–1977.) Subtract the hits from the total bases and multiply the resulting extra bases by .31 and the hits by .47. This may introduce small variations from a more rigorous formula that includes differing run values for the differing periods or even for single years (generally amounting to a fraction of a run), but the calculation is much snappier for those without a computer.

The Batting Runs formula may be long, even in its condensed form, but it calls for only addition, subtraction, and multiplication and thus is as simple as Slugging Average, whose incorrect weights (1, 2, 3, and 4) it revises and expands upon. Each event has a value and frequency, just as in Slugging Average, yet in Batting Runs outs are treated as offensive events with a run value of their own (albeit a negative one). Just as the run potential for a team in a given half-inning is boosted by a man reaching base, it is diminished by a man being retired; not only has he failed to brighten the situation on the bases but he has deprived his team of the services of a man further down the order who might have come up in this half-inning, either with men on base and/or with scores already in.

The Batting Runs stat treats every offensive event in terms of its impact upon the team—an *average* team, so that a man does not benefit in his individual record for having the good fortune to bat cleanup with the Red Sox or suffer for batting cleanup with the White Sox. The relationship of individual performance to team play is stated poorly or not at all in conventional baseball statistics. In Batting Runs it is crystal clear.

Recognizing that some readers will wish to keep track of batting performance by compiling Batting Runs themselves over the course of a season and that they may be frustrated by the difficulty of separating out pitcher batting or of calculating the (At-Bats − Hits) factor for the league, we advise that using the fixed value of −.25 for outs will tend to work quite well if you wish to include pitcher batting performance, and a fixed value of −.27 will serve if you wish to exclude it. Actually, any fixed value will suffice in midseason; it's only when all the numbers are in and you care to compare this year's results with last year's (or, e.g., with those of the 1927 Yankees) that more precision is desirable. At that point the value of the out may be calculated by the more ambitious among you, but, ideally, the sporting press will provide accurate Batting Runs figures. (Who calculates ERA for himself?) Batting Runs are abbreviated as BR.

Batting Wins Adjusted Batting Runs divided by the number of runs required to create an additional win beyond average (see *Runs Per Win*). That average is defined as a team record of .500 because a league won-lost average must be .500, or as an individual record of zero because the value of the out for a given year is calculated to establish a baseline of zero. Abbreviated as BW.

Calculated Stat One or more counting stats (see below) subjected to a mathematical process such as averaging.

Chances Accepted Putouts and assists, minus errors.

Clutch Hitting Index Calculated for individuals, actual RBIs over expected RBIs, adjusted for league average and slot in batting order; 100 is a league-average performance. The spot in the batting order is figured as

$$5 - (9 \times \text{BFPGP} - \text{BFPGT})$$

where BFPGP is the batters facing pitcher per game for the player, or plate appearances divided by games, and BFPGT is the batters facing pitcher per game of the entire team.

Expected RBIs are calculated as

$$(.25 \text{ singles} + .50 \text{ doubles} + .75 \text{ triples} + 1.75 \text{ homers}) \times \text{LGAV} \times \text{EXPSL}$$

where LGAV (league average) = league RBIs divided by (.25 singles + .50 doubles + .75 triples + 1.75 homers), and EXPSL (expected RBI by slot number) = .88 for the leadoff batter, and for the remaining slots, descending to ninth, .90, .98, 1.08, 1.08, 1.04, 1.04, 1.04, and 1.02.

Calculated for teams, Clutch Hitting Index is actual runs scored over Batting Runs. Abbreviated as CHI.

Clutch Pitching Index Expected runs allowed over actual runs allowed, with 100 being a league-average performance. Expected runs are figured on the basis of the pitcher's opposing at-bats, hits, walks, and hit batsmen (doubles and triples estimated at league average). Abbreviated as CPI.

Counting Stat A raw figure that tells how many of an item have been accumulated, as opposed to a calculated or derived figure such as an average.

Differential The difference between a team's actual won-lost record and that predicted by the total of its Pitching Wins, Batting Wins, Fielding Wins, and Stolen Base Wins; this measure indicates the extent to which a team outperformed or underperformed its talent. Abbreviated as DIF.

Earned Run Average Calculated as earned runs times nine, divided by innings pitched. For a few years after being introduced as an official stat in the National League in 1912 and the American League in 1913, runs aided by stolen bases were not counted as earned (see Chronology of Scoring Rules in Appendix 1, Rules and Scoring). For years before 1912, ERA has been constructed from raw data, but for some teams in some seasons, earned runs cannot be identified with perfect certainty. For those teams, we use the estimating procedure created by Information Concepts, Inc., of assigning to those runs whose earned/unearned status is unknown the percentage of earned runs to runs that characterize the team's known runs. In *Total Baseball*, we have created an Adjusted ERA by normalizing to the league average—which is done by dividing the league average ERA by the individual ERA—and then factoring in home park.

Expected Wins Calculated for the team based on its actual runs scored and allowed, not its predicted runs scored and allowed. A team that allows exactly as many runs as it scores is predicted to play .500 ball. The equation for expected wins is:

$$\frac{(\text{Runs Scored} - \text{Runs Allowed})}{\text{Runs Per Win}} + \frac{(\text{Wins} + \text{Losses})}{2}$$

Abbreviated as W− EXP.

Fielding Average Defined as putouts and assists divided by the total of putouts, assists, and errors. The weakness of this stat is that it values a player with minimal range but good hands over another player who may accept many more chances but mishandle a few of these. Abbreviated as FA. See *Range Factor, Total Chances*.

Fielding Runs The Linear Weights measure of runs saved *beyond* what a league-average player at that position might have saved, defined as zero; this stat is calculated to take account of the particular demands of the different positions.

For second basemen, shortstops, and third basemen, the formula begins by calculating the league average for the position:

$$\text{AVG} \begin{array}{c} \text{pos.} \\ \text{lg.} \end{array} = \left(\frac{.20 \, (\text{PO} + 2\text{A} - \text{E} + \text{DP}) \text{ league at position}}{\text{PO league total} - \text{K league total}} \right)$$

where A = assists, PO = putouts, E = errors, DP = double plays, and K = strikeouts. Then we estimate the number of innings for each player at each position based upon each player's entire fielding record and his number of plate appearances. So, if the team played 1,500 innings and one player was calculated to have played 1,000 of those innings at a given position, his Fielding Runs (FR) would be calculated as:

$$FR = .20\,(PO + 2A - E + DP)\,\text{player} - \text{avg. pos. lg.} \times \left(\frac{PO}{\text{team}} - \frac{K}{\text{team}}\right)\frac{\text{innings, player}}{\text{innings, team}}$$

Assists are doubly weighted because more fielding skill is generally required to get one than to record a putout.

For catchers, the above formula is modified by removing strikeouts from their formulas and subtracting not only errors but also passed balls divided by two. Also incorporated in the catcher's Fielding Runs is one tenth of the adjusted Pitching Runs for the team, times the percentage of games behind the plate by that catcher.

For pitchers, the above formula is modified to subtract individual pitcher strikeouts from the total number of potential outs (otherwise, exceptional strikeout pitchers like Nolan Ryan or Bob Feller would see their Fielding Runs artificially depressed). Also, pitchers' chances are weighted less than infielders' assists because a pitcher's style may produce fewer ground balls. Thus the formula for pitchers is .10(PO + 2A − E + DP), whereas for second basemen, shortstops, and third basemen it is .20(PO + 2A − E + DP).

For first basemen, because putouts and double plays require so little skill in all but the odd case, these plays are eliminated, leaving only .20(2A − E) in the numerator.

For outfielders, the formula becomes .20(PO + 4A − E + 2DP). The weighting for assists is boosted here because a good outfielder can prevent runs through the threat of assists that are never made; for them, unlike infielders, the assist is essentially an elective play, like the stolen base. Outfielders' Fielding Runs were subject to some degree of error because outfielders sometimes switch fields within a game or season (Babe Ruth, for example, was positioned in the field that required the lesser range—right field in Yankee Stadium, left field in most road parks). Also, short distances to left- or right-field walls in some parks tend to depress putout totals.

Since the third edition of *Total Baseball,* however, we have researched and obtained breakouts of all outfielders' games in left, center, and right fields. Center fielders now have higher ratings than they did in the first and second editions. Abbreviated as FR.

Fielding Wins Fielding Runs divided by the number of runs required to create an additional win beyond average. That average is defined as a team record of .500 because a league won-lost average must be .500. Abbreviated as FW. See *Runs Per Win.*

Games Behind Figured by adding the difference in wins between a trailing team and the leader to the difference in losses, and dividing by two. Thus a team that is three games behind may trail by three in the win column and three in the loss column, or four and two, or any other combination of wins and losses totaling six. Abbreviated as GB.

Game-Winning Run Batted In Credited to the batter who drives in a run that gives his club a lead that it never relinquishes, no matter when that run is driven in nor what the final score is. Introduced in 1980 as an official stat and later disowned, the GWRBI is not recorded in this volume.

Grounded into Double Play Kept officially since 1993 in the NL and 1939 in the AL (though the NL data of 1933-38 made no distinction between lined-into double plays and grounded-into double plays, and the AL data of 1939 was not published). This stat tends to be overvalued by the general public as an indicator of rally-killing ineptitude. Instead, it is largely a function of high totals of at-bats, which tend to be accumulated by the game's best players, not its worst. Abbreviated as GIDP.

Hands Out The original 1840s scoring term for batters producing outs either at the plate or on the bases. On a force out, the runner retired on the bases would be charged with a hand out, not the batter. Also called Hands Lost, and abbreviated as HO or HL.

Hit by Pitch A batter struck by a pitched ball was not awarded first base until 1884 in the American Association and 1887 in the National League. Reconstruction of stats for batters and pitchers in the years 1897-1908 has been accomplished. Abbreviated as HBP.

Hits Bases on balls originally counted as hits in 1887, but are recorded in this volume as neither hits nor at-bats.

Home Run Factor A measure of the home runs hit in a given ballpark, with 100 representing the average home park and the highest figure above that representing the best home-run park. Computed in the same manner as Home Run Batter Rating (see above). Abbreviated as HRF.

Home Run Percentage Home runs per 100 at-bats.

Home Run Pitcher Rating A measure of a team's ability to prevent home runs, taking into account the Home Run Factor (see above) of the park and the team's not having to face its own batters. The average mark is represented as 100, and the lowest figure beneath that indicates the best.

Home Runs When is a home run not a home run? Before 1920, not if it came with men on base in the ultimate inning and created a margin of victory greater than one run. A ruling of the Special Baseball Records Committee in 1969 reversed its earlier decision that had made home runs of 37 disputed final-inning, game-winning base hits. In accordance with the practice of the day, such a hit, even if it sailed out of the park, would be credited with only as many bases as necessary to plate the winning run. Thus Babe Ruth's "715th home run," hit on July 8, 1918, to win a game against Cleveland, remained a triple, and Jimmy Collins and Sherry Magee were each deprived of two home runs.

Innings Pitched Official baseball practice was, until 1982, to round off fractional innings for individuals to the next highest inning. Since then fractional innings have been kept for individuals and teams. In this volume fractional innings are supplied for all individuals and all teams in all years. Those men who took a turn on the mound but failed to retire a batter are credited with no innings pitched and, if they allowed a runner or runners to score, an ERA of infinity.

Intentional Bases on Balls Recorded only since 1955.

Isolated Power Total bases minus hits, divided by at-bats; in other words, Slugging Average minus Batting Average. Appears to have been created by Allan Roth and Branch Rickey in the 1950s.

League-Average Replacement Player That model player who performs at precisely the league average, creating a baseline against which to measure others.

League Performance: Because the caliber of play in the Union Association of 1884 and the Federal League of 1914-15 was substantially below that of its rivals in those years, we have made an upward adjustment to overall league performance, thus lowering individual ratings or computed stats, while leaving unaffected the raw statistics of Organized Baseball. League at bats were reduced to 80 percent for the UA and 90 percent for the FL.

We tested all players who appeared in at least 30 games for the UA in 1884 and 30 or more games in the NL or AA in the 1883-85 period. There were 31 players who played 2,182 games in the UA and had a Total Player Rating 2.6 wins higher per 112 games in the UA. There were 17 pitchers who pitched 3,678 innings in the UA with at least 30 innings in the UA and 30 innings in other leagues in the 1883-85 period). These pitchers had a Total Pitcher Index 0.8 wins higher in the UA per 112 innings.

For the Federal League, there were 54 players with 30 games in the FL and at least 30 games in other leagues in the 1913-16 period. These players had 10,401 games in the FL and had a Total Player Rating 1.26 wins higher per 154 games. For pitchers, there were 39 with 30 or more innings in the FL and 30 innings in other leagues in the 1913-16 period). These pitchers had 13,872 innings and a Total Pitcher Index .49 wins higher in the FL per 154 innings.

Actually, the calculations for the UA produced a .76 multiplier for on base percentage and slugging, which we have rounded to .80. The calculations for the FL produced a .90 multiplier for on base percentage and slugging, which we have incorporated. UA pitchers had an .875 multiplier for earned run average, which we have expressed as .80 for consistency with the batting figure. FL pitchers had a multiplier of .924, which we have rounded to .90.

Linear Weights A system created by Pete Palmer to measure all the events on a ballfield in terms of runs. At the root of this system, as with other sabermetric figures such as Runs Created, is the knowledge that wins and losses are what the game of baseball is about, that wins and losses are proportional in some way to runs scored and runs allowed, and that runs in turn are proportional to the events that go into their making.

Normalizing Restating a figure as a ratio by comparing it to the league average, or norm.

On Base Percentage Created by Roth and Rickey in its current form—hits plus walks plus hit by pitch, divided by at-bats plus walks plus hit by pitch—in the early 1950s, although there were nineteenth-century forebears such as "Reached First Base." When OBP, as it is abbreviated, was adopted as an official stat in 1984, the denominator was expanded to include sacrifice flies. The effect is to penalize a batter in his on base percentage by giving him a plate appearance while at the same time crediting him in his batting average by deleting the plate appearance. In this book we calculate OBP without considering sacrifice flies, which in any event are calculable on a continuing basis only since 1954.

On Base plus Slugging See *Production*.

Opponents' Batting Average Hits allowed divided by at-bats allowed (or, if at-bats allowed is unknown, then at-bats equals hits plus inning times "K," where "K" is the league average of at-bats minus hits, all over innings). Abbreviated as OAV.

Opponents' On Base Percentage For years before 1908 in the American League and 1903 in the National League, the number of batters facing a pitcher has been constructed from the available raw data. We have subtracted league base hits from league at-bats, divided by league innings pitched, multiplied by the pitcher's innings, and added his hits and walks allowed and hit by pitch and sacrifices, if available. Abbreviated as OOB.

Outs Until 1883, included catching a ball on one bounce in foul ground. Not credited after three strikes in 1887, when the rule was "four strikes and yer out"—as it was, in fact, from 1871–1881, when batters commonly received "warning pitches" rather than called strikes.

Outs Per Game The 1860s successor to Hands Out (see above), it joined with Runs Per Game to form the batting record before the rise of professional league play.

Park Factor Calculated separately for batters and pitchers. Above 100 signifies a park favorable to hitters; below 100 signifies a park favorable to pitchers. The computation of PF is admittedly daunting, and what follows is probably of interest to the merest handful of readers, but we feel obliged to state the mathematical underpinnings for those few who may care. We use a three-year average Park Factor for players and teams unless they change home parks. Then a two-year average is used, unless the park existed for only one year. Then a one-year mark is used. If a team started up in Year 1, played two years in the first park, one in the next, and three in the park after that and then stopped play, the average would be as follows (where F*n* is the one-year park factor for year *n*):

Year 1 and 2 = (F1 + F2)/2   Year 4 = (F4 + F5)/2
Year 3   = F3   Year 5 = (F4 + F5 + F6)/3
                                    Year 6 = (F5 + F6)/2

Step 1. Find games, losses, and runs scored and allowed for each team at home and on the road. Take runs per game scored and allowed at home over runs per game scored and allowed on the road. This is the initial figure, but we must make two corrections to it.

Step 2. The first correction is for innings pitched at home and on the road. This is a bit complicated, so the mathematically faint of heart may want to head back at this point. First, find the team's home winning percentage (wins at home over games at home). Do the same for road games. Calculate the Innings Pitched Corrector (IPC) shown below. If it is greater than 1, this means the innings pitched on the road are higher because the other team is batting more often in the last of the ninth. This rating is divided by the Innings Pitched Corrector, like so:

$$IPC = \frac{(18.5 - \text{Wins at home} / \text{Games at home})}{(18.5 - \text{Losses on road} / \text{Games on road})}$$

Note: 18.5 is the average number of half-innings per game if the home team always bats in the ninth.

Step 3. Make corrections for the fact that the other road parks' total difference from the league average is offset by the park rating of the club that is being rated. Multiply rating by this Other Parks Corrector (OPC):

$$OPC = \frac{\text{No. of teams}}{\text{No. of teams} - 1 + \text{Run Factor, team}}$$

(Note that this OPC differs from that presented earlier in *The Hidden Game of Baseball*, for in preparing the pre-1900 data for *Total Baseball*, we discovered that for some parks with extreme characteristics, like Chicago's Lake Front Park of 1884, which had a Home Run Factor of nearly 5, the earlier formula produced wrong results. For parks with factors of 1.5 or less, either formula works well.)

Example. In 1982, Atlanta scored 388 runs and allowed 387 runs at home in 81 games, and scored 351 and allowed 315 on the road in 81 games. The initial factor is $(775/81) \div (666/81) = 1.164$. The Braves' home record was 42–39, or .519, and their road record was 47–34, or .580. Thus the IPC $= (18.5 - .519) \div (18.5 - .420) = .995$. The team rating is now $1.164/.995 = 1.170$. The OPC $= (12) \div (12 - 1 + 1.170) = .986$. The final runs-allowed rating is $1.170 \times .986$, or 1.154.

We warned you it wouldn't be easy!

The batter adjustment factor is composed of two parts, one the park factor and the other the fact that a batter does not have to face his own team's pitchers. The initial correction takes care of only the second factor. Start with the following (SF = Scoring Factor, previously determined [for Atlanta, 1.154], and SF1 = Scoring Factor of the other clubs [NT = number of teams]):

$$1 - \frac{SF - 1}{NT - 1}$$

Next is an iterative process in which the initial team pitching rating is assumed to be 1, and the following factors are employed:

RHT, RAT = Runs per game scored at home (H) and away (A), by team
OHT, OAT = Runs per game allowed at home, away, by team
RAL = Runs per game by both teams

Now, with the Team Pitching Rating (TPR) = 1, we proceed to calculate Team Batting Rating (TBR):

$$TBR = \left(\frac{RAT}{SF1} + \frac{RHT}{SF} \right) \left(1 + \frac{TPR - 1}{NT - 1} \right) \Big/ RAL$$

$$TPR = \left(\frac{OAT}{SF1} + \frac{OHT}{SF} \right) \left(1 + \frac{TBR - 1}{NT - 1} \right) \Big/ RAL$$

The last two steps are repeated three more times. The final Batting Corrector, or Batters' Park Factor (BPF) is

$$BPF = \frac{(SF + SF1)}{\left(2 \times \left[1 + \frac{TPR - 1}{NT - 1} \right] \right)}$$

Similarly, the final Pitching Corrector, or Pitchers' Park Factor (PPF) is

$$PPF = \frac{(SF + SF1)}{\left(2 \times \left[1 + \frac{TBR - 1}{NT - 1} \right] \right)}$$

Now an example, using the 1982 Atlanta Braves once again.

$$RHT - \frac{388}{81} - 4.79 \qquad RAT - \frac{351}{81} - 4.33$$

$$OHT = \frac{387}{81} = 4.78 \qquad OAT = \frac{315}{81} = 3.89$$

$$RAL = \frac{7947}{972} = 8.18 \qquad NT = 12$$

$$SF = 1.154 \qquad\qquad SF1 = 1 - \left(\frac{1.154 - 1}{11}\right) = .986$$

$$TBR = \left(\frac{4.33}{.986} + \frac{4.79}{1.154}\right)\left(1 + \frac{1-1}{11}\right)\bigg/ 8.18 = 1.044$$

$$TPR = \left(\frac{3.89}{.986} + \frac{4.78}{1.154}\right)\left(1 + \frac{1.044-1}{11}\right)\bigg/ 8.18 = .993$$

Repeating these steps gives a TBR of 1.04 and a TPR of .97. The Batters' Park Factor is

$$BPF = \frac{(1.170 + .986)}{\left(2 \times \left[1 + \frac{.99 - 1}{11}\right]\right)} = 1.07$$

This is not a great deal removed from taking the original ratio,

$$\frac{1.170 + 1}{2}, \text{ which is 1.08.}$$

The Pitchers' Park Factor may be calculated in analogous fashion.

To apply the Batters' Park Factor to Batting Runs, one must use this formula:

$$\frac{BR}{corr.} = \frac{BR}{uncorr.}\bigg/ \frac{Runs(league)}{AB+BB+HBP} - \frac{Runs(league)}{AB+BB+HBP} \times (BPF - 1) \times \frac{AB+BB+HBP}{(player\ or\ team)}$$
(league)   (league)

For example, if a player produces 20 runs above average in 700 plate appearances with a Batters' Park Factor of 1.10, and the league average of runs produced per plate appearance is .11, this means that the player's uncorrected Batting Runs is 20 over the zero point of 700 × .11 (77 runs). In other words, 77 runs is the average run contribution expected of this batter were he playing in an average home park. But because his Batters' Park Factor is 1.10, which means his home park was 10 percent kinder to hitters (than the average), you would really expect an average run production of 1.1 × 77, or 85 runs. Thus the player whose uncorrected Batting Runs is 97 with a BF of 1.1 is only +10 runs rather than +20, and 10 is his Park Adjusted Batting Runs (in the Player Register, BR/A):

$$10 = 20/1.10 - .11 \times (1.10 - 1) \times 700.$$

Percentage of Team Wins A simple but deceiving measure of a good pitcher's contribution to a bad club; in this, it shares the virtues and flaws of Ted Oliver's Weighted Rating System and, to a lesser degree, our own Wins Above Team (both of which see). Steve Carlton had the highest single-season rating in this century when, in 1972, he went 27–10 for a Phillie club that won only 59 games. Yet his mark of 45.8 percent of his team's wins would not make the top 100 list of seasons since 1876, making this stat nearly useless for historical analysis.

Pitcher Defense Abbreviated as PD. See *Fielding Runs*.

Pitchers' Park Factor The same as the Park Factor shown in the pitchers' section of the team statistics portion of the Annual Record and in the Pitcher Register; above 100 means a pitcher was hurt by playing half his games in a good hitting park. See *Park Factor*.

Pitcher Strikeouts Made tougher or easier by cyclically varying rules and conditions. For instance, foul tips did not count as strikes for many years, even when deliberate, as with bunts; fouls caught on a bounce were outs until 1883; the ball-strike count underwent much experimentation until settling at four balls and three strikes in

1889; not to mention the high-low strike zone, warning pitches, varying pitching distances, and restricted deliveries. It helps to know some history before rattling off stats to prove this or that, but normalizing a stat to its league helps, even with counting stats such as strikeouts.

Pitching Runs The Linear Weights measure of runs saved *beyond* what a league-average pitcher or team might have saved, defined as zero. The math is simple: *Pitching Runs = Innings Pitched × (League ERA/9) – Earned Runs Allowed*. An alternate version is: *Innings Pitched/9 × (League ERA – Individual ERA)*. Abbreviated as PR.

Pitching Wins Park Adjusted Pitching Runs divided by the number of runs required to create an additional win beyond average. That average is defined as a team record of .500 because a league won-lost average must be .500. Abbreviated as PW. See *Pitching Runs*, above, and *Runs Per Win*.

Player Win Averages The title of a 1970 book issued by the Mills brothers, Harlan and Eldon, as well as the name of their overall method of determining not only the *what* of baseball statistics but also the *when*, or clutch element. Computerizing complete play-by-play data for a full season for their book, they assigned "Win Points"—reflective of that event's potential impact on the team's prospects of victory—to *every* event on a baseball field.

Positional Adjustment A key factor in the Total Player Rating that addresses the relative worth to a ball club of the defensive positions. A man who bats .270, hits 25 homers, and drives in 80 runs may be an average performer in left field, no matter how good his glove; but credit those batting stats to a shortstop or second baseman and you have a star, because the defensive demands of the position are so much greater. To balance the abundance of good-hitting outfielders or first basemen against the scarcity of such players at catcher or shortstop, we created a positional adjustment expressed in terms of the average batting skill needed to hold down a major league spot at that position.

To determine the average defensive skill required of a position, simply subtract the average batting skill at that position from his Total Player Rating. This may seem strange at first glance, but it does put, for example, shortstops, first basemen, and left fielders on the same footing. The explanation that follows represents a change from previous editions, in which players were measured against only those who played their position in their league in that year. We have now redefined the positional adjustment as an average over *both* leagues for a three-year period centered on the measured year. This raised the ratings for Lou Gehrig and Jimmie Foxx by a win or two, as they are now compared with sixteen first basemen over three years (a total of forty-eight) rather than just eight. In the 1950–1970 period, AL outfielders averaged a few more Batting Runs per season than their counterparts in the NL. When both leagues were counted, NL players dropped a few Wins and AL players gained. Hank Aaron lost 4 Wins for this reason.

In the years since 1977 the positional adjustment for, say a National League first baseman, will be in the context of the batting records of not merely twelve men, but twenty-six—times three, or seventy-eight—obviously, a much broader base of comparison. For each edition, the concluding season's positional adjustments are based on the average of that year and the preceding season.

Let's say that last year all major league left fielders accounted for 198 batting runs. The positional adjustment, or factor for average defensive skill, for a left fielder who played in all 162 games would be 162 × 198/3,202 (which calculates to 10), where 3,202 is the number of games played in both leagues by all left fielders (or any other position, obviously). Thus a left fielder who played in all his team's games would have 10 runs subtracted from the sum of his Batting Runs, Stolen Base Runs, and Fielding Runs. If all major league shortstops last year accounted for 158 Batting Runs below average, the adjustment for a shortstop would be figured in the same way, multiplying his games played by – 158/3,202, or – 8 runs, meaning that 8 runs (minus a minus 8) would be *added* to his Total Player Rating.

Production On Base Percentage plus Slugging Average: a simple but elegant measure of batting prowess, in that the weaknesses of one-half of the formulation, On Base Percentage, are countered by the strengths of the other, Slugging Average, and vice versa. When PRO, as it is abbreviated, is adjusted for home park and normalized to league average to become PRO⁺, the calculation is modified slightly to create a baseline of 100 for a league-average performance. For PRO⁺, the calculation is

$$\frac{\text{Player On Base Pct.}}{\text{League On Base Pct.}} + \frac{\text{Player Slugging Avg.}}{\text{League Slugging Avg.}} - 1$$

This produces a figure with a decimal point—an above-average figure, like 1.46, or a below-average figure, like 0.82. For ease of display, in this book we drop the decimal and express these as 146 and 82.

Putout Average Putouts divided by games played; a stat created by Philadelphia baseball writer Al Wright in 1875.

Quality Start A game started in which a pitcher lasts for six innings or more and allows three runs or less.

Ratio Hits plus walks plus hit batsmen allowed per nine innings. Abbreviated as RAT.

RBI Opportunities An official American League stat for the first three weeks of 1918, until the league saw how much work it involved and scrapped it. Still a good idea, sort of, and the folks at the Elias Sports Bureau have tracked this type of "situational stat" since 1975.

Reached First Base A precursor of the On Base Percentage, this stat was introduced as an official National League measure in 1879, its one and only year of existence. It included times reached via hits, walks, and errors, but not hit by pitch because putting their bodies on the line did not yet, in 1879, send batters to first base. Trivia: the league leader in this stat's lone year of life was Paul Hines, with 193.

Relative Batting Average Pioneered by David Shoebotham in a *Baseball Research Journal* article in 1976, this was the first traditional stat normalized to league average so as to permit cross-era comparison. Most folks who have employed this measure simply divide individual batting average by league batting average. Shoebotham's original computation was more precise:

$$\text{RBA} = \frac{\text{player's hits}}{\text{player's AB}} \Big/ \frac{\text{league hits} - \text{player's hits}}{\text{league AB} - \text{player's AB}}$$

In this manner a player's own performance would not be compared with itself.

Relief Points Relief wins plus saves minus losses was the original formula used as the basis for the Rolaids Company's annual award to the top reliever in each league. Recently the formula has been changed to include a debit for blown saves.

Relief Ranking Takes *Relief Runs* (which see), adjusts them for home park, then weights them by a factor (F in the formula below) reflecting the greater value of the innings pitched by a bullpen "closer." Relief Runs, which weights all innings identically, will tend to benefit long and middle relievers who are effective over many innings, while Relief Ranking—which was initially designed for those men who pitch less than three innings per game over a season or career—will tend to benefit relievers who may have fewer innings but who have more saves and decisions. The formula is

$$(\text{Relief Runs}) \times \text{F where the Factor} = \frac{9 \times (\text{Wins} + \text{Losses} + .25\,[\text{Saves}])}{\text{IP}}$$

The multiplier, or Factor, is usually around 1, but can get up to 1.5 or even 2 for some relievers, and can get down as low as 0.8 for some starters who have a lot of no-decision games.

Relief Runs Identical to Pitching Runs but confined to relief pitchers, defined as those who average less than three innings per appearance. Abbreviated as RR. See *Relief Ranking*.

Run Batted In Though widely regarded as a good measure of a batter's overall productivity and value to his team, the RBI is extremely situation-dependent, denying equal access to opportunity on the basis of a player's team, slot in the batting order, and

particularly the men surrounding him in the batting order.

Run Factor A measure of the run scoring in a given ballpark compared to other ballparks, with 100 representing the average home park and the highest figure above that representing the best hitters' park. Abbreviated as RF, it is computed on the basis of comparing runs scored and allowed per inning at home and on the road. Innings are estimated from the number of games and games won, allowing for the home team not batting in the final inning of a game in which it leads. The resulting Run Factor is then compared to the league average.

Run Rating for Batters A measure of a team's run-scoring ability, taking into account the park's *Run Factor* (see above) and the team's batters not having to face its own pitchers, with 100 representing the average and the highest figure above that representing the best. Abbreviated as RB.

Run Rating for Pitchers A measure of a team's run-prevention ability, taking into account the *Run Factor* (see above) and the team's pitchers not having to face its own batters, with 100 representing the average and the lowest figure beneath that representing the best. Abbreviated as RP.

Runs Created Bill James's formulation for run contribution from a variety of batting and baserunning events. Many different formulas are used, depending upon data available. In its basic expression, the formula is:

$$\frac{(\text{Hits} + \text{Walks})\,(\text{Total Bases})}{\text{At-Bats} + \text{Walks}}$$

The essence of this formulation is that the ability to get on base and the ability to push baserunners around fairly describes offensive ability. James later refined the formula with a "stolen base version":

$$\frac{(\text{Hits} + \text{Walks} - \text{Caught Stealing})\,(\text{Total Bases} + .55 \times \text{Stolen Bases})}{\text{At-Bats} + \text{Walks}}$$

Next came the "technical version": a longer formulation, presented below using the standard abbreviations for the various offensive events (the two elements multiplied in the numerator are referred to below as "A" and "B," and the denominator is referred to as "C"):

$$\frac{(\text{H} + \text{BB} + \text{HBP} - \text{CS} - \text{GIDP})\,(\text{TB} + .26[\text{BB} - \text{IBB} + \text{HBP}] + .52[\text{SH} + \text{SF} + \text{SB}])}{\text{AB} + \text{BB} + \text{HBP} + \text{SH} + \text{SF}}$$

From this technical version (Tech-1), James spun off 13 additional technical versions. "The reason that we have to do this," he wrote in *The Bill James Historical Baseball Abstract*, "is that the data set changes and evolves rapidly throughout the century, or at least up until about 1955, when the progress of evolution in statistical information came to a temporary halt (it stopped moving forward until Bill James and Pete Palmer came around, about twenty years later). In 1900 we have no data for how many times a player grounded into a double play, how many times he was hit by a pitch, how many of his walks might have been intentional, how many times he was caught stealing, or how many sacrifice flies he hit." Accordingly, James adjusted his Runs Created formula to fit the available data; some versions, such as Tech-3, cover as much as a decade in a given league, while others, such as Tech-4, are in force for only a single league season. In *Total Baseball*, we have computed Runs Created values for all players since 1876 using the version most applicable to the period, with the single exception of Tech-9, which James applied only to the American League of 1916 but which we use for 1914–1916 in the AL and 1915–1916 in the NL because we have discovered additional caught-stealing data. (For those players whose careers began before 1900, James used the Tech-11 formula "to estimate how many runs they had created," but appended a note saying that "these estimates were of indeterminate accuracy.")

Here are the formulas for Runs Created (RC) technical versions

2–14 (Tech-1 was used for both leagues in 1955–1988):

Tech-2 (1954)
Factors A and C of Tech-1 remain the same, while Part B simply drops Intentional Bases on Balls.

Tech-3 (AL 1940–1953; NL 1951–1953)
Factor A remains the same, while SF is dropped from Factor C; Factor B changes to: 1.025 TB + .26(BB + HBP) + .52(SH + SB).

Tech-4 (AL 1939)
Factors A and C remain the same, while B becomes: TB + .26(BB + HBP) + .52(SH + SB).

Tech-5 (AL 1931–1938)
Factors B and C remain the same, while A becomes: .96(H + BB + HBP − CS).

Tech-6 (AL 1920–1930; NL 1920–1925)
Factors A and C remain the same, while B changes only in the value placed on the sacrifice hit and stolen base, which declines from .52 to .51.

Tech-7 (NL 1926–1930)
C remains the same, while A changes to: .93(H + BB + HBP), and B becomes: TB + .26(BB + HBP) + .46(SH).

Tech-8 (AL 1913, 1917–1919; NL 1913–1914, 1917–1919)
C remains the same, while A becomes: H + W + HBP − .02(AB), and B becomes: TB + .85(SH + SB).

Tech-9 (AL 1914–1916; NL 1915–1916)
B and C are the same, while A becomes: H + BB + HBP − CS.

Tech-10 (AL, NL 1908–1912)
A and C remain the same, while B becomes: 1.025(TB + SB) + .75(SH).

Tech-11 (AL, NL 1900–1907)
B and C remain the same, while A becomes: H + BB + HBP.

Tech-12 (NL 1939–1950)
A Factor: H + BB + HBP − GIDP
B Factor: TB + .26(BB +HBP) + .52(SH)

Tech-13 (NL 1933–1938)
A and C remain the same as above, while B becomes: 1.025(TB) + .26(BB + HBP) + .52(SH)

Tech-14 (NL 1931–1932)
B and C remain the same, but A becomes: .95(H + BB + HBP).

Runs Per Game With its mate *Outs Per Game* (which see), this was the precursor, in the 1860s, of the batting average; by the end of that decade it gave way to Hits Per Game.

Runs Per Win Branch Rickey and Allan Roth first stated the proportional nature of runs and wins in their 1954 article in *Life*. Since then the point has been expanded upon by George Lindsey, Pete Palmer, Bill James, and every sabermetrician worth his salt: the point being that just as runs scored and allowed are the key to victory in a given game, so are they the key to success over the course of a season and the predictors of won-lost record with a surprising degree of precision. In 1982, Palmer wrote in *The National Pastime*, "My work showed that as a rough rule of thumb, each additional ten runs scored (or ten less runs allowed) produced one extra win. . . . However, breaking the teams into groups showed that high-scoring teams needed more runs to produce a win. This runs-per-win factor I determined to be ten times the square root of the average number of runs scored per inning by both teams. Thus in normal play, when 4.5 runs per game are scored by each club, each team scores .5 runs per inning—totaling one run, the square root of which is one, times ten."

For *Total Baseball*, we have improved the Runs Per Win figure used in calculating the overall win figures in the Total Player Rating and the Total Pitcher Index. Rather than using 10 times the square root of the average number of runs scored per inning by both teams, we use adjusted runs per inning based on what the player or pitcher rating is. A hitter will increase the figure by adding in his rating over the number of games played, while a pitcher will have his rating subtracted. Say the average number of runs scored per inning is 1, as in the model above; then Runs Per Win = 10. Take a pitcher who allows 45 runs less than average in 25 games. This lowers the runs per game by 1.8, or runs per inning by .2, so the new Runs Per Win figure is 10 times the square root of the average number of runs scored per inning by both teams, *minus the pitcher's rating*. So we take from the one run per inning the .2 run saved by the pitcher, giving a result of 0.8. Ten times the square root of 0.8 is 8.9, so the pitcher gets 45/8.9, or 5.1, wins instead of 4.5. A hitter with plus 45 runs in 150 games, or .3 runs per game, contributes .03 runs per inning. His Runs Per Win is now 10 times the square root of the average number of runs scored per inning *plus the batter's rating*. So we add to the 1 run per inning the .03 runs added by the batter, giving a result of 10.1. Ten times the square root of 10.1 gives the batter 4.4 wins. (This method makes makes more of a difference in pitching because the runs are contributed over fewer games. With the same run contribution—45 beyond average—the pitcher gains 0.7 wins over the batter. This is because when the total number of runs scored is lowered, the value of each run is greater).

Runs Produced Runs batted in plus runs scored minus home runs.

Sabermetrics Defined by Bill James, who coined the term in honor of the Society for American Baseball Research, as "the search for objective knowledge about baseball" and, earlier, as "the mathematical and statistical analysis of baseball records."

SABR Pronounced "saber," this is the acronym for the Society for American Baseball Research, the organization that has, since its founding by Bob Davids in 1971, steadily advanced the state of baseball knowledge.

Sacrifice Fly First recognized as an event in 1908 but indistinguishable in the official records from sacrifice hits until 1954. There has been much flip-flopping since 1930 on whether to credit the sacrifice flier with an at-bat or an RBI or whether a fly ball that advances a runner to a base other than home plate also should exempt a man from an at-bat.

Sacrifice Hits Invented in the 1860s, recorded since 1889; sacrificer charged with an at-bat until 1894. Sabermetricians frown on the strategy because all the studies show that the trading of an out for a base advanced is a losing strategy—lowering the run expectations of the team that attempts it—in all but the most unusual of cases . . . even if the sacrifice "succeeds."

Sacrifice Hits Allowed Computed officially in the National League since 1913 but not published until 1916, and kept in the American League since 1921 but not published until 1922; what it signified about anything is unclear.

Save Created by Jerome Holtzman of the Chicago *Sun-Times*, the save began to be reported by *The Sporting News* on a regular basis in 1960. The major leagues adopted the save in 1969, at which time it was credited to a reliever who finished a game that his team won. In 1973 the save was redefined so that a reliever had not only to finish the game but also to find the potential tying or winning run on base or at the plate, or, alternately, to pitch the final three innings of a victorious contest. In 1975 the rule was liberalized to include a reliever's appearance of one inning or more in which he protects a lead of three runs or less; or he enters the game with the tying or winning run on base, at bat, or on deck; or he pitches three innings to the game's conclusion. In this book, the 1969 definition is applied to all games before 1969; otherwise the rule in force at the time prevails. Abbreviated as SV.

Shutouts On an individual basis, credited only to pitchers of complete-game scoreless victories; former practice was to credit combined shutouts to the starting pitcher if he had pitched most of the way. Abbreviated as SH.

Situational Statistics How does a batter perform with the bases loaded? At night? On artificial turf? With no one on base? After the seventh inning when his team is tied or trails? The specialty of Baseball Workshop, Stats, Inc., and the Elias Sports Bureau.

Slugging Average Total bases divided by at-bats; combines nicely with On Base Percentage to create *Production* (which see). Abbreviated as SLG.

Starter Runs Identical to *Pitching Runs* (which see) but confined to starting pitchers, defined as those who average more than three innings per appearance. Abbreviated as SR.

Stolen Base Average Stolen bases divided by attempts; its computation is dependent upon the availability of caught-stealing numbers. Abbreviated as SBA.

Stolen Base Runs For teams, the Linear Weights measure of runs contributed *beyond* what a league-average basestealing team might have gained, defined as zero; for individuals, Stolen Base Runs are calculated on the basis of the 66.7 percent success rate that sabermetric studies have shown to be the break-even point for producing runs beyond the average. Availability dependent upon caught stealing data as with Stolen Base Average. The formula is simple: .30(Stolen Bases) − .60(Caught Stealing). A man who steals two bases in three attempts is merely spinning his wheels in terms of value to his team, and even a man who succeeds at an 80 percent clip will have to steal a lot of bases—about 65—to create just one win beyond average. Abbreviated as SBR.

Stolen Base Wins Stolen Base Runs divided by the number of runs required to create an additional win beyond average. Those runs are generally around around 10—historically in the range of 9–11. Abbreviated as SBW. See *Runs Per Win*.

Stolen Bases Recorded since 1886, but until 1898 steals are thought to have included a variety of daring baserunning exploits, such as going from first to third on a single or advancing an extra base on an out. Abbreviated as SB.

Strikeouts Varying rules concerning the strike zone, the foul strike, and the warning pitch—not to mention the fourth strike of 1887—all contribute to making the cross-era comparison of strikeout accomplishments a very sticky business. Abbreviated as SO.

Strikeout Percentage A batters' stat: fewest strikeouts per 100 at bats.

Total Average Tom Boswell's formulation for offensive contribution from a variety of batting and baserunning events; as with Runs Created, we have calculated Total Average to make use of the maximum available data in a given year. The concept of the numerator is bases gained, that of the denominator is outs made:

$$\frac{\text{(Total Bases + Steals + Walks + HBP − Caught Stealing)}}{\text{(At-Bats − Hits + Caught Stealing + GIDP)}}$$

Abbreviated as TA. See *Base-Out Percentage*.

Total Baseball Ranking The "MVP" of statistics, this ranks pitchers and position players by their total wins contributed in all their endeavors, revealing the most valuable performers in a given year. Abbreviated as TBR, it is not a computed stat but a sorting of players and pitchers by, respectively, the sum of their Total Batter Rating and Total Pitcher Index.

Total Bases Average Henry Chadwick's measure that divided total bases by games played; a forerunner of the Slugging Average.

Total Bases Run A silly stat of one year's duration, 1880, this was sort of an RBI in reverse, from the runner's perspective. Also called "Bases Touched," it was nothing more than that and signified nothing about individual talent. Trivia: the National League's leader in 1880 was Abner Dalrymple, with 501 bases touched.

Total Chances Putouts plus assists plus errors; in other words, total chances offered, not total chances accepted.

Total Pitcher Index The sum of a pitcher's Pitching Runs—expressed as Ranking Runs, employing the same formula used to compute Relief Ranking Runs—Batting Runs (in the AL since 1973, zero), and Fielding Runs, all divided by the Runs Per Win factor for that year (generally around 10, historically in the 9–11 range); abbreviated as TPI. See *Runs Per Win, Relief Ranking*.

Total Player Rating The sum of a player's Adjusted Batting Runs, Fielding Runs, and Base Stealing Runs, minus his positional adjustment, all divided by the Runs Per Win factor for that year

(generally around 10, historically in the 9–11 range). See *Runs Per Win*.

Triple Crown Long regarded as consisting of batting average, home runs, and RBIs, but was not always so. In the early years of this century, newspapers spoke of Ty Cobb shooting for the "triple crown" of batting average, runs, and hits.

Weighted Average The next step in statistical sophistication after first, counting and, next, averaging. Chadwick's Total Bases Average was probably the first weighted average, in that it assigned values of 1 to a single, 2 to a double, 3 to a triple, and 4 to a home run.

Weighted Rating System Ted Oliver's invention, promoted in a 1944 self-published booklet called *Kings of the Mound*. We have modified Oliver's pioneering effort to create *Wins Above Team* (see below), which entry presents a discussion of Oliver's effort.

Win Points See *Player Win Averages*.

Wins Above League A pitcher's won-lost record restated by adding his Pitching Wins above the league average to the record that a league-average pitcher would have had with his number of decisions. Example: Tom Seaver has a hard-luck season, going only 16–14 despite a 1.76 ERA and five Pitching Wins; applying the five wins to a league-average 15–15 mark in the same 30 decisions results in a WAL of 20-10.

Wins Above Team How many wins a pitcher garnered beyond those expected of an average pitcher for that team. As the editors of this volume, in their earlier *Hidden Game of Baseball*, modified Ted Oliver's *Weighted Rating System* (see above), they now improve this statistic thanks to Bill Deane's corrective for its tendency to overvalue the contributions of good pitchers on awful teams.

Oliver's Weighted Rating System for pitchers was motivated by the inadequacies of both the won-lost percentage and the ERA when it came to evaluating pitchers laboring for poor teams. The Oliver formula, ingenious if flawed, was: pitcher's won-lost percentage minus the team's won-lost percentage—after removing the pitcher's decisions from the team's record—then multiplying the difference by the pitcher's number of decisions. Here is an example of the Oliver method as applied to Bobby Castillo, who in 1982 pitched very well in going 13–11 for a very bad Minnesota club (60–102; without him, 47–91):

$$\left(\frac{13}{24} - \frac{47}{138}\right) \times 24$$

or

$$(.542 - .341) \times 24$$

or

$$.201 \times 24 = 4.824$$

The figure of 4.824 would have been represented by Ted Oliver as "4,824 points"; he did not seem to recognize that had he retained the decimal point, his rating would have been expressed directly in *wins*. Thus the number of wins Castillo accounted for in his 24 decisions that an average Minnesota pitcher would *not* have gained was 4.8.

Thanks to a key modification of our earlier formula for Wins Above Team, abbreviated as WAT, we now propose the following: calculate the pitcher's won-lost percentage and the team's winning percentage after his decisions have been set aside. If the pitcher's percentage is higher, then WAT is

$$\text{Pitcher decisions} \times \left(\frac{\text{Pitcher pct. − Team pct.}}{2 - 2 \times \text{Team pct.}}\right)$$

If the pitcher's percentage is lower, then WAT is

$$\text{Pitcher decisions} \times \left(\frac{\text{Pitcher pct. − Team pct.}}{2 \times \text{Team pct.}}\right)$$

Won-lost percentage Computed as wins over decisions.

Team and League Abbreviations

These are the 146 franchises, seven principal leagues, and their abbreviations as used throughout this book.

NATIONAL ASSOCIATION, 1871–1875 (shown as n or NA)

Abbrev.	First	Last	Team
ATH n	1871	1875	Philadelphia Athletics
ATL n	1872	1875	Brooklyn Atlantics
BAL n	1872	1874	Baltimore Lord Baltimores
BOS n	1871	1875	Boston Red Stockings
CEN n	1875	1875	Philadelphia Centennials
CHI n	1871	1871	Chicago White Stockings
CHI n	1874	1875	Chicago White Stockings
CLE n	1871	1872	Cleveland Forest City
ECK n	1872	1872	Brooklyn Eckfords
HAR n	1874	1875	Hartford Dark Blues
KEK n	1871	1871	Fort Wayne Kekiongas
MAN n	1872	1872	Middletown (Conn.) Mansfields
MAR n	1873	1873	Baltimore Marylands
MUT n	1871	1875	New York Mutuals
NAT n	1872	1872	Washington, D.C., Nationals
NH n	1875	1875	New Haven Elm City
OLY n	1871	1872	Washington, D.C., Olympics
PHI n	1873	1875	Philadelphia White Stockings
RES n	1873	1873	Elizabeth (N.J.) Resolutes
ROK n	1871	1871	Rockford (Ill.) Forest City
RS n	1875	1875	St. Louis Red Stockings
STL n	1875	1875	St. Louis Brown Stockings
TRO n	1871	1872	Troy Haymakers
WAS n	1873	1873	Washington Washingtons
WAS n	1875	1875	Washington Washingtons
WES n	1875	1875	Keokuk (Iowa) Westerns

NATIONAL LEAGUE, 1876– (shown as N or NL)

Abbrev.	First	Last	Team
ATL N	1966		Atlanta
BAL N	1892	1899	Baltimore
BOS N	1876	1952	Boston (transferred to Milwaukee)
BRO N	1890	1957	Brooklyn (transferred to Los Angeles)
BUF N	1879	1885	Buffalo
CHI N	1876		Chicago
CIN N	1876	1880	Cincinnati
CIN N	1890		Cincinnati
CLE N	1879	1884	Cleveland
CLE N	1889	1899	Cleveland
COL N	1993		Colorado
DET N	1881	1888	Detroit
FLA N	1993		Florida
HAR N	1876	1877	Hartford (played in Brooklyn in 1877)
HOU N	1962		Houston
IND N	1878	1878	Indianapolis
IND N	1887	1889	Indianapolis
KC N	1886	1886	Kansas City
LA N	1958		Los Angeles
LOU N	1876	1877	Louisville
LOU N	1892	1899	Louisville
MIL N	1878	1878	Milwaukee
MIL N	1953	1965	Milwaukee (transferred to Atlanta)
MON N	1969		Montreal
NY N	1876	1876	New York (played in Brooklyn)
NY N	1883	1957	New York (transferred to San Francisco)
NY N	1962		New York
PHI N	1876	1876	Philadelphia
PHI N	1883		Philadelphia
PIT N	1887		Pittsburgh
PRO N	1878	1885	Providence
STL N	1876	1877	St. Louis
STL N	1885	1886	St. Louis
STL N	1892		St. Louis
SD N	1969		San Diego
SF N	1958		San Francisco
SYR N	1879	1879	Syracuse
TRO N	1879	1882	Troy (N.Y.)
WAS N	1886	1889	Washington, D.C.
WAS N	1892	1899	Washington, D.C.
WOR N	1880	1882	Worcester (Mass.)

AMERICAN ASSOCIATION, 1882–1891 (shown as a or AA)

Abbrev.	First	Last	Team
BAL a	1882	1889	Baltimore
BAL a	1890	1890	Baltimore (combined with Brooklyn, shown as BB)
BAL a	1891	1891	Baltimore (transferred to National League)
BOS a	1891	1891	Boston
BRO a	1884	1889	Brooklyn (transferred to National League)
BRO a	1890	1890	Brooklyn (combined with Baltimore, shown as BB)
CIN a	1882	1889	Cincinnati (transferred to National League)
CIN a	1891	1891	Cincinnati
CLE a	1887	1888	Cleveland (transferred to National League)
COL a	1883	1884	Columbus (Ohio)
COL a	1889	1891	Columbus (Ohio)
IND a	1884	1884	Indianapolis
KC a	1888	1889	Kansas City
LOU a	1882	1891	Louisville (transferred to National League)
MIL a	1891	1891	Milwaukee
NY a	1883	1887	New York
PHI a	1882	1891	Philadelphia
PIT a	1882	1886	Pittsburgh (transferred to National League)
RIC a	1884	1884	Richmond
ROC a	1890	1890	Rochester
STL a	1882	1891	St. Louis (transferred to National League)
SYR a	1890	1890	Syracuse
TOL a	1884	1884	Toledo
TOL a	1890	1890	Toledo
WAS a	1884	1884	Washington, D.C.
WAS a	1891	1891	Washington, D.C. (transferred to National League)

UNION ASSOCIATION, 1884 (shown as U or UA)

Abbrev.	First	Last	Team
ALT U	1884	1884	Altoona (Pa.)
BAL U	1884	1884	Baltimore
BOS U	1884	1884	Boston
CHI U	1884	1884	Chicago (combined with Pittsburgh, shown as CP)
CIN U	1884	1884	Cincinnati
KC U	1884	1884	Kansas City
MIL U	1884	1884	Milwaukee
PHI U	1884	1884	Philadelphia
PIT U	1884	1884	Pittsburgh (combined with Chicago, shown as CP)
STL U	1884	1884	St. Louis
STP U	1884	1884	St. Paul (Minn.)
WAS U	1884	1884	Washington, D.C.
WIL U	1884	1884	Wilmington (Del.)

PLAYERS LEAGUE, 1890 (shown as P or PL)

Abbrev.	First	Last	Team
BOS P	1890	1890	Boston
BRO P	1890	1890	Brooklyn
BUF P	1890	1890	Buffalo
CHI P	1890	1890	Chicago
CLE P	1890	1890	Cleveland
NY P	1890	1890	New York
PHI P	1890	1890	Philadelphia
PIT P	1890	1890	Pittsburgh

AMERICAN LEAGUE, 1901– (shown as A or AL)

Abbrev.	First	Last	Team
BAL A	1901	1902	Baltimore (replaced by New York)
BAL A	1954		Baltimore
BOS A	1901		Boston
CAL A	1965		California
CHI A	1901		Chicago
CLE A	1901		Cleveland
DET A	1901		Detroit
KC A	1955	1967	Kansas City (transferred to Oakland)
KC A	1969		Kansas City
LA A	1961	1964	Los Angeles (transferred to California)
MIL A	1901	1901	Milwaukee (replaced by St. Louis)
MIL A	1970		Milwaukee
MIN A	1961		Minnesota
NY A	1903		New York
OAK A	1968		Oakland
PHI A	1901	1954	Philadelphia (transferred to Kansas City)
STL A	1902	1953	St. Louis (transferred to Baltimore)
SEA A	1969	1969	Seattle (transferred to Milwaukee)
SEA A	1977		Seattle
TEX A	1972		Texas
TOR A	1977		Toronto
WAS A	1901	1960	Washington, D.C. (transferred to Minnesota)
WAS A	1961	1971	Washington, D.C. (transferred to Texas)

FEDERAL LEAGUE, 1914-1915 (shown as F or FL)

Abbrev.	First	Last	Team
BAL F	1914	1915	Baltimore
BRO F	1914	1915	Brooklyn
BUF F	1914	1915	Buffalo
CHI F	1914	1915	Chicago
IND F	1914	1914	Indianapolis (transferred to Newark)
KC F	1914	1915	Kansas City
NEW F	1915	1915	Newark
PIT F	1914	1915	Pittsburgh
STL F	1914	1915	St. Louis